How to use this book

This book provides information about prescription and over-the-counter medicines. It is written in everyday language, making it a valuable reference guide for consumers.

On this page, you'll find general information about how to use this book. An illustration showing how the listings are organized appears on the back of this page.

About the entries

The drug entries are arranged alphabetically like an encyclopedia. ***If you already know what entry the drug belongs to,*** you can turn directly to it.

If you know only the drug's generic or brand name, the best way to find your information is to use the index at the front of this book. It will tell you what entry includes that drug and the page number on which the entry starts.

For more information

For general guidelines about medicines, see *To the Reader* (page v), which also discusses this book's content and USP in-depth. In addition to the entries, this book contains general information about the use of medicines, a glossary with over 400 medical terms plus a four-color medicine chart and the following supplemental appendixes:

- ***Appendix 1*** *Introductory Version Leaflets*
- ***Appendix 2*** *Additional Products and Uses*
- ***Appendix 3*** *Poison Control Center Listing*
- ***Appendix 4*** *USP People*

See illustration on the back of this page.

Sample entry

Title section: lists the drug's commonly used brand names in both the United States and Canada.

Precautions: tells you what to avoid or be careful of when using the drug, and when medical supervision is required.

Proper use of this medicine: tells how to store and use the drug, including usual doses and information such as what to do if you miss a dose.

Additional Information: when necessary, gives details about other uses that are not shown in the product labeling.

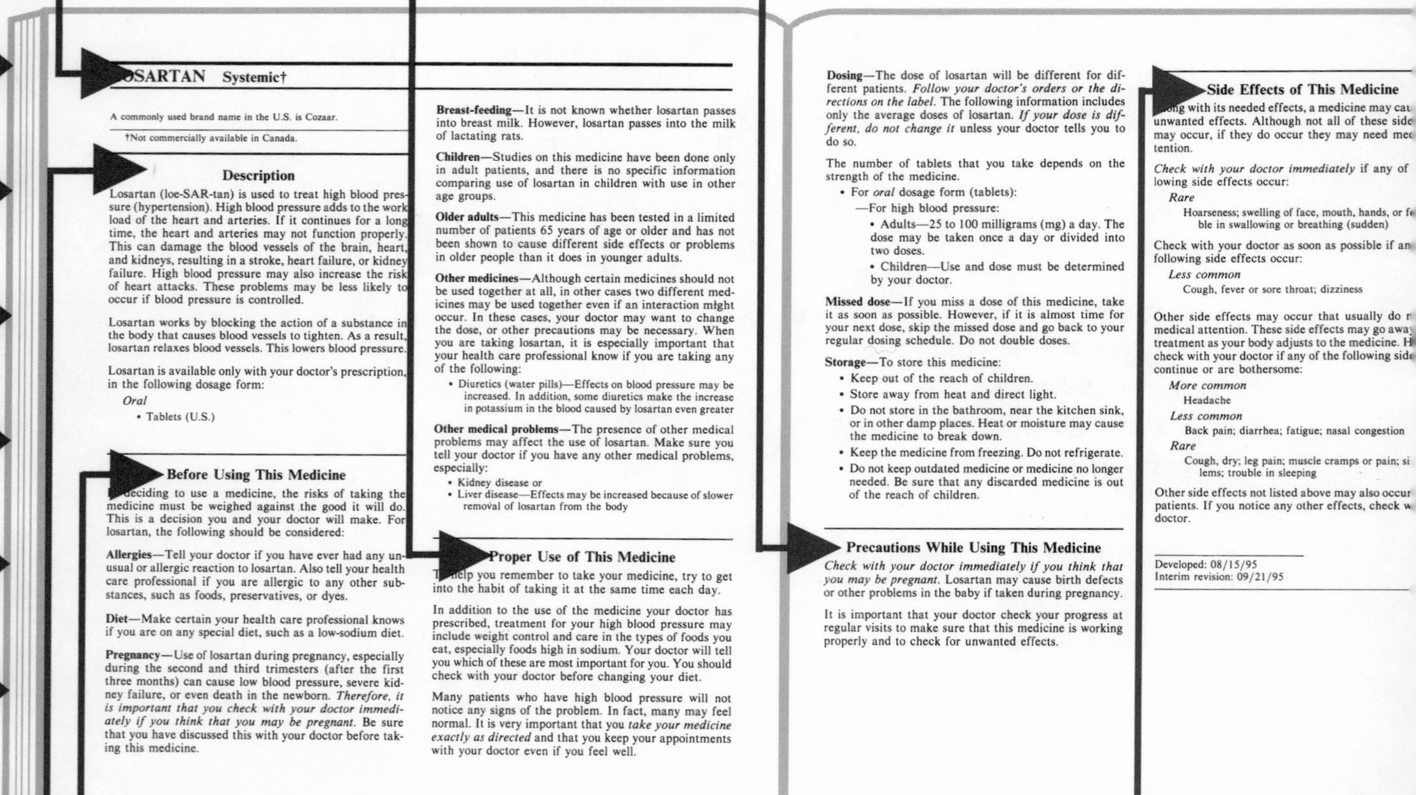

LOSARTAN Systemic†

A commonly used brand name in the U.S. is Cozaar.

†Not commercially available in Canada.

Description

Losartan (loe-SAR-tan) is used to treat high blood pressure (hypertension). High blood pressure adds to the work load of the heart and arteries. If it continues for a long time, the heart and arteries may not function properly. This can damage the blood vessels of the brain, heart, and kidneys, resulting in a stroke, heart failure, or kidney failure. High blood pressure may also increase the risk of heart attacks. These problems may be less likely to occur if blood pressure is controlled.

Losartan works by blocking the action of a substance in the body that causes blood vessels to tighten. As a result, losartan relaxes blood vessels. This lowers blood pressure.

Losartan is available only with your doctor's prescription, in the following dosage form:

Oral

- Tablets (U.S.)

Before Using This Medicine

In deciding to use a medicine, the risks of taking the medicine must be weighed against the good it will do. This is a decision you and your doctor will make. For losartan, the following should be considered:

Allergies—Tell your doctor if you have ever had any unusual or allergic reaction to losartan. Also tell your health care professional if you are allergic to any other substances, such as foods, preservatives, or dyes.

Diet—Make certain your health care professional knows if you are on any special diet, such as a low-sodium diet.

Pregnancy—Use of losartan during pregnancy, especially during the second and third trimesters (after the first three months) can cause low blood pressure, severe kidney failure, or even death in the newborn. *Therefore, it is important that you check with your doctor immediately if you think that you may be pregnant.* Be sure that you have discussed this with your doctor before taking this medicine.

Breast-feeding—It is not known whether losartan passes into breast milk. However, losartan passes into the milk of lactating rats.

Children—Studies on this medicine have been done only in adult patients, and there is no specific information comparing use of losartan in children with use in other age groups.

Older adults—This medicine has been tested in a limited number of patients 65 years of age or older and has not been shown to cause different side effects or problems in older people than it does in younger adults.

Other medicines—Although certain medicines should not be used together at all, in other cases two different medicines may be used together even if an interaction might occur. In these cases, your doctor may want to change the dose, or other precautions may be necessary. When you are taking losartan, it is especially important that your health care professional know if you are taking any of the following:

- Diuretics (water pills)—Effects on blood pressure may be increased. In addition, some diuretics make the increase in potassium in the blood caused by losartan even greater

Other medical problems—The presence of other medical problems may affect the use of losartan. Make sure you tell your doctor if you have any other medical problems, especially:

- Kidney disease or
- Liver disease—Effects may be increased because of slower removal of losartan from the body

Proper Use of This Medicine

To help you remember to take your medicine, try to get into the habit of taking it at the same time each day.

In addition to the use of the medicine your doctor has prescribed, treatment for your high blood pressure may include weight control and care in the types of foods you eat, especially foods high in sodium. Your doctor will tell you which of these are most important for you. You should check with your doctor before changing your diet.

Many patients who have high blood pressure will not notice any signs of the problem. In fact, many may feel normal. It is very important that you *take your medicine exactly as directed* and that you keep your appointments with your doctor even if you feel well.

Dosing—The dose of losartan will be different for different patients. *Follow your doctor's orders or the directions on the label.* The following information includes only the average doses of losartan. *If your dose is different, do not change it* unless your doctor tells you to do so.

The number of tablets that you take depends on the strength of the medicine.

- For *oral* dosage form (tablets):
  - —For high blood pressure:
    - Adults—25 to 100 milligrams (mg) a day. The dose may be taken once a day or divided into two doses.
    - Children—Use and dose must be determined by your doctor.

Missed dose—If you miss a dose of this medicine, take it as soon as possible. However, if it is almost time for your next dose, skip the missed dose and go back to your regular dosing schedule. Do not double doses.

Storage—To store this medicine:

- Keep out of the reach of children.
- Store away from heat and direct light.
- Do not store in the bathroom, near the kitchen sink, or in other damp places. Heat or moisture may cause the medicine to break down.
- Keep the medicine from freezing. Do not refrigerate.
- Do not keep outdated medicine or medicine no longer needed. Be sure that any discarded medicine is out of the reach of children.

Precautions While Using This Medicine

Check with your doctor immediately if you think that you may be pregnant. Losartan may cause birth defects or other problems in the baby if taken during pregnancy.

It is important that your doctor check your progress at regular visits to make sure that this medicine is working properly and to check for unwanted effects.

Side Effects of This Medicine

Along with its needed effects, a medicine may cau[se] unwanted effects. Although not all of these side [effects] may occur, if they do occur they may need me[dical at]tention.

Check with your doctor immediately if any of [the fol]lowing side effects occur:

Rare

Hoarseness; swelling of face, mouth, hands, or fe[et]; [trou]ble in swallowing or breathing (sudden)

Check with your doctor as soon as possible if an[y of the] following side effects occur:

Less common

Cough, fever or sore throat; dizziness

Other side effects may occur that usually do n[ot need] medical attention. These side effects may go away [during] treatment as your body adjusts to the medicine. H[owever,] check with your doctor if any of the following side [effects] continue or are bothersome:

More common

Headache

Less common

Back pain; diarrhea; fatigue; nasal congestion

Rare

Cough, dry; leg pain; muscle cramps or pain; si[nus prob]lems; trouble in sleeping

Other side effects not listed above may also occur [in some] patients. If you notice any other effects, check w[ith your] doctor.

Developed: 08/15/95
Interim revision: 09/21/95

Before using this medicine: explains what you and your health care professional should consider in advance, such as allergies and special diet restrictions.

Side effects: lists both common and rare side effects of the drug and whether they require medical attention.

Description: tells how to pronounce the drug's name, what the drug is used for, what dosage forms are available, and if a doctor must prescribe the drug.

PLEASE HELP US

Dear Reader:

Thank you for purchasing the *1998 Complete Drug Reference* from *Consumer Reports*. We hope you find it useful. To help us make it even more useful in the future, please share your comments and opinions below. If you mail this back by August 15, 1998, and include your name and address at the bottom, we'll send you a dollar as a THANK YOU for your help.

Lloyd Wohlner

Lloyd Wohlner for *Consumer Reports*

Where did you buy this book?

☐ Chain bookstore → name ____________

☐ Independent bookstore → name ____________

☐ Mail-order offer

☐ Ordered through *Consumer Reports*

☐ Discount store ☐ Other ____________

When did you buy this book?

Month __________ Year _________

How did you find out about this book?

☐ Saw in store ☐ Librarian recommended

☐ Friend told me ☐ Ad in *Consumer Reports*

☐ Doctor/pharmacist recommended

☐ TV / Radio

☐ Other ________________________________

Most people buy a book like this to have as a reference at home. Why else did you buy this book? Check as many as apply.

☐ Gain information about new drug(s)

☐ Replace an older, out-of-date reference

☐ Answer specific question about a drug

☐ Check up on a medication I am taking

☐ Check up on a medication a relative/friend is taking

☐ Other ________________________________

How easy is it to understand the information in this book? Circle the answer that best matches your experience.

Too technical   About right   Not technical enough

When did you last buy a drug reference like this?

19 ______ or ☐ Never bought one before

Would you have bought this book if the retail price was $44.95? ☐ Yes ☐ No

What suggestions do you have to make this book better?

____

____

Do you think you will buy next year's edition of this *CDR*?

Yes, definitely   Probably   Probably not   Definitely not

Why do you say that? ____________________

____

Please tell us a little about yourself so your answers can be compared to others.

Are you: ☐ Male ☐ Female

Do you read *Consumer Reports* magazine?

☐ **Current subscriber → How many years?** ____

☐ **Buy on newsstand → Number of copies a year?** ____

☐ **Read friend's copy / read at library**

☐ **Former subscriber → Why did you stop?** ____________

____

☐ **Don't read *Consumer Reports***

What is the highest education level you have completed?

☐ High school graduate or less

☐ Trade school or some college

☐ College graduate / BA / BS

☐ Some post-graduate school

☐ Post graduate degree

Are you trained in / working in a health-care field?

☐ Yes ☐ No

If yes, what field? ____________________

What year were you born? 19 _________

Please fill in your name and address below to receive your $1 THANK YOU. U.S. residents only, please. Please respond by August 15, 1998.

Mr. / Miss / Mrs. / Ms / Dr. [PLEASE CIRCLE ONE]

Name ________________________________

Address ________________________________

City ________________________________

State ______________ ZIP ____________

98CDRP1

FOLD HERE

NO POSTAGE NECESSARY IF MAILED IN THE UNITED STATES

POSTAGE WILL BE PAID BY ADDRESSEE

Lloyd Wohlner
CONSUMER REPORTS
PO BOX 2015
YONKERS NY 10703-9938

FOLD HERE

COMPLETE DRUG REFERENCE

1998 Edition

United States Pharmacopeia

Consumer Reports
A Division of Consumers Union

Yonkers, New York

Library of Congress Catalog Card Number: 81-640842
ISBN: 0-89043-850-1

First printing, November 1997

Manufactured in the United States of America

Published simultaneously by USPC, Inc., under the title *USP DI, Volume II (Advice for the Patient), Eighteenth* Edition, 1998. Previous editions of this book appeared under the title *United States Pharmacopeia Drug Information for the Consumer*.

The *Complete Drug Reference*, 1998 Edition, is published by Consumers Reports, a division of Consumers Union, U.S. Inc. Consumers Union is a nonprofit, independent organization established in 1936 to provide consumers with information and advice on products, services, health, and personal finance. It is chartered under the Not-For-Profit Corporation Law of the State of New York. Consumers Union derives its income mainly from the sale of *Consumer Reports* magazine and other publications and services, such as Consumer Reports on Health, Consumer Reports Travel Letter, Consumer Reports Television, and Consumer Reports TV News. Income is also derived from nonrestrictive, noncommercial contributions, grants, and fees.

Consumers Union accepts no advertising or product samples and is not beholden in any way to any commercial or Federal interest. Its Ratings and reports are solely for the use of the readers of its publicaions. Neither the Ratings nor the reports nor any Consumers Reports publication, including this book, may be used in advertising or for any commercial purpose. Consumers Union will take all steps available to it to prevent such uses of its material, its name, or the name of Consumer Reports.

NOTICE AND WARNING

Concerning U.S. Patent or Trademark Rights

Inclusion in the *Complete Drug Reference* of any article in respect to which patent or trademark rights may exist shall not be deemed, and is not intended as, a grant of, or authority to exercise, any right or privilege protected by such patent or trademark. All such rights and privileges are vested in the patent or trademark owner, and no other person may exercise the same without express permission, authority, or license secured from such patent or trademark owner.

The listing of selected brand names is intended only for ease of reference. The inclusion of a brand name does not mean the USPC or Consumers Union has any particular knowledge that the brand listed has properties different from other brands of the same drug, nor should it be interpreted as an endorsement by the USPC or by Consumers Union. Similarly, the fact that a particular brand has not been included does not indicate that the product has been judged to be unsatisfactory or unacceptable.

Check the Index first. It's on page 1.

Contents

Complete Drug Reference

Foreword to the Consumer Reports Edition

The *1998 Complete Drug Reference* is a consumer's guide to prescription and over-the-counter drugs published by Consumer Reports, a division of Consumers Union of the U.S., Inc., in partnership with the United States Pharmacopeia Convention (USPC). This uinque partnership brings together two independent, nonprofit organizations dedicated to the consumer's well-being.

The USPC has set official standards of strength, quality, purity, packaging, and labeling for medical products in the United States for more than a hundred years. And for more than 60 years Consumers Union, through its magazine *Consumer Reports* and other information services, has served as this country's foremost source for authoritative, reliable, and unbiased product testing and buying guidance.

At one time or another, most of us find it necessary to use some type of medication. In fact, many people feel that medical treatment is only effective when it includes drug therapy, even though this is not always the case. At the same time, studies show many prescriptions are taken incorrectly, possibly because many patients receive little or no counseling about drug usage, including interactions with food or other drugs, and possible side effects. That's how this straightforward, objective guide to drugs can help.

The *Complete Drug Reference* lists almost every medicine—prescription and nonprescription—available in the United States and Canada. It provides consumers with up-to-date information about drug usage and potential side effects. Organized alphabetically by generic or family name, each entry includes different dosage forms and common brand names—more than 10,000 different brand and generic entries in all. It is thoroughly indexed according to both generic and brand names, making it easy to look up any medication. Most important, unlike other drug information books available to the consumer—notably the *Physicians' Desk Reference*—the information presented in this guide is not a replication of the drug manufacturers' package inserts. Rather, the *Complete Drug Reference* is a consensus book put together by many experts—physicians, pharmacists, pharmacologists, dentists, nurses, chemists, microbiologists, and other individuals particularly qualified to judge drugs—and is supported by 35 advisory panels representing different medical specialties, health professionals, and consumers. The database on which this guide is based is constantly in revision, which allows it to contain the latest precautions and side effects of a particular drug, sometimes even before the information is readily available elsewhere.

Consumers can help in that review, too. Even the exacting approval process undertaken by the U.S. Food and Drug Administration cannot possibly predict all effects of drugs on the market. It's important that patients report any side effects of drugs to their physicians and that physicians relay that information to the FDA.

The material contained in this book is presented in a direct, factual manner. Each profile of a specific drug lists indications, proper usage, precautions, and side effects. The language is easily understood and targeted specifically to the patient. The *Complete Drug Reference* is the most comprehensive drug information book available to the public, and we are proud to present it to our readers.

To The Reader

When purchasing a medicine, whether over-the-counter (nonprescription) or with a doctor's prescription, you may have questions about its usefulness to you, the best way to take it, possible side effects, and precautions to take to avoid complications. For instance, some medicines should be taken with meals, others between meals. Some may make you drowsy while others may tend to keep you awake. Alcoholic or other beverages, other medicines, certain foods, or smoking may affect the way your medicine works. As for side effects, some are merely bothersome and may go away while others may require medical attention.

Complete Drug Reference contains information which may provide general answers to some of your questions as well as suggestions for the correct use of your medicine. *It is important to remember, however, that the human body is very complex and medicines may act differently on different people—and even in the same person at different times. If you want additional information about your medicine or its possible side effects, ask your doctor, nurse, pharmacist, or other health care provider. They are there to help you.*

How to Use This Book

Complete Drug Reference contains a section of general information about the appropriate use of any medicine, as well as individual discussions of a wide variety of commonly and not so commonly used medicines. *You should read both the general information and the information specific to the medicine you are taking.* See page 115 for this general information.

Each medicine has a generic name that all manufacturers who make that medicine must use. Some manufacturers also create a brand name to put on the label and to use in advertising. *Look in the index* for the generic name or the brand name of the medicine about which you have questions. We have put the generic names and common brand names in the same index, so you do not have to know whether the name you have is a generic name or a brand name. However, it is a good idea for you to learn both the generic and the brand names of the medicines you are using and to write them down and keep them for future use.

Although the informational monographs generally appear in alphabetical order by generic name, there are numerous occasions when closely related medicines are grouped under a family name. Therefore, the surest way to quickly find the page number of the information about each medicine is to *look in the index first.*

The information for each medicine is presented according to the area of the body which is affected. As a general rule, information for one type of use will not be the same as for other types of use. For example, if you take tetracycline capsules by mouth for their systemic effect in treating an infection, the information will not be the same as for tetracycline ointment, which is applied directly to the skin for its topical effects. And both of these will be different from the information for tetracyclines used in the eye. The common divisions used in this publication are:

- *BUCCAL*—For general effects throughout the body when a medicine is placed in the cheek pocket and slowly absorbed.
- *DENTAL*—For local effects when applied to the teeth or gums.
- *INHALATION*—For local, and in some cases systemic, effects when inhaled into the lungs.
- *INTRA-AMNIOTIC*—For local effects when a medicine is injected into the sac that contains the fetus and amniotic fluid.
- *INTRACAVERNOSAL*—For local effects in the penis when a medicine is given by injection.
- *LINGUAL*—For general effects throughout the body when a medicine is absorbed through the lining of the mouth.
- *MUCOSAL*—For local effects when applied directly to mucous membranes (for example, the inside of the mouth).
- *NASAL*—For local effects when used in the nose.
- *OPHTHALMIC*—For local effects when applied directly to the eyes.
- *ORAL-LOCAL*—For local effects in the gastrointestinal tract when taken by mouth (i.e., not absorbed into the body).
- *OTIC*—For local effects when used in the ear.
- *PARENTERAL-LOCAL*—For local effects in a specific area of the body when given by injection.
- *RECTAL*—For local, and in some cases systemic, effects when used in the rectum.
- *SUBLINGUAL*—For general effects throughout the body when a medicine is placed under the tongue and slowly absorbed.
- *SYSTEMIC*—For general effects throughout the body; applies to most medicines when taken by mouth or given by injection or transdermal patch.
- *TOPICAL*—For local effects when applied directly to the skin.
- *VAGINAL*—For local, and in some cases systemic, effects when used in the vagina.

Notice:

The information about the drugs contained herein is general in nature and is intended to be used in consultation with your health care providers. It is not intended to replace specific instructions or directions or warnings given to you by your physician or other prescriber or accompanying a particular product. The information is selective and it is not claimed that it includes all known precautions, contraindications, effects, or interactions possibly related to the use of a drug. The information may differ from that contained in the product labeling which is required by law. The information is not sufficient to make an evaluation as to the risks and benefits of taking a particular drug in a particular case and is not medical advice for individual problems and should not alone be relied upon for these purposes. Since the inclusion or exclusion of particular information about a drug is judgmental in nature and since opinion as to drug usage may differ, you may wish to consult additional sources. Should you desire additional information or if you have any questions as to how this information may relate to you in particular, ask your doctor, nurse, pharmacist, or other health care provider.

Since new drugs are constantly being marketed and since previously unreported side effects, newly recognized precautions, or other new information for any given drug may come to light at any time, continuously updated drug information sources should be consulted as necessary.

There are many brands of drugs on the market. The listing of selected brand names is intended only for ease of reference. The inclusion of a brand name does not mean the USP or Consumers Union has any particular knowledge that the brand listed has properties different from other brands of the same drug, nor should it be interpreted as an endorsement by the USP or Consumers Union. Similarly, the fact that a brand name has not been included does not indicate that that particular brand has been judged to be unsatisfactory or unacceptable.

If any of the information in this book causes you special concern, do not decide against taking any medicine prescribed for you without first checking with your doctor.

About USP

The information in this volume is prepared by the United States Pharmacopeia (USP), the organization that sets the official standards of strength, quality, purity, packaging, and labeling for medical products used in the United States.

The United States Pharmacopeia is an independent, not-for-profit corporation composed of delegates from the accredited colleges of medicine and pharmacy in the U.S.; state medical and pharmaceutical associations; many national associations concerned with medicines, such as the American Medical Association, the American Nurses Association, the American Dental Association, the National Association of Retail Druggists, and the American Pharmaceutical Association; and various departments of the federal government, including the Food and Drug Administration. Other members represent the public. USP was established 178 years ago, and is the only national body that represents the professions of both pharmacy and medicine.

The first convention came into being on January 1, 1820, and within the year published the first national drug formulary of the United States. The *U.S. Pharmacopeia* of 1820 contained 217 drug names, divided into two groups according to the level of general acceptance and usage.

When Congress passed the first major drug safety law in 1906, the standards recognized by that statute were those set forth in the *United States Pharmacopeia* and in the *National Formulary*. Today, the *USP* and *NF* continue to be the official U.S. compendia for standards for drugs and for the inactive ingredients in drug dosage forms. The *United States Pharmacopeia* is the world's oldest regularly revised national pharmacopeia and is generally accepted as being the most influential.

The work of the USP is carried out by the Committee of Revision. This committee of experts is elected by the members and currently consists of 128 outstanding physicians, pharmacists, dentists, nurses, chemists, microbiologists, and other individuals particularly qualified to judge the merits of drugs and the standards and information that should apply to them. Committee members serve without pay, are subject to conflict-of-interest requirements, and are assisted by numerous advisory panels, other outside reviewers, and USP staff.

Index

Brand names are in *italics*. There are many brands and different manufacturers of drugs and the listing of selected American and Canadian brand names and manufacturers is intended only for ease of reference. There are additional brands and manufacturers that have not been included. The inclusion of a brand name does not mean the USP has any particular knowledge that the brand listed has properties different from other brands of the same drug, nor should it be interpreted as an endorsement by the USP. Similarly, the fact that a particular brand has not been included does not indicate that the product has been judged to be unsatisfactory or unacceptable. The page numbers MC-1 to MC-32 refer to the product identification photographs in The Medicine Chart.

A

B

C

D

Darvon Compound-65—Propoxyphene, Aspirin, and Caffeine—*See* Narcotic Analgesics and Aspirin (Systemic), 1153
Darvon-N—Propoxyphene—*See* Narcotic Analgesics—For Pain Relief (Systemic), 1140
Darvon-N with A.S.A.—Propoxyphene and Aspirin—*See* Narcotic Analgesics and Aspirin (Systemic), 1153
Darvon-N Compound—Propoxyphene, Aspirin, and Caffeine—*See* Narcotic Analgesics and Aspirin (Systemic), 1153
Datril Extra-Strength—Acetaminophen (Systemic), 129
Daunorubicin (Systemic), 657
Daypro—Oxaprozin—*See* Anti-inflammatory Drugs, Nonsteroidal (Systemic), 301, MC-7, MC-23; Oxaprozin (Systemic), 1735
Dayto Himbin—Yohimbine (Systemic), 1645
Dazamide—Acetazolamide—*See* Carbonic Anhydrase Inhibitors (Systemic), 465
2′DCF—*See* Pentostatin (Systemic), 1258
DC Softgels—Docusate—*See* Laxatives (Oral), 980
DDAVP—Desmopressin (Systemic), 667, 1729, MC-8
DDAVP Nasal Spray—Desmopressin (Systemic), 667
DDAVP Rhinal Tube—Desmopressin (Systemic), 667
DDAVP Rhinyle Nasal Solution—Desmopressin (Systemic), 667
DDAVP Spray—Desmopressin (Systemic), 667
ddC—*See* Zalcitabine (Systemic), 1648
ddI—*See* Didanosine (Systemic), 676
DDS—*See* Dapsone (Systemic), 655
Debetrol—Dextrothyroxine (Systemic), 670
Debrisoquine (Systemic), 1729
Decaderm—Dexamethasone—*See* Corticosteroids—Low Potency (Topical), 600
Decadrol—Dexamethasone—*See* Corticosteroids—Glucocorticoid Effects (Systemic), 595
Decadron—Dexamethasone—*See* Corticosteroids (Ophthalmic), 591; Corticosteroids (Otic), 593; Corticosteroids—Glucocorticoid Effects (Systemic), 595, MC-8; Corticosteroids—Low Potency (Topical), 600
Decadron-LA—Dexamethasone—*See* Corticosteroids—Glucocorticoid Effects (Systemic), 595
Decadron Phosphate—Dexamethasone—*See* Corticosteroids—Glucocorticoid Effects (Systemic), 595
Decadron Respihaler—Dexamethasone—*See* Corticosteroids (Inhalation), 582
Decadron Turbinaire—Dexamethasone—*See* Corticosteroids (Nasal), 588
Deca-Durabolin—Nandrolone—*See* Anabolic Steroids (Systemic), 185
Decaject—Dexamethasone—*See* Corticosteroids—Glucocorticoid Effects (Systemic), 595
Decaject-L.A.—Dexamethasone—*See* Corticosteroids—Glucocorticoid Effects (Systemic), 595
Decaspray—Dexamethasone—*See* Corticosteroids—Low Potency (Topical), 600
Decholin—Dehydrocholic Acid—*See* Laxatives (Oral), 980
Declinax—Debrisoquine (Systemic), 1729
Declomycin—Demeclocycline—*See* Tetracyclines (Systemic), 1533, MC-8
Decofed—Pseudoephedrine (Systemic), 1354
Decohistine DH—Chlorpheniramine, Pseudoephedrine, and Codeine—*See* Cough/Cold Combinations (Systemic), 606
De-Comberol—Testosterone and Estradiol—*See* Androgens and Estrogens (Systemic), 193
Deconamine—Chlorpheniramine and Pseudoephedrine—*See* Antihistamines and Decongestants (Systemic), 281
Deconamine CX—Pseudoephedrine, Hydrocodone, and Guaifenesin—*See* Cough/Cold Combinations (Systemic), 606
Deconamine SR—Chlorpheniramine and Pseudoephedrine—*See* Antihistamines and Decongestants (Systemic), 281
Decongestabs—Chlorpheniramine, Phenyltoloxamine, Phenylephrine, and Phenylpropanolamine—*See* Antihistamines and Decongestants (Systemic), 281
Decongestants and Analgesics (Systemic), 659
Deconhist—Chlorpheniramine, Phenylephrine, Phenylpropanolamine, Atropine, Hyoscyamine, and Scopolamine—*See* Antihistamines, Decongestants, and Anticholinergics (Systemic), 291
Deconomed SR—Chlorpheniramine and Pseudoephedrine—*See* Antihistamines and Decongestants (Systemic), 281
Deconsal II—Pseudoephrine and Guaifenesin—*See* Cough/Cold Combinations (Systemic), 606
Deconsal Pediatric—Phenylephrine and Guaifenesin—*See* Cough/Cold Combinations (Systemic), 606
Deconsal Sprinkle—Phenylephrine and Guaifenesin—*See* Cough/Cold Combinations (Systemic), 606
Decylenes Powder—Undecylenic Acid, Compound (Topical), 1605
Deep Woods OFF—Diethyltoluamide (Topical), 681
Deep Woods OFF For Sportsmen—Diethyltoluamide (Topical), 681
DEET—*See* Diethyltoluamide (Topical), 681
Deferoxamine (Systemic), 664
Deficol—Bisacodyl—*See* Laxatives (Oral), 980; Laxatives (Rectal), 986
Degas—Simethicone (Oral), 1736
Degest 2—Naphazoline (Ophthalmic), 1139
Dehist—Brompheniramine—*See* Antihistamines (Systemic), 274
Dehydrocholic Acid—*See* Laxatives (Oral), 980
Dehydrocholic Acid and Docusate—*See* Laxatives (Oral), 980
Dehydrocholic Acid, Docusate, and Phenolphthalein—*See* Laxatives (Oral), 980
Delacort—Hydrocortisone—*See* Corticosteroids—Low Potency (Topical), 600
Deladumone—Testosterone and Estradiol—*See* Androgens and Estrogens (Systemic), 193
Del-Aqua-5 Gel—Benzoyl Peroxide (Topical), 377
Del-Aqua-10 Gel—Benzoyl Peroxide (Topical), 377
Delatest—Testosterone—*See* Androgens (Systemic), 188
Delatestadiol—Testosterone and Estradiol—*See* Androgens and Estrogens (Systemic), 193
Delatestryl—Testosterone—*See* Androgens (Systemic), 188
Delestrogen—Estradiol—*See* Estrogens (Systemic), 766
Delfen—Nonoxynol 9—*See* Spermicides (Vaginal), 1464
Delhistine D—Pheniramine, Phenyltoloxamine, Pyrilamine, and Phenylpropanolamine—*See* Antihistamines and Decongestants (Systemic), 281
Deliver 2.0—Enteral Nutrition Formula, Polymeric—*See* Enteral Nutrition Formulas (Systemic), 741
Delsym—Dextromethorphan (Systemic), 669
Delta-Cortef—Prednisolone—*See* Corticosteroids—Glucocorticoid Effects (Systemic), 595
Deltasone—Prednisone—*See* Corticosteroids—Glucocorticoid Effects (Systemic), 595, MC-25
Delta-9-tetrahydrocannabinol (THC)—*See* Dronabinol (Systemic), 733
Delta-Tritex—Triamcinolone—*See* Corticosteroids—Medium to Very High Potency (Topical), 602
Demadex—Torsemide (Systemic), 1580, MC-31
Demazin—Chlorpheniramine and Phenylpropanolamine—*See* Antihistamines and Decongestants (Systemic), 281
Demazin Repetabs—Chlorpheniramine and Phenylpropanolamine—*See* Antihistamines and Decongestants (Systemic), 281
Demecarium—*See* Antiglaucoma Agents, Cholinergic, Long-acting (Ophthalmic), 269
Demeclocycline—*See* Tetracyclines (Systemic), 1533, MC-8
Demerol—Meperidine—*See* Narcotic Analgesics—For Pain Relief (Systemic), 1140, MC-18; Narcotic Analgesics—For Surgery and Obstetrics (Systemic), 1147
Demi-Regroton—Reserpine and Chlorthalidone—*See* Rauwolfia Alkaloids and Thiazide Diuretics (Systemic), 1385, MC-27
Demser—Metyrosine (Systemic), 1099
Demulen 1/35—Ethynodiol Diacetate and Ethinyl Estradiol—*See* Estrogens and Progestins (Oral Contraceptives) (Systemic), 774, MC-12
Demulen 1/50—Ethynodiol Diacetate and Ethinyl Estradiol—*See* Estrogens and Progestins (Oral Contraceptives) (Systemic), 774, MC-12
Demulen 30—Ethynodiol Diacetate and Ethinyl Estradiol—*See* Estrogens and Progestins (Oral Contraceptives) (Systemic), 774
Demulen 50—Ethynodiol Diacetate and Ethinyl Estradiol—*See* Estrogens and Progestins (Oral Contraceptives) (Systemic), 774
Denorex—Coal Tar (Topical), 558
Denorex Extra Strength Medicated Shampoo—Coal Tar (Topical), 558
Denorex Extra Strength Medicated Shampoo with Conditioners—Coal Tar (Topical), 558
Denorex Medicated Shampoo—Coal Tar (Topical), 558
Denorex Medicated Shampoo and Conditioner—Coal Tar (Topical), 558
Denorex Mountain Fresh Herbal Scent Medicated Shampoo—Coal Tar (Topical), 558
Dentapaine—Benzocaine—*See* Anesthetics (Dental), 197
Dentocaine—Benzocaine—*See* Anesthetics (Dental), 197
Dent-Zel-Ite—Benzocaine—*See* Anesthetics (Dental), 197
2′-deoxycoformycin—*See* Pentostatin (Systemic), 1258
Depacon—Valproate Sodium—*See* Valproic Acid (Systemic), 1611
Depakene—Valproic Acid (Systemic), 1611, MC-32
Depakote—Divalproex—*See* Valproic Acid (Systemic), 1611, MC-10
Depakote Sprinkle—Divalproex—*See* Valproic Acid (Systemic), 1611, MC-10
depAndro 100—Testosterone—*See* Androgens (Systemic), 188
depAndro 200—Testosterone—*See* Androgens (Systemic), 188
depAndrogyn—Testosterone and Estradiol—*See* Androgens and Estrogens (Systemic), 193
Depen—Penicillamine (Systemic), 1242
depGynogen—Estradiol—*See* Estrogens (Systemic), 766
depMedalone 40—Methylprednisolone—*See* Corticosteroids—Glucocorticoid Effects (Systemic), 595
depMedalone 80—Methylprednisolone—*See* Corticosteroids—Glucocorticoid Effects (Systemic), 595
Depo-Estradiol—Estradiol—*See* Estrogens (Systemic), 766
Depogen—Estradiol—*See* Estrogens (Systemic), 766
Depoject-40—Methylprednisolone—*See* Corticosteroids—Glucocorticoid Effects (Systemic), 595
Depoject-80—Methylprednisolone—*See* Corticosteroids—Glucocorticoid Effects (Systemic), 595
Depo-Medrol—Methylprednisolone—*See* Corticosteroids—Glucocorticoid Effects (Systemic), 595
Deponit—Nitroglycerin—*See* Nitrates—Oral (Systemic), 1186; Nitroglycerin Transdermal Patches—*See* Nitrates—Topical (Systemic), 1192
Depopred-40—Methylprednisolone—*See* Corticosteroids—Glucocorticoid Effects (Systemic), 595
Depopred-80—Methylprednisolone—*See* Corticosteroids—Glucocorticoid Effects (Systemic), 595
Depo-Predate 40—Methylprednisolone—*See* Corticosteroids—Glucocorticoid Effects (Systemic), 595
Depo-Predate 80—Methylprednisolone—*See* Corticosteroids—Glucocorticoid Effects (Systemic), 595
Depo-Provera—Medroxyprogesterone—*See* Progestins—For Noncontraceptive Use (Systemic), 1347
Depo-Provera Contraceptive Injection—Medroxyprogesterone—*See* Progestins—For Contraceptive Use (Systemic), 1343
Depotest—Testosterone—*See* Androgens (Systemic), 188
Depo-Testadiol—Testosterone and Estradiol—*See* Androgens and Estrogens (Systemic), 193
Depotestogen—Testosterone and Estradiol—*See* Androgens and Estrogens (Systemic), 193
Depo-Testosterone—Testosterone—*See* Androgens (Systemic), 188
Depo-Testosterone Cypionate—Testosterone—*See* Androgens (Systemic), 188
Deprenil—*See* Selegiline (Systemic), 1435
Deprenyl—*See* Selegiline (Systemic), 1435
Deproic—Valproic Acid (Systemic), 1611
Deproist Expectorant with Codeine—Pseudoephedrine, Codeine, and Guaifenesin—*See* Cough/Cold Combinations (Systemic), 606
Derbac-M—Malathion (Topical), 1027
Dermabet—Betamethasone—*See* Corticosteroids—Medium to Very High Potency (Topical), 602
Dermacomb—Nystatin and Triamcinolone (Topical), 1201

E

F

G

H

J

K

L

M

Maolate—Chlorphenesin—*See* Skeletal Muscle Relaxants (Systemic), 1448
Maox—Magnesium Oxide—*See* Antacids (Oral), 219; Magnesium Supplements (Systemic), 1024
Maox 420—Magnesium Oxide—*See* Antacids (Oral), 219; Laxatives (Oral), 980
Mapap Cold Formula—Chlorpheniramine, Pseudoephedrine, Dextromethorphan, and Acetaminophen—*See* Cough/Cold Combinations (Systemic), 606
Maprotiline (Systemic), 1030, MC-18
Marax—Theophylline, Ephedrine, and Hydroxyzine (Systemic), 1543
Marax-DF—Theophylline, Ephedrine, and Hydroxyzine (Systemic), 1543
Marblen—Calcium and Magnesium Carbonates—*See* Antacids (Oral), 219
Marcaine—Bupivacaine—*See* Anesthetics (Parenteral-Local), 202
Marcaine Spinal—Bupivacaine—*See* Anesthetics (Parenteral-Local), 202
Marcof Expectorant—Hydrocodone and Potassium Guaiacolsulfonate—*See* Cough/Cold Combinations (Systemic), 606
Marezine—Cyclizine—*See* Meclizine/Buclizine/Cyclizine (Systemic), 1044
Margesic #3—Acetaminophen and Codeine—*See* Narcotic Analgesics and Acetaminophen (Systemic), 1149
Margesic-H—Hydrocodone and Acetaminophen—*See* Narcotic Analgesics and Acetaminophen (Systemic), 1149
Marinol—Dronabinol (Systemic), 733
Marmine—Dimenhydrinate—*See* Antihistamines (Systemic), 274
Marnal—Butalbital, Aspirin, and Caffeine—*See* Butalbital and Aspirin (Systemic), 431
Marplan—Isocarboxazid—*See* Antidepressants, Monoamine Oxidase (MAO) Inhibitor (Systemic), 242
Marthritic—Salsalate—*See* Salicylates (Systemic), 1421
Marvelon—Desogestrel and Ethinyl Estradiol—*See* Estrogens and Progestins (Oral Contraceptives) (Systemic), 774
Marzine—Cyclizine—*See* Meclizine/Buclizine/Cyclizine (Systemic), 1044
Masoprocol (Topical), 1032
Masporin Otic—Neomycin, Polymyxin B, and Hydrocortisone (Otic), 1172
Matulane—Procarbazine (Systemic), 1337
Mavik—Trandolapril (Systemic), MC-31
Maxafil—Menthyl Anthranilate—*See* Sunscreen Agents (Topical), 1510
Maxair—Pirbuterol—*See* Bronchodilators, Adrenergic (Inhalation), 406
Maxair Autohaler—Pirbuterol—*See* Bronchodilators, Adrenergic (Inhalation), 406
Maxaquin—Lomefloxacin—*See* Fluoroquinolones (Systemic), 815, MC-17
Max-Caro—Beta-carotene (Systemic), 392
Maxenal—Pseudoephedrine (Systemic), 1354
Maxeran—Metoclopramide (Systemic), 1091
Maxidex—Dexamethasone—*See* Corticosteroids (Ophthalmic), 591
Maxiflor—Diflorasone—*See* Corticosteroids—Medium to Very High Potency (Topical), 602
Maximum Strength Arthritis Foundation Safety Coated Aspirin—Aspirin—*See* Salicylates (Systemic), 1421
Maximum Strength Ascriptin—Aspirin, Buffered—*See* Salicylates (Systemic), 1421
Maximum Strength Cortaid—Hydrocortisone—*See* Corticosteroids—Low Potency (Topical), 600
Maximum Strength Doan's Analgesic Caplets—Magnesium Salicylate—*See* Salicylates (Systemic), 1421
Maximum Strength Gas Relief—Simethicone (Oral), 1446
Maximum Strength Mylanta Gas Relief—Simethicone (Oral), 1446
Maximum Strength Phazyme—Simethicone (Oral), 1446
Maxivate—Betamethasone—*See* Corticosteroids—Medium to Very High Potency (Topical), 602
MAXX—Latex Condoms—*See* Condoms, 571
MAXX Plus—Latex Condoms and Nonoxynol 9—*See* Condoms, 571
Maxzide—Triamterene and Hydrochlorothiazide—*See* Diuretics, Potassium-sparing and Hydrochlorothiazide (Systemic), 716, MC-31
Mazanor—Mazindol—*See* Appetite Suppressants (Systemic), 319
Mazindol—*See* Appetite Suppressants (Systemic), 319
MC 903—*See* Calcipotriene (Topical), 442
MCT Oil—Enteral Nutrition Formula, Modular—*See* Enteral Nutrition Formulas (Systemic), 741
m-DET—*See* Diethyltoluamide (Topical), 681
Measles, Mumps, and Rubella Virus Vaccine Live (Systemic), 1034
Measles and Rubella Virus Vaccine Live (Systemic), 1035
Measles Virus Vaccine Live (Systemic), 1037
Mebaral—Mephobarbital—*See* Barbiturates (Systemic), 352
Mebendazole (Systemic), 1038
Mecamylamine (Systemic), 1040
Mechlorethamine (Systemic), 1042
Meclan—Meclocycline—*See* Tetracyclines (Topical), 1538
Meclizine—*See* Meclizine/Buclizine/Cyclizine (Systemic), 1044, MC-18
Meclizine/Buclizine/Cyclizine (Systemic), 1044
Meclocycline—*See* Tetracyclines (Topical), 1538
Meclofenamate—*See* Anti-inflammatory Drugs, Nonsteroidal (Systemic), 301, MC-18
Meclofenamic acid—Meclofenamate—*See* Anti-inflammatory Drugs, Nonsteroidal (Systemic), 301
Meclomen—Meclofenamate—*See* Anti-inflammatory Drugs, Nonsteroidal (Systemic), 301
Meda Syrup Forte—Chlorpheniramine, Phenylephrine, Dextromethorphan, and Guaifenesin—*See* Cough/Cold Combinations (Systemic), 606
Med-Hist—Chlorpheniramine and Pseudoephedrine—*See* Antihistamines and Decongestants (Systemic), 281
Med-Hist Exp—Pseudoephedrine, Hydrocodone, and Guaifenesin—*See* Cough/Cold Combinations (Systemic), 606
Med-Hist HC—Chlorpheniramine, Phenylephrine, and Hydrocone—*See* Cough/Cold Combinations (Systemic), 606
Medi-Flu—Chlorpheniramine, Pseudoephedrine, Dextromethorphan, and Acetaminophen—*See* Cough/Cold Combinations (Systemic), 606
Medi-Flu Caplets—Chlorpheniramine, Pseudoephedrine, Dextromethorphan, and Acetaminophen—*See* Cough/Cold Combinations (Systemic), 606
Medigesic—Butalbital, Acetaminophen, and Caffeine—*See* Butalbital and Acetaminophen (Systemic), 428
Medihaler Ergotamine—Ergotamine—*See* Headache Medicines, Ergot Derivative–containing (Systemic), 879
Medihaler-Iso—Isoproterenol—*See* Bronchodilators, Adrenergic (Inhalation), 406
Medilax—Phenolphthalein—*See* Laxatives (Oral), 980
Mediplast—Salicylic Acid (Topical), 1429
Medipren—Ibuprofen—*See* Anti-inflammatory Drugs, Nonsteroidal (Systemic), 301
Medipren Caplets—Ibuprofen—*See* Anti-inflammatory Drugs, Nonsteroidal (Systemic), 301
Mediquell—Dextromethorphan (Systemic), 669
Mediquell Decongestant Formula—Pseudoephedrine and Dextromethorphan—*See* Cough/Cold Combinations (Systemic), 606
Medotar—Coal Tar (Topical), 558
Medralone-40—Methylprednisolone—*See* Corticosteroids—Glucocorticoid Effects (Systemic), 595
Medralone-80—Methylprednisolone—*See* Corticosteroids—Glucocorticoid Effects (Systemic), 595
Medrogestone—*See* Progestins—For Noncontraceptive Use (Systemic), 1347
Medrol—Methylprednisolone—*See* Corticosteroids—Glucocorticoid Effects (Systemic), 595, MC-19
Medrol Enpak—Methylprednisolone—*See* Corticosteroids—Glucocorticoid Effects (Systemic), 595
Medroxyprogesterone—*See* Conjugated Estrogens and Medroxyprogesterone for Ovarian Hormone Therapy (OHT) (Systemic), 574; *See also* Progestins—For Contraceptive Use (Systemic), 1343; Progestins—For Noncontraceptive Use (Systemic), 1347, MC-18
Medrysone—*See* Corticosteroids (Ophthalmic), 591
Med Tamoxifen—Tamoxifen (Systemic), 1520
Med Timolol—Timolol (Ophthalmic), 1737
Med Valproic—Valproic Acid (Systemic), 1611
Mefenamic Acid—*See* Anti-inflammatory Drugs, Nonsteroidal (Systemic), 301
Mefloquine (Systemic), 1046, MC-18
Mefoxin—Cefoxitin—*See* Cephalosporins (Systemic), 474
Mega-C/A Plus—Ascorbic Acid (Vitamin C) (Systemic), 324
Megace—Megestrol—*See* Progestins—For Noncontraceptive Use (Systemic), 1347, MC-18
Megace OS—Megestrol (Systemic), 1734
Megacillin—Penicillin G—*See* Penicillins (Systemic), 1245
Megestrol (Systemic), 1734; *See* also Progestins—For Noncontraceptive Use (Systemic), 1347, MC-18
Megral—Ergotamine, Caffeine, and Cyclizine—*See* Headache Medicines, Ergot Derivative–containing (Systemic), 879
Melfiat-105 Unicelles—Phendimetrazine—*See* Appetite Suppressants (Systemic), 319
Mellaril—Thioridazine—*See* Phenothiazines (Systemic), 1268, MC-30
Mellaril Concentrate—Thioridazine—*See* Phenothiazines (Systemic), 1268
Mellaril-S—Thioridazine—*See* Phenothiazines (Systemic), 1268
Melphalan (Systemic), 1049, 1734, MC-18
Menadiol—*See* Vitamin K (Systemic), 1638
Menaval-20—Estradiol—*See* Estrogens (Systemic), 766
Menest—Esterified Estrogens—*See* Estrogens (Systemic), 766, MC-11
Meni-D—Meclizine—*See* Meclizine/Buclizine/Cyclizine (Systemic), 1044
Meningococcal Polysaccharide Vaccine (Systemic), 1051
Menoject-L.A.—Testosterone and Estradiol—*See* Androgens and Estrogens (Systemic), 193
Menomune—Meningococcal Polysaccharide Vaccine (Systemic), 1051
Menotrophin—*See* Menotropins (Systemic), 1052
Menotropins (Systemic), 1052
Mentax—Butenafine (Topical), 1727
Mentholatum—Padimate O—*See* Sunscreen Agents (Topical), 1510
Menthyl Anthranilate—*See* Sunscreen Agents (Topical), 1510
Menthyl Anthranilate, Octocrylene, and Octyl Methoxycinnamate—*See* Sunscreen Agents (Topical), 1510
Menthyl Anthranilate, Octocrylene, Octyl Methoxycinnamate, and Oxybenzone—*See* Sunscreen Agents (Topical), 1510
Menthyl Anthranilate and Octyl Methoxycinnamate—*See* Sunscreen Agents (Topical), 1510
Menthyl Anthranilate, Octyl Methoxycinnamate, and Octyl Salicylate—*See* Sunscreen Agents (Topical), 1510
Menthyl Anthranilate, Octyl Methoxycinnamate, Octyl Salicylate, and Oxybenzone—*See* Sunscreen Agents (Topical), 1510
Menthyl Anthranilate, Octyl Methoxycinnamate, and Oxybenzone—*See* Sunscreen Agents (Topical), 1510
Menthyl Anthranilate and Padimate O—*See* Sunscreen Agents (Topical), 1510
Menthyl Anthranilate and Titanium Dioxide—*See* Sunscreen Agents (Topical), 1510
Menu Magic Instant Breakfast—Enteral Nutrition Formula, Milk-based—*See* Enteral Nutrition Formulas (Systemic), 741
Menu Magic Milk Shake—Enteral Nutrition Formula, Milk-based—*See* Enteral Nutrition Formulas (Systemic), 741
Mepacrine—*See* Quinacrine (Systemic), 1368
Mepenzolate—*See* Anticholinergics/Antispasmodics (Systemic), 225
Meperidine—*See* Narcotic Analgesics—For Pain Relief (Systemic), 1140, MC-18; *See also* Narcotic Analgesics—For Surgery and Obstetrics (Systemic), 1147
Mephenytoin—*See* Anticonvulsants, Hydantoin (Systemic), 235
Mephobarbital—*See* Barbiturates (Systemic), 352
Mephyton—Phytonadione—*See* Vitamin K (Systemic), 1638
Mepivacaine—*See* Anesthetics (Parenteral-Local), 202
Meprobamate (Systemic), 1054
Meprobamate and Aspirin (Systemic), 1056
Meprogesic—Meprobamate and Aspirin (Systemic), 1056
Meprogesic Q—Meprobamate and Aspirin (Systemic), 1056
Meprolone—Methylprednisolone—*See* Corticosteroids—Glucocorticoid Effects (Systemic), 595
Mepron—Atovaquone (Systemic), 333

N

Novo-rythro—Erythromycin Estolate—*See* Erythromycins (Systemic), 757; Erythromycin Stearate—*See* Erythromycins (Systemic), 757
Novo-rythro Encap—Erythromycin Base—*See* Erythromycins (Systemic), 757
Novo-Salmol—Albuterol—*See* Bronchodilators, Adrenergic (Inhalation), 406; Bronchodilators, Adrenergic (Oral/Injection), 412
Novosecobarb—Secobarbital—*See* Barbiturates (Systemic), 352
Novo-selegiline—Selegiline (Systemic), 1435
Novosemide—Furosemide—*See* Diuretics, Loop (Systemic), 709
Novosorbide—Isosorbide Dinitrate—*See* Nitrates—Oral (Systemic), 1186
Novo-Soxazole—Sulfisoxazole—*See* Sulfonamides (Systemic), 1493
Novospiroton—Spironolactone—*See* Diuretics, Potassium-sparing (Systemic), 713
Novo-Spirozine—Spironolactone and Hydrochlorothiazide—*See* Diuretics, Potassium-sparing and Hydrochlorothiazide (Systemic), 716
Novo-Sundac—Sulindac—*See* Anti-inflammatory Drugs, Nonsteroidal (Systemic), 301
Novo-Tamoxifen—Tamoxifen (Systemic), 1520
Novo-Terfenadine—Terfenadine—*See* Antihistamines (Systemic), 274
Novotetra—Tetracycline—*See* Tetracyclines (Systemic), 1533
Novo-Thalidone—Chlorthalidone—*See* Diuretics, Thiazide (Systemic), 719
Novo-Timol—Timolol—*See* Beta-adrenergic Blocking Agents (Systemic), 382; Timolol (Ophthalmic), 1737
Novo-Tolmetin—Tolmetin—*See* Anti-inflammatory Drugs, Nonsteroidal (Systemic), 301
Novo-Triamzide—Triamterene and Hydrochlorothiazide—*See* Diuretics, Potassium-sparing and Hydrochlorothiazide (Systemic), 716
Novo-Trimel—Sulfamethoxazole and Trimethoprim—*See* Sulfonamides and Trimethoprim (Systemic), 1501
Novo-Trimel D.S.—Sulfamethoxazole and Trimethoprim—*See* Sulfonamides and Trimethoprim (Systemic), 1501
Novo-Triolam—Triazolam—*See* Benzodiazepines (Systemic), 368
Novo-Tripramine—Trimipramine—*See* Antidepressants, Tricyclic (Systemic), 245
Novotriptyn—Amitriptyline—*See* Antidepressants, Tricyclic (Systemic), 245
Novo-Valproic—Valproic Acid (Systemic), 1611
Novo-Veramil—Verapamil—*See* Calcium Channel Blocking Agents (Systemic), 446
Novoxapam—Oxazepam—*See* Benzodiazepines (Systemic), 368
Noxzema Anti-Acne Gel—Salicylic Acid (Topical), 1429
Noxzema Anti-Acne Pads Maximum Strength—Salicylic Acid (Topical), 1429
Noxzema Anti-Acne Pads Regular Strength—Salicylic Acid (Topical), 1429
Noxzema Clear-ups Maximum Strength 10 Lotion—Benzoyl Peroxide (Topical), 377
Noxzema Clear-ups On-The-Spot 10 Lotion—Benzoyl Peroxide (Topical), 377
Noxzema Moisturizer—Octyl Methoxycinnamate and Phenylbenzimidazole—*See* Sunscreen Agents (Topical), 1510
Nozinan—Methotrimeprazine—*See* Phenothiazines (Systemic), 1268
Nozinan Liquid—Methotrimeprazine—*See* Phenothiazines (Systemic), 1268
Nozinan Oral Drops—Methotrimeprazine—*See* Phenothiazines (Systemic), 1268
NP-27 Cream—Tolnaftate (Topical), 1578
NPH Iletin—Insulin, Isophane—*See* Insulin (Systemic), 923
NPH Iletin I—Insulin, Isophane—*See* Insulin (Systemic), 923
NPH Iletin II—Insulin, Isophane—*See* Insulin (Systemic), 923
NPH Insulin—Insulin, Isophane—*See* Insulin (Systemic), 923
NPH insulin, NPH—Insulin, Isophane—*See* Insulin (Systemic), 923; Insulin, Isophane, Human—*See* Insulin (Systemic), 923
NPH-N—Insulin, Isophane—*See* Insulin (Systemic), 923
NP-27 Powder—Tolnaftate (Topical), 1578
NP-27 Solution—Tolnaftate (Topical), 1578
NP-27 Spray Powder—Tolnaftate (Topical), 1578
NTS—Nitroglycerin Transdermal Patches—*See* Nitrates—Topical (Systemic), 1192
NTZ Long Acting Decongestant Nasal Spray—Oxymetazoline (Nasal), 1225
NTZ Long Acting Decongestant Nose Drops—Oxymetazoline (Nasal), 1225
Nu-Alpraz—Alprazolam—*See* Benzodiazepines (Systemic), 368
Nu-Amoxi—Amoxicillin—*See* Penicillins (Systemic), 1245; Amoxicillin (Systemic), 1726
Nu-Ampi—Ampicillin—*See* Penicillins (Systemic), 1245
Nubain—Nalbuphine—*See* Narcotic Analgesics—For Pain Relief (Systemic), 1140; Narcotic Analgesics—For Surgery and Obstetrics (Systemic), 1147
NuBasics—Enteral Nutrition Formula, Polymeric—*See* Enteral Nutrition Formulas (Systemic), 741
NuBasics with Fiber—Enteral Nutrition Formula, Fiber-containing—*See* Enteral Nutrition Formulas (Systemic), 741
NuBasics Plus—Enteral Nutrition Formula, Polymeric—*See* Enteral Nutrition Formulas (Systemic), 741
NuBasics VHP—Enteral Nutrition Formula, Polymeric—*See* Enteral Nutrition Formulas (Systemic), 741
Nu-Cal—Calcium Carbonate—*See* Calcium Supplements (Systemic), 451
Nu-Carbamazepine—Carbamazepine (Systemic), 459
Nu-Cephalex—Cephalexin—*See* Cephalosporins (Systemic), 474
Nu-Cloxi—Cloxacillin—*See* Penicillins (Systemic), 1245
Nucochem—Pseudoephedrine and Codeine—*See* Cough/Cold Combinations (Systemic), 606
Nucochem Expectorant—Pseudoephedrine, Codeine, and Guaifenesin—*See* Cough/Cold Combinations (Systemic), 606
Nucochem Pediatric Expectorant—Pseudoephedrine, Codeine, and Guaifenesin—*See* Cough/Cold Combinations (Systemic), 606
Nucofed—Pseudoephedrine and Codeine—*See* Cough/Cold Combinations (Systemic), 606
Nucofed Expectorant—Pseudoephedrine, Codeine, and Guaifenesin—*See* Cough/Cold Combinations (Systemic), 606
Nucofed Pediatric Expectorant—Pseudoephedrine, Codeine, and Guaifenesin—*See* Cough/Cold Combinations (Systemic), 606
Nu-Cotrimox—Sulfamethoxazole and Trimethoprim—*See* Sulfonamides and Trimethoprim (Systemic), 1501
Nu-Cotrimox DS—Sulfamethoxazole and Trimethoprim—*See* Sulfonamides and Trimethoprim (Systemic), 1501
Nucotuss Expectorant—Pseudoephedrine, Codeine, and Guaifenesin—*See* Cough/Cold Combinations (Systemic), 606
Nucotuss Pediatric Expectorant—Pseudoephedrine, Codeine, and Guaifenesin—*See* Cough/Cold Combinations (Systemic), 606
Nu-Diclo—Diclofenac—*See* Anti-inflammatory Drugs, Nonsteroidal (Systemic), 301
Nu-Diltiaz—Diltiazem—*See* Calcium Channel Blocking Agents (Systemic), 446
Nu-Flurbiprofen—Flurbiprofen—*See* Anti-inflammatory Drugs, Nonsteroidal (Systemic), 301
Nu-Glyburide—Glyburide—*See* Antidiabetic Agents, Sulfonylurea (Systemic), 251
Nu-Ibuprofen—Ibuprofen—*See* Anti-inflammatory Drugs, Nonsteroidal (Systemic), 301
Nu-Indo—Indomethacin—*See* Anti-inflammatory Drugs, Nonsteroidal (Systemic), 301
Nu-Iron—Iron-Polysaccharide—*See* Iron Supplements (Systemic), 946
Nu-Iron 150—Iron-Polysaccharide—*See* Iron Supplements (Systemic), 946
Nujol—Mineral Oil—*See* Laxatives (Oral), 980
Nu-Levocarb—Carbidopa and Levodopa (Systemic), 1727
Nu-Loraz—Lorazepam—*See* Benzodiazepines (Systemic), 368
NuLYTELY—Polyethylene Glycol and Electrolytes (Local), 1309
NuLYTELY, Cherry Flavor—Polyethylene Glycol and Electrolytes (Local), 1309
Nu-Medopa—Methyldopa (Systemic), 1082, 1734
Nu-Metop—Metoprolol (Systemic), 1734
Numorphan—Oxymorphone—*See* Narcotic Analgesics—For Pain Relief (Systemic), 1140
Numzident—Benzocaine—*See* Anesthetics (Dental), 197
Num-Zit Gel—Benzocaine—*See* Anesthetics (Dental), 197
Num-Zit Lotion—Benzocaine—*See* Anesthetics (Dental), 197
Nu-Naprox—Naproxen—*See* Anti-inflammatory Drugs, Nonsteroidal (Systemic), 301
Nu-Nifed—Nifedipine—*See* Calcium Channel Blocking Agents (Systemic), 446
Nu-Pen-VK—Penicillin V—*See* Penicillins (Systemic), 1245
Nupercainal—Dibucaine—*See* Anesthetics (Rectal), 204
Nupercainal Cream—Dibucaine—*See* Anesthetics (Topical), 206
Nupercainal Ointment—Dibucaine—*See* Anesthetics (Topical), 206
Nu-Pirox—Piroxicam—*See* Anti-inflammatory Drugs, Nonsteroidal (Systemic), 301
Nuprin—Ibuprofen—*See* Anti-inflammatory Drugs, Nonsteroidal (Systemic), 301
Nuprin Caplets—Ibuprofen—*See* Anti-inflammatory Drugs, Nonsteroidal (Systemic), 301
Nursoy—Infant Formulas, Soy-based—*See* Infant Formulas (Systemic), 920
Nu-Tetra—Tetracycline—*See* Tetracyclines (Systemic), 1533
Nu-Timolol—Timolol (Ophthalmic), 1737
Nutracort—Hydrocortisone—*See* Corticosteroids—Low Potency (Topical), 600
Nutramigen—Infant Formulas, Hypoallergenic—*See* Infant Formulas (Systemic), 920
Nutren 1.0—Enteral Nutrition Formula, Polymeric—*See* Enteral Nutrition Formulas (Systemic), 741
Nutren 1.5—Enteral Nutrition Formula, Polymeric—*See* Enteral Nutrition Formulas (Systemic), 741
Nutren 2.0—Enteral Nutrition Formula, Disease-specific—*See* Enteral Nutrition Formulas (Systemic), 741; Enteral Nutrition Formula, Polymeric—*See* Enteral Nutrition Formulas (Systemic), 741
Nutren 1.0 with Fiber—Enteral Nutrition Formula, Fiber-containing—*See* Enteral Nutrition Formulas (Systemic), 741
Nu-Triazo—Triazolam—*See* Benzodiazepines (Systemic), 368
NutriHep—Enteral Nutrition Formula, Disease-specific—*See* Enteral Nutrition Formulas (Systemic), 741
Nutrilan—Enteral Nutrition Formula, Polymeric—*See* Enteral Nutrition Formulas (Systemic), 741
NutriSource—Enteral Nutrition Formula, Fiber-containing—*See* Enteral Nutrition Formulas (Systemic), 741
NutriSource HN—Enteral Nutrition Formula, Fiber-containing—*See* Enteral Nutrition Formulas (Systemic), 741
NutriVent—Enteral Nutrition Formula, Disease-specific—*See* Enteral Nutrition Formulas (Systemic), 741
Nutropin—Somatropin, Recombinant—*See* Growth Hormone (Systemic), 856; Somatropin, Recombinant (Systemic), 1736
Nutropin AQ—Somatropin, Recombinant (Systemic), 1736
Nu-Verap—Verapamil—*See* Calcium Channel Blocking Agents (Systemic), 446
Nyaderm—Nystatin (Topical), 1199; Nystatin (Vaginal), 1200
Nydrazid—Isoniazid (Systemic), 952
Nystatin (Oral), 1197
Nystatin (Topical), 1199, 1735
Nystatin (Vaginal), 1200
Nystatin and Triamcinolone (Topical), 1201
Nystex—Nystatin (Oral), 1197; Nystatin (Topical), 1199
Nystop—Nystatin (Topical), 1735
Nytcold Medicine—Doxylamine, Pseudoephedrine, Dextromethorphan, and Acetaminophen—*See* Cough/Cold Combinations (Systemic), 606
Nytilax—Sennosides—*See* Laxatives (Oral), 980
Nytime Cold Medicine Liquid—Doxylamine, Pseudoephedrine, Dextromethorphan, and Acetaminophen—*See* Cough/Cold Combinations (Systemic), 606
Nytol with DPH—Diphenhydramine—*See* Antihistamines (Systemic), 274
Nytol Maximum Strength—Diphenhydramine—*See* Antihistamines (Systemic), 274

O

OB—Testosterone and Estradiol—*See* Androgens and Estrogens (Systemic), 193
Obalan—Phendimetrazine—*See* Appetite Suppressants (Systemic), 319
Obe-Nix—Phentermine—*See* Appetite Suppressants (Systemic), 319

P

Pherazine DM—Promethazine and Dextromethorphan—*See* Cough/Cold Combinations (Systemic), 606
Pherazine VC—Promethazine and Phenylephrine—*See* Antihistamines and Decongestants (Systemic), 281
Pherazine VC with Codeine—Promethazine, Phenylephrine, and Codeine—*See* Cough/Cold Combinations (Systemic), 606
Pheryl-E—Vitamin E (Systemic), 1635
Phillips'—Magnesium Hydroxide—*See* Antacids (Oral), 219
Phillips' Chewable—Magnesium Hydroxide—*See* Antacids (Oral), 219; Laxatives (Oral), 980
Phillips' Chewable Tablets—Magnesium Hydroxide—*See* Magnesium Supplements (Systemic), 1024
Phillips' Concentrated—Magnesium Hydroxide—*See* Laxatives (Oral), 980
Phillips' Concentrated Double Strength—Magnesium Hydroxide—*See* Antacids (Oral), 219
Phillips' Gelcaps—Phenolphthalein and Docusate—*See* Laxatives (Oral), 980
Phillips' LaxCaps—Phenolphthalein and Docusate—*See* Laxatives (Oral), 980
Phillips' Magnesia Tablets—Magnesium Hydroxide—*See* Laxatives (Oral), 980; Magnesium Supplements (Systemic), 1024
Phillips' Milk of Magnesia—Magnesium Hydroxide—*See* Laxatives (Oral), 980; Magnesium Supplements (Systemic), 1024
pHisoAc BP 10 Cream—Benzoyl Peroxide (Topical), 377
Phos-Flur—Sodium Fluoride (Systemic), 1454
PhosLo—Calcium Acetate (Oral), 1684; Calcium Acetate (Systemic), MC-4
Phosphates (Systemic), 1287
Phosphocol P 32—Chromic Phosphate P 32 (Therapeutic), 513
Phospholine Iodide—Echothiophate—*See* Antiglaucoma Agents, Cholinergic, Long-acting (Ophthalmic), 269
Phosphonoformic acid—*See* Foscarnet (Systemic), 827
Photofrin—Profimer (Injection), 1712
Photoplex Plus Sunscreen—Avobenzone, Octocrylene, Octyl Salicylate, and Oxybenzone—*See* Sunscreen Agents (Topical), 1510
Phrenilin—Butalbital and Acetaminophen (Systemic), 428
Phrenilin Forte—Butalbital and Acetaminophen (Systemic), 428
Phyllocontin—Aminophylline—*See* Bronchodilators, Theophylline (Systemic), 418
Phyllocontin-350—Aminophylline—*See* Bronchodilators, Theophylline (Systemic), 418
Physostigmine (Ophthalmic), 1291
Phytomenadione—Phytonadione—*See* Vitamin K (Systemic), 1638
Phytonadione—*See* Vitamin K (Systemic), 1638
Pilagan—Pilocarpine (Ophthalmic), 1292
Pilocar—Pilocarpine (Ophthalmic), 1292
Pilocarpine (Ophthalmic), 1292
Pilocarpine (Systemic), 1295
Pilopine HS—Pilocarpine (Ophthalmic), 1292
Piloptic—Pilocarpine (Ophthalmic), 1292
Piloptic-1—Pilocarpine (Ophthalmic), 1292
Piloptic-2—Pilocarpine (Ophthalmic), 1292
Piloptic-3—Pilocarpine (Ophthalmic), 1292
Piloptic-4—Pilocarpine (Ophthalmic), 1292
Piloptic-6—Pilocarpine (Ophthalmic), 1292
Pilostat—Pilocarpine (Ophthalmic), 1292
Pima—Potassium Iodide (Systemic), 1310
Pimaricin—*See* Natamycin (Ophthalmic), 1159
Pimozide (Systemic), 1296
Pindolol—*See* Beta-adrenergic Blocking Agents (Systemic), 382, MC-25
Pindolol and Hydrochlorothiazide—*See* Beta-adrenergic Blocking Agents and Thiazide Diuretics (Systemic), 388
Piperacillin—*See* Penicillins (Systemic), 1245
Piperacillin and Tazobactam—*See* Penicillins and Beta-lactamase Inhibitors (Systemic), 1251
Piperazine (Systemic), 1299
Piperazine estrone sulfate—Estropipate—*See* Estrogens (Systemic), 766; Estrogens (Vaginal), 771
Piportil L_4—Pipotiazine—*See* Phenothiazines (Systemic), 1268
Pipotiazine—*See* Phenothiazines (Systemic), 1268
Pipracil—Piperacillin—*See* Penicillins (Systemic), 1245
Pirbuterol—*See* Bronchodilators, Adrenergic (Inhalation), 406
Pirenzepine—*See* Anticholinergics/Antispasmodics (Systemic), 225
Piroxicam—*See* Anti-inflammatory Drugs, Nonsteroidal (Systemic), 301, MC-25
Pitocin—Oxytocin (Systemic), 1228
Pitressin—Vasopressin (Systemic), 1617
Pitrex Cream—Tolnaftate (Topical), 1578
Pivampicillin—*See* Penicillins (Systemic), 1245
Pivmecillinam—*See* Penicillins (Systemic), 1245
Pizotyline (Systemic), 1736
Placidyl—Ethchlorvynol (Systemic), 782
Plague Vaccine (Systemic), 1301
Plaquenil—Hydroxychloroquine (Systemic), 901, MC-14
Plasma thromboplastin component (PTC)—*See* Factor IX (Systemic), 793
Platinol—Cisplatin (Systemic), 523
Platinol-AQ—Cisplatin (Systemic), 523
Plegine—Phendimetrazine—*See* Appetite Suppressants (Systemic), 319
Plendil—Felodipine—*See* Calcium Channel Blocking Agents (Systemic), 446, MC-12
Plicamycin (Systemic), 1302
PMS-Acetaminophen with Codeine—Acetaminophen and Codeine—*See* Narcotic Analgesics and Acetaminophen (Systemic), 1149
PMS Alumina, Magnesia, and Simethicone—Alumina, Magnesia, and Simethicone—*See* Antacids (Oral), 219
PMS-ASA—Aspirin—*See* Salicylates (Systemic), 1421
PMS-Baclofen—Baclofen (Systemic), 350
PMS Benztropine—Benztropine—*See* Antidyskinetics (Systemic), 257
PMS-Bisacodyl—Bisacodyl—*See* Laxatives (Oral), 980, 986; Laxatives (Rectal), 986
PMS-Bismuth Subsalicylate—Bismuth Subsalicylate (Oral), 397
PMS-Chloral Hydrate—Chloral Hydrate (Systemic), 484
PMS-Dexamethasone Sodium Phosphate—Dexamethasone—*See* Corticosteroids (Ophthalmic), 591
PMS Diazepam—Diazepam—*See* Benzodiazepines (Systemic), 368
PMS-Dimenhydrinate—Dimenhydrinate—*See* Antihistamines (Systemic), 274
PMS-Docusate Calcium—Docusate—*See* Laxatives (Oral), 980
PMS-Docusate Sodium—Phenolphthalein and Docusate—*See* Laxatives (Oral), 980
PMS Dopazide—Methyldopa and Hydrochlorothiazide—*See* Methyldopa and Thiazide Diuretics (Systemic), 1084
PMS Egozinc—Zinc Sulfate—*See* Zinc Supplements (Systemic), 1652
PMS-Ferrous Sulfate—Ferrous Sulfate—*See* Iron Supplements (Systemic), 946
PMS Haloperidol—Haloperidol (Systemic), 874
PMS-Hydromorphone—Hydromorphone—*See* Narcotic Analgesics—For Pain Relief (Systemic), 1140
PMS-Hydromorphone Syrup—Hydromorphone—*See* Narcotic Analgesics—For Pain Relief (Systemic), 1140
PMS Isoniazid—Isoniazid (Systemic), 952
PMS-Lactulose—Lactulose—*See* Laxatives (Oral), 980
PMS Levazine—Perphenazine and Amitriptyline (Systemic), 1264
PMS-Levothyroxine Sodium—Levothyroxine—*See* Thyroid Hormones (Systemic), 1568
PMS Lindane—Lindane (Topical), 1005
PMS-Loperamide Hydrochloride—Loperamide (Oral), 1013
PMS-Methylphenidate—Methylphenidate (Systemic), 1087
PMS Nystatin—Nystatin (Oral), 1197
PMS-Oxtriphylline—Oxtriphylline—*See* Bronchodilators, Xanthine-derivative (Systemic), 418
PMS Perphenazine—Perphenazine—*See* Phenothiazines (Systemic), 1268
PMS-Phosphates—Sodium Phosphate—*See* Laxatives (Oral), 980
PMS-Piroxicam—Piroxicam—*See* Anti-inflammatory Drugs, Nonsteroidal (Systemic), 301
PMS Primidone—Primidone (Systemic), 1327
PMS Prochlorperazine—Prochlorperazine—*See* Phenothiazines (Systemic), 1268
PMS Procyclidine—Procyclidine—*See* Antidyskinetics (Systemic), 257
PMS-Progesterone—Progesterone—*See* Progestins—For Noncontraceptive Use (Systemic), 1347
pms Propranolol—Propranolol—*See* Beta-adrenergic Blocking Agents (Systemic), 382
pms-Pyrazinamide—Pyrazinamide (Systemic), 1357
PMS-Sennosides—Sennosides—*See* Laxatives (Oral), 980
PMS-Sodium cromoglycate—Cromolyn (Inhalation), 619
PMS-Sulfasalazine—Sulfasalazine (Systemic), 1486
PMS-Sulfasalazine E.C.—Sulfasalazine (Systemic), 1486
PMS-Theophylline—Theophylline—*See* Bronchodilators, Theophylline (Systemic), 418
PMS Thioridazine—Thioridazine—*See* Phenothiazines (Systemic), 1268
PMS Trifluoperazine—Trifluoperazine—*See* Phenothiazines (Systemic), 1268
PMS Trihexyphenidyl—Trihexyphenidyl—*See* Antidyskinetics (Systemic), 257
pms-Valproic Acid—Valproic Acid (Systemic), 1611
pms-Valproic Acid E.C.—Valproic Acid (Systemic), 1611
PMS-Yohimbine—Yohimbine (Systemic), 1645
Pneumococcal Vaccine Polyvalent (Systemic), 1304
Pneumomist—Guaifenesin (Systemic), 858
Pneumopent—Pentamidine (Inhalation), 1254
Pneumotussin HC—Hydrocodone and Guaifenesin—*See* Cough/Cold Combinations (Systemic), 606
Pneumovax 23—Pneumococcal Vaccine Polyvalent (Systemic), 1304
P.N. Ophthalmic—Neomycin, Polymyxin B, and Gramicidin (Ophthalmic), 1169
Pnu-Imune 23—Pneumococcal Vaccine Polyvalent (Systemic), 1304
Podocon-25—Podophyllum (Topical), 1305
Podofilox (Topical), 1736
Podofin—Podophyllum (Topical), 1305
Podophyllum (Topical), 1305
Poladex T.D.—Dexchlorpheniramine—*See* Antihistamines (Systemic), 274
Polaramine—Dexchlorpheniramine—*See* Antihistamines (Systemic), 274
Polaramine Expectorant—Dexchlorpheniramine, Pseudoephedrine, and Guaifenesin—*See* Cough/Cold Combinations (Systemic), 606
Polaramine Repetabs—Dexchlorpheniramine—*See* Antihistamines (Systemic), 274
Poliovirus Vaccine (Systemic), 1307
Poliovirus Vaccine Inactivated—*See* Poliovirus Vaccine (Systemic), 1307
Poliovirus Vaccine Inactivated Enhanced Potency—*See* Poliovirus Vaccine (Systemic), 1307
Poliovirus Vaccine Live Oral—*See* Poliovirus Vaccine (Systemic), 1307
Polocaine—Mepivacaine—*See* Anesthetics (Parenteral-Local), 202
Polocaine-MPF—Mepivacaine—*See* Anesthetics (Parenteral-Local), 202
Poloxamer 188—*See* Laxatives (Oral), 980
Polycarbophil—*See* Laxatives (Oral), 980
Polycillin—Ampicillin—*See* Penicillins (Systemic), 1245
Polycillin-N—Ampicillin—*See* Penicillins (Systemic), 1245
Polycitra-K—Potassium Citrate and Citric Acid—*See* Citrates (Systemic), 525
Polycitra-K Crystals—Potassium Citrate and Citric Acid—*See* Citrates (Systemic), 525
Polycitra-LC—Tricitrates—*See* Citrates (Systemic), 525
Polycitra Syrup—Tricitrates—*See* Citrates (Systemic), 525
Polycose—Enteral Nutrition Formula, Modular—*See* Enteral Nutrition Formulas (Systemic), 741
Poly-D—Pheniramine, Phenyltoloxamine, Pyrilamine, and Phenylpropanolamine—*See* Antihistamines and Decongestants (Systemic), 281
Poly D—Pheniramine, Phenyltoloxamine, Pyrilamine, and Phenylpropanolamine—*See* Antihistamines and Decongestants (Systemic), 281
Polydimethylsiloxane—*See* Silicone Oil 5000 Centistokes (Parenteral-Local), 1443
Polyethylene Glycol and Electrolytes (Local), 1309
Polygam—Immune Globulin Intravenous (Human) (Systemic), 917
Polygesic—Hydrocodone and Acetaminophen—*See* Narcotic Analgesics and Acetaminophen (Systemic), 1149
Poly Hist Forte—Chlorpheniramine, Pyrilamine, Phenylephrine, and Phenylpropanolamine—*See* Antihistamines and Decongestants (Systemic), 281

R

S

Synphasic—Norethindrone and Ethinyl Estradiol—*See* Estrogens and Progestins (Oral Contraceptives) (Systemic), 774
Syn-Pindolol—Pindolol—*See* Beta-adrenergic Blocking Agents (Systemic), 382
SYN-Rx AM Treatment—Pseudoephedrine and Guaifenesin—*See* Cough/Cold Combinations (Systemic), 606
Synthroid—Levothyroxine—*See* Thyroid Hormones (Systemic), 1568, MC-17
Syntocinon—Oxytocin (Systemic), 1228
Synvinolin—Simvastatin—*See* HMG-CoA Reductase Inhibitors (Systemic), 893
Syprine—Trientine (Systemic), 1589
Syracol CF—Dextromethorphan and Guaifenesin—*See* Cough/Cold Combinations (Systemic), 606

T

206 Shake—Enteral Nutrition Formula, Milk-based—*See* Enteral Nutrition Formulas (Systemic), 741
217—Aspirin and Caffeine—*See* Salicylates (Systemic), 1421
217 Strong—Aspirin and Caffeine—*See* Salicylates (Systemic), 1421
222—Aspirin, Codeine, and Caffeine—*See* Narcotic Analgesics and Aspirin (Systemic), 1153
282—Aspirin, Codeine, and Caffeine—*See* Narcotic Analgesics and Aspirin (Systemic), 1153
292—Aspirin, Codeine, and Caffeine—*See* Narcotic Analgesics and Aspirin (Systemic), 1153
Tac-3—Triamcinolone—*See* Corticosteroids—Glucocorticoid Effects (Systemic), 595
Tacaryl—Methdilazine—*See* Antihistamines, Phenothiazine-derivative (Systemic), 295
TACE—Chlorotrianisene—*See* Estrogens (Systemic), 766
Tacrine (Systemic), 1516, MC-29
Tacrolimus (Systemic), 1518, MC-29
Tagamet—Cimetidine—*See* Histamine H_2-receptor Antagonists (Systemic), 889, MC-7
Tagamet HB 200—Cimetidine—*See* Histamine H_2-receptor Antagonists (Systemic), 889
Tagamet HB—Cimetidine—*See* Histamine H_2-receptor Antagonists (Systemic), 889
Talacen—Pentazocine and Acetaminophen—*See* Narcotic Analgesics and Acetaminophen (Systemic), 1149, MC-24
Talwin—Pentazocine—*See* Narcotic Analgesics—For Pain Relief (Systemic), 1140
Talwin Compound—Pentazocine and Aspirin—*See* Narcotic Analgesics and Aspirin (Systemic), 1153
Talwin-Nx—Pentazocine—*See* Narcotic Analgesics—For Pain Relief (Systemic), 1140, MC-24
Tambocor—Flecainide (Systemic), 807, MC-12
Tamine S.R.—Brompheniramine, Phenylephrine, and Phenylpropanolamine—*See* Antihistamines and Decongestants (Systemic), 281
Tamofen—Tamoxifen (Systemic), 1520
Tamone—Tamoxifen (Systemic), 1520
Tamoplex—Tamoxifen (Systemic), 1520
Tamoxifen (Systemic), 1520, MC-29
Tanafed—Chlorpheniramine and Pseudoephedrine—*See* Antihistamines and Decongestants (Systemic), 281
Tanoral—Chlorpheniramine, Pyrilamine, and Phenylephrine—*See* Antihistamines and Decongestants (Systemic), 281
Tantacol DM—Pheniramine, Pyrilamine, Phenylpropanolamine, and Dextromethorphan—*See* Cough/Cold Combinations (Systemic), 606
Tanta Cough Syrup—Dextromethorphan and Guaifenesin—*See* Cough/Cold Combinations (Systemic), 606
Tantum—Benzydamine (Oral), 1726
Tapanol Extra Strength Caplets—Acetaminophen (Systemic), 129
Tapanol Extra Strength Tablets—Acetaminophen (Systemic), 129
Tapazole—Methimazole—*See* Antithyroid Agents (Systemic), 316
Taractan—Chlorprothixene—*See* Thioxanthenes (Systemic), 1563
Taraphilic—Coal Tar (Topical), 558
Tarbonis—Coal Tar (Topical), 558
Tar Doak—Coal Tar (Topical), 558
Tarka—Trandolapril and Verapamil (Systemic), MC-31
Tarpaste—Coal Tar (Topical), 558
Tarpaste 'Doak'—Coal Tar (Topical), 558
Tasty Shake—Enteral Nutrition Formula, Milk-based—*See* Enteral Nutrition Formulas (Systemic), 741
Tavist—Clemastine—*See* Antihistamines (Systemic), 274
Tavist-1—Clemastine—*See* Antihistamines (Systemic), 274
Tavist-D—Clemastine and Phenylpropanolamine—*See* Antihistamines and Decongestants (Systemic), 281
Taxol—Paclitaxel (Systemic), 1230
Tazicef—Ceftazidime—*See* Cephalosporins (Systemic), 474
Tazidime—Ceftazidime—*See* Cephalosporins (Systemic), 474
Tazocin—Piperacillin and Tazobactam—*See* Penicillins and Beta-lactamase Inhibitors (Systemic), 1251
3TC—Lamivudine (Systemic), 975
T-Cypionate—Testosterone—*See* Androgens (Systemic), 188
Td—Tetanus and Diphtheria Toxoids for Adult Use—*See* Diphtheria and Tetanus Toxoids (Systemic), 695
T/Derm Tar Emollient—Coal Tar (Topical), 558
T-Diet—Phentermine—*See* Appetite Suppressants (Systemic), 319
Tearisol—Hydroxypropyl Methylcellulose (Ophthalmic), 905
Tears Naturale—Hydroxypropyl Methylcellulose (Ophthalmic), 905
Tears Naturale II—Hydroxypropyl Methylcellulose (Ophthalmic), 905
Tears Naturale Free—Hydroxypropyl Methylcellulose (Ophthalmic), 905
Tears Renewed—Hydroxypropyl Methylcellulose (Ophthalmic), 905
Tebamide—Trimethobenzamide (Systemic), 1593
Tebrazid—Pyrazinamide (Systemic), 1357
Technetium Tc 99m Albumin—*See* Radiopharmaceuticals (Diagnostic), 1380
Technetium Tc 99m Albumin Aggregated—*See* Radiopharmaceuticals (Diagnostic), 1380
Technetium Tc 99m Albumin Colloid—*See* Radiopharmaceuticals (Diagnostic), 1380
Technetium Tc 99m Arcitumomab (Systemic), 1737
Technetium Tc 99m Bicisate—*See* Radiopharmaceuticals (Diagnostic), 1380
Technetium Tc 99m Disofenin—*See* Radiopharmaceuticals (Diagnostic), 1380
Technetium Tc 99m Exametazime—*See* Radiopharmaceuticals (Diagnostic), 1380
Technetium Tc 99m Gluceptate—*See* Radiopharmaceuticals (Diagnostic), 1380
Technetium Tc 99m Lidofenin—*See* Radiopharmaceuticals (Diagnostic), 1380
Technetium Tc 99m Mebrofenin—*See* Radiopharmaceuticals (Diagnostic), 1380
Technetium Tc 99m Medronate—*See* Radiopharmaceuticals (Diagnostic), 1380
Technetium Tc 99m Mertiatide—*See* Radiopharmaceuticals (Diagnostic), 1380
Technetium Tc 99m Nofetumomab Merpentan (Systemic), 1737
Technetium Tc 99m Oxidronate—*See* Radiopharmaceuticals (Diagnostic), 1380
Technetium Tc 99m Pentetate—*See* Radiopharmaceuticals (Diagnostic), 1380
Technetium Tc 99m Pyrophosphate—*See* Radiopharmaceuticals (Diagnostic), 1380
Technetium Tc 99m (Pyro- and trimeta-) Phosphates—*See* Radiopharmaceuticals (Diagnostic), 1380
Technetium Tc 99m Sestamibi—*See* Radiopharmaceuticals (Diagnostic), 1380
Technetium Tc 99m Succimer—*See* Radiopharmaceuticals (Diagnostic), 1380
Technetium Tc 99m Sulfur Colloid—*See* Radiopharmaceuticals (Diagnostic), 1380
Technetium Tc 99m Teboroxime—*See* Radiopharmaceuticals (Diagnostic), 1380
Technetium Tc 99m Tetrofosmin —*See* Radiopharmaceuticals (Diagnostic), 1380
Tecnal—Butalbital, Aspirin, and Caffeine—*See* Butalbital and Aspirin (Systemic), 431
Tecnal-C 1/4—Butalbital, Aspirin, Caffeine, and Codeine—*See* Barbiturates, Aspirin, and Codeine (Systemic), 358
Tecnal-C 1/2—Butalbital, Aspirin, Caffeine, and Codeine—*See* Barbiturates, Aspirin, and Codeine (Systemic), 358
Tedelparin—*See* Dalteparin (Systemic), 649
Tedrigen—Theophylline, Ephedrine, and Phenobarbital (Systemic), 1546
Teejel—Choline Salicylate and Cetyl-dimethylbenzyl-ammonium Chloride (Oral), 1728
Teev—Testosterone and Estradiol—*See* Androgens and Estrogens (Systemic), 193
Tegamide—Trimethobenzamide (Systemic), 1593
Tega-Vert—Dimenhydrinate—*See* Antihistamines (Systemic), 274
Tegison—Etretinate (Systemic), 789
Tegopen—Cloxacillin—*See* Penicillins (Systemic), 1245
Tegretol—Carbamazepine (Systemic), 459, MC-5
Tegretol Chewtabs—Carbamazepine (Systemic), 459
Tegretol CR—Carbamazepine (Systemic), 459
Tegretol-XR—Carbamazepine (Systemic), 459, MC-5
Tegrin Lotion for Psoriasis—Coal Tar (Topical), 558
Tegrin Medicated Cream Shampoo—Coal Tar (Topical), 558
Tegrin Medicated Shampoo Concentrated Gel—Coal Tar (Topical), 558
Tegrin Medicated Shampoo Extra Conditioning Formula—Coal Tar (Topical), 558
Tegrin Medicated Shampoo Herbal Formula—Coal Tar (Topical), 558
Tegrin Medicated Shampoo Original Formula—Coal Tar (Topical), 558
Tegrin Medicated Soap for Psoriasis—Coal Tar (Topical), 558
Tegrin Skin Cream for Psoriasis—Coal Tar (Topical), 558
Telachlor—Chlorpheniramine—*See* Antihistamines (Systemic), 274
Teladar—Betamethasone—*See* Corticosteroids—Medium to Very High Potency (Topical), 602
Teldrin—Chlorpheniramine—*See* Antihistamines (Systemic), 274
Teldrin 12 Hour Allergy Relief—Chlorpheniramine and Phenylpropanolamine—*See* Antihistamines and Decongestants (Systemic), 281
Telepaque—Iopanoic Acid—*See* Cholecystographic Agents, Oral (Diagnostic), 508
Temaril—Trimeprazine—*See* Antihistamines, Phenothiazine-derivative (Systemic), 295
Temazepam—*See* Benzodiazepines (Systemic), 368, MC-29
Temazin Cold—Chlorpheniramine and Phenylpropanolamine—*See* Antihistamines and Decongestants (Systemic), 281
Temovate—Clobetasol—*See* Corticosteroids—Medium to Very High Potency (Topical), 602
Temovate Scalp Application—Clobetasol—*See* Corticosteroids—Medium to Very High Potency (Topical), 602
Tempo—Alumina, Magnesia, Calcium Carbonate, and Simethicone—*See* Antacids (Oral), 219
Tempra—Acetaminophen (Systemic), 129
Tempra Caplets—Acetaminophen (Systemic), 129
Tempra Chewable Tablets—Acetaminophen (Systemic), 129
Tempra Drops—Acetaminophen (Systemic), 129
Tempra D.S.—Acetaminophen (Systemic), 129
Tempra, Infants'—Acetaminophen (Systemic), 129
Tempra Syrup—Acetaminophen (Systemic), 129
Tencet—Butalbital, Acetaminophen, and Caffeine—*See* Butalbital and Acetaminophen (Systemic), 428
Tencon—Butalbital and Acetaminophen (Systemic), 428
Tenex—Guanfacine (Systemic), 868, MC-14
Teniposide (Injection), 1718
Teniposide (Systemic), 1737
Ten-K—Potassium Chloride—*See* Potassium Supplements (Systemic), 1313
Tenoretic—Atenolol and Chlorthalidone—*See* Beta-adrenergic Blocking Agents and Thiazide Diuretics (Systemic), 388, MC-3
Tenormin—Atenolol—*See* Beta-adrenergic Blocking Agents (Systemic), 382, MC-3
Tenoxicam—*See* Anti-inflammatory Drugs, Nonsteroidal (Systemic), 301
Tenuate—Diethylpropion—*See* Appetite Suppressants (Systemic), 319, MC-9
Tepanil Ten-Tab—Diethylpropion—*See* Appetite Suppressants (Systemic), 319
Teramine—Phentermine—*See* Appetite Suppressants (Systemic), 319
Terazol 3—Terconazole—*See* Antifungals, Azole (Vaginal), 266
Terazol 7—Terconazole—*See* Antifungals, Azole (Vaginal), 266
Terazol 3 Dual-Pak—Terconazole—*See* Antifungals, Azole (Vaginal), 266
Terazol 3 Vaginal Ovules—Terconazole—*See* Antifungals, Azole (Vaginal), 266
Terazosin (Systemic), 1522, MC-29
Terbinafine (Systemic), 1524, 1737, MC-29

Tussirex—Pheniramine, Phenylephrine, Codeine, Sodium Citrate, Sodium Salicylate, and Caffeine—*See* Cough/Cold Combinations (Systemic), 606
Tuss-LA—Pseudoephedrine and Guaifenesin—*See* Cough/Cold Combinations (Systemic), 606
Tusso-DM—Dextromethorphan and Iodinated Glycerol—*See* Cough/Cold Combinations (Systemic), 606
Tussogest—Phenylpropanolamine and Caramiphen—*See* Cough/Cold Combinations (Systemic), 606
Tuss-Ornade Spansules—Chlorpheniramine, Phenylpropanolamine, and Caramiphen—*See* Cough/Cold Combinations (Systemic), 606
Tusstat—Diphenhydramine—*See* Antihistamines (Systemic), 274
Twilite Caplets—Diphenhydramine—*See* Antihistamines (Systemic), 274
Twin-K—Potassium Gluconate and Potassium Citrate—*See* Potassium Supplements (Systemic), 1313
TwoCal HN—Enteral Nutrition Formula, Polymeric—*See* Enteral Nutrition Formulas (Systemic), 741
Two-Dyne—Butalbital, Acetaminophen, and Caffeine—*See* Butalbital and Acetaminophen (Systemic), 428
Ty-Cold Cold Formula—Chlorpheniramine, Pseudoephedrine, Dextromethorphan, and Acetaminophen—*See* Cough/Cold Combinations (Systemic), 606
Tylenol Allergy Sinus Medication Extra Strength Caplets—Chlorpheniramine, Pseudoephedrine, and Acetaminophen—*See* Antihistamines, Decongestants, and Analgesics (Systemic), 286
Tylenol Allergy Sinus Medication Maximum Strength Caplets—Chlorpheniramine, Pseudoephedrine, and Acetaminophen—*See* Antihistamines, Decongestants, and Analgesics (Systemic), 286
Tylenol Allergy Sinus Medication Maximum Strength Gelcaps—Chlorpheniramine, Pseudoephedrine, and Acetaminophen—*See* Antihistamines, Decongestants, and Analgesics (Systemic), 286
Tylenol Allergy Sinus Medication Maximum Strength Geltabs—Chlorpheniramine, Pseudoephedrine, and Acetaminophen—*See* Antihistamines, Decongestants, and Analgesics (Systemic), 286
Tylenol Allergy Sinus Night Time Medicine Maximum Strength Caplets—Diphenhydramine, Pseudoephedrine, and Acetaminophen—*See* Cough/Cold Combinations (Systemic), 286
Tylenol Caplets—Acetaminophen (Systemic), 129
Tylenol Children's Chewable Tablets—Acetaminophen (Systemic), 129
Tylenol Children's Cold DM Medication—Chlorpheniramine, Pseudoephedrine, Dextromethorphan, and Acetaminophen—*See* Cough/Cold Combinations (Systemic), 606
Tylenol Children's Elixir—Acetaminophen (Systemic), 129
Tylenol Children's Suspension Liquid—Acetaminophen (Systemic), 129
Tylenol with Codeine Elixir—Acetaminophen and Codeine—*See* Narcotic Analgesics and Acetaminophen (Systemic), 1149
Tylenol with Codeine No.1—Acetaminophen, Codeine, and Caffeine—*See* Narcotic Analgesics and Acetaminophen (Systemic), 1149, MC-1
Tylenol with Codeine No.2—Acetaminophen and Codeine—*See* Narcotic Analgesics and Acetaminophen (Systemic), 1149, MC-1; Acetaminophen, Codeine, and Caffeine—*See* Narcotic Analgesics and Acetaminophen (Systemic), 1149
Tylenol with Codeine No.3—Acetaminophen and Codeine—*See* Narcotic Analgesics and Acetaminophen (Systemic), 1149, MC-1; Acetaminophen, Codeine, and Caffeine—*See* Narcotic Analgesics and Acetaminophen (Systemic), 1149
Tylenol with Codeine No.4—Acetaminophen and Codeine—*See* Narcotic Analgesics and Acetaminophen (Systemic), 1149, MC-1
Tylenol with Codeine No.1 Forte—Acetaminophen, Codeine, and Caffeine—*See* Narcotic Analgesics and Acetaminophen (Systemic), 1149
Tylenol Cold and Flu—Chlorpheniramine, Pseudoephedrine, Dextromethorphan, and Acetaminophen—*See* Cough/Cold Combinations (Systemic), 606
Tylenol Cold and Flu No Drowsiness Powder—Pseudoephedrine, Dextromethorphan, and Acetaminophen—*See* Cough/Cold Combinations (Systemic), 606
Tylenol Cold Medication—Chlorpheniramine, Pseudoephedrine, Dextromethorphan, and Acetaminophen—*See* Cough/Cold Combinations (Systemic), 606
Tylenol Cold Medication Caplets—Chlorpheniramine, Pseudoephedrine, Dextromethorphan, and Acetaminophen—*See* Cough/Cold Combinations (Systemic), 606
Tylenol Cold Medication Children's—Chlorpheniramine, Pseudoephedrine, and Acetaminophen—*See* Antihistamines, Decongestants, and Analgesics (Systemic), 286
Tylenol Cold Medication Extra Strength Daytime Caplets—Pseudoephedrine, Dextromethorphan, and Acetaminophen—*See* Cough/Cold Combinations (Systemic), 606
Tylenol Cold Medication Extra Strength Nighttime Caplets—Chlorpheniramine, Pseudoephedrine, Dextromethorphan, and Acetaminophen—*See* Cough/Cold Combinations (Systemic), 606
Tylenol Cold Medication, Non-Drowsy Caplets—Pseudoephedrine, Dextromethorphan, and Acetaminophen—*See* Cough/Cold Combinations (Systemic), 606
Tylenol Cold Medication, Non-Drowsy Gelcaps—Pseudoephedrine, Dextromethorphan, and Acetaminophen—*See* Cough/Cold Combinations (Systemic), 606
Tylenol Cold Medication Regular Strength Daytime Caplets—Pseudoephedrine, Dextromethorphan, and Acetaminophen—*See* Cough/Cold Combinations (Systemic), 606
Tylenol Cold Medication Regular Strength Nighttime Caplets—Chlorpheniramine, Pseudoephedrine, Dextromethorphan, and Acetaminophen—*See* Cough/Cold Combinations (Systemic), 606
Tylenol Cold Multi-Symptom—Chlorpheniramine, Pseudoephedrine, Dextromethorphan, and Acetaminophen—*See* Cough/Cold Combinations (Systemic), 606
Tylenol Cough with Decongestant Maximum Strength—Pseudoephedrine, Dextromethorphan, and Acetaminophen—*See* Cough/Cold Combinations (Systemic), 606
Tylenol Cough Extra Strength Caplets—Dextromethorphan and Acetaminophen—*See* Cough/Cold Combinations (Systemic), 606
Tylenol Cough Medication with Decongestant, Regular Strength—Pseudoephedrine, Dextromethorphan, and Acetaminophen—*See* Cough/Cold Combinations (Systemic), 606
Tylenol Cough Medication Regular Strength—Dextromethorphan and Acetaminophen—*See* Cough/Cold Combinations (Systemic), 606
Tylenol Drops—Acetaminophen (Systemic), 129
Tylenol Elixir—Acetaminophen (Systemic), 129
Tylenol Extra Strength Adult Liquid Pain Reliever—Acetaminophen (Systemic), 129
Tylenol Extra Strength Caplets—Acetaminophen (Systemic), 129
Tylenol Extra Strength Cold and Flu Medication Powder—Chlorpheniramine, Pseudoephedrine, Dextromethorphan, and Acetaminophen—*See* Cough/Cold Combinations (Systemic), 606
Tylenol Extra Strength Gelcaps—Acetaminophen (Systemic), 129
Tylenol Extra Strength Tablets—Acetaminophen (Systemic), 129
Tylenol Flu Medication Extra Strength Gelcaps—Diphenhydramine, Pseudoephedrine, and Acetaminophen—*See* Antihistamines, Decongestants, and Analgesics (Systemic), 286
Tylenol Flu NightTime Hot Medication Maximum Strength—Diphenhydramine, Pseudoephedrine, and Acetaminophen—*See* Antihistamines, Decongestants, and Analgesics (Systemic), 286
Tylenol Flu NightTime Medication Maximum Strength Gelcaps—Diphenhydramine, Pseudoephedrine, and Acetaminophen—*See* Antihistamines, Decongestants, and Analgesics (Systemic), 286
Tylenol Gelcaps—Acetaminophen (Systemic), 129
Tylenol Infants' Drops—Acetaminophen (Systemic), 129
Tylenol Infants' Suspension Drops—Acetaminophen (Systemic), 129
Tylenol Junior Strength Caplets—Acetaminophen (Systemic), 129
Tylenol Junior Strength Chewable Tablets—Acetaminophen (Systemic), 129
Tylenol Junior Strength Cold DM Medication—Chlorpheniramine, Pseudoephedrine, Dextromethorphan, and Acetaminophen—*See* Cough/Cold Combinations (Systemic), 606
Tylenol Maximum Strength Cough—Dextromethorphan and Acetaminophen—*See* Cough/Cold Combinations (Systemic), 606
Tylenol Maximum Strength Flu Gelcaps—Pseudoephedrine, Dextromethorphan, and Acetaminophen—*See* Cough/Cold Combinations (Systemic), 606
Tylenol Multi-Symptom Cough—Promethazine and Potassium Guaiacolsulfonate—*See* Cough/Cold Combinations (Systemic), 606
Tylenol Multi-Symptom Cough with Decongestant—Pseudoephedrine, Dextromethorphan, and Acetaminophen—*See* Cough/Cold Combinations (Systemic), 606
Tylenol No.1—Acetaminophen, Codeine, and Caffeine—*See* Narcotic Analgesics and Acetaminophen (Systemic), 1149
Tylenol Regular Strength Caplets—Acetaminophen (Systemic), 129
Tylenol Regular Strength Tablets—Acetaminophen (Systemic), 129
Tylenol Sinus Maximum Strength—Pseudoephedrine and Acetaminophen—*See* Decongestants and Analgesics (Systemic), 659
Tylenol Sinus Maximum Strength Caplets—Pseudoephedrine and Acetaminophen—*See* Decongestants and Analgesics (Systemic), 659
Tylenol Sinus Maximum Strength Gelcaps—Pseudoephedrine and Acetaminophen—*See* Decongestants and Analgesics (Systemic), 659
Tylenol Sinus Maximum Strength Geltabs—Pseudoephedrine and Acetaminophen—*See* Decongestants and Analgesics (Systemic), 659
Tylenol Sinus Medication Extra Strength Caplets—Pseudoephedrine and Acetaminophen—*See* Decongestants and Analgesics (Systemic), 659
Tylenol Sinus Medication Regular Strength Caplets—Pseudoephedrine and Acetaminophen—*See* Decongestants and Analgesics (Systemic), 659
Tylenol Tablets—Acetaminophen (Systemic), 129
Tylosterone—Diethylstilbestrol and Methyltestosterone—*See* Androgens and Estrogens (Systemic), 193
Tylox—Oxycodone and Acetaminophen—*See* Narcotic Analgesics and Acetaminophen (Systemic), 1149, MC-23
Typhim Vi—Typhoid Vi Polysaccharide Vaccine (Systemic), 1603
Typhoid Vi Polysaccharide Vaccine (Systemic), 1603
Tyrodone—Pseudoephedrine and Hydrocodone—*See* Cough/Cold Combinations (Systemic), 606
Tyropanoate—*See* Cholecystographic Agents, Oral (Diagnostic), 508

U

UAA—Atropine, Hyoscyamine, Methenamine, Methylene Blue, Phenyl Salicylate, and Benzoic Acid (Systemic), 337
UAD Otic—Neomycin, Polymyxin B, and Hydrocortisone (Otic), 1172
Ucephan—Sodium Benzoate and Sodium Phenylacetate (Systemic), 1451
UDCA—*See* Ursodiol (Systemic), 1608
Ugesic—Hydrocodone and Acetaminophen—*See* Narcotic Analgesics and Acetaminophen (Systemic), 1149
ULR-LA—Phenylpropanolamine and Guaifenesin—*See* Cough/Cold Combinations (Systemic), 606
Ultane—Sevoflurane (Inhalation-Systemic), 1442
ULTRAbrom—Brompheniramine and Pseudoephedrine—*See* Antihistamines and Decongestants (Systemic), 281
ULTRAbrom PD—Brompheniramine and Pseudoephedrine—*See* Antihistamines and Decongestants (Systemic), 281
Ultracal—Enteral Nutrition Formula, Fiber-containing—*See* Enteral Nutrition Formulas (Systemic), 741
Ultracef—Cefadroxil—*See* Cephalosporins (Systemic), 474
Ultralan—Enteral Nutrition Formula, Polymeric—*See* Enteral Nutrition Formulas (Systemic), 741
Ultralente Insulin—Insulin Zinc, Extended—*See* Insulin (Systemic), 923

Ultralente insulin, U—Insulin Zinc, Extended— *See* Insulin (Systemic), 923; Insulin Zinc, Extended, Human—*See* Insulin (Systemic), 923
Ultram—Tramadol (Systemic), 1583, MC-31
Ultra MOP—Methoxsalen (Systemic), 1078
UltraMOP Lotion—Methoxsalen (Topical), 1080
Ultra Muskol—Diethyltoluamide (Topical), 681
Ultra Pep-Back—Caffeine (Systemic), 439
Ultra Pred—Prednisolone—*See* Corticosteroids (Ophthalmic), 591
Ultrase MT 12—Pancrelipase (Systemic), 1233
Ultrase MT 20—Pancrelipase (Systemic), 1233
Ultra Tears—Hydroxypropyl Methylcellulose (Ophthalmic), 905
Ultravate—Halobetasol—*See* Corticosteroids—Medium to Very High Potency (Topical), 602
Ultrazine-10—Prochlorperazine—*See* Phenothiazines (Systemic), 1268
Unasyn—Ampicillin and Sulbactam—*See* Penicillins and Beta-lactamase Inhibitors (Systemic), 1251
Undecylenic Acid, Compound (Topical), 1605
Uni-Bent Cough—Diphenhydramine—*See* Antihistamines (Systemic), 274
Uni-Bronchial—Theophylline and Guaifenesin (Systemic), 1548
Unicort—Hydrocortisone—*See* Corticosteroids—Low Potency (Topical), 600
Uni-Decon—Chlorpheniramine, Phenyltoloxamine, Phenylephrine, and Phenylpropanolamine—*See* Antihistamines and Decongestants (Systemic), 281
Uni-Dur—Theophylline—*See* Bronchodilators, Theophylline (Systemic), 418
Unilax—Phenolphthalein and Docusate—*See* Laxatives (Oral), 980
Uni-Multihist D—Pheniramine, Phenyltoloxamine, Pyrilamine, and Phenylpropanolamine—*See* Antihistamines and Decongestants (Systemic), 281
Unipen—Nafcillin—*See* Penicillins (Systemic), 1245
Uniphyl—Theophylline—*See* Bronchodilators, Theophylline (Systemic), 418, MC-29
Unipres—Reserpine, Hydralazine, and Hydrochlorothiazide (Systemic), 1390
Uniretic—Moexipril and Hydrochlorothiazide (Systemic), MC-20
Unisom Nighttime Sleep Aid—Doxylamine—*See* Antihistamines (Systemic), 274
Unisom SleepGels Maximum Strength—Diphenhydramine—*See* Antihistamines (Systemic), 274
Unituss HC—Chlorpheniramine, Phenylephrine, and Hydrocone—*See* Cough/Cold Combinations (Systemic), 606
Uni-tussin—Guaifenesin (Systemic), 858
Uni-tussin DM—Dextromethorphan and Guaifenesin—*See* Cough/Cold Combinations (Systemic), 606
Univasc—Moexipril (Systemic), 1115, MC-20
Univol—Alumina and Magnesia—*See* Antacids (Oral), 219
Unproco—Dextromethorphan and Guaifenesin—*See* Cough/Cold Combinations (Systemic), 606
Urabeth—Bethanechol (Systemic), 394
Urecholine—Bethanechol (Systemic), 394
Urex—Methenamine (Systemic), 1071
Uridon—Chlorthalidone—*See* Diuretics, Thiazide (Systemic), 719
Uridon Modified—Atropine, Hyoscyamine, Methenamine, Methylene Blue, Phenyl Salicylate, and Benzoic Acid (Systemic), 337
Urimed—Atropine, Hyoscyamine, Methenamine, Methylene Blue, Phenyl Salicylate, and Benzoic Acid (Systemic), 337
Urinary Antiseptic No. 2—Atropine, Hyoscyamine, Methenamine, Methylene Blue, Phenyl Salicylate, and Benzoic Acid (Systemic), 337
Urised—Atropine, Hyoscyamine, Methenamine, Methylene Blue, Phenyl Salicylate, and Benzoic Acid (Systemic), 337
Uriseptic—Atropine, Hyoscyamine, Methenamine, Methylene Blue, Phenyl Salicylate, and Benzoic Acid (Systemic), 337
Urispas—Flavoxate (Systemic), 805
Uritab—Atropine, Hyoscyamine, Methenamine, Methylene Blue, Phenyl Salicylate, and Benzoic Acid (Systemic), 337
Uritin—Atropine, Hyoscyamine, Methenamine, Methylene Blue, Phenyl Salicylate, and Benzoic Acid (Systemic), 337
Uritol—Furosemide—*See* Diuretics, Loop (Systemic), 709
Urobak—Sulfamethoxazole—*See* Sulfonamides (Systemic), 1493
Urocit-K—Potassium Citrate—*See* Citrates (Systemic), 525
Urodine—Phenazopyridine (Systemic), 1267
Urofollitrophin—*See* Urofollitropin (Systemic), 1606
Urofollitropin (Systemic), 1606
Urogesic—Phenazopyridine (Systemic), 1267
Urokinase—*See* Thrombolytic Agents (Systemic), 1566
Uro-KP-Neutral—Potassium and Sodium Phosphates—*See* Phosphates (Systemic), 1287
Uro-Mag—Magnesium Oxide—*See* Antacids (Oral), 219; Magnesium Supplements (Systemic), 1024
Uromitexan—Mesna (Systemic), 1065
Uro-Ves—Atropine, Hyoscyamine, Methenamine, Methylene Blue, Phenyl Salicylate, and Benzoic Acid (Systemic), 337
Urozide—Hydrochlorothiazide—*See* Diuretics, Thiazide (Systemic), 719
Ursinus Inlay—Pseudoephedrine and Aspirin—*See* Decongestants and Analgesics (Systemic), 659
Ursodeoxycholic acid—*See* Ursodiol (Systemic), 1608
Ursodiol (Systemic), 1608, MC-32
Ursofalk—Ursodiol (Systemic), 1608
Utex-S.R.—Phenylpropanolamine and Guaifenesin—*See* Cough/Cold Combinations (Systemic), 606
Uticort—Betamethasone—*See* Corticosteroids—Medium to Very High Potency (Topical), 602

Vagistat-1—Tioconazole—*See* Antifungals, Azole (Vaginal), 266
Vagitrol—Sulfanilamide—*See* Sulfonamides (Vaginal), 1496
Valacyclovir (Systemic), 1610, 1738, MC-32
Valergen-10—Estradiol—*See* Estrogens (Systemic), 766
Valergen-20—Estradiol—*See* Estrogens (Systemic), 766
Valergen-40—Estradiol—*See* Estrogens (Systemic), 766
Valertest No. 1—Testosterone and Estradiol—*See* Androgens and Estrogens (Systemic), 193
Valertest No. 2—Testosterone and Estradiol—*See* Androgens and Estrogens (Systemic), 193
Valisone—Betamethasone—*See* Corticosteroids—Medium to Very High Potency (Topical), 602
Valisone Reduced Strength—Betamethasone—*See* Corticosteroids—Medium to Very High Potency (Topical), 602
Valisone Scalp Lotion—Betamethasone—*See* Corticosteroids—Medium to Very High Potency (Topical), 602
Valium—Diazepam—*See* Benzodiazepines (Systemic), 368, MC-8
Valnac—Betamethasone—*See* Corticosteroids—Medium to Very High Potency (Topical), 602
Valorin—Acetaminophen (Systemic), 129
Valorin Extra—Acetaminophen (Systemic), 129
Valproate—*See* Valproic Acid (Systemic), 1611, MC-32
Valproic Acid (Systemic), 1611, MC-32
Valrelease—Diazepam—*See* Benzodiazepines (Systemic), 368
Valtrex—Valacyclovir (Systemic), 1610, 1738, MC-32
Vanacet—Hydrocodone and Acetaminophen—*See* Narcotic Analgesics and Acetaminophen (Systemic), 1149
Vanadom—Carisoprodol—*See* Skeletal Muscle Relaxants (Systemic), 1448
Vancenase—Beclomethasone—*See* Corticosteroids (Nasal), 588
Vancenase AQ—Beclomethasone—*See* Corticosteroids (Nasal), 588
Vanceril—Beclomethasone—*See* Corticosteroids (Inhalation), 582
Vancocin—Vancomycin (Oral), 1614; Vancomycin (Systemic), 1615
Vancoled—Vancomycin (Systemic), 1615
Vancomycin (Oral), 1614
Vancomycin (Systemic), 1615
Vanex Expectorant—Pseudoephedrine, Hydrocodone, and Guaifenesin—*See* Cough/Cold Combinations (Systemic), 606
Vanex Forte Caplets—Chlorpheniramine, Pyrilamine, Phenylephrine, and Phenylpropanolamine—*See* Antihistamines and Decongestants (Systemic), 281
Vanex Grape—Chlorpheniramine, Phenylephrine, Phenylpropanolamine, and Dihydrocodeine—*See* Cough/Cold Combinations (Systemic), 606
Vanex-HD—Chlorpheniramine, Phenylephrine, and Hydrocodone—*See* Cough/Cold Combinations (Systemic), 606
Vanoxide 5 Lotion—Benzoyl Peroxide (Topical), 377
Vanquin—Pyrvinium (Oral), 1365
Vanquish Caplets—Acetaminophen, Aspirin, and Caffeine, Buffered—*See* Acetaminophen and Salicylates (Systemic), 132
Vanseb Cream Dandruff Shampoo—Salicylic Acid and Sulfur (Topical), 1432
Vanseb Lotion Dandruff Shampoo—Salicylic Acid and Sulfur (Topical), 1432
Vanseb-T—Salicylic Acid, Sulfur, and Coal Tar (Topical), 1434
Vansil—Oxamniquine (Systemic), 1219
Vantin—Cefpodoxime—*See* Cephalosporins (Systemic), 474, MC-5
Vaponefrin—Racepinephrine—*See* Bronchodilators, Adrenergic (Inhalation), 406
Vaqta—Hepatitis A Vaccine Inactivated (Systemic), 886
Vascor—Bepridil—*See* Calcium Channel Blocking Agents (Systemic), 446, MC-3
Vaseline Baby Sunblock—Titanium Dioxide and Zinc Oxide—*See* Sunscreen Agents (Topical), 1510
Vaseline Broad Spectrum Sunblock—Avobenzone and Octyl Methoxycinnamate—*See* Sunscreen Agents (Topical), 1510
Vaseline Extra Defense for Hand and Body—Octyl Methoxycinnamate and Oxybenzone—*See* Sunscreen Agents (Topical), 1510
Vaseline Intensive Care Active Sport—Octyl Methoxycinnamate and Oxybenzone—*See* Sunscreen Agents (Topical), 1510
Vaseline Intensive Care Baby Moisturizing Sunblock—Octyl Methoxycinnamate, Octyl Salicylate, Oxybenzone, and Titanium Dioxide—*See* Sunscreen Agents (Topical), 1510; Titanium Dioxide—*See* Sunscreen Agents (Topical), 1510
Vaseline Intensive Care Baby Sunblock—Octyl Methoxycinnamate, Octyl Salicylate, Oxybenzone, and Titanium Dioxide—*See* Sunscreen Agents (Topical), 1510
Vaseline Intensive Care Blockout Moisturizing—Octyl Methoxycinnamate, Octyl Salicylate, Oxybenzone, Padimate O, and Titanium Dioxide—*See* Sunscreen Agents (Topical), 1510; Octyl Methoxycinnamate, Octyl Salicylate, Oxybenzone, and Titanium Dioxide—*See* Sunscreen Agents (Topical), 1510
Vaseline Intensive Care Lip Therapy—Octyl Methoxycinnamate and Oxybenzone—*See* Sunscreen Agents (Topical), 1510
Vaseline Intensive Care Moisturizing Sunblock—Octyl Methoxycinnamate, Octyl Salicylate, and Oxybenzone—*See* Sunscreen Agents (Topical), 1510; Octyl Methoxycinnamate and Oxybenzone—*See* Sunscreen Agents (Topical), 1510
Vaseline Intensive Care Moisturizing Sunscreen—Octyl Methoxycinnamate and Octyl Salicylate—*See* Sunscreen Agents (Topical), 1510
Vaseline Kids Sunblock—Octyl Methoxycinnamate, Octyl Salicylate, and Oxybenzone—*See* Sunscreen Agents (Topical), 1510; Octyl Methoxycinnamate and Oxybenzone—*See* Sunscreen Agents (Topical), 1510
Vaseline Lip Therapy—Octyl Methoxycinnamate and Oxybenzone—*See* Sunscreen Agents (Topical), 1510
Vaseline Moisturizing Sunscreen—Octyl Methoxycinnamate and Oxybenzone—*See* Sunscreen Agents (Topical), 1510
Vaseline Sports Sunscreen—Octyl Methoxycinnamate and Oxybenzone—*See* Sunscreen Agents (Topical), 1510
Vaseline Sport Sunblock—Octyl Methoxycinnamate and Oxybenzone—*See* Sunscreen Agents (Topical), 1510
Vaseline Sunblock—Octyl Methoxycinnamate, Octyl Salicylate, and Oxybenzone—*See* Sunscreen Agents (Topical), 1510; Octyl Methoxycinnamate, Octyl Salicylate, Oxybenzone, and Padimate O—*See* Sunscreen Agents (Topical), 1510; Octyl Methoxycinnamate and Oxybenzone—*See* Sunscreen Agents (Topical), 1510
Vaseline Sunscreen—Octyl Methoxycinnamate and Oxybenzone—*See* Sunscreen Agents (Topical), 1510

Vaseline Ultraviolet Daily Defense for Hand and Body—Octyl Methoxycinnamate and Oxybenzone—*See* Sunscreen Agents (Topical), 1510
Vaseretic—Enalapril and Hydrochlorothiazide—*See* Angiotensin-converting Enzyme (ACE) Inhibitors and Hydrochlorothiazide (Systemic), 215, MC-11; Enalapril and Hydrochlorothiazide (Systemic), 1730
VasoClear—Naphazoline (Ophthalmic), 1139
VasoClear A—Naphazoline (Ophthalmic), 1139
Vasocon—Naphazoline (Ophthalmic), 1139
Vasocon Regular—Naphazoline (Ophthalmic), 1139
Vasodilan—Isoxsuprine (Systemic), 958
Vasofrinic—Chlorpheniramine and Pseudoephedrine—*See* Antihistamines and Decongestants (Systemic), 281
Vasopressin (Systemic), 1617
Vasotate HC—Hydrocortisone and Acetic Acid (Otic), 1732
Vasotec—Enalapril—*See* Angiotensin-converting Enzyme (ACE) Inhibitors (Systemic), 212, MC-10; Enalaprilat—*See* Angiotensin-converting Enzyme (ACE) Inhibitors (Systemic), 212
VCF—Nonoxynol 9—*See* Spermicides (Vaginal), 1464
V-Cillin K—Penicillin V—*See* Penicillins (Systemic), 1245, MC-24
V-Dec-M—Pseudoephedrine and Guaifenesin—*See* Cough/Cold Combinations (Systemic), 606
Veetids—Penicillin V—*See* Penicillins (Systemic), 1245, MC-24
Velban—Vinblastine (Systemic), 1621
Velbe—Vinblastine (Systemic), 1621
Velosef—Cephradine—*See* Cephalosporins (Systemic), 474, MC-6
Velosulin BR—Insulin Human, Buffered—*See* Insulin (Systemic), 923
Velosulin Human—Insulin Human, Buffered—*See* Insulin (Systemic), 923
Velsar—Vinblastine (Systemic), 1621
Veltane—Brompheniramine—*See* Antihistamines (Systemic), 274
Vendone—Hydrocodone and Acetaminophen—*See* Narcotic Analgesics and Acetaminophen (Systemic), 1149
Venlafaxine (Systemic), 1618, MC-32
Venoglobulin-I—Immune Globulin Intravenous (Human) (Systemic), 917
Ventodisk—Albuterol—*See* Bronchodilators, Adrenergic (Inhalation), 406
Ventolin—Albuterol—*See* Bronchodilators, Adrenergic (Inhalation), 406; Bronchodilators, Adrenergic (Oral/Injection), 412, MC-1
Ventolin Nebules—Albuterol—*See* Bronchodilators, Adrenergic (Inhalation), 406
Ventolin Nebules P.F.—Albuterol—*See* Bronchodilators, Adrenergic (Inhalation), 406
Ventolin Rotacaps—Albuterol—*See* Bronchodilators, Adrenergic (Inhalation), 406
VePesid—Etoposide (Systemic), 787
Veracolate—Cascara Sagrada and Phenolphthalein—*See* Laxatives (Oral), 980
Verapamil—*See* Calcium Channel Blocking Agents (Systemic), 446, MC-32
Verazinc—Zinc Sulfate—*See* Zinc Supplements (Systemic), 1652
Verelan—Verapamil—*See* Calcium Channel Blocking Agents (Systemic), 446, MC-32
Verluma—Technetium Tc 99m Nofetumomab Merpentan (Systemic), 1737
Vermox—Mebendazole (Systemic), 1038
Versacaps—Pseudoephedrine and Guaifenesin—*See* Cough/Cold Combinations (Systemic), 606
Versed—Midazolam (Systemic), 1104
Versel Lotion—Selenium Sulfide (Topical), 1437
Vertab—Dimenhydrinate—*See* Antihistamines (Systemic), 274
Verukan-HP Topical Solution—Salicylic Acid (Topical), 1429
Verukan Topical Solution—Salicylic Acid (Topical), 1429
Vesanoid—Tretinoin (Oral), 1722; Tretinoin (Systemic), MC-31
Vesprin—Triflupromazine—*See* Phenothiazines (Systemic), 1268
Vexol—Rimexolone (Ophthalmic), 1716
V-Gan-25—Promethazine—*See* Antihistamines, Phenothiazine-derivative (Systemic), 295
V-Gan-50—Promethazine—*See* Antihistamines, Phenothiazine-derivative (Systemic), 295
Vi-Atro—Diphenoxylate and Atropine (Systemic), 692
Vibal—Cyanocobalamin—*See* Vitamin B_{12} (Systemic), 1629
Vibal LA—Hydroxocobalamin—*See* Vitamin B_{12} (Systemic), 1629
Vibramycin—Doxycycline—*See* Tetracyclines (Systemic), 1533, MC-10
Vibra-tabs—Doxycycline—*See* Tetracyclines (Systemic), 1533, MC-10
Vibutal—Butalbital, Aspirin, and Caffeine—*See* Butalbital and Aspirin (Systemic), 431
Vicks Children's DayQuil Allergy Relief—Chlorpheniramine and Pseudoephedrine—*See* Antihistamines and Decongestants (Systemic), 281
Vicks Children's NyQuil—Chlorpheniramine, Pseudoephedrine, and Dextromethorphan—*See* Cough/Cold Combinations (Systemic), 606
Vicks Children's NyQuil Cold/Cough Relief—Chlorpheniramine, Pseudoephedrine, and Dextromethorphan—*See* Cough/Cold Combinations (Systemic), 606
Vicks 44 Cough and Cold Relief LiquiCaps—Pseudoephedrine and Dextromethorphan—*See* Cough/Cold Combinations (Systemic), 606
Vicks 44 Cough and Cold Relief Non-Drowsy Liqui-Caps—Pseudoephedrine and Dextromethorphan—*See* Cough/Cold Combinations (Systemic), 606
Vicks Cough Syrup—Ephedrine, Carbetapentane, and Guaifenesin—*See* Cough/Cold Combinations (Systemic), 606
Vicks DayQuil 4 Hour Allergy Relief—Brompheniramine and Phenylpropanolamine—*See* Antihistamines and Decongestants (Systemic), 281
Vicks DayQuil 12 Hour Allergy Relief—Brompheniramine and Phenylpropanolamine—*See* Antihistamines and Decongestants (Systemic), 281
Vicks DayQuil Liquicaps—Pseudoephedrine, Dextromethorphan, Guaifenesin, and Acetaminophen—*See* Cough/Cold Combinations (Systemic), 606
Vicks DayQuil Multi-Symptom Cold/Flu Liquicaps—Pseudoephedrine, Dextromethorphan, Guaifenesin, and Acetaminophen—*See* Cough/Cold Combinations (Systemic), 606
Vicks DayQuil Multi-Symptom Cold/Flu Relief—Pseudoephedrine, Dextromethorphan, Guaifenesin, and Acetaminophen—*See* Cough/Cold Combinations (Systemic), 606
Vicks DayQuil Non-Drowsy Cold/Flu—Pseudoephedrine, Dextromethorphan, Guaifenesin, and Acetaminophen—*See* Cough/Cold Combinations (Systemic), 606
Vicks DayQuil Sinus Pressure and Congestion Relief Caplets—Phenylpropanolamine and Guaifenesin—*See* Cough/Cold Combinations (Systemic), 606
Vicks DayQuil Sinus Pressure & Pain Relief Caplets—Pseudoephedrine and Ibuprofen—*See* Decongestants and Analgesics (Systemic), 659
Vicks 44D Cough and Head Congestion—Pseudoephedrine and Dextromethorphan—*See* Cough/Cold Combinations (Systemic), 606
Vicks 44D Dry Hacking Cough and Head Congestion—Pseudoephedrine and Dextromethorphan—*See* Cough/Cold Combinations (Systemic), 606
Vicks 44E Cough & Chest Congestion—Dextromethorphan and Guaifenesin—*See* Cough/Cold Combinations (Systemic), 606
Vicks Formula 44-D—Pseudoephedrine and Dextromethorphan—*See* Cough/Cold Combinations (Systemic), 606
Vicks Formula 44-d Pediatric—Pseudoephedrine and Dextromethorphan—*See* Cough/Cold Combinations (Systemic), 606
Vicks Formula 44E—Dextromethorphan and Guaifenesin—*See* Cough/Cold Combinations (Systemic), 606
Vicks Formula 44e Pediatric—Dextromethorphan and Guaifenesin—*See* Cough/Cold Combinations (Systemic), 606
Vicks Formula 44M—Chlorpheniramine, Pseudoephedrine, Dextromethorphan, and Acetaminophen—*See* Cough/Cold Combinations (Systemic), 606
Vicks Formula 44 Pediatric Formula—Dextromethorphan (Systemic), 669
Vicks 44M Cough, Cold and Flu Relief—Chlorpheniramine, Pseudoephedrine, Dextromethorphan, and Acetaminophen—*See* Cough/Cold Combinations (Systemic), 606
Vicks 44M Cough, Cold and Flu Relief LiquiCaps—Chlorpheniramine, Pseudoephedrine, Dextromethorphan, and Acetaminophen—*See* Cough/Cold Combinations (Systemic), 606
Vicks NyQuil—Doxylamine, Pseudoephedrine, Dextromethorphan, and Acetaminophen—*See* Cough/Cold Combinations (Systemic), 606
Vicks NyQuil Hot Therapy—Doxylamine, Pseudoephedrine, Dextromethorphan, and Acetaminophen—*See* Cough/Cold Combinations (Systemic), 606
Vicks NyQuil Liqui-Caps—Doxylamine, Pseudoephedrine, Dextromethorphan, and Acetaminophen—*See* Cough/Cold Combinations (Systemic), 606
Vicks NyQuil Multi-Symptom Cold/Flu LiquiCaps—Doxylamine, Pseudoephedrine, Dextromethorphan, and Acetaminophen—*See* Cough/Cold Combinations (Systemic), 606
Vicks NyQuil Multi-Symptom Cold/Flu Relief—Doxylamine, Pseudoephedrine, Dextromethorphan, and Acetaminophen—*See* Cough/Cold Combinations (Systemic), 606
Vicks Pediatric 44D Cough & Head Congestion—Pseudoephedrine and Dextromethorphan—*See* Cough/Cold Combinations (Systemic), 606
Vicks Pediatric 44E—Dextromethorphan and Guaifenesin—*See* Cough/Cold Combinations (Systemic), 606
Vicks Pediatric 44M Multi-Symptom Cough & Cold—Chlorpheniramine, Pseudoephedrine, and Dextromethorphan—*See* Cough/Cold Combinations (Systemic), 606
Vicks Sinex—Phenylephrine (Nasal), 1281
Vicks Sinex Long-Acting 12-Hour Formula Decongestant Nasal Spray—Oxymetazoline (Nasal), 1225
Vicks Sinex Long-Acting 12-Hour Formula Decongestant Ultra Fine Mist—Oxymetazoline (Nasal), 1225
Vicodin—Hydrocodone and Acetaminophen—*See* Narcotic Analgesics and Acetaminophen (Systemic), 1149, MC-14
Vicodin ES—Hydrocodone and Acetaminophen—*See* Narcotic Analgesics and Acetaminophen (Systemic), 1149, MC-14
Vicodin HP—Hydrocodone and Acetaminophen (Systemic), MC-14
Vicodin Tuss—Hydrocodone and Guaifenesin—*See* Cough/Cold Combinations (Systemic), 606
Vidarabine (Ophthalmic), 1620
Vi-Daylin/F—Multiple Vitamins and Fluoride—*See* Vitamins and Fluoride (Systemic), 1640
Videx—Didanosine (Systemic), 676, MC-9
Vinblastine (Systemic), 1621
Vincasar PFS—Vincristine (Systemic), 1623
Vincol—Tiopronin (Systemic), 1572
Vincrex—Vincristine (Systemic), 1623
Vincristine (Systemic), 1623
Vindesine (Systemic), 1738
Vinorelbine (Injection), 1724
Vioform—Clioquinol (Topical), 537
Vioform-Hydrocortisone Cream—Clioquinol and Hydrocortisone (Topical), 538
Vioform-Hydrocortisone Lotion—Clioquinol and Hydrocortisone (Topical), 538
Vioform-Hydrocortisone Mild Cream—Clioquinol and Hydrocortisone (Topical), 538
Vioform-Hydrocortisone Mild Ointment—Clioquinol and Hydrocortisone (Topical), 538
Vioform-Hydrocortisone Ointment—Clioquinol and Hydrocortisone (Topical), 538
Viokase—Pancrelipase (Systemic), 1233
Viprynium—*See* Pyrvinium (Oral), 1365
Vira-A—Vidarabine (Ophthalmic), 1620
Viracept—Nelfinavir (Oral), 1706
Viramune—Nevirapine (Oral), 1707
Viranol—Salicylic Acid (Topical), 1429
Viranol Ultra—Salicylic Acid (Topical), 1429
Virazid—Ribavirin (Systemic), 1397
Virazole—Ribavirin (Systemic), 1397
Viridium—Phenazopyridine (Systemic), 1267
Virilon—Methyltestosterone—*See* Androgens (Systemic), 188
Virilon IM—Testosterone—*See* Androgens (Systemic), 188
Viroptic—Trifluridine (Ophthalmic), 1590
Visine L.R.—Oxymetazoline (Ophthalmic), 1227, 1735
Viskazide—Pindolol and Hydrochlorothiazide—*See* Beta-adrenergic Blocking Agents and Thiazide Diuretics (Systemic), 388
Visken—Pindolol—*See* Beta-adrenergic Blocking Agents (Systemic), 382, MC-25
Vistacrom—Cromolyn (Ophthalmic), 625
Vistaject-25—Hydroxyzine—*See* Antihistamines (Systemic), 274
Vistaject-50—Hydroxyzine—*See* Antihistamines (Systemic), 274

THE MEDICINE CHART

The Medicine Chart presents photographs of the most frequently prescribed medicines in the United States. In general, commonly used brand name products and a representative sampling of generic products have been included. The pictorial listing is not intended to be inclusive and does not represent all products on the market. Only selected solid oral dosage forms (capsules and tablets) have been included. The inclusion of a product does not mean the USPC has any particular knowledge that the product included has properties different from other products, nor should it be interpreted as an endorsement by USPC. Similarly, the fact that a particular product has not been included does not indicate that the product has been judged by the USPC to be unsatisfactory or unacceptable.

The drug products in *The Medicine Chart* are listed alphabetically by generic name of active ingredient(s). To quickly locate a particular medicine, check the product listing index that follows. This listing provides brand and generic names and directs the user to the appropriate page and chart location. In addition, any identifying code found on the surface of a capsule or tablet that might be useful in making a correct identification is included in the parentheses that follow the product's index entry. Only the identifying alphanumeric codes have been indexed; if a product also bears the brand name or manufacturer's name, this information has not been indexed. Please note that these codes may change as manufacturers reformulate or redesign their products. In addition, some companies may not manufacture all of their own products. In some of these cases, the imprinting on the tablet or capsule may be that of the actual manufacturer and not of the company marketing the product.

An imprint index has also been included to help identify products based on the identifying codes imprinted or otherwise marked on the products. These codes may not be unique to a given product; they are intended for use in initial identification only. In this index, the codes are listed first in alphanumeric order, accompanied by their generic or brand names and page and chart location.

Brand names are in *italics*. An asterisk next to the generic name of the active ingredient(s) indicates that the solid oral dosage forms containing the ingredient(s) are available only from a single source with no generic equivalents currently available in the U.S. Where multiple source products are shown, it must be kept in mind that other products may also be available.

The size and color of the products shown are intended to match the actual product as closely as possible; however, there may be some differences due to variations caused by the photographic process. Also, manufacturers may occasionally change the color, imprinting, or shape of their products, and for a period of time both the ''old'' and the newly changed dosage forms may be on the market. Such changes may not occur uniformly thoughout the different dosages of the product. These types of changes will be incorporated in subsequent versions of the chart as they are brought to our attention.

Use of this chart is limited to serving as an initial guide in identifying drug products. The identity of a product should be verified further before any action is taken.

Acarbose................MC-1, A1
Accolate Tablets—
20 mg (ZENECA/ ACCOLATE 20).......MC-32, C7
Accupril Tablets—
5 mg (PD 527/5).......MC-27, B1
10 mg (PD 530/10)....MC-27, B1
20 mg (PD 532/20)....MC-27, B2
40 mg (PD 535/40)....MC-27, B2
Accutane Capsules—
10 mg (ACCUTANE 10 ROCHE)..............MC-16, A7
20 mg (ACCUTANE 20 ROCHE)..............MC-16, A7
40 mg (ACCUTANE 40 ROCHE)..............MC-16, A7
Acebutolol..............MC-1, A2-4
Mylan Capsules—
200 mg (MYLAN 1200/ MYLAN 1200).........MC-1, A2
400 mg (MYLAN 1400/ MYLAN 1400).........MC-1, A2
Watson Capsules—
200 mg (WATSON 437/ 200 mg)..............MC-1, A3
400 mg (WATSON 438/ 400 mg)..............MC-1, A3
Aceon Tablets—
2 mg (Logo (rpr)/162)..MC-24, D1
4 mg (Logo (rpr)/164)..MC-24, D1
8 mg (Logo (rpr)/168)..MC-24, D1
Acetaminophen and Codeine.............MC-1, A5-B1
Purepac Tablets—
300/30 mg (Logo 001/3)..................MC-1, A7
300/60 mg (Logo 003/4)..................MC-1, A7
Acetohexamide..........MC-1, B2
Barr Tablets—
250 mg (barr 442)......MC-1, B2
500 mg (barr 443)......MC-1, B2
Achromycin V Capsules—
250 mg (Lederle 250 mg/ Lederle A3)..........MC-29, D2
500 mg (Lederle 500 mg/ Lederle A5)..........MC-29, D2
Actigall Capsules—
300 mg (ACTIGALL/ 300 mg)..............MC-32, A5
Acyclovir..............MC-1, B3-4
Adalat Capsules—
10 mg (ADALAT 10)...MC-21, D1
20 mg (ADALAT 20)...MC-21, D1
Adalat CC Extended-release Tablets—
30 mg (ADALAT CC/30)...............MC-21, D2
60 mg (ADALAT CC/60)...............MC-21, D2
90 mg (ADALAT CC/90)...............MC-21, D3
Albuterol..............MC-1, B5-C1
Schein Tablets—
2 mg (DAN 2/5710).....MC-1, B6
4 mg (DAN 4/5711).....MC-1, B6
UDL Tablets—
2 mg..................MC-1, C1
4 mg..................MC-1, C1
Aldactazide Tablets—
25/25 mg (SEARLE 1011/ ALDACTAZIDE 25)....MC-28, C3
50/50 mg (SEARLE 1021/ ALDACTAZIDE 50)....MC-28, C3
Aldactone Tablets—
25 mg (SEARLE 1001/ ALDACTONE 25).....MC-28, C1
50 mg (SEARLE 1041/ ALDACTONE 50).....MC-28, C1
100 mg (SEARLE 1031/ ALDACTONE 100)....MC-28, C1
Aldomet Tablets—
125 mg (MSD 135/ ALDOMET)...........MC-19, A7
250 mg (MSD 140/ ALDOMET)...........MC-19, A7
500 mg (MSD 516/ ALDOMET)...........MC-19, A7
Aldoril Tablets—
250/15 mg (MSD 423/ ALDORIL).............MC-19, B1
250/25 mg (MSD 456/ ALDORIL).............MC-19, B1
500/30 mg (MSD 694/ ALDORIL).............MC-19, B2
500/50 mg (MSD 935/ ALDORIL).............MC-19, B2
Alendronate..............MC-1, C2
Alkeran Tablets—
2 mg (ALKERAN A2A)..MC-18, C1
Allegra Capsules—
60 mg (60 mg/1102)...MC-12, D1
Allopurinol.............MC-1, C3-5
Mutual Tablets—
100 mg (Logo 71).....MC-1, C4
300 mg (Logo 80).....MC-1, C4
Mylan Tablets—
100 mg (M 31).......MC-1, C5
300 mg (M 71).......MC-1, C5
Alprazolam...........MC-1, C6-D1
Lederle Tablets—
0.25 mg (Logo/A 51)...MC-1, C6
0.5 mg (Logo/A 52)....MC-1, C6
1 mg (Logo/A 53)......MC-1, C6
2 mg (Logo/A 54)......MC-1, C6
Purepac Tablets—
0.25 mg (Logo/027)....MC-1, D1
0.5 mg (Logo/029).....MC-1, D1
1 mg (Logo/031).......MC-1, D1
2 mg (Logo/039).......MC-1, D1
Altace Capsules—
1.25 mg (HOECHST/ ALTACE 1.25 mg)....MC-27, C1
2.5 mg (HOECHST/ ALTACE 2.5 mg).....MC-27, C1
5 mg (HOECHST/ ALTACE 5 mg).......MC-27, C1
10 mg (HOECHST/ ALTACE 10 mg)......MC-27, C1
Alupent Tablets—
10 mg (BI 74).........MC-18, D1
20 mg (BI 72).........MC-18, D1
Amantadine...........MC-1, D2-4
Medirex Capsules—
100 mg (INV 211/ INV 211)...............MC-1, D3
UDL Capsules—
100 mg (C-122)........MC-1, D4
Amaryl Tablets—
1 mg (Logo/AMA RYL)..................MC-13, C6
2 mg (Logo/AMA RYL)..................MC-13, C6
4 mg (Logo/AMA RYL)..................MC-13, C6
Ambien Tablets—
5 mg (AMB 5/5401)....MC-32, D4
10 mg (AMB 10/5421) MC-32, D4
Amicar Tablets—
500 mg (Logo (LL)/ A 10)..................MC-2, A1
Amiloride..................MC-1, D5
Amiloride and Hydrochlorothiazide..MC-1, D6-7
Barr Tablets—
5/50 mg (barr/555 483)..................MC-1, D6
Aminocaproic Acid.......MC-2, A1
Amiodarone..............MC-2, A2
Amitriptyline...........MC-2, A3-6
Rugby Tablets—
10 mg (RUGBY/3071)..MC-2, A3
25 mg (RUGBY/3072)..MC-2, A3
50 mg (RUGBY/3073)..MC-2, A3
75 mg (RUGBY/3074)..MC-2, A4
100 mg (RUGBY/ 3075)..................MC-2, A4
150 mg (RUGBY/M39)..MC-2, A4
Amlodipine..............MC-2, A7
Amoxapine.............MC-2, B1-3
Schein Tablets—
50 mg (DAN 50/5714)..MC-2, B3
100 mg (DAN 100/ 5715)..................MC-2, B3
Amoxicillin............MC-2, B4-C1
Novopharm Capsules—
250 mg (N 724/250)....MC-2, B5
500 mg (N 176/500)....MC-2, B5

Amoxicillin and Clavulanate MC-2, C2-4
Amoxil Capsules—
250 mg (AMOXIL 250)...MC-2, B6
500 mg (AMOXIL 500)...MC-2, B6
Amoxil Chewable Tablets—
125 mg (AMOXIL/125) ...MC-2, B7
250 mg (AMOXIL/250) ...MC-2, B7
Ampicillin MC-2, C5-D1
Warner Chilcott Capsules—
500 mg (WC 404) MC-2, C6
Warner Chilcott Chewable Tablets—
250 mg (B L/222)...... MC-2, C7
Anafranil Capsules—
25 mg (ANAFRANIL 25 mg).............. MC-7, C4
50 mg (ANAFRANIL 50 mg).............. MC-7, C4
75 mg (ANAFRANIL 75 mg).............. MC-7, C4
Anaprox Tablets—
275 mg (ANAPROX/ ROCHE) MC-21, B45
50 mg (ANAPROX DS/ ROCHE) MC-21, B4
Anastrozole MC-2, D2
Ancobon Capsules—
250 mg (ANCOBON 250 ROCHE) MC-12, D6
500 mg (ANCOBON 500 ROCHE) MC-12, D6
Ansaid Tablets—
50 mg (ANSAID 50 mg)............... MC-13, B1
100 mg (ANSAID 100 mg)............... MC-13, B1
Antivert Tablets—
12.5 mg (ANTIVERT/ 210).................. MC-18, B1
25 mg (ANTIVERT/ 211).................. MC-18, B1
50 mg (ANTIVERT/ 214).................. MC-18, B1
Apresazide Capsules—
25/25 mg (CIBA 139/ APRESAZIDE 25/25).. MC-14, B3
50/50 mg (CIBA 149/ APRESAZIDE 50/50).. MC-14, B3
100/50 mg (CIBA 159/ APRESAZIDE 100/50) MC-14, B4
Apresoline Tablets—
10 mg (CIBA/37)....... MC-14, B2
25 mg (CIBA/39)....... MC-14, B2
50 mg (CIBA/73)....... MC-14, B2
100 mg (CIBA/101) MC-14, B2
Aricept Tablets—
10 mg (E 246/10)...... MC-10, B4
Arimidex Tablets—
1 mg (Logo/Adx 1)...... MC-2, D2
Asacol Delayed-release Tablets—
400 mg (ASACOL NE) MC-18, C6
Asendin Tablets—
50 mg (LL 50/A 15) MC-2, B2
Aspirin and Codeine MC-2, D4
URL Tablets—
325/30 mg (Z 3984/3) MC-2, D4
Aspirin, Caffeine, and Dihydrocodeine......... MC-2, D3
Astemizole MC-2, D5
Atarax Tablets—
10 mg (ATARAX 10)... MC-15, A4
25 mg (ATARAX 25)... MC-15, A4
50 mg (ATARAX 50)... MC-15, A4
100 mg (ATARAX 100).................. MC-15, A4
Atenolol MC-2, D6-MC-3, A1
Lederle Tablets—
25 mg (Logo/A7)........ MC-2, D6
50 mg (Logo/A 49) MC-2, D6
100 mg (Logo/A 71) MC-2, D6
Mutual Tablets—
25 mg (Logo 9)........ MC-2, D7
50 mg (Logo 146) MC-2, D7
100 mg (Logo 147).... MC-2, D7
Atenolol and Chlorthalidone........MC-3, A2-4
Mutual Tablets—
50/25 mg (Logo 153) ...MC-3, A2
100/25 mg (Logo 152)..MC-3, A2
Mylan Tablets—
50/25 mg (M 63) MC-3, A3
100/25 mg (M 64) MC-3, A3
Ativan Tablets—
0.5 mg (WYETH 81/ Logo)................. MC-17, D6
1 mg (WYETH 64/ Logo)................. MC-17, D6
2 mg (WYETH 65/ Logo 2) MC-17, D6
Atorvastatin MC-3, A5-6
Atropine, Hyoscyamine, Scopolamine, and Phenobarbital.......... MC-3, A7-B2
Augmentin Chewable Tablets—
125/31.25 mg (BMP 189) MC-2, C4
250/62.5 mg (BMP 190) MC-2, C4
Augmentin Tablets—
875/125 mg (AUGMENTIN 875).............. MC-2, C2
250/125 mg (AUGMENTIN 250/125).............. MC-2, C2
500/125 mg (AUGMENTIN 500/125).............. MC-2, C3
Axid Capsules—
150 mg (Lilly 3144/ AXID 150 mg) MC-22, B2
300 mg (Lilly 3145/ AXID 300 mg) MC-22, B2
Azatadine MC-3, B3
Azatadine and Pseudoephedrine.......MC-3, B4
Azathioprine MC-3, B5-6
Roxane Tablets—
50 mg (54 043)..........MC-3, B6
Azithromycin...............MC-3, B7
Azulfidine Tablets—
500 mg (Logo/101)..... MC-28, D4
Azulfidine EN-Tabs Enteric-coated Tablets—
500 mg (Logo/102)..... MC-28, D5
Baclofen MC-3, C1-2
Rugby Tablets—
10 mg (RUGBY/4959) MC-3, C2
20 mg (RUGBY/4960) MC-3, C2
Bactrim Tablets—
400/80 mg (ROCHE/ BACTRIM)............. MC-28, D2
800/160 mg (ROCHE/ BACTRIM-DS)............. MC-28, D2
Benazepril................ MC-3, C3
Benazepril and Hydrochlorothiazide .. MC-3, C4-5
Bendroflumethiazide..... MC-3, C6
Bentyl Capsules—
10 mg (BENTYL 10) MC-9, A4
Bentyl Tablets—
20 mg (BENTYL 20)......MC-9, A5
Benzphetamine MC-3, C7
Benztropine MC-3, D1-3
Goldline Tablets—
1 mg (par 165) MC-3, D1
2 mg (INV 210)......... MC-3, D1
Mutual Tablets—
1 mg (Logo 44)......... MC-3, D3
2 mg (Logo 142) MC-3, D3
Bepridil................... MC-3, D4
Betapace Tablets—
80 mg (BETAPACE/ 80 mg).............. MC-28, B4
120 mg (BETAPACE/ 120 mg).............. MC-28, B4
160 mg (BETAPACE/ 160 mg).............. MC-28, B5
240 mg (BETAPACE/ 240 mg).............. MC-28, B5
Betaxolol MC-3, D5
Biaxin Tablets—
250 mg (Logo KT) MC-7, B6
500 mg (Logo KL) MC-7, B6
Bicalutamide MC-3, D6
Bismuth Subsalicylate... MC-3, D7
Bisoprolol..................MC-4, A1
Bisoprolol and Hydrochlorothiazide MC-4, A2
Blocadren Tablets—
5 mg (MSD 59/ BLOCADREN)......... MC-30, C7
10 mg (MSD 136/ BLOCADREN)......... MC-30, C7
20 mg (MSD 437/ BLOCADREN)......... MC-30, C7
Brethine Tablets—
2.5 mg (Geigy 72) MC-29, C3
5 mg (Geigy 105)....... MC-29, C3
Bromocriptine...........MC-4, A3-4
Bumetanide MC-4, A5-6
0.5 mg (MYLAN/245).......MC-4, A5
Mylan Tablets—
1 mg (MYLAN/370) MC-4, A5
2 mg (MYLAN/417) MC-4, A5
Bumex Tablets—
0.5 mg (ROCHE/BUMEX 0.5) MC-4, A6
1 mg (ROCHE/BUMEX 1) MC-4, A6
2 mg (ROCHE/BUMEX 2) MC-4, A6
Bupropion............. MC-4, A7-B2
BuSpar Tablets—
5 mg (MJ5/BUSPAR) MC-4, B3
10 mg (MJ10/BUSPAR) ...MC-4, B3
Buspirone..................MC-4, B3
Busulfan MC-4, B4
Butalbital, Acetaminophen, and Caffeine.............. MC-4, B5-C1
Lemmon Tablets—
50/325/50 mg (West-Ward 787).....................MC-4, B5
Qualitest Capsules—
50/325/40 mg (59743/ 004).....................MC-4, B7
Qualitest Tablets—
50/325/40 mg (HD 567) MC-4, C1
Butalbital, Acetaminophen, Caffeine, and Codeine MC-4, C2
Butalbital, Aspirin, and Caffeine.............. MC-4, C3-6
Qualitest Tablets—
50/325/40 mg (West-Ward 785).................. MC-4, C5
URL Capsules—
50/325/40 mg (LANNETT 0527/1552)............ MC-4, C6
Butalbital, Aspirin, Caffeine, and Codeine..............MC-4, C7-D1
Watson Capsules—
50/325/40/30 mg (WATSON/425) MC-4, D1
Calan Tablets—
40 mg (CALAN/40)....... MC-32, B7
80 mg (CALAN/80)....... MC-32, B7
120 mg (CALAN 120).. MC-32, B7
Calan SR Extended-release Tablets—
120 mg (CALAN/ SR 120).............. MC-32, C1
180 mg (CALAN/ SR 180).............. MC-32, C1
240 mg (CALAN/ SR 240).............. MC-32, C1
Calcitriol MC-4, D2
Calcium Acetate MC-4, D3
Capoten Tablets—
12.5 mg (CAPOTEN/ 12.5) MC-4, D5
25mg (CAPOTEN 25) ... MC-4, D5
50 mg (CAPOTEN 50)... MC-4, D6
100 mg (CAPOTEN 100)...................... MC-4, D6
Capozide Tablets—
25/15 mg (CAPOZIDE 25/15) MC-4, D7
50/15 mg (CAPOZIDE 50/15) MC-4, D7
25/25 mg (CAPOZIDE 25/25) MC-5, A1
50/25 mg (CAPOZIDE 50/25) MC-5, A1
Captopril MC-4, D4-6
Apothecon Tablets—
25 mg (AP 7046)...... MC-4, D4
50 mg (AP 7047)...... MC-4, D4
Captopril and Hydrochlorothiazide MC-4, D7-MC-5, A1
Carafate Tablets—
1 gram (CARAFATE/ 1712).................... MC-28, C6
Carbamazepine MC-5, A2-6
Purepac Tablets—
200 mg (Logo/143).......MC-5, A5
Warner Chilcott Chewable Tablets—
100 mg (WC 242) MC-5, A6
Carbenicillin..............MC-5, A7
Carbidopa and Levodopa MC-5, B1-4
Purepac Tablets—
10/100 mg (93 292) MC-5, B3
25/100 mg (Logo/539)...MC-5, B3
25/250 mg (Logo/540) ..MC-5, B4
Carbinoxamine and Pseudoephedrine..........MC-5, B5
Cardene Capsules—
20 mg (CARDENE 20 mg/ ROCHE) MC-21, C5
30 mg (CARDENE 30 mg/ ROCHE) MC-21, C5
Cardene SR Extended-release Capsules—
30 mg (CARDENE SR 30 mg/ROCHE) MC-21, C6
45 mg (CARDENE 45 mg/ROCHE) MC-21, C6
60 mg (CARDENE SR 60 mg/ROCHE) MC-21, C7
Cardizem Tablets—
30 mg (MARION/1771)... MC-9, C5
60 mg (MARION/1772).. MC-9, C5
90 mg (CARDIZEM/ 90 mg).................. MC-9, C6
120 mg (CARDIZEM/ 120 mg)................ MC-9, C6
Cardizem CD Capsules—
120 mg (Logo/cardizem CD 120 mg) MC-9, C2
180 mg (Logo/cardizem CD 180 mg) MC-9, C2
240 mg (Logo/cardizem CD 240 mg) MC-9, C3
300 mg (Logo/cardizem CD 300 mg) MC-9, C3
Cardizem SR Extended-release Capsules—
60 mg (Logo/cardizem SR 60 mg)............ MC-9, C4
90 mg (Logo/cardizem SR 90 mg)............ MC-9, C4
120 mg (Logo/cardizem SR 120 mg) MC-9, C4
Cardura Tablets—
1 mg (CARDURA/ 1 mg)................... MC-10, B5
2 mg (CARDURA/ 2 mg)................... MC-10, B5
4 mg (CARDURA/ 4 mg)................... MC-10, B5
8 mg (CARDURA/ 8 mg)................... MC-10, B5
Carisoprodol MC-5, B6-7
Mutual Tablets—
350 mg (Logo 58) MC-5, B6
Carisoprodol and Aspirin..................MC-5, C1-2
Qualitest Tablets—
200/325 mg (par 246) MC-5, C1
Carisoprodol, Aspirin, and Codeine.................. MC-5, C3
Carteolol MC-5, C4
Cartrol Tablets—
2.5 mg (Logo 1A)....... MC-5, C4
5 mg (Logo 1C)......... MC-5, C4
Carvedilol MC-5, C5-6
Casodex Tablets—
50 mg (Logo/Cdx 50) ... MC-3, D6
Catapres Tablets—
0.1 mg (BI 6)............ MC-7, C7
0.2 mg (BI 7)............ MC-7, C7
0.3 mg (BI 11)........... MC-7, C7

Ceclor Capsules—
250 mg (Lilly 3061/ CECLOR 250 mg)..... MC-5, C7
500 mg (Lilly 3062/ CECLOR 500 mg)..... MC-5, C7
Cedax Capsules—
400 mg (Cedax/ 400 mg)..................MC-6, A1
Cefaclor...............MC-5, C7-D1
Mylan Capsules—
250 mg (MYLAN 7250)................ MC-5, D1
500 mg (MYLAN 7500)................ MC-5, D1
Cefadroxil.............. MC-5, D2-4
Apothecon Capsules—
500 mg (500 mg/ BRISTOL 7271)....... MC-5, D2
Cefixime................. MC-5, D5
Cefpodoxime............. MC-5, D6
Cefprozil................ MC-5, D7
Ceftibuten.................MC-6, A1
Ceftin Tablets—
125 mg (Glaxo/395)......MC-6, A2
250 mg (Glaxo/387)......MC-6, A2
500 mg (Glaxo/394)......MC-6, A3
Cefuroxime Axetil MC-6, A2-3
Cefzil Tablets—
250 mg (7720 BMS 250)................... MC-5, D7
500 mg (7721 BMS 500)................... MC-5, D7
CellCept Capsules—
250 mg (CellCept 250/ Roche)................ MC-20, D4
Cephalexin..............MC-6, A4-7
Apothecon Capsules—
250 mg (SQUIBB 181)..................MC-6, A4
500 mg (SQUIBB 239)....................MC-6, A4
Barr Capsules—
250 mg (barr/514).......MC-6, A5
500 mg (barr/515).......MC-6, A5
Biocraft Capsules—
250 mg (biocraft 115)...MC-6, A6
500 mg (biocraft 117)...MC-6, A6
Novopharm Capsules—
250 mg (N 084/250)....MC-6, A7
500 mg (N 114/500)....MC-6, A7
Cephradine..............MC-6, B1-2
Biocraft Capsules—
250 mg (biocraft 112)...MC-6, B2
500 mg (biocraft 113)...MC-6, B2
Cetirizine.................MC-6, B3
Chlor-Trimeton Tablets—
8 mg (Logo 374)........ MC-6, C4
12 mg (Logo 009) MC-6, C4
Chlorambucil..............MC-6, B4
Chlordiazepoxide MC-6, B5-6
Barr Capsules—
5 mg (barr/158)..........MC-6, B5
10 mg (barr/033)........MC-6, B5
25 mg (barr/159)........MC-6, B5
Chlordiazepoxide and Amitriptyline.........MC-6, B7-C1
Mylan Tablets—
5/12.5 mg (MYLAN/ 211).................MC-6, B7
10/25 mg (MYLAN/ 277)...................MC-6, B7
Chlordiazepoxide and Clidinium MC-6, C2-3
Chlorpheniramine........ MC-6, C4
Chlorpheniramine, Phenylpropanolamine, Phenylephrine, and Phenyltoloxamine....... MC-6, C5
Geneva Extended-release Tablets—
5/15/10/40 mg (GG 118)............ MC-6, C5
Chlorpheniramine, Phenyltoloxamine, Phenylephrine, and Phenylpropanolamine............MC-6, C6
Chlorpheniramine, Pyrilamine, and Phenylephrine..........MC-6, C7
Chlorpromazine........ MC-6, D1-5
UDL Tablets—
10 mg (832 10)........ MC-6, D4
25 mg (832 25)........ MC-6, D4
50 mg (832 50)........ MC-6, D4
100 mg (832 100) MC-6, D5
Chlorpropamide........ MC-6, D6-7
UDL Tablets—
100 mg (MYLAN 197/100).............. MC-6, D7
250 mg (MYLAN 210/250) MC-6, D7
Chlorthalidone MC-7, A1-3
Barr Tablets—
25 mg (Barr/267).......MC-7, A1
50 mg (Barr/268).......MC-7, A1
Chlorzoxazone MC-7, A4-6
Barr Tablets—
500 mg (barr/555 585)......................MC-7, A4
Mutual Tablets—
500 mg (Logo 74) MC-7, A6
Cimetidine MC-7, A7-B2
Mylan Tablets—
200 mg (M/53)...........MC-7, A7
300 mg (M/317)..........MC-7, A7
400 mg (M/372)..........MC-7, A7
800 mg (M 541)..........MC-7, A7
Cipro Tablets—
100 mg (CIPRO/100).....MC-7, B3
250 mg (CIPRO/250).....MC-7, B3
500 mg (CIPRO/500).....MC-7, B4
750 mg (CIPRO/750).....MC-7, B4
Ciprofloxacin.............MC-7, B3-4
Cisapride.................MC-7, B5
Clarithromycin MC-7, B6
Claritin Tablets—
10 mg (CLARITIN 10/458).................. MC-17, D2
Claritin-D Tablets—
5/120 mg (CLARITIN D)................... MC-17, D3
Cleocin Capsules—
75 mg (CLEOCIN 75 mg)..................... MC-7, C1
150 mg (CLEOCIN 150 mg)................... MC-7, C1
300 mg (CLEOCIN 300 mg).................... MC-7, C2
Clindamycin..........MC-7, B7-C2
Biocraft Capsules—
150 mg (biocraft 149)...MC-7, B7
Clindex Capsules—
5/2.5 mg (RUGBY 3490)................. MC-6, C3
Clinoril Tablets—
150 mg (MSD 941/ CLINORIL) MC-29, A2
200 mg (MSD 942/ CLINORIL) MC-29, A2
Clomid Tablets—
50 mg (CLOMID 50).... MC-7, C3
Clomiphene MC-7, C3
Clomipramine MC-7, C4
Clonazepam............ MC-7, C5-6
Lemmon Tablets—
0.5 mg (93 832) MC-7, C5
2 mg (93 834)......... MC-7, C5
Clonidine..............MC-7, C7-D4
Lederle Tablets—
0.1 mg (Logo/C 42)... MC-7, D1
0.2 mg (Logo/C 43)... MC-7, D1
0.3 mg (Logo/C 44)... MC-7, D1
Mylan Tablets—
0.1 mg (MYLAN 152).. MC-7, D2
0.2 mg (MYLAN 186).. MC-7, D2
0.3 mg (MYLAN 199).. MC-7, D2
Purepac Tablets—
0.1 mg (Logo/127) MC-7, D3
0.2 mg (Logo/128) MC-7, D3
0.3 mg (Logo/129) MC-7, D3
Schein Tablets—
0.1 mg (DAN 5609).... MC-7, D4
Clonidine and Chlorthalidone........ MC-7, D5-6
Mylan Tablets—
0.1/15 mg (M 1)......... MC-7, D6
0.2/15 mg (M 27)....... MC-7, D6
0.3/15 mg (M 72)....... MC-7, D6
Clorazepate MC-7, D7-MC-8, A2
Mylan Tablets—
3.75 mg (M 30)...........MC-8, A2
7.5 mg (M 40)............MC-8, A2
15 mg (M 70)..............MC-8, A2
Clotrimazole...............MC-8, A3
Clozapine MC-8, A4
Clozaril Tablets—
25 mg (CLOZARIL/25) ...MC-8, A4
100 mg (CLOZARIL/ 100)......................MC-8, A4
Cogentin Tablets—
0.5 mg (MSD 21/ COGENTIN)........... MC-3, D2
1 mg (MSD 635/ COGENTIN)............ MC-3, D2
2 mg (COGENTIN/60)... MC-3, D2
Cognex Capsules—
10 mg (COGNEXr 10) MC-29, A6
20 mg (COGNEXr 20) MC-29, A6
30 mg (COGNEXr 30) MC-29, A7
40 mg (COGNEXr 40) MC-29, A7
Colestid Tablets—
1000 mg (1 gm) (U) MC-8, A5
Colestipol...................MC-8, A5
Combipres Tablets—
0.1/15 mg (BI 8)......... MC-7, D5
0.2/15 mg (BI 9)......... MC-7, D5
0.3/15 mg (BI 10)....... MC-7, D5
Compazine Extended-release Capsules—
10 mg (SKF C44)...... MC-26, B1
15 mg (SKF C46)...... MC-26, B1
Compazine Tablets—
5 mg (SKF C66) MC-26, B2
10 mg (SKF C67)....... MC-26, B2
Cordarone Tablets—
200 mg (WYETH 4188/ 200)........................MC-2, A2
Coreg Tablets—
3.125 mg (SB/39) MC-5, C5
6.25 mg (SB 4140) MC-5, C5
12.5 mg (SB 4141) MC-5, C6
25 mg (SB 4142) MC-5, C6
Corgard Tablets—
20 mg (CORGARD 20/BL 232)............. MC-21, A1
40 mg (CORGARD 40/BL 207)............. MC-21, A1
80 mg (CORGARD 80/BL 241)............. MC-21, A1
120 mg (CORGARD 120 MG/BL 208)...... MC-21, A2
160 mg (CORGARD 160 MG/BL 246)...... MC-21, A2
Cortef Tablets—
5 mg (CORTEF 5)........ MC-14, D3
10 mg (CORTEF 10) ... MC-14, D3
20 mg (CORTEF 20) .. MC-14, D3
Corzide Tablets—
80/5 mg (CORZIDE 80-5/PPP284) MC-21, A3
40/5 mg (CORZIDE 40-5/PPP 283)........ MC-21, A3
Cotazym Capsules—
8/30/30 units (Organon (Logo)/381)............. MC-24, A6
Coumadin Tablets—
2 mg (DuPont/COUMADIN 2)............................ MC-32, C5
2.5 mg (DuPont/ COUMADIN 21/2)....... MC-32, C5
5 mg (DuPont/COUMADIN 5)............................ MC-32, C5
7.5 mg (DuPont/ COUMADIN 71/2)....... MC-32, C6
10 mg (DuPont/ COUMADIN 10)........... MC-32, C6
Covera-HS Extended-release Tablets—
180 mg (COVERA-HS 2011)................... MC-32, C2
240 mg (COVERA-HS 2021)................... MC-32, C2
Cozaar Tablets—
25 mg (MRK/951)....... MC-17, D7
50 mg (MRK952/ COZAAR) MC-17, D7
Creon Capsules—
5/16.6/18.75 (000) units (SOLVAY/1205) MC-24, A2
10/32.2/37.5 (000) units (SOLVAY/1210) MC-24, A2
20/66.4/75 (000) units (SOLVAY/1220) MC-24, A3
Crixivan Capsules—
200 mg (CRIXIVAN 200 mg)................... MC-15, C6
400 mg (CRIXIVAN 400 mg)................... MC-15, C6
Cyclobenzaprine MC-8, A6-B1
Endo Tablets—
10 mg (WPPh/156) MC-8, A6
Mylan Tablets—
10 mg (Logo/751).......MC-8, B1
Cyclophosphamide MC-8, B2
Cyclosporine............MC-8, B3-5
Cylert Chewable Tablets—
37.5 mg (Logo/TK) MC-24, B3
Cylert Tablets—
18.75 mg (Logo/TH).... MC-24, B2
37.5 mg (Logo/TI) MC-24, B2
75 mg (Logo/TJ) MC-24, B2
Cytotec Tablets—
0.1 mg (SEARLE/ 1451).................... MC-20, C2
0.2 mg (Logo/SEARLE 1461).................... MC-20, C2
Cytovene Capsules—
250 mg (CYTOVENE 250 mg)................... MC-13, C2
Cytoxan Tablets—
50 mg (MJ (Logo) 503/50)......................MC-8, B2
Dalmane Capsules—
15 mg (DALMANE 15 ROCHE) MC-13, A6
30 mg (DALMANE 30 ROCHE) MC-13, A6
Danazol MC-8, B6
Danocrine Capsules—
50 mg (Logo D 03/ DANOCRINE 50 mg)....MC-8, B6
100 mg (Logo D 04/ DANOCRINE 100 mg)..MC-8, B6
200 mg (Logo D 05/ DANOCRINE 200 mg)..MC-8, B6
Dantrium Capsules—
25 mg (DANTRIUM 25 mg/0149 0030) MC-8, B7
50 mg (DANTRIUM 50 mg/0149 0031) MC-8, B7
100 mg (DANTRIUM 100 mg/0149 0033)......MC-8, B7
Dantrolene MC-8, B7
Daraprim Tablets—
25 mg (DARAPRIM A3A) MC-27, A6
Darvocet-N Tablets—
50/325 mg (Lilly DARVOCET-N 50)..... MC-26, C1
100/650 mg (Lilly/ DARVOCET-N 100).... MC-26, C1
Daypro Tablets—
600 mg (SEARLE/ 1381)..................... MC-23, B7
DDAVP Tablets—
0.1 mg (Logo/ DDAVP 0.1)............ MC-8, C5
0.2 mg (Logo/ DDAVP 0.2)............ MC-8, C5
Decadron Tablets—
0.5 mg (MSD 41/ DECADRON)............ MC-8, D1
0.75 mg (MSD 63/ DECADRON)............ MC-8, D1
1.5 mg (MSD 95/ DECADRON)............ MC-8, D1
4 mg (MSD 97/ DECADRON)............ MC-8, D1
Declomycin Tablets—
150 mg (LL/D 11)....... MC-8, C1
300 mg (LL/D12)........ MC-8, C1

Deltasone Tablets—
2.5 mg (DELTASONE 2.5) MC-25, D1
5 mg (DELTASONE 5) MC-25, D1
10 mg (DELTASONE 10) MC-25, D1
20 mg (DELTASONE 20) MC-25, D2
50 mg (DELTASONE 50) MC-25, D2
Demadex Tablets—
5 mg (Logo 102/5) MC-31, A7
10 mg (Logo 103/10) .. MC-31, A7
20 mg (Logo 104/20) .. MC-31, B1
100 mg (Logo 105/ 100) MC-31, B1
Demeclocycline MC-8, C1
Demerol Tablets—
50 mg (Logo/D35) MC-18, C3
100 mg (Logo/D37) MC-18, C3
Demi-Regroton Tablets—
0.125/25 mg (R 32) MC-27, C6
Demulen 1/35-21 and -28 Tablets—
1/0.035 mg (SEARLE/ 151) MC-12, A4
Inert (SEARLE/P) MC-12, A4
Demulen 1/50-21 and -28 Tablets—
1/0.05 mg (SEARLE/ 71) MC-12, A5
Inert (SEARLE/P) MC-12, A5
Depakene Delayed-release Capsules—
250 mg (DEPAKENE) .. MC-32, A7
Depakote Delayed-release Tablets—
125 mg (Logo NT) MC-10, B2
250 mg (Logo NR) MC-10, B2
500 mg (Logo NS) MC-10, B3
Depakote Sprinkle Delayed-release Capsules—
125 mg (DEPAKOTE SPRINKLE 125 mg/ THIS END UP) MC-10, B1
Desipramine MC-8, C2-4
Geneva Tablets—
100 mg (GG 167) MC-8, C2
150 mg (GG 168) MC-8, C2
Desmopressin MC-8, C5
0.15/0.03 mg (ORGANON*/ TR 5) MC-8, C6
Inert (ORGANON*/ KH 2) MC-8, C6
Desogen Tablets—
Desogestrel and Ethinyl Estradiol MC-8, C6-7
Desyrel Tablets—
50 mg (DESYREL MJ775) MC-31, B7
100 mg (DESYREL MJ776) MC-31, B7
150 mg (Logo/778) MC-31, C1
Dexamethasone MC-8, D1-2
Roxane Tablets—
0.5 mg (54 299) MC-8, D2
0.75 mg (54 960) MC-8, D2
1 mg (54 489) MC-8, D2
1.5 mg (54 943) MC-8, D2
2 mg (54 662) MC-8, D2
4 mg (54 892) MC-8, D2
Dexfenfluramine MC-8, D3
DiaBeta Tablets—
1.25 mg (HOECHST/ Dia) MC-13, D4
2.5 mg (HOECHST/ Dia) MC-13, D4
5 mg (HOECHST/ Dia) MC-13, D4
Diabinese Tablets—
100 mg (PFIZER 393) .. MC-6, D6
250 mg (PFIZER 394) .. MC-6, D6
Diazepam MC-8, D4-6
Barr Tablets—
5 mg (barr/555 363) ... MC-8, D4
10 mg (barr/555 164) .. MC-8, D4
Purepac Tablets—
2 mg (Logo/051) MC-8, D5
5 mg (Logo/052) MC-8, D5
10 mg (Logo/053) MC-8, D5
Diclofenac Sodium MC-8, D7-MC-9, A3
Geneva Enteric-coated Tablets—
50 mg (GG 738) MC-9, A2
75 mg (GG 739) MC-9, A1
Purepac Delayed-release Tablets—
50 mg (Logo/550) MC-9, A3
75 mg (Logo/551) MC-9, A3
Dicyclomine MC-9, A4-7
Rugby Capsules—
10 mg (RUGBY 3367/ RUGBY 3367) MC-9, A6
Rugby Tablets—
20 mg (RUGBY/3377) .. MC-9, A7
Didanosine MC-9, B1-2
Didrex Tablets—
50 mg (DIDREX 50) ... MC-3, C7
Didronel Tablets—
200 mg (P&GP 402) ... MC-12, A6
Diethylpropion MC-9, B3-4
Diflucan Tablets—
50 mg (ROERIG/DIFLUCAN 50) MC-12, D4
100 mg (ROERIG/DIFLUCAN 100) MC-12, D4
150 mg (ROERIG/DIFLUCAN 150) MC-12, D5
200 mg (ROERIG/DIFLUCAN 200) MC-12, D5
Diflunisal MC-9, B5-6
Roxane Tablets—
250 mg (54 010) MC-9, B6
500 mg (54 093) MC-9, B6
Digoxin MC-9, B7-C1
Dilantin Kapseals Extended-release Capsules—
30 mg (P-D 365) MC-25, A4
100 mg (P-D 362) MC-25, A4
Dilantin Infatabs Chewable Tablets—
50 mg (P-D 007) MC-25, A3
Dilatrate-SR Extended-release Capsules—
40 mg (Logo/0920) MC-15, D5
Dilaudid Tablets—
2 mg (Logo/2) MC-14, D4
4 mg (Logo/4) MC-14, D4
8 mg (Logo Logo/8) MC-14, D4
Diltiazem MC-9, C2-D2
Mylan Tablets—
30 mg (M 23) MC-9, C7
60 mg (M 45) MC-9, C7
Rugby Tablets—
30 mg (BRL 30/3101) .. MC-9, D1
60 mg (BRL 60/3102) .. MC-9, D1
90 mg (BRL 90/3103) .. MC-9, D2
120 mg (BRL 120/ 3104) MC-9, D2
Dipentum Capsules—
250 mg (DIPENTUM 250mg) MC-23, B4
Diphenhist Tablets—
25 mg (RUGBY/3597) ... MC-9, D5
Diphenhydramine MC-9, D3-5
Purepac Capsules—
25 mg (Logo/191) MC-9, D3
50 mg (Logo/192) MC-9, D3
Rugby Capsules—
25 mg (RUGBY 3758/ RUGBY 3758) MC-9, D4
50 mg (RUGBY 3762/ RUGBY 3762) MC-9, D4
Diphenoxylate and Atropine MC-9, D6-7
Mylan Tablets—
2.5/0.025 mg (M 15) ... MC-9, D6
Dipyridamole MC-10, A1-3
Barr Tablets—
25 mg (Logo/252) MC-10, A1
50 mg (Logo/285) MC-10, A1
75 mg (BARR/286) MC-10, A1
Purepac Tablets—
25 mg (Logo/193) MC-10, A3
50 mg (Logo183) MC-10, A3
75 mg (Logo185) MC-10, A3
Dirithromycin MC-10, A4
Disopyramide MC-10, A5-7
Geneva Capsules—
100 mg (GG 56) MC-10, A5
150 mg (GG 57) MC-10, A5
Ditropan Tablets—
5 mg (DITROPAN/ 13 75) MC-23, C4
Divalproex MC-10, B1-3
Dolobid Tablets—
250 mg (MSD 675/ DOLOBID) MC-9, B5
500 mg (MSD 697/ DOLOBID) MC-9, B5
Donepezil MC-10, B4
Donnatal Capsules—
0.0194/0.1037/0.0065/16.2 mg (AHR 4207) MC-3, A7
Donnatal Extended-release Tablets—
0.0582/0.3111/0.0195/48.6 mg (AHR DONNATAL EXTEN- TAB) MC-3, B2
Donnatal Tablets—
0.0194/0.1037/0.0065/ 16.2 mg (R 4250) MC-3, B1
Doral Tablets—
7.5 mg (DORAL/7.5) ... MC-27, A7
15 mg (DORAL/15) MC-27, A7
Doxazosin MC-10, B5
Doxepin MC-10, B6-C6
Mylan Capsules—
10 mg (MYLAN 1049) MC-10, B6
25 mg (MYLAN 3125) MC-10, B6
50 mg (MYLAN 4250) MC-10, B6
75mg (MYLAN 5375) MC-10, B7
100 mg (MYLAN 6410) MC-10, B7
Par Capsules—
10 mg (par 217) MC-10, C1
25 mg (par 218) MC-10, C1
50 mg (par 219) MC-10, C1
75 mg (par 220) MC-10, C2
100 mg (par 221) MC-10, C2
150 mg (par 222) MC-10, C2
Rugby Capsules—
10 mg (RUGBY 4563) MC-10, C5
25 mg (RUGBY 4564) MC-10, C5
50 mg (RUGBY 4565) MC-10, C5
75 mg (RUGBY 3737) MC-10, C6
100 mg (RUGBY 4566) MC-10, C6
150 mg (RUGBY 3738) MC-10, C6
Doxycycline MC-10, C7-D4
Purepac Delayed-release Capsules—
100 mg (Logo 2598) .. MC-10, D2
Rugby Capsules—
50 mg (RUGBY/ 0280) MC-10, D3
100 mg (RUGBY/ 0230) MC-10, D3
Zenith Capsules—
100 mg (Logo 2985) .. MC-10, D4
Drisdol Capsules—
1.25 mg (W (Logo)/ D92) MC-11, A4
Duricef Capsules—
500 mg (MJ 784) MC-5, D3
Duricef Tablets—
1 gram (MJ 785) MC-5, D4
Dyazide Capsules—
37.5/25 mg (DYAZIDE Logo) MC-31, D3
Dynabac Tablets—
250 mg (DYNABAC UC5364) MC-10, A4
DynaCirc Capsules—
2.5 mg (Logo 2.5/DynaCirc Logo) MC-16, B1
5 mg (Logo 5/DynaCirc Logo) MC-16, B1
Dyphylline MC-10, D5
Dyphylline and Guaifenesin MC-10, D6
Dyphylline/GG Tablets—
200/200 mg (EL 522) .. MC-10, D6
Dyrenium Capsules—
50 mg (DYRENIUM 50 SKF) MC-31, C6
100 mg (DYRENIUM 100 SKF) MC-31, C6
E-C Naprosyn Delayed-release Tablets—
375 mg (EC-NAPROSYN/ 375) MC-21, B2
500 mg (EC-NAPROSYN/ 500) MC-21, B2
E-Mycin Delayed-release Tablets—
250 mg (E-MYCIN 250mg) MC-11, B7
333 mg (E-MYCIN 333mg) MC-11, B7
E.E.S. Tablets—
400 mg (Logo EE) MC-11, C6
Effexor Tablets—
25 mg (Logo 25/701) .. MC-32, B2
37.5 mg (Logo 37.5/ 781) MC-32, B2
50 mg (Logo 50/703) .. MC-32, B2
75 mg (Logo 75/704) .. MC-32, B3
100 mg (Logo 100/ 705) MC-32, B3
Elavil Tablets—
10 mg (MSD 23/ ELAVIL) MC-2, A5
25 mg (MSD 45/ ELAVIL) MC-2, A5
50 mg (MSD 102/ ELAVIL) MC-2, A5
75 mg (MSD 430/ ELAVIL) MC-2, A6
100 mg (MSD 435/ ELAVIL) MC-2, A6
150 mg (MSD 673/ ELAVIL) MC-2, A6
Eldepryl Capsules—
5 mg (Logo Somerset/ Eldeprylr 5 mg) MC-28, B1
Elmiron Capsules—
100 mg (BNP 7600) ... MC-24, C5
Enalapril MC-10, D7
Enalapril and Felodipine MC-11, A1
Enalapril and Hydrochlorothiazide ... MC-11, A2
Enduron Tablets—
2.5 mg (Logo ENDURON) MC-19, A4
5 mg (Logo ENDURON) MC-19, A4
Enoxacin MC-11, A3
Entex Capsules—
5/45/200 mg (ENTEX/ 0149 0412) MC-24, D7
Entex LA Extended-release Tablets—
75/400mg (entexLA/ 0149 0436) MC-25, A1
Entex PSE Tablets—
120/600 mg (entex PSE) MC-27, A4
Epivir Tablets—
150 mg (GX CJ7/150) MC-16, C4
Ercaf Tablets—
1/100 mg (Logo/400) ... MC-11, B1
Ergocalciferol MC-11, A4
Ergoloid Mesylates ... MC-11, A5-7
Mutual Tablets—
1 mg (Logo 20) MC-11, A5
Ergotamine and Caffeine MC-11, B1
Ery-Tab Delayed-release Tablets—
250 mg (Logo EC) MC-11, B5
333 mg (Logo EH) MC-11, B5
500 mg (Logo ED) MC-11, B5
Eryc Delayed-release Capsules—
250 mg (Eryc/P-D 696) MC-11, C2
EryPed Chewable Tablets—
200 mg (Logo/ CHEW EZ) MC-11, C7

Erythrocin Tablets—
250 mg (Logo/ES) MC-11, D1
500 mg (Logo/ET)...... MC-11, D1
Erythromycin.........MC-11, B2-C2
Abbott Delayed-release Capsules—
250 mg (Logo ER).... MC-11, B2
Abbott Tablets—
250 mg (Logo EB).... MC-11, B3
500 mg (Logo/EA) MC-11, B3
Barr Delayed-release Capsules—
250 mg (barr/584)..... MC-11, B6
Purepac Delayed-release Capsules—
250 mg (Logo 553)... MC-11, C1
Erythromycin Estolate............. MC-11, C3-5
Barr Capsules—
250 mg (barr 230).... MC-11, C3
Erythromycin Ethylsuccinate....... MC-11, C6-7
Erythromycin Stearate.. MC-11, D1
Esidrix Tablets—
25 mg (CIBA/22)...... MC-14, C1
50 mg (CIBA/46)...... MC-14, C1
100 mg (CIBA/192) MC-14, C1
Eskalith Capsules—
300 mg (ESKALITH SKF/ ESKALITH SKF) MC-17, C1
Eskalith CR Extended-release Tablets—
450 mg (SKF J10)..... MC-17, C2
Estazolam.............. MC-11, D2
Estrace Tablets—
0.5 mg (Logo 021) MC-11, D3
1 mg (Logo 755)...... MC-11, D3
2 mg (Logo 756)...... MC-11, D3
Estradiol........... MC-11, D3-4
Watson Tablets—
0.5 mg (WATSON 528)................. MC-11, D4
1 mg (WATSON 487).................. MC-11, D4
2 mg (WATSON 488)................. MC-11, D4
Estratab Tablets—
0.3 mg (SOLVAY 1014).................. MC-12, A1
0.625 mg (SOLVAY 1022)................ MC-12, A1
2.5 mg (SOLVAY 1025).................. MC-12, A1
Estratest Tablets—
1.25/0.625 mg (SOLVAY 1023)................. MC-19, C4
2.5/1.25 mg (SOLVAY 1026)................. MC-19, C4
Estrogens, Conjugated MC-11, D5-6
Estrogens, Esterified .. MC-11, D7-MC-12, A1
Estropipate........... MC-12, A2-3
Watson Tablets—
.75 mg (WATSON 414).................. MC-12, A3
1.5 mg (WATSON 415).................. MC-12, A3
3 mg (WATSON 416)................. MC-12, A3
Estrostep Fe Tablets—
1/0.035 mg............. MC-22, D3
1/0.03mg MC-22, D3
75 mg..................... MC-22, D3
1/0.02 mg MC-22, D3
Ethmozine Tablets—
200 mg (ETHMOZINE 200).................. MC-20, C5
250 mg (ETHMOZINE 250).................. MC-20, C5
300 mg (ETHMOZINE 300).................. MC-20, C6
Ethynodiol Diacetate and Ethinyl Estradiol MC-12, A4-5
Etidronate............... MC-12, A6
Etodolac MC-12, A7-B1
Famciclovir........... MC-12, B2-3
Famotidine.............. MC-12, B4
Famvir Tablets—
125 mg (FAMVIR/125) MC-12, B2
250 mg (FAMVIR/250) MC-12, B2
500 mg (FAMVIR/500) MC-12, B2

Fansidar Tablets—
500/25 mg (FANSIDAR ROCHE) MC-28, C7
Felbamate.............. MC-12, B5
Felbatol Tablets—
400 mg (WALLACE/ 0430)................ MC-12, B5
600 mg (WALLACE/ 0431)................ MC-12, B5
Feldene Capsules—
10 mg (PFIZER 322/ FELDENE) MC-25, B1
20 mg (PFIZER 323/ FELDENE) MC-25, B1
Felodipine............ MC-12, B6-7
Fenfluramine............ MC-12, C1
Fenoprofen............ MC-12, C2-6
Geneva Capsules—
300 mg (GG 559/ GG 559) MC-12, C3
Geneva Tablets—
600 mg (GG 254) MC-12, C4
Goldline Tablets—
600 mg (Logo 4141/ 600)................. MC-12, C5
Purepac Tablets—
600 mg (Logo 317)... MC-12, C6
Ferrous Sulfate MC-12, C7
Paddock Tablets—
324 mg (B-3) MC-12, C7
Fexofenadine............ MC-12, D1
Finasteride MC-12, D2
Fioricet Tablets—
50/325/40 mg (Logo/ 78-84) MC-4, B6
Fioricet with Codeine Capsules—
50/325/40/30 mg (Logo/ Fioricet Codeine) MC-4, C2
Fiorinal Capsules—
50/325/40 mg (FIORINAL 78-103)................ MC-4, C3
Fiorinal Tablets—
50/325/40 mg (FIORINAL/ 78-104)................ MC-4, C4
Fiorinal with Codeine Capsules—
50/325/40/30 mg (Logo F-C/SANDOZ 78-107).. MC-4, C7
Flagyl Tablets—
250 mg (SEARLE 1831/ FLAGYL 250) MC-20, A6
500 mg (FLAGYL/ 500).................... MC-20, A6
Flagyl® 375 Capsules—
375 mg (FLAGYL/ 375 mg).............. MC-20, A5
Flecainide............... MC-12, D3
Flexeril Tablets—
10 mg (MSD 931/ FLEXERIL) MC-8, A7
Floxin Tablets—
200 mg (FLOXIN 200 mg)............. MC-23, A7
300 mg (FLOXIN 300 mg)............. MC-23, A7
400 mg (FLOXIN 400 mg)............. MC-23, B1
Fluconazole........... MC-12, D4-5
Flucytosine.............. MC-12, D6
Flumadine Tablets—
100 mg (FLUMADINE 100/FOREST) MC-28, A1
Fluoxetine............... MC-12, D7
Fluoxymesterone MC-13, A1
Fluphenazine......... MC-13, A2-4
Mylan Tablets—
1 mg (MYLAN/4)...... MC-13, A3
2.5 mg (MYLAN/9).... MC-13, A3
5 mg (MYLAN/74) MC-13, A4
10 mg (MYLAN/97) MC-13, A4
Flurazepam MC-13, A5-6
Purepac Capsules—
15 mg (Logo-021)...... MC-13, A5
30 mg (Logo-022)...... MC-13, A5
Flurbiprofen..........MC-13, A7-B1
Mylan Tablets—
50 mg (M 76).......... MC-13, A7
100 mg (M 93) MC-13, A7

Fluvastatin MC-13, B2
Fluvoxamine MC-13, B3
Fosamax Tablets—
10 mg (Logo MRK 936).................... MC-1, C2
40 mg (MRK 212) MC-1, C2
Fosinopril MC-13, B4
Furosemide MC-13, B5-6
Schein Tablets—
20 mg (M2) MC-13, B6
40 mg (DAN 5575) MC-13, B6
80 mg (WATSON 302)................. MC-13, B6
Gabapentin...........MC-13, B7-C1
Ganciclovir............. MC-13, C2
Gemfibrozil........... MC-13, C3-5
Purepac Tablets—
600 mg (Logo/552).... MC-13, C4
Rugby Tablets—
600 mg (RUGBY/ 3854) MC-13, C5
Genora 0.5/35-28 Tablets—
0.5/0.035 mg (SGP/ 0.5/35) MC-22, C1
Inert (SGP)............. MC-22, C1
Inert (SGP)............. MC-22, C2
Genora 1/35-28 Tablets—
1/0.035 mg (SFP/ 1/35) MC-22, C2
Inert (SGP)............. MC-22, C2
Genora 1/50-28 Tablets—
1/0.05 mg (SGP/ 1/50) MC-22, C4-5
Inert (S G P).......... MC-22, C4-5
Geocillin Tablets—
382 mg (ROERIG/143)...MC-5, A7
Glimepiride.............. MC-13, C6
Glipizide.............MC-13, C7-D2
Mylan Tablets—
5 mg (MYLAN G1) ... MC-13, C7
10 mg (MYLAN G2) .. MC-13, C7
Glucophage Tablets—
500 mg (BMS 6060/ 500).................... MC-18, D3
850 mg (BMS 6070/ 850).................... MC-18, D3
Glucotrol Tablets—
5 mg (PFIZER 411).... MC-13, D1
10 mg (PFIZER 412) .. MC-13, D1
Glucotrol XL Extended-release Tablets—
5 mg (GLUCOTROL XL 5) MC-13, D2
10 mg (GLUCOTROL XL 10) MC-13, D2
Glyburide MC-13, D3-5
Geneva Tablets—
2.5 mg (GG 239)..... MC-13, D3
5 mg (GG 240)........ MC-13, D3
Granisetron MC-13, D6
Grifulvin V Tablets—
250 mg (Ortho 211)..... MC-14, A1
500 mg (Ortho 214).... MC-14, A1
Griseofulvin .. MC-13, D7-MC-14, A1
ESI Tablets—
500 mg (59911 5808).................. MC-13, D7
Guaifen PSE Tablets—
120/600 mg (V/6211)... MC-27, A5
Guanabenz.............. MC-14, A2
Guanfacine............ MC-14, A3-4
Watson Tablets—
1 mg (WATSON 444) ..MC-14, A4
2 mg (WATSON 453) ..MC-14, A4
Halcion Tablets—
0.125 mg (HALCION 0.125)................ MC-31, D4
0.25 mg (HALCION 0.25) MC-31, D4
Haldol Tablets—
0.5 mg (McNEIL/ HALDOL).............. MC-14, A5
1 mg (McNEIL/ HALDOL 1) MC-14, A5
2 mg (McNEIL/ HALDOL 2) MC-14, A5
5 mg (McNEIL/ HALDOL 5) MC-14, A6

Haldol Tablets *(continued)*
10 mg (McNEIL/ HALDOL 10).......... MC-14, A6
20 mg (McNEIL/ HALDOL 20).......... MC-14, A6
Haloperidol........... MC-14, A5-7
Mylan Tablets—
0.5 mg (MYLAN 351) ..MC-14, A7
1 mg (MYLAN 257) MC-14, A7
2 mg (MYLAN 214) MC-14, A7
5 mg (MYLAN 327) MC-14, A7
Halotestin Tablets—
2 mg (HALOTESTIN 2) MC-13, A1
5 mg (HALOTESTIN 5) MC-13, A1
10 mg (HALOTESTIN 10) MC-13, A1
Helidac Therapy Capsules—
500 mg (PG 12) MC-29, D3
Helidac Therapy Chewable Tablets—
262.4 mg (PG 11) MC-3, D7
Helidac Therapy Tablets—
250 mg (PG 10) MC-20, A3
Hismanal Tablets—
10 mg (JANSSEN/ Ast 10)................. MC-2, D5
0.75 mg (ROCHE/HIVID 0.750).................. MC-32, D1
Hivid Tablets—
Hydergine Tablets—
1 mg (Logo/ HYDERGINE 1) MC-11, A7
Hydergine LC Capsules—
1 mg (Logo/HYDERGINE LC 1 mg) MC-11, A6
Hydralazine MC-14, B1-2
Lederle Tablets—
25 mg (Logo/H11) MC-14, B1
50 mg (Logo/H12) MC-14, B1
Hydralazine and Hydrochlorothiazide MC-14, B3-4
Hydrea Capsules—
500 mg (HYDREA 830/HYDREA 830)................. MC-14, D7
Hydrochlorothiazide .. MC-14, B5-C1
Geneva Tablets—
25 mg (GG 28)....... MC-14, B6
50 mg (GG 27)....... MC-14, B6
Hydrocodone and Acetaminophen.....MC-14, C2-D1
Watson Tablets—
2.5/500 mg (WATSON 388).................. MC-14, C7
5/500 mg (WATSON 349).................. MC-14, C7
7.5/500 mg (WATSON 385).................. MC-14, C7
7.5/650 mg (WATSON 502).................. MC-14, D1
7.5/750 mg (WATSON 387).................. MC-14, C7
10/650 mg (WATSON 503).................. MC-14, D1
Hydrocortisone MC-14, D2-3
Hydrocortone Tablets—
10 mg (HYDROCORTONE/ MSD 619)............. MC-14, D2
HydroDIURIL Tablets—
25 mg (MSD 42/ HYDRODIURIL) MC-14, B7
50 mg (MSD 105/ HYDRODIURIL) MC-14, B7
Hydromorphone MC-14, D4
Hydroxychloroquine .. MC-14, D5-6
Invamed Tablets—
200 mg (INV 250) MC-14, D5
Hydroxyurea.. MC-14, D7-MC-15, A1
Roxane Capsules—
500 mg (54 072) MC-15, A1
Hydroxyzine........... MC-15, A2-4
Barr Capsules—
25 mg (barr 323/25) .. MC-15, A2
100 mg (barr 324/ 100)................. MC-15, A2
Hygroton Tablets—
25 mg (Logo/H 22r)......MC-7, A3
50 mg (Logo/H 20r)......MC-7, A3
100 mg (Logo/21) MC-7, A3

Hyoscyamine Sulfate ... MC-15, A5
Hytrin Capsules—
1 mg (Logo/DF) ... MC-29, B7
2 mg (Logo/HY) ... MC-29, B7
5 mg (Logo/HK) ... MC-29, C1
10 mg (Logo/HN) ... MC-29, C1
Hyzaar Tablets—
50/12.5 mg (MRK 717/ HYZAAR) ... MC-18, A1
Ibuprofen ... MC-15, A6-B6
Mylan Tablets—
400 mg (MYLAN 1401) ... MC-15, A6
800 mg (MYLAN 1801) ... MC-15, A7
Rugby Tablets—
400 mg (RUGBY/ 4604) ... MC-15, B3
600 mg (RUGBY/ 4605) ... MC-15, B3
800 mg (RUGBY/ 4606) ... MC-15, B4
Schein Tablets—
200 mg (DAN/5585) .. MC-15, B5
400 mg (DAN/5584) .. MC-15, B5
600 mg (DAN/5586) .. MC-15, B6
800 mg (DAN/5644) .. MC-15, B6
Ilosone Capsules—
250 mg (DISTA H09/ ILOSONE 250 mg) ... MC-11, C4
Ilosone Tablets—
500 mg (DISTA U26) .. MC-11, C5
Imipramine ... MC-15, B7-C3
Geneva Tablets—
10 mg (GG/41) ... MC-15, C3
25 mg (GG/47) ... MC-15, C3
Imitrex Tablets—
25 mg (Logo/25) ... MC-29, A5
50 mg (Imitrex/50) ... MC-29, A5
Imodium Capsules—
2 mg (JANSSEN/ IMODIUM) ... MC-17, C7
Imuran Tablets—
50 mg (IMURAN 50) ... MC-3, B5
Indapamide ... MC-15, C4-5
UDL Tablets—
2.5 mg (M/80) ... MC-15, C5
Inderal Tablets—
10 mg (Logo/INDERAL 10) ... MC-26, D2
20 mg (Logo/INDERAL 20) ... MC-26, D2
40 mg (Logo/INDERAL 40) ... MC-26, D2
60 mg (Logo/INDERAL 60) ... MC-26, D2
80 mg (Logo/INDERAL 80) ... MC-26, D2
Inderal LA Extended-release Capsules—
60 mg (INDERAL LA 60) ... MC-26, C7
80 mg (INDERAL LA 80) ... MC-26, C7
120 mg (INDERAL LA 120) ... MC-26, D1
160 mg (INDERAL LA 160) ... MC-26, D1
Inderide Tablets—
40/25 mg (Logo/INDERIDE 40/25) ... MC-27, A1
80/25 mg (Logo/INDERIDE 80/25) ... MC-27, A1
Inderide LA Extended-release Capsules—
80/50 mg (INDERIDE LA 80/50) ... MC-26, D6
120/50 mg (INDERIDE LA 120/50) ... MC-26, D6
160/50 mg (INDERIDE LA 160/50) ... MC-26, D7
Indinavir ... MC-15, C6
Indocin Capsules—
25 mg (MSD 25/ INDOCIN) ... MC-15, D1
50 mg (MSD 50/ INDOCIN) ... MC-15, D1
Indocin SR Extended-release Capsules—
75 mg (MSD 693/ INDOCIN SR) ... MC-15, D2
Indomethacin ... MC-15, C7-D2
Geneva Capsules—
25 mg (GG 517) ... MC-15, C7
50 mg (GG 518) ... MC-15, C7
Invirase Capsules—
200 mg (ROCHE 0245) ... MC-28, A6
ISMO Tablets—
20 mg (Logo/ISMO 20) ... MC-16, A6
Isoniazid ... MC-15, D3-4
Barr Tablets—
100 mg (Barr 066/ 100) ... MC-15, D3
300 mg (Barr 071/ 300) ... MC-15, D3
Paddock Tablets—
300 mg (Logo 4350) .. MC-15, D4
Isoptin SR Extended-release Tablets—
120 mg (KNOLL/ 120 SR) ... MC-32, B4
180 mg (ISOPTIN SR/180 MG) ... MC-32, B4
240 mg (Logo Logo/ ISOPTIN SR) ... MC-32, B4
Isordil Extended-release Tablets—
40 mg (WYETH/4125) .. MC-15, D7
Isordil Sublingual Tablets—
2.5 mg (W/2.5) ... MC-16, A1
5 mg (W/5) ... MC-16, A1
10 mg (WYETH/10) ... MC-16, A1
Isordil Tablets—
5 mg (WYETH 4152) .. MC-15, D6
10 mg (WYETH 4153) ... MC-15, D6
20 mg (WYETH 4154) ... MC-15, D6
30 mg (WYETH 4159) ... MC-15, D6
40 mg (WYETH 4192) ... MC-15, D6
Isosorbide Dinitrate ... MC-15, D5-MC-16, A4
Isosorbide Mononitrate ... MC-16, A5-6
Isotretinoin ... MC-16, A7
Isradipine ... MC-16, B1
Itraconazole ... MC-16, B2
K-Dur Extended-release Tablets—
750 mg (K-DUR 10) .. MC-25, B4
1500 mg (K-DUR 20) .. MC-25, B4
K-Tab Extended-release Tablets—
750 mg (K-TAB) ... MC-25, B2
Kerlone Tablets—
10 mg (KERLONE 10) .. MC-3, D5
20 mg (Logo/KERLONE 20) ... MC-3, D5
Ketoconazole ... MC-16, B3
Ketoprofen ... MC-16, B4-7
Ketorolac ... MC-16, C1
Klonopin Tablets—
0.5 mg (KLONOPIN 0.5 ROCHE) ... MC-7, C6
1 mg (KLONOPIN 1 ROCHE) ... MC-7, C6
2 mg (KLONOPIN 2 ROCHE) ... MC-7, C6
Klor-Con Extended-release Tablets—
600 mg (KLOR-CON 8) ... MC-25, B7
750 mg (KLOR-CON 10) ... MC-25, B7
Klotrix Extended-release Tablets—
750 mg (Logo KLOTRIX 10 mEq 710) ... MC-25, B3
Kytril Tablets—
1 mg (K1) ... MC-13, D6
Labetalol ... MC-16, C2-3
Lamictal Tablets—
25 mg (LAMICTAL 25) ... MC-16, C5
100 mg (LAMICTAL 100) ... MC-16, C5
Lamictal Tablets *(continued)*
150 mg (LAMICTAL 150) ... MC-16, C6
200 mg (LAMICTAL 200) ... MC-16, C6
Lamisil Tablets—
250 mg (LAMISIL/250) MC-29, C2
Lamivudine ... MC-16, C4
Lamotrigine ... MC-16, C5-6
Lanoxicaps Capsules—
0.05 mg (A2C) ... MC-9, B7
0.1 mg (B2C) ... MC-9, B7
0.2 mg (C2C) ... MC-9, B7
Lanoxin Tablets—
0.125 mg (LANOXIN Y3B) ... MC-9, C1
0.25 mg (LANOXIN X3A) ... MC-9, C1
Lansoprazole ... MC-16, C7
Lariam Tablets—
250 mg (LARIAM ROCHE 250) ... MC-18, B5
Lasix Tablets—
20 mg (HOECHST/ LASIX®) ... MC-13, B5
40 mg (HOECHST/ LASIX® 40) ... MC-13, B5
80 mg (HOESCHST/ LASIX® 80) ... MC-13, B5
Ledercillin VK Tablets—
250 mg (Logo/L10) ... MC-24, B6
500 mg (Logo/L9) ... MC-24, B6
Lescol Capsules—
20 mg (Logo 20/LESCOL Logo) ... MC-13, B2
40 mg (Logo 40/LESCOL Logo) ... MC-13, B2
Leucovorin ... MC-16, D1-3
Barr Tablets—
5 mg (Logo/484) ... MC-16, D1
25 mg (Logo/485) ... MC-16, D1
Immunex Tablets—
5 mg (LL 5/C 33) ... MC-16, D3
15 mg (LL 15/C 35) .. MC-16, D3
Leukeran Tablets—
2 mg (635) ... MC-6, B4
Levaquin Tablets—
250 mg (McNEIL 1520/ 250) ... MC-16, D4
Levatol Tablets—
20 mg (Logo 22) ... MC-24, B4
Levbid Extended-release Tablets—
0.375 mg (SP 538) ... MC-15, A5
Levlen 21 and 28 Tablets—
0.15/0.03 mg (B/21) ... MC-16, D5
Inert (B/28) ... MC-16, D5
Levofloxacin ... MC-16, D4
Levonorgestrel and Ethinyl Estradiol ... MC-16, D5-MC-17, A1
Levothyroxine ... MC-17, A2-6
Rugby Tablets—
0.1 mg (RUGBY/ 3952) ... MC-17, A6
0.15 mg (RUGBY/ 3953) ... MC-17, A6
0.2 mg (RUGBY/ 4381) ... MC-17, A6
0.3 mg (RUGBY/ 3958) ... MC-17, A6
Levoxyl Tablets—
0.025 mg (LEVOXYL/ Logo 25) ... MC-17, A2
0.05 mg (LEVOXYL/ Logo 50) ... MC-17, A2
0.075 mg (LEVOXYL/ Logo 75) ... MC-17, A2
0.088 mg (LEVOXYL/ Logo 88) ... MC-17, A2
0.1 mg (LEVOXYL/ Logo 100) ... MC-17, A2
0.112 mg (LEVOXYL/ Logo 112) ... MC-17, A2
0.125 mg (LEVOXYL/ Logo 125) ... MC-17, A3
0.137 mg (LEVOXYL/Logo 137) ... MC-17, A3
0.15 mg (LEVOXYL/Logo 150) ... MC-17, A3
0.175 mg (LEVOXYL/Logo 175) ... MC-17, A3
Levoxyl Tablets *(continued)*
0.2 mg (LEVOXYL/Logo 200) ... MC-17, A3
0.3 mg (LEVOXYL/Logo 300) ... MC-17, A3
Lexxel Extended-release Tablets—
5/5 mg (LEXXEL 1 5-5) ... MC-11, A1
Librax Capsules—
5/2.5 mg (ROCHE LIBRAX®) ... MC-6, C2
Librium Capsules—
5 mg (ROCHE/ LIBRIUM® 5) ... MC-6, B6
10 mg (ROCHE/ LIBRIUM® 10) ... MC-6, B6
25 mg (ROCHE/ LIBRIUM® 25) ... MC-6, B6
Limbitrol Tablets—
5/12.5 mg (ROCHE/ LIMBITROL®) ... MC-6, C1
10/25 mg (ROCHE/ LIMBITROL® DS) ... MC-6, C1
Lioresal Tablets—
10 mg (Geigy 23) ... MC-3, C1
20 mg (Geigy/33) ... MC-3, C1
Lipitor Tablets—
10 mg (PD155/10) ... MC-3, A5
20 mg (PD156) ... MC-3, A5
40 mg (PD 157/40) ... MC-3, A6
Lisinopril ... MC-17, A7-B3
Lisinopril and Hydrochlorothiazide MC-17, B4-5
Lithium ... MC-17, B6-C5
Roxane Capsules—
150 mg (54 213) ... MC-17, B6
300 mg (54 463) ... MC-17, B6
600 mg (54 702/) ... MC-17, B6
Roxane Tablets—
300 mg (54 452) ... MC-17, B7
Lithobid Extended-release Tablets—
300 mg (SOLVAY 4492) ... MC-17, C5
Lithonate Capsules—
300 mg (SOLVAY/ 7512) ... MC-17, C3
Lithotab Tablets—
300 mg (SOLVAY 7516) ... MC-17, C4
Lo-Ovral-21 and -28 Tablets—
0.3/0.03 mg (WYETH/ 78) ... MC-23, A1
Inert (WYETH/486) ... MC-23, A1
Lodine Capsules—
200 mg (LODINE 200) ... MC-12, A7
300 mg (LODINE 300) ... MC-12, A7
Lodine Tablets—
400 mg (LODINE 400) ... MC-12, B1
500 mg (LODINE 500) ... MC-12, B1
Loestrin 21 1/20 Tablets—
1/0.02 mg (P-D 915) ... MC-22, C6
Loestrin 21 1.5/30 Tablets—
1.5/0.03mg (P-D 916) .. MC-22, C7
Loestrin Fe 1/20 Tablets—
75 mg (P-D 622) ... MC-22, D1
1/0.02 mg (P-D 915) ... MC-22, D1
Loestrin Fe 1.5/30 Tablets—
75 mg (P-D 622) ... MC-22, D2
1.5/0.03 mg (P-D 916) ... MC-22, D2
Lomefloxacin ... MC-17, C6
Lomotil Tablets—
2.5/0.025 mg (Searle/ 61) ... MC-9, D7
Loniten Tablets—
2.5 mg (U121/2) ... MC-20, B6
10 mg (LONITEN 10) .. MC-20, B6
Loperamide ... MC-17, C7
Lopid Tablets—
600 mg (Lopid) ... MC-13, C3
Lopressor Tablets—
50 mg (GEIGY/51) ... MC-19, D3
100 mg (GEIGY/71) ... MC-19, D3

Lopressor HCT Tablets—
100/25 mg (GEIGY/ 53).................. MC-20, A2
100/50 mg (GEIGY/ 73).................. MC-20, A2
Lorabid Capsules—
200 mg (Lilly 3170/LORABID 200 mg).............. MC-17, D1
400 mg (Lilly 3171/LORABID 400 mg).............. MC-17, D1
Loracarbef MC-17, D1
Loratadine MC-17, D2
Loratadine and Pseudoephedrine...... MC-17, D3
Lorazepam MC-17, D4-6
Mylan Tablets—
0.5 mg (M/321) MC-17, D4
1 mg (MYLAN 457)... MC-17, D4
2 mg (MYLAN 777)... MC-17, D4
Purepac Tablets—
0.5 mg (Logo/57) MC-17, D5
1 mg (Logo/59) MC-17, D5
2 mg (Logo/063) MC-17, D5
Lortab Tablets—
2.5/500 mg (ucb/901)... MC-14, C5
5/500 mg (ucb/902) MC-14, C5
7.5/500 mg (ucb/903)... MC-14, C6
10/500 (ucb/910) MC-14, C6
Losartan MC-17, D7
Losartan and Hydrochlorothiazide... MC-18, A1
Lotensin Tablets—
5 mg (LOTENSIN/5) MC-3, C3
10 mg (LOTENSIN/10).. MC-3, C3
20 mg (LOTENSIN/20).. MC-3, C3
40 mg (LOTENSIN/40).. MC-3, C3
Lotensin HCT Tablets—
5/6.25 mg (LOTENSIN HCT/57)............... MC-3, C4
10/12.5 mg (LOTENSIN HCT/72)............... MC-3, C4
20/12.5 mg (LOTENSIN HCT/74)............... MC-3, C5
20/25 mg (LOTENSIN HCT/75)............... MC-3, C5
Lotrel Capsules—
2.5/10 mg (LOTREL 2255).................MC-2, B1
5/20 mg (LOTREL 2265).................MC-2, B1
5/10 mg (LOTREL 2260).................MC-2, B1
Lovastatin............... MC-18, A2
Loxapine............... MC-18, A3-5
Watson Capsules—
5 mg (WATSON 369/ 5 mg)............... MC-18, A4
10 mg (WATSON 370/ 10 mg)............... MC-18, A4
25 mg (WATSON 371/ 25 mg)............... MC-18, A5
50 mg (WATSON 372/ 50 mg)............... MC-18, A5
Loxitane Capsules—
25 mg (Lederle L3/ 25 mg)............... MC-18, A3
Lozol Tablets—
1.25 mg (R/7).......... MC-15, C4
2.5 mg (R/8).......... MC-15, C4
Ludiomil Tablets—
25 mg (CIBA/110)....... MC-18, A6
50 mg (CIBA/26)....... MC-18, A6
75 mg (CIBA/135)....... MC-18, A6
Lufyllin Tablets—
200 mg (WALLACE 521).................... MC-10, D
400 mg (WALLACE 731)..................MC-10, D5
Luvox Tablets—
25 mg (SOLVAY 4202).................. MC-13, B3
50 mg (SOLVAY 4205).................. MC-13, B3
100 mg (SOLVAY 4210).................. MC-13, B3
Macrobid Capsules—
100 mg (Norwich Eaton/ Macrobid) MC-22, A4
Macrodantin Capsules—
25 mg (MACRODANTIN 25 mg/0149 0007) MC-22, A5
50 mg (MACRODANTIN 50 mg/0149 0008) MC-22, A5
100 mg (MACRODANTIN 100 mg/0149 0009)... MC-22, A5
Maprotiline MC-18, A6
Mavik Tablets—
1 mg (KNOLL 1)....... MC-31, B3
2 mg (KNOLL 2)....... MC-31, B3
4 mg (KNOLL 4)....... MC-31, B3
Maxaquin Tablets—
400 mg (MAXAQUIN 400)................ MC-17, C6
Maxzide Tablets—
37.5/25 mg (Logo M9/ MAXIDE)............. MC-31, D2
75/50 mg (Logo M8/ MAXIDE)............. MC-31, D2
Meclizine.............MC-18, A7-B1
Geneva Tablets—
12.5 mg (GG 141)...... MC-18, A7
25 mg (GG 261)...... MC-18, A7
Meclofenamate........ MC-18, B2-3
Mylan Capsules—
50 mg (MYLAN 2150/ MYLAN 2150) MC-18, B2
100 mg (MYLAN 3000/ MYLAN 3000) MC-18, B2
Schein Capsules—
50 mg (DAN 5636/ DAN 5636).......... MC-18, B3
100 mg (DAN 5637/ DAN 5637) MC-18, B3
Medrol Tablets—
2 mg (MEDROL 2) MC-19, C1
4 mg (MEDROL 4) MC-19, C1
8 mg (MEDROL 8) MC-19, C1
16 mg (MEDROL 16).. MC-19, C2
24 mg (MEDROL 24).. MC-19, C2
32 mg (MEDROL 32).. MC-19, C2
Medroxyprogesterone .. MC-18, B4
Mefloquine.............. MC-18, B5
Megace Tablets—
20 mg (MJ 595) MC-18, B7
40 mg (MEGACE/40) .. MC-18, B7
Megestrol MC-18, B6-7
Barr Tablets—
40 mg (barr/555 607).................. MC-18, B6
Mellaril Tablets—
10 mg (Logo/78-2) MC-30, B6
15 mg (Logo/78-8) MC-30, B6
25 mg (Logo/MELLARIL 25)..................... MC-30, B6
50 mg (Logo/MELLARIL 50)..................... MC-30, B6
100 mg (Logo/MELLARIL 100)..................... MC-30, B7
150 mg (Logo/MELLARIL 150)..................... MC-30, B7
200 mg (Logo/MELLARIL 200)..................... MC-30, B7
Melphalan.............. MC-18, C1
Menest Tablets—
0.625 mg (BMP 126) .. MC-11, D7
Meperidine MC-18, C2-3
Barr Tablets—
50 mg (Logo/381)...... MC-18, C2
100 mg (barr/382)...... MC-18, C2
Mercaptopurine MC-18, C4
Mesalamine MC-18, C5-6
Mesoridazine........... MC-18, C7
Metaproterenol....... MC-18, D1-2
Goldline Tablets—
10 mg (BL/132)....... MC-18, D2
Metformin MC-18, D3
Methergine Tablets—
0.2 mg (SANDOZ/ 78 54) MC-19, B5
Methocarbamol MC-18, D4-5
Geneva Tablets—
500 mg (GG 190) MC-18, D4
750 mg (GG 101) MC-18, D4
Methocarbamol and Aspirin............ MC-18, D6-7
Zenith Tablets—
400/325 mg (Z 2813).. MC-18, D7
Methotrexate.......... MC-19, A1-3
Barr Tablets—
2.5 mg (Logo 572).... MC-19, A1
Roxane Tablets—
2.5 mg (54 323)...... MC-19, A2
Methyclothiazide...... MC-19, A4-5
Geneva Tablets—
2.5 mg (GG 244) MC-19, A5
5 mg (GG 242)...... MC-19, A5
Methyldopa............ MC-19, A6-7
Goldline Tablets—
250 mg (Z 2931) MC-19, A6
500 mg (Z 2932)...... MC-19, A6
Methyldopa and Hydrochlorothiazide MC-19, B1-4
Qualitest Tablets—
250/15 mg (par 186).. MC-19, B3
250/25 mg (INV 206) MC-19, B3
Schein Tablets—
250/15 mg MC-19, B4
Methylergonovine....... MC-19, B5
Methylphenidate MC-19, B6-7
Methylprednisolone... MC-19, C1-3
URL Tablets—
4 mg (Logo 301) MC-19, C3
Methyltestosterone and Esterified Estrogens........... MC-19, C4
Metoclopramide....... MC-19, C5-7
Purepac Tablets—
10 mg (Logo/269)...... MC-19, C5
Rugby Tablets—
10 mg (RUGBY/ 4042) MC-19, C7
Metoprolol Succinate MC-19, D1-2
Metoprolol Tartrate ... MC-19, D3-MC-20, A1
Geneva Tablets—
50 mg (GG 414)...... MC-19, D4
100 mg (GG 415) MC-19, D4
Mutual Tablets—
50 mg (Logo 184) MC-19, D5
100 mg (Logo 185)... MC-19, D5
Mylan Tablets—
100 mg (M 47) MC-19, D6
Novopharm Tablets—
100 mg (N 734/100).. MC-19, D7
Purepac Tablets—
50 mg (Logo/554)..... MC-20, A1
100 mg (Logo/555).... MC-20, A1
Metoprolol and Hydrochlorothiazide .. MC-20, A2
Metronidazole......... MC-20, A3-6
Rugby Tablets—
250 mg (RUGBY/ 4018) MC-20, A4
500 mg (RUGBY/ 4019)................ MC-20, A4
Mevacor Tablets—
10 mg (MSD 730/ MEVACOR) MC-18, A2
20 mg (MSD 731/ MEVACOR)............ MC-18, A2
40 mg (MSD 732/ MEVACOR)............ MC-18, A2
Mexiletine MC-20, A7-B1
Roxane Capsules—
150 mg (54 523/54 523).................. MC-20, A7
200 mg (54/632)...... MC-20, A7
250 mg (54/959)....... MC-20, B1
Mibefradil MC-20, B2
Micro-K Extended-release Capsules—
600 mg (MICRO-K/AHR 5720)................... MC-25, B5
750 mg (MICRO-K 10/AHR 5730)................... MC-25, B5
Micronase Tablets—
1.25 mg (MICRONASE 1.25) MC-13, D5
2.5 mg (MICRONASE 2.5) MC-13, D5
5 mg (MICRONASE 5) MC-13, D5
Midamor Tablets—
5 mg (MSD 92/ MIDAMOR)............ MC-1, D5
Minipress Capsules—
1 mg (PFIZER 431/ MINIPRESS) MC-25, C3
2 mg (PFIZER 437/ MINIPRESS) MC-25, C3
5 mg (PFIZER 438/ MINIPRESS) MC-25, C4
Minizide Capsules—
1/0.5 mg (PFIZER 430/ MINIZIDE).............. MC-25, C6
2/0.5 mg (PFIZER 432/ MINIZIDE).............. MC-25, C6
5/0.5 mg (PFIZER 436/ MINIZIDE).............. MC-25, C7
Minocin Capsules—
50 mg (Lederle M45/ 50 mg)............ MC-20, B3
100 mg (Lederle M46/ 100 mg)............ MC-20, B3
Minocycline MC-20, B3-5
Lederle Tablets—
50 mg (Logo/M 45)... MC-20, B4
100 mg (Logo/M 46)... MC-20, B4
Warner Chilcott Capsules—
50 mg (WC 615/ WC 615)............ MC-20, B5
100 mg (WC 616/ WC 616)............ MC-20, B5
Minoxidil MC-20, B6-7
Schein Tablets—
2.5 mg (DAN 5642)... MC-20, B7
10 mg (DAN 5643)... MC-20, B7
Mirtazapine............... MC-20, C1
Misoprostol MC-20, C2
Moduretic Tablets—
5/50 mg (MSD 917/ Logo).................... MC-1, D7
Moexipril MC-20, C3
Moexipril and Hydrochlorothiazide... MC-20, C4
Monoket Tablets—
10 mg (Schwarz 610/ 10)..................... MC-16, A5
20 mg (Schwarz 620/ 20)..................... MC-16, A5
Monopril Tablets—
10 mg (BMS/MONOPRIL 10)..................... MC-13, B4
20 mg (BMS/MONOPRIL 20)..................... MC-13, B4
Moricizine............... MC-20, C5-6
Morphine............MC-20, C7-D3
Motrin Tablets—
300 mg (MOTRIN 300 mg)............... MC-15, B1
400 mg (MOTRIN 400 mg)............... MC-15, B1
600 mg (MOTRIN 600 mg)............... MC-15, B2
800 mg (MOTRIN 800 mg)............... MC-15, B2
MS Contin Extended-release Tablets—
15 mg (PF/M 15) MC-20, D2
30 mg (PF/M 30) MC-20, D2
60 mg (PF/M 60) MC-20, D2
100 mg (PF/100)....... MC-20, D3
200 mg (PF/M 200)...... MC-20, D3
MSIR Capsules—
15 mg (PF MSIR 15/ THIS END UP) MC-20, C7
30 mg (PF MSIR 30/ THIS END UP) MC-20, C7
MSIR Tablets—
15 mg (PF/MI 15)...... MC-20, D1
30 mg (PF/MI 30)...... MC-20, D1
Mycelex Troche Lozenges—
10 mg (MYCELEX 10)...MC-8, A3
Mycobutin Capsules—
150 mg (Adria MYCOBUTIN) MC-27, D2
Mycophenolate........... MC-20, D4
Myleran Tablets—
2 mg (MYLERAN K2A) ..MC-4, B4
Nabumetone MC-20, D5-6
Nadolol...... MC-20, D7-MC-21, A2
Apothecon Tablets—
20 mg (AP 2461)..... MC-20, D7
40 mg (AP 2462)..... MC-20, D7
120 mg (AP 2464)..... MC-20, D7

Nadolol and Bendroflumethiazide ... MC-21, A3
Nalfon Capsules—
200 mg (DISTA H76/ NALFON 200) ... MC-12, C2
300 mg (DISTA H77/ NALFON) ... MC-12, C2
Nalidixic Acid ... MC-21, A4
Naprelan Extended-release Tablets—
375 mg (W/901) ... MC-21, B5
500 mg (W/902) ... MC-21, B5
Naprosyn Tablets—
250 mg (SYNTEX/NAPROSYN 250) ... MC-21, B1
375 mg (NAPROSYN/ 375) ... MC-21, B1
500 mg (NAPROSYN/ 500) ... MC-21, B1
Naproxen ... MC-21, A5-B2
Lemmon Tablets—
250 mg (93/147) ... MC-21, A5
375 mg (93/148) ... MC-21, A5
Mylan Tablets—
250 mg (MYLAN/ 377) ... MC-21, A6
375 mg (MYLAN/ 555) ... MC-21, A6
500 mg (MYLAN/ 451) ... MC-21, A6
Purepac Tablets—
250 mg (Logo/521) ... MC-21, A7
375 mg (Logo/522) ... MC-21, A7
500 mg (Logo/523) ... MC-21, A7
Naproxen Sodium ... MC-21, B3-5
Purepac Tablets—
275 mg (Logo/547) ... MC-21, B3
550 mg (Logo/548) ... MC-21, B3
Naturetin Tablets—
5 mg (PPP 606/ NATURETIN 5) ... MC-3, C6
10 mg (PPP 618/ NATURETIN 10) ... MC-3, C6
Navane Capsules—
1 mg (ROERIG 571/ NAVANE) ... MC-30, C2
2 mg (ROERIG 572/ NAVANE) ... MC-30, C2
5 mg (ROERIG 573/ NAVANE) ... MC-30, C2
10 mg (ROERIG 574/ NAVANE) ... MC-30, C3
20 mg (ROERIG 577/ NAVANE) ... MC-30, C3
Nefazodone ... MC-21, B6-7
NegGram Tablets—
250 mg (Logo/N 21) ... MC-21, A4
500 mg (Logo/N 22) ... MC-21, A4
1 gram (Logo/N 23) ... MC-21, A4
Neoral Capsules—
25 mg (NEORAL 25 mg) ... MC-8, B3
100 mg (NEORAL 100 mg) ... MC-8, B3
Neurontin Capsules—
100 mg (Logo/Neurotonin® 100 mg) ... MC-13, B7
300 mg (Logo/Neurotonin® 300 mg) ... MC-13, B7
400 mg (Logo/Neurotonin® 400 mg) ... MC-13, C1
Niacin ... MC-21, C1-4
Nicardipine ... MC-21, C5-7
Nicobid Extended-release Capsules—
125 mg (Logo/NICOBID 125 mg) ... MC-21, C1
250 mg (Logo/NICOBID 250 mg) ... MC-21, C1
500 mg (RORER/ NICOBID 500) ... MC-21, C2
Nicolar Tablets—
500 mg (Logo/ Logo NE) ... MC-21, C3
Nifedipine ... MC-21, D1-6
Purepac Capsules—
10 mg (Logo 497) ... MC-21, D6
20 mg (Logo 530) ... MC-21, D6
Nilandron Tablets—
50 mg (Logo/168) ... MC-21, D7
Nilutamide ... MC-21, D7
Nimodipine ... MC-22, A1
Nimotop Capsules—
30 mg (NIMOTOP) ... MC-22, A1
Nisoldipine ... MC-22, A2-3
Nitrofurantoin ... MC-22, A4-6
Schein Capsules—
25 mg (DAN 25 mg/ NITROFURANTOIN MACROCRYSTALS) ... MC-22, A6
50 mg (DAN 50 mg/ NITROFURANTOIN MACROCRYSTALS) ... MC-22, A6
100 mg (DAN 100 mg/ NITROFURANTOIN MACROCRYSTALS) ... MC-22, A6
Nitroglycerin ... MC-22, A7-B1
Goldline Extended-release Capsules—
6.5 mg (TCL/1222) ... MC-22, A7
9 mg (TCL/1223) ... MC-22, A7
Nitrostat Sublingual Tablets—
0.3 mg ... MC-22, B1
0.4 mg ... MC-22, B1
0.6 mg ... MC-22, B1
Nizatidine ... MC-22, B2
Nizoral Tablets—
200 mg (JANSSEN/NI- ZORAL) ... MC-16, B3
Nolvadex Tablets—
10 mg (NOLVADEX 600) ... MC-29, B3
20 mg (Logo/NOLVADEX 604) ... MC-29, B3
Nordette-21 and -28 Tablets—
0.15/0.03 mg (WYETH/ 75) ... MC-16, D7
Inert (WYETH/ 486) ... MC-16, D7
Norethindrone and Ethinyl Estradiol ... MC-22, B3-C2
Norethindrone and Mestranol ... MC-22, C3-5
Norethindrone Acetate and Ethinyl Estradiol ... MC-22, C6-7
Norethindrone Acetate/Ethinyl Estradiol and Ferrous Fumarate ... MC-22, D1-3
Norfloxacin ... MC-22, D4
Norgestimate and Ethinyl Estradiol ... MC-22, D5-7
Norgestrel and Ethinyl Estradiol ... MC-23, A1-2
Normodyne Tablets—
100 mg (SCHERING 244/ NORMODYNE 100) ... MC-16, C3
200 mg (SCHERING 752/ NORMODYNE 200) ... MC-16, C3
300 mg (SCHERING 438/ NORMODYNE 300) ... MC-16, C3
Noroxin Tablets—
400 mg (MSD 705/ NOROXIN) ... MC-22, D4
Norpace Capsules—
100 mg (SEARLE 2752/ NORPACE 100 mg) ... MC-10, A6
150 mg (SEARLE 2762/ NORPACE 150 mg) ... MC-10, A6
Norpace CR Extended-release Capsules—
100 mg (SEARLE 2732/ NORPACE CR 100 mg) ... MC-10, A7
150 mg (SEARLE 2742/ NORPACE CR 150 mg) ... MC-10, A7
Norpramin Tablets—
10 mg (68-7) ... MC-8, C3
25 mg (NORPRAMIN 25) ... MC-8, C3
50 mg (NORPRAMIN 50) ... MC-8, C3
75 mg (NORPRAMIN 75) ... MC-8, C4
100 mg (NORPRAMIN 100) ... MC-8, C4
150 mg (NORPRAMIN 150) ... MC-8, C4
Nortriptyline ... MC-23, A3-6
Mylan Capsules—
10 mg (MYLAN 1410) ... MC-23, A3
25 mg (MYLAN 2325) ... MC-23, A3
50 mg (MYLAN 3250) ... MC-23, A4
75 mg (MYLAN 4175) ... MC-23, A4
Norvasc Tablets—
2.5 mg (NORVASC/2.5) ... MC-2, A7
5 mg (NORVASC 5) ... MC-2, A7
10 mg (NORVASC 10) ... MC-2, A7
Ofloxacin ... MC-23, A7-B1
Olanzapine ... MC-23, B2-3
Olsalazine ... MC-23, B4
Omeprazole ... MC-23, B5
Omnipen Capsules—
250 mg (Wyeth/53) ... MC-2, D1
500 mg (Wyeth/309) ... MC-2, D1
Ondansetron ... MC-23, B6
Optimine Tablets—
1 mg (SCHERING Logo/ 282) ... MC-3, B3
Oretic Tablets—
25 mg (Logo) ... MC-14, B5
50 mg (Logo) ... MC-14, B5
Orinase Tablets—
500 mg (ORINASE 500) ... MC-30, D7
Ortho-Cyclen Tablets—
0.250/0.035 mg (Ortho 250) ... MC-22, D5
Inert (Ortho) ... MC-22, D5
Ortho-Cept Tablets—
0.15/ 0.03 mg (ORTHO/ D 150) ... MC-8, C7
Inert (ORTHO P) ... MC-8, C7
Ortho-Est Tablets—
0.625 mg (Ortho 1801) ... MC-12, A2
1.25 mg (Ortho 1800) ... MC-12, A2
Ortho-Novum 1/35-21 and -28 Tablets—
1/0.035 mg (Ortho 135) ... MC-22, B5
Inert (Ortho) ... MC-22, B5
Ortho-Novum 1/50-21 and -28 Tablets—
1/0.05 mg (Ortho 150) ... MC-22, C3
Inert (Ortho) ... MC-22, C3
Ortho-Novum 7/7/7-21 and -28 Tablets—
0.5/ 0.035 mg (Ortho 535) ... MC-22, B6
0.75/0.035 mg (Ortho 75) ... MC-22, B6
1/0.035 mg (Ortho 135) ... MC-22, B7
Inert (Ortho) ... MC-22, B7
Ortho Tri-Cyclen Tablets—
0.180/0.035 mg (Ortho 180) ... MC-22, D6
0.215/0.035 mg (Ortho 215) ... MC-22, D6
0.25/0.035 mg (Ortho 250) ... MC-22, D7
Inert (Ortho) ... MC-22, D7
Orudis Capsules—
25 mg (WYETH 4186/ ORUDIS® 25) ... MC-16, B4
50 mg (WYETH 4181/ ORUDIS® 50) ... MC-16, B4
75 mg (WYETH 4187/ ORUDIS® 75) ... MC-16, B5
Oruvail Extended-release Capsules—
100 mg (ORUVAIL 100) ... MC-16, B6
150 mg (ORUVAIL 150) ... MC-16, B6
200 mg (ORUVAIL 200) ... MC-16, B7
Ovcon 35-21 and -28 Tablets—
0.4/0.035 mg (MJ/583) ... MC-22, B3
Inert (MJ/850) ... MC-22, B3
Ovcon 50-21 and -28 Tablets—
1/0.05 mg (MJ/584) ... MC-22, B4
Inert (MJ/850) ... MC-22, B4
Ovral-21 and -28 Tablets—
0.5/0.05 mg (WYETH/ 56) ... MC-23, A2
0.5/0.05 mg (WYETH/ 56) ... MC-23, A2
Oxaprozin ... MC-23, B7
Oxazepam ... MC-23, C1-3
Purepac Capsules—
10 mg (Logo-067) ... MC-23, C1
15 mg (Logo-069) ... MC-23, C1
30 mg (Logo-073) ... MC-23, C1
Oxybutynin ... MC-23, C4-5
Qualitest Tablets—
5 mg (SL 456) ... MC-23, C5
Oxycodone ... MC-23, C6-D2
Oxycodone and Acetaminophen ... MC-23, D3-5
Oxycodone and Aspirin ... MC-23, D6-MC-24, A1
OxyContin Extended-release Tablets—
10 mg (OC/10) ... MC-23, C7
20 mg (OC/20) ... MC-23, C7
40 mg (OC/40) ... MC-23, D1
80 mg (OC/80) ... MC-23, D1
OxyIR Capsules—
5 mg (O-IR/PF 5 mg) ... MC-23, C6
Pamelor Capsules—
10 mg (Logo SANDOZ/ Logo PAMELOR) ... MC-23, A5
25 mg (Logo SANDOZ/ PAMELOR) ... MC-23, A5
50 mg (Logo SANDOZ/ PAMELOR) ... MC-23, A6
75 mg (Logo SANDOZ/ PAMELOR) ... MC-23, A6
Pancrease Delayed-release Capsules—
4/12/12 (McNEILPancrease MT 4) ... MC-24, A4
4/20/25 (McNEIL/ Pancrease) ... MC-24, A4
10/30/30 (McNEIL/Pancrease MT 10) ... MC-24, A4
16/48/48 (McNEIL/Pancrease MT 16) ... MC-24, A5
25/75/75 (McNEIL/Pancrease MT 25) ... MC-24, A5
Pancreatin ... MC-24, A2-3
Pancrelipase ... MC-24, A4-6
Panmycin Capsules—
250 mg (PANMYCIN 250 mg/ PANMYCIN 250 mg) ... MC-29, D4
Parafon Forte DSC Tablets—
500 mg (McNEIL/ PARAFON FORTE DSC) ... MC-7, A5
Parlodel Capsules—
5 mg (Logo/PARLODEL 5 mg) ... MC-4, A3
Parlodel Tablets—
2.5 mg (PARLODEL 2 1/2) ... MC-4, A4
Parnate Tablets—
10 mg (PARNATE SKF) ... MC-31, B6
Paroxetine ... MC-24, A7-B1
Paxil Tablets—
10 mg (PAXIL/10) ... MC-24, A7
20 mg (PAXIL/20) ... MC-24, A7
30 mg (PAXIL/30) ... MC-24, B1
40 mg (PAXIL/40) ... MC-24, B1
PCE Tablets—
333 mg (Logo PCE) ... MC-11, B4
500 mg (Logo EK) ... MC-11, B4
Pemoline ... MC-24, B2-3
Pen-Vee K Tablets—
250 mg (WYETH/59) ... MC-24, C2
500 mg (WYETH/390) ... MC-24, C2
Penbutolol ... MC-24, B4
Penetrex Tablets—
200 mg (Logo/5100) ... MC-11, A3
400 mg (Logo/5140) ... MC-11, A3
Penicillin V ... MC-24, B5-C2
Warner Chilcott Tablets—
250 mg (WC648) ... MC-24, C1
500 mg (WC673) ... MC-24, C1

Pentasa Extended-release Capsules—
250 mg (Logo 2010/PENTASA 250 mg Logo)......... MC-18, C5
Pentazocine and Acetaminophen........ MC-24, C3
Pentazocine and Naloxone............ MC-24, C4
Pentosan................ MC-24, C5
Pentoxifylline MC-24, C6
Pepcid Tablets—
20 mg (PEPCID/ MSD 963)............. MC-12, B4
40 mg (PEPCID/ MSD 964)............. MC-12, B4
Percocet Tablets—
5/325 mg (DuPont/ PERCOCET)......... MC-23, D3
Percodan Tablets—
4.88/325 mg (DuPont/ PERCODAN).......... MC-23, D6
Percodan-Demi Tablets—
2.44/325 mg (DuPont/ PERCODAN DEMI) ... MC-23, D7
Pergolide............. MC-24, C7
Perindopril MC-24, D1
Permax Tablets—
0.25 mg (Logo (A) 625).................. MC-24, C7
0.05 mg (A615) MC-24, C7
1 mg (A630) MC-24, C7
Perphenazine and Amitriptyline......... MC-24, D2-3
Mylan Tablets—
2/10 mg (MYLAN/ 330).................. MC-24, D2
2/25 mg (MYLAN/ 442).................. MC-24, D2
4/25 mg (MYLAN/ 574).................. MC-24, D2
4/10 mg (MYLAN/ 727).................. MC-24, D3
4/50 mg (MYLAN/73) MC-24, D3
Persantine Tablets—
25 mg (BI/17).......... MC-10, A2
50 mg (BI/18).......... MC-10, A2
75 mg (BI/19).......... MC-10, A2
Phenaphen with Codeine Capsules—
325/15 mg (AHR 6242) ...MC-1, B1
325/30 mg (AHR 6257) ...MC-1, B1
Phendimetrazine........ MC-24, D4
Phenergan Tablets—
12.5 mg (WYETH/19).. MC-26, B4
25 mg (WYETH 27) ... MC-26, B4
50 mg (WYETH/227)... MC-26, B4
Phenobarbital......... MC-24, D5-6
Lilly Tablets—
15 mg (Lilly J31) MC-24, D5
Warner Chilcott Tablets—
15 mg (WC 699) MC-24, D6
30 mg (WC 700) MC-24, D6
60 mg (WC 607) MC-24, D6
100 mg (WC 698) MC-24, D6
Phenylephrine, Phenylpropanolamine, and Guaifenesin........... MC-24, D7
Phenylpropanolamine and Guaifenesin.......... MC-25, A1-2
Sidmak Extended-release Tablets—
75/400 mg (SL 385) .. MC-25, A2
Phenytoin MC-25, A3-4
PhosLo Tablets—
667 mg (BRA 200)...... MC-4, D3
Pindolol............... MC-25, A5-6
Mutual Tablets—
5 mg (Logo 178) MC-25, A5
10 mg (Logo 183) MC-25, A5
Piroxicam MC-25, A7-B1
Mylan Capsules—
10 mg (MYLAN 1010/ MYLAN 1010) MC-25, A7
20 mg (MYLAN 2020/ MYLAN 2020) MC-25, A7
Plaquenil Tablets—
200 mg (PLAQUENIL) MC-14, D6
Plendil Extended-release Tablets—
2.5 mg (PLENDIL/450) MC-12, B6
5 mg (PLENDIL/451)... MC-12, B6
10 mg (PLENDIL/452).. MC-12, B7
Pondimin Tablets—
20 mg (AHR 6447) MC-12, C1
Posicor Tablets—
50 mg (ROCHE/POSICOR 50).................. MC-20, B2
100 mg (ROCHE/POSICOR 100).................. MC-20, B2
Potassium Chloride .. MC-25, B2-7
Pravachol Tablets—
10 mg (Logo/PRAVACHOL 10) MC-25, C1
20 mg (PRAVACHOL 20/ Logo).................. MC-25, C1
40 mg (Logo/PRAVACHOL 40) MC-25, C1
Pravastatin............. MC-25, C1
Prazosin.............. MC-25, C2-5
Mylan Capsules—
1 mg (MYLAN 1101) MC-25, C2
2 mg (MYLAN 2302) MC-25, C2
5 mg (MYLAN 3205) MC-25, C2
Purepac Capsules—
1 mg (Logo-500)...... MC-25, C5
2 mg (Logo-501)...... MC-25, C5
5 mg (Logo-502)...... MC-25, C5
Prazosin and Polythiazide.......... MC-25, C6-7
Precose Tablets—
50 mg (PRECOSE 50)...MC-1, A1
100 mg (PRECOSE 100).....................MC-1, A1
Prednisone............ MC-25, D1-5
Purepac Tablets—
5 mg (Logo/336)...... MC-25, D3
10 mg (Logo/338)..... MC-25, D3
20 mg (Logo/337)..... MC-25, D3
Roxane Tablets—
1 mg (54 092)......... MC-25, D4
2.5 mg (54 339)...... MC-25, D4
5 mg (54 612)........ MC-25, D4
10 mg (54 899)....... MC-25, D4
20 mg (54 760)....... MC-25, D4
50 mg (54 343)....... MC-25, D4
Rugby Tablets—
5 mg (Logo 189) MC-25, D5
10 mg (RUGBY/ 4325) MC-25, D5
20 mg (RUGBY/ 4326) MC-25, D5
50 mg (Logo 527) MC-25, D5
Prelu-2 Extended-release Capsules—
105 mg (BI/64)......... MC-24, D4
Premarin Tablets—
0.3 mg (PREMARIN 0.3) MC-11, D5
0.625 mg (PREMARIN 0.625)................. MC-11, D5
0.9 mg (PREMARIN 0.9) MC-11, D5
1.25 mg (PREMARIN 1.25) MC-11, D6
2.5 mg (PREMARIN 2.5) MC-11, D6
Prevacid Delayed-release Capsules—
15 mg (Logo/PREVACID 15) MC-16, C7
30 mg (Logo/PREVACID 30) MC-16, C7
Prilosec Delayed-release Capsules—
10 mg (PRILOSEC 10/ 606)................. MC-23, B5
20 mg (PRILOSEC 20/ 742)................. MC-23, B5
Principen Capsules—
250 mg (BRISTOL 7992)................ MC-2, C5
500 mg (BRISTOL 7993)................ MC-2, C5
Prinivil Tablets—
2.5 mg (MSD/15)....... MC-17, A7
5 mg (MSD 19/ PRINIVIL) MC-17, A7
Prinivil Tablets *(continued)*
10 mg (MSD 106/ PRINIVIL) MC-17, A7
20 mg (MSD 207/ PRINIVIL) MC-17, B1
40 mg (MSD 237/ PRINIVIL) MC-17, B1
Prinzide Tablets—
10/12.5 mg (MSD 145/ PRINZIDE) MC-17, B4
20/12.5 mg (MSD 140/ PRINZIDE) MC-17, B4
20/25 mg (MSD 142/ PRINZIDE) MC-17, B4
Pro-Banthine Tablets—
7.5 mg (SEARLE/611).. MC-26, B6
15 mg (SEARLE/601) .. MC-26, B6
Procainamide MC-25, D6-MC-26, A7
Copley Extended-release Tablets—
500 mg (COPLEY/ 188)................. MC-26, A3
750 mg (COPLEY/ 114)................. MC-26, A3
Qualitest Capsules—
250 mg (Logo 2345).. MC-26, A5
500 mg (Logo 2347).. MC-26, A5
Qualitest Extended-release Tablets—
750 mg (COPLEY/ 114)................. MC-26, A6
UDL Capsules—
250 mg (DAN 5026).. MC-26, A7
500 mg (Logo 2347)...MC-26, A7
Procanbid Extended-release Tablets—
500 mg (Procanbid/ 500)................ MC-26, A4
1000 mg (Procanbid/ 1000)................ MC-26, A4
Procardia Capsules—
10 mg (PROCARDIA PFIZER 260).......... MC-21, D4
20 mg (PROCARDIA 20 PFIZER 261).......... MC-21, D4
Procardia XL Extended-release Tablets—
30 mg (PROCARDIA XL 30) MC-21, D5
60 mg (PROCARDIA XL/60)................. MC-21, D5
90 mg (PROCARDIA XL 90) MC-21, D5
Prochlorperazine...... MC-26, B1-2
Prograf Capsules—
1 mg (1 mg/Logo 617)................. MC-29, B1
Prolixin Tablets—
1 mg (PPP 863) MC-13, A2
2.5 mg (PPP 864) MC-13, A2
5 mg (PPP 877) MC-13, A2
10 mg (PPP 956)...... MC-13, A2
Proloprim Tablets—
100 mg (PROLOPRIM 09A).................. MC-32, A1
200 mg (PROLOPRIM 200)................. MC-32, A1
Promethazine MC-26, B3-4
ESI Tablets—
12.5 mg (59911/ 5871) MC-26, B3
25 mg (59911 5872).. MC-26, B3
Pronestyl Capsules—
250 mg (SQUIBB 758)................. MC-25, D6
375 mg (SQUIBB 756)................. MC-25, D6
500 mg (SQUIBB 757)................. MC-25, D7
Pronestyl Tablets—
250 mg (SQUIBB 431)................. MC-26, A1
375 mg (SQUIBB 434)................. MC-26, A1
500 mg (SQUIBB 438)................. MC-26, A1
Pronestyl-SR Extended-release Tablets—
500 mg (PPP 775)..... MC-26, A2
Propafenone MC-26, B5
Propantheline MC-26, B6-7
Roxane Tablets—
15 mg (54 303)...... MC-26, B7
Propoxyphene Napsylate and Acetaminophen...... MC-26, C1-3
Mylan Tablets—
100/650 mg (1155).... MC-26, C2
Purepac Tablets—
100/650 mg (Logo/ 085)................. MC-26, C3
Propranolol MC-26, C4-D2
Lederle Tablets—
20 mg (Logo/P 45) ... MC-26, C4
40 mg (Logo/P 46) ... MC-26, C4
80 mg (Logo/P 47) ... MC-26, C4
Purepac Tablets—
10 mg (Logo/27)...... MC-26, C5
20 mg (Logo/29)...... MC-26, C5
40 mg (Logo/331)..... MC-26, C5
60 mg (Logo/321)..... MC-26, C5
80 mg (Logo/333)..... MC-26, C5
Rugby Tablets—
10 mg (RUGBY/4309) MC-26, C6
20 mg (RUGBY/4313) MC-26, C6
40 mg (RUGBY/4314) MC-26, C6
60 mg (RUGBY/4315) MC-26, C6
80 mg (RUGBY/4316) MC-26, C6
Propranolol and Hydrochlorothiazide .. MC-26, D3-MC-27, A1
Barr Tablets—
40/25 mg (barr/ 555 427)............. MC-26, D3
80/25 mg (barr/ 555 428)............. MC-26, D3
Purepac Tablets—
40/25 mg (Logo/358).. MC-26, D4
80/25 mg (Logo/360).. MC-26, D4
Rugby Tablets—
40/25 mg (RUGBY/ 4402) MC-26, D5
80/25 mg (RUGBY/ 4403) MC-26, D5
Propulsid Tablets—
10 mg (JANSSEN/P10) ..MC-7, B5
20 mg (JANSSEN/P20) ..MC-7, B5
Proscar Tablets—
5 mg (MSD 72/ PROSCAR) MC-12, D2
ProSom Tablets—
1 mg (Logo UC) MC-11, D2
2 mg (Logo UD) MC-11, D2
Protriptyline........... MC-27, A2-3
Sidmak Tablets—
5 mg (SL 523)........ MC-27, A3
10 mg (SL 524) MC-27, A3
Proventil Extended-release Tablets—
4 mg (Logo 431).........MC-1, B7
Provera Tablets—
2.5 mg (PROVERA 2.5) MC-18, B4
5 mg (PROVERA 5) ... MC-18, B4
10 mg (PROVERA 10) MC-18, B4
Prozac Capsules—
10 mg (DISTA 3104/ PROZAC 10 mg) ... MC-12, D7
20 mg (DISTA 3105/ PROZAC 20 mg) MC-12, D7
Pseudoephedrine and Guaifenesin.......... MC-27, A4-5
Purinethol Tablets—
50 mg (PURINETHOL 04A).................. MC-18, C4
Pyrimethamine......... MC-27, A6
Quazepam.............. MC-27, A7
Quibron Capsules—
150/90 mg (BRISTOL 516)................. MC-30, B2
300/180 mg (BRISTOL 515)................. MC-30, B2
Quibron-T Dividose Tablets—
300 mg (BL 512) MC-30, A5
Quibron-T/SR Dividose Extended-release Tablets—
300 mg (BL 519) MC-30, A6

Quinaglute Dura-Tabs Extended-release Tablets—
324 mg (Logo/Clockface) MC-27, B3
Quinapril MC-27, B1-2
Quinidex Extended-release Tablets—
300 mg (AHR QUIN-IDEX) MC-27, B6
Quinidine Gluconate .. MC-27, B3-5
Mutual Extended-release Tablets—
324 mg (Logo 66) MC-27, B4
Schein Extended-release Tablets—
324 mg (DAN/5538) .. MC-27, B5
Quinidine Sulfate MC-27, B6-7
Roxane Tablets—
300 mg (54 053/300) MC-27, B7
Ramipril MC-27, C1
Ranitidine MC-27, C2-4
Ranitidine Bismuth Citrate MC-27, C5
Redux Capsules—
15 mg (REDUX) MC-8, D3
Reglan Tablets—
5 mg (AHR/REGLAN 5) MC-19, C6
10 mg (AHR 10/REGLAN) MC-19, C6
Regroton Tablets—
0.25/50 mg (R 31) MC-27, C7
Relafen Tablets—
500 mg (RELAFEN/500) MC-20, D5
750 mg (RELAFEN/750) MC-20, D6
Remeron Tablets—
15 mg (Organon/TZ 3 TZ 3) MC-20, C1
Reserpine and Chlorthalidone MC-27, C6-7
Reserpine, Hydralazine, and Hydrochlorothiazide ... MC-27, D1
Restoril Capsules—
7.5 mg (RESTORIL 7.5mg/FOR SLEEP) MC-29, B5
15 mg (RESTORIL 15 mg/FOR SLEEP) MC-29, B5
30 mg (RESTORIL 30 mg/FOR SLEEP) MC-29, B5
Retrovir Capsules—
100 mg (Logo Wellcome/Y9C 100) MC-32, D2
Retrovir Tablets—
300 mg (GX CW3/300) MC-32, D3
Rezulin Tablets—
200 mg (PD 352/200) .. MC-32, A4
400 mg (PD 353/400) .. MC-32, A4
Rheumatrex Tablets—
2.5 mg (Logo/M 1) MC-19, A3
Rifabutin MC-27, D2
Rifadin Capsules—
150 mg (RIFADIN 150) MC-27, D3
300 mg (RIFADIN 300) MC-27, D3
Rifamate Capsules—
300/150 mg (RIFAMATE/RIFAMATE) MC-27, D5
Rifampin MC-27, D3-4
Rifampin and Isoniazid MC-27, D5
Rifampin, Isoniazid, and Pyrazinamide MC-27, D6
Rifater Tablets—
120/50/300 mg (RIFATER) MC-27, D6
Rilutek Tablets—
50 mg (RPR 202) MC-27, D7
Riluzole MC-27, D7
Rimactane Capsules—
300 mg (CIBA 154/CIBA 154) MC-27, D4
Rimantadine MC-28, A1
Risperdal Tablets—
1 mg (JANSSEN/R 1) .. MC-28, A2
2 mg (JANSSEN/R 2) .. MC-28, A2
3 mg (JANSSEN/R 3) .. MC-28, A3
4 mg (JANSSEN/R 4) .. MC-28, A3
Risperidone MC-28, A2-3
Ritalin Tablets—
5 mg (CIBA/7) MC-19, B6
10 mg (CIBA/3) MC-19, B6
20 mg (CIBA/34) MC-19, B6
Ritalin-SR Extended-release Tablets—
20 mg (CIBA 16) MC-19, B7
Robaxin Tablets—
500 mg (AHR/ROBAXIN) MC-18, D5
750 mg (AHR/ROBAXIN 750) MC-18, D5
Robaxisal Tablets—
400/325 mg (AHR ROBAXISAL) MC-18, D6
Rocaltrol Capsules—
0.25 mcg (ROCALTROL 0.25 ROCHE) MC-4, D2
0.5 mcg (ROCALTROL 0.5 ROCHE) MC-4, D2
Rondec-TR Tablets—
8/120 mg (R/6240) MC-5, B5
Roxicet Tablets—
5/325 mg (54 543) MC-23, D5
5/500 mg (54 730) MC-23, D5
Roxicodone Tablets—
5 mg (54 582) MC-23, D2
Roxiprin Tablets—
4.88/325 mg (54 902) .. MC-24, A1
Rynatan Tablets—
8/25/25 mg (WALLACE 713) MC-6, C7
Rythmol Tablets—
150 mg (Logo 150) MC-26, B5
225 mg (Logo/225) MC-26, B5
300 mg (Logo 300) MC-26, B5
Salsalate MC-28, A4-5
Mutual Tablets—
500 mg (Logo 174) ... MC-28, A4
750 mg (Logo 177) ... MC-28, A4
Sidmak Tablets—
500 mg (SL 390) MC-28, A5
Sandimmune SGC Capsules—
25 mg (Logo 78 240) MC-8, B4
50 mg (Logo 78 242) MC-8, B4
100 mg (Logo 78 241) MC-8, B5
Saquinavir MC-28, A6
Sectral Capsules—
200 mg (WYETH 4177/SECTRAL 200) MC-1, A4
400 mg (WYETH 4179/SECTRAL 400) MC-1, A4
Seldane Tablets—
60 mg (SELDANE) MC-29, C4
Seldane-D Tablets—
60/120 mg (SELDANE D) MC-29, C5
Selegiline MC-28, A7-B1
Novopharm Tablets—
5 mg (N 179/5) MC-28, A7
Septra Tablets—
400/80 mg (SEPTRA Y2B) MC-28, D1
800/160 mg (SEPTRA DS 02C) MC-28, D1
Ser-Ap-Es Tablets—
0.1/25/15 mg (CIBA/71) MC-27, D1
Serax Capsules—
10 mg (WYETH-51 Logo/SERAX 10) MC-23, C2
15 mg (WYETH-6 Logo/SERAX 15) MC-23, C2
30 mg (WYETH-52 Logo/SERAX 30) MC-23, C2
Serax Tablets—
15 mg (WYETH 317/15) MC-23, C3
Serentil Tablets—
10 mg (BI/10) MC-18, C7
25 mg (BI/25) MC-18, C7
50 mg (BI/50) MC-18, C7
Sertraline MC-28, B2
Serzone Tablets—
100 mg (BMS 100/32) MC-21, B6
150 mg (BMS 150/39) MC-21, B6
200 mg (BMS 200/33) MC-21, B7
250 mg (BMS 250/41) MC-21, B7
Simvastatin MC-28, B3
Sinemet Tablets—
10/100 mg (SINEMET/647) MC-5, B1
25/100 mg (SINEMET/650) MC-5, B1
25/250 mg (SINEMET/654) MC-5, B1
Sinemet CR Extended-release Tablets—
25/100 mg (SINEMET CR/601) MC-5, B2
50/200 mg (SINEMET CR/521) MC-5, B2
Sinequan Capsules—
10 mg (SINEQUAN/ROERIG 534) MC-10, C3
25 mg (SINEQUAN/ROERIG 535) MC-10, C3
50 mg (SINEQUAN/ROERIG 536) MC-10, C3
75 mg (SINEQUAN/ROERIG 539) MC-10, C4
100 mg (SINEQUAN/ROERIG 538) MC-10, C4
150 mg (SINEQUAN/ROERIG 537) MC-10, C4
Slo-bid Extended-release Capsules—
50 mg (RORER/Slo-bid 50) MC-30, A1
75 mg (Logo/Slo-bid 75 mg) MC-30, A1
100 mg (Logo/Slo-bid 100 mg) MC-30, A1
125 mg (Logo/Slo-bid 125 mg) MC-30, A2
200 mg (Logo/Slo-bid 200 mg) MC-30, A2
300 mg (Logo/Slo-bid 300 mg) MC-30, A2
Slo-Niacin Extended-release Tablets—
250 mg (250) MC-21, C4
500 mg (500) MC-21, C4
750 mg (750) MC-21, C4
Slo-Phyllin Extended-release Capsules—
60 mg (WHR 1354) MC-30, A3
125 mg (Logo/Slo-Phyllin 125 mg) MC-30, A3
250 mg (WHR 1356) MC-30, A3
Slo-Phyllin Tablets—
100 mg (Logo 351) MC-30, A4
200 mg (Logo 352) MC-30, A4
Slow-K Extended-release Tablets—
600 mg (Slow-K) MC-25, B6
Soma Tablets—
350 mg (37 WALLACE 2001/SOMA) MC-5, B7
Soma Compound Tablets—
200/325 mg (WALLACE 2103/SOMA C) MC-5, C2
Soma Compound with Codeine Tablets—
200/325/16 mg (WALLACE 2403/SOMA CC) MC-5, C3
Sorbitrate Chewable Tablets—
5 mg (S/810) MC-16, A3
10 mg (S/815) MC-16, A3
Sorbitrate Sublingual Tablets—
2.5 mg (S/853) MC-16, A4
5 mg (S/760) MC-16, A4
Sorbitrate Tablets—
5 mg (S/770) MC-16, A2
10 mg (S/780) MC-16, A2
20 mg (S/820) MC-16, A2
30 mg (S/773) MC-16, A2
40 mg (S/774) MC-16, A2
Sotalol MC-28, B4-5
Sparfloxacin MC-28, B6
Spironolactone MC-28, B7-C1
Purepac Tablets—
25 mg (Logo/338) MC-28, B7
Spironolactone and Hydrochlorothiazide MC-28, C2-4
Geneva Tablets—
25/25 mg (GG 95) MC-28, C2
URL Tablets—
25/25 mg (Logo 40) .. MC-28, C4
Sporanox Capsules—
100 mg (JANSSEN SPORANOX 100) MC-16, B2
Stavudine MC-28, C5
Stelazine Tablets—
2 mg (SKF 504) MC-31, D7
Sucralfate MC-28, C6
Sular Extended-release Tablets—
10 mg (ZENECA 10/891) MC-22, A2
20 mg (ZENECA 20/892) MC-22, A2
30 mg (ZENECA 30/893) MC-22, A3
40 mg (ZENECA 40/894) MC-22, A3
Sulfadoxine & Pyrimethamine MC-28, C7
Sulfamethoxazole and Trimethoprim MC-28, D1-3
Schein Tablets—
400/80 mg (DAN 5546) MC-28, D3
800/160 mg (DAN 5547) MC-28, D3
Sulfasalazine MC-28, D4-6
Rugby Tablets—
500 mg (RUGBY/4617) MC-28, D6
Sulfinpyrazone MC-28, D7-MC-29, A1
Barr Capsules—
200 mg (barr/272) MC-28, D7
Barr Tablets—
100 mg (barr/555 271) MC-29, A1
Sulindac MC-29, A2-4
Mutual Tablets—
150 mg (Logo 112) ... MC-29, A3
200 mg (Logo 116) ... MC-29, A3
Schein Tablets—
150 mg (DAN/5661) .. MC-29, A4
200 mg (DAN 5660) .. MC-29, A4
Sumatriptan MC-29, A5
Sumycin Capsules—
250 mg (SQUIBB 655) MC-29, C6
500 mg (SQUIBB 763) MC-29, C6
Sumycin Tablets—
250 mg (SQUIBB 663) MC-29, C7
500 mg (SQUIBB 603) MC-29, C7
Suprax Tablets—
200 mg (Logo 200/SUPRAX) MC-5, D5
400 mg (Logo 400/SUPRAX) MC-5, D5
Surmontil Capsules—
25 mg (WYETH/4132) .. MC-32, A3
50 mg (WYETH/4133) .. MC-32, A3
100 mg (WYETH/4158) MC-32, A3
Symmetrel Capsules—
100 mg (DuPont/SYMMETREL) MC-1, D2
Synalgos-DC Capsules—
356.4/30/16 mg (WYETH/4191) MC-2, D4
Synthroid Tablets—
0.025 mg (FLINT/25) ... MC-17, A4
0.05 mg (FLINT/50) ... MC-17, A4
0.075 mg (FLINT/75) ... MC-17, A4
0.088 mg (FLINT/88) ... MC-17, A4
0.1 mg (FLINT/100) ... MC-17, A4
0.112 mg (FLINT/112) .. MC-17, A4
0.125 mg (FLINT/125) .. MC-17, A5
0.15 mg (FLINT/150) ... MC-17, A5
0.175 mg (FLINT/175) .. MC-17, A5
0.2 mg (FLINT/200) MC-17, A5
0.3 mg (FLINT/300) MC-17, A5
Tacrine MC-29, A6-7
Tacrolimus MC-29, B1
Tagamet Tablets—
200 mg (TAGAMET 200 SKF) MC-7, B1
300 mg (TAGAMET 300 SB) MC-7, B1

Tagamet Tablets *(continued)*
400 mg (TAGAMET 400 SB)................MC-7, B2
800 mg (TAGAMET 800 SB)................MC-7, B2
Talacen Tablets—
25/650 mg (Winthrop/ T37).................. MC-24, C3
Talwin-Nx Tablets—
50/0.5 mg (Logo/ T 51).................. MC-24, C4
Tambocor Tablets—
50 mg (3M/TR 50)..... MC-12, D3
100 mg (3M/TR 100) .. MC-12, D3
Tamoxifen............ MC-29, B2-3
Barr Tablets—
10 mg (barr/446)...... MC-29, B2
Tarka Extended-release Tablets—
1/240 mg (Logo 241/ TARKA)............... MC-31, B4
2/180 mg (Logo 182/ TARKA)............... MC-31, B5
2/240 mg (Logo 242/ TARKA)............... MC-31, B4
4/240 mg (Logo 244/ TARKA)............... MC-31, B5
Tegretol Chewable Tablets—
100 mg (TEGRETOL/ 52 52)..................MC-5, A3
Tegretol Tablets—
200 mg (TEGRETOL/ 27 27)..................MC-5, A2
Tegretol-XR Extended-release Tablets—
200 mg (T (Logo)/ 200 mg)..................MC-5, A4
Temazepam........... MC-29, B4-6
Mylan Capsules—
15 mg (MYLAN 4010)............... MC-29, B4
30 mg (MYLAN 5050)............... MC-29, B4
Purepac Capsules—
15 mg (Logo-076)..... MC-29, B6
30 mg (Logo-077)..... MC-29, B6
Tenex Tablets—
1 mg (AHR 1/ TENEX)............... MC-14, A3
2 mg (AHR 2/ TENEX)............... MC-14, A3
Tenoretic Tablets—
50/25 mg (TENORETIC/ 115)..................MC-3, A4
100/25 mg (TENORETIC/ 117)..................MC-3, A4
Tenormin Tablets—
25 mg (Logo/107)........MC-3, A1
50 mg (TENORMIN/ 105)..................MC-3, A1
100 mg (TENORMIN/ 101)..................MC-3, A1
Tenuate Extended-release Tablets—
75 mg (TENUATE 75) ...MC-9, B4
Tenuate Tablets—
25 mg (TENUATE 25) ...MC-9, B3
Terazosin............MC-29, B7-C1
Terbinafine............. MC-29, C2
Terbutaline............. MC-29, C3
Terfenadine............. MC-29, C4
Terfenadine and Pseudoephedrine...... MC-29, C5
Tetracycline..........MC-29, C6-D5
Barr Capsules—
250 mg (barr/011)..... MC-29, D1
500 mg (barr/010)..... MC-29, D1
Purepac Capsules—
250 mg (Logo-404) ... MC-29, D5
500 mg (Logo-406) ... MC-29, D5
Thalitone Tablets—
25 mg (BI/76)..................MC-7, A2
Theo-24 Extended-release Capsules—
100 mg (ucb 2832/Theo-24 100).................. MC-30, A7
200 mg (ucb 2842/Theo-24 200).................. MC-30, A7
300 mg (ucb 2852/Theo-24 300).................. MC-30, B1
400 mg (ucb 2902/Theo-24 400).................. MC-30, B1
Theo-Dur Extended-release Tablets—
100 mg (THEO-DUR 100).................. MC-29, D6
200 mg (THEO-DUR 200).................. MC-29, D6
300 mg (THEO-DUR 300).................. MC-29, D6
Theophylline........... MC-29, D6-MC-30, B1
Theophylline and Guaifenesin.......... MC-30, B2
Thioridazine.......... MC-30, B3-7
Creighton Tablets—
10 mg (Logo/264)..... MC-30, B3
25 mg (Logo/266)..... MC-30, B3
100 mg (CP/268) MC-30, B3
Geneva Tablets—
150 mg (GG 35)...... MC-30, B4
200 mg (GG 36)...... MC-30, B4
Mylan Tablets—
10 mg (M 54/10) MC-30, B5
25 mg (M 58/25) MC-30, B5
50 mg (M 59/50) MC-30, B5
100 mg (M 61/100)... MC-30, B5
Thiothixene.......... MC-30, C1-5
Geneva Capsules—
1 mg (GG 589)....... MC-30, C1
2 mg (GG 596)....... MC-30, C1
5 mg (GG 597)....... MC-30, C1
10 mg (GG 598)...... MC-30, C1
Schein Capsules—
1 mg (DAN 5593) MC-30, C4
2 mg (DAN 5592) MC-30, C4
5 mg (DAN 5595) MC-30, C5
10 mg (DAN 5594) ... MC-30, C5
Thorazine Extended-release Capsules—
75 mg (SKF T64)....... MC-6, D1
150 mg (SKF T66)....... MC-6, D1
Thorazine Tablets—
10 mg (SKF T73)....... MC-6, D2
25 mg (SKF T74)....... MC-6, D2
50 mg (SKF T76)....... MC-6, D3
Ticlid Tablets—
250 mg (Ticlid/250)..... MC-30, C6
Ticlopidine............... MC-30, C6
Timolol..............MC-30, C7-D1
Mylan Tablets—
5 mg (M 55).......... MC-30, D1
10 mg (M 221) MC-30, D1
20 mg (M 715) MC-30, D1
Tizanidine................ MC-30, D2
Tocainide................ MC-30, D3
Tofranil Tablets—
10 mg (GEIGY/32) MC-15, C2
25 mg (GEIGY/140).... MC-15, C2
50 mg (GEIGY/136).... MC-15, C2
Tofranil-PM Capsules—
75 mg (GEIGY/20)...... MC-15, B7
100 mg (GEIGY/40)..... MC-15, B7
125 mg (GEIGY/45)..... MC-15, C1
150 mg (GEIGY/22)..... MC-15, C1
Tolazamide........... MC-30, D4-5
Zenith Tablets—
100 mg (Z 2978) MC-30, D5
250 mg (Z 2979) MC-30, D5
Tolbutamide........... MC-30, D6-7
Mylan Tablets—
500 mg (M 13) MC-30, D6
Tolectin Tablets—
200 mg (McNEIL/TOLECTIN 200).................. MC-31, A2
600 mg (McNEIL 600 TOLECTIN)............ MC-31, A2
Tolectin DS Capsules—
400 mg (McNEIL/TOLECTIN DS) MC-31, A1
Tolinase Tablets—
100 mg (TOLINASE 100).................. MC-30, D4
250 mg (TOLINASE 250).................. MC-30, D4
500 mg (TOLINASE 500).................. MC-30, D4
Tolmetin............... MC-31, A1-6
Mutual Capsules—
400 mg (MUTUAL 179).................. MC-31, A3
Mutual Tablets—
200 mg (Logo 50) MC-31, A4
Purepac Capsules—
400 mg (Logo-520) ... MC-31, A5
Purepac Tablets—
600 mg (Logo/480).... MC-31, A6
Tonocard Tablets—
400 mg (TONOCARD/ 707).................. MC-30, D3
600 mg (TONOCARD/ 709).................. MC-30, D3
Toprol XL Extended-release Tablets—
50 mg (A MO) MC-19, D1
100 mg (A MS) MC-19, D1
200 mg (A MY) MC-19, D2
Toradol Tablets—
10 mg (TORADOL/ SYNTEX).............. MC-16, C1
Torsemide............MC-31, A7-B1
Tramadol.................. MC-31, B2
Trandate Tablets—
100 mg (TRANDATE 100).................. MC-16, C2
200 mg (TRANDATE 200).................. MC-16, C2
300 mg (TRANDATE 300).................. MC-16, C2
Trandolapril.............. MC-31, B3
Trandolapril and Verapamil............ MC-31, B4-5
Tranxene SD Tablets—
11.25 mg (Logo TX) MC-7, D7
22.5 mg (Logo TY) MC-7, D7
Tranxene T-Tab Tablets—
3.75 mg (Logo/TL) MC-8, A1
7.5 mg (Logo/TM).........MC-8, A1
15 mg (Logo/TN)..........MC-8, A1
Tranylcypromine........ MC-31, B6
Trazodone.............MC-31, B7-C4
Barr Tablets—
50 mg (barr/555 489).................. MC-31, C2
100 mg (barr/555 490).................. MC-31, C2
Mutual Tablets—
50 mg (Logo 118) MC-31, C3
100 mg (Logo 114).... MC-31, C3
150 mg (MP 168/25-25 50-50)................ MC-31, C3
Purepac Tablets—
50 mg (Logo/439)..... MC-31, C4
100 mg (Logo/441)..... MC-31, C4
Trental Extended-release Tablets—
400 mg (HOECHST/TREN-TAL) MC-24, C6
Tretinoin.................. MC-31, C5
Tri-Levlen 21 and 28 Tablets—
0.05/0.03 mg (B/95).... MC-16, D6
0.075/0.04 mg (B/96)... MC-16, D6
0.125/0.03 mg (B/97)... MC-16, D6
Inert (B/11)............ MC-16, D6
Tri-phen-mine Extended-release Tablets—
5/15/10/40 mg (832 PPPC) MC-6, C6
Triamterene............... MC-31, C6
Triamterene and Hydrochlorothiazide....... MC-31, C7-D3
Barr Tablets—
75/50 mg (barr/555 444).................. MC-31, C7
Geneva Tablets—
75/50 mg (GG 172)... MC-31, D1
Triazolam............. MC-31, D4-5
Qualitest Tablets—
0.25 mg (Logo/ TR 250) MC-31, D5
Trifluoperazine....... MC-31, D6-7
Geneva Tablets—
1 mg (GG 51/1) MC-31, D6
2 mg (GG 53/2) MC-31, D6
5 mg (GG 55/5) MC-31, D6
10 mg (GG 58/10).... MC-31, D6
Trimethoprim.......... MC-32, A1-2
Schein Tablets—
100 mg (DAN DAN/ 5571)................ MC-32, A2
Trimipramine............ MC-32, A3
Trimox Capsules—
250 mg (BRISTOL 7278/ BRISTOL 7278).........MC-2, B4
500 mg (BRISTOL 7279/ BRISTOL 7279).........MC-2, B4
Trinalin Extended-release Tablets—
1/120 mg (TRINALIN 703)..................MC-3, B4
Triphasil-21 and -28 Tablets—
0.05/0.03 mg (Logo/ 641).................. MC-17, A10
.075/0.04 mg (Logo/ 642).................. MC-17, A1
0.125/0.03 mg (Logo/ 643)................... MC-17, A1
Inert (Logo/650) MC-17, A1
Tritec Tablets—
400 mg (Logo/ TRITEC) MC-27, C5
Troglitazone............. MC-32, A4
Tylenol with Codeine Tablets—
300/7.5 mg (McNEIL/TYLENOL CODEINE 1)............MC-1, A5
300/15 mg (McNEIL/TYLENOL CODEINE 2)............MC-1, A5
300/30 mg (McNEIL/TYLENOL CODEINE 3)............MC-1, A6
300/60 mg (McNEIL/TYLENOL CODEINE 4)............MC-1, A6
Tylox Capsules—
5/500 mg (TYLOX McNEIL/ TYLOX McNEIL) MC-23, D4
Ultram Tablets—
50 mg (McNEIL/659)... MC-31, B2
Uniphyl Extended-release Tablets—
400 mg (PF/U 400) MC-29, D7
600 mg (PF/U 600) MC-29, D7
Uniretic Tablets—
7.5/12.5 mg (S P/712) MC-20, C4
15/25 mg (S P/725).... MC-20, C4
Univasc Tablets—
7.5 mg (SP 7.5/707) ... MC-20, C3
15 mg (SP 15/715) MC-20, C3
Ursodiol................. MC-32, A5
V-Cillin K Tablets—
250 mg (V-CILLIN K 250 Lilly).................. MC-24, B7
500 mg (V-CILLIN K 500 Lilly).................. MC-24, B7
Valacyclovir............ MC-32, A6
Valium Tablets—
2 mg (ROCHE ROCHE/ 2 Valium®) MC-8, D6
5 mg (ROCHE ROCHE/ 5 Valium®) MC-8, D6
10 mg (ROCHE ROCHE/ 10 Valium®)............ MC-8, D6
Valproic Acid........MC-32, A7-B1
Goldline Capsules—
250 mg (0665 4120).. MC-32, B1
Valtrex Tablets—
500 mg (VALTREX 500 mg).............. MC-32, A6
1 gram (VALTREX 1 gram) MC-32, A6
Vantin Tablets—
100 mg (U 3617) MC-5, D6
200 mg (U 3618) MC-5, D6
Vascor Tablets—
200 mg (VASCOR 200) ..MC-3, D4
300 mg (VASCOR 300) ..MC-3, D4
400 mg (VASCOR 400) ..MC-3, D4

Vaseretic Tablets—
5/12.5 mg (MSD/173).... MC-11, A2
10/25 mg (MSD 720/ VASERETIC) MC-11, A2
Vasotec Tablets—
2.5 mg (MSD 14/ VASOTEC) MC-10, D7
5 mg (MSD 712/ VASOTEC) MC-10, D7
10 mg (MSD 713/ VASOTEC) MC-10, D7
20 mg (MSD 714/ VASOTEC) MC-10, D7
Veetids Tablets—
250 mg (BL V1)........ MC-24, B5
500 mg (BL V2)........ MC-24, B5
Velosef Capsules—
250 mg (SQUIBB 113).................... MC-6, B1
500 mg (SQUIBB 114).................... MC-6, B1
Venlafaxine........... MC-32, B2-3
Ventolin Tablets—
2 mg (Glaxo/ VENTOLIN 2) MC-1, B5
4 mg (Glaxo/ VENTOLIN 4) MC-1, B5
Verapamil MC-32, B4-C4
Purepac Tablets—
80 mg (Logo/473) MC-32, B5
120 mg (Logo/475).... MC-32, B5
Rugby Tablets—
80 mg (RUGBY/ 4812) MC-32, B6
120 mg (RUGBY/ 4932) MC-32, B6
Verelan Extended-release Capsules—
120 mg (Lederle V8/VERELAN 120 mg)............... MC-32, C3
180 mg (Lederle V7/VERELAN 180 mg)............... MC-32, C3
240 mg (Lederle V9/VERELAN 240 mg)............... MC-32, C4
360 mg (Lederle V6/VERELAN 360 mg)............... MC-32, C4
Vesanoid Capsules—
10 mg (VESANOID 10 ROCHE) MC-31, C5
Vibra-tabs Tablets—
100 mg (PFIZER 099/ VIBRA-TAB)........... MC-10, D1

Vibramycin Capsules—
50 mg (VIBRA/PFIZER 094)..................... MC-10, C7
100 mg (VIBRA/PFIZER 095)..................... MC-10, C7
Vicodin Tablets—
5/500 mg (VICODIN)... MC-14, C2
Vicodin ES Tablets—
7.5/750 mg (VICODIN ES)..................... MC-14, C3
Vicodin HP Tablets—
10/600 mg (VICODIN HP)..................... MC-14, C4
Videx Chewable Tablets—
100 mg (VIDEX/100) MC-9, B1
150 mg (VIDEX/150) MC-9, B2
Visken Tablets—
5 mg (VISKEN 5)...... MC-25, A6
10 mg (VISKEN 10/V) MC-25, A6
Vistaril Capsules—
25 mg (PFIZER 541/ VISTARIL)............ MC-15, A3
50 mg (PFIZER 542/ VISTARIL)............ MC-15, A3
100 mg (PFIZER 543/ VISTARIL)............ MC-15, A3
Vivactil Tablets—
5 mg (MSD 26/ VIVACTIL)............ MC-27, A2
Voltaren Tablets—
25 mg (VOLTAREN 25) MC-8, D7
50 mg (VOLARTEN 50) MC-8, D7
75 mg (VOLTAREN 75) MC-8, D7
Warfarin Sodium...... MC-32, C5-6
Wellbutrin Tablets—
75 mg (WELLBUTRIN 75) MC-4, A7
100 mg (WELLBUTRIN 100)..................... MC-4, A7
Wellbutrin SR Extended-release Tablets—
100 mg (WELLBUTRIN SR 100)................. MC-4, B2
150 mg (WELLBUTRIN SR 150)................. MC-4, B2
Wellcovorin Tablets—
5 mg (WELLCOVORIN 5) MC-16, D2
25 mg (WELLCOVORIN 25) MC-16, D2

Wymox Capsules—
250 mg (WYETH 559) .. MC-2, C1
500 mg (WYETH 560) .. MC-2, C1
Wytensin Tablets—
4 mg (WYETH 73/ W4) MC-14, A2
8 mg (WYETH 74/ W8) MC-14, A2
Xanax Tablets—
0.25 mg (XANAX 0.25) MC-1, C7
0.5 mg (XANAX 0.5).... MC-1, C7
1 mg (XANAX 1.0)...... MC-1, C7
2 mg (XANAX/2) MC-1, C7
Zafirlukast............ MC-32, C7
Zagam Tablets—
200 mg (RPR 201) MC-28, B6
Zalcitabine MC-32, D1
Zanaflex Tablets—
4 mg (Logo/594) MC-30, D2
Zantac Tablets—
150 mg (Glaxo/ZANTAC 150)................. MC-27, C3
300 mg (Glaxo/ZANTAC 300)................. MC-27, C3
Zantac EFFERdose Effervescent Tablets—
150 mg (ZANTAC 150/ 427)................. MC-27, C4
Zantac Geldose Capsules—
150 mg (Glaxo/ZANTAC 150)................. MC-27, C2
300 mg (Glaxo/ZANTAC 300)................. MC-27, C2
Zebeta Tablets—
5 mg (Logo/B1) MC-4, A1
10 mg (Logo/B3) MC-4, A1
Zerit Capsules—
30 mg (BMS 1966/30) MC-28, C5
40 mg (BMS 1967/40) MC-28, C5
Zestoretic Tablets—
10/12.5 mg (STUART 141/ ZESTORETIC) MC-17, B5
20/12.5 mg (STUART 142)................. MC-17, B5
20/25 mg (STUART 145)................. MC-17, B5
Zestril Tablets—
2.5 mg (Zestril 2/135) .. MC-17, B2
5 mg (ZESTRIL/130) ... MC-17, B2
10 mg (ZESTRIL 10/ 131)................. MC-17, B2

Zestril Tablets *(continued)*
20 mg (ZESTRIL 20/ 132)................. MC-17, B3
40 mg (ZESTRIL 40/ 134)................. MC-17, B3
Ziac Tablets—
2.5/6.25 mg (Logo/B12) .. MC-4, A2
5/6.25 mg (Logo/B13) MC-4, A2
10/6.25 mg (Logo/B14).... MC-4, A2
Zidovudine........... MC-32, D2-3
Zithromax Capsules—
250 mg (PFIZER 305) .. MC-3, B7
Zocor Tablets—
5 mg (MSD 726/ ZOCOR) MC-28, B3
10 mg (MSD 735/ ZOCOR) MC-28, B3
20 mg (MSD 740/ ZOCAR)............ MC-28, B3
40 mg (MSD 749/ ZOCOR) MC-28, B3
Zofran Tablets—
4 mg (Glaxo/4)......... MC-23, B6
8 mg (Glaxo/8)......... MC-23, B6
Zoloft Tablets—
50 mg (ZOLOFT/ 50 MG)............ MC-28, B2
100 mg (ZOLOFT/ 100 MG)............ MC-28, B2
Zolpidem............. MC-32, D4
Zovirax Capsules—
200 mg (Logo Wellcome/ ZOVIRAX 200).......... MC-1, B3
Zovirax Tablets—
400 mg (Logo/ ZOVIRAX)................ MC-1, B4
800 mg (ZOVIRAX 800)................ MC-1, B4
Zyban Extended-release Tablets—
150 mg (ZYBAN 150).... MC-4, B1
Zyloprim Tablets—
100 mg (ZYLOPRIM 100)................ MC-1, C3
300 mg (ZYLOPRIM 300)................ MC-1, C3
Zyprexa Tablets—
2.5 mg (LILLY 4112).... MC-23, B2
5 mg (LILLY 4115).... MC-23, B2
7.5 mg (LILLY 4116).... MC-23, B3
10 mg (LILLY 4117) ... MC-23, B3
Zyrtec Tablets—
5 mg (PFIZER/550) MC-6, B3
10 mg (PFIZER/551) MC-6, B3

*Single source product for solid oral dosage forms in the U.S.

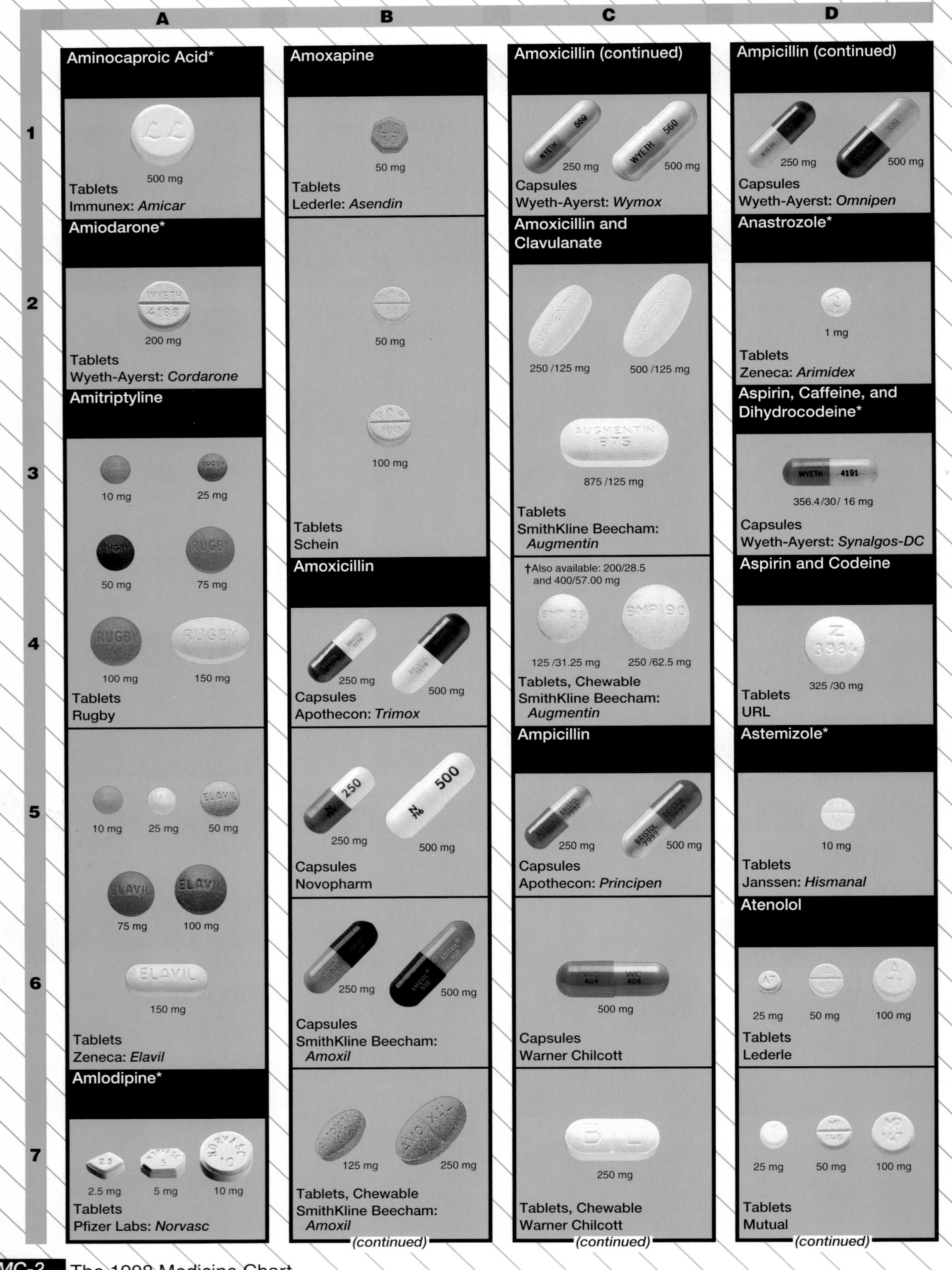

*Single source product for solid oral dosage forms in the U.S.

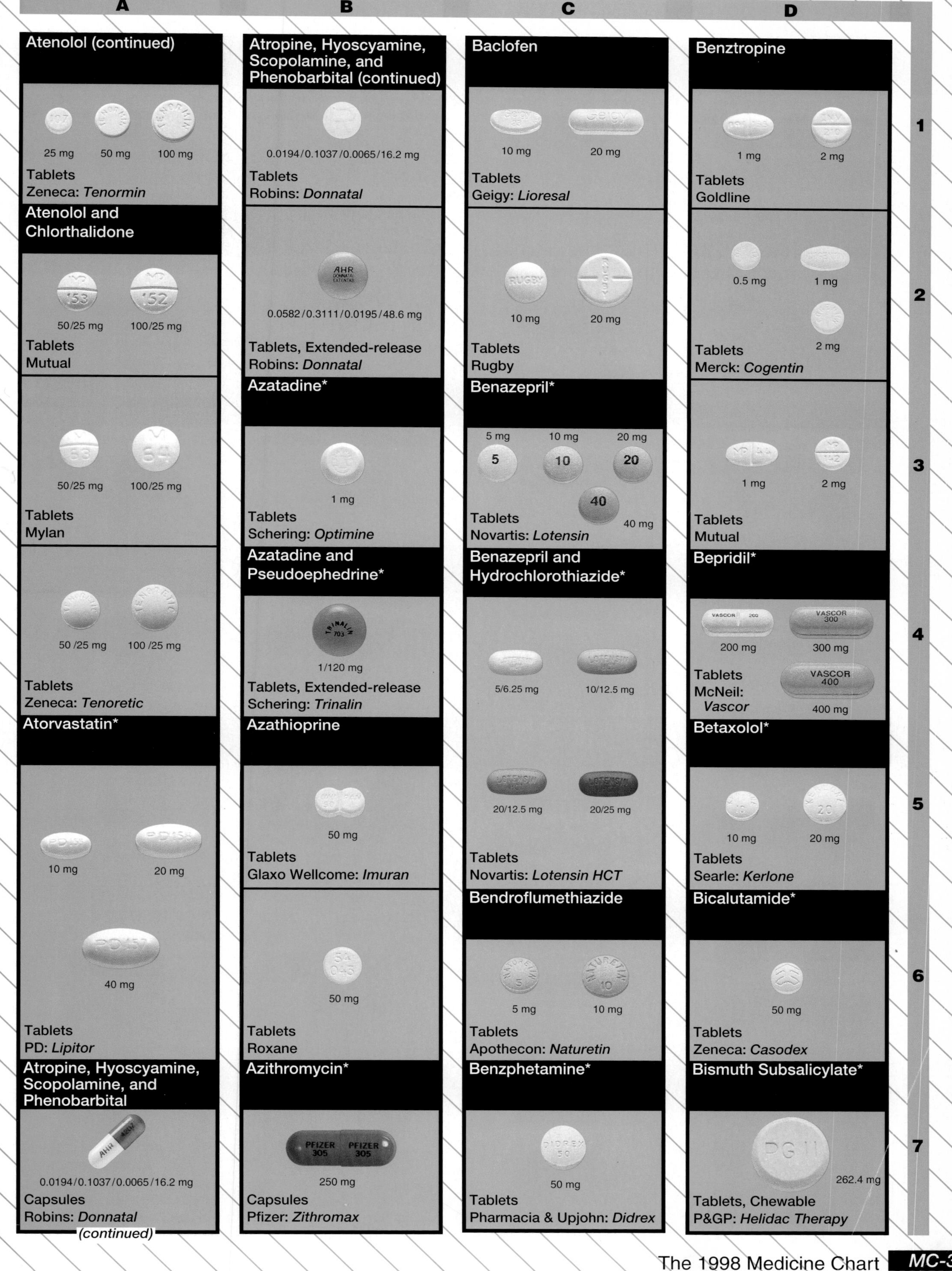

*Single source product for solid oral dosage forms in the U.S.

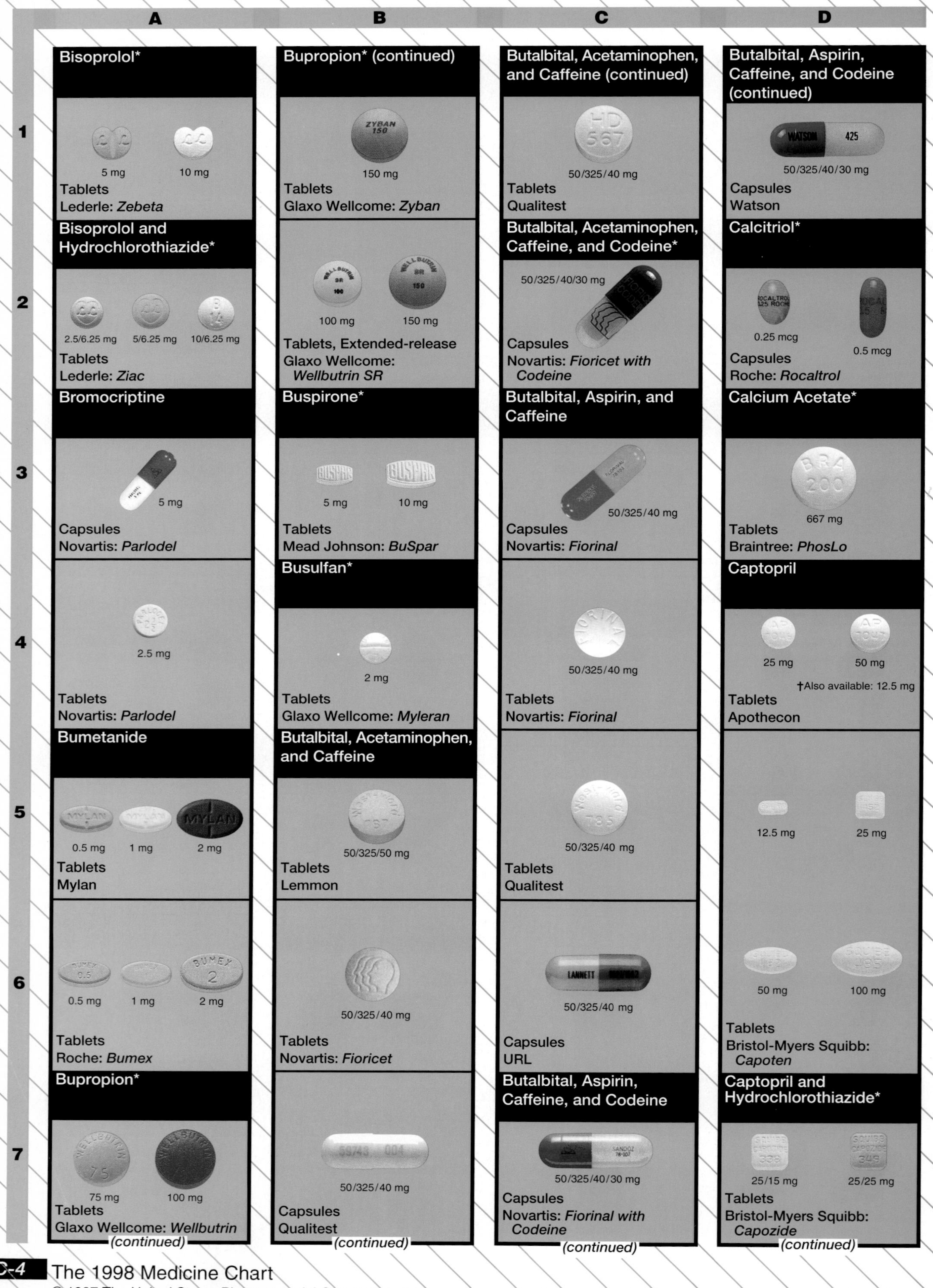

*Single source product for solid oral dosage forms in the U.S.

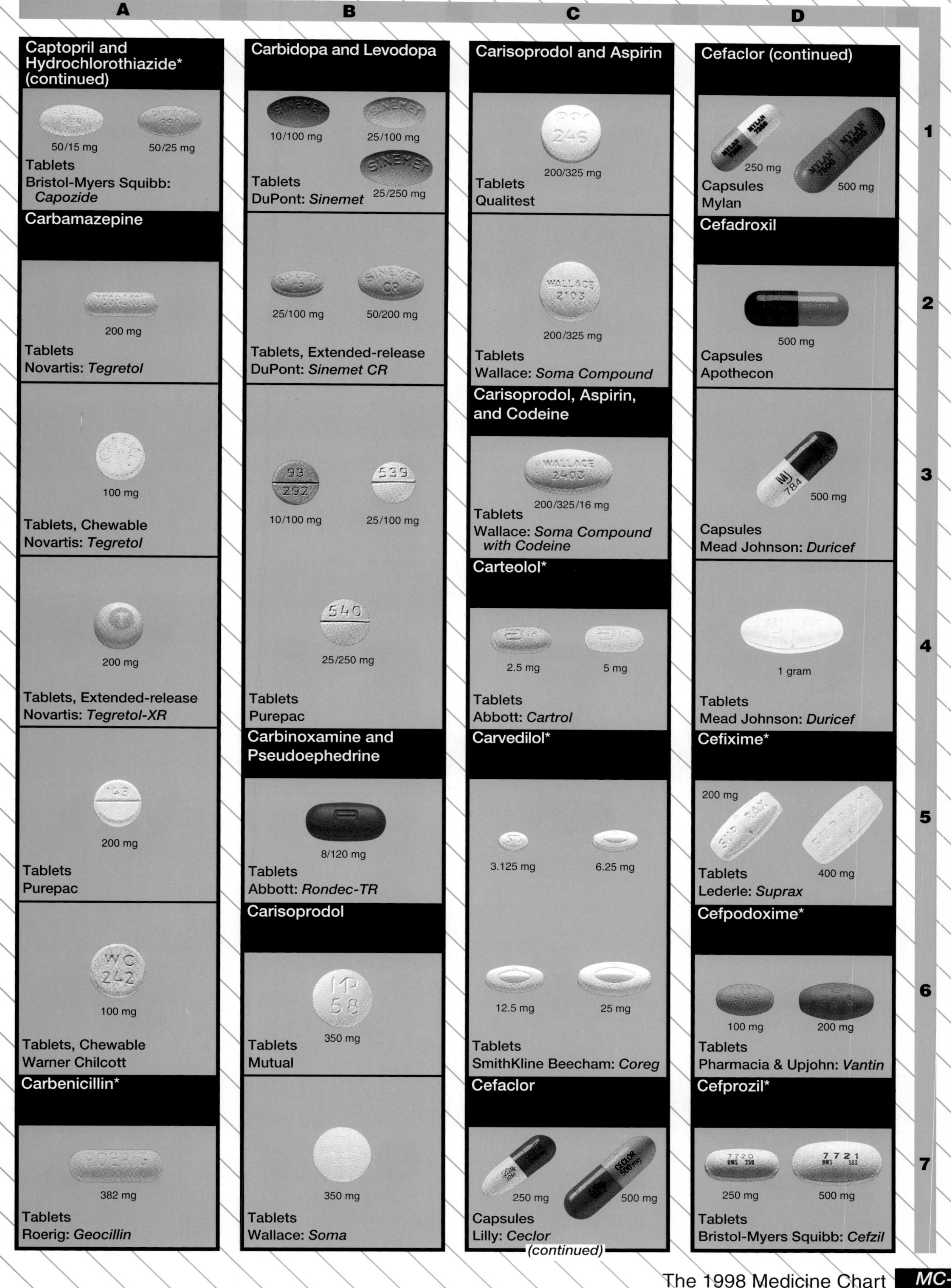

*Single source product for solid oral dosage forms in the U.S.

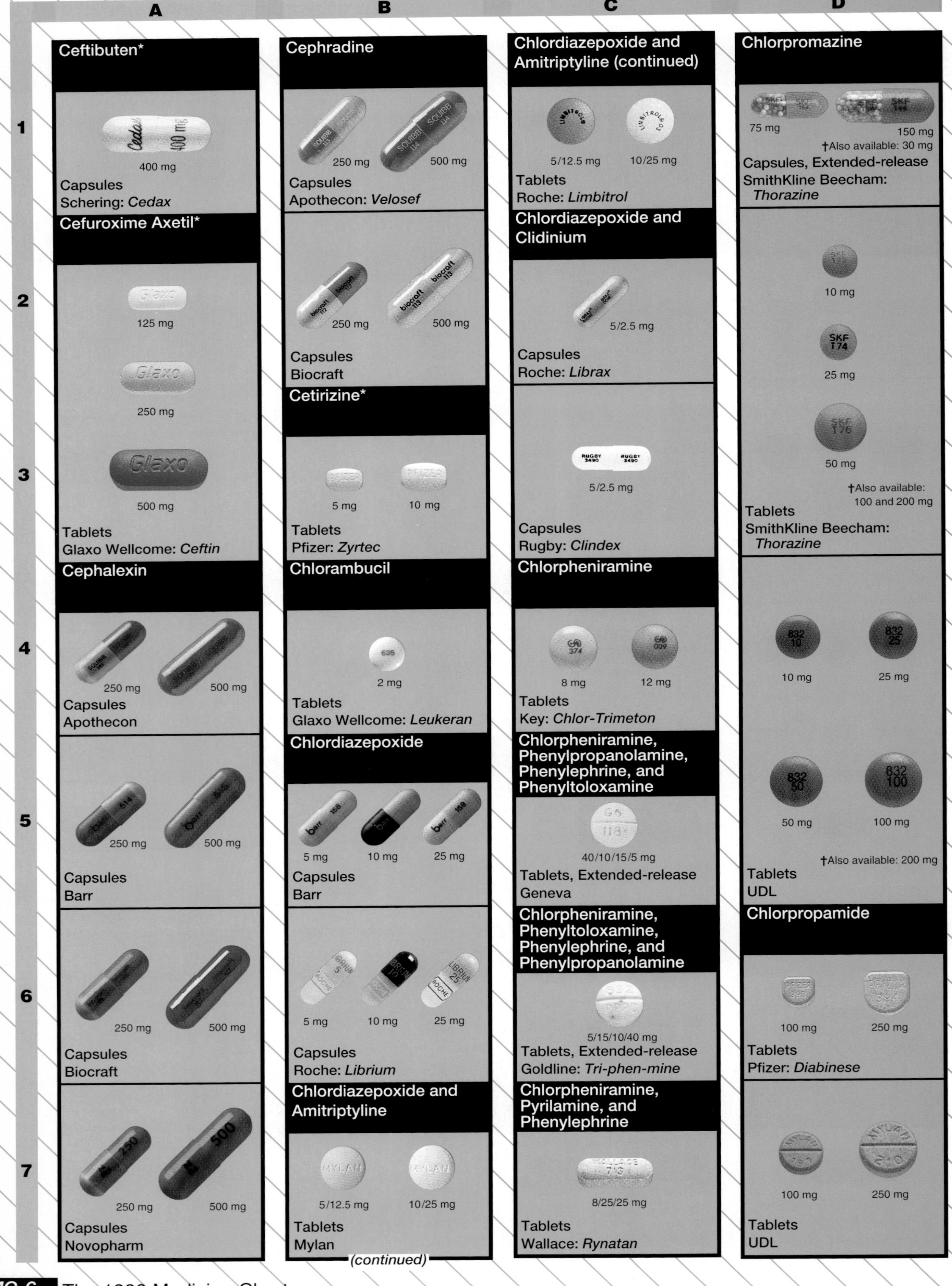

*Single source product for solid oral dosage forms in the U.S.

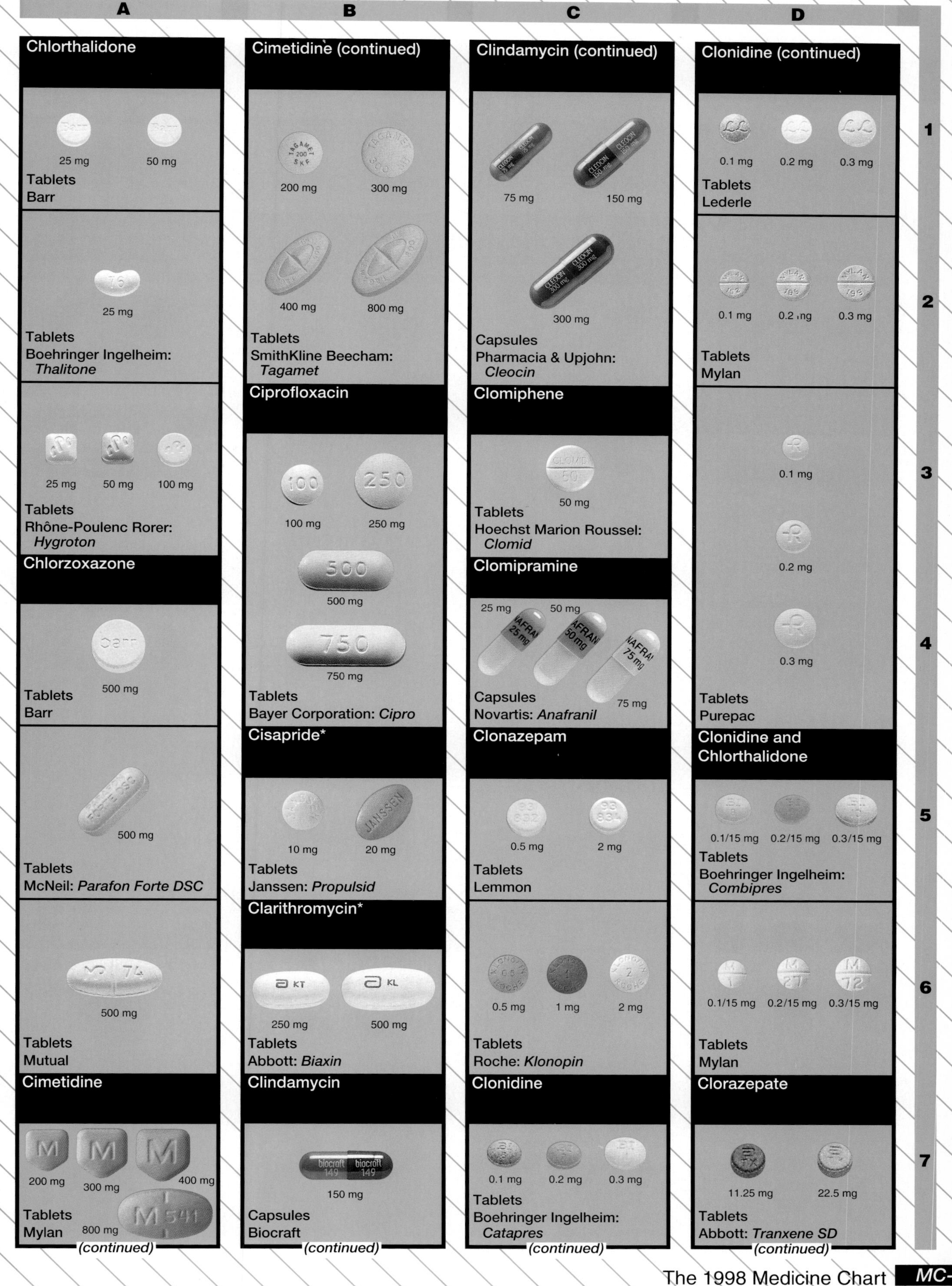

*Single source product for solid oral dosage forms in the U.S.

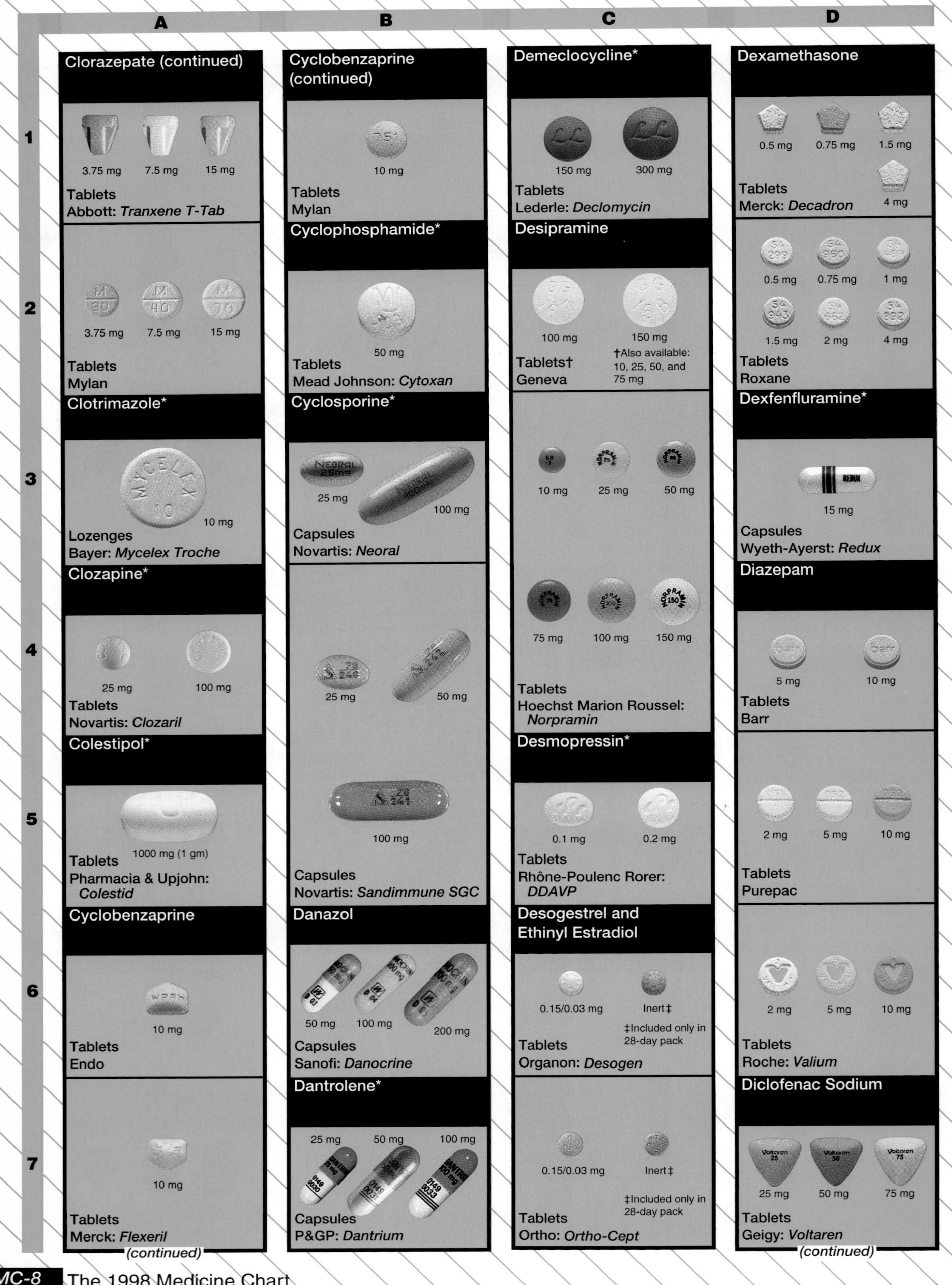

*Single source product for solid oral dosage forms in the U.S.

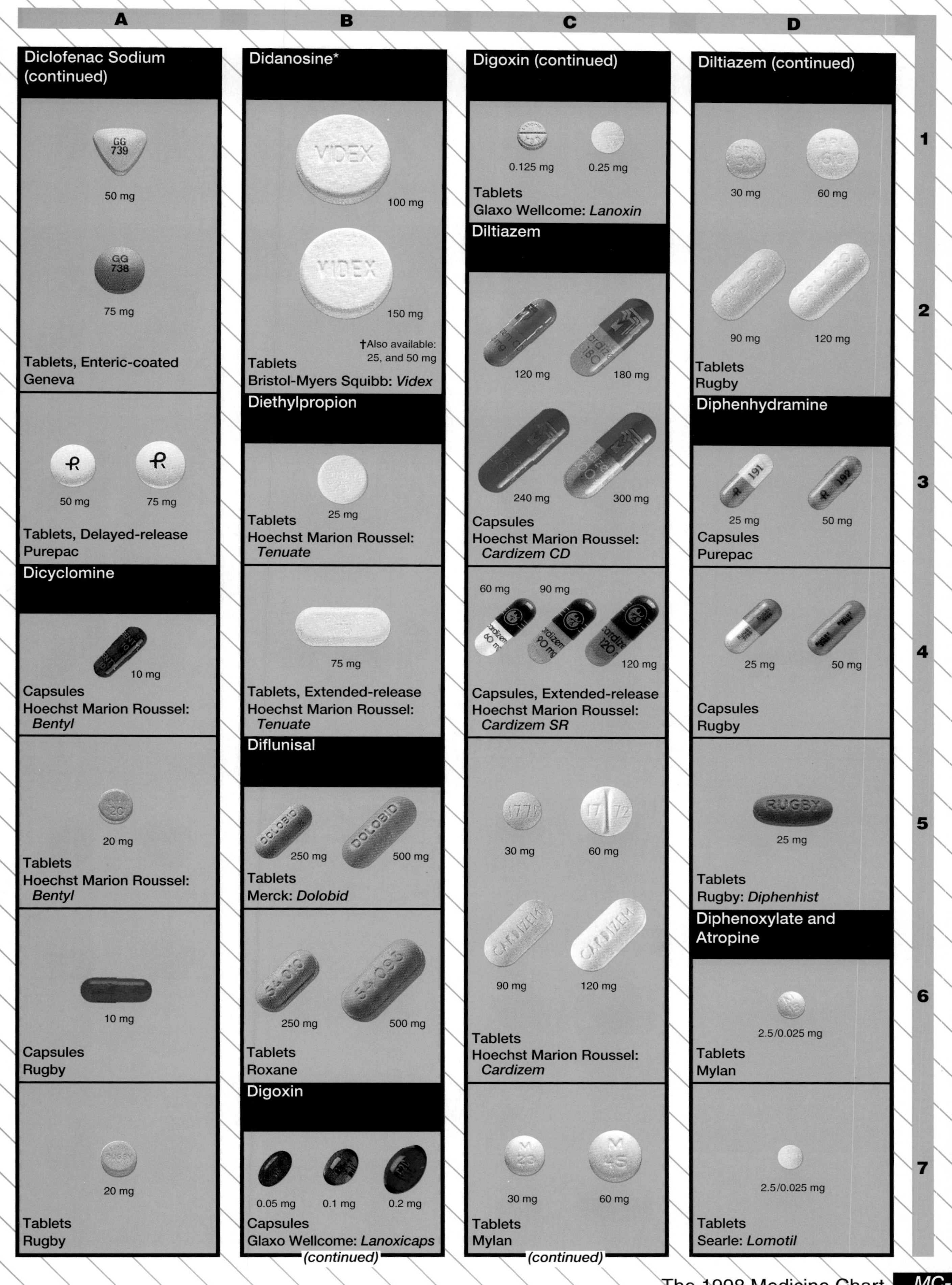

*Single source product for solid oral dosage forms in the U.S.

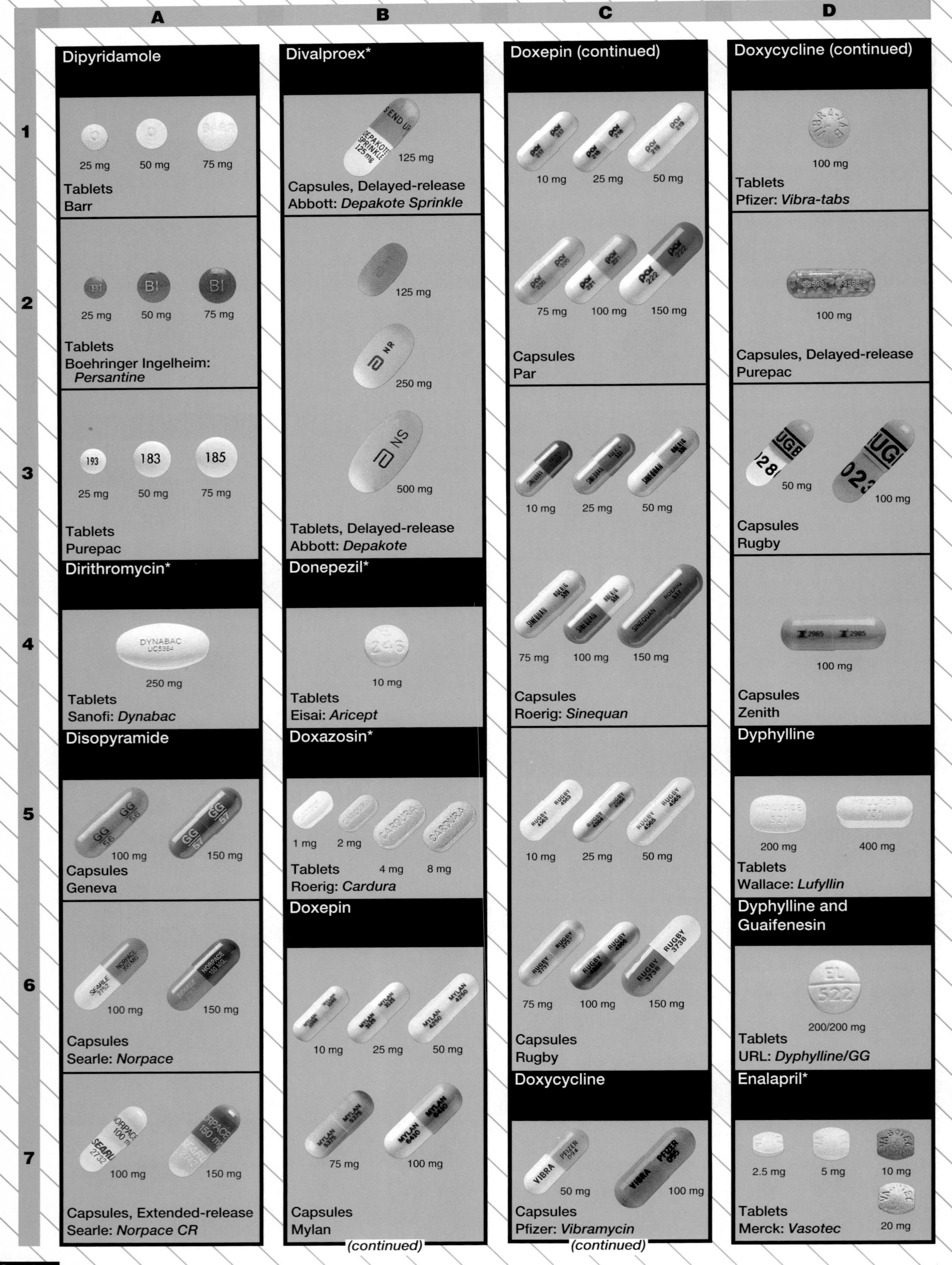

*Single source product for solid oral dosage forms in the U.S.

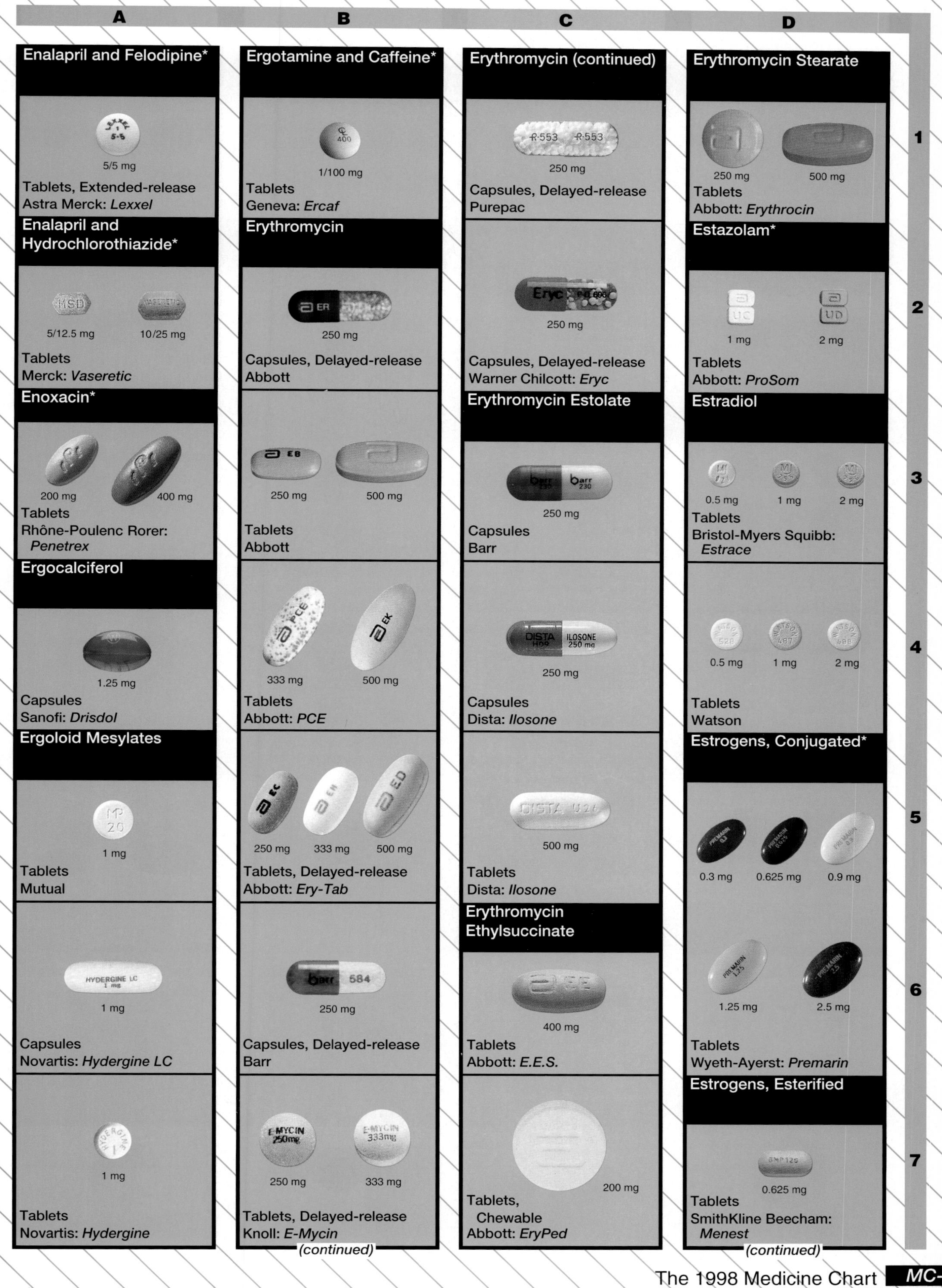

*Single source product for solid oral dosage forms in the U.S.

A
B
C
D
1
2
3
4
5
6
7
Estrogens, Esterified (continued)
0.3 mg
0.625 mg
2.5 mg
Tablets
Solvay: Estratab
Estropipate
0.625 mg (equivalent to 0.75 mg estropipate)
1.25 mg (equivalent to 1.5 mg estropipate)
Tablets
Ortho: Ortho-Est
.75 mg
1.5 mg
3 mg
Tablets
Watson
Ethynodiol Diacetate and Ethinyl Estradiol
1/0.035 mg
Inert ‡
‡ Included only in 28-day pack
Tablets:
Searle: Demulen 1/35-21 and -28
1/0.05 mg
Inert ‡
‡ Included only in 28-day pack
Tablets
Searle: Demulen 1/50-21 and -28
Etidronate*
200 mg
Tablets
P&GP: Didronel
Etodolac*
200 mg
300 mg
Capsules
Wyeth-Ayerst: Lodine
(continued)
Etodolac* (continued)
400 mg
500 mg
Tablets
Wyeth-Ayerst: Lodine
Famciclovir*
125 mg
250 mg
500 mg
Tablets
SmithKline Beecham: Famvir
Famotidine*
20 mg
40 mg
Tablets
Merck: Pepcid
Felbamate*
400 mg
600 mg
Tablets
Wallace: Felbatol
Felodipine*
2.5 mg
5 mg
10 mg
Tablets, Extended-release
Astra Merck: Plendil
Fenfluramine*
20 mg
Tablets
Wyeth-Ayerst: Pondimin
Fenoprofen
200 mg
300 mg
Capsules
Dista: Nalfon
300 mg
Capsules
Geneva
600 mg
Tablets
Geneva
600 mg
Tablets
Goldline
600 mg
Tablets
Purepac
Ferrous Sulfate
324 mg
Tablets
Paddock
Fexofenadine*
60 mg
Capsules
Hoechst Marion Roussel: Allegra
Finasteride*
5 mg
Tablets
Merck: Proscar
Flecainide*
50 mg
100 mg
Tablets
3M: Tambocor
Fluconazole*
50 mg
100 mg
150 mg
200 mg
Tablets
Roerig: Diflucan
Flucytosine*
250 mg
500 mg
Capsules
Roche: Ancobon
Fluoxetine*
10 mg
20 mg
Capsules
Dista: Prozac
*Single source product for solid oral dosage forms in the U.S.

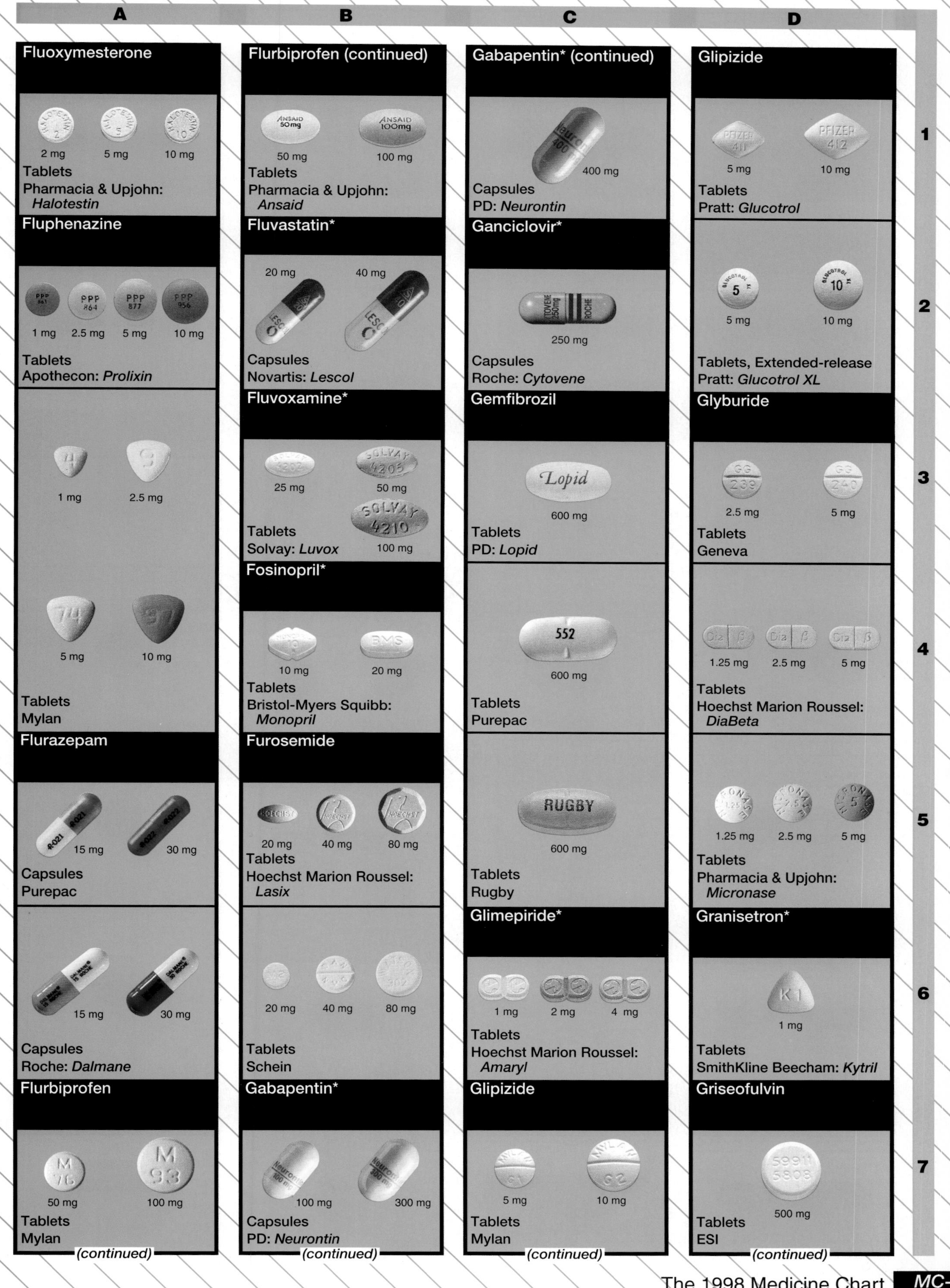

*Single source product for solid oral dosage forms in the U.S.

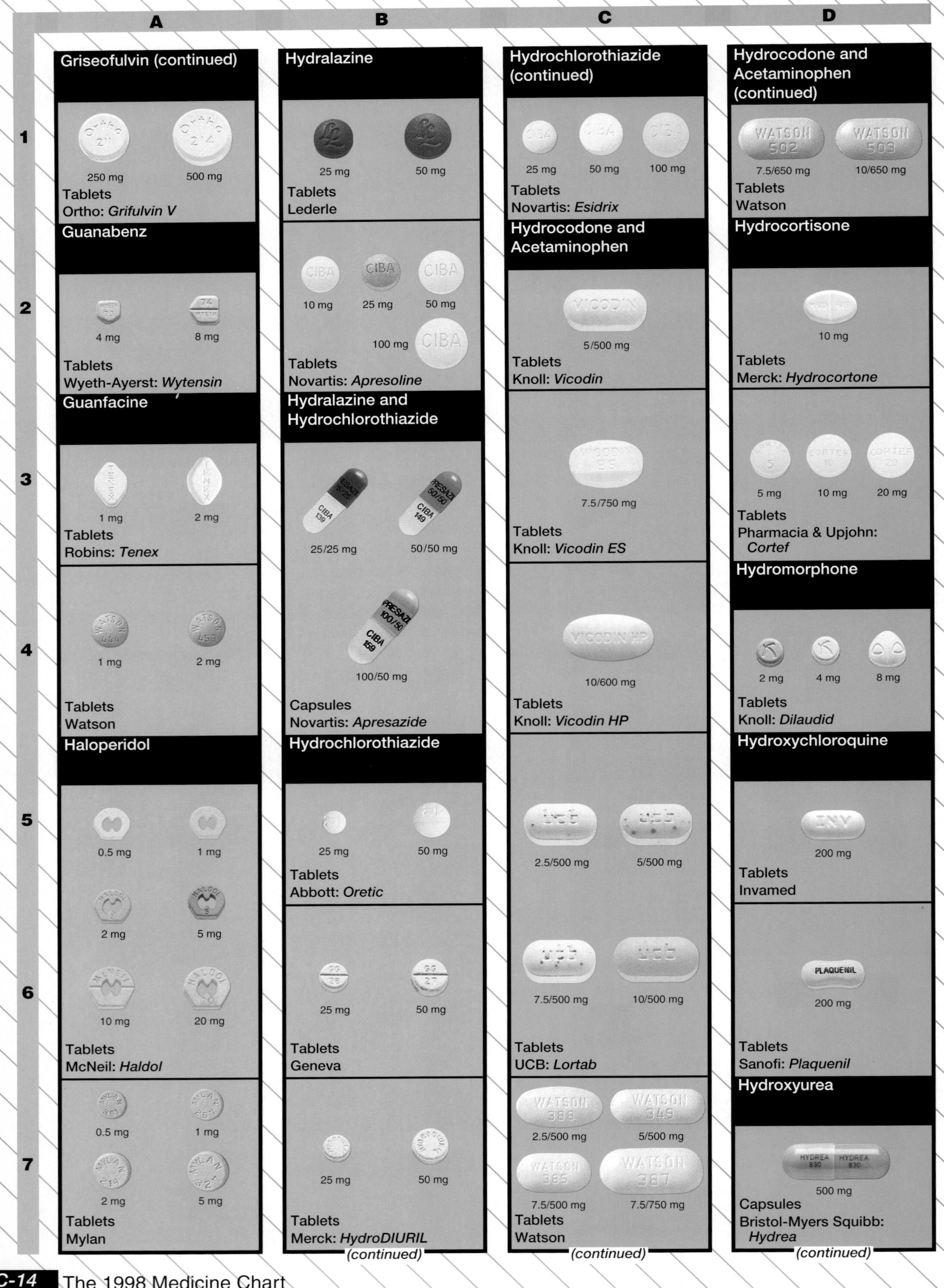

*Single source product for solid oral dosage forms in the U.S.

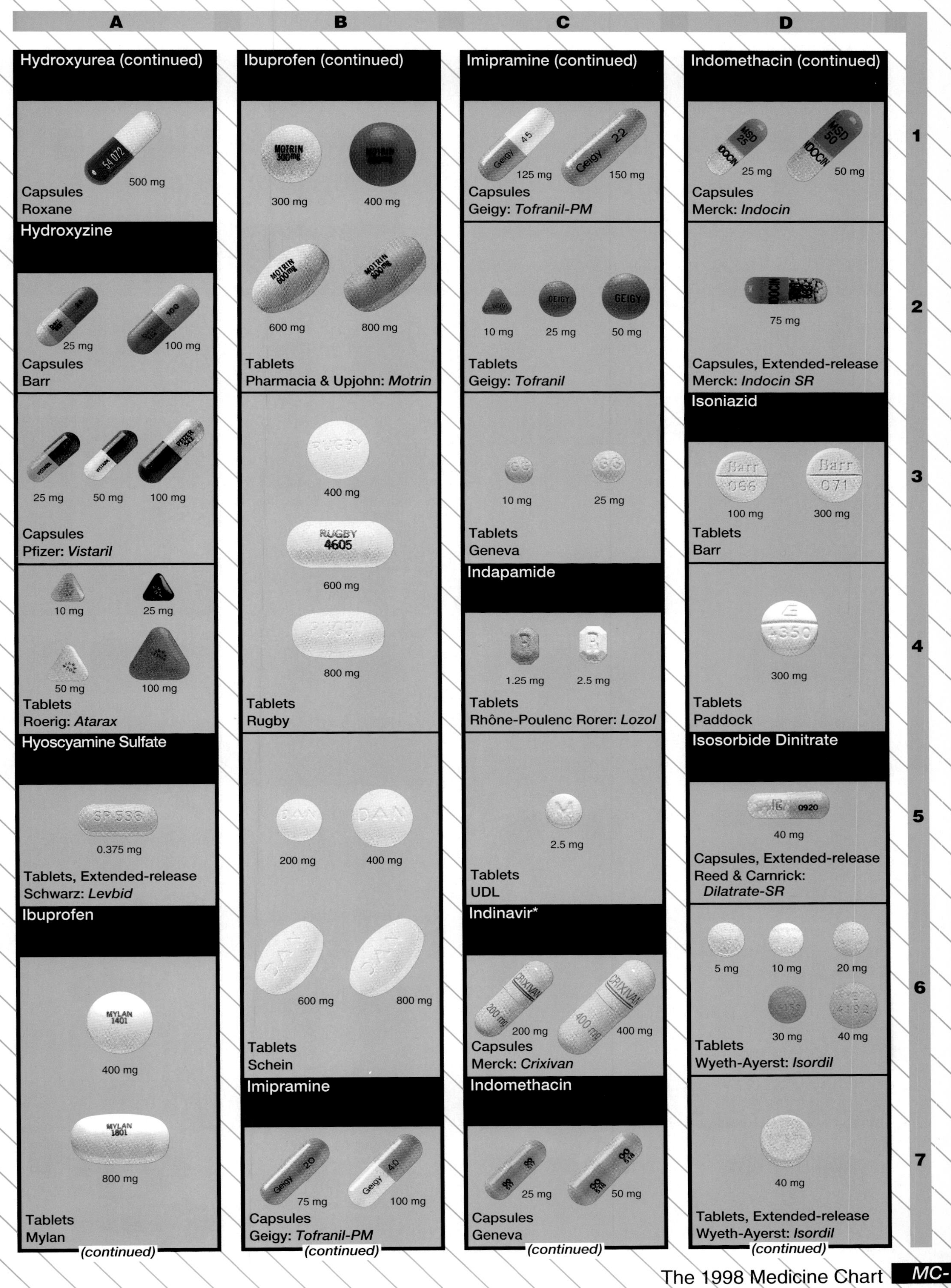

*Single source product for solid oral dosage forms in the U.S.

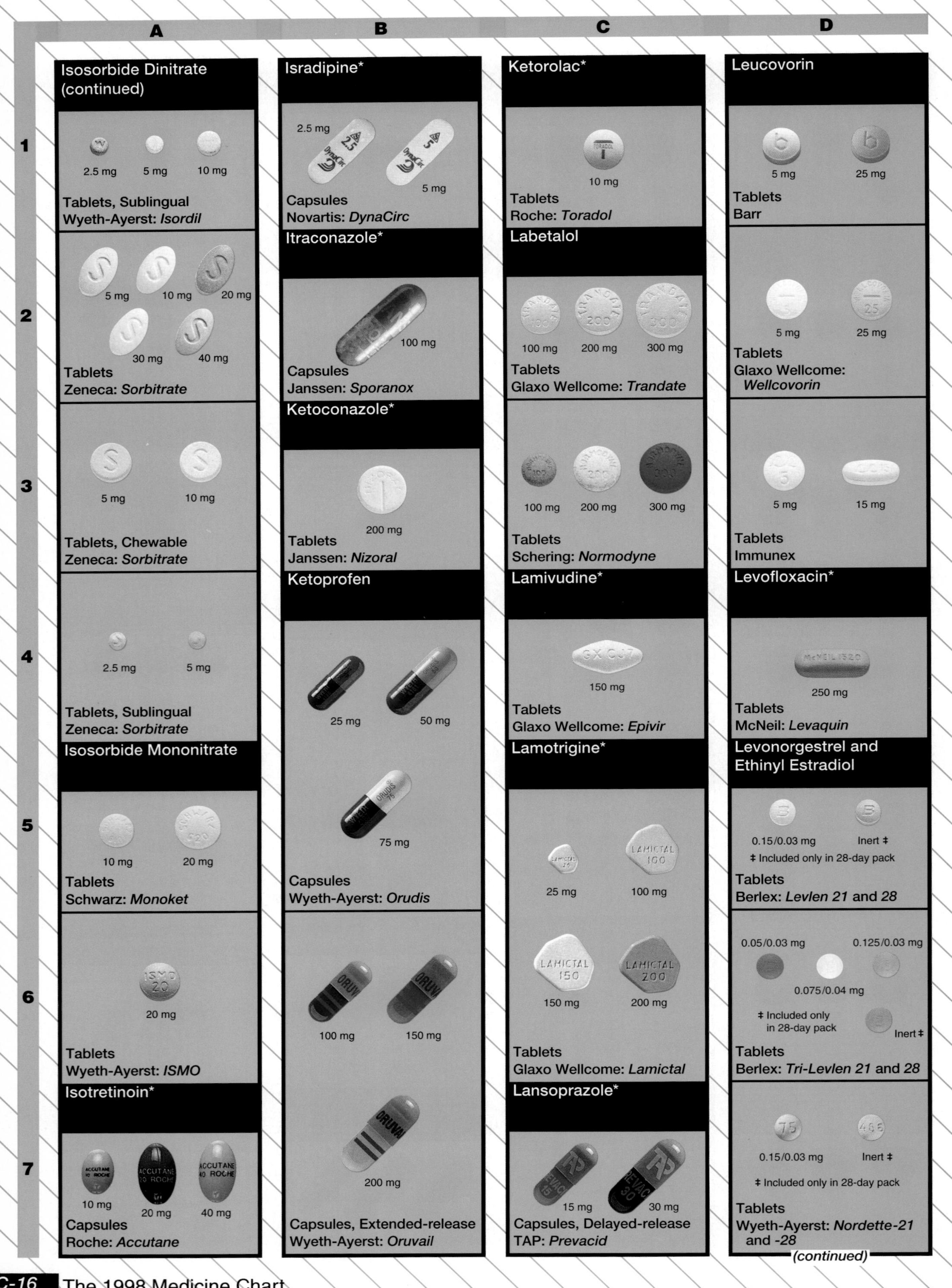

*Single source product for solid oral dosage forms in the U.S.

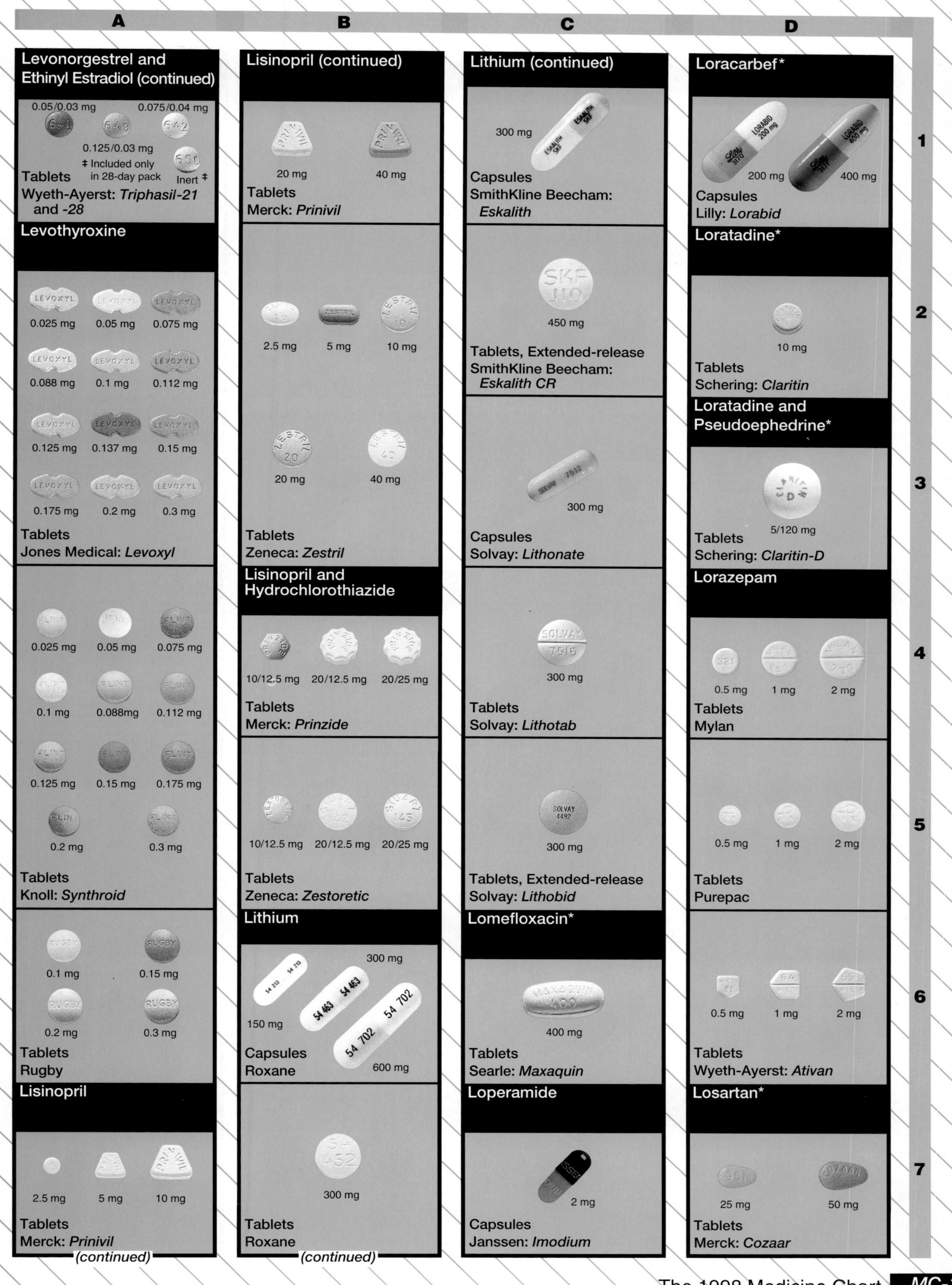

*Single source product for solid oral dosage forms in the U.S.

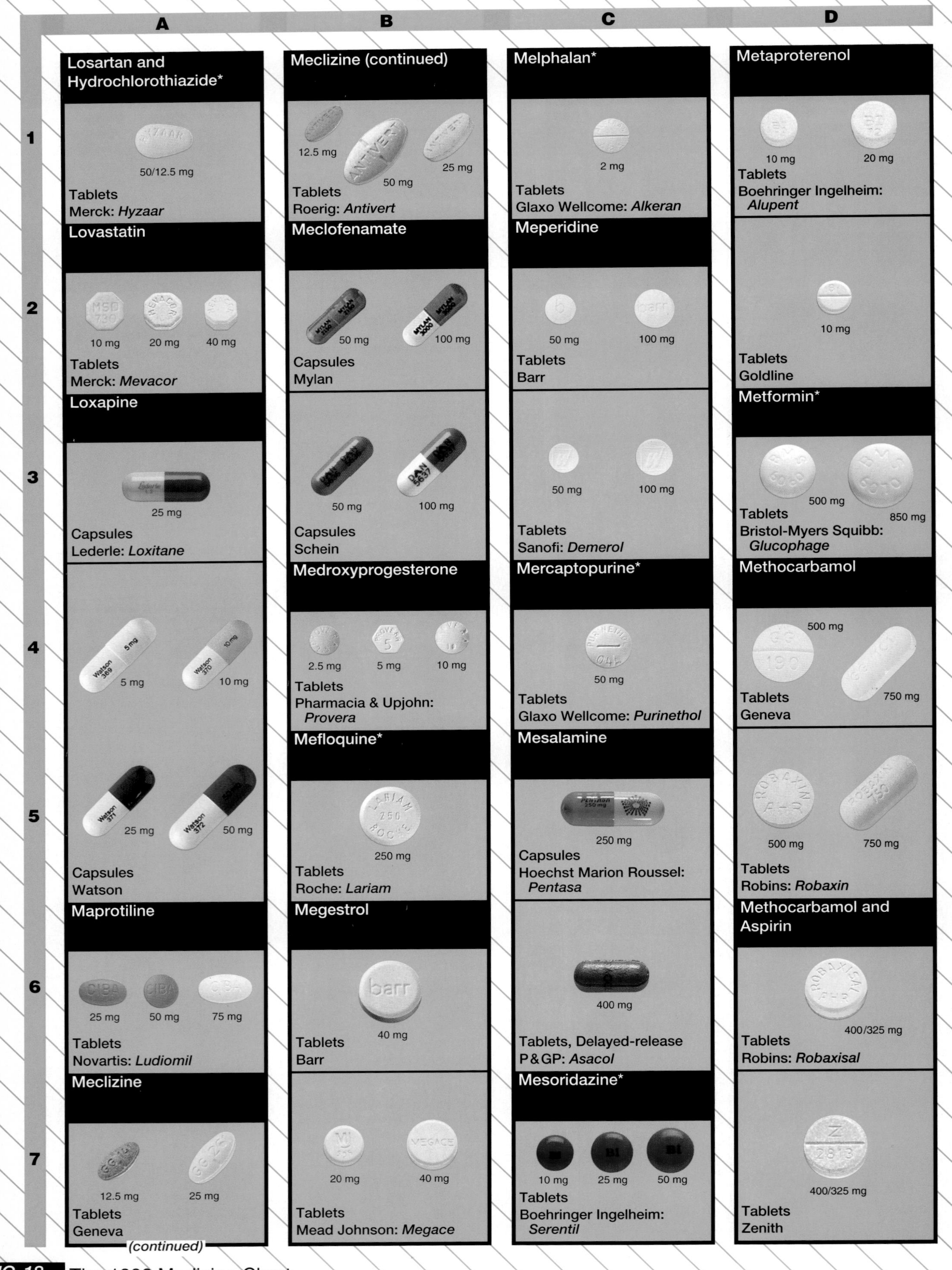

*Single source product for solid oral dosage forms in the U.S.

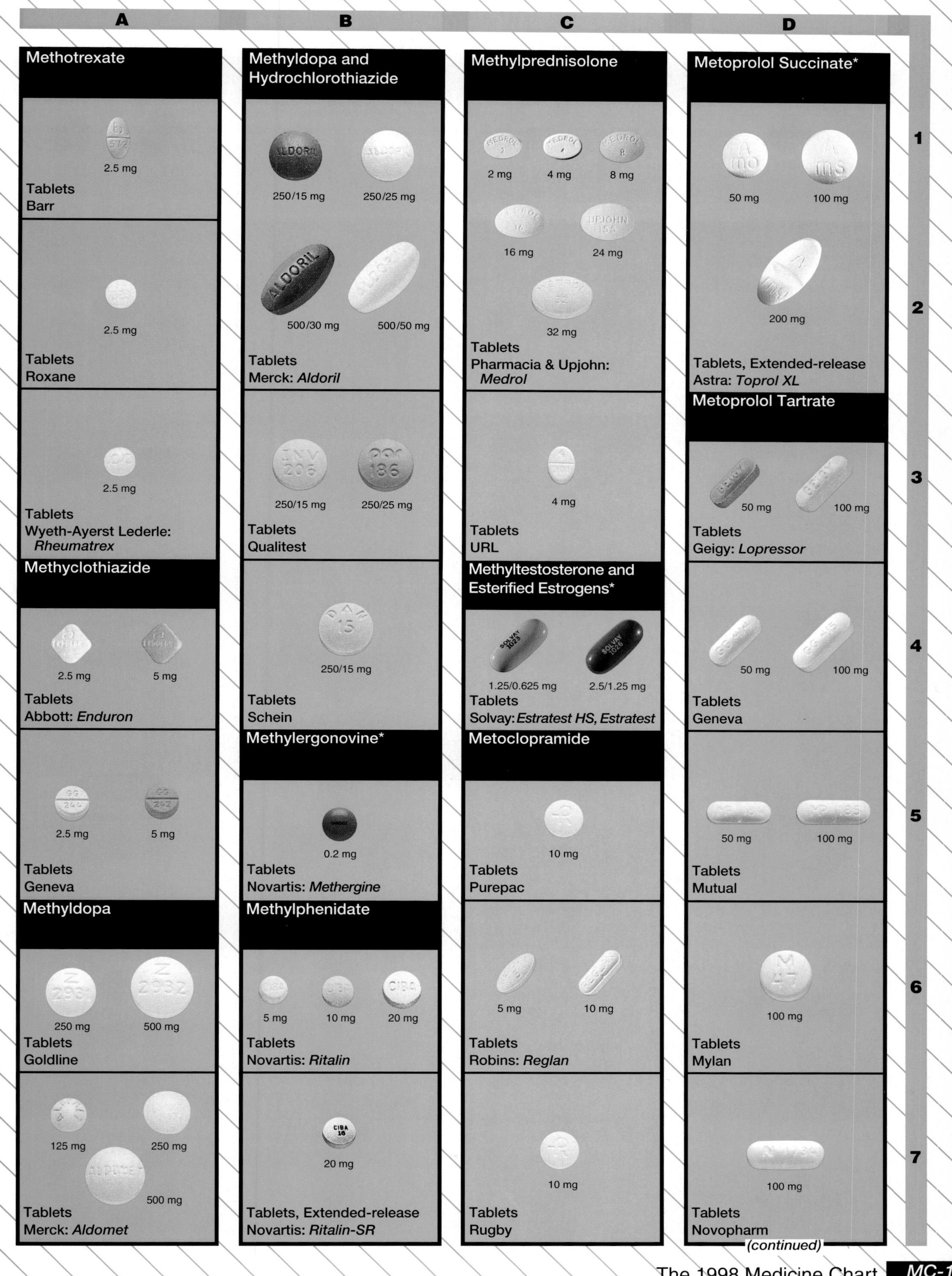
A
B
C
D
1
2
3
4
5
6
7
Methotrexate
2.5 mg
Tablets
Barr
2.5 mg
Tablets
Roxane
2.5 mg
Tablets
Wyeth-Ayerst Lederle: Rheumatrex
Methyclothiazide
2.5 mg
5 mg
Tablets
Abbott: Enduron
2.5 mg
5 mg
Tablets
Geneva
Methyldopa
250 mg
500 mg
Tablets
Goldline
125 mg
250 mg
500 mg
Tablets
Merck: Aldomet
Methyldopa and Hydrochlorothiazide
250/15 mg
250/25 mg
500/30 mg
500/50 mg
Tablets
Merck: Aldoril
250/15 mg
250/25 mg
Tablets
Qualitest
250/15 mg
Tablets
Schein
Methylergonovine*
0.2 mg
Tablets
Novartis: Methergine
Methylphenidate
5 mg
10 mg
20 mg
Tablets
Novartis: Ritalin
20 mg
Tablets, Extended-release
Novartis: Ritalin-SR
Methylprednisolone
2 mg
4 mg
8 mg
16 mg
24 mg
32 mg
Tablets
Pharmacia & Upjohn: Medrol
4 mg
Tablets
URL
Methyltestosterone and Esterified Estrogens*
1.25/0.625 mg
2.5/1.25 mg
Tablets
Solvay: Estratest HS, Estratest
Metoclopramide
10 mg
Tablets
Purepac
5 mg
10 mg
Tablets
Robins: Reglan
10 mg
Tablets
Rugby
Metoprolol Succinate*
50 mg
100 mg
200 mg
Tablets, Extended-release
Astra: Toprol XL
Metoprolol Tartrate
50 mg
100 mg
Tablets
Geigy: Lopressor
50 mg
100 mg
Tablets
Geneva
50 mg
100 mg
Tablets
Mutual
100 mg
Tablets
Mylan
100 mg
Tablets
Novopharm
(continued)
*Single source product for solid oral dosage forms in the U.S.

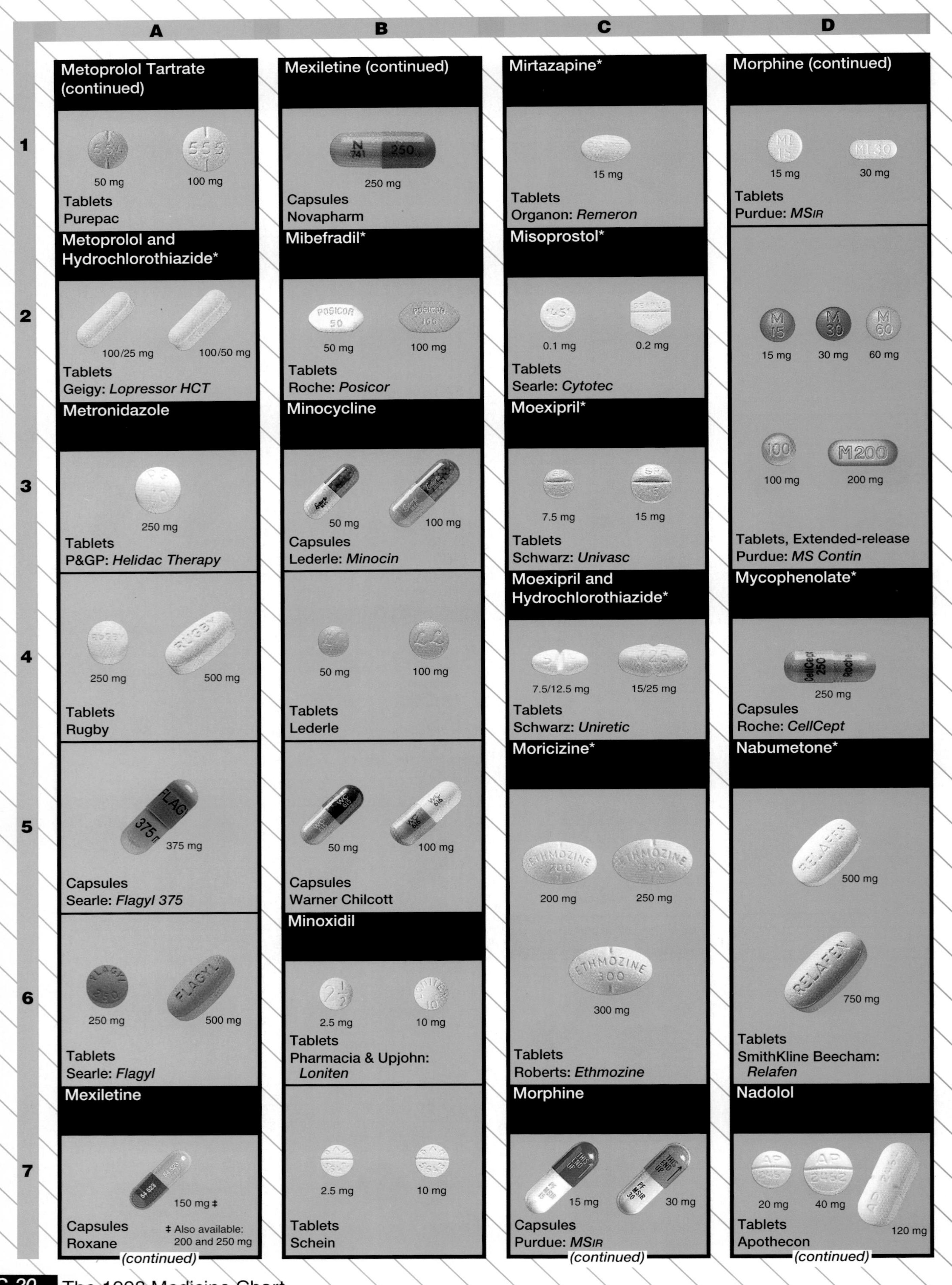

*Single source product for solid oral dosage forms in the U.S.

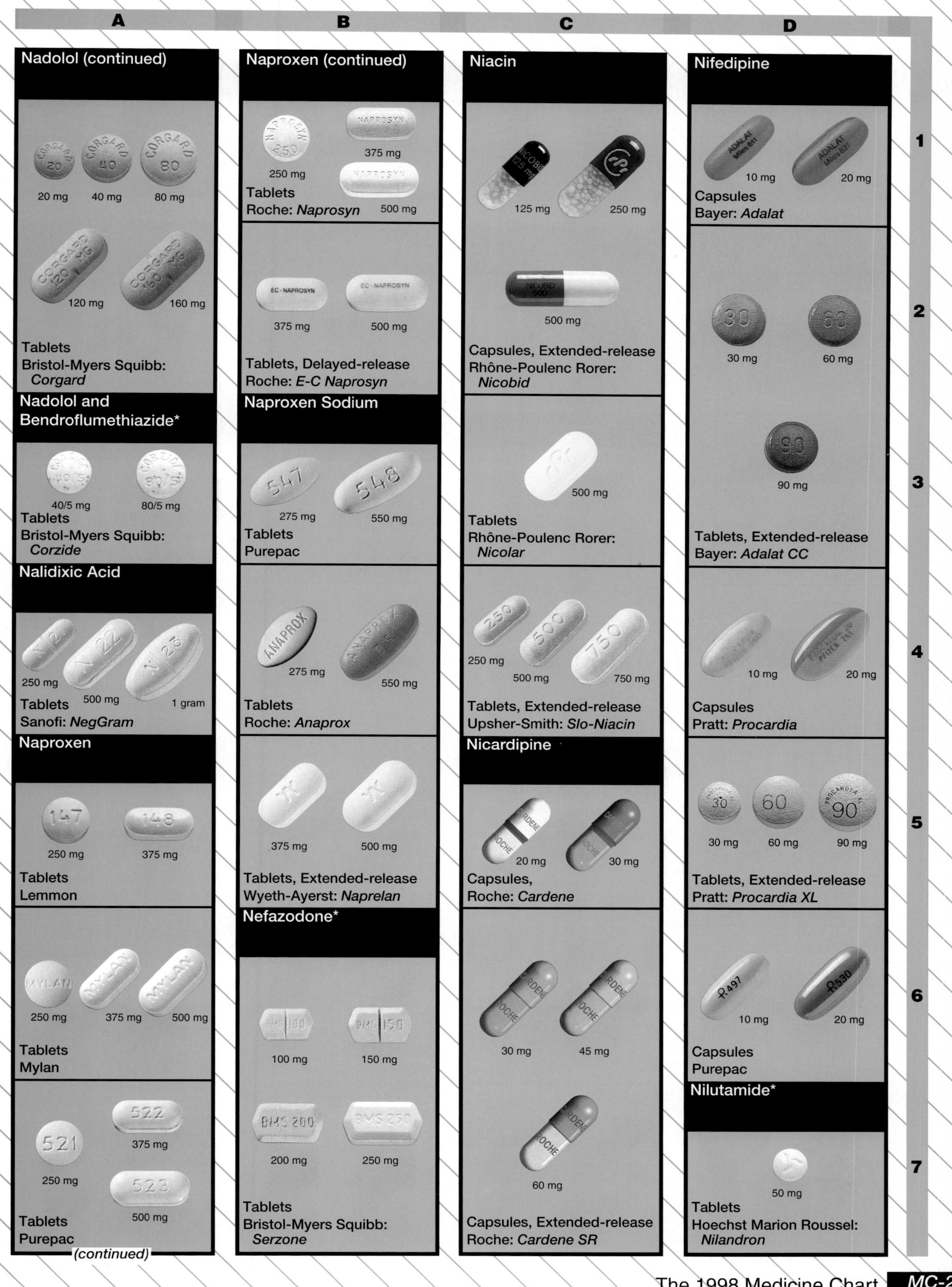

*Single source product for solid oral dosage forms in the U.S.

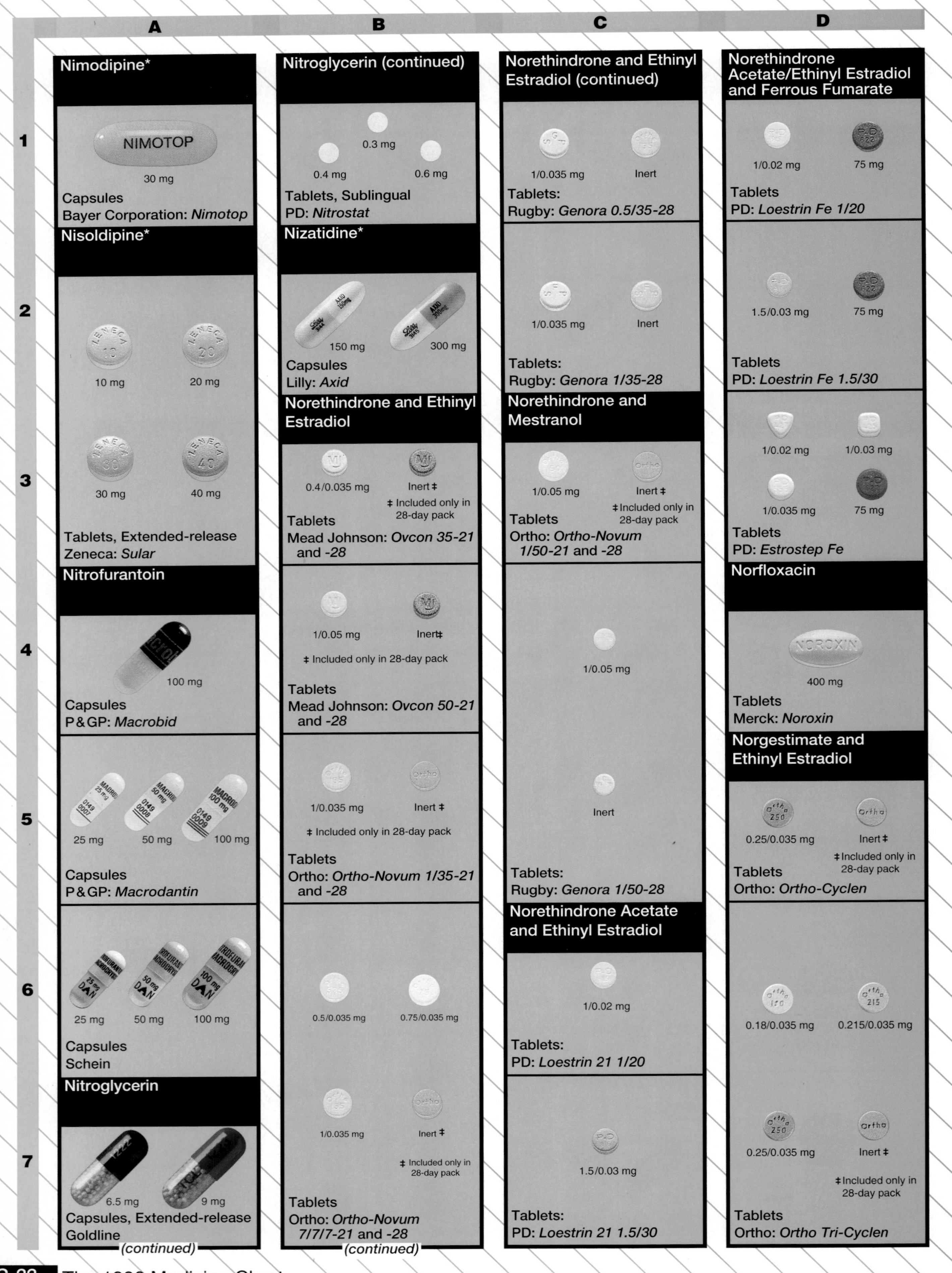

*Single source product for solid oral dosage forms in the U.S.

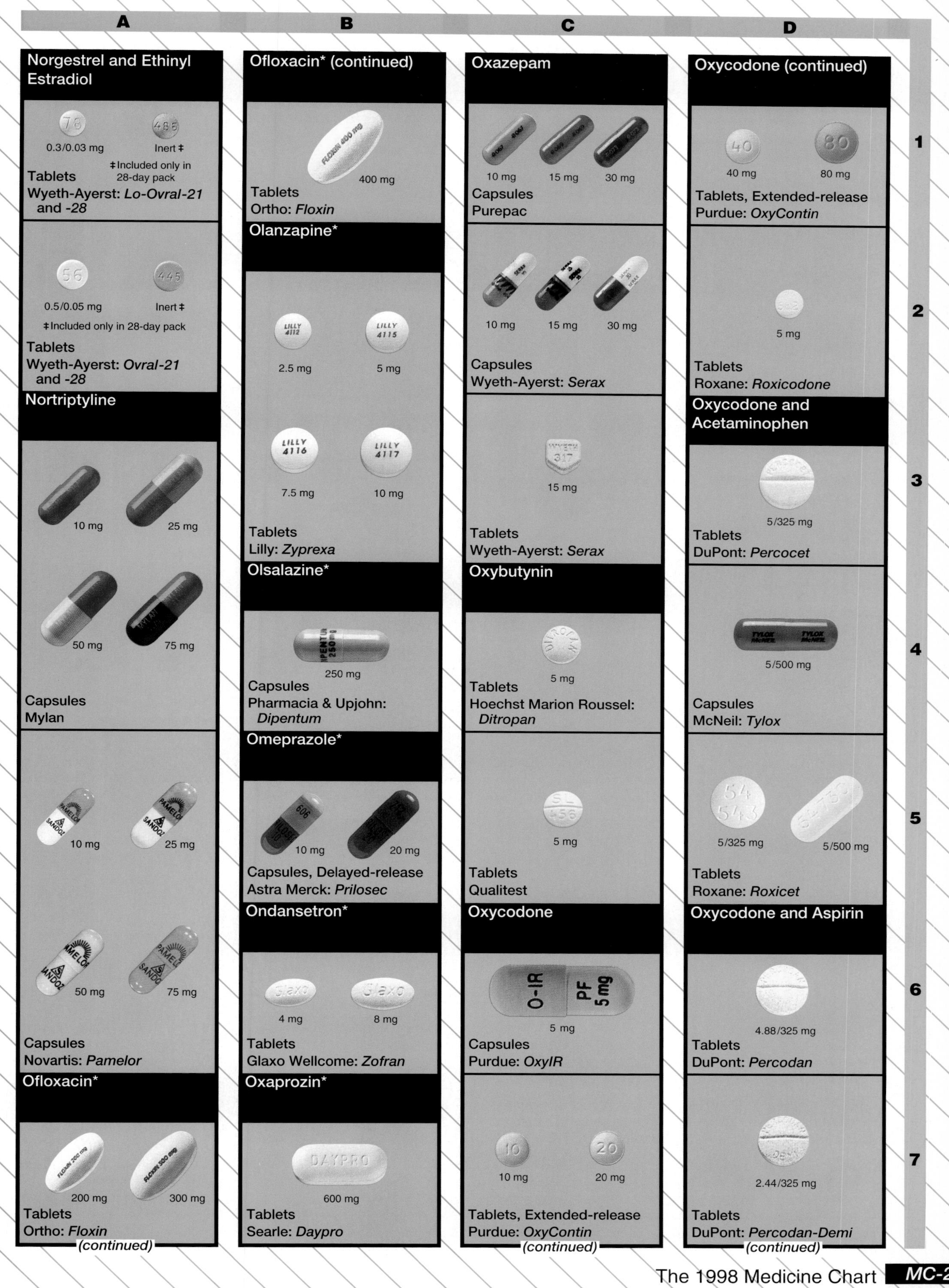

*Single source product for solid oral dosage forms in the U.S.

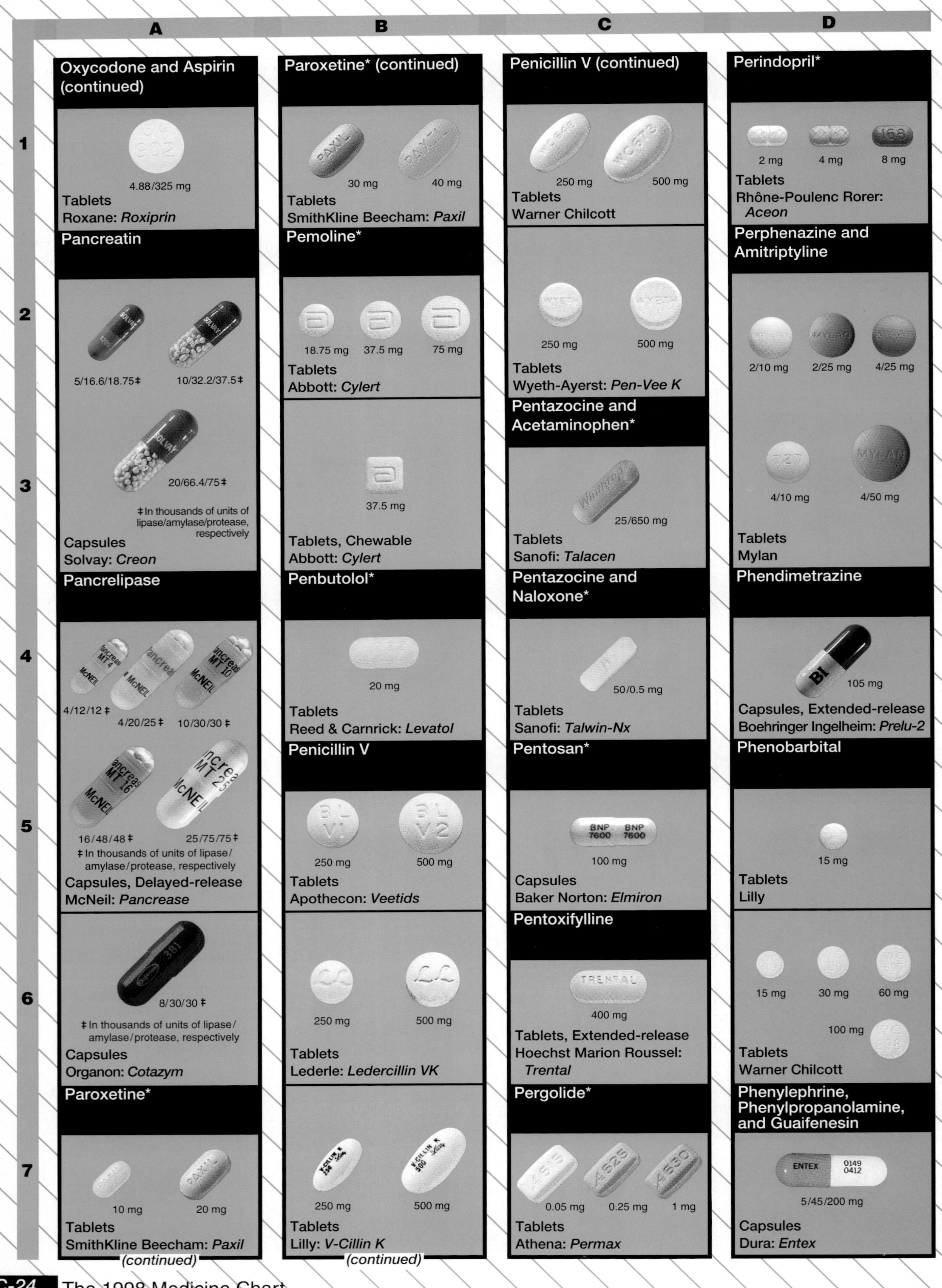

*Single source product for solid oral dosage forms in the U.S.

*Single source product for solid oral dosage forms in the U.S.

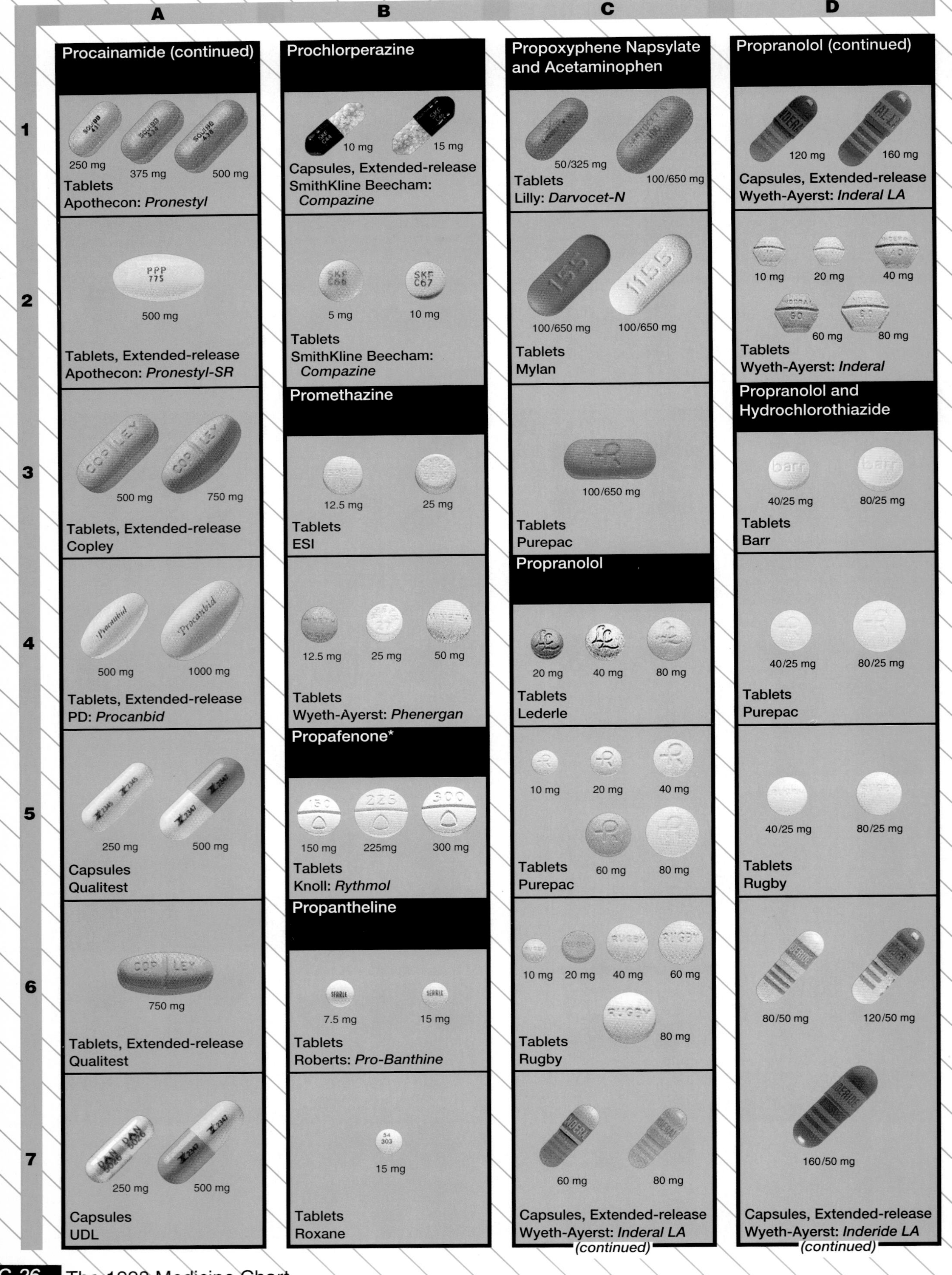

*Single source product for solid oral dosage forms in the U.S.

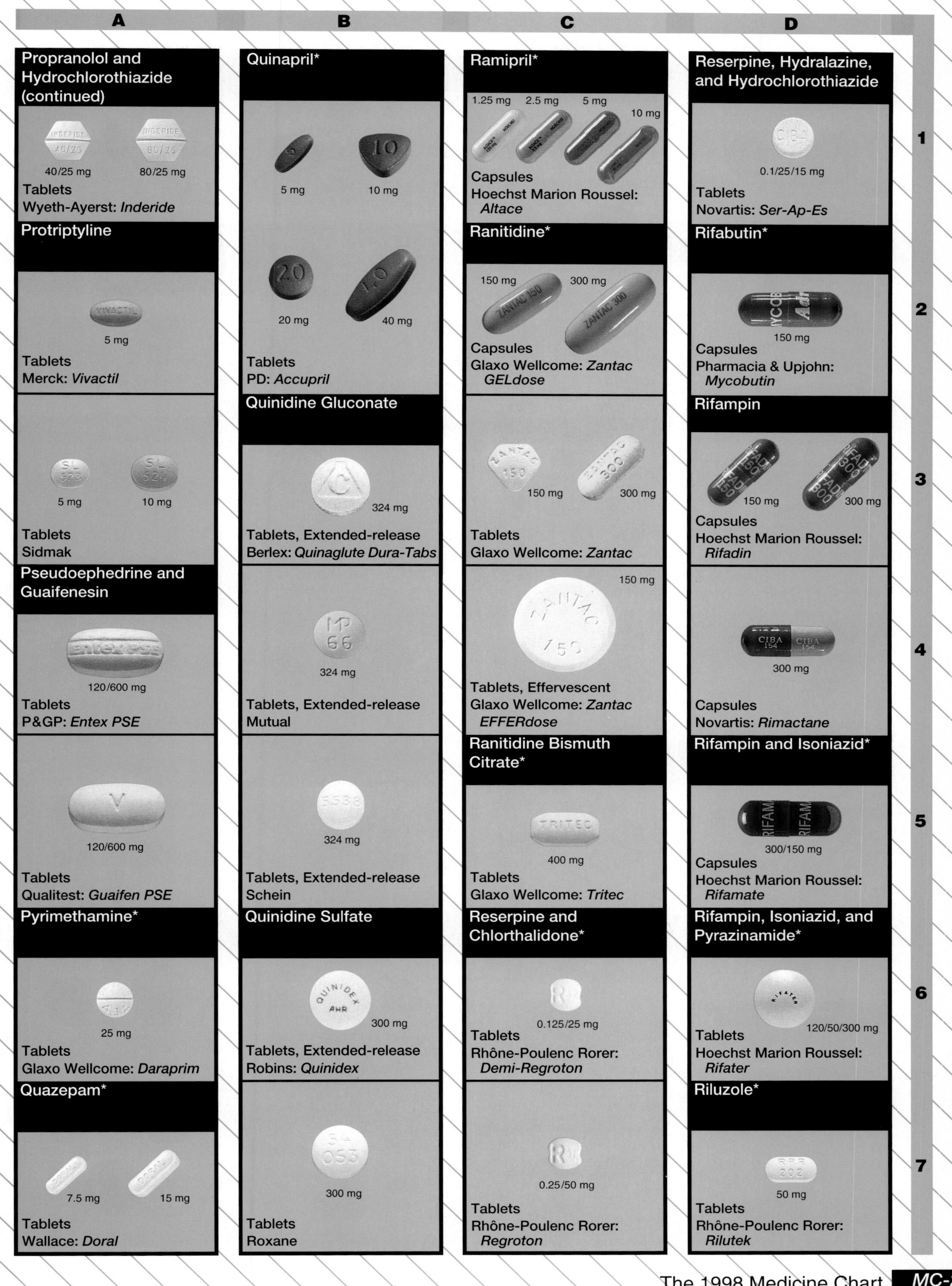

*Single source product for solid oral dosage forms in the U.S.

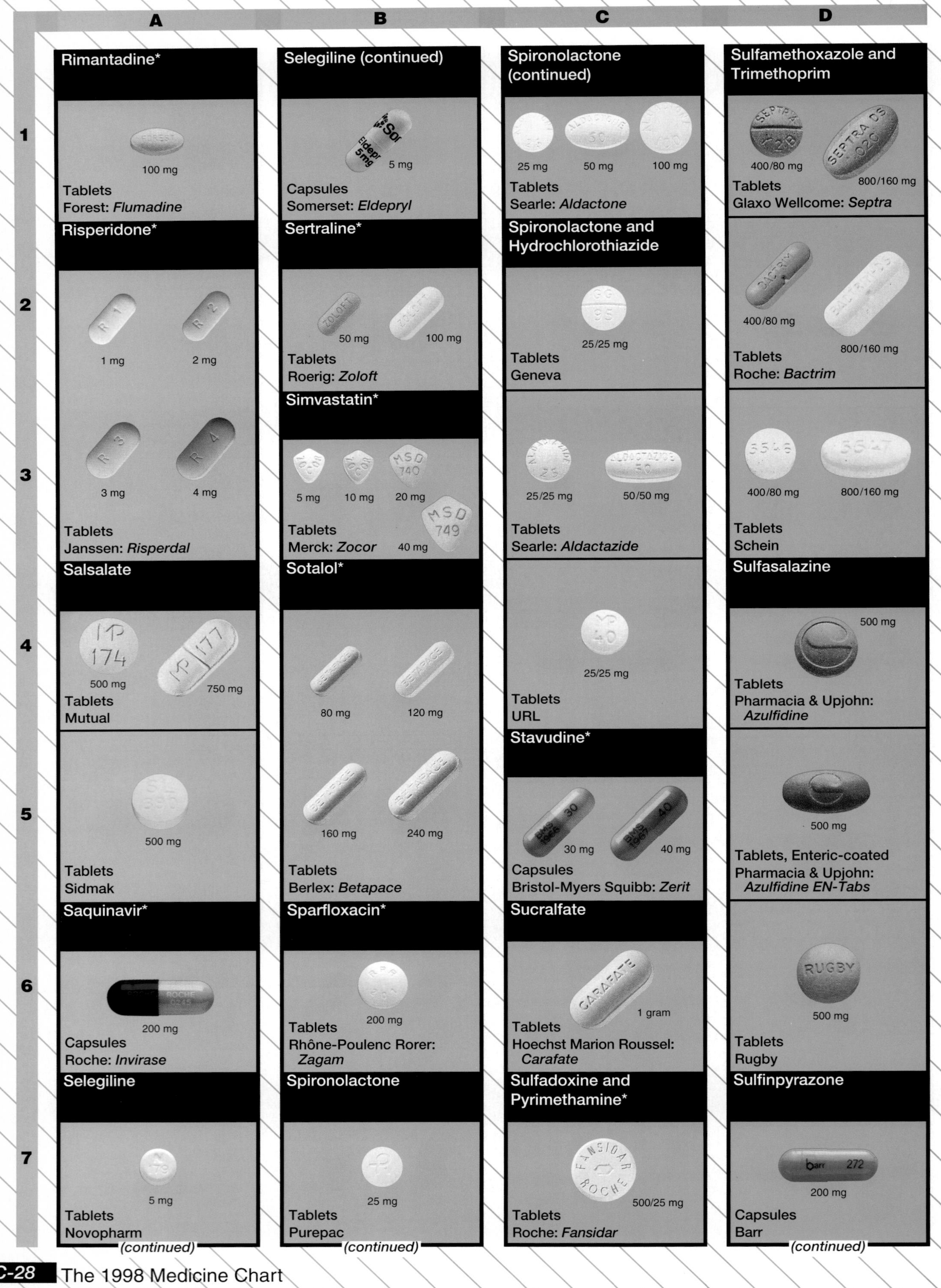

*Single source product for solid oral dosage forms in the U.S.

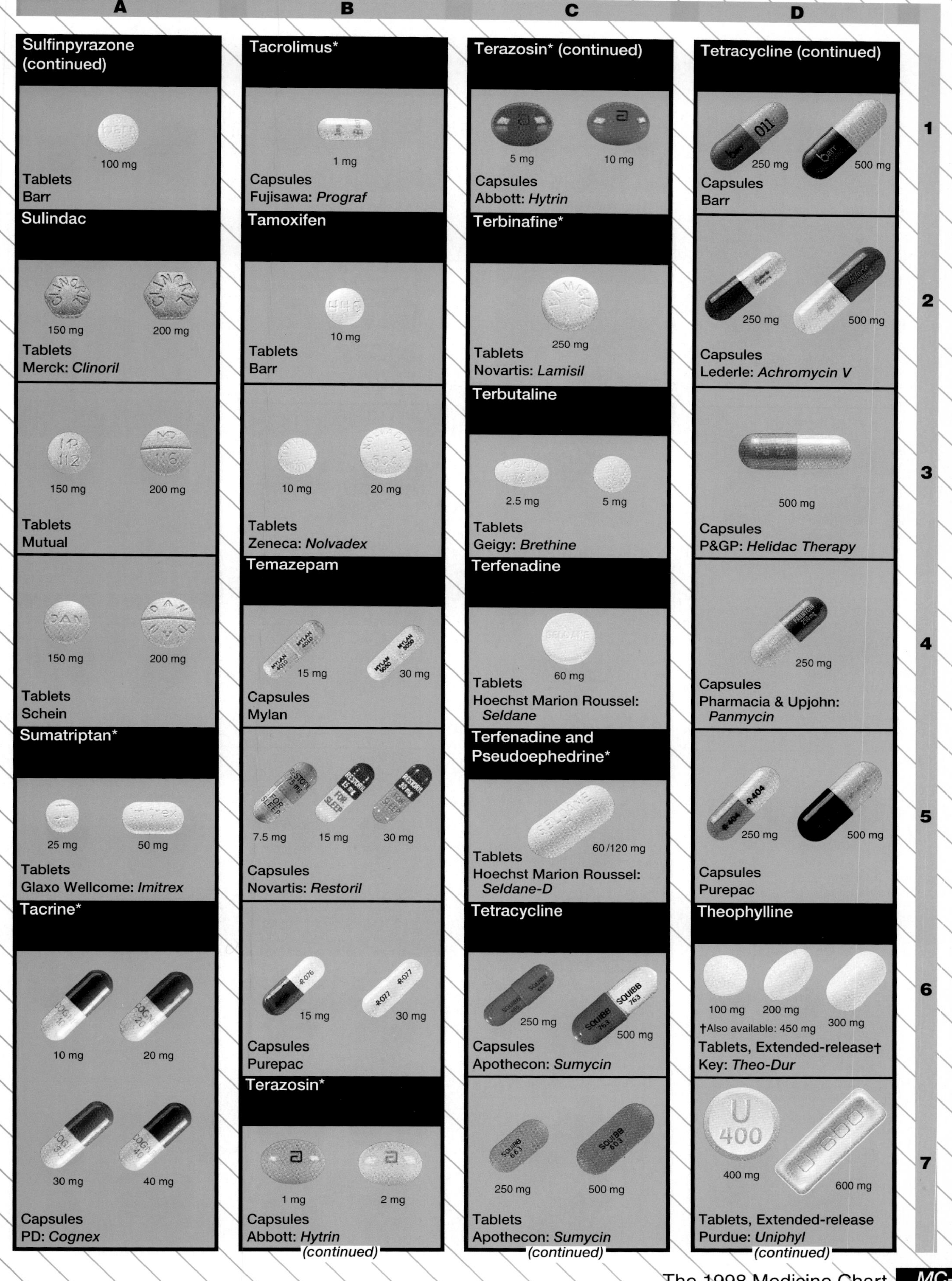

*Single source product for solid oral dosage forms in the U.S.

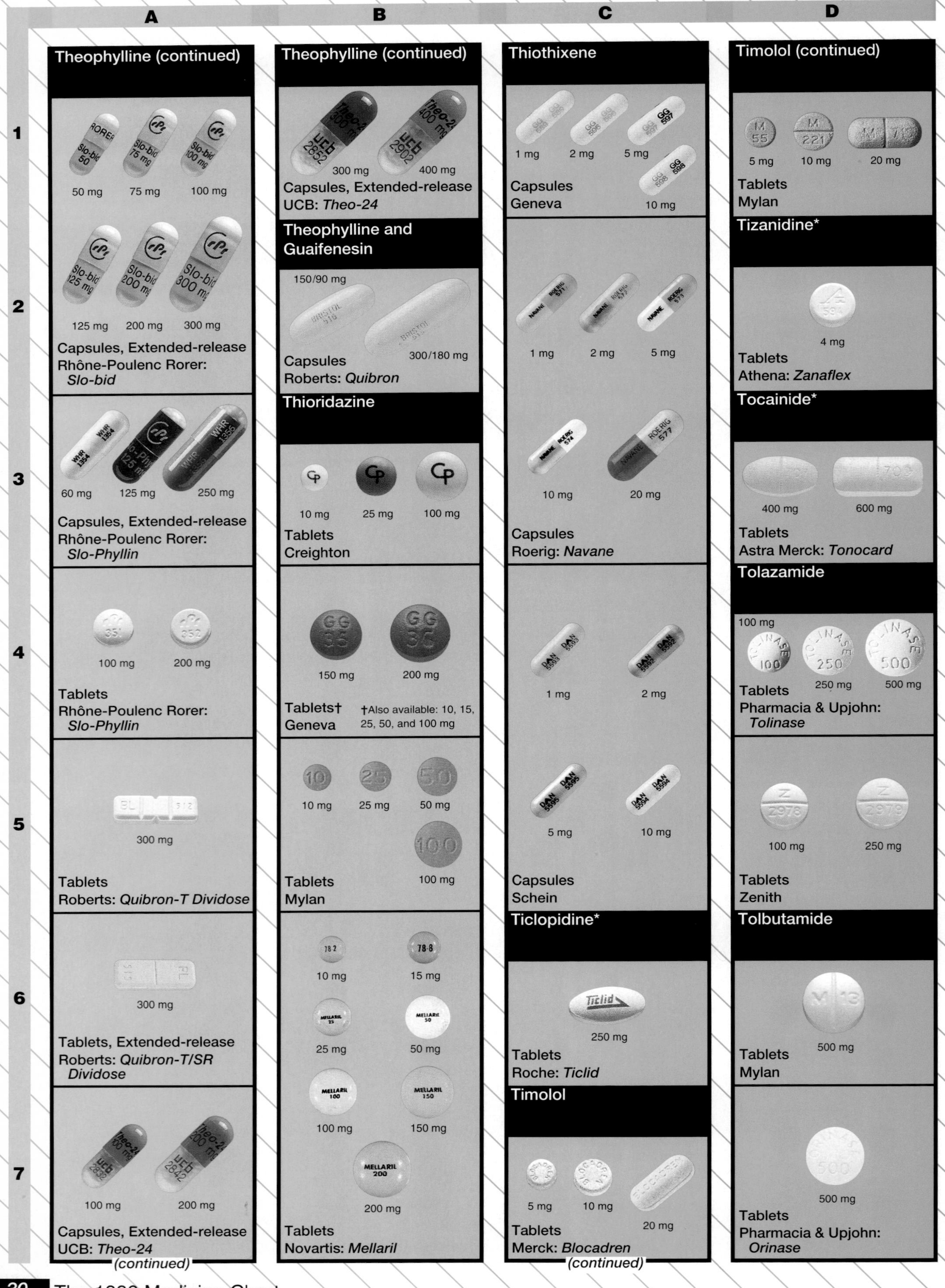

*Single source product for solid oral dosage forms in the U.S.

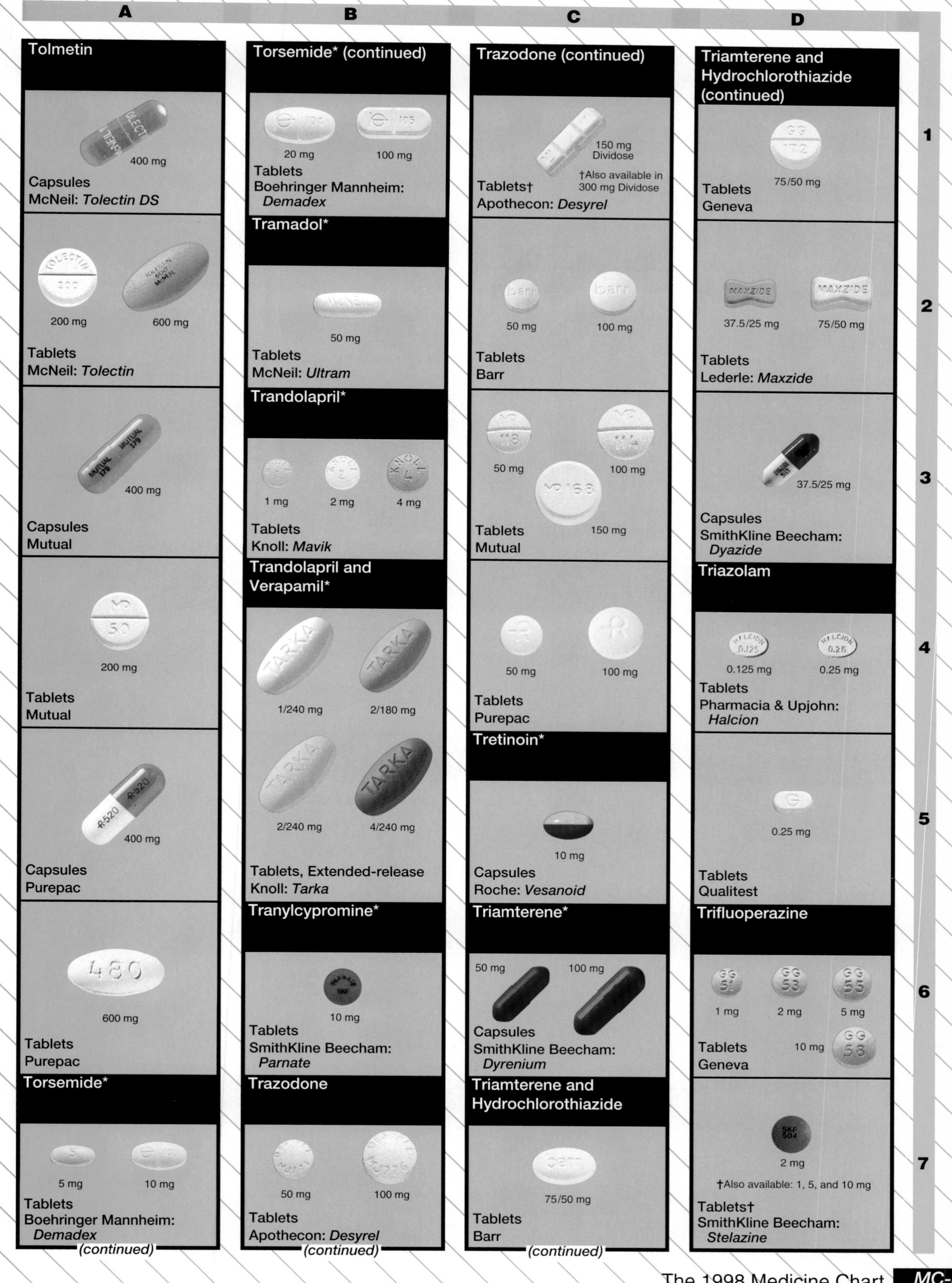

*Single source product for solid oral dosage forms in the U.S.

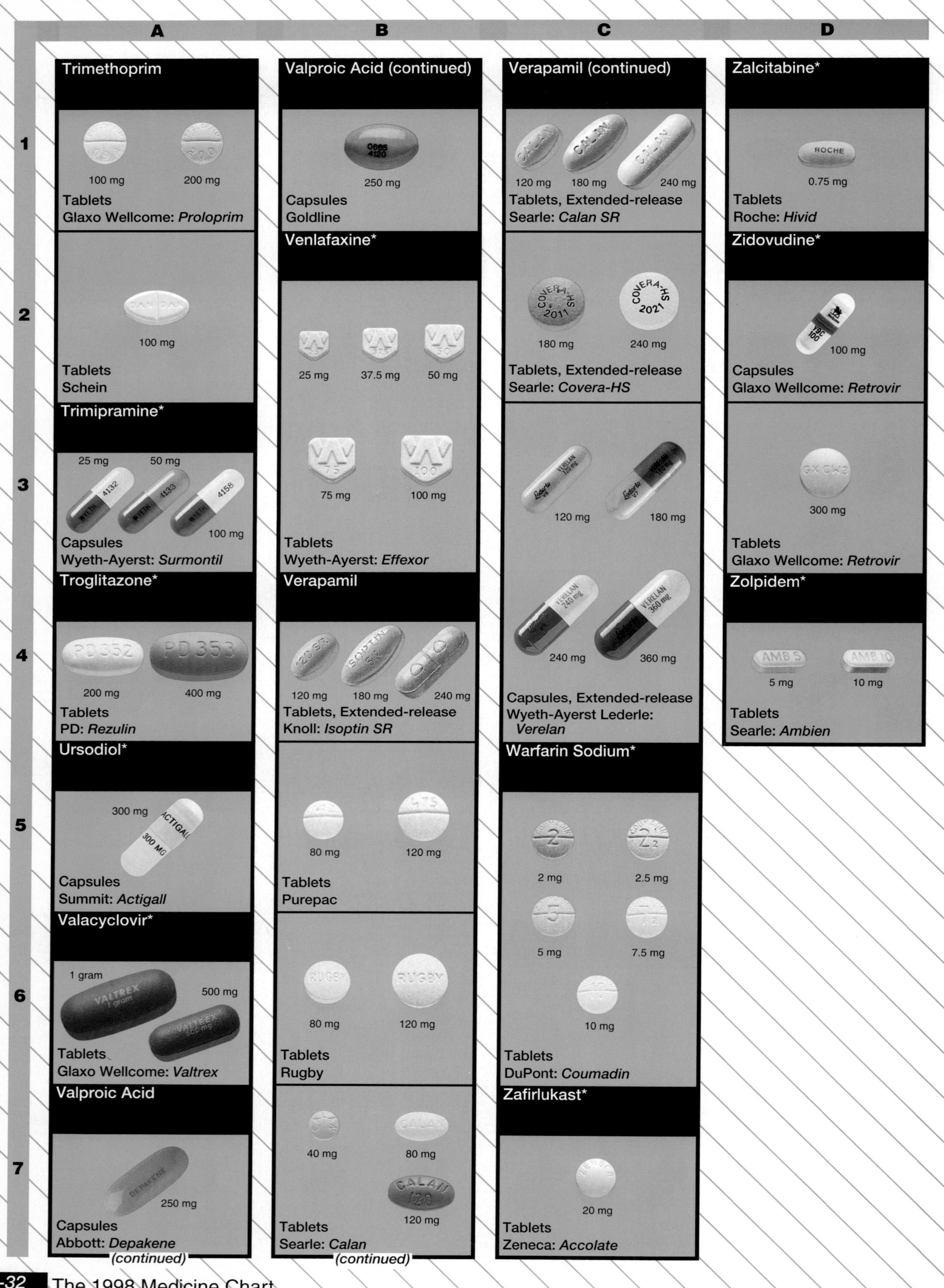

*Single source product for solid oral dosage forms in the U.S.

General Information

GENERAL INFORMATION ABOUT USE OF MEDICINES

There are two kinds of information about the proper use of medicines. One type applies to a certain medicine or group of medicines only. The other type is more general and applies to the use of any medicine.

The information that follows is general in nature. For your own safety, health, and well-being, however, it is important that you learn about the proper use of your specific medicines as well. You can get this information from your health care professional, or find it in the individual listings of this book.

Before Using Your Medicine

Before you use any medicine, tell your health care professional:

—if you have ever had an allergic or unusual reaction to any medicine, food, or other substance, such as yellow dye or sulfites.

—if you are on a low-salt, low-sugar, or any other special diet. Most medicines contain more than their active ingredient, and many liquid medicines contain alcohol.

—if you are pregnant or if you plan to become pregnant. Certain medicines may cause birth defects or other problems in the unborn child. For other medicines, safe use during pregnancy has not been established. *The use of any medicine during pregnancy must be carefully considered* and should be discussed with a health care professional.

—if you are breast-feeding. Some medicines may pass into the breast milk and cause unwanted effects in the baby.

—if you are now taking or have taken any medicines or dietary supplements in the recent past. Do not forget over-the-counter (nonprescription) medicines such as pain relievers, laxatives, and antacids or dietary supplements.

—if you have any medical problems other than the one(s) for which your medicine was prescribed.

—if you have difficulty remembering things or reading labels.

Storage of Your Medicine

It is important to store your medicines properly. Guidelines for proper storage include:

- *Keep out of the reach of children.*
- Keep medicines in their original containers.
- Store away from heat and direct light.
- Do not store capsules or tablets in the bathroom, near the kitchen sink, or in other damp places. Heat or moisture may cause the medicine to break down. Also, do not leave the cotton plug in a medicine container that has been opened, since it may draw moisture into the container.
- Keep liquid medicines from freezing.
- Do not store medicines in the refrigerator unless directed to do so.
- Do not leave your medicines in an automobile for long periods of time.
- Do not keep outdated medicine or medicine that is no longer needed. Be sure that any discarded medicine is out of the reach of children.

Proper Use of Your Medicine

Take medicine only as directed, at the right time, and for the full length of your prescribed treatment. If you are using an over-the-counter (nonprescription) medicine, follow the directions on the label unless otherwise directed by your health care professional. If you feel that your medicine is not working for you, check with your health care professional.

Unless your pharmacist has packaged different medicines together in a ''bubble-pack,'' different medicines should never be mixed in one container. It is best to keep your medicines tightly capped in their original containers when not in use. Do not remove the label since directions for use and other important information may appear on it.

To avoid mistakes, do not take medicine in the dark. Always read the label before taking, especially noting the expiration date and any directions for use.

For oral (by mouth) medicines:

- In general, it is best to take oral medicines with a full glass of water. However, follow your health care professional's directions. Some medicines should be taken with food, while others should be taken on an empty stomach.
- When taking most long-acting forms of a medicine, each dose should be swallowed whole. Do not break, crush, or chew before swallowing unless you have been specifically told that it is all right to do so.
- If you are taking liquid medicines, you should consider using a specially marked measuring spoon or other device to measure each dose accurately. Ask your pharmacist about these devices. The average household teaspoon may not hold the right amount of liquid.
- Oral medicine may come in a number of different dosage forms, such as tablets, capsules, and liquids. If you have trouble swallowing the dosage form prescribed for you, check with your health care professional. Another dosage form that you can swallow more easily may be available.
- Child-resistant caps on medicine containers have decreased greatly the number of accidental poisonings that occur each year. Use of these caps is required by law. However, if you find it hard to open such caps, you may ask your pharmacist for a regular, easier-to-open cap. He or she can provide you with a regular cap if you request it. However, you must make this request each time you get a prescription filled.

For skin patches:

- Apply the patch to a clean, dry skin area that has little or no hair and is free of scars, cuts, or irritation. Remove the previous patch before applying a new one.
- Apply a new patch if the first one becomes loose or falls off.
- Apply each patch to a different area of skin to prevent skin irritation or other problems.
- Do not try to trim or cut the adhesive patch to adjust the dosage. Check with your health care professional if you think the medicine is not working as it should.

For inhalers:

- Medicines that come in inhalers usually come with patient directions. *Read the directions carefully before using the medicine.* If you do not understand the directions, or if you are not sure how to use the inhaler, check with your health care professional.
- Since different types of inhalers may be used in different ways, it is very important to follow carefully the directions given to you.

For ophthalmic (eye) drops:

- To prevent contamination, do not let the tip of the eye drop applicator touch any surface (including the eye) and keep the container tightly closed.
- The bottle may not be full; this is to provide proper drop control.
- How to apply: First, wash your hands. Tilt your head back and, with the index finger, pull the lower eyelid away from the eye to form a pouch. Drop the medicine into the pouch and gently close your eyes. Do not blink. Keep your eyes closed for 1 to 2 minutes.
- If your medicine is for glaucoma or inflammation of the eye: Follow the directions for application that are listed above. However, immediately after placing the drops in your eye, apply pressure to the inside corner of the eye with your middle finger. Continue to apply pressure for 1 to 2 minutes after the medicine has been placed in the eye. This will help prevent the medicine from being absorbed into the body and causing side effects.
- After applying the eye drops, wash your hands to remove any medicine.

For ophthalmic (eye) ointments:

- To prevent contamination of the eye ointment, do not let the tip of the applicator touch any surface (including the eye). After using, wipe the tip of the ointment tube with a clean tissue and keep the tube tightly closed.
- How to apply: First, wash your hands. Pull the lower eyelid away from the eye to form a pouch. Squeeze a thin strip of ointment into the pouch. A 1-cm (approximately 1/3-inch) strip of ointment is usually enough unless otherwise directed. Gently close your eyes and keep them closed for 1 to 2 minutes.
- After applying the eye ointment, wash your hands to remove any medicine.

For nasal (nose) drops:

- How to use: Blow your nose gently, without squeezing. Tilt your head back while standing or sitting up, or lie down on your back on a bed and hang your head over the side. Place the drops into each nostril and keep your head tilted back for a few minutes to allow the medicine to spread throughout the nose.
- Rinse the dropper with hot water and dry with a clean tissue. Replace the cap right after use. To avoid the spread of infection, do not use the container for more than one person.

For nasal (nose) spray:

- How to use: Blow your nose gently, without squeezing. With your head upright, spray the medicine into each nostril. Sniff briskly while squeezing the bottle quickly and firmly.
- Rinse the tip of the spray bottle with hot water, taking care not to suck water into the bottle, and dry with a clean tissue. Replace the cap right after cleaning. To avoid the spread of infection, do not use the container for more than one person.

For otic (ear) drops:

- To prevent contamination of the ear drops, do not touch the applicator tip to any surface (including the ear).
- The bottle may not be full; this is to provide proper drop control.
- How to apply: Lie down or tilt the head so the ear needing treatment faces up. For adults, gently pull the earlobe up and back (pull down and back for children). Drop the medicine into the ear canal. Keep the ear facing up for about 5 minutes so the medicine can run to the bottom of the ear canal. (For young children and other patients who cannot stay still for 5 minutes, try to keep the ear facing up for at least 1 or 2 minutes.)
- Do not rinse the dropper after use. Wipe the tip of the dropper with a clean tissue and keep the container tightly closed.

For rectal suppositories:

- How to insert suppository: First, wash your hands. Remove the foil wrapper and moisten the suppository with water. Lie down on your side. Push the suppository well up into the rectum with your finger. If the suppository is too soft to insert, chill it in the refrigerator for 30 minutes or run cold water over it before removing the foil wrapper.
- Wash your hands after you have inserted the suppository.

For rectal cream or ointment:

- Clean and dry the rectal area. Apply a small amount of cream or ointment and rub it in gently.
- If your health care professional wants you to insert the medicine into the rectum: First, attach the plastic applicator tip onto the opened tube. Insert the applicator tip into the rectum and gently squeeze the tube to deliver the cream. Remove the applicator tip from the tube and wash with hot, soapy water. Replace the cap of the tube after use.
- Wash your hands after you have inserted the medicine.

For vaginal medicines:

- How to insert the medicine: First, wash your hands. Use the special applicator. Follow any special directions that are provided by the manufacturer. If you are pregnant, however, check with your health care professional before using the applicator to insert the medicine.
- Lie on your back, with your knees drawn up. Using the applicator, insert the medicine into the vagina as far as you can without using force or causing discomfort. Release the medicine by pushing on the plunger. Wait several minutes before getting up.
- Wash the applicator and your hands with soap and warm water.

Precautions While Using Your Medicine

Never give your medicine to anyone else. It has been prescribed for your personal medical problem or condition and may be harmful to another person.

Many medicines should not be taken with other medicines or with alcoholic beverages. Follow your health care professional's directions to help avoid problems.

Before having any kind of surgery (including dental surgery) or emergency treatment, tell the physician or dentist about any medicine you are taking.

If you think you have taken an overdose of any medicine or if a child has taken a medicine by accident: Call your poison control center or your health care professional at once. Keep those telephone numbers handy. Also, keep a bottle of Ipecac Syrup safely stored in your home in case you are told to cause vomiting. Read the directions on the label of Ipecac Syrup before using.

Side Effects of Your Medicine

Along with its intended effects, a medicine may cause some unwanted effects. Some of these side effects may need medical attention, while others may not. It is important for you to know what side effects may occur and what you should do if you notice signs of them. Check with your health care professional about the possible side effects of the medicines you are taking, or if you notice any unusual reactions or side effects.

Additional Information

It is a good idea for you to learn both the generic and brand names of your medicine and even to write them down for future use.

Many prescriptions may not be refilled until your pharmacist checks with your health care professional. *To save time, do not wait until you have run out of medicine before requesting a refill.* This is especially important if you must take your medicine every day.

When traveling:

- Carry your medicine with you rather than putting it in your checked luggage. Checked luggage may get lost or stored in very cold or very hot areas.
- Make sure a source of medicine is available where you are traveling, or take a large enough supply to last during your visit. It is also a good idea to take a copy of your written prescription with you.

If you want more information about your medicines, ask your health care professional. *Do not be embarrassed to ask questions* about any medicine you are taking. To help you remember, it may be useful to write down any questions and bring them with you on your next visit to your health care professional.

AVOIDING MEDICINE MISHAPS

Tips Against Tampering

Over-the-counter (OTC) or nonprescription medicines are now packaged so that it will be easier to notice signs of tampering. A tamper-evident package is required either to be unique so that it cannot be copied easily, or to have a barrier or indicator (with an identifying characteristic, such as a pattern, picture, or logo) that will be easily noticed if broken. For two-piece, unsealed, hard gelatin capsules, two tamper-evident features are required. Improved packaging also includes using special wrappers, seals, or caps on the outer and/or inner containers, or sealing each dose in its own pouch.

Even with such packaging, however, no system is completely safe. It is important that you do your part by checking for signs of tampering whenever you buy or use a medicine.

The following information may help you detect possible signs of tampering.

Protecting yourself

General common sense suggestions include the following:

- When buying a drug product, *consider* the dosage form (for example, capsules, tablets, syrup), the type of packaging, and the tamper-evident features. Ask yourself: Would it be easy for someone to tamper with this product? Will I be able to determine whether or not this product has been tampered with?
- *Look very carefully* at the outer packaging of the drug product before you buy it. After you buy it, also check the inner packaging as soon as possible.
- If the medicine has a protective packaging feature, it should be described in the labeling. This description is required to be placed so that it will not be affected if the feature is broken or missing. If the feature is broken or missing, *do not buy or use* the product. If you have already purchased the product, return it to the store. Always be sure to tell someone in charge about any problems.

• *Do not take* medicines that show even the slightest signs of tampering or do not seem quite right.

• Never take medicines in the dark or in poor lighting. *Read* the label and check each dose of medicine before you take it.

What to look for

Packaging

• Are there breaks, cracks, or holes in the outer or inner wrapping or protective cover or seal?

• Does the outer or inner covering appear to have been disturbed, unwrapped, or replaced?

• Does a plastic or other shrink band (tight-fitting wrap) around the top of the bottle appear distorted or stretched, as though it had been rolled down and then put back into place? Is the band missing? Has the band been slit and retaped?

• Is the bottom of the container intact?

• Does the container appear to be too full or not full enough?

• Is the cap on tight?

• Are there bits of paper or glue stuck on the rim of the container (does it seem like the container once had a bottle seal)?

• Is the cotton plug or filler in the bottle torn, sticky, or stained, or does it appear to have been taken out and put back?

• Do eye drops have a protective seal? All eye drops must be sealed when they are made, in order to keep them germ-free. Do not use if there is any sign of a broken or removed seal.

• Check the bottom as well as the top of a tube. Is the tube properly sealed? Metal tubes crimped up from the bottom like a tube of toothpaste should be firmly sealed.

• Are the expiration date, lot number, and other information the same on both the container and its outer wrapping or box?

Liquids

• Is the medicine the usual color? Thickness?

• Is a normally clear liquid cloudy or colored?

• Are there particles (small pieces) in the bottom of the bottle or floating in the solution? For some liquids, called suspensions, floating particles are normal.

• Does the medicine have a strange or different taste or odor (for example, bleach, acid, gasoline-like, or other pungent or sharp odor)? Do not taste the medicine if it has a strange odor.

Tablets

• Do the tablets look different than they usually do? Do they have unusual spots or markings? If they normally are shiny and smooth, are some dull or rough? Is there anything unusual about the color?

• Are the tablets all the same size and thickness?

• If there is printing on the tablets, do they all have the same imprint? Is the imprint missing from any?

• Do the tablets have a strange or different odor or taste?

• Are any of the tablets broken?

Capsules

• Do the capsules look different than they usually do? Are any cracked or dented? Are they all the same size and color?

• Do they have their normal shiny appearance or are some dull? Do some have fingerprints on them as though they have been handled?

• Are the capsules all the same length?

• If there is printing on the capsules, do they all have the same imprint? Is the imprint missing from any? Do the imprints all line up the same way?

• Do the capsules have an unexpected or unusual odor or taste?

Tubes and jars (ointments, creams, pastes, etc.)

• Does the product or container look different than usual?

• Are ointments and creams smooth and non-gritty? Have they separated?

Be a wise consumer. Look for signs of tampering before you buy a medicine and again each time you take a dose. Also, pay attention to the daily news in order to learn about any reported tampering.

It is important to understand that a change in the appearance or condition of a product may not mean that the package has been tampered with. The manufacturer may have changed the color of a medicine or its packaging. Also, the product may be breaking down with age or it may have had rough or unusual handling in shipping. In addition, some minor product variations may be normal.

Whenever you suspect that something is unusual about a medicine or its packaging, take it to your pharmacist. He or she is familiar with most products and their packaging. If there are serious concerns or problems, your pharmacist should report it to the USP Practitioners' Reporting Network℠ (USP PRN) at 1-800-487-7776, or other appropriate authorities.

Unintentional Poisoning

According to information provided by the American Association of Poison Control Centers, over one million children 6 years of age and under were unintentionally poisoned in 1995.

Adults also may be unintentionally poisoned. This happens most often through carelessness or lack of information. For example, people can be poisoned by taking medicines in the dark and getting the wrong one, or taking medicine prescribed for a friend to treat ''the same symptoms.''

Drug poisoning from an unintentional overdose is 1 type of accidental poisoning contributing to these figures. Other causes include household chemical poisoning from unintentional ingestion or contact, and inhaled poisoning—for example, carbon monoxide from a car.

Children are ready victims

The natural curiosity of children makes them ready victims of poisoning. Children explore everywhere and investigate their environment. What they find frequently goes into their mouths. They do not understand danger and possibly cannot read warning labels.

Accidental poisoning from medicine is especially dangerous in small children because a medicine's strength is usually based on its use in adults. Even a small quantity of an adult dose can sometimes poison a child.

Preventing poisoning from medicines

- Store medicines out of the sight and reach of children, preferably in a locked cabinet—not in the bathroom medicine cabinet or in a food cabinet. Always store your medicines in a secure place.
- If you have children living with you or as occasional guests, you should have child-resistant caps on your medicine containers. These will help ensure that an accidental poisoning does not occur in your home. (Adults who have difficulty opening child-resistant closures may request traditional, easy-to-open packaging for their medicines.)
- If you are called to the telephone or to answer the door while you are taking a medicine, take the container with you or put the medicine out of the reach of small children. Children act quickly—usually when no one is watching.
- Always replace lids and return medicines to their storage place after use, even if you will be using them again soon.
- Date medicines when purchased and clean out your medicines periodically. Discard prescription medicines that are past their expiration or ''beyond use'' date. As medicines grow old, the chemicals in them may change. In general, medicines that do not have an expiration date should not be kept for more than 1 year. Carefully discard any medicines so children cannot get them. Rinse containers well before discarding in the trash.
- Take only those medicines prescribed for you and give medicines only to those for whom they are prescribed. A medicine that worked well for one person may harm another.
- It is best to keep all medicines in their original containers with their labels intact. The label contains valuable information for taking the medicine properly. Also, in case of accidental poisoning, it is important to know the ingredients in a drug product and any emergency instructions from the manufacturer. While prescription medicines usually do not list ingredients, information on the label makes it possible for your pharmacist to identify the contents.
- Ask your pharmacist to include on the label the number of tablets or capsules that he or she put in the container. In case of poisoning, it may be important to know roughly how many tablets or capsules were taken.
- Do not trust your memory—read the label before using the medicine, and take it as directed.
- If a medicine container has no label or the label has been defaced so you are not absolutely sure what it says, do not use it.
- Turn on a light when taking or giving medicines at night or in a dark room.
- Label medicine containers with poison symbols, especially if you have children, individuals with poor vision, or other persons in your home who cannot read well.
- Teach children that medicine is not candy by calling each medicine by its proper name.
- Do not take medicines in front of children. They may wish to imitate you.
- Communicate these safety rules to any babysitters you have and remember them if you babysit or are visiting a house with children. Children are naturally curious and can get into a pocketbook, briefcase, or overnight bag that contains medicines.

What to do if a poisoning happens

Remember:

- There may be no immediate, significant symptoms or warning signs, particularly in a child.
- Nothing you can give will work equally well in all cases of poisoning. In fact, one ''antidote'' may counteract the effects of another.
- Many poisons act quickly, leaving little time for treatment.

Therefore:

- If you think someone has swallowed medicine or a household product, and the person is unconscious, having seizures (convulsions), or is not breathing, immediately call for an ambulance. Otherwise, do not wait to see what effect the poison will have or if symptoms of overdose develop; immediately call a poison control center (listed in the white pages of your telephone book under ''Poison Control'' or inside the front cover with other emergency numbers). These numbers should be posted beside every telephone in the house, as should those of your pharmacist, the police, the fire department, and ambulance services. (Some poison control centers have TTY capability for the deaf. Check with your local center if you or someone in your family requires this service.)
- Have the container with you when you call so you can read the label on the product for ingredients.
- Describe what, when, and how much was taken and the age and condition of the person poisoned—for example, if the person is vomiting, choking, drowsy, shows a change in color or temperature of skin, is conscious or unconscious, or is convulsing.
- *Do not induce vomiting* unless instructed by medical personnel. *Do not induce vomiting or force liquids* into a person who is convulsing, unconscious, or very drowsy.
- Stay calm and in control of the situation.

Keep a bottle of Ipecac Syrup stored in a secure place in your home for emergency use. It is available at pharmacies in 1 ounce bottles without prescription. Ipecac Syrup is often recommended to induce vomiting in cases of poisoning.

Activated Charcoal also is sometimes recommended in certain types of poisoning and you may wish to add a supply to your emergency medicines. It is available without a prescription. Before using this medicine for poisoning, however, call a poison control center for advice.

GETTING THE MOST OUT OF YOUR MEDICINES

To get the most out of your medicines, there are certain things that you must do. Your health care professionals will be working with you, but you also have a responsibility for your own health.

Communicating With Your Health Care Provider

Communication between you and your health care professional is central to good medical care. Your health care professional needs to know about you, your medical history, and your current problems. In turn, you need to understand the recommendations he or she is making and what you will need to do to follow the treatment. You will have to ask questions—and answer some too. Communication is a two-way process.

Giving information

Your health care professional needs to know some details about your past and present medical history. In discussing these details, you should always be completely open and honest. Your health professional's diagnosis and treatment will be based in part on the information that you provide. A complete list of the details that should be included in a full medical history is provided below.

''Medical history'' checklist

A ''medical history'' checklist covers the following information:

- All the serious illnesses you have ever had and the approximate dates.
- Your current symptoms, if any.
- **All** the medicines and dietary supplements you are taking or have taken in the recent past. This includes prescription and nonprescription medicines (such as pain relievers, antacids, laxatives, and cold medicines, etc.) and home remedies. This is especially important if you are seeing more than one health care professional; if you are having surgery, including dental or emergency treatment; or if you get your medicines from more than one source.
- **Any** allergies or sensitivities to medicines, foods, or other substances.
- Your smoking, drinking, and exercise habits.
- Any recent changes in your lifestyle or personal habits. New job? Retired? Change of residence? Death in family? Married? Divorced? Other?
- Any special diet you are on—low-sugar, low-sodium, low-fat, or a diet to lose or gain weight.
- If you are pregnant, plan to become pregnant, or if you are breast-feeding.
- All the vaccinations and vaccination boosters you have had, with dates if possible.
- Any operations you have had, including dental and those performed on an outpatient basis, and any accidents that have required hospitalization.
- Illnesses or conditions that run in your family.
- Cause of death of closest relatives.

Remember, be sure to tell your health care professional at each visit if there have been any changes since your last visit.

Medical history forms

Many health care professionals have a standard ''medical history'' form they will ask you to fill out when they see you for the first time. Some may ask the questions and write down the answers for you. If you will be visiting a health care professional for the first time, prepare yourself before you go by thinking about the questions that might be asked and jotting down the answers—including dates—so that you will not forget an important detail. Once your ''medical history'' is in the files, subsequent visits will take less time.

You will have to supply each health care provider you see—every time you see one—with complete information about what happened since your last visit. It is important that your records are updated so he or she can make sound recommendations for your continued treatment, or treatment of any new problems.

Medical history file

It will simplify things if you develop a ''medical history'' file at home for yourself and each family member for whom you are responsible. Setting up the file will take time. However, once it is established, you need only to keep it up-to-date and remember to take it with you when you see a health care professional. This will be easier than having to repeat the information each time and running the risk of confusing or forgetting details.

It is also a good idea to carry in your wallet a card that summarizes your chronic medical conditions, the medicines you are taking, and your allergies and drug sensitivities. You should keep this card as up-to-date as possible. Many pharmacists provide these cards as a service.

Getting information

In order to benefit from your health care professional's advice you must understand completely everything that he or she tells you. Do not be embarrassed to ask questions, or to ask him or her to explain again any instruction or detail that you do not understand. Then it is up to you to carry out those instructions precisely. If there is a failure in any part of this system, you will pay an even higher price—physically and financially—for your health care.

Your health care professional may provide instructions to you in written form. If he or she does not, you may want to write them down or ask the health care professional to write them down for you. If you do not have time to jot down everything while you are still with your health care professional, sit down in the waiting room before you leave and write down the information while it is still fresh in your mind and you can still ask questions. If you have been given a prescription, ask for written information about the drug and how to take it. Your pharmacist can also answer questions when you have your prescription filled.

What you need to know about your medicines

There are a number of things that you should know about each medicine you are taking. These include:

- The medicine's generic and brand name.
- How the medicine will help you and the expected results. How it makes you feel. How long it takes to begin working.
- How much to take at one time.
- How often to take the medicine.
- How long it will be necessary to take the medicine.
- When to take it. Before, during, after meals? At bedtime? At any other special times?
- How to take it. With water? With fruit juice? With food?
- What to do if you forget to take it (miss a dose).
- Foods, drinks, or other medicines that you should not take while taking the medicine.
- Restrictions on activities while taking the medicine, such as driving a car or operating other motor vehicles.
- Possible side effects. What to do if they appear. How to minimize the side effects. How soon they will go away.
- When to seek help if there are problems.
- How long to wait before reporting no change in your symptoms.
- How to store the medicine.
- The expiration date.
- The cost of the medicine.
- How to have your prescription refilled, if necessary.

Other information

Following are some other issues and information that you may want to consider:

- Ask your health care professional about the ingredients in the medicines (both prescription and over-the-counter [OTC]) you are taking and whether there may be a conflict with other medicines. Your health care professional can help you avoid dangerous combinations or drug products that contain ingredients to which you are allergic or sensitive.
- Ask your health care professional for help in developing a system for taking your medicines properly, particularly if you are taking a number of them on a daily basis. (When you are a patient in a hospital, ask for instructions before you are discharged.) Do not hesitate or be embarrassed to ask questions or ask for help.
- If you are over 60 years of age, ask your health care professional if the dose of the medicine is right for you. Some medicines should be given in lower doses to certain older individuals.
- If you are taking several different medicines, ask your health care professional if all of them are necessary for you. You should take only those medicines that you need.
- Medicines should be kept in the container they came in. If this is not possible when you are at work or away from home, ask your pharmacist to provide or recommend a container to transport your medicines safely. The use of "pill boxes" can also cause some problems, such as broken or chipped tablets, mistaking one medicine for another, and even interactions between the medicine and the metal of these boxes.
- Some people have trouble taking tablets or capsules. Your health care professional will know if another dosage form is available, and if tablet or capsule contents can be taken in a liquid. If this is an ongoing problem, ask your prescriber to write the prescription for the dosage form you can take most comfortably.
- To protect children from accidental poisoning, child-resistant caps are required by law on most oral prescription medicines. These containers are designed so children will have difficulty opening them. Since many adults also find these containers hard to open, the law allows consumers to request traditional, easy-to-open packaging for their drugs. If you do not use child-resistant packaging, make sure that your medicines are stored where small children cannot see or reach them. If you use child-resistant containers, ask your pharmacist to show you how to open them.

Consumer education is one of your health care professional's most important responsibilities. To supplement what you learn during your visit, ask if there is any written information about your medicines that you can take home with you. Your health care professional may also have available various reference books or computerized drug information that you can consult for details about precautions, side effects, and proper use of your medicines.

Your Health Care Team

Your health care team will be made up of several different health care professionals. Each of these individuals will play an important part in the overall provision of your health care. It is important that you understand the roles of each of these providers and what you should be able to expect from each of them.

Your dentist

In addition to providing care and maintenance of your mouth, teeth, and gums, your dentist is also an essential member of your overall health care team since your oral health and general health often affect one another.

In providing dental treatment, your dentist should base his or her decisions upon an extensive knowledge of your current condition and past medical and dental history. Because the dentist is a prescriber of medications, it is very important that he or she is aware of your **full** medical and dental history. A complete medical and dental history should include the information that is listed in the ''Medical history checklist'' section above. Even if you do not consider this information important, you should inform your dentist as fully as possible.

In the treatment of any dental/oral problem your dentist should make every effort to inform you as fully as possible about the nature of the problem. He or she should explain why this problem has occurred, the advantages and disadvantages of available treatments (including no treatment), and what types of preventive measures can be employed to avoid future problems. These measures may include periodic visits to the dentist, and a general awareness of the manner in which dental and overall health may affect one another. In any type of treatment, your dentist should always allow you to ask questions, and should be willing to answer them to your satisfaction.

In selecting a dentist, it is important to keep in mind the role of the dentist as a member of the health care team, and the extent of the information that he or she should be asking for and providing. There are also several practical issues that you should consider, such as:

- Is the dentist a specialist or general practitioner?
- What are the office hours?
- Is the dentist or his/her associates available after office hours by phone? In emergencies, will you be able to contact a dentist?
- What is the office policy on cancellations?
- What types of payment are accepted at the office?
- What is the office policy on x-ray procedures?
- Is the dentist willing to work with other medical and/or dental specialists that you may be seeing?

Your dentist should be an integral part of your health care team. In treating problems and providing general maintenance of your oral health, your dentist should base decisions upon a full dental and medical history. He or she should also be willing to answer any questions that you have regarding your oral health, any medications prescribed, and preventive measures to avoid future problems.

Your nurse

Depending upon the setting, type of therapy being administered, and state regulations, the role of the nurse in your health care team may vary. Registered nurses practice in diverse health care settings, such as hospitals, out-patient clinics or physicians' offices, schools, workplaces, homes, and long-term care facilities like nursing homes and retirement centers. Some nurses, including certified nurse practitioners and midwives, hold a master's degree in nursing and may assume the role of primary health care professional, either in practice by themselves or in joint practices with physicians. In most states, nurse practitioners may prescribe selected medications. Clinical nurse specialists also have a master's degree in nursing and specialize in a particular area of health care. In some hospitals, long-term care facilities, and out-patient care settings, licensed practical nurses (LPNs) have certain responsibilities in administering medication to patients. LPNs usually work under the supervision of a RN or physician. Nursing aides assist RNs and LPNs with different kinds of patient care activities. In most places where people receive health care, RNs may be the primary source of information for drug therapies and other medical treatments. It is important that you be aware of the roles and responsibilities of the nurses participating in your health care.

Professional nurses participate with other health professionals to ensure that your medication therapy is safe and effective and to monitor any effects (both desired and negative) from the medication. You may be admitted to the hospital so that nurses can administer medications and monitor your response to therapy. In hospitals or long-term care facilities, nurses are responsible for administering your medications in their proper dosage form and dose, and at correct time intervals, as well as monitoring your response to these medications. At home or in outpatient settings, nurses should ensure that you have the proper information and support of others, if needed, to get the medication and take it as prescribed. When nurses administer medication, they should explain why you are receiving this medication, how it works, any possible side effects, special precautions or actions that you must take while using the medication, and any potential interactions with other medications.

If you experience any side effects or symptoms from a medication, you should always tell your health care provider. It is important that these reactions be detected before they become serious or permanent. You can seek advice about possible ways to minimize these side effects from your nurse. Your health care professional should also be made aware of any additional medical problems or conditions (such as pregnancy) that you may have, since these can also affect the safety and effectiveness of a medication.

The professional nurse is someone who can help to clarify drug information. In most health care settings, nurses are accessible and can answer your questions or direct you to others who can assist you. Professional nurses are skilled in the process of patient teaching. To make sure that patients learn important information about their health problem and its treatment, RNs often use a combination of teaching methods, such as verbal instruction, written materials, demonstration, and audio-visual instructions. Above all, professional nurses should teach at a pace and level that are appropriate for you. RNs can also help you design a medication schedule that fits your lifestyle and may be less likely to cause unwanted side effects.

Your pharmacist

Your pharmacist is an important member of your health care team. In addition to performing traditional services, such as dispensing medications, your pharmacist can help you understand your medications and how to take them safely and effectively. By keeping accurate and up-to-date records and monitoring your use of medications, your pharmacist can help to protect you from improper medication therapy, unwanted side effects, and dangerous drug interactions. Because your pharmacist can play a vital role in protecting and improving your health, you should seek a pharmacist who will provide these services.

To provide you with the best possible care, your pharmacist should be informed about your current condition and medication history. Your personal medication history should include the information that is listed in the ''Medical history checklist'' section above. Your pharmacist should also be aware of any special packaging needs that you may have (such as child-resistant or easy-to-open containers). Your pharmacist should keep accurate and up-to-date records that contain this information. If you visit a new pharmacy that does not have access to your medication records, it is important that you inform that pharmacist as fully as possible about your medical history or provide him or her with a copy of your medication records from your previous pharmacy. In general, in order to get the most out of your pharmacy services, it is best to get all of your medications (including OTCs) from the same pharmacy.

Your pharmacist should be a knowledgeable and approachable source of information about your medications. Some of the information that your pharmacist should explain is listed in the ''What you need to know about your medicines'' section above. Ideally, this information should also be provided in written form, so that you may refer to it later if you have any questions or problems. The pharmacist should always be willing to answer any questions that you have regarding your medications, and should also be willing to contact your physician or other health care professionals (dentist, nurses, etc.) on your behalf if necessary.

Your pharmacist can also help you with information on the costs of your medicines. Many medicines are available from more than one company. They may have equal effects but different costs. Your insurance company, HMO, or other third-party payment group may reimburse you for only some of these medications or only for part of their costs. Your pharmacist will be able to tell you which of these medications are covered by your payment plan or which cost less.

In selecting a pharmacist, it is important that you understand the role of the pharmacist as a member of your health care team and the extent of information that he or she should be asking for and providing. Because pharmacies can offer different types of services and have different policies regarding patient information, some of the issues that you should consider in selecting a pharmacist also relate to the pharmacy where that person practices. There are several issues regarding the pharmacist and pharmacy that you should consider, such as:

- Does the pharmacy offer written information that you can take home? Home delivery?
- Are you able to talk to your pharmacist without other people hearing you?
- Can the pharmacist be reached easily by phone? In an emergency, is a pharmacist available twenty-four hours (including weekends and holidays) by phone?
- What types of payment are accepted in the pharmacy?
- Does the pharmacy accept your HMO or third-party payment plan?
- Does the pharmacy offer any specialized services, such as diabetes education?

You should select your pharmacist and pharmacy as carefully as you select your physician, and stay with the same pharmacy so that all of your medication records are in the same place. This will help to ensure that your records are accurate and up-to-date and will allow you to develop a beneficial relationship with your pharmacist.

Your physician

One of the most important health care decisions that you will make is your choice of a personal physician. The physician is central to your health care team, and is responsible for helping you maintain your overall health. In addition to detecting and treating ailments or adverse conditions, your physician and his or her coworkers should also serve as primary sources of health care information. Because the physician plays such an important role in your overall health care, it is important that you understand the full range of the physician's role as health care and information provider.

In providing any type of treatment or counseling, your physician should base his or her decisions upon an extensive knowledge of your current condition and past medical history. A complete medical history should include the information that is listed in the ''Medical history checklist'' section above. Your physician should keep accurate and comprehensive medical records containing this information. Because your treatment (and your health) is dependent upon a full disclosure of your medical history, as well as any factors that may currently be affecting your health (i.e., stress, smoking, drug use, etc.), it is important that you inform your physician as fully as possible, even if you might not consider this information important.

It is important that you inform your personal physician of any other physicians (such as specialists or subspecialists), dentists, or other health care professionals that you are seeing. You should also inform your physician of the pharmacy that you use or intend to use, so that he or she can contact the pharmacist if necessary.

In treating any health problem, your physician should make every effort to help you understand completely the nature of the problem and its treatment. He or she should take the time to explain the problem, why it may have occurred, and what preventive measures (if any) can be taken to avoid it in the future. Your physician should explain fully the reasons for any prescribed treatment. He or she should also be willing to discuss alternative therapies, especially if you are uncomfortable with the one that has been prescribed. Your physician should always be willing to answer all of your questions to your satisfaction.

In selecting a physician, you should look for one who will provide a full range of services. Asking for a full medical history and providing complete information about your treatment and medications are some of these services. There are several other issues that you may want to consider. Does your physician:

- Inquire about your general health as well as specific problems?
- Have a good working relationship with your pharmacist? With the nurses and staff at his/her office?
- Periodically have you bring in bottles or labels from all of the medications (prescription and nonprescription) that you are taking or have at home?

• Periodically check the status of your vaccinations?

• Consult peers with specialty training for difficult problems?

You may also want to consider your physician's medical credentials. Your local medical society should be able to provide specific facts about your physician's training, experience, and membership in professional societies.

Cost and payment are two of the most important issues in contemporary health care. Your physician should be sensitive to the costs of your treatment and the manner in which you intend to pay for this and related medications. If you belong to an HMO or third-party payment plan, be sure that your physician is aware of your involvement in the plan. You should also be aware of the different types of payment that are accepted at the physician's office.

In prescribing medications, your physician should take into account the manner in which you intend to pay for your drugs, and should be aware of any specific concerns regarding the costs of your treatment and medication. He or she should also explain why brand or generic medication may be preferable in certain situations.

In selecting a physician, there are also several practical issues and matters of convenience that you should consider, such as:

• Is the office convenient to your home or work?

• What are the office hours?

• Is your physician or his/her associates or partners available (twenty-four hours) by phone? In emergencies, will you be able to contact a physician?

• Are you able to arrange appointments to fit your schedule? What is the office policy on cancellations?

• Is the physician well regarded in the community? Does he or she have a reputation for listening to patients and answering questions?

• Does the physician have admitting privileges at a hospital of your preference?

• Does he/she participate in your health plan?

In addition to the considerations already mentioned, your physician should be sensitive to the special concerns of treating the elderly. Older patients can present disease processes differently from younger adults, can react differently to certain drugs and dosages, and may have preexisting conditions that require special treatments to be prescribed.

There are also several special issues to consider in your selection of a pediatrician or family physician. If your child is not old enough to understand all instructions and information, it is important that your child's physician explain to you any information about a problem and all instructions for treatment. When your child is of school age, the physician should speak directly to the child as well, asking and answering questions, and providing information about cause and prevention of medical problems and the use of medications. He or she should choose a dosage form and dose that is appropriate for your child's age and explain what to do if the child has certain symptoms, such as fever, vomiting, etc. (including the amount and type of medicine to give, if any, and when to call him or her for advice).

Your physician should be a primary source of information about your health and any medications that you are taking. In providing treatment for medical problems or conditions, the physician should base decisions on a full medical history and be willing to answer any questions that you have regarding your health, treatment, and medications.

Managing Your Medicines

To get the full benefit and reduce risks in taking your medicines, it is important to follow instructions exactly. This means taking the right medicine and dose, at correct time intervals, for the length of time prescribed. Bad effects can result from taking too much or too little of a medicine, or taking it too often or not often enough.

Establishing a system

Whether you are taking one or several medicines, you should develop a system for taking them. It can be just as difficult to remember whether you took your once-a-day medicine as it can be to keep track of a number of medicines that need to be taken several times a day. Many medicines also have special instructions that can further complicate proper use.

Establish a way of knowing whether you took your medicines properly, then make that a part of your daily routine. If you take 1 or 2 medicines a day, you may only need to take them at the same time that you perform some other regular task, such as brushing your teeth or getting dressed.

For most people, a check-off record can also be a handy way of managing multiple medicines. Keep your medicine record in a handy, visible place next to where you take your medicines. Check off each dose as you take it. If you miss a dose, make a note about what happened and what you did on the back of the record or the bottom of the sheet.

Be sure to note any unwanted effects or anything unusual that you think may be connected with your medicines. Also note if a medicine does not do what you expect, but remember that some medicines take a while before having a noticeable effect.

If you keep a check-off record faithfully, you will know for sure whether or not you took your medicine. You will also have a complete record for your health care professionals to review when you visit them again. This information can help them determine if the medicine is working properly or causing unwanted side effects, or whether adjustments should be made in your medicines and/or doses.

If your medicines or the instructions for taking them are changed, correct your record or make a new one. Keep the old record until you are sure this information is no longer needed.

You might want to color code your medicine containers to help tell them apart. If you are having trouble reading labels or if you are color-blind, codes that can be recognized by touch (rubber bands, a cotton ball, or a piece of emery board, for instance) can be attached to the container. If you code your medicines, be sure these identifications are included on any medicine record you use. If necessary, ask your pharmacist to type medicine labels in large letters for easier reading.

A check-off list is not the only method for recording medicine use. If this system does not work for you, ask your health care professional for help in developing an alternative. Be sure he or she knows all the medicines prescribed for you and any nonprescription medicines you take regularly, the hours you usually eat your meals, and any special diet you are following.

Informed management

Your medicines have been prescribed for you and your condition. Ask your health care professional what benefits to expect, what side effects may occur, and when to report any side effects. If your symptoms go away, do not decide you are well and stop taking your medicine. If you stop too soon, the symptoms may come back. Finish all of the medicine if you have been told to do so. However, if you develop diarrhea or other unpleasant side effects, do not continue with the medicine; call your health care professional and report these effects. A change in dose or in the kind of medicine you are taking may be necessary.

When you are given a prescription for a medicine, ask the person who wrote it to explain it to you. For example, does "four times a day" mean one in the morning, one at noon, one in the evening, and one at bedtime; or does it mean every six hours around the clock? When a prescription says "take as needed," ask how close together the doses can be taken and what the maximum number of doses you can take in one day should be. Does "take with liquids" mean with water, milk, or something else? Are there some liquids that should avoided? What does "take with food" mean? At every meal time (some people must eat six meals a day), or with a snack? Do not trust your memory—have the instructions written down. You must understand exactly what the prescriber wants you to do in order to "take as directed."

When the pharmacist dispenses your medicine, you have another opportunity to clarify information or to ask other questions. Before you leave, check the label on your medicine to be sure it matches the prescription and your understanding of what you are to do. If it does not, ask more questions.

The key to getting the most from your prescribed treatments is following instructions accurately and intelligently. If you have questions or doubts about the prescribed treatment, do not decide not to take the medicine or fail to follow the prescribed regimen. Discuss your questions and doubts with your health care professional.

The time and effort put into setting up a system to manage your medicines and establishing a routine for taking them will pay off by relieving anxiety and helping you get the most from your prescribed treatment.

Taking Your Medicine

To take medicines safely and get the greatest benefit from them, it is important to establish regular habits so you are less likely to make mistakes.

Before taking any medicine, read the label and any accompanying information. You can also consult books to learn more about the medicine. If you have unanswered questions, check with your health care professional.

The label on the container of a prescription medicine should bear your first and last name; the name of the prescriber; the pharmacy address and telephone number; the prescription number; the date of dispensing; and directions for use. Some states or provinces may have additional requirements. If the name of the drug product is not on the label, ask the pharmacist to include the brand (if any) and generic names. An expiration date may also appear. All of this information is important in identifying your medicines and using them properly. The labels on containers should never be removed and all medicines should be kept in their original containers.

Some tips for taking medicines safely and accurately include the following:

- Read the label of each medicine container three times:
  - —before you remove it from its storage place,
  - —before you take the lid off the container to remove the dose, and
  - —before you replace the container in its storage place.
- Never take medicines in the dark, even if you think you know exactly where to find them.
- Use standard measuring devices to take your medicines (household teaspoons, cups, or glasses vary widely in the amount they hold). Ask your pharmacist for help with measuring.
- Set bottles and boxes of medicines on a clear area, well back from the edge of the surface to prevent containers and/or caps from being knocked to the floor.
- When pouring liquid medicines, pick up the container with the label against the palm of your hand to protect it from being stained by dripping medicine.
- Wipe off the top and neck of bottles of liquid medicines to keep labels from being obscured, and to make it less likely that the lid will stick.
- Shake all liquid suspensions of drug products before pouring so that ingredients are mixed thoroughly.
- If you are taking medicine with water, use a full, 8 ounce glassful, not just enough to get it down. Too little liquid with some medicines can prevent the medicine from working properly, and can cause throat irritation if the medicine does not get completely to the stomach.
- To avoid accidental confusion of lids, labels, and medicines, replace the lid on one container before opening another.
- When you are interrupted while taking your medicine, take the container with you or put the medicine out of the reach of small children. It only takes a second for them to take an overdose. When you return, check the label of the medicine to be sure you have the right one.
- Only crush tablets or open capsules to take with food or beverages if your health care professional has told you that this will not affect the way the medicine works. If you have difficulty swallowing a tablet or capsule, check with your health care professional about the availability of a different dosage form.
- Follow any diet instructions or other treatment measures prescribed by your health care professional.

- If at any point you realize you have taken the wrong medicine or the wrong amount, call your health care professional immediately. In an emergency, call your local emergency number.

When you have finished taking your medicines, mark it down immediately on your medication calendar to avoid ''double dosing.'' Also make note of any unusual changes in your body, including change in weight, color or amount of urine, perspiration, or sputum; as well as your pulse, temperature, or any other items you may have been instructed to observe for your condition or your medicine.

Try to take your medicines on time, but a half hour early or late will usually not upset your schedule. If you are more than several hours late and are getting close to your next scheduled dose, check any instructions that were given to you by your health care professional. If you did not receive instructions about missed doses, check with your health care professional. You may also find missed dose information in the entries included in this book.

When your medicines are being managed by someone else (for example, when you are a patient in a hospital or nursing home), question what is happening to you and communicate what you know about your previous drug therapy or any other treatments. If you know you always take 1, not 2, of a certain tablet, say so and ask that your record be checked before you take the medicine. If you think you are receiving the wrong treatment or medication, do not hesitate to say so. You should always remain involved in your own therapy.

Many hospitals and nursing homes now offer counseling in medicine management as part of their discharge planning for patients. If you or a family member are getting ready to come home, ask your health care professional if you can be part of such instruction.

The ''Expiration Date'' on Medicine Labels

To assure that a drug product meets applicable standards of identity, strength, quality, and purity at the time of use, an ''expiration date'' is added by the manufacturer to the label of most prescription and nonprescription drug products.

The expiration date on a drug product is valid only as long as the product is stored in the original, unopened container under the storage conditions specified by the manufacturer. Among other things, drugs can be affected by humidity, temperature, light, and even air. A medicine taken after the expiration date may have changed in potency or may have formed harmful material as it deteriorates. Contamination with germs can also occur. The safest rule is not to use any medicine beyond the expiration date.

Preventing deterioration

A drug begins to deteriorate the minute it is made. This rate of deterioration is factored in by the manufacturer in calculating the expiration date. Keeping the drug product in the container supplied by the pharmacist helps slow down deterioration. Storing the drug in a proper manner—for example, in a light-resistant container or in a cool, dry place (not the bathroom medicine cabinet)—also helps. The need for medicines to be kept in their containers and stored properly cannot be overstressed.

Patients sometimes ask their health care professionals to prescribe a large quantity of a particular medicine in order to ''economize.'' Although this may be all right in some cases, this practice may backfire. If you have a large supply of your medicine and it deteriorates before you can use it all, or if your doctor changes your medicine, you may lose out.

Sometimes deterioration can be recognized by physical changes in the drug, such as a change in odor or appearance. For example, aspirin tablets develop a vinegar odor when they break down. These changes are not true of all drugs, however, and the absence of physical changes should not be assumed to mean that no deterioration has occurred.

Some liquid medicines mixed at the pharmacy will have a ''beyond use'' date on the label. This is an expiration date that is calculated from the date of preparation in the pharmacy. This is a definite date, after which you should throw away any remaining medicine.

If your prescription medicines do not bear an ''expiration'' or ''beyond use'' date, your dispensing pharmacist is the best person to advise you about how long they can be safely used.

ABOUT THE MEDICINES YOU ARE TAKING

New Drugs—From Idea to Marketplace

To be sold legitimately in the United States, new drugs must pass through a rigorous system of approval specified in the Food, Drug, and Cosmetic Act and supervised by the Food and Drug Administration (FDA). Except for certain drugs subject to other regulatory provisions, no new drug for human use may be marketed in this country unless FDA has approved a ''New Drug Application'' (NDA) for it.

The idea

The creation of a new drug usually starts with an idea. Most likely that idea results from the study of a disease or group of symptoms. Ideas can also come from observations of clinical research. This may involve many years of study, or the idea may occur from an accidental discovery in a research laboratory. Some may be coincidental discoveries, as in the case of penicillin.

Idea development takes place most often in the laboratory of a pharmaceutical company, but may also happen in laboratories at research institutions like the National Institutes of Health, at medical centers and universities, or in the laboratory of a chemical company.

Animal testing

A new drug is first tested on animals to help determine how toxic the substance may be. Most drugs interfere in some way with normal body functions. These animal studies are designed to discover the degree of that interference and the extent of the toxic effects.

After successful animal testing, perhaps over several years, the sponsors of the new drug apply to the FDA for an Investigational New Drug (IND) application. This status allows the drug to be tested in humans. As part of their request, the sponsoring manufacturer must submit the results of the animal studies, plus a detailed outline of the proposed human testing and information about the researchers that will be involved.

Human testing

Drug testing in humans usually consists of three consecutive phases. ''Informed consent'' must be secured from all volunteers participating in this testing.

Phase I testing is most often done on young, healthy adults. This testing is done on a relatively small number of subjects, generally between 20 and 80. Its purpose is to learn more about the biochemistry of the drug: how it acts on the body and how the body reacts to it. The procedure differs for some drugs, however. For example, Phase I testing of cancer drugs involves actual cancer patients from the beginning of testing.

During Phase II, small controlled clinical studies are designed to test the effectiveness and relative safety of the drug. These are done on closely monitored patients who have the disease for which the drug is being tested. Their numbers seldom go beyond 100 to 200 patients. Some volunteers for Phase II testing who have severely complicating conditions may be excluded.

A ''control'' group of people of comparable physical and disease types is used to do double-blind, controlled experiments for most drugs. These are conducted by medical investigators thoroughly familiar with the disease and this type of research. In a double-blind experiment, the patient, the health professional, and other personnel do not know whether the patient is receiving the drug being tested, another active drug, or no medicine at all (a placebo or ''sugar pill''). This helps eliminate bias and assures the accuracy of results. The findings of these tests are statistically analyzed to determine whether they are ''significant'' or due to chance alone.

Phase III consists of larger studies. This testing is performed after effectiveness of the drug has been established and is intended to gather additional evidence of effectiveness for specific uses of the drug. These studies also help discover adverse drug reactions that may occur with the drug. Phase III studies involve a few hundred to several thousand patients who have the disease the drug is intended to treat.

Patients with additional diseases or those receiving other therapy may be included in later Phase II and Phase III studies. They would be expected to be representative of certain segments of the population who would receive the drug following approval for marketing.

Final approval

When a sponsor believes the investigational studies on a drug have shown it to be safe and effective in treating specific conditions, a New Drug Application (NDA) is submitted to FDA. This application is accompanied by all the documentation from the company's research, including complete records of all the animal and human testing. This documentation can run to many thousands of pages.

The NDA application and its documentation must then be reviewed by FDA physicians, pharmacologists, chemists, statisticians, and other professionals experienced in evaluating new drugs. Proposed labeling information for the physician and pharmacist is also screened for accuracy, completeness, and conformity to FDA-approved wording.

Regulations call for the FDA to review an NDA within 180 days. This period may be extended if additional data is required and, in some cases, may take several years. When all research phases are considered, the actual time it takes from idea to marketplace may be 8 to 10 years or even longer. However, for drugs representing major therapeutic advances, FDA may ''fast-track'' the approval process to try to get those drugs to patients who need them as soon as possible.

After approval

After a drug is marketed, the manufacturer must inform the FDA of any unexpected side effects or toxicity that comes to its attention. Consumers and health care professionals have an important role in helping to identify any previously unreported effects. If new evidence indicates that the drug may present an ''imminent hazard,'' the FDA can withdraw approval for marketing or add new information to the drug's labeling at any time.

Generic drugs

After a new drug is approved for marketing, a patent will generally protect the financial interests of the drug's developer for a number of years. The traditional protection period is for 17 years. In reality, however, the period is much less due to the extended period of time needed to gain approval before marketing can begin. Recognizing that a considerable part of a drug's patent life may be tied up in the approval process, in 1984 the U.S. Congress passed a law providing patent extension for drugs whose commercial sale may have been unduly delayed by the approval process.

Any manufacturer can apply for permission to produce and market a drug after the patent for the drug has expired. Following a procedure called an Abbreviated New Drug Application (ANDA), the applicant must show that its product is bioequivalent to the original product. Although the extensive clinical testing completed by the originator during the drug's development does not have to be repeated, comparative testing between the products must be done.

Drug Names

Every drug must have a nonproprietary name, a name that is available for each manufacturer to use. These names are commonly called generic names.

The FDA requires the generic name of a drug product to be placed on its labeling. However, manufacturers often use brand names in promoting their products. In general, brand names are shorter and easier to use than the corresponding generic name. The manufacturer then emphasizes its brand name (which cannot be used by anyone else) in advertising and other promotions. Often, the consumer may not realize that a brand name drug is also available under other brand names or by generic name. Ask your pharmacist if you have any questions about the names of your medicines.

Drug Quality

After an NDA or an ANDA has been approved for a product, the manufacturer must then meet all requirements relating to production. These include the FDA's current Good Manufacturing Practice regulations and any applicable standards relating to strength, quality, purity, packaging, and labeling that are established by the *United States Pharmacopeia* (USP).

Routine product testing by the manufacturer is required by the Good Manufacturing Practice regulations of the FDA (the FDA itself does not routinely test all products, except in cases where there is a suspicion that something may be wrong). In addition to governmental requirements, drug products must meet public standards of strength, quality, and purity that are developed by USP. In order to market their products, all manufacturers in the United States must meet USP-established standards unless they specifically choose not to meet the standards for a particular product. In this case, that product's label must state that it is ''not USP'' and how it differs from USP standards (this occurs very rarely).

Differences in Drug Products

Although standards to ensure strength, quality, purity, and bioequivalence exist, the standards allow for variations in certain factors that may produce other differences from product to product. These product variations may be important to some patients, since not all patients are ''equivalent.'' For example, the size, shape, and coating may vary and, therefore, be harder or easier for some patients to swallow; an oral liquid will taste good to some patients and bad to others; one manufacturer may use lactose as an inactive ingredient in its product, while another product may contain a different inactive ingredient; one product may contain sugar or alcohol while another product does not.

In deciding to use one therapeutically equivalent product over another, consumers should keep the following in mind:

- Consider convenience factors of drug products (for example, ease of taking a particular dosage form).
- Don't overlook the convenience of the package. The package must protect the drug in accordance with USP requirements, but packages can be quite different in their ease of carrying, storing, opening, and measuring.
- If you have an allergy or any type of dietary restriction, you need to be aware of the ''inactive'' ingredients that may be present in different medicines. These inactive ingredients may vary from product to product.
- Price is always a consideration. The price difference between products (e.g., different brands, or brands versus generics) may be a major factor in the overall price of a prescription. Talk to your pharmacist about price considerations. Some states require that the pharmacist dispense exactly what is prescribed. However, other states allow the pharmacist to dispense less expensive medicines when appropriate.

Aside from differences in the drug product, there are many other factors that may influence the effectiveness of a medicine. For example, your diet, body chemistry, medical conditions, or other drugs you are taking may affect how much of a dose of a particular medicine gets into the body.

For the majority of drugs, slight differences in the amount of drug made available to the body will not make any therapeutic difference. For other drugs, the precise amount that gets into the body is more critical. For example, some heart or epilepsy medicines may create problems for the patient if the dose delivered to the body varies for some reason.

For those drugs in the critical category, it is a good idea to stay on the specific product you started on. Changes should only be made after a consultation with the health care professional who prescribed the medicine. If you feel that a certain batch of your medicine is more potent or does not work as well as other batches, or if you have other questions, check with your health care professional.

ACETAMINOPHEN Systemic

Some commonly used brand names are:

In the U.S.—

Aceta Elixir[1]
Aceta Tablets[1]
Acetaminophen Uniserts[1]
Actamin[1]
Actamin Extra[1]
Actamin Super[2]
Aminofen[1]
Aminofen Max[1]
Apacet Capsules[1]
Apacet Elixir[1]
Apacet Extra Strength Caplets[1]
Apacet Extra Strength Tablets[1]
Apacet, Infants'[1]
Apacet Regular Strength Tablets[1]
Aspirin Free Anacin Maximum Strength Caplets[1]
Aspirin Free Anacin Maximum Strength Gel Caplets[1]
Aspirin Free Anacin Maximum Strength Tablets[1]
Aspirin-Free Excedrin Caplets[2]
Banesin[1]
Bayer Select Maximum Strength Headache Pain Relief Formula[2]
Dapa[1]
Dapa X-S[1]
Datril Extra-Strength[1]
Feverall, Children's[1]
Feverall, Infants'[1]
Feverall Junior Strength[1]
Feverall Sprinkle Caps, Children's[1]
Feverall Sprinkle Caps Junior Strength[1]
Genapap Children's Elixir[1]
Genapap Children's Tablets[1]
Genapap Extra Strength Caplets[1]
Genapap Extra Strength Tablets[1]
Genapap, Infants'[1]
Genapap Regular Strength Tablets[1]
Genebs Extra Strength Caplets[1]
Genebs Regular Strength Tablets[1]
Genebs X-Tra[1]
Liquiprin Children's Elixir[1]
Liquiprin Infants' Drops[1]
Neopap[1]
Oraphen-PD[1]
Panadol, Children's[1]
Panadol, Infants'[1]
Panadol Junior Strength Caplets[1]
Panadol Maximum Strength Caplets[1]
Panadol Maximum Strength Tablets[1]
Phenaphen Caplets[1]
Redutemp[1]
Snaplets-FR[1]
St. Joseph Aspirin-Free Fever Reducer for Children[1]
Suppap-120[1]
Suppap-325[1]
Suppap-650[1]
Tapanol Extra Strength Caplets[1]
Tapanol Extra Strength Tablets[1]
Tempra[1]
Tempra D.S.[1]
Tempra, Infants'[1]
Tempra Syrup[1]
Tylenol Children's Chewable Tablets[1]
Tylenol Children's Elixir[1]
Tylenol Children's Suspension Liquid[1]
Tylenol Extra-Strength Adult Liquid Pain Reliever[1]
Tylenol Extra Strength Caplets[1]
Tylenol Extra Strength Gelcaps[1]
Tylenol Extra Strength Tablets[1]
Tylenol Infants' Drops[1]
Tylenol Infants' Suspension Drops[1]
Tylenol Junior Strength Caplets[1]
Tylenol Junior Strength Chewable Tablets[1]
Tylenol Regular Strength Caplets[1]
Tylenol Regular Strength Tablets[1]
Valorin[1]
Valorin Extra[1]

In Canada—

Abenol[1]
Actimol Chewable Tablets[1]
Actimol Children's Suspension[1]
Actimol Infants' Suspension[1]
Actimol Junior Strength Caplets[1]
Anacin-3[1]
Anacin-3 Extra Strength[1]
Apo-Acetaminophen[1]
Atasol Caplets[1]
Atasol Drops[1]
Atasol Forte Caplets[1]
Atasol Forte Tablets[1]
Atasol Oral Solution[1]
Atasol Tablets[1]
Excedrin Caplets[2]
Excedrin Extra Strength Caplets[2]
Exdol[1]
Exdol Strong[1]
Panadol[1]
Panadol Extra Strength[1]
Robigesic[1]
Rounox[1]
Tempra Caplets[1]
Tempra Chewable Tablets[1]
Tempra Drops[1]
Tempra Syrup[1]
Tylenol Caplets[1]
Tylenol Children's Chewable Tablets[1]
Tylenol Drops[1]
Tylenol Elixir[1]
Tylenol Gelcaps[1]
Tylenol Junior Strength Caplets[1]
Tylenol Tablets[1]

Other commonly used names are APAP and paracetamol.

This information applies to the following medicines:

1. Acetaminophen (a-seat-a-MIN-oh-fen)‡§
2. Acetaminophen and Caffeine (kaf-EEN)

‡Generic name product may also be available in the U.S.
§Generic name product may also be available in Canada.

Description

Acetaminophen is used to relieve pain and reduce fever. Unlike aspirin, it does not relieve the redness, stiffness, or swelling caused by rheumatoid arthritis. However, it may relieve the pain caused by mild forms of arthritis.

This medicine is available without a prescription; however, your medical doctor or dentist may have special instructions on the proper dose of acetaminophen for your medical condition.

Acetaminophen is available in the following dosage forms:

Oral

Acetaminophen
- Capsules (U.S.)
- Oral granules (in packets) (U.S.)
- Oral liquid (drops) for babies (U.S. and Canada)
- Oral liquid for children (U.S. and Canada)
- Oral liquid for adults (U.S.)
- Oral powders (in capsules) (U.S.)
- Oral suspension (drops) for babies (U.S. and Canada)
- Oral suspension (liquid) for children (U.S. and Canada)
- Tablets (U.S. and Canada)
- Chewable tablets (U.S. and Canada)

Acetaminophen and Caffeine
- Tablets (U.S. and Canada)

Rectal

Acetaminophen
- Suppositories (U.S. and Canada)

Before Using This Medicine

If you are taking this medicine without a prescription, carefully read and follow any precautions on the label. For acetaminophen, the following should be considered:

Allergies—Tell your doctor if you have ever had any unusual or allergic reaction to acetaminophen or aspirin. Also tell your health care professional if you are allergic to any other substances, such as foods, preservatives, or dyes.

Pregnancy—Although studies have not been done in pregnant women, acetaminophen has not been reported to cause birth defects or other problems.

Breast-feeding—Although acetaminophen passes into the breast milk in small amounts, it has not been reported to cause problems in nursing babies.

Children—This medicine has been tested in children and has not been shown to cause different side effects or problems than it does in adults. However, some children's products containing acetaminophen also contain aspartame, which may be dangerous if it is given to children with phenylketonuria.

Older adults—Acetaminophen has been tested and has not been shown to cause different side effects or problems in older people than it does in younger adults.

Other medicines—Although certain medicines should not be used together at all, in other cases two different medicines may be used together even if an interaction might occur. In these cases, your doctor may want to change the dose, or other precautions may be necessary. Tell your health care professional if you are taking any other prescription or nonprescription (over-the-counter [OTC]) medicine.

Other medical problems—The presence of other medical problems may affect the use of acetaminophen. Make sure you tell your doctor if you have any other medical problems, especially:

- Alcohol abuse or
- Kidney disease (severe) or
- Hepatitis or other liver disease—The chance of serious side effects may be increased
- Phenylketonuria—Some brands of acetaminophen contain aspartame, which can make your condition worse

Proper Use of This Medicine

Unless otherwise directed by your medical doctor or dentist:

- *Do not take more of this medicine than is recommended on the package label.* If too much is taken, liver and kidney damage may occur.
- *Children up to 12 years of age should not take this medicine more than 5 times a day.*

To use *acetaminophen oral granules* (e.g., Snaplets-FR):

- Just before the medicine is to be taken, open the number of packets needed for one dose. Mix the granules inside of the packets with a small amount of soft food, such as applesauce, ice cream, or jam. Eat the acetaminophen granules along with the food.

To use *acetaminophen oral powders* (e.g., Feverall Sprinkle Caps [Children's or Junior Strength]):

- These capsules are not intended to be swallowed whole. Instead, just before the medicine is to be taken, open the number of capsules needed for one dose. Empty the powder from each capsule into 1 teaspoonful of water or other liquid. Drink the medicine along with the liquid. You may drink more liquid after taking the medicine. You may also mix the powder with a small amount of soft food, such as applesauce, ice cream, or jam. Eat the acetaminophen powder along with the food.

For patients using *acetaminophen suppositories:*

- If the suppository is too soft to insert, chill it in the refrigerator for 30 minutes or run cold water over it before removing the foil wrapper.
- To insert the suppository:

  —First remove the foil wrapper and moisten the suppository with cold water. Lie down on your side and use your finger to push the suppository well up into the rectum.

Dosing—The dose of acetaminophen will be different for different patients. *Follow your doctor's orders or the directions on the label.* The following information includes only the average doses of acetaminophen. *If your dose is different, do not change it* unless your doctor tells you to do so.

The number of capsules, tablets, teaspoonfuls of oral solution or suspension that you take, the amount of oral granules or powders that you take, or the number of suppositories that you use, depends on the strength of the medicine. Also, the number of doses you use each day and the time allowed between doses depend on the strength of the medicine.

- For *oral* dosage forms (capsules, granules, powders, solution, suspension, or tablets) and *rectal* dosage forms (suppositories):
  —For pain or fever:
  - Adults and teenagers—325 or 500 milligrams (mg) every three or four hours, 650 mg every four to six hours, or 1000 mg every six hours as needed. For short-term treatment (up to ten days), the total dose should not be more than 4000 mg (for example, eight 500-mg tablets) a day. For long-term treatment, the total dose should not be more than 2600 mg (for example, eight 325-mg tablets) a day.
  - Children—Acetaminophen dose is based on the child's age.
    —Infants up to 3 months of age: 40 mg every four hours as needed.
    —Infants 4 to 12 months of age: 80 mg every four hours as needed.
    —Children 1 to 2 years of age: 120 mg every four hours as needed.
    —Children 2 to 4 years of age: 160 mg every four hours as needed.
    —Children 4 to 6 years of age: 240 mg every four hours as needed.
    —Children 6 to 9 years of age: 320 mg every four hours as needed.
    —Children 9 to 11 years of age: 320 to 400 mg every four hours as needed.
    —Children 11 to 12 years of age: 320 to 480 mg every four hours as needed.

Storage—To store this medicine:

- Keep out of the reach of children.
- Store away from heat and direct light.
- Do not store acetaminophen tablets (including caplets and gelcaps), capsules, or granules in the bathroom,

near the kitchen sink, or in other damp places. Heat or moisture may cause the medicine to break down.
- Keep the liquid and suppository forms of this medicine from freezing.
- Do not keep outdated medicine or medicine no longer needed. Be sure that any discarded medicine is out of the reach of children.

Precautions While Using This Medicine

If you will be taking this medicine for a long time, especially in high doses (more than eight 325-mg or five 500-mg doses a day), your doctor should check your progress at regular visits.

Check with your medical doctor or dentist:
- If you are taking this medicine to relieve pain, including arthritis pain, and the pain lasts for more than 10 days for adults or 5 days for children or if the pain gets worse, new symptoms occur, or the painful area is red or swollen. These could be signs of a serious condition that needs medical or dental treatment.
- If you are taking this medicine to bring down a fever, and the fever lasts for more than 3 days or returns, the fever gets worse, new symptoms occur, or redness or swelling is present. These could be signs of a serious condition that needs treatment.
- If you are taking this medicine for a sore throat, and the sore throat is very painful, lasts for more than 2 days, or occurs together with or is followed by fever, headache, skin rash, nausea, or vomiting.

Check the labels of all prescription and nonprescription (over-the-counter [OTC]) medicines you now take. If any contain acetaminophen, check with your health care professional. Taking them together with this medicine may cause an overdose.

If you will be taking more than an occasional 1 or 2 doses of acetaminophen, *do not drink alcoholic beverages.* To do so may increase the chance of liver damage, especially if you drink large amounts of alcoholic beverages regularly, if you take more acetaminophen than is recommended on the package label, or if you take it regularly for a long time.

Taking certain other medicines together with acetaminophen may increase the chance of unwanted effects. The risk will depend on how much of each medicine you take every day, and on how long you take the medicines together. If your medical doctor or dentist directs you to take these medicines together on a regular basis, follow his or her directions carefully. However, *do not take any of the following medicines together with acetaminophen for more than a few days, unless your doctor has directed you to do so and is following your progress:*

Aspirin or other salicylates
Diclofenac (e.g., Voltaren)
Diflunisal (e.g., Dolobid)
Etodolac (e.g., Lodine)
Fenoprofen (e.g., Nalfon)
Floctafenine (e.g., Idarac)
Flurbiprofen, oral (e.g., Ansaid)
Ibuprofen (e.g., Motrin)
Indomethacin (e.g., Indocin)
Ketoprofen (e.g., Orudis)
Ketorolac (e.g., Toradol)
Meclofenamate (e.g., Meclomen)
Mefenamic acid (e.g., Ponstel)
Nabumetone (e.g., Relafen)
Naproxen (e.g., Naprosyn)
Oxaprozin (e.g., Daypro)
Phenylbutazone (e.g., Butazolidin)
Piroxicam (e.g., Feldene)
Sulindac (e.g., Clinoril)
Tenoxicam (e.g., Mobiflex)
Tiaprofenic acid (e.g., Surgam)
Tolmetin (e.g., Tolectin)

Acetaminophen may interfere with the results of some medical tests. Before you have any medical tests, tell the person in charge if you have taken acetaminophen within the past 3 or 4 days. If possible, it is best to call the laboratory where the test will be done about 4 days ahead of time, to find out whether this medicine may be taken during the 3 or 4 days before the test.

For *diabetic patients:*
- Acetaminophen may cause false results with some blood glucose (sugar) tests. If you notice any change in your test results, or if you have any questions about this possible problem, check with your health care professional. This is especially important if your diabetes is not well-controlled.

For patients taking one of the products that contain *caffeine* in addition to acetaminophen:
- Caffeine may interfere with the results of a test that uses adenosine (e.g., Adenocard) or dipyridamole (e.g., Persantine) to help find out how well your blood is flowing through certain blood vessels. Therefore, you should not have any caffeine for 8 to 12 hours before the test.

If you think that you or anyone else may have taken an overdose of acetaminophen, get emergency help at once, even if there are no signs of poisoning. Signs of severe poisoning may not appear for 2 to 4 days after the overdose is taken, but treatment to prevent liver damage or death must be started as soon as possible. Treatment started more than 24 hours after the overdose is taken may not be effective.

Side Effects of This Medicine

Along with its needed effects, a medicine may cause some unwanted effects. Although not all of these side effects may occur, if they do occur they may need medical attention.

Check with your doctor immediately if any of the following side effects occur:

Rare

Yellow eyes or skin

Symptoms of overdose

Diarrhea; increased sweating; loss of appetite; nausea or vomiting; stomach cramps or pain; swelling, pain, or tenderness in the upper abdomen or stomach area

Also, check with your doctor as soon as possible if any of the following side effects occur:

Rare

Bloody or black, tarry stools; bloody or cloudy urine; fever with or without chills (not present before treatment and not caused by the condition being treated); pain in lower back and/or side (severe and/or sharp); pinpoint red spots on skin; skin rash, hives, or itching; sores, ulcers, or white spots on lips or in mouth; sore throat (not present before treatment and not caused by the condition being treated); sudden decrease in amount of urine; unusual bleeding or bruising; unusual tiredness or weakness

Other side effects not listed above may also occur in some patients. If you notice any other effects, check with your doctor.

Revised: 07/12/94

ACETAMINOPHEN AND SALICYLATES Systemic

Some commonly used brand names are:

In the U.S.—

Buffets II[3]
Duoprin[6]
Duradyne[2]
Excedrin Extra-Strength Caplets[2]
Excedrin Extra-Strength Tablets[2]
Gelpirin[3]
Gemnisyn[1]
Goody's Extra Strength Tablets[2]
Goody's Headache Powders[2]
Presalin[5]
Rid-A-Pain Compound[7]
S-A-C[7]
Saleto[4]
Supac[3]
Tri-Pain Caplets[4]
Vanquish Caplets[3]

Note: In Canada, Excedrin contains acetaminophen and caffeine, but no aspirin.

This information applies to the following medicines:

1. Acetaminophen and Aspirin (a-seat-a-MIN-oh-fen and AS-pir-in)†
2. Acetaminophen, Aspirin, and Caffeine (kaf-EEN)†
3. Acetaminophen, Aspirin, and Caffeine, Buffered†
4. Acetaminophen, Aspirin, Salicylamide (sal-i-SILL-a-mide), and Caffeine†
5. Acetaminophen, Aspirin, and Salicylamide, Buffered†
6. Acetaminophen and Salicylamide†
7. Acetaminophen, Salicylamide, and Caffeine†

†Not commercially available in Canada.

Description

Acetaminophen and salicylate combination medicines relieve pain and reduce fever. They may be used to relieve occasional pain caused by mild inflammation or arthritis (rheumatism). However, neither acetaminophen nor salicylamide is as effective as aspirin for treating chronic or severe pain, or other symptoms, caused by inflammation or arthritis. Some of these combination medicines do not contain any aspirin. Even those that do contain aspirin may not contain enough to be effective in treating these conditions.

A few reports have suggested that acetaminophen and salicylates used together may cause kidney damage or cancer of the kidney or urinary bladder. This may occur if large amounts of both medicines are taken together for a very long time. However, taking usual amounts of these combination medicines for a short time has not been shown to cause these unwanted effects. Also, these effects are not likely to occur with either acetaminophen or a salicylate used alone, even if large amounts have been taken for a long time. Therefore, for long-term use, it may be best to use either acetaminophen or a salicylate, but not both, unless you are under a doctor's care.

Before giving any of these combination medicines to a child, check the package label very carefully. Some of these medicines are too strong for use in children. If you are not certain whether a specific product can be given to a child, or if you have any questions about the amount to give, check with your health care professional.

These medicines are available without a prescription. However, your doctor may have special instructions on the proper dose of these medicines for your medical condition.

These medicines are available in the following dosage forms:

Oral

Acetaminophen and Aspirin
- Tablets (U.S.)

Acetaminophen, Aspirin, and Caffeine
- Oral powders (U.S.)
- Tablets (U.S.)

Acetaminophen, Aspirin, and Caffeine, Buffered
- Tablets (U.S.)

Acetaminophen, Aspirin, Salicylamide, and Caffeine
- Tablets (U.S.)

Acetaminophen, Aspirin, and Salicylamide, Buffered
- Tablets (U.S.)

Acetaminophen and Salicylamide
- Capsules (U.S.)

Acetaminophen, Salicylamide, and Caffeine
- Capsules (U.S.)
- Tablets (U.S.)

Before Using This Medicine

If you are taking this medicine without a prescription, carefully read and follow any precautions on the label. For acetaminophen and salicylate combinations, the following should be considered:

Allergies—Tell your doctor if you have ever had any unusual or allergic reaction to acetaminophen, aspirin or other salicylates including methyl salicylate (oil of wintergreen), or to any of the following medicines:

Diclofenac (e.g., Voltaren)
Diflunisal (e.g., Dolobid)
Etodolac (e.g., Lodine)
Fenoprofen (e.g., Nalfon)
Floctafenine (e.g., Idarac)

Flurbiprofen, oral (e.g., Ansaid)
Ibuprofen (e.g., Motrin)
Indomethacin (e.g., Indocin)
Ketoprofen (e.g., Orudis)
Ketorolac (e.g., Toradol)
Meclofenamate (e.g., Meclomen)
Mefenamic acid (e.g., Ponstel)
Nabumetone (e.g., Relafen)
Naproxen (e.g., Naprosyn)
Oxaprozin (e.g., Daypro)
Oxyphenbutazone (e.g., Tandearil)
Phenylbutazone (e.g., Butazolidin)
Piroxicam (e.g., Feldene)
Sulindac (e.g., Clinoril)
Suprofen (e.g., Suprol)
Tenoxicam (e.g., Mobiflex)
Tiaprofenic acid (e.g., Surgam)
Tolmetin (e.g., Tolectin)
Zomepirac (e.g., Zomax)

Also tell your health care professional if you are allergic to any other substances, such as foods, preservatives, or dyes.

Pregnancy—

- *For Acetaminophen*: Studies on birth defects have not been done in humans. However, acetaminophen has not been reported to cause birth defects or other problems.
- *For Aspirin*: Studies in humans have not shown that aspirin causes birth defects. However, aspirin has been shown to cause birth defects in animals.

  Do not take aspirin during the last 3 months of pregnancy unless it has been ordered by your doctor. Some reports have suggested that too much use of aspirin late in pregnancy may cause a decrease in the newborn's weight and possible death of the fetus or newborn infant. However, the mothers in these reports had been taking much larger amounts of aspirin than are usually recommended. Studies of mothers taking aspirin in the doses that are usually recommended did not show these unwanted effects. However, there is a chance that regular use of aspirin late in pregnancy may cause unwanted effects on the heart or blood flow in the fetus or newborn infant.

  Use of aspirin during the last 2 weeks of pregnancy may cause bleeding problems in the fetus before or during delivery, or in the newborn infant. Also, too much use of aspirin during the last 3 months of pregnancy may increase the length of pregnancy, prolong labor, cause other problems during delivery, or cause severe bleeding in the mother before, during, or after delivery.
- *For Salicylamide*: Studies on birth defects have not been done in humans.
- *For Caffeine*: Studies in humans have not shown that caffeine causes birth defects. However, use of large amounts of caffeine by the mother during pregnancy may cause problems with the heart rhythm of the fetus and may affect the growth of the fetus. Studies in animals have shown that caffeine causes birth defects when given in very large doses (amounts equal to the amount of caffeine in 12 to 24 cups of coffee a day).

Breast-feeding—

- *For Acetaminophen and for Aspirin:* Acetaminophen and aspirin pass into the breast milk; however, they have not been reported to cause problems in nursing babies.
- *For Caffeine:* Caffeine (contained in some of these combination medicines) passes into the breast milk in small amounts. Taking caffeine in the amounts present in these medicines has not been reported to cause problems in nusing babies. However, studies have shown that babies may appear jittery and have trouble in sleeping when their mothers drink large amounts of caffeine-containing beverages. Therefore, breast-feeding mothers who use these medicines should probably limit the amount of caffeine they take in from other medicines or from beverages.

Children—

- *For Acetaminophen*: Acetaminophen has been tested in children and, in effective doses, has not been shown to cause different side effects or problems than it does in adults.
- *For Aspirin and for Salicylamide*: *Do not give a medicine containing aspirin or salicylamide to a child with symptoms of a virus infection, especially flu or chickenpox, without first discussing its use with your child's doctor.* This is very important because aspirin may cause a serious illness called Reye's syndrome in children with fever caused by a virus infection, especially flu or chickenpox. Children who do not have a virus infection may also be more sensitive to the effects of aspirin, especially if they have a fever or have lost large amounts of body fluid because of vomiting, diarrhea, or sweating. This may increase the chance of side effects during treatment.
- *For Caffeine*: There is no specific information comparing use of caffeine in children up to 12 years of age with use in other age groups. However, caffeine is not expected to cause different side effects or problems in children than it does in adults.

Teenagers—*Teenagers with fever or other symptoms of a virus infection, especially flu or chickenpox, should check with a doctor before taking this medicine.* Aspirin and salicylamide may cause a serious illness called Reye's syndrome in teenagers with fever caused by a virus infection, especially flu or chickenpox.

Older adults—Elderly people may be more likely than younger adults to develop serious kidney problems if they take large amounts of these combination medicines for a long time. Therefore, it is best that elderly people not take this medicine for more than 5 days in a row unless they are under a doctor's care.

- *For Acetaminophen*: Acetaminophen has been tested and, in effective doses, has not been shown to cause different side effects or problems in older people than it does in younger adults.
- *For Aspirin*: People 60 years of age and older are especially sensitive to the effects of aspirin. This may increase the chance of side effects during treatment.
- *For Caffeine*: Many medicines have not been studied specifically in older people. Therefore, it may not be

known whether they work exactly the same way they do in younger adults or if they cause different side effects or problems in older people. There is no specific information comparing use of caffeine in the elderly with use in other age groups.

Other medicines—Although certain medicines should not be used together at all, in other cases two different medicines may be used together even if an interaction might occur. In these cases, your doctor may want to change the dose, or other precautions may be necessary. When you are taking an acetaminophen and salicylate combination, it is especially important that your health care professional know if you are taking any of the following:

- Anticoagulants (blood thinners) or
- Carbenicillin by injection (e.g., Geopen) or
- Cefamandole (e.g., Mandol) or
- Cefoperazone (e.g., Cefobid) or
- Cefotetan (e.g., Cefotan) or
- Dipyridamole (e.g., Persantine) or
- Divalproex (e.g., Depakote) or
- Heparin or
- Inflammation or pain medicine, except narcotics, or
- Pentoxifylline (e.g., Trental) or
- Plicamycin (e.g., Mithracin) or
- Ticarcillin (e.g., Ticar) or
- Valproic acid (e.g., Depakene)—Taking these medicines together with aspirin (present in some of these combination medicines) may increase the chance of serious bleeding
- Antidiabetics, oral (diabetes medicine you take by mouth)—Aspirin (present in some of these combination medicines) may increase the effects of the antidiabetic medicine; a change in dose may be needed if aspirin is taken regularly
- Ciprofloxacin (e.g., Cipro) or
- Enoxacin (e.g., Penetrex) or
- Itraconazole (e.g., Sporanox) or
- Ketoconazole (e.g., Nizoral) or
- Lomefloxacin (e.g., Maxaquin) or
- Norfloxacin (e.g., Noroxin) or
- Ofloxacin (e.g., Floxin) or
- Tetracyclines (medicine for infection), taken by mouth—Antacids (present in buffered forms of acetaminophen and salicylate combination medicines) can keep these other medicines from working properly if the medicines are taken too close together
- Methotrexate (e.g., Mexate)—Taking aspirin (present in some of these combination medicines) together with methotrexate may increase the chance of serious side effects
- Probenecid (e.g., Benemid)—Aspirin (present in some of these combination medicines) can keep probenecid from working properly for treating gout
- Sulfinpyrazone (e.g., Anturane)—Aspirin (present in some of these combination medicines) can keep sulfinpyrazone from working properly for treating gout; also, taking aspirin together with sulfinpyrazone may increase the chance of bleeding
- Urinary alkalizers (medicine that makes the urine less acid, such as acetazolamide [e.g., Diamox], calcium- and/or magnesium-containing antacids, dichlorphenamide [e.g., Daranide], methazolamide [e.g., Neptazane], potassium or sodium citrate and/or citric acid, sodium bicarbonate [baking soda])—These medicines may make aspirin (present in some of these combination medicines) less effective by causing it to be removed from the body more quickly

Other medical problems—The presence of other medical problems may affect the use of acetaminophen and salicylate combinations. Make sure you tell your doctor if you have any other medical problems, especially:

- Alcohol abuse or
- Asthma, allergies, and nasal polyps (history of) or
- Hepatitis or other liver disease or
- Kidney disease—The chance of serious side effects may be increased
- Anemia or
- Stomach ulcer or other stomach problems—Aspirin (present in some of these combination medicines) may make these conditions worse
- Gout—Aspirin (present in some of these combination medicines) can make this condition worse and can also lessen the effects of some medicines used to treat gout
- Heart disease—Caffeine (present in some of these combination medicines) can make your condition worse
- Hemophilia or other bleeding problems—Aspirin (present in some of these combination medicines) increases the chance of serious bleeding

Proper Use of This Medicine

Take this medicine with food or a full glass (8 ounces) of water to lessen the chance of stomach upset.

Unless otherwise directed by your doctor:

- *Do not take more of this medicine than directed on the package label.* Taking too much acetaminophen may cause liver damage or lead to other medical problems because of an overdose. Also, taking too much aspirin can cause stomach problems or lead to other medical problems because of an overdose.
- *Children up to 12 years of age should not take this medicine more often than 5 times a day.*

Check with your doctor before taking one of these combination medicines to treat severe or chronic inflammation or arthritis (rheumatism). These combination medicines may not relieve the severe pain, redness, swelling, or stiffness caused by these conditions unless very large amounts are taken for a long time. *It is best not to take acetaminophen and salicylate combination medicines in large amounts for a long time* unless you are under a doctor's care.

If a combination medicine containing aspirin has a strong vinegar-like odor, do not use it. This odor means the medicine is breaking down. If you have any questions about this, check with your pharmacist.

Dosing—The dose of acetaminophen and salicylate combination medicines will be different for different patients. *Follow your doctor's orders or the directions on the label.* The following information includes only the average doses of these combination medicines. *If your dose is different, do not change it* unless your doctor tells you to do so.

The number of capsules, tablets (including caplets), or packets of oral powders that you take depends on the total amount of acetaminophen and salicylate (aspirin and/or salicylamide) in one capsule, tablet, or packet of oral powder. Also, the number of doses you take each day and the time allowed between doses depend on the strength of the medicine.

- For *oral capsule or tablet (including caplet)* dosage forms:
  —For pain, fever, or mild arthritis symptoms:
    - Adults and teenagers—The usual dose is 1 or 2 capsules or tablets every three, four, or six hours, depending on the strength of the product. Do not take any of these combination medicines for more than ten days, unless otherwise directed by your doctor.
    - Children—Use and dose must be determined by your doctor.
- For *oral powder* dosage form:
  —For pain, fever, or mild arthritis symptoms:
    - Adults and teenagers—This medicine is very strong. Each packet of powder contains 260 mg of acetaminophen and 500 mg of aspirin (a total of 760 mg of both medicines). The usual dose is one packet of powder every six hours. Do not take this medicine for more than ten days, unless otherwise directed by your doctor.
    - Children—The oral powder dosage form is too strong to use in children 12 years of age or younger.

Storage—To store this medicine:

- Keep out of the reach of children. Overdose of the salicylates in these combination medicines is very dangerous in young children.
- Store away from heat and direct light.
- Do not store tablets (including caplets), capsules, or powders in the bathroom, near the kitchen sink, or in other damp places. Heat or moisture may cause the medicine to break down.
- Do not keep outdated medicine or medicine no longer needed. Be sure that any discarded medicine is out of the reach of children.

Precautions While Using This Medicine

If you will be taking this medicine for a long time, or in high doses, *your doctor should check your progress at regular visits*. This is especially important for elderly people, who may be more likely than younger adults to develop serious kidney problems if they take large amounts of this medicine for a long time.

Check with your doctor:

- If you are taking this medicine to relieve pain and the pain lasts for more than 10 days (5 days for children), if the pain gets worse, if new symptoms occur, or if the painful area is red or swollen. These could be signs of a serious condition that needs treatment.
- If you are taking this medicine to bring down a fever, and the fever lasts for more than 3 days or returns, if your fever gets worse, if new symptoms occur, or if redness or swelling is present. These could be signs of a serious condition that needs treatment.
- If you are taking this medicine for a sore throat, and the sore throat is very painful, lasts for more than 2 days, or occurs together with or is followed by fever, headache, skin rash, nausea, or vomiting.

Do not take any of the combination medicines containing aspirin for 5 days before any surgery, including dental surgery, unless otherwise directed by your medical doctor or dentist. Taking aspirin during this time may cause bleeding problems.

Check the label of all over-the-counter (OTC), nonprescription, and prescription medicines you now take. If any of them contain acetaminophen, aspirin, other salicylates such as bismuth subsalicylate (e.g., Pepto Bismol) or magnesium salicylate (e.g., Nuprin Backache Caplets), or salicylic acid (present in some shampoos and skin products), *check with your health care professional. Using any of them together with this medicine may cause an overdose.*

If you will be taking more than an occasional 1 or 2 doses of this medicine, do not drink alcoholic beverages. Stomach problems may be more likely to occur if you drink alcoholic beverages while you are taking aspirin. Also, liver damage may be more likely to occur if you drink large amounts of alcoholic beverages while you are taking acetaminophen.

Taking certain other medicines together with acetaminophen and salicylates may increase the chance of unwanted effects. The risk will depend on how much of each medicine you take every day, and on how long you take the medicines together. If your medical doctor or dentist directs you to take these medicines together on a regular basis, follow his or her directions carefully. However, *do not take any of the following medicines together with any of these combination medicines for more than a few days, unless your doctor has directed you to do so and is following your progress:*

Diclofenac (e.g., Voltaren)
Diflunisal (e.g., Dolobid)
Etodolac (e.g., Lodine)
Fenoprofen (e.g., Nalfon)
Floctafenine (e.g., Idarac)
Flurbiprofen, oral (e.g., Ansaid)
Ibuprofen (e.g., Motrin)
Indomethacin (e.g., Indocin)
Ketoprofen (e.g., Orudis)
Ketorolac (e.g., Toradol)
Meclofenamate (e.g., Meclomen)
Mefenamic acid (e.g., Ponstel)
Nabumetone (e.g., Relafen)
Naproxen (e.g., Naprosyn)
Oxaprozin (e.g., Daypro)
Phenylbutazone (e.g., Butazolidin)
Piroxicam (e.g., Feldene)
Sulindac (e.g., Clinoril)
Tenoxicam (e.g., Mobiflex)
Tiaprofenic acid (e.g., Surgam)
Tolmetin (e.g., Tolectin)

The antacid present in buffered forms of these combination medicines can keep other medicines from working properly. If you need to take a buffered form of this medicine, and you are also taking one of the following medicines, *be sure to take the buffered acetaminophen and salicylate combination medicine:*

- *At least 6 hours before or 2 hours after taking ciprofloxacin (e.g., Cipro) or lomefloxacin (e.g., Maxaquin).*
- *At least 8 hours before or 2 hours after taking enoxacin (e.g., Penetrex).*
- *At least 2 hours after taking itraconazole (e.g., Sporanox).*
- *At least 3 hours before or after taking ketoconazole (e.g., Nizoral).*
- *At least 2 hours before or after taking norfloxacin (e.g., Noroxin) or ofloxacin (e.g., Floxin).*
- *At least 3 or 4 hours before or after taking a tetracycline antibiotic by mouth.*
- *At least 1 or 2 hours before or after taking any other medicine by mouth.*

If you are taking a laxative containing cellulose, do not take it within 2 hours of taking this medicine. Taking the laxative and this medicine close together may make this medicine less effective by preventing the salicylate in it from being absorbed by your body.

Acetaminophen and salicylate combinations may interfere with the results of some medical tests. Before you have any medical tests, tell the person in charge if you have taken any of these combination medicines within the past 3 or 4 days. If possible, it is best to call the laboratory where the test will be done about 4 days ahead of time, to find out whether the medicine may be taken during the 3 or 4 days before the test.

For diabetic patients:

- Acetaminophen and salicylate combinations may cause false results with some blood and urine glucose (sugar) tests. If you notice any change in your test results, or if you have any questions about this possible problem, check with your health care professional. This is especially important if your diabetes is not well-controlled.

For patients taking one of the products that contain *caffeine:*

- Caffeine may interfere with the results of a test that uses adenosine (e.g., Adenocard) or dipyridamole (e.g., Persantine) to help find out how well your blood is flowing through certain blood vessels. Therefore, you should not have any caffeine for 8 to 12 hours before the test.

If you think that you or anyone else may have taken an overdose of this medicine, get emergency help at once. Taking an overdose of a salicylate may cause unconsciousness or death. The first symptom of an aspirin overdose may be ringing or buzzing in the ears. Other signs include convulsions (seizures), hearing loss, confusion, severe drowsiness or tiredness, severe excitement or nervousness, and unusually fast or deep breathing. Signs of severe acetaminophen overdose may not appear until 2 to 4 days after the overdose is taken, but treatment to prevent liver damage or death must be started within 24 hours or less after the overdose is taken.

Side Effects of This Medicine

Along with its needed effects, a medicine may cause some unwanted effects. Although not all of these side effects may occur, if they do occur they may need medical attention.

Check with your doctor immediately if any of the following side effects occur:

Less common or rare

Difficulty in swallowing; dizziness, lightheadedness, or feeling faint (severe); flushing, redness, or other change in skin color; shortness of breath, troubled breathing, tightness in chest, or wheezing; sudden decrease in amount of urine; swelling of eyelids, face, or lips

Signs and symptoms of overdose

Agitation, anxiety, excitement, irritability, nervousness, or restlessness; any loss of hearing; bloody urine; confusion or delirium; convulsions (seizures); diarrhea (severe or continuing); dizziness or lightheadedness; drowsiness (severe); fast or deep breathing; fast or irregular heartbeat (for medicines containing caffeine); frequent urination (for medicines containing caffeine); hallucinations (seeing, hearing, or feeling things that are not there); headache (severe or continuing); increased sensitivity to touch or pain (for medicines containing caffeine); increased sweating; increased thirst; loss of appetite; muscle trembling or twitching (for medicines containing caffeine); nausea or vomiting (continuing, sometimes with blood); ringing or buzzing in ears (continuing); seeing flashes of ''zig-zag'' lights (for medicines containing caffeine); stomach cramps or pain (severe or continuing); swelling, pain, or tenderness in the upper abdomen or stomach area; trouble in sleeping (for medicines containing caffeine); uncontrollable flapping movements of the hands, especially in elderly patients; unexplained fever; vision problems

Signs of overdose in children

Changes in behavior; drowsiness or tiredness (severe); fast or deep breathing

Also, check with your doctor as soon as possible if any of the following side effects occur:

Less common or rare

Bloody or black, tarry stools; bloody or cloudy urine; fever with or without chills (not present before treatment and not caused by the condition being treated); pain in lower back and/or side (severe and/or sharp); pinpoint red spots on skin; skin rash, hives, or itching; sores, ulcers, or white spots on lips or in mouth; sore throat (not present before treatment and not caused by the condition being treated); swelling of face, fingers, feet, or lower legs; unusual bleeding or bruising; unusual tiredness or weakness; vomiting of blood or material that looks like coffee grounds; weight gain; yellow eyes or skin

Other side effects may occur that usually do not need medical attention. These side effects may go away during treatment as your body adjusts to the medicine. However, check with your doctor if any of the following side effects continue or are bothersome:

More common

Heartburn or indigestion (for medicines containing aspirin); nausea, vomiting, or stomach pain (for medicines containing aspirin)

Less common

Drowsiness (for medicines containing salicylamide); trouble in sleeping, nervousness, or jitters (for medicines containing caffeine)

Some side effects may occur after you have stopped taking these combination medicines, especially if you have taken large amounts of them for a long time. *Check with your doctor immediately* if any of these side effects occur after you have stopped taking these medicines:

Rare

Bloody or cloudy urine; decreased urination; swelling of face, fingers, feet, or lower legs; weight gain

Other side effects not listed above may also occur in some patients. If you notice any other effects, check with your doctor.

Revised: 07/12/94

ACETAMINOPHEN, SODIUM BICARBONATE, AND CITRIC ACID Systemic†

A commonly used brand name in the U.S. is Bromo-Seltzer.

†Not commercially available in Canada.

Description

Acetaminophen, sodium bicarbonate, and citric acid (a-seat-a-MIN-oh-fen, SOE-dee-um bi-KAR-boe-nate, and SI-trik AS-id) combination is used to relieve pain occurring together with heartburn, sour stomach, or acid indigestion. The acetaminophen in this combination medicine is the pain reliever. The sodium bicarbonate in this medicine is an antacid. It neutralizes stomach acid by combining with it to form a new substance that is not an acid.

This medicine is available without a prescription; however, your doctor may have special instructions on the proper dose for your medical condition.

Acetaminophen, sodium bicarbonate, and citric acid combination is available in the following dosage form:

Oral

- Effervescent granules (U.S.)

Before Using This Medicine

If you are taking this medicine without a prescription, carefully read and follow any precautions on the label. For acetaminophen, sodium bicarbonate, and citric acid combination, the following should be considered:

Allergies—Tell your doctor if you have ever had any unusual or allergic reaction to acetaminophen or aspirin, or to sodium bicarbonate. Also tell your health care professional if you are allergic to any other substances, such as foods, preservatives, or dyes.

Diet—Make certain your health care professional knows if you are on a low-sodium, low-sugar, or any other special diet. This medicine contains a large amount of sodium (more than 750 mg for each 325 mg of acetaminophen).

Pregnancy—Although studies on birth defects have not been done in humans, the ingredients in this combination medicine have not been reported to cause birth defects in humans. However, you should avoid this medicine if you tend to retain (keep) body water because the sodium in it can cause the body to hold water. This can result in swelling and weight gain.

Breast-feeding—Acetaminophen passes into the breast milk in small amounts. However, acetaminophen, sodium bicarbonate, and citric acid have not been reported to cause problems in nursing babies.

Children—Acetaminophen has been tested in children and has not been shown to cause different side effects or problems than it does in adults. However, sodium bicarbonate should not be given to young children (under 6 years of age) unless ordered by their doctor. Small children with stomach problems usually cannot describe their symptoms very well. They should be checked by a doctor, because they may have a condition that needs other treatment.

Older adults—Acetaminophen has been tested and has not been shown to cause different side effects or problems in older people than it does in younger adults. However, the large amount of sodium in this combination medicine can be harmful to some elderly people. Therefore, it is best that older people not use this medicine for more than 5 days in a row, unless otherwise directed by their doctor.

Other medicines—Although certain medicines should not be used together at all, in other cases two different medicines may be used together even if an interaction might occur. In these cases, your doctor may want to change the dose, or other precautions may be necessary. When you are taking this combination medicine, it is especially important that your health care professional know if you are taking any of the following:

- Alcohol—The chance of liver damage may be increased
- Ciprofloxacin (e.g., Cipro) or
- Enoxacin (e.g., Penetrex) or
- Itraconazole (e.g., Sporanox) or
- Ketoconazole (e.g., Nizoral) or
- Lomefloxacin (e.g., Maxaquin) or
- Methenamine (e.g., Mandelamine) or
- Norfloxacin (e.g., Noroxin) or
- Ofloxacin (e.g., Floxin) or
- Tetracyclines (medicine for infection), taken by mouth—Sodium bicarbonate can keep these medicines from working properly
- Mecamylamine (e.g., Inversine)—Sodium bicarbonate can increase the risk of unwanted effects by causing mecamylamine to stay in your body longer than usual

Other medical problems—The presence of other medical problems may affect the use of acetaminophen, sodium bicarbonate, and citric acid combination. Make sure you tell your doctor if you have any other medical problems, especially:

- Alcohol abuse or
- Hepatitis or other liver disease—The chance of serious side effects, including liver damage, may be increased
- Appendicitis (symptoms of, such as stomach or lower abdominal pain, cramping, bloating, soreness, nausea, or vomiting)—Sodium bicarbonate can make your condition worse; also, people who may have appendicitis need medical attention and should not try to treat themselves
- Edema (swelling of face, fingers, feet, or lower legs caused by too much water in the body) or
- Heart disease or
- High blood pressure or
- Toxemia of pregnancy—The sodium in this combination medicine can make these conditions worse
- Kidney disease—The chance of serious side effects may be increased

Proper Use of This Medicine

Unless otherwise directed by your doctor, do not take more of this medicine than is recommended on the package label. If too much is taken, liver damage or other serious side effects may occur.

To use this medicine:

- This medicine must be taken in the form of a liquid that is made from the effervescent granules. Do not swallow the granules themselves.
- To make the liquid, pour the amount of effervescent granules directed on the package into a glass. Then add 1/2 glass (4 ounces) of cool water.
- Drink all of the liquid. You may drink the liquid while it is still fizzing or after the fizzing stops.
- Add a little more water to the glass and drink that, to make sure that you get the full amount of the medicine.

Dosing—The dose of this combination medicine will be different for different people. *Follow your doctor's orders or the directions on the label.* The following information includes only the average doses of the acetaminophen in this combination medicine. *If your dose is different, do not change it* unless your doctor tells you to do so.

- For *oral* dosage form (effervescent granules):
  - —For pain and upset stomach:
    - Adults and teenagers—325 to 650 milligrams (mg) of acetaminophen, dissolved in water, every four hours as needed. The bottle cap can be used to measure the dose. There are 325 mg of acetaminophen in three-fourths of a capful.
    - Children—Use and dose must be determined by your doctor.

Missed dose—If your doctor has directed you to take this medicine according to a regular schedule and you miss a dose, take it as soon as you remember. However, if it is almost time for your next dose, skip the missed dose and go back to your regular dosing schedule. Do not double doses.

Storage—To store this medicine:

- Keep out of the reach of children.
- Store away from heat and direct light.
- Do not store this medicine in the bathroom, near the kitchen sink, or in other damp places. Heat or moisture may cause the medicine to break down.
- Do not keep outdated medicine or medicine no longer needed. Be sure that any discarded medicine is out of the reach of children.

Precautions While Using This Medicine

If you will be taking this medicine for a long time (more than 10 days in a row), your doctor should check your progress at regular visits.

Check with your doctor if your pain and/or upset stomach last for more than 10 days or if they get worse, if new symptoms occur, or if the painful area is red or swollen. These could be signs of a serious condition that needs medical treatment.

The sodium bicarbonate in this combination medicine can keep other medicines from working properly if the 2 medicines are taken too close together. *Always take this medicine:*

- *At least 6 hours before or 2 hours after taking ciprofloxacin (e.g., Cipro) or lomefloxacin (e.g., Maxaquin).*
- *At least 8 hours before or 2 hours after taking enoxacin (e.g., Penetrex).*
- *At least 2 hours after taking itraconazole (e.g., Sporanox).*
- *At least 3 hours before or after taking ketoconazole (e.g., Nizoral).*
- *At least 2 hours before or after taking norfloxacin (e.g., Noroxin) or ofloxacin (e.g., Floxin).*
- *At least 3 or 4 hours before or after taking a tetracycline antibiotic by mouth.*
- *At least 1 or 2 hours before or after taking any other medicine by mouth.*

Check the labels of all nonprescription (over-the-counter [OTC]) and prescription medicines you now take. If any contain acetaminophen or sodium, check with your health care professional. Taking them together with this medicine may cause an overdose.

Taking certain other medicines together with acetaminophen may increase the chance of unwanted effects. The risk will depend on how much of each medicine you take every day, and on how long you take the medicines together. If your medical doctor or dentist directs you to take these medicines together on a regular basis, follow his or her directions carefully. However, *do not take any of the following medicines together with acetaminophen for more than a few days, unless your doctor has directed you to do so and is following your progress:*

Aspirin or other salicylates
Diclofenac (e.g., Voltaren)
Diflunisal (e.g., Dolobid)
Etodolac (e.g., Lodine)
Fenoprofen (e.g., Nalfon)

Floctafenine (e.g., Idarac)
Flurbiprofen, oral (e.g., Ansaid)
Ibuprofen (e.g., Motrin)
Indomethacin (e.g., Indocin)
Ketoprofen (e.g., Orudis)
Ketorolac (e.g., Toradol)
Meclofenamate (e.g., Meclomen)
Mefenamic acid (e.g., Ponstel)
Nabumetone (e.g., Relafen)
Naproxen (e.g., Naprosyn)
Oxaprozin (e.g., Daypro)
Phenylbutazone (e.g., Butazolidin)
Piroxicam (e.g., Feldene)
Sulindac (e.g., Clinoril)
Tenoxicam (e.g., Mobiflex)
Tiaprofenic acid (e.g., Surgam)
Tolmetin (e.g., Tolectin)

If you will be taking more than an occasional 1 or 2 doses of this medicine:

- *Do not drink alcoholic beverages.* Drinking alcoholic beverages while you are taking acetaminophen may increase the chance of liver damage, especially if you drink large amounts of alcoholic beverages regularly, if you take more acetaminophen than is recommended on the package label, or if you take it regularly for a long time.
- *Do not also drink a lot of milk or eat a lot of milk products.* To do so may increase the chance of side effects.
- To prevent side effects caused by too much sodium in the body, you may need to limit the amount of sodium in the foods you eat. Some foods that contain large amounts of sodium are canned soup, canned vegetables, pickles, ketchup, green and ripe (black) olives, relish, frankfurters and other sausage-type meats, soy sauce, and carbonated beverages. If you have any questions about this, check with your health care professional.

Acetaminophen may interfere with the results of some medical tests. Before you have any medical tests, tell the person in charge if you have taken acetaminophen within the past 3 or 4 days. If possible, it is best to call the laboratory where the test will be done about 4 days ahead of time, to find out whether this medicine may be taken during the 3 or 4 days before the test.

For diabetic patients:

- Acetaminophen may cause false results with some blood glucose (sugar) tests. If you notice any change in your test results, or if you have any questions about this possible problem, check with your health care professional. This is especially important if your diabetes is not well-controlled.

If you think that you or anyone else may have taken an overdose of this medicine, get emergency help at once, even if there are no signs of poisoning. Signs of severe acetaminophen poisoning may not appear for 2 to 4 days after the overdose is taken, but treatment to prevent liver damage or death must be started as soon as possible. Treatment started more than 24 hours after the overdose is taken may not be effective.

Side Effects of This Medicine

Along with its needed effects, a medicine may cause some unwanted effects. Although the following side effects occur very rarely when 1 or 2 doses of this combination medicine is taken occasionally, they may be more likely to occur if:

- too much medicine is taken.
- the medicine is taken several times a day.
- the medicine is taken for more than a few days in a row.

Check with your doctor immediately if any of the following side effects occur:

Rare
Yellow eyes or skin

Symptoms of overdose
Diarrhea; increased sweating; loss of appetite; nausea or vomiting; stomach cramps or pain; swelling, pain, or tenderness in the upper abdomen or stomach area

Also, check with your doctor as soon as possible if any of the following side effects occur:

Less common or rare
Bloody or black, tarry stools; bloody or cloudy urine, frequent urge to urinate, or sudden decrease in amount of urine; fever with or without chills (not present before treatment and not caused by the condition being treated); headache (continuing); increased blood pressure; mood or mental changes; muscle pain or twitching; nervousness or restlessness; pain (severe and/or sharp) in lower back and/or side; skin rash, hives, or itching; slow breathing; sores, ulcers, or white spots on lips or in mouth; sore throat (not present before treatment and not caused by the condition being treated); swelling of face, fingers, ankles, feet, or lower legs; unpleasant taste; unusual bleeding or bruising; unusual tiredness or weakness; weight gain

Other side effects may occur that usually do not need medical attention. These side effects may go away during treatment as your body adjusts to the medicine. However, check with your doctor if any of the following side effects continue or are bothersome:

Less common
Increased thirst

Other side effects not listed above may also occur in some patients. If you notice any other effects, check with your doctor.

Revised: 07/12/94

ACETOHYDROXAMIC ACID Systemic†

A commonly used brand name in the U.S. is Lithostat.

†Not commercially available in Canada.

Description

Acetohydroxamic acid (a-SEE-toe-hye-drox-AM-ik AS-id) is used to keep kidney stones from forming and to stop the growth of existing stones. Such stone build-up is often caused by certain bacterial infections.

The bacteria produce an enzyme that makes the urine too alkaline. Under such conditions, kidney stones tend to form and, once formed, to grow in size. Acetohydroxamic acid stops the enzyme action and so reduces the chance for stones to form. This medicine is not used to dissolve existing stones and is not used in place of surgery. It is sometimes used to make antibiotics or similar medicines work better when treating kidney or urinary tract infections.

Acetohydroxamic acid is available only with your doctor's prescription, in the following dosage form:

Oral

- Tablets (U.S.)

Before Using This Medicine

In deciding to use a medicine, the risks of taking the medicine must be weighed against the good it will do. This is a decision you and your doctor will make. For acetohydroxamic acid, the following should be considered:

Allergies—Tell your doctor if you have ever had any unusual or allergic reaction to acetohydroxamic acid. Also tell your health care professional if you are allergic to any other substances, such as foods, preservatives, or dyes.

Pregnancy—Acetohydroxamic acid should not be used during pregnancy since it has been shown to cause serious birth defects in animals. Effective methods of contraception (birth control) must be used during treatment with this medicine to prevent a pregnancy that could result in birth defects. Be sure you have discussed this with your doctor.

Breast-feeding—It is not known whether acetohydroxamic acid passes into the breast milk. Although no problems have been reported in nursing babies, its use in breast-feeding mothers is not recommended.

Children—Although there is no specific information comparing use of acetohydroxamic acid in children with use in other age groups, it is not expected to cause different side effects or problems in children than it does in adults.

Older adults—Many medicines have not been studied specifically in older people. Therefore, it may not be known whether they work exactly the same way they do in younger adults or if they cause different side effects or problems in older people. There is no specific information comparing use of acetohydroxamic acid in the elderly with use in other age groups.

Other medicines—Although certain medicines should not be used together at all, in many cases two different medicines may be used together even if an interaction might occur. In these cases, your doctor may want to change the dose, or other precautions may be necessary. When you are taking acetohydroxamic acid it is especially important that your health care professional know if you are taking the following:

- Iron supplements or any other medicine containing iron, taken by mouth—Use with acetohydroxamic acid may decrease effects of both medicines; iron supplements by injection may be needed

Other medical problems—The presence of other medical problems may affect the use of acetohydroxamic acid. Make sure you tell your doctor if you have any other medical problems, especially:

- Anemia or other blood disorders or
- Blood clots (history of) or
- Phlebitis (vein inflammation)—If you have one of these conditions, use of acetohydroxamic acid increases the risk of problems occurring
- Other kidney disorders—Higher blood levels of acetohydroxamic acid may result and a change in your dose may be needed

Proper Use of This Medicine

Acetohydroxamic acid works best when taken on an empty stomach. Take the medicine 1 hour before or 2 hours after meals if possible.

Take this medicine exactly as ordered by your doctor. This is especially important because it is used along with antibiotics or other medicine to clear up the infection.

Do not miss any doses. Skipped doses may delay treatment progress and your recovery. When too many doses are missed, stone formation and growth may start again. Remember that this medicine is intended to prevent kidney stones and the surgery that is sometimes required to remove them.

Dosing—The dose of acetohydroxamic acid will be different for different patients. *Follow your doctor's orders or the directions on the label.* The following information includes only the average doses of acetohydroxamic acid. *If your dose is different, do not change it* unless your doctor tells you to do so.

- *To prevent kidney stones:*
  - —For *oral* dosage form (tablets):
    - Adults—250 milligrams (mg) taken every six to eight hours. The dose is usually not more than 1500 mg a day.
    - Children—Dose is based on body weight and must be determined by your doctor. The dose is usually 10 mg per kilogram (kg) (4.5 mg per pound) of body weight a day.

Missed dose—If you miss a dose of acetohydroxamic acid, take it as soon as possible. Then go back to your regular dosing schedule. Do not double doses.

Storage—To store this medicine:

- Keep out of the reach of children.
- Store away from heat and direct light.

- Do not store in the bathroom, near the kitchen sink, or in other damp places. Heat or moisture may cause the medicine to break down.
- Do not keep outdated medicine or medicine no longer needed. Be sure that any discarded medicine is out of the reach of children.

Precautions While Using This Medicine

Your doctor should check your progress at regular visits to make sure that this medicine is working properly and does not cause unwanted effects.

Do not take any form of iron by mouth while you are taking acetohydroxamic acid. Taking the 2 medicines together will keep both medicines from working properly.

Do not drink alcoholic beverages while you are taking acetohydroxamic acid. To do so may cause a rash to appear on the arms and face about 30 to 45 minutes after you drink the alcohol. Also, the skin may become flushed and feel warm and tingling. This reaction lasts about 30 minutes and can be very strong in some patients.

If you suspect you may have become pregnant during treatment with acetohydroxamic acid, stop taking the medicine immediately and check with your doctor.

Side Effects of This Medicine

Along with its needed effects, a medicine may cause some unwanted effects. The following side effects may be caused by blood clots. If they occur, they need immediate medical attention. *Stop taking this medicine and get emergency help immediately* if any of the following side effects occur:

More common

Headache (severe or sudden); loss of coordination (sudden); pains in chest, groin, or legs (especially in calves of legs); shortness of breath (sudden); slurred speech (sudden); vision changes (sudden)

Other side effects may occur that require medical attention. Check with your doctor as soon as possible if any of the following side effects occur:

More common

Anxiety, confusion, or mental depression; loss of appetite; nausea or vomiting; nervousness, shakiness, or tremors; unusual tiredness or weakness

Other side effects may occur that usually do not need medical attention. These side effects may go away during treatment as your body adjusts to the medicine. However, check with your doctor if any of the following side effects continue or are bothersome:

More common

General feeling of discomfort or illness; headache (mild)

Less common

Hair loss; skin rash (non-itching) on arms and face

Other side effects not listed above may also occur in some patients. If you notice any other effects, check with your doctor at once.

Revised: 12/11/92
Interim revision: 06/13/94

ACETYLCYSTEINE Inhalation

Some commonly used brand names are:

In the U.S.—

Mucomyst
Mucomyst-10
Mucosil

Generic name product may also be available.

In Canada—

Mucomyst

Another commonly used name is *N*-acetylcysteine.

Description

Acetylcysteine (a-se-teel-SIS-teen) is a mucolytic (medicine that destroys or dissolves mucus). It is usually given by inhalation but may be given in other ways in a hospital.

Acetylcysteine is used for certain lung conditions when increased amounts of mucus make breathing difficult. Acetylcysteine liquefies (thins) or dissolves mucus so that it may be coughed up. Sometimes the mucus may have to be removed by suction.

This medicine is available only with your doctor's prescription, in the following dosage form:

Inhalation

- Solution (U.S. and Canada)

Before Using This Medicine

In deciding to use a medicine, the risks of taking the medicine must be weighed against the good it will do. This is a decision you and your doctor will make. For acetylcysteine, the following should be considered:

Allergies—Tell your doctor if you have ever had any unusual or allergic reaction to acetylcysteine. Also tell your health care professional if you are allergic to any other substances, such as foods, preservatives, or dyes.

Pregnancy—Acetylcysteine has not been studied in pregnant women. However, acetylcysteine has not been shown to cause birth defects or other problems in animal studies when given in doses larger than the recommended human dose.

Breast-feeding—It is not known whether acetylcysteine passes into the breast milk. Although most medicines pass into breast milk in small amounts, many of them may be used safely while breast-feeding. Mothers who are taking this medicine and who wish to breast-feed should discuss this with their doctor.

Children—Although there is no specific information comparing use of acetylcysteine in children with use in other age groups, this medicine is not expected to cause different side effects or problems in children than it does in adults.

Older adults—Many medicines have not been studied specifically in older people. Therefore, it may not be known whether they work exactly the same way they do in younger adults or if they cause different side effects or problems in older people. There is no specific information comparing use of acetylcysteine in the elderly with use in other age groups.

Other medical problems—The presence of other medical problems may affect the use of acetylcysteine. Make sure you tell your doctor if you have any other medical problems, especially:

- Asthma—Acetylcysteine may make the condition worse
- Decreased ability to cough—The mucus may have to be removed by suctioning

Proper Use of This Medicine

Use acetylcysteine only as directed. Do not use more of it and do not use it more often than your doctor ordered. To do so may increase the chance of side effects.

If you are using this medicine at home, make sure you understand exactly how to use it. If you have any questions about this, check with your doctor.

After using acetylcysteine, try to cough up the loosened or thinned mucus. If this does not work, it may have to be suctioned out. This will prevent too much mucus from building up in the lungs. If you have any questions about this, check with your doctor.

Dosing—The dose of acetylcysteine will be different for different patients. *Follow your doctor's orders or the directions on the label.* The following information includes only the average doses of acetylcysteine. *If your dose is different, do not change it* unless your doctor tells you to do so.

The amount of solution that you use depends on the strength of the medicine and the method of inhalation used. Also, *the number of doses you use each day, the time allowed between doses, and the length of time you use the medicine depend on the medical problem for which you are using acetylcysteine.*

- For *inhalation* dosage form (solution):
  - —To thin or dissolve mucus in lung diseases:
    - Adults and children—
      - —3 to 5 milliliters (mL) of a 20% solution or 6 to 10 mL of a 10% solution used in a nebulizer three or four times a day. The medicine is inhaled through a face mask, mouthpiece, or tracheostomy.
      - —The 10 or 20% solution may be used for inhalation as a heavy mist in a tent or croupette.
      - —Sometimes the 10 or 20% solution is placed directly into the trachea or through a catheter into the trachea for certain conditions.
  - —For use in tests to diagnose lung problems:
    - Adults and children—1 to 2 mL of a 20% solution or 2 to 4 mL of a 10% solution used for inhalation or placed directly into the trachea two or three times before the test.

Missed dose—If you miss a dose of this medicine, use it as soon as possible. Then use any remaining doses for that day at regularly spaced intervals.

Storage—To store this medicine:

- Keep out of the reach of children.
- Before the container is opened, store it away from heat and direct light.
- After the container is opened, store it in the refrigerator. However, keep the medicine from freezing. The opened container should be discarded after 4 days.
- Do not keep outdated medicine or medicine no longer needed. Be sure that any discarded medicine is out of the reach of children.

Precautions While Using This Medicine

If your condition does not improve or if it becomes worse, check with your doctor.

Side Effects of This Medicine

Along with its needed effects, a medicine may cause some unwanted effects. Although not all of these side effects may occur, if they do occur they may need medical attention.

Check with your doctor as soon as possible if any of the following side effects occur:

Less common

Wheezing, tightness in chest, or difficulty in breathing (especially in asthma patients)

Rare

Skin rash or other irritation

Other side effects may occur that usually do not need medical attention. These side effects may go away during treatment as your body adjusts to the medicine. However, check with your doctor if any of the following side effects continue or are bothersome:

Less common

Clammy skin; fever; increase in amount of mucus in lungs; irritation or soreness of mouth, throat, or lungs; nausea or vomiting; runny nose

For patients using a face mask for inhalation of acetylcysteine:

- The mask may leave a stickiness on your face. This can be removed with water.

When you use acetylcysteine, you may notice that the medicine has an unpleasant odor at first. However, this smell will go away soon after you use the medicine.

Other side effects not listed above may also occur in some patients. If you notice any other effects, check with your doctor.

Revised: 05/14/97

ACYCLOVIR Systemic

Some commonly used brand names are:

In the U.S.—
Zovirax

In Canada—
Avirax Zovirax

Another commonly used name is aciclovir.

Description

Acyclovir (ay-SYE-kloe-veer) belongs to the family of medicines called antivirals, which are used to treat infections caused by viruses. Usually these medicines work for only one kind or group of virus infections.

Acyclovir is used to treat the symptoms of herpes virus infections of the genitals (sex organs), the skin, the brain, and mucous membranes (lips and mouth). Acyclovir is also used to treat chickenpox and shingles. Although acyclovir will not cure herpes, it does help relieve the pain and discomfort and helps the sores (if any) heal faster.

Acyclovir may also be used for other virus infections as determined by your doctor. However, it does not work in treating certain viruses, such as the common cold.

Acyclovir is available only with your doctor's prescription, in the following dosage forms:

Oral
- Capsules (U.S. and Canada)
- Oral suspension (U.S. and Canada)
- Tablets (U.S. and Canada)

Parenteral
- Injection (U.S. and Canada)

Before Using This Medicine

In deciding to use a medicine, the risks of taking the medicine must be weighed against the good it will do. This is a decision you and your doctor will make. For acyclovir, the following should be considered:

Allergies—Tell your doctor if you have ever had any unusual or allergic reaction to acyclovir or ganciclovir. Also tell your health care professional if you are allergic to any other substances, such as foods, sulfites or other preservatives, or dyes.

Pregnancy—Acyclovir has been used in pregnant women and has not been reported to cause birth defects or other problems. However, studies have not been done in humans. Studies in rabbits have shown that acyclovir given by injection may keep the fetus from becoming attached to the lining of the uterus (womb). However, acyclovir has not been shown to cause birth defects or other problems in mice given many times the usual human dose, or in rats or rabbits given several times the usual human dose.

Breast-feeding—Acyclovir passes into the breast milk. However, it has not been reported to cause problems in nursing babies.

Children—A limited number of studies have been done using oral acyclovir in children, and it has not caused different effects or problems in children than it does in adults.

Older adults—Acyclovir has been used in the elderly and has not been shown to cause different side effects or problems in older people than it does in younger adults.

Other medicines—Although certain medicines should not be used together at all, in many cases two different medicines may be used together even if an interaction might occur. In these cases, changes in dose or other precautions may be necessary. If you are receiving acyclovir by injection it is especially important that your health care professional know if you are taking any of the following:

- Carmustine (e.g., BiCNU) or
- Cisplatin (e.g., Platinol) or
- Combination pain medicine containing acetaminophen and aspirin (e.g., Excedrin) or other salicylates or
- Cyclosporine (e.g., Sandimmune) or
- Deferoxamine (e.g., Desferal) (with long-term use) or
- Gold salts (medicine for arthritis) or
- Inflammation or pain medicine, except narcotics, or
- Lithium (e.g., Lithane) or
- Methotrexate (Mexate) or
- Other medicine for infection or
- Penicillamine (e.g., Cuprimine) or
- Plicamycin (e.g., Mithracin) or
- Streptozocin (e.g., Zanosar) or
- Tiopronin (Thiola)—Concurrent use of these medicines with acyclovir by injection may increase the chance for side effects, especially when kidney disease is present

Other medical problems—The presence of other medical problems may affect the use of acyclovir. Make sure you tell your doctor if you have any other medical problems, especially:

- Kidney disease—Kidney disease may increase blood levels of acyclovir, increasing the chance of side effects
- Nerve disease—Acyclovir by injection may increase the chance for nervous system side effects

Proper Use of This Medicine

Patient information about the treatment of herpes is available with this medicine. Read it carefully before using this medicine.

Acyclovir is best used as soon as possible after the symptoms of herpes infection (for example, pain, burning, blisters) begin to appear.

Acyclovir capsules, tablets, and oral suspension may be taken with meals.

If you are taking acyclovir for the *treatment of chickenpox*, it is best to start taking acyclovir as soon as possible after the first sign of the chickenpox rash, usually within one day.

If you are using *acyclovir oral suspension*, use a specially marked measuring spoon or other device to measure each dose accurately. The average household teaspoon may not hold the right amount of liquid.

Acyclovir is best taken with a full glass (8 ounces) of water.

To help clear up your herpes infection, *keep taking acyclovir for the full time of treatment,* even if your symptoms begin to clear up after a few days. *Do not miss any doses.* However, *do not use this medicine more often or for a longer time than your doctor ordered.*

Dosing—The dose of acyclovir will be different for different patients. *Follow your doctor's orders or the directions on the label.* The following information includes only the average doses of acyclovir. Your dose may be different if you have kidney disease. *If your dose is different, do not change it* unless your doctor tells you to do so.

The number of capsules or tablets or teaspoonfuls of suspension that you take depends on the strength of the medicine. Also, *the number of doses you take each day, the time allowed between doses, and the length of time you take the medicine depend on the medical problem for which you are taking acyclovir.*

- For *oral* dosage forms (capsules, oral suspension, or tablets):
  - —For treatment of herpes of the genitals or mucous membranes, or for shingles:
    - Adults and children 12 years of age and older—200 to 800 milligrams (mg) two to five times a day for up to ten days.
    - Children younger than 12 years of age—Use and dose must be determined by the doctor.
  - —For treatment of chickenpox:
    - Adults and children 2 years of age and older—Dose is based on body weight. The usual dose is 20 mg per kilogram (kg) of body weight, up to 800 mg, four times a day for five days.
    - Children younger than 2 years of age—Use and dose must be determined by the doctor.
- For *injection* dosage form:
  - —For treatment of herpes of the genitals or mucous membranes, or for shingles:
    - Adults and children 12 years of age and older—Dose is based on body weight. The usual dose is 5 to 10 mg of acyclovir per kg (2.3 to 4.6 mg per pound) of body weight, injected slowly into a vein over at least a one-hour period, and repeated every eight hours for five to ten days.
    - Children younger than 12 years of age—Dose is based on body weight or body size. The medicine is injected slowly into a vein over at least a one-hour period and repeated every eight hours for five to ten days.

Missed dose—If you do miss a dose of this medicine, take it as soon as possible. However, if it is almost time for your next dose, skip the missed dose and go back to your regular dosing schedule. Do not double doses.

Storage—To store this medicine:

- Keep out of the reach of children.
- Store away from heat and direct light.
- Do not store the capsule or tablet form of this medicine in the bathroom, near the kitchen sink, or in other damp places. Heat or moisture may cause the medicine to break down.
- Do not keep outdated medicine or medicine no longer needed. Be sure that any discarded medicine is out of the reach of children.

Precautions While Using This Medicine

Women with genital herpes may be more likely to get cancer of the cervix (entrance to the womb). Therefore, it is very important that a Pap test be taken at least once a year to check for cancer. Cervical cancer can be cured if found and treated early.

If your symptoms do not improve within a few days, or if they become worse, check with your doctor.

The areas affected by herpes should be kept as clean and dry as possible. Also, wear loose-fitting clothing to avoid irritating the sores (blisters).

It is important to remember that acyclovir will not keep you from spreading herpes to others.

Herpes infection of the genitals can be caught from or spread to your partner during any sexual activity. Even though you may get herpes if your partner has no symptoms, the infection is more likely to be spread if sores are present. This is true until the sores are completely healed and the scabs have fallen off. *Therefore, it is best to avoid any sexual activity if either you or your sexual partner has any symptoms of herpes.* The use of a latex condom (''rubber'') may help prevent the spread of herpes. However, spermicidal (sperm-killing) jelly or a diaphragm will probably not help.

Side Effects of This Medicine

Along with its needed effects, a medicine may cause some unwanted effects. Although not all of these side effects may occur, if they do occur they may need medical attention.

Check with your doctor immediately if any of the following side effects occur:

For acyclovir injection only

More common

Pain, swelling, or redness at place of injection

Less common (more common with rapid injection)

Abdominal or stomach pain; decreased frequency of urination or amount of urine; increased thirst; loss of appetite; nausea or vomiting; unusual tiredness or weakness

Rare

Confusion; convulsions (seizures); hallucinations (seeing, hearing, or feeling things that are not there); trembling

Other side effects may occur that usually do not need medical attention. These side effects may go away during treatment as your body adjusts to the medicine. However,

check with your doctor if any of the following side effects continue or are bothersome:

For oral acyclovir only

Less common (especially seen with long-term use or high doses)

Diarrhea; headache; lightheadedness; nausea or vomiting

Other side effects not listed above may also occur in some patients. If you notice any other effects, check with your doctor.

Additional Information

Once a medicine has been approved for marketing for a certain use, experience may show that it is also useful for other medical problems. Although not specifically included in product labeling, acyclovir by injection is used in certain patients with the following medical conditions:

- Disseminated neonatal herpes simplex (widespread infection in the newborn)
- Herpes simplex (prevention of repeated infections)

Other than the above information, there is no additional information relating to proper use, precautions, or side effects for these uses.

Revised: 06/22/94

ACYCLOVIR Topical

A commonly used brand name in the U.S. and Canada is Zovirax. Other commonly used names are aciclovir and acycloguanosine.

Description

Acyclovir (ay-SYE-kloe-veer) belongs to the family of medicines called antivirals. Antivirals are used to treat infections caused by viruses. Usually they work for only one kind or group of virus infections.

Topical acyclovir is used to treat the symptoms of herpes simplex virus infections of the skin, mucous membranes, and genitals (sex organs). Although topical acyclovir will not cure herpes simplex, it may help relieve the pain and discomfort and may help the sores (if any) heal faster. Topical acyclovir may also be used for other conditions as determined by your doctor.

Acyclovir is available only with your doctor's prescription, in the following dosage form:

Topical

- Ointment (U.S. and Canada)

Before Using This Medicine

In deciding to use a medicine, the risks of using the medicine must be weighed against the good it will do. This is a decision you and your doctor will make. For acyclovir, the following should be considered:

Allergies—Tell your doctor if you have ever had any unusual or allergic reaction to acyclovir. Also tell your health care professional if you are allergic to any other substances, such as preservatives or dyes.

Pregnancy—Topical acyclovir has not been studied in pregnant women. However, this medication has not been shown to cause birth defects or other problems in animal studies using mice, rats, or rabbits.

Breast-feeding—It is not known whether topical acyclovir passes into the breast milk. However, acyclovir ointment has not been reported to cause problems in nursing babies, even though small amounts of topical acyclovir are absorbed through the mother's skin and mucous membranes.

Children—Although there is no specific information comparing the use of topical acyclovir in children with use in other age groups, this medicine is not expected to cause different side effects or problems in children than it does in adults.

Older adults—Many medicines have not been studied specifically in older people. Therefore, it may not be known whether they work exactly the same way they do in younger adults. Although there is no specific information comparing the use of topical acyclovir in the elderly with use in other age groups, this medicine is not expected to cause different side effects or problems in older people than it does in younger adults.

Other medicines—Although certain medicines should not be used together at all, in other cases two different medicines may be used together even if an interaction might occur. In these cases, your doctor may want to change the dose, or other precautions may be necessary. Tell your health care professional if you are using any other topical prescription or nonprescription (over-the-counter [OTC]) medicine that is to be applied to the same area of the skin.

Proper Use of This Medicine

Acyclovir may come with patient information about herpes simplex infections. Read this information carefully. If you have any questions, check with your health care professional.

Do not use this medicine in the eyes.

Acyclovir is best used as soon as possible after the symptoms of herpes infection (for example, pain, burning, or blisters) begin to appear.

Use a finger cot or rubber glove when applying this medicine. This will help keep you from spreading the infection to other areas of your body. Apply enough medicine to completely cover all the sores (blisters). A 1.25-cm (approximately 1/2-inch) strip of ointment applied to each area of the affected skin measuring 5 × 5 cm (approximately 2 × 2 inches) is usually enough, unless otherwise directed by your doctor.

To help clear up your herpes infection, *continue using acyclovir for the full time of treatment,* even if your symptoms begin to clear up after a few days. *Do not miss any doses.* However, *do not use this medicine more often or for a longer time than your doctor ordered.*

Dosing—The dose of topical acyclovir will be different for different patients. *Follow your doctor's orders or the directions on the label.* The following information includes only the average dose of topical acyclovir. *If your dose is different, do not change it* unless your doctor tells you to do so.

- For *topical* dosage form (ointment):
  - —For herpes simplex infection:
    - Adults and children—Apply to the affected area(s) of the skin and mucous membranes, every three hours, for a total of six times a day, for seven days.

Missed dose—If you miss a dose of this medicine, apply it as soon as possible. However, if it is almost time for your next dose, skip the missed dose and go back to your regular dosing schedule.

Storage—To store this medicine:

- Keep out of the reach of children.
- Store away from heat and direct light.
- Keep the medicine from freezing.
- Do not keep outdated medicine or medicine no longer needed. Be sure that any discarded medicine is out of the reach of children.

Precautions While Using This Medicine

Women with genital herpes may be more likely to get cancer of the cervix (opening to the womb). Therefore, it is very important that Pap tests be taken at least once a year to check for cancer. Cervical cancer can be cured if found and treated early.

If your symptoms do not improve within 1 week, or if they become worse, check with your doctor.

The areas affected by herpes should be kept as clean and dry as possible. Also, wear loose-fitting clothing to avoid irritating the sores (blisters).

Herpes infection of the genitals can be caught from or spread to your partner during any sexual activity. Although you may get herpes even though your sexual partner has no symptoms, the infection is more likely to be spread if sores are present. This is true until the sores are completely healed and the scabs have fallen off. The use of a condom (prophylactic) may help prevent the spread of herpes. However, spermicidal (sperm-killing) jelly or a diaphragm will not help prevent the spread of herpes. *Therefore, it is best to avoid any sexual activity if either you or your partner has any symptoms of herpes. It is also important to remember that acyclovir will not keep you from spreading herpes to others.*

Side Effects of This Medicine

Along with its needed effects, a medicine may cause some unwanted effects. The following side effects may go away during treatment as your body adjusts to the medicine. However, check with your doctor if any of these effects continue or are bothersome:

More common
Mild pain, burning, or stinging

Less common
Itching

Rare
Skin rash

Other side effects not listed above may also occur in some patients. If you notice any other effects, check with your doctor.

Revised: 01/15/92
Interim revision: 05/10/94

ADAPALENE Topical

A commonly used brand name in the U.S. and Canada is Differin.

Description

Adapalene (a-DAP-a-leen) is used to treat acne. It works partly by keeping skin pores clear.

Adapalene is available only with your doctor's prescription, in the following dosage form:

Topical
- Gel (U.S. and Canada)

Before Using This Medicine

In deciding to use a medicine, the risks of applying the medicine must be weighed against the good it will do. This is a decision you and your doctor will make. For adapalene, the following should be considered:

Allergies—Tell your doctor if you have ever had any unusual or allergic reaction to adapalene. Also tell your health care professional if you are allergic to any other substances, such as foods, preservatives, or dyes.

Pregnancy—Adapalene has not been studied in pregnant women. It is not recommended for use during pregnancy. Adapalene in large doses has been shown to cause some bone problems in the fetuses of some animals. Before using this medicine, make sure your doctor knows if you are pregnant or if you are trying to become pregnant.

Breast-feeding—It is not known if adapalene passes into breast milk.

Children—Studies of this medicine have been done only in adult patients, and there is no specific information comparing use of adapalene in children up to 12 years of age with use in other age groups. In teenagers, adapalene is not expected to cause different side effects or problems than it does in adults.

Older adults—Many medicines have not been studied specifically in older people. Therefore, it may not be known whether they work exactly the same way they do in younger adults or if they cause different side effects or problems in older people. There is no specific information comparing use of adapalene in the elderly with use in other age groups. Older adults are not likely to develop acne.

Other medicines—Although certain medicines should not be used together at all, in other cases two different medicines may be used together even if an interaction might occur. In these cases, your doctor may want to change the dose, or other precautions may be necessary. Tell your doctor and pharmacist if you are using any other topical prescription or nonprescription (over-the-counter [OTC]) medicine that is to be applied to the same area of the skin.

Other medical problems—The presence of other medical problems may affect the use of adapalene. Make sure you tell your doctor if you have any other medical problems, especially:

- Eczema or
- Seborrheic dermatitis—Use of this medicine may cause or increase the irritation associated with eczema or seborrheic dermatitis

Proper Use of This Medicine

It is very important that you use this medicine only as directed. Do not use more of it, do not use it more often, and do not use it for a longer time than your doctor ordered. To do so may cause irritation of the skin.

Do not apply this medicine to windburned or sunburned skin or on open wounds.

Do not use this medicine in or around the eyes, lips, or inside of the nose. Spread the medicine away from these areas when applying. If the medicine accidently gets on these areas, wash with water at once.

Apply the medicine to clean, dry areas of the skin affected by acne. Rub in gently and well. Wash your hands afterwards to remove any medicine that may remain on them.

To help clear up your acne completely, *it is very important that you keep using this medicine for the full time of treatment,* even if your symptoms begin to clear up after a short time. If you stop using this medicine too soon, your acne may return or get worse.

Dosing—*Follow your doctor's orders or the directions on the label.* The following information includes only the average doses of adapalene. *If your dose is different, do not change it* unless your doctor tells you to do so.

- For *topical* dosage form (gel):
  - —For acne:
    - Adults and teenagers—Apply a small amount as a thin film once a day, at least one hour before bedtime. Apply the medicine to dry, clean areas affected by acne. Rub in gently and well.
    - Children—Use and dose must be determined by your doctor.

Missed dose—If you miss a dose of this medicine, skip the missed dose and go back to your regular dosing schedule. Do not double doses.

Storage—To store this medicine:

- Keep out of the reach of children.
- Do not keep outdated medicine or medicine no longer needed. Be sure that any discarded medicine is out of the reach of children.

Precautions While Using This Medicine

During the first 3 weeks you are using adapalene, your acne may seem to get worse before it gets better. Full improvement should be seen within 12 weeks, especially if you use the medicine every day. You should not stop using adapalene if your acne seems worse at first, unless irritation or other symptoms become severe. Check with your doctor if your acne does not improve within 8 to 12 weeks.

Do not apply any topical product to the same area where you are using adapalene, unless otherwise directed by your doctor. If applied to the same area treated with adapalene, the following products may cause mild to severe irritation of the skin:

- Hair products that irritate the skin, such as permanents or hair removal products
- Skin products for acne (such as clindamycin or erythromycin) or other skin products containing a peeling agent (such as benzoyl peroxide, resorcinol, salicylic acid, or sulfur)
- Skin products that cause one to be more sensitive to the sun, such as those containing spices or lime
- Skin products that are too drying or that contain a large amount of alcohol, such as astringents, cosmetics, shaving creams, or after-shave lotions
- Skin products that are abrasive, such as some soaps or skin cleansers

Your doctor may ask you to use other topical products, such as benzoyl peroxide, clindamycin, or erythromycin, during your treatment with adapalene. Applying the products at different times of the day will lessen the chance of causing skin irritation.

If your skin becomes too dry or red at any time, discuss with your doctor whether you should continue using adapalene. Applying creams, lotions, or moisturizers as needed helps lessen these skin problems.

During treatment with this medicine, avoid getting too much sun on treated areas and do not use sunlamps. Since your skin may be more prone to sunburn or skin irritation, use sunscreen or sunblocking lotions regularly with a sun protection factor (SPF) of 15 or more. Wear protective clothing against sun, wind, and cold weather.

Side Effects of This Medicine

Along with its needed effects, a medicine may cause some unwanted effects. Although not all of these side effects may occur, if they do occur, they may need medical attention.

Check with your doctor as soon as possible if any of the following side effects occur:

More common—especially during the first month of use

Burning sensation or stinging of skin; dryness and peeling of skin; itching of skin; redness of skin

Other side effects may occur that usually do not need medical attention. These side effects may go away during treatment as your body adjusts to the medicine. However, check with your doctor if the following side effect continues or is bothersome:

Rare—more common during the first month of use
Worsening of acne

Other side effects not listed above may also occur in some patients. If you notice any other effects, check with your doctor.

Developed: 06/02/97

ALCOHOL AND SULFUR Topical

Some commonly used brand names are:

In the U.S.—
Acne Lotion 10
Liquimat Light
Liquimat Medium

In Canada—
Postacne

Description

Alcohol and sulfur (AL-koe-hol and SUL-fur) combination is used in the treatment of acne and oily skin. Some of the products are tinted a flesh color and can be used as a makeup or cover-up.

This medicine is available without a doctor's prescription; however, your doctor may have special instructions on the proper use of this medicine for your medical condition.

Alcohol and sulfur combination is available in the following dosage forms:

Topical
- Lotion (U.S. and Canada)

Before Using This Medicine

If you are using this medicine without a prescription, carefully read and follow any precautions on the label. For alcohol and sulfur combination, the following should be considered:

Allergies—Tell your doctor if you have ever had any unusual or allergic reaction to alcohol or sulfur. Also tell your health care professional if you are allergic to any other substances, such as preservatives or dyes.

Pregnancy—Topical alcohol and sulfur combination has not been shown to cause birth defects or other problems in humans.

Breast-feeding—Topical alcohol and sulfur combination has not been reported to cause problems in nursing babies.

Children—This medicine should not be used for children up to 8 years of age. In older children, although there is no specific information comparing use of alcohol and sulfur with use in other age groups, this medicine is not expected to cause different side effects or problems than it does in adults.

Older adults—Many medicines have not been studied specifically in older people. Therefore, it may not be known whether they work exactly the same way they do in younger adults. Although there is no specific information comparing use of alcohol and sulfur in the elderly with use in other age groups, this medicine is not expected to cause different side effects or problems in older people than it does in younger adults.

Other medicines—Although certain medicines should not be used together at all, in other cases two different medicines may be used together even if an interaction might occur. In these cases, your doctor may want to change the dose, or other precautions may be necessary. Tell your health care professional if you are using any other topical prescription or nonprescription (over-the-counter [OTC]) medicine that is to be applied to the same area of the skin.

Proper Use of This Medicine

Before using this medicine, wash or cleanse the affected areas thoroughly and gently pat dry. Then apply a small amount of this medicine to the affected areas and rub in gently.

Keep this medicine away from the eyes, the inside of the nose, and the lips. If you accidentally get some in your eyes, inside your nose, or on your lips, flush them thoroughly with water.

This medicine is flammable. Do not use near heat, near open flame, or while smoking.

Use this medicine only as directed. Do not use it more often than recommended on the label, unless otherwise directed by your doctor.

Dosing—The dose of alcohol and sulfur combination will be different for different patients. *Follow your doctor's orders or the directions on the label.* The following information includes only the average dose of alcohol and sulfur combination. *If your dose is different, do not change it* unless your doctor tells you to do so.

- For *topical* dosage form (lotion):
  —For acne or oily skin:
    - Adults and children 8 years of age and older—Apply to the affected area(s) of the skin one or two times a day.
    - Children up to 8 years of age—Use is not recommended.

Missed dose—If you miss a dose of this medicine, apply it as soon as possible. Then go back to your regular dosing schedule.

Storage—To store this medicine:
- Keep out of the reach of children.
- Store away from heat and direct light.

- Keep the medicine from freezing.
- Do not keep outdated medicine or medicine no longer needed. Be sure that any discarded medicine is out of the reach of children.

Precautions While Using This Medicine

When using alcohol and sulfur combination, do not use any of the following preparations on the same affected area, unless otherwise directed by your doctor.

Abrasive soaps or cleansers
Any other topical acne preparation or preparation containing a peeling agent (for example, benzoyl peroxide, resorcinol, salicylic acid, or tretinoin [vitamin A acid])
Cosmetics or soaps that dry the skin
Medicated cosmetics
Other alcohol-containing preparations
Other topical medicine for the skin

To use any of the above preparations on the same affected area as this medicine may cause severe irritation of the skin.

Do not use any topical mercury-containing preparation, such as ammoniated mercury ointment, on the same affected area as this medicine. To do so may cause a foul odor, may be irritating to the skin, and may stain the skin black. If you have any questions about this, check with your health care professional.

Side Effects of This Medicine

Along with its needed effects, a medicine may cause some unwanted effects. Although not all of these side effects may occur, if they do occur they may need medical attention.

Check with your doctor as soon as possible if the following side effect occurs:

Skin irritation not present before use of this medicine

Other side effects may occur that usually do not need medical attention. These side effects may go away during treatment as your body adjusts to the medicine. However, check with your health care professional if any of the following side effects continue or are bothersome:

Burning or stinging of skin; dryness or peeling of skin (may occur after a few days)

Other side effects not listed above may also occur in some patients. If you notice any other effects, check with your health care professional.

Revised: 08/02/95

ALDESLEUKIN Systemic†

A commonly used brand name in the U.S. is Proleukin.
Other commonly used names are interleukin-2 and IL-2.

†Not commercially available in Canada.

Description

Aldesleukin (al-des-LOO-kin) is a synthetic (man-made) version of a substance called interleukin-2. Interleukins are produced naturally by cells in the body to help white blood cells work. Aldesleukin is used to treat cancer of the kidney.

Aldesleukin causes some other very serious effects in addition to its helpful effects. Some effects can be fatal. For that reason, aldesleukin is given only in the hospital. If severe side effects occur, which is common, treatment in an intensive care unit (ICU) may be necessary. Other effects may not be serious but may cause concern. Before you begin treatment with aldesleukin, you and your doctor should talk about the good this medicine will do as well as the risks of using it.

Aldesleukin is to be administered only by or under the immediate supervision of your doctor. It is available in the following dosage form:

Parenteral
- Injection (U.S.)

Before Using This Medicine

In deciding to use a medicine, the risks of taking the medicine must be weighed against the good it will do. This is a decision you and your doctor will make. For aldesleukin, the following should be considered:

Allergies—Tell your doctor if you have ever had any unusual or allergic reaction to aldesleukin.

Pregnancy—Aldesleukin has not been studied in humans or in animals. However, because this medicine may cause serious side effects, use during pregnancy is usually not recommended.

Be sure that you have discussed this with your doctor before receiving this medicine.

Breast-feeding—It is not known whether aldesleukin passes into breast milk.

Children—There is no specific information comparing use of aldesleukin in children with use in other age groups.

Older adults—Many medicines have not been studied specifically in older people. Therefore, it may not be known whether they work exactly the same way they do in younger adults. There is no specific information comparing use of aldesleukin in the elderly with use in other age groups.

Other medicines—Although certain medicines should not be used together at all, in other cases two different medicines may be used together even if an interaction might occur. In these cases, your doctor may want to change the dose, or other precautions may be necessary. Tell your health care professional if you are taking *any* other medicine.

Other medical problems—The presence of other medical problems may affect the use of aldesleukin. Make sure you

tell your doctor if you have any other medical problems, especially:

- Chickenpox (including recent exposure) or
- Herpes zoster (shingles)—Risk of severe disease affecting other parts of the body
- Heart disease or
- Immune system problems or
- Liver disease or
- Lung disease or
- Psoriasis or
- Underactive thyroid—May be worsened by aldesleukin
- Infection—Aldesleukin may decrease your body's ability to fight infection
- Kidney disease—Effects of aldesleukin may be increased because of slower removal from the body
- Mental problems—Aldesleukin may make them worse
- Seizures (history of)—Aldesleukin can cause seizures

Proper Use of This Medicine

Dosing—The dose of aldesleukin will be different for different patients. The dose that is used may depend on a number of things, including what the medicine is being used for, the patient's weight, and whether or not other medicines are also being taken. Because this medicine can cause very serious side effects, your doctor will be watching your dose very carefully and may change it as needed. If you have any questions about the proper dose of aldesleukin, ask your doctor.

Precautions While Using This Medicine

Aldesleukin can temporarily affect the white blood cells in your blood, increasing the chance of getting an infection. It can also lower the number of platelets, which are necessary for proper blood clotting. If this occurs, there are certain precautions you can take, especially when your blood count is low, to reduce the risk of infection or bleeding:

- If you can, avoid people with infections. *Check with your doctor immediately* if you think you are getting an infection or if you get a fever or chills, cough or hoarseness, lower back or side pain, or painful or difficult urination.
- *Check with your doctor immediately* if you notice any unusual bleeding or bruising; black, tarry stools; blood in urine or stools; or pinpoint red spots on your skin.
- Be careful when using a regular toothbrush, dental floss, or toothpick. Your medical doctor, dentist, or nurse may recommend other ways to clean your teeth and gums. Check with your medical doctor before having any dental work done.
- Do not touch your eyes or the inside of your nose unless you have just washed your hands and have not touched anything else in the meantime.
- Be careful not to cut yourself when you are using sharp objects such as a safety razor or fingernail or toenail cutters.
- Avoid contact sports or other situations where bruising or injury could occur.

Side Effects of This Medicine

Along with its needed effects, a medicine may cause some unwanted effects. Some side effects will have signs or symptoms that you can see or feel. Your doctor may watch for others by doing certain tests.

Check with your doctor or nurse immediately if any of the following side effects occur:

More common

Fever or chills; shortness of breath

Less common

Black, tarry stools; blisters on skin; blood in urine; bloody vomit; chest pain; cough or hoarseness; lower back or side pain; painful or difficult urination; pinpoint red spots on skin; stomach pain (severe); unusual bleeding or bruising

Check with your health care professional as soon as possible if any of the following side effects occur:

More common

Agitation; confusion; diarrhea; dizziness; drowsiness; mental depression; nausea and vomiting; sores in mouth and on lips; tingling of hands or feet; unusual decrease in urination; unusual tiredness; weight gain of 5 to 10 pounds or more

Less common

Bloating and stomach pain; blurred or double vision; faintness; fast or irregular heartbeat; loss of taste; rapid breathing; redness, swelling, and soreness of tongue; trouble in speaking; yellow eyes and skin

Rare

Changes in menstrual periods; clumsiness; coldness; convulsions (seizures); listlessness; muscle aches; pain or redness at site of injection; sudden inability to move; swelling in the front of the neck; swelling of feet or lower legs; weakness

This medicine may also cause the following side effects that your doctor will watch for:

More common

Anemia; heart problems; kidney problems; liver problems; low blood pressure; low platelet counts in blood; low white blood cell counts; other blood problems; underactive thyroid

Other side effects may occur that usually do not need medical attention. These side effects may go away during treatment as your body adjusts to the medicine. Also, your health care professional may be able to tell you about ways to prevent or reduce some of these side effects. Check with your health care professional if any of the following side effects continue or are bothersome or if you have any questions about them:

More common

Dry skin; loss of appetite; skin rash or redness with burning or itching, followed by peeling; unusual feeling of discomfort or illness

Less common

Constipation; headache; joint pain; muscle pain

Other side effects not listed above may also occur in some patients. If you notice any other effects, check with your doctor.

Developed: 09/15/93
Interim revision: 08/08/94

ALENDRONATE Systemic

A commonly used brand name in the U.S. and Canada is Fosamax.

Description

Alendronate (a-LEN-dro-nate) is used to treat osteoporosis (thinning of the bone) in women after menopause. It may also be used to treat Paget's disease of bone.

Alendronate is available only with your doctor's prescription, in the following dosage form:

Oral
- Tablets (U.S. and Canada)

Before Using This Medicine

In deciding to use a medicine, the risks of taking the medicine must be weighed against the good it will do. This is a decision you and your doctor will make. For alendronate, the following should be considered:

Allergies—Tell your doctor if you have ever had any unusual or allergic reaction to alendronate. Also tell your health care professional if you are allergic to any other substances, such as foods, preservatives, or dyes.

Diet—Make certain your health care professional knows if you are on any special diet, such as a low-sodium or low-sugar diet. Your doctor may recommend that you eat a balanced diet with an adequate amount of calcium and vitamin D (found in milk or other dairy products).

Pregnancy—Alendronate has not been studied in pregnant women. However, studies in animals have shown that alendronate causes birth defects and other pregnancy problems. Before taking this medicine, make sure your doctor knows if you are pregnant or if you may become pregnant.

Breast-feeding—It is not known whether alendronate passes into breast milk. However, this medicine has been reported to pass into the milk of lactating rats.

Children—Studies on this medicine have been done only in adult patients and there is no specific information comparing use of alendronate in children with use in other age groups.

Older adults—This medicine has been tested and has not been shown to cause different side effects or problems in older people than it does in younger adults.

Other medicines—Although certain medicines should not be used together at all, in other cases two different medicines may be used together even if an interaction might occur. In these cases, your doctor may want to change the dose, or other precautions may be necessary. When you are taking alendronate, it is especially important that your health care professional know if you are taking the following:

- Aspirin or products that contain aspirin—Use with alendronate may cause or make esophagus, intestine, or stomach problems worse

Other medical problems—The presence of other medical problems may affect the use of alendronate. Make sure you tell your doctor if you have any other medical problems, especially:

- Digestion problems—Taking alendronate may be harmful to the esophagus, intestine, or stomach
- Esophagus problems or
- Intestine problems or
- Stomach problems—Alendronate may make these conditions worse
- Kidney problems—The effects of alendronate may be increased

Proper Use of This Medicine

Take alendronate with a full glass (6 to 8 ounces) of plain water on an empty stomach. It should be taken in the morning at least 30 minutes before any food, beverage, or other medicines. Food and beverages, such as mineral water, coffee, tea, or juice, will decrease the amount of alendronate absorbed by the body. Waiting longer than 30 minutes will allow more of the drug to be absorbed. Medicines such as antacids or calcium or vitamin supplements will also decrease the absorption of alendronate.

Do not lie down for 30 minutes after taking alendronate. This will help alendronate reach your stomach faster. It will also help prevent irritation to your esophagus.

Your doctor may recommend that you eat a balanced diet with an adequate amount of calcium and vitamin D (found in milk or other dairy products). However, do not take any food, beverages, or calcium or vitamin supplements within 30 minutes or longer of taking alendronate. To do so may keep this medicine from working properly.

Dosing—The dose of alendronate will be different for different patients. *Follow your doctor's orders or the directions on the label.* The following information includes only the average doses of alendronate. *If your dose is different, do not change it* unless your doctor tells you to do so.

—For Paget's disease of bone:

- Adults—40 milligrams (mg) once a day in the morning, taken at least thirty minutes before the first food, beverage, or medication. You should take alendronate with six to eight ounces of plain water. Your treatment may continue for six months. Your doctor may repeat the treatment.
- Children—Use and dose must be determined by your doctor.

—For postmenopausal osteoporosis (thinning of bone):

- Adults—10 mg once a day in the morning, taken at least thirty minutes before the first food, beverage, or medication. You should take alendronate with six to eight ounces of plain water.

Missed dose—If you miss a dose of this medicine, do not take it later in the day. Resume your usual schedule the next morning. Do not double doses.

Storage—To store this medicine:
- Keep out of the reach of children.
- Store away from heat and direct light.
- Do not store in the bathroom, near the kitchen sink, or in other damp places. Heat or moisture may cause the medicine to break down.
- Keep the medicine from freezing. Do not refrigerate.
- Do not keep outdated medicine or medicine no longer needed. Be sure that any discarded medicine is out of the reach of children.

Side Effects of This Medicine

Along with its needed effects, a medicine may cause some unwanted effects. Although not all of these side effects may occur, if they do occur they may need medical attention.

Check with your doctor as soon as possible if any of the following side effects occur:

More common
Abdominal pain

Less common
Difficulty in swallowing; heartburn; irritation or pain of the esophagus; muscle pain

Rare
Skin rash

Other side effects may occur that usually do not need medical attention. These side effects may go away during treatment as your body adjusts to the medicine. However, check with your doctor if any of the following side effects continue or are bothersome:

Less common
Constipation; diarrhea; full or bloated feeling; gas; headache; nausea

Other side effects not listed above may also occur in some patients. If you notice any other effects, check with your doctor.

Developed: 01/06/97

ALGLUCERASE Systemic

A commonly used brand name in the U.S. and Canada is Ceredase.

Description

Alglucerase (al-GLOO-ser-ace) is used to treat Gaucher's disease caused by the lack of a certain enzyme, glucocerebrosidase, in the body. This enzyme is necessary for your body to use fats.

Alglucerase is made from human placenta tissue that is collected after a baby is born. Before it is used, the tissue is tested for hepatitis and human immunodeficiency virus (HIV). This is similar to the testing that a blood bank does on donated blood before it is given to anyone else.

Alglucerase is available with your doctor's prescription, in the following dosage form:

Parenteral
- Injection (U.S. and Canada)

Before Receiving This Medicine

In deciding to use a medicine, the risks of receiving the medicine must be weighed against the good it will do. This is a decision you and your doctor will make. For alglucerase, the following should be considered:

Allergies—Tell your doctor if you have ever had any unusual or allergic reaction to alglucerase. Also tell your health care professional if you are allergic to any other substances, such as foods, preservatives, or dyes.

Pregnancy—Studies have not been done in either humans or animals.

Breast-feeding—It is not known whether alglucerase passes into human breast milk.

Children—This medicine has been tested in a limited number of children. In effective doses, the medicine has not been shown to cause different side effects or problems than it does in adults.

Older adults—Many medicines have not been studied specifically in older people. Therefore, it may not be known whether they work exactly the same way they do in younger adults or if they cause different side effects or problems in older people. There is no specific information comparing use of alglucerase in the elderly with use in other age groups.

Other medicines—Although certain medicines should not be used together at all, in other cases two different medicines may be used together even if an interaction might occur. In these cases, your doctor may want to change the dose, or other precautions may be necessary. Tell your health care professional if you are taking any other prescription or nonprescription (over-the-counter [OTC]) medicines.

Proper Use of This Medicine

This medicine will not cure Gaucher's disease but it does help control it. Therefore, you must continue to receive it if you expect to keep your condition under control. You may have to receive alglucerase for the rest of your life. If Gaucher's disease is not treated, it can cause serious blood, liver, skeletal, or spleen problems.

Dosing—The dose of alglucerase will be different for different patients. *Follow your doctor's orders.* The following information includes only the average doses of alglucerase.

- For Gaucher's disease:
  - —For *injection* dosage form:
    - Adults and children—The dose is based on body weight. It is injected slowly into a vein over one to two hours. To start, some patients may receive 1.15 Units per kilogram (kg) (0.52 Units per pound) of body weight three times a week. Other patients may receive up to 60 Units per kg

(27 Units per pound) of body weight as often as once a week or as seldom as every four weeks. Later, your doctor may raise or lower your dose.

Precautions While Receiving This Medicine

It is important that your doctor check your progress while you are receiving alglucerase to make sure that the dosage is correct for you.

Side Effects of This Medicine

Since alglucerase is made from human tissue, it is possible that diseases caused by viruses could be passed on. Examples of such diseases are hepatitis and HIV infection. These problems have not been reported to date, however, and are unlikely since the tissue is tested before being used. If you have questions or concerns about this, check with your doctor.

Along with its needed effects, a medicine may cause some unwanted effects. The following side effects may go away during treatment as your body adjusts to the medicine. However, check with your doctor if any of these effects continue or are bothersome:

Less common

Abdominal discomfort; chills; fever; nausea and vomiting; swelling at place of injection

Other side effects not listed above may also occur in some patients. If you notice any other effects, check with your doctor.

Revised: 01/18/93
Interim revision: 09/15/95; 07/17/96

ALLOPURINOL Systemic

Some commonly used brand names are:

In the U.S.—

Lopurin
Zyloprim

Generic name product may also be available.

In Canada—

Apo-Allopurinol
Zyloprim
Purinol

Description

Allopurinol (al-oh-PURE-i-nole) is used to treat chronic gout (gouty arthritis). This condition is caused by too much uric acid in the blood.

This medicine works by causing less uric acid to be produced by the body. Allopurinol will not relieve a gout attack that has already started. Also, it does not cure gout, but it will help prevent gout attacks. However, it works only after you have been taking it regularly for a few months. Allopurinol will help prevent gout attacks only as long as you continue to take it.

Allopurinol is also used to prevent or treat other medical problems that may occur if too much uric acid is present in the body. These include certain kinds of kidney stones or other kidney problems.

Certain medicines or medical treatments can greatly increase the amount of uric acid in the body. This can cause gout or kidney problems in some people. Allopurinol is also used to prevent these problems.

Allopurinol is available only with your doctor's prescription in the following dosage form:

Oral

- Tablets (U.S. and Canada)

Before Using This Medicine

In deciding to use a medicine, the risks of taking the medicine must be weighed against the good it will do. This is a decision you and your doctor will make. For allopurinol, the following should be considered:

Allergies—Tell your doctor if you have ever had any unusual or allergic reaction to allopurinol. Also tell your health care professional if you are allergic to any other substances, such as foods, preservatives, or dyes.

Pregnancy—Although studies on birth defects have not been done in pregnant women, allopurinol has not been reported to cause problems in humans. In one study in mice, large amounts of allopurinol caused birth defects and other unwanted effects. However, allopurinol did not cause birth defects or other problems in rats or rabbits given doses up to 20 times the amount usually given to humans.

Breast-feeding—Allopurinol passes into the breast milk. Mothers who are taking this medicine and who wish to breast-feed should discuss this with their doctor.

Children—This medicine has been tested in children and, in effective doses, has not been shown to cause different side effects or problems than it does in adults.

Older adults—Many medicines have not been studied specifically in older people. Therefore, it may not be known whether they work exactly the same way they do in younger adults or if they cause different side effects or problems in older people. There is no specific information comparing use of allopurinol in the elderly with use in other age groups.

Other medicines—Although certain medicines should not be used together at all, in other cases two different medicines may be used together even if an interaction might occur. In these cases, your doctor may want to change the dose, or other precautions may be necessary. When you are taking allopurinol, it is especially important that your doctor and pharmacist know if you are taking any of the following:

- Anticoagulants (blood thinners)—Allopurinol may increase the chance of bleeding; changes in the dose of the anticoagulant may be needed, depending on blood test results

- Azathioprine (e.g., Imuran) or
- Mercaptopurine (e.g., Purinethol)—Allopurinol may cause higher blood levels of azathioprine or mercaptopurine, leading to an increased chance of serious side effects

Other medical problems—The presence of other medical problems may affect the use of allopurinol. Make sure you tell your doctor if you have any other medical problems, especially:

- Congestive heart disease or
- Diabetes mellitus (sugar diabetes) or
- High blood pressure or
- Kidney disease—There is an increased risk of severe allergic reactions or other serious effects; a change in the dose of allopurinol may be needed

Proper Use of This Medicine

If this medicine upsets your stomach, it may be taken after meals. If stomach upset (indigestion, nausea, vomiting, diarrhea, or stomach pain) continues, check with your doctor.

In order for this medicine to help you, it must be taken regularly as ordered by your doctor.

To help prevent kidney stones while taking allopurinol, adults should drink at least 10 to 12 full glasses (8 ounces each) of fluids each day unless otherwise directed by their doctor. Check with the doctor about the amount of fluids that children should drink each day while receiving this medicine. Also, your doctor may want you to take another medicine to make your urine less acid. It is important that you follow your doctor's instructions very carefully.

For patients taking allopurinol for *chronic gout:*

- After you begin to take allopurinol, gout attacks may continue to occur for a while. However, if you take this medicine regularly as directed by your doctor, the attacks will gradually become less frequent and less painful. After you have been taking allopurinol regularly for several months, the attacks may stop completely.
- Allopurinol is used to help prevent gout attacks. It will not relieve an attack that has already started. *Even if you take another medicine for gout attacks, continue to take this medicine also.*

Dosing—The dose of allopurinol will be different for different patients. *Follow your doctor's orders or the directions on the label.* The following information includes only the average doses of allopurinol. *If your dose is different, do not change it* unless your doctor tells you to do so.

The number of tablets that you take each day and the number of times that you take the medicine every day depend on the strength of the medicine, on the dose that you need, and on the reason you are taking allopurinol. Up to 300 milligrams (mg) of allopurinol can be taken at one time. Doses larger than 300 mg a day should be divided into smaller amounts that are taken two, three, or even four times a day.

- For the *oral* dosage form (tablets):
  - —For gout:
    - Adults—At first, most people will take 100 mg a day. After about a week, your doctor will probably increase the dose gradually until the amount of uric acid in your blood has been lowered to normal levels. The total amount of allopurinol is usually not more than 800 mg a day. After the uric acid has remained at normal levels for a while, your doctor may lower your dose gradually until you are taking the smallest amount of medicine that will keep the uric acid from increasing again.
    - Children and teenagers—Use and dose must be determined by the doctor.
  - —For kidney stones:
    - Adults—100 to 800 mg a day, depending on the kind of kidney stones.
    - Children and teenagers—Use and dose must be determined by the doctor.
  - —For preventing or treating medical problems that may occur if certain treatments increase the amount of uric acid in the blood:
    - Adults—600 to 800 mg a day, starting one to three days before the treatment.
    - Children—The dose depends on the child's age.
      - —Children up to 6 years of age: 50 mg (one-half of a 100-mg tablet) three times a day.
      - —Children 6 to 10 years of age: One 100-mg tablet three times a day or one 300-mg tablet a day.
      - —Children 11 years of age and older: The dose may be the same as for adults.

Missed dose—If you miss a dose of this medicine, take it as soon as possible. However, if it is almost time for your next dose, skip the missed dose and go back to your regular dosing schedule. Do not double doses.

Storage—To store this medicine:

- Keep out of the reach of children.
- Store away from heat and direct light.
- Do not store this medicine in the bathroom, near the kitchen sink, or in other damp places. Heat or moisture may cause the medicine to break down.
- Do not keep outdated medicine or medicine no longer needed. Be sure that any discarded medicine is out of the reach of children.

Precautions While Using This Medicine

Your doctor should check your progress at regular visits. Blood tests may be needed to make sure that this medicine is working properly and is not causing unwanted effects.

Drinking too much alcohol may increase the amount of uric acid in the blood and lessen the effects of allopurinol. Therefore, people with gout and other people with too much uric acid in the body should be careful to limit the amount of alcohol they drink.

Taking too much vitamin C may make the urine more acidic and increase the possibility of kidney stones forming while you are taking allopurinol. Therefore, check with your doctor before you take vitamin C while taking this medicine.

Check with your doctor immediately:

- *If you notice a skin rash, hives, or itching while you are taking allopurinol.*
- *If chills, fever, joint pain, muscle aches or pains, sore throat, or nausea or vomiting occur, especially if they occur together with or shortly after a skin rash.*

Very rarely, these effects may be the first signs of a serious reaction to the medicine.

Allopurinol may cause some people to become drowsy or less alert than they are normally. *Make sure you know how you react to this medicine before you drive, use machines, or do anything else that could be dangerous if you are not alert.*

Side Effects of This Medicine

Along with its needed effects, a medicine may cause some unwanted effects. Although not all of these side effects may occur, if they do occur they may need medical attention.

Stop taking this medicine and check with your doctor immediately if any of the following side effects occur:

More common

Skin rash or sores, hives, or itching

Rare

Black, tarry stools; bleeding sores on lips; blood in urine or stools; chills, fever, muscle aches or pains, nausea, or vomiting—especially if occurring with or shortly after a skin rash; difficult or painful urination; pinpoint red spots on skin; redness, tenderness, burning, or peeling of skin; red and/or irritated eyes; red, thickened, or scaly skin; shortness of breath, troubled breathing, tightness in chest, or wheezing; sores, ulcers, or white spots in mouth or on lips; sore throat and fever; sudden decrease in amount of urine; swelling in upper abdominal (stomach) area; swelling of face, fingers, feet, or lower legs; swollen and/or painful glands; unusual bleeding or bruising; unusual tiredness or weakness; weight gain (rapid); yellow eyes or skin

Also, check with your doctor as soon as possible if any of the following side effects occur:

Rare

Loosening of fingernails; numbness, tingling, pain, or weakness in hands or feet; pain in lower back or side; unexplained nosebleeds

Other side effects may occur that usually do not need medical attention. These side effects may go away during treatment as your body adjusts to the medicine. However, check with your doctor if any of the following side effects continue or are bothersome:

Less common or rare

Diarrhea; drowsiness; headache; indigestion; nausea or vomiting occurring without a skin rash or other side effects; stomach pain occurring without other side effects; unusual hair loss

Other side effects not listed above may also occur in some patients. If you notice any other effects, check with your doctor.

Revised: 08/25/94

ALPHA$_1$-PROTEINASE INHIBITOR, HUMAN Systemic

A commonly used brand name in the U.S. and Canada is Prolastin. Another commonly used name is alpha$_1$-antitrypsin.

Description

Alpha$_1$-proteinase (AL-fa wun PRO-teen-ayce) inhibitor (alpha$_1$-PI) is used to treat emphysema caused by the lack of a certain protein, alpha$_1$-antitrypsin, in the body. This medicine replaces the protein when the body does not produce enough by itself.

Alpha$_1$-PI is prepared from human blood received from many donors. Each donor's blood is tested for human immunodeficiency virus (HIV) and hepatitis B virus before it is used to prepare this medicine. Also, alpha$_1$-PI is treated with heat to further reduce the risk of transmission of virus infections. However, no procedure has been found to be totally effective in removing viruses from blood products.

There have not been any reports of hepatitis developing in any patients receiving alpha$_1$-PI. However, as a precaution, before you receive this medicine, you should be vaccinated with hepatitis B vaccine. This will help prevent infection by any hepatitis virus that may have been in the blood used to prepare alpha$_1$-PI. In some cases, there may not be enough time for the vaccine to take effect before the alpha$_1$-PI is given. Therefore, you may be given hepatitis B immune globulin at the same time that you receive the hepatitis B vaccine.

Alpha$_1$-PI is given once a week. Your doctor may want you to receive this medicine regularly for a long time. However, it is not known what the effects of this medicine are when it is used regularly to treat emphysema caused by lack of alpha$_1$-antitrypsin. Be sure you have discussed this with your doctor.

Alpha$_1$-PI is administered only by or under the immediate supervision of your doctor. It is available in the following dosage form:

Parenteral

- Injection (U.S. and Canada)

Before Receiving This Medicine

In deciding to use a medicine, the risks of using the medicine must be weighed against the good it will do. This is

a decision you and your doctor will make. For alpha$_1$-proteinase inhibitor, the following should be considered:

Allergies—Tell your doctor if you have ever had any unusual or allergic reaction to alpha$_1$-proteinase inhibitor. Also tell your health care professional if you are allergic to any other substances, such as foods, preservatives, or dyes.

Pregnancy—Studies on effects in pregnancy have not been done in either humans or animals.

Breast-feeding—It is not known whether alpha$_1$-proteinase inhibitor passes into breast milk. Although most medicines pass into breast milk in small amounts, many of them may be used safely while breast-feeding. Mothers who are taking this medicine and who wish to breast-feed should discuss this with their doctor.

Children—Studies on this medicine have been done only in adult patients, and there is no specific information comparing use of alpha$_1$-proteinase inhibitor in children with use in other age groups.

Older adults—Many medicines have not been studied specifically in older people. Therefore, it may not be known whether they work exactly the same way they do in younger adults or if they cause different side effects or problems in older people. There is no specific information comparing use of alpha$_1$-proteinase inhibitor in the elderly with use in other age groups.

Other medicines—Although certain medicines should not be used together at all, in other cases two different medicines may be used together even if an interaction might occur. In these cases, your doctor may want to change the dose, or other precautions may be necessary. Tell your health care professional if you are taking any other prescription or nonprescription (over-the-counter [OTC]) medicine.

Proper Use of This Medicine

In order for alpha$_1$-proteinase inhibitor (alpha$_1$-PI) to work properly, it is important that you receive this medicine once a week on a regular schedule. If you have any questions about this, check with your doctor.

Dosing—The dose of alpha$_1$-proteinase inhibitor will be different for different patients. *Follow your doctor's orders or the directions on the label.* The following information includes only the average dose of alpha$_1$-proteinase inhibitor. *If your dose is different, do not change it* unless your doctor tells you to do so.

- For *emphysema caused by lack of the protein alpha$_1$-antitrypsin in the body:*
  - —For *injection* dosage form:
    - Adults—Dose is based on body weight and must be determined by your doctor. The usual dose is 60 milligrams (mg) per kilogram (kg) (27 mg per pound) of body weight, slowly injected into a vein over a period of several minutes. This dose is given once a week.
    - Children—Use and dose must be determined by your doctor.

Side Effects of This Medicine

Along with its needed effects, a medicine may cause some unwanted effects. The following side effects usually do not require medical attention. However, check with your doctor if any of these effects continue or are bothersome:

Less common or rare

Chills and fever; dizziness or lightheadedness; fever up to 102 °F (38.9 °C)

Note: Chills and fever may occur several hours after you receive this medicine but are usually mild and only temporary. Also, fever up to 102 °F (38.9 °C) may occur up to 12 hours after you receive this medicine and will disappear within about 24 hours.

Other side effects not listed above may also occur in some patients. If you notice any other effects, check with your doctor.

Revised: 08/09/94

ALPROSTADIL Local

Some commonly used brand names are:

In the U.S.—

Caverject
Edex
Muse
Prostin VR Pediatric

In Canada—

Caverject
Prostin VR

Other commonly used names are PGE_1 and prostaglandin E_1.

Description

Alprostadil (al-PROS-ta-dil) belongs to the group of medicines called vasodilators that can increase blood flow by expanding blood vessels. Alprostadil is used to produce erections in some men who need treatment for erectile dysfunction (sexual impotence). This medicine causes an erection because it increases the blood flow to the penis.

Alprostadil injection should not be used as a sexual aid by men who do not have erectile dysfunction. If the medicine is not used properly, permanent damage to the penis and loss of the ability to have erections could result.

Alprostadil is used alone or with medical tests to help diagnose erectile dysfunction that may be caused by nerve or blood vessel problems in the penis.

Alprostadil is available only with your doctor's prescription, in the following dosage forms:

Intraurethral
- Suppositories (U.S.)

Parenteral
- Injection (U.S. and Canada)

Before Using This Medicine

In deciding to use a medicine, the risks of using the medicine must be weighed against the good it will do. This is

a decision you and your doctor will make. For alprostadil, the following should be considered:

Allergies—Tell your doctor if you have ever had any unusual or allergic reaction to alprostadil. Also tell your health care professional if you are allergic to any other substances, such as foods, preservatives, or dyes.

Older adults—This medicine has been tested and has not been shown to cause different side effects or problems in older people than it does in younger adults.

Other medicines—Although certain medicines should not be used together at all, in other cases two different medicines may be used together even if an interaction might occur. In these cases, your doctor may want to change the dose, or other precautions may be necessary. Tell your health care professional if you are taking any other prescription or nonprescription (over-the-counter [OTC]) medicine.

Other medical problems—The presence of other medical problems may affect the use of alprostadil. Make sure you tell your doctor if you have any other medical problems, especially:

- Abnormal penis, including curved penis and birth defects of the penis—Chance of problems occurring may be increased
- Bleeding problems—Chance of bleeding at the place of injection may be increased
- Infection of penis or
- Red or itchy (inflamed) penis—Conditions may worsen with the use of alprostadil suppositories. Also, local skin problems and minor bleeding from inserting the suppository may occur
- Conditions causing thickened blood or slower blood flow, including leukemia; multiple myeloma (tumors of the bone marrow); polycythemia, sickle cell disease, or thrombocythemia (blood problems) or
- Priapism (history of)—Patients with these conditions have an increased risk of priapism (erection lasting longer than 6 hours) while using alprostadil

Proper Use of This Medicine

Special patient directions come with the suppositories and some of the injection medicines. *Read the directions carefully before using the medicine.*

For the injections—

These are several alprostadil products that can be injected. Although the injection method is the same, the mixing procedures are different. *Be sure you know which of these products you will be using and the proper way to mix the injection.*

- One product called Alprostadil for Injection (brand names *Caverject* and *Edex*) is available as a powder in an injection bottle (vial). *Caverject* must be mixed with a solution called Bacteriostatic Water for Injection USP. *Edex* must be mixed with a solution called Sodium Chloride Injection USP. The solution for mixing comes with your product and may be already loaded into a syringe or contained in another injection bottle (vial).
- Another product is called Alprostadil Injection (brand names *Prostin VR Pediatric* and *Prostin VR*). Although the medicine is already in solution, it is much too strong to be injected into the penis. The solution must be mixed (diluted) with another liquid that is sold as a separate prescription, called 0.9% Sodium Chloride Injection USP. In most cases, a pharmacist will make this solution for you, giving you the proper strength that you need. Check with your doctor or pharmacist to make sure the solution has been diluted before using it.

It is important to follow several steps to prepare your alprostadil injection correctly. Before drawing up the medicine into the syringe:

- Wash your hands with soap and water.
- Set the bottles on a clean surface. Wipe the top of the injection bottles with an alcohol swab. *Do not wipe the needle.* Throw away the alcohol swab.
- You may need to attach the needle to the syringe. Do not take the cap off yet.

How to mix Caverject:

- If the syringe already contains the Bacteriostatic Water for Injection USP, then you need only add the plunger to the syringe. To do this:
  —Pick up the rod-like plunger and place it within the barrel of the syringe until it touches the rubber piece. Gently screw the plunger into the rubber piece until it seems secure. Do not use a lot of force.

  —Hold the syringe by the barrel (not the plunger) and take the cap off the needle.

  —You are now ready to mix the water and the powder. Skip to the directions under the title, "*To mix the water and powder.*"
- If the syringe does not already contain the Bacteriostatic Water for Injection USP, you must withdraw 1 milliliter (mL) of it from the bottle provided. To do this:
  —Pick up the syringe and take the cap off the needle.

  —Pull the plunger back to the 1-mL mark on the syringe. This pulls air into the syringe. Insert the needle into rubber top of the bottle while it is upright and inject the 1 mL of air into the bottle.

  —Turn the bottle upside down using one hand. Be sure the tip of the needle is covered by solution.

  —With your other hand, pull the plunger back slowly to withdraw 1 mL of solution into the syringe. Remove the needle and skip to the directions under the title, "*To mix the water and powder.*"
- *To mix the water and powder:*
  —Insert the needle into the bottle of alprostadil and inject 1 milliliter of Bacteriostatic Water for Injection USP from your syringe into the bottle of alprostadil.

  —Remove the needle from the bottle, holding the barrel of the syringe.

—Gently swirl the bottle to mix the powder into the solution, turning it upside down to wet all the powder in the bottle.

—Follow the directions below, "*How to draw your dose into the syringe.*"

How to mix Edex:

- The syringe already contains the Sodium Chloride Injection USP. You need only attach the needle to the syringe and add the plunger. To do this:

  —Remove the needle from its package. Do not remove the needle cap. Gently screw the needle into place on the syringe tip.

  —Pick up the rod-like plunger and place it within the barrel of the syringe until it touches the rubber piece. Gently screw the plunger into the rubber piece until it seems secure. Do not use a lot of force.

  —Hold the syringe by the barrel (not the plunger) and take the cap off the needle.

  —You are now ready to mix the Sodium Chloride Injection USP and the powder.

  —Insert the needle into the bottle of alprostadil and inject 1.2 milliliters of the Sodium Chloride Injection USP from your syringe into the bottle of alprostadil.

  —Remove the needle from the bottle, holding the barrel of the syringe.

  —Gently swirl the bottle to mix the powder into the solution, turning it upside down to wet all the powder in the bottle.

  —Follow the directions below, "*How to draw your dose into the syringe.*"

How to mix Prostin VR or Prostin VR Pediatric:

- You will need to get exact mixing instructions from your doctor or pharmacist if you are given two solutions to be mixed. Follow them carefully, asking the pharmacist or doctor any questions that you might have before injecting the medicine.
- After you or the pharmacist has mixed these solutions, follow the directions below, "*How to draw your dose into the syringe.*"

How to draw your dose into the syringe (for all injection products):

- Check the solution to make sure it is clear. *Do not use the mixture if you can see anything solid in the solution or if the solution is cloudy or colored.*
- After the alprostadil solution is mixed and the needle is inserted into the alprostadil bottle, turn the bottle with the syringe as a unit upside down in one hand. Be sure the tip of the needle is covered by the solution. With your other hand, pull the plunger back slowly to draw the correct dose of the medicine into the syringe.
- Hold the syringe with the measuring scale at eye level to see that the proper dose is withdrawn and to check for air bubbles. To remove air bubbles, tap gently on the measuring scale of the syringe to move any bubbles to the top of the syringe near the needle.
- If your dose measures too low in the syringe, withdraw more solution from the bottle. If there is too much medicine in the syringe, put some back into the bottle. Then check your dose again.
- Remove the needle from the bottle, holding the barrel of the syringe, not the plunger.
- Place the cover back on the needle. You are now ready to inject your dose. Follow the directions below, "*How to give the alprostadil injection.*"

How to give the alprostadil injection:

- Choose a spot on your penis as directed by your doctor where you will give the injection.
- Clean the injection site with alcohol. Sitting upright or slightly reclined, hold your penis against the side of your thigh so that it cannot move.
- Remove the cover from the needle and hold the needle at a 90-degreee angle to the place of injection.
- Insert the needle until almost all of the metal part of the needle is inserted into the penis.
- Do not inject the medicine just under the surface of the skin, at the top or head of the penis, or at the base of the penis near the scrotum or testes. Avoid injecting the medicine into blood vessels that you can see.
- Press the plunger down slowly, taking 5 to 10 seconds to release the dose into the penis.
- The injection is usually not painful. If the injection is very painful or if you notice bruising or swelling at the place of injection, that means you are injecting the medicine under the skin. Stop, withdraw the needle, and reposition it properly before continuing with the injection.
- Remove the needle and recap it.
- After you have completed the injection, put pressure on the place of injection for about 5 minutes or until any bleeding stops. This will prevent bruising. Then massage your penis as instructed by your doctor. This helps the medicine spread to all parts of the penis, so that the medicine will work better.

Choose a different place of injection each time you use the medicine to prevent skin problems. This includes switching the place of injection from the right side of the penis for one injection to the left side for the next injection.

After a single-use injection is mixed, the medicine must be used immediately. Throw away any unused mixture in the syringe. It cannot be stored for a later injection.

Do not reuse your needles.

How to throw away the syringes and bottles safely:

Dispose of your materials properly. *Caverject* comes in a plastic case that can be permanently locked with the red locking device that is included with the packaging. When the case label is removed, you can see a hole in the center of the case. The red locking device can be inserted and, by firmly pressing it down with your thumb, you will permanently lock the case. The locked case is safe to be thrown away.

If you do not have the plastic case or are using *Prostin VR* or *Prostin VR Pediatric* injection, unscrew the needle from the barrel of the syringe. Then bend, break, or cut the needle into two pieces with wire cutters. The pieces can be placed in a heavy plastic container, such as a bleach container, and thrown away. Or you may give them to a health care professional to throw away. If you have any questions about disposing of the syringe and needles, ask your health care professional.

For suppositories—

Before inserting the suppository, you should urinate. The small amount of urine normally left in your urethra will help dissolve the suppository after it is inserted.

How to insert suppositories:

- Remove the delivery device containing the suppository from the foil. Remove the cap from the applicator stem.
- Stretch your penis upward to extend its length, pressing your penis top and bottom. Gently insert the delivery stem up to its collar into your urethra (located at the top of the penis). *If you have pain or a pulling feeling in the penis, withdraw the device and start again.*
- Press the button down slowly as far as it will go. This releases the suppository into the urethra. After holding the delivery device within your penis still for 5 seconds, carefully rock the penis and delivery device as a unit from side to side. This helps remove the suppository from the device.
- Remove the delivery device while your penis is upright. Look at the device to make sure that the suppository was completely released.
- Repeat the process if a part of the suppository remains in the device.
- After the suppository is completely released, roll your penis between your hands for 10 seconds. This helps to dissolve the suppository. If you feel any stinging, continue this motion to help stop it.
- Sitting, standing, or walking for 10 minutes while an erection is developing helps increase the blood flow to your penis to gain a proper erection.

How to throw away the suppository delivery device safely:

- Replace the cap on the delivery device. After storing it in the foil, fold and throw away.

For injections or suppositories—

This medicine usually begins to work in about 5 to 10 minutes. You should attempt intercourse within 10 to 30 minutes after using the medicine. An erection may continue after ejaculation.

Dosing—The dose of alprostadil will be different for different patients. *Follow your doctor's orders or the directions on the label.* The following information includes only the average doses of alprostadil. *If your dose is different, do not change it* unless your doctor tells you to do so.

- For the treatment of erectile dysfunction:
  - —For *injection* dosage form:
    - Adults—1.25 to 60 micrograms (mcg) as a single dose once a day. Your exact dose will be determined by your doctor. Inject this medicine very slowly into your penis as shown to you by your doctor ten to thirty minutes before intercourse. Allow five to ten seconds to completely inject the dose. Do not inject more than one dose within twenty-four hours. Also, do not use this medicine for more than two days in a row or more than three times a week.
  - —For *suppository* dosage form:
    - Adults—125, 250, 500, or 1000 mcg as a single dose once a day. Your exact dose will be determined by your doctor. Insert this medicine into the urethra of your penis as shown to you by your doctor ten to thirty minutes before intercourse. Do not insert more than two doses within twenty-four hours.

Storage—To store this medicine:

- Keep out of the reach of children.
- Refrigerate Alprostadil Injection USP. Keep the medicine from freezing.
- Alprostadil for Injection while in the powder form can be stored at room temperature (between 15 and 25°C or 59 and 77°F) for 3 months. After it is mixed, the solution must be used immediately.
- Refrigerate alprostadil suppositories. Keep from freezing. They may be stored at room temperature for 14 days.
- Do not keep outdated medicine or medicine no longer needed. Be sure that any discarded medicine is out of the reach of children.

Precautions While Using This Medicine

Do not use alprostadil if you have a penile implant unless advised by your doctor.

If using the alprostadil suppository, use a condom when having sexual intercourse with a pregnant female. Although harm to the fetus is unlikely, using a condom will protect the fetus from exposure to this medicine. *If a woman can become pregnant, use of contraceptive methods is recommended* because the effects of this medicine on early pregnancy are not known.

Use alprostadil injection exactly as directed by your doctor. Do not use more of it and do not use it more often than your doctor ordered. If too much is used, the erection lasts too long and does not reverse when it should. This condition is called priapism. If the erection is not reversed, the blood supply to the penis may be cut off and permanent damage may occur.

Contact your doctor immediately if the erection lasts longer than 4 hours or if it becomes painful. This may be a sign of priapism and must be treated right away to prevent permanent damage.

If you notice bleeding at the place where you injected the medicine, put pressure on the spot until the bleeding stops.

If it doesn't stop within 10 minutes, check with your doctor.

Side Effects of This Medicine

Along with its needed effects, a medicine may cause some unwanted effects. Although not all of these side effects may occur, if they do occur they may need medical attention.

Check with your doctor immediately if the following side effects occur:

Rare

Curving of penis with pain during erection; erection continuing for 4 to 6 hours; erection continuing longer than 6 hours with severe and continuing pain of the penis; swelling in or pain of the testes

Symptoms of too much medicine being absorbed into the body

Dizziness; faintness; pelvic pain; flu-like symptoms

Other side effects may occur that usually do not need medical attention. These side effects may go away during treatment as your body adjusts to the medicine. However, check with your doctor if any of the following side effects continue or are bothersome:

More common

Bleeding at place of injection, short-term; mild bleeding or spotting from urethra (suppository only); pain at place of injection; painful erection; stinging of urethra (suppository only)

Rare

Bruising or clotted blood in penis at place of injection, usually caused by an incorrect injection

Female partners may experience itching or stinging of vagina when you first begin using the alprostadil suppository. These side effects may not be caused from the medicine but may result if female partner has not had frequent or recent sexual intercourse.

Other side effects not listed above may also occur in some patients. If you notice any other effects, check with your doctor.

Revised: 08/18/97

ALTRETAMINE Systemic

Some commonly used brand names are:

In the U.S.

Hexalen

In Canada

Hexastat

Another commonly used name is hexamethylmelamine.

Description

Altretamine (al-TRET-a-meen) belongs to the group of medicines called antineoplastics. It is used to treat cancer of the ovaries.

Altretamine interferes with the growth of cancer cells, which are eventually destroyed. Since the growth of normal body cells may also be affected by altretamine, other effects will also occur. Some of these may be serious and must be reported to your doctor. Other effects may not be serious but may cause concern. Some effects may not occur for months or years after the medicine is used.

Before you begin treatment with altretamine, you and your doctor should talk about the good this medicine will do as well as the risks of using it.

Altretamine is available only with your doctor's prescription in the following dosage form:

Oral

- Capsules (U.S. and Canada)

Before Using This Medicine

In deciding to use a medicine, the risks of taking the medicine must be weighed against the good it will do. This is a decision you and your doctor will make. For altretamine, the following should be considered:

Allergies—Tell your doctor if you have ever had any unusual or allergic reaction to altretamine.

Pregnancy—There is a chance that this medicine may cause birth defects if either the male or female is taking it at the time of conception or if it is taken during pregnancy. In addition, many cancer medicines may cause sterility which could be permanent. Although sterility has not been reported with this medicine, it does occur in animals and the possibility should be kept in mind.

Be sure that you have discussed this with your doctor before taking this medicine. It is best to use some kind of birth control while you are taking altretamine. Tell your doctor right away if you think you have become pregnant while taking altretamine.

Breast-feeding—Because altretamine may cause serious side effects, breast-feeding is generally not recommended while you are taking it.

Children—There is no specific information comparing use of altretamine in children with use in other age groups.

Older adults—Many medicines have not been studied specifically in older people. Therefore, it may not be known whether they work exactly the same way they do in younger adults. Although there is no specific information comparing use of altretamine in the elderly with use in other age groups, this medicine is not expected to cause different side effects or problems in older people than it does in younger adults.

Other medicines—Although certain medicines should not be used together at all, in other cases two different medicines may be used together even if an interaction might occur. In these cases, your doctor may want to change the dose, or other precautions may be necessary. When you are taking altretamine, it is especially important that your

health care professional know if you are taking any of the following:

- Amphotericin B by injection (e.g., Fungizone) or
- Antithyroid agents (medicine for overactive thyroid) or
- Azathioprine (e.g., Imuran) or
- Chloramphenicol (e.g., Chloromycetin) or
- Colchicine or
- Flucytosine (e.g., Ancobon) or
- Ganciclovir (e.g., Cytovene) or
- Interferon (e.g., Intron A, Roferon-A) or
- Plicamycin (e.g., Mithracin) or
- Zidovudine (e.g., AZT, Retrovir) or
- If you have ever been treated with radiation or cancer medicines—Altretamine may increase the effects of these medicines or radiation therapy on the blood
- Monoamine oxidase (MAO) inhibitors (furazolidone [e.g., Furoxone], isocarboxazid [e.g., Marplan], phenelzine [e.g., Nardil], procarbazine [e.g., Matulane], selegiline [e.g., Eldepryl], tranylcypromine [e.g., Parnate])—Taking altretamine while you are taking MAO inhibitors may cause a severe drop in blood pressure

Other medical problems—The presence of other medical problems may affect the use of altretamine. Make sure you tell your doctor if you have any other medical problems, especially:

- Chickenpox (including recent exposure) or
- Herpes zoster (shingles)—Risk of severe disease affecting other parts of the body
- Nervous system problems—May be worsened by altretamine
- Infection—Altretamine may decrease your body's ability to fight infection
- Kidney disease—Effects of altretamine may be increased because of slower removal from the body
- Liver disease—Effects may be changed because altretamine is activated and cleared from the body by the liver

Proper Use of This Medicine

This medicine often causes nausea and vomiting. However, it is very important that you continue to receive the medicine even if you begin to feel ill. Taking this medicine after meals will lessen stomach upset. Ask your health care professional for other ways to lessen these effects.

Dosing—The dose of altretamine will be different for different patients. The dose that is used may depend on a number of things, including what the medicine is being used for, the patient's size, and whether or not other medicines are also being taken. *If you are taking altretamine at home, follow your doctor's orders or the directions on the label.* If you have any questions about the proper dose of altretamine, ask your doctor.

Missed dose—If you miss a dose of this medicine, take it as soon as possible. However, if it is almost time for your next dose, skip the missed dose and go back to your regular dosing schedule. Do not double doses.

Storage—To store this medicine:

- Keep out of the reach of children.
- Store away from heat and direct light.
- Do not store in the bathroom, near the kitchen sink, or in other damp places. Heat or moisture may cause the medicine to break down.
- Do not keep outdated medicine or medicine no longer needed. Be sure that any discarded medicine is out of the reach of children.

Precautions While Using This Medicine

It is very important that your doctor check your progress at regular visits to make sure that this medicine is working properly and to check for unwanted effects.

While you are being treated with altretamine, and after you stop treatment with it, *do not have any immunizations (vaccinations) without your doctor's approval.* Altretamine may lower your body's resistance and there is a chance you might get the infection the immunization is meant to prevent. In addition, other persons living in your household should not take oral polio vaccine since there is a chance they could pass the polio virus on to you. Also, avoid persons who have taken oral polio vaccine. Do not get close to them and do not stay in the same room with them for very long. If you cannot take these precautions, you should consider wearing a protective face mask that covers the nose and mouth.

Altretamine can temporarily lower the number of white blood cells in your blood, increasing the chance of getting an infection. It can also lower the number of platelets, which are necessary for proper blood clotting. If this occurs, there are certain precautions you can take, especially when your blood count is low, to reduce the risk of infection or bleeding:

- If you can, avoid people with infections. *Check with your doctor immediately* if you think you are getting an infection or if you get a fever or chills, cough or hoarseness, lower back or side pain, or painful or difficult urination.
- *Check with your doctor immediately* if you notice any unusual bleeding or bruising; black, tarry stools; blood in urine or stools; or pinpoint red spots on your skin.
- Be careful when using a regular toothbrush, dental floss, or toothpick. Your medical doctor, dentist, or nurse may recommend other ways to clean your teeth and gums. Check with your medical doctor before having any dental work done.
- Do not touch your eyes or the inside of your nose unless you have just washed your hands and have not touched anything else in the meantime.
- Be careful not to cut yourself when you are using sharp objects such as a safety razor or fingernail or toenail cutters.
- Avoid contact sports or other situations where bruising or injury could occur.

Side Effects of This Medicine

Along with its needed effects, a medicine may cause some unwanted effects. Although not all of these side effects may occur, if they do occur they may need medical attention.

Also, because of the way these medicines act on the body, there is a chance that they might cause other unwanted effects that may not occur until months or years after the medicine is used. These delayed effects may include certain types of cancer, such as leukemia. Discuss these possible effects with your doctor.

Check with your doctor or nurse immediately if any of the following side effects occur:

Less common or rare

Black, tarry stools; blood in urine or stools; cough or hoarseness; fever or chills; lower back or side pain; painful or difficult urination; pinpoint red spots on skin; unusual bleeding or bruising; unusual tiredness

Check with your doctor as soon as possible if any of the following side effects occur:

More common

Anxiety; clumsiness; confusion; dizziness; mental depression; numbness in arms or legs; weakness

Rare

Convulsions (seizures); skin rash or itching

Other side effects may occur that usually do not need medical attention. These side effects may go away during treatment as your body adjusts to the medicine. Also, your health care professional may be able to tell you about ways to prevent or reduce some of these side effects. Check with your doctor if any of the following side effects continue or are bothersome or if you have any questions about them:

More common

Nausea and vomiting

Less common

Diarrhea; loss of appetite; stomach cramps

Other side effects not listed above may also occur in some patients. If you notice any other effects, check with your doctor.

Revised: 07/23/92
Interim revision: 04/29/94

AMANTADINE Systemic

Some commonly used brand names are:

In the U.S.—

Symadine
Symmetrel

Generic name product may also be available.

In Canada—

Symmetrel

Description

Amantadine (a-MAN-ta-deen) is an antiviral. It is used to prevent or treat certain influenza (flu) infections (type A). It may be given alone or along with flu shots. Amantadine will not work for colds, other types of flu, or other virus infections.

Amantadine also is an antidyskinetic. It is used to treat Parkinson's disease, sometimes called paralysis agitans or shaking palsy. It may be given alone or with other medicines for Parkinson's disease. By improving muscle control and reducing stiffness, this medicine allows more normal movements of the body as the disease symptoms are reduced. Amantadine is also used to treat stiffness and shaking caused by certain medicines used to treat nervous, mental, and emotional conditions.

Amantadine may be used for other conditions as determined by your doctor.

Amantadine is available only with your doctor's prescription, in the following dosage forms:

Oral

- Capsules (U.S. and Canada)
- Syrup (U.S. and Canada)

Before Using This Medicine

In deciding to use a medicine, the risks of taking the medicine must be weighed against the good it will do. This is a decision you and your doctor will make. For amantadine, the following should be considered:

Allergies—Tell your doctor if you have ever had any unusual or allergic reaction to amantadine. Also tell your health care professional if you are allergic to any other substances, such as foods, preservatives, or dyes.

Pregnancy—Studies have not been done in humans. However, studies in some animals have shown that amantadine is harmful to the fetus and causes birth defects.

Breast-feeding—Amantadine passes into breast milk. However, the effects of amantadine in newborn babies and infants are not known.

Children—This medicine has been tested in children over one year of age and has not been shown to cause different side effects or problems in these children than it does in adults. There is no specific information comparing the use of amantadine in children under one year of age with use in other age groups.

Older adults—Elderly people are especially sensitive to the effects of amantadine. Confusion, difficult urination, blurred vision, constipation, and dry mouth, nose, and throat may be especially likely to occur.

Other medicines—Although certain medicines should not be used together at all, in other cases two different medicines may be used together even if an interaction might occur. In these cases, your doctor may want to change the dose, or other precautions may be necessary. When you are taking amantadine, it is especially important that your health care professional know if you are taking any of the following:

- Amphetamines or
- Appetite suppressants (diet pills), except fenfluramine (e.g., Pondimin), or
- Caffeine (e.g., NoDoz) or

- Chlophedianol (e.g., Ulone) or
- Cocaine or
- Medicine for asthma or other breathing problems or
- Medicine for colds, sinus problems, or hay fever or other allergies (including nose drops or sprays) or
- Methylphenidate (e.g., Ritalin) or
- Nabilone (e.g., Cesamet) or
- Pemoline (e.g., Cylert)—The use of amantadine with these medicines may increase the chance of unwanted effects such as nervousness, irritability, trouble in sleeping, and possibly seizures or irregular heartbeat
- Anticholinergics (medicine for abdominal or stomach spasms or cramps)—The use of amantadine with these medicines may increase the chance of unwanted effects such as blurred vision, dryness of the mouth, confusion, hallucinations, and nightmares

Other medical problems—The presence of other medical problems may affect the use of amantadine. Make sure you tell your doctor if you have any other medical problems, especially:

- Eczema (recurring)—Amantadine may cause or worsen eczema
- Epilepsy or other seizures (history of)—Amantadine may increase the frequency of convulsions (seizures) in patients with a seizure disorder
- Heart disease or other circulation problems or
- Swelling of feet and ankles—Amantadine may increase the chance of swelling of the feet and ankles, and may worsen heart disease or circulation problems
- Kidney disease—Amantadine is removed from the body by the kidneys; patients with kidney disease will need to receive a lower dose of amantadine
- Mental or emotional illness—Higher doses of amantadine may cause confusion, hallucinations, and nightmares

Proper Use of This Medicine

For patients *taking amantadine to prevent or treat flu infections:*

- Talk to your doctor about the possibility of getting a flu shot if you have not had one yet.
- This medicine is *best taken before exposure, or as soon as possible after exposure,* to people who have the flu.
- To help keep yourself from getting the flu, *keep taking this medicine for the full time of treatment.* Or if you already have the flu, continue taking this medicine for the full time of treatment even if you begin to feel better after a few days. This will help to clear up your infection completely. If you stop taking this medicine too soon, your symptoms may return. This medicine should be taken for at least 2 days after all your flu symptoms have disappeared.
- This medicine works best when there is a constant amount in the blood. *To help keep the amount constant, do not miss any doses. Also, it is best to take the doses at evenly spaced times day and night.* For example, if you are to take 2 doses a day, the doses should be spaced about 12 hours apart. If this interferes with your sleep or other daily activities, or if you need help in planning the best times to take your medicine, check with your health care professional.
- If you are using the oral liquid form of amantadine, use a specially marked measuring spoon or other device to measure each dose accurately. The average household teaspoon may not hold the right amount of liquid.

For patients *taking amantadine for Parkinson's disease or movement problems* caused by certain medicines used to treat nervous, mental, and emotional conditions:

- *Take this medicine exactly as directed by your doctor.* Do not miss any doses and do not take more medicine than your doctor ordered.
- Improvement in the symptoms of Parkinson's disease usually occurs in about 2 days. However, in some patients this medicine must be taken for up to 2 weeks before full benefit is seen.

Dosing—The dose of amantadine will be different for different patients. *Follow your doctor's orders or the directions on the label.* The following information includes only the average doses of amantadine. Your dose may be different if you have kidney disease. *If your dose is different, do not change it* unless your doctor tells you to do so.

- The number of capsules or teaspoonfuls of suspension that you take depends on the strength of the medicine. Also, *the number of doses you take each day, the time allowed between doses, and the length of time you take the medicine depend on the medical problem for which you are taking amantadine.*
- For the *treatment or prevention of flu:*
  - —Older adults: 100 milligrams once a day.
  - —Adults and children 12 years of age and older: 200 milligrams once a day, or 100 milligrams two times a day.
  - —Children 9 to 12 years of age: 100 milligrams two times a day.
  - —Children 1 to 9 years of age: Dose is based on body weight and must be determined by the doctor.
- For the *treatment of Parkinson's disease or movement problems:*
  - —Older adults: 100 milligrams once a day to start. The dose may be increased slowly over time, if needed.
  - —Adults: 100 milligrams one or two times a day.
  - —Children: Dose has not been determined.

Missed dose—If you miss a dose of this medicine, take it as soon as possible. This will help to keep a constant amount of medicine in the blood. However, if it is almost time for your next dose, skip the missed dose and go back to your regular dosing schedule. Do not double doses.

Storage—To store this medicine:

- Keep out of the reach of children.
- Store away from heat and direct light.
- Do not store the capsule form of this medicine in the bathroom, near the kitchen sink, or in other damp places. Heat or moisture may cause the medicine to break down.
- Keep the oral liquid form of this medicine from freezing.

- Do not keep outdated medicine or medicine no longer needed. Be sure that any discarded medicine is out of the reach of children.

Precautions While Using This Medicine

Drinking alcoholic beverages while taking this medicine may cause increased side effects such as circulation problems, dizziness, lightheadedness, fainting, or confusion. Therefore, *do not drink alcoholic beverages while you are taking this medicine.*

This medicine may cause some people to become dizzy, confused, or lightheaded, or to have blurred vision or trouble concentrating. *Make sure you know how you react to this medicine before you drive, use machines, or do anything else that could be dangerous if you are dizzy or are not alert or able to see well.* If these reactions are especially bothersome, check with your doctor.

Getting up suddenly from a lying or sitting position may also be a problem because of the dizziness, lightheadedness, or fainting that may be caused by this medicine. Getting up slowly may help. If this problem continues or gets worse, check with your doctor.

Amantadine may cause dryness of the mouth, nose, and throat. For temporary relief of mouth dryness, use sugarless candy or gum, melt bits of ice in your mouth, or use a saliva substitute. However, if your mouth continues to feel dry for more than 2 weeks, check with your doctor or dentist. Continuing dryness of the mouth may increase the chance of dental disease, including tooth decay, gum disease, and fungus infections.

This medicine may cause purplish red, net-like, blotchy spots on the skin. This problem occurs more often in females and usually occurs on the legs and/or feet after this medicine has been taken regularly for a month or more. Although the blotchy spots may remain as long as you are taking this medicine, they usually go away gradually within 2 to 12 weeks after you stop taking the medicine. If you have any questions about this, check with your doctor.

For patients *taking amantadine to prevent or treat flu infections:*

- If your symptoms do not improve within a few days, or if they become worse, check with your doctor.

For patients *taking amantadine for Parkinson's disease or movement problems* caused by certain medicines used to treat nervous, mental, and emotional conditions:

- *Patients with Parkinson's disease must be careful not to overdo physical activities as their condition improves and body movements become easier* since injuries resulting from falls may occur. Such activities must be gradually increased to give your body time to adjust to changing balance, circulation, and coordination.
- Some patients may notice that this medicine gradually loses its effect while they are taking it regularly for a few months. If you notice this, check with your doctor. Your doctor may want to adjust the dose or stop the medicine for a while and then restart it to restore its effect.
- *Do not suddenly stop taking this medicine without first checking with your doctor* since your Parkinson's disease may get worse very quickly. Your doctor may want you to reduce your dose gradually before stopping the medicine completely.

Side Effects of This Medicine

Along with its needed effects, a medicine may cause some unwanted effects. Although not all of these side effects may occur, if they do occur they may need medical attention.

Check with your doctor immediately if any of the following side effects occur:

Less common

Blurred vision; confusion (especially in elderly patients); difficult urination (especially in elderly patients); fainting; hallucinations (seeing, hearing, or feeling things that are not there)

Rare

Convulsions (seizures); decreased vision or any change in vision; difficulty in coordination; irritation and swelling of the eye; mental depression; skin rash; swelling of feet or lower legs; unexplained shortness of breath

Other side effects may occur that usually do not need medical attention. These side effects may go away during treatment as your body adjusts to the medicine. However, check with your doctor if any of the following side effects continue or are bothersome:

More common

Difficulty concentrating; dizziness or lightheadedness; headache; irritability; loss of appetite; nausea; nervousness; purplish red, net-like, blotchy spots on skin; trouble in sleeping or nightmares

Less common or rare

Constipation; dryness of the mouth, nose, and throat; vomiting

Other side effects not listed above may also occur in some patients. If you notice any other effects, check with your doctor.

Additional Information

Once a medicine has been approved for marketing for a certain use, experience may show that it is also useful for other medical problems. Although this use is not included in product labeling, amantadine is used in certain patients with the following medical condition:

- Unusual tiredness or weakness associated with multiple sclerosis

Other than the above information, there is no additional information relating to proper use, precautions, or side effects for this use.

Revised: 02/23/93

AMINOBENZOATE POTASSIUM Systemic

Some commonly used brand names in the U.S. and Canada are Potaba, Potaba Envules, and Potaba Powder.

Other commonly used names are KPAB, potassium aminobenzoate, and potassium para-aminobenzoate.

Description

Aminobenzoate potassium (a-mee-noe-BEN-zoe-ate poe-TAS-ee-um) is used to treat fibrosis, a condition in which the skin and underlying tissues tighten and become less flexible. This condition occurs in such diseases as dermatomyositis, morphea, Peyronie's disease, scleroderma, and linear scleroderma.

Aminobenzoate potassium is also used to treat a certain type of inflammation (nonsuppurative inflammation) that occurs in such diseases as dermatomyositis, pemphigus, and Peyronie's disease.

This medicine is available only with your doctor's prescription in the following dosage forms:

Oral
- Capsules (U.S. and Canada)
- Powder for oral solution (U.S. and Canada)
- Tablets (U.S. and Canada)

Before Using This Medicine

In deciding to use a medicine, the risks of taking the medicine must be weighed against the good it will do. This is a decision you and your doctor will make. For aminobenzoate potassium, the following should be considered:

Allergies—Tell your doctor if you have ever had any unusual or allergic reaction to aminobenzoate potassium or aminobenzoic acid (PABA). Also tell your health care professional if you are allergic to any other substances, such as foods, preservatives, or dyes.

Diet—Make certain your health care professional knows if you are on any special diet, such as a low-sodium or low-sugar diet.

Pregnancy—Studies on effects in pregnancy have not been done in either humans or animals.

Breast-feeding—Aminobenzoate potassium has not been reported to cause problems in nursing babies.

Children—Although there is no specific information comparing use of aminobenzoate potassium in children with use in other age groups, this medicine is not expected to cause different side effects or problems in children than it does in adults.

Older adults—Elderly people may be more sensitive to certain symptoms of the low blood sugar side effect. These symptoms include confusion, difficulty in concentration, and headache. In addition, these symptoms may be harder to detect in elderly persons than in younger adults. This may increase the chance of problems during treatment with this medicine.

Other medicines—Although certain medicines should not be used together at all, in other cases two different medicines may be used together even if an interaction might occur. In these cases, your doctor may want to change the dose, or other precautions may be necessary. When you are taking aminobenzoate potassium, it is especially important that your health care professional know if you are taking any of the following:

- Aminosalicylates or
- Sulfonamides (sulfa medicine)—Aminobenzoate potassium may decrease the effects of these medicines

Other medical problems—The presence of other medical problems may affect the use of aminobenzoate potassium. Make sure you tell your doctor if you have any other medical problems, especially:

- Diabetes mellitus (sugar diabetes) or
- Hypoglycemia (low blood sugar)—The risk of the medicine causing hypoglycemia (low blood sugar) may be increased
- Kidney disease—Aminobenzoate potassium is removed from the body by the kidneys; higher blood levels of the medicine may occur if kidney disease is present, which may increase the chance of side effects

Proper Use of This Medicine

Take this medicine with meals or snacks to lessen the possibility of stomach upset. If stomach upset continues, check with your doctor.

For patients taking the *capsule or tablet form* of aminobenzoate potassium:

- Take each dose with a full glass (8 ounces) of water or milk to lessen the possibility of stomach upset.
- Patients using the tablets should dissolve them in water before taking. This will help lessen the possibility of stomach upset.

For patients using the *powder form* of this medicine:

- This medicine should never be taken in its dry form. Instead, always mix it with water or citrus juice, as directed.
- To cover up the taste of aminobenzoate potassium, you may dissolve the powder in citrus drinks instead of in water. However, if you do dissolve the powder in water, drinking a citrus juice or a carbonated beverage immediately after each dose of medicine will also help cover up the taste.
- The flavor of this medicine is improved if the solution is chilled before you take it.
- For patients using the *two-gram individual packets of powder*:

  —Dissolve one packet (2 grams) of aminobenzoate potassium in a full glass (8 ounces) of water or citrus juice.

  —Stir well to dissolve the powder.
- For patients using the *bulk powder form* of this medicine:

  —Use a specially marked measuring spoon or other device to measure out the correct amount of medicine. Your health care professional can help you with this.

—To make a 10-percent solution of this medicine:
- Choose a container that is resistant to light, such as an amber glass container, a metal container, or a plastic container that you cannot see through. Make sure the container is large enough to measure one liter (approximately one quart).
- Place 100 grams (approximately 3 ounces) of aminobenzoate potassium powder in the container.
- Add enough water or citrus juice to make one liter (approximately one quart) of solution and stir well.
- Store the solution in a container that is resistant to light, such as an amber glass container, a metal container, or a plastic container that you cannot see through.
- Keep the solution refrigerated. Stir well before pouring each dose. Discard the unused portion after one week.

For this medicine to be effective, it must be taken every day as ordered by your doctor. It may take 3 or more months before you begin to see an improvement in your condition.

Dosing—The dose of aminobenzoate potassium will be different for different patients. *Follow your doctor's orders or the directions on the label.* The following information includes only the average dose of aminobenzoate potassium. *If your dose is different, do not change it* unless your doctor tells you to do so.

- For *oral* dosage forms (capsules, powder for oral solution, and tablets):
  - —For fibrosis:
    - Adults—12 grams a day, divided into four to six doses and taken with meals or snacks.
    - Children—Dose is based on body weight and must be determined by your doctor. The usual dose is 220 milligrams (mg) per kilogram (kg) (100 mg per pound) of body weight a day. This is divided into four to six doses and taken with meals or snacks.

Missed dose—If you miss a dose of this medicine, take it as soon as possible. However, if it is within 2 hours of your next dose, skip the missed dose and go back to your regular dosing schedule. Do not double doses.

Storage—To store this medicine:
- Keep out of the reach of children.
- Store away from heat and direct light.
- Do not store the medicine in the bathroom, near the kitchen sink, or in other damp places. Heat or moisture may cause the medicine to break down.
- Store the liquid form of this medicine in the refrigerator. However, keep the medicine from freezing. Store the liquid form of this medicine in a container that is resistant to light, such as an amber glass container, a metal container, or a plastic container that you cannot see through.
- Discard the unused portion of the liquid form of this medicine after one week.
- Do not keep outdated medicine or medicine no longer needed. Be sure that any discarded medicine is out of the reach of children.

Precautions While Using This Medicine

While you are taking this medicine, it is important that your doctor check your progress at regular visits.

Check with your doctor right away if you cannot eat normally while taking this medicine because of nausea, loss of appetite, or for any other reason. Taking this medicine when you have not been eating normally for several days may cause low blood sugar (hypoglycemia).

If symptoms of low blood sugar (hypoglycemia) appear, stop taking this medicine, eat or drink something containing sugar, and check with your doctor right away. Good sources of sugar are table sugar mixed in water, sugar cubes, orange juice, corn syrup, or honey. One popular source of sugar is a glassful of orange juice containing 2 or 3 teaspoonfuls of table sugar.
- *Tell someone ahead of time to take you to your doctor or to a hospital right away if you begin to feel that you may pass out. If you do pass out, emergency help should be gotten at once.*
- *Even if you correct the symptoms of low blood sugar by eating or drinking something with sugar, it is very important to call your doctor right away. The effects this medicine has on low blood sugar may last for a few days, and the symptoms may return often during this period of time.*

Side Effects of This Medicine

Along with its needed effects, a medicine may cause some unwanted effects. Although not all of these side effects may occur, if they do occur they may need medical attention.

Check with your doctor as soon as possible if any of the following side effects occur:

Less common or rare
Chills; fever; skin rash; sore throat

Symptoms of low blood sugar
Anxiety; chills; cold sweats; confusion; cool pale skin; difficulty in concentration; drowsiness; excessive hunger; fast heartbeat; headache; nervousness; shakiness; unsteady walk; unusual tiredness or weakness

Other side effects may occur that usually do not need medical attention. These side effects may go away during treatment as your body adjusts to the medicine. However, check with your doctor if either of the following side effects continues or is bothersome:

More common
Loss of appetite; nausea

Other side effects not listed above may also occur in some patients. If you notice any other effects, check with your doctor.

Revised: 07/06/94

AMINOGLUTETHIMIDE Systemic

A commonly used brand name in the U.S. and Canada is Cytadren.

Description

Aminoglutethimide (a-mee-noe-gloo-TETH-i-mide) acts on a part of the body called the adrenal cortex. It affects production of steroids and also has some other effects. Aminoglutethimide is used to treat some kinds of tumors that affect the adrenal cortex. Also, it is sometimes used when the adrenal cortex is overactive without being cancerous.

In addition, aminoglutethimide is sometimes used to treat certain other conditions as determined by your doctor.

Aminoglutethimide is available only with your doctor's prescription, in the following dosage form:

Oral

- Tablets (U.S. and Canada)

Before Using This Medicine

In deciding to use a medicine, the risks of taking the medicine must be weighed against the good it will do. This is a decision you and your doctor will make. For aminoglutethimide, the following should be considered:

Allergies—Tell your doctor if you have ever had any unusual or allergic reaction to glutethimide or aminoglutethimide. Also tell your health care professional if you are allergic to any other substances, such as foods, preservatives, or dyes.

Pregnancy—Aminoglutethimide has been shown to cause birth defects in humans and animals. However, this medicine may be needed in serious diseases or in other situations that threaten the mother's life. Be sure you have discussed this with your doctor before taking this medicine.

Breast-feeding—It is not known whether aminoglutethimide passes into breast milk. However, this medicine has not been reported to cause problems in nursing babies.

Children—There is no specific information comparing use of aminoglutethimide in children with use in other age groups. However, there is a chance that aminoglutethimide could cause premature growth and sexual development in males or development of male features in females.

Older adults—Lack of energy is more likely to occur in the elderly, who are usually more sensitive to the effects of aminoglutethimide.

Other medicines—Although certain medicines should not be used together at all, in other cases two different medicines may be used together even if an interaction might occur. In these cases, your doctor may want to change the dose, or other precautions may be necessary. When you are taking aminoglutethimide it is especially important that your health care professional know if you are taking any of the following:

- Dexamethasone (e.g., Decadron)—Aminoglutethimide increases the rate at which dexamethasone is removed from the body

Other medical problems—The presence of other medical problems may affect the use of aminoglutethimide. Make sure you tell your doctor if you have any other medical problems, especially:

- Chickenpox (including recent exposure) or
- Herpes zoster (shingles)—Risk of severe disease affecting other parts of the body
- Infection—May affect the adrenal cortex. If a steroid supplement is being used, a change in dose may be needed
- Kidney disease or
- Liver disease—Effects of aminoglutethimide may be increased because of slower removal from the body
- Underactive thyroid—Aminoglutethimide can cause underactive thyroid

Proper Use of This Medicine

Take this medicine only as directed by your doctor. Do not take more or less of it, and do not take it more often than your doctor ordered.

This medicine sometimes causes nausea and vomiting. This effect usually goes away or lessens after you have taken the medicine for a while. It is very important that you continue to use this medicine even if you begin to feel ill. Ask your health care provider for ways to lessen these effects. *Do not stop taking this medicine without first checking with your doctor.*

If you vomit shortly after taking a dose of aminoglutethimide, check with your doctor. You will be told whether to take the dose again or to wait until the next scheduled dose.

Dosing—The dose of aminoglutethimide will be different for different patients. The dose that is used may depend on a number of things, including what the medicine is being used for, the patient's weight, and whether or not other medicines are also being taken. *If you are taking aminoglutethimide at home, follow your doctor's orders or the directions on the label.* If you have any questions about the proper dose of aminoglutethimide, ask your doctor.

Missed dose—If you miss a dose of this medicine and remember within 2 to 4 hours of the missed dose, take it as soon as possible. Then go back to your regular dosing schedule. However, if it is almost time for your next dose, skip the missed dose and go back to your regular dosing schedule. Do not double doses.

Storage—To store this medicine:

- Keep out of the reach of children.
- Store away from heat and direct light.
- Do not store in the bathroom, near the kitchen sink, or in other damp places. Heat or moisture may cause the medicine to break down.
- Do not keep outdated medicine or medicine no longer needed. Be sure that any discarded medicine is out of the reach of children.

Precautions While Using This Medicine

It is very important that your doctor check your progress at regular visits to make sure that the medicine is working properly and does not cause unwanted effects.

Your doctor may want you to carry a medical identification card or wear a bracelet stating that you are taking this medicine.

Before you have any kind of surgery (including dental surgery) or emergency treatment, tell the medical doctor or dentist in charge that you are taking this medicine. Because this medicine affects the adrenal gland, extra steroids may be needed.

Check with your doctor right away if you get an injury, infection, or illness of any kind. This medicine may weaken your body's defenses against infection or inflammation.

This medicine may cause some people to become dizzy, drowsy, or less alert than they are normally. *Make sure you know how you react to this medicine before you drive, use machines, or do anything else that could be dangerous if you are dizzy or are not alert.*

Side Effects of This Medicine

Along with its needed effects, a medicine may cause some unwanted effects. Some side effects will have signs or symptoms that you can see or feel. Your doctor may watch for others by doing certain tests. Some of the unwanted effects that may be caused by aminoglutethimide are listed below. Although not all of these side effects may occur, if they do occur they may need medical attention.

Check with your doctor immediately if any of the following side effects occur:

Rare

Black, tarry stools; blood in urine or stools; cough or hoarseness; fever or chills; lower back or side pain; painful or difficult urination; pinpoint red spots on skin; unusual bleeding or bruising; yellow eyes or skin

Check with your doctor as soon as possible if the following side effects occur:

Less common

Darkening of skin; mental depression

Rare

Neck tenderness or swelling

This medicine may also cause the following side effects that your doctor will watch for:

More common

Low red blood cell count; low white blood cell count

Other side effects may occur that usually do not need medical attention. These side effects may go away during treatment as your body adjusts to the medicine. However, check with your health care professional if any of the following side effects continue or are bothersome:

More common

Clumsiness; dizziness or lightheadedness (especially when getting up from a lying or sitting position); drowsiness; lack of energy; loss of appetite; measles-like skin rash or itching on face and/or palms of hands; nausea; uncontrolled eye movements

Less common or rare

Deepening of voice in females; headache; increased hair growth in females; irregular menstrual periods; mental depression; muscle pain; vomiting

Other side effects not listed above may also occur in some patients. If you notice any other effects, check with your doctor.

Additional Information

Once a medicine has been approved for marketing for a certain use, experience may show that it is also useful for other medical problems. Although these uses are not included in product labeling, aminoglutethimide is used in certain patients with the following medical conditions:

- Breast cancer
- Prostate cancer

Other than the above information, there is no additional information relating to proper use, precautions, or side effects for these uses.

Revised: 04/09/93
Interim revision: 04/29/94

AMINOGLYCOSIDES Systemic

Some commonly used brand names are:

In the U.S.—

Amikin[1]
Garamycin[2]
G-Mycin[2]
Jenamicin[2]
Kantrex[3]
Nebcin[7]
Netromycin[5]

In Canada—

Amikin[1]
Cidomycin[2]
Garamycin[2]
Nebcin[7]
Netromycin[5]

Note: For quick reference, the following aminoglycosides are numbered to match the corresponding brand names.

This information applies to the following medicines:

1. Amikacin (am-i-KAY-sin)‡
2. Gentamicin (jen-ta-MYE-sin)‡
3. Kanamycin (kan-a-MYE-sin)†‡
4. Neomycin (nee-oh-MYE-sin)†‡
5. Netilmicin (ne-til-MYE-sin)
6. Streptomycin (strep-toe-MYE-sin)‡§
7. Tobramycin (toe-bra-MYE-sin)‡

†Not commercially available in Canada.
‡Generic name product may also be available in the U.S.
§Generic name product may also be available in Canada.

Description

Aminoglycosides (a-mee-noe-GLYE-koe-sides) are used to treat serious bacterial infections. They work by killing bacteria or preventing their growth.

Aminoglycosides are given by injection to treat serious bacterial infections in many different parts of the body. In addition, some aminoglycosides may be given by irrigation (applying a solution of the medicine to the skin or mucous membranes or washing out a body cavity) or by inhalation into the lungs. Streptomycin may also be given for tuberculosis (TB). These medicines may be given with 1 or more other medicines for bacterial infections, or they may be given alone. Aminoglycosides may also be used for other conditions as determined by your doctor. However, aminoglycosides will not work for colds, flu, or other virus infections.

Aminoglycosides given by injection are usually used for serious bacterial infections for which other medicines may not work. However, aminoglycosides may also cause some serious side effects, including damage to your hearing, sense of balance, and kidneys. These side effects may be more likely to occur in elderly patients and newborn infants. *You and your doctor should talk about the good these medicines may do as well as the risks of receiving them.*

Aminoglycosides are to be administered only by or under the immediate supervision of your doctor. They are available in the following dosage forms:

Inhalation

Amikacin
- Inhalation solution (U.S.)

Gentamicin
- Inhalation solution (U.S.)

Kanamycin
- Inhalation solution (U.S.)

Tobramycin
- Inhalation solution (U.S.)

Irrigation

Kanamycin
- Irrigation solution (U.S.)

Parenteral

Amikacin
- Injection (U.S. and Canada)

Gentamicin
- Injection (U.S. and Canada)

Kanamycin
- Injection (U.S.)

Neomycin
- Injection (U.S.)

Netilmicin
- Injection (U.S. and Canada)

Streptomycin
- Injection (U.S. and Canada)

Tobramycin
- Injection (U.S. and Canada)

Before Receiving This Medicine

In deciding to use a medicine, the risks of taking the medicine must be weighed against the good it will do. This is a decision you and your doctor will make. For aminoglycosides, the following should be considered:

Allergies—Tell your doctor if you have ever had any unusual or allergic reaction to any of the aminoglycosides. Also tell your health care professional if you are allergic to any other substances, such as foods, sulfites, or other preservatives.

Pregnancy—Studies on most of the aminoglycosides have not been done in pregnant women. Some reports have shown that aminoglycosides, especially streptomycin and tobramycin, may cause damage to the infant's hearing, sense of balance, and kidneys if the mother was receiving the medicine during pregnancy. However, this medicine may be needed in serious diseases or other situations that threaten the mother's life. Be sure you have discussed this with your doctor.

Breast-feeding—Aminoglycosides pass into breast milk in small amounts. However, they are not absorbed very much when taken by mouth. To date, aminoglycosides have not been reported to cause problems in nursing babies.

Children—Children are especially sensitive to the effects of aminoglycosides. Damage to hearing, sense of balance, and kidneys is more likely to occur in premature infants and neonates.

Older adults—Elderly people are especially sensitive to the effects of aminoglycosides. Serious side effects, such as damage to hearing, sense of balance, and kidneys may occur in elderly patients.

Other medicines—Although certain medicines should not be used together at all, in other cases two different medicines may be used together even if an interaction might occur. In these cases, your doctor may want to change the dose, or other precautions may be necessary. When you are receiving aminoglycosides it is especially important that your health care professional knows if you are taking any of the following:

- Aminoglycosides, used on the skin or mucous membranes and by injection at the same time; or more than one aminoglycoside at a time or
- Anti-infectives by mouth or by injection (medicine for infection) or
- Capreomycin (e.g., Capastat) or
- Carmustine (e.g., BiCNU) or
- Chloroquine (e.g., Aralen) or
- Cisplatin (e.g., Platinol) or
- Combination pain medicine containing acetaminophen and aspirin (e.g., Excedrin) or other salicylates (with large amounts taken regularly) or
- Cyclosporine (e.g., Sandimmune) or
- Deferoxamine (e.g., Desferal) (with long-term use) or
- Gold salts (medicine for arthritis) or
- Hydroxychloroquine (e.g., Plaquenil) or
- Inflammation or pain medicine, except narcotics, or
- Lithium (e.g., Lithane) or
- Methotrexate (e.g., Mexate) or
- Penicillamine (e.g., Cuprimine) or
- Plicamycin (e.g., Mithracin) or
- Quinine (e.g., Quinamm) or
- Streptozocin (e.g., Zanosar) or

- Tiopronin (e.g., Thiola)—Use of any of these medicines with aminoglycosides may increase the chance of hearing, balance, or kidney side effects

Other medical problems—The presence of other medical problems may affect the use of the aminoglycosides. Make sure you tell your doctor if you have any other medical problems, especially:

- Kidney disease—Patients with kidney disease may have increased aminoglycoside blood levels and increased chance of side effects
- Loss of hearing and/or balance (eighth-cranial-nerve disease)—High aminoglycoside blood levels may cause hearing loss or balance disturbances
- Myasthenia gravis or
- Parkinson's disease—Aminoglycosides may cause muscular problems, resulting in further muscle weakness

Proper Use of This Medicine

To help clear up your infection completely, *aminoglycosides must be given for the full time of treatment,* even if you begin to feel better after a few days. Also, this medicine works best when there is a certain amount in the blood or urine. To help keep the correct level, aminoglycosides must be given on a regular schedule.

Dosing—The dose of aminoglycosides will be different for different patients. *Follow your doctor's orders or the directions on the label.* The following information includes only the average doses of aminoglycosides. Your dose may be different if you have kidney disease. *If your dose is different, do not change it* unless your doctor tells you to do so.

The dose of most aminoglycosides is based on body weight and must be determined by your doctor. The medicine is injected into a muscle or vein. Depending on the aminoglycoside prescribed, doses are given at different times and for different lengths of time. These times are as follows:

For amikacin

- For *all* dosage forms:
  - —Adults and children: The dose is given every eight or twelve hours for seven to ten days.
  - —Newborn babies: The dose is given every twelve hours for seven to ten days.
  - —Premature babies: The dose is given every eighteen to twenty-four hours for seven to ten days.

For gentamicin

- For *all* dosage forms:
  - —Adults and children: The dose is given every eight hours for seven to ten days or more.
  - —Infants: The dose is given every eight to sixteen hours for seven to ten days or more.
  - —Premature and full-term newborn babies: The dose is given every twelve to twenty-four hours for seven to ten days or more.

For kanamicin

- For *all* dosage forms:
  - —Adults and children: The dose is given every eight or twelve hours for seven to ten days.

For netilmicin

- For *all* dosage forms:
  - —Adults and children: The dose is given every eight or twelve hours for seven to fourteen days.

For tobramycin

- For *all* dosage forms:
  - —Adults and adolescents: The dose is given every six to eight hours for seven to ten days or more.
  - —Older infants and children: The dose is given every six to sixteen hours.
  - —Premature and full-term newborn babies: The dose is given every twelve to twenty-four hours.

For streptomycin

- For *all* dosage forms—The dose of streptomycin is often not based on body weight and the amount given depends on the disease being treated.
  - —*Treatment of tuberculosis (TB):*
    - Adults and adolescents: 1 gram injected into a muscle once a day. This will be reduced to two or three times a week, if possible. This medicine must be given with other medicines for tuberculosis (TB).
    - Children: Dose is based on body weight and must be determined by your doctor. This dose is injected into a muscle once a day. This medicine must be given with other medicines for tuberculosis (TB).
  - —*Treatment of bacterial infections:*
    - Adults and adolescents: 250 milligrams to 1 gram of streptomycin is injected into a muscle every six to twelve hours.
    - Children: Dose is based on body weight and must be determined by your doctor. This dose is injected into a muscle every six to twelve hours.

Side Effects of This Medicine

Along with its needed effects, a medicine may cause some unwanted effects. Although not all of these side effects may occur, if they do occur they may need medical attention.

Check with your health care professional immediately if any of the following side effects occur:

More common

Any loss of hearing; clumsiness or unsteadiness; dizziness; greatly increased or decreased frequency of urination or amount of urine; increased thirst; loss of appetite; nausea or vomiting; numbness, tingling, or burning of face or mouth (streptomycin only); muscle twitching, or convulsions (seizures); ringing or buzzing or a feeling of fullness in the ears

Less common

Any loss of vision (streptomycin only); skin rash, itching, redness, or swelling

Rare

Difficulty in breathing; drowsiness; weakness

In addition, leg cramps, skin rash, fever, and convulsions (seizures) may occur when gentamicin is given by injection into the muscle or a vein, and into the spinal fluid.

For up to several weeks after you stop receiving this medicine, it may still cause some side effects that need medical attention. Check with your doctor if you notice any of the following side effects or if they get worse:

Any loss of hearing; clumsiness or unsteadiness; dizziness; greatly increased or decreased frequency of urination or amount of urine; increased thirst; loss of appetite; nausea or vomiting; ringing or buzzing or a feeling of fullness in the ears

Other side effects not listed above may also occur in some patients. If you notice any other effects, check with your doctor.

Revised: 02/23/93

AMINOSALICYLATE SODIUM Systemic

Some commonly used brand names are:

In the U.S.—
Tubasal

In Canada—
Nemasol Sodium

Another commonly used name is PAS.

Description

Aminosalicylate sodium (a-mee-noe-sal-I-si-late soe-dee-um) belongs to the family of medicines called anti-infectives. It is used with other medicines, to help the body overcome tuberculosis (TB). It will not work for colds, flu, or other virus infections.

To help clear up your tuberculosis (TB) completely, you must keep taking this medicine for the full time of treatment, even if you begin to feel better. This is very important. It is also important that you do not miss any doses.

Aminosalicylate sodium is available only with your doctor's prescription, in the following dosage form:

Oral

- Tablets (U.S. and Canada)

Before Using This Medicine

In deciding to use a medicine, the risks of taking the medicine must be weighed against the good it will do. This is a decision you and your doctor will make. For aminosalicylate sodium, the following should be considered:

Allergies—Tell your doctor if you have ever had any unusual or allergic reaction to aminosalicylate sodium, aspirin or other salicylates, including methyl salicylate (oil of wintergreen), or to other related medicines such as sulfonamides (sulfa medicine). Also tell your health care professional if you are allergic to any other substances, such as foods, preservatives, or dyes.

Pregnancy—In one study where aminosalicylates were taken with other medicines for tuberculosis, there was an increase in birth defects. However, other studies have not shown aminosalicylates to cause birth defects.

Breast-feeding—Aminosalicylate sodium passes into the breast milk. However, this medicine has not been reported to cause problems in nursing babies.

Children—There is no specific information comparing use of aminosalicylate sodium in children with use in other age groups.

Older adults—Many medicines have not been studied specifically in older people. Therefore, it may not be known whether they work exactly the same way they do in younger adults or if they cause different side effects or problems in older people. There is no specific information comparing use of aminosalicylate sodium in the elderly with use in other age groups.

Other medicines—Although certain medicines should not be used together at all, in other cases two different medicines may be used together even if an interaction might occur. In these cases, your doctor may want to change the dose, or other precautions may be necessary. When you are taking aminosalicylate sodium, it is especially important that your health care professional know if you are taking any of the following:

- Aminobenzoates (e.g., Potaba)—Use of aminosalicylate sodium with aminobenzoates may decrease the effectiveness of aminosalicylate sodium

Other medical problems—The presence of other medical problems may affect the use of aminosalicylate sodium. Make sure you tell your doctor if you have any other medical problems, especially:

- Glucose-6-phosphate dehydrogenase (G6PD) deficiency—Aminosalicylate sodium may cause or worsen this blood problem
- Heart disease or other circulation problems—The sodium in aminosalicylate sodium may cause or worsen heart or circulation problems
- Kidney disease (severe)—Patients with kidney disease may have an increase in side effects
- Liver disease (severe)—Patients with severe liver disease may have an increase in side effects
- Stomach ulcer—Aminosalicylate sodium may cause stomach irritation

Proper Use of This Medicine

Aminosalicylate sodium may be taken with or after meals or with an antacid if it upsets your stomach.

To help clear up your tuberculosis (TB) completely, *it is important that you keep taking this medicine for the full time of treatment* even if you begin to feel better after a few weeks. Since TB may take a long time to clear up, you may have to take the medicine every day for as long as 1 to 2 years or more. If you stop taking this medicine too soon, your symptoms may return.

This medicine works best when there is a constant amount in the blood. *To help keep the amount constant, do not miss any doses. Also, it is best to take the doses at evenly spaced times day and night.* For example, if you are to take 3 doses a day, doses should be spaced about 8 hours apart. If this interferes with your sleep or other daily activities, or if you need help in planning the best times to take your medicine, check with your health care professional.

Dosing—The dose of aminosalicylate sodium will be different for different patients. *Follow your doctor's orders or the directions on the label.* The following information includes only the average doses of aminosalicylate sodium. This medicine comes in tablets as aminosalicylate sodium (the salt form), but your doctor bases the dose on the amount of aminosalicylate acid (the acid form of the medicine) in the tablet. *If your dose is different, do not change it* unless your doctor tells you to do so.

- For the *tablet* dosage form:
  - —For the treatment of tuberculosis:
    - Adults and children 12 years of age and older—3.3 to 4 grams (aminosalicylate acid) every eight hours, or 5 to 6 grams (aminosalicylate acid) every twelve hours. This medicine must be taken with other medicines used to treat tuberculosis (TB).
    - Younger children—The dose is based on body weight and must be determined by the doctor. Depending on the size of the dose, the medicine may be given every six or eight hours. This medicine must be taken with other medicines used to treat tuberculosis (TB).

Missed dose—If you do miss a dose of this medicine, take it as soon as possible. This will help to keep a constant amount of medicine in the blood. However, if it is almost time for your next dose, skip the missed dose and go back to your regular dosing schedule. Do not double doses.

Storage—To store this medicine:
- Keep out of the reach of children.
- Store away from heat and direct light.
- Do not store in the bathroom, near the kitchen sink, or in other damp places. Heat or moisture may cause the medicine to break down.
- Do not keep outdated medicine or medicine no longer needed. Be sure that any discarded medicine is out of the reach of children.

Precautions While Using This Medicine

If your symptoms do not improve within 2 to 3 weeks, or if they become worse, check with your doctor.

Do not take aminosalicylate sodium within 6 hours of taking rifampin. Taking the 2 medicines too close together may keep rifampin from working properly.

For diabetic patients:
- *This medicine may cause false test results with some urine sugar tests.* Check with your doctor before changing your diet or the dosage of your diabetes medicine.

Side Effects of This Medicine

Along with its needed effects, a medicine may cause some unwanted effects. Although not all of these side effects may occur, if they do occur they may need medical attention.

Check with your doctor immediately if any of the following side effects occur:

More common

Fever; joint pains; skin rash or itching; unusual tiredness or weakness

Less common

Abdominal pain (severe); backache; headache; lower back pain; pain or burning while urinating; paleness of skin; sore throat; yellow eyes or skin

Check with your doctor as soon as possible if any of the following side effects occur:

Less common—with long-term, high-dose therapy

Changes in menstrual periods; decreased sexual ability in males; dry, puffy skin; swelling of front part of neck; weight gain (unusual)

Other side effects may occur that usually do not need medical attention. These side effects may go away during treatment as your body adjusts to the medicine. However, check with your doctor if any of the following side effects continue or are bothersome:

More common

Diarrhea; loss of appetite; nausea and vomiting; stomach pain (mild)

Other side effects not listed above may also occur in some patients. If you notice any other effects, check with your doctor.

Revised: 05/02/94

AMIODARONE Systemic

A commonly used brand name in the U.S. and Canada is Cordarone.

Description

Amiodarone (am-ee-OH-da-rone) belongs to the group of medicines known as antiarrhythmics. It is used to correct irregular heartbeats to a normal rhythm.

Amiodarone produces its helpful effects by slowing nerve impulses in the heart and acting directly on the heart tissues.

This medicine is available only with your doctor's prescription, in the following dosage form:

Oral
- Tablets (U.S. and Canada)

Before Using This Medicine

In deciding to use a medicine, the risks of taking the medicine must be weighed against the good it will do. This is

a decision you and your doctor will make. For amiodarone, the following should be considered:

Allergies—Tell your doctor if you have ever had any unusual or allergic reaction to amiodarone. Also tell your health care professional if you are allergic to any other substances, such as foods, preservatives, or dyes.

Pregnancy—Amiodarone has been shown to cause thyroid problems in babies whose mothers took amiodarone when pregnant. In addition, there is concern that amiodarone could cause slow heartbeat in the newborn. However, this medicine may be needed in serious situations that threaten the mother's life. Be sure you have discussed this with your doctor before taking this medicine.

Breast-feeding—Although amiodarone passes into breast milk, it has not been shown to cause problems in nursing babies. However, amiodarone has been shown to cause growth problems in rats. It may be necessary for you to stop breast-feeding during treatment. Be sure you have discussed the risks and benefits of the medicine with your doctor.

Children—Amiodarone can cause serious side effects in any patient. Therefore, it is especially important that you discuss with the child's doctor the good that this medicine may do as well as the risks of using it.

Older adults—Elderly patients may be more likely to get thyroid problems with this medicine. Also, difficulty in walking and numbness, tingling, trembling, or weakness in hands or feet are more likely to occur in the elderly.

Other medicines—Although certain medicines should not be used together at all, in other cases two different medicines may be used together even if an interaction might occur. In these cases, your doctor may want to change the dose, or other precautions may be necessary. When you are taking amiodarone, it is especially important that your health care professional knows if you are taking any of the following:

- Anticoagulants (blood thinners) or
- Other heart medicine or
- Phenytoin (e.g., Dilantin)—Effects may be increased

Other medical problems—The presence of other medical problems may affect the use of amiodarone. Make sure you tell your doctor if you have any other medical problems, especially:

- Liver disease—Effects may be increased because of slower removal from the body
- Thyroid problems—Risk of overactive or underactive thyroid is increased

Proper Use of This Medicine

Take amiodarone exactly as directed by your doctor even though you may feel well. Do not take more medicine than ordered and do not miss any doses.

Dosing—The dose of amiodarone will be different for different patients. *Follow your doctor's orders or the directions on the label.* The following information includes only the average doses of amiodarone. *If your dose is different, do not change it* unless your doctor tells you to do so:

- For *oral* dosage form (tablets):
  - —For treatment of *ventricular arrhythmias:*
    - Adults—At first, 800 to 1600 milligrams (mg) per day taken in divided doses. Then, 600 to 800 mg per day for one month. Then, 400 mg per day.
    - Children—Dose is based on body weight and must be determined by your doctor. The dose for the first ten days is usually 10 mg per kilogram (4.55 mg per pound) of body weight per day. Then, the dose is decreased to 5 mg per kilogram (2.27 mg per pound) of body weight per day. After several weeks, the dose is then decreased to 2.5 mg per kilogram (1.14 mg per pound) of body weight per day.

Missed dose—If you miss a dose of this medicine, do not take the missed dose at all and do not double the next one. Instead, go back to your regular dosing schedule. If you miss two or more doses in a row, check with your doctor.

Storage—To store this medicine:

- Keep out of the reach of children.
- Store away from heat and direct light.
- Do not store in the bathroom, near the kitchen sink, or in other damp places. Heat or moisture may cause the medicine to break down.
- Do not keep outdated medicine or medicine no longer needed. Be sure that any discarded medicine is out of the reach of children.

Precautions While Using This Medicine

It is important that your doctor check your progress at regular visits to make sure the medicine is working properly. This will allow for changes to be made in the amount of medicine you are taking, if necessary.

Your doctor may want you to carry a medical identification card or bracelet stating that you are taking this medicine.

Before having any kind of surgery (including dental surgery) or emergency treatment, tell the medical doctor or dentist in charge that you are taking this medicine.

Amiodarone increases the sensitivity of your skin to sunlight; too much exposure could cause a serious burn. Your skin may continue to be sensitive to sunlight for several months after treatment with this medicine is stopped. A burn can occur even through window glass or thin cotton clothing. If you must go out in the sunlight, *cover your skin and wear a wide-brimmed hat. A special sun-blocking cream should also be used;* it must contain zinc or titanium oxide because other sunscreens will not work. *In case of a severe burn, check with your doctor.*

After you have taken this medicine for a long time, it may cause a blue-gray color to appear on your skin, especially in areas exposed to the sun, such as your face, neck, and arms. This color will usually fade after treatment with amiodarone has ended, although it may take several months. However, check with your doctor if this effect occurs.

Side Effects of This Medicine

Along with its needed effects, a medicine may cause some unwanted effects. Although not all of these side effects may occur, if they do occur they may need medical attention. Also, some side effects may not appear until several weeks or months, or even years, after you start taking amiodarone.

Check with your doctor immediately if any of the following side effects occur:

More common

Cough; painful breathing; shortness of breath

Check with your doctor as soon as possible if any of the following side effects occur:

More common

Fever (slight); numbness or tingling in fingers or toes; sensitivity of skin to sunlight; trembling or shaking of hands; trouble in walking; unusual and uncontrolled movements of the body; weakness of arms or legs

Less common

Blue-gray coloring of skin on face, neck, and arms; blurred vision or blue-green halos seen around objects; coldness; dry eyes; dry, puffy skin; fast or irregular heartbeat; nervousness; pain and swelling in scrotum; sensitivity of eyes to light; sensitivity to heat; slow heartbeat; sweating; swelling of feet or lower legs; trouble in sleeping; unusual tiredness; weight gain or loss

Rare

Skin rash; yellow eyes or skin

Other side effects may occur that usually do not need medical attention. These side effects may go away during treatment as your body adjusts to the medicine. However, check with your doctor if any of the following side effects continue or are bothersome:

More common

Constipation; headache; loss of appetite; nausea and vomiting

Less common

Bitter or metallic taste; decreased sexual ability in males; decrease in sexual interest; dizziness; flushing of face

After you stop using this medicine, your body may need time to adjust. The length of time this takes depends on the amount of medicine you were using and how long you used it. During this period of time check with your doctor if you notice any of the following side effects:

Cough; fever (slight); painful breathing; shortness of breath

Other side effects not listed above may also occur in some patients. If you notice any other effects, check with your doctor.

Revised: 04/13/93

AMLODIPINE Systemic†

A commonly used brand name in the U.S. is Norvasc.

†Not commercially available in Canada.

Description

Amlodipine (am-LOE-di-peen) is a calcium channel blocker used to treat angina (chest pain) and high blood pressure. Amlodipine affects the movement of calcium into the cells of the heart and blood vessels. As a result, amlodipine relaxes blood vessels and increases the supply of blood and oxygen to the heart while reducing its workload.

High blood pressure adds to the workload of the heart and arteries. If it continues for a long time, the heart and arteries may not function properly. This can damage the blood vessels of the brain, heart, and kidneys, resulting in a stroke, heart failure, or kidney failure. High blood pressure may also increase the risk of heart attacks. These problems may be less likely to occur if blood pressure is controlled.

This medicine is available only with your doctor's prescription, in the following dosage form:

Oral

- Tablets (U.S.)

Before Using This Medicine

In deciding to use a medicine, the risks of taking the medicine must be weighed against the good it will do. This is a decision you and your doctor will make. For amlodipine, the following should be considered:

Allergies—Tell your doctor if you have ever had any unusual or allergic reaction to amlodipine. Also tell your health care professional if you are allergic to any other substances, such as foods, preservatives, or dyes.

Pregnancy—Amlodipine has not been studied in pregnant women. However, studies in animals have shown that, at very high doses, amlodipine may cause fetal death. Before taking this medicine, make sure your doctor knows if you are pregnant or if you may become pregnant.

Breast-feeding—It is not known whether amlodipine passes into breast milk. Although most medicines pass into breast milk in small amounts, many of them may be used safely while breast-feeding. Mothers who are taking this medicine and who wish to breast-feed should discuss this with their doctor.

Children—Studies on this medicine have been done only in adult patients, and there is no specific information comparing use of amlodipine in children with use in other age groups.

Older adults—Elderly people may be especially sensitive to the effects of amlodipine. This may increase the chance of side effects during treatment.

Other medicines—Although certain medicines should not be used together at all, in other cases two different medicines may be used together even if an interaction might occur. In these cases, your doctor may want to change the dose, or other precautions may be necessary. Tell your health care professional if you are using any other prescription or nonprescription (over-the-counter [OTC]) medicine.

Other medical problems—The presence of other medical problems may affect the use of amlodipine. Make sure you tell your doctor if you have any other medical problems, especially:

- Congestive heart failure—There is a small chance that amlodipine may make this condition worse
- Liver disease—Higher blood levels of amlodipine may result and a smaller dose may be needed
- Very low blood pressure—Amlodipine may make this condition worse

Proper Use of This Medicine

Take this medicine exactly as directed even if you feel well and do not notice any chest pain. Do not take more of this medicine and do not take it more often than your doctor ordered. Do not miss any doses.

For patients taking this medicine *for high blood pressure:*

- In addition to the use of the medicine your doctor has prescribed, treatment for your high blood pressure may include weight control and care in the types of food you eat, especially foods high in sodium (salt). Your doctor will tell you which of these are most important for you. You should check with your doctor before changing your diet.
- Many patients who have high blood pressure will not notice any signs of the problem. In fact, many may feel normal. It is very important that you *take your medicine exactly as directed* and that you keep your appointments with your doctor even if you feel well.
- Remember that this medicine will not cure your high blood pressure but it does help control it. Therefore, you must continue to take it as directed if you expect to lower your blood pressure and keep it down. *You may have to take high blood pressure medicine for the rest of your life.* If high blood pressure is not treated, it can cause serious problems such as heart failure, blood vessel disease, stroke, or kidney disease.

Dosing—The dose of amlodipine will be different for different patients. *Follow your doctor's orders or the directions on the label.* The following information includes only the average doses of amlodipine. *If your dose is different, do not change it* unless your doctor tells you to do so.

The number of tablets that you take depends on the strength of the medicine.

- For *oral* dosage form (tablets):
  - —For angina (chest pain):
    - Adults—5 to 10 milligrams (mg) once a day.
    - Children—Use must be determined by your doctor.
  - —For high blood pressure:
    - Adults—2.5 to 10 mg once a day.
    - Children—Use must be determined by your doctor.

Missed dose—If you miss a dose of this medicine, take it as soon as possible. However, if it is almost time for your next dose, skip the missed dose and go back to your regular dosing schedule. Do not double doses.

Storage—To store this medicine:

- Keep out of the reach of children.
- Store away from heat and direct light.
- Do not store in the bathroom, near the kitchen sink, or in other damp places. Heat or moisture may cause the medicine to break down.
- Keep the medicine from freezing. Do not refrigerate.
- Do not keep outdated medicine or medicine no longer needed. Be sure that any discarded medicine is out of the reach of children.

Precautions While Using This Medicine

It is important that your doctor check your progress at regular visits. This will allow your doctor to make sure the medicine is working properly and to change the dosage if needed.

If you have been using this medicine regularly for several weeks, do not suddenly stop using it. Stopping suddenly may cause your chest pain or high blood pressure to come back or get worse. Check with your doctor for the best way to reduce gradually the amount you are taking before stopping completely.

Chest pain resulting from exercise or physical exertion usually is reduced or prevented by this medicine. This may tempt you to be too active. *Make sure you discuss with your doctor a safe amount of exercise for your medical problem.*

After taking a dose of this medicine you may get a headache that lasts for a short time. This should become less noticeable after you have taken this medicine for a while. If this effect continues, or if the headaches are severe, check with your doctor.

In some patients, tenderness, swelling, or bleeding of the gums may appear soon after treatment with this medicine is started. Brushing and flossing your teeth carefully and regularly and massaging your gums may help prevent this. *See your dentist regularly* to have your teeth cleaned. Check with your medical doctor or dentist if you have any questions about how to take care of your teeth and gums, or if you notice any tenderness, swelling, or bleeding of your gums.

For patients taking this medicine *for high blood pressure:*

- *Do not take other medicines unless they have been discussed with your doctor.* This especially includes over-the-counter (nonprescription) medicines for appetite control, asthma, colds, cough, hay fever, or sinus problems, since they may tend to increase your blood pressure.

Side Effects of This Medicine

Along with its needed effects, a medicine may cause some unwanted effects. Although not all of these side effects may occur, if they do occur they may need medical attention.

Check with your doctor as soon as possible if any of the following side effects occur:

More common
Swelling of ankles or feet

Less common
Dizziness; pounding heartbeat

Rare
Chest pain; dizziness or lightheadedness when getting up from a lying or sitting position; slow heartbeat

Other side effects may occur that usually do not need medical attention. These side effects may go away during treatment as your body adjusts to the medicine. However, check with your doctor if any of the following side effects continue or are bothersome:

More common
Flushing; headache

Less common
Nausea; unusual tiredness or weakness

Other side effects not listed above may also occur in some patients. If you notice any other effects, check with your doctor.

Revised: 08/12/93

AMMONIA SPIRIT, AROMATIC Inhalation†

Available in the U.S. as generic name product.
Another commonly used name is smelling salts.

†Not commercially available in Canada.

Description

Aromatic (air-a-MAT-ik) ammonia (a-MOAN-ya) spirit (SPIR-it) is used to prevent or treat fainting.

Fainting may be caused by some kinds of medicine, by an unpleasant or stressful event, or by a serious medical problem, such as heart disease. Fainting in an older person is often more serious than fainting in a younger person. Older people and people with a history of heart problems should seek medical attention as soon as possible after fainting.

Aromatic ammonia spirit is available without a doctor's prescription in the following dosage forms:

Inhalation
- Inhalants (U.S.)
- Solution (U.S.)

Before Using This Medicine

If you are using this medicine without a prescription, carefully read and follow any precautions on the label. For aromatic ammonia spirit, the following should be considered:

Allergies—Tell your doctor if you have ever had any unusual or allergic reaction to aromatic ammonia spirit. Also tell your health care professional if you are allergic to any other substances, such as foods, preservatives, or dyes.

Pregnancy—Studies on effects in pregnancy have not been done in either humans or animals.

Breast-feeding—It is not known whether aromatic ammonia spirit passes into breast milk. However, this medicine has not been reported to cause problems in nursing babies.

Children—This medicine has been tested in children and, in effective doses, has not been shown to cause different side effects or problems than it does in adults. However, this medicine should not be given to children without first checking with their doctor.

Older adults—Many medicines have not been studied specifically in older people. Therefore, it may not be known whether they work exactly the same way they do in younger adults. Although there is no specific information comparing use of aromatic ammonia spirit in the elderly with use in other age groups, this medicine is not expected to cause different side effects or problems in older people than it does in younger adults.

Other medicines—Although certain medicines should not be used together at all, in other cases two different medicines may be used together even if an interaction might occur. In these cases, your doctor may want to change the dose, or other precautions may be necessary. Tell your health care professional if you are taking any other prescription or nonprescription (over-the-counter [OTC]) medicine.

Other medical problems—The presence of other medical problems may affect the use of aromatic ammonia spirit. Make sure you tell your doctor if you have any other medical problems, especially:

- Asthma, bronchitis, emphysema, or other chronic lung disease, or
- Eye problems—This medicine may make these conditions worse
- Flushed face—The cause of the fainting may be a serious condition that should be treated by a doctor

Proper Use of This Medicine

Dosing—*Follow your doctor's orders or the directions on the label.* The following information includes only the average doses of aromatic ammonia spirit. *If your dose is different, do not change it* unless your doctor tells you to do so.

- For preventing or treating fainting:
  - —For *inhalation* dosage form (inhalants):
    - Adults and teenagers—The inhalant should be held away from the face and crushed between the

fingers. The inhalant should then be held about four inches away from the nostrils, and the vapor slowly inhaled until the patient awakens or no longer feels faint.

• Children—Use and dose must be determined by your doctor.

—For *inhalation* dosage form (solution):

• Adults and teenagers—After the top is taken off the container, the vapor may be slowly inhaled until the patient awakens or no longer feels faint.

• Children—Use and dose must be determined by your doctor.

Storage—To store this medicine:

- Keep out of the reach of children.
- Store away from heat and direct light.
- Do not store inhalants in the bathroom, near the kitchen sink, or in other damp places. Heat or moisture may cause the medicine to break down.
- Keep the medicine from freezing. Do not refrigerate.
- Keep the container of liquid tightly closed.
- Do not keep outdated medicine or medicine no longer needed. Be sure that any discarded medicine is out of the reach of children.

Precautions While Using This Medicine

Fainting in older people may be a sign of a serious medical problem. *Older people and people with heart problems should check with their doctor as soon as possible after fainting.*

Keep this medicine away from your eyes and skin. If aromatic ammonia spirit comes into contact with your eyes or skin, burns and irritation may occur. Burns in the eyes may cause blindness.

If this medicine gets into your eyes:

- Rinse your eyes with a gentle stream of water for 20 minutes. Hold the eyelid away from the eyeball to allow complete rinsing.
- Call a poison control center, your doctor, or a hospital emergency room immediately.

If this medicine comes into contact with your skin:

- Remove any clothing on which aromatic ammonia spirit has spilled.
- Rinse the skin with large amounts of water.
- Do not rub or apply ointment to the skin.
- Call your doctor if skin irritation continues.

If a large amount of this medicine is taken orally:

- Drink a glass (8 ounces) of water.
- Call a poison control center, your doctor, or a hospital emergency room immediately.

Side Effects of This Medicine

Along with its needed effects, a medicine may cause some unwanted effects. Although not all of these side effects may occur, if they do occur they may need medical attention.

Check with your doctor as soon as possible if any of the following side effects occur:

Less common

Cough; diarrhea; difficulty in breathing; headache; vomiting

Other side effects not listed above may also occur in some patients. If you notice any other effects, check with your doctor.

Developed: 06/23/95

AMPHETAMINES Systemic

Some commonly used brand names are:

In the U.S.—

Desoxyn[3]
Desoxyn Gradumet[3]
Dexedrine[2]
Dexedrine Spansule[2]
DextroStat[2]

In Canada—

Dexedrine[2]
Dexedrine Spansule[2]

Note: For quick reference, the following amphetamines are numbered to match the corresponding brand names.

This information applies to the following medicines:

1. Amphetamine (am-FET-a-meen)†‡
2. Dextroamphetamine (dex-troe-am-FET-a-meen)‡
3. Methamphetamine (meth-am-FET-a-meen)†

†Not commercially available in Canada.
‡Generic name product may also be available in the U.S.
§Generic name product may also be available in Canada.

Description

Amphetamines (am-FET-a-meens) belong to the group of medicines called central nervous system (CNS) stimulants. They are used to treat attention-deficit hyperactivity disorder (ADHD). Amphetamines increase attention and decrease restlessness in patients who are overactive, unable to concentrate for very long or are easily distracted, and have unstable emotions. These medicines are used as part of a total treatment program that also includes social, educational, and psychological treatment.

Amphetamine and dextroamphetamine are also used in the treatment of narcolepsy (uncontrollable desire for sleep or sudden attacks of deep sleep).

Amphetamines should not be used for weight loss or weight control or to combat unusual tiredness or weakness or replace rest. When used for these purposes, they may be dangerous to your health.

Amphetamines may also be used for other conditions as determined by your doctor.

These medicines are available only with a doctor's prescription. Prescriptions cannot be refilled. A new prescription must be obtained from your doctor each time you or your child needs this medicine.

Amphetamines are available in the following dosage forms:

Oral

Amphetamine
- Tablets (U.S.)

Dextroamphetamine
- Extended-release capsules (U.S. and Canada)
- Tablets (U.S. and Canada)

Methamphetamine
- Tablets (U.S.)
- Extended-release tablets (U.S.)

Before Using This Medicine

In deciding to use a medicine, the risks of taking the medicine must be weighed against the good it will do. This is a decision you and your doctor will make. For amphetamines, the following should be considered:

Allergies—Tell your doctor if you have ever had any unusual or allergic reaction to amphetamine, dextroamphetamine, ephedrine, epinephrine, isoproterenol, metaproterenol, methamphetamine, norepinephrine, phenylephrine, phenylpropanolamine, pseudoephedrine, or terbutaline. Also tell your health care professional if you are allergic to any other substances, such as foods, preservatives, or dyes.

Pregnancy—Studies have not been done in humans. However, animal studies have shown that amphetamines may increase the chance of birth defects if taken during the early months of pregnancy.

In addition, overuse of amphetamines during pregnancy may increase the chances of a premature delivery and of having a baby with a low birth weight. Also, the baby may become dependent on amphetamines and experience withdrawal effects such as agitation and drowsiness.

Breast-feeding—Amphetamines pass into breast milk. Although this medicine has not been reported to cause problems in nursing babies, it is best not to breast-feed while you are taking an amphetamine. Be sure you have discussed this with your doctor.

Children—When amphetamines are used for long periods of time in children, they may cause unwanted effects on behavior and growth. Before these medicines are given to a child, you should discuss their use with your child's doctor.

Older adults—Many medicines have not been studied specifically in older people. Therefore, it may not be known whether they work exactly the same way they do in younger adults or if they cause different side effects or problems in older people. There is no specific information comparing use of amphetamines in the elderly with use in other age groups.

Other medicines—Although certain medicines should not be used together at all, in many cases 2 different medicines may be used together even if an interaction might occur. In these cases, changes in dose or other precautions may be necessary. When you are taking amphetamines, it is especially important that your health care professional know if you are taking any of the following:

- Amantadine (e.g., Symmetrel) or
- Caffeine (e.g., NoDoz) or
- Chlophedianol (e.g., Ulone) or
- Methylphenidate (e.g., Ritalin) or
- Nabilone (e.g., Cesamet) or
- Pemoline (e.g., Cylert)—Use of these medicines may increase the CNS stimulation effects of amphetamines and cause unwanted effects such as nervousness, irritability, trouble in sleeping, and possibly convulsions (seizures)
- Appetite suppressants (diet pills), except fenfluramine (e.g., Pondimin), or
- Medicine for asthma or other breathing problems or
- Medicine for colds, sinus problems, or hay fever or other allergies (including nose drops or sprays)—Use of these medicines may increase the CNS stimulation effects of amphetamines and cause unwanted effects such as nervousness, irritability, trouble in sleeping, and possibly convulsions (seizures), as well as unwanted effects on the heart and blood vessels
- Beta-adrenergic blocking agents (acebutolol [e.g., Sectral], atenolol [e.g., Tenormin], betaxolol [e.g., Kerlone], carteolol [e.g., Cartrol], labetalol [e.g., Normodyne], metoprolol [e.g., Lopressor], nadolol [e.g., Corgard], oxprenolol [e.g., Trasicor], penbutolol [e.g., Levatol], pindolol [e.g., Visken], propranolol [e.g., Inderal], sotalol [e.g., Sotacor], timolol [e.g., Blocadren])—Use of amphetamines with beta-blocking agents may increase the chance of high blood pressure and heart problems
- Cocaine—Use by persons taking amphetamines may cause a severe increase in blood pressure and other unwanted effects, including nervousness, irritability, trouble in sleeping, and possible convulsions (seizures)
- Digitalis glycosides (heart medicine)—Amphetamines may cause additive effects, resulting in irregular heartbeat
- Meperidine—Use of meperidine by persons taking amphetamines is not recommended because the chance of serious side effects (such as high fever, convulsions, and coma) may be increased
- Monoamine oxidase (MAO) inhibitors (furazolidone [e.g., Furoxone], isocarboxazid [e.g., Marplan], phenelzine [e.g., Nardil], procarbazine [e.g., Matulane], selegiline [e.g., Eldepryl], tranylcypromine [e.g., Parnate])—Taking amphetamines while you are taking or within 2 weeks of taking monoamine oxidase (MAO) inhibitors may increase the chance of serious side effects such as sudden and severe high blood pressure or fever
- Thyroid hormones—The effects of either these medicines or amphetamines may be increased; unwanted effects may occur in patients with heart or blood vessel disease
- Tricyclic antidepressants (amitriptyline [e.g., Elavil], amoxapine [e.g., Asendin], clomipramine [e.g., Anafranil], desipramine [e.g., Pertofrane], doxepin [e.g., Sinequan], imipramine [e.g., Tofranil], nortriptyline [e.g., Aventyl], protriptyline [e.g., Vivactil], trimipramine [e.g., Surmontil])—Although tricyclic antidepressants may be used with amphetamines to help make them work better, using the 2 medicines together may increase the chance of fast or irregular heartbeat, severe high blood pressure, or high fever

Other medical problems—The presence of other medical problems may affect the use of amphetamines.Make sure

you tell your doctor if you have any other medical problems, especially:

- Anxiety or tension (severe) or
- Drug abuse or dependence, (history of) or
- Glaucoma or
- Heart or blood vessel disease or
- High blood pressure or
- Mental illness (severe), especially in children, or
- Overactive thyroid or
- Tourette's syndrome (history of) or other tics—Amphetamines may make the condition worse

Proper Use of This Medicine

Take this medicine only as directed by your doctor. Do not take more or less of it, do not take it more often, and do not take it for a longer time than your doctor ordered. If too much is taken, it may become habit-forming (causing mental or physical dependence).

If you think this medicine is not working properly after you have taken it for several weeks, *do not increase the dose.* Instead, check with your doctor.

For patients taking *the short-acting form* of this medicine:

- Take the last dose for each day at least 6 hours before bedtime to help prevent trouble in sleeping.

For patients taking *the long-acting form* of this medicine:

- Take the daily dose about 10 to 14 hours before bedtime to help prevent trouble in sleeping.
- These capsules or tablets should be swallowed whole. Do not break, crush, or chew them before swallowing.

Amphetamines may be taken with or without food or on a full or empty stomach. However, if your doctor tells you to take the medicine a certain way, take it exactly as directed.

Dosing—The dose of amphetamines will be different for different patients. *Follow your doctor's orders or the directions on the label.* The following information includes only the average doses of amphetamines. *If your dose is different, do not change it* unless your doctor tells you to do so.

The number of capsules or tablets that you take depends on the strength of the medicine. Also, *the number of doses you take each day, the time allowed between doses, and the length of time you take the medicine depend on the medical problem for which you are taking amphetamines.*

For amphetamine

- For *oral* dosage form (tablets):
  - —For attention-deficit hyperactivity disorder:
    - Adults—At first, 5 milligrams (mg) one to three times a day. Your doctor may increase your dose if needed.
    - Children 6 years of age and over—At first, 5 mg one or two times a day. Your doctor may increase your dose if needed.
    - Children 3 to 6 years of age—At first, 2.5 mg once a day. Your doctor may increase your dose if needed.
    - Children up to 3 years of age—Use is not recommended.
  - —For narcolepsy:
    - Adults—At first, 5 mg one to three times a day. Your doctor may increase your dose if needed.
    - Children 12 years of age and over—At first, 5 mg two times a day. Your doctor may increase your dose if needed.
    - Children 6 to 12 years of age—At first, 2.5 mg two times a day. Your doctor may increase your dose if needed.
    - Children up to 6 years of age—Dose must be determined by your doctor.

For dextroamphetamine

- For *oral extended-release capsule* dosage form:
  - —For attention-deficit hyperactivity disorder:
    - Adults—5 to 60 milligrams (mg) a day.
    - Children 6 years of age and over—At first, 5 mg one or two times a day. Your doctor may increase your dose if needed.
    - Children 3 to 6 years of age—At first, 2.5 mg a day. Your doctor may increase your dose if needed.
    - Children up to 3 years of age—Use is not recommended.
  - —For narcolepsy:
    - Adults—5 to 60 mg a day.
    - Children 12 years of age and over—At first, 10 mg a day. Your doctor may increase your dose if needed.
    - Children 6 to 12 years of age—At first, 5 mg a day. Your doctor may increase your dose if needed.
    - Children 3 to 6 years of age—Dose must be determined by your doctor.
    - Children up to 3 years of age—Use is not recommended.
- For *oral tablet* dosage form:
  - —For attention-deficit hyperactivity disorder:
    - Adults—5 to 60 mg a day.
    - Children 6 years of age and over—At first, 5 mg one or two times a day. Your doctor may increase your dose if needed.
    - Children 3 to 5 years of age—At first, 2.5 mg a day. Your doctor may increase your dose if needed.
    - Children up to 3 years of age—Use is not recommended.
  - —For narcolepsy:
    - Adults—5 to 60 mg a day.
    - Children 12 years of age and over—At first, 10 mg a day. Your doctor may increase your dose if needed.
    - Children 6 to 12 years of age—At first, 5 mg a day. Your doctor may increase your dose if needed.

• Children up to 6 years of age—Dose must be determined by your doctor.

For methamphetamine

• For *oral tablet* dosage form:

—For attention-deficit hyperactivity disorder:

• Children 6 years of age and over—At first, 5 milligrams (mg) one or two times a day. Your doctor may increase your dose if needed.

• Children up to 6 years of age—Use is not recommended.

• For *oral extended-release tablet* dosage form:

—For attention-deficit hyperactivity disorder:

• Children 6 years of age and over—20 to 25 mg a day.

• Children up to 6 years of age—Use is not recommended.

Missed dose—If you miss a dose of this medicine and your dosing schedule is:

- One dose a day—Take the missed dose as soon as possible, but not later than stated above, to prevent trouble in sleeping. However, if you do not remember the missed dose until the next day, skip it and go back to your regular dosing schedule. Do not double doses.
- Two or three doses a day—If you remember within an hour or so of the missed dose, take the dose right away. However, if you do not remember until later, skip it and go back to your regular dosing schedule. Do not double doses.

Storage—To store this medicine:

- Keep out of the reach of children.
- Store away from heat and direct light.
- Do not store the capsule or tablet form of this medicine in the bathroom, near the kitchen sink, or in other damp places. Heat or moisture may cause the medicine to break down.
- Keep the liquid form of this medicine from freezing.
- Do not keep outdated medicine or medicine no longer needed. Be sure that any discarded medicine is out of the reach of children.

Precautions While Using This Medicine

Your doctor should check your progress at regular visits to make sure that this medicine does not cause unwanted effects.

If you will be taking this medicine in large doses for a long time, *do not stop taking it without first checking with your doctor.* Your doctor may want you to reduce gradually the amount you are taking before stopping completely.

This medicine may cause some people to feel a false sense of well-being or to become dizzy, lightheaded, or less alert than they are normally. *Make sure you know how you react to this medicine before you drive, use machines, or do anything else that could be dangerous if you are dizzy or are not alert.*

Before you have any medical tests, tell the medical doctor in charge that you are taking this medicine. The results of the metyrapone test may be affected by this medicine.

If you have been using this medicine for a long time and you think you may have become mentally or physically dependent on it, check with your doctor. Some signs of dependence on amphetamines are:

- A strong desire or need to continue taking the medicine.
- A need to increase the dose to receive the effects of the medicine.
- Withdrawal effects (for example, mental depression, nausea or vomiting, stomach cramps or pain, trembling, unusual tiredness or weakness) occurring after the medicine is stopped.

Side Effects of This Medicine

Along with its needed effects, a medicine may cause some unwanted effects. Although not all of these side effects may occur, if they do occur they may need medical attention.

Check with your doctor as soon as possible if any of the following side effects occur:

More common

Irregular heartbeat

Rare

Chest pain; fever, unusually high; skin rash or hives; uncontrolled movements of head, neck, arms, and legs

With long-term use or high doses

Difficulty in breathing; dizziness or feeling faint; increased blood pressure; mood or mental changes; pounding heartbeat; unusual tiredness or weakness

Other side effects may occur that usually do not need medical attention. These side effects may go away during treatment as your body adjusts to the medicine. However, check with your doctor if any of the following side effects continue or are bothersome:

More common

False sense of well-being; irritability; nervousness; restlessness; trouble in sleeping

Note: After these stimulant effects have worn off, drowsiness, trembling, unusual tiredness or weakness, or mental depression may occur.

Less common

Blurred vision; changes in sexual desire or decreased sexual ability; constipation; diarrhea; dizziness or lightheadedness; dryness of mouth or unpleasant taste; fast or pounding heartbeat; headache; increased sweating; loss of appetite; nausea or vomiting; stomach cramps or pain; weight loss

After you stop using this medicine, your body may need time to adjust. The length of time this takes depends on the amount of medicine you were using and how long you used it. During this period of time check with your doctor if you notice any of the following side effects:

Mental depression; nausea or vomiting; stomach cramps or pain; trembling; unusual tiredness or weakness

Other side effects not listed above may also occur in some patients. If you notice any other effects check with your doctor.

Revised: 08/18/94

AMPHOTERICIN B Systemic

Some commonly used brand names are:

In the U.S.—

Amphocin
Fungizone Intravenous

In Canada—

Fungizone Intravenous

Generic name product may also be available in the U.S.

Description

Amphotericin (am-foe-TER-i-sin) B is an antifungal. It is used to help the body overcome serious fungus infections. It may also be used for other problems as determined by your doctor.

Amphotericin B is available only with your doctor's prescription. It is available in the following dosage form:

Parenteral

- Injection (U.S. and Canada)

Before Receiving This Medicine

In deciding to use a medicine, the risks of taking the medicine must be weighed against the good it will do. This is a decision you and your doctor will make. For amphotericin B, the following should be considered:

Allergies—Tell your doctor if you have ever had any unusual or allergic reaction to amphotericin B. Also tell your health care professional if you are allergic to any other substances, such as foods, preservatives, or dyes.

Pregnancy—Amphotericin B has not been reported to cause birth defects or other problems in humans.

Breast-feeding—Amphotericin B has not been reported to cause problems in nursing babies.

Children—Although there is no specific information comparing use of amphotericin B in children with use in other age groups, this medicine is not expected to cause different side effects or problems in children than it does in adults.

Older adults—Many medicines have not been studied specifically in older people. Therefore, it may not be known whether they work exactly the same way they do in younger adults or if they cause different side effects or problems in older people. There is no specific information comparing use of amphotericin B in the elderly with use in other age groups.

Other medicines—Although certain medicines should not be used together at all, in other cases two different medicines may be used together even if an interaction might occur. In these cases, your doctor may want to change the dose, or other precautions may be necessary. When you are taking amphotericin B, it is especially important that your health care professional knows if you are taking any of the following:

- Antineoplastics (cancer medicine) or
- Antithyroid agents (medicine for overactive thyroid) or
- Azathioprine (e.g., Imuran) or
- Chloramphenicol (e.g., Chloromycetin) or
- Colchicine or
- Cyclophosphamide (e.g., Cytoxan) or
- Flucytosine (e.g., Ancobon) or
- Ganciclovir (e.g., Cytovene) or
- Interferon (e.g., Intron A, Roferon-A) or
- Mercaptopurine (e.g., Purinethol) or
- Zidovudine (e.g., AZT, Retrovir) or
- X-ray treatment—Use of amphotericin B with any of these medicines or x-ray treatment may increase the chance of side effects affecting the blood
- Bumetanide (e.g., Bumex) or
- Carmustine (e.g., BiCNU) or
- Cisplatin (e.g., Platinol) or
- Combination pain medicine containing acetaminophen and aspirin (e.g., Excedrin) or other salicylates (with large amounts taken regularly) or
- Cyclosporine (e.g., Sandimmune) or
- Deferoxamine (e.g., Desferal) (with long-term use) or
- Ethacrynic acid (e.g., Edecrin) or
- Furosemide (e.g., Lasix) or
- Gold salts (medicine for arthritis) or
- Indapamide (e.g., Lozol) or
- Inflammation or pain medicine, except narcotics, or
- Lithium (e.g., Lithane) or
- Other medicine for infection or
- Plicamycin (e.g., Mithracin) or
- Streptozocin (e.g., Zanosar) or
- Tiopronin (e.g., Thiola) or
- Thiazide diuretics (water pills)—Using these medicines with amphotericin B may increase the risk of side effects affecting the kidneys
- Corticosteroids (cortisone-like medicine) or
- Corticotropin (ACTH)—Use of amphotericin B with these medicines may cause changes in the blood that may increase the chance for heart problems
- Digitalis glycosides (heart medicine)—Use of amphotericin B with digitalis medicines (such as digoxin) may cause changes in the blood that may increase the chance of heart problems
- Methotrexate (e.g., Mexate) or
- Penicillamine (e.g., Cuprimine)—Using these medicines with amphotericin B may increase the risk of side effects affecting the blood and the kidneys

Other medical problems—The presence of other medical problems may affect the use of amphotericin B. Make sure

you tell your doctor if you have any other medical problems, especially:

- Kidney disease—Amphotericin B may cause side effects affecting the kidneys

Proper Use of This Medicine

Dosing—The dose of amphotericin B will be different for different patients. The following information includes only the average doses of amphotericin B. Your dose may be different if you have kidney disease.

- For the *injection* dosage form:
  —Adults and children: A small test dose is usually given first to see how you react to the medicine. The dose is then slowly increased, depending on what your infection is and how well you tolerate the medicine. The dose must be determined by your doctor.

Side Effects of This Medicine

Along with its needed effects, a medicine may cause some unwanted effects. Although not all of these side effects may occur, if they do occur they may need medical attention.

Check with your health care professional immediately if any of the following side effects occur:

More common

With intravenous injection

Fever and chills; headache; increased or decreased urination; irregular heartbeat; muscle cramps or pain; nausea; pain at the place of injection; unusual tiredness or weakness; vomiting

Less common or rare

With intravenous injection

Blurred or double vision; convulsions (seizures); numbness, tingling, pain, or weakness in hands or feet; shortness of breath, troubled breathing, wheezing, or tightness in chest; skin rash or itching; sore throat and fever; unusual bleeding or bruising

With spinal injection

Blurred vision or any change in vision; difficult urination; numbness, tingling, pain, or weakness

Other side effects may occur that usually do not need medical attention. These side effects may go away during treatment as your body adjusts to the medicine. However, check with your doctor if any of the following side effects continue or are bothersome:

More common

With intravenous injection

Diarrhea; headache; indigestion; loss of appetite; nausea or vomiting; stomach pain

Less common

With spinal injection

Back, leg, or neck pain; dizziness or lightheadedness; headache; nausea or vomiting

Other side effects not listed above may also occur in some patients. If you notice any other effects, check with your doctor.

Revised: 02/23/93
Interim revision: 04/19/95

AMPHOTERICIN B Topical†

A commonly used brand name in the U.S. is Fungizone.

†Not commericially available in Canada.

Description

Amphotericin (am-foe-TER-i-sin) B belongs to the family of medicines called antifungals. Amphotericin B topical preparations are used to treat fungus infections.

Amphotericin B is available only with your doctor's prescription, in the following dosage forms:

Topical

- Cream (U.S.)
- Lotion (U.S.)
- Ointment (U.S.)

Before Using This Medicine

In deciding to use a medicine, the risks of using the medicine must be weighed against the good it will do. This is a decision you and your doctor will make. For amphotericin B, the following should be considered:

Allergies—Tell your doctor if you have ever had any unusual or allergic reaction to amphotericin B. Also tell your health care professional if you are allergic to any other substances, such as preservatives or dyes.

Pregnancy—Amphotericin B topical preparations have not been shown to cause birth defects or other problems in humans.

Breast-feeding—Amphotericin B topical preparations have not been reported to cause problems in nursing babies.

Children—Although there is no specific information comparing use of amphotericin B topical preparations in children with use in other age groups, this medicine is not expected to cause different side effects or problems in children than it does in adults.

Older adults—Many medicines have not been studied specifically in older people. Therefore, it may not be known whether they work exactly the same way they do in younger adults. Although there is no specific information comparing use of topical amphotericin B preparations in the elderly with use in other age groups, these preparations are not expected to cause different side effects or problems in older people than they do in younger adults.

Other medicines—Although certain medicines should not be used together at all, in other cases two different medicines may be used together even if an interaction might occur. In these cases, your doctor may want to change the dose, or other precautions may be necessary. Tell your

health care professional if you are using any other topical prescription or nonprescription (over-the-counter [OTC]) medicine that is to be applied to the same area of the skin.

Proper Use of This Medicine

Apply enough amphotericin B to cover the affected areas, and rub in gently.

Do not apply an occlusive dressing (airtight covering such as kitchen plastic wrap) over this medicine since it may cause irritation of the skin. If you have any questions about this, check with your doctor.

To help clear up your infection completely, *it is very important that you keep using this medicine for the full time of treatment,* even if your symptoms begin to clear up after a few days. Since fungus infections may be very slow to clear up, you may have to continue using this medicine every day for several months or longer. If you stop using this medicine too soon, your symptoms may return. *Do not miss any doses.*

Dosing—The dose of topical amphotericin B will be different for different patients. *Follow your doctor's orders or the directions on the label.* The following information includes only the average doses of topical amphotericin B. *If your dose is different, do not change it* unless your doctor tells you to do so.

- For *topical* dosage forms (cream, lotion, and ointment):
  —For fungus infections:
    - Adults and children—Apply to the affected area(s) of the skin two to four times a day.

Missed dose—If you miss a dose of this medicine, apply it as soon as possible. Then go back to your regular dosing schedule.

Storage—To store this medicine:

- Keep out of the reach of children.
- Store away from heat and direct light.
- Keep the medicine from freezing.
- Do not keep outdated medicine or medicine no longer needed. Be sure that any discarded medicine is out of the reach of children.

Precautions While Using This Medicine

If your skin problem does not improve within 1 to 2 weeks, or if it becomes worse, check with your doctor.

When amphotericin B is rubbed into the affected skin areas, it may stain the skin slightly, especially if it is applied to areas on or around the nails. It may also stain the nails.

For patients using the *cream or lotion form* of this medicine:

- If either of these forms stain your clothing, the stain may be removed by hand-washing the clothing with soap and warm water.

For patients using the *ointment form* of this medicine:

- If this form stains your clothing, the stain may be removed with a standard cleaning fluid.

Side Effects of This Medicine

Along with its needed effects, a medicine may cause some unwanted effects. Although not all of these side effects may occur, if they do occur they may need medical attention.

Check with your doctor as soon as possible if any of the following side effects occur:

Less common

Burning, itching, redness, or other sign of irritation not present before use of this medicine

Rare

Skin rash

Other side effects may occur that usually do not need medical attention. These side effects may go away during treatment as your body adjusts to the medicine. However, check with your doctor if the following side effect continues or is bothersome:

Less common—for cream only

Dryness of skin

Other side effects not listed above may also occur in some patients. If you notice any other effects, check with your doctor.

Revised: 07/25/94

AMYL NITRITE Systemic

Generic name product available in the U.S. and Canada.

Description

Amyl nitrite (AM-il NYE-trite) is related to the nitrate medicines and is used by inhalation to relieve the pain of angina attacks. It works by relaxing blood vessels and increasing the supply of blood and oxygen to the heart while reducing its work load.

Amyl nitrite may also be used for other conditions as determined by your doctor.

This medicine comes in a glass capsule covered by a protective cloth. The cloth covering allows you to crush the glass capsule between your fingers without cutting yourself.

On the street, this medicine and others like it are sometimes called ''poppers.'' They have been used by some people to cause a ''high'' or to improve sex. Use in this way is not recommended. Amyl nitrite can cause serious harmful effects if too much is inhaled.

Amyl nitrite is available only with your doctor's prescription, in the following dosage form:

Inhalation

- Glass capsules (U.S. and Canada)

Before Using This Medicine

In deciding to use a medicine, the risks of taking the medicine must be weighed against the good it will do. This is a decision you and your doctor will make. For amyl nitrite, the following should be considered:

Allergies—Tell your doctor if you have ever had any unusual or allergic reaction to amyl nitrite or nitrates. Also tell your health care professional if you are allergic to any other substances, such as foods or dyes.

Pregnancy—Studies on effects in pregnancy have not been done in either humans or animals. However, use of amyl nitrite is not recommended during pregnancy because it could cause serious problems in the unborn baby.

Breast-feeding—It is not known whether amyl nitrite passes into breast milk. However, use of amyl nitrite is not recommended during breast-feeding, because it may cause unwanted effects in nursing babies.

Children—Studies on this medicine have been done only in adult patients and there is no specific information comparing use of amyl nitrite in children with use in other age groups.

Older adults—Dizziness or lightheadedness may be more likely to occur in the elderly, who are usually more sensitive to the effects of amyl nitrite.

Other medicines—Although certain medicines should not be used together at all, in other cases two different medicines may be used together even if an interaction might occur. In these cases, your doctor may want to change the dose, or other precautions may be necessary. When you are taking amyl nitrite, it is especially important that your health care professional knows if you are taking any of the following:

- Amantadine (e.g., Symmetrel) or
- Antidepressants (medicine for depression) or
- Antihypertensives (high blood pressure medicine) or
- Antipsychotics (medicine for mental illness) or
- Bromocriptine (e.g., Parlodel) or
- Diuretics (water pills) or
- Levodopa (e.g., Dopar) or
- Medicine for heart disease or
- Nabilone (e.g., Cesamet)—in high doses or
- Narcotic pain medicine or
- Nimodipine (e.g., Nimotop) or
- Pentamidine (e.g., Pentam) or
- Pimozide (e.g., Orap) or
- Promethazine (e.g., Phenergan) or
- Trimeprazine (e.g., Temaril)—May increase dizziness or lightheadedness when getting up from a lying or sitting position

It is also important that your health care professional knows if you are using any of the following medicines in the eye:

- Levobunolol (e.g., Betagan) or
- Metipranolol (e.g., Optipranolol) or
- Timolol (e.g., Timoptic)—May increase dizziness or lightheadedness when getting up from a lying or sitting position

Other medical problems—The presence of other medical problems may affect the use of amyl nitrite. Make sure you tell your doctor if you have any other medical problems, especially:

- Anemia (severe)
- Glaucoma—Amyl nitrite may make this condition worse
- Overactive thyroid
- Recent stroke, heart attack, or head injury

Proper Use of This Medicine

To use amyl nitrite:

- *When you begin to feel an attack of angina starting (chest pains or a tightness or squeezing in the chest), sit down. Then crush the cloth-covered glass capsule containing amyl nitrite between your finger and thumb. Pass it back and forth close to your nose and inhale the vapor several (1 to 6) times.* Since you may become dizzy, lightheaded, or faint soon after using amyl nitrite, it is best to sit or lie down rather than stand while the medicine is working. If you become dizzy or faint while sitting, take several deep breaths of air and either bend forward with your head between your knees or lie down with your feet elevated.
- Remain calm and you should feel better in a few minutes.

Use this medicine exactly as directed by your doctor, and do not use more than your doctor ordered. Using too much amyl nitrite may cause a dangerous overdose. If the medicine does not seem to be working as well after you have used it for a while, check with your doctor. *Do not increase the dose on your own.*

Dosing—*Follow your doctor's orders or the directions on the label.* The following information includes only the average doses of amyl nitrite:

- For *inhalation* dosage form:
  —Adults: 0.18 or 0.3 milliliter (1 ampul) taken by inhaling the vapor of amyl nitrite through the nose. Dose may be repeated within 1 to 5 minutes if pain is not relieved. *If you still have chest pain after a total of 2 doses in a 10-minute period, contact your doctor or have someone take you to a hospital emergency room without delay.*

Storage—To store this medicine:

- Keep out of the reach of children.
- Store away from heat and direct light.
- Do not store in the bathroom or in the kitchen. Heat may cause the medicine to break down.
- Do not keep outdated medicine or medicine no longer needed. Be sure that any discarded medicine is out of the reach of children.

Precautions While Using This Medicine

Amyl nitrite is extremely flammable. Keep it away from heat or any open flame, especially when crushing the capsule. Amyl nitrite can catch fire very easily and cause serious burns.

Dizziness or lightheadedness may occur, especially when you get up from a lying or sitting position. Getting up slowly may help, but if the problem continues or gets worse, check with your doctor.

Drinking alcohol while you are taking this medicine may make the dizziness or lightheadedness worse and may cause a serious drop in blood pressure. Check with your doctor before drinking alcoholic beverages.

After using a dose of amyl nitrite, you may get a mild headache that lasts for a short time. This is a common side effect and is no cause for alarm. However, if this effect continues, or if the headaches are severe, check with your doctor.

Side Effects of This Medicine

Along with its needed effects, a medicine may cause some unwanted effects. Although not all of these side effects may occur, if they do occur they may need medical attention.

Check with your doctor as soon as possible if any of the following side effects occur:

Rare

Skin rash; unusual tiredness or weakness

Signs and symptoms of overdose

Bluish-colored lips, fingernails, or palms of hands; dizziness (extreme) or fainting; feeling of extreme pressure in head; shortness of breath; unusual tiredness or weakness; weak and fast heartbeat

Other side effects may occur that usually do not need medical attention. These side effects may go away during treatment as your body adjusts to the medicine. However, check with your doctor if any of the following side effects continue or are bothersome:

More common

Dizziness or lightheadedness, especially when getting up from a lying or sitting position; fast pulse; flushing of face and neck; headache (mild); nausea or vomiting; restlessness

Other side effects not listed above may also occur in some patients. If you notice any other effects, check with your doctor.

Revised: 04/12/93

ANABOLIC STEROIDS Systemic

Some commonly used brand names are:

In the U.S.—

Deca-Durabolin[1]
Durabolin[1]
Durabolin-50[1]
Hybolin Decanoate[1]
Hybolin-Improved[1]
Kabolin[1]
Oxandrin[2]
Winstrol[4]

In Canada—

Anapolon 50[3]
Deca-Durabolin[1]

Note: For quick reference, the following anabolic steroids are numbered to match the corresponding brand names.

This information applies to the following medicines:

1. Nandrolone (NAN-droe-lone)‡
2. Oxandrolone (ox-AN-droe-lone)†
3. Oxymetholone (ox-i-METH-oh-lone)*
4. Stanozolol (stan-OH-zoe-lole)†

*Not commercially available in the U.S.
†Not commercially available in Canada.
‡Generic name product may also be available in the U.S.

Description

This medicine belongs to the group of medicines known as anabolic (an-a-BOL-ik) steroids. They are related to testosterone, a male sex hormone. Anabolic steroids help to rebuild tissues that have become weak because of serious injury or illness. A diet high in proteins and calories is necessary with anabolic steroid treatment.

Anabolic steroids are used for several reasons:

- to help patients gain weight after a severe illness, injury, or continuing infection. They also are used when patients fail to gain or maintain normal weight because of unexplained medical reasons.
- to treat certain types of anemia.
- to treat certain kinds of breast cancer in some women.
- to treat hereditary angioedema, which causes swelling of the face, arms, legs, throat, windpipe, bowels, or sexual organs.

Anabolic steroids may also be used for other conditions as determined by your doctor.

Anabolic steroids are available only with your doctor's prescription, in the following dosage forms:

Oral

Oxandrolone
- Tablets (U.S.)

Oxymetholone
- Tablets (Canada)

Stanozolol
- Tablets (U.S.)

Parenteral

Nandrolone
- Injection (U.S. and Canada)

Before Using This Medicine

In deciding to use a medicine, the risks of taking the medicine must be weighed against the good it will do. This is a decision you and your doctor will make. For anabolic steroids, the following should be considered:

Allergies—Tell your doctor if you have ever had any unusual or allergic reaction to anabolic steroids or androgens (male sex hormones). Also tell your health care professional if you are allergic to any other substances, such as foods, preservatives, or dyes.

Pregnancy—Anabolic steroids are not recommended during pregnancy. They may cause the development of male features in the female fetus and premature growth and development of male features in the male fetus. Be sure you have discussed this with your doctor.

Breast-feeding—It is not known whether anabolic steroids can cause problems in nursing babies. There is very little experience with their use in mothers who are breast-feeding.

Children—Anabolic steroids may cause children to stop growing. In addition, they may make male children develop too fast sexually and may cause male-like changes in female children.

Older adults—When elderly male patients are treated with anabolic steroids, they may have an increased risk of enlarged prostate or cancer of the prostate.

Other medicines—Although certain medicines should not be used together at all, in other cases two different medicines may be used together even if an interaction might occur. In these cases, your doctor may want to change the dose, or other precautions may be necessary. When you are taking anabolic steroids, it is especially important that your health care professional know if you are taking any of the following:

- Acetaminophen (e.g., Tylenol) (with long-term, high-dose use) or
- Amiodarone (e.g., Cordarone) or
- Androgens (male hormones) or
- Anti-infectives by mouth or by injection (medicine for infection) or
- Antithyroid agents (medicine for overactive thyroid) or
- Carbamazepine (e.g., Tegretol) or
- Carmustine (e.g., BiCNU) or
- Chloroquine (e.g., Aralen) or
- Dantrolene (e.g., Dantrium) or
- Daunorubicin (e.g., Cerubidine) or
- Disulfiram (e.g., Antabuse) or
- Divalproex (e.g., Depakote) or
- Estrogens (female hormones) or
- Etretinate (e.g., Tegison) or
- Gold salts (medicine for arthritis) or
- Hydroxychloroquine (e.g., Plaquenil) or
- Mercaptopurine (e.g., Purinethol) or
- Methotrexate (e.g., Mexate) or
- Methyldopa (e.g., Aldomet) or
- Naltrexone (e.g., Trexan) (with long-term, high-dose use) or
- Oral contraceptives (birth control pills) containing estrogen or
- Phenothiazines (acetophenazine [e.g., Tindal], chlorpromazine [e.g., Thorazine], fluphenazine [e.g., Prolixin], mesoridazine [e.g., Serentil], perphenazine [e.g., Trilafon], prochlorperazine [e.g., Compazine], promazine [e.g., Sparine], promethazine [e.g., Phenergan], thioridazine [e.g., Mellaril], trifluoperazine [e.g., Stelazine], triflupromazine [e.g., Vesprin], trimeprazine [e.g., Temaril]) or
- Phenytoin (e.g., Dilantin) or
- Plicamycin (e.g., Mithracin) or
- Valproic acid (e.g., Depakene)—Taking anabolic steroids with any of these medicines may increase the chances of liver damage. Your doctor may want you to have extra blood tests to check for this if you must take both medicines
- Anticoagulants, oral (blood thinners you take by mouth)—Anabolic steroids can increase the effect of these medicines and possibly cause excessive bleeding

Other medical problems—The presence of other medical problems may affect the use of anabolic steroids. Make sure you tell your doctor if you have any other medical problems, especially:

- Breast cancer (in males and some females)
- Diabetes mellitus (sugar diabetes)—Anabolic steroids can decrease blood sugar levels
- Enlarged prostate or
- Prostate cancer—Anabolic steroids may make these conditions worse by causing more enlargement of the prostate or more growth of a tumor
- Heart or blood vessel disease—Anabolic steroids can worsen these conditions by increasing blood cholesterol levels
- Kidney disease
- Liver disease
- Too much calcium in the blood (or history of) (in females)—Anabolic steroids may worsen this condition by raising the amount of calcium in the blood even more

Proper Use of This Medicine

Take this medicine only as directed. Do not take more of it and do not take it more often than your doctor ordered. To do so may increase the chance of side effects.

In order for this medicine to work properly, it is important that you follow a diet high in proteins and calories. If you have any questions about this, check with your health care professional.

Dosing—The dose of these medicines will be different for different patients. *Follow your doctor's orders or the directions on the label.* The following information includes only the average doses of these medicines. *If your dose is different, do not change it* unless your doctor tells you to do so.

The number of tablets that you take depends on the strength of the medicine. Also, *the number of doses you take each day, the time allowed between doses, and the length of time you take the medicine depend on the medical problem for which you are taking the anabolic steroid.*

For nandrolone decanoate

- For *injection* dosage form:
  - —For treatment of certain types of anemia:
    - Women and girls 14 years of age and older—50 to 100 milligrams (mg) injected into a muscle every one to four weeks.
    - Men and boys 14 years of age and older—50 to 200 mg injected into a muscle every one to four weeks.

    Your doctor may want to continue treatment for up to twelve weeks. After a four-week rest period without receiving this medicine, your doctor may want you to repeat the cycle.
    - Children up to 2 years of age—Dose must be determined by your doctor.
    - Children 2 to 13 years of age—25 to 50 mg injected into a muscle every three to four weeks.

For nandrolone phenpropionate

- For *injection* dosage form:
  - —For treatment of certain breast cancers in women:
    - Adults—25 to 100 milligrams (mg) injected into a muscle once a week for up to twelve weeks. After a four-week rest period without receiving this medicine, your doctor may want you to repeat the cycle.

• Children—Dose must be determined by your doctor.

For oxandrolone

• For *oral* dosage form (tablets):

—For treatment in rebuilding tissue after a serious illness or injury:

• Adults and teenagers—2.5 milligrams (mg) two to four times a day for up to four weeks. Your doctor may increase your dose up to 20 mg a day.

• Children—Dose is based on body weight and must be determined by your doctor. The usual dose is 0.25 mg per kilogram (kg) (0.11 mg per pound) of body weight a day.

For oxymetholone

• For *oral* dosage form (tablets):

—For treatment of certain types of anemia:

• Adults, teenagers, children, and older infants—Dose is based on body weight and must be determined by your doctor. The usual dose is 1 to 5 milligrams (mg) per kilogram (kg) (0.45 to 2.3 mg per pound) of body weight a day.

• Premature and newborn infants—Dose is based on body weight or size and must be determined by your doctor. The usual dose is 0.175 mg per kg (0.08 mg per pound) of body weight once a day.

For stanozolol

• For *oral* dosage form (tablets):

—To prevent hereditary angioedema, which causes swelling of the face, arms, legs, throat, windpipe, bowels, or sexual organs:

• Adults and teenagers—At first, 2 milligrams (mg) three times a day to 4 mg four times a day for five days. Then, your doctor may slowly lower the dose to 2 mg once a day or once every other day.

Missed dose—If you miss a dose of this medicine and your dosing schedule is:

- One dose a day—Take the missed dose as soon as possible. However, if you do not remember it until the next day, skip the missed dose and go back to your regular dosing schedule. Do not double doses.
- More than one dose a day—Take the missed dose as soon as possible. However, if it is almost time for your next dose, skip the missed dose and go back to your regular dosing schedule. Do not double doses.

If you have any questions about this, check with your doctor.

Storage—To store this medicine:

- Keep out of the reach of children.
- Store away from heat and direct light.
- Do not store the tablet form of this medicine in the bathroom, near the kitchen sink, or in other damp places. Heat or moisture may cause the medicine to break down.
- Keep the liquid form of this medicine from freezing.
- Do not keep outdated medicine or medicine no longer needed. Be sure that any discarded medicine is out of the reach of children.

Precautions While Using This Medicine

Your doctor should check your progress at regular visits to make sure that this medicine does not cause unwanted effects.

For diabetic patients:

- This medicine may affect blood sugar levels. If you notice a change in the results of your blood or urine sugar tests or if you have any questions, check with your doctor.

Side Effects of This Medicine

Tumors of the liver, liver cancer, or peliosis hepatis, a form of liver disease, have occurred during long-term, high-dose therapy with anabolic steroids. Although these effects are rare, they can be very serious and may cause death. Discuss these possible effects with your doctor.

Along with its needed effects, a medicine may cause some unwanted effects. Although not all of these side effects may occur, if they do occur they may need medical attention.

Check with your doctor immediately if any of the following side effects occur:

For both females and males

Less common

Yellow eyes or skin

Rare (with long-term use)

Black, tarry, or light-colored stools; dark-colored urine; purple- or red-colored spots on body or inside the mouth or nose; sore throat and/or fever; vomiting of blood

Also, check with your doctor as soon as possible if any of the following side effects occur:

For both females and males

Less common

Bone pain; nausea or vomiting; sore tongue; swelling of feet or lower legs; unusual bleeding; unusual weight gain

Rare (with long-term use)

Abdominal or stomach pain; feeling of discomfort (continuing); headache (continuing); hives; loss of appetite (continuing); unexplained weight loss; unpleasant breath odor (continuing)

For females only

More common

Acne or oily skin; enlarging clitoris; hoarseness or deepening of voice; irregular menstrual periods; unnatural hair growth; unusual hair loss

Less common

Mental depression; unusual tiredness

For young males (boys) only

More common

Acne; enlarging penis; increased frequency of erections; unnatural hair growth

Less common

Unexplained darkening of skin

For sexually mature males only
More common
Enlargement of breasts or breast soreness; frequent or continuing erections; frequent urge to urinate
For elderly males only
Less common
Difficult or frequent urination

Other side effects may occur that usually do not need medical attention. These side effects may go away during treatment as your body adjusts to the medicine. However, check with your doctor if any of the following side effects continue or are bothersome:

For both females and males
Less common
Chills; diarrhea; feeling of abdominal or stomach fullness; muscle cramps; trouble in sleeping; unusual decrease or increase in sexual desire
For males only
More common
Acne
Less common
Decreased sexual ability

Other side effects not listed above may also occur in some patients. If you notice any other effects, check with your doctor.

Additional Information

Once a medicine has been approved for marketing for a certain use, experience may show that it is also useful for other medical problems. Although these uses are not included in product labeling, anabolic steroids may be used in certain patients with the following medical conditions:

- Certain blood clotting diseases
- Growth failure
- Turner's syndrome

Other than the above information, there is no additional information relating to proper use, precautions, or side effects for these uses.

Revised: 06/20/92
Interim revision: 06/08/94; 06/23/97

ANDROGENS Systemic

Some commonly used brand names are:

In the U.S.—

Androderm[3]
Android[2]
Android-F[1]
Andro L.A. 200[3]
Andronate 100[3]
Andronate 200[3]
Andropository 200[3]
Andryl 200[3]
Delatest[3]
Delatestryl[3]
Depotest[3]
Depo-Testosterone[3]
Everone 200[3]
Halotestin[1]
ORETON Methyl[2]
T-Cypionate[3]
Testamone 100[3]
Testaqua[3]
Testex[3]
Testoderm[3]
Testoderm with Adhesives[3]
Testopel Pellets[3]
Testred[2]
Testred Cypionate 200[3]
Testrin-P.A.[3]
Virilon[2]
Virilon IM[3]

In Canada—

Delatestryl[3]
Depo-Testosterone Cypionate[3]
Halotestin[1]
Malogen in Oil[3]
Metandren[2]

Note: For quick reference, the following androgens are numbered to match the corresponding brand names.

This information applies to the following medicines:

1. Fluoxymesterone (floo-ox-i-MES-te-rone)‡
2. Methyltestosterone (meth-il-tes-TOS-te-rone)‡
3. Testosterone (tes-TOS-te-rone)‡

‡Generic name product may also be available in the U.S.

Description

Androgens (AN-droe-jens) are male hormones. Some androgens are naturally produced in the body and are necessary for the normal sexual development of males.

Androgens are used for several reasons, such as:

- to replace the hormone when the body is unable to produce enough on its own.
- to stimulate the beginning of puberty in certain boys who are late starting puberty naturally.
- to treat certain types of breast cancer in females.

In addition, some of these medicines may be used for other conditions as determined by your doctor.

Androgens are available only with your doctor's prescription, in the following dosage forms:

Oral
Fluoxymesterone
- Tablets (U.S. and Canada)

Methyltestosterone
- Capsules (U.S.)
- Tablets (U.S. and Canada)

Parenteral
Testosterone
- Injection (U.S. and Canada)

Subcutaneous
Testosterone
- Implants (Pellets) (U.S.)

Topical
Testosterone
- Ointment
- Transdermal systems (skin patches) (U.S.)

Before Using This Medicine

In deciding to use a medicine, the risks of taking the medicine must be weighed against the good it will do. This is a decision you and your doctor will make. For androgens, the following should be considered:

Allergies—Tell your doctor if you have ever had any unusual or allergic reaction to androgens. Also tell your health care professional if you are allergic to any other substances, such as foods, preservatives, or dyes.

Pregnancy—Androgens are not recommended during pregnancy. When given to pregnant women, the medicine has caused male features to develop in female babies.

Breast-feeding—Use is not recommended in nursing mothers, since androgens may pass into the breast milk and may cause unwanted effects in the nursing baby, such as premature (too early) sexual development in males and development of male features in female babies.

Children—Androgens may cause children to stop growing. In addition, androgens may make male children develop too fast sexually and may cause male-like changes in female children.

Older adults—When older male patients are treated with androgens, they may have an increased risk of enlarged prostate (a male gland) or their existing prostate cancer may get worse. For these reasons, a prostate examination and a blood test to check for prostate cancer is often done before androgens are prescribed for men over the age of 50 years. These examinations may be repeated during treatment.

The reservoir-type (nonscrotal) patch should not be applied to the backs of men older than 65 years of age because the medicine is not absorbed as well at that location.

Other medicines—Although certain medicines should not be used together at all, in other cases two different medicines may be used together even if an interaction might occur. In these cases, your doctor may want to change the dose, or other precautions may be necessary. When you are taking androgens, it is especially important that your health care professional know if you are taking any of the following:

- Acetaminophen (e.g., Tylenol) (with long-term, high-dose use) or
- Amiodarone (e.g., Cordarone) or
- Anabolic steroids (nandrolone [e.g., Anabolin], oxandrolone [e.g., Anavar], oxymetholone [e.g., Anadrol], stanozolol [e.g., Winstrol]) or
- Anti-infectives by mouth or by injection (medicines for infection) or
- Antithyroid agents (medicines for overactive thyroid) or
- Carbamazepine (e.g., Tegretol) or
- Carmustine (e.g., BiCNU) or
- Chloroquine (e.g., Aralen) or
- Dantrolene (e.g., Dantrium) or
- Daunorubicin (e.g., Cerubidine) or
- Disulfiram (e.g., Antabuse) or
- Divalproex (e.g., Depakote) or
- Estrogens (female hormones) or
- Etretinate (e.g., Tegison) or
- Gold salts (medicines for arthritis) or
- Hydroxychloroquine (e.g., Plaquenil) or
- Mercaptopurine (e.g., Purinethol) or
- Methotrexate (e.g., Mexate) or
- Methyldopa (e.g., Aldomet) or
- Naltrexone (e.g., Trexan) (with long-term, high-dose use) or
- Oral contraceptives (birth control pills) containing estrogen or
- Phenothiazines (acetophenazine [e.g., Tindal], chlorpromazine [e.g., Thorazine], fluphenazine [e.g., Prolixin], mesoridazine [e.g., Serentil], perphenazine [e.g., Trilafon], prochlorperazine [e.g., Compazine], promazine [e.g., Sparine], promethazine [e.g., Phenergan], thioridazine [e.g., Mellaril], trifluoperazine [e.g., Stelazine], triflupromazine [e.g., Vesprin], trimeprazine [e.g., Temaril]) or
- Phenytoin (e.g., Dilantin) or
- Plicamycin (e.g., Mithracin) or
- Valproic acid (e.g., Depakene)—Use of these medicines with androgens may increase the chance of liver problems. Your doctor may want you to have extra blood tests that check your liver while you are taking any of these medicines with an androgen
- Anticoagulants (blood thinners)—Androgens can increase the effect of these medicines and possibly cause excessive bleeding

Other medical problems—The presence of other medical problems may affect the use of androgens. Make sure you tell your doctor if you have any other medical problems, especially:

- Breast cancer (in males) or
- Prostate cancer—Androgens can cause growth of these tumors
- Breast cancer (in females)—Androgens may cause high calcium levels in the blood to become worse
- Diabetes mellitus (sugar diabetes)—Androgens can increase or decrease blood sugar levels. Careful monitoring of blood glucose should be done
- Edema (swelling of face, hands, feet, or lower legs) or
- Kidney disease or
- Liver disease—These conditions can be worsened by the fluid retention (keeping too much water in the body) that can be caused by androgens. Also, liver disease can prevent the body from removing the medicine from the bloodstream as fast as it normally would. This could increase the chance of side effects occurring
- Enlarged prostate—Androgens can cause further enlargement of the prostate
- Heart or blood vessel disease—Androgens can make these conditions worse because androgens may increase blood cholesterol levels. Also, androgens can cause fluid retention (keeping too much water in the body), which also can worsen heart or blood vessel disease

Proper Use of This Medicine

Take this medicine only as directed. Do not take more of it and do not take it more often than your doctor ordered. Doing so may increase the chance of side effects.

There are two types of testosterone skin patches. The matrix-type is applied to skin of the scrotum. The reservoir-type is never applied to the skin of the scrotum. It is applied to the abdomen, back, thighs, or upper arms. Be sure you know which type you are using so that you will apply it properly. These skin patches come with patient directions. Read them carefully before using the patch.

For patients taking *fluoxymesterone* or *methyltestosterone*:

- Take this medicine with food to lessen possible stomach upset, unless otherwise directed by your doctor.

For patients using the *matrix-type skin patch of testosterone (Testoderm):*

- You must apply the patch to the scrotum because the medicine easily passes into your body at this area. Other areas of your skin are too thick for the medicine to work properly.

- Wash and dry your hands thoroughly before and after handling the patch.
  —Before applying the patch:
  - Clean and dry your scrotum.
  - You should also dry-shave this area once a week by using a shaver only (no soap or water). To dry-shave, stretch the skin of your scrotum with your fingers. Use short gentle strokes with no pressure on the razor to remove the hair. Do not use shaving cream or hair-removing creams (e.g., Nair).
  - You may sit with your legs apart or stand while applying the patch.

  —To apply the patch:
  - Open the wrapper containing the patch at the point shown on the package.
  - Carefully remove the patch from its protective plastic liner by peeling the patch from the liner starting at the corner.
  - Warm your scrotum for a few seconds before applying the patch to achieve the best results. Stretch the skin of your scrotum gently to remove the folds by pulling the penis up and to the side. Another way is to pull your scrotum down. Use your first and middle fingers to stretch the skin of your scrotum.
  - Place the shiny side of the patch onto the warm stretched skin of your scrotum.
  - Press the shiny side of the patch firmly in place with the palm of your hand for about 10 seconds. Make sure there is good contact, especially around the edges. The patch should stick to your scrotum and show the natural wrinkles of your scrotum.
  - Put on comfortable, close-fitting briefs (underwear) after applying the patch.
  - If a patch becomes loose or falls off, you may reapply it or discard it and apply a new patch.

  —To remove the skin patch:
  - Gently peel the patch from the skin.
  - You may reuse the patch after removing it for swimming, bathing, showering, or sexual activity. First, remove the patch and place the shiny (sticky) side up on a counter. Before you reapply the patch, be sure the skin on your scrotum is dry. Then, follow the directions to reapply the patch.
  - When the wearing period is over, fold the patch in half with the sticky sides together. Place the folded, used patch in its protective pouch or in aluminum foil. Be sure to throw it away out of the reach of children and pets.

For patients using the *reservoir-type skin patch of testosterone (Androderm):*

- Apply the patch to the abdomen, back, thighs, or arms. Men over 65 years of age should not apply it to the back because the medicine is not absorbed as well at that location. Do not apply the patch to the scrotum. Do not apply the patch to areas of the body that seem bony, such as the top of the shoulders or near the elbows, or to areas that may have to support your body while sleeping or sitting, such as the hips or shoulder blades. Apply each new patch to a different place. Do not reapply a patch to the same area of skin for 7 days.
- Wash and dry your hands thoroughly before and after handling the patch.
  —Before applying the patch, clean and dry the application site.
  —To apply the patch:
  - Open the wrapper containing the patch at the point shown on the package.
  - Carefully remove the patch from its protective plastic liner by peeling the patch from the liner, starting at the corner.
  - Place the shiny side of the patch onto the skin.
  - Press the shiny side of the patch firmly in place with the palm of you hand for about 10 seconds. Be sure there is good contact, especially around the edges.
  - If a patch becomes loose or falls off, you may reapply it or discard it and apply a new patch.

  —To remove the skin patch:
  - Gently peel the patch from the skin.
  - You do not need to remove this patch for swimming, bathing, showering, or sexual activity.
  - When the wearing period is over, fold the patch in half with the sticky sides together. Place the folded, used patch in its protective pouch or in aluminum foil. Be sure to throw it away out of the reach of children and pets.

Dosing—The dose of these medicines will be different for different patients. *Follow your doctor's orders or the directions on the label.* The following information includes only the average doses of these medicines. *If your dose is different, do not change it* unless your doctor tells you to do so.

The number of capsules or tablets that you take depends on the strength of the medicine. Also, *the number of doses you take each day, the time between doses, and the length of time you take the medicine depend on the medical problem for which you are taking the androgen.*

For fluoxymesterone

- For *oral* dosage form (tablets):
  —For androgen hormone replacement in men:
  - Adults—5 milligrams (mg) one to four times a day.

  —For treatment of breast cancer in women:
  - Adults—10 to 40 mg a day in divided doses.

  —For treatment of delayed sexual development in boys:
  - Children—2.5 to 10 mg a day for four to six months.

For methyltestosterone

- For *oral* dosage forms (capsules or tablets):
  —For androgen hormone replacement in men:
  - Adults—10 to 50 milligrams (mg) a day.

  —For treatment of breast cancer in women:
  - Adults—50 mg one to four times a day. Your doctor may decrease your dose to 50 mg two times a day after two to four weeks.

—For treatment of delayed sexual development in boys:

• Children—5 to 25 mg a day for four to six months.

For testosterone

• For *injection* dosage form:

—For androgen hormone replacement in men:

• Adults—25 to 50 milligrams (mg) injected into a muscle two or three times a week.

—For treatment of breast cancer in women:

• Adults—50 to 100 mg injected into a muscle three times a week.

—For treatment of delayed sexual development in boys:

• Children—Up to 100 mg injected into a muscle once a month for four to six months.

• For *subcutaneous* dosage form (implants):

—For androgen hormone replacement in men:

• Adults—150 to 450 milligram (mg) (two to six implants) inserted into the skin every three to six months.

—For treatment of delayed sexual development in boys:

• Children—Use and dose must be determined by your doctor.

• For *topical* dosage forms (patches):

—For androgen hormone replacement in men:

When using the brand name Testoderm patches (matrix-type)

• Adults—4 or 6 mg (one patch) applied to your scrotum once a day. The patch should be worn at least twenty-two of the twenty-four hours in a day.

• Children—Use and dose must be determined by your doctor.

When using the brand name Androderm patches (reservoir-type)

• Adults and teenagers 15 years of age and older—2.5 to 7.5 mg (one to three patches) applied to the abdomen, back, thighs, or upper arms once a day. The patch(es) should be worn at least twenty-two of the twenty-four hours in a day. Do not apply to the back if you are older than 65 years of age.

• Children up to 15 years of age—Use and dose must be determined by your doctor.

For testosterone cypionate or *testosterone enanthate*

• For *injection* dosage form:

—For androgen hormone replacement in men:

• Adults—50 to 400 milligrams (mg) injected into a muscle every two to four weeks.

—For treatment of breast cancer in women:

• Adults—200 to 400 mg injected into a muscle every two to four weeks.

—For treatment of delayed sexual development in boys:

• Children—Up to 100 mg injected into a muscle once a month for four to six months.

For testosterone propionate

• For *injection* dosage form:

—For androgen hormone replacement in men:

• Adults—25 to 50 milligrams (mg) injected into a muscle two or three times a week.

—For treatment of breast cancer in women:

• Adults—50 to 100 mg injected into a muscle three times a week.

—For treatment of delayed sexual development in boys:

• Children—Up to 100 milligrams (mg) injected into a muscle once a month for four to six months.

Missed dose—If you miss a dose of this medicine and your dosing schedule is:

• One dose a day—Take, use, or apply the missed dose as soon as possible. However, if you do not remember it until the next day, skip the missed dose and go back to your regular dosing schedule. Do not double doses.

• More than one dose a day—Take or use the missed dose as soon as possible. However, if it is almost time for your next dose, skip the missed dose and go back to your regular dosing schedule. Do not double doses.

If you have any questions about this, check with your doctor.

Storage—To store this medicine:

• Keep out of the reach of children.

• Store away from heat and direct light.

• Do not store in the bathroom, near the kitchen sink, or in other damp places. Heat or moisture may cause the medicine to break down.

• Keep the injection form of this medicine from freezing.

• Do not keep outdated medicine or medicine no longer needed. Be sure that any discarded medicine is out of the reach of children.

Precautions While Using This Medicine

Your doctor should check your progress at regular visits to make sure this medicine does not cause unwanted effects.

For patients with diabetes mellitus (sugar diabetes):

• This medicine may affect blood sugar levels. If you notice a change in the results of your blood or urine sugar tests or if you have any questions, check with your doctor.

For patients using the brand name, Testoderm patches (matrix-type):

• In some cases, this medicine can pass from you to your sexual partner. Tell your doctor if your female sex partner has a great increase in acne. Also, tell your doctor if her hair begins to grow in odd places like her upper lip, chest, or back. This will not occur if you are using the reservoir-type skin patch because it is not applied to the scrotum and because it has a protective liner.

Side Effects of This Medicine

Discuss these possible effects with your doctor:

- Tumors of the liver, liver cancer, or peliosis hepatis (a form of liver disease) have occurred during long-term, high-dose therapy with androgens. Although these effects are rare, they can be very serious and may cause death.
- Androgens can stimulate existing prostate cancer in men who already have it but have not yet been diagnosed. Also, the prostate (a male gland) may become enlarged. Enlargement of the prostate does not mean that cancer will develop. If enlargement occurs and you have difficulty in urinating, it it a good idea to be checked by your doctor.
- When androgens are used in women, especially in high doses, male-like changes may occur, such as hoarseness or deepening of the voice, unnatural hair growth, or unusual hair loss. Most of these changes will go away if the medicine is stopped as soon as the changes are noticed. However, some changes, such as voice changes or enlarged clitoris, may not go away.
- When androgens are used in high doses in males, they interfere with the production of sperm. This effect is usually temporary and only happens during the time you are taking the medicine. However, discuss this possible effect with your doctor if you are planning on having children.

Along with its needed effects, a medicine may cause some unwanted effects. Although not all of these side effects appear very often, when they do occur they may require medical attention.

Check with your doctor as soon as possible if any of the following side effects occur:

More common

For females only

Acne or oily skin; decreased breast size; irregular menstrual cycles; hoarseness or deepening of voice; increase in size of female genitals; increase in unnatural hair growth or male pattern baldness

Note: These symptoms may occur in females whose male sexual partner uses a scrotal patch.

For males only

Blistering of skin under patch (especially when the nonscrotal patch is applied to bony areas of the skin); breast soreness or enlargement; frequent or continuing erection of penis lasting up to 4 hours or painful penile erections lasting longer than 4 hours; frequent urge to urinate; itching or redness of skin under patch (less likely with nonscrotal patch) or at site of implants, mild to severe

For prepubertal boys only

Acne; early growth of pubic hair; enlargement of penis; frequent or continuing erections

Less common

For males or females

Dizziness; frequent or continuing headache; nausea; overall body flushing, redness, or itching of skin; rapid weight gain; swelling of feet or lower legs; unusual bleeding; unusual tiredness; vomiting; yellow skin or eyes (occurring with fluoxymesterone or methyltestosterone more often than with testosterone)

For females with breast cancer or bedridden males or females—in addition to the side effects listed above

Confusion or mental depression; constipation; increased thirst; increased urge to urinate or increased amount of urine

For males only

Burning sensation or hardening or thickening of skin under patch; chills; continuing pain at site of implants; difficulty in urinating; itching, skin redness, or rash under patch, severe (less likely with nonscrotal patch); pain in scrotum or groin

Rare

For males or females—more likely with oral androgens or long-term or high doses of androgens

Abdominal or stomach pain, continuing; bad breath odor, continuing; black, tarry or light-colored stools or dark urine; fever; hives; loss of appetite, continuing; purple or red spots on body or inside the mouth or nose; sore throat; swelling, pain, or tenderness of abdomen; vomiting of blood

Other side effects may occur that usually do not need medical attention. These side effects may go away during treatment as your body adjusts to the medicine. However, check with your doctor if any of the following side effects continue or are bothersome:

Less common

For both males and females

Acne, mild; diarrhea; increase in pubic hair growth; infection, pain, redness, or other irritation at site of injection; decrease or increase in sexual desire or drive; stomach pain; trouble in sleeping

For males only

Decrease in testicle size

Other side effects not listed above may also occur in some patients. If you notice any other effects, check with your doctor.

Additional Information

Once a medicine has been approved for marketing for a certain use, experience may show that it is also useful for other medical problems. Although these uses are not included in product labeling, androgens are used in certain patients with the following medical conditions:

- Anemias (blood problems)
- Delayed growth spurt
- Development of male features in transsexuals
- Microphallus (underdevelopment of the penis)
- Lichen sclerosus (a skin problem of the vulva)

Other than the above information, there is no additional information relating to proper use, precautions, or side effects for these uses.

Revised: 08/24/97

ANDROGENS AND ESTROGENS Systemic

Some commonly used brand names are:

In the U.S.—

Andrest 90-4[5]	Estratest[3]
Andro-Estro 90-4[5]	Estratest H.S.[3]
Androgyn L.A.[5]	Halodrin[4]
De-Comberol[5]	Menoject-L.A.[5]
Deladumone[5]	OB[5]
Delatestadiol[5]	Premarin with Methyltestosterone[2]
depAndrogyn[5]	
Depo-Testadiol[5]	Teev[5]
Depotestogen[5]	Tes Est Cyp[5]
Duo-Cyp[5]	Test-Estro Cypionate[5]
Duo-Gen L.A.[5]	Tylosterone[1]
Dura-Dumone 90/4[5]	Valertest No. 1[5]
Duratestin[5]	Valertest No. 2[5]

In Canada—

Climacteron[5]	Premarin with Methyltestosterone[2]
Duogex L.A.[5]	
Neo-Pause[5]	

Another commonly used name for diethylstilbestrol is DES.

Note: For quick reference, the following androgens and estrogens are numbered to match the corresponding brand names.

This information applies to the following medicines:

1. Diethylstilbestrol (dye-eth-il-stil-BESS-trole) and Methyltestosterone (meth-il-tes-TOSS-ter-one)
2. Estrogens, Conjugated (ESS-troe-jenz, CON-ju-gate-ed), and Methyltestosterone
3. Estrogens, Esterified (ess-TAIR-i-fyed), and Methyltestosterone
4. Fluoxymesterone (floo-ox-e-MESS-ter-own) and Ethinyl Estradiol (ETH-in-il ess-tra-DYE-ole)
5. Testosterone (tess-TOSS-ter-own) and Estradiol‡

‡Generic name product may also be available in the U.S.

Description

Androgens (AN-droe-jens) and estrogens (ESS-troe-jens) are hormones. Estrogens are produced by the body in greater amounts in females. They are necessary for normal sexual development of the female and for regulation of the menstrual cycle during the childbearing years. Androgens are produced by the body in greater amounts in males. However, androgens are also present in females in small amounts.

The ovaries and adrenal glands begin to produce less of these hormones after menopause. This combination product is prescribed to make up for this lower production of hormones. This may relieve signs of menopause, such as hot flashes and unusual sweating, chills, faintness, or dizziness.

Androgens and estrogens may also be used for other conditions as determined by your doctor.

There is no medical evidence to support the belief that the use of estrogens (contained in this combination medicine) will keep the patient feeling young, keep the skin soft, or delay the appearance of wrinkles. Nor has it been proven that the use of estrogens during the menopause will relieve emotional and nervous symptoms, unless these symptoms are caused by other menopausal symptoms, such as hot flashes.

A paper called "Information for the Patient" should be given to you with your prescription. Read this carefully.

Also, before you use an androgen and estrogen product, you and your doctor should discuss the good that it will do as well as the risks of using it.

This medicine is available only with your doctor's prescription, in the following dosage forms:

Oral

Diethylstilbestrol and Methyltestosterone
- Tablets (U.S.)

Estrogens, Conjugated, and Methyltestosterone
- Tablets (U.S. and Canada)

Estrogens, Esterified, and Methyltestosterone
- Tablets (U.S.)

Fluoxymesterone and Ethinyl Estradiol
- Tablets (U.S.)

Parenteral

Testosterone and Estradiol
- Injection (U.S. and Canada)

Before Using This Medicine

In deciding to use a medicine, the risks of taking the medicine must be weighed against the good it will do. This is a decision you and your doctor will make. For androgen and estrogen combination products, the following should be considered:

Allergies—Tell your doctor if you have ever had any unusual or allergic reaction to androgens, anabolic steroids, or estrogens. Also tell your health care professional if you are allergic to any other substances, such as foods, preservatives, or dyes.

Pregnancy—Estrogens (contained in this combination medicine) are not recommended for use during pregnancy, since some estrogens have been shown to cause serious birth defects in humans. Some daughters of women who took diethylstilbestrol (DES) during pregnancy have developed reproductive (genital) tract problems and, rarely, cancer of the vagina and/or uterine cervix when they reached childbearing age. Some sons of women who took DES during pregnancy have developed urinary-genital tract problems.

Androgens (contained in this combination medicine) should not be used during pregnancy because they may cause male-like changes in a female baby.

Breast-feeding—Use of this medicine is not recommended in nursing mothers. Estrogens pass into the breast milk and their possible effect on the baby is not known. It is not known if androgens pass into breast milk. However, androgens may cause unwanted effects in nursing babies such as too early sexual development in males or male-like changes in females.

Older adults—This medicine has been tested and has not been shown to cause different side effects or problems in older women than it does in younger females.

Other medicines—Although certain medicines should not be used together at all, in other cases two different medicines may be used together even if an interaction might occur. In these cases, your doctor may want to change the

dose, or other precautions may be necessary. When you are taking an androgen and estrogen combination product, it is especially important that your health care professional know if you are taking any of the following:

- Acetaminophen (e.g., Tylenol) (with long-term, high-dose use) or
- Amiodarone (e.g., Cordarone) or
- Anabolic steroids (nandrolone [e.g., Anabolin], oxandrolone [e.g., Anavar], oxymetholone [e.g., Anadrol], stanozolol [e.g., Winstrol]) or
- Anti-infectives by mouth or by injection (medicine for infection) or
- Antithyroid agents (medicine for overactive thyroid) or
- Carbamazepine (e.g., Tegretol) or
- Carmustine (e.g., BiCNU) or
- Chloroquine (e.g., Aralen) or
- Dantrolene (e.g., Dantrium) or
- Daunorubicin (e.g., Cerubidine) or
- Disulfiram (e.g., Antabuse) or
- Divalproex (e.g., Depakote) or
- Etretinate (e.g., Tegison) or
- Gold salts (medicine for arthritis) or
- Hydroxychloroquine (e.g., Plaquenil) or
- Mercaptopurine (e.g., Purinethol) or
- Methotrexate (e.g., Mexate) or
- Methyldopa (e.g., Aldomet) or
- Naltrexone (e.g., Trexan) (with long-term, high-dose use) or
- Phenothiazines (acetophenazine [e.g., Tindal], chlorpromazine [e.g., Thorazine], fluphenazine [e.g., Prolixin], mesoridazine [e.g., Serentil], perphenazine [e.g., Trilafon], prochlorperazine [e.g., Compazine], promazine [e.g., Sparine], promethazine [e.g., Phenergan], thioridazine [e.g., Mellaril], trifluoperazine [e.g., Stelazine], triflupromazine [e.g., Vesprin], trimeprazine [e.g., Temaril]) or
- Phenytoin (e.g., Dilantin) or
- Plicamycin (e.g., Mithracin) or
- Valproic acid (e.g., Depakene)—Androgens, estrogens, and all of these medicines can cause liver damage. Your doctor may want you to have extra blood tests that tell about your liver, while you are taking any of these medicines with an androgen and estrogen combination product.
- Anticoagulants (blood thinners)—Androgens can cause an increased effect of blood thinners, which could lead to uncontrolled or excessive bleeding
- Cyclosporine (e.g., Sandimmune)—Estrogens can increase the chances of toxic effects to the kidney or liver from cyclosporine because estrogens can interfere with the body's ability to get the cyclosporine out of the bloodstream as it normally would

Other medical problems—The presence of other medical problems may affect the use of androgen and estrogen combination products. Make sure you tell your doctor if you have any other medical problems, especially:

- Blood clots (or history of during previous estrogen therapy)—Estrogens may worsen blood clots or cause new clots to form
- Breast cancer (active or suspected)—Estrogens may cause growth of the tumor
- Changes in vaginal bleeding of unknown causes—Some irregular vaginal bleeding is a sign that the lining of the uterus is growing too much or is a sign of cancer of the uterus lining; estrogens may make these conditions worse
- Diabetes mellitus (sugar diabetes)—Androgens can decrease blood sugar levels
- Edema (swelling of feet or lower legs caused by retaining [keeping] too much body water) or
- Heart or circulation disease or
- Kidney disease or
- Liver disease—Androgens can worsen these conditions because androgens cause the body to retain extra fluid (keep too much body water). Also, heart or circulation disease can be worsened by androgens because androgens may increase blood cholesterol levels
- Endometriosis—Estrogens may worsen endometriosis by causing growth of endometriosis implants
- Fibroid tumors of the uterus—Estrogens may cause fibroid tumors to increase in size
- Gallbladder disease or gallstones (or history of)—There is no clear evidence as to whether estrogens increase the risk of gallbladder disease or gallstones
- Jaundice (or history of during pregnancy)—Estrogens use may worsen or cause jaundice in these patients
- Liver disease—Toxic drug effects may occur in patients with liver disease because the body is not able to get this medicine out of the bloodstream as it normally would
- Porphyria—Estrogens can worsen porphyria

Proper Use of This Medicine

For patients taking any of the androgen and estrogen products by mouth:

- *Take this medicine only as directed by your doctor. Do not take more of it and do not take it for a longer time than your doctor ordered.*
- Try to take the medicine at the same time each day to reduce the possibility of side effects and to allow it to work better.
- Nausea may occur during the first few weeks after you start taking estrogens. This effect usually disappears with continued use. If the nausea is bothersome, it can usually be prevented or reduced by taking each dose with food or immediately after food.

Dosing—The dose of these medicines will be different for different patients. *Follow your doctor's orders or the directions on the label.* The following information includes only the average doses of these medicines. *If your dose is different, do not change it* unless your doctor tells you to do so.

The number of tablets that you take depends on the strength of the medicine. Also, *the number of doses you take each day, the time allowed between doses, and the length of time you take the medicine depend on the medical problem for which you are taking combinations of androgen and estrogen.*

For diethylstilbestrol and methyltestosterone

- For *oral* dosage form (tablets):
  —For treatment of certain signs of menopause, such as hot flashes and unusual sweating, chills, faintness, or dizziness:
    - Adults—0.25 milligrams (mg) of diethylstilbestrol and 5 mg of methyltestosterone once a day for twenty-one days. Stop the medicine for seven days, then repeat the twenty-one day cycle. After a while, your doctor may decrease your dose to 0.125 mg of diethylstilbestrol and 2.5 mg of

methyltestosterone once a day for twenty-one days. Again, after stopping for seven days, you will then repeat the cycle.

For conjugated estrogens and methyltestosterone

- For *oral* dosage form (tablets):
  - —For treatment of certain signs of menopause, such as hot flashes and unusual sweating, chills, faintness, or dizziness:
    - Adults—1.25 milligrams (mg) of conjugated estrogens and 10 mg of methyltestosterone once a day for twenty-one days. Stop the medicine for seven days, then repeat the twenty-one day cycle.

For esterified estrogens and methyltestosterone

- For *oral* dosage form (tablets):
  - —For treatment of certain signs of menopause, such as hot flashes and unusual sweating, chills, faintness, or dizziness:
    - Adults—0.625 to 2.5 mg of esterified estrogens and 1.25 to 5 mg of methyltestosterone once a day for twenty-one days. Stop the medicine for seven days, then repeat the twenty-one day cycle.

For fluoxymesterone and ethinyl estradiol

- *For oral* dosage form (tablets):
  - —For treatment of certain signs of menopause, such as hot flashes and unusual sweating, chills, faintness, or dizziness:
    - Adults—1 to 2 milligrams (mg) of fluoxymesterone and 0.02 to 0.04 mg of ethinyl estradiol two times a day for twenty-one days. Stop the medicine for seven days, then repeat the twenty-one day cycle.

For testosterone cypionate and estradiol cypionate

- For *injection* dosage form:
  - —For treatment of certain signs of menopause, such as hot flashes and unusual sweating, chills, faintness, or dizziness:
    - Adults—50 milligrams (mg) of testosterone cypionate and 2 mg of estradiol cypionate injected into a muscle once every four weeks.

For testosterone enanthate and estradiol valerate

- For *injection* dosage form:
  - —For treatment of certain signs of menopause, such as hot flashes and unusual sweating, chills, faintness, or dizziness:
    - Adults—90 milligrams (mg) of testosterone enanthate and 4 mg of estradiol valerate injected into a muscle once every four weeks.

For testosterone enanthate benzilic acid hydrazone, estradiol dienanthate, and estradiol benzoate

- For *injection* dosage form:
  - —For treatment of bone loss (osteoporosis) or certain signs of menopause, such as hot flashes and unusual sweating, chills, faintness, or dizziness:
    - Adults—150 milligrams (mg) of testosterone enanthate benzilic acid hydrazone, 7.5 mg of estradiol dienanthate, and 1 mg of estradiol benzoate injected into a muscle once every four to eight weeks or less.

Missed dose—If you miss a dose of this medicine and your dosing schedule is:

- One dose a day—Take the missed dose as soon as possible. However, if you do not remember it until the next day, skip the missed dose and go back to your regular dosing schedule. Do not double doses.
- More than one dose a day—Take the missed dose as soon as possible. However, if it is almost time for your next dose, skip the missed dose and go back to your regular dosing schedule. Do not double doses.

If you have any questions about this, check with your doctor.

Storage—To store this medicine:

- Keep out of the reach of children.
- Store away from heat and direct light.
- Do not store in the bathroom medicine cabinet because the heat or moisture may cause the medicine to break down.
- Keep the injectable form of this medicine from freezing.
- Do not keep outdated medicine or medicine no longer needed. Be sure that any discarded medicine is out of the reach of children.

Precautions While Using This Medicine

It is very important that your doctor check your progress at regular visits to make sure this medicine does not cause unwanted effects. These visits will usually be every 6 to 12 months, but many doctors require them more often.

It is not yet known whether the use of estrogen increases the risk of breast cancer in women. Therefore, it is very important that you regularly check your breasts for any unusual lumps or discharge. You should also have a mammogram (x-ray picture of the breasts) done if your doctor recommends it.

In some patients using estrogens, tenderness, swelling, or bleeding of the gums may occur. Brushing and flossing your teeth carefully and regularly and massaging your gums may help prevent this. See your dentist regularly to have your teeth cleaned. Check with your medical doctor or dentist if you have any questions about how to take care of your teeth and gums, or if you notice any tenderness, swelling, or bleeding of your gums.

For diabetic patients:

- This medicine may affect blood sugar levels. If you notice a change in the results of your blood or urine sugar tests or if you have any questions, check with your doctor.

If you think that you may have become pregnant, check with your doctor immediately. Continued use of this medicine during pregnancy may cause birth defects or future health problems in the child.

In studies with oral contraceptives (birth control pills) containing estrogens, cigarette smoking during the use of estrogens was shown to cause an increased risk of serious side effects affecting the heart or blood circulation, such as dangerous blood clots, heart attack, or stroke. The risk increased as the amount of smoking and the age of the smoker increased. Women aged 35 and over were at greatest risk when they smoked while using oral contraceptives containing estrogens. It is not known if this risk exists with the use of androgens and estrogens for symptoms of menopause. However, smoking may make estrogens less effective.

Do not give this medicine to anyone else. Your doctor has prescribed it specifically for you after studying your health record and the results of your physical examination. Androgens and estrogens may be dangerous for some people because of differences in their health and body chemistry.

Side Effects of This Medicine

Discuss these possible effects with your doctor:

- Tumors of the liver, liver cancer, and peliosis hepatis (a form of liver disease) have occurred during long-term, high-dose therapy with androgens. Although these effects are rare, they can be very serious and may cause death.
- When androgens are used in women, especially in high doses, male-like changes may occur, such as hoarseness or deepening of the voice, unnatural hair growth, or unusual hair loss. Most of these changes will go away if the medicine is stopped as soon as the changes are noticed. However, some changes, such as voice changes, may not go away.
- The prolonged use of estrogens has been reported to increase the risk of endometrial cancer (cancer of the uterus lining) in women after menopause. The risk seems to increase as the dose and the length of use increase. When estrogens are used in low doses for less than one year, there is less risk. The risk is also reduced if a progestin (another female hormone) is added to, or replaces part of, your estrogen dose. If the uterus has been removed by surgery (total hysterectomy), there is no risk of endometrial cancer.
- It is not yet known whether the use of estrogens increases the risk of breast cancer in women. Although some large studies show an increased risk, most studies and information gathered to date do not support this idea.

Along with its needed effects, a medicine may cause some unwanted effects. Although not all of these side effects may occur, if they do occur they may need medical attention.

Check with your doctor immediately if any of the following side effects occur:

Less common

Yellow eyes or skin

Rare

Uncontrolled jerky muscle movements; vomiting of blood (with long-term use or high doses)

Also, check with your doctor as soon as possible if any of the following side effects occur:

More common

Acne or oily skin (severe); breast pain or tenderness; changes in vaginal bleeding (spotting, breakthrough bleeding, prolonged or heavier bleeding, or complete stoppage of bleeding); enlarged clitoris; enlargement or decrease in size of breasts; hoarseness or deepening of voice; swelling of feet or lower legs; unnatural hair growth; unusual hair loss; weight gain (rapid)

Less common or rare

Confusion; dizziness; flushing or redness of skin; headaches (frequent or continuing); hives (especially at place of injection); shortness of breath (unexplained); skin rash, hives, or itching; unusual bleeding; unusual tiredness or drowsiness

With long-term use or high doses

Black, tarry, or light-colored stools; dark-colored urine; general feeling of discomfort or illness (continuing); hives (frequent or continuing); loss of appetite (continuing); lump in, or discharge from breast; nausea (severe); pain, swelling, or tenderness in stomach or upper abdomen (continuing); purple- or red-colored spots on body or inside the mouth or nose; sore throat or fever (continuing); unpleasant breath odor (continuing); vomiting (severe)

Other side effects may occur that usually do not need medical attention. These side effects may go away during treatment as your body adjusts to the medicine. However, check with your doctor if any of the following side effects continue or are bothersome:

More common

Bloating of abdomen or stomach; cramps of abdomen or stomach; loss of appetite (temporary); nausea (mild); stomach pain (mild); unusual increase in sexual desire; vomiting (mild)

Less common

Constipation; diarrhea (mild); dizziness (mild); headaches (mild); infection, redness, pain, or other irritation at place of injection; migraine headaches; problems in wearing contact lenses; trouble in sleeping

Also, many women who are taking a progestin (another type of female hormone) with this medicine will begin to have monthly vaginal bleeding again, similar to menstrual periods. This effect will continue for as long as this medicine is used. However, monthly bleeding will not occur in women who have had the uterus removed by surgery (total hysterectomy).

Other side effects not listed above may also occur in some patients. If you notice any other effects, check with your doctor.

Revised: 06/30/92
Interim revision: 06/21/94

ANESTHETICS Dental

Some commonly used brand names are:

In the U.S.—

Anbesol, Baby[1]
Anbesol Maximum Strength Gel[1]
Anbesol Maximum Strength Liquid[1]
Anbesol Regular Strength Gel[3]
Anbesol Regular Strength Liquid[3]
Benzodent[1]
Chloraseptic Lozenges[2]
Chloraseptic Lozenges, Children's[1]
Dentapaine[1]
Dent-Zel-Ite[1]
Hurricaine[1]
Numzident[1]
Num-Zit Gel[1]
Num-Zit Lotion[1]
Orabase, Baby[1]
Orabase-B with Benzocaine[1]
Orajel, Baby[1]
Orajel Maximum Strength[1]
Orajel Nighttime Formula, Baby[1]
Oratect Gel[1]
Rid-A-Pain[1]
SensoGARD Canker Sore Relief[1]
Spec-T Sore Throat Anesthetic[1]
Sucrets, Children's[4]
Sucrets Maximum Strength[4]
Sucrets Regular Strength[4]
Xylocaine[5]
Xylocaine Viscous[5]
Zilactin-L[5]

In Canada—

Anbesol Baby Jel[1]
Anbesol Gel[3]
Anbesol Liquid[3]
Anbesol Maximum Strength Liquid[3]
Chloraseptic Lozenges Cherry Flavor[2]
Dentocaine[1]
Orajel, Baby[1]
Orajel Extra Strength[1]
Orajel Liquid[1]
Supracaine[6]*
Topicaine[1]
Xylocaine[5]
Xylocaine Viscous[5]

Other commonly used names are:

amethocaine[6]
dyclocaine[4]
ethyl aminobenzoate[1]
lignocaine[5]

Note: For quick reference, the following anesthetics are numbered to match the corresponding brand names.

This information applies to the following medicines:

1. Benzocaine (BEN-zoe-kane)
2. Benzocaine and Menthol (MEN-thole)
3. Benzocaine and Phenol (FEE-nole)
4. Dyclonine (DYE-kloe-neen)
5. Lidocaine (LYE-doe-kane)‡
6. Tetracaine (TET-ra-kane)

*Not commercially available in the U.S.
‡Generic name product may also be available in the U.S.

Description

Dental anesthetics (an-ess-THET-iks) are used in the mouth to relieve pain or irritation caused by many conditions. Examples include toothache, teething, and sores in or around the mouth, such as cold sores, canker sores, and fever blisters. Also, some of these medicines are used to relieve pain or irritation caused by dentures or other dental appliances, including braces. However, if you have an infection or a lot of large sores in your mouth, check with your medical doctor or dentist before using a dental anesthetic because other kinds of treatment may be needed. Also, the chance of side effects is increased.

One form of lidocaine is also used to relieve pain caused by certain throat conditions. Some forms of benzocaine, benzocaine and menthol combination, and dyclonine are also used to relieve sore throat pain.

Some of these medicines are available only with your medical doctor's or dentist's prescription. Others are available without a prescription; however, your medical doctor or dentist may have special instructions on the proper use and dose for your medical problem. Some nonprescription (over-the-counter [OTC]) aerosols, gels, liquids, or ointments that contain a local anesthetic are not meant to be used in or around the mouth. If you have any questions about which product to use, check with your pharmacist.

These medicines are available in the following dosage forms:

Dental

Benzocaine
- Aerosol spray (U.S.)
- Dental paste (U.S.)
- Film-forming gel (U.S.)
- Gel (U.S. and Canada)
- Lozenges (U.S.)
- Ointment (U.S. and Canada)
- Solution (liquid) (U.S. and Canada)

Benzocaine and Menthol
- Lozenges (U.S. and Canada)

Benzocaine and Phenol
- Gel (U.S. and Canada)
- Solution (liquid) (U.S. and Canada)

Dyclonine
- Lozenges (U.S.)

Lidocaine
- Aerosol spray (U.S. and Canada)
- Ointment (U.S. and Canada)
- Solution (U.S. and Canada)
- Viscous (very thick) solution (U.S. and Canada)

Tetracaine
- Aerosol spray (Canada)

Before Using This Medicine

If you are taking this medicine without a prescription, carefully read and follow any precautions on the label. For dental anesthetics, the following should be considered:

Allergies—Tell your doctor if you have ever had any unusual or allergic reaction to a local anesthetic, especially one that was applied to any part of the body as a liquid, cream, ointment, or spray. Also tell your health care professional if you are allergic to any other substances, such as foods, preservatives, or dyes.

Pregnancy—Dental anesthetics have not been reported to cause birth defects or other problems in humans.

Breast-feeding—Dental anesthetics have not been reported to cause problems in nursing babies.

Children—Children may be especially sensitive to the effects of dental anesthetics. This may increase the chance of unwanted effects, some of which can be serious, during treatment. When using a dental anesthetic for a child, be very careful not to use more of the medicine than directed on the label, unless otherwise directed by your health care professional. Teething medicines that contain benzocaine may be used in babies 4 months of age and older. One product that contains benzocaine (Orabase-B with Benzocaine) may be used in children 6 years of age and older. Most of the other nonprescription (over-the-counter [OTC]) medicines that contain a dental anesthetic may be used in children 2 years of age and older. However, these other nonprescription products should not be used in infants or children younger than 2 years of age unless prescribed by a health care professional.

Older adults—Elderly people are especially sensitive to the effects of many local anesthetics. This may increase the chance of side effects during treatment, especially with lidocaine. Nonprescription (over-the-counter [OTC]) products containing local anesthetics are not likely to cause problems. However, elderly people should be especially careful not to use more medicine than directed on the package label, unless otherwise directed by a medical doctor or a dentist.

Other medicines—Although certain medicines should not be used together at all, in other cases two different medicines may be used together even if an interaction might occur. In these cases, your doctor may want to change the dose, or other precautions may be necessary. Before you use a dental anesthetic, check with your medical doctor, dentist, or pharmacist if you are taking any other prescription or nonprescription (over-the-counter [OTC]) medicine.

Proper Use of This Medicine

For safe and effective use of this medicine:

- Follow your medical doctor's or dentist's instructions if this medicine was prescribed.
- Follow the manufacturer's package directions if you are treating yourself.
- *Do not use more of this medicine, do not use it more often, and do not use it for a longer time than directed.* To do so may increase the chance of absorption into the body and the risk of side effects. This is particularly important for young children and elderly patients, especially with lidocaine.
- Dental anesthetics should be used only for conditions being treated by your medical doctor or dentist or for problems listed in the package directions. *Do not use any of them for other problems without first checking with your medical doctor or dentist.* These medicines should not be used if certain kinds of infections are present.

To use *the viscous (very thick) liquid form of lidocaine* (e.g., Xylocaine Viscous):

- This medicine may cause serious side effects if too much of it is swallowed. Be certain that you understand exactly how you are to use this medicine, and whether or not you are to swallow it. Follow your medical doctor's or dentist's directions very carefully. Also, *be very careful to measure the exact amount of medicine that you are to use.* Use a special measuring spoon to measure the amount; regular household teaspoons or soup spoons that you use at the table may not measure the amount correctly. These measures are especially important when this medicine is used for young children, who are especially sensitive to its effects.
- If you are using this medicine for a problem in the mouth, you may apply it to the sore places with a cotton-tipped applicator. Or, you may swish the measured amount of medicine around in your mouth until you are certain that it has reached all of the sore places. *Do not swallow the medicine unless your medical doctor or dentist has told you to do so.*
- If you are using this medicine for a problem in the throat, gargle with the measured amount of medicine as directed by your doctor. *Do not swallow the medicine unless your doctor has told you to do so.*

To use *benzocaine film-forming gel* (e.g., Oratect Gel):

- Children may find it difficult to apply this medicine correctly. They should be helped by an adult.
- First, dry the area where the medicine is needed, using a swab included in the package.
- Apply the gel to a second swab. Then roll the swab over the dried area.
- Keep your mouth open and dry for about 30 to 60 seconds after applying the medicine. A film will form where you placed the medicine.
- Do not remove the film. It will slowly disappear and should be gone about 6 hours after the medicine was applied.

To use *other gel or liquid forms of a dental anesthetic:*

- Apply the medicine to the sore places with a clean finger, a cotton-tipped applicator, or a piece of gauze.
- When relieving pain caused by dentures or other dental appliances, *do not apply this medicine directly to the appliance, and do not place the appliance in your mouth while the medicine is there,* unless directed to do so by your dentist. Instead, apply the medicine to the sore areas in your mouth and wait until the pain is relieved. Then rinse your mouth with water before replacing the appliance.

To use *benzocaine dental paste* (e.g., Orabase-B with Benzocaine):

- Use a cotton-tipped applicator to dab small amounts of the medicine onto the sore places. Do not rub or try to spread the medicine with your finger while you are applying it, because the medicine will become crumbly and gritty.

To use *aerosol or spray forms of a dental anesthetic:*

- To help prevent unwanted effects, be very careful not to inhale (breathe in) the medicine. Also, do not spray the back of your mouth or throat with it unless your medical doctor or dentist directs you to do so.

To use *lozenge forms of benzocaine, benzocaine and menthol, or dyclonine:*

- These lozenges should be dissolved slowly in the mouth. Do not bite or chew them or swallow them whole. Before giving a lozenge to a young child, be sure that the child understands these directions and will follow them.

Dosing—The dose of these medicines will be different for different patients. *Follow your health care professional's orders or the directions on the label.* The following information includes only the average doses of these medicines. *If your dose is different, do not change it* unless your medical doctor or dentist tells you to do so.

For benzocaine

- For *dental paste* dosage form:
  —For sores in and around the mouth, sore gums, or pain caused by dental appliances:
  - Adults, teenagers, and children 6 years of age and older—Apply a small amount of the medicine to the painful areas.
  - Children up to 6 years of age—Use and dose must be determined by your health care professional.
- For *film-forming gel, liquid, and ointment* dosage forms:
  —For sores in and around the mouth, toothache, sore gums, or pain caused by dental appliances:
  - Adults, teenagers, and children 2 years of age and older—Apply a small amount of medicine to the painful areas up to four times a day.
  - Children up to 2 years of age—Use and dose must be determined by your health care professional.
- For *gel* dosage form:
  —For sores in and around the mouth, toothache, sore gums, or pain caused by dental appliances:
  - Adults, teenagers, and children 2 years of age and older—Apply a small amount of medicine to the painful areas up to four times a day.
  - Children up to 2 years of age—Use and dose must be determined by your health care professional.

  —For teething pain:
  - Infants up to 4 months of age—Use and dose must be determined by your health care professional.
  - Infants and children 4 months to 2 years of age—Apply a small amount of the 7.5% or 10% benzocaine gel to sore gums up to four times a day.
  - Children 2 years of age and older—Apply any strength of benzocaine gel to sore gums up to four times a day.
- For *lozenge* dosage form:
  —For pain in the mouth or throat:
  - Adults and teenagers—One lozenge, dissolved slowly in the mouth every two hours as needed.
  - Children up to 2 years of age—Use and dose must be determined by your health care professional.
  - Children 2 years of age and older—One children's strength (5-milligram [mg]) lozenge, dissolved slowly in the mouth every two hours as needed.
- For *aerosol spray* dosage form:
  —For pain in the mouth:
  - Adults and teenagers—One or 2 sprays, pointed at the sore places. Each spray should last about one second.
  - Children—Use and dose must be determined by your dentist.

For benzocaine and menthol combination

- For *lozenge* dosage form:
  —For pain in the mouth or throat:
  - Adults, teenagers, and children 2 years of age and older—One lozenge, dissolved slowly in the mouth every two hours as needed.
  - Children up to 2 years of age—Use and dose must be determined by your health care professional.

For benzocaine and phenol combination

- For *gel* dosage form:
  —For sores in and around the mouth, teething, toothache, sore gums, or pain caused by dental appliances:
  - Adults, teenagers, and children 2 years of age and older—Apply a small amount of medicine to the painful areas up to four times a day.
  - Children up to 2 years of age—Use and dose must be determined by your health care professional.
- For *liquid* dosage form:
  —For sores in and around the mouth, toothache, sore gums, or pain caused by dental appliances:
  - Adults, teenagers, and children 2 years of age and older—Apply a small amount of medicine to the painful areas up to four times a day.
  - Children up to 2 years of age—Use and dose must be determined by your health care professional.

For dyclonine

- For *lozenge* dosage form:
  —For pain in the mouth or throat:
  - Adults and teenagers—One 2-milligram (mg) or 3-mg lozenge, dissolved slowly in the mouth every two hours as needed.
  - Children up to 2 years of age—Use and dose must be determined by your health care professional.
  - Children 2 years of age and older—One children's strength (1.2-mg) lozenge, dissolved slowly in the mouth every two hours as needed.

For lidocaine

- For *dental liquid* dosage form (e.g., Zilactin-L):
  —For sores on the lips and around the mouth:
  - Adults and teenagers—Apply to sores every one or two hours for the first three days. Then apply as needed.
  - Children—Dose must be determined by your health care professional.
- For *dental ointment* dosage form:
  —For gum pain:
  - Adults—Apply a small amount of medicine to the sore places. Do not apply the ointment directly to dentures, braces, or other dental appliances, unless your dentist has directed you to do so.

- Children—Use and dose must be determined by your health care professional.

- For *aerosol spray* dosage form:
  - —For pain in the mouth:
    - Adults and teenagers—Two sprays, pointed at the sore places. Do not use more than twenty sprays a day.
    - Children—Use and dose must be determined by your health care professional.
- For *viscous (very thick) solution* dosage form (e.g., Xylocaine Viscous):
  - —For pain in the mouth:
    - Adults and teenagers—One tablespoonful of medicine (or less), swished around in the mouth, then spit out. Or, apply a total of 1 tablespoonful (or less) to the sore places with a cotton-tipped applicator. This medicine should not be used more often than every three hours.
    - Infants and children up to 3 years of age—Apply a total of one-fourth of a teaspoonful (or less) to the sore places with a cotton-tipped applicator. This medicine should not be used more often than every three hours.
    - Children 3 years of age and older—Apply a small amount of medicine to the sore places with a cotton-tipped applicator. The largest amount that can be used must be determined by your health care professional.
  - —For sore throat pain:
    - Adults and teenagers—One tablespoonful, used as a gargle. Swallow after gargling only if directed to do so by your doctor. Otherwise, spit out the medicine after gargling with it.
    - Children—Dose must be determined by your doctor.

For tetracaine

- For *aerosol spray* dosage form:
  - —For pain in the mouth:
    - Adults and teenagers—Two sprays, pointed at the sore places.
    - Children—Dose must be determined by your health care professional.

Missed dose—If your health care professional has directed you to use this medicine on a regular schedule, and you miss a dose, use it as soon as possible. However, if it is almost time for your next dose, skip the missed dose and go back to your regular dosing schedule. Do not double doses.

Storage—To store this medicine:

- Keep out of the reach of children.
- Store away from heat and direct light.
- Do not store throat lozenge forms of benzocaine, benzocaine and menthol combination, or dyclonine in the bathroom, near the kitchen sink, or in other damp places. Heat or moisture may cause the medicine to break down.
- Keep the medicine from freezing.
- Do not puncture, break, or burn aerosol containers, even when they are empty.
- Do not keep outdated medicine or medicine no longer needed. Be sure that any discarded medicine is out of the reach of children.

Precautions While Using This Medicine

Check with your medical doctor:

- If you are using this medicine for a sore throat and your sore throat is severe or lasts for more than 2 days.
- If other symptoms, such as fever, headache, skin rash, swelling, nausea, or vomiting, are also present.

You may have a condition that needs other treatment.

Check with your health care professional:

- If you are using this medicine for pain or sores in or around the mouth and your condition does not get better within 7 days or gets worse.
- If you notice other symptoms, such as swelling, rash, or fever.

You may have a condition that needs other treatment.

Check with your dentist:

- If you are using this medicine for a toothache. This medicine should not be used for a long time. It is meant to relieve toothache pain temporarily, until the problem causing the toothache can be corrected. Arrange for treatment as soon as possible.
- If you are using this medicine to relieve pain caused by new dentures or other dental appliances. An adjustment to your appliance may be needed to prevent more soreness. Also, if your dentist has ordered you to apply this medicine to the appliance before inserting it or to keep the appliance in your mouth while using the medicine, he or she will want to make sure that the medicine is not causing any unwanted effects.

False test results may occur if benzocaine, lidocaine, or tetracaine is present in your body when a certain laboratory test is done. This test uses a medicine called bentiromide (e.g., Chymex) to show how well your pancreas is working. You should not use any products containing benzocaine, lidocaine, or tetracaine for about 72 hours (3 days) before this test is done.

If you are using this medicine in the back of the mouth, or in the throat, *do not eat or drink anything for one hour after using it.* When this medicine is applied to these areas, it may interfere with swallowing and cause choking.

Do not chew gum or food while your mouth or throat feels numb after you use this medicine. To do so may cause an injury. You may accidentally bite your tongue or the inside of your cheeks.

Side Effects of This Medicine

Along with its needed effects, a medicine may cause some unwanted effects. Although not all of these side effects may occur, if they do occur they may need medical attention.

Stop using this medicine and check with your medical doctor or dentist immediately if any of the following side effects occur:

Less common

Large swellings that look like hives on skin or in mouth or throat

Signs and symptoms of too much medicine being absorbed by the body

Blurred or double vision; confusion; convulsions (seizures); dizziness or lightheadedness; drowsiness; feeling hot, cold, or numb; headache; increased sweating; ringing or buzzing in the ears; shivering or trembling; slow or irregular heartbeat; troubled breathing; unusual anxiety, excitement, nervousness, or restlessness; unusual paleness; unusual tiredness or weakness

Also, check with your health care professional as soon as possible if any of the following side effects occur:

Less common

Burning, stinging, swelling, or tenderness not present before treatment; skin rash, redness, itching, or hives in or around the mouth

Other side effects not listed above may also occur in some patients. If you notice any other effects, check with your medical doctor or dentist.

Revised: 09/01/94

ANESTHETICS Ophthalmic

Some commonly used brand names are:

In the U.S.—

Ak-Taine[1]
Ak-T-Caine[2]
Alcaine[1]
Ocu-Caine[1]
Ophthaine[1]
Ophthetic[1]
Opticaine[2]
Pontocaine[2]
Spectro-Caine[1]

In Canada—

Alcaine[1]
Diocaine[1]
Minims Tetracaine[2]
Ophthetic[1]
Pontocaine[2]

Other commonly used names are:

Amethocaine[2]
Proxymetacaine[1]

Note: For quick reference, the following anesthetics are numbered to match the corresponding brand names.

This information applies to the following medicines:

1. Proparacaine (proe-PARE-a-kane)‡
2. Tetracaine (TET-ra-kane)‡§

‡Generic name product may also be available in the U.S.
§Generic name product may also be available in Canada.

Description

Proparacaine and tetracaine are local anesthetics that are used in the eye to cause numbness or loss of feeling. They are used before certain procedures such as measuring of eye pressure, removing foreign objects or sutures (stitches) from the eye, and performing certain eye examinations.

These medicines are to be administered only by or under the immediate supervision of your doctor. They are available in the following dosage forms:

Ophthalmic

Proparacaine
- Ophthalmic solution (U.S. and Canada)

Tetracaine
- Ophthalmic ointment (U.S.)
- Ophthalmic solution (U.S. and Canada)

Before Receiving This Medicine

In deciding to use a medicine, the risks of using the medicine must be weighed against the good it will do. This is a decision you and your doctor will make. For local anesthetics used in the eye, the following should be considered:

Allergies—Tell your doctor if you have ever had any unusual or allergic reaction after use of a local anesthetic in the eye. Such a reaction may include severe itching, pain, redness, or swelling of the eye or eyelid, or severe and continuing watering of the eyes.

Also, tell your doctor if you have ever had any unusual or allergic reaction to tetracaine or other local anesthetics, such as benzocaine, butacaine, butamben, chloroprocaine, procaine, or propoxycaine, when given by injection or applied to the skin.

In addition, tell your doctor if you have ever had an allergic reaction to aminobenzoic acid (also called para-aminobenzoic acid [PABA]), or if you are allergic to any other substances, such as foods, preservatives, or dyes.

Pregnancy—Although studies on effects in pregnancy have not been done in either humans or animals, proparacaine and tetracaine have not been reported to cause birth defects or other problems in humans.

Breast-feeding—It is not known whether proparacaine or tetracaine passes into breast milk. Although most medicines pass into breast milk in small amounts, many of them may be used safely while breast-feeding. Mothers who receive this medicine and who wish to breast-feed should discuss this with their doctor.

Children—Although there is no specific information comparing use of ophthalmic anesthetics in children with use in other age groups, these medicines are not expected to cause different side effects or problems in children than they do in adults.

Older adults—Many medicines have not been studied specifically in older people. Therefore, it may not be known whether they work exactly the same way they do in younger adults. Although there is no specific information comparing use of ophthalmic anesthetics in the elderly with use in other age groups, these medicines are not expected to cause different side effects or problems in older people than they do in younger adults.

Other medicines—Although certain medicines should not be used together at all, in other cases two different medicines may be used together even if an interaction might occur. In these cases, your doctor may want to change the dose, or other precautions may be necessary. Before receiving a local anesthetic in the eye, tell your doctor if you are taking any other prescription or nonprescription (over-the-counter [OTC]) medicine.

Other medical problems—The presence of other medical problems may affect the use of local anesthetics in the eye. Make sure you tell your doctor if you have any other medical problems, especially:

- Allergies—The risk of unwanted effects may be increased

Proper Use of This Medicine

Dosing—The dose of proparacaine or tetracaine will be different for different people. It will depend on the reason the anesthetic is being used. Your health care professional will apply the medicine.

For proparacaine or tetracaine

- For *ophthalmic drops* dosage form (eye drops):
  - —For causing loss of feeling in the eye:
    - Adults and teenagers—For most procedures, one or two drops will be all that is needed. However, for some other procedures, several applications of the medicine may be needed, usually five or ten minutes apart.
    - Children—Use and dose must be determined by the doctor.

For tetracaine

- For *ophthalmic ointment* dosage form (eye ointment):
  - —For causing loss of feeling in the eye:
    - Adults and teenagers—Your health care professional will apply a small amount of the ointment to the lower eyelid.
    - Children—Use and dose must be determined by the doctor.

Precautions After Receiving This Medicine

After a local anesthetic is applied to the eye, *do not rub or wipe the eye until the anesthetic has worn off and feeling in the eye returns.* To do so may cause injury or damage to the eye. The effects of these medicines usually last for about 20 minutes. However, if more than one dose is applied, the effects may last longer.

If you get one of these medicines on your fingers, it may cause a rash with dryness and cracking of the skin. If you touch your eye after this medicine has been applied, wash your hands as soon as possible.

Side Effects of This Medicine

Along with its needed effects, a medicine may cause some unwanted effects. Although not all of these side effects may occur, if they do occur they may need medical attention.

Tell your doctor immediately if any of the following side effects occur shortly after this medicine has been applied:

Symptoms of too much medicine being absorbed into the body—very rare

Dizziness or drowsiness; increased sweating; irregular heartbeat; muscle twitching or trembling; nausea or vomiting; shortness of breath or troubled breathing; unusual excitement, nervousness, or restlessness; unusual tiredness or weakness

Other side effects may occur that usually do not need medical attention. Mild stinging or eye irritation may occur as soon as tetracaine is applied or up to several hours after proparacaine is applied. Although these side effects usually are not serious, *check with your doctor as soon as possible if any of the following side effects are severe,* because you may be having an allergic reaction to the medicine. Also, check with your doctor if any of these effects continue or are bothersome:

Less common

Burning, stinging, redness, or other irritation of eye

Rare

Itching, pain, redness, or swelling of the eye or eyelid; watering of eyes

Other side effects not listed above may also occur in some patients. If you notice any other effects, check with your doctor.

Revised: 08/25/94
Interim revision: 07/11/95

ANESTHETICS Parenteral-Local

Some commonly used brand names are:

In the U.S.—

Carbocaine[5]
Carbocaine with Neo-Cobefrin[5]
Citanest Forte[6]
Citanest Plain[6]
Dalcaine[4]
Dilocaine[4]
Duranest[4]
Duranest-MPF[3]
Isocaine[5]
L-Caine[4]
Lidoject-1[4]
Lidoject-2[4]
Marcaine[1]
Marcaine Spinal[1]
Nervocaine[4]
Nesacaine[2]
Nesacaine-MPF[2]
Novocain[7]
Octocaine[4]
Polocaine[5]
Polocaine-MPF[5]
Pontocaine[9]
Ravocaine and Novocain with Levophed[8]
Ravocaine and Novocain with Neo-Cobefrin[8]
Sensorcaine[1]
Sensorcaine-MPF[1]
Sensorcaine-MPF Spinal[1]
Xylocaine[4]
Xylocaine-MPF[4]
Xylocaine-MPF with Glucose[4]

In Canada—

Carbocaine[5]
Citanest Forte[6]
Citanest Plain[6]
Isocaine 2%[5]
Isocaine 3%[5]
Marcaine[1]
Nesacaine-CE[2]
Novocain[7]
Octocaine-50[4]
Octocaine-100[4]
Polocaine[5]
Pontocaine[9]
Xylocaine[4]
Xylocaine with Glucose[4]
Xylocaine Test Dose[4]

Another commonly used name for lidocaine is lignocaine.

Note: For quick reference, the following anesthetics are numbered to match the corresponding brand names.

This information applies to the following medicines:

1. Bupivacaine (byoo-PIV-a-kane)‡
2. Chloroprocaine (klor-oh-PROE-kane)‡
3. Etidocaine (e-TI-doe-kane)
4. Lidocaine (LYE-doe-kane)‡§
5. Mepivacaine (me-PIV-a-kane)‡
6. Prilocaine (PRIL-oh-kane)§
7. Procaine (PROE-kane)‡
8. Propoxycaine and Procaine (proe-POX-i-kane)
9. Tetracaine (TET-ra-kane)

‡Generic name product may also be available in the U.S.
§Generic name product may also be available in Canada.

Description

Parenteral-local anesthetics (an-ess-THET-iks) are given by injection to cause loss of feeling before and during surgery, dental procedures (including dental surgery), or labor and delivery. These medicines do not cause loss of consciousness.

These medicines are given only by or under the immediate supervision of a medical doctor or dentist, or by a specially trained nurse, in the doctor's office or in a hospital.

These medicines are available in the following dosage forms:

Parenteral

Bupivacaine
- Injection (U.S. and Canada)

Chloroprocaine
- Injection (U.S. and Canada)

Etidocaine
- Injection (U.S.)

Lidocaine
- Injection (U.S. and Canada)

Mepivacaine
- Injection (U.S. and Canada)

Prilocaine
- Injection (U.S. and Canada)

Procaine
- Injection (U.S. and Canada)

Propoxycaine and Procaine
- Injection (U.S.)

Tetracaine
- Injection (U.S. and Canada)

Before Receiving This Medicine

In deciding to use a medicine, the risks of using the medicine must be weighed against the good it will do. This is a decision you and your medical doctor, dentist, or nurse will make. For local anesthetics, the following should be considered:

Allergies—Tell your medical doctor, dentist, or nurse if you have ever had any unusual or allergic reaction to a local anesthetic or to epinephrine (e.g., Adrenalin). Also tell your medical doctor, dentist, nurse, or pharmacist if you are allergic to any other substances, such as sulfites or other preservatives, especially aminobenzoic acid (also called para-aminobenzoic acid [PABA]).

Pregnancy—Local anesthetics have not been reported to cause birth defects in humans.

Use of a local anesthetic during labor and delivery may rarely cause unwanted effects. These medicines may increase the length of labor by making it more difficult for the mother to bear down (push). They may also cause unwanted effects in the fetus or newborn baby, especially if certain medical problems are present at the time of delivery. Before receiving a local anesthetic for labor and delivery, you should discuss with your doctor the good that this medicine will do as well as the risks of receiving it.

Breast-feeding—It is not known whether local anesthetics pass into the breast milk. However, these medicines have not been reported to cause problems in nursing babies.

Children—Children may be especially sensitive to the effects of parenteral-local anesthetics. This may increase the chance of side effects.

Older adults—Elderly people are especially sensitive to the effects of parenteral-local anesthetics. This may increase the chance of side effects.

Other medicines—Although certain medicines should not be used together at all, in other cases two different medicines may be used together even if an interaction might occur. In these cases, your medical doctor, dentist, or nurse may want to change the dose, or other precautions may be necessary. It is very important that you tell the person in charge if you are taking:

- Any other medicine, prescription or nonprescription (over-the-counter [OTC]), or
- "Street" drugs, such as amphetamines ("uppers"), barbiturates ("downers"), cocaine (including "crack"), marijuana, phencyclidine (PCP, "angel dust"), and heroin or other narcotics—Serious side effects may occur if anyone gives you a local anesthetic without knowing that you have taken another medicine

Other medical problems—The presence of other medical problems may affect the use of local anesthetics. Make sure you tell your medical doctor, dentist, or nurse if you have *any* other medical problems, especially:

- Malignant hyperthermia (very high fever, fast and irregular heartbeat, muscle spasms or tightness, and breathing problems occurring during, or soon after, use of an anesthetic) (history of, in yourself or in any close relative)—The chance of an attack of malignant hyperthermia is increased. Some anesthetics are more likely than others to cause this unwanted effect. Your medical doctor, dentist, or nurse will want to avoid using them

Proper Use of This Medicine

Dosing—The dose of a local anesthetic will be different for different patients. Your health care professional will decide on the right amount for you, depending on:

- Your age;
- Your general physical condition;
- The reason the local anesthetic is being given; and
- Other medicines you are taking or will receive before or after the local anesthetic is given.

Precautions After Receiving This Medicine

For patients going home before the numbness or loss of feeling caused by a local anesthetic wears off:

- During the time that the injected area feels numb, serious injury can occur without your knowing about it. Be especially careful to avoid injury until the anesthetic wears off or feeling returns to the area.

- If you have received a local anesthetic injection in your mouth, do not chew gum or food while your mouth feels numb. You may injure yourself by biting your tongue or the inside of your cheeks.

Side Effects of This Medicine

Along with its needed effects, a medicine may cause some unwanted effects. Although not all of these side effects may occur, if they do occur they may need medical attention. While you are in the hospital or your medical doctor's or dentist's office, your medical doctor, dentist, or nurse will carefully follow the effects of any medicine you have received. However, some effects may not be noticed until later.

Check with your doctor immediately if any of the following side effects occur:

Less common or rare

Skin rash, hives, or itching

Also, check with your dentist if you have received a local anesthetic for dental work, and the feeling of numbness or tingling in your lips and mouth does not go away within a few hours, or if you have difficulty in opening your mouth.

Other side effects not listed above may also occur in some patients. If you notice any other effects, check with your medical doctor or dentist.

Revised: 01/30/92
Interim revision: 08/14/94

ANESTHETICS Rectal

Some commonly used brand names are:

In the U.S.—

Americaine Hemorrhoidal[1]
Nupercainal[2]
Fleet Relief[3]
Pontocaine Cream[4]†
Pontocaine Ointment[5]
ProctoFoam/non-steroid[3]
Tronolane[3]
Tronothane[3]

In Canada—

Nupercainal[2]
Tronothane[3]

Other commonly used names are:

amethocaine[4]
cinchocaine[2]
ethyl aminobenzoate[1]
pramocaine[3]

Note: For quick reference, the following anesthetics are numbered to match the corresponding brand names.

This information applies to the following medicines:

1. Benzocaine (BEN-zoe-kane)
2. Dibucaine (DYE-byoo-kane)‡
3. Pramoxine (pra-MOX-een)
4. Tetracaine (TET-ra-kane)
5. Tetracaine and Menthol (MEN-thol)

†Not commercially available in Canada.
‡Generic name product may also be available in the U.S.

Description

Rectal anesthetics (an-ess-THET-iks) are used to relieve the pain and itching of hemorrhoids (piles) and other problems in the rectal area. However, if you have hemorrhoids that bleed, especially after a bowel movement, check with your doctor before using this medicine. Bleeding may mean that you have a condition that needs other treatment.

These medicines are available without a prescription; however, your doctor may have special instructions on the proper use and dose for your medical problem.

These medicines are available in the following dosage forms:

Rectal

Benzocaine
- Ointment (U.S.)

Dibucaine
- Ointment (U.S. and Canada)

Pramoxine
- Aerosol foam (U.S.)
- Cream (U.S. and Canada)
- Ointment (U.S.)

Tetracaine
- Cream (U.S.)

Tetracaine and Menthol
- Ointment (U.S.)

Before Using This Medicine

If you are using this medicine without a prescription, carefully read and follow any precautions on the label. For rectal anesthetics, the following should be considered:

Allergies—Tell your doctor if you have ever had any unusual or allergic reaction to a local anesthetic, especially one that was applied to any part of the body as a liquid, cream, ointment, or spray. Also tell your health care professional if you are allergic to any other substances, such as foods, preservatives, or dyes.

Pregnancy—Rectal anesthetics have not been reported to cause birth defects or other problems in humans.

Breast-feeding—Rectal anesthetics have not been reported to cause problems in nursing babies.

Children—Children may be especially sensitive to the effects of local anesthetics. This may increase the chance of side effects during treatment.

Older adults—Elderly people are especially sensitive to the effects of local anesthetics. This may increase the chance of side effects during treatment.

Other medicines—Although certain medicines should not be used together at all, in other cases two different medicines may be used together even if an interaction might occur. In these cases, your doctor may want to change the dose, or other precautions may be necessary. Before you use a rectal anesthetic, check with your health care professional if you are taking any other prescription or nonprescription (over-the-counter [OTC]) medicine.

Other medical problems—The presence of other medical problems may affect the use of rectal anesthetics. Make sure you tell your doctor if you have any other medical problems, especially:

- Infection at or near place of treatment or
- Large sores, broken skin, or severe injury at or near place of treatment—The chance of unwanted effects may be increased

Proper Use of This Medicine

For safe and effective use of this medicine:

- Rectal anesthetics usually come with patient directions. Read them carefully before using the medicine, even if it was prescribed by your doctor. Check with your pharmacist if you have any questions about how to use the product.
- Follow your doctor's instructions if this medicine was prescribed.
- Follow the manufacturer's package directions if you are treating yourself.
- *Do not use more of this medicine, do not use it more often, and do not use it for a longer time than directed.* To do so may increase the chance of absorption into the body and the chance of unwanted effects.

This medicine should be used only for conditions being treated by your doctor or for problems listed on the package label. *Do not use it for other problems without first checking with your doctor.* This medicine should not be used if certain kinds of infections are present.

For *applying a rectal anesthetic to the area around the rectum:*

- First, clean the area, using mild soap and water or a cleansing wipe. Rinse the area carefully and dry it gently with a soft towel or toilet paper.
- Apply a small amount of medicine to the sore area, using a piece of gauze, a tissue, or a ''finger cot.''

For *inserting a rectal cream or ointment inside the rectum:*

- Use only products that come packaged in pre-filled applicators or that come packaged with a special inserter called a rectal tube.
- If you are using a product that has an inserter (rectal tube) packaged separately from the tube of cream or ointment:

  —Remove the cap from the tube of cream or ointment. Attach the inserter to the top of the tube. Squeeze the tube until a little cream or ointment comes out on the inserter. Then spread the cream or ointment over the inserter.

  —Place the inserter into your rectum and squeeze the tube until a small amount of medicine comes out. Then remove the inserter from your body.

  —Remove the inserter from the tube and replace the cap. Then wash the applicator carefully.
- If you are using the product that comes in pre-filled applicators:

  —Follow the manufacturer's directions for using the applicator and inserting the medicine. Each applicator is meant to be used only once. Throw the applicator away after using it.

For *inserting the rectal aerosol foam (e.g., Proctofoam/nonsteroid) into the rectum:*

- Do not insert the container itself into your rectum. Use the applicator provided.
- To fill the container—First, shake the container hard for several seconds. Then, holding the container upright, insert it into the applicator. Press the cap of the container until the foam reaches the fill line of the applicator. Remove the applicator from the container.
- To use the medicine—Place a small amount of foam on the tip of the applicator. Insert the applicator into your rectum, then push the plunger as far as possible. Remove the applicator. Then take it apart and wash it carefully.

Dosing—The dose of rectal anesthetics will be different for different patients. *Follow your doctor's orders or the directions on the label.* The following information includes only the average doses of these medicines. *If your dose is different, do not change it* unless your doctor tells you to do so.

For benzocaine

- For pain and itching of hemorrhoids or other problems in the rectal area:

  —For *rectal ointment* dosage form:

  - Adults—Apply a small amount of ointment to the area around the rectum up to six times a day.
  - Children—Use and dose must be determined by the doctor.

For dibucaine

- For pain and itching of hemorrhoids or other problems in the rectal area:

  —For *rectal ointment* dosage form:

  - Adults—Insert a small amount of ointment into the rectum three or four times a day, in the morning, in the evening, and after bowel movements. Or, apply a small amount of ointment to the area around the rectum three or four times a day.
  - Children—Use and dose must be determined by the doctor.

For pramoxine

- For pain and itching of hemorrhoids or other problems in the rectal area:

  —For *rectal cream* dosage form:

  - Adults—Apply a small amount to the area around the rectum up to five times a day, in the morning, in the evening, and after bowel movements.
  - Children—Use and dose must be determined by the doctor.

  —For *rectal ointment* dosage form:

  - Adults—Insert a small amount of ointment into the rectum up to five times a day, in the morning, in the evening, and after bowel movements. Or, apply a small amount to the area around the rectum up to five times a day, in the morning, in the evening, and after bowel movements.

—For the *rectal aerosol foam* dosage form:

• Adults—Insert 1 applicatorful into the rectum two or three times a day. Or, apply a small amount to the area around the rectum two or three times a day.

• Children—Use and dose must be determined by the doctor.

For tetracaine and for tetracaine and menthol

• For pain and itching of hemorrhoids or other problems in the rectal area:

—For the *rectal cream* or *rectal ointment* dosage form:

• Adults—Insert a small amount into the rectum up to six times a day. Or, apply a small amount to the area around the rectum up to six times a day.

• Children—Use and dose must be determined by the doctor.

Missed dose—If your doctor has directed you to use this medicine on a regular schedule and you miss a dose, use it as soon as possible. However, if it is almost time for your next dose, skip the missed dose and go back to your regular dosing schedule.

Storage—To store this medicine:

- Keep out of the reach of children.
- Store away from heat and direct light.
- Keep the medicine from freezing.
- Do not puncture, break, or burn the pramoxine aerosol foam container, even after it is empty.
- Do not keep outdated medicine or medicine no longer needed. Be sure that any discarded medicine is out of the reach of children.

Precautions While Using This Medicine

Check with your doctor:

- If your condition does not improve after you have been using this medicine regularly for 7 days, or if it becomes worse.
- If any bleeding from the rectum occurs.
- If you notice any rash, redness, or irritation that was not present before you started using this medicine.

False test results may occur if benzocaine or tetracaine is present in your body when a certain laboratory test is done. This test uses a medicine called bentiromide (e.g., Chymex) to show how well your pancreas is working. You should not use any products containing benzocaine or tetracaine for about 72 hours (3 days) before this test is done.

Side Effects of This Medicine

Along with its needed effects, a medicine may cause some unwanted effects. Although not all of these side effects may occur, if they do occur they may need medical attention.

Stop using this medicine and check with your doctor immediately if any of the following side effects occur:

Signs and symptoms of too much medicine being absorbed by the body

Blurred or double vision; confusion; convulsions (seizures); dizziness or lightheadedness; drowsiness; feeling hot, cold, or numb; increased sweating; ringing or buzzing in ears; shivering or trembling; slow or irregular heartbeat; unusual anxiety, excitement, nervousness, or restlessness; unusual paleness

Also, check with your doctor as soon as possible if any of the following side effects occur:

Less common

Burning, stinging, swelling, or tenderness not present before treatment; skin rash, redness, itching, or hives at or near place of application

Other side effects not listed above may also occur in some patients. If you notice any other effects, check with your doctor.

Revised: 09/01/94

ANESTHETICS Topical

Some commonly used brand names are:

In the U.S.—

Almay Anti-itch Lotion[7]
Americaine Topical Anesthetic First Aid Ointment[1]
Americaine Topical Anesthetic Spray[1]
Butesin Picrate[3]
DermaFlex[5]
Dermoplast[2]
Lagol[1]
Nupercainal Cream[4]
Nupercainal Ointment[4]
Pontocaine Cream[8]
Pontocaine Ointment[9]
Pramegel[7]
Prax[6]
Tronothane[6]
Xylocaine[5]

In Canada—

After Burn Double Strength Gel[5]
After Burn Double Strength Spray[5]
After Burn Gel[5]
After Burn Spray[5]
Alphacaine[5]
Dermoplast[2]
Endocaine[1]
Norwood Sunburn Spray[5]
Nupercainal Ointment[4]
Pramegel[7]
Shield Burnasept Spray[1]
Tronothane[6]
Xylocaine[5]

Other commonly used names are:

Amethocaine[8]
Butyl aminobenzoate[2]
Cinchocaine[4]
Ethyl aminobenzoate[1]
Lignocaine[5]
Pramocaine[6]

Note: For quick reference, the following anesthetics are numbered to match the corresponding brand names.

This information applies to the following medicines:

1. Benzocaine (BEN-zoe-kane)‡
2. Benzocaine and Menthol (MEN-thol)
3. Butamben (byoo-TAM-ben)
4. Dibucaine (DYE-byoo-kane)‡
5. Lidocaine (LYE-doe-kane)‡
6. Pramoxine (pra-MOX-een)
7. Pramoxine and Menthol
8. Tetracaine (TET-ra-kane)
9. Tetracaine and Menthol

‡Generic name product may also be available in the U.S.

Description

This medicine belongs to a group of medicines known as topical local anesthetics (an-ess-THET-iks). Topical anesthetics are used to relieve pain and itching caused by conditions such as sunburn or other minor burns, insect bites or stings, poison ivy, poison oak, poison sumac, and minor cuts and scratches.

Topical anesthetics deaden the nerve endings in the skin. They do not cause unconsciousness as do general anesthetics used for surgery.

Most topical anesthetics are available without a prescription; however, your doctor may have special instructions on the proper use and dose for your medical problem.

These medicines are available in the following dosage forms:

Topical

Benzocaine
- Cream (U.S.)
- Ointment (U.S.)
- Topical aerosol (U.S.)
- Topical spray solution (Canada)

Benzocaine and Menthol
- Lotion (U.S.)
- Topical aerosol solution (U.S. and Canada)

Butamben
- Ointment (U.S.)

Dibucaine
- Cream (U.S.)
- Ointment (U.S. and Canada)

Lidocaine
- Film-forming gel (U.S.)
- Jelly (Canada)
- Ointment (U.S. and Canada)
- Topical aerosol (Canada)
- Topical spray solution (Canada)

Pramoxine
- Cream (U.S. and Canada)
- Lotion (U.S.)

Pramoxine and Menthol
- Gel (U.S. and Canada)
- Lotion (U.S.)

Tetracaine
- Cream (U.S.)

Tetracaine and Menthol
- Ointment (U.S.)

Before Using This Medicine

If you are using this medicine without a prescription, carefully read and follow any precautions on the label. For topical anesthetics, the following should be considered:

Allergies—Tell your doctor if you have ever had any unusual or allergic reaction to a local anesthetic, especially when applied to the skin or other areas of the body. Also tell your health care professional if you are allergic to any other substances, such as foods, preservatives, or dyes, especially aminobenzoic acid (also called para-aminobenzoic acid [PABA]), to parabens (preservatives in many foods and medicines), or to paraphenylenediamine (a hair dye).

Pregnancy—Although studies on effects in pregnancy have not been done in humans, topical anesthetics have not been reported to cause problems in humans. Lidocaine has not been shown to cause birth defects or other problems in animal studies. Other topical anesthetics have not been studied in animals.

Breast-feeding—Topical anesthetics have not been reported to cause problems in nursing babies.

Children—Benzocaine may be absorbed through the skin of young children and cause unwanted effects. There is no specific information comparing use of other topical anesthetics in children with use in other age groups, but it is possible that they may also cause unwanted effects in young children. Check with your doctor before using any product that contains a topical anesthetic for a child younger than 2 years of age.

Older adults—Many medicines have not been studied specifically in older people. Therefore, it may not be known whether they work exactly the same way they do in younger adults or if they cause different side effects or problems in older people. There is no specific information comparing use of topical anesthetics in the elderly with use in other age groups.

Other medicines—Although certain medicines should not be used together at all, in other cases two different medicines may be used together even if an interaction might occur. In these cases, your doctor may want to change the dose, or other precautions may be necessary. Tell your health care professional if you are taking any other prescription or nonprescription (over-the-counter [OTC]) medicine.

Other medical problems—The presence of other medical problems may affect the use of topical anesthetics. Before using a topical anesthetic, check with your health care professional if you have any other medical problems, especially:

- Infection at or near the place of application or
- Large sores, broken skin, or severe injury at the area of application—The chance of side effects may be increased

Proper Use of This Medicine

For safe and effective use of this medicine:

- Follow your doctor's instructions if this medicine was prescribed.
- Follow the manufacturer's package directions if you are treating yourself.

- Unless otherwise directed by your doctor, *do not use this medicine on large areas, especially if the skin is broken or scraped. Also, do not use it more often than directed on the package label, or for more than a few days at a time.* To do so may increase the chance of absorption through the skin and the chance of unwanted effects. This is especially important when benzocaine is used for children younger than 2 years of age.

This medicine should be used only for problems being treated by your doctor or conditions listed in the package directions. *Check with your doctor before using it for other problems, especially if you think that an infection may be present.* This medicine should not be used to treat certain kinds of skin infections or serious problems, such as severe burns.

Read the package label very carefully to see if the product contains any alcohol. Alcohol is flammable and can catch on fire. *Do not use any product containing alcohol near a fire or open flame, or while smoking. Also, do not smoke after applying one of these products until it has completely dried.*

If you are using this medicine on your face, *be very careful not to get it in your eyes, mouth, or nose.* If you are using an aerosol or spray form of this medicine, do not spray it directly on your face. Instead, use your hand or an applicator (for example, a sterile gauze pad or a cotton swab) to apply the medicine.

For patients using *butamben:*

- Butamben may stain clothing and discolor hair. It may not be possible to remove the stains. To avoid this, do not touch your clothing or your hair while applying the medicine. Also, cover the treated area with a loose bandage after applying butamben, to protect your clothes.

To use *lidocaine film-forming gel* (e.g., DermaFlex):

- First dry the area with a clean cloth or a piece of gauze. Then apply the medicine. The medicine should dry, forming a clear film, after about 1 minute.

Dosing—The dose of a topical anesthetic will be different for different patients. *Follow your doctor's orders or the directions on the label.* The following information includes only the average doses of these medicines. *If your dose is different, do not change it* unless your doctor tells you to do so.

For benzocaine and for benzocaine and menthol combination

- For *topical* dosage forms (aerosol solution, cream, lotion, ointment, and spray solution):
  - —For pain and itching caused by minor skin conditions:
    - Adults and children 2 years of age and older—Apply to the affected area three or four times a day as needed.
    - Children younger than 2 years of age—Dose must be determined by your doctor.

For butamben

- For *topical* dosage form (ointment):
  - —For pain and itching caused by minor skin conditions:
    - Adults—Apply to the affected area three or four times a day as needed.
    - Children—Dose must be determined by your doctor.

For dibucaine

- For *topical cream* dosage form:
  - —For pain and itching caused by minor skin conditions:
    - Adults and children 2 years of age and older—Apply to the affected area three or four times a day as needed.
    - Children up to 2 years of age—Dose must be determined by your doctor.
- For *topical ointment* dosage form:
  - —For pain and itching caused by minor skin conditions:
    - Adults—Apply to the affected area three or four times a day as needed. The largest amount that may be used in a twenty-four-hour period is 30 grams, but much smaller amounts are usually enough.
    - Children 2 years of age and older—Apply to the affected area three or four times a day as needed. Do not use more than 7.5 grams in a twenty-four-hour period.
    - Children up to 2 years of age—Dose must be determined by your doctor.

For lidocaine

- For *topical* dosage forms (aerosol solution, film-forming gel, jelly, ointment, and spray solution):
  - —For pain and itching caused by minor skin conditions:
    - Adults—Apply to the affected area three or four times a day as needed.
    - Children—Dose must be determined by your doctor.

For pramoxine and for pramoxine and menthol combination

- For *topical* dosage forms (cream, gel, and lotion):
  - —For pain and itching caused by minor skin conditions:
    - Adults and children 2 years of age and older—Apply to the affected area three or four times a day as needed.
    - Children younger than 2 years of age—Dose must be determined by your doctor.

For tetracaine and for tetracaine and menthol combination

- For *topical* dosage forms (cream and ointment):
  - —For pain and itching caused by minor skin conditions:
    - Adults and teenagers—Apply to the affected area three or four times a day as needed. The

largest amount that may be used in a twenty-four-hour period is 30 grams (a whole tube of the medicine), but much smaller amounts are usually enough.

• Children 2 years of age and older—Apply to the affected area three or four times a day as needed. Do not use more than 7 grams (about one-fourth of a tube of the medicine) in a twenty-four-hour period.

• Children younger than 2 years of age—Dose must be determined by your doctor.

Missed dose—If your doctor has ordered you to use this medicine according to a regular schedule and you miss a dose, use it as soon as possible. However, if it is almost time for your next dose, skip the missed dose and use your next dose at the regularly scheduled time.

Storage—To store this medicine:

- Keep out of the reach of children.
- Store away from heat and direct light.
- Keep the medicine from freezing.
- Do not puncture, break, or burn aerosol containers, even when they are empty.
- Do not keep outdated medicine or medicine no longer needed. Be sure that any discarded medicine is out of the reach of children.

Precautions While Using This Medicine

After applying this medicine to the skin of a child, *watch the child carefully to make sure that he or she does not get any of the medicine into his or her mouth.* Topical anesthetics can cause serious side effects, especially in children, if any of the medicine gets into the mouth or is swallowed.

Stop using this medicine and check with your doctor:

- *If your condition does not improve within 7 days, or if it gets worse.*
- *If the area you are treating becomes infected.*
- *If you notice a skin rash, burning, stinging, swelling, or any other sign of irritation that was not present when you began using this medicine.*
- *If you swallow any of the medicine.*

Side Effects of This Medicine

Along with its needed effects, a medicine may cause some unwanted effects. Although not all of these side effects may occur, if they do occur they may need medical attention.

Check with your doctor immediately if any of the following side effects occur:

Less common

Large swellings that look like hives on the skin or in the mouth or throat

Symptoms of too much medicine being absorbed by the body—very rare

Blurred or double vision; confusion; convulsions (seizures); dizziness or lightheadedness; drowsiness; feeling hot, cold, or numb; headache; increased sweating; ringing or buzzing in the ears; shivering or trembling; slow or irregular heartbeat; troubled breathing; unusual anxiety, excitement, nervousness, or restlessness; unusual paleness; unusual tiredness or weakness

Also, check with your doctor as soon as possible if any of the following side effects occur:

Burning, stinging, or tenderness not present before treatment; skin rash, redness, itching, or hives

Other side effects not listed above may also occur in some patients. If you notice any other effects, check with your doctor.

Revised: 08/29/94

ANESTHETICS, GENERAL Systemic

Some commonly used brand names are:

In the U.S.—

Amidate[2]
Brevital[6]
Diprivan[9]
Ethrane[1]
Fluothane[3]
Forane[4]
Ketalar[5]
Penthrane[7]
Pentothal[10]

In Canada—

Brietal[6]
Diprivan[9]
Ethrane[1]
Fluothane[3]
Forane[4]
Ketalar[5]
Pentothal[10]
Somnothane[3]

Other commonly used names are:

Methohexitone[6]
Thiopentone[10]

Note: For quick reference, the following general anesthetics are numbered to match the corresponding brand names.

This information applies to the following medicines:

1. Enflurane (EN-floo-rane)‡
2. Etomidate (e-TOM-i-date)†
3. Halothane (HA-loe-thane)‡
4. Isoflurane (eye-soe-FLURE-ane)
5. Ketamine (KEET-a-meen)
6. Methohexital (meth-oh-HEX-i-tal)
7. Methoxyflurane (meth-ox-ee-FLOO-rane)
8. Nitrous (NYE-trus) Oxide‡§
9. Propofol (PROE-po-fole)
10. Thiopental (thye-oh-PEN-tal)‡

†Not commercially available in Canada.
‡Generic name product may also be available in the U.S.
§Generic name product may also be available in Canada.

Description

General anesthetics (an-ess-THET-iks) are normally used to produce loss of consciousness before and during surgery. However, for obstetrics (labor and delivery) or certain minor procedures, an anesthetic may be given in small amounts to relieve anxiety or pain without causing unconsciousness. Also, some of the anesthetics may be used for certain procedures in a medical doctor's or dentist's office.

Thiopental is also sometimes used to control convulsions (seizures) caused by certain medicines or seizure disorders. Thiopental may be used to reduce pressure on the brain in certain conditions. Thiopental may also be used for other conditions as determined by your doctor.

General anesthetics are usually given by inhalation or by injection into a vein. However, certain anesthetics may be given rectally to help produce sleep before surgery or certain procedures. Although most general anesthetics can be used by themselves in producing loss of consciousness, some are often used together. This allows for more effective anesthesia in certain patients.

General anesthetics are given only by or under the immediate supervision of a medical doctor or dentist trained to use them. If you will be receiving a general anesthetic during surgery, your doctor or anesthesiologist will give you the medicine and closely follow your progress.

General anesthetics are available in the following dosage forms:

Inhalation
- Enflurane
  - Inhalation (U.S. and Canada)
- Halothane
  - Inhalation (U.S. and Canada)
- Isoflurane
  - Inhalation (U.S. and Canada)
- Methoxyflurane
  - Inhalation (U.S.)
- Nitrous oxide
  - Inhalation (U.S. and Canada)

Parenteral
- Etomidate
  - Injection (U.S.)
- Ketamine
  - Injection (U.S. and Canada)
- Methohexital
  - Injection (U.S. and Canada)
- Propofol
  - Injection (U.S. and Canada)
- Thiopental
  - Injection (U.S. and Canada)

Rectal
- Methohexital
  - Rectal solution (U.S. and Canada)
- Thiopental
  - Rectal solution (U.S. and Canada)
  - Rectal suspension (U.S.)

Before Receiving This Medicine

In deciding to use a medicine, the risks of taking the medicine must be weighed against the good it will do. This is a decision you and your doctor will make. For general anesthetics, the following should be considered:

Allergies—Tell your doctor if you have ever had any unusual or allergic reaction to barbiturates or general anesthetics. Also tell your health care professional if you are allergic to any other substances, such as foods, preservatives, or dyes.

Pregnancy—
- *For barbiturate anesthetics (methohexital and thiopental)*—Methohexital has not been studied in pregnant women. However, it has not been shown to cause birth defects or other problems in animal studies. Studies on effects in pregnancy with thiopental have not been done in either humans or animals. However, use of barbiturate anesthetics during pregnancy may affect the nervous system in the fetus.
- *For etomidate*—Etomidate has not been studied in pregnant women. Although studies in animals have not shown etomidate to cause birth defects, it has been shown to cause other unwanted effects in the animal fetus when given in doses usually many times the human dose.
- *For inhalation anesthetics (enflurane, halothane, isoflurane, methoxyflurane, and nitrous oxide)*—Enflurane, halothane, isoflurane, methoxyflurane, and nitrous oxide have not been studied in pregnant women. However, studies in animals have shown that inhalation anesthetics may cause birth defects or other harm to the fetus.

  When used as an anesthetic for an abortion, enflurane, halothane, or isoflurane may cause increased bleeding.

  When used in small doses to relieve pain during labor and delivery, halothane may slow delivery and increase bleeding in the mother after the baby is born. These effects do not occur with small doses of enflurane, isoflurane, or methoxyflurane. However, they may occur with large doses of these anesthetics.
- *For ketamine*—Ketamine has not been studied in pregnant women. Studies in animals have not shown that ketamine causes birth defects, but it caused damage to certain tissues when given in large amounts for a long period of time.
- *For propofol*—Propofol has not been studied in pregnant women. Although studies in animals have not shown propofol to cause birth defects, it has been shown to cause deaths in nursing mothers and their offspring when given in doses usually many times the human dose.

General anesthetics may cause unwanted effects, such as drowsiness, in the newborn baby if large amounts are given to the mother during labor and delivery.

Breast-feeding—Barbiturate anesthetics (methohexital and thiopental), halothane, and propofol pass into the breast milk. However, general anesthetics have not been reported to cause problems in nursing babies.

Children—Anesthetics given by inhalation and ketamine have been tested in children and have not been shown to cause different side effects or problems in children than they do in adults.

Although there is no specific information comparing use of barbiturate anesthetics (methohexital and thiopental), etomidate, or propofol in children with use in other age groups, these medicines are not expected to cause different side effects or problems in children than they do in adults.

Older adults—Elderly people are especially sensitive to the effects of the barbiturate anesthetics (methohexital and thiopental), etomidate, propofol, and anesthetics given by inhalation. This may increase the chance of side effects.

Ketamine has not been shown to cause different side effects or problems in older people than it does in younger adults.

Other medicines—Although certain medicines should not be used together at all, in other cases 2 different medicines may be used together even if an interaction might occur. In these cases, your doctor may want to change the dose, or other precautions may be necessary. When you are receiving general anesthetics, it is especially important that your health care professional know if you are taking *any other medicine*, including any of the following:

- "Street" drugs, such as amphetamines ("uppers"), barbiturates ("downers"), cocaine, marijuana, phencyclidine (PCP or "angel dust"), and heroin or other narcotics—Serious, possibly fatal, side effects may occur if your medical doctor or dentist gives you an anesthetic without knowing that you have taken another medicine

Other medical problems—The presence of other medical problems may affect the use of general anesthetics. Make sure you tell your doctor if you have any other medical problems, especially:

- Malignant hyperthermia, during or shortly after receiving an anesthetic (history of, or family history of). Signs of malignant hyperthermia include very high fever, fast and irregular heartbeat, muscle spasms or tightness, and breathing problems—This side effect may occur again

Proper Use of This Medicine

Dosing—The dose of a general anesthetic will be different for different patients. Your doctor will decide on the right amount for you. The dose will depend on:

- Your age;
- Your general physical condition;
- The kind of surgery or other procedure you are having; and
- Other medicines you are taking or will receive before and during surgery.

Precautions After Receiving This Medicine

For patients going home within 24 hours after receiving a general anesthetic:

- General anesthetics may cause you to feel drowsy, tired, or weak for up to a few days after they have been given. They may also cause problems with coordination and your ability to think. Therefore, for at least 24 hours (or longer if necessary) after receiving a general anesthetic, *do not drive, use machines, or do anything else that could be dangerous if you are not alert*.
- Unless otherwise directed by your medical doctor or dentist, *do not drink alcoholic beverages or take other CNS depressants (medicines that slow down the nervous system, possibly causing drowsiness) for about 24 hours after you have received a general anesthetic*. To do so may add to the effects of the anesthetic. Some examples of CNS depressants are antihistamines or medicine for hay fever, other allergies, or colds; other sedatives, tranquilizers, or sleeping medicine; prescription pain medicine or narcotics; other barbiturates; medicine for seizures; and muscle relaxants.

Side Effects of This Medicine

Along with its needed effects, a medicine may cause some unwanted effects. Although not all of these side effects may occur, if they do occur they may need medical attention. While you are receiving a general anesthetic, your doctor will closely follow its effects. However, some effects may not be noticed until later.

Check with your doctor as soon as possible if any of the following side effects occur within 2 weeks after you have received an anesthetic:

Rare

Abdominal or stomach pain; back or leg pain; black or bloody vomit; fever; headache (severe); increase or decrease in amount of urine; loss of appetite; nausea (severe); pale skin; unusual tiredness or weakness; weakness of wrist and fingers; weight loss (unusual); yellow eyes or skin

Other side effects may occur that usually do not need medical attention. The following side effects should go away as the effects of the anesthetic wear off. However, check with your doctor if any of the following side effects continue or are bothersome:

More common

Shivering or trembling

Less common

Blurred or double vision or other vision problems; dizziness, lightheadedness, or feeling faint; drowsiness; headache; mood or mental changes; nausea (mild) or vomiting; nightmares or unusual dreams

Other side effects not listed above may also occur in some patients. If you notice any other effects, check with your doctor.

Additional Information

Once a medicine has been approved for marketing for a certain use, experience may show that it is also useful for other medical problems. Although these uses are not included in product labeling, thiopental is used in certain patients with the following medical conditions:

- Hypoxia, cerebral (shortage of oxygen supplied to the brain) or
- Ischemia, cerebral (shortage of blood supplied to the brain)

Other than the above information, there is no additional information relating to proper use, precautions, or side effects for these uses.

Revised: 08/26/94

ANGIOTENSIN-CONVERTING ENZYME (ACE) INHIBITORS Systemic

Some commonly used brand names are:

In the U.S.—

Accupril[7]	Monopril[5]
Altace[8]	Prinivil[6]
Capoten[2]	Vasotec[3,4]
Lotensin[1]	Zestril[6]

In Canada—

Capoten[2]	Vasotec[3,4]
Prinivil[6]	Zestril[6]

Note: For quick reference, the following angiotensin-converting enzyme (ace) inhibitors are numbered to match the corresponding brand names.

This information applies to the following medicines:

1. Benazepril (ben-AY-ze-pril)†
2. Captopril (KAP-toe-pril)
3. Enalapril (e-NAL-a-pril)
4. Enalaprilat (e-NAL-a-pril-at)
5. Fosinopril (foe-SIN-oh-pril)†
6. Lisinopril (lyse-IN-oh-pril)
7. Quinapril (KWIN-a-pril)†
8. Ramipril (ra-MI-pril)†

†Not commercially available in Canada.

Description

ACE inhibitors belong to the class of medicines called high blood pressure medicines (antihypertensives). They are used to treat high blood pressure (hypertension).

High blood pressure adds to the work load of the heart and arteries. If it continues for a long time, the heart and arteries may not function properly. This can damage the blood vessels of the brain, heart, and kidneys, resulting in a stroke, heart failure, or kidney failure. High blood pressure may also increase the risk of heart attacks. These problems may be less likely to occur if blood pressure is controlled.

Captopril is used in some patients after a heart attack. After a heart attack, some of the heart muscle is damaged and weakened. The heart muscle may continue to weaken as time goes by. This makes it more difficult for the heart to pump blood. Captopril helps slow down the further weakening of the heart.

Captopril is also used to treat kidney problems in some diabetic patients who use insulin to control their diabetes. Over time, these kidney problems may get worse. Captopril may help slow down the further worsening of kidney problems.

In addition, some ACE inhibitors are used to treat congestive heart failure or may be used for other conditions as determined by your doctor.

The exact way that these medicines work is not known. They block an enzyme in the body that is necessary to produce a substance that causes blood vessels to tighten. As a result, they relax blood vessels. This lowers blood pressure and increases the supply of blood and oxygen to the heart.

These medicines are available only with your doctor's prescription, in the following dosage forms:

Oral

- Benazepril
  - Tablets (U.S.)
- Captopril
  - Tablets (U.S. and Canada)
- Enalapril
  - Tablets (U.S. and Canada)
- Fosinopril
  - Tablets (U.S.)
- Lisinopril
  - Tablets (U.S. and Canada)
- Quinapril
  - Tablets (U.S.)
- Ramipril
  - Capsules (U.S.)

Parenteral

- Enalaprilat
  - Injection (U.S. and Canada)

Before Using This Medicine

In deciding to use a medicine, the risks of taking the medicine must be weighed against the good it will do. This is a decision you and your doctor will make. For the angiotensin-converting enzyme (ACE) inhibitors, the following should be considered:

Allergies—Tell your doctor if you have ever had any unusual or allergic reaction to benazepril, captopril, enalapril, fosinopril, lisinopril, quinapril, or ramipril. Also tell your health care professional if you are allergic to any other substances, such as foods, preservatives, or dyes.

Pregnancy—Use of angiotensin-converting enzyme (ACE) inhibitors during pregnancy, especially in the second and third trimesters (after the first three months) can cause low blood pressure, severe kidney failure, too much potassium, or even death in the newborn. *Therefore, it is important that you check with your doctor immediately if you think that you may be pregnant.* Be sure that you have discussed this with your doctor before taking this medicine. In addition, if you are taking:

- *Benazepril*—Benazepril has not been shown to cause birth defects in animals when given in doses more than 3 times the highest recommended human dose.
- *Captopril*—Studies in rabbits and rats at doses up to 400 times the recommended human dose have shown that captopril causes an increase in deaths of the fetus and newborn. Also, captopril has caused deformed skulls in the offspring of rabbits given doses 2 to 70 times the recommended human dose.
- *Enalapril*—Studies in rats at doses many times the recommended human dose have shown that use of enalapril causes the fetus to be smaller than normal. Studies in rabbits have shown that enalapril causes an increase in fetal death. Enalapril has not been shown to cause birth defects in rats or rabbits.
- *Fosinopril*—Studies in rats have shown that fosinopril causes the fetus to be smaller than normal. Studies in rabbits have shown that fosinopril causes fetal

death, probably due to extremely low blood pressure. In rats, birth defects such as skeletal and facial deformities were seen. However, it is not clear that the deformities were related to fosinopril. Birth defects were not seen in rabbits.

- *Lisinopril*—Studies in mice and rats at doses many times the recommended human dose have shown that use of lisinopril causes a decrease in successful pregnancies, a decrease in the weight of infants, and an increase in infant deaths. It has also caused a decrease in successful pregnancies and abnormal bone growth in rabbits. Lisinopril has not been shown to cause birth defects in mice, rats, or rabbits.
- *Quinapril*—Studies in rats have shown that quinapril causes lower birth weights and changes in kidney structure of the fetus. However, birth defects were not seen in rabbits given quinapril.
- *Ramipril*—Studies in animals have shown that ramipril causes lower birth weights.

Breast-feeding—

- *Benazepril, captopril, and fosinopril*—These medicines pass into breast milk.
- *Enalapril, lisinopril, quinapril, or ramipril*—It is not known whether these medicines pass into breast milk. However, these medicines have not been reported to cause problems in nursing babies.

Children—Children may be especially sensitive to the blood pressure–lowering effect of ACE inhibitors. This may increase the chance of side effects or other problems during treatment. Therefore, it is especially important that you discuss with the child's doctor the good that this medicine may do as well as the risks of using it.

Older adults—This medicine has been tested in a limited number of patients 65 years of age or older and has not been shown to cause different side effects or problems in older people than it does in younger adults.

Other medicines—Although certain medicines should not be used together at all, in other cases two different medicines may be used together even if an interaction might occur. In these cases, your doctor may want to change the dose, or other precautions may be necessary. When you are taking or receiving ACE inhibitors it is especially important that your health care professional know if you are taking any of the following:

- Diuretics (water pills)—Effects on blood pressure may be increased. In addition, some diuretics make the increase in potassium in the blood caused by ACE inhibitors even greater
- Potassium-containing medicines or supplements or
- Salt substitutes or
- Low-salt milk—Use of these substances with ACE inhibitors may result in an unusually high potassium level in the blood, which can lead to heart rhythm and other problems

Other medical problems—The presence of other medical problems may affect the use of the ACE inhibitors. Make sure you tell your doctor if you have any other medical problems, especially:

- Diabetes mellitus (sugar diabetes)—Increased risk of potassium levels in the body becoming too high
- Heart or blood vessel disease or
- Heart attack or stroke (recent)—Lowering blood pressure may make problems resulting from these conditions worse
- Kidney disease or
- Liver disease—Effects may be increased because of slower removal of medicine from the body
- Kidney transplant—Increased risk of kidney disease caused by ACE inhibitors
- Systemic lupus erythematosus (SLE)—Increased risk of blood problems caused by ACE inhibitors
- Previous reaction to any ACE inhibitor involving hoarseness; swelling of face, mouth, hands, or feet; or sudden trouble in breathing—Reaction is more likely to occur again

Proper Use of This Medicine

To help you remember to take your medicine, try to get into the habit of taking it at the same time each day.

For patients taking *captopril:*

- This medicine is best taken on an empty stomach 1 hour before meals, unless you are otherwise directed by your doctor.

For patients taking this medicine *for high blood pressure:*

- In addition to the use of the medicine your doctor has prescribed, treatment for your high blood pressure may include weight control and care in the types of foods you eat, especially foods high in sodium. Your doctor will tell you which of these are most important for you. You should check with your doctor before changing your diet.
- Many patients who have high blood pressure will not notice any signs of the problem. In fact, many may feel normal. It is very important that you *take your medicine exactly as directed* and that you keep your appointments with your doctor even if you feel well.
- Remember that this medicine will not cure your high blood pressure but it does help control it. Therefore, you must continue to take it as directed if you expect to lower your blood pressure and keep it down. *You may have to take high blood pressure medicine for the rest of your life.* If high blood pressure is not treated, it can cause serious problems such as heart failure, blood vessel disease, stroke, or kidney disease.

Dosing—The dose of the ACE inhibitor will be different for different patients. *Follow your doctor's orders or the directions on the label.* The following information includes only the average doses. *If your dose is different, do not change it* unless your doctor tells you to do so.

The number of capsules or tablets that you take depends on the strength of the medicine. Also, *the number of doses you take each day, the time allowed between doses, and the length of time you take the medicine depend on the medical problem for which you are taking the ACE inhibitor.*

For benazepril

- For *oral* dosage form (tablets):
  - —For high blood pressure:
    - Adults—10 milligrams (mg) once a day at first. Then, your doctor may increase your dose to 20 to 40 mg a day taken as a single dose or divided into two doses.
    - Children—Use and dose must be determined by your doctor.

For captopril

- For *oral* dosage form (tablets):
  - —For congestive heart failure:
    - Adults—12.5 to 100 mg two or three times a day.
    - Children—Dose must be determined by your doctor.
  - —For high blood pressure:
    - Adults—12.5 to 25 mg two or three times a day.
    - Children—Dose must be determined by your doctor.
  - —For kidney problems related to diabetes:
    - Adults—25 mg three times a day.
  - —For treatment after a heart attack:
    - Adults—12.5 to 50 mg three times a day.

For enalapril

- For *oral* dosage form (tablets):
  - —For congestive heart failure:
    - Adults—2.5 mg once a day or two times a day at first. Your doctor may increase your dose to 5 to 20 mg a day taken as a single dose or divided into two doses.
    - Children—Use and dose must be determined by your doctor.
  - —For high blood pressure:
    - Adults—5 mg once a day at first. Then, your doctor may increase your dose to 10 to 40 mg a day taken as a single dose or divided into two doses.
    - Children—Use and dose must be determined by your doctor.
  - —For treating weakened heart muscle:
    - Adults—2.5 mg two times a day at first. Then, your doctor may increase your dose up to 20 mg a day taken in divided doses.
- For *injection* dosage form:
  - —For high blood pressure:
    - Adults—1.25 mg every six hours injected into a vein.
    - Children—Use and dose must be determined by your doctor.

For fosinopril

- For *oral* dosage form (tablets):
  - —For high blood pressure:
    - Adults—10 to 40 mg once a day.
    - Children—Use and dose must be determined by your doctor.

For lisinopril

- For *oral* dosage form (tablets):
  - —For congestive heart failure:
    - Adults—2.5 to 20 mg once a day.
    - Children—Use and dose must be determined by your doctor.
  - —For high blood pressure:
    - Adults—10 to 40 mg once a day.
    - Children—Use and dose must be determined by your doctor.

For quinapril

- For *oral* dosage form (tablets):
  - —For high blood pressure:
    - Adults—10 mg once a day at first. Then, your doctor may increase your dose to 20 to 80 mg a day taken as a single dose or divided into two doses.
    - Children—Use and dose must be determined by your doctor.

For ramipril

- For *oral* dosage form (capsules):
  - —For high blood pressure:
    - Adults—2.5 mg once a day at first. Then, your doctor may increase your dose up to 20 mg a day taken as a single dose or divided into two doses.
    - Children—Use and dose must be determined by your doctor.

Missed dose—If you miss a dose of this medicine, take it as soon as possible. However, if it is almost time for your next dose, skip the missed dose and go back to your regular dosing schedule. Do not double doses.

Storage—To store this medicine:

- Keep out of the reach of children.
- Store away from heat and direct light.
- Do not store in the bathroom, near the kitchen sink, or in other damp places. Heat or moisture may cause the medicine to break down.
- Do not keep outdated medicine or medicine no longer needed. Be sure that any discarded medicine is out of the reach of children.

Precautions While Using This Medicine

It is important that your doctor check your progress at regular visits to make sure that this medicine is working properly and to check for unwanted effects.

For patients taking this medicine *for high blood pressure:*

- *Do not take other medicines unless they have been discussed with your doctor.* This especially includes over-the-counter (nonprescription) medicines for appetite control, asthma, colds, cough, hay fever, or sinus problems, since they may tend to increase your blood pressure.

Dizziness or lightheadedness may occur after the first dose of this medicine, especially if you have been taking a diuretic (water pill). Make sure you know how you react to this medicine before you drive, use machines, or do anything else that could be dangerous if you are dizzy.

Check with your doctor right away if you become sick while taking this medicine, especially with severe or continuing nausea and vomiting or diarrhea. These conditions may cause you to lose too much water and lead to low blood pressure.

Dizziness, lightheadedness, or fainting may also occur if you exercise or if the weather is hot. Heavy sweating can cause loss of too much water and low blood pressure. Use extra care during exercise or hot weather.

Avoid alcoholic beverages until you have discussed their use with your doctor. Alcohol may make the low blood pressure effect worse and/or increase the possibility of dizziness or fainting.

Before having any kind of surgery (including dental surgery) or emergency treatment, tell the medical doctor or dentist in charge that you are taking this medicine.

For patients taking *captopril or fosinopril:*

- Before you have any medical tests, tell the doctor in charge that you are taking this medicine. The results of some tests may be affected by this medicine.

Side Effects of This Medicine

Along with its needed effects, a medicine may cause some unwanted effects. Although not all of these side effects may occur, if they do occur they may need medical attention.

Check with your doctor immediately if any of the following side effects occur:

Rare

Fever and chills; hoarseness; swelling of face, mouth, hands, or feet; trouble in swallowing or breathing (sudden); stomach pain, itching of skin, or yellow eyes or skin

Check with your doctor as soon as possible if any of the following side effects occur:

Less common

Dizziness, lightheadedness, or fainting; skin rash, with or without itching, fever, or joint pain

Rare

Abdominal pain, abdominal distention, fever, nausea, or vomiting; chest pain

Signs and symptoms of too much potassium in the body

Confusion; irregular heartbeat; nervousness; numbness or tingling in hands, feet, or lips; shortness of breath or difficulty breathing; weakness or heaviness of legs

Other side effects may occur that usually do not need medical attention. These side effects may go away during treatment as your body adjusts to the medicine. However, check with your doctor if any of the following side effects continue or are bothersome:

More common

Cough (dry, continuing)

Less common

Diarrhea; headache; loss of taste; nausea; unusual tiredness

Other side effects not listed above may also occur in some patients. If you notice any other effects, check with your doctor.

Additional Information

Once a medicine has been approved for marketing for a certain use, experience may show that it is also useful for other medical problems. Although these uses are not included in product labeling, ACE inhibitors are used in certain patients with the following medical conditions:

- Hypertension in scleroderma (high blood pressure in patients with hardening and thickening of the skin)
- Renal crisis in scleroderma (kidney problems in patients with hardening and thickening of the skin)

Other than the above information, there is no additional information relating to proper use, precautions, or side effects for these uses.

Revised: 07/12/92
Interim revision: 08/04/93; 07/12/94

ANGIOTENSIN-CONVERTING ENZYME (ACE) INHIBITORS AND HYDROCHLOROTHIAZIDE Systemic†

Some commonly used brand names are:

In the U.S.—

Capozide[1] Vaseretic[2]
Prinzide[3] Zestoretic[3]

Note: For quick reference, the following medicines are numbered to match the corresponding brand names.

This information applies to the following medicines:

1. Captopril (KAP-toe-pril) and Hydrochlorothiazide (hye-droe-klor-oh-THYE-a-zide)†
2. Enalapril (e-NAL-a-pril) and Hydrochlorothiazide†
3. Lisinopril (lyse-IN-oh-pril) and Hydrochlorothiazide†

†Not commercially available in Canada.

Description

This combination belongs to the class of medicines called high blood pressure medicines (antihypertensives). It is used to treat high blood pressure (hypertension).

High blood pressure adds to the workload of the heart and arteries. If it continues for a long time, the heart and arteries may not function properly. This can damage the blood vessels of the brain, heart, and kidneys, resulting in a stroke, heart failure, or kidney failure. High blood pressure may also increase the risk of heart attacks. These

problems may be less likely to occur if blood pressure is controlled.

The exact way in which captopril, enalapril, and lisinopril work is not known. They block an enzyme in the body that is necessary to produce a substance that causes blood vessels to tighten. As a result, they relax blood vessels. This lowers blood pressure and increases the supply of blood and oxygen to the heart. Hydrochlorothiazide helps reduce the amount of salt and water in the body by acting on the kidneys to increase the flow of urine; this also helps to lower blood pressure.

This combination may also be used for other conditions as determined by your doctor.

This medicine is available only with doctor's prescription, in the following dosage forms:

Oral

Captopril and Hydrochlorothiazide
- Tablets (U.S.)

Enalapril and Hydrochlorothiazide
- Tablets (U.S.)

Lisinopril and Hydrochlorothiazide
- Tablets (U.S.)

Before Using This Medicine

In deciding to use a medicine, the risks of taking the medicine must be weighed against the good it will do. This is a decision you and your doctor will make. For the angiotensin-converting enzyme (ACE) inhibitors and hydrochlorothiazide, the following should be considered:

Allergies—Tell your doctor if you have ever had any unusual or allergic reaction to enalapril, captopril, lisinopril, sulfonamides (sulfa drugs), bumetanide, furosemide, acetazolamide, dichlorphenamide, or methazolamide or to hydrochlorothiazide or any of the other thiazide diuretics (water pills). Also tell your health care professional if you are allergic to any other substances, such as foods, sulfites or other preservatives, or dyes.

Pregnancy—Studies with this combination medicine have not been done in pregnant women. However, use of any of the ACE inhibitors (captopril, enalapril, lisinopril) during pregnancy, especially in the second and third trimesters (after the first three months) can cause low blood pressure, kidney failure, too much potassium, or even death in newborns. *Therefore, it is important that you check with your doctor immediately if you think that you may be pregnant.* Be sure that you have discussed this with your doctor before taking this medicine. In addition, if your medicine contains:

- *Captopril*—Studies in rabbits and rats at doses up to 400 times the recommended human dose have shown that captopril causes an increase in death of the fetus and newborn. Also, captopril has caused deformed skulls in the offspring of rabbits given doses 2 to 70 times the recommended human dose.
- *Enalapril*—Studies in rats at doses many times the recommended human dose have shown that use of enalapril causes the fetus to be smaller than normal. Studies in rabbits have shown that enalapril causes an increase in fetal death. Enalapril has not been shown to cause birth defects in rats or rabbits.
- *Lisinopril*—Studies in mice and rats at doses many times the recommended human dose have shown that use of lisinopril causes a decrease in successful pregnancies, a decrease in the weight of infants, and an increase in infant deaths. It has also caused a decrease in successful pregnancies and abnormal bone growth in rabbits. Lisinopril has not been shown to cause birth defects in mice, rats, or rabbits.
- *Hydrochlorothiazide*—Hydrochlorothiazide has not been shown to cause birth defects or other problems in animal studies. However, when hydrochlorothiazide is used during pregnancy, it may cause side effects including jaundice, blood problems, and low potassium in the newborn baby.

Breast-feeding—
- *Captopril*—Passes into breast milk. However, this medicine has not been reported to cause problems in nursing babies.
- *Enalapril or lisinopril*—It is not known whether enalapril or lisinopril passes into breast milk. However, these medicines have not been reported to cause problems in nursing babies.
- *Hydrochlorothiazide*—Passes into breast milk. However, this medicine has not been reported to cause problems in nursing babies.

Children—Children may be especially sensitive to the blood pressure–lowering effect of ACE inhibitors. This may increase the chance of side effects or other problems during treatment. Extra caution may be necessary when using hydrochlorothiazide in infants with jaundice because it can make this condition worse. Therefore, it is especially important that you discuss with the child's doctor the good that this medicine may do as well as the risks of using it.

Older adults—Dizziness or lightheadedness and symptoms of too much potassium loss may be more likely to occur in the elderly, who may be more sensitive to the effects of this medicine.

Other medicines—Although certain medicines should not be used together at all, in other cases two different medicines may be used together even if an interaction might occur. In these cases, your doctor may want to change the dose, or other precautions may be necessary. When taking ACE inhibitors and hydrochlorothiazide it is especially important that your health care professional know if you are taking any of the following:

- Cholestyramine or
- Colestipol—Use with thiazide diuretics may prevent the diuretic from working properly; the diuretic should be taken at least 1 hour before or 4 hours after cholestyramine or colestipol
- Digitalis glycosides (heart medicine)—If potassium levels in the body are decreased, symptoms of digitalis toxicity may occur
- Diuretics (water pills)—Effects on blood pressure may be increased
- Lithium (e.g., Lithane)—Risk of lithium overdose, even at low doses, may be increased
- Potassium-containing medicines or supplements or

- Salt substitutes or
- Low-salt milk—Use of these substances with ACE inhibitors may result in an unusually high potassium level in the blood, which can lead to heart rhythm and other problems

Other medical problems—The presence of other medical problems may affect the use of the ACE inhibitors. Make sure you tell your doctor if you have any other medical problems, especially:

- Diabetes mellitus (sugar diabetes)—Increased risk of potassium levels in the body becoming too high
- Gout (or history of)—Hydrochlorothiazide may increase the amount of uric acid in the body, which can lead to gout
- Heart or blood vessel disease or
- Heart attack or stroke (recent)—Lowering blood pressure may make problems resulting from these conditions worse
- Kidney disease or
- Liver disease—Effects may be increased because of slower removal from the body
- Kidney transplant—Increased risk of kidney disease caused by ACE inhibitors
- Pancreatitis (inflammation of the pancreas)—Hydrochlorothiazide can make this condition worse
- Systemic lupus erythematosus (SLE) (or history of)—Hydrochlorothiazide may worsen the condition, and there is an increased risk of blood problems caused by ACE inhibitors
- Previous reaction to captopril, enalapril, or lisinopril involving hoarseness; swelling of face, mouth, hands, or feet; or sudden trouble in breathing—Reaction is more likely to occur again

Proper Use of This Medicine

To help you remember to take your medicine, try to get into the habit of taking it at the same time each day.

For patients taking *captopril and hydrochlorothiazide:*

- This medicine is best taken on an empty stomach 1 hour before meals, unless you are otherwise directed by your doctor.

For patients taking this medicine *for high blood pressure:*

- In addition to the use of the medicine your doctor has prescribed, treatment for your high blood pressure may include weight control and care in the types of foods you eat, especially foods high in sodium. Your doctor will tell you which of these are most important for you. You should check with your doctor before changing your diet.
- Many patients who have high blood pressure will not notice any signs of the problem. In fact, many may feel normal. It is very important that you *take your medicine exactly as directed* and that you keep your appointments with your doctor even if you feel well.
- Remember that this medicine will not cure your high blood pressure but it does help control it. Therefore, you must continue to take it as directed if you expect to lower your blood pressure and keep it down. *You may have to take high blood pressure medicine for the rest of your life.* If high blood pressure is not treated, it can cause serious problems such as heart failure, blood vessel disease, stroke, or kidney disease.

This medicine may cause you to have an unusual feeling of tiredness when you begin to take it. You may also notice an increase in the amount of urine or in your frequency of urination. After you have taken the medicine for a while, these effects should lessen. In general, to keep the increase in urine from affecting your sleep:

- If you are to take a single dose a day, take it in the morning after breakfast.
- If you are to take more than one dose a day, take the last dose no later than 6 p.m., unless otherwise directed by your doctor.

However, it is best to plan your dose or doses according to a schedule that will least affect your personal activities and sleep. Ask your health care professional to help you plan the best time to take this medicine.

Dosing—The dose of these medicines will be different for different patients. *Follow your doctor's orders or the directions on the label.* The following information includes only the average doses of these medicines. *If your dose is different, do not change it* unless your doctor tells you to do so.

The number of tablets that you take depends on the strength of the medicine.

For captopril and hydrochlorothiazide combination

- For *oral* dosage form (tablets):
  - —For high blood pressure:
    - Adults—1 tablet two or three times a day.
    - Children—Dose is based on body weight and must be determined by your doctor.

For enalapril and hydrochlorothiazide combination

- For *oral* dosage form (tablets):
  - —For high blood pressure:
    - Adults—1 tablet once a day.
    - Children—Dose is based on body weight and must be determined by your doctor.

For lisinopril and hydrochlorothiazide combination

- For *oral* dosage form (tablets):
  - —For high blood pressure:
    - Adults—1 or 2 tablets once a day.
    - Children—Dose must be determined by your doctor.

Missed dose—If you miss a dose of this medicine, take it as soon as possible. However, if it is almost time for your next dose, skip the missed dose and go back to your regular dosing schedule. Do not double doses.

Storage—To store this medicine:

- Keep out of the reach of children.
- Store away from heat and direct light.
- Do not store in the bathroom, near the kitchen sink, or in other damp places. Heat or moisture may cause the medicine to break down.
- Do not keep outdated medicine or medicine no longer needed. Be sure that any discarded medicine is out of the reach of children.

Precautions While Using This Medicine

It is important that your doctor check your progress at regular visits to make sure that this medicine is working properly and to check for unwanted effects.

Dizziness or lightheadedness may occur, especially after the first dose of this medicine. Make sure you know how you react to the medicine before you drive, use machines, or do anything else that could be dangerous if you are dizzy.

Check with your doctor right away if you become sick while taking this medicine, especially with severe or continuing nausea and vomiting or diarrhea. These conditions may cause you to lose too much water and lead to low blood pressure.

Dizziness, lightheadedness, or fainting may also occur if you exercise or if the weather is hot. Heavy sweating can cause loss of too much water and low blood pressure. Use extra care during exercise or hot weather.

Avoid alcoholic beverages until you have discussed their use with your doctor. Alcohol may make the low blood pressure effect worse and/or increase the possibility of dizziness or fainting.

Before having any kind of surgery (including dental surgery) or emergency treatment, tell the medical doctor or dentist in charge that you are taking this medicine.

For patients taking *captopril and hydrochlorothiazide:*

- Before you have any medical tests, tell the doctor in charge that you are taking this medicine. The results of some tests may be affected by this medicine.

For patients taking this medicine *for high blood pressure:*

- *Do not take other medicines unless they have been discussed with your doctor.* This especially includes over-the-counter (nonprescription) medicines for appetite control, asthma, colds, cough, hay fever, or sinus problems, since they may tend to increase your blood pressure.

For *diabetic patients:*

- Hydrochlorothiazide (contained in this combination medicine) may raise blood sugar levels. While you are taking this medicine, be especially careful in testing for sugar in your urine.

Hydrochlorothiazide (contained in this combination medicine) may cause your skin to be more sensitive to sunlight than it is normally. Exposure to sunlight, even for brief periods of time, may cause a skin rash, itching, redness or other discoloration of the skin, or a severe sunburn. When you first begin taking this medicine:

- Stay out of direct sunlight, especially between the hours of 10:00 a.m. and 3:00 p.m., if possible.
- Wear protective clothing, including a hat. Also, wear sunglasses.
- Apply a sun block product that has a skin protection factor (SPF) of at least 15. Some patients may require a product with a higher SPF number, especially if they have a fair complexion. If you have any questions about this, check with your health care professional.
- Apply a sun block lipstick that has an SPF of at least 15 to protect your lips.
- Do not use a sunlamp or tanning bed or booth.

If you have a severe reaction from the sun, check with your doctor.

Before you have any medical tests, tell the doctor in charge that you are taking this medicine. The results of some tests may be affected by this medicine.

Side Effects of This Medicine

Along with its needed effects, a medicine may cause some unwanted effects. Although not all of these side effects may occur, if they do occur they may need medical attention.

Check with your doctor immediately if any of the following side effects occur:

Rare

Fever and chills; hoarseness; swelling of face, mouth, hands, or feet; trouble in swallowing or breathing (sudden)

Check with your doctor as soon as possible if any of the following side effects occur:

Less common

Dizziness, lightheadedness, or fainting; skin rash, with or without itching, fever, or joint pain

Rare

Chest pain; joint pain; lower back or side pain; stomach pain (severe) with nausea and vomiting; unusual bleeding or bruising; yellow eyes or skin

Signs and symptoms of too much or too little potassium in the body

Dryness of mouth; increased thirst; irregular heartbeats; mood or mental changes; muscle cramps or pain; numbness or tingling in hands, feet, or lips; weakness or heaviness of legs; weak pulse

Other side effects may occur that usually do not need medical attention. These side effects may go away during treatment as your body adjusts to the medicine. However, check with your doctor if any of the following side effects continue or are bothersome:

More common

Cough (dry, continuing)

Less common

Diarrhea; headache; increased sensitivity of skin to sunlight (skin rash, itching, redness or other discoloration of skin or severe sunburn after exposure to sunlight); loss of appetite; loss of taste; stomach upset; unusual tiredness

Other side effects not listed above may also occur in some patients. If you notice any other effects, check with your doctor.

Additional Information

Once a medicine has been approved for marketing for a certain use, experience may show that it is also useful for other medical problems. Although this use is not included in product labeling, ACE inhibitors and hydrochlorothiazide are used in certain patients with the following medical condition:

- Congestive heart failure

Other than the above information, there is no additional information relating to proper use, precautions, or side effects for this use.

Revised: 07/28/92
Interim revision: 06/29/94

ANTACIDS Oral

Some commonly used brand names are:

In the U.S.—

Advanced Formula Di-Gel[16]
Alamag[1a]
Alamag Plus[5]
Alenic Alka[7, 11]
Alenic Alka Extra Strength[9]
Alka-Mints[14]
Alkets[14]
Alkets Extra Strength[14]
Almacone[5]
Almacone II[5]
AlternaGEL[11a]
Alu-Cap[13]
Aludrox[5]
Alu-Tab[13]
Amitone[14]
Amphojel[13]
Antacid Gelcaps[18]
Antacid Liquid[5]
Antacid Liquid Double Strength[5]
Basaljel[12]
Calglycine[14]
Chooz[14]
Dicarbosil[14]
Di-Gel[5]
Equilet[14]
Foamicon[10]
Gaviscon[7, 11]
Gaviscon-2[11]
Gaviscon Extra Strength Relief Formula[8, 9]
Gelusil[5]
Genaton[7, 11]
Genaton Extra Strength[9]
Kudrox Double Strength[5]
Losopan[20]
Losopan Plus[21]
Lowsium Plus[21]
Maalox[1a]
Maalox Antacid Caplets[18]
Maalox Heartburn Relief Formula[7]
Maalox Plus[5]
Maalox Plus, Extra Strength[5]
Maalox TC[1a]
Magnalox[5]
Magnalox Plus[5]
Mag-Ox 400[24]
Mallamint[14]
Maox 420[24]
Marblen[18]
Mi-Acid[5, 18]
Mi-Acid Double Strength[5]
Mintox[1a]
Mintox Extra Strength[5]
Mygel[5]
Mygel II[5]
Mylanta[5, 14, 15]
Mylanta Double Strength[5, 15]
Mylanta Gelcaps[15]
Nephrox[13]
Phillips'[23]
Phillips' Chewable[23]
Phillips' Concentrated Double Strength[23]
Riopan[20]
Riopan Plus[21]
Riopan Plus Double Strength[21]
Rolaids[15]
Rulox[1a]
Rulox No. 1[1a]
Rulox No. 2[1a]
Rulox Plus[5]
Simaal Gel[5]
Simaal 2 Gel[5]
Tempo[2]
Titralac[14]
Titralac Extra Strength[14]
Titralac Plus[17]
Tums[14]
Tums Anti-gas/Antacid[17]
Tums E-X[14]
Tums Ultra[14]
Uro-Mag[24]

In Canada—

Almagel 200[1a]
Alugel[13]
Alu-Tab[13]
Amphojel[13]
Amphojel 500[1a]
Amphojel Plus[4, 5]
Basaljel[13]
Diovol[3, 5]
Diovol Caplets[1a]
Diovol Ex[1a]
Diovol Plus[4, 5]
Diovol Plus AF[16]
Gasmas[4]
Gaviscon Acid Plus Gas Relief[16]
Gaviscon Acid Relief[15]
Gaviscon Extra Strength Acid Relief[15]
Gaviscon Heartburn Relief[13,22]
Gaviscon Heartburn Relief Extra Strength[13]
Gelusil[1a]
Gelusil Extra Strength[1a]
Life Antacid[1a]
Life Antacid Plus[5]
Maalox[1a]
Maalox Antacid Caplets[18]
Maalox HRF[6]
Maalox Plus[5]
Maalox Plus, Extra Strength[5]
Maalox TC[1a]
Mylanta[5]
Mylanta Double Strength[5]
Mylanta Double Strength Plain[1a]
Mylanta Extra Strength[5]
Neutralca-S[1a]
Phillips'[23]
PMS Alumina, Magnesia, and Simethicone[5]
Rafton[1, 11b]
Riopan[20]
Riopan Extra Strength[20]
Riopan Plus[21]
Riopan Plus Extra Strength[21]
Rolaids[15]
Rolaids Extra Strength[15]
Trial[14]
Tums[14]
Tums Extra Strength[14]
Tums Ultra[14]
Univol[1a]

Note: For quick reference the following antacids are numbered to match the corresponding brand names.

This information applies to the following medicines:

1. Alumina (a-LOO-mi-na), Calcium Carbonate (KAL-see-um KAR-bon-ate), and Sodium Bicarbonate (SOE-dee-um bi-KAR-bon-ate)*
1a. Alumina and Magnesia (mag-NEE-zha)*†
2. Alumina, Magnesia, Calcium Carbonate, and Simethicone (Si-METH-i-kone)
3. Alumina, Magnesia, and Magnesium (mag-NEE-zhum) Carbonate
4. Alumina, Magnesia, Magnesium Carbonate, and Simethicone
5. Alumina, Magnesia, and Simethicone*†
6. Alumina, Magnesium Alginate (al-JI-nate), and Magnesium Carbonate
7. Alumina and Magnesium Carbonate
8. Alumina, Magnesium Carbonate, and Simethicone
9. Alumina, Magnesium Carbonate, and Sodium Bicarbonate
10. Alumina and Magnesium Trisilicate (trye-SILL-i-kate)
11. Alumina, Magnesium Trisilicate, and Sodium Bicarbonate
11a. Alumina and Simethicone
11b. Alumina and Sodium Bicarbonate
12. Aluminum (a-LOO-mi-num) Carbonate, Basic
12a. Aluminum Carbonate, Basic, and Simethicone
13. Aluminum Hydroxide (hye-DROX-ide)*†
14. Calcium Carbonate*
15. Calcium Carbonate and Magnesia
16. Calcium Carbonate, Magnesia, and Simethicone
17. Calcium Carbonate and Simethicone
18. Calcium and Magnesium Carbonates
20. Magaldrate (MAG-al-drate)*
21. Magaldrate and Simethicone*

22. Magnesium Carbonate and Sodium Bicarbonate
23. Magnesium Hydroxide*†
24. Magnesium Oxide (OX-ide)

*Generic name product may also be available in U.S.
†Generic name product available in Canada.

Description

Antacids are taken by mouth to relieve heartburn, sour stomach, or acid indigestion. They work by neutralizing excess stomach acid. Some antacid combinations also contain simethicone, which may relieve the symptoms of excess gas. Antacids alone or in combination with simethicone may also be used to treat the symptoms of stomach or duodenal ulcers.

With larger doses than those used for the antacid effect, magnesium hydroxide (magnesia) and magnesium oxide antacids produce a laxative effect. The information that follows applies only to their use as an antacid.

Some antacids, like aluminum carbonate and aluminum hydroxide, may be prescribed with a low-phosphate diet to treat hyperphosphatemia (too much phosphate in the blood). Aluminum carbonate and aluminum hydroxide may also be used with a low-phosphate diet to prevent the formation of some kinds of kidney stones. Aluminum hydroxide may also be used for other conditions as determined by your doctor.

These medicines are available without a prescription. However, your doctor may have special instructions on the proper use and dose of these medicines for your medical problem. They are available in the following dosage forms:

Oral

Alumina, Calcium Carbonate, and Sodium Bicarbonate
- Oral suspension (Canada)

Alumina and Magnesia
- Oral suspension (U.S. and Canada)
- Tablets (Canada)
- Chewable tablets (U.S. and Canada)

Alumina, Magnesia, Calcium Carbonate, and Simethicone
- Chewable tablets (U.S.)

Alumina, Magnesia, and Magnesium Carbonate
- Chewable tablets (Canada)

Alumina, Magnesia, Magnesium Carbonate, and Simethicone
- Chewable tablets (Canada)

Alumina, Magnesia, and Simethicone
- Oral suspension (U.S. and Canada)
- Chewable tablets (U.S. and Canada)

Alumina, Magnesium Alginate, and Magnesium Carbonate
- Oral suspension (Canada)
- Chewable tablets (Canada)

Alumina and Magnesium Carbonate
- Oral suspension (U.S.)
- Chewable tablets (U.S.)

Alumina, Magnesium Carbonate, and Simethicone
- Oral suspension (U.S.)

Alumina, Magnesium Carbonate, and Sodium Bicarbonate
- Chewable tablets (U.S.)

Alumina and Magnesium Trisilicate
- Chewable tablets (U.S.)

Alumina, Magnesium Trisilicate, and Sodium Bicarbonate
- Chewable tablets (U.S.)

Alumina and Simethicone
- Gel (U.S.)

Alumina and Sodium Bicarbonate
- Chewable tablets (Canada)

Aluminum Carbonate, Basic
- Capsules (U.S.)
- Tablets (U.S.)

Aluminum Carbonate, Basic, and Simethicone
- Oral suspension (U.S.)

Aluminum Hydroxide
- Capsules (U.S. and Canada)
- Oral suspension (U.S. and Canada)
- Gel (U.S. and Canada)
- Tablets (U.S. and Canada)
- Chewable tablets (Canada)

Calcium Carbonate
- Chewing gum (U.S.)
- Lozenges (U.S.)
- Oral suspension (U.S.)
- Tablets (U.S.)
- Chewable tablets (U.S. and Canada)

Calcium Carbonate and Magnesia
- Oral suspension (Canada)
- Tablets (U.S.)
- Chewable tablets (U.S. and Canada)

Calcium Carbonate, Magnesia, and Simethicone
- Oral suspension (Canada)
- Chewable tablets (U.S. and Canada)

Calcium Carbonate and Simethicone
- Oral suspension (U.S.)
- Chewable tablets (U.S.)

Calcium and Magnesium Carbonates
- Oral suspension (U.S.)
- Tablets (U.S. and Canada)

Magaldrate
- Oral suspension (U.S. and Canada)
- Chewable tablets (Canada)

Magaldrate and Simethicone
- Oral suspension (U.S. and Canada)
- Chewable tablets (U.S. and Canada)

Magnesium Carbonate and Sodium Bicarbonate
- Chewable tablets (Canada)

Magnesium Hydroxide
- Milk of magnesia (U.S. and Canada)
- Chewable tablets (U.S. and Canada)

Magnesium Oxide
- Capsules (U.S.)
- Tablets (U.S.)

Before Using This Medicine

If you are taking this medicine without a prescription, carefully read and follow any precautions on the label. For antacids, the following should be considered:

Allergies—Tell your health care professional if you have ever had any unusual or allergic reaction to aluminum-, calcium-, magnesium-, simethicone-, or sodium bicarbonate–containing medicines. Also, tell your health care professional if you are allergic to any other substances, such as foods, preservatives, or dyes.

Diet—Make certain your health care professional knows if you are on a low-sodium diet. Some antacids contain large amounts of sodium.

Pregnancy—Studies on effects in pregnancy have not been done in either humans or animals. However, there have been reports of antacids causing side effects in babies whose mothers took antacids for a long time, especially in high doses during pregnancy. Also, sodium-containing medicines should be avoided if you tend to retain (keep) body water.

Breast-feeding—Some aluminum-, calcium-, or magnesium-containing antacids may pass into breast milk. However, these medicines have not been reported to cause problems in nursing babies.

Children—Antacids should not be given to young children (under 6 years of age) unless ordered by their doctor. Since children cannot usually describe their symptoms very well, a doctor should first check the child. The child may have a condition that needs other treatment. If so, antacids will not help and may even cause unwanted effects or make the condition worse. In addition, aluminum- or magnesium-containing medicines should not be given to premature or very young children because they may cause serious side effects, especially when given to children who have kidney disease or who are dehydrated.

Older adults—Aluminum-containing antacids should not be used by elderly persons with bone problems or with Alzheimer's disease. The aluminum may cause their condition to get worse.

Other medicines—Although certain medicines should not be used together at all, in other cases two different medicines may be used together even if an interaction might occur. In these cases, your doctor may want to change the dose, or other precautions may be necessary. When you are taking antacids, it is especially important that your health care professional know if you are taking any of the following:

- Cellulose sodium phosphate (e.g., Calcibind)—Calcium-containing antacids may decrease the effects of cellulose sodium phosphate; use with magnesium-containing antacids may prevent either medicine from working properly; antacids should not be taken within 1 hour of cellulose sodium phosphate
- Fluoroquinolones (medicine for infection)—Antacids may decrease the effects of these medicines
- Isoniazid taken by mouth (e.g., INH)—Aluminum-containing antacids may decrease the effects of isoniazid; isoniazid should be taken at least 1 hour before or after the antacid
- Ketoconazole (e.g., Nizoral) or
- Methenamine (e.g., Mandelamine)—Antacids may decrease the effects of ketoconazole or methenamine; these medicines should be taken 3 hours before the antacid
- Mecamylamine (e.g., Inversine)—Antacids may increase the effects and possibly the side effects of mecamylamine
- Sodium polystyrene sulfonate resin (SPSR) (e.g., Kayexalate)—This medicine may decrease the effects of antacids
- Tetracyclines (medicine for infection) taken by mouth—Use with antacids may decrease the effects of both medicines; antacids should not be taken within 3 to 4 hours of tetracyclines

Other medical problems—The presence of other medical problems may affect the use of antacids. Make sure you tell your doctor if you have any other medical problems, especially:

- Alzheimer's disease (for aluminum-containing antacids only) or
- Appendicitis (or signs of) or
- Bone fractures or
- Colitis or
- Constipation (severe and continuing) or
- Hemorrhoids or
- Intestinal blockage or
- Intestinal or rectal bleeding—Antacids may make these conditions worse
- Colostomy or
- Ileostomy or
- Inflamed bowel—Use of antacids may cause the body to retain (keep) water and electrolytes such as sodium and/or potassium
- Diarrhea (continuing)—Aluminum-containing antacids may cause the body to lose too much phosphorus; magnesium-containing antacids may make diarrhea worse
- Edema (swelling of feet or lower legs) or
- Heart disease or
- Liver disease or
- Toxemia of pregnancy—Use of sodium-containing antacids may cause the body to retain (keep) water
- Kidney disease—Antacids may cause higher blood levels of aluminum, calcium, or magnesium, which may increase the risk of serious side effects
- Sarcoidosis—Use of calcium-containing antacids may cause kidney problems or too much calcium in the blood
- Underactive parathyroid glands—Use with calcium-containing antacids may cause too much calcium in the blood

Proper Use of This Medicine

For patients taking the *chewable tablet form* of this medicine:

- Chew the tablets well before swallowing. This is to allow the medicine to work faster and be more effective.

For patients taking this medicine for a *stomach or duodenal ulcer:*

- *Take it exactly as directed and for the full time of treatment as ordered by your doctor,* to obtain maximum relief of your symptoms.
- Take it 1 and 3 hours after meals and at bedtime for best results, unless otherwise directed by your doctor.

For patients taking *aluminum carbonate* or *aluminum hydroxide* to *prevent kidney stones:*

- Drink plenty of fluids for best results, unless otherwise directed by your doctor.

For patients taking *aluminum carbonate* or *aluminum hydroxide* for *hyperphosphatemia* (too much phosphate in the blood):

- Your doctor may want you to follow a low-phosphate diet. If you have any questions about this, check with your doctor.

Dosing—The dose of an antacid will be different for different patients. *Follow your doctor's orders or the directions on the label.*

Missed dose—If your doctor has told you to take this medicine on a regular schedule and you miss a dose, take it as soon as possible. However, if it is almost time for your next dose, skip the missed dose and go back to your regular dosing schedule. Do not double doses.

Storage—To store this medicine:

- Keep out of the reach of children.
- Store away from heat and direct light.
- Do not store the capsule, tablet, or lozenge form of this medicine in the bathroom, near the kitchen sink, or in other damp places. Heat or moisture may cause the medicine to break down.
- Keep the liquid or gel form of this medicine from freezing.
- Do not keep outdated medicine or medicine no longer needed. Be sure that any discarded medicine is out of the reach of children.

Precautions While Using This Medicine

If this medicine has been ordered by your doctor and you will be taking it in large doses, or for a long time, your doctor should check your progress at regular visits. This is to make sure the medicine does not cause unwanted effects.

Some tests may be affected by this medicine. Tell the doctor in charge that you are taking this medicine before you have any tests to determine how much acid your stomach produces.

Do not take this medicine:

- *if you have any signs of appendicitis or inflamed bowel* (such as stomach or lower abdominal pain, cramping, bloating, soreness, nausea, or vomiting). Instead, check with your doctor as soon as possible.
- *within 1 to 2 hours or more of taking other medicine by mouth.* To do so may keep the other medicine from working properly.

For patients on a *sodium-restricted diet:*

- Some antacids (especially those containing sodium bicarbonate) contain a large amount of sodium. If you have any questions about this, check with your health care professional.

For patients taking this medicine for increased stomach acid:

- *Do not take it for more than 2 weeks unless otherwise directed by your doctor.* Antacids should be used only for occasional relief.
- If your stomach problem is not helped by the antacid or if it keeps coming back, check with your doctor.
- Using magnesium- or sodium bicarbonate–containing antacids too often, or in high doses, may produce a laxative effect. This happens fairly often and depends on the individual's sensitivity to the medicine.

For patients taking *aluminum-containing antacids* (including magaldrate):

- Before you have any test in which a radiopharmaceutical will be used, tell the doctor in charge that you are taking this medicine. The results of the test may be affected by aluminum-containing antacids.

For patients taking *calcium-* or *sodium bicarbonate–containing antacids:*

- *Do not take the antacid with large amounts of milk or milk products.* To do so may increase the chance of side effects.

Side Effects of This Medicine

Along with its needed effects, a medicine may cause some unwanted effects. Although the following side effects occur very rarely when this medicine is taken as recommended, they may be more likely to occur if:

- too much medicine is taken.
- it is taken in large doses.
- it is taken for a long time.
- it is taken by patients with kidney disease.

Check with your doctor as soon as possible if any of the following side effects (which may be signs of overdose) occur:

For aluminum-containing antacids (including magaldrate)

Bone pain; constipation (severe and continuing); feeling of discomfort (continuing); loss of appetite (continuing); mood or mental changes; muscle weakness; swelling of wrists or ankles; weight loss (unusual)

For calcium-containing antacids

Constipation (severe and continuing); difficult or painful urination; frequent urge to urinate; headache (continuing); loss of appetite (continuing); mood or mental changes; muscle pain or twitching; nausea or vomiting; nervousness or restlessness; slow breathing; unpleasant taste; unusual tiredness or weakness

For magnesium-containing antacids (including magaldrate)

Difficult or painful urination (with magnesium trisilicate); dizziness or lightheadedness; feeling of discomfort (continuing); irregular heartbeat; loss of appetite (continuing); mood or mental changes; muscle weakness; unusual tiredness or weakness; weight loss (unusual)

For sodium bicarbonate–containing antacids

Frequent urge to urinate; headache (continuing); loss of appetite (continuing); mood or mental changes; muscle pain or twitching; nausea or vomiting; nervousness or restlessness; slow breathing; swelling of feet or lower legs; unpleasant taste; unusual tiredness or weakness

Other side effects may occur that usually do not need medical attention. These side effects may go away during treatment as your body adjusts to the medicine. However, check with your doctor if any of the following side effects continue or are bothersome:

More common

Chalky taste

Less common

Constipation (mild); diarrhea or laxative effect; increased thirst; speckling or whitish discoloration of stools; stomach cramps

Other side effects not listed above may also occur in some patients. If you notice any other effects, check with your doctor.

Revised: 08/15/95
Interim revision: 07/18/96

ANTHRALIN Topical

Some commonly used brand names are:

In the U.S.—

Anthra-Derm	Lasan
Anthra-Tex	Lasan 0.1
Drithocreme	Lasan 0.2
Drithocreme HP	Lasan 0.4
Dritho-Scalp	Lasan HP-1

In Canada—

Anthraforte 1	Anthranol 0.2
Anthraforte 2	Anthranol 0.4
Anthraforte 3	Anthrascalp
Anthranol 0.1	

Another commonly used name is dithranol.

Description

Anthralin (AN-thra-lin) is used to treat psoriasis. It may also be used to treat other skin conditions as determined by your doctor.

In the U.S., this medicine is available only with your doctor's prescription. In Canada, this medicine should be used only on the advice of your doctor.

This medicine is available in the following dosage forms:

Topical

- Cream (U.S. and Canada)
- Ointment (U.S. and Canada)

Before Using This Medicine

In deciding to use a medicine, the risks of using the medicine must be weighed against the good it will do. This is a decision you and your doctor will make. For anthralin, the following should be considered:

Allergies—Tell your doctor if you have ever had any unusual or allergic reaction to anthralin. Also tell your health care professional if you are allergic to any other substances, such as preservatives or dyes.

Pregnancy—Anthralin may be absorbed through the skin. However, studies on effects in pregnancy have not been done in either humans or animals.

Breast-feeding—Anthralin may be absorbed through the mother's skin. However, it is not known whether anthralin passes into the breast milk. Although most medicines pass into breast milk in small amounts, many of them may be used safely while breast-feeding. Mothers who are using this medicine and who wish to breast-feed should discuss this with their doctor.

Children—Studies on this medicine have been done only in adult patients, and there is no specific information comparing use of anthralin in children with use in other age groups.

Older adults—Many medicines have not been studied specifically in older people. Therefore, it may not be known whether they work exactly the same way they do in younger adults or if they cause different side effects or problems in older people. There is no specific information comparing use of anthralin in the elderly with use in other age groups.

Other medicines—Although certain medicines should not be used together at all, in other cases two different medicines may be used together even if an interaction might occur. In these cases, your doctor may want to change the dose, or other precautions may be necessary. Tell your health care professional if you are using any other prescription or nonprescription (over-the-counter [OTC]) medicine.

Other medical problems—The presence of other medical problems may affect the use of anthralin. Make sure you tell your doctor if you have any other medical problems, especially:

- Skin diseases or problems (other)—Anthralin may make the condition worse

Proper Use of This Medicine

Keep this medicine away from the eyes and other mucous membranes, such as the mouth and the inside of the nose.

Do not apply this medicine to blistered, raw, or oozing areas of the skin or scalp.

Do not use this medicine on your face or sex organs or in the folds and creases of your skin. If you have any questions about this, check with your doctor.

Use this medicine only as directed. Do not use more of it, do not use it more often, and do not use it for a longer time than your doctor ordered. To do so may increase the chance of side effects.

Anthralin may be used in different ways. In some cases, it is applied at night and allowed to remain on the affected areas overnight, then washed off the next morning or before the next application. In other cases, it may be applied and allowed to remain on the affected areas for a short period of time (usually 10 to 30 minutes), then washed off. (This is called short contact treatment.) Make sure you understand exactly how you are to use this medicine. If you have any questions about this, check with your doctor.

Anthralin may cause irritation of normal skin. If it does, petrolatum may be applied to the skin or scalp around the affected areas for protection.

Apply a thin layer of anthralin to only the affected area of the skin or scalp and rub in gently.

Immediately after applying this medicine, wash your hands to remove any medicine that may be on them.

For patients using *anthralin for short contact* (usually 10 to 30 minutes) treatment:

- After applying anthralin, allow the medicine to remain on the affected area for 10 to 30 minutes or as directed by your doctor. Then remove the medicine by bathing, if the anthralin was applied to the skin, or by shampooing, if it was applied to the scalp.

For patients using the *cream form* of anthralin for overnight treatment:

- If anthralin cream is applied to the skin, any medicine remaining on the affected areas the next morning should be removed by bathing.
- If anthralin cream is applied to the scalp, shampoo to remove the scales and any medicine remaining on the affected areas from the previous application. Dry the hair and, after parting, rub the cream into the affected areas. Check with your doctor to see when the cream should be removed.

For patients using the *ointment form* of anthralin for overnight treatment:

- If anthralin ointment is applied to the skin at night, any ointment remaining on the affected areas the next morning should be removed with warm liquid petrolatum followed by bathing.
- If anthralin ointment is applied to the scalp at night, use a shampoo the next morning to clean the scalp.

Dosing—The dose of anthralin will be different for different patients. *Follow your doctor's orders or the directions on the label.* The following information includes only the average doses of anthralin. *If your dose is different, do not change it* unless your doctor tells you to do so.

- For psoriasis:
  - —For *cream* dosage form:
    - Adults—Apply to the affected area(s) of the skin once a day.
    - Children—Use and dose must be determined by your doctor.
  - —For *ointment* dosage form:
    - Adults—Apply to the affected area(s) of the skin one or two times a day.
    - Children—Use and dose must be determined by your doctor.

Missed dose—If you miss a dose of this medicine, apply it as soon as possible. However, if it is almost time for your next dose, skip the missed dose and go back to your regular dosing schedule. Do not double doses.

Storage—To store this medicine:

- Keep out of the reach of children.
- Store away from heat and direct light.
- Keep the medicine from freezing.
- Do not keep outdated medicine or medicine no longer needed. Be sure that any discarded medicine is out of the reach of children.

Precautions While Using This Medicine

Anthralin may stain the skin, hair, fingernails, clothing, bed linens, or bathtub or shower:

- Avoid getting the medicine on your clothing or on bed linens. Protective dressings may be used, unless you have been otherwise directed by your doctor.
- The stain on the skin or hair will wear off in several weeks after you stop using this medicine.
- To prevent staining of your hands, you may wear plastic gloves when you apply this medicine.
- If the medicine is applied to the scalp at night, check with your doctor to see if you may wear a plastic cap to prevent staining of the pillow.
- To remove any medicine on the surface of the bathtub or shower, wash it with hot water immediately after bathing or showering. Then use a household cleanser to remove any remaining deposit of the medicine on the bathtub or shower.

Side Effects of This Medicine

Anthralin has been shown to cause tumors (some cancerous) in animals. However, there have been no reports of anthralin causing tumors in humans.

Along with its needed effects, a medicine may cause some unwanted effects. Although not all of these side effects may occur, if they do occur they may need medical attention.

Check with your doctor as soon as possible if any of the following side effects occur:

More common

Redness or other skin irritation not present before use of this medicine

Rare

Skin rash

Other side effects not listed above may also occur in some patients. If you notice any other effects, check with your doctor.

Additional Information

Once a medicine has been approved for marketing for a certain use, experience may show that it is also useful for other medical problems. Although this use is not included in product labeling, anthralin is used in certain patients with the following medical condition:

- Alopecia areata (a certain type of baldness)

Other than the above information, there is no additional information relating to proper use, precautions, or side effects for this use.

Revised: 08/15/95

ANTICHOLINERGICS/ANTISPASMODICS Systemic

Some commonly used brand names are:

In the U.S.—

Anaspaz[8]
Antispas[5]
A-Spas[5]
Banthine[10]
Bentyl[5]
Cantil[9]
Cystospaz[8]
Cystospaz-M[8]
Di-Spaz[5]
Dibent[5]
Gastrosed[8]
Homapin[7]
Levsin[8]
Levsinex Timecaps[8]
Levsin/SL[8]
Neoquess[5,8]
Or-Tyl[5]
Pamine[11]
Pro-Banthine[13]
Quarzan[4]
Robinul[6]
Robinul Forte[6]
Spasmoject[5]
Transderm-Scōp[14]

In Canada—

Bentylol[5]
Buscopan[14]
Formulex[5]
Gastrozepin[12]
Levsin[8]
Lomine[5]
Pro-Banthine[13]
Propanthel[13]
Robinul[6]
Robinul Forte[6]
Spasmoban[5]
Transderm-V[14]

Other commonly used names are:

dicycloverine[5]
glycopyrronium bromide[6]
hyoscine hydrobromide[14]
hyoscine methobromide[11]
methanthelinium[10]
octatropine[1]

Note: For quick reference, the following anticholinergics/antispasmodics are numbered to match the corresponding brand names.

This information applies to the following medicines:

1. Anisotropine (an-iss-oh-TROE-peen)†‡
2. Atropine (A-troe-peen)‡§
3. Belladonna (bell-a-DON-a)†‡
4. Clidinium (kli-DI-nee-um)†
5. Dicyclomine (dye-SYE-kloe-meen)‡
6. Glycopyrrolate (glye-koe-PYE-roe-late)‡
7. Homatropine (hoe-MA-troe-peen)†
8. Hyoscyamine (hye-oh-SYE-a-meen)‡
9. Mepenzolate (me-PEN-zoe-late)†
10. Methantheline (meth-AN-tha-leen)†
11. Methscopolamine (meth-skoe-POL-a-meen)†
12. Pirenzepine (peer-EN-ze-peen)*
13. Propantheline (proe-PAN-the-leen)‡
14. Scopolamine (scoe-POL-a-meen)‡

*Not commercially available in the U.S.
†Not commercially available in Canada.
‡Generic name product may be available in the U.S.
§Generic name product may be available in Canada.

Description

The anticholinergics/antispasmodics are a group of medicines that include the natural belladonna alkaloids (atropine, belladonna, hyoscyamine, and scopolamine) and related products.

The anticholinergics/antispasmodics are used to relieve cramps or spasms of the stomach, intestines, and bladder. Some are used together with antacids or other medicine in the treatment of peptic ulcer. Others are used to prevent nausea, vomiting, and motion sickness.

Anticholinergics/antispasmodics are also used in certain surgical and emergency procedures. In surgery, some are given by injection before anesthesia to help relax you and to decrease secretions, such as saliva. During anesthesia and surgery, atropine, glycopyrrolate, hyoscyamine, and scopolamine are used to help keep the heartbeat normal. Atropine is also given by injection to help relax the stomach and intestines for certain types of examinations. Some anticholinergics are also used to treat poisoning caused by medicines such as neostigmine and physostigmine, certain types of mushrooms, and poisoning by ''nerve'' gases or organic phosphorous pesticides (for example, demeton [Systox], diazinon, malathion, parathion, and ronnel [Trolene]). Also, anticholinergics can be used for painful menstruation, runny nose, and to prevent urination during sleep.

These medicines may also be used for other conditions as determined by your doctor.

The anticholinergics/antispasmodics are available only with your doctor's prescription in the following dosage forms:

Oral

Anisotropine
- Tablets (U.S.)

Atropine
- Tablets (U.S.)
- Soluble tablets (U.S.)

Belladonna
- Tincture (U.S.)

Clidinium
- Capsules (U.S.)

Dicyclomine
- Capsules (U.S. and Canada)
- Syrup (U.S. and Canada)
- Tablets (U.S. and Canada)
- Extended-release Tablets (Canada)

Glycopyrrolate
- Tablets (U.S. and Canada)

Homatropine
- Tablets (U.S.)

Hyoscyamine
- Extended-release capsules (U.S.)
- Elixir (U.S.)
- Oral solution (U.S. and Canada)
- Tablets (U.S.)

Mepenzolate
- Tablets (U.S.)

Methantheline
- Tablets (U.S.)

Methscopolamine
- Tablets (U.S.)

Pirenzepine
- Tablets (Canada)

Propantheline
- Tablets (U.S. and Canada)

Scopolamine
- Tablets (Canada)

Parenteral

Atropine
- Injection (U.S. and Canada)

Dicyclomine
- Injection (U.S. and Canada)

Glycopyrrolate
- Injection (U.S. and Canada)

Hyoscyamine
- Injection (U.S. and Canada)

Scopolamine
- Injection (U.S. and Canada)

Rectal

Scopolamine
- Suppositories (Canada)

Transdermal

Scopolamine
- Transdermal disk (U.S. and Canada)

Before Using This Medicine

In deciding to use a medicine, the risks of taking the medicine must be weighed against the good it will do. This is a decision you and your doctor will make. For anticholinergics/antispasmodics the following should be considered:

Allergies—Tell your doctor if you have ever had any unusual or allergic reaction to any of the natural belladonna alkaloids (atropine, belladonna, hyoscyamine, and scopolamine), or any related products. Also, tell your health care professional if you are allergic to any other substances, such as foods, preservatives, or dyes.

Pregnancy—If you are pregnant or if you may become pregnant, make sure your doctor knows if your medicine contains any of the following:

- *Atropine*—Atropine has not been shown to cause birth defects or other problems in animals. However, when injected into humans during pregnancy, atropine has been reported to increase the heartbeat of the fetus.
- *Belladonna*—Studies on effects in pregnancy have not been done in either humans or animals.
- *Clidinium*—Clidinium has not been studied in pregnant women. However, clidinium has not been shown to cause birth defects or other problems in animal studies.
- *Dicyclomine*—Dicyclomine has been associated with a few cases of human birth defects but dicyclomine has not been confirmed as the cause.
- *Glycopyrrolate*—Glycopyrrolate has not been studied in pregnant women. However, glycopyrrolate did not cause birth defects in animal studies, but did decrease the chance of becoming pregnant and in the newborn's chance of surviving after weaning.
- *Hyoscyamine*—Studies on effects in pregnancy have not been done in either humans or animals. However, when injected into humans during pregnancy, hyoscyamine has been reported to increase the heartbeat of the fetus.
- *Mepenzolate*—Mepenzolate has not been studied in pregnant women. However, studies in animals have not shown that mepenzolate causes birth defects or other problems.
- *Propantheline*—Studies on effects in pregnancy have not been done in either humans or animals.
- *Scopolamine*—Studies on effects in pregnancy have not been done in either humans or animals.

Breast-feeding—Although these medicines may pass into the breast milk, they have not been reported to cause problems in nursing babies. However, the flow of breast milk may be reduced in some patients. The use of dicyclomine in nursing mothers has been reported to cause breathing problems in infants.

Children—Unusual excitement, nervousness, restlessness, or irritability and unusual warmth, dryness, and flushing of skin are more likely to occur in children, who are usually more sensitive to the effects of anticholinergics. Also, when anticholinergics are given to children during hot weather, a rapid increase in body temperature may occur. In infants and children, especially those with spastic paralysis or brain damage, this medicine may be more likely to cause severe side effects. Shortness of breath or difficulty in breathing has occurred in children taking dicyclomine.

Older adults—Confusion or memory loss; constipation; difficult urination; drowsiness; dryness of mouth, nose, throat, or skin; and unusual excitement, nervousness, restlessness, or irritability may be more likely to occur in the elderly, who are usually more sensitive than younger adults to the effects of anticholinergics. Also, eye pain may occur, which may be a sign of glaucoma.

Other medicines—Although certain medicines should not be used together at all, in other cases two different medicines may be used together even if an interaction might occur. In these cases, your doctor may want to change the dose, or other precautions may be necessary. When you are taking anticholinergics/antispasmodics, it is especially important that your health care professional know if you are taking any of the following:

- Antacids or
- Diarrhea medicine containing kaolin or attapulgite or
- Ketoconazole (e.g., Nizoral)—Using these medicines with an anticholinergic may lessen the effects of the anticholinergic
- Central nervous system (CNS) depressants (medicines that cause drowsiness)—Taking scopolamine with CNS depressants may increase the effects of either medicine
- Other anticholinergics (medicine for abdominal or stomach spasms or cramps) or
- Tricyclic antidepressants (amitriptyline [e.g., Elavil], amoxapine [e.g., Asendin], clomipramine [e.g., Anafranil], desipramine [e.g., Pertofrane], doxepin [e.g., Sinequan], imipramine [e.g., Tofranil], nortriptyline [e.g., Aventyl], protriptyline [e.g., Vivactil], trimipramine [e.g., Surmontil])—Taking anticholinergics with tricyclic antidepressants or other anticholinergics may cause an increase in the effects of the anticholinergic
- Potassium chloride (e.g., Kay Ciel)—Using this medicine with an anticholinergic may make gastrointestinal problems caused by potassium worse

Other medical problems—The presence of other medical problems may affect the use of anticholinergics/antispasmodics. Make sure you tell your doctor if you have any other medical problems, especially:

- Bleeding problems (severe)—These medicines may increase heart rate, which would make bleeding problems worse
- Brain damage (in children)—May increase the CNS effects of this medicine
- Colitis (severe) or
- Dryness of mouth (severe and continuing) or
- Enlarged prostate or
- Fever or

- Glaucoma or
- Heart disease or
- Hernia (hiatal) or
- High blood pressure (hypertension) or
- Intestinal blockage or other intestinal problems or
- Lung disease (chronic) or
- Myasthenia gravis or
- Toxemia of pregnancy or
- Urinary tract blockage or difficult urination—These medicines may make these conditions worse
- Down's syndrome (mongolism)—These medicines may cause an increase in pupil dilation and heart rate
- Kidney disease or
- Liver disease—Higher blood levels may occur and cause an increase in side effects
- Overactive thyroid—These medicines may further increase heart rate
- Spastic paralysis (in children)—This condition may increase the effects of the anticholinergic

Proper Use of This Medicine

Take this medicine only as directed. Do not take more of it, do not take it more often, and do not take it for a longer time than your doctor ordered. To do so may increase the chance of side effects.

Dosing—The dose of the anticholinergic/antispasmodic will be different for different patients. *Follow your doctor's orders or the directions on the label.* The following information includes only the average doses of your medicine. *If your dose is different, do not change it* unless your doctor tells you to do so.

The number of capsules or tablets or teaspoonfuls of solution or syrup that you take depends on the strength of the medicine. Also, *the number of doses you take each day, the time allowed between doses, and the length of time you take the medicine depends on the medical problem for which you are taking this medicine.*

For anisotropine

- For *oral* dosage forms (tablets):
  —To treat duodenal or stomach ulcers:
  - Older adults, adults, and teenagers—50 milligrams (mg) three times a day. Your doctor may change the dose if needed.
  - Children—Dose must be determined by your doctor.

For atropine

- For *oral* dosage form (tablets):
  —To treat duodenal or stomach ulcers, intestine problems, or urinary problems:
  - Older adults, adults, and teenagers—300 to 1200 micrograms (mcg) every four to six hours.
  - Children—Dose is based on body weight. The usual dose is 10 mcg per kilogram (kg) (4.5 mcg per pound) of body weight every four to six hours. However, the dose will not be more than 400 mcg every four to six hours.
- For *injectable* dosage form:
  —To treat duodenal or stomach ulcers or intestine problems:
  - Older adults, adults, and teenagers—400 to 600 mcg injected into a muscle, vein, or under the skin every four to six hours.
  - Children—The dose is based on body weight. The usual dose is 10 mcg per kilogram (kg) (4.5 mcg per pound) of body weight injected under the skin every four to six hours. However, the dose will not be more than 400 mcg every every four to six hours.

  —To treat heart problems:
  - Older adults, adults, and teenagers—400 to 1000 mcg injected into a vein every one to two hours as needed. The total dose will not be more than 2 mg.
  - Children—The dose is based on body weight. The usual dose is 10 to 30 mcg per kilogram (kg) (4.5 to 13.6 mcg per pound) of body weight injected under the skin.

For belladonna

- For *oral* dosage form (oral solution):
  —To treat duodenal or stomach ulcers or intestine problems:
  - Older adults, adults, and teenagers—180 to 300 micrograms (mcg) three or four times a day. The dose should be taken 30 to 60 minutes before meals and at bedtime. Your doctor may change the dose if needed.
  - Children—The dose is based on body weight. The usual dose is 9 mcg per kilogram (kg) (4 mcg per pound) of body weight three or four times a day.

For clidinium

- For *oral* dosage form (capsules):
  —To treat duodenal or stomach ulcers:
  - Older adults, adults, and teenagers—2.5 to 5 milligrams (mg) three or four times a day. The dose should be taken before meals and at bedtime. Your doctor may change the dose if needed.
  - Children—Dose must be determined by your doctor.

For dicyclomine

- For *oral* dosage forms (capsules, extended-release tablets, syrup, tablets):
  —To treat intestine problems:
  - Older adults, adults, and teenagers—10 to 20 milligrams (mg) three or four times a day. Some people may take 30 mg two times a day. Your doctor may change the dose if needed. Your dose will not be more than 160 mg a day.
  - Children 2 years of age and older—5 to 10 mg three or four times a day. Your doctor may change the dose if needed.
  - Children 6 months to 2 years of age—5 to 10 mg of the syrup three or four times a day. Your doctor may change the dose if needed.

- Children up to 6 months of age—Use is not recommended.
- For *injectable* dosage form:
  —To treat intestine problems:
  - Older adults, adults, and teenagers—20 mg injected into a muscle every four to six hours. Your doctor may change the dose if needed.
  - Children—Dose must be determined by your doctor.

For glycopyrrolate

- For *oral* dosage form (tablets):
  —To treat duodenal or stomach ulcers:
  - Older adults, adults, and teenagers—To start, 1 to 2 milligrams (mg) two or three times a day. Some people may also take 2 mg at bedtime. Your doctor may change the dose if needed. However, your dose will not be more than 8 mg a day.
  - Children—Dose must be determined by your doctor.
- For *injectable* dosage form:
  —To treat duodenal or stomach ulcers:
  - Older adults, adults, and teenagers—100 to 200 micrograms (mcg) injected into a muscle or vein. The dose may be repeated every four hours up to four times a day.
  - Children—Dose must be determined by your doctor.

For homatropine

- For *oral* dosage form:
  —To treat duodenal or stomach ulcers:
  - Older adults, adults, and teenagers—5 to 10 milligrams (mg) three or four times a day. Your doctor may change the dose if needed.
  - Children—Dose must be determined by your doctor.

For hyoscyamine

- For *oral* dosage forms (capsules, elixir, oral solution, tablets):
  —To treat duodenal or stomach ulcers, intestine problems, or urinary problems:
  - Older adults, adults, and teenagers—125 to 500 micrograms (mcg) four to six times a day. Some people may take 375 mcg two times a day. The tablets should be taken 30 to 60 minutes before meals. Your doctor may change the dose if needed.
  - Children—Dose is based on body weight. The usual dose is 12.5 to 187 mcg every four hours if needed.
- For *injectable* dosage form:
  —To treat duodenal or stomach ulcers or intestine problems:
  - Older adults, adults, and teenagers—250 to 500 mcg injected into a muscle, vein, or under the skin every four to six hours.
  - Children—Dose must be determined by your doctor.

For mepenzolate

- For *oral* dosage form (tablets):
  —To treat duodenal or stomach ulcers or intestine problems:
  - Older adults, adults, and teenagers—25 to 50 milligrams (mg) four times a day, with meals and at bedtime. Your doctor may change the dose if needed.
  - Children—Dose must be determined by your doctor

For methantheline

- For *oral* dosage form (tablets):
  —To treat intestine or stomach ulcers, intestine problems, or urinary problems:
  - Older adults, adults, and teenagers—50 to 100 milligrams (mg) every six hours. Your doctor may change the dose if needed.
  - Children 1 year of age and older—12.5 to 50 mg four times a day. Your doctor may change the dose if needed.
  - Children 1 month to 1 year of age—12.5 mg four times a day. Your doctor may change the dose if needed.
  - Children up to 1 month of age—12.5 mg two times a day. Your doctor may change the dose if needed.

For methscopolamine

- For *oral* dosage form (tablets):
  —To treat duodenal or stomach ulcers or intestine problems:
  - Older adults, adults, and teenagers—2.5 to 5 milligrams (mg) four times a day, one-half hour before meals and at bedtime. Your doctor may change the dose if needed.
  - Children—Dose is based on body weight. The usual dose is 200 micrograms (mcg) per kilogram (kg) (90.9 mcg per pound) of body weight four times a day. The dose should be taken before meals and at bedtime.

For pirenzepine

- For *oral* dosage form (tablets):
  —To treat duodenal or stomach ulcers or intestine problems:
  - Older adults, adults, and teenagers—50 milligrams (mg) two times a day, in the morning and at bedtime. Your doctor may change the dose if needed.
  - Children—Dose must be determined by your doctor.

For propantheline

- For *oral* dosage form (tablets):
  —To treat dudenal or stomach ulcers:
  - Older adults, adults, and teenagers—7.5 to 15 milligrams (mg) three times a day, one-half hour before meals, and 30 mg at bedtime. Your doctor may change the dose if needed.
  - Children—Dose is based on body weight (kg) 375 micrograms (mcg) per kilogram (kg) (170

mcg per pound) of body weight four times a day. Your doctor may change the dose if needed.

For scopolamine

- For *oral* dosage form (tablets):

—To treat urinary problems or intestine problems or painful menstruation:

- Older adults, adults, and teenagers—10 to 20 milligrams (mg) three or four times a day. Your doctor may change the dose if needed.
- Children—Dose must be determined by your doctor.

- For *injectable* dosage form:

—To treat urinary problems or intestine problems:

- Older adults, adults, and teenagers—10 to 20 mg three or four times a day. Your doctor may change the dose if needed.
- Children—Dose must be determined by your doctor.

- For *rectal* dosage form (suppository):

—To treat urinary problems or intestine problems or painful menstruation:

- Older adults, adults, and teenagers—Insert one 10 mg suppository rectally three or four times a day. Your doctor may change the dose if needed.
- Children—Dose must be determined by your doctor.

- For *transdermal* dosage form (patch):

—To treat motion sickness:

- Older adults, adults, and teenagers—Apply one 500 to 1000 microgram (mcg) patch behind ear at least four to twelve hours (depending on the product) before antinausea effect is needed.
- Children—Use is not recommended.

Missed dose—If you miss a dose of this medicine, take it as soon as possible. However, if it is almost time for your next dose, skip the missed dose and go back to your regular dosing schedule. Do not double doses.

For patients *taking any of these medicines by mouth:*

- Take this medicine 30 minutes to 1 hour before meals unless otherwise directed by your doctor.

To use the *rectal suppository* form of *scopolamine:*

- If the suppository is too soft to insert, chill it in the refrigerator for 30 minutes or run cold water over it before removing the foil wrapper.
- To insert the suppository: First remove the foil wrapper and moisten the suppository with cold water. Lie down on your side and use your finger to push the suppository well up into the rectum.

To use the *transdermal disk* form of *scopolamine:*

- This medicine usually comes with patient directions. Read them carefully before using this medicine.
- Wash and dry your hands thoroughly before and after handling.
- Apply the disk to the hairless area of skin behind the ear. Do not place over any cuts or irritations.

Storage—To store this medicine:

- Keep out of the reach of children. Overdose is especially dangerous in young children.
- Store away from heat and direct light.
- Do not store the capsule or tablet form of this medicine in the bathroom, near the kitchen sink, or in other damp places. Heat or moisture may cause the medicine to break down.
- Keep the liquid form of this medicine tightly closed and keep it from freezing. Do not refrigerate the syrup form of this medicine.
- Do not keep outdated medicine or medicine no longer needed. Be sure that any discarded medicine is out of the reach of children.

Precautions While Using This Medicine

If you think you or someone else may have taken an overdose, get emergency help at once. Taking an overdose of any of the belladonna alkaloids or taking scopolamine with alcohol or other CNS depressants may lead to unconsciousness and possibly death. Some signs of overdose are clumsiness or unsteadiness; dizziness; severe drowsiness; fever; hallucinations (seeing, hearing, or feeling things that are not there); confusion; shortness of breath or troubled breathing; slurred speech; unusual excitement, nervousness, restlessness, or irritability; fast heartbeat; and unusual warmth, dryness, and flushing of skin.

These medicines may make you sweat less, causing your body temperature to increase. *Use extra care not to become overheated during exercise or hot weather while you are taking this medicine,* since overheating may result in heat stroke. Also, hot baths or saunas may make you dizzy or faint while you are taking this medicine.

Check with your doctor before you stop using this medicine. Your doctor may want you to reduce gradually the amount you are using before stopping completely. Stopping this medicine may cause withdrawal side effects such as vomiting, sweating, and dizziness.

Anticholinergics may cause some people to have blurred vision. *Make sure your vision is clear before you drive or do anything else that could be dangerous if you are not able to see well.* These medicines may also cause your eyes to become more sensitive to light than they are normally. Wearing sunglasses may help lessen the discomfort from bright light.

These medicines, especially in high doses, may cause some people to become dizzy or drowsy. *Make sure you know how you react to this medicine before you drive, use machines, or do anything else that could be dangerous if you are dizzy or are not alert.*

Dizziness, lightheadedness, or fainting may occur, especially when you get up from a lying or sitting position. Getting up slowly may help lessen this problem.

These medicines may cause dryness of the mouth, nose, and throat. For temporary relief of mouth dryness, use sugarless candy or gum, melt bits of ice in your mouth, or use a saliva substitute. However, if your mouth continues to feel dry for more than 2 weeks, check with your medical doctor or dentist. Continuing dryness of the mouth may increase the chance of dental disease, including tooth decay, gum disease, and fungus infections.

For patients taking *scopolamine:*
- This medicine will add to the effects of alcohol and other CNS depressants (medicines that slow down the nervous system, possibly causing drowsiness). Some examples of CNS depressants are antihistamines or medicine for hay fever, other allergies, or colds; sedatives, tranquilizers, or sleeping medicine; prescription pain medicine or narcotics; barbiturates; medicine for seizures; muscle relaxants; or anesthetics, including some dental anesthetics. *Check with your doctor before taking any of the above while you are using this medicine.*

For patients *taking any of these medicines by mouth:*
- Do not take this medicine within 2 or 3 hours of taking antacids or medicine for diarrhea. Taking antacids or antidiarrhea medicines and this medicine too close together may prevent this medicine from working properly.

Side Effects of This Medicine

Along with its needed effects, a medicine may cause some unwanted effects. Although not all of these side effects may occur, if they do occur they may need medical attention.

Check with your doctor as soon as possible if any of the following side effects occur:

Rare

Confusion (especially in the elderly); dizziness, lightheadedness (continuing), or fainting; eye pain; skin rash or hives

Symptoms of overdose

Blurred vision (continuing) or changes in near vision; clumsiness or unsteadiness; confusion; convulsions (seizures); difficulty in breathing, muscle weakness (severe), or tiredness (severe); dizziness; drowsiness (severe); dryness of mouth, nose, or throat (severe); fast heartbeat; fever; hallucinations (seeing, hearing, or feeling things that are not there); slurred speech; unusual excitement, nervousness, restlessness, or irritability; unusual warmth, dryness, and flushing of skin

Other side effects may occur that usually do not need medical attention. These side effects may go away during treatment as your body adjusts to the medicine. However, check with your doctor if any of the following side effects continue or are bothersome:

More common

Constipation (less common with hyoscyamine); decreased sweating; dryness of mouth, nose, throat, or skin

Less common or rare

Bloated feeling; blurred vision; decreased flow of breast milk; difficult urination; difficulty in swallowing; drowsiness (more common with high doses of any of these medicines and with usual doses of scopolamine when given by mouth or by injection); false sense of well-being (for scopolamine only); headache; increased sensitivity of eyes to light; lightheadedness (with injection); loss of memory; nausea or vomiting; redness or other signs of irritation at place of injection; trouble in sleeping (for scopolamine only); unusual tiredness or weakness

For patients using *scopolamine:*
- After you stop using scopolamine, your body may need time to adjust. The length of time this takes depends on the amount of scopolamine you were using and how long you used it. During this period of time check with your doctor if you notice any of the following side effects:

  Anxiety; irritability; nightmares; trouble in sleeping

For patients using the *transdermal disk* of *scopolamine:*
- While using the disk or even after removing it, your eyes may become more sensitive to light than usual. You may also notice the pupil in one eye is larger than the other. Check with your doctor if this side effect continues or is bothersome.

Other side effects not listed above may also occur in some patients. If you notice any other effects, check with your doctor.

Additional Information

Once a medicine has been approved for marketing for a certain use, experience may show that it is also useful for other medical problems. Although these uses are not included in product labeling, anticholinergics/antispasmodics are used in certain patients with the following medical conditions:
- Diarrhea
- Excessive watering of mouth

Other than the above information, there is no additional information relating to proper use, precautions, or side effects for these uses.

Revised: 01/29/92
Interim revision: 07/19/95

ANTICOAGULANTS Systemic

Some commonly used brand names are:

In the U.S.—

Coumadin[3] Panwarfin[3]
Miradon[1] Sofarin[3]

In Canada—

Coumadin[3] Warfilone[3]

Note: For quick reference, the following anticoagulants are numbered to match the corresponding brand names.

This information applies to the following medicines:
1. Anisindione (an-iss-in-DYE-one)†
2. Dicumarol (dye-KOO-ma-role)†‡
3. Warfarin (WAR-far-in)‡

This information does *not* apply to heparin.

†Not commercially available in Canada.
‡Generic name product may also be available in the U.S.

Description

Anticoagulants decrease the clotting ability of the blood and therefore help to prevent harmful clots from forming in the blood vessels. These medicines are sometimes called blood thinners, although they do not actually thin the blood. They also will not dissolve clots that already have formed, but they may prevent the clots from becoming larger and causing more serious problems. They are often used as treatment for certain blood vessel, heart, and lung conditions.

In order for an anticoagulant to help you without causing serious bleeding, it must be used properly and all of the precautions concerning its use must be followed exactly. Be sure that you have discussed the use of this medicine with your doctor. It is very important that you understand all of your doctor's orders and that you are willing and able to follow them exactly.

Anticoagulants are available only with your doctor's prescription, in the following dosage forms:

Oral
- Anisindione
  - Tablets (U.S.)
- Dicumarol
  - Tablets (U.S.)
- Warfarin
  - Tablets (U.S. and Canada)

Parenteral
- Warfarin
  - Injection (U.S.)

Before Using This Medicine

In deciding to use a medicine, the risks of taking the medicine must be weighed against the good it will do. This is a decision you and your doctor will make. For anticoagulants, the following should be considered:

Allergies—Tell your doctor if you have ever had any unusual or allergic reaction to an anticoagulant. Also tell your health care professional if you are allergic to any other substances, such as foods, preservatives, or dyes.

Pregnancy—Anticoagulants may cause birth defects. They may also cause other problems affecting the physical or mental growth of the fetus or newborn baby. In addition, use of this medicine during the last 6 months of pregnancy may increase the chance of severe, possibly fatal, bleeding in the fetus. If taken during the last few weeks of pregnancy, anticoagulants may cause severe bleeding in both the fetus and the mother before or during delivery and in the newborn infant.

Do not begin taking this medicine during pregnancy, and do not become pregnant while taking it, unless you have first discussed the possible effects of this medicine with your doctor. Also, if you suspect that you may be pregnant and you are already taking an anticoagulant, check with your doctor at once. Your doctor may suggest that you take a different anticoagulant that is less likely to harm the fetus or the newborn infant during all or part of your pregnancy. Anticoagulants may also cause severe bleeding in the mother if taken soon after the baby is born.

Breast-feeding—Warfarin is not likely to cause problems in nursing babies. Other anticoagulants may pass into the breast milk. A blood test can be done to see if unwanted effects are occurring in the nursing baby. If necessary, another medicine that will overcome any unwanted effects of the anticoagulant can be given to the baby.

Children—Very young babies may be especially sensitive to the effects of anticoagulants. This may increase the chance of bleeding during treatment.

Older adults—Elderly people are especially sensitive to the effects of anticoagulants. This may increase the chance of bleeding during treatment.

Other medicines—Although certain medicines should not be used together at all, in other cases two different medicines may be used together even if an interaction might occur. In these cases, your doctor may want to change the dose, or other precautions may be necessary. *Many different medicines can affect the way anticoagulants work in your body.* Therefore, it is very important that your health care professional knows if you are taking *any* other prescription or nonprescription (over-the-counter [OTC]) medicine, even aspirin, laxatives, vitamins, or antacids.

Other medical problems—The presence of other medical problems may affect the use of anticoagulants. Make sure you tell your doctor if you have *any* other medical problems, or if you are now being treated by any other medical doctor or dentist. Many medical problems and treatments will affect the way your body responds to this medicine.

Also, it is important that you tell your doctor if you have recently had any of the following conditions or medical procedures:

- Childbirth or
- Falls or blows to the body or head or
- Fever lasting more than a couple of days or
- Heavy or unusual menstrual bleeding or
- Insertion of intrauterine device (IUD) or
- Medical or dental surgery or
- Severe or continuing diarrhea or
- Spinal anesthesia or
- X-ray (radiation) treatment—The risk of serious bleeding may be increased

Proper Use of This Medicine

Take this medicine only as directed by your doctor. Do not take more or less of it, do not take it more often, and do not take it for a longer time than your doctor ordered. This is especially important for elderly patients, who are especially sensitive to the effects of anticoagulants.

Your doctor should check your progress at regular visits. A blood test must be taken regularly to see how fast your blood is clotting. This will help your doctor decide on the proper amount of anticoagulant you should be taking each day.

Dosing—The dose of these medicines will be different for different patients. *Follow your doctor's orders or the directions on the label.* The following information includes only the average doses of these medicines. *If your dose is different, do not change it* unless your doctor tells you to do so.

For anisindione

- For *oral* dosage form (tablets):
  - —For preventing harmful blood clots:
    - Adults and teenagers—The usual dose is 25 to 250 milligrams (mg) per day.
    - Children—Dose must be determined by your doctor.

For dicumarol

- For *oral* dosage form (tablets):
  - —For preventing harmful blood clots:
    - Adults and teenagers—The usual dose is 25 to 200 milligrams (mg) per day.
    - Children—Dose must be determined by your doctor.

For warfarin

- For *oral* dosage form (tablets):
  - —For preventing harmful blood clots:
    - Adults and teenagers—The starting dose is usually 10 to 15 milligrams (mg) per day for two to four days. Then, your doctor may decrease the dose to 2 to 10 mg per day, depending on your condition.
    - Children—Dose must be determined by your doctor.
- For *injection* dosage form:
  - —For preventing harmful blood clots:
    - Adults and teenagers—The starting dose is usually 10 to 15 mg, injected into a muscle or a vein, once a day for two to four days. Then, your doctor may decrease the dose to 2 to 10 mg per day, depending on your condition.
    - Children—Dose must be determined by your doctor.

Missed dose—If you miss a dose of this medicine, take it as soon as possible. Then go back to your regular dosing schedule. If you do not remember until the next day, do not take the missed dose at all and do not double the next one. *Doubling the dose may cause bleeding.* Instead, go back to your regular dosing schedule. It is recommended that you keep a record of each dose as you take it to avoid mistakes. Also, be sure to give your doctor a record of any doses you miss. If you have any questions about this, check with your doctor.

Storage—To store this medicine:

- Keep out of the reach of children.
- Store away from heat and direct light.
- Do not store this medicine in the bathroom, near the kitchen sink, or in other damp places. Heat or moisture may cause the medicine to break down.
- Do not keep outdated medicine or medicine no longer needed. Be sure that any discarded medicine is out of the reach of children.

Precautions While Using This Medicine

Tell all medical doctors, dentists, and pharmacists you go to that you are taking this medicine.

Check with your health care professional before you start or stop taking any other medicine. This includes any nonprescription (over-the-counter [OTC]) medicine, even aspirin or acetaminophen. Many medicines change the way this medicine affects your body. You may not be able to take the other medicine, or the dose of your anticoagulant may need to be changed.

It is important that you carry identification stating that you are using this medicine. If you have any questions about what kind of identification to carry, check with your health care professional.

While you are taking this medicine, it is very important that you avoid sports and activities that may cause you to be injured. Report to your doctor any falls, blows to the body or head, or other injuries, since serious internal bleeding may occur without your knowing about it.

Be careful to avoid cutting yourself. This includes taking special care in brushing your teeth and in shaving. Use a soft toothbrush and floss gently. Also, it is best to use an electric shaver rather than a blade.

Drinking too much alcohol may change the way this anticoagulant affects your body. You should not drink regularly on a daily basis or take more than 1 or 2 drinks at any time. If you have any questions about this, check with your doctor.

The foods that you eat may also affect the way this medicine affects your body. Eat a normal, balanced diet while you are taking this medicine. Do not go on a reducing diet, make other changes in your eating habits, start taking vitamins, or begin using other nutrition supplements unless you have first checked with your health care professional. Also, check with your doctor if you are unable to eat for several days or if you have continuing stomach upset, diarrhea, or fever. These precautions are important because the effects of the anticoagulant depend on the amount of vitamin K in your body. Therefore, it is best to have the same amount of vitamin K in your body every day. Some multiple vitamins and some nutrition supplements contain vitamin K. Vitamin K is also present in meats, dairy products (such as milk, cheese, and yogurt), and green, leafy vegetables (such as broccoli, cabbage, collard greens, kale, lettuce, and spinach). It is especially important that you do not make large changes in the amounts of these foods that you eat every day while you are taking an anticoagulant.

After you stop taking this medicine, your body will need time to recover before your blood clotting ability returns to normal. Your health care professional can tell you how long this will take depending on which anticoagulant you were taking. Use the same caution during this period of time as you did while you were taking the anticoagulant.

Side Effects of This Medicine

Along with its needed effects, a medicine may cause some unwanted effects. Although not all of these side effects may occur, if they do occur they may need medical attention.

Check with your doctor immediately if any of the following side effects occur:

Less common or rare

Blue or purple color of toes and pain in toes; cloudy or dark urine; difficult or painful urination; sores, ulcers, or white spots in mouth or throat; sore throat and fever or chills; sudden decrease in amount of urine; swelling of face, feet, or lower legs; unusual tiredness or weakness; unusual weight gain; yellow eyes or skin

Since many things can affect the way your body reacts to this medicine, you should always watch for signs of unusual bleeding. Unusual bleeding may mean that your body is getting more medicine than it needs. *Check with your doctor immediately if any of the following signs of overdose occur:*

Bleeding from gums when brushing teeth; unexplained bruising or purplish areas on skin; unexplained nosebleeds; unusually heavy bleeding or oozing from cuts or wounds; unusually heavy or unexpected menstrual bleeding

Signs and symptoms of bleeding inside the body

Abdominal or stomach pain or swelling; back pain or backaches; blood in urine; bloody or black tarry stools; constipation; coughing up blood; dizziness; headache (severe or continuing); joint pain, stiffness, or swelling; vomiting blood or material that looks like coffee grounds

Also, check with your doctor as soon as possible if any of the following side effects occur:

Less common or rare

Diarrhea (more common with dicumarol); nausea or vomiting; skin rash, hives, or itching; stomach cramps or pain

For patients taking *anisindione* (e.g., Miradon):

- Depending on your diet, this medicine may cause your urine to turn orange. Since it may be hard to tell the difference between blood in the urine and this normal color change, check with your doctor if you notice any color change in your urine.

Other side effects may occur that usually do not need medical attention. These side effects may go away during treatment as your body adjusts to the medicine. However, check with your doctor if any of the following side effects continue or are bothersome:

More common

Bloated feeling or gas (with dicumarol)

Less common

Blurred vision or other vision problems (with anisindione); loss of appetite; unusual hair loss

Other side effects not listed above may also occur in some patients. If you notice any other effects, check with your doctor.

Revised: June 1990
Interim revision: 07/28/94

ANTICONVULSANTS, DIONE Systemic

Other commonly used names for trimethadione are TMO, trimethadionum, trimethinum, and troxidone.

This information applies to the following medicines:

Paramethadione (par-a-meth-a-DYE-one)*†
Trimethadione (trye-meth-a-DYE-one)*†

*Not commercially available in the U.S.
†Not commercially available in Canada.

Description

Dione anticonvulsants are used to control certain types of seizures in the treatment of epilepsy. They act on the central nervous system (CNS) to reduce the number of seizures. These medicines cannot cure epilepsy and will only work to control seizures for as long as you continue to take them.

Before Using This Medicine

In deciding to use a medicine, the risks of taking the medicine must be weighed against the good it will do. This is a decision you and your doctor will make. For dione anticonvulsants, the following should be considered:

Allergies—Tell your doctor if you have ever had any unusual or allergic reaction to anticonvulsant medicines. Also tell your health care professional if you are allergic to any other substances, such as foods, preservatives, or dyes.

Pregnancy—There have been reports of increased birth defects when dione anticonvulsants were used during pregnancy. The use of an effective method of birth control is recommended during treatment with dione anticonvulsants. Be sure you have discussed this with your doctor before taking this medicine. Dione anticonvulsants may also cause a bleeding problem in the mother during delivery and in the newborn. Doctors can help prevent this by giving vitamin K to the mother before and during delivery, and to the baby immediately after birth.

Breast-feeding—It is not known whether this medicine passes into breast milk. However, dione anticonvulsants may have serious unwanted effects, and breast-feeding is not recommended.

Children—Although there is no specific information comparing use of dione anticonvulsants in children with use in other age groups, these medicines are not expected to cause different side effects or problems in children than they do in adults.

Older adults—This medicine has been tested in a very small number of older people. Dione anticonvulsants are removed from the body more slowly in older people than in younger people. Higher blood levels of the medicine may occur, which may increase the chance of unwanted effects. Your doctor may give you a different dose than a younger person would receive.

Other medicines—Although certain medicines should not be used together at all, in other cases 2 different medicines may be used together even if an interaction might occur. In these cases, your doctor may want to change the dose, or other precautions may be necessary. When you are taking dione anticonvulsants, it is especially important that your health care professional know if you are taking any of the following:

- Central nervous system (CNS) depressants (medicine that causes drowsiness) or
- Tricyclic antidepressants (medicine for depression)—Using these medicines together may increase the CNS depressant effects

Other medical problems—The presence of other medical problems may affect the use of the dione anticonvulsants. Make sure you tell your doctor if you have any other medical problems, especially:

- Blood disease or
- Diseases of the eye or optic nerve or
- Kidney disease or
- Liver disease—Dione anticonvulsants may make the condition worse. Liver disease may cause higher blood levels of this medicine, which may increase the chance of side effects
- Porphyria—Trimethadione may make the condition worse

Proper Use of This Medicine

For patients taking *paramethadione capsules:*

- Swallow the capsules whole. Do not crush, chew, or break them before swallowing.

For patients taking *trimethadione solution:*

- Use a specially marked measuring spoon, a plastic syringe, or a small marked measuring cup to measure each dose accurately. The average household teaspoon may not hold the right amount of liquid.

For patients taking *trimethadione chewable tablets:*

- The tablets should be crushed and dissolved in a small amount of water or chewed before they are swallowed.

If this medicine upsets your stomach, take it with a small amount of food or milk unless otherwise directed by your doctor.

Take this medicine only as directed by your doctor, to benefit your condition as much as possible. Do not take more or less of it and do not take it more or less often than your doctor ordered.

Dosing—The dose of dione anticonvulsants will be different for different patients. *Follow your doctor's orders or the directions on the label.* The following information includes only the average doses of paramethadione and trimethadione. *If your dose is different, do not change it* unless your doctor tells you to do so.

The number of tablets or capsules or teaspoonfuls of solution that you take depends on the strength of the medicine.

For paramethadione

- For *oral* dosage forms (capsules):
  - —Adults and teenagers: To start, 300 milligrams (mg) three times a day. Your doctor may increase your dose by 300 mg every week until seizures are controlled or side effects appear. However, the dose is usually not more than 2400 mg a day, taken in three or four smaller doses.
  - —Children 6 years of age and over: 300 mg three times a day.
  - —Children 2 to 6 years of age: 200 mg three times a day.
  - —Children up to 2 years of age: 100 mg three times a day.

For trimethadione

- For *oral* dosage forms (capsules, solution, tablets):
  - —Adults and teenagers: To start, 300 milligrams (mg) three times a day. Your doctor may increase your dose by 300 mg every week until seizures are controlled or side effects appear. However, the dose is usually not more than 2400 mg a day, taken in three or four smaller doses.
  - —Children 6 years of age and over: 300 mg three or four times a day.
  - —Children 2 to 6 years of age: 200 mg three times a day.
  - —Children up to 2 years of age: 100 mg three times a day.

Missed dose—If you miss a dose of this medicine, take it as soon as possible. However, if it is almost time for your next dose, skip the missed dose and go back to your regular dosing schedule. If only one dose is missed, it may be taken at bedtime.

Storage—To store this medicine:

- Keep out of the reach of children.
- Store away from heat and direct light.
- Do not store the capsule form of this medicine in the bathroom, near the kitchen sink, or in other damp places. Heat or moisture may cause the medicine to break down.
- Store trimethadione chewable tablets in the refrigerator.
- Keep the liquid form of this medicine from freezing.
- Do not keep outdated medicine or medicine no longer needed. Be sure that any discarded medicine is out of the reach of children.

Precautions While Using This Medicine

It is very important that your doctor check your progress at regular visits. This is necessary to allow dose adjustments and to test for serious unwanted effects.

Tell your doctor as soon as possible if you have a sore throat, fever, or general feeling of tiredness, or if you notice any unusual bleeding or bruising, such as red or purple spots on the skin, nosebleed, or bleeding gums.

Dione anticonvulsants may cause your eyes to become more sensitive to bright light than they are normally, making it difficult for you to see well. Wearing sunglasses and avoiding too much exposure to bright light may help lessen the discomfort. You may also have difficulty seeing in light that changes in brightness. If you notice this effect, be especially careful when driving at night.

This medicine will add to the effects of alcohol and other CNS depressants (medicines that slow down the nervous system, possibly causing drowsiness). Some examples of CNS depressants are antihistamines or medicine for hay fever, other allergies, or colds; sedatives, tranquilizers, or sleeping medicine; prescription pain medicine or narcotics; barbiturates; medicine for seizures; muscle relaxants; or anesthetics, including some dental anesthetics. *Check with your doctor before taking any of the above while you are using this medicine.*

Dione anticonvulsants may cause some people to become drowsy or less alert than they are normally. *Make sure you know how you react to this medicine before you drive, use machines, or do anything else that could be dangerous if you are not alert.* After you have taken this medicine for a while, this effect may not be so bothersome.

Before having any kind of surgery, dental treatment, or emergency treatment, tell the medical doctor or dentist in charge that you are taking this medicine. Taking dione anticonvulsants together with medicines that are used during surgery or dental or emergency treatments may increase the CNS depressant effects.

Check with your doctor as soon as possible if you suspect you have become pregnant.

Do not stop taking dione anticonvulsant medicines without first checking with your doctor. Your doctor may want to reduce your dose gradually. Stopping this medicine suddenly may cause seizures.

Side Effects of This Medicine

Along with its needed effects, a medicine may cause some unwanted effects. Although not all of these side effects may occur, if they do occur they may need medical attention.

Check with your doctor as soon as possible if any of the following side effects occur:

More common

Changes in vision, especially night blindness, glare or snowy image caused by bright light, or double vision

Rare

Confusion; convulsions (seizures); dark or cloudy urine; dizziness; fever; loss of appetite or weight; muscle weakness (severe), especially drooping eyelids, or difficulty in chewing, swallowing, talking, or breathing; nausea or vomiting; pain in abdomen, chest, muscles or joints; shortness of breath; skin rash or itching; sore throat and fever; swelling of face, hands, legs, and feet; swollen lymph nodes; unusual bleeding or bruising, such as recurring nosebleeds, bleeding gums, or vaginal bleeding, or red or purple spots on skin; unusual tiredness or weakness; yellow eyes or skin

Symptoms of overdose

Clumsiness or unsteadiness; coma; dizziness (severe); drowsiness (severe); nausea (severe); problems with vision

Other side effects may occur that usually do not need medical attention. These side effects may go away during treatment as your body adjusts to the medicine. However, check with your doctor if any of the following side effects continue or are bothersome:

More common

Dizziness; drowsiness; headache; increased sensitivity of eyes to light; irritability

Less common

Behavior or mood changes; blood pressure changes; hair loss; hiccups; loss of appetite; stomach pain, nausea, or vomiting; tingling, burning, or prickly sensations; trouble in sleeping; unusual weight loss

Other side effects not listed above may also occur in some patients. If you notice any other effects, check with your doctor.

Revised: 12/4/95

ANTICONVULSANTS, HYDANTOIN Systemic

Some commonly used brand names are:

In the U.S.—

Cerebyx[2]
Dilantin[4]
Dilantin-125[4]
Dilantin Infatabs[4]
Dilantin Kapseals[4]
Mesantoin[3]
Peganone[1]
Phenytex[4]

In Canada—

Dilantin[4]
Dilantin-30[4]
Dilantin-125[4]
Dilantin Infatabs[4]

Another commonly used name for phenytoin is diphenylhydantoin.

Note: For quick reference, the following hydantoin anticonvulsants are numbered to match the corresponding brand names.

This information applies to the following medicines:

1. Ethotoin (ETH-oh-toyn)†
2. Fosphenytoin (fos-FEN-i-toyn)†
3. Mephenytoin (me-FEN-i-toyn)†
4. Phenytoin (FEN-i-toyn)‡

†Not commercially available in Canada.
‡Generic name product may also be available in the U.S.

Description

Hydantoin anticonvulsants (hye-DAN-toyn an-tye-kon-VUL-sants) are used most often to control certain convulsions or seizures in the treatment of epilepsy. Phenytoin also may be used for other conditions as determined by your doctor.

In seizure disorders, these medicines act on the central nervous system (CNS) to reduce the number and severity of seizures. Hydantoin anticonvulsants may also produce some unwanted effects. These depend on the patient's individual condition, the amount of medicine taken, and how long it has been taken. It is important that you know what the side effects are and when to call your doctor if they occur.

Hydantoin anticonvulsants are available only with your doctor's prescription, in the following dosage forms:

Oral
- Ethotoin
  - Tablets (U.S.)
- Mephenytoin
  - Tablets (U.S.)
- Phenytoin
  - Extended capsules (U.S. and Canada)
  - Prompt capsules (U.S.)
  - Oral suspension (U.S. and Canada)
  - Chewable tablets (U.S. and Canada)

Parenteral
- Fosphenytoin
  - Injection (U.S.)
- Phenytoin
  - Injection (U.S. and Canada)

Note: Because fosphenytoin is converted to phenytoin in your body, it has the same effects as those listed for phenytoin in the following sections.

Before Using This Medicine

In deciding to use a medicine, the risks of taking the medicine must be weighed against the good it will do. This is a decision you and your doctor will make. For hydantoin anticonvulsants, the following should be considered:

Allergies—Tell your doctor if you have ever had any unusual or allergic reaction to any hydantoin anticonvulsant medicine. Also tell your health care professional if you are allergic to any other substance, such as foods, preservatives, or dyes.

Pregnancy—Although most mothers who take medicine for seizure control deliver normal babies, there have been reports of increased birth defects when these medicines were used during pregnancy. It is not definitely known if any of these medicines are the cause of such problems.

Also, pregnancy may cause a change in the way hydantoin anticonvulsants are absorbed in your body. You may have more seizures, even though you are taking your medicine regularly. Your doctor may need to increase the anticonvulsant dose during your pregnancy.

In addition, when taken during pregnancy, this medicine may cause a bleeding problem in the mother during delivery and in the newborn. This may be prevented by giving vitamin K to the mother during delivery, and to the baby immediately after birth.

Breast-feeding—Ethotoin and phenytoin pass into the breast milk in small amounts. It is not known whether mephenytoin passes into breast milk. Be sure you have discussed the risks and benefits of the medicine with your doctor.

Children—Some side effects, especially bleeding, tender, or enlarged gums and enlarged facial features, are more likely to occur in children and young adults. Also, unusual and excessive hair growth may occur, which is more noticeable in young girls. In addition, some children may not do as well in school after using high doses of this medicine for a long time.

Older adults—Some medicines may affect older patients differently than they do younger patients. Overdose is more likely to occur in elderly patients and in patients with liver disease.

Other medicines—Although certain medicines should not be used together at all, in other cases two different medicines may be used together even if an interaction might occur. In these cases, your doctor may want to change the dose, or other precautions may be necessary. When you are taking or receiving hydantoin anticonvulsants, it is especially important that your health care professional know if you are taking any of the following:

- Alcohol or
- Central nervous system (CNS) depressants (medicine that causes drowsiness)—Long-term use of alcohol may decrease the blood levels of hydantoin anticonvulsants, resulting in decreased effects; use of hydantoin anticonvulsants in cases where a large amount of alcohol is consumed may increase the blood levels of the hydantoin, resulting in an increased risk of side effects

- Amiodarone (e.g., Cordarone)—Use with phenytoin and possibly with other hydantoin anticonvulsants may increase blood levels of the hydantoin, resulting in an increase in serious side effects

- Antacids or
- Medicine containing calcium—Use of antacids or calcium supplements may decrease the absorption of phenytoin; doses of antacids and phenytoin or calcium supplements and phenytoin should be taken 2 to 3 hours apart

- Anticoagulants (blood thinners) or
- Chloramphenicol (e.g., Chloromycetin) or
- Cimetidine (e.g., Tagamet) or
- Disulfiram (e.g., Antabuse) (medicine for alcoholism) or
- Isoniazid (INH) (e.g., Nydrazid) or
- Fluconazole (e.g., Diflucan) or
- Fluoxetine (e.g., Prozac) or
- Itraconazole (e.g., Sporanox) or
- Ketoconazole (e.g., Nizoral) or
- Miconazole (e.g., Monistat) or
- Phenylbutazone (e.g., Butazolidin) or
- Sulfonamides (sulfa drugs)—Blood levels of hydantoin anticonvulsants may be increased, increasing the risk of serious side effects; hydantoin anticonvulsants may increase the effects of the anticoagulants at first, but with continued use may decrease the effects of these medicines

- Corticosteroids (cortisone-like medicines) or
- Estrogens (female hormones) or
- Oral contraceptives (birth-control pills) containing estrogens or progestins or
- Progestin injection contraceptives (e.g., Depo-Provera) or
- Progestin implant contraceptives (e.g., Norplant)—Hydantoin anticonvulsants may decrease the effects of these medicines; use of hydantoin anticonvulsants with estrogen- or progestin-containing contraceptives may result in breakthrough bleeding and contraceptive failure; additional birth control measures may be needed to decrease the risk of pregnancy

- Diazoxide (e.g., Proglycem)—Use with hydantoin anticonvulsants may decrease the effects of both medicines; therefore, these medicines should not be taken together

- Felbamate (e.g., Felbatrol)—Blood levels of hydantoin anticonvulsants may be increased, and blood levels of felbamate may be decreased. Your doctor may need to adjust your dosage
- Lidocaine—Risk of slow heartbeat may be increased. Other effects of lidocaine may be decreased because hydantoin anticonvulsants may cause it to be removed from the body more quickly
- Methadone (e.g., Dolophine, Methadose)—Long-term use of phenytoin may bring on withdrawal symptoms in patients being treated for drug dependence
- Phenacemide (e.g., Phenurone)—Use with hydantoin anticonvulsants may increase the risk of serious side effects
- Rifampin (e.g., Rifadin)—Use with phenytoin may decrease the effects of phenytoin; your doctor may need to adjust your dosage
- Streptozocin (e.g., Zanosar)—Phenytoin may decrease the effects of streptozocin; therefore, these medicines should not be used together
- Sucralfate (e.g., Carafate)—Use of sucralfate may decrease the absorption of hydantoin anticonvulsants
- Theophylline (e.g., Theo-Dur)—Hydantoin anticonvulsants may make this medicine less effective
- Valproic acid (e.g., Depakene, Depakote)—Use with phenytoin, and possibly other hydantoin anticonvulsants, may increase seizure frequency and increase the risk of serious side effects affecting the liver, especially in infants

Other medical problems—The presence of other medical problems may affect the use of hydantoin anticonvulsants. Make sure you tell your doctor if you have any other medical problems, especially:

- Alcohol abuse—Blood levels of phenytoin may be decreased, decreasing its effects
- Blood disease—Risk of serious infections rarely may be increased by hydantoin anticonvulsants
- Diabetes mellitus (sugar diabetes) or
- Porphyria or
- Systemic lupus erythematosus—Hydantoin anticonvulsants may make the condition worse
- Fever above 101 °F for longer than 24 hours—Blood levels of hydantoin anticonvulsants may be decreased, decreasing the medicine's effects
- Heart disease—Administration of phenytoin by injection may change the rhythm of the heart
- Kidney disease or
- Liver disease—Blood levels of hydantoin anticonvulsants may be increased, leading to an increase in serious side effects
- Thyroid disease—Blood levels of thyroid hormones may be decreased

Proper Use of This Medicine

For patients taking the *liquid form* of this medicine:

- Shake the bottle well before using.
- Use a specially marked measuring spoon, a plastic syringe, or a small measuring cup to measure each dose accurately. The average household teaspoon may not hold the right amount of liquid.

For patients taking the *chewable tablet form* of this medicine:

- Tablets may be chewed or crushed before they are swallowed, or may be swallowed whole.

For patients taking the *capsule form* of this medicine:

- Swallow the capsule whole.

If this medicine upsets your stomach, take it with food, unless otherwise directed by your doctor. The medicine should always be taken at the same time in relation to meals to make sure that it is absorbed in the same way.

To control your medical problem, *take this medicine every day* exactly as ordered by your doctor. Do not take more or less of it than your doctor ordered. To help you remember to take the medicine at the correct times, try to get into the habit of taking it at the same time each day.

Dosing—The dose of hydantoin anticonvulsants will be different for different patients. *Follow your doctor's orders or the directions on the label.* The following information includes only the average doses of ethotoin, fosphenytoin, mephenytoin, and phenytoin. *If your dose is different, do not change it* unless your doctor tells you to do so.

The number of capsules or tablets or teaspoonfuls of suspension that you take or the number of injections you receive depends on the strength of the medicine. Also, *the number of doses you take each day, the time allowed between doses, and the length of time you take the medicine depend on the medical problem for which you are using a hydantoin anticonvulsant.*

For ethotoin

- For *oral* dosage form (tablets):
  —As an anticonvulsant:
    - Adults and teenagers—To start, 125 to 250 milligrams (mg) four to six times a day. Your doctor may increase your dose gradually over several days if needed. However, the dose is usually not more than 3000 mg a day.
    - Children—To start, up to 750 mg a day, based on the age and weight of the child. The doctor may increase the dose gradually if needed.

For fosphenytoin—

- For *injection* dosage form:
  —As an anticonvulsant:
    - Adults and children—Dose is based on the illness being treated, and the body weight or size of the patient. The medicine is injected into a vein or muscle.

For mephenytoin

- For *oral* dosage form (tablets):
  —As an anticonvulsant:
    - Adults and teenagers—To start, 50 to 100 milligrams (mg) once a day. Your doctor may increase your dose by 50 to 100 mg a day at weekly intervals if needed. However, the dose is usually not more than 1200 mg a day.
    - Children—To start, 25 to 50 mg once a day. The doctor may increase the dose by 25 to 50 mg a day at weekly intervals if needed. However, the dose is usually not more than 400 mg a day.

For phenytoin

- For *oral* dosage forms (capsules, chewable tablets, or suspension):
  —As an anticonvulsant:
  - Adults and teenagers—To start, 100 to 125 milligrams (mg) three times a day. Your doctor may adjust your dose at intervals of seven to ten days if needed.
  - Children—Dose is based on body weight or body surface area. The usual dose is 5 mg of phenytoin per kilogram (kg) (2.3 mg per pound) of body weight to start. The doctor may adjust the dose if needed.
  - Older adults—Dose is based on body weight. The usual dose is 3 mg per kg (1.4 mg per pound) of body weight. The doctor may need to adjust the dose based on your response to the medicine.
- For *injection* dosage form:
  —As an anticonvulsant:
  - Adults and children—Dose is based on the illness being treated, and the body weight or size of the patient. The medicine is usually injected into a vein.

Missed dose—*If you miss a dose of this medicine* and your dosing schedule is:

- One dose a day—Take the missed dose as soon as possible. However, if you do not remember the missed dose until the next day, skip it and go back to your regular dosing schedule. Do not double doses.
- More than one dose a day—Take the missed dose as soon as possible. However, if it is within 4 hours of your next dose, skip the missed dose and go back to your regular dosing schedule. Do not double doses.

If you miss doses for 2 or more days in a row, check with your doctor.

Storage—To store this medicine:

- Keep out of the reach of children.
- Store away from heat and direct light.
- Do not store in the bathroom, near the kitchen sink, or in other damp places. Heat or moisture may cause the medicine to break down.
- Keep the liquid form of this medicine from freezing. Do not refrigerate.
- Do not keep outdated medicine or medicine no longer needed. Be sure any discarded medicine is out of the reach of children.

Precautions While Using This Medicine

Your doctor should check your progress at regular visits, especially during the first few months of treatment with this medicine. During this time the amount of medicine you are taking may have to be changed often to meet your individual needs.

Do not start or stop taking any other medicine without your doctor's advice. Other medicines may affect the way this medicine works.

This medicine will add to the effects of alcohol and other CNS depressants (medicines that may make you drowsy or less alert). Some examples of CNS depressants are antihistamines or medicine for hay fever, other allergies, or colds; sedatives, tranquilizers, or sleeping medicine; prescription pain medicine or narcotics; barbiturates; other medicine for seizures; muscle relaxants; or anesthetics, including some dental anesthetics. *Check with your doctor before taking any of the above while you are using this medicine.*

Do not take this medicine within 2 to 3 hours of taking antacids or medicine for diarrhea. Taking these medicines and hydantoin anticonvulsants too close together may make the hydantoins less effective.

Do not change brands or dosage forms of phenytoin without first checking with your doctor. Different products may not work the same way. If you refill your medicine and it looks different, check with your pharmacist.

If you have been taking this medicine regularly for several weeks or more, do not suddenly stop taking it. Your doctor may want you to reduce gradually the amount you are taking before stopping completely.

Your doctor may want you to carry a medical identification card or bracelet stating that you are taking this medicine.

For diabetic patients:

- This medicine may affect blood sugar levels. If you notice a change in the results of your blood or urine sugar tests or if you have any questions, check with your doctor.

Before you have any medical tests, tell the doctor in charge that you are taking this medicine. The results of some tests (including the dexamethasone, metyrapone, or Schilling tests, and certain thyroid function tests) may be affected by this medicine.

Before having any kind of surgery, dental treatment, or emergency treatment, tell the medical doctor or dentist in charge that you are taking this medicine. Taking hydantoin anticonvulsants together with medicines that are used during surgery or dental or emergency treatments may cause increased side effects.

This medicine may cause some people to become dizzy, lightheaded, drowsy, or less alert than they are normally. After you have taken this medicine for a while, this effect may not be so bothersome. However, *make sure you know how you react to this medicine before you drive, use machines, or do anything else that could be dangerous if you are dizzy or are not alert.*

Oral contraceptives (birth control pills) containing estrogen or progestin, contraceptive progestin injections (e.g., Depo-Provera), and implant contraceptive forms of progestin (e.g., Norplant) may not work properly if you take them while you are taking hydantoin anticonvulsants. Unplanned pregnancies may occur. You should use a different or additional means of birth control while you are taking hydantoin anticonvulsants. If you have any questions about this, check with your health care professional.

For patients taking *phenytoin* or *mephenytoin*:

- In some patients (usually younger patients), tenderness, swelling, or bleeding of the gums (gingival hyperplasia) may appear soon after phenytoin or mephenytoin treatment is started. To help prevent this, brush and floss your teeth carefully and regularly and massage your gums. Also, *see your dentist every 3 months to have your teeth cleaned. If you have any questions about how to take care of your teeth and gums, or if you notice any tenderness, swelling, or bleeding of your gums, check with your doctor or dentist.*

Side Effects of This Medicine

Along with its needed effects, a medicine may cause some unwanted effects. Although not all of these side effects may occur, if they do occur they may need medical attention.

Check with your doctor as soon as possible if any of the following side effects or signs of overdose occur:

More common

Bleeding, tender, or enlarged gums (rare with ethotoin); burning, tingling, pain, or itching, especially in the groin—following fosphenytoin injection; clumsiness or unsteadiness; confusion; continuous, uncontrolled back-and-forth and/or rolling eye movements—may be sign of overdose; swollen glands in neck or underarms; fever; muscle pain; skin rash or itching; slurred speech or stuttering—may be sign of overdose; sore throat; trembling—may be sign of overdose; unusual excitement, nervousness, or irritability

Rare

Bone malformations; burning pain at place of injection; chest discomfort; chills and fever; dark urine; dizziness; frequent breaking of bones; headache; joint pain; learning difficulties—in children taking high doses for a long time; light gray–colored stools; loss of appetite; nausea or vomiting; pain of penis on erection; restlessness or agitation; slowed growth; stomach pain (severe); troubled or quick, shallow breathing; uncontrolled jerking or twisting movements of hands, arms, or legs; uncontrolled movements of lips, tongue, or cheeks; unusual bleeding (such as nosebleeds) or bruising; unusual tiredness or weakness; weight loss (unusual); yellow eyes or skin

Rare (with long-term use of phenytoin)

Numbness, tingling, or pain in hands or feet

Symptoms of overdose

Blurred or double vision; clumsiness or unsteadiness (severe); confusion (severe); dizziness or drowsiness (severe); seizures; staggering walk; stuttering or slurred speech

Other side effects may occur that usually do not need medical attention. These side effects may go away during treatment as your body adjusts to the medicine. However, check with your doctor if any of the following side effects continue or are bothersome:

More common

Constipation; dizziness (mild); drowsiness (mild)

Less common

Diarrhea (with ethotoin); enlargement of jaw; muscle twitching; swelling of breasts—in males; thickening of lips; trouble in sleeping; unusual and excessive hair growth on body and face (more common with phenytoin); widening of nose tip

Other side effects not listed above may also occur in some patients. If you notice any other effects, check with your doctor.

Additional Information

Once a medicine has been approved for marketing for a certain use, experience may show that it is also useful for other medical problems. Although these uses are not included in product labeling, phenytoin is used in certain patients with the following medical conditions:

- Cardiac arrhythmias (changes in your heart rhythm) caused by digitalis medicine
- Myotonia congenita or
- Myotonic muscular dystrophy or
- Neuromyotonia (certain muscle disorders)
- Paroxysmal choreoathetosis (certain movement disorders)
- Tricyclic antidepressant poisoning
- Trigeminal neuralgia (tic douloureux)

Other than the above information, there is no additional information relating to proper use, precautions, or side effects for these uses.

Revised: 08/11/97

ANTICONVULSANTS, SUCCINIMIDE Systemic

Some commonly used brand names are:

In the U.S.—

Celontin[2]
Milontin[3]
Zarontin[1]

In Canada—

Celontin[2]
Zarontin[1]

Note: For quick reference, the following succinimide anticonvulsants are numbered to match the corresponding brand names.

This information applies to the following medicines:

1. Ethosuximide (eth-oh-SUX-i-mide)‡
2. Methsuximide (meth-SUX-i-mide)
3. Phensuximide (fen-SUX-i-mide)†

†Not commercially available in Canada.
‡Generic name product may also be available in the U.S.

Description

Succinimide anticonvulsants are used to control certain seizures in the treatment of epilepsy. These medicines act on the central nervous system (CNS) to reduce the number and severity of seizures.

This medicine is available only with your doctor's prescription, in the following dosage forms:

Oral

Ethosuximide
- Capsules (U.S. and Canada)
- Syrup (U.S. and Canada)

Methsuximide
- Capsules (U.S. and Canada)

Phensuximide
- Capsules (U.S.)

Before Using This Medicine

In deciding to use a medicine, the risks of taking the medicine must be weighed against the good it will do. This is a decision you and your doctor will make. For succinimide anticonvulsants, the following should be considered:

Allergies—Tell your doctor if you have ever had any unusual or allergic reaction to anticonvulsant medicines. Also tell your health care professional if you are allergic to any other substances, such as foods, preservatives, or dyes.

Pregnancy—Although succinimide anticonvulsants have not been shown to cause problems in humans, there have been unproven reports of increased birth defects associated with the use of other anticonvulsant medicines.

Breast-feeding—Ethosuximide passes into breast milk. It is not known whether methsuximide or phensuximide passes into breast milk. However, these medicines have not been reported to cause problems in nursing babies.

Children—Succinimide anticonvulsants are not expected to cause different side effects or problems in children than they do in adults.

Older adults—Many medicines have not been studied specifically in older people. Therefore, it may not be known whether they work exactly the same way they do in younger adults. Although there is no specific information comparing use of succinimide anticonvulsants in the elderly to use in other age groups, they are not expected to cause different side effects or problems in older people than they do in younger adults.

Other medicines—Although certain medicines should not be used together at all, in other cases two different medicines may be used together even if an interaction might occur. In these cases, your doctor may want to change the dose, or other precautions may be necessary. When you are taking succinimide anticonvulsants, it is especially important that your health care professional know if you are taking any of the following:

- Central nervous system (CNS) depressants (medicines that cause drowsiness)—Using these medicines together may increase CNS depressant effects
- Haloperidol (e.g., Haldol)—A change in the pattern and/or the frequency of seizures may occur; the dose of either medicine may need to be changed

Other medical problems—The presence of other medical problems may affect the use of succinimide anticonvulsants. Make sure you tell your doctor if you have any other medical problems, especially:

- Blood disease or
- Intermittent porphyria or
- Kidney disease (severe) or
- Liver disease—Succinimide anticonvulsants may make the condition worse

Proper Use of This Medicine

This medicine must be taken every day in regularly spaced doses as ordered by your doctor. Do not take more or less of it than your doctor ordered.

If this medicine upsets your stomach, take it with food or milk unless otherwise directed by your doctor.

Dosing—The dose of succinimide anticonvulsants will be different for different patients. *Follow your doctor's orders or the directions on the label.* The following information includes only the average doses of ethosuximide, methsuximide, and phensuximide. *If your dose is different, do not change it* unless your doctor tells you to do so.

The number of capsules or teaspoonfuls of syrup that you take depends on the strength of the medicine. Also, *the number of doses you take each day, the time allowed between doses, and the length of time you take the medicine depend on the medical problem for which you are taking a succinimide anticonvulsant.*

For ethosuximide
- For *oral* dosage form (capsules or syrup):
  - —As an anticonvulsant:
    - Adults and children 6 years of age and over—To start, 250 milligrams (mg) twice a day. Your doctor may increase your dose gradually if needed. However, the dose is usually not more than 1500 mg a day.
    - Children up to 6 years of age—To start, 250 mg once a day. Your doctor may increase your dose gradually if needed. However, the dose is usually not more than 1000 mg a day.

For methsuximide
- For *oral* dosage form (capsules):
  - —As an anticonvulsant:
    - Adults, teenagers, and children—To start, 300 milligrams (mg) once a day. Your doctor may increase your dose gradually if needed. However, the dose is usually not more than 1200 mg a day.

For phensuximide
- For *oral* dosage form (capsules):
  - —As an anticonvulsant:
    - Adults, teenagers, and children—To start, 500 milligrams (mg) two or three times a day. Your doctor may increase your dose gradually if needed. However, the dose is usually not more than 3000 mg a day.

Missed dose—If you miss a dose of this medicine, take it as soon as possible. However, if it is within 4 hours of your next dose, skip the missed dose and go back to your regular dosing schedule. Do not double doses.

Storage—To store this medicine:
- Keep out of the reach of children.
- Store away from heat and direct light.
- Do not store the capsule form of this medicine in the bathroom, near the kitchen sink, or in other damp places. Heat or moisture may cause the medicine to break down.
- Keep the liquid form of this medicine from freezing. Do not refrigerate.
- Do not keep outdated medicine or medicine that is no longer needed. Be sure any discarded medicine is out of the reach of children.

Precautions While Using This Medicine

Your doctor should check your progress at regular visits, especially during the first few months of treatment with this medicine. During this time the amount of medicine you are taking may have to be changed often to meet your individual needs.

If you have been taking a succinimide anticonvulsant regularly, do not stop taking it without first checking with your doctor. Your doctor may want you to reduce gradually the amount you are taking before stopping completely. Stopping this medicine suddenly may cause seizures.

Do not start or stop taking any other medicine without your doctor's advice. Other medicines may affect the way this medicine works.

This medicine will add to the effects of alcohol and other CNS depressants (medicines that slow down the nervous system, possibly causing drowsiness). Some examples of CNS depressants are antihistamines or medicine for hay fever, other allergies, or colds; sedatives, tranquilizers, or sleeping medicine; prescription pain medicine or narcotics; barbiturates; medicine for seizures; muscle relaxants; or anesthetics, including some dental anesthetics. *Check with your doctor before taking any of the above while you are using this medicine.*

This medicine may cause some people to become drowsy or less alert than they are normally. *Make sure you know how you react to this medicine before you drive, use machines, or do anything else that could be dangerous if you are not alert.* After you have taken this medicine for a while, this effect may lessen.

Before having any kind of surgery, dental treatment, or emergency treatment, tell the medical doctor or dentist in charge that you are taking this medicine. Taking succinimide anticonvulsants together with medicines that are used during surgery or dental or emergency treatments may increase the CNS depressant effects.

Your doctor may want you to carry a medical identification card or bracelet stating that you are taking this medicine.

For patients taking *methsuximide*:
- Do not use capsules that are not full or in which the contents have melted, because they may not work properly.

Side Effects of This Medicine

Along with its needed effects, a medicine may cause some unwanted effects. Although not all of these side effects may occur, if they do occur they may need medical attention.

Check with your doctor as soon as possible if any of the following side effects occur:

More common
Muscle pain; skin rash and itching; swollen glands; sore throat and fever

Less common
Aggressiveness; difficulty in concentration; mental depression; nightmares

Rare
Chills; increased chance of certain types of seizures; mood or mental changes; nosebleeds or other unusual bleeding or bruising; shortness of breath; sores, ulcers, or white spots on lips or in mouth; unusual tiredness or weakness; wheezing, tightness in chest, or troubled breathing

Symptoms of overdose
Drowsiness (severe); nausea and vomiting (severe); troubled breathing

Other side effects may occur that usually do not need medical attention. These side effects may go away during treatment as your body adjusts to the medicine. However, check with your doctor if any of the following side effects continue or are bothersome:

More common
Clumsiness or unsteadiness; dizziness; drowsiness; headache; hiccups; loss of appetite; nausea or vomiting; stomach cramps

Less common
Irritability

Phensuximide may cause the urine to turn pink, red, or red-brown. This is harmless and is to be expected while you are taking this medicine.

Other side effects not listed above may also occur in some patients. If you notice any other effects, check with your doctor.

Revised: 05/23/94

ANTIDEPRESSANTS, MONOAMINE OXIDASE (MAO) INHIBITOR Systemic

Some commonly used brand names are:

In the U.S.—

Marplan[1] Parnate[3]
Nardil[2]

In Canada—

Marplan[1] Parnate[3]
Nardil[2]

Note: For quick reference, the following antidepressants are numbered to match the corresponding brand names.

This information applies to the following medicines:

1. Isocarboxazid (eye-soe-kar-BOX-a-zid)
2. Phenelzine (FEN-el-zeen)
3. Tranylcypromine (tran-ill-SIP-roe-meen)

Note: This information does *not* apply to furazolidone, procarbazine, or selegiline.

Description

Monoamine oxidase (MAO) inhibitors are used to relieve certain types of mental depression. They work by blocking the action of a chemical substance known as monoamine oxidase (MAO) in the nervous system.

Although these medicines are very effective for certain patients, they may also cause some unwanted reactions if not taken in the right way. It is very important to avoid certain foods, beverages, and medicines while you are being treated with an MAO inhibitor. Your health care professional will help you obtain a list to carry in your wallet or purse as a reminder of which products you should avoid.

MAO inhibitors are available only with your doctor's prescription, in the following dosage forms:

Oral

Isocarboxazid
- Tablets (U.S. and Canada)

Phenelzine
- Tablets (U.S. and Canada)

Tranylcypromine
- Tablets (U.S. and Canada)

Before Using This Medicine

In deciding to use a medicine, the risks of taking the medicine must be weighed against the good it will do. This is a decision you and your doctor will make. For monoamine oxidase (MAO) inhibitors, the following should be considered:

Allergies—Tell your doctor if you have ever had any unusual or allergic reaction to any MAO inhibitor. Also tell your health care professional if you are allergic to any other substances, such as foods, preservatives, or dyes.

Diet—Dangerous reactions such as sudden high blood pressure may result when MAO inhibitors are taken with certain foods or drinks. The following foods should be avoided:

- Foods that have a high tyramine content (most common in foods that are aged or fermented to increase their flavor), such as cheeses; fava or broad bean pods; yeast or meat extracts; smoked or pickled meat, poultry, or fish; fermented sausage (bologna, pepperoni, salami, summer sausage) or other fermented meat; sauerkraut; or any overripe fruit. If a list of these foods and beverages is not given to you, ask your health care professional to provide one.
- Alcoholic beverages or alcohol-free or reduced-alcohol beer and wine.
- Large amounts of caffeine-containing food or beverages such as coffee, tea, cola, or chocolate.

Pregnancy—A limited study in pregnant women showed an increased risk of birth defects when these medicines were taken during the first 3 months of pregnancy. In animal studies, MAO inhibitors caused a slowing of growth and increased excitability in the newborn when very large doses were given to the mother during pregnancy.

Breast-feeding—Tranylcypromine passes into the breast milk; it is not known whether isocarboxazid or phenelzine passes into breast milk. Problems in nursing babies have not been reported.

Children—Studies on these medicines have been done only in adult patients, and there is no specific information comparing use of MAO inhibitors in children with use in other age groups. However, animal studies have shown that these medicines may slow growth in the young. Therefore, be sure to discuss with your doctor the use of these medicines in children.

Older adults—Dizziness or lightheadedness may be especially likely to occur in elderly patients, who are usually more sensitive than younger adults to these effects of MAO inhibitors.

Other medicines—Although certain medicines should not be used together at all, in other cases 2 different medicines may be used together even if an interaction might occur. In these cases, your doctor may want to change the dose, or other precautions may be necessary. When you are taking MAO inhibitors, it is especially important that your health care professional know if you are taking any of the following:

- Amphetamines or
- Antihypertensives (high blood pressure medicine) or
- Appetite suppressants (diet pills) or
- Cyclobenzaprine (e.g., Flexeril) or
- Fluoxetine (e.g., Prozac) or
- Levodopa (e.g., Dopar, Larodopa) or
- Maprotiline (e.g., Ludiomil) or
- Medicine for asthma or other breathing problems or
- Medicines for colds, sinus problems, or hay fever or other allergies (including nose drops or sprays) or
- Meperidine (e.g., Demerol) or
- Methylphenidate (e.g., Ritalin) or
- Monoamine oxidase (MAO) inhibitors, other, including furazolidone (e.g., Furoxone), procarbazine (e.g., Matulane), or selegiline (e.g., Eldepryl), or
- Paroxetine (e.g., Paxil), or
- Sertraline (e.g., Zoloft), or
- Tricyclic antidepressants (amitriptyline [e.g., Elavil], amoxapine [e.g., Asendin], clomipramine [e.g., Anafranil], desipramine [e.g., Pertofrane], doxepin [e.g., Sinequan], imipramine [e.g., Tofranil], nortriptyline [e.g., Aventyl], protriptyline [e.g., Vivactil], trimipramine [e.g., Surmon-

til])—Using these medicines while you are taking or within 2 weeks of taking MAO inhibitors may cause serious side effects such as sudden rise in body temperature, extremely high blood pressure, severe convulsions, and death; however, sometimes certain of these medicines may be used with MAO inhibitors under close supervision by your doctor

- Antidiabetics, oral (diabetes medicine you take by mouth) or
- Insulin—MAO inhibitors may change the amount of antidiabetic medicine you need to take
- Bupropion (e.g., Wellbutrin)—Using bupropion while you are taking or within 2 weeks of taking MAO inhibitors may cause serious side effects such as seizures
- Buspirone (e.g., BuSpar)—Use with MAO inhibitors may cause high blood pressure
- Carbamazepine (e.g., Tegretol)—Use with MAO inhibitors may increase seizures
- Central nervous system (CNS) depressants (medicines that cause drowsiness)—Using these medicines with MAO inhibitors may increase the CNS and other depressant effects
- Cocaine—Cocaine use by persons taking MAO inhibitors, including furazolidone and procarbazine, may cause a severe increase in blood pressure
- Dextromethorphan—Use with MAO inhibitors may cause excitement, high blood pressure, and fever
- Trazodone or
- Tryptophan used as a food supplement or a sleep aid—Use of these medicines by persons taking MAO inhibitors, including furazolidone and procarbazine, may cause mental confusion, excitement, shivering, trouble in breathing, or fever

Other medical problems—The presence of other medical problems may affect the use of MAO inhibitors. Make sure you tell your doctor if you have any other medical problems, especially:

- Alcohol abuse—Drinking alcohol while you are taking an MAO inhibitor may cause serious side effects
- Angina (chest pain) or
- Headaches (severe or frequent)—These conditions may interfere with warning signs of serious side effects of MAO inhibitors
- Asthma or bronchitis—Some medicines used to treat these conditions may cause serious side effects when used while you are taking an MAO inhibitor
- Diabetes mellitus (sugar diabetes)—These medicines may change the amount of insulin or oral antidiabetic medication that you need
- Epilepsy—Seizures may occur more often
- Heart or blood vessel disease or
- Liver disease or
- Mental illness (or history of) or
- Parkinson's disease or
- Recent heart attack or stroke—MAO inhibitors may make the condition worse
- High blood pressure—Condition may be affected by these medicines
- Kidney disease—Higher blood levels of MAO inhibitors may occur, which increases the chance of side effects
- Overactive thyroid or
- Pheochromocytoma (PCC)—Serious side effects may occur

Proper Use of This Medicine

Sometimes this medicine must be taken for several weeks before you begin to feel better. Your doctor should check your progress at regular visits, especially during the first few months of treatment, to make sure that this medicine is working properly and to check for unwanted effects.

Take this medicine only as directed by your doctor. Do not take more of it, do not take it more often, and do not take it for a longer time than your doctor ordered.

MAO inhibitors may be taken with or without food or on a full or empty stomach. However, if your doctor tells you to take the medicine a certain way, take it exactly as directed.

Dosing—The dose of MAO inhibitors will be different for different patients. *Follow your doctor's orders or the directions on the label.* The following information includes only the average doses of isocarboxazid, phenelzine, and tranylcypromine. *If your dose is different, do not change it* unless your doctor tells you to do so.

The number of tablets that you take depends on the strength of the medicine. Also, *the number of doses you take each day, the time allowed between doses, and the length of time you take the medicine depend on the medical problem for which you are using an MAO inhibitor.*

For isocarboxazid

- For *oral* dosage form (tablets):
  - —For treatment of depression:
    - Adults—To start, 30 milligrams (mg) a day. Your doctor may decrease or increase your dose as needed. However, the dose is usually not more than 60 mg a day.
    - Children up to 16 years of age—Use and dose must be determined by the doctor.

For phenelzine

- For *oral* dosage form (tablets):
  - —For treatment of depression:
    - Adults—Dose is based on your body weight. To start, the usual dose is 1 milligram (mg) per kilogram (kg) of body weight (0.45 mg per pound) a day. Your doctor may decrease or increase your dose as needed. However, the dose is usually not more than 90 mg a day.
    - Children up to 16 years of age—Use and dose must be determined by the doctor.
    - Older adults—To start, 15 mg in the morning. Your doctor may increase your dose gradually as needed. However, the dose is usually not more than 60 mg a day.

For tranylcypromine

- For *oral* dosage form (tablets):
  - —For treatment of depression:
    - Adults—To start, 30 milligrams (mg) a day. Your doctor may increase your dose gradually as needed. However, the dose is usually not more than 60 mg a day.

- Children up to 16 years of age—Use and dose must be determined by the doctor.
- Older adults—To start, 2.5 to 5 mg a day. The doctor may increase your dose as needed. However, the dose is usually not more than 45 mg a day.

Missed dose—If you miss a dose of this medicine, take it as soon as possible. However, if it is within 2 hours of your next dose, skip the missed dose and go back to your regular dosing schedule. Do not double doses.

Storage—To store this medicine:
- Keep out of the reach of children.
- Store away from heat and direct light.
- Do not store in the bathroom, near the kitchen sink, or in other damp places. Heat or moisture may cause the medicine to break down.
- Do not keep outdated medicine or medicine no longer needed. Be sure that any discarded medicine is out of the reach of children.

Precautions While Using This Medicine

When taken with certain foods, drinks, or other medicines, MAO inhibitors can cause very dangerous reactions such as sudden high blood pressure (also called hypertensive crisis). To avoid such reactions, *obey the following rules of caution:*
- Do not eat foods that have a high tyramine content (most common in foods that are aged or fermented to increase their flavor), such as cheeses; fava or broad bean pods; yeast or meat extracts; smoked or pickled meat, poultry, or fish; fermented sausage (bologna, pepperoni, salami, and summer sausage) or other fermented meat; sauerkraut; or any overripe fruit. If a list of these foods is not given to you, ask your health care professional to provide one.
- Do not drink alcoholic beverages or alcohol-free or reduced-alcohol beer and wine.
- Do not eat or drink large amounts of caffeine-containing food or beverages such as coffee, tea, cola, or chocolate.
- Do not take any other medicine unless approved or prescribed by your doctor. This especially includes nonprescription (over-the-counter [OTC]) medicine, such as that for colds (including nose drops or sprays), cough, asthma, hay fever, and appetite control; ''keep awake'' products; or products that make you sleepy.

This medicine will add to the effects of alcohol and other CNS depressants (medicines that slow down the nervous system, possibly causing drowsiness). Some examples of CNS depressants are antihistamines or medicine for hay fever, other allergies, or colds; sedatives, tranquilizers, or sleeping medicine; prescription pain medicine or narcotics; barbiturates; medicine for seizures; muscle relaxants; or anesthetics, including some dental anesthetics. *Check with your doctor before taking any of the above while you are using this medicine.*

Check with your doctor or hospital emergency room immediately if severe headache, stiff neck, chest pains, fast heartbeat, or nausea and vomiting occur while you are taking this medicine. These may be symptoms of a serious side effect that should have a doctor's attention.

Do not stop taking this medicine without first checking with your doctor. Your doctor may want you to reduce gradually the amount you are using before stopping completely.

Dizziness, lightheadedness, or fainting may occur, especially when you get up from a lying or sitting position. *Getting up slowly may help.* When you get up from lying down, sit on the edge of the bed with your feet dangling for 1 or 2 minutes. Then stand up slowly. If the problem continues or gets worse, check with your doctor.

This medicine may cause blurred vision or make some people drowsy or less alert than they are normally. *Make sure you know how you react to this medicine before you drive, use machines, or do anything else that could be dangerous if you are unable to see well or are not alert.*

Before having any kind of surgery, dental treatment, or emergency treatment, tell the medical doctor or dentist in charge that you are using this medicine or have used it within the past 2 weeks. Taking MAO inhibitors together with medicines that are used during surgery or dental or emergency treatments may increase the risk of serious side effects.

Your doctor may want you to carry an identification card stating that you are using this medicine.

For patients with *angina* (chest pain):
- This medicine may cause you to have an unusual feeling of good health and energy. However, *do not suddenly increase the amount of exercise you get without discussing it with your doctor.* Too much activity could bring on an attack of angina.

For *diabetic* patients:
- This medicine may affect blood sugar levels. While you are using this medicine, be especially careful in testing for sugar in your blood or urine. If you have any questions about this, check with your doctor.

After you stop using this medicine, you must continue to obey the rules of caution for at least 2 weeks concerning food, drink, and other medicine, since these things may continue to react with MAO inhibitors.

Side Effects of This Medicine

Along with its needed effects, a medicine may cause some unwanted effects. Although not all of these side effects may occur, if they do occur they may need medical attention.

Stop taking this medicine and get emergency help immediately if any of the following side effects occur:

Symptoms of unusually high blood pressure (hypertensive crisis)

Chest pain (severe); enlarged pupils; fast or slow heartbeat; headache (severe); increased sensitivity of eyes to light; increased sweating (possibly with fever or cold, clammy skin); nausea and vomiting; stiff or sore neck

Check with your doctor as soon as possible if any of the following side effects occur:

More common

Dizziness or lightheadedness (severe), especially when getting up from a lying or sitting position

Less common

Diarrhea; fast or pounding heartbeat; swelling of feet or lower legs; unusual excitement or nervousness

Rare

Dark urine; fever; skin rash; slurred speech; sore throat; staggering walk; yellow eyes or skin

Symptoms of overdose

Anxiety (severe); confusion; convulsions (seizures); cool, clammy skin; dizziness (severe); drowsiness (severe); fast and irregular pulse; fever; hallucinations (seeing, hearing, or feeling things that are not there); headache (severe); high or low blood pressure; muscle stiffness; sweating; troubled breathing; trouble in sleeping (severe); unusual irritability

Other side effects may occur that usually do not need medical attention. These side effects may go away during treatment as your body adjusts to the medicine. However, check with your doctor if any of the following side effects continue or are bothersome:

More common

Blurred vision; decreased amount of urine; decreased sexual ability; dizziness or lightheadedness (mild), especially when getting up from a lying or sitting position; drowsiness; headache (mild); increased appetite (especially for sweets) or weight gain; increased sweating; muscle twitching during sleep; restlessness; shakiness or trembling; tiredness and weakness; trouble in sleeping

Less common or rare

Chills; constipation; decreased appetite; dryness of mouth

Other side effects not listed above may also occur in some patients. If you notice any other effects, check with your doctor.

Additional Information

Once a medicine has been approved for marketing for a certain use, experience may show that it is also useful for other medical problems. Although these uses are not included in product labeling, phenelzine and tranylcypromine are used in certain patients with the following medical conditions:

- Headache
- Panic disorder

Other than the above information, there is no additional information relating to proper use, precautions, or side effects for these uses.

Revised: 05/23/94

ANTIDEPRESSANTS, TRICYCLIC Systemic

Some commonly used brand names are:

In the U.S.—

Anafranil[3]
Asendin[2]
Aventyl[7]
Elavil[1]
Endep[1]
Norfranil[6]
Norpramin[4]
Pamelor[7]
Sinequan[5]
Surmontil[9]
Tipramine[6]
Tofranil[6]
Tofranil-PM[6]
Vivactil[8]

In Canada—

Anafranil[3]
Apo-Amitriptyline[1]
Apo-Imipramine[6]
Apo-Trimip[9]
Asendin[2]
Aventyl[7]
Elavil[1]
Impril[6]
Levate[1]
Norpramin[4]
Novo-Doxepin[5]
Novopramine[6]
Novo-Tripramine[9]
Novotriptyn[1]
Pertofrane[4]
Rhotrimine[9]
Sinequan[5]
Surmontil[9]
Tofranil[6]
Triadapin[5]
Triptil[8]

Note: For quick reference, the following tricyclic antidepressants are numbered to match the corresponding brand names.

This information applies to the following medicines:

1. Amitriptyline (a-mee-TRIP-ti-leen)‡§
2. Amoxapine (a-MOX-a-peen)‡
3. Clomipramine (cloe-MIP-ra-meen)‡
4. Desipramine (dess-IP-ra-meen)‡§
5. Doxepin (DOX-e-pin)‡
6. Imipramine (im-IP-ra-meen)‡
7. Nortriptyline (nor-TRIP-ti-leen)‡
8. Protriptyline (proe-TRIP-ti-leen)‡
9. Trimipramine (trye-MIP-ra-meen)‡

‡Generic name product may also be available in the U.S.
§Generic name product may also be available in Canada.

Description

Tricyclic antidepressants are used to relieve mental depression.

One form of this medicine (imipramine) is also used to treat enuresis (bedwetting) in children. Another form (clomipramine) is used to treat obsessive-compulsive disorders. Tricyclic antidepressants may be used for other conditions as determined by your doctor.

These medicines are available only with your doctor's prescription, in the following dosage forms:

Oral

Amitriptyline
- Syrup (Canada)
- Tablets (U.S. and Canada)

Amoxapine
- Tablets (U.S. and Canada)

Clomipramine
- Capsules (U.S.)
- Tablets (Canada)

Desipramine
- Tablets (U.S. and Canada)

Doxepin
- Capsules (U.S. and Canada)
- Oral solution (U.S.)

Imipramine
- Capsules (U.S.)
- Tablets (U.S. and Canada)

Nortriptyline
- Capsules (U.S. and Canada)
- Oral solution (U.S.)

Protriptyline
- Tablets (U.S. and Canada)

Trimipramine
- Capsules (U.S. and Canada)
- Tablets (Canada)

Parenteral

Amitriptyline
- Injection (U.S.)

Imipramine
- Injection (U.S.)

Before Using This Medicine

In deciding to use a medicine, the risks of taking the medicine must be weighed against the good it will do. This is a decision you and your doctor will make. For tricyclic antidepressants, the following should be considered:

Allergies—Tell your doctor if you have ever had any unusual or allergic reaction to any tricyclic antidepressant or to carbamazepine, maprotiline, or trazodone. Also tell your health care professional if you are allergic to any other substances, such as foods, preservatives, or dyes.

Pregnancy—Studies have not been done in pregnant women. However, there have been reports of newborns suffering from muscle spasms and heart, breathing, and urinary problems when their mothers had taken tricyclic antidepressants immediately before delivery. Also, studies in animals have shown that some tricyclic antidepressants may cause unwanted effects in the fetus.

Breast-feeding—Tricyclic antidepressants pass into the breast milk. Doxepin has been reported to cause drowsiness in the nursing baby.

Children—Children are especially sensitive to the effects of this medicine. This may increase the chance of side effects during treatment. However, side effects in children taking this medicine for bedwetting usually disappear upon continued use. The most common of these are nervousness, sleeping problems, tiredness, and mild stomach upset. If these side effects continue or are bothersome, check with your doctor.

Older adults—Drowsiness, dizziness, confusion, vision problems, dryness of mouth, constipation, and problems in urinating are more likely to occur in elderly patients, who are usually more sensitive than younger adults to the effects of tricyclic antidepressants.

Other medicines—Although certain medicines should not be used together at all, in other cases 2 different medicines may be used together even if an interaction might occur. In these cases, your doctor may want to change the dose, or other precautions may be necessary. When you are taking a tricyclic antidepressant, it is especially important that your health care professional know if you are taking any of the following:

- Amphetamines or
- Appetite suppressants (diet pills) or
- Ephedrine or
- Epinephrine (e.g., Adrenalin) or
- Isoproterenol (e.g., Isuprel) or
- Medicine for asthma or other breathing problems or
- Medicine for colds, sinus problems, or hay fever or other allergies or
- Phenylephrine (e.g., Neo-Synephrine)—Using these medicines with tricyclic antidepressants may increase the risk of serious effects on the heart
- Antipsychotics (medicine for mental illness) or
- Clonidine (e.g., Catapres)—Using these medicines with tricyclic antidepressants may increase the CNS depressant effects and increase the chance of serious side effects
- Antithyroid agents (medicine for overactive thyroid) or
- Cimetidine (e.g., Tagamet)—Using these medicines with tricyclic antidepressants may increase the chance of serious side effects
- Central nervous system (CNS) depressants (medicine that causes drowsiness)—Using these medicines with tricyclic antidepressants may increase the CNS depressant effects
- Guanadrel (e.g., Hylorel) or
- Guanethidine (e.g., Ismelin)—Tricyclic antidepressants may keep these medicines from working as well
- Methyldopa (e.g., Aldomet) or
- Metoclopramide (e.g., Reglan) or
- Metyrosine (e.g., Demser) or
- Pemoline (e.g., Cylert) or
- Pimozide (e.g., Orap) or
- Promethazine (e.g., Phenergan) or
- Rauwolfia alkaloids (alseroxylon [e.g., Rauwiloid], deserpidine [e.g., Harmonyl], rauwolfia serpentina [e.g., Raudixin], reserpine [e.g., Serpasil]) or
- Trimeprazine (e.g., Temaril)—Tricyclic antidepressants may cause certain side effects to be more severe and occur more often
- Metrizamide—The risk of seizures may be increased
- Monoamine oxidase (MAO) inhibitors (furazolidone [e.g., Furoxone], isocarboxazid [e.g., Marplan], phenelzine [e.g., Nardil], procarbazine [e.g., Matulane], selegiline [e.g., Eldepryl], tranylcypromine [e.g., Parnate])—Taking tricyclic antidepressants while you are taking or within 2 weeks of taking MAO inhibitors may cause sudden high body temperature, extremely high blood pressure, severe convulsions, and death; however, sometimes certain of these medicines may be used together under close supervision by your doctor

Other medical problems—The presence of other medical problems may affect the use of tricyclic antidepressants. Make sure you tell your doctor if you have any other medical problems, especially:

- Alcohol abuse (or history of)—Drinking alcohol may cause increased CNS depressant effects
- Asthma or
- Bipolar disorder (manic-depressive illness) or
- Blood disorders or
- Convulsions (seizures) or
- Difficult urination or
- Enlarged prostate or
- Glaucoma or increased eye pressure or
- Heart disease or
- High blood pressure (hypertension) or
- Schizophrenia—Tricyclic antidepressants may make the condition worse
- Kidney disease or
- Liver disease—Higher blood levels of tricyclic antidepressants may result, increasing the chance of side effects
- Overactive thyroid or
- Stomach or intestinal problems—Tricyclic antidepressants may cause an increased chance of serious side effects

Proper Use of This Medicine

To lessen stomach upset, take this medicine with food, even for a daily bedtime dose, unless your doctor has told you to take it on an empty stomach.

Take this medicine only as directed by your doctor, to benefit your condition as much as possible. Do not take more of it, do not take it more often, and do not take it for a longer time than your doctor ordered.

Sometimes this medicine must be taken for several weeks before you begin to feel better. Your doctor should check your progress at regular visits.

To use *doxepin oral solution:*

- This medicine is to be taken by mouth even though it comes in a dropper bottle. The amount you should take should be measured with the dropper provided with your prescription and diluted just before you take each dose. Dilute each dose with about one-half glass (4 ounces) of water, milk, citrus fruit juice, tomato juice, or prune juice. Do not mix this medicine with grape juice or carbonated beverages since these may decrease the medicine's effectiveness.
- Doxepin oral solution must be mixed immediately before you take it. Do not prepare it ahead of time.

Dosing—The dose of tricyclic antidepressants will be different for different patients. *Follow your doctor's orders or the directions on the label.* The following information includes only the average doses of tricyclic antidepressants. *If your dose is different, do not change it* unless your doctor tells you to do so.

The number of capsules or tablets, or the amount of solution or syrup that you take depends on the strength of the medicine. Also, *the number of doses you take each day, the time allowed between doses, and the length of time you take the medicine depend on the medical problem for which you are taking tricyclic antidepressants.*

For amitriptyline

- For *tablet* dosage form:
  - —For depression:
    - Adults—At first, 25 milligrams (mg) two to four times a day. Your doctor may increase your dose gradually as needed. However, the dose is usually not more than 150 mg a day, unless you are in the hospital. Some hospitalized patients may need higher doses.
    - Teenagers—At first, 10 mg three times a day, and 20 mg at bedtime. Your doctor may increase your dose gradually as needed. However, the dose is usually not more than 100 mg a day.
    - Children 6 to 12 years of age—10 to 30 mg a day.
    - Children up to 6 years of age—Use and dose must be determined by your doctor.
    - Older adults— At first, 25 mg at bedtime. Your doctor may increase your dose gradually as needed. However, the dose is usually not more than 100 mg a day.
- For *syrup* dosage form:
  - —For depression:
    - Adults—At first, 25 mg two to four times a day. Your doctor may increase your dose gradually as needed.
    - Teenagers—At first, 10 mg three times a day, and 20 mg at bedtime. Your doctor may increase your dose gradually as needed. However, the dose is usually not more than 100 mg a day.
    - Children 6 to 12 years of age—10 to 30 mg a day.
    - Children up to 6 years of age—Use and dose must be determined by your doctor.
    - Older adults—At first, 10 mg three times a day, and 20 mg at bedtime. Your doctor may increase your dose gradually as needed. However, the dose is usually not more than 100 mg a day.
- For *injection* dosage form:
  - —For depression:
    - Adults—20 to 30 mg four times a day, injected into a muscle.
    - Children up to 12 years of age—Use and dose must be determined by your doctor.

For amoxapine

- For *tablet* dosage form:
  - —For depression:
    - Adults—At first, 50 milligrams (mg) two to three times a day. Your doctor may increase your dose gradually as needed.
    - Children up to 16 years of age—Use and dose must be determined by your doctor.
    - Older adults—At first, 25 mg two to three times a day. Your doctor may increase your dose gradually as needed.

For clomipramine

- For *capsule or tablet* dosage forms:
  - —For obsessive-compulsive disorders:
    - Adults—At first, 25 milligrams (mg) once a day. Your doctor may increase your dose gradually as needed. However, the dose is usually not more than 250 mg a day, unless you are in the hospital. Some hospitalized patients may need higher doses.
    - Teenagers and children 10 years of age and over—At first, 25 mg once a day. Your doctor may increase your dose gradually as needed. However, the dose is usually not more than 200 mg a day.
    - Children up to 10 years of age—Use and dose must be determined by your doctor.
    - Older adults—At first, 20 to 30 mg a day. Your doctor may increase your dose gradually as needed.

For desipramine

- For *tablet* dosage form:
  - —For depression:
    - Adults—100 to 200 milligrams (mg) a day. Your doctor may increase your dose gradually as needed. However, the dose is usually not more than 300 mg a day.
    - Teenagers—25 to 50 mg a day. Your doctor may increase your dose gradually as needed. However, the dose is usually not more than 100 mg a day.
    - Children 6 to 12 years of age—10 to 30 mg a day.
    - Older adults—25 to 50 mg a day. Your doctor may increase your dose gradually as needed. However, the dose is usually not more than 150 mg a day.

For doxepin

- For *capsule or solution* dosage forms:
  - —For depression:
    - Adults—At first, 25 milligrams (mg) three times a day. Your doctor may increase your dose gradually as needed. However, the dose is usually not more than 150 mg a day, unless you are in the hospital. Some hospitalized patients may need higher doses.
    - Children up to 12 years of age—Use and dose must be determined by your doctor.
    - Older adults—At first, 25 to 50 mg a day. Your doctor may increase your dose gradually as needed.

For imipramine

- For *tablet* dosage form:
  - —For depression:
    - Adults—25 to 50 milligrams (mg) three to four times a day. Your doctor may increase your dose gradually as needed. However, the dose is usually not more than 200 mg a day, unless you are in the hospital. Some hospitalized patients may need higher doses.
    - Adolescents—25 to 50 mg a day. Your doctor may increase your dose gradually as needed. However, the dose is usually not more than 100 mg a day.
    - Children 6 to 12 years of age—10 to 30 mg a day.
    - Children up to 6 years of age—Use and dose must be determined by your doctor.
    - Older adults—At first, 25 mg at bedtime. Your doctor may increase your dose gradually as needed. However, the dose is usually not more than 100 mg a day.
  - —For bedwetting:
    - Children—25 mg once a day, taken one hour before bedtime. Your doctor may increase the dose as needed, based on the child's age.
- For *capsule* dosage form:
  - —For depression:
    - Adults—At first, 75 mg a day taken at bedtime. Your doctor may increase your dose gradually as needed. However, the dose is usually not more than 200 mg a day, unless you are in the hospital. Some hospitalized patients may need higher doses.
    - Children up to 12 years of age—Use and dose must be determined by your doctor.
- For *injection* dosage form:
  - —For depression:
    - Adults—Dose must be determined by your doctor. It is injected into a muscle. The dose is usually not more than 300 mg a day.
    - Children up to 12 years of age—Use and dose must be determined by your doctor.

For nortriptyline

- For *capsule or solution* dosage forms:
  - —For depression:
    - Adults—25 milligrams (mg) three to four times a day. Your doctor may increase your dose gradually as needed. However, the dose is usually not more than 150 mg a day.
    - Teenagers—25 to 50 mg a day. Your doctor may increase your dose gradually as needed.
    - Children 6 to 12 years of age—10 to 20 mg a day.
    - Older adults—30 to 50 mg a day. Your doctor may increase your dose gradually as needed.

For protriptyline

- For *tablet* dosage form:
  - —For depression:
    - Adults—At first, 5 to 10 milligrams (mg) three to four times a day. Your doctor may increase your dose gradually as needed. However, the dose is usually not more than 60 mg a day.
    - Teenagers—At first, 5 mg three times a day. Your doctor may increase your dose gradually as needed.
    - Children up to 12 years of age—Use and dose must be determined by your doctor.
    - Older adults—At first, 5 mg three times a day. Your doctor may increase your dose gradually as needed.

For trimipramine

- For *capsule or tablet* dosage forms:
  - —For depression:
    - Adults—At first, 75 milligrams (mg) a day. Your doctor may increase your dose as needed. However, the dose is usually not more than 200 mg a day, unless you are hospitalized. Some hospitalized patients may need higher doses.
    - Teenagers—At first, 50 mg a day. Your doctor may increase your dose gradually as needed. However, the dose is usually not more than 100 mg a day.

- Children up to 12 years of age—Use and dose must be determined by your doctor.
- Older adults—At first, 50 mg a day. Your doctor may increase your dose gradually as needed. However, the dose is usually not more than 100 mg a day.

Missed dose—If you miss a dose of this medicine and your dosing schedule is:

- One dose a day at bedtime—Do not take the missed dose in the morning since it may cause disturbing side effects during waking hours. Instead, check with your doctor.
- More than one dose a day—Take the missed dose as soon as possible. However, if it is almost time for your next dose, skip the missed dose, and go back to your regular dosing schedule. Do not double doses.

If you have any questions about this, check with your doctor.

Storage—To store this medicine:

- Keep out of the reach of children. Overdose of this medicine is very dangerous in young children.
- Store away from heat and direct light.
- Do not store the tablet or capsule form of this medicine in the bathroom, near the kitchen sink, or in other damp places. Heat or moisture may cause the medicine to break down.
- Keep the liquid form of this medicine from freezing.
- Do not keep outdated medicine or medicine no longer needed. Be sure that any discarded medicine is out of the reach of children.

Precautions While Using This Medicine

It is very important that your doctor check your progress at regular visits to allow dosage adjustments and to help reduce side effects.

This medicine will add to the effects of alcohol and other CNS depressants (medicines that make you drowsy or less alert). Some examples of CNS depressants are antihistamines or medicine for hay fever, other allergies, or colds; sedatives, tranquilizers, or sleeping medicine; prescription pain medicine or narcotics; barbiturates; medicine for seizures; muscle relaxants; or anesthetics, including some dental anesthetics. *Check with your medical doctor or dentist before taking any of the above while you are taking this medicine.*

This medicine may cause some people to become drowsy. *If this occurs, do not drive, use machines, or do anything else that could be dangerous if you are not alert.*

Dizziness, lightheadedness, or fainting may occur, especially when you get up from a lying or sitting position. Getting up slowly may help. If this problem continues or gets worse, check with your doctor.

This medicine may cause dryness of the mouth. For temporary relief, use sugarless gum or candy, melt bits of ice in your mouth, or use a saliva substitute. However, if your mouth continues to feel dry for more than 2 weeks, check with your medical doctor or dentist. Continuing dryness of the mouth may increase the chance of dental disease, including tooth decay, gum disease, and fungus infections.

Tricyclic antidepressants may cause your skin to be more sensitive to sunlight than it is normally. Exposure to sunlight, even for brief periods of time, may cause a skin rash, itching, redness or other discoloration of the skin, or a severe sunburn. When you begin taking this medicine:

- Stay out of direct sunlight, especially between the hours of 10:00 a.m. and 3:00 p.m., if possible.
- Wear protective clothing, including a hat. Also, wear sunglasses.
- Apply a sun block product that has a skin protection factor (SPF) of at least 15. Some patients may require a product with a higher SPF number, especially if they have a fair complexion. If you have any questions about this, check with your health care professional.
- Apply a sun block lipstick that has an SPF of at least 15 to protect your lips.
- Do not use a sunlamp or tanning bed or booth.

If you have a severe reaction from the sun, check with your doctor.

Before you have any medical tests, tell the medical doctor in charge that you are taking this medicine. The results of the metyrapone test may be affected by this medicine.

Before having any kind of surgery, dental treatment, or emergency treatment, tell the medical doctor or dentist in charge that you are using this medicine. Taking tricyclic antidepressants together with medicines used during surgery or dental or emergency treatments may increase the risk of side effects.

For diabetic patients:

- This medicine may affect blood sugar levels. If you notice a change in the results of your blood or urine sugar tests or if you have any questions, check with your doctor.

Do not stop taking this medicine without first checking with your doctor. Your doctor may want you to reduce gradually the amount you are using before stopping completely. This may help prevent a possible worsening of your condition and reduce the possibility of withdrawal symptoms such as headache, nausea, and/or an overall feeling of discomfort.

The effects of this medicine may last for 3 to 7 days after you have stopped taking it. Therefore, all the precautions stated here must be observed during this time.

For patients taking protriptyline:

- If taken late in the day, protriptyline may interfere with nighttime sleep.

Side Effects of This Medicine

Along with its needed effects, a medicine may cause some unwanted effects. Although not all of these side effects may occur, if they do occur they may need medical attention.

Stop taking this medicine and get emergency help immediately if any of the following side effects occur:

Reported for amoxapine only—rare

Convulsions (seizures); difficult or fast breathing; fever with increased sweating; high or low (irregular) blood pressure; loss of bladder control; muscle stiffness (severe); pale skin; unusual tiredness or weakness

Check with your doctor as soon as possible if any of the following side effects occur:

Less common

Blurred vision; confusion or delirium; constipation (especially in the elderly); decreased sexual ability (more common with amoxapine and clomipramine); difficulty in speaking or swallowing; eye pain; fainting; fast or irregular heartbeat (pounding, racing, skipping); hallucinations; loss of balance control; mask-like face; nervousness or restlessness; problems in urinating; shakiness or trembling; shuffling walk; slowed movements; stiffness of arms and legs

Reported for amoxapine only (in addition to the above)—less common

Lip smacking or puckering; puffing of cheeks; rapid or worm-like movements of tongue; uncontrolled chewing movements; uncontrolled movements of hands, arms, or legs

Rare

Anxiety; breast enlargement in both males and females; hair loss; inappropriate secretion of milk—in females; increased sensitivity to sunlight; irritability; muscle twitching; red or brownish spots on skin; ringing, buzzing, or other unexplained sounds in the ears; seizures (more common with clomipramine); skin rash and itching; sore throat and fever; swelling of face and tongue; swelling of testicles (more common with amoxapine); trouble with teeth or gums (more common with clomipramine); weakness; yellow eyes or skin

Symptoms of acute overdose

Confusion; convulsions (seizures); disturbed concentration; drowsiness (severe); enlarged pupils; fast, slow, or irregular heartbeat; fever; hallucinations (seeing, hearing, or feeling things that are not there); restlessness and agitation; shortness of breath or troubled breathing; unusual tiredness or weakness (severe); vomiting

Other side effects may occur that usually do not need medical attention. These side effects may go away during treatment as your body adjusts to the medicine. However, check with your doctor if any of the following side effects continue or are bothersome:

More common

Dizziness; drowsiness; dryness of mouth; headache; increased appetite (may include craving for sweets); nausea; tiredness or weakness (mild); unpleasant taste; weight gain

Less common

Diarrhea; heartburn; increased sweating; trouble in sleeping (more common with protriptyline, especially when taken late in the day); vomiting

Certain side effects of this medicine may occur after you have stopped taking it. Check with your doctor if you notice any of the following effects:

Headache; irritability; nausea, vomiting, or diarrhea; restlessness; trouble in sleeping, with vivid dreams; unusual excitement

Reported for amoxapine only (in addition to the above)

Lip smacking or puckering; puffing of cheeks; rapid or worm-like movements of the tongue; uncontrolled chewing movements; uncontrolled movements of arms or legs

Other side effects not listed above also may occur in some patients. If you notice any other effects, check with your doctor.

Additional Information

Once a medicine has been approved for marketing for a certain use, experience may show that it is also useful for other medical problems. Although these uses are not included in product labeling, tricyclic antidepressants are used in certain patients with the following medical conditions:

- Attention deficit hyperactivity disorder (hyperactivity in children) (desipramine, imipramine, and protriptyline)
- Bulimia (uncontrolled eating, followed by vomiting) (amitriptyline, clomipramine, desipramine, and imipramine)
- Cocaine withdrawal (desipramine and imipramine)
- Headache prevention (for certain types of frequent or continuing headaches) (most tricyclic antidepressants)
- Itching with hives due to cold temperature exposure (doxepin)
- Narcolepsy (extreme tendency to fall asleep suddenly) (clomipramine, desipramine, imipramine, and protriptyline)
- Neurogenic pain (a type of continuing pain) (amitriptyline, clomipramine, desipramine, doxepin, imipramine, nortriptyline, and trimipramine)
- Panic disorder (clomipramine, desipramine, doxepin, nortriptyline, and trimipramine)
- Stomach ulcer (amitriptyline, doxepin, and trimipramine)
- Urinary incontinence (imipramine)

Other than the above information, there is no additional information relating to proper use, precautions, or side effects for these uses.

Revised: 05/22/92
Interim revision: 06/01/92; 03/01/93; 04/29/94; 08/08/97

ANTIDIABETIC AGENTS, SULFONYLUREA Systemic

Some commonly used brand names are:

In the U.S.—

DiaBeta[5]	Micronase[5]
Diabinese[2]	Orinase[7]
Dymelor[1]	Tolinase[6]
Glucotrol[4]	Tol-Tab[7]
Glucotrol XL[4]	
Glynase PresTab[5]	

In Canada—

Albert Glyburide[5]	Euglucon[5]
Apo-Chlorpropamide[2]	Gen-Glybe[5]
Apo-Glyburide[5]	Mobenol[7]
Apo-Tolbutamide[7]	Novo-Butamide[7]
DiaBeta[5]	Novo-Glyburide[5]
Diabinese[2]	Novo-Propamide[2]
Diamicron[3]	Nu-Glyburide[5]
Dimelor[1]	Orinase[7]

Another commonly used name for glyburide is glibenclamide.

Note: For quick reference, the following oral antidiabetics are numbered to match the corresponding brand names.

This information applies to the following medicines:

1. Acetohexamide (a-set-oh-HEX-a-mide)‡
2. Chlorpropamide (klor-PROE-pa-mide)‡§
3. Gliclazide (GLIK-la-zide)*
4. Glipizide (GLIP-i-zide)†‡
5. Glyburide (GLYE-byoo-ride)‡
6. Tolazamide (tole-AZ-a-mide)†‡
7. Tolbutamide (tole-BYOO-ta-mide)‡§

*Not commercially available in the US.
†Not commercially available in Canada.
‡Generic name product may also be available in the U.S.
§Generic name product may also be available in Canada.

Description

Sulfonylurea antidiabetic agents (also known as sulfonylureas) are used to treat a certain type of diabetes mellitus (sugar diabetes) called non–insulin-dependent diabetes (NIDDM) or Type II diabetes. When you have NIDDM, insulin is still being produced by your pancreas. Sometimes the amount of insulin you produce may not be enough or your body may not be using it properly and you may still need more. Sulfonylureas work by causing your pancreas to release more insulin into the bloodstream. All of the cells in your body need insulin to help turn the food you eat into energy. This is done by using sugar (or glucose) in the blood as quick energy. Or you can store the sugar in the form of fats, sugars, and proteins for use later, such as for energy between meals.

Sometimes insulin that is being produced by the body is not able to help sugar get inside the body's cells. Sulfonylureas help insulin get into the cells where it can work properly to lower blood sugar. In this way, sulfonylureas will help lower blood sugar and help restore the way you use food to make energy.

Many people with NIDDM can be controlled with diet or diet and exercise alone. Following a diabetes diet plan and exercising will always be important with any type of diabetes. To work properly, the amount of sulfonylurea you use must be balanced against the amount and type of food you eat and the amount of exercise you do. If you change your diet, your exercise, or both, you will want to test your blood sugar level so that it doesn't drop too low (hypoglycemia) or rise too high (hyperglycemia). Your health care professional will teach you what to do if this happens.

Sometimes patients with NIDDM might need to change to treatment with insulin for a short period of time during pregnancy or for a serious medical condition, such as diabetic coma; ketoacidosis; severe injury, burn, or infection; or major surgery. In these conditions, insulin and blood sugar can change fast and blood sugar can be best controlled with insulin instead of a sulfonylurea.

At some point, a sulfonylurea may stop working as well and your blood sugar will go up. You will need to know if this happens and what to do. Instead of taking more of this medicine, your doctor may change you to another sulfonylurea. Or your doctor may have you inject small doses of insulin or take another oral antidiabetic medicine called metformin along with your sulfonylurea to help the insulin you make work better. If that doesn't bring down the amount of sugar in your blood, your doctor may have you stop taking the oral antidiabetic agents and begin receiving only insulin injections.

Chlorpropamide may also be used for other conditions as determined by your doctor.

Oral antidiabetic medicines do not help diabetic patients who have insulin-dependent diabetes mellitus (IDDM) or Type I diabetes because these patients cannot produce or release insulin from their pancreas gland. Their blood sugar is best controlled by insulin injections.

Sulfonylureas are available only with your doctor's prescription, in the following dosage forms:

Oral

Acetohexamide
- Tablets (U.S. and Canada)

Chlorpropamide
- Tablets (U.S. and Canada)

Gliclazide
- Tablets (Canada)

Glipizide
- Extended-release Tablets (U.S.)
- Tablets (U.S.)

Glyburide
- Micronized Tablets (U.S.)
- Tablets (U.S. and Canada)

Tolazamide
- Tablets (U.S.)

Tolbutamide
- Tablets (U.S. and Canada)

Before Using This Medicine

In deciding to use a medicine, the risks of taking the medicine must be weighed against the good it will do. This is a decision you and your doctor will make. For sulfonylurea medicines, the following should be considered:

Allergies—Tell your doctor if you have ever had any unusual or allergic reaction to sulfonylureas, or to sulfonamide-type (sulfa) medicines, including thiazide diuretics (a certain type of water pill). Also tell your health care professional if you are allergic to any other substances, such as foods, preservatives, or dyes.

Pregnancy— Sulfonylureas are rarely used during pregnancy. The amount of insulin you need changes during and after pregnancy. For this reason, it is easier to control your blood sugar using injections of insulin, rather than with the use of sulfonylureas. Close control of your blood sugar can reduce the chance of your baby gaining too much weight, having birth defects, or having high blood sugar during the pregnancy. Be sure to tell your doctor if you plan to become pregnant or if you think you are pregnant. If insulin is not available or cannot be used and sulfonylureas are used during pregnancy, they should be stopped at least 2 weeks before the delivery date (one month before for chlorpropamide and glipizide). Lowering of blood sugar can occur as a rebound effect at delivery and for several days following birth and will be watched closely by your health care professionals.

Breast-feeding—Chlorpropamide and tolbutamide pass into the breast milk. Chlorpropamide is not recommended but, in some cases, tolbutamide has been used. It is not known if other sulfonylureas pass into breast milk. Check with your doctor if you are thinking about breast-feeding.

Children—There is little information about the use of sulfonylureas in children. Type II diabetes is unusual in this age group.

Older adults—Some elderly patients may be more sensitive than younger adults to the effects of sulfonylureas, especially when more than one antidiabetic medicine is being taken or if other medicines that affect blood sugar are also being taken. This may increase the chance of low blood sugar during treatment. Furthermore, the first signs of low or high blood sugar are not easily seen or do not occur at all in older patients. This may increase the chance of low blood sugar developing during treatment.

Also, elderly patients who take chlorpropamide are more likely to hold too much body water.

Other medicines—Although certain medicines should not be used together at all, in other cases two different medicines may be used together even if an interaction might occur. In these cases, your doctor may want to change the dose, or other precautions may be necessary. *Do not take any other medicine, unless prescribed or approved by your doctor.* When you are taking sulfonylurea antidiabetic drugs, it is especially important that your health care professional know if you are taking any of the following:

- Alcohol—When low blood sugar occurs, it may last longer than usual if more than a small amount of alcohol is taken, especially on an empty stomach. Small amounts of alcohol at meal time usually do not cause problems with your blood sugar but may cause a redness (called flushing) in the face, arms, and neck that can be uncomfortable. This can occur with most of the sulfonylureas but is most likely to occur with chlorpropamide and has occurred up to 12 hours after alcohol was taken during chlorpropamide use
- Anticoagulants (blood thinners)—The effect of either the blood thinner or the antidiabetic medicine may be increased or decreased if the 2 medicines are used together
- Antifungal azoles (miconazole [e.g., Monistat I.V.], fluconazole [e.g., Diflucan], ketoconazole [e.g., Nizoral]) or
- Aspirin or other salicylates or
- Chloramphenicol (e.g., Chloromycetin) or
- Cimetidine (e.g., Tagamet) or
- Ciprofloxacin (e.g., Cipro) or
- Quinidine (e.g., Quinidex) or
- Quinine (e.g., Q-Vel) or
- Ranitidine (e.g., Zantac)—These medicines may increase the chances of low blood sugar
- Asparaginase (e.g., Elspar) or
- Corticosteroids (cortisone-like medicine) or
- Lithium (e.g., Lithonate) or
- Thiazide diuretics (e.g., Dyazide)—These medicines may increase the chances of high blood sugar
- Asthma medicines or
- Cough or cold medicines or
- Hay fever or allergy medicines—Many medicines (including nonprescription [over-the-counter]) products can affect the control of your blood sugar
- Beta-blockers (acebutolol [e.g., Sectral], atenolol [e.g., Tenormin], carteolol [e.g., Cartrol], labetalol [e.g., Normodyne], metoprolol [e.g., Lopressor], nadolol [e.g., Corgard], oxprenolol [e.g., Trasicor], penbutolol [e.g., Levatol], pindolol [e.g., Visken], propranolol [e.g., Inderal], sotalol [e.g., Sotacor], timolol [e.g., Blocadren])—Beta-blockers may increase the chance that high or low blood sugar can occur. Also, they can hide symptoms of low blood sugar (such as fast heartbeat). Because of this, a person with diabetes mellitus might not recognize that he or she has low blood sugar and might not take immediate steps to treat it. Beta-blockers can also cause low blood sugar to last longer than normal
- Cyclosporine [e.g., Sandimmune]—Sulfonylureas can increase the effects of cyclosporine
- Guanethidine (e.g., Ismelin) or
- Monoamine oxidase (MAO) inhibitors (furazolidone [e.g., Furoxone], isocarboxazid [e.g., Marplan], phenelzine [e.g., Nardil], procarbazine [e.g., Matulane], selegiline [e.g. Eldepryl], or tranylcypromine [e.g., Parnate])—Taking a sulfonylurea while you are taking (or within 2 weeks of taking) these medicines may increase the chances of low blood sugar occurring
- Octreotide (e.g., Sandostatin) or
- Pentamidine (e.g., Pentam)—Use of these medicines with sulfonylureas may increase the chance of either high or low blood sugar occurring

Other medical problems—The presence of other medical problems may affect the use of the sulfonylurea antidiabetic medicines. Make sure you tell your doctor if you have any other medical problems, especially:

- Acid in the blood (acidosis) or
- Diabetic coma or
- Fever, high, or
- Injury, severe, or
- Ketones in the blood (diabetic ketoacidosis) or
- Surgery, major, or
- Any other condition in which insulin needs change rapidly—Insulin may be needed temporarily to control diabetes mellitus in patients with these conditions because changes in blood sugar may occur rapidly and without

much warning; also, your blood sugar may need to be tested more often

- Diarrhea, continuing, or
- Female hormone changes for some women (e.g., during puberty, pregnancy, or menstruation) or
- Mental stress, severe, or
- Problems with intestines, severe, or
- Slow stomach emptying or
- Vomiting, continuing, or
- Any other condition that causes severe blood sugar changes—Insulin may be needed temporarily to control diabetes mellitus in patients with these conditions because changes in blood sugar may occur rapidly and without much warning; also, your blood sugar may need to be tested more often
- Heart disease—Chlorpropamide or tolbutamide causes some patients to retain (keep) more body water than usual. Heart disease may be worsened by this extra body water
- Kidney disease—Your blood sugar may be increased or decreased, partly because of slower removal of the medicine from the body; this may change the amount of sulfonylurea you need
- Liver disease—Your blood sugar may be increased or decreased, partly because of slower removal of sulfonylurea from the body; this may change the amount of sulfonylurea you need
- Overactive thyroid, not properly controlled—Your blood sugar may be increased or decreased, partly because of faster removal of the medicine from the body. Until your thyroid condition is controlled, the amount of sulfonylurea you need may change, Also, your blood sugar may need to be tested more often
- Underactive adrenal gland, not properly controlled, or
- Underactive pituitary gland, not properly controlled, or
- Undernourished condition or
- Weakened physical condition or
- Any other condition that causes low blood sugar—Patients with these conditions may be more likely to develop low blood sugar while taking sulfonylureas

Proper Use of This Medicine

Use this medicine only as directed even if you feel well and do not notice any signs of high blood sugar. Do not take more of this medicine and do not take it more often than your doctor ordered. To do so may increase the chance of serious side effects.

Remember that this medicine will not cure your diabetes but it does help control it. Therefore, you must continue to take it as directed if you expect to lower your blood sugar and keep it low. *You may have to take an antidiabetic medicine for the rest of your life.* If high blood sugar is not treated, it can cause serious problems, such as heart failure, blood vessel disease, eye disease, or kidney disease.

Your doctor will give you instructions about diet, exercise, how to test your blood sugar levels, and how to adjust your dose when you are sick.

- Diet—The daily number of calories in the meal plan should be adjusted by your doctor or a registered dietitian to help you reach and maintain a healthy body weight. In addition, regular meals and snacks are arranged to meet the energy needs of your body at different times of the day. *It is very important that you carefully follow your meal plan.*
- Exercise—Ask your doctor what kind of exercise to do, the best time to do it, and how much you should do each day.
- Blood tests—This is the best way to tell whether your diabetes is being controlled properly. Blood sugar testing helps you and your health care team adjust the dose of your medicine, meal plan, or exercise schedule.
- On sick days—When you become sick with a cold, fever, or the flu, you need to take your usual dose of sulfonylurea, even if you feel too ill to eat. This is especially true if you have nausea, vomiting, or diarrhea. Infection usually increases your need to produce more insulin. Sometimes you may need to be switched from your sulfonylurea to insulin for a short period of time while you are sick to properly control blood sugar. Call your doctor for specific instructions.

  Continue taking your sulfonylurea and try to stay on your regular meal plan. If you have trouble eating solid food, drink fruit juices, non-diet soft drinks, or clear soups, or eat small amounts of bland foods. A dietitian or your health care professional can give you a list of foods and the amounts to use for sick days.

  Test your blood sugar level at least every 4 hours while you are awake and check your urine for ketones. If ketones are present, call your doctor at once. If you have severe or prolonged vomiting, check with your doctor. Even when you start feeling better, let your doctor know how you are doing.

For patients taking *glipizide extended-release tablets:*

- Swallow the tablet whole, without breaking, crushing, or chewing it.
- You may sometimes notice what looks like a tablet in your stool. Do not worry. After you swallow the tablet, the medicine in the tablet is absorbed inside your body. Then the tablet passes into your stool without changing its shape. The medicine has entered your body and will work properly.

Dosing—The dose of these medicines will be different for different patients. *Follow your doctor's orders or the directions on the label.* The following information includes only the average doses of these medicines. *If your dose is different, do not change it* unless your doctor tells you to do so.

The number of tablets that you take depends on the strength of the medicine. Also, *the number of doses you take each day, the time allowed between doses, and the length of time you take the medicine depend on the amount of sugar in your blood or urine.*

For acetohexamide

- For *oral* dosage form (tablets):
  - —For treating sugar diabetes (diabetes mellitus):
    - Adults—At first, 250 milligrams (mg) once a day. Some elderly people may need a lower dose at first. Then, your doctor may change your dose a little at a time if needed. The dose is usually

not more than 1.5 grams a day. If your dose is 1 gram or more, the dose is usually divided into two doses. These doses are taken before the morning and evening meals.

- Children—The type of diabetes treated with this medicine is rare in children. However, if a child needs this medicine, the dose would have to be determined by the doctor.

For chlorpropamide

- For *oral* dosage form (tablets):
  —For treating sugar diabetes (diabetes mellitus):
  - Adults—At first, 250 milligrams (mg) once a day. Some elderly people may need a lower dose of 100 to 125 mg a day at first. Then, your doctor may change your dose a little at a time if needed. The dose is usually not more than 750 mg a day.
  - Children—The type of diabetes treated with this medicine is rare in children. However, if a child needs this medicine, the dose would have to be determined by the doctor.

For gliclazide

- For *oral* dosage form (tablets):
  —For treating sugar diabetes (diabetes mellitus):
  - Adults— 80 mg a day with a meal as a single dose or 160 to 320 milligrams (mg) divided into two doses taken with the morning and evening meals.
  - Children—The type of diabetes treated with this medicine is rare in children. However, if a child needs this medicine, the dose would have to be determined by the doctor.

For glipizide

- For *oral* dosage form (extended-release tablets):
  —For treating sugar diabetes (diabetes mellitus):
  - Adults—At first, 5 to 10 milligrams (mg) once a day with breakfast. Then, your doctor may change your dose a little at a time if needed. The dose is usually not more than 20 mg a day.
  - Children—The type of diabetes treated with this medicine is rare in children. However, if a child needs this medicine, the dose would have to be determined by the doctor.
- For *oral* dosage form (tablets):
  —For treating sugar diabetes (diabetes mellitus):
  - Adults—At first, 5 milligrams (mg) once a day. Some elderly people may need a lower dose of 2.5 mg a day at first. Then, your doctor may change your dose a little at a time if needed. The dose is usually not more than 40 mg a day. If your dose is 15 mg or more, the dose is usually divided into two doses. These doses are taken before the morning and evening meals.
  - Children—The type of diabetes treated with this medicine is rare in children. However, if a child needs this medicine, the dose would have to be determined by the doctor.

For glyburide

- For *oral* dosage form (micronized tablets):
  —For treating sugar diabetes (diabetes mellitus):
  - Adults—At first, 0.75 to 12 milligrams (mg) a day. Some elderly people may need a low dose of 0.75 to 3 mg a day at first. Then, your doctor may change your dose a little at a time if needed. The dose is usually not more than 12 mg a day. If your dose is 6 mg or more, the dose is usually divided into two doses. These doses are taken with the morning and evening meals. A single dose is taken with breakfast or with the first meal.
  - Children—The type of diabetes treated with this medicine is rare in children. However, if a child needs this medicine, the dose would have to be determined by the doctor.
- For *oral* dosage form (nonmicronized tablets):
  —For treating sugar diabetes (diabetes mellitus):
  - Adults—At first, 2.5 to 5 milligrams (mg) once a day. Some elderly people may need a lower dose of 1.25 to 2.5 mg a day at first. Then, your doctor may change your dose a little at a time if needed. The dose is usually not more than 20 mg a day. If your dose is 10 mg or more, the dose usually is divided into two doses. These doses are taken with the morning and evening meals.
  - Children—The type of diabetes treated with this medicine is rare in children. However, if a child needs this medicine, the dose would have to be determined by the doctor.

For tolazamide

- For *oral* dosage form (tablets):
  —For treating sugar diabetes (diabetes mellitus):
  - Adults—At first, 100 to 250 milligrams (mg) once a day in the morning. Then, your doctor may change your dose a little at a time if needed. The dose is usually not more than 1 gram a day. If your dose is 500 mg or more, the dose is usually divided into two doses. These doses are taken with the morning and evening meals.
  - Children—The type of diabetes treated with this medicine is rare in children. However, if a child needs this medicine, the dose would have to be determined by the doctor.

For tolbutamide

- For *oral* dosage form (tablets):
  —For treating sugar diabetes (diabetes mellitus):
  - Adults—At first, 1000 to 2000 milligrams (mg) a day. Some elderly people may need lower doses to start. The dose is usually divided into two doses. These doses are taken before the morning and evening meals. Your doctor may change your dose a little at a time if needed. The dose is usually not more than 3000 mg a day.
  - Children—The type of diabetes treated with this medicine is rare in children. However, if a child needs this medicine, the dose would have to be determined by the doctor.

Missed dose—If you miss a dose of this medicine, take it as soon as possible. However, if it is almost time for your next dose, skip the missed dose and go back to your regular dosing schedule. Do not double doses.

Storage—To store this medicine:

- Keep out of the reach of children.
- Store away from heat and direct light.
- Do not store in the bathroom, near the kitchen sink, or in other damp places. Heat or moisture may cause the medicine to break down.
- Do not keep outdated medicine or medicine no longer needed. Be sure that any discarded medicine is out of the reach of children.

Precautions While Using This Medicine

Your doctor will want to check your progress at regular visits, especially during the first few weeks that you take this medicine.

It is very important to follow carefully any instructions from your health care team about:

- Alcohol—Drinking alcohol may cause severe low blood sugar. Discuss this with your health care team.
- Tobacco—If you have been smoking for a long time and suddenly stop, your dosage of sulfonylurea may need to be reduced. If you decide to quit, tell your doctor first.
- Other medicines—Do not take other medicines unless they have been discussed with your doctor. This especially includes nonprescription medicines such as aspirin, and medicines for appetite control, asthma, colds, cough, hay fever, or sinus problems.
- Counseling—Other family members need to learn how to prevent side effects or help with side effects if they occur. Also, diabetics, especially teenagers, may need special counseling about sulfonylurea or insulin dosing changes that might occur because of lifestyle changes, such as changes in exercise and diet. Furthermore, counseling on contraception and pregnancy may be needed because of the problems that can occur in pregnancy for diabetics.
- Travel—Carry a recent prescription and your medical history. Be prepared for an emergency as you would normally. Make allowances for changing time zones, and keep your meal times as close as possible to your usual meal times.
- Protecting skin from sunlight—Sulfonylureas can make you more sensitive to the sun. Use of sunblock products that have a skin protection factor (SPF) of at least 15 on your skin and lips can help to prevent sunburn. Do not use a sunlamp or tanning bed or booth.

In case of emergency—There may be a time when you need emergency help for a problem caused by your diabetes. You need to be prepared for these emergencies. It is a good idea to:

- Wear a medical identification (I.D.) bracelet or neck chain at all times. Also, carry an I.D. card in your wallet or purse that says that you have diabetes and a list of all of your medicines.
- Have a glucagon kit and a syringe and needle available in case severe low blood sugar occurs. Check and replace any expired kits regularly.
- Keep some kind of quick-acting sugar handy to treat low blood sugar.

Too much of a sulfonylurea can cause low blood sugar (also called hypoglycemia). *Symptoms of low blood sugar must be treated before they lead to unconsciousness (passing out).* Different people may feel different symptoms of low blood sugar. *It is important that you learn which symptoms of low blood sugar you usually have so that you can treat it quickly.*

- Symptoms of low blood sugar can include: Anxious feeling, behavior change similar to being drunk, blurred vision, cold sweats, confusion, cool pale skin, difficulty in concentrating, drowsiness, excessive hunger, headache, nausea, nervousness, rapid heartbeat, shakiness, unusual tiredness or weakness.
- The symptoms of low blood sugar may develop quickly and may result from:
  - —delaying or missing a scheduled meal or snack.
  - —exercising more than usual.
  - —drinking a significant amount of alcohol.
  - —taking certain medicines.
  - —taking too high a dose of sulfonylurea.
  - —if using insulin, using too much insulin.
  - —sickness (especially with vomiting or diarrhea).
- Know what to do if symptoms of low blood sugar occur. Eating some form of quick-acting sugar when symptoms of low blood sugar first appear will usually prevent them from getting worse.

  Good sources of sugar include:
  - —Glucagon is used in emergency situations such as unconsciousness. Have a glucagon kit available, along with a syringe and needle, and know how to prepare and use it. Members of your household also should know how and when to use it.
  - —Glucose tablets or gel, fruit juice or non-diet soft drink (4 to 6 ounces [one-half cup]), corn syrup or honey (1 tablespoon), sugar cubes (6 one-half-inch sized), or table sugar (dissolved in water).
  - Do not use chocolate because its fat slows down the sugar entering the bloodstream.
  - If a snack is not scheduled for an hour or more you should also eat a light snack, such as crackers or a half sandwich, or drink an 8-ounce glass of milk.

High blood sugar (hyperglycemia) is another problem related to uncontrolled diabetes. *If you have any symptoms of high blood sugar, contact your health care team right away.* If high blood sugar is not treated, severe hyperglycemia can occur, leading to ketoacidosis (diabetic coma) and death.

- Symptoms of high blood sugar appear more slowly than those of low blood sugar. Symptoms can include: Blurred vision, drowsiness, dry mouth, flushed and dry skin, fruit-like breath odor, increased urination, loss of appetite, nausea or vomiting, sleepiness, stomachache, tiredness, troubled breathing (rapid and deep), unusual thirst.

- Symptoms of severe high blood sugar (called ketoacidosis or diabetic coma) that need immediate hospitalization include: Flushed dry skin, fruit-like breath odor, ketones in urine, passing out, troubled breathing (rapid and deep).
- High blood sugar symptoms may occur if you:
  —have a fever, diarrhea, or an infection.
  —if using insulin, do not take enough insulin or skip a dose of insulin.
  —do not exercise as much as usual.
  —overeat or do not follow your meal plan.
- Know what to do if high blood sugar occurs. Your doctor may recommend changes in your sulfonylurea dose or meal plan to avoid high blood sugar. Symptoms of high blood sugar must be corrected before they progress to more serious conditions. Check with your doctor often to make sure you are controlling your blood sugar, *but don't change your dose without checking with your doctor*. Your doctor might discuss the following with you:

  —Decreasing your dose for a short time for special needs, such as when you can't exercise as you normally do.

  —Increasing your dose when you plan to eat an unusually large dinner, such as on holidays. This type of increase is called an anticipatory dose.

  —Delaying a meal if your blood sugar is over 200 mg/dL to allow time for your blood sugar to go down. An extra dose or an injection of insulin may be needed if your blood sugar does not come down shortly.

  —Not exercising if your blood sugar is over 240 mg/dL and reporting this to your doctor immediately.

  —Being hospitalized if ketoacidosis or diabetic coma occurs with a possible change of treatment.

Side Effects of This Medicine

The use of sulfonylurea antidiabetics has been reported, but not proven in all studies, to increase the risk of death from heart and blood vessel disease. Diabetics are already more likely to have these problems if they do not control their blood sugar. Some sulfonylureas, such as glyburide and gliclazide, can have a positive effect on heart and blood vessel disease. It is important to know that problems can occur, but it is also not known if other sulfonylureas, particularly tolbutamide, help to cause these problems. It is known that if blood sugar is not controlled, such problems can occur.

Along with their needed effects, sulfonylureas may cause some unwanted effects. Although not all of these side effects may occur, if they do occur they may need medical attention.

Check with your doctor immediately if any of the following side effects occur:

More common
Convulsions (seizures), fainting or unconsciousness

Also, check with your doctor as soon as possible if any of the following side effects occur:

More common
Low blood sugar, including anxious feeling, behavior change similar to being drunk, blurred vision, cold sweats, confusion, cool pale skin, difficulty in concentrating, drowsiness, excessive hunger, fast heartbeat, headache, nausea, nervousness, nightmares, restless sleep, shakiness, slurred speech, unusual tiredness or weakness; or unusual weight gain

Rare
Chest pain; chills; coughing up blood; dark urine; fever; fluid-filled skin blisters; general feeling of illness; increased amounts of sputum (phlegm); increased sweating; itching of the skin; light-colored stools; pale skin; sensitivity to the sun; shortness of breath; sore throat; thinning of the skin; unusual bleeding or bruising; unusual tiredness or weakness; yellow eyes or skin

Other side effects may occur that usually do not need medical attention. These side effects may go away during treatment as your body adjusts to the medicine. However, check with your doctor if any of the following side effects continue or are bothersome:

More common
Changes in taste; constipation; diarrhea; dizziness; drowsiness (mild); increased amount of urine or more frequent urination; headache; heartburn; increased or decreased appetite; nausea; stomach pain, fullness, or discomfort; vomiting

Less common or rare
Increased sensitivity of skin to sun

For patients taking chlorpropamide or tolbutamide:

- Rarely, some patients who take chlorpropamide may retain (keep) more body water than usual. This happens even less often with tolbutamide. Check with your doctor as soon as possible if any of the following signs occur:
  Breathing difficulty; shortness of breath

Other side effects not listed above may also occur in some patients. If you notice any other effects, check with your doctor.

Additional Information

Once a medicine has been approved for marketing for a certain use, experience may show that it is also useful for other medical problems. Although this use is not included in product labeling, chlorpropamide is used in certain patients with the following medical condition:

- Diabetes insipidus (water diabetes)

If you are taking this medicine for water diabetes, the advice listed above that relates to diet for patients with *sugar* diabetes *does not apply to you.* However, the advice about hypoglycemia (low blood sugar) *does* apply to you. Call your doctor right away if you feel any of the symptoms described.

Other than the above information, there is no additional information relating to its proper use, precautions, or side effects for this use.

Revised: 08/03/95

ANTIDYSKINETICS Systemic

Some commonly used brand names are:

In the U.S.—

Akineton[2]	Kemadrin[4]
Artane[5]	Parsidol[3]
Artane Sequels[5]	Trihexane[5]
Cogentin[1]	Trihexy[5]

In Canada—

Akineton[2]	Kemadrin[4]
Apo-Benztropine[1]	Parsitan[3]
Apo-Trihex[5]	PMS Benztropine[1]
Artane[5]	PMS Procyclidine[4]
Artane Sequels[5]	PMS Trihexyphenidyl[5]
Cogentin[1]	Procyclid[4]

Other commonly used names are:

Benzatropine[1]	Profenamine[3]

Note: For quick reference, the following antidyskinetics are numbered to match the corresponding brand names.

This information applies to the following medicines:

1. Benztropine (BENZ-troe-peen)‡§
2. Biperiden (bye-PER-i-den)
3. Ethopropazine (eth-oh-PROE-pa-zeen)
4. Procyclidine (proe-SYE-kli-deen)
5. Trihexyphenidyl (trye-hex-ee-FEN-i-dill)‡

Note: This information does *not* apply to Amantadine, Carbidopa and Levodopa, Diphenhydramine, Haloperidol, and Levodopa.

‡Generic name product may also be available in the U.S.
§Generic name product may also be available in Canada.

Description

Antidyskinetics are used to treat Parkinson's disease, sometimes referred to as "shaking palsy." By improving muscle control and reducing stiffness, this medicine allows more normal movements of the body as the disease symptoms are reduced. It is also used to control severe reactions to certain medicines such as reserpine (e.g., Serpasil) (medicine to control high blood pressure) or phenothiazines, chlorprothixene (e.g., Taractan), thiothixene (e.g., Navane), loxapine (e.g., Loxitane), and haloperidol (e.g., Haldol) (medicines for nervous, mental, and emotional conditions).

Antidyskinetics may also be used for other conditions as determined by your doctor.

These medicines are available only with your doctor's prescription in the following dosage forms:

Oral

Benztropine
- Tablets (U.S. and Canada)

Biperiden
- Tablets (U.S. and Canada)

Ethopropazine
- Tablets (U.S. and Canada)

Procyclidine
- Elixir (Canada)
- Tablets (U.S. and Canada)

Trihexyphenidyl
- Extended-release capsules (U.S. and Canada)
- Elixir (U.S. and Canada)
- Tablets (U.S. and Canada)

Parenteral

Benztropine
- Injection (U.S. and Canada)

Biperiden
- Injection (U.S.)

Before Using This Medicine

In deciding to use a medicine, the risks of taking the medicine must be weighed against the good it will do. This is a decision you and your doctor will make. For antidyskinetics, the following should be considered:

Allergies—Tell your doctor if you have ever had any unusual or allergic reaction to antidyskinetics. Also tell your health care professional if you are allergic to any other substances, such as foods, preservatives, or dyes.

Pregnancy—Studies on effects in pregnancy have not been done in either humans or animals. However, antidyskinetics have not been shown to cause problems in humans.

Breast-feeding—It is not known if antidyskinetics pass into breast milk. Although most medicines pass into breast milk in small amounts, many of them may be used safely while breast-feeding. Mothers who are taking these medicines and who wish to breast-feed should discuss this with their doctor.

Since antidyskinetics tend to decrease the secretions of the body, it is possible that the flow of breast milk may be reduced in some patients.

Children—Children may be especially sensitive to the effects of antidyskinetics. This may increase the chance of side effects during treatment.

Older adults—Agitation, confusion, disorientation, hallucinations, memory loss, and mental changes are more likely to occur in elderly patients, who are usually more sensitive to the effects of antidyskinetics.

Other medicines—Although certain medicines should not be used together at all, in other cases 2 different medicines may be used together even if an interaction might occur. In these cases, your doctor may want to change the dose, or other precautions may be necessary. When you are taking an antidyskinetic, it is especially important that your

health care professional know if you are taking any of the following:

- Anticholinergics (medicine for abdominal or stomach spasms or cramps) or
- Central nervous system (CNS) depressants (medicine that causes drowsiness) or
- Tricyclic antidepressants (medicine for depression)—Using these medicines together with antidyskinetics may result in additive effects, increasing the chance of unwanted effects

Other medical problems—The presence of other medical problems may affect the use of antidyskinetics. Make sure you tell your doctor if you have any other medical problems, especially:

- Difficult urination or
- Enlarged prostate or
- Glaucoma or
- Heart or blood vessel disease or
- High blood pressure or
- Intestinal blockage or
- Myasthenia gravis or
- Uncontrolled movements of hands, mouth, or tongue—Antidyskinetics may make the condition worse
- Kidney disease or
- Liver disease—Higher blood levels of the antidyskinetics may result, increasing the chance of side effects

Proper Use of This Medicine

Take this medicine only as directed by your doctor. Do not take more of it, do not take it more often, and do not take it for a longer period of time than your doctor ordered. To do so may increase the chance of side effects.

To lessen stomach upset, take this medicine with meals or immediately after meals, unless otherwise directed by your doctor.

Dosing—The dose of antidyskinetics will be different for different patients. *Follow your doctor's orders or the directions on the label.* The following information includes only the average doses of benztropine, biperiden, ethopropazine, procyclidine, and trihexyphenidyl. *If your dose is different, do not change it* unless your doctor tells you to do so.

The number of capsules, tablets, or teaspoonfuls of elixir that you take depends on the strength of the medicine. Also, *the number of doses you take each day, the time allowed between doses, and the length of time you take the medicine depend on the medical problem for which you are taking antidyskinetics.*

For benztropine

- For *oral* dosage forms (tablets):
  - —For Parkinson's disease or certain severe side effects caused by some other medicines:
    - Adults—To start, 0.5 to 4 milligrams (mg) a day, depending on your condition. Your doctor will adjust your dose as needed; however, the dose is usually not more than 6 mg a day.
    - Children—Use and dose must be determined by your doctor.
- For *injection* dosage form:
  - —For Parkinson's disease or certain severe side effects caused by some other medicines:
    - Adults—1 to 4 mg a day, depending on your condition. Your doctor will adjust your dose as needed; however, the dose is usually not more than 6 mg a day.
    - Children—Use and dose must be determined by your doctor.

For biperiden

- For *oral* dosage forms (tablets):
  - —For Parkinson's disease or certain severe side effects caused by some other medicines:
    - Adults—2 mg up to four times a day. Your doctor will adjust your dose, depending on your condition; however, the dose is usually not more than 16 mg a day.
    - Children—Use and dose must be determined by your doctor.
- For *injection* dosage form:
  - —For Parkinson's disease or certain severe side effects caused by some other medicines:
    - Adults—2 mg, injected into a muscle or vein. The dose may be repeated if needed; however, the dose is usually not given more than four times a day.
    - Children—Use and dose is based on body weight and must be determined by your doctor.

For ethopropazine

- For *oral* dosage forms (tablets):
  - —For Parkinson's disease or certain severe side effects caused by some other medicines:
    - Adults—50 mg one or two times a day. Your doctor will adjust your dose as needed; however, the dose is usually not more than 600 mg a day.
    - Children—Use and dose must be determined by your doctor.

For procyclidine

- For *oral* dosage forms (elixir or tablets):
  - —For Parkinson's disease or certain severe side effects caused by some other medicines:
    - Adults—To start, 2.5 mg three times a day after meals. Your doctor may need to adjust your dose, depending on your condition.
    - Children—Use and dose must be determined by your doctor.

For trihexyphenidyl

- For *extended-release oral* dosage forms (extended-release capsules):
  - —For Parkinson's disease or certain severe side effects caused by some other medicines:
    - Adults—5 mg after breakfast. Your doctor may add another 5 mg dose to be taken twelve hours later, depending on your condition.
    - Children: Use and dose must be determined by your doctor.

- For other *oral* dosage forms (elixir or tablets):
  —For Parkinson's disease or certain severe side effects caused by some other medicines:
    - Adults—To start, 1 to 2 mg a day. Your doctor may adjust your dose as needed; however, the dose is usually not more than 15 mg a day.
    - Children—Use and dose must be determined by your doctor.

Missed dose—If you miss a dose of this medicine, take it as soon as possible. However, if it is within 2 hours of your next dose, skip the missed dose and go back to your regular dosing schedule. Do not double doses.

Storage—To store this medicine:
- Keep out of the reach of children.
- Store away from heat and direct light.
- Do not store the capsule or tablet form of this medicine in the bathroom, near the kitchen sink, or in other damp places. Heat or moisture may cause the medicine to break down.
- Keep the liquid form of this medicine from freezing.
- Do not keep outdated medicine or medicine no longer needed. Be sure that any discarded medicine is out of the reach of children.

Precautions While Using This Medicine

Your doctor should check your progress at regular visits, especially for the first few months you take this medicine. This will allow your dosage to be changed as necessary to meet your needs.

Your doctor may want you to have your eyes examined by an ophthalmologist (eye doctor) before and also sometime later during treatment.

Do not stop taking this medicine without first checking with your doctor. Your doctor may want you to reduce gradually the amount you are taking before stopping completely, to prevent side effects or the worsening of your condition.

This medicine will add to the effects of alcohol and other CNS depressants (medicines that slow down the nervous system, possibly causing drowsiness). Some examples of CNS depressants are antihistamines or medicine for hay fever, other allergies, or colds; sedatives, tranquilizers, or sleeping medicine; prescription pain medicine or narcotics; barbiturates; medicine for seizures; muscle relaxants; or anesthetics, including some dental anesthetics. *Check with your doctor before taking any of the above while you are using this medicine.*

Do not take this medicine within 1 hour of taking medicine for diarrhea. Taking these medicines too close together will make this medicine less effective.

If you think you or anyone else has taken an overdose of this medicine, get emergency help at once. Taking an overdose of this medicine may lead to unconsciousness. Some signs of an overdose are clumsiness or unsteadiness; seizures; severe drowsiness; severe dryness of mouth, nose and throat; fast heartbeat; hallucinations (seeing, hearing, or feeling things that are not there); mood or mental changes; shortness of breath or troubled breathing; trouble in sleeping; and unusual warmth, dryness, and flushing of skin.

This medicine may cause your eyes to become more sensitive to light than they are normally. Wearing sunglasses and avoiding too much exposure to bright light may help lessen the discomfort.

This medicine may cause some people to have blurred vision or to become drowsy, dizzy, or less alert than they are normally. *Make sure you know how you react to this medicine before you drive, use machines, or do anything else that could be dangerous if you are dizzy or are not alert or able to see well.*

Dizziness, lightheadedness, or fainting may occur, especially when you get up from lying or sitting. Getting up slowly may help. If the problem continues or gets worse, check with your doctor.

This medicine may make you sweat less, causing your body temperature to increase. *Use extra care to avoid becoming overheated during exercise or hot weather while you are taking this medicine, since overheating may result in heat stroke.* Also, hot baths or saunas may make you feel dizzy or faint while you are taking this medicine.

This medicine may cause dryness of the mouth. For temporary relief, use sugarless candy or gum, melt bits of ice in your mouth, or use a saliva substitute. However, if your mouth continues to feel dry for more than 2 weeks, check with your medical doctor or dentist. Continuing dryness of the mouth may increase the chance of dental disease, including tooth decay, gum disease, and fungus infections.

Side Effects of This Medicine

Along with its needed effects, a medicine may cause some unwanted effects. Although not all of these side effects may occur, if they do occur they may need medical attention.

Check with your doctor as soon as possible if any of the following side effects occur:

Rare

Confusion (more common in the elderly or with high doses); eye pain; skin rash

Symptoms of overdose

Clumsiness or unsteadiness; drowsiness (severe); dryness of mouth, nose, or throat (severe); fast heartbeat; hallucinations (seeing, hearing, or feeling things that are not there); mood or mental changes; seizures; shortness of breath or troubled breathing; trouble in sleeping; warmth, dryness, and flushing of skin

Other side effects may occur that usually do not need medical attention. These side effects may go away during treatment as your body adjusts to the medicine. However, check with your doctor if any of the following side effects continue or are bothersome:

More common

Blurred vision; constipation; decreased sweating; difficult or painful urination (especially in older men); drowsiness; dryness of mouth, nose, or throat; increased sensitivity of eyes to light; nausea or vomiting

Less common or rare

Dizziness or lightheadedness when getting up from a lying or sitting position; false sense of well-being (especially in the elderly or with high doses); headache; loss of memory (especially in the elderly); muscle cramps; nervousness; numbness or weakness in hands or feet; soreness of mouth and tongue; stomach upset or pain; unusual excitement (more common with large doses of trihexyphenidyl)

After you stop using this medicine, your body may need time to adjust. The length of time this takes depends on the amount of medicine you were using and how long you used it. During this period of time check with your doctor if you notice any of the following side effects:

Anxiety; difficulty in speaking or swallowing; dizziness or lightheadedness when getting up from a lying or sitting position; fast heartbeat; loss of balance control; mask-like face; muscle spasms, especially of face, neck, and back; restlessness or desire to keep moving; shuffling walk; stiffness of arms or legs; trembling and shaking of hands and fingers; trouble in sleeping; twisting movements of body

Other side effects not listed above may also occur in some patients. If you notice any other effects, check with your doctor.

Revised: 05/11/93

ANTIFIBRINOLYTIC AGENTS Systemic

Some commonly used brand names are:

In the U.S.—

Amicar[1]
Cyklokapron[2]

In Canada—

Amicar[1]
Cyklokapron[2]

Another commonly used name for aminocaproic acid is epsilon-aminocaproic acid[1].

This information applies to the following medicines:

1. Aminocaproic Acid (a-mee-noe-ka-PROE-ik ASS-id)‡
2. Tranexamic Acid (tran-ex-AM-ik ASS-id)

‡Generic name product may also be available in the U.S.

Description

Antifibrinolytic (an-tee-fye-bri-noh-LIT-ik) agents are used to treat serious bleeding, especially when the bleeding occurs after dental surgery (particularly in patients with hemophilia) or certain other kinds of surgery. These medicines are also sometimes given before an operation to prevent serious bleeding in patients with medical problems that increase the chance of serious bleeding.

Antifibrinolytic agents may also be used for other conditions as determined by your doctor.

Antifibrinolytic agents are available only with your doctor's prescription, in the following dosage forms:

Oral

Aminocaproic acid
- Syrup (U.S. and Canada)
- Tablets (U.S. and Canada)

Tranexamic acid
- Tablets (U.S. and Canada)

Parenteral

Aminocaproic acid
- Injection (U.S. and Canada)

Tranexamic acid
- Injection (U.S. and Canada)

Before Using This Medicine

In deciding to use a medicine, the risks of taking the medicine must be weighed against the good it will do. This is a decision you and your doctor will make. For antifibrinolytic agents, the following should be considered:

Allergies—Tell your doctor if you have ever had any unusual or allergic reaction to aminocaproic acid or tranexamic acid. Also tell your health care professional if you are allergic to any other substances, such as foods, preservatives, or dyes.

Pregnancy—Studies on birth defects have not been done in humans. However, these medicines have been given to pregnant women without causing birth defects or other problems.

Studies on effects of aminocaproic acid in pregnancy have not been done in animals. Tranexamic acid has not been shown to cause birth defects or other problems in animal studies.

Breast-feeding—These medicines have not been reported to cause problems in nursing babies. However, small amounts of tranexamic acid pass into the breast milk.

Children—Although there is no specific information comparing use of aminocaproic acid or tranexamic acid in children with use in other age groups, these medicines are not expected to cause different side effects or problems in children than they do in adults.

Older adults—

- *For aminocaproic acid*: Although there is no specific information comparing use of aminocaproic acid in the elderly with use in other age groups, this medicine is not expected to cause different side effects or problems in older people than it does in younger adults.
- *For tranexamic acid*: Tranexamic acid has been tested and has not been shown to cause different side effects or problems in older people than it does in younger adults.

Other medicines—Although certain medicines should not be used together at all, in other cases two different medicines may be used together even if an interaction might occur. In these cases, your doctor may want to change the dose, or other precautions may be necessary. Tell your

health care professional if you are taking any other prescription or nonprescription (over-the-counter [OTC]) medicine.

Other medical problems—The presence of other medical problems may affect the use of antifibrinolytic agents. Make sure you tell your doctor if you have any other medical problems, especially:

- Blood clots or a history of medical problems caused by blood clots or
- Blood in the urine or
- Color vision problems or
- Heart disease or
- Kidney disease or
- Liver disease—The chance of side effects may be increased

Proper Use of This Medicine

Take this medicine only as directed by your doctor. Do not take more or less of it, do not take it more often, and do not take it for a longer time than your doctor ordered. To do so may increase the chance of unwanted effects.

Dosing—The dose of these medicines will be different for different patients. *Follow your doctor's orders or the directions on the label.* The following information includes only the average doses of these medicines. *If your dose is different, do not change it* unless your doctor tells you to do so.

For aminocaproic acid

- To prevent or treat serious bleeding:
  —For *oral* dosage forms (syrup or tablets):
  - Adults—For the first hour, the dose is 5 grams. Then the dose is 1 or 1.25 grams per hour for eight hours.
  - Children—Dose is based on body weight or size and must be determined by your doctor. For the first hour, the dose is usually 100 milligrams (mg) per kilogram (kg) (45.4 mg per pound) of body weight. Then the dose is 33.3 mg per kg (15.1 mg per pound) of body weight per hour.

  —For *injection* dosage form:
  - Adults—At first, the dose is 4 to 5 grams injected into a vein, over a period of one hour. Then the dose is 1 gram per hour, injected into a vein over a period of eight hours.
  - Children—Dose is based on body weight or size and must be determined by your doctor. At first, the dose is usually 100 mg per kg (45.4 mg per pound) of body weight, injected into a vein over a period of one hour. Then the dose is 33.3 mg per kg (15.1 mg per pound) of body weight per hour, injected into a vein.

For tranexamic acid

- To prevent or treat serious bleeding after dental surgery:
  —For *oral* dosage form (tablets):
  - Adults and children—Dose is based on body weight and must be determined by your doctor. The dose is usually 25 milligrams (mg) per kilogram (kg) (11.4 mg per pound) of body weight every six to eight hours, beginning one day before surgery. After surgery, the dose is usually 25 mg per kg (11.4 mg per pound) of body weight every six to eight hours for seven to ten days.

  —For *injection* dosage form:
  - Adults and children—Dose is based on body weight and must be determined by your doctor. The dose is usually 10 mg per kg (4.5 mg per pound) of body weight, injected into a vein just before surgery. After surgery, the dose is usually 10 mg per kg (4.5 mg per pound) of body weight, injected into a vein every six to eight hours for seven to ten days.

Missed dose—

- *For aminocaproic acid* (e.g., Amicar): If you miss a dose, take it as soon as possible. However, if you do not remember until it is almost time for your next dose, double the next dose. Then go back to your regular dosing schedule.
- *For tranexamic acid* (e.g., Cyklokapron): If you miss a dose, take it as soon as possible. Then take any remaining doses for the day at regularly spaced times. Do not double doses. If you have any questions about this, check with your doctor.

Storage—To store this medicine:

- Keep out of the reach of children.
- Store away from heat and direct light.
- Do not store the tablet form of this medicine in the bathroom, near the kitchen sink, or in other damp places. Heat or moisture may cause the medicine to break down.
- Do not keep outdated medicine or medicine no longer needed. Be sure that any discarded medicine is out of the reach of children.

Precautions While Using This Medicine

If you will be taking tranexamic acid for longer than several days, your doctor may want you to have your eyes checked regularly by an ophthalmologist (eye doctor). This will allow your doctor to check for unwanted effects that may be caused by this medicine.

If you are using aminocaproic acid syrup as a mouth rinse to control oral bleeding, and you are in the first or second trimester of pregnancy, you should spit out the syrup after rinsing without swallowing it.

Side Effects of This Medicine

Along with its needed effects, a medicine may cause some unwanted effects. Although not all of these side effects may occur, if they do occur they may need medical attention.

The same effect that makes aminocaproic acid or tranexamic acid help prevent or stop bleeding also may cause blood clots that could be dangerous. Check with your doctor immediately if any of the following possible signs and symptoms of blood clots occur:

Less common or rare

Headache (severe and sudden); loss of coordination (sudden); pains in chest, groin, or legs, especially the calves; shortness of breath (sudden); slurred speech (sudden); vision changes (sudden); weakness or numbness in arm or leg

Also, check with your doctor as soon as possible if any of the following side effects occur:

Less common or rare

For aminocaproic acid

Dizziness; headache; muscle pain or weakness (severe and continuing); ringing or buzzing in ears; skin rash; slow or irregular heartbeat—with the injection only; stomach cramps or pain; stuffy nose; sudden decrease in amount of urine; swelling of face, feet, or lower legs; unusual tiredness or weakness; weight gain (rapid)

For tranexamic acid

Blurred vision or other changes in vision; dizziness or lightheadedness; unusual tiredness or weakness

Other side effects may occur that usually do not need medical attention. These side effects may go away during treatment as your body adjusts to the medicine. However, check with your doctor if any of the following side effects continue or are bothersome:

Diarrhea; dry ejaculation; nausea or vomiting; unusual menstrual discomfort; watery eyes

Other side effects not listed above may also occur in some patients. If you notice any other effects, check with your doctor.

Revised: 08/13/97

ANTIFUNGALS, AZOLE Systemic

Some commonly used brand names are:

In the U.S.—

Diflucan[1]	Nizoral[3]
Monistat i.v.[4]	Sporanox[2]

In Canada—

Diflucan[1]	Nizoral[3]
Diflucan-150[1]	Sporanox[2]

Note: For quick reference, the following antifungals are numbered to match the corresponding brand names.

This information applies to the following medicines:

1. Fluconazole (floo-KOE-na-zole)
2. Itraconazole (i-tra-KOE-na-zole)
3. Ketoconazole (kee-toe-KON-a-zole)
4. Miconazole (mi-KON-a-zole)†

†Not commercially available in Canada.

Description

Azole antifungals are used to treat serious fungus infections that may occur in different parts of the body. These medicines may also be used for other problems as determined by your doctor.

Azole antifungals are available only with your doctor's prescription, in the following dosage forms:

Oral

Fluconazole
- Capsules (Canada)
- Oral suspension (U.S. and Canada)
- Tablets (U.S. and Canada)

Itraconazole
- Capsules (U.S. and Canada)
- Oral solution (U.S.)

Ketoconazole
- Oral suspension (Canada)
- Tablets (U.S. and Canada)

Parenteral

Fluconazole
- Injection (U.S. and Canada)

Miconazole
- Injection (U.S.)

Before Using This Medicine

In deciding to use a medicine, the risks of taking the medicine must be weighed against the good it will do. This is a decision you and your doctor will make. For the azole antifungals, the following should be considered:

Allergies—Tell your doctor if you have ever had any unusual or allergic reaction to any of the azole antifungals. Also tell your health care professional if you are allergic to any other substances, such as foods, preservatives, or dyes.

Pregnancy—Studies have not been done in pregnant women. However, studies in some animals have shown that azole antifungals, taken in high doses, may cause harm to the mother and the fetus. They have caused birth defects in animals. Before taking these medicines, make sure your doctor knows if you are pregnant or if you may become pregnant.

Breast-feeding—Azole antifungals pass into breast milk. Mothers who are taking these medicines and who wish to breast-feed should discuss this with their doctors.

Children—A small number of children have been safely treated with azole antifungals. Be sure to discuss with your child's doctor the use of these medicines in children.

Older adults—Many medicines have not been studied specifically in older people. Therefore, it may not be known whether they work exactly the same way they do in younger adults or if they cause different side effects or problems in older people. There is no specific information comparing use of azole antifungals in the elderly with use in other age groups.

Other medicines—Although certain medicines should not be used together at all, in other cases two different medicines may be used together even if an interaction might occur. In these cases, your doctor may want to change the dose, or other precautions may be necessary. When you are taking azole antifungals, it is especially important that your health care professional know if you are taking any of the following:

- Acetaminophen (e.g., Tylenol) (with long-term, high-dose use) or
- Amiodarone (e.g., Cordarone) or
- Anabolic steroids (nandrolone [e.g., Anabolin], oxandrolone [e.g., Anavar], oxymetholone [e.g., Anadrol], stanozolol [e.g., Winstrol]) or
- Androgens (male hormones) or
- Antithyroid agents (medicine for overactive thyroid) or
- Carmustine (e.g., BiCNU) or
- Chloroquine (e.g., Aralen) or
- Dantrolene (e.g., Dantrium) or
- Daunorubicin (e.g., Cerubidine) or
- Disulfiram (e.g., Antabuse) or
- Divalproex (e.g., Depakote) or
- Estrogens (female hormones) or
- Etretinate (e.g., Tegison) or
- Gold salts (medicine for arthritis) or
- Hydroxychloroquine (e.g., Plaquenil) or
- Mercaptopurine (e.g., Purinethol) or
- Methotrexate (e.g., Mexate) or
- Methyldopa (e.g., Aldomet) or
- Naltrexone (e.g., Trexan) (with long-term, high-dose use) or
- Oral contraceptives (birth control pills) containing estrogen or
- Other anti-infectives by mouth or by injection (medicine for infection) or
- Phenothiazines (acetophenazine [e.g., Tindal], chlorpromazine [e.g., Thorazine], fluphenazine [e.g., Prolixin], mesoridazine [e.g., Serentil], perphenazine [e.g., Trilafon], prochlorperazine [e.g., Compazine], promazine [e.g., Sparine], promethazine [e.g., Phenergan], thioridazine [e.g., Mellaril], trifluoperazine [e.g., Stelazine], triflupromazine [e.g., Vesprin], trimeprazine [e.g., Temaril]) or
- Plicamycin (e.g., Mithracin) or
- Valproic acid (e.g., Depakene)—Use of these medicines with azole antifungals may increase the chance of side effects affecting the liver

- Amantadine (e.g., Symmetrel) or
- Antacids or
- Anticholinergics (medicine for abdominal or stomach spasms or cramps) or
- Antidepressants (medicine for depression) or
- Antidyskinetics (medicine for Parkinson's disease or other conditions affecting control of muscles) or
- Antihistamines or
- Antipsychotics (medicine for mental illness) or
- Buclizine (e.g., Bucladin) or
- Cimetidine (e.g., Tagamet) or
- Cyclizine (e.g., Marezine) or
- Cyclobenzaprine (e.g., Flexeril) or
- Disopyramide (e.g., Norpace) or
- Famotidine (e.g., Pepcid) or
- Flavoxate (e.g., Urispas) or
- Ipratropium (e.g., Atrovent) or
- Meclizine (e.g., Antivert) or
- Methylphenidate (e.g., Ritalin) or
- Nizatidine (e.g., Axid) or
- Omeprazole (e.g., Prilosac) or
- Orphenadrine (e.g., Norflex) or
- Oxybutynin (e.g., Ditropan) or
- Procainamide (e.g., Pronestyl) or
- Promethazine (e.g., Phenergan) or
- Quinidine (e.g., Quinidex) or
- Ranitidine (e.g., Zantac) or
- Sucralfate (e.g., Carafate) or
- Trimeprazine (e.g., Temaril)—Use of these medicines may decrease the effects of itraconazole and ketoconazole; these medicines should be taken at least 2 hours after itraconazole or ketoconazole

- Antidiabetic agents, oral (chlorpropamide [e.g., Diabinese], glipizide [e.g., Glucotrol], glyburide [e.g., DiaBeta, Micronase], tolbutamide [e.g., Orinase]) or
- Cyclosporine (e.g., Sandimmune) or
- Digoxin (e.g., Lanoxin) or
- Warfarin (e.g., Coumadin)—Azole antifungals may increase the effects of these medicines, which may increase the chance of side effects

- Astemizole (e.g., Hismanal) or
- Terfenadine (e.g., Seldane)—These medicines should not be taken with fluconazole, itraconazole, or ketoconazole; these azole antifungals may increase the chance of serious side effects of astemizole or terfenadine

- Carbamazepine (e.g., Tegretol) or
- Isoniazid or
- Rifampin (e.g., Rifadin)—These medicines may decrease the effects of azole antifungals

- Cisapride (e.g., Propulsid)—Cisapride should not be taken with oral itraconazole, oral ketoconazole, or miconazole injection; these azole antifungals may increase the chance of serious side effects of cisapride

- Didanosine (e.g., ddI, Videx)—Use of didanosine with itraconazole or ketoconazole may decrease the effects of both itraconazole and ketoconazole, as well as didanosine. Itraconazole and ketoconazole should be taken at least 2 hours before or 2 hours after didanosine is given

- Indinavir (e.g., Crixivan)—Use of indinavir with ketoconazole may increase the effects of indinavir

- Lovastatin (e.g., Mevacor) or
- Simvastatin (e.g., Zocor)—Use of these medicines with itraconazole may increase the effects of lovastatin or simvastatin

- Midazolam (e.g., Versed) or
- Triazolam (e.g., Halcion)—Use of these medicines with itraconazole or ketoconazole may increase the effects of midazolam or triazolam

- Phenytoin (e.g., Dilantin)—Use of phenytoin with azole antifungals may increase the effects of the azole antifungals, increase side effects of azole antifungals affecting the liver, and increase the chance of phenytoin side effects

Other medical problems—The presence of other medical problems may affect the use of azole antifungals. Make sure you tell your doctor if you have any other medical problems, especially:

- Achlorhydria (absence of stomach acid) or
- Hypochlorhydria (decreased amount of stomach acid)—Itraconazole and ketoconazole may not be absorbed from the stomach as well in patients who have low levels of or no stomach acid

- Alcohol abuse (or history of) or
- Liver disease—Alcohol abuse or liver disease may increase the chance of side effects caused by azole antifungals

- Kidney disease—The effects of fluconazole may be increased in patients with kidney disease

Proper Use of This Medicine

Ketoconazole and the capsule form of itraconazole should be taken with a meal or a snack. The oral solution form of itraconazole should be taken on an empty stomach. If you have any questions about the antifungal medicine you are taking, check with your health care professional.

For patients taking the *oral liquid form of fluconazole, itraconazole, or ketoconazole:*

- Use a specially marked measuring spoon or other device to measure each dose accurately. The average household teaspoon may not hold the right amount of liquid.

If you have achlorhydria (absence of stomach acid) or hypochlorhydria (decreased amount of stomach acid), and you are taking itraconazole or ketoconazole, your doctor may want you to take your medicine with an acidic drink. You may dissolve your medicine in cola or seltzer water and drink the solution, or your may take your medicine with a glass of cola or seltzer water. Your doctor may suggest that you dissolve each capsule or tablet in a teaspoonful of weak hydrochloric acid solution to help you absorb the medicine better. Your health care professional can prepare the solution for you. After you dissolve the tablet in the acid solution, add this mixture to a small amount (1 or 2 teaspoonfuls) of water in a glass. Drink the mixture through a plastic or glass drinking straw. Place the straw behind your teeth, as far back in your mouth as you can. This will keep the acid from harming your teeth. Be sure to drink all the liquid to get the full dose of medicine. Next, swish around in your mouth about 1/2 glass of water and then swallow it. This will help wash away any acid that may remain in your mouth or on your teeth.

To help clear up your infection completely, *it is very important that you keep taking this medicine for the full time of treatment,* even if your symptoms begin to clear up or you begin to feel better after a few days. Since fungus infections may be very slow to clear up, you may have to continue taking this medicine every day for as long as 6 months to a year or more. Some fungus infections never clear up completely and require continuous treatment. If you stop taking this medicine too soon, your symptoms may return.

This medicine works best when there is a constant amount in the blood. *To help keep the amount constant, do not miss any doses. Also, it is best to take each dose at the same time every day.* If you need help in planning the best time to take your medicine, check with your health care professional.

Dosing—The dose of azole antifungals may be different for different patients. *Follow your doctor's orders or the directions on the label.* The following information includes only the average doses of azole antifungals. Your dose of fluconazole may be different if you have kidney disease. *If your dose is different, do not change it* unless your doctor tells you to do so.

The number of capsules, tablets, or the amount of oral suspension that you take depends on the strength of the medicine. Also, *the number of doses you take each day, the time allowed between doses, and the length of time you take the medicine depend on the medical problem for which you are taking azole antifungals.*

For fluconazole

- For fungus infections:
  - —For *capsule* dosage form:
    - Adults—150 milligrams (mg) as a single dose to treat vaginal yeast infections.
    - Children up to 18 years of age—Dose must be determined by your doctor.
  - —For *oral suspension* and *tablet* dosage forms:
    - Adults and teenagers—200 to 400 mg on the first day, then 100 to 400 mg once a day for weeks or months, depending on the medical problem being treated. A vaginal yeast infection is treated with a single dose of 150 mg.
    - Children 6 months of age and older—6 to 12 mg per kilogram (mg/kg) (2.7 to 5.4 mg per pound) of body weight on the first day, then 3 to 12 mg/kg (1.35 to 5.4 mg per pound) of body weight once a day for weeks or months, depending on the medical problem being treated.
    - Children up to 6 months of age—Dose must be determined by your doctor.
  - —For *injection* dosage form:
    - Adults and teenagers—200 to 400 mg on the first day, then 100 to 400 mg once a day, injected into a vein, for weeks or months, depending on the medical problem being treated.
    - Children 6 months of age and older—6 to 12 mg per kilogram (mg/kg) (2.7 to 5.4 mg per pound) of body weight on the first day, then 3 to 12 mg/kg (1.35 to 5.4 mg per pound) of body weight once a day, injected into a vein, for weeks or months, depending on the medical problem being treated.
    - Children up to 6 months of age—Dose must be determined by your doctor.

For itraconazole

- For fungus infections:
  - —For *capsule* dosage form:
    - Adults and teenagers—200 milligrams (mg) once a day, which may be increased up to 400 mg once a day for weeks or months, depending on the medical problem being treated. Fingernail and toenail infections are treated with 200 mg two or four times a day for weeks or months.
    - Children up to 16 years of age—Dose must be determined by your doctor.
  - —For *oral solution* dosage form:
    - Adults and teenagers—100 to 200 mg once a day for days or weeks, depending on the medical problem being treated.
    - Children up to 12 years of age—Dose must be determined by your doctor.

For ketoconazole

- For fungus infections:
  - —For *oral* dosage form (oral suspension and tablets):
    - Adults and teenagers—200 to 400 milligrams (mg) once a day for days or weeks, depending on the medical problem being treated.

• Children over 2 years of age—3.3 to 6.6 mg per kilogram (1.5 to 3 mg per pound) of body weight once a day for days or weeks, depending on the medical problem being treated.

• Children up to 2 years of age—Dose must be determined by your doctor.

For miconazole

- For fungus infections:
  - —For *injection* dosage form:
    - Adults and teenagers—200 milligrams (mg) to 1.2 grams three times a day, injected into a vein, for weeks or months, depending on the medical problem being treated.
    - Children 1 year of age and over—20 to 40 mg per kilogram (9.1 to 18.2 mg per pound) of body weight per day, given in two or three doses, for weeks or months, depending on the medical problem being treated.
    - Children up to 1 year of age—Dose must be determined by your doctor.

Missed dose—If you miss a dose of this medicine, take it as soon as possible. This will help to keep a constant amount of medicine in the blood. However, if it is almost time for your next dose, skip the missed dose and go back to your regular dosing schedule. Do not double doses.

Storage—To store this medicine:

- Keep out of the reach of children.
- Store away from heat and direct light.
- Do not store the capsule or tablet form of this medicine in the bathroom, near the kitchen sink, or in other damp places. Heat or moisture may cause the medicine to break down.
- Keep the oral liquid form of this medicine from freezing.
- Do not keep outdated medicine or medicine no longer needed. Be sure that any discarded medicine is out of the reach of children.

Precautions While Using This Medicine

It is important that your doctor check your progress at regular visits. This will allow your doctor to check for any unwanted effects.

If your symptoms do not improve within a few weeks (or months for some infections), or if they become worse, check with your doctor.

*These medicines should **not** be taken with astemizole (e.g., Hismanal), cisapride (e.g., Propulsid), or terfenadine (e.g., Seldane).* Doing so may increase the risk of serious side effects affecting the heart.

Liver problems may be more likely to occur if you drink alcoholic beverages while you are taking ketoconazole. Alcoholic beverages may also cause stomach pain, nausea, vomiting, headache, or flushing or redness of the face. Other alcohol-containing preparations (for example, elixirs, cough syrups, tonics) may also cause problems. These problems may occur for at least a day after you stop taking ketoconazole. Therefore, *you should not drink alcoholic beverages or use alcohol-containing preparations while you are taking this medicine and for at least a day after you stop taking it.*

If you are taking antacids, cimetidine (e.g., Tagamet), famotidine (e.g., Pepcid), nizatidine (e.g., Axid), omeprazole (e.g., Prilosec), or ranitidine (e.g., Zantac) while you are taking itraconazole or ketoconazole, take the other medicine at least 2 hours after you take itraconazole or ketoconazole. If you take these medicines at the same time that you take itraconazole or ketoconazole, they will keep your antifungal medicine from working properly.

Ketoconazole may cause your eyes to become more sensitive to light than they are normally. Wearing sunglasses and avoiding too much exposure to bright light may help lessen the discomfort.

Side Effects of This Medicine

Along with its needed effects, a medicine may cause some unwanted effects. Although not all of these effects may occur, if they do occur they may need medical attention.

Check with your doctor immediately if any of the following side effects occur:

More common—for miconazole

Redness, swelling, or pain at the place of injection

Less common

Fever and chills; skin rash or itching

Rare

Dark or amber urine; fever and sore throat; loss of appetite; pale stools; reddening, blistering, peeling, or loosening of skin and mucous membranes; stomach pain; unusual bleeding or bruising; unusual tiredness or weakness; yellow eyes or skin

Other side effects may occur that usually do not need medical attention. These side effects may go away during treatment as your body adjusts to the medicine. However, check with your doctor if any of the following side effects continue or are bothersome:

Less common

Constipation; diarrhea; dizziness; drowsiness; flushing or redness of the face or skin; headache; nausea; vomiting

Rare—for ketoconazole

Decreased sexual ability in males; enlargement of the breasts in males; increased sensitivity of the eyes to light; menstrual irregularities

Other side effects not listed above may also occur in some patients. If you notice any other effects, check with your doctor.

Revised: 05/20/94
Interim revision: 11/14/94; 04/18/95; 08/14/97

ANTIFUNGALS, AZOLE Vaginal

Some commonly used brand names are:

In the U.S.—

FemCare[2]
Femizole-7[2]
Femstat 3[1]
Gyne-Lotrimin[2]
Gyne-Lotrimin Combination Pack[2]
Gyne-Lotrimin3[2]
Gyne-Lotrimin3 Combination Pack[2]
Miconazole-7[4]
Monistat 3[4]
Monistat 3 Combination Pack[4]
Monistat 5 Tampon[4]
Monistat 7[4]
Monistat 7 Combination Pack[4]
Mycelex-7[2]
Mycelex-G[2]
Mycelex Twin Pack[2]
Terazol 3[5]
Terazol 7[5]
Vagistat-1[6]

In Canada—

Canesten Combi-Pak 1-Day Therapy[2]
Canesten Combi-Pak 3-Day Therapy[2]
Canesten 1-Day Cream Combi-Pak[2]
Canesten 1-Day Therapy[2]
Canesten 3-Day Therapy[2]
Canesten 6-Day Therapy[2]
Clotrimaderm[2]
Ecostatin Vaginal Ovules[3]
GyneCure[6]
GyneCure Ovules[6]
GyneCure Vaginal Ointment Tandempak[6]
GyneCure Vaginal Ovules Tandempak[6]
Monistat 3 Dual-Pak[4]
Monistat 3 Vaginal Ovules[4]
Monistat 7[4]
Monistat 7 Dual-Pak[4]
Monistat 7 Vaginal Suppositories[4]
Myclo-Gyne[2]
Novo-Miconazole Vaginal Ovules[4]
Terazol 3[5]
Terazol 3 Dual Pak[5]
Terazol 3 Vaginal Ovules[5]
Terazol 7[5]

Note: For quick reference, the following azole antifungals are numbered to match the corresponding brand names.

This information applies to the following medicines:

1. Butoconazole (byoo-toe-KON-a-zole)†
2. Clotrimazole (kloe-TRIM-a-zole)‡
3. Econazole (e-KON-a-zole)*
4. Miconazole (mi-KON-a-zole)‡
5. Terconazole (ter-KON-a-zole)
6. Tioconazole (tye-oh-KON-a-zole)

*Not commercially available in the U.S.
†Not commercially available in Canada.
‡Generic name product may be available in the U.S.

Description

Vaginal azoles (A-zoles) are used to treat yeast (fungus) infections of the vagina.

Some vaginal azoles are available only with your doctor's prescription. Most are available without a prescription; however, your doctor may have special instructions on the proper use of this medicine.

Vaginal azoles are available in the following dosage forms:

Vaginal
- Butoconazole
  - Cream (U.S.)
- Clotrimazole
  - Cream (U.S. and Canada)
  - Tablets (U.S. and Canada)
- Econazole
  - Suppositories (Canada)
- Miconazole
  - Cream (U.S. and Canada)
  - Suppositories (U.S. and Canada)
  - Tampons (U.S.—California only)
- Terconazole
  - Cream (U.S. and Canada)
  - Suppositories (U.S. and Canada)
- Tioconazole
  - Ointment (U.S. and Canada)
  - Suppositories (Canada)

Before Using This Medicine

In deciding to use a medicine, the risks of using the medicine must be weighed against the good it will do. This is a decision you and your doctor will make. For vaginal azoles, the following should be considered:

Allergies—Tell your doctor if you have ever had any unusual or allergic reaction to any of the azoles. Also tell your health care professional if you are allergic to any other substances, such as foods, preservatives, or dyes.

Pregnancy—Studies have not been done in humans during the first trimester of pregnancy. Vaginal azoles have not been shown to cause birth defects or other problems in humans when used during the second and third trimesters.

Breast-feeding—It is not known whether vaginal azoles pass into the breast milk. However, these medicines have not been shown to cause problems in nursing babies.

Children—Studies on these medicines have been done only in adult patients, and there is no specific information comparing use of vaginal azoles in children with use in other age groups.

Older adults—Many medicines have not been studied specifically in older people. Therefore, it may not be known whether they work exactly the same way they do in younger adults. Although there is no specific information comparing use of vaginal azoles in the elderly with use in other age groups, they are not expected to cause different side effects or problems in older people than they do in younger adults.

Other medicines—Although certain medicines should not be used together at all, in other cases two different medicines may be used together even if an interaction might occur. In these cases, your doctor may want to change the dose, or other precautions may be necessary. Tell your health care professional if you are using any other vaginal prescription or nonprescription (over-the-counter [OTC]) medicine.

Proper Use of This Medicine

Vaginal azoles usually come with patient directions. Read them carefully before using this medicine.

Use this medicine at bedtime, unless otherwise directed by your doctor. The vaginal tampon form of miconazole should be left in the vagina overnight and removed the next morning.

This medicine is usually inserted into the vagina with an applicator. However, if you are pregnant, check with your doctor before using the applicator.

Some of the vaginal suppositories or tablets come packaged with a small tube of cream. This cream can be applied outside of the vagina in the genital area to treat itching. The packages are called combination, dual, or twin packs.

To help clear up your infection completely, *it is very important that you keep using this medicine for the full time of treatment,* even if your symptoms begin to clear up after a few days. If you stop using this medicine too soon, your symptoms may return. *Do not miss any doses. Also, do not stop using this medicine if your menstrual period starts during the time of treatment.*

Dosing—The dose of these medicines will be different for different patients. *Follow your doctor's orders or the directions on the label.* The following information includes only the average doses of these medicines. *If your dose is different, do not change it* unless your doctor tells you to do so.

For butoconazole

- For yeast infection:
  - —For *vaginal cream* dosage form:
    - Adults and teenagers:
      - —Women who are not pregnant: 100 milligrams (mg) (one applicatorful) of 2% cream inserted into the vagina at bedtime for three nights in a row.
      - —Pregnant women, after the third month: 100 mg (one applicatorful) of 2% cream inserted into the vagina at bedtime for six nights in a row.
    - Children—Dose must be determined by your doctor.
  - —For *vaginal suppository* dosage form:
    - Adults and teenagers:
      - —Women who are not pregnant: 100 mg (one suppository) inserted into the vagina at bedtime for three nights in a row.

For clotrimazole

- For yeast infection:
  - —For *vaginal cream* dosage form:
    - Adults and teenagers—The dose depends on the strength of the cream.
      - —1% cream: 50 mg (one applicatorful) inserted into the vagina at bedtime for six to fourteen nights in a row.
      - —2% cream: 100 mg (one applicatorful) inserted into the vagina at bedtime for three nights in a row.
      - —10% cream: 500 mg (one applicatorful) inserted into the vagina at bedtime for one night only.
    - Children—Dose must be determined by your doctor.
  - —For *vaginal tablet* dosage form:
    - Adults and teenagers—The dose depends on the strength of the vaginal tablet.
      - —Women who are not pregnant:
        - 100-mg tablet: Insert one tablet into the vagina at bedtime for six or seven nights in a row.
        - 200-mg tablet: Insert one tablet into the vagina at bedtime for three nights in a row.
        - 500-mg tablet: Insert one tablet into the vagina at bedtime as a single dose.
      - —Pregnant women: 100 mg (one vaginal tablet) inserted into the vagina at bedtime for seven nights in a row.
    - Children—Dose must be determined by your doctor.

For econozole

- For yeast infection:
  - —For *vaginal suppository* dosage form:
    - Adults and teenagers—150 milligrams (mg) (one vaginal suppository) inserted into the vagina at bedtime for three nights in a row.
    - Children—Dose must be determined by your doctor.

For miconazole

- For yeast infection:
  - —For *vaginal cream* dosage form:
    - Adults and teenagers—One applicatorful inserted into the vagina at bedtime for seven or fourteen nights in a row.
    - Children—Dose must be determined by your doctor.
  - —For *vaginal suppository* dosage form:
    - Adults and teenagers—The dose depends on the strength of the suppository.
      - —100-mg suppository: Insert one vaginal suppository into the vagina at bedtime for seven nights in a row.
      - —200-mg suppository or
      - —400-mg suppository: Insert one vaginal suppository into the vagina at bedtime for three nights in a row.
    - Children—Dose must be determined by your doctor.
  - —For *tampon* dosage form:
    - Adults and teenagers—100 mg (one tampon) inserted into the vagina at bedtime and then removed the next morning. This is repeated every night for five nights in a row.
    - Children—Dose must be determined by your doctor.

For terconazole

- For yeast infection:
  - —For *vaginal cream* dosage form:
    - Adults and teenagers—The dose depends on the strength of the cream.
      - —0.4% cream: 20 mg (one applicatorful) inserted into the vagina at bedtime for seven nights in a row.

—0.8% cream: 40 mg (one applicatorful) inserted into the vagina at bedtime for three nights in a row.
- Children—Dose must be determined by your doctor.

—For *vaginal suppository* dosage form:
- Adults and teenagers—80 mg (one vaginal suppository) inserted into the vagina at bedtime for three nights in a row.
- Children—Dose must be determined by your doctor.

For tioconazole
- For yeast infection:
  —For *vaginal ointment* dosage form:
  - Adults and teenagers—300 mg (one applicatorful) of 6.5% ointment inserted into the vagina at bedtime for one night only.
  - Children—Dose must be determined by your doctor.

  —For *vaginal suppository* dosage form:
  - Adults and teenagers—300 mg (one vaginal suppository) inserted into the vagina at bedtime for one night only.
  - Children—Dose must be determined by your doctor.

Missed dose—If you miss a dose of this medicine, insert it as soon as possible. However, if it is almost time for your next dose, skip the missed dose and go back to your regular dosing schedule.

Storage—To store this medicine:
- Keep out of the reach of children.
- Store away from heat and direct light.
- Do not store the vaginal suppository or vaginal tablet form of this medicine in the bathroom, near the kitchen sink, or in other damp places. Heat or moisture may cause the medicine to break down.
- Keep the vaginal cream, ointment, and suppository forms of this medicine from freezing.
- Do not keep outdated medicine or medicine no longer needed. Be sure that any discarded medicine is out of the reach of children.

Precautions While Using This Medicine

If your symptoms do not improve within a few days, or if they become worse, check with your doctor.

Vaginal medicines usually will come out of the vagina during treatment. To keep the medicine from getting on your clothing, wear a minipad or sanitary napkin. The use of nonmedicated tampons (like those used for menstrual periods) is not recommended since they may soak up the medicine.

To help clear up your infection completely and to help make sure it does not return, good health habits are also required.
- Wear cotton panties (or panties or pantyhose with cotton crotches) instead of synthetic (for example, nylon or rayon) panties.
- Wear only clean panties.

If you have any questions about this, check with your health care professional.

Many vaginal infections are spread by having sex. A male sexual partner may carry the yeast on or in his penis. *While you are using this medicine, it may be a good idea for your partner to wear a condom during sex to avoid reinfection. Also, it may be necessary for your partner to be treated.*

Certain brands of vaginal azoles contain oils in the cream. Oils can weaken latex rubber condoms, diaphragms, or cervical caps. This increases the chances of a condom breaking during sexual intercourse. The rubber in cervical caps or diaphragms may break down faster and wear out sooner. Check with your health care professional to make sure the vaginal azole product you are using can be used with latex rubber birth control devices.

Some women may want to use a douche before the next dose. Some doctors will allow the use of a vinegar-and-water douche or other douche. However, others do not allow any douching. If you do use a douche, *do not overfill the vagina.* To do so may push the douche up into the uterus and possibly cause inflammation or infection. Also, *do not douche if you are pregnant, since this may harm the fetus.* If you have any questions about this, check with your health care professional.

Side Effects of This Medicine

Along with its needed effects, a medicine may cause some unwanted effects. Although not all of these side effects may occur, if they do occur they may need medical attention.

Check with your doctor as soon as possible if any of the following side effects occur:

Less common

Vaginal burning, itching, discharge, or other irritation not present before use of this medicine

Rare

Skin rash or hives

Other side effects may occur that usually do not need medical attention. These side effects may go away during treatment as your body adjusts to the medicine. However, check with your doctor if any of the following side effects continue or are bothersome:

Less common or rare

Abdominal or stomach cramps or pain; burning or irritation of penis of sexual partner; headache

Other side effects not listed above may also occur in some patients. If you notice any other effects, check with your doctor.

Revised: 04/21/92
Interim revision: 07/23/92; 07/12/94; 06/07/95; 07/15/96; 08/11/97

ANTIGLAUCOMA AGENTS, CHOLINERGIC, LONG-ACTING Ophthalmic

Some commonly used brand names are:

In the U.S.—

Floropryl[3]
Humorsol[1]
Phospholine Iodide[2]

In Canada—

Phospholine Iodide[2]

Other commonly used names are:

DFP[3]
difluorophate[3]
dyflos[3]
ecothiopate[2]

Note: For quick reference, the following medicines are numbered to match the corresponding brand names.

This information applies to the following medicines:

1. Demecarium (dem-e-KARE-ee-um)
2. Echothiophate (ek-oh-THYE-oh-fate)
3. Isoflurophate (eye-soe-FLURE-oh-fate)

Description

Demecarium, echothiophate, and isoflurophate are used in the eye to treat certain types of glaucoma and other eye conditions, such as accommodative esotropia. They may also be used in the diagnosis of certain eye conditions, such as accommodative esotropia.

These medicines are available only with your doctor's prescription, in the following dosage forms:

Ophthalmic

Demecarium
- Ophthalmic solution (eye drops) (U.S.)

Echothiophate
- Ophthalmic solution (eye drops) (U.S. and Canada)

Isoflurophate
- Ophthalmic ointment (eye ointment) (U.S.)

Before Using This Medicine

In deciding to use a medicine, the risks of taking the medicine must be weighed against the good it will do. This is a decision you and your doctor will make. For demecarium, echothiophate, or isoflurophate, the following should be considered:

Allergies—Tell your doctor if you have ever had any unusual or allergic reaction to demecarium, echothiophate, or isoflurophate. Also tell your health care professional if you are allergic to any other substances, such as preservatives.

Pregnancy—Because of the toxicity of these medicines in general, demecarium, echothiophate, and isoflurophate are not recommended during pregnancy.

Breast-feeding—Demecarium, echothiophate, and isoflurophate may be absorbed into the body. These medicines are not recommended during breast-feeding, because they may cause unwanted effects in nursing babies. It may be necessary for you to use another medicine or to stop breast-feeding during treatment. Be sure you have discussed the risks and benefits of the medicine with your doctor.

Children—Demecarium, echothiophate, or isoflurophate can cause serious side effects in any patient. When this medicine is used for a long time, eye cysts may occur. These eye cysts occur more often in children than in adults. Therefore, it is especially important that you discuss with the child's doctor the good that this medicine may do as well as the risks of using it.

Older adults—Many medicines have not been studied specifically in older people. Therefore, it may not be known whether they work exactly the same way they do in younger adults or if they cause different side effects or problems in older people. There is no specific information comparing use of these medicines in the elderly with use in other age groups. However, demecarium, echothiophate, or isoflurophate can cause serious side effects in any patient.

Other medicines—Although certain medicines should not be used together at all, in other cases two different medicines may be used together even if an interaction might occur. In these cases, your doctor may want to change the dose, or other precautions may be necessary. When you are taking demecarium, echothiophate, or isoflurophate, it is especially important that your health care professional know if you are taking any of the following:

- Amantadine (e.g., Symmetrel) or
- Anticholinergics (medicine for abdominal or stomach spasms or cramps) or
- Antidepressants (medicine for depression) or
- Antidyskinetics (medicine for Parkinson's disease or other conditions affecting control of muscles) or
- Antihistamines or
- Antimyasthenics (ambenonium [e.g., Mytelase], neostigmine [e.g., Prostigmin], pyridostigmine [e.g., Mestinon]) or
- Antipsychotics (medicine for mental illness) or
- Buclizine (e.g., Bucladin) or
- Carbamazepine (e.g., Tegretol) or
- Cyclizine (e.g., Marezine) or
- Cyclobenzaprine (e.g., Flexeril) or
- Disopyramide (e.g., Norpace) or
- Flavoxate (e.g., Urispas) or
- Ipratropium (e.g., Atrovent) or
- Meclizine (e.g., Antivert) or
- Methylphenidate (e.g., Ritalin) or
- Orphenadrine (e.g., Norflex) or
- Oxybutynin (e.g., Ditropen) or
- Procainamide (e.g., Pronestyl) or
- Promethazine (e.g., Phenergan) or
- Quinidine (e.g., Quinidex) or
- Trimeprazine (e.g., Temaril)—May increase the possibility of side effects or toxic effects; use of these medicines with demecarium, echothiophate, or isoflurophate is not recommended except under close supervision by your doctor
- Malathion (topical) (e.g., Prioderm)—May increase the possibility of side effects or toxic effects, especially if large amounts of malathion are used

Pesticides or insecticides—Make sure you tell your doctor if you have been exposed recently to pesticides or insecticides.

Other medical problems—The presence of other medical problems may affect the use of demecarium, echothiophate, or isoflurophate. Make sure you tell your doctor if you have any other medical problems, especially:

- Asthma or
- Epilepsy or
- Heart disease or
- High blood pressure or
- Myasthenia gravis or
- Overactive thyroid or
- Parkinsonism or
- Stomach ulcer or other stomach problems or
- Urinary tract blockage—If this medicine is absorbed into the body, it may make the condition worse
- Down's syndrome (mongolism)—This medicine may cause these children to become hyperactive
- Eye disease or problems (other)—May increase absorption of this medicine into the body or this medicine may make the condition worse

Proper Use of This Medicine

To use the *ophthalmic solution (eye drops) form* of this medicine:

- First, wash your hands. Tilt the head back and, pressing your finger gently on the skin just beneath the lower eyelid, pull the lower eyelid away from the eye to make a space. Drop the medicine into this space. Let go of the eyelid and gently close the eyes. Do not blink. Keep the eyes closed and apply pressure to the inner corner of the eye with your finger for 1 or 2 minutes to allow the medicine to be absorbed by the eye.
- Remove any excess solution around the eye with a clean tissue, being careful not to touch the eye.
- Immediately after using the eye drops, wash your hands to remove any medicine that may be on them.
- To keep the medicine as germ-free as possible, do not touch the applicator tip to any surface (including the eye). Also, keep the container tightly closed.

To use the *ophthalmic ointment (eye ointment) form* of this medicine:

- First, wash your hands. Tilt the head back and, pressing your finger gently on the skin just beneath the lower eyelid, pull the lower eyelid away from the eye to make a space. Squeeze a thin strip of ointment into this space. A 1/2-cm (approximately 1/4-inch) strip of ointment is usually enough, unless you have been told by your doctor to use a different amount. Let go of the eyelid and gently close the eyes. Keep the eyes closed for 1 to 2 minutes to allow the medicine to be absorbed by the eye.
- Immediately after using the eye ointment, wash your hands to remove any medicine that may be on them.
- Since isoflurophate loses its effectiveness when exposed to moisture, do not wash the tip of the ointment tube or allow it to touch any moist surface (including the eye).
- To keep the medicine as germ-free as possible, do not touch the applicator tip to any surface (including the eye). After using this eye ointment, wipe the tip of the ointment tube with a clean tissue and keep the tube tightly closed.
- Since an eye ointment usually causes blurred vision for a short time after you use it, ask your doctor if the dose (or one of the doses if you use more than 1 dose a day) can be used at bedtime.

It is very important that you use this medicine only as directed. Do not use more of it and do not use it more often than your doctor ordered. To do so may increase the chance of too much medicine being absorbed into the body and the chance of side effects.

Dosing—The doses of these medicines will be different for different patients. *Follow your doctor's orders or the directions on the label.* The following information includes only the average doses of these medicines. *If your dose is different, do not change it* unless your doctor tells you to do so.

For demecarium

- For *ophthalmic solution (eye drops)* dosage form:
  - —For glaucoma:
    - Adults and older children—Use one drop in the eye one or two times a day.
    - Infants and young children—Use and dose must be determined by your doctor.
  - —For treatment of accommodative esotropia:
    - Adults and older children—Use one drop in the eye once a day for two to three weeks, then one drop in the eye once every two days for three to four weeks, then use as determined by the doctor.
    - Infants and young children—Use and dose must be determined by your doctor.
  - —For diagnosis of accommodative esotropia:
    - Adults and older children—Use one drop in the eye once a day for two weeks, then one drop in the eye once every two days for two to three weeks.
    - Infants and young children—Use and dose must be determined by your doctor.

For echothiophate

- For *ophthalmic solution (eye drops)* dosage form:
  - —For glaucoma:
    - Adults and older children—Use one drop in the eye one or two times a day.
    - Infants and younger children—Use and dose must be determined by your doctor.
  - —For treatment of accommodative esotropia:
    - Adults and older children—Use one drop in the eye once a day or one drop in the eye once every two days.
    - Infants and young children—Use and dose must be determined by your doctor.

—For diagnosis of accommodative esotropia:
- Adults and older children—Use one drop in the eye once a day at bedtime for two to three weeks.
- Infants and young children—Use and dose must be determined by your doctor.

For isoflurophate
- For *ophthalmic ointment* dosage form:
  —For glaucoma:
  - Adults and older children—Use the ointment in the eyes once every three days or as often as three times a day as directed by the doctor.
  - Infants and young children—Use and dose must be determined by your doctor.

  —For treatment of accommodative esotropia:
  - Adults and older children—Use the ointment in the eyes once a day at bedtime for two weeks, then once a week or as often as once every two days as directed by the doctor.
  - Infants and young children—Use and dose must be determined by your doctor.

  —For diagnosis of accommodative esotropia:
  - Adults and older children—Use the ointment in the eyes once a day at bedtime for two weeks.
  - Infants and young children—Use and dose must be determined by your doctor.

Missed dose—If you miss a dose of this medicine and your dosing schedule is:
- One dose every other day—Use the missed dose as soon as possible if you remember it on the day it should be used. However, if you do not remember the missed dose until the next day, use it at that time. Then skip a day and start your dosing schedule again. Do not double doses.
- One dose a day—Use the missed dose as soon as possible. However, if you do not remember the missed dose until the next day, skip the missed dose and go back to your regular dosing schedule. Do not double doses.
- More than one dose a day—Use the missed dose as soon as possible. However, if it is almost time for your next dose, skip the missed dose and go back to your regular dosing schedule. Do not double doses.

If your dosing schedule is different from all of the above and you miss a dose of this medicine, or if you have any questions about this, check with your doctor.

Storage—To store this medicine:
- Keep out of the reach of children. Overdose of demecarium, echothiophate, or isoflurophate is very dangerous in young children.
- Store away from heat and direct light.
- Keep this medicine from freezing.
- Do not keep outdated medicine or medicine no longer needed. Be sure that any discarded medicine is out of the reach of children.

Precautions While Using This Medicine

If you are using this medicine for glaucoma, your doctor should check your eye pressure at regular visits to make sure the medicine is working.

If you will be using this medicine for a long time, your doctor should examine your eyes at regular visits to make sure this medicine does not cause unwanted effects.

Before you have any kind of surgery (including eye surgery), dental treatment, or emergency treatment, tell the medical doctor or dentist in charge and the anesthesiologist or anesthetist (the person who puts you to sleep) that you are using this medicine or have used it within the past month.

Avoid breathing in even small amounts of carbamate- or organophosphate-type insecticides or pesticides (for example, carbaryl [Sevin], demeton [Systox], diazinon, malathion, parathion, ronnel [Trolene], or TEPP). They may add to the effects of this medicine. Farmers, gardeners, residents of communities undergoing insecticide or pesticide spraying or dusting, workers in plants manufacturing such products, or other persons exposed to such poisons should protect themselves by wearing a mask over the nose and mouth, changing clothes frequently, and washing hands often.

Make sure your vision is clear before you drive, use machines, or do anything else that could be dangerous if you are not able to see well. This is because:
- After you apply this medicine to your eyes, your pupils may become unusually small. This may cause you to see less well at night or in dim light.
- After you begin using this medicine, your vision may be blurred or there may be a change in your near or distance vision.
- The eye ointment form of this medicine usually causes blurred vision for a short time after you apply it.

Side Effects of This Medicine

Along with its needed effects, a medicine may cause some unwanted effects. Although not all of these side effects may occur, if they do occur they may need medical attention.

Check with your doctor immediately if any of the following side effects occur:

Rare

Veil or curtain appearing across part of vision

Symptoms of too much medicine being absorbed into the body

Increased sweating; loss of bladder control; muscle weakness; nausea, vomiting, diarrhea, or stomach cramps or pain; shortness of breath, tightness in chest, or wheezing; slow or irregular heartbeat; unusual tiredness or weakness; watering of mouth

Note: The most common of these symptoms, especially in children, are nausea, vomiting, diarrhea, and stomach cramps or pain.

Too much medicine being absorbed is rare with the eye ointment form of this medicine.

Check with your doctor as soon as possible if any of the following side effects occur:

Rare
Burning, redness, stinging, or other eye irritation; eye pain

Other side effects may occur that usually do not need medical attention. These side effects may go away during treatment as your body adjusts to the medicine. However, check with your doctor if any of the following side effects continue or are bothersome:

Blurred vision or change in near or distance vision; difficulty in seeing at night or in dim light; headache or browache; twitching of eyelids; watering of eyes

Other side effects not listed above may also occur in some patients. If you notice any other effects, check with your doctor.

Revised: 06/21/94

ANTIHEMOPHILIC FACTOR Systemic

Some commonly used brand names are:

In the U.S.—

Alphanate	Hyate:C
Bioclate	Koate-HP
Helixate	Kogenate
Hemofil M	Monoclate-P
Humate-P	Recombinate

Generic name product may also be available.

In Canada—

Hemofil M	Kogenate
Hyate:C	Recombinate
Koate-HP	

Generic name product may also be available.

Other commonly used names are AHF and factor VIII.

Description

Antihemophilic (an-tee-hee-moe-FIL-ik) factor (AHF) is a protein produced naturally in the body. It helps the blood form clots to stop bleeding.

Hemophilia A, also called classical hemophilia, is a condition in which the body does not make enough AHF. If you do not have enough AHF and you become injured, your blood will not form clots as it should, and you may bleed into and damage your muscles and joints. One type of AHF is used to treat another condition called von Willebrand disease, in which there is a risk of bleeding. AHF also may be used for other conditions as determined by your doctor.

The AHF that your doctor will give you is obtained naturally from human or pig blood or artificially by a man-made process.

AHF obtained from human blood has been treated. It is not likely to contain harmful viruses such as hepatitis B virus; hepatitis C virus (non-A, non-B hepatitis); or human immunodeficiency virus (HIV), the virus that causes acquired immunodeficiency syndrome (AIDS). The man-made and pork AHF products do not contain these viruses.

AHF is available only with your doctor's prescription, in the following dosage form:

Parenteral
- Injection (U.S. and Canada)

Before Using This Medicine

In deciding to use a medicine, the risks of taking the medicine must be weighed against the good it will do. This is a decision you and your doctor will make. For antihemophilic factor (AHF), the following should be considered:

Allergies—Tell your doctor if you have ever had any unusual or allergic reaction to AHF. Also tell your health care professional if you are allergic to any other substances, such as foods, preservatives, or dyes.

Pregnancy—Studies on effects in pregnancy have not been done in either humans or animals.

Breast-feeding—It is not known whether AHF passes into breast milk. Although most medicines pass into breast milk in small amounts, many of them may be used safely while breast-feeding. Mothers who are using this medicine and who wish to breast-feed should discuss this with their doctor.

Children—This medicine has been tested in children and, in effective doses, has not been shown to cause different side effects or problems than it does in adults.

Older adults—This medicine has been tested and has not been shown to cause different side effects or problems in older people than it does in younger adults.

Other medicines—Although certain medicines should not be used together at all, in other cases two different medicines may be used together even if an interaction might occur. In these cases, your doctor may want to change the dose, or other precautions may be necessary. Tell your health care professional if you are using any other prescription or nonprescription (over-the-counter [OTC]) medicine.

Other medical problems—The presence of other medical problems may affect the use of AHF. Make sure you tell your doctor if you have any other medical problems.

Proper Use of This Medicine

Some medicines given by injection may sometimes be given at home to patients who do not need to be in the hospital. If you are using this medicine at home, your health care professional will teach you how to prepare and inject the medicine. You will have a chance to practice preparing and injecting it. *Be certain that you understand exactly how the medicine is to be prepared and injected.*

To prepare this medicine:

- Take the dry medicine and the liquid (diluent) out of the refrigerator or freezer and bring them to room temperature, as directed by your doctor.
- When injecting the liquid (diluent) into the dry medicine, *aim the stream of liquid (diluent) against the wall of the container of dry medicine* to prevent foaming.
- *Swirl the container gently to dissolve the medicine. Do not shake the container.*

Use this medicine right away. It should not be kept longer than 1 or 3 hours after it has been prepared, as directed on the package or by your doctor.

A plastic disposable syringe and filter needle must be used with this medicine. The medicine may stick to the inside of a glass syringe, and you may not receive a full dose.

Do not reuse syringes and needles. Put used syringes and needles in a puncture-resistant disposable container, or dispose of them as directed by your health care professional.

Dosing—The dose of antihemophilic factor (AHF) will be different for different patients. The dose you receive will be based on:

- Your body weight.
- The amount of AHF your body is able to make.
- How much, how often, and where in your body you are bleeding.
- Whether or not your body has built up a defense (antibody) against this medicine.

Your dose of this medicine may even be different at different times. It is important that you *follow your doctor's orders.*

Missed dose—If you miss a dose of this medicine, check with your doctor as soon as possible for instructions. If you cannot reach your doctor, use your usual dose as soon as you remember.

Storage—To store this medicine:

- Keep out of the reach of children.
- Some AHF products must be stored in the refrigerator and some in the freezer. However, some of them may be kept at room temperature for short periods of time. Store this medicine as directed by your doctor or by the manufacturer.
- Do not keep outdated medicine or medicine no longer needed. Be sure that any discarded medicine is out of the reach of children.

Precautions While Using This Medicine

If you were recently diagnosed with hemophilia A, you should receive hepatitis A and hepatitis B vaccines to reduce even further your risk of getting hepatitis A or B from antihemophilic factor.

It is recommended that you carry identification stating that you have hemophilia A, and what medicine you are using. If you have any questions about what kind of identification to carry, check with your health care professional.

After a while, your body may build up a defense (antibody) against this medicine. *Tell your doctor if this medicine seems to be less effective than usual.*

Side Effects of This Medicine

Along with its needed effects, a medicine may cause some unwanted effects. Some side effects will have signs or symptoms that you can see or feel. Your doctor may watch for others by doing certain tests.

Check with your doctor immediately if any of the following side effects occur, because they may mean that you are having a serious allergic reaction to the medicine:

Less common or rare

Changes in facial skin color; fast or irregular breathing; puffiness or swelling of the eyelids or around the eyes; shortness of breath, troubled breathing, tightness in chest, and/or wheezing; skin rash, hives, and/or itching

Also, check with your doctor as soon as possible if any of the following occur:

Less common or rare

Chills; fever; nausea; tenderness, pain, swelling, warmth, skin discoloration, and noticeable veins over affected area; unusual bleeding or bruising; unusual tiredness or weakness

Other side effects may occur that usually do not need medical attention. These side effects may go away during treatment as your body adjusts to the medicine. However, check with your doctor if any of the following side effects continue or are bothersome:

Less common

Burning, stinging, or swelling at place of injection; dizziness or lightheadedness; dry mouth or bad taste in mouth; headache; nosebleed; redness of face; vomiting

Other side effects not listed above may also occur in some patients. If you notice any other effects, check with your doctor.

Revised: 08/15/97

ANTIHISTAMINES Systemic

Some commonly used brand names are:

In the U.S.—

Aller-Chlor[8]
AllerMax Caplets[13]
Aller-med[13]
Anxanil[16]
Atarax[16]
Banophen[13]
Banophen Caplets[13]
Beldin[13]
Belix[13]
Bena-D 10[13]
Bena-D 50[13]
Benadryl[13]
Benadryl 25[13]
Benadryl Kapseals[13]
Benahist 10[13]
Benahist 50[13]
Ben-Allergin-50[13]
Benoject-10[13]
Benoject-50[13]
Benylin Cough[13]
Bromphen[5]
Bydramine Cough[13]
Calm X[12]
Children's Dramamine[12]
Chlo-Amine[8]
Chlor-100[8]
Chlorate[8]
Chlor-Niramine[8]
Chlorphed[5]
Chlor-Pro[8]
Chlor-Pro 10[8]
Chlorspan-12 [8]
Chlortab-4[8]
Chlortab-8[8]
Chlor-Trimeton[8]
Chlor-Trimeton Allergy[8]
Chlor-Trimeton Repetabs[8]
Claritin[17]
Codimal-A[5]
Compoz[13]
Conjec-B[5]
Contac 12 Hour Allergy[9]
Cophene-B[5]
Dehist[5]
Dexchlor[11]
Diamine T.D.[5]
Dimetabs[12]
Dimetane[5]
Dimetane Extentabs[5]
Dimetapp Allergy[5]
Dimetapp Allergy Liqui-Gels[5]
Dinate[12]
Diphenacen-50[13]
Diphenadryl[13]
Diphen Cough[13]
Diphenhist[13]
Diphenhist Captabs[13]
Dommanate[12]
Dormarex 2[13]
Dormin[13]
Dramamine[12]
Dramamine Chewable[12]
Dramamine Liquid[12]
Dramanate[12]
Dramocen[12]
Dramoject[12]
Dymenate[12]
E-Vista[16]
Fynex[13]
Genahist[13]
Gen-Allerate[8]
Gen-D-phen[13]
Hismanal[2]
Histaject Modified[5]
Hydramine[13]
Hydramine Cough[13]
Hydramyn[13]
Hydrate[12]
Hydril[13]
Hydroxacen[16]
Hyrexin-50[13]
Hyzine-50[16]
Marmine[12]
Myidil[22]
Nasahist B[5]
ND-Stat Revised[5]
Nervine Nighttime Sleep-Aid[13]
Nico-Vert [12]
Nidryl [13]
Nisaval[19]
Nolahist[18]
Noradryl[13]
Nordryl[13]
Nordryl Cough[13]
Nytol with DPH[13]
Nytol Maximum Strength[13]
Optimine[3]
Oraminic II[5]
PBZ[21]
PBZ-SR[21]
PediaCare Allergy Formula[8]
Pelamine[21]
Periactin[10]
Pfeiffer's Allergy[8]
Phendry[13]
Phendry Children's Allergy Medicine[13]
Phenetron[8]
Phenetron Lanacaps[8]
Poladex T.D.[11]
Polaramine[11]
Polaramine Repetabs[11]
Quiess[16]
Seldane[20]
Siladryl[13]
Silphen Cough Syrup[13]
Sleep-Eze 3[13]
Sominex Formula 2[13]
Tavist[9]
Tavist-1[9]
Tega-Vert[12]
Telachlor[8]
Teldrin[8]
Triptone Caplets[12]
Trymegen[8]
Tusstat[13]
Twilite Caplets[13]
Uni-Bent Cough[13]
Unisom Nighttime Sleep Aid[15]
Unisom SleepGels Maximum Strength[13]
Veltane[5]
Vertab[12]
Vistaject-25[16]
Vistaject-50[16]
Vistaril[16]
Vistazine 50[16]
Wehdryl-10[13]
Wehdryl-50[13]

In Canada—

Allerdryl[13]
Apo-Dimenhydrinate[12]
Apo-Hydroxyzine[16]
Atarax[16]
Benadryl[13]
Chlor-Tripolon[8]
Claritin[17]
Dimetane[5]
Dimetane Extentabs[5]
Dommanate[12]
Gravol[12]
Gravol L/A[12]
Hismanal[2]
Insomnal[13]
Multipax[16]
Nauseatol[12]
Novo-Dimenate[12]
Novo-Hydroxyzin[16]
Novo-Pheniram[8]
Novo-Terfendadine[20]
Optimine[3]
Periactin[10]
PMS-Dimenhydrinate[12]
Polaramine[11]
Polaramine Repetabs[11]
Pyribenzamine[21]
Reactine[7]
Seldane[20]
Seldane Caplets[20]
Tavist[9]
Travamine[12]
Traveltabs[12]

Note: For quick reference, the following antihistamines are numbered to match the corresponding brand names.

This information applies to the following medicines:

1. Acrivastine (AK-ri-vas-teen)
2. Astemizole (a-STEM-mi-zole)
3. Azatadine (a-ZA-ta-deen)
4. Bromodiphenhydramine (broe-moe-dye-fen-HYE-dra-meen)‡
5. Brompheniramine (brome-fen-EER-a-meen)‡
6. Carbinoxamine (kar-bi-NOX-a-meen)‡
7. Cetirizine (se-TI-ra-zeen)*
8. Chlorpheniramine (klor-fen-EER-a-meen)‡
9. Clemastine (KLEM-as-teen)‡
10. Cyproheptadine (si-proe-HEP-ta-deen)‡
11. Dexchlorpheniramine (dex-klor-fen-EER-a-meen)‡
12. Dimenhydrinate (dye-men-HYE-dri-nate)‡§
13. Diphenhydramine (dye-fen-HYE-dra-meen)‡§
14. Diphenylpyraline (dye-fen-il-PEER-a-leen)§
15. Doxylamine (dox-ILL-a-meen)†
16. Hydroxyzine (hye-DROX-i-zeen)‡§
17. Loratadine (lor-AT-a-deen)
18. Phenindamine (fen-IN-da-meen)†
19. Pyrilamine (peer-ILL-a-meen)†‡
20. Terfenadine (ter-FEN-a-deen)
21. Tripelennamine (tri-pel-ENN-a-meen)‡
22. Triprolidine (trye-PROE-li-deen)†‡

*Not commercially available in the U.S.
†Not commercially available in Canada.
‡Generic name product may also be available in the U.S.
§Generic name product may also be available in Canada.

Description

Antihistamines are used to relieve or prevent the symptoms of hay fever and other types of allergy. They work by preventing the effects of a substance called histamine, which is produced by the body. Histamine can cause itching, sneezing, runny nose, and watery eyes. Also, in some persons histamine can close up the bronchial tubes (air passages of the lungs) and make breathing difficult.

Some of the antihistamines are also used to prevent motion sickness, nausea, vomiting, and dizziness. In patients with Parkinson's disease, diphenhydramine may be used to decrease stiffness and tremors. Also, the syrup form of diphenhydramine is used to relieve the cough due to colds or hay fever. In addition, since antihistamines may cause drowsiness as a side effect, some of them may be used to help people go to sleep.

Hydroxyzine is used in the treatment of nervous and emotional conditions to help control anxiety. It can also be used to help control anxiety and produce sleep before surgery. Antihistamines may also be used for other conditions as determined by your doctor.

Some antihistamine preparations are available only with your doctor's prescription. Others are available without a prescription. However, your doctor may have special instructions on the proper dose of the medicine for your medical condition.

These medicines are available in the following dosage forms:

Oral

Astemizole
- Oral suspension (Canada)
- Tablets (U.S. and Canada)

Azatadine
- Tablets (U.S. and Canada)

Brompheniramine
- Capsules (U.S.)
- Elixir (U.S. and Canada)
- Tablets (U.S. and Canada)
- Extended-release tablets (U.S. and Canada)

Cetirizine
- Tablets (Canada)

Chlorpheniramine
- Extended-release capsules (U.S.)
- Syrup (U.S. and Canada)
- Tablets (U.S. and Canada)
- Chewable tablets (U.S.)
- Extended-release tablets (U.S. and Canada)

Clemastine
- Syrup (U.S. and Canada)
- Tablets (U.S. and Canada)

Cyproheptadine
- Syrup (U.S. and Canada)
- Tablets (U.S. and Canada)

Dexchlorpheniramine
- Syrup (U.S. and Canada)
- Tablets (U.S. and Canada)
- Extended-release tablets (U.S. and Canada)

Dimenhydrinate
- Capsules (U.S.)
- Extended-release capsules (Canada)
- Elixir (U.S. and Canada)
- Syrup (U.S.)
- Tablets (U.S. and Canada)
- Chewable tablets (U.S.)

Diphenhydramine
- Capsules (U.S. and Canada)
- Elixir (U.S. and Canada)
- Syrup (U.S.)
- Tablets (U.S.)

Doxylamine
- Tablets (U.S.)

Hydroxyzine
- Capsules (U.S. and Canada)
- Oral suspension (U.S.)
- Syrup (U.S. and Canada)
- Tablets (U.S.)

Loratadine
- Syrup (Canada)
- Tablets (U.S. and Canada)

Phenindamine
- Tablets (U.S.)

Pyrilamine
- Tablets (U.S.)

Terfenadine
- Oral suspension (Canada)
- Tablets (U.S. and Canada)

Tripelennamine
- Elixir (U.S.)
- Tablets (U.S. and Canada)
- Extended-release tablets (U.S.)

Triprolidine
- Syrup (U.S.)

Rectal

Dimenhydrinate
- Suppositories (Canada)

Before Using This Medicine

In deciding to use a medicine, the risks of taking the medicine must be weighed against the good it will do. This is a decision you and your doctor will make. For antihistamines, the following should be considered:

Allergies—Tell your doctor if you have ever had any unusual or allergic reaction to antihistamines. Also tell your health care professional if you are allergic to any other substances, such as foods, preservatives, or dyes.

Diet—Make certain your health care professional knows if you are on a low-sodium, low-sugar, or any other special diet. Most medicines contain more than their active ingredient, and many liquid medicines contain alcohol.

Do not take terfenadine (e.g., Seldane) with grapefruit juice. To do so may cause heart rhythm problems.

Pregnancy—Most antihistamines have not been studied in pregnant women. Although these antihistamines have not been shown to cause problems in humans, studies in animals have shown that some other antihistamines, such as meclizine (e.g., Antivert) and cyclizine (e.g., Marezine), may cause birth defects. Also, studies in animals have shown that terfenadine, when given in doses several times the human dose, lowers the birth weight and increases the risk of death of the offspring.

Cetirizine and hydroxyzine are not recommended for use in the first months of pregnancy since they have been shown to cause birth defects in animal studies when given in doses many times higher than the usual human dose. Be sure you have discussed this with your doctor.

Breast-feeding—Small amounts of antihistamines pass into the breast milk. Use is not recommended since babies are more susceptible to the side effects of antihistamines, such as unusual excitement or irritability. Also, since these medicines tend to decrease the secretions of the body, it is possible that the flow of breast milk may be reduced in some patients. It is not known yet whether astemizole, cetirizine, loratadine, and terfenadine cause these same side effects.

Children—Serious side effects, such as convulsions (seizures), are more likely to occur in younger patients and would be of greater risk to infants than to older children or adults. In general, children are more sensitive to the effects of antihistamines. Also, nightmares or unusual excitement, nervousness, restlessness, or irritability may be more likely to occur in children.

Older adults—Elderly patients are usually more sensitive to the effects of antihistamines. Confusion; difficult or painful urination; dizziness; drowsiness; feeling faint; or dryness of mouth, nose, or throat may be more likely to occur in elderly patients. Also, nightmares or unusual excitement, nervousness, restlessness, or irritability may be more likely to occur in elderly patients.

Other medicines—Although certain medicines should not be used together at all, in other cases different medicines may be used together even if an interaction might occur. In these cases, your doctor may want to change the dose, or other precautions may be necessary. When you are taking antihistamines it is especially important that your health care professional knows if you are taking any of the following:

- Anticholinergics (medicine for abdominal or stomach spasms or cramps)—Side effects, such as dryness of mouth, of antihistamines or anticholinergics may be more likely to occur

- Azithromycin (e.g., Zithromax) or
- Clarithromycin (e.g., Biaxin) or
- Erythromycin (e.g., E-Mycin) or
- Itraconazole (e.g., Sporanox) or
- Ketoconazole (e.g., Nizoral)—Use of these medicines with astemizole and terfenadine may cause heart problems, such as an irregular heartbeat; these medicines should not be used together

- Bepridil (e.g., Vascor) or
- Disopyramide (e.g., Norpace) or
- Maprotiline (e.g., Ludiomil) or
- Phenothiazines (acetophenazine [e.g., Tindal], chlorpromazine [e.g., Thorazine], fluphenazine [e.g., Prolixin], mesoridazine [e.g., Serentil], perphenazine [e.g., Trilafon], prochlorperazine [e.g., Compazine], promazine [e.g., Sparine], promethazine [e.g., Phenergan], thioridazine [e.g. Mellaril], trifluoperazine [e.g., Stelazine], triflupromazine [e.g., Vesprin], trimeprazine [e.g., Temaril]) or
- Pimozide (e.g., Orap) or
- Procainamide (e.g., Pronestyl) or
- Quinidine (e.g., Quinaglute Dura-tabs) or
- Tricyclic antidepressants (amitriptyline [e.g., Elavil], amoxapine [e.g., Asendin], clomipramine [e.g., Anafranil], desipramine [e.g., Pertofrane], doxepin [e.g., Sinequan], imipramine [e.g., Tofranil], nortriptyline [e.g., Aventyl], protriptyline [e.g., Vivactil], trimipramine [e.g., Surmontil])—Use of these medicines with astemizole or terfenadine may increase the risk of heart rhythm problems

- Cisapride (e.g., Propulsid) or
- HIV protease inhibitors (indinavir [e.g., Crixivan], nelfinavir [e.g., Viracept], ritonavir [e.g., Norvir], saquinavir [e.g., Invirase]) or
- Mibefradil (e.g., Posicor) or
- Serotonin reuptake inhibitors (fluvoxamine [e.g., Luvox], nefazodone [e.g., Serzone], sertraline [e.g., Zoloft]) or
- Sparfloxacin (e.g., Zagam) or
- Zileuton (e.g., Zyflo)—Use of these medicines with terfenadine may cause heart problems; these medicines should not be used with terfenadine

- Central nervous system (CNS) depressants—Effects, such as drowsiness, of CNS depressants or antihistamines may be worsened; also, taking maprotiline or tricyclic antidepressants may cause some side effects of either of these medicines, such as dryness of mouth, to become more severe
- Monoamine oxidase (MAO) inhibitors (furazolidone [e.g., Furoxone], isocarboxazid [e.g., Marplan], phenelzine [e.g., Nardil], procarbazine [e.g., Matulane], tranylcypromine [e.g., Parnate])—If you are now taking, or have taken within the past 2 weeks, any of the MAO inhibitors, the side effects of the antihistamines, such as drowsiness and dryness of mouth, may become more severe; these medicines should not be used together
- Quinine—Use of this medicine with astemizole may cause heart problems, such as irregular heartbeat; these medicines should not be used together

Other medical problems—The presence of other medical problems may affect the use of antihistamines. Make sure you tell your doctor if you have any other medical problems, especially:

- Enlarged prostate or
- Urinary tract blockage or difficult urination—Antihistamines may make urinary problems worse
- Glaucoma—These medicines may cause a slight increase in inner eye pressure that may make the condition worse
- Heart rhythm problems (history of) or
- Low potassium blood levels—Use of astemizole or terfenadine can cause serious heart rhythm problems
- Liver disease—Higher blood levels of astemizole or terfenadine may result, which may increase the chance of heart problems

Proper Use of This Medicine

Antihistamines are used to relieve or prevent the symptoms of your medical problem. Take them only as directed. Do not take more of them and do not take them more often than recommended on the label, unless otherwise directed by your doctor. To do so may increase the chance of side effects.

Dosing—The dose of an antihistamine will be different for different patients. *Follow your doctor's orders or the directions on the label.* The following information includes only the average doses of antihistamines. *If your dose is different, do not change it* unless your doctor tells you to do so.

The number of capsules or tablets or teaspoonfuls of liquid that you take or the number of suppositories you use depends on the strength of the medicine. Also, *the number of doses you take each day and the time between doses depends on whether you are taking a short-acting or long-acting form of antihistamine.*

- For use as an antihistamine:

  For astemizole

  - For *oral* dosage forms (tablets or liquid):

    —Adults and teenagers: 10 milligrams (mg) once a day.

    —Children younger than 6 years of age: 0.2 mg per kilogram (kg) (0.1 mg per pound) of body weight once a day.

    —Children 6 to 12 years of age: 5 mg once a day.

For azatadine

• For *oral* dosage form (tablets):
—Adults: 1 to 2 milligrams (mg) every eight to twelve hours as needed.
—Children younger than 12 years of age: Use and dose must be determined by your doctor.
—Children 12 years of age and older: 0.5 mg to 1 mg two times a day as needed.

For brompheniramine

• For *regular (short-acting) oral* dosage forms (capsules, tablets, or liquid):
—Adults and teenagers: 4 milligrams (mg) every four to six hours as needed.
—Children 2 to 6 years of age: 1 mg every four to six hours as needed.
—Children 6 to 12 years of age: 2 mg every four to six hours as needed.

• For *long-acting oral* dosage form (tablets):
—Adults: 8 milligrams (mg) every eight or twelve hours, or 12 mg every twelve hours as needed.
—Children younger than 6 years of age: Use and dose must be determined by your doctor.
—Children 6 years of age and older: 8 or 12 mg every twelve hours as needed.

• For *injection* dosage form:
—Adults and teenagers: 10 milligrams (mg) injected into a muscle, under the skin, or into a vein every eight to twelve hours.
—Children younger than 12 years of age: 0.125 mg per kilogram (0.06 mg per pound) of body weight injected into a muscle, under the skin, or into a vein three or four times a day as needed.

For cetirizine

• For *oral* dosage form (tablets):
—Adults: 5 to 10 milligrams (mg) once a day.
—Children: Use and dose must be determined by your doctor.

For chlorpheniramine

• For *regular (short-acting) oral* dosage forms (tablets or liquid):
—Adults and teenagers: 4 milligrams (mg) every four to six hours as needed.
—Children younger than 6 years of age: Use and dose must be determined by your doctor.
—Children 6 to 12 years of age: 2 mg three or four times a day as needed.

• For *long-acting oral* dosage forms (capsules or tablets):
—Adults: 8 or 12 milligrams (mg) every eight to twelve hours as needed.
—Children younger than 12 years of age: Use and dose must be determined by your doctor.
—Children 12 years of age and older: 8 mg every twelve hours as needed.

• For *injection* dosage form:
—Adults: 5 to 40 milligrams (mg) injected into a muscle, into a vein, or under the skin.
—Children: 0.0875 mg per kilogram (0.04 mg per pound) of body weight injected under the skin every six hours as needed.

For clemastine

• For *oral* dosage forms (tablets or liquid):
—Adults and teenagers: 1.34 milligrams (mg) two times a day or 2.68 mg one to three times a day as needed.
—Children younger than 6 years of age: Use and dose must be determined by your doctor.
—Children 6 to 12 years of age: 0.67 to 1.34 mg two times a day.

For cyproheptadine

• For *oral* dosage forms (tablets or liquid):
—Adults and children 14 years of age and older: 4 milligrams (mg) every eight hours. The doctor may increase the dose if needed.
—Children 2 to 6 years of age: 2 mg every eight to twelve hours as needed.
—Children 6 to 14 years of age: 4 mg every eight to twelve hours as needed.

For dexchlorpheniramine

• For *regular (short-acting) oral* dosage forms (tablets or liquid):
—Adults and teenagers: 2 milligrams (mg) every four to six hours as needed.
—Children 2 to 5 years of age: 0.5 mg every four to six hours as needed.
—Children 5 to 12 years of age: 1 mg every four to six hours as needed.

• For *long-acting oral* dosage form (tablets):
—Adults: 4 or 6 milligrams (mg) every eight to twelve hours as needed.
—Children: Use and dose must be determined by your doctor.

For diphenhydramine

• For *oral* dosage forms (capsules, tablets, or liquid):
—Adults and teenagers: 25 to 50 milligrams (mg) every four to six hours as needed.
—Children younger than 6 years of age: 6.25 to 12.5 mg every four to six hours.
—Children 6 to 12 years of age: 12.5 to 25 mg every four to six hours.

• For *injection* dosage form:
—Adults: 10 to 50 milligrams (mg) injected into a muscle or into a vein.
—Children: 1.25 mg per kg (0.6 mg per pound) of body weight injected into a muscle four times a day.

For doxylamine

• For *oral* dosage form (tablets):
—Adults and teenagers: 12.5 to 25 milligrams (mg) every four to six hours as needed.
—Children younger than 6 years of age: Use and dose must be determined by your doctor.
—Children 6 to 12 years of age: 6.25 to 12.5 mg every four to six hours as needed.

For hydroxyzine
- For *oral* dosage forms (capsules, tablets, or liquid):
  —Adults and teenagers: 25 to 100 milligrams (mg) three or four times a day as needed.
  —Children younger than 12 years of age: 0.5 mg per kg (0.2 mg per pound) of body weight every six hours as needed.

For loratadine
- For *oral* dosage forms (tablets or liquid):
  —Adults and children 10 years of age and older: 10 milligrams (mg) once a day.
  —Children 2 to 9 years of age: 5 mg once a day.

For phenindamine
- For *oral* dosage form (tablets):
  —Adults and teenagers: 25 milligrams (mg) every four to six hours as needed.
  —Children younger than 6 years of age: Use and dose must be determined by your doctor.
  —Children 6 to 12 years of age: 12.5 mg every four to six hours as needed.

For pyrilamine
- For *oral* dosage form (tablets):
  —Adults: 25 to 50 milligrams (mg) every eight hours as needed.
  —Children 2 to 6 years of age: Use and dose must be determined by your doctor.
  —Children 6 years of age and older: 12.5 to 25 mg every eight hours as needed.

For terfenadine
- For *oral* dosage forms (tablets or liquid):
  —Adults and teenagers: 60 milligrams (mg) every twelve hours.
  —Children 3 to 6 years of age: 15 mg every twelve hours as needed.
  —Children 7 to 12 years of age: 30 mg every twelve hours as needed.

For tripelennamine
- For *regular (short-acting) oral* dosage forms (tablets or liquid):
  —Adults: 25 to 50 milligrams (mg) every four to six hours as needed.
  —Children: 1.25 mg per kilogram (kg) (0.6 mg per pound) of body weight every six hours as needed.
- For *long-acting oral* dosage form (tablets):
  —Adults: 100 milligrams (mg) every eight to twelve hours as needed.
  —Children: Use and dose must be determined by your doctor.

For triprolidine
- For *oral* dosage forms (liquid):
  —Adults and teenagers: 2.5 milligrams (mg) every four to six hours as needed.
  —Children 4 months to 2 years of age: 0.312 mg (1/4 teaspoonful) every six to eight hours as needed.
  —Children 2 to 4 years of age: 0.625 mg (1/2 teaspoonful) every six to eight hours as needed.
  —Children 4 to 6 years of age: 0.937 mg (3/4 teaspoonful) every six to eight hours as needed.
  —Children 6 to 12 years of age: 1.25 mg (1 teaspoonful) every six to eight hours as needed.

- For nausea, vomiting, and vertigo (only dimenhydrinate and diphenhydramine are used for vertigo):

  For dimenhydrinate
  - For *regular (short-acting) oral* dosage forms (capsules, tablets, or liquid):
    —Adults and teenagers: 50 to 100 milligrams (mg) every four hours as needed.
    —Children 2 to 6 years of age: 12.5 to 25 mg every six to eight hours as needed.
    —Children 6 to 12 years of age: 25 to 50 mg every six to eight hours as needed.
  - For *long-acting oral* dosage form (capsules):
    —Adults: 1 capsule (contains 25 milligrams [mg] for immediate action and 50 mg for long action) every twelve hours.
    —Children: Use and dose must be determined by your doctor.
  - For *injection* dosage form:
    —Adults: 50 milligrams (mg) injected into a muscle or into a vein every four hours as needed.
    —Children: 1.25 mg per kg (0.6 mg per pound) of body weight injected into a muscle or into a vein every six hours as needed.
  - For *suppository* dosage form:
    —Adults: 50 to 100 milligrams (mg) inserted into the rectum every six to eight hours as needed.
    —Children younger than 6 years of age: Use and dose must be determined by your doctor.
    —Children 6 to 8 years of age: 12.5 to 25 mg inserted into the rectum every eight to twelve hours as needed.
    —Children 8 to 12 years of age: 25 to 50 mg inserted into the rectum every eight to twelve hours as needed.
    —Children 12 years of age and older: 50 mg inserted into the rectum every eight to twelve hours as needed.

  For diphenhydramine
  - For *oral* dosage forms (capsules, tablets, or liquid):
    —Adults: 25 to 50 milligrams (mg) every four to six hours as needed.
    —Children: 1 to 1.5 mg per kg (0.45 to 0.7 mg per pound) of body weight every four to six hours as needed.
  - For *injection* dosage form:
    —Adults: 10 milligrams (mg) injected into a muscle or into a vein. Dose may be increased to 25 to 50 mg every two to three hours.
    —Children: 1 to 1.5 mg per kg (0.45 to 0.68 mg per pound) of body weight injected into a muscle every six hours.

For hydroxyzine

- For *oral* dosage forms (capsules, tablets, or liquid):
  - —Adults: 25 to 100 milligrams (mg) three or four times a day as needed.
  - —Children younger than 6 years of age: 12.5 mg every six hours as needed.
  - —Children 6 years of age and older: 12.5 to 25 mg every six hours as needed.
- For *injection* dosage form:
  - —Adults: 25 to 100 milligrams (mg) injected into a muscle.
  - —Children: 1 mg per kg (0.45 mg per pound) of body weight injected into a muscle.

- For Parkinson's disease:

  For diphenhydramine

  - For *oral* dosage forms (capsules, tablets, or liquid):
    - —Adults: 25 milligrams (mg) three times a day when starting treatment. Your doctor may increase the dose gradually later if needed.
  - For *injection* dosage form:
    - —Adults: 10 to 50 milligrams (mg) injected into a muscle or into a vein.
    - —Children: 1.25 mg per kg (0.6 mg per pound) of body weight four times a day injected into a muscle.

- For use as a sedative (to help sleep):

  For diphenhydramine

  - For *oral* dosage forms (capsules, tablets, or liquid):
    - —Adults: 50 milligrams (mg) twenty to thirty minutes before bedtime if needed.

  For doxylamine

  - For *oral* dosage form (tablets):
    - —Adults: 25 milligrams (mg) thirty minutes before bedtime if needed.
    - —Children: Use and dose must be determined by your doctor.

  For hydroxyzine

  - For *oral* dosage forms (capsules, tablets, or liquid):
    - —Adults: 50 to 100 milligrams (mg).
    - —Children: 0.6 mg per kg (0.3 mg per pound) of body weight.
  - For *injection* dosage form:
    - —Adults: 50 milligrams (mg) injected into a muscle.

- For cough:

  For diphenhydramine

  - For *oral* dosage form (liquid):
    - —Adults and teenagers: 25 milligrams (mg) every four to six hours.
    - —Children younger than 2 years of age: Use and dose must be determined by your doctor.
    - —Children 2 to 6 years of age: 6.25 mg (1/2 teaspoonful) every four to six hours as needed.
    - —Children 6 to 12 years of age: 12.5 mg (1 teaspoonful) every four to six hours as needed.

- For anxiety:

  For hydroxyzine

  - For *oral* dosage forms (capsules, tablets, or liquid):
    - —Adults: 50 to 100 milligrams (mg).
    - —Children: 0.6 mg per kilogram (0.3 mg per pound) of body weight.
  - For *injection* dosage form:
    - —Adults: 50 to 100 milligrams (mg) injected into a muscle every four to six hours as needed.
    - —Children: 1 mg per kilogram (0.45 mg per pound) of body weight injected into a muscle.

Missed dose—If you are taking this medicine regularly and you miss a dose, take it as soon as possible. However, if it is almost time for your next dose, skip the missed dose and go back to your regular dosing schedule. Do not double doses.

For patients *taking this medicine by mouth:*

- Antihistamines can be taken with food or a glass of water or milk to lessen stomach irritation if necessary. However, food may change the amount of astemizole that is absorbed. For this reason, astemizole should be taken on an empty stomach.
- If you are taking the extended-release tablet form of this medicine, swallow the tablets whole. Do not break, crush, or chew before swallowing.

For patients taking *dimenhydrinate or diphenhydramine for motion sickness:*

- Take this medicine at least 30 minutes or, even better, 1 to 2 hours before you begin to travel.

For patients using the *suppository form of this medicine:*

- To insert suppository: First remove the foil wrapper and moisten the suppository with cold water. Lie down on your side and use your finger to push the suppository well up into the rectum. If the suppository is too soft to insert, chill the suppository in the refrigerator for 30 minutes or run cold water over it before removing the foil wrapper.

For patients using the *injection form of this medicine:*

- If you will be giving yourself the injections, make sure you understand exactly how to give them. If you have any questions about this, check with your health care professional.

Storage—To store this medicine:

- Keep out of the reach of children, since overdose may be very dangerous in children.
- Store away from heat and direct light.
- Do not store the capsule or tablet form of this medicine in the bathroom medicine cabinet, near the kitchen sink, or in other damp places. Heat or moisture may cause the medicine to break down.
- Keep the liquid form of this medicine from freezing.
- Do not keep outdated medicine or medicine no longer needed. Be sure that any discarded medicine is out of the reach of children.

Precautions While Using This Medicine

Before you have any skin tests for allergies, tell the doctor in charge that you are taking this medicine. The results of the test may be affected by this medicine.

When taking antihistamines on a regular basis, make sure your doctor knows if you are taking large amounts of aspirin at the same time (as for arthritis or rheumatism). Effects of too much aspirin, such as ringing in the ears, may be covered up by the antihistamine.

Antihistamines will add to the effects of alcohol and other CNS depressants (medicines that slow down the nervous system, possibly causing drowsiness). Some examples of CNS depressants are sedatives, tranquilizers, or sleeping medicine; prescription pain medicine or narcotics; barbiturates; medicine for seizures; muscle relaxants; or anesthetics, including some dental anesthetics. *Check with your doctor before taking any of the above while you are using this medicine.*

This medicine may cause some people to become drowsy or less alert than they are normally. Even if taken at bedtime, it may cause some people to feel drowsy or less alert on arising. Some antihistamines are more likely to cause drowsiness than others. Drowsiness is less likely with cetirizine, and rare with astemizole, loratadine, and terfenadine. *Make sure you know how you react to the antihistamine you are taking before you drive, use machines, or do anything else that could be dangerous if you are not alert.*

Antihistamines may cause dryness of the mouth, nose, and throat. Some antihistamines are more likely to cause dryness of the mouth than others (astemizole, cetirizine, loratadine, and terfenadine, for example, rarely produce this effect). For temporary relief of mouth dryness, use sugarless candy or gum, melt bits of ice in your mouth, or use a saliva substitute. However, if your mouth continues to feel dry for more than 2 weeks, check with your medical doctor or dentist. Continuing dryness of the mouth may increase the chance of dental disease, including tooth decay, gum disease, and fungus infections.

For patients using *dimenhydrinate, diphenhydramine, or hydroxyzine:*

- This medicine controls nausea and vomiting. For this reason, it may cover up the signs of overdose caused by other medicines or the symptoms of appendicitis. This will make it difficult for your doctor to diagnose these conditions. Make sure your doctor knows that you are taking this medicine if you have other symptoms of appendicitis such as stomach or lower abdominal pain, cramping, or soreness. Also, if you think you may have taken an overdose of any medicine, tell your doctor that you are taking this medicine.

For patients using *diphenhydramine or doxylamine as a sleeping aid:*

- If you are already taking a sedative or tranquilizer, do not take this medicine without consulting your doctor first.

Side Effects of This Medicine

Along with its needed effects, a medicine may cause some unwanted effects. Although not all of these side effects may occur, if they do occur they may need medical attention.

Check with your doctor immediately if the following side effect occurs:

Less common or rare—with high doses of astemizole or terfenadine only

Fast or irregular heartbeat

Also, check with your doctor as soon as possible if any of the following side effects occur:

Less common or rare

Sore throat and fever; unusual bleeding or bruising; unusual tiredness or weakness

Symptoms of overdose

Clumsiness or unsteadiness; convulsions (seizures); drowsiness (severe); dryness of mouth, nose, or throat (severe); feeling faint; flushing or redness of face; hallucinations (seeing, hearing, or feeling things that are not there); shortness of breath or troubled breathing; trouble in sleeping

Other side effects may occur that usually do not need medical attention. These side effects may go away during treatment as your body adjusts to the medicine. However, check with your health care professional if any of the following side effects continue or are bothersome:

More common—less common with cetirizine; rare with astemizole, loratadine, and terfenadine

Drowsiness; thickening of mucus

Less common or rare

Blurred vision or any change in vision; confusion; difficult or painful urination; dizziness; dryness of mouth, nose, or throat; fast heartbeat; increased sensitivity of skin to sun; increased sweating; loss of appetite (increased appetite with astemizole, cetirizine, cyproheptadine, loratadine, and terfenadine); nightmares; ringing or buzzing in ears; skin rash; stomach upset or stomach pain (more common with pyrilamine and tripelennamine); unusual excitement, nervousness, restlessness, or irritability; weight gain (with astemizole and cyproheptadine only)

Other side effects not listed above may also occur in some patients. If you notice any other effects, check with your health care professional.

Additional Information

Once a medicine has been approved for marketing for a certain use, experience may show that it is also useful for

other medical problems. Although this use is not included in product labeling, astemizole, cetirizine, loratadine, and terfenadine are used in certain patients with asthma together with asthma medicines. The antihistamine is used before and during exposure to substances that cause reactions, to prevent or reduce bronchospasm (wheezing or difficulty in breathing).

Other than the above information, there is no additional information relating to proper use, precautions, or side effects for this use.

Revised: 07/26/94
Interim revision: 07/10/96

ANTIHISTAMINES AND DECONGESTANTS Systemic

Some commonly used brand names are:

In the U.S.—

Actagen[25]
Actifed[25]
Actifed Allergy Nighttime Caplets[19]
Alcomed[4]
Alcomed 2-60[18]
Allent[6]
Allercon[25]
Allerest Maximum Strength[14]
Allerfrim[25]
Allerphed[25]
Amilon[8]
Anamine[14]
Anamine T.D.[14]
Andec[7]
Andec-TR[7]
Aprodrine[25]
A.R.M. Maximum Strength Caplets[11]
Atrofed[25]
Atrohist Pediatric[14, 15]
Banophen[19]
Benadryl Allergy Decongestant Liquid Medication[19]
Biohist-LA[7]
Brexin L.A.[14]
Brofed Liquid[6]
Bromadrine PD[6]
Bromadrine TR[6]
Bromaline[4]
Bromanate[4]
Bromatapp[4]
Bromfed[6]
Bromfed-PD[6]
Bromfenex[6]
Bromfenex PD[6]
Bromophen T.D.[3]
Brompheril[18]
Carbiset[7]
Carbiset-TR[7]
Carbodec[7]
Carbodec TR[7]
Cardec[7]
Cardec-S[7]
Cenafed Plus[25]
Chemdec[7]
C-Hist-SR[12]
Chlorafed[14]
Chlorafed H.S. Timecelles[14]
Chlorafed Timecelles[14]
Chlordrine S.R.[14]
Chlorfed[14]
Chlorfed II[14]
Chlorphedrine SR[14]
Chlor-Rest[11]
Chlortox[12]
Chlor-Trimeton 4 Hour Relief[14]
Chlor-Trimeton 12 Hour Relief[14]
Claritin-D[19a]
Codimal-L.A.[14]
Codimal-L.A. Half[14]
Cold and Allergy[4]
Cold-Gest Cold[11]
Colfed-A[14]
Comhist[12]
Comhist LA[12]
Contac 12-Hour[11]
Contac Maximum Strength 12-Hour Caplets[11]
Cophene No. 2[14]
Co-Pyronil 2[14]
CP Oral[7]
Dallergy Jr.[6]
Deconamine[14]
Deconamine SR[14]
Decongestabs[13]
Deconomed SR[14]
Delhistine D[20]
Demazin[11]
Demazin Repetabs[11]
Dexaphen SA[18]
Dexophed[18]
Dimaphen[4]
Dimaphen S.A.[4]
Dimetane Decongestant[2]
Dimetane Decongestant Caplets[2]
Dimetapp[3, 4]
Dimetapp Cold and Allergy[4]
Dimetapp Cold & Allergy Quick Dissolve[4]
Dimetapp Extentabs[4]
Dimetapp 4-Hour[4]
Disobrom[18]
Disophrol Chronotabs[18]
Dorcol Children's Cold Formula[14]
Drixomed[18]
Drixoral Cold and Allergy[18]
Drize[11]
Duralex[14]
Dura-Tap PD[14]
Dura-Vent/A[11]
Ed A-Hist[9]
Endafed[6]
E.N.T[4]
Fedahist[14]
Fedahist Gyrocaps[14]
Fedahist Timecaps[14]
Genac[25]
Genamin[11]
Genatap[4]
Gencold[11]
Hayfebrol[14]
Histalet[14]
Histalet Forte[16]
Histatab Plus[9]
Histatan[15]
Hista-Vadrin[10]
Histor-D[9]
Iofed[6]
Iofed PD[6]
Iohist-D[20]
Klerist-D[14]
Kronofed-A Jr. Kronocaps[14]
Kronofed-A Kronocaps[14]
Linhist-L.A.[12]
Liqui-Histine-D[20]
Liqui-Minic Infant Drops[21]
Lodrane LD[6]
Lodrane Liquid[6]
Med-Hist[14]
Metahistine D[20]
M-Hist[6]
Mooredec[7]
Myphetapp[4]
Nalda-Relief Pediatric Drops[13]
Naldecon[13]
Naldecon Pediatric Drops[13]
Naldecon Pediatric Syrup[13]
Naldelate[13]
Naldelate Pediatric Drops[13]
Naldelate Pediatric Syrup[13]
Nalex-A[12]
Nalfed[6]
Nalfed-PD[6]
Nalgest[13]
Nalgest Pediatric[13]
Nalphen[13]
Nalphen Pediatric[13]
ND Clear T.D.[14]
Nolamine[8]
Novafed A[14]
Novahistine[9]
Ornade Spansules[11]
PediaCare Cold-Allergy[14]
PediaCare Cold Formula[14]
Phenergan VC[22]
Pherazine VC[22]
Poly D[20]
Poly-D[20]
Poly Hist Forte[16]
Poly-Histine-D[20]
Poly-Histine-D Ped[20]
Promethazine VC[22]
Prometh VC Plain[22]
Prop-a-Hist[13]
Pseudo-Chlor[14]
Pseudo-gest Plus[14]
Q-Hist LA[12]
Resaid S.R.[11]
Rescon[11, 14]
Rescon-ED[14]
Rescon JR[14]
Respahist[6]
Rhinatate[15]
Rhinolar-EX[11]
Rhinolar-EX 12[11]
Rhinosyn[14]
Rhinosyn-PD[14]
Ricobid[9]
Ricobid Pediatric[9]
Rinade B.I.D.[14]
Rolatuss Plain[9]
Rondamine[7]
Rondec[7]
Rondec Drops[7]
Rondec-TR[7]
R-Tannamine[15]
R-Tannamine Pediatric[15]
R-Tannate[15]
R-Tannate Pediatric[15]
Ru-Tuss[9]
Ryna[14]
Rynatan[15]
Rynatan Pediatric[15]
Rynatan-S Pediatric[15]
Seldane-D[24]
Semprex-D[1]
Shellcap[6]
Shellcap PD[6]
Silafed[25]
Silaminic[11]
Sinucon[13]
Sinucon Pediatric Drops[13]
Sudafed Plus[14]
Tamine S.R.[3]
Tanafed[14]
Tanoral[15]
Tavist-D[17]
Teldrin 12 Hour Allergy Relief[11]
Temazin Cold[11]
Touro A&H[6]
Triaminic[11]
Triaminic-12[11]
Triaminic Allergy[11]
Triaminic Chewables[11]
Triaminic Cold[11]
Triaminic Oral Infant Drops[21]

Triaminic TR[21]
Trihist-D[20]
Trinalin Repetabs[1a]
Tri-Nefrin Extra Strength[11]
Triofed[25]
Triotann[15]
Triotann Pediatric[15]
Triotann-S Pediatric[15]
Tri-Phen-Chlor[13]
Tri-Phen-Chlor Pediatric[13]
Tri-Phen-Chlor T.R.[13]
Tri-Phen-Mine Pediatric Drops[13]
Tri-Phen-Mine Pediatric Syrup[13]
Tri-Phen-Mine S.R.[13]
Triphenyl[11]
Triposed[25]
Tritan[15]
Tri-Tannate[15]
Tri-Tannate Pediatric[15]
ULTRAbrom[6]
ULTRAbrom PD[6]
Uni-Decon[13]
Uni-Multihist D[20]
Vanex Forte Caplets[16]
Vicks Children's DayQuil Allergy Relief[14]
Vicks DayQuil 4 Hour Allergy Relief[4]
Vicks DayQuil 12 Hour Allergy Relief[4]
West-Decon[13]

In Canada—

Actifed[25]
Chlor-Tripolon Decongestant[11]
Chlor-Tripolon N.D.[19a]
Claritin Extra[19a]
Coricidin D Long Acting[11]
Corsym[11]
Dimetapp[3]
Dimetapp Chewables[4]
Dimetapp Clear[4]
Dimetapp Extentabs[3]
Dimetapp Liqui-Fills[4]
Dimetapp Oral Infant Drops[3]
Drixoral[18]
Drixoral Night[18]
Drixtab[18]
Neo Citran A[19b]
Novahistex[14]
Ornade[11]
Ornade-A.F.[11]
Ornade Spansules[11]
Triaminic[11, 21]
Trinalin Repetabs[1a]
Vasofrinic[14]

Note: For quick reference the following antihistamine and decongestant combinations are numbered to match the corresponding brand names.

This information applies to the following medicines:

1. Acrivastine (AK-ri-vas-teen) and Pseudoephedrine (soo-doe-e-FED-rin)†
1a. Azatadine (a-ZA-ta-deen) and Pseudoephedrine
2. Brompheniramine (brome-fen-EER-a-meen) and Phenylephrine (fen-ill-EF-rin)†
3. Brompheniramine, Phenylephrine, and Phenylpropanolamine (fen-ill-proe-pa-NOLE-a-meen)
4. Brompheniramine and Phenylpropanolamine‡
5. No product available
6. Brompheniramine and Pseudoephedrine†‡
7. Carbinoxamine (kar-bi-NOX-a-meen) and Pseudoephedrine†
8. Chlorpheniramine (klor-fen-EER-a-meen), Phenindamine (fen-IN-da-meen), and Phenylpropanolamine†
9. Chlorpheniramine and Phenylephrine†
10. Chlorpheniramine, Phenylephrine, and Phenylpropanolamine†
11. Chlorpheniramine and Phenylpropanolamine‡
12. Chlorpheniramine, Phenyltoloxamine (fen-ill-toe-LOX-a-meen), and Phenylephrine†
13. Chlorpheniramine, Phenyltoloxamine, Phenylephrine, and Phenylpropanolamine†
14. Chlorpheniramine and Pseudoephedrine‡
15. Chlorpheniramine, Pyrilamine (peer-ILL-a-meen), and Phenylephrine†
16. Chlorpheniramine, Pyrilamine, Phenylephrine, and Phenylpropanolamine†
17. Clemastine (KLEM-as-teen) and Phenylpropanolamine†
18. Dexbrompheniramine (dex-brom-fen-EER-a-meen) and Pseudoephedrine
19. Diphenhydramine (dye-fen-HYE-dra-meen) and Pseudoephedrine
19a. Loratadine (lor-AT-a-deen) and Pseudoephedrine
19b. Pheniramine (fen-EER-a-meen) and Phenylephrine*
20. Pheniramine, Phenyltoloxamine, Pyrilamine, and Phenylpropanolamine†
21. Pheniramine, Pyrilamine, and Phenylpropanolamine
22. Promethazine (proe-METH-a-zeen) and Phenylephrine†‡
23. No product available
24. Terfenadine (ter-FEN-a-deen) and Pseudoephedrine†
25. Triprolidine (trye-PROE-li-deen) and Pseudoephedrine‡

*Not commercially available in the U.S.
†Not commercially available in Canada.
‡Generic name product may be available in the U.S.
§Generic name product may be available in Canada.

Description

Antihistamine and decongestant combinations are used to treat the nasal congestion (stuffy nose), sneezing, and runny nose caused by colds and hay fever.

Some of these combinations are available only with your doctor's prescription. Others are available without a prescription; however, your doctor may have special instructions on the proper dose of the medicine for your medical condition. They are available in the following dosage forms:

Oral

Acrivastine and Pseudoephedrine
- Capsules (U.S.)

Azatadine and Pseudoephedrine
- Extended-release tablets (U.S. and Canada)

Brompheniramine and Phenylephrine
- Elixir (U.S.)
- Tablets (U.S.)

Brompheniramine, Phenylephrine, and Phenylpropanolamine
- Elixir (U.S. and Canada)
- Oral solution (Canada)
- Tablets (Canada)
- Extended-release tablets (U.S. and Canada)

Brompheniramine and Phenylpropanolamine
- Capsules (Canada)
- Elixir (U.S.)
- Oral Solution (U.S. and Canada)
- Tablets (U.S.)
- Chewable tablets (U.S. and Canada)
- Extended-release tablets (U.S.)

Brompheniramine and Pseudoephedrine
- Extended-release capsules (U.S.)
- Oral solution (U.S.)
- Syrup (U.S.)
- Tablets (U.S.)

Carbinoxamine and Pseudoephedrine
- Oral solution (U.S.)
- Syrup (U.S.)
- Tablets (U.S.)
- Extended-release tablets (U.S.)

Chlorpheniramine, Phenindamine, and Phenylpropanolamine
- Extended-release tablets (U.S.)

Chlorpheniramine and Phenylephrine
- Elixir (U.S.)
- Oral solution (U.S.)
- Oral suspension (U.S.)
- Syrup (U.S.)
- Tablets (U.S.)
- Extended-release tablets (U.S.)

Chlorpheniramine, Phenylephrine, and Phenylpropanolamine
- Tablets (U.S.)

Chlorpheniramine and Phenylpropanolamine
- Extended-release capsules (U.S. and Canada)
- Oral solution (U.S. and Canada)
- Extended-release oral suspension (Canada)
- Syrup (U.S. and Canada)
- Tablets (U.S.)
- Extended-release tablets (U.S. and Canada)

Chlorpheniramine, Phenyltoloxamine, and Phenylephrine
- Extended-release capsules (U.S.)
- Tablets (U.S.)
- Extended-release tablets (U.S.)

Chlorpheniramine, Phenyltoloxamine, Phenylephrine, and Phenylpropanolamine
- Oral solution (U.S.)
- Syrup (U.S.)
- Extended-release tablets (U.S.)

Chlorpheniramine and Pseudoephedrine
- Capsules (U.S.)
- Extended-release capsules (U.S. and Canada)
- Oral solution (U.S. and Canada)
- Oral suspension (U.S.)
- Syrup (U.S.)
- Tablets (U.S.)
- Chewable tablets (U.S.)
- Extended-release tablets (U.S.)

Chlorpheniramine, Pyrilamine, and Phenylephrine
- Oral suspension (U.S.)
- Tablets (U.S.)

Chlorpheniramine, Pyrilamine, Phenylephrine, and Phenylpropanolamine
- Tablets (U.S.)
- Extended-release tablets (U.S.)

Clemastine and Phenylpropanolamine
- Extended-release tablets (U.S. and Canada)

Dexbrompheniramine and Pseudoephedrine
- Tablets (U.S. and Canada)
- Extended-release tablets (U.S. and Canada)

Diphenhydramine and Pseudoephedrine
- Capsules (U.S.)
- Oral solution (U.S.)
- Tablets (U.S. and Canada)

Loratadine and Pseudoephedrine
- Extended-release tablets (U.S. and Canada)

Pheniramine and Phenylephrine
- for Oral solution (Canada)

Pheniramine, Phenyltoloxamine, Pyrilamine, and Phenylpropanolamine
- Extended-release capsules (U.S.)
- Elixir (U.S.)

Pheniramine, Pyrilamine, and Phenylpropanolamine
- Oral solution (U.S.)
- Extended-release tablets (U.S. and Canada)

Promethazine and Phenylephrine
- Syrup (U.S.)

Terfenadine and Pseudoephedrine
- Extended-release tablets (U.S.)

Triprolidine and Pseudoephedrine
- Syrup (U.S. and Canada)
- Tablets (U.S. and Canada)

Before Using This Medicine

If you are taking this medicine without a prescription, carefully read and follow any precautions on the label. For antihistamine and decongestant combinations, the following should be considered:

Allergies—Tell your doctor if you have ever had any unusual or allergic reaction to antihistamines or to amphetamine, dextroamphetamine (e.g., Dexedrine), ephedrine (e.g., Ephed II), epinephrine (e.g., Adrenalin), isoproterenol (e.g., Isuprel), metaproterenol (e.g., Alupent), methamphetamine (e.g., Desoxyn), norepinephrine (e.g., Levophed), phenylephrine (e.g., Neo-Synephrine), pseudoephedrine (e.g., Sudafed), PPA (e.g., Dexatrim), or terbutaline (e.g., Brethine).

Diet—Do not take terfenadine (e.g., Seldane with grapefruit juice. To do so may cause heart rhythm problems.

Pregnancy—The occasional use of antihistamine and decongestant combinations is not likely to cause problems in the fetus or in the newborn baby. However, when these medicines are used at higher doses and/or for a long time, the chance that problems might occur may increase. For the individual ingredients of these combinations, the following apply:

- *Alcohol*—Some of these combination medicines contain alcohol. Too much use of alcohol during pregnancy may cause birth defects.
- *Antihistamines*—Antihistamines have not been shown to cause problems in humans.
- *Phenylephrine*—Studies on birth defects have not been done in either humans or animals with phenylephrine.
- *Phenylpropanolamine*—Studies on birth defects have not been done in either humans or animals with phenylpropanolamine. However, it seems that women who take phenylpropanolamine in the weeks following delivery are more likely to suffer mental or mood changes.
- *Promethazine*—Phenothiazines, such as promethazine (contained in some of these combination medicines [e.g., Phenergan-D]), have been shown to cause jaundice and muscle tremors in a few newborn infants whose mothers received phenothiazines during pregnancy. Also, the newborn baby may have blood clotting problems if promethazine is taken by the mother within 2 weeks before delivery.
- *Pseudoephedrine*—Studies on birth defects with pseudoephedrine have not been done in humans. In animal studies pseudoephedrine did not cause birth defects but did cause a decrease in average weight, length, and rate of bone formation in the animal fetus when administered in high doses.

Breast-feeding—Small amounts of antihistamines and decongestants pass into the breast milk. Use is not recommended since the chances are greater for this medicine to cause side effects, such as unusual excitement or irritability, in the nursing baby. Also, since antihistamines tend to decrease the secretions of the body, it is possible that the flow of breast milk may be reduced in some patients. It is not known yet whether loratadine or terfenadine causes these same side effects.

Children—Very young children are usually more sensitive to the effects of this medicine. Increases in blood pressure, nightmares or unusual excitement, nervousness, restlessness, or irritability may be more likely to occur in children. Also, mental changes may be more likely to occur in young children taking combination medicines that contain phenylpropanolamine. *Before giving any of these* *combination medicines to a child, check the package label very carefully. Some of these medicines are too strong for use in children.* If you are not certain whether a specific product can be given to a child, or if you have any questions about the amount to give, check with your health care professional.

Older adults—Confusion, difficult and painful urination, dizziness, drowsiness, dryness of mouth, or convulsions (seizures) may be more likely to occur in the elderly, who are usually more sensitive to the effects of this medicine. Also, nightmares or unusual excitement, nervousness, restlessness, or irritability may be more likely to occur in elderly patients.

Other medicines—Although certain medicines should not be used together at all, in other cases different medicines may be used together even if an interaction might occur. In these cases, your doctor may want to change the dose, or other precautions may be necessary. When you are taking antihistamines it is especially important that your health care professional know if you are taking any of the following:

- Anticholinergics (medicine for abdominal or stomach spasms or cramps)—Side effects, such as dryness of mouth, of antihistamines or anticholinergics may be more likely to occur
- Azithromycin (e.g., Zithromax) or
- Clarithromycin (e.g., Biaxin) or
- Erythromycin (e.g., E-Mycin) or
- Itraconazole (e.g., Sporanox) or
- Ketoconazole (e.g., Nizoral)—Use of these medicines with the terfenadine-containing combination may cause heart problems, such as an irregular heartbeat; these medicines should not be used together
- Central nervous system (CNS) depressants—Effects, such as drowsiness, of CNS depressants or antihistamines may be worsened
- Cisapride (e.g., Propulsid) or
- HIV protease inhibitors (indinavir [e.g., Crixivan], nelfinavir [e.g., Viracept], ritonavir [e.g., Norvir], saquinavir [e.g., Invirase]) or
- Mibefradil (e.g., Posicor) or
- Serotonin reuptake inhibitors (fluvoxamine [e.g., Luvox], nefazodone [e.g., Serzone], sertraline [e.g., Zoloft]) or
- Sparfloxacin (e.g., Zagam) or
- Zileuton (e.g., Zyflo)—Use of these medicines with terfenadine may cause heart problems; these medicines should not be used with terfenadine
- Maprotiline (e.g., Ludiomil) or
- Tricyclic antidepressants (amitriptyline [e.g., Elavil], amoxapine [e.g., Asendin], clomipramine [e.g., Anafranil], desipramine [e.g., Pertofrane], doxepin [e.g., Sinequan], imipramine [e.g., Tofranil], nortriptyline [e.g., Aventyl], protriptyline [e.g., Vivactil], trimipramine [e.g., Surmontil])—Effects, such as drowsiness, of CNS depressants or antihistamines may be worsened; also, taking these medicines together may cause some of their side effects, such as dryness of mouth, to become more severe
- Monoamine oxidase (MAO) inhibitors (furazolidone [e.g., Furoxone], isocarboxazid [e.g., Marplan], phenelzine [e.g., Nardil], procarbazine [e.g., Matulane], selegiline [e.g., Eldepryl], tranylcypromine [e.g., Parnate])—If you are now taking, or have taken within the past 2 weeks, any of the MAO inhibitors, the side effects of the antihistamines may become more severe; these medicines should not be used together
- Rauwolfia alkaloids (alseroxylon [e.g., Rauwiloid], deserpidine [e.g., Harmonyl], rauwolfia serpentina [e.g., Raudixin], reserpine [e.g., Serpasil])—These medicines may increase or decrease the effect of the decongestant

Also, if you are taking one of the combinations containing phenylpropanolamine or pseudoephedrine and are also taking:

- Amantadine (e.g., Symmetrel) or
- Amphetamines or
- Appetite suppressants (diet pills), except fenfluramine (e.g., Pondimin) or
- Caffeine (e.g., NoDoz) or
- Chlophedianol (e.g., Ulone) or
- Medicine for asthma or other breathing problems or
- Medicine for colds, sinus problems, or hay fever or other allergies (including nose drops or sprays) or
- Methylphenidate (e.g., Ritalin) or
- Nabilone (e.g., Cesamet) or
- Pemoline (e.g., Cylert)—Using any of these medicines together with an antihistamine and decongestant combination may cause excessive stimulant side effects, such as difficulty in sleeping, heart rate problems, nervousness, and irritability
- Beta-adrenergic blocking agents (acebutolol [e.g., Sectral], atenolol [e.g., Tenormin], betaxolol [e.g., Kerlone], bisoprolol [e.g., Zebeta], carteolol [e.g., Cartrol], labetalol [e.g., Normodyne], metoprolol [e.g., Lopressor], nadolol [e.g., Corgard], oxprenolol [e.g., Trasicor], penbutolol [e.g., Levatol], pindolol [e.g., Visken], propanolol [e.g., Inderal], sotalol [e.g., Sotacor], timolol [e.g., Blocadren])—Using any of these medicines together with an antihistamine and decongestant combination may cause high blood pressure and heart problems (e.g., unusually slow heartbeat)

Other medical problems—The presence of other medical problems may affect the use of antihistamine and decongestant combinations. Make sure you tell your doctor if you have any other medical problems, especially:

- Diabetes mellitus (sugar diabetes)—The decongestant in this medicine may put diabetic patients at a greater risk of having heart or blood vessel disease
- Enlarged prostate or
- Urinary tract blockage or difficult urination—Some of the effects of antihistamines may make urinary problems worse
- Glaucoma—A slight increase in inner eye pressure may occur
- Heart or blood vessel disease or
- High blood pressure—The decongestant in this medicine may cause the blood pressure to increase and may also speed up the heart rate
- Liver disease—Higher blood levels of terfenadine may result, which may increase the chance of heart problems (for terfenadine-containing combination only)

- Overactive thyroid—If the overactive thyroid has caused a fast heart rate, the decongestant in this medicine may cause the heart rate to speed up further

Proper Use of This Medicine

Take this medicine only as directed. Do not take more of it and do not take it more often than recommended on the label, unless otherwise directed by your doctor. To do so may increase the chance of side effects.

If this medicine irritates your stomach, you may take it with food or a glass of water or milk, to lessen the irritation.

For patients *taking the extended-release capsule or tablet form of this medicine:*
- Swallow it whole.
- Do not crush, break, or chew before swallowing.
- If the capsule is too large to swallow, you may mix the contents of the capsule with applesauce, jelly, honey, or syrup and swallow without chewing.

Dosing—There is a large variety of antihistamine and decongestant combination products on the market. Some products are for use in adults only, while others may be used in children. If you have any questions about this, check with your health care professional.

The dose of antihistamines and decongestants will be different for different products. The number of capsules or tablets or teaspoonfuls of liquid or granules that you take depends on the strengths of the medicines. Also, *the number of doses you take each day and the time between doses depends on whether you are taking a short-acting or long-acting form of antihistamine and decongestant. Follow your doctor's orders if this medicine was prescribed. Or, follow the directions on the box if you are buying this medicine without a prescription.*

Missed dose—If you are taking this medicine regularly and you miss a dose, take it as soon as possible. However, if it is almost time for your next dose, skip the missed dose and go back to your regular dosing schedule. Do not double doses.

Storage—To store this medicine:
- Keep out of the reach of children.
- Store away from heat and direct light.
- Do not store in the bathroom, near the kitchen sink, or in other damp places. Heat or moisture may cause the medicine to break down.
- Keep the liquid form of this medicine from freezing.
- Do not keep outdated medicine or medicine no longer needed. Be sure that any discarded medicine is out of the reach of children.

Precautions While Using This Medicine

Before you have any skin tests for allergies, tell the doctor in charge that you are taking this medicine. The results of the test may be affected by the antihistamine in this medicine.

When taking antihistamines (contained in this combination medicine) on a regular basis, make sure your doctor knows if you are taking large amounts of aspirin at the same time (as for arthritis or rheumatism). Effects of too much aspirin, such as ringing in the ears, may be covered up by the antihistamine.

The antihistamine in this medicine will add to the effects of alcohol and other CNS depressants (medicines that slow down the nervous system, possibly causing drowsiness). Some examples of CNS depressants are other antihistamines or medicine for hay fever, other allergies, or colds; sedatives, tranquilizers, or sleeping medicine; prescription pain medicine or narcotics; barbiturates; medicine for seizures; muscle relaxants; or anesthetics, including some dental anesthetics. *Check with your doctor before taking any of the above while you are taking this medicine.*

The antihistamine in this medicine may cause some people to become drowsy, dizzy, or less alert than they are normally. *Some antihistamines are more likely to cause drowsiness than others (loratadine and terfenadine, for example, rarely produce this effect). Make sure you know how you react before you drive, use machines, or do anything else that could be dangerous if you are dizzy or are not alert.*

The decongestant in this medicine may add to the central nervous system (CNS) stimulant and other effects of phenylpropanolamine (PPA)-containing diet aids. *Do not use medicines for diet or appetite control while taking this medicine unless you have checked with your doctor.*

The decongestant in this medicine may cause some people to be nervous or restless or to have trouble in sleeping. If you have trouble in sleeping, *take the last dose of this medicine for each day a few hours before bedtime.* If you have any questions about this, check with your doctor.

Antihistamines may cause dryness of the mouth, nose, and throat. Some antihistamines are more likely to cause dryness of the mouth than others (loratadine and terfenadine, for example, rarely produce this effect). For temporary relief, use sugarless candy or gum, melt bits of ice in your mouth, or use a saliva substitute. However, if your mouth continues to feel dry for more than 2 weeks, check with your dentist. Continuing dryness of the mouth may increase the chance of dental disease, including tooth decay, gum disease, and fungus infections.

For patients *using promethazine-containing medicine:*
- This medicine controls nausea and vomiting. For this reason, it may cover up the signs of overdose caused by other medicines or the symptoms of intestinal blockage. This will make it difficult for your doctor to diagnose these conditions. Make sure your doctor knows that you are taking this medicine if you have other symptoms such as stomach or lower abdominal pain, cramping, or soreness. Also, if you think you may have taken an overdose of any medicine, tell your doctor that you are taking this medicine.

Side Effects of This Medicine

Along with its needed effects, a medicine may cause some unwanted effects. Although serious side effects occur rarely when this medicine is taken as recommended, they may be more likely to occur if:

- too much medicine is taken.
- it is taken in large doses.
- it is taken for a long period of time.

Get emergency help immediately if any of the following symptoms of overdose occur:

Clumsiness or unsteadiness; convulsions (seizures); drowsiness (severe); dryness of mouth, nose, or throat (severe); flushing or redness of face; hallucinations (seeing, hearing, or feeling things that are not there); headache (continuing); shortness of breath or troubled breathing; slow, fast, or irregular heartbeat; trouble in sleeping

For promethazine only

Muscle spasms (especially of neck and back); restlessness; shuffling walk; tic-like (jerky) movements of head and face; trembling and shaking of hands

Also, check with your doctor as soon as possible if any of the following side effects occur:

Rare

Mood or mental changes; sore throat and fever; tightness in chest; unusual bleeding or bruising; unusual tiredness or weakness

Other side effects may occur that usually do not need medical attention. These side effects may go away during treatment as your body adjusts to the medicine. However, check with your health care professional if any of the following side effects continue or are bothersome:

More common—rare with loratadine- or terfenadine–containing combination

Drowsiness; thickening of the bronchial secretions

Less common—more common with high doses

Blurred vision; confusion; difficult or painful urination; dizziness; dryness of mouth, nose, or throat; headache; loss of appetite; nightmares; pounding heartbeat; ringing or buzzing in ears; skin rash; stomach upset or pain (more common with pyrilamine and tripelennamine); unusual excitement, nervousness, restlessness, or irritability

Other side effects not listed above may also occur in some patients. If you notice any other effects, check with your doctor.

Revised: 07/19/94
Interim revision: 07/25/95; 08/28/96

ANTIHISTAMINES, DECONGESTANTS, AND ANALGESICS Systemic

Some commonly used brand names are:

In the U.S.—

Aclophen[5]
Actifed Cold & Sinus[24]
Actifed Cold & Sinus Caplets[24]
Actifed Sinus Nighttime[18]
Actifed Sinus Nighttime Caplets[18]
Alka-Seltzer Plus Allergy Medicine Liqui-Gels[13]
Alka-Seltzer Plus Cold Medicine[10]
Alka-Seltzer Plus Cold Medicine Liqui-Gels[13]
Allerest Sinus Pain Formula Caplets[13]
Alumadrine[8]
BC Multi Symptom Cold Powder[10]
Benadryl Allergy/Cold[18]
Benadryl Allergy/Sinus Headache Caplets[18]
BQ Cold[8]
Children's Tylenol Cold Multi-Symptom[13]
Chlor-Trimeton Allergy-Sinus Caplets[8]
Codimal[13]
Co-Hist[13]
Comtrex Allergy-Sinus[13]
Comtrex Allergy-Sinus Caplets[13]
Congestant D[8]
Contac Allergy/Sinus Night Caplets[18]
Contac Cold/Flu Night Caplets[18]
Coridicin D[8]
Covangesic[15]
Dapacin Cold[8]
Dimetapp Allergy Sinus Caplets[2]
Dimetapp Cold & Fever Suspension[4]
Dristan Cold Maximum Strength Caplets[4]
Dristan Cold Multi-Symptom Formula[5]
Drixoral Allergy-Sinus[16]
Drixoral Cold and Flu[16]
Duadacin[8]
Gendecon[5]
Histagesic Modified[5]
Histosal[23]
Kolephrin Caplets[13]
ND-Gesic[14]
Night-Time Effervescent Cold[17]
Norel Plus[12]
Phenate T.D.[8]
Pyrroxate Caplets[8]
Scot-Tussin Original 5-Action Cold Formula[20]
Simplet[13]
Sinapils[9]
Sinarest[13]
Sinarest Extra Strength Caplets[13]
Sine-Off Sinus Medicine Caplets[13]
Singlet for Adults[13]
Sinulin[8]
Sinus Headache & Congestion[13]
Sinutab Sinus Allergy Maximum Strength[13]
Sinutab Sinus Allergy Maximum Strength Caplets[13]
TheraFlu/Flu and Cold Medicine[13]
TheraFlu/Flu and Cold Medicine for Sore Throat[13]
Triaminicin Cold, Allergy, Sinus[8]
Tylenol Allergy Sinus Medication Maximum Strength Caplets[13]
Tylenol Allergy Sinus Medication Maximum Strength Gelcaps[13]
Tylenol Allergy Sinus Medication Maximum Strength Geltabs[13]
Tylenol Allergy Sinus Night Time Medicine Maximum Strength Caplets[18]
Tylenol Flu NightTime Hot Medication Maximum Strength[18]
Tylenol Flu NightTime Medication Maximum Strength Gelcaps[18]

In Canada—

Actifed Plus Extra Strength Caplets[24]
Alka-Seltzer Plus Cold Medicine[10]
Coricidin D[10]
Dristan[5]
Dristan Extra Strength Caplets[5]
Dristan Formula P[22]
Neo Citran Colds and Flu[19]
Neo Citran Colds and Flu Calorie Reduced[19]
Neo Citran Extra Strength Colds and Flu[19]
Oradrine-2[18a]
Sinutab Extra Strength Caplets[13]
Sinutab Regular Caplets[13]
Sinutab SA[21]
Triaminicin[20a]
Tylenol Allergy Sinus Medication Extra Strength Caplets[13]
Tylenol Cold Medication Children's[13]
Tylenol Flu Medication Extra Strength Gelcaps[18]

Note: For quick reference, the following antihistamines, decongestants, and analgesics are numbered to match the corresponding brand names.

This information applies to the following medicines:

1. No product available
2. Brompheniramine (brome-fen-IR-a-meen), Phenylpropanolamine (fen-ill-proe-pa-NOLE-a-meen), and Acetaminophen (a-set-a-MIN-oh-fen)†
3. No product available
4. Brompheniramine, Pseudoephedrine (soo-doe-e-FED-rin), and Acetaminophen†
5. Chlorpheniramine (klor-fen-EER-a-meen), Phenylephrine (fen-il-EF-rin), and Acetaminophen
6. No product available
7. No product available
8. Chlorpheniramine, Phenylpropanolamine, and Acetaminophen

9. Chlorpheniramine, Phenylpropanolamine, Acetaminophen, and Caffeine (kaf-EEN)†
10. Chlorpheniramine, Phenylpropanolamine, and Aspirin
11. No product available
12. Chlorpheniramine, Phenyltoloxamine (fen-ill-tole-OX-a-meen), Phenylpropanolamine, and Acetaminophen†
13. Chlorpheniramine, Pseudoephedrine, and Acetaminophen
14. Chlorpheniramine, Pyrilamine (peer-ILL-a-meen), Phenylephrine, and Acetaminophen†
15. Chlorpheniramine, Pyrilamine, Phenylephrine, Phenylpropanolamine, and Acetaminophen†
16. Dexbrompheniramine (dex-brome-fen-EER-a-meen), Pseudoephedrine, and Acetaminophen†
17. Diphenhydramine (dye-fen-HYE-dra-meen), Phenylpropanolamine, and Aspirin†
18. Diphenhydramine, Pseudoephedrine, and Acetaminophen†

18a. Diphenylpyraline (dye-fen-il-PEER-a-leen), Phenylpropanolamine, Acetaminophen, and Caffeine*

19. Pheniramine (fen-EER-a-meen), Phenylephrine, and Acetaminophen*
20. Pheniramine, Phenylephrine, Sodium Salicylate (SOE-dee-um sa-LI-si-late), and Caffeine†

20a. Pheniramine, Pyrilamine, Phenylpropanolamine, Acetaminophen, and Caffeine*

21. Phenyltoloxamine, Phenylpropanolamine, and Acetaminophen*
22. Pyrilamine, Phenylephrine, Aspirin, and Caffeine*
23. Pyrilamine, Phenylpropanolamine, Acetaminophen, and Caffeine†
24. Triprolidine (trye-PROE-li-deen), Pseudoephedrine, and Acetaminophen

*Not commercially available in the U.S.
†Not commercially available in Canada.

Description

Antihistamine, decongestant, and analgesic combinations are taken by mouth to relieve the sneezing, runny nose, sinus and nasal congestion (stuffy nose), fever, headache, and aches and pain, of colds, influenza, and hay fever. These combinations do not contain any ingredient to relieve coughs.

Antihistamines are used to relieve or prevent the symptoms of hay fever and other types of allergy. They may also help relieve some symptoms of the common cold, such as sneezing and runny nose. They work by preventing the effects of a substance called histamine, which is produced by the body. Antihistamines contained in these combinations are: brompheniramine, chlorpheniramine, dexbrompheniramine, diphenhydramine, pheniramine, phenyltoloxamine, pyrilamine, and triprolidine.

Decongestants, such as phenylephrine, phenylpropanolamine (also known as PPA), and pseudoephedrine, produce a narrowing of blood vessels. This leads to clearing of nasal congestion, but it may also cause an increase in blood pressure in patients who have high blood pressure.

Analgesics, such as acetaminophen and salicylates (e.g., aspirin, sodium salicylate), are used in these combination medicines to help relieve fever, headache, aches, and pain.

Some of these medicines are available without a prescription. However, your doctor may have special instructions on the proper dose of these medicines for your medical condition. These medicines are available in the following dosage forms:

Oral

Brompheniramine, Phenylpropanolamine, and Acetaminophen
- Tablets (U.S.)

Brompheniramine, Pseudoephedrine, and Acetaminophen
- Oral suspension (U.S.)
- Tablets (U.S.)

Chlorpheniramine, Phenylephrine, and Acetaminophen
- Capsules (Canada)
- Tablets (U.S. and Canada)
- Extended-release tablets (U.S.)

Chlorpheniramine, Phenylpropanolamine, and Acetaminophen
- Capsules (U.S.)
- Tablets (U.S.)
- Extended-release tablets (U.S.)

Chlorpheniramine, Phenylpropanolamine, Acetaminophen, and Caffeine
- Tablets (U.S.)

Chlorpheniramine, Phenylpropanolamine, and Aspirin
- Effervescent tablets (U.S. and Canada)
- For oral solution (U.S.)
- Tablets (Canada)

Chlorpheniramine, Phenyltoloxamine, Phenylpropanolamine, and Acetaminophen
- Capsules (U.S.)

Chlorpheniramine, Pseudoephedrine, and Acetaminophen
- Capsules (U.S. and Canada)
- For oral solution (U.S.)
- Oral solution (U.S. and Canada)
- Tablets (U.S. and Canada)
- Chewable tablets (U.S. and Canada)

Chlorpheniramine, Pyrilamine, Phenylephrine, and Acetaminophen
- Tablets (U.S.)

Chlorpheniramine, Pyrilamine, Phenylephrine, Phenylpropanolamine, and Acetaminophen
- Tablets (U.S.)

Dexbrompheniramine, Pseudoephedrine, and Acetaminophen
- Extended-release tablets (U.S.)

Diphenhydramine, Phenylpropanolamine, and Aspirin
- Effervescent tablets (U.S.)

Diphenhydramine, Pseudoephedrine, and Acetaminophen
- For oral solution (U.S.)
- Tablets (U.S. and Canada)

Diphenylpyraline, Phenylpropanolamine, Acetaminophen, and Caffeine
- Tablets (Canada)

Pheniramine, Phenylephrine, and Acetaminophen
- For oral solution (Canada)

Pheniramine, Phenylephrine, Sodium Salicylate, and Caffeine
- Oral solution (U.S.)

Pheniramine, Pyrilamine, Phenylpropanolamine, Acetaminophen, and Caffeine
- Tablets (Canada)

Phenyltoloxamine, Phenylpropanolamine, and Acetaminophen
- Extended-release tablets (Canada)

Pyrilamine, Phenylephrine, Aspirin, and Caffeine
- Tablets (Canada)

Pyrilamine, Phenylpropanolamine, Acetaminophen, and Caffeine
- Tablets (U.S.)

Triprolidine, Pseudoephedrine, and Acetaminophen
- Tablets (U.S. and Canada)

Before Using This Medicine

If you are taking this medicine without a prescription, carefully read and follow any precautions on the label. For antihistamine, decongestant, and analgesic combinations, the following should be considered:

Allergies—Tell your doctor if you have ever had any unusual or allergic reaction to any of the ingredients contained in this medicine. If this medicine contains *aspirin* or *another salicylate*, before taking it, check with your doctor if you have ever had any unusual or allergic reaction to any of the following medicines:

Diclofenac (e.g., Voltaren)
Diflunisal (e.g., Dolobid)
Etodolac (e.g., Lodine)
Fenoprofen (e.g., Nalfon)
Floctafenine
Flurbiprofen, by mouth (e.g., Ansaid)
Ibuprofen (e.g., Motrin)
Indomethacin (e.g., Indocin)
Ketoprofen (e.g., Orudis)
Meclofenamate (e.g., Meclomen)
Mefenamic acid (e.g., Ponstel)
Methyl salicylate (oil of wintergreen)
Nabumetone (e.g., Relafen)
Naproxen (e.g., Naprosyn)
Oxaprozin (e.g., Daypro)
Oxyphenbutazone (e.g., Tandearil)
Phenylbutazone (e.g., Butazolidin)
Piroxicam (e.g., Feldene)
Sulindac (e.g., Clinoril)
Suprofen (e.g., Suprol)
Tenoxicam (e.g., Mobiflex)
Tiaprofenic acid (e.g., Surgam)
Tolmetin (e.g., Tolectin)
Zomepirac (e.g., Zomax)

Also tell your health care professional if you are allergic to any other substances, such as foods, preservatives, or dyes.

Pregnancy—The occasional use of antihistamine, decongestant, and analgesic combinations is not likely to cause problems in the fetus or in the newborn baby. However, when these medicines are used at higher doses and/or for a long time, the chance that problems might occur may increase. For the individual ingredients of these combinations, the following apply:

- *Acetaminophen*—Acetaminophen has not been shown to cause birth defects or other problems in humans. However, studies on birth defects have not been done in humans.
- *Alcohol*—Some of these combination medicines contain large amounts of alcohol. Too much use of alcohol during pregnancy may cause birth defects.
- *Antihistamines*—Antihistamines have not been shown to cause problems in humans.
- *Caffeine*—Studies in humans have not shown that caffeine causes birth defects. However, studies in animals have shown that caffeine causes birth defects when given in very large doses (amounts equal to the amount of caffeine contained in 12 to 24 cups of coffee a day).
- *Phenylephrine*—Studies on birth defects have not been done in either humans or animals with phenylephrine.
- *Phenylpropanolamine*—Studies on birth defects have not been done in either humans or animals with phenylpropanolamine. However, it seems that women who take phenylpropanolamine in the weeks following delivery are more likely to suffer mental or mood changes.
- *Pseudoephedrine*—Studies on birth defects with pseudoephedrine have not been done in humans. In animal studies pseudoephedrine did not cause birth defects but did cause a decrease in average weight, length, and rate of bone formation in the animal fetus when administered in high doses.
- *Salicylates (e.g., aspirin)*—Salicylates have not been shown to cause birth defects in humans. Studies on birth defects in humans have been done with aspirin. However, salicylates have been shown to cause birth defects in animals.

  Regular use of salicylates late in pregnancy may cause unwanted effects on the heart or blood flow in the fetus or newborn baby. Use of salicylates during the last 2 weeks of pregnancy may cause bleeding problems in the fetus before or during delivery, or in the newborn baby. Also, too much use of salicylates during the last 3 months of pregnancy may increase the length of pregnancy, prolong labor, cause other problems during delivery, or cause severe bleeding in the mother before, during, or after delivery. *Do not take aspirin during the last 3 months of pregnancy unless it has been ordered by your doctor.*

Breast-feeding—If you are breast-feeding the chance that problems might occur depends on the ingredients of the combination. For the individual ingredients of these combinations, the following apply:

- *Acetaminophen*—Acetaminophen passes into the breast milk. However, it has not been shown to cause problems in nursing babies.
- *Alcohol*—Alcohol passes into the breast milk. However, the amount of alcohol in recommended doses of this medicine does not usually cause problems in nursing babies.
- *Antihistamines*—Use is not recommended since the chances are greater for this medicine to cause side effects, such as unusual excitement or irritability, in the nursing baby. Also, since antihistamines tend to decrease the secretions of the body, it is possible that the flow of breast milk may be reduced in some women.
- *Caffeine*—Small amounts of caffeine pass into the breast milk and may build up in the nursing baby. However, the amount of caffeine in recommended doses of this medicine does not usually cause problems in nursing babies.
- *Decongestants (e.g., phenylephrine, phenylpropanolamine, pseudoephedrine)*—Decongestants may pass into the breast milk and may cause unwanted effects in nursing babies of mothers taking this medicine.
- *Salicylates (e.g., aspirin, sodium salicylate)*—Salicylates pass into the breast milk. Although salicylates have not been reported to cause problems in nursing babies, it is possible that problems may occur if large amounts are taken regularly.

Children—Very young children are usually more sensitive to the effects of this medicine. Increases in blood pressure, nightmares, unusual excitement, nervousness, restlessness, or irritability may be more likely to occur in children. Also, mental changes may be more likely to occur in young children taking these combination medicines.

Before giving any of these combination medicines to a child, check the package label very carefully. Some of these medicines are too strong for use in children. If you are not certain whether a specific product can be given to a child, or if you have any questions about the amount to give, check with your health care professional.

Do not give aspirin or other salicylates to a child with a fever or other symptoms of a virus infection, especially flu or chickenpox, without first discussing their use with your child's doctor. This is very important because salicylates may cause a serious illness called Reye's syndrome in children with fever caused by a virus infection, especially flu or chickenpox. Also, children may be more sensitive to the aspirin or other salicylates contained in some of these medicines, especially if they have a fever or have lost large amounts of body fluid because of vomiting, diarrhea, or sweating.

Teenagers—*Do not give aspirin or other salicylates to a teenager with a fever or other symptoms of a virus infection, especially flu or chickenpox, without first discussing their use with your child's doctor.* This is very important because salicylates may cause a serious illness called Reye's syndrome in teenagers with fever caused by a virus infection, especially flu or chickenpox.

Older adults—The elderly are usually more sensitive to the effects of this medicine. Confusion, difficult or painful urination, dizziness, drowsiness, feeling faint, or dryness of mouth, nose, or throat may be more likely to occur in elderly patients. Also, nightmares or unusual excitement, nervousness, restlessness, or irritability may be more likely to occur in the elderly.

Other medicines—Although certain medicines should not be used together at all, in other cases two different medicines may be used together even if an interaction might occur. In these cases, your doctor may want to change the dose, or other precautions may be necessary. When you are taking antihistamine, decongestant, and analgesic combinations it is especially important that your health care professional know if you are taking *any* other prescription or nonprescription (over-the-counter [OTC]) medicine, for example, aspirin or other medicine for allergies. Some medicines may change the way this medicine affects your body. Also, the effect of other medicines may be increased or reduced by some of the ingredients in this medicine.

Other medical problems—The presence of other medical problems may affect the use of antihistamine, decongestant, and analgesic combinations. Make sure you tell your doctor if you have any other medical problems, especially:

- Alcohol abuse—Acetaminophen-containing medicines increase the chance of liver damage
- Anemia—Taking a salicylate-containing medicine may make the anemia worse
- Asthma, allergies, and nasal polyps, history of, or
- Asthma attacks—Taking a salicylate-containing medicine may cause an allergic reaction in which breathing becomes difficult; also, although antihistamines open tightened bronchial passages, other effects of the antihistamines may cause secretions to become thick so that during an asthma attack it might be difficult to cough them up
- Diabetes mellitus (sugar diabetes)—The decongestant in this medicine may put the patient with diabetes at a greater risk of having heart or blood vessel disease
- Enlarged prostate or
- Urinary tract blockage or difficult urination—Some of the effects of antihistamines may cause urinary problems to get worse
- Glaucoma—A slight increase in inner eye pressure may occur
- Gout—Aspirin- or sodium salicylate–containing medicine may make the gout worse and reduce the benefit of the medicines used for gout
- Hemophilia or other bleeding problems—Aspirin- or sodium salicylate–containing medicine may increase the chance of bleeding
- Hepatitis or other liver disease—There is a greater chance of side effects because the medicine is not broken down and may build up in the body; also, if liver disease is severe there is a greater chance that aspirin-containing medicine may cause bleeding
- Heart or blood vessel disease or
- High blood pressure—The decongestant in this medicine may cause the blood pressure to increase and may also speed up the heart rate; also, caffeine-containing medicine, if taken in large amounts, may have a similar effect on the heart
- Kidney disease (severe)—The kidneys may be affected, especially if too much of this medicine is taken for a long time
- Overactive thyroid—If the overactive thyroid has caused a fast heart rate, the decongestant in this medicine may cause the heart rate to speed up further
- Stomach ulcer or other stomach problems—Salicylate-containing medicine may make the ulcer worse or cause bleeding of the stomach

Proper Use of This Medicine

Take this medicine only as directed. Do not take more of it and do not take it more often than recommended on the label, unless otherwise directed by your doctor. To do so may increase the chance of side effects.

If this medicine irritates your stomach, you may take it with food or a glass of water or milk, to lessen the irritation.

For patients taking the extended-release tablet form of this medicine:

- Swallow the tablets whole.
- Do not crush, break, or chew before swallowing.

If a combination medicine containing aspirin has a strong vinegar-like odor, do not use it. This odor means the medicine is breaking down. If you have any questions about this, check with your pharmacist.

Dosing—The dose of these combination medicines will be different for different products. *Follow the directions on the box if you are taking this medicine without a pre-*

scription. Or, follow your doctor's orders if this medicine was prescribed. The following information includes only the average doses for these combinations.

The number of capsules or tablets or teaspoonfuls of liquid that you take depends on the strength of the medicine.

There is a large variety of antihistamine, decongestant, and analgesic combination products on the market. Some products are for use in adults only, while others may be used in children. If you have any questions about this, check with your health care professional.

For cold symptoms and sinus pain and congestion:

- For *regular (short-acting) oral* dosage forms (chewable tablets, capsules, liquid, or tablets):
  —Adults and children 12 years of age and older: Usually the dose is 1 to 2 capsules or tablets, or 1 teaspoonful of liquid, every four to six hours.
  —Children 6 to 12 years of age: Usually the dose is 1 tablet, 4 chewable tablets, or 1 to 2 teaspoonfuls of liquid every four hours.
  —Children up to 6 years of age: Use and dose must be determined by your doctor.
- For *oral* dosage forms that *must be dissolved* (effervescent tablets or powder):
  —Adults and children 12 years of age and older: Usually the dose is 2 effervescent tablets or the contents of 1 packet of powder dissolved as directed on the package.
  —Children up to 12 years of age: Use and dose must be determined by your doctor.
- For *long-acting oral* dosage form (tablets):
  —Adults and children 12 years of age and older: Usually the dose is 1 to 2 tablets every 12 hours.
  —Children up to 12 years of age: Use and dose must be determined by your doctor.

Missed dose—If you must take this medicine regularly and you miss a dose, take it as soon as possible. However, if it is almost time for your next dose, skip the missed dose and go back to your regular dosing schedule. Do not double doses.

Storage—To store this medicine:

- Keep this medicine out of the reach of children. Overdose is very dangerous in young children.
- Store away from heat and direct light.
- Do not store the capsule or tablet form of this medicine in the bathroom, near the kitchen sink, or in other damp places. Heat or moisture may cause the medicine to break down.
- Keep the liquid form of this medicine from freezing.
- Do not keep outdated medicine or medicine no longer needed. Be sure that any discarded medicine is out of the reach of children.

Precautions While Using This Medicine

Before you have any skin tests for allergies, tell the doctor in charge that you are taking this medicine. The results of the test may be affected by the antihistamine in this medicine.

Check with your doctor if your symptoms do not improve or become worse, or if you have a high fever.

The antihistamine in this medicine will add to the effects of alcohol and other central nervous system (CNS) depressants (medicines that slow down the nervous system, possibly causing drowsiness). Some examples of CNS depressants are other antihistamines or medicine for hay fever, other allergies, or colds; sedatives, tranquilizers, or sleeping medicine; prescription pain medicine or narcotics; barbiturates; medicine for seizures; muscle relaxants; or anesthetics, including some dental anesthetics. *Check with your doctor before taking any of the above while you are taking this medicine.*

Also, stomach problems may be more likely to occur if you drink alcoholic beverages while taking a medicine that contains aspirin. In addition, drinking large amounts of alcoholic beverages while taking a medicine that contains acetaminophen may cause liver damage.

The antihistamine in this medicine may cause some people to become drowsy, dizzy, or less alert than they are normally. *Make sure you know how you react to this medicine before you drive, use machines, or do anything else that could be dangerous if you are dizzy or are not alert.*

The decongestant in this medicine may cause some people to become nervous or restless or to have trouble in sleeping. If you have trouble in sleeping, *take the last dose of this medicine for each day a few hours before bedtime.* If you have any questions about this, check with your doctor.

Also, this medicine may add to the CNS stimulant and other effects of phenylpropanolamine (PPA)-containing diet aids. *Do not use medicines for diet or appetite control while taking this medicine unless you have checked with your doctor.*

Before having any kind of surgery (including dental surgery) or emergency treatment, tell the medical doctor or dentist in charge that you are taking this medicine.

Antihistamines may cause dryness of the mouth, nose, and throat. For temporary relief of mouth dryness, use sugarless candy or gum, melt bits of ice in your mouth, or use a saliva substitute. However, if your mouth continues to feel dry for more than 2 weeks, check with your dentist. Continuing dryness of the mouth may increase the chance of dental disease, including tooth decay, gum disease, and fungus infections.

Check the label of all over-the-counter (OTC), nonprescription, and prescription medicines you now take. If any contain acetaminophen or aspirin or other salicylates, including diflunisal or bismuth subsalicylate (e.g., Pepto-Bismol), be especially careful. This combination medicine contains acetaminophen and/or a salicylate. Therefore, taking it while taking any other medicine that contains these drugs may lead to overdose. If you have any questions about this, check with your health care professional.

For patients taking *aspirin-containing medicine*:

- Do not take aspirin-containing medicine within 5 days before any surgery, including dental surgery, unless otherwise directed by your medical doctor or dentist. Taking aspirin during this time may cause bleeding problems.

For diabetic patients taking *salicylate-containing medicine,* false urine sugar test results may occur:
- If you take 8 or more 325-mg (5-grain) doses of aspirin every day for several days in a row.
- If you take 8 or more 325-mg (5-grain), or 4 or more 500-mg (10-grain), doses of sodium salicylate a day.

Smaller doses or occasional use usually will not affect urine sugar tests. If you have any questions about this, check with your health care professional, especially if your diabetes is not well controlled.

Side Effects of This Medicine

Along with its needed effects, a medicine may cause some unwanted effects. Although serious side effects occur rarely when this medicine is taken as recommended, they may be more likely to occur if:
- too much medicine is taken.
- it is taken in large doses.
- it is taken for a long time.

Get emergency help immediately if any of the following symptoms of overdose occur:

For all combinations

Clumsiness or unsteadiness; convulsions (seizures); drowsiness (severe); dryness of mouth, nose, or throat (severe); fast heartbeat; flushing or redness of face; hallucinations (seeing, hearing, or feeling things that are not there); headache (continuing and/or severe); increased sweating; nausea or vomiting (severe or continuing); shortness of breath or troubled breathing; stomach cramps or pain (severe or continuing); trouble in sleeping

For acetaminophen-containing only

Diarrhea; loss of appetite; swelling or tenderness in the upper abdomen or stomach area

Note: Signs of severe acetaminophen overdose may not appear until 2 to 4 days after the overdose is taken, but treatment to prevent liver damage or death must be started within 24 hours or less after the overdose is taken.

For salicylate-containing only

Any loss of hearing; bloody urine; changes in behavior (in children); confusion; diarrhea (severe or continuing); drowsiness or tiredness (severe, especially in children); fast or deep breathing (especially in children); fever; ringing or buzzing in ears (continuing); uncontrollable flapping movements of the hands (especially in elderly patients); unusual thirst; vision problems

Also, check with your doctor as soon as possible if any of the following side effects occur:

More common

Nausea or vomiting; stomach pain (mild)

Less common or rare

Bloody or black tarry stools; changes in urine or problems with urination; skin rash, hives, or itching; sore throat and fever; swelling of face, feet, or lower legs; tightness in chest; unusual bleeding or bruising; unusual tiredness or weakness; vomiting of blood or material that looks like coffee grounds; weight gain (unusual); yellow eyes or skin

Other side effects may occur that usually do not need medical attention. These side effects may go away during treatment as your body adjusts to the medicine. However, check with your doctor if any of the following side effects continue or are bothersome:

More common

Drowsiness; heartburn or indigestion (for salicylate-containing medicines); thickening of mucus

Less common—more common with high doses

Blurred vision; confusion; difficult or painful urination; dizziness; dryness of mouth, nose, or throat; headache; loss of appetite; nightmares; pounding heartbeat; ringing or buzzing in ears; skin rash; stomach upset or stomach pain; unusual excitement, nervousness, restlessness, or irritability

Not all of the side effects listed above have been reported for each of these medicines, but they have been reported for at least one of them. There are some similarities among these combination medicines, so many of the above side effects may occur with any of these medicines.

Other side effects not listed above may also occur in some patients. If you notice any other effects, check with your doctor.

Revised: 08/30/94
Interim revision: 07/18/95; 05/30/96

ANTIHISTAMINES, DECONGESTANTS, AND ANTICHOLINERGICS Systemic†

Some commonly used brand names are:

In the U.S.—

AH-chew[1]
Atrohist Plus[2]
D.A. Chewable[1]
Dallergy[1]
Dallergy Caplets[1]
Deconhist[2]
Dura-Vent/DA[1]
Extendryl[1]
Extendryl JR[1]
Extendryl SR[1]
Mescolor[4]
OMNIhist L.A.[1]
Pannaz[3]
Phenahist-TR[2]
Phenchlor S.H.A.[2]
Pre-Hist-D[1]
Pro-Tuss[2]
Q-Tuss[2]
Rolatuss SR[2]
Ru-Tab[2]
Ru-Tuss[2]
Stahist[2]
Tuss Delay[2]

Note: For quick reference the following antihistamine, decongestant, and anticholinergic combinations are numbered to match the corresponding brand names.

This information applies to the following medicines:
1. Chlorpheniramine (klor-fen-EER-a-meen), Phenylephrine (fen-ill-EF-rin), and Methscopolamine (meth-skoe-POL-a-meen)
2. Chlorpheniramine, Phenylephrine, Phenylpropanolamine (fen-ill-proe-pa-NOLE-a-meen), Atropine (A-troe-peen), Hyoscyamine (hye-oh-SYE-a-meen), and Scopolamine (skoe-POL-a-meen)
3. Chlorpheniramine, Phenylpropanolamine, and Methscopolamine
4. Chlorpheniramine, Pseudoephedrine (soo-doe-e-FED-rin), and Methscopolamine

†Not commercially available in Canada.

Description

Antihistamine, decongestant, and anticholinergic combinations are used to treat the nasal congestion (stuffy nose) and runny nose caused by allergies.

Antihistamines work by preventing the effects of a substance called histamine, which is produced by the body. Histamine can cause itching, sneezing, runny nose, and watery eyes. The antihistamine contained in these combinations is chlorpheniramine.

The decongestants in these combinations, phenylephrine, phenylpropanolamine (also known as PPA), and pseudoephedrine produce a narrowing of blood vessels. This leads to clearing of nasal congestion, but it may also cause an increase in blood pressure in patients who have high blood pressure.

Anticholinergics, such as atropine, hyoscyamine, methscopolamine, and scopolamine may help produce a drying effect in the nose and chest.

These combinations are available only with your doctor's prescription in the following dosage forms:

Oral

Chlorpheniramine, Phenylephrine, and Methscopolamine
- Extended-release capsules (U.S.)
- Syrup (U.S.)
- Tablets (U.S.)
- Chewable tablets (U.S.)
- Extended-release tablets (U.S.)

Chlorpheniramine, Phenylephrine, Phenylpropanolamine, Atropine, Hyoscyamine, and Scopolamine
- Extended-release tablets (U.S.)

Chlorpheniramine, Phenylpropanolamine, and Methscopolamine
- Extended-release tablets (U.S.)

Chlorpheniramine, Pseudoephedrine, and Methscopolamine
- Extended-release tablets (U.S.)

Before Using This Medicine

In deciding to use a medicine, the risks of taking the medicine must be weighed against the good it will do. This is a decision you and your doctor will make. For antihistamine, decongestant, and anticholinergic combinations, the following should be considered:

Allergies—Tell your doctor if you have ever had any unusual or allergic reaction to antihistamines or anticholinergics, or to amphetamine, dextroamphetamine (e.g., Dexedrine), ephedrine (e.g., Ephed II), epinephrine (e.g., Adrenalin), isoproterenol (e.g., Isuprel), metaproterenol (e.g., Alupent), methamphetamine (e.g., Desoxyn), norepinephrine (e.g., Levophed), phenylephrine (e.g., Neo-Synephrine), phenylpropanolamine [PPA] (e.g., Dexatrim), pseudoephedrine (e.g., Sudafed), or terbutaline (e.g., Brethine). Also, tell your health care professional if you are allergic to any other substances, such as foods, preservatives, or dyes.

Pregnancy—For the individual ingredients of these combinations, the following apply:

- *Antihistamines*—Antihistamines have not been shown to cause problems in humans.
- *Atropine*—Studies on effects in pregnancy have not been done in humans. Atropine has not been shown to cause birth defects or other problems in animals.
- *Hyoscyamine*—Studies on effects in pregnancy have not been done in either humans or animals.
- *Methscopolamine*—Studies on effects in pregnancy have not been done in either humans or animals.
- *Phenylephrine*—Studies on birth defects have not been done in either humans or animals.
- *Phenylpropanolamine*—Studies on birth defects have not been done in either humans or animals. However, it seems that some women who take phenylpropanolamine in the weeks following delivery are more likely to suffer mental or mood changes.
- *Pseudoephedrine*—Studies on birth defects have not been done in humans. Pseudoephedrine has not been shown to cause birth defects in animal studies. However, studies in animals have shown that pseudoephedrine causes a reduction in average weight, length, and rate of bone formation in the animal fetus.
- *Scopolamine*—Studies on effects in pregnancy have not been done in pregnant women. However, studies in animals at doses many times the human dose have shown that scopolamine causes a small increase in the number of fetal deaths.

Breast-feeding—Small amounts of antihistamines, decongestants, and anticholinergics may pass into the breast milk. Use is not recommended since this medicine may cause side effects, such as unusual excitement or irritability, in the nursing baby. Also, since this medicine tends to decrease the secretions of the body, it is possible that the flow of breast milk may be reduced in some women.

Children—Very young children are usually more sensitive than adults to the effects of this medicine. Increases in blood pressure, nightmares or unusual excitement, nervousness, restlessness, or irritability may be more likely to occur in children. Also, mental changes may be more likely to occur in young children taking combination medicines that contain phenylpropanolamine. Also, when anticholinergics are given to children during hot weather, a rapid increase in body temperature may occur, which may lead to heat stroke. In infants and children, especially those with spastic paralysis or brain damage, this medicine may be especially likely to cause severe side effects.

Older adults—Confusion or memory loss, difficult and painful urination, dizziness, drowsiness, dryness of mouth, or convulsions (seizures) may be more likely to occur in the elderly, who are usually more sensitive than younger adults to the effects of this medicine. Also, nightmares or unusual excitement, nervousness, restlessness, or irritability may be more likely to occur in elderly patients. In addition, eye pain may occur, which may be a sign of glaucoma.

Other medicines—Although certain medicines should not be used together at all, in other cases different medicines may be used together even if an interaction might occur. In these cases, your doctor may want to change the dose, or other precautions may be necessary. When you are taking this medicine it is especially important that your health care professional know if you are taking any of the following:

- Amantadine (e.g., Symmetrel) or
- Amphetamines or
- Appetite suppressants (diet pills), except fenfluramine (e.g., Pondimin), or
- Beta-adrenergic blocking agents (acebutolol [e.g., Sectral], atenolol [e.g., Tenormin], betaxolol [e.g., Kerlone], bisoprolol [e.g., Zebeta], carteolol [e.g., Cartrol], labetalol [e.g., Normodyne], metoprolol [e.g., Lopressor], nadolol [e.g., Corgard], oxprenolol [e.g., Trasicor], penbutolol [e.g., Levatol], pindolol [e.g., Visken], propranolol [e.g., Inderal], sotalol [e.g., Sotacor], timolol [e.g., Blocadren]) or
- Caffeine (e.g., NoDoz) or
- Chlophedianol (e.g., Ulone) or
- Cocaine or
- Digitalis medicine (heart medicine) or
- Medicine for asthma or other breathing problems or
- Medicine for colds, sinus problems, or hay fever or other allergies (including nose drops or sprays) or
- Methylphenidate (e.g., Ritalin) or
- Nabilone (e.g., Cesamet) or
- Pemoline (e.g., Cylert)—Using any of these medicines together with a decongestant-containing combination may cause excessive stimulant side effects, such as difficulty in sleeping, heart rate problems, nervousness, and irritability
- Central nervous system (CNS) depressants—Using these combinations with CNS depressants may worsen the effects (e.g., drowsiness) of CNS depressants or antihistamines
- Monoamine oxidase (MAO) inhibitors (furazolidone [e.g., Furoxone], isocarboxazid [e.g., Marplan], phenelzine [e.g., Nardil], procarbazine [e.g., Matulane], selegiline [e.g., Eldepryl], tranylcypromine [e.g., Parnate])—Taking an antihistamine, decongestant, and anticholinergic combination while you are taking or within 2 weeks of taking MAO inhibitors, may make the side effects of the antihistamines, decongestants, and anticholinergics more severe; these medicines should not be used together
- Other anticholinergics (medicine for abdominal or stomach spasms or cramps)—Side effects of antihistamines or anticholinergics, such as dryness of mouth, may be more likely to occur
- Potassium chloride (e.g., Kay Ciel)—Using this medicine with an anticholinergic-containing medicine may make gastrointestinal problems caused by potassium worse
- Rauwolfia alkaloids (alseroxylon [e.g., Rauwiloid], deserpidine [e.g., Harmonyl], rauwolfia serpentina [e.g., Raudixin], reserpine [e.g., Serpasil])—These medicines may increase or decrease the effect of the decongestant in this medicine
- Tricyclic antidepressants (amitriptyline [e.g., Elavil], amoxapine [e.g., Asendin], clomipramine [e.g., Anafranil], desipramine [e.g., Pertofrane], doxepin [e.g., Sinequan], imipramine [e.g., Tofranil], nortriptyline [e.g., Aventyl], protriptyline [e.g., Vivactil], trimipramine [e.g., Surmontil])—Effects, such as drowsiness, may be worsened; also, taking these medicines together may make some of the anticholinergic side effects, such as dryness of mouth, more severe

Other medical problems—The presence of other medical problems may affect the use of antihistamine, decongestant, and anticholinergic combinations. Make sure you tell your doctor if you have any other medical problems, especially:

- Brain damage in children or
- Down's syndrome or
- Dryness of mouth (severe and continuing) or
- Enlarged prostate or
- Fever or
- Glaucoma or
- Intestinal blockage or other intestinal problems or
- Kidney disease or
- Liver disease or
- Lung disease or
- Mental or emotional problems or
- Myasthenia gravis or
- Toxemia of pregnancy or
- Urinary tract blockage or difficult urination—These medicines may make these conditions worse
- Diabetes mellitus (sugar diabetes)—The decongestant in this medicine may put diabetic patients at greater risk of having heart or blood vessel disease
- Heart or blood vessel disease or
- High blood pressure—The decongestant and anticholinergic in this medicine may cause the blood pressure to increase and may also speed up the heart rate
- Overactive thyroid—If the overactive thyroid has caused a fast heartbeat, the decongestant and anticholinergic in this medicine may cause the heart rate to speed up further

Proper Use of This Medicine

Take this medicine only as directed. Do not take more of it and do not take it more often than recommended on the label, unless otherwise directed by your doctor. To do so may increase the chance of side effects.

If this medicine irritates your stomach, you may take it with food or a glass of water or milk, to lessen the irritation.

For patients *taking the extended-release capsule or extended-release tablet form of this medicine:*

- Swallow the capsule or tablet whole.
- Do not crush, break, or chew before swallowing.
- If the capsule is too large to swallow, you may mix the contents of the capsule with applesauce, jelly, honey, or syrup and swallow without chewing.

Dosing—The dose of these combination medicines will be different for different patients. *Follow your doctor's orders or the directions on the label.* The following information includes only the average doses for these combinations. *If your dose is different, do not change it* unless your doctor tells you to do so.

The number of capsules or tablets or teaspoonfuls of syrup that you take depends on the strength of the medicine. Also, the number of doses you take each day and the time between doses depend on whether you are taking a short-acting or a long-acting form of this medicine.

- For *regular (short-acting)* dosage forms (syrup, tablets, or chewable tablets):
  —For allergy and cold symptoms:
    - Adults and children 12 years of age and older—1 or 2 tablets or chewable tablets, or 1 to 2 teaspoonfuls of syrup every four to six hours.
    - Children up to 6 years of age—Use and dose must be determined by your doctor.
    - Children 6 to 12 years of age—1 chewable tablet or 1 teaspoonful of syrup every four hours.
- For *long-acting* dosage forms (extended-release capsules or tablets):
  —For allergy and cold symptoms:
    - Adults and children 12 years of age and older—1 capsule or tablet every twelve hours.
    - Children up to 12 years of age—Use and dose must be determined by your doctor.

Missed dose—If you miss a dose of this medicine, take it as soon as possible. However, if it is almost time for your next dose, skip the missed dose and go back to your regular dosing schedule. Do not double doses.

Storage—To store this medicine:
- Keep out of the reach of children.
- Store away from heat and direct light.
- Do not store in the bathroom, near the kitchen sink, or in other damp places. Heat or moisture may cause the medicine to break down.
- Keep the liquid form of this medicine from freezing.
- Do not keep outdated medicine or medicine no longer needed. Be sure that any discarded medicine is out of the reach of children.

Precautions While Using This Medicine

Check with your doctor if your symptoms do not improve or become worse, or if you have a high fever.

Before you have any skin tests for allergies, tell the doctor in charge that you are taking this medicine. The results of the test may be affected by the antihistamine in this medicine.

These medicines may make you sweat less, causing your body temperature to increase. *Use extra care not to become overheated during exercise or hot weather while you are taking this medicine,* since overheating may result in heat stroke. Also hot baths or saunas may make you dizzy or faint while you are taking this medicine.

The anticholinergic contained in this medicine may cause some people to have blurred vision. *Make sure your vision is clear before you drive or do anything else that could be dangerous if you are not able to see well.* These medicines may also cause your eyes to become more sensitive to light than they are normally. Wearing sunglasses may help lessen the discomfort from bright light.

These medicines may cause some people to become dizzy or drowsy. *Make sure you know how you react to this medicine before you drive, use machines, or do anything else that could be dangerous if you are dizzy or are not alert.*

The decongestant in this medicine may cause some people to be nervous or restless or to have trouble in sleeping. If you have trouble in sleeping, *take the last dose of this medicine for each day a few hours before bedtime.* If you have any questions about this, check with your doctor.

The decongestant in this medicine may add to the central nervous system (CNS) stimulant and other effects of phenylpropanolamine (PPA)-containing diet aids. *Do not use medicines for diet or appetite control while taking this medicine unless you have checked with your doctor.*

Before having any kind of surgery (including dental surgery) or emergency treatment, tell the medical doctor or dentist in charge that you are taking this medicine.

This medicine may cause dryness of the mouth, nose, and throat. For temporary relief, use sugarless candy or gum, melt bits of ice in your mouth, or use a saliva substitute. However, if your mouth continues to feel dry for more than 2 weeks, check with your dentist. Continuing dryness of the mouth may increase the chance of dental disease, including tooth decay, gum disease, and fungus infections.

If you think you or someone else may have taken an overdose, get emergency help at once. Taking an overdose of this medicine or taking this medicine with alcohol or other CNS depressants may lead to unconsciousness and possibly death.

Side Effects of This Medicine

Along with its needed effects, a medicine may cause some unwanted effects. Although not all of these side effects may occur, if they do occur they may need medical attention.

Get emergency help immediately if any of the following symptoms of overdose occur:

Clumsiness or unsteadiness; convulsions (seizures); drowsiness (severe); dryness of mouth, nose, or throat (severe); fast heartbeat; flushing or redness of face; hallucinations (seeing, hearing, or feeling things that are not there); headache (continuing); shortness of breath or troubled breathing; trouble in sleeping

For pseudoephedrine only

Unusual nervousness, restlessness, or excitement

Also, check with your doctor as soon as possible if any of the following side effects occur:

Rare

Irregular or slow heartbeat; mood or mental changes; skin rash, hives, or itching; sore throat and fever; tightness in chest; unusual bleeding or bruising; unusual tiredness or weakness

Other side effects may occur that usually do not need medical attention. These side effects may go away during treatment as your body adjusts to the medicine. However, check with your health care professional if any of the following side effects continue or are bothersome:

More common

Drowsiness; nervousness; restlessness; thickening of mucus, trouble in sleeping

Less common—more common with high doses

Blurred vision; confusion; difficult or painful urination; dizziness; dryness of mouth, nose, or throat; fast or pounding heartbeat; headache; increased sweating, loss of appetite; nausea or vomiting, nightmares; ringing or buzzing in ears; trembling; unusual excitement, nervousness, restlessness, or irritability; unusual paleness; weakness

Other side effects not listed above may also occur in some patients. If you notice any other effects, check with your doctor.

Revised: 07/19/94
Interim revision: 07/18/95; 05/31/96

ANTIHISTAMINES, PHENOTHIAZINE-DERIVATIVE Systemic

Some commonly used brand names are:

In the U.S.—

Anergan 25[2]	Promacot[2]
Anergan 50[2]	Pro-Med 50[2]
Antinaus 50[2]	Promet[2]
Pentazine[2]	Prorex-25[2]
Phenazine 25[2]	Prorex-50[2]
Phenazine 50[2]	Prothazine[2]
Phencen-50[2]	Prothazine Plain[2]
Phenergan[2]	Shogan[2]
Phenergan Fortis[2]	Tacaryl[1]
Phenergan Plain[2]	Temaril[3]
Phenerzine[2]	V-Gan-25[2]
Phenoject-50[2]	V-Gan-50[2]
Pro-50[2]	

In Canada—

Histantil[2]	Phenergan[2]
Panectyl[3]	

Another commonly used name for trimeprazine is alimemazine.

Note: For quick reference, the following antihistamines, are numbered to match the corresponding brand names.

This information applies to the following medicines:

1. Methdilazine (meth-DILL-a-zeen)†
2. Promethazine (proe-METH-a-zeen)‡§
3. Trimeprazine (trye-MEP-ra-zeen)‡

†Not commercially available in Canada.
‡Generic name product may also be available in the U.S.
§Generic name product may also be available in Canada.

Description

Phenothiazine (FEE-noe-THYE-a-zeen)-derivative antihistamines are used to relieve or prevent the symptoms of hay fever and other types of allergy. They work by preventing the effects of a substance called histamine, which is produced by the body. Histamine can cause itching, sneezing, runny nose, and watery eyes. Also, in some persons histamine can close up the bronchial tubes (air passages of the lungs) and make breathing difficult.

Some of these antihistamines are also used to prevent motion sickness, nausea, vomiting, and dizziness. In addition, some of them may be used to help people go to sleep and control their anxiety before or after surgery.

Phenothiazine-derivative antihistamines may also be used for other conditions as determined by your doctor.

In the U.S. these antihistamines are available only with your doctor's prescription. In Canada some are available without a prescription. However, your doctor may have special instructions on the proper dose of the medicine for your medical condition.

These medicines are available in the following dosage forms:

Oral

Methdilazine
- Syrup (U.S.)
- Tablets (U.S.)
- Chewable tablets (U.S.)

Promethazine
- Syrup (U.S. and Canada)
- Tablets (U.S. and Canada)

Trimeprazine
- Extended-release capsules (U.S.)
- Syrup (U.S. and Canada)
- Tablets (U.S. and Canada)

Parenteral

Promethazine
- Injection (U.S. and Canada)

Rectal

Promethazine
- Suppositories (U.S.)

Before Using This Medicine

In deciding to use a medicine, the risks of taking the medicine must be weighed against the good it will do. This is a decision you and your doctor will make. For phenothiazine-derivative antihistamines, the following should be considered:

Allergies—Tell your doctor if you have ever had any unusual or allergic reaction to these medicines or to phenothiazines. Also tell your health care professional if you are allergic to any other substances, such as foods, preservatives, or dyes.

Pregnancy—Methdilazine, promethazine, and trimeprazine have not been studied in pregnant women. In animal studies, promethazine has not been shown to cause birth defects. However, other phenothiazine medicines caused jaundice and muscle tremors in a few newborn babies whose mothers received these medicines during pregnancy. Also, the newborn baby may have blood clotting problems if promethazine is taken by the mother within 2 weeks before delivery.

Breast-feeding—Small amounts of antihistamines pass into the breast milk. Use by nursing mothers is not recommended since babies are more sensitive to the side effects of antihistamines, such as unusual excitement or irritability. Also, with the use of phenothiazine-derivative antihistamines there is the chance that the nursing baby may be more at risk of having difficulty in breathing while sleeping or of the sudden infant death syndrome (SIDS). However, more studies are needed to confirm this.

In addition, since these medicines tend to decrease the secretions of the body, it is possible that the flow of breast milk may be reduced in some patients.

Children—Serious side effects, such as convulsions (seizures), are more likely to occur in younger patients and would be of greater risk to infants than to older children or adults. In general, children are more sensitive to the effects of antihistamines. Also, nightmares or unusual excitement, nervousness, restlessness, or irritability may be more likely to occur in children. *The use of phenothiazine-derivative antihistamines is not recommended in children who have a history of difficulty in breathing while sleeping, or a family history of sudden infant death syndrome (SIDS).*

Children who show signs of Reye's syndrome should not be given phenothiazine-derivative antihistamines, especially by injection. Uncontrolled movements that may occur with phenothiazine-derivative antihistamines may be mistakenly confused with symptoms of Reye's syndrome.

Adolescents—Adolescents who show signs of Reye's syndrome should not be given phenothiazine-derivative antihistamines, especially by injection. Uncontrolled movements that may occur with phenothiazine-derivative antihistamines may be mistakenly confused with symptoms of Reye's syndrome.

Older adults—Elderly patients are especially sensitive to the effects of antihistamines. Confusion; difficult or painful urination; dizziness; drowsiness; feeling faint; or dryness of the mouth, nose, or throat may be more likely to occur in elderly patients. Also, nightmares or unusual excitement, nervousness, restlessness, or irritability may be more likely to occur in elderly patients. In addition, uncontrolled movements may be more likely to occur in elderly patients taking phenothiazine-derivative antihistamines.

Other medicines—Although certain medicines should not be used together at all, in other cases two different medicines may be used together even if an interaction might occur. In these cases, your doctor may want to change the dose, or other precautions may be necessary. When taking phenothiazine-derivative antihistamines, it is especially important that your health care professional know if you are taking/receiving any of the following:

- Amoxapine (e.g., Asendin) or
- Antipsychotics (medicine for mental illness) or
- Methyldopa (e.g., Aldomet) or
- Metoclopramide (e.g., Reglan) or
- Metyrosine (e.g., Demser) or
- Pemoline (e.g., Cylert) or
- Pimozide (e.g., Orap) or
- Rauwolfia alkaloids (alseroxylon [e.g., Rauwiloid], deserpidine [e.g., Harmonyl], rauwolfia serpentina [e.g., Raudixin], reserpine [e.g., Serpasil])—Side effects of these medicines, such as uncontrolled body movements, may become more severe and frequent if they are used together with phenothiazine-derivative antihistamines
- Anticholinergics (medicine for abdominal or stomach spasms or cramps)—Side effects of phenothiazine-derivative antihistamines or anticholinergics, such as dryness of mouth, may be more likely to occur
- Central nervous system (CNS) depressants (medicines that cause drowsiness) or
- Maprotiline or
- Tricyclic antidepressants (medicine for depression)—Effects of CNS depressants or antihistamines, such as drowsiness, may become more severe; also, taking maprotiline or tricyclic antidepressants may cause some side effects of antihistamines, such as dryness of mouth, to become more severe
- Contrast agent, injected into spinal canal—If you are having an x-ray test of the head, spinal canal, or nervous system for which you are going to receive an injection into the spinal canal, phenothiazine-derivative antihistamines may increase the chance of seizures; stop taking any phenothiazine-derivative antihistamine 48 hours before the test and do not start taking it until 24 hours after the test
- Levodopa—When used together with phenothiazine-derivative antihistamines, the levodopa may not work as it should
- Monoamine oxidase (MAO) inhibitors (furazolidone [e.g., Furoxone], isocarboxazid [e.g., Marplan], phenelzine [e.g., Nardil], procarbazine [e.g., Matulane], selgiline [e.g., Eldepryl], tranylcypromine [e.g., Parnate])—If you are now taking or have taken within the past 2 weeks any of the MAO inhibitors, the side effects of the phenothiazine-derivative antihistamines may become more severe; these medicines should not be used together

Other medical problems—The presence of other medical problems may affect the use of antihistamines. Make sure you tell your doctor if you have any other medical problems, especially:

- Blood disease or
- Heart or blood vessel disease—These medicines may cause more serious conditions to develop
- Enlarged prostate or
- Urinary tract blockage or difficult urination—Phenothiazine-derivative antihistamines may cause urinary problems to become worse
- Epilepsy—Phenothiazine-derivative antihistamines, especially promethazine given by injection, may increase the chance of seizures
- Glaucoma—These medicines may cause a slight increase in inner eye pressure that may worsen the condition
- Jaundice—Phenothiazine-derivative antihistamines may make the condition worse
- Liver disease—Phenothiazine-derivative antihistamines may build up in the body, which may increase the chance of side effects such as muscle spasms
- Reye's syndrome—Phenothiazine-derivative antihistamines, especially promethazine given by injection, may increase the chance of uncontrolled movements

Proper Use of This Medicine

Antihistamines are used to relieve or prevent the symptoms of your medical problem. Take them only as directed. Do not take more of them and do not take them more often than recommended on the label, unless otherwise directed by your doctor. To do so may increase the chance of side effects.

For patients *taking this medicine by mouth:*

- Antihistamines can be taken with food or a glass of water or milk to lessen stomach irritation if necessary.

- If you are taking the *extended-release capsule* form of this medicine, swallow it whole. Do not break, crush, or chew before swallowing.

For patients taking *promethazine for motion sickness:*
- Take this medicine 30 minutes to 1 hour before you begin to travel.

For patients using the *suppository form of this medicine:*
- To insert suppository: First remove the foil wrapper and moisten the suppository with cold water. Lie down on your side and use your finger to push the suppository well up into the rectum. If the suppository is too soft to insert, chill the suppository in the refrigerator for 30 minutes or run cold water over it before removing the foil wrapper.

For patients using the *injection form of this medicine:*
- If you will be giving yourself the injections, make sure you understand exactly how to give them. If you have any questions about this, check with your health care professional.

Dosing—The dose of an antihistamine will be different for different patients. *Follow your doctor's orders or the directions on the label.* The following information includes only the average doses of antihistamines. *If your dose is different, do not change it* unless your doctor tells you to do so.

The number of capsules or tablets or teaspoonfuls of liquid that you take depends on the strength of the medicine. Also, *the number of doses you take each day and the time between doses depends on whether you are taking a short-acting or long-acting form of antihistamine.*

For methdilazine
- For *regular (short-acting) oral* dosage forms (tablets or liquid):
  —For allergy symptoms:
  - Adults and teenagers—8 milligrams (mg) every six to twelve hours as needed.
  - Children younger than 3 years of age—Use and dose must be determined by your doctor.
  - Children 3 to 12 years of age—4 mg every six to twelve hours as needed.

For promethazine
- For *regular (short-acting) oral* dosage forms (tablets or liquid):
  —For allergy symptoms:
  - Adults and teenagers—10 to 12.5 mg four times a day before meals and at bedtime; or 25 mg at bedtime as needed.
  - Children younger than 2 years of age—Use and dose must be determined by your doctor.
  - Children 2 years of age and older—Your doctor will determine dose based on the weight and/or size of the child. Children usually are given 5 to 12.5 mg three times a day or 25 mg at bedtime as needed.

  —For nausea and vomiting:
  - Adults and teenagers—25 mg for the first dose, then 10 to 25 mg every four to six hours if needed.
  - Children younger than 2 years of age—Use and dose must be determined by your doctor.
  - Children 2 years of age and older—Your doctor will determine dose based on the weight and/or size of the child. Children usually are given 10 to 25 mg every four to six hours as needed.

  —For prevention of motion sickness:
  - Adults and teenagers—25 mg taken one-half to one hour before traveling. The dose may be repeated eight to twelve hours later if needed.
  - Children younger than 2 years of age—Use and dose must be determined by your doctor.
  - Children 2 years of age and older—Your doctor will determine dose based on the weight and/or size of the child. Children usually are given 10 to 25 mg one-half to one hour before traveling. The dose may be repeated eight to twelve hours later if needed.

  —For vertigo (dizziness):
  - Adults and teenagers—25 mg two times a day as needed.
  - Children younger than 2 years of age—Use and dose must be determined by your doctor.
  - Children 2 years of age and older—Your doctor will determine dose based on the weight and/or size of the child. Children usually are given 10 to 25 mg two times a day as needed.

  —For use as a sedative:
  - Adults and teenagers—25 to 50 mg.
  - Children younger than 2 years of age—Use and dose must be determined by your doctor.
  - Children 2 years of age and older—Your doctor will determine dose based on the weight and/or size of the child. Children usually are given 10 to 25 mg.

- For *injection* dosage form:
  —For allergy symptoms:
  - Adults and teenagers—25 mg injected into a muscle or into a vein.
  - Children younger than 2 years of age—Use and dose must be determined by your doctor.
  - Children 2 years of age and older—Your doctor will determine dose based on the weight and/or size of the child. Children usually are given 6.25 to 12.5 mg injected into a muscle three times a day or 25 mg at bedtime as needed.

  —For nausea and vomiting:
  - Adults and teenagers—12.5 to 25 mg injected into a muscle or into a vein every four hours as needed.
  - Children younger than 2 years of age—Use and dose must be determined by your doctor.

• Children 2 years of age and older—Your doctor will determine dose based on the weight and/or size of the child. Children usually are given 12.5 to 25 mg injected into a muscle every four to six hours as needed.

—For use as a sedative:

• Adults and teenagers—25 to 50 mg injected into a muscle or into a vein.

• Children younger than 2 years of age—Use and dose must be determined by your doctor.

• Children 2 years of age and older—Your doctor will determine dose based on the weight and/or size of the child. Children usually are given 12.5 to 25 mg injected into a muscle.

• For *suppository* dosage form:

—For allergy symptoms:

• Adults and teenagers—25 mg inserted in rectum. Another 25-mg suppository may be inserted two hours later if needed.

• Children younger than 2 years of age—Use and dose must be determined by your doctor.

• Children 2 years of age and older—Your doctor will determine dose based on the weight and/or size of the child. Children usually are given 6.25 to 12.5 mg inserted into the rectum three times a day or 25 mg at bedtime as needed.

—For nausea and vomiting:

• Adults and teenagers—25 mg inserted into the rectum for the first dose, then 12.5 to 25 mg every four to six hours if needed.

• Children younger than 2 years of age—Use and dose must be determined by your doctor.

• Children 2 years of age and older—Your doctor will determine dose based on the weight and/or size of the child. Children usually are given 12.5 to 25 mg inserted into the rectum every four to six hours as needed.

—For vertigo (dizziness):

• Adults and teenagers—25 mg inserted into the rectum, two times a day as needed.

• Children younger than 2 years of age—Use and dose must be determined by your doctor.

• Children 2 years of age and older—Your doctor will determine dose based on the weight and/or size of the child. Children usually are given 12.5 to 25 mg inserted into the rectum two times a day as needed.

—For use as a sedative:

• Adults and teenagers—25 to 50 mg inserted into the rectum.

• Children younger than 2 years of age—Use and dose must be determined by your doctor.

• Children 2 years of age and older—Your doctor will determine dose based on the weight and/or size of the child. Children usually are given 12.5 to 25 mg inserted into the rectum.

For trimeprazine

• For *regular (short-acting) oral* dosage forms (tablets or liquid):

—For allergy symptoms:

• Adults and teenagers—2.5 mg four times a day as needed.

• Children younger than 2 years of age—Use and dose must be determined by your doctor.

• Children 2 to 3 years of age—1.25 mg at bedtime or three times a day as needed.

• Children 3 to 12 years of age—2.5 mg at bedtime or three times a day as needed.

• For *long-acting oral* dosage forms (extended-release capsules):

—For allergy symptoms:

• Adults and teenagers—5 mg every twelve hours as needed.

• Children younger than 6 years of age—Use and dose must be determined by your doctor.

• Children 6 to 12 years of age—5 mg once a day as needed.

Missed dose—If you are taking this medicine regularly and you miss a dose, take it as soon as possible. However, if it is almost time for your next dose, skip the missed dose and go back to your regular dosing schedule. Do not double doses.

Storage—To store this medicine:

- Keep out of the reach of children, since overdose may be very dangerous in children.
- Store away from heat and direct light.
- Do not store the capsule or tablet form of this medicine in the bathroom medicine cabinet, near the kitchen sink, or in other damp places. Heat or moisture may cause the medicine to break down.
- Keep the liquid form of this medicine from freezing.
- Do not keep outdated medicine or medicine no longer needed. Be sure that any discarded medicine is out of the reach of children.

Precautions While Using This Medicine

Tell the doctor in charge that you are taking this medicine before you have any skin tests for allergies. The results of the tests may be affected by this medicine.

When taking phenothiazine-derivative antihistamines on a regular basis, make sure your doctor knows if you are taking large amounts of aspirin at the same time (as for arthritis or rheumatism). Effects of too much aspirin, such as ringing in the ears, may be covered up by the antihistamine.

Phenothiazine-derivative antihistamines will add to the effects of alcohol and other CNS depressants (medicines that slow down the nervous system, possibly causing drowsiness). Some examples of CNS depressants are sedatives, tranquilizers, or sleeping medicine; prescription pain medicine or narcotics; barbiturates; medicine for seizures; muscle relaxants; or anesthetics, including some dental anesthetics. *Check with your doctor before taking any of the above while you are using this medicine.*

This medicine may cause some people to become drowsy or less alert than they are normally. Even if taken at bedtime, it may cause some people to feel drowsy or less alert on arising. *Make sure you know how you react to the phenothiazine-derivative antihistamine you are taking before you drive, use machines, or do anything else that could be dangerous if you are not alert.*

Phenothiazine-derivative antihistamines may cause dryness of the mouth, nose, and throat. For temporary relief of mouth dryness, use sugarless candy or gum, melt bits of ice in your mouth, or use a saliva substitute. However, if your mouth continues to feel dry for more than 2 weeks, check with your medical doctor or dentist. Continuing dryness of the mouth may increase the chance of dental disease, including tooth decay, gum disease, and fungus infections.

This medicine controls nausea and vomiting. For this reason, it may cover up some of the signs of overdose caused by other medicines or the symptoms of appendicitis. This will make it difficult for your doctor to diagnose these conditions. Make sure your doctor knows that you are taking this medicine if you have other symptoms of appendicitis such as stomach or lower abdominal pain, cramping, or soreness. Also, if you think you may have taken an overdose of any medicine, tell your doctor that you are taking this medicine.

Side Effects of This Medicine

Along with its needed effects, a medicine may cause some unwanted effects. Although not all of these side effects may occur, if they do occur they may need medical attention.

Check with your doctor as soon as possible if any of the following side effects occur:

Less common or rare

Sore throat and fever; unusual bleeding or bruising; unusual tiredness or weakness

Symptoms of overdose

Clumsiness or unsteadiness; convulsions (seizures); drowsiness (severe); dryness of mouth, nose, or throat (severe); feeling faint; flushing or redness of face; hallucinations (seeing, hearing, or feeling things that are not there); muscle spasms (especially of neck and back); restlessness; shortness of breath or troubled breathing; shuffling walk; tic-like (jerky) movements of head and face; trembling and shaking of hands; trouble in sleeping

Other side effects may occur that usually do not need medical attention. These side effects may go away during treatment as your body adjusts to the medicine. However, check with your health care professional if any of the following side effects continue or are bothersome:

More common

Drowsiness (less common with methdilazine); thickening of mucus

Less common or rare

Blurred vision or any change in vision; burning or stinging of rectum (with rectal suppository); confusion; difficult or painful urination; dizziness; dryness of mouth, nose, or throat; fast heartbeat; feeling faint; increased sensitivity of skin to sun; increased sweating; loss of appetite; nightmares; ringing or buzzing in ears; skin rash; unusual excitement, nervousness, restlessness, or irritability

Other side effects not listed above may also occur in some patients. If you notice any other effects, check with your health care professional.

Revised: 07/26/94

ANTI-INFLAMMATORY DRUGS, NONSTEROIDAL Ophthalmic

Some commonly used brand names are:

In the U.S.—

Ocufen[2]
Profenal[4]
Voltaren Ophthalmic[1]

In Canada—

Indocid[3]
Ocufen[2]
Voltaren Ophtha[1]

Another commonly used name for indomethacin is indomethacin.

Note: For quick reference, the following nonsteroidal anti-inflammatory drugs are numbered to match the corresponding brand names.

This information applies to the following medicines:

1. Diclofenac (dye-KLOE-fen-ak)
2. Flurbiprofen (flure-BI-proe-fen)
3. Indomethacin (in-doe-METH-a-sin)*
4. Suprofen (soo-PROE-fen)†

*Not commercially available in the U.S.
†Not commercially available in Canada.

Description

Ophthalmic anti-inflammatory medicines are used in the eye to lessen problems that can occur during or after some kinds of eye surgery. Sometimes, the pupil of the eye gets smaller during an operation. This makes it more difficult for the surgeon to reach some areas of the eye. Some of these medicines are used to help prevent this. Also, some of them are used after eye surgery, to relieve effects such as inflammation or edema (too much fluid in the eye).

These medicines may also be used for other conditions, as determined by your ophthalmologist (eye doctor).

These medicines are available only with your doctor's prescription, in the following dosage forms:

Ophthalmic

Diclofenac
- Ophthalmic solution (U.S. and Canada)

Flurbiprofen
- Ophthalmic solution (U.S. and Canada)

Indomethacin
- Ophthalmic suspension (Canada)

Suprofen
- Ophthalmic solution (U.S.)

Before Using This Medicine

In deciding to use a medicine, the risks of taking the medicine must be weighed against the good it will do. This is a decision you and your doctor will make. For ophthalmic anti-inflammatory medicines, the following should be considered:

Allergies—Tell your doctor if you have ever had any unusual or allergic reaction to one of the ophthalmic anti-inflammatory medicines or other serious reactions, especially asthma or wheezing, runny nose, or hives, to any of the following medicines:

Aspirin or other salicylates
Diclofenac (e.g., Voltaren)
Diflunisal (e.g., Dolobid)
Etodolac (e.g., Lodine)
Fenoprofen (e.g., Nalfon)
Floctafenine (e.g., Idarac)
Flurbiprofen, oral (e.g., Ansaid)
Ibuprofen (e.g., Motrin)
Indomethacin (e.g., Indocin)
Ketoprofen (e.g., Orudis)
Ketorolac (e.g., Toradol)
Meclofenamate (e.g., Meclomen)
Mefenamic acid (e.g., Ponstel)
Nabumetone (e.g., Relafen)
Naproxen (e.g., Naprosyn)
Oxyphenbutazone (e.g., Tandearil)
Phenylbutazone (e.g., Butazolidin)
Piroxicam (e.g., Feldene)
Sulindac (e.g., Clinoril)
Suprofen (e.g., Suprol)
Tenoxicam (e.g., Mobiflex)
Tiaprofenic acid (e.g., Surgam)
Tolmetin (e.g., Tolectin)
Zomepirac (e.g., Zomax)

Also tell your health care professional if you are allergic to any other substances, such as foods, preservatives, or dyes.

Pregnancy—Although studies on birth defects have not been done in pregnant women after use of these medicines in the eye, ophthalmic anti-inflammatory medicines have not been reported to cause birth defects or other problems. Studies have been done in animals receiving anti-inflammatory medicines by mouth in amounts that are much greater than the amounts used in the eye. These medicines did not cause birth defects in these studies. However, they decreased the weight or slowed the growth of the fetus and caused other, more serious, harmful effects on the fetus when they were given in amounts that were large enough to cause harmful effects in the mother. Also, when these medicines were given to animals late in pregnancy, they increased the length of pregnancy or prolonged labor.

Breast-feeding—It is not known whether any of these medicines pass into the breast milk after they are placed in the eye. Diclofenac, indomethacin, and suprofen pass into the breast milk when they are are taken by mouth. It is not known whether flurbiprofen passes into the breast milk when it is taken by mouth. However, these medicines have not been shown to cause problems in nursing babies.

Children—These medicines have been studied only in adults, and there is no specific information about their use in children.

Older adults—These medicines have been tested and have not been shown to cause different side effects or problems in older people than they do in younger adults.

Other medical problems—The presence of other medical problems may affect the use of these medicines. Make sure you tell your doctor if you have any other medical problems, especially:

- Hemophilia or other bleeding problems—The possibility of bleeding may be increased

Proper Use of This Medicine

To use:

- First, wash your hands. Tilt the head back and, pressing your finger gently on the skin just beneath the lower eyelid, pull the lower eyelid away from the eye to make a space. Drop the medicine into this space. Let go of the eyelid and gently close the eyes. Do not blink. Keep the eyes closed and apply pressure to the inner corner of the eye with your finger for 1 or 2 minutes to allow the medicine to be absorbed by the eye.
- Immediately after using the eye drops, wash your hands to remove any medicine that may be on them.
- To keep the medicine as germ-free as possible, do not touch the applicator tip to any surface (including the eye). Also, always keep the container tightly closed.

Do not use this medicine more often or for a longer time than your doctor ordered. To do so may increase the chance of side effects.

Do not use any leftover medicine for future eye problems without first checking with your doctor. If certain kinds of infection are present, using this medicine may make the infection worse and possibly lead to eye damage.

Dosing—The dose of these medicines will be different for different patients. *Follow your doctor's orders or the directions on the label.* The following information includes only the average doses of these medicines. *If your dose is different, do not change it* unless your doctor tells you to do so.

For diclofenac

- Adults:
  —For use before an eye operation: Your doctor or nurse will probably give you the medicine before your operation.
  —To relieve inflammation or edema in the eye: 1 drop in the eye 3 to 5 times a day.
- Children: To be determined by the doctor.

For flurbiprofen

- Adults:
  —For use before an eye operation: Your health care professional will probably give you the medicine before your operation.
  —To relieve inflammation: 1 drop in the eye every 4 hours.
- Children: To be determined by the doctor.

For indomethacin
- Adults:
  - —For use before an eye operation: Your health care professional will probably give you the medicine before your operation.
  - —To relieve inflammation or edema in the eye: 1 drop in the eye 4 times a day.
- Children: To be determined by the doctor.

For suprofen
- Adults:
  - —For use before an eye operation: Your health care professional will probably give you the medicine before your operation.
  - —To relieve inflammation or edema in the eye: To be determined by the doctor.
- Children: To be determined by the doctor.

Missed dose—If you miss a dose of this medicine, apply it as soon as possible. But if it is almost time for your next dose, skip the missed dose and go back to your regular dosing schedule.

Storage—To store this medicine:
- Keep out of the reach of children.
- Store away from heat and direct light.
- Keep the medicine from freezing.
- Do not keep outdated medicine or medicine no longer needed. Be sure that any discarded medicine is out of the reach of children.

Precautions While Using This Medicine

Wearing soft (hydrogel) contact lenses during treatment with diclofenac has caused severe irritation (redness and itching) in some people. Therefore, *do not wear soft contact lenses during the time that you are being treated with diclofenac.*

Side Effects of This Medicine

Along with its needed effects, a medicine may cause some unwanted effects. Check with your doctor as soon as possible if any of the following side effects occur:

Less common or rare

Bleeding in the eye or redness or swelling of the eye or the eyelid (not present before you started using this medicine or becoming worse while you are using this medicine); itching or tearing

Other side effects may occur that usually do not need medical attention. The following side effects usually do not need medical attention. However, check with your doctor if they continue or are bothersome.

More common

Burning or stinging after application

Other side effects not listed above may also occur in some patients. If you notice any other effects, check with your doctor.

Revised: 09/08/92
Interim revision: 08/17/93; 01/24/95

ANTI-INFLAMMATORY DRUGS, NONSTEROIDAL Systemic

Some commonly used brand names are:

In the U.S.—

Actron[9]
Advil[7]
Advil Caplets[7]
Advil, Children's[7]
Aleve[13]
Anaprox[13]
Anaprox DS[13]
Ansaid[6]
Bayer Select Ibuprofen Pain Relief Formula Caplets[7]
Cataflam[1]
Clinoril[17]
Cotylbutazone[15]
Cramp End[7]
Daypro[14]
Dolgesic[7]
Dolobid[2]
EC-Naprosyn[13]
Excedrin IB[7]
Excedrin IB Caplets[7]
Feldene[16]
Genpril[7]
Genpril Caplets[7]
Haltran[7]
Ibifon 600 Caplets[7]
Ibren[7]
Ibu[7]
Ibu-200[7]
Ibu-4[7]
Ibu-6[7]
Ibu-8[7]
Ibuprin[7]
Ibuprohm[7]
Ibuprohm Caplets[7]
Ibu-Tab[7]
Indocin[8]
Indocin SR[8]
Lodine[3]
Meclomen[10]
Medipren[7]
Medipren Caplets[7]
Midol IB[7]
Motrin[7]
Motrin Chewables[7]
Motrin, Children's[7]
Motrin, Children's Oral Drops[7]
Motrin-IB[7]
Motrin-IB Caplets[7]
Motrin, Junior Strength Caplets[7]
Nalfon[4]
Nalfon 200[4]
Naprosyn[13]
Nuprin[7]
Nuprin Caplets[7]
Orudis[9]
Orudis KT[9]
Oruvail[9]
Pamprin-IB[7]
Ponstel[11]
Q-Profen[7]
Relafen[12]
Rufen[7]
Tolectin 200[20]
Tolectin 600[20]
Tolectin DS[20]
Trendar[7]
Voltaren[1]

In Canada—

Actiprofen Caplets[7]
Advil[7]
Advil Caplets[7]
Albert Tiafen[19]
Alka Butazolidin[15]
Anaprox[13]
Anaprox DS[13]
Ansaid[6]
Apo-Diclo[1]
Apo-Diflunisal[2]
Apo-Flurbiprofen[6]
Apo-Ibuprofen[7]
Apo-Indomethacin[8]
Apo-Keto[9]
Apo-Keto-E[9]
Apo-Napro-Na[13]
Apo-Napro-Na DS[13]
Apo-Naproxen[13]
Apo-Phenylbutazone[15]
Apo-Piroxicam[16]
Apo-Sulin[17]
Butazolidin[15]
Clinoril[17]
Dolobid[2]
Feldene[16]
Froben[6]
Froben SR[6]
Idarac[5]
Indocid[8]
Indocid SR[8]
Medipren Caplets[7]
Mobiflex[18]
Motrin[7]
Motrin-IB[7]
Nalfon[4]
Naprosyn[13]
Naprosyn-E[13]
Naprosyn-SR[13]
Naxen[13]
Novo-Difenac[1]
Novo-Difenac SR[1]
Novo-Diflunisal[2]
Novo-Flurprofen[6]
Novo-Keto-EC[9]
Novo-Methacin[8]
Novo-Naprox[13]
Novo-Naprox Sodium[13]
Novo-Naprox Sodium DS[13]
Novo-Pirocam[16]
Novo-Profen[7]
Novo-Sundac[17]
Novo-Tolmetin[20]
Nu-Diclo[11]
Nu-Flurbiprofen[6]
Nu-Ibuprofen[7]
Nu-Indo[8]
Nu-Naprox[13]
Nu-Pirox[16]

Orudis[9]
Orudis-E[9]
Orudis-SR[9]
Oruvail[9]
PMS-Piroxicam[16]
Ponstan[11]
Relafen[12]
Rhodis[9]
Rhodis-EC[9]
Surgam[19]
Surgam SR[19]
Synflex[13]
Synflex DS[13]
Tolectin 200[20]
Tolectin 400[20]
Tolectin 600[20]
Voltaren[1]
Voltaren Rapide[1]
Voltaren SR[1]

Other commonly used names are:
Etodolic acid[3]
Indometacin[8]
Meclofenamic acid[10]

Note: For quick reference, the following nonsteroidal anti-inflammatory drugs are numbered to match the corresponding brand names.

This information applies to the following medicines:

1. Diclofenac (dye-KLOE-fen-ak)
2. Diflunisal (dye-FLOO-ni-sal)‡
3. Etodolac (ee-TOE-doe-lak)†
4. Fenoprofen (fen-oh-PROE-fen)‡
5. Floctafenine (flok-ta-FEN-een)*
6. Flurbiprofen (flure-BI-proe-fen)‡§
7. Ibuprofen (eye-byoo-PROE-fen)‡§
8. Indomethacin (in-doe-METH-a-sin)‡
9. Ketoprofen (kee-toe-PROE-fen)‡
10. Meclofenamate (me-kloe-FEN-am-ate)†‡
11. Mefenamic (me-fe-NAM-ik) Acid
12. Nabumetone (na-BYOO-me-tone)
13. Naproxen (na-PROX-en)‡
14. Oxaprozin (ox-a-PROE-zin)†
15. Phenylbutazone (fen-ill-BYOO-ta-zone)‡
16. Piroxicam (peer-OX-i-kam)‡
17. Sulindac (sul-IN-dak)‡
18. Tenoxicam (ten-OX-i-kam)*
19. Tiaprofenic (tie-a-pro-FEN-ik) Acid*
20. Tolmetin (TOLE-met-in)‡

This information does *not* apply to aspirin or other salicylates or to ketorolac (e.g., Toradol).

*Not commercially available in the U.S.
†Not commercially available in Canada.
‡Generic name product may also be available in the U.S.
§Generic name product may also be available in the Canada.

Description

Nonsteroidal anti-inflammatory drugs (also called NSAIDs) are used to relieve some symptoms caused by arthritis (rheumatism), such as inflammation, swelling, stiffness, and joint pain. However, this medicine does not cure arthritis and will help you only as long as you continue to take it.

Some of these medicines are also used to relieve other kinds of pain or to treat other painful conditions, such as:

- gout attacks;
- bursitis;
- tendinitis;
- sprains, strains, or other injuries; or
- menstrual cramps.

Ibuprofen and naproxen are also used to reduce fever.

Meclofenamate is also used to reduce the amount of bleeding in some women who have very heavy menstrual periods.

Nonsteroidal anti-inflammatory drugs may also be used to treat other conditions as determined by your doctor.

Any nonsteroidal anti-inflammatory drug can cause side effects, especially when it is used for a long time or in large doses. Some of the side effects are painful or uncomfortable. Others can be more serious, resulting in the need for medical care and sometimes even death. If you will be taking this medicine for more than one or two months or in large amounts, you should discuss with your doctor the good that it can do as well as the risks of taking it. Also, it is a good idea to ask your doctor about other forms of treatment that might help to reduce the amount of this medicine that you take and/or the length of treatment.

One of the nonsteroidal anti-inflammatory drugs, phenylbutazone, is especially likely to cause very serious side effects. These serious side effects are more likely to occur in patients 40 years of age or older than in younger adults, and the risk becomes greater as the patient's age increases. Before you take phenylbutazone, be sure that you have discussed its use with your doctor. *Also, do not use phenylbutazone to treat any painful condition other than the one for which it was prescribed by your doctor.*

Although ibuprofen and naproxen may be used instead of aspirin to treat many of the same medical problems, they must not be used by people who are allergic to aspirin.

The 200-mg strength of ibuprofen and the 220-mg strength of naproxen are available without a prescription. However, your health care professional may have special instructions on the proper dose of these medicines for your medical condition.

Other nonsteroidal anti-inflammatory drugs and other strengths of ibuprofen and naproxen are available only with your medical doctor's or dentist's prescription. These medicines are available in the following dosage forms:

Oral

Diclofenac
- Tablets (U.S. and Canada)
- Delayed-release tablets (U.S. and Canada)
- Extended-release tablets (Canada)

Diflunisal
- Tablets (U.S. and Canada)

Etodolac
- Capsules (U.S.)
- Tablets (U.S.)

Fenoprofen
- Capsules (U.S. and Canada)
- Tablets (U.S. and Canada)

Floctafenine
- Tablets (Canada)

Flurbiprofen
- Extended-release capsules (Canada)
- Tablets (U.S. and Canada)

Ibuprofen
- Oral suspension (U.S.)
- Tablets (U.S. and Canada)
- Chewable tablets (U.S.)

Indomethacin
- Capsules (U.S. and Canada)
- Extended-release capsules (U.S. and Canada)
- Oral suspension (U.S.)

Ketoprofen
- Capsules (U.S. and Canada)
- Extended-release capsules (U.S. and Canada)

- Tablets (U.S.)
- Delayed-release tablets (Canada)
- Extended-release tablets (Canada)

Meclofenamate
- Capsules (U.S.)

Mefenamic Acid
- Capsules (U.S. and Canada)

Nabumetone
- Tablets (U.S. and Canada)

Naproxen
- Oral suspension (U.S. and Canada)
- Tablets (U.S. and Canada)
- Delayed-release tablets (U.S. and Canada)
- Extended-release tablets (Canada)

Oxaprozin
- Tablets (U.S.)

Phenylbutazone
- Capsules (U.S.)
- Tablets (U.S. and Canada)
- Buffered tablets (Canada)

Piroxicam
- Capsules (U.S. and Canada)

Sulindac
- Tablets (U.S. and Canada)

Tenoxicam
- Tablets (Canada)

Tiaprofenic Acid
- Extended-release capsules (Canada)
- Tablets (Canada)

Tolmetin
- Capsules (U.S. and Canada)
- Tablets (U.S. and Canada)

Rectal

Diclofenac
- Suppositories (Canada)

Indomethacin
- Suppositories (U.S. and Canada)

Ketoprofen
- Suppositories (Canada)

Naproxen
- Suppositories (Canada)

Piroxicam
- Suppositories (Canada)

Before Using This Medicine

In deciding to use a medicine, the risks of taking the medicine must be weighed against the good it will do. This is a decision you and your health care professional will make. For the nonsteroidal anti-inflammatory drugs, the following should be considered:

Allergies—Tell your health care professional if you have ever had any unusual or allergic reaction to any of the nonsteroidal anti-inflammatory drugs, or to any of the following medicines:

- Aspirin or other salicylates
- Ketorolac (e.g., Toradol)
- Oxyphenbutazone (e.g., Oxalid, Tandearil)
- Suprofen (e.g., Suprol)
- Zomepirac (e.g., Zomax)

Also tell your health care professional if you are allergic to any other substances, such as foods, preservatives, or dyes.

Diet—Make certain your health care professional knows if you are on any special diet, such as a low-sodium or low-sugar diet. Some of these medicines contain sodium or sugar.

Pregnancy—Studies on birth defects with these medicines have not been done in humans. However, there is a chance that these medicines may cause unwanted effects on the heart or blood flow of the fetus or newborn baby if they are taken regularly during the last few months of pregnancy. Also, studies in animals have shown that these medicines, if taken late in pregnancy, may increase the length of pregnancy, prolong labor, or cause other problems during delivery. If you are pregnant, do not take any of these medicines, including nonprescription (over-the-counter [OTC]) ibuprofen or naproxen, without first discussing its use with your doctor.

Studies in animals have not shown that fenoprofen, floctafenine, flurbiprofen, ibuprofen, ketoprofen, nabumetone, naproxen, phenylbutazone, piroxicam, tiaprofenic acid, or tolmetin causes birth defects. Diflunisal caused birth defects of the spine and ribs in rabbits, but not in mice or rats. Diclofenac and meclofenamate caused unwanted effects on the formation of bones in animals. Etodolac and oxaprozin caused birth defects in animals. Indomethacin caused slower development of bones and damage to nerves in animals. In some animal studies, sulindac caused unwanted effects on the development of bones and organs. Studies on birth defects with mefenamic acid have not been done in animals.

Even though most of these medicines did not cause birth defects in animals, many of them did cause other harmful or toxic effects on the fetus, usually when they were given in such large amounts that the pregnant animals became sick.

Breast-feeding—

- *For indomethacin:* Indomethacin passes into the breast milk and has been reported to cause unwanted effects in nursing babies.
- *For meclofenamate:* Use of meclofenamate by nursing mothers is not recommended because in animal studies it caused unwanted effects on the newborn's development.
- *For phenylbutazone:* Phenylbutazone passes into the breast milk and may cause unwanted effects, such as blood problems, in nursing babies.
- *For piroxicam:* Studies in animals have shown that piroxicam may decrease the amount of milk.

Although other anti-inflammatory analgesics have not been reported to cause problems in nursing babies, diclofenac, diflunisal, fenoprofen, flurbiprofen, meclofenamate, mefenamic acid, naproxen, piroxicam, and tolmetin pass into the breast milk. It is not known whether etodolac, floctafenine, ibuprofen, ketoprofen, nabumetone, oxaprozin, sulindac, or tiaprofenic acid passes into human breast milk.

Children—

- *For ibuprofen:* Ibuprofen has been tested in children 6 months of age and older. It has not been shown to cause different side effects or problems than it does in adults.

- *For indomethacin and for tolmetin:* Indomethacin and tolmetin have been tested in children 2 years of age and older and have not been shown to cause different side effects or problems than they do in adults.
- *For naproxen:* Studies with naproxen in children 2 years of age and older have shown that skin rash may be more likely to occur.
- *For oxaprozin:* Oxaprozin has been used in children with arthritis. However, there is no specific information comparing use of this medicine in children with use in other age groups.
- *For phenylbutazone:* Use of phenylbutazone in children up to 15 years of age is not recommended.
- *For other anti-inflammatory analgesics:* There is no specific information on the use of other anti-inflammatory analgesics in children.

Most of these medicines, especially indomethacin and phenylbutazone, can cause serious side effects in any patient. Therefore, it is especially important that you discuss with the child's doctor the good that this medicine may do as well as the risks of using it.

Older adults—Certain side effects, such as confusion, swelling of the face, feet, or lower legs, or sudden decrease in the amount of urine, may be especially likely to occur in elderly patients, who are usually more sensitive than younger adults to the effects of nonsteroidal anti-inflammatory drugs. Also, elderly people are more likely than younger adults to get very sick if these medicines cause stomach problems. With phenylbutazone, blood problems may also be more likely to occur in the elderly.

Other medicines—Although certain medicines should not be used together at all, in other cases two different medicines may be used together even if an interaction might occur. In these cases, your doctor may want to change the dose, or other precautions may be necessary. When you are taking a nonsteroidal anti-inflammatory drug, it is especially important that your health care professional know if you are taking any of the following:

- Anticoagulants (blood thinners) or
- Cefamandole (e.g., Mandol) or
- Cefoperazone (e.g., Cefobid) or
- Cefotetan (e.g., Cefotan) or
- Heparin or
- Plicamycin (e.g., Mithracin) or
- Valproic acid—The chance of bleeding may be increased
- Aspirin—The chance of serious side effects may be increased if aspirin is used together with a nonsteroidal anti-inflammatory drug on a regular basis
- Ciprofloxacin (e.g., Cipro) or
- Enoxacin (e.g., Penetrex) or
- Itraconazole (e.g., Sporanox) or
- Ketoconazole (e.g., Nizoral) or
- Lomefloxacin (e.g., Maxaquin) or
- Norfloxacin (e.g., Noroxin) or
- Ofloxacin (e.g., Floxin) or
- Tetracyclines, oral—The buffered form of phenylbutazone (e.g., Alka Butazolidin) may keep these medicines from working properly if the 2 medicines are taken too close together
- Cyclosporine (e.g., Sandimmune) or
- Digitalis glycosides (heart medicine) or
- Lithium (e.g., Lithane) or
- Methotrexate (e.g., Mexate) or
- Phenytoin (e.g., Dilantin)—Higher blood levels of these medicines and an increased chance of side effects may occur
- Penicillamine (e.g., Cuprimine)—The chance of serious side effects may be increased, especially with phenylbutazone (e.g., Cotylbutazone)
- Probenecid (e.g., Benemid)—Higher blood levels of the nonsteroidal anti-inflammatory drug and an increased chance of side effects may occur
- Triamterene (e.g., Dyrenium)—The chance of kidney problems may be increased, especially with indomethacin
- Zidovudine (e.g., AZT, Retrovir)—The chance of serious side effects may be increased, especially with indomethacin

Other medical problems—The presence of other medical problems may affect the use of nonsteroidal anti-inflammatory drugs. Make sure you tell your doctor if you have any other medical problems, especially:

- Alcohol abuse or
- Bleeding problems or
- Colitis, Crohn's disease, diverticulitis, stomach ulcer, or other stomach or intestinal problems or
- Diabetes mellitus (sugar diabetes) or
- Hemorrhoids or
- Hepatitis or other liver disease or
- Kidney disease (or history of) or
- Rectal irritation or bleeding, recent, or
- Systemic lupus erythematosus (SLE) or
- Tobacco use (or recent history of)—The chance of side effects may be increased

- Anemia or
- Asthma or
- Epilepsy or
- Fluid retention (swelling of feet or lower legs) or
- Heart disease or
- High blood pressure or
- Kidney stones (or history of) or
- Low platelet count or
- Low white blood cell count or
- Mental illness or
- Parkinson's disease or
- Polymyalgia rheumatica or
- Porphyria or
- Temporal arteritis—Some nonsteroidal anti-inflammatory drugs may make these conditions worse
- Ulcers, sores, or white spots in mouth—Ulcers, sores, or white spots in the mouth sometimes mean that the medicine is causing serious side effects; if these sores or spots are already present before you start taking the medicine, it will be harder for you and your doctor to recognize that these side effects might be occurring

Proper Use of This Medicine

For patients taking *a capsule, tablet (including caplet), or liquid form* of this medicine:

- *Take tablet or capsule forms of these medicines with a full glass (8 ounces) of water.* Also, do not lie down for about 15 to 30 minutes after taking the medicine. This helps to prevent irritation that may lead to trouble in swallowing.
- To lessen stomach upset, these medicines should be taken with food or an antacid. This is especially im-

portant when you are taking indomethacin, mefenamic acid, phenylbutazone, or piroxicam, which should always be taken with food or an antacid. Taking the extended-release tablet dosage form of flurbiprofen or naproxen and taking nabumetone with food may also help the medicine be absorbed into your body more quickly. However, your doctor may want you to take the first 1 or 2 doses of other nonsteroidal anti-inflammatory drugs 30 minutes before meals or 2 hours after meals. This helps the medicine start working a little faster when you first begin to take it. However, after the first few doses, take the medicine with food or an antacid.

- It is not necessary to take delayed-release (enteric-coated) tablets with food or an antacid, because the enteric coating helps protect your stomach from the irritating effects of the medicine. Also, it is not necessary to take ketoprofen extended-release capsules (e.g., Oruvail) with food or an antacid, because the medicine inside the capsules is enteric coated.
- If you will be taking your medicine together with an antacid, one that contains magnesium and aluminum hydroxides (e.g., Maalox) may be the best kind of antacid to use, unless your doctor has directed you to use another antacid. However, do not mix the liquid form of ibuprofen, indomethacin, or naproxen together with an antacid, or any other liquid, before taking it. To do so may cause the medicine to break down. If stomach upset (indigestion, nausea, vomiting, stomach pain, or diarrhea) continues or if you have any questions about how you should be taking this medicine, check with your health care professional.
- Some of these medicines must be swallowed whole. Tablets should not be crushed, chewed, or broken, and capsules should not be emptied out, before you take the medicine. These include delayed-release (enteric-coated) or extended-release tablets or capsules, diflunisal tablets (e.g., Dolobid), and phenylbutazone tablets (e.g., Butazolidin). If you are not sure whether you are taking a delayed-release or extended-release form of your medicine, check with your pharmacist.

For patients using *a suppository form* of this medicine:

- If the suppository is too soft to insert, chill it in the refrigerator for 30 minutes or run cold water over it before removing the foil wrapper.
- To insert the suppository: First remove the foil wrapper and moisten the suppository with cold water. Lie down on your side and use your finger to push the suppository well up into the rectum.
- Indomethacin suppositories should be kept inside the rectum for at least one hour so that all of the medicine can be absorbed by your body. This helps the medicine work better.

For patients taking *nonprescription (over-the-counter [OTC]) ibuprofen or naproxen:*

- This medicine comes with a patient information sheet. Read it carefully. If you have any questions about this information, check with your health care professional.

For safe and effective use of this medicine, do not take more of it, do not take it more often, and do not take it for a longer time than ordered by your health care professional or directed on the nonprescription (over-the-counter [OTC]) package label. Taking too much of any of these medicines may increase the chance of unwanted effects, especially in elderly patients.

When used for severe or continuing arthritis, a nonsteroidal anti-inflammatory drug must be taken regularly as ordered by your doctor in order for it to help you. These medicines usually begin to work within one week, but in severe cases up to two weeks or even longer may pass before you begin to feel better. Also, several weeks may pass before you feel the full effects of the medicine.

For patients taking *mefenamic acid:*

- *Always take mefenamic acid with food or antacids.*
- *Do not take mefenamic acid for more than 7 days at a time* unless otherwise directed by your doctor. To do so may increase the chance of side effects, especially in elderly patients.

For patients taking *phenylbutazone:*

- Phenylbutazone is intended to treat your current medical problem only. *Do not take it for any other aches or pains.* Also, phenylbutazone should be used for the shortest time possible because of the chance of serious side effects, especially in patients who are 40 years of age or older.

Dosing—The dose of these medicines will be different for different patients. *Follow your doctor's orders or the directions on the label.* The following information includes only the average doses of these medicines. *If your dose is different, do not change it* unless your doctor tells you to do so.

The number of capsules or tablets or teaspoonfuls of suspension that you take, or the number of suppositories that you use, depends on the strength of the medicine. Also, *the number of doses you take each day, the time allowed between doses, and the length of time you take the medicine depend on the medical problem for which you are taking the medicine.*

People with arthritis usually need to take more of a nonsteroidal anti-inflammatory drug during a ''flare-up'' than they do between ''flare-ups'' of arthritis symptoms. Therefore, your dose may need to be increased or decreased as your condition changes.

For diclofenac

- For *tablet* dosage form:
  - —For relieving pain or menstrual cramps:
    - Adults—50 milligrams (mg) three times a day as needed. Your doctor may direct you to take 100 mg for the first dose only.
    - Children—Use and dose must be determined by your doctor.

—For rheumatoid arthritis:

- Adults—At first, 50 mg three or four times a day. Your doctor may increase the dose, if necessary, up to a total of 225 mg a day. After your condition improves your doctor may direct you to take a lower dose.
- Children—Use and dose must be determined by your doctor.

—For osteoarthritis:

- Adults—At first, 50 mg two or three times a day. Usually, no more than a total of 150 mg a day should be taken. After your condition improves your doctor may direct you to take a lower dose.
- Children—Use and dose must be determined by your doctor.

—For spondylitis (lower back pain):

- Adults—At first, 25 mg four or five times a day. After your condition improves your doctor may direct you to take a lower dose.
- Children—Use and dose must be determined by your doctor.

• For *delayed-release tablet* dosage form:

—For rheumatoid arthritis:

- Adults—At first, 50 mg three or four times a day. Your doctor may increase the dose, if necessary, up to a total of 225 mg a day. After your condition improves your doctor may direct you to take a lower dose.
- Children—Use and dose must be determined by your doctor.

—For osteoarthritis:

- Adults—At first, 50 mg two or three times a day. Usually, no more than a total of 150 mg a day should be taken. After your condition improves your doctor may direct you to take a lower dose.
- Children—Use and dose must be determined by your doctor.

—For spondylitis (lower back pain):

- Adults—At first, 25 mg four or five times a day. After your condition improves your doctor may direct you to take a lower dose.
- Children—Use and dose must be determined by your doctor.

• For *extended-release tablet* dosage form:

—For rheumatoid arthritis, osteoarthritis, or spondylitis:

- Adults—Usually 75 or 100 mg once a day, in the morning or evening. Some people may need 75 mg twice a day, in the morning and evening. Take the medicine at the same time every day.
- Children—Use and dose must be determined by your doctor.

• For *rectal* dosage form (suppositories):

—For rheumatoid arthritis, osteoarthritis, or spondylitis:

- Adults—One 50-mg or 100-mg suppository, inserted into the rectum. The suppository is usually used only at night by people who take tablets during the day. Usually, no more than a total of 150 mg of diclofenac should be used in a day from all dosage forms combined.
- Children—Use and dose must be determined by your doctor.

For diflunisal

• For *oral* dosage form (tablets):

—For pain:

- Adults—1000 milligrams (mg) for the first dose, then 500 mg every eight to twelve hours as needed. Some people may need only 500 mg for the first dose, then 250 mg every eight to twelve hours as needed. Usually, no more than a total of 1500 mg a day should be taken.
- Children—Dose must be determined by your doctor.

—For rheumatoid arthritis or osteoarthritis:

- Adults—At first, 250 or 500 mg twice a day. Your doctor may increase the dose, if necessary, up to a total of 1500 mg a day. After your condition improves your doctor may direct you to take a lower dose.
- Children—Dose must be determined by your doctor.

For etodolac

• For *oral* dosage forms (capsules or tablets):

—For pain:

- Adults—400 milligrams (mg) for the first dose, then 200 to 400 mg every six to eight hours as needed. Usually, no more than a total of 1200 mg a day should be taken.
- Children—Use and dose must be determined by your doctor.

—For osteoarthritis:

- Adults—At first, 400 mg two or three times a day or 300 mg three or four times a day. Usually, no more than a total of 1200 mg a day should be taken. After your condition improves your doctor may direct you to take a lower dose.
- Children—Use and dose must be determined by your doctor.

For fenoprofen

• For *oral* dosage forms (capsules or tablets):

—For pain:

- Adults—200 milligrams (mg) every four to six hours as needed.
- Children—Use and dose must be determined by your doctor.

—For arthritis:

- Adults—At first, 300 to 600 mg three or four times a day. Your doctor may increase the dose, if necessary, up to a total of 3200 mg a day. After your condition improves your doctor may direct you to take a lower dose.

• Children—Use and dose must be determined by your doctor.

For floctafenine

• For *oral* dosage form (tablets):

—For pain:

• Adults—200 to 400 milligrams (mg) every six to eight hours, as needed. Usually, no more than 1200 mg a day should be taken.

• Children—Use is not recommended.

For flurbiprofen

• For *oral tablet* dosage form:

—For menstrual cramps:

• Adults—50 milligrams (mg) four times a day.

• Children—Use and dose must be determined by your doctor.

—For bursitis, tendinitis, or athletic injuries:

• Adults—50 mg every four to six hours as needed.

• Children—Use and dose must be determined by your doctor.

—For rheumatoid arthritis or osteoarthritis:

• Adults—At first, 200 to 300 mg a day, divided into smaller amounts that are taken two to four times a day. Usually, no more than a total of 300 mg a day should be taken. After your condition improves your doctor may direct you to take a lower dose.

• Children—Use and dose must be determined by your doctor.

—For spondylitis (lower back pain):

• Adults—At first, 50 mg four times a day. Your doctor may increase the dose, if necessary, up to a total of 300 mg a day. After your condition improves your doctor may direct you to take a lower dose.

• Children—Use and dose must be determined by your doctor.

• For *extended-release capsule* dosage form:

—For arthritis:

• Adults—200 mg once a day, in the evening. Take the medicine at the same time every day.

• Children—Use and dose must be determined by your doctor.

For ibuprofen

• For *oral* dosage forms (oral suspension, tablets, chewable tablets):

—For pain or menstrual cramps:

• Adults and teenagers—200 to 400 milligrams (mg) every four to six hours as needed. If you are taking the medicine without a prescription from your health care professional, do not take more than a total of 1200 mg (six 200-mg tablets) a day.

• Children up to 12 years of age—Use and dose must be determined by your doctor.

—For fever:

• Adults and teenagers—200 to 400 mg every four to six hours as needed. If you are taking the medicine without a prescription from your health care professional, do not take more than a total of 1200 mg (six 200-mg tablets) a day.

• Children 6 months to 12 years of age—The medicine should be used only with a prescription from your doctor. The dose is based on body weight and on the body temperature. For fevers lower than 102.5 °F (39.2 °C) the dose is 5 mg per kilogram (kg) (about 2.2 mg per pound) of body weight. For higher fevers the dose is 10 mg per kg (about 4.5 mg per pound) of body weight.

• Infants younger than 6 months of age—Use and dose must be determined by your doctor.

—For arthritis:

• Adults and teenagers—At first, a total of 1200 to 3200 mg a day, divided into smaller amounts that are taken three or four times a day. After your condition improves your doctor may direct you to take a lower dose.

• Children 6 months to 12 years of age—The dose is based on body weight. At first, a total of 30 to 40 mg per kg (about 13.6 to 18 mg per pound) of body weight a day, divided into smaller amounts that are taken three or four times a day. Your doctor may increase the dose, if necessary, up to a total of 50 mg per kg (about 21 mg per pound) of body weight a day. After your condition improves your doctor may direct you to take a lower dose.

• Infants younger than 6 months of age—Use and dose must be determined by your doctor.

For indomethacin

• For *capsule or oral suspension* dosage forms:

—For arthritis:

• Adults—At first, 25 or 50 milligrams (mg) two to four times a day. Your doctor may increase the dose, if necessary, up to a total of 200 mg a day. After your condition improves your doctor may direct you to take a lower dose.

• Children—The dose is based on body weight. At first, 1.5 to 2.5 mg per kilogram (kg) (about 0.7 to 1.1 mg per pound) of body weight a day, divided into smaller amounts that are taken three or four times a day. Your doctor may increase the dose, if necessary, up to a total of 4 mg per kg (about 1.8 mg per pound) of body weight or 200 mg a day, whichever is less. After your condition improves your doctor may direct you to take a lower dose.

—For gout:

• Adults—100 mg for the first dose, then 50 mg three times a day. After the pain is relieved, your doctor may direct you to take a lower dose for a while before stopping treatment completely.

• Children—Use and dose must be determined by your doctor.

—For bursitis or tendinitis:

• Adults—25 mg three or four times a day or 50 mg three times a day.

• Children—Use and dose must be determined by your doctor.

• For *extended-release capsule* dosage form:

—For arthritis:

• Adults—75 mg once a day, in the morning or evening. Some people may need to take 75 mg twice a day, in the morning and evening. Take the medicine at the same time each day.

• Children—Dose must be determined by your doctor.

• For *rectal suppository* dosage form:

—For arthritis, bursitis, tendinitis, or gout:

• Adults—One 50-mg suppository, inserted into the rectum up to four times a day.

• Children—One 50-mg suppository, inserted into the rectum up to four times a day. The suppository dosage form is too strong for small children. However, the suppositories may be used for large or heavy children if they need doses as large as 50 mg.

For ketoprofen

• For *capsule, tablet, or delayed-release tablet* dosage forms:

—For pain or menstrual cramps:

• Adults—25 to 50 milligrams (mg) every six to eight hours as needed. Some people may need to take as much as 75 mg every six to eight hours. Doses larger than 75 mg are not likely to give better relief.

• Over the counter medication—12.5 mg every 4 to 6 hours.

• Children—Use and dose must be determined by your doctor.

—For arthritis:

• Adults—At first, 50 mg four times a day or 75 mg three times a day. Your doctor may increase the dose, if necessary, up to a total of 300 mg a day. After your condition improves your doctor may direct you to take a lower dose.

• Children—Use and dose must be determined by your doctor.

• For *extended-release capsule or extended-release tablet* dosage forms:

—For arthritis:

• Adults—150 or 200 mg once a day, in the morning or evening. Take the medicine at the same time every day.

• Children—Use and dose must be determined by your doctor.

• For *rectal suppository* dosage form:

—For arthritis:

• Adults—50 or 100 mg twice a day, inserted into the rectum, in the morning and evening. Sometimes, the suppository is used only at night by people who take an oral dosage form (capsules or delayed-release tablets) during the day. Usually, no more than a total of 300 mg of ketoprofen should be used in a day from all dosage forms combined.

• Children—Use and dose must be determined by your doctor.

For meclofenamate

• For *oral* dosage form (capsules):

—For arthritis:

• Adults and teenagers 14 years of age and older—At first, 50 milligrams (mg) four times a day. Your doctor may increase the dose, if necessary, up to a total of 400 mg a day. After your condition improves your doctor may direct you to take a lower dose.

• Children up to 14 years of age—Use and dose must be determined by your doctor.

—For pain:

• Adults and teenagers 14 years of age and older—50 mg every four to six hours. Some people may need as much as 100 mg every four to six hours.

• Children up to 14 years of age—Use and dose must be determined by your doctor.

—For menstrual cramps and heavy menstrual bleeding:

• Adults and teenagers 14 years of age and older—100 mg three times a day for up to six days.

• Children up to 14 years of age—Use and dose must be determined by your doctor.

For mefenamic acid

• For *oral* dosage form (capsules):

—For pain and for menstrual cramps:

• Adults and teenagers 14 years of age and older—500 milligrams (mg) for the first dose, then 250 mg every six hours as needed for up to seven days.

• Children up to 14 years of age—Use and dose must be determined by your doctor.

For nabumetone

• For *oral* dosage form (tablets):

—For arthritis:

• Adults—At first, 1000 milligrams (mg) once a day, in the morning or evening, or 500 mg twice a day, in the morning and evening. Your doctor may increase the dose, if necessary, up to a total of 2000 mg a day. After your condition improves your doctor may direct you to take a lower dose.

• Children—Use and dose must be determined by your doctor.

For naproxen

- For *naproxen (e.g., Naprosyn) tablet, oral suspension, and delayed-release tablet* dosage forms:
  —For arthritis:
  • Adults—At first, 250, 375, or 500 milligrams (mg) two times a day, in the morning and evening. Your doctor may increase the dose, if necessary, up to a total of 1500 mg a day. After your condition improves your doctor may direct you to take a lower dose.
  • Children—The dose is based on body weight. At first, 5 mg per kilogram (kg) (about 2.25 mg per pound) of body weight twice a day. After your condition improves your doctor may direct you to take a lower dose.
  —For bursitis, tendinitis, menstrual cramps, and other kinds of pain:
  • Adults—500 mg for the first dose, then 250 mg every six to eight hours as needed.
  • Children—Use and dose must be determined by your doctor.
  —For gout:
  • Adults—750 mg for the first dose, then 250 mg every eight hours until the attack is relieved.
  • Children—Use and dose must be determined by your doctor.
- For *naproxen extended-release tablet (e.g., Naprosyn-E)* dosage form:
  —For arthritis:
  • Adults—750 mg once a day, in the morning or evening.
  • Children—The extended-release tablets are too strong for use in children.
- For *naproxen (e.g., Naprosyn) rectal suppository* dosage form:
  —For arthritis:
  • Adults—One 500-mg suppository, inserted into the rectum at bedtime. The suppository is usually used only at night by people who take an oral dosage form (tablets, oral suspension, or delayed-release tablets) during the day. Usually, no more than a total of 1500 mg of naproxen should be used in a day from all dosage forms combined.
  • Children—The suppositories are too strong for use in children.
- For *naproxen sodium (e.g., Aleve, Anaprox) tablet* dosage form:
  —For arthritis:
  • Adults—At first, 275 or 550 mg two times a day, in the morning and evening, or 275 mg in the morning and 550 mg in the evening. Your doctor may increase the dose, if necessary, up to a total of 1650 mg a day. After your condition improves your doctor may direct you to take a lower dose.
  • Children—Naproxen sodium tablets are too strong for most children. Naproxen (e.g., Naprosyn) tablets or oral suspension are usually used for children.
  —For bursitis and tendinitis:
  • Adults—550 mg for the first dose, then 275 mg every six to eight hours as needed.
  • Children—Use and dose must be determined by your doctor. Naproxen sodium tablets are too strong for most children.
  —For gout:
  • Adults—825 mg for the first dose, then 275 mg every eight hours until the attack is relieved.
  • Children—Use and dose must be determined by your doctor. Naproxen sodium tablets are too strong for most children.
  —For pain, fever, and menstrual cramps:
  • Adults and children 12 years of age or older—For nonprescription (over-the-counter [OTC]) use: 220 mg (one tablet) every eight to twelve hours as needed. Some people may get better relief if they take 440 mg (two tablets) for the first dose, then 220 mg twelve hours later on the first day only. If you are taking this medicine without a prescription from your health care professional, do not take more than three 220-mg tablets a day. If you are older than 65 years of age, do not take more than two 220-mg tablets a day. Your health care professional may direct you to take larger doses.
  • Children up to 12 years of age—Use and dose must be determined by your doctor.

For oxaprozin

- For *oral* dosage form (tablets):
  —For arthritis:
  • Adults—At first, 600 milligrams (mg) once or twice a day, or 1200 mg once a day. Some people may need a larger amount for the first dose only. Your doctor may increase the dose, if necessary, up to 1800 mg a day. This large dose should always be divided into smaller amounts that are taken two or three times a day. After your condition improves your doctor may direct you to take a lower dose.
  • Children—Use and dose must be determined by your doctor.

For phenylbutazone

- For *oral* dosage forms (capsules, tablets, and buffered tablets):
  —For severe arthritis:
  • Adults and teenagers 15 years of age and older—At first, 100 milligrams (mg) three or four times a day. Some people may need a higher dose of 200 mg three times a day. After your condition improves your doctor may direct you to take a lower dose for a while before stopping treatment completely. This medicine should not be taken for longer than a few weeks.
  • Children up to 15 years of age—Use is not recommended.

—For gout:

- Adults—400 mg for the first dose, then 100 mg every four hours for one week or less.
- Children up to 15 years of age—Use is not recommended.

For piroxicam

- For *oral* dosage form (capsules):
  —For arthritis:
  - Adults—20 milligrams (mg) once a day or 10 mg twice a day.
  - Children—Dose must be determined by your doctor.

  —For menstrual cramps:
  - Adults—40 mg once a day for one day only, then 20 mg once a day if needed.
  - Children—Dose must be determined by your doctor.
- For *rectal* dosage form (suppositories):
  —For arthritis:
  - Adults—20 mg once a day or 10 mg twice a day.
  - Children—Dose must be determined by your doctor.

For sulindac

- For *oral* dosage form (tablets):
  —For arthritis:
  - Adults—At first, 150 or 200 milligrams (mg) twice a day. After your condition improves, your doctor may direct you to take a lower dose.
  - Children—Use and dose must be determined by your doctor.

  —For gout, bursitis, or tendinitis:
  - Adults—At first, 200 mg twice a day. After the pain is relieved, your doctor may direct you to take a lower dose for a while before treatment is stopped completely.
  - Children—Use and dose must be determined by your doctor.

For tenoxicam

- For *oral* dosage form (tablets):
  —For arthritis:
  - Adults and teenagers 16 years of age and older—At first, 20 milligrams (mg) once a day, at the same time each day. For some people, a smaller dose of 10 mg (one-half tablet) a day may be enough.
  - Children and teenagers up to 16 years of age—Dose must be determined by your doctor.

For tiaprofenic acid

- For *oral tablet* dosage form:
  —For arthritis:
  - Adults—At first, 200 milligrams (mg) three times a day or 300 mg twice a day. After your condition improves, your doctor may direct you to take a lower dose.
  - Children—Use and dose must be determined by your doctor.
- For *extended-release capsule* dosage form:
  —For arthritis:
  - Adults—600 mg (two capsules) once a day, at the same time each day.
  - Children—Use and dose must be determined by your doctor.

For tolmetin

- For *oral* dosage forms (capsules or tablets):
  —For arthritis:
  - Adults—At first, 400 milligrams (mg) three times a day. Your doctor may increase the dose, if necessary, up to a total of 1800 mg a day. After your condition improves, your doctor may direct you to take a lower dose.
  - Children 2 years of age and older—The dose is based on body weight. At first, 20 mg per kilogram (kg) (about 9 mg per pound) of body weight a day, divided into smaller amounts that are taken three or four times a day. Your doctor may increase the dose, if necessary, up to 30 mg per kg (about 13.5 mg per pound) of body weight a day. After your condition improves, your doctor may direct you to take a lower dose.
  - Children up to 2 years of age—Dose must be determined by your doctor.

Missed dose—If your health care professional has ordered you to take this medicine according to a regular schedule, and you miss a dose, take it as soon as you remember. However, if it is almost time for your next dose, skip the missed dose and go back to your regular dosing schedule. (For long-acting medicines or extended-release dosage forms that are only taken once or twice a day, take the missed dose only if you remember within an hour or two after the dose should have been taken. If you do not remember until later, skip the missed dose and go back to your regular dosing schedule.) Do not double doses.

Storage—To store this medicine:

- Keep out of the reach of children.
- Store away from heat and direct light.
- Do not store tablets or capsules in the bathroom, near the kitchen sink, or in other damp places. Heat or moisture may cause the medicine to break down.
- Keep liquid and suppository forms of this medicine from freezing.
- Do not keep outdated medicine or medicine no longer needed. Be sure that any discarded medicine is out of the reach of children.

Precautions While Using This Medicine

If you will be taking this medicine for a long time, as for arthritis (rheumatism), your doctor should check your progress at regular visits. Your doctor may want to do certain tests to find out if unwanted effects are occurring, especially if you are taking phenylbutazone. The tests are very important because serious side effects, including ulcers, bleeding, or blood problems, can occur without any warning.

Stomach problems may be more likely to occur if you drink alcoholic beverages while being treated with this medicine. Also, alcohol may add to the depressant side effects of phenylbutazone. Therefore, *do not regularly drink alcoholic beverages while taking this medicine,* unless otherwise directed by your doctor.

Taking two or more of the nonsteroidal anti-inflammatory drugs together on a regular basis may increase the chance of unwanted effects. Also, taking acetaminophen, aspirin or other salicylates, or ketorolac (e.g., Toradol) regularly while you are taking a nonsteroidal anti-inflammatory drug may increase the chance of unwanted effects. The risk will depend on how much of each medicine you take every day, and on how long you take the medicines together. If your health care professional directs you to take these medicines together on a regular basis, follow his or her directions carefully. However, *do not take acetaminophen or aspirin or other salicylates together with this medicine for more than a few days, and do not take any ketorolac (e.g., Toradol) while you are taking this medicine, unless your doctor has directed you to do so and is following your progress.*

Before having any kind of surgery (including dental surgery), tell the medical doctor or dentist in charge that you are taking this medicine. If possible, this should be done when your surgery is first being planned. Some of the nonsteroidal anti-inflammatory drugs can increase the chance of bleeding during and after surgery. It may be necessary for you to stop treatment for a while, or to change to a different nonsteroidal anti-inflammatory drug that is less likely to cause bleeding.

This medicine may cause some people to become confused, drowsy, dizzy, lightheaded, or less alert than they are normally. It may also cause blurred vision or other vision problems in some people. *Make sure you know how you react to this medicine before you drive, use machines, or do anything else that could be dangerous if you are confused, dizzy, or drowsy, or if you are not alert and able to see well.* If these reactions are especially bothersome, check with your doctor.

For patients taking *the buffered form of phenylbutazone (e.g., Alka-Butazolidin):*

- This medicine contains antacids that can keep other medicines from working properly if the 2 medicines are taken too close together. *Always take this medicine:*

  —At least 6 hours before or 2 hours after taking ciprofloxacin (e.g., Cipro) or lomefloxacin (e.g., Maxaquin).

  —At least 8 hours before or 2 hours after taking enoxacin (e.g., Penetrex).

  —At least 2 hours after taking itraconazole (e.g., Sporanox).

  —At least 3 hours before or after taking ketoconazole (e.g., Nizoral).

  —At least 2 hours before or after taking norfloxacin (e.g., Noroxin) or ofloxacin (e.g., Floxin).

  —At least 1 to 3 hours before or after taking a tetracycline antibiotic by mouth.

  —At least 1 or 2 hours before or after taking any other medicine by mouth.

For patients taking *mefenamic acid:*

- If diarrhea occurs while you are using this medicine, *stop taking it and check with your doctor immediately. Do not take it again without first checking with your doctor,* because severe diarrhea may occur each time you take it.

Some people who take nonsteroidal anti-inflammatory drugs may become more sensitive to sunlight than they are normally. Exposure to sunlight, even for brief periods of time, may cause severe sunburn; blisters on the skin; skin rash, redness, itching, or discoloration; or vision changes. When you begin taking this medicine:

- Stay out of direct sunlight, especially between the hours of 10:00 a.m. and 3:00 p.m., if possible.
- Wear protective clothing, including a hat and sunglasses.
- Apply a sun block product that has a skin protection factor (SPF) of at least 15. Some patients may require a product with a higher SPF number, especially if they have a fair complexion. If you have any questions about this, check with your health care professional.
- Do not use a sunlamp or tanning bed or booth.

If you have a severe reaction from the sun, check with your doctor.

Serious side effects, including ulcers or bleeding, can occur during treatment with this medicine. Sometimes serious side effects can occur without any warning. However, possible warning signs often occur, including severe abdominal or stomach cramps, pain, or burning; black, tarry stools; severe, continuing nausea, heartburn, or indigestion; and/or vomiting of blood or material that looks like coffee grounds. *Stop taking this medicine and check with your doctor immediately if you notice any of these warning signs.*

Check with your doctor immediately if chills, fever, muscle aches or pains, or other influenza-like symptoms occur, especially if they occur shortly before, or together with, a skin rash. Very rarely, these effects may be the first signs of a serious reaction to this medicine.

Nonsteroidal anti-inflammatory drugs may cause a serious type of allergic reaction called anaphylaxis. Although this is rare, it may occur more often in patients who are allergic to aspirin or to any of the nonsteroidal anti-inflammatory drugs. *Anaphylaxis requires immediate medical attention.* The most serious signs of this reaction are very fast or irregular breathing, gasping for breath, wheezing, or fainting. Other signs may include changes in color of the skin of the face; very fast but irregular heartbeat or pulse; hive-like swellings on the skin; and puffiness or swellings of the eyelids or around the eyes. If these effects occur, get emergency help at once. Ask someone to drive you to the nearest hospital emergency room. If this is not possible, do not try to drive yourself. Call an ambulance, lie down, cover yourself to keep warm, and prop your feet higher than your head. Stay in that position until help arrives.

For patients taking *ibuprofen* or *naproxen* without a prescription:

- Check with your medical doctor or dentist:
  —if your symptoms do not improve or if they get worse.
  —if you are using this medicine to bring down a fever and the fever lasts more than 3 days or returns.
  —if the painful area is red or swollen.

Side Effects of This Medicine

Along with its needed effects, a medicine may cause some unwanted effects. Although not all of these side effects may occur, if they do occur they may need medical attention.

Stop taking this medicine and get emergency help right away if any of the following side effects occur:

Rare—For all nonsteroidal anti-inflammatory drugs
Fainting; fast or irregular breathing; fast, irregular heartbeat or pulse; hive-like swellings (large) on face, eyelids, mouth, lips, or tongue; puffiness or swelling of the eyelids or around the eyes; shortness of breath, troubled breathing, wheezing, or tightness in chest

Also, stop taking this medicine and check with your doctor immediately if any of the following side effects occur:

More common—for mefenamic acid only
Diarrhea

More common—for phenylbutazone only
Swelling of face, hands, feet, or lower legs; weight gain (rapid)

Symptoms of phenylbutazone overdose
Bluish color of fingernails, lips, or skin; headache (severe and continuing)

Rare—for all nonsteroidal anti-inflammatory drugs
Abdominal or stomach pain, cramping, or burning (severe); bloody or black, tarry stools; chest pain; convulsions (seizures); fever with or without chills; nausea, heartburn, and/or indigestion (severe and continuing); pinpoint red spots on skin; sores, ulcers, or white spots on lips or in mouth; spitting up blood; unexplained nosebleeds; unusual bleeding or bruising; vomiting of blood or material that looks like coffee grounds

Also, check with your doctor as soon as possible if any of the following side effects occur:

More common
Bleeding from rectum (with suppositories); headache (severe), especially in the morning (for indomethacin only); skin rash

Less common or rare
Bladder pain; bleeding from cuts or scratches that lasts longer than usual; bleeding or crusting sores on lips; bloody or cloudy urine or any problem with urination, such as difficult, burning, or painful urination; change in urine color or odor; frequent urge to urinate; sudden, large increase or decrease in the amount of urine; or loss of bladder control; blurred vision or any change in vision; burning feeling in throat, chest, or stomach; confusion, forgetfulness, mental depression, or other mood or mental changes; cough or hoarseness; decreased hearing, any other change in hearing, or ringing or buzzing in ears; difficulty in swallowing; eye pain, irritation, dryness, redness, and/or swelling; hallucinations (seeing, hearing, or feeling things that are not there); headache (severe), throbbing, or with stiff neck or back; hives, itching of skin, or any other skin problem, such as blisters, redness or other color change, tenderness, burning, peeling, thickening, or scaliness; increased blood pressure; irritated tongue; light-colored stools; loosening or splitting of fingernails; muscle cramps, pain, or weakness; numbness, tingling, pain, or weakness in hands or feet; pain in lower back and/or side (severe); swelling and/or tenderness in upper abdominal or stomach area; swelling of face, feet, or lower legs (if taking phenylbutazone, stop taking it and check with your doctor immediately); swelling of lips or tongue; swollen and/or painful glands (especially in the neck or throat area); thirst (continuing); trouble in speaking; unexplained runny nose or sneezing; unexplained, unexpected, or unusually heavy vaginal bleeding; unusual tiredness or weakness; weight gain (rapid) (if taking phenylbutazone, stop taking it and check with your doctor immediately); yellow eyes or skin

Other side effects may occur that usually do not need medical attention. These side effects may go away during treatment as your body adjusts to the medicine. However, check with your doctor if any of the following side effects continue or are bothersome:

More common
Abdominal or stomach cramps, pain, or discomfort (mild to moderate); diarrhea (if taking mefenamic acid, stop taking it and check with your doctor immediately); dizziness, drowsiness, or lightheadedness; headache (mild to moderate); heartburn, indigestion, nausea, or vomiting

Less common or rare
Bitter taste or other taste change; bloated feeling, gas, or constipation; decreased appetite or loss of appetite; fast or pounding heartbeat; flushing or hot flashes; general feeling of discomfort or illness; increased sensitivity of eyes to light; increased sensitivity of skin to sunlight; increased sweating; irritation, dryness, or soreness of mouth; nervousness, anxiety, irritability, trembling, or twitching; rectal irritation (with suppositories); trouble in sleeping; unexplained weight loss; unusual tiredness or weakness without any other symptoms

Although not all of the side effects listed above have been reported for all of these medicines, they have been reported for at least one of them. However, since all anti-inflammatory analgesics are very similar, it is possible that any of the above side effects may occur with any of these medicines.

Some side effects may occur many days or weeks after you have stopped using phenylbutazone. During this time *check with your doctor immediately* if you notice any of the following side effects:

Sore throat and fever; ulcers, sores, or white spots in mouth; unusual bleeding or bruising; unusual tiredness or weakness

Other side effects not listed above may also occur in some patients. If you notice any other effects, check with your doctor.

Revised: 09/13/94
Interim revision: 05/09/95; 07/24/96

ANTIMYASTHENICS Systemic

Some commonly used brand names are:

In the U.S.—

Mestinon[3]
Mestinon Timespans[3]
Mytelase Caplets[1]
Prostigmin[2]
Regonol[3]

In Canada—

Mestinon[3]
Mestinon-SR[3]
Prostigmin[2]
Regonol[3]

Note: For quick reference, the following antimyasthenics are numbered to match the corresponding brand names.

This information applies to the following medicines:

1. Ambenonium (am-be-NOE-nee-um)†
2. Neostigmine (nee-oh-STIG-meen)‡
3. Pyridostigmine (peer-id-oh-STIG-meen)

†Not commercially available in Canada.
‡Generic name product may also be available in the U.S.

Description

Antimyasthenics are given by mouth or by injection to treat myasthenia gravis. Neostigmine may also be given by injection as a test for myasthenia gravis. Sometimes neostigmine is given by injection to prevent or treat certain urinary tract or intestinal disorders. In addition, neostigmine or pyridostigmine may be given by injection as an antidote to certain types of muscle relaxants used in surgery.

These medicines are available only with your doctor's prescription in the following dosage forms:

Oral

Ambenonium
- Tablets (U.S.)

Neostigmine
- Tablets (U.S. and Canada)

Pyridostigmine
- Syrup (U.S.)
- Tablets (U.S. and Canada)
- Extended-release tablets (U.S. and Canada)

Parenteral

Neostigmine
- Injection (U.S. and Canada)

Pyridostigmine
- Injection (U.S. and Canada)

Before Using This Medicine

In deciding to use a medicine, the risks of taking the medicine must be weighed against the good it will do. This is a decision you and your doctor will make. For the antimyasthenics, the following should be considered:

Allergies—Tell your doctor if you have ever had any unusual or allergic reaction to ambenonium, bromides, neostigmine, or pyridostigmine. Also tell your health care professional if you are allergic to any other substances, such as foods, preservatives, or dyes.

Pregnancy—Antimyasthenics have not been reported to cause birth defects; however, muscle weakness has occurred temporarily in some newborn babies whose mothers took antimyasthenics during pregnancy.

Breast-feeding—Antimyasthenics have not been reported to cause problems in nursing babies.

Children—Although there is no specific information comparing use of antimyasthenics in children with use in other age groups, these medicines are not expected to cause different side effects or problems in children than they do in adults.

Older adults—Many medicines have not been studied specifically in older people. Therefore, it may not be known whether they work exactly the same way they do in younger adults. Although there is not much information comparing use of antimyasthenics in the elderly with use in other age groups, these medicines are not expected to cause different side effects or problems in older people than they do in younger adults.

Other medicines—Although certain medicines should not be used together at all, in other cases 2 different medicines may be used together even if an interaction might occur. In these cases, your doctor may want to change the dose, or other precautions may be necessary. When you are taking an antimyasthenic, it is especially important that your health care professional knows if you are using any of the following:

- Demecarium (e.g., Humorsol) or
- Echothiophate (e.g., Phospholine Iodide) or
- Isoflurophate (e.g., Floropryl) or
- Malathion (e.g., Prioderm)—Using these medicines with antimyasthenics may result in serious side effects
- Guanadrel (e.g., Hylorel) or
- Guanethidine (e.g., Ismelin) or
- Mecamylamine (e.g., Inversine) or
- Procainamide (e.g., Pronestyl) or
- Trimethaphan (e.g., Arfonad)—The effects of these medicines may interfere with the actions of the antimyasthenics

Other medical problems—The presence of other medical problems may affect the use of the antimyasthenics. Make sure you tell your doctor if you have any other medical problems, especially:

- Intestinal blockage or
- Urinary tract blockage or
- Urinary tract infection—These medicines may make the condition worse

Proper Use of This Medicine

Your doctor may want you to take this medicine with food or milk to help lessen the chance of side effects. If you have any questions about how you should be taking this medicine, check with your doctor.

Take this medicine only as directed. Do not take more of it, do not take it more often, and do not take it for a longer time than your doctor ordered. To do so may increase the chance of side effects.

If you are taking this medicine *for myasthenia gravis*:

- When you first begin taking this medicine, your doctor may want you to keep a daily record of:
  - —the time you take each dose.
  - —how long you feel better after taking each dose.
  - —how long you feel worse.
  - —any side effects that occur.

This is to help your doctor decide whether the dose of this medicine should be increased or decreased and how often the medicine should be taken in order for it to be most effective in your condition.

Dosing—The dose of these medicines will be different for different patients. *Follow your doctor's orders or the directions on the label.* The following information includes only the average doses of these medicines. *If your dose is different, do not change it* unless your doctor tells you to do so.

The number of tablets or teaspoonfuls of syrup that you take depends on the strength of the medicine. Also, *the number of doses you take each day, the time allowed between doses, and the length of time you take the medicine depend on the medical problem for which you are taking these medicines.*

For ambenonium

- For *oral* dosage form (tablets):
  - —For myasthenia gravis:
    - Adults and teenagers—At first, the dose is 5 milligrams (mg) three or four times per day. Then, if needed, the dose will be adjusted by your doctor.
    - Children—The dose is based on body weight or size and must be determined by your doctor. The total daily dose is usually 300 micrograms (mcg) per kilogram (kg) (136 mcg per pound) of body weight or 10 mg per square meter of body surface area. This dose may be divided into three or four smaller doses. If needed, the total daily dose will be increased to 1.5 mg per kg (0.68 mg per pound) of body weight or 50 mg per square meter of body surface area. This dose may be divided into three or four smaller doses.

For neostigmine

- For *oral* dosage form (tablets):
  - —For myasthenia gravis:
    - Adults and teenagers—At first, the dose is 15 milligrams (mg) every three or four hours. Then, the dose is 150 mg taken over a twenty-four-hour period.
    - Children—The dose is based on body weight or size and must be determined by your doctor. The total daily dose is usually 2 mg per kilogram (kg) (0.91 mg per pound) of body weight or 60 mg per square meter of body surface area. This dose may be divided into six to eight smaller doses.
- For *injection* dosage form:
  - —For myasthenia gravis:
    - Adults and teenagers—The usual dose is 500 micrograms (mcg) injected into a muscle or under the skin.
    - Children—The dose is based on body weight and must be determined by your doctor. It is usually 10 to 40 mcg per kg (4.5 to 18.2 mcg per pound) of body weight, injected into a muscle or under the skin, every two or three hours.
  - —For urinary tract or intestinal disorders:
    - Adults and teenagers—The usual dose is 250 to 500 mcg, injected into a muscle or under the skin, as needed.
    - Children—Use and dose must be determined by your doctor.

For pyridostigmine

- For *oral* dosage forms (syrup and tablets):
  - —For myasthenia gravis:
    - Adults and teenagers—At first, the dose is 30 to 60 milligrams (mg) every three or four hours. Then, the dose is 60 mg to 1.5 grams (usually 600 mg) per day.
    - Children—The dose is based on body weight or size and must be determined by your doctor. The total daily dose is usually 7 mg per kilogram (kg) (3.2 mg per pound) of body weight or 200 mg per square meter of body surface area. This dose may be divided into five or six smaller doses.
- For *long-acting oral* dosage form (extended-release tablets):
  - —For myasthenia gravis:
    - Adults and teenagers—The usual dose is 180 to 540 mg one or two times per day.
    - Children—Dose must be determined by your doctor.
- For *injection* dosage form:
  - —For myasthenia gravis:
    - Adults and teenagers—The usual dose is 2 mg, injected into a muscle or vein, every two or three hours.
    - Children—The dose is based on body weight and must be determined by your doctor. It is usually 50 to 150 micrograms (mcg) per kg (22.7 to 68.1 mcg per pound) of body weight, injected into a muscle every four to six hours.

Missed dose—If you miss a dose of this medicine, take it as soon as you remember. However, if it is almost time for your next dose, skip the missed dose and go back to your regular dosing schedule. Do not double doses.

Storage—To store this medicine:
- Keep out of the reach of children.
- Store away from heat and direct light.
- Do not store the tablet form of this medicine in the bathroom, near the kitchen sink, or in other damp places. Heat or moisture may cause the medicine to break down.
- Keep the syrup form of pyridostigmine from freezing.
- Do not keep outdated medicine or medicine no longer needed. Be sure that any discarded medicine is out of the reach of children.

Side Effects of This Medicine

Along with its needed effects, a medicine may cause some unwanted effects. Although not all of these side effects may occur, if they do occur they may need medical attention.

Check with your doctor immediately if any of the following side effects occur:

Symptoms of overdose

Blurred vision; clumsiness or unsteadiness; confusion; convulsions (seizures); diarrhea (severe); increase in bronchial secretions or watering of mouth (excessive); increasing muscle weakness (especially in the arms, neck, shoulders, and tongue); muscle cramps or twitching; nausea or vomiting (severe); shortness of breath, troubled breathing, wheezing, or tightness in chest; slow heartbeat; slurred speech; stomach cramps or pain (severe); unusual irritability, nervousness, restlessness, or fear; unusual tiredness or weakness

Also, check with your doctor as soon as possible if any of the following side effects occur:

Rare

Redness, swelling, or pain at place of injection (for pyridostigmine injection only); skin rash (does not apply to ambenonium)

Other side effects may occur that usually do not need medical attention. These side effects may go away during treatment as your body adjusts to the medicine. However, check with your doctor if any of the following side effects continue or are bothersome:

More common

Diarrhea; increased sweating; increased watering of mouth; nausea or vomiting; stomach cramps or pain

Less common

Frequent urge to urinate; increase in bronchial secretions; unusually small pupils; unusual watering of eyes

Other side effects not listed above may also occur in some patients. If you notice any other effects, check with your doctor.

Revised: 09/30/91
Interim revision: 07/18/94

ANTIPYRINE AND BENZOCAINE Otic

Some commonly used brand names are:

In the U.S.—

A/B Otic	Aurodex
Allergen	Auroto
Analgesic Otic	Dolotic
Antiben	Ear Drops
Auralgan	Otocalm

Generic name product may be available.

In Canada—

Auralgan
Earache Drops

Another commonly used name for antipyrine is phenazone. Another commonly used name for benzocaine is ethyl aminobenzoate.

Description

Antipyrine (an-tee-PYE-reen) and benzocaine (BEN-zoe-kane) combination is used in the ear to help relieve the pain, swelling, and congestion of some ear infections. It will not cure the infection itself. An antibiotic will be needed to treat the infection. This medicine is also used to soften earwax so that the earwax can be washed away more easily.

In the U.S., this medicine is available only with your doctor's prescription. In Canada, this medicine is available without a prescription. However, your doctor may have special instructions on the proper dose for your ear problem. This medicine is available in the following dosage form:

Otic
- Otic solution (ear drops) (U.S. and Canada)

Before Using This Medicine

In deciding to use a medicine, the risks of using the medicine must be weighed against the good it will do. This is a decision you and your doctor will make. For antipyrine and benzocaine combination, the following should be considered:

Allergies—Tell your doctor if you have ever had any unusual or allergic reaction to antipyrine or benzocaine or other local anesthetics. Also tell your health care professional if you are allergic to any other substances, such as foods, preservatives, or dyes.

Pregnancy—Although studies on effects in pregnancy have not been done in either humans or animals, this medicine has not been reported to cause problems in humans.

Breast-feeding—It is not known whether this medicine passes into the breast milk. Although most medicines pass into breast milk in small amounts, many of them may be used safely while breast-feeding. Mothers who are using this medicine and who wish to breast-feed should discuss this with their doctor.

Children—Infants, especially infants up to 3 months of age, may be especially sensitive to the effects of the benzocaine in this combination medicine. This may increase the chance of side effects. However, this medicine is not expected to cause different side effects or problems in older children than it does in adults.

Older adults—Many medicines have not been studied specifically in older people. Therefore, it may not be known whether they work exactly the same way they do in younger adults. Although there is no specific information comparing use of antipyrine and benzocaine in the elderly with use in other age groups, this medicine is not expected to cause different side effects or problems in older people than it does in younger adults.

Other medical problems—The presence of other medical problems may affect the use of antipyrine and benzocaine combination. Make sure you tell your doctor if:

- Your ear is draining—The chance of unwanted effects may be increased

Proper Use of This Medicine

You may warm the ear drops to body temperature (37 °C or 98.6 °F) by holding the bottle in your hand for a few minutes before applying the drops.

To use:

- Lie down or tilt the head so that the affected ear faces up. Gently pull the earlobe up and back for adults (down and back for children) to straighten the ear canal. Drop the medicine into the ear canal. Keep the ear facing up for about 5 minutes to allow the medicine to coat the ear canal. (For young children and other patients who cannot stay still for 5 minutes, try to keep the ear facing up for at least 1 or 2 minutes.) A sterile cotton plug may be moistened with a few drops of this medicine and gently placed at the ear opening for no longer than 5 to 10 minutes to help keep the medicine from leaking out. If you have any questions about this, check with your doctor.
- To keep the medicine as germ-free as possible, do not touch the dropper to any surface (including the ear).
- *Do not rinse the dropper after use.* Wipe the tip of the dropper with a clean tissue and keep the container tightly closed.

If you are using this medicine to help remove earwax, the ear should be flushed with warm water after you have used this medicine for 2 or 3 days. This is usually done by your doctor. If you have been directed to flush the ear out yourself, make sure that you have learned how to do it correctly. Follow the instructions carefully.

Dosing—The dose of this medicine will be different for different patients. *Follow your doctor's orders or the directions on the label.* The following information includes only the average amounts of this medicine. *If your dose is different, do not change it* unless your doctor tells you to do so.

- For *otic* dosage form (ear drops):
  - —Adults and children:
    - For ear pain caused by an infection—Use enough medicine to fill the entire ear canal every one or two hours until the pain is relieved.
    - For softening earwax before removal—Use enough medicine to fill the entire ear canal three times a day for two or three days.

Missed dose—If you miss a dose of this medicine, use it as soon as you remember. However, if it is almost time for your next dose, skip the missed dose and go back to your regular dosing schedule.

Storage—To store this medicine:

- Keep out of the reach of children.
- Store away from heat and direct light.
- Keep the medicine from freezing.
- Do not keep outdated medicine or medicine no longer needed. Be sure that any discarded medicine is out of the reach of children.

Side Effects of This Medicine

Along with its needed effects, a medicine may cause some unwanted effects. The following side effects may mean that you are having an allergic reaction to the medicine. Stop using the medicine right away if any of them occur. Check with your doctor if any of the following effects continue or are bothersome:

Itching, burning, redness, or oozing sores in the ear

Other side effects not listed above may also occur in some patients. If you notice any other effects, check with your doctor.

Revised: 07/14/95

ANTITHYROID AGENTS Systemic

Some commonly used brand names are:

In the U.S.—

Tapazole[1]

In Canada—

Propyl-Thyracil[2] Tapazole[1]

Another commonly used name for methimazole is thiamazole.

Note: For quick reference, the following antithyroid agents are numbered to match the corresponding brand names.

This information applies to the following medicines:

1. Methimazole (meth-IM-a-zole)
2. Propylthiouracil (proe-pill-thye-oh-YOOR-a-sill)‡

‡Generic name product may also be available in the U.S.

Description

Methimazole and propylthiouracil are used to treat conditions in which the thyroid gland produces too much thyroid hormone.

These medicines work by making it harder for the body to use iodine to make thyroid hormone. They do not block the effects of thyroid hormone that was made by the body before their use was begun.

Methimazole and propylthiouracil are available only with your doctor's prescription, in the following dosage forms:

Oral

Methimazole
- Tablets (U.S. and Canada)

Propylthiouracil
- Tablets (U.S. and Canada)

Before Using This Medicine

In deciding to use a medicine, the risks of taking the medicine must be weighed against the good it will do. This is a decision you and your doctor will make. For antithyroid agents, the following should be considered:

Allergies—Tell your doctor if you have ever had any unusual or allergic reaction to methimazole or propylthiouracil. Also tell your health care professional if you are allergic to any other substances, such as foods, preservatives, or dyes.

Pregnancy—Use of too large a dose during pregnancy may cause problems in the fetus. However, use of the proper dose, with careful monitoring by the doctor, is not likely to cause problems.

Breast-feeding—These medicines pass into breast milk. (Methimazole passes into breast milk more freely and in higher amounts than propylthiouracil.) However, your doctor may allow you to continue to breast-feed, if your dose is low and the infant gets frequent check-ups. If you are taking a large dose, it may be necessary for you to stop breast-feeding during treatment.

Children—This medicine has been used in children and, in effective doses, has not been shown to cause different side effects or problems in children than it does in adults.

Teenagers—This medicine has been used in teenagers and, in effective doses, has not been shown to cause different side effects or problems in teenagers than it does in adults.

Older adults—Elderly people may have an increased chance of certain side effects during treatment. Your doctor may need to take special precautions while you are taking this medicine.

Other medicines—Although certain medicines should not be used together at all, in other cases two different medicines may be used together even if an interaction might occur. In these cases, your doctor may want to change the dose, or other precautions may be necessary. When you are taking antithyroid agents, it is especially important that your health care professional know if you are taking any of the following:

- Amiodarone or
- Iodinated glycerol or
- Potassium iodide (e.g., Pima)—The use of these medicines may change the effect of antithyroid agents
- Anticoagulants (blood thinners)—The use of antithyroid agents may affect the way anticoagulants work in your body
- Digitalis glycosides—The use of antithyroid agents may affect the amount of digitalis glycosides in the bloodstream

Other medical problems—The presence of other medical problems may affect the use of antithyroid agents. Make sure you tell your doctor if you have any other medical problems, especially:

- Liver disease—The body may not get this medicine out of the bloodstream at the usual rate, which may increase the chance of side effects

Proper Use of This Medicine

Use this medicine only as directed by your doctor. Do not use more or less of it and do not use it more often or for a longer time than your doctor ordered. To do so may increase the chance of side effects.

This medicine works best when there is a constant amount in the blood. *To help keep the amount constant, do not miss any doses. Also, if you are taking more than one dose a day, it is best to take the doses at evenly spaced times day and night.* For example, if you are to take 3 doses a day, the doses should be spaced about 8 hours apart. If this interferes with your sleep or other daily activities, or if you need help in planning the best times to take your medicine, check with your health care professional.

Food in your stomach may change the amount of methimazole that is able to enter the bloodstream. To make sure that you always get the same effects, try to take methimazole at the same time in relation to meals every day. That is, always take it with meals or always take it on an empty stomach.

Dosing—The dose of these medicines will be different for different patients. *Follow your doctor's orders or the directions on the label.* The following information includes only the average doses of these medicines. *If your dose is different, do not change it* unless your doctor tells you to do so.

The number of tablets that you take or the number of suppositories that you use depends on the strength of the medicine. Also, *the number of doses you take each day, the time allowed between doses, and the length of time you take the medicine depend on the medical problem for which you are taking antithyroid agents.*

For methimazole

- For *oral* dosage form (tablets):
  - —For treatment of hyperthyroidism (overactive thyroid):
    - Adults and teenagers—At first, 15 to 60 milligrams (mg) a day for up to six to eight weeks. Later, your doctor may want to lower your dose to 5 to 30 mg a day. This may be taken once a day or it may be divided into two doses a day.
    - Children—Dose is based on body weight and must be determined by your doctor. The usual dose is 0.4 mg per kilogram (kg) (0.18 mg per pound) of body weight a day. Later, your doctor may want to lower the dose to 0.2 mg per kg (0.09 mg per pound) of body weight a day. The dose may be taken once a day or it may be divided into two doses a day.

—For treatment of thyrotoxicosis (a thyroid emergency):

• Adults and teenagers—15 to 20 mg every four hours.

• For *rectal* dosage form (suppositories):

—For treatment of thyrotoxicosis (a thyroid emergency):

• Adults and teenagers—15 to 20 mg inserted into the rectum every four hours. Your doctor may change your dose as needed.

• Children—The dose is based on body weight and must be determined by your doctor. The usual dose is 0.4 mg per kg (0.18 mg per pound) of body weight inserted into the rectum a day. This may be used as a single dose or or it may be divided into two doses a day.

For propylthiouracil

• For *oral* dosage form (tablets):

—For treatment of hyperthyroidism (overactive thyroid):

• Adults and teenagers—At first, 300 to 900 milligrams (mg) a day. Some people may need up to 1200 mg a day. This may be taken as a single dose or it may be divided into two to four doses in a day. Later, your doctor may lower your dose to 50 to 600 mg a day.

• Children 6 to 10 years of age—At first, 50 to 150 mg a day. This may be taken as a single dose or it may be divided into two to four doses in a day. Later, your doctor may change your dose as needed.

• Children 10 years of age and older—At first, 50 to 300 mg a day. This may be taken as a single dose or it may be divided into two to four doses in a day. Then, your doctor may change your dose as needed.

—For treatment of thyrotoxicosis (a thyroid emergency):

• Adults and teenagers—200 to 400 mg every four hours. Your doctor will lower your dose as needed.

• Newborn infants—Dose is based on body weight and must be determined by your doctor. The usual dose is 10 mg per kilogram (kg) (4.5 mg per pound) of body weight a day. This is usually divided into more than one dose a day.

• For *rectal* dosage forms (enemas or suppositories):

—For treatment of thyrotoxicosis (a thyroid emergency):

• Adults and teenagers—200 to 400 mg inserted into the rectum every four hours. Your doctor may change your dose as needed.

• Children 6 to 10 years of age—50 to 150 mg inserted into the rectum a day. This dose may be used as a single dose or it may be divided into two to four doses in a day. Your doctor may change your dose as needed.

• Children 10 years of age and older—50 to 300 mg inserted into the rectum a day. This dose may be used as a single dose or it may be divided into two to four doses in a day. Your doctor may change your dose as needed.

• Newborn infants—Dose is based on body weight and must be determined by your doctor. The usual dose is 10 mg per kg (4.5 mg per pound) of body weight inserted into the rectum. This is usually divided into more than one dose a day. Your doctor may change your dose as needed.

Missed dose—If you miss a dose of this medicine, take it as soon as possible. If it is almost time for your next dose, take both doses together. Then go back to your regular dosing schedule. If you miss more than one dose or if you have any questions about this, check with your doctor.

Storage—To store this medicine:

• Keep out of the reach of children.

• Store away from heat and direct light.

• Do not store in the bathroom, near the kitchen sink, or in other high-moisture areas. Heat or moisture may cause the medicine to break down.

• Do not keep outdated medicine or medicine no longer needed. Be sure that any discarded medicine is out of the reach of children.

Precautions While Using This Medicine

It is very important that your doctor check your progress at regular visits to make sure that this medicine is working properly and to check for unwanted effects.

It may take several days or weeks for this medicine to work. However, *do not stop taking this medicine without first checking with your doctor.* Some medical problems may require several years of continuous treatment.

Before having any kind of surgery (including dental surgery) or emergency treatment, *tell the medical doctor or dentist in charge that you are taking this medicine.*

Check with your doctor right away if you get an injury, infection, or illness of any kind. Your doctor may want you to stop taking this medicine or change the amount you are taking.

While you are being treated with antithyroid agents, and after you stop treatment with it, *do not have any immunizations (vaccinations) without your doctor's approval.* Antithyroid agents may lower your body's resistance and there is a chance you might get the infection the immunization is meant to prevent. In addition, other persons living in your household should not take or have recently taken oral polio vaccine since there is a chance they could pass the polio virus on to you. Also, avoid other persons who have taken oral polio vaccine. Do not get close to them, and do not stay in the same room with them for very long. If you cannot take these precautions, you should consider wearing a protective face mask that covers the nose and mouth.

Before you have any medical tests, tell the doctor in charge that you are taking this medicine. The results of some tests may be affected by this medicine.

Side Effects of This Medicine

Along with its needed effects, a medicine may cause some unwanted effects. Although not all of these side effects may occur, if they do occur they may need medical attention.

Check with your doctor immediately if any of the following side effects occur:

Less common

Cough; fever or chills (continuing or severe); general feeling of discomfort, illness or weakness; hoarseness; mouth sores; pain, swelling, or redness in joints; throat infection

Rare

Yellow eyes or skin

Check with your doctor as soon as possible if any of the following side effects occur:

More common

Fever (mild and temporary); skin rash or itching

Rare

Backache; black, tarry stools; blood in urine or stools; shortness of breath; increase in bleeding or bruising; increase or decrease in urination; numbness or tingling of fingers, toes, or face; pinpoint red spots on skin; swelling of feet or lower legs; swollen lymph nodes; swollen salivary glands

Symptoms of overdose

Changes in menstrual periods; coldness; constipation; dry, puffy skin; headache; listlessness or sleepiness; muscle aches; swelling in the front of the neck; unusual tiredness or weakness; weight gain (unusual)

Other side effects may occur that usually do not need medical attention. These side effects may go away during treatment as your body adjusts to the medicine. However, check with your doctor if any of the following side effects continue or are bothersome:

Less common

Dizziness; loss of taste (for methimazole); nausea; stomach pain; vomiting

Other side effects not listed above may also occur in some patients. If you notice any other effects, check with your doctor.

Revised: 04/21/92
Interim revision: 06/03/94

APPETITE SUPPRESSANTS Systemic

Some commonly used brand names are:

In the U.S.—

Adipex-P[5]
Adipost[4]
Anorex SR[4]
Appecon[4]
Bontril PDM[4]
Bontril Slow-Release[4]
Didrex[1]
Fastin[5]
Ionamin[5]
Mazanor[3]
Melfiat-105 Unicelles[4]
Obalan[4]
Obe-Nix[5]
Obezine[4]
OBY-CAP[5]
Panshape M[5]
Parzine[4]
Phendiet[4]
Phendiet-105[4]
Phendimet[4]
Phentercot[5]
Phentride[5]
Plegine[4]
Prelu-2[4]
PT 105[4]
Rexigen Forte[4]
Sanorex[3]
T-Diet[5]
Tenuate[2]
Tenuate Dospan[2]
Tepanil Ten-Tab[2]
Teramine[5]
Wehless[4]
Wehless-105 Timecelles[4]
Zantryl[5]

In Canada—

Fastin[5]
Ionamin[5]
Sanorex[3]
Tenuate[2]
Tenuate Dospan[2]

Other commonly used brand names are:

Amfepramone[2]
Benzfetamine[1]

Note: For quick reference, the following appetite suppressants are numbered to match the corresponding brand names.

This information applies to the following medicines:

1. Benzphetamine (benz-FET-a-meen)†
2. Diethylpropion (dye-eth-il-PROE-pee-on)‡
3. Mazindol (MAY-zin-dole)
4. Phendimetrazine (fen-dye-MET-ra-zeen)†‡
5. Phentermine (FEN-ter-meen)‡

Note: This information does *not* apply to Fenfluramine or Phenylpropanolamine.

†Not commercially available in Canada.
‡Generic name product may also be available in the U.S.

Description

Appetite suppressants are used in the short-term treatment of obesity. For a few weeks, these medicines in combination with dieting, exercise, and changes in eating habits can help obese patients lose weight. However, since their appetite-reducing effect is only temporary, they are useful only for the first few weeks of dieting until new eating habits are established.

These medicines are available only with your doctor's prescription, in the following dosage forms:

Oral

Benzphetamine
- Tablets (U.S.)

Diethylpropion
- Tablets (U.S. and Canada)
- Extended-release tablets (U.S. and Canada)

Mazindol
- Tablets (U.S. and Canada)

Phendimetrazine
- Capsules (U.S.)
- Extended-release capsules (U.S.)
- Tablets (U.S.)
- Extended-release tablets (U.S.)

Phentermine
- Capsules (U.S. and Canada)
- Resin capsules (U.S. and Canada)
- Tablets (U.S.)

Before Using This Medicine

In deciding to use a medicine, the risks of taking the medicine must be weighed against the good it will do. This is a decision you and your doctor will make. For appetite suppressants, the following should be considered:

Allergies—Tell your doctor if you have ever had any unusual or allergic reaction to this medicine or amphetamine, dextroamphetamine, ephedrine, epinephrine, isoproterenol, metaproterenol, methamphetamine, norepinephrine, phenylephrine, phenylpropanolamine, pseudoephedrine, terbutaline, or other appetite suppressants. Also tell your health care professional if you are allergic to any other substances, such as foods, preservatives, or dyes.

Pregnancy—

- *Benzphetamine*—Benzphetamine must not be used during pregnancy because it may harm the fetus. Be sure you have discussed this with your doctor. If you think you may have become pregnant during treatment with benzphetamine, tell your doctor immediately.
- *Diethylpropion*—Diethylpropion has not been reported to cause birth defects or other problems in human and animal studies.
- *Mazindol*—Studies in animals have shown that mazindol increases the chance of rib malformations, and also increases the chance of death in the newborn when given in large doses.
- *Phendimetrazine* and *phentermine*—These medicines have not been shown to cause birth defects or other problems in humans.

Breast-feeding—Diethylpropion and benzphetamine pass into breast milk. It is not known if other appetite suppressants pass into breast milk. However, problems in nursing babies have not been reported.

Children—Appetite suppressants should not be used by children up to 12 years of age.

Older adults—Many medicines have not been studied specifically in older people. Therefore, it may not be known whether they work exactly the same way they do in younger adults or if they cause different side effects or problems in older people. There is no specific information comparing use of appetite suppressants in the elderly to use in other age groups.

Other medicines—Although certain medicines should not be used together at all, in other cases two different medicines may be used together even if an interaction might occur. In these cases, your doctor may want to change the dose, or other precautions may be necessary. When you are taking appetite suppressants, it is especially important that your health care professional know if you are taking any of the following:

- Amantadine (e.g., Symmetrel) or
- Amphetamines or
- Caffeine (e.g., NoDoz) or
- Chlophedianol (e.g., Ulone) or
- Cocaine or
- Medicine for asthma or other breathing problems or
- Medicine for colds, sinus problems, or hay fever or other allergies (including nose drops or sprays) or
- Methylphenidate (e.g., Ritalin) or
- Nabilone (e.g., Cesamet) or
- Other appetite suppressants (diet pills) or
- Pemoline (e.g., Cylert)—Using these medicines with appetite suppressants may increase the CNS stimulant effects
- Monoamine oxidase (MAO) inhibitors (furazolidone [e.g., Furoxone], isocarboxazid [e.g., Marplan], phenelzine [e.g., Nardil], procarbazine [e.g., Matulane], selegiline [e.g., Eldepryl], tranylcypromine [e.g., Parnate])—Taking appetite suppressants while you are taking or within 2 weeks of taking monoamine oxidase (MAO) inhibitors may cause sudden extremely high blood pressure; at least 14 days should be allowed between stopping treatment with one medicine and starting treatment with the other

Other medical problems—The presence of other medical problems may affect the use of appetite suppressants. Make sure you tell your doctor if you have any other medical problems, especially:

- Alcohol abuse (or history of) or
- Drug abuse or dependence (or history of)—Dependence on appetite suppressants may develop
- Diabetes mellitus (sugar diabetes)—The amount of insulin or oral antidiabetic medicine that you need to take may change
- Epilepsy—Diethylpropion may increase the risk of seizures
- Glaucoma or
- Heart or blood vessel disease or
- High blood pressure or
- Mental illness (severe) or
- Overactive thyroid—Appetite suppressants may make the condition worse
- Kidney disease—Higher blood levels of mazindol may occur, increasing the chance of serious side effects

Proper Use of This Medicine

For patients taking the *short-acting form* of this medicine:

- Take the last dose for each day about 4 to 6 hours before bedtime to help prevent trouble in sleeping.

For patients taking the *long-acting form* of this medicine:

- Take the daily dose about 10 to 14 hours before bedtime to help prevent trouble in sleeping.
- These capsules or tablets are to be swallowed whole. Do not break, crush, or chew before swallowing.

For patients taking *mazindol:*

- To help prevent trouble in sleeping, if you are taking this medicine in a:

  —*1-mg tablet,* take the last dose for each day about 4 to 6 hours before bedtime.

  —*2-mg tablet,* take the dose once each day about 10 to 14 hours before bedtime.

Take this medicine only as directed by your doctor. Do not take more of it, do not take it more often, and do not take it for a longer time than your doctor ordered. If too much is taken, it may become habit-forming.

If you think this medicine is not working properly after you have taken it for a few weeks, *do not increase the dose.* Instead, check with your doctor.

Dosing—The dose of appetite suppressants will be different for different patients. *Follow your doctor's orders or the directions on the label.* The following information includes only the average doses of appetite suppressants. *If your dose is different, do not change it* unless your doctor tells you to do so.

For benzphetamine

- For *oral* dosage form (tablets):
  - —For appetite suppression:
    - Adults—At first, 25 to 50 milligrams (mg) once a day, taken at midmorning or midafternoon. Your doctor may need to adjust your dose.
    - Children up to 12 years of age—Use is not recommended.

For diethylpropion

- For *oral tablet* dosage form:
  - —For appetite suppression:
    - Adults—25 milligrams (mg) three times a day, taken one hour before meals.
    - Children up to 12 years of age—Use is not recommended.
- For *oral extended-release tablet* dosage form:
  - —For appetite suppression:
    - Adults—75 mg once a day, taken at midmorning.
    - Children up to 12 years of age—Use is not recommended.

For mazindol

- For *oral* dosage form (tablets):
  - —For appetite suppression:
    - Adults—At first, 1 milligram (mg) once a day, taken one hour before your first meal of the day. Your doctor may need to adjust your dose.
    - Children up to 12 years of age—Use is not recommended.

For phendimetrazine

- For *oral capsule* dosage form:
  - —For appetite suppression:
    - Adults—35 milligrams (mg) two or three times a day, taken one hour before meals.
    - Children up to 12 years of age—Use is not recommended.
- For *oral extended-release capsule or tablet* dosage forms:
  - —For appetite suppression:
    - Adults—105 mg once a day, taken thirty to sixty minutes before the morning meal.
    - Children up to 12 years of age—Use is not recommended.
- For *oral tablet* dosage form:
  - —For appetite suppression:
    - Adults—17.5 to 35 mg two or three times a day, taken one hour before meals.
    - Children up to 12 years of age—Use is not recommended.

For phentermine

- For *oral capsule* dosage form:
  - —For appetite suppression:
    - Adults—15 to 37.5 milligrams (mg) once a day, taken before breakfast or one to two hours after breakfast.
    - Children up to 12 years of age—Use is not recommended.
- For *oral tablet* dosage form:
  - —For appetite suppression:
    - Adults—15 to 37.5 mg once a day, taken before breakfast or one to two hours after breakfast. Instead of taking it once a day, your doctor may tell you to take a smaller dose thirty minutes before meals.
    - Children up to 12 years of age—Use is not recommended.
- For *oral resin capsule* dosage form:
  - —For appetite suppression:
    - Adults—15 to 30 mg once a day, taken before breakfast.
    - Children up to 12 years of age—Use is not recommended.

Storage—To store this medicine:

- Keep out of the reach of children.
- Store away from heat and direct light.
- Do not store in the bathroom, near the kitchen sink, or in other damp places. Heat or moisture may cause the medicine to break down.
- Do not keep outdated medicine or medicine no longer needed. Be sure that any discarded medicine is out of the reach of children.

Precautions While Using This Medicine

Your doctor should check your progress at regular visits to make sure that this medicine does not cause unwanted effects.

This medicine may cause some people to feel a false sense of well-being or to become dizzy, lightheaded, drowsy, or less alert than they are normally. *Make sure you know how you react to this medicine before you drive, use machines, or do anything else that could be dangerous if you are dizzy or are not alert.*

Before having any kind of surgery, dental treatment, or emergency treatment, tell the medical doctor or dentist in charge that you are using this medicine. Taking appetite suppressants together with medicines that are used during surgery or dental or emergency treatments may cause serious side effects.

Check with your doctor immediately if you notice a decrease in your ability to exercise, if you faint, or if you have chest pain, swelling of your feet or lower legs, or trouble in breathing. These may be symptoms of very serious heart or lung problems.

If you have been taking this medicine for a long time or in large doses and *you think you may have become mentally or physically dependent on it, check with your doctor.*

- Some signs of dependence on appetite suppressants are:

  —a strong desire or need to continue taking the medicine.

  —a need to increase the dose to receive the effects of the medicine.

  —withdrawal side effects (for example, mental depression, nausea or vomiting, stomach cramps or pain, trembling, unusual tiredness or weakness when you stop taking the medicine).

For *diabetic patients:*

- This medicine may affect blood sugar levels. If you notice a change in the results of your urine or blood sugar test or if you have any questions, check with your doctor.

If you have been taking this medicine in large doses for a long time, *do not stop taking it without first checking with your doctor.* Your doctor may want you to reduce gradually the amount you are taking before stopping completely.

Side Effects of This Medicine

Appetite suppressants may cause some serious side effects, including heart and lung problems. *You and your doctor should discuss the good this medicine may do as well as the risks of taking it.*

Along with its needed effects, a medicine may cause some unwanted effects. Although not all of these side effects may occur, if they do occur they may need medical attention.

Check with your doctor immediately if any of the following side effects occur:

Rare

Chest pain; decreased ability to exercise; fainting; swelling of feet or lower legs; trouble in breathing

Check with your doctor as soon as possible if any of the following side effects occur:

More common

Increased blood pressure

Less common or rare

Confusion or mental depression; mental illness; skin rash or hives; sore throat and fever; unusual bleeding or bruising

Symptoms of overdose

Abdominal or stomach cramps; diarrhea (severe); fast breathing; fever; hallucinations (seeing, hearing or feeling things that are not there); high or low blood pressure; hostility; irregular heartbeat; nausea or vomiting (severe); panic state; restlessness; tremor

Other side effects may occur that usually do not need medical attention. These side effects may go away during treatment as your body adjusts to the medicine. However, check with your doctor if any of the following side effects continue or are bothersome:

More common

False sense of well-being; irritability; nervousness or restlessness; trouble in sleeping

Note: After these stimulant effects have worn off, drowsiness, trembling, unusual tiredness or weakness, or mental depression may occur.

Less common or rare

Blurred vision; changes in sexual desire or decreased sexual ability; constipation; diarrhea; difficult or painful urination; dizziness or lightheadedness; drowsiness; dryness of mouth; fast or pounding heartbeat; frequent urge to urinate or increased urination; headache; increased sweating; nausea or vomiting; stomach cramps or pain; unpleasant taste

Although not all of the side effects listed above have been reported for all of these medicines, they have been reported for at least one of them. However, since all of the appetite suppressants are very similar, any of the above side effects may occur with any of these medicines.

After you stop using this medicine, your body may need time to adjust. The length of time this takes depends on the amount of medicine you were using and how long you used it. During this time check with your doctor if you notice any of the following side effects:

Mental depression; nausea or vomiting; stomach cramps or pain; trembling; unusual tiredness or weakness

Other side effects not listed above may also occur in some patients. If you notice any other effects, check with your doctor.

Revised: 08/29/94
Interim revision: 06/30/95; 08/15/97

APRACLONIDINE Ophthalmic

A commonly used brand name in the U.S. and Canada is Iopidine.

Other commonly used names are aplonidine and p-aminoclonidine.

Description

Apraclonidine (a-pra-KLON-i-deen) 0.5% is used to treat glaucoma when the medications you have been using for glaucoma do not reduce your eye pressure enough.

Apraclonidine 1% is used just before and after certain types of eye surgery (argon laser trabeculoplasty, argon laser iridotomy, and Nd:YAG laser posterior capsulotomy). The medicine is used to control or prevent a rise in pressure within the eye (ocular hypertension) that can occur after this type of surgery.

Apraclonidine 0.5% is available only with your doctor's prescription. Apraclonidine 1% is given in the hospital at the time of the surgery. This medicine is available in the following dosage form:

Ophthalmic

- Ophthalmic solution (eye drops) (U.S. and Canada)

Before Using This Medicine

In deciding to use a medicine, the risks of using the medicine must be weighed against the good it will do. This is a decision you and your doctor will make. For apraclonidine, the following should be considered:

Allergies—Tell your doctor if you have ever had any unusual or allergic reaction to apraclonidine or clonidine. Also tell your health care professional if you are allergic to any other substances, such as preservatives.

Pregnancy—Apraclonidine has not been studied in pregnant women. However, apraclonidine has been shown to cause death of the fetus when given by mouth to pregnant rabbits in doses that are many times larger than the human dose. Before using this medicine, make sure your doctor knows if you are pregnant or if you may become pregnant.

Breast-feeding—It is not known whether apraclonidine passes into the breast milk. Although most medicines pass into breast milk in small amounts, many of them may be used safely while breast-feeding. Mothers who are using 0.5% apraclonidine and who wish to breast-feed should discuss this with their doctor. For mothers who are to be treated with 1% apraclonidine during eye surgery, your doctor may want you to stop breast-feeding during the day of your surgery.

Children—Studies on this medicine have been done only in adult patients, and there is no specific information comparing use of apraclonidine in children with use in other age groups.

Older adults—Many medicines have not been studied specifically in older people. Therefore, it may not be known whether they work exactly the same way they do in younger adults or if they cause different side effects or problems in older people. There is no specific information comparing use of apraclonidine in the elderly with use in other age groups.

Other medicines—Although certain medicines should not be used together at all, in other cases two different medicines may be used together even if an interaction might occur. In these cases, your doctor may want to change the dose, or other precautions may be necessary. Tell your health care professional if you are using any other prescription or nonprescription (over-the-counter [OTC]) medicine.

Other medical problems—The presence of other medical problems may affect the use of apraclonidine. Make sure you tell your doctor if you have any other medical problems, especially:

- Depression or
- Heart or blood vessel disease or
- High blood pressure—Apraclonidine may make the condition worse
- Kidney disease or
- Liver disease—Higher blood levels of apraclonidine may result, which may lead to increased side effects
- Unusual reaction to a medicine that reduces the pressure within the eye—Apraclonidine is a strong reducer of eye pressure and could also cause this reaction
- Vasovagal attack (history of)—The signs and symptoms are paleness, nausea, sweating, slow heartbeat, sudden and severe tiredness or weakness, and possibly fainting, usually brought on by emotional stress caused by fear or pain. Apraclonidine may cause this reaction to happen again

Proper Use of This Medicine

If your doctor ordered two different eye drops to be used together, wait at least 10 minutes between the times you apply the medicines. This will help to keep the second medicine from "washing out" the first one.

To use the *eye drops:*

- First, wash your hands. Tilt the head back and, pressing your finger gently on the skin just beneath the lower eyelid, pull the lower eyelid away from the eye to make a space. Drop the medicine into this space. Let go of the eyelid and gently close the eyes. Do not blink. Keep the eyes closed and apply pressure to the inner corner of the eye with your finger for 1 or 2 minutes to allow the medicine to be absorbed by the eye.
- If you think you did not get the drop of medicine into your eye properly, use another drop.
- To keep the medicine as germ-free as possible, do not touch the applicator tip to any surface (including the eye). Also, keep the container tightly closed.

Use this medicine only as directed. Do not use more of it and do not use it more often than your doctor ordered. To do so may increase the chance of too much medicine being absorbed into the body and the chance of side effects.

It is important that your doctor check your progress at regular visits. This is to make sure the medicine is working properly.

Dosing—The dose of ophthalmic apraclonidine will be different for different patients. *Follow the doctor's orders or the directions on the label.* The following information includes only the average doses of ophthalmic apraclonidine. *If your dose is different, do not change it unless your doctor tells you to do so.*

- For *ophthalmic solution (eye drops)* dosage form:
  - —For glaucoma (0.5% apraclonidine):
    - Adults—Use one drop in each eye two or three times a day.
    - Children—Use and dose must be determined by your doctor.
  - —For preventing ocular hypertension before and after eye surgery (1% apraclonidine):
    - Adults—One drop is placed in the affected eye one hour before surgery, then one drop in the same eye immediately after surgery.
    - Children—Use and dose must be determined by your doctor.

Missed dose—If you are using this medicine regularly and you miss a dose, use it as soon as possible. However, if it is almost time for your next dose, skip the missed dose and go back to your regular dosing schedule. Do not double doses.

Storage—To store this medicine:
- Keep out of the reach of children.
- Store away from heat and direct light.
- The 0.5% eye drops may be stored in the refrigerator. However, keep the medicine from freezing.
- Do not keep outdated medicine or medicine no longer needed. Be sure that any discarded medicine is out of the reach of children.

Precautions While Using This Medicine

This medicine may cause some people to become dizzy, drowsy, or less alert than they are normally. *Make sure you know how you react to this medicine before you drive, use machines, or do anything else that could be dangerous if you are not alert.*

Apraclonidine may cause your eyes to become more sensitive to light than they are normally. Wearing sunglasses and avoiding too much exposure to bright light may help lessen the discomfort.

Side Effects of This Medicine

Along with its needed effects, a medicine may cause some unwanted effects. Although not all of these side effects may occur, if they do occur they may need medical attention.

Check with your doctor or nurse as soon as possible if the following side effects occur:

For 0.5% apraclonidine

More common

Allergic reaction (redness, itching, tearing of eye)

Less common or rare

Blurred vision or change in vision; chest pain; clumsiness or unsteadiness; depression; dizziness; eye discharge, irritation, or pain; irregular heartbeat; numbness or tingling in fingers or toes; raising of upper eyelid; rash around eyes; redness of eyelid, or inner lining of eyelid; swelling of eye, eyelid, or inner lining of eyelid; swelling of face, hands, or feet; wheezing or troubled breathing

For 1% apraclonidine

Less common or rare

Allergic reaction (redness of eye or inner lining of eyelid, swelling of eyelid, watering of eye); irregular heartbeat

Other side effects may occur that usually do not need medical attention. These side effects may go away during treatment as your body adjusts to the medicine. However, check with your doctor or nurse if any of the following side effects continue or are bothersome:

For 0.5% apraclonidine

More common

Dryness of mouth; eye discomfort

Less common or rare

Change in taste or smell; constipation; crusting or scales on eyelid or corner of eye; discoloration of white part of eye; drowsiness or sleepiness; dry nose or eyes; general feeling of discomfort or illness; headache; increased sensitivity of eyes to light; muscle aches; nausea; nervousness; paleness of eye or inner lining of eyelid; runny nose; sore throat; tiredness or weakness; trouble in sleeping

For 1% apraclonidine

More common

Increase in size of pupil of eye; paleness of eye or inner lining of eyelid; raising of upper eyelid

Less common or rare

Runny nose

Other side effects not listed above may also occur in some patients. If you notice any other effects, check with your doctor or nurse.

Revised: 06/21/94
Interim revision: 07/03/95

ASCORBIC ACID (Vitamin C) Systemic

Some commonly used brand names are:

In the U.S.—

Ascorbicap
Cebid Timecelles
Cecon
Cecore 500
Cee-500
Cemill
Cenolate
Cetane
Cevi-Bid
Flavorcee
Mega-C/A Plus
Ortho/CS
Sunkist

Generic name product may also be available.

In Canada—

Apo-C

Generic name product may also be available.

Description

Vitamins (VYE-ta-mins) are compounds that you *must* have for growth and health. They are needed in small amounts only and are usually available in the foods that you eat. Ascorbic (a-SKOR-bik) acid, also known as vitamin C, is necessary for wound healing. It is needed for many functions in the body, including helping the body use carbohydrates, fats, and protein. Vitamin C also strengthens blood vessel walls.

Lack of vitamin C can lead to a condition called scurvy, which causes muscle weakness, swollen and bleeding gums, loss of teeth, and bleeding under the skin, as well as tiredness and depression. Wounds also do not heal easily. Your health care professional may treat scurvy by prescribing vitamin C for you.

Some conditions may increase your need for vitamin C. These include:
- AIDS (acquired immune deficiency syndrome)
- Alcoholism
- Burns
- Cancer

- Diarrhea (prolonged)
- Fever (prolonged)
- Infection (prolonged)
- Intestinal diseases
- Overactive thyroid (hyperthyroidism)
- Stomach ulcer
- Stress (continuing)
- Surgical removal of stomach
- Tuberculosis

Also, the following groups of people may have a deficiency of vitamin C:

- Infants receiving unfortified formulas
- Smokers
- Patients using an artificial kidney (on hemodialysis)
- Patients who undergo surgery
- Individuals who are exposed to long periods of cold temperatures

Increased need for vitamin C should be determined by your health care professional.

Vitamin C may be used for other conditions as determined by your health care professional.

Claims that vitamin C is effective for preventing senility and the common cold, and for treating asthma, some mental problems, cancer, hardening of the arteries, allergies, eye ulcers, blood clots, gum disease, and pressure sores have not been proven. Although vitamin C is being used to reduce the risk of cardiovascular disease and certain types of cancer, there is not enough information to show that these uses are effective.

Injectable vitamin C is given by or under the supervision of a health care professional. Other forms of vitamin C are available without a prescription.

Vitamin C is available in the following dosage forms:

Oral

- Extended-release capsules (U.S.)
- Oral solution (U.S.)
- Syrup (U.S.)
- Tablets (U.S. and Canada)
- Chewable tablets (U.S. and Canada)
- Effervescent tablets (U.S.)
- Extended-release tablets (U.S. and Canada)

Parenteral

- Injection (U.S.)

Importance of Diet

For good health, it is important that you eat a balanced and varied diet. Follow carefully any diet program your health care professional may recommend. For your specific dietary vitamin and/or mineral needs, ask your health care professional for a list of appropriate foods. If you think that you are not getting enough vitamins and/or minerals in your diet, you may choose to take a dietary supplement.

Vitamin C is found in various foods, including citrus fruits (oranges, lemons, grapefruit), green vegetables (peppers, broccoli, cabbage), tomatoes, and potatoes. It is best to eat fresh fruits and vegetables whenever possible since they contain the most vitamins. Food processing may destroy some of the vitamins. For example, exposure to air, drying, salting, or cooking (especially in copper pots), mincing of fresh vegetables, or mashing potatoes may reduce the amount of vitamin C in foods. Freezing does not usually cause loss of vitamin C unless foods are stored for a very long time.

Vitamins alone will not take the place of a good diet and will not provide energy. Your body also needs other substances found in food such as protein, minerals, carbohydrates, and fat. Vitamins themselves often cannot work without the presence of other foods.

The daily amount of vitamin C needed is defined in several different ways.

For U.S.—

- Recommended Dietary Allowances (RDAs) are the amount of vitamins and minerals needed to provide for adequate nutrition in most healthy persons. RDAs for a given nutrient may vary depending on a person's age, sex, and physical condition (e.g., pregnancy).
- Daily Values (DVs) are used on food and dietary supplement labels to indicate the percent of the recommended daily amount of each nutrient that a serving provides. DV replaces the previous designation of United States Recommended Daily Allowances (USRDAs).

For Canada—

- Recommended Nutrient Intakes (RNIs) are used to determine the amounts of vitamins, minerals, and protein needed to provide adequate nutrition and lessen the risk of chronic disease.

Normal daily recommended intakes for vitamin C are generally defined as follows:

Persons	U.S. (mg)	Canada (mg)
Infants and children		
Birth to 3 years of age	30–40	20
4 to 6 years of age	45	25
7 to 10 years of age	45	25
Adolescent and adult males	50–60	25–40
Adolescent and adult females	50–60	25–30
Pregnant females	70	30–40
Breast-feeding females	90–95	55
Smokers	100	45–60

Before Using This Dietary Supplement

If you are taking this dietary supplement without a prescription, carefully read and follow any precautions on the label. For vitamin C, the following should be considered:

Allergies—Tell your health care professional if you have ever had any unusual or allergic reaction to ascorbic acid. Also, tell your health care professional if you are allergic to any other substances, such as foods, sulfites or other preservatives, or dyes.

Pregnancy—It is especially important that you are receiving enough vitamins when you become pregnant and that you continue to receive the right amount of vitamins throughout your pregnancy. Healthy fetal growth and development depend on a steady supply of nutrients from mother to fetus.

However, taking too much vitamin C daily throughout pregnancy may harm the fetus.

Breast-feeding—It is especially important that you receive the right amounts of vitamins so that your baby will also get the vitamins needed to grow properly. You should also check with your doctor if you are giving your baby an unfortified formula. In that case, the baby must get the vitamins needed some other way. However, taking large amounts of a dietary supplement while breast-feeding may be harmful to the mother and/or baby and should be avoided.

Children—Problems in children have not been reported with intake of normal daily recommended amounts.

Older adults—Problems in older adults have not been reported with intake of normal daily recommended amounts.

Medicines or other dietary supplements—Although certain medicines or dietary supplements should not be used together at all, in other cases they may be used together even if an interaction might occur. In these cases, your health care professional may want to change the dose, or other precautions may be necessary. Tell your health care professional if you are taking any other dietary supplement or any prescription or nonprescription (over-the-counter [OTC]) medicine.

Other medical problems—The presence of other medical problems may affect the use of vitamin C. Make sure you tell your health care professional if you have any other medical problems, especially:

- Blood problems—High doses of vitamin C may cause certain blood problems
- Diabetes mellitus (sugar diabetes)—Very high doses of vitamin C may interfere with tests for sugar in the urine
- Glucose-6-phosphate dehydrogenase (G6PD) deficiency—High doses of vitamin C may cause hemolytic anemia
- Kidney stones (history of)—High doses of vitamin C may increase risk of kidney stones in the urinary tract

Proper Use of This Dietary Supplement

Dosing—The amount of vitamin C needed to meet normal daily recommended intakes will be different for different individuals. The following information includes only the average amounts of vitamin C.

- For *oral* dosage form (capsules, tablets, oral solution, syrup):
  —To prevent deficiency, the amount taken by mouth is based on normal daily recommended intakes:
  For the U.S.
  - Adult and teenage males—50 to 60 milligrams (mg) per day.
  - Adult and teenage females—50 to 60 mg per day.
  - Pregnant females—70 mg per day.
  - Breast-feeding females—90 to 95 mg per day.
  - Smokers—100 mg per day.
  - Children 4 to 10 years of age—45 mg per day.
  - Children birth to 3 years of age—30 to 40 mg per day.

  For Canada
  - Adult and teenage males—25 to 40 mg per day.
  - Adult and teenage females—25 to 30 mg per day.
  - Pregnant females—30 to 40 mg per day.
  - Breast-feeding females—55 mg per day.
  - Smokers—45 to 60 mg per day.
  - Children 4 to 10 years of age—25 mg per day.
  - Children birth to 3 years of age—20 mg per day.

  —To treat deficiency:
  - Adults and teenagers—Treatment dose is determined by prescriber for each individual based on the severity of deficiency. The following dose has been determined for scurvy: 500 mg a day for at least 2 weeks.
  - Children—Treatment dose is determined by prescriber for each individual based on the severity of deficiency. The following dose has been determined for scurvy: 100 to 300 mg a day for at least 2 weeks.

For those individuals taking the *oral liquid form* of vitamin C:

- This preparation is to be taken by mouth even though it comes in a dropper bottle.
- This dietary supplement may be dropped directly into the mouth or mixed with cereal, fruit juice, or other food.

Missed dose—If you miss taking a vitamin for one or more days there is no cause for concern, since it takes some time for your body to become seriously low in vitamins. However, if your health care professional has recommended that you take this vitamin, try to remember to take it as directed every day.

Storage—To store this dietary supplement:

- Keep out of the reach of children.
- Store away from heat and direct light.
- Do not store in the bathroom, near the kitchen sink, or in other damp places. Heat or moisture may cause the dietary supplement to break down.
- Keep the oral liquid form of this dietary supplement from freezing.
- Do not keep outdated dietary supplements or those no longer needed. Be sure that any discarded dietary supplement is out of the reach of children.

Precautions While Using This Dietary Supplement

Vitamin C is not stored in the body. If you take more than you need, the extra vitamin C will pass into your urine.

Very large doses may also interfere with tests for sugar in diabetics and with tests for blood in the stool.

Side Effects of This Dietary Supplement

Along with its needed effects, a dietary supplement may cause some unwanted effects. Although not all of these side effects may occur, if they do occur, they may need medical attention.

Check with your health care professional as soon as possible if the following side effect occurs:

Less common or rare—with high doses

Side or lower back pain

Other side effects may occur that usually do not need medical attention. These side effects may go away during treatment as your body adjusts to the dietary supplement. However, check with your health care professional as soon as possible if any of the following side effects continue or are bothersome:

Less common or rare—with high doses

Diarrhea; dizziness or faintness (with the injection only); flushing or redness of skin; headache; increase in urination (mild); nausea or vomiting; stomach cramps

Other side effects not listed above may also occur in some individuals. If you notice any other effects, check with your health care professional.

Additional Information

Once a medicine or dietary supplement has been approved for marketing for a certain use, experience may show that it is also useful for other medical problems. Although these uses are not included in product labeling, vitamin C is used in certain patients with the following medical conditions:

- Overdose of iron (to help another drug in decreasing iron levels in the body)
- Methemoglobinemia (a blood disease)

Other than the above information, there is no additional information relating to proper use, precautions, or side effects for these uses.

Revised: 05/01/95

ASPARAGINASE Systemic

Some commonly used brand names are:

In the U.S.—
Elspar

In Canada—
Kidrolase

Another commonly used name is colaspase.

Description

Asparaginase (a-SPARE-a-gin-ase) belongs to the group of medicines known as enzymes. It is used to treat some kinds of cancer.

All cells need a chemical called asparagine to stay alive. Normal cells can make this chemical for themselves, while cancer cells cannot. Asparaginase breaks down asparagine in the body. Since the cancer cells cannot make more asparagine, they die.

Before you begin treatment with asparaginase, you and your doctor should talk about the good this medicine will do as well as the risks of using it.

Asparaginase is to be administered only by or under the supervision of your doctor. It is available in the following dosage form:

Parenteral

- Injection (U.S. and Canada)

Before Using This Medicine

In deciding to use a medicine, the risks of taking the medicine must be weighed against the good it will do. This is a decision you and your doctor will make. For asparaginase, the following should be considered:

Allergies—Tell your doctor if you have ever had any unusual or allergic reaction to asparaginase.

Pregnancy—Asparaginase has not been studied in pregnant women. However, studies in mice and rats have shown that asparaginase in doses 5 times the usual human dose slows the weight gain of infants and may also increase the risk of birth defects or cause a decrease in successful pregnancies. In addition, doses slightly less than the human dose have caused birth defects in rabbits.

It is best to use some kind of birth control while you are receiving asparaginase. Tell your doctor right away if you think you have become pregnant while receiving asparaginase.

Breast-feeding—It is not known whether asparaginase passes into breast milk. However, because asparaginase may cause serious side effects, breast-feeding is generally not recommended while you are receiving it.

Children—This medicine has been tested in children and has not been shown to cause different side effects or problems than it does in adults. In fact, the side effects of this medicine seem to be less severe in children than in adults.

Older adults—Many medicines have not been studied specifically in older people. Therefore, it may not be known whether they work exactly the same way they do in younger adults or if they cause different side effects or problems in older people. There is no specific information comparing use of asparaginase in the elderly with use in other age groups.

Other medicines—Although certain medicines should not be used together at all, in other cases two different medicines may be used together even if an interaction might occur. In these cases, your doctor may want to change the dose, or other precautions may be necessary. When you are receiving asparaginase it is especially important that your health care professional know if you are taking any of the following:

- Probenecid (e.g., Benemid) or
- Sulfinpyrazone (e.g., Anturane)—Asparaginase may raise the concentration of uric acid in the blood. Since these medicines are used to lower uric acid levels, they may not work as well in patients receiving asparaginase
- If you have ever been treated with radiation or cancer medicines—Asparaginase may increase the total effects of these medications and radiation therapy

Other medical problems—The presence of other medical problems may affect the use of asparaginase. Make sure you tell your doctor if you have any other medical problems, especially:

- Chickenpox (including recent exposure) or
- Herpes zoster (shingles)—Risk of severe disease affecting other parts of the body
- Diabetes mellitus (sugar diabetes)—Asparaginase may increase glucose (sugar) in the blood
- Gout or
- Kidney stones—Asparaginase may increase levels of uric acid in the body, which can cause gout or kidney stones
- Infection—Asparaginase can reduce your body's ability to fight infection
- Liver disease—Asparaginase may worsen the condition
- Pancreatitis (inflammation of the pancreas)—Asparaginase may cause pancreatitis

Proper Use of This Medicine

This medicine is usually given together with certain other medicines. If you are using a combination of medicines, it is important that you receive each one at the proper time. If you are taking some of these medicines by mouth, ask your health care professional to help you plan a way to remember to take them at the right times.

While you are using this medicine, your doctor may want you to drink extra fluids so that you will pass more urine. This will help prevent kidney problems and keep your kidneys working well.

This medicine often causes nausea, vomiting, and loss of appetite. However, it is very important that you continue to receive the medicine, even if you begin to feel ill. After several doses, your stomach upset should lessen. Ask your health care professional for ways to lessen these effects.

Dosing—The dose of asparaginase will be different for different patients. The dose that is used may depend on a number of things, including what the medicine is being used for, the patient's weight, and whether or not other medicines are also being taken. *If you are receiving asparaginase at home, follow your doctor's orders or the directions on the label.* If you have any questions about the proper dose of asparaginase, ask your doctor.

Precautions While Using This Medicine

It is very important that your doctor check your progress at regular visits to make sure that this medicine is working properly and to check for unwanted effects.

While you are being treated with asparaginase, and after you stop treatment with it, *do not have any immunizations (vaccinations) without your doctor's approval.* Asparaginase may lower your body's resistance and there is a chance you might get the infection the immunization is meant to prevent. In addition, other persons living in your household should not take oral polio vaccine since there is a chance they could pass the polio virus on to you. Also, avoid persons who have taken oral polio vaccine. Do not get close to them, and do not stay in the same room with them for very long. If you cannot take these precautions, you should consider wearing a protective face mask that covers the nose and mouth.

Before you have any medical tests, tell the medical doctor in charge that you are receiving this medicine. The results of thyroid tests may be affected by this medicine.

Side Effects of This Medicine

Along with its needed effects, a medicine may cause some unwanted effects. Some side effects will have signs or symptoms that you can see or feel. Your doctor may watch for others by doing certain tests. Some of the unwanted effects that may be caused by asparaginase are listed below. Although not all of these effects may occur, if they do occur, they may need medical attention.

Also, because of the way these medicines act on the body, there is a chance that they might cause other unwanted effects that may not occur until months or years after the medicine is used. These delayed effects may include certain types of cancer, such as leukemia. Discuss these possible effects with your doctor.

Check with your doctor or nurse immediately if any of the following side effects occur:

More common

Joint pain; puffy face; skin rash or itching; stomach pain (severe) with nausea and vomiting; trouble in breathing

Rare

Fever or chills; headache (severe); inability to move arm or leg; unusual bleeding or bruising

Check with your health care professional as soon as possible if any of the following side effects occur:

Less common

Confusion; drowsiness; frequent urination; hallucinations (seeing, hearing, or feeling things that are not there); lower back or side pain; mental depression; nervousness; sores in mouth or on lips; swelling of feet or lower legs; unusual thirst; unusual tiredness

Rare

Convulsions (seizures); pain in lower legs

This medicine may also cause the following side effect that your doctor will watch for:

More common

Liver problems

Other side effects may occur that usually do not need medical attention. These side effects may go away during treatment as your body adjusts to the medicine. Also, your health care professional may be able to tell you about ways to prevent or reduce some of these side effects. Check with your health care professional if any of the

following side effects continue or are bothersome or if you have any questions about them:

More common

Headache (mild); loss of appetite; nausea or vomiting; stomach cramps; weight loss

After you stop receiving asparaginase, it may still produce some side effects that need attention. During this period of time, *check with your doctor or nurse immediately* if any of the following side effects occur:

Headache (severe); inability to move arm or leg; stomach pain (severe) with nausea and vomiting

Other side effects not listed above may also occur in some patients. If you notice any other effects, check with your health care professional.

Revised: 04/09/93
Interim revision: 04/29/94

ASPIRIN, SODIUM BICARBONATE, AND CITRIC ACID Systemic

Some commonly used brand names in the U.S. and Canada are Alka-Seltzer Effervescent Pain Reliever and Antacid and Flavored Alka-Seltzer Effervescent Pain Reliever and Antacid.

Other commonly used names for aspirin are acetylsalicylic acid and ASA. Because Aspirin is a brand name in Canada, ASA is the term that commonly appears on Canadian product labels.

Description

Aspirin, sodium bicarbonate, and citric acid (AS-pir-in, SOE-dee-um bye-KAR-boe-nate, and SI-trik AS-id) combination is used to relieve pain occurring together with heartburn, sour stomach, or acid indigestion.

The aspirin in this combination is the pain reliever. Aspirin belongs to the group of medicines known as salicylates (sa-LISS-ih-lates) and to the group of medicines known as anti-inflammatory analgesics. The sodium bicarbonate in this medicine is an antacid. It neutralizes stomach acid by combining with it to form a new substance that is not an acid.

Aspirin, sodium bicarbonate, and citric acid combination may also be used to lessen the chance of heart attack, stroke, or other problems that may occur when a blood vessel is blocked by blood clots. The aspirin in this medicine helps prevent dangerous blood clots from forming. However, this effect of aspirin may increase the chance of serious bleeding in some people. Therefore, aspirin should be used for this purpose only when your doctor decides, after studying your medical condition and history, that the danger of blood clots is greater than the risk of bleeding. *Do not take aspirin to prevent blood clots or a heart attack unless it has been ordered by your doctor.*

This combination medicine is available without a prescription. However, your doctor may have special instructions on the proper dose for your medical condition.

Aspirin, sodium bicarbonate, and citric acid combination is available in the following dosage form:

Oral

- Effervescent tablets (U.S. and Canada)

Before Using This Medicine

If you are taking this medicine without a prescription, carefully read and follow any precautions on the label. For aspirin, sodium bicarbonate, and citric acid combination, the following should be considered:

Allergies—Tell your doctor if you have ever had any unusual or allergic reaction to aspirin or other salicylates, including methyl salicylate (oil of wintergreen), or to any of the following medicines:

Diclofenac (e.g., Voltaren)
Diflunisal (e.g., Dolobid)
Etodolac (e.g., Lodine)
Fenoprofen (e.g., Nalfon)
Floctafenine (e.g., Idarac)
Flurbiprofen, oral (e.g., Ansaid)
Ibuprofen (e.g., Motrin)
Indomethacin (e.g., Indocin)
Ketoprofen (e.g., Orudis)
Ketorolac (e.g., Toradol)
Meclofenamate (e.g., Meclomen)
Mefenamic acid (e.g., Ponstel)
Nabumetone (e.g., Relafen)
Naproxen (e.g., Naprosyn)
Oxaprozin (e.g., Daypro)
Oxyphenbutazone (e.g., Tandearil)
Phenylbutazone (e.g., Butazolidin)
Piroxicam (e.g., Feldene)
Sulindac (e.g., Clinoril)
Suprofen (e.g., Suprol)
Tenoxicam (e.g., Mobiflex)
Tiaprofenic acid (e.g., Surgam)
Tolmetin (e.g., Tolectin)
Zomepirac (e.g., Zomax)

Also tell your health care professional if you are allergic to any other substances, such as foods, preservatives, or dyes.

Diet—Make certain your health care professional knows if you are on any special diet, such as a low-sodium or low-sugar diet. This medicine contains a large amount of sodium (more than 500 mg in each tablet).

Pregnancy—Studies in humans have not shown that aspirin causes birth defects in humans. However, it has been shown to cause birth defects in animal studies.

Do not take aspirin during the last 3 months of pregnancy unless it has been ordered by your doctor. Some reports have suggested that too much use of aspirin late in pregnancy may cause a decrease in the newborn's weight and possible death of the fetus or newborn infant. However, the mothers in these reports had been taking much larger amounts of aspirin than are usually recommended. Studies of mothers taking aspirin in the doses that are usually recommended did not show these unwanted effects. However, there is a chance that regular use of aspirin late in pregnancy may cause unwanted effects on the heart or blood flow in the fetus or in the newborn infant.

Use of aspirin during the last 2 weeks of pregnancy may cause bleeding problems in the fetus before or during delivery or in the newborn infant. Also, too much use of aspirin during the last 3 months of pregnancy may increase the length of pregnancy, prolong labor, cause other problems during delivery, or cause severe bleeding in the mother before, during, or after delivery.

The sodium in this combination medicine can cause your body to hold water. This may result in swelling and weight gain. Therefore, you should not use this combination medicine if you tend to hold body water.

Breast-feeding—Aspirin passes into the breast milk. However, aspirin (in the amounts used to relieve pain or prevent blood clots), sodium bicarbonate, and citric acid have not been reported to cause problems in nursing babies.

Children—*Do not give any medicine containing aspirin to a child with fever or other symptoms of a virus infection, especially flu or chickenpox, without first discussing its use with your child's doctor.* This is very important because aspirin may cause a serious illness called Reye's syndrome in children with fever caused by a virus infection, especially flu or chickenpox. Children who do not have a virus infection may also be more sensitive to the effects of aspirin, especially if they have a fever or have lost large amounts of body fluid because of vomiting, diarrhea, or sweating. This may increase the chance of side effects during treatment.

Teenagers—*Teenagers with fever or other symptoms of a virus infection, especially flu or chickenpox, should check with a doctor before taking this medicine.* The aspirin in this combination medicine may cause a serious illness called Reye's syndrome in teenagers with fever caused by a virus infection, especially flu or chickenpox.

Older adults—People 60 years of age and older are especially sensitive to the effects of aspirin. This may increase the chance of side effects during treatment. Also, the sodium in this combination medicine can be harmful to some elderly people, especially if large amounts of the medicine are taken regularly. Therefore, it is best that older people not use this medicine for more than 5 days in a row, unless otherwise directed by their doctor.

Other medicines—Although certain medicines should not be used together at all, in other cases two different medicines may be used together even if an interaction might occur. In these cases, your doctor may want to change the dose, or other precautions may be necessary. When you are taking this combination medicine, it is especially important that your health care professional know if you are taking any of the following:

- Anticoagulants (blood thinners) or
- Carbenicillin by injection (e.g., Geopen) or
- Cefamandole (e.g., Mandol) or
- Cefoperazone (e.g., Cefobid) or
- Cefotetan (e.g., Cefotan) or
- Dipyridamole (e.g., Persantine) or
- Divalproex (e.g., Depakote) or
- Heparin or
- Pentoxifylline (e.g., Trental) or
- Plicamycin (e.g., Mithracin) or
- Ticarcillin (e.g., Ticar) or
- Valproic acid (e.g., Depakene)—Use of these medicines together with aspirin may increase the chance of bleeding
- Antidiabetics, oral (diabetes medicine you take by mouth)—Aspirin may increase the effects of these medicines; a change in dose may be needed
- Ciprofloxacin (e.g., Cipro) or
- Enoxacin (e.g, Penetrex) or
- Itraconazole (e.g., Sporanox) or
- Ketoconazole (e.g., Nizoral) or
- Lomefloxacin (e.g., Maxaquin) or
- Methenamine (e.g., Mandelamine) or
- Norfloxacin (e.g., Noroxin) or
- Ofloxacin (e.g., Floxin) or
- Tetracyclines (medicine for infection), taken by mouth—Sodium bicarbonate can keep these medicines from working properly
- Mecamylamine (e.g., Inversine)—Sodium bicarbonate may increase the chance of unwanted effects by causing mecamylamine to stay in your body longer than usual
- Medicine for pain and/or inflammation (except narcotics) or
- Methotrexate (e.g., Mexate) or
- Vancomycin (e.g., Vancocin)—The chance of serious side effects may be increased
- Probenecid (e.g., Benemid) or
- Sulfinpyrazone (e.g., Anturane)—Aspirin can keep these medicines from working properly when they are used to treat gout

Other medical problems—The presence of other medical problems may affect the use of this combination medicine. Make sure you tell your doctor if you have any other medical problems, especially:

- Anemia or
- Stomach ulcer or other stomach problems—Aspirin can make these conditions worse
- Appendicitis (symptoms of, such as stomach or lower abdominal pain, cramping, bloating, soreness, nausea, or vomiting)—Sodium bicarbonate can make your condition worse; also, people who may have appendicitis need medical attention and should not try to treat themselves
- Asthma, allergies, and nasal polyps (history of) or
- Kidney disease or
- Liver disease—The chance of serious side effects may be increased
- Edema (swelling of face, fingers, feet, or lower legs caused by too much water in the body) or
- Heart disease or
- High blood pressure or
- Toxemia of pregnancy—The sodium in this combination medicine can make these conditions worse
- Gout—Aspirin can make this condition worse and can also keep some medicines used to treat gout from working properly
- Hemophilia or other bleeding problems—Aspirin increases the chance of serious bleeding

Proper Use of This Medicine

Unless otherwise directed by your doctor, do not take more of this medicine than is recommended on the package label. If too much is taken, serious side effects may occur.

To use this medicine:

- The tablets must be dissolved in water before taking. Do not swallow the tablets or any pieces of the tablets.
- Place the number of tablets needed for one dose (1 or 2 tablets) into a glass. Then add 1/2 glass (4 ounces) of cool water.
- Check to be sure that the tablets have disappeared completely. This shows that all of the medicine is in the liquid. Then drink all of the liquid. You may drink the liquid while it is still fizzing or after the fizzing stops.
- Add a little more water to the glass and drink that, to make sure that you get the full amount of the medicine.

Dosing—The dose of this combination medicine will be different for different people. *Follow your doctor's orders or the directions on the label.* The following information includes only the average doses of this combination medicine. *If your dose is different, do not change it* unless your doctor tells you to do so.

- For *oral* dosage forms (effervescent tablets):
  —For pain and upset stomach:
    - Adults and teenagers—One or two regular-strength (325-milligram [mg]) tablets every four to six hours as needed, one extra-strength (500-mg) tablet every four to six hours as needed, or two extra-strength (500-mg) tablets every six hours as needed, dissolved in water. Elderly people should not take more than four regular-strength or extra-strength tablets a day. Other adults and teenagers should not take more than 6 regular-strength flavored tablets, 8 regular-strength unflavored tablets, or 7 extra-strength tablets a day.
    - Children—The dose depends on the child's age.
      —Children younger than 3 years of age: Use and dose must be determined by your doctor.
      —Children 3 to 5 years of age: One-half of a regular-strength (325-mg) tablet, dissolved in water, every four to six hours as needed.
      —Children 6 to 12 years of age: One regular-strength (325-mg) tablet, dissolved in water, every four to six hours as needed.

  —For reducing the chance of heart attack, stroke, or other problems that may occur when a blood vessel is blocked by blood clots:
    - Adults—One regular-strength (325-mg) tablet a day, dissolved in water.
    - Children and teenagers—Use and dose must be determined by your doctor.

Missed dose—If your doctor has ordered you to take this medicine according to a regular schedule and you miss a dose, take it as soon as you remember. However, if it is almost time for your next dose, skip the missed dose and go back to your regular dosing schedule. Do not double doses.

Storage—To store this medicine:

- Keep out of the reach of children. Overdose is very dangerous in young children.
- Store away from heat and direct light.
- Do not store in the bathroom, near the kitchen sink, or in other damp places. Heat or moisture may cause the medicine to break down.
- Do not keep outdated medicine or medicine no longer needed. Be sure that any discarded medicine is out of the reach of children.

Precautions While Using This Medicine

If you will be taking this medicine for a long time (more than 5 days in a row for children or 10 days in a row for adults), your doctor should check your progress at regular visits.

Check with your doctor if your pain and/or upset stomach last for more than 10 days for adults or 5 days for children or if they get worse, if new symptoms occur, or if the painful area is red or swollen. These could be signs of a serious condition that needs medical treatment.

The sodium bicarbonate in this combination medicine can keep other medicines from working properly if the 2 medicines are taken too close together. *Always take this medicine:*

- *At least 6 hours before or 2 hours after taking ciprofloxacin (e.g., Cipro) or lomefloxacin (e.g., Maxaquin).*
- *At least 8 hours before or 2 hours after taking enoxacin (e.g., Penetrex).*
- *At least 2 hours after taking itraconazole (e.g., Sporanox).*
- *At least 3 hours before or after taking ketoconazole (e.g., Nizoral).*
- *At least 2 hours before or after taking norfloxacin (e.g., Noroxin) or ofloxacin (e.g., Floxin).*
- *At least 3 or 4 hours before or after taking a tetracycline antibiotic by mouth.*
- *At least 1 or 2 hours before or after taking any other medicine by mouth.*

If you are also taking a laxative that contains cellulose, take this combination medicine at least 2 hours before or after you take the laxative. Taking the medicines too close together may lessen the effects of aspirin.

Check the labels of all nonprescription (over-the-counter [OTC]) and prescription medicines you now take. If any contain aspirin or other salicylates, including bismuth subsalicylate (e.g., Pepto-Bismol), magnesium salicylate (e.g., Nuprin Backache Caplets), or salsalate (e.g., Disalcid); if any contain salicylic acid (present in some shampoos or medicines for your skin); or if any contain sodium, *check with your health care professional.* Taking other salicylate-containing or other sodium-containing products together with this medicine may cause an overdose.

Do not take aspirin for 5 days before any surgery, including dental surgery, unless otherwise directed by your medical doctor or dentist. Taking aspirin during this time may cause bleeding problems.

For patients taking this medicine to lessen the chance of a heart attack, stroke, or other problems caused by blood clots:

- *Take only the amount of aspirin ordered by your doctor.* If you need a medicine to relieve pain, a fever, or arthritis, your doctor may not want you to take extra aspirin. It is a good idea to discuss this with your doctor, so that you will know ahead of time what medicine to take.
- *Do not stop taking this medicine for any reason without first checking with the doctor who directed you to take it.*

Taking certain other medicines together with a salicylate may increase the chance of unwanted effects. The risk will depend on how much of each medicine you take every day, and on how long you take the medicines together. If your doctor directs you to take these medicines together on a regular basis, follow his or her directions carefully. However, *do not take any of the following medicines together with a salicylate for more than a few days, unless your doctor has directed you to do so and is following your progress*:

Acetaminophen (e.g., Tylenol)
Diclofenac (e.g., Voltaren)
Diflunisal (e.g., Dolobid)
Etodolac (e.g., Lodine)
Fenoprofen (e.g., Nalfon)
Floctafenine (e.g., Idarac)
Flurbiprofen, oral (e.g., Ansaid)
Ibuprofen (e.g., Motrin)
Indomethacin (e.g., Indocin)
Ketoprofen (e.g., Orudis)
Ketorolac (e.g., Toradol)
Meclofenamate (e.g., Meclomen)
Mefenamic acid (e.g., Ponstel)
Nabumetone (e.g., Relafen)
Naproxen (e.g., Naprosyn)
Oxaprozin (e.g., Daypro)
Phenylbutazone (e.g., Butazolidin)
Piroxicam (e.g., Feldene)
Sulindac (e.g., Clinoril)
Tenoxicam (e.g., Mobiflex)
Tiaprofenic acid (e.g., Surgam)
Tolmetin (e.g., Tolectin)

If you will be taking more than an occasional 1 or 2 doses of this medicine:

- *Do not drink alcoholic beverages.* Drinking alcoholic beverages while you are taking aspirin, especially if you take aspirin regularly or in large amounts, may increase the chance of stomach problems.
- *Do not drink a lot of milk or eat a lot of milk products.* To do so may increase the chance of side effects.
- To prevent side effects caused by too much sodium in the body, you may need to limit the amount of sodium in the foods you eat. Some foods that contain large amounts of sodium are canned soup, canned vegetables, pickles, ketchup, green and ripe (black) olives, relish, frankfurters and other sausage-type meats, soy sauce, and carbonated beverages. If you have any questions about this, check with your health care professional.

Before you have any medical tests, tell the person in charge that you are taking this medicine. The results of some tests may be affected by the aspirin in this combination medicine.

For *diabetic patients:*

- Aspirin can cause false urine glucose (sugar) test results if you regularly take 8 or more 324-mg, or 4 or more 500-mg (extra-strength), tablets a day. Smaller amounts or occasional use of aspirin usually will not affect the test results. However, check with your health care professional if you notice any change in your urine glucose test results. This is especially important if your diabetes is not well-controlled.

If you think that you or anyone else may have taken an overdose, get emergency help at once. Taking an overdose of aspirin may cause unconsciousness or death, especially in young children. Signs of overdose include convulsions (seizures), hearing loss, confusion, ringing or buzzing in the ears, severe drowsiness or tiredness, severe excitement or nervousness, and fast or deep breathing.

Side Effects of This Medicine

Along with its needed effects, a medicine may cause some unwanted effects. Although the following side effects occur very rarely when 1 or 2 doses of this combination medicine is taken occasionally, they may be more likely to occur if:

- too much medicine is taken.
- the medicine is taken several times a day.
- the medicine is taken for more than a few days in a row.

Get emergency help immediately if any of the following side effects occur:

Any loss of hearing; bloody urine; confusion; convulsions (seizures); diarrhea (severe or continuing); difficulty in swallowing; dizziness, lightheadedness, or feeling faint (severe); drowsiness (severe); excitement or nervousness (severe); fast or deep breathing; flushing, redness, or other change in skin color; hallucinations (seeing, hearing, or feeling things that are not there); nausea or vomiting (severe or continuing); shortness of breath, troubled breathing, tightness in chest, or wheezing; stomach pain (severe or continuing); swelling of eyelids, face, or lips; unexplained fever; uncontrollable flapping movements of the hands (especially in elderly patients); vision problems

Signs of overdose in children

Changes in behavior; drowsiness or tiredness (severe); fast or deep breathing

Also, check with your doctor as soon as possible if any of the following side effects occur:

Less common or rare

Bloody or black, tarry stools; frequent urge to urinate; headache (severe or continuing); increased blood pressure; loss of appetite (continuing); mood or mental changes; muscle pain or twitching; ringing or buzzing in ears (continuing); skin rash, hives, or itching; slow breathing; swelling of face, fingers, ankles, feet, or lower legs; unpleasant taste; unusual tiredness or weakness; vomiting of blood or material that looks like coffee grounds; weight gain (unusual)

Other side effects may occur that usually do not need medical attention. These side effects may go away during treatment as your body adjusts to the medicine. However, check with your health care professional if any of the following side effects continue or are bothersome:

Heartburn or indigestion; increased thirst; nausea or vomiting; stomach pain (mild)

Other side effects not listed above may also occur in some patients. If you notice any other effects, check with your doctor.

Revised: 08/29/94

ATOVAQUONE Systemic

A commonly used brand name in the U.S. and Canada is Mepron.

Description

Atovaquone (a-TOE-va-kwone) is used to treat *Pneumocystis* (noo-moe-SISS-tis) *carinii* pneumonia (PCP), a very serious kind of pneumonia. This particular kind of pneumonia occurs commonly in patients whose immune systems are not working normally, such as cancer patients, transplant patients, and patients with acquired immune deficiency syndrome (AIDS).

This medicine is available only with your doctor's prescription, in the following dosage form:

Oral

- Oral suspension (U.S.)
- Tablets (Canada)

Before Receiving This Medicine

In deciding to use a medicine, the risks of taking the medicine must be weighed against the good it will do. This is a decision you and your doctor will make. For atovaquone, the following should be considered:

Allergies—Tell your doctor if you have ever had any unusual or allergic reaction to atovaquone. Also tell your health care professional if you are allergic to any other substances, such as foods, preservatives, or dyes.

Diet—Make certain your health care professional knows if you are on any special diet. This medicine must be taken with balanced meals so that it can work properly.

Pregnancy—Atovaquone has not been studied in pregnant women. However, studies in rabbits have shown an increase in miscarriages and other harmful effects in the mother and fetus. Before taking this medicine, make sure your doctor knows if you are pregnant or if you may become pregnant.

Breast-feeding—It is not known whether atovaquone passes into human breast milk. However, it was found in the milk of rats. Be sure you have discussed the risks and benefits of atovaquone with your doctor.

Children—Atovaquone has been tested in a limited number of children 1 month of age to 13 years old. It is not known if this medicine causes different side effects or problems in children than it does in adults.

Older adults—Many medicines have not been studied specifically in older people. Therefore, it may not be known whether they work exactly the same way they do in younger adults or if they cause different side effects or problems in older people. There is no specific information comparing use of atovaquone in the elderly with use in other age groups.

Other medicines—Although certain medicines should not be used together at all, in other cases two different medicines may be used together even if an interaction might occur. In these cases, your doctor may want to change the dose, or other precautions may be necessary. When you are taking atovaquone, it is especially important that your health care professional know if you are taking any of the following:

- Rifampin (e.g., Rifadin)—Use of rifampin with atovaquone may decrease the amount of atovaquone in the blood and keep it from working properly

Other medical problems—The presence of other medical problems may affect the use of atovaquone. Make sure you tell your doctor if you have any other medical problems, especially:

- Stomach or intestinal disorders—Atovaquone may not work properly in patients with some kinds of stomach or intestinal problems

Proper Use of This Medicine

It is *important that you take atovaquone with a balanced meal*. This is to make sure the medicine is fully absorbed into the body and will work properly.

Atovaquone tablets may be crushed if necessary to make it easier to swallow the tablets.

Because atovaquone tablets and oral suspension do not produce the same amount of medicine in the blood, the *tablets and the suspension cannot be switched and used in place of each other.*

For patients taking the *oral liquid* form of this medicine:

- This medicine is to be taken by mouth. Use a specially marked measuring spoon or other device to measure each dose accurately. The average household teaspoon may not hold the right amount of liquid.
- Do not use after the expiration date on the label since the medicine may not work properly after that date. Check with your pharmacist if you have any questions about this.

To help clear up your infection completely, *keep taking your medicine for the full time of treatment,* even if you begin to feel better after a few days. If you stop taking this medicine too soon, your symptoms may return.

Atovaquone works best when there is a constant amount in the blood. *To help keep the amount constant, do not miss any doses.*

Dosing—The dose of atovaquone may be different for different patients. *Follow your doctor's orders or the directions on the label.* The following information includes only the average doses of atovaquone. *If your dose is different, do not change it* unless your doctor tells you to do so.

- For treatment of *Pneumocystis carinii* pneumonia (PCP):
  - —For *oral suspension* dosage form:
    - Adults and teenagers—750 milligrams (mg) taken with a meal two times a day for twenty-one days.
    - Children—Use and dose must be determined by your doctor.
  - —For *tablet* dosage form:
    - Adults and teenagers—750 mg taken with a meal three times a day for twenty-one days.
    - Children—Use and dose must be determined by your doctor.

Missed dose—If you miss a dose of this medicine, take it as soon as possible. This will help to keep a constant amount of medicine in the blood. However, if it is almost time for your next dose, skip the missed dose and go back to your regular dosing schedule. Do not double doses.

Storage—To store this medicine:
- Keep out of the reach of children.
- Store away from heat and direct light.
- Do not store in the bathroom, near the kitchen sink, or in other damp places. Heat or moisture may cause the medicine to break down.
- Do not keep outdated medicine or medicine no longer needed. Be sure that any discarded medicine is out of the reach of children.
- Do not freeze.

Precautions While Using This Medicine

If your symptoms do not improve within a few days, or if they become worse, check with your doctor.

Side Effects of This Medicine

Along with its needed effects, a medicine may cause some unwanted effects. Although not all of these side effects may occur, if they do occur they may need medical attention.

Check with your doctor immediately if any of the following side effects occur:

More common

Fever; skin rash

Other side effects may occur that usually do not need medical attention. These side effects may go away during treatment as your body adjusts to the medicine. However, check with your doctor if any of the following side effects continue or are bothersome:

More common

Cough; diarrhea; headache; nausea; trouble in sleeping; vomiting

Other side effects not listed above may also occur in some patients. If you notice any other effects, check with your doctor.

Revised: 08/14/95

ATROPINE/HOMATROPINE/SCOPOLAMINE Ophthalmic

Some commonly used brand names are:

In the U.S.—

AK-Homatropine[2]
Atropair[1]
Atropine Care[1]
Atropine Sulfate S.O.P.[1]
Atropisol[1]
Atrosulf[1]
I-Homatrine[2]
Isopto Atropine[1]
Isopto Homatropine[2]
Isopto Hyoscine[3]
I-Tropine[1]
Ocu-Tropine[1]
Spectro-Homatropine[2]

In Canada—

Atropisol[1]
Isopto Atropine[1]
Isopto Homatropine[2]
Minims Atropine[1]
Minims Homatropine[2]

Another commonly used name for scopolamine is hyoscine.

Note: For quick reference, the following medicines are numbered to match the corresponding brand names.

This information applies to the following medicines:

1. Atropine (A-troe-peen)‡§
2. Homatropine (hoe-MA-troe-peen)‡§
3. Scopolamine (skoe-POL-a-meen)†

†Not commercially available in Canada.
‡Generic name product may also be available in the U.S.
§Generic name product may also be available in Canada.

Description

Ophthalmic atropine, homatropine, and scopolamine are used to dilate (enlarge) the pupil of the eye. They are used before eye examinations, before and after eye surgery, and to treat certain eye conditions, such as uveitis or posterior synechiae.

These medicines are available only with your doctor's prescription, in the following dosage forms:

Ophthalmic

Atropine
- Ophthalmic ointment (U.S. and Canada)
- Ophthalmic solution (eye drops) (U.S. and Canada)

Homatropine
- Ophthalmic solution (eye drops) (U.S. and Canada)

Scopolamine
- Ophthalmic solution (eye drops) (U.S.)

Before Using This Medicine

In deciding to use a medicine, the risks of using the medicine must be weighed against the good it will do. This is a decision you and your doctor will make. For ophthalmic atropine, homatropine, and scopolamine, the following should be considered:

Allergies—Tell your doctor if you have ever had any unusual or allergic reaction to atropine, homatropine, or scopolamine. Also tell your health care professional if you are allergic to any other substances, such as certain preservatives.

Pregnancy—Studies on effects in pregnancy have not been done in either humans or animals. However, these medicines may be absorbed into the body.

Breast-feeding—These medicines may be absorbed into the body. Atropine passes into the breast milk in very small amounts and may cause side effects, such as fast pulse, fever, or dry skin, in babies of nursing mothers using ophthalmic atropine. It is not known whether homatropine or scopolamine passes into breast milk. Although most medicines pass into breast milk in small amounts, many of them may be used safely while breast-feeding. Mothers who are using one of these medicines and who wish to breast-feed should discuss this with their doctor.

Children—Infants and young children and children with blond hair or blue eyes may be especially sensitive to the effects of atropine, homatropine, or scopolamine. This may increase the chance of side effects during treatment.

Older adults—Elderly people are especially sensitive to the effects of atropine, homatropine, or scopolamine. This may increase the chance of side effects during treatment.

Other medicines—Although certain medicines should not be used together at all, in other cases two different medicines may be used together even if an interaction might occur. In these cases, your doctor may want to change the dose, or other precautions may be necessary. Tell your health care professional if you are using any other prescription or nonprescription (over-the-counter [OTC]) medicine.

Other medical problems—The presence of other medical problems may affect the use of ophthalmic atropine, homatropine, or scopolamine. Make sure you tell your doctor if you have any other medical problems, especially:

- Brain damage (in children) or
- Down's syndrome (mongolism) (in children and adults) or
- Glaucoma or
- Other eye diseases or problems or
- Spastic paralysis (in children)—Use of ophthalmic atropine, homatropine, or scopolamine may make the condition worse

Proper Use of This Medicine

To use the ophthalmic solution *(eye drops) form* of this medicine:

- First, wash your hands. Tilt the head back and, pressing your finger gently on the skin just beneath the lower eyelid, pull the lower eyelid away from the eye to make a space. Drop the medicine into this space. Let go of the eyelid and gently close the eyes. Do not blink. Keep the eyes closed and apply pressure to the inner corner of the eye with your finger for 2 or 3 minutes to allow the medicine to be absorbed by the eye.
- Immediately after using the eye drops, wash your hands to remove any medicine that may be on them. If you are using the eye drops for an infant or child, be sure to wash his or her hands immediately afterwards also, and do not let any of the medicine get in his or her mouth. In addition, wipe off any medicine that may have accidentally gotten on the infant or child, including his or her face or eyelids.
- To keep the medicine as germ-free as possible, do not touch the applicator tip to any surface (including the eye). Also, keep the container tightly closed.

To use the *ointment form* of this medicine:

- First, wash your hands. Tilt the head back and, pressing your finger gently on the skin just beneath the lower eyelid, pull the lower eyelid away from the eye to make a space. Squeeze a thin strip of ointment into this space. A 1/3- to 1/2-cm (approximately 1/8-inch in infants and young children and 1/4-inch in older children and adults) strip of ointment is usually enough, unless you have been told by your doctor to use a different amount. Let go of the eyelid and gently close the eyes. Keep the eyes closed for 1 or 2 minutes to allow the medicine to be absorbed by the eye.
- Immediately after using the eye ointment, wash your hands to remove any medicine that may be on them. If you are using the eye ointment for an infant or child, be sure to wash his or her hands immediately afterwards also, and do not let any of the medicine get in his or her mouth. In addition, wipe off any medicine that may have accidentally gotten on the infant or child, including his or her face or eyelids.
- To keep the medicine as germ-free as possible, do not touch the applicator tip to any surface (including the eye). After using the eye ointment, wipe the tip of the ointment tube with a clean tissue and keep the tube tightly closed.

Use this medicine only as directed. Do not use more of it and do not use it more often than your doctor ordered. To do so may increase the chance of too much medicine being absorbed into the body and the chance of side effects. *This is especially important when this medicine is used in infants and children, since overdose is very dangerous in infants and children.*

Dosing—The doses of these medicines will be different for different patients. *Follow your doctor's orders or the directions on the label.* The following information includes only the average doses of these medicines. *If your dose is different, do not change it* unless your doctor tells you to do so.

The number of doses you use each day, the time allowed between doses, and the length of time you use the medicine depend on the medical problem for which you are using atropine, homatropine, or scopolamine.

For atropine

- For *ophthalmic ointment* dosage form:
  - —For uveitis:
    - Adults—Use a thin strip of the ointment in the eye one or two times a day.
    - Children—Use a thin strip of the ointment in the eye one to three times a day.
  - —For eye examinations:
    - Adults—Use and dose must be determined by your doctor.
    - Children—Use a thin strip of the ointment in the eye three times a day for one to three days before the examination.
- For *ophthalmic solution (eye drops)* dosage form:
  - —For uveitis:
    - Adults—Use one drop in the eye one or two times a day.
    - Children—Use one drop in the eye one to three times a day.
  - —For eye examinations:
    - Adults—Use and dose must be determined by your doctor.
    - Children—Use one drop in the eye two times a day for one to three days before the examination.

For homatropine

- For *ophthalmic solution (eye drops)* dosage form:
  - —For uveitis:
    - Adults and children—Use one drop in the eye two or three times a day.
  - —For eye examinations:
    - Adults—Use one drop in the eye. May be repeated every five to ten minutes for two or three doses.
    - Children—Use one drop in the eye every ten minutes for two or three doses.

For scopolamine

- For *ophthalmic solution (eye drops)* dosage form:
  - —For uveitis:
    - Adults and children—Use one drop in the eye up to four times a day.
  - —For eye examinations:
    - Adults—Use one drop in the eye one hour before the examination.
    - Children—Use one drop in the eye two times a day for two days before the examination.
  - —For posterior synechiae:
    - Adults—Use one drop in the eye every ten minutes for three doses.
    - Children—Use and dose must be determined by your doctor.
  - —For use before and after surgery:
    - Adults and children—Use one drop in the eye one to four times a day.

Missed dose—If you miss a dose of this medicine and your dosing schedule is:

- One dose a day—Apply the missed dose as soon as possible. However, if you do not remember the missed dose until the next day, skip the missed dose and go back to your regular dosing schedule. Do not double doses.
- More than one dose a day—Apply the missed dose as soon as possible. However, if it is almost time for your next dose, skip the missed dose and go back to your regular dosing schedule. Do not double doses.

Storage—To store this medicine:

- Keep out of the reach of children. Overdose of this medicine is very dangerous for infants and children.
- Store away from heat and direct light.
- Keep this medicine from freezing.
- Do not keep outdated medicine or medicine no longer needed. Be sure that any discarded medicine is out of the reach of children.

Precautions While Using This Medicine

After you apply this medicine to your eyes:

- Your pupils will become unusually large and you will have blurring of vision, especially for close objects. *Make sure your vision is clear before you drive, use machines, or do anything else that could be dangerous if you are not able to see well.*
- Your eyes will become more sensitive to light than they are normally. *Wear sunglasses to protect your eyes from sunlight and other bright lights.*

These effects may continue for several days after you stop using this medicine. However, check with your doctor if they continue longer than:

- 14 days if you are using atropine.
- 3 days if you are using homatropine.
- 7 days if you are using scopolamine.

Side Effects of This Medicine

Along with its needed effects, a medicine may cause some unwanted effects. Although not all of these side effects may occur, if they do occur they may need medical attention.

Check with your doctor immediately if any of the following side effects occur:

Symptoms of too much medicine being absorbed into the body

Clumsiness or unsteadiness; confusion or unusual behavior; dizziness; dryness of skin; fast or irregular heartbeat; fever; flushing or redness of face; hallucinations (seeing, hearing, or feeling things that are not there); skin rash; slurred speech; swollen stomach in infants; thirst or unusual dryness of mouth; unusual drowsiness, tiredness, or weakness

Other side effects may occur that usually do not need medical attention. These side effects may go away during treatment as your body adjusts to the medicine. However,

check with your doctor if any of the following side effects continue or are bothersome:

Blurred vision; eye irritation not present before use of this medicine; increased sensitivity of eyes to light; swelling of the eyelids

Other side effects not listed above may also occur in some patients. If you notice any other effects, check with your doctor.

Revised: 06/21/94
Interim revision: 05/01/95

ATROPINE, HYOSCYAMINE, METHENAMINE, METHYLENE BLUE, PHENYL SALICYLATE, AND BENZOIC ACID Systemic†

Some commonly used brand names are:

In the U.S.—

Atrosept	Urimed
Dolsed	Urinary Antiseptic No. 2
Hexalol	Urised
Prosed/DS	Uriseptic
Trac Tabs 2X	Uritab
UAA	Uritin
Uridon Modified	Uro-Ves

†Not commercially available in Canada.

Description

Atropine (A-troe-peen), hyoscyamine (hye-oh-SYE-a-meen), methenamine (meth-EN-a-meen), methylene (METH-i-leen) blue, phenyl salicylate (FEN-ill sa-LI-si-late), and benzoic acid (ben-ZOE-ik AS-id) combination medicine is an anticholinergic, anti-infective, and analgesic. It is given by mouth to help relieve the discomfort caused by urinary tract infections; however, it will not cure the infection itself. This combination medicine may also be used for other conditions as determined by your doctor.

This medicine is available only with your doctor's prescription in the following dosage form:

Oral

- Tablets (U.S.)

Before Using This Medicine

In deciding to use a medicine, the risks of taking the medicine must be weighed against the good it will do. This is a decision you and your doctor will make. For this combination medicine, the following should be considered:

Allergies—Tell your doctor if you have ever had any unusual or allergic reaction to any of the belladonna alkaloids such as atropine, hyoscyamine, and scopolamine, or to aspirin or other salicylates. Also tell your health care professional if you are allergic to any other substances, such as foods, preservatives, or dyes.

Diet—While you are taking this combination medicine, it is important for your urine to be acidic. To do this, your doctor may recommend that you eat more protein and such foods as cranberries (especially cranberry juice with vitamin C added), plums, or prunes. You should avoid foods that make the urine more alkaline, such as most fruits (especially citrus fruits and juices), milk, and other dairy products.

Pregnancy—Studies have not been done in either humans or animals.

Breast-feeding—Although methenamine and very small amounts of atropine and hyoscyamine (contained in this combination medicine) pass into the breast milk, this medicine has not been reported to cause problems in nursing babies.

Children—Unusual excitement, nervousness, restlessness or irritability, and unusual warmth, dryness, and flushing of skin are more likely to occur in children, who are usually more sensitive to the effects of atropine and hyoscyamine (contained in this combination medicine). Also, when atropine and hyoscyamine are given to children during hot weather, a rapid increase in body temperature may occur. In infants and children, especially those with spastic paralysis or brain damage, this medicine may be more likely to cause severe side effects.

Older adults—Confusion or memory loss, constipation, difficult urination, excitement, agitation, drowsiness, or dryness of mouth may be more likely to occur in elderly patients, who are usually more sensitive than younger adults to the effects of atropine and hyoscyamine. Also, this combination medicine may cause eye pain in patients who have untreated glaucoma.

Other medicines—Although certain medicines should not be used together at all, in other cases two different medicines may be used together even if an interaction might occur. In these cases, your doctor may want to change the dose, or other precautions may be necessary. When you are taking this combination medicine, it is especially important that your health care professional know if you are taking any of the following:

- Antacids or
- Diarrhea medicine containing kaolin or attapulgite or
- Thiazide diuretics (water pills) or
- Urinary alkalizers (medicine that makes the urine less acid, such as acetazolamide [e.g., Diamox], calcium- and/or magnesium-containing antacids, dichlorphenamide [e.g., Daranide], methazolamide [e.g., Neptazone], potassium or sodium citrate and/or citric acid, sodium bicarbonate [baking soda])—Use with these medicines may decrease the effects of this combination medicine
- Ketoconazole (e.g., Nizoral)—Use with this combination medicine may reduce the effects of ketoconazole
- Other anticholinergics (medicine for abdominal or stomach spasms or cramps)—Use with these medicines may increase the effects of atropine and hyoscyamine
- Potassium chloride (e.g., Slow K or K-Dur)—May worsen or cause an increase in lesions (sores) of the stomach or intestine

- Sulfonamides (sulfa medicine)—Use with this combination medicine may increase the risk of crystals forming in the urine

Other medical problems—The presence of other medical problems may affect the use of this combination medicine. Make sure you tell your doctor if you have any other medical problems, especially:

- Bleeding problems (severe)—This combination medicine may increase heart rate, which would make bleeding problems worse
- Brain damage (in children)—May increase the central nervous system (CNS) effects of this combination medicine
- Colitis (severe) or
- Dryness of mouth (severe or continuing) or
- Enlarged prostate or
- Fever or
- Glaucoma or
- Heart disease or
- Hernia (hiatal) or
- High blood pressure or
- Intestinal blockage or other intestinal or stomach problems or
- Lung disease or
- Myasthenia gravis or
- Toxemia of pregnancy or
- Urinary tract blockage or difficult urination—This combination medicine may make these conditions worse
- Dehydration or
- Kidney disease or
- Liver disease—Higher levels of medicine may result and increase the risk of side effects
- Overactive thyroid—May increase the heart rate

Proper Use of This Medicine

Take this medicine only as directed. Do not take more of it, do not take it more often, and do not take it for a longer time than your doctor ordered. To do so may increase the chance of side effects.

Each dose should be taken with a full glass (8 ounces) of water or other liquid (except citrus juices and milk). Drink plenty of water or other liquids every day, unless otherwise directed by your doctor. Drinking enough liquids will help your kidneys work better and lessen your discomfort.

To help clear up your infection completely, *keep taking this medicine for the full time of treatment* even if you begin to feel better after a few days. *Do not miss any doses.*

In order for this medicine to work well, your urine must be acid (pH 5.5 or below). To make sure that your urine is acid:

- Before you start taking this medicine, check your urine with phenaphthazine paper or another test to see if it is acid. If you have any questions about this, check with your health care professional.
- You may need to change your diet; however, check with your doctor first if you are on a special diet (for example, for diabetes). To help make your urine more acid you should avoid most fruits (especially citrus fruits and juices), milk and other dairy products, and other foods which make the urine more alkaline. Eating more protein and foods such as cranberries (especially cranberry juice with vitamin C added), plums, or prunes may also help. If your urine is still not acid enough, check with your doctor.

Dosing—The dose of this combination medicine will be different for different patients. *Follow your doctor's orders or the direction on the label.* The following information includes only the average doses of this combination medicine. *If your dose is different, do not change it* unless your doctor tells you to do so.

- For *oral* dosage form (tablets):
  - —For relief of urinary tract symptoms:
    - Adults and children 12 years of age and older—1 to 2 tablets four times a day.
    - Children 6 to 12 years of age—Dose must be determined by the doctor.
    - Children up to 6 years of age—Use is not recommended.

Missed dose—If you miss a dose of this medicine, take it as soon as possible. However, if it is almost time for your next dose, skip the missed dose and go back to your regular dosing schedule. Do not double doses.

Storage—To store this medicine:

- Keep out of the reach of children.
- Store away from heat and direct light.
- Do not store this medicine in the bathroom, near the kitchen sink, or in other damp places. Heat or moisture may cause the medicine to break down.
- Do not keep outdated medicine or medicine no longer needed. Be sure that any discarded medicine is out of the reach of children.

Precautions While Using This Medicine

If your symptoms do not improve within a few days or if they become worse, check with your doctor.

These medicines may make you sweat less, causing your body temperature to increase. *Use extra care not to become overheated during exercise or hot weather while you are taking this medicine,* since overheating may result in heat stroke. Also, hot baths or saunas may make you dizzy or faint while you are taking this medicine.

This medicine may cause some people to have blurred vision. *Make sure you know how you react to this medicine before you drive, use machines, or do anything else that could be dangerous if you are not able to see well. If your vision continues to be blurred, check with your doctor.*

This medicine may cause dryness of the mouth. For temporary relief, use sugarless candy or gum, melt bits of ice in your mouth, or use a saliva substitute. However, if your mouth continues to feel dry for more than 2 weeks, check with your dentist. Continuing dryness of the mouth may increase the chance of dental disease, including tooth decay, gum disease, and fungus infections.

Do not take this medicine within 2 or 3 hours of taking antacids or medicine for diarrhea. Taking antacids or antidiarrhea medicines and this medicine too close together may prevent this medicine from working properly.

Side Effects of This Medicine

Along with its needed effects, a medicine may cause some unwanted effects. Although not all of these side effects may occur, if they do occur they may need medical attention.

Check with your doctor as soon as possible if any of the following side effects occur:

Less common or rare

Blurred vision; eye pain; skin rash or hives

Symptoms of overdose

Blood in urine and/or stools; diarrhea; dizziness; drowsiness (severe); fast heartbeat; flushing or redness of face; headache (severe or continuing); lower back pain; pain or burning while urinating; ringing or buzzing in the ears; shortness of breath or troubled breathing; sweating; unusual tiredness or weakness

Other side effects may occur that usually do not need medical attention. These side effects may go away during treatment as your body adjusts to the medicine. However, check with your doctor if any of the following side effects continue or are bothersome:

Less common

Difficult urination (more common with large doses taken over a prolonged period of time); dryness of mouth, nose, or throat; nausea or vomiting; stomach upset or pain (more common with large doses taken over a prolonged period of time)

This medicine may cause your urine and/or stools to turn blue or blue-green. This is to be expected while you are taking this medicine.

Other side effects not listed above may also occur in some patients. If you notice any other effects, check with your doctor.

Revised: 05/11/93

ATTAPULGITE Oral

Some commonly used brand names are:

In the U.S.—

Diar-Aid	Kaopectate Advanced Formula
Diarrest	Kaopectate Maximum Strength
Diasorb	Kaopek
Diatrol	K-Pek
Donnagel	Parepectolin
Kaopectate	Rheaban

In Canada—

Fowler's	Kaopectate

Description

Attapulgite (at-a-PULL-gite) is taken by mouth to treat diarrhea. Attapulgite is a clay-like powder believed to work by adsorbing the bacteria or germ that may be causing the diarrhea.

This medicine is available without a prescription; however, the product's directions and warnings should be carefully followed. In addition, your doctor may have special instructions on the proper dose or use of attapulgite medicine for your medical condition.

Attapulgite is available in the following dosage forms:

Oral

Attapulgite

- Oral suspension (U.S. and Canada)
- Tablets (U.S. and Canada)
- Chewable tablets (U.S. and Canada)

Before Using This Medicine

If you are taking this medicine without a prescription, carefully read and follow any precautions on the label. For attapulgite, the following should be considered:

Pregnancy—This medicine is not absorbed into the body and is not likely to cause problems.

Breast-feeding—This medicine is not absorbed into the body and is not likely to cause problems.

Children—The fluid loss caused by diarrhea may result in a severe condition. For this reason, antidiarrheals must not be given to young children (under 3 years of age) without first checking with their doctor. In older children with diarrhea, antidiarrheals may be used, but it is also very important that a sufficient amount of liquids be given to replace the fluid lost by the body. If you have any questions about this, check with your health care professional.

Older adults—The fluid loss caused by diarrhea may result in a severe condition. For this reason, elderly persons with diarrhea, in addition to using an antidiarrheal, must receive a sufficient amount of liquids to replace the fluid lost by the body. If you have any questions about this, check with your health care professional.

Other medicines—Although certain medicines should not be used together at all, in other cases two different medicines may be used together even if an interaction might occur. In these cases, your doctor may want to change the dose, or other precautions may be necessary. *If you are taking any other medicine, do not take it within 2 to 3 hours of attapulgite.* Taking the medicines at the same time may prevent the other medicine from being absorbed by your body. If you have any questions about this, check with your health care professional.

Other medical problems—The presence of other medical problems may affect the use of attapulgite. Make sure you tell your doctor if you have any other medical problems, especially:

- Dysentery—This condition may get worse; a different kind of treatment may be needed

Proper Use of This Medicine

Do not use attapulgite to treat your diarrhea if you have a fever or if there is blood or mucus in your stools. Contact your doctor.

Take this medicine after each loose bowel movement following the directions in the product package, unless otherwise directed by your doctor.

Importance of diet and fluid intake while treating diarrhea:

- *In addition to using medicine for diarrhea, it is very important that you replace the fluid lost by the body and follow a proper diet.* For the first 24 hours you should eat gelatin and drink plenty of clear liquids, such as ginger ale, decaffeinated cola, decaffeinated tea, and broth. During the next 24 hours you may eat bland foods, such as cooked cereals, bread, crackers, and applesauce. Fruits, vegetables, fried or spicy foods, bran, candy, and caffeine and alcoholic beverages may make the condition worse.
- If too much fluid has been lost by the body due to the diarrhea a serious condition may develop. Check with your doctor as soon as possible if any of the following occurs:

  Decreased urination
  Dizziness and lightheadedness
  Dryness of mouth
  Increased thirst
  Wrinkled skin

Dosing—The dose of attapulgite will be different for different patients. *Follow your doctor's orders or the directions on the label.* The following information includes only the average doses of attapulgite.

The number of tablets or teaspoonfuls of suspension that you take depends on the strength of the medicine.

- For diarrhea:
  - —For *oral* dosage form (suspension):
    - Adults and children 12 years of age and older—The usual dose is 1200 to 1500 milligrams (mg) taken after each loose bowel movement. No more than 9000 mg should be taken in twenty-four hours.
    - Children 6 to 12 years of age—The usual dose is 600 mg taken after each loose bowel movement. No more than 4200 mg should be taken in twenty-four hours.
    - Children 3 to 6 years of age—The usual dose is 300 mg taken after each loose bowel movement. No more than 2100 mg should be taken in twenty-four hours.
    - Children up to 3 years of age—Use and dose must be determined by your doctor.
  - —For *oral* dosage form (tablets):
    - Adults and children 12 years of age and older—The usual dose is 1200 to 1500 mg taken after each loose bowel movement. No more than 9000 mg should be taken in twenty-four hours.
    - Children 6 to 12 years of age—The usual dose is 750 mg taken after each loose bowel movement. No more than 4500 mg should be taken in twenty-four hours.
    - Children 3 to 6 years of age—The oral suspension dosage form should be used in this age group.
  - —For *oral* dosage form (chewable tablets):
    - Adults and children 12 years of age and older—The usual dose is 1200 mg taken after each loose bowel movement. No more than 8400 mg should be taken in twenty-four hours.
    - Children 6 to 12 years of age—The usual dose is 600 mg taken after each loose bowel movement. No more than 4200 mg should be taken in twenty-four hours.
    - Children 3 to 6 years of age—The usual dose is 300 mg taken after each loose bowel movement. No more than 2100 mg should be taken in twenty-four hours.
    - Children up to 3 years of age—Use and dose must be determined by your doctor.

Storage—To store this medicine:

- Keep out of the reach of children.
- Store away from heat and direct light.
- Keep the liquid form of this medicine from freezing.
- Do not keep outdated medicine or medicine no longer needed. Be sure that any discarded medicine is out of the reach of children.

Precautions While Using This Medicine

Check with your doctor if your diarrhea does not stop after 1 or 2 days or if you develop a fever.

Side Effects of This Medicine

Along with its needed effects, a medicine may cause some unwanted effects. No serious side effects have been reported for this medicine. However, constipation may occur in some patients, especially if they take a lot of it. Check with your doctor as soon as possible if constipation continues or is bothersome.

Other side effects not listed above may also occur in some patients. If you notice any other effects, check with your doctor.

Revised: 08/12/94
Interim revision: 04/27/95

AZATHIOPRINE Systemic

In the U.S.—
Imuran

Generic name product may be available.

In Canada—
Imuran

Description

Azathioprine (ay-za-THYE-oh-preen) belongs to the group of medicines known as immunosuppressive agents. It is used to reduce the body's natural immunity in patients who receive organ transplants. It is also used to treat rheumatoid arthritis. Azathioprine may also be used for other conditions as determined by your doctor.

Azathioprine is a very strong medicine. You and your doctor should talk about the need for this medicine and its risks. Even though azathioprine may cause side effects that could be very serious, remember that it may be required to treat your medical problem.

Azathioprine is available only with your doctor's prescription, in the following dosage forms:

Oral
- Tablets (U.S. and Canada)

Parenteral
- Injection (U.S. and Canada)

Before Using This Medicine

In deciding to use a medicine, the risks of taking the medicine must be weighed against the good it will do. This is a decision you and your doctor will make. For azathioprine, the following should be considered:

Allergies—Tell your doctor if you have ever had any unusual or allergic reaction to azathioprine. Also tell your health care professional if you are allergic to any other substances, such as foods, preservatives, or dyes.

Pregnancy—Use of azathioprine is not recommended during pregnancy. It may cause birth defects if either the male or the female is using it at the time of conception. The use of birth control methods is recommended. If you have any questions about this, check with your doctor.

Breast-feeding—Azathioprine passes into breast milk. Because this medicine may cause serious side effects, breast-feeding is generally not recommended while you are using it.

Children—This medicine has been tested in children and, in effective doses, has not been shown to cause different side effects or problems than it does in adults.

Older adults—Many medicines have not been studied specifically in older people. Therefore, it may not be known whether they work exactly the same way they do in younger adults. Although there is no specific information comparing use of azathioprine in the elderly with use in other age groups, this medicine is not expected to cause different side effects or problems in older people than it does in younger adults.

Other medicines—Although certain medicines should not be used together at all, in other cases two different medicines may be used together even if an interaction might occur. In these cases, your doctor may want to change the dose, or other precautions may be necessary. When you are taking or receiving azathioprine it is especially important that your health care professional know if you are taking any of the following:

- Allopurinol (e.g., Zyloprim)—May interfere with removal of azathioprine from the body; effects of azathioprine (including toxicity) may be increased
- Chlorambucil (e.g., Leukeran) or
- Corticosteroids (cortisone-like medicine) or
- Cyclophosphamide (e.g., Cytoxan) or
- Cyclosporine (e.g., Sandimmune) or
- Mercaptopurine (e.g., Purinethol) or
- Muromonab-CD3 (monoclonal antibody) (e.g., Orthoclone OKT3)—There may be an increased risk of infection and cancer because azathioprine reduces the body's ability to fight them

Other medical problems—The presence of other medical problems may affect the use of azathioprine. Make sure you tell your doctor if you have any other medical problems, especially:

- Chickenpox (including recent exposure) or
- Herpes zoster (shingles)—Risk of severe disease affecting other parts of the body
- Gout—Allopurinol (used to treat gout) may increase wanted and unwanted effects of azathioprine
- Infection—Azathioprine decreases your body's ability to fight infection
- Kidney disease or
- Liver disease—Effects of azathioprine may be increased because of slower removal from the body
- Pancreatitis (inflammation of the pancreas)—Azathioprine can cause pancreatitis

Proper Use of This Medicine

Use this medicine only as directed by your doctor. Do not use more or less of it, and do not use it more often than your doctor ordered. The exact amount of medicine you need has been carefully worked out. Taking too much may increase the chance of side effects, while taking too little may not properly treat your condition.

This medicine is sometimes given together with certain other medicines. If you are using a combination of medicines, make sure that you take each one at the proper time and do not mix them up. Ask your health care professional to help you plan a way to remember to take your medicines at the right times.

Do not stop taking this medicine without first checking with your doctor.

Azathioprine sometimes causes nausea or vomiting. Taking this medicine after meals or at bedtime may lessen stomach upset. Ask your health care professional for other ways to lessen these effects.

If you vomit shortly after taking a dose of azathioprine, check with your doctor. You will be told whether to take the dose again or to wait until the next scheduled dose.

Dosing—The dose of azathioprine will be different for different patients. Follow your doctor's orders or the directions on the label. The following information includes only the average doses of azathioprine. *If your dose is different, do not change it* unless your doctor tells you to do so.

The number of doses you take each day, the time allowed between doses, and the length of time you take the medicine depend on the medical problem for which you are taking azathioprine.

- For *oral* dosage form (tablets):
  —For transplant rejection:
    - Adults, teenagers, and children: Dose is based on body weight or size. The usual beginning dose is 3 to 5 milligrams (mg) per kilogram (kg) (1.5 to 2 mg per pound) of body weight a day. As time goes on, your doctor may lower your dose to 1 to 2 mg per kg (0.5 to 1 mg per pound) a day.

  —For rheumatoid arthritis:
    - Adults, teenagers, and children: Dose is based on body weight or size. The usual beginning dose is 1 mg per kg (0.5 mg per pound) of body weight a day. Your doctor will increase this dose as needed. The highest dose is usually not more than 2.5 mg per kg (1 mg per pound) a day. Your doctor may then lower your dose as needed.
- For *injection* dosage form:
  —For transplant rejection:
    - Adults, teenagers, and children: Dose is based on body weight or size. The usual beginning dose is 3 to 5 milligrams (mg) per kilogram (kg) (1.5 to 2 mg per pound) of body weight a day. As time goes on, your doctor may lower your dose to 1 to 2 mg per kg (0.5 to 1 mg per pound) a day.

Missed dose—If you miss a dose of this medicine and your dosing schedule is:
- One dose a day—Do not take the missed dose at all and do not double the next one. Instead, go back to your regular dosing schedule and check with your doctor.
- More than one dose a day—Take the missed dose as soon as you remember it. If it is time for your next dose, take both doses together, then go back to your regular dosing schedule. If you miss more than one dose, check with your doctor.

Storage—To store this medicine:
- Keep out of the reach of children.
- Store away from heat and direct light.
- Do not store in the bathroom, near the kitchen sink, or in other damp places. Heat or moisture may cause the medicine to break down.
- Do not keep outdated medicine or medicine no longer needed. Be sure that any discarded medicine is out of the reach of children.

Precautions While Using This Medicine

It is very important that your doctor check your progress at regular visits to make sure that this medicine is working properly and to check for unwanted effects.

While you are being treated with azathioprine, and after you stop treatment with it, *do not have any immunizations (vaccinations) without your doctor's approval.* Azathioprine lowers your body's resistance and there is a chance you might get the infection the immunization is meant to prevent. In addition, other persons living in your household should not take oral polio vaccine since there is a chance they could pass the polio virus on to you. Also, avoid persons who have recently taken oral polio vaccine. Do not get close to them, and do not stay in the same room with them for very long. If you cannot take these precautions, you should consider wearing a protective face mask that covers the nose and mouth.

Azathioprine can temporarily lower the number of white blood cells in your blood, increasing the chance of getting an infection. It can also lower the number of platelets, which are necessary for proper blood clotting. If this occurs, there are certain precautions you can take, especially when your blood count is low, to reduce the risk of infection or bleeding:
- If you can, avoid people with infections. *Check with your doctor immediately* if you think you are getting an infection or if you get a fever or chills, cough or hoarseness, lower back or side pain, or painful or difficult urination.
- *Check with your doctor immediately* if you notice any unusual bleeding or bruising; black, tarry stools; blood in urine or stools; or pinpoint red spots on your skin.
- Be careful when using a regular toothbrush, dental floss, or toothpick. Your medical doctor, dentist, or nurse may recommend other ways to clean your teeth and gums. Check with your health care professional before having any dental work done.
- Do not touch your eyes or the inside of your nose unless you have just washed your hands and have not touched anything else in the meantime.
- Be careful not to cut yourself when you are using sharp objects such as a safety razor or fingernail or toenail cutters.
- Avoid contact sports or other situations where bruising or injury could occur.

Side Effects of This Medicine

Along with its needed effects, a medicine may cause some unwanted effects. Some side effects will have signs or symptoms that you can see or feel. Your doctor will watch for others by doing certain tests.

Also, because of the way these medicines act on the body, there is a chance that they might cause other unwanted effects that may not occur until months or years after the medicine is used. These delayed effects may include certain types of cancer, such as leukemia, lymphoma, or skin cancer. However, the risk of cancer seems to be lower in people taking azathioprine for arthritis. Discuss these possible effects with your doctor.

Check with your doctor immediately if any of the following side effects occur:

More common

Unusual tiredness or weakness

Less common

Cough or hoarseness; fever or chills; lower back or side pain; painful or difficult urination

Rare

Black, tarry stools; blood in urine or stools; fast heartbeat; fever (sudden); muscle or joint pain; nausea, vomiting, and diarrhea (severe); pinpoint red spots on skin; redness or blisters on skin; stomach pain (severe) with nausea and vomiting; unusual bleeding or bruising; unusual feeling of discomfort or illness (sudden)

Check with your doctor as soon as possible if any of the following side effects occur:

Rare

Shortness of breath; sores in mouth and on lips; stomach pain; swelling of feet or lower legs

This medicine may also cause the following side effect that your doctor will watch for:

Less common

Liver problems

For patients taking this medicine *for rheumatoid arthritis:*

- Signs and symptoms of blood problems (black, tarry stools; blood in urine or stools; cough or hoarseness; fever or chills; lower back or side pain; painful or difficult urination; pinpoint red spots on skin; unusual tiredness or weakness; or unusual bleeding or bruising) are less likely to occur in patients taking azathioprine for rheumatoid arthritis than for transplant rejection. This is because lower doses are often used.

Other side effects may occur that usually do not need medical attention. These side effects may go away during treatment as your body adjusts to the medicine. However, check with your doctor if any of the following side effects continue or are bothersome:

More common

Loss of appetite; nausea or vomiting

Less common

Skin rash

After you stop using this medicine, it may still produce some side effects that need attention. During this period of time *check with your doctor immediately* if you notice any of the following:

Black, tarry stools; blood in urine; cough or hoarseness; fever or chills; lower back or side pain; painful or difficult urination; pinpoint red spots on skin; unusual bleeding or bruising

Other side effects not listed above may also occur in some patients. If you notice any other effects, check with your doctor.

Additional Information

Once a medicine has been approved for marketing for a certain use, experience may show that it is also useful for other medical problems. Although these uses are not included in product labeling, azathioprine is used in certain patients with the following medical conditions:

- Bowel disease, inflammatory
- Hepatitis, chronic active
- Cirrhosis, biliary
- Lupus erythematosus, systemic
- Glomerulonephritis
- Nephrotic syndrome
- Myopathy, inflammatory
- Myasthenia gravis
- Dermatomyositis, systemic
- Pemphigoid
- Pemphigus

Other than the above information, there is no additional information relating to proper use, precautions, or side effects for these uses.

Revised: 05/06/93
Interim revision: 04/29/94; 07/30/97

AZELAIC ACID Topical†

A commonly used brand name in the U.S. is Azelex.

†Not commercially available in Canada.

Description

Azelaic (ay-ze-LAY-ik) acid is used to treat mild to moderate acne. It works in part by stopping the growth of skin bacteria that can help cause acne. Azelaic acid also helps to lessen acne by keeping skin pores (tiny openings on the skin's surface) clear.

It may also be used to treat other conditions as determined by your doctor.

Azelaic acid is available only with your doctor's prescription, in the following dosage form:

Topical

- Cream (U.S.)

Before Using This Medicine

In deciding to use a medicine, the risks of taking the medicine must be weighed against the good it will do. This is a decision you and your doctor will make. For azelaic acid, the following should be considered:

Allergies—Tell your doctor if you have ever had any unusual or allergic reaction to azelaic acid. Also tell your

health care professional if you are allergic to any other substances, such as foods, preservatives, or dyes.

Pregnancy—Azelaic acid has not been studied in pregnant women.

Breast-feeding—Small amounts of azelaic acid are absorbed through the skin into the bloodstream. It is possible that tiny amounts of the medicine may pass into the breast milk. However, this medicine has not been reported to cause problems in nursing babies.

Children—Studies of this medicine have been done only in adult patients, and there is no specific information comparing use of azelaic acid in children with use in other age groups.

Older adults—Many medicines have not been studied specifically in older people. Therefore, it may not be known whether they work exactly the same way they do in younger adults or if they cause different side effects or problems in older people. There is no specific information comparing use of azelaic acid in the elderly with use in other age groups.

Other medicines—Although certain medicines should not be used together at all, in other cases two different medicines may be used together even if an interaction might occur. In these cases, your doctor may want to change the dose, or other precautions may be necessary. Tell your doctor and pharmacist if you are using any other topical prescription or nonprescription (over-the-counter [OTC]) medicine that is to be applied to the same area of the skin.

Proper Use of This Medicine

When applying the cream, use only a small amount of medicine and apply a thin film to clean, dry skin that is affected by acne. It is important to rub it in gently but well.

After applying azelaic acid cream, wash your hands well to remove any medicine that may remain on them.

Keep this medicine away from the eyes, other mucous membranes, such as the mouth, lips, and inside of the nose, and sensitive areas of the neck. If the medicine accidently gets on these areas, wash with water at once.

To help clear up your acne completely, *it is very important that you keep using this medicine for the full time of treatment,* even if your symptoms begin to clear up after a short time. If you stop using this medicine too soon, your acne may return or get worse.

Dosing—The dose of azelaic acid will be different for different patients. *Follow your doctor's orders or the directions on the label.* The following information includes only the average doses of azelaic acid. *If your dose is different, do not change it* unless your doctor tells you to do so.

- For *topical* dosage form (cream):
  - For acne:
    - Adults and teenagers—Apply a small amount two times a day, usually in the morning and the evening, to areas affected by acne. Rub in gently but well. When you are just beginning to use the medicine, your doctor may want you to apply the medicine only one time a day for a few days, to reduce the chance of skin irritation.
    - Children—Use and dose must be determined by your doctor.

Missed dose—If you miss a dose of this medicine, use it as soon as possible. However, if it is almost time for your next dose, skip the missed dose and go back to your regular dosing schedule. Do not double doses.

Storage—To store this medicine:

- Keep out of the reach of children.
- Store away from heat and direct light.
- Keep the medicine from freezing. Do not refrigerate.
- Do not keep outdated medicine or medicine no longer needed. Be sure that any discarded medicine is out of the reach of children.

Precautions While Using This Medicine

If your acne does not improve within 4 weeks, or if it becomes worse, check with your health care professional. However, it may take longer than 4 weeks before you notice full improvement in your acne even if you use the medicine every day.

If this medicine causes too much redness, peeling, or dryness of your skin, check with your doctor. It may be necessary for you to reduce the number of times a day that you use the medicine or to stop using the medicine for a short time until your skin is less irritated.

If your doctor has ordered another medicine to be applied to the skin along with this medicine, it is best to apply them at different times. This may help keep your skin from becoming too irritated. Also, if the medicines are used at or near the same time, they may not work properly.

You may continue to use cosmetics (make-up) while you are using this medicine for acne. However, it is best to use only water-base cosmetics. Also, it is best not to use cosmetics too heavily or too often. They may make your acne worse. If you have any questions about this, check with your doctor.

Side Effects of This Medicine

Along with its needed effects, a medicine may cause some unwanted effects. Although not all of these side effects may occur, if they do occur, they may need medical attention.

Check with your doctor as soon as possible if any of the following side effects occur:

Rare

White spots or lightening of treated areas of dark skin—in patients with dark complexions, although usually not lightened beyond normal skin color

Other side effects may occur that usually do not need medical attention. These side effects may go away during treatment as your body adjusts to the medicine. However,

check with your doctor if any of the following side effects continue or are bothersome:

More common

Burning, stinging, or tingling of skin, mild; dryness of skin; itching of skin; peeling of skin; redness of skin

Other side effects not listed above may also occur in some patients. If you notice any other effects, check with your doctor.

Additional Information

Once a medicine has been approved for marketing for a certain use, experience may show that it is also useful for other medical problems. Although this use is not included in product labeling, azelaic acid is used in certain patients with the following medical condition:

- Melasma

Other than the above information, there is no additional information relating to proper use, precautions, or side effects for this use.

Developed: 06/27/96

AZITHROMYCIN Systemic

A commonly used brand name in the U.S. and Canada is Zithromax.

Description

Azithromycin (az-ith-roe-MYE-sin) is used to treat bacterial infections in many different parts of the body. It works by killing bacteria or preventing their growth. However, this medicine will not work for colds, flu, or other virus infections. Azithromycin may be used for other problems as determined by your doctor.

Azithromycin is available only with your doctor's prescription, in the following dosage form:

Oral

- Capsules (U.S. and Canada)

Before Using This Medicine

In deciding to use a medicine, the risks of taking the medicine must be weighed against the good it will do. This is a decision you and your doctor will make. For azithromycin, the following should be considered:

Allergies—Tell your doctor if you have ever had any unusual or allergic reaction to azithromycin or to any related medicines such as erythromycin. Also tell your health care professional if you are allergic to any other substances, such as foods, preservatives, or dyes.

Pregnancy—Azithromycin has not been studied in pregnant women. However, azithromycin has not been shown to cause birth defects or other problems in animal studies.

Breast-feeding—It is not known whether azithromycin passes into breast milk. Although most medicines pass into breast milk in small amounts, many of them may be used safely while breast-feeding. Mothers who are taking this medicine and who wish to breast-feed should discuss this with their doctor.

Children—This medicine has been tested in a limited number of children up to the age of 16. In effective doses, the medicine has not been shown to cause different side effects or problems than it does in adults.

Older adults—This medicine has been tested in a limited number of elderly patients and has not been shown to cause different side effects or problems in older people than it does in younger adults.

Other medicines—Although certain medicines should not be used together at all, in other cases two different medicines may be used together even if an interaction might occur. In these cases, your doctor may want to change the dose, or other precautions may be necessary. When you are taking azithromycin, it is especially important that your health care professional know if you are taking any of the following:

- Antacids, aluminum- and magnesium-containing—Antacids may decrease the amount of azithromycin in the blood, which may decrease its effects. To avoid problems, azithromycin should be taken at least 1 hour before or at least 2 hours after antacids

Other medical problems—The presence of other medical problems may affect the use of azithromycin. Make sure you tell your doctor if you have any other medical problems, especially:

- Liver disease—Patients with severe liver disease may have an increased chance of side effects

Proper Use of This Medicine

Azithromycin should be taken at least one hour before or at least 2 hours after meals. Taking azithromycin with food may decrease the amount of medicine that gets into your blood and keep the medicine from working properly.

To help clear up your infection completely, *keep taking azithromycin for the full time of treatment,* even if you begin to feel better after a few days. If you stop taking this medicine too soon, your symptoms may return.

Dosing—The dose of azithromycin will be different for different patients. *Follow your doctor's orders or the directions on the label.* The following information includes only the average doses of azithromycin. *If your dose is different, do not change it* unless your doctor tells you to do so.

The number of capsules that you take depends on the medical problem for which you are taking azithromycin.

- For *oral* dosage form (capsules):
  - —For bronchitis, strep throat, pneumonia, and skin infections:
    - Adults and children 16 years of age and older—500 milligrams (mg) on the first day, then 250 mg once a day on the second through fifth days.

- Children up to 16 years of age—Use and dose must be determined by your doctor.

—For chlamydia infections:

- Adults and children 16 years of age and older—1000 mg taken once as a single dose.
- Children up to 16 years of age—Use and dose must be determined by your doctor.

Missed dose—If you miss a dose of this medicine, take it as soon as possible. However, if it is almost time for your next dose, skip the missed dose and go back to your regular dosing schedule. Do not double doses.

Storage—To store this medicine:

- Keep out of the reach of children.
- Store away from heat and direct light.
- Do not store in the bathroom, near the kitchen sink, or in other damp places. Heat or moisture may cause the medicine to break down.
- Do not keep outdated medicine or medicine no longer needed. Be sure that any discarded medicine is out of the reach of children.

Precautions While Using This Medicine

If your symptoms do not improve within a few days, or if they become worse, check with your doctor.

Side Effects of This Medicine

Along with its needed effects, a medicine may cause some unwanted effects. Although not all of these side effects may occur, if they do occur they may need medical attention.

Stop taking this medicine and get emergency help immediately if any of the following side effects occur:

Rare

Difficulty in breathing; fever; joint pain; skin rash; swelling of face, mouth, neck, hands, and feet

Other side effects may occur that usually do not need medical attention. These side effects may go away during treatment as your body adjusts to the medicine. However, check with your doctor if any of the following side effects continue or are bothersome:

Less common

Diarrhea; nausea; stomach pain or discomfort; vomiting

Rare

Dizziness; headache

Other side effects not listed above may also occur in some patients. If you notice any other effects, check with your doctor.

Additional Information

Once a medicine has been approved for marketing for a certain use, experience may show that it is also useful for other medical problems. Although this use is not included in product labeling, azithromycin is used in certain patients with the following medical condition:

- Mycoplasmal pneumonia

Other than the above information, there is no additional information relating to proper use, precautions, or side effects for this use.

Revised: 05/27/94
Interim revision: 06/28/94

AZTREONAM Systemic†

A commonly used brand name in the U.S. is Azactam.

†Not commercially available in Canada.

Description

Aztreonam (az-TREE-oh-nam) is an antibiotic that is used to treat infections caused by bacteria. It works by killing bacteria or preventing their growth.

Aztreonam is used to treat bacterial infections in many different parts of the body. It is sometimes given with other antibiotics. This medicine will not work for colds, flu, or other virus infections.

This medicine is available only with your doctor's prescription. It is available in the following dosage form:

Parenteral

- Injection (U.S.)

Before Receiving This Medicine

In deciding to use a medicine, the risks of taking the medicine must be weighed against the good it will do. This is a decision you and your doctor will make. For aztreonam, the following should be considered:

Allergies—Tell your doctor if you have ever had any unusual or allergic reaction to aztreonam. Also tell your health care professional if you are allergic to any other substances, such as foods, preservatives, or dyes.

Pregnancy—Studies have not been done in humans. However, aztreonam has not been shown to cause birth defects or other problems in studies in rabbits and rats given up to 15 times the highest human daily dose.

Breast-feeding—Aztreonam passes into the breast milk in small amounts. However, this medicine is not absorbed when taken by mouth, and problems have not been seen in nursing babies.

Children—This medicine has been tested in a limited number of children up to 12 years of age and has not been shown to cause different side effects or problems in children than it does in adults.

Older adults—Aztreonam has been tested in a limited number of patients 65 years of age or older and has not been shown to cause different side effects or problems in older people than it does in younger adults.

Other medicines—Although certain medicines should not be used together at all, in other cases two different medicines may be used together even if an interaction might occur. In these cases, your doctor may want to change the

dose, or other precautions may be necessary. Tell your health care professional if you are taking any other prescription or nonprescription (over-the-counter [OTC]) medicine.

Other medical problems—The presence of other medical problems may affect the use of aztreonam. Make sure you tell your doctor if you have any other medical problems, especially:

- Cirrhosis (liver disease)—Patients receiving high doses of aztreonam for a long time, who also have severe liver disease, may have an increased chance of side effects
- Kidney disease—Patients with kidney disease may have an increased chance of side effects

Proper Use of This Medicine

To help clear up your infection completely, *aztreonam must be given for the full time of treatment,* even if you begin to feel better after a few days. Also, this medicine works best when there is a constant amount in the blood or urine. To help keep the amount constant, aztreonam must be given on a regular schedule.

Dosing—The dose of aztreonam will be different for different patients. *Follow your doctor's orders or the directions on the label.* The following information includes only the average doses of aztreonam. Your dose may be different if you have kidney disease. *If your dose is different, do not change it* unless your doctor tells you to do so.

- For *injection* dosage form:
  —Adults and children 12 years of age and older: 1 to 2 grams injected slowly into a vein over a twenty- to sixty-minute period. This is repeated every six to twelve hours.
  —Children up to 12 years of age: Dosage is based on body weight and must be determined by your doctor.

Side Effects of This Medicine

Along with its needed effects, a medicine may cause some unwanted effects. Although not all of these side effects may occur, if they do occur they may need medical attention.

Check with your doctor immediately if any of the following side effects occur:

Less common

Pain, swelling, or redness at place of injection; skin rash, redness, or itching

Other side effects may occur that usually do not need medical attention. These side effects may go away during treatment as your body adjusts to the medicine. However, check with your doctor if any of the following side effects continue or are bothersome:

Less common or rare

Abdominal or stomach cramps; nausea, vomiting, or diarrhea

Other side effects not listed above may also occur in some patients. If you notice any other effects, check with your doctor.

Revised: 02/23/93

BACILLUS CALMETTE-GUÉRIN (BCG) LIVE Mucosal-Local

Some commonly used brand names are:

In the U.S.—
TheraCys
TICE BCG

In Canada—
ImmuCyst

Description

Bacillus Calmette-Guérin (BCG) is used as a solution that is run through a tube (instilled through a catheter) into the bladder to treat bladder cancer. The exact way it works against cancer is not known, but it may work by stimulating the body's immune system.

BCG is to be administered only by or under the immediate supervision of your doctor. It is available in the following dosage form:

Mucosal-Local
- Bladder instillation (U.S. and Canada)

Before Receiving This Medicine

In deciding to use a medicine, the risks of taking the medicine must be weighed against the good it will do. This is a decision you and your doctor will make. For BCG, the following should be considered:

Allergies—Tell your doctor if you have ever had any unusual or allergic reaction to BCG.

Pregnancy—BCG has not been studied in pregnant women or animals. Make sure your doctor knows if you are pregnant or if you may become pregnant before receiving BCG.

Breast-feeding—It is not known whether BCG passes into the breast milk.

Children—There is no specific information comparing use of BCG for treatment of cancer in children with use in other age groups.

Older adults—This medicine has been tested and has not been shown to cause different side effects or problems in older people than it does in younger adults.

Other medicines—Although certain medicines should not be used together at all, in other cases two different medicines may be used together even if an interaction might occur. In these cases, your doctor may want to change the dose, or other precautions may be necessary. When receiving BCG it is especially important that your health care professional know if you are taking any of the following:

- Amphotericin B by injection (e.g., Fungizone) or
- Antineoplastics (cancer medicine) or
- Antithyroid agents (medicine for overactive thyroid) or
- Azathioprine (e.g., Imuran) or
- Chlorambucil (e.g., Leukeran) or
- Chloramphenicol (e.g., Chloromycetin) or
- Colchicine or
- Corticosteroids (cortisone-like medicine) or
- Cyclophosphamide (e.g., Cytoxan) or
- Cyclosporine (e.g., Sandimmune) or
- Flucytosine (e.g., Ancobon) or
- Ganciclovir (e.g., Cytovene) or
- Interferon (e.g., Intron A, Roferon-A) or
- Mercaptopurine (e.g., Purinethol) or
- Methotrexate (e.g., Mexate) or
- Muromonab-CD3 (e.g., Orthoclone OKT3) or
- Plicamycin (e.g., Mithracin) or
- Zidovudine (e.g., AZT, Retrovir)—Because these medicines reduce the body's natural immunity, they may prevent BCG from stimulating the immune system and will cause it to be less effective. In addition, the risk of infection may be increased

Other medical problems—The presence of other medical problems may affect the use of BCG. Make sure you tell your doctor if you have any other medical problems, especially:

- Fever—Infection may be present and could cause problems
- Immunity problems—BCG treatment is less effective and there is a risk of infection
- Urinary tract infection—Infection and irritation of the bladder may occur

Proper Use of This Medicine

Your doctor will ask you to empty your bladder completely before the solution is instilled into it.

Follow your doctor's instructions carefully about how long to hold the solution in your bladder:

- The solution should be held in your bladder for 2 hours. If you think you cannot hold it, tell your health care professional.
- During the first hour, your doctor may have you lie for 15 minutes each on your stomach, back, and each side.
- When you do empty your bladder, you should be sitting down.

It is important that you drink extra fluids for several hours after each treatment with BCG so that you will pass more urine. Also, empty your bladder frequently. This will help prevent bladder problems.

BCG is a live product. In other words, it contains active bacteria that can cause infection. Some bacteria will be present for several hours in urine that you pass after each treatment with BCG. Any urine that you pass during the first 6 hours after each treatment should be disinfected with an equal amount (usually about 1 cup) of undiluted household bleach. After the bleach is added to the urine, it should be allowed to sit for 15 minutes before it is flushed. If you have any questions about this, check with your doctor.

Dosing—The dose of BCG will be different for different patients. The dose that is used may depend on a number of things. *If you are receiving BCG at home, follow your doctor's orders or the directions on the label.* If you have any questions about the proper dose of BCG, ask your doctor.

Precautions While Using This Medicine

While you are being treated with BCG, and for 6 to 12 weeks after you stop treatment with it, avoid contact with people who have tuberculosis. If you think you have been exposed to someone with tuberculosis, tell your doctor.

While you are being treated with BCG and for a few weeks after you stop treatment with it, do not have any immunizations (vaccinations) without your doctor's approval.

Side Effects of This Medicine

Along with its needed effects, a medicine may cause some unwanted effects. Although not all of these side effects may occur, if they do occur they may need medical attention.

Check with your doctor as soon as possible if any of the following side effects occur:

More common

Blood in urine; fever and chills; frequent urge to urinate; increased frequency of urination; joint pain; nausea and vomiting; painful urination (severe or continuing)

Rare

Cough; skin rash

Other side effects may occur that usually do not need medical attention. These side effects may go away during treatment as your body adjusts to the medicine. However, check with your doctor if any of the following side effects continue or are bothersome or if you have any questions about them:

More common

Burning during first urination after treatment

After you stop using this medicine, your body may need time to adjust. The length of time this takes depends on the amount of medicine you were using and how long you used it. During this period of time (up to 6 months after treatment with BCG) check with your doctor if you notice any of the following side effects:

Cough; fever

Other side effects not listed above may also occur in some patients. If you notice any other effects, check with your doctor.

Revised: 07/11/94

BACILLUS CALMETTE-GUÉRIN (BCG) LIVE Systemic

A commonly used brand name in the U.S. is TICE BCG

Description

Bacillus Calmette-Guérin (Ba-SIL'es Kal-met Geh-rin) (BCG) vaccine is given by injection to help prevent tuberculosis (TB). TB is a serious disease that can cause severe illness. It is spread by close contact with people who already have TB, such as people living in the same house. Some infected people do not appear to be sick, but they can still spread TB to others. BCG vaccine does not provide 100% protection. Therefore it is important to avoid people with TB, even if you have received the vaccine.

BCG vaccine is to be administered only by or under the direct supervision of a doctor. It is available in the following dosage forms:

Parenteral

- Multiple-puncture device (U.S.)
- Injection (Canada)

Before Receiving This Vaccine

In deciding to use a medicine, the risks of taking the medicine must be weighed against the good it will do. This is a decision you and your doctor will make. For BCG vaccine, the following should be considered:

Allergies—Tell your doctor if you have ever had any unusual or allergic reaction to BCG vaccine. Also tell your health care professional if you are allergic to any other substances, such as foods, preservatives, or dyes.

Pregnancy—Studies on effects in pregnancy have not been done in either humans or animals. Before you receive BCG vaccine, make sure your doctor knows if you are pregnant or if you may become pregnant.

Breast-feeding—It is not known whether BCG vaccine passes into the breast milk. Although most medicines pass into breast milk in small amounts, many of them may be used safely while breast-feeding. Mothers who will receive or have received BCG vaccine and who wish to breast-feed should discuss this with their doctor.

Children—BCG vaccine has been used widely in children, and it has not been reported to cause different side effects or problems in children than it does in adults.

Older adults—Many medicines have not been studied specifically in older people. Therefore, it may not be known whether they work exactly the same way they do in younger adults or if they cause different side effects or problems in older people. There is no specific information comparing use of BCG vaccine in the elderly with use in other age groups.

Other medicines—Although certain medicines should not be used together at all, in other cases two different medicines may be used together even if an interaction might occur. In these cases, your doctor may want to change the dose, or other precautions may be necessary. When you are going to receive BCG vaccine, it is especially important that your health care professional know if you are taking any of the following:

- Antituberculosis medicines (rifampin [e.g., Rifadin], isoniazid [e.g., Nydrazid])—These medicines may prevent BCG vaccine from working properly

- Corticosteroids (e.g., cortisone-like medicine)—Concurrent administration may result in increased risk of systemic infection
- Immunosuppressants (e.g., Sandimmune, Imuran)—Because these medicines reduce the body's natural immunity, they may prevent BCG from working properly. Also, the risk of infection may be increased
- Virus vaccines (e.g., Poliovax)—Concurrent administration with BCG is not recommended

Other medical problems—The presence of other medical problems may affect the use of BCG vaccine. Make sure you tell your doctor if you have any other medical problems, especially:

- Fever—If an infection is present, the chance of side effects from BCG vaccine may be increased
- Immunity problems—BCG vaccine may not work properly in persons with decreased natural immunity; also, the risk of side effects from BCG vaccine may be increased.
- Widespread skin infections

Proper Use of This Vaccine

Dosing—The dose of BCG vaccine may be different for different patients.

Side Effects of This Vaccine

Along with its needed effects, a medicine may cause some unwanted effects. Although not all of these side effects may occur, if they do occur they may need medical attention.

More common

Accumulation of pus; peeling or scaling of the skin; sores at place of injection; sores at different sites of the skin; swollen lymph glands

Rare

Cough; fever; increase in bone pain; skin rash

Other side effects not listed above may also occur in some patients. If you notice any other effects, check with your doctor.

Developed: 07/20/95

BACLOFEN Systemic

Some commonly used brand names are:

In the U.S.—

Lioresal

Generic name product may also be available.

In Canada—

Alpha-Baclofen
PMS-Baclofen
Lioresal

Description

Baclofen (BAK-loe-fen) is used to help relax certain muscles in your body. It relieves the spasms, cramping, and tightness of muscles caused by medical problems such as multiple sclerosis or certain injuries to the spine. Baclofen does not cure these problems, but it may allow other treatment, such as physical therapy, to be more helpful in improving your condition.

Baclofen acts on the central nervous system (CNS) to produce its muscle relaxant effects. Its actions on the CNS may also cause some of the medicine's side effects. Baclofen may also be used to relieve other conditions as determined by your doctor.

This medicine is available only with your doctor's prescription, in the following dosage form:

Oral

- Tablets (U.S. and Canada)

Before Using This Medicine

In deciding to use a medicine, the risks of taking the medicine must be weighed against the good it will do. This is a decision you and your doctor will make. For baclofen, the following should be considered:

Allergies—Tell your doctor if you have ever had any unusual or allergic reaction to baclofen. Also tell your health care professional if you are allergic to any other substances, such as foods, preservatives, or dyes.

Pregnancy—Studies on birth defects with baclofen have not been done in humans. However, studies in animals have shown that baclofen, when given in doses several times the human dose, increases the chance of hernias and incomplete or slow development of bones in the fetus, and of lower birth weight.

Breast-feeding—Baclofen passes into the breast milk. However, this medicine has not been reported to cause problems in nursing babies.

Children—Studies on this medicine have been done only in adult patients, and there is no specific information comparing use of baclofen in children with use in other age groups.

Older adults—Side effects such as hallucinations, confusion or mental depression, other mood or mental changes, and severe drowsiness may be especially likely to occur in elderly patients, who are usually more sensitive than younger adults to the effects of baclofen.

Other medicines—Although certain medicines should not be used together at all, in other cases two different medicines may be used together even if an interaction might occur. In these cases, your doctor may want to change the dose, or other precautions may be necessary. When you are taking baclofen, it is especially important that your health care professional know if you are taking any of the following:

- Antidepressants, tricyclic (amitriptyline [e.g., Elavil], amoxapine [e.g., Asendin], clomipramine [e.g., Anafranil], desipramine [e.g., Pertofrane], doxepin [e.g., Sinequan], imipramine [e.g., Tofranil], nortriptyline [e.g., Av-

entyl], protriptyline [e.g., Vivactil], trimipramine [e.g., Surmontil]) or
- Central nervous system (CNS) depressants—The chance of side effects may be increased

Other medical problems—The presence of other medical problems may affect the use of baclofen. Make sure you tell your doctor if you have any other medical problems, especially:
- Diabetes mellitus (sugar diabetes)—Baclofen may raise blood sugar levels
- Epilepsy or
- Kidney disease or
- Mental or emotional problems or
- Stroke or other brain disease—The chance of side effects may be increased

Proper Use of This Medicine

Dosing—The dose of baclofen will be different for different patients. *Follow your doctor's orders or the directions on the label.* The following information includes only the average doses of baclofen. *If your dose is different, do not change it* unless your doctor tells you to do so.
- For *oral* dosage form (tablets):
  —For muscle relaxation:
    - Adults and teenagers—At first, the dose is 5 milligrams (mg) three times a day. Then, each dose may be increased by 5 mg every three days until the desired response is reached. No more than 80 mg should be taken within a twenty-four hour period.
    - Children—Use and dose must be determined by your doctor.

Missed dose—If you miss a dose of this medicine, and you remember within an hour or so of the missed dose, take it as soon as you remember. However, if you do not remember until later, skip the missed dose and go back to your regular dosing schedule. Do not double doses.

Storage—To store this medicine:
- Keep out of the reach of children.
- Store away from heat and direct light.
- Do not store in the bathroom, near the kitchen sink, or in other damp places. Heat or moisture may cause the medicine to break down.
- Do not keep outdated medicine or medicine no longer needed. Be sure that any discarded medicine is out of the reach of children.

Precautions While Using This Medicine

Do not suddenly stop taking this medicine. Unwanted effects may occur if the medicine is stopped suddenly. Check with your doctor for the best way to reduce gradually the amount you are taking before stopping completely.

This medicine will add to the effects of alcohol and other CNS depressants (medicines that slow down the nervous system, possibly causing drowsiness). Some examples of CNS depressants are antihistamines or medicine for hay fever, other allergies, or colds; sedatives, tranquilizers, or sleeping medicine; prescription pain medicine or narcotics; barbiturates; medicine for seizures; other muscle relaxants; or anesthetics, including some dental anesthetics. *Check with your doctor before taking any of the above while you are using baclofen.*

This medicine may cause drowsiness, dizziness, vision problems, or clumsiness or unsteadiness in some people. *Make sure you know how you react to this medicine before you drive, use machines, or do anything else that could be dangerous if you are not alert, well-coordinated, and able to see well.*

For *diabetic patients:*
- This medicine may cause your blood sugar levels to rise. If you notice a change in the results of your blood or urine sugar test or if you have any questions about this, check with your doctor.

Side Effects of This Medicine

Along with its needed effects, a medicine may cause some unwanted effects. Although not all of these side effects may occur, if they do occur they may need medical attention.

Check with your doctor as soon as possible if any of the following side effects occur:

Rare

Bloody or dark urine; chest pain; fainting; hallucinations (seeing or hearing things that are not there); mental depression or other mood changes; ringing or buzzing in the ears; skin rash or itching

Symptoms of overdose

Blurred or double vision; convulsions (seizures); muscle weakness (severe); shortness of breath or unusually slow or troubled breathing; vomiting

Other side effects may occur that usually do not need medical attention. These side effects may go away during treatment as your body adjusts to the medicine. However, check with your doctor if any of the following side effects continue or are bothersome:

More common

Confusion; dizziness or lightheadedness; drowsiness; nausea; unusual weakness, especially muscle weakness

Less common or rare

Abdominal or stomach pain or discomfort; clumsiness, unsteadiness, trembling, or other problems with muscle control; constipation; diarrhea; difficult or painful urination or decrease in amount of urine; false sense of well-being; frequent urge to urinate or uncontrolled urination; headache; loss of appetite; low blood pressure; muscle or joint pain; numbness or tingling in hands or feet; pounding heartbeat; sexual problems in males; slurred speech or other speech problems; stuffy nose; swelling of ankles; trouble in sleeping; unexplained muscle stiffness; unusual excitement; unusual tiredness; weight gain

Some side effects may occur after you have stopped taking this medicine, especially if you stop taking it suddenly. *Check with your doctor immediately* if any of the following effects occur:

Convulsions (seizures); hallucinations (seeing or hearing things that are not there); increase in muscle spasm, cramping, or tightness; mood or mental changes; unusual nervousness or restlessness

Other side effects not listed above may also occur in some patients. If you notice any other effects, check with your doctor.

Additional Information

Once a medicine has been approved for marketing for a certain use, experience may show that it is also useful for other medical problems. Although this use is not included in product labeling, baclofen is used in certain patients with trigeminal neuralgia (severe burning or stabbing pain along the nerves in the face); also called ''tic douloureux.''

There is no additional information relating to proper use, precautions, or side effects for this use of baclofen.

Revised: 07/09/91
Interim revision: 06/13/95

BARBITURATES Systemic

Some commonly used brand names are:

In the U.S.—

Alurate[2]
Amytal[1]
Barbita[7]
Busodium[3]
Butalan[3]
Butisol[3]
Luminal[7]
Mebaral[4]
Nembutal[6]
Sarisol No. 2[3]
Seconal[8]
Solfoton[7]
Tuinal[9]

In Canada—

Amytal[1]
Ancalixir[7]
Butisol[3]
Mebaral[4]
Nembutal[6]
Nova Rectal[6]
Novopentobarb[6]
Novosecobarb[8]
Seconal[8]
Tuinal[9]

In other countries—

Gemonil[5]

Note: For quick reference, the following barbiturates are numbered to match the corresponding brand names.

This information applies to the following medicines:

1. Amobarbital (am-oh-BAR-bi-tal)‡
2. Aprobarbital (a-proe-BAR-bi-tal)†
3. Butabarbital (byoo-ta-BAR-bi-tal)‡
4. Mephobarbital (me-foe-BAR-bi-tal)
5. Metharbital (meth-AR-bi-tal)*†
6. Pentobarbital (pen-toe-BAR-bi-tal)‡
7. Phenobarbital (fee-noe-BAR-bi-tal)‡§
8. Secobarbital (see-koe-BAR-bi-tal)‡
9. Secobarbital and Amobarbital (see-koe-BAR-bi-tal and am-oh-BAR-bi-tal)

*Not commercially available in the U.S.
†Not commercially available in Canada.
‡Generic name product may also be available in the U.S.
§Generic name product may also be available in Canada.

Description

Barbiturates (bar-BI-tyoo-rates) belong to the group of medicines called central nervous system (CNS) depressants (medicines that cause drowsiness). They act on the brain and CNS to produce effects that may be helpful or harmful. This depends on the individual patient's condition and response and the amount of medicine taken.

Some of the barbiturates may be used before surgery to relieve anxiety or tension. In addition, some of the barbiturates are used as anticonvulsants to help control seizures in certain disorders or diseases, such as epilepsy. Barbiturates may also be used for other conditions as determined by your doctor.

The barbiturates have been used to treat insomnia (trouble in sleeping); but if they are used regularly (for example, every day) for insomnia, they are usually not effective for longer than 2 weeks. The barbiturates have also been used to relieve nervousness or restlessness during the daytime. However, the barbiturates have generally been replaced by safer medicines for the treatment of insomnia and daytime nervousness or tension.

If too much of a barbiturate is used, it may become habit-forming.

Barbiturates should not be used for anxiety or tension caused by the stress of everyday life.

These medicines are available only with your doctor's prescription, in the following dosage forms:

Oral

Amobarbital
- Capsules (U.S. and Canada)
- Tablets (U.S. and Canada)

Aprobarbital
- Elixir (U.S.)

Butabarbital
- Capsules (U.S.)
- Elixir (U.S.)
- Tablets (U.S. and Canada)

Mephobarbital
- Tablets (U.S. and Canada)

Metharbital
- Tablets (Other countries)

Pentobarbital
- Capsules (U.S. and Canada)
- Elixir (U.S.)

Phenobarbital
- Capsules (U.S.)
- Elixir (U.S. and Canada)
- Tablets (U.S. and Canada)

Secobarbital
- Capsules (U.S. and Canada)

Secobarbital and Amobarbital
- Capsules (U.S. and Canada)

Parenteral

Amobarbital
- Injection (U.S. and Canada)

Pentobarbital
- Injection (U.S. and Canada)

Phenobarbital
- Injection (U.S. and Canada)

Secobarbital
- Injection (U.S.)

Rectal

Pentobarbital
- Suppositories (U.S. and Canada)

Before Using This Medicine

In deciding to use a medicine, the risks of taking the medicine must be weighed against the good it will do. This is a decision you and your doctor will make. For barbiturates, the following should be considered:

Allergies—Tell your doctor if you have ever had any unusual or allergic reaction to barbiturates. Also tell your health care professional if you are allergic to any other substances, such as foods, preservatives, or dyes.

Pregnancy—Barbiturates have been shown to increase the chance of birth defects in humans. However, this medicine may be needed in serious diseases or other situations that threaten the mother's life. Be sure you have discussed this and the following information with your doctor:

- Taking barbiturates regularly during pregnancy may cause bleeding problems in the newborn infant. In addition, taking barbiturates regularly during the last 3 months of pregnancy may cause the baby to become dependent on the medicine. This may lead to withdrawal side effects in the baby after birth.
- One study in humans has suggested that barbiturates taken during pregnancy may increase the chance of brain tumors in the baby.
- Barbiturates taken for anesthesia during labor and delivery may reduce the force and frequency of contractions of the uterus; this may prolong labor and delay delivery.
- Use of barbiturates during labor may cause breathing problems in the newborn infant.

Breast-feeding—Barbiturates pass into the breast milk and may cause drowsiness, slow heartbeat, shortness of breath, or troubled breathing in babies of nursing mothers taking this medicine.

Children—Unusual excitement may be more likely to occur in children, who are usually more sensitive than adults to the effects of barbiturates.

Older adults—Confusion, mental depression, and unusual excitement may be more likely to occur in the elderly, who are usually more sensitive than younger adults to the effects of barbiturates.

Other medicines—Although certain medicines should not be used together at all, in other cases 2 different medicines may be used together even if an interaction might occur. In these cases, your doctor may want to change the dose, or other precautions may be necessary. When you are taking a barbiturate, it is especially important that your health care professional know if you are taking any of the following:

- Adrenocorticoids (cortisone-like medicine) or
- Anticoagulants (blood thinners) or
- Carbamazepine or
- Corticotropin (ACTH)—Barbiturates may decrease the effects of these medicines
- Central nervous system (CNS) depressants (medicines that cause drowsiness)—Using these medicines with barbiturates may result in increased CNS depressant effects
- Divalproex sodium or
- Valproic acid—Using these medicines with barbiturates may change the amount of either medicine that you need to take
- Oral contraceptives (birth control pills) containing estrogens—Barbiturates may decrease the effectiveness of these oral contraceptives, and you may need to change to a different type of birth control

Other medical problems—The presence of other medical problems may affect the use of barbiturates. Make sure you tell your doctor if you have any other medical problems, especially:

- Alcohol abuse (or history of) or
- Drug abuse or dependence (or history of)—Dependence on barbiturates may develop
- Anemia (severe) or
- Asthma (history of), emphysema, or other chronic lung disease or
- Diabetes mellitus (sugar diabetes) or
- Hyperactivity (in children) or
- Mental depression or
- Overactive thyroid or
- Porphyria (or history of)—Barbiturates may make the condition worse
- Kidney disease or
- Liver disease—Higher blood levels of barbiturates may result, increasing the chance of side effects
- Pain—Barbiturates may cause unexpected excitement or mask important symptoms of more serious problems
- Underactive adrenal gland—Barbiturates may interfere with the effects of other medicines needed for this condition

Proper Use of This Medicine

For patients taking the *extended-release capsule or tablet form* of this medicine:

- These capsules or tablets are to be swallowed whole. Do not break, crush, or chew before swallowing.

For patients using the *rectal suppository form* of this medicine:

- To insert the suppository: First remove the foil wrapper and moisten the suppository with cold water. Lie down on your side and use your finger to push the suppository well up into the rectum.
- Wash your hands with soap and water.

Use this medicine only as directed by your doctor. Do not use more of it, do not use it more often, and do not use it for a longer time than your doctor ordered. If too much is used, it may become habit-forming (causing mental or physical dependence).

If you think this medicine is not working properly after you have taken it for a few weeks, *do not increase the dose.* To do so may increase the chance of your becoming dependent on the medicine. Instead, check with your doctor.

If you are taking this medicine for epilepsy, it must be taken every day in regularly spaced doses as ordered by your doctor in order for it to control your seizures. This is necessary to keep a constant amount of medicine in the blood. To help keep the amount constant, do not miss any doses.

Dosing—The dose of barbiturates will be different for different patients. *Follow your doctor's orders or the directions on the label.* The following information includes only the average doses of barbiturates. *If your dose is different, do not change it* unless your doctor tells you to do so.

The number of capsules, tablets, or teaspoonfuls of elixir that you take, the number of suppositories you use, or the number of injections you receive depends on the strength of the medicine. Also, *the number of doses you take each day, the time allowed between doses, and the length of time you take the medicine depend on the medical problem for which you are taking barbiturates.*

For amobarbital

- For *oral* dosage form (tablets or capsules):
  - —For trouble in sleeping:
    - Adults—65 to 200 milligrams (mg) at bedtime.
    - Children—Dose must be determined by your doctor.
  - —For daytime sedation:
    - Adults—50 to 300 mg, taken in smaller doses during the day.
    - Children—Dose is based on body weight or size and must be determined by your doctor. The usual dose is 2 mg per kilogram (kg) (0.9 mg per pound) of body weight taken three times a day.
  - —For sedation before surgery:
    - Adults—200 mg taken one to two hours before surgery.
    - Children—Dose is based on body weight and must be determined by your doctor. The usual dose is 2 to 6 mg per kg (0.9 to 2.7 mg per pound) of body weight, taken before surgery. However, the dose is usually not more than 100 mg.
  - —For sedation during labor:
    - Adults—200 to 400 mg every one to three hours if needed. However, the total dose is usually not more than 1000 mg.
- For *injection* dosage form:
  - —For trouble in sleeping:
    - Adults—65 to 200 mg, injected into a muscle or vein.
    - Children up to 6 years of age—Dose is based on body weight and must be determined by your doctor. The usual dose is 2 to 3 mg per kg (0.9 to 1.4 mg per pound) of body weight, injected into a muscle.
    - Children 6 years of age and over—Dose is based on body weight and must be determined by your doctor. The usual dose is 2 to 3 mg per kg (0.9 to 1.4 mg per pound) of body weight, injected into a muscle, or 65 to 500 mg injected into a vein.
  - —For daytime sedation:
    - Adults—30 to 50 mg two or three times a day, injected into a muscle or vein.
  - —For sedation before surgery:
    - Children—Dose is based on body weight and must be determined by your doctor. The usual dose is 3 to 5 mg per kg (1.4 to 2.3 mg per pound) of body weight or 65 to 500 mg per dose, injected into a vein.
  - —For control of seizures:
    - Adults and children 6 years of age and over—65 to 500 mg per dose, injected into a vein.
    - Children up to 6 years of age—Dose is based on body weight or size and must be determined by your doctor. The usual dose is 3 to 5 mg per kg (1.4 to 2.3 mg per pound) of body weight, injected into a muscle or vein.

For aprobarbital

- For *oral* dosage form (elixir):
  - —For trouble in sleeping:
    - Adults—40 to 160 milligrams (mg) at bedtime.
    - Children—Dose must be determined by your doctor.
  - —For daytime sedation:
    - Adults—40 mg three times a day.
    - Children—Dose must be determined by your doctor.

For butabarbital

- For *oral* dosage form (elixir or tablets):
  - —For trouble in sleeping:
    - Adults—50 to 100 milligrams (mg) at bedtime.
    - Children—Dose must be determined by your doctor.
  - —For daytime sedation:
    - Adults—15 to 30 mg three or four times a day.
    - Children—Dose is based on body weight or size and must be determined by your doctor. The usual dose is 2 mg per kilogram (kg) (0.9 mg per pound) of body weight three times a day.
  - —For sedation before surgery:
    - Adults—50 to 100 mg sixty to ninety minutes before surgery.
    - Children—Dose is based on body weight and must be determined by your doctor. The usual dose is 2 to 6 mg per kg (0.9 to 2.7 mg per pound) of body weight. However, the dose is usually not more than 100 mg.

For mephobarbital

- For *oral* dosage form (tablets):
  - —For daytime sedation:
    - Adults—32 to 100 milligrams (mg) three or four times a day.
    - Children—16 to 32 mg three or four times a day.

—For control of seizures:

• Adults—200 to 600 mg a day, taken in smaller doses during the day.

• Children up to 5 years of age—16 to 32 mg three or four times a day.

• Children 5 years of age and over—32 to 64 mg three or four times a day.

For metharbital

• For *oral* dosage form (tablets):

—For control of seizures:

• Adults—At first, 100 milligrams (mg) one to three times a day. Your doctor may increase your dose if needed. However, the dose is usually not more than 800 mg a day.

• Children—50 mg one to three times a day.

For pentobarbital

• For *oral* dosage form (elixir or capsules):

—For trouble in sleeping:

• Adults—100 milligrams (mg) at bedtime.

• Children—Dose must be determined by your doctor.

—For daytime sedation:

• Adults—20 mg three or four times a day.

• Children—Dose is based on body weight and must be determined by your doctor. The usual dose is 2 to 6 mg per kilogram (kg) (0.9 to 2.7 mg per pound) of body weight per day.

—For sedation before surgery:

• Adults—100 mg before surgery.

• Children—Dose is based on body weight and must be determined by your doctor. The usual dose is 2 to 6 mg per kilogram (0.9 to 2.7 mg per pound) of body weight, taken before surgery. However, the dose is usually not more than 100 mg.

• For *injection* dosage form:

—For trouble in sleeping:

• Adults—150 to 200 mg, injected into a muscle. Or, 100 mg injected into a vein, with additional small doses given if needed. However, the dose is usually not more than 500 mg.

• Children—Dose is based on body weight and must be determined by your doctor. The usual dose is 2 to 6 mg per kg (0.9 to 2.7 mg per pound) of body weight, injected into a muscle. Or, 50 mg injected into a vein, with additional small doses given if needed.

—For sedation before surgery:

• Adults—150 to 200 mg, injected into a muscle.

• Children—Dose is based on body weight and must be determined by your doctor. The usual dose is 2 to 6 mg per kg (0.9 to 2.7 mg per pound) of body weight, injected into a muscle. However, the dose is usually not more than 100 mg.

—For control of seizures:

• Adults—At first, 100 mg injected into a vein. Additional small doses may be given if needed. However, the dose is usually not more than 500 mg.

• Children—At first, 50 mg injected into a muscle or vein. Additional small doses may be given if needed.

• For *rectal* dosage form (suppositories):

—For trouble in sleeping:

• Adults—120 to 200 mg inserted into the rectum at bedtime.

• Children up to 2 months of age—Dose must be determined by your doctor.

• Children 2 months to 1 year of age—30 mg inserted into the rectum at bedtime.

• Children 1 to 4 years of age—30 or 60 mg inserted into the rectum at bedtime.

• Children 5 to 12 years of age—60 mg inserted into the rectum at bedtime.

• Children 12 to 14 years of age—60 or 120 mg inserted into the rectum at bedtime.

—For daytime sedation:

• Adults—30 mg inserted into the rectum two to four times a day.

• Children—Dose is based on body weight or size and must be determined by your doctor. The usual dose is 2 mg per kg (0.9 mg per pound) of body weight, inserted into the rectum three times a day.

—For sedation before surgery:

• Children up to 2 months of age—Dose must be determined by your doctor.

• Children 2 months to 1 year of age—30 mg inserted into the rectum.

• Children 1 to 4 years of age—30 or 60 mg inserted into the rectum.

• Children 5 to 12 years of age—60 mg inserted into the rectum.

• Children 12 to 14 years of age—60 or 120 mg inserted into the rectum.

For phenobarbital

• For *oral* dosage form (elixir, capsules, or tablets):

—For trouble in sleeping:

• Adults—100 to 320 milligrams (mg) at bedtime.

• Children—Dose must be determined by your doctor.

—For daytime sedation:

• Adults—30 to 120 mg a day, taken in smaller doses two or three times during the day.

• Children—Dose is based on body weight or size and must be determined by your doctor. The usual dose is 2 mg per kilogram (kg) (0.9 mg per pound) of body weight three times a day.

—For sedation before surgery:

• Children—Dose is based on body weight and must be determined by your doctor. The usual dose is 1 to 3 mg per kg (0.45 to 1.4 mg per pound) of body weight.

—For control of seizures:

• Adults—60 to 250 mg a day.

• Children—Dose is based on body weight and must be determined by your doctor. The usual dose is 1 to 6 mg per kg (0.45 to 2.7 mg per pound) of body weight a day.

• For *injection* dosage form:

—For trouble in sleeping:

• Adults—100 to 325 mg, injected into a muscle or vein, or under the skin.

• Children—Dose must be determined by your doctor.

—For daytime sedation:

• Adults—30 to 120 mg a day, injected into a muscle or a vein, or under the skin, in smaller doses two or three times during the day,

• Children—Dose must be determined by your doctor.

—For sedation before surgery:

• Adults—130 to 200 mg, injected into a muscle sixty to ninety minutes before surgery.

• Children—Dose is based on body weight and must be determined by your doctor. The usual dose is 1 to 3 mg per kg (0.45 to 1.4 mg per pound) of body weight, injected into a muscle or vein sixty to ninety minutes before surgery.

—For control of seizures:

• Adults—100 to 320 mg injected into a vein. The dose may be repeated if needed, but is usually not more than 600 mg a day. However, higher doses may be needed for certain types of continuing seizures.

• Children—Dose is based on body weight and must be determined by your doctor. At first, the usual dose is 10 to 20 mg per kg (4.5 to 9 mg per pound) of body weight, injected into a vein. Later, 1 to 6 mg per kg (0.45 to 2.7 mg per pound) of body weight a day, injected into a vein. Higher doses may be needed for certain types of continuing seizures.

For secobarbital

• For *oral* dosage form (capsules):

—For trouble in sleeping:

• Adults—100 milligrams (mg) at bedtime.

• Children—Dose must be determined by your doctor.

—For daytime sedation:

• Adults—30 to 50 mg three or four times a day.

• Children—Dose is based on body weight or size and must be determined by your doctor. The usual dose is 2 mg per kilogram (kg) (0.9 mg per pound) of body weight three times a day.

—For sedation before surgery:

• Adults—200 to 300 mg one or two hours before surgery.

• Children—Dose is based on body weight and must be determined by your doctor. The usual dose is 2 to 6 mg per kg (0.9 to 2.7 mg per pound) of body weight one or two hours before surgery. However, the dose is usually not more than 100 mg.

• For *injection* dosage form:

—For trouble in sleeping:

• Adults—100 to 200 mg injected into a muscle, or 50 to 250 mg injected into a vein.

• Children—Dose is based on body weight or size and must be determined by your doctor. The usual dose is 3 to 5 mg per kg (1.4 to 2.3 mg per pound) of body weight, injected into a muscle. However, the dose is usually not more than 100 mg.

—For sedation before dental procedures:

• Adults—Dose is based on body weight and must be determined by your doctor. The usual dose is 1.1 to 2.2 mg per kg (0.5 to 1 mg per pound) of body weight, injected into a muscle ten to fifteen minutes before the procedure.

• Children—Dose must be determined by your dentist.

—For sedation before a nerve block:

• Adults—100 to 150 mg, injected into a vein.

—For sedation before surgery:

• Children—Dose is based on body weight and must be determined by your doctor. The usual dose is 4 to 5 mg per kg (1.8 to 2.3 mg per pound) of body weight, injected into a muscle.

—For seizures from tetanus:

• Adults—Dose is based on body weight and must be determined by your doctor. The usual dose is 5.5 mg per kg (2.5 mg per pound) of body weight, injected into a muscle or vein. Dose may be repeated every three to four hours if needed.

• Children—Dose is based on body weight and must be determined by your doctor. The usual dose is 3 to 5 mg per kg (1.4 to 2.3 mg per pound) of body weight, injected into a muscle or vein.

For secobarbital and amobarbital combination

• For *oral* dosage form (capsules):

—For trouble in sleeping:

• Adults—1 capsule at bedtime.

• Children—Dose must be determined by your doctor.

—For sedation before surgery:

• Adults—1 capsule taken one hour before surgery.

• Children—Dose must be determined by your doctor.

Missed dose—If you are taking this medicine regularly (for example, every day as in epilepsy) and you do miss a dose, take it as soon as possible. However, if it is almost time for your next dose, skip the missed dose and go back to your regular dosing schedule. Do not double doses.

Storage—To store this medicine:
- Keep out of the reach of children since overdose is especially dangerous in children.
- Store away from heat and direct light.
- Do not store the capsule or tablet form of this medicine in the bathroom, near the kitchen sink, or in other damp places. Heat or moisture may cause the medicine to break down.
- Keep the liquid form of this medicine from freezing.
- Store the suppository form of this medicine in the refrigerator.
- Do not keep outdated medicine or medicine no longer needed. Be sure that any discarded medicine is out of the reach of children.

Precautions While Using This Medicine

If you will be using this medicine regularly for a long time:
- Your doctor should check your progress at regular visits.
- Do not stop using it without first checking with your doctor. Your doctor may want you to reduce gradually the amount you are using before stopping completely.

This medicine will add to the effects of alcohol and other CNS depressants (medicines that slow down the nervous system, possibly causing drowsiness). Some examples of CNS depressants are antihistamines or medicine for hay fever, other allergies, or colds; sedatives, tranquilizers, or sleeping medicine; prescription pain medicine or narcotics; medicine for seizures; muscle relaxants; or anesthetics, including some dental anesthetics. *Check with your doctor before taking any of the above while you are using this medicine.*

Before you have any medical tests, tell the medical doctor in charge that you are taking this medicine. The results of the metyrapone test may be affected by this medicine.

If you have been using this medicine for a long time and you think that you may have become mentally or physically dependent on it, check with your doctor. Some signs of mental or physical dependence on barbiturates are:
- a strong desire or need to continue taking the medicine.
- a need to increase the dose to receive the effects of the medicine.
- withdrawal side effects (for example, anxiety or restlessness, convulsions [seizures], feeling faint, nausea or vomiting, trembling of hands, trouble in sleeping) occurring after the medicine is stopped.

If you think you or someone else may have taken an overdose of this medicine, get emergency help at once. Taking an overdose of a barbiturate or taking alcohol or other CNS depressants with the barbiturate may lead to unconsciousness and possibly death. Some signs of an overdose are severe drowsiness, severe confusion, severe weakness, shortness of breath or slow or troubled breathing, slurred speech, staggering, and slow heartbeat.

This medicine may cause some people to become dizzy, lightheaded, drowsy, or less alert than they are normally. Even if taken at bedtime, it may cause some people to feel drowsy or less alert on arising. *Make sure you know how you react to this medicine before you drive, use machines, or do anything else that could be dangerous if you are dizzy or are not alert.*

Oral contraceptives (birth control pills) containing estrogen may not work properly if you take them while you are taking barbiturates. Unplanned pregnancies may occur. You should use a different or additional means of birth control while you are taking barbiturates. If you have any questions about this, check with your health care professional.

Side Effects of This Medicine

Along with its needed effects, a medicine may cause some unwanted effects. Although not all of these side effects may occur, if they do occur they may need medical attention.

Check with your doctor immediately if any of the following side effects occur:

Rare

Bleeding sores on lips; chest pain; fever; muscle or joint pain; red, thickened, or scaly skin; skin rash or hives; sores, ulcers, or white spots in mouth (painful); sore throat and/or fever; swelling of eyelids, face, or lips; wheezing or tightness in chest

Also, check with your doctor as soon as possible if any of the following side effects occur:

Less common

Confusion; mental depression; unusual excitement

Rare

Hallucinations (seeing, hearing, or feeling things that are not there); unusual bleeding or bruising; unusual tiredness or weakness

With long-term or chronic use

Bone pain, tenderness, or aching; loss of appetite; muscle weakness; weight loss (unusual); yellow eyes or skin

Symptoms of overdose

Confusion (severe); decrease in or loss of reflexes; drowsiness (severe); fever; irritability (continuing); low body temperature; poor judgment; shortness of breath or slow or troubled breathing; slow heartbeat; slurred speech; staggering; trouble in sleeping; unusual movements of the eyes; weakness (severe)

Other side effects may occur that usually do not need medical attention. These side effects may go away during treatment as your body adjusts to the medicine. However, check with your doctor if any of the following side effects continue or are bothersome:

More common

Clumsiness or unsteadiness; dizziness or lightheadedness; drowsiness; "hangover" effect

Less common
Anxiety or nervousness; constipation; feeling faint; headache; irritability; nausea or vomiting; nightmares or trouble in sleeping

For very ill patients:
- Confusion, mental depression, and unusual excitement may be more likely to occur in very ill patients.

After you stop using this medicine, your body may need time to adjust. If you took this medicine in high doses or for a long time, this may take up to about 15 days. During this period of time check with your doctor if any of the following side effects occur (usually occur within 8 to 16 hours after medicine is stopped):
Anxiety or restlessness; convulsions (seizures); dizziness or lightheadedness; feeling faint; hallucinations (seeing, hearing, or feeling things that are not there); muscle twitching; nausea or vomiting; trembling of hands; trouble in sleeping, increased dreaming, or nightmares; vision problems; weakness

Other side effects not listed above may also occur in some patients. If you notice any other effects, check with your doctor.

Additional Information

Once a medicine has been approved for marketing for a certain use, experience may show that it is also useful for other medical problems. Although this use is not included in product labeling, phenobarbital is used in certain patients with the following medical condition:
- Hyperbilirubinemia (high amount of bile pigments in the blood that may lead to jaundice)

Other than the above information, there is no additional information relating to proper use, precautions, or side effects for these uses.

Revised: 01/27/92
Interim revision: 08/29/94

BARBITURATES, ASPIRIN, AND CODEINE Systemic

Some commonly used brand names are:

In the U.S.—
Ascomp with Codeine No.3[1]
Butalbital Compound with Codeine[1]
Butinal with Codeine No.3[1]
Fiorinal with Codeine No.3[1]
Idenal with Codeine[1]
Isollyl with Codeine[1]

In Canada—
Fiorinal-C 1/4[1]
Fiorinal-C 1/2[1]
Phenaphen with Codeine No.2[2]
Phenaphen with Codeine No.3[2]
Phenaphen with Codeine No.4[2]
Tecnal-C 1/4[1]
Tecnal-C 1/2[1]

Note: For quick reference, the following combination medicines are numbered to match the corresponding brand names.

This information applies to the following medicines:
1. Butalbital (byoo-TAL-bi-tal), Aspirin (AS-pir-in), and Codeine (KOE-deen)‡
2. Phenobarbital (fee-noe-BAR-bi-tal), Aspirin, and Codeine*‡

*Not commercially available in the U.S.
‡In Canada, *Aspirin* is a brand name. Acetylsalicylic acid is the generic name in Canada. ASA, a synonym for acetylsalicylic acid, is the term that commonly appears on Canadian product labels.

Description

Barbiturate (bar-BI-tyoo-rate), aspirin, and codeine combinations are used to relieve headaches and other kinds of pain. These combination medicines may provide better pain relief than either aspirin or codeine used alone. In some cases, relief of pain may come at lower doses of each medicine.

Codeine is a narcotic analgesic (nar-KOT-ik an-al-JEE-zik) that acts in the central nervous system (CNS) to relieve pain. Many of its side effects are also caused by actions in the CNS. Butalbital and phenobarbital belong to the group of medicines called barbiturates. Barbiturates also act in the CNS to produce their effects.

When you use a barbiturate or codeine for a long time, your body may get used to the medicine so that larger amounts are needed to produce the same effects. This is called tolerance to the medicine. Also, barbiturates and codeine may become habit-forming (causing mental or physical dependence) when they are used for a long time or in large doses. Physical dependence may lead to withdrawal symptoms when you stop taking the medicine. In patients who get headaches, the first symptom of withdrawal may be new (rebound) headaches.

The butalbital, aspirin, and codeine combination also contains caffeine (kaf-EEN). Caffeine may help to relieve headaches. However, caffeine can also cause physical dependence when it is used for a long time. This may lead to withdrawal (rebound) headaches when you stop taking it.

Aspirin is not a narcotic and does not cause physical dependence. However, it may cause other unwanted effects if too much is taken.

These combination medicines are available only with your doctor's prescription, in the following dosage forms:

Oral
Butalbital, Aspirin, Caffeine, and Codeine
- Capsules (U.S. and Canada)
- Tablets (U.S.)

Phenobarbital, Aspirin, and Codeine
- Capsules (Canada)

Before Using This Medicine

In deciding to use a medicine, the risks of taking the medicine must be weighed against the good it will do. This is a decision you and your doctor will make. For barbiturate, aspirin, and codeine combinations, the following should be considered:

Allergies—Tell your doctor if you have ever had any unusual or allergic reaction to aspirin or other salicylates including methyl salicylate (oil of wintergreen); butalbital, phenobarbital, or other barbiturates; caffeine; codeine; or any of the following medicines:

Diclofenac (e.g., Voltaren)
Diflunisal (e.g., Dolobid)
Etodolac (e.g., Lodine)
Fenoprofen (e.g., Nalfon)
Floctafenine (e.g., Idarac)
Flurbiprofen, oral (e.g., Ansaid)
Ibuprofen (e.g., Motrin)
Indomethacin (e.g., Indocin)
Ketoprofen (e.g., Orudis)
Ketorolac (e.g., Toradol)
Meclofenamate (e.g., Meclomen)
Mefenamic acid (e.g., Ponstel)
Nabumetone (e.g., Relafen)
Naproxen (e.g., Naprosyn)
Oxaprozin (e.g., Daypro)
Oxyphenbutazone (e.g., Tandearil)
Phenylbutazone (e.g., Butazolidin)
Piroxicam (e.g., Feldene)
Sulindac (e.g., Clinoril)
Suprofen (e.g., Suprol)
Tenoxicam (e.g., Mobiflex)
Tiaprofenic acid (e.g., Surgam)
Tolmetin (e.g., Tolectin)
Zomepirac (e.g., Zomax)

Also tell your health care professional if you are allergic to any other substances, such as foods, preservatives, or dyes.

Pregnancy—

- *For butalbital or phenobarbital:* Barbiturates have been shown to increase the chance of birth defects in humans. Also, one study in humans has suggested that barbiturates taken during pregnancy may increase the chance of brain tumors in the baby. Barbiturates may cause breathing problems in the newborn baby if taken just before or during delivery.
- *For aspirin:* Although studies in humans have not shown that aspirin causes birth defects, aspirin has caused birth defects in animal studies.

  Do not take aspirin during the last 3 months of pregnancy unless it has been ordered by your doctor. Some reports have suggested that use of aspirin late in pregnancy may cause a decrease in the newborn's weight and possible death of the fetus or newborn baby. However, the mothers in these reports had been taking much larger amounts of aspirin than are usually recommended. Studies of mothers taking aspirin in the doses that are usually recommended did not show these unwanted effects.

  There is a chance that regular use of aspirin late in pregnancy may cause unwanted effects on the heart or blood flow in the fetus or in the newborn baby. Also, use of aspirin during the last 2 weeks of pregnancy may cause bleeding problems in the fetus before or during delivery or in the newborn baby. In addition, too much use of aspirin during the last 3 months of pregnancy may increase the length of pregnancy, prolong labor, cause other problems during delivery, or cause severe bleeding in the mother before, during, or after delivery.
- *For codeine:* Although studies on birth defects with codeine have not been done in pregnant women, it has not been reported to cause birth defects. However, it may cause breathing problems in the newborn baby if taken just before or during delivery. Codeine did not cause birth defects in animal studies, but it caused slower development of bones and other harmful effects in the fetus.
- *For caffeine:* Studies in humans have not shown that caffeine causes birth defects. However, use of large amounts of caffeine during pregnancy may cause problems with the heart rhythm and the growth of the fetus. Also, studies in animals have shown that caffeine causes birth defects when given in very large doses (amounts equal to those in 12 to 24 cups of coffee a day).

Breast-feeding—Although this combination medicine has not been reported to cause problems, the chance always exists, especially if the medicine is taken for a long time or in large amounts.

- *For butalbital or phenobarbital:* Barbiturates pass into the breast milk and may cause drowsiness, unusually slow heartbeat, shortness of breath, or troubled breathing in nursing babies.
- *For aspirin:* Aspirin passes into the breast milk. However, taking aspirin in the amount present in these combination medicines has not been reported to cause problems in nursing babies.
- *For codeine:* Codeine passes into the breast milk in small amounts. However, it has not been reported to cause problems in nursing babies.
- *For caffeine:* The caffeine in the butalbital, aspirin, and codeine combination medicine passes into the breast milk in small amounts. Taking caffeine in the amounts present in this combination medicine has not been reported to cause problems in nursing babies. However, studies have shown that nursing babies may appear jittery when their mothers drink large amounts of caffeine-containing beverages. Therefore, breast-feeding mothers who use caffeine-containing medicines should probably limit the amount of caffeine they take in from other medicines or from beverages.

Children—

- *For butalbital or phenobarbital:* Although barbiturates often cause drowsiness, some children become excited after taking them.
- *For aspirin: Do not give a medicine containing aspirin to a child with fever or other symptoms of a virus infection, especially flu or chickenpox, without first discussing its use with your child's doctor.* This is very important because aspirin may cause a serious illness called Reye's syndrome in children with fever caused by a virus infection, especially flu or chickenpox. Children who do not have a virus infection may also be more sensitive to the effects of aspirin, especially if they have a fever or have lost large amounts of body fluid because of vomiting, diarrhea, or sweating. This may increase the chance of side effects during treatment.

- *For caffeine:* There is no specific information comparing use of caffeine in children up to 12 years of age with use in other age groups. However, caffeine is not expected to cause different side effects or problems in children than it does in adults.

Teenagers—*Teenagers with fever or other symptoms of a virus infection, especially flu or chickenpox, should check with a doctor before taking this medicine.* The aspirin in this combination medicine may cause a serious illness called Reye's syndrome in teenagers with fever caused by a virus infection, especially flu or chickenpox.

Older adults—
- *For butalbital or phenobarbital:* Confusion, depression, or excitement may be especially likely to occur in elderly patients, who are usually more sensitive than younger adults to the effects of barbiturates.
- *For aspirin:* Elderly patients are more sensitive than younger adults to the effects of aspirin. This may increase the chance of side effects during treatment.
- *For codeine:* Breathing problems may be especially likely to occur in elderly patients, who are usually more sensitive than younger adults to the effects of codeine.
- *For caffeine:* Many medicines have not been studied specifically in older people.Therefore, it may not be known whether they work exactly the same way they do in younger adults or if they cause different side effects or problems in older people. There is no specific information comparing use of caffeine in the elderly with use in other age groups.

Other medicines—Although certain medicines should not be used together at all, in other cases two different medicines may be used together even if an interaction might occur. In these cases, your doctor may want to change the dose, or other precautions may be necessary. When you are taking this combination medicine, it is especially important that your health care professional know if you are taking any of the following:
- Antacids, large amounts taken regularly, especially calcium- and/or magnesium-containing antacids or sodium bicarbonate (baking soda), or
- Urinary alkalizers (medicine that makes the urine less acid, such as acetazolamide [e.g., Diamox], dichlorphenamide [e.g., Daranide], methazolamide [e.g., Neptazane], potassium or sodium citrate and/or citric acid)—These medicines may cause aspirin to be removed from the body faster than usual, which may shorten the length of time that aspirin is effective; acetazolamide, dichlorphenamide, and methazolamide may also increase the chance of side effects when taken together with aspirin
- Anticoagulants (blood thinners) or
- Heparin—Use of these medicines together with aspirin may increase the chance of bleeding; also, barbiturates, especially phenobarbital, may decrease the effects of anticoagulants
- Antidepressants, tricyclic (amitriptyline [e.g., Elavil], amoxapine [e.g., Asendin], clomipramine [e.g., Anafranil], desipramine [e.g., Pertofrane], doxepin [e.g., Sinequan], imipramine [e.g., Tofranil], nortriptyline [e.g., Aventyl], protriptyline [e.g., Vivactil], trimipramine [e.g., Surmontil]) or
- Central nervous system (CNS) depressants (medicines that often cause drowsiness)—These medicines may add to the effects of barbiturates and codeine and increase the chance of drowsiness or other side effects
- Carbamazepine or
- Contraceptives, oral (birth control pills) containing estrogens or
- Corticosteroids (cortisone-like medicines) or
- Corticotropin (ACTH)—Barbiturates, especially phenobarbital, may make these medicines less effective
- Divalproex (e.g., Depakote) or
- Methotrexate (e.g., Mexate) or
- Valproic acid (e.g., Depakene) or
- Vancomycin (e.g., Vancocin)—The chance of serious side effects may be increased
- Naltrexone (e.g., Trexan)—Naltrexone blocks the pain-relieving effect of codeine
- Probenecid (e.g., Benemid) or
- Sulfinpyrazone (e.g., Anturane)—Aspirin can keep these medicines from working properly for treating gout

Other medical problems—The presence of other medical problems may affect the use of butalbital, aspirin, and codeine combination. Make sure you tell your doctor if you have any other medical problems, especially:
- Alcohol abuse (or history of) or
- Drug abuse or dependence (or history of)—Dependence on barbiturates and/or codeine may develop
- Asthma, especially if occurring together with other allergies and nasal polyps (history of), or
- Brain disease or head injury or
- Colitis or
- Convulsions (seizures) (history of) or
- Emphysema or other chronic lung disease or
- Enlarged prostate or problems with urination or
- Gallbladder disease or gallstones or
- Hyperactivity (in children) or
- Kidney disease or
- Liver disease—The chance of serious side effects may be increased
- Diabetes mellitus (sugar diabetes) or
- Mental depression or
- Overactive thyroid or
- Porphyria (or history of)—Barbiturates can make these conditions worse
- Gout—Aspirin can make this condition worse and can also lessen the effects of some medicines used to treat gout
- Heart disease (severe)—The caffeine in the butalbital, aspirin, and codeine combination can make some kinds of heart disease worse
- Hemophilia or other bleeding problems or
- Vitamin K deficiency—Aspirin increases the chance of serious bleeding
- Stomach ulcer, especially with a history of bleeding, or other stomach problems—Aspirin can make your condition worse

Proper Use of This Medicine

Take this medicine with food or a full glass (8 ounces) of water to lessen stomach irritation.

Do not take this medicine if it has a strong vinegar-like odor. This odor means the aspirin in it is breaking down. If you have any questions about this, check with your health care professional.

Take this medicine only as directed by your doctor. Do not take more of it, do not take it more often, and do not take it for a longer time than your doctor ordered. If a barbiturate or codeine is taken regularly (for example, every day), it may become habit-forming (causing mental or physical dependence). Regular use of caffeine can also cause physical dependence. Dependence is especially likely to occur in people who take these medicines to relieve frequent headaches. Also, taking too much of this combination medicine may cause stomach problems or other medical problems.

This medicine will relieve a headache best if you *take it as soon as the headache begins.* If you get warning signs of a migraine, take this medicine as soon as you are sure that the migraine is coming. This may even stop the headache pain from occurring. *Lying down in a quiet, dark room for a while after taking the medicine also helps to relieve headaches.*

People who get a lot of headaches may need to take a different medicine to help prevent headaches. *It is important that you follow your doctor's directions about taking the other medicine, even if your headaches continue to occur.* Headache-preventing medicines may take several weeks to start working. Even after they do start working, your headaches may not go away completely. However, your headaches should occur less often, and they should be less severe and easier to relieve than before. This will reduce the amount of headache relievers that you need. If you do not notice any improvement after several weeks of headache-preventing treatment, check with your doctor.

Dosing—The dose of these medicines will be different for different patients. *Follow your doctor's orders or the directions on the label.* The following information includes only the average doses of these medicines. *If your dose is different, do not change it* unless your doctor tells you to do so.

The number of capsules or tablets that you take depends on the strength of the medicine.

For Butalbital, Aspirin, and Codeine combination

- For *oral* dosage forms (capsules and tablets):
  - —For relieving pain:
    - Adults—One or 2 capsules or tablets every four hours as needed. You should not take more than six capsules or tablets a day.
    - Children—Dose must be determined by your doctor.

For Phenobarbital, Aspirin, and Codeine combination

- For *oral* dosage form (capsules):
  - —For relieving pain:
    - Adults—One or 2 capsules every three or four hours as needed.
    - Children—Dose must be determined by your doctor.

Missed dose—If your doctor has ordered you to take this medicine according to a regular schedule and you miss a dose, take it as soon as you remember. However, if it is almost time for your next dose, skip the missed dose and go back to your regular dosing schedule. Do not double doses.

Storage—To store this medicine:

- Keep out of the reach of children. Overdose is especially dangerous in young children.
- Store away from heat and direct light.
- Do not store this medicine in the bathroom, near the kitchen sink, or in other damp places. Heat or moisture may cause the medicine to break down.
- Do not keep outdated medicine or medicine no longer needed. Be sure that any discarded medicine is out of the reach of children.

Precautions While Using This Medicine

Check with your doctor:

- If the medicine stops working as well as it did when you first started using it. This may mean that you are in danger of becoming dependent on the medicine. *Do not try to get better pain relief by increasing the dose.*
- *If you are having headaches more often than you did before you started using this medicine.* This is especially important if a new headache occurs within 1 day after you took your last dose of headache medicine, headaches begin to occur every day, or a headache continues for several days in a row. This may mean that you are dependent on the headache medicine. *Continuing to take this medicine will cause even more headaches later on.* Your doctor can give you advice on how to relieve the headaches.

Check the labels of all nonprescription (over-the-counter [OTC]) and prescription medicines you now take. If any contain a narcotic, a barbiturate, aspirin, or other salicylates, including diflunisal, check with your doctor or pharmacist. Taking them together with this medicine may cause an overdose.

The barbiturate and the codeine in this medicine will add to the effects of alcohol and other CNS depressants (medicines that slow down the nervous system, possibly causing drowsiness). Some examples of CNS depressants are antihistamines or medicine for hay fever, other allergies, or colds; sedatives, tranquilizers, or sleeping medicine; other prescription pain medicine or narcotics; other barbiturates; medicine for seizures; muscle relaxants; or anesthetics, including some dental anesthetics. Also, stomach problems may be more likely to occur if you drink alcoholic beverages while you are taking aspirin. Therefore, *do not drink alcoholic beverages, and check with your doctor before taking any of the medicines listed above, while you are using this medicine.*

This medicine may cause some people to become drowsy, dizzy, or lightheaded, or to feel a false sense of well-being. *Make sure you know how you react to this medicine before you drive, use machines, or do anything else that could be dangerous if you are dizzy or are not alert and clearheaded.*

Dizziness, lightheadedness, or fainting may occur, especially when you get up suddenly from a lying or sitting position. Getting up slowly may help lessen this problem. Lying down for a while may relieve these effects.

Nausea or vomiting may occur, especially after the first couple of doses. This effect may go away if you lie down for a while. However, if nausea or vomiting continues, check with your doctor.

Before having any kind of surgery (including dental surgery) or emergency treatment, tell the medical doctor or dentist in charge that you are taking this medicine. Serious side effects can occur if your medical doctor or dentist gives you certain medicines without knowing that you have taken a barbiturate or codeine.

Do not take this medicine for 5 days before any planned surgery, including dental surgery, unless otherwise directed by your medical doctor or dentist. Taking aspirin during this time may cause bleeding problems.

Before you have any medical tests, tell the person in charge that you are taking this medicine. The caffeine in the butalbital, aspirin, and codeine combination interferes with the results of certain tests that use dipyridamole (e.g., Persantine) to help show how well blood is flowing to your heart. Caffeine should not be taken for 8 to 12 hours before the test. The results of some other tests may also be affected by this medicine.

If you have been taking large amounts of this medicine, or if you have been taking it regularly for several weeks or more, *do not suddenly stop using it without first checking with your doctor.* Your doctor may want you to reduce gradually the amount you are taking before stopping completely, to lessen the chance of withdrawal side effects.

If you think you or anyone else may have taken an overdose of this medicine, get emergency help at once. Taking an overdose of this medicine or taking alcohol or CNS depressants with this medicine may lead to unconsciousness or death. Signs of overdose of this medicine include convulsions (seizures); hearing loss; confusion; ringing or buzzing in the ears; severe excitement, nervousness, or restlessness; severe dizziness; severe drowsiness; unusually slow or troubled breathing; and severe weakness.

Side Effects of This Medicine

Along with its needed effects, a medicine may cause some unwanted effects. Although not all of these side effects may occur, if they do occur they may need medical attention.

The following side effects may mean that a serious allergic reaction is occurring. Check with your doctor or get emergency help immediately if they occur, especially if several of them occur at the same time.

Less common or rare

Bluish discoloration or flushing or redness of skin (occurring together with other effects listed in this section); coughing, shortness of breath, troubled breathing, tightness in chest, or wheezing; difficulty in swallowing; dizziness or feeling faint (severe); hive-like swellings (large) on eyelids, face, lips, or tongue; skin rash, itching, or hives; stuffy nose (occurring together with other effects listed in this section)

Also check with your doctor immediately if any of the following side effects occur, especially if several of them occur together:

Rare

Bleeding or crusting sores on lips; chest pain; fever with or without chills; red, thickened, or scaly skin; sores, ulcers, or white spots in mouth (painful); sore throat (unexplained); tenderness, burning, or peeling of skin

Symptoms of overdose

Anxiety, confusion, excitement, irritability, nervousness, restlessness, or trouble in sleeping (severe, especially with products containing caffeine); cold, clammy skin; convulsions (seizures); diarrhea (severe or continuing); dizziness, lightheadedness, drowsiness, or weakness (severe); frequent urination (for products containing caffeine); hallucinations (seeing, hearing, or feeling things that are not there); increased sensitivity to touch or pain (for products containing caffeine); increased thirst; low blood pressure; muscle trembling or twitching (for products containing caffeine); nausea or vomiting (severe or continuing), sometimes with blood; pinpoint pupils of eyes; ringing or buzzing in ears (continuing) or hearing loss; seeing flashes of "zig-zag" lights (for products containing caffeine); slow, fast, or irregular heartbeat; slow, fast, irregular, or troubled breathing; slurred speech; staggering; stomach pain (severe); uncontrollable flapping movements of the hands (especially in elderly patients); unusual movements of the eyes; vision problems

Also, check with your doctor as soon as possible if any of the following side effects occur:

Less common or rare

Bloody or black, tarry stools; bloody urine; confusion or mental depression; pinpoint red spots on skin; skin rash, hives, or itching (without other signs of an allergic reaction to aspirin listed above); sore throat and fever; stomach pain (severe); swollen or painful glands; trembling or uncontrolled muscle movements; unusual bleeding or bruising; unusual excitement (mild); unusual tiredness or weakness (mild)

Other side effects may occur that usually do not need medical attention. These side effects may go away during treatment as your body adjusts to the medicine. However, check with your doctor if any of the following side effects continue or are bothersome:

More common

Bloated or "gassy" feeling; dizziness, lightheadedness, or drowsiness (mild); heartburn or indigestion; nausea, vomiting, or stomach pain (occurring without other symptoms of overdose)

Other side effects not listed above may also occur in some patients. If you notice any other effects, check with your doctor.

Revised: 07/14/92
Interim revision: 07/19/94

BARIUM SULFATE Diagnostic

Description

Barium sulfate is a radiopaque agent. Radiopaque agents are used to help diagnose certain medical problems. Since radiopaque agents are opaque to (block) x-rays, the areas of the body in which they are localized will appear white on the x-ray film. This creates the needed distinction, or contrast, between one organ and other tissues. The contrast will help the doctor see any special conditions that may exist in that organ or part of the body.

Barium sulfate is taken by mouth or given rectally by enema. If taken by mouth, it makes the esophagus, the stomach, and/or the small intestine opaque to the x-rays so that they can be ''photographed.'' If it is given by enema, the colon and/or the small intestine can be seen and photographed by x-rays.

The dose of barium sulfate will be different for different patients and depends on the type of test. The strength of the suspension and tablet is determined by how much barium they contain. Different tests will require a different strength and amount of suspension (some may require the tablet form), depending on the age of the patient, the contrast needed, and the x-ray equipment used.

Barium sulfate is to be used only by or under the direct supervision of a doctor.

Before Having This Test

In deciding to use a diagnostic test, any risks of the test must be weighed against the good it will do. This is a decision you and your doctor will make. Also, test results may be affected by other things. For barium sulfate, the following should be considered:

Allergies—Tell your doctor if you have ever had any unusual or allergic reaction to barium sulfate. Also, tell your doctor if you are allergic to any other substances, such as foods, preservatives, or dyes.

Pregnancy—X-rays of the abdomen are usually not recommended during pregnancy. This is to avoid exposing the fetus to radiation. Be sure you have discussed this with your doctor.

Breast-feeding—Barium sulfate does not pass into the breast milk. This medicine has not been reported to cause problems in nursing babies.

Children—Although there is no specific information comparing use of barium sulfate in children with use in other age groups, this agent is not expected to cause different side effects or problems in children than it does in adults.

Older adults—This contrast agent has been used in older people and has not been shown to cause different side effects or problems in them than it does in younger adults.

Other medical problems—The presence of other medical problems may affect the use of barium sulfate. Make sure you tell your doctor if you have any other medical problems, especially:

- Asthma, hay fever, or other allergies (history of)—If you have a history of these conditions, the risk of having a reaction, such as an allergic reaction to the additives in the barium sulfate preparation, is greater
- Cystic fibrosis—The risk of blockage in the small bowel is greater
- Dehydration—Barium sulfate may cause severe constipation
- Intestinal blockage or perforation—Barium sulfate may make this condition worse

Preparation For This Test

Your doctor may have special instructions for you in preparation for your test. If you have not received such instructions or if you do not understand them, check with your doctor in advance.

For some tests your doctor may tell you not to eat after 8 the evening before the test. You may be allowed to drink small amounts of clear liquids until midnight; however, check first with your doctor. For other tests you may need to eat meals free of fiber and bulk the day before the test. You may also need to use a laxative.

Precautions After Having This Test

Make sure to drink plenty of liquids after the test. Otherwise, barium sulfate may cause severe constipation.

Side Effects of This Medicine

Along with its needed effects, a radiopaque agent may cause some unwanted effects. Although not all of these side effects may occur, if they do occur they may need medical attention.

Check with your doctor immediately if any of the following side effects occur:

Rare

Bloating; constipation (severe, continuing); cramping (severe); nausea or vomiting; stomach or lower abdominal pain; tightness in chest or troubled breathing; wheezing

Other side effects may occur that usually do not need medical attention. These side effects may go away as your body adjusts to this agent. However, check with your doctor if any of the following side effects continue or are bothersome:

More common

Constipation or diarrhea; cramping

Other side effects not listed above may also occur in some patients. If you notice any other effects, check with your doctor.

Revised: 07/26/94

BELLADONNA ALKALOIDS AND BARBITURATES Systemic

Some commonly used brand names are:

In the U.S.—

Antrocol[2]
Barbidonna[1]
Barbidonna No. 2[1]
Barophen[1]
Bellalphen[1]
Butibel[3]
Chardonna-2[4]
Donnamor[1]
Donnapine[1]
Donnatal[1]
Donnatal Extentabs[1]
Donnatal No. 2[1]
Donphen[1]
Hyosophen[1]
Kinesed[1]
Levsin-PB[5]
Levsin with Phenobarbital[5]
Malatal[1]
Relaxadon[1]
Spaslin[1]
Spasmolin[1]
Spasmophen[1]
Spasquid[1]
Susano[1]

In Canada—

Donnatal[1]
Donnatal Extentabs[1]

Note: For quick reference, the following belladonna alkaloids and barbiturates are numbered to match the corresponding brand names.

This information applies to the following medicines:

1. Atropine (A-troe-peen), Hyoscyamine (hye-oh-SYE-a-meen), Scopolamine (skoe-POL-a-meen), and Phenobarbital (fee-noe-BAR-bi-tal)†
2. Atropine and Phenobarbital†
3. Belladonna and Butabarbital (byoo-ta-BAR-bi-tal)†
4. Belladonna and Phenobarbital†
5. Hyoscyamine and Phenobarbital†

†Not commercially available in Canada.
‡Generic name product may also be available in the U.S.
§Generic name product may also be available in Canada.

Description

Belladonna alkaloids and barbiturates are combination medicines taken to relieve cramping and spasms of the stomach and intestines. They are used also to decrease the amount of acid formed in the stomach.

These medicines are available only with your doctor's prescription in the following dosage forms:

Oral

Atropine, Hyoscyamine, Scopolamine, and Phenobarbital
- Capsules (U.S.)
- Elixir (U.S. and Canada)
- Tablets (U.S. and Canada)
- Chewable tablets (U.S.)
- Extended-release tablets (U.S. and Canada)

Atropine and Phenobarbital
- Capsules (U.S.)
- Elixir (U.S.)
- Tablets (U.S.)

Belladonna and Butabarbital
- Elixir (U.S.)
- Tablets (U.S.)

Belladonna and Phenobarbital
- Tablets (U.S.)

Hyoscyamine and Phenobarbital
- Elixir (U.S.)
- Oral solution (U.S.)
- Tablets (U.S.)

Before Using This Medicine

In deciding to use a medicine, the risks of taking the medicine must be weighed against the good it will do. This is a decision you and your doctor will make. For belladona alkaloids and barbiturates, the following should be considered:

Allergies—Tell your doctor if you have ever had any unusual or allergic reaction to belladonna alkaloids (atropine, belladonna, hyoscyamine, and scopolamine) or to barbiturates (butabarbital, phenobarbital). Also, tell your health care professional if you are allergic to any other substances, such as foods, preservatives, or dyes.

Pregnancy—Belladonna alkaloids have not been shown to cause problems in humans. However, barbiturates (contained in this medicine) have been shown to increase the chance of birth defects in humans. Also, when taken during pregnancy, barbiturates may cause bleeding problems in the newborn baby. Be sure that you have discussed this with your doctor before taking this medicine.

Breast-feeding—Belladonna alkaloids or barbiturates have not been shown to cause problems in nursing babies. However, traces of the belladonna alkaloids and barbiturates pass into the breast milk. Also, because the belladonna alkaloids tend to decrease the secretions of the body, it is possible that the flow of breast milk may be reduced in some patients.

Children—Severe side effects may be more likely to occur in infants and children, especially those with spastic paralysis or brain damage. Unusual excitement, nervousness, restlessness, or irritability and unusual warmth, dryness, and flushing of skin are more likely to occur in children, who are usually more sensitive to the effects of belladonna alkaloids. Also, when belladonna alkaloids are given to children during hot weather, a rapid increase in body temperature may occur. In addition, the barbiturate in this medicine could cause some children to become hyperactive.

Older adults—Confusion or memory loss; constipation; difficult urination; drowsiness; dryness of mouth, nose, throat, or skin; and unusual excitement, nervousness, restlessness, or irritability may be more likely to occur in the elderly, who are usually more sensitive than younger adults to the effects of belladonna alkaloids and barbiturates. Also, eye pain may occur, which may be a sign of glaucoma.

Other medicines—Although certain medicines should not be used together at all, in other cases two different medicines may be used together even if an interaction might occur. In these cases, your doctor may want to change the dose, or other precautions may be necessary. When you are taking belladonna alkaloids and barbiturates, it is especially important that your health care professional know if you are taking any of the following:

- Adrenocorticoids (cortisone-like medicine) or
- Corticotropin (ACTH)—Belladonna alkaloids and barbiturates may decrease the response to these medicines
- Antacids or
- Diarrhea medicine containing kaolin or attapulgite—These medications may decrease the response to belladonna alkaloids

- Anticholinergics (medicine for abdominal or stomach spasms or cramps)—Belladonna alkaloids and barbiturates may increase the response to anticholinergics
- Anticoagulants (blood thinners)—Belladonna alkaloids and barbiturates may decrease the effect of this medicine
- Central nervous system (CNS) depressants (medicines that cause drowsiness)—The CNS effects of either medicine could be increased
- Ketoconazole (e.g., Nizoral)—Using ketoconazole with this combination medicine may lessen the effects of ketoconazole and barbiturates
- Monoamine oxidase (MAO) inhibitors (furazolidone [e.g., Furoxone], isocarboxazid [e.g., Marplan], phenelzine [e.g., Nardil], procarbazine [e.g., Matulane], selegiline [Eldepryl]; tranylcypromine [e.g., Parnate])—Taking belladonna alkaloids and barbiturates while you are taking or within 2 weeks of taking monoamine oxidase inhibitors may increase the effects of the barbiturates
- Potassium chloride (e.g., Slow K or K-Dur)—May cause an increase in lesions (sores) of the stomach or intestine

Other medical problems—The presence of other medical problems may affect the use of belladonna alkaloids and barbiturates. Make sure you tell your doctor if you have any other medical problems, especially:

- Asthma, emphysema, or other chronic lung disease or
- Dryness of mouth (severe and continuing) or
- Enlarged prostate or
- Glaucoma or
- Heart disease or
- Hyperactivity (in children) or
- Intestinal blockage or other intestinal problems or
- Urinary tract blockage or difficult urination—Belladonna alkaloids and barbiturates may make these conditions worse
- Brain damage (in children) or
- Spastic paralysis (in children)—These conditions may increase the effects of the medicine
- Down's syndrome (mongolism)—This condition may increase the side effects of the medicine
- Kidney disease or
- Liver disease—Higher levels of the belladonna alkaloid and barbiturate may result, possibly leading to increased side effects

Proper Use of This Medicine

Take this medicine about 1/2 to 1 hour before meals, unless otherwise directed by your doctor.

Take this medicine only as directed. Do not take more or less of it, do not take it more often, and do not take it for a longer time than your doctor ordered. To do so may increase the chance of side effects.

Dosing—The dose of belladonna alkaloids and barbiturates combination will be different for different patients. *Follow your doctor's orders or the directions on the label.* The following information includes only the average doses of these combination medicines. *If your dose is different, do not change it* unless your doctor tells you to do so.

The number of capsules or tablets or the amount of solution you take depends on the strength of the medicine. Also, *the number of doses you take each day, the time allowed between doses, and the length of time you take the medicine depend on the medical problem for which you are taking these combination products.*

For atropine, hyoscyamine, scopolamine, and phenobarbital combination

- For stomach or intestine problems:
  - —For *oral* dosage form (capsules or tablets):
    - Older adults, adults, and teenagers—1 or 2 capsules two to four times a day. Your doctor may change the dose if needed.
    - Children—Dose must be determined by your doctor.
  - —For *oral* dosage form (solution):
    - Adults and teenagers—The usual dose is 1 to 2 teaspoonfuls (5 to 10 milliliters [mL]) three or four times a day. Your doctor may change the dose if needed.
    - Children—Dose is based on body weight and must be determined by your doctor. The usual dose is 0.5 to 7.5 mL every four to six hours. Your doctor may change the dose if needed.
  - —For *oral* dosage form (chewable tablets):
    - Older adults, adults, and teenagers—Chew 1 or 2 tablets three or four times a day. Your doctor may change the dose if needed.
    - Children up to 2 years of age—Use is not recommended.
    - Children 2 to 12 years of age—1/2 to 1 tablet three or four times a day. Your doctor may change the dose if needed.
  - —For *oral* dosage form (extended-release tablets):
    - Older adults, adults, and teenagers—1 tablet every eight to twelve hours. Your doctor may change the dose if needed.
    - Children—Use is not recommended.

For atropine and phenobarbital

- For stomach or intestine problems:
  - —For *oral* dosage form (capsules or tablets):
    - Older adults, adults, and teenagers—1 or 2 capsules or tablets two to four times a day. Your doctor may change the dose if needed.
    - Children—Dose must be determined by your doctor.
  - —For *oral* dosage form (solution):
    - Older adults, adults, and teenagers—1 to 2 teaspoonfuls (5 to 10 milliliters [mL]) three or four times a day. Your doctor may change the dose if needed.
    - Children—Dose is based on body weight and must be determined by your doctor. The usual dose is 0.5 to 3 mL every four to six hours. Your doctor may change the dose if needed.

For belladonna and butabarbital

- For stomach or intestine problems:
  - —For *oral* dosage form (solution):
    - Older adults, adults and teenagers—1 to 2 teaspoonfuls (5 to 10 milliliters [mL]) three or four

times a day. Your doctor may change the dose if needed.

• Children up to 6 years of age—1.25 to 2.5 mL three or four times a day. Your doctor may change the dose if needed.

• Children 6 to 12 years of age—2.5 to 5 mL three or four times a day. Your doctor may change the dose if needed.

—For *oral* dosage form (tablets):

• Older adults, adults, and teenagers—1 or 2 tablets three or four times a day. Your doctor may change the dose if needed.

• Children—Dose must be determined by your doctor.

For belladonna and phenobarbital

- For stomach or intestine problems:

—For *oral* dosage form (tablets):

• Older adults, adults, and teenagers—1 or 2 tablets two to four times a day. Your doctor may change the dose if needed.

• Children—Dose must be determined by your doctor.

For hyoscyamine and phenobarbital

- For stomach or intestine problems:

—For *oral* dosage form (elixir):

• Older adults, adults, and children older than 10 years of age—The usual dose is 1 to 2 teaspoonfuls (5 to 10 milliliters [mL]) every four hours. Your doctor may change the dose if needed.

• Children up to 2 years of age—1.25 to 2.5 mL every four hours. Your doctor may change the dose if needed.

• Children 2 to 10 years of age—2.5 to 5 mL every four hours. Your doctor may change the dose if needed

—For *oral* dosage form (solution):

• Older adults, adults, and children over 10 years of age—1 to 2 mL every four hours. Your doctor may change the dose if needed.

• Children up to 1 year of age—0.1 to 0.5 mL every four hours. Your doctor may change the dose if needed.

• Children 1 to 10 years of age—0.5 to 1 mL every four hours. Your doctor may change the dose if needed.

—For *oral* dosage form (tablets):

• Older adults, adults, and teenagers—1 or 2 tablets three or four times a day. Your doctor may change the dose if needed.

• Children—Dose must be determined by your doctor.

Missed dose—If you miss a dose of this medicine, take it as soon as possible. However, if it is almost time for your next dose, skip the missed dose and go back to your regular dosing schedule. Do not double doses.

Storage—To store this medicine:

- Keep this medicine out of the reach of children. Overdose of belladonna alkaloids and barbiturates is especially dangerous in young children.
- Store away from heat and direct light.
- Do not store the capsule or tablet form of this medicine in the bathroom, near the kitchen sink, or in other damp places. Heat or moisture may cause the medicine to break down.
- Keep the liquid form of this medicine from freezing.
- Do not keep outdated medicine or medicine no longer needed. Be sure that any discarded medicine is out of the reach of children.

Precautions While Using This Medicine

This medicine will add to the effects of alcohol and other CNS depressants (medicines that slow down the nervous system, possibly causing drowsiness). Some examples of CNS depressants are antihistamines or medicine for hay fever, other allergies, or colds; sedatives, tranquilizers, or sleeping medicine; prescription pain medicine or narcotics; barbiturates; medicine for seizures; muscle relaxants; or anesthetics, including some dental anesthetics. *Check with your doctor before taking any of the above while you are taking this medicine.*

Do not take this medicine within 1 hour of taking antacids or medicine for diarrhea. Taking them too close together will make the belladonna alkaloids less effective.

Belladonna alkaloids will often make you sweat less, causing your body temperature to increase. *Use extra care not to become overheated during exercise or hot weather while you are taking this medicine,* as overheating could possibly result in heat stroke. This is especially important in children taking belladonna alkaloids.

This medicine may cause your eyes to become more sensitive to light than they are normally. Wearing sunglasses and avoiding too much exposure to bright light may help lessen the discomfort.

This medicine may cause some people to have blurred vision or to become drowsy, dizzy, or less alert than they are normally. *Make sure you know how you react to this medicine before you drive, use machines, or do anything else that could be dangerous if you are not alert or able to see well.*

This medicine may cause dryness of the mouth, nose, and throat. For temporary relief of mouth dryness, use sugarless candy or gum, melt bits of ice in your mouth, or use a saliva substitute. However, if your mouth continues to feel dry for more than 2 weeks, check with your dentist. Continuing dryness of the mouth may increase the chance of dental disease, including tooth decay, gum disease, and fungus infections.

Side Effects of This Medicine

Along with its needed effects, a medicine may cause some unwanted effects. Although not all of these side effects may occur, if they do occur they may need medical attention.

Check with your doctor as soon as possible if any of the following side effects occur:

Rare

Eye pain; skin rash or hives; sore throat and fever; unusual bleeding or bruising; yellow eyes or skin

Symptoms of overdose

Blurred vision (continuing) or changes in near vision; clumsiness or unsteadiness; confusion; convulsions (seizures); dizziness (continuing); drowsiness (severe); dryness of mouth, nose, or throat (severe); fast heartbeat; fever; hallucinations (seeing, hearing, or feeling things that are not there); shortness of breath or troubled breathing; slurred speech; unusual excitement, nervousness, restlessness, or irritability; unusual warmth, dryness, and flushing of skin

Other side effects may occur that usually do not need medical attention. These side effects may go away during treatment as your body adjusts to the medicine. However, check with your doctor if any of the following side effects continue or are bothersome:

More common

Constipation; decreased sweating; dizziness; drowsiness; dryness of mouth, nose, throat, or skin

Less common or rare

Bloated feeling; blurred vision; decreased flow of breast milk; difficult urination; difficulty in swallowing; headache; increased sensitivity of eyes to sunlight; loss of memory; nausea or vomiting; unusual tiredness or weakness

Other side effects not listed above may also occur in some patients. If you notice any other effects, check with your doctor.

Revised: 01/13/92
Interim revision: 08/29/94

BENTOQUATAM Topical†

A commonly used brand name in the U.S. is IvyBlock.

†Not commercially available in Canada.

Description

Bentoquatam (BEN-toe-kwa-tam) protects the skin like a shield against poison ivy, poison oak, and poison sumac by physically blocking skin contact with their resin. The best protection against getting these conditions is to avoid contact with these plants. This medicine does not dry oozing and weeping caused by the rash of poison ivy, poison oak, or poison sumac.

Bentoquatam is available without prescription in the following dosage form:

Topical

- Lotion (U.S.)

Before Using This Medicine

If you are using this medicine without a prescription, carefully read and follow any precautions on the label. For bentoquatam, the following should be considered:

Allergies—Tell your doctor if you have ever had any unusual or allergic reaction to bentoquatam. Also tell your health care professional if you are allergic to any other substances, such as foods, preservatives, or dyes.

Pregnancy—Studies on effects in pregnancy have not been done in humans.

Breast-feeding—Bentoquatam has not been reported to cause problems in nursing babies.

Children—Although there is no specific information comparing use of bentoquatam in children 6 years of age or older with use in other age groups, this medicine is not expected to cause different side effects or problems in these children than it does in adults. Use is not recommended for children up to 6 years of age.

Older adults—Many medicines have not been studied specifically in older people. Therefore, it may not be known whether they work exactly the same way they do in younger adults. Although there is no specific information comparing use of bentoquatam in the elderly with use in other age groups, this medicine is not expected to cause different side effects or problems in older people than it does in younger adults.

Other medicines—Although certain medicines should not be used together at all, in other cases two different medicines may be used together even if an interaction might occur. In these cases, your doctor may want to change the dose, or other precautions may be necessary. Tell your health care professional if you are using any other topical prescription or nonprescription (over-the-counter [OTC]) medicine that is to be applied to the same area of the skin.

Other medical problems—The presence of other medical problems may affect the use of bentoquatam. Make sure you tell your doctor if you have any other medical problems, especially:

- Contact dermatitis, allergic, due to poison ivy, poison oak, or poison sumac—Bentoquatam should not be applied to the rash of poison ivy, poison oak, or poison sumac and should be discontinued if such rash develops

Proper Use of This Medicine

Although this medicine provides some protection, avoiding contact with poison ivy, poison oak, or poison sumac is best.

Do not use this medicine in or near the eyes. If this medicine does get into your eyes, wash them out immediately for 20 minutes with large amounts of cool tap water. If your eyes still burn or are painful, check with your doctor.

To use *bentoquatam lotion:*

- Shake the lotion well before using.
- Rub on enough lotion to leave a smooth wet film on skin.

- Allow the medicine to dry on the skin at least 15 minutes before being exposed to poison ivy, poison oak, or poison sumac.
- Maximum protection lasts for 4 hours but lotion must be reapplied whenever the dried film on the skin cannot be seen.
- Remove medicine with soap and water when it is no longer needed.

Dosing—*Follow your doctor's orders or the directions on the label.* The following information includes only the average dose of bentoquatam. *If your dose is different, do not change it* unless your doctor tells you to do so.

- For prevention of skin irritation from poison ivy, poison oak, or poison sumac (allergic contact dermatitis):
  —For *topical* dosage form (lotion):
    - Adults and children six years of age and older—Apply to the area(s) of skin that may be affected at least fifteen minutes before exposure. Reapply whenever dry film is not seen or every four hours as needed.
    - Children up to six years of age—Use must be determined by the doctor.

Storage—To store this medicine:
- Keep out of the reach of children.
- Store away from heat and direct light.
- Keep the medicine from freezing. Do not refrigerate.
- Do not keep outdated medicine or medicine no longer needed. Be sure that any discarded medicine is out of the reach of children.

Precautions While Using This Medicine

If a rash or irritation occurs, stop using bentoquatam and check with your health care professional.

Side Effects of This Medicine

Along with its needed effects, a medicine may cause some unwanted effects. Although not all of these side effects may occur, if they do occur they may need medical attention.

Check with your doctor as soon as possible if any of the following side effects occur:

Rare

Mild redness of skin

Other side effects not listed above may also occur in some patients. If you notice any other effects, check with your doctor.

Developed: 05/07/97

BENZODIAZEPINES Systemic

Some commonly used brand names are:

In the U.S.—

Alprazolam Intensol[1]
Ativan[11]
Centrax[14]
Dalmane[8]
Diazepam Intensol[6]
Doral[15]
D-Val[6]
Gen-XENE[5]
Halcion[17]
Klonopin[4]
Libritabs[3]
Librium[3]
Lorazepam Intensol[11]
Paxipam[9]
Poxi[3]
ProSom[7]
Restoril[16]
Serax[13]
Tranxene-SD[5]
Tranxene T-Tab[5]
Valium[6]
Valrelease[6]
Xanax[1]
Zetran[6]

In Canada—

Apo-Alpraz[1]
Apo-Chlordiazepoxide[3]
Apo-Clorazepate[5]
Apo-Diazepam[6]
Apo-Flurazepam[8]
Apo-Lorazepam[11]
Apo-Oxazepam[13]
Apo-Triazo[17]
Ativan[11]
Dalmane[8]
Diazemuls[6]
Gen-Triazolam[17]
Halcion[17]
Lectopam[2]
Librium[3]
Loftran[10]
Mogadon[12]
Novo-Alprazol[1]
Novo-Clopate[5]
Novodipam[6]
Novoflupam[8]
Novo-Lorazem[11]
Novopoxide[3]
Novo-Triolam[17]
Novoxapam[13]
Nu-Alpraz[1]
Nu-Loraz[11]
Nu-Triazo[17]
PMS-Diazepam[6]
Restoril[16]
Rivotril[4]
Serax[13]
Solium[3]
Somnol[8]
Syn-Clonazepam[4]
Tranxene[5]
Valium[6]
Vivol[6]
Xanax[1]
Xanax TS[1]

Note: For quick reference, the following benzodiazepines are numbered to match the corresponding brand names.

This information applies to the following medicines:

1. Alprazolam (al-PRAZ-oh-lam)‡§
2. Bromazepam (broe-MA-ze-pam)*
3. Chlordiazepoxide (klor-dye-az-e-POX-ide)‡
4. Clonazepam (kloe-NA-ze-pam)
5. Clorazepate (klor-AZ-e-pate)‡
6. Diazepam (dye-AZ-e-pam)‡
7. Estazolam (ess-TA-zoe-lam)†
8. Flurazepam (flure-AZ-e-pam)‡
9. Halazepam (hal-AZ-e-pam)†
10. Ketazolam (kee-TAY--zoe-lam)*
11. Lorazepam (lor-AZ-e-pam)‡
12. Nitrazepam (nye-TRA-ze-pam)*
13. Oxazepam (ox-AZ-e-pam)‡
14. Prazepam (PRAZ-e-pam)†‡
15. Quazepam (KWA-ze-pam)†
16. Temazepam (tem-AZ-e-pam)‡
17. Triazolam (trye-AY-zoe-lam)§

*Not commercially available in the U.S.
†Not commercially available in Canada.
‡Generic name product may also be available in the U.S.
§Generic name product may also be available in Canada.

Description

Benzodiazepines (ben-zoe-dye-AZ-e-peens) belong to the group of medicines called central nervous system (CNS) depressants (medicines that slow down the nervous system).

Some benzodiazepines are used to relieve nervousness or tension. Others are used in the treatment of insomnia (trouble in sleeping). However, if used regularly (for example, every day) for insomnia, they are usually not effective for more than a few weeks.

One of the benzodiazepines, diazepam, is also used to help relax muscles or relieve muscle spasm. Another benzodiazepine, alprazolam, is also used in the treatment of panic disorder. Clonazepam, clorazepate, and diazepam are also used to treat certain convulsive (seizure) disorders, such as epilepsy. The benzodiazepines may also be used for other conditions as determined by your doctor.

Benzodiazepines should not be used for nervousness or tension caused by the stress of everyday life.

These medicines are available only with your doctor's prescription, in the following dosage forms:

Oral

Alprazolam
- Oral solution (U.S.)
- Tablets (U.S. and Canada)

Bromazepam
- Tablets (Canada)

Chlordiazepoxide
- Capsules (U.S. and Canada)
- Tablets (U.S.)

Clonazepam
- Tablets (U.S. and Canada)

Clorazepate
- Capsules (U.S. and Canada)
- Tablets (U.S.)

Diazepam
- Extended-release capsules (U.S.)
- Oral solution (U.S. and Canada)
- Tablets (U.S. and Canada)

Estazolam
- Tablets (U.S.)

Flurazepam
- Capsules (U.S. and Canada)
- Tablets (Canada)

Halazepam
- Tablets (U.S.)

Ketazolam
- Capsules (Canada)

Lorazepam
- Oral solution (U.S.)
- Tablets (U.S. and Canada)
- Sublingual tablets (Canada)

Nitrazepam
- Tablets (Canada)

Oxazepam
- Capsules (U.S.)
- Tablets (U.S. and Canada)

Prazepam
- Capsules (U.S.)
- Tablets (U.S.)

Quazepam
- Tablets (U.S.)

Temazepam
- Capsules (U.S. and Canada)
- Tablets (U.S.)

Triazolam
- Tablets (U.S. and Canada)

Parenteral

Chlordiazepoxide
- Injection (U.S. and Canada)

Diazepam
- Injection (U.S. and Canada)

Lorazepam
- Injection (U.S. and Canada)

Rectal

Diazepam
- For rectal solution (U.S. and Canada)

Before Using This Medicine

In deciding to use a medicine, the risks of taking the medicine must be weighed against the good it will do. This is a decision you and your doctor will make. For benzodiazepines, the following should be considered:

Allergies—Tell your doctor if you have ever had any unusual or allergic reaction to benzodiazepines. Also tell your health care professional if you are allergic to any other substances, such as foods, preservatives, or dyes.

Pregnancy—Chlordiazepoxide and diazepam have been reported to increase the chance of birth defects when used during the first 3 months of pregnancy. Although similar problems have not been reported with the other benzodiazepines, the chance always exists since all of the benzodiazepines are related.

Studies in animals have shown that clonazepam, lorazepam, and temazepam cause birth defects or other problems, including death of the animal fetus.

Too much use of benzodiazepines during pregnancy may cause the baby to become dependent on the medicine. This may lead to withdrawal side effects after birth. Also, use of benzodiazepines during pregnancy, especially during the last weeks, may cause drowsiness, slow heartbeat, shortness of breath, or troubled breathing in the newborn infant.

Benzodiazepines given just before or during labor may cause weakness in the newborn infant. When diazepam is given in high doses (especially by injection) within 15 hours before delivery, it may cause breathing problems, muscle weakness, difficulty in feeding, and body temperature problems in the newborn infant.

Breast-feeding—Benzodiazepines may pass into the breast milk and cause drowsiness, slow heartbeat, shortness of breath, or troubled breathing in nursing babies of mothers taking this medicine.

Children—Most of the side effects of these medicines are more likely to occur in children, especially the very young. These patients are usually more sensitive than adults to the effects of benzodiazepines.

When clonazepam is used for long periods of time in children, it may cause unwanted effects on physical and mental growth. These effects may not be noticed until many years later. Before this medicine is given to children for long periods of time, you should discuss its use with your child's doctor.

Older adults—Most of the side effects of these medicines are more likely to occur in the elderly, who are usually more sensitive to the effects of benzodiazepines.

Taking benzodiazepines for trouble in sleeping may cause more daytime drowsiness in elderly patients than in younger adults. In addition, falls and related injuries may be more likely to occur in elderly patients taking benzodiazepines.

Other medicines—Although certain medicines should not be used together at all, in other cases 2 different medicines may be used together even if an interaction might occur. In these cases, your doctor may want to change the dose, or other precautions may be necessary. When you are taking or receiving benzodiazepines it is especially important that your health care professional know if you are taking any of the following:

- Central nervous system (CNS) depressants (medicine that causes drowsiness)—The CNS depressant effects of either these medicines or benzodiazepines may be increased; your doctor may want to change the dose of either or both medicines

Other medical problems—The presence of other medical problems may affect the use of benzodiazepines. Make sure you tell your doctor if you have any other medical problems, especially:

- Alcohol abuse (or history of) or
- Drug abuse or dependence (or history of)—Dependence on benzodiazepines may develop
- Brain disease—CNS depression and other side effects of benzodiazepines may be more likely to occur
- Difficulty in swallowing (in children) or
- Emphysema, asthma, bronchitis, or other chronic lung disease or
- Glaucoma or
- Hyperactivity or
- Mental depression or
- Mental illness (severe) or
- Myasthenia gravis or
- Porphyria or
- Sleep apnea (temporarily stopping of breathing during sleep)—Benzodiazepines may make the condition worse
- Epilepsy or history of seizures—Although clonazepam and diazepam are used in treating epilepsy, starting or suddenly stopping treatment with these medicines may increase seizures
- Kidney or liver disease—Higher blood levels of benzodiazepines may result, increasing the chance of side effects

Proper Use of This Medicine

For patients taking *diazepam extended-release capsules:*

- Swallow capsules whole.
- Do not crush, break, or chew the capsules before swallowing.

For patients taking *lorazepam oral solution:*

- Each dose may be diluted with water, soda or soda-like beverages, or semisolid food, such as applesauce or pudding.

For patients taking *lorazepam sublingual tablets:*

- Do not chew or swallow the tablet. This medicine is meant to be absorbed through the lining of the mouth. Place the tablet under your tongue (sublingual) and let it slowly dissolve there. Do not swallow for at least 2 minutes.

Take this medicine only as directed by your doctor. Do not take more of it, do not take it more often, and do not take it for a longer time than your doctor ordered. If too much is taken, it may become habit-forming (causing mental or physical dependence).

If you think this medicine is not working properly after you have taken it for a few weeks, *do not increase the dose.* Instead, check with your doctor.

For patients taking this medicine *for epilepsy or other seizure disorder:*

- *In order for this medicine to control your seizures, it must be taken every day in regularly spaced doses as ordered by your doctor.* This is necessary to keep a constant amount of the medicine in the blood. To help keep the amount constant, do not miss any doses.

For patients taking this medicine *for insomnia:*

- *Do not take this medicine when your schedule does not permit you to get a full night's sleep (7 to 8 hours).* If you must wake up before this, you may continue to feel drowsy and may experience memory problems, because the effects of the medicine have not had time to wear off.

For patients taking *flurazepam:*

- *When you begin to take this medicine, your sleeping problem will improve somewhat the first night. However, 2 or 3 nights may pass before you receive the full effects of this medicine.*

Dosing—The dose of benzodiazepines will be different for different patients. *Follow your doctor's orders or the directions on the label.* The following information includes only the average doses of benzodiazepines. *If your dose is different, do not change it* unless your doctor tells you to do so.

The number of capsules or tablets, or the amount of solution that you take, or the number of injections you receive, depends on the strength of the medicine. Also, *the number of doses you take each day, the time allowed between doses, and the length of time you take the medicine depend on the medical problem for which you are taking benzodiazepines.*

For alprazolam

- For *oral* dosage form (solution or tablets):
  - —For anxiety:
    - Adults—At first, 0.25 to 0.5 milligrams (mg) three times a day. Your doctor may increase your dose if needed. However, the dose is usually not more than 4 mg a day.
    - Children up to 18 years of age—Use and dose must be determined by your doctor.
    - Older adults—At first, 0.25 mg two to three times a day. Your doctor may increase your dose if needed.

—For panic disorder:

• Adults—At first, 0.5 mg three times a day. Your doctor may increase your dose if needed. However, the dose is usually not more than 10 mg a day.

• Children up to 18 years of age—Use and dose must be determined by your doctor.

For bromazepam

• For *oral* dosage form (tablets):

—For anxiety:

• Adults—6 to 30 milligrams (mg) a day, taken in smaller doses during the day.

• Children up to 18 years of age—Use and dose must be determined by your doctor.

• Older adults—At first, up to 3 mg a day. Your doctor may change your dose if needed.

For chlordiazepoxide

• For *oral* dosage form (capsules or tablets):

—For anxiety:

• Adults—5 to 25 milligrams (mg) three or four times a day.

• Children 6 years of age and over—5 mg two to four times a day. Your doctor may increase your dose if needed.

• Children up to 6 years of age—Use and dose must be determined by your doctor.

• Older adults—At first, 5 mg two to four times a day. Your doctor may increase your dose if needed.

—For sedation during withdrawal from alcohol:

• Adults—At first, 50 to 100 mg, repeated if needed. However, the dose is usually not more than 400 mg a day.

• Children—Use and dose must be determined by your doctor.

• For *injection* dosage form:

—For anxiety:

• Adults—At first, 50 to 100 mg, injected into a muscle or vein. Then, if needed, 25 to 50 mg three or four times a day.

• Teenagers—25 to 50 mg, injected into a muscle or vein.

• Children up to 12 years of age—Use and dose must be determined by your doctor.

• Older adults—25 to 50 mg, injected into a muscle or vein.

—For sedation during withdrawal from alcohol:

• Adults—At first, 50 to 100 mg, injected into a muscle or vein. If needed, the dose may be repeated in two to four hours.

• Children—Use and dose must be determined by your doctor.

For clonazepam

• For *oral* dosage form (tablets):

—For control of seizures:

• Adults—At first, 0.5 milligrams (mg) three times a day. Your doctor may increase your dose if needed. However, the dose is usually not more than 20 mg a day.

• Infants and children up to 10 years of age—Dose is based on weight and must be determined by your doctor.

For clorazepate

• For *oral* dosage form (capsules or tablets):

—For anxiety:

• Adults and teenagers—7.5 to 15 milligrams (mg) two to four times a day. Or your doctor may want you to start by taking 15 mg at bedtime.

• Children up to 12 years of age—Use and dose must be determined by your doctor.

• Older adults—At first, 3.75 to 15 mg a day. Your doctor may increase your dose if needed.

—For sedation during withdrawal from alcohol:

• Adults and teenagers—At first, 30 mg. Your doctor will set up a schedule that will gradually reduce your dose.

• Children up to 12 years of age—Use and dose must be determined by your doctor.

—For control of seizures:

• Adults and teenagers—At first, up to 7.5 mg taken three times a day. Your doctor may increase your dose if needed. However, the dose is usually not more than 90 mg a day.

• Children 9 to 12 years of age—At first, 7.5 mg two times a day. Your doctor may increase your dose if needed. However, the dose is usually not more than 60 mg a day.

• Children up to 9 years of age—Use and dose must be determined by your doctor.

For diazepam

• For *oral* dosage form (extended-release capsules):

—For anxiety:

• Adults—15 to 30 milligrams (mg) once a day.

• Children 6 months of age and over—15 mg once a day.

• Children up to 6 months of age—Use is not recommended.

• Older adults—15 mg once a day.

—For relaxing muscles:

• Adults—15 to 30 mg once a day.

• Children 6 months of age and over—15 mg once a day.

• Children up to 6 months of age—Use is not recommended.

• Older adults—15 mg once a day.

- For *oral* dosage form (solution or tablets):
  - —For anxiety:
    - Adults—2 to 10 mg two to four times a day.
    - Children 6 months of age and over—Dose is based on body weight or size and must be determined by your doctor.
    - Children up to 6 months of age—Use is not recommended.
    - Older adults—2 to 2.5 mg one or two times a day. Your doctor may increase your dose if needed.
  - —For sedation during withdrawal from alcohol:
    - Adults—At first, 10 mg three or four times a day. Your doctor will set up a schedule that will gradually decrease your dose.
    - Children—Use and dose must be determined by your doctor.
  - —For control of seizures:
    - Adults—2 to 10 mg taken two to four times a day.
    - Children 6 months of age and over—Dose is based on body weight or size and must be determined by your doctor.
    - Children up to 6 months of age—Use is not recommended.
    - Older adults—2 to 2.5 mg one or two times a day. Your doctor may increase your dose if needed.
  - —For relaxing muscles:
    - Adults—2 to 10 mg three or four times a day.
    - Children 6 months of age and over—Dose is based on body weight or size and must be determined by your doctor.
    - Children up to 6 months of age—Use is not recommended.
    - Older adults—2 to 2.5 mg one or two times a day. Your doctor may increase your dose if needed.
- For *injection* dosage form:
  - —For anxiety:
    - Adults—2 to 10 mg, injected into a muscle or vein.
    - Children—Use and dose must be determined by your doctor.
    - For older adults—2 to 5 mg, injected into a muscle or vein.
  - —For sedation during withdrawal from alcohol:
    - Adults—At first, 10 mg injected into a muscle or vein. If needed, 5 to 10 mg may be given three or four hours later.
    - Children—Use and dose must be determined by your doctor.
  - —For sedation before surgery or other procedures:
    - Adults—5 to 20 mg, injected into a muscle or vein.
    - Children—Use and dose must be determined by your doctor.
    - Older adults—2 to 5 mg, injected into a muscle or vein.
  - —For control of seizures:
    - Adults—At first, 5 to 10 mg, usually injected into a vein. If needed, the dose may be repeated.
    - Children 5 years of age and older—At first, 1 mg injected into a vein every two to five minutes. The dose may need to be repeated.
    - Infants over 30 days of age and children up to 5 years of age—At first, 0.2 to 0.5 mg injected into a vein every two to five minutes. The dose may need to be repeated.
    - Newborns and infants up to 30 days of age: Use and dose must be determined by your doctor.
    - Older adults—2 to 5 mg, injected into a muscle or vein.
  - —For relaxing muscle spasms:
    - Adults—At first, 5 to 10 mg injected into a muscle or vein. The dose may be repeated in three or four hours.
    - Children: Use and dose must be determined by your doctor.
    - Older adults—2 to 5 mg, injected into a muscle or vein.
  - —For relaxing muscles in tetanus:
    - Adults—At first, 5 to 10 mg injected into a muscle or vein. Your doctor may increase your dose if needed.
    - Children 5 years of age and older—5 to 10 mg, injected into a muscle or vein. The dose may be repeated every three to four hours if needed.
    - Infants over 30 days of age and children up to 5 years of age—1 to 2 mg, injected into a muscle or vein. The dose may be repeated every three to four hours if needed.
    - Newborns and infants up to 30 days of age: Use and dose must be determined by your doctor.
- For *rectal* dosage form (solution):
  - —For control of seizures:
    - Adults and teenagers—Dose is based on body weight and must be determined by your doctor.
    - Children—Dose is based on body weight and must be determined by your doctor.

For estazolam

- For *oral* dosage form (tablets):
  - —For trouble in sleeping:
    - Adults—1 milligram (mg) at bedtime.
    - Children up to 18 years of age—Use and dose must be determined by your doctor.

For flurazepam
- For *oral* dosage form (capsules or tablets):
  - —For trouble in sleeping:
    - Adults—15 or 30 milligrams (mg) at bedtime.
    - Children up to 15 years of age—Use and dose must be determined by your doctor.
    - Older adults—At first, 15 mg at bedtime. Your doctor may increase your dose if needed.

For halazepam
- For *oral* dosage form (tablets):
  - —For anxiety:
    - Adults—20 to 40 milligrams (mg) three or four times a day.
    - Children up to 18 years of age—Use and dose must be determined by your doctor.
    - Older adults—20 mg one or two times a day.

For ketazolam
- For *oral* dosage form (capsules):
  - —For anxiety:
    - Adults—15 milligrams (mg) one or two times a day. Your doctor may increase your dose if needed.
    - Children up to 18 years of age—Use and dose must be determined by your doctor.
    - Infants—Use is not recommended.
    - Older adults—15 mg once a day.

For lorazepam
- For *oral* dosage form (solution or tablets):
  - —For anxiety:
    - Adults—1 to 3 milligrams (mg) two or three times a day.
    - Children up to 12 years of age—Use and dose must be determined by your doctor.
    - Older adults—0.5 to 2 mg a day, taken in smaller doses during the day.
  - —For trouble in sleeping:
    - Adults—2 to 4 mg taken at bedtime.
    - Children up to 12 years of age—Use and dose must be determined by your doctor.
- For *sublingual tablet* dosage form:
  - —For anxiety:
    - Adults—2 to 3 mg a day, in smaller doses placed under the tongue during the day. Your doctor may increase your dose if needed. However, the dose is usually not more than 6 mg a day.
    - Children 6 to 18 years of age—Use and dose must be determined by your doctor.
    - Children up to 6 years of age—Use is not recommended.
    - Older adults—At first, 0.5 mg a day. Your doctor may increase your dose if needed.
  - —For sedation before surgery:
    - Adults—Dose is based on body weight and is usually 0.05 mg per kilogram (0.023 mg per pound) of body weight, placed under the tongue, one to two hours before surgery. The dose is usually not more than 4 mg.
    - Children—Use and dose must be determined by your doctor.
- For *injection* dosage form:
  - —For sedation before surgery or other procedures:
    - Adults—Dose is based on body weight and will be determined by your doctor. However, the dose is usually not more than 4 mg, injected into a muscle or vein.
    - Children up to 18 years of age—Use and dose must be determined by your doctor.

For nitrazepam
- For *oral* dosage form (tablets):
  - —For trouble in sleeping:
    - Adults—5 to 10 milligrams (mg) at bedtime.
    - Children—Use and dose must be determined by your doctor.
    - Older adults—At first, 2.5 mg taken at bedtime. Your doctor may increase your dose if needed.
  - —For control of seizures:
    - Children up to 30 kilograms (66 pounds) of body weight—Dose is based on body weight and is usually 0.3 to 1 mg per kilogram (0.14 to 0.45 mg per pound) of body weight per day, taken in smaller doses three times during the day. Your doctor may increase your dose if needed.

For oxazepam
- For *oral* dosage form (capsules or tablets):
  - —For anxiety:
    - Adults—10 to 30 milligrams (mg) three or four times a day.
    - Children 6 to 12 years of age—Use and dose must be determined by your doctor.
    - Children up to 6 years of age—Use is not recommended.
    - Older adults—At first, 10 mg three times a day.Your doctor may increase your dose if needed. However, the dose is usually not more than 15 mg taken four times a day.
  - —For sedation during withdrawal from alcohol:
    - Adults—15 to 30 mg three or four times a day.
    - Children—Use and dose must be determined by your doctor.

For prazepam
- For *oral* dosage form (capsules or tablets):
  - —For anxiety:
    - Adults—10 milligrams (mg) three times a day, or 20 to 40 mg taken at bedtime.
    - Children—Use and dose must be determined by your doctor.
    - Older adults—At first, 10 to 15 mg a day, taken in smaller doses during the day. Your doctor may increase your dose if needed.

For quazepam
- For *oral* dosage form (tablets):
 —For trouble in sleeping:
  - Adults—7.5 to 15 milligrams (mg) taken at bedtime.
  - Children up to 18 years of age—Use and dose must be determined by your doctor.

For temazepam
- For *oral* dosage form (capsules or tablets):
 —For trouble in sleeping:
  - Adults—15 milligrams (mg) taken at bedtime.
  - Children up to 18 years of age—Use and dose must be determined by your doctor.
  - Older adults—At first, 7.5 mg at bedtime. Your doctor may increase your dose if needed.

For triazolam
- For *oral* dosage form (tablets):
 —For trouble in sleeping:
  - Adults—125 to 250 micrograms (mcg) taken at bedtime.
  - Children up to 18 years of age—Use and dose must be determined by your doctor.
  - Older adults—At first, 125 mcg at bedtime. Your doctor may increase your dose if needed.

Missed dose—If you are taking this medicine regularly (for example, every day as for epilepsy) and you miss a dose, take it right away if you remember within an hour or so of the missed dose. However, if you do not remember until later, skip the missed dose and go back to your regular dosing schedule. Do not double doses.

Storage—To store this medicine:
- Keep out of the reach of children. Overdose of benzodiazepines may be especially dangerous in children.
- Store away from heat and direct light.
- Do not store the capsule or tablet form of this medicine in the bathroom, near the kitchen sink, or in other damp places. Heat or moisture may cause the medicine to break down.
- Keep the liquid form of this medicine from freezing.
- Do not keep outdated medicine or medicine no longer needed. Be sure that any discarded medicine is out of the reach of children.

Precautions While Using This Medicine

If you will be *taking this medicine regularly for a long time:*
- Your doctor should check your progress at regular visits to make sure that this medicine does not cause unwanted effects. If you are taking clonazepam, this is also important during the first few months of treatment.
- If you are taking this medicine for nervousness or tension or for panic disorder, check with your doctor at least every 4 months to make sure you need to continue taking this medicine.
- If you are taking estazolam, flurazepam, quazepam, temazepam, or triazolam for insomnia (trouble in sleeping), and you think you need this medicine for more than 7 to 10 days, be sure to discuss it with your doctor. Insomnia that lasts longer than this may be a sign of another medical problem.

If you will be taking this medicine in large doses or for a long time, do not stop taking it without first checking with your doctor. Your doctor may want you to reduce gradually the amount you are taking before stopping completely. Stopping this medicine suddenly may cause withdrawal side effects. Also, if you are taking this medicine for epilepsy or another seizure disorder, stopping this medicine suddenly may cause seizures.

For patients taking this medicine *for epilepsy or another seizure disorder:*
- Your doctor may want you to carry a medical identification card or bracelet stating that you are taking this medicine.

This medicine will add to the effects of alcohol and other CNS depressants (medicines that slow down the nervous system, possibly causing drowsiness). Some examples of CNS depressants are antihistamines or medicine for hay fever, other allergies, or colds; sedatives, tranquilizers, or sleeping medicine; prescription pain medicine or narcotics; barbiturates; medicine for seizures; muscle relaxants; or anesthetics, including some dental anesthetics. This effect may last for a few days after you stop taking this medicine. *Check with your doctor before taking any of the above while you are taking this medicine.*

If you think you or someone else may have taken an overdose of this medicine, get emergency help at once. Taking an overdose of a benzodiazepine or taking alcohol or other CNS depressants with the benzodiazepine may lead to unconsciousness and possibly death. Some signs of an overdose are continuing slurred speech or confusion, severe drowsiness, severe weakness, and staggering.

Before you have any medical tests, tell the medical doctor in charge that you are taking this medicine. The results of the metyrapone test may be affected by chlordiazepoxide.

If you develop any unusual and strange thoughts or behavior while you are taking this medicine, be sure to discuss it with your doctor. Some changes that have occurred in people taking this medicine are like those seen in people who drink alcohol and then act in a manner that is not normal. Other changes may be more unusual and extreme, such as confusion, agitation, and hallucinations (seeing, hearing, or feeling things that are not there).

This medicine may cause some people, especially older persons, to become drowsy, dizzy, lightheaded, clumsy or unsteady, or less alert than they are normally. Even if taken at bedtime, it may cause some people to feel drowsy or less alert on arising. *Make sure you know how you react to this medicine before you drive, use machines, or do anything else that could be dangerous if you are dizzy or are not alert.*

If you have been taking this medicine for insomnia, you may have difficulty sleeping (rebound insomnia) for the first few nights after you stop taking the medicine.

Side Effects of This Medicine

Along with its needed effects, a medicine may cause some unwanted effects. Although not all of these side effects may occur, if they do occur they may need medical attention.

Check with your doctor as soon as possible if any of the following side effects occur:

Less common or rare

Behavior problems, including difficulty in concentrating and outbursts of anger; confusion or mental depression; convulsions (seizures); hallucinations (seeing, hearing, or feeling things that are not there); hypotension (low blood pressure); impaired memory—may be more common with triazolam; muscle weakness; skin rash or itching; sore throat, fever, and chills; trouble in sleeping; ulcers or sores in mouth or throat (continuing); uncontrolled movements of body, including the eyes; unusual bleeding or bruising; unusual excitement, nervousness, or irritability; unusual tiredness or weakness (severe); yellow eyes or skin

Symptoms of overdose

Confusion (continuing); drowsiness (severe); shakiness; slow heartbeat, shortness of breath, or troubled breathing; slow reflexes; slurred speech (continuing); staggering; weakness (severe)

Other side effects may occur that usually do not need medical attention. These side effects may go away during treatment as your body adjusts to the medicine. However, check with your doctor if any of the following side effects continue or are bothersome:

More common

Clumsiness or unsteadiness; dizziness or lightheadedness; drowsiness; slurred speech

Less common or rare

Abdominal or stomach cramps or pain; blurred vision or other changes in vision; changes in sexual drive or performance; constipation; diarrhea; dryness of mouth or increased thirst; false sense of well-being; fast or pounding heartbeat; headache; increased bronchial secretions or watering of mouth; muscle spasm; nausea or vomiting; problems with urination; trembling; unusual tiredness or weakness

Not all of the side effects listed above have been reported for each of these medicines, but they have been reported for at least one of them. All of the benzodiazepines are similar, so any of the above side effects may occur with any of these medicines.

For patients having *chlordiazepoxide, diazepam, or lorazepam injected:*

- Check with your doctor if there is redness, swelling, or pain at the place of injection.

After you stop using this medicine, your body may need time to adjust. If you took this medicine in high doses or for a long time, this may take up to 3 weeks. During this period of time check with your doctor if you notice any of the following side effects:

More common

Irritability; nervousness; trouble in sleeping

Less common

Abdominal or stomach cramps; confusion; fast or pounding heartbeat; increased sense of hearing; increased sensitivity to touch and pain; increased sweating; loss of sense of reality; mental depression; muscle cramps; nausea or vomiting; sensitivity of eyes to light; tingling, burning, or prickly sensations; trembling

Rare

Confusion as to time, place, or person; convulsions (seizures); feelings of suspicion or distrust; hallucinations (seeing, hearing, or feeling things that are not there)

Other side effects not listed above may also occur in some patients. If you notice any other effects, check with your doctor.

Additional Information

Once a medicine has been approved for marketing for a certain use, experience may show that it is also useful for other medical problems. Although these uses are not included in product labeling, some of the benzodiazepines are used in certain patients with the following medical conditions:

- Nausea and vomiting caused by cancer chemotherapy
- Tension headache
- Tremors

Other than the above information, there is no additional information relating to proper use, precautions, or side effects for these uses.

Revised: 08/04/92
Interim revision: 08/17/94

BENZONATATE Systemic

A commonly used brand name in the U.S. and Canada is Tessalon. Generic name product may also be available in the U.S.

Description

Benzonatate (ben-ZOE-na-tate) is used to relieve coughs due to colds or influenza (flu). It is not to be used for chronic cough that occurs with smoking, asthma, or emphysema or when there is an unusually large amount of mucus or phlegm (pronounced flem) with the cough.

Benzonatate relieves cough by acting directly on the lungs and the breathing passages. It may also act on the cough center in the brain.

This medicine is available only with your doctor's prescription, in the following dosage form:

Oral

- Capsules (U.S. and Canada)

Before Using this Medicine

In deciding to use a medicine, the risks of taking the medicine must be weighed against the good it will do. This is a decision you and your doctor will make. For benzonatate, the following should be considered:

Allergies—Tell your doctor if you have ever had any unusual or allergic reaction to benzonatate or to tetracaine or other local anesthetics. Also tell your health care professional if you are allergic to any other substances, such as foods, preservatives, or dyes.

Pregnancy—Studies on effects in pregnancy have not been done in either humans or animals.

Breast-feeding—It is not known whether benzonatate passes into breast milk. Although most medicines pass into breast milk in small amounts, many of them may be used safely while breast-feeding. Mothers who are taking this medicine and who wish to breast-feed should discuss this with their doctor.

Children—Children may tend to chew the capsule before swallowing it. This may cause numbness (loss of feeling) in the mouth and throat, and choking may occur.

Older adults—Many medicines have not been studied specifically in older people. Therefore, it may not be known whether they work exactly the same way they do in younger adults or if they cause different side effects or problems in older people. There is no specific information comparing use of benzonatate in the elderly with use in other age groups.

Other medicines—Although certain medicines should not be used together at all, in other cases 2 different medicines may be used together even if an interaction might occur. In these cases, your doctor may want to change the dose, or other precautions may be necessary. Tell your health care professional if you are taking any other prescription or nonprescription (over-the-counter [OTC]) medicine.

Other medical problems—The presence of other medical problems may affect the use of benzonatate. Make sure you tell your doctor if you have any other medical problems, especially:

- Mucus or phlegm with cough—Since benzonatate decreases coughing, it makes it difficult to get rid of the mucus that may collect in the lungs and airways with some diseases

Proper Use of This Medicine

Do not chew the capsules before swallowing them. If the benzonatate contained in the capsules comes in contact with the mouth, it may cause the mouth and throat to become numb (loss of feeling) and choking may occur.

Dosing—The dose of benzonatate will be different for different patients. *Follow your doctor's orders or the directions on the label.* The following information includes only the average doses of benzonatate. *If your dose is different, do not change it* unless your doctor tells you to do so.

- For *oral* dosage form (capsules):
  - —For cough:
    - Adults—100 milligrams (mg) three times a day as needed.
    - Children—

      Up to 10 years of age: Use is not recommended.

      10 years of age and older: 100 mg three times a day as needed.

Missed dose—If you must take this medicine regularly and you miss a dose, take it as soon as possible. However, if it is almost time for your next dose, skip the missed dose and go back to your regular dosing schedule. Do not double doses.

Storage—To store this medicine:

- Store away from heat and direct light.
- Keep out of the reach of children.
- Do not store this medicine in the bathroom, near the kitchen sink, or in other damp places. Heat or moisture may cause the medicine to break down.
- Do not keep outdated medicine or medicine no longer needed. Be sure that any discarded medicine is out of the reach of children.

Precautions While Using This Medicine

If your cough has not become better after 7 days or if you have a high fever, skin rash, or continuing headache with the cough, check with your doctor. These signs may mean that you have other medical problems.

Side Effects of This Medicine

Along with its needed effects, a medicine may cause some unwanted effects. Although not all of these side effects may occur, if they do occur they may need medical attention.

Check with your doctor as soon as possible if any of the following side effects occur:

Symptoms of overdose

Convulsions (seizures); restlessness; trembling

Other side effects may occur that usually do not need medical attention. These side effects may go away during treatment as your body adjusts to the medicine. However, check with your health care professional if any of the following side effects continue or are bothersome:

Less common or rare

Constipation; dizziness (mild); drowsiness (mild); nausea or vomiting; skin rash; stuffy nose

Other side effects not listed above may also occur in some patients. If you notice any other effects, check with your doctor.

Revised: 02/23/94

BENZOYL PEROXIDE Topical

Some commonly used brand names are:

In the U.S.—

Acne Aid 10 Cream
Acne-5 Lotion
Acne-10 Lotion
Ben-Aqua-2½ Gel
Ben-Aqua-5 Gel
Ben-Aqua-10 Gel
Ben-Aqua-5 Lotion
Ben-Aqua-10 Lotion
Ben-Aqua Masque 5
Benoxyl 5 Lotion
Benoxyl 10 Lotion
Benzac Ac 2½ Gel
Benzac Ac 5 Gel
Benzac Ac 10 Gel
Benzac 5 Gel
Benzac 10 Gel
Benzac W 2½ Gel
Benzac W 5 Gel
Benzac W 10 Gel
Benzac W Wash 5
Benzac W Wash 10
BenzaShave 5 Cream
BenzaShave 10 Cream
Brevoxyl 4 Gel
Clearasil Maximum Strength Medicated Anti-Acne 10 Tinted Cream
Clearasil Maximum Strength Medicated Anti-Acne 10 Vanishing Cream
Clearasil Maximum Strength Medicated Anti-Acne 10 Vanishing Lotion
Clear By Design 2.5 Gel
Cuticura Acne 5 Cream
Del-Aqua-5 Gel
Del-Aqua-10 Gel
Desquam-E 2.5 Gel
Desquam-E 5 Gel
Desquam-E 10 Gel
Desquam-X 10 Bar
Desquam-X 2.5 Gel
Desquam-X 5 Gel
Desquam-X 10 Gel
Desquam-X 5 Wash
Desquam-X 10 Wash
Dry and Clear Double Strength 10 Cream
Dry and Clear 5 Lotion
Dryox 5 Gel
Dryox 10 Gel
Dryox 20 Gel
Dryox Wash 5
Dryox Wash 10
Fostex 10 Bar
Fostex 10 Cream
Fostex 5 Gel
Fostex 10 Gel
Fostex 10 Wash
Loroxide 5.5 Lotion
Neutrogena Acne Mask 5
Noxzema Clear-ups Maximum Strength 10 Lotion
Noxzema Clear-ups On-The-Spot 10 Lotion
Oxy 10 Daily Face Wash
Oxy 5 Tinted Lotion
Oxy 10 Tinted Lotion
Oxy 5 Vanishing Lotion
Oxy 10 Vanishing Lotion
PanOxyl AQ 2½ Gel
PanOxyl AQ 5 Gel
PanOxyl AQ 10 Gel
PanOxyl 5 Bar
PanOxyl 10 Bar
PanOxyl 5 Gel
PanOxyl 10 Gel
Persa-Gel 5
Persa-Gel 10
Persa-Gel W 5
Persa-Gel W 10
pHisoAc BP 10 Cream
Propa P.H. 10 Acne Cover Stick
Propa P.H. 10 Liquid Acne Soap
Stri-Dex Maximum Strength Treatment 10 Cream
Theroxide 5 Lotion
Theroxide 10 Lotion
Theroxide 10 Wash
Topex 10 Lotion
Vanoxide 5 Lotion
Xerac BP 5 Gel
Xerac BP 10 Gel
Zeroxin-5 Gel
Zeroxin-10 Gel

Generic name product may also be available.

In Canada—

Acetoxyl 2.5 Gel
Acetoxyl 5 Gel
Acetoxyl 10 Gel
Acetoxyl 20 Gel
Acnomel B.P. 5 Lotion
Benoxyl 5 Lotion
Benoxyl 10 Lotion
Benoxyl 20 Lotion
Benoxyl 5 Wash
Benoxyl 10 Wash
Benzac W 5 Gel
Benzac W 10 Gel
Benzagel 5 Acne Lotion
Benzagel 5 Acne Wash
Benzagel 5 Gel
Benzagel 10 Gel
Clearasil BP Plus 5 Cream
Clearasil BP Plus 5 Lotion
Dermoxyl Aqua 5 Gel
Dermoxyl 2.5 Gel
Dermoxyl 5 Gel
Dermoxyl 10 Gel
Dermoxyl 20 Gel
Desquam-X 5 Bar
Desquam-X 5 Gel
Desquam-X 10 Gel
Desquam-X 5 Wash
Desquam-X 10 Wash
H_2Oxyl 2.5 Gel
H_2Oxyl 5 Gel
H_2Oxyl 10 Gel
H_2Oxyl 20 Gel
Loroxide 5 Lotion with Flesh-Tinted Base
Oxyderm 5 Lotion
Oxyderm 10 Lotion
Oxyderm 20 Lotion
Oxy 5 Vanishing Formula Lotion
PanOxyl 5 Bar
PanOxyl 10 Bar
PanOxyl 5 Gel
PanOxyl 10 Gel
PanOxyl 15 Gel
PanOxyl 20 Gel
Topex 5 Lotion

Description

Benzoyl peroxide (BEN-zoe-ill per-OX-ide) is used to treat acne. It may also be used for other conditions as determined by your doctor.

Some of these preparations are available only with your doctor's prescription. Others are available without a prescription; however, your doctor may have special instructions on the proper use of benzoyl peroxide for your medical condition.

Benzoyl peroxide is available in the following dosage forms:

Topical

- Cleansing bar (U.S. and Canada)
- Cream (U.S. and Canada)
- Gel (U.S. and Canada)
- Lotion (U.S. and Canada)
- Cleansing lotion (U.S. and Canada)
- Facial mask (U.S.)
- Stick (U.S.)

Before Using This Medicine

If you are using this medicine without a prescription, carefully read and follow any precautions on the label. For benzoyl peroxide, the following should be considered:

Allergies—Tell your doctor if you have ever had any unusual or allergic reaction to benzoyl peroxide. Also tell your health care professional if you are allergic to any other substances, such as preservatives or dyes.

Pregnancy—Studies on effects in pregnancy have not been done in either humans or animals. However, benzoyl peroxide may be absorbed through the skin.

Breast-feeding—Benzoyl peroxide may be absorbed through the mother's skin. It is not known whether it passes into the breast milk. However, this medicine has not been reported to cause problems in nursing babies.

Children—For children up to 12 years of age: Studies on this medicine have been done only in adult patients, and there is no specific information comparing use of benzoyl peroxide with use in other age groups. For children 12 years of age and older: Although there is no specific information comparing use of benzoyl peroxide in children with use in other age groups, this medicine is not expected to cause different side effects or problems in children 12 years of age and older than it does in adults.

Older adults—Many medicines have not been studied specifically in older people. Therefore, it may not be known whether they work exactly the same way they do in younger adults. Although there is no specific information comparing use of benzoyl peroxide in the elderly with use in other age groups, this medicine is not expected to cause different side effects or problems in older people than it does in younger adults.

Other medicines—Although certain medicines should not be used together at all, in other cases two different medicines may be used together even if an interaction might occur. In these cases, your doctor may want to change the dose, or other precautions may be necessary. Tell your health care professional if you are using any other topical prescription or nonprescription (over-the-counter [OTC]) medicine that is to be applied to the same area of the skin.

Other medical problems—The presence of other medical problems may affect the use of benzoyl peroxide. Make sure you tell your doctor if you have any other medical problems, especially:

- Red or raw skin—Irritation will occur if benzoyl peroxide is used on red or raw skin

Proper Use of This Medicine

To use the *cream, gel, lotion, or stick form* of benzoyl peroxide:

- Before applying, wash the affected area with non-medicated soap and water or with a degreasing cleanser and then gently pat dry with a towel.
- Apply enough medicine to cover the affected areas, and rub in gently.

To use the *shave cream form* of benzoyl peroxide:

- Wet the area to be shaved.
- Apply a small amount of the shave cream and gently rub over entire area.
- Shave.
- Rinse the area and pat dry.
- After-shave lotions or other drying face products should not be used without checking with your doctor first.

To use the *cleansing bar, cleansing lotion, or soap form* of benzoyl peroxide:

- Use to wash the affected areas as directed.

To use the *facial mask form* of benzoyl peroxide:

- Before applying, wash the affected area with a non-medicated cleanser. Then rinse and pat dry.
- Using a circular motion, apply a thin layer of the mask evenly over the affected area.
- Allow the mask to dry for 15 to 25 minutes.
- Then rinse thoroughly with warm water and pat dry.

Use benzoyl peroxide only as directed. Do not use more of it and do not use it more often than recommended on the label, unless otherwise directed by your doctor.

Keep this medicine away from the eyes, other mucous membranes, such as the mouth, lips, and inside of the nose, and sensitive areas of the neck.

Do not apply benzoyl peroxide to raw or irritated skin.

Dosing—The dose of benzoyl peroxide will be different for different patients. *Follow your doctor's orders or the directions on the label.* The following information includes only the average doses of benzoyl peroxide. *If your dose is different, do not change it* unless your doctor tells you to do so.

- For acne:
  - —For *cleansing bar* dosage form:
    - Adults and children 12 years of age and over—Use two or three times a day, or as directed by your doctor.
    - Children up to 12 years of age—Use and dose must be determined by your doctor.
  - —For *cleansing lotion, cream,* or *gel* dosage forms:
    - Adults and children 12 years of age and over—Use on the affected area(s) of the skin one or two times a day.
    - Children up to 12 years of age—Use and dose must be determined by your doctor.
  - —For *lotion* dosage form:
    - Adults and children 12 years of age and over—Use on the affected area(s) of the skin one to four times a day.
    - Children up to 12 years of age—Use and dose must be determined by your doctor.
  - —For *facial mask* dosage form:
    - Adults and children 12 years of age and over—Use one time a week or as directed by your doctor.
    - Children up to 12 years of age—Use and dose must be determined by your doctor.
  - —For *stick* dosage form:
    - Adults and children 12 years of age and over—Use on the affected area(s) of the skin one to three times a day.
    - Children up to 12 years of age—Use and dose must be determined by your doctor.

Missed dose—If you miss a dose of this medicine, apply or use it as soon as possible. Then go back to your regular dosing schedule.

Storage—To store this medicine:

- Keep out of the reach of children.
- Store away from heat and direct light.
- Keep the cream, gel, or liquid form of this medicine from freezing.
- Do not keep outdated medicine or medicine no longer needed. Be sure that any discarded medicine is out of the reach of children.

Precautions While Using This Medicine

If your skin problem has not improved within 4 to 6 weeks, check with your doctor.

If this medicine causes too much redness, peeling, or dryness of your skin, check with your doctor. It may be necessary for you to reduce the number of times a day that you use the medicine and/or use a weaker strength of the medicine.

When using benzoyl peroxide, do not use any of the following preparations on the same affected area as this medicine, unless otherwise directed by your doctor:

- Abrasive soaps or cleansers
- Alcohol-containing preparations
- Any other topical acne preparation or preparation containing a peeling agent (for example, resorcinol, salicylic acid, sulfur, or tretinoin [vitamin A acid])
- Cosmetics or soaps that dry the skin
- Medicated cosmetics
- Other topical medicine for the skin

To use any of the above preparations on the same affected area as benzoyl peroxide may cause severe irritation of the skin.

This medicine may bleach hair or colored fabrics.

Side Effects of This Medicine

Along with its needed effects, a medicine may cause some unwanted effects. Although not all of these side effects may occur, if they do occur they may need medical attention.

Check with your doctor as soon as possible if any of the following side effects occur:

Less common or rare

Painful irritation of skin, including burning, blistering, crusting, itching, severe redness, or swelling; skin rash

Symptoms of overdose

Burning, itching, scaling, redness, or swelling of skin (severe)

Other side effects may occur that usually do not need medical attention. These side effects may go away during treatment as your body adjusts to the medicine. However, check with your health care professional if any of the following side effects continue or are bothersome:

Less common

Dryness or peeling of skin (may occur after a few days); feeling of warmth, mild stinging, and redness of skin

Other side effects not listed above may also occur in some patients. If you notice any other effects, check with your health care professional.

Additional Information

Once a medicine has been approved for marketing for a certain use, experience may show that it is also useful for other medical problems. Although these uses are not included in product labeling, benzoyl peroxide is used in certain patients with the following medical conditions:

- Decubital ulcer (bed sores)
- Stasis ulcer (a certain type of ulcer)

Other than the above information, there is no additional information relating to proper use, precautions, or side effects for these uses.

Revised: 01/15/92
Interim revision: 05/20/94

BETA-ADRENERGIC BLOCKING AGENTS Ophthalmic

Some commonly used brand names are:

In the U.S.—

- Betagan C Cap B.I.D.[3]
- Betagan C Cap Q.D.[3]
- Betagan Standard Cap[3]
- Betoptic[1]
- Betoptic S[1]
- Ocupress[2]
- OptiPranolol[4]
- Timoptic[5]
- Timoptic in Ocudose[5]

In Canada—

- Apo-Timop[5]
- Betagan C Cap B.I.D.[3]
- Betagan Standard Cap[3]
- Betoptic[1]
- Gen-Timolol[5]
- Timoptic[5]

Note: For quick reference, the following beta-adrenergic blocking agents are numbered to match the corresponding brand names.

This information applies to the following medicines:

1. Betaxolol (be-TAX-oh-lol)
2. Carteolol (KAR-tee-oh-lole)†
3. Levobunolol (lee-voe-BYOO-noe-lole)
4. Metipranolol (met-i-PRAN-oh-lol)†
5. Timolol (TYE-moe-lole)

†Not commercially available in Canada.

Description

Betaxolol, carteolol, levobunolol, metipranolol, and timolol are used to treat certain types of glaucoma. They appear to work by reducing the production of fluid in the eye. This lowers the pressure in the eye.

These medicines are available only with your doctor's prescription, in the following dosage forms:

Ophthalmic

- Betaxolol
  - Ophthalmic solution (eye drops) (U.S. and Canada)
  - Ophthalmic suspension (eye drops) (U.S.)
- Carteolol
  - Ophthalmic solution (eye drops) (U.S.)
- Levobunolol
  - Ophthalmic solution (eye drops) (U.S. and Canada)
- Metipranolol
  - Ophthalmic solution (eye drops) (U.S.)
- Timolol
  - Ophthalmic solution (eye drops) (U.S. and Canada)

Before Using This Medicine

In deciding to use a medicine, the risks of taking the medicine must be weighed against the good it will do. This is a decision you and your doctor will make. For ophthalmic beta-adrenergic blocking agents, the following should be considered:

Allergies—Tell your doctor if you have ever had any unusual or allergic reaction to any of the beta-adrenergic blocking agents, either ophthalmic or systemic, such as acebutolol, atenolol, betaxolol, bisoprolol, carteolol, labetalol, levobunolol, metipranolol, metoprolol, nadolol, oxprenolol, penbutolol, pindolol, propranolol, sotalol, or timolol. Also tell your health care professional if you are allergic to any other substances, such as sulfites or preservatives.

Pregnancy—Ophthalmic beta-adrenergic blocking agents may be absorbed into the body. These medicines have not been studied in pregnant women. Studies in animals have not shown that betaxolol, levobunolol, metipranolol, or timolol causes birth defects. However, very large doses of carteolol given by mouth to pregnant rats have been shown to cause wavy ribs in rat babies. In addition, some studies in animals have shown that beta-adrenergic blocking agents increase the chance of death in the animal fetus. Before using ophthalmic beta-adrenergic blocking agents, make sure your doctor knows if you are pregnant or if you may become pregnant.

Breast-feeding—Betaxolol and timolol, and maybe other beta-adrenergic blocking agents, when taken by mouth, may pass into the breast milk. Since ophthalmic beta-adrenergic blocking agents may be absorbed into the body, they, too, may pass into the breast milk. However, it is not known whether ophthalmic beta-adrenergic blocking agents pass into the breast milk, and these medicines have not been reported to cause problems in nursing babies.

Children—Infants may be especially sensitive to the effects of ophthalmic beta-adrenergic blocking agents. This may increase the chance of side effects during treatment.

Older adults—Elderly people are especially sensitive to the effects of ophthalmic beta-adrenergic blocking agents. If too much medicine is absorbed into the body, the chance of side effects during treatment may be increased.

Other medicines—Although certain medicines should not be used together at all, in other cases two different medicines may be used together even if an interaction might occur. In these cases, your doctor may want to change the dose, or other precautions may be necessary. Tell your health care professional if you are using any other prescription or nonprescription (over-the-counter [OTC]) medicine.

Other medical problems—The presence of other medical problems may affect the use of ophthalmic beta-adrenergic blocking agents. Make sure you tell your doctor if you have any other medical problems, especially:

- Asthma (or history of), chronic bronchitis, emphysema, or other lung disease—Severe breathing problems, including death due to bronchospasm (spasm of the bronchial tubes), have been reported in patients with asthma following use of some ophthalmic beta-adrenergic blocking agents (carteolol, levobunolol, metipranolol, and timolol). Although most often not a problem, the possibility of wheezing or troubled breathing also exists with betaxolol
- Diabetes mellitus (sugar diabetes) or
- Hypoglycemia (low blood sugar)—Ophthalmic beta-adrenergic blocking agents may cover up some signs and symptoms of hypoglycemia (low blood sugar), such as fast heartbeat and trembling, although they do not cover up other signs, such as dizziness or sweating
- Heart or blood vessel disease—Ophthalmic beta-adrenergic blocking agents may decrease heart activity
- Overactive thyroid—Ophthalmic beta-adrenergic blocking agents may cover up certain signs and symptoms of hyperthyroidism (overactive thyroid). Suddenly stopping the use of ophthalmic beta-adrenergic blocking agents may cause a sudden and dangerous increase in thyroid symptoms

Proper Use of This Medicine

To use:

- First, wash your hands. With the middle finger, apply pressure to the inside corner of the eye (and continue to apply pressure for 1 or 2 minutes after the medicine has been placed in the eye). *This is especially important if the ophthalmic beta-adrenergic blocking agent is used to treat infants and children.* Tilt the head back and with the index finger of the same hand, pull the lower eyelid away from the eye to form a pouch. Drop the medicine into the pouch and gently close the eyes. Do not blink. Keep the eyes closed for 1 or 2 minutes to allow the medicine to be absorbed.
- Immediately after using the eye drops, wash your hands to remove any medicine that may be on them.
- To keep the medicine as germ-free as possible, do not touch the applicator tip to any surface (including the eye). Also, keep the container tightly closed.
- If you are using the medication with the compliance cap (C Cap):

  —Before using the eye drops for the first time, make sure the number 1 or the correct day of the week appears in the window on the cap.

  —Remove the cap and use the eye drops as directed.

  —Replace the cap. Holding the cap between your thumb and forefinger, rotate the bottle until the cap clicks to the next position. This will tell you the time of your next dose.

  —After every dose, rotate the bottle until the cap clicks to the position that tells you the time of your next dose.

Use this medicine only as directed. Do not use more of it and do not use it more often than your doctor ordered. To do so may increase the chance of too much medicine being absorbed into the body and the chance of side effects.

Dosing—The dose of betaxolol, carteolol, levobunolol, metipranolol, or timolol will be different for different patients. *Follow your doctor's orders or the directions on the label.* The following information includes only the average doses. *If your dose is different, do not change it* unless your doctor tells you to do so.

The number of doses of medicine that you use also depends on the strength of the medicine.

For betaxolol, carteolol, or metipranolol

- For *ophthalmic drops* dosage forms:

  —For glaucoma:

  - Adults and older children—Topical, to the conjunctiva, 1 drop two times a day.
  - Infants and younger children—Dose must be determined by the doctor.

For levobunolol or timolol

- For *ophthalmic drops* dosage forms:
  —For glaucoma:
    - Adults and older children—Topical, to the conjunctiva, 1 drop one or two times a day.
    - Infants and younger children—Dose must be determined by the doctor.

Missed dose—If you miss a dose of this medicine and your dosing schedule is:

- One dose a day—Use the missed dose as soon as possible. However, if you do not remember the missed dose until the next day, skip the missed dose and go back to your regular dosing schedule. Do not double doses.
- More than one dose a day—Use the missed dose as soon as possible. However, if it is almost time for your next dose, skip the missed dose and go back to your regular dosing schedule. Do not double doses.

If you have any questions about this, check with your doctor.

Storage—To store this medicine:

- Keep out of the reach of children.
- Store away from heat and direct light.
- Keep this medicine from freezing.
- Do not keep outdated medicine or medicine no longer needed. Be sure that any discarded medicine is out of the reach of children.

Precautions While Using This Medicine

Your doctor should check your eye pressure at regular visits to make certain that your glaucoma is being controlled.

Before you have any kind of surgery, dental treatment, or emergency treatment, tell the medical doctor or dentist in charge that you are using this medicine. Using an ophthalmic beta-adrenergic blocking agent during this time may cause an increased risk of side effects.

For diabetic patients:

- *Ophthalmic beta-adrenergic blocking agents may affect blood sugar levels. They may also cover up some signs of hypoglycemia (low blood sugar),* such as trembling or increase in pulse rate or blood pressure. However, other signs of low blood sugar, such as dizziness or sweating, are not affected. If you notice a change in the results of your blood or urine sugar tests or if you have any questions, check with your doctor.

Some ophthalmic beta-adrenergic blocking agents (betaxolol, carteolol, and metipranolol) may cause your eyes to become more sensitive to light than they are normally. Wearing sunglasses and avoiding too much exposure to bright light may help lessen the discomfort.

Side Effects of This Medicine

Along with its needed effects, a medicine may cause some unwanted effects. Although not all of these side effects may occur, if they do occur they may need medical attention.

Check with your doctor as soon as possible if any of the following side effects occur:

More common

Redness of eyes or inside of eyelids

Less common or rare

Blurred vision or other change in vision; different size pupils of the eyes; discoloration of the eyeball; droopy upper eyelid; eye pain; redness or irritation of the tongue; seeing double; swelling, irritation or inflammation of eye or eyelid (severe)

Symptoms of too much medicine being absorbed into the body

Anxiety or nervousness; burning or prickling feeling on body; change in taste; chest pain; clumsiness or unsteadiness; confusion or mental depression; coughing, wheezing, or troubled breathing; decreased sexual ability; diarrhea; dizziness or feeling faint; drowsiness; hair loss; hallucinations (seeing, hearing, or feeling things that are not there); headache; irregular, slow, or pounding heartbeat; muscle or joint aches or pain; nausea or vomiting; raw or red areas of the skin; runny, stuffy, or bleeding nose; skin rash, hives, or itching; swelling of feet, ankles, or lower legs; trouble in sleeping; unusual tiredness or weakness

Other side effects may occur that usually do not need medical attention. These side effects may go away during treatment as your body adjusts to the medicine. However, check with your doctor if any of the following side effects continue or are bothersome:

More common

Decreased night vision; stinging of eye or other eye irritation (when medicine is applied)

Less common or rare

Browache; crusting of eyelashes; dryness of eye; increased sensitivity of eye to light; redness, itching, stinging, burning, or watering of eye or other eye irritation

Other side effects not listed above may also occur in some patients. If you notice any other effects, check with your doctor.

Revised: 05/12/93

BETA-ADRENERGIC BLOCKING AGENTS Systemic

Some commonly used brand names are:

In the U.S.—

Betapace[13]
Blocadren[14]
Cartrol[5]
Corgard[8]
Inderal[12]
Inderal LA[12]
Kerlone[3]
Levatol[10]
Lopressor[7]
Normodyne[6]
Sectral[1]
Tenormin[2]
Toprol-XL[7]
Trandate[6]
Visken[11]
Zebeta[4]

In Canada—

Apo-Atenolol[2]
Apo-Metoprolol[7]
Apo-Metoprolol (Type L)[7]
Apo-Propranolol[12]
Apo-Timol[14]
Betaloc[7]
Betaloc Durules[7]
Blocadren[14]
Corgard[8]
Detensol[12]
Inderal[12]
Inderal LA[12]
Lopresor[7]
Lopresor SR[7]
Monitan[1]
Novo-Atenol[2]
Novometoprol[7]
Novo-Pindol[11]
Novo-Timol[14]
Novopranol[12]
pms Propranolol[12]
Sectral[1]
Slow-Trasicor[9]
Sotacor[13]
Syn-Nadolol[8]
Syn-Pindolol[11]
Tenormin[2]
Trandate[6]
Trasicor[9]
Visken[11]

Note: For quick reference, the following beta-adrenergic blocking agents are numbered to match the corresponding brand names.

This information applies to the following medicines:

1. Acebutolol (a-se-BYOO-toe-lole)‡
2. Atenolol (a-TEN-oh-lole)‡
3. Betaxolol (be-TAX-oh-lol)†
4. Bisoprolol (bis-OH-proe-lol)†
5. Carteolol (KAR-tee-oh-lole)†
6. Labetalol (la-BET-a-lole)
7. Metoprolol (met-oh-PROE-lol)‡§
8. Nadolol (nay-DOE-lole)§
9. Oxprenolol (ox-PREN-oh-lole)*
10. Penbutolol (pen-BYOO-toe-lole)†
11. Pindolol (PIN-doe-lole)
12. Propranolol (proe-PRAN-oh-lole)‡§
13. Sotalol (SOE-ta-lole)
14. Timolol (TYE-moe-lole)‡

*Not commercially available in the U.S.
†Not commercially available in Canada.
‡Generic name product may be available in the U.S.
§Generic name product may be available in Canada.

Description

This group of medicines is known as beta-adrenergic blocking agents, beta-blocking agents, or, more commonly, beta-blockers. Beta-blockers are used in the treatment of high blood pressure (hypertension). Some beta-blockers are also used to relieve angina (chest pain) and in heart attack patients to help prevent additional heart attacks. Beta-blockers are also used to correct irregular heartbeat, prevent migraine headaches, and treat tremors. They may also be used for other conditions as determined by your doctor.

Beta-blockers work by affecting the response to some nerve impulses in certain parts of the body. As a result, they decrease the heart's need for blood and oxygen by reducing its workload. They also help the heart to beat more regularly.

Beta-adrenergic blocking agents are available only with your doctor's prescription, in the following dosage forms:

Oral

Acebutolol
- Capsules (U.S.)
- Tablets (Canada)

Atenolol
- Tablets (U.S. and Canada)

Betaxolol
- Tablets (U.S.)

Bisoprolol
- Tablets (U.S.)

Carteolol
- Tablets (U.S.)

Labetalol
- Tablets (U.S. and Canada)

Metoprolol
- Tablets (U.S. and Canada)
- Extended-release tablets (U.S. and Canada)

Nadolol
- Tablets (U.S. and Canada)

Oxprenolol
- Tablets (Canada)
- Extended-release tablets (Canada)

Penbutolol
- Tablets (U.S.)

Pindolol
- Tablets (U.S. and Canada)

Propranolol
- Extended-release capsules (U.S. and Canada)
- Oral solution (U.S.)
- Tablets (U.S. and Canada)

Sotalol
- Tablets (U.S. and Canada)

Timolol
- Tablets (U.S. and Canada)

Parenteral

Atenolol
- Injection (U.S.)

Labetalol
- Injection (U.S. and Canada)

Metoprolol
- Injection (U.S. and Canada)

Propranolol
- Injection (U.S. and Canada)

Before Using This Medicine

In deciding to use a medicine, the risks of taking the medicine must be weighed against the good it will do. This is a decision you and your doctor will make. For the beta-blockers, the following should be considered:

Allergies—Tell your doctor if you have ever had any unusual or allergic reaction to the beta-blocker medicine prescribed. Also tell your health care professional if you are allergic to any other substances, such as foods, preservatives, or dyes.

Pregnancy—Use of some beta-blockers during pregnancy has been associated with low blood sugar, breathing problems, a lower heart rate, and low blood pressure in the newborn infant. Other reports have not shown unwanted effects on the newborn infant. Animal studies have shown some beta-blockers to cause problems in pregnancy when used in doses many times the usual human dose. Before taking any of these medicines, make sure your doctor knows if you are pregnant or if you may become pregnant.

Breast-feeding—It is not known whether bisoprolol, carteolol, or penbutolol passes into breast milk. All other beta-blockers pass into breast milk. Problems such as slow heartbeat, low blood pressure, and trouble in breathing have been reported in nursing babies. Mothers who are taking beta-blockers and who wish to breast-feed should discuss this with their doctor.

Children—Some of these medicines have been used in children and, in effective doses, have not been shown to cause different side effects or problems in children than they do in adults.

Older adults—Some side effects are more likely to occur in the elderly, who are usually more sensitive to the effects of beta-blockers. Also, beta-blockers may reduce tolerance to cold temperatures in elderly patients.

Other medicines—Although certain medicines should not be used together at all, in other cases two different medicines may be used together even if an interaction might occur. In these cases, your doctor may want to change the dose, or other precautions may be necessary. When you are taking or receiving a beta-blocker it is especially important that your health care professional know if you are taking any of the following:

- Allergen immunotherapy (allergy shots) or
- Allergen extracts for skin testing—Beta-blockers may increase the risk of serious allergic reaction to these medicines

- Aminophylline (e.g., Somophyllin) or
- Caffeine (e.g., NoDoz) or
- Dyphylline (e.g., Lufyllin) or
- Oxtriphylline (e.g., Choledyl) or
- Theophylline (e.g., Somophyllin-T)—The effects of both these medicines and beta-blockers may be blocked; in addition, theophylline levels in the body may be increased, especially in patients who smoke

- Antidiabetics, oral (diabetes medicine you take by mouth) or
- Insulin—There is an increased risk of hyperglycemia (high blood sugar); beta-blockers may cover up certain symptoms of hypoglycemia (low blood sugar) such as increases in pulse rate and blood pressure, and may make the hypoglycemia last longer

- Calcium channel blockers (bepridil [e.g., Bepadin], diltiazem [e.g., Cardizem], felodipine [e.g., Plendil], flunarizine [e.g., Sibelium], isradipine [e.g., DynaCirc], nicardipine [e.g., Cardene], nifedipine [e.g., Procardia], nimodipine [e.g., Nimotop], verapamil [e.g., Calan]) or
- Clonidine (e.g., Catapres) or
- Guanabenz (e.g., Wytensin)—Effects on blood pressure may be increased. In addition, unwanted effects may occur if clonidine, guanabenz, or a beta-blocker is stopped suddenly after use together. Unwanted effects on the heart may occur when beta-blockers are used with calcium channel blockers

- Cocaine—Cocaine may block the effects of beta-blockers; in addition, there is an increased risk of high blood pressure, fast heartbeat, and possibly heart problems if you use cocaine while taking a beta-blocker

- Monoamine oxidase (MAO) inhibitors (furazolidone [e.g., Furoxone], isocarboxazid [e.g., Marplan], phenelzine [e.g., Nardil], procarbazine [e.g., Matulane], selegiline [e.g., Eldepryl], tranylcypromine [e.g., Parnate])—Taking beta-blockers while you are taking or within 2 weeks of taking monoamine oxidase (MAO) inhibitors may cause severe high blood pressure

Other medical problems—The presence of other medical problems may affect the use of the beta blockers. Make sure you tell your doctor if you have any other medical problems, especially:

- Allergy, history of (asthma, eczema, hay fever, hives), or
- Bronchitis or
- Emphysema—Severity and duration of allergic reactions to other substances may be increased; in addition, beta-blockers can increase trouble in breathing

- Bradycardia (unusually slow heartbeat) or
- Heart or blood vessel disease—There is a risk of further decreased heart function; also, if treatment is stopped suddenly, unwanted effects may occur

- Diabetes mellitus (sugar diabetes)—Beta-blockers may cause hyperglycemia (high blood sugar) and circulation problems; in addition, if your diabetes medicine causes your blood sugar to be too low, beta-blockers may cover up some of the symptoms (fast heartbeat), although they will not cover up other symptoms such as dizziness or sweating

- Kidney disease or
- Liver disease—Effects of beta-blockers may be increased because of slower removal from the body

- Mental depression (or history of)—May be increased by beta-blockers

- Myasthenia gravis or
- Psoriasis—Beta-blockers may make these conditions worse

- Overactive thyroid—Stopping beta-blockers suddenly may increase symptoms; beta-blockers may cover up fast heartbeat, which is a sign of overactive thyroid

Proper Use of This Medicine

For patients taking the *extended-release capsule or tablet* form of this medicine:

- Swallow the capsule or tablet whole.
- Do not crush, break (except metoprolol succinate extended-release tablets, which may be broken in half), or chew before swallowing.

For patients taking the *concentrated oral solution* form of *propranolol:*

- This medicine is to be taken by mouth even though it comes in a dropper bottle. The amount you should take is to be measured only with the specially marked dropper.
- Mix the medicine with some water, juice, or a carbonated drink. After drinking all the liquid containing the medicine, rinse the glass with a little more liquid and drink that also, to make sure you get all the medicine.

  If you prefer, you may mix this medicine with applesauce or pudding instead.
- Mix the medicine immediately before you are going to take it. Throw away any mixed medicine that you do not take immediately. Do not save medicine that has been mixed.

Ask your doctor about checking your pulse rate before and after taking beta-blocking agents. If your doctor tells you to check your pulse regularly while you are taking this medicine, and it is much slower than the rate your doctor has designated, check with your doctor. A pulse rate that is too slow may cause circulation problems.

To help you remember to take your medicine, try to get into the habit of taking it at the same time each day.

For patients taking this medicine *for high blood pressure:*

- In addition to the use of the medicine your doctor has prescribed, treatment for your high blood pressure may include weight control and care in the types of foods you eat, especially foods high in sodium. Your doctor will tell you which of these are most important for you. You should check with your doctor before changing your diet.
- Many patients who have high blood pressure will not notice any signs of the problem. In fact, many may feel normal. However, if high blood pressure is not treated, it can cause serious problems such as heart failure, blood vessel disease, stroke, or kidney disease.
- Remember that this medicine will not cure your high blood pressure but it does help control it. It is very important that you *take your medicine exactly as directed*, even if you feel well. You must continue to take it as directed if you expect to lower your blood pressure and keep it down. *You may have to take high blood pressure medicine for the rest of your life.* Also, it is very important to keep your appointments with your doctor, even if you feel well.

Dosing—The dose of beta-blocker will be different for different patients. *Follow your doctor's orders or the directions on the label.* The following information includes only the average doses. *If your dose is different, do not change it* unless your doctor tells you to do so.

The number of capsules or tablets or teaspoonfuls of solution that you take depends on the strength of the medicine. Also, *the number of doses you take each day, the time allowed between doses, and the length of time you take the medicine depend on the medical problem for which you are taking the beta-blocker.*

For acebutolol

- For *oral* dosage forms (capsules and tablets):
  - —For angina (chest pain) or irregular heartbeat:
    - Adults—200 milligrams (mg) two times a day. The dose may be increased up to a total of 1200 mg a day.
    - Children—Dose must be determined by your doctor.
  - —For high blood pressure:
    - Adults—200 to 800 mg a day as a single dose or divided into two daily doses.
    - Children—Dose must be determined by your doctor.

For atenolol

- For *oral* dosage form (tablets):
  - —For angina (chest pain):
    - Adults—50 to 100 mg once a day.
  - —For high blood pressure:
    - Adults—25 to 100 mg once a day.
    - Children—Dose must be determined by your doctor.
  - —For treatment after a heart attack:
    - Adults—50 mg ten minutes after the last intravenous dose, followed by another 50 mg twelve hours later. Then 100 mg once a day or 50 mg two times a day for six to nine days or until discharge from hospital.
- For *injection* dosage form:
  - —For treatment of heart attacks:
    - Adults—5 mg given over 5 minutes. The dose is repeated ten minutes later.

For betaxolol

- For *oral* dosage form (tablets):
  - —For high blood pressure:
    - Adults—10 mg once a day. Your doctor may double your dose after seven to fourteen days.
    - Children—Dose must be determined by your doctor.

For bisoprolol

- For *oral* dosage form (tablets):
  - —For high blood pressure:
    - Adults—5 to 10 mg once a day.
    - Children—Dose must be determined by your doctor.

For carteolol

- For *oral* dosage form (tablets):
  - —For high blood pressure:
    - Adults—2.5 to 10 mg once a day.
    - Children—Dose must be determined by your doctor.

For labetalol

- For *oral* dosage form (tablets):
  - —For high blood pressure:
    - Adults—100 to 400 mg two times a day.
    - Children—Dose must be determined by your doctor.
- For *injection* dosage form:
  - —For high blood pressure:
    - Adults—20 mg injected slowly over two minutes with additional injections of 40 and 80 mg given every ten minutes if needed, up to a total of 300 mg; may be given instead as an infusion at a rate of 2 mg per minute to a total dose of 50 to 300 mg.
    - Children—Dose must be determined by your doctor.

For metoprolol

- For *regular (short-acting) oral* dosage form (tablets):
  - —For high blood pressure or angina (chest pain):
    - Adults—100 to 450 mg a day, taken as a single dose or in divided doses.
    - Children—Dose must be determined by your doctor.
  - —For treatment after a heart attack:
    - Adults—50 mg every six hours starting fifteen minutes after last intravenous dose. Then 100 mg two times a day for three months to 1 to 3 years.
- For *long-acting oral* dosage forms (extended-release tablets):
  - —For high blood pressure or angina (chest pain):
    - Adults—Up to 400 mg once a day.
    - Children—Dose must be determined by your doctor.
- For *injection* dosage form:
  - —For treatment of a heart attack:
    - Adults—5 mg every two minutes for three doses.

For nadolol

- For *oral* dosage form (tablets):
  - —For angina (chest pain):
    - Adults—40 to 240 mg once a day.
  - —For high blood pressure:
    - Adults—40 to 320 mg once a day.
    - Children—Dose must be determined by your doctor.

For oxprenolol

- For *regular (short-acting) oral* dosage form (tablets):
  - —For high blood pressure:
    - Adults—20 mg three times a day. Your doctor may increase your dose up to 480 mg a day.
    - Children—Dose must be determined by your doctor.
- For *long-acting oral* dosage form (extended-release tablets):
  - —For high blood pressure:
    - Adults—120 to 320 mg once a day.
    - Children—Dose must be determined by your doctor.

For penbutolol

- For *oral* dosage form (tablets):
  - —For high blood pressure:
    - Adults—20 mg once a day.
    - Children—Dose must be determined by your doctor.

For pindolol

- For *oral* dosage form (tablets):
  - —For high blood pressure:
    - Adults—5 mg two times a day. Your doctor may increase your dose up to 60 mg a day.
    - Children—Dose must be determined by your doctor.

For propranolol

- For *regular (short-acting) oral* dosage forms (tablets and oral solution):
  - —For angina (chest pain):
    - Adults—80 to 320 mg a day taken in two, three, or four divided doses.
  - —For irregular heartbeat:
    - Adults—10 to 30 mg three or four times a day.
    - Children—500 micrograms (0.5 mg) to 4 mg per kilogram of body weight a day taken in divided doses.
  - —For high blood pressure:
    - Adults—40 mg two times a day. Your doctor may increase your dose up to 640 mg a day.
    - Children—500 micrograms (0.5 mg) to 4 mg per kilogram of body weight a day taken in divided doses.
  - —For diseased heart muscle (cardiomyopathy):
    - Adults—20 to 40 mg three or four times a day.
  - —For treatment after a heart attack:
    - Adults—180 to 240 mg a day taken in divided doses.
  - —For treating pheochromocytoma:
    - Adults—30 to 160 mg a day taken in divided doses.
  - —For preventing migraine headaches:
    - Adults—20 mg four times a day. Your doctor may increase your dose up to 240 mg a day.
  - —For trembling:
    - Adults—40 mg two times a day. Your doctor may increase your dose up to 320 mg a day.
- For *long-acting oral* dosage form (extended-release capsules):
  - —For high blood pressure:
    - Adults—80 to 160 mg once a day. Doses up to 640 mg once a day may be needed in some patients.
  - —For angina (chest pain):
    - Adults—80 to 320 mg once a day.
  - —For preventing migraine headaches:
    - Adults—80 to 240 mg once a day.
- For *injection* dosage form:
  - —For irregular heartbeat:
    - Adults—1 to 3 mg given at a rate not greater than 1 mg per minute. Dose may be repeated after two minutes and again after four hours if needed.
    - Children—10 to 100 micrograms (0.01 to 0.1 mg) per kilogram of body weight given intravenously every six to eight hours.

For sotalol

- For *oral* dosage form (tablets):
  - —For irregular heartbeat:
    - Adults—80 mg two times a day. Your doctor may increase your dose up to 320 mg per day taken in two or three divided doses.
    - Children—Dose must be determined by your doctor.

For timolol

- For *oral* dosage form (tablets):
  - —For high blood pressure:
    - Adults—10 mg two times a day. Your doctor may increase your dose up 60 mg per day taken as a single dose or in divided doses.
    - Children—Dose must be determined by your doctor.
  - —For treatment after a heart attack:
    - Adults—10 mg two times a day.
  - —For preventing migraine headaches:
    - Adults—10 mg two times a day. Your doctor may increase your dose up to 30 mg once a day or in divided doses.

Missed dose—Do not miss any doses. This is especially important when you are taking only one dose per day. Some conditions may become worse if this medicine is not taken regularly.

If you do miss a dose of this medicine, take it as soon as possible. However, if it is within 4 hours of your next dose (8 hours when using atenolol, betaxolol, bisoprolol, carteolol, labetalol, nadolol, penbutolol, sotalol, or extended-release [long-acting] metoprolol, oxprenolol, or propranolol), skip the missed dose and go back to your regular dosing schedule. Do not double doses.

Storage—To store this medicine:

- Keep out of the reach of children.
- Store away from heat and direct light.
- Do not store in the bathroom, near the kitchen sink, or in other damp places. Heat or moisture may cause the medicine to break down.
- Do not keep outdated medicine or medicine no longer needed. Be sure that any discarded medicine is out of the reach of children.

Precautions While Using This Medicine

It is important that your doctor check your progress at regular visits. This is to make sure the medicine is working for you and to allow the dosage to be changed if needed.

Do not stop taking this medicine without first checking with your doctor. Your doctor may want you to reduce gradually the amount you are taking before stopping completely. Some conditions may become worse when the medicine is stopped suddenly, and the danger of heart attack is increased in some patients.

Make sure that you have enough medicine on hand to last through weekends, holidays, or vacations. You may want to carry an extra written prescription in your billfold or purse in case of an emergency. You can then have it filled if you run out of medicine while you are away from home.

Your doctor may want you to carry medical identification stating that you are taking this medicine.

Before having any kind of surgery (including dental surgery) or emergency treatment, tell the medical doctor or dentist in charge that you are taking this medicine.

For *diabetic patients:*

- *This medicine may cause your blood sugar levels to rise.* Also, *this medicine may cover up signs of hypoglycemia (low blood sugar),* such as change in pulse rate.

This medicine may cause some people to become dizzy, drowsy, or lightheaded. *Make sure you know how you react to this medicine before you drive, use machines, or do anything else that could be dangerous if you are dizzy or are not alert.* If the problem continues or gets worse, check with your doctor.

Beta-blockers may make you more sensitive to cold temperatures, especially if you have blood circulation problems. Beta-blockers tend to decrease blood circulation in the skin, fingers, and toes. Dress warmly during cold weather and be careful during prolonged exposure to cold, such as in winter sports.

Chest pain resulting from exercise or physical exertion is usually reduced or prevented by this medicine. This may tempt a patient to be overly active. *Make sure you discuss with your doctor a safe amount of exercise for your medical problem.*

Before you have any medical tests, tell the doctor in charge that you are taking this medicine. The results of some tests may be affected by this medicine.

Before you have any allergy shots, tell the doctor in charge that you are taking a beta-blocker. Beta-blockers may cause you to have a serious reaction to the allergy shot.

For patients with *allergies to foods, medicines, or insect stings:*

- There is a chance that this medicine will cause allergic reactions to be worse and harder to treat. If you have a severe allergic reaction while you are being treated with this medicine, check with a doctor right away so that it can be treated. Be sure to tell the doctor that you are taking a beta-blocker.

For patients taking this medicine *for high blood pressure:*

- *Do not take other medicines unless they have been discussed with your doctor.* This especially includes over-the-counter (nonprescription) medicines for appetite control, asthma, colds, cough, hay fever, or sinus problems since they may tend to increase your blood pressure.

For patients taking *labetalol by mouth:*

- *Dizziness, lightheadedness, or fainting may occur, especially when you get up from a lying or sitting position.* This is more likely to occur when you first start taking labetalol or when the dose is increased. *Getting up slowly may help.* When you get up from lying down, sit on the edge of the bed with your feet dangling for 1 to 2 minutes. Then stand up slowly. If the problem continues or gets worse, check with your doctor.

- The dizziness, lightheadedness, or fainting is also more likely to occur if you drink alcohol, stand for long periods of time, or exercise, or if the weather is hot. *While you are taking this medicine, be careful to limit the amount of alcohol you drink. Also, use extra care during exercise or hot weather or if you must stand for long periods of time.*

For patients receiving *labetalol by injection:*

- It is very important that you lie down flat while receiving labetalol and for up to 3 hours afterward. If you try to get up too soon, you may become dizzy or faint. *Do not try to sit or stand until your doctor or nurse tells you to do so.*

Side Effects of This Medicine

Along with its needed effects, a medicine may cause some unwanted effects. Although not all of these side effects may occur, if they do occur they may need medical attention.

Check with your doctor as soon as possible if any of the following side effects occur:

Less common

Breathing difficulty and/or wheezing; cold hands and feet; mental depression; shortness of breath; slow heartbeat (especially less than 50 beats per minute); swelling of ankles, feet, and/or lower legs

Rare

Back pain or joint pain; chest pain; confusion (especially in elderly patients); dark urine—for acebutolol, bisoprolol, or labetalol; dizziness or lightheadedness when getting up from a lying or sitting position; fever and sore throat; hallucinations (seeing, hearing, or feeling things that are not there); irregular heartbeat; red, scaling, or crusted skin; skin rash; unusual bleeding and bruising; yellow eyes or skin—for acebutolol, bisoprolol, or labetalol

Signs and symptoms of overdose (in the order in which they may occur)

Slow heartbeat; dizziness (severe) or fainting; fast or irregular heartbeat; difficulty in breathing; bluish-colored fingernails or palms of hands; convulsions (seizures)

Other side effects may occur that usually do not need medical attention. These side effects may go away during treatment as your body adjusts to the medicine. However, check with your doctor if any of the following side effects continue or are bothersome:

More common

Decreased sexual ability; dizziness or lightheadedness; drowsiness (slight); trouble in sleeping; unusual tiredness or weakness

Less common or rare

Anxiety and/or nervousness; changes in taste—for labetalol only; constipation; diarrhea; dry, sore eyes; frequent urination—for acebutolol and carteolol only; itching of skin; nausea or vomiting; nightmares and vivid dreams; numbness and/or tingling of fingers and/or toes; numbness and/or tingling of skin, especially on scalp—for labetalol only; stomach discomfort; stuffy nose

Although not all of the side effects listed above have been reported for all of these medicines, they have been reported for at least one of them. Since all of the beta-adrenergic blocking agents are very similar, any of the above side effects may occur with any of these medicines. However, they may be more or less common with some agents than with others.

After you have been taking a beta-blocker for a while, it may cause unpleasant or even harmful effects if you stop taking it too suddenly. After you stop taking this medicine or while you are gradually reducing the amount you are taking, check with your doctor right away if any of the following occur:

Chest pain; fast or irregular heartbeat; general feeling of discomfort or illness or weakness; headache; shortness of breath (sudden); sweating; trembling

For patients taking *labetalol:*

- You may notice a tingling feeling on your scalp when you first begin to take labetalol. This is to be expected and usually goes away after you have been taking labetalol for a while.

Other side effects not listed above may also occur in some patients. If you notice any other effects, check with your doctor.

Additional Information

Once a medicine has been approved for marketing for a certain use, experience may show that it is also useful for other medical problems. Although these uses are not included in product labeling, some beta-blockers are used in certain patients with the following medical conditions:

- Glaucoma
- Neuroleptic-induced akathisia (restlessness or the need to keep moving caused by some medicines used to treat nervousness or mental and emotional disorders)

Other than the above information, there is no additional information relating to proper use, precautions, or side effects for these uses.

Revised: 05/13/93
Interim revision: 08/18/97

BETA-ADRENERGIC BLOCKING AGENTS AND THIAZIDE DIURETICS Systemic

Some commonly used brand names are:

In the U.S.—

Corzide[4]
Inderide[6]
Inderide LA[6]
Lopressor HCT[3]
Tenoretic[1]
Timolide[7]
Ziac[2]

In Canada—

Corzide[4]
Inderide[6]
Tenoretic[1]
Timolide[7]
Viskazide[5]

Note: For quick reference, the following beta-adrenergic blocking agents and thiazide diuretics are numbered to match the corresponding brand names.

This information applies to the following medicines:

1. Atenolol (a-TEN-oh-lole) and Chlorthalidone (klor-THAL-i-doan)‡
2. Bisoprolol (bis-OH-proe-lol) and Hydrochlorothiazide (hye-droe-klor-oh-THYE-a-zide)†
3. Metoprolol (me-TOE-proe-lole) and Hydrochlorothiazide†
4. Nadolol (NAY-doe-lole) and Bendroflumethiazide (ben-droe-floo-meth-EYE-a-zide)
5. Pindolol (PIN-doe-lole) and Hydrochlorothiazide*
6. Propranolol (proe-PRAN-oh-lole) and Hydrochlorothiazide‡
7. Timolol (TIM-oh-lole) and Hydrochlorothiazide

*Not commercially available in the U.S.
†Not commercially available in Canada.
‡Generic name product may also be available in the U.S.

Description

Beta-adrenergic blocking agent (more commonly, beta-blockers) and thiazide diuretic combinations belong to the group of medicines known as antihypertensives (high blood pressure medicine). Both ingredients of the combination control high blood pressure, but they work in different ways. Beta-blockers (atenolol, bisoprolol, metoprolol, nadolol, pindolol, propranolol, and timolol) reduce the work load on the heart as well as having other effects. Thiazide diuretics (bendroflumethiazide, chlorthalidone, and hydrochlorothiazide) reduce the amount of fluid pressure in the body by increasing the flow of urine.

High blood pressure adds to the work load of the heart and arteries. If it continues for a long time, the heart and arteries may not function properly. This can damage the blood vessels of the brain, heart, and kidneys, resulting in a stroke, heart failure, or kidney failure. High blood pressure may also increase the risk of heart attacks. These problems may be less likely to occur if blood pressure is controlled.

Beta-blocker and thiazide diuretic combinations are available only with your doctor's prescription, in the following dosage forms:

Oral

Atenolol and chlorthalidone
- Tablets (U.S. and Canada)

Bisoprolol and hydrochlorothiazide
- Tablets (U.S.)

Metoprolol and hydrochlorothiazide
- Tablets (U.S.)

Nadolol and bendroflumethiazide
- Tablets (U.S. and Canada)

Pindolol and hydrochlorothiazide
- Tablets (Canada)

Propranolol and hydrochlorothiazide
- Extended-release capsules (U.S.)
- Tablets (U.S. and Canada)

Timolol and hydrochlorothiazide
- Tablets (U.S. and Canada)

Before Using This Medicine

In deciding to use a medicine, the risks of taking the medicine must be weighed against the good it will do. This is a decision you and your doctor will make. For the beta-blocker and thiazide diuretic combinations, the following should be considered:

Allergies—Tell your doctor if you have ever had any unusual or allergic reaction to beta-blockers, sulfonamides (sulfa drugs), bumetanide, furosemide, acetazolamide, dichlorphenamide, methazolamide, or any of the thiazide diuretics. Also tell your health care professional if you are allergic to any other substances, such as foods, preservatives, or dyes.

Pregnancy—Use of some beta-blockers during pregnancy has been associated with low blood sugar, breathing problems, a slower heart rate, and low blood pressure in the newborn infant. Other reports have not shown unwanted effects in the newborn infant. Animal studies have shown some beta-blockers to cause problems in pregnancy when used in doses many times the usual human dose.

Studies with thiazide diuretics have not been done in pregnant women. However, use of thiazide diuretics during pregnancy may cause side effects such as jaundice, blood problems, and low potassium in the newborn infant. Animal studies have not shown thiazide diuretic medicines to cause birth defects even when used in doses several times the usual human dose.

Before taking a beta-blocker and thiazide diuretic combination, make sure your doctor knows if you are pregnant or if you may become pregnant.

Breast-feeding—Atenolol, metoprolol, nadolol, propranolol, pindolol, timolol, and thiazide diuretics pass into breast milk. It is not known whether bisoprolol passes into breast milk. Thiazide diuretics may decrease the flow of breast milk.

Children—Although there is no specific information comparing use of this combination medicine in children with use in other age groups, this medicine is not expected to cause different side effects or problems in children than it does in adults. However, extra caution may be necessary in infants with jaundice, because these medicines can make the condition worse.

Older adults—Some side effects, especially dizziness or lightheadedness and signs and symptoms of too much potassium loss, may be more likely to occur in the elderly, who are usually more sensitive to the effects of this medicine. Also, beta-blockers may reduce tolerance to cold temperatures in elderly patients.

Other medicines—Although certain medicines should not be used together at all, in other cases 2 different medicines may be used together even if an interaction might occur. In these cases, your doctor may want to change the dose, or other precautions may be necessary. When you are taking beta-blocker and thiazide diuretic combinations, it is especially important that your health care professional know if you are taking any of the following:

- Allergy shots or
- Allergy skin tests—The beta-blocker contained in this medicine may increase the risk of a serious allergic reaction to these medicines
- Aminophylline (e.g., Somophyllin) or
- Caffeine (e.g., NoDoz) or
- Dyphylline (e.g., Lufylline) or
- Oxtriphylline (e.g., Choledyl) or
- Theophylline (e.g., Somophyllin-T)—The effects of these medicines and beta-blockers may be blocked; in addition, theophylline levels in the body may be increased, especially in patients who smoke
- Antidiabetics, oral (diabetes medicine you take by mouth) or
- Insulin—There is an increased risk of hyperglycemia (high blood sugar); the beta-blocker contained in this medicine may also cover up certain symptoms of hypoglycemia (low blood sugar), such as increases in pulse rate and blood pressure, and may make the hypoglycemia last longer
- Calcium channel blockers (amlodipine [e.g., Norvasc], bepridil [e.g., Bepadin], diltiazem [e.g., Cardizem], felodipine [e.g., Plendil], flunarizine [e.g., Sibelium], isradipine [e.g., DynaCirc], nicardipine [e.g., Cardene], nifedipine [e.g., Procardia], nimodipine [e.g., Nimotop], verapamil [e.g., Calan]) or
- Clonidine (e.g., Catapres) or
- Guanabenz (e.g., Wytensin)—Effects on blood pressure may be increased. In addition, unwanted effects may occur if clonidine, guanabenz, or a beta-blocker are stopped suddenly after use together. Unwanted effects on the heart may occur when beta-blocker and thiazide diuretic combinations are used with calcium channel blockers
- Cocaine—Cocaine may block the effects of beta-blockers; in addition, there is an increased risk of high blood pressure, fast heartbeat, and possibly heart problems if you use cocaine while taking a beta-blocker and thiazide diuretic combination
- Digitalis glycosides (heart medicine)—Use with beta-blocker and thiazide diuretic combinations may cause high blood levels of digoxin, which may increase the chance of side effects
- Lithium—The thiazide diuretic contained in this combination may cause high blood levels of lithium, which may increase the chance of side effects
- Monoamine oxidase (MAO) inhibitors (furazolidone [e.g., Furoxone], isocarboxazid [e.g., Marplan], phenelzine [e.g., Nardil], procarbazine [e.g., Matulane], selegiline [e.g., Eldepryl], tranylcypromine [e.g., Parnate])—Taking a beta-blocker and thiazide diuretic combination while you are taking or within 2 weeks of taking monoamine oxidase (MAO) inhibitors may cause severe high blood pressure

Other medical problems—The presence of other medical problems may affect the use of the beta-blockers and thiazide diuretics. Make sure you tell your doctor if you have any other medical problems, especially:

- Allergy, history of (asthma, eczema, hay fever, hives), or
- Bronchitis or
- Emphysema—This combination medicine may make allergic reactions to other substances more severe or make the reaction last longer; in addition, the beta-blocker contained in this combination can increase trouble in breathing
- Bradycardia (unusually slow heartbeat) or
- Heart or blood vessel disease—This combination medicine may make these heart problems worse; also, if treatment is stopped suddenly, unwanted effects may occur
- Diabetes mellitus (sugar diabetes)—The beta-blocker contained in this medicine may cause hyperglycemia (high blood sugar) and circulation problems; in addition, if your diabetes medicine causes your blood sugar to be too low, beta-blockers may cover up some of the symptoms (fast heartbeat), although they will not cover up other symptoms such as dizziness or sweating; the thiazide diuretic contained in this medicine may increase the amount of sugar in the blood
- Gout (history of) or
- Lupus erythematosus (history of) or
- Pancreatitis (inflammation of the pancreas)—The thiazide diuretic contained in this medicine may make these conditions worse
- Kidney disease or
- Liver disease—Effects of this medicine may be increased because of slower removal from the body
- Mental depression (or history of) or
- Myasthenia gravis or
- Pheochromocytoma or
- Psoriasis or
- Raynaud's syndrome—The beta-blocker contained in this medicine may make these conditions worse
- Overactive thyroid—Stopping this medicine suddenly may increase symptoms of overactive thyroid; the beta-blocker contained in this medicine may cover up fast heartbeat, which is a sign of overactive thyroid

Proper Use of This Medicine

In addition to the use of the medicine your doctor has prescribed, treatment for your high blood pressure may include weight control and care in the types of foods you eat, especially foods high in sodium. Your doctor will tell you which of these are most important for you. You should check with your doctor before changing your diet.

Many patients who have high blood pressure will not notice any signs of the problem. In fact, many may feel normal. It is very important that you *take your medicine exactly as directed* and that you keep your appointments with your doctor even if you feel well.

Remember that this medicine will not cure your high blood pressure but it does help control it. Therefore, you must continue to take it as directed if you expect to lower your blood pressure and keep it down. *You may have to take high blood pressure medicine for the rest of your life.* If high blood pressure is not treated, it can cause serious problems such as heart failure, blood vessel disease, stroke, or kidney disease.

For patients taking the *extended-release tablet* form of this medicine:

- Swallow the tablet whole.
- Do not crush, break, or chew before swallowing.

To help you remember to take your medicine, try to get into the habit of taking it at the same time each day.

Ask your doctor about checking your pulse rate before and after taking beta-blocking agents. Then, while you are taking this medicine, check your pulse regularly. If it is much slower than your usual rate (or less than 50 beats per minute), check with your doctor. A pulse rate that is too slow may cause circulation problems.

The thiazide diuretic (e.g., bendroflumethiazide, chlorthalidone, or hydrochlorothiazide) contained in this combination medicine may cause you to have an unusual feeling of tiredness when you begin to take it. You may also notice an increase in the amount of urine or in your frequency of urination. After you take the medicine for a while, these effects should lessen. To keep the increase in urine from affecting your sleep:

- If you are to take a single dose a day, take it in the morning after breakfast.
- If you are to take more than one dose a day, take the last dose no later than 6 p.m., unless otherwise directed by your doctor.

However, it is best to plan your dose or doses according to a schedule that will least affect your personal activities and sleep. Ask your health care professional to help you plan the best time to take this medicine.

Do not miss any doses. This is especially important when you are taking only one dose per day. Some conditions may become worse when this medicine is not taken regularly.

Dosing—The dose of beta-blocker and thiazide diuretic combinations will be different for different patients. *Follow your doctor's orders or the directions on the label.* The following information includes only the average doses of beta-blocker and thiazide diuretic combinations. *If your dose is different, do not change it* unless your doctor tells you to do so.

The number of capsules or tablets that you take depends on the strength of the medicine.

For atenolol and chlorthalidone combination

- For *oral* dosage form (tablets):
  - —For high blood pressure:
    - Adults—1 or 2 tablets once a day.
    - Children—Dose must be determined by your doctor.

For bisoprolol and hydrochlorothiazide combination

- For *oral* dosage form (tablets):
  - —For high blood pressure:
    - Adults—1 or 2 tablets once a day.
    - Children—Dose must be determined by your doctor.

For metoprolol and hydrochlorothiazide combination

- For *oral* dosage form (tablets):
  - —For high blood pressure:
    - Adults—1 or 2 tablets a day.
    - Children—Dose must be determined by your doctor.

For nadolol and bendroflumethiazide combination

- For *oral* dosage form (tablets):
  - —For high blood pressure:
    - Adults—1 tablet once a day.
    - Children—Dose must be determined by your doctor.

For pindolol and hydrochlorothiazide combination

- For *oral* dosage form (tablets):
  - —For high blood pressure:
    - Adults—1 or 2 tablets once a day.
    - Children—Dose must be determined by your doctor.

For propranolol and hydrochlorothiazide combination

- For *regular (short-acting) oral* dosage form (tablets):
  - —For high blood pressure:
    - Adults—1 or 2 tablets two times a day.
    - Children—Dose must be determined by your doctor.
- For *long-acting oral* dosage form (capsules):
  - —For high blood pressure:
    - Adults—1 capsule a day.
    - Children—Dose must be determined by your doctor.

For timolol and hydrochlorothiazide combination

- For *oral* dosage form (tablets):
  - —For high blood pressure:
    - Adults—1 tablet two times a day or 2 tablets once a day.
    - Children—Dose must be determined by your doctor.

Missed dose—If you miss a dose of this medicine, take it as soon as possible. However, if it is within 4 hours of your next dose (8 hours if you are using atenolol and chlorthalidone, bisoprolol and hydrochlorothiazide, nadolol and bendroflumethiazide, or extended-release propranolol and hydrochlorothiazide), skip the missed dose and go back to your regular dosing schedule. Do not double doses.

Storage—To store this medicine:

- Keep out of the reach of children.
- Store away from heat and direct light.
- Do not store in the bathroom, near the kitchen sink, or in other damp places. Heat or moisture may cause the medicine to break down.
- Do not keep outdated medicine or medicine no longer needed. Be sure that any discarded medicine is out of the reach of children.

Precautions While Using This Medicine

It is important that your doctor check your progress at regular visits. This is to make sure the medicine is properly controlling your blood pressure and to allow the dosage to be changed if needed.

Do not stop taking this medicine without first checking with your doctor. Your doctor may want you to reduce gradually the amount you are taking before stopping completely. Some conditions may become worse when the medicine is stopped suddenly, and the risk of heart attack is increased in some patients.

Make sure that you have enough medicine on hand to last through weekends, holidays, or vacations. You may want to carry an extra written prescription in your billfold or purse in case of an emergency. You can then have it filled if you run out of medicine while you are away from home.

Your doctor may want you to carry medical identification stating that you are taking this medicine.

Do not take other medicines unless they have been discussed with your doctor. This especially includes over-the-counter (nonprescription) medicines for appetite control, asthma, colds, cough, hay fever, or sinus problems since they may increase your blood pressure.

Before having any kind of surgery (including dental surgery) or emergency treatment, tell the medical doctor or dentist in charge that you are taking this medicine.

For *diabetic patients*:
- *This medicine may increase your blood sugar levels.* Also, *this medicine may cover up signs of hypoglycemia (low blood sugar),* such as change in pulse rate. While you are taking this medicine, be especially careful in testing for sugar in your urine. If you have any questions about this, check with your doctor.

The thiazide diuretic contained in this medicine may cause a loss of potassium from your body.
- To help prevent this, your doctor may want you to:
  —eat or drink foods that have a high potassium content (for example, orange or other citrus fruit juices), or
  —take a potassium supplement, or
  —take another medicine to help prevent the loss of the potassium in the first place.
- It is very important to follow these directions. Also, it is important not to change your diet on your own. This is more important if you are already on a special diet (as for diabetes), or if you are taking a potassium supplement or a medicine to reduce potassium loss. Extra potassium may not be necessary and, in some cases, too much potassium could be harmful.

Check with your doctor if you become sick and have severe or continuing vomiting or diarrhea. These problems may cause you to lose additional water and potassium.

This medicine may cause some people to become dizzy, drowsy, lightheaded, or less alert than they are normally. *Make sure you know how you react to this medicine before you drive, use machines, or do anything else that could be dangerous if you are dizzy or are not alert.* If the problem continues or gets worse, check with your doctor.

The beta-blocker (atenolol, bisoprolol, metoprolol, nadolol, pindolol, propranolol, or timolol) contained in this medicine may make you more sensitive to cold temperatures, especially if you have blood circulation problems. Beta-blockers tend to decrease blood circulation in the skin, fingers, and toes. Dress warmly during cold weather and be careful during prolonged exposure to cold, such as in winter sports.

This medicine may cause your skin to be more sensitive to sunlight than it is normally. Exposure to sunlight, even for brief periods of time, may cause a skin rash, itching, redness or other discoloration of the skin, or a severe sunburn. When you begin taking this medicine:
- Stay out of direct sunlight, especially between the hours of 10:00 a.m. and 3:00 p.m., if possible.
- Wear protective clothing, including a hat. Also, wear sunglasses.
- Apply a sun block product that has a skin protection factor (SPF) of at least 15. Some patients may require a product with a higher SPF number, especially if they have a fair complexion. If you have any questions about this, check with your health care professional.
- Apply a sun block lipstick that has an SPF of at least 15 to protect your lips.
- Do not use a sunlamp or tanning bed or booth.

If you have a severe reaction from the sun, check with your doctor.

Before you have any medical tests, tell the doctor in charge that you are taking this medicine. The results of some tests may be affected by this medicine.

For patients with allergies to foods, medicines, or insect stings:
- There is a chance that this medicine will make allergic reactions worse and harder to treat. If you have a severe allergic reaction while you are being treated with this medicine, check with a doctor right away so that it can be treated.

Side Effects of This Medicine

Along with its needed effects, a medicine may cause some unwanted effects. Although not all of these side effects may occur, if they do occur they may need medical attention.

Check with your doctor as soon as possible if any of the following side effects occur:

Less common

Breathing difficulty and/or wheezing; cold hands and feet; mental depression; slow heartbeat (especially less than 50 beats per minute); swelling of ankles, feet, and/or lower legs

Rare

Black, tarry stools; blood in urine or stools; chest pain; dark urine; fever, chills, cough, or sore throat; hallucinations (seeing, hearing, or feeling things that are not there); joint pain; lower back or side pain; pinpoint red spots on skin; red, scaling, or crusted skin; skin rash or hives; stomach pain (severe) with nausea and vomiting; unusual bleeding or bruising; or yellow eyes or skin

Signs and symptoms of too much potassium or sodium loss

Confusion; convulsions (seizures); dryness of mouth; increased thirst; irregular heartbeats; irritability, mood or mental changes; muscle cramps or pain; nausea or vomiting, unusual tiredness or weakness; weak pulse

Signs and symptoms of overdose (in the order in which they may occur)

Slow heartbeat; dizziness (severe) or fainting; difficulty in breathing; bluish-colored fingernails or palms of hands; convulsions (seizures)

Other side effects may occur that usually do not need medical attention. These side effects may go away during treatment as your body adjusts to the medicine. However, check with your doctor if any of the following side effects continue or are bothersome:

More common

Decreased sexual ability; dizziness or lightheadedness; drowsiness (mild); trouble in sleeping

Less common

Anxiety or nervousness; constipation; diarrhea; increased sensitivity of skin to sunlight (skin rash, itching, redness or other discoloration of skin, or severe sunburn); loss of appetite; numbness or tingling of fingers and toes; stomach discomfort or upset; stuffy nose

Rare

Changes in taste; dry, sore eyes; itching of skin; nightmares and vivid dreams

Although not all of the above side effects have been reported for all of these medicines, they have been reported for at least one of the beta-blockers or thiazide diuretics. Since all of the beta-blockers are very similar and the thiazide diuretics are also very similar, any of the above side effects may occur with any of these medicines. However, they may be more common with some combinations than with others.

After you have been taking this medicine for a while, it may cause unpleasant or even harmful effects if you stop taking it too suddenly. After you stop taking this medicine or while you are gradually reducing the amount you are taking, check with your doctor right away if any of the following occur:

Chest pain; fast or irregular heartbeat; general feeling of discomfort, illness, or weakness; headache; shortness of breath (sudden); sweating; trembling

Other side effects not listed above may also occur in some patients. If you notice any other effects, check with your doctor.

Revised: 08/23/94

BETA-CAROTENE Systemic

Some commonly used brand names are:

In the U.S.—

Lumitene
Max-Caro

Generic name product may be available.

Description

Vitamins (VYE-ta-mins) are compounds that you *must* have for growth and health. They are needed in small amounts only and are usually available in the foods that you eat. Beta-carotene (bay-ta-KARE-oh-teen) is converted in the body to vitamin A, which is necessary for healthy eyes and skin.

A lack of vitamin A may cause a rare condition called night blindness (problems seeing in the dark). It may also cause dry eyes, eye infections, skin problems, and slowed growth. Your health care professional may treat these problems by prescribing either beta-carotene, which your body can change into vitamin A, or vitamin A for you.

Some conditions may increase your need for vitamin A. These include:

- Cystic fibrosis
- Diarrhea, continuing
- Illness, long-term
- Injury, serious
- Liver disease
- Malabsorption problems
- Pancreas disease

Increased need for vitamin A should be determined by your health care professional.

Claims that beta-carotene is effective as a sunscreen have not been proven. Although beta-carotene supplements are being studied for their ability to reduce the risk of certain types of cancer and possibly heart disease, there is not enough information to show that this is effective.

Beta-carotene may be used to treat other conditions as determined by your doctor.

Beta-carotene is available without a prescription in the following dosage forms:

Oral

- Capsules (U.S. and Canada)
- Tablets (U.S. and Canada)
- Chewable tablets (Canada)

Importance of Diet

For good health, it is important that you eat a balanced and varied diet. Follow carefully any diet program your health care professional may recommend. For your specific dietary vitamin and/or mineral needs, ask your health care professional for a list of appropriate foods. If you think that you are not getting enough vitamins and/or minerals in your diet, you may choose to take a dietary supplement.

It is documented that people who consume diets high in fruits and vegetables have a reduced risk of heart disease and certain cancers. Fruits and vegetables are rich in beta-carotene and other nutrients that may be beneficial.

Beta-carotene is found in carrots; dark-green leafy vegetables, such as spinach and green leaf lettuce; sweet potatoes; broccoli; cantaloupe; and winter squash. The body converts beta-carotene into vitamin A. Ordinary cooking does not destroy beta-carotene.

Vitamins alone will not take the place of a good diet and will not provide energy. Your body needs other substances found in food, such as protein, minerals, carbohydrates, and fat. Vitamins themselves often cannot work without the presence of other foods. For example, some fat is needed so that beta-carotene can be absorbed into the body.

Before Using This Dietary Supplement

If you are taking this dietary supplement without a prescription, carefully read and follow any precautions on the label. For beta-carotene, the following should be considered:

Allergies—Tell your health care professional if you have ever had any unusual or allergic reaction to beta-carotene. Also tell your health care professional if you are allergic to any other substances, such as foods, preservatives, or dyes.

Pregnancy—It is especially important that you are receiving enough vitamins when you become pregnant and that you continue to receive the right amount of vitamins throughout your pregnancy. The healthy growth and development of the fetus depend on a steady supply of nutrients from the mother.

Beta-carotene has not been studied in pregnant women. However, no problems with fertility or pregnancy have been reported in women taking up to 30 milligrams (mg) of beta-carotene a day. The effects of taking more than 30 mg a day are not known.

Breast-feeding—It is especially important that you receive the right amounts of vitamins so that your baby will also get the vitamins needed to grow properly. However, taking large amounts of a dietary supplement while breast-feeding may be harmful to the mother and/or baby and should be avoided.

Children—Problems in children have not been documented with intake of normal daily recommended amounts.

Older adults—Problems in older adults have not been documented with intake of normal daily recommended amounts.

Medicines or other dietary supplements—Although certain medicines or dietary supplements should not be used together at all, in other cases they may be used together even if an interaction might occur. In these cases, your health care professional may want to change the dose, or other precautions may be necessary. Tell your health care professional if you are taking any other dietary supplement or any prescription or nonprescription (over-the-counter [OTC]) medicine.

Other medical problems—The presence of other medical problems may affect the use of beta-carotene. Make sure you tell your health care professional if you have any other medical problems, especially:

- Eating disorders or
- Kidney disease or
- Liver disease—These conditions may cause high blood levels of beta-carotene, which may increase the chance of side effects

Proper Use of This Dietary Supplement

Dosing—For use as a dietary supplement:

- For *oral* dosage forms (capsules or chewable tablets):
  - —Adults and teenagers: 6 to 15 milligrams (mg) of beta-carotene (the equivalent of 10,000 to 25,000 Units of vitamin A activity) per day.
  - —Children: 3 to 6 mg of beta-carotene (the equivalent of 5000 to 10,000 Units of vitamin A activity) per day.

If you have high blood levels of vitamin A, your body will convert less beta-carotene to vitamin A.

Missed dose—If you miss taking a vitamin for one or more days there is no cause for concern, since it takes some time for your body to become seriously low in vitamins. However, if your health care professional has recommended that you take this vitamin, try to remember to take it as directed every day.

Storage—To store this dietary supplement:

- Keep out of the reach of children.
- Store away from heat and direct light.
- Do not store in the bathroom, near the kitchen sink, or in other damp places. Heat or moisture may cause the dietary supplement to break down.
- Keep the dietary supplement from freezing. Do not refrigerate.
- Do not keep outdated dietary supplements or those no longer needed. Be sure that any discarded dietary supplement is out of the reach of children.

Precautions While Using This Dietary Supplement

Use of beta-carotene has been associated with an increased risk of lung cancer in people who smoke or who have been exposed to asbestos. One study of 29,000 male smokers found an 18% increase in lung cancer in the group receiving 20 mg of beta-carotene a day for 5 to 8 years. Another study of 18,000 people found 28% more lung cancers in people with a history of smoking and/or asbestos exposure. These people took 30 mg of beta-carotene in addition to 25,000 Units of retinol (a form of vitamin A) a day for 4 years. However, one study of 22,000 male physicians, some of them smokers or former smokers, found no increase in lung cancer. These people took 50 mg of beta-carotene every other day for 12 years.

If you smoke or have a history of smoking or asbestos exposure, you should not take large amounts of beta-carotene supplements for long periods of time. However, foods that are rich in beta-carotene are considered safe and appear to lower the risk of some types of cancer and possibly heart disease.

Side Effects of This Dietary Supplement

Along with its needed effects, a dietary supplement may cause some unwanted effects. The following side effects may go away during treatment as your body adjusts to the dietary supplement. However, check with your health care professional if any of the following side effects continue or are bothersome:

More common

Yellowing of palms, hands, or soles of feet, and to a lesser extent the face (this may be a sign that your dose of beta-carotene as a nutritional supplement is too high)

Rare

Diarrhea; dizziness; joint pain; unusual bleeding or bruising

Other side effects not listed above may also occur in some individuals. If you notice any other effects, check with your health care professional.

Additional Information

Once a product has been approved for marketing for a certain use, experience may show that it is also useful for other medical problems. Although this use is not included in product labeling, beta-carotene is used in certain patients with the following medical conditions:

- Polymorphous light eruption (a type of reaction to sun)
- Erythropoietic protoporphyria photosensitivity reaction (a type of reaction to sun)

Breast-feeding—Beta-carotene has not been reported to cause problems in nursing babies.

Children—This medicine has been tested in children and, in effective doses, has not been shown to cause different side effects or problems in children than it does in adults.

Older adults—Many medicines have not been studied specifically in older people. Therefore, it may not be known whether they work exactly the same way they do in younger adults. Although there is no specific information comparing use of beta-carotene in the elderly with use in other age groups, it is not expected to cause different side effects or problems in older people than it does in younger adults.

Dosing—The dose of beta-carotene will be different for different patients. *Follow your doctor's orders or the directions on the label.* The following information includes only the average doses of beta-carotene. *If your dose is different, do not change it* unless your doctor tells you to do so.

- For *oral* dosage forms (capsules or tablets):
  —To treat or prevent a reaction to sun in patients with erythropoietic protoporphyria:
  - Adults and teenagers—30 to 300 milligrams (mg) of beta-carotene (the equivalent of 50,000 to 500,000 Units of vitamin A activity) a day.
  - Children—30 to 150 mg of beta-carotene (the equivalent of 50,000 to 250,000 Units of vitamin A activity) a day.

  —To treat or prevent a reaction to sun in patients with polymorphous light eruption:
  - Adults and teenagers—75 to 180 mg of beta-carotene (the equivalent of 125,000 to 300,000 Units of vitamin A acitivity) a day.
  - Children—30 to 150 mg of beta-carotene (the equivalent of 50,000 to 250,000 Units of vitamin A activity) a day.

Missed dose—If you miss a dose of this medicine, take it as soon as possible. However, if it is almost time for your next dose, skip the missed dose and go back to your regular dosing schedule. Do not double doses.

Other than the above information, there is no additional information relating to proper use, precautions, or side effects for these uses.

Revised: 07/09/97

BETHANECHOL Systemic

Some commonly used brand names are:

In the U.S.—

Duvoid	Urecholine
Urabeth	

Generic name product may also be available.

In Canada—

Duvoid	Urecholine

Description

Bethanechol (be-THAN-e-kole) is taken to treat certain disorders of the urinary tract or bladder. It helps to cause urination and emptying of the bladder. Bethanechol may also be used for other conditions as determined by your doctor.

Bethanechol is available only with your doctor's prescription in the following dosage forms:

Oral

- Tablets (U.S. and Canada)

Parenteral

- Injection (U.S. and Canada)

Before Using This Medicine

In deciding to use a medicine, the risks of taking the medicine must be weighed against the good it will do. This is a decision you and your doctor will make. For bethanechol, the following should be considered:

Allergies—Tell your doctor if you have ever had any unusual or allergic reaction to bethanechol. Also tell your

health care professional if you are allergic to any other substances, such as foods, preservatives, or dyes.

Pregnancy—Studies on effects in pregnancy have not been done in either humans or animals.

Breast-feeding—It is not known whether bethanechol passes into the breast milk.

Children—Although there is no specific information comparing use of bethanechol in children with use in other age groups, this medicine is not expected to cause different side effects or problems in children than it does in adults.

Older adults—Many medicines have not been studied specifically in older people. Therefore, it may not be known whether they work exactly the same way they do in younger adults. Although there is no specific information comparing use of bethanechol in the elderly with use in other age groups, it is not expected to cause different side effects or problems in older people than it does in younger adults.

Other medicines—Although certain medicines should not be used together at all, in other cases two different medicines may be used together even if an interaction might occur. In these cases, your doctor may want to change the dose, or other precautions may be necessary. Tell your health care professional if you are taking any other prescription or nonprescription (over-the-counter [OTC]) medicine.

Other medical problems—The presence of other medical problems may affect the use of bethanechol. Make sure you tell your doctor if you have any other medical problems, especially:

- Asthma or
- Epilepsy or
- Heart or blood vessel disease or
- Intestinal blockage or
- Low blood pressure or
- Parkinson's disease or
- Recent bladder or intestinal surgery or
- Stomach ulcer or other stomach problems or
- Urinary tract blockage or difficult urination—Bethanechol may make these conditions worse
- High blood pressure—Bethanechol may cause a rapid fall in blood pressure
- Overactive thyroid—Bethanechol may further increase the chance of heart problems

Proper Use of This Medicine

Take this medicine on an empty stomach (either 1 hour before or 2 hours after meals) to lessen the possibility of nausea and vomiting, unless otherwise directed by your doctor.

Take this medicine only as directed. Do not take more of it, do not take it more often, and do not take it for a longer time than your doctor ordered. To do so may increase the chance of side effects.

Dosing—The dose of bethanechol will be different for different patients. *Follow your doctor's orders or the directions on the label.* The following information includes only the average doses of bethanechol. *If your dose is different, do not change it* unless your doctor tells you to do so.

- To empty the bladder:
  - —For *oral* dosage form (tablets):
    - Adults—25 to 50 milligrams (mg) three or four times a day.
    - Children—Dose is based on body weight and must be determined by your doctor. The usual dose is 0.6 mg per kilogram (kg) (0.27 mg per pound) of body weight a day. This dose is divided into smaller doses and taken three or four times a day.
  - —For *injection* dosage form:
    - Adults—5 mg injected under the skin three or four times a day.
    - Children—Dose is based on body weight and must be determined by your doctor. The usual dose is 0.2 mg per kg (0.09 mg per pound) of body weight a day. This dose is divided into smaller doses, which are injected under the skin three or four times a day.

Missed dose—If you miss a dose of this medicine and you remember within an hour or so of the missed dose, take it right away. However, if you do not remember until 2 or more hours after, skip the missed dose and go back to your regular dosing schedule. Do not double doses.

Storage—To store this medicine:

- Keep out of the reach of children.
- Store away from heat and direct light.
- Do not store the tablet form of this medicine in the bathroom, near the kitchen sink, or in other damp places. Heat or moisture may cause the medicine to break down.
- Do not keep outdated medicine or medicine no longer needed. Be sure that any discarded medicine is out of the reach of children.

Precautions While Using This Medicine

Dizziness, lightheadedness, or fainting may occur, especially when you get up from a lying or sitting position. Getting up slowly may help lessen this problem.

Side Effects of This Medicine

Along with its needed effects, a medicine may cause some unwanted effects. Although not all of these side effects may occur, if they do occur they may need medical attention.

Check with your doctor as soon as possible if any of the following side effects occur:

Rare—more common with the injection
Shortness of breath, wheezing, or tightness in chest

Other side effects may occur that usually do not need medical attention. These side effects may go away during treatment as your body adjusts to the medicine. However, check with your doctor if any of the following side effects continue or are bothersome:

Less common or rare—more common with the injection
Belching; blurred vision or change in near or distance vision; diarrhea; dizziness or lightheadedness; feeling

faint; frequent urge to urinate; headache; increased watering of mouth or sweating; nausea or vomiting; redness or flushing of skin or feeling of warmth; seizures; sleeplessness, nervousness, or jitters; stomach discomfort or pain

Other side effects not listed above may also occur in some patients. If you notice any other effects, check with your doctor.

Additional Information

Once a medicine has been approved for marketing for a certain use, experience may show that it is also useful for other medical problems. Although these uses are not included in product labeling, bethanechol is used in certain patients with the following medical conditions:

- Certain stomach problems
- Gastroesophageal reflux (caused by acid in the stomach washing back up into the esophagus)
- Megacolon (an abnormally large or dilated colon)

Other than the above information, there is no additional information relating to proper use, precautions, or side effects for these uses.

Revised: 05/12/93
Interim revision: 06/27/94

BIOTIN Systemic

Generic name product is available in the U.S. and Canada.

Other commonly used names are vitamin H, coenzyme R, or vitamin Bw.

Description

Biotin (BYE-oh-tin) supplements are used to prevent or treat biotin deficiency.

Vitamins (VYE-ta-mins) are compounds that you must have for growth and health. They are needed in only small amounts and are usually available in the foods that you eat. Biotin is necessary for formation of fatty acids and glucose, which are used as fuels by the body. It is also important for the metabolism of amino acids and carbohydrates.

A lack of biotin is rare. However, if it occurs it may lead to skin rash, loss of hair, high blood levels of cholesterol, and heart problems.

Some conditions may increase your need for biotin. These include:

- Genetic disorder of biotin deficiency
- Seborrheic determatitis in infants
- Surgical removal of the stomach

Increased need for biotin should be determined by your health care professional.

Claims that biotin supplements are effective in the treatment of acne, eczema (a type of skin disorder), or hair loss have not been proven.

Biotin supplements are available without a prescription in the following dosage forms:

Oral
- Capsules (U.S.)
- Tablets (U.S. and Canada)

Importance of Diet

For good health, it is important that you eat a balanced and varied diet. Follow carefully any diet program your health care professional may recommend. For your specific vitamin and/or mineral needs, ask your health care professional for a list of appropriate foods. If you think that you are not getting enough vitamins and/or minerals in your diet, you may choose to take a dietary supplement.

Biotin is found in various foods, including liver, cauliflower, salmon, carrots, bananas, soy flour, cereals, and yeast. Biotin content of food is reduced by cooking and preserving.

Vitamins alone will not take the place of a good diet and will not provide energy. Your body needs other substances found in food, such as protein, minerals, carbohydrates, and fat. Vitamins themselves cannot work without the presence of other foods.

The daily amount of biotin needed is defined in several different ways.

For U.S.—
- Recommended Dietary Allowances (RDAs) are the amount of vitamins and minerals needed to provide for adequate nutrition in most healthy persons. RDAs for a given nutrient may vary depending on a person's age, sex, and physical condition (e.g., pregnancy).
- Daily Values (DVs) are used on food and dietary supplement labels to indicate the percent of the recommended daily amount of each nutrient that a serving provides. DVs replace the previous designation of United States Recommended Daily Allowances (USRDAs).

For Canada—
- Recommended Nutrient Intakes (RNIs) are used to determine the amounts of vitamins, minerals, and protein needed to provide adequate nutrition and lessen the risk of chronic disease.

Because lack of biotin is rare, there is no RDA or RNI for it. Normal daily recommended intakes for biotin are generally defined as follows:

Infants and children—
Birth to 3 years of age: 10 to 20 micrograms (mcg).
4 to 6 years of age: 25 mcg.

7 to 10 years of age: 30 mcg.
Adolescents and adults—30 to 100 mcg.

Before Using This Dietary Supplement

If you are taking this dietary supplement without a prescription, carefully read and follow any precautions on the label. For biotin, the following should be considered:

Allergies—Tell your health care professional if you have ever had any unusual or allergic reaction to biotin. Also tell your health care professional if you are allergic to any other substances, such as foods, preservatives, or dyes.

Pregnancy—It is especially important that you are receiving enough vitamins and minerals when you become pregnant and that you continue to receive the right amount of vitamins and minerals throughout your pregnancy. The healthy growth and development of the fetus depend on a steady supply of nutrients from the mother. However, taking large amounts of a dietary supplement in pregnancy may be harmful to the mother and/or fetus and should be avoided.

Breast-feeding—It is especially important that you receive the right amounts of vitamins so that your baby will also get the vitamins needed to grow properly. However, taking large amounts of a dietary supplement while breast-feeding may be harmful to the mother and/or baby and should be avoided.

Children—Problems in children have not been reported with intake of normal daily recommended amounts.

Older adults—Problems in older adults have not been reported with intake of normal daily recommended amounts.

Proper Use of This Dietary Supplement

Dosing—The amount of biotin to meet normal daily recommended intakes will be different for different individuals. The following information includes only the average amounts of biotin.

- For *oral* dosage form (capsules or tablets):
  - —To prevent deficiency, the amount taken by mouth is based on normal daily recommended intakes:
    - Adults and teenagers—30 to 100 micrograms (mcg) per day.
    - Children 7 to 10 years of age—30 mcg per day.
    - Children 4 to 6 years of age—25 mcg per day.
    - Children birth to 3 years of age—10 to 20 mcg per day.
  - —To treat deficiency:
    - Adults, teenagers, and children—Treatment dose is determined by prescriber for each individual based on severity of deficiency.

Missed dose—If you miss taking biotin supplements for one or more days there is no cause for concern, since it takes some time for your body to become seriously low in biotin. However, if your health care professional has recommended that you take biotin, try to remember to take it as directed every day.

Storage—To store this dietary supplement:

- Keep out of the reach of children.
- Store away from heat and direct light.
- Do not store in the bathroom, near the kitchen sink, or in other damp places. Heat or moisture may cause the dietary supplement to break down.
- Keep the dietary supplement from freezing. Do not refrigerate.
- Do not keep outdated dietary supplements or those no longer needed. Be sure that any discarded dietary supplement is out of the reach of children.

Side Effects of This Dietary Supplement

No side effects have been reported for biotin in amounts up to 10 milligrams a day. However, check with your health care professional if you notice any unusual effects while you are taking it.

Revised: 09/26/91
Interim revision: 06/02/92; 04/25/95

BISMUTH SUBSALICYLATE Oral

Some commonly used brand names are:

In the U.S.—

Bismatrol
Bismatrol Extra Strength
Pepto-Bismol
Pepto-Bismol Easy-to-Swallow Caplets
Pepto-Bismol Maximum Strength

Generic name product may also be available.

In Canada—

Bismed
Pepto-Bismol
PMS-Bismuth Subsalicylate

Description

Bismuth subsalicylate (BIS-muth sub-sa-LIS-a-late) is used to treat diarrhea. It is also used to relieve the symptoms of an upset stomach, such as heartburn, indigestion, and nausea.

This medicine is available without a prescription; however, your doctor may have special instructions on the proper use and dose for your medical problem. Bismuth subsalicylate is available in the following dosage forms:

Oral

- Oral suspension (U.S. and Canada)
- Tablets (U.S.)
- Chewable tablets (U.S. and Canada)

Before Using This Medicine

If you are taking this medicine without a prescription, carefully read and follow any precautions on the label. For bismuth subsalicylate, the following should be considered:

Allergies—Tell your doctor if you have ever had any unusual or allergic reaction to bismuth subsalicylate or to other salicylates, such as aspirin, including methyl salicylate (oil of wintergreen), or to any of the following medicines:

- Carprofen (e.g., Rimadyl)
- Diclofenac (e.g., Voltaren)
- Diflunisal (e.g., Dolobid)
- Fenoprofen (e.g., Nalfon)
- Floctafenine (e.g., Idarac)
- Flurbiprofen taken by mouth (e.g., Ansaid)
- Ibuprofen (e.g., Motrin)
- Indomethacin (e.g., Indocin)
- Ketoprofen (e.g., Orudis)
- Ketorolac (e.g., Toradol)
- Meclofenamate (e.g., Meclomen)
- Mefenamic acid (e.g., Ponstel)
- Naproxen (e.g., Naprosyn)
- Oxyphenbutazone (e.g., Tandearil)
- Phenylbutazone (e.g., Butazolidin)
- Piroxicam (e.g., Feldene)
- Sulindac (e.g., Clinoril)
- Suprofen (e.g., Suprol)
- Tiaprofenic acid (e.g., Surgam)
- Tolmetin (e.g., Tolectin)
- Zomepirac (e.g., Zomax)

Also tell your health care professional if you are allergic to any other substances, such as certain foods, sulfites or other preservatives, or dyes.

Diet—Make certain your health care professional knows if you are on any special diet, such as a low-sodium or low-sugar diet.

Pregnancy—The occasional use of bismuth subsalicylate is not likely to cause problems in the fetus or in the newborn baby. However, based on what is known about the use of other salicylates, especially at high doses and for long periods of time, the following information may also apply for bismuth subsalicylate.

Salicylates have not been shown to cause birth defects in humans. However, studies in animals have shown that salicylates may cause birth defects.

There is a chance that regular use of salicylates late in pregnancy may cause unwanted effects on the heart or blood flow in the fetus or in the newborn infant.

Use of salicylates during the last 2 weeks of pregnancy may cause bleeding problems in the fetus before or during delivery or in the newborn infant. Also, too much use of salicylates during the last 3 months of pregnancy may increase the length of pregnancy, prolong labor, cause other problems during delivery, or cause severe bleeding in the mother before, during, or after delivery.

Breast-feeding—Salicylates pass into the breast milk. Although they have not been shown to cause problems in nursing babies, it is possible that problems may occur if large amounts of salicylates are taken regularly.

Children—The fluid loss caused by diarrhea may result in a severe condition. For this reason, medicine for diarrhea must not be given to young children (under 3 years of age) without first checking with their doctor. In older children with diarrhea, medicine for diarrhea may be used, but it is also very important that a sufficient amount of liquids be given to replace the fluid lost by the body. If you have any questions about this, check with your health care professional.

Also, children are usually more sensitive to the effects of salicylates, especially if they have a fever or have lost large amounts of body fluid because of vomiting, diarrhea, or sweating.

The bismuth in this medicine may cause severe constipation in children.

In addition, do not use this medicine to treat nausea or vomiting in children or teenagers who have or are recovering from the flu or chickenpox. If nausea or vomiting is present, check with the child's doctor because this could be an early sign of Reye's syndrome.

Older adults—The fluid loss caused by diarrhea may result in a severe condition. For this reason, elderly persons with diarrhea should not take this medicine without first checking with their doctor. It is also very important that a sufficient amount of liquids be taken to replace the fluid lost by the body. If you have any questions about this, check with your health care professional.

Also, the elderly may be more sensitive to the effects of salicylates. This may increase the chance of side effects during treatment. In addition, the bismuth in this medicine may cause severe constipation in the elderly.

Other medicines—Although certain medicines should not be used together at all, in other cases two different medicines may be used together even if an interaction might occur. In these cases, your doctor may want to change the dose, or other precautions may be necessary. When taking bismuth subsalicylate it is especially important that your health care professional know if you are taking any of the following:

- Anticoagulants (blood thinners) or
- Heparin—The salicylate in this medicine may increase the chance of bleeding
- Antidiabetics, oral (diabetes medicine you take by mouth)—This medicine may make the levels of sugar in the blood become too low
- Medicine for pain and/or inflammation (except narcotics)—If these medicines contain salicylates, use of bismuth subsalicylate (which also contains salicylate) may lead to increased side effects and overdose
- Probenecid (e.g., Benemid) or
- Sulfinpyrazone (e.g., Anturane)—Bismuth subsalicylate may make these medicines less effective for treating gout
- Tetracyclines by mouth (medicine for infection)—The tablet form of bismuth subsalicylate should be taken at least 1 to 3 hours before or after tetracyclines; otherwise it may decrease the effectiveness of the tetracycline

Other medical problems—The presence of other medical problems may affect the use of bismuth subsalicylate.

Make sure you tell your doctor if you have any other medical problems, especially:

- Dysentery—This condition may get worse; a different kind of treatment may be needed
- Gout—The salicylate in this medicine may worsen the gout and make the medicines taken for gout less effective
- Hemophilia or other bleeding problems—The salicylate in this medicine may increase the chance of bleeding
- Kidney disease—There is a greater chance of side effects because the body may be unable to get rid of the bismuth subsalicylate
- Stomach ulcer—Use of this medicine may make the ulcer worse

Proper Use of This Medicine

For safe and effective use of this medicine:

- Follow your doctor's instructions if this medicine was prescribed.
- Follow the manufacturer's package directions if you are treating yourself.

For patients using this medicine to treat diarrhea:

- *It is very important that the fluid lost by the body be replaced and that a proper diet be followed.* For the first 24 hours you should drink plenty of clear liquids, such as ginger ale, decaffeinated cola, decaffeinated tea, broth, and gelatin. During the next 24 hours you may eat bland foods, such as cooked cereals, bread, crackers, and applesauce. Fruits, vegetables, fried or spicy foods, bran, candy, and caffeine and alcoholic beverages may make the diarrhea worse.
- If too much fluid has been lost by the body due to the diarrhea a serious condition may develop. Check with your doctor as soon as possible if any of the following signs of too much fluid loss occur:

  Decreased urination
  Dizziness and lightheadedness
  Dryness of mouth
  Increased thirst
  Wrinkled skin

Dosing—The dose of bismuth subsalicylate will be different for different patients. *Follow your doctor's orders or the directions on the label.* The following information includes only the average doses of bismuth subsalicylate. *If your dose is different, do not change it* unless your doctor tells you to do so.

The number of tablets or tablespoonfuls or teaspoonfuls of suspension that you take depends on the strength of the medicine.

- For *oral* dosage form (suspension):
  - —For diarrhea or upset stomach:
    - Adults and teenagers—The usual dose is 2 tablespoonfuls every half-hour to one hour if needed. You should not take more than 16 tablespoonfuls of the regular-strength suspension or 8 tablespoonfuls of the concentrate in twenty-four hours.
    - Children 9 to 12 years of age—The usual dose is 1 tablespoonful every half-hour to one hour. You should not take more than 8 tablespoonfuls of the regular-strength suspension or 4 tablespoonfuls of the concentrate in twenty-four hours.
    - Children 6 to 9 years of age—The usual dose is 2 teaspoonfuls every half-hour to one hour. You should not take more than 16 teaspoonfuls of the regular-strength suspension or 8 teaspoonfuls of the concentrate in twenty-four hours.
    - Children 3 to 6 years of age—The usual dose is 1 teaspoonful every half-hour to one hour. You should not take more than 8 teaspoonfuls of the regular-strength suspension or 4 teaspoonfuls of the concentrate in twenty-four hours.
    - Children up to 3 years of age—Dose is based on body weight:
      - —For children weighing 6.4 to 8 kilograms (kg) (14 to 18 pounds): The usual dose is 1/2 teaspoonful of the regular-strength suspension or 1/4 teaspoonful of the concentrate.
      - —For children weighing over 13 kg (29 pounds): The usual dose is 1 teaspoonful of the regular-strength suspension or 1/2 teaspoonful of the concentrate.
- For *oral* dosage forms (tablets or chewable tablets):
  - —For diarrhea or upset stomach:
    - Adults and teenagers—The usual dose is 2 tablets every half-hour to one hour. You should not take more than 16 tablets in twenty-four hours.
    - Children 9 to 12 years of age—The usual dose is 1 tablet every half-hour to one hour. You should not take more than 8 tablets in twenty-four hours.
    - Children up to 9 years of age—The oral suspension is the preferred dosage form for this age group.

Missed dose—If your doctor has ordered you to take this medicine according to a regular schedule and you miss a dose, take it as soon as you remember. However, if it is almost time for your next dose, skip the missed dose and go back to your regular dosing schedule. Do not double doses.

Storage—To store this medicine:

- Keep out of the reach of children. Overdose is very dangerous in young children.
- Store away from heat and direct light.
- Do not store the tablet form of this medicine in the bathroom, near the kitchen sink, or in other damp places. Heat or moisture may cause the medicine to break down.
- Keep the liquid form of this medicine from freezing.
- Do not keep outdated medicine or medicine no longer needed. Be sure that any discarded medicine is out of the reach of children.

Precautions While Using This Medicine

Check the labels of all over-the-counter (OTC), nonprescription, and prescription medicines you now take. If any contain aspirin or other salicylates, be especially careful. Using other salicylate-containing products while taking this medicine may lead to overdose. If you have any questions about this, check with your health care professional.

For diabetic patients:

- False urine sugar test results may occur if you are regularly taking large amounts of bismuth subsalicylate or other salicylates.
- Smaller doses or occasional use of bismuth subsalicylate usually will not affect urine sugar tests. However, check with your health care professional (especially if your diabetes is not well-controlled) if:
  —you are not sure how much salicylate you are taking every day.
  —you notice any change in your urine sugar test results.
  —you have any other questions about this possible problem.

If you think that you or anyone else may have taken an overdose, get emergency help at once. Taking an overdose of this medicine may cause unconsciousness or death. Signs of overdose include convulsions (seizures), hearing loss, confusion, ringing or buzzing in the ears, severe drowsiness or tiredness, severe excitement or nervousness, and fast or deep breathing.

If you are taking this medicine for diarrhea, check with your doctor:

- if your symptoms do not improve within 2 days or if they become worse.
- if you also have a high fever.

Side Effects of This Medicine

Along with its needed effects, a medicine may cause some unwanted effects. Although not all of these side effects may occur, if they do occur they may need medical attention.

When this medicine is used occasionally or for short periods of time at low doses, side effects usually are rare. However, check with your doctor immediately if any of the following side effects occur, since they may indicate that too much medicine is being taken:

Anxiety; any loss of hearing; confusion; constipation (severe); diarrhea (severe or continuing); difficulty in speaking or slurred speech; dizziness or lightheadedness; drowsiness (severe); fast or deep breathing; headache (severe or continuing); increased sweating; increased thirst; mental depression; muscle spasms (especially of face, neck, and back); muscle weakness; nausea or vomiting (severe or continuing); ringing or buzzing in ears (continuing); stomach pain (severe or continuing); trembling; uncontrollable flapping movements of the hands (especially in elderly patients) or other uncontrolled body movements; vision problems

In some patients bismuth subsalicylate may cause dark tongue and/or grayish black stools. This is only temporary and will go away when you stop taking this medicine.

Other side effects not listed above may also occur in some patients. If you notice any other effects, check with your doctor.

Revised: 02/03/92
Interim revision: 09/01/94

BLEOMYCIN Systemic

A commonly used brand name in the U.S. and Canada is Blenoxane.

Description

Bleomycin (blee-oh-MYE-sin) belongs to the general group of medicines called antineoplastics. It is used to treat some kinds of cancer.

Bleomycin seems to act by interfering with the growth of cancer cells, which are eventually destroyed. Since the growth of normal body cells may also be affected by bleomycin, other effects will also occur. Some of these may be serious and must be reported to your doctor. Other effects, like darkening of skin or hair loss, may not be serious but may cause concern. Some effects may not occur for months or years after the medicine is used.

This medicine may also be used for other conditions, as determined by your doctor.

Before you begin treatment with bleomycin, you and your doctor should talk about the good this medicine will do as well as the risks of using it.

Bleomycin is to be administered only by or under the immediate supervision of your doctor. It is available in the following dosage form:

Parenteral

- Injection (U.S. and Canada)

Before Using This Medicine

In deciding to use a medicine, the risks of taking the medicine must be weighed against the good it will do. This is a decision you and your doctor will make. For bleomycin, the following should be considered:

Allergies—Tell your doctor if you have ever had any unusual or allergic reaction to bleomycin.

Pregnancy—Studies have not been done in pregnant women. However, there is a chance that this medicine may cause birth defects if either the male or female is receiving it at the time of conception or if it is used during pregnancy. Studies in mice given large doses of bleomycin have shown that it causes birth defects. In addition, many cancer medicines may cause sterility which could be permanent. Although sterility has not been reported with this medicine, the possibility should be kept in mind.

Be sure that you have discussed this with your doctor before receiving this medicine. It is best to use some kind of birth control while you are receiving bleomycin. Tell your doctor right away if you think you have become pregnant while receiving bleomycin.

Breast-feeding—Because bleomycin may cause serious side effects, breast-feeding is generally not recommended while you are receiving it.

Children—Although there is no specific information comparing use of bleomycin in children with use in other age groups, this medicine is not expected to cause different side effects or problems in children than it does in adults.

Older adults—Lung problems are more likely to occur in elderly patients (over 70 years of age), who are usually more sensitive to the effects of bleomycin.

Other medical problems—The presence of other medical problems may affect the use of bleomycin. Make sure you tell your doctor if you have any other medical problems, especially:

- Kidney disease—Effects of bleomycin may be increased because of slower removal from the body
- Liver disease—Bleomycin can cause liver problems
- Lung disease—Bleomycin may worsen the condition

Smoking—Tell your doctor if you smoke. The risk of lung problems is increased in people who smoke.

Proper Use of This Medicine

Bleomycin is sometimes given together with certain other medicines. If you are using a combination of medicines, it is important that you receive each medicine at the proper time. If you are taking some of these medicines by mouth, ask your health care professional to help you plan a way to take them at the right times.

Bleomycin often causes nausea, vomiting, and loss of appetite. However, it is very important that you continue to receive the medicine, even if you begin to feel ill. Ask your health care professional for ways to lessen these effects.

Dosing—The dose of bleomycin will be different for different patients. The dose that is used may depend on a number of things, including what the medicine is being used for, the patient's weight, and whether or not other medicines are also being taken. *If you are receiving bleomycin at home, follow your doctor's orders or the directions on the label.* If you have any questions about the proper dose of bleomycin, ask your doctor.

Precautions While Using This Medicine

It is very important that your doctor check your progress at regular visits to make sure that this medicine is working properly and to check for unwanted effects.

Before having any kind of surgery (including dental surgery) or emergency treatment, *tell the medical doctor or dentist in charge that you are receiving or have received this medicine.*

Side Effects of This Medicine

Along with its needed effects, a medicine may cause some unwanted effects. Although not all of these side effects may occur, if they do occur they may need medical attention.

Also, because of the way these medicines act on the body, there is a chance that they might cause other unwanted effects that may not occur until months or years after the medicine is used. These delayed effects may include certain types of cancer, such as leukemia. Discuss these possible effects with your doctor.

Check with your doctor or nurse immediately if the following side effects occur:

More common

Fever and chills (occurring within 3 to 6 hours after a dose)

Less common

Confusion; faintness; wheezing

Rare

Chest pain (sudden severe); weakness in arms or legs (sudden)

Check with your health care professional as soon as possible if any of the following side effects occur:

More common

Cough; shortness of breath; sores in mouth and on lips

Other side effects may occur that usually do not need medical attention. These side effects may go away during treatment as your body adjusts to the medicine. Also, your health care professional may be able to tell you about ways to prevent or reduce some of these side effects. Check with your health care professional if any of the following side effects continue or are bothersome or if you have any questions about them:

More common

Darkening or thickening of skin; dark stripes on skin; itching of skin; skin rash or colored bumps on fingertips, elbows, or palms; skin redness or tenderness; swelling of fingers; vomiting and loss of appetite

Less common

Changes in fingernails or toenails; weight loss

Bleomycin may cause a temporary loss of hair in some people. After treatment has ended, normal hair growth should return, although it may take several months.

Side effects that affect your lungs (for example, cough and shortness of breath) may be more likely to occur if you smoke.

After you stop receiving bleomycin, it may still produce some side effects that need attention. During this period of time, check with your health care professional *immediately* if you notice either of the following:

Cough; shortness of breath

Other side effects not listed above may also occur in some patients. If you notice any other effects, check with your health care professional.

Additional Information

Once a medicine has been approved for marketing for a certain use, experience may show that it is also useful for other medical problems. Although this use is not included in product labeling, bleomycin is used in certain patients with the following medical condition:

- Verruca vulgaris (warts)

For patients being treated with bleomycin for warts:

- Bleomycin is used to treat severe cases of warts when other treatments have not worked.
- Before using bleomycin, tell your doctor if you have problems with circulation. Bleomycin can cause paleness or coldness in fingers treated for warts.
- Bleomycin is injected directly into the wart. Because it is not absorbed into the body, it does not cause loss of hair, lung problems, or other unwanted effects described above. However, it may cause burning or pain at the place of injection. Skin rash or itching, nail loss, and pain or coldness in the finger where bleomycin was injected have also been reported.

Other than the above information, there is no additional information relating to proper use, precautions, or side effects for these uses.

Revised: 07/11/94

BOTULINUM TOXIN TYPE A Parenteral-Local

A commonly used brand name in the U.S. and Canada is Botox.

Description

Botulinum toxin type A (BOT-yoo-lye-num) is used to treat certain eye conditions, such as:

- Blepharospasm—A condition in which the eyelid will not stay open, because of a spasm of a muscle of the eye.
- Strabismus—A condition in which the eyes do not line up properly.

Botulinum toxin type A is injected into the surrounding muscle or tissue of the eye, but not into the eye itself. Depending on your condition, more than one treatment may be required.

This medicine is to be administered only by, or under the immediate supervision of, your doctor. It is available in the following dosage form:

Parenteral-Local

- Injection (U.S. and Canada)

Before Receiving This Medicine

In deciding to receive a medicine, the risks of receiving the medicine must be weighed against the good it will do. This is a decision you and your doctor will make. For botulinum toxin type A, the following should be considered:

Allergies—Tell your doctor if you have ever had any unusual or allergic reaction to botulinum toxin type A. Also tell your health care professional if you are allergic to any other substances.

Pregnancy—Studies on effects in pregnancy have not been done in either humans or animals.

Breast-feeding—It is not known whether botulinum toxin type A passes into the breast milk. However, this medicine has not been reported to cause problems in nursing babies.

Children—Studies on this medicine have been done only in adult patients, and there is no specific information comparing use of botulinum toxin type A in children up to 12 years of age with use in other age groups.

Older adults—Many medicines have not been studied specifically in older people. Therefore, it may not be known whether they work exactly the same way they do in younger adults. Although there is no specific information comparing use of botulinum toxin type A in the elderly with use in other age groups, this medicine is not expected to cause different side effects or problems in older people than it does in younger adults.

Other medicines—Although certain medicines should not be used together at all, in other cases two different medicines may be used together even if an interaction might occur. In these cases, your doctor may want to change the dose, or other precautions may be necessary. Tell your health care professional if you are using any other ophthalmic prescription or nonprescription (over-the-counter [OTC]) medicine.

Other medical problems—The presence of other medical problems may affect the use of botulinum toxin type A. Make sure you tell your doctor if you have any other medical problems, especially:

- Heart problems or other medical conditions that may worsen with rapidly increasing activity—Treatment with botulinum toxin type A may give you better vision and the desire to become more active in your daily life; this may put a strain on your heart and body
- Infection with *Clostridium botulinum* toxin (botulism poisoning), history of—Persons with a history of infection with *Clostridium botulinum* toxin (botulism poisoning) may have produced antibodies that may interfere with botulinum toxin type A therapy and make it less effective

Proper Use of This Medicine

Dosing—The dose of botulinum toxin type A will be different for different patients. The following information includes only the average doses of botulinum toxin type A.

- For *injection* dosage form:
  - —For certain eye conditions:
    - Adults and children 12 years of age and older—One or more injections into the muscles around the eyes one or more times, depending on the condition being treated.
    - Children up to 12 years of age—Use and dose must be determined by your doctor.

Precautions After Receiving This Medicine

After you have received this medicine and your vision is better, you may find that you are a lot more active than you were before. You should increase your activities slowly and carefully to allow your heart and body time to get stronger. Also, before you start any exercise program, check with your doctor.

Side Effects of This Medicine

Along with its needed effects, a medicine may cause some unwanted effects. Although not all of these side effects may occur, if they do occur they may need medical attention.

Check with your doctor as soon as possible if any of the following side effects occur:

More common

Dryness of the eye; inability to close the eyelid completely

Less common or rare

Decreased blinking; irritation of the cornea (colored portion) of the eye; turning outward or inward of the edge of the eyelid

Other side effects may occur that usually do not need medical attention. These side effects may go away as your body adjusts to the medicine. However, check with your doctor if any of the following side effects continue or are bothersome:

More common

Blue or purplish bruise on eyelid; drooping of the upper eyelid; eye pointing upward or downward instead of straight ahead; irritation or watering of the eye; sensitivity of the eye to light

Less common or rare

Difficulty finding the location of objects; double vision; skin rash; swelling of the eyelid skin

Other side effects not listed above may also occur in some patients. If you notice any other effects, check with your doctor.

Additional Information

Once a medicine has been approved for marketing for a certain use, experience may show that it is also useful for other medical problems. Although these uses are not included in product labeling, botulinum toxin type A is used in certain patients with the following medical conditions:

- Spasms of the face
- Spasms of the neck

Revised: 01/09/92
Interim revision: 10/28/93

BROMOCRIPTINE Systemic

Some commonly used brand names are:

In the U.S.—

Parlodel
Parlodel SnapTabs

Generic name product may be available.

In Canada—

Alti-Bromocriptine
Apo-Bromocriptine
Parlodel

Generic name product may be available.

Description

Bromocriptine (broe-moe-KRIP-teen) belongs to the group of medicines known as ergot alkaloids. Bromocriptine blocks release of a hormone called prolactin from the pituitary gland. Prolactin affects the menstrual cycle and milk production. Bromocriptine is used to treat certain menstrual problems or to stop milk production in some women or men who have abnormal milk leakage. It is also used to treat infertility in both men and women that occurs because the body made too much prolactin.

Bromocriptine is also used to treat some people who have Parkinson's disease. It works by stimulating certain parts of the brain and nervous system that are involved in this disease.

Bromocriptine is also used to treat acromegaly (overproduction of growth hormone) and pituitary prolactinomas (tumors of the pituitary gland).

Bromocriptine may also be used for other conditions as determined by your doctor.

Bromocriptine is available only with your doctor's prescription, in the following dosage forms:

Oral

- Capsules (U.S. and Canada)
- Tablets (U.S. and Canada)

Before Using This Medicine

In deciding to use a medicine, the risks of taking the medicine must be weighed against the good it will do. This is a decision you and your doctor will make. For bromocriptine, the following should be considered:

Allergies—Tell your doctor if you have ever had any unusual or allergic reaction to bromocriptine or other ergot medicines such as ergotamine. Also tell your health care professional if you are allergic to any other substances, such as foods, preservatives, or dyes.

Pregnancy—Bromocriptine is not generally recommended for use during pregnancy. However, bromocriptine can be used during pregnancy in certain patients who are closely monitored by their doctor.

Breast-feeding—This medicine stops milk from being produced.

Children—Studies of this medicine have been done only in teenagers over 15 years of age and adult patients. There is no specific information comparing use of bromocriptine in children with use in other age groups.

Teenagers—This medicine has been tested in a limited number of teenagers 15 years of age and older. In effective doses, the medicine has not been shown to cause different side effects or problems than it does in adults. Appropriate studies have not been done in teenagers younger than 15 years of age, and there is no specific information comparing use of bromocriptine in these teenagers with use in other age groups.

Older adults—Confusion, hallucinations, or uncontrolled body movements may be more likely to occur in elderly patients, who are usually more sensitive than younger adults to the effects of bromocriptine.

Other medicines—Although certain medicines should not be used together at all, in other cases two different medicines may be used together even if an interaction might occur. In these cases, your doctor may want to change the dose, or other precautions may be necessary. When you are taking bromocriptine, it is especially important that your health care professional know if you are taking any of the following:

- Ergot alkaloids (dihydroergotamine [e.g., D.H.E. 45], ergoloid mesylates [e.g., Hydergine], ergonovine [e.g., Ergotrate], ergotamine [e.g., Gynergen], methylergonovine [e.g., Methergine], methysergide [e.g., Sansert])—Severe cases of high blood pressure have occurred with the use of bromocriptine. This may be made worse with the use of ergot alkaloids
- Erythromycin (e.g., E.E.S. or Erytab) or
- Risperidone (e.g., Risperdal) or
- Ritonavir (e.g., Norvir)—Use of these medications with bromocriptine may greatly increase the effects of bromocriptine

Other medical problems—The presence of other medical problems may affect the use of bromocriptine. Make sure you tell your doctor if you have any other medical problems, especially:

- High blood pressure (or history of) or
- Pregnancy-induced high blood pressure (history of)—Rarely, bromocriptine can make the high blood pressure worse
- Liver disease—Toxic effects of bromocriptine may occur in patients with liver disease because the body is not able to remove bromocriptine from the bloodstream as it normally would
- Mental problems (history of)—Bromocriptine may make certain mental problems worse

Proper Use of This Medicine

If bromocriptine upsets your stomach, it may be taken with meals or milk. Also, taking the dose at bedtime may help to lessen nausea if it occurs. If stomach upset continues, check with your doctor. Your doctor may recommend that you take the first doses vaginally.

Dosing—The dose of bromocriptine will be different for different patients. *Follow your doctor's orders or the directions on the label.* The following information includes only the average doses of bromocriptine. *If your dose is different, do not change it* unless your doctor tells you to do so.

The number of capsules or tablets that you take depends on the strength of the medicine. Also, *the number of doses you take each day, the time allowed between doses, and the length of time you take the medicine depend on the medical problem for which you are taking bromocriptine.*

- For *oral* dosage forms (capsules and tablets):
  - —For infertility, male hormone problem (male hypogonadism), starting the menstrual cycle (amenorrhea), or stopping abnormal milk secretion from nipples (galactorrhea):
    - Adults and teenagers 15 years of age or older—At first, 1.25 to 2.5 milligrams (mg) once a day taken at bedtime with a snack. Then your doctor may change your dose by 2.5 mg every three to seven days as needed. Doses greater than 5 mg a day are taken in divided doses with meals or at bedtime with a snack.
    - Teenagers less than 15 years of age and children—Use and dose must be determined by your doctor.
  - —For lowering growth hormone (acromegaly):
    - Adults and teenagers 15 years of age or older—At first, 1.25 to 2.5 milligrams (mg) once a day taken at bedtime with a snack for three days. Then your doctor may change your dose by 1.25 or 2.5 mg every three to seven days as needed. Doses greater than 5 mg are divided into smaller doses and taken with meals or at bedtime with a snack.
    - Teenagers less than 15 years of age and children—Use and dose must be determined by your doctor.
  - —For Parkinson's disease:
    - Adults and teenagers 15 years of age or older—At first, 1.25 milligrams (mg) one or two times a day taken with meals or at bedtime with a snack. Then your doctor may change your dose over several weeks as needed.
    - Teenagers less than 15 years of age and children—Use and dose must be determined by your doctor.
  - —For pituitary tumors:
    - Adults and teenagers 15 years of age or older—At first, 1.25 milligrams (mg) two or three times a day taken with meals. Then your doctor may change your dose over several weeks as needed.
    - Teenagers less than 15 years of age and children—Use and dose must be determined by your doctor.

Missed dose—If you miss a dose of this medicine and remember it within 4 hours, take the missed dose when you remember it. However, if a longer time has passed, skip the missed dose and go back to your regular dosing schedule. Do not double doses.

Storage—To store this medicine:

- Keep out of the reach of children.
- Store away from heat and direct light.
- Do not store in the bathroom, near the kitchen sink, or in other damp places. Heat or moisture may cause the medicine to break down.

- Do not keep outdated medicine or medicine no longer needed. Be sure that any discarded medicine is out of the reach of children.

Precautions While Using This Medicine

It is important that your doctor check your progress at regular visits, to make sure that this medicine is working properly and to check for unwanted effects.

This medicine may cause some people to become drowsy, dizzy, or less alert than they are normally. *Make sure you know how you react to this medicine before you drive, use machines, or do anything else that could be dangerous if you are dizzy or are not alert.*

Dizziness is more likely to occur after the first dose of bromocriptine. Taking the first dose at bedtime or when you are able to lie down may lessen problems. It may also be helpful if you get up slowly from a lying or sitting position. Your doctor may also recommend that you take the first dose vaginally.

Bromocriptine may cause dryness of the mouth. For temporary relief, use sugarless candy or gum, melt bits of ice in your mouth, or use a saliva substitute. However, *if dry mouth continues for more than 2 weeks, check with your medical doctor or dentist.* Continuing dryness of the mouth may increase the chance of dental disease, including tooth decay, gum disease, and fungus infections.

It may take several weeks for bromocriptine to work. Do not stop taking this medicine or reduce the amount you are taking without first checking with your doctor.

Drinking alcohol while you are taking bromocriptine may cause you to have a certain reaction. *Avoid alcoholic beverages until you have discussed this with your doctor.* Some of the symptoms you may have if you drink any alcohol while you are taking this medicine are blurred vision, chest pain, confusion, fast or pounding heartbeat, flushing or redness of face, nausea, severe weakness, sweating, throbbing headache, or vomiting.

For females who are able to bear children and who are *taking this medicine for menstrual or infertility problems, to stop milk production, or to treat acromegaly or pituitary tumors:*

- It is best to use some type of birth control while you are taking bromocriptine. However, do not use oral contraceptives (''the Pill'') since they may prevent this medicine from working. For women using bromocriptine for infertility, tell your doctor when your normal menstrual cycle returns. If you wish to become pregnant, you and your doctor should decide on the best time for you to stop using birth control. Tell your doctor right away if you think you have become pregnant while taking this medicine. You and your doctor should discuss whether or not you should continue to take bromocriptine during pregnancy.
- *Check with your doctor right away* if you develop blurred vision, a sudden headache, or severe nausea and vomiting.

Side Effects of This Medicine

Along with its needed effects, a medicine may cause some unwanted effects. Although not all of these side effects may occur, if they do occur they may need medical attention.

Some serious side effects have occurred during the use of bromocriptine to stop milk flow after pregnancy or abortion. These side effects have included strokes, seizures (convulsions), and heart attacks. Some deaths have also occurred. You should discuss with your doctor the good that this medicine will do as well as the risks of using it.

Check with your doctor immediately if any of the following side effects occur:

Rare

Black, tarry stools; bloody vomit; chest pain (severe); convulsions (seizures); fainting; fast heartbeat; headache (unusual); increased sweating; nausea and vomiting (continuing or severe); nervousness; shortness of breath (unexplained); vision changes (such as blurred vision or temporary blindness); weakness (sudden)

Check with your doctor as soon as possible if any of the following side effects occur:

Less common—reported more often in patients with Parkinson's disease

Confusion; hallucinations (seeing, hearing, or feeling things that are not there); uncontrolled movements of the body, such as the face, tongue, arms, hands, head, and upper body

Rare—reported more often in patients taking large doses

Abdominal or stomach pain (continuing or severe); increased frequency of urination; loss of appetite (continuing); lower back pain; runny nose (continuing); weakness

Other side effects may occur that usually do not need medical attention. These side effects may go away during treatment as your body adjusts to the medicine. However, check with your doctor if any of the following side effects continue or are bothersome:

More common

Dizziness or lightheadedness, especially when getting up from a lying or sitting position; nausea

Less common

Constipation; diarrhea; drowsiness or tiredness; dry mouth; leg cramps at night; loss of appetite; mental depression; stomach pain; stuffy nose; tingling or pain in fingers and toes when exposed to cold; vomiting

Some side effects may be more likely to occur in patients who are taking bromocriptine for Parkinson's disease, acromegaly, or pituitary tumors since they may be taking larger doses.

Other side effects not listed above may also occur in some patients. If you notice any other effects, check with your doctor.

Additional Information

Once a medicine has been approved for marketing for a certain use, experience may show that it is also useful for other medical problems. Although these uses are not in-

cluded in product labeling, bromocriptine is used in certain patients with the following medical conditions:
- To stop milk production after an abortion or miscarriage or in women after a delivery who should not breast-feed for medical reasons
- Neuroleptic malignant syndrome

Other than the above information, there is no additional information relating to proper use, precautions, or side effects for these uses.

Revised: 08/09/95
Interim revision: 08/16/97

BRONCHODILATORS, ADRENERGIC Inhalation

Some commonly used brand names are:

In the U.S.—

Adrenalin Chloride[3]
Airet[1]
Alupent[7]
Arm-a-Med Isoetharine[5]
Arm-a-Med Metaproterenol[7]
Asthmahaler Mist[3]
AsthmaNefrin[3]
Beta-2[5]
Brethaire[11]
Bronkaid Mist[3]
Bronkaid Suspension Mist[3]
Bronkometer[5]
Bronkosol[5]
Dey-Lute Isoetharine[5]
Dey-Lute Metaproterenol[7]
Isuprel[6]
Isuprel Mistometer[6]
Maxair[8]
Maxair Autohaler[8]
Medihaler-Iso[6]
microNefrin[3]
Nephron[3]
Primatene Mist[3]
Proventil[1]
Proventil HFA[1]
S-2[3]
Serevent[10]
Tornalate[2]
Vaponefrin[3]
Ventolin[1]
Ventolin Nebules[1]
Ventolin Rotacaps[1]

In Canada—

Alupent[7]
Apo-Salvent[1]
Berotec[4]
Bricanyl Turbuhaler[11]
Bronkaid Mistometer[3]
Gen-Salbutamol Sterinebs P.F.[1]
Isuprel[6]
Isuprel Mistometer[6]
Maxair[8]
Novo-Salmol[1]
Pro-Air[9]
Serevent[10]
Vaponefrin[3]
Ventodisk[1]
Ventolin[1]
Ventolin Nebules P.F.[1]
Ventolin Rotacaps[1]

Other commonly used names are:
Adrenaline[3]
Orciprenaline[7]
Salbutamol[1]

Note: For quick reference, the following adrenergic bronchodilators are numbered to match the corresponding brand names.

This information applies to the following medicines:
1. Albuterol (al-BYOO-ter-ole)‡§
2. Bitolterol (bye-TOLE-ter-ole)†
3. Epinephrine (ep-i-NEF-rin)‡
4. Fenoterol (fen-OH-ter-ole)*
5. Isoetharine (eye-soe-ETH-a-reen)†‡
6. Isoproterenol (eye-soe-proe-TER-e-nole)‡
7. Metaproterenol (met-a-proe-TER-e-nole)‡
8. Pirbuterol (peer-BYOO-ter-ole)
9. Procaterol (proe-KAY-ter-ole)*
10. Salmeterol (sal-ME-te-role)
11. Terbutaline (ter-BYOO-ta-leen)

*Not commercially available in the U.S.
†Not commercially available in Canada.
‡Generic name product may also be available in the U.S.
§Generic name product may also be available in Canada.

Description

Adrenergic bronchodilators are medicines that are breathed in through the mouth to open up the bronchial tubes (air passages) of the lungs. Some of these medicines are used to treat the symptoms of asthma, chronic bronchitis, emphysema, and other lung diseases, while others are used to prevent the symptoms.

Salmeterol is a long-acting bronchodilator that is used with anti-inflammatory medication to prevent asthma attacks. *Salmeterol is different from the other adrenergic bronchodilators because it does not act quickly enough to relieve an asthma attack that has already started.*

Some of these medicines are also breathed in through the mouth to prevent bronchospasm (wheezing or difficulty in breathing) caused by exercise. Also, epinephrine may be used in the treatment of croup.

All of these medicines, except some epinephrine preparations, are available only with your doctor's prescription. Although some of the epinephrine preparations are available without a prescription, your doctor may have special instructions on the proper dose of epinephrine for your medical condition.

These medicines are available in the following dosage forms:

Inhalation

Albuterol
- Inhalation aerosol (U.S. and Canada)
- Inhalation solution (U.S. and Canada)
- Powder for inhalation (U.S. and Canada)

Bitolterol
- Inhalation aerosol (U.S.)
- Inhalation solution (U.S.)

Epinephrine
- Inhalation aerosol (U.S. and Canada)
- Inhalation solution (U.S. and Canada)

Fenoterol
- Inhalation aerosol (Canada)
- Inhalation solution (Canada)

Isoetharine
- Inhalation aerosol (U.S.)
- Inhalation solution (U.S.)

Isoproterenol
- Inhalation aerosol (U.S. and Canada)
- Inhalation solution (U.S. and Canada)

Metaproterenol
- Inhalation aerosol (U.S. and Canada)
- Inhalation solution (U.S. and Canada)

Pirbuterol
- Inhalation aerosol (U.S. and Canada)

Procaterol
- Inhalation aerosol (Canada)

Salmeterol
- Inhalation aerosol (U.S. and Canada)
- Powder for inhalation (Canada)

Terbutaline
- Inhalation aerosol (U.S. and Canada)

Before Using This Medicine

In deciding to use a medicine, the risks of taking the medicine must be weighed against the good it will do. This is a decision you and your doctor will make. For inhalation adrenergic bronchodilators, the following should be considered:

Allergies—Tell your doctor if you have ever had any unusual or allergic reaction to albuterol, bitolterol, epinephrine, fenoterol, isoetharine, isoproterenol, metaproterenol, pirbuterol, procaterol, salmeterol, terbutaline, or other inhalation medicines. Also tell your health care professional if you are allergic to sulfites, which may be used as a preservative in some of these medicines.

Pregnancy—

- *For albuterol, bitolterol, metaproterenol, and salmeterol:* These medicines are used to treat asthma in pregnant women. Although there are no studies on birth defects in humans, problems have not been reported. Some studies in animals have shown that they cause birth defects when given in doses many times higher than the human dose.
- *For epinephrine:* Women given epinephrine subcutaneously (under the skin) during pregnancy have been studied. The babies of these women had more birth defects than expected, although the severity of the mother's asthma may have contributed to this result.
- *For fenoterol, isoproterenol, pirbuterol, procaterol, and terbutaline:* These medicines are used to treat asthma in pregnant women. Although there are no studies on birth defects in humans, problems have not been reported. These medicines have not been shown to cause birth defects in animal studies when given in doses many times higher than the human dose.
- *For isoetharine:* Studies on birth defects have not been done in either humans or animals.

Breast-feeding—It is not known whether these medicines pass into the breast milk. Although most medicines pass into breast milk in small amounts, many of them may be used safely while breast-feeding. Mothers who are using these medicines and who wish to breast-feed should discuss this with their doctor.

Children—Appropriate studies performed to date have not demonstrated pediatrics-specific problems that would limit the usefulness of these medicines in children. However, isoetharine is not recommended for use in children.

Older adults—

- *For albuterol, bitolterol, epinephrine, fenoterol, isoetharine, isoproterenol, metaproterenol, pirbuterol, procaterol, and terbutaline:* These medicines have not been studied specifically in older people. Therefore, it may not be known whether they work exactly the same way they do in younger adults or if they cause different side effects or problems in older people. There is no specific information comparing use of inhalation adrenergic bronchodilators in the elderly with use in other age groups.
- *For salmeterol:* This medicine has been tested in a limited number of patients 65 years of age or older. It has not been shown to cause different side effects or problems in older people than it does in younger adults.

Other medicines—Although certain medicines should not be used together at all, in other cases two different medicines may be used together even if an interaction might occur. In these cases, your doctor may want to change the dose, or other precautions may be necessary. When you are using inhalation adrenergic bronchodilators, it is especially important that your health care professional know if you are taking any of the following:

- Beta-adrenergic blocking agents (acebutolol [e.g., Sectral], atenolol [e.g., Tenormin], betaxolol [e.g., Kerlone], carteolol [e.g., Cartrol], labetalol [e.g., Normodyne], metoprolol [e.g., Lopressor], nadolol [e.g., Corgard], oxprenolol [e.g., Trasicor], penbutolol [e.g., Levatol], pindolol [e.g., Visken], propranolol [e.g., Inderal], sotalol [e.g., Sotacor], timolol [e.g., Blocadren])—These medicines may make your condition worse and prevent the adrenergic bronchodilators from working properly

Other medical problems—The presence of other medical problems may affect the use of inhalation adrenergic bronchodilators. Make sure you tell your doctor if you have any other medical problems, especially:

- Heart or blood vessel disease—These medicines may make these conditions worse
- High blood pressure, not well controlled—Epinephrine may make this condition worse
- Overactive thyroid—The chance of side effects may be increased

Proper Use of This Medicine

These medicines come with patient directions. Read them carefully before using the medicine. If you do not understand the directions or if you are not sure how to use the medicine, ask your health care professional to show you what to do. Also, ask your health care professional to check regularly how you use the medicine to make sure you are using it properly.

Use this medicine only as directed. Do not use more of it and do not use it more often than recommended on the label, unless otherwise directed by your doctor. Using the medicine more often may increase the chance of serious unwanted effects. Deaths have occurred when too much inhalation bronchodilator medicine was used.

Keep the spray away from your eyes because it may cause irritation.

Salmeterol is used to prevent asthma attacks. It is not used to relieve an attack that has already started. For relief of an asthma attack that has already started, you should use a medicine that starts working faster than salmeterol does. *If you do not have another medicine to use for an attack or if you have any questions about this, check with your doctor.* Because the effects of salmeterol usually last about 12 hours, doses should never be taken more than two times a day or less than 12 hours apart.

Some *epinephrine* preparations are available without a doctor's prescription. However, *do not use this medicine unless you are seeing a doctor about asthma. Do not use this medicine* if you have been hospitalized for asthma treatment or if you are taking a prescription medicine for asthma, unless you have been told to do so by a doctor.

When you use the inhaler for the first time, or if you have not used it in a while, the inhaler may not deliver the right amount of medicine with the first puff. Therefore, before using the inhaler, you may have to test or prime it.

- *To test or prime most inhalers:*

—Insert the medicine container (canister) firmly into the clean mouthpiece according to the manufacturer's directions. Check to make sure it is placed properly into the mouthpiece.

—Take the cap off the mouthpiece and shake the inhaler three or four times.

—Hold the inhaler well away from you at arm's length and press the top of the canister, spraying the medicine into the air *two* times. The inhaler will now be ready to provide the right amount of medicine when you use it.

- *To use most inhalers:*

—Using your thumb and one or two fingers, hold the inhaler upright, with the mouthpiece end down and pointing toward you.

—Take the cap off the mouthpiece. Check the mouthpiece to make sure it is clear. Then, gently shake the inhaler three or four times.

—Breathe out slowly to the end of a normal breath.

—Use the inhalation method recommended by your doctor:

• Open-mouth method—Place the mouthpiece about 1 to 2 inches (2 fingerwidths) in front of your widely opened mouth. Make sure the inhaler is aimed into your mouth so the spray does not hit the roof of your mouth or your tongue.

• Closed-mouth method—Place the mouthpiece in your mouth between your teeth and over your tongue with your lips closed tightly around it. Make sure your tongue or teeth are not blocking the opening.

—Start to breathe in slowly through your mouth. At the same time, press the top of the canister one time to get 1 puff of medicine. Continue to breathe in slowly for 3 to 5 seconds. Count the seconds while breathing in. It is important to press the canister and breathe in slowly at the same time so the medicine gets into your lungs. This step may be difficult at first. If you are using the closed-mouth method and you see a fine mist coming from your mouth or nose, the inhaler is not being used correctly.

—Hold your breath as long as you can up to 10 seconds. This gives the medicine time to settle into your airways and lungs.

—Take the mouthpiece away from your mouth and breathe out slowly.

—If your doctor has told you to inhale more than 1 puff of medicine at each dose, gently shake the inhaler again and take the next puff following exactly the same steps you used for the first puff. Press the canister one time for each puff of medicine.

—When you are done, wipe off the mouthpiece and replace the cap.

Your doctor, nurse, or pharmacist may want you to use a spacer or holding chamber with the inhaler. A spacer helps get the medicine into the lungs and reduces the amount of medicine that stays in your mouth and throat.

To use a spacer with the inhaler:

- Attach the spacer to the inhaler according to the manufacturer's directions. There are different types of spacers available, but the method of breathing is the same with most spacers.
- Gently shake the inhaler and spacer three or four times.
- Hold the mouthpiece of the spacer away from your mouth and breathe out slowly to the end of a normal breath.
- Place the mouthpiece into your mouth between your teeth and over your tongue with your lips closed around it.
- Press down on the canister top one time to release 1 puff of medicine into the spacer. Within one or two seconds, begin to breathe in slowly through your mouth for three to five seconds. Do not breathe in through your nose. Count the seconds while inhaling.
- Hold your breath as long as you can up to ten seconds (count slowly to ten).
- Breathe out slowly. Do not remove the mouthpiece from your mouth. Breathe in and out slowly two or three times to make sure the spacer is emptied.
- If your doctor has told you to take more than 1 puff of medicine at each dose, gently shake the inhaler and spacer again, and take the next puff, following exactly the same steps you used for the first puff. Do not put more than 1 puff of medicine into the spacer at a time.
- If you rinse your mouth with water after you have finished, be sure to spit out the rinse water. Do not swallow it.
- When you are finished, remove the spacer from the inhaler. Wipe off the mouthpiece and replace the cap.
- Clean the inhaler and mouthpiece at least once a week.

—*To clean the inhaler:*

• Remove the canister from the inhaler and set the canister aside.

• Wash the mouthpiece and cap with warm, soapy water. Then, rinse well with warm, running water.

• Shake off the excess water and let the inhaler parts air dry completely before putting the inhaler back together.

- Save your inhaler. Refill units may be available.

For patients using the powder for inhalation dosage form:

- These medicines are used with a special device. If you do not understand the directions that come with the inhaler or if you are not sure how to use the inhaler, ask your health care professional to show you how to use it. Also, ask your health care professional to check regularly how you use the inhaler to make sure you are using it properly.

For patients using the inhalation solution dosage form:

- If you are using this medicine in a nebulizer, make sure you understand exactly how to use it. If you have any questions about this, check with your health care professional.
- Do not use if solution turns pinkish to brownish in color or if it becomes cloudy.
- Do not mix another inhalation medicine with an adrenergic bronchodilator medicine in the nebulizer unless told to do so by your health care professional.

Dosing—The dose of these medicines will be different for different patients. *Follow your doctor's orders or the directions on the label.* The following information includes only the average doses of these medicines. *If your dose is different, do not change it* unless your doctor tells you to do so.

The number of inhalations or the amount of medicine that you use depends on the strength of the medicine. Also, *the number of doses you take each day, the time allowed between doses, and the length of time you take the medicine depend on the medical problem for which you are taking the adrenergic bronchodilator.*

For albuterol

- For *inhalation aerosol* dosage form:
  —For preventing or treating bronchospasm:
  - Adults and children 4 years of age and older—2 inhalations (puffs) every four to six hours.
  - Children up to 4 years of age—Dose must be determined by your doctor.

  —For preventing bronchospasm caused by exercise:
  - Adults and children 4 years of age and older—2 inhalations (puffs) taken fifteen minutes before you start to exercise.
  - Children up to 4 years of age—Dose must be determined by your doctor.
- For *inhalation solution* dosage form:
  —For preventing or treating bronchospasm:
  - Adults and children 12 years of age and older—This medicine is used in a nebulizer and is taken by inhalation over five to fifteen minutes. The usual dose is 2.5 milligrams (mg) of albuterol taken every four to six hours if needed.
  - Children up to 12 years of age—This medicine is used in a nebulizer and is taken by inhalation over five to fifteen minutes. The usual dose is 1.25 to 2.5 milligrams (mg) of albuterol taken every four to six hours if needed.
- For *capsules (powder) for inhalation* dosage form:
  —For preventing or treating bronchospasm:
  - Adults and children 4 years of age and older—200 or 400 mcg taken by inhalation every four to six hours.
  - Children up to 4 years of age—Dose must be determined by your doctor.

  —For preventing bronchospasm caused by exercise:
  - Adults and children 4 years of age and older—200 mcg taken by inhalation fifteen minutes before you start to exercise.
  - Children up to 4 years of age—Dose must be determined by your doctor.

For albuterol sulfate

- For *inhalation aerosol* dosage form:
  —For treating bronchospasm:
  - Adults and children 12 years of age and older—2 inhalations (puffs) every four to six hours.
  - Children up to 12 years of age—Dose must be determined by your doctor.

For bitolterol

- For *inhalation aerosol* dosage form:
  —For preventing or treating bronchospasm:
  - Adults and children 12 years of age and older—2 inhalations (puffs) every eight hours or 2 inhalations (puffs) at first, allowing one to three minutes between each puff. This dose may be followed by another puff, if needed. However, the dose taken each day should not be more than 2 puffs every four hours or 3 puffs every six hours.
  - Children up to 12 years of age—Dose must be determined by your doctor.

  —For preventing bronchospasm caused by exercise:
  - Adults and teenagers—2 inhalations (puffs) taken five minutes before you start to exercise.
  - Children—1 or 2 inhalations (puffs) taken five minutes before you start to exercise.
- For *inhalation solution* dosage form:
  —For preventing or treating bronchospasm:
  - Adults and children 12 years of age and older—This medicine is used in a nebulizer and is taken by inhalation over ten to fifteen minutes. The usual dose is 1 to 2.5 milligrams (mg) of bitolterol taken three or four times a day. Doses should be taken at least four hours apart.
  - Children up to 12 years of age—Dose must be determined by your doctor.

For epinephrine

- For treating bronchospasm:
  —For *inhalation aerosol* dosage form:
  - Adults and children 4 years of age and older—1 inhalation (puff). The dose may be repeated after at least one minute, if needed. Doses should be taken at least three hours apart.

- Children up to 4 years of age—Dose must be determined by your doctor.

—For *inhalation solution* dosage form:

- Adults and children 4 years of age and older—This medicine should be used in a hand-bulb nebulizer. The usual dose is 1 to 3 inhalations (puffs) of a 1% solution. Doses should be taken at least three hours apart.
- Children up to 4 years of age—Dose must be determined by your doctor.

For fenoterol

- For *inhalation aerosol* dosage form:

—For preventing or treating bronchospasm:

- Adults and children 12 years of age and older—100 or 200 micrograms (mcg), repeated three or four times a day if needed. This medicine should not be taken more often than every four hours. The total dose should not be more than 8 puffs a day of the 100 mcg per spray product or 6 puffs of the 200 mcg per spray product.
- Children up to 12 years of age—Dose must be determined by your doctor.

- For *inhalation solution* dosage form:

—For preventing or treating bronchospasm:

- Adults and children 12 years of age and older—This medicine is used in a nebulizer and is taken by inhalation over ten to fifteen minutes. The usual dose is 0.5 to 1 milligram (mg) of fenoterol taken every six hours if needed.
- Children up to 12 years of age—Dose must be determined by your doctor.

For isoetharine

- For *inhalation solution* dosage form:

—For treating bronchospasm:

- Adults—This medicine is used in a nebulizer and is taken by inhalation over fifteen to twenty minutes. The amount of medicine you use and whether it requires dilution depends on the product ordered by your doctor. The usual dose is 2.5 to 10 milligrams (mg). This medicine usually should not be used more often than every four hours.
- Children—Use is not recommended.

- For *inhalation aerosol* dosage form:

—For treating bronchospasm:

- Adults and teenagers—1 or 2 inhalations (puffs). This dose may be repeated every four hours as necessary.
- Children—Use is not recommended.

For isoproterenol

- For *inhalation solution* dosage form:

—For treating bronchospasm:

- Adults and teenagers—This medicine is used in a nebulizer and is taken by inhalation over ten to twenty minutes. The usual dose is 2.5 milligrams (mg). This medicine usually should not be used more often than every four hours.
- Children—This medicine is used in a nebulizer and is taken by inhalation over ten to twenty minutes. The usual dose is 0.05 to 0.1 milligram (mg) per kilogram (kg) of body weight, up to 1.25 mg, diluted. The dose may be repeated every four hours, if needed.

For isoproterenol hydrochloride

- For *inhalation aerosol* dosage form:

—For treating bronchospasm:

- Adults and children 12 years of age and older—1 inhalation (puff), repeated after two to five minutes if needed. This dose is taken every three to four hours.
- Children up to 12 years of age—Use is not recommended.

For isoproterenol sulfate

- For *inhalation aerosol* dosage form:

—For treating bronchospasm:

- Adults and children 12 years of age and older—1 inhalation (puff), repeated after two to five minutes if needed. This dose is taken every four to six hours.
- Children up to 12 years of age—Dose must be determined by your doctor.

For metaproterenol

- For *inhalation aerosol* dosage form:

—For preventing and treating bronchospasm:

- Adults and children 12 years of age and older—2 or 3 inhalations (puffs) every three to four hours. The total dose should not be more than 12 puffs a day.
- Children up to 12 years of age—1 to 3 inhalations (puffs) every three to four hours. The total dose should not be more than 12 puffs a day.

- For *inhalation solution* dosage form:

—For preventing or treating bronchospasm:

- Adults and children 6 years of age and older—This medicine is used in a nebulizer and is taken by inhalation. The amount of medicine you use and whether it requires dilution depends on the product ordered by your doctor. The usual dose is 10 to 15 milligrams (mg) taken three or four times a day. Doses should be taken at least four hours apart.
- Children up to 6 years of age—This medicine is used in a nebulizer and is taken by inhalation. The amount of medicine you use and whether it requires dilution depends on the product ordered by your doctor. The usual dose is 5 to 15 milligrams (mg) taken three or four times a day, at least four hours apart.

For pirbuterol

- For *inhalation aerosol* dosage form:

—For preventing and treating bronchospasm:

- Adults and children—1 or 2 inhalations (puffs) every four to six hours. The total dose should not be more than 12 puffs a day.

—For preventing bronchospasm caused by exercise:

• Adults and children—2 inhalations (puffs) taken five minutes before you start to exercise.

For procaterol

• For *inhalation aerosol* dosage form:

—For preventing and treating bronchospasm:

• Adults and children 12 years of age and older—1 or 2 inhalations (puffs) three times a day.

• Children up to 12 years of age—Dose must be determined by your doctor.

—For preventing bronchospasm caused by exercise:

• Adults and children 12 years of age and older—1 or 2 inhalations (puffs) taken at least fifteen minutes before you start to exercise.

For salmeterol

• For the *inhalation aerosol* dosage form:

—For preventing bronchospasm:

• Adults and children 12 years of age and older—2 inhalations (puffs) two times a day, in the morning and evening. Doses should be taken about twelve hours apart.

• Children up to 12 years of age—Dose must be determined by your doctor.

—For preventing bronchospasm caused by exercise:

• Adults and children 12 years of age and older—2 inhalations (puffs) taken at least thirty to sixty minutes before you start to exercise. If you are already using salmeterol two times a day to treat your asthma, you do not need to use additional salmeterol before you exercise.

• Children up to 12 years of age—Dose must be determined by your doctor.

• For the *powder for inhalation* dosage form:

—For preventing bronchospasm:

• Adults and children 12 years of age and older—1 inhalation (the contents of one blister) two times a day, in the morning and evening. Doses should be taken about twelve hours apart.

• Children up to 12 years of age—Dose must be determined by your doctor.

For terbutaline

• For *inhalation aerosol* dosage form:

—For preventing or treating bronchospasm:

• Adults and children—

—For the 200 microgram (mcg) per metered spray product: 2 inhalations (puffs) every four to six hours.

—For the 500 mcg per metered spray product: 1 inhalation (puff), repeated after five minutes if needed. The total dose should not be more than 6 puffs a day.

—For preventing bronchospasm caused by exercise:

• Adults and children—

—For the 200 microgram (mcg) per metered spray product: 2 inhalations (puffs) taken five to fifteen minutes before you start to exercise.

Missed dose—

• *For salmeterol:* If you use salmeterol inhalation regularly and you miss a dose of this medicine, use it as soon as possible. Then go back to your regular schedule. Do not double doses. If you have wheezing or breathlessness before the next dose is due, you should use another inhaled bronchodilator that starts to work faster than salmeterol does to relieve the attack.

• *For all other adrenergic bronchodilators:* If you are using one of these medicines regularly and you miss a dose, use it as soon as possible. Then use any remaining doses for that day at regularly spaced intervals. Do not double doses.

Storage—To store this medicine:

• Keep out of the reach of children.
• Store away from heat.
• Store the solution form of this medicine away from direct light. Store the inhalation aerosol form of this medicine away from direct sunlight.
• Keep the medicine from freezing.
• Store canister with the nozzle end down.
• Do not store the powder for inhalation forms of these medicines in the bathroom, near the kitchen sink, or in other damp places. Moisture may cause the medicine to break down.
• Do not puncture, break, or burn the inhalation aerosol container, even if it is empty.
• Do not keep outdated medicine or medicine no longer needed. Be sure that any discarded medicine is out of the reach of children.

Precautions While Using This Medicine

It is important that your doctor check your progress at regular intervals to make sure that your medicine is working properly.

If you still have trouble breathing after using one of these medicines, or if your condition becomes worse, check with your doctor at once.

You may also be taking an anti-inflammatory medicine for asthma along with this medicine. *Do not stop taking the anti-inflammatory medicine even if your asthma seems better, unless you are told to do so by your doctor.*

For patients using *salmeterol*, check with your doctor:

• If you need to use 4 or more inhalations (puffs) a day of a fast-acting inhaled bronchodilator for 2 or more days in a row to relieve asthma attacks.
• If you need to use more than 1 canister (a total of 200 inhalations per canister) of a fast-acting inhaled bronchodilator in a 2-month period to relieve asthma attacks.

For patients using *any of these medicines except salmeterol, check with your doctor:*

• If you need more inhalations (puffs) than usual of a fast-acting beta-adrenergic bronchodilator to relieve an acute attack

- If not using an anti-inflammatory medicine and using a fast-acting beta-adrenergic bronchodilator to relieve symptoms more than two times per week
- If you are using an anti-inflammatory medicine and you also are using more than 1 canister per month of a fast-acting beta-adrenergic bronchodilator to relieve symptoms

Side Effects of This Medicine

Along with its needed effects, a medicine may cause some unwanted effects. Although not all of these side effects may occur, if they do occur they may need medical attention.

Check with your doctor immediately if any of the following side effects occur:

Rare

Dizziness, severe; feeling of choking, irritation, or swelling in throat; flushing or redness of skin; hives; increased shortness of breath; skin rash; swelling of face, lips, or eyelids; tightness in chest or wheezing, troubled breathing

Other side effects may occur that usually do not need medical attention. These side effects may go away during treatment as your body adjusts to the medicine. However, check with your doctor if any of the following side effects continue or are bothersome:

More common

Fast heartbeat; headache; nervousness; trembling

Less common

Coughing or other bronchial irritation; dizziness or lightheadedness; dryness or irritation of mouth or throat

Rare

Chest discomfort or pain; drowsiness or weakness; irregular heartbeat; muscle cramps or twitching; nausea and/or vomiting; restlessness; trouble in sleeping

Not all of the side effects listed above have been reported for each of these medicines, but they have been reported for at least one of them. All of the adrenergic bronchodilators are similar, so any of the above side effects may occur with any of these medicines.

While you are using an adrenergic bronchodilator, you may notice an unusual or unpleasant taste. This may be expected and will go away when you stop using the medicine.

Isoproterenol may cause the saliva to turn pinkish to red. This is to be expected while you are taking this medicine.

Other side effects not listed above may also occur in some patients. If you notice any other effects, check with your doctor.

Revised: 7/20/97

BRONCHODILATORS, ADRENERGIC Oral/Injection

Some commonly used brand names are:

In the U.S.—

Adrenalin Chloride Solution[3]
Alupent[7]
Ana-Guard[3]
Brethine[8]
Bricanyl[8]
Bronkephrine[4]
EpiPen Auto-Injector[3]
EpiPen Jr. Auto-Injector[3]
Isuprel[6]
Isuprel Glossets[6]
Metaprel[7]
Prometa[7]
Proventil[1]
Proventil Repetabs[1]
Sus-Phrine[3]
Ventolin[1]
Volmax[1]

In Canada—

Adrenalin[3]
Alupent[7]
Berotec[5]
Bricanyl[8]
EpiPen Auto-Injector[3]
EpiPen Jr. Auto-Injector[3]
Isuprel[6]
Novo-Salmol[1]
Ventolin[1]
Volmax[1]

Other commonly used names are:

Salbutamol[1]
Orciprenaline[7]

Note: For quick reference the following adrenergic bronchodilators are numbered to match the corresponding brand names.

This information applies to the following medicines:

1. Albuterol (al-BYOO-ter-ole)‡
2. Ephedrine (e-FED-rin)‡§
3. Epinephrine (ep-i-NEF-rin)‡§
4. Ethylnorepinephrine (ETH-il-nor-ep-i-NEF-rin)†
5. Fenoterol (fen-OH-ter-ole)*
6. Isoproterenol (eye-soe-proe-TER-e-nole)‡
7. Metaproterenol (met-a-proe-TER-e-nole)‡
8. Terbutaline (ter-BYOO-ta-leen)

*Not commercially available in the U.S.
†Not commercially available in Canada.
‡Generic name product may also be available in the U.S.
§Generic name product may also be available in Canada.

Description

Adrenergic bronchodilators are medicines that open up the bronchial tubes (air passages) of the lungs. They are used to treat the symptoms of bronchial asthma, chronic bronchitis, emphysema, and other lung diseases. They relieve cough, wheezing, shortness of breath, and troubled breathing by increasing the flow of air through the bronchial tubes.

Ephedrine may also be used for the relief of nasal congestion in hay fever or other allergies. In addition, ephedrine may be used in the treatment of narcolepsy (uncontrolled desire for sleep or sudden attacks of sleep) and certain types of mental depression.

Epinephrine injection (not including the auto-injector or the sterile suspension) may be used in eye surgery to stop bleeding, reduce congestion, and dilate the pupil. It may also be applied topically to the skin or mucous membranes to stop bleeding.

Epinephrine injection (including the auto-injector but not the sterile suspension) is used in the emergency treatment of allergic reactions to insect stings, medicines, foods, or other substances. It relieves skin rash, hives, and itching; wheezing; and swelling of the lips, eyelids, tongue, and inside of nose.

Adrenergic bronchodilators may be used for other conditions as determined by your doctor.

Ephedrine capsules are available without a prescription. However, your doctor may have special instructions on the proper dose of ephedrine for your medical condition.

All of the other adrenergic bronchodilators are available only with your doctor's prescription.

These medicines are available in the following dosage forms:

Oral

Albuterol
- Oral solution (Canada)
- Syrup (U.S.)
- Tablets (U.S. and Canada)
- Extended-release tablets (U.S. and Canada)

Ephedrine
- Capsules (U.S.)

Fenoterol
- Tablets (Canada)

Isoproterenol
- Tablets (U.S.)

Metaproterenol
- Syrup (U.S. and Canada)
- Tablets (U.S. and Canada)

Terbutaline
- Tablets (U.S. and Canada)

Parenteral

Albuterol
- Injection (Canada)

Ephedrine
- Injection (U.S. and Canada)

Epinephrine
- Injection (U.S. and Canada)

Ethylnorepinephrine
- Injection (U.S.)

Isoproterenol
- Injection (U.S. and Canada)

Terbutaline
- Injection (U.S.)

Before Using This Medicine

In deciding to use a medicine, the risks of taking the medicine must be weighed against the good it will do. This is a decision you and your doctor will make. For adrenergic bronchodilators taken by mouth or given by injection, the following should be considered:

Allergies—Tell your doctor if you have ever had any unusual or allergic reaction to albuterol, ephedrine, epinephrine, ethylnorepinephrine, fenoterol, isoproterenol, metaproterenol, or terbutaline. Also tell your health care professional if you are allergic to any other substances, such as foods, preservatives, or dyes.

Pregnancy—
- *For albuterol:* Albuterol has not been studied in pregnant women. However, studies in animals have shown that albuterol causes birth defects when given in doses many times the usual human dose. In addition, although albuterol has been reported to delay preterm labor when taken by mouth, it has not been shown to stop preterm labor or prevent labor at term.
- *For ephedrine:* Studies on birth defects with ephedrine have not been done in either humans or animals. When ephedrine is used just before or during labor, its effects on the newborn infant or on the growth and development of the child are not known.
- *For epinephrine:* Epinephrine has not been studied in pregnant women. However, studies in animals have shown that epinephrine causes birth defects when given in doses many times the usual human dose. Also, use of epinephrine during pregnancy may decrease the supply of oxygen to the fetus. Epinephrine is not recommended for use during labor since it may delay the second stage of labor. In addition, high doses of epinephrine that decrease contractions of the uterus may result in excessive bleeding when used during labor and delivery.
- *For ethylnorepinephrine and isoproterenol:* Studies on birth defects with ethylnorepinephrine or isoproterenol have not been done in either humans or animals.
- *For fenoterol:* Fenoterol has not been shown to cause birth defects or other problems in humans.
- *For metaproterenol:* Metaproterenol has not been studied in pregnant women. However, studies in animals have shown that metaproterenol causes birth defects when given in doses many times the usual human dose. Also, studies in animals have shown that metaproterenol causes death of the animal fetus when given in doses many times the usual human dose.
- *For terbutaline:* Terbutaline has not been studied in pregnant women. It has not been shown to cause birth defects in animal studies when given in doses many times the usual human dose. However, terbutaline given by injection during pregnancy has been reported to cause an unusually fast heartbeat in the fetus. Although terbutaline is used to delay preterm labor, it may also delay labor at term.

Breast-feeding—
- *For albuterol, fenoterol, isoproterenol, and metaproterenol:* It is not known whether albuterol, fenoterol, isoproterenol, or metaproterenol passes into the breast milk. Although most medicines pass into breast milk in small amounts, many of them may be used safely while breast-feeding. Mothers who are taking this medicine and who wish to breast-feed should discuss this with their doctor.
- *For ephedrine and epinephrine:* Ephedrine and epinephrine pass into the breast milk and may cause unwanted side effects in babies of mothers using ephedrine or epinephrine.
- *For terbutaline:* Terbutabline passes into the breast milk. Although most medicines pass into breast milk in small amounts, many of them may be used safely while breast-feeding. Mothers who are taking this medicine and who wish to breast-feed should discuss this with their doctor.

Children—Although there is no specific information comparing use of albuterol, ethylnorepinephrine, fenoterol, isoproterenol, metaproterenol, or terbutaline in children with use in other age groups, these medicines are not expected to cause different side effects or problems in children than they do in adults.

Infants may be especially sensitive to the effects of ephedrine.

Infants and children may be especially sensitive to the effects of epinephrine. Fainting has occurred after epinephrine was given to children with asthma.

Older adults—Many medicines have not been studied specifically in older people. Therefore, it may not be known whether they work exactly the same way they do in younger adults or if they cause different side effects or problems in older people. There is no specific information comparing use of adrenergic bronchodilators in the elderly with use in other age groups.

Other medicines—Although certain medicines should not be used together at all, in other cases two different medicines may be used together even if an interaction might occur. In these cases, your doctor may want to change the dose, or other precautions may be necessary. When you are taking adrenergic bronchodilators, it is especially important that your health care professional know if you are taking any of the following:

- Beta-blockers (acebutolol [e.g., Sectral], atenolol [e.g., Tenormin], betaxolol [e.g., Betoptic, Kerlone], bisoprolol [e.g., Zebeta], carteolol [e.g., Cartrol], labetalol [e.g., Normodyne], levobunolol [e.g., Betagan], metoprolol [e.g., Lopressor], nadolol [e.g., Corgard], oxprenolol [e.g., Trasicor], penbutolol [e.g., Levatol], pindolol [e.g., Visken], propranolol [e.g., Inderal], sotalol [e.g., Sotacor], timolol [e.g., Blocadren, Timoptic])—These medicines may prevent the adrenergic bronchodilators from working properly
- Cocaine or
- Ergoloid mesylates (e.g., Hydergine) or
- Ergotamine (e.g., Gynergen) or
- Maprotiline (e.g., Ludiomil) or
- Tricyclic antidepressants (medicine for depression)—The effects of these medicines on the heart and blood vessels may be increased
- Digitalis glycosides (heart medicine)—The chance of irregular heartbeat may be increased
- Monoamine oxidase (MAO) inhibitors (furazolidone [e.g., Furoxone], isocarboxazid [e.g., Marplan], phenelzine [e.g., Nardil], procarbazine [e.g., Matulane], tranylcypromine [e.g., Parnate])—Taking adrenergic bronchodilators while you are taking or within 2 weeks of taking monoamine oxidase (MAO) inhibitors may increase the effects of MAO inhibitors

Other medical problems—The presence of other medical problems may affect the use of adrenergic bronchodilators. Make sure you tell your doctor if you have any other medical problems, especially:

- Brain damage
- Convulsions (seizures) (history of)
- Diabetes mellitus (sugar diabetes)—Adrenergic bronchodilators may make the condition worse; your doctor may need to change the dose of your diabetes medicine
- Enlarged prostate—Ephedrine may make the condition worse
- Heart or blood vessel disease or
- High blood pressure—Adrenergic bronchodilators may make the condition worse
- Mental disease—Epinephrine may make the condition worse
- Overactive thyroid—The chance of side effects may be increased
- Parkinson's disease—Epinephrine may temporarily increase certain symptoms of Parkinson's disease, such as rigidity and tremor

Proper Use of This Medicine

For patients taking *albuterol extended-release tablets:*

- Swallow the tablet whole.
- Do not crush, break, or chew before swallowing.

For patients taking *ephedrine:*

- Ephedrine may cause trouble in sleeping. To help prevent this, *take the last dose of ephedrine for each day a few hours before bedtime*. If you have any questions about this, check with your doctor.

For patients taking *isoproterenol sublingual tablets*:

- Do not chew or swallow the tablet. This medicine is meant to be absorbed through the lining of the mouth. Place the tablet under your tongue (sublingual) and let it slowly dissolve there. Do not swallow until the tablet has dissolved completely.

For patients using the *injection* form of this medicine:

- Do not use the epinephrine solution or suspension if it turns pinkish to brownish in color or if the solution becomes cloudy.
- *Use this medicine only for the conditions for which it was prescribed by your doctor.*
- Keep this medicine ready for use at all times. Also, keep the telephone numbers for your doctor and the nearest hospital emergency room readily available.
- Check the expiration date on the injection regularly. Replace the medicine before that date.
- This medicine is for injection only. If you will be giving yourself the injections, make sure you understand exactly how to give them. If you have any questions about this, check with your doctor.

For patients using *epinephrine injection* for an *allergic reaction emergency*:

- If an allergic reaction as described by your doctor occurs, *use the epinephrine injection immediately.*
- Notify your doctor immediately or go to the nearest hospital emergency room. If you have used the epinephrine injection, be sure to tell your doctor.
- If you have been stung by an insect, remove the insect's stinger with your fingernails, if possible. Be careful not to squeeze, pinch, or push it deeper into the skin. Ice packs or sodium bicarbonate (baking soda) soaks, if available, may then be applied to the area stung.
- If you are using the epinephrine auto-injector (automatic injection device):
  —It is important that you do not remove the safety cap on the auto-injector until you are ready to use

it. This prevents accidental activation of the device during storage and handling.

—Epinephrine auto-injector comes with patient directions. Read them carefully before you actually need to use this medicine. Then, when an emergency arises, you will know how to inject the epinephrine.

—To use the epinephrine auto-injector:

- Remove the gray safety cap.
- Place the black tip on the thigh, at a right angle to the leg.
- Press hard into the thigh until the auto-injector functions. Hold in place for several seconds. Then remove the auto-injector and discard.
- Massage the injection area for 10 seconds.

Use this medicine only as directed. Do not use more of it and do not use it more often than your doctor ordered, or more than recommended on the label unless otherwise directed by your doctor. To do so may increase the chance of side effects.

Dosing—The dose of these medicines will be different for different patients. *Follow your doctor's orders or the directions on the label.* The following information includes only the average doses of these medicines. *If your dose is different, do not change it* unless your doctor tells you to do so.

The number of capsules or tablets, teaspoonfuls of solution or syrup, or amount of injection that you take depends on the strength of the medicine. Also, *the number of doses you take each day, the time allowed between doses, and the length of time you take the medicine depend on the medical problem for which you are taking the adrenergic bronchodilator.*

For albuterol

- For symptoms of bronchial asthma, chronic bronchitis, emphysema, or other lung disease:
  - —For *solution* dosage form:
    - Adults—2 to 4 milligrams (mg) of albuterol three or four times a day.
    - Children 6 to 12 years of age—2 mg of albuterol three or four times a day.
    - Children 2 to 6 years of age—Dose is based on body weight and must be determined by your doctor. The usual dose is 100 micrograms (mcg) of albuterol per kilogram (kg) (45 mcg per pound) of body weight three or four times a day.
    - Children up to 2 years of age—Dose must be determined by your doctor.
  - —For *syrup* dosage form:
    - Adults and children 14 years of age and older—At first, 2 to 6 mg of albuterol three or four times a day. Then your doctor may increase your dose, if needed, up to 8 mg four times a day.
    - Children 6 to 14 years of age—At first, 2 mg of albuterol three or four times a day. Then your doctor may increase your dose, if needed, up to 24 mg a day taken in divided doses.
    - Children 2 to 6 years of age—Dose is based on body weight and must be determined by your doctor. At first, the usual dose is 100 mcg of albuterol per kg (45 mcg per pound) of body weight. Then your doctor may increase your dose, if needed, up to 200 mcg per kg (90 mcg per pound) of body weight. However, the dose should not be more than 4 mg three times a day.
    - Children up to 2 years of age—Dose must be determined by your doctor.
  - —For *tablet* dosage form:
    - Older adults—At first, 2 mg of albuterol three or four times a day. Then your doctor may increase your dose, if needed, up to 8 mg three or four times a day.
    - Adults and children 12 years of age and older—At first, 2 to 6 mg of albuterol three or four times a day. Then your doctor may increase your dose, if needed, up to 8 mg four times a day.
    - Children 6 to 12 years of age—At first, 2 mg of albuterol three or four times a day. Then your doctor may increase your dose, if needed, up to 24 mg a day taken in divided doses.
    - Children up to 6 years of age—Dose must be determined by your doctor.
  - —For *extended-release tablet* dosage form:
    - Adults and children 12 years of age and older—4 or 8 mg of albuterol every twelve hours.
    - Children up to 12 years of age—Dose must be determined by your doctor.
  - —For *injection* dosage form:
    - Dose is usually based on body weight and must be determined by your doctor. Depending on your condition, this medicine is injected into either a muscle or vein or injected slowly into a vein over a period of time.
    - —Adults:
      - The usual dose injected into a muscle is 8 mcg of albuterol per kg (3.6 mcg per pound) of body weight every four hours as needed, up to a total dose of 2 mg a day.
      - The usual dose injected into a vein is 4 mcg per kg (1.8 mcg per pound) of body weight, given over a period of two to five minutes. The dose may be repeated after fifteen minutes, if needed, up to a total dose of 1 mg a day.
      - When albuterol is injected slowly into a vein, it is given at a rate of 5 mcg per minute. Your doctor may increase the rate to 10 mcg per minute and then 20 mcg per minute every fifteen to thirty minutes, if needed.
    - —Children: Dose must be determined by your doctor.

For ephedrine

- For *capsule* dosage form:
  - —For nasal congestion, narcolepsy (uncontrolled desire for sleep), or symptoms of bronchial asthma, chronic bronchitis, emphysema, or other lung disease:
    - Adults—25 or 50 milligrams (mg) every three or four hours, if needed.
    - Children—Dose is based on body weight or size and must be determined by your doctor. The usual dose is 3 mg per kg (1.3 mg per pound) of body weight a day. This dose is divided into four to six doses.
- For *injection* dosage form:
  - —For symptoms of bronchial asthma, chronic bronchitis, emphysema, or other lung disease:
    - Adults—12.5 to 25 mg injected into a muscle, a vein, or under the skin. Your doctor may give you another dose, if needed.
    - Children—Dose is based on body weight and must be determined by your doctor. The usual dose is 3 mg per kg (1.3 mg per pound) of body weight a day. This dose is divided into four to six doses.

For epinephrine

- For *injection* dosage form:
  - —For symptoms of bronchial asthma, chronic bronchitis, emphysema, or other lung disease:
    - Adults and teenagers—200 to 500 micrograms (mcg) injected under the skin. The dose may be repeated every twenty minutes to four hours as needed. Your doctor may increase your dose up to 1 mg a dose, if needed.
    - Children—Dose is based on body weight or size and must be determined by your doctor. The usual dose is 10 mcg per kilogram (kg) (4.5 mcg per pound) of body weight, up to 500 mcg a dose. The dose may be repeated every fifteen minutes for two doses, then every four hours as needed.
  - —For allergic reactions:
    - Adults—At first, 200 to 500 mcg injected into a muscle or under the skin. Then the dose may be repeated every ten to fifteen minutes as needed. Your doctor may increase your dose up to 1 mg a dose, if needed.
    - Children—Dose is based on body weight or size and must be determined by your doctor. The usual dose is 10 mcg per kg (4.5 mcg per pound) of body weight, up to 500 mcg a dose. The dose may be repeated every fifteen minutes for two doses, then every four hours as needed.
- For *sterile suspension (injection)* dosage form:
  - —For symptoms of bronchial asthma, chronic bronchitis, emphysema, or other lung disease:
    - Adults—At first, 500 mcg injected under the skin. Then 500 mcg to 1.5 milligrams (mg) injected no more often than every six hours as needed.
    - Children—Dose is based on body weight or size and must be determined by your doctor. The usual dose is 25 mcg per kg (11 mcg per pound) of body weight. The dose may be repeated, if needed, but not more often than every six hours.

For ethylnorepinephrine

- For *injection* dosage form:
  - —For symptoms of bronchial asthma, chronic bronchitis, emphysema, or other lung disease:
    - Adults—1 to 2 milligrams (mg) injected into a muscle or under the skin.
    - Children—200 micrograms (mcg) to 1 mg injected into a muscle or under the skin.

For fenoterol

- For *tablet* dosage form:
  - —For symptoms of bronchial asthma, chronic bronchitis, emphysema, or other lung disease:
    - Adults and children 12 years of age and older—At first, 2.5 milligrams (mg) two times a day. Then your doctor may increase your dose up to 5 mg three times a day, if needed. However, the medicine should not be taken more often than every six hours.
    - Children up to 12 years of age—Dose must be determined by your doctor.

For isoproterenol

- For *tablet* dosage form:
  - —For symptoms of bronchial asthma, chronic bronchitis, emphysema, or other lung disease:
    - Adults—10 to 15 milligrams (mg) dissolved under the tongue three or four times a day.
    - Children—5 to 10 mg dissolved under the tongue three times a day.

For metaproterenol

- For *oral* dosage form (syrup or tablets):
  - —For symptoms of bronchial asthma, chronic bronchitis, emphysema, or other lung disease:
    - Adults and children 9 years of age and older or weighing 27 kilograms (kg) (59 pounds) or more—20 milligrams (mg) three or four times a day.
    - Children 6 to 9 years of age and older or weighing up to 27 kg (59 pounds)—10 mg three or four times a day.
    - Children up to 6 years of age—Dose must be determined by your doctor.

For terbutaline

- For symptoms of bronchial asthma, chronic bronchitis, emphysema, or other lung disease:
  - —For *tablet* dosage form:
    - Adults—2.5 to 5 milligrams (mg) three times a day, taken about every six hours.
    - Children 12 to 15 years of age—2.5 mg three times a day, taken about every six hours.
    - Children up to 12 years of age—Dose must be determined by your doctor.

—For *injection* dosage form:

- Adults—250 micrograms (mcg) injected under the skin. The dose may be repeated after fifteen to thirty minutes, if needed. However, not more than 500 mcg should be taken within a four-hour period.
- Children up to 12 years of age—Dose must be determined by your doctor.

Missed dose—If you are using this medicine regularly and you miss a dose, use it as soon as possible. Then use any remaining doses for that day at regularly spaced intervals. Do not double doses.

Storage—To store this medicine:

- Keep out of the reach of children.
- Store away from heat and direct light.
- Do not store the capsule or tablet form of this medicine in the bathroom, near the kitchen sink, or in other damp places. Heat or moisture may cause the medicine to break down.
- Keep the injection or syrup form of this medicine from freezing.
- Store the suspension form of epinephrine injection in the refrigerator.
- Do not keep outdated medicine or medicine no longer needed. Be sure that any discarded medicine is out of the reach of children.

Precautions While Using This Medicine

If after using this medicine for asthma or other breathing problems you still have trouble breathing, or if your condition becomes worse, check with your doctor at once.

For *diabetic patients* using *epinephrine:*

- This medicine may cause your blood sugar levels to rise. If you notice a change in the results of your blood or urine sugar tests or if you have any questions, check with your doctor.

For patients using *epinephrine injection* (including the auto-injector but not the sterile suspension) or *ethylnorepinephrine injection:*

- Some of the injection preparations may contain sulfites as a preservative. Sulfites may cause an allergic reaction in some people. If you know that you are allergic to sulfites, carefully read the label on the injection or check with your health care professional to find out if the injection contains sulfites.
- Although epinephrine injection may contain sulfites, it is still used to treat serious allergic reactions or other emergency conditions because other medicines may not work properly in a life-threatening situation.
- If you have any questions about when or whether you should use an epinephrine injection that contains sulfites, check with your doctor.
- Signs of an allergic reaction to sulfites include bluish coloration of skin; severe dizziness or feeling faint; continuing flushing or redness of face or skin; increased wheezing or difficulty in breathing; skin rash, hives, or itching; or swelling of face, lips, or eyelids. *If any of these signs occur, check with your doctor immediately.*

Side Effects of This Medicine

In some animal studies, albuterol and terbutaline were shown to increase the chance of benign (not cancerous) tumors. Terbutaline was also shown to increase the chance of ovarian cysts. The doses given were many times the oral dose of albuterol or terbutaline given to humans. It is not known if albuterol or terbutaline increases the chance of tumors in humans, or if terbutaline increases the chance of ovarian cysts in humans.

Along with its needed effects, a medicine may cause some unwanted effects. Although not all of these side effects may occur, if they do occur they may need medical attention.

Check with your doctor immediately if any of the following side effects occur:

Bluish coloration of skin; dizziness (severe) or feeling faint; flushing or redness of face or skin (continuing); increased wheezing or difficulty in breathing; skin rash, hives, or itching; swelling of face, lips, or eyelids

Check with your doctor as soon as possible if any of the following side effects occur:

Rare

Chest discomfort or pain; irregular heartbeat

With high doses

Hallucinations (seeing, hearing, or feeling things that are not there); mood or mental changes (reported for ephedrine only)

Symptoms of overdose

Bluish coloration of skin; chest discomfort or pain (continuing or severe); chills or fever; convulsions (seizures); dizziness or lightheadedness (continuing or severe); fast or slow heartbeat (continuing); headache (continuing or severe); increase or decrease in blood pressure (severe); irregular or pounding heartbeat (continuing or severe); muscle cramps (severe); nausea or vomiting (continuing or severe); shortness of breath or troubled breathing (severe); trembling (severe); unusual anxiety, nervousness, or restlessness; unusually large pupils or blurred vision; unusual paleness and coldness of skin; weakness (severe)

Other side effects may occur that usually do not need medical attention. These side effects may go away during treatment as your body adjusts to the medicine. However, check with your doctor if any of the following side effects continue or are bothersome:

More common

Nervousness or restlessness; trembling

Less common

Difficult or painful urination; dizziness or lightheadedness; drowsiness; fast or pounding heartbeat; flushing or redness of face or skin; headache; heartburn; increased sweating; increase in blood pressure; loss of appetite; muscle cramps or twitching; nausea or vomiting; trouble in sleeping; unusual paleness; weakness

Not all of the side effects listed above have been reported for each of these medicines, but they have been reported for at least one of them. All of the adrenergic bronchodilators are similar, so any of the above side effects may occur with any of these medicines.

While you are using albuterol, fenoterol, metaproterenol, or terbutaline, you may notice an unusual or unpleasant taste. This may be expected and will go away when you stop using the medicine.

Isoproterenol sublingual (under-the-tongue) tablets may cause the saliva to turn pinkish to red. This is to be expected while you are using this medicine.

Other side effects not listed above may also occur in some patients. If you notice any other effects, check with your doctor.

Additional Information

Once a medicine has been approved for marketing for a certain use, experience may show that it is also useful for other medical problems. Although these uses are not included in product labeling, some of the adrenergic bronchodilators are used in certain patients with the following medical conditions:

- Premature labor (terbutaline)
- Urticaria (hives) (ephedrine)
- Hemorrhage (bleeding) of gums and teeth (epinephrine)
- Priapism (prolonged abnormal erection of penis) (epinephrine)

Other than the above information, there is no additional information relating to proper use, precautions, or side effects for these uses.

Revised: July 1990
Interim revision: 09/12/94

BRONCHODILATORS, THEOPHYLLINE Systemic

Some commonly used brand names are:

In the U.S.—

Aerolate Sr[3]
Asmalix[3]
Choledyl[2]
Choledyl SA[2]
Elixophyllin[3]
Lanophyllin[3]
Phyllocontin[1]
Quibron-T Dividose[3]
Quibron-T/SR Dividose[3]
Respbid[3]
Slo-Bid Gyrocaps[3]
Slo-Phyllin[3]
Theo-24[3]
Theobid Duracaps[3]
Theochron[3]
Theoclear-80[3]
Theoclear L.A.-260[3]
Theo-Dur[3]
Theolair[3]
Theolair-SR[3]
Theo-Time[3]
Theovent Long-Acting[3]
Theo-X[3]
T-Phyl[3]
Truphylline[1]
Truxophyllin[3]
Uni-Dur[3]
Uniphyl[3]

In Canada—

Apo-Oxtriphylline[2]
Apo-Theo LA[3]
Choledyl[2]
Choledyl SA[2]
Phyllocontin[1]
Phyllocontin-350[1]
PMS Oxtriphylline[2]
PMS Theophylline[3]
Pulmophylline[3]
Quibron-T/SR Dividose[3]
Slo-Bid Gyrocaps[3]
Theochron[3]
Theo-Dur[3]
Theolair[3]
Theolair-SR[3]
Theo-SR[3]
Uniphyl[3]

Note: For quick reference, the following theophylline bronchodilators are numbered to match the corresponding brand names.

This information applies to the following medicines:

1. Aminophylline (am-in-OFF-i-lin)‡§
2. Oxtriphylline (ox-TRYE-fi-lin)§
3. Theophylline (thee-OFF-i-lin)‡§

‡Generic name product may be available in the U.S.
§Generic name product may be available in Canada.

Description

Aminophylline, oxtriphylline, and theophylline are used to treat and/or prevent the symptoms of bronchial asthma, chronic bronchitis, and emphysema. These medicines relieve cough, wheezing, shortness of breath, and troubled breathing. They work by opening up the bronchial tubes (air passages of the lungs) and increasing the flow of air through them.

Aminophylline and theophylline may also be used for other conditions as determined by your doctor.

The oral liquid, tablet, and capsule dosage forms of these medicines may be used for treatment of the acute attack or for chronic (long-term) treatment. The enteric-coated and extended-release dosage forms are usually used only for chronic treatment. Sometimes, aminophylline suppositories may be used but they are generally not recommended because of possible poor absorption.

These medicines are available only with your doctor's prescription, in the following dosage forms:

Oral

Aminophylline
- Oral solution (U.S.)
- Tablets (U.S. and Canada)
- Extended-release tablets (U.S. and Canada)

Oxtriphylline
- Oral solution (Canada)
  Syrup (Canada)
- Tablets (U.S. and Canada)
  Delayed-release tablets (U.S.)
- Extended-release tablets (U.S. and Canada)

Theophylline
- Capsules (U.S.)
- Extended-release capsules (U.S. and Canada)
- Elixir (U.S. and Canada)
- Oral solution (U.S. and Canada)
- Syrup (U.S.)
- Tablets (U.S. and Canada)
- Extended-release tablets (U.S. and Canada)

Parenteral

Aminophylline
- Injection (U.S. and Canada)

Theophylline
- Injection (U.S. and Canada)

Rectal
Aminophylline
• Suppositories (U.S.)

Before Using This Medicine

In deciding to use a medicine, the risks of taking the medicine must be weighed against the good it will do. This is a decision you and your doctor will make. For aminophylline, oxtriphylline, or theophylline, the following should be considered:

Allergies—Tell your doctor if you have ever had any unusual or allergic reaction to aminophylline, ethylenediamine (contained in aminophylline), oxtriphylline, or theophylline.

Diet—Make certain your health care professional knows if you are on any special diet, such as a high-protein, low-carbohydrate or a low-protein, high-carbohydrate diet.

Pregnancy—Aminophylline, oxtriphylline, and theophylline are frequently used to treat asthma in pregnant women. Although there are no studies on birth defects in humans, problems have not been reported. Some studies in animals have shown that aminophylline, oxtriphylline, and theophylline can cause birth defects when given in doses many times the human dose.

Because your ability to clear theophylline from your body may decrease later in pregnancy, your doctor may want to take blood samples during your pregnancy to measure the amount of medicine in the blood. This will help your doctor decide whether the dose of this medicine should be changed.

Theophylline crosses the placenta. Use of aminophylline, oxtriphylline, or theophylline during pregnancy may cause unwanted effects such as fast heartbeat, irritability, jitteriness, or vomiting in the newborn infant if the amount of medicine in your blood is too high.

Breast-feeding—Theophylline passes into the breast milk and may cause irritability in nursing babies of mothers taking aminophylline, oxtriphylline, or theophylline.

Children—Very young children and newborn infants require a lower dose than older children. If the amount of theophylline in the blood is too high, side effects are more likely to occur. Your doctor may want to take blood samples to determine whether a dose change is needed.

Older adults—Patients older than 60 years of age are likely to require a lower dose than younger adults. If the amount of theophylline is too high, side effects are more likely to occur. Your doctor may want to take blood samples to determine whether a dose change is needed.

Other medicines—Although certain medicines should not be used together at all, in other cases two different medicines may be used together even if an interaction might occur. In these cases, your doctor may want to change the dose, or other precautions may be necessary. When you are taking aminophylline, oxtriphylline, or theophylline, it is especially important that your health care professional know if you are taking any of the following:

- Beta-adrenergic blocking agents including those used in the eyes (acebutolol [e.g., Sectral], atenolol [e.g., Tenormin], betaxolol [e.g., Betoptic, Kerlone], bisoprolol [e.g., Zebeta], carteolol [e.g., Cartrol], labetalol [e.g., Normodyne], levobunolol [e.g., Betagan], metipranolol [e.g., OptiPranolol], metoprolol [e.g., Lopressor], nadolol [e.g., Corgard], oxprenolol [e.g., Trasicor], penbutolol [e.g., Levatol], pindolol [e.g., Visken], propranolol [e.g., Inderal], sotalol [e.g., Sotacor], timolol [e.g., Blocadren, Timoptic])—These medicines may prevent aminophylline, oxtriphylline, or theophylline from working properly
- Cimetidine (e.g., Tagamet) or
- Ciprofloxacin (e.g., Cipro) or
- Clarithromycin (e.g., Biaxin) or
- Enoxacin (e.g., Penetrex) or
- Erythromycin (e.g., E-Mycin) or
- Fluvoxamine (e.g., Luvox) or
- Mexiletine (e.g., Mexitil) or
- Pentoxifylline (e.g., Trental) or
- Propranolol (e.g., Inderal) or
- Tacrine (e.g., Cognex) or
- Thiabendazole or
- Ticlopidine (e.g., Ticlid) or
- Troleandomycin (e.g., TAO)—These medicines may increase the effects of aminophylline, oxtriphylline, or theophylline
- Moricizine (e.g., Ethmozine) or
- Phenytoin (e.g., Dilantin) or
- Rifampin (e.g., Rifadin)—These medicines may decrease the effects of aminophylline, oxtriphylline, or theophylline
- Smoking tobacco or marijuana—Starting or stopping smoking may change the effectiveness of these medicines

Other medical problems—The presence of other medical problems may affect the use of aminophylline, oxtriphylline, or theophylline. Make sure you tell your doctor if you have any other medical problems, especially:

- Convulsions (seizures)—Aminophylline, oxtriphylline, or theophylline may make this condition worse
- Heart failure or
- Liver disease or
- Underactive thyroid—The effects of aminophylline, oxtriphylline, or theophylline may be increased

Proper Use of This Medicine

For patients *taking this medicine by mouth:*

- If you are taking the *capsule, tablet, liquid, or extended-release (not including the once-a-day capsule or tablet) form* of this medicine, *it works best when taken with a glass of water on an empty stomach* (either 30 minutes to 1 hour before meals or 2 hours after meals). In some cases your doctor may want you to take this medicine with meals or right after meals to lessen stomach upset. If you have any questions about how you should be taking this medicine, check with your doctor.

- If you are taking the *once-a-day capsule or tablet form* of this medicine, *some products are to be taken each morning after fasting overnight and at least 1 hour before eating. However, other products are to be taken in the morning or evening with or without food. Be sure you understand exactly how to take the medicine prescribed for you.* Try to take the medicine about the same time each day.

- There are several different forms of aminophylline, oxtriphylline, and theophylline capsules and tablets. If you are taking:
  —*Enteric-coated or delayed-release tablets,* swallow the tablets whole. Do not crush, break, or chew before swallowing.
  —*Extended-release capsules,* swallow the capsule whole. Do not crush, break, or chew before swallowing. Do not open the capsule and sprinkle the beads onto food unless told to do so by your health care professional.
  —*Extended-release tablets,* swallow the tablets whole. Do not break (unless tablet is scored for breaking), crush, or chew before swallowing.

Use this medicine only as directed by your doctor. Do not use more of it, do not use it more often, and do not use it for a longer time than your doctor ordered. To do so may increase the chance of serious side effects.

In order for this medicine to help your medical problem, it must be taken every day in regularly spaced doses as ordered by your doctor. This is necessary to keep a constant amount of this medicine in the blood. To help keep the amount constant, do not miss any doses.

Dosing—When you are taking aminophylline, oxtriphylline, or theophylline, it is very important that you get the exact amount of medicine that you need. The dose of these medicines will be different for different patients. Your doctor will determine the proper dose of these medicines for you. *Follow your doctor's orders or the directions on the label.*

After you begin taking aminophylline, oxtriphylline, or theophylline, it is very important that your doctor check the level of medicine in your blood at regular intervals to find out if your dose needs to be changed. *Do not change your dose of aminophylline, oxtriphylline, or theophylline unless your doctor tells you to do so.*

The number of capsules or tablets or teaspoonfuls of solution or syrup that you take depends on the strength of the medicine. Also, *the number of doses you take each day and the time between doses depend on whether you are taking a short-acting or long-acting form of aminophylline, oxtriphylline, or theophylline.*

Missed dose—If you miss a dose of this medicine, take it as soon as possible. However, if it is almost time for your next dose, skip the missed dose and go back to your regular dosing schedule. Do not double doses.

Storage—To store this medicine:
- Keep out of the reach of children.
- Store away from heat and direct light.
- Do not store the capsule or tablet form of this medicine in the bathroom, near the kitchen sink, or in other damp places. Heat or moisture may cause the medicine to break down.
- Keep the liquid form of this medicine from freezing.
- Do not keep outdated medicine or medicine no longer needed. Be sure that any discarded medicine is out of the reach of children.

Precautions While Using This Medicine

Your doctor should check your progress at regular visits, especially for the first few weeks after you begin using this medicine. A blood test may be taken to help your doctor decide whether the dose of this medicine should be changed.

Do not change brands or dosage forms of this medicine without first checking with your doctor. Different products may not work the same way. If you refill your medicine and it looks different, check with your pharmacist.

A change in your usual behavior or physical well-being may affect the way this medicine works in your body. *Check with your doctor if you:*
- have a fever of 102 °F or higher for at least 24 hours or higher than 100 °F for longer than 24 hours.
- start or stop smoking.
- start or stop taking another medicine.
- change your diet for a long time.

This medicine may add to the central nervous system (CNS) stimulant effects of caffeine-containing foods or beverages such as chocolate, cocoa, tea, coffee, and cola drinks. Avoid eating or drinking large amounts of these foods or beverages while using this medicine. If you have questions about this, check with your doctor.

Before you have myocardial perfusion studies (a medical test that shows how well blood is flowing to your heart), tell the medical doctor in charge that you are taking this medicine. The results of the test may be affected by this medicine.

Side Effects of This Medicine

Along with its needed effects, a medicine may cause some unwanted effects. Although not all of these side effects may occur, if they do occur they may need medical attention.

Check with your doctor as soon as possible if any of the following side effects occur:

Less common

Heartburn and/or vomiting

Rare

Hives, skin rash, or sloughing of skin (with aminophylline only)

Symptoms of toxicity

Abdominal pain, continuing or severe; confusion or change in behavior; convulsions (seizures); dark or bloody vomit; diarrhea; dizziness or lightheadedness; fast and/or irregular heartbeat; nervousness or restlessness, continuing; trembling, continuing

Other side effects may occur that usually do not need medical attention. These side effects may go away during treatment as your body adjusts to the medicine. However, check with your doctor if any of the following side effects continue or are bothersome:

Less common

Headache; fast heartbeat; increased urination; nausea; nervousness; trembling; trouble in sleeping

Other side effects not listed above may also occur in some patients. If you notice any other effects, check with your doctor.

Additional Information

Once a medicine has been approved for marketing for a certain use, experience may show that it is also useful for other medical problems. Although this use is not included in product labeling, aminophylline and theophylline are used in certain patients with the following medical condition:

- Apnea (breathing problem) in newborns

Other than the above information, there is no additional information relating to proper use, precautions, or side effects for this use.

Revised: 8/11/95

BUPROPION Systemic†

A commonly used brand name in the U.S. is Wellbutrin.
Another commonly used name is amfebutamone.

†Not commercially available in Canada.

Description

Bupropion (byoo-PROE-pee-on) is used to relieve mental depression.

This medicine is available only with your doctor's prescription, in the following dosage form:

Oral

- Tablets (U.S.)

Before Using This Medicine

In deciding to use a medicine, the risks of taking the medicine must be weighed against the good it will do. This is a decision you and your doctor will make. For bupropion, the following should be considered:

Allergies—Tell your doctor if you have ever had any unusual or allergic reaction to bupropion. Also tell your health care professional if you are allergic to any other substances, such as foods, preservatives, or dyes.

Pregnancy—Studies have not been done in pregnant women. However, bupropion has not been reported to cause birth defects or other problems in animal studies.

Breast-feeding—Bupropion passes into breast milk. Because it may cause unwanted effects in nursing babies, use of bupropion is not recommended during breast-feeding.

Children—Studies on this medicine have been done only in adult patients, and there is no specific information comparing use of bupropion in children with use in other age groups.

Older adults—This medicine has been tested in a limited number of patients 60 years of age and older and has not been shown to cause different side effects or problems in older people than it does in younger adults.

Other medicines—Although certain medicines should not be used together at all, in other cases two different medicines may be used together even if an interaction might occur. In these cases, your doctor may want to change the dose, or other precautions may be necessary. When you are taking bupropion, it is especially important that your health care professional know if you are taking any of the following:

- Alcohol or
- Antipsychotics (medicine for mental illness) or
- Fluoxetine (e.g., Prozac) or
- Lithium (e.g., Lithane) or
- Maprotiline (e.g., Ludiomil) or
- Trazodone (e.g., Desyrel) or
- Tricyclic antidepressants (amitriptyline [e.g., Elavil], amoxapine [e.g., Asendin], clomipramine [e.g., Anafranil], desipramine [e.g., Pertofrane], doxepin [e.g., Sinequan], imipramine [e.g., Tofranil], nortriptyline [e.g., Aventyl], protriptyline [e.g., Vivactil], trimipramine [e.g., Surmontil])—Using these medicines with bupropion may increase the risk of seizures
- Monoamine oxidase (MAO) inhibitors (furazolidone [e.g., Furoxone], isocarboxazid [e.g., Marplan], phenelzine [e.g., Nardil], procarbazine [e.g., Matulane], selegiline [e.g., Eldepryl], tranylcypromine [e.g., Parnate])—Taking bupropion while you are taking or within 2 weeks of taking MAO inhibitors may increase the chance of side effects; at least 14 days should be allowed between stopping treatment with one medicine and starting treatment with the other

Other medical problems—The presence of other medical problems may affect the use of bupropion. Make sure you tell your doctor if you have any other medical problems, especially:

- Anorexia nervosa or
- Brain tumor or
- Bulimia or
- Head injury, history of, or
- Seizure disorder—The risk of seizures may be increased when bupropion is taken by patients with these conditions
- Bipolar disorder (manic-depressive illness) or
- Other nervous, mental, or emotional conditions—Bupropion may make the condition worse
- Heart attack (recent) or heart disease—Bupropion may cause unwanted effects on the heart
- Kidney disease or
- Liver disease—Higher blood levels of bupropion may result, increasing the chance of side effects

Proper Use of This Medicine

Use bupropion only as directed by your doctor. Do not use more of it, do not use it more often, and do not use it for a longer time than your doctor ordered. To do so may increase the chance of side effects.

To lessen stomach upset, this medicine may be taken with food, unless your doctor has told you to take it on an empty stomach.

Usually this medicine must be taken for several weeks before you feel better. Your doctor should check your progress at regular visits.

Dosing—The dose of bupropion will be different for different patients. *Follow your doctor's orders or the directions on the label.* The following information includes only the average doses of bupropion. *If your dose is different, do not change it* unless your doctor tells you to do so.

The number of tablets that you take depends on the strength of the medicine. Also, *the number of doses you take each day, the time allowed between doses, and the length of time you take the medicine depend on the medical problem for which you are taking bupropion.*

- For *oral* dosage form (tablets):
  - —For depression:
    - Adults—At first, 100 milligrams (mg) twice a day. Your doctor may increase your dose as needed. However, the dose is usually not more than 450 mg a day.
    - Children—Use and dose must be determined by your doctor.

Missed dose—If you miss a dose of this medicine, take it as soon as possible. However, if it is within 4 hours of your next dose, skip the missed dose and go back to your regular dosing schedule. Do not double doses.

Storage—To store this medicine:
- Keep out of the reach of children.
- Store away from heat and direct light.
- Do not store in the bathroom, near the kitchen sink, or in other damp places. Heat or moisture may cause the medicine to break down.
- Do not keep outdated medicine or medicine no longer needed. Be sure that any discarded medicine is out of the reach of children.

Precautions While Using This Medicine

Your doctor should check your progress at regular visits, especially during the first few months of treatment with this medicine. The amount of bupropion you take may have to be changed often to meet the needs of your condition and to help avoid unwanted effects.

If you have been taking this medicine regularly, do not stop taking it without first checking with your doctor. Your doctor may want you to reduce gradually the amount you are taking before stopping completely. This will help reduce the possibility of side effects.

Drinking of alcoholic beverages should be limited or avoided, if possible, while taking bupropion. This will help prevent unwanted effects.

This medicine may cause some people to feel a false sense of well-being, or to become drowsy, dizzy, or less alert than they are normally. *Make sure you know how you react to this medicine before you drive, use machines, or do anything else that could be dangerous if you are dizzy or are not alert and clearheaded.*

Side Effects of This Medicine

Along with its needed effects, a medicine may cause some unwanted effects. Although not all of these side effects may occur, if they do occur they may need medical attention.

Check with your doctor as soon as possible if any of the following side effects occur:

More common

Agitation or excitement; anxiety; confusion; fast or irregular heartbeat; headache (severe); restlessness; trouble in sleeping

Less common

Hallucinations; skin rash

Rare

Fainting; seizures (convulsions), especially with higher doses

Other side effects may occur that usually do not need medical attention. These side effects may go away during treatment as your body adjusts to the medicine. However, check with your doctor if any of the following side effects continue or are bothersome:

More common

Constipation; decrease in appetite; dizziness; dryness of mouth; increased sweating; nausea or vomiting; tremor; weight loss (unusual)

Less common

Blurred vision; difficulty concentrating; drowsiness; fever or chills; hostility or anger; tiredness; sleep disturbances; unusual feeling of well-being

Other side effects not listed above may also occur in some patients. If you notice any other effects, check with your doctor.

Revised: 07/29/94

BUSERELIN Systemic*

A commonly used brand name in Canada is Suprefact.

*Not commercially available in the U.S.

Description

Buserelin (BYOO-se-rel-in) is used to treat cancer of the prostate gland.

It is similar to a hormone normally released from the hypothalamus gland. When given regularly, buserelin decreases testosterone levels. Reducing the amount of testosterone in the body is one way of treating cancer of the prostate.

Buserelin is available only with your doctor's prescription, in the following dosage forms:

Nasal
- Nasal solution (Canada)

Parenteral
- Injection (Canada)

Before Using This Medicine

In deciding to use a medicine, the risks of taking the medicine must be weighed against the good it will do. This is a decision you and your doctor will make. For buserelin, the following should be considered:

Allergies—Tell your doctor if you have ever had any unusual or allergic reaction to buserelin.

Fertility—Buserelin causes sterility which may be permanent. If you intend to have children, discuss this with your doctor before receiving this medicine.

Older adults—Many medicines have not been studied specifically in older people. Therefore, it may not be known whether they work exactly the same way they do in younger adults. Although there is no specific information comparing use of buserelin in the elderly to use in other age groups, it has been used mostly in elderly patients and is not expected to cause different side effects or problems in older people than it does in younger adults.

Proper Use of This Medicine

Buserelin comes with patient directions. Read these instructions carefully.

For patients using the *injection* form of this medicine:
- Use the syringes provided in the kit. Other syringes may not provide the correct dose. These disposable syringes and needles are already sterilized and designed to be used one time only and then discarded. If you have any questions about the use of disposable syringes, check with your health care professional.
- After use, dispose of the syringes and needles in a safe manner. If a special container is not provided, ask your health care professional about the best way to dispose of syringes and needles.

For patients using the *nasal solution* form of this medicine:
- Use the nebulizer (spray pump) provided. Directions about how to use it are included. If you have any questions about the use of the nebulizer, check with your health care professional.

Use this medicine only as directed by your doctor. Do not use more or less of it, and do not use it more often than your doctor ordered. The exact amount of medicine you need has been carefully worked out. Using too much may increase the chance of side effects, while using too little may not improve your condition.

Buserelin sometimes causes unwanted effects such as hot flashes or decreased sexual ability. It may also cause a temporary increase in pain, trouble in urinating, or weakness in your legs when you begin to use it. However, it is very important that you continue to use the medicine, even after you begin to feel better. *Do not stop using this medicine without first checking with your doctor.*

Dosing—The dose of buserelin will be different for different patients. *Follow your doctor's orders or the directions on the label.* The following information includes only the average doses of buserelin. *If your dose is different, do not change it* unless your doctor tells you to do so.

The number of doses you use each day, the time allowed between doses, and the length of time you use the medicine depend on the medical problem for which you are using buserelin.

- For prostate cancer:
  - —For *nasal* dosage forms:
    - Adults: 200 micrograms (mcg) (2 sprays) into each nostril every eight hours.
  - —For *injection* dosage forms:
    - Adults: In the beginning, 500 mcg (0.5 milligrams [mg]) injected under the skin every eight hours. After a time, your doctor may lower your dose to 200 mcg (0.2 mg) once a day.

Missed dose—If you miss a dose of this medicine, use it as soon as possible. However, if it is almost time for the next dose, skip the missed dose and go back to your regular dosing schedule. Do not double doses.

Storage—To store this medicine:
- Keep out of the reach of children.
- Store away from heat and direct light.
- Keep the medicine from freezing.
- Do not keep outdated medicine or medicine no longer needed. Dispose of used syringes properly in the container provided. Be sure that any discarded medicine is out of the reach of children.

Precautions While Using This Medicine

It is very important that your doctor check your progress at regular visits to make sure that this medicine is working properly and to check for unwanted effects.

Side Effects of This Medicine

Along with its needed effects, a medicine may cause some unwanted effects. Although not all of these side effects may occur, if they do occur they may need medical attention.

The following side effects are symptoms of a flareup of your condition that may occur during the first few days of treatment. After a few days, these symptoms should lessen. However, they may require medical attention. Check with your doctor if any of the following side effects occur or get worse:

Bone pain; numbness or tingling of hands or feet; trouble in urinating; weakness in legs

Other side effects may occur that usually do not need medical attention. These side effects may go away during treatment as your body adjusts to the medicine. However,

check with your doctor if any of the following side effects continue or are bothersome:

More common

Decrease in sexual desire; impotence; sudden sweating and feelings of warmth (''hot flashes'')

Less common

Burning, itching, redness, or swelling at place of injection; diarrhea; dry or sore nose (with nasal solution); headache (with nasal solution); increased sweating (with nasal solution); loss of appetite; nausea or vomiting; swelling and increased tenderness of breasts; swelling of feet or lower legs

Other side effects not listed above may also occur in some patients. If you notice any other effects, check with your doctor.

Revised: 07/11/94

BUSPIRONE Systemic

A commonly used brand name in the U.S. and Canada is BuSpar.

Description

Buspirone (byoo-SPYE-rone) is used to treat certain anxiety disorders or to relieve the symptoms of anxiety. However, buspirone is usually not used for anxiety or tension caused by the stress of everyday life.

It is not known exactly how buspirone works to relieve the symptoms of anxiety.

Buspirone is available only with your doctor's prescription, in the following dosage form:

Oral

- Tablets (U.S. and Canada)

Before Using This Medicine

In deciding to use a medicine, the risks of taking the medicine must be weighed against the good it will do. This is a decision you and your doctor will make. For buspirone, the following should be considered:

Allergies—Tell your doctor if you have ever had any unusual or allergic reaction to buspirone. Also tell your health care professional if you are allergic to any other substances, such as foods, preservatives, or dyes.

Pregnancy—Buspirone has not been studied in pregnant women. However, buspirone has not been shown to cause birth defects or other problems in animal studies.

Breast-feeding—It is not known whether buspirone passes into the breast milk of humans.

Children—Studies on this medicine have been done only in adult patients, and there is no specific information comparing use of buspirone in children up to 18 years of age with use in other age groups.

Older adults—This medicine has been tested and has not been shown to cause different side effects or problems in older people than it does in younger adults.

Other medicines—Although certain medicines should not be used together at all, in other cases 2 different medicines may be used together even if an interaction might occur. In these cases, your doctor may want to change the dose, or other precautions may be necessary. When you are taking buspirone, it is especially important that your health care professional know if you are taking any of the following:

- Monoamine oxidase (MAO) inhibitors (furazolidone [e.g., Furoxone], isocarboxazid [e.g., Marplan], phenelzine [e.g., Nardil], procarbazine [e.g., Matulane], selegiline at doses more than 10 mg a day [e.g., Eldepryl], tranylcypromine [e.g., Parnate])—Taking buspirone while you are taking or within 2 weeks of taking monoamine oxidase (MAO) inhibitors may cause high blood pressure

Other medical problems—The presence of other medical problems may affect the use of buspirone. Make sure you tell your doctor if you have any other medical problems, especially:

- Drug abuse or dependence (history of)—There is a possibility that buspirone could become habit-forming, causing mental or physical dependence
- Kidney disease or
- Liver disease—The effects of buspirone may be increased, which may increase the chance of side effects

Proper Use of This Medicine

Take buspirone only as directed by your doctor. Do not take more of it, do not take it more often, and do not take it for a longer time than your doctor ordered. To do so may increase the chance of unwanted effects.

After you begin taking buspirone, 1 to 2 weeks may pass before you feel the full effects of this medicine.

Dosing—The dose of buspirone will be different for different patients. *Follow your doctor's orders or the directions on the label.* The following information includes only the average doses of buspirone. *If your dose is different, do not change it* unless your doctor tells you to do so.

The number of tablets that you take depends on the strength of the medicine. Also, *the number of doses you take each day, the time allowed between doses, and the length of time you take the medicine depend on the medical problem for which you are taking buspirone.*

- For *oral* dosage forms (tablets):
  —Adults: To start, 5 milligrams three times a day. Your doctor may increase your dose by 5 milligrams a day every few days if needed. However, the dose is usually not more than 60 milligrams a day.
  —Children up to 18 years of age: Dose must be determined by the doctor.

Missed dose—If you are taking this medicine regularly and you miss a dose, take it as soon as possible. However, if it is almost time for your next dose, skip the missed dose and go back to your regular dosing schedule. Do not double doses.

Storage—To store this medicine:
- Keep out of the reach of children.
- Store away from heat and direct light.
- Do not store in the bathroom, near the kitchen sink, or in other damp places. Heat or moisture may cause the medicine to break down.
- Do not keep outdated medicine or medicine no longer needed. Be sure that any discarded medicine is out of the reach of children.

Precautions While Using This Medicine

If you will be using buspirone regularly for a long time, your doctor should check your progress at regular visits to make sure the medicine does not cause unwanted effects.

Buspirone, when taken with alcohol or other CNS depressants (medicines that slow down the nervous system, possibly causing drowsiness), may increase the chance of drowsiness. Some examples of CNS depressants are antihistamines or medicine for hay fever, other allergies, or colds; sedatives, tranquilizers, or sleeping medicine; prescription pain medicine or narcotics; barbiturates; medicine for seizures; muscle relaxants; or anesthetics, including some dental anesthetics. Check with your doctor before taking any of the above while you are taking this medicine.

Buspirone may cause some people to become dizzy, lightheaded, drowsy, or less alert than they are normally. *Make sure you know how you react to this medicine before you drive, use machines, or do anything else that could be dangerous if you are dizzy or are not alert.*

If you think you or someone else may have taken an overdose of buspirone, get emergency help at once. Some symptoms of an overdose are severe dizziness or drowsiness; severe stomach upset, including nausea or vomiting; or unusually small pupils.

Side Effects of This Medicine

Along with its needed effects, a medicine may cause some unwanted effects. Although not all of these side effects may occur, if they do occur they may need medical attention.

Check with your doctor as soon as possible if any of the following side effects occur:

Rare

Chest pain; confusion or mental depression; fast or pounding heartbeat; muscle weakness; numbness, tingling, pain, or weakness in hands or feet; sore throat or fever; uncontrolled movements of the body

Symptoms of overdose

Dizziness (severe); drowsiness (severe); stomach upset, including nausea or vomiting (severe); unusually small pupils

Other side effects may occur that usually do not need medical attention. These side effects may go away during treatment as your body adjusts to the medicine. However, check with your doctor if any of the following side effects continue or are bothersome:

More common

Dizziness or lightheadedness; headache; nausea; restlessness, nervousness, or unusual excitement

Less common or rare

Blurred vision; decreased concentration; drowsiness (more common with doses of more than 20 mg per day); dryness of mouth; muscle pain, spasms, cramps, or stiffness; ringing in the ears; stomach upset; trouble in sleeping, nightmares, or vivid dreams; unusual tiredness or weakness

Other side effects not listed above may also occur in some patients. If you notice any other effects, check with your doctor.

Revised: 03/09/93

BUSULFAN Systemic

A commonly used brand name in the U.S. and Canada is Myleran.

Description

Busulfan (byoo-SUL-fan) belongs to the group of medicines known as alkylating agents. It is used to treat some kinds of cancer.

Busulfan seems to act by interfering with the function of the bone marrow. Since the growth of normal body cells may also be affected by busulfan, other effects will also occur. Some of these may be serious and must be reported to your doctor. Other effects may not be serious but may cause concern. Some effects may not occur for months or years after the medicine is used.

Before you begin treatment with busulfan, you and your doctor should talk about the good this medicine will do as well as the risks of using it.

Busulfan is available only with your doctor's prescription, in the following dosage form:

Oral
- Tablets (U.S. and Canada)

Before Using This Medicine

In deciding to use a medicine, the risks of taking the medicine must be weighed against the good it will do. This is a decision you and your doctor will make. For busulfan, the following should be considered:

Allergies—Tell your doctor if you have ever had any unusual or allergic reaction to busulfan.

Pregnancy—Although only one case has been reported, there is a chance that this medicine may cause birth defects if either the male or the female is taking it at the time of conception or if it is taken during pregnancy. In addition, many cancer medicines may cause sterility which could be permanent. Sterility may occur with busulfan and the possibility should be kept in mind.

Be sure that you have discussed this with your doctor before taking this medicine. It is best to use some kind of birth control while you are taking busulfan. Tell your doctor right away if you think you have become pregnant while taking busulfan.

Breast-feeding—It is not known whether busulfan passes into breast milk. However, because this medicine may cause serious side effects, breast-feeding is generally not recommended while you are taking it.

Children—Although there is no specific information comparing use of busulfan in children with use in other age groups, this medicine is not expected to cause different side effects or problems in children than it does in adults.

Older adults—Many medicines have not been studied specifically in older people. Therefore, it may not be known whether they work exactly the same way they do in younger adults. Although there is no specific information comparing use of busulfan in the elderly with use in other age groups, this medicine is not expected to cause different side effects or problems in older people than it does in younger adults.

Other medicines—Although certain medicines should not be used together at all, in other cases two different medicines may be used together even if an interaction might occur. In these cases, your doctor may want to change the dose, or other precautions may be necessary. When taking busulfan it is especially important that your health care professional know if you are taking any of the following:

- Amphotericin B by injection (e.g., Fungizone) or
- Antithyroid agents (medicine for overactive thyroid) or
- Azathioprine (e.g., Imuran) or
- Chloramphenicol (e.g., Chloromycetin) or
- Colchicine or
- Flucytosine (e.g., Ancobon) or
- Ganciclovir (e.g., Cytovene) or
- Interferon (e.g., Intron A, Roferon-A) or
- Plicamycin (e.g., Mithracin) or
- Zidovudine (e.g., AZT, Retrovir) or
- If you have ever been treated with radiation or cancer medicines—Busulfan may increase the effects of these medicines or radiation therapy on the blood
- Probenecid (e.g., Benemid) or
- Sulfinpyrazone (e.g., Anturane)—Busulfan may raise the amount of uric acid in the blood. Since these medicines are used to lower uric acid levels, they may not be as effective in patients taking busulfan

Other medical problems—The presence of other medical problems may affect the use of busulfan. Make sure you tell your doctor if you have any other medical problems, especially:

- Chickenpox (including recent exposure) or
- Herpes zoster (shingles)—Risk of severe disease affecting other parts of the body
- Gout (history of) or
- Kidney stones (or history of)—Busulfan may increase levels of uric acid in the body, which can cause gout or kidney stones
- Head injury or
- Convulsions (history of)—Very high doses of busulfan can cause convulsions
- Infection—Busulfan may decrease your body's ability to fight infection

Proper Use of This Medicine

Take this medicine only as directed by your doctor. Do not take more or less of it, and do not take it more often than your doctor ordered. The exact amount of medicine you need has been carefully worked out. Taking too much may increase the chance of side effects, while taking too little may not improve your condition.

Take each dose at the same time each day to make sure it has the best effect.

While you are taking this medicine, your doctor may want you to drink extra fluids so that you will pass more urine. This will help prevent kidney problems and keep your kidneys working well.

This medicine sometimes causes nausea and vomiting. However, it is very important that you continue to use the medicine, even if you begin to feel ill. *Do not stop taking this medicine without first checking with your doctor.* Ask your health care professional for ways to lessen these effects.

If you vomit shortly after taking a dose of busulfan, check with your doctor. You will be told whether to take the dose again or to wait until the next scheduled dose.

Dosing—The dose of busulfan will be different for different patients. The dose that is used may depend on a number of things, including what the medicine is being used for, the patient's weight, and whether or not other medicines are also being taken. *If you are taking busulfan at home, follow your doctor's orders or the directions on the label.* If you have any questions about the proper dose of busulfan, ask your doctor.

Missed dose—If you miss a dose of this medicine, skip the missed dose and go back to your regular dosing schedule. Do not double doses.

Storage—To store this medicine:

- Keep out of the reach of children.
- Store away from heat and direct light.
- Do not store in the bathroom, near the kitchen sink, or in other damp places. Heat or moisture may cause the medicine to break down.
- Do not keep outdated medicine or medicine no longer needed. Be sure that any discarded medicine is out of the reach of children.

Precautions While Using This Medicine

It is very important that your doctor check your progress at regular visits to make sure that this medicine is working properly and to check for unwanted effects.

While you are being treated with busulfan, and after you stop treatment with it, *do not have any immunizations (vaccinations) without your doctor's approval.* Busulfan may lower your body's resistance and there is a chance you might get the infection the immunization is meant to prevent. In addition, other persons living in your household should not take oral polio vaccine since there is a chance they could pass the polio virus on to you. Also, avoid persons who have recently taken oral polio vaccine. Do not get close to them, and do not stay in the same room with them for very long. If you cannot take these precautions, you should consider wearing a protective face mask that covers the nose and mouth.

Busulfan can temporarily lower the number of white blood cells in your blood, increasing the chance of getting an infection. It can also lower the number of platelets, which are necessary for proper blood clotting. If this occurs, there are certain precautions you can take, especially when your blood count is low, to reduce the risk of infection or bleeding:

- If you can, avoid people with infections. *Check with your doctor immediately* if you think you are getting an infection or if you get a fever or chills, cough or hoarseness, lower back or side pain, or painful or difficult urination.
- *Check with your doctor immediately* if you notice any unusual bleeding or bruising; black, tarry stools; blood in urine or stools; or pinpoint red spots on your skin.
- Be careful when using a regular toothbrush, dental floss, or toothpick. Your medical doctor, dentist, or nurse may recommend other ways to clean your teeth and gums. Check with your medical doctor before having any dental work done.
- Do not touch your eyes or the inside of your nose unless you have just washed your hands and have not touched anything else in the meantime.
- Be careful not to cut yourself when you are using sharp objects such as a safety razor or fingernail or toenail cutters.
- Avoid contact sports or other situations where bruising or injury could occur.

Before you have any medical tests, tell the medical doctor in charge that you are taking this medicine. The results of some body tissue studies may be affected by this medicine.

Side Effects of This Medicine

Along with its needed effects, a medicine may have some unwanted effects. Although not all of these side effects may occur, if they do occur they may need medical attention.

Also, because of the way these medicines act on the body, there is a chance that they might cause other unwanted effects that may not occur until months or years after the medicine is used. These delayed effects may include certain types of cancer, such as leukemia. Discuss these possible effects with your doctor.

Check with your doctor or nurse immediately if any of the following side effects occur:

More common

Black, tarry stools; blood in urine or stools; pinpoint red spots on skin; unusual bleeding or bruising

Less common

Cough or hoarseness; fever or chills; lower back or side pain; painful or difficult urination

Check with your doctor as soon as possible if any of the following side effects occur:

Less common

Joint pain; shortness of breath; sores in mouth and on lips; swelling of feet or lower legs

Rare

Blurred vision

Other side effects may occur that usually do not need medical attention. These side effects may go away during treatment as your body adjusts to the medicine. Also, your health care professional may be able to tell you about ways to prevent or reduce some of these side effects. Check with your health care professional if any of the following side effects continue or are bothersome or if you have any questions about them:

More common

Darkening of skin; missed or irregular menstrual periods

Less common

Confusion; diarrhea; dizziness; loss of appetite; nausea and vomiting; unusual tiredness or weakness; weight loss (sudden)

After you stop taking busulfan, it may still produce some side effects that need attention. During this period of time, check with your doctor if you notice any of the following:

Black, tarry stools; blood in urine or stools; cough or hoarseness; fever or chills; lower back or side pain; painful or difficult urination; pinpoint red spots on skin; shortness of breath; unusual bleeding or bruising

Other side effects not listed above may also occur in some patients. If you notice any other effects, check with your doctor.

Revised: 06/12/92
Interim revision: 05/02/94

BUTALBITAL AND ACETAMINOPHEN Systemic†

Some commonly used brand names are:

In the U.S.—

Amaphen[2]	Isocet[2]
Anolor-300[2]	Isopap[2]
Anoquan[2]	Medigesic[2]
Arcet[2]	Pacaps[2]
Bancap[1]	Pharmagesic[2]
Bucet[1]	Phrenilin[1]
Butace[2]	Phrenilin Forte[1]
Conten[1]	Repan[2]
Dolmar[2]	Sedapap[1]
Endolor[2]	Tencet[2]
Esgic[2]	Tencon[1]
Esgic-Plus[2]	Triad[2]
Ezol[2]	Triaprin[1]
Femcet[2]	Two-Dyne[2]
Fioricet[2]	

Note: For quick reference, the following butalbital and acetaminophens are numbered to match the corresponding brand names.

This information applies to the following medicines:

1. Butalbital and Acetaminophen†‡
2. Butalbital, Acetaminophen, and Caffeine†‡

†Not commercially available in Canada.
‡Generic name product may also be available in the U.S.

Description

Butalbital (byoo-TAL-bi-tal) and acetaminophen (a-seat-a-MIN-oh-fen) combination is a pain reliever and relaxant. It is used to treat tension headaches. Butalbital belongs to the group of medicines called barbiturates (bar-BI-tyoo-rates). Barbiturates act in the central nervous system (CNS) to produce their effects.

When you take butalbital for a long time, your body may get used to it so that larger amounts are needed to produce the same effects. This is called tolerance to the medicine. Also, butalbital may become habit-forming (causing mental or physical dependence) when it is used for a long time or in large doses. Physical dependence may lead to withdrawal side effects when you stop taking the medicine. In patients who get headaches, the first symptom of withdrawal may be new (rebound) headaches.

Some butalbital and acetaminophen combinations also contain caffeine (kaf-EEN). Caffeine may help to relieve headaches. However, caffeine can also cause physical dependence when it is used for a long time. This may lead to withdrawal (rebound) headaches when you stop taking it.

Butalbital and acetaminophen combination may also be used for other kinds of headaches or other kinds of pain as determined by your doctor.

Butalbital and acetaminophen combinations are available only with your doctor's prescription in the following dosage forms:

Oral

Butalbital and Acetaminophen
- Capsules (U.S.)
- Tablets (U.S.)

Butalbital, Acetaminophen, and Caffeine
- Capsules (U.S.)
- Tablets (U.S.)

Before Using This Medicine

In deciding to use a medicine, the risks of taking the medicine must be weighed against the good it will do. This is a decision you and your doctor will make. For butalbital and acetaminophen combinations, the following should be considered:

Allergies—Tell your doctor if you have ever had any unusual or allergic reaction to butalbital or other barbiturates, or to acetaminophen, aspirin, or caffeine. Also tell your health care professional if you are allergic to any other substances, such as foods, preservatives, or dyes.

Pregnancy—

- *For butalbital:* Barbiturates such as butalbital have been shown to increase the chance of birth defects in humans. Also, one study in humans has suggested that barbiturates taken during pregnancy may increase the chance of brain tumors in the baby.

  Butalbital may cause breathing problems in the newborn baby if taken just before or during delivery.
- *For acetaminophen:* Although studies on birth defects with acetaminophen have not been done in pregnant women, it has not been reported to cause birth defects or other problems.
- *For caffeine:* Studies in humans have not shown that caffeine (contained in some of these combination medicines) causes birth defects. However, use of large amounts of caffeine during pregnancy may cause problems with the heart rhythm and the growth of the fetus. Also, studies in animals have shown that caffeine causes birth defects when given in very large doses (amounts equal to those present in 12 to 24 cups of coffee a day).

Breast-feeding—

- *For butalbital:* Barbiturates such as butalbital pass into the breast milk and may cause drowsiness, unusually slow heartbeat, shortness of breath, or troubled breathing in nursing babies.
- *For acetaminophen:* Although acetaminophen has not been shown to cause problems in nursing babies, it passes into the breast milk in small amounts.
- *For caffeine:* Caffeine (present in some butalbital and acetaminophen combinations) passes into the breast milk in small amounts. Taking caffeine in the amounts present in these medicines has not been shown to cause problems in nursing babies. However, studies have shown that nursing babies may appear jittery and have trouble in sleeping when their mothers drink large amounts of caffeine-containing beverages. Therefore, breast-feeding mothers who use caffeine-containing medicines should probably limit the amount of caffeine they take in from other medicines or from beverages.

Children—

- *For butalbital:* Although barbiturates such as butalbital often cause drowsiness, some children become excited after taking them.
- *For acetaminophen:* Acetaminophen has been tested in children and, in effective doses, has not been shown to cause different side effects or problems than it does in adults.
- *For caffeine:* There is no specific information comparing use of caffeine in children up to 12 years of age with use in other age groups. However, caffeine is not expected to cause different side effects or problems in children than it does in adults.

Older adults—

- *For butalbital:* Certain side effects, such as confusion, excitement, or mental depression, may be especially likely to occur in elderly patients, who are usually more sensitive than younger adults to the effects of the butalbital in this combination medicine.
- *For acetaminophen:* Acetaminophen has been tested and has not been shown to cause different side effects or problems in older people than it does in younger adults.
- *For caffeine:* Many medicines have not been studied specifically in older people. Therefore, it may not be known whether they work exactly the same way they do in younger adults or if they cause different side effects or problems in older people. There is no specific information comparing use of caffeine in the elderly with use in other age groups.

Other medicines—Although certain medicines should not be used together at all, in other cases two different medicines may be used together even if an interaction might occur. In these cases, your doctor may want to change the dose, or other precautions may be necessary. When you are taking a butalbital and acetaminophen combination, it is especially important that your health care professional know if you are taking any of the following:

- Anticoagulants (blood thinners), or
- Carbamazepine (e.g., Tegretol) or
- Contraceptives, oral (birth control pills) containing estrogen, or
- Corticosteroids (cortisone-like medicines) or
- Corticotropin (e.g., ACTH)—Butalbital may make these medicines less effective
- Antidepressants, tricyclic (amitriptyline [e.g., Elavil], amoxapine [e.g., Asendin], clomipramine [e.g., Anafranil], desipramine [e.g., Pertofrane], doxepin [e.g., Sinequan], imipramine [e.g., Tofranil], nortriptyline [e.g., Aventyl], protriptyline [e.g., Vivactil], trimipramine [e.g., Surmontil]) or
- Central nervous system (CNS) depressants (medicines that often cause drowsiness)—These medicines may add to the effects of butalbital and increase the chance of drowsiness or other side effects
- Divalproex (e.g., Depakote) or
- Valproic acid (e.g., Depakene)—The chance of side effects may be increased

Other medical problems—The presence of other medical problems may affect the use of butalbital and acetaminophen combinations. Make sure you tell your doctor if you have any other medical problems, especially:

- Alcohol abuse (or history of) or
- Drug abuse or dependence (or history of)—Dependence on butalbital may develop; also, acetaminophen may cause liver damage in people who abuse alcohol
- Asthma (or history of), emphysema, or other chronic lung disease or
- Hepatitis or other liver disease or
- Hyperactivity (in children) or
- Kidney disease—The chance of serious side effects may be increased
- Diabetes mellitus (sugar diabetes) or
- Mental depression or
- Overactive thyroid or
- Porphyria (or history of)—Butalbital can make these conditions worse
- Heart disease (severe)—The caffeine in some butalbital and acetaminophen combinations can make some kinds of heart disease worse

Proper Use of This Medicine

Take this medicine only as directed by your doctor. Do not take more of it, do not take it more often, and do not take it for a longer time than your doctor ordered. If butalbital and acetaminophen combination is taken regularly (for example, every day), it may become habit-forming (causing mental or physical dependence). The caffeine in some butalbital and acetaminophen combinations can also increase the chance of dependence. Dependence is especially likely to occur in patients who take these medicines to relieve frequent headaches. Taking too much of this medicine may also lead to liver damage or other medical problems.

This medicine will relieve a headache best if you *take it as soon as the headache begins.* If you get warning signs of a migraine, take this medicine as soon as you are sure that the migraine is coming. This may even stop the headache pain from occurring. *Lying down in a quiet, dark room for a while after taking the medicine also helps to relieve headaches.*

People who get a lot of headaches may need to take a different medicine to help prevent headaches. *It is important that you follow your doctor's directions about taking the other medicine, even if your headaches continue to occur.* Headache-preventing medicines may take several weeks to start working. Even after they do start working, your headaches may not go away completely. However, your headaches should occur less often, and they should be less severe and easier to relieve than before. This will reduce the amount of headache relievers that you need. If you do not notice any improvement after several weeks of headache-preventing treatment, check with your doctor.

Dosing—The dose of butalbital and acetaminophen combination medicines will be different for different patients. *Follow your doctor's orders or the directions on the label.* The following information includes only the average doses of these medicines. *If your dose is different, do not change it* unless your doctor tells you to do so.

The number of capsules or tablets that you take depends on the strength of the medicine.

- For *oral* dosage forms (capsules or tablets):
  —For tension headaches:
    - Adults—One or 2 capsules or tablets every four hours as needed. If your medicine contains 325 or 500 milligrams (mg) of acetaminophen in each capsule or tablet, you should not take more than six capsules or tablets a day. If your medicine contains 650 mg of acetaminophen in each capsule or tablet, you should not take more than four capsules or tablets a day.
    - Children—Dose must be determined by your doctor.

Missed dose—If your doctor has ordered you to take this medicine according to a regular schedule and you miss a dose, take it as soon as you remember. However, if it is almost time for your next dose, skip the missed dose and go back to your regular dosing schedule. *Do not double doses.*

Storage—To store this medicine:

- Keep out of the reach of children. Overdose is especially dangerous in young children.
- Store away from heat and direct light.
- Do not store this medicine in the bathroom, near the kitchen sink, or in other damp places. Heat or moisture may cause the medicine to break down.
- Do not keep outdated medicine or medicine no longer needed. Be sure that any discarded medicine is out of the reach of children.

Precautions While Using This Medicine

Check with your doctor:

- If the medicine stops working as well as it did when you first started using it. This may mean that you are in danger of becoming dependent on the medicine. *Do not try to get better pain relief by increasing the dose.*
- *If you are having headaches more often than you did before you started taking this medicine.* This is especially important if a new headache occurs within 1 day after you took your last dose of this medicine, headaches begin to occur every day, or a headache continues for several days in a row. This may mean that you are dependent on the medicine. *Continuing to take this medicine will cause even more headaches later on.* Your doctor can give you advice on how to relieve the headaches.

Check the labels of all nonprescription (over-the-counter [OTC]) or prescription medicines you now take. If any contain a barbiturate or acetaminophen, check with your health care professional. Taking them together with this medicine may cause an overdose.

The butalbital in this medicine will add to the effects of alcohol and other CNS depressants (medicines that slow down the nervous system, possibly causing drowsiness). Some examples of CNS depressants are antihistamines or medicine for hay fever, other allergies, or colds; sedatives, tranquilizers, or sleeping medicine; other prescription pain medicine; narcotics; other barbiturates; medicine for seizures; muscle relaxants; or anesthetics, including some dental anesthetics. Also, drinking large amounts of alcoholic beverages regularly while taking this medicine may increase the chance of liver damage, especially if you take more of this medicine than your doctor ordered or if you take it regularly for a long time. *Therefore, do not drink alcoholic beverages, and check with your doctor before taking any of the medicines listed above, while you are using this medicine.*

This medicine may cause some people to become drowsy, dizzy, or lightheaded. *Make sure you know how you react to this medicine before you drive, use machines, or do anything else that could be dangerous if you are dizzy or are not alert and clearheaded.*

Before you have any medical tests, tell the person in charge that you are taking this medicine. Caffeine (present in some butalbital and acetaminophen combinations) interferes with the results of certain tests that use dipyridamole (e.g., Persantine) to help show how well blood is flowing to your heart. Caffeine should not be taken for 8 to 12 hours before the test. The results of other tests may also be affected by butalbital and acetaminophen combinations.

Before having any kind of surgery (including dental surgery) or emergency treatment, tell the medical doctor or dentist in charge that you are taking this medicine. Serious side effects can occur if your medical doctor or dentist gives you certain medicines without knowing that you have taken butalbital.

If you have been taking large amounts of this medicine, or if you have been taking it regularly for several weeks or more, *do not suddenly stop taking it without first checking with your doctor.* Your doctor may want you to reduce gradually the amount you are taking before stopping completely in order to lessen the chance of withdrawal side effects.

If you think you or anyone else may have taken an overdose of this medicine, get emergency help at once. Taking an overdose of this medicine or taking alcohol or CNS depressants with this medicine may lead to unconsciousness or possibly death. Signs of butalbital overdose include severe drowsiness, confusion, severe weakness, shortness of breath or unusually slow or troubled breathing, slurred speech, staggering, and unusually slow heartbeat. Signs of severe acetaminophen poisoning may not occur until 2 to 4 days after the overdose is taken, but treatment to prevent liver damage or death must be started within 24 hours or less after the overdose is taken.

Side Effects of This Medicine

Along with its needed effects, a medicine may cause some unwanted effects. Although not all of these side effects may occur, if they do occur they may need medical attention.

Check with your doctor immediately if any of the following side effects occur, especially if several of them occur together:

Rare

Bleeding or crusting sores on lips; chest pain; fever with or without chills; hive-like swellings (large) on eyelids, face, lips, and/or tongue; muscle cramps or pain; red, thickened, or scaly skin; shortness of breath, troubled breathing, tightness in chest, or wheezing; skin rash, itching, or hives; sores, ulcers, or white spots in mouth (painful); sore throat

Symptoms of overdose

Anxiety, confusion, excitement, irritability, nervousness, restlessness, or trouble in sleeping (severe, especially with products containing caffeine); convulsions (seizures) (for products containing caffeine); diarrhea, especially if occurring together with increased sweating, loss of appetite, and stomach cramps or pain; dizziness, lightheadedness, drowsiness, or weakness, (severe); frequent urination (for products containing caffeine); hallucinations (seeing, hearing, or feeling things that are not there); increased sensitivity to touch or pain (for products containing caffeine); muscle trembling or twitching (for products containing caffeine); nausea or vomiting, sometimes with blood; ringing or other sounds in ears (for products containing caffeine); seeing flashes of "zig-zag" lights (for products containing caffeine); shortness of breath or unusually slow or troubled breathing; slow, fast, or irregular heartbeat; slurred speech; staggering; swelling, pain, or tenderness in the upper abdomen or stomach area; unusual movements of the eyes

Also, check with your doctor as soon as possible if any of the following side effects occur:

Less common

Confusion (mild); mental depression; unusual excitement (mild)

Rare

Bloody or black, tarry stools; bloody urine; pinpoint red spots on skin; swollen or painful glands; unusual bleeding or bruising; unusual tiredness or weakness (mild)

Other side effects may occur that usually do not need medical attention. These side effects may go away during treatment as your body adjusts to the medicine. However, check with your doctor if any of the following side effects continue or are bothersome:

More common

Bloated or "gassy" feeling; dizziness or lightheadedness (mild); drowsiness (mild); nausea, vomiting, or stomach pain (occurring without other symptoms of overdose)

Other side effects not listed above may also occur in some patients. If you notice any other effects, check with your doctor.

Revised: 07/14/92
Interim revision: 07/15/94

BUTALBITAL AND ASPIRIN Systemic

Some commonly used brand names are:

In the U.S.—

Axotal[1]	Isobutyl[2]
Butalgen[2]	Isolin[2]
Fiorgen[2]	Isollyl[2]
Fiorinal[2]	Laniroif[2]
Fiormor[2]	Lanorinal[2]
Fortabs[2]	Marnal[2]
Isobutal[2]	Vibutal[2]

In Canada—

Fiorinal[2]	Tecnal[2]

Other commonly used names for the butalbital, aspirin, and caffeine combination medicine are butalbital-AC and butalbital compound.

Note: For quick reference, the following medicines are numbered to match the corresponding brand names.

This information applies to the following medicines:

1. For Butalbital and Aspirin†
2. For Butalbital, Aspirin#, and Caffeine‡

†Not commercially available in Canada.
‡Generic name product may also be available in the U.S.
#In Canada, *Aspirin* is a brand name. Acetylsalicylic acid is the generic name in Canada. ASA, a synonym for acetylsalicylic acid, is the term that commonly appears on Canadian product labels.

Description

Butalbital (byoo-TAL-bi-tal) and aspirin (AS-pir-in) combination is a pain reliever and relaxant. It is used to treat tension headaches. Butalbital belongs to the group of medicines called barbiturates (bar-BI-tyoo-rates). Barbiturates act in the central nervous system (CNS) to produce their effects.

When you use butalbital for a long time, your body may get used to it so that larger amounts are needed to produce the same effects. This is called tolerance to the medicine. Also, butalbital may become habit-forming (causing mental or physical dependence) when it is used for a long time or in large doses. Physical dependence may lead to withdrawal side effects when you stop taking the medicine. In patients who get headaches, the first symptom of withdrawal may be new (rebound) headaches.

Some of these medicines also contain caffeine (kaf-EEN). Caffeine may help to relieve headaches. However, caffeine can also cause physical dependence when it is used for a long time. This may lead to withdrawal (rebound) headaches when you stop taking it.

Butalbital and aspirin combination is sometimes also used for other kinds of headaches or other kinds of pain, as determined by your doctor.

Butalbital and aspirin combination is available only with your doctor's prescription, in the following dosage forms:

Oral

Butalbital and Aspirin

- Tablets (U.S.)

Butalbital, Aspirin, and Caffeine
- Capsules (U.S. and Canada)
- Tablets (U.S. and Canada)

Before Using This Medicine

In deciding to use a medicine, the risks of taking the medicine must be weighed against the good it will do. This is a decision you and your doctor will make. For butalbital and aspirin combinations, the following should be considered:

Allergies—Tell your doctor if you have ever had any unusual or allergic reaction to butalbital or other barbiturates; aspirin or other salicylates, including methyl salicylate (oil of wintergreen); caffeine; or any of the following medicines:

Diclofenac (e.g., Voltaren)
Diflunisal (e.g., Dolobid)
Etodolac (e.g., Lodine)
Fenoprofen (e.g., Nalfon)
Floctafenine (e.g., Idarac)
Flurbiprofen, oral (e.g., Ansaid)
Ibuprofen (e.g., Motrin)
Indomethacin (e.g., Indocin)
Ketoprofen (e.g., Orudis)
Ketorolac (e.g., Toradol)
Meclofenamate (e.g., Meclomen)
Mefenamic acid (e.g., Ponstel)
Nabumetone (e.g., Relafen)
Naproxen (e.g., Naprosyn)
Oxaprozin (e.g., Daypro)
Oxyphenbutazone (e.g., Tandearil)
Phenylbutazone (e.g., Butazolidin)
Piroxicam (e.g., Feldene)
Sulindac (e.g., Clinoril)
Suprofen (e.g., Suprol)
Tenoxicam (e.g., Mobiflex)
Tiaprofenic acid (e.g., Surgam)
Tolmetin (e.g., Tolectin)
Zomepirac (e.g., Zomax)

Also tell your health care professional if you are allergic to any other substances, such as foods, preservatives, or dyes.

Pregnancy—
- *For butalbital:* Barbiturates such as butalbital have been shown to increase the chance of birth defects in humans. Also, one study in humans has suggested that barbiturates taken during pregnancy may increase the chance of brain tumors in the baby. Butalbital may cause breathing problems in the newborn baby if taken just before or during delivery.
- *For aspirin:* Although studies in humans have not shown that aspirin causes birth defects, it has caused birth defects in animal studies.

  Do not take aspirin during the last 3 months of pregnancy unless it has been ordered by your doctor. Some reports have suggested that use of aspirin late in pregnancy may cause a decrease in the newborn's weight and possible death of the fetus or newborn baby. However, the mothers in these reports had been taking much larger amounts of aspirin than are usually recommended. Studies of mothers taking aspirin in the doses that are usually recommended did not show these unwanted effects.

  There is a chance that regular use of aspirin late in pregnancy may cause unwanted effects on the heart or blood flow in the fetus or in the newborn baby. Also, use of aspirin during the last 2 weeks of pregnancy may cause bleeding problems in the fetus before or during delivery or in the newborn baby. In addition, too much use of aspirin during the last 3 months of pregnancy may increase the length of pregnancy, prolong labor, cause other problems during delivery, or cause severe bleeding in the mother before, during, or after delivery.
- *For caffeine:* Studies in humans have not shown that caffeine causes birth defects. However, use of large amounts of caffeine during pregnancy may cause problems with the heart rhythm and the growth of the fetus. Also, studies in animals have shown that caffeine causes birth defects when given in very large doses (amounts equal to the amount in 12 to 24 cups of coffee a day).

Breast-feeding—Although this combination medicine has not been reported to cause problems, the chance always exists, especially if the medicine is taken for a long time or in large amounts.
- *For butalbital:* Barbiturates such as butalbital pass into the breast milk and may cause drowsiness, unusually slow heartbeat, shortness of breath, or troubled breathing in nursing babies.
- *For aspirin:* Aspirin passes into the breast milk. However, taking aspirin in the amounts present in these combination medicines has not been reported to cause problems in nursing babies.
- *For caffeine:* The caffeine in some of these combination medicines passes into the breast milk in small amounts. Taking caffeine in the amounts present in these medicines has not been reported to cause problems in nursing babies. However, studies have shown that nursing babies may appear jittery and have trouble in sleeping when their mothers drink large amounts of caffeine-containing beverages. Therefore, breast-feeding mothers who use caffeine-containing medicines should probably limit the amount of caffeine they take in from other medicines or from beverages.

Children—
- *For butalbital:* Although barbiturates such as butalbital often cause drowsiness, some children become excited after taking them.
- *For aspirin: Do not give a medicine containing aspirin to a child with fever or other symptoms of a virus infection, especially flu or chickenpox, without first discussing its use with your child's doctor.* This is very important because aspirin may cause a serious illness called Reye's syndrome in children with fever caused by a virus infection, especially flu or chickenpox. Children who do not have a virus infection may also be more sensitive to the effects of aspirin, especially if they have a fever or have lost large amounts of body fluid because of vomiting, diarrhea,

or sweating. This may increase the chance of side effects during treatment.

- *For caffeine:* There is no specific information comparing use of caffeine in children up to 12 years of age with use in other age groups. However, caffeine is not expected to cause different side effects or problems in children than it does in adults.

Teenagers—*Teenagers with fever or other symptoms of a virus infection, especially flu or chickenpox, should check with a doctor before taking this medicine.* The aspirin in this combination medicine may cause a serious illness called Reye's syndrome in teenagers with fever caused by a virus infection, especially flu or chickenpox.

Older adults—

- *For butalbital:* Confusion, depression, or excitement may be especially likely to occur in elderly patients, who are usually more sensitive than younger adults to the effects of butalbital.
- *For aspirin:* Elderly patients are more sensitive than younger adults to the effects of aspirin. This may increase the chance of side effects during treatment.
- *For caffeine:* Many medicines have not been studied specifically in older people. Therefore, it may not be known whether they work exactly the same way they do in younger adults or if they cause different side effects or problems in older people. There is no specific information comparing use of caffeine in the elderly with use in other age groups.

Other medicines—Although certain medicines should not be used together at all, in other cases two different medicines may be used together even if an interaction might occur. In these cases, your doctor may want to change the dose, or other precautions may be necessary. When you are taking a butalbital and aspirin combination, it is especially important that your health care professional know if you are taking any of the following:

- Antacids, large amounts taken regularly, especially calcium- and/or magnesium-containing antacids or sodium bicarbonate (baking soda), or
- Urinary alkalizers (medicine that makes the urine less acid, such as acetazolamide [e.g., Diamox], dichlorphenamide [e.g., Daranide], methazolamide [e.g., Neptazane], potassium or sodium citrate and/or citric acid)—These medicines may cause aspirin to be removed from the body faster than usual, which may shorten the time that aspirin is effective; acetazolamide, dichlorphenamide, and methazolamide may also increase the chance of side effects when taken together with aspirin

- Anticoagulants (blood thinners) or
- Heparin—Use of these medicines together with aspirin may increase the chance of bleeding; also, butalbital may cause anticoagulants to be less effective

- Antidepressants, tricyclic (amitriptyline [e.g., Elavil], amoxapine [e.g., Asendin], clomipramine [e.g., Anafranil], desipramine [e.g., Pertofrane], doxepin [e.g., Sinequan], imipramine [e.g., Tofranil], nortriptyline [e.g., Aventyl], protriptyline [e.g., Vivactil], trimipramine [e.g., Surmontil]) or
- Central nervous system (CNS) depressants (medicines that often cause drowsiness)—These medicines may add to the effects of butalbital and increase the chance of drowsiness or other side effects
- Carbamazepine (e.g., Tegretol) or
- Contraceptives, oral (birth control pills), containing estrogen or
- Corticosteroids (cortisone-like medicines) or
- Corticotropin (e.g., ACTH)—Butalbital may make these medicines less effective
- Divalproex (e.g., Depakote) or
- Methotrexate (e.g., Folex, Mexate) or
- Valproic acid (e.g., Depakene) or
- Vancomycin (e.g., Vancocin)—The chance of serious side effects may be increased

- Probenecid (e.g., Benemid) or
- Sulfinpyrazone (e.g., Anturane)—Aspirin can keep these medicines from working properly for treating gout

Other medical problems—The presence of other medical problems may affect the use of butalbital and aspirin combinations. Make sure you tell your doctor if you have any other medical problems, especially:

- Alcohol abuse (or history of) or
- Drug abuse or dependence (or history of)—Dependence on butalbital may develop
- Asthma, especially if occurring together with other allergies and nasal polyps (or history of), or
- Emphysema or other chronic lung disease or
- Hyperactivity (in children) or
- Kidney disease or
- Liver disease—The chance of serious side effects may be increased
- Diabetes mellitus (sugar diabetes) or
- Mental depression or
- Overactive thyroid or
- Porphyria (or history of)—Butalbital may make these conditions worse

- Gout—Aspirin can make this condition worse and can also lessen the effects of some medicines used to treat gout
- Heart disease (severe)—The caffeine in some of these combination medicines can make some kinds of heart disease worse

- Hemophilia or other bleeding problems or
- Vitamin K deficiency—Aspirin increases the chance of serious bleeding

- Stomach ulcer, especially with a history of bleeding, or other stomach problems—Aspirin can make your condition worse

Proper Use of This Medicine

Take this medicine with food or a full glass (8 ounces) of water to lessen stomach irritation.

Do not take this medicine if it has a strong vinegar-like odor. This odor means the aspirin in it is breaking down. If you have any questions about this, check with your health care professional.

Take this medicine only as directed by your doctor. Do not take more of it, do not take it more often, and do not take it for a longer time than your doctor ordered. If butalbital and aspirin combination is taken regularly (for example, every day), it may become habit-forming (causing mental or physical dependence). The caffeine in some butalbital and aspirin combinations can also increase the chance of dependence. Dependence is especially likely to occur in patients who take this medicine to relieve frequent headaches. Taking too much of this combination medicine can also lead to stomach problems or to other medical problems.

This medicine will relieve a headache best if you *take it as soon as the headache begins.* If you get warning signs of a migraine, take this medicine as soon as you are sure that the migraine is coming. This may even stop the headache pain from occurring. *Lying down in a quiet, dark room for a while after taking the medicine also helps to relieve headaches.*

People who get a lot of headaches may need to take a different medicine to help prevent headaches. *It is important that you follow your doctor's directions about taking the other medicine, even if your headaches continue to occur.* Headache-preventing medicines may take several weeks to start working. Even after they do start working, your headaches may not go away completely. However, your headaches should occur less often, and they should be less severe and easier to relieve than before. This will reduce the amount of headache relievers that you need. If you do not notice any improvement after several weeks of headache-preventing treatment, check with your doctor.

Dosing—The dose of butalbital and aspirin combination medicines will be different for different patients. *Follow your doctor's orders or the directions on the label.* The following information includes only the average doses of the medicine. *If your dose is different, do not change it* unless your doctor tells you to do so.

For Butalbital and Aspirin combination

- For *oral* dosage form (tablets):
  - —For tension headaches:
    - Adults—One tablet every four hours as needed. You should not take more than six tablets a day.
    - Children—Dose must be determined by your doctor.

For Butalbital, Aspirin, and Caffeine combination

- For *oral* dosage forms (capsules or tablets):
  - —For tension headaches:
    - Adults—One or 2 capsules or tablets every four hours as needed. You should not take more than six capsules or tablets a day.
    - Children—Dose must be determined by your doctor.

Missed dose—If your doctor has ordered you to take this medicine according to a regular schedule and you miss a dose, take it as soon as you remember. However, if it is almost time for your next dose, skip the missed dose and go back to your regular dosing schedule. Do not double doses.

Storage—To store this medicine:

- Keep out of the reach of children. Overdose is especially dangerous in young children.
- Store away from heat and direct light.
- Do not store this medicine in the bathroom, near the kitchen sink, or in other damp places. Heat or moisture may cause the medicine to break down.
- Do not keep outdated medicine or medicine no longer needed. Be sure that any discarded medicine is out of the reach of children.

Precautions While Using This Medicine

Check with your doctor:

- If the medicine stops working as well as it did when you first started using it. This may mean that you are in danger of becoming dependent on the medicine. *Do not try to get better pain relief by increasing the dose.*
- *If you are having headaches more often than you did before you started using this medicine.* This is especially important if a new headache occurs within 1 day after you took your last dose of headache medicine, headaches begin to occur every day, or a headache continues for several days in a row. This may mean that you are dependent on the headache medicine. *Continuing to take this medicine will cause even more headaches later on.* Your doctor can give you advice on how to relieve the headaches.

Check the labels of all nonprescription (over-the-counter [OTC]) and prescription medicines you now take. If any contain a barbiturate, aspirin, or other salicylates, including diflunisal, check with your health care professional. Taking them together with this medicine may cause an overdose.

The butalbital in this medicine will add to the effects of alcohol and other CNS depressants (medicines that slow down the nervous system, possibly causing drowsiness). Some examples of CNS depressants are antihistamines or medicine for hay fever, other allergies, or colds; sedatives, tranquilizers, or sleeping medicine; other prescription pain medicine or narcotics; other barbiturates; medicine for seizures; muscle relaxants; or anesthetics, including some dental anesthetics. Also, stomach problems may be more likely to occur if you drink alcoholic beverages while you are taking aspirin. Therefore, *do not drink alcoholic beverages, and check with your doctor before taking any of the medicines listed above, while you are using this medicine.*

This medicine may cause some people to become drowsy, dizzy, or lightheaded. *Make sure you know how you react to this medicine before you drive, use machines, or do anything else that could be dangerous if you are dizzy or are not alert and clearheaded.*

Before having any kind of surgery (including dental surgery) or emergency treatment, tell the medical doctor or dentist in charge that you are taking this medicine. Serious side effects may occur if your medical doctor or dentist gives you certain other medicines without knowing that you have taken butalbital.

Do not take this medicine for 5 days before any planned surgery, including dental surgery, unless otherwise directed by your medical doctor or dentist. Taking aspirin during this time may cause bleeding problems.

Before you have any medical tests, tell the person in charge that you are taking this medicine. Caffeine (present in some butalbital and aspirin combinations) interferes with the results of certain tests that use dipyridamole (e.g., Persantine) to help show how well blood is flowing to your heart. Caffeine should not be taken for 8 to 12 hours before the test. The results of some other tests may also be affected by butalbital and aspirin combinations.

If you have been taking large amounts of this medicine, or if you have been taking it regularly for several weeks or more, *do not suddenly stop using it without first checking with your doctor.* Your doctor may want you to reduce gradually the amount you are taking before stopping completely, to lessen the chance of withdrawal side effects.

If you think you or anyone else may have taken an overdose of this medicine, get emergency help at once. Taking an overdose of this medicine or taking alcohol or CNS depressants with this medicine may lead to unconsciousness or death. Symptoms of overdose of this medicine include convulsions (seizures); hearing loss; confusion; ringing or buzzing in the ears; severe excitement, nervousness, or restlessness; severe dizziness; severe drowsiness; shortness of breath or troubled breathing; and severe weakness.

Side Effects of This Medicine

Along with its needed effects, a medicine may cause some unwanted effects. Although not all of these side effects may occur, if they do occur they may need medical attention.

The following side effects may mean that a serious allergic reaction is occurring. Check with your doctor or get emergency help immediately if they occur, especially if several of them occur at the same time.

Less common or rare

Bluish discoloration or flushing or redness of skin (occurring together with other effects listed in this section); coughing, shortness of breath, troubled breathing, tightness in chest, or wheezing; difficulty in swallowing; dizziness or feeling faint (severe); hive-like swellings (large) on eyelids, face, lips, or tongue; skin rash, itching, or hives; stuffy nose (occurring together with other effects listed in this section)

Also check with your doctor immediately if any of the following side effects occur, especially if several of them occur together:

Rare

Bleeding or crusting sores on lips; chest pain; fever with or without chills; red, thickened, or scaly skin; sores, ulcers, or white spots in mouth (painful); sore throat (unexplained); tenderness, burning, or peeling of skin

Symptoms of overdose

Anxiety, confusion, excitement, irritability, nervousness, restlessness, or trouble in sleeping (severe, especially with products containing caffeine); convulsions (seizures, with products containing caffeine); diarrhea (severe or continuing); dizziness, lightheadedness, drowsiness, or weakness (severe); frequent urination (for products containing caffeine); hallucinations (seeing, hearing, or feeling things that are not there); increased sensitivity to touch or pain (for products containing caffeine); increased thirst; muscle trembling or twitching (for products containing caffeine); nausea or vomiting (severe or continuing), sometimes with blood; ringing or buzzing in ears (continuing) or hearing loss; seeing flashes of "zig-zag" lights (for products containing caffeine); slow, fast, or irregular heartbeat; slow, fast, irregular, or troubled breathing; slurred speech; staggering; stomach pain (severe); uncontrollable flapping movements of the hands, especially in elderly patients; unusual movements of the eyes; vision problems

Also, check with your doctor as soon as possible if any of the following side effects occur:

Less common or rare

Bloody or black, tarry stools; bloody urine; confusion or mental depression; muscle cramps or pain; pinpoint red spots on skin; swollen or painful glands; unusual bleeding or bruising; unusual excitement (mild)

Other side effects may occur that usually do not need medical attention. These side effects may go away during treatment as your body adjusts to the medicine. However, check with your doctor if any of the following side effects continue or are bothersome:

More common

Bloated or "gassy" feeling; dizziness or lightheadedness (mild); drowsiness (mild); heartburn or indigestion; nausea, vomiting, or stomach pain (occurring without other symptoms of overdose)

Other side effects not listed above may also occur in some patients. If you notice any other effects, check with your doctor.

Revised: 07/14/92
Interim revision: 07/12/94

BUTORPHANOL Nasal-Systemic

A commonly used brand name in the U.S. and Canada is Stadol NS.

Description

Butorphanol (byoo-TOR-fa-nole) is a narcotic analgesic (pain medicine) that is sprayed into the nose. It is used to relieve moderate or severe pain. It is also used to relieve pain that occurs after an operation.

Narcotic analgesics act in the central nervous system (CNS) to relieve pain. Some of their side effects are also caused by actions in the CNS.

If a narcotic is used for a long time, it may become habit-forming (causing mental or physical dependence). Physical dependence may lead to withdrawal side effects when you stop taking the medicine.

This medicine is available only with your doctor's or dentist's prescription, in the following dosage form:

Nasal
- Nasal solution (U.S. and Canada)

Before Using This Medicine

In deciding to use a medicine, the risks of taking the medicine must be weighed against the good it will do. This is a decision you and your doctor will make. For butorphanol, the following should be considered:

Allergies—Tell your doctor if you have ever had any unusual or allergic reaction to butorphanol or any other narcotic analgesic. Also tell your health care professional if you are allergic to any other substances, such as foods, preservatives, or dyes.

Pregnancy—Nasal butorphanol has not been studied in pregnant women. However, studies in animals have shown that butorphanol causes a decrease pregnancy rate and an increase in stillbirths. Before taking this medicine make sure your doctor knows if you are pregnant or if you may become pregnant.

Too much use of butorphanol during pregnancy may cause the baby to become dependent on the medicine. This may lead to withdrawal side effects after birth.

Breast-feeding—Although butorphanol may pass into the breast milk, it is not expected to cause problems in nursing babies.

Children—Studies on this medicine have been done only in adult patients, and there is no specific information comparing use of butorphanol in children with use in other age groups.

Older adults—Elderly people are especially sensitive to the effects of butorphanol. This may increase the chance of side effects, especially dizziness, during treatment. Studies in older adults show that butorphanol stays in the body for a longer time than it does in younger adults. Your doctor will consider this when deciding on your dose.

Other medicines—Although certain medicines should not be used together at all, in other cases two different medicines may be used together even if an interaction might occur. In these cases, your doctor may want to change the dose, or other precautions may be necessary. When you are taking butorphanol it is especially important that your health care professional know if you are taking any of the following:

- Central nervous system (CNS) depressants (medicines that make you drowsy or less alert) or
- Tricyclic antidepressants (medicines for depression) (amitriptyline [e.g., Elavil], amoxapine [e.g., Asendin], clomipramine [e.g., Anafranil], desipramine [e.g., Pertofrane], doxepin [e.g., Sinequan], imipramine [e.g., Tofranil], nortriptyline [e.g., Aventyl], protriptyline [e.g., Vivactil], trimipramine [e.g., Surmontil])—The chance of side effects may be increased
- Narcotic pain medicine, other—Withdrawal symptoms may occur if a narcotic you are dependent on is replaced by butorphanol.

Other medical problems—The presence of other medical problems may affect the use of butorphanol. Make sure you tell your doctor if you have any other medical problems, especially:

- CNS disease affecting breathing or
- Emphysema, asthma, or other chronic lung disease or
- Head injury—Some of the side effects of butorphanol can be dangerous if you have any of these conditions
- Drug dependence, especially narcotic abuse, or history of, or
- Emotional problems—The chance of side effects may be increased; also, withdrawal symptoms may occur if a narcotic you are dependent on is replaced by butorphanol
- Heart disease or
- Kidney disease or
- Liver disease—The chance of side effects may be increased

Proper Use of This Medicine

You will be given an instruction sheet with your prescription for butorphanol that explains how to use the pump spray unit. If you have any questions about using the unit, ask your health care professional.

To use:

- *Use this medicine only as directed by your medical doctor or dentist.* Do not use more of it, do not use it more often, and do not use it for a longer time than your medical doctor or dentist told you. This is especially important for elderly patients, who may be more sensitive to the effects of butorphanol. If too much is used, the medicine may become habit-forming (causing mental or physical dependence) or lead to medical problems because of an overdose.
- Remove the protective cover and clip. Before you use each new bottle of butorphanol, the spray pump needs to be started. To do this, point the sprayer away from you and other people or pets. Pump the spray unit firmly about 7 or 8 times. A fine, wide spray should come out by the seventh or eighth time you pump the unit. If the unit is not used for 48 hours or longer, the spray pump should be started again by pumping it 1 or 2 times only.
- Before each use, blow your nose gently.
- For a 1-mg dose, insert the spray tip into one nostril. Close off the other nostril by pressing the side of your nose with your index finger. Tilt your head slightly forward and spray one time. Sniff gently with your mouth closed.
- Remove the spray tip from your nostril. Tilt your head back and sniff gently.
- For a 2-mg dose, repeat these steps using the other nostril.
- Replace the protective cover and clip after each use.

Dosing—The dose of butorphanol will be different for different patients. *Follow your doctor's or dentist's orders or the directions on the label.* The following information includes only the average doses of butorphanol. *If your dose is different, do not change it* unless your doctor or dentist tells you to do so.

- For *nasal* dosage form:
  - —For pain:
    - Adults—1 mg (one spray in one nostril). If pain is not relieved within sixty to ninety minutes,

another spray (1 mg) in one nostril may be used. This dosing procedure may be repeated in three to four hours as needed. However, if pain is severe, a 2-mg dose (one spray in each nostril) may be used every three to four hours, but it is important to remain lying down if drowsiness or dizziness occurs.

• Children and teenagers—Use and dose must be determined by your doctor.

Missed dose—If your medical doctor or dentist has told you to use this medicine on a regular schedule and you miss a dose, use it as soon as you remember. However, if it is almost time for your next dose, skip the missed dose and go back to your regular dosing schedule. *Do not double doses.*

Storage—To store this medicine:

- Keep out of the reach of children. Overdose is very dangerous in young children.
- Store away from heat and direct light.
- Keep the medicine from freezing.
- Do not keep outdated medicine or medicine no longer needed. Be sure that any discarded medicine is out of the reach of children.

Precautions While Using This Medicine

Butorphanol will add to the effects of alcohol and other CNS depressants (medicines that make you drowsy or less alert). Some examples of CNS depressants are antihistamines or medicine for hay fever, other allergies, or colds; sedatives, tranquilizers, or sleeping medicine; other prescription pain medicines, including other narcotics; barbiturates; medicine for seizures; muscle relaxants; or anesthetics, including some dental anesthetics. *Do not drink alcoholic beverages, and check with your medical doctor or dentist before taking any of the medicines listed above, while you are using this medicine.*

This medicine may cause some people to become drowsy, dizzy, or lightheaded, or to feel a false sense of well-being. *Make sure you know how you react to this medicine before you drive, use machines, or do anything else that could be dangerous if you are dizzy or are not alert and clearheaded.*

Dizziness, lightheadedness, or fainting may occur, especially in the first hour after use or when you get up suddenly from a lying or sitting position. Getting up slowly may help lessen this problem.

Before having any kind of surgery (including dental surgery) or emergency treatment, tell the medical doctor or dentist in charge that you are using this medicine.

Butorphanol may cause dryness of the mouth. For temporary relief, use sugarless candy or gum, melt bits of ice in your mouth, or use a saliva substitute. However, if dry mouth continues for more than 2 weeks, check with your dentist. Continuing dryness of the mouth may increase the chance of dental disease, including tooth decay, gum disease, and fungus infections.

If you have been using this medicine regularly for several weeks or more, *do not suddenly stop using it without first checking with your doctor.* Your doctor may want you to reduce gradually the amount you are using before stopping completely, in order to lessen the chance of withdrawal side effects.

If you think you or someone else may have used an overdose, get emergency help at once. Using an overdose of this medicine or taking alcohol or CNS depressants with this medicine may lead to unconsciousness or death. Signs of overdose include convulsions (seizures), confusion, severe nervousness or restlessness, severe dizziness, severe drowsiness, slow or troubled breathing, and severe weakness.

Side Effects of This Medicine

Along with its needed effects, a medicine may cause some unwanted effects. Although not all of these side effects may occur, if they do occur they may need medical attention.

Get emergency help immediately if any of the following symptoms of overdose occur:

Cold, clammy skin; confusion; convulsions (seizures); dizziness (severe); drowsiness (severe); nervousness, restlessness, or weakness (severe); small pupils; slow heartbeat; slow or troubled breathing

Also, check with your doctor as soon as possible if any of the following side effects occur:

More common

Difficulty in breathing; fever; nosebleeds; ringing or buzzing in ears; runny nose; sinus congestion; sneezing; sore throat

Less common or rare

Blurred vision; congestion in chest; cough; difficulty in urinating; difficult or painful breathing; ear pain; fainting; hallucinations; itching; sinus congestion with pain; skin rash or hives

Other side effects may occur that usually do not need medical attention. These side effects may go away during treatment as your body adjusts to the medicine. However, check with your doctor if any of the following side effects continue or are bothersome:

More common

Confusion; constipation; dizziness; drowsiness; dry mouth; flushing; headache; irritation inside nose; loss of appetite; nasal congestion; nausea or vomiting; sweating or clammy feeling; trouble in sleeping; unpleasant taste; weakness (severe)

Less common or rare

Anxious feeling; behavior changes; burning, crawling, or prickling feeling on skin; false sense of well-being; feeling hot; floating feeling; nervousness, sometimes with restlessness; pounding heartbeat; stomach pain; strange dreams; trembling

After you stop using this medicine, your body may need time to adjust. The length of time this takes depends on the amount of medicine you were using and how long you used it. During this period of time, check with your doctor if you notice any of the following side effects:

Anxious feeling; diarrhea; nervousness and restlessness

Other side effects not listed above may also occur in some patients. If you notice any other effects, check with your doctor.

Developed: 12/02/96

CAFFEINE Systemic

Some commonly used brand names are:

In the U.S.—

Caffedrine[1]
Caffedrine Caplets[1]
Dexitac[1]
Enerjets[1]
Keep Alert[1]
NoDoz[1]
NoDoz Maximum Strength Caplets[1]
Pep-Back[1]
Quick Pep[1]
Ultra Pep-Back[1]
Vivarin[1]

In Canada—

Caffedrine[1]
Wake-Up[1]

Note: For quick reference, the following caffeine are numbered to match the corresponding brand names.

This information applies to the following medicines:

1. Caffeine (kaf-FEEN)
2. Citrated Caffeine (SIH-tray-ted)‡
3. Caffeine and Sodium Benzoate (SOE-dee-um BEN-zo-ate)†‡

†Not commercially available in Canada.
‡Generic name product may also be available in the U.S.

Description

Caffeine (kaf-FEEN) belongs to the group of medicines called central nervous system (CNS) stimulants. It is used to help restore mental alertness when unusual tiredness or weakness or drowsiness occurs. Caffeine's use as an alertness aid should be only occasional. It is not intended to replace sleep and should not be used regularly for this purpose.

Caffeine is also used in combination with ergotamine (for treatment of migraine and cluster headaches) or with certain pain relievers, such as aspirin or aspirin and acetaminophen. When used in this way, caffeine may increase the effectiveness of the other medicines. Caffeine is sometimes used in combination with an antihistamine to overcome the drowsiness caused by the antihistamine.

Caffeine may also be used for other conditions as determined by your doctor.

Caffeine is present in coffee, tea, soft drinks, cocoa, and chocolate.

As a medicine, it is available without a prescription; however, your health care professional may have special instructions on its proper use. Caffeine is available in the following dosage forms:

Oral

Caffeine
- Extended-release capsules (U.S.)
- Tablets (U.S. and Canada)

Citrated caffeine
- Tablets (U.S.)

Before Using This Medicine

If you are taking this medicine without a prescription, carefully read and follow any precautions on the label. For caffeine, the following should be considered:

Allergies—Tell your doctor if you have ever had any unusual or allergic reaction to aminophylline, caffeine, dyphylline, oxtriphylline, theobromine (also found in cocoa or chocolate), or theophylline. Also tell your health care professional if you are allergic to any other substances, such as foods, preservatives, or dyes.

Pregnancy—Studies in humans have shown that caffeine may cause miscarriage or may slow the growth of a developing fetus when given in doses greater than 300 mg a day. In addition, use of large amounts of caffeine by the mother during pregnancy may cause problems with the heart rhythm of the fetus. Therefore, it is recommended that pregnant women consume less than 300 mg of caffeine (an amount equal to 3 cups of coffee) a day. Studies in animals have shown that caffeine causes birth defects when given in very large doses (amounts equal to 12 to 24 cups of coffee a day) and problems with bone growth when given in smaller doses.

Breast-feeding—Caffeine passes into breast milk in small amounts and may build up in the nursing baby. Studies have shown that babies may appear jittery and have trouble in sleeping when their mothers drink large amounts of caffeine-containing beverages.

Children—With the exception of infants, there is no specific information comparing use of caffeine in children with use in other age groups. However, this medicine is not expected to cause different side effects or problems in children than it does in adults.

Older adults—Many medicines have not been studied specifically in older people. Therefore, it may not be known whether they work exactly the same way they do in younger adults or if they cause different side effects or problems in older people. There is no specific information comparing use of caffeine in the elderly with use in other age groups.

Other medicines—Although certain medicines should not be used together at all, in other cases 2 different medicines may be used together even if an interaction might occur. In these cases, your doctor may want to change the dose, or other precautions may be necessary. When you are taking caffeine, it is especially important that your health care professional know if you are taking any of the following:

- Amantadine (e.g., Symmetrel) or
- Amphetamines (e.g., Desoxyn, Dexedrine) or
- Appetite suppressants (diet pills), except fenfluramine (e.g., Pondimin), or
- Chlophedianol (e.g., Ulone) or
- Cocaine or
- Medicine for asthma or other breathing problems or
- Medicine for colds, sinus problems, hay fever or other allergies (including nose drops or sprays) or
- Methylphenidate (e.g., Ritalin) or
- Nabilone (e.g., Cesamet) or
- Other medicines or beverages containing caffeine or
- Pemoline (e.g., Cylert)—Using these medicines with caffeine may increase the CNS-stimulant effects, such as nervousness, irritability, or trouble in sleeping, or possibly cause convulsions (seizures) or changes in the rhythm of your heart
- Monoamine oxidase (MAO) inhibitors (furazolidone [e.g., Furoxone], isocarboxazid [e.g., Marplan], phenelzine [e.g., Nardil], procarbazine [e.g., Matulane], selegiline

[e.g., Eldepryl], tranylcypromine [e.g., Parnate])—Taking large amounts of caffeine while you are taking or within 2 weeks of taking monoamine oxidase (MAO) inhibitors may cause extremely high blood pressure or dangerous changes in the rhythm of your heart; taking small amounts of caffeine may cause mild high blood pressure and fast heartbeat

Other medical problems—The presence of other medical problems may affect the use of caffeine. Make sure you tell your doctor if you have any other medical problems, especially:

- Agoraphobia (fear of being in open places) or
- Anxiety or
- Heart disease or
- High blood pressure or
- Panic attacks or
- Trouble in sleeping—Caffeine may make the condition worse
- Liver disease—Higher blood levels of caffeine may result, increasing the chance of side effects

Proper Use of This Medicine

For patients taking the *extended-release form* of this medicine:

- Swallow the capsule whole.
- Do not break, crush, or chew the capsule before swallowing.

Take caffeine in capsule or tablet form only as directed. Do not take more of it, do not take it more often, and do not take it for a longer time than directed. Taking too much may increase the chance of side effects. It may also become habit-forming.

If you think this medicine is not working properly after you have taken it for a long time, *do not increase the dose.* To do so may increase the chance of side effects.

Dosing—The dose of caffeine will be different for different patients. *Follow the directions on the label.*

- For unusual tiredness or weakness, or drowsiness:
  - —For *long-acting* dosage forms (extended-release capsules):
    - Adults and children 12 years of age and older—The usual dose is 200 to 250 milligrams (mg) of caffeine every three or four hours. You should not take more than 1 gram in twenty-four hours.
    - Children up to 12 years of age—Use is not recommended.
  - —For *regular* (short-acting) dosage forms (tablets):
    - Adults and children 12 years of age and older—The usual dose is 100 to 200 mg of caffeine every three or four hours. You should not take more than 1 gram in twenty-four hours.
    - Children up to 12 years of age—Use is not recommended.
  - —For citrated caffeine (tablets):
    - Adults and children 12 years of age and older—The usual dose is 65 to 325 mg of caffeine three times a day, as needed. You should not take more than 1 gram in twenty-four hours.
    - Children up to 12 years of age—Use is not recommended.

Storage—To store this medicine:

- Keep out of the reach of children.
- Store away from heat and direct light.
- Do not store in the bathroom, near the kitchen sink, or in other damp places. Heat or moisture may cause the medicine to break down.
- Do not keep outdated medicine or medicine no longer needed. Be sure that any discarded medicine is out of the reach of children.

Precautions While Using This Medicine

Capsules or tablets containing caffeine are for occasional use only. They are not intended to replace sleep and should not be used regularly for this purpose. If unusual tiredness or weakness or drowsiness continues or returns often, check with your doctor.

The recommended dose of this medicine contains about the same amount of caffeine as a cup of coffee. Do not drink large amounts of caffeine-containing coffee, tea, or soft drinks while you are taking this medicine. Also, do not take large amounts of other medicines that contain caffeine. To do so may cause unwanted effects.

The amount of caffeine in some common foods and beverages is as follows:

- Coffee, brewed—40 to 180 milligrams (mg) per cup.
- Coffee, instant—30 to 120 mg per cup.
- Coffee, decaffeinated—3 to 5 mg per cup.
- Tea, brewed American—20 to 90 mg per cup.
- Tea, brewed imported—25 to 110 mg per cup.
- Tea, instant—28 mg per cup.
- Tea, canned iced—22 to 36 mg per 12 ounces.
- Cola and other soft drinks, caffeine-containing—36 to 90 mg per 12 ounces.
- Cola and other soft drinks, decaffeinated—0 mg per 12 ounces.
- Cocoa—4 mg per cup.
- Chocolate, milk—3 to 6 mg per ounce.
- Chocolate, bittersweet—25 mg per ounce.

Caffeine may cause nervousness or irritability, trouble in sleeping, dizziness, or a fast or pounding heartbeat. If these effects occur, discontinue the use of caffeine-containing beverages or medicines, or large amounts of chocolate-containing products.

To prevent trouble in sleeping, do not take caffeine-containing beverages or medicines too close to bedtime.

Side Effects of This Medicine

Along with its needed effects, a medicine may cause some unwanted effects. Although not all of these side effects may occur, they may be more likely to occur if caffeine is taken in large doses or more often than recommended. If they do occur, they may need medical attention.

Check with your doctor as soon as possible if any of the following side effects occur:

More common

Diarrhea; dizziness; fast heartbeat; irritability, nervousness, or severe jitters in newborn babies; nausea (severe); tremors; trouble in sleeping; vomiting

Symptoms of overdose

Abdominal or stomach pain; agitation, anxiety, excitement, or restlessness; confusion or delirium; convulsions (seizures)—in acute overdose; fast or irregular heartbeat; fever; frequent urination; headache; increased sensitivity to touch or pain; irritability; muscle trembling or twitching; nausea and vomiting, sometimes with blood; painful, swollen abdomen or vomiting in newborn babies; ringing or other sounds in ears; seeing flashes of ''zig-zag'' lights; trouble in sleeping; whole-body tremors in newborn babies

Other side effects may occur that usually do not need medical attention. These side effects may go away during treatment as your body adjusts to the medicine. However, check with your doctor if any of the following side effects continue or are bothersome:

More common

Nausea (mild); nervousness or jitters (mild)

After you stop using this medicine, your body may need time to adjust. The length of time this takes depends on the amount of medicine you were using and how long you used it. During this time check with your doctor if you notice any of the following side effects:

More common

Anxiety; dizziness; headache; irritability; muscle tension; nausea; nervousness; stuffy nose; unusual tiredness

Other side effects not listed above may also occur in some patients. If you notice any other effects, check with your doctor.

Additional Information

Once a medicine has been approved for marketing for a certain use, experience may show that it is also useful for other medical problems. Although these uses are not included in product labeling, caffeine is used in certain patients with the following medical conditions:

- Neonatal apnea (breathing problems in newborn babies)
- Postoperative infant apnea (breathing problems after surgery in young babies)
- Psychiatric disorders requiring electroconvulsive or shock therapy (ECT)

Other than the above information, there is no additional information relating to proper use, precautions, or side effects for these uses.

Revised: 07/12/94

CALAMINE Topical

Some commonly used brand names are:

In the U.S.—

Calamox

Generic name product may be available.

In Canada—

Diaper Rash Ointment

Onguent de Calamine

Generic name product may be available.

Description

Calamine (KAL-a-meen) is used to relieve the itching, pain, and discomfort of minor skin irritations, such as those caused by poison ivy, poison oak, and poison sumac. This medicine also dries oozing and weeping caused by poison ivy, poison oak, and poison sumac.

Calamine is available without prescription in the following dosage forms:

Topical

- Lotion (U.S. and Canada)
- Ointment (U.S. and Canada)

Before Using This Medicine

If you are using this medicine without a prescription, carefully read and follow any precautions on the label. For calamine, the following should be considered:

Allergies—Tell your doctor if you have ever had any unusual or allergic reaction to calamine. Also tell your health care professional if you are allergic to any other substances, such as foods, preservatives, or dyes.

Pregnancy—Calamine has not been shown to cause birth defects or other problems in humans.

Breast-feeding—Calamine has not been reported to cause problems in nursing babies.

Children—Although there is no specific information comparing use of calamine in children with use in other age groups, this medicine is not expected to cause different side effects or problems in children than it does in adults.

Older adults—Many medicines have not been studied specifically in older people. Therefore, it may not be known whether they work exactly the same way they do in younger adults. Although there is no specific information comparing use of calamine in the elderly with use in other age groups, this medicine is not expected to cause different side effects or problems in older people than it does in younger adults.

Other medicines—Although certain medicines should not be used together at all, in other cases two different medicines may be used together even if an interaction might occur. In these cases, your doctor may want to change the dose, or other precautions may be necessary. Tell your health care professional if you are using any other topical prescription or nonprescription (over-the-counter [OTC]) medicine that is to be applied to the same area of the skin.

Proper Use of This Medicine

Calamine is for external use only. Do not swallow it and do not use it on the eyes or mucous membranes such as the inside of the mouth, nose, genital (sex organs), or anal areas.

To use *calamine lotion:*
- Shake the lotion well before using.
- Moisten a pledget of cotton with the lotion.
- Use the moistened pledget to apply the lotion to the affected skin area(s).
- Allow the medicine to dry on the skin.

To use *calamine ointment:*
- Apply enough medicine to cover affected skin area(s) and rub in gently.

Dosing—*Follow your doctor's orders or the directions on the label.* The following information includes only the average dose of calamine. *If your dose is different, do not change it* unless your doctor tells you to do so.

- For minor skin irritations:
  - —For *topical* dosage forms (lotion, ointment):
    - Adults and children—Apply to the affected area(s) of skin as often as needed.

Storage—To store this medicine:
- Keep out of the reach of children.
- Store away from heat and direct light.
- Keep the medicine from freezing. Do not refrigerate.
- Do not keep outdated medicine or medicine no longer needed. Be sure that any discarded medicine is out of the reach of children.

Precautions While Using This Medicine

If your condition gets worse or if it does not improve within 7 days, or if rash or irritation develops, stop using calamine and check with your doctor.

Developed: 05/26/95

CALCIPOTRIENE Topical

A commonly used brand name in the U.S. and Canada is Dovonex. Another commonly used name is MC 903.

Description

Calcipotriene (kal-si-poe-TRY-een) is used to treat psoriasis. It works by controlling the overproduction of skin cells in areas affected by psoriasis.

Calcipotriene is available only with your doctor's prescription in the following dosage forms:

Topical
- Cream (U.S. and Canada)
- Ointment (U.S. and Canada)
- Solution (U.S. and Canada)

Before Using This Medicine

In deciding to use a medicine, the risks of using the medicine must be weighed against the good it will do. This is a decision you and your doctor will make. For calcipotriene, the following should be considered:

Allergies—Tell your doctor if you have ever had any unusual or allergic reaction to calcipotriene or to other ingredients of the preparation, which you may find listed on the label. Also tell your health care professional if you are allergic to any other substances, such as foods, preservatives, or dyes.

Pregnancy—Calcipotriene has not been studied in pregnant women. However, studies in animals have shown that calcipotriene taken in high doses by mouth causes problems in the mother and the fetus, including birth defects. Before using this medicine, make sure your doctor knows if you are pregnant or if you may become pregnant.

Breast-feeding—It is not known whether calcipotriene passes into breast milk. Although most medicines pass into breast milk in small amounts, many of them may be used safely while breast-feeding. Mothers who are using this medicine and who wish to breast-feed should discuss this with their doctor.

Children—This medicine has been tested in a limited number of children 2 to 14 years of age with psoriasis on less than 30% of the body. When used for 8 weeks or less, the medicine has not been shown to cause different side effects or problems than it does in adults. However, more studies are needed.

Older adults—Skin-related side effects caused by calcipotriene may be more severe when they occur in patients over 65 years of age.

Other medicines—Although certain medicines should not be used together at all, in other cases two different medicines may be used together even if an interaction might occur. In these cases, your doctor may want to change the dose, or other precautions may be necessary. Tell your health care professional if you are taking or using any other prescription or nonprescription (over-the-counter [OTC]) medicine.

Other medical problems—The presence of other medical problems may affect the use of calcipotriene. Make sure you tell your doctor if you have any other medical problems, especially:
- Highly irritated areas of psoriasis on the scalp—Calcipotriene topical solution may increase the skin irritation because of the alcohol in the product
- Hypercalcemia (high blood levels of calcium) or
- Hypercalciuria (high urine levels of calcium) or
- Hypervitaminosis D (high blood levels of vitamin D)—Calcipotriene may increase the chance of kidney stone formation
- Kidney stones (or history of)—Calcipotriene may make this condition worse

Proper Use of This Medicine

Calcipotriene is for external use only. Do not use this medicine orally and do not apply it in your vagina. Use this medicine only as directed. Do not use more of it, do not use it more often, and do not use it for a longer time than your doctor ordered. To do so may increase the chance of side effects.

To help clear up your skin problem completely, it is very important that you keep using calcipotriene for the full time of treatment. Do not miss any doses.

Unless otherwise directed by your doctor, *do not use more than 100 grams of calcipotriene ointment or cream in 1 week* (that is, one 100-gram tube or three 30-gram tubes or six 15-gram tubes in 1 week). Do not use more than 60 milliliters of the topical solution for the scalp in 1 week.

Do not use this medicine on your face, near the eyes, inside your nose or mouth, or on unaffected areas of the skin. If you accidentally get some on these areas, wash it off with water right away.

Use this medicine sparingly in the folds of your skin because it is more likely to cause irritation there.

Wash your hands after using this medicine to avoid accidentally getting the medicine on your face or on unaffected areas of the skin.

Do not use this medicine for treating skin problems other than the one for which it was prescribed by your doctor.

For *cream* and *ointment* dosage forms:

- Apply enough medicine to cover the areas of your skin affected by psoriasis and rub in gently and well. *The treated areas should not be covered (for instance, with a bandage or plastic wrap) after the medicine is applied.*
- If you are being treated with calcipotriene ointment in combination with ultraviolet light (found in sunlight and some special lamps), *do not apply the morning dose of calcipotriene before being treated with the ultraviolet light. It can be applied afterwards.*

For *solution* dosage form:

- Before applying the medicine to your scalp, comb your dry hair to remove any flakes, then part your hair so that you can see the scalp lesions. Apply the solution to the lesions and rub it in gently but completely. *Do not apply the medicine if the lesions are very irritated* because the alcohol in the product may make the irritation worse. Try not to get any medicine on your forehead.

Dosing—*Follow your doctor's orders or the directions on the label.* The following information includes only the average dose of calcipotriene. *If your dose is different, do not change it* unless your doctor tells you to do so.

The length of time you use the medicine depends on the severity of your psoriasis.

- For *topical* dosage form (cream):
  - —For psoriasis:
    - Adults—Apply to the affected area(s) of the skin two times a day, in the morning and evening. Treatment may be continued for six to eight weeks or as determined by your doctor.
    - Children—Use and dose must be determined by your doctor.
- For *topical* dosage form (ointment):
  - —For psoriasis:
    - Adults—Apply to the affected area(s) of the skin one or two times a day, in the morning and evening. Treatment may be continued for six to eight weeks or as determined by your doctor.
    - Children—Use and dose must be determined by your doctor.
- For *topical* dosage form (solution):
  - —For psoriasis:
    - Adults—Apply to the affected area(s) of the scalp two times a day, in the morning and evening. Treatment may be continued for six to eight weeks or as determined by your doctor.
    - Children—Use and dose must be determined by your doctor.

Missed dose—If you miss a dose of this medicine, apply it as soon as possible. However, if it is almost time for your next dose, skip the missed dose and go back to your regular dosing schedule. Do not double doses.

Storage—To store this medicine:

- Keep out of the reach of children.
- Store away from heat and direct light.
- Keep the medicine from freezing. Do not refrigerate.
- Do not keep outdated medicine or medicine no longer needed. Be sure that any discarded medicine is out of the reach of children.
- Keep the topical solution away from open flame.

Precautions While Using This Medicine

Calcipotriene may cause irritation of the affected area(s) of your skin for a short time after you have applied it. Sometimes it may also cause irritation of the surrounding normal skin. If this happens, try not to scratch the area.

If the irritation continues, if you develop rash on your face, or if the medicine causes any other problems for you, *stop using the medicine and check with your doctor.*

You may have to see your doctor regularly while using this medicine so that your doctor can check for any side effects, especially an increase in the level of calcium in your blood or urine, because this may lead to kidney stone formation.

Your doctor may tell you when you should expect to notice an improvement in your condition (usually within 2 to 8 weeks). If your condition has not improved by then or if it becomes worse, check with your doctor.

Side Effects of This Medicine

Along with its needed effects, a medicine may cause some unwanted effects. Although not all of these side effects may occur, if they do occur they may need medical attention.

Check with your doctor as soon as possible if any of the following side effects occur:

More common

Redness and swelling of skin with itching; skin rash; worsening of psoriasis, including spreading to the face and scalp

Rare—for ointment dosage form only

Abdominal or stomach pain, constipation, depression, loss of appetite, loss of weight, muscle weakness, nausea, thirst, tiring easily, and vomiting; burning, itching, and pain in hairy areas; pus in the hair follicles; thinning, weakness, or wasting away of skin

Other side effects may occur that usually do not need medical attention. These side effects may go away during treatment as your body adjusts to the medicine. However, check with your doctor if any of the following side effects continue or are bothersome:

More common

Burning, dryness, irritation, peeling, or redness of skin

Less common or rare—for cream and ointment dosage forms only

Darkening of treated areas of skin

Other side effects not listed above may also occur in some patients. If you notice any other effects, check with your doctor.

Revised: 08/20/97

CALCITONIN Systemic

Some commonly used brand names are:

In the U.S.—

Calcimar[2]
Cibacalcin[1]
Miacalcin[2]

In Canada—

Calcimar[2]

Note: For quick reference, the following calcitonin are numbered to match the corresponding brand names.

This information applies to the following medicines:

1. Calcitonin-Human†
2. Calcitonin-Salmon

†Not commercially available in Canada.

Description

Calcitonin (kal-si-TOE-nin) is used to treat Paget's disease of bone. It also may be used to prevent continuing bone loss in women with postmenopausal osteoporosis and to treat hypercalcemia (too much calcium in the blood). This medicine may be used to treat other conditions as determined by your doctor.

Calcitonin is available only with your doctor's prescription, in the following dosage forms:

Parenteral

Calcitonin-Human
- Injection (U.S.)

Calcitonin-Salmon
- Injection (U.S. and Canada)

Before Using This Medicine

In deciding to use a medicine, the risks of taking the medicine must be weighed against the good it will do. This is a decision you and your doctor will make. For calcitonin, the following should be considered:

Allergies—Tell your doctor if you have ever had any unusual or allergic reaction to calcitonin or other proteins. Also tell your health care professional if you are allergic to any other substances, such as foods, preservatives, or dyes.

Diet—Make certain your health care professional knows if your diet includes large amounts of calcium-containing foods and/or vitamin D–containing foods, such as milk or other dairy products. Calcium and vitamin D may cause the calcitonin to be less effective in treating a high blood calcium. Also let your health care professional know if you are on any special diet, such as low-sodium or low-sugar diet.

Pregnancy—Calcitonin has not been studied in pregnant women. However, in animal studies, calcitonin has been shown to lower the birth weight of the baby when the mother was given a dose of calcitonin many times the human dose.

Breast-feeding—Calcitonin has not been reported to cause problems in nursing babies. However, studies in animals have shown that calcitonin may decrease the flow of breast milk.

Children—Studies on this medicine have been done only in adult patients, and there is no specific information comparing the use of calcitonin in children with use in other age groups. Therefore, be sure to discuss with your doctor the use of this medicine in children.

Older adults—Many medicines have not been studied specifically in older people. Therefore, it may not be known whether they work exactly the same way they do in younger adults. Although there is no specific information comparing the use of calcitonin in the elderly with use in other age groups, this medicine is not expected to cause different side effects or problems in older people than it does in younger adults. Calcitonin is often used in elderly patients.

Other medicine—Although certain medicines should not be used together at all, in other cases two different medicines may be used together even if an interaction might occur. In these cases, your doctor may want to change the dose, or other precautions may be necessary. Tell your health care professional if you are using any other prescription or nonprescription (over-the-counter [OTC]) medicine.

Proper Use of This Medicine

This medicine is for injection only. If you will be giving yourself the injections, make sure you understand exactly how to give them, including how to fill the syringe before injection. If you have any questions about this, check with your doctor.

Use the calcitonin only when the contents of the syringe are clear and colorless. Do not use it if it looks grainy or discolored.

Dosing—The dose of calcitonin will be different for different patients. *Follow your doctor's orders or the directions on the label.* The following information includes only the average doses of calcitonin. *If your dose is different, do not change it* unless your doctor tells you to do so.

The number of doses you receive, the time allowed between doses, and the length of time you receive the medicine depends on the medical problem for which you are receiving calcitonin.

For calcitonin-human

- For *injection* dosage form:
  - —For Paget's disease of bone:
    - Adults—To start, 500 micrograms (mcg) injected under the skin once a day. Your doctor may reduce your dose or increase the time between doses. Or, your doctor may give you a smaller dose to start and increase your dose over two weeks.
    - Children—Dose must be determined by your doctor.

For calcitonin-salmon

- For *injection* dosage form:
  - —For Paget's disease of bone:
    - Adults—To start, 100 Units injected into a muscle or under the skin once a day, once every other day, or three times a week. Your doctor may reduce your dose or increase the time between doses.
    - Children—Dose must be determined by your doctor.
  - —For hypercalcemia (too much calcium in the blood):
    - Adults—To start, 4 Units per kilogram (kg) (1.8 Units per pound) of body weight injected into a muscle or under the skin every twelve hours. Your doctor may increase your dose or increase the time between doses.
    - Children—Dose must be determined by your doctor.
  - —For postmenopausal osteoporosis:
    - Adults—100 Units injected into a muscle or under the skin once a day, once every other day, or three times a week. Or, your doctor may give you a smaller dose to start and increase your dose over two weeks.
    - Children—Dose must be determined by your doctor.

Missed dose—If you miss a dose of this medicine and your dosing schedule is:

- Two doses a day—If you remember within 2 hours of the missed dose, give it right away. Then go back to your regular dosing schedule. But if you do not remember the missed dose until later, skip it and go back to your regular dosing schedule. Do not double doses.
- One dose a day—Give the missed dose as soon as possible. Then go back to your regular dosing schedule. If you do not remember the missed dose until the next day, skip it and go back to your regular dosing schedule. Do not double doses.
- One dose every other day—Give the missed dose as soon as possible if you remember it on the day it should be given. Then go back to your regular dosing schedule. If you do not remember the missed dose until the next day, give it at that time. Then skip a day and start your dosing schedule again.
- One dose three times a week—Give the missed dose the next day. Then set each injection back a day for the rest of the week. Go back to your regular Monday-Wednesday-Friday schedule the following week. Do not double doses.

If you have any questions about this, check with your doctor.

Storage—To store this medicine:

- Keep out of the reach of children.
- Store away from heat and direct light.
- Store *calcitonin-human* at a temperature below 77 °F. Do not refrigerate. Use prepared solution within 6 hours.
- Store *calcitonin-salmon* in the refrigerator. However, keep it from freezing.
- Do not keep outdated medicine or medicine no longer needed. Be sure that any discarded medicine is out of the reach of children.

Precautions While Using This Medicine

Your doctor should check your progress at regular visits to make sure that this medicine does not cause unwanted effects.

If you are using this medicine for hypercalcemia (too much calcium in the blood), your doctor may want you to follow a low-calcium diet. If you have any questions about this, check with your doctor.

Side Effects of This Medicine

Along with its needed effects, a medicine may cause some unwanted effects. Although not all of these side effects may occur, if they do occur they may need medical attention.

Check with your doctor as soon as possible if either of the following side effects occurs:

Rare

Skin rash or hives

Other side effects may occur that usually do not need medical attention. These side effects may go away during treatment as your body adjusts to the medicine. However,

check with your doctor if any of the following side effects continue or are bothersome:

More common

Diarrhea; flushing or redness of face, ears, hands, or feet; loss of appetite; nausea or vomiting; pain, redness, soreness, or swelling at place of injection; stomach pain

Less common

Increased frequency of urination

Rare

Chills; dizziness; headache; pressure in chest; stuffy nose; tenderness or tingling of hands or feet; trouble in breathing; weakness

Other side effects not listed above may also occur in some patients. If you notice any other effects, check with your doctor.

Additional Information

Once a medicine has been approved for marketing for a certain use, experience may show that it is also useful for other medical problems. Although this use is not included in product labeling, calcitonin is used in certain patients with the following medical condition:

- Osteoporosis caused by hormone problems, certain drugs, and other causes

Other than the above information, there is no additional information relating to proper use, precautions, or side effects for this use.

Revised: 05/13/92
Interim revision: 06/27/94

CALCIUM CHANNEL BLOCKING AGENTS Systemic

Some commonly used brand names are:

In the U.S.—

Adalat[7]
Adalat CC[7]
Bepadin[1]
Calan[9]
Calan SR[9]
Cardene[6]
Cardizem[2]
Cardizem CD[2]
Cardizem SR[2]
Dilacor-XR[2]
DynaCirc[5]
Isoptin[9]
Isoptin SR[9]
Nimotop[8]
Plendil[3]
Procardia[7]
Procardia XL[7]
Vascor[1]
Verelan[9]

In Canada—

Adalat[7]
Adalat FT[7]
Adalat P.A.[7]
Apo-Diltiaz[2]
Apo-Nifed[7]
Apo-Verap[9]
Cardene[6]
Cardizem[2]
Cardizem SR[2]
Isoptin[9]
Isoptin SR[9]
Nimotop[8]
Novo-Diltazem[2]
Novo-Nifedin[7]
Novo-Veramil[9]
Nu-Diltiaz[2]
Nu-Nifed[7]
Nu-Verap[9]
Plendil[3]
Renedil[3]
Sibelium[4]
Syn-Diltiazem[2]

Note: For quick reference, the following calcium channel blocking agents are numbered to match the corresponding brand names.

This information applies to the following medicines:

1. Bepridil (BE-pri-dil)†
2. Diltiazem (dil-TYE-a-zem)‡§
3. Felodipine (fe-LOE-di-peen)
4. Flunarizine (floo-NAR-i-zeen)*
5. Isradipine (is-RA-di-peen)†
6. Nicardipine (nye-KAR-de-peen)
7. Nifedipine (nye-FED-i-peen)‡
8. Nimodipine (nye-MOE-di-peen)
9. Verapamil (ver-AP-a-mil)‡§

*Not commercially available in the U.S.
†Not commercially available in Canada.
‡Generic name product may also be available in the U.S.
§Generic name product may also be available in Canada.

Description

Bepridil, diltiazem, felodipine, flunarizine, isradipine, nicardipine, nifedipine, nimodipine, and verapamil belong to the group of medicines called calcium channel blockers.

Calcium channel blocking agents affect the movement of calcium into the cells of the heart and blood vessels. As a result, they relax blood vessels and increase the supply of blood and oxygen to the heart while reducing its workload.

Some of the calcium channel blocking agents are used to relieve and control angina pectoris (chest pain).

Some are also used to treat high blood pressure (hypertension). High blood pressure adds to the workload of the heart and arteries. If it continues for a long time, the heart and arteries may not function properly. This can damage the blood vessels of the brain, heart, and kidneys, resulting in a stroke, heart failure, or kidney failure. High blood pressure may also increase the risk of heart attacks. These problems may be less likely to occur if blood pressure is controlled.

Flunarizine is used to prevent migraine headaches.

Nimodipine is used to prevent and treat problems caused by a burst blood vessel in the head (also known as a ruptured aneurysm or subarachnoid hemorrhage).

Other calcium channel blocking agents may also be used for these and other conditions as determined by your doctor.

These medicines are available only with your doctor's prescription, in the following dosage forms:

Oral

Bepridil
- Tablets (U.S.)

Diltiazem
- Extended-release capsules (U.S. and Canada)
- Tablets (U.S. and Canada)

Felodipine
- Extended-release tablets (U.S. and Canada)

Flunarizine
- Capsules (Canada)

Isradipine
- Capsules (U.S.)

Nicardipine
- Capsules (U.S. and Canada)

Nifedipine
- Capsules (U.S. and Canada)
- Tablets (Canada)
- Extended-release tablets (U.S. and Canada)

Nimodipine
- Capsules (U.S. and Canada)

Verapamil
- Extended-release capsules (U.S.)
- Tablets (U.S. and Canada)
- Extended-release tablets (U.S. and Canada)

Parenteral

Diltiazem
- Injection (U.S.)

Verapamil
- Injection (U.S. and Canada)

Before Using This Medicine

In deciding to use a medicine, the risks of taking the medicine must be weighed against the good it will do. This is a decision you and your doctor will make. For the calcium channel blocking agents, the following should be considered:

Allergies—Tell your doctor if you have ever had any unusual or allergic reaction to bepridil, diltiazem, felodipine, flunarizine, isradipine, nicardipine, nifedipine, nimodipine, or verapamil. Also tell your health care professional if you are allergic to any other substances, such as foods, preservatives, or dyes.

Pregnancy—Calcium channel blockers have not been studied in pregnant women. However, studies in animals have shown that large doses of calcium channel blockers cause birth defects, prolonged pregnancy, poor bone development, and stillbirth.

Breast-feeding—Although bepridil, diltiazem, nifedipine, verapamil, and possibly other calcium channel blockers, pass into breast milk, they have not been reported to cause problems in nursing babies.

Children—Although there is no specific information comparing use of this medicine in children with use in other age groups, it is not expected to cause different side effects or problems in children than it does in adults.

Older adults—Elderly people may be especially sensitive to the effects of calcium channel blockers. This may increase the chance of side effects during treatment.

Other medicines—Although certain medicines should not be used together at all, in other cases two different medicines may be used together even if an interaction might occur. In these cases, your doctor may want to change the dose, or other precautions may be necessary. When taking calcium channel blockers it is especially important that your health care professional know if you are taking any of the following:

- Acetazolamide (e.g., Diamox) or
- Amphotericin B by injection (e.g., Fungizone) or
- Corticosteroids (cortisone-like medicine) or
- Dichlorphenamide (e.g., Daranide) or
- Diuretics (water pills) or
- Methazolamide (e.g., Naptazane)—These medicines can cause hypokalemia (low levels of potassium in the body), which can increase the unwanted effects of bepridil
- Beta-blockers (acebutolol [e.g., Sectral], atenolol [e.g., Tenormin], betaxolol [e.g., Kerlone], carteolol [e.g., Cartrol], labetalol [e.g., Normodyne], metoprolol [e.g., Lopressor], nadolol [e.g., Corgard], oxprenolol [e.g., Trasicor], penbutolol [e.g., Levatol], pindolol [e.g., Visken], propranolol [e.g., Inderal], sotalol [e.g., Sotacor], timolol [e.g., Blocadren])—Effects of both may be increased. In addition, unwanted effects may occur if a calcium channel blocker or a beta-blocker is stopped suddenly after use together
- Carbamazepine (e.g., Tegretol) or
- Cyclosporine (e.g., Sandimmune) or
- Procainamide (e.g., Pronestyl) or
- Quinidine (e.g., Quinidex)—Effects of these medicines may be increased if they are used with some calcium channel blockers
- Digitalis glycosides (heart medicine)—Effects of these medicines may be increased if they are used with some calcium channel blockers
- Disopyramide (e.g., Norpace)—Effects of some calcium channel blockers on the heart may be increased

Also, tell your health care professional if you are using any of the following medicines in the eye:

- Betaxolol (e.g., Betoptic) or
- Levobunolol (e.g., Betagan) or
- Metipranolol (e.g., OptiPranolol) or
- Timolol (e.g., Timoptic)—Effects on the heart and blood pressure may be increased

Other medical problems—The presence of other medical problems may affect the use of the calcium channel blockers. Make sure you tell your doctor if you have any other medical problems, especially:

- Heart rhythm problems (history of)—Bepridil can cause serious heart rhythm problems
- Kidney disease or
- Liver disease—Effects of the calcium channel blocker may be increased
- Mental depression (history of)—Flunarizine may cause mental depression
- Parkinson's disease or similar problems—Flunarizine can cause parkinsonian-like effects
- Other heart or blood vessel disorders—Calcium channel blockers may make some heart conditions worse

Proper Use of This Medicine

Take this medicine exactly as directed even if you feel well and do not notice any signs of chest pain. Do not take more of this medicine and do not take it more often than your doctor ordered. Do not miss any doses.

For patients taking *bepridil:*
- If this medicine causes upset stomach, it can be taken with meals or at bedtime.

For patients taking *diltiazem extended-release capsules:*
- Swallow the capsule whole, without crushing or chewing it.
- *Do not change to another brand without checking with your physician.* Different brands have different doses. If you refill your medicine and it looks different, check with your pharmacist.

For patients taking *nifedipine or verapamil extended-release capsules:*
- Swallow the capsule whole, without crushing or chewing it.

For patients taking *regular nifedipine or extended-release felodipine or nifedipine tablets:*
- Swallow the tablet whole, without breaking, crushing, or chewing it.
- If you are taking *Procardia XL*, you may sometimes notice what looks like a tablet in your stool. That is just the empty shell that is left after the medicine has been absorbed into your body.

For patients taking *verapamil extended-release tablets:*
- Swallow the tablet whole, without crushing or chewing it. However, if your doctor tells you to, you may break the tablet in half.
- Take the medicine with food or milk.

For patients taking this medicine *for high blood pressure:*
- In addition to the use of the medicine your doctor has prescribed, appropriate treatment for your high blood pressure may include weight control and care in the types of food you eat, especially foods high in sodium (salt). Your doctor will tell you which factors are most important for you. You should check with your doctor before changing your diet.
- Many patients who have high blood pressure will not notice any signs of the problem. In fact, many may feel normal. It is very important that you *take your medicine exactly as directed* and that you keep your appointments with your doctor even if you feel well.
- Remember that this medicine will not cure your high blood pressure but it does help control it. Therefore, you must continue to take it as directed if you expect to lower your blood pressure and keep it down. *You may have to take high blood pressure medicine for the rest of your life.* If high blood pressure is not treated, it can cause serious problems such as heart failure, blood vessel disease, stroke, or kidney disease.

Dosing—The dose of these medicines will be different for different patients. *Follow your doctor's orders or the directions on the label.* The following information includes only the average doses of these medicines. *If your dose is different, do not change it* unless your doctor tells you to do so.

The number of capsules or tablets that you take depends on the strength of the medicine. Also, *the number of doses you take each day, the time allowed between doses, and the length of time you take the medicine depend on the medical problem for which you are taking calcium channel blocking agents.*

For bepridil
- For *oral* dosage form (tablets):
  —For angina (chest pain):
    - Adults—200 to 300 milligrams (mg) once a day.
    - Children—Use and dose must be determined by your doctor.

For diltiazem
- For *long-acting oral* dosage form (extended-release capsules):
  —For high blood pressure:
    - Adults and teenagers—
      —For *Cardizem CD* or *Dilacor-XR:* 180 to 240 milligrams (mg) once a day.
      —For *Cardizem SR:* 60 to 120 mg two times a day.
    - Children—Dose must be determined by your doctor.
- For *regular (short-acting) oral* dosage form (tablets):
  —For angina (chest pain):
    - Adults and teenagers—30 mg three or four times a day. Your doctor may gradually increase your dose as needed.
    - Children—Dose must be determined by your doctor.
- For *injection* dosage form:
  —For arrhythmias (irregular heartbeat):
    - Adults and teenagers—Dose is based on body weight and must be determined by your doctor.
    - Children—Use and dose must be determined by your doctor.

For felodipine
- For *long-acting oral* dosage form (extended-release tablets):
  —For high blood pressure:
    - Adults—5 to 10 milligrams (mg) once a day.
    - Children—Use and dose must be determined by your doctor.
  —For angina (chest pain):
    - Adults—10 mg once a day.
    - Children—Use and dose must be determined by your doctor.

For flunarizine
- For *oral* dosage form (capsules):
  —To prevent headaches:
    - Adults—10 milligrams (mg) once a day in the evening.
    - Children—Dose must be determined by your doctor.

For isradipine
- For *oral* dosage form (capsules):
  —For high blood pressure:
    - Adults—2.5 milligrams (mg) two times a day. Your doctor may increase your dose as needed.
    - Children—Use and dose must be determined by your doctor.

For nicardipine
- For *oral* dosage form (capsules):
  —For high blood pressure or angina (chest pain):
    - Adults and teenagers—20 milligrams (mg) three times a day.
    - Children—Dose must be determined by your doctor.

For nifedipine

- For *regular (short-acting) oral* dosage form (capsules or tablets):
  - —For high blood pressure or angina (chest pain):
    - Adults and teenagers—10 milligrams (mg) three times a day. Your doctor may increase your dose as needed.
    - Children—Dose must be determined by your doctor.
- For *long-acting oral* dosage form (extended-release tablets):
  - —For high blood pressure or angina (chest pain):
    - Adults and teenagers—
      - —For *Adalat CC* or *Procardia XL:* 30 or 60 mg once a day. Your doctor may increase your dose as needed.
      - —For *Adalat P.A.:* 20 mg two times a day. Your doctor may increase your dose as needed.
    - Children—Dose must be determined by your doctor.

For nimodipine

- For *oral* dosage form (capsules):
  - —To treat a burst blood vessel in the head:
    - Adults—60 milligrams (mg) every four hours.
    - Children—Dose must be determined by your doctor.

For verapamil

- For *regular (short-acting) oral* dosage form (tablets):
  - —For angina (chest pain), arrhythmias (irregular heartbeat), or high blood pressure:
    - Adults and teenagers—40 to 120 milligrams (mg) three times a day. Your doctor may increase your dose as needed.
    - Children—Dose is based on body weight and must be determined by your doctor. The usual dose is 4 to 8 mg per kilogram (kg) (1.82 to 3.64 mg per pound) of body weight a day. This is divided into smaller doses.
- For *long-acting oral* dosage form (extended-release capsules):
  - —For high blood pressure:
    - Adults and teenagers—240 to 480 mg once a day.
    - Children—Dose must be determined by your doctor.
- For *long-acting oral* dosage form (extended-release tablets):
  - —For high blood pressure:
    - Adults and teenagers—120 mg once a day to 240 mg every twelve hours.
    - Children—Dose must be determined by your doctor.
- For *injection* dosage form:
  - —For arrhythmias (irregular heartbeat):
    - Adults—5 to 10 mg slowly injected into a vein. The dose may be repeated after thirty minutes.
    - Children—Dose is based on body weight and must be determined by your doctor.
      - —Infants up to 1 year of age: 100 to 200 micrograms (mcg) per kg (45.5 to 90.9 mcg per pound) of body weight injected slowly into a vein. The dose may be repeated after thirty minutes.
      - —Children 1 to 15 years of age: 100 to 300 mcg per kg (45.5 to 136.4 mcg per pound) of body weight injected slowly into a vein. The dose may be repeated after thirty minutes.

Missed dose—If you miss a dose of this medicine, take it as soon as possible. However, if it is almost time for your next dose, skip the missed dose and go back to your regular dosing schedule. Do not double doses.

Storage—To store this medicine:

- Keep out of the reach of children.
- Store away from heat and direct light.
- Do not store in the bathroom, near the kitchen sink, or in other damp places. Heat or moisture may cause the medicine to break down.
- Do not keep outdated medicine or medicine no longer needed. Be sure that any discarded medicine is out of the reach of children.

Precautions While Using This Medicine

It is important that your doctor check your progress at regular visits. This will allow your doctor to make sure the medicine is working properly and to change the dosage if needed.

If you have been using this medicine regularly for several weeks, do not suddenly stop using it. Stopping suddenly may bring on your previous problem. Check with your doctor for the best way to reduce gradually the amount you are taking before stopping completely.

Chest pain resulting from exercise or physical exertion is usually reduced or prevented by this medicine. This may tempt you to be overly active. *Make sure you discuss with your doctor a safe amount of exercise for your medical problem.*

After taking a dose of this medicine you may get a headache that lasts for a short time. This effect is more common if you are taking felodipine, isradipine, or nifedipine. This should become less noticeable after you have taken this medicine for a while. If this effect continues or if the headaches are severe, check with your doctor.

In some patients, tenderness, swelling, or bleeding of the gums may appear soon after treatment with this medicine is started. Brushing and flossing your teeth carefully and regularly and massaging your gums may help prevent this. *See your dentist regularly to have your teeth cleaned. Check with your medical doctor or dentist if you have any questions about how to take care of your teeth and gums, or if you notice any tenderness, swelling, or bleeding of your gums.*

For patients taking *bepridil, diltiazem,* or *verapamil:*

- *Ask your doctor how to count your pulse rate. Then, while you are taking this medicine, check your pulse regularly.* If it is much slower than your usual rate, or less than 50 beats per minute, check with your doctor. A pulse rate that is too slow may cause circulation problems.

For patients taking *flunarizine:*

- This medicine may cause some people to become drowsy or less alert than they are normally. This is more likely to happen when you begin to take it or when you increase the amount of medicine you are taking. *Make sure you know how you react to this medicine before you drive, use machines, or do anything else that could be dangerous if you are not alert.*

For patients taking this medicine *for high blood pressure:*

- *Do not take other medicines unless they have been discussed with your doctor.* This especially includes over-the-counter (nonprescription) medicines for appetite control, asthma, colds, cough, hay fever, or sinus problems, since they may tend to increase your blood pressure.

Side Effects of This Medicine

Along with its needed effects, a medicine may cause some unwanted effects. Although not all of these side effects may occur, if they do occur they may need medical attention.

Not all of the side effects listed below have been reported for each of these medicines, but they have been reported for at least one of them. Since many of the effects of calcium channel blockers are similar, some of these side effects may occur with any of these medicines. However, they may be more common with some of these medicines than with others.

Check with your doctor as soon as possible if any of the following side effects occur:

Less common

Breathing difficulty, coughing, or wheezing; irregular or fast, pounding heartbeat; skin rash; slow heartbeat (less than 50 beats per minute—bepridil, diltiazem, and verapamil only); swelling of ankles, feet, or lower legs (more common with felodipine and nifedipine)

For flunarizine only—less common

Loss of balance control; mask-like face; mental depression; shuffling walk; stiffness of arms or legs; trembling and shaking of hands and fingers; trouble in speaking or swallowing

Rare

Bleeding, tender, or swollen gums; chest pain (may appear about 30 minutes after medicine is taken); fainting; painful, swollen joints (for nifedipine only); trouble in seeing (for nifedipine only)

For flunarizine and verapamil only—rare

Unusual secretion of milk

Other side effects may occur that usually do not need medical attention. These side effects may go away during treatment as your body adjusts to the medicine. However, check with your doctor if any of the following side effects continue or are bothersome:

More common

Drowsiness (for flunarizine only); increased appetite and/or weight gain (for flunarizine only)

Less common

Constipation; diarrhea; dizziness or lightheadedness (more common with bepridil and nifedipine); dryness of mouth (for flunarizine only); flushing and feeling of warmth (more common with nicardipine and nifedipine); headache (more common with felodipine, isradipine, and nifedipine); nausea (more common with bepridil and nifedipine); unusual tiredness or weakness

Other side effects not listed above may also occur in some patients. If you notice any other effects, check with your doctor.

Additional Information

Once a medicine has been approved for marketing for a certain use, experience may show that it is also useful for other medical problems. Although these uses are not included in product labeling, calcium channel blockers are used in certain patients with the following medical conditions:

- Hypertrophic cardiomyopathy (a heart condition) (verapamil)
- Raynaud's phenomenon (circulation problems) (nicardipine and nifedipine)

Other than the above information, there is no additional information relating to proper use, precautions, or side effects for these uses.

Revised: 08/21/92
Interim revision: 09/07/94; 04/13/95

CALCIUM SUPPLEMENTS Systemic

Some commonly used brand names are:

In the U.S.—

Alka-Mints[2]
Amitone[2]
Calcarb 600[2]
Calci-Chew[2]
Calciday 667[2]
Calcilac[2]
Calci-Mix[2]
Calcionate[5]
Calcium 600[2]
Calglycine[2]
Calphosan[8]
Cal-Plus[2]
Caltrate 600[2]
Caltrate Jr.[2]
Chooz[2]
Citracal[4]
Citracal Liquitabs[4]
Dicarbosil[2]
Gencalc 600[2]
Liquid-Cal[2]
Liquid Cal-600[2]
Maalox Antacid Caplets[2]
Mallamint[2]
Neo-Calglucon[5]
Nephro-Calci[2]
Os-Cal 500[2]
Os-Cal 500 Chewable[2]
Oysco[2]
Oysco 500 Chewable[2]
Oyst-Cal 500[2]
Oystercal 500[2]
Posture[12]
Rolaids Calcium Rich[2]
Titralac[2]
Tums[2]
Tums 500[2]
Tums E-X[2]

In Canada—

Apo-Cal[2]
Calciject[3]
Calcite 500[2]
Calcium-Sandoz[5]
Calcium-Sandoz Forte[10]
Calcium Stanley[6]
Calsan[2]
Caltrate 600[2]
Gramcal[10]
Nu-Cal[2]
Os-Cal[2]
Os-Cal Chewable[2]
Tums Extra Strength[2]
Tums Regular Strength[2]

Note: For quick reference, the following calcium supplements are numbered to match the corresponding brand names.

This information applies to the following:

1. Calcium Acetate (KAL-see-um ASa-tate)†
2. Calcium Carbonate (KAR-boh-nate)‡§
3. Calcium Chloride (KLOR-ide)‡§
4. Calcium Citrate (SIH-trayt)†‡
5. Calcium Glubionate (gloo-BY-oh-nate)§
6. Calcium Gluceptate and Calcium Gluconate (GLOO-coh-nate)*
7. Calcium Gluconate‡§
8. Calcium Glycerophosphate (gliss-er-o-FOS-fate) and Calcium Lactate (LAK-tate)†
9. Calcium Lactate‡§
10. Calcium Lactate-Gluconate and Calcium Carbonate*
11. Dibasic (dy-BAY-sic) Calcium Phosphate (FOS-fate)†‡
12. Tribasic (try-BAY-sic) Calcium Phosphate†

Note: This information does *not* apply to calcium carbonate used as an antacid.

*Not commercially available in the U.S.
†Not commercially available in Canada.
‡Generic name product may also be available in the U.S.
§In Canada, calcium glubionate is known as calcium glucono-galacto gluconate.

Description

Calcium supplements are taken by individuals who are unable to get enough calcium in their regular diet or who have a need for more calcium. They are used to prevent or treat several conditions that may cause hypocalcemia (not enough calcium in the blood). The body needs calcium to make strong bones. Calcium is also needed for the heart, muscles, and nervous system to work properly.

The bones serve as a storage site for the body's calcium. They are continuously giving up calcium to the bloodstream and then replacing it as the body's need for calcium changes from day to day. When there is not enough calcium in the blood to be used by the heart and other organs, your body will take the needed calcium from the bones. When you eat foods rich in calcium, the calcium will be restored to the bones and the balance between your blood and bones will be maintained.

Pregnant women, nursing mothers, children, and adolescents may need more calcium than they normally get from eating calcium-rich foods. Adult women may take calcium supplements to help prevent a bone disease called osteoporosis. Osteoporosis, which causes thin, porous, easily broken bones, may occur in women after menopause, but may sometimes occur in elderly men also. Osteoporosis in women past menopause is thought to be caused by a reduced amount of ovarian estrogen (a female hormone). However, a diet low in calcium for many years, especially in the younger adult years, may add to the risk of developing it. Other bone diseases in children and adults are also treated with calcium supplements.

Calcium supplements may also be used for other conditions as determined by your health care professional.

Injectable calcium is administered only by or under the supervision of your health care professional. Other forms of calcium are available without a prescription.

Calcium supplements are available in the following dosage forms:

Oral

Calcium Carbonate
- Capsules (U.S. and Canada)
- Oral suspension (U.S.)
- Tablets (U.S. and Canada)
- Chewable tablets (U.S. and Canada)

Calcium Citrate
- Tablets (U.S.)
- Tablets for solution (U.S.)

Calcium Glubionate
- Syrup (U.S. and Canada)

Calcium Gluceptate and Calcium Gluconate
- Oral solution (Canada)

Calcium Gluconate
- Tablets (U.S. and Canada)
- Chewable tablets (U.S.)

Calcium Lactate
- Tablets (U.S. and Canada)

Calcium Lactate-Gluconate and Calcium Carbonate
- Tablets for solution (Canada)

Dibasic Calcium Phosphate
- Tablets (U.S.)

Tribasic Calcium Phosphate
- Tablets (U.S.)

Parenteral

Calcium Acetate
- Injection (U.S.)

Calcium Chloride
- Injection (U.S. and Canada)

Calcium Glubionate
- Injection (Canada)

Calcium Gluceptate
- Injection (U.S.)

Calcium Gluconate
- Injection (U.S. and Canada)

Calcium Glycerophosphate and Calcium Lactate
- Injection (U.S.)

A calcium "salt" contains calcium along with another substance, such as carbonate or gluconate. Some calcium salts have more calcium (elemental calcium) than others. For example, the amount of calcium in calcium carbonate is greater than that in calcium gluconate. To give you an idea of how different calcium supplements vary in calcium content, the following chart explains how many tablets of each type of supplement will provide 1000 milligrams of elemental calcium. When you look for a calcium supplement, be sure the number of milligrams on the label refers to the amount of elemental calcium, and not to the strength of each tablet.

Calcium supplement	Strength of each tablet (in milligrams)	Amount of elemental calcium per tablet (in milligrams)	Number of tablets to provide 1000 milligrams of calcium
Calcium carbonate	625	250	4
	650	260	4
	750	300	4
	835	334	3
	1250	500	2
	1500	600	2
Calcium citrate	950	200	5
Calcium gluconate	500	45	22
	650	58	17
	1000	90	11
Calcium lactate	325	42	24
	650	84	12
Calcium phosphate, dibasic	500	115	9
Calcium phosphate, tribasic	800	304	4
	1600	608	2

Importance of Diet

For good health, it is important that you eat a balanced and varied diet. Follow carefully any diet program your health care professional may recommend. For your specific dietary vitamin and/or mineral needs, ask your health care professional for a list of appropriate foods. If you think that you are not getting enough vitamins and/or minerals in your diet, you may choose to take a dietary supplement.

The daily amount of calcium needed is defined in several different ways.

For U.S.—
- Recommended Dietary Allowances (RDAs) are the amount of vitamins and minerals needed to provide for adequate nutrition in most healthy persons. RDAs for a given nutrient may vary depending on a person's age, sex, and physical condition (e.g., pregnancy).
- Daily Values (DVs) are used on food and dietary supplement labels to indicate the percent of the recommended daily amount of each nutrient that a serving provides. DV replaces the previous designation of United States Recommended Daily Allowances (USRDAs).

For Canada—
- Recommended Nutrient Intakes (RNIs) are used to determine the amounts of vitamins, minerals, and protein needed to provide adequate nutrition and lessen the risk of chronic disease.

Normal daily recommended intakes in milligrams (mg) for calcium are generally defined as follows:

Persons	U.S. (mg)	Canada (mg)
Infants and children		
Birth to 3 years of age	400–800	250–550
4 to 6 years of age	800	600
7 to 10 years of age	800	700–1100
Adolescent and adult males	800–1200	800–1100
Adolescent and adult females	800–1200	700–1100
Pregnant females	1200	1200–1500
Breast-feeding females	1200	1200–1500

Getting the proper amount of calcium in the diet every day and participating in weight-bearing exercise (walking, dancing, bicycling, aerobics, jogging), especially during the early years of life (up to about 35 years of age) is most important in helping to build and maintain bones as dense as possible to prevent the development of osteoporosis in later life.

The following table includes some calcium-rich foods. The calcium content of these foods can supply the daily RDA or RNI for calcium if the foods are eaten regularly in sufficient amounts.

Food (amount)	Milligrams of calcium
Nonfat dry milk, reconstituted (1 cup)	375
Lowfat, skim, or whole milk (1 cup)	290 to 300
Yogurt (1 cup)	275 to 400
Sardines with bones (3 ounces)	370
Ricotta cheese, part skim (1/2 cup)	340
Salmon, canned, with bones (3 ounces)	285
Cheese, Swiss (1 ounce)	272
Cheese, cheddar (1 ounce)	204
Cheese, American (1 ounce)	174
Cottage cheese, lowfat (1 cup)	154
Tofu (4 ounces)	154
Shrimp (1 cup)	147
Ice milk (3/4 cup)	132

Vitamin D helps prevent calcium loss from your bones. It is sometimes called "the sunshine vitamin" because it is made in your skin when you are exposed to sunlight. If you get outside in the sunlight every day for 15 to 30 minutes, you should get all the vitamin D you need. However, in northern locations in winter, the sunlight may be too weak to make vitamin D in the skin. Vitamin D may also be obtained from your diet or from multivitamin preparations. Most milk is fortified with vitamin D.

Do not use bonemeal or dolomite as a source of calcium. The Food and Drug Administration has issued warnings that bonemeal and dolomite could be dangerous because these products may contain lead.

Before Using This Dietary Supplement

If you are taking this dietary supplement without a prescription, carefully read and follow any precautions on the label. For calcium supplements, the following should be considered:

Pregnancy—It is especially important that you are receiving enough calcium when you become pregnant and that you continue to receive the right amount of calcium throughout your pregnancy. The healthy growth and development of the fetus depend on a steady supply of nutrients from the mother. However, taking large amounts of a dietary supplement during pregnancy may be harmful to the mother and/or fetus and should be avoided.

Breast-feeding—It is especially important that you receive the right amount of calcium so that your baby will also get the calcium needed to grow properly. However, taking large amounts of a dietary supplement while breast-feeding may be harmful to the mother and/or baby and should be avoided.

Children—Problems in children have not been reported with intake of normal daily recommended amounts. Injectable forms of calcium should not be given to children because of the risk of irritating the injection site.

Older adults—Problems in older adults have not been reported with intake of normal daily recommended amounts. It is important that older people continue to receive enough calcium in their daily diets. However, some older people may need to take extra calcium or larger doses because they do not absorb calcium as well as younger people. Check with your health care professional if you have any questions about the amount of calcium you should be taking in each day.

Medicines or other dietary supplements—Although certain medicines or dietary supplements should not be used together at all, in other cases they may be used together even if an interaction might occur. In these cases, your health care professional may want to change the dose, or other precautions may be necessary. When you are taking calcium supplements, it is especially important that your health care professional know if you are taking any of the following:

- Calcium-containing medicines, other—Taking excess calcium may cause too much calcium in the blood or urine and lead to medical problems
- Cellulose sodium phosphate (e.g., Calcibind)—Use with calcium supplements may decrease the effects of cellulose sodium phosphate
- Digitalis glycosides (heart medicine)—Use with calcium supplements by injection may increase the chance of irregular heartbeat
- Etidronate (e.g., Didronel)—Use with calcium supplements may decrease the effects of etidronate; etidronate should not be taken within 2 hours of calcium supplements
- Gallium nitrate (e.g., Ganite)—Use with calcium supplements may cause gallium nitrate to not work properly
- Magnesium sulfate (for injection)—Use with calcium supplements may cause either medicine to be less effective
- Phenytoin (e.g., Dilantin)—Use with calcium supplements may decrease the effects of both medicines; calcium supplements should not be taken within 1 to 3 hours of phenytoin
- Tetracyclines (medicine for infection) taken by mouth—Use with calcium supplements may decrease the effects of tetracycline; calcium supplements should not be taken within 1 to 3 hours of tetracyclines

Other medical problems—The presence of other medical problems may affect the use of calcium supplements. Make sure you tell your health care professional if you have any other medical problems, especially:

- Diarrhea or
- Stomach or intestinal problems—Extra calcium or specific calcium preparations may be necessary in these conditions
- Heart disease—Calcium by injection may increase the chance of irregular heartbeat
- Hypercalcemia (too much calcium in the blood) or
- Hypercalciuria (too much calcium in the urine)—Calcium supplements may make these conditions worse
- Hyperparathyroidism or
- Sarcoidosis—Calcium supplements may increase the chance of hypercalcemia (too much calcium in the blood)
- Hypoparathyroidism—Use of calcium phosphate may cause high blood levels of phosphorus which could increase the chance of side effects
- Kidney disease or stones—Too much calcium may increase the chance of kidney stones

Proper Use of This Dietary Supplement

Dosing—The amount of calcium needed to meet normal daily recommended intakes will be different for different individuals. The following information includes only the average amounts of calcium.

- For *oral* dosage form (capsules, chewable tablets, lozenges, oral solution, oral suspension, syrup, tablets, extended-release tablets, tablets for solution):
  —To prevent deficiency, the amount taken by mouth is based on normal daily recommended intakes (Note that the normal daily recommended intakes are expressed as an actual amount of calcium. The salt form [e.g., calcium carbonate, calcium gluconate, etc.] has a different strength):

  For the U.S.
  - Adults and teenagers—800 to 1200 milligrams (mg) per day.
  - Pregnant and breast-feeding females—1200 mg per day.
  - Children 4 to 10 years of age—800 mg per day.
  - Children birth to 3 years of age—400 to 800 mg per day.

  For Canada
  - Adult and teenage males—800 to 1100 mg per day.
  - Adult and teenage females—700 to 1100 mg per day.
  - Pregnant and breast-feeding females—1200 to 1500 mg per day.
  - Children 7 to 10 years of age—700 to 1100 mg per day.

- Children 4 to 6 years of age—600 mg per day.
- Children birth to 3 years of age—250 to 550 mg per day.

—To treat deficiency:
- Adults, teenagers, and children—Treatment dose is determined by prescriber for each individual based on severity of deficiency.

Drink a full glass (8 ounces) of water or juice when taking a calcium supplement. However, if you are taking calcium carbonate as a phosphate binder in kidney dialysis, it is not necessary to drink a glass of water.

This dietary supplement is best taken 1 to 1½ hours after meals, unless otherwise directed by your health care professional. However, patients with a condition known as achlorhydria may not absorb calcium supplements on an empty stomach and should take them with meals.

For individuals taking *the chewable tablet form* of this dietary supplement:
- Chew the tablets completely before swallowing.

For individuals taking *the syrup form* of this dietary supplement:
- Take the syrup before meals. This will allow the dietary supplement to work faster.
- Mix in water or fruit juice for infants or children.

Take this dietary supplement only as directed. Do not take more of it and do not take it more often than recommended on the label. To do so may increase the chance of side effects.

Missed dose—If you are taking this dietary supplement on a regular schedule and you miss a dose, take it as soon as possible, then go back to your regular dosing schedule.

Storage—To store this dietary supplement:
- Keep out of the reach of children.
- Store away from heat and direct light.
- Do not store in the bathroom, near the kitchen sink, or in other damp places. Heat or moisture may cause the dietary supplement to break down.
- Keep the liquid form of this dietary supplement from freezing.
- Do not keep outdated dietary supplements or those no longer needed. Be sure that any discarded dietary supplement is out of the reach of children.

Precautions While Using This Dietary Supplement

If this dietary supplement has been ordered for you by your health care professional and you will be taking it in large doses or for a long time, your health care professional should check your progress at regular visits. This is to make sure the calcium is working properly and does not cause unwanted effects.

Do not take calcium supplements within 1 to 2 hours of taking other medicine by mouth. To do so may keep the other medicine from working properly.

Unless you are otherwise directed by your health care professional, to make sure that calcium is used properly by your body:
- *Do not take other medicines or dietary supplements containing large amounts of calcium, phosphates, magnesium, or vitamin D unless your health care professional has told you to do so or approved.*
- *Do not take calcium supplements within 1 to 2 hours of eating large amounts of fiber-containing foods, such as bran and whole-grain cereals or breads, especially if you are being treated for hypocalcemia (not enough calcium in your blood).*
- *Do not drink large amounts of alcohol or caffeine-containing beverages (usually more than 8 cups of coffee a day), or use tobacco.*

Some calcium carbonate tablets have been shown to break up too slowly in the stomach to be properly absorbed into the body. If the calcium carbonate tablets you purchase are not specifically labeled as being "USP," check with your pharmacist. He or she may be able to help you determine which tablets are best.

Side Effects of This Dietary Supplement

Along with its needed effects, a dietary supplement may cause some unwanted effects. Although the following side effects occur very rarely when the calcium supplement is taken as recommended, they may be more likely to occur if:
- It is taken in large doses.
- It is taken for a long time.
- It is taken by patients with kidney disease.

Check with your health care professional as soon as possible if any of the following side effects occur:

More common (for injection form only)

Dizziness; flushing and/or sensation of warmth or heat; irregular heartbeat; nausea or vomiting; skin redness, rash, pain, or burning at injection site; sweating; tingling sensation

Rare

Difficult or painful urination; drowsiness; nausea or vomiting (continuing); weakness

Early signs of overdose

Constipation (severe); dryness of mouth; headache (continuing); increased thirst; irritability; loss of appetite; mental depression; metallic taste; unusual tiredness or weakness

Late signs of overdose

Confusion; drowsiness (severe); high blood pressure; increased sensitivity of eyes or skin to light; irregular, fast, or slow heartbeat; unusually large amount of urine or increased frequency of urination

Other side effects not listed above may also occur in some patients. If you notice any other effects, check with your health care professional.

Additional Information

Once a medicine or dietary supplement has been approved for marketing for a certain use, experience may show that it is also useful for other medical problems. Although this use is not included in product labeling, calcium supplements are used in certain patients with the following medical condition:

• Hyperphosphatemia (too much phosphate in the blood)

Other than the above information, there is no additional information relating to proper use, precautions, or side effects for this use.

Revised: 06/10/92
Interim revision: 08/22/94; 07/18/95

CAPREOMYCIN Systemic

A commonly used brand name in the U.S. and Canada is Capastat.

Description

Capreomycin (kap-ree-oh-MYE-sin) is used to treat tuberculosis (TB). It is given with other medicines for TB.

To help clear up your tuberculosis (TB) completely, you must keep taking this medicine for the full time of treatment, even if you begin to feel better. This is very important. It is also important that you do not miss any doses.

Capreomycin is available only with your doctor's prescription, in the following dosage form:

Parenteral
- Injection (U.S. and Canada)

Before Receiving This Medicine

In deciding to use a medicine, the risks of taking the medicine must be weighed against the good it will do. This is a decision you and your doctor will make. For capreomycin, the following should be considered:

Allergies—Tell your doctor if you have ever had any unusual or allergic reaction to capreomycin. Also tell your health care professional if you are allergic to any other substances, such as foods, preservatives, or dyes.

Pregnancy—Capreomycin has not been studied in pregnant women. However, studies in rats given $3^1/_2$ times the human dose have shown that capreomycin may cause birth defects.

Breast-feeding—It is not known whether capreomycin passes into breast milk. Although most medicines pass into breast milk in small amounts, many of them may be used safely while breast-feeding. Mothers who are taking this medicine and who wish to breast-feed should discuss this with their doctor.

Children—Studies on this medicine have been done only in adult patients, and there is no specific information comparing use of capreomycin in children with use in other age groups.

Older adults—Many medicines have not been studied specifically in older people. Therefore, it may not be known whether they work exactly the same way they do in younger adults or if they cause different side effects or problems in older people. There is no specific information comparing use of capreomycin in the elderly with use in other age groups.

Other medicines—Although certain medicines should not be used together at all, in other cases two different medicines may be used together even if an interaction might occur. In these cases, your doctor may want to change the dose, or other precautions may be necessary. When you are receiving capreomycin, it is especially important that your health care professional know if you are taking any of the following:

- Aminoglycosides by injection (amikacin [e.g., Amikin], gentamicin [e.g., Garamycin], kanamycin [e.g., Kantrex], neomycin [e.g., Mycifradin], netilmicin [e.g., Netromycin], streptomycin, tobramycin [e.g., Nebcin]) or
- Anti-infectives by mouth or by injection (medicine for infection) or
- Carmustine (e.g., BiCNU) or
- Chloroquine (e.g., Aralen) or
- Cisplatin (e.g., Platinol) or
- Combination pain medicine containing acetaminophen and aspirin (e.g., Excedrin) or other salicylates (with large amounts taken regularly) or
- Cyclosporine (e.g., Sandimmune) or
- Deferoxamine (e.g., Desferal) (with long-term use) or
- Gold salts (medicine for arthritis) or
- Hydroxychloroquine (e.g., Plaquenil) or
- Inflammation or pain medicines, except narcotics, or
- Lithium (e.g., Lithane) or
- Methotrexate (e.g., Mexate) or
- Penicillamine (e.g., Cuprimine) or
- Plicamycin (e.g., Mithracin) or
- Quinine (e.g., Quinamm) or
- Streptozocin (e.g., Zanosar) or
- Tiopronin (e.g., Thiola)—Use of any of these medicines with capreomycin may increase the chance of hearing, balance, or kidney side effects

Other medical problems—The presence of other medical problems may affect the use of capreomycin. Make sure you tell your doctor if you have any other medical problems, especially:

- Eighth-cranial-nerve disease (loss of hearing and/or balance)—Capreomycin may cause hearing and balance side effects
- Kidney disease—Capreomycin may cause serious side effects affecting the kidneys
- Myasthenia gravis or
- Parkinson's disease—Capreomycin may cause muscular weakness

Proper Use of This Medicine

To help clear up your infection completely, *it is very important that you keep taking this medicine for the full time of treatment,* even if you begin to feel better after a few weeks. You may have to use it every day for as long as 1 to 2 years or more. If you stop using this medicine too soon, your symptoms may return.

Dosing—The dose of capreomycin will be different for different patients. The following information includes only the average doses of capreomycin. Your dose may be different if you have kidney disease.

- For *injection* dosage form:
  - —For treatment of tuberculosis (TB):
    - Adults and adolescents—1 gram of capreomycin injected into the muscle once a day for 60 to 120 days. After this time, 1 gram of capreomycin is injected into the muscle 2 or 3 times a week. This medicine must be given with other medicines to treat tuberculosis (TB).
    - Children—Dose has not been determined.

Side Effects of This Medicine

Along with its needed effects, a medicine may cause some unwanted effects. Although not all of these side effects may occur, if they do occur they may need medical attention.

Check with your doctor as soon as possible if any of the following side effects occur:

More common

Greatly increased or decreased frequency of urination or amount of urine; increased thirst; loss of appetite; nausea; vomiting

Less common

Any loss of hearing; clumsiness or unsteadiness; difficulty in breathing; dizziness; drowsiness; fever; irregular heartbeat; itching; muscle cramps or pain; pain, redness, hardness, unusual bleeding, or a sore at the place of injection; ringing or buzzing or a feeling of fullness in the ears; skin rash; swelling; unusual tiredness or weakness

Other side effects not listed above may also occur in some patients. If you notice any other effects, check with your doctor.

Revised: 06/27/94

CAPSAICIN Topical

Some commonly used brand names are:

In the U.S.—

Zostrix
Zostrix–HP

In Canada—

Axsain
Zostrix

Description

Capsaicin (cap-SAY-sin) is used to help relieve a certain type of pain known as neuralgia (new-RAL-ja). Capsaicin is also used to temporarily help relieve the pain from osteoarthritis (OS-te-o-ar-THRI-tis) or rheumatoid arthritis (ROO-ma-toid ar-THRI-tis). This medicine will not cure any of these conditions.

Neuralgia is a pain from the nerves near the surface of your skin. This pain may occur after an infection with herpes zoster (shingles). It may also occur if you have diabetic neuropathy (di-a-BET-ick new-ROP-a-thee). Diabetic neuropathy is a condition that occurs in some persons with diabetes. The condition causes tingling and pain in the feet and toes. Capsaicin will help relieve the pain of diabetic neuropathy, but it will not cure diabetic neuropathy or diabetes.

Capsaicin may also be used for neuralgias caused by other conditions as determined by your doctor.

Capsaicin is available without a prescription; however, your doctor may have special instructions on the proper use of this medicine.

Topical

- Cream (U.S. and Canada)

Before Using This Medicine

If you are using this medicine without a prescription, carefully read and follow any precautions on the label. For capsaicin, the following should be considered:

Allergies—Tell your health care professional if you have ever had any unusual or allergic reaction to capsaicin or to the fruit of capsicum plants (for example, hot peppers). Also tell your health care professional if you are allergic to any other substances, such as foods, preservatives, or dyes.

Pregnancy—Capsaicin has not been reported to cause birth defects or other problems in humans.

Breast-feeding—Capsaicin has not been reported to cause problems in nursing babies.

Children—Use is not recommended for infants and children up to 2 years of age, except as directed by your doctor. In children 2 years of age and older, this medicine is not expected to cause different side effects or problems than it does in adults.

Older adults—Many medicines have not been studied specifically in older people. Therefore, it may not be known whether they work exactly the same way they do in younger adults. Although there is no specific information comparing use of capsaicin in the elderly with use in other age groups, this medicine is not expected to cause different side effects or problems in older people than it does in younger adults.

Other medical problems—The presence of other medical problems may affect the use of capsaicin. Make sure you tell your health care professional if you have any other medical problems, especially:

- Broken or irritated skin on area to be treated with capsaicin

Proper Use of This Medicine

If you are using capsaicin for the treatment of neuralgia caused by herpes zoster, do not apply the medicine until the zoster sores have healed.

It is not necessary to wash the areas to be treated before you apply capsaicin, but doing so will not cause harm.

Apply a small amount of cream and use your fingers to rub it well into the affected area so that little or no cream is left on the surface of the skin afterwards.

Wash your hands with soap and water after applying capsaicin to avoid getting the medicine in your eyes or on other sensitive areas of the body. However, if you are using capsaicin for arthritis in your hands, do not wash your hands for at least 30 minutes after applying the cream.

If a bandage is being used on the treated area, it should not be applied tightly.

When you first begin to use capsaicin, a warm, stinging, or burning sensation (feeling) may occur. This sensation is related to the action of capsaicin on the skin, and is to be expected. Although this sensation usually disappears after the first several days of treatment, it may last 2 to 4 weeks or longer. Heat, humidity, clothing, bathing in warm water, or sweating may increase the sensation. However, the sensation usually occurs less often and is less severe the longer you use the medicine. Reducing the number of doses of capsaicin that you use each day will not lessen the sensation, and may lengthen the period of time that you get the sensation. Also, reducing the number of doses you use may reduce the amount of pain relief that you get.

Capsaicin must be used regularly every day as directed if it is to work properly. Even then, it may not relieve your pain right away. The length of time it takes to work depends on the type of pain you have. In persons with arthritis, pain relief usually begins within 1 to 2 weeks. In most persons with neuralgia, relief usually begins within 2 to 4 weeks, although with head and neck neuralgias, relief may take as long as 4 to 6 weeks.

Once capsaicin has begun to relieve pain, you must continue to use it regularly 3 or 4 times a day to keep the pain from returning. If you stop using capsaicin and your pain returns, you can begin using it again.

Dosing—The dose of capsaicin may be different for different patients. *Follow your doctor's orders or the directions on the label.* The following information includes only the average dose of capsaicin. *If your dose is different, do not change it* unless your doctor tells you to do so:

- Apply regularly 3 or 4 times a day and rub in well.

Missed dose—If you miss a dose of this medicine, use it as soon as possible. However, if it is almost time for your next dose, skip the missed dose and go back to your regular dosing schedule. Do not double doses.

Storage—To store this medicine:

- Keep out of the reach of children.
- Store away from heat and direct light.
- Keep the medicine from freezing. Do not refrigerate.
- Do not keep outdated medicine or medicine no longer needed. Be sure that any discarded medicine is out of the reach of children.

Precautions While Using This Medicine

If capsaicin gets into your eyes or on other sensitive areas of the body, it will cause a burning sensation. If capsaicin gets into your eyes, flush your eyes with water. If capsaicin gets on other sensitive areas of your body, wash the areas with warm (not hot) soapy water.

If your condition gets worse, or does not improve after 1 month, stop using this medicine and check with your doctor.

Side Effects of This Medicine

Along with its needed effects, a medicine may cause some unwanted effects. Although not all of these side effects may occur, if they do occur they may need medical attention. Some side effects may occur that usually do not need medical attention. These side effects may go away during treatment as your body adjusts to the medicine. However, check with your doctor if any of the following side effects continue or are bothersome:

More common

Warm, stinging, or burning feeling at the place of treatment

Other side effects not listed above may also occur in some patients. If you notice any other effects, check with your doctor.

Revised: 07/14/92

CARBACHOL Ophthalmic

Some commonly used brand names are:

In the U.S.—

Carboptic
Isopto Carbachol
Miostat

In Canada—

Isopto Carbachol
Miostat

Another commonly used name is carbamylcholine.

Description

Carbachol (KAR-ba-kole) is used in the eye to treat glaucoma. Sometimes it is also used in eye surgery.

This medicine is available only with your doctor's prescription, in the following dosage forms:

Ophthalmic
- Intraocular solution (U.S. and Canada)
- Ophthalmic solution (eye drops) (U.S. and Canada)

Before Using This Medicine

In deciding to use a medicine, the risks of taking the medicine must be weighed against the good it will do. This is a decision you and your doctor will make. For carbachol, the following should be considered:

Allergies—Tell your doctor if you have ever had any unusual or allergic reaction to carbachol. Also tell your health care professional if you are allergic to any other substances, such as preservatives.

Pregnancy—Studies on effects in pregnancy have not been done in either humans or animals. However, carbachol may be absorbed into the body.

Breast-feeding—Carbachol may be absorbed into the mother's body. However, it is not known whether carbachol passes into breast milk. Although most medicines pass into breast milk in small amounts, many of them may be used safely while breast-feeding. Mothers who are using this medicine and who wish to breast-feed should discuss this with their doctor.

Children—Although there is no specific information comparing use of carbachol in children with use in other age groups, this medicine is not expected to cause different side effects or problems in children than it does in adults.

Older adults—Many medicines have not been studied specifically in older people. Therefore, it may not be known whether they work exactly the same way they do in younger adults. Although there is no specific information comparing use of carbachol in the elderly with use in other age groups, this medicine is not expected to cause different side effects or problems in older people than it does in younger adults.

Other medicines—Although certain medicines should not be used together at all, in other cases two different medicines may be used together even if an interaction might occur. In these cases, your doctor may want to change the dose, or other precautions may be necessary. Tell your health care professional if you are using any other prescription or nonprescription (over-the-counter [OTC]) medicine.

Other medical problems—The presence of other medical problems may affect the use of carbachol. Make sure you tell your doctor if you have any other medical problems, especially:
- Asthma or
- Eye problems (other) or
- Heart disease or
- Overactive thyroid or
- Parkinson's disease or
- Stomach ulcer or other stomach problems or
- Urinary tract blockage—Carbachol may make the condition worse

Proper Use of This Medicine

Use this medicine only as directed. Do not use more of it and do not use it more often than your doctor ordered. To do so may increase the chance of too much medicine being absorbed into the body and the chance of side effects.

To use:
- First, wash your hands. Tilt the head back and, pressing your finger gently on the skin just beneath the lower eyelid, pull the lower eyelid away from the eye to make a space. Drop the medicine into this space. Let go of the eyelid and gently close the eyes. Do not blink. Keep the eyes closed and apply pressure to the inner corner of the eye with your finger for 1 or 2 minutes to allow the medicine to be absorbed by the eye.
- Immediately after using the eye drops, wash your hands to remove any medicine that may be on them.
- To keep the medicine as germ-free as possible, do not touch the applicator tip to any surface (including the eye). Also, keep the container tightly closed.

Dosing—The dose of carbachol will be different for different patients. *Follow your doctor's orders or the directions on the label.* The following information includes only the average doses of carbachol. If your dose is different, do not change it unless your doctor tells you to do so.

- For glaucoma:
  - —For *ophthalmic solution (eye drops)* dosage form:
    - Adults and children—Use one drop in the eye one to three times a day.
- For use during surgery:
  - —For *intraocular solution* dosage form:
    - Adults and children—Up to 0.5 milliliter (mL), used in the eye during surgery.

Missed dose—If you miss a dose of this medicine, apply it as soon as possible. However, if it is almost time for your next dose, skip the missed dose and go back to your regular dosing schedule. Do not double doses.

Storage—To store this medicine:
- Keep out of the reach of children.
- Store away from heat and direct light.
- Keep the medicine from freezing.
- Do not keep outdated medicine or medicine no longer needed. Be sure that any discarded medicine is out of the reach of children.

Precautions While Using This Medicine

Your doctor should check your eye pressure at regular visits.

After you apply this medicine to your eyes, your pupils may become unusually small. This may cause you to see less well at night or in dim light. *Be especially careful if you drive, use machines, or do anything else at night or in dim light that could be dangerous if you are not able to see well.*

Also, for a short time after you apply this medicine, your vision may be blurred or there may be a change in your near or distance vision. *Make sure your vision is clear before you drive, use machines, or do anything else that could be dangerous if you are not able to see well.*

Side Effects of This Medicine

Along with its needed effects, a medicine may cause some unwanted effects. Although not all of these side effects may occur, if they do occur they may need medical attention.

Check with your doctor as soon as possible if any of the following side effects occur:

Rare

Veil or curtain appearing across part of vision

Symptoms of too much medicine being absorbed into the body

Diarrhea, stomach cramps or pain, or vomiting; fainting; flushing or redness of face; frequent urge to urinate; increased sweating; irregular heartbeat; shortness of breath, wheezing, or tightness in chest; unusual tiredness or weakness; watering of mouth

Other side effects may occur that usually do not need medical attention. These side effects may go away during treatment as your body adjusts to the medicine. However, check with your doctor if any of the following side effects continue or are bothersome:

More common

Blurred vision or change in near or distance vision; eye pain; stinging or burning of the eye

Less common

Headache; irritation or redness of eyes; twitching of eyelids

Other side effects not listed above may also occur in some patients. If you notice any other effects, check with your doctor.

Revised: 06/21/94
Interim revision: 05/01/95

CARBAMAZEPINE Systemic

Some commonly used brand names are:

In the U.S.—

Atretol	Tegretol
Epitol	Tegretol-XR

Generic name product may also be available.

In Canada—

Apo-Carbamazepine	Tegretol
Novo-Carbamaz	Tegretol Chewtabs
Nu-Carbamazepine	Tegretol CR

Description

Carbamazepine (kar-ba-MAZ-e-peen) is used to control some types of seizures in the treatment of epilepsy. It is also used to relieve pain due to trigeminal neuralgia (tic douloureux). It should not be used for other more common aches or pains.

Carbamazepine may also be used for other conditions as determined by your doctor.

This medicine is available only with your doctor's prescription, in the following dosage forms:

Oral

- Oral Suspension (U.S.)
- Tablets (U.S. and Canada)
- Chewable tablets (U.S. and Canada)
- Extended-release tablets (U.S. and Canada)

Before Using This Medicine

In deciding to use a medicine, the risks of taking the medicine must be weighed against the good it will do. This is a decision you and your doctor will make. For carbamazepine, the following should be considered:

Allergies—Tell your doctor if you have ever had any unusual or allergic reaction to carbamazepine or to any of the tricyclic antidepressants, such as amitriptyline, amoxapine, clomipramine, desipramine, doxepin, imipramine, nortriptyline, protriptyline, or trimipramine. Also tell your health care professional if you are allergic to any other substances, such as foods, preservatives, or dyes.

Pregnancy—Carbamazepine has not been studied in pregnant women. However, there have been reports of babies having low birth weight, small head size, skull and facial defects, underdeveloped fingernails, and delays in growth when their mothers had taken carbamazepine in high doses during pregnancy. In addition, birth defects have been reported in some babies when the mothers took other medicines for epilepsy during pregnancy. Also, studies in animals have shown that carbamazepine causes birth defects when given in large doses. Therefore, the use of carbamazepine during pregnancy should be discussed with your doctor.

Breast-feeding—Carbamazepine passes into the breast milk, and in some cases the baby may receive enough of it to cause unwanted effects. In animal studies, carbamazepine has affected the growth and appearance of the nursing babies.

Children—Behavior changes are more likely to occur in children.

Older adults—Confusion; restlessness and nervousness; irregular, pounding, or unusually slow heartbeat; and chest pain may be especially likely to occur in elderly patients, who are usually more sensitive than younger adults to the effects of carbamazepine.

Other medicines—Although certain medicines should not be used together at all, in other cases two different medicines may be used together even if an interaction might occur. In these cases, your doctor may want to change the dose, or other precautions may be necessary. When you are taking carbamazepine, it is especially important that your health care professional know if you are taking any of the following:

- Anticoagulants (blood thinners)—The effects of anticoagulants may be decreased; monitoring of blood clotting time may be necessary during and after carbamazepine treatment

- Cimetidine (e.g., Tagamet)—Blood levels of carbamazepine may be increased, leading to an increase in serious side effects
- Clarithromycin (e.g., Biaxin)—Blood levels of carbamazepine may be increased, increasing the risk of unwanted effects
- Corticosteroids (cortisone-like medicine)—The effects of corticosteroids may be decreased
- Diltiazem (e.g., Cardizem) or
- Erythromycin (e.g., E-Mycin, Erythrocin, Ilosone) or
- Propoxyphene (e.g., Darvon) or
- Verapamil (e.g., Calan)—Blood levels of carbamazepine may be increased; these medicines should not be used with carbamazepine
- Estrogens (female hormones) or
- Oral contraceptives (birth control pills) containing estrogen or
- Quinidine—The effects of these medicines may be decreased; use of a nonhormonal method of birth control or an oral contraceptive containing only a progestin may be necessary
- Isoniazid (e.g., INH)—The risk of serious side effects may be increased
- Monoamine oxidase (MAO) inhibitors (furazolidone [e.g., Furoxone], isocarboxazid [e.g., Marplan], phenelzine [e.g., Nardil], procarbazine [e.g., Matulane], selegiline [e.g., Eldepryl], tranylcypromine [e.g., Parnate])—Taking carbamazepine while you are taking or within 2 weeks of taking monoamine oxidase (MAO) inhibitors may cause sudden high body temperature, extremely high blood pressure, and severe convulsions; at least 14 days should be allowed between stopping treatment with one medicine and starting treatment with the other
- Other anticonvulsants (seizure medicine)—The effects of these medicines may be decreased; in addition, if these medicines and carbamazepine are used together during pregnancy, the risk of birth defects may be increased
- Risperidone [e.g., Risperdal]—The effects of risperidone may be decreased
- Tricyclic antidepressants (amitriptyline [e.g., Elavil], amoxapine [e.g., Asendin], clomipramine [e.g., Anafranil], desipramine [e.g., Pertofrane], doxepin [e.g., Sinequan], imipramine [e.g., Tofranil], nortriptyline [e.g., Aventyl], protriptyline [e.g., Vivactil], trimipramine [e.g., Surmontil])—Central nervous system depressant effects of carbamazepine may be increased while the anticonvulsant effects of carbamazepine may be decreased; seizures may occur more frequently

Other medical problems—The presence of other medical problems may affect the use of carbamazepine. Make sure you tell your doctor if you have any other medical problems, especially:

- Alcohol abuse (or history of) —Drinking alcohol may decrease the effectiveness of carbamazepine
- Anemia or other blood problems or
- Behavioral problems or
- Glaucoma or
- Heart or blood vessel disease or
- Problems with urination—Carbamazepine may make the condition worse
- Diabetes mellitus (sugar diabetes)—Carbamazepine may cause increased urine glucose levels
- Kidney disease or
- Liver disease—Higher blood levels of carbamazepine may result, increasing the chance of side effects

Proper Use of This Medicine

Carbamazepine should be taken with meals to lessen the chance of stomach upset (nausea and vomiting).

It is very important that you take this medicine exactly as directed by your doctor to obtain the best results and lessen the chance of serious side effects. Do not take more of it, do not take it more often, and do not take it for a longer time than your doctor ordered.

If you are taking this medicine for pain relief:

- Carbamazepine is *not* an ordinary pain reliever. It should be used only when a doctor prescribes it for certain kinds of pain. *Do not take carbamazepine for any other aches or pains.*

If you are taking this medicine for epilepsy:

- *Do not suddenly stop taking this medicine without first checking with your doctor.* To keep your seizures under control, it is usually best to gradually reduce the amount of carbamazepine you are taking before stopping completely.

Dosing—The dose of carbamazepine will be different for different patients. *Follow your doctor's orders or the directions on the label.* The following information includes only the average doses of carbamazepine. *If your dose is different, do not change it* unless your doctor tells you to do so.

The number of tablets or teaspoonfuls of suspension that you take depends on the strength of the medicine. Also, *the number of doses you take each day, the time allowed between doses, and the length of time you take the medicine depend on the medical problem for which you are taking carbamazepine.*

- For *oral* dosage form (suspension):
  - —For epilepsy:
    - Adults and teenagers—At first, 100 milligrams (mg) taken up to four times a day. Your doctor may increase your dose if needed. However, the dose is usually not more than 1200 mg a day.
    - Children 6 to 12 years of age—At first, 50 mg taken four times a day. Your doctor may increase your dose if needed. However, the dose is usually not more than 1000 mg a day.
    - Children up to 6 years of age—Dose is based on body weight and will be determined by your doctor.
  - —For trigeminal neuralgia:
    - Adults and teenagers—At first, 50 mg four times a day. Your doctor may increase your dose if needed. However, the dose is usually not more than 1200 mg a day.
    - Children—Use and dose must be determined by your doctor.

- For *oral* dosage form (tablets and chewable tablets):
  —For epilepsy:
    - Adults and teenagers—At first, 200 mg taken two times a day. Your doctor may increase your dose if needed. However, the dose is usually not more than 1200 mg a day.
    - Children 6 to 12 years of age—At first, 100 mg taken two times a day. Your doctor may increase your dose if needed. However, the dose is usually not more than 1000 mg a day.
    - Children up to 6 years of age—Dose is based on body weight and will be determined by your doctor.

  —For trigeminal neuralgia:
    - Adults and teenagers—At first, 100 mg taken two times a day. Your doctor may increase your dose if needed. However, the dose is usually not more than 1200 mg a day.
    - Children—Use and dose must be determined by your doctor.
- For *oral extended-release tablet* dosage form:
  —For epilepsy:
    - Adults and teenagers—At first, 100 to 200 mg taken one or two times a day with meals. Your doctor may increase your dose if needed. However, the dose is usually not more than 1200 mg a day.
    - Children 6 to 12 years of age—At first, 100 to 200 mg taken in smaller doses during the day. Your doctor may increase your dose if needed. However, the dose is usually not more than 1000 mg a day.
    - Children up to 6 years of age—Use and dose must be determined by your doctor.

  —For trigeminal neuralgia:
    - Adults and teenagers—At first, 100 mg taken two times a day. Your doctor may increase your dose if needed. However, the dose is usually not more than 1200 mg a day.
    - Children—Use and dose must be determined by your doctor.

Missed dose—If you miss a dose of this medicine, take it as soon as possible. However, if it is almost time for your next dose, skip the missed dose and go back to your regular dosing schedule. Do not double doses. However, if you miss more than one dose a day, check with your doctor.

Storage—To store this medicine:
- Keep out of the reach of children.
- Store away from heat and direct light.
- *Do not store the tablet forms of carbamazepine in the bathroom, near the kitchen sink, or in other damp places. Heat or moisture may cause the medicine to break down and become less effective.*
- Keep the liquid form of this medicine from freezing.
- Do not keep outdated medicine or medicine no longer needed. Be sure that any discarded medicine is out of the reach of children.

Precautions While Using This Medicine

It is very important that your doctor check your progress at regular visits. Your doctor may want to have certain tests done to see if you are receiving the right amount of medicine or if certain side effects may be occurring without your knowing it. Also, the amount of medicine you are taking may have to be changed often.

This medicine will add to the effects of alcohol and other CNS depressants (medicines that cause drowsiness). Some examples of CNS depressants are antihistamines or medicine for hay fever, other allergies, or colds; sedatives, tranquilizers, or sleeping medicine; prescription pain medicine or narcotics; barbiturates; medicine for seizures; muscle relaxants; or anesthetics, including some dental anesthetics. *Check with your doctor before taking any of the above while you are using this medicine.*

This medicine may cause some people to become drowsy, dizzy, lightheaded, or less alert than they are normally, especially when they are starting treatment or increasing the dose. It may also cause blurred or double vision, weakness, or loss of muscle control in some people. *Make sure you know how you react to this medicine before you drive, use machines, or do anything else that could be dangerous if you are not alert and well-coordinated or able to see well.*

Some people who take carbamazepine may become more sensitive to sunlight than they are normally. Exposure to sunlight, even for brief periods of time, may cause a skin rash, itching, redness or other discoloration of the skin, or a severe sunburn. When you begin taking this medicine:
- Stay out of direct sunlight, especially between the hours of 10:00 a.m. and 3:00 p.m., if possible.
- Wear protective clothing, including a hat. Also, wear sunglasses.
- Apply a sun block product that has a skin protection factor (SPF) of at least 15. Some patients may require a product with a higher SPF number, especially if they have a fair complexion. If you have any questions about this, check with your health care professional.
- Apply a sun block lipstick that has an SPF of at least 15 to protect your lips.
- Do not use a sunlamp or tanning bed or booth.

If you have a severe reaction from the sun, check with your doctor.

Oral contraceptives (birth control pills) containing estrogen may not work properly if you take them while you are taking carbamazepine. Unplanned pregnancies may occur. You should use a different or additional means of birth control while you are taking carbamazepine. If you have any questions about this, check with your health care professional.

For diabetic patients:
- Carbamazepine may affect urine sugar levels. While you are using this medicine, be especially careful when testing for sugar in your urine. If you notice a change in the results of your urine sugar tests or have any questions about this, check with your doctor.

Before having any medical tests, tell the medical doctor in charge that you are taking this medicine. The results of some pregnancy tests and the metyrapone test may be affected by this medicine.

Before having any kind of surgery, dental treatment, or emergency treatment, tell the medical doctor or dentist in charge that you are taking this medicine. Taking carbamazepine together with medicines that are used during surgery or dental or emergency treatments may increase the CNS depressant effects.

Your doctor may want you to carry a medical identification card or bracelet stating that you are taking this medicine.

Side Effects of This Medicine

Along with its needed effects, a medicine may cause some unwanted effects. Although not all of these side effects may occur, if they do occur they may need medical attention.

Check with your doctor immediately if any of the following side effects occur:

Rare

Black, tarry stools; blood in urine or stools; bone or joint pain; cough or hoarseness; darkening of urine; lower back or side pain; nosebleeds or other unusual bleeding or bruising; painful or difficult urination; pain, tenderness, swelling, or bluish color in leg or foot; pale stools; pinpoint red spots on skin; shortness of breath or cough; sores, ulcers, or white spots on lips or in the mouth; sore throat, chills, and fever; swollen or painful glands; unusual tiredness or weakness; wheezing, tightness in chest, or troubled breathing; yellow eyes or skin

Symptoms of overdose

Body spasm in which head and heels are bent backward and body is bowed forward; clumsiness or unsteadiness; convulsions (seizures)—especially in small children; dizziness (severe) or fainting; drowsiness (severe); fast or irregular heartbeat; high or low blood pressure (hypertension or hypotension); irregular, slow, or shallow breathing; large pupils; nausea or vomiting (severe); overactive reflexes followed by underactive reflexes; poor control in body movements (for example, when reaching or stepping); sudden decrease in amount of urine; trembling, twitching, or abnormal body movements

In addition, check with your doctor as soon as possible if any of the following side effects occur:

More common

Blurred vision or double vision; continuous back-and-forth eye movements

Less common

Behavioral changes (especially in children); confusion, agitation, or hostility (especially in the elderly); diarrhea (severe); headache (continuing); increase in seizures; nausea and vomiting (severe); skin rash, hives, or itching; unusual drowsiness

Rare

Chest pain; difficulty in speaking or slurred speech; fainting; frequent urination; irregular, pounding, or unusually slow heartbeat; mental depression with restlessness and nervousness or other mood or mental changes; muscle or stomach cramps; numbness, tingling, pain, or weakness in hands and feet; rapid weight gain; rigidity; ringing, buzzing, or other unexplained sounds in the ears; sudden decrease in amount of urine; swelling of face, hands, feet, or lower legs; trembling; uncontrolled body movements; visual hallucinations (seeing things that are not there)

Other side effects may occur that usually do not need medical attention. These side effects may go away during treatment as your body adjusts to the medicine. However, check with your doctor if any of the following side effects continue or are bothersome:

More common

Clumsiness or unsteadiness; dizziness (mild); drowsiness (mild); lightheadedness; nausea or vomiting (mild)

Less common or rare

Aching joints or muscles; constipation; diarrhea; dryness of mouth; headache; increased sensitivity of skin to sunlight (skin rash, itching, redness or other discoloration of skin, or severe sunburn); increased sweating; irritation or soreness of tongue or mouth; loss of appetite; loss of hair; sexual problems in males; stomach pain or discomfort

Other side effects not listed above may also occur in some patients. If you notice any other effects, check with your doctor.

Additional Information

Once a medicine has been approved for marketing for a certain use, experience may show that it is also useful for other medical problems. Although these uses are not included in product labeling, carbamazepine is used in certain patients with the following medical conditions:
- Neurogenic pain (a type of continuing pain)
- Bipolar disorder (manic-depressive illness)
- Central partial diabetes insipidus (water diabetes)
- Alcohol withdrawal
- Psychotic disorders (severe mental illness)

Other than the above information, there is no additional information relating to proper use, precautions, or side effects for these uses.

Revised: 07/26/96

CARBOHYDRATES AND ELECTROLYTES Systemic

Some commonly used brand names are:

In the U.S.—

Infalyte[3]
Kao Lectrolyte[1]
Naturalyte[1]
Oralyte[1]
Pedialyte[1]
Rehydralyte[1]
Resol‡[1]

In Canada—

Lytren[1]
Gastrolyte[2]
Pedialyte[1]
Rapolyte[2]

Other commonly used names are oral rehydration salts, ORS-bicarbonate, and ORS-citrate.§

Note: For quick reference, the following are numbered to match the corresponding brand names.

This information applies to the following medicines:

1. Dextrose and Electrolytes (DEX-trose and ee-LEK-tro-lites)#
2. Oral Rehydration Salts (OR-al ree-hi-DRA-shen solts)*§
3. Rice Syrup Solids and Electrolytes (RIS SIR-ep SOL-ids and ee-LEK-tro-lites)†

*Not commercially available in the U.S.
†Not commercially available in Canada.
‡Resol is available to hospitals only.
§Distributed by the World Health Organization (WHO).
#Generic name product may also be available in the U.S.

Description

Carbohydrate and electrolytes combination is used to treat or prevent dehydration (the loss of too much water from the body) that may occur with severe diarrhea, especially in babies and young children. Although this medicine does not immediately stop the diarrhea, it replaces the water and some important salts (electrolytes), such as sodium and potassium, that are lost from the body during diarrhea, and helps prevent more serious problems. Some carbohydrate and electrolytes solutions may also be used after surgery when food intake has been stopped.

This medicine is available without a prescription; however, your doctor may have special instructions on the proper use and dose for you or your child.

Carbohydrate and electrolytes combination is available in the following dosage forms:

Oral
- Solution (U.S. and Canada)
- Powder for oral solution (Canada)

Before Using This Medicine

If you are taking this medicine without a prescription, carefully read and follow any precautions on the label. For carbohydrate and electrolytes solutions, the following should be considered:

Allergies—Tell your health care professional if you have ever had any unusual or allergic reaction to medicines containing potassium, sodium, citrates, rice, or sugar. Also tell your health care professional if you are allergic to any other substances, such as foods, preservatives, or dyes.

Pregnancy—Carbohydrate and electrolytes solutions have not been shown to cause birth defects or other problems in humans.

Breast-feeding—This medicine has not been reported to cause problems in nursing babies. Breast-feeding should continue, if possible, during treatment with carbohydrate and electrolytes solution.

Children—This medicine has been tested in children and, in effective doses, appears to be safe and effective in children. This medicine has not been tested in premature infants.

Older adults—This medicine has been tested and has been shown to be well tolerated by older people.

Other medicines—Although certain medicines should not be used together at all, in other cases two different medicines may be used together even if an interaction might occur. In these cases, your doctor may want to change the dose, or other precautions may be necessary. Tell your health care professional if you are taking any other prescription or nonprescription (over-the-counter [OTC]) medicine.

Other medical problems—The presence of other medical problems may affect the use of carbohydrate and electrolytes solutions. Make sure you tell your doctor if you have any other medical problems, especially:

- Difficult urination—This condition may prevent the carbohydrate and electrolytes solution from working properly
- Inability to drink or
- Vomiting (severe and continuing)—Treatment by injection may need to be given to patients with these conditions
- Intestinal blockage—Carbohydrate and electrolytes solution may be harmful if given to patients with this condition

Proper Use of This Medicine

For patients using the *commercial powder form* of this medicine:

- Add 7 ounces of boiled, cooled tap water to the entire contents of one powder packet. Shake or stir the container for 2 or 3 minutes until all the powder is dissolved.
- Do not add more water to the solution after it is mixed.
- Do not boil the solution.
- Make and use a fresh solution each day.

For patients using the *powder form* of this medicine *distributed by the World Health Organization (WHO):*

- Add the entire contents of one powder packet to enough drinking water to make one quart (32 ounces) or liter of solution. Shake the container for 2 or 3 minutes until all the powder is dissolved.
- Do not add more water to the solution after it is mixed.
- Do not boil the solution.
- Make and use a fresh solution each day.

Babies and small children should be given the solution slowly, in small amounts, with a spoon, as often as possible, during the first 24 hours of diarrhea.

Take as directed. Do not take it for a longer time than your doctor has recommended. To do so may increase the chance of side effects.

Dosing—The dose of these combination medicines will be different for different patients. *Follow your doctor's orders or the directions on the label.* The following information includes only the average doses of these medicines. *If your dose is different, do not change it* unless your doctor tells you to do so.

For dextrose and electrolytes and for rice syrup solids and electrolytes

- For rehydration (to replace the water and some important salts [electrolytes]):
  —For *oral* dosage form (solution):
  - Adults and children over 10 years of age—Dose is based on body weight and must be determined by your doctor. At first, the usual dose is 50 to 100 milliliters (mL) per kilogram (kg) (23 to 45 mL per pound) of body weight taken over four to six hours. Your doctor may change the dose depending on your thirst and your response to the treatment.
  - Children up to 2 years of age—The dose is based on body weight and must be determined by your doctor. At first, the usual dose is 75 mL per kg (34 mL per pound) of body weight during the first eight hours and 75 mL per kg (34 mL per pound) of body weight during the next sixteen hours. Your doctor may change the dose depending on your thirst and your response to the treatment. However, the dose is usually not more than 100 mL in any 20-minute period.
  - Children 2 to 10 years of age—Dose is based on body weight and must be determined by your doctor. At first, the usual dose is 50 mL per kg (23 mL per pound) of body weight taken over the first four to six hours. Then, the dose is 100 mL per kg (45 mL per pound) of body weight taken over the next eighteen to twenty-four hours. Your doctor may change the dose depending on your thirst and your response to the treatment. However, the dose is usually not more than 100 mL in any 20-minute period.

For oral rehydration salts

- For rehydration (to replace the water and some important salts [electrolytes]):
  —For *oral* dosage form (solution):
  - Adults and teenagers—Dose is based on body weight and must be determined by your doctor. At first, the usual dose is 50 to 100 milliliters (mL) of solution per kilogram (kg) (23 to 45 mL per pound) of body weight taken over four to six hours. Your doctor may change the dose depending on your thirst and your response to the treatment.
  - Children—Dose is based on body weight and must be determined by your doctor. At first, the usual dose is 50 to 100 mL per kg (23 to 46 mL per pound) of body weight taken over the first four hours. Your doctor may change the dose depending on your thirst and your response to the treatment.

Storage—To store this medicine:

- Keep out of the reach of children.
- Store away from heat and direct light.
- Do not store the powder packets in the bathroom, near the kitchen sink, or in other damp places. Heat or moisture may cause the medicine to break down.
- Store the liquid in the refrigerator. However, keep the medicine from freezing.
- Make a fresh solution each day. Discard unused solution at the end of each day. Be sure that any discarded medicine is out of the reach of children.

Precautions While Using This Medicine

Eat soft foods, if possible, such as rice cereal, bananas, cooked peas or beans, and potatoes to keep up nutrition until the diarrhea stops and regular food and milk can be taken again. Breast-fed infants should be given breast milk between doses of the solution.

If your diarrhea does not improve in 1 or 2 days, or if it becomes worse, check with your doctor.

Also, *check with your doctor immediately* if your baby or child appears to have severe thirst, doughy skin, sunken eyes, dizziness or lightheadedness, tiredness or weakness, irritability, difficult urination, loss of weight, or convulsions (seizures). These signs may mean that too much water has been lost from the body.

For patients (except nursing babies) using the *powder form* of this medicine:

- Drink plain water whenever thirsty between doses of solution.

For patients taking the *premixed liquid form* of this medicine:

- Do not drink fruit juices or eat foods containing added salt until the diarrhea has stopped.

Side Effects of This Medicine

Along with its needed effects, a medicine may cause some unwanted effects. Although not all of these side effects may occur, if they do occur they may need medical attention.

Check with your doctor as soon as possible if any of the following side effects occur:

Symptoms of too much sodium (salt) in the body
Convulsions (seizures); dizziness; fast heartbeat; high blood pressure; irritability; muscle twitching; restlessness; swelling of feet or lower legs; weakness

Symptoms of too much fluid in the body
Puffy eyelids

Other side effects may occur that usually do not need medical attention. These side effects may go away during treatment as your body adjusts to the medicine. However, check with your doctor if the following side effect continues or is bothersome:

More common

Vomiting (mild)

Other side effects not listed above may also occur in some patients. If you notice any other effects, check with your doctor.

Revised: 12/02/92
Interim revision: 07/20/95; 08/11/97

CARBONIC ANHYDRASE INHIBITORS Systemic

Some commonly used brand names are:

In the U.S.—

Ak-Zol[1]
Daranide[2]
Dazamide[1]
Diamox[1]
Diamox Sequels[1]
MZM[3]
Neptazane[3]
Storzolamide[1]

In Canada—

Acetazolam[1]
Apo-Acetazolamide[1]
Diamox[1]
Diamox Sequels[1]
Neptazane[3]

Another commonly used name for dichlorphenamide is diclofenamide.

Note: For quick reference, the following carbonic anhydrase inhibitors are numbered to match the corresponding brand names.

This information applies to the following medicines:

1. Acetazolamide (a-set-a-ZOLE-a-mide)‡
2. Dichlorphenamide (dye-klor-FEN-a-mide)†
3. Methazolamide (meth-a-ZOLE-a-mide)‡

†Not commercially available in Canada.
‡Generic name product may also be available in U.S.

Description

Carbonic anhydrase inhibitors are used to treat glaucoma. Acetazolamide is also used as an anticonvulsant to control certain seizures in the treatment of epilepsy. It is also sometimes used to prevent or lessen some effects in mountain climbers who climb to high altitudes, and to treat other conditions as determined by your doctor.

These medicines are available only with your doctor's prescription, in the following dosage forms:

Oral

Acetazolamide
- Extended-release capsules (U.S. and Canada)
- Tablets (U.S. and Canada)

Dichlorphenamide
- Tablets (U.S.)

Methazolamide
- Tablets (U.S. and Canada)

Parenteral

Acetazolamide
- Injection (U.S. and Canada)

Before Using This Medicine

In deciding to use a medicine, the risks of taking the medicine must be weighed against the good it will do. This is a decision you and your doctor will make. For carbonic anhydrase inhibitors, the following should be considered:

Allergies—Tell your doctor if you have ever had any unusual or allergic reaction to carbonic anhydrase inhibitors, sulfonamides (sulfa drugs), or thiazide diuretics (a type of water pill). Also tell your health care professional if you are allergic to any other substances, such as foods, preservatives, or dyes.

Pregnancy—Carbonic anhydrase inhibitors have not been studied in pregnant women. However, studies in animals have shown that carbonic anhydrase inhibitors cause birth defects. Before taking this medicine, make sure your doctor knows if you are pregnant or if you may become pregnant.

Breast-feeding—Carbonic anhydrase inhibitors may pass into the breast milk. These medicines are not recommended during breast-feeding, because they may cause unwanted effects in nursing babies. It may be necessary for you to use another medicine or to stop breast-feeding during treatment. Be sure you have discussed this with your doctor.

Children—Although there is no specific information comparing use of carbonic anhydrase inhibitors in children with use in other age groups, these medicines are not expected to cause different side effects or problems in children than they do in adults.

Older adults—Many medicines have not been studies specifically in older people. Therefore, it may not be known whether they work exactly the same way they do in younger adults. Although there is no specific information comparing use of carbonic anhydrase inhibitors in the elderly with use in other age groups, these medicines are not expected to cause different side effects or problems in older people than they do in younger adults.

Other medicines—Although certain medicines should not be used together at all, in other cases two different medicines may be used together even if an interaction might occur. In these cases, your doctor may want to change the dose, or other precautions may be necessary. When you are using carbonic anhydrase inhibitors, it is especially important that your health care professional know if you are using any of the following:

- Amphetamines or
- Mecamylamine (e.g., Inversine) or
- Quinidine (e.g., Quinidex)—Use of carbonic anhydrase inhibitors may increase the chance of side effects
- Methenamine (e.g., Mandelamine)—Use of carbonic anhydrase inhibitors may decrease the effectiveness of methenamine

Other medical problems—The presence of other medical problems may affect the use of carbonic anhydrase inhibitors. Make sure you tell your doctor if you have any other medical problems, especially:

- Diabetes mellitus (sugar diabetes)—Use of carbonic anhydrase inhibitors may increase the patient's blood and urine sugar concentrations
- Emphysema or other chronic lung disease—Use of carbonic anhydrase inhibitors may increase the risk of acidosis (shortness of breath, troubled breathing)
- Gout or
- Low blood levels of potassium or sodium—Use of carbonic anhydrase inhibitors may make the condition worse
- Kidney disease or stones—Higher blood levels of carbonic anhydrase inhibitors may result, which may increase the chance of side effects; also, these medicines may make the condition worse
- Liver disease—Use of carbonic anhydrase inhibitors may increase the risk of electrolyte imbalance and may make the condition worse
- Underactive adrenal gland (Addison's disease)—Use of carbonic anhydrase inhibitors may increase the risk of electrolyte imbalance

Proper Use of This Medicine

Take this medicine only as directed. Do not take more of it and do not take it more often than your doctor ordered. To do so may increase the chance of side effects without increasing the effectiveness of this medicine.

This medicine may be taken with meals to lessen the chance of stomach upset. However, if stomach upset (nausea or vomiting) continues, check with your doctor.

This medicine may cause an increase in the amount of urine or in your frequency of urination. If you continue to take the medicine every day, these effects should lessen or stop. To keep the increase in urine from affecting your nighttime sleep:

- If you are to take a single dose a day, take it in the morning after breakfast.
- If you are to take more than one dose a day, take the last dose no later than 6 p.m., unless otherwise directed by your doctor.

However, it is best to plan your dose or doses according to a schedule that will least affect your personal activities and sleep. Ask your health care professional to help you plan the best time to take this medicine.

Dosing—The doses of carbonic anhydrase inhibitors will be different for different patients. *Follow your doctor's orders or the directions on the label.* The following information includes only the average doses of these medicines. *If your dose is different, do not change it* unless your doctor tells you to do so.

The number of capsules or tablets that you take depends on the strength of the medicine. Also, *the number of doses you take each day, the time allowed between doses, and the length of time you take the medicine depend on the medical problem for which you are taking the carbonic anhydrase inhibitor.*

For acetazolamide

- For *oral* dosage form (extended-release capsules):
  - —For glaucoma:
    - Adults—500 milligrams (mg) two times a day, in the morning and evening.
    - Children—Use and dose must be determined by your doctor.
  - —For altitude sickness:
    - Adults—500 mg one or two times a day.
    - Children—Use and dose must be determined by your doctor.
- For *oral* dosage form (tablets):
  - —For glaucoma:
    - Adults—250 mg one to four times a day.
    - Children—Dose is based on body weight and must be determined by your doctor. The usual dose is 10 to 15 mg per kilogram (kg) (4.5 to 6.8 mg per pound) of body weight a day in divided doses.
  - —For epilepsy:
    - Adults and children—Dose is based on body weight and must be determined by your doctor. The usual dose is 10 mg per kg (4.5 mg per pound) of body weight a day in divided doses.
  - —For altitude sickness:
    - Adults—250 mg two to four times a day.
    - Children—Use and dose must be determined by your doctor.
- For *injection* dosage form:
  - —For glaucoma:
    - Adults—500 mg, injected into a muscle or vein, for one dose.
    - Children—Dose is based on body weight and must be determined by your doctor. The usual dose is 5 to 10 mg per kg (2.3 to 4.5 mg per pound) of body weight every six hours, injected into a muscle or vein.

For dichlorphenamide

- For *oral* dosage form (tablets):
  - —For glaucoma:
    - Adults—25 to 50 milligrams (mg) one to three times a day.
    - Children—Use and dose must be determined by your doctor.

For methazolamide

- For *oral* dosage form (tablets):
  - —For glaucoma:
    - Adults—50 to 100 milligrams (mg) two or three times a day.
    - Children—Use and dose must be determined by your doctor.

Missed dose—If you miss a dose of this medicine, take it as soon as possible. However, if it is almost time for your next dose, skip the missed dose and go back to your regular dosing schedule. Do not double doses.

Storage—To store this medicine:

- Keep out of the reach of children.
- Store away from heat and direct light.
- Do not store the capsule or tablet form of this medicine in the bathroom, near the kitchen sink, or in other damp places. Heat or moisture may cause the medicine to break down.
- Do not keep outdated medicine or medicine no longer needed. Be sure that any discarded medicine is out of the reach of children.

Precautions While Using This Medicine

This medicine may cause some people to feel drowsy, dizzy, lightheaded, or more tired than they are normally. *Make sure you know how you react to this medicine before you drive, use machines, or do anything else that could be dangerous if you are not alert.*

It is important that your doctor check your progress at regular visits. Your doctor may want to do certain tests to see if the medicine is working properly or to see if certain side effects may be occurring without your knowing it.

This medicine may cause a loss of potassium from your body. To help prevent this, your doctor may want you to eat or drink foods that have a high potassium content (for example, orange or other citrus fruit juices) or take a potassium supplement. It is very important to follow these directions. Also, it is important not to change your diet on your own. This is more important if you are already on a special diet (as for diabetes) or if you are taking a potassium supplement. Extra potassium may not be necessary and, in some cases, too much potassium could be harmful.

For *diabetic patients:*

- This medicine may raise blood and urine sugar levels. While you are using this medicine, be especially careful in testing for sugar in your blood or urine. If you have any questions about this, check with your doctor.

Your doctor may want you to increase the amount of fluids you drink while you are taking this medicine. This is to prevent kidney stones. However, do not increase the amount of fluids you drink without first checking with your doctor.

For patients taking *acetazolamide as an anticonvulsant*:

- *If you have been taking acetazolamide regularly for several weeks or more, do not suddenly stop taking it.* Your doctor may want you to reduce gradually the amount you are taking before stopping completely.

Side Effects of This Medicine

Along with its needed effects, a medicine may cause some unwanted effects. Although not all of these side effects may occur, if they do occur they may need medical attention.

Check with your doctor immediately if either of the following side effects occurs:

Rare

Shortness of breath or trouble in breathing

Also, check with your doctor as soon as possible if any of the following side effects occur:

More common

Unusual tiredness or weakness

Less common

Blood in urine; difficult urination; mental depression; pain in lower back; pain or burning while urinating; sudden decrease in amount of urine

Rare

Bloody or black, tarry stools; clumsiness or unsteadiness; confusion; convulsions (seizures); darkening of urine; fever; hives, itching of skin, skin rash, or sores; muscle weakness (severe); pale stools; ringing or buzzing in the ears; sore throat; trembling; unusual bruising or bleeding; yellow eyes or skin

Symptoms of too much potassium loss

Dryness of mouth; increased thirst; irregular heartbeats; mood or mental changes; muscle cramps or pain; nausea or vomiting; unusual tiredness or weakness; weak pulse

Also, check with your doctor if you have any changes in your vision (especially problems with seeing faraway objects) when you first begin taking this medicine.

Other side effects may occur that usually do not need medical attention. These side effects may go away during treatment as your body adjusts to the medicine. However, check with your doctor if any of the following side effects continue or are bothersome:

More common

Diarrhea; general feeling of discomfort or illness; increase in frequency of urination or amount of urine (rare with methazolamide); loss of appetite; metallic taste in mouth; nausea or vomiting; numbness, tingling, or burning in hands, fingers, feet, toes, mouth, lips, tongue, or anus; weight loss

Less common or rare

Constipation; dizziness or lightheadedness; drowsiness; feeling of choking or lump in the throat; headache; increased sensitivity of eyes to sunlight; loss of taste and smell; nervousness or irritability

Other side effects not listed above may also occur in some patients. If you notice any other effects, check with your doctor.

Revised: 06/21/94
Interim revision: 01/24/95

CARBOPLATIN Systemic

Some commonly used brand names are:

In the U.S.—
Paraplatin

In Canada—
Paraplatin
Paraplatin-AQ

Description

Carboplatin (KAR-boe-pla-tin) belongs to the group of medicines known as alkylating agents. It is used to treat some kinds of cancer.

Carboplatin interferes with the growth of cancer cells, which are eventually destroyed. Since the growth of normal body cells may also be affected by carboplatin, other effects will also occur. Some of these may be serious and must be reported to your doctor. Other effects may not be serious but may cause concern. Some effects may not occur for months or years after the medicine is used.

Before you begin treatment with carboplatin, you and your doctor should talk about the good this medicine will do as well as the risks of using it.

Carboplatin is to be administered only by or under the immediate supervision of your doctor. It is available in the following dosage form:

Parenteral
- Injection (U.S. and Canada)

Before Using This Medicine

In deciding to use a medicine, the risks of taking the medicine must be weighed against the good it will do. This is a decision you and your doctor will make. For carboplatin, the following should be considered:

Allergies—Tell your doctor if you have ever had any unusual or allergic reaction to carboplatin, cisplatin, or any other platinum-containing substance.

Pregnancy—There is a chance that this medicine may cause birth defects if either the male or female is taking it at the time of conception or if it is taken during pregnancy. Carboplatin causes toxic or harmful effects and birth defects in rats. In addition, many cancer medicines may cause sterility which could be permanent. Although sterility has not been reported with this medicine, the possibility should be kept in mind.

Be sure that you have discussed these possible effects with your doctor before receiving this medicine. It is best to use some kind of birth control while you are receiving carboplatin. Tell your doctor right away if you think you have become pregnant while receiving carboplatin. Before receiving carboplatin, make sure your doctor knows if you are pregnant or if you may become pregnant.

Breast-feeding—Because carboplatin may cause serious side effects, breast-feeding is generally not recommended while you are receiving it.

Children—Studies on this medicine have been done only in adult patients and there is no specific information comparing use of carboplatin in children with use in other age groups.

Older adults—Some side effects of carboplatin (especially blood problems or numbness or tingling in fingers or toes) may be more likely to occur in the elderly.

Other medicines—Although certain medicines should not be used together at all, in other cases two different medicines may be used together even if an interaction might occur. In these cases, your doctor may want to change the dose, or other precautions may be necessary. When receiving carboplatin it is especially important that your health care professional know if you have every been treated with radiation or cancer medicines or if you are taking any of the following:

- Amphotericin B by injection (e.g., Fungizone) or
- Antithyroid agents (medicine for overactive thyroid) or
- Azathioprine (e.g., Imuran) or
- Chloramphenicol (e.g., Chloromycetin) or
- Colchicine or
- Flucytosine (e.g., Ancobon) or
- Ganciclovir (e.g., Cytovene) or
- Interferon (e.g., Intron A, Roferon-A) or
- Plicamycin (e.g., Mithracin) or
- Zidovudine (e.g., AZT, Retrovir)—Carboplatin may increase the effects of these medicines or radiation on the blood

Other medical problems—The presence of other medical problems may affect the use of carboplatin. Make sure you tell your doctor if you have any other medical problems, especially:

- Chickenpox (including recent exposure) or
- Herpes zoster (shingles)—Risk of severe disease affecting other parts of the body
- Hearing problems—May be worsened by carboplatin
- Infection—Carboplatin decreases your body's ability to fight infection
- Kidney disease—Effects may be increased because of slower removal from the body

Proper Use of This Medicine

This medicine is sometimes given together with certain other medicines. If you are using a combination of medicines, it is important that you receive each one at the proper time. If you are taking some of these medicines by mouth, ask your health care professional to help you plan a way to take them at the right times.

This medicine usually causes nausea and vomiting that may sometimes be severe. However, it is very important that you continue to receive the medicine, even if you begin to feel ill. Ask your health care professional for ways to lessen these effects, especially if they are severe.

Dosing—The dose of carboplatin will be different for different patients. The dose that is used may depend on a number of things, including what the medicine is being used for, the patient's size, and whether or not other medicines are also being taken. *If you are receiving carboplatin at home, follow your doctor's orders or the directions* *on the label.* If you have any questions about the proper dose of carboplatin, ask your doctor.

Precautions While Using This Medicine

It is very important that your doctor check your progress at regular visits to make sure that this medicine is working properly and to check for unwanted effects.

While you are being treated with carboplatin, and after you stop treatment with it, *do not have any immunizations (vaccinations) without your doctor's approval.* Carboplatin may lower your body's resistance and there is a chance you might get the infection the immunization is meant to prevent. In addition, other persons living in your household should not take oral polio vaccine since there is a chance they could pass the polio virus on to you. Also, avoid persons who have taken oral polio vaccine. Do not get close to them, and do not stay in the same room with them for very long. If you cannot take these precautions, you should consider wearing a protective face mask that covers the nose and mouth.

Carboplatin can temporarily lower the number of white blood cells in your blood, increasing the chance of getting an infection. It can also lower the number of platelets, which are necessary for proper blood clotting. If this occurs, there are certain precautions you can take, especially when your blood count is low, to reduce the risk of infection or bleeding:

- If you can, avoid people with infections. *Check with your doctor immediately* if you think you are getting an infection or if you get a fever or chills, cough or hoarseness, lower back or side pain, or painful or difficult urination.
- *Check with your doctor immediately* if you notice any unusual bleeding or bruising; black, tarry stools; blood in urine or stools; or pinpoint red spots on your skin.
- Be careful when using a regular toothbrush, dental floss, or toothpick. Your medical doctor, dentist, or nurse may recommend other ways to clean your teeth and gums. Check with your health care professional before having any dental work done.
- Do not touch your eyes or the inside of your nose unless you have just washed your hands and have not touched anything else in the meantime.
- Be careful not to cut yourself when you are using sharp objects such as a safety razor or fingernail or toenail cutters.
- Avoid contact sports or other situations where bruising or injury could occur.

Side Effects of This Medicine

Along with its needed effects, a medicine may cause some unwanted effects. Although not all of these side effects may occur, if they do occur they may need medical attention.

Also, because of the way these medicines act on the body, there is a chance that they might cause other unwanted effects that may not occur until months or years after the medicine is used. These delayed effects may include certain types of cancer, such as leukemia. Discuss these possible effects with your doctor.

Check with your doctor or nurse immediately if any of the following side effects occur:

Less common

Black, tarry stools; blood in urine or stools; cough or hoarseness; fever or chills; lower back or side pain; painful or difficult urination; pinpoint red spots on skin; skin rash or itching; unusual bleeding or bruising

Rare

Wheezing

Check with your doctor as soon as possible if any of the following side effects occur:

More common

Pain at place of injection

Less common

Numbness or tingling in fingers or toes

Rare

Blurred vision; ringing in ears; sores in mouth and on lips

Other side effects may occur that usually do not need medical attention. These side effects may go away during treatment as your body adjusts to the medicine. Also, your health care professional may be able to tell you about ways to prevent or reduce some of these side effects. Check with your health care professional if any of the following side effects continue or are bothersome or if you have any questions about them:

More common

Nausea and vomiting; unusual tiredness or weakness

Less common

Constipation or diarrhea; loss of appetite

This medicine may cause a temporary loss of hair in some people. After treatment with carboplatin has ended, normal hair growth should return.

Other side effects not listed above may also occur in some patients. If you notice any other effects, check with your doctor.

Revised: 06/03/92
Interim revision: 05/02/94

CARBOPROST Systemic

Some commonly used brand names are:

In the U.S.—
Hemabate

In Canada—
Prostin/15M

Description

DescriptionCarboprost (KAR-boe-prost) is given by injection to cause abortion. It is an oxytocic, which means it acts by causing the uterus to contract the way it does during labor and also helps the cervix to dilate.

Carboprost may also be used for other purposes as determined by your doctor.

Carboprost is to be administered only by or under the immediate care of your doctor. It is available in the following dosage form:

Parenteral

- Injection (U.S. and Canada)

Before Receiving This Medicine

In deciding to use a medicine, the risks of taking the medicine must be weighed against the good it will do. This is a decision you and your doctor will make. For carboprost, the following should be considered:

Allergies—Tell your doctor if you have ever had any unusual or allergic reaction to carboprost or other oxytocics (medicines that stimulate the uterus to contract). Also tell your health care professional if you are allergic to any other substances, such as foods, preservatives, or dyes.

Other medicines—Although certain medicines should not be used together at all, in other cases two different medicines may be used together even if an interaction might occur. In these cases, your doctor may want to change the dose, or other precautions may be necessary. Tell your doctor if you are taking any prescription or nonprescription (over-the-counter [OTC]) medicine.

Other medical problems—The presence of other medical problems may affect the use of carboprost. Make sure you tell your doctor if you have any other medical problems, especially:

- Adrenal gland disease (history of)—Carboprost stimulates the body to produce steroids
- Anemia—In some patients, abortion with carboprost may result in loss of blood that may require a transfusion
- Asthma (or history of) or
- Lung disease—Carboprost may cause narrowing of the blood vessels in the lungs or narrowing of the lung passages
- Diabetes mellitus (sugar diabetes) (history of)
- Epilepsy (or history of)—Rarely, seizures have occurred with use of carboprost
- Fibroid tumors of the uterus or
- Uterus surgery (history of)—There is an increased risk of rupture of the uterus
- Glaucoma—Rarely, the pressure within the eye has increased during use of carboprost
- Heart or blood vessel disease (or history of) or
- High blood pressure (or history of) or
- Low blood pressure (or history of)—Carboprost may cause changes in heart function or blood pressure changes
- Jaundice (history of)
- Kidney disease (or history of)
- Liver disease (or history of)—The body may not get carboprost out of the bloodstream at the usual rate, which may make the medicine work longer or cause toxic effects

Proper Use of This Medicine

Dosing—The dose of carboprost will be different for different patients. Your doctor will give you the dose of this medicine and follow your care in a hospital or another health care setting. The following information includes only the average doses of carboprost.

- For *injection* dosage form:
  - —For causing an abortion in the second trimester of pregnancy (13th to 24th week):
    - Adults—At first, 100 to 250 micrograms (mcg) injected deep into a muscle. Then, 250 to 500 mcg every one and one-half to three and one-half hours for up to two days.
  - —For bleeding of the uterus after pregnancy:
    - Adults—250 mcg injected deep into a muscle. Your doctor may repeat this dose every fifteen to ninety minutes as needed.

Side Effects of This Medicine

Along with its needed effects, a medicine may cause some unwanted effects. Although not all of these side effects may occur, if they do occur they may need medical attention.

Tell the health care professional immediately if any of the following side effects occur:

Less common or rare

Fast or slow heartbeat; headache (severe and continuing); hives or skin rash; increased pain of the uterus; pale, cool, blotchy skin on arms or legs; pressing or painful feeling in chest; shortness of breath; swelling of face, inside the nose, and eyelids; tightness in chest; trouble in breathing; weak or absent pulse in arms or legs; wheezing

Check with the health care professional as soon as possible if any of the following side effects occur:

Constipation; pain or inflammation at place of injection; tender or mildly bloated abdomen or stomach

Other side effects may occur that usually do not need medical attention. These side effects usually go away after the medicine is stopped. However, let the health care professional know if any of the following side effects continue or are bothersome:

More common

Diarrhea; nausea; vomiting

Less common or rare

Chills or shivering; dizziness; fever (temporary); flushing or redness of face; headache; stomach cramps or pain

This procedure may result in some effects, which occur after the procedure is completed, that need medical attention. Check with your doctor if you notice any of the following:

Chills or shivering (continuing); fever (continuing); foul-smelling vaginal discharge; increase in uterus bleeding; pain in lower abdomen

Other side effects not listed above may also occur in some patients. If you notice any other effects, check with your health care professional.

Revised: 10/26/92
Interim revision: 06/08/94

CARMUSTINE Systemic

A commonly used brand name in the U.S. and Canada is BiCNU. Another commonly used name is BCNU.

Description

Carmustine (kar-MUS-teen) belongs to the group of medicines known as alkylating agents. It is used to treat some kinds of cancer.

Carmustine interferes with the growth of cancer cells, which are eventually destroyed. Since the growth of normal body cells may also be affected by carmustine, other effects will also occur. Some of these may be serious and must be reported to your doctor. Other effects, like hair loss, may not be serious but may cause concern. Some effects may not occur for months or years after the medicine is used.

Before you begin treatment with carmustine, you and your doctor should talk about the good this medicine will do as well as the risks of using it.

Carmustine is to be administered only by or under the immediate supervision of your doctor. It is available in the following dosage form:

Parenteral
- Injection (U.S. and Canada)

Before Using This Medicine

In deciding to use a medicine, the risks of taking the medicine must be weighed against the good it will do. This is a decision you and your doctor will make. For carmustine, the following should be considered:

Allergies—Tell your doctor if you have ever had any unusual or allergic reaction to carmustine.

Pregnancy—There is a chance that this medicine may cause birth defects if either the male or female is taking it at the time of conception or if it is taken during pregnancy. Carmustine causes toxic or harmful effects in the fetus of rats and rabbits and causes birth defects in rats at doses about the same as the human dose. In addition, many cancer medicines may cause sterility which could be permanent. Although this has only been reported in animals with this medicine, the possibility should be kept in mind.

Be sure that you have discussed this with your doctor before receiving this medicine. It is best to use some kind of birth control while you are receiving carmustine. Tell your doctor right away if you think you have become pregnant while receiving carmustine.

Breast-feeding—Because carmustine may cause serious side effects, breast-feeding is generally not recommended while you are receiving it.

Children—Although there is no specific information comparing use of carmustine in children with use in other age groups, this medicine is not expected to cause different side effects or problems in children than it does in adults.

Older adults—Many medicines have not been studied specifically in older people. Therefore, it may not be known whether they work exactly the same way they do in younger adults or if they cause different side effects or problems in older people. There is no specific information comparing use of carmustine in the elderly with use in other age groups.

Other medicines—Although certain medicines should not be used together at all, in other cases two different medicines may be used together even if an interaction might occur. In these cases, your doctor may want to change the dose, or other precautions may be necessary. When you are receiving carmustine, it is especially important that your health care professional know if you are taking any of the following:

- Amphotericin B by injection (e.g., Fungizone) or
- Antithyroid agents (medicine for overactive thyroid) or
- Azathioprine (e.g., Imuran) or
- Chloramphenicol (e.g., Chloromycetin) or
- Colchicine or
- Flucytosine (e.g., Ancobon) or
- Ganciclovir (e.g., Cytovene) or
- Interferon (e.g., Intron A, Roferon-A) or
- Plicamycin (e.g., Mithramycin) or
- Zidovudine (e.g., AZT, Retrovir) or
- If you have ever been treated with radiation or cancer medicines—Carmustine may increase the effects of these medicines or radiation therapy on the blood

Other medical problems—The presence of other medical problems may affect the use of carmustine. Make sure you tell your doctor if you have any other medical problems, especially:

- Chickenpox (including recent exposure) or
- Herpes zoster (shingles)—Risk of severe disease affecting other parts of the body
- Infection—Carmustine decreases your body's ability to fight infection
- Kidney disease—Effects of carmustine may be increased because of slower removal from the body
- Liver disease—Carmustine may cause side effects to the liver
- Lung disease—Risk of lung problems caused by carmustine may be increased

Smoking—Increased risk of lung problems.

Proper Use of This Medicine

Carmustine is sometimes given together with certain other medicines. If you are using a combination of medicines, it is important that you receive each one at the proper time. If you are taking some of these medicines by mouth, ask your health care professional to help you plan a way to take them at the right times.

This medicine often causes nausea and vomiting, which usually last no longer than 4 to 6 hours. It is very important that you continue to receive the medicine, even if you begin to feel ill. Ask your health care professional for ways to lessen these effects.

Dosing—The dose of carmustine will be different for different patients. The dose that is used may depend on a number of things, including what the medicine is being used for, the patient's size, and whether or not other medicines are also being taken. *If you are receiving carmustine at home, follow your doctor's orders or the directions on the label.* If you have any questions about the proper dose of carmustine, ask your doctor.

Precautions While Using This Medicine

It is very important that your doctor check your progress at regular visits to make sure that this medicine is working properly and to check for unwanted effects.

While you are being treated with carmustine, and after you stop treatment with it, *do not have any immunizations (vaccinations) without your doctor's approval.* Carmustine may lower your body's resistance and there is a chance you might get the infection the immunization is meant to prevent. In addition, other persons living in your household should not take oral polio vaccine since there is a chance they could pass the polio virus on to you. Also, avoid persons who have taken oral polio vaccine. Do not get close to them, and do not stay in the same room with them for very long. If you cannot take these precautions, you should consider wearing a protective face mask that covers the nose and mouth.

Carmustine can temporarily lower the number of white blood cells in your blood, increasing the chance of getting an infection. It can also lower the number of platelets, which are necessary for proper blood clotting. If this occurs, there are certain precautions you can take, especially when your blood count is low, to reduce the risk of infection or bleeding:

- If you can, avoid people with infections. *Check with your doctor immediately* if you think you are getting an infection or if you get a fever or chills, cough or hoarseness, lower back or side pain, or painful or difficult urination.
- *Check with your doctor immediately* if you notice any unusual bleeding or bruising; black, tarry stools; blood in urine or stools; or pinpoint red spots on your skin.
- Be careful when using a regular toothbrush, dental floss, or toothpick. Your medical doctor, dentist, or nurse may recommend other ways to clean your teeth and gums. Check with your medical doctor before having any dental work done.
- Do not touch your eyes or the inside of your nose unless you have just washed your hands and have not touched anything else in the meantime.
- Be careful not to cut yourself when you are using sharp objects such as a safety razor or fingernail or toenail cutters.
- Avoid contact sports or other situations where bruising or injury could occur.

If carmustine accidentally seeps out of the vein into which it is injected, it may damage some tissues and cause scarring. *Tell the doctor or nurse right away if you notice redness, pain, or swelling at the place of injection.*

Side Effects of This Medicine

Along with its needed effects, a medicine may cause some unwanted effects. Some side effects will have signs or symptoms that you can see or feel. Your doctor may watch for others by doing certain tests. Some of the unwanted effects that may be caused by carmustine are listed below. Although not all of these effects may occur, if they do occur, they may need medical attention.

Also, because of the way these medicines act on the body, there is a chance that they might cause other unwanted effects that may not occur until months or years after the medicine is used. These delayed effects may include certain types of cancer, such as leukemia. Discuss these possible effects with your doctor.

Check with your doctor or nurse immediately if any of the following side effects occur:

More common

Pain or redness at place of injection

Less common

Black, tarry stools; blood in urine or stools; cough or hoarseness; fever or chills; lower back or side pain; painful or difficult urination; pinpoint red spots on skin; unusual bleeding or bruising

Check with your health care professional as soon as possible if any of the following side effects occur:

More common

Shortness of breath

Less common

Flushing of face; sores in mouth and on lips; unusual tiredness or weakness

Rare

Decrease in urination; swelling of feet or lower legs

This medicine may also cause the following side effects that your doctor will watch for:

More common

Low red blood cell count; low white blood cell count

Rare

Liver problems; lung problems

Other side effects may occur that usually do not need medical attention. These side effects may go away during treatment as your body adjusts to the medicine. Also, your health care professional may be able to tell you about ways to prevent or reduce some of these side effects. Check with your health care professional if any of the following side effects continue or are bothersome or if you have any questions about them:

More common

Nausea and vomiting (usually lasting no longer than 4 to 6 hours)

Less common

Diarrhea; discoloration of skin along vein of injection; dizziness; loss of appetite; skin rash and itching; trouble in swallowing; trouble in walking

This medicine may cause a temporary loss of hair in some people. After treatment with carmustine has ended, normal hair growth should return.

Side effects that affect your lungs (for example, cough and shortness of breath) may be more likely to occur if you smoke.

After you stop receiving carmustine, it may still produce some side effects that need attention. During this period of time check with your health care professional if you notice any of the following:

Black, tarry stools; blood in urine or stools; cough or hoarseness; fever or chills; lower back or side pain; painful or difficult urination; pinpoint red spots on skin; shortness of breath; unusual bleeding or bruising

Other side effects not listed above may also occur in some patients. If you notice any other effects, check with your health care professional.

Revised: 07/15/94

CELLULOSE SODIUM PHOSPHATE Systemic†

A commonly used brand name in the U.S. is Calcibind.

†Not commercially available in Canada.

Description

Cellulose sodium phosphate (SELL-u-lose SO-dee-um FOS-fate) is used to prevent the formation of calcium-containing kidney stones. It is used in patients whose bodies absorb too much calcium from their food.

Cellulose sodium phosphate works by combining with the calcium and some other minerals in food. This prevents the calcium from reaching the kidneys where the stones are formed.

Cellulose sodium phosphate is available only with your doctor's prescription, in the following dosage form:

Oral

- Powder for oral suspension (U.S.)

Before Using This Medicine

In deciding to use a medicine, the risks of taking the medicine must be weighed against the good it will do. This is a decision you and your doctor will make. For cellulose sodium phosphate, the following should be considered:

Allergies—Tell your doctor if you have ever had any unusual or allergic reaction to cellulose sodium phosphate. Also tell your health care professional if you are allergic to any other substances, such as foods, preservatives, or dyes.

Diet—Make certain your health care professional knows if you are on any special diet, such as a low-sodium or low-sugar diet. Also tell your health care professional if your diet contains large amounts of milk or other dairy products, spinach (or other dark green leafy vegetables), chocolate, brewed tea, or rhubarb or if you are taking vitamin C or magnesium supplements.

Pregnancy—Studies have not been done in either humans or animals. However, pregnant women usually need more calcium in their diet, and should not take cellulose sodium phosphate unless it is clearly needed. Be sure you have discussed the risks and benefits with your doctor.

Breast-feeding—It is not known whether cellulose sodium phosphate passes into breast milk. However, this medicine has not been reported to cause problems in nursing babies.

Children—Although there is no specific information comparing use of cellulose sodium phosphate in children with use in any other age group, its use is not recommended in children up to 16 years of age because of the increased need for calcium in growing children.

Older adults—Many medicines have not been studied specifically in older people. Therefore, it may not be known whether they work exactly the same way they do in younger adults or if they cause different side effects or problems in older people. There is no specific information comparing use of cellulose sodium phosphate in the elderly with use in other age groups.

Other medicines—Although certain medicines should not be used together at all, in other cases two different medicines may be used together even if an interaction might occur. In these cases, your doctor may want to change the dose, or other precautions may be necessary. When you are taking cellulose sodium phosphate, it is especially important that your health care professional know if you are taking any of the following:

- Calcium supplements, or calcium containing antacids or laxatives—Use may lead to too much calcium in the body, preventing the cellulose sodium phosphate from working properly
- Magnesium supplements, or magnesium containing antacids or laxatives—Cellulose sodium phosphate and magnesium should not be taken within 1 hour of each other

Other medical problems—The presence of other medical problems may affect the use of cellulose sodium phosphate. Make sure you tell your doctor if you have any other medical problems, especially:

- Bone disease—Cellulose sodium phosphate may make the condition worse
- Edema or swelling or
- Heart disease—The high sodium content of cellulose sodium phosphate may cause the body to hold water
- Intestinal problems or
- Parathyroid disease or problems—Cellulose sodium phosphate may increase the risk of bone problems

Proper Use of This Medicine

Take this medicine mixed in a full glass (8 ounces) of water, soft drink, or fruit juice. After drinking all the liquid containing the medicine, rinse the glass with a little more liquid. Drink that also to make sure you get all the medicine.

It is very important that you take cellulose sodium phosphate with meals. If this medicine is taken an hour or more after a meal, it will not work properly.

Take cellulose sodium phosphate only as directed. Do not take more of it, do not take it more often, and do not take it for a longer time than your doctor ordered. To do so may increase the chance of side effects.

Drink at least a full glass (8 ounces) of water, a soft drink, or fruit juice every hour while you are awake, unless otherwise directed by your doctor. This also will help prevent kidney stones while you are taking cellulose sodium phosphate.

Dosing—The dose of cellulose sodium phosphate will be different for different patients. *Follow your doctor's orders or the directions on the label.* The following information includes only the average doses of cellulose sodium phosphate. *If your dose is different, do not change it* unless your doctor tells you to do so.

- To prevent kidney stones:
  - —Adults: At first, 10 to 15 grams a day (3.3 to 5 grams three times a day with meals). Then, your doctor may reduce your dose.
  - —Children: Use is not recommended.

Missed dose—If you miss a dose of this medicine, skip the missed dose and go back to your regular dosing schedule. Do not double doses.

Storage—To store this medicine:
- Keep out of the reach of children.
- Store away from heat and direct light.
- Do not store in the bathroom, near the kitchen sink, or in other damp places. Heat or moisture may cause the medicine to break down.
- Do not keep outdated medicine or medicine no longer needed. Be sure that any discarded medicine is out of the reach of children.

Precautions While Using This Medicine

It is important that your doctor check your progress at regular visits. This is to make sure cellulose sodium phosphate is working properly and does not cause unwanted effects.

If you are taking a magnesium supplement, take it at least one hour before or after you take cellulose sodium phosphate. Otherwise, the magnesium may combine with this medicine and keep it from working properly.

Do not take vitamin C, or eat spinach (or other dark green leafy vegetables), chocolate, brewed tea, or rhubarb while you are taking cellulose sodium phosphate. They may increase the chance of kidney stones.

Do not drink milk or eat milk products (for example, cheese, ice cream, and yogurt) while you are taking this medicine, because dairy products are high in calcium. Drinking milk or eating milk products may keep cellulose sodium phosphate from working properly.

While you are taking cellulose sodium phosphate, do not eat salty foods or use extra salt on foods. To do so may increase the chance of unwanted effects.

For patients on a low-sodium diet:
- This medicine contains sodium. If you have any questions about this, check with your health care professional.

Side Effects of This Medicine

Along with its needed effects, a medicine may cause some unwanted effects. Although not all of these side effects may occur, if they do occur they may need medical attention.

Check with your doctor as soon as possible if any of the following side effects occur:

With long-term use

Convulsions (seizures); drowsiness; loss of appetite; mood or mental changes; muscle spasms or twitching; nausea or vomiting; trembling; unusual tiredness or weakness

Other side effects may occur that usually do not need medical attention. These side effects may go away during treatment as your body adjusts to the medicine. However, check with your doctor if any of the following side effects continue or are bothersome:

More common

Abdominal or stomach discomfort; loose bowel movements or diarrhea

Other side effects not listed above may also occur in some patients. If you notice any other effects, check with your doctor.

Revised: 12/02/92
Interim revision: 05/13/94

CEPHALOSPORINS Systemic

Some commonly used brand names are:

In the U.S.—

Ancef[4]
Ceclor[1]
Cefadyl[20]
Cefanex[18]
Cefizox[15]
Cefobid[8]
Cefotan[10]
Ceftin[17]
Cefzil[13]
Ceptaz[14]
Claforan[9]
C-Lexin[18]
Duricef[2]
Fortaz[14]
Keflex[18]
Keflin[19]
Keftab[18]
Kefurox[17]
Kefzol[4]
Mandol[3]
Mefoxin[11]
Monocid[7]
Rocephin[16]
Suprax[5]
Tazicef[14]
Tazidime[14]
Ultracef[2]
Vantin[12]
Velosef[21]
Zefazone[6]
Zinacef[17]
Zolicef[4]

In Canada—

Ancef[4]
Apo-Cephalex[18]
Ceclor[1]
Cefizox[15]
Cefobid[8]
Cefotan[10]
Ceftin[17]
Ceptaz[14]
Claforan[9]
Duricef[2]

Fortaz[14]	Novo-Lexin[18]
Gen-Cefazolin[4]	Nu-Cephalex[18]
Keflex[18]	Rocephin[16]
Keflin[19]	Suprax[5]
Kefurox[17]	Tazidime[14]
Kefzol[4]	Velosef[21]
Mandol[3]	Zinacef[17]
Mefoxin[11]	

Note: For quick reference, the following cephalosporins are numbered to match the corresponding brand names.

This information applies to the following medicines:

1. Cefaclor (SEF-a-klor)
2. Cefadroxil (sef-a-DROX-ill)‡
3. Cefamandole (sef-a-MAN-dole)
4. Cefazolin (sef-A-zoe-lin)‡
5. Cefixime (sef-IX-eem)
6. Cefmetazole (sef-MET-a-zole)†
7. Cefonicid (se-FON-i-sid)†
8. Cefoperazone (sef-oh-PER-a-zone)
9. Cefotaxime (sef-oh-TAKS-eem)
10. Cefotetan (sef-oh-TEE-tan)
11. Cefoxitin (se-FOX-i-tin)
12. Cefpodoxime (sef-pode-OX-eem)†
13. Cefprozil (sef-PROE-zil)†
14. Ceftazidime (sef-TAY-zi-deem)
15. Ceftizoxime (sef-ti-ZOX-eem)
16. Ceftriaxone (sef-try-AX-one)
17. Cefuroxime (se-fyoor-OX-eem)
18. Cephalexin (sef-a-LEX-in)‡
19. Cephalothin (sef-A-loe-thin)‡
20. Cephapirin (sef-a-PYE-rin)†‡
21. Cephradine (SEF-ra-deen)‡

†Not commercially available in Canada.
‡Generic name product may also be available in the U.S.

Description

Cephalosporins (sef-a-loe-SPOR-ins) are used in the treatment of infections caused by bacteria. They work by killing bacteria or preventing their growth.

Cephalosporins are used to treat infections in many different parts of the body. They are sometimes given with other antibiotics. Some cephalosporins are also given by injection to prevent infections before, during, and after surgery. However, cephalosporins will not work for colds, flu, or other virus infections.

Cephalosporins are available only with your doctor's prescription, in the following dosage forms:

Oral

- Cefaclor
  - Capsules (U.S. and Canada)
  - Oral suspension (U.S. and Canada)
- Cefadroxil
  - Capsules (U.S. and Canada)
  - Oral suspension (U.S.)
  - Tablets (U.S.)
- Cefixime
  - Oral suspension (U.S. and Canada)
  - Tablets (U.S. and Canada)
- Cefpodoxime
  - Oral suspension (U.S.)
  - Tablets (U.S.)
- Cefprozil
  - Oral suspension (U.S.)
  - Tablets (U.S.)
- Cefuroxime
  - Oral suspension (U.S.)
  - Tablets (U.S. and Canada)
- Cephalexin
  - Capsules (U.S. and Canada)
  - Oral suspension (U.S. and Canada)
  - Tablets (U.S. and Canada)
- Cephradine
  - Capsules (U.S. and Canada)
  - Oral suspension (U.S.)

Parenteral

- Cefamandole
  - Injection (U.S. and Canada)
- Cefazolin
  - Injection (U.S. and Canada)
- Cefmetazole
  - Injection (U.S.)
- Cefonicid
  - Injection (U.S.)
- Cefoperazone
  - Injection (U.S. and Canada)
- Cefotaxime
  - Injection (U.S. and Canada)
- Cefotetan
  - Injection (U.S. and Canada)
- Cefoxitin
  - Injection (U.S. and Canada)
- Ceftazidime
  - Injection (U.S. and Canada)
- Ceftizoxime
  - Injection (U.S. and Canada)
- Ceftriaxone
  - Injection (U.S. and Canada)
- Cefuroxime
  - Injection (U.S. and Canada)
- Cephalothin
  - Injection (U.S. and Canada)
- Cephapirin
  - Injection (U.S.)
- Cephradine
  - Injection (U.S.)

Before Using This Medicine

In deciding to use a medicine, the risks of taking the medicine must be weighed against the good it will do. This is a decision you and your doctor will make. For the cephalosporins, the following should be considered:

Allergies—Tell your doctor if you have ever had any unusual or allergic reaction to any of the cephalosporins, penicillins, penicillin-like medicines, or penicillamine. Also tell your health care professional if you are allergic to any other substances, such as foods, preservatives, or dyes.

Pregnancy—Studies have not been done in humans. However, most cephalosporins have not been reported to cause birth defects or other problems in animal studies. Studies in rabbits have shown that cefoxitin may increase the risk of miscarriages and cause other problems.

Breast-feeding—Most cephalosporins pass into human breast milk, usually in small amounts. However, cephalosporins have not been reported to cause problems in nursing babies.

Children—Many cephalosporins have been tested in children and, in effective doses, have not been shown to cause different side effects or problems than they do in adults. However, there are some cephalosporins that have not been tested in children up to 1 year of age.

Older adults—Cephalosporins have been used in the elderly, and they are not expected to cause different side effects or problems in older people than they do in younger adults.

Other medicines—Although certain medicines should not be used together at all, in other cases 2 different medicines may be used together even if an interaction might occur. In these cases, your doctor may want to change the dose, or other precautions may be necessary. When you are taking a cephalosporin, it is especially important that your health care professional know if you are taking any of the following:

- Alcohol and alcohol-containing medicine (cefamandole, cefmetazole, cefoperazone, and cefotetan only)—Using alcohol and these cephalosporins together may cause abdominal or stomach cramps, nausea, vomiting, headache, dizziness or lightheadedness, shortness of breath, sweating, or facial flushing; this reaction usually begins within 15 to 30 minutes after alcohol is consumed and usually goes away over several hours
- Anticoagulants (blood thinners) or
- Carbenicillin by injection (e.g., Geopen) or
- Dipyridamole (e.g., Persantine) or
- Divalproex (e.g., Depakote) or
- Heparin (e.g., Panheprin) or
- Pentoxifylline (e.g., Trental) or
- Plicamycin (e.g., Mithracin) or
- Sulfinpyrazone (e.g., Anturane) or
- Ticarcillin (e.g., Ticar) or
- Thrombolytic agents or
- Valproic acid (e.g., Depakene)—Any of these medicines may increase the chance of bleeding, especially when used with cefamandole, cefmetazole, cefoperazone, or cefotetan
- Probenecid (e.g., Benemid) (except cefoperazone, ceftazidime, or ceftriaxone)—Probenecid increases the blood level of many cephalosporins. Although probenecid may be given with a cephalosporin by your doctor purposely to increase the blood level to treat some infections, in other cases this effect may be unwanted and may increase the chance of side effects

Other medical problems—The presence of other medical problems may affect the use of cephalosporins. Make sure you tell your doctor if you have any other medical problems, especially:

- Bleeding problems, history of (cefamandole, cefmetazole, cefoperazone, and cefotetan only)—These medicines may increase the chance of bleeding
- Kidney disease—Some cephalosporins need to be given at a lower dose to people with kidney disease. Also, cephalothin, especially, may increase the chance of kidney damage
- Liver disease (cefoperazone only)—Cefoperazone needs to be given at a lower dose to people with liver and kidney disease
- Phenylketonuria—Cefprozil oral suspension contains phenylalanine
- Stomach or intestinal disease, history of (especially colitis, including colitis caused by antibiotics, or enteritis)—Cephalosporins may cause colitis in some patients

Proper Use of This Medicine

Cephalosporins may be taken on a full or empty stomach. If this medicine upsets your stomach, it may help to take it with food.

Cefuroxime axetil tablets and cefpodoxime should be taken with food to increase absorption of the medicine.

For patients taking the *oral liquid* form of this medicine:

- This medicine is to be taken by mouth even if it comes in a dropper bottle. If this medicine does not come in a dropper bottle, use a specially marked measuring spoon or other device to measure each dose accurately. The average household teaspoon may not hold the right amount of liquid.
- Do not use after the expiration date on the label since the medicine may not work properly after that date. Check with your pharmacist if you have any questions about this.

For patients unable to swallow *cefuroxime axetil tablets* whole ask your doctor for suggestions.

To help clear up your infection completely, *keep taking this medicine for the full time of treatment,* even if you begin to feel better after a few days. *If you have a "strep" infection, you should keep taking this medicine for at least 10 days. This is especially important in "strep" infections since serious heart or kidney problems could develop later* if your infection is not cleared up completely. Also, if you stop taking this medicine too soon, your symptoms may return.

This medicine works best when there is a constant amount in the blood or urine. *To help keep the amount constant, do not miss any doses. Also, it is best to take the doses at evenly spaced times, day and night.* For example, if you are to take 4 doses a day, the doses should be spaced about 6 hours apart. If this interferes with your sleep or other daily activities, or if you need help in planning the best times to take your medicine, check with your health care professional.

Dosing—The dose of these medicines will be different for different patients. *Follow your doctor's orders or the directions on the label.* The following information includes only the average doses of these medicines. Your dose may be different if you have kidney disease. *If your dose is different, do not change it* unless your doctor tells you to do so.

The number of capsules or tablets or teaspoonfuls of suspension that you take depends on the strength of the medicine. Also, *the number of doses you take each day, the time allowed between doses, and the length of time you take the medicine depend on the medical problem for which you are taking a cephalosporin.*

For cefaclor

- For bacterial infections:
  - —For *oral* dosage form (capsules or oral suspension):
    - Adults and teenagers—250 to 500 milligrams (mg) every eight hours.
    - Infants and children 1 month of age and older—6.7 to 13.4 mg per kilogram (kg) (3 to 6 mg per pound) of body weight every eight hours, or 10 to 20 mg per kg (4.5 to 9 mg per pound) of body weight every twelve hours.

For cefadroxil

- For bacterial infections:
  - —For *oral* dosage form (capsules, tablets, or oral suspension):
    - Adults and teenagers—500 milligrams (mg) every twelve hours, or 1 to 2 grams once a day.
    - Children—15 mg per kilogram (kg) (6.8 mg per pound) of body weight every twelve hours, or 30 mg per kg (13.6 mg per pound) of body weight once a day.

For cefamandole

- For bacterial infections:
  - —For *injection* dosage form:
    - Adults and teenagers—500 milligrams (mg) to 2 grams every four to eight hours, injected into a muscle or vein.
    - Infants and children 1 month of age and older—8.3 to 33.3 mg per kilogram (kg) (3.8 to 15.1 mg per pound) of body weight every four to eight hours, injected into a muscle or vein.

For cefazolin

- For bacterial infections:
  - —For *injection* dosage form:
    - Adults and teenagers—250 milligrams (mg) to 1.5 grams every six to eight hours, injected into a vein.
    - Infants and children 1 month of age and older—6.25 to 25 mg per kilogram (kg) (2.8 to 11.4 mg per pound) of body weight every six hours, or 8.3 to 33.3 mg per kg (3.8 to 15.1 mg per pound) of body weight every eight hours, injected into a vein.

For cefixime

- For bacterial infections:
  - —For *oral* dosage form (tablets or oral suspension):
    - Adults and teenagers—200 milligrams (mg) every twelve hours, or 400 mg once a day. Gonorrhea is treated with a single, oral dose of 400 mg.
    - Children 6 months of age to 12 years of age—4 mg per kilogram (kg) (1.8 mg per pound) of body weight every twelve hours, or 8 mg per kg (3.6 mg per pound) of body weight once a day.

For cefmetazole

- For bacterial infections:
  - —For *injection* dosage form:
    - Adults and teenagers—2 grams every six to twelve hours, injected into a vein, for five to fourteen days. Gonorrhea is treated with a single dose of 1 gram, injected into the muscle, along with a single, oral 1 gram dose of probenecid.
    - Children—Dose must be determined by your doctor.

For cefonicid

- For bacterial infections:
  - —For *injection* dosage form:
    - Adults and teenagers—500 milligrams (mg) to 1 gram every twenty-four hours, injected into a vein or muscle.
    - Children—Dose must be determined by your doctor.

For cefoperazone

- For bacterial infections:
  - —For *injection* dosage form:
    - Adults and teenagers—1 to 6 grams every twelve hours, or 2 to 4 grams every eight hours, injected into a vein.
    - Children—Dose must be determined by your doctor.

For cefotaxime

- For bacterial infections:
  - —For *injection* dosage form:
    - Adults and teenagers—1 to 2 grams every four to twelve hours. Gonorrhea is usually treated with a single dose of 250 milligrams (mg), injected into a muscle.
    - Newborns up to 1 week of age—50 mg per kilogram (kg) (22.7 mg per pound) of body weight every twelve hours, injected into a vein.
    - Newborns 1 to 4 weeks of age—50 mg per kg (22.7 mg per pound) of body weight every eight hours, injected into a vein.
    - Infants and children up to 50 kg of body weight (110 pounds)—8.3 to 30 mg per kg (3.8 to 13.6 mg per pound) of body weight every four hours, or 12.5 to 45 mg per kg (5.7 to 20.4 mg per pound) of body weight every six hours, injected into a vein.
    - Children over 50 kg of body weight (110 pounds)—1 to 2 grams every four to twelve hours.

For cefotetan

- For bacterial infections:
  - —For *injection* dosage form:
    - Adults and teenagers—1 to 3 grams every twelve hours, injected into a vein or muscle.
    - Children—Dose must be determined by your doctor.

For cefoxitin

- For bacterial infections:
  - —For *injection* dosage form:
    - Adults and teenagers—1 to 3 grams every four to eight hours, injected into a vein. Gonorrhea is treated with a single dose of 2 grams, injected into a muscle, and given along with a single, oral 1 gram dose of probenecid.
    - Infants and children 3 months of age and over—13.3 to 26.7 milligrams (mg) per kilogram (kg) (6 to 12 mg per pound) of body weight every

four hours, or 20 to 40 mg per kg (9 to 18 mg per pound) of body weight every six hours.

For cefpodoxime

- For bacterial infections:
  —For *oral* dosage forms (tablets or oral suspension):
  - Adults and teenagers—100 to 400 milligrams (mg) every twelve hours for seven to fourteen days. Gonorrhea is treated with a single, oral dose of 200 mg.
  - Infants and children 6 months to 12 years of age—5 mg per kilogram (kg) (2.3 mg per pound) of body weight every twelve hours for ten days.
  - Infants up to 6 months of age—Dose must be determined by your doctor.

For cefprozil

- For bacterial infections:
  —For *oral* dosage forms (tablets or oral suspension):
  - Adults and teenagers—250 to 500 milligrams (mg) every twelve to twenty-four hours for ten days.
  - Children 2 to 12 years of age—7.5 mg per kilogram (kg) (3.4 mg per pound) of body weight every twelve hours for ten days.
  - Infants and children 6 months to 12 years of age—15 mg per kg (6.8 mg per pound) of body weight every twelve hours for ten days.

For ceftazidime

- For bacterial infections:
  —For *injection* dosage form:
  - Adults and teenagers—500 milligrams (mg) to 2 grams every eight to twelve hours.
  - Newborns up to 4 weeks of age—30 mg per kilogram (kg) (13.6 mg per pound) of body weight every twelve hours, injected into a vein.
  - Infants and children 1 month to 12 years of age—30 mg to 50 mg per kg (13.6 to 22.7 mg per pound) of body weight every eight hours, injected into a vein.

For ceftizoxime

- For bacterial infections:
  —For *injection* dosage form:
  - Adults and teenagers—1 to 4 grams every eight to twelve hours injected into a vein.
  - Infants and children 6 months of age and older—50 milligrams (mg) per kilogram (kg) (22.7 mg per pound) of body weight every six to eight hours, injected into a vein.

For ceftriaxone

- For bacterial infections:
  —For *injection* dosage form:
  - Adults and teenagers—1 to 2 grams every twenty-four hours, or 500 milligrams (mg) to 1 gram every twelve hours, injected into a vein or muscle. Gonorrhea is treated with a single 250 mg dose injected into a muscle.
  - Infants and children—25 to 50 mg per kilogram (kg) (11.4 to 22.7 mg per pound) of body weight every twelve hours, or 50 to 75 mg per kg (22.7 to 34.1 mg per pound) of body weight once a day, injected into a vein. Meningitis is treated with an initial dose of 100 mg per kg, then, 100 mg per kg once a day injected into a vein.

For cefuroxime

- For bacterial infections:
  —For *oral suspension* dosage form:
  - Adults and teenagers—The oral suspension is usually used only in children. Refer to the dosing for cefuroxime tablets.
  - Children up to 12 years of age—10 to 15 milligrams (mg) per kilogram (kg) (4.5 to 6.8 mg per pound) of body weight every twelve hours for ten days.

  —For *tablet* dosage form:
  - Adults and teenagers—125 to 500 mg every twelve hours. Gonorrhea is treated with a single, oral 1 gram dose.
  - Children up to 12 years of age—125 mg every twelve hours.

  —For *injection* dosage form:
  - Adults and teenagers—750 mg to 1.5 grams every eight hours injected into a vein or a muscle. Gonorrhea is treated with a single dose of 1.5 grams, injected into a muscle; the total 1.5-gram dose is divided into two doses and injected into muscles at two separate places on the body, and given along with a single oral 1 gram dose of probenecid.
  - Newborns—10 to 33.3 mg per kg (4.5 to 15.1 mg per pound) of body weight every eight hours, or 15 to 50 mg per kg (6.8 to 22.7 mg per pound) of body weight every twelve hours, injected into a muscle or a vein.
  - Infants and children 3 months of age and over—16.7 to 33.3 mg per kg (7.6 to 15.1 mg per pound) of body weight every eight hours, injected into a muscle or a vein.

For cephalexin

- For bacterial infections:
  —For *oral* dosage form (capsules, oral suspension, or tablets):
  - Adults and teenagers—250 to 500 milligrams (mg) every six to twelve hours.
  - Children—6.25 to 25 mg per kilogram (kg) (1.6 to 11.4 mg per pound) of body weight every six hours, or 12.5 to 50 mg per kg (5.7 to 22.7 mg per pound) of body weight every twelve hours.

For cephalothin

- For bacterial infections:
  —For *injection* dosage form:
  - Adults and teenagers—500 milligrams (mg) to 2 grams every four to six hours, injected into a vein.

• Children—13.3 to 26.6 mg per kilogram (kg) (6 to 12 mg per pound) of body weight every four hours, or 20 to 40 mg per kg (9.1 to 18.2 mg per pound) of body weight every six hours, injected into a vein.

For cephapirin

- For bacterial infections:
  —For *injection* dosage form:
    - Adults and teenagers—500 milligrams (mg) to 1 gram every four to six hours, injected into a muscle or a vein.
    - Infants and children 3 months of age and over—10 to 20 mg per kilogram (kg) (4.5 to 9.1 mg per pound) of body weight every six hours, injected into a muscle or a vein.

For cephradine

- For bacterial infections:
  —For *oral* dosage forms (capsules or oral suspension):
    - Adults and teenagers—250 to 500 milligrams (mg) every six hours, or 500 mg to 1 gram every twelve hours.
    - Children—6.25 to 25 mg per kilogram (kg) (2.8 to 11.4 mg per pound) of body weight every six hours.
  —For *injection* dosage form:
    - Adults and teenagers—500 mg to 1 gram every six hours, injected into a muscle or a vein.
    - Children 1 year of age and over—12.5 to 25 mg per kg (5.7 to 11.4 mg per pound) of body weight every six hours, injected into a muscle or a vein.

Missed dose—If you miss a dose of this medicine, take it as soon as possible. This will help to keep a constant amount of medicine in the blood or urine. However, if it is almost time for your next dose, skip the missed dose and go back to your regular dosing schedule. Do not double doses.

Storage—To store this medicine:

- Keep out of the reach of children.
- Store away from heat and direct light.
- Do not store the capsule or tablet form of this medicine in the bathroom, near the kitchen sink, or in other damp places. Heat or moisture may cause the medicine to break down.
- Store the oral liquid form of most cephalosporins in the refrigerator because heat will cause this medicine to break down. However, keep the medicine from freezing. Follow the directions on the label. Cefixime oral suspension (Suprax) does not need to be refrigerated.
- Do not keep outdated medicine or medicine no longer needed. Be sure that any discarded medicine is out of the reach of children.

Precautions While Using This Medicine

If your symptoms do not improve within a few days, or if they become worse, check with your doctor.

For diabetic patients:

- *This medicine may cause false test results with some urine sugar tests.* Check with your doctor before changing your diet or the dosage of your diabetes medicine.

For patients with phenylketonuria (PKU):

- Cefprozil oral suspension contains phenylalanine. Check with your doctor before taking this medicine.

In some patients, cephalosporins may cause diarrhea:

- Severe diarrhea may be a sign of a serious side effect. *Do not take any diarrhea medicine without first checking with your doctor.* Diarrhea medicines may make your diarrhea worse or make it last longer.
- For mild diarrhea, diarrhea medicine containing kaolin or attapulgite (e.g., Kaopectate tablets, Diasorb) may be taken. However, other kinds of diarrhea medicine should not be taken. They may make your diarrhea worse or make it last longer.
- If you have any questions about this or if mild diarrhea continues or gets worse, check with your health care professional.

For patients receiving *cefamandole, cefmetazole, cefoperazone, or cefotetan by injection:*

- Drinking alcoholic beverages or taking other alcohol-containing preparations (for example, elixirs, cough syrups, tonics, or injections of alcohol) while receiving these medicines may cause problems. The problems may occur if you consume alcohol even several days after you stop taking the cephalosporin. Drinking alcoholic beverages may result in increased side effects such as abdominal or stomach cramps, nausea, vomiting, headache, fainting, fast or irregular heartbeat, difficult breathing, sweating, or redness of the face or skin. These effects usually start within 15 to 30 minutes after you drink alcohol and may not go away for up to several hours. Therefore, *you should not drink alcoholic beverages or take other alcohol-containing preparations while you are receiving these medicines and for several days after stopping them.*

Side Effects of This Medicine

Along with its needed effects, a medicine may cause some unwanted effects. Although not all of these side effects may occur, if they do occur they may need medical attention.

Check with your doctor immediately if any of the following side effects occur:

Less common or rare

Abdominal or stomach cramps and pain (severe); fever; watery and severe diarrhea, which may also be bloody; (these side effects may also occur up to several weeks after you stop taking this medicine); unusual bleeding or bruising (more common for cefamandole, cefmetazole, cefoperazone, and cefotetan)

Rare

Blistering, peeling, or loosening of skin; convulsions (seizures); decrease in urine output; dizziness or lightheadedness; joint pain; loss of appetite; pain, redness, and swelling at place of injection; skin rash, itching, redness, or swelling; trouble in breathing; unusual tiredness or weakness; yellowing of the eyes or skin

Other side effects may occur that usually do not need medical attention. These side effects may go away during treatment as your body adjusts to the medicine. However, check with your doctor if any of the following side effects continue or are bothersome:

More common (less common with some cephalosporins)
Diarrhea (mild); nausea and vomiting; sore mouth or tongue; stomach cramps (mild)

Less common or rare
Vaginal itching or discharge

Other side effects not listed above may also occur in some patients. If you notice any other effects, check with your doctor.

Revised: 02/28/94
Interim revision: 06/26/95

CHARCOAL, ACTIVATED Oral

Some commonly used brand names are:

In the U.S.—

- Actidose-Aqua[1]
- Actidose with Sorbitol[2]
- Charcoaid[2]
- CharcoAid 2000[1]
- Charcocaps[1]
- Insta-Char Aqueous[1]
- Insta-Char with Sorbitol[2]
- Liqui-Char[1]
- Liqui-Char with Sorbitol[2]
- Pediatric Aqueous Insta-Char[1]

In Canada—

- Aqueous Charcodote[1]
- Charac-50[1]
- Charac-tol 50[2]
- Charcodote[2]
- Charcodote TFS-25[2]
- Charcodote TFS-50[2]
- Insta-Char Aqueous[1]
- Pediatric Aqueous Charcodote[1]
- Pediatric Charcodote[2]

Note: For quick reference, the following medicines are numbered to match the corresponding brand names.

This information applies to the following medicines:

1. Activated Charcoal (AK-ti-vay-ted CHAR-kole)‡§
2. Activated Charcoal and Sorbitol (SOR-bi-tole)

‡Generic name product may be available in the U.S.
§Generic name product may be available in Canada.

Description

Activated charcoal is used in the emergency treatment of certain kinds of poisoning. It helps prevent the poison from being absorbed by the body. Ordinarily, this medicine should not be used in poisoning if corrosive agents such as alkalis (lye) and strong acids, iron, boric acid, lithium, petroleum products (e.g., kerosene, gasoline, coal oil, fuel oil, paint thinner, cleaning fluid), ethyl alcohol, or methyl alcohol have been swallowed, since it will not prevent these poisons from being absorbed into the body.

Some activated charcoal products contain sorbitol. Sorbitol is a sweetener. It also works as a laxative, for the elimination of the poison from the body. *Products that contain sorbitol should be given only under the direct supervision of a doctor because severe diarrhea and vomiting may result.*

Activated charcoal (without sorbitol) may also be used to relieve diarrhea and intestinal gas.

Activated charcoal is available without a doctor's prescription; however, before using this medicine for poisoning, call a poison control center, your doctor, or an emergency room for advice. Also, your doctor may have special instructions on the proper use of this medicine for diarrhea or intestinal gas. Activated charcoal is available in the following dosage forms:

Oral

Activated Charcoal
- Capsules (U.S. and Canada)
- Powder (U.S. and Canada)
- Oral suspension (U.S. and Canada)
- Tablets (U.S.)

Activated Charcoal and Sorbitol
- Oral suspension (U.S. and Canada)

Before Using This Medicine

In deciding to use a medicine, the risks of taking the medicine must be weighed against the good it will do. This is a decision you and your doctor will make. Before you use activated charcoal *for diarrhea or intestinal gas*, the following should be considered:

Allergies—Tell your doctor if you have ever had any unusual or allergic reaction to activated charcoal. Also tell your health care professional if you are allergic to any other substances, such as foods, preservatives, or dyes.

Diet—Make certain your health care professional knows if you are on a low-sodium, low-sugar, or any other special diet. Most medicines contain more than their active ingredient.

Pregnancy—Activated charcoal has not been reported to cause birth defects or other problems in humans.

Breast-feeding—Activated charcoal has not been reported to cause problems in nursing babies.

Children—In babies and children under 3 years of age, activated charcoal should not be used regularly to relieve diarrhea and gas, since it may affect the child's nutrition. Also, the fluid loss caused by diarrhea may result in a severe condition. For this reason, a medicine for diarrhea must not be given to children without first checking with their doctor. If medicine for diarrhea is used, it is also very important that a sufficient amount of liquids be given to replace the fluid lost by the body. If you have any questions about this, check with your health care professional.

Older adults—Many medicines have not been studied specifically in older people. Therefore, it may not be known whether they work exactly the same way they do in younger adults. Although there is no specific information comparing the use of activated charcoal in the elderly, this medicine is not expected to cause different side effects or problems in older people than it does in younger adults.

However, the fluid loss caused by diarrhea may result in a severe condition. For this reason, elderly persons with diarrhea, in addition to using a medicine for diarrhea, must receive a sufficient amount of liquids to replace the fluid lost by the body. If you have any questions about this, check with your health care professional.

Other medicines—Although certain medicines should not be used together at all, in other cases two different medicines may be used together even if an interaction might occur. In these cases, your doctor may want to change the dose, or other precautions may be necessary. Tell your health care professional if you are taking any other prescription or nonprescription (over-the-counter [OTC]) medicine.

Other medical problems—The presence of other medical problems may affect the use of activated charcoal to relieve diarrhea. Make sure you tell your doctor if you have any other medical problems, especially:

- Dysentery—This condition may get worse; a different kind of treatment may be needed

Proper Use of This Medicine

Do not take this medicine mixed with chocolate syrup, ice cream, or sherbet, since it may prevent the medicine from working properly.

For patients taking this medicine *for poisoning*:

- *Before taking this medicine for the treatment of poisoning, call a poison control center, your doctor, or an emergency room for advice.* It is a good idea to have these telephone numbers readily available.
- *It is very important that you shake the liquid form of this medicine well before taking it, some might have settled in the bottom. Be sure to drink all the liquid to get the full dose of activated charcoal.*
- If you have been told to take both this medicine and ipecac syrup to treat the poisoning, *do not take this medicine until after you have taken the ipecac syrup to cause vomiting and the vomiting has stopped. This is usually about 30 minutes.*

For patients taking this medicine *for diarrhea or intestinal gas:*

- *If you are taking any other medicine, do not take it within 2 hours of the activated charcoal.* Taking other medicines together with activated charcoal may prevent the other medicine from being absorbed by your body. If you have any questions about this, check with your health care professional.

Importance of diet and fluid intake while treating diarrhea:

- *In addition to using medicine for diarrhea, it is very important that you replace the fluid lost by the body and follow a proper diet.* For the first 24 hours you should drink plenty of caffeine-free clear liquids, such as ginger ale, decaffeinated cola, decaffeinated tea, broth, or gelatin. During the next 24 hours you may eat bland foods, such as cooked cereals, bread, crackers, and applesauce. Fruits, vegetables, fried or spicy foods, bran, candy, caffeine, and alcoholic beverages may make the condition worse.
- If too much fluid has been lost by the body due to the diarrhea, a serious condition may develop. Check with your doctor as soon as possible if any of the following signs of too much fluid loss occur:

  Decreased urination
  Dizziness and lightheadedness
  Dryness of mouth
  Increased thirst
  Wrinkled skin

Dosing—The dose of these medicines will be different for different patients. *Follow your doctor's orders or the directions on the label.* The following information includes only the average doses of these medicines. *If your dose is different, do not change it* unless your doctor tells you to do so.

For activated charcoal

- For *oral* dosage form (powder):
  - —For treatment of poisoning:
    - Adults and teenagers—Dose is usually 25 to 100 grams mixed with water.
    - Children—Dose is based on body weight and must be determined by your doctor or other health care professional. It is usually 1 gram per kilogram (kg) (0.454 gram per pound) of body weight mixed with water. Or, the dose may be 25 to 50 grams mixed with water.
- For *oral* dosage form (capsules):
  - —For treatment of diarrhea:
    - Adults and children 3 years of age and older—Dose is usually 520 milligrams (mg) repeated every thirty minutes to one hour, as needed. No more than 4.16 grams (4160 mg) should be taken within a twenty-four hour period.
    - Children up to 3 years of age—Dose must be determined by your doctor.
  - —For treatment of intestinal gas:
    - Adults and teenagers—Dose is usually 1.04 to 3.9 grams (1040 to 3900 mg) three times a day after meals.
    - Children—Dose must be determined by your doctor.
- For *oral* dosage form (oral suspension):
  - —For treatment of poisoning:
    - Adults and teenagers—Dose is usually 25 to 100 grams given one time.
    - Children 1 to 12 years of age—Dose is usually 25 to 50 grams given one time.
    - Children up to 1 year of age—Dose is based on body weight and must be determined by your doctor or other health care professional. It is usually 1 gram per kg (0.454 gram per pound) of body weight given one time.

• For *oral* dosage form (tablets):
—For treatment of intestinal gas:
• Adults and teenagers—Dose is usually 975 mg to 3.9 grams (3900 mg) three times a day after meals.
• Children—Dose must be determined by your doctor.

For activated charcoal and sorbitol
• For *oral* dosage form (oral suspension):
—For treatment of poisoning:
• Adults and teenagers—Dose is usually 50 grams of activated charcoal given one time.
• Children 1 to 12 years of age—Dose is usually 25 to 50 grams of activated charcoal given one time.
• Children up to 1 year of age—Use is not recommended.

Storage—To store this medicine:
- Keep out of the reach of children.
- Store away from heat and direct light.
- Do not store the capsule, tablet, or powder form of this medicine in the bathroom, near the kitchen sink, or in other damp places. Heat or moisture may cause the medicine to break down.
- Keep the liquid form of this medicine from freezing.
- Do not keep outdated medicine or medicine no longer needed. Be sure that any discarded medicine is out of the reach of children.

Precautions While Using This Medicine

For patients taking this medicine *for diarrhea or intestinal gas:*
- If you are taking this medicine for intestinal gas and your condition has not improved after 7 days, check with your doctor.
- If you are taking this medicine for diarrhea and your condition has not improved after 2 days or if you have fever with the diarrhea, check with your doctor.

Side Effects of This Medicine

Along with its needed effects, a medicine may cause some unwanted effects. Although not all of these side effects may occur, if they do occur they may need medical attention.

Check with your doctor as soon as possible if the following side effect occurs:

Rare
Swelling or pain in stomach

Other side effects may occur that usually do not need medical attention. These side effects may go away during treatment as your body adjusts to the medicine. However, check with your doctor if any of the following side effects continue:

More common (for sorbitol-containing preparations only)
Diarrhea; vomiting

Activated charcoal will cause your stools to turn black. This is to be expected while you are taking this medicine.

There have not been any other side effects reported with this medicine. However, if you notice any other effects, check with your doctor.

Revised: 08/16/91
Interim revision: 06/14/95

CHENODIOL Systemic*†

A commonly used name is chenodeoxycholic acid.

*Not commercially available in the U.S.
†Not commercially available in Canada.

Description

Chenodiol (kee-noe-DYE-ole) is used in the treatment of gallstone disease. It is taken by mouth to dissolve the gallstones.

Chenodiol is used in patients who do not need to have their gallbladder removed or in those in whom surgery is best avoided because of other medical problems. However, chenodiol works only in those patients who have a working gallbladder and whose gallstones are made of cholesterol. Chenodiol works best when these stones are small and of the ''floating'' type.

Chenodiol is available only with your doctor's prescription, in the following dosage form:

Oral
• Tablets

Before Using This Medicine

In deciding to use a medicine, the risks of taking the medicine must be weighed against the good it will do. This is a decision you and your doctor will make. For chenodiol, the following should be considered:

Allergies—Tell your doctor if you have ever had any unusual or allergic reaction to chenodiol or to other bile acid products.

Diet—If you have gallstones, your doctor may prescribe chenodiol and a personal high-fiber diet for you. Some foods that are high in fiber are whole grain breads and cereals, bran, fruit, and green, leafy vegetables. It has been found that such a diet may help dissolve the stones faster and may keep new stones from forming.

It may also be important for you to go on a reducing diet. However, check with your doctor before going on any diet.

Pregnancy—Chenodiol is not recommended for use during pregnancy. It has been shown to cause liver and kidney problems in animals when given in doses many times the human dose. Be sure you have discussed this with your doctor.

Breast-feeding—It is not known whether chenodiol passes into breast milk. Although most medicines pass into breast milk in small amounts, many of them may be used safely while breast-feeding. Mothers who are taking this medicine and who wish to breast-feed should discuss this with their doctor.

Children—Studies on this medicine have been done only in adult patients, and there is no specific information comparing use of chenodiol in children with use in other age groups.

Older adults—Many medicines have not been studied specifically in older people. Therefore, it may not be known whether they work exactly the same way they do in younger adults. Although there is no specific information comparing use of chenodiol in the elderly with use in other age groups, this medicine is not expected to cause different side effects or problems in older people than it does in younger adults.

Other medicines—Although certain medicines should not be used together at all, in other cases two different medicines may be used together even if an interaction might occur. In these cases, your doctor may want to change the dose, or other precautions may be necessary. Tell your health care professional if you are taking any other prescription or nonprescription (over-the-counter [OTC]) medicine.

Other medical problems—The presence of other medical problems may affect the use of chenodiol. Make sure you tell your doctor if you have any other medical problems, especially:

- Biliary tract problems or
- Blood vessel disease or
- Pancreatitis (inflammation of pancreas)—These conditions may make it necessary to have surgery since treatment with chenodiol would take too long
- Liver disease—Liver disease may become worse with use of chenodiol

Proper Use of This Medicine

Take chenodiol with food or milk for best results, unless otherwise directed by your doctor.

Take chenodiol for the full time of treatment, even if you begin to feel better. If you stop taking this medicine too soon, the gallstones may not dissolve as fast or may not dissolve at all.

Dosing—The dose of chenodiol will be different for different patients. *Follow your doctor's orders or the directions on the label.* The following information includes only the average doses of chenodiol. *If your dose is different, do not change it unless your doctor tells you to do so:*

- For *oral* dosage forms (tablets):
  - —For gallstone disease:
    - Adults and children 12 years of age and older—250 milligrams (mg) a day for the first two weeks of treatment. Your doctor may then increase the dose by 250 mg a day until the proper treatment dose is reached. The treatment dose is based on body weight. It is usually 13 to 16 mg per kilogram (6 to 7 mg per pound) of body weight a day, divided into two doses, taken in the morning and at night. Each dose should be taken with food or milk.
    - Children up to 12 years of age—Use and dose must be determined by your doctor.

Missed dose—If you miss a dose of this medicine, take it as soon as possible. However, if it is almost time for your next dose, skip the missed dose and go back to your regular dosing schedule. Do not double doses.

Storage—To store this medicine:

- Keep out of the reach of children.
- Store away from heat and direct light.
- Do not store in the bathroom, near the kitchen sink, or in other damp places. Heat or moisture may cause the medicine to break down.
- Do not keep outdated medicine or medicine no longer needed. Be sure that any discarded medicine is out of the reach of children.

Precautions While Using This Medicine

Do not take aluminum-containing antacids (e.g., ALternaGel, Maalox) while taking chenodiol. To do so may keep the chenodiol from working properly.

It is important that your doctor check your progress at regular visits. Laboratory tests will have to be done every few months while you are taking this medicine to make sure that the gallstones are dissolving and your liver is working properly.

Check with your doctor immediately if severe abdominal or stomach pain, especially toward the upper right side, and severe nausea and vomiting occur. These symptoms may mean that you have other medical problems or that your gallstone condition needs your doctor's attention.

Side Effects of This Medicine

Along with its needed effects, a medicine may cause some unwanted effects. Although not all of these side effects may occur, if they do occur they may need medical attention.

Check with your doctor as soon as possible if the following side effect occurs:

Less common or rare
Diarrhea (severe)

Other side effects may occur that usually do not need medical attention. These side effects may go away during treatment as your body adjusts to the medicine. However, check with your doctor if any of the following side effects continue or are bothersome:

More common
Diarrhea (mild)

Less common or rare
Constipation; frequent urge for bowel movement; gas or indigestion (usually disappears within 2 to 4 weeks

after the beginning of treatment); loss of appetite; nausea or vomiting; stomach cramps or pain

Other side effects not listed above may also occur in some patients. If you notice any other effects, check with your doctor.

Revised: 04/27/94

CHLORAL HYDRATE Systemic

Some commonly used brand names are:

In the U.S.—
- Aquachloral Supprettes
- Generic name product may also be available.

In Canada—
- Novo-Chlorhydrate
- PMS-Chloral Hydrate
- Generic name product may also be available.

Description

Chloral hydrate (KLOR-al HYE-drate) belongs to the group of medicines called sedatives and hypnotics. It is sometimes used before surgery or certain procedures to relieve anxiety or tension or to produce sleep. If your child is to take this medicine before a dental or medical procedure, it should be given to the child only at the health care facility where the procedure is to be done. This will allow the health care professional to monitor your child.

Chloral hydrate has been used in the treatment of insomnia (trouble in sleeping) and to help calm or relax patients who are nervous or tense. However, this medicine has generally been replaced by other medicines for the treatment of insomnia and nervousness or tension.

Chloral hydrate has also been used with analgesics (pain medicine) for control of pain following surgery. However, this medicine has generally been replaced by other medicines for control of pain following surgery.

Chloral hydrate comes in different strengths. Serious problems, including deaths, have occurred when children were given the wrong strength. *Make sure your doctor has told your pharmacist both how many milligrams (mg) and how many capsules, teaspoonfuls, or suppositories should be used.* This information is needed to be sure the right amount is given.

This medicine is available only with your doctor's prescription, in the following dosage forms:

Oral
- Capsules (U.S. and Canada)
- Syrup (U.S. and Canada)

Rectal
- Suppositories (U.S.)

Before Using This Medicine

In deciding to use a medicine, the risks of taking the medicine must be weighed against the good it will do. This is a decision you and your doctor will make. For chloral hydrate, the following should be considered:

Allergies—Tell your doctor if you have ever had any unusual or allergic reaction to chloral hydrate. Also tell your health care professional if you are allergic to any other substances, such as foods, preservatives, or dyes.

Pregnancy—Studies on birth defects have not been done in either humans or animals. Too much use of chloral hydrate during pregnancy may cause the baby to become dependent on the medicine. This may lead to withdrawal side effects after birth.

Breast-feeding—Chloral hydrate passes into the breast milk and may cause drowsiness in babies of mothers using this medicine.

Children—This medicine comes in different strengths. Serious problems, including deaths, have occurred when children were given the wrong strength. *Make sure your doctor has told your pharmacist both how many milligrams (mg) and how many capsules, teaspoonfuls, or suppositories your child should receive.* This information is needed to be sure the right amount is given. With proper use, this medicine is not expected to cause different side effects or problems in children than it does in adults.

Older adults—Many medicines have not been studied specifically in older people. Therefore, it may not be known whether they work exactly the same way they do in younger adults. Although there is no specific information comparing use of chloral hydrate in the elderly with use in other age groups, this medicine is not expected to cause different side effects or problems in older people than it does in younger adults.

Other medicines—Although certain medicines should not be used together at all, in other cases two different medicines may be used together even if an interaction might occur. In these cases, your doctor may want to change the dose, or other precautions may be necessary. When you are taking chloral hydrate, it is especially important that your health care professional know if you are taking any of the following:

- Anticoagulants (blood thinners)—Chloral hydrate may change the amount of anticoagulant you need to take
- Central nervous system (CNS) depressants (medicine that causes drowsiness) or
- Tricyclic antidepressants (medicine for depression)—Using these medicines and chloral hydrate together may increase the CNS and other depressant effects

Other medical problems—The presence of other medical problems may affect the use of chloral hydrate. Make sure you tell your doctor if you have any other medical problems, especially:

- Alcohol abuse or dependence (or history of) or
- Drug abuse or dependence (or history of)—Dependence on chloral hydrate may develop

- Colitis or
- Proctitis or inflammation of the rectum—Chloral hydrate used rectally may make the condition worse
- Esophagitis or inflammation of the esophagus, or
- Gastritis or inflammation of the stomach, or
- Stomach ulcers—Chloral hydrate taken by mouth may make the condition worse
- Heart disease—Chloral hydrate may make the condition worse
- Kidney disease or
- Liver disease—Higher blood levels of chloral hydrate may occur, increasing the chance of side effects
- Porphyria—Acute attacks may be set off by chloral hydrate
- Sleep problems in children (especially in those with enlarged tonsils)—Risk of breathing problems may be increased

Proper Use of This Medicine

Use this medicine only as directed by your doctor. Do not use more of it, do not use it more often, and do not use it for a longer time than your doctor ordered. If too much is used, it may become habit-forming.

For patients taking *chloral hydrate capsules:*

- Swallow the capsule whole. Do not chew since the medicine may cause an unpleasant taste.
- Take this medicine with a full glass (8 ounces) of water, fruit juice, or ginger ale to lessen stomach upset.

For patients taking *chloral hydrate syrup:*

- Take each dose of medicine mixed with clear liquid, such as water, apple juice, or ginger ale. This will help to improve flavor and lessen stomach upset.

For patients using *chloral hydrate rectal suppositories:*

- If the suppository is too soft to insert, chill it in the refrigerator for 30 minutes or run cold water over it before removing the foil wrapper.
- To insert suppository–First remove the foil wrapper and moisten the suppository with cold water. Lie down on your side and use your finger to push the suppository well up into the rectum.

Dosing—The dose of chloral hydrate will be different for different patients. *Follow your doctor's orders or the directions on the label.* The following information includes only the average doses of chloral hydrate. *If your dose is different, do not change it* unless your doctor tells you to do so.

This medicine comes in different strengths. *Make sure your doctor has told your pharmacist both how many milligrams (mg) and how many capsules, teaspoonfuls, or suppositories should be used.* This information is needed to be sure the right amount is given.

The number of capsules or teaspoonfuls of syrup that you take, or suppositories that you use, depends on the strength of the medicine. Also, *the number of doses you use each day, the time allowed between doses, and the length of time you use the medicine depend on the medical problem for which you are using chloral hydrate.*

- For *oral* dosage form (capsules or syrup):
  - —For trouble in sleeping or sedation before surgery:
    - Adults—500 to 1000 milligrams (mg) taken thirty minutes before bedtime or surgery.
  - —For daytime sedation:
    - Adults—250 mg taken three times a day after meals.
  - —For sedation before a dental or medical procedure:
    - Children—Dose is based on body weight and must be determined by your doctor. The dose is usually 50 mg per kilogram (kg) (23 mg per pound) of body weight.
  - —For sedation before an electroencephalograph (EEG) test:
    - Children—Dose is based on body weight and must be determined by your doctor. The usual dose is 25 mg per kg (11 mg per pound) of body weight.
- For *rectal* dosage form (suppositories):
  - —For trouble in sleeping:
    - Adults—500 to 1000 mg at bedtime.
  - —For daytime sedation:
    - Adults—325 mg three times a day.
  - —For sedation before a dental or medical procedure:
    - Children—Dose is based on body weight and must be determined by your doctor. The dose is usually 50 mg per kg (23 mg per pound) of body weight.
  - —For sedation before an electroencephalograph (EEG) test:
    - Children—Dose is based on body weight and must be determined by your doctor. The dose is usually 25 mg per kg (11 mg per pound) of body weight.

Missed dose—If you miss a dose of this medicine, skip the missed dose and go back to your regular dosing schedule. Do not double doses.

Storage—To store this medicine:

- Keep out of the reach of children. Overdose of chloral hydrate is especially dangerous in children.
- Store away from heat and direct light.
- Do not store the capsule form of this medicine in the bathroom, near the kitchen sink, or in other damp places. Heat or moisture may cause the medicine to break down.
- Keep the syrup form of this medicine from freezing.
- Do not keep outdated medicine or medicine no longer needed. Be sure that any discarded medicine is out of the reach of children.

Precautions While Using This Medicine

If you will be using this medicine regularly for a long time:

- Your doctor should check your progress at regular visits to make sure that this medicine does not cause unwanted effects.

- Do not stop using it without first checking with your doctor. Your doctor may want you to reduce gradually the amount you are using before stopping completely.

This medicine will add to the effects of alcohol and other CNS depressants (medicines that slow down the nervous system, possibly causing drowsiness). Some examples of CNS depressants are antihistamines or medicine for hay fever, other allergies, or colds; sedatives, tranquilizers, or sleeping medicine; prescription pain medicine or narcotics; barbiturates; medicine for seizures; muscle relaxants; or anesthetics, including some dental anesthetics. *Check with your doctor before taking any of the above while you are using this medicine.*

If you think you or someone else may have taken an overdose of this medicine, get emergency help at once. Taking an overdose of chloral hydrate or taking alcohol or other CNS depressants with chloral hydrate may lead to unconsciousness and possibly death. Some signs of an overdose are continuing confusion, difficulty in swallowing, convulsions (seizures), severe drowsiness, severe weakness, shortness of breath or troubled breathing, staggering, and slow or irregular heartbeat.

This medicine may cause some people to become dizzy, lightheaded, drowsy, or less alert than they are normally. Even if taken at bedtime, it may cause some people to feel drowsy or less alert on arising. *Make sure you know how you react to this medicine before you drive, use machines, or do anything else that could be dangerous if you are dizzy or are not alert.*

Side Effects of This Medicine

Along with its needed effects, a medicine may cause some unwanted effects. Although not all of these side effects may occur, if they do occur they may need medical attention.

Check with your doctor as soon as possible if any of the following side effects occur:

Less common

Skin rash or hives

Rare

Confusion; hallucinations (seeing, hearing, or feeling things that are not there); unusual excitement

Symptoms of overdose

Confusion (continuing); convulsions (seizures); difficulty in swallowing; drowsiness (severe); low body temperature; nausea, vomiting, or stomach pain (severe); shortness of breath or troubled breathing; slow or irregular heartbeat; slurred speech; staggering; weakness (severe)

Other side effects may occur that do not need medical attention. These side effects may go away during treatment as your body adjusts to the medicine. However, check with your doctor if any of the following side effects continue or are bothersome:

More common

Nausea; stomach pain; vomiting

Less common

Clumsiness or unsteadiness; diarrhea; dizziness or lightheadedness; drowsiness; "hangover" effect

After you stop using this medicine, your body may need time to adjust. The length of time this takes depends on the amount of medicine you were using and how long you used it. During this period of time, check with your doctor if you notice any of the following side effects:

Confusion; hallucinations (seeing, hearing, or feeling things that are not there); nausea or vomiting; nervousness; restlessness; stomach pain; trembling; unusual excitement

Other side effects not listed above may also occur in some patients. If you notice any other effects, check with your doctor.

Revised: 08/02/94
Interim revision: 03/31/95

CHLORAMBUCIL Systemic

A commonly used brand name in the U.S. and Canada is Leukeran.

Description

Chlorambucil (klor-AM-byoo-sill) belongs to the group of medicines called alkylating agents. It is used to treat some kinds of cancer.

Chlorambucil interferes with the growth of cancer cells, which are eventually destroyed. Since the growth of normal body cells may also be affected by chlorambucil, other effects will also occur. Some of these may be serious and must be reported to your doctor. Other effects may not be serious but may cause concern. Some effects may not occur for months or years after the medicine is used.

Before you begin treatment with chlorambucil, you and your doctor should talk about the good this medicine will do as well as the risks of using it.

Chlorambucil may also be used for other conditions as determined by your doctor.

Chlorambucil is available only with your doctor's prescription, in the following dosage form:

Oral

- Tablets (U.S. and Canada)

Before Using This Medicine

In deciding to use a medicine, the risks of taking the medicine must be weighed against the good it will do. This is a decision you and your doctor will make. For chlorambucil, the following should be considered:

Allergies—Tell your doctor if you have ever had any unusual or allergic reaction to chlorambucil or other cancer medicines.

Pregnancy—This medicine may cause birth defects if either the male or female is taking it at the time of conception or if it is taken during pregnancy. In addition, many cancer medicines may cause sterility which could be permanent. Sterility has been reported with this medicine and the possibility should be kept in mind.

Be sure that you have discussed this with your doctor before taking this medicine. It is best to use some kind of birth control while you are taking chlorambucil. Tell your doctor right away if you think you have become pregnant while taking chlorambucil.

Breast-feeding—Because chlorambucil may cause serious side effects, breast-feeding is generally not recommended while you are taking it.

Children—In general, this medicine has not been shown to cause different side effects or problems in children than it does in adults. However, some children with nephrotic syndrome (a kidney disease) may be more likely to have convulsions (seizures).

Older adults—Many medicines have not been studied specifically in older people. Therefore, it may not be known whether they work exactly the same way they do in younger adults or if they cause different side effects or problems in older people. There is no specific information comparing use of chlorambucil in the elderly with use in other age groups.

Other medicines—Although certain medicines should not be used together at all, in other cases two different medicines may be used together even if an interaction might occur. In these cases, your doctor may want to change the dose, or other precautions may be necessary. When you are taking chlorambucil it is especially important that your health care professional know if you are taking any of the following:

- Amphotericin B by injection (e.g., Fungizone) or
- Antithyroid agents (medicine for overactive thyroid) or
- Chloramphenicol (e.g., Chloromycetin) or
- Colchicine or
- Flucytosine (e.g., Ancobon) or
- Ganciclovir (e.g., Cytovene) or
- Interferon (e.g., Intron A, Roferon-A) or
- Plicamycin (e.g., Mithracin) or
- Zidovudine (e.g., AZT, Retrovir) or
- If you have ever been treated with radiation or cancer medicines—Chlorambucil may increase the effects of these medicines or radiation therapy on the blood
- Azathioprine (e.g., Imuran) or
- Corticosteroids (cortisone-like medicine) or
- Cyclophosphamide (e.g., Cytoxan) or
- Cyclosporine (e.g., Sandimmune) or
- Cytarabine (e.g., Cytosar-U) or
- Mercaptopurine (e.g., Purinethol) or
- Muromonab-CD3 (monoclonal antibody) (e.g., Orthoclone OKT3) or
- Tacrolimus (e.g., Prograf)—There may be an increased risk of infection and development of cancer because chlorambucil decreases the body's ability to fight them
- Probenecid (e.g., Benemid) or
- Sulfinpyrazone (e.g., Anturane)—Chlorambucil may increase the amount of uric acid in the blood. Since these medicines are used to lower uric acid levels, they may not work as well in patients taking chlorambucil

Other medical problems—The presence of other medical problems may affect the use of chlorambucil. Make sure you tell your doctor if you have any other medical problems, especially:

- Chickenpox (including recent exposure) or
- Herpes zoster (shingles)—Risk of severe disease affecting other parts of the body
- Convulsions (seizures) (history of) or
- Head injury—Increased risk of seizures
- Gout or
- Kidney stones (history of)—Chlorambucil may increase levels of uric acid in the body, which can cause gout or kidney stones
- Infection—Chlorambucil decreases your body's ability to fight infection

Proper Use of This Medicine

Take this medicine only as directed by your doctor. Do not take more or less of it, and do not take it more often than your doctor ordered. The exact amount of medicine you need has been carefully worked out. Taking too much may increase the chance of side effects, while taking too little may not improve your condition.

Chlorambucil is sometimes given together with certain other medicines. If you are using a combination of medicines, make sure that you take each one at the proper time and do not mix them. Ask your health care professional to help you plan a way to remember to take your medicines at the right times.

While you are using chlorambucil, your doctor may want you to drink extra fluids so that you will pass more urine. This will help prevent kidney problems and keep your kidneys working well.

This medicine sometimes causes nausea and vomiting. However, it is very important that you continue to use the medicine, even if you begin to feel ill. *Do not stop using this medicine without first checking with your doctor.* Ask your health care professional for ways to lessen these effects.

If you vomit shortly after taking a dose of chlorambucil, check with your doctor. You will be told whether to take the dose again or to wait until the next scheduled dose.

Dosing—The dose of chlorambucil will be different for different patients. The dose that is used may depend on a number of things, including what the medicine is being used for, the patient's weight, and whether or not other medicines are also being taken. *If you are taking chlorambucil at home, follow your doctor's orders or the directions on the label.* If you have any questions about the proper dose of chlorambucil, ask your doctor.

Missed dose—If you miss a dose of this medicine and your dosing schedule is:

- One dose a day—Take the missed dose as soon as possible. Then go back to your regular dosing schedule. However, if you do not remember the missed dose until the next day, do not take it at all. Instead, take your regularly scheduled dose. Do not double doses.

- More than one dose a day—Take the missed dose as soon as possible. Then go back to your regular dosing schedule. However, if it is almost time for your next dose, skip the missed dose and go back to your regular dosing schedule. Do not double doses.

Storage—To store this medicine:
- Keep out of the reach of children.
- Store away from heat and direct light.
- Do not store in the bathroom, near the kitchen sink, or in other damp places. Heat or moisture may cause the medicine to break down.
- Do not keep outdated medicine or medicine no longer needed. Be sure that any discarded medicine is out of the reach of children.

Precautions While Using This Medicine

It is very important that your doctor check your progress at regular visits to make sure this medicine is working properly and to check for unwanted effects.

While you are being treated with chlorambucil, and after you stop treatment with it, *do not have any immunizations (vaccinations) without your doctor's approval.* Chlorambucil may lower your body's resistance and there is a chance you might get the infection the immunization is meant to prevent. In addition, other persons living in your household should not take oral polio vaccine since there is a chance they could pass the polio virus on to you. Also, avoid persons who have recently taken oral polio vaccine. Do not get close to them, and do not stay in the same room with them for very long. If you cannot take these precautions, you should consider wearing a protective face mask that covers the nose and mouth.

Chlorambucil can temporarily lower the number of white blood cells in your blood, increasing the chance of getting an infection. It can also lower the number of platelets, which are necessary for proper blood clotting. If this occurs, there are certain precautions you can take, especially when your blood count is low, to reduce the risk of infection or bleeding:
- If you can, avoid people with infections. *Check with your doctor immediately* if you think you are getting an infection or if you get a fever or chills, cough or hoarseness, lower back or side pain, or painful or difficult urination.
- *Check with your doctor immediately* if you notice any unusual bleeding or bruising; black, tarry stools; blood in urine or stools; or pinpoint red spots on your skin.
- Be careful when using a regular toothbrush, dental floss, or toothpick. Your medical doctor, dentist, or nurse may recommend other ways to clean your teeth and gums. Check with your medical doctor before having any dental work done.
- Do not touch your eyes or the inside of your nose unless you have just washed your hands and have not touched anything else in the meantime.
- Be careful not to cut yourself when you are using sharp objects such as a safety razor or fingernail or toenail cutters.
- Avoid contact sports or other situations where bruising or injury could occur.

Side Effects of This Medicine

Along with its needed effects, a medicine may have some unwanted effects. Although not all of these side effects may occur, if they do occur they may need medical attention.

Also, because of the way these medicines act on the body, there is a chance that they might cause other unwanted effects that may not occur until months or years after the medicine is used. These delayed effects may include certain types of cancer, such as leukemia. Discuss these possible effects with your doctor.

Check with your doctor or nurse immediately if any of the following side effects occur:

Less common

Black, tarry stools; blood in urine or stools; cough or hoarseness; fever or chills; lower back or side pain; painful or difficult urination; pinpoint red spots on skin; sores in mouth and on lips; unusual bleeding or bruising

Check with your doctor as soon as possible if any of the following side effects occur:

Less common

Joint pain; skin rash; swelling of feet or lower legs

Rare

Agitation; blisters on skin; confusion; convulsions (seizures); hallucinations (seeing, hearing, or feeling things that are not there); muscle twitching; peeling or scaling of skin; shortness of breath; skin rash (severe); tremors; trouble in walking; weakness (severe) or paralysis; yellow eyes or skin

Symptoms of overdose (in the order of frequency)

Black, tarry stools; blood in urine or stools; cough or hoarseness; fever or chills; lower back or side pain; painful or difficult urination; pinpoint red spots on skin; unusual bleeding or bruising; agitation; convulsions (seizures); trouble in walking

Other side effects may occur that usually do not need medical attention. These side effects may go away during treatment as your body adjusts to the medicine. Also, your health care professional may be able to tell you about ways to prevent or reduce some of these side effects. Check with your health care professional if any of the following side effects continue or are bothersome or if you have any questions about them:

Less common

Changes in menstrual period; itching of skin; nausea and vomiting

After you stop using chlorambucil, it may still produce some side effects that need attention. During this period of time, check with your doctor if you notice any of the following side effects:

Black, tarry stools; blood in urine or stools; cough or hoarseness; fever or chills; lower back or side pain; painful or difficult urination; pinpoint red spots on skin; shortness of breath; unusual bleeding or bruising

Other side effects not listed above may also occur in some patients. If you notice any other effects, check with your doctor.

Additional Information

Once a medicine has been approved for marketing for a certain use, experience may show that it is also useful for other medical problems. Although these uses are not included in product labeling, chlorambucil is used in certain patients with the following medical conditions:

- Polycythemia vera
- Nephrotic syndrome

Other than the above information, there is no additional information relating to proper use, precautions, or side effects for these uses.

Revised: 07/15/94

CHLORAMPHENICOL Ophthalmic

Some commonly used brand names are:

In the U.S.—

- Ak-Chlor Ophthalmic Ointment
- Ak-Chlor Ophthalmic Solution
- Chloracol Ophthalmic Solution
- Chlorofair Ophthalmic Ointment
- Chlorofair Ophthalmic Solution
- Chloromycetin Ophthalmic Ointment
- Chloromycetin for Ophthalmic Solution
- Chloroptic Ophthalmic Solution
- Chloroptic S.O.P.
- Econochlor Ophthalmic Ointment
- Econochlor Ophthalmic Solution
- I-Chlor Ophthalmic Solution
- Ocu-Chlor Ophthalmic Ointment
- Ocu-Chlor Ophthalmic Solution
- Ophthochlor Ophthalmic Solution
- Spectro-Chlor Ophthalmic Ointment
- Spectro-Chlor Ophthalmic Solution

In Canada—

- Ak-Chlor Ophthalmic Solution
- Chloromycetin Ophthalmic Ointment
- Chloromycetin for Ophthalmic Solution
- Chloroptic Ophthalmic Solution
- Chloroptic S.O.P.
- Fenicol Ophthalmic Ointment
- Ophtho-Chloram Ophthalmic Solution
- Pentamycetin Ophthalmic Ointment
- Pentamycetin Ophthalmic Solution
- Sopamycetin Ophthalmic Ointment
- Sopamycetin Ophthalmic Solution

Description

Chloramphenicol (klor-am-FEN-i-kole) belongs to the family of medicines called antibiotics. Chloramphenicol ophthalmic preparations are used to treat infections of the eye. This medicine may be given alone or with other medicines that are taken by mouth for eye infections.

Chloramphenicol is available only with your doctor's prescription, in the following dosage forms:

Ophthalmic

- Ophthalmic ointment (eye ointment) (U.S. and Canada)
- Ophthalmic solution (eye drops) (U.S. and Canada)

Before Using This Medicine

In deciding to use a medicine, the risks of taking the medicine must be weighed against the good it will do. This is a decision you and your doctor will make. For chloramphenicol, the following should be considered:

Allergies—Tell your doctor if you have ever had any unusual or allergic reaction to chloramphenicol. Also tell your health care professional if you are allergic to any other substances, such as preservatives.

Pregnancy—Chloramphenicol ophthalmic preparations have not been shown to cause birth defects or other problems in humans.

Breast-feeding—Chloramphenicol ophthalmic preparations have not been reported to cause problems in nursing babies.

Children—Studies on this medicine have been done only in adult patients, and there is no specific information comparing use of this medicine in children with use in other age groups.

Older adults—Many medicines have not been studied specifically in older people. Therefore, it may not be known whether they work exactly the same way they do in younger adults or if they cause different side effects or problems in older people. There is no specific information comparing use of this medicine in the elderly with use in other age groups.

Other medicines—Although certain medicines should not be used together at all, in other cases two different medicines may be used together even if an interaction might occur. In these cases, your doctor may want to change the dose, or other precautions may be necessary. Tell your health care professional if you are using any other prescription or nonprescription (over-the-counter [OTC]) medicine.

Proper Use of This Medicine

For patients using the *eye drop form* of chloramphenicol:

- Although the bottle may not be full, it contains exactly the amount of medicine your doctor ordered.
- To use:

  —First, wash your hands. Tilt the head back and, pressing your finger gently on the skin just beneath the lower eyelid, pull the lower eyelid away from the eye to make a space. Drop the medicine into this space. Let go of the eyelid and gently close the eyes. Do not blink. Keep the eyes closed and apply pressure to the inner corner of the eye with your finger for 1 or 2 minutes to allow the medicine to come into contact with the infection.

  —If you think you did not get the drop of medicine into your eye properly, use another drop.

  —To keep the medicine as germ-free as possible, do not touch the applicator tip or dropper to any surface (including the eye). Also, keep the container tightly closed.

To use the *eye ointment form* of chloramphenicol:

- First, wash your hands. Tilt the head back and, pressing your finger gently on the skin just beneath the

lower eyelid, pull the lower eyelid away from the eye to make a space. Squeeze a thin strip of ointment into this space. A 1-cm (approximately 1/3-inch) strip of ointment is usually enough, unless you have been told by your doctor to use a different amount. Let go of the eyelid and gently close the eyes. Keep the eyes closed for 1 or 2 minutes to allow the medicine to come into contact with the infection.
- To keep the medicine as germ-free as possible, do not touch the applicator tip to any surface (including the eye). After using chloramphenicol eye ointment, wipe the tip of the ointment tube with a clean tissue and keep the tube tightly closed.

To help clear up your infection completely, *keep using this medicine for the full time of treatment*, even if your symptoms begin to clear up after a few days. If you stop using this medicine too soon, your symptoms may return. *Do not miss any doses.*

Dosing—The dose of chloramphenicol will be different for different patients. *Follow your doctor's orders or the directions on the label.* The following information includes only the average doses of chloramphenicol. *If your dose is different, do not change it unless your doctor tells you to do so.*

- For eye infection:
  - For *ophthalmic ointment* dosage form:
    - Adults and children—Use every three hours.
  - For *ophthalmic solution (eye drops)* dosage form:
    - Adults and children—One drop every one to four hours.

Missed dose—If you miss a dose of this medicine, apply it as soon as possible. However, if it is almost time for your next dose, skip the missed dose and go back to your regular dosing schedule.

Storage—To store this medicine:
- Keep out of the reach of children.
- Store away from heat and direct light.
- Keep the medicine from freezing.
- Do not keep outdated medicine or medicine no longer needed. Be sure that any discarded medicine is out of the reach of children.

Precautions While Using This Medicine

If your symptoms do not improve within a few days, or if they become worse, check with your doctor.

Side Effects of This Medicine

Along with its needed effects, a medicine may cause some unwanted effects. Although not all of these side effects may occur, if they do occur they may need medical attention.

Check with your doctor immediately if any of the following side effects occur:

Rare

Pale skin; sore throat and fever; unusual bleeding or bruising; unusual tiredness or weakness (the above side effects may also occur weeks or months after you stop using this medicine)

Check with your doctor as soon as possible if any of the following side effects occur:

Less common

Itching, redness, skin rash, swelling, or other sign of irritation not present before use of this medicine

Other side effects may occur that usually do not need medical attention. These side effects may go away during treatment as your body adjusts to the medicine. However, check with your doctor if either of the following side effects continues or is bothersome:

Less common

Burning or stinging

After application, eye ointments may be expected to cause your vision to blur for a few minutes.

Other side effects not listed above may also occur in some patients. If you notice any other effects, check with your doctor.

Revised: 01/15/92
Interim revision: 09/30/93; 12/13/93

CHLORAMPHENICOL Otic

Some commonly used brand names are:

In the U.S.—
Chloromycetin
Generic name product may also be available.

In Canada—
Chloromycetin
Sopamycetin

Description

Chloramphenicol (klor-am-FEN-i-kole) belongs to the family of medicines called antibiotics. Chloramphenicol otic drops are used to treat infections of the ear canal. This medicine may be used alone or with other medicines that are taken by mouth for ear canal infections.

Chloramphenicol is available only with your doctor's prescription, in the following dosage form:

Otic
- Solution (U.S. and Canada)

Before Using This Medicine

In deciding to use a medicine, the risks of using the medicine must be weighed against the good it will do. This is a decision you and your doctor will make. For chloramphenicol otic, the following should be considered:

Allergies—Tell your doctor if you have ever had any unusual or allergic reaction to chloramphenicol. Also tell your health care professional if you are allergic to any other substances, such as preservatives.

Pregnancy—Chloramphenicol otic drops have not been shown to cause birth defects or other problems in humans.

Breast-feeding—Chloramphenicol otic drops have not been reported to cause problems in nursing babies.

Children—Although there is no specific information comparing use of chloramphenicol otic drops in children with use in other age groups, this medicine is not expected to cause different side effects or problems in children than it does in adults.

Older adults—Many medicines have not been studied specifically in older people. Therefore, it may not be known whether they work exactly the same way they do in younger adults or if they cause different side effects or problems in older people. There is no specific information comparing use of this medicine in the elderly with use in other age groups.

Other medicines—Although certain medicines should not be used together at all, in other cases two different medicines may be used together even if an interaction might occur. In these cases, your doctor may want to change the dose, or other precautions may be necessary. Tell your health care professional if you are using any other prescription or nonprescription (over-the-counter [OTC]) medicine.

Other medical problems—The presence of other medical problems may affect the use of chloramphenicol ear drops. Make sure you tell your doctor if you have any other medical problems, especially:

- Opening in your ear drum—This medicine may cause unwanted effects if it goes past the ear drum into the middle ear

Proper Use of This Medicine

To use:

- Lie down or tilt the head so that the infected ear faces up. Gently pull the earlobe up and back for adults (down and back for children) to straighten the ear canal. Drop the medicine into the ear canal. Keep the ear facing up for about 1 or 2 minutes to allow the medicine to come into contact with the infection. A sterile cotton plug may be gently inserted into the ear opening to prevent the medicine from leaking out.
- To keep the medicine as germ-free as possible, do not touch the dropper to any surface (including the ear). Also, keep the container tightly closed.

To help clear up your infection completely, *keep using this medicine for the full time of treatment,* even if your symptoms begin to clear up after a few days. If you stop using this medicine too soon, your symptoms may return. *Do not miss any doses.*

Dosing—The dose of otic chloramphenicol will be different for different patients. *Follow your doctor's orders or the directions on the label.* The following information includes only the average doses of otic chloramphenicol. *If your dose is different, do not change it* unless your doctor tells you to do so.

- For *otic solution (ear drops)* dosage form:
  - —For infections of the ear canal:
    - Adults and children—Use two or three drops in the ear every six to eight hours.

Missed dose—If you miss a dose of this medicine, apply it as soon as possible. However, if it is almost time for your next dose, skip the missed dose and go back to your regular dosing schedule.

Storage—To store this medicine:

- Keep out of the reach of children.
- Store away from heat and direct light.
- Keep the medicine from freezing.
- Do not keep outdated medicine or medicine no longer needed. Be sure that any discarded medicine is out of the reach of children.

Precautions While Using This Medicine

If your symptoms do not improve within a few days, or if they become worse, check with your doctor.

Side Effects of This Medicine

Along with its needed effects, a medicine may cause some unwanted effects. Although not all of these side effects may occur, if they do occur they may need medical attention.

Check with your doctor immediately if any of the following side effects occur:

Rare

Pale skin; sore throat and fever; unusual bleeding or bruising; unusual tiredness or weakness (the above side effects may also occur weeks or months after you stop using this medicine)

Check with your doctor as soon as possible if any of the following side effects occur:

Less common

Burning, itching, redness, skin rash, swelling, or other sign of irritation not present before use of this medicine

Other side effects not listed above may also occur in some patients. If you notice any other effects, check with your doctor.

Revised: 02/10/92
Interim revision: 02/17/94

CHLORAMPHENICOL Systemic

Some commonly used brand names are:

In the U.S.—

Chloromycetin

Generic name product may also be available.

In Canada—

Chloromycetin Novochlorocap

Description

Chloramphenicol (klor-am-FEN-i-kole) is used in the treatment of infections caused by bacteria. It works by killing bacteria or preventing their growth.

Chloramphenicol is used to treat serious infections in different parts of the body. It is sometimes given with other antibiotics. However, chloramphenicol should not be used for colds, flu, other virus infections, sore throats or other minor infections, or to prevent infections.

Chloramphenicol should only be used for serious infections in which other medicines do not work. This medicine may cause some serious side effects, including blood problems and eye problems. Symptoms of the blood problems include pale skin, sore throat and fever, unusual bleeding or bruising, and unusual tiredness or weakness. *You and your doctor should talk about the good this medicine will do as well as the risks of taking it.*

Chloramphenicol is available only with your doctor's prescription, in the following dosage forms:

Oral

- Capsules (U.S. and Canada)
- Oral suspension (U.S.)

Parenteral

- Injection (U.S. and Canada)

Before Using This Medicine

In deciding to use a medicine, the risks of taking the medicine must be weighed against the good it will do. This is a decision you and your doctor will make. For chloramphenicol, the following should be considered:

Allergies—Tell your doctor if you have ever had any unusual or allergic reaction to chloramphenicol. Also tell your health care professional if you are allergic to any other substances, such as foods, preservatives, or dyes.

Pregnancy—Chloramphenicol has not been shown to cause birth defects in humans. However, use is not recommended within a week or two of your delivery date. Chloramphenicol may cause gray skin color, low body temperature, bloated stomach, uneven breathing, drowsiness, pale skin, sore throat and fever, unusual bleeding or bruising, unusual tiredness or weakness, or other problems in the infant.

Breast-feeding—Chloramphenicol passes into the breast milk and has been shown to cause unwanted effects, such as pale skin, sore throat and fever, unusual bleeding or bruising, unusual tiredness or weakness, or other problems in nursing babies. It may be necessary for you to take another medicine or to stop breast-feeding during treatment. Be sure you have discussed the risks and benefits of the medicine with your doctor.

Children—Newborn infants are especially sensitive to the side effects of chloramphenicol because they cannot remove the medicine from their body as well as older children and adults.

Older adults—Many medicines have not been studied specifically in older people. Therefore, it may not be known whether they work exactly the same way they do in younger adults or if they cause different side effects or problems in older people. There is no specific information comparing use of chloramphenicol in the elderly with use in other age groups.

Other medicines—Although certain medicines should not be used together at all, in other cases two different medicines may be used together even if an interaction might occur. In these cases, your doctor may want to change the dose, or other precautions may be necessary. When you are taking chloramphenicol, it is especially important that your health care professional know if you are taking any of the following:

- Alfentanil or
- Antidiabetics, oral (diabetes medicine you take by mouth) or
- Phenobarbital or
- Warfarin (e.g., Coumadin)—Use of chloramphenicol with these medicines may increase the chance of side effects of these medicines

- Amphotericin B by injection (e.g., Fungizone) or
- Antineoplastics (cancer medicine) or
- Antithyroid agents (medicine for overactive thyroid) or
- Azathioprine (e.g., Imuran) or
- Colchicine or
- Cyclophosphamide (e.g., Cytoxan) or
- Ethotoin (e.g., Peganone) or
- Flucytosine (e.g., Ancobon) or
- Ganciclovir (e.g., Cytovene) or
- Interferon (e.g., Intron A, Roferon-A) or
- Mephenytoin (e.g., Mesantoin) or
- Mercaptopurine (e.g., Purinethol) or
- Methotrexate (e.g., Mexate) or
- Phenytoin (e.g., Dilantin) or
- Plicamycin (e.g., Mithracin) or
- Zidovudine (e.g., AZT, Retrovir) or
- X-ray treatment—Use of chloramphenicol with any of these medicines or with x-ray treatment may increase the risk of blood problems

- Clindamycin (e.g., Cleocin) or
- Erythromycins (medicine for infection) or
- Lincomycin (e.g., Lincocin)—Use of chloramphenicol with any of these medicines may decrease the effectiveness of these medicines

- Phenytoin (e.g., Dilantin)—Use of chloramphenicol with phenytoin may increase the chance of blood problems or increase the side effects of phenytoin

Other medical problems—The presence of other medical problems may affect the use of chloramphenicol. Make sure you tell your doctor if you have any other medical problems, especially:

- Anemia, bleeding, or other blood problems—Chloramphenicol may cause blood problems
- Liver disease—Patients with liver disease may have an increased risk of side effects

Proper Use of This Medicine

Chloramphenicol is best taken with a full glass (8 ounces) of water on an empty stomach (either 1 hour before or 2 hours after meals), unless otherwise directed by your doctor.

For patients taking the oral liquid form of this medicine:

- Use a specially marked measuring spoon or other device to measure each dose accurately. The average household teaspoon may not hold the right amount of liquid.

To help clear up your infection completely, *keep taking this medicine for the full time of treatment,* even if you begin to feel better after a few days. *Do not miss any doses.*

Dosing—The dose of chloramphenicol will be different for different patients. *Follow your doctor's orders or the directions on the label.* The following information includes only the average doses of chloramphenicol. *If your dose is different, do not change it* unless your doctor tells you to do so.

The number of capsules or teaspoonfuls of suspension that you take depends on the strength of the medicine. Also, *the number of doses you take each day, the time allowed between doses, and the length of time you take the medicine depend on the medical problem for which you are taking chloramphenicol.*

- For infections caused by bacteria:
  - —For *oral* dosage forms (capsules and suspension):
    - Adults and teenagers—Dose is based on body weight. The usual dose is 12.5 milligrams (mg) per kilogram (kg) (5.7 mg per pound) of body weight every six hours.
    - Children—
      - —Infants up to 2 weeks of age: Dose is based on body weight. The usual dose is 6.25 mg per kg (2.8 mg per pound) of body weight every six hours.
      - —Infants 2 weeks of age and older: Dose is based on body weight. The usual dose is 12.5 mg per kg (5.7 mg per pound) of body weight every six hours; or 25 mg per kg (11.4 mg per pound) of body weight every twelve hours.
  - —For *injection* dosage form:
    - Adults and teenagers—Dose is based on body weight. The usual dose is 12.5 mg per kg (5.7 mg per pound) of body weight every six hours.
    - Children—
      - —Infants up to 2 weeks of age: Dose is based on body weight. The usual dose is 6.25 mg per kg (2.8 mg per pound) of body weight every six hours.
      - —Infants 2 weeks of age and older: Dose is based on body weight. The usual dose is 12.5 mg per kg (5.7 mg per pound) of body weight every six hours; or 25 mg per kg (11.4 mg per pound) of body weight every twelve hours.

Missed dose—If you miss a dose of this medicine, take it as soon as possible. However, if it is almost time for your next dose, skip the missed dose and go back to your regular dosing schedule. Do not double doses.

Storage—To store this medicine:

- Keep out of the reach of children.
- Store away from heat and direct light.
- Do not store the capsule form of this medicine in the bathroom, near the kitchen sink, or in other damp places. Heat or moisture may cause the medicine to break down.
- Keep the oral liquid form of this medicine from freezing.
- Do not keep outdated medicine or medicine no longer needed. Be sure that any discarded medicine is out of the reach of children.

Precautions While Using This Medicine

If your symptoms do not improve within a few days, or if they become worse, check with your doctor.

It is very important that your doctor check you at regular visits for any blood problems that may be caused by this medicine.

Chloramphenicol may cause blood problems. These problems may result in a greater chance of infection, slow healing, and bleeding of the gums. Therefore, you should be careful when using regular toothbrushes, dental floss, and toothpicks. Dental work, whenever possible, should be done before you begin taking this medicine or delayed until your blood counts have returned to normal. Check with your medical doctor or dentist if you have any questions about proper oral hygiene (mouth care) during treatment.

For diabetic patients:

- *This medicine may cause false test results with urine sugar tests.* Check with your doctor before changing your diet or the dosage of your diabetes medicine.

Side Effects of This Medicine

Along with its needed effects, a medicine may cause some serious unwanted effects. Although not all of these side effects may occur, if they do occur they may need medical attention.

Stop taking this medicine and get emergency help immediately if any of the following side effects occur:

Rare—in babies only

Bloated stomach; drowsiness; gray skin color; low body temperature; uneven breathing; unresponsiveness

Also, *check with your doctor immediately* if any of the following side effects occur:

Less common

Pale skin; sore throat and fever; unusual bleeding or bruising; unusual tiredness or weakness (the above side effects may also occur up to weeks or months after you stop taking this medicine)

Rare

Confusion, delirium, or headache; eye pain, blurred vision, or loss of vision; numbness, tingling, burning pain, or weakness in the hands or feet; skin rash, fever, or difficulty in breathing

Other side effects may occur that usually do not need medical attention. These side effects may go away during treatment as your body adjusts to the medicine. However, check with your doctor if any of the following side effects continue or are bothersome:

Less common

Diarrhea; nausea or vomiting

Other side effects not listed above may also occur in some patients. If you notice any other effects, check with your doctor.

Revised: 05/13/92
Interim revision: 03/17/94; 06/20/95

CHLORAMPHENICOL Topical

A commonly used brand name in the U.S. and Canada is Chloromycetin.

Description

Chloramphenicol (klor-am-FEN-i-kole) belongs to the family of medicines called antibiotics. Chloramphenicol cream is used to treat infections of the skin. It may be used alone or with other medicines that are taken by mouth for skin infections.

Chloramphenicol is available only with your doctor's prescription, in the following dosage form:

Topical

- Cream (U.S. and Canada)

Before Using This Medicine

In deciding to use a medicine, the risks of using the medicine must be weighed against the good it will do. This is a decision you and your doctor will make. For chloramphenicol, the following should be considered:

Allergies—Tell your doctor if you have ever had any unusual or allergic reaction to chloramphenicol. Also tell your health care professional if you are allergic to any other substances, such as preservatives or dyes.

Pregnancy—Topical chloramphenicol has not been shown to cause birth defects or other problems in humans.

Breast-feeding—Topical chloramphenicol has not been reported to cause problems in nursing babies.

Children—Although there is no specific information comparing use of topical chloramphenicol in children with use in other age groups, this medicine is not expected to cause different side effects or problems in children than it does in adults.

Older adults—Many medicines have not been studied specifically in older people. Therefore, it may not be known whether they work exactly the same way they do in younger adults or if they cause different side effects or problems in older people. There is no specific information comparing use of this medicine in the elderly with use in other age groups.

Other medicines—Although certain medicines should not be used together at all, in other cases two different medicines may be used together even if an interaction might occur. In these cases, your doctor may want to change the dose, or other precautions may be necessary. Tell your health care professional if you are using any other prescription or nonprescription (over-the-counter [OTC]) medicine.

Proper Use of This Medicine

Before applying this medicine, wash the affected area with soap and water, and dry thoroughly.

To help clear up your infection completely, *keep using this medicine for the full time of treatment,* even if your symptoms begin to clear up after a few days. If you stop using this medicine too soon, your symptoms may return. *Do not miss any doses.* However, *do not use this medicine more often or for a longer time than your doctor ordered.*

Dosing—The dose of topical chloramphenicol will be different for different patients. *Follow your doctor's orders or the directions on the label.* The following information includes only the average dose of topical chloramphenicol. *If your dose is different, do not change it* unless your doctor tells you to do so.

- For *topical* dosage form (cream):
  - —For bacterial skin infections:
    - Adults and children—Apply to the affected area(s) of the skin three or four times a day.

Missed dose—If you miss a dose of this medicine, apply it as soon as possible. However, if it is almost time for your next dose, skip the missed dose and go back to your regular dosing schedule.

Storage—To store this medicine:

- Keep out of the reach of children.
- Store away from heat and direct light.
- Keep the medicine from freezing.
- Do not keep outdated medicine or medicine no longer needed. Be sure that any discarded medicine is out of the reach of children.

Precautions While Using This Medicine

If your skin problem does not improve within 1 week, or if it becomes worse, check with your doctor.

Side Effects of This Medicine

Along with its needed effects, a medicine may cause some unwanted effects. Although not all of these side effects may occur, if they do occur they may need medical attention.

Check with your doctor immediately if any of the following side effects occur:

Rare

Pale skin; sore throat and fever; unusual bleeding or bruising; unusual tiredness or weakness (the above side effects may also occur weeks or months after you stop using this medicine)

Check with your doctor as soon as possible if any of the following side effects occur:

More common

Burning, itching, redness, skin rash, swelling, or other signs of irritation not present before use of this medicine

Other side effects not listed above may also occur in some patients. If you notice any other effects, check with your doctor.

Revised: 02/10/92
Interim revision: 06/13/94

CHLORDIAZEPOXIDE AND AMITRIPTYLINE Systemic†

Some commonly used brand names in the U.S. are Limbitrol and Limbitrol DS.

Generic name product may also be available.

†Not commercially available in Canada.

Description

Chlordiazepoxide (klor-dy-az-e-POX-ide) and amitriptyline (a-mee-TRIP-ti-leen) combination is used to treat mental depression that occurs with anxiety or nervous tension.

This medicine is available only with your doctor's prescription, in the following dosage form:

Oral

- Tablets (U.S.)

Before Using This Medicine

In deciding to use a medicine, the risks of taking the medicine must be weighed against the good it will do. This is a decision you and your doctor will make. For chlordiazepoxide and amitriptyline combination, the following should be considered:

Allergies—Tell your doctor if you have ever had any unusual or allergic reaction to chlordiazepoxide (e.g., Librium) or other benzodiazepines (such as alprazolam [e.g., Xanax], bromazepam [e.g., Lectopam], clonazepam [e.g., Klonopin], clorazepate [e.g., Tranxene], diazepam [e.g., Valium], estazolam [e.g., ProSom], flurazepam [e.g., Dalmane], halazepam [e.g., Paxipam], ketazolam [e.g., Loftran], lorazepam [e.g., Ativan], midazolam [e.g., Versed], nitrazepam [e.g., Mogadon], oxazepam [e.g., Serax], prazepam [e.g., Centrax], quazepam [e.g., Doral], temazepam [e.g., Restoril], triazolam [e.g., Halcion]) or to amitriptyline (e.g., Elavil) or other tricyclic antidepressants (such as amoxapine [e.g., Asendin], clomipramine [e.g., Anafranil], desipramine [e.g., Pertofrane], doxepin [e.g., Sinequan], imipramine [e.g., Tofranil], nortriptyline [e.g., Aventyl], protriptyline [e.g., Vivactil], trimipramine [e.g., Surmontil]).

Also tell your health care professional if you are allergic to any other substances, such as foods, preservatives, or dyes.

Pregnancy—

- *Chlordiazepoxide*: Chlordiazepoxide has been reported to increase the chance of birth defects when used during the first 3 months of pregnancy.

  In addition, overuse of chlordiazepoxide during pregnancy may cause the baby to become dependent on the medicine. This may lead to withdrawal side effects in the baby after birth.

  Use of chlordiazepoxide during pregnancy, especially during the last weeks, may cause drowsiness, slow heartbeat, shortness of breath, or troubled breathing in the newborn baby. Chlordiazepoxide given just before or during labor may cause weakness in the newborn baby.
- *Amitriptyline*: Studies with amitriptyline have not been done in pregnant women. However, studies in animals have shown amitriptyline to cause birth defects when used in doses many times the human dose. Also, there have been reports of newborns suffering from muscle spasms and heart, breathing, and urinary problems when their mothers had taken tricyclic antidepressants (such as amitriptyline) immediately before delivery.

Breast-feeding—Chlordiazepoxide may pass into the breast milk and cause drowsiness, slow heartbeat, shortness of breath, or troubled breathing in babies of mothers taking this medicine. Although amitriptyline has also been found in breast milk, it has not been reported to cause problems in nursing babies.

Children—Children may be especially sensitive to the effects of chlordiazepoxide and amitriptyline combination. This may increase the chance of side effects during treatment.

Older adults—Elderly people are especially sensitive to the effects of chlordiazepoxide and amitriptyline combination. This may increase the chance of side effects during treatment.

Other medicines—Although certain medicines should not be used together at all, in other cases 2 different medicines may be used together even if an interaction might occur. In these cases, your doctor may want to change the dose, or other precautions may be necessary. When you are taking chlordiazepoxide and amitriptyline combination, it is especially important that your health care professional know if you are taking any of the following:

- Alcohol or

- Central nervous system (CNS) depressants (medicines that cause drowsiness)—Using these medicines with chlordiazepoxide and amitriptyline combination may increase the CNS depressant effects
- Amphetamines or
- Appetite suppressants (diet pills) or
- Medicine for asthma or other breathing problems or
- Medicine for colds, sinus problems, or hay fever or other allergies (including nose drops or sprays)—Using these medicines with chlordiazepoxide and amitriptyline combination may increase the risk of serious effects on your heart
- Antacids—Taking these medicines with chlordiazepoxide and amitriptyline combination may delay the combination medicine's effects
- Antihypertensives (high blood pressure medicine)—Taking these medicines with chlordiazepoxide and amitriptyline combination may increase the chance of low blood pressure (hypotension)
- Antithyroid agents (medicine for overactive thyroid) or
- Cimetidine (e.g., Tagamet)—Taking these medicines with chlordiazepoxide and amitriptyline combination may increase the chance of serious side effects
- Monoamine oxidase (MAO) inhibitors (furazolidone [e.g., Furoxone], isocarboxazid [e.g., Marplan], phenelzine [e.g., Nardil], procarbazine [e.g., Matulane], selegiline [e.g., Eldepryl], tranylcypromine [e.g., Parnate])—Taking chlordiazepoxide and amitriptyline combination while you are taking or within 2 weeks of taking monoamine oxidase (MAO) inhibitors may cause sudden very high body temperature, extremely high blood pressure, and severe convulsions; however, sometimes certain of these medicines may be used with this combination medicine under close supervision by your doctor

Other medical problems—The presence of other medical problems may affect the use of chlordiazepoxide and amitriptyline combination. Make sure you tell your doctor if you have any other medical problems, especially:

- Alcohol abuse (or history of) or
- Drug abuse or dependence (or history of)—Dependence on this medicine may develop
- Bipolar disorder (manic-depressive illness) or
- Blood problems or
- Difficulty in urinating or
- Emphysema, asthma, bronchitis, or other chronic lung disease or
- Enlarged prostate or
- Glaucoma or increased eye pressure or
- Heart disease or
- Mental illness (severe) or
- Myasthenia gravis or
- Porphyria—Chlordiazepoxide and amitriptyline combination may make the condition worse
- Epilepsy or history of seizures—The risk of seizures may be increased
- Hyperactivity—Chlordiazepoxide and amitriptyline combination may cause unexpected effects
- Kidney disease or
- Liver disease—Higher blood levels of chlordiazepoxide and amitriptyline may occur, increasing the chance of side effects
- Overactive thyroid or
- Stomach or intestinal problems—Use of this combination medicine may result in more serious problems

Proper Use of This Medicine

To reduce stomach upset, take this medicine immediately after meals or with food unless your doctor has told you to take it on an empty stomach.

Sometimes this medicine must be taken for several weeks before you begin to feel better. Your doctor should check your progress at regular visits.

Take this medicine only as directed by your doctor. Do not take more of it, do not take it more often, and do not take it for a longer period of time than your doctor ordered. If too much is taken, it may increase unwanted effects or become habit-forming (causing mental or physical dependence).

If you think this medicine is not working properly after you have taken it for a few weeks, *do not increase the dose.* Instead, check with your doctor.

Dosing—The dose of chlordiazepoxide and amitriptyline combination will be different for different patients. *Follow your doctor's orders or the directions on the label.* The following information includes only the average doses of chlordiazepoxide and amitriptyline combination. *If your dose is different, do not change it* unless your doctor tells you to do so.

The number of tablets that you take depends on the strength of the medicine. Also, *the number of doses you take each day, the time allowed between doses, and the length of time you take the medicine depend on the medical problem for which you are taking chlordiazepoxide and amitriptyline combination.*

- For *oral* dosage forms (tablets):
  —Adults and adolescents: To start, 5 milligrams of chlordiazepoxide and 12.5 milligrams of amitriptyline or 10 milligrams of chlordiazepoxide and 25 milligrams of amitriptyline, taken three or four times a day. The doctor may adjust your dose if needed. However, the dose is usually not greater than 10 milligrams of chlordiazepoxide and 25 milligrams of amitriptyline taken six times a day.
  —Children up to 12 years of age: Dose must be determined by the doctor.

Missed dose—If you miss a dose of this medicine, skip the missed dose and go back to your regular dosing schedule. Do not double doses.

Storage—To store this medicine:

- Keep out of the reach of children. Overdose of this medicine is very dangerous in young children.
- Store away from heat and direct light.
- Do not store in the bathroom, near the kitchen sink, or in other damp places. Heat or moisture may cause the medicine to break down.
- Do not keep outdated medicine or medicine no longer needed. Be sure that any discarded medicine is out of the reach of children.

Precautions While Using This Medicine

It is very important that your doctor check your progress at regular visits to allow dose adjustments and help reduce side effects.

Do not stop taking this medicine without first checking with your doctor. Your doctor may want you to reduce gradually the amount you are using before stopping completely. This may help prevent a possible worsening of your condition and reduce the possibility of withdrawal symptoms such as headache, nausea, and/or an overall feeling of discomfort.

This medicine will add to the effects of alcohol and other CNS depressants (medicines that slow down the nervous system, possibly causing drowsiness). Some examples of CNS depressants are antihistamines or medicine for hay fever, other allergies, or colds; sedatives, tranquilizers, or sleeping medicine; prescription pain medicine or narcotics; barbiturates; medicine for seizures; muscle relaxants; or anesthetics, including some dental anesthetics. This effect may last for a few days after you stop taking this medicine. *Check with your doctor before taking any of the above while you are using this medicine.*

For diabetic patients:

- This medicine may affect blood sugar levels. If you notice a change in the results of your blood or urine sugar tests or if you have any questions, check with your doctor.

Before you have any medical tests, tell the medical doctor in charge that you are taking this medicine. The results of the metyrapone test may be affected by this medicine.

Before having any surgery, any dental treatment, or emergency treatment, tell the medical doctor or dentist in charge that you are using this medicine. Taking chlordiazepoxide and amitriptyline combination together with medicines that are used during surgery or dental or emergency treatments may increase the CNS depressant effects.

This medicine may cause some people to become dizzy, lightheaded, drowsy, or less alert than they are normally. Even if taken at bedtime, it may cause some people to feel drowsy or less alert on arising. *Make sure you know how you react to this medicine before you drive, use machines, or do anything else that could be dangerous if you are dizzy or are not alert.*

Dizziness, lightheadedness, or fainting may occur when you get up from a lying or sitting position. Getting up slowly may help. If this problem continues or gets worse, check with your doctor.

Chlordiazepoxide and amitriptyline combination may cause dryness of the mouth. For temporary relief, use sugarless candy or gum, melt bits of ice in your mouth, or use a saliva substitute. However, if your mouth continues to feel dry for more than 2 weeks, check with your medical doctor or dentist. Continuing dryness of the mouth may increase the chance of dental disease, including tooth decay, gum disease, and fungus infections.

Chlordiazepoxide and amitriptyline combination may cause your skin to be more sensitive to sunlight than it is normally. Exposure to sunlight, even for brief periods of time, may cause a skin rash, itching, redness or other discoloration of the skin, or a severe sunburn. When you begin taking this medicine:

- Stay out of direct sunlight, especially between the hours of 10:00 a.m. and 3:00 p.m., if possible.
- Wear protective clothing, including a hat. Also, wear sunglasses.
- Apply a sun block product that has a skin protection factor (SPF) of at least 15. Some patients may require a product with a higher SPF number, especially if they have a fair complexion. If you have any questions about this, check with your health care professional.
- Apply a sun block lipstick that has an SPF of at least 15 to protect your lips.
- Do not use a sunlamp or tanning bed or booth.

If you have a severe reaction from the sun, check with your doctor.

Side Effects of This Medicine

Along with its needed effects, a medicine may cause some unwanted effects. Although not all of these side effects may occur, if they do occur they may need medical attention.

Check with your doctor as soon as possible if any of the following side effects occur:

Less common

Blurred vision or other changes in vision; confusion or hallucinations (seeing, hearing, or feeling things that are not there); constipation; difficulty in urinating; eye pain; fainting; irregular heartbeat; mental depression; shakiness; trouble in sleeping; unusual excitement, nervousness, or irritability

Rare

Convulsions (seizures); increased sensitivity to sunlight; skin rash and itching; sore throat and fever; yellow eyes or skin

Symptoms of overdose

Agitation; confusion; convulsions (seizures); dizziness or lightheadedness (severe); drowsiness (severe); enlarged pupils; fast or irregular heartbeat; fever; hallucinations; muscle stiffness or rigidity; vomiting (severe)

Other side effects may occur that usually do not need medical attention. These side effects may go away during treatment as your body adjusts to the medicine. However, check with your doctor if any of the following side effects continue or are bothersome:

More common

Bloating; clumsiness or unsteadiness; dizziness or lightheadedness; drowsiness; dryness of mouth or unpleasant taste; headache; weight gain

Less common

Diarrhea; nausea or vomiting; unusual tiredness or weakness

After you stop using this medicine, your body may need time to adjust. If you took this medicine in high doses or for a long time, this may take up to 2 weeks. *During this time check with your doctor if you notice any of the following side effects:*

Convulsions (seizures); headache; increased sweating; irritability or restlessness; muscle cramps; nausea or vomiting;

stomach cramps; trembling; trouble in sleeping, with vivid dreams

Other side effects not listed above may also occur in some patients. If you notice any other effects, check with your doctor.

Revised: 03/19/93

CHLORDIAZEPOXIDE AND CLIDINIUM Systemic

Some commonly used brand names are:

In the U.S.—

Clindex	Lidox
Clinoxide	Lidoxide
Clipoxide	Zebrax
Librax	

Generic name product may also be available.

In Canada—

Apo-Chlorax	Librax
Corium	

Description

Chlordiazepoxide (klor-dye-az-e-POX-ide) and clidinium (kli-DI-nee-um) is a combination of medicines used to relax the digestive system and to reduce stomach acid. It is used to treat stomach and intestinal problems such as ulcers and colitis.

Chlordiazepoxide belongs to the group of medicines known as benzodiazepines. It is a central nervous system (CNS) depressant (a medicine that slows down the nervous system).

Clidinium belongs to the group of medicines known as anticholinergics. It helps lessen the amount of acid formed in the stomach. Clidinium also helps relieve abdominal or stomach spasms or cramps.

This combination is available only with your doctor's prescription, in the following dosage form:

Oral

- Capsules (U.S. and Canada)

Before Using This Medicine

In deciding to use a medicine, the risks of taking the medicine must be weighed against the good it will do. This is a decision you and your doctor will make. For chlordiazepoxide and clidinium, the following should be considered:

Allergies—Tell your doctor if you have ever had any unusual or allergic reaction to benzodiazepines such as alprazolam [e.g., Xanax], bromazepam [e.g., Lectopam], chlordiazepoxide [e.g., Librium], clonazepam [e.g., Klonopin], clorazepate [e.g., Tranxene], diazepam [e.g., Valium], flurazepam [e.g., Dalmane], halazepam [e.g., Paxipam], ketazolam [e.g., Loftran], lorazepam [e.g., Ativan], midazolam [e.g., Versed], nitrazepam [e.g., Mogadon], oxazepam [e.g., Serax], prazepam [e.g., Centrax], temazepam [e.g., Restoril], or triazolam [e.g., Halcion], or to clidinium or any of the belladonna alkaloids (atropine, belladonna, hyoscyamine, and scopolamine). Also tell your health care professional if you are allergic to any other substances, such as foods, preservatives, or dyes.

Pregnancy—Clidinium (contained in this combination) has not been studied in pregnant women. However, clidinium has not been shown to cause birth defects or other problems in animal studies. Chlordiazepoxide (contained also in this combination) may cause birth defects if taken during the first 3 months of pregnancy. In addition, too much use of this medicine during pregnancy may cause the baby to become dependent on the medicine. This may lead to withdrawal side effects after birth. Make sure your doctor knows if you are pregnant or if you may become pregnant before taking chlordiazepoxide and clidinium.

Breast-feeding—Chlordiazepoxide may pass into the breast milk and cause unwanted effects, such as excessive drowsiness, in nursing babies. Also, because clidinium tends to decrease the secretions of the body, it is possible that the flow of breast milk may be reduced in some patients.

Children—There is no specific information comparing use of chlordiazepoxide and clidinium in children with use in other age groups. However, children are especially sensitive to the effects of chlordiazepoxide and clidinium. Therefore, this may increase the chance of side effects during treatment.

Older adults—Confusion or memory loss; constipation; difficult urination; drowsiness; dryness of mouth, nose, throat, or skin; and unusual excitement or agitation may be more likely to occur in the elderly, who are usually more sensitive than younger adults to the effects of chlordiazepoxide and clidinium.

Other medicines—Although certain medicines should not be used together at all, in other cases 2 different medicines may be used together even if an interaction might occur. In these cases, your doctor may want to change the dose, or other precautions may be necessary. When you are taking chlordiazepoxide and clidinium it is especially important that your health care professional know if you are taking any of the following:

- Antacids or
- Diarrhea medicine containing kaolin or attapulgite—These medicines may reduce the blood levels of chlordiazepoxide and clidinium, which may decrease their effects; they should be taken at least 2 to 3 hours before or after the chlordiazepoxide and clidinium combination
- Central nervous system (CNS) depressants (medicines that cause drowsiness) or
- Other anticholinergics (medicines for abdominal or stomach spasms or cramps)—Use with chlordiazepoxide and clidinium may increase the side effects of either medicine
- Ketoconazole (e.g., Nizoral)—Chlordiazepoxide and clidinium may reduce the blood level of ketoconazole, which

may decrease its effects; therefore, chlordiazepoxide and clidinium should be taken at least 2 hours after ketoconazole

• Potassium chloride (e.g., Kay Ciel)—Use of chlordiazepoxide and clidinium may worsen or cause sores of the stomach or intestine

Other medical problems—The presence of other medical problems may affect the use of chlordiazepoxide and clidinium. Make sure you tell your doctor if you have any other medical problems, especially:

• Difficult urination or
• Dryness of mouth (severe and continuing) or
• Emphysema, asthma, bronchitis, or other chronic lung disease or
• Enlarged prostate or
• Glaucoma or
• Hiatal hernia or
• High blood pressure (hypertension) or
• Intestinal blockage or
• Mental depression or
• Mental illness (severe) or
• Myasthenia gravis or
• Ulcerative colitis (severe)—Use of chlordiazepoxide and clidinium may make these conditions worse
• Drug abuse or dependence—Taking chlordiazepoxide (contained in this combination) may become habit-forming, causing mental or physical dependence
• Kidney disease or
• Liver disease—Higher blood levels of chlordiazepoxide and clidinium may result, possibly increasing the chance of side effects
• Overactive thyroid—Use of chlordiazepoxide and clidinium may further increase the heart rate

Proper Use of This Medicine

Take this medicine about 1/2 to 1 hour before meals unless otherwise directed by your doctor.

Take this medicine only as directed by your doctor. Do not take more of it, do not take it more often, and do not take it for a longer time than your doctor ordered. If too much is taken, it may become habit-forming.

Dosing—The dose of chlordiazepoxide and clidinium combination will be different for different people. *Follow your doctor's orders or the directions on the label.* The following information includes only the average doses of this combination medicine. *If your dose is different, do not change it* unless your doctor tells you to do so.

• For *oral* dosage form (capsules)
—To relax the digestive system and to reduce stomach acid:
• Adults—1 or 2 capsules one to four times a day, thirty to sixty minutes before meals or food. Your doctor may change the dose if needed. However, most people usually will not take more than 8 capsules a day.
• Children—Dose must be determined by your doctor.
• Older adults—To start, 1 capsule two times a day. Your doctor may change the dose if needed.

Missed dose—If you miss a dose of this medicine, take it as soon as possible. However, if it is almost time for your next dose, skip the missed dose and go back to your regular dosing schedule. Do not double doses.

Storage—To store this medicine:

• Keep out of the reach of children.
• Store away from heat and direct light.
• Do not store the capsule form of this medicine in the bathroom, near the kitchen sink, or in other damp places. Heat or moisture may cause the medicine to break down.
• Do not keep outdated medicine or medicine no longer needed. Be sure that any discarded medicine is out of the reach of children.

Precautions While Using This Medicine

If you will be taking this medicine regularly for a long time your doctor should check your progress at regular visits.

Do not take this medicine within an hour of taking medicine for diarrhea. Taking them too close together will make this medicine less effective.

This medicine may cause some people to have blurred vision or to become dizzy, lightheaded, drowsy, or less alert than they are normally. *Make sure you know how you react to this medicine before you drive, use machines, or do anything else that could be dangerous if you are dizzy or are not alert or able to see well.*

This medicine will add to the effects of alcohol and other CNS depressants (medicines that slow down the nervous system, possibly causing drowsiness). Some examples of CNS depressants are sedatives, tranquilizers, or sleeping medicine; prescription pain medicine or narcotics; barbiturates; medicine for seizures; muscle relaxants; or anesthetics, including some dental anesthetics. *Check with your doctor before taking any of the above while you are using this medicine and also for a few days after you stop taking it.*

This medicine will often make you sweat less, causing your body temperature to increase. *Use extra care not to become overheated during exercise or hot weather while you are taking this medicine* as this could possibly result in heat stroke. Also, hot baths or saunas may make you feel dizzy or faint while you are taking this medicine.

Your mouth, nose, and throat may feel very dry while you are taking this medicine. For temporary relief of mouth dryness, use sugarless candy or gum, melt bits of ice in your mouth, or use a saliva substitute. However, if your mouth continues to feel dry for more than 2 weeks, check with your dentist. Continuing dryness of the mouth may increase the chance of dental disease, including tooth decay, gum disease, and fungus infections.

Check with your doctor if you develop intestinal problems such as constipation. This is especially important if you are taking other medicine while you are taking chlordiazepoxide and clidinium. If these problems are not corrected, serious complications may result.

If you will be taking this medicine in large doses or for a long time, do not stop taking it without first checking with your doctor. Your doctor may want you to reduce gradually the amount you are taking before stopping completely.

Side Effects of This Medicine

Along with its needed effects, a medicine may cause some unwanted effects. Although not all of these side effects may occur, if they do occur they may need medical attention.

Check with your doctor as soon as possible if any of the following side effects occur:

Less common or rare

Constipation; eye pain; mental depression; skin rash or hives; slow heartbeat, shortness of breath, or troubled breathing; sore throat and fever; trouble in sleeping; unusual excitement, nervousness, or irritability; yellow eyes or skin

Symptoms of overdose

Confusion; difficult urination; drowsiness (severe); dryness of mouth, nose, or throat (severe); fast heartbeat; unusual warmth, dryness, and flushing of skin

Other side effects may occur that usually do not need medical attention. These side effects may go away during treatment as your body adjusts to the medicine. However, check with your doctor if any of the following side effects continue or are bothersome:

More common

Bloated feeling; decreased sweating; dizziness; drowsiness; dryness of mouth; headache

Less common

Blurred vision; decreased sexual ability; loss of memory; nausea; unusual tiredness or weakness

After you stop using this medicine, your body may need time to adjust. The length of time this takes depends on the amount of medicine you were using and how long you used it. During this time check with your doctor if you notice any of the following side effects:

Convulsions (seizures); muscle cramps; nausea or vomiting; stomach cramps; trembling

Other side effects not listed above may also occur in some patients. If you notice any other effects, check with your doctor.

Revised: 01/29/92
Interim revision: 08/10/94

CHLORHEXIDINE Dental†

Some commonly used brand names in the U.S. are Peridex and PerioGard.

†Not commercially available in Canada.

Description

Chlorhexidine (klor-HEX-i-deen) is used to treat gingivitis. It helps to reduce the inflammation (redness) and swelling of your gums and to reduce gum bleeding.

Gingivitis is caused by the bacteria that grow in the coating (plaque) that forms on your teeth between tooth brushings. Chlorhexidine destroys the bacteria, thereby preventing the gingivitis from occurring. However, chlorhexidine does *not* prevent plaque and tartar from forming; proper tooth brushing and flossing are still necessary and important.

Chlorhexidine is available only with your dentist's or medical doctor's prescription, in the following dosage form:

Dental

- Oral rinse (U.S.)

Before Using This Medicine

In deciding to use a medicine, the risks of using the medicine must be weighed against the good it will do. This is a decision you and your dentist or medical doctor will make. For chlorhexidine, the following should be considered:

Allergies—Tell your dentist or medical doctor if you have ever had any unusual or allergic reaction to this medicine or to skin disinfectants containing chlorhexidine. Also tell your dentist or medical health care professional if you are allergic to any other substances, such as foods, preservatives, or dyes.

Pregnancy—Chlorhexidine has not been studied in pregnant women. However, chlorhexidine has not been shown to cause birth defects or other problems in animal studies.

Breast-feeding—It is not known whether chlorhexidine passes into the breast milk. Although most medicines pass into breast milk in small amounts, many of them may be used safely while breast-feeding. Mothers who are taking this medicine and who wish to breast-feed should discuss this with their dentist or medical doctor.

Children—Studies on this medicine have been done only in adult patients, and there is no specific information comparing use of this medicine in children with use in other age groups.

Older adults—Many medicines have not been studied specifically in older people. Therefore, it may not be known whether they work exactly the same way they do in younger adults or if they cause different side effects or problems in older people. There is no specific information comparing use of this medicine in the elderly with use in other age groups.

Other medicines—Although certain medicines should not be used together at all, in other cases two different medicines may be used together even if an interaction might occur. In these cases, your dentist or medical doctor may want to change the dose, or other precautions may be necessary. Tell your dentist or health care professional if you are using any other prescription or nonprescription (over-the-counter [OTC]) medicine that is to be used in the mouth.

Other medical problems—The presence of other medical problems may affect the use of chlorhexidine. Make sure you tell your dentist or medical doctor if you have any other medical problems, especially:

- Front-tooth fillings (especially those having rough surfaces)—Chlorhexidine may cause staining that, in some cases, may be impossible to remove and may require replacement of the filling
- Gum problems (other)—Use of chlorhexidine may make other gum problems, such as periodontitis, worse

Proper Use of This Medicine

Chlorhexidine oral rinse should be used after you have brushed and flossed your teeth. Rinse the toothpaste completely from your mouth with water before using the oral rinse. Do not eat or drink for several hours after using the oral rinse.

The cap on the original container of chlorhexidine can be used to measure the 15 mL (1/2 fluid ounce) dose of this medicine. Fill the cap to the "fill line." If you do not receive the dental rinse in its original container, make sure you have a measuring device to measure out the correct dose. Your pharmacist can help you with this.

Swish chlorhexidine around in the mouth for 30 seconds. Then spit out. *Use the medicine full strength.* Do not mix with water before using. *Do not swallow the medicine.*

Dosing—The dose of chlorhexidine oral rinse will be different for different patients. *Follow your dentist's or medical doctor's orders or the directions on the label.* The following information includes only the average doses of chlorhexidine oral rinse. *If your dose is different, do not change it* unless your dentist or medical doctor tells you to do so.

- For *oral rinse* dosage form:
  - —For gingivitis:
    - Adults—Use 15 milliliters (mL) as a mouth wash for 30 seconds two times a day.
    - Children up to 18 years of age—Use and dose must be determined by your dentist or medical doctor.

Missed dose—If you miss a dose of this medicine, use it as soon as possible. However, if it is almost time for your next dose, skip the missed dose and go back to your regular dosing schedule. Do not double doses.

Storage—To store this medicine:

- Keep out of the reach of children.
- Store away from heat and direct light.
- Keep the medicine from freezing.
- Do not keep outdated medicine or medicine that is no longer needed. Be sure any discarded medicine is out of the reach of children.

Precautions While Using This Medicine

Chlorhexidine may have a bitter aftertaste. Do not rinse your mouth with water immediately after using chlorhexidine, since doing so will increase the bitterness. Rinsing may also decrease the effect of the medicine.

Chlorhexidine may change the way foods taste to you. Sometimes this effect may last up to 4 hours after you use the oral rinse. In most cases, this effect will become less noticeable as you continue to use the medicine. When you stop using chlorhexidine, your taste should return to normal.

Chlorhexidine may cause staining and an increase in tartar (calculus) on your teeth. Brushing with a tartar-control toothpaste and flossing your teeth daily may help reduce this tartar build-up and staining. In addition, you should visit your dentist at least every 6 months to have your teeth cleaned and your gums examined.

If you think that a child weighing 22 pounds (10 kilograms) or less has swallowed more than 4 ounces of the dental rinse, *get emergency help at once.* In addition, if a child of any age drinks the dental rinse and has symptoms of alcohol intoxication, such as slurred speech, sleepiness, or a staggering or stumbling walk, *get emergency help at once.*

Side Effects of This Medicine

Along with its needed effects, a medicine may cause some unwanted effects. Although not all of these side effects may occur, if they do occur they may need medical attention.

Check with your doctor immediately if any of the following side effects occur:

Rare

Signs of allergic reaction, such as nasal congestion; shortness of breath or troubled breathing; skin rash, hives, or itching; or swelling of face

Other side effects may occur that usually do not need medical attention. These side effects may go away during treatment as your body adjusts to the medicine. However, check with your dentist or medical doctor if any of the following side effects continue or are bothersome:

More common

Change in taste; increase in tartar (calculus) on teeth; staining of teeth, mouth, tooth fillings, and dentures or other mouth appliances

Less common or rare

Mouth irritation; swollen glands on side of face or neck; tongue tip irritation

Other side effects not listed above may also occur in some patients. If you notice any other effects, check with your dentist or medical doctor.

Revised: 05/16/94
Interim revision: 08/22/94

CHLOROQUINE Systemic

Some commonly used brand names are:

In the U.S.—
- Aralen
- Aralen HCl
- Generic name product may also be available.

In Canada—
- Aralen

Description

Chloroquine (KLOR-oh-kwin) is a medicine used to prevent and treat malaria and to treat some conditions such as liver disease caused by protozoa (tiny one-celled animals).

This medicine may be given alone or with one or more other medicines. It may also be used for other conditions as determined by your doctor.

Chloroquine is available only with your doctor's prescription, in the following dosage forms:

Oral
- Tablets (U.S. and Canada)

Parenteral
- Injection (U.S.)

Before Using This Medicine

In deciding to use a medicine, the risks of taking the medicine must be weighed against the good it will do. This is a decision you and your doctor will make. For chloroquine, the following should be considered:

Allergies—Tell your doctor if you have ever had any unusual or allergic reaction to chloroquine or hydroxychloroquine. Also tell your health care professional if you are allergic to any other substances, such as foods, preservatives, or dyes.

Pregnancy—Unless you are taking it for malaria or liver disease caused by protozoa, use of this medicine is not recommended during pregnancy. In animal studies, chloroquine has been shown to cause damage to the central nervous system (brain and spinal cord) of the fetus, including damage to hearing, sense of balance, bleeding inside the eyes, and other eye problems. However, when given in low doses (once a week) to prevent malaria, this medicine has not been shown to cause birth defects or other problems in humans.

Breast-feeding—Chloroquine passes into the breast milk. Chloroquine has not been reported to cause problems in nursing babies to date. However, babies and children are especially sensitive to the effects of chloroquine.

Children—Children are especially sensitive to the effects of chloroquine. This may increase the chance of side effects during treatment. Overdose is especially dangerous in children. Taking as little as 1 tablet (300-mg strength) has resulted in the death of a small child.

Older adults—Many medicines have not been studied specifically in older people. Therefore, it may not be known whether they work exactly the same way they do in younger adults or if they cause different side effects or problems in older people. There is no specific information comparing use of chloroquine in the elderly with use in other age groups.

Other medicines—Although certain medicines should not be used together at all, in other cases 2 different medicines may be used together even if an interaction might occur. In these cases, your doctor may want to change the dose, or other precautions may be necessary. Tell your health care professional if you are taking any other prescription or nonprescription (over-the-counter [OTC]) medicine.

Other medical problems—The presence of other medical problems may affect the use of chloroquine. Make sure you tell your doctor if you have any other medical problems, especially:

- Blood disease (severe)—Chloroquine may cause blood disorders
- Eye or vision problems—Chloroquine may cause serious eye side effects, especially in high doses
- Glucose-6-phosphate dehydrogenase (G6PD) deficiency—Chloroquine may cause serious blood side effects in patients with this deficiency
- Liver disease—May decrease the removal of chloroquine from the blood, increasing the chance of side effects
- Nerve or brain disease (severe), including convulsions (seizures)—Chloroquine may cause muscle weakness and, in high doses, seizures
- Porphyria—Chloroquine may cause episodes of porphyria to occur more frequently
- Psoriasis—Chloroquine may bring on severe attacks of psoriasis
- Stomach or intestinal disease (severe)—Chloroquine may cause stomach or intestinal irritation

Proper Use of This Medicine

Take this medicine with meals or milk to lessen possible stomach upset, unless otherwise directed by your doctor.

Keep this medicine out of the reach of children. Children are especially sensitive to the effects of chloroquine and overdose is especially dangerous in children. Taking as little as 1 tablet (300-mg strength) has resulted in the death of a small child.

It is very important that you *take this medicine only as directed.* Do not take more of it, do not take it more often, and do not take it for a longer time than your doctor ordered. To do so may increase the chance of serious side effects.

If you are taking this medicine to help keep you from getting malaria, *keep taking it for the full time of treatment.* If you already have malaria, you should still keep taking this medicine for the full time of treatment even if you begin to feel better after a few days. This will help to clear up your infection completely. If you stop taking this medicine too soon, your symptoms may return.

Chloroquine works best when you take it on a regular schedule. For example, if you are to take it once a week to prevent malaria, it is best to take it on the same day each week. Or if you are to take 2 doses a day, 1 dose may be taken with breakfast and the other with the evening meal. *Make sure that you do not miss any doses.* If you have any questions about this, check with your health care professional.

For patients taking chloroquine *to prevent malaria:*
- Your doctor may want you to start taking this medicine 1 to 2 weeks before you travel to an area where there is a chance of getting malaria. This will help you to see how you react to the medicine. Also, it will allow time for your doctor to change to another medicine if you have a reaction to this medicine.
- Also, you should keep taking this medicine while you are in the area and for 4 weeks after you leave the area. No medicine will protect you completely from malaria. However, to protect you as completely as possible, *it is important to keep taking this medicine for the full time your doctor ordered.* Also, if fever develops during your travels or within 2 months after you leave the area, *check with your doctor immediately.*

Dosing—The dose of chloroquine will be different for different patients. *Follow your doctor's orders or the directions on the label.* The following information includes only the average doses of chloroquine. *If your dose is different, do not change it* unless your doctor tells you to do so.

The number of tablets that you take depends on the strength of the medicine. Also, *the number of doses you take each day, the time allowed between doses, and the length of time you take the medicine depend on the medical problem for which you are taking chloroquine.*
- For *oral* dosage form (tablets):
  - —For prevention of malaria:
    - Adults—500 milligrams (mg) once every seven days.
    - Children—Dose is based on body weight and must be determined by your doctor. The usual dose is 8.3 mg per kilogram (kg) (3.7 mg per pound) of body weight once every seven days.
  - —For treatment of malaria:
    - Adults—At first, start with 1 gram. Then, 500 mg six to eight hours after the first dose, and 500 mg once a day on the second and third days of treatment.
    - Children—Dose is based on body weight and must be determined by your doctor. The usual dose is 41.7 mg per kg (18.9 mg per pound) of body weight divided up over three days. This dose is given as follows: Start with 16.7 mg per kg (7.5 mg per pound) of body weight, then 8.3 mg per kg (3.7 mg per pound) six hours, twenty-four hours, and forty-eight hours after the first dose.
  - —For treatment of liver disease caused by protozoa:
    - Adults—At first, start with 250 mg four times a day for two days. Then 250 mg two times a day for at least two to three weeks.
    - Children—Dose is based on body weight and must be determined by your doctor. The usual dose is 10 mg per kg (4.5 mg per pound) of body weight a day for three weeks.
- For *injection* dosage form:
  - —For treatment of malaria:
    - Adults—200 to 250 mg injected into a muscle. This dose may be repeated in six hours if needed.
    - Children—Dose is based on body weight and must be determined by your doctor. The usual dose is 4.4 mg per kg (2 mg per pound) of body weight injected into a muscle or under the skin. This dose may be repeated in six hours if needed. Chloroquine may also be injected slowly into a vein. If the medicine is given in this way, the dose must be determined by your doctor.
  - —For treatment of liver disease caused by protozoa:
    - Adults—200 to 250 mg a day injected into a muscle for ten to twelve days.
    - Children—Dose is based on body weight and must be determined by your doctor. The usual dose is 7.5 mg per kg (3.4 mg per pound) of body weight a day for ten to twelve days.

Missed dose—If you miss a dose of this medicine and your dosing schedule is:
- One dose every seven days—Take the missed dose as soon as possible. Then go back to your regular dosing schedule.
- One dose a day—Take the missed dose as soon as possible. But if you do not remember until the next day, skip the missed dose and go back to your regular dosing schedule. Do not double doses.
- More than one dose a day—Take it right away if you remember within an hour or so of the missed dose. But if you do not remember until later, skip the missed dose and go back to your regular dosing schedule. Do not double doses.

If you have any questions about this, check with your doctor.

Storage—To store this medicine:
- Keep out of the reach of children. Overdose of chloroquine is very dangerous in children.
- Store away from heat and direct light.
- Do not store in the bathroom, near the kitchen sink, or in other damp places. Heat or moisture may cause the medicine to break down.
- Do not keep outdated medicine or medicine no longer needed. Be sure that any discarded medicine is out of the reach of children.

Precautions While Using This Medicine

If you will be taking this medicine for a long time, *it is very important that your doctor check you at regular visits* for any blood problems or muscle weakness that may be caused by this medicine. In addition, *check with your doctor immediately if blurred vision, difficulty in reading, or any other change in vision occurs during or after treatment.* Your doctor may want you to have your eyes checked by an ophthalmologist (eye doctor).

If your symptoms do not improve within a few days or if they become worse, check with your doctor.

Chloroquine may cause blurred vision, difficulty in reading, or other change in vision. It may also cause some people to become lightheaded. *Make sure you know how you react to this medicine before you drive, use machines, or do anything else that could be dangerous if you are not able to see well.* If these reactions are especially bothersome, check with your doctor.

Malaria is spread by mosquitoes. If you are living in, or will be traveling to, an area where there is a chance of getting malaria, the following mosquito-control measures will help to prevent infection:

- Avoid going out between dusk and dawn because it is at these times when mosquitoes most commonly bite.
- If possible, sleep in a screened or air-conditioned room or under mosquito netting sprayed with insecticide to avoid being bitten by malaria-carrying mosquitoes.
- Wear long-sleeved shirts or blouses and long trousers to protect your arms and legs, especially from dusk through dawn when mosquitoes are out.
- Apply mosquito repellent to uncovered areas of the skin from dusk through dawn when mosquitoes are out.
- Use mosquito coils or sprays to kill mosquitoes in living and sleeping quarters during evening and night-time hours.

Side Effects of This Medicine

Along with its needed effects, a medicine may cause some unwanted effects. Although not all of these side effects may occur, if they do occur they may need medical attention. When this medicine is used for short periods of time, side effects usually are rare. However, when it is used for a long time and/or in high doses, side effects are more likely to occur and may be serious.

Check with your doctor immediately if any of the following side effects occur:

Less common

Blurred vision or any other change in vision

Note: The above side effects may also occur or get worse after you stop taking this medicine.

Rare

Convulsions (seizures); fatigue; feeling faint or lightheaded; increased muscle weakness; mood or other mental changes; ringing or buzzing in ears or any loss of hearing; sore throat and fever; unusual bleeding or bruising; weakness

Symptoms of overdose

Drowsiness; headache; increased excitability

Other side effects may occur that usually do not need medical attention. These side effects may go away during treatment as your body adjusts to the medicine. However, check with your doctor if any of the following side effects continue or are bothersome:

More common

Diarrhea; difficulty in seeing to read; headache; itching (more common in black patients); loss of appetite; nausea or vomiting; stomach cramps or pain

Less common

Bleaching of hair or increased hair loss; blue-black discoloration of skin, fingernails, or inside of mouth; skin rash

Other side effects not listed above may also occur in some patients. If you notice any other effects, check with your doctor.

Additional Information

Once a medicine has been approved for marketing for a certain use, experience may show that it is also useful for other medical problems. Although these uses are not included in product labeling, chloroquine is used in certain patients with the following medical conditions:

- Arthritis in children
- High levels of calcium in the blood associated with sarcoidosis
- Rheunatoid arthritis
- Systemic lupus erythematosus (lupus; SLE)
- Various skin disorders

For patients taking chloroquine *for arthritis or lupus:*

- This medicine must be taken regularly as ordered by your doctor in order for it to help you. It may take up to several weeks before you begin to feel better. It may take up to 6 months before you feel the full benefit of this medicine.
- If your symptoms of arthritis do not improve within a few weeks or months, or if they become worse, check with your doctor.

Other than the above information, there is no additional information relating to proper use, precautions, or side effects for these uses.

Revised: 8/11/95

CHLOROXINE Topical†

A commonly used brand name in the U.S. is Capitrol.

†Not commercially available in Canada.

Description

Chloroxine (klor-OX-een) is used in the treatment of dandruff and seborrheic dermatitis of the scalp.

This medicine is available only with your doctor's prescription, in the following dosage form:

Topical

- Lotion shampoo (U.S.)

Before Using This Medicine

In deciding to use a medicine, the risks of using the medicine must be weighed against the good it will do. This is a decision you and your doctor will make. For chloroxine, the following should be considered:

Allergies—Tell your doctor if you have ever had any unusual or allergic reaction to chloroxine, clioquinol (iodochlorhydroxyquin), iodoquinol (diiodohydroxyquin), or edetate disodium. Also tell your health care professional if you are allergic to any other substances, such as preservatives or dyes.

Pregnancy—Studies on effects in pregnancy have not been done in either humans or animals.

Breast-feeding—It is not known whether chloroxine passes into the breast milk. However, this medicine has not been reported to cause problems in nursing babies.

Children—Studies on this medicine have been done only in adult patients, and there is no specific information comparing use of this medicine in children with use in other age groups.

Older adults—Many medicines have not been studied specifically in older people. Therefore, it may not be known whether they work exactly the same way they do in younger adults or if they cause different side effects or problems in older people. There is no specific information comparing use of this medicine in the elderly with use in other age groups.

Other medicines—Although certain medicines should not be used together at all, in other cases two different medicines may be used together even if an interaction might occur. In these cases, your doctor may want to change the dose, or other precautions may be necessary. Tell your health care professional if you are using any other topical prescription or nonprescription (over-the-counter [OTC]) medicine that is to be applied to the same area of the skin.

Proper Use of This Medicine

Do not use this medicine if blistered, raw, or oozing areas are present on your scalp, unless otherwise directed by your doctor.

Keep this medicine away from the eyes. If you should accidentally get some in your eyes, flush them thoroughly with cool water. Check with your doctor if eye irritation continues or is bothersome.

To use:

- Wet the hair and scalp with lukewarm water. Apply enough chloroxine to the scalp to work up a lather, and rub in well. Allow the lather to remain on the scalp for about 3 minutes, then rinse. Apply the medicine again and rinse thoroughly. Use the medicine two times a week or as directed by your doctor.

Dosing—The dose of chloroxine will be different for different patients. *Follow your doctor's orders or the directions on the label.* The following information includes only the average doses of chloroxine. *If your dose is different, do not change it* unless your doctor tells you to do so.

- For *topical* dosage form (lotion shampoo):
  - —For dandruff or seborrheic dermatitis of the scalp:
    - Adults—Use two times a week.
    - Children—Use and dose must be determined by your doctor.

Missed dose—If you miss a dose of this medicine, apply it as soon as possible.

Storage—To store this medicine:

- Keep out of the reach of children.
- Store away from heat and direct light.
- Keep the medicine from freezing.
- Do not keep outdated medicine or medicine no longer needed. Be sure that any discarded medicine is out of the reach of children.

Precautions While Using This Medicine

This medicine may slightly discolor light-colored hair (for example, bleached, blond, or gray).

Side Effects of This Medicine

Along with its needed effects, a medicine may cause some unwanted effects. Although not all of these side effects may occur, if they do occur they may need medical attention.

Check with your doctor as soon as possible if any of the following side effects occur:

Irritation or burning of scalp not present before use of this medicine; skin rash

Other side effects may occur that usually do not need medical attention. However, check with your doctor if either of the following side effects continues or is bothersome:

Dryness or increased itching of scalp

Other side effects not listed above may also occur in some patients. If you notice any other effects, check with your doctor.

Revised: 01/21/94

CHLORZOXAZONE AND ACETAMINOPHEN Systemic*

A commonly used brand name in Canada is Parafon Forte.

Another commonly used name for this combination medicine is chlorzoxazone with APAP.

*Not commercially available in the U.S.

Description

Chlorzoxazone (klor-ZOX-a-zone) and acetaminophen (a-seat-a-MIN-oh-fen) combination medicine is used to help relax certain muscles in your body and relieve the pain and discomfort caused by strains, sprains, or other injuries to your muscles. However, this medicine does not take the place of rest, exercise or physical therapy, or other treatment that your doctor may recommend for your medical problem.

Chlorzoxazone acts in the central nervous system (CNS) to produce its muscle relaxant effects. Its actions in the CNS may also produce some of its side effects.

In Canada, this medicine is available without a prescription.

This medicine is available in the following dosage forms:

Oral

- Tablets (Canada)

Before Using This Medicine

If you are taking this medicine without a prescription, carefully read and follow any precautions on the label. For chlorzoxazone and acetaminophen combination, the following should be considered:

Allergies—Tell your doctor if you have ever had any unusual or allergic reaction to acetaminophen, chlorzoxazone, or aspirin. Also tell your health care professional if you are allergic to any other substances, such as foods, preservatives, or dyes.

Pregnancy—Although studies on birth defects with chlorzoxazone or acetaminophen have not been done in pregnant women, these medicines have not been reported to cause birth defects or other problems.

Breast-feeding—Chlorzoxazone and acetaminophen have not been shown to cause problems in nursing babies. However, acetaminophen passes into the breast milk in small amounts.

Children—Studies on this combination medicine have been done only in adult patients, and there is no specific information about its use in children. However, chlorzoxazone and acetaminophen have been tested separately in children. In effective doses, these medicines have not been shown to cause different side effects or problems in children than they do in adults.

Older adults—Many medicines have not been studied specifically in older people. Therefore, it may not be known whether they work exactly the same way they do in younger adults or if they cause different side effects or problems in older people. There is no specific information comparing use of chlorzoxazone and acetaminophen combination, or of chlorzoxazone alone, in the elderly with use in other age groups. However, acetaminophen has been tested and has not been shown to cause different side effects or problems in older people than it does in younger adults.

Other medicines—Although certain medicines should not be used together at all, in other cases two different medicines may be used together even if an interaction might occur. In these cases, your doctor may want to change the dose, or other precautions may be necessary. When you are taking chlorzoxazone and acetaminophen combination, it is especially important that your health care professional know if you are taking any of the following:

- Antidepressants, tricyclic (amitriptyline [e.g., Elavil], amoxapine [e.g., Asendin], clomipramine [e.g., Anafranil], desipramine [e.g., Pertofrane], doxepin [e.g., Sinequan], imipramine [e.g., Tofranil], nortriptyline [e.g., Aventyl], protriptyline [e.g., Vivactil], trimipramine [e.g., Surmontil]) or
- Central nervous system (CNS) depressants (medicines that often cause drowsiness)—These medicines may add to the effects of chlorzoxazone and increase the chance of drowsiness or other side effects

Other medical problems—The presence of other medical problems may affect the use of chlorzoxazone and acetaminophen combination. Make sure you tell your doctor if you have any other medical problems, especially:

- Alcohol abuse or
- Allergies (asthma, eczema, hay fever, hives) or
- Hepatitis or other liver disease or
- Kidney disease—The chance of side effects may be increased

Proper Use of This Medicine

Take this medicine only as directed. Do not take more of it, do not take it more often, and do not take it for a longer time than directed on the package label or by your doctor. To do so may increase the chance of side effects. This medicine may cause liver damage if too much is taken.

Dosing—The dose of chlorzoxazone and acetaminophen combination will be different for different patients. *Follow your doctor's orders or the directions on the label.* The following information includes only the average doses of this medicine. *If your dose is different, do not change it* unless your doctor tells you to do so.

- For *oral* dosage form (tablets):
  - —For relieving painful, stiff muscles:
    - Adults—Two tablets four times a day.
    - Children—Use and dose must be determined by your doctor.

Missed dose—If you miss a dose of this medicine, take it as soon as you remember. However, if it is almost time for your next dose, skip the missed dose and go back to your regular dosing schedule. Do not double doses.

Storage—To store this medicine:

- Keep out of the reach of children.
- Store away from heat and direct light.
- Do not store this medicine in the bathroom, near the kitchen sink, or in other damp places. Heat or moisture may cause the medicine to break down.
- Do not keep outdated medicine or medicine no longer needed. Be sure that any discarded medicine is out of the reach of children.

Precautions While Using This Medicine

If you will be taking this medicine for a long time (for example, for several months at a time), your doctor should check your progress at regular visits.

Check the labels of all nonprescription (over-the-counter [OTC]) and prescription medicines you now take. If any of them contain chlorzoxazone or acetaminophen, check with your doctor or pharmacist. Using any of them together with this medicine may cause an overdose.

This medicine will add to the effects of alcohol and other CNS depressants (medicines that slow down the nervous system, possibly causing drowsiness). Some examples of CNS depressants are antihistamines or medicine for hay fever, other allergies, or colds; sedatives, tranquilizers, or sleeping medicine; prescription pain medicine or narcotics; barbiturates; medicine for seizures; or anesthetics, including some dental anesthetics. Also, the risk of liver damage from acetaminophen may be greater if you use large amounts of alcoholic beverages with acetaminophen. Therefore, *do not drink alcoholic beverages, and check with your doctor before taking any of the medicines listed above, while you are taking this medicine.*

Taking the acetaminophen in this combination medicine together with certain other medicines may increase the chance of unwanted effects. The risk will depend on how much of each medicine you take every day, and on how long you take the medicines together. If your medical doctor or dentist directs you to take these medicines together on a regular basis, follow his or her directions carefully. However, *do not take any of the following medicines together with chlorzoxazone and acetaminophen combination for more than a few days, unless your doctor has directed you to do so and is following your progress.*

Aspirin or other salicylates
Diclofenac (e.g., Voltaren)
Diflunisal (e.g., Dolobid)
Etodolac (e.g., Lodine)
Fenoprofen (e.g., Nalfon)
Floctafenine (e.g., Idarac)
Flurbiprofen, oral (e.g., Ansaid)
Ibuprofen (e.g., Motrin)
Indomethacin (e.g., Indocin)
Ketoprofen (e.g., Orudis)
Ketorolac (e.g., Toradol)
Meclofenamate (e.g., Meclomen)
Mefenamic acid (e.g., Ponstel)
Nabumetone (e.g., Relafen)
Naproxen (e.g., Naprosyn)
Oxaprozin (e.g., Daypro)
Phenylbutazone (e.g., Butazolidin)
Piroxicam (e.g., Feldene)
Sulindac (e.g., Clinoril)
Tenoxicam (e.g., Mobiflex)
Tiaprofenic acid (e.g., Surgam)
Tolmetin (e.g., Tolectin)

This medicine may cause some people to become drowsy, dizzy, or less alert than they are normally. *Make sure you know how you react to this medicine before you drive, use machines, or do anything else that could be dangerous if you are dizzy or are not alert.*

Acetaminophen may interfere with the results of some medical tests. Before you have any medical tests, tell the doctor in charge if you have taken acetaminophen within the past 3 or 4 days. If possible, it is best to check with the doctor first, to find out whether this medicine may be taken during the 3 or 4 days before the test.

For *diabetic patients:*

- Acetaminophen may cause false results with some blood glucose (sugar) tests. If you notice any change in your test results, or if you have any questions about this possible problem, check with your health care professional. This is especially important if your diabetes is not well-controlled.

If you think that you or anyone else may have taken an overdose of this medicine, get emergency help at once. Signs of overdose of this medicine include fast or irregular breathing and severe muscle weakness. Signs of severe acetaminophen poisoning may not appear for 2 to 4 days after the overdose is taken, but treatment to prevent liver damage or death must be started within 24 hours or less after the overdose is taken.

Side Effects of This Medicine

Along with its needed effects, a medicine may cause some unwanted effects. Although not all of these side effects may occur, if they do occur they may need medical attention.

Check with your doctor immediately if any of the following side effects occur:

Rare

Hive-like swellings (large) on face, eyelids, mouth, lips, or tongue; sudden decrease in amount of urine

Symptoms of overdose

Diarrhea; fast or irregular breathing; increased sweating; loss of appetite; muscle weakness (severe); nausea or vomiting; pain, tenderness, or swelling in upper abdomen or stomach area; stomach cramps or pain

Also, check with your doctor as soon as possible if any of the following side effects occur:

Rare

Bloody or black, tarry stools; bloody or cloudy urine; pain in lower back and/or side (severe and/or sharp); pinpoint red spots on skin; skin rash, hives, itching, or redness; sore throat and fever; unusual bleeding or bruising; unusual tiredness or weakness; yellow eyes or skin

Other side effects may occur that usually do not need medical attention. These side effects may go away during treatment as your body adjusts to the medicine. However, check with your doctor if any of the following side effects continue or are bothersome:

More common

Dizziness or lightheadedness; drowsiness

Less common

Constipation; headache; heartburn; unusual excitement, nervousness, restlessness, or irritability

This medicine sometimes causes the urine to turn orange or reddish purple. This is not harmful and will go away when you stop taking the medicine. If you have any questions about this, check with your doctor.

Other side effects not listed above may also occur in some patients. If you notice any other effects, check with your doctor.

Revised: 08/29/94

CHOLECYSTOGRAPHIC AGENTS, ORAL Diagnostic

Some commonly used brand names are:

In the U.S.—

Bilivist[3]	Oragrafin Calcium[3]
Bilopaque[4]	Oragrafin Sodium[3]
Cholebrine[1]	Telepaque[2]

In Canada—

Telepaque[2]

Other—

Biloptin[3]	Felombrine[2]
Cistobil[2]	Jopanonsyre[2]
Colebrin[1]	Lumopaque[4]
Colebrina[1]	Neocontrast[2]
Colegraf[2]	

Another commonly used name for tyropanoate is sodium tyropanoate.

Note: For quick reference, the following oral cholecystographic agents are numbered to match the corresponding brand names.

This information applies to the following medicines:

1. Iocetamic Acid (eye-oh-se-TAM-ik)†
2. Iopanoic Acid (eye-oh-pa-NOE-ik)
3. Ipodate (EYE-poe-date)†
4. Tyropanoate (tye-roe-pa-NOE-ate)†

†Not commercially available in Canada.

Description

Oral cholecystographic (ko-le-sis-to-GRAF-ik) agents are radiopaque agents. Radiopaque agents are drugs used to help diagnose certain medical problems. These agents contain iodine, which blocks x-rays. Depending on how the radiopaque agent is given, it localizes or builds up in certain areas of the body. When radiopaque agents are inside the body they will appear white on the x-ray film. This creates the needed distinction, or contrast, between one organ and other tissues. This will help the doctor see any special conditions that may exist in that organ or part of the body.

The oral cholecystographic agents are taken by mouth before x-ray tests to help check for problems of the gallbladder and the biliary tract. Ipodate may also be used for other conditions as determined by your doctor.

These radiopaque agents are to be given only by or under the direct supervision of a doctor. They are available in the following dosage forms:

Oral

Iocetamic acid
- Tablets (U.S.)

Iopanoic acid
- Tablets (U.S. and Canada)

Ipodate
- Capsules (U.S.)
- Oral suspension (U.S.)

Tyropanoate
- Capsules (U.S.)

Before Having This Test

In deciding to use a diagnostic test, any risks of the test must be weighed against the good it will do. This is a decision you and your doctor will make. Also, test results may be affected by other things. For cholecystographic agents, the following should be considered:

Allergies—Tell your doctor if you have ever had any unusual or allergic reaction to iodine, to products containing iodine (for example, iodine-containing foods, such as seafoods, cabbage, kale, rape [turnip-like vegetable], turnips, or iodized salt), or to other radiopaque agents. Also tell your doctor if you are allergic to any other substances, such as preservatives.

Pregnancy—Studies on effects in pregnancy have not been done in humans with any of these agents. Studies in animals have been done only with iocetamic acid, which has not been shown to cause birth defects or other problems. However, on rare occasions, other radiopaque agents containing iodine have caused hypothyroidism (underactive thyroid) in the baby when given in late pregnancy. Also, x-rays of the abdomen are usually not recommended during pregnancy. This is to avoid exposing the fetus to radiation. Be sure you have discussed this with your doctor.

Breast-feeding—Iocetamic acid, iopanoic acid, and tyropanoate pass into the breast milk, and the other agents may pass into the breast milk also. However, these radiopaque agents have not been reported to cause problems in nursing babies.

Children—Although there is no specific information comparing use of cholecystographic agents in children with use in other age groups, tests using iopanoic acid and ipodate in children have not shown that these agents cause different side effects or problems in children than they do in adults.

Older adults—Many medicines have not been studied specifically in older people. Therefore, it may not be known whether they work exactly the same way they do in younger adults. Although there is no specific information comparing use of cholecystographic agents in the elderly with use in other age groups, these agents are not expected to cause different side effects or problems in older people than they do in younger adults.

Other medicines—Although certain medicines should not be used together at all, in other cases two different medicines may be used together even if an interaction might occur. In these cases, your doctor may want to change the dose, or other precautions may be necessary. Tell your doctor if you are taking any other prescription or nonprescription (over-the-counter [OTC]) medicine.

Other medical problems—The presence of other medical problems may affect the use of cholecystographic agents. Make sure you tell your doctor if you have any other medical problems, especially:

- Asthma, hay fever, or other allergies (history of) or
- Previous reaction to penicillins or to a skin test for allergies—Patients with these conditions have a greater chance of having a reaction, such as an allergic reaction
- Heart disease—Other problems, such as low blood pressure or slow heartbeat, may occur

- Kidney disease or
- Liver disease (severe)—Serious kidney problems may result
- Overactive thyroid—A sudden increase in symptoms, such as fast heartbeat or palpitations, fatigue, nervousness, excessive sweating, and muscle weakness may occur

Preparation For This Test

Dosing—Take this radiopaque agent with water after dinner the evening or evenings before the examination, following the directions of your doctor. Keep drinking an adequate amount of water, unless otherwise directed by your doctor.

Do not eat or drink anything but water after taking the medicine. Also, avoid smoking or chewing gum.

Your doctor may order a special diet or use of a laxative or enema in preparation for your test, depending on the type of test. If you have not received such instructions or if you do not understand them, check with your doctor in advance.

Precautions After Having This Test

Make sure your doctor knows if you are planning to have any future thyroid tests. The results of the thyroid test may be affected, even weeks or months later, by the iodine in this agent.

Side Effects of This Medicine

Along with its needed effects, a medicine may cause some unwanted effects. Although not all of these side effects may occur, if they do occur they may need medical attention.

Check with your health care professional immediately if any of the following side effects occur:

Rare

Itching; skin rash or hives; swelling of skin; unusual bleeding or bruising (with iopanoic acid only)

Symptoms of overdose

Diarrhea (severe); nausea and vomiting (severe); problems with urination

Other side effects may occur that usually do not need medical attention. These side effects should go away as the effects of the radiopaque agent wear off. However, check with your doctor if any of the following side effects continue or are bothersome:

More common

Diarrhea (mild); nausea and vomiting (mild to moderate)

Less common

Abdominal or stomach spasms or cramps; diarrhea (severe); difficult or painful urination; dizziness; frequent urge to urinate; headache; heartburn; nausea and vomiting (severe or continuing)

Other side effects not listed above may also occur in some patients. If you notice any other effects, check with your doctor.

Additional Information

Once a medicine has been approved for marketing for a certain use, experience may show that it is also useful for other medical problems. Although not specifically included in product labeling, ipodate is used in certain patients with the following medical condition:

- Graves' disease

In addition to the above information, for patients with Graves' disease taking ipodate:

- Ipodate is used in patients with Graves' disease, who have an overactive thyroid, to reduce the amount of thyroid hormone produced by the thyroid gland.
- *Use this medicine only as directed by your doctor.* Do not take more of it, do not take it more often, and do not take it for a longer period of time than your doctor ordered. To do so may increase the chance of side effects.
- In order for it to work properly, *ipodate must be taken every day, as ordered by your doctor.*
- The information given above in the section *Preparation For This Test* will not apply to you.

Other than the above information, there is no additional information relating to proper use, precautions, or side effects for these uses.

Revised: 06/29/95

CHOLESTYRAMINE Oral

Some commonly used brand names in the U.S. and Canada are Questran and Questran Light.

Description

Cholestyramine (koe-less-TEAR-a-meen) is used to lower high cholesterol levels in the blood. This may help prevent medical problems caused by cholesterol clogging the blood vessels. Cholestyramine is also used to remove substances called bile acids from your body. With some liver problems, there is too much bile acid in your body and this can cause severe itching.

Cholestyramine works by attaching to certain substances in the intestine. Since cholestyramine is not absorbed into the body, these substances also pass out of the body without being absorbed.

Cholestyramine may also be used for other conditions as determined by your doctor.

Cholestyramine is available only with your doctor's prescription, in the following dosage form:

Oral

- Powder (U.S. and Canada)

Before Using This Medicine

In deciding to use a medicine, the risks of taking the medicine must be weighed against the good it will do. This is a decision you and your doctor will make. For cholestyramine, the following should be considered:

Allergies—Tell your doctor if you have ever had any unusual or allergic reaction to cholestyramine. Also tell your health care professional if you are allergic to any other substances, such as foods, preservatives, or dyes.

Pregnancy—Cholestyramine is not absorbed into the body and is not likely to cause problems. However, it may reduce absorption of vitamins into the body. Ask your doctor whether you need to take extra vitamins.

Breast-feeding—Cholestyramine is not absorbed into the body and is not likely to cause problems. However, the reduced absorption of vitamins by the mother may affect the nursing infant.

Children—This medicine has been tested in a limited number of children. In effective doses, the medicine has not been shown to cause different side effects or problems than it does in adults.

Older adults—Side effects may be more likely to occur in patients over 60 years of age, who are usually more sensitive to the effects of cholestyramine.

Other medicines—Although certain medicines should not be used together at all, in other cases two different medicines may be used together even if an interaction might occur. In these cases, your doctor may want to change the dose, or other precautions may be necessary. When you are taking cholestyramine it is especially important that your health care professional know if you are taking any of the following:

- Anticoagulants (blood thinners)—The effects of the anticoagulant may be changed and this may increase the chance of bleeding.
- Digitalis glycosides (heart medicine) or
- Diuretics (water pills) or
- Penicillin G, taken by mouth or
- Phenylbutazone or
- Propranolol (e.g., Inderal) or
- Tetracyclines, taken by mouth (medicine for infection) or
- Thyroid hormones or
- Vancomycin, taken by mouth—Cholestyramine may prevent these medicines from working properly

Other medical problems—The presence of other medical problems may affect the use of cholestyramine. Make sure you tell your doctor if you have any other medical problems, especially:

- Bleeding problems or
- Constipation or
- Gallstones or
- Heart or blood vessel disease or
- Hemorrhoids or
- Stomach ulcer or other stomach problems or
- Underactive thyroid—Cholestyramine may make these conditions worse
- Kidney disease—There is an increased risk of developing electrolyte problems (problems in the blood)
- Phenylketonuria—Phenylalanine in aspartame is included in the sugar-free brand of cholestyramine and should be avoided. Aspartame can cause problems in people with phenylketonuria. Therefore, it is best if you avoid using the sugar-free product.

Proper Use of This Medicine

Take this medicine exactly as directed by your doctor. Try not to miss any doses and do not take more medicine than your doctor ordered.

This medicine should never be taken in its dry form, since it could cause you to choke. Instead, always mix as follows:

- Place the medicine in 2 ounces of any beverage and mix thoroughly. Then add an additional 2 to 4 ounces of beverage and again mix thoroughly (it will not dissolve) before drinking. After drinking all the liquid containing the medicine, rinse the glass with a little more liquid and drink that also, to make sure you get all the medicine.
- You may also mix this medicine with milk in hot or regular breakfast cereals, or in thin soups such as tomato or chicken noodle soup. Or you may add it to some pulpy fruits such as crushed pineapple, pears, peaches, or fruit cocktail.

For patients taking this medicine *for high cholesterol:*

- Importance of diet—Before prescribing medicine for your condition, your doctor will probably try to control your condition by prescribing a personal diet for you. Such a diet may be low in fats, sugars, and/or cholesterol. Many people are able to control their condition by carefully following their doctor's orders for proper diet and exercise. Medicine is prescribed only when additional help is needed. *Follow carefully the special diet your doctor gave you,* since the medicine is effective only when a schedule of diet and exercise is properly followed.
- Also, this medicine is less effective if you are greatly overweight. It may be very important for you to go on a reducing diet. However, check with your doctor before going on any diet.
- Remember that this medicine will not cure your cholesterol problem but it will help control it. Therefore, you must continue to take it as directed if you expect to lower your cholesterol level.

Dosing—The dose of cholestyramine will be different for different patients. *Follow your doctor's orders or the directions on the label.* The following information includes only the average doses of cholestyramine. *If your dose is different, do not change it* unless your doctor tells you to do so.

- For *oral* dosage form (powder for oral suspension):
  —For high cholesterol or pruritus (itching) related to biliary obstruction:
  - Adults—At first, 4 grams one or two times a day before meals. Then, your doctor may increase your dose to 8 to 24 grams a day. This is divided into two to six doses.
  - Children—At first, 4 grams a day. This is divided into two doses and taken before meals. Then, your doctor may increase your dose to 8 to

24 grams a day. This is divided into two or more doses.

Missed dose—If you miss a dose of this medicine, take it as soon as possible. Then go back to your regular dosing schedule. However, if it is almost time for your next dose, skip the missed dose and go back to your regular dosing schedule. Do not double doses.

Storage—To store this medicine:
- Keep out of the reach of children.
- Store away from heat and direct light.
- Do not store in the bathroom, near the kitchen sink, or in other damp places. Heat or moisture may cause the medicine to break down.
- Do not keep outdated medicine or medicine no longer needed. Be sure that any discarded medicine is out of the reach of children.

Precautions While Using This Medicine

It is very important that your doctor check your progress at regular visits. This will allow your doctor to see if the medicine is working properly and to decide if you should continue to take it.

Do not take any other medicine unless prescribed by your doctor since cholestyramine may change the effect of other medicines.

Do not stop taking this medicine without first checking with your doctor. When you stop taking this medicine, your blood cholesterol levels may increase again. Your doctor may want you to follow a special diet to help prevent this from happening.

Side Effects of This Medicine

In some animal studies, cholestyramine was found to cause tumors. It is not known whether cholestyramine causes tumors in humans.

Along with its needed effects, a medicine may cause some unwanted effects. Although not all of these side effects may occur, if they do occur they may need medical attention.

Check with your doctor immediately if any of the following side effects occur:

Rare

Black, tarry stools; stomach pain (severe) with nausea and vomiting

Check with your doctor as soon as possible if any of the following side effects occur:

More common

Constipation

Rare

Loss of weight (sudden)

Other side effects may occur that usually do not need medical attention. These side effects may go away during treatment as your body adjusts to the medicine. However, check with your doctor if any of the following side effects continue or are bothersome:

More common

Heartburn or indigestion; nausea or vomiting; stomach pain

Less common

Belching; bloating; diarrhea; dizziness; headache

Other side effects not listed above may also occur in some patients. If you notice any other effects, check with your doctor.

Additional Information

Once a medicine has been approved for marketing for a certain use, experience may show that it is also useful for other medical problems. Although these uses are not included in product labeling, cholestyramine is used in certain patients with the following medical conditions:
- Digitalis glycoside overdose
- Excess oxalate in the urine

Other than the above information, there is no additional information relating to proper use, precautions, or side effects for these uses.

Revised: 08/02/94

CHORIONIC GONADOTROPIN Systemic

Some commonly used brand names are:

In the U.S.—

A.P.L.
Profasi
Pregnyl

Generic name product may also be available.

In Canada—

A.P.L.
Profasi HP

Generic name product may also be available.

Another commonly used name is human chorionic gonadotropin (hCG).

Description

Chorionic gonadotropin (kor-ee-ON-ik goe-NAD-oh-troe-pin) is a drug whose actions are almost the same as those of luteinizing (loo-te-in-eye-ZING) hormone (LH), which is produced by the pituitary gland. It is a hormone also normally produced by the placenta in pregnancy. Chorionic gonadotropin has different uses for females and males.

In females, chorionic gonadotropin is used to help conception occur. It is usually given in combination with other drugs such as menotropins and urofollitropin. Many women being treated with these drugs usually have already tried clomiphene alone (e.g., Serophene) and have not been able to conceive yet. Chorionic gonadotropin is also used in *in vitro* fertilization (IVF) programs.

In males, LH and chorionic gonadotropin stimulate the testes to produce male hormones such as testosterone. Testosterone causes the enlargement of the penis and testes and the growth of pubic and underarm hair. It also increases the production of sperm.

Although chorionic gonadotropin has been prescribed to help some patients lose weight, it should *never* be used this way. When used improperly, chorionic gonadotropin can cause serious problems.

Chorionic gonadotropin is to be administered only by or under the immediate supervision of your doctor. It is available in the following dosage form:

Parenteral
- Injection (U.S. and Canada)

Before Using This Medicine

In deciding to use a medicine, the risks of taking the medicine must be weighed against the good it will do. This is a decision you and your doctor will make. For chorionic gonadotropin, the following should be considered:

Allergies—Tell your doctor if you have ever had any unusual or allergic reaction to chorionic gonadotropin. Also tell your health care professional if you are allergic to any other substances, such as foods, preservatives, or dyes.

Pregnancy—If you become pregnant as a result of using this medicine with menotropins (e.g., Pergonal) or urofollitropin (e.g., Metrodin), there is an increased chance of a multiple pregnancy (for example, twins, triplets).

Children—Chorionic gonadotropin, when used for treating cryptorchidism (a birth defect where the testes remain inside the body), has caused the sexual organs of some male children to develop too rapidly.

Other medicines—Although certain medicines should not be used together at all, in other cases two different medicines may be used together even if an interaction might occur. In these cases, your doctor may want to change the dose, or other precautions may be necessary. Tell your health care professional if you are taking any prescription or nonprescription (over-the-counter [OTC]) medicine.

Other medical problems—The presence of other medical problems may affect the use of chorionic gonadotropin. Make sure you tell your doctor if you have any other medical problems, especially:

- Cancer of the prostate—Increases in the amount of testosterone in the bloodstream may make this condition worse
- Cyst on ovary or
- Fibroid tumors of the uterus—Chorionic gonadotropin can cause further growth of cysts on the ovary or fibroid tumors of the uterus
- Pituitary gland enlargement or tumor—Chorionic gonadotropin can cause the pituitary gland or a pituitary tumor to increase in size
- Unusual vaginal bleeding—Irregular vaginal bleeding is a sign that the endometrium is growing too much, of endometrial cancer, or of other hormone imbalances; the increases in estrogen production caused by ovulation can aggravate these problems of the endometrium. If other hormone imbalances are present, they should be treated before beginning ovulation induction

Proper Use of This Medicine

Dosing—The dose of chorionic gonadotropin will be different for different patients. *Follow your doctor's orders or the directions on the label.* The following information includes only the average doses for chorionic gonadotropin. *If your dose is different, do not change it* unless your doctor tells you to do so.

The number of doses you receive each day, the time allowed between doses, and the length of time you receive the medicine depend on the medical problem for which you are receiving chorionic gonadotropin.

- For *injection* dosage form:
  - —For treating men with problems related to low levels of male hormones:
    - Adults—1000 to 4000 Units injected into the muscle two to three times a week. You may need to receive this medicine for several weeks, months, or longer. If you are being treated for a low sperm count and have been on this medicine for six months, your doctor may give you another hormone medicine (menotropin or urofollitropin injection). You may need to receive both of these medicines together for up to twelve more months.
  - —To help pregnancy occur in women:
    - Adults—5000 to 10,000 Units injected into the muscle on a day chosen by your doctor. The dose and day will depend on your hormone levels and the other medicines that you have been using.
  - —For the treatment of cryptorchidism (condition where testes do not develop properly):
    - Children—1000 to 5000 Units injected into the muscle two to three times a week for up to ten doses.

Precautions While Using This Medicine

It is very important that your doctor check your progress at regular visits to make sure that the medicine is working and to check for unwanted effects.

For women *taking this medicine to become pregnant:*

- Record your basal body temperature every day if told to do so by your doctor, so that you will know if you have begun to ovulate. It is important that intercourse take place around the time of ovulation to give you the best chance of becoming pregnant. Your doctor will likely want to monitor the development of the ovarian follicle(s) by measuring the amount of estrogen in your bloodstream and by checking the size of the follicle(s) with ultrasound examinations.

Side Effects of This Medicine

Along with its needed effects, a medicine may cause some other effects. Although not all of these side effects may occur, if they do occur they may need medical attention.

Check with your doctor as soon as possible if any of the following side effects occur:

For females only

More common

Bloating (mild); stomach or pelvic pain

Less common or rare

Abdominal or stomach pain (severe); bloating (moderate to severe); decreased amount of urine; feeling of indigestion; nausea, vomiting, or diarrhea (continuing or severe); pelvic pain (severe); shortness of breath; swelling of feet or lower legs; weight gain (rapid)

For boys only

Less common

Acne; enlargement of penis and testes; growth of pubic hair; increase in height (rapid)

Other side effects may occur that usually do not need medical attention. These side effects may go away during treatment as your body adjusts to the medicine. However, check with your doctor if any of the following side effects continue or are bothersome:

Less common

Enlargement of breasts; headache; irritability; mental depression; pain at place of injection; tiredness

After you stop receiving this medicine, it may continue to cause some side effects which require medical attention. During this period of time check with your doctor if you notice either of the following side effects:

For females only

Less common or rare

Abdominal or stomach pain (severe); bloating (moderate to severe); decreased amount of urine; feeling of indigestion; nausea, vomiting, or diarrhea (continuing or severe); pelvic pain (severe); shortness of breath; weight gain (rapid)

Other side effects not listed above may also occur in some patients. If you notice any other effects, check with your doctor.

Revised: 07/26/92
Interim revision: 06/03/94

CHROMIC PHOSPHATE P 32 Therapeutic

A commonly used brand name in the U.S. is Phosphocol P 32.

Description

Chromic phosphate (KROME-ik FOS-fate) P 32 is a radiopharmaceutical (ray-dee-oh-far-ma-SOO-ti-kal). Radiopharmaceuticals are agents used to diagnose certain medical problems or treat certain diseases.

Chromic phosphate P 32 is used to treat cancer or related problems. It is put by catheter into the pleura (sac that contains the lungs) or into the peritoneum (sac that contains the liver, stomach, and intestines) to treat the leaking of fluid inside these areas that is caused by cancer. It may also be given by injection to treat cancer in certain organs such as the ovaries and prostate.

Chromic phosphate P 32 is to be given only by or under the direct supervision of a doctor with specialized training in nuclear medicine. It is available in the following dosage form:

Parenteral

- Suspension (U.S.)

Before Using This Medicine

In deciding to use a medicine, the risks of taking the medicine must be weighed against the good it will do. This is a decision you and your doctor will make. For chromic phosphate P 32, the following should be considered:

Pregnancy—Radiopharmaceuticals are usually not recommended for use during pregnancy to avoid exposing the fetus to radiation. However, some treatment using radiopharmaceuticals may be required even during pregnancy. Be sure you have discussed this with your doctor.

Breast-feeding—Chromic phosphate P 32 passes into the breast milk. If you must receive this radiopharmaceutical, it may be necessary for you to stop breast-feeding during treatment. Be sure you have discussed this with your doctor.

Children—There is no specific information comparing use of chromic phosphate P 32 in children with use in other age groups.

Older adults—Many medicines have not been studied specifically in older people. Therefore, it may not be known whether they work exactly the same way they do in younger adults. Although there is no specific information comparing use of chromic phosphate P 32 in the elderly with use in other age groups, this medicine is not expected to cause different side effects or problems in older people than it does in younger adults.

Preparation for This Treatment

Your doctor may have special instructions for you in preparation for your treatment. If you have not received such instructions or if you do not understand them, check with your doctor in advance.

Side Effects of This Medicine

Along with its needed effects, a medicine may cause some unwanted effects. Although not all of these side effects may occur, if they do occur they may need medical attention.

Check with your health care professional immediately if any of the following side effects occur:

Less common or rare

Abdominal or stomach pain (severe); chest pain; chills and/or fever; dry cough; nausea and vomiting (severe); sore throat and fever; troubled breathing; unusual bleeding or bruising; unusual tiredness or weakness

Other side effects may occur that usually do not need medical attention. These side effects may go away during treatment as your body adjusts to the medicine. However,

check with your doctor if any of the following side effects continue or are bothersome:

More common

Abdominal or stomach cramps; diarrhea; feeling of discomfort; loss of appetite; nausea and vomiting; weakness

Other side effects not listed above may also occur in some patients. If you notice any other effects, check with your doctor.

Revised: 05/18/92

CHROMIUM SUPPLEMENTS Systemic

A commonly used brand name is:

In the U.S.—

Chroma-Pak[1]

Note: For quick reference, the following chromium supplements are numbered to match the corresponding brand name.

This information applies to the following:

1. Chromic Chloride (KROME-ik KLOR-ide)†‡
2. Chromium (KROH-mee-um)‡§

†Not commercially available in Canada.
‡Generic name product may also be available in the U.S.
§Generic name product may also be available in Canada.

Description

Chromium supplements are used to prevent or treat chromium deficiency.

The body needs chromium for normal growth and health. For patients who are unable to get enough chromium in their regular diet or who have a need for more chromium, chromium supplements may be necessary. They are generally taken by mouth but some patients may have to receive them by injection. Chromium helps your body use sugar properly. It is also needed for the breakdown of proteins and fats.

Lack of chromium may lead to nerve problems and may decrease the body's ability to use sugar properly.

There is not enough evidence to show that taking chromium supplements improves the way your body uses sugar (glucose tolerance).

Injectable chromium is given by or under the supervision of a health care professional. Other forms are available without a prescription.

Chromium supplements are available in the following dosage forms:

Oral

Chromium
- Capsules (U.S.)
- Tablets (U.S. and Canada)

Parenteral

Chromic Chloride
- Injection (U.S.)

Importance of Diet

For good health, it is important that you eat a balanced and varied diet. Follow carefully any diet program your health care professional may recommend. For your specific dietary vitamin and/or mineral needs, ask your health care professional for a list of appropriate foods. If you think that you are not getting enough vitamins and/or minerals in your diet, you may choose to take a dietary supplement.

Chromium is found in various foods, including brewer's yeast, calf liver, American cheese, and wheat germ.

The daily amount of chromium needed is defined in several different ways.

For U.S.—

- Recommended Dietary Allowances (RDAs) are the amount of vitamins and minerals needed to provide for adequate nutrition in most healthy persons. RDAs for a given nutrient may vary depending on a person's age, sex, and physical condition (e.g., pregnancy).
- Daily Values (DVs) are used on food and dietary supplement labels to indicate the percent of the recommended daily amount of each nutrient that a serving provides. DV replaces the previous designation of United States Recommended Daily Allowances (USRDAs).

For Canada—

- Recommended Nutrient Intakes (RNIs) are used to determine the amounts of vitamins, minerals, and protein needed to provide adequate nutrition and lessen the risk of chronic disease.

Because a lack of chromium is rare, there is no RDA or RNI for it. Normal daily recommended intakes for chromium are generally defined as follows:

- Infants and children—
  Birth to 3 years of age: 10 to 80 micrograms (mcg) a day.
  4 to 6 years of age: 30 to 120 mcg a day.
  7 to 10 years of age: 50 to 200 mcg a day.
- Adolescents and adults—50 to 200 mcg a day.

Before Using This Dietary Supplement

If you are taking this dietary supplement without a prescription, carefully read and follow any precautions on the label. For chromium, the following should be considered:

Allergies—Tell your health care professional if you have ever had any unusual or allergic reaction to chromium. Also tell your health care professional if you are allergic to any other substances, such as foods, preservatives, or dyes.

Pregnancy—It is especially important that you are receiving enough vitamins and minerals when you become pregnant and that you continue to receive the right amount of vitamins and minerals throughout your pregnancy. The healthy growth and development of the fetus depend on a steady supply of nutrients from the mother. However, taking large amounts of a dietary supplement during pregnancy may be harmful to the mother and/or fetus and should be avoided.

Breast-feeding—It is important that you receive the right amounts of vitamins and minerals so that your baby will also get the vitamins and minerals needed to grow properly. However, taking large amounts of a dietary supplement while breast-feeding may be harmful to the mother and/or baby and should be avoided.

Children—Problems in children have not been reported with intake of normal daily recommended amounts.

Older adults—Problems in older adults have not been reported with intake of normal daily recommended amounts.

Medicines or other dietary supplements—Although certain medicines or dietary supplements should not be used together at all, in other cases they may be used together even if an interaction might occur. In these cases, your health care professional may want to change the dose, or other precautions may be necessary. Tell your health care professional if you are using any other dietary supplement or any prescription or over-the-counter (OTC) medication.

Other medical problems—The presence of other medical problems may affect the use of chromium. Make sure you tell your health care professional if you have any other medical problems, especially:

- Diabetes mellitus (sugar diabetes)—Taking chromium supplements when you have a chromium deficiency may cause a change in the amount of insulin you need

Proper Use of This Dietary Supplement

Dosing—The amount of chromium needed to meet normal daily recommended intakes will be different for different individuals. The following information includes only the average amounts of chromium.

- For *oral* dosage forms (capsules and tablets):
  - —To prevent deficiency, the amount taken by mouth is based on normal daily recommended intakes:
    - Adults and teenagers—50 to 200 micrograms (mcg) per day.
    - Children 7 to 10 years age—50 to 200 mcg per day.
    - Children 4 to 6 years of age—30 to 120 mcg per day.
    - Children birth to 3 years of age—10 to 80 mcg per day.
  - —To treat deficiency:
    - Adults, teenagers, and children—Treatment dose is determined by prescriber for each individual based on severity of deficiency.

Missed dose—If you miss taking chromium supplements for one or more days there is no cause for concern, since it takes some time for your body to become seriously low in chromium. However, if your health care professional has recommended that you take chromium, try to remember to take it as directed every day.

Storage—To store this dietary supplement:

- Keep out of the reach of children.
- Store away from heat and direct light.
- Do not store in the bathroom, near the kitchen sink, or in other damp places. Heat or moisture may cause the dietary supplement to break down.
- Keep the dietary supplement from freezing. Do not refrigerate.
- Do not keep outdated dietary supplements or those no longer needed. Be sure that any discarded dietary supplement is out of the reach of children.

Side Effects of This Dietary Supplement

No side effects or overdoses have been reported for chromium. However, check with your health care professional if you notice any unusual effects while you are taking it.

Revised: 03/24/92
Interim revision: 08/01/94; 05/26/95

CHYMOPAPAIN Parenteral-Local

A commonly used brand name in the U.S. and Canada is Chymodiactin.

Description

Chymopapain (kye-mo-PA-pane) is injected directly into a herniated (''slipped'') disk in the spine to dissolve part of the disk and relieve the pain and other problems caused by the disk pressing on a nerve. Before you receive chymopapain, you will be given an anesthetic (either a general anesthetic to put you to sleep or a local anesthetic).

Very rarely, use of chymopapain may cause serious side effects, including paralysis of the legs or death. Another dangerous side effect of chymopapain injection is a severe allergic reaction called anaphylaxis. This side effect occurs in less than 1% of the patients receiving the medicine, but it occurs more often in women than in men. Before receiving chymopapain, you should discuss its use, and the possibility of anaphylaxis or other serious side effects, with your doctor.

Chymopapain injections are given only in a hospital, usually in an operating room, by your surgeon. This medicine is available in the following dosage form:

Parenteral

- Injection (U.S. and Canada)

Before Receiving This Medicine

In deciding to use a medicine, the risks of receiving the medicine must be weighed against the good it will do. This is a decision you and your doctor will make. For chymopapain, the following should be considered:

Allergies—Tell your doctor if you have ever had any unusual or allergic reaction to chymopapain, papaya, meat tenderizer, contact lens cleaning solutions, beer, or iodine. Also tell your doctor if you are allergic to any other substances, such as foods, preservatives, or dyes.

Pregnancy—Studies on effects of pregnancy have not been done in either humans or animals.

Breast-feeding—It is not known whether chymopapain passes into breast milk. Although most medicines pass into breast milk in small amounts, many of them may be used safely while breast-feeding. Mothers who are receiving this medicine and who wish to breast-feed should discuss this with their doctor.

Children—Studies on this medicine have been done only in adult patients, and there is no specific information comparing use of chymopapain in children with use in other age groups.

Older adults—Many medicines have not been studied specifically in older people. Therefore, it may not be known whether they work exactly the same way they do in younger adults or if they cause different side effects or problems in older people. There is no specific information comparing use of chymopapain in the elderly with use in other age groups.

Other medicines—Although certain medicines should not be used together at all, in other cases two different medicines may be used together even if an interaction might occur. In these cases, your doctor may want to change the dose, or other precautions may be necessary. Tell your doctor if you are taking any other prescription or nonprescription (over-the-counter [OTC]) medicine.

Other medical problems—The presence of other medical problems may affect the use of chymopapain. Make sure you tell your doctor if you have ever received an injection of chymopapain, if you have had back surgery, or if you have any other medical problems, especially:

- Allergies or
- Stroke or bleeding in the brain (or if any member of your family has ever had these problems) or
- High blood pressure (hypertension)—The chance of side effects may be increased

Proper Use of This Medicine

Dosing—The dose of chymopapain will be different for different patients and must be determined by your doctor.

Side Effects of This Medicine

Along with its needed effects, a medicine may cause some unwanted effects. Very rarely, use of chymopapain has caused serious side effects, including paralysis of the legs or death. Also, this medicine may cause dangerous allergic reactions, especially in women.

Although not all of the following side effects may occur, if they do occur they may need medical attention. Tell your health care professional if any of the following side effects occur:

Rare

Abdominal or stomach cramps or pain; changes of skin color, hot skin, pain, tenderness, or swelling of leg or foot; constipation (severe); decreased or uncontrolled urination; fast or irregular breathing; headache (sudden, severe, and continuing); puffiness or swelling of the eyelids or around the eyes; runny nose; shortness of breath, troubled breathing, tightness in chest, or wheezing; skin rash, redness, hives, or itching; swelling of abdomen or stomach; uncontrolled bowel movements; vomiting; weakness in legs (severe) or problems with moving legs

Other side effects may occur that usually do not need medical attention. Pain and muscle spasms in the lower back may last for several days after you have received this medicine. Stiffness or soreness in the back may last for several months. Other side effects may go away after a short time. However, check with your doctor if any of the following side effects continue or are bothersome:

More common

Back pain, stiffness, or soreness; muscle spasms in lower back

Less common or rare

Cramps, pain, or mild weakness in legs; dizziness; feeling of burning in lower back; headache; nausea; numbness or tingling in legs or toes

Some side effects may not appear until several days or weeks after you have received chymopapain. Check with your doctor as soon as possible if any of the following side effects occur within 1 month after you have received this medicine:

Back pain or muscle weakness (sudden and severe); skin rash, hives, or itching

Other side effects not listed above may also occur in some patients. If you notice any other effects, check with your doctor.

Revised: 07/26/94

CICLOPIROX Topical

A commonly used brand name in the U.S. and Canada is Loprox.

Description

Ciclopirox (sye-kloe-PEER-ox) is used to treat infections caused by fungus. It works by killing the fungus or preventing its growth.

Ciclopirox is applied to the skin to treat:
- ringworm of the body (tinea corporis);
- ringworm of the foot (tinea pedis; athlete's foot);
- ringworm of the groin (tinea cruris; jock itch);
- ''sun fungus'' (tinea versicolor; pityriasis versicolor); and
- certain other fungus infections, such as Candida (Monilia) infections.

Ciclopirox is available only with your doctor's prescription, in the following dosage forms:

Topical
- Cream (U.S. and Canada)
- Lotion (U.S. and Canada)

Before Using This Medicine

In deciding to use a medicine, the risks of taking the medicine must be weighed against the good it will do. This is a decision you and your doctor will make. For ciclopirox, the following should be considered:

Allergies—Tell your doctor if you have ever had any unusual or allergic reaction to ciclopirox. Also tell your health care professional if you are allergic to any other substances, such as preservatives or dyes.

Pregnancy—Ciclopirox has not been studied in pregnant women. However, this medication has not been shown to cause birth defects or other problems in animal studies.

Breast-feeding—It is not known whether ciclopirox passes into breast milk. Although most medicines pass into breast milk in small amounts, many of them may be used safely while breast-feeding. Mothers who are using this medicine and who wish to breast-feed should discuss this with their doctor.

Children—Studies on this medicine have been done only in adult patients, and there is no specific information comparing use of ciclopirox in children under the age of 10 with use in other age groups.

Older adults—Many medicines have not been studied specifically in older people. Therefore, it may not be known whether they work exactly the same way they do in younger adults. Although there is no specific information comparing use of ciclopirox in the elderly with use in other age groups, this medicine is not expected to cause different side effects or problems in older people than it does in younger adults.

Other medicines—Although certain medicines should not be used together at all, in other cases two different medicines may be used together even if an interaction might occur. In these cases, your doctor may want to change the dose, or other precautions may be necessary. Tell your health care professional if you are using any other topical prescription or nonprescription (over-the-counter [OTC]) medicine that is to be applied to the same area of the skin.

Proper Use of This Medicine

Apply enough ciclopirox to cover the affected and surrounding skin areas and rub in gently.

Keep this medicine away from the eyes.

When ciclopirox is used to treat certain types of fungus infections of the skin, an occlusive dressing (airtight covering, such as kitchen plastic wrap) should *not* be applied over the medicine. To do so may irritate the skin. *Do not apply an airtight covering over this medicine unless you have been directed to do so by your doctor.*

To help clear up your infection completely, *it is very important that you keep using ciclopirox for the full time of treatment,* even if your symptoms begin to clear up after a few days. Since fungus infections may be very slow to clear up, you may have to continue using this medicine every day for several weeks or more. If you stop using this medicine too soon, your symptoms may return. *Do not miss any doses.*

Dosing—The dose of topical ciclopirox will be different for different patients. *Follow your doctor's orders or the directions on the label.* The following information includes only the average doses of topical ciclopirox. *If your dose is different, do not change it* unless your doctor tells you to do so.

- For *topical* dosage forms (cream and lotion):
  - —Fungus infections (treatment):
    - Adults and children 10 years of age and over—Apply two times a day, morning and evening.
    - Children up to 10 years of age—Use and dose must be determined by your doctor.

Missed dose—If you miss a dose of this medicine, apply it as soon as possible. However, if it is almost time for your next dose, skip the missed dose and go back to your regular dosing schedule.

Storage—To store this medicine:
- Keep out of the reach of children.
- Store away from heat and direct light.
- Keep the medicine from freezing.
- Do not keep outdated medicine or medicine no longer needed. Be sure that any discarded medicine is out of the reach of children.

Precautions While Using This Medicine

If your skin problem does not improve within 2 to 4 weeks, or if it becomes worse, check with your doctor.

To help clear up your infection completely and to help make sure it does not return, good health habits are also required. The following measures will help reduce chafing and irritation and will also help keep the area cool and dry.

- *For patients using ciclopirox for ringworm of the groin (tinea cruris):*
  —Avoid wearing underwear that is tight-fitting or made from synthetic materials (for example, rayon or nylon). Instead, wear loose-fitting, cotton underwear.
  —Use a bland, absorbent powder (for example, talcum powder) or an antifungal powder (for example, tolnaftate) on the skin. It is best to use the powder between applications of ciclopirox.
- *For patients using ciclopirox for ringworm of the foot (tinea pedis):*
  —Carefully dry the feet, especially between the toes, after bathing.
  —Avoid wearing socks made from wool or synthetic materials (for example, rayon or nylon). Instead, wear clean, cotton socks and change them daily or more often if the feet sweat freely.
  —Wear sandals or well-ventilated shoes (for example, shoes with holes on top or on the side).
  —Use a bland, absorbent powder (for example, talcum powder) or an antifungal powder (for example, tolnaftate) between the toes, on the feet, and in socks and shoes freely once or twice a day. It is best to use the powder between applications of ciclopirox.

If you have any questions about these measures, check with your health care professional.

Side Effects of This Medicine

Along with its needed effects, a medicine may cause some unwanted effects. Although not all of these side effects may occur, if they do occur they may need medical attention.

Check with your doctor as soon as possible if any of the following side effects occur:

Rare

Burning, itching, redness, swelling, or other signs of irritation not present before use of this medicine

Other side effects not listed above may also occur in some patients. If you notice any other effects, check with your doctor.

Revised: 05/26/94

CINOXACIN Systemic†

A commonly used brand name in the U.S. is Cinobac.

Generic name product may also be available in the U.S.

†Not commercially available in Canada.

Description

Cinoxacin (sin-OX-a-sin) is used to prevent and treat infections of the urinary tract. It will not work for other infections or for colds, flu, or other virus infections.

Cinoxacin is available only with your doctor's prescription, in the following dosage form:

Oral

- Capsules (U.S.)

Before Using This Medicine

In deciding to use a medicine, the risks of taking the medicine must be weighed against the good it will do. This is a decision you and your doctor will make. For cinoxacin, the following should be considered:

Allergies—Tell your doctor if you have ever had any unusual or allergic reaction to cinoxacin or to any related medicines such as ciprofloxacin (e.g., Cipro), enoxacin (e.g., Penetrex), lomefloxacin (e.g., Maxaquin), nalidixic acid (e.g., NegGram), norfloxacin (e.g., Noroxin), or ofloxacin (e.g., Floxin). Also tell your health care professional if you are allergic to any other substances, such as foods, preservatives, or dyes.

Pregnancy—Studies have not been done in humans. However, use is not recommended during pregnancy since cinoxacin has been shown to cause bone development problems in young animals.

Breast-feeding—It is not known whether cinoxacin passes into the breast milk. However, other related medicines do pass into the breast milk. Since cinoxacin has been shown to cause bone development problems in young animals, use is not recommended in nursing mothers.

Children—Since this medicine has been shown to cause bone development problems in young animals, its use is not recommended in children up to 18 years of age.

Older adults—Many medicines have not been studied specifically in older people. Therefore, it may not be known whether they work exactly the same way they do in younger adults. Although there is no specific information comparing use of cinoxacin in the elderly with use in other age groups, this medicine is not expected to cause different side effects or problems in older people than it does in younger adults.

Other medical problems—The presence of other medical problems may affect the use of cinoxacin. Make sure you tell your doctor if you have any other medical problems, especially:

- Kidney disease—Patients with kidney disease may have an increased risk of side effects

Proper Use of This Medicine

Cinoxacin may be taken with food, unless you are otherwise directed by your doctor.

Do not give this medicine to infants or children under 18 years of age, unless otherwise directed by your doctor. It has been shown to cause bone development problems in young animals.

To help clear up your infection completely, *keep taking this medicine for the full time of treatment,* even if you begin to feel better after a few days. If you stop taking this medicine too soon, your symptoms may return.

This medicine works best when there is a constant amount in the urine. *To help keep the amount constant, do not miss any doses. Also, it is best to take the doses at evenly spaced times, day and night.* For example, if you are to take 4 doses a day, the doses should be spaced about 6 hours apart. If this interferes with your sleep or other daily activities, or if you need help in planning the best times to take your medicine, check with your health care professional.

Dosing—The dose of cinoxacin will be different for different patients. *Follow your doctor's orders or the directions on the label.* The following information includes only the average doses of cinoxacin. Your dose may be different if you have kidney disease. *If your dose is different, do not change it* unless your doctor tells you to do so.

The number of capsules that you take depends on the strength of the medicine. Also, *the number of doses you take each day, the time allowed between doses, and the length of time you take the medicine depend on whether you are using cinoxacin to prevent or to treat urinary tract infections.*

- For *capsule* dosage form:
  - —For the *prevention* of urinary tract infections:
    - Adults—250 milligrams (mg) at bedtime for up to five months.
    - Children up to 18 years of age—Use is generally not recommended because it may cause bone development problems.
  - —For the *treatment* of urinary tract infections:
    - Adults—250 mg every six hours; or 500 mg every twelve hours for seven to fourteen days.
    - Children up to 18 years of age—Use is generally not recommended because it may cause bone development problems.

Missed dose—If you miss a dose of this medicine, take it as soon as possible. This will help to keep a constant amount of medicine in the urine. However, if it is almost time for your next dose, skip the missed dose and go back to your regular dosing schedule. Do not double doses.

Storage—To store this medicine:

- Keep out of the reach of children.
- Store away from heat and direct light.
- Do not store in the bathroom, near the kitchen sink, or in other damp places. Heat or moisture may cause the medicine to break down.
- Do not keep outdated medicine or medicine no longer needed. Be sure that any discarded medicine is out of the reach of children.

Precautions While Using This Medicine

If your symptoms do not improve within a few days, or if they become worse, check with your doctor.

This medicine may also cause some people to become dizzy. *Make sure you know how you react to this medicine before you drive, use machines, or do anything else that could be dangerous if you are dizzy.* If this reaction is especially bothersome, check with your doctor.

Some people who take cinoxacin may become more sensitive to sunlight than they are normally. Exposure to sunlight, even for brief periods of time, may cause severe sunburn; skin rash, redness, itching, or discoloration; or vision changes. When you begin taking this medicine:

- Stay out of direct sunlight, especially between the hours of 10:00 a.m. and 3:00 p.m., if possible.
- Wear protective clothing, including a hat and sunglasses.
- Apply a sun block product that has a skin protection factor (SPF) of at least 15. Some patients may require a product with a higher SPF number, especially if they have a fair complexion. If you have any questions about this, check with your health care professional.
- Do not use a sunlamp or tanning bed or booth.

If you have a severe reaction from the sun, check with your doctor.

Side Effects of This Medicine

Along with its needed effects, a medicine may cause some unwanted effects. Although not all of these side effects may occur, if they do occur they may need medical attention.

Check with your doctor as soon as possible if any of the following side effects occur:

Less common

Skin rash, itching, redness, or swelling

Rare

Dizziness; headache; increased sensitivity of skin to sunlight

Other side effects may occur that usually do not need medical attention. These side effects may go away during treatment as your body adjusts to the medicine. However, check with your doctor if any of the following side effects continue or are bothersome:

Less common

Diarrhea; loss of appetite; nausea; stomach cramps; vomiting

Other side effects not listed above may also occur in some patients. If you notice any other effects, check with your doctor.

Revised: 07/19/95

CIPROFLOXACIN Ophthalmic

A commonly used brand name in the U.S. and Canada is Ciloxan.

Description

Ophthalmic ciprofloxacin (sip-roe-FLOX-a-sin) is used in the eye to treat bacterial infections of the eye and corneal ulcers of the eye. Ophthalmic ciprofloxacin works by killing bacteria.

Ciprofloxacin ophthalmic preparation is available only with your doctor's prescription, in the following dosage form:

Ophthalmic
- Ophthalmic solution (eye drops) (U.S. and Canada)

Before Using This Medicine

In deciding to use a medicine, the risks of using the medicine must be weighed against the good it will do. This is a decision you and your doctor will make. For ophthalmic ciprofloxacin, the following should be considered:

Allergies—Tell your doctor if you have ever had any unusual or allergic reaction to ophthalmic or systemic ciprofloxacin (e.g., Cipro) or any related medicines, such as cinoxacin (e.g., Cinobac), norfloxacin (e.g., Chibroxin or Noroxin), ofloxacin (e.g., Floxin), or nalidixic acid (e.g., NegGram). Also tell your health care professional if you are allergic to any other substances, such as foods, preservatives, or dyes.

Pregnancy—Ciprofloxacin has not been studied in pregnant women. However, studies in animals have not shown that ciprofloxacin causes birth defects.

Breast-feeding—It is not known whether ophthalmic ciprofloxin passes into breast milk. However, ciprofloxacin given by mouth does pass into breast milk. Although most medicines pass into breast milk in small amounts, many of them may be used safely while breast-feeding. Mothers who are using this medicine and who wish to breast-feed should discuss this with their doctor.

Children—Use is not recommended in infants and children up to 12 years of age. In children 12 years of age and older, this medicine is not expected to cause different side effects or problems than it does in adults.

Older adults—Many medicines have not been studied specifically in older people. Therefore, it may not be known whether they work exactly the same way they do in younger adults or if they cause different side effects or problems in older people. There is no specific information comparing use of ophthalmic ciprofloxacin in the elderly with use in other age groups.

Other medicines—Although certain medicines should not be used together at all, in other cases two different medicines may be used together even if an interaction might occur. In these cases, your doctor may want to change the dose, or other precautions may be necessary. Tell your health care professional if you using any other prescription or nonprescription (over-the-counter [OTC]) medicine that is to be used in the eye.

Proper Use of This Medicine

To use:
- First, wash your hands. Then tilt the head back and pull the lower eyelid away from the eye to form a pouch. Drop the medicine into the pouch and gently close the eyes. Do not blink. Keep the eyes closed for 1 or 2 minutes to allow the medicine to come into contact with the infection.
- If you think you did not get the drop of medicine into your eyes properly, use another drop.
- To keep the medicine as germ-free as possible, do not touch the applicator tip to any surface (including the eye). Also, keep the container tightly closed.

To help clear up your eye infection completely, *keep using ophthalmic ciprofloxacin for the full time of treatment*, even if your symptoms have disappeared. *Do not miss any doses.*

Dosing—The dose of ophthalmic ciprofloxacin will be different for different patients. *Follow your doctor's orders or the directions on the label.* The following information includes only the average doses of ophthalmic ciprofloxacin. *If your dose is different, do not change it* unless your doctor tells you to do so.

The number of doses you use each day, the time allowed between doses, and the length of time you use the medicine depend on the medical problem for which you are using ophthalmic ciprofloxacin.

- For *ophthalmic solution* dosage form:
  - —For bacterial conjunctivitis:
    - Adults and children 12 years of age and older—Use 1 drop in each eye every two hours, while you are awake, for two days. Then use 1 drop in each eye every four hours, while you are awake, for the next five days.
    - Infants and children up to 12 years of age—Use and dose must be determined by your doctor.
  - —For corneal ulcers:
    - Adults and children 12 years of age and older—On day one, use 1 drop in the affected eye every fifteen minutes for six hours, then 1 drop every thirty minutes for the rest of the day, while you are awake. On day two, use 1 drop every hour, while you are awake. On days three through fourteen, use 1 drop every four hours, while you are awake.
    - Infants and children up to 12 years of age—Use and dose must be determined by your doctor.

Missed dose—If you miss a dose of this medicine, use it as soon as possible. However, if it is almost time for your next dose, skip the missed dose and go back to your regular dosing schedule.

Storage—To store this medicine:
- Keep out of the reach of children.
- Store away from heat and direct light.

- Keep the medicine from freezing. Do not refrigerate.
- Do not keep outdated medicine or medicine no longer needed. Be sure that any discarded medicine is out of the reach of children.

Precautions While Using This Medicine

If your eye infection does not improve within a few days, or if it becomes worse, check with your doctor.

This medicine may cause your eyes to become more sensitive to light than they are normally. Wearing sunglasses and avoiding too much exposure to bright light may help lessen the discomfort.

Side Effects of This Medicine

Along with its needed effects, a medicine may cause some unwanted effects. Although not all of these side effects may occur, if they do occur they may need medical attention.

Check with your doctor as soon as possible if any of the following side effects occur:

Rare

Blurred vision or other change in vision; irritation (severe) or redness of eye; nausea; skin rash

Other side effects may occur that usually do not need medical attention. These side effects may go away during treatment as your body adjusts to the medicine. However, check with your doctor if any of the following side effects continue or are bothersome:

More common

Burning or other discomfort of eye; crusting or crystals in corner of eye

Less common

Bad taste following use in the eye; feeling of something in eye; itching of eye; redness of the lining of the eyelids

Rare

Increased sensitivity of eyes to light; swelling of eyelid; tearing of eye

Other side effects not listed above may also occur in some patients. If you notice any other effects, check with your doctor.

Revised: 07/29/93

CISAPRIDE Systemic

Some commonly used brand names are:

In the U.S.—

Propulsid

In Canada—

Prepulsid

Description

Cisapride (SIS-a-pride) is a medicine that increases the movements or contractions of the stomach and intestines. It is used to treat symptoms such as heartburn caused by a backward flow of stomach acid into the esophagus.

Cisapride is available only with your doctor's prescription. It is available in the following dosage forms:

Oral

- Oral suspension (U.S. and Canada)
- Tablets (U.S. and Canada)

Before Using This Medicine

In deciding to use a medicine, the risks of taking the medicine must be weighed against the good it will do. This is a decision you and your doctor will make. For cisapride, the following should be considered:

Allergies—Tell your doctor if you have ever had any unusual or allergic reaction to cisapride. Also tell your health care professional if you are allergic to any other substances, such as foods, preservatives, or dyes.

Pregnancy—Cisapride has not been studied in pregnant women. However, studies in animals have shown that cisapride causes harm to the fetus. Before taking this medicine, make sure your doctor knows if you are pregnant or if you may become pregnant.

Breast-feeding—Although cisapride passes into the breast milk, it has not been shown to cause problems in nursing babies.

Children—This medicine has been tested in a limited number of children. In effective doses, the medicine has not been shown to cause different side effects or problems than it does in adults.

Older adults—Elderly people are especially sensitive to the effects of cisapride. Cisapride stays in the body longer so the dose may be different than in younger people.

Other medicines—Although certain medicines should not be used together at all, in other cases two different medicines may be used together even if an interaction might occur. In these cases, your doctor may want to change the dose, or other precautions may be necessary. When you are taking cisapride, it is especially important that your health care professional know if you are taking any of the following:

- Amantadine (e.g., Symmetrel) or
- Anticholinergics (medicine for abdominal or stomach spasms or cramps) or
- Antidepressants (medicine for depression) or
- Antidyskinetics (medicine for Parkinson's disease or other conditions affecting control of muscles) or
- Antihistamines or
- Antipsychotics (medicine for mental illness) or
- Buclizine (e.g., Bucladin) or
- Carbamazepine (e.g., Tegretol) or
- Cyclizine (e.g., Marezine) or
- Cyclobenzaprine (e.g., Flexeril) or
- Disopyramide (e.g., Norpace) or
- Flavoxate (e.g., Urispas) or
- Ipratropium (e.g., Atrovent) or

- Meclizine (e.g., Antivert) or
- Methylphenidate (e.g., Ritalin) or
- Orphenadrine (e.g., Norflex) or
- Oxybutynin (e.g., Ditropen) or
- Procainamide (e.g., Pronestyl) or
- Promethazine (e.g., Phenergan) or
- Quinidine (e.g., Quinidex) or
- Trimeprazine (e.g., Temaril)—Cisapride may decrease the absorption of these medicines and cause them to be less effective
- Clarithromycin (e.g., Biaxin) or
- Erythromycin (e.g., E-Mycin) or
- Fluconazole (e.g., Diflucan) or
- Itraconazole (e.g., Sporanox) or
- Ketoconazole (e.g., Nizoral) or
- Miconazole (e.g., Monistat i.v.) or
- Troleandomycin (e.g., Tao)—These medicines may increase the chance of serious side effects and should not be taken with cisapride

Other medical problems—The presence of other medical problems may affect the use of cisapride. Make sure you tell your doctor if you have any other medical problems, especially:

- Abdominal or stomach bleeding or
- Intestinal blockage—Cisapride may make these conditions worse
- Epilepsy or history of seizures—Cisapride has been reported to cause seizures in patients with a history of seizures
- Heart disease—Cisapride may increase the chance of side effects in patients with a history of an irregular heartbeat
- Kidney disease or
- Liver disease—Higher blood levels of cisapride may result and increase the chance of side effects

Proper Use of This Medicine

Take this medicine 15 minutes before meals and at bedtime with a beverage, unless otherwise directed by your doctor.

Dosing—The dose of cisapride will be different for different patients. *Follow your doctor's orders or the directions on the label.* The following information includes only the average doses of cisapride. *If your dose is different, do not change it* unless your doctor tells you to do so.

- For *oral* dosage forms (tablets and suspension):
  - —For heartburn caused by gastroesophageal reflux:
    - Adults and children 12 years of age and older—5 to 20 milligrams (mg) of cisapride two to four times a day. Cisapride should be taken fifteen minutes before meals and at bedtime.
    - Children up to 12 years of age—Dose is based on body weight and must be determined by your doctor. The dose is usually 0.15 to 0.3 mg of cisapride per kilogram (0.07 to 0.14 mg per pound) of body weight three to four times a day, fifteen minutes before meals.

Missed dose—If you miss a dose of this medicine, take it as soon as possible. However, if it is almost time for your next dose, skip the missed dose and go back to your regular dosing schedule. Do not double doses.

Storage—To store this medicine:

- Keep out of the reach of children.
- Store away from heat and direct light.
- Do not store in the bathroom, near the kitchen sink, or in other damp places. Heat or moisture may cause the medicine to break down.
- Do not keep outdated medicine or medicine no longer needed. Be sure that any discarded medicine is out of the reach of children.

Precautions While Using This Medicine

This medicine may cause your body to absorb alcohol more quickly than you normally would. Therefore, you may notice the effects sooner. *Check with your doctor before drinking alcohol while you are using this medicine.*

This medicine may cause some people to become drowsy or less alert than they are normally. *Make sure you know how you react to this medicine before you drive, use machines, or do anything else that could be dangerous if you are dizzy or are not alert.*

Side Effects of This Medicine

Along with its needed effects, a medicine may cause some unwanted effects. Although not all of these side effects may occur, if they do occur they may need medical attention.

Check with your doctor immediately if the following side effect occurs:

Rare

Seizures

Note: Seizures have occurred only in patients with a history of seizures.

Other side effects may occur that usually do not need medical attention. These side effects may go away during treatment as your body adjusts to the medicine. However, check with your doctor if any of the following side effects continue or are bothersome:

Less common

Abdominal cramping, constipation, diarrhea, drowsiness, headache, nausea, unusual tiredness or weakness

Other side effects not listed above may also occur in some patients. If you notice any other effects, check with your doctor.

Additional Information

Once a medicine has been approved for marketing for a certain use, experience may show that it is also useful for other medical problems. Although this use is not included in product labeling, cisapride is used in certain patients with the following medical condition:

- Gastroparesis (stomach condition)

Other than the above information, there is no additional information relating to proper use, precautions, or side effects for this use.

Revised: 07/29/96

CISPLATIN Systemic

Some commonly used brand names are:

In the U.S.—
- Platinol
- Platinol-AQ

In Canada—
- Platinol
- Platinol-AQ

Generic name product may also be available.

Description

Cisplatin (sis-PLA-tin) belongs to the group of medicines known as alkylating agents. It is used to treat some kinds of cancer.

Cisplatin interferes with the growth of cancer cells, which are eventually destroyed. Since the growth of normal body cells may also be affected by cisplatin, other effects will also occur. Some of these may be serious and must be reported to your doctor. Other effects may not be serious but may cause concern. Some effects may not occur for months or years after the medicine is used.

Before you begin treatment with cisplatin, you and your doctor should talk about the good this medicine will do as well as the risks of using it.

Cisplatin is to be administered only by or under the immediate supervision of your doctor. It is available in the following dosage form:

Parenteral
- Injection (U.S. and Canada)

Before Using This Medicine

In deciding to use a medicine, the risks of taking the medicine must be weighed against the good it will do. This is a decision you and your doctor will make. For cisplatin, the following should be considered:

Allergies—Tell your doctor if you have ever had any unusual or allergic reaction to cisplatin.

Pregnancy—There is a chance that this medicine may cause birth defects if either the male or female is taking it at the time of conception or if it is taken during pregnancy. Cisplatin causes toxic or harmful effects in the fetus in humans and birth defects in mice. In addition, many cancer medicines may cause sterility which could be permanent. Although sterility has not been reported with this medicine, the possibility should be kept in mind.

Be sure that you have discussed this with your doctor before receiving this medicine. It is best to use some kind of birth control while you are receiving cisplatin. Tell your doctor right away if you think you have become pregnant while receiving cisplatin.

Breast-feeding—Because cisplatin may cause serious side effects, breast-feeding is generally not recommended while you are receiving it.

Children—Hearing problems and loss of balance are more likely to occur in children, who are usually more sensitive to the effects of cisplatin.

Older adults—Many medicines have not been studied specifically in older people. Therefore, it may not be known whether they work exactly the same way they do in younger adults or if they cause different side effects or problems in older people. There is no specific information comparing use of cisplatin in the elderly with use in other age groups.

Other medicines—Although certain medicines should not be used together at all, in other cases two different medicines may be used together even if an interaction might occur. In these cases, your doctor may want to change the dose, or other precautions may be necessary. When you are receiving cisplatin, it is especially important that your health care professional know if you are taking any of the following:

- Amphotericin B by injection (e.g., Fungizone) or
- Antithyroid agents (medicine for overactive thyroid) or
- Azathioprine (e.g., Imuran) or
- Chloramphenicol (e.g., Chloromycetin) or
- Colchicine or
- Flucytosine (e.g., Ancobon) or
- Ganciclovir (e.g., Cytovene) or
- Interferon (e.g., Intron A, Roferon-A) or
- Plicamycin (e.g., Mithracin) or
- Zidovudine (e.g., AZT, Retrovir) or
- If you have ever been treated with radiation or cancer medicines—Cisplatin may increase the effects of these medicines or radiation therapy on the blood
- Anti-infectives by mouth or by injection (medicine for infection) or
- Chloroquine (e.g., Aralen) or
- Combination pain medicine containing acetaminophen and aspirin (e.g., Excedrin) or other salicylates (with large amounts taken regularly) or
- Cyclosporine (e.g., Sandimmune) or
- Deferoxamine (e.g., Desferal) (with long-term use) or
- Gold salts (medicine for arthritis) or
- Hydroxychloroquine (e.g., Plaquenil) or
- Inflammation or pain medicine, except narcotics, or
- Lithium (e.g., Lithane) or
- Penicillamine (e.g., Cuprimine) or
- Plicamycin (e.g., Mithracin) or
- Quinine (e.g., Quinamm) or
- Tiopronin (e.g., Thiola)—Risk of ear and kidney problems caused by cisplatin is increased
- Probenecid (e.g., Benemid) or
- Sulfinpyrazone (e.g., Anturane)—Cisplatin may raise the amount of uric acid in the blood. Since these medicines are used to lower uric acid levels, they may not work as well in patients receiving cisplatin

Other medical problems—The presence of other medical problems may affect the use of cisplatin. Make sure you tell your doctor if you have any other medical problems, especially:

- Chickenpox (including recent exposure) or
- Herpes zoster (shingles)—Risk of severe disease affecting other parts of the body
- Gout (history of) or
- Kidney stones (history of)—Cisplatin may increase levels of uric acid in the body, which can cause gout or kidney stones

- Hearing problems—May be worsened by cisplatin
- Infection—Cisplatin decreases your body's ability to fight infection
- Kidney disease—Effects of cisplatin may be increased because of slower removal from the body

Proper Use of This Medicine

This medicine is sometimes given together with certain other medicines. If you are using a combination of medicines, it is important that you receive each one at the proper time. If you are taking some of these medicines by mouth, ask your health care professional to help you plan a way to take them at the right times.

While you are receiving this medicine, your doctor may want you to drink extra fluids so that you will pass more urine. This will help prevent kidney problems and keep your kidneys working well.

This medicine usually causes nausea and vomiting that may be severe. However, it is very important that you continue to receive the medicine, even if you begin to feel ill. Ask your health care professional for ways to lessen these effects, especially if they are severe.

Dosing—The dose of cisplatin will be different for different patients. The dose that is used may depend on a number of things, including what the medicine is being used for, the patient's size, and whether or not other medicines are also being taken. *If you are receiving cisplatin at home, follow your doctor's orders or the directions on the label.* If you have any questions about the proper dose of cisplatin, ask your doctor.

Precautions While Using This Medicine

It is very important that your doctor check your progress at regular visits to make sure that this medicine is working properly and to check for unwanted effects.

While you are being treated with cisplatin, and after you stop treatment with it, *do not have any immunizations (vaccinations) without your doctor's approval.* Cisplatin may lower your body's resistance and there is a chance you might get the infection the immunization is meant to prevent. In addition, other persons living in your household should not take oral polio vaccine since there is a chance they could pass the polio virus on to you. Also, avoid persons who have recently taken oral polio vaccine. Do not get close to them, and do not stay in the same room with them for very long. If you cannot take these precautions, you should consider wearing a protective face mask that covers the nose and mouth.

Cisplatin can temporarily lower the number of white blood cells in your blood, increasing the chance of getting an infection. It can also lower the number of platelets, which are necessary for proper blood clotting. If this occurs, there are certain precautions you can take, especially when your blood count is low, to reduce the risk of infection or bleeding:

- If you can, avoid people with infections. *Check with your doctor immediately* if you think you are getting an infection or if you get a fever or chills, cough or hoarseness, lower back or side pain, or painful or difficult urination.
- *Check with your doctor immediately* if you notice any unusual bleeding or bruising; black, tarry stools; blood in urine or stools; or pinpoint red spots on your skin.
- Be careful when using a regular toothbrush, dental floss, or toothpick. Your medical doctor, dentist, or nurse may recommend other ways to clean your teeth and gums. Check with your medical doctor before having any dental work done.
- Do not touch your eyes or the inside of your nose unless you have just washed your hands and have not touched anything else in the meantime.
- Be careful not to cut yourself when you are using sharp objects such as a safety razor or fingernail or toenail cutters.
- Avoid contact sports or other situations where bruising or injury could occur.

If cisplatin accidentally seeps out of the vein into which it is injected, it may damage some tissues and cause scarring. *Tell the doctor or nurse right away if you notice redness, pain, or swelling at the place of injection.*

Side Effects of This Medicine

Along with its needed effects, a medicine may cause unwanted effects. Although not all of these side effects may occur, if they do occur they may need medical attention.

Also, because of the way cancer medicines act on the body, there is a chance that they might cause other unwanted effects that may not occur until months or years after the medicine is used. These delayed effects may include certain types of cancer, such as leukemia. Discuss these possible effects with your doctor.

Check with your doctor or nurse immediately if any of the following side effects occur:

Less common

Black, tarry stools; blood in urine or stools; cough or hoarseness; dizziness or faintness (during or shortly after a dose); fast heartbeat (during or shortly after a dose); fever or chills; lower back or side pain; painful or difficult urination; pain or redness at place of injection; pinpoint red spots on skin; swelling of face (during or shortly after a dose); unusual bleeding or bruising; wheezing (during or shortly after a dose)

Check with your doctor as soon as possible if any of the following side effects occur:

More common

Joint pain; loss of balance; ringing in ears; swelling of feet or lower legs; trouble in hearing; unusual tiredness or weakness

Less common

Convulsions (seizures); loss of reflexes; loss of taste; numbness or tingling in fingers or toes; trouble in walking

Rare

Agitation or confusion; blurred vision; change in ability to see colors (especially blue or yellow); muscle cramps; sores in mouth and on lips

Other side effects may occur that usually do not need medical attention. These side effects may go away during treatment as your body adjusts to the medicine. Also, your health care professional may be able to tell you about ways to prevent or reduce some of these side effects. Check with your health care professional if any of the following side effects continue or are bothersome or if you have any questions about them:

More common

Nausea and vomiting (severe)

Less common

Loss of appetite

After you stop receiving cisplatin, it may still produce some side effects that need attention. During this period of time check with your doctor if you notice any of the following side effects:

Black, tarry stools; blood in urine or stools; convulsions (seizures); cough or hoarseness; decrease in urination; fever or chills; loss of balance; loss of reflexes; loss of taste; lower back or side pain; numbness or tingling in fingers or toes; painful or difficult urination; pinpoint red spots on skin; ringing in ears; swelling of feet or lower legs; trouble in hearing; trouble in walking; unusual bleeding or bruising

Other side effects not listed above may also occur in some patients. If you notice any other effects, check with your doctor.

Revised: 08/12/94

CITRATES Systemic

Some commonly used brand names are:

In the U.S.—

Bicitra[4]
Citrolith[3]
Oracit[4]
Polycitra-K[2]
Polycitra-K Crystals[2]
Polycitra-LC[5]
Polycitra Syrup[5]
Urocit-K[1]

In Canada—

Oracit[4]

Other commonly used names for sodium citrate and citric acid are Albright's solution and modified Shohl's solution.

Note: For quick reference, the following citrates are numbered to match the corresponding brand names.

This information applies to the following medicines:

1. Potassium Citrate (poe-TASS-ee-um SIH-trayt)
2. Potassium Citrate and Citric Acid (SIH-trik A-sid)
3. Potassium Citrate and Sodium (SOE-dee-um) Citrate
4. Sodium Citrate and Citric Acid
5. Tricitrates (Try-SIH-trayts)

Description

Citrates (SIH-trayts) are used to make the urine more alkaline (less acid). This helps prevent certain kinds of kidney stones. Citrates are sometimes used with other medicines to help treat kidney stones that may occur with gout. They are also used to make the blood more alkaline in certain conditions.

Citrates are available only with your doctor's prescription, in the following dosage forms:

Oral

Potassium Citrate
- Tablets (U.S.)

Potassium Citrate and Citric Acid
- Oral solution (U.S.)
- Crystals for oral solution (U.S.)

Potassium Citrate and Sodium Citrate
- Tablets (U.S.)

Sodium Citrate and Citric Acid
- Oral solution (U.S. and Canada)

Tricitrates
- Oral solution (U.S.)

Before Using This Medicine

In deciding to use a medicine, the risks of taking the medicine must be weighed against the good it will do. This is a decision you and your doctor will make. For citrates, the following should be considered:

Allergies—Tell your doctor if you have ever had any unusual or allergic reaction to potassium citrate or potassium. Also tell your health care professional if you are allergic to any other substances, such as foods, preservatives, or dyes.

Pregnancy—Studies on effects in pregnancy have not been done in either humans or animals.

Breast-feeding—Although it is not known whether citrates pass into the breast milk, this medicine has not been reported to cause problems in nursing babies.

Children—Although there is no specific information comparing use of citrates in children with use in other age groups, these medicines are not expected to cause different side effects or problems in children than they do in adults.

Older adults—Many medicines have not been studied specifically in older people. Therefore, it may not be known whether they work exactly the same way they do in younger adults or if they cause different side effects or problems in older people. There is no specific information comparing use of citrates in the elderly with use in other age groups.

Other medicines—Although certain medicines should not be used together at all, in other cases two different medicines may be used together even if an interaction might occur. In these cases, your doctor may want to change the dose, or other precautions may be necessary. When you are taking citrates, it is especially important that your health care professional know if you are taking any of the following:

- Amiloride (e.g., Midamor) or
- Benazepril (e.g., Lotensin) or
- Captopril (e.g., Capoten) or
- Digitalis glycosides (heart medicine) or
- Enalapril (e.g., Vasotec) or
- Fosinopril (e.g., Monotril) or
- Heparin (e.g., Panheprin) or
- Lisinopril (e.g., Prinivil; Zestril) or
- Medicines for inflammation or pain (except narcotics) or

- Potassium-containing medicines (other) or
- Quinapril (e.g., Accuprol) or
- Ramipril (e.g., Altase) or
- Salt substitutes, low-salt foods or milk or
- Spironolactone (e.g., Aldactone) or
- Triamterene (e.g., Dyrenium)—Use with potassium-containing citrates may further increase potassium blood levels, possibly leading to serious side effects
- Antacids, especially those containing aluminum or sodium bicarbonate—Use with citrates may increase the risk of kidney stones; also, citrates may increase the amount of aluminum in the blood and cause serious side effects, especially in patients with kidney problems
- Methenamine (e.g., Mandelamine)—Use with citrates may make the methenamine less effective
- Quinidine (e.g., Quinidex)—Use with citrates may cause quinidine to build up in the bloodstream, possibly leading to serious side effects

Other medical problems—The presence of other medical problems may affect the use of citrates. Make sure you tell your doctor if you have any other medical problems, especially:

- Addison's disease (underactive adrenal glands) or
- Diabetes mellitus (sugar diabetes) or
- Kidney disease—The potassium in potassium-containing citrates may worsen or cause heart problems in patients with these conditions
- Diarrhea (chronic)—Treatment with citrates may not be effective; a change in dose of citrate may be needed
- Edema (swelling of the feet or lower legs) or
- High blood pressure or
- Toxemia of pregnancy—The sodium in sodium-containing citrates may cause the body to retain (keep) water
- Heart disease—The sodium in sodium-containing citrates may cause the body to retain (keep) water; the potassium in potassium-containing citrates may make heart disease worse
- Intestinal or esophageal blockage—Potassium citrate tablets may cause irritation of the stomach or intestines
- Stomach ulcer or other stomach problems—Potassium citrate–containing products may make these conditions worse
- Urinary tract infection—Citrates may make conditions worse

Proper Use of This Medicine

For patients taking the *tablet form of this medicine:*

- Swallow the tablets whole. Do not crush, chew, or suck the tablet.
- Take with a full glass (8 ounces) of water.
- *If you have trouble swallowing the tablets or they seem to stick in your throat, check with your doctor at once.* If this medicine is not completely swallowed and not properly dissolved, it can cause severe irritation.

For patients taking the *liquid form of this medicine:*

- Dilute with a full glass (6 ounces) of water or juice and drink; follow with additional water, if desired.
- Chill, but do *not* freeze, this medicine before taking it, for a better taste.

For patients taking the *crystals form of this medicine:*

- Add the contents of one packet to at least 6 ounces of cool water or juice.
- Stir well to make sure the crystals are completely dissolved.
- Drink all the mixture to be sure you are taking the correct dose. Follow with additional water or juice, if desired.

Take each dose immediately after a meal or within 30 minutes after a meal or bedtime snack. This helps prevent the medicine from causing stomach pain or a laxative effect.

Drink at least a full glass (8 ounces) of water or other liquid (except milk) every hour during the day (about 3 quarts a day), unless otherwise directed by your doctor. This will increase the flow of urine and help prevent kidney stones.

Take this medicine only as directed by your doctor. Do not take more of it, do not take it more often, and do not take it for a longer time than your doctor ordered. *This is especially important if you are also taking a diuretic (water pill) or digitalis medicine for your heart.*

Dosing—The dose of these single or combination medicines will be different for different patients. *Follow your doctor's orders or the directions on the label.* The following information includes only the average doses of these medicines. *If your dose is different, do not change it* unless your doctor tells you to do so.

The number of tablets that you take or of teaspoonfuls or ounces of solution that you drink depends on the strength of the single or combination medicine. *Also, the number of doses you take each day, the time allowed between doses, and the length of time you take the medicine depend on the medical problem for which you are taking this single or combination medicine.*

For potassium citrate

- For *oral* dosage form (tablets):
  - —To make the urine more alkaline (less acidic) and to prevent kidney stones:
    - Adults—At first, 1.08 to 2.16 grams three times a day with meals. Some people may take 1.62 grams four times a day with meals or within thirty minutes after a meal or bedtime snack. Your doctor may change your dose if needed. However, most people usually will not take more than 10.8 grams a day.
    - Children—Dose must be determined by your doctor.

For potassium citrate and citric acid

- For *oral* dosage form (solution):
  - —To make the urine or blood more alkaline (less acidic) and to prevent kidney stones:
    - Adults—At first, 2 to 3 teaspoonfuls of solution, mixed with water or juice, four times a day, after meals and at bedtime. Your doctor may change the dose if needed.

—To make the urine more alkaline (less acidic):

- Children—At first, 1 to 3 teaspoonfuls of solution, mixed with water or juice, four times a day after meals and at bedtime. Your doctor may change the dose if needed.

- For *oral* dosage form (crystals for solution):

—To make the urine or blood more alkaline (less acidic) and to prevent kidney stones:

- Adults—At first, 3.3 grams of potassium citrate, mixed with water or juice, four times a day, after meals and at bedtime. Your doctor may change the dose if needed.
- Children—Use is not recommended.

For potassium citrate and sodium citrate

- For *oral* dosage form (tablets):

—To make the urine more alkaline (less acidic) and to prevent kidney stones:

- Adults—At first, 1 to 4 tablets after meals and at bedtime.
- Children—Dose must be determined by your doctor.

For sodium citrate and citric acid

- For *oral* dosage form (solution):

—To make the urine and blood more alkaline (less acidic) and to prevent kidney stones:

- Adults—At first, 2 to 6 teaspoonfuls of solution four times a day, after meals and at bedtime. The solution should be mixed in one to three ounces of water. Your doctor may change the dose if needed. However, most people will usually not take more than five ounces a day.

—To make the contents of the stomach less acidic before surgery:

- Adults—1 to 2 tablespoonfuls as a single dose. You may mix it in one to two tablespoonfuls of water.

—To make the blood more alkaline (less acidic):

- Children—At first, 1 to 3 teaspoonfuls of solution four times a day, after meals and at bedtime. The solution should be mixed in one to three ounces of water. Your doctor may change the dose if needed.

For tricitrates

- *For oral* dosage form (solution):

—To make the urine and blood more alkaline (less acidic) and to prevent kidney stones:

- Adults—At first, 1 to 2 tablespoonfuls of solution four times a day, after meals and at bedtime. Your doctor may change the dose if needed.

—To make the contents of the stomach less acidic before surgery:

- Adults—1 tablespoonful as a single dose. You should mix the solution in one tablespoonful of water.

—To make the urine or blood more alkaline (less acidic):

- Children—At first, 5 to 10 mL four times a day after meals and at bedtime. Your doctor may change the dose if needed.

Missed dose—If you miss a dose of this medicine, take it as soon as possible if remembered within 2 hours. However, if it is almost time for your next dose, skip the missed dose and go back to your regular dosing schedule. Do not double doses.

Storage—To store this medicine:

- Keep out of the reach of children.
- Store away from heat and direct light.
- Do not store in the bathroom, near the kitchen sink, or in other damp places. Heat or moisture may cause the medicine to break down.
- Keep the liquid form of this medicine from freezing.
- Do not keep outdated medicine or medicine no longer needed. Be sure that any discarded medicine is out of the reach of children.

Precautions While Using This Medicine

It is important that your doctor check your progress at regular visits. This is to make sure the medicine is working properly and to check for unwanted effects.

Do not eat salty foods or use extra table salt on your food while you are taking citrates. This will help prevent kidney stones and unwanted effects.

Check with your doctor before starting any strenuous physical exercise, especially if you are out of condition and are taking any other medication. Exercise and certain medications may increase the amount of potassium in the blood.

For patients taking *potassium citrate–containing medicines:*

- Do not use salt substitutes and low-salt milk unless told to do so by your doctor. They may contain potassium.
- *Check with your doctor at once if you are taking the tablet form and notice black, tarry stools or other signs of stomach or intestinal bleeding.*
- Do not be alarmed if you notice what appears to be a whole tablet in the stool after taking potassium citrate tablets. Your body has received the proper amount of medicine from the tablet and has expelled the tablet shell. However, it is a good idea to check with your doctor also.
- If you are on a potassium-rich or potassium-restricted diet, check with your health care professional. Potassium citrate–containing medicines contain a large amount of potassium.

For patients taking *sodium citrate–containing medicines:*

- If you are on a sodium-restricted diet, check with your health care professional. Sodium citrate–containing medicines contain a large amount of sodium.

Side Effects of This Medicine

Along with its needed effects, a medicine may cause some unwanted effects. Although not all of these side effects may occur, if they do occur they may need medical attention.

Stop taking this medicine and check with your doctor immediately if any of the following side effects occur:

Rare

Abdominal or stomach pain or cramping (severe); black, tarry stools; vomiting (severe), sometimes with blood

Also, check with your doctor as soon as possible if any of the following side effects occur:

Confusion; convulsions (seizures); dizziness; high blood pressure; irregular or fast heartbeat; irritability; mood or mental changes; muscle pain or twitching; nervousness or restlessness; numbness or tingling in hands, feet, or lips; shortness of breath, difficult breathing, or slow breathing; swelling of feet or lower legs; unexplained anxiety; unpleasant taste; unusual tiredness or weakness; weakness or heaviness of legs

Other side effects may occur that usually do not need medical attention. These side effects may go away during treatment as your body adjusts to the medicine. However, check with your doctor if any of the following side effects continue or are bothersome:

Less common

Abdominal or stomach soreness or pain (mild); diarrhea or loose bowel movements; nausea or vomiting

Other side effects not listed above may also occur in some patients. If you notice any other effects, check with your doctor.

Revised: 01/18/93
Interim revision: 08/29/94

CLADRIBINE Systemic

A commonly used brand name in the U.S. and Canada is Leustatin.

Other commonly used names are 2-chlorodeoxyadenosine and 2-CdA.

Description

Cladribine (KLAD-ri-been) belongs to the group of medicines called antimetabolites. It is used to treat hairy cell leukemia. It is also sometimes used to treat other kinds of cancer, as determined by your doctor.

Cladribine interferes with the growth of cancer cells, which are eventually destroyed. Since the growth of normal body cells may also be affected by cladribine, other effects will also occur. Some of these may be serious and must be reported to your doctor. Other effects may not be serious but may cause concern. Some effects may not occur for months or years after the medicine is used.

Before you begin treatment with cladribine, you and your doctor should talk about the good this medicine will do as well as the risks of using it.

Cladribine is to be administered only by or under the immediate supervision of your doctor. It is available in the following dosage form:

Parenteral

- Injection (U.S. and Canada)

Before Using This Medicine

In deciding to use a medicine, the risks of taking the medicine must be weighed against the good it will do. This is a decision you and your doctor will make. For cladribine, the following should be considered:

Allergies—Tell your doctor if you have ever had any unusual or allergic reaction to cladribine.

Pregnancy—There is a chance that this medicine may cause birth defects if either the male or female is taking it at the time of conception or if it is taken during pregnancy. Cladribine has been shown to cause birth defects in mice and rabbits. In addition, many cancer medicines may cause sterility which could be permanent. Although sterility has not been reported with this medicine, fertility problems do occur in male monkeys and the possibility should be kept in mind.

Be sure that you have discussed this with your doctor before receiving this medicine. It is best to use some kind of birth control while you are receiving cladribine. Tell your doctor right away if you think you have become pregnant while receiving cladribine.

Breast-feeding—It is not known whether cladribine passes into breast milk. However, because this medicine may cause serious side effects, breast-feeding is generally not recommended while you are receiving it.

Children—There is no specific information comparing use of cladribine in children with use in other age groups.

Older adults—Many medicines have not been studied specifically in older people. Therefore, it may not be known whether they work exactly the same way they do in younger adults. Although there is no specific information comparing use of cladribine in the elderly with use in other age groups, it is not expected to cause different side effects or problems in older people than it does in younger adults.

Other medicines—Although certain medicines should not be used together at all, in other cases two different medicines may be used together even if an interaction might occur. In these cases, your doctor may want to change the dose, or other precautions may be necessary. When you are receiving cladribine it is especially important that your health care professional know if you are taking any of the following:

- Amphotericin B by injection (e.g., Fungizone) or
- Antithyroid agents (medicine for overactive thyroid) or
- Azathioprine (e.g., Imuran) or

- Chloramphenicol (e.g., Chloromycetin) or
- Colchicine or
- Flucytosine (e.g., Ancobon) or
- Ganciclovir (e.g., Cytovene) or
- Interferon (e.g., Intron A, Roferon-A) or
- Plicamycin (e.g., Mithracin) or
- Zidovudine (e.g., AZT, Retrovir) or
- If you have ever been treated with radiation or cancer medicines—Cladribine may increase the effects of these medicines or radiation therapy on the blood
- Probenecid (e.g., Benemid) or
- Sulfinpyrazone (e.g., Anturane)—Cladribine may raise the amount of uric acid in the blood. Since these medicines are used to lower uric acid levels, they may not be as effective in patients receiving cladribine

Other medical problems—The presence of other medical problems may affect the use of cladribine. Make sure you tell your doctor if you have any other medical problems, especially:

- Chickenpox (including recent exposure) or
- Herpes zoster (shingles)—Risk of severe disease affecting other parts of the body
- Gout (history of) or
- Kidney stones (history of)—Cladribine may increase levels of uric acid in the body, which can cause gout or kidney stones
- Infection—Cladribine may decrease your body's ability to fight infection

Proper Use of This Medicine

This medicine may cause mild nausea and may also cause vomiting. However, it is very important that you continue to receive the medicine even if you begin to feel ill. Ask your health care professional for ways to lessen these effects.

Dosing—The dose of cladribine will be different for different patients. The dose that is used may depend on a number of things, including what the medicine is being used for, the patient's weight, and whether or not other medicines are also being taken. *If you are receiving cladribine at home, follow your doctor's orders or the directions on the label.* If you have any questions about the proper dose of cladribine, ask your doctor.

Precautions While Using This Medicine

It is very important that your doctor check your progress at regular visits to make sure that this medicine is working properly and to check for unwanted effects.

While you are being treated with cladribine, and after you stop treatment with it, *do not have any immunizations (vaccinations) without your doctor's approval.* Cladribine may lower your body's resistance and there is a chance you might get the infection the immunization is meant to prevent. In addition, other persons living in your household should not take oral polio vaccine since there is a chance they could pass the polio virus on to you. Also, avoid persons who have taken oral polio vaccine. Do not get close to them and do not stay in the same room with them for very long. If you cannot take these precautions, you should consider wearing a protective face mask that covers the nose and mouth.

Cladribine can temporarily lower the number of white blood cells in your blood, increasing the chance of getting an infection. It can also lower the number of platelets, which are necessary for proper blood clotting. If this occurs, there are certain precautions you can take, especially when your blood count is low, to reduce the risk of infection or bleeding:

- If you can, avoid people with infections, colds, or flu. *Check with your doctor immediately* if you think you are getting an infection or if you get a fever or chills, cough or hoarseness, lower back or side pain, or painful or difficult urination.
- *Check with your doctor immediately* if you notice any unusual bleeding or bruising; black, tarry stools; blood in urine or stools; or pinpoint red spots on your skin.
- Be careful when using a regular toothbrush, dental floss, or toothpick. Your medical doctor, dentist, or nurse may recommend other ways to clean your teeth and gums. Check with your medical doctor before having any dental work done.
- Do not touch your eyes or the inside of your nose unless you have just washed your hands and have not touched anything else in the meantime.
- Be careful not to cut yourself when you are using sharp objects such as a safety razor or fingernail or toenail cutters.
- Avoid contact sports or other situations where bruising or injury could occur.

Side Effects of This Medicine

Along with its needed effects, a medicine may cause some unwanted effects. Some side effects will have signs or symptoms that you can see or feel. Your doctor may watch for others by doing certain tests.

Also, because of the way cancer medicines act on the body, there is a chance that they might cause other unwanted effects that may not occur until months or years after the medicine is used. These delayed effects may include certain types of cancer. Discuss these possible effects with your doctor.

Check with your doctor or nurse immediately if any of the following side effects occur:

More common

Black, tarry stools; blood in urine; cough or hoarseness; chills; fever; lower back or side pain; painful or difficult urination; pinpoint red spots on skin; unusual bleeding or bruising

Check with your health care professional as soon as possible if any of the following side effects occur:

More common

Skin rash

Less common

Pain or redness at place of injection; shortness of breath; stomach pain; swelling of feet or lower legs; unusually fast heartbeat

This medicine may also cause the following side effects that your doctor will watch out for:

More common

Anemia; low white cell counts in blood

Other side effects may occur that usually do not need medical attention. These side effects may go away during treatment as your body adjusts to the medicine. Also, your health care professional may be able to tell you about ways to prevent or reduce some of these side effects. Check with your health care professional if any of the following side effects continue or are bothersome or if you have any questions about them:

More common

Headache; loss of appetite; nausea; unusual tiredness; vomiting

Less common

Constipation; diarrhea; dizziness; general feeling of discomfort or illness; itching; muscle or joint pain; sweating; trouble in sleeping; weakness

Other side effects not listed above may also occur in some patients. If you notice any other effects, check with your doctor.

Developed: 07/26/94
Interim revision: 08/15/94

CLARITHROMYCIN Systemic

A commonly used brand name in the U.S. and Canada is Biaxin.

Description

Clarithromycin (kla-RITH-roe-mye-sin) is used to treat bacterial infections in many different parts of the body. It works by killing bacteria or preventing their growth. It is also used to treat *Mycobacterium avium* complex (MAC) infection. However, this medicine will not work for colds, flu, or other virus infections. Clarithromycin may be used for other problems as determined by your doctor.

Clarithromycin is available only with your doctor's prescription, in the following dosage forms:

Oral

- Oral suspension (U.S.)
- Tablets (U.S. and Canada)

Before Using This Medicine

In deciding to use a medicine, the risks of taking the medicine must be weighed against the good it will do. This is a decision you and your doctor will make. For clarithromycin, the following should be considered:

Allergies—Tell your doctor if you have ever had any unusual or allergic reaction to clarithromycin or to any related medicines, such as erythromycin. Also tell your health care professional if you are allergic to any other substances, such as foods, preservatives, or dyes.

Pregnancy—Clarithromycin has not been studied in pregnant women. However, studies in animals have shown that clarithromycin causes birth defects and other problems. Before taking this medicine, make sure your doctor knows if you are pregnant or if you may become pregnant.

Breast-feeding—Clarithromycin passes into breast milk.

Children—Studies on this medicine have not been done in children up to 6 months of age. In effective doses, the medicine has not been shown to cause different side effects or problems in children over the age of 6 months than it does in adults.

Older adults—This medicine has been tested in a limited number of elderly patients and has not been shown to cause different side effects or problems in older people than it does in younger adults.

Other medicines—Although certain medicines should not be used together at all, in other cases two different medicines may be used together even if an interaction might occur. In these cases, your doctor may want to change the dose, or other precautions may be necessary. When you are taking clarithromycin, it is especially important that your health care professional know if you are taking any of the following:

- Carbamazepine (e.g., Tegretol) or
- Digoxin (e.g., Lanoxin) or
- Terfenadine (e.g., Seldane) or
- Theophylline (e.g., Theodur, Slo-Bid) or
- Warfarin (e.g., Coumadin)—Clarithromycin may increase the chance of side effects of these medicines
- Rifabutin (e.g., Mycobutin) or
- Rifampin (e.g., Rifadin)—Rifabutin or rifampin may decrease the amount of clarithromycin in the blood
- Zidovudine (e.g., Retrovir)—Clarithromycin may decrease the amount of zidovudine in the blood

Other medical problems—The presence of other medical problems may affect the use of clarithromycin. Make sure you tell your doctor if you have any other medical problems, especially:

- Kidney disease—Patients with severe kidney disease may have an increased chance of side effects

Proper Use of This Medicine

Clarithromycin may be taken with meals or milk or on an empty stomach.

To help clear up your infection completely, *keep taking clarithromycin for the full time of treatment,* even if you begin to feel better after a few days. If you stop taking this medicine too soon, your symptoms may return.

If you are using *clarithromycin oral suspension,* use a specially marked measuring spoon or other device to measure each dose accurately. The average household teaspoon may not hold the right amount of liquid.

Dosing—The dose of clarithromycin will be different for different patients. *Follow your doctor's orders or the directions on the label.* The following information includes only the average doses of clarithromycin. Your dose may be different if you have kidney disease. *If your dose is different, do not change it* unless your doctor tells you to do so.

The number of tablets or teaspoonfuls of suspension that you take depends on the strength of the medicine.

- For *oral* dosage forms (suspension and tablets):
  - —For bacterial infections:
    - Adults and teenagers—250 to 500 milligrams (mg) every twelve hours for seven to fourteen days.
    - Children 6 months of age and older—7.5 mg per kilogram (kg) (3.4 mg per pound) of body weight every twelve hours for ten days.
  - —For treatment of *Mycobacterium avium* complex (MAC):
    - Adults and teenagers—500 mg every twelve hours.
    - Children 6 months of age and older—7.5 mg per kg (3.4 mg per pound) of body weight, up to 500 mg, every twelve hours.

Missed dose—If you miss a dose of this medicine, take it as soon as possible. However, if it is almost time for your next dose, skip the missed dose and go back to your regular dosing schedule. Do not double doses.

Storage—To store this medicine:

- Keep out of the reach of children.
- Store away from heat and direct light.
- Do not store in the bathroom, near the kitchen sink, or in other damp places. Heat or moisture may cause the medicine to break down.
- Do not keep outdated medicine or medicine no longer needed. Be sure that any discarded medicine is out of the reach of children.
- Do not store suspension in the refrigerator.

Precautions While Using This Medicine

If your symptoms do not improve within a few days, or if they become worse, check with your doctor.

Side Effects of This Medicine

Along with its needed effects, a medicine may cause some unwanted effects. Although neither of these side effects may occur, if they do occur they may need medical attention. Check with your doctor as soon as possible if either of the following side effects occur:

Rare

Abdominal tenderness; fever; nausea and vomiting; severe abdominal or stomach cramps and pain; shortness of breath; skin rash and itching; unusual bleeding or bruising; watery and severe diarrhea, which may also be bloody; yellow eyes or skin

Other side effects may occur that usually do not need medical attention. These side effects may go away during treatment as your body adjusts to the medicine. However, check with your doctor if any of the following side effects continue or are bothersome:

Less common

Abnormal taste; diarrhea; headache

Other side effects not listed above may also occur in some patients. If you notice any other effects, check with your doctor.

Additional Information

Once a medicine has been approved for marketing for a certain use, experience may show that it is also useful for other medical problems. Although this use is not included in product labeling, clarithromycin is used in certain patients with the following medical condition:

- Legionnaires' disease

Other than the above information, there is no additional information relating to proper use, precautions, or side effects for this use.

Revised: 07/24/95

CLINDAMYCIN Systemic

Some commonly used brand names are:

In the U.S.—

Cleocin
Cleocin Pediatric

Generic name product may also be available.

In Canada—

Dalacin C
Dalacin C Palmitate
Dalacin C Phosphate

Description

Clindamycin (klin-da-MYE-sin) is used to treat bacterial infections. It will not work for colds, flu, or other virus infections.

Clindamycin is available only with your doctor's prescription, in the following dosage forms:

Oral

- Capsules (U.S. and Canada)
- Oral solution (U.S. and Canada)

Parenteral

- Injection (U.S. and Canada)

Before Using This Medicine

In deciding to use a medicine, the risks of taking the medicine must be weighed against the good it will do. This is a decision you and your doctor will make. For clindamycin, the following should be considered:

Allergies—Tell your doctor if you have ever had any unusual or allergic reaction to clindamycin, lincomycin, or doxorubicin. Also tell your health care professional if you are allergic to any other substances, such as foods, preservatives, or dyes.

Pregnancy—Clindamycin has not been reported to cause birth defects or other problems in humans.

Breast-feeding—Clindamycin passes into the breast milk. However, clindamycin has not been reported to cause problems in nursing babies.

Children—This medicine has been tested in children and, in effective doses, has not been reported to cause different side effects or problems than it does in adults.

Older adults—Many medicines have not been studied specifically in older people. Therefore, it may not be known whether they work exactly the same way they do in younger adults or if they cause different side effects or problems in older people. There is no specific information comparing use of clindamycin in the elderly with use in other age groups.

Other medicines—Although certain medicines should not be used together at all, in other cases two different medicines may be used together even if an interaction might occur. In these cases, your doctor may want to change the dose, or other precautions may be necessary. When you are taking clindamycin, it is especially important that your health care professional know if you are taking any of the following:

- Chloramphenicol (e.g., Chloromycetin) or
- Diarrhea medicine containing kaolin or attapulgite or
- Erythromycins (medicine for infection)—Taking these medicines along with clindamycin may decrease the effects of clindamycin

Other medical problems—The presence of other medical problems may affect the use of clindamycin. Make sure you tell your doctor if you have any other medical problems, especially:

- Kidney disease (severe) or
- Liver disease (severe)—Severe kidney or liver disease may increase blood levels of this medicine, increasing the chance of side effects
- Stomach or intestinal disease, history of (especially colitis, including colitis caused by antibiotics, or enteritis)—Patients with a history of stomach or intestinal disease may have an increased chance of side effects

Proper Use of This Medicine

For patients taking the *capsule form* of clindamycin:

- *The capsule form of clindamycin should be taken with a full glass (8 ounces) of water or with meals* to prevent irritation of the esophagus (tube between the throat and stomach).

For patients taking the *oral liquid form* of clindamycin:

- Use a specially marked measuring spoon or other device to measure each dose accurately. The average household teaspoon may not hold the right amount of liquid.
- Do not use after the expiration date on the label. The medicine may not work properly after this date. Check with your pharmacist if you have any questions about this.

To help clear up your infection completely, *keep taking this medicine for the full time of treatment,* even if you begin to feel better after a few days. *If you have a ''strep'' infection, you should keep taking this medicine for at least 10 days. This is especially important in ''strep'' infections. Serious heart problems could develop later* if your infection is not cleared up completely. Also, if you stop taking this medicine too soon, your symptoms may return.

This medicine works best when there is a constant amount in the blood. *To help keep the amount constant, do not miss any doses. Also, it is best to take each dose at evenly spaced times day and night.* For example, if you are to take 4 doses a day, doses should be spaced about 6 hours apart. If this interferes with your sleep or other daily activities, or if you need help in planning the best times to take your medicine, check with your health care professional.

Dosing—The dose of clindamycin will be different for different patients. *Follow your doctor's orders or the directions on the label.* The following information includes only the average doses of clindamycin. *If your dose is different, do not change it* unless your doctor tells you to do so.

The number of capsules or teaspoonfuls of solution that you take depends on the strength of the medicine. Also, *the number of doses you take each day, the time allowed between doses, and the length of time you take the medicine depend on the medical problem for which you are taking clindamycin.*

- For bacterial infection:
  - —For *oral* dosage forms (capsules and solution):
    - Adults and teenagers—150 to 300 milligrams (mg) every six hours.
    - Children—
      - —Infants up to 1 month of age: Use and dose must be determined by your doctor.
      - —Infants and children 1 month of age and older: Dose is based on body weight. The usual dose is 2 to 5 mg per kilogram (kg) (0.9 to 2.3 mg per pound) of body weight every six hours; or 2.7 to 6.7 mg per kg (1.2 to 3.0 mg per pound) of body weight every eight hours.
  - —For *injection* dosage form:
    - Adults and teenagers—300 to 600 mg every six to eight hours injected into a muscle or vein; or 900 mg every eight hours injected into a muscle or vein.
    - Children—
      - —Infants up to 1 month of age: Dose is based on body weight. The usual dose is 3.75 to 5 mg per kg (1.7 to 2.3 mg per pound) of body weight every six hours injected into a muscle or vein; or 5 to 6.7 mg per kg (2.3 to 3.0 mg per pound) of body weight every eight hours injected into a muscle or vein.
      - —Infants and children 1 month of age and older: Dose is based on body weight. The usual dose is 3.75 to 10 mg per kg (1.7 to 4.5

mg per pound) of body weight every six hours injected into a muscle or vein; or 5 to 13.3 mg per kg (2.3 to 6.0 mg per pound) of body weight every eight hours injected into a muscle or vein.

Missed dose—If you miss a dose of this medicine, take it as soon as possible. This will help to keep a constant amount of medicine in the blood. However, if it is almost time for your next dose, skip the missed dose and go back to your regular dosing schedule. Do not double doses.

Storage—To store this medicine:
- Keep out of the reach of children.
- Store away from heat and direct light.
- Do not store the capsule form of this medicine in the bathroom, near the kitchen sink, or in other damp places. Heat or moisture may cause the medicine to break down.
- Do not refrigerate the oral liquid form of clindamycin. If chilled, the liquid may thicken and be difficult to pour. Follow the directions on the label.
- Do not keep outdated medicine or medicine no longer needed. Be sure that any discarded medicine is out of the reach of children.

Precautions While Using This Medicine

It is important that your doctor check your progress at regular visits.

If your symptoms do not improve within a few days, or if they become worse, check with your doctor.

In some patients, clindamycin may cause diarrhea.
- Severe diarrhea may be a sign of a serious side effect. *Do not take any diarrhea medicine without first checking with your doctor.* Diarrhea medicines, such as loperamide (Imodium A-D) or diphenoxylate and atropine (Lomotil), may make your diarrhea worse or make it last longer.
- For mild diarrhea, diarrhea medicine containing attapulgite (e.g., Kaopectate tablets, Diasorb) may be taken. However, attapulgite may keep clindamycin from being absorbed into the body. Therefore, these diarrhea medicines should be taken at least 2 hours before or 3 to 4 hours after you take clindamycin by mouth.
- If you have any questions about this or if mild diarrhea continues or gets worse, check with your health care professional.

Before having surgery (including dental surgery) with a general anesthetic, tell the medical doctor or dentist in charge that you are taking clindamycin.

Side Effects of This Medicine

Along with its needed effects, a medicine may cause some unwanted effects. Although not all of these side effects may occur, if they do occur they may need medical attention.

Check with your doctor immediately if any of the following side effects occur:

More common

Abdominal or stomach cramps and pain (severe); abdominal tenderness; diarrhea (watery and severe), which may also be bloody; fever
(the above side effects may also occur up to several weeks after you stop taking this medicine)

Less common

Sore throat and fever; skin rash, redness, and itching; unusual bleeding or bruising

Other side effects may occur that usually do not need medical attention. These side effects may go away during treatment as your body adjusts to the medicine. However, check with your doctor if any of the following side effects continue or are bothersome:

More common

Diarrhea (mild); nausea and vomiting; stomach pain

Less common

Itching of rectal, or genital (sex organ) areas

Other side effects not listed above may also occur in some patients. If you notice any other effects, check with your doctor.

Revised: 08/12/92
Interim revision: 03/18/94; 04/19/95

CLINDAMYCIN Topical

Some commonly used brand names are:

In the U.S.

Cleocin T Gel
Cleocin T Lotion
Cleocin T Topical Solution
Clinda-Derm

Generic name product may also be available.

In Canada

Dalacin T Topical Solution

Description

Clindamycin (klin-da-MYE-sin) belongs to the family of medicines called antibiotics. Topical clindamycin is used to help control acne. It may be used alone or with one or more other medicines that are used on the skin or taken by mouth for acne. Topical clindamycin may also be used for other problems as determined by your doctor.

Clindamycin is available only with your doctor's prescription, in the following dosage forms:

Topical
- Gel (U.S.)
- Solution (U.S. and Canada)
- Suspension (U.S.)

Before Using This Medicine

In deciding to use a medicine, the risks of using the medicine must be weighed against the good it will do. This is

a decision you and your doctor will make. For topical clindamycin, the following should be considered:

Allergies—Tell your doctor if you have ever had any unusual or allergic reaction to this medicine or any of the other clindamycins (by mouth or by injection) or to lincomycin. Also tell your health care professional if you are allergic to any other substances, such as preservatives or dyes.

Pregnancy—Clindamycin has not been studied in pregnant women. However, this medicine has not been shown to cause birth defects or other problems in animal studies.

Breast-feeding—Small amounts of topical clindamycin are absorbed through the skin. It is possible that small amounts of the medicine may pass into the breast milk. However, this medicine has not been reported to cause problems in nursing babies.

Children—Studies on this medicine have been done only in adult patients, and there is no specific information comparing use of this medicine in children up to 12 years of age with use in other age groups.

Older adults—Many medicines have not been studied specifically in older people. Therefore, it may not be known whether they work exactly the same way they do in younger adults. Although there is no specific information comparing use of this medicine in the elderly with use in other age groups, this medicine is not expected to cause different side effects or problems in older people than it does in younger adults.

Other medicines—Although certain medicines should not be used together at all, in other cases two different medicines may be used together even if an interaction might occur. In these cases, your doctor may want to change the dose, or other precautions may be necessary. Tell your health care professional if you are using any other prescription or nonprescription (over-the-counter [OTC]) medicine.

Other medical problems—The presence of other medical problems may affect the use of topical clindamycin. Make sure you tell your doctor if you have any other medical problems, especially:

- History of stomach or intestinal disease (especially colitis, including colitis caused by antibiotics, or enteritis)—These conditions may increase the chance of side effects that affect the stomach and intestines

Proper Use of This Medicine

Before applying this medicine, thoroughly wash the affected areas with warm water and soap, rinse well, and pat dry.

When applying the medicine, use enough to cover the affected area lightly. *You should apply the medicine to the whole area usually affected by acne, not just to the pimples themselves.* This will help keep new pimples from breaking out.

You should avoid washing the acne-affected areas too often. This may dry your skin and make your acne worse. Washing with a mild, bland soap 2 or 3 times a day should be enough, unless you have oily skin. If you have any questions about this, check with your doctor.

Topical clindamycin will not cure your acne. However, to help keep your acne under control, *keep using this medicine for the full time of treatment,* even if your symptoms begin to clear up after a few days. You may have to continue using this medicine every day for months or even longer in some cases. If you stop using this medicine too soon, your symptoms may return. *It is important that you do not miss any doses.*

For patients using the *topical solution form* of clindamycin:

- After washing or shaving, it is best to wait 30 minutes before applying this medicine. The alcohol in it may irritate freshly washed or shaved skin.
- This medicine contains alcohol and is flammable. *Do not use near heat, near open flame, or while smoking.*
- To apply this medicine:

  —This medicine comes in a bottle with an applicator tip, which may be used to apply the medicine directly to the skin. Use the applicator with a dabbing motion instead of a rolling motion (not like a roll-on deodorant, for example). Tilt the bottle and press the tip firmly against your skin. If needed, you can make the medicine flow faster from the applicator tip by slightly increasing the pressure against the skin. If the medicine flows too fast, use less pressure. If the applicator tip becomes dry, turn the bottle upside down and press the tip several times to moisten it.

  —Since this medicine contains alcohol, it will sting or burn. In addition, it has an unpleasant taste if it gets on the mouth or lips. Therefore, *do not get this medicine in the eyes, nose, or mouth, or on other mucous membranes.* Spread the medicine away from these areas when applying. If this medicine does get in the eyes, wash them out immediately, but carefully, with large amounts of cool tap water. If your eyes still burn or are painful, check with your doctor.
- It is important that you do not use this medicine more often than your doctor ordered. It may cause your skin to become too dry or irritated.

For patients using the *topical suspension form* of clindamycin:

- *Shake well* before applying.

Dosing—The dose of topical clindamycin will be different for different patients. *Follow your doctor's orders or the directions on the label.* The following information includes only the average doses of topical clindamycin. *If your dose is different, do not change it* unless your doctor tells you to do so.

The number of doses you use each day, the time allowed between doses, and the length of time you use the medicine depend on the medical problem for which you are using clindamycin.

- For *topical* dosage forms (gel, solution, and suspension):
  —For acne:
  - Adults and children 12 years of age and over—Apply two times a day to areas affected by acne.
  - Infants and children up to 12 years of age—Use and dose must be determined by your doctor.

Missed dose—If you miss a dose of this medicine, apply it as soon as possible. However, if it is almost time for your next dose, skip the missed dose and go back to your regular dosing schedule.

Storage—To store this medicine:
- Keep out of the reach of children.
- Store away from heat and direct light.
- Keep the medicine from freezing.
- Do not keep outdated medicine or medicine no longer needed. Be sure that any discarded medicine is out of the reach of children.

Precautions While Using This Medicine

If your acne does not improve within about 6 weeks, or if it becomes worse, check with your health care professional. However, treatment of acne may take up to 8 to 12 weeks before full improvement is seen.

If your doctor has ordered another medicine to be applied to the skin along with this medicine, it is best to apply them at different times. This may help keep your skin from becoming too irritated. Also, if the medicines are used at or near the same time, they may not work properly.

For patients using the *topical solution form* of clindamycin:
- This medicine may cause the skin to become unusually dry, even with normal use. If this occurs, check with your doctor.

In some patients, clindamycin may cause diarrhea.
- Severe diarrhea may be a sign of a serious side effect. *Do not take any diarrhea medicine without first checking with your doctor.* Diarrhea medicines may make your diarrhea worse or make it last longer.
- For mild diarrhea, only diarrhea medicine containing attapulgite (e.g., Kaopectate, Diasorb) may be taken. Other kinds of diarrhea medicine (e.g., Imodium A.D. or Lomotil) should not be taken. They may make your condition worse or make it last longer.
- If you have any questions about this or if mild diarrhea continues or gets worse, check with your health care professional.

You may continue to use cosmetics (make-up) while you are using this medicine for acne. However, it is best to use only ''water-base'' cosmetics. Also, it is best not to use cosmetics too heavily or too often. They may make your acne worse. If you have any questions about this, check with your doctor.

Side Effects of This Medicine

Along with its needed effects, a medicine may cause some unwanted effects. Although not all of these side effects may occur, if they do occur they may need medical attention.

Check with your doctor immediately if any of the following side effects occur:

Rare

Abdominal or stomach cramps, pain, and bloating (severe); diarrhea (watery and severe), which may also be bloody; fever; increased thirst; nausea or vomiting; unusual tiredness or weakness; weight loss (unusual)—these side effects may also occur up to several weeks after you stop using this medicine

Also, check with your doctor as soon as possible if any of the following side effects occur:

Less common

Skin rash, itching, redness, swelling, or other sign of irritation not present before use of this medicine

Other side effects may occur that usually do not need medical attention. These side effects may go away during treatment as your body adjusts to the medicine. However, check with your doctor if any of the following side effects continue or are bothersome:

More common

Dryness, scaliness, or peeling of skin (for the topical solution)

Less common

Abdominal pain; diarrhea (mild); irritation or oiliness of skin; stinging or burning feeling of skin

Other side effects not listed above may also occur in some patients. If you notice any other effects, check with your doctor.

Revised: 02/22/94

CLINDAMYCIN Vaginal

Some commonly used brand names are:

In the U.S.—
Cleocin

In Canada—
Dalacin

Description

Clindamycin (klin-da-MYE-sin) is used to treat certain vaginal infections. It works by killing the bacteria. This medicine will not work for vaginal fungus or yeast infections.

Clindamycin is available only with your doctor's prescription, in the following dosage form:

Vaginal

- Cream (U.S. and Canada)

Before Using This Medicine

In deciding to use a medicine, the risks of taking the medicine must be weighed against the good it will do. This is a decision you and your doctor will make. For vaginal clindamycin, the following should be considered:

Allergies—Tell your doctor if you have ever had any unusual or allergic reaction to clindamycin or lincomycin (e.g., Lincocin). Also tell your health care professional if you are allergic to any other substances, such as foods, preservatives, or dyes.

Pregnancy—Vaginal clindamycin is used during the second trimester of pregnancy. It was found to cause birth defects in one strain of mouse, but has not caused problems in other animials. Vaginal clindamycin has not been reported to cause birth defects or other problems in humans.

Breast-feeding—It is not known whether clindamycin used vaginally passes into the breast milk. Clindamycin taken by mouth does pass into the breast milk and has not been reported to cause problems in nursing babies. Although most medicines pass into the breast milk in small amounts, many of them may be used safely while breast-feeding. Mothers who are using this medicine and who wish to breast-feed should discuss this with their doctor.

Children—Studies on this medicine have been done only in adult patients, and there is no specific information comparing use of vaginal clindamycin in children with use in other age groups.

Older adults—Many medicines have not been studied specifically in older people. Therefore, it may not be known whether they work exactly the same way they do in younger adults or if they cause different side effects or problems in older people. There is no specific information comparing use of vaginal clindamycin in the elderly with use in other age groups.

Other medicines—Although certain medicines should not be used together at all, in other cases two different medicines may be used together even if an interaction might occur. In these cases, your doctor may want to change the dose, or other precautions may be necessary. Tell your health care professional if you are taking or using any other prescription or nonprescription (over-the-counter [OTC]) medicine.

Other medical problems—The presence of other medical problems may affect the use of vaginal clindamycin. Make sure you tell your doctor if you have any other medical problems, especially:

- Stomach or intestinal disease, history of (especially colitis, including colitis caused by antibiotics, or enteritis)—Patients with a history of stomach or intestinal disease may have an increased chance of side effects including diarrhea

Proper Use of This Medicine

Wash your hands before and after using this medicine.

Avoid getting this medicine in your eyes. If this medicine does get into your eyes, rinse them immediately with large amounts of cool tap water. If your eyes still burn or are painful, check with your doctor.

Vaginal clindamycin usually comes with patient directions. Read them carefully before using this medicine.

Use clindamycin vaginal cream exactly as directed by your doctor.

- *To fill the applicator*
  - —Remove cap from the tube.
  - —Screw one of the applicators onto the tube. Always use a new applicator. Never use one that has been used before.
  - —Squeeze the medicine into the applicator slowly until it is full.
  - —Remove the applicator from the tube. Replace the cap on the tube.
- *To insert the vaginal cream using the applicator*
  - —Relax while lying on your back with your knees bent.
  - —Hold the full applicator in one hand. Insert it slowly into the vagina. Stop before it becomes uncomfortable.
  - —Slowly press the plunger until it stops.
  - —Withdraw the applicator. The medicine will be left behind in the vagina.
- *To care for the applicator*
  - —Throw the applicator away after you use it.

To help clear up your infection completely, *it is very important that you keep using this medicine for the full time of treatment,* even if your symptoms begin to clear up after a few days. If you stop using this medicine too soon, your symptoms may return. *Do not miss any doses.* Also, *continue using this medicine even if your menstrual period starts during the time of treatment.*

Dosing—The dose of vaginal clindamycin will be different for different patients. The following information includes only the average dose of vaginal clindamycin. *If your dose is different, do not change it* unless your doctor tells you to do so.

- For *vaginal cream* dosage form:
  - —For bacterial vaginosis:
    - Adults and teenagers—One applicatorful (100 milligrams [mg]) inserted into the vagina once a day, usually at bedtime, for seven days.
    - Children—Use and dose must be determined by your doctor.

Missed dose—If you miss a dose of this medicine, use it as soon as possible. However, if it is almost time for your next dose, skip the missed dose and go back to your regular dosing schedule. Do not double doses.

Storage—To store this medicine:
- Keep out of the reach of children.
- Store away from heat and direct light.
- Keep the medicine from freezing. Do not refrigerate.
- Do not keep outdated medicine or medicine no longer needed. Be sure that any discarded medicine is out of the reach of children.

Precautions While Using This Medicine

If your symptoms do not improve within a few days, or if they become worse, check with your doctor.

It is important that you visit your doctor after you have used all your medicine to make sure that the infection is gone.

This medicine may cause some people to become dizzy. Make sure you know how you react to this medicine before you drive, use machines, or do anything else that could be dangerous if you are dizzy.

Vaginal medicines usually leak out of the vagina during treatment. To keep the medicine from getting on your clothing, wear a minipad or sanitary napkin. Do not use tampons since they may soak up the medicine.

To help clear up your infection completely and make sure it does not return, good health habits are also required.
- Wear cotton panties (or panties or pantyhose with cotton crotches) instead of synthetic (for example, nylon or rayon) panties.
- Wear only freshly washed panties daily.

Do not have sexual intercourse while you are using this medicine. Having sexual intercourse may reduce the strength of the medicine. This may cause the medicine to not work as well.

Do not use latex (rubber) contraceptive products such as condoms, diaphragms, or cervical caps for 72 hours after stopping treatment with vaginal clindamycin cream. The cream contains oils that weaken or harm the latex products, causing them to not work properly to prevent pregnancy. If you have any questions about this, check with your health care professional.

Side Effects of This Medicine

Along with its needed effects, a medicine may cause some unwanted effects. Although not all of these side effects may occur, if they do occur they may need medical attention.

Check with your doctor as soon as possible if any of the following side effects occur:

More common

Itching of the vagina or genital area; pain during sexual intercourse; thick, white vaginal discharge with no odor or with mild odor

Less common

Diarrhea; dizziness; headache; nausea or vomiting; stomach pain or cramps

Rare

Burning, itching, rash, redness, swelling or other signs of skin problems not present before use of this medicine

After you stop using this medicine, your body may need time to adjust. The length of time this takes depends on the amount of medicine you were using and how long you used it. During this period of time, check with your doctor if you notice any of the following side effects:

Itching of the vagina or genital area; pain during sexual intercourse; thick, white vaginal discharge with no odor or with mild odor

Other side effects not listed above may also occur in some patients. If you notice any other effects, check with your doctor.

Revised: 08/19/97

CLIOQUINOL Topical

A commonly used brand name in the U.S. and Canada is Vioform.

Another commonly used name is iodochlorhydroxyquin.

Description

Clioquinol (klye-oh-KWIN-ole) belongs to the family of medicines called anti-infectives. Clioquinol topical preparations are used to treat skin infections.

Clioquinol is available without a prescription; however, your doctor may have special instructions on the proper use of this medicine for your medical problem. It is available in the following dosage forms:

Topical
- Cream (U.S. and Canada)
- Ointment (U.S. and Canada)

Before Using This Medicine

If you are using this medicine without a prescription, carefully read and follow any precautions on the label. For clioquinol, the following should be considered:

Allergies—Tell your doctor if you have ever had any unusual or allergic reaction to clioquinol, chloroxine (e.g., capitrol), iodine, or iodine-containing preparations. Also tell your health care professional if you are allergic to any other substances, such as preservatives or dyes.

Pregnancy—Clioquinol topical preparations have not been shown to cause birth defects or other problems in humans.

Breast-feeding—Clioquinol topical preparations have not been reported to cause problems in nursing babies.

Children—Clioquinol is not recommended in children under 2 years of age. Although there is no specific information comparing use of this medicine in children 2 years of age and over with use in other age groups, this medicine is not expected to cause different side effects or problems in children than it does in adults.

Older adults—Many medicines have not been studied specifically in older people. Therefore, it may not be known whether they work exactly the same way they do in younger adults. Although there is no specific information comparing use of this medicine in the elderly with use in other age groups, this medicine is not expected to cause different side effects or problems in older people than it does in younger adults.

Other medicines—Although certain medicines should not be used together at all, in other cases two different medicines may be used together even if an interaction might occur. In these cases, your doctor may want to change the dose, or other precautions may be necessary. Tell your health care professional if you are using any other prescription or nonprescription (over-the-counter [OTC]) medicine.

Proper Use of This Medicine

Before applying this medicine, wash the affected area with soap and water, and dry thoroughly.

Do not use this medicine in or around the eyes.

To use the *cream form* of this medicine:

- Apply a thin layer of cream to the affected area and rub in gently until the cream disappears.

To use the *ointment form* of this medicine:

- Apply a thin layer of ointment to the affected area and rub in gently.

To help clear up your infection completely, *keep using this medicine for the full time of treatment,* even if your symptoms have disappeared. *Do not miss any doses.*

Dosing—The dose of clioquinol will be different for different patients. *Follow your doctor's orders or the directions on the label.* The following information includes only the average dose of clioquinol. *If your dose is different, do not change it* unless your doctor tells you to do so.

- For *topical* dosage forms (cream or ointment):
  - —For bacterial or fungus infections:
    - Adults and children 2 years of age and over—Apply to the affected area(s) of the skin two or three times a day.
    - Children up to 2 years of age—Use is not recommended.

Missed dose—If you miss a dose of this medicine, apply it as soon as possible. However, if it is almost time for your next dose, skip the missed dose and go back to your regular dosing schedule.

Storage—To store this medicine:

- Keep out of the reach of children.
- Store away from heat and direct light.
- Keep the medicine from freezing.
- Do not keep outdated medicine or medicine no longer needed. Be sure that any discarded medicine is out of the reach of children.

Precautions While Using This Medicine

If your skin problem does not improve within 1 to 2 weeks, or if it becomes worse, check with your doctor.

This medicine may stain clothing, skin, hair, and nails yellow. Avoid getting this medicine on your clothing since bleaching may not remove the stain.

Before you have any medical tests, tell the doctor in charge that you are using this medicine. The results of some tests may be affected by this medicine.

Side Effects of This Medicine

Along with its needed effects, a medicine may cause some unwanted effects. Although not all of these side effects may occur, if they do occur they may need medical attention.

Check with your doctor immediately if any of the following side effects occur:

Rare

Itching, rash, redness, swelling, or other sign of skin irritation not present before use of this medicine

Other side effects not listed above may also occur in some patients. If you notice any other effects, check with your doctor.

Revised: 02/10/92
Interim revision: 06/03/94

CLIOQUINOL AND HYDROCORTISONE Topical

Some commonly used brand names are:

In the U.S.—

Vioform-Hydrocortisone Cream
Vioform-Hydrocortisone Lotion
Vioform-Hydrocortisone Mild Cream
Vioform-Hydrocortisone Mild Ointment
Vioform-Hydrocortisone Ointment

In Canada—

Vioform-Hydrocortisone Cream
Vioform-Hydrocortisone Mild Cream
Vioform-Hydrocortisone Ointment

Another commonly used name is iodochlorhyroxyquin and hydrocortisone.

Description

Clioquinol (klye-oh-KWIN-ole) and hydrocortisone (hye-droe-KOR-ti-sone) is a combined anti-infective and cortisone-like medicine. Clioquinol and hydrocortisone topical preparations are used to treat infections of the skin and to help provide relief from the redness, itching, and discomfort of many skin problems.

Clioquinol and hydrocortisone combination is available only with your doctor's prescription, in the following dosage forms:

Topical
- Cream (U.S. and Canada)
- Lotion (U.S.)
- Ointment (U.S. and Canada)

Before Using This Medicine

In deciding to use a medicine, the risks of taking the medicine must be weighed against the good it will do. This is a decision you and your doctor will make. For clioquinol and hydrocortisone combination, the following should be considered:

Allergies—Tell your doctor if you have ever had any unusual or allergic reaction to clioquinol, hydrocortisone, chloroxine (e.g., Capitrol), iodine, or iodine-containing preparations. Also tell your health care professional if you are allergic to any other substances, such as preservatives or dyes.

Pregnancy—Clioquinol and hydrocortisone topical preparations may be absorbed through the mother's skin. This medicine has not been shown to cause birth defects or other problems in humans. However, studies in animals have shown that it causes birth defects. Use of large amounts on the skin or use for a long time is not recommended during pregnancy.

Breast-feeding—Clioquinol and hydrocortisone topical preparations have not been reported to cause problems in nursing babies.

Children—Clioquinol and hydrocortisone combination is not recommended in children up to 2 years of age. Although there is no specific information comparing use of clioquinol and hydrocortisone combination in children over 2 years of age with use in other age groups, this medicine is not expected to cause different side effects or problems in these children than it does in adults.

Older adults—Many medicines have not been studied specifically in older people. Therefore, it may not be known whether they work exactly the same way they do in younger adults. Although there is no specific information comparing use of clioquinol and hydrocortisone combination in the elderly with use in other age groups, this medicine is not expected to cause different side effects or problems in older people than it does in younger adults.

Other medicines—Although certain medicines should not be used together at all, in other cases two different medicines may be used together even if an interaction might occur. In these cases, your doctor may want to change the dose, or other precautions may be necessary. Tell your health care professional if you are using any other prescription or nonprescription (over-the-counter [OTC]) medicine.

Other medical problems—The presence of other medical problems may affect the use of clioquinol and hydrocortisone topical preparations. Make sure you tell your doctor if you have any other medical problems, especially:

- Skin infection (other)—Use of clioquinol and hydrocortisone topical preparations may make the condition worse

Proper Use of This Medicine

Before applying this medicine, wash the affected area with soap and water, and dry thoroughly.

Do not use this medicine in or around the eyes or on infants and children up to 2 years of age.

To use the *cream form* of this medicine:
- Apply a thin layer of cream to the affected area and rub in gently until cream disappears.

To use the *lotion form* of this medicine:
- Gently squeeze bottle and apply a few drops of lotion to the affected area. Rub in gently until lotion disappears.

To use the *ointment form* of this medicine:
- Apply a thin layer of ointment to the affected area and rub in gently.

Do not bandage or otherwise wrap the area of the skin being treated unless directed to do so by your doctor.

Check with your doctor before using this medicine on any other skin problems. It should not be used on certain kinds of bacterial, virus, or fungus skin infections.

To help clear up your infection completely, *keep using this medicine for the full time of treatment,* even if your symptoms have disappeared. *Do not miss any doses.* However, *do not use this medicine more often or for a longer time than your doctor ordered.* To do so may increase the chance of absorption through the skin and the chance of side effects. In addition, too much use, especially on thin skin areas (for example, face, armpits, groin), may result in thinning of the skin and stretch marks.

Dosing—The dose of clioquinol and hydrocortisone combination will be different for different patients. *Follow your doctor's orders or the directions on the label.* The following information includes only the average dose of clioquinol and hydrocortisone combination. *If your dose is different, do not change it* unless your doctor tells you to do so.

- For *topical* dosage forms (cream, lotion, or ointment):
  - —For bacterial and fungus infections:
    - Adults, teenagers, and children 2 years of age and over—Apply to the affected area(s) of the skin three or four times a day.
    - Children up to 2 years of age—Use is not recommended.

Missed dose—If you miss a dose of this medicine, apply it as soon as possible. However, if it is almost time for your next dose, skip the missed dose and go back to your regular dosing schedule.

Storage—To store this medicine:
- Keep out of the reach of children.
- Store away from heat and direct light.
- Keep the medicine from freezing.
- Do not keep outdated medicine or medicine no longer needed. Be sure that any discarded medicine is out of the reach of children.

Precautions While Using This Medicine

If your skin problem does not improve within 1 to 2 weeks, or if it becomes worse, check with your doctor.

This medicine may be absorbed through the skin, and too much use can affect growth. *Children who must use this medicine should be followed closely by their doctor.*

This medicine may stain clothing, skin, hair, and nails yellow. Avoid getting this medicine on your clothing. Bleaching may not remove the stain.

Side Effects of This Medicine

Along with its needed effects, a medicine may cause some unwanted effects. Although not all of these side effects may occur, if they do occur they may need medical attention.

Check with your doctor immediately if any of the following side effects occur:

Rare

Blistering, burning, itching, peeling, skin rash, redness, swelling, or other sign of irritation not present before use of this medicine

With prolonged use

Thinning of skin with easy bruising

Other side effects not listed above may also occur in some patients. If you notice any other effects, check with your doctor.

Revised: 02/10/92
Interim revision: 07/14/94

CLOFAZIMINE Systemic†

A commonly used brand name in the U.S. is Lamprene.

†Not commercially available in Canada.

Description

Clofazimine (kloe-FA-zi-meen) is taken to treat leprosy (Hansen's disease). It is sometimes given with other medicines for leprosy. When this medicine is used to treat "flare-ups" of leprosy, it may be given with a cortisone-like medicine. Clofazimine may also be used for other problems as determined by your doctor.

This medicine is available only with your doctor's prescription, in the following dosage form:

Oral
- Capsules (U.S.)

Before Using This Medicine

In deciding to use a medicine, the risks of taking the medicine must be weighed against the good it will do. This is a decision you and your doctor will make. For clofazimine, the following should be considered:

Allergies—Tell your doctor if you have ever had any unusual or allergic reaction to clofazimine. Also tell your health care professional if you are allergic to any other substances, such as foods, preservatives, or dyes.

Pregnancy—Clofazimine has not been studied in pregnant women. Although the skin of babies born to mothers who took clofazimine during pregnancy was deeply discolored, this medicine has not been shown to cause birth defects or other problems in humans. A gradual fading of the discoloration may occur over a period of about a year. Some animal studies have not shown that clofazimine causes birth defects. However, studies in mice have shown that clofazimine may cause slow bone formation of the skull and a decrease in successful pregnancies. Before you take clofazimine, make sure your doctor knows if you are pregnant or if you may become pregnant.

Breast-feeding—Clofazimine passes into the breast milk. Use is not recommended in nursing mothers.

Children—Studies on this medicine have been done only in adult patients, and there is no specific information comparing use of clofazimine in children with use in other age groups.

Older adults—Many medicines have not been studied specifically in older people. Therefore, it may not be known whether they work exactly the same way they do in younger adults or if they cause different side effects or problems in older people. There is no specific information comparing use of clofazimine in the elderly with use in other age groups.

Other medicines—Although certain medicines should not be used together at all, in other cases two different medicines may be used together even if an interaction might occur. In these cases, your doctor may want to change the dose, or other precautions may be necessary. Tell your health care professional if you are taking any other prescription or nonprescription (over-the-counter [OTC]) medicine.

Other medical problems—The presence of other medical problems may affect the use of clofazimine. Make sure you tell your doctor if you have any other medical problems, especially:
- Liver disease—Clofazimine may on rare occasion cause hepatitis and liver disease
- Stomach or intestinal problems, history of—Clofazimine often causes some stomach upset, but on rare occasion may cause severe, sharp abdominal pain and burning, which may be a sign of a serious side effect

Proper Use of This Medicine

Clofazimine should be taken with meals or milk.

To help clear up your leprosy completely, *it is very important that you keep taking clofazimine for the full time of treatment,* even if you begin to feel better after a few months. You may have to take it every day for as long as 2 years to life. If you stop taking this medicine too soon, your symptoms may return.

This medicine works best when there is a constant amount in the blood. *To help keep the amount constant, do not miss any doses. Also, it is best to take each dose at the same time every day.* If you need help in planning the best time to take your medicine, check with your health care professional.

Dosing—The dose of clofazimine will be different for different patients. *Follow your doctor's orders or the directions on the label.* The following information includes only the average doses of clofazimine. *If your dose is different, do not change it* unless your doctor tells you to do so.

The number of capsules that you take depends on the strength of the medicine. Also, *the number of doses you take each day, the time allowed between doses, and the length of time you take the medicine depend on the medical problem for which you are taking clofazimine.*

- For the *treatment of leprosy (Hansen's disease):*
  - —Adults and teenagers: 50 to 100 milligrams once a day. This medicine must be taken with other medicines for the treatment of Hansen's disease.
  - —Children: Dose must be determined by the doctor.

Missed dose—If you miss a dose of this medicine, take it as soon as possible. However, if it is almost time for your next dose, skip the missed dose and go back to your regular dosing schedule. Do not double doses.

Storage—To store this medicine:

- Keep out of the reach of children.
- Store away from heat and direct light.
- Do not store in the bathroom, near the kitchen sink, or in other damp places. Heat or moisture may cause the medicine to break down.
- Do not keep outdated medicine or medicine no longer needed. Be sure that any discarded medicine is out of the reach of children.

Precautions While Using This Medicine

If your symptoms do not improve within 1 to 3 months, or if they become worse, check with your doctor. It may take up to 6 months before the full benefit of this medicine is seen.

Clofazimine may cause pink or red to brownish-black discoloration of the skin within a few weeks after you start taking it. Because of the skin discoloration, some patients may become depressed. The discoloration will go away when you stop taking this medicine. However, it may take several months or years for the skin to clear up completely. *If skin discoloration causes you to feel very depressed or to have thoughts of suicide, check with your doctor immediately.*

This medicine may cause some people to become dizzy, drowsy, or less alert than they are normally. *Make sure you know how you react to this medicine before you drive, use machines, or do anything else that could be dangerous if you are dizzy or are not alert or able to see well.* If these reactions are especially bothersome, check with your doctor.

Clofazimine may cause your skin to become more sensitive to sunlight than it is normally. Exposure to sunlight, even for brief periods of time, may cause a skin rash, itching, redness, or other discoloration of the skin, or a severe sunburn. When you begin taking this medicine:

- Stay out of direct sunlight, especially between the hours of 10:00 a.m. and 3:00 p.m., if possible.
- Wear protective clothing, including a hat. Also, wear sunglasses.
- Apply a sun block product that has a skin protection factor (SPF) of at least 15. Some patients may require a product with a higher SPF number, especially if they have a fair complexion. If you have any questions about this, check with your health care professional.
- Apply a sun block lipstick that has an SPF of at least 15 to protect your lips.
- Do not use a sunlamp or tanning bed or booth.

If you have a severe reaction, check with your doctor.

Clofazimine may also cause dry, rough, or scaly skin. A skin cream, lotion, or oil may help to treat this problem.

Side Effects of This Medicine

Along with its needed effects, a medicine may cause some unwanted effects. Although not all of these side effects may occur, if they do occur they may need medical attention.

Check with your doctor immediately if any of the following side effects occur:

Rare

Bloody or black, tarry stools; colicky or burning abdominal or stomach pain; mental depression; yellow eyes or skin—may be an orange color if already have a pink to brownish-black skin or eye discoloration

Other side effects may occur that usually do not need medical attention. These side effects may go away during treatment as your body adjusts to the medicine. However, check with your doctor if any of the following side effects continue or are bothersome:

More common

Diarrhea; dry, rough, or scaly skin; loss of appetite; nausea or vomiting; pink or red to brownish-black discoloration of skin and eyes; skin rash and itching

Less common or rare

Changes in taste; dryness, burning, itching, or irritation of the eyes; increased sensitivity of skin to sunlight

Clofazimine commonly causes discoloration of the feces, lining of the eyelids, sputum, sweat, tears, and urine. Usually this side effect does not require medical attention, but the discoloration may not go away. However, *clofazimine may also cause bloody or black, tarry stools. This side effect may be a symptom of serious bleeding problems that do require medical attention.*

Other side effects not listed above may also occur in some patients. If you notice any other effects, check with your doctor.

Revised: 02/23/93

CLOFIBRATE Systemic

Some commonly used brand names are:

In the U.S.—

Abitrate

Atromid-S

Generic name product may also be available.

In Canada—

Atromid-S

Claripex

Novofibrate

Description

Clofibrate (kloe-FYE-brate) is used to lower cholesterol and triglyceride (fat-like substances) levels in the blood. This may help prevent medical problems caused by such substances clogging the blood vessels.

Clofibrate may also be used for other conditions as determined by your doctor.

Clofibrate is available only with your doctor's prescription, in the following dosage form:

Oral

- Capsules (U.S. and Canada)

Before Using This Medicine

In addition to its helpful effects in treating your medical problem, this medicine may have some harmful effects.

You may have read or heard about a study called the World Health Organization (WHO) Study. This study compared the effects in patients who used clofibrate with effects in those who used a placebo (sugar pill). The results of this study suggested that clofibrate might increase the patient's risk of cancer, liver disease, and pancreatitis (inflammation of the pancreas), although it might also decrease the risk of heart attack. It may also increase the risk of gallstones and problems from gallbladder surgery. Other studies have not found all of these effects. Be sure you have discussed this with your doctor before taking this medicine.

In deciding to use a medicine, the risks of taking the medicine must be weighed against the good it will do. This is a decision you and your doctor will make. For clofibrate, the following should be considered:

Allergies—Tell your doctor if you have ever had any unusual or allergic reaction to clofibrate. Also tell your health care professional if you are allergic to any other substances, such as foods, preservatives, or dyes.

Diet—Before prescribing medicine for your condition, your doctor will probably try to control your condition by prescribing a personal diet for you. Such a diet may be low in fats, sugars, and/or cholesterol. Many people are able to control their condition by carefully following their doctors' orders for proper diet and exercise. *Medicine is prescribed only when additional help is needed* and is effective only when a schedule of diet and exercise is properly followed.

Also, this medicine is less effective if you are greatly overweight. It may be very important for you to go on a reducing diet. However, check with your doctor before going on any diet.

Make certain your health care professional knows if you are on a low-sodium, low-sugar, or any other special diet. Most medicines contain more than their active ingredient.

Pregnancy—Use of clofibrate is not recommended during pregnancy. Although studies have not been done in pregnant women, studies in rabbits have shown that the fetus may not be able to break down and get rid of this medicine as well as the mother. Because of this, it is possible that clofibrate may be harmful to the fetus if you take it while you are pregnant or for up to several months before you become pregnant. Be sure that you have discussed this with your doctor before taking this medicine, especially if you plan to become pregnant in the near future.

Breast-feeding—Clofibrate passes into breast milk. This medicine is not recommended during breast-feeding because it may cause unwanted effects in nursing babies.

Children—Studies on this medicine have been done only in adult patients, and there is no specific information comparing use of clofibrate in children with use in other age groups. However, use is not recommended in children under 2 years of age since cholesterol is needed for normal development.

Older adults—Many medicines have not been studied specifically in older people. Therefore, it may not be known whether they work exactly the same way they do in younger adults. Although there is no specific information comparing use of clofibrate in the elderly with use in other age groups, this medicine is not expected to cause different side effects or problems in older people than it does in younger adults.

Other medicines—Although certain medicines should not be used together at all, in other cases two different medicines may be used together even if an interaction might occur. In these cases, your doctor may want to change the dose, or other precautions may be necessary. When you are taking clofibrate, it is especially important that your health care professional knows if you are taking the following:

- Anticoagulants (blood thinners)—Use with clofibrate may increase the effects of the anticoagulant

Other medical problems—The presence of other medical problems may affect the use of clofibrate. Make sure you tell your doctor if you have any other medical problems, especially:

- Gallstones or
- Stomach or intestinal ulcer—May make these conditions worse
- Heart disease or
- Kidney disease or
- Liver disease—Higher blood levels may result and increase the risk of side effects
- Underactive thyroid—Clofibrate may cause or make muscle disease worse

Proper Use of This Medicine

Use this medicine only as directed by your doctor. Do not use more or less of it, and do not use it more often or for a longer time than your doctor ordered.

Follow carefully the special diet your doctor gave you. This is the most important part of controlling your condition and is necessary if the medicine is to work properly.

Stomach upset may occur but usually lessens after a few doses. Take this medicine with food or immediately after meals to lessen possible stomach upset.

Dosing—The dose of clofibrate will be different for different patients. *Follow your doctor's orders or the directions on the label.* The following information includes only the average doses of clofibrate. *If your dose is different, do not change it* unless your doctor tells you to do so.

The number of capsules that you take depends on the strength of the medicine.

- For *oral* dosage form (capsules):
  - —For high cholesterol:
    - Adults—1.5 to 2 grams a day. This is divided into two to four doses.
    - Children—Dose must be determined by your doctor.

Missed dose—If you miss a dose of this medicine, take it as soon as possible. However, if it is almost time for your next dose, skip the missed dose and go back to your regular dosing schedule. Do not double doses.

Storage—To store this medicine:

- Keep out of the reach of children.
- Store away from heat and direct light.
- Do not store in the bathroom, near the kitchen sink, or in other damp places. Heat or moisture may cause the medicine to break down.
- Do not keep outdated medicine or medicine no longer needed. Be sure that any discarded medicine is out of the reach of children.

Precautions While Using This Medicine

It is very important that your doctor check your progress at regular visits. This will allow your doctor to see if the medicine is working properly to lower your cholesterol and triglyceride levels and to decide if you should continue to take it.

Do not stop taking this medicine without first checking with your doctor. When you stop taking this medicine, your blood fat levels may increase again. Your doctor may want you to follow a special diet to help prevent that.

Side Effects of This Medicine

Along with its needed effects, a medicine may cause some unwanted effects. Although not all of these side effects may occur, if they do occur they may need medical attention.

Check with your doctor immediately if you think you have taken an overdose or if any of the following side effects occur:

Rare

Chest pain; irregular heartbeat; shortness of breath; stomach pain (severe) with nausea and vomiting

Check with your doctor as soon as possible if any of the following side effects occur:

Rare

Blood in urine; cough or hoarseness; decrease in urination; fever or chills; lower back or side pain; painful or difficult urination; swelling of feet or lower legs

Other side effects may occur that usually do not need medical attention. These side effects may go away during treatment as your body adjusts to the medicine. However, check with your doctor if any of the following side effects continue or are bothersome:

More common

Diarrhea; nausea

Less common or rare

Decreased sexual ability; headache; increased appetite or weight gain (slight); muscle aches or cramps; sores in mouth and on lips; stomach pain, gas, or heartburn; unusual tiredness or weakness; vomiting

Other side effects not listed above may also occur in some patients. If you notice any other effects, check with your doctor.

Additional Information

Once a medicine has been approved for marketing for a certain use, experience may show that it is also useful for other medical problems. Although this use is not included in product labeling, clofibrate is used in certain patients with the following medical condition:

- Certain types of diabetes insipidus (water diabetes)

Other than the above information, there is no additional information relating to proper use, precautions, or side effects for this use.

Revised: 11/24/92
Interim revision: 04/14/94

CLOMIPHENE Systemic

Some commonly used brand names are:

In the U.S.—

Clomid
Milophene
Serophene

Generic name product may also be available.

In Canada—

Clomid
Serophene

Other commonly used names are clomifene and clomifene citrate.

Description

Clomiphene (KLOE-mi-feen) is used as a fertility medicine in some women who are unable to become pregnant.

Clomiphene probably works by changing the hormone balance of the body. In women, this causes ovulation to occur and prepares the body for pregnancy.

Clomiphene may also be used for other conditions in both females and males as determined by your doctor.

The following information applies only to female patients taking clomiphene. Check with your doctor if you are a male and have any questions about the use of clomiphene.

Clomiphene is available only with your doctor's prescription, in the following dosage form:

Oral

- Tablets (U.S. and Canada)

Before Using This Medicine

In deciding to use a medicine, the risks of taking the medicine must be weighed against the good it will do. This is a decision you and your doctor will make. For clomiphene, the following should be considered:

Allergies—Tell your doctor if you have ever had any unusual or allergic reaction to clomiphene. Also tell your health care professional if you are allergic to any other substances, such as foods, preservatives, or dyes.

Pregnancy—There is a chance that clomiphene may cause birth defects if it is taken after you become pregnant. *Stop taking this medicine and tell your doctor immediately if you think you have become pregnant* while still taking clomiphene.

If you become pregnant as a result of using this medicine, there is a chance of a multiple birth (for example, twins, triplets) occurring.

Breast-feeding—It is not known if clomiphene passes into breast milk. However, this medicine stops milk from being produced.

Other medicines—Although certain medicines should not be used together at all, in other cases two different medicines may be used together even if an interaction might occur. In these cases, your doctor may want to change the dose, or other precautions may be necessary. When you are taking clomiphene, it is especially important that your health care professional know if you are taking any other prescription or nonprescription (over-the-counter [OTC]) medicine.

Other medical problems—The presence of other medical problems may affect the use of clomiphene. Make sure you tell your doctor if you have any other medical problems, especially:

- Unusually large ovary or
- Cyst on ovary—Clomiphene may cause the cyst to increase in size
- Endometriosis—Inducing ovulation (including using clomiphene) may worsen endometriosis because the body estrogen level is increased; estrogen can cause growth of endometriosis implants
- Fibroid tumors of the uterus—Clomiphene may cause fibroid tumors to increase in size
- Inflamed veins due to blood clots—Clomiphene may make condition worse
- Liver disease (or history of)—Clomiphene may make any liver disease worse
- Mental depression—Existing depression may become worse because of hormone changes caused by clomiphene
- Unusual vaginal bleeding—Some irregular vaginal bleeding is a sign that the lining of the uterus is growing too much or is a sign of cancer of the uterus lining; these problems must be ruled out before clomiphene is used because clomiphene can make these conditions worse

Proper Use of This Medicine

Take this medicine only as directed by your doctor. If you are to begin on Day 5, count the first day of your menstrual period as Day 1. Beginning on Day 5, take the correct dose every day for as many days as your doctor ordered. To help you to remember to take your dose of medicine, take it at the same time every day.

Dosing—The dose of clomiphene will be different for different patients. *Follow your doctor's orders or the directions on the label.* The following information includes only the average doses of clomiphene. *If your dose is different, do not change it* unless your doctor tells you to do so.

- For *oral* dosage form (tablets):
  - —For treating infertility:
    - Adults—50 milligrams (mg) a day for five days of a menstrual cycle. The treatment is usually started on the fifth day of your menstrual period. If you do not have menstrual cycles, you can begin taking your medicine at any time. If you do not become pregnant after the first course, your doctor may increase your dose a little at a time up to 250 mg a day. Your treatment may be repeated until you do become pregnant or for up to four treatment cycles.

Missed dose—If you miss a dose of this medicine, take it as soon as possible. If you do not remember until it is time for the next dose, take both doses together; then go back to your regular dosing schedule. If you miss more than one dose, check with your doctor.

Storage—To store this medicine:

- Keep out of the reach of children.
- Store away from heat and direct light.
- Do not store in the bathroom, near the kitchen sink, or in other damp places. Heat or moisture may cause the medicine to break down.
- Do not keep outdated medicine or medicine no longer needed. Be sure that any discarded medicine is out of the reach of children.

Precautions While Using This Medicine

It is very important that your doctor check your progress at regular visits to make sure this medicine is working and to check for unwanted effects.

At certain times in your menstrual cycle, your doctor may want you to use an ovulation prediction test kit. *Follow your doctor's instructions carefully.* Ovulation is controlled by luteinizing hormone (LH). LH is present in the blood and urine in very small amounts during most of the menstrual cycle but rises suddenly for a short time in the middle of the menstrual cycle. This sharp rise, the LH surge, usually causes ovulation within about 30 hours. A woman is most likely to become pregnant if she has intercourse within the 24 hours after detecting the LH surge. Ovulation prediction test kits are used to test for this large amount of LH in the urine. This method is better for predicting ovulation than measuring daily basal body temperature. It is important that intercourse take place at the correct time to give you the best chance of becoming pregnant.

There is a chance that clomiphene may cause birth defects if it is taken after you become pregnant. *Stop taking this medicine and tell your doctor immediately if you think you have become pregnant* while still taking clomiphene.

This medicine may cause blurred vision, difficulty in reading, or other changes in vision. It may also cause some people to become dizzy or lightheaded. *Make sure you know how you react to this medicine before you drive, use machines, or do anything else that could be dangerous if you are not clear-headed or able to see well.* If these reactions are especially bothersome, check with your doctor.

Side Effects of This Medicine

Along with its needed effects, a medicine may cause some unwanted effects. Although not all of these side effects may occur, if they do occur they may need medical attention.

When this medicine is used for a short time at low doses, serious side effects usually are rare. *However, check with your doctor immediately* if any of the following side effects occur:

More common

Bloating; stomach or pelvic pain

Check with your doctor as soon as possible if any of the following side effects occur:

Less common or rare

Blurred vision; decreased or double vision or other vision problems; seeing flashes of light; sensitivity of eyes to light; yellow eyes or skin

Other side effects may occur that usually do not need medical attention. These side effects may go away during treatment as your body adjusts to the medicine. However, check with your doctor if any of the following side effects continue or are bothersome:

More common

Hot flashes

Less common or rare

Breast discomfort; dizziness or lightheadedness; headache; heavy menstrual periods or bleeding between periods; mental depression; nausea or vomiting; nervousness; restlessness; tiredness; trouble in sleeping

Other side effects not listed above may also occur in some patients. If you notice any other effects, check with your doctor.

Additional Information

Once a medicine has been approved for marketing for a certain use, experience may show that it is also useful for other medical problems. Although these uses are not included in product labeling, clomiphene is used in certain patients with the following medical conditions:

- Certain problems of the male sexual organs caused by pituitary or hypothalamus gland problems (diagnosis)
- Male infertility caused by low production of sperm
- Problems with the corpus luteum (mature egg)

For males taking this medicine for treatment of infertility caused by low sperm production:

- To help decide on the best treatment for your medical problem, tell your doctor:
  —if you have ever had any unusual or allergic reaction to clomiphene.
  —if you have either of the following medical problems:
    - Liver disease
    - Mental depression
    - Thrombophlebitis
- If you miss a dose of this medicine, take it as soon as possible. If you do not remember until it is time for the next dose, take both doses together; then go back to your regular dosing schedule. If you miss more than one dose, check with your doctor.
- *It is important that your doctor check your progress at regular visits to find out if clomiphene is working and to check for unwanted effects.*
- This medicine may cause vision problems, dizziness, or lightheadedness. *Make sure you know how you react to this medicine before you drive, use machines, or do anything else that could be dangerous if you are not clear-headed or able to see well.*
- Along with its needed effects, a medicine may cause some unwanted effects. Although not all of these side effects may occur, if they do occur they may need medical attention. When this medicine is used for short periods of time at low doses, serious side effects usually are rare. However, check with your doctor if any of the following side effects occur:

  Less common or rare

  Blurred vision; decreased or double vision or other vision problems; seeing flashes of light; sensitivity of eyes to light; yellow eyes or skin

- Other side effects may occur that usually do not need medical attention. These side effects may go away during treatment as your body adjusts to the medicine. However, check with your doctor if any of the following side effects continue or are bothersome:

  Less common or rare

  Breast enlargement; dizziness or lightheadedness; headache; mental depression; nausea or vomiting; nervousness; restlessness; tiredness; trouble in sleeping

Other than the above information, there is no additional information relating to proper use, precautions, or side effects for these uses.

Revised: 08/08/95

CLONIDINE Systemic

Some commonly used brand names are:

In the U.S.—

Catapres
Catapres-TTS

Generic name product may also be available.

In Canada—

Catapres
Dixarit

Description

Clonidine (KLOE-ni-deen) belongs to the general class of medicines called antihypertensives. It is used to treat high blood pressure (hypertension).

High blood pressure adds to the work load of the heart and arteries. If it continues for a long time, the heart and arteries may not function properly. This can damage the blood vessels of the brain, heart, and kidneys, resulting in a stroke, heart failure, or kidney failure. Hypertension may also increase the risk of heart attacks. These problems may be less likely to occur if blood pressure is controlled.

Clonidine works by controlling nerve impulses along certain nerve pathways. As a result, it relaxes blood vessels so that blood passes through them more easily. This helps to lower blood pressure.

Clonidine may also be used for other conditions as determined by your doctor.

Clonidine is available only with your doctor's prescription, in the following dosage forms:

Oral

- Tablets (U.S. and Canada)

Transdermal

- Skin patch (U.S.)

Before Using This Medicine

In deciding to use a medicine, the risks of taking the medicine must be weighed against the good it will do. This is a decision you and your doctor will make. For clonidine, the following should be considered:

Allergies—Tell your doctor if you have ever had any unusual or allergic reaction to clonidine. Also tell your health care professional if you are allergic to any other substance, such as foods, preservatives, or dyes.

Pregnancy—Clonidine has not been studied in pregnant women. However, studies in animals have shown that clonidine causes harmful effects in the fetus, but not birth defects.

Breast-feeding—Although clonidine passes into breast milk, it has not been reported to cause problems in nursing babies.

Children—Children may be more sensitive than adults to clonidine. Clonidine overdose has been reported when children accidentally took this medicine.

Older adults—Dizziness or faintness may be more likely to occur in the elderly, who are more sensitive than younger adults to the effects of clonidine.

Other medicines—Although certain medicines should not be used together at all, in other cases two different medicines may be used together even if an interaction might occur. In these cases, your doctor may want to change the dose, or other precautions may be necessary. When you are taking clonidine, it is especially important that your health care professional know if you are taking any of the following:

- Beta-blockers (acebutolol [e.g., Sectral], atenolol [e.g., Tenormin], betaxolol [e.g., Kerlone], carteolol [e.g., Cartrol], labetalol [e.g., Normodyne], metoprolol [e.g., Lopressor], nadolol [e.g., Corgard], oxprenolol [e.g., Trasicor], penbutolol [e.g., Levatol], pindolol [e.g., Visken], propranolol [e.g., Inderal], sotalol [e.g., Sotacor], timolol [e.g., Blocadren])—These medicines may increase the risk of harmful effects when clonidine treatment is stopped suddenly
- Tricyclic antidepressants (amitriptyline [e.g., Elavil], amoxapine [e.g., Asendin], clomipramine [e.g., Anafranil], desipramine [e.g., Pertofrane], doxepin [e.g., Sinequan], imipramine [e.g., Tofranil], nortriptyline [e.g., Aventyl], protriptyline [e.g., Vivactil], trimipramine [e.g., Surmontil])—These medicines may decrease clonidine's effects on blood pressure

Other medical problems—The presence of other medical problems may affect the use of clonidine. Make sure you tell your doctor if you have any other medical problems, especially:

- Heart or blood vessel disease—Clonidine may make these conditions worse
- Irritated or scraped skin (with transdermal system [skin patch] only)—The effects of clonidine may be increased if the skin patch is placed on an area of scraped or irritated skin because more medicine is absorbed into the body
- Kidney disease—Effects of clonidine may be increased because of slower removal of clonidine from the body
- Mental depression (history of) or
- Raynaud's syndrome—Clonidine may make these conditions worse
- Polyarteritis nodosa or

- Scleroderma or
- Systemic lupus erythematosus (SLE)—with transdermal system (skin patch) only—Effects of clonidine may be decreased because absorption of this medicine into the body is blocked

Proper Use of This Medicine

For patients taking this medicine *for high blood pressure:*

- In addition to the use of the medicine your doctor has prescribed, treatment for your high blood pressure may include weight control and care in the types of foods you eat, especially foods high in sodium. Your doctor will tell you which of these are most important for you. You should check with your doctor before changing your diet.
- Many patients who have high blood pressure will not notice any signs of the problem. In fact, many may feel normal. It is very important that you *take your medicine exactly as directed* and that you keep your appointments with your doctor even if you feel well.
- Remember that this medicine will not cure your high blood pressure but it does help control it. Therefore, you must continue to use it as directed if you expect to lower your blood pressure and keep it down. *You may have to take high blood pressure medicine for the rest of your life.* If high blood pressure is not treated, it can cause serious problems such as heart failure, blood vessel disease, stroke, or kidney disease.

For patients using the *transdermal system (skin patch):*

- *Use this medicine exactly as directed by your doctor.* It will work only if applied correctly. *This medicine usually comes with patient instructions. Read them carefully before using.*
- Do not try to trim or cut the adhesive patch to adjust the dosage. Check with your doctor if you think the medicine is not working as it should.
- Apply the patch to a clean, dry area of skin on your upper arm or chest. Choose an area with little or no hair and free of scars, cuts, or irritation.
- The system should stay in place even during showering, bathing, or swimming. If the patch becomes loose, cover it with the extra adhesive overlay provided. Apply a new patch if the first one becomes too loose or falls off.
- Each dose is best applied to a different area of skin to prevent skin problems or other irritation.
- After removing a used patch, fold the patch in half with the sticky sides together. Make sure to dispose of it out of the reach of children.

To help you remember to use your medicine, try to get into the habit of using it at regular times. If you are taking the tablets, take them at the same time each day. If you are using the transdermal system (skin patch), try to change it at the same time and day of the week.

Dosing—The dose of clonidine will be different for different patients. *Follow your doctor's orders or the directions on the label.* The following information includes only the average doses of clonidine used for the treatment of high blood pressure. *If your dose is different, do not change it* unless your doctor tells you to do so:

- For *oral* dosage form (tablets):
  - —For high blood pressure:
    - Adults—100 mcg (0.1 mg) two times a day. Your doctor may increase your dose up to 200 mcg (0.2 mg) to 600 mcg (0.6 mg) a day taken in divided doses.
    - Children—Use and dose must be determined by your doctor.
- For *transdermal* dosage form (skin patch):
  - —For high blood pressure:
    - Adults—One transdermal dosage system (skin patch) applied once a week.
    - Children—Use and dose must be determined by your doctor.

Missed dose—If you miss a dose of this medicine, take it or use it as soon as possible. Then go back to your regular dosing schedule. *If you miss 2 or more doses of the tablets in a row or if you miss changing the transdermal patch for 3 or more days, check with your doctor right away.* If your body goes without this medicine for too long, your blood pressure may go up to a dangerously high level and some unpleasant effects may occur.

Storage—To store this medicine:

- Keep out of the reach of children.
- Store away from heat and direct light.
- Do not store in the bathroom, near the kitchen sink, or in other damp places. Heat or moisture may cause the medicine to break down.
- Do not keep outdated medicine or medicine no longer needed. Be sure that any discarded medicine is out of the reach of children.

Precautions While Using This Medicine

It is important that your doctor check your progress at regular visits to make sure that this medicine is working properly.

Check with your doctor before you stop using this medicine. Your doctor may want you to reduce gradually the amount you are using before stopping completely.

Make sure that you have enough clonidine on hand to last through weekends, holidays, or vacations. You should not miss any doses. You may want to ask your doctor for another written prescription for clonidine to carry in your wallet or purse. You can then have it filled if you run out of medicine when you are away from home.

For patients taking this medicine *for high blood pressure:*

- *Do not take other medicines unless they have been discussed with your doctor.* This especially includes over-the-counter (nonprescription) medicines for appetite control, asthma, colds, cough, hay fever, or sinus problems, since they may tend to increase your blood pressure.

Clonidine will add to the effects of alcohol and other CNS depressants (medicines that slow down the nervous system, possibly causing drowsiness). Some examples of

CNS depressants are antihistamines or medicine for hay fever, other allergies, or colds; sedatives, tranquilizers, or sleeping medicine; prescription pain medicine or narcotics; barbiturates; medicine for seizures; muscle relaxants; or anesthetics, including some dental anesthetics. *Check with your doctor before taking any of the above while you are using this medicine.*

Clonidine may cause some people to become drowsy or less alert than they are normally. This is more likely to happen when you begin to take it or when you increase the amount of medicine you are taking. *Make sure you know how you react to this medicine before you drive, use machines, or do anything else that could be dangerous if you are not alert.*

Before having any kind of surgery (including dental surgery) or emergency treatment, *tell the medical doctor or dentist in charge that you are using this medicine.*

Dizziness, lightheadedness, or fainting may occur after you take this medicine, especially when you get up from a lying or sitting position. Getting up slowly may help, but if the problem continues or gets worse, check with your doctor.

The dizziness, lightheadedness, or fainting is also more likely to occur if you drink alcohol, stand for long periods of time, exercise, or if the weather is hot. While you are taking clonidine, be careful to limit the amount of alcohol you drink. Also, use extra care during exercise or hot weather or if you must stand for a long time.

Clonidine may cause dryness of the mouth. For temporary relief, use sugarless candy or gum, melt bits of ice in your mouth, or use a saliva substitute. However, if your mouth continues to feel dry for more than 2 weeks, check with your medical doctor or dentist. Continuing dryness of the mouth may increase the chance of dental disease, including tooth decay, gum disease, and fungus infections.

Side Effects of This Medicine

Along with its needed effects, a medicine may cause some unwanted effects. Although not all of these side effects may occur, if they do occur they may need medical attention.

Check with your doctor immediately if any of the following side effects occur:

Signs and symptoms of overdose

Difficulty in breathing; dizziness (extreme) or faintness; pinpoint pupils of eyes; slow heartbeat; unusual tiredness or weakness (extreme)

Check with your doctor as soon as possible if any of the following side effects occur:

More common—with transdermal system (skin patch) only

Itching or redness of skin

Less common

Mental depression; swelling of feet and lower legs

Rare

Paleness or cold feeling in fingertips and toes; vivid dreams or nightmares

Other side effects may occur that usually do not need medical attention. These side effects may go away during treatment as your body adjusts to the medicine. However, check with your doctor if any of the following side effects continue or are bothersome:

More common

Constipation; dizziness; drowsiness; dryness of mouth; unusual tiredness or weakness

Less common

Darkening of skin—with transdermal system (skin patch) only; decreased sexual ability; dizziness, lightheadedness, or fainting, especially when getting up from a lying or sitting position; dry, itching, or burning eyes; loss of appetite; nausea or vomiting; nervousness

After you have been using this medicine for a while, it may cause unpleasant or even harmful effects if you stop taking it too suddenly. After you stop taking this medicine, *check with your doctor immediately* if any of the following occur:

Anxiety or tenseness; chest pain; fast or pounding heartbeat; headache; increased salivation; nausea; nervousness; restlessness; shaking or trembling of hands and fingers; stomach cramps; sweating; trouble in sleeping; vomiting

Other side effects not listed above may also occur in some patients. If you notice any other effects, check with your doctor.

Additional Information

Once a medicine has been approved for marketing for a certain use, experience may show that it is also useful for other medical problems. Although these uses are not included in product labeling, clonidine is used in certain patients with the following medical conditions:

- Migraine headache
- Symptoms associated with menopause or menstrual discomfort
- Symptoms of withdrawal associated with alcohol, nicotine, or narcotics
- Gilles de la Tourette's syndrome

Other than the above information, there is no additional information relating to proper use, precautions, or side effects for these uses.

Revised: 05/17/93

CLONIDINE AND CHLORTHALIDONE Systemic

A commonly used brand name in the U.S. and Canada is Combipres. Generic name product may also be available in the U.S.

Description

Clonidine (KLOE-ni-deen) and chlorthalidone (klor-THAL-i-done) combinations are used in the treatment of high blood pressure (hypertension).

High blood pressure adds to the work load of the heart and arteries. If it continues for a long time, the heart and arteries may not function properly. This can damage the blood vessels of the brain, heart, and kidneys resulting in a stroke, heart failure, or kidney failure. Hypertension may also increase the risk of heart attacks. These problems may be less likely to occur if blood pressure is controlled.

Clonidine works by controlling nerve impulses along certain body nerve pathways. As a result, it relaxes blood vessels so that blood passes through them more easily. The chlorthalidone in this combination is a diuretic (water pill) that helps reduce the amount of water in the body by increasing the flow of urine.

Clonidine and chlorthalidone combination is available only with your doctor's prescription, in the following dosage form:

Oral

- Tablets (U.S. and Canada)

Before Using This Medicine

In deciding to use a medicine, the risks of taking the medicine must be weighed against the good it will do. This is a decision you and your doctor will make. For clonidine and chlorthalidone, the following should be considered:

Allergies—Tell your doctor if you have ever had any unusual or allergic reaction to clonidine, chlorthalidone, sulfonamides (sulfa drugs), or other thiazide diuretics (water pills). Also tell your health care professional if you are allergic to any other substance, such as foods, preservatives, or dyes.

Pregnancy—Clonidine has not been studied in pregnant women. However, studies in animals have shown that clonidine does not cause birth defects but does cause other harmful effects in the fetus. When chlorthalidone is used during pregnancy, it may cause side effects including jaundice, blood problems, and low potassium in the newborn infant. Be sure you have discussed this with your doctor before taking this medicine.

Breast-feeding—Both clonidine and chlorthalidone pass into breast milk. Chlorthalidone may decrease the flow of breast milk. Therefore, you should avoid use of clonidine and chlorthalidone combination during the first month of breast-feeding.

Children—Studies on this medicine have been done only in adult patients, and there is no specific information comparing use of clonidine and chlorthalidone combination in children with use in other age groups. However, children may be more sensitive than adults to clonidine. Clonidine overdose has been reported when children accidentally took this medicine.

Older adults—Dizziness or lightheadedness and signs of too much potassium loss may be more likely to occur in the elderly, who are more sensitive to the effects of clonidine and chlorthalidone.

Other medicines—Although certain medicines should not be used together at all, in other cases two different medicines may be used together even if an interaction might occur. In these cases, your doctor may want to change the dose, or other precautions may be necessary. When you are taking clonidine and chlorthalidone, it is especially important that your health care professional know if you are taking any of the following:

- Beta-blockers (acebutolol [e.g., Sectral], atenolol [e.g., Tenormin], betaxolol [Kerlone], bisoprolol [Zebeta], carteolol [e.g., Cartrol], labetalol [e.g., Normodyne], metoprolol [e.g., Lopressor], nadolol [e.g., Corgard], oxprenolol [e.g., Trasicor], penbutolol [e.g., Levatol], pindolol [e.g., Visken], propranolol [e.g., Inderal], sotalol [e.g., Sotacor], timolol [e.g., Blocadren])—These medicines may increase the risk of harmful effects when clonidine and chlorthalidone combination treatment is stopped suddenly
- Cholestyramine or
- Colestipol—Use with clonidine and chlorthalidone combination may prevent the chlorthalidone portion of the medicine from working properly; take clonidine and chlorthalidone combination at least 1 hour before or 4 hours after cholestyramine or colestipol
- Digitalis glycosides (heart medicine)—This medicine may cause low potassium in the blood, which may increase the chance of side effects of digitalis glycosides
- Lithium (e.g., Lithane)—Use with clonidine and chlorthalidone combination may cause high blood levels of lithium, which may increase the chance of side effects
- Tricyclic antidepressants (amitriptyline [e.g., Elavil], amoxapine [e.g., Asendin], clomipramine [e.g., Anafranil], desipramine [e.g., Pertofrane], doxepin [e.g., Sinequan], imipramine [e.g., Tofranil], nortriptyline [e.g., Aventyl], protriptyline [e.g., Vivactil], trimipramine [e.g., Surmontil])—These medicines may decrease the effects of clonidine and chlorthalidone combination on blood pressure

Other medical problems—The presence of other medical problems may affect the use of clonidine and chlorthalidone. Make sure you tell your doctor if you have any other medical problems, especially:

- Diabetes mellitus (sugar diabetes)—This medicine may change the amount of diabetes medicine needed
- Gout—This medicine may increase the amount of uric acid in the blood, which can lead to gout
- Heart or blood vessel disease or
- Lupus erythematosus (history of) or
- Mental depression (history of) or
- Pancreatitis (inflammation of the pancreas) or
- Raynaud's syndrome—This medicine may make these conditions worse
- Kidney disease—Effects of this medicine may be increased because of slower removal from the body. If severe, the chlorthalidone portion of this medicine may not work

- Liver disease—If this medicine causes loss of too much water from the body, liver disease can become much worse

Proper Use of This Medicine

This medicine may cause you to have an unusual feeling of tiredness when you begin to take it. You may also notice an increase in the amount of urine or in your frequency of urination. After taking the medicine for a while, these effects should lessen. It is best to plan your doses according to a schedule that will least affect your personal activities and sleep. Ask your health care professional to help you plan the best time to take this medicine.

In addition to the use of the medicine your doctor has prescribed, appropriate treatment for your high blood pressure may include weight control and care in the types of foods you eat, especially foods high in sodium. Your doctor will tell you which factors are most important for you. You should check with your doctor before changing your diet.

Many patients who have high blood pressure will not notice any signs of the problem. In fact, many may feel normal. It is very important that you *take your medicine exactly as directed* and that you keep your appointments with your doctor even if you feel well.

Remember that this medicine will not cure your high blood pressure but it does help control it. Therefore, you must continue to take it as directed if you expect to lower your blood pressure and keep it down. *You may have to take high blood pressure medicine for the rest of your life.* If high blood pressure is not treated, it can cause serious problems such as heart failure, blood vessel disease, stroke, or kidney disease.

To help you remember to take your medicine, try to get into the habit of taking it at the same time each day.

Dosing—The dose of clonidine and chlorthalidone combination will be different for different patients. *Follow your doctor's orders or the directions on the label.* The following information includes only the average doses of clonidine and chlorthalidone combination. *If your dose is different, do not change it* unless your doctor tells you to do so.

The number of tablets that you take depends on the strength of the medicine.

- For *oral* dosage form (tablets):
  - —For high blood pressure:
    - Adults—1 or 2 tablets two to four times a day.
    - Children—Dose must be determined by your doctor.

Missed dose—If you miss a dose of this medicine, take it as soon as possible. Then go back to your regular dosing schedule. *If you miss two or more doses in a row, check with your doctor right away.* If your body goes without this medicine for too long, your blood pressure may go up to a dangerously high level and some unpleasant effects may occur.

Storage—To store this medicine:

- Keep out of the reach of children.
- Store away from heat and direct light.
- Do not store in the bathroom, near the kitchen sink, or in other damp places. Heat or moisture may cause the medicine to break down.
- Do not keep outdated medicine or medicine no longer needed. Be sure that any discarded medicine is out of the reach of children.

Precautions While Using This Medicine

It is important that your doctor check your progress at regular visits to make sure that this medicine is working properly.

Check with your doctor before you stop taking this medicine. Your doctor may want you to reduce gradually the amount you are taking before stopping completely.

Make sure that you have enough medicine on hand to last through weekends, holidays, or vacations. You should not miss taking any doses. You may want to ask your doctor for another written prescription to carry in your wallet or purse. You can then have it filled if you run out of medicine when you are away from home.

Before having any kind of surgery (including dental surgery) or emergency treatment, *make sure the medical doctor or dentist in charge knows that you are taking this medicine.*

Do not take other medicines unless they have been discussed with your doctor. This especially includes over-the-counter (nonprescription) medicines for appetite control, asthma, colds, cough, hay fever, or sinus problems, since they may tend to increase your blood pressure.

This medicine will add to the effects of alcohol and other CNS depressants (medicines that slow down the nervous system, possibly causing drowsiness). Some examples of CNS depressants are antihistamines or medicine for hay fever, other allergies, or colds; sedatives, tranquilizers, or sleeping medicine; prescription pain medicine or narcotics; barbiturates; medicine for seizures; muscle relaxants; or anesthetics, including some dental anesthetics. *Check with your doctor before taking any of the above while you are using this medicine.*

This medicine may cause some people to become drowsy or less alert than they are normally. This is more likely to happen when you begin to take it or when you increase the amount of medicine you are taking. *Make sure you know how you react to this medicine before you drive, use machines, or do anything else that could be dangerous if you are not alert.*

Dizziness, lightheadedness, or fainting may occur, especially when you get up from a lying or sitting position. Getting up slowly may help, but if the problem continues or gets worse, check with your doctor.

The dizziness, lightheadedness, or fainting is also more likely to occur if you drink alcohol, stand for long periods of time, exercise, or if the weather is hot. Drinking alcoholic beverages may also make the drowsiness worse. While you are taking this medicine, be careful to limit the amount of alcohol you drink. Also, use extra care during exercise or hot weather or if you must stand for long periods of time.

This medicine may cause a loss of potassium from your body.

- To help prevent this, your doctor may want you to:
  —eat or drink foods that have a high potassium content (for example, orange or other citrus fruit juices), or
  —take a potassium supplement, or
  —take another medicine to help prevent the loss of the potassium in the first place.
- It is very important to follow these directions. Also, it is important not to change your diet on your own. This is more important if you are already on a special diet (as for diabetes), or if you are taking a potassium supplement or a medicine to reduce potassium loss. Extra potassium may not be necessary and, in some cases, too much potassium could be harmful.

Check with your doctor if you become sick and have severe or continuing vomiting or diarrhea. These problems may cause you to lose additional water and potassium.

For *diabetic patients:*

- The chlorthalidone contained in this medicine may raise blood sugar levels. While you are using this medicine, be especially careful in testing for sugar in your urine.

This medicine may cause your skin to be more sensitive to sunlight than it is normally. Exposure to sunlight, even for brief periods of time, may cause a skin rash, itching, redness or other discoloration of the skin, or a severe sunburn. When you begin taking this medicine:

- Stay out of direct sunlight, especially between the hours of 10:00 a.m. and 3:00 p.m., if possible.
- Wear protective clothing, including a hat. Also, wear sunglasses.
- Apply a sun block product that has a skin protection factor (SPF) of at least 15. Some patients may require a product with a higher SPF number, especially if they have a fair complexion. If you have any questions about this, check with your health care professional.
- Apply a sun block lipstick that has an SPF of at least 15 to protect your lips.
- Do not use a sunlamp or tanning bed or booth.

If you have a severe reaction from the sun, check with your doctor.

This medicine may cause dryness of the mouth. For temporary relief, use sugarless candy or gum, melt bits of ice in your mouth, or use a saliva substitute. However, if your mouth continues to feel dry for more than 2 weeks, check with your medical doctor or dentist. Continuing dryness of the mouth may increase the chance of dental disease, including tooth decay, gum disease, and fungus infections.

Side Effects of This Medicine

Along with its needed effects, a medicine may cause some unwanted effects. Although not all of these side effects may occur, if they do occur they may need medical attention.

Check with your doctor immediately if any of the following side effects occur:

Signs and symptoms of overdose
Difficulty in breathing; dizziness (extreme) or faintness; feeling cold; pinpoint pupils of eyes; slow heartbeat; unusual tiredness or weakness (extreme)

Check with your doctor as soon as possible if any of the following side effects occur:

Signs and symptoms of too much potassium loss
Dryness of mouth; increased thirst; irregular heartbeat; mood or mental changes; muscle cramps or pain; nausea or vomiting; weak pulse

Signs and symptoms of too much sodium loss
Confusion; convulsions (seizures); decreased mental activity; irritability; muscle cramps; unusual tiredness or weakness

Less common
Mental depression; swelling of feet and lower legs

Rare
Black, tarry stools; blood in urine or stools; cough or hoarseness; fever or chills; joint pain; lower back or side pain; paleness or cold feeling in fingertips and toes; pinpoint red spots on skin; skin rash or hives; stomach pain (severe) with nausea and vomiting; unusual bleeding or bruising; vivid dreams or nightmares; yellow eyes or skin

Other side effects may occur that usually do not need medical attention. These side effects may go away during treatment as your body adjusts to the medicine. However, check with your doctor if any of the following side effects continue or are bothersome:

More common
Constipation; dizziness; drowsiness; dryness of mouth; unusual tiredness or weakness

Less common
Decreased sexual ability; diarrhea; dizziness or lightheadedness when getting up from a lying or sitting position; dry, itching, or burning eyes; increased sensitivity of skin to sunlight; loss of appetite; nausea or vomiting; nervousness; upset stomach

After you have been using this medicine for a while, it may cause unpleasant or even harmful effects if you stop taking it too suddenly. After you stop taking this medicine, check with your doctor if any of the following occur:

Anxiety or tenseness; chest pain; fast or irregular heartbeat; headache; increased salivation; nausea; nervousness; restlessness; shaking or trembling of hands and fingers; stomach cramps; sweating; trouble in sleeping; vomiting

Other side effects not listed above may also occur in some patients. If you notice any other effects, check with your doctor.

Revised: 08/02/94

CLOTRIMAZOLE Oral†

A commonly used brand name in the U.S. is Mycelex Troches.

†Not commercially available in Canada.

Description

Clotrimazole (kloe-TRIM-a-zole) lozenges are dissolved slowly in the mouth to prevent and treat thrush. Thrush, also called candidiasis or white mouth, is a fungus infection of the mouth and throat. This medicine may also be used for other problems as determined by your doctor.

Clotrimazole is available only with your doctor's prescription, in the following dosage form:

Oral
- Lozenges (U.S.)

Before Using This Medicine

In deciding to use a medicine, the risks of taking the medicine must be weighed against the good it will do. This is a decision you and your doctor will make. For clotrimazole, the following should be considered:

Allergies—Tell your doctor if you have ever had any unusual or allergic reaction to clotrimazole. Also tell your health care professional if you are allergic to any other substances, such as foods, preservatives, or dyes.

Pregnancy—Studies have not been done in humans. Studies in mice, rats, and rabbits given very high doses have not shown that clotrimazole causes birth defects. However, studies in rats and mice given high doses have shown that clotrimazole lozenges may cause other harmful effects in the fetus.

Breast-feeding—It is not known whether clotrimazole passes into breast milk. However, only small amounts of clotrimazole are absorbed into the mother's body. Clotrimazole has not been reported to cause problems in nursing babies.

Children—Although this medicine has not been shown to cause different side effects or problems in children than it does in adults, it should not be given to children under 5 years of age since they may be too young to use the lozenges safely.

Older adults—Many medicines have not been studied specifically in older people. Therefore, it may not be known whether they work exactly the same way they do in younger adults. Although there is no specific information comparing use of clotrimazole lozenges in the elderly with use in other age groups, this medicine is not expected to cause different side effects or problems in older people than it does in younger adults.

Proper Use of This Medicine

Clotrimazole lozenges should be held in the mouth and allowed to dissolve slowly and completely, then swallowed. This may take 15 to 30 minutes. *Do not chew the lozenges or swallow them whole.*

Do not give clotrimazole lozenges to infants or children under 5 years of age. They may be too young to use the lozenges safely.

To help clear up your infection completely, *it is very important that you keep using clotrimazole for the full time of treatment,* even if your symptoms begin to clear up after a few days. Since fungus infections may be very slow to clear up, you may have to continue using this medicine every day for two weeks or more. If you stop using this medicine too soon, your symptoms may return. *Do not miss any doses.*

Dosing—The dose of clotrimazole lozenges will be different for different patients. *Follow your doctor's orders or the directions on the label.* The following information includes only the average doses of clotrimazole lozenges. *If your dose is different, do not change it* unless your doctor tells you to do so.

- For the *treatment of thrush*:
  - —Adults and children 5 years of age and older: Dissolve one 10-milligram lozenge slowly and completely in your mouth; this dose should be taken five times a day for at least fourteen days.
  - —Children up to 5 years of age: This medicine is not recommended in children under 5 years of age since they may be too young to use the lozenges safely.
- For the *prevention of thrush*:
  - —Adults and children 5 years of age and older: Dissolve one 10-milligram lozenge slowly and completely in your mouth; this dose should be taken three times a day.
  - —Children up to 5 years of age: This medicine is not recommended in children under 5 years of age since they may be too young to use the lozenges safely.

Missed dose—If you miss a dose of this medicine, take it as soon as possible. However, if it is almost time for your next dose, skip the missed dose and go back to your regular dosing schedule.

Storage—To store this medicine:
- Keep out of the reach of children.
- Store away from heat and direct light.
- Do not store in the bathroom, near the kitchen sink, or in other damp places. Heat or moisture may cause the medicine to break down.
- Do not keep outdated medicine or medicine no longer needed. Be sure that any discarded medicine is out of the reach of children.

Precautions While Using This Medicine

If your symptoms do not improve within 1 week, or if they become worse, check with your doctor.

Side Effects of This Medicine

Along with its needed effects, a medicine may cause some unwanted effects. The following side effects may go away during treatment as your body adjusts to the medicine. However, check with your doctor if any of these effects continue or are bothersome:

More common—when swallowed

Abdominal or stomach cramping or pain; diarrhea; nausea or vomiting

Other side effects not listed above may also occur in some patients. If you notice any other effects, check with your doctor.

Revised: 02/23/93

CLOTRIMAZOLE Topical

Some commonly used brand names are:

In the U.S.—

Lotrimin AF Cream
Lotrimin AF Lotion
Lotrimin AF Solution
Lotrimin Cream
Lotrimin Lotion
Lotrimin Solution
Mycelex Cream
Mycelex Solution

Generic name product may also be available.

In Canada—

Canesten Cream
Canesten Solution
Canesten Solution with Atomizer
Clotrimaderm Cream
Myclo Cream
Myclo Solution
Myclo Spray Solution
Neo-Zol Cream

Description

Clotrimazole (kloe-TRIM-a-zole) topical preparations are used to treat fungus infections.

Some of these preparations are available only with your doctor's prescription. Others are available without a prescription; however, your doctor may have special instructions on the proper dose for your medical condition.

Clotrimazole is available in the following dosage forms:

Topical

- Cream (U.S. and Canada)
- Lotion (U.S.)
- Solution (U.S. and Canada)

Before Using This Medicine

If you are using this medicine without a prescription, carefully read and follow any precautions on the label. For topical clotrimazole, the following should be considered:

Allergies—Tell your doctor if you have ever had any unusual or allergic reaction to clotrimazole. Also tell your health care professional if you are allergic to any other substances, such as preservatives or dyes.

Pregnancy—Clotrimazole has not been studied in pregnant women during the first trimester (3 months). However, clotrimazole used vaginally during the second and third trimesters has not been shown to cause birth defects or other problems in humans.

Breast-feeding—It is not known whether topical clotrimazole passes into the breast milk. Although most medicines pass into breast milk in small amounts, many of them may be used safely while breast-feeding. Mothers who are using this medicine and who wish to breast-feed should discuss this with their doctor.

Children—This medicine has been tested in children and, in effective doses, has not been shown to cause different side effects or problems than it does in adults.

Older adults—Many medicines have not been studied specifically in older people. Therefore, it may not be known whether they work exactly the same way they do in younger adults. Although there is no specific information comparing use of topical clotrimazole in the elderly with use in other age groups, this medicine is not expected to cause different side effects or problems in older people than it does in younger adults.

Other medicines—Although certain medicines should not be used together at all, in other cases two different medicines may be used together even if an interaction might occur. In these cases, your doctor may want to change the dose, or other precautions may be necessary. Tell your health care professional if you are using any other topical prescription or nonprescription (over-the-counter [OTC]) medicine that is to be applied to the same area of the skin.

Proper Use of This Medicine

Apply enough clotrimazole to cover the affected and surrounding skin areas, and rub in gently.

Keep this medicine away from the eyes.

When clotrimazole is used to treat certain types of fungus infections of the skin, an occlusive dressing (airtight covering, such as kitchen plastic wrap) should *not* be applied over the medicine. To do so may cause irritation of the skin. *Do not apply an occlusive dressing over this medicine unless you have been directed to do so by your doctor.*

To help clear up your infection completely, *it is very important that you keep using this medicine for the full time of treatment,* even if your symptoms begin to clear up after a few days. Since fungus infections may be very slow to clear up, you may have to continue using this medicine every day for several weeks or more. If you stop using this medicine too soon, your symptoms may return. *Do not miss any doses.*

Dosing—The dose of topical clotrimazole will be different for different patients. *Follow your doctor's orders or the directions on the label.* The following information includes only the average doses of topical clotrimazole.

your dose is different, do not change it unless your doctor tells you to do so:

The number of doses you use each day, the time allowed between doses, and the length of time you use the medicine depend on the medical problem for which you are using clotrimazole.

- For *topical* dosage forms (cream, lotion, and solution):
  - —Fungal infections (treatment):
    - Adults and children—Use two times a day, morning and evening.

Missed dose—If you miss a dose of this medicine, apply it as soon as possible. However, if it is almost time for your next dose, skip the missed dose and go back to your regular dosing schedule.

Storage—To store this medicine:
- Keep out of the reach of children.
- Store away from heat and direct light.
- Keep the medicine from freezing.
- Do not keep outdated medicine or medicine no longer needed. Be sure that any discarded medicine is out of the reach of children.

Precautions While Using This Medicine

If your skin problem does not improve within 4 weeks, or if it becomes worse, check with your doctor.

Side Effects of This Medicine

Along with its needed effects, a medicine may cause some unwanted effects. Although not all of these side effects may occur, if they do occur they may need medical attention.

Check with your doctor as soon as possible if any of the following side effects occur:

Skin rash, hives, blistering, burning, itching, peeling, redness, stinging, swelling, or other sign of skin irritation not present before use of this medicine

Other side effects not listed above may also occur in some patients. If you notice any other effects, check with your doctor.

Revised: 03/29/94

CLOTRIMAZOLE AND BETAMETHASONE Topical

Some commonly used brand names are:

In the U.S.—
Lotrisone

In Canada—
Lotriderm

Description

Clotrimazole (kloe-TRIM-a-zole) and betamethasone (bay-ta-METH-a-sone) combination is used to treat fungus infections. Clotrimazole works by killing the fungus or preventing its growth. Betamethasone, a corticosteroid (cortisone-like medicine or steroid), is used to help relieve redness, swelling, itching, and other discomfort of fungus infections.

Clotrimazole and betamethasone cream is applied to the skin to treat:
- athlete's foot (ringworm of the foot; tinea pedis);
- jock itch (ringworm of the groin; tinea cruris); and
- ringworm of the body (tinea corporis).

This medicine may also be used for other fungus infections of the skin as determined by your doctor.

This medicine is available only with your doctor's prescription, in the following dosage form:

Topical
- Cream (U.S. and Canada)

Before Using This Medicine

In deciding to use a medicine, the risks of using the medicine must be weighed against the good it will do. This is a decision you and your doctor will make. For clotrimazole and betamethasone combination, the following should be considered:

Allergies—Tell your doctor if you have ever had any unusual or allergic reaction to this medicine or to clotrimazole (e.g., Gyne-Lotrimin, Lotrimin), betamethasone (e.g., Valisone), butoconazole (e.g., Femstat), econazole (e.g., Ecostatin, Spectazole), ketoconazole (e.g., Nizoral), miconazole (e.g., Monistat, Monistat-Derm), terconazole (e.g., Terazol 7), or to any of the other corticosteroids. Also tell your health care professional if you are allergic to any other substances, such as preservatives or dyes.

Pregnancy—Clotrimazole and betamethasone combination has not been studied in pregnant women. However, for the individual medicines:
- *Clotrimazole*—Clotrimazole (e.g., Gyne-Lotrimin), used in the vagina, has not been shown to cause birth defects or other problems in studies in rats or humans. However, clotrimazole (e.g., Mycelex), given by mouth, has been shown to cause a decrease in successful pregnancies, but no birth defects, in rats and mice.
- *Betamethasone*—Studies in animals have shown that corticosteroids, given by mouth or by injection, may cause birth defects, even at low doses. Also, some of the stronger corticosteroids have been shown to cause birth defects when applied to the skin of animals.

Therefore, this medicine should not be used on large areas of the skin, in large amounts, or for a long time in pregnant patients. Before using this medicine, make sure your doctor knows if you are pregnant or if you may become pregnant.

Breast-feeding—It is not known whether topical clotrimazole and betamethasone combination passes into the breast milk, but it has not been reported to cause problems in nursing babies. However, clotrimazole and betamethasone may be absorbed into the mother's body.

- *Betamethasone*—Corticosteroids, given by mouth or by injection, do pass into the breast milk. They may cause unwanted effects, such as slower growth rate of nursing babies.

Children—Clotrimazole and betamethasone combination may rarely cause serious side effects. Some of these side effects may be more likely to occur in children, who may absorb greater amounts of this medicine than adults do. Long-term use in children may affect growth and development as well. Therefore, it is especially important that you discuss with the child's doctor the good that this medicine may do, as well as the risks of using it.

Older adults—Many medicines have not been studied specifically in older people. Therefore, it may not be known whether they work exactly the same way they do in younger adults or if they cause different side effects or problems in older people. There is no specific information comparing use of clotrimazole and betamethasone combination in the elderly with use in other age groups.

Other medicines—Although certain medicines should not be used together at all, in other cases two different medicines may be used together even if an interaction might occur. In these cases, your doctor may want to change the dose, or other precautions may be necessary. Tell your health care professional if you are using any other prescription or nonprescription (over-the-counter [OTC]) medicine.

Other medical problems—The presence of other medical problems may affect the use of clotrimazole and betamethasone combination. Make sure you tell your doctor if you have any other medical problems, especially:

- Herpes or
- Vaccinia (cowpox) or
- Varicella (chickenpox) or
- Other virus infections of the skin—Betamethasone may speed up the spread of virus infections
- Tuberculosis (TB) of the skin—Betamethasone may make a TB infection worse

Proper Use of This Medicine

Before applying this medicine, wash the affected area with soap and water, and dry thoroughly.

Do not use this medicine in the eyes.

To use:

- *Check with your doctor before using this medicine on any other skin problems.* It should not be used on bacterial or virus infections. Also, it should only be used on certain kinds of fungus infections of the skin.
- Apply a thin layer of this medicine to the affected area(s) and surrounding skin. Rub in gently and thoroughly.

The use of any kind of occlusive dressing (airtight covering, such as kitchen plastic wrap) over this medicine may increase absorption of the medicine and the chance of irritation and other side effects. Therefore, *do not bandage, wrap, or apply any occlusive dressing over this medicine* unless directed by your doctor. Also, wear loose-fitting clothing when using this medicine on the groin area. When using this medicine on the diaper area of children, *avoid tight-fitting diapers and plastic pants.*

To help clear up your skin infection completely, *keep using this medicine for the full time of treatment,* even if your symptoms have disappeared. *Do not miss any doses.* However, *do not use this medicine more often or for a longer time than your doctor ordered.* To do so may increase absorption through your skin and the chance of side effects. In addition, too much use, especially on thin skin areas (for example, face, armpits, genitals [sex organs], between the toes, groin), may result in thinning of the skin and stretch marks.

Dosing—*Follow your doctor's orders or the directions on the label.* The following information includes only the average dose of clotrimazole and betamethasone combination. *If your dose is different, do not change it* unless your doctor tells you to do so.

- For *topical cream* dosage form:
  —For fungus infections:
    - Adults and children 12 years of age and over—Apply to the affected area(s) of the skin two times a day, morning and evening.
    - Children up to 12 years of age—Use and dose must be determined by your doctor.

Missed dose—If you miss a dose of this medicine, apply it as soon as possible. However, if it is almost time for your next dose, skip the missed dose and go back to your regular dosing schedule.

Storage—To store this medicine:

- Keep out of the reach of children.
- Store away from heat and direct light.
- Keep the medicine from freezing.
- Do not keep outdated medicine or medicine no longer needed. Be sure that any discarded medicine is out of the reach of children.

Precautions While Using This Medicine

If your skin infection does not improve within a few days, or if it becomes worse, check with your doctor.

To help clear up your skin infection completely and to help make sure it does not return, the following good health habits are important:

- For patients using this medicine *for athlete's foot:*
  —Carefully dry the feet, especially between the toes, after bathing.
  —Avoid wearing socks made from wool or synthetic materials (for example, rayon or nylon). Instead, wear clean, cotton socks and change them daily or more often if your feet sweat freely.
  —Wear well-ventilated shoes (for example, shoes with holes) or sandals.

—Use a bland, absorbent powder (for example, talcum powder) or an antifungal powder freely between the toes, on the feet, and in socks and shoes once or twice a day. Be sure to use the powder after clotrimazole and betamethasone cream has been applied and has disappeared into the skin. Do not use the powder as the only treatment for your fungus infection.

These measures will help keep the feet cool and dry.

- For patients using this medicine *for jock itch:*

—Carefully dry the groin area after bathing.

—Avoid wearing underwear that is tight-fitting or made from synthetic materials (for example, rayon or nylon). Instead, wear loose-fitting, cotton underwear.

—Use a bland, absorbent powder (for example, talcum powder) or an antifungal powder freely once or twice a day. Be sure to use the powder after clotrimazole and betamethasone cream has been applied and has disappeared into the skin. Do not use the powder as the only treatment for your fungus infection.

These measures will help reduce chafing and irritation and will also help keep the groin area cool and dry.

- For patients using this medicine *for ringworm of the body:*

—Carefully dry yourself after bathing.

—Avoid too much heat and humidity if possible. Try to keep moisture from building up on affected areas of the body.

—Wear well-ventilated clothing.

—Use a bland, absorbent powder (for example, talcum powder) or an antifungal powder freely once or twice a day. Be sure to use the powder after clotrimazole and betamethasone cream has been applied and has disappeared into the skin. Do not use the powder as the only treatment for your fungus infection.

These measures will help keep the affected areas cool and dry.

If you have any questions about this, check with your health care professional

For diabetic patients:

- *Rarely, the corticosteroid in this medicine may cause higher blood and urine sugar levels. This is more likely to occur if you have severe diabetes and are using large amounts of this medicine.* Check with your doctor before changing your diet or the dosage of your diabetes medicine.

Side Effects of This Medicine

Along with its needed effects, a medicine may cause some unwanted effects. Although not all of these side effects may occur, if they do occur they may need medical attention.

Check with your doctor immediately if any of the following side effects occur:

Less common

Blistering, burning, itching, peeling, dryness, redness, or other sign of skin irritation not present before use of this medicine

Additional side effects may occur if you use this medicine for a long time. Check with your doctor as soon as possible if any of the following side effects occur:

Acne or oily skin; increased hair growth, especially on the face; increased loss of hair, especially on the scalp; reddish purple lines on arms, face, legs, trunk, or groin; thinning of skin with easy bruising

Other side effects not listed above may also occur in some patients. If you notice any other effects, check with your doctor.

Revised: 02/10/92
Interim revision: 07/01/94

CLOZAPINE Systemic

Some commonly used brand names are:

In the U.S. and Canada—
Clozaril

Other—
Leponex

Description

Clozapine (KLOE-za-peen) is used to treat schizophrenia in patients who have not been helped by or are unable to take other medicines.

Clozapine is only available from pharmacies that agree to participate with your doctor in a plan to monitor your blood tests. You will need to have blood tests done every week, and you will receive a 7-day supply of clozapine only if the results of your blood tests show that it is safe for you to take this medicine.

Clozapine is available in the following dosage form:

Oral

- Tablets (U.S. and Canada)

Before Using This Medicine

In deciding to use a medicine, the risks of taking the medicine must be weighed against the good it will do. This is a decision you and your doctor will make. For clozapine, the following should be considered:

Allergies—Tell your doctor if you have ever had any unusual or allergic reaction to clozapine. Also tell your health care professional if you are allergic to any other substance, such as foods, preservatives, or dyes.

Pregnancy—Clozapine has not been studied in pregnant women. However, clozapine has not been shown to cause birth defects or other problems in animal studies.

Breast-feeding—Clozapine may pass into breast milk and cause sedation, decreased suckling, restlessness or irritability, seizures, or heart or blood vessel problems in nursing babies.

Children—Studies on this medicine have been done only in adult patients, and there is no specific information comparing use of clozapine in children with use in other age groups.

Older adults—Many medicines have not been tested in older people. Therefore, it may not be known whether they work exactly the same way they do in younger adults. Clozapine may be more likely to cause side effects in the elderly, including dizziness and fainting, low blood pressure, and confusion or excitement.

Other medicines—Although certain medicines should not be used together at all, in other cases 2 different medicines may be used together even if an interaction might occur. In these cases, your doctor may want to change the dose, or other precautions may be necessary. When you are taking clozapine, it is especially important that your health care professional know if you are taking any of the following:

- Alcohol or
- Central nervous system (CNS) depressants (medicines that cause drowsiness) or
- Tricyclic antidepressants (medicine for depression)—Clozapine may cause an increase in sedation or effects on the heart, or increase the risk of seizures
- Amphotericin B by injection (e.g., Fungizone) or
- Antineoplastics (cancer medicine) or
- Antithyroid agents (medicine for overactive thyroid) or
- Azathioprine (e.g., Imuran) or
- Chlorambucil (e.g., Leukeran) or
- Chloramphenicol (e.g., Chloromycetin) or
- Colchicine or
- Cyclophosphamide (e.g., Cytoxan) or
- Flucytosine (e.g., Ancobon) or
- Interferon (e.g., Intron A, Roferon-A) or
- Mercaptopurine (e.g., Purinethol) or
- Methotrexate (e.g., Mexate) or
- Plicamycin (e.g., Mithracin) or
- Zidovudine (e.g., Retrovir)—Taking clozapine with any of these medicines may cause increased blood problems
- Lithium—Using clozapine with lithium may increase the risk of seizures, or cause confusion or body movement disorders

Other medical problems—The presence of other medical problems may affect the use of clozapine. Make sure you tell your doctor if you have any other medical problems, especially:

- Blood diseases or
- Enlarged prostate or difficult urination or
- Gastrointestinal problems or
- Heart or blood vessel problems—Clozapine may make the condition worse
- Epilepsy or other seizure disorder—Clozapine may increase the risk of seizures
- Kidney or liver disease—Higher blood levels of clozapine may occur, increasing the chance of side effects

Proper Use of This Medicine

Take this medicine exactly as directed. Do not take more of this medicine and do not take it more often than your doctor ordered. Do not miss any doses.

This medicine has been prescribed for your current medical problem only. It must not be given to other people or used for other problems unless you are directed to do so by your doctor.

Dosing—The dose of clozapine will be different for different patients. *Follow your doctor's orders or the directions on the label.* The following information includes only the average doses of clozapine. *If your dose is different, do not change it* unless your doctor tells you to do so.

The number of tablets that you take depends on the strength of the medicine. Also, *the number of doses you take each day, the time allowed between doses, and the length of time you take the medicine depend on your special needs.*

- For *oral* dosage form (tablets):
  - —For schizophrenia:
    - Adults—At first, 25 milligrams (mg) once or twice a day. Your doctor may increase your dose as needed. However, the dose is usually not more than 900 mg a day.
    - Children up to 16 years of age—Use and dose must be determined by your doctor.

Missed dose—If you miss a dose of this medicine, take it as soon as possible. However, if it is almost time for your next dose, skip the missed dose and go back to your regular dosing schedule. Do not double doses.

Storage—To store this medicine:

- Keep out of the reach of children.
- Store away from heat and direct light.
- Do not store in the bathroom, near the kitchen sink, or in other damp places. Heat or moisture may cause the medicine to break down.
- Do not keep outdated medicine or medicine no longer needed. Be sure that any discarded medicine is out of the reach of children.

Precautions While Using This Medicine

It is important that you have your blood tests done weekly and that your doctor check your progress at regular visits. This will allow your doctor to make sure the medicine is working properly and to change the dosage if needed.

If you have been using this medicine regularly, do not stop taking it without first checking with your doctor. Your doctor may want you to reduce gradually the amount you are taking before stopping completely.

This medicine will add to the effects of alcohol and other CNS depressants (medicines that slow down the nervous system, possibly causing drowsiness). Some examples of CNS depressants are antihistamines or medicine for hay fever, other allergies, or colds; sedatives, tranquilizers, or sleeping medicine; prescription pain medicine or narcotics; barbiturates; medicine for seizures; muscle relaxants;

or anesthetics, including some dental anesthetics. *Check with your doctor before taking any of the above while you are using this medicine.*

Clozapine may cause drowsiness, blurred vision or convulsions (seizures). *Do not drive, climb, swim, operate machines or do anything else that could be dangerous* while you are taking this medicine.

Dizziness, lightheadedness, or fainting may occur, especially when you get up from a lying or sitting position. Getting up slowly may help. If this problem continues or gets worse, check with your doctor.

In some patients, clozapine may cause increased watering of the mouth. Other patients, however, may get dryness of the mouth. For temporary relief of mouth dryness, use sugarless gum or candy, melt bits of ice in your mouth, or use a saliva substitute. However, if your mouth continues to feel dry for more than 2 weeks, check with your medical doctor or dentist. Continuing dryness of the mouth may increase the chance of dental disease, including tooth decay, gum disease, and fungus infections.

Side Effects of This Medicine

Along with its needed effects, a medicine may cause some unwanted effects. Although not all of these side effects may occur, if they do occur they may need medical attention.

Check with your doctor immediately if any of the following side effects occur:

More common
Fast or irregular heartbeat; fever; low blood pressure

Less common
High blood pressure

Rare
Chills; convulsions (seizures); difficult or fast breathing; increased sweating; loss of bladder control; muscle stiffness (severe); sore throat; sores, ulcers, or white spots on lips or in mouth; unusual bleeding or bruising; unusual tiredness or weakness; unusually pale skin

Check with your doctor as soon as possible if any of the following side effects occur:

More common
Dizziness or fainting

Less common
Blurred vision; confusion; restlessness or need to keep moving; trembling; unusual anxiety, nervousness, or irritability

Rare
Absence of or decrease in movement; decreased sexual ability; difficulty in sleeping; difficulty in urinating; headache (severe or continuing); lip smacking or puckering; mental depression; puffing of cheeks; rapid or worm-like movements of tongue; uncontrolled chewing movements; uncontrolled movements of arms and legs

Symptoms of overdose
Dizziness or fainting; drowsiness (severe); fast, slow, or irregular heartbeat; hallucinations (seeing, hearing, or feeling things that are not there); increased watering of mouth (severe); slow, irregular, or troubled breathing; unusual excitement, nervousness, or restlessness

Other side effects may occur that usually do not need medical attention. These side effects may go away during treatment as your body adjusts to the medicine. However, check with your doctor if any of the following side effects continue or are bothersome:

More common
Constipation; dizziness or lightheadedness (mild); drowsiness; headache (mild); increased watering of mouth; nausea or vomiting; unusual weight gain

Less common
Abdominal discomfort or heartburn; dryness of mouth

Other side effects not listed above may also occur in some patients. If you notice any other effects, check with your doctor.

Revised: 07/17/91
Interim revision: 03/25/92; 06/08/94

COAL TAR Topical

Some commonly used brand names are:

In the U.S.—

Alphosyl
Aquatar
Balnetar Therapeutic Tar Bath
Cutar Water Dispersible Emollient Tar
Denorex Extra Strength Medicated Shampoo
Denorex Extra Strength Medicated Shampoo with Conditioners
Denorex Medicated Shampoo
Denorex Medicated Shampoo and Conditioner
Denorex Mountain Fresh Herbal Scent Medicated Shampoo
DHS Tar Gel Shampoo
DHS Tar Shampoo
Doak Oil Forte Therapeutic Bath Treatment
Doak Oil Therapeutic Bath Treatment For All-Over Body Care
Doak Tar Lotion
Doak Tar Shampoo
Doctar Hair & Scalp Shampoo and Conditioner
Doctar Shampoo
Estar
Fototar
Ionil T Plus
Lavatar
Medotar
Pentrax Anti-Dandruff Tar Shampoo
Psorigel
PsoriNail Topical Solution
Taraphilic
Tarbonis
Tarpaste 'Doak'
T/Derm Tar Emollient
Tegrin Lotion for Psoriasis
Tegrin Medicated Cream Shampoo
Tegrin Medicated Shampoo Concentrated Gel
Tegrin Medicated Shampoo Extra Conditioning Formula
Tegrin Medicated Shampoo Herbal Formula
Tegrin Medicated Shampoo Original Formula
Tegrin Medicated Soap for Psoriasis
Tegrin Skin Cream for Psoriasis
Tersa-Tar Soapless Tar Shampoo
T/Gel Therapeutic Conditioner
T/Gel Therapeutic Shampoo
Theraplex T Shampoo
Zetar Emulsion
Zetar Medicated Antiseborrheic Shampoo

In Canada—

- Alphosyl
- Balnetar
- Denorex
- Doak Oil
- Doak Oil Forte
- Estar
- Lavatar
- Liquor Carbonis Detergens
- Pentrax Extra-Strength Therapeutic Tar Shampoo
- Psorigel
- Tar Doak
- Tarpaste
- Tersa-Tar Mild Therapeutic Shampoo with Protein and Conditioner
- Tersa-Tar Therapeutic Shampoo
- T-Gel
- Zetar Emulsion
- Zetar Shampoo

Description

Coal tar is used to treat eczema, psoriasis, seborrheic dermatitis, and other skin disorders.

Some of these preparations are available only with your doctor's prescription. Others are available without a prescription; however, your doctor may have special instructions on the proper use of coal tar for your medical condition.

Coal tar is available in the following dosage forms:

Topical
- Cleansing bar (U.S.)
- Cream (U.S. and Canada)
- Gel (U.S. and Canada)
- Lotion (U.S. and Canada)
- Ointment (U.S. and Canada)
- Shampoo (U.S. and Canada)
- Topical solution (U.S. and Canada)
- Topical suspension (U.S. and Canada)

Before Using This Medicine

If you are using this medicine without a prescription, carefully read and follow any precautions on the label. For coal tar, the following should be considered:

Allergies—Tell your doctor if you have ever had any unusual or allergic reaction to coal tar or to any other tar. Also tell your health care professional if you are allergic to any other substances, such as preservatives or dyes.

Pregnancy—Studies on effects in pregnancy have not been done in either humans or animals.

Breast-feeding—It is not known whether coal tar passes into the breast milk. However, this medicine has not been reported to cause problems in nursing babies.

Children—Coal tar products should not be used on infants, unless otherwise directed by your doctor. Studies on this medicine have been done only in adult patients, and there is no specific information comparing use of this medicine in children with use in other age groups.

Older adults—Many medicines have not been studied specifically in older people. Therefore, it may not be known whether they work exactly the same way they do in younger adults or if they cause different side effects or problems in older people. There is no specific information comparing use of this medicine in the elderly with use in other age groups.

Other medicines—Although certain medicines should not be used together at all, in other cases two different medicines may be used together even if an interaction might occur. In these cases, your doctor may want to change the dose, or other precautions may be necessary. Tell your health care professional if you are using any other topical prescription or nonprescription (over-the-counter [OTC]) medicine that is to be applied to the same area of the skin.

Proper Use of This Medicine

Use this medicine only as directed. Do not use more of it and do not use it more often than recommended on the label, unless otherwise directed by your doctor. To do so may increase the chance of side effects.

After applying coal tar, *protect the treated area from direct sunlight and do not use a sunlamp for 72 hours,* unless otherwise directed by your doctor, since a severe reaction may occur. Also, make sure you have removed all the coal tar medicine from your skin before you go back into direct sunlight or use a sunlamp.

Do not apply this medicine to infected, blistered, raw, or oozing areas of the skin.

Keep this medicine away from the eyes. If you should accidentally get some in your eyes, flush them thoroughly with water at once.

To use the *cream or ointment form* of this medicine:
- Apply enough medicine to cover the affected area, and rub in gently.

To use the *gel form* of this medicine:
- Apply enough gel to cover the affected area, and rub in gently. Allow the gel to remain on the affected area for 5 minutes, then remove excess gel by patting with a clean tissue.

To use the *shampoo form* of this medicine:
- Wet the scalp and hair with lukewarm water. Apply a generous amount of shampoo and rub into the scalp, then rinse. Apply the shampoo again, working up a rich lather, and allow to remain on the scalp for 5 minutes. Then rinse thoroughly.

To use the *nonshampoo liquid form* of this medicine:
- Some of these preparations are to be applied directly to dry or wet skin, some are to be added to lukewarm bath water, and some may be applied directly to dry or wet skin or added to lukewarm bath water. Make sure you know exactly how you should use this medicine. If you have any questions about this, check with your health care professional.
- If this medicine is to be applied directly to the skin, apply enough to cover the affected area, and rub in gently.
- Some of these preparations contain alcohol and are flammable. Do not use near heat, near open flame, or while smoking.

Dosing—The dose of coal tar will be different for different patients. *Follow your doctor's orders or the directions on the label.* The following information includes only the average doses of coal tar. *If your dose is different, do not change it* unless your doctor tells you to do so.

- For eczema, psoriasis, seborrheic dermatitis, and other skin disorders:
  —For *cleansing bar* dosage form:
    - Adults—Use one or two times a day, or as directed by your doctor.
    - Children—Use and dose must be determined by your doctor.
  —For *cream* dosage form:
    - Adults—Apply to the affected area(s) of the skin up to four times a day.
    - Children—Use and dose must be determined by your doctor.
  —For *gel* dosage form:
    - Adults—Apply to the affected area(s) of the skin one or two times a day.
    - Children—Use and dose must be determined by your doctor.
  —For *lotion* dosage form:
    - Adults—Apply directly to the affected area(s) of the skin or use as a bath, hand or foot soak, or as a hair rinse, depending on the product.
    - Children—Use and dose must be determined by your doctor.
  —For *ointment* dosage form:
    - Adults—Apply to the affected area(s) of the skin two or three times a day.
    - Children—Use and dose must be determined by your doctor.
  —For *shampoo* dosage form:
    - Adults—Use once a day to once a week or as directed by your doctor.
    - Children—Use and dose must be determined by your doctor.
  —For *topical solution* dosage form:
    - Adults—Apply to wet the skin or scalp, or use as a bath, depending on the product.
    - Children—Use and dose must be determined by your doctor.
  —For *topical suspension* dosage form:
    - Adults—Use as a bath.
    - Children—Use and dose must be determined by your doctor.

Missed dose—If you miss a dose of this medicine, apply it as soon as possible. However, if it is almost time for your next dose, skip the missed dose and go back to your regular dosing schedule. Do not double doses.

Storage—To store this medicine:
- Keep out of the reach of children.
- Store away from heat and direct light.
- Keep the medicine from freezing.
- Do not keep outdated medicine or medicine no longer needed. Be sure that any discarded medicine is out of the reach of children.

Precautions While Using This Medicine

If this medicine is used on the scalp, it may temporarily discolor blond, bleached, or tinted hair.

Coal tar may stain the skin or clothing. Avoid getting it on your clothing. The stain on the skin will wear off after you stop using the medicine.

Side Effects of This Medicine

In animal studies, coal tar has been shown to increase the chance of skin cancer.

Along with its needed effects, a medicine may cause some unwanted effects. Although not all of these side effects may occur, if they do occur they may need medical attention.

Check with your doctor as soon as possible if either of the following side effects occurs:

Rare

Skin irritation not present before use of this medicine; skin rash

Other side effects may occur that usually do not need medical attention. These side effects may go away during treatment as your body adjusts to the medicine. However, check with your health care professional if the following side effect continues or is bothersome:

More common

Stinging (mild)—especially for gel and solution dosage forms

Other side effects not listed above may also occur in some patients. If you notice any other effects, check with your health care professional.

Revised: 03/04/92
Interim revision: 06/03/94

COCAINE Mucosal-Local

Description

Cocaine (KOE-kane) is a local anesthetic. It is applied to certain areas of the body (for example, the nose, mouth, or throat) to cause loss of feeling. This allows some kinds of examinations or surgery to be done without causing pain.

Cocaine can cause psychological dependence (a strong desire to continue using the medicine because of the ''high'' feeling it produces). This may lead to cocaine abuse (more frequent use and/or use of larger amounts of cocaine) and to an increased chance of serious side effects. Cocaine abuse has caused death from heart or breathing failure.

Use of cocaine as a local anesthetic for an examination or surgery is not likely to cause psychological dependence or other serious side effects. However, if cocaine is absorbed into the body too quickly, serious side effects can occur. Also, some people are especially sensitive to the effects of cocaine. Unwanted effects may occur in these people even with small amounts of the medicine. Before receiving cocaine as a local anesthetic, you should discuss its use with your doctor.

Cocaine is applied only by or under the immediate supervision of your doctor. It is available in the following dosage forms:

Mucosal-Local

- Crystals (U.S. and Canada)
- Solution (U.S.)

Before Receiving This Medicine

In deciding to use a medicine, the risks of taking the medicine must be weighed against the good it will do. This is a decision you and your doctor will make. For cocaine, the following should be considered:

Allergies—Tell your doctor if you have ever had any unusual or allergic reaction to cocaine. Also tell your health care professional if you are allergic to any other substances, such as foods, preservatives, or dyes.

Pregnancy—Studies on birth defects or other problems have not been done in pregnant women receiving cocaine as a local anesthetic. However, studies in women who abused cocaine during pregnancy have shown that cocaine may cause birth defects, decreased birth weight and size, and problems affecting the baby's nervous system. These studies have also shown that too much use of cocaine may cause the baby to be born too soon, sometimes too soon to survive. Cocaine has also been shown to cause birth defects and other unwanted effects in animal studies.

Breast-feeding—Cocaine passes into the breast milk and may cause unwanted effects such as convulsions (seizures), high blood pressure, fast heartbeat, breathing problems, trembling, and unusual irritability in nursing babies. Therefore, after receiving this medicine you should stop breast-feeding your baby for about 2 days.

Children—Cocaine can cause serious side effects in any patient. Therefore, it is especially important that you discuss with the child's doctor the good that this medicine may do as well as the risks of using it.

Older adults—Side effects, including dizziness or lightheadedness or fast or irregular heartbeat, may be especially likely to occur in elderly patients, who are usually more sensitive than younger adults to the effects of cocaine.

Other medicines—Although certain medicines should not be used together at all, in other cases two different medicines may be used together even if an interaction might occur. In these cases, your doctor may want to change the dose, or other precautions may be necessary. When you are receiving cocaine, it is especially important that your health care professional know if you are taking any of the following:

- Amantadine (e.g., Symmetrel) or
- Amphetamines or
- Antimyasthenics (ambenonium [e.g., Mytelase], neostigmine [e.g., Prostigmin], pyridostigmine [e.g., Mestinon]) or
- Appetite suppressants (diet pills), except fenfluramine (e.g., Pondimin), or
- Beta-blockers (acebutolol [e.g., Sectral], atenolol [e.g., Tenormin], betaxolol [e.g., Kerlone], carteolol [e.g., Cartrol], labetalol [e.g., Normodyne], metoprolol [e.g., Lopressor], nadolol [e.g., Corgard], oxprenolol [e.g., Trasicor], penbutolol [e.g., Levatol], pindolol [e.g., Visken], propranolol [e.g., Inderal], sotalol [e.g., Sotacor], timolol [e.g., Blocadren]) or
- Betaxolol (ophthalmic) (e.g., Betoptic) or
- Caffeine (e.g., NoDoz) or
- Chlophedianol (e.g., Ulone) or
- Cyclophosphamide (e.g., Cytoxan) or
- Demecarium (e.g., Humorsol) or
- Echothiophate (e.g., Phospholine Iodide) or
- Guanadrel (e.g., Hylorel) or
- Guanethidine (e.g., Ismelin) or
- Isoflurophate (e.g., Floropryl) or
- Levobunolol (e.g., Betagan) or
- Levodopa (e.g., Dopar) or
- Malathion (e.g., Prioderm) or
- Medicine for asthma or other breathing problems or
- Medicine for colds, sinus problems, or hay fever or other allergies (including nose drops or sprays) or
- Methyldopa (e.g., Aldomet) or
- Methylphenidate (e.g., Ritalin) or
- Metipranolol (e.g., OptiPranolol) or
- Nabilone (e.g., Cesamet) or
- Pemoline (e.g., Cylert) or
- Thiotepa or
- Timolol (ophthalmic) (e.g., Timoptic)—The chance of serious side effects may be increased
- Monoamine oxidase (MAO) inhibitors (furazolidone [e.g., Furoxone], isocarboxazid [e.g., Marplan], phenelzine [e.g., Nardil], procarbazine [e.g., Matulane], selegiline [e.g., Eldepryl], tranylcypromine [e.g., Parnate])—Receiving cocaine while you are taking or within 2 weeks after you have taken an MAO inhibitor may increase the chance of serious side effects.

Also tell your doctor if you have recently used an insecticide (insect killer) or if you have been in an area that was recently treated with an insecticide. Some insecticides can slow the breakdown of cocaine in your body. This increases the chance of serious side effects.

Other medical problems—The presence of other medical problems may affect the use of cocaine. Make sure you tell your doctor if you have any other medical problems, especially:

- Cancer or
- Chest pain, or history of, or
- Convulsions (seizures), history of, or
- Fast or irregular heartbeat or
- Heart or blood vessel disease or
- High blood pressure or
- Liver disease or
- Myocardial infarction (''heart attack''), history of, or
- Overactive thyroid—The chance of serious side effects may be increased

- Tourette's syndrome—Cocaine can make your condition worse

Proper Use of This Medicine

Dosing—The dose of cocaine will be different for different patients. It will depend on the reason a local anesthetic is needed and on the size of the area to which it is being applied. Your doctor or nurse will apply the medicine.

- For *mucosal-local* dosage forms (crystals or solution):
  - —For causing loss of feeling before examinations or surgery:
    - Adults and teenagers—Your doctor or nurse will apply the smallest amount of cocaine that will produce the needed effect. The largest amount that is usually used is 400 milligrams (mg).
    - Children up to 12 years of age—Use and dose must be determined by your doctor.

Precautions After Receiving This Medicine

Cocaine and some of its metabolites (substances to which cocaine is broken down in the body) will appear in your blood and urine for several days after you have received the medicine. Tests for possible drug use will then be "positive" for cocaine. If you must have such a test within 5 days or so after receiving cocaine, be sure to tell the person in charge that you have recently received cocaine for medical reasons. It may be helpful to have written information from your doctor stating why the medicine was used, the date on which you received it, and the amount you received.

Side Effects of This Medicine

Along with its needed effects, a medicine may cause some unwanted effects. Although not all of these side effects may occur, if they do occur they may need medical attention.

After cocaine has been applied, your doctor or nurse will closely follow its effects. However, *tell your doctor or nurse immediately* if any of the following side effects occur:

Signs and symptoms of too much medicine being absorbed into the body

Abdominal or stomach pain; chills; confusion; dizziness or lightheadedness; excitement, nervousness, restlessness, or any mood or mental changes; fast or irregular heartbeat; general feeling of discomfort or illness; hallucinations (seeing, hearing, or feeling things that are not there); headache (sudden); increased sweating; nausea

Other side effects may occur that usually do not need medical attention. However, check with your doctor if the following side effects continue or are bothersome:

More common

Loss of sense of taste or smell (after application to the nose or mouth)

Other side effects not listed above may also occur in some patients. If you notice any other effects, *tell your doctor or nurse immediately.*

Revised: 08/08/92
Interim revision: 07/14/94

COLCHICINE Systemic

Description

Colchicine (KOL-chi-seen) is used to prevent or treat attacks of gout (also called gouty arthritis). People with gout have too much uric acid in their blood and joints. An attack of gout occurs when uric acid causes inflammation (pain, redness, swelling, and heat) in a joint. Colchicine does not cure gout or take the place of other medicines that lower the amount of uric acid in the body. It prevents or relieves gout attacks by reducing inflammation. Colchicine is not an ordinary pain reliever and will not relieve most kinds of pain.

Colchicine may also be used for other conditions as determined by your doctor.

Colchicine may be used in 2 ways. Most people take small amounts of it regularly for a long time (months or even years) to prevent severe attacks or other problems caused by inflammation. Other people take large amounts of colchicine during a short period of time (several hours) only when the medicine is needed to relieve an attack that is occurring. The chance of serious side effects is much lower with the first (preventive) kind of treatment.

Because some of colchicine's side effects can be very serious, you should discuss with your doctor the good that this medicine can do as well as the risks of using it. Make sure you understand exactly how you are to use it, and follow the instructions carefully, to lessen the chance of unwanted effects.

This medicine is available only with your doctor's prescription, in the following dosage forms:

Oral

- Tablets (U.S. and Canada)

Parenteral

- Injection (U.S.)

Before Using This Medicine

In deciding to use a medicine, the risks of taking the medicine must be weighed against the good it will do. This is a decision you and your doctor will make. For colchicine, the following should be considered:

Allergies—Tell your doctor if you have ever had any unusual or allergic reaction to colchicine. Also tell your health care professional if you are allergic to any other substances, such as foods, preservatives, or dyes.

Pregnancy—Studies in humans taking large amounts of colchicine to relieve attacks have not been done. Fertility problems have occurred in some men taking small amounts of colchicine regularly (preventive treatment), but these problems went away after treatment was stopped. Many other men taking preventive amounts of colchicine have fathered children without stopping treatment. Also, many women receiving preventive treatment with colchicine have become pregnant and given birth to normal, healthy babies. Some women receive preventive amounts of colchicine regularly for a medical condition that can cause fertility problems or miscarriages. Treatment with colchicine does not increase, and may actually decrease, the occurrence of these problems in women with this condition.

Colchicine has caused birth defects and other problems in animal studies.

Breast-feeding—Colchicine passes into breast milk. When breast-feeding mothers receive preventive treatment with one 0.6-milligram (mg) tablet twice a day, the amount that appears in the breast milk is not likely to cause problems in nursing babies. There is no information about whether colchicine can cause problems in nursing babies when the mother takes larger amounts of it. Mothers who are taking this medicine and who wish to breast-feed should discuss this with their doctor.

Children—Studies on the effects of colchicine in patients with gout have been done only in adults. Gout is very rare in children. However, colchicine is used in children 3 years of age and older who need preventive treatment for other medical conditions. It has not been reported to cause different side effects or problems in these children than it does in adults.

Older adults—Elderly people are especially sensitive to the effects of colchicine. Also, colchicine may stay in the body longer in older patients than it does in younger adults. This may increase the chance of side effects during treatment.

Other medicines—Although certain medicines should not be used together at all, in other cases two different medicines may be used together even if an interaction might occur. In these cases, your doctor may want to change the dose, or other precautions may be necessary. When you are taking colchicine, it is especially important that your health care professional know if you are taking any of the following:

- Amphotericin B by injection (e.g., Fungizone) or
- Antineoplastics (cancer medicine) or
- Antithyroid agents (medicine for overactive thyroid) or
- Azathioprine (e.g., Imuran) or
- Chloramphenicol (e.g., Chloromycetin) or
- Cyclophosphamide (e.g., Cytoxan) or
- Flucytosine (e.g., Ancobon) or
- Ganciclovir (e.g., Cytovene) or
- Interferon (e.g., Intron A, Roferon-A) or
- Mercaptopurine (e.g., Purinethol) or
- Methotrexate (e.g., Mexate) or
- Phenylbutazone (e.g., Butazolidin) or
- Plicamycin (e.g., Mithracin) or
- Zidovudine (e.g., Retrovir)—The chance of serious side effects caused by a decrease in the numbers of certain blood cells may be increased

Other medical problems—The presence of other medical problems may affect the use of colchicine. Make sure you tell your doctor if you have any other medical problems, especially:

- Alcohol abuse or
- Intestinal disease or
- Stomach ulcer or other stomach problems—The chance of stomach upset may be increased. Also, colchicine can make some kinds of stomach or intestinal problems worse
- Heart disease or
- Kidney disease or
- Liver disease—The chance of serious side effects may be increased because these conditions can cause colchicine to build up in the body
- Low white blood cell count or
- Low platelet count—The chance of serious side effects may be increased because colchicine can make these conditions worse

Proper Use of This Medicine

Colchicine can build up in the body and cause serious side effects if too much of it is taken or if it is taken too often. Therefore, *do not take more of this medicine, and do not take it more often, than directed by your doctor*. This is especially important for elderly patients, who are more likely than younger adults to have colchicine build up in the body and who are also more sensitive to its effects.

For patients *taking small amounts of colchicine regularly (preventive treatment):*

- Take this medicine regularly as directed by your doctor, even if you feel well. If you are taking colchicine to prevent gout attacks, and you are also taking another medicine to reduce the amount of uric acid in your body, you probably will be able to stop taking colchicine after a while. However, if you stop taking it too soon, your attacks may return or get worse. If you are taking colchicine for certain other medical conditions, you may need to keep taking it for the rest of your life.
- If you are taking colchicine to prevent gout attacks, ask your doctor to recommend other medicine to be taken if an attack occurs. Most people receiving preventive amounts of colchicine should not take extra colchicine to relieve an attack. However, some people cannot take the other medicines that are used for gout attacks and will have to take extra colchicine. If you are one of these people, ask your doctor to tell you the largest amount of colchicine you should take for an attack and how long you should wait before starting to take the smaller preventive amounts again. Be sure to follow these directions carefully.

For patients *taking large amounts of colchicine only when needed to relieve an attack:*

- Start taking this medicine at the first sign of the attack for best results.
- *Stop taking this medicine as soon as the pain is relieved or at the first sign of nausea, vomiting, stomach pain, or diarrhea.* Also, stop taking colchicine

when you have taken the largest amount that your doctor ordered for each attack, even if the pain is not relieved or none of these side effects occurs.

- The first few times you take colchicine, keep a record of each dose as you take it. Then, whenever stomach upset (nausea, vomiting, stomach pain, or diarrhea) occurs, count the number of doses you have taken. The next time you need colchicine, stop taking it before that number of doses is reached. For example, if diarrhea occurs after your fifth dose of medicine, take no more than four doses the next time. If taking fewer doses does not prevent stomach upset from occurring after a few treatments, check with your doctor.
- After taking colchicine tablets to treat an attack, *do not take any more colchicine for at least 3 days. Also, after receiving the medicine by injection for an attack, do not take any more colchicine (tablets or injection) for at least 7 days.* Elderly patients may have to wait even longer between treatments and should check with their doctor for directions.
- If you are taking colchicine for an attack of gout, and you are also taking other medicine to reduce the amount of uric acid in your body, *do not stop taking the other medicine.* Continue taking the other medicine as directed by your doctor.

Dosing—The dose of colchicine will be different for different patients. *Follow your doctor's orders or the directions on the label.* The following information includes only the average doses of colchicine. *If your dose is different, do not change it* unless your doctor tells you to do so.

The number of doses you take each day, the time allowed between doses, and the length of time you take the medicine depend on how often your attacks occur and on whether you are taking the medicine to prevent or to relieve attacks. The amount of medicine you take will also depend on how you react to the medicine.

- For *oral* dosage form (tablets):
  - —Adults:
    - For *preventing gout attacks*—Most people start with one 0.5-milligram (mg) or 0.6-mg tablet a day. If gout attacks continue to occur, the doctor may direct you to increase the dose to one tablet two or even three times a day for a while. Some people with mild gout may need only one tablet every other day, or even less.
    - For *treating a gout attack that has already started*—Your doctor will probably recommend one of the following treatment plans:

      —One or two 0.5-mg or 0.6-mg tablets for the first dose, then one 0.5-mg or 0.6-mg tablet every one or two hours, or

      —Two 0.5-mg or 0.6-mg tablets or one 1-mg tablet every two hours.

      For both plans, *stop taking this medicine after you have taken the largest amount ordered by your doctor.* If your doctor has not told you the largest amount that you should take for one attack, *do not take more than 6 mg of this medicine* (a total of twelve 0.5-mg tablets, ten 0.6-mg tablets, or six 1-mg tablets, spread over a period of several hours).
  - —Children: Use and dose must be determined by the doctor.
- For *parenteral* dosage form (injection):
  - —Adults:
    - For *preventing gout attacks*—0.5 or 1 mg one or two times a day, injected into a vein.
    - For *treating an attack of gout that has already started*—1 or 2 mg for the first dose, then 0.5 mg or 1 mg every six to twelve hours, injected into a vein. *After a total of 4 mg has been given, no more colchicine (tablets or injections) should be given for at least seven days.*
  - —Children: Use and dose must be determined by the doctor.

Missed dose—If you are taking colchicine regularly (for example, every day) and you miss a dose, take it as soon as possible. However, if it is almost time for your next dose, skip the missed dose and go back to your regular dosing schedule. Do not double doses.

Storage—To store this medicine:

- Keep out of the reach of children.
- Store away from heat and direct light.
- Do not store this medicine in the bathroom, near the kitchen sink, or in other damp places. Heat or moisture may cause the medicine to break down.
- Do not keep outdated medicine or medicine no longer needed. Be sure that any discarded medicine is out of the reach of children.

Precautions While Using This Medicine

If you must take colchicine for a long time (preventive treatment), your doctor may want to check your progress at regular visits. He or she may also want to check for certain side effects. Finding these side effects early can help to keep them from becoming serious.

Stomach problems may be more likely to occur if you drink large amounts of alcoholic beverages while taking colchicine. Also, drinking too much alcohol may increase the amount of uric acid in your blood. This may lessen the effects of colchicine when it is used to prevent gout attacks. Therefore, people who take colchicine should be careful to limit the amount of alcohol they drink.

For patients taking *small amounts of colchicine regularly (preventive treatment):*

- Attacks of gout or other problems caused by inflammation may continue to occur during treatment. However, the attacks or other problems should occur less often, and they should not be as severe as they were before you started taking colchicine. Even if you think the colchicine is not working, *do not stop taking it and do not increase the dose.* Check with your doctor instead.

Side Effects of This Medicine

Along with its needed effects, a medicine may cause some unwanted effects. Although not all of these side effects may occur, if they do occur they may need medical attention.

Stop taking this medicine immediately if any of the following side effects occur:

More common

Diarrhea; nausea or vomiting; stomach pain

If any of these side effects continue for 3 hours or longer after you have stopped taking colchicine, check with your doctor.

Also, *check with your doctor immediately* if any of the following side effects occur:

Rare

Black, tarry stools; blood in urine or stools; difficulty in breathing when exercising; fever with or without chills; headache; large, hive-like swellings on the face, eyelids, mouth, lips, and/or tongue; pinpoint red spots on skin; sores, ulcers, or white spots on lips or in mouth; sore throat; unusual bleeding or bruising; unusual tiredness or weakness

Signs and symptoms of overdose

Burning feeling in the stomach, throat, or skin; diarrhea (severe or bloody); nausea, stomach pain, or vomiting (severe)

Note: These side effects are usually the first signs of an overdose of colchicine tablets. They are not likely to occur when too much colchicine has been given by injection. Other signs and symptoms that may occur after an overdose of either the tablets or the injection include bleeding; fast, shallow breathing; convulsions (seizures); fever; and very severe muscle weakness. An overdose of colchicine can cause damage to the blood, heart, intestines, kidneys, liver, lungs, and muscles.

The following side effects may occur after an injection of colchicine. Check with your doctor as soon as possible if any of the following occur at or near the place of injection:

Rare

Burning, ''crawling,'' or tingling feeling in the skin; pain; peeling of skin; redness; swelling; tenderness

Also, check with your doctor as soon as possible if any of the following side effects occur:

Rare

Muscle weakness; numbness in fingers or toes (usually mild); skin rash or hives

Other side effects may occur that usually do not need medical attention. However, check with your doctor if either of the following side effects continues or is bothersome:

Less common

Loss of appetite

With long-term use

Loss of hair

Other side effects not listed above may also occur in some patients. If you notice any other effects, check with your doctor.

Additional Information

Once a medicine has been approved for marketing for a certain use, experience may show that it is also useful for other medical problems. Although these uses are not included in product labeling, colchicine is used in certain patients with the following medical conditions:

- Amyloidosis
- Behçet's syndrome
- Calcium pyrophosphate deposition disease (pseudogout)
- Cirrhosis of the liver
- Familial Mediterranean fever
- Pericarditis
- Sarcoid arthritis

If you are taking colchicine for any of these conditions, the following information may apply:

- For all of these conditions, colchicine is usually given regularly in small amounts to reduce inflammation (preventive treatment). This usually decreases the occurrence of severe attacks or other problems caused by inflammation.
- Colchicine is not a cure for these conditions. It will help prevent problems caused by inflammation only as long as you continue to take it.
- Some patients with calcium pyrophosphate deposition disease (pseudogout) or familial Mediterranean fever may take larger amounts of colchicine only when an attack occurs, to relieve the attack.

For patients taking colchicine for *familial Mediterranean fever:*

- Preventive treatment with colchicine may be helping you even if it does not reduce the number of severe attacks. Colchicine helps prevent other serious problems, such as kidney disease, that can occur in people with this condition. Therefore, even if you think that the colchicine isn't working, *do not stop taking it*. Check with your doctor instead.

Other than the above information, there is no additional information relating to proper use, precautions, or side effects for these uses.

Revised: 01/31/94

COLESTIPOL Oral

A commonly used brand name is:

In the U.S.—
Colestid

In Canada—
Colestid

Description

Colestipol (koe-LES-ti-pole) is used to lower high cholesterol levels in the blood. This may help prevent medical problems caused by cholesterol clogging the blood vessels.

Colestipol works by attaching to certain substances in the intestine. Since colestipol is not absorbed into the body, these substances also pass out of the body without being absorbed.

Colestipol may also be used for other conditions as determined by your doctor.

Colestipol is available only with your doctor's prescription, in the following dosage form:

Oral
- Powder (U.S. and Canada)

Before Using This Medicine

In deciding to use a medicine, the risks of taking the medicine must be weighed against the good it will do. This is a decision you and your doctor will make. For colestipol, the following should be considered:

Allergies—Tell your doctor if you have ever had any unusual or allergic reaction to colestipol. Also tell your health care professional if you are allergic to any substances, such as foods, preservatives, or dyes.

Diet—Before prescribing medicine for your condition, your doctor will probably try to control your condition by prescribing a personal diet for you. Such a diet may be low in fats, sugars, and/or cholesterol. Many people are able to control their condition by carefully following their doctor's orders for proper diet and exercise. Medicine is prescribed only when additional help is needed and is effective only when a schedule of diet and exercise is properly followed.

Also, this medicine is less effective if you are greatly overweight. It may be very important for you to go on a reducing diet. However, check with your doctor before going on any diet.

Make certain your health care professional knows if you are on a low-sodium, low-sugar, or any other special diet.

Pregnancy—Colestipol is not absorbed into the body and is not likely to cause problems. However, it may reduce absorption of vitamins into the body. Ask your doctor whether you need to take extra vitamins.

Breast-feeding—Colestipol is not absorbed into the body and is not likely to cause problems.

Children—There is no specific information comparing use of colestipol in children with use in other age groups. However, use is not recommended in children under 2 years of age since cholesterol is needed for normal development.

Older adults—Side effects may be more likely to occur in patients over 60 years of age, who are usually more sensitive to the effects of colestipol.

Other medicines—Although certain medicines should not be used together at all, in other cases two different medicines may be used together even if an interaction might occur. In these cases, your doctor may want to change the dose, or other precautions may be necessary. When you are taking colestipol it is especially important that your health care professional knows if you are taking any of the following:

- Anticoagulants (blood thinners)—The effects of the anticoagulant may be altered
- Digitalis glycosides (heart medicine) or
- Diuretics (water pills) or
- Penicillin G, taken by mouth, or
- Propranolol, taken by mouth, or
- Tetracyclines (medicine for infection), taken by mouth, or
- Thyroid hormones or
- Vancomycin, taken by mouth—Colestipol may cause these medicines to be less effective; these medicines should be taken 4 to 5 hours apart from colestipol

Other medical problems—The presence of other medical problems may affect the use of colestipol. Make sure you tell your doctor if you have any other medical problems, especially:

- Bleeding problems or
- Constipation or
- Gallstones or
- Heart or blood vessel disease or
- Hemorrhoids or
- Stomach ulcer or other stomach problems or
- Underactive thyroid—Colestipol may make these conditions worse
- Kidney disease—There is an increased risk of developing electrolyte problems
- Liver disease—Cholesterol levels may be raised

Proper Use of This Medicine

Take this medicine exactly as directed by your doctor. Try not to miss any doses and do not take more medicine than your doctor ordered.

Follow carefully the special diet your doctor gave you. This is the most important part of controlling your condition and is necessary if the medicine is to work properly.

This medicine should never be taken in its dry form, since it could cause you to choke. Instead, always mix as follows:

- Add this medicine to 3 ounces or more of water, milk, flavored drink, or your favorite juice or carbonated drink. If you use a carbonated drink, slowly mix in the powder in a large glass to prevent too much foaming. Stir until it is completely mixed (it will *not* dissolve) before drinking. After drinking all the liquid containing the medicine, rinse the glass with a little more liquid and drink that also, to make sure you get all the medicine.
- You may also mix this medicine with milk in hot or regular breakfast cereals, or in thin soups such as tomato or chicken noodle soup. Or you may add it to some pulpy fruits such as crushed pineapple, pears, peaches, or fruit cocktail.

Dosing—The dose of colestipol will be different for different patients. *Follow your doctor's orders or the directions on the label.* The following information includes only the average doses of colestipol. *If your dose is different, do not change it* unless your doctor tells you to do so.

• For *oral* dosage form (powder for oral suspension):
—For high cholesterol:
• Adults—15 to 30 grams a day. This is divided into two to four doses and taken before meals.
• Children—Use and dose must be determined by your doctor.

Missed dose—If you miss a dose of this medicine, take it as soon as possible. Then go back to your regular dosing schedule. However, if it is almost time for your next dose, skip the missed dose and go back to your regular dosing schedule. Do not double doses.

Storage—To store this medicine:
• Keep out of the reach of children.
• Store away from heat and direct light.
• Do not store in the bathroom, near the kitchen sink or in other damp places. Heat or moisture may cause the medicine to break down.
• Do not keep outdated medicine or medicine no longer needed. Be sure that any discarded medicine is out of the reach of children.

Precautions While Using This Medicine

It is very important that your doctor check your progress at regular visits. This will allow your doctor to see if the medicine is working properly to lower your cholesterol levels and to decide if you should continue to take it.

Do not stop taking this medicine without first checking with your doctor. When you stop taking this medicine, your blood cholesterol levels may increase again. Your doctor may want you to follow a special diet to help prevent this from happening.

Do not take any other medicine unless prescribed by your doctor since colestipol may interfere with other medicines.

Side Effects of This Medicine

Along with its needed effects, a medicine may cause some unwanted effects. Although not all of these side effects may occur, if they do occur they may need medical attention.

Check with your doctor immediately if either of the following side effects occurs:
Rare
Black, tarry stools; stomach pain (severe) with nausea and vomiting

Check with your doctor as soon as possible if either of the following side effects occurs:
More common
Constipation
Rare
Loss of weight (sudden)

Other side effects may occur that usually do not need medical attention. These side effects may go away during treatment as your body adjusts to the medicine. However, check with your doctor if any of the following side effects continue or are bothersome:
Less common
Belching; bloating; diarrhea; dizziness; headache; nausea or vomiting; stomach pain

Other side effects not listed above may also occur in some patients. If you notice any other effects, check with your doctor.

Additional Information

Once a medicine has been approved for marketing for a certain use, experience may show that it is also useful for other medical problems. Although these uses are not included in product labeling, colestipol is used in certain patients with the following medical conditions:
• Diarrhea caused by bile acids
• Digitalis glycoside overdose
• Excess oxalate in the urine
• Itching (pruritus) associated with partial biliary obstruction

Other than the above information, there is no additional information relating to proper use, precautions, or side effects for these uses.

Revised: 10/21/92
Interim revision: 04/14/94

COLISTIN, NEOMYCIN, AND HYDROCORTISONE Otic

Some commonly used brand names are:

In the U.S.—
Coly-Mycin S Otic

In Canada—
Coly-Mycin Otic

Description

Colistin (koe-LIS-tin), neomycin (nee-oh-MYE-sin), and hydrocortisone (hye-droe-KOR-ti-sone) combination contains two antibiotics and a cortisone-like medicine. It is used in the ear to treat infections of the ear canal and to help provide relief from redness, irritation, and discomfort of certain ear problems.

Colistin, neomycin, and hydrocortisone combination is available only with your doctor's prescription, in the following dosage form:
Otic
• Suspension (U.S. and Canada)

Before Using This Medicine

In deciding to use a medicine, the risks of taking the medicine must be weighed against the good it will do. This is a decision you and your doctor will make. For colistin, neomycin, and hydrocortisone combination, the following should be considered:

Allergies—Tell your doctor if you have ever had any unusual or allergic reaction to this medicine or to any related antibiotics such as amikacin (e.g., Amikin), colistin by mouth or by injection (e.g., Coly-Mycin), gentamicin (e.g., Garamycin), kanamycin (e.g., Kantrex), neomycin by mouth or by injection (e.g., Mycifradin), netilmicin (e.g., Netromycin), paromomycin (e.g., Humatin), polymyxin B (e.g., Aerosporin), streptomycin, or tobramycin (e.g., Nebcin). Also tell your health care professional if you are allergic to any other substances, such as thimerosal or other preservatives.

Pregnancy—Colistin, neomycin, and hydrocortisone otic drops have not been shown to cause birth defects or other problems in humans.

Breast-feeding—Colistin, neomycin, and hydrocortisone otic drops have not been reported to cause problems in nursing babies.

Children—Although there is no specific information comparing use of colistin, neomycin, and hydrocortisone combination in children with use in other age groups, this medicine is not expected to cause different side effects or problems in children than it does in adults.

Older adults—Many medicines have not been studied specifically in older people. Therefore, it may not be known whether they work exactly the same way they do in younger adults. Although there is no specific information comparing use of colistin, neomycin, and hydrocortisone combination in the elderly with use in other age groups, this medicine is not expected to cause different side effects or problems in older people than it does in younger adults.

Other medicines—Although certain medicines should not be used together at all, in other cases two different medicines may be used together even if an interaction might occur. In these cases, your doctor may want to change the dose, or other precautions may be necessary. Tell your health care professional if you are using any other prescription or nonprescription (over-the-counter [OTC]) medicine that is to be used in the ear.

Other medical problems—The presence of other medical problems may affect the use of colistin, neomycin, and hydrocortisone combination. Make sure you tell your doctor if you have any other medical problems, especially:

- Other ear infection or problem, including punctured eardrum—Use of colistin, neomycin, and hydrocortisone combination may make the condition worse or may increase the chance of side effects
- Herpes simplex—Use of hydrocortisone may make the condition worse

Proper Use of This Medicine

Before applying this medicine, thoroughly clean the ear canal and dry it with a sterile cotton applicator.

You may warm the ear drops to body temperature (37 °C or 98.6 °F), but no higher, by holding the bottle in your hand for a few minutes before applying. If this medicine gets too warm, it may break down and not work properly.

To apply this medicine:

- Lie down or tilt the head so that the infected ear faces up. Gently pull the earlobe up and back for adults (down and back for children) to straighten the ear canal. Drop the medicine into the ear canal. Keep the ear facing up for about 5 minutes to allow the medicine to coat the ear canal. (For young children and other patients who cannot stay still for 5 minutes, try to keep the ear facing up for at least 1 or 2 minutes.) Your doctor may have inserted a gauze or cotton wick into your ear and may want you to keep the wick moistened with this medicine. Your doctor also may have other directions for you, such as how long you should keep the wick in your ear or when you should return to your doctor to have the wick replaced. If you have any questions about this, check with your doctor.

To keep the medicine as germ-free as possible, do not touch the dropper to any surface (including the ear). Also, keep the container tightly closed.

Do not use this medicine for more than 10 days unless otherwise directed by your doctor.

To help clear up your infection completely, *keep using this medicine for the full time of treatment,* even if your symptoms begin to clear up after a few days. If you stop using this medicine too soon, your symptoms may return. *Do not miss any doses.*

Dosing—The dose of otic colistin, neomycin, and hydrocortisone combination will be different for different patients. *Follow your doctor's orders or the directions on the label.* The following information includes only the average doses of otic colistin, neomycin, and hydrocortisone combination. *If your dose is different, do not change it* unless your doctor tells you to do so.

- For *otic suspension (ear drops)* dosage form:
  —For infections of the ear canal:
    - Adults—Use four drops in the ear every six to eight hours.
    - Children—Use up to three drops in the ear every six to eight hours.

Missed dose—If you miss a dose of this medicine, apply it as soon as possible. However, if it is almost time for your next dose, skip the missed dose and go back to your regular dosing schedule.

Storage—To store this medicine:

- Keep out of the reach of children.
- Store away from heat and direct light.
- Keep the medicine from freezing
- Do not keep outdated medicine or medicine no longer needed. Be sure that any discarded medicine is out of the reach of children.

Precautions While Using This Medicine

If your symptoms do not improve within 1 week, or if they become worse, check with your doctor immediately.

Side Effects of This Medicine

Along with its needed effects, a medicine may cause some unwanted effects. Although not all of these side effects may occur, if they do occur they may need medical attention.

Check with your doctor immediately if any of the following side effects occur:

More common

Itching, skin rash, redness, swelling, or other sign of irritation not present before use of this medicine

Other side effects not listed above may also occur in some patients. If you notice any other effects, check with your doctor.

Revised: 05/25/95

COLONY STIMULATING FACTORS Systemic

Some commonly used brand names are:

In the U.S.—

Neupogen[1]

Leukine[2]

In Canada—

Neupogen[1]

Other commonly used names are:

Granulocyte colony stimulating factor (G-CSF)[1]

Granulocyte-macrophage colony stimulating factor (GM-CSF)[2]

Note: For quick reference, the following colony stimulating factors are numbered to match the corresponding brand names.

This information applies to the following medicines:

1. Filgrastim (fil-GRA-stim)
2. Sargramostim (sar-GRAM-o-stim)†

†Not commercially available in Canada.

Description

Filgrastim and sargramostim are synthetic (man-made) versions of substances naturally produced in your body. These substances, called colony stimulating factors, help the bone marrow to make new white blood cells.

When certain cancer medicines fight your cancer cells, they also affect those white blood cells that fight infection. To help prevent infections when these cancer medicines are used, colony stimulating factors may also be given.

Colony stimulating factors are available only with your doctor's prescription, in the following dosage form:

Parenteral

Filgrastim

- Injection (U.S. and Canada)

Sargramostim

- Injection (U.S.)

Before Using This Medicine

In deciding to use a medicine, the risks of taking the medicine must be weighed against the good it will do. This is a decision you and your doctor will make. For colony stimulating factors, the following should be considered:

Allergies—Tell your doctor if you have ever had any unusual or allergic reaction to the colony stimulating factor. Also tell your health care professional if you are allergic to any other substances, such as foods, preservatives, or dyes.

Pregnancy—Colony stimulating factors have not been studied in pregnant women.

- *Filgrastim*—In studies in rabbits, filgrastim did not cause birth defects but did cause internal defects, a decrease in average weight, and death of the fetus in high doses.
- *Sargramostim*—Studies on birth defects have not been done in animals.

Breast-feeding—It is not known whether colony stimulating factors pass into the breast milk. However, these medicines have not been reported to cause problems in nursing babies.

Children—Although there is no specific information comparing use of colony stimulating factors in children with use in other age groups, this medicine is not expected to cause different side effects or problems in children than it does in adults.

Older adults—Many medicines have not been studied specifically in older people. Therefore, it may not be known whether they work exactly the same way they do in younger adults. Although there is no specific information comparing use of colony stimulating factors in the elderly with use in other age groups, this medicine has been used in many elderly patients and is not expected to cause different side effects or problems in older people than it does in younger adults.

Other medicines—Although certain medicines should not be used together at all, in other cases two different medicines may be used together even if an interaction might occur. In these cases, your doctor may want to change the dose, or other precautions may be necessary. Tell your health care professional if you are taking any other prescription or nonprescription (over-the-counter [OTC]) medicine.

Other medical problems—The presence of other medical problems may affect the use of colony stimulating factors. Make sure you tell your doctor if you have any other medical problems, especially:

- Conditions caused by inflammation or immune system problems—There is a chance these may be worsened by colony stimulating factor
- Heart disease—Risk of some unwanted effects (heart rhythm problems, retaining water) may be increased
- Kidney disease or
- Liver disease—May sometimes be worsened by colony stimulating factor
- Lung disease—Colony stimulating factor may cause shortness of breath

Proper Use of This Medicine

If you are injecting this medicine yourself, *use it exactly as directed by your doctor*. Do not use more or less of it, and do not use it more often than your doctor ordered.

The exact amount of medicine you need has been carefully worked out. Using too much will increase the risk of side effects, while using too little may not improve your condition.

If you are injecting this medicine yourself, each package of colony stimulating factor will contain a patient instruction sheet. Read this sheet carefully and make sure you understand:
- How to prepare the injection.
- Proper use of disposable syringes.
- How to give the injection.
- How long the injection is stable.

If you have any questions about any of this, check with your health care professional.

Dosing—The dose of colony stimulating factors will be different for different patients. The dose that is used may depend on a number of things, including what the medicine is being used for, the patient's body weight or size, and whether or not other medicines are also being taken. *If you are receiving colony stimulating factors at home, follow your doctor's orders or the directions on the label.* If you have any questions about the proper dose of colony stimulating factors, ask your doctor.

Missed dose—If you miss a dose of this medicine, check with your doctor.

Storage—To store this medicine:
- Keep out of the reach of children.
- Store in the refrigerator.
- Keep the medicine from freezing.
- Do not keep outdated medicine or medicine no longer needed. Ask your health care professional how you should dispose of any medicine you do not use. Be sure that any discarded medicine is out of the reach of children.

Precautions While Using This Medicine

It is very important that your doctor check your progress at regular visits to make sure that this medicine is working properly and to check for unwanted effects.

Colony stimulating factors are used to prevent or reduce the risk of infection while you are being treated with cancer medicines. Because your body's ability to fight infection is reduced, *it is very important that you call your doctor at the first sign of any infection* (for example, if you get a fever or chills) so you can start antibiotic treatment right away.

Colony stimulating factors commonly cause mild bone pain, usually in the lower back or pelvis, about the time the white blood cells start to come back in your bone marrow. The pain is usually mild and lasts only a few days. Your doctor will probably prescribe a mild analgesic (painkiller) for you to take during that time. If you find that the analgesic is not strong enough, talk with your doctor about using something that will make you more comfortable.

Side Effects of This Medicine

Along with its needed effects, a medicine may cause some unwanted effects. Although not all of these side effects may occur, if they do occur they may need medical attention.

The side effects listed below include only those that might be caused by colony stimulating factors. To find out about other side effects that may be caused by the cancer medicines you are also receiving, look under the information about those specific medicines.

Check with your doctor as soon as possible if any of the following side effects occur:

For filgrastim

Less common

Redness or pain at the site of subcutaneous (under the skin) injection

Rare

Fever; rapid or irregular heartbeat; sores on skin; wheezing

For sargramostim

Less common

Fever; redness or pain at the site of subcutaneous (under the skin) injection; shortness of breath; swelling of feet or lower legs; weight gain (sudden)

Rare

Chest pain; rapid or irregular heartbeat; sores on skin; wheezing

Other side effects may occur that usually do not need medical attention. These side effects may go away during treatment as your body adjusts to the medicine. However, check with your doctor if any of the following side effects continue or are bothersome:

For both filgrastim and sargramostim

More common

Headache; pain in joints or muscles; pain in lower back or pelvis; skin rash or itching

Less common

Pain in arms or legs

For sargramostin only (in addition to the above)

Less common or rare

Dizziness or faintness after first dose of medicine; flushing of face after first dose of medicine; weakness

Other side effects not listed above may also occur in some patients. If you notice any other effects, check with your doctor.

Revised: 08/07/92
Interim revision: 04/22/93; 07/14/94

CONDOMS

Some commonly used brand names are:

In the U.S.—

Beyond Seven[3]
Beyond Seven Plus[4]
Class Act Ribbed & Sensitive[3]
Class Act Ultra Thin & Sensitive[3]
Class Act Ultra Thin & Sensitive Spermicidal Lubricated[4]
Crown[3]
Crown Plus[4]
Embrace[3]
Excita Fiesta[3]
Excita Sensitrol[3]
Fourex Natural Skins[1]
Fourex Natural Skins Spermicidally Lubricated[2]
Gold Circle Coin[3]
Gold Circle Rainbow Coin[3]
Kimono[3]
Kimono Microthins[3]
Kimono Microthins Plus[4]
Kimono Plus[4]
Kimono Sensation[3]
Kimono Sensation Plus[4]
Kling-Tite Naturalamb[1]
Kling-Tite Naturalamb with Spermicide Lubricant[2]
LifeStyles Assorted Colors[3]
LifeStyles Extra Strength with Spermicide[4]
LifeStyles Form Fitting[3]
LifeStyles Lubricated[3]
LifeStyles Non-Lubricated[3]
LifeStyles Spermicidally Lubricated[4]
LifeStyles Ultra Sensitive[3]
LifeStyles Ultra Sensitive with Spermicide[4]
LifeStyles Vibra-Ribbed[3]
LifeStyles Vibra-Ribbed with Spermicide[4]
MAXX[3]
MAXX Plus[4]
Ramses Extra[4]
Ramses Extra Ribbed[4]
Ramses Extra Strength[4]
Ramses Non-Lubricated[3]
Ramses Ribbed[4]
Ramses Safe Play[3]
Ramses Sensitol[3]
Ramses Ultra Thin[3]
Ramses with Spermicidal Lubricant[4]
Ramses Ultra Thin Ribbed with Spermicide[4]
Ramses Ultra Thin with Spermicide[4]
Saxon Gold Rainbow Ultra Spermicidal[4]
Saxon Gold Ultra Sensitive[3]
Saxon Gold Ultra Spermicidal[4]
Sheik Classic Lubricated[3]
Sheik Classic Non-Lubricated[3]
Sheik Classic Spermicidally Lubricated[4]
Sheik Excita Extra[4]
Sheik Fiesta Colors[3]
Sheik Super Thin Lubricated[3]
Sheik Super Thin Ribbed Lubricated[3]
Sheik Super Thin Ribbed Spermicidally Lubricated[4]
Sheik Super Thin Spermicidally Lubricated[4]
Touch Lubricated[3]
Touch Non-Lubricated[3]
Touch Ribbed Lubricated[3]
Touch Sunrise Colors[3]
Touch Spermicidally Lubricated[4]
Touch Thins Lubricated[3]
Trojan-Enz Large Lubricated[3]
Trojan-Enz Large with Spermicidal Lubricant[4]
Trojan-Enz Lubricated[3]
Trojan-Enz Nonlubricated[3]
Trojan-Enz with Spermicidal Lubricant[4]
Trojan Extra Strength Lubricated[3]
Trojan Magnum[3]
Trojan Magnum Spermicidal Lubricant[4]
Trojan Naturalube Ribbed[3]
Trojan Plus[3]
Trojan Plus 2[4]
Trojan Ribbed[3]
Trojan Ribbed with Spermicidal Lubricant[4]
Trojans[3]
Trojan Ultra Texture Lubricant[3]
Trojan Ultra Texture with Spermicidal Lubricant[4]
Trojan Very Sensitive with Lubricant[3]
Trojan Very Sensitive with Spermicidal Lubricant[4]
Trojan Very Thin with Lubricant[3]
Trojan Very Thin with Spermicidal Lubricant[4]

Generic name product may be available.

In Canada—

Embrace[3]
Fourex Natural Skins[1]
Gold Circle Coin[3]
Kling-Tite Naturalamb[1]
LifeStyles Extra Strength with Spermicide[4]
LifeStyles Form Fitting[3]
LifeStyles Lubricated[3]
LifeStyles Lubricated with Spermicide[4]
LifeStyles Ultra Sensitive[3]
LifeStyles Vibra-Ribbed[3]
Ortho Shields Lubricated[3]
Ortho Shields Non-Lubricated[3]
Ortho Shields Plus[4]
Ortho Shields X[3]
Ortho Supreme[3]
Ramses Extra[4]
Ramses Extra-15[4]
Ramses Non-Lubricated[3]
Ramses Ribbed[4]
Ramses Sensitol[3]
Ramses Thin Lub[3]
Ramses Thin Spermicidal Lub[4]
Ramses Ultra[3]
Ramses Ultra-15[4]
Sheik Denim[3]
Sheik Elite[4]
Sheik Excita[4]
Sheik Non-Lubricated[3]
Sheik Sensi-Creme[3]
Sheik Thin Lub[3]
Sheik Thin Spermicidal Lub[4]
Titan Lubricated[3]
Titan Ribbed[3]
Titan with Silicone Spermicidal Lubricant[4]
Trojan[3]
Trojan-Enz[3]
Trojan-Enz Large Lubricated[3]
Trojan-Enz Large with Spermicidal Lube[4]
Trojan-Enz Lubricated[3]
Trojan-Enz with Spermicidal Lubricant[4]
Trojan Naturalube Ribbed[3]
Trojan Plus[3]
Trojan Ribbed[3]
Trojan Ribbed with Spermicidal Lube[4]

Note: For quick reference, the following condoms are numbered to match the corresponding brand names.

This information applies to the following products:
1. Lamb Cecum Condoms
2. Lamb Cecum Condoms and Nonoxynol 9
3. Latex Condoms
4. Latex Condoms and Nonoxynol 9

Description

Condoms (KON-dums) are used by a male partner during sexual intercourse as a form of birth control. Latex rubber condoms are also used during anal, vaginal, or oral sex to help protect against sexually transmitted diseases such as AIDS (HIV infection), genital herpes (herpes simplex II), gonorrhea, syphilis, chlamydia, genital warts, and hepatitis.

Condoms can be a highly effective form of birth control when they are used properly. However, pregnancy usually occurs in 12 of each 100 women during the first year of condom use. You can discuss with your doctor what your options are for birth control and the pros and cons of using each method.

Condoms work to protect against sexually transmitted diseases (STDs) and as a birth control method by acting as barrier (wall) to keep blood, semen, and other fluids from passing from one partner to the other. The germs that can cause STDs are present in these fluids. With the proper use of latex condoms, these fluids are trapped inside the condom, along with sperm and any germs that may be present.

Latex rubber condoms are preferred for the prevention of STDs. Even though lamb intestine condoms are as effective as latex condoms in preventing pregnancy, it is not known whether they are as effective as latex condoms in protecting against all of the STDs, especially AIDS. Therefore, lamb intestine condoms should be used to protect against STDs *only* if you (or your partner) are allergic or sensitive to latex rubber condoms.

The use of a spermicide along with a condom increases the condom's ability to prevent pregnancy. Also, *laboratory studies* have shown that the spermicide nonoxynol 9 kills or stops the growth of the AIDS virus (HIV) and herpes simplex I and II viruses. It was also shown to be effective against other types of germs that cause gonorrhea, chlamydia, syphilis, trichomoniasis, and other STDs. *Although this has not been proven in human studies, some scientists believe that spermicides put into the vagina or on the outside of a latex condom may kill these germs before they are able to come in contact with the vagina or rectum (lower bowel).* Spermicides also provide a back-up in case the condom breaks, slips, or leaks during sexual intercourse.

The most effective way to protect yourself against STDs (such as AIDS) is by abstinence (not having sexual intercourse) or by having only one partner and making sure that person is not already infected and is *not* going to get an STD. However, if any of these methods are not likely or possible, using latex rubber condoms with an extra spermicide product is the best way to protect yourself. This is especially important if you cannot be sure a partner does not have an STD.

The use of a condom is recommended even when you are using other methods of birth control, such as birth control pills (the Pill), the cervical cap, the contraceptive sponge, diaphragm, and the intrauterine device (IUD), since these methods do not offer any protection from STDs.

The safety of using condoms with spermicides in the rectum (lower bowel), anus, or rectal area is not known. No side effects have been reported that are different from those reported for use in the vagina. However, some studies have reported that latex condoms are more likely to break during anal intercourse.

Condoms are available without a prescription in the following product forms:

- Lamb intestine condoms (U.S. and Canada)
- Lamb intestine condoms and nonoxynol 9 (a spermicide) (U.S.)
- Latex condoms (U.S. and Canada)
- Latex condoms and nonoxynol 9 (U.S. and Canada)

Before Using This Product

In deciding to use condoms as a method of birth control or to prevent STDs, you need to consider the pros and cons involved with their use. This is a decision you and your sexual partner will make. The following information may help you in making your decision. Ask your health care professional for more information if you have any questions.

Allergies—If you have ever had any unusual or allergic reaction to condoms or other rubber products, it is best to check with your doctor before using latex condoms. Also, it is a good idea to check with your doctor before using condoms with nonoxynol 9 if you have ever had an allergic or unusual reaction to spermicides.

Adolescents—These products are frequently used by teenagers and have not been shown to cause different problems than they do in adults. However, some younger or first time users may need extra counseling and information on the importance of using condoms exactly as they are supposed to be used so they will work properly.

Proper Use of This Product

Some condoms have a dry or wet lubricant applied to them. Use of a lubricant may help prevent condoms from breaking or slipping and prevent irritation to the vagina, anus, or rectum. It may be especially important to use a lubricant during anal intercourse, since some studies have shown that latex condoms break more often during anal intercourse. This is because there is greater friction (rubbing force) during anal intercourse, as compared with vaginal or oral intercourse. *If you need an extra lubricant, make sure it is a water-based product safe for use with condoms, cervical caps, or diaphragms.* Spermicides, especially gels and jellies, also provide some lubrication during sexual intercourse. *Oil-based products such as hand, face, or body cream; petroleum jelly; cooking oils or shortenings; or mineral or baby oil should not be used because they weaken the latex rubber.* (Even some products that easily rinse away with water are oil-based and should not be used.) This increases the chances of the condom breaking during sexual intercourse.

To use:

- *Before **any** genital contact occurs:*

—Open the condom wrapper carefully, making sure you do not damage it before use. Always handle the unwrapped condom carefully. If the wrapper was already open, do not use the condom because the condom may be damaged or weakened.

—Look at the unrolled condom before it is placed on the penis, to check it for any damage or defects. Occasionally, a condom may be damaged from improper storage, opening, or manufacturing. If the condom feels sticky, brittle, dried out, or gummy, do not use it. Also, check the tip for tears or holes. However, do not unroll the condom to look at it before you are ready to use it. Also, do not fill it with water to check it for leaks. Both of these actions will weaken the condom. When handling the condom, be careful also not to tear it with sharp or jagged fingernails and sharp rings or jewelry. Use a different condom if you have any doubts about any condom's quality or condition.

—Place the unrolled condom over the tip of the erect (hard) penis. Check the condom to make sure the correct side is touching the penis. If you accidentally put on the unrolled condom with the wrong side out, it should not be used. There is a chance that germs or sperm could get on the tip of the condom. If you then reversed the condom and unrolled it correctly, your partner would be in contact with the germs or sperm.

—Pinch the end of the condom to leave a half-inch of space for the semen to collect in. If the condom has a reservoir, pinch this reservoir to get rid of any air. Leaving this extra space will keep semen and other fluids from spilling out during intercourse.

—While still pinching the tip of the condom, completely unroll the condom down the length of the penis to its base. If the penis is uncircumcised, the foreskin should be pulled back before the condom is unrolled. To be most effective in preventing STDs, the condom must cover the entire penis.

—If you are using extra spermicide or lubricant, carefully spread some on the outside of the condom. It is a good idea to check the rest of the condom for any defects or damage at this time. A female partner should also use a spermicide inside the vagina.

- *After genital contact occurs:*

—If a condom breaks during intercourse, immediately put on a new condom. Also, apply more spermicide or lubricant.

—Immediately after ejaculation and before the penis becomes soft, firmly grasp the ring of the condom at the base of the penis. Carefully withdraw the penis to avoid tearing the condom or spilling semen. Discard the used condom properly.

—You must use a new condom each time you repeat intercourse. *Condoms should never be reused.* Spermicide or lubricant should also be re-applied outside of the new condom. A female partner should also put more spermicide in the vagina each time she has intercourse.

For females using condoms with extra spermicide:

- Condoms do not have to be used with spermicides, but the spermicide may provide a back-up in case the condom leaks or breaks.
- It is very important that the spermicide be placed properly in the vagina. It should be put deep into the vagina, directly on the cervix (opening to the uterus). The written instructions about how the product container and the applicator work, how much spermicide to use each time, and how long each application remains effective may be different for each product. Make sure you carefully read and follow the instructions that come with each product.
- *Make sure the spermicide you choose is labeled as being safe for use with latex diaphragms, cervical caps, or condoms.* Otherwise, it may cause the condom to weaken and leak or even break during intercourse.

Storage—To store:

- Store in a dark, cool, dry place. Avoid extreme temperatures and direct light. If you carry a condom with you, keep it in a wallet, loose pocket, or purse for no more than a few hours at time.
- Do not store in the bathroom or in other damp places. Heat or moisture may weaken condoms.
- Keep the product from freezing.
- Do not use outdated condoms or condoms that are clearly old or that have no date on the package. Only latex condoms with a pre-applied spermicide have an expiration date. After this time, the maker cannot guarantee the spermicide potency. Other condoms should have the date that they were made on the box. It is best if you do not buy condoms long before you use them, in case the storage has not been ideal. The best way to make sure you are using fresh condoms is to buy them only a short time before they will be used. Older condoms are more likely to break during sexual intercourse. If you have any questions about the storage and expiration dating of condoms, ask your health care professional.
- Be sure that any discarded condoms are out of the reach of children. Used condoms should be wrapped in tissue or paper. Discard them in the trash so that others will not accidentally handle them.

Side Effects of This Product

Condoms occasionally cause allergies or local irritation in some people. They may cause itching, burning, stinging, or a rash. These reactions could be due to the latex itself, the lubricant, or the spermicide. Changing to a different brand of condom may solve this problem. Also, using a weaker strength of vaginal spermicide (if you are using extra spermicide) may be necessary, although it will be less effective. If any of these effects continue after you have changed products, you may have an allergy to these products or an infection and should contact a doctor as soon as possible.

Very rarely, some people may have a severe allergic reaction to latex rubber. *Check with a doctor immediately* if any of the following effects occur:

Rare

For latex condoms only

Difficulty in breathing; hives; swelling of the face or inside of the throat

Also, check with a doctor as soon as possible if any of the following effects occur:

Rare

For latex condoms only

For females and males

Redness of the inside of the eyelids; skin rash, redness, swelling, irritation, local swelling, or itching that occurs each time a latex condom is used; stuffy nose after using latex condoms

For females only

Vaginal bleeding, irritation, redness, rash, dryness, or whitish discharge that occurs each time a latex condom is used (signs of vaginal allergy)

For latex condoms containing spermicide only

For females only

Bladder pain; cloudy or bloody urine; increased frequency of urination; pain on urination

Other side effects may occur that usually do not need medical attention. Using a different brand of condom may help to eliminate these effects. However, check with your doctor if any of the following side effects continue or are bothersome:

Less common

Burning, stinging, warmth, itching, or other irritation of the skin, penis, rectum, or vagina; vaginal dryness or odor

Other side effects not listed above may also occur in some people. If you notice any other effects, check with your doctor.

Revised: 03/04/93
Interim revision: 07/18/95

CONJUGATED ESTROGENS AND MEDROXYPROGESTERONE FOR OVARIAN HORMONE THERAPY (OHT) Systemic†

Some commonly used brand names are:

In the U.S.—

Premphase[1]
Prempro[2]

Note: For quick reference, the following estrogens are numbered to match the corresponding brand names.

This information applies to the following medicines:

1. Conjugated Estrogens, and Conjugated Estrogens and Medroxyprogesterone (CON-ju-gate-ed ES-troe-jenz, and CON-ju-gate-ed ES-troe-jenz and me-DROX-ee-proe-JES-te-rone)†
2. Conjugated Estrogens and Medroxyprogesterone (CON-ju-gate-ed ES-troe-jenz and me-DROX-ee-proe-JES-te-rone)†

†Not commercially available in Canada.

Description

Conjugated estrogens and medroxyprogesterone (CON-ju-gate-ed ES-troe-jenz and me-DROX-ee-proe-JES-te-rone) are estrogen and progestin hormones. Along with other effects, estrogens help females develop sexually at puberty and regulate the menstrual cycle. Progestin lowers the effect of estrogen on the uterus and keeps estrogen-related problems from developing.

Around the time of menopause, the ovaries produce less estrogen. Estrogens are given to:

- Relieve the signs of menopause (vasomotor symptoms of menopause), such as hot flashes and unusual sweating, chills, faintness, or dizziness.
- Treat inflammation of the vagina (atrophic vaginitis) and of the genital area (atrophy of the vulva) by keeping these areas from becoming too dry, itchy, or painful.
- Prevent the loss of bone that begins at the time of menopause. Keeping bones strong lowers the chance of developing weak bones that easily break (osteoporosis). Estrogen use is most effective when it is taken for more than 7 years while getting regular exercise and extra calcium. Protection from bone loss can then last for many years after you stop taking the medicine.

There is *no* medical evidence to support the belief that the use of estrogens will keep the patient feeling young, keep the skin soft, or delay the appearance of wrinkles. Nor has it been proven that the use of estrogens during menopause will relieve emotional and nervous symptoms, unless these symptoms are related to the menopausal symptoms, such as hot flashes.

Progestins are not needed if the uterus has been removed (by a surgical method called hysterectomy). In that case, it may be better to receive estrogens alone without the progestin.

Conjugated estrogens and medroxyprogesterone are available only with your doctor's prescription, in the following dosage forms:

Oral

Conjugated Estrogens; Conjugated Estrogens and Medroxyprogesterone
- Tablets (U.S.)

Conjugated Estrogens and Medroxyprogesterone
- Tablets (U.S.)

Before Using This Medicine

In deciding to use a medicine, the risks of taking the medicine must be weighed against the good it will do. This is a decision you and your doctor will make. For conjugated estrogens and medroxyprogesterone, the following should be considered:

Allergies—Tell your doctor if you have ever had any unusual or allergic reaction to estrogens or progestins. Also tell your health care professional if you are allergic to any other substances, such as foods, preservatives, or dyes.

Pregnancy—Conjugated estrogens and medroxyprogesterone are not recommended for use during pregnancy. Becoming pregnant or maintaining a pregnancy is not likely to occur around the time of menopause. Tell your doctor right away if you suspect you are pregnant.

Breast-feeding—Conjugated estrogens and medroxyprogesterone pass into the breast milk. This medicine is not recommended for use during breast-feeding.

Other medicines—Although certain medicines should not be used together at all, in other cases two different medicines may be used together even if an interaction might occur. In these cases, your doctor may want to change the dose, or other precautions may be necessary. When you are taking conjugated estrogens and medroxyprogesterone, it is especially important that your health care professional know if you are taking any of the following:

- Acetaminophen (e.g., Tylenol) (with long-term, high-dose use) or
- Amiodarone (e.g., Cordarone) or
- Anabolic steroids (nandrolone [e.g., Anabolin], oxandrolone [e.g., Anavar], oxymetholone [e.g., Anadrol], stanozolol [e.g., Winstrol]) or
- Androgens (male hormones) or

- Anti-infectives by mouth or by injection (medicine for infection) or
- Antithyroid agents (medicine for overactive thyroid) or
- Carmustine (e.g., BiCNU) or
- Chloroquine (e.g., Aralen) or
- Dantrolene (e.g., Dantrium) or
- Daunorubicin (e.g., Cerubidine) or
- Disulfiram (e.g., Antabuse) or
- Divalproex (e.g., Depakote) or
- Etretinate (e.g., Tegison) or
- Gold salts (medicine for arthritis) or
- Hydroxychloroquine (e.g., Plaquenil) or
- Isoniazid or
- Mercaptopurine (e.g., Purinethol) or
- Methotrexate (e.g., Mexate) or
- Methyldopa (e.g., Aldomet) or
- Naltrexone (e.g., Trexan) (with long-term, high-dose use) or
- Phenothiazines (acetophenazine [e.g., Tindal], chlorpromazine [e.g., Thorazine], fluphenazine [e.g., Prolixin], mesoridazine [e.g., Serentil], perphenazine [e.g., Trilafon], prochlorperazine [e.g., Compazine], promazine [e.g., Sparine], promethazine [e.g., Phenergan], thioridazine [e.g., Mellaril], trifluoperazine [e.g., Stelazine], triflupromazine [e.g., Vesprin], trimeprazine [e.g., Temaril]) or
- Plicamycin (e.g., Mithracin)—Use of these medicines with conjugated estrogens and medroxyprogesterone may increase the chance of problems occurring that affect the liver
- Aminoglutethimide (e.g., Cytadren) or
- Barbiturates, especially phenobarbital or
- Carbamazepine (e.g., Tegretol) or
- Phenytoin (e.g., Dilantin) or
- Rifampin (e.g., Rifadin)—These medicines may decrease the effect of conjugated estrogens or medroxyprogesterone
- Cyclosporine (e.g., Sandimmune)—Conjugated estrogens can prevent cyclosporine's removal from the body; this can lead to cyclosporine causing kidney or liver problems
- Protease inhibitors, such as ritonavir (e.g., Norvir)—May decrease the effect of conjugated estrogens

Other medical problems—The presence of other medical problems may affect the use of conjugated estrogens and medroxyprogesterone. Make sure you tell your doctor if you have any other medical problems, especially:

- Asthma or
- Heart problems or
- Epilepsy or
- High blood pressure or
- Kidney problems, severe or
- Migraine headaches—Rarely, water retention caused by conjugated estrogens or medroxyprogesterone may worsen these conditions; on the other hand, blood pressure and some heart or blood vessel problems can improve for most patients
- Blood clotting problems (or history of during previous estrogen therapy)—Estrogens usually are not used until blood clotting problems stop; using estrogens is usually not a problem for most patients without a history of blood clotting problems due to estrogen use
- Bone cancer or
- Breast cancer or
- Cancer of the uterus (active or suspected) or
- Fibroid tumors of the uterus—Estrogens may interfere with the treatment of breast or bone cancer, worsen cancer of the uterus, or increase the size of fibroid tumors
- Changes in genital or vaginal bleeding of unknown causes—Estrogens may make these conditions worse; some irregular vaginal bleeding may be a sign that the lining of the uterus may be growing too much or is a sign of cancer of the uterus lining
- Diabetes mellitus (sugar diabetes)—Conjugated estrogens or medroxyprogesterone may slightly change the amount of blood sugar for some patients, but for most patients with sugar diabetes, there is no change in blood sugar
- Endometriosis or
- Gallbladder disease or gallstones (or history of) or
- High cholesterol or triglycerides (or family history of) or
- Liver disease, including jaundice (or history of) or
- Pancreatitis (inflammation of pancreas)—Conjugated estrogens or medroxyprogesterone may worsen these conditions; however, using estrogens can lower blood cholesterol in many patients with high cholestrol

Proper Use of This Medicine

Conjugated estrogens and medroxyprogesterone usually come with patient directions. Read them carefully before taking this medicine.

Take this medicine only as directed by your doctor. Do not take more of it and do not take it for longer period of time than your doctor ordered. The length of time you take the medicine will depend on the medical problem for which you are taking conjugated estrogens and medroxyprogesterone. Discuss with your doctor how long you will need to take these medicines.

If you are taking the estrogen or progestin hormones in a certain order (conjugated estrogens tablets followed by conjugated estrogens and medroxyprogesterone tablets), *be sure you know in which order you need to take the medicines.* If you have questions about this, ask your health care professional.

Nausea may occur during the first few weeks after you start taking estrogens. This effect usually disappears with continued use. If the nausea is bothersome, it can usually be prevented or reduced by taking each dose with food or immediately after food.

Dosing—The dose of these medicines will be different for different patients. *Follow your doctor's orders or the directions on the label.* The following information includes only the average doses of these medicines. *If your dose is different, do not change it* unless your doctor tells you to do so.

For conjugated estrogens, and conjugated estrogens and medroxyprogesterone

- For *oral* dosage form (tablets):
  - —To prevent loss of bone (osteoporosis) or for treating itching or dryness of the genital area (atrophy of the vulva), inflammation of the vagina (atrophic vaginitis), or symptoms of menopause:
    - Adults—One tablet (containing 0.625 mg conjugated estrogens) once a day on Days 1 through 14; then, one tablet (containing 0.625 mg conjugated estrogens and 5 mg medroxyprogesterone) once a day on Days 15 through 28. Repeat cycle.

For conjugated estrogens and medroxyprogesterone

- For *oral* dosage form (tablets):
  - —To prevent loss of bone (osteoporosis) or for treating itching or dryness of the genital area (atrophy of the vulva), inflammation of the vagina (atrophic vaginitis), or symptoms of menopause:
    - Adults—One tablet (containing 0.625 mg conjugated estrogens and 2.5 mg medroxyprogesterone) once a day for twenty-eight days. Repeat cycle.

Missed dose—If you miss a dose of this medicine, take it as soon as possible. However, if it is almost time for your next dose, skip the missed dose and go back to your regular dosing schedule. Do not double doses.

Storage—To store this medicine:

- Keep out of the reach of children.
- Store away from heat and direct light.
- Do not store in the bathroom, near the kitchen sink, or in other damp places. Heat or moisture may cause the medicine to break down.
- Do not keep outdated medicine or medicine no longer needed. Be sure that any discarded medicine is out of the reach of children.

Precautions While Using This Medicine

It is very important that your doctor check your progress at regular visits to make sure this medicine does not cause unwanted effects. Plan on going to see your doctor every year, but some doctors require visits more often.

Although the risk for developing breast problems or breast cancer is low, it is still important that you regularly check your breasts for any unusual lumps or discharge, and report any problems to your doctor. You should also have a mammogram (x-ray pictures of the breasts) and breast examination done by your doctor whenever your doctor recommends it.

If your menstrual periods have stopped, they may start again once you begin taking this medicine. This effect will continue for as long as the medicine is taken. However, if taking the continuous treatment (0.625 mg conjugated estrogens and 2.5 mg medroxyprogesterone once a day), monthly bleeding usually stops within ten months.

Also, vaginal bleeding between your regular menstrual periods may occur during the first three months of use. *Do not stop taking your medicine. Check with your doctor* if bleeding continues for an unusually long time, if your period has not started within 45 days of your last period, or if you think you are pregnant.

Tell the doctor in charge that you are taking this medicine before having any laboratory test, because some test results may be affected.

Side Effects of This Medicine

Healthy women rarely have a severe side effects from taking conjugated estrogens or medroxyprogesterone to replace estrogen.

Check with your doctor as soon as possible if any of the following side effects occur:

More common

Menstrual periods beginning again, including changing menstrual bleeding pattern for up to six months (spotting, breakthrough bleeding, prolonged or heavier vaginal bleeding, or vaginal bleeding completely stopping by ten months); vaginal itching or irritation, or thick, white vaginal discharge

Less common

Breast lumps; discharge from breast

Rare

Pain in stomach, side, or abdomen; yellow eyes or skin

Other side effects may occur that usually do not need medical attention. These side effects may go away during treatment as your body adjusts to the medicine. However, check with your doctor if any of the following side effects continue or are bothersome:

More common

Abdominal cramps; nausea

Less common

Bloating or swelling of face, ankles, or feet; breast pain or tenderness; enlarged breasts; increase in sexual desire; headaches; weight gain or loss

Rare

Dizziness; insomnia; mental depression; mood changes; nervousness; tiredness; vomiting

Other side effects not listed above may also occur in some patients. If you notice any other effects, check with your doctor.

Developed: 08/24/97

COPPER INTRAUTERINE DEVICES (IUDs)

Some commonly used brand names are:

In U.S.—

ParaGard-T 380A[3]

In Canada—

Gyne-T[1]

Gyne-T 380 Slimline[4]

Nova-T[2]

Note: For quick reference, the following copper intrauterine devices are numbered to match the corresponding brand names.

This information applies to the following devices:

1. Copper-T 200 IUD*
2. Copper-T 200Ag IUD*
3. Copper-T 380A IUD†
4. Copper-T 380S IUD*

*Not commercially available in the U.S.

†Not commercially available in Canada.

Description

A copper intrauterine device (KOP-er IN-tra-YOU-ta-rin de-VICE) (also called an IUD) is inserted by a health care professional into a woman's uterus as a long-term contraceptive (birth control method).

The copper-T IUD works by causing changes in the uterus that make becoming pregnant (conception) harder. The fertilization of the woman's egg with her partner's sperm is less likely with an IUD in place, but it can occur. Even so, the IUD makes it harder for the fertilized egg to become attached to the uterus walls making it hard to become pregnant. Having copper on the IUD is believed to improve the effects of the device. After the IUD is removed, most women can become pregnant.

Studies have shown that pregnancy can occur in up to 4 of each 100 women using copper-T IUDs during the first year of use. Other birth control methods such as not having intercourse, taking birth control pills (the Pill), or having surgery to become sterile are as effective or more effective. Methods that do not work as well include using condoms, diaphragms, vaginal sponges, or spermicides. Discuss with your health care professional what your options are for birth control and the risks and benefits of each method.

IUDs do not protect a woman from sexually transmitted diseases (STDs), including human immunodeficiency virus (HIV) or acquired immunodeficiency syndrome (AIDS). The use of latex (rubber) condoms or abstinence is recommended for protection from these diseases.

Your lifestyle will determine how safe and reliable the copper-T IUD will be for you. Problems that may occur with use of an IUD are far less likely to occur in women who have a long-term relationship with one sexual partner. Also, it is important that your sexual partner not have any other sexual partners. If you or your partner has more than one sexual partner it increases *your* chance of getting an infection in the vagina. If an infection is present in the vagina or uterus when the IUD is in the uterus it may make an infection more serious. *If your lifestyle changes while you are using an IUD or you get or are exposed to an STD, call your health care professional.*

Copper-T IUDs are available only from your doctor or other authorized health care professional in the following forms:

- Copper-T 200 Intrauterine Device (Canada)
- Copper-T 200Ag Intrauterine Device (Canada)
- Copper-T 380A Intrauterine Device (U.S.)
- Copper-T 380S Intrauterine Device (Canada)

Before Receiving This Device

In deciding whether to use a copper-T IUD as a method of birth control, you need to consider the risks of using it as well as the good it can do. This is a decision you, your sexual partner, and your health care professional will make. For copper-T IUDs, the following should be considered:

Allergies—Tell your health care professional if you have ever had any unusual or allergic reaction to copper.

Pregnancy—IUD use is not recommended during pregnancy or if you plan to become pregnant in the near future. It is also not recommended in women who have had a pregnancy develop outside of the uterus (ectopic pregnancy).

There is a rare chance that a woman can become pregnant with the IUD in the uterus. If this happens, it is recommended that the IUD be removed or that the pregnancy be ended within the first 3 months. If the pregnancy continues, removing the IUD decreases the chance of a problem developing. However, whether the IUD is removed or not, some problems can occur. Some of these problems include miscarriage, premature labor and delivery, infection, and, very rarely, death of the mother.

Your health care professional will help you decide on the proper time to begin using an IUD after delivering a baby. Sometimes problems can occur if you start using the IUD too soon after delivery. These problems include having the IUD move out of place or having it press into the walls of the uterus or the cervix (opening to the uterus). These problems may harm the cervix or uterus, causing pain or unusual vaginal bleeding. *Call your health care professional immediately* if you have any problems.

Breast-feeding—The copper from an IUD has not been shown to cause problems in nursing babies.

Teenagers—Sexually active teenagers may need to use a contraceptive method that protects them against sexually transmitted diseases (STDs).

Teenagers who have not had children usually have more side effects than teenagers or adults who have had children. In some of these women, the IUD may move out of place. This may harm the uterus or cervix. Abdominal pain and increased menstrual bleeding also are more common in teenagers than in women who are older and have had children.

Other medical problems—The presence of other medical problems may affect the use of copper-T IUDs. Make sure you tell your health care professional if you have any othe medical problems, especially:

- Abnormal uterus—May decrease the IUD's ability tc vent pregnancy or may increase the chance of prc such as the IUD moving out of the uterus or through the cervix or uterus
- Acquired immunodeficiency syndrome (AID mune diseases, treatable cancer, suspected c cer of the uterus or cervix, or any other may decrease the ability of the body to These conditions may increase the ch infection occurring with the use of ar
- Anemia or
- Bleeding problems, especially he riods or bleeding between peri make these conditions worse, may cause the IUD to move
- Diabetes, insulin-dependent c
- Heart defect—If an infection the infection may become in these patients

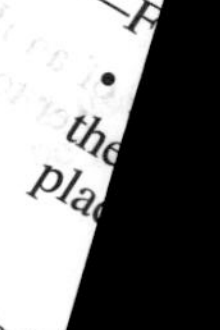

- Ectopic pregnancy (pregnancy not in the uterus), history of—The chance of an ectopic pregnancy may be increased if contraception fails during IUD use
- Fainting (history of) or
- Slow heartbeat (history of)—The chance of problems may be increased when, or soon after, the IUD is inserted
- Infection in the vagina or uterus or
- Recent infected abortion or
- Sexually transmitted disease in the last 12 months—Use of an IUD may make an infection worse
- Surgery involving the uterus or fallopian tubes—Certain surgeries done on the uterus or the fallopian tubes may increase the chance of problems if an IUD is present in the uterus
- Wilson's disease—Use of a copper IUD can make this condition worse

Proper Use of This Device

IUDs come with patient information. *You must understand this information.* You should keep a copy for reference. *Be sure you understand possible problems with the copper-T IUD, especially side effects, risks, and warning signs of trouble.*

Spermicides such as contraceptive foams or creams are not needed to prevent pregnancy with a properly placed copper-T IUD.

It is important that you check for the IUD threads every month (if not more often) especially after each menstrual period. Feeling the IUD threads near the cervix lets you know that the copper-T IUD is still in place.

To check for the IUD threads:

- Wash your hands thoroughly.
- Squat and, using your middle finger, find the cervix high in the vagina.
- The IUD threads should hang down from the cervix.
- *Do not pull on the threads.*

Dosing—The length of time that you will be using the copper-T IUD depends on the device that you are using. *Follow your health care professional's orders to schedule the proper time to remove and replace your copper-T IUD.* You and your health care professional may choose to replace it sooner or begin a new method of birth control.

- For preventing pregnancy:
  - —For copper-T 200 dosage form:
    - Adults and teenagers—One device inserted into the vagina by a health care professional and replaced within 24 months of use.
  - —For copper-T 200Ag dosage form:
    - Adults and teenagers—One device inserted into the vagina by a health care professional and replaced within 30 months of use.
  - —For copper-T 380A dosage form:
    - Adults and teenagers—One device inserted into the vagina by a health care professional and replaced within 10 years of use.
  - —For copper-T 380S dosage form:
    - Adults and teenagers—One device inserted into the vagina by a health care professional and replaced within 30 months of use.

Precautions While Using This Device

It is very important to keep all medical appointments with your health care professional during the first year of IUD use. After the first year, your health care professional will probably want to check your progress once a year. This will allow the health care professional to make sure that the device is still in place and working properly.

Check with your medical doctor if you plan to have surgery of the uterus or fallopian tubes. Your doctor may remove your IUD before the surgery. *Also, tell your health care professional if you plan to get heat or radiation therapy.* Some types of therapy such as treatments used in sports medicine may heat the copper on the IUD. This may cause harm to the area directly around the IUD. Your doctor may take the IUD out or help you choose another type of treatment.

Tell your doctor immediately if you think that the IUD has moved out of place. Do not try to put the IUD back into place inside the uterus. Do not try to remove the IUD.

Although IUDs are very reliable, there is a rare chance that the IUD may fail to protect some people from becoming pregnant. Very rarely a pregnancy can occur outside of the uterus; this is called an ectopic pregnancy. It can be hard to tell if an ectopic pregnancy has occurred. Unlike a normal pregnancy in the uterus which stops the menstrual period, some people can still have a menstrual period with an ectopic pregnancy. These women may not think they are pregnant.

Notify your doctor immediately if you feel many of the following changes that can occur with a pregnancy: Enlarged or tender breasts, lack of menstrual period, lower abdominal pain or cramping (possibly severe), sore abdomen, unusual tiredness or weakness, unusual vaginal bleeding (in some cases, very heavy).

If you think you are pregnant or if you miss a period while you are using the IUD, tell your health care professional. Until your doctor is able to see you, use another birth control method, such as condoms, to prevent pregnancy just in case you are not pregnant.

Also, notify your doctor and use another birth control method, such as condoms, if:

- you have unusual vaginal bleeding
- you are exposed to or get a sexually transmitted disease (STD)
- you feel the tip of the IUD at the cervix or you or your partner feels pain during sexual intercourse
- you cannot find the threads from the IUD or think that the thread length is different
- you or your sexual partner's lifestyle changes and one or both of you have more than one sexual partner

- you have unusual or severe lower abdominal pain or cramping, possibly with a fever
- you develop vaginal discharge or sores in the vaginal area

You can use other products in the vagina, such as tampons or condoms, while you are using a copper-T IUD.

Side Effects of This Device

Along with its needed effects, a device may cause some unwanted effects. Although not all of these side effects may occur, if any do occur they may need medical attention.

Get emergency help immediately if any of the following side effects occur:

Rare

Abdominal pain or cramping (severe); vaginal bleeding (unexpected, heavy)

Check with your health care professional immediately if any of the following side effects occur:

More common

Faintness, dizziness, or sharp pain at time of IUD insertion; increased amount of menstrual bleeding at regular monthly periods; normal menstrual bleeding occurring earlier or lasting longer than expected

Less common

Abnormal vaginal bleeding (mild to moderate) not associated with a menstrual period; abdominal pain (dull or aching), odorous vaginal discharge, pain on urination with increased urge to urinate, and unusual vaginal bleeding

Rare

Abdominal pain or cramping, fever, nausea, and vomiting; painful sexual intercourse; unusual tiredness or weakness, and increased menstrual bleeding

Other side effects may occur that usually do not need medical attention. These side effects may go away during treatment as your body adjusts to the device. However, check with your health care professional if the following side effect continues or is bothersome:

More common

Increased abdominal pain and cramping at menstrual periods

After you stop using this device, you may become pregnant. The contraceptive effect of copper-T IUDs is usually reversible. If you stop using an IUD and still do not want to become pregnant, you should begin using another contraceptive method immediately to prevent pregnancy.

Other side effects not listed above may also occur in some patients. If you notice any other effects, check with your health care professional.

Developed: 06/29/94

COPPER SUPPLEMENTS Systemic

A commonly used brand name is:

In the U.S.—

Cupri-Pak[2]

Note: For quick reference, the following copper supplements are numbered to match the corresponding brand names.

This information applies to the following:

1. Copper Gluconate (KOP-er GLOO-coh-nate)†‡
2. Cupric Sulfate (KYOO-prik SUL-fate)†‡

†Not commercially available in Canada.
‡Generic name product may also be available in the U.S.

Description

Copper supplements are used to prevent or treat copper deficiency.

The body needs copper for normal growth and health. For patients who are unable to get enough copper in their regular diet or who have a need for more copper, copper supplements may be necessary. They are generally taken by mouth but some patients may have to receive them by injection. Copper is needed to help your body use iron. It is also important for nerve function, bone growth, and to help your body use sugar.

Lack of copper may lead to anemia and osteoporosis (weak bones).

Some conditions may increase your need for copper. These include:

- Burns
- Diarrhea
- Intestine disease
- Kidney disease
- Pancreas disease
- Stomach removal
- Stress, continuing

In addition, premature infants may need additional copper.

Increased need for copper should be determined by your health care professional.

Claims that copper supplements are effective in the treatment of arthritis or skin conditions have not been proven. Use of copper supplements to cause vomiting has caused death and should be avoided.

Injectable copper is given by or under the supervision of a health care professional. Another form of copper is available without a prescription.

Copper supplements are available in the following dosage forms:

Oral

Copper Gluconate

- Tablets (U.S.)

Parenteral
Cupric Sulfate
• Injection (U.S.)

Importance of Diet

For good health, it is important that you eat a balanced and varied diet. Follow carefully any diet program your health care professional may recommend. For your specific dietary vitamin and/or mineral needs, ask your health care professional for a list of appropriate foods. If you think that you are not getting enough vitamins and/or minerals in your diet, you may choose to take a dietary supplement.

Copper is found in various foods, including organ meats (especially liver), seafoods, beans, nuts, and whole-grains. Additional copper can come from drinking water from copper pipes, using copper cookware, and eating farm products sprayed with copper-containing chemicals. Copper may be decreased in foods that have high acid content and are stored in tin cans for a long time.

The daily amount of copper needed is defined in several different ways.

For U.S.—
- Recommended Dietary Allowances (RDAs) are the amount of vitamins and minerals needed to provide for adequate nutrition in most healthy persons. RDAs for a given nutrient may vary depending on a person's age, sex, and physical condition (e.g., pregnancy).
- Daily Values (DVs) are used on food and dietary supplement labels to indicate the percent of the recommended daily amount of each nutrient that a serving provides. DV replaces the previous designation of United States Recommended Daily Allowances (USRDAs).

For Canada—
- Recommended Nutrient Intakes (RNIs) are used to determine the amounts of vitamins, minerals, and protein needed to provide adequate nutrition and lessen the risk of chronic disease.

There is no RDA or RNI for copper. However, normal daily recommended intakes are generally defined as follows:
- Infants and children—
  Birth to 3 years of age: 0.4 to 1 milligram (mg) per day.
  4 to 6 years of age: 1 to 1.5 mg per day.
  7 to 10 years of age: 1 to 2 mg per day.
- Adolescent and adult males—1.5 to 2.5 mg per day.
- Adolescent and adult females—1.5 to 3 mg per day.

Before Using This Dietary Supplement

If you are taking this dietary supplement without a prescription, carefully read and follow any precautions on the label. For copper supplements, the following should be considered:

Allergies—Tell your health care professional if you are allergic to any substances, such as foods, preservatives, or dyes.

Pregnancy—It is especially important that you are receiving enough vitamins and minerals when you become pregnant and that you continue to receive the right amount of vitamins and minerals throughout your pregnancy. The healthy growth and development of the fetus depend on a steady supply of nutrients from the mother. However, taking large amounts of a dietary supplement in pregnancy may be harmful to the mother and/or fetus and should be avoided.

Breast-feeding—It is important that you receive the right amounts of vitamins and minerals so that your baby will also get the vitamins and minerals needed to grow properly. However, taking large amounts of a dietary supplement while breast-feeding may be harmful to the mother and/or baby and should be avoided.

Children—Problems in children have not been reported with intake of normal daily recommended amounts.

Older adults—Problems in older adults have not been reported with intake of normal daily recommended amounts.

Medicines or other dietary supplements—Although certain medicines or dietary supplements should not be used together at all, in other cases they may be used together even if an interaction might occur. In these cases, your health care professional may want to change the dose, or other precautions may be necessary. When you are taking copper supplements, it is especially important that your health care professional know if you are taking any of the following:
- Penicillamine or
- Trientine or
- Zinc supplements (taken by mouth)—Use with copper supplements may decrease the amount of copper that gets into the body; copper supplements should be taken at least 2 hours after penicillamine, trientine, or zinc supplements

Other medical problems—The presence of other medical problems may affect the use of copper supplements. Make sure you tell your health care professional if you have any other medical problems, especially:
- Biliary disease or
- Liver disease—Taking copper supplements may cause high blood levels of copper, and dosage for copper may have to be changed
- Wilson's disease (too much copper in the body)—Copper supplements may make this condition worse

Proper Use of This Dietary Supplement

Dosing—The amount of copper needed to meet normal daily recommended intakes will be different for different individuals. The following information includes only the average amounts of copper.
- For *oral* dosage form (tablets):
  —To prevent deficiency, the amount taken by mouth is based on normal daily recommended intakes:
  - Adult and teenage males—1.5 to 2.5 milligrams (mg) per day.
  - Adult and teenage females—1.5 to 3 mg per day.

• Children 7 to 10 years of age—1 to 2 mg per day.
• Children 4 to 6 years of age—1 to 1.5 mg per day.
• Children birth to 3 years of age—0.4 to 1 mg per day.

—To treat deficiency:
• Adults, teenagers, and children—Treatment dose is determined by prescriber for each individual based on the severity of deficiency.

Missed dose—If you miss taking copper supplements for one or more days there is no cause for concern, since it takes some time for your body to become seriously low in copper. However, if your health care professional has recommended that you take copper try to remember to take it as directed every day.

Storage—To store this dietary supplement:
- Keep out of the reach of children.
- Store away from heat and direct light.
- Do not store in the bathroom, near the kitchen sink, or in other damp places. Heat or moisture may cause the dietary supplement to break down.
- Keep the dietary supplement from freezing. Do not refrigerate.
- Do not keep outdated dietary supplements or those no longer needed. Be sure that any discarded dietary supplement is out of the reach of children.

Precautions While Using This Dietary Supplement

Do not take copper supplements and zinc supplements at the same time. It is best to take your copper supplement 2 hours after zinc supplements, to get the full benefit of each.

Side Effects of This Dietary Supplement

Along with its needed effects, a dietary supplement may cause some unwanted effects. Although copper supplements have not been reported to cause any side effects, *check with your health care professional immediately* if any of the following side effects occur as a result of an overdose:

Symptoms of overdose

Black or bloody vomit; blood in urine; coma; diarrhea; dizziness or fainting; headache (severe or continuing); heartburn; loss of appetite; lower back pain; metallic taste; nausea (severe or continuing); pain or burning while urinating; vomiting; yellow eyes or skin

Other side effects not listed above may also occur in some individuals. If you notice any other effects, check with your health care professional.

Revised: 09/01/91
Interim revision: 06/25/92; 08/17/94; 05/26/95

CORTICOSTEROIDS Dental

Some commonly used brand names are:

In the U.S.—

Kenalog in Orabase[2]
Orabase-HCA[1]
Oracort[2]
Oralone[2]

In Canada—

Kenalog in Orabase[2]

Another commonly used name for hydrocortisone is cortisol.

Note: For quick reference, the following corticosteroids are numbered to match the corresponding brand names.

This information applies to the following medicines:

1. Hydrocortisone (hye-droe-KOR-ti-sone)
2. Triamcinolone (trye-am-SIN-oh-lone)

Description

Dental corticosteroids (kor-ti-ko-STER-oyds) are used to relieve the discomfort and redness of some mouth and gum problems. These medicines are like cortisone. They belong to the general family of medicines called steroids.

Dental corticosteroids are available only with your medical doctor's or dentist's prescription in the following dosage forms:

Dental

Hydrocortisone
• Paste (U.S.)

Triamcinolone
• Paste (U.S. and Canada)

Before Using This Medicine

In deciding to use a medicine, the risks of taking the medicine must be weighed against the good it will do. This is a decision you and your doctor or dentist will make. For dental corticosteroids, the following should be considered:

Allergies—Tell your doctor if you have ever had any unusual or allergic reaction to corticosteroids. Also tell your health care professional if you are allergic to any other substances, such as foods, preservatives, or dyes.

Pregnancy—When used properly, these medicines have not been shown to cause problems in humans. Studies on birth defects with dental corticosteroids have not been done in humans. However, studies in animals have shown that topical corticosteroids, such as the hydrocortisone or triamcinolone in this medicine, when applied to the skin in large amounts or used for a long time, could cause birth defects. Studies with dental paste have not been done in animals.

Breast-feeding—When used properly, dental corticosteroids have not been reported to cause problems in nursing babies.

Children—Children and teenagers who must use this medicine should be checked often by their doctor. Dental corticosteroids may be absorbed through the lining of the mouth and, if used too often or for too long a time, may interfere with growth in children. Before using this medicine in children, you should discuss its use with your child's medical doctor or dentist.

Older adults—Although there is no specific information comparing use of dental corticosteroids in the elderly with use in other age groups, these medicines are not expected to cause different side effects or problems in older people than they do in younger adults.

Other medicines—Although certain medicines should not be used together at all, in many cases two different medicines may be used together even if an interaction might occur. In these cases, your doctor or dentist may want to change the dose, or other precautions may be necessary. Tell your doctor, dentist, and pharmacist if you are taking or using any other prescription or nonprescription (over-the-counter [OTC]) medicine.

Other medical problems—The presence of other medical problems may affect the use of dental corticosteroids. Make sure you tell your doctor or dentist if you have any other medical problems, especially:

- Diabetes mellitus (sugar diabetes)—Too much use of corticosteroids may cause a loss of control of diabetes by increasing blood and urine glucose. However, this is not likely to happen when dental corticosteroids are used for a short period of time
- Herpes sores or
- Infection or sores of the mouth or throat or
- Tuberculosis—Corticosteroids may make existing infections worse or cause new infections

Proper Use of This Medicine

To use hydrocortisone or triamcinolone:

- Using a cotton swab, press (do not rub) a small amount of paste onto the area to be treated until the paste sticks and a smooth, slippery film forms. Do not try to spread the medicine because it will become crumbly and gritty. Apply the paste at bedtime so the medicine can work overnight. The other applications of the paste should be made following meals.

Do not use corticosteroids more often or for a longer time than your medical doctor or dentist ordered. To do so may increase the chance of absorption through the lining of the mouth and the chance of side effects.

Do not use any leftover medicine for future mouth problems without first checking with your medical doctor or dentist. This medicine should *not* be used on many kinds of bacterial, virus, or fungus infections.

Missed dose—If your medical doctor or dentist has ordered you to use this medicine according to a regular schedule and you miss a dose, use it as soon as you remember. However, if it is almost time for your next dose, skip the missed dose and go back to your regular dosing schedule.

Storage—To store this medicine:

- Keep out of the reach of children.
- Store away from heat and direct light.
- Keep the medicine from freezing.
- Do not keep outdated medicine or medicine no longer needed. Be sure that any discarded medicine is out of the reach of children.

Precautions While Using This Medicine

Check with your medical doctor or dentist:

- if your symptoms do not improve within 1 week.
- if your condition gets worse.

Side Effects of This Medicine

Along with its needed effects, a medicine may cause some unwanted effects. Although not all of these side effects may occur, if they do occur they may need medical attention.

Check with your medical doctor or dentist as soon as possible if the following side effects occur:

Signs of infection or irritation such as burning, itching, blistering, or peeling not present before use of this medicine

Other side effects not listed above may also occur in some patients. If you notice any other effects, check with your medical doctor or dentist.

Revised: 11/18/92

CORTICOSTEROIDS Inhalation

Some commonly used brand names are:

In the U.S.—

AeroBid[4]
AeroBid-M[4]
Azmacort[5]
Beclovent[1]
Decadron Respihaler[3]
Vanceril[1]

In Canada—

Azmacort[5]
Beclodisk[1]
Becloforte[1]
Beclovent[1]
Beclovent Rotacaps[1]
Bronalide[4]
Pulmicort Nebuamp[2]
Pulmicort Turbuhaler[2]
Vanceril[1]

Other commonly used names are:

Beclomethasone dipropionate[1]
Beclometasone[1]
Beclometasone dipropionate[1]

Note: For quick reference, the following corticosteroids are numbered to match the corresponding brand names.

This information applies to the following medicines:

1. Beclomethasone (be-kloe-METH-a-sone)
2. Budesonide (byoo-DESS-oh-nide)*
3. Dexamethasone (dex-a-METH-a-sone)†
4. Flunisolide (floo-NISS-oh-lide)
5. Triamcinolone (trye-am-SIN-oh-lone)

*Not commercially available in the U.S.
†Not commercially available in Canada.

Description

Inhalation corticosteroids (kor-ti-koe-STER-oids) are cortisone-like medicines. They are used to help prevent the symptoms of asthma. When used regularly every day, inhalation corticosteroids decrease the number and severity of asthma attacks. However, they will not relieve an asthma attack that has already started.

Inhaled corticosteroids work by preventing certain cells in the lungs and breathing passages from releasing substances that cause asthma symptoms.

This medicine may be used with other asthma medicines, such as bronchodilators (medicines that open up narrowed breathing passages) or other corticosteroids taken by mouth.

Inhalation corticosteroids are available only with your doctor's prescription, in the following dosage forms:

Inhalation

Beclomethasone
- Aerosol (U.S. and Canada)
- Capsules for inhalation (Canada)
- Powder for inhalation (Canada)

Budesonide
- Powder for inhalation (Canada)
- Suspension for inhalation (Canada)

Dexamethasone
- Aerosol (U.S.)

Flunisolide
- Aerosol (U.S. and Canada)

Triamcinolone
- Aerosol (U.S. and Canada)

Before Using This Medicine

In deciding to use a medicine, the risks of taking the medicine must be weighed against the good it will do. This is a decision you and your doctor will make. For inhalation corticosteroids, the following should be considered:

Pregnancy—When used in regular daily doses during pregnancy to keep the mother's asthma under control, these medicines have not been reported to cause breathing problems or birth defects in the baby.

Breast-feeding—It is not known whether inhaled corticosteroids pass into breast milk. Although most medicines pass into breast milk in small amounts, many of them may be used safely while breast-feeding. Mothers who are using this medicine and who wish to breast-feed should discuss this with their doctor.

Children—Inhalation corticosteroids have been tested in children and, in low effective doses, have not been shown to cause different side effects or problems than they do in adults.

There have been a few reports of slowed growth or reduced adrenal gland function in some children using inhaled corticosteroids in recommended doses. However, poorly contolled asthma may cause slowed growth, especially when corticosteroids taken by mouth are needed often. Your doctor will want you to use the lowest possible dose of an inhaled corticosteroid that controls asthma. This will lessen the chance of an effect on growth or adrenal gland function.

Regular use of inhaled corticosteroids may allow some children to stop using or decrease the amount of corticosteroids taken by mouth. This also will reduce the risk of slowed growth or reduced adrenal function.

Children who are using inhaled corticosteroids in large doses should avoid exposure to chickenpox or measles. When a child is exposed or the disease develops, the doctor's directions should be followed carefully.

Before this medicine is given to a child, you and your child's doctor should talk about the good this medicine will do as well as the risks of using it. Follow the doctor's directions very carefully to lessen the chance that unwanted effects will occur.

Older adults—Many medicines have not been studied specifically in older people. Therefore, it may not be known whether they work exactly the same way they do in younger adults. Although there is no specific information comparing use of inhaled corticosteroids in the elderly with use in other age groups, this medicine is not expected to cause different side effects or problems in older people than it does in younger adults.

Other medicines—Although certain medicines should not be used together at all, in other cases two different medicines may be used together even if an interaction might occur. In these cases, your doctor may want to change the dose, or other precautions may be necessary. Tell your health care professional if you are taking any other prescription or nonprescription (over-the-counter [OTC]) medicine.

Other medical problems—The presence of other medical problems may affect the use of inhaled corticosteroids. Make sure you tell your doctor if you have any other medical problems, especially:

- Osteoporosis (bone disease)—Inhaled corticosteroids in high doses may make this condition worse in women who are past menopause and who are not receiving an estrogen replacement
- Tuberculosis (history of)—Use of this medicine may cause a tuberculosis infection to occur again

Proper Use of This Medicine

Inhaled corticosteroids will not relieve an asthma attack that has already started. However, your doctor may want you to continue taking this medicine at the usual time, even if you use another medicine to relieve the asthma attack.

Use this medicine only as directed. Do not use more of it and do not use it more often than your doctor ordered. To do so may increase the chance of side effects.

In order for this medicine to help prevent asthma attacks, it must be used every day in regularly spaced doses, as ordered by your doctor. Up to four weeks may pass before you begin to notice improvement in your condition. It may take several months before you feel the full effects of this medicine. This may not take as long if you have already been taking certain other medicines for your asthma.

Gargling and rinsing your mouth with water after each dose may help prevent hoarseness, throat irritation, and infection in the mouth. However, do not swallow the water after rinsing. Your doctor may also want you to use a spacer device to lessen these problems.

Inhaled corticosteroids are used with a special inhaler and usually come with patient directions. *Read the directions carefully before using this medicine.* If you do not understand the directions or you are not sure how to use the inhaler, ask your health care professional to show you what to do. Also, *ask your health care professional to check regularly how you use the inhaler to make sure you are using it properly.*

For patients using *beclomethasone, flunisolide, or triamcinolone inhalation aerosol:*

- When you use the inhaler for the first time, it may not deliver the right amount of medicine with the first puff. Therefore, before using the inhaler, test it to make sure it works properly.
- *To test the inhaler:*

  —Insert the metal canister firmly into the clean mouthpiece according to the manufacturer's instructions. Check to make sure the canister is placed properly into the mouthpiece.

  —Take the cover off the mouthpiece and shake the inhaler three or four times.

  —Hold the canister well away from you against a light background and press the top of the canister, spraying the medicine once into the air. If you see a fine mist, you will know the inhaler is working properly to provide the right amount of medicine when you use it. If you do not see a fine mist, try a second time.
- *To use the inhaler:*

  —Using your thumb and one or two fingers, hold the inhaler upright with the mouthpiece end down and pointing toward you.

  —Take the cover off the mouthpiece. Check the mouthpiece and remove any foreign objects. Then gently shake the inhaler three or four times.

  —Hold the mouthpiece away from your mouth and breathe out slowly and completely.

  —Use the inhalation method recommended by your doctor.

  - Open-mouth method—Place the mouthpiece about 1 or 2 inches (2 fingerwidths) in front of your widely opened mouth. Make sure the inhaler is aimed into your mouth so that the spray does not hit the roof of your mouth or your tongue.
  - Closed-mouth method—Place the mouthpiece in your mouth between your teeth and over your tongue with your lips closed tightly around it. Do not block the mouthpiece with your teeth or tongue.

  —Tilt your head back a little. Start to breathe in slowly and deeply through your mouth and, at the same time, press the top of the canister one time to get one puff of medicine. Continue to breathe in slowly for 5 to 10 seconds. Count the seconds while inhaling. It is important to press the top of the canister and breathe in slowly at the same time so the medicine is pulled into your lungs. This step may be difficult at first. If you are using the closed-mouth method and you see a fine mist coming from your mouth or nose, the inhaler is not being used correctly.

  —Hold your breath as long as you can up to 10 seconds. This gives the medicine time to settle in your airways and lungs.

  —Take the mouthpiece away from your mouth and breathe out slowly.

  —If your doctor has told you to inhale more than one puff of medicine at each dose, gently shake the inhaler again, and take the second puff following exactly the same steps you used for the first puff.

  —When you are finished, wipe off the mouthpiece and replace the cover to keep the mouthpiece clean and free of foreign objects.
- Your doctor may want you to use a spacer device with the inhaler. A spacer makes the inhaler easier to use. With a spacer, more of the medicine is able to reach your lungs, and less of it stays in the mouth and throat.

  —To use a spacer device with the inhaler:

  - Attach the spacer to the inhaler according to the manufacturer's directions. There are different types of spacers available, but the method of breathing remains the same with most spacers.
  - Gently shake the inhaler and spacer three or four times.
  - Hold the mouthpiece of the spacer away from your mouth and breathe out slowly to the end of a normal breath.
  - Place the mouthpiece into your mouth between your teeth and over your tongue with your lips closed around it.
  - Press down on the canister top once to release one puff of medicine into the spacer. Within one or two seconds, start to breathe in slowly and deeply through your mouth for 5 to 10 seconds. Count the seconds while inhaling. Do not breathe in through your nose.
  - Then hold your breath as long as you can up to 10 seconds.
  - Breathe out slowly. Do not remove the mouthpiece from your mouth. Breathe in and out slowly two or three times to make sure the spacer device is emptied.
  - If your doctor has told you to take more than one puff of medicine at each dose, gently shake the inhaler and spacer again and take the second puff, following exactly the same steps you used for the first puff. Do not spray more than one puff at a time into the spacer.
  - When you are finished, remove the spacer device from the inhaler and replace the cover of the mouthpiece.
- Clean the inhaler, mouthpiece, and spacer at least twice a week to prevent build-up of medicine and blockage of the mouthpiece.

—*To clean the inhaler:*

• Remove the metal canister from the inhaler and set it aside.

• Wash the mouthpiece and cover, the plastic case, and spacer with soap and warm water. Rinse well with warm, running water.

• Shake off the excess water and let the inhaler parts air dry completely before replacing the metal canister and cover.

- Check with your pharmacist to see if you should save the inhaler piece that comes with this medicine after the medicine is used up. Refill units may be available at a lower cost. However, remember that the inhaler is meant to be used only for the medicine that comes with it. Do not use the inhaler for any other inhalation aerosol medicine, even if the cartridge fits.

For patients using *beclomethasone capsules for inhalation:*

- *Do not swallow the capsules. The medicine will not work if you swallow it.*
- *To load the inhaler:*

—Make sure your hands are clean and dry.

—Do not insert the capsule into the inhaler until just before you are ready to use this medicine.

—Take the inhaler from its container. Hold the inhaler by the mouthpiece and twist the barrel in either direction until it stops.

—Take a capsule from its container. Hold the inhaler upright with the mouthpiece pointing downward. Press the capsule, with the clear end first, firmly into the raised small hole.

—Make sure the top of the capsule is even with the top of the hole. This will push the old used capsule shell, if there is one, into the inhaler.

—Hold the inhaler on its side with the white dot facing up. Twist the barrel quickly until it stops. This will break the capsule into two halves so the powder can be inhaled.

- *To use the inhaler:*

—Hold the inhaler away from your mouth and breathe out slowly to the end of a normal breath.

—Keep the inhaler on its side and place the mouthpiece in your mouth. Close your lips around it, and tilt your head slightly back. Do not block the mouthpiece with your teeth or tongue.

—Breathe in slowly through your mouth until you have taken a full deep breath.

—Take the inhaler from your mouth and hold your breath as long as you can up to 10 seconds. This gives the medicine time to settle in your airways and lungs.

—Hold the inhaler well away from your mouth and breathe out to the end of a normal breath.

—If your doctor has told you to use a second capsule, follow the same steps you used for the first capsule.

—When you have finished using the inhaler, pull the two halves of the inhaler apart and throw away the empty capsule shells. There is no need to remove the shell left in the small hole, except before cleaning.

—Put the two halves of the inhaler back together again and place it into its container to keep it clean.

- *To clean the inhaler:*

—Every two weeks, take the inhaler apart and wash the two halves of the inhaler in clean, warm water. Make sure the empty capsule shell is removed from the small raised hole.

—Shake out the excess water.

—Allow all parts of the inhaler to dry before you put it back together.

- The inhaler should be replaced every 6 months.

For patients using *beclomethasone powder for inhalation:*

- *To load the inhaler:*

—Make sure your hands are clean and dry.

—Do not insert the cartridge until just before you are ready to use this medicine.

—Take off the dark brown mouthpiece cover and make sure the mouthpiece is clean.

—Hold the white cartridge by the exposed corners and gently pull it out until you see the ribbed sides of the cartridge.

—Squeeze the ribbed sides and take out the cartridge unit from the body of the inhaler.

—Place the disk containing the medicine onto the white wheel with the numbers facing up. Allow the underside of the disk to fit into the holes of the wheel.

—Slide the cartridge unit with wheel and disk back into the body of the inhaler. Gently push the cartridge in and pull it out again. The disk will turn.

—Continue to turn the disk in this way until the number 8 appears in the side indicator window. Each disk has eight blisters containing the medicine. The window will display how many doses you have left after you use it each time, by counting down from 8. For example, when you see the number 1, you have one dose left.

—To replace the empty disk with a full disk, follow the same steps you used to load the inhaler. Do not throw away the wheel when you discard the empty disk.

- *To use the inhaler:*

—Hold the inhaler flat in your hand. Lift the rear edge of the lid until it is fully upright.

—The plastic needle on the front of the lid will break the blister containing one inhalation of medicine. When the lid is raised as far as it will go, both the upper and the lower surfaces of the blister will be pierced. Do not lift the lid if the cartridge is not in the inhaler. Doing this will break the needle and you will need a new inhaler.

—After the blister is broken open, close the lid. Keeping the inhaler flat and well away from your mouth, breathe out to the end of a normal breath.

—Raise the inhaler to your mouth, and place the mouthpiece in your mouth.

—Close your lips around the mouthpiece and tilt your head slightly back. Do not block the mouthpiece with your teeth or tongue. Do not cover the air holes on the side of the mouthpiece.

—Breathe in through your mouth as fast as you can until you have taken a full deep breath.

—Hold your breath and remove the mouthpiece from your mouth. Continue holding your breath as long as you can up to 10 seconds before breathing out. This gives the medicine time to settle in your airways and lungs.

—Hold the inhaler well away from your mouth and breathe out to the end of a normal breath.

—Prepare the cartridge for your next inhalation. Pull the cartridge out once and push it in once. The disk will turn to the next numbered dose as seen in the indicator window. Do not pierce the blister until just before the inhalation.

- *To clean the inhaler:* Brush away the loose powder each day with the brush provided.
- The inhaler should be replaced every 6 months.

For patients using *budesonide powder for inhalation:*

- *To load the inhaler:*

—Unscrew the cover of the inhaler and lift it off.

—Hold the inhaler upright with the brown piece pointing downward. Turn the brown piece of the inhaler in one direction as far as it will go. Then twist it back until it clicks.

- *To use the inhaler:*

—Hold the inhaler away from your mouth and breathe out slowly to the end of a normal breath.

—Place the mouthpiece in your mouth and close your lips around it. Tilt your head slightly back. Do not block the mouthpiece with your teeth or tongue.

—Breathe in quickly and evenly through your mouth until you have taken a full deep breath.

—Hold your breath and remove the inhaler from your mouth. Continue holding your breath as long as you can up to 10 seconds before breathing out. This gives the medicine time to settle in your airways and lungs.

—Hold the inhaler well away from your mouth and breathe out to the end of a normal breath.

—Replace the cover on the mouthpiece to keep it clean.

- When the indicator window begins to show a red mark, there are about 20 doses left. When the red mark covers the window, the inhaler is empty.

For patients using *budesonide suspension for inhalation:*

- This medicine is to be used in a power-operated nebulizer equipped with a face mask or mouthpiece. Your doctor will advise you on which nebulizer to use. Make sure you understand how to use the nebulizer. If you have any questions about this, check with your doctor.
- Any opened ampul should be protected from light. The medicine in an open ampul must be used within 12 hours after the ampul is opened. Ampuls should be used within 3 months after the envelope containing them is opened.
- *To prepare the medicine for use in the nebulizer:*

—Remove one ampul from the sheet of five units and shake it gently.

—Hold the ampul upright. Open it by twisting off the wing.

—Squeeze the contents of the ampul into the cup of the nebulizer. If you use only half of the contents of an ampul, add enough of the sodium chloride solution provided to dilute the solution.

—Gently shake the nebulizer. Then attach the face mask to the nebulizer and connect the nebulizer to the air pump.

- *To use the medicine in the nebulizer:*

—This medicine should be inhaled over a period of 10 to 15 minutes.

—Breathe slowly and evenly, in and out, until no more mist is left in the nebulizer cup.

—Rinse your mouth when you are finished with the treatment. Wash your face if you used a face mask.

- *To clean the nebulizer:*

—After each treatment, wash the cup of the nebulizer and the mask or mouthpiece in warm water with a mild detergent.

—Allow the nebulizer parts to dry before putting them back together again.

Dosing—The dose of these medicines will be different for different patients. *Follow your doctor's orders or the directions on the label.* The following information includes only the average doses of these medicines. *If your dose is different, do not change it* unless your doctor tells you to do so.

For beclomethasone

- For inhalation *aerosol:*

—For bronchial asthma:

  - Adults and children 12 years of age and older—84 to 100 micrograms (mcg) (2 puffs) three or four times a day, or 168 to 200 mcg (4 puffs) two times a day. In severe asthma, your doctor may want you to take a higher dose.
  - Children 6 to 12 years of age—42 to 100 mcg (1 or 2 puffs) three or four times a day, or 168 to 200 mcg (4 puffs) two times a day.
  - Children up to 6 years of age—Use and dose must be determined by the doctor.

- For *capsules* for inhalation or *powder* for inhalation:

—For bronchial asthma:

  - Adults and teenagers 14 years of age and older—At first, 200 mcg three or four times a day. Then your doctor may reduce the dose, based on your condition.

• Children 6 to 14 years of age—At first, 100 mcg two to four times a day. Then your doctor may reduce the dose, based on your condition.

• Children up to 6 years of age—Use and dose must be determined by the doctor.

For budesonide

• For *powder* for inhalation:

—For bronchial asthma:

• Adults and children 12 years of age and older—At first, 400 to 2400 micrograms (mcg) a day, divided into two to four doses. The higher dose is usually used for treatment of severe asthma or when the dose of corticosteroids taken by mouth is being reduced or stopped. Later, your doctor may reduce the dose to 200 to 400 mcg two times a day.

• Children 6 to 12 years of age—At first, 100 to 200 mcg two times a day. The higher dose is usually used for treatment of severe asthma or when the dose of corticosteroids taken by mouth is being reduced or stopped.

• Children up to 6 years of age—Use and dose must be determined by the doctor.

• For *suspension* for inhalation:

—For bronchial asthma:

• Adults and children 12 years of age and older—500 to 2000 micrograms (mcg) mixed with enough sterile sodium chloride solution for inhalation, if necessary, to make 2 to 4 milliliters (mL). This solution is used in a nebulizer for a period of ten to fifteen minutes. The medicine should be used two times a day.

• Children 3 months to 12 years of age—250 to 1000 mcg mixed with enough sterile sodium chloride solution for inhalation, if necessary, to make 2 to 4 mL. This solution is used in a nebulizer for a period of ten to fifteen minutes. The medicine should be used two times a day.

• Children up to 3 months of age—Use and dose must be determined by the doctor.

For flunisolide

• For inhalation *aerosol:*

—For bronchial asthma:

• Adults and children 4 years of age and older—500 micrograms (mcg) (2 puffs) two times a day, morning and evening.

• Children up to 4 years of age—Use and dose must be determined by the doctor.

For triamcinolone

• For inhalation *aerosol:*

—For bronchial asthma:

• Adults and children 12 years of age and older—At first, 200 micrograms (mcg) (2 puffs) two to four times a day. Then your doctor may reduce the dose, based on your condition. In severe asthma, your doctor may want you to take a higher dose.

• Children 6 to 12 years of age—At first, 100 to 200 mcg (1 or 2 puffs) three or four times a day. Then your doctor may adjust your dose, based on your condition.

• Children up to 6 years of age—Use and dose must be determined by the doctor.

Missed dose—If you miss a dose of this medicine, use it as soon as possible. Then use any remaining doses for that day at regularly spaced times.

Storage—To store this medicine:

• Keep out of the reach of children.
• Store away from heat and direct light.
• Do not store the capsule form of this medicine in the bathroom, near the kitchen sink, or in other damp places. Heat or moisture may cause the medicine to break down.
• Keep the aerosol or suspension form of this medicine from getting too cold or freezing. This medicine may be less effective if the container is cold when you use it.
• Do not puncture, break, or burn the aerosol container, even after it is empty.
• Do not keep outdated medicine or medicine no longer needed. Be sure that any discarded medicine is out of the reach of children.

Precautions While Using This Medicine

Check with your doctor if:

• *You go through a period of unusual stress to your body, such as surgery, injury, or infection.*
• *You have an asthma attack* that does not improve after you take a bronchodilator medicine.
• *Signs of mouth, throat, or lung infection occur.*
• *Your symptoms do not improve or if your condition gets worse.*

Your doctor may want you to carry a medical identification card stating that you are using this medicine and that you may need additional medicine during times of emergency, a severe asthma attack or other illness, or unusual stress.

Before you have any kind of surgery (including dental surgery) or emergency treatment, tell the medical doctor or dentist in charge that you are using this medicine.

For patients who are also regularly taking a corticosteroid by mouth in tablet or liquid form:

• *Do not stop taking the corticosteroid taken by mouth without your doctor's advice, even if your asthma seems better.* Your doctor may want you to reduce gradually the amount you are taking before stopping completely to lessen the chance of unwanted effects.
• When your doctor tells you to reduce the dose, or to stop taking the corticosteroid taken by mouth, follow the directions carefully. Your body may need time to adjust to the change. The length of time this takes may depend on the amount of medicine you were taking and how long you took it. *It is especially im-*

portant that your doctor check your progress at regular visits during this time. Ask your doctor if there are special directions you should follow if you have a severe asthma attack, if you need any other medical or surgical treatment, or if certain side effects occur. Be certain that you understand these directions, and follow them carefully.

Side Effects of This Medicine

Along with its needed effects, a medicine may cause some unwanted effects. Although not all of these side effects may occur, if they do occur they may need medical attention.

Check with your doctor immediately if any of the following side effects occur just after you use this medicine:

Rare
Troubled breathing, tightness in chest, or wheezing

Also, check with your doctor as soon as possible if any of the following side effects occur:

Less common
Creamy white, curd-like patches in the mouth or throat and/or pain when eating or swallowing

Rare
Behavior changes; mental depression; nervousness; restlessness; pain or burning in the chest

Other side effects may occur that usually do not need medical attention. These side effects may go away during treatment as your body adjusts to the medicine. However, check with your doctor if any of the following side effects continue or are bothersome:

More common
Cough; dry mouth; hoarseness or other voice changes; sore throat

Less common or rare
Dry throat; headache; nausea; skin bruising or thinning; unpleasant taste

Other side effects not listed above may also occur in some patients. If you notice any other effects, check with your doctor.

Revised: 09/02/94

CORTICOSTEROIDS Nasal

Some commonly used brand names are:

In the U.S.—

Beconase[1]
Beconase AQ[1]
Decadron Turbinaire[3]
Nasacort[5]
Nasalide[4]
Vancenase[1]
Vancenase AQ[1]

In Canada—

Beconase[1]
Beconase AQ[1]
Nasacort[5]
Rhinalar[4]
Rhinocort Aqua[2]
Rhinocort Turbuhaler[2]
Vancenase[1]

Another commonly used name for beclomethasone is beclometasone.

Note: For quick reference, the following corticosteroids are numbered to match the corresponding brand names.

This information applies to the following medicines:

1. Beclomethasone (be-kloe-METH-a-sone)§
2. Budesonide (byoo-DES-oh-nide)*
3. Dexamethasone (dex-a-METH-a-sone)†
4. Flunisolide (floo-NISS-oh-lide)
5. Triamcinolone (trye-am-SIN-oh-lone)

*Not commercially available in the U.S.
†Not commercially available in the Canada.
§Generic name product may also be available in Canada.

Description

Nasal corticosteroids (kor-ti-ko-STER-oids) are cortisone-like medicines. They belong to the family of medicines called steroids. These medicines are sprayed or inhaled into the nose to help relieve the stuffy nose, irritation, and discomfort of hay fever, other allergies, and other nasal problems. These medicines are also used to prevent nasal polyps from growing back after they have been removed by surgery.

These medicines are available only with your doctor's prescription, in the following dosage forms:

Nasal

Beclomethasone
- Aerosol (U.S. and Canada)
- Solution (U.S. and Canada)

Budesonide
- Powder (Canada)
- Solution (Canada)

Dexamethasone
- Aerosol (U.S.)

Flunisolide
- Solution (U.S. and Canada)

Triamcinolone
- Aerosol (U.S. and Canada)

Before Using This Medicine

In deciding to use a medicine, the risks of taking the medicine must be weighed against the good it will do. This is a decision you and your doctor will make. For corticosteroids, the following should be considered:

Allergies—Tell your doctor if you have ever had any unusual or allergic reaction to corticosteroids. Also tell your health care professional if you are allergic to any other substances, such as foods, preservatives, or dyes.

Pregnancy—In one human study, use of beclomethasone oral inhalation by pregnant women did not cause birth defects or other problems. Studies on birth defects with budesonide, dexamethasone, flunisolide, or triamcinolone have not been done in humans.

In animal studies, corticosteroids taken by mouth or injection during pregnancy were shown to cause birth defects. Also, too much use of corticosteroids during pregnancy may cause other unwanted effects in the infant, such as slower growth and reduced adrenal gland function.

If corticosteroids are medically necessary during pregnancy to control nasal problems, nasal corticosteroids are generally considered safer than corticosteroids taken by mouth or injection. Also, use of nasal corticosteroids may allow some patients to stop using or decrease the amount of corticosteroids taken by mouth or injection.

Breast-feeding—Use of dexamethasone is not recommended in nursing mothers, since dexamethasone passes into breast milk and may affect the infant's growth.

It is not known whether beclomethasone, budesonide, flunisolide, or triamcinolone passes into breast milk. Although most medicines pass into breast milk in small amounts, many of them may be used safely while breast-feeding. Mothers who are taking this medicine and who wish to breast-feed should discuss this with their doctor.

Children—Corticosteroids taken by mouth or injection have been shown to slow or stop growth in children and cause reduced adrenal gland function. If corticosteroids are medically necessary to control nasal problems in a child, nasal corticosteroids are generally considered to be safer than corticosteroids taken by mouth or injection. Most nasal corticosteroids have not been shown to affect growth. Also, use of most nasal corticosteroids may allow some children to stop using or decrease the amount of corticosteroids taken by mouth or injection.

Before this medicine is given to a child, you and your child's doctor should talk about the good this medicine will do as well as the risks of using it. Follow the doctor's directions very carefully to lessen the chance of unwanted effects.

Older adults—Although there is no specific information comparing use of nasal corticosteroids in the elderly with use in other age groups, they are not expected to cause different side effects or problems in older people than they do in younger adults.

Other medicines—Although certain medicines should not be used together at all, in other cases two different medicines may be used together even if an interaction might occur. In these cases, your doctor may want to change the dose, or other precautions may be necessary. Tell your health care professional if you are taking any prescription or nonprescription (over-the-counter [OTC]) medicines.

Other medical problems—The presence of other medical problems may affect the use of corticosteroids. Make sure you tell your doctor if you have any other medical problems, especially:

- Amebiasis—Nasal corticosteroids may make this condition worse
- Glaucoma—Long-term use of nasal corticosteroids may worsen glaucoma by increasing the pressure within the eye
- Herpes simplex (virus) infection of the eye or
- Infections (virus, bacteria, or fungus)—Nasal corticosteroids may cover up the signs of these conditions
- Injury to the nose (recent) or
- Nose surgery (recent) or
- Sores in the nose—Nasal corticosteroids may prevent proper healing of these conditions
- Liver disease
- Tuberculosis (active or history of)
- Underactive thyroid

Proper Use of This Medicine

This medicine usually comes with patient directions. *Read them carefully before using the medicine.* Beclomethasone, budesonide, dexamethasone, and triamcinolone are used with a special inhaler. If you do not understand the directions, or if you are not sure how to use the inhaler, check with your health care professional.

Before using this medicine, clear the nasal passages by blowing your nose. Then, with the nosepiece inserted into the nostril, aim the spray towards the inner corner of the eye.

In order for this medicine to help you, it must be used regularly as ordered by your doctor. This medicine usually begins to work in about 1 week, but up to 3 weeks may pass before you feel its full effects.

Use this medicine only as directed. Do not use more of it and do not use it more often than your doctor ordered. To do so may increase the chance of absorption through the lining of the nose and the chance of unwanted effects.

Check with your doctor before using this medicine for nasal problems other than the one for which it was prescribed, since it should not be used on many bacterial, virus, or fungus nasal infections.

Save the inhaler that comes with beclomethasone or dexamethasone, since refill units may be available at lower cost.

Dosing—The dose of nasal corticosteroids will be different for different patients. *Follow your doctor's orders or the directions on the label.* The following information includes only the average doses of nasal corticosteroids. *If your dose is different, do not change it* unless your doctor tells you to do so.

For beclomethasone

- For allergies or other nasal conditions:
  - —For *nasal aerosol* dosage form:
    - Adults and children 6 years of age and older—One spray in each nostril two to four times a day.
    - Children up to 6 years of age—Use and dose must be determined by your doctor.
  - —For *nasal solution* dosage form:
    - Adults and children 6 years of age and older—One or two sprays in each nostril two times a day.
    - Children up to 6 years of age—Use and dose must be determined by your doctor.

For budesonide

- For allergies or other nasal conditions:
  - —For *nasal powder* dosage form:
    - Adults and children 6 years of age and older—Two inhalations in each nostril once a day in the morning.
    - Children up to 6 years of age—Use and dose must be determined by your doctor.

—For *nasal solution* dosage form:

• Adults and children 6 years of age and older—One or two sprays in each nostril one or two times a day.

• Children up to 6 years of age—Use and dose must be determined by your doctor.

For dexamethasone

• For allergies or other nasal conditions:

—For *nasal aerosol* dosage form:

• Adults and children 6 years of age and older—One or two sprays in each nostril two or three times a day for up to two weeks.

• Children up to 6 years of age—Use and dose must be determined by your doctor.

For flunisolide

• For allergies or other nasal conditions:

—For *nasal solution* dosage form:

• Adults and children 6 years of age and older—One or two sprays in each nostril one to three times a day.

• Children up to 6 years of age—Use and dose must be determined by your doctor.

For triamcinolone

• For allergies or other nasal conditions:

—For *nasal aerosol* dosage form:

• Adults and children 12 years of age and older—Two sprays in each nostril once a day.

• Children up to 12 years of age—Use and dose must be determined by your doctor.

Missed dose—If you miss a dose of this medicine and remember within an hour or so, use it right away. However, if you do not remember until later, skip the missed dose and go back to your regular dosing schedule. Do not double doses.

Storage—To store this medicine:

- Keep out of the reach of children.
- Store away from heat and direct light.
- Do not store budesonide powder in the bathroom, near the kitchen sink, or in other damp places, especially if the cap has not been tightly screwed back on. Moisture may cause the medicine to break down.
- Keep the medicine from getting too cold or freezing. This medicine may be less effective if it is too cold when you use it.
- Do not puncture, break, or burn the beclomethasone, dexamethasone, or triamcinolone aerosol container, even after it is empty.
- Do not keep outdated medicine or medicine no longer needed. Also, discard any unused flunisolide or beclomethasone solution 3 months after you open the package. Be sure that any discarded medicine is out of the reach of children.

Precautions While Using This Medicine

If you will be using this medicine for more than a few weeks, your doctor should check your progress at regular visits.

Check with your doctor:

- *if signs of a nose, sinus, or throat infection occur.*
- *if your symptoms do not improve within 7 days (for dexamethasone) or within 3 weeks (for beclomethasone, budesonide, flunisolide, or triamcinolone).*
- *if your condition gets worse.*

Side Effects of This Medicine

Along with its needed effects, a medicine may cause some unwanted effects. Although not all of these side effects may occur, if they do occur they may need medical attention.

Check with your doctor as soon as possible if any of the following side effects occur:

Less common or rare

Bad smell; bloody mucus or unexplained nosebleeds; burning or stinging after use of spray or irritation inside nose (continuing); crusting, white patches, or sores inside nose; eye pain; gradual loss of vision; headache; hives; lightheadedness or dizziness; loss of sense of taste or smell; nausea or vomiting; shortness of breath, troubled breathing, tightness in chest, or wheezing; skin rash; sore throat, cough, or hoarseness; stomach pains; stuffy, dry, or runny nose or watery eyes (continuing); swelling of eyelids, face, or lips; unusual tiredness or weakness; white patches in throat

Symptoms of overdose

Acne; fullness or rounding of the face; menstrual changes

Other side effects may occur that usually do not need medical attention. These side effects may go away during treatment as your body adjusts to the medicine. However, check with your doctor if any of the following side effects continue or are bothersome:

More common

Burning, dryness, or other irritation inside the nose (mild, lasting only a short time); increase in sneezing; irritation of throat

Less common

Throat discomfort or itching

Not all of the side effects listed above have been reported for each of these medicines, but they have been reported for at least one of them. All of the nasal corticosteroids are very similar, so any of the above side effects may occur with any of these medicines.

Other side effects not listed above may also occur in some patients. If you notice any other effects, check with your doctor.

Revised: 05/16/94

CORTICOSTEROIDS Ophthalmic

Some commonly used brand names are:

In the U.S.—

AK-Dex[2]
AK-Pred[6]
AK-Tate[6]
Baldex[2]
Decadron[2]
Dexair[2]
Dexotic[2]
Econopred[6]
Econopred Plus[6]
Eflone[3]
Flarex[3]
Fluor-Op[3]
FML Forte[3]
FML Liquifilm[3]
FML S.O.P.[3]
HMS Liquifilm[5]
Inflamase Forte[6]
Inflamase Mild[6]
I-Pred[6]
Lite Pred[6]
Maxidex[2]
Ocu-Dex[2]
Ocu-Pred[6]
Ocu-Pred-A[6]
Ocu-Pred Forte[6]
Predair[6]
Predair A[6]
Predair Forte[6]
Pred Forte[6]
Pred Mild[6]
Storz-Dexa[2]
Ultra Pred[6]

In Canada—

AK-Tate[6]
Betnesol[1]
Cortamed[4]
Decadron[2]
Diodex[2]
Flarex[3]
FML Forte[3]
FML Liquifilm[3]
HMS Liquifilm[5]
Inflamase Forte[6]
Inflamase Mild[6]
Maxidex[2]
Ophtho-Tate[6]
PMS-Dexamethasone Sodium Phosphate[2]
Pred Forte[6]
Pred Mild[6]
R.O.-Dexasone[2]
Spersadex[2]

Another commonly used name for hydrocortisone is cortisol.

Note: For quick reference, the following corticosteroids are numbered to match the corresponding brand names.

This information applies to the following medicines:

1. Betamethasone (bay-ta-METH-a-sone)*
2. Dexamethasone (dex-a-METH-a-sone)‡
3. Fluorometholone (flure-oh-METH-oh-lone)
4. Hydrocortisone (hye-droe-KOR-ti-sone)*
5. Medrysone (ME-dri-sone)
6. Prednisolone (pred-NISS-oh-lone)‡§

*Not commercially available in the U.S.
‡Generic name product may also be available in U.S.
§Generic name product may also be available in Canada.

Description

Ophthalmic corticosteroids (kor-ti-ko-STER-oids) (cortisone-like medicines) are used to prevent permanent damage to the eye, which may occur with certain eye problems. They also provide relief from redness, irritation, and other discomfort.

Corticosteroids for use in the eye are available only with your doctor's prescription, in the following dosage forms:

Ophthalmic

Betamethasone
- Solution (eye drops) (Canada)

Dexamethasone
- Ointment (U.S. and Canada)
- Solution (eye drops) (U.S. and Canada)
- Suspension (eye drops) (U.S. and Canada)

Fluorometholone
- Ointment (U.S.)
- Suspension (eye drops) (U.S. and Canada)

Hydrocortisone
- Ointment (Canada)

Medrysone
- Suspension (eye drops) (U.S. and Canada)

Prednisolone
- Solution (eye drops) (U.S. and Canada)
- Suspension (eye drops) (U.S. and Canada)

Before Using This Medicine

In deciding to use a medicine, the risks of taking the medicine must be weighed against the good it will do. This is a decision you and your doctor will make. For ophthalmic corticosteroids, the following should be considered:

Allergies—Tell your doctor if you have ever had any unusual or allergic reaction to corticosteroids. Also tell your health care professional if you are allergic to any other substances, such as foods, preservatives, or dyes.

Pregnancy—Although studies on birth defects with ophthalmic corticosteroids have not been done in humans, these medicines have not been reported to cause birth defects or other problems. However, in animal studies, dexamethasone, fluorometholone, hydrocortisone, and prednisolone caused birth defects when applied to the eyes of pregnant animals. Also, fluorometholone and medrysone caused other unwanted effects in the animal fetus.

Breast-feeding—Ophthalmic corticosteroids have not been reported to cause problems in nursing babies.

Children—Children less than 2 years of age may be especially sensitive to the effects of ophthalmic corticosteroids. This may increase the chance of side effects. If this medicine has been ordered for a young child, you should discuss its use with your child's doctor. Be sure you follow all of the doctor's instructions very carefully.

Older adults—Although there is no specific information about the use of ophthalmic corticosteroids in the elderly, they are not expected to cause different side effects or problems in older people than they do in younger adults.

Other medicines—Although certain medicines should not be used together at all, in other cases two different medicines may be used together even if an interaction might occur. In these cases, your doctor may want to change the dose, or other precautions may be necessary. Tell your health care professional if you are using any other prescription or nonprescription (over-the-counter [OTC]) ophthalmic medicine.

Other medical problems—The presence of other medical problems may affect the use of ophthalmic corticosteroids. Make sure you tell your doctor if you have any other medical problems, especially:

- Cataracts—Corticosteroids may cause cataracts or make them worse
- Diabetes mellitus (sugar diabetes)—Patients with diabetes may be more likely to develop cataracts or glaucoma with the use of corticosteroids
- Glaucoma (or family history of)—Corticosteroids may cause glaucoma or make it worse
- Herpes infection of the eye or
- Tuberculosis of the eye (active or history of) or
- Any other eye infection—Ophthalmic corticosteroids may make existing infections worse or cause new infections

Proper Use of This Medicine

For patients who wear *contact lenses:*

- Use of ophthalmic corticosteroids while you are wearing contact lenses (either hard lenses or soft lenses) may increase the chance of infection. Therefore, do not apply this medicine while you are wearing contact lenses. Also, check with an ophthalmologist (eye doctor) for advice on how long to wait after applying this medicine before inserting your contact lenses. It is possible that you may be directed not to wear contact lenses at all during the entire time of treatment and for a day or two after treatment has been stopped.

For patients using an *ophthalmic solution or suspension (eye drop) form* of this medicine:

- If you are using a suspension form of this medicine, always shake the container very well just before applying the eye drops.
- To use:
  —First, wash your hands. Tilt the head back and, pressing your finger gently on the skin just beneath the lower eyelid, pull the lower eyelid away from the eye to make a space. Drop the medicine into this space. Let go of the eyelid and gently close the eyes. Do not blink. Keep the eyes closed and apply pressure to the inner corner of the eye with your finger for 1 or 2 minutes to allow the medicine to be absorbed by the eye.
  —If you think you did not get the drop of medicine into your eye properly, use another drop.
  —Immediately after using the eye drops, wash your hands to remove any medicine that may be on them.
  —To keep the medicine as germ-free as possible, do not touch the dropper or the applicator tip to any surface (including the eye). Always keep the container tightly closed.

For patients using an *ointment form* of this medicine:

- To use:
  —First, wash your hands. Tilt the head back and, pressing your finger gently on the skin just beneath the lower eyelid, pull the lower eyelid away from the eye to make a space. Squeeze a thin strip of ointment into this space. A 1-cm (approximately 1/3 inch) strip of ointment is usually enough, unless you have been told by your doctor to use a different amount. Let go of the eyelid and gently close the eyes. Keep the eyes closed for 1 or 2 minutes to allow the medicine to come into contact with the irritation.
  —To keep the medicine as germ-free as possible, do not touch the applicator tip to any surface (including the eye). After using the eye ointment, wipe the tip of the ointment tube with a clean tissue. Do not wash the tip with water. Always keep the tube tightly closed.

Do not use corticosteroids more often or for a longer time than your doctor ordered. To do so may increase the chance of side effects, especially in children 2 years of age or younger.

Do not use any leftover medicine for future eye problems without first checking with your doctor. This medicine should not be used if certain kinds of infections are present. To do so may make the infection worse and possibly lead to eye damage.

Dosing—The dose of ophthalmic corticosteroids will be different for different patients. *Follow your doctor's orders or the directions on the label.* The following information includes only the average doses of ophthalmic corticosteroids. *If your dose is different, do not change it* unless your doctor tells you to do so.

For betamethasone
- For eye disorders:
  —For *ophthalmic solution (eye drops)* dosage form:
    - Adults and children—Use one or two drops in the eye every one or two hours, then space the doses further apart as the eye gets better.

For dexamethasone
- For eye disorders:
  —For *ophthalmic ointment* dosage form:
    - Adults and children—Use the ointment in the eye three or four times a day, then space the doses further apart as the eye gets better.

  —For *ophthalmic solution (eye drops)* dosage form:
    - Adults and children—Use one or two drops in the eye up to six times a day.

  —For *ophthalmic suspension (eye drops)* dosage form:
    - Adults and children—Use one or two drops in the eye four to six times a day.

For fluorometholone
- For eye disorders:
  —For *ophthalmic ointment* dosage form:
    - Adults and children—Use the ointment in the eye one to three times a day.

  —For *ophthalmic suspension (eye drops)* dosage form:
    - Adults and children—Use one or two drops in the eye two to four times a day.

For hydrocortisone
- For eye disorders:
  —For *ophthalmic ointment* dosage form:
    - Adults and children—Use the ointment in the eye three or four times a day, then space the doses further apart as the eye gets better.

For medrysone
- For eye disorders:
  —For *ophthalmic suspension (eye drops)* dosage form:
    - Adults and children—Use one drop in the eye up to every four hours.

For prednisolone
- For eye disorders:
  —For *ophthalmic solution (eye drops)* dosage form:
  - Adults and children—Use one or two drops in the eye up to six times a day.

  —For *ophthalmic suspension (eye drops)* dosage form:
  - Adults and children—Use one or two drops in the eye two to four times a day.

Missed dose—If you miss a dose of this medicine, apply it as soon as possible. However, if it is almost time for your next dose, skip the missed dose and go back to your regular dosing schedule.

Storage—To store this medicine:
- Keep out of the reach of children.
- Store away from heat and direct light.
- Keep the medicine from freezing.
- Do not keep outdated medicine or medicine no longer needed. Be sure that any discarded medicine is out of the reach of children.

Precautions While Using This Medicine

If you will be using this medicine for more than a few weeks, an ophthalmologist (eye doctor) should examine your eyes at regular visits to make sure it does not cause unwanted effects.

If your eye condition does not improve after 5 to 7 days, or if it becomes worse, check with your doctor.

Side Effects of This Medicine

Along with its needed effects, a medicine may cause some unwanted effects. Although not all of these side effects may occur, if they do occur they may need medical attention. Check with your doctor as soon as possible if any of the following side effects occur:

Less common or rare
Decreased vision; eye pain; gradual blurring or loss of vision; vomiting

Other side effects may occur that usually do not need medical attention. These side effects may go away during treatment as your body adjusts to the medicine. However, check with your doctor if any of the following side effects continue or are bothersome:

More frequent
Blurred vision (mild and temporary, occurs after use of ointments)

Less common or rare
Burning, stinging, redness, or watering of eyes

Other side effects not listed above may also occur in some patients. If you notice any other effects, check with your doctor.

Revised: 01/05/94
Interim revision: 05/16/94; 01/27/95

CORTICOSTEROIDS Otic

Some commonly used brand names are:

In the U.S.—
AK-Dex[2]
Decadron[2]
I-Methasone[2]

In Canada—
AK-Dex[2]
Betnesol[1]
Cortamed[3]
Decadron[2]

Another commonly used name for hydrocortisone is cortisol.

Note: For quick reference, the following corticosteroids are numbered to match the corresponding brand names.

This information applies to the following medicines:
1. Betamethasone (bay-ta-METH-a-sone)*
2. Dexamethasone (dex-a-METH-a-sone)
3. Hydrocortisone (hye-droe-KOR-ti-sone)*

*Not commercially available in the U.S.

Description

Otic corticosteroids (kor-ti-koe-STE-roids) (cortisone-like medicines) are used in the ear to relieve the redness, itching, and swelling caused by certain ear problems.

Otic corticosteroids are available only with your doctor's prescription, in the following dosage forms:

Otic
Betamethasone
- Solution (Canada)

Dexamethasone
- Solution (U.S. and Canada)

Hydrocortisone
- Ointment (Canada)

Before Using This Medicine

In deciding to use a medicine, the risks of taking the medicine must be weighed against the good it will do. This is a decision you and your doctor will make. For otic corticosteroids, the following should be considered:

Allergies—Tell your doctor if you have ever had any unusual or allergic reaction to corticosteroids. Also tell your health care professional if you are allergic to any other substances, such as certain preservatives or dyes.

Pregnancy—Otic corticosteroids have not been shown to cause birth defects or other problems in pregnant women.

Breast-feeding—Otic corticosteroids have not been reported to cause problems in nursing infants.

Children—Although there is no specific information about the use of otic corticosteroids in children, they are not expected to cause different side effects or problems in children than they do in adults.

Older adults—Although there is no specific information about the use of otic corticosteroids in the elderly, they are not expected to cause different side effects or problems in older people than they do in younger adults.

Other medical problems—The presence of other medical problems may affect the use of otic corticosteroids. Make sure you tell your doctor if you have ... other medical problems, especially:

- Any other ear infection or conditi... r history of)—Otic corticosteroids may worsen ex... infections or cause new infections
- Punctured ear drum—Usin... corticosteroids with a punctured ear drum may ... the ear

Proper Use ...s Medicine

To use *ear drops*:

- Lie down or tilt t... o that the affected ear faces up. Gently pul... be up and back for adults (down and b... ildren) to straighten the ear canal. Drop... e into the ear canal. Keep the ear facing... ral (about 5) minutes to allow the med... o the bottom of the ear canal. A sterile... ay be gently inserted into the ear open... the medicine from leaking out. At firs... nay want you to put more medicine ...g during the day to keep it moist.

To... ...ol amount of ointment to the area just ...r canal, using a clean finger or a piece ...uze. Do not use a cotton-tipped swab un... ...doctor has directed you to do so and has ... exactly how to use it.

... medicine as germ-free as possible, do not ...opper or applicator tip to any surface (includ- ...). Also, keep the container tightly closed.

...*e corticosteroids more often or for a longer time ...ur doctor ordered.* To do so may increase the ... of side effects.

...*ot use any leftover medicine for future ear problems ...out first checking with your doctor.* This medicine ...uld not be used if certain kinds of infections are pres-... To do so may make the infection worse.

...osing—The dose of otic corticosteroids will be different for different patients. *Follow your doctor's orders or the directions on the label.* The following information includes only the average doses of otic corticosteroids. *If your dose is different, do not change it* unless your doctor tells you to do so.

For betamethasone

- For *otic solution (ear drops)* dosage form:
  - —For redness, itching, and swelling:
    - Adults and children—Use two or three drops in the ear every two or three hours. After symptoms are relieved, your doctor may lower the dose.

For dexamethasone

- For *otic solution (ear drops)* dosage form:
  - —For redness, itching, and swelling:
    - Adults and children—Use three or four drops in the ear two or three times a day. After symptoms are relieved, your doctor may lower the dose.

For hydrocortisone

- For *otic ointment (ear ointment)* dosage form:
  - —For redness, itching, and swelling:
    - Adults and children 2 years of age and older—Use two or three times a day in the ear. After symptoms are relieved, your doctor may lower the dose.
    - Children up to 2 years of age—Use and dose must be determined by your doctor.

Missed dose—If you miss a dose of this medicine, use it as soon as you remember. However, if it is almost time for your next dose, skip the missed dose and go back to your regular dosing schedule. Do not double doses.

Storage—To store this medicine:

- Keep out of the reach of children.
- Store away from heat and direct light.
- Keep the medicine from freezing.
- Do not keep outdated medicine or medicine no longer needed. Be sure that any discarded medicine is out of the reach of children.

Precautions While Using This Medicine

If your condition does not improve within 5 to 7 days, or if it becomes worse, check with your doctor.

Side Effects of This Medicine

Along with its needed effects, a medicine may cause some unwanted effects. The following side effects usually do not need medical attention and may go away during treatment as your body adjusts to the medicine. However, check with your doctor if either of the following side effects continues or is bothersome:

Less common

Burning or stinging of the ear

There have not been any other common or important side effects reported with this medicine. However, if you notice any unusual effects, check with your doctor.

Revised: 03/31/92
Interim revision: 02/17/94

CORTICOSTEROIDS—Glucocorticoid Effects Systemic

Some commonly used brand names are:

In the U.S.—

A-hydroCort[4]
AK-Dex[3]
Amcort[8]
A-methaPred[5]
Aristocort[8]
Aristocort Forte[8]
Aristocort Intralesional[8]
Aristospan Intra-articular[8]
Aristospan Intralesional[8]
Articulose-50[6]
Articulose-L.A.[8]
Celestone[1]
Celestone Phosphate[1]
Celestone Soluspan[1]
Cenocort A-40[8]
Cenocort Forte[8]
Cinalone 40[8]
Cinonide 40[8]
Cortef[4]
Cortenema[4]
Cortifoam[4]
Cortone Acetate[2]
Dalalone[3]
Dalalone D.P.[3]
Dalalone L.A.[3]
Decadrol[3]
Decadron[3]
Decadron-LA[3]
Decadron Phosphate[3]
Decaject[3]
Decaject-L.A.[3]
Delta-Cortef[6]
Deltasone[7]
depMedalone 40[5]
depMedalone 80[5]
Depoject-40[5]
Depoject-80[5]
Depo-Medrol[5]
Depopred-40[5]
Depopred-80[5]
Depo-Predate 40[5]
Depo-Predate 80[5]
Deronil[3]
Dexacen-4[3]
Dexacen LA-8[3]
Dexamethasone Intensol[3]
Dexasone[3]
Dexasone-LA[3]
Dexone[3]
Dexone 0.5[3]
Dexone 0.75[3]
Dexone 1.5[3]
Dexone 4[3]
Dexone LA[3]
Duralone-40[5]
Duralone-80[5]
Hexadrol[3]
Hexadrol Phosphate[3]
Hydeltrasol[6]
Hydeltra-T.B.A.[6]
Hydrocortone[4]
Hydrocortone Acetate[4]
Hydrocortone Phosphate[4]
Kenacort[8]
Kenacort Diacetate[8]
Kenaject-40[8]
Kenalog-10[8]
Kenalog-40[8]
Key-Pred 25[6]
Key-Pred 50[6]
Key-Pred SP[6]
Liquid Pred[7]
Medralone-40[5]
Medralone-80[5]
Medrol[5]
Medrol Enpak[5]
Meprolone[5]
Meticorten[7]
Mymethasone[3]
Nor-Pred T.B.A.[6]
Orasone 1[7]
Orasone 5[7]
Orasone 10[7]
Orasone 20[7]
Orasone 50[7]
Pediapred[6]
Predaject-50[6]
Predalone 50[6]
Predalone T.B.A.[6]
Predate 50[6]
Predate S[6]
Predate TBA[6]
Predcor-25[6]
Predcor-50[6]
Predcor-TBA[6]
Predicort-50[6]
Predicort-RP[6]
Prednicen-M[7]
Prednisone Intensol[7]
Prelone[6]
Rep-Pred 40[5]
Rep-Pred 80[5]
Selestoject[1]
Solu-Cortef[4]
Solu-Medrol[5]
Solurex[3]
Solurex-LA[3]
Sterapred[7]
Sterapred DS[7]
Tac-3[8]
Triam-A[8]
Triam-Forte[8]
Triamolone 40[8]
Triamonide 40[8]
Tri-Kort[8]
Trilog[8]
Trilone[8]
Tristoject[8]

In Canada—

Apo-Prednisone[7]
Aristocort[8]
Aristocort Forte[8]
Aristocort Intralesional[8]
Aristospan Intra-articular[8]
Betnelan[1]
Betnesol[1]
Celestone[1]
Celestone Soluspan[1]
Cortef[4]
Cortenema[4]
Cortifoam[4]
Cortone[2]
Decadron[3]
Decadron Phosphate[3]
Deltasone[7]
Depo-Medrol[5]
Deronil[3]
Dexasone[3]
Hexadrol[3]
Kenacort[8]
Kenalog-10[8]
Kenalog-40[8]
Medrol[5]
Oradexon[3]
Solu-Cortef[4]
Solu-Medrol[5]
Winpred[7]

Another commonly used name for hydrocortisone is cortisol.

Note: For quick reference, the following corticosteroids are numbered to match the corresponding brand names.

This information applies to the following medicines:

1. Betamethasone (bay-ta-METH-a-sone)‡
2. Cortisone (KOR-ti-sone)‡§
3. Dexamethasone (dex-a-METH-a-sone)‡§
4. Hydrocortisone (hye-droe-KOR-ti-sone)
5. Methylprednisolone (meth-ill-pred-NISS-oh-lone)‡
6. Prednisolone (pred-NISS-oh-lone)‡
7. Prednisone (PRED-ni-sone)‡§
8. Triamcinolone (trye-am-SIN-oh-lone)‡§

The following information does *not* apply to desoxycorticosterone or fludrocortisone.

‡Generic name product may also be available in the U.S.
§Generic name product may also be available in Canada.

Description

Corticosteroids (kor-ti-koe-STER-oyds) (cortisone-like medicines) are used to provide relief for inflamed areas of the body. They lessen swelling, redness, itching, and allergic reactions. They are often used as part of the treatment for a number of different diseases, such as severe allergies or skin problems, asthma, or arthritis. Corticosteroids may also be used for other conditions as determined by your doctor.

Your body naturally produces certain cortisone-like hormones that are necessary to maintain good health. If your body does not produce enough, your doctor may have prescribed this medicine to help make up the difference.

Corticosteroids are very strong medicines. In addition to their helpful effects in treating your medical problem, they have side effects that can be very serious. If your adrenal glands are not producing enough cortisone-like hormones, taking this medicine is not likely to cause problems unless you take too much of it. If you are taking this medicine to treat another medical problem, be sure that you discuss the risks and benefits of this medicine with your doctor.

These medicines are available only with your doctor's prescription, in the following dosage forms:

Oral

Betamethasone
- Syrup (U.S.)
- Tablets (U.S. and Canada)
- Effervescent tablets (Canada)
- Extended-release tablets (Canada)

Cortisone
- Tablets (U.S. and Canada)

Dexamethasone
- Elixir (U.S.)
- Oral solution (U.S.)
- Tablets (U.S. and Canada)

Hydrocortisone
- Oral suspension (U.S.)
- Tablets (U.S. and Canada)

Methylprednisolone
- Tablets (U.S. and Canada)

Prednisolone
- Oral solution (U.S.)
- Syrup (U.S.)
- Tablets (U.S.)

Prednisone
- Oral solution (U.S.)
- Syrup (U.S.)
- Tablets (U.S. and Canada)

Triamcinolone
- Syrup (U.S. and Canada)
- Tablets (U.S. and Canada)

Parenteral

Betamethasone
- Injection (U.S. and Canada)

Cortisone
- Injection (U.S. and Canada)

Dexamethasone
- Injection (U.S. and Canada)

Hydrocortisone
- Injection (U.S. and Canada)

Methylprednisolone
- Injection (U.S. and Canada)

Prednisolone
- Injection (U.S.)

Triamcinolone
- Injection (U.S. and Canada)

Rectal

Betamethasone
- Enema (Canada)

Hydrocortisone
- Aerosol foam (U.S. and Canada)
- Enema (U.S. and Canada)

Methylprednisolone
- Enema (U.S.)

Before Using This Medicine

In deciding to use a medicine, the risks of taking the medicine must be weighed against the good it will do. This is a decision you and your doctor will make. For corticosteroids, the following should be considered:

Allergies—Tell your doctor if you have ever had any unusual or allergic reaction to corticosteroids. Also tell your health care professional if you are allergic to any other substances, such as foods, preservatives, or dyes.

Diet—If you will be using this medicine for a long time, your doctor may want you to:

- Follow a low-salt diet and/or a potassium-rich diet.
- Watch your calories to prevent weight gain.
- Add extra protein to your diet. Make certain your health care professional knows if you are already on any special diet, such as a low-sodium or low-sugar diet.

Pregnancy—Studies on birth defects with corticosteroids have not been done in humans. However, too much use of corticosteroids during pregnancy may cause the baby to have problems after birth, such as slower growth. Also, studies in animals have shown that corticosteroids cause birth defects.

Breast-feeding—Corticosteroids pass into breast milk and may cause problems with growth or other unwanted effects in nursing babies. Depending on the amount of medicine you are taking every day, it may be necessary for you to take another medicine or to stop breast-feeding during treatment.

Children—Corticosteroids may cause infections such as chickenpox or measles to be more serious in children who catch them. These medicines can also slow or stop growth in children and in growing teenagers, especially when they are used for a long time. Before this medicine is given to children or teenagers, you should discuss its use with your child's doctor and then carefully follow the doctor's instructions.

Older adults—Older patients may be more likely to develop high blood pressure or bone disease from corticosteroids. Women are especially at risk of developing bone disease.

Other medicines—Although certain medicines should not be used together at all, in other cases two different medicines may be used together even if an interaction might occur. In these cases, your doctor may want to change the dose, or other precautions may be necessary. When you are taking corticosteroids, it is especially important that your health care professional know if you are taking any of the following:

- Aminoglutethimide or
- Antacids (in large amounts) or
- Barbiturates, except butalbital, or
- Carbamazepine (e.g., Tegretol) or
- Griseofulvin (e.g., Fulvicin) or
- Mitotane (e.g., Lysodren) or
- Phenylbutazone (e.g., Butazolidin) or
- Phenytoin (e.g., Dilantin) or
- Primidone (e.g., Mysoline) or
- Rifampin (e.g., Rifadin)—Use of these medicines may make certain corticosteroids less effective
- Amphotericin B by injection (e.g., Fungizone)—Corticosteroids and this medicine decrease the amount of potassium in the blood. Serious side effects could occur if the level of potassium gets too low
- Antidiabetics, oral (diabetes medicine taken by mouth) or
- Insulin—Corticosteroids may increase blood glucose (sugar) levels
- Digitalis glycosides (heart medicine)—Corticosteroids decrease the amount of potassium in the blood. Digitalis can cause an irregular heartbeat or other problems more commonly if the blood potassium gets too low
- Diuretics (water pills) or

- Medicine containing potassium—Using corticosteroids with diuretics may cause the diuretic to be less effective. Also, corticosteroids may increase the risk of low blood potassium, which is also a problem with certain diuretics. Potassium supplements or a different type of diuretic is used in treating high blood pressure in those people who have problems keeping their blood potassium at a normal level. Corticosteroids may make these medicines less able to do this
- Immunizations (vaccinations)—While you are being treated with this medicine, and even after you stop taking it, do not have any immunizations without your doctor's approval. Also, other people living in your home should not receive oral polio vaccine, since there is a chance they could pass the polio virus on to you. In addition, you should avoid close contact with other people at school or work who have recently taken oral polio vaccine
- Skin test injections—Corticosteroids may cause false results in skin tests
- Sodium-containing medicine—Corticosteroids cause the body to retain (keep) more salt and water. Too much sodium may cause high blood sodium, high blood pressure, and excess body water

Other medical problems—The presence of other medical problems may affect the use of corticosteroids. Make sure you tell your doctor if you have any other medical problems, especially:

- Bone disease—These medicines may worsen bone disease because they cause the body to lose more calcium
- Chickenpox (including recent exposure) or
- Measles (including recent exposure)—Risk of severe disease affecting other parts of the body
- Colitis or
- Diverticulitis or
- Stomach ulcer or other stomach or intestine problems—These medicines may cover up symptoms of a worsening stomach or intestinal condition. A patient would not know if his/her condition was getting worse and would not get medical help when needed
- Diabetes mellitus (sugar diabetes)—Corticosteroids may cause a loss of control of diabetes by increasing blood glucose (sugar)
- Fungus infection or any other infection or
- Herpes simplex infection of the eye or
- Infection at the place of treatment or
- Recent surgery or serious injury or
- Tuberculosis (active TB, nonactive TB, or past history of)—These medicines can cause slower healing, worsen existing infections, or cause new infections
- Glaucoma—Corticosteroids may cause the pressure within the eye to increase
- Heart disease or
- High blood pressure or
- Kidney disease (especially if you are receiving dialysis) or
- Kidney stones—These medicines cause the body to retain (keep) more salt and water. These conditions may be made worse by this extra body water
- High cholesterol levels—Corticosteroids may increase blood cholesterol levels
- Liver disease or
- Overactive thyroid or
- Underactive thyroid—With these conditions, the body may not eliminate the corticosteroid at the usual rate, which may change the medicine's effect
- Myasthenia gravis—When these medicines are first started, muscle weakness may occur. Your doctor may want to take special precautions because this could cause problems with breathing
- Systemic lupus erythematosus (SLE)—This condition may cause certain side effects of corticosteroids to occur more easily

Proper Use of This Medicine

For patients taking this medicine by mouth:

- *Take this medicine with food* to help prevent stomach upset. If stomach upset, burning, or pain continues, check with your doctor.
- Stomach problems may be more likely to occur if you drink alcoholic beverages while being treated with this medicine. You should not drink alcoholic beverages while taking this medicine, unless you have first checked with your doctor.

For patients using this medicine rectally:

- This medicine usually comes with patient directions. Read them carefully before using this medicine.
- For patients using hydrocortisone enema:

  —Each bottle contains a single dose. Use it all, unless otherwise directed by your doctor.

  —For best results, use this medicine right after a bowel movement. Lie down on your left side when giving the enema.

  —Insert the rectal tip of the enema applicator gently to prevent damage to the rectal wall.

  —Stay on your left side for at least 30 minutes after the enema is given so the medicine can work. If you can, keep the medicine inside the rectum all night.
- For patients using hydrocortisone acetate rectal aerosol foam:

  —This medicine is used with a special applicator. Do not insert any part of the aerosol container into the rectum.
- For patients using methylprednisolone acetate for enema:

  —Each bottle contains a single dose. Use it all, unless otherwise directed by your doctor.

  —Insert the rectal tip of the enema applicator gently to prevent damage to the rectal wall.

  —If you have been directed to use this enema slowly (not all at once), shake the bottle once in a while while you are giving the enema.

  —Save your applicator. Refill units of this medicine may be available at a lower cost.

Use this medicine only as directed by your doctor. Do not use more or less of it, do not use it more often, and do not use it for a longer time than your doctor ordered. To do so may increase the chance of side effects.

Dosing—The dose of these medicines will be different for different patients. *Follow your doctor's orders or the directions on the label.* The following information gives the range of doses of these medicines for all uses, which can vary widely. The dose that you are receiving may be very different. *If your dose is different, do not change it* unless your doctor tells you to do so.

The number of capsules, tablets, teaspoonfuls of liquid or amount of injection that you use depends on the strength of the medicine. Also, *the number of doses you take each day, the time allowed between doses, and the length of time you take the medicine depend on the medical problem for which you are taking the corticosteroid. In addition, your doctor may need to change the dose from time to time.*

For betamethasone

- For *oral* dosage forms:
  - —Syrup, tablets, effervescent tablets:
    - Adults and teenagers—Dose may range from 0.6 milligrams (mg) to 7.2 mg a day.
    - Children—Dose is based on body weight or size and must be determined by your doctor.
  - —Extended-release tablets:
    - Adults and teenagers—2 to 6 mg a day.
    - Children—Dose is based on body weight or size and must be determined by your doctor.
- For *injection* dosage form:
  - —Adults and teenagers: Up to 9 mg (betamethasone) a day, injected into a muscle, vein, joint, or lesion.
  - —Children: Dose is based on body weight or size and must be determined by your doctor.
- For *rectal* dosage form (enema):
  - —Adults and teenagers: 5 mg (betamethasone), given as directed, each night.
  - —Children: Dose must be determined by your doctor.

For cortisone

- For *oral* dosage form (tablets):
  - —Adults and teenagers: 25 to 300 milligrams (mg) a day, as a single dose or divided into several doses.
  - —Children: Dose is based on body weight or size and must be determined by your doctor.
- For *injection* dosage form:
  - —Adults and teenagers: 20 to 300 mg a day, injected into a muscle.
  - —Children: Dose is based on body weight or size and must be determined by your doctor.

For dexamethasone

- For *oral* dosage forms (elixir, solution, tablets):
  - —Adults and teenagers: 0.5 to 9 milligrams (mg) a day, as a single dose or divided into several doses.
  - —Children: Dose is based on body weight or size and must be determined by your doctor.
- For *injection* dosage form:
  - —Adults and teenagers: 0.2 to 16 mg (dexamethasone or dexamethasone phosphate) every three days to three weeks as needed. It is injected into a muscle, joint, or lesion.
  - —Children: Dose is based on body weight or size and must be determined by your doctor.

For hydrocortisone

- For *oral* dosage forms (tablets, suspension):
  - —Adults and teenagers: 20 to 240 milligrams (mg) (hydrocortisone) a day, as a single dose or divided into several doses.
  - —Children: Dose is based on body weight or size and must be determined by your doctor.
- For *injection* dosage form:
  - —Adults and teenagers:
    - 15 to 240 mg a day, injected into a muscle; or
    - 5 to 75 mg every two to three weeks, injected into a joint or lesion; or
    - 100 to 500 mg (hydrocortisone) every two to six hours as needed, injected into a muscle or vein or under the skin.
  - —Children: Dose is based on body weight or size and must be determined by your doctor.
- For *rectal* dosage forms (enema, aerosol foam):
  - —Enema:
    - Adults and teenagers—100 mg, given as directed, every night.
    - Children—Dose must be determined by your doctor.
  - —Aerosol foam:
    - Adults and teenagers—90 mg (one applicatorful) one or two times a day.
    - Children—Dose must be determined by your doctor.

For methylprednisolone

- For *oral* dosage form (tablets):
  - —Adults and teenagers: 4 to 160 milligrams (mg) a day, as a single dose or divided into several doses.
  - —Children: Dose is based on body weight or size and must be determined by your doctor.
- For *injection* dosage form:
  - —Adults and teenagers:
    - 4 to 120 mg every one day to five weeks as needed, injected into a muscle, joint, or lesion; or
    - 10 to 160 mg (methylprednisolone) repeated as needed, injected into a muscle or vein.
  - —Children: Dose is based on body weight or size and must be determined by your doctor.
- For *rectal* dosage form (enema):
  - —Adults and teenagers: 40 mg, given as directed, three to seven times a week.
  - —Children: Dose is based on body weight or size and must be determined by your doctor.

For prednisolone

- For *oral* dosage forms (solution, syrup, tablets):
  - —Adults and teenagers: 5 to 200 milligrams (mg) (prednisolone) a day, as needed, as a single dose or divided into several doses.
  - —Children: Dose is based on body weight or size and must be determined by your doctor.

- For *injection* dosage form:

  —Adults and teenagers: 2 to 100 mg (prednisolone or prednisolone phosphate) a day as needed, injected into a muscle, vein, joint, or lesion.

  —Children: Dose is based on body weight or size and must be determined by your doctor.

For prednisone

- For *oral* dosage forms (solution, syrup, tablets):

  —Adults and teenagers: 5 to 200 milligrams (mg) a day, as needed, as a single dose or divided into several doses.

  —Children: Dose is usually based on body weight or size and must be determined by your doctor.

For triamcinolone

- For *oral* dosage forms (syrup, tablets):

  —Adults and teenagers: 4 to 60 milligrams (mg) (triamcinolone) a day, as needed, as a single dose or divided into several doses.

  —Children: Dose is based on body weight or size and must be determined by your doctor.

- For *injection* dosage form:

  —Adults and teenagers: 0.5 to 80 mg repeated as needed, injected into a muscle, joint, or lesion, or under the skin.

  —Children: Dose is usually based on body weight or size and must be determined by your doctor.

Missed dose—If you miss a dose of this medicine and your dosing schedule is:

- One dose every other day—Take the missed dose as soon as possible if you remember it the same morning, then go back to your regular dosing schedule. If you do not remember the missed dose until later, wait and take it the following morning. Then skip a day and start your regular dosing schedule again.
- One dose a day—Take the missed dose as soon as possible, then go back to your regular dosing schedule. If you do not remember until the next day, skip the missed dose and do not double the next one.
- Several doses a day—Take the missed dose as soon as possible, then go back to your regular dosing schedule. If you do not remember until your next dose is due, double the next dose.

If you have any questions about this, check with your health care professional.

Storage—To store this medicine:

- Keep out of the reach of children.
- Store away from heat and direct light.
- Do not store tablets in the bathroom, near the kitchen sink, or in other damp places. Heat or moisture may cause the medicine to break down.
- Keep the liquid dosage forms of this medicine, including enemas, and hydrocortisone rectal aerosol foam from freezing.
- Do not puncture, break, or burn the hydrocortisone rectal aerosol foam container, even when it is empty.
- Do not keep outdated medicine or medicine no longer needed. Be sure that any discarded medicine is out of the reach of children.

Precautions While Using This Medicine

Your doctor should check your progress at regular visits. Also, your progress may have to be checked after you have stopped using this medicine, since some of the effects may continue.

Do not stop using this medicine without first checking with your doctor. Your doctor may want you to reduce gradually the amount you are using before stopping completely.

Check with your doctor if your condition reappears or worsens after the dose has been reduced or treatment with this medicine is stopped.

If you will be using corticosteroids for a long time:

- *Your doctor may want you to follow a low-salt diet and/or a potassium-rich diet.*
- Your doctor may want you to watch your calories to prevent weight gain.
- Your doctor may want you to add extra protein to your diet.
- Your doctor may want you to have your eyes examined by an ophthalmologist (eye doctor) before and also sometime later during treatment.
- Your doctor may want you to carry a medical identification card stating that you are using this medicine.

Tell the doctor in charge that you are using this medicine:

- *Before having skin tests.*
- *Before having any kind of surgery (including dental surgery) or emergency treatment.*
- *If you get a serious infection or injury.*

Avoid close contact with anyone who has chickenpox or measles. This is especially important for children. *Tell your doctor right away if you think you have been exposed to chickenpox or measles.*

While you are being treated with this medicine, and after you stop taking it, *do not have any immunizations without your doctor's approval*. Also, other people living in your home should not receive oral polio vaccine, since there is a chance they could pass the polio virus on to you. In addition, you should avoid close contact with other people at school or work who have recently taken oral polio vaccine.

For *diabetic patients:*

- This medicine may affect blood sugar levels. If you notice a change in the results of your blood or urine sugar tests or if you have any questions, check with your doctor.

For patients having this medicine *injected into their joints:*

- If this medicine is injected into one of your joints, you should be careful not to put too much stress or strain on that joint for a while, even if it begins to

- feel better. Make sure your doctor has told you how much you are allowed to move this joint while it is healing.
- If redness or swelling occurs at the place of injection, and continues or gets worse, check with your doctor.

For patients using this medicine *rectally:*

- Check with your doctor if you notice rectal bleeding, pain, burning, itching, blistering, or any other sign of irritation not present before you started using this medicine, or if signs of infection occur.

Side Effects of This Medicine

Corticosteroids may lower your resistance to infections. Also, any infection you get may be harder to treat. Always check with your doctor as soon as possible if you notice any signs of a possible infection, such as sore throat, fever, sneezing, or coughing.

Along with its needed effects, a medicine may cause some unwanted effects. Although not all of these side effects may occur, if they do occur they may need medical attention. When this medicine is used for short periods of time, side effects usually are rare. However, check with your doctor as soon as possible if any of the following side effects occur:

Less common

Decreased or blurred vision; frequent urination; increased thirst; rectal bleeding, blistering, burning, itching, or pain not present before use of this medicine (when used rectally)

Rare

Blindness (sudden, when injected in the head or neck area); confusion; excitement; false sense of well-being; hallucinations (seeing, hearing, or feeling things that are not there); mental depression; mood swings (sudden and wide); mistaken feelings of self-importance or being mistreated; redness, swelling, pain, or other sign of allergy or infection at place of injection; restlessness

Additional side effects may occur if you take this medicine for a long time. Check with your doctor if any of the following side effects occur:

Abdominal or stomach pain or burning (continuing); acne or other skin problems; bloody or black, tarry stools; filling or rounding out of the face; irregular heartbeat; menstrual problems; muscle cramps or pain; muscle weakness; nausea; pain in back, hips, ribs, arms, shoulders, or legs; pitting, scarring, or depression of skin at place of injection; reddish purple lines on arms, face, legs, trunk, or groin; swelling of feet or lower legs; thin, shiny skin; unusual bruising; unusual tiredness or weakness; vomiting; weight gain (rapid); wounds that will not heal

Other side effects may occur that usually do not need medical attention. These side effects may go away during treatment as your body adjusts to the medicine. However, check with your doctor if any of the following side effects continue or are bothersome:

More common

Increased appetite; indigestion; loss of appetite (for triamcinolone only); nervousness or restlessness; trouble in sleeping

Less common or rare

Darkening or lightening of skin color; dizziness; flushing of face or cheeks (after injection into the nose); headache; increased joint pain (after injection into a joint); increased sweating; lightheadedness; nosebleeds (after injection into the nose); unusual increase in hair growth on body or face

After you stop using this medicine, your body may need time to adjust. The length of time this takes depends on the amount of medicine you were using and how long you used it. If you have taken large doses of this medicine for a long time, your body may need one year to adjust. During this time, *check with your doctor immediately if any of the following side effects occur:*

Abdominal, stomach, or back pain; dizziness; fainting; fever; loss of appetite (continuing); muscle or joint pain; nausea; reappearance of disease symptoms; shortness of breath; unexplained headaches (frequent or continuing); unusual tiredness or weakness; vomiting; weight loss (rapid)

Other side effects not listed above may also occur in some patients. If you notice any other effects, check with your doctor.

Revised: 04/14/92
Interim revision: 08/09/94; 04/01/96

CORTICOSTEROIDS—Low Potency Topical

Some commonly used brand names are:

In the U.S.—

Aclovate[1]
Acticort 100[7]
Aeroseb-Dex[4]
Aeroseb-HC[7]
Ala-Cort[7]
Ala-Scalp HP[7]
Allercort[7]
Alphaderm[7]
Bactine[7]
Beta-HC[7]
CaldeCORT Anti-Itch[7,8]
CaldeCORT Light[8]
Carmol-HC[8]
Cetacort[7]
Cloderm[2]
Cortaid[7,8]
Cort-Dome[7]
Cortef Feminine Itch[8]
Corticaine[8]
Cortifair[7]
Cortril[7]
Decaderm[4]
Decadron[4]
Decaspray[4]
Delacort[7]
Dermacort[7]
Dermarest DriCort[7]
DermiCort[7]
Dermtex HC[7]
DesOwen[3]
Epifoam[8]
FoilleCort[8]
Gly-Cort[7]
Gynecort[8]
Gynecort 10[8]
Hi-Cor 1.0[7]
Hi-Cor 2.5[7]
Hydro-Tex[7]
Hytone[7]
LactiCare-HC[7]
Lanacort[8]
Lanacort 10[8]
Lemoderm[7]
Maximum Strength Cortaid[7]
MyCort[7]
9-1-1[8]
Nutracort[7]
Penecort[7]
Pentacort[7]
Pharma-Cort[8]
Rederm[7]
Rhulicort[8]
S-T Cort[7]
Synacort[7]
Texacort[7]
Tridesilon[3]

In Canada—

Barriere-HC[7]
Cortacet[8]
Cortate[7]
Cortef[7,8]
Corticreme[8]
Cortoderm[8]
Drenison-1/4[6]
Emo-Cort[7]
Emo-Cort Scalp Solution[7]
Hyderm[8]
Locacorten[5]
Novohydrocort[8]
Prevex HC[7]
Sarna HC 1.0%[7]
Sential[7]
Tridesilon[3]
Unicort[7]

Other commonly used names are:
cortisol[7]
flumetasone[5]

Note: For quick reference, the following low potency corticosteroids are numbered to match the corresponding brand names.

This information applies to the following medicines:

1. Alclometasone (al-kloe-MET-a-sone)†
2. Clocortolone (kloe-KOR-toe-lone)†
3. Desonide (DESS-oh-nide)‡
4. Dexamethasone (dex-a-METH-a-sone)†
5. Flumethasone (floo-METH-a-sone)*
6. Flurandrenolide (flure-an-DREN-oh-lide) (Drenison-1/4 only)
7. Hydrocortisone (hye-droe-KOR-ti-sone)‡
8. Hydrocortisone acetate (hye-droe-KOR-ti-sone AS-a-tate)‡

*Not commercially available in the U.S.
†Not commercially available in Canada.
‡Generic name product may also be available in the U.S.

Description

Topical corticosteroids (kor-ti-ko-STER-oyds) are used to help relieve redness, swelling, itching, and discomfort of many skin problems. These medicines are like cortisone. They belong to the general family of medicines called steroids.

Most corticosteroids are available only with your doctor's prescription. Some strengths of hydrocortisone are available without a prescription; however, your doctor may have special instructions on the proper use for your medical condition.

Topical corticosteroids are available in the following dosage forms:

Topical

Alclometasone
- Cream (U.S.)
- Ointment (U.S.)

Clocortolone
- Cream (U.S.)

Desonide
- Cream (U.S. and Canada)
- Lotion (U.S.)
- Ointment (U.S. and Canada)

Dexamethasone
- Cream (U.S.)
- Gel (U.S.)
- Topical aerosol (U.S.)

Flumethasone
- Cream (Canada)
- Ointment (Canada)

Flurandrenolide
- Cream 0.0125% (Canada)
- Ointment 0.0125% (Canada)

Hydrocortisone
- Cream (U.S. and Canada)
- Lotion (U.S. and Canada)
- Ointment (U.S. and Canada)
- Topical solution (U.S. and Canada)

Hydrocortisone acetate
- Cream (U.S. and Canada)
- Topical aerosol foam (U.S.)
- Lotion (U.S.)
- Ointment (U.S. and Canada)

Before Using This Medicine

In deciding to use a medicine, the risks of taking the medicine must be weighed against the good it will do. This is a decision you and your doctor will make. For topical corticosteroids, the following should be considered:

Allergies—Tell your doctor if you have ever had any unusual or allergic reaction to corticosteroids. Also tell your health care professional if you are allergic to any other substances, such as foods, preservatives, or dyes.

Pregnancy—When used properly, these medicines have not been shown to cause problems in humans. Studies on birth defects have not been done in humans. However, studies in animals have shown that topical corticosteroids, when applied to the skin in large amounts or used for a long time, could cause birth defects.

Breast-feeding—Topical corticosteroids have not been reported to cause problems in nursing babies when used properly. However, corticosteroids should not be applied to the breasts just before nursing.

Children—Children and teenagers who must use this medicine for a long time should be checked often by their doctor. Other more potent corticosteroids are absorbed through the skin and can affect growth or cause other unwanted effects. Topical corticosteroids can also be absorbed if they are applied to large areas of skin. These effects are less likely to occur with the use of the lower potency corticosteroids. However, before using this medicine in children, you should discuss its use with your child's doctor.

Older adults—This medicine is not expected to cause different side effects or problems in older people than it does in younger adults.

Other medical problems—The presence of other medical problems may affect the use of topical corticosteroids. Make sure you tell your doctor if you have any other medical problems, especially:

- Diabetes mellitus (sugar diabetes)—Too much use of corticosteroids may cause a loss of control of diabetes by increasing blood and urine glucose. However, this is not likely to happen when topical corticosteroids are used for a short time
- Infection or sores at the place of treatment or
- Tuberculosis—Corticosteroids may make existing infections worse or cause new infections
- Skin conditions that cause thinning of skin with easy bruising—Corticosteroids may make thinning of the skin worse

Proper Use of This Medicine

Be very careful not to get this medicine in your eyes. Wash your hands after using your finger to apply the medicine. If you accidentally get this medicine in your eyes, flush them with water.

Do not bandage or otherwise wrap the skin being treated unless directed to do so by your doctor.

If your doctor has ordered an occlusive dressing (airtight covering, such as kitchen plastic wrap or a special patch) to be applied over this medicine, make sure you know how to apply it. Since occlusive dressings increase the amount of medicine absorbed through your skin and the possibility of side effects, use them only as directed. If you have any questions about this, check with your doctor.

For patients using the *topical aerosol form* of this medicine:

- This medicine usually comes with patient directions. Read them carefully before using this medicine.
- It is important to avoid breathing in the vapors from the spray or getting them in your eyes. If you accidentally get this medicine in your eyes, flush them with water.
- Do not use near heat, near an open flame, or while smoking.

Do not use this medicine more often or for a longer time than your doctor ordered or than recommended on the package label. To do so may increase the chance of absorption through the skin and the chance of side effects.

If this medicine has been prescribed for you, it is meant to treat a specific skin problem. *Do not use it for other skin problems, and do not use nonprescription hydrocortisone for skin problems that are not listed on the package label, without first checking with your doctor.* Topical corticosteroids should not be used on many kinds of bacterial, virus, or fungus skin infections.

Missed dose—If your doctor has ordered you to use this medicine on a regular schedule and you miss a dose, apply it as soon as possible. But if it is almost time for your next dose, skip the missed dose and apply it at the next regularly scheduled time.

Storage—To store this medicine:

- Keep out of the reach of children.
- Store away from heat and direct light.
- Keep the medicine from freezing.
- Do not puncture, break, or burn aerosol containers, even after they are empty.
- Do not keep outdated medicine or medicine no longer needed. Be sure that any discarded medicine is out of the reach of children.

Precautions While Using This Medicine

Avoid using tight-fitting diapers or plastic pants on a child if this medicine is being used on the child's diaper area. Plastic pants and tight-fitting diapers may increase the chance of absorption of the medicine through the skin and the chance of side effects.

Side Effects of This Medicine

Along with its needed effects, a medicine may cause some unwanted effects. Although not all of these side effects may occur, if they do occur they may need medical attention.

Check with your doctor as soon as possible if any of the following side effects occur:

Less common or rare

Lack of healing of skin condition; skin pain, redness, itching, or pus-containing blisters; severe burning and continued itching of skin

Some side effects may occur that usually do not need medical attention. These side effects may go away during treatment as your body adjusts to the medicine. However, check with your doctor if any of the following side effects continue or are bothersome:

Less common or rare

Burning, dryness, irritation, itching, or redness of skin; increased redness or scaling of skin sores; skin rash

When the gel, solution, lotion, or aerosol form of this medicine is applied, a mild, temporary stinging may be expected.

Other side effects not listed above may also occur in some patients. If you notice any other effects, check with your doctor.

Revised: 11/18/92

CORTICOSTEROIDS—Medium to Very High Potency Topical

Some commonly used brand names or other names are:

In the U.S.—

Alphatrex[3]
Aristocort[18]
Aristocort A[18]
Betatrex[3]
Beta-Val[3]
Bio-Syn[9]
Cordran[11]
Cordran SP[11]
Cutivate[12]
Cyclocort[1]
Delta-Tritex[18]
Dermabet[3]
Diprolene[3]
Diprolene AF[3]
Diprosone[3]
Elocon[17]
Florone[7]
Florone E[7]
Fluocet[9]
Fluocin[10]
Fluonid[9]
Flurosyn[9]
Flutex[18]
Halog[13]
Halog-E[13]
Kenac[18]
Kenalog[18]
Kenalog-H[18]
Kenonel[18]
Licon[10]
Lidex[10]
Lidex-E[10]
Locoid[15]
Maxiflor[7]
Maxivate[3]
Psorcon[7]
Synalar[9]
Synalar-HP[9]
Synemol[9]
Teladar[3]
Temovate[4]
Temovate Scalp Application[4]
Topicort[6]
Topicort LP[6]
Triacet[18]
Triderm[18]
Ultravate[14]
Uticort[3]
Valisone[3]
Valisone Reduced Strength[3]
Valnac[3]
Westcort[16]

In Canada—

Aristocort C[18]
Aristocort D[18]
Aristocort R[18]
Beben[3]
Betacort Scalp Lotion[3]
Betaderm[3]
Betaderm Scalp Lotion[3]
Betnovate[3]
Betnovate-1/2[3]
Celestoderm-V[3]
Celestoderm-V/2[3]
Cyclocort[1]
Dermovate[4]
Dermovate Scalp Lotion[4]
Diprolene[3]
Diprosone[3]
Drenison[11]
Ectosone Mild[3]
Ectosone Regular[3]
Ectosone Scalp Lotion[3]
Elocom[17]
Eumovate[5]
Florone[7]
Fluoderm[9]
Fluolar[9]
Fluonide[9]
Halog[13]
Kenalog[18]
Lidemol[10]
Lidex[10]
Lyderm[10]
Metaderm Mild[3]
Metaderm Regular[3]
Nerisone[8]
Nerisone Oily[8]
Novobetamet[3]
Prevex B[3]
Propaderm[2]
Synalar[9]
Synamol[9]
Topicort[6]
Topicort Mild[6]
Topilene[3]
Topisone[3]
Topsyn[10]
Triaderm[18]
Trianide Mild[18]
Trianide Regular[18]
Valisone Scalp Lotion[3]
Westcort[16]

Other commonly used names are:

beclometasone[2]
fludroxycortide[11]

Note: For quick reference, the following medium to very high potency corticosteroids are numbered to match the corresponding brand names.

This information applies to the following medicines:

1. Amcinonide (am-SIN-oh-nide)
2. Beclomethasone (be-kloe-METH-a-sone)*
3. Betamethasone (bay-ta-METH-a-sone)‡
4. Clobetasol (kloe-BAY-ta-sol)
5. Clobetasone (kloe-BAY-ta-sone)*
6. Desoximetasone (des-ox-i-MET-a-sone)‡
7. Diflorasone (dye-FLOR-a-sone)
8. Diflucortolone (di-floo-KOR-toe-lone)*
9. Fluocinolone (floo-oh-SIN-oh-lone)‡
10. Fluocinonide (floo-oh-SIN-oh-nide)‡
11. Flurandrenolide (flure-an-DREN-oh-lide) (except Drenison-1/4)‡
12. Fluticasone (floo-TIK-a-sone)†
13. Halcinonide (hal-SIN-oh-nide)
14. Halobetasol (hal-oh-BAY-ta-sol)†
15. Hydrocortisone butyrate (hye-droe-KOR-ti-sone bue-TEAR-ate)
16. Hydrocortisone valerate (hye-droe-KOR-ti-sone val-AIR-ate)
17. Mometasone (moe-MET-a-sone)
18. Triamcinolone (trye-am-SIN-oh-lone)‡

*Not commercially available in the U.S.
†Not commercially available in Canada.
‡Generic name product may also be available in the U.S.

Description

Topical corticosteroids (kor-ti-ko-STER-oyds) are used to help relieve redness, swelling, itching, and discomfort of many skin problems. These medicines are like cortisone. They belong to the general family of medicines called steroids.

These corticosteroids are available only with your doctor's prescription. Topical corticosteroids are available in the following dosage forms:

Topical

Amcinonide
- Cream (U.S. and Canada)
- Lotion (U.S. and Canada)
- Ointment (U.S. and Canada)

Beclomethasone
- Cream (Canada)
- Lotion (Canada)
- Ointment (Canada)

Betamethasone
- Cream (U.S. and Canada)
- Gel (U.S. and Canada)
- Lotion (U.S. and Canada)
- Ointment (U.S. and Canada)
- Topical aerosol (U.S.)

Clobetasol
- Cream (U.S. and Canada)
- Ointment (U.S. and Canada)
- Solution (U.S. and Canada)

Clobetasone
- Cream (Canada)
- Ointment (Canada)

Desoximetasone
- Cream (U.S. and Canada)
- Gel (U.S. and Canada)
- Ointment (U.S.)

Diflorasone
- Cream (U.S. and Canada)
- Ointment (U.S. and Canada)

Diflucortolone
- Cream (Canada)
- Ointment (Canada)

Fluocinolone
- Cream (U.S. and Canada)
- Ointment (U.S. and Canada)
- Topical solution (U.S. and Canada)

Fluocinonide
- Cream (U.S. and Canada)
- Gel (U.S. and Canada)
- Ointment (U.S. and Canada)
- Topical solution (U.S. and Canada)

Flurandrenolide
- Cream (U.S. and Canada)
- Lotion (U.S.)
- Ointment (U.S. and Canada)
- Tape (U.S. and Canada)

Fluticasone
- Cream (U.S.)
- Ointment (U.S.)

Halcinonide
- Cream (U.S. and Canada)
- Ointment (U.S. and Canada)
- Topical solution (U.S. and Canada)

Halobetasol
- Cream (U.S.)
- Ointment (U.S.)

Hydrocortisone butyrate
- Cream (U.S.)
- Ointment (U.S.)

Hydrocortisone valerate
- Cream (U.S. and Canada)
- Ointment (U.S. and Canada)

Mometasone
- Cream (U.S. and Canada)
- Lotion (U.S. and Canada)
- Ointment (U.S. and Canada)

Triamcinolone
- Cream (U.S. and Canada)
- Lotion (U.S.)
- Ointment (U.S. and Canada)
- Topical aerosol (U.S.)

Before Using This Medicine

In deciding to use a medicine, the risks of taking the medicine must be weighed against the good it will do. This is a decision you and your doctor will make. For corticosteroids, the following should be considered:

Allergies—Tell your doctor if you have ever had any unusual or allergic reaction to corticosteroids. Also tell your health care professional if you are allergic to any other substances, such as foods, preservatives, or dyes.

Pregnancy—When used properly, these medicines have not been shown to cause problems in humans. Studies on birth defects have not been done in humans. However, studies in animals have shown that topical corticosteroids, when applied to the skin in large amounts or used for a long time, could cause birth defects.

Breast-feeding—Topical corticosteroids have not been reported to cause problems in nursing babies when used properly. However, corticosteroids should not be applied to the breasts before nursing.

Children—Children and teenagers who must use this medicine should be checked often by their doctor since this medicine may be absorbed through the skin and can affect growth or cause other unwanted effects.

Older adults—Certain side effects may be more likely to occur in elderly patients since the skin of older adults may be naturally thin. These unwanted effects may include tearing of the skin or blood-containing blisters on the skin.

Other medicines—Although certain medicines should not be used together at all, in other cases two different medicines may be used together even if an interaction might occur. In these cases, your doctor may want to change the dose, or other precautions may be necessary. Tell your health care professional if you are taking or using any other prescription or nonprescription (over-the-counter [OTC]) medicine.

Other medical problems—The presence of other medical problems may affect the use of topical corticosteroids. Make sure you tell your doctor if you have any other medical problems, especially:

- Cataracts or
- Glaucoma—Corticosteroids may make these medical problems worse, especially when stronger corticosteroids are used in the eye area
- Diabetes mellitus (sugar diabetes)—Too much use of corticosteroids may cause a loss of control of diabetes by increasing blood and urine glucose. However, this is not likely to happen when topical corticosteroids are used for a short time
- Infection or sores at the place of treatment (unless your doctor also prescribed medicine for the infection) or
- Tuberculosis—Corticosteroids may make existing infections worse or cause new infections

Proper Use of This Medicine

Be very careful not to get this medicine in your eyes. Wash your hands after using your finger to apply the medicine. If you accidentally get this medicine in your eyes, flush them with water.

Do not bandage or otherwise wrap the skin being treated unless directed to do so by your doctor.

If your doctor has ordered an occlusive dressing (airtight covering, such as kitchen plastic wrap or a special patch) to be applied over this medicine, make sure you know how to apply it. Since occlusive dressings increase the amount of medicine absorbed through your skin and the possibility of side effects, use them only as directed. If you have any questions about this, check with your doctor.

For patients using the *topical aerosol form* of this medicine:

- This medicine usually comes with patient directions. Read them carefully before using this medicine.
- It is important to avoid breathing in the vapors from the spray or getting them in your eyes. If you accidentally get this medicine in your eyes, flush them with water.
- Do not use near heat, near an open flame, or while smoking.

For patients using *flurandrenolide tape:*

- This medicine usually comes with patient directions. Read them carefully before using this medicine.

Do not use this medicine more often or for a longer time than your doctor ordered. To do so may increase the chance of absorption through the skin and the chance of side effects. In addition, too much use, especially on areas with thinner skin (for example, face, armpits, groin), may result in thinning of the skin and stretch marks or other unwanted effects.

Do not use any leftover medicine for other skin problems without first checking with your doctor. Topical corticosteroids should not be used on many kinds of bacterial, virus, or fungus skin infections.

Missed dose—If your doctor has ordered you to use this medicine on a regular schedule and you miss a dose, apply it as soon as possible. However, if it is almost time for your next dose, skip the missed dose and apply it at the next regularly scheduled time.

Storage—To store this medicine:

- Keep out of the reach of children.
- Store away from heat and direct light.
- Keep the medicine from freezing.
- Do not puncture, break, or burn aerosol containers, even after they are empty.
- Do not keep outdated medicine or medicine no longer needed. Be sure that any discarded medicine is out of the reach of children.

Precautions While Using This Medicine

Avoid using tight-fitting diapers or plastic pants on a child if this medicine is being used on the child's diaper area. Plastic pants or tight-fitting diapers may increase the chance of absorption of the medicine through the skin and the chance of side effects.

Side Effects of This Medicine

Along with its needed effects, a medicine may cause some unwanted effects. Although not all of these side effects may occur, if they do occur they may need medical attention.

Check with your doctor as soon as possible if any of the following side effects occur:

Less frequent or rare

Blood-containing blisters on skin; increased skin sensitivity (for some brands of betamethasone lotion); lack of healing of skin condition; loss of top skin layer (for tape dosage forms); numbness in fingers; raised, dark red, wart-like spots on skin; skin pain, redness, itching or pus-containing blisters; severe burning and continued itching of skin; thinning of skin with easy bruising

Additional side effects may occur if you use this medicine improperly or for a long time. Check with your doctor if any of the following side effects occur:

Rare

Acne or oily skin; backache; blurring or loss of vision (occurs gradually if certain products have been used near the eye); burning and itching of skin with pinhead-sized red blisters; eye pain (if certain products have been used near the eye); filling or rounding out of the face; increased blood pressure; irregular heartbeat; irregular menstrual periods; irritability; irritation of skin around mouth; loss of appetite (continuing); mental depression; muscle cramps, pain, or weakness; nausea; rapid weight gain or loss; reddish purple lines (stretch marks) on arms, face, legs, trunk, or groin; skin color changes; softening of skin; stomach bloating, pain, cramping, or burning; swelling of feet or lower legs; tearing of the skin; unusual decrease in sexual desire or ability (in men); unusual increase in hair growth, especially on the face; unusual loss of hair, especially on the scalp; unusual tiredness or weakness; vomiting; weakness of the arms, legs, or trunk (severe); worsening of infections

Some side effects may occur that usually do not need medical attention. These side effects may go away during treatment as your body adjusts to the medicine. However, check with your doctor if any of the following side effects continue or are bothersome:

Less frequent or rare

Burning, dryness, irritation, itching, or redness of skin; increased redness or scaling of skin sores; skin rash

When the gel, solution, lotion, or aerosol form of this medicine is applied, a mild, temporary stinging may be expected.

Other side effects not listed above may also occur in some patients. If you notice any other effects, check with your doctor.

Revised: 11/18/92

CORTICOSTEROIDS AND ACETIC ACID Otic

Some commonly used brand names are:

In the U.S.—

Otic Tridesilon Solution[1]
VõSol HC[2]

In Canada—

VõSol HC[2]

Another commonly used name for hydrocortisone is cortisol.

Note: For quick reference, the following corticosteroids and acetic acid combinations are numbered to match the corresponding brand names.

This information applies to the following medicines:

1. Desonide (DESS-oh-nide) and Acetic Acid (a-SEAT-ic AS-id)
2. Hydrocortisone (hye-droe-KOR-ti-sone) and Acetic Acid

Description

Corticosteroid (kor-ti-koe-STE-roid) and acetic acid combinations are used to treat certain problems of the ear canal. They also help relieve the redness, itching, and swelling that may accompany these conditions.

These medicines may also be used for other conditions as determined by your doctor.

Corticosteroid and acetic acid combinations are available only with your doctor's prescription, in the following dosage forms:

Otic

Desonide and Acetic Acid
- Solution (U.S.)

Hydrocortisone and Acetic Acid
- Solution (U.S. and Canada)

Before Using This Medicine

In deciding to use a medicine, the risks of using the medicine must be weighed against the good it will do. This is a decision you and your doctor will make. For otic corticosteroids with acetic acid, the following should be considered:

Allergies—Tell your doctor if you have ever had any unusual or allergic reaction to corticosteroids or acetic acid. Also tell your health care professional if you are allergic to any other substances, such as certain preservatives or dyes.

Pregnancy—Corticosteroid and acetic acid combinations used in the ear have not been shown to cause birth defects or other problems in humans.

Breast-feeding—Otic corticosteroid and acetic acid combinations have not been reported to cause problems in nursing babies.

Children—Although there is no specific information comparing the use of otic corticosteroids in children with use in other age groups, this combination medicine is not expected to cause different side effects or problems in children than it does in adults.

Older adults—Although there is no specific information comparing the use of otic corticosteroids in the elderly with use in other age groups, they are not expected to cause different side effects or problems in older people than they do in younger adults.

Other medical problems—The presence of other medical problems may affect the use of otic corticosteroids. Make sure you tell your doctor if you have any other medical problems, especially:

- Any other ear infection or condition—Otic corticosteroids may worsen existing infections or cause new infections
- Punctured ear drum—Using otic corticosteroids when you have a punctured ear drum may damage the ear

Proper Use of This Medicine

To use:

- Lie down or tilt the head so that the affected ear faces up. Gently pull the ear lobe up and back for adults (down and back for children) to straighten the ear canal. Drop the medicine into the ear canal. Keep the ear facing up for several (about 5) minutes to allow the medicine to run to the bottom of the ear canal. A sterile cotton plug may be gently inserted into the ear opening to prevent the medicine from leaking out. At first, your doctor may want you to put more medicine on the cotton plug during the day to keep it moist.

To keep the medicine as germ-free as possible, avoid touching the dropper or applicator tip to any surface as much as possible (including the ear). Also, always keep the container tightly closed.

For patients using *hydrocortisone and acetic acid ear drops:*

- *Do not wash the dropper or applicator tip,* because water may get into the medicine and make it weaker. If necessary, you may wipe the dropper or applicator tip with a clean tissue.

Do not use corticosteroids more often or for a longer time than your doctor ordered. To do so may increase the chance of side effects.

Do not use any leftover medicine for future ear problems without first checking with your doctor. This medicine should not be used if certain kinds of infections are present. To do so may make the infection worse.

Dosing—The dose of otic corticosteroid and acetic acid combination will be different for different patients. *Follow your doctor's orders or the directions on the label.* The following information includes only the average doses of otic corticosteroid and acetic acid combination. *If your dose is different, do not change it* unless your doctor tells you to do so.

For desonide and acetic acid

- For *ear drops* dosage form:
  - —For ear infections:
    - Adults and children—Use three or four drops in the ear three or four times a day.

For hydrocortisone and acetic acid

- For *ear drops* dosage form:
  - —For ear infections:
    - Adults and children—Use two to five drops in the ear three or four times a day.

Missed dose—If you miss a dose of this medicine, apply it as soon as possible. However, if it is almost time for your next dose, skip the missed dose and go back to your regular dosing schedule.

Storage—To store this medicine:

- Keep out of the reach of children.
- Store away from heat and direct light.
- Keep the medicine from freezing.
- Do not keep outdated medicine or medicine no longer needed. Be sure that any discarded medicine is out of the reach of children.

Precautions While Using This Medicine

If your condition does not improve within 5 to 7 days, or if it becomes worse, check with your doctor.

Side Effects of This Medicine

Along with its needed effects, a medicine may cause some unwanted effects. The following side effects usually do not need medical attention and may go away during treatment as your body adjusts to the medicine or your condition improves. However, check with your doctor if any of the following side effects continue or are bothersome:

Less common

Stinging, itching, irritation or burning of the ear

There have not been any other side effects reported with this medicine. However, if you notice any other effects, check with your doctor.

Revised: 03/31/92
Interim revision: 04/01/94

COUGH/COLD COMBINATIONS Systemic

Some commonly used brand names are:

In the U.S.—

Actagen-C Cough[41]
Actifed with Codeine Cough[41]
Alka-Seltzer Plus Cold and Cough[49]
Alka-Seltzer Plus Cold and Cough Medicine Liqui-Gels[50]
Alka-Seltzer Plus Flu & Body Aches[48]
Alka-Seltzer Plus Flu & Body Aches Medicine Liqui-Gels[108]
Alka-Seltzer Plus Night-Time Cold[51]
Alka-Seltzer Plus Night-Time Cold Liqui-Gels[52]
Allerfrin with Codeine[41]
All-Nite Cold Formula[52]
Ambenyl Cough[1]
Ambenyl-D Decongestant Cough Formula[114]
Ambophen[1]
Amgenal Cough[1]
Ami-Tex[120a]
Ami-Tex LA[121]
Anaplex HD[23]
Anatuss[112 116]
Anatuss DM[114]
Anatuss LA[122]
Anti-Tuss DM Expectorant[94]
Aprodine with Codeine[41]
Atuss DM[22]
Atuss EX[97]
Atuss HD[23]
Banex-LA[121]
Banex Liquid[120a]
Benylin Expectorant[94]
Benylin Multi-Symptom[114]
Bromanate DC Cough[19]
Bromanyl[1]

Bromarest DX Cough[19b]
Bromatane DX Cough[19b]
Bromfed-DM[19b]
Bromotuss with Codeine[1]
Bromphen DC with Codeine Cough[19]
Bromphen DX Cough[19b]
Broncholate[118]
Bronkotuss Expectorant[82]
Brontex[91]
Brotane DX Cough[19b]
Calcidrine[90]
Carbinoxamine Compound[20]
Carbinoxamine Compound-Drops[20]
Carbodec DM[20]
Carbodec DM Drops[20]
Cardec DM[20]
Cardec DM Drops[20]
Cardec DM Pediatric[20]
Cerose-DM[22]
Cheracol[91]
Cheracol D Cough[94]
Cheracol Plus[27]
Children's Formula Cough[94]
Children's Tylenol Cold Plus Cough Multi Symptom[50]
Chlorgest-HD[23]
Citra Forte[15 44]
Co-Apap[50]
Co-Complex DM Caplets[108]
Codamine[103]
Codamine Pediatric[103]
Codan[89]
Codegest Expectorant[111]
Codehist DH[28]
Codiclear DH[97]
Codimal DH[40]
Codimal DM[39]
Codimal PH[38]
Comtrex Cough Formula[117]
Comtrex Daytime Caplets[108]
Comtrex Daytime Maximum Strength Cold, Cough, and Flu Relief[108]
Comtrex Daytime Maximum Strength Cold and Flu Relief[108]
Comtrex Maximum Strength Multi-Symptom Liqui-Gels[48]
Comtrex Multi-Symptom Cold Reliever[48]
Comtrex Multi-Symptom Maximum Strength Non-Drowsy Caplets[108]
Comtrex Nighttime[50]
Comtrex Nighttime Maximum Strength Cold, Cough and Flu Relief[50]
Comtrex Nighttime Maximum Strength Cold and Flu Relief[50]
Concentrin[114]
Conex[121]
Conex with Codeine Liquid[111]
Congess JR[122]
Congess SR[122]
Congestac Caplets[122]
Contac Cold/Flu Day Caplets[108]
Contac Severe Cold & Flu Caplets[48]
Contac Severe Cold & Flu Non-Drowsy Caplets[108]
Contuss[120a]
Cophene-S[26]
Cophene-X[109a]
Cophene XP[115]
Cophene-XP[64]
Co-Tuss V[97]
C-Tussin Expectorant[111]
Decohistine DH[28]
Deconamine CX[115]
Deconsal II[122]
Deconsal Pediatric[120]
Deproist Expectorant with Codeine[113]
Despec[120a]
Despec SF[120a]
Despec-SR Caplets[121]
De-Tuss[106]
Detussin Expectorant[115]
Detussin Liquid[106]
Dexafed Cough[109]
Diabetic Tussin DM[94]
Dihistine DH[28]
Dihistine Expectorant[113]
Dilaudid Cough[99]
Dimacol Caplets[114]
Dimetane-DC Cough[19]
Dimetane-DX Cough[19b]
Dimetapp DM[19a]
Dimetapp DM Cold & Cough[19a]
Dimetapp Maximum Strength Cold & Cough Liqui-Gels[19a]
Donatussin[62]
Donatussin DC[110]
Donatussin Drops[83]
Dondril[22]
Dorcol Children's Cough[114]
Drixoral Cough & Congestion Liquid Caps[105]
Drixoral Cough & Sore Throat Liquid Caps[88b]
Dura-Gest[120a]
Duratex[120a]
Duratuss[122]
Duratuss HD[115]
Dura-Vent[121]
ED-TLC[23]
ED Tuss HC[23]
Effective Strength Cough Formula[3]
Effective Strength Cough Formula with Decongestant [105]
Endagen-HD[23]
Endal[120]
Endal Expectorant[111]
Endal-HD[23]
Endal-HD Plus[23]
Enomine[120a]
Entex[120a]
Entex LA[121]
Entex Liquid[120a]
Entex PSE[122]
Entuss-D[115 115a]
Entuss-D Jr.[115]
Entuss Expectorant[97 98]
Eudal-SR[122]
Exgest LA[121]
Expressin 400 Caplets[122]
Extra Action Cough[94]
Father John's Medicine Plus[63]
Fendol[123]
Fenesin DM[94]
Gelpirin-CCF[88a]
Genatuss DM[94]
Genite[52]
Glycofed[122]
Glycotuss-dM[94]
Glydeine Cough[91]
GP-500[122]
Guaifed[122]
Guaifed-PD[122]
Guaifenex PPA 75[121]
Guaifenex PSE 60[122]
Guaifenex PSE 120[122]
GuaiMAX-D[122]
Guaipax[121]
Guaitab[122]
Guaivent[122]
Guaivent PD[122]
Guai-Vent/PSE[122]
GuiaCough CF[112]
GuiaCough PE[122]
Guiamid D.M. Liquid[94]
Guiatuss A.C.[91]
Guiatuss CF[112]
Guiatuss DAC[113]
Guiatuss-DM[94]
Guiatussin with Codeine Liquid[91]
Guiatussin DAC[113]
Guiatussin w/ Dextromethorphan[94]
Guiatuss PE[122]
Halotussin-DM[94]
Histinex DM[19a]
Histinex HC[23]
Histinex PV[30]
Histussin HC[23]
Humibid DM[94]
Humibid DM Pediatric[94]
Hycodan[89]
Hycomine[103]
Hycomine Compound[47]
Hycomine Pediatric[103]
Hycotuss Expectorant[97]
Hydromet[89]
Hydromine[103]
Hydromine Pediatric[103]
Hydropane[89]
Hydrophen[103]
Improved Sino-Tuss[46]
Iobid DM[94]
Iodal HD[23]
Iohist DM[19a]
Iophen-C Liquid[92]
Iophen DM[95]
Iosal II[122]
Iotussin HC[23]
Ipsatol Cough Formula for Children and Adults[112]
Kiddy Koff[112]
KIE[119]
Kolephrin/DM Cough and Cold Medication[50]
Kolephrin GG/DM[94]
Kophane Cough and Cold Formula[27]
Kwelcof Liquid[97]
Lanatuss Expectorant[85]
Liqui-Histine DM[19a]
Mapap Cold Formula[50]
Marcof Expectorant[98]
Med-Hist Exp[115]
Med-Hist HC[23]
Midahist DH[28]
Muco-Fen DM[94]
Myminic Expectorant[121]
Myminicol[27]
Myphetane DC Cough[19]
Myphetane DX Cough[19b]
Mytussin AC[91]
Mytussin DAC[113]
Mytussin DM[94]
Naldecon-CX Adult Liquid[111]
Naldecon-DX Adult Liquid[112]
Naldecon-DX Children's Syrup[112]
Naldecon-DX Pediatric Drops[112]
Naldecon-EX Children's Syrup[121]
Naldecon-EX Pediatric Drops[121]
Naldecon Senior DX[94]
Nalex[122]
Nalex DH[100a]
Nalex Jr.[122]
Nasabid[122]
Nasatab LA[122]
Nasatuss[23]
Norel[120a]
Novagest Expectorant w/Codeine[113]
Novahistine DH Liquid[28]
Novahistine DMX Liquid[114]
Novahistine Expectorant[113]
Nucochem Expectorant[113]
Nucochem Pediatric Expectorant[113]
Nucofed[104]
Nucofed Expectorant[113]
Nucofed Pediatric Expectorant[113]
Nucotuss Expectorant[113]
Nucotuss Pediatric Expectorant[113]
Nytcold Medicine[52]
Nytime Cold Medicine Liquid[52]
Omnicol[43]
Ordrine AT[101]
Ornex Severe Cold No Drowsiness Caplets[108]
Para-Hist HD[23]
Partuss LA[121]
PediaCare Cough-Cold[29]
PediaCare Night Rest Cough-Cold Liquid[29]
Pediacof Cough[61]
PediaPressin Pediatric Drops[114]
Pedituss Cough[61]
Pentazine VC w/ Codeine[5]
Phanatuss[94]
Phanatussin[72a]
Phenameth DM[6]
Phenameth VC with Codeine[37]
Phenergan with Codeine[5]
Phenergan with Dextromethorphan[6]
Phenergan VC with Codeine[37]
Phenhist DH w/ Codeine[28]
Phenhist Expectorant[113]
Phenylfenesin L.A.[121]
Pherazine w/Codeine[5]
Pherazine DM[6]
Pherazine VC with Codeine[37]
Pneumotussin HC[97]
Polaramine Expectorant[87]
Poly-Histine-CS[19]
Poly-Histine-DM[19a]
Primatuss Cough Mixture 4[3]
Primatuss Cough Mixture 4D[114]
Profen II[121]
Profen-LA[121]
Promethazine DM[6]
Promethazine VC w/ Codeine[37]
Prometh w/ Dextromethorphan[6]
Promethist w/Codeine[37]
Prometh VC with Codeine[37]
Prominic Expectorant[121]
Prominicol Cough[69]
Promist HD Liquid[30]
Protuss-D[115a]
Pseudo-Car DM[20]
P-V-Tussin[30 106]
Quelidrine Cough[57]
Rentamine Pediatric [21]
Rescaps-D S.R.[101]
Rescon-DM[29]
Rescon-GG[120]
Respa-1st[122]
Respa-DM[94]
Respaire-60 SR[122]
Respaire-120 SR[122]
Rhinosyn-DM[29]
Rhinosyn-DMX Expectorant[94]
Rhinosyn-X[114]
Robafen AC Cough[91]
Robafen CF[112]
Robafen DAC[113]
Robafen DM[94]
Robitussin A-C[91]
Robitussin-CF[112]
Robitussin Cold and Cough Liqui-Gels[114]
Robitusssin Cold, Cough & Flu Liqui-Gels[117]
Robitussin-DAC[113]
Robitussin-DM[94]
Robitussin Maximum Strength Cough and Cold[105]
Robitussin Night Relief[54]
Robitussin Night-Time Cold Formula[52]
Robitussin-PE[122]
Robitussin Pediatric Cough & Cold[105]
Robitussin Severe Congestion Liqui-Gels[122]
Rolatuss Expectorant[60]
Rolatuss w/ Hydrocodone[34]
Rondamine-DM Drops[20]
Rondec-DM[20]
Rondec-DM Drops[20]
Ru-Tuss DE[122]
Ru-Tuss Expectorant[114]
Ru-Tuss with Hydrocodone Liquid[34]
Rymed[122]
Rymed Liquid[122]
Rymed-TR Caplets[121]
Ryna-C Liquid[28]
Ryna-CX Liquid[113]
Rynatuss[21]
Rynatuss Pediatric[21]
Safe Tussin 30[94]
Saleto-CF[107]
Scot-Tussin DM[3]
Scot-Tussin Senior Clear[94]
Silaminic Expectorant[121]
Sildec-DM[20]
Sildec-DM Oral Drops[20]
Sildicon-E Pediatric Drops[121]
Silexin Cough[94]
Siltapp w/ Dextromethorphan Cough & Cold[19a]
Sil-Tex[120a]
Siltussin-CF[112]
Siltussin DM[94]
Sinufed Timecelles[122]
Sinupan[120]
Sinutab Non-Drying No Drowsiness Liquid Caps[122]
SINUvent[121]
Snaplets-DM[102]
Snaplets-EX[121]
Snaplets-Multi[27]
SRC Expectorant[115]
Stamoist E[122]
Stamoist LA[121]
Status Expectorant[111]
Statuss Green[34]
S-T Forte[71a]
S-T Forte 2[3a]
Sudafed Children's Non-Drowsy Cold & Cough[114]
Sudafed Cold & Cough Liquid Caps[117]
Sudafed Children's Cold & Cough[114]
Sudafed Non-Drowsy Non-Drying Sinus Liquid Caps[122]
Sudafed Severe Cold Formula[108]
Sudafed Severe Cold Formula Caplets[108]
Sudal 60/500[122]
Sudal 120/600[122]
Suppressin DM[94]
Suppressin DM Caplets[94]
Suppressin DM Plus[109]
Syracol CF[94]
TheraFlu Flu, Cold & Cough Medicine [50]
TheraFlu Maximum Strength Non-Drowsy Formula Flu, Cold & Cough Medicine[108]
TheraFlu Maximum Strength Non-Drowsy Formula Flu, Cold & Cough Medicine Caplets[108]
TheraFlu Nighttime Maximum Strength Flu, Cold & Cough[50]
Threamine DM[27]
T-Koff[24]
Tolu-Sed Cough[91]
Tolu-Sed DM[94]
Touro LA Caplets[122]
Triacin C Cough[41]
Triafed w/Codeine[41]
Triaminic AM Non-Drowsy Cough and Decongestant[105]

Triaminic-DM Cough Relief[102]
Triaminic Expectorant[121]
Triaminic Expectorant with Codeine[111]
Triaminic Expectorant DH[71]
Triaminic Night Time[29]
Triaminicol Multi-Symptom Cold and Cough Medicine[27]
Triaminic Sore Throat Formula[108]
Triaminic Triaminicol[27]
Tricodene[7]
Tricodene Forte[27]
Tricodene NN[27]
Tricodene Pediatric[102]
Tricodene Sugar Free[3]
Trifed-C Cough[41]
Triminol Cough[27]
Triphenyl Expectorant[121]
Tri-Tannate Plus Pediatric[21]
Tusquelin[58]
Tuss-Ade[101]
Tussafed[20]
Tussafed Drops[20]
Tussafin Expectorant[115]
Tuss-Allergine Modified T.D.[101]
Tussar-2[113]
Tussar DM[29]
Tussar SF[113]
Tuss-DA[105]
Tuss-DM[94]
Tussex Cough[109]
Tussigon[89]
Tussionex Pennkinetic[3a]
Tussi-Organidin DM NR Liquid[94]
Tussi-Organidin DM-S NR Liquid[94]
Tussi-Organidin NR Liquid[91]
Tussi-Organidin-S NR Liquid[91]
Tussirex[78]
Tuss-LA[122]
Tusso-DM[95]
Tussogest[101]
Tylenol Cold and Flu No Drowsiness Powder[108]
Tylenol Cold Medication[50]
Tylenol Cold Medication Caplets[50]
Tylenol Cold Medication, Non-Drowsy Caplets[108]
Tylenol Cold Medication, Non-Drowsy Gelcaps[108]
Tylenol Cold Multi-Symptom[50]
Tylenol Maximum Strength Flu Gelcaps[108]
Tylenol Multi-Symptom Cough[88b]
Tylenol Multi-Symptom Cough with Decongestant[108]
Tyrodone[106]
ULR-LA[121]
Unituss HC[23]
Uni-tussin DM[94]
Unproco[94]
Vanex Expectorant[115]
Vanex Grape[26]
Vanex-HD[23]
V-Dec-M[122]
Versacaps[122]
Vicks Children's NyQuil Cold/Cough Relief[29]
Vicks 44 Cough and Cold Relief Non-Drowsy LiquiCaps[105]
Vicks 44D Cough and Head Congestion[105]
Vicks DayQuil Multi-Symptom Cold/Flu LiquiCaps[117]
Vicks DayQuil Multi-Symptom Cold/Flu Relief[117]
Vicks DayQuil Sinus Pressure and Congestion Relief Caplets[121]
Vicks 44E Cough & Chest Congestion[94]
Vicks 44M Cough, Cold and Flu Relief[50]
Vicks 44M Cough, Cold and Flu Relief LiquiCaps[50]
Vicks NyQuil Hot Therapy[52]
Vicks NyQuil Multi-Symptom Cold/Flu LiquiCaps[52]
Vicks NyQuil Multi-Symptom Cold/Flu Relief[52]
Vicks Pediatric 44D Cough & Head Decongestion[105]
Vicks Pediatric 44E[94]
Vicks Pediatric 44M Multi-Symptom Cough & Cold[29]
Vicodin Tuss[97]
Zephrex[122]
Zephrex-LA[122]

In Canada—

Actifed DM[42]
Ambenyl Cough[9]
Benylin Codeine D-E[113]
Benylin DM-D[105]
Benylin DM-D for Children[105]
Benylin DM-D-E[114]
Benylin DM-D-E Extra Strength[114]
Benylin DM-E[94]
Benylin DM-E Extra Strength[94]
Benylin 4 Flu[117]
Biohisdex DM[32]
Biohisdine DM[32]
Buckley's DM[105]
Caldomine-DH Forte[36]
Caldomine-DH Pediatric[36]
Calmydone[33]
Calmylin #2[105]
Calmylin #3[114]
Calmylin #4[12]
Calmylin Codeine D-E[113]
Calmylin Cough & Flu[117]
Calmylin DM-D-E Extra Strength[114]
Calmylin DM-E[94]
Calmylin Original with Codeine[11]
Calmylin Pediatric[105]
Cheracol[89a]
CoActifed[41]
CoActifed Expectorant[73]
Coristex-DH[100a]
Coristine-DH[100a]
CoSudafed[104]
CoSudafed Expectorant[113]
Cotridin[41]
Cotridin Expectorant[73]
Dimetane Expectorant[80]
Dimetane Expectorant-C[55]
Dimetane Expectorant-DC[56]
Dimetapp-C[17]
Dimetapp-DM[18]
Entex LA[121]
Histenol[108]
Hycodan[89]
Hycomine[72]
Hycomine-S Pediatric[72]
Mercodol with Decapryn[33]
Mersyndol with Codeine[8]
Neo Citran Day Caps Extra Strength Caplets[108]
NeoCitran DM Coughs and Colds[33a]
Novahistex C[100]
Novahistex DH[100a]
Novahistex DH Expectorant[110]
Novahistex DM w/ Decongestant[105]
Novahistex DM Expectorant w/ Decongestant[114]
Novahistex Expectorant w/ Decongestant[122]
Novahistine DH[100a]
Novahistine DM w/ Decongestant[105]
Novahistine DM Expectorant w/ Decongestant[114]
Omni-Tuss[67]
Ornade-DM 10[27]
Ornade-DM 15[27]
Ornade-DM 30[27]
Ornade Expectorant[84]
Penntuss[2]
Pharmasave Children's Cough Syrup[105]
Pharmasave DM+ Decongestant/ Expectorant[114]
Pharmasave DM+ Expectorant[94]
Phenergan Expectorant[88b]
Phenergan Expectorant w/ Codeine[16]
Phenergan VC Expectorant[88]
Phenergan VC Expectorant w/Codeine[71b]
Promatussin DM[37a]
Promatussin DM Children's Syrup[37a]
Robitussin A-C[14]
Robitussin-CF[112]
Robitussin with Codeine[14]
Robitussin Cough & Cold[114]
Robitussin Cough & Cold Liqui-Fills[114]
Robitussin-DM[94]
Robitussin-PE[122]
Robitussin Pediatric Cough & Cold[105]
Sinutab with Codeine[49a]
Sudafed Cold & Flu Gelcaps[117]
Sudafed Cough & Cold Extra Strength Caplets[108]
Sudafed DM[105]
Tantacol DM[35]
Tanta Cough Syrup[94]
Triaminic DM Day Time for Children[112]
Triaminic-DM Expectorant[68]
Triaminic DM Night-Time for Children[29]
Triaminic Expectorant[86]
Triaminic Expectorant DH[71]
Triaminicol DM[29]
Tussaminic C Forte[34a]
Tussaminic C Pediatric[34a]
Tussaminic DH Forte[36]
Tussaminic DH Pediatric[36]
Tussilyn DM[29]
Tussionex[4]
Tuss-Ornade Spansules[26a]
Tylenol Children's Cold DM Medication[50]
Tylenol Cold and Flu[50]
Tylenol Cold Medication Extra Strength Daytime Caplets[108]
Tylenol Cold Medication Extra Strength Nighttime Caplets[50]
Tylenol Cold Medication Regular Strength Daytime Caplets[108]
Tylenol Cold Medication Regular Strength Nighttime Caplets[50]
Tylenol Cough Extra Strength Caplets[88c]
Tylenol Cough Medication with Decongestant, Regular Strength[108]
Tylenol Cough Medication Regular Strength[88c]
Tylenol Extra Strength Cold and Flu Medication Powder[50]
Tylenol Junior Strength Cold DM Medication[50]
Vicks Children's NyQuil[29]
Vicks Cough Syrup[108a]
Vicks DayQuil Liquicaps[117]
Vicks Formula 44-D[105]
Vicks Formula 44-d Pediatric[105]
Vicks Formula 44E[94]
Vicks Formula 44e Pediatric[94]
Vicks Formula 44M[50]
Vicks NyQuil[52]
Vicks NyQuil LiquiCaps[52]

Note: For quick reference the following cough/cold combinations are numbered to match the preceding corresponding brand names.

Antihistamine and antitussive combinations—

1. Bromodiphenhydramine and Codeine†‡
2. Chlorpheniramine and Codeine*
3. Chlorpheniramine and Dextromethorphan†
3a. Chlorpheniramine and Hydrocodone†
4. Phenyltoloxamine and Hydrocodone*
5. Promethazine and Codeine†‡
6. Promethazine and Dextromethorphan†
7. Pyrilamine and Codeine†

Antihistamine, antitussive, and analgesic combinations—

8. Doxylamine, Codeine, and Acetaminophen*

Antihistamine, antitussive, and expectorant combinations—

9. Bromodiphenhydramine, Diphenhydramine, Codeine, Ammonium Chloride, and Potassium Guaiacolsulfonate*
10. No product available
11. Diphenhydramine, Codeine, and Ammonium Chloride*
12. Diphenhydramine, Dextromethorphan, and Ammonium Chloride*
13. No product available
14. Pheniramine, Codeine, and Guaifenesin*
15. Pheniramine, Pyrilamine, Hydrocodone, Potassium Citrate, and Ascorbic Acid†
16. Promethazine, Codeine, and Potassium Guaiacolsulfonate*

Antihistamine, decongestant, and antitussive combinations—

17. Brompheniramine, Phenylephrine, Phenylpropanolamine, and Codeine*
18. Brompheniramine, Phenylephrine, Phenylpropanolamine, and Dextromethorphan*
19. Brompheniramine, Phenylpropanolamine, and Codeine†
19a. Brompheniramine, Phenylpropanolamine, and Dextromethorphan†
19b. Brompheniramine, Pseudoephedrine, and Dextromethorphan†
20. Carbinoxamine, Pseudoephedrine, and Dextromethorphan†
21. Chlorpheniramine, Ephedrine, Phenylephrine, and Carbetapentane†
22. Chlorpheniramine, Phenylephrine, and Dextromethorphan†

23. Chlorpheniramine, Phenylephrine, and Hydrocodone†
24. Chlorpheniramine, Phenylephrine, Phenylpropanolamine, and Codeine†
25. No product
26. Chlorpheniramine, Phenylephrine, Phenylpropanolamine, and Dihydrocodeine†
26a. Chlorpheniramine, Phenylpropanolamine, and Caramiphen*
27. Chlorpheniramine, Phenylpropanolamine, and Dextromethorphan
28. Chlorpheniramine, Pseudoephedrine, and Codeine†
29. Chlorpheniramine, Pseudoephedrine, and Dextromethorphan
30. Chlorpheniramine, Pseudoephedrine, and Hydrocodone†
31. No product available
32. Diphenylpyraline, Phenylephrine, and Dextromethorphan*
33. Doxylamine, Etafedrine, and Hydrocodone*
33a. Pheniramine, Phenylephrine, and Dextromethorphan*
34. Pheniramine, Pyrilamine, Phenylephrine, Phenylpropanolamine, and Hydrocodone†
34a. Pheniramine, Pyrilamine, Phenylpropanolamine, and Codeine*
35. Pheniramine, Pyrilamine, Phenylpropanolamine, and Dextromethorphan*
36. Pheniramine, Pyrilamine, Phenylpropanolamine, and Hydrocodone*
37. Promethazine, Phenylephrine, and Codeine†
37a. Promethazine, Pseudoephedrine, and Dextromethorphan*
38. Pyrilamine, Phenylephrine, and Codeine†
39. Pyrilamine, Phenylephrine, and Dextromethorphan†
40. Pyrilamine, Phenylephrine, and Hydrocodone†
41. Triprolidine, Pseudoephedrine, and Codeine
42. Triprolidine, Pseudoephedrine, and Dextromethorphan*

Antihistamine, decongestant, antitussive, and analgesic combinations—

43. Chlorpheniramine, Phenindamine, Phenylephrine, Dextromethorphan, Acetaminophen, Salicylamide, Caffeine, and Ascorbic Acid†
44. Chlorpheniramine, Pheniramine, Pyrilamine, Phenylephrine, Hydrocodone, Salicylamide, Caffeine, and Ascorbic Acid†
45. No product available
46. Chlorpheniramine, Phenylephrine, Dextromethorphan, Acetaminophen, and Salicylamide†
47. Chlorpheniramine, Phenylephrine, Hydrocodone, Acetaminophen, and Caffeine†
48. Chlorpheniramine, Phenylpropanolamine, Dextromethorphan, and Acetaminophen†
49. Chlorpheniramine, Phenylpropanolamine, Dextromethorphan, and Aspirin†
49a. Chlorpheniramine, Pseudoephedrine, Codeine, and Acetaminophen*
50. Chlorpheniramine, Pseudoephedrine, Dextromethorphan, and Acetaminophen
51. Doxylamine, Phenylpropanolamine, Dextromethorphan, and Aspirin†
52. Doxylamine, Pseudoephedrine, Dextromethorphan, and Acetaminophen
53. No product available
54. Pyrilamine, Pseudoephedrine, Dextromethorphan, and Acetaminophen†

Antihistamine, decongestant, antitussive, and expectorant combinations—

55. Brompheniramine, Phenylephrine, Phenylpropanolamine, Codeine, and Guaifenesin*
56. Brompheniramine, Phenylephrine, Phenylpropanolamine, Hydrocodone, and Guaifenesin*
57. Chlorpheniramine, Ephedrine, Phenylephrine, Dextromethorphan, Ammonium Chloride, and Ipecac†
58. Chlorpheniramine, Phenylephrine, Phenylpropanolamine, Dextromethorphan, Potassium Guaiacolsulfonate, and Ipecac†
59. No product available
60. Chlorpheniramine, Phenylephrine, Codeine and Ammonium Chloride†
61. Chlorpheniramine, Phenylephrine, Codeine, and Potassium Iodide†
62. Chlorpheniramine, Phenylephrine, Dextromethorphan, and Guaifenesin†
63. Chlorpheniramine, Phenylephrine, Dextromethorphan, Guaifenesin, and Ammonium Chloride†
64. Chlorpheniramine, Phenylephrine, Phenylpropanolamine, Carbetapentane, and Potassium Guaiacolsulfonate†
65. No product available
66. No product available
67. Chlorpheniramine, Phenyltoloxamine, Ephedrine, Codeine, and Guaiacol Carbonate*
68. Chlorpheniramine, Pseudoephedrine, Dextromethorphan, and Guaifenesin*
69. Pheniramine, Pyrilamine, Phenylpropanolamine, Dextromethorphan, and Ammonium Chloride†
70. No product available
71. Pheniramine, Pyrilamine, Phenylpropanolamine, Hydrocodone, and Guaifenesin
71a. Pheniramine, Phenylephrine, Phenylpropanolamine, Hydrocodone, and Guaifenesin†
71b. Promethazine, Phenylephrine, Codeine, and Potassium Guaiacolsulfonate*
72. Pyrilamine, Phenylephrine, Hydrocodone, and Ammonium Chloride*
72a. Pyrilamine, Phenylpropanolamine, Dextromethorphan, Guaifenesin, Potassium Citrate, and Citric Acid†
73. Triprolidine, Pseudoephedrine, Codeine, and Guaifenesin*

Antihistamine, decongestant, antitussive, expectorant, and analgesic combinations—

74. No product available
75. No product available
76. No product available
77. No product available
78. Pheniramine, Phenylephrine, Codeine, Sodium Citrate, Sodium Salicylate, and Caffeine†
79. No product available

Antihistamine, decongestant, and expectorant combinations—

80. Brompheniramine, Phenylephrine, Phenylpropanolamine, and Guaifenesin*
81. No product available
82. Chlorpheniramine, Ephedrine, and Guaifenesin†
83. Chlorpheniramine, Phenylephrine, and Guaifenesin†
84. Chlorpheniramine, Phenylpropanolamine, and Guaifenesin*
85. Chlorpheniramine, Phenylpropanolamine, Guaifenesin, Sodium Citrate, and Citric Acid†
86. Chlorpheniramine, Pseudoephedrine, and Guaifenesin*
87. Dexchlorpheniramine, Pseudoephedrine, and Guaifenesin†
88. Promethazine, Phenylephrine, and Potassium Guaiacolsulfonate*

Antihistamine, decongestant, expectorant, and analgesic combinations—

88a. Chlorpheniramine, Phenylpropanolamine, Guaifenesin, and Acetaminophen†

Antihistamine and expectorant combination—

88b. Promethazine and Potassium Guaiacolsulfonate*

Antitussive and analgesic combination—

88c. Dextromethorphan and Acetaminophen

Antitussive and anticholinergic combination—

89. Hydrocodone and Homatropine‡§

Antitussive and expectorant combinations—

89a. Codeine, Ammonium Chloride, and Guaifenesin*
90. Codeine and Calcium Iodide†
91. Codeine and Guaifenesin†‡
92. Codeine and Iodinated Glycerol†
93. No product available
94. Dextromethorphan and Guaifenesin
95. Dextromethorphan and Iodinated Glycerol†
96. No product available
97. Hydrocodone and Guaifenesin†‡
98. Hydrocodone and Potassium Guaiacolsulfonate†
99. Hydromorphone and Guaifenesin†

Decongestant and antitussive combinations—

100. Phenylephrine and Codeine*
100a. Phenylephrine and Hydrocodone
101. Phenylpropanolamine and Caramiphen†
102. Phenylpropanolamine and Dextromethorphan†

103. Phenylpropanolamine and Hydrocodone†‡
104. Pseudoephedrine and Codeine
105. Pseudoephedrine and Dextromethorphan
106. Pseudoephedrine and Hydrocodone†

Decongestant, antitussive, and analgesic combinations—

107. Phenylpropanolamine, Dextromethorphan, and Acetaminophen†
108. Pseudoephedrine, Dextromethorphan, and Acetaminophen

Decongestant, antitussive, and expectorant combinations—

108a. Ephedrine, Carbetapentane, and Guaifenesin*
109. Phenylephrine, Dextromethorphan, and Guaifenesin†
109a. Phenylephrine, Phenylpropanolamine, Carbetapentane, and Potassium Guaiacolsulfonate†
110. Phenylephrine, Hydrocodone, and Guaifenesin
111. Phenylpropanolamine, Codeine, and Guaifenesin†
112. Phenylpropanolamine, Dextromethorphan, and Guaifenesin†
113. Pseudoephedrine, Codeine, and Guaifenesin‡
114. Pseudoephedrine, Dextromethorphan, and Guaifenesin
115. Pseudoephedrine, Hydrocodone, and Guaifenesin†
115a. Pseudoephedrine, Hydrocodone, and Potassium Guaiacolsulfonate†

Decongestant, antitussive, expectorant, and analgesic combinations—

116. Phenylpropanolamine, Dextromethorphan, Guaifenesin, and Acetaminophen†
117. Pseudoephedrine, Dextromethorphan, Guaifenesin, and Acetaminophen

Decongestant and expectorant combinations—

118. Ephedrine and Guaifenesin†
119. Ephedrine and Potassium Iodide†
120. Phenylephrine and Guaifenesin†
120a. Phenylephrine, Phenylpropanolamine, and Guaifenesin†
121. Phenylpropanolamine and Guaifenesin‡
122. Pseudoephedrine and Guaifenesin‡

Decongestant, expectorant, and analgesic combination—

123. Phenylephrine, Guaifenesin, Acetaminophen, Salicylamide and Caffeine†

---

*Not commercially available in the U.S.
†Not commercially available in Canada.
‡Generic name product available in the U.S.
§Canadian product does not contain Homatropine.

Description

Cough/cold combinations are used mainly to relieve the cough due to colds, influenza, or hay fever. They are not to be used for the chronic cough that occurs with smoking, asthma, or emphysema or when there is an unusually large amount of mucus or phlegm (pronounced flem) with the cough.

Cough/cold combination products contain more than one ingredient. For example, some products may contain an antihistamine, a decongestant, and an analgesic, in addition to a medicine for coughing. If you are treating yourself, it is important to select a product that is best for your symptoms. Also, in general, it is best to buy a product that includes only those medicines you really need. If you have questions about which product to buy, check with your pharmacist.

Since different products contain ingredients that will have different precautions and side effects, it is important that you know the ingredients of the medicine you are taking. The different kinds of ingredients that may be found in cough/cold combinations include:

Antihistamines—Antihistamines are used to relieve or prevent the symptoms of hay fever and other types of allergy. They also help relieve some symptoms of the common cold, such as sneezing and runny nose. They work by preventing the effects of a substance called histamine, which is produced by the body. Some examples of antihistamines contained in these combinations are: bromodiphenhydramine (broe-moe-dye-fen-HYE-dra-meen), brompheniramine (brome-fen-EER-a-meen), carbinoxamine (kar-bi-NOX-a-meen), chlorpheniramine (klor-fen-EER-a-meen), dexchlorpheniramine (dex-klor-fen-EER-a-meen), diphenhydramine (dye-fen-HYE-dra-meen), doxylamine (dox-ILL-a-meen), phenindamine (fen-IN-da-meen), pheniramine (fen-EER-a-meen), phenyltoloxamine (fen-ill-tole-OX-a-meen), pyrilamine (peer-ILL-a-meen), promethazine (proe-METH-a-zeen), and triprolidine (trye-PROE-li-deen).

Decongestants—Decongestants, such as ephedrine (e-FED-rin), phenylephrine (fen-ill-EF-rin), phenylpropanolamine (fen-ill-proe-pa-NOLE-a-meen), and pseudoephedrine (soo-doe-e-FED-rin), produce a narrowing of blood vessels. This leads to clearing of nasal congestion. However, this effect may also increase blood pressure in patients who have high blood pressure.

Antitussives—To help relieve coughing these combinations contain either a narcotic (codeine [KOE-deen], dihydrocodeine [dye-hye-droe-KOE-deen], hydrocodone [hye-droe-KOE-done] or hydromorphone [hye-droe-MOR-fone]) or a non-narcotic (carbetapentane [kar-bay-ta-PEN-tane], caramiphen [kar-AM-i-fen], or dextromethorphan [dex-troe-meth-OR-fan]) antitussive. These antitussives act directly on the cough center in the brain. Narcotics may become habit-forming, causing mental or physical dependence, if used for a long time. Physical dependence may lead to withdrawal side effects when you stop taking the medicine.

Expectorants—Guaifenesin (gwye-FEN-e-sin) works by loosening the mucus or phlegm in the lungs. Other ingredients added as expectorants (for example, ammonium chloride, calcium iodide, iodinated glycerol, ipecac, potassium guaiacolsulfonate, potassium iodide, and sodium citrate) have not been proven to be effective. In general, the best thing you can do to loosen mucus or phlegm is to drink plenty of water.

Analgesics—Analgesics, such as acetaminophen (a-seat-a-MIN-oh-fen), aspirin, and other salicylates (such as salicylamide [sal-i-SILL-a-mide] and sodium salicylate [SOE-dee-um sa-LI-sill-ate]) are used in these combination medicines to help relieve the aches and pain that may occur with the common cold.

The use of too much acetaminophen and salicylates at the same time may cause kidney damage or cancer of the kidney or urinary bladder. This may occur if large amounts of both medicines are taken together for a long time. However, taking the recommended amounts of combination medicines that contain both acetaminophen and a salicylate for short periods of time has not been shown to cause these unwanted effects.

Anticholinergics—Anticholinergics such as homatropine (hoe-MA-troe-peen) may help produce a drying effect in the nose and chest.

Some of these combinations are available only with your doctor's prescription. Others are available without a prescription; however, your health care professional may have special instructions on the proper dose of the medicine for your medical condition.

Cough/cold combinations are available in the following dosage forms:

Antihistamine and antitussive combinations—

Oral

Bromodiphenhydramine and Codeine
- Syrup (U.S.)

Chlorpheniramine and Codeine
- Oral suspension (Canada)

Chlorpheniramine and Dextromethorphan
- Oral solution (U.S.)

Chlorpheniramine and Hydrocodone
- Oral solution (U.S.)
- Oral suspension (U.S.)

Phenyltoloxamine and Hydrocodone
- Oral suspension (Canada)
- Tablets (Canada)

Promethazine and Codeine
- Oral solution (U.S.)
- Syrup (U.S.)

Promethazine and Dextromethorphan
- Oral solution (U.S.)
- Syrup (U.S.)

Pyrilamine and Codeine
- Oral solution (U.S.)

Antihistamine, antitussive, and analgesic combinations—

Oral

Doxylamine, Codeine, and Acetaminophen
- Tablets (Canada)

Antihistamine, antitussive, and expectorant combinations—

Oral

Bromodiphenhydramine, Diphenhydramine, Codeine, Ammonium Chloride, and Potassium Guaiacolsulfonate
- Syrup (Canada)

Diphenhydramine, Codeine, and Ammonium Chloride
- Syrup (Canada)

Diphenhydramine, Dextromethorphan, and Ammonium Chloride
- Syrup (Canada)

Pheniramine, Codeine, and Guaifenesin
- Syrup (Canada)

Pheniramine, Pyrilamine, Hydrocodone, Potassium Citrate, and Ascorbic Acid
- Syrup (U.S.)

Promethazine, Codeine, and Potassium Guaiacolsulfonate
- Syrup (Canada)

Antihistamine, decongestant, and antitussive combinations—

Oral

Brompheniramine, Phenylephrine, Phenylpropanolamine, and Codeine
- Syrup (Canada)

Brompheniramine, Phenylephrine, Phenylpropanolamine, and Dextromethorphan
- Elixir (Canada)
- Tablets (Canada)

Brompheniramine, Phenylpropanolamine, and Codeine
- Syrup (U.S.)

Brompheniramine, Phenylpropanolamine, and Dextromethorphan
- Capsules (U.S.)
- Elixir (U.S.)
- Oral solution (U.S.)
- Syrup (U.S.)

Brompheniramine, Pseudoephedrine, and Dextromethorphan
- Syrup (U.S.)

Carbinoxamine, Pseudoephedrine, and Dextromethorphan
- Oral solution (U.S.)
- Syrup (U.S.)

Chlorpheniramine, Ephedrine, Phenylephrine, and Carbetapentane
- Oral suspension (U.S.)
- Tablets (U.S.)

Chlorpheniramine, Phenylephrine, and Dextromethorphan
- Oral solution (U.S.)
- Syrup (U.S.)
- Tablets (U.S.)

Chlorpheniramine, Phenylephrine, and Hydrocodone
- Oral solution (U.S.)
- Syrup (U.S.)

Chlorpheniramine, Phenylephrine, Phenylpropanolamine, and Codeine
- Oral solution (U.S.)

Chlorpheniramine, Phenylephrine, Phenylpropanolamine, and Dihydrocodeine
- Oral solution (U.S.)
- Syrup (U.S.)

Chlorpheniramine, Phenylpropanolamine, and Caramiphen
- Extended-release capsules (Canada)

Chlorpheniramine, Phenylpropanolamine, and Dextromethorphan
- Granules (U.S.)
- Oral solution (U.S. and Canada)
- Syrup (U.S.)
- Tablets (U.S.)

Chlorpheniramine, Pseudoephedrine, and Codeine
- Elixir (U.S.)
- Oral solution (U.S.)

Chlorpheniramine, Pseudoephedrine, and Dextromethorphan
- Chewable tablets (U.S.)
- Oral solution (U.S. and Canada)
- Syrup (U.S. and Canada)

Chlorpheniramine, Pseudoephedrine, and Hydrocodone
- Oral solution (U.S.)
- Syrup (U.S.)

Diphenylpyraline, Phenylephrine, and Dextromethorphan
- Oral solution (Canada)

Doxylamine, Etafedrine, and Hydrocodone
- Syrup (Canada)

Pheniramine, Phenylephrine, and Dextromethorphan
- Oral solution (Canada)

Pheniramine, Pyrilamine, Phenylephrine, Phenylpropanolamine, and Hydrocodone
- Oral solution (U.S.)

Pheniramine, Pyrilamine, Phenylpropanolamine, and Codeine
- Syrup (Canada)

Pheniramine, Pyrilamine, Phenylpropanolamine, and Dextromethorphan
- Syrup (Canada)

Pheniramine, Pyrilamine, Phenylpropanolamine, and Hydrocodone
- Oral solution (Canada)
- Syrup (Canada)

Promethazine, Phenylephrine, and Codeine
- Oral solution (U.S.)
- Syrup (U.S.)

Promethazine, Pseudoephedrine, and Dextromethorphan
- Syrup (Canada)

Pyrilamine, Phenylephrine, and Codeine
- Syrup (U.S.)

Pyrilamine, Phenylephrine, and Dextromethorphan
- Syrup (U.S.)

Pyrilamine, Phenylephrine, and Hydrocodone
- Syrup (U.S.)

Triprolidine, Pseudoephedrine, and Codeine
- Oral solution (Canada)
- Syrup (U.S.)
- Tablets (Canada)

Triprolidine, Pseudoephedrine, and Dextromethorphan
- Oral solution (Canada)
- Tablets (Canada)

Antihistamine, decongestant, antitussive, and analgesic combinations—

Oral

Chlorpheniramine, Phenindamine, Phenylephrine, Dextromethorphan, Acetaminophen, Salicylamide, Caffeine, and Ascorbic Acid
- Tablets (U.S.)

Chlorpheniramine, Pheniramine, Pyrilamine, Phenylephrine, Hydrocodone, Salicylamide, Caffeine, and Ascorbic Acid
- Capsules (U.S.)

Chlorpheniramine, Phenylephrine, Dextromethorphan, Acetaminophen, and Salicylamide
- Tablets (U.S.)

Chlorpheniramine, Phenylephrine, Hydrocodone, Acetaminophen, and Caffeine
- Tablets (U.S.)

Chlorpheniramine, Phenylpropanolamine, Dextromethorphan, and Acetaminophen
- Capsules (U.S.)
- Effervescent tablets (U.S.)
- Oral solution (U.S.)
- Tablets (U.S.)

Chlorpheniramine, Phenylpropanolamine, Dextromethorphan, and Aspirin
- Effervescent tablets (U.S.)

Chlorpheniramine, Pseudoephedrine, Codeine, and Acetaminophen
- Tablets (Canada)

Chlorpheniramine, Pseudoephedrine, Dextromethorphan, and Acetaminophen
- Capsules (U.S.)
- Chewable tablets (U.S. and Canada)
- Oral solution (U.S. and Canada)
- Syrup (Canada)
- Tablets (U.S. and Canada)

Doxylamine, Phenylpropanolamine, Dextromethorphan, and Aspirin
- Effervescent tablets (U.S.)

Doxylamine, Pseudoephedrine, Dextromethorphan, and Acetaminophen
- Capsules (U.S.)
- Oral solution (U.S.)

Pyrilamine, Pseudoephedrine, Dextromethorphan, and Acetaminophen
- Oral solution (U.S.)

Antihistamine, decongestant, antitussive, and expectorant combinations—

Oral

Brompheniramine, Phenylephrine, Phenylpropanolamine, Codeine, and Guaifenesin
- Oral solution (Canada)

Brompheniramine, Phenylephrine, Phenylpropanolamine, Hydrocodone, and Guaifenesin
- Oral solution (Canada)

Chlorpheniramine, Ephedrine, Phenylephrine, Dextromethorphan, Ammonium Chloride, and Ipecac
- Syrup (U.S.)

Chlorpheniramine, Phenylephrine, Codeine, and Ammonium Chloride
- Oral solution (U.S.)

Chlorpheniramine, Phenylephrine, Codeine, and Potassium Iodide
- Syrup (U.S.)

Chlorpheniramine, Phenylephrine, Dextromethorphan, and Guaifenesin
- Syrup (U.S.)

Chlorpheniramine, Phenylephrine, Dextromethorphan, Guaifenesin, and Ammonium Chloride
- Oral solution (U.S.)

Chlorpheniramine, Phenylephrine, Phenylpropanolamine, Carbetapentane, and Potassium Guaiacolsulfonate
- Syrup (U.S.)

Chlorpheniramine, Phenylephrine, Phenylpropanolamine, Dextromethorphan, Potassium Guaicolsulfonate, and Ipecac
- Syrup (U.S.)

Chlorpheniramine, Phenyltoloxamine, Ephedrine, Codeine, and Guaiacol Carbonate
- Oral suspension (Canada)

Chlorpheniramine, Pseudoephedrine, Dextromethorphan, and Guaifenesin
- Oral solution (Canada)

Pheniramine, Pyrilamine, Phenylpropanolamine, Dextromethorphan, and Ammonium Chloride
- Syrup (U.S.)

Pheniramine, Pyrilamine, Phenylpropanolamine, Hydrocodone, and Guaifenesin
- Oral solution (U.S.)
- Elixir (Canada)

Pheniramine, Phenylephrine, Phenylpropanolamine, Hydrocodone, and Guaifenesin
- Oral solution (U.S.)
- Syrup (U.S.)

Promethazine, Phenylephrine, Codeine, and Potassium Guaiacolsulfonate
- Syrup (Canada)

Pyrilamine, Phenylephrine, Hydrocodone, and Ammonium Chloride
- Syrup (Canada)

Pyrilamine, Phenylpropanolamine, Dextromethorphan, Guaifenesin, Potassium Citrate, and Citric Acid
- Syrup (U.S.)

Triprolidine, Pseudoephedrine, Codeine, and Guaifenesin
- Oral solution (Canada)

Antihistamine, decongestant, antitussive, expectorant, and analgesic combinations—

Oral

Pheniramine, Phenylephrine, Codeine, Sodium Citrate, Sodium Salicylate, and Caffeine
- Oral solution (U.S.)

Antihistamine, decongestant, and expectorant combinations—

Oral

Brompheniramine, Phenylephrine, Phenylpropanolamine, and Guaifenesin
- Oral solution (Canada)

Chlorpheniramine, Ephedrine, and Guaifenesin
- Oral solution (U.S.)

Chlorpheniramine, Phenylephrine, and Guaifenesin
- Oral solution (U.S.)

Chlorpheniramine, Phenylpropanolamine, and Guaifenesin
- Oral solution (Canada)

Chlorpheniramine, Phenylpropanolamine, Guaifenesin, Sodium Citrate, and Citric Acid
- Oral solution (U.S.)

Chlorpheniramine, Pseudoephedrine, and Guaifenesin
- Extended-release tablets (Canada)
- Oral solution (Canada)

Dexchlorpheniramine, Pseudoephedrine, and Guaifenesin
- Oral solution (U.S.)

Promethazine, Phenylephrine, and Potassium Guaiacolsulfonate
- Syrup (Canada)

Antihistamine, decongestant, expectorant, and analgesic combinations—
Oral

Chlorpheniramine, Phenylpropanolamine, Guaifenesin, and Acetaminophen
- Tablets (U.S.)

Antitussive and analgesic combination—
Oral

Dextromethorphan and Acetaminophen
- Capsules (U.S.)
- Oral solution (U.S.)
- Oral suspension (Canada)
- Tablets (U.S.)

Antitussive and anticholinergic combination—
Oral

Hydrocodone and Homatropine§
- Syrup (U.S. and Canada)
- Tablets (U.S. and Canada)

Antitussive and expectorant combinations—
Oral

Codeine, Ammonium Chloride, and Guaifenesin
- Syrup (Canada)

Codeine and Calcium Iodide
- Syrup (U.S.)

Codeine and Guaifenesin
- Oral solution (U.S.)
- Syrup (U.S.)
- Tablets (U.S.)

Codeine and Iodinated Glycerol
- Oral solution (U.S.)

Dextromethorphan and Guaifenesin
- Capsules (U.S.)
- Extended-release capsules (U.S.)
- Oral solution (U.S.)
- Syrup (U.S. and Canada)
- Tablets (U.S.)
- Extended-release tablets (U.S.)

Dextromethorphan and Iodinated Glycerol
- Oral solution (U.S.)

Hydrocodone and Guaifenesin
- Oral solution (U.S.)
- Syrup (U.S.)
- Tablets (U.S.)

Hydrocodone and Potassium Guaiacolsulfonate
- Oral solution (U.S.)
- Syrup (U.S.)

Hydromorphone and Guaifenesin
- Syrup (U.S.)

Decongestant and antitussive combinations—
Oral

Phenylephrine and Codeine
- Oral solution (Canada)

Phenylephrine and Hydrocodone
- Oral solution (Canada)
- Syrup (Canada)

Phenylpropanolamine and Caramiphen
- Extended-release capsules (U.S.)

Phenylpropanolamine and Dextromethorphan
- Granules (U.S.)
- Oral solution (U.S.)
- Syrup (U.S.)

Phenylpropanolamine and Hydrocodone
- Oral solution (U.S.)
- Syrup (U.S.)

Pseudoephedrine and Codeine
- Capsules (U.S.)
- Syrup (U.S. and Canada)
- Tablets (Canada)

Pseudoephedrine and Dextromethorphan
- Capsules (U.S.)
- Oral solution (U.S. and Canada)
- Syrup (Canada)

Pseudoephedrine and Hydrocodone
- Oral solution (U.S.)
- Syrup (U.S.)
- Tablets (U.S.)

Decongestant, antitussive, and analgesic combinations—
Oral

Phenylpropanolamine, Dextromethorphan, and Acetaminophen
- Tablets (U.S.)

Pseudoephedrine, Dextromethorphan, and Acetaminophen
- Capsules (U.S.)
- Oral solution (U.S.)
- Oral suspension (Canada)
- Tablets (U.S. and Canada)

Decongestant, antitussive, and expectorant combinations—
Oral

Ephedrine, Carbetapentane, and Guaifenesin
- Syrup (Canada)

Phenylephrine, Dextromethorphan, and Guaifenesin
- Syrup (U.S.)

Phenylephrine, Phenylpropanolamine, Carbetapentane and Potassium Guaiacolsulfonate
- Capsules (U.S.)

Phenylephrine, Hydrocodone, and Guaifenesin
- Oral solution (Canada)
- Syrup (U.S.)

Phenylpropanolamine, Codeine, and Guaifenesin
- Oral solution (U.S.)
- Syrup (U.S.)

Phenylpropanolamine, Dextromethorphan, and Guaifenesin
- Oral solution (U.S.)
- Syrup (U.S. and Canada)

Pseudoephedrine, Codeine, and Guaifenesin
- Oral solution (U.S. and Canada)
- Syrup (U.S. and Canada)

Pseudoephedrine, Dextromethorphan, and Guaifenesin
- Capsules (U.S. and Canada)
- Oral solution (U.S. and Canada)
- Syrup (U.S. and Canada)
- Tablets (U.S.)

Pseudoephedrine, Hydrocodone, and Guaifenesin
- Elixir (U.S.)
- Oral solution (U.S.)
- Syrup (U.S.)
- Tablets (U.S.)

Pseudoephedrine, Hydrocodone, and Potassium Guaiacolsulfonate
- Oral solution (U.S.)

Decongestant, antitussive, expectorant, and analgesic combinations—
Oral

Phenylpropanolamine, Dextromethorphan, Guaifenesin, and Acetaminophen
- Tablets (U.S.)

Pseudoephedrine, Dextromethorphan, Guaifenesin, and Acetaminophen
- Capsules (U.S.)
- Oral solution (U.S. and Canada)
- Syrup (Canada)
- Tablets (U.S.)

Decongestant and expectorant combinations—
Oral

Ephedrine and Guaifenesin
- Syrup (U.S.)

Ephedrine and Potassium Iodide
- Syrup (U.S.)

Phenylephrine and Guaifenesin
- Oral solution (U.S.)
- Extended-release capsules (U.S.)
- Extended-release tablets (U.S.)

Phenylephrine, Phenylpropanolamine, and Guaifenesin
- Capsules (U.S.)
- Oral solution (U.S.)

Phenylpropanolamine and Guaifenesin
- Granules (U.S.)
- Oral solution (U.S.)
- Syrup (U.S.)
- Tablets (U.S.)
- Extended-release tablets (U.S. and Canada)

Pseudoephedrine and Guaifenesin
- Capsules (U.S.)
- Extended-release capsules (U.S.)
- Oral solution (U.S. and Canada)
- Syrup (U.S. and Canada)
- Tablets (U.S.)
- Extended-release tablets (U.S.)

Decongestant, expectorant, and analgesic combination—
Oral

Phenylephrine, Guaifenesin, Acetaminophen, Salicylamide and Caffeine
- Tablets (U.S.)

Before Using This Medicine

If you are taking this medicine without a prescription, carefully read and follow any precautions on the label. For cough/cold combinations, the following should be considered:

Allergies—Tell your doctor if you have ever had any unusual or allergic reaction to any of the ingredients contained in this medicine. Also tell your health care professional if you are allergic to any other substances, such as foods, preservatives, or dyes. In addition, if this medicine contains *aspirin or other salicylates*, before taking it, check with your doctor if you have ever had any unusual or allergic reaction to any of the following medicines:

Aspirin or other salicylates
Diclofenac (e.g., Voltaren)
Diflunisal (e.g., Dolobid)
Fenoprofen (e.g., Nalfon)
Floctafenine
Flurbiprofen, by mouth (e.g., Ansaid)
Ibuprofen (e.g., Motrin)
Indomethacin (e.g., Indocin)
Ketoprofen (e.g., Orudis)
Ketorolac (e.g., Toradol)
Meclofenamate (e.g., Meclomen)
Mefenamic acid (e.g., Ponstel)
Methyl salicylate (oil of wintergreen)
Naproxen (e.g., Naprosyn)
Oxyphenbutazone (e.g., Tandearil)
Phenylbutazone (e.g., Butazolidin)
Piroxicam (e.g., Feldene)
Sulindac (e.g., Clinoril)
Suprofen (e.g., Suprol)
Tiaprofenic acid (e.g., Surgam)
Tolmetin (e.g., Tolectin)
Zomepirac (e.g., Zomax)

Diet—Make certain your health care professional knows if you are on any special diet, such as a low-sodium or low-sugar diet.

Pregnancy—The occasional use of a cough/cold combination is not likely to cause problems in the fetus or in the newborn baby. However, when these medicines are used at higher doses and/or for a long time, the chance that problems might occur may increase. For the individual ingredients of these combinations, the following information should be considered before you decide to use a particular cough/cold combination:

- *Acetaminophen*—Studies on birth defects have not been done in humans. However, acetaminophen has not been shown to cause birth defects or other problems in humans.
- *Alcohol*—Some of these combination medicines contain a large amount of alcohol. Too much use of alcohol during pregnancy may cause birth defects.
- *Antihistamines*—Antihistamines have not been shown to cause problems in humans.
- *Caffeine*—Studies in humans have not shown that caffeine causes birth defects. However, studies in animals have shown that caffeine causes birth defects when given in very large doses (amounts equal to the amount of caffeine contained in 12 to 24 cups of coffee a day).
- *Codeine*—Although studies on birth defects with codeine have not been done in humans, it has not been reported to cause birth defects in humans. Codeine has not been shown to cause birth defects in animal studies, but it caused other unwanted effects. Also, regular use of narcotics during pregnancy may cause the baby to become dependent on the medicine. This may lead to withdrawal side effects after birth. In addition, narcotics may cause breathing problems in the newborn baby if taken by the mother just before delivery.

- *Hydrocodone*—Although studies on birth defects with hydrocodone have not been done in humans, it has not been reported to cause birth defects in humans. However, hydrocodone has been shown to cause birth defects in animals when given in very large doses. Also, regular use of narcotics during pregnancy may cause the baby to become dependent on the medicine. This may lead to withdrawal side effects after birth. In addition, narcotics may cause breathing problems in the newborn baby if taken by the mother just before delivery.
- *Iodides (e.g., calcium iodide and iodinated glycerol)*—Not recommended during pregnancy. Iodides have caused enlargement of the thyroid gland in the fetus and resulted in breathing problems in newborn babies whose mothers took iodides in large doses for a long period of time.
- *Phenylephrine*—Studies on birth defects with phenylephrine have not been done in either humans or animals.
- *Phenylpropanolamine*—Studies on birth defects with phenylpropanolamine have not been done in either humans or animals. However, it seems that women who take phenylpropanolamine in the weeks following delivery are more likely to suffer mental or mood changes.
- *Pseudoephedrine*—Studies on birth defects with pseudoephedrine have not been done in humans. In animal studies pseudoephedrine did not cause birth defects but did cause a decrease in average weight, length, and rate of bone formation in the animal fetus when given in high doses.
- *Salicylates (e.g., aspirin)*—Studies on birth defects in humans have been done with aspirin, but not with salicylamide or sodium salicylate. Salicylates have not been shown to cause birth defects in humans. However, salicylates have been shown to cause birth defects in animals.

  Some reports have suggested that too much use of aspirin late in pregnancy may cause a decrease in the newborn's weight and possible death of the fetus or newborn infant. However, the mothers in these reports had been taking much larger amounts of aspirin than are usually recommended. Studies of mothers taking aspirin in the doses that are usually recommended did not show these unwanted effects. However, there is a chance that regular use of salicylates late in pregnancy may cause unwanted effects on the heart or blood flow in the fetus or newborn baby.

  Use of salicylates, especially aspirin, during the last 2 weeks of pregnancy may cause bleeding problems in the fetus before or during delivery, or in the newborn baby. Also, too much use of salicylates during the last 3 months of pregnancy may increase the length of pregnancy, prolong labor, cause other problems during delivery, or cause severe bleeding in the mother before, during, or after delivery. *Do not take aspirin during the last 3 months of pregnancy unless it has been ordered by your doctor.*

Breast-feeding—If you are breast-feeding, the chance that problems might occur depends on the ingredients of the combination. For the individual ingredients of these combinations, the following apply:

- *Acetaminophen*—Acetaminophen passes into the breast milk. However, it has not been reported to cause problems in nursing babies.
- *Alcohol*—Alcohol passes into the breast milk. However, the amount of alcohol in recommended doses of this medicine does not usually cause problems in nursing babies.
- *Antihistamines*—Small amounts of antihistamines pass into the breast milk. Antihistamine-containing medicine is not recommended for use while breast-feeding since most antihistamines are especially likely to cause side effects, such as unusual excitement or irritability, in the baby. Also, since antihistamines tend to decrease the secretions of the body, the flow of breast milk may be reduced in some patients.
- *Caffeine*—Small amounts of caffeine pass into the breast milk and may build up in the nursing baby. However, the amount of caffeine in recommended doses of this medicine does not usually cause problems in nursing babies.
- *Decongestants (e.g., ephedrine, phenylephrine, phenylpropanolamine, pseudoephedrine)*—Phenylephrine and phenylpropanolamine have not been reported to cause problems in nursing babies. Ephedrine and pseudoephedrine pass into the breast milk and may cause unwanted effects in nursing babies (especially newborn and premature babies).
- *Iodides (e.g., calcium iodide and iodinated glycerol)*—These medicines pass into the breast milk and may cause unwanted effects, such as underactive thyroid, in the baby.
- *Narcotic antitussives (e.g., codeine, dihydrocodeine, hydrocodone, and hydromorphone)*—Small amounts of codeine have been shown to pass into the breast milk. However, the amount of codeine or other narcotic antitussives in recommended doses of this medicine has not been reported to cause problems in nursing babies.
- *Salicylates (e.g., aspirin)*—Salicylates pass into the breast milk. Although salicylates have not been reported to cause problems in nursing babies, it is possible that problems may occur if large amounts are taken regularly.

Children—Very young children are usually more sensitive to the effects of this medicine. *Before giving any of these combination medicines to a child, check the package label very carefully. Some of these medicines are too strong for use in children.* If you are not certain whether a specific product can be given to a child, or if you have any questions about the amount to give, check with your health care professional, especially if it contains:

- *Antihistamines*—Nightmares, unusual excitement, nervousness, restlessness, or irritability may be more likely to occur in children taking antihistamines.

- *Decongestants (e.g., ephedrine, phenylephrine, phenylpropanolamine, pseudoephedrine)*—Increases in blood pressure may be more likely to occur in children taking decongestants. Also, mental changes may be more likely to occur in young children taking phenylpropanolamine-containing combinations.
- *Narcotic antitussives (e.g., codeine, hydrocodeine, hydrocodone, and hydromorphone)*—Breathing problems may be especially likely to occur in children younger than 2 years of age taking narcotic antitussives. Also, unusual excitement or restlessness may be more likely to occur in children receiving these medicines.
- *Salicylates (e.g., aspirin)—Do not give medicines containing aspirin or other salicylates to a child with a fever or other symptoms of a virus infection, especially flu or chickenpox, without first discussing its use with your child's doctor.* This is very important because salicylates may cause a serious illness called Reye's syndrome in children with fever caused by a virus infection, especially flu or chickenpox. Also, children may be more sensitive to the aspirin or other salicylates contained in some of these medicines, especially if they have a fever or have lost large amounts of body fluid because of vomiting, diarrhea, or sweating.

Teenagers—*Do not give medicines containing aspirin or other salicylates to a teenager with a fever or other symptoms of a virus infection, especially flu or chickenpox, without first discussing its use with your child's doctor.* This is very important because salicylates may cause a serious illness called Reye's syndrome in teenagers with fever caused by a virus infection, especially flu or chickenpox.

Older adults—The elderly are usually more sensitive to the effects of this medicine, especially if it contains:

- *Antihistamines*—Confusion, difficult or painful urination, dizziness, drowsiness, feeling faint, or dryness of mouth, nose, or throat may be more likely to occur in elderly patients. Also, nightmares or unusual excitement, nervousness, restlessness, or irritability may be more likely to occur in the elderly taking antihistamines.
- *Decongestants (e.g., ephedrine, phenylephrine, phenylpropanolamine, pseudoephedrine)*—Confusion, hallucinations, drowsiness, or convulsions (seizures) may be more likely to occur in the elderly, who are usually more sensitive to the effects of this medicine. Also, increases in blood pressure may be more likely to occur in elderly persons taking decongestants.

Other medicines—Although certain medicines should not be used together at all, in other cases two different medicines may be used together even if an interaction might occur. In these cases, your doctor may want to change the dose, or other precautions may be necessary. Tell your health care professional if you are taking *any* other prescription or nonprescription (over-the-counter [OTC]) medicine, for example, aspirin or other medicine for allergies. Some medicines may change the way this medicine affects your body. Also, the effect of other medicines may be increased or reduced by some of the ingredients in this medicine. Check with your health care professional about which medicines you should not take with this medicine.

Other medical problems—The presence of other medical problems may affect the use of the cough/cold combination medicine. Make sure you tell your doctor if you have any other medical problems, especially:

- Alcohol abuse (or history of)—Acetaminophen-containing medicines increase the chance of liver damage; also, some of the liquid medicines contain a large amount of alcohol
- Anemia or
- Gout or
- Hemophilia or other bleeding problems or
- Stomach ulcer or other stomach problems—These conditions may become worse if you are taking a combination medicine containing aspirin or another salicylate
- Brain disease or injury or
- Colitis or
- Convulsions (seizures) (history of) or
- Diarrhea or
- Gallbladder disease or gallstones—These conditions may become worse if you are taking a combination medicine containing codeine, dihydrocodeine, hydrocodone, or hydromorphone
- Cystic fibrosis (in children)—Side effects of iodinated glycerol may be more likely in children with cystic fibrosis
- Diabetes mellitus (sugar diabetes)—Decongestants may put diabetic patients at greater risk of having heart or blood vessel disease
- Emphysema, asthma, or chronic lung disease (especially in children)—Salicylate-containing medicine may cause an allergic reaction in which breathing becomes difficult
- Enlarged prostate or
- Urinary tract blockage or difficult urination—Some of the effects of anticholinergics (e.g., homatropine) or antihistamines may make urinary problems worse
- Glaucoma—A slight increase in inner eye pressure may occur with the use of anticholinergics (e.g., homatropine) or antihistamines, which may make the condition worse
- Heart or blood vessel disease or
- High blood pressure—Decongestant-containing medicine may increase the blood pressure and speed up the heart rate; also, caffeine-containing medicine, if taken in large amounts, may speed up the heart rate
- Kidney disease—This condition may increase the chance of side effects of this medicine because the medicine may build up in the body
- Liver disease—Liver disease increases the chance of side effects because the medicine may build up in the body; also, if liver disease is severe, there is a greater chance that aspirin-containing medicine may cause bleeding
- Thyroid disease—If an overactive thyroid has caused a fast heart rate, the decongestant in this medicine may cause the heart rate to speed up further; also, if the medicine contains narcotic antitussives (e.g., codeine), iodides (e.g., iodinated glycerol), or salicylates, the thyroid problem may become worse

Proper Use of This Medicine

To help loosen mucus or phlegm in the lungs, *drink a glass of water after each dose of this medicine*, unless otherwise directed by your doctor.

Take this medicine only as directed. Do not take more of it and do not take it more often than recommended on the label, unless otherwise directed by your doctor. To do so may increase the chance of side effects.

For patients *taking the extended-release capsule or tablet form of this medicine:*

- Swallow the capsule or tablet whole.
- Do not crush, break, or chew before swallowing.
- If the capsule is too large to swallow, you may mix the contents of the capsule with applesauce, jelly, honey, or syrup and swallow without chewing.

For patients *taking a combination medicine containing an antihistamine and/or aspirin or other salicylate:*

- Take with food or a glass of water or milk to lessen stomach irritation, if necessary.

If a combination medicine containing aspirin has a strong vinegar-like odor, do not use it. This odor means the medicine is breaking down. If you have any questions about this, check with your pharmacist.

Missed dose—If you must take this medicine regularly and you miss a dose, take it as soon as possible. However, if it is almost time for your next dose, skip the missed dose and go back to your regular dosing schedule. Do not double doses.

Storage—To store this medicine:

- Keep this medicine out of the reach of children. Overdose is very dangerous in young children.
- Store away from heat and direct light.
- Do not store the capsule or tablet form of this medicine in the bathroom, near the kitchen sink, or in other damp places. Heat or moisture may cause the medicine to break down.
- Keep the liquid form of this medicine from freezing. Do not refrigerate the syrup.
- Do not keep outdated medicine or medicine no longer needed. Be sure that any discarded medicine is out of the reach of children.

Precautions While Using This Medicine

If your cough has not improved after 7 days or if you have a high fever, skin rash, continuing headache, or sore throat with the cough, check with your doctor. These signs may mean that you have other medical problems.

For patients *taking antihistamine-containing medicine:*

- Before you have any skin tests for allergies, tell the doctor in charge that you are taking this medicine. The results of the test may be affected by the antihistamine in this medicine.
- This medicine will add to the effects of alcohol and other CNS depressants (medicines that slow down the nervous system, possibly causing drowsiness). Some examples of CNS depressants are antihistamines or medicine for hay fever, other allergies, or colds; sedatives, tranquilizers, or sleeping medicine; prescription pain medicine or narcotics; barbiturates; medicine for seizures; muscle relaxants; or anesthetics, including some dental anesthetics. *Check with your doctor before taking any of the above while you are taking this medicine.*
- This medicine may cause some people to become drowsy, dizzy, or less alert than they are normally. *Make sure you know how you react to this medicine before you drive, use machines, or do anything else that could be dangerous if you are dizzy or are not alert.*
- When taking antihistamines on a regular basis, make sure your doctor knows if you are taking large amounts of aspirin at the same time (as in arthritis or rheumatism). Effects of too much aspirin, such as ringing in the ears, may be covered up by the antihistamine.
- Antihistamines may cause dryness of the mouth. For temporary relief, use sugarless candy or gum, melt bits of ice in your mouth, or use a saliva substitute. However, if your mouth continues to feel dry for more than 2 weeks, check with your medical doctor or dentist. Continuing dryness of the mouth may increase the chance of dental disease, including tooth decay, gum disease, and fungus infections.

For patients *taking decongestant-containing medicine:*

- This medicine may add to the central nervous system (CNS) stimulant and other effects of phenylpropanolamine (PPA)-containing diet aids. *Do not use medicines for diet or appetite control while taking this medicine unless you have checked with your doctor.*
- This medicine may cause some people to be nervous or restless or to have trouble in sleeping. If you have trouble in sleeping, *take the last dose of this medicine for each day a few hours before bedtime.* If you have any questions about this, check with your doctor.
- Before having any kind of surgery (including dental surgery) or emergency treatment, tell the medical doctor or dentist in charge that you are taking this medicine.

For patients *taking narcotic antitussive (codeine, dihydrocodeine, hydrocodone, or hydromorphone)–containing medicine:*

- This medicine will add to the effects of alcohol and other CNS depressants (medicines that slow down the nervous system, possibly causing drowsiness). Some examples of CNS depressants are antihistamines or medicine for hay fever, other allergies, or colds; sedatives, tranquilizers, or sleeping medicine; prescription pain medicine or narcotics; barbiturates; medicine for seizures; muscle relaxants; or anesthetics, including some dental anesthetics. *Check with your doctor before taking any of the above while you are taking this medicine.*
- This medicine may cause some people to become drowsy, dizzy, less alert than they are normally, or to feel a false sense of well-being. *Make sure you know how you react to this medicine before you drive, use machines, or do anything else that could be dangerous if you are dizzy or are not alert and clearheaded.*

- Nausea or vomiting may occur after taking a narcotic antitussive. This effect may go away if you lie down for a while. However, if nausea or vomiting continues, check with your doctor.
- Dizziness, lightheadedness, or fainting may be especially likely to occur when you get up suddenly from a lying or sitting position. Getting up slowly may help lessen this problem.
- Before having any kind of surgery (including dental surgery) or emergency treatment, tell the medical doctor or dentist in charge that you are taking this medicine.

For patients *taking iodide (calcium iodide, iodinated glycerol, or potassium iodide)-containing medicine:*

- Make sure your doctor knows if you are planning to have any future thyroid tests. The results of the thyroid test may be affected by the iodine in this medicine.

For patients *taking analgesic-containing medicine:*

- *Check the label of all nonprescription (over-the-counter [OTC]), and prescription medicines you now take.* If any contain acetaminophen or aspirin or other salicylates, including diflunisal or bismuth subsalicylate, be especially careful. Taking them while taking a cough/cold combination medicine that already contains them may lead to overdose. If you have any questions about this, check with your health care professional.
- Do not take aspirin-containing medicine for 5 days before any surgery, including dental surgery, unless otherwise directed by your medical doctor or dentist. Taking aspirin during this time may cause bleeding problems.

For *diabetic patients taking aspirin- or sodium salicylate–containing medicine:*

- False urine sugar test results may occur:

  —If you take 8 or more 325-mg (5-grain) doses of aspirin every day for several days in a row.

  —If you take 8 or more 325-mg (5-grain), or 4 or more 500-mg (10-grain) doses of sodium salicylate.
- Smaller doses or occasional use of aspirin or sodium salicylate usually will not affect urine sugar tests. If you have any questions about this, check with your health care professional, especially if your diabetes is not well controlled.

For patients *taking homatropine-containing medicine:*

- This medicine may make you sweat less, causing your body temperature to increase. *Use extra care not to become overheated during exercise or hot weather while you are taking this medicine,* since overheating may result in heat stroke. Also, hot baths or saunas may make you feel dizzy or faint while you are taking this medicine.

Side Effects of This Medicine

Along with its needed effects, a medicine may cause some unwanted effects. Although serious side effects occur rarely when this medicine is taken as recommended, they may be more likely to occur if:

- too much medicine is taken.
- it is taken in large doses.
- it is taken for a long period of time.

Get emergency help immediately if any of the following symptoms of overdose occur:

For narcotic antitussive (codeine, dihydrocodeine, hydrocodone, or hydromorphone)–containing

Cold, clammy skin; confusion (severe); convulsions (seizures); drowsiness or dizziness (severe); nervousness or restlessness (severe); pinpoint pupils of eyes; slow heartbeat; slow or troubled breathing; weakness (severe)

For acetaminophen-containing

Diarrhea; increased sweating; loss of appetite; nausea or vomiting; stomach cramps or pain; swelling or tenderness in the upper abdomen or stomach area

For salicylate-containing

Any loss of hearing; bloody urine; confusion; convulsions (seizures); diarrhea (severe or continuing); dizziness or lightheadedness; drowsiness (severe); excitement or nervousness (severe); fast or deep breathing; fever; hallucinations (seeing, hearing, or feeling things that are not there); increased sweating; nausea or vomiting (severe or continuing); shortness of breath or troubled breathing (for salicylamide only); stomach pain (severe or continuing); uncontrollable flapping movements of the hands, especially in elderly patients; unusual thirst; vision problems

For decongestant-containing

Fast, pounding, or irregular heartbeat; headache (continuing and severe); nausea or vomiting (severe); nervousness or restlessness (severe); shortness of breath or troubled breathing (severe or continuing)

Also, check with your doctor as soon as possible if any of the following side effects occur:

For all combinations

Skin rash, hives, and/or itching

For antihistamine- or anticholinergic-containing

Clumsiness or unsteadiness; convulsions (seizures); drowsiness (severe); dryness of mouth, nose, or throat (severe); flushing or redness of face; hallucinations (seeing, hearing, or feeling things that are not there); restlessness (severe); shortness of breath or troubled breathing; slow or fast heartbeat

For iodine-containing

Headache (continuing); increased watering of mouth; loss of appetite; metallic taste; skin rash, hives, or redness; sore throat; swelling of face, lips, or eyelids

For acetaminophen-containing

Unexplained sore throat and fever; unusual tiredness or weakness; yellow eyes or skin

Other side effects may occur that usually do not need medical attention. These side effects may go away during treatment as your body adjusts to the medicine. However, check with your doctor if any of the following side effects continue or are bothersome:

Constipation; decreased sweating; difficult or painful urination; dizziness or lightheadedness; drowsiness; dryness of mouth, nose, or throat; false sense of well-being; increased sensitivity of skin to sun; nausea or vomiting; nightmares; stomach pain; thickening of mucus; trouble in sleeping;

unusual excitement, nervousness, restlessness, or irritability; unusual tiredness or weakness

Not all of the side effects listed above have been reported for each of these medicines, but they have been reported for at least one of them. There are some similarities among these combination medicines, so many of the above side effects may occur with any of these medicines.

Other side effects not listed above may also occur in some patients. If you notice any other effects, check with your doctor.

Revised: 09/03/92
Interim revision: 08/11/95; 08/28/96

CROMOLYN Inhalation

Some commonly used brand names are:

In the U.S.—
Intal

Generic name product may also be available.

In Canada—
Intal
Novo-cromolyn
PMS-Sodium Cromoglycate

Other commonly used names are cromoglicic acid, cromoglycic acid, sodium cromoglicate, and sodium cromoglycate.

Description

Cromolyn (KROE-moe-lin) is used to prevent the symptoms of asthma. When it is used regularly, cromolyn lessens the number and severity of asthma attacks by reducing inflammation in the lungs. Cromolyn is also used just before exposure to conditions or substances (for example, exercise, allergens, chemicals, cold air, or air pollutants) that cause bronchospasm (wheezing or difficulty in breathing). Cromolyn will not help an asthma or bronchospasm attack that has already started.

Cromolyn may be used alone or with other asthma medicines, such as bronchodilators (medicines that open up narrowed breathing passages) or corticosteroids (cortisone-like medicines).

Cromolyn inhalation works by acting on certain inflammatory cells in the lungs to prevent them from releasing substances that cause asthma symptoms or bronchospasm.

This medicine is available only with your doctor's prescription, in the following dosage forms:

Inhalation
- Capsules for inhalation (Canada)
- Inhalation aerosol (U.S. and Canada)
- Inhalation solution (U.S. and Canada)

Before Using This Medicine

In deciding to use a medicine, the risks of using the medicine must be weighed against the good it will do. This is a decision you and your doctor will make. For cromolyn inhalation, the following should be considered:

Allergies—Tell your doctor if you have ever had any unusual or allergic reaction to cromolyn or to any other inhalation aerosol medicine.

Pregnancy—Cromolyn has not been studied in pregnant women. However, when taken during pregnancy to control the mother's asthma, cromolyn has not been shown to cause problems in the baby. Studies in animals have shown that cromolyn causes a decrease in successful pregnancies and a decrease in the weight of the animal fetus only when given by injection in very large amounts.

Breast-feeding—It is not known whether cromolyn passes into the breast milk. However, this medicine has not been reported to cause problems in nursing babies. Although most medicines pass into breast milk in small amounts, many of them may be used safely while breast-feeding. Mothers who are using this medicine and who wish to breast-feed should discuss this with their doctor.

Children—This medicine has been tested in children and, in effective doses, has not been shown to cause different side effects or problems than it does in adults.

Older adults—Many medicines have not been studied specifically in older people. Therefore, it may not be known whether they work exactly the same way they do in younger adults. Although there is no specific information comparing the use of cromolyn inhalation in the elderly with use in other age groups, this medicine is not expected to cause different side effects or problems in older people than it does in younger adults.

Proper Use of This Medicine

Cromolyn oral inhalation is used to help prevent symptoms of asthma or bronchospasm (wheezing or difficulty in breathing). Cromolyn will not relieve an asthma or a bronchospasm attack that has already started.

Use cromolyn inhalation only as directed. Do not use more of it and do not use it more often than your doctor ordered. To do so may increase the chance of side effects.

Cromolyn inhalation usually comes with patient directions. Read them carefully before using this medicine. If you do not understand the directions that come with the inhaler or if you are not sure how to use the inhaler, ask your health care professional to show you how to use it. Also, ask your health care professional to check regularly how you use the inhaler to make sure you are using it properly.

For patients using *cromolyn inhalation aerosol:*
- The cromolyn aerosol canister provides about 112 or 200 inhalations, depending on the size of the canister your doctor ordered. You should try to keep a record of the number of inhalations you use so you will know when the canister is almost empty. This canister, unlike some other aerosol canisters, cannot be floated in water to test its fullness.

- When you use the inhaler for the first time, or if you have not used it in a while, the inhaler may not deliver the right amount of medicine with the first puff. Therefore, before using the inhaler, test or prime it.
- *To test or prime the inhaler:*

  —Insert the medicine container (canister) firmly into the clean mouthpiece according to the manufacturer's directions. Check to make sure the canister is placed properly into the mouthpiece.

  —Take the cap off the mouthpiece and shake the inhaler 3 or 4 times.

  —Hold the inhaler well away from you at arm's length and press the top of the canister, spraying the medicine one time into the air. The inhaler will now be ready to provide the right amount of medicine when you use it.
- *To use the inhaler:*

  —Using your thumb and one or two fingers, hold the inhaler upright, with the mouthpiece end down and pointing toward you.

  —Take the cap off the mouthpiece. Check the mouthpiece to make sure it is clear. Do not use the inhaler with any other mouthpieces.

  —Gently shake the inhaler 3 or 4 times.

  —Hold the mouthpiece away from your mouth and breathe out slowly and completely to the end of a normal breath.

  —Use the inhalation method recommended by your doctor.
  - Open-mouth method: Place the mouthpiece about 1 to 2 inches (2 fingerwidths) in front of your widely opened mouth. Make sure the inhaler is aimed into your mouth so the spray does not hit the roof of your mouth or your tongue.
  - Closed-mouth method: Place the mouthpiece in your mouth between your teeth and over your tongue with your lips closed tightly around it. Make sure your tongue or teeth are not blocking the opening.

  —Tilt your head back a little. Start to breathe in slowly through your mouth. At the same time, press the top of the canister once to get one puff of medicine. Continue to breathe in slowly for 3 to 4 seconds until you have taken a full deep breath. It is important to press down on the canister and breathe in slowly at the same time so the medicine gets into your lungs. This step may be difficult at first. If you are using the closed-mouth method and you see a fine mist coming from your mouth or nose, the inhaler is not being used correctly.

  —Hold your breath as long as you can up to 10 seconds (count slowly to ten). This gives the medicine time to settle into your airways and lungs.

  —Take the mouthpiece away from your mouth and breathe out slowly.

  —If your doctor has told you to inhale more than 1 puff of medicine at each dose, wait about 1 minute between puffs. Then, gently shake the inhaler again, and take the second puff following exactly the same steps you used for the first puff. Breathe in only one puff at a time.

  —When you are finished using the inhaler, wipe off the mouthpiece and replace the cap.

Your doctor may want you to use a spacer device with the inhaler. A spacer makes the inhaler easier to use. It allows more of the medicine to reach your lungs, rather than staying in your mouth and throat.

- *To use a spacer device with the inhaler:*

  —Attach the spacer to the inhaler according to the manufacturer's directions. There are different types of spacers available, but the method of breathing remains the same with most spacers.

  —Gently shake the inhaler and spacer well.

  —Hold the mouthpiece of the spacer away from your mouth and breathe out slowly and completely.

  —Place the mouthpiece of the spacer into your mouth between your teeth and over your tongue with your lips closed around it.

  —Press down on the canister top once to release one puff of medicine into the spacer. Then, within one or two seconds, begin to breathe in slowly and deeply through your mouth for 5 to 10 seconds. Count the seconds while inhaling.

  —Hold your breath as long as you can up to 10 seconds (count slowly to 10).

  —Breathe out slowly.

  —Wait a minute between puffs. Then, gently shake the inhaler and spacer again and take the second puff, following exactly the same steps you used for the first puff. Do not spray more than one puff at a time into the spacer.

  —When you are finished using the inhaler, remove the spacer device from the inhaler and replace the cap.

Clean the inhaler, mouthpiece, and spacer at least once a week.

- *To clean the inhaler:*

  —Remove the canister from the inhaler and set the canister aside. Do not get the canister wet.

  —Wash the mouthpiece, cap, and the spacer in warm soapy water. Rinse well with warm, running water.

  —Shake off the excess water and let the inhaler parts air dry completely before putting the inhaler back together.

For patients using *cromolyn capsules for inhalation:*

- *Do not swallow the capsules. The medicine will not work if you swallow it.*
- This medicine is used with a special inhaler, either the *Spinhaler* or the *Halermatic*. If you do not understand the directions that come with the inhaler or if you are not sure how to use the inhaler, ask your health care professional to show you how to use it. Also, ask your health care professional to check reg-

ularly how you use the inhaler to make sure you are using it properly.

- If you are using *cromolyn capsules for inhalation* with the *Spinhaler:*
  —*To load the Spinhaler:*
    - Make sure your hands are clean and dry.
    - Insert the capsule into the inhaler just before using this medicine.
    - Hold the inhaler upright with the mouthpiece pointing down. Unscrew the body of the inhaler from the mouthpiece.
    - Keep the mouthpiece pointing down and the propeller on the spindle. Remove the foil from the capsule and insert the colored end of the cromolyn capsule firmly into the cup of the propeller. Avoid too much handling of the capsule, because moisture from your hands may make the capsule soft.
    - Make sure the propeller moves freely.
    - Screw the body of the inhaler back into the mouthpiece and make certain that it is fastened well.
    - While keeping the inhaler upright with the mouthpiece pointing down, slide the grey outer sleeve down firmly until it stops. This will puncture the capsule. Then slide the sleeve up as far as it will go. This step may be repeated a second time to make sure the capsule is punctured.

  —*To use the Spinhaler:*
    - Check to make sure the mouthpiece is properly attached to the body of the inhaler.
    - Hold the inhaler away from your mouth and breathe out slowly to the end of a normal breath.
    - Place the mouthpiece in your mouth, close your lips around it, and tilt your head back. Do not block the mouthpiece with your teeth or tongue.
    - Take a deep and rapid breath. You should hear and feel the vibrations of the rotating propeller as you breathe in.
    - Take the inhaler from your mouth and hold your breath for a few seconds or as long as possible.
    - Hold the inhaler away from your mouth and breathe out slowly and completely to the end of a normal breath. Do not breathe out through the inhaler because this may prevent the inhaler from working properly.
    - Keep taking inhalations of this medicine until all the powder from the capsule is inhaled. A light dusting of powder remaining in the capsule is normal and is not a sign that the inhaler is not working properly.
    - Throw away the empty capsule. Then return the inhaler to the container and replace the lid on the container.

  —*To clean the Spinhaler:*
    - At least once a week, brush off any powder left sticking to the propeller.
    - Take the inhaler apart and wash the parts of the inhaler with clean, warm water.
    - Wash the inside of the propeller shaft by moving the propeller on and off the steel spindle under water.
    - Shake out the excess water.
    - Allow all parts of the inhaler to dry completely before putting it back together.
    - The Spinhaler should be replaced after 6 months.

- If you are using *cromolyn capsules for inhalation* with the *Halermatic:*
  —*To load the Halermatic:*
    - Make sure your hands are clean and dry.
    - Insert the capsule cartridge into the inhaler just before using this medicine.
    - Remove the mouthpiece cover. Then pull off the mouthpiece.
    - Push a cromolyn capsule cartridge firmly down to the bottom of the slot.
    - Slide the mouthpiece back on the body of the inhaler. Push down slowly as far as the mouthpiece will go. This punctures the capsule cartridge and lifts it into the rotation chamber. Do not repeat this step because the capsule cartridge needs to be punctured only once.

  —*To use the Halermatic:*
    - Hold the inhaler away from your mouth and breathe out slowly to the end of a normal breath.
    - Place the mouthpiece in your mouth, close your lips around it, and tilt your head back. Do not block the flow of medicine into the lungs with your teeth or tongue.
    - Breathe in quickly and steadily through the mouthpiece.
    - Hold your breath for a few seconds to keep the medicine in the lungs as long as possible. Then take the inhaler away from your mouth.
    - Hold the inhaler well away from your mouth and breathe out to the end of a normal breath. Do not breathe out through the inhaler because this may prevent the inhaler from working properly.
    - Keep taking inhalations of this medicine until all the powder from the capsule is inhaled. A light dusting of powder remaining in the capsule is normal and is not a sign that the inhaler is not working properly.
    - Throw away the empty capsule cartridge.

  —*To clean the Halermatic:*
    - Brush away powder deposits each day with a brush.
    - When powder deposits build up, wipe them away with a slightly damp cloth.

- The mouthpiece may be washed separately if necessary. However, do not wet the blue-based body of the inhaler. Be sure the mouthpiece grid is dry before putting the inhaler back together.
- The Halermatic should be replaced every 6 months.

For patients using *cromolyn inhalation solution:*
- Cromolyn inhalation solution comes in a small glass container called an ampul. The ampul must be broken gently to empty the contents. If you do not understand the manufacturer's directions, ask your health care professional to show you what to do.
- Do not use the solution in the ampul if it is cloudy or contains particles.
- *To break and empty the ampul:*

  —The glass ampul is weak at each end so the ends can be broken easily by hand.

  —Hold the ampul away from the nebulizer and your face when you break it. Hold the ampul at an angle and carefully break off the lower end. No solution will come out.

  —Turn the ampul over so the open end faces up. Place a forefinger carefully over the open end.

  —Keep your finger firmly in place and break off the lower end of the ampul.

  —To empty the ampul, hold it over the bowl of the nebulizer unit and remove your finger to let the solution flow out.

  —Throw away any solution left in the nebulizer after you have taken your treatment.
- Use this medicine only in a power-operated nebulizer that has an adequate flow rate and is equipped with a face mask or mouthpiece. Your doctor will advise you on which nebulizer to use. Make sure you understand exactly how to use it. Hand-squeezed bulb nebulizers cannot be used with this medicine. If you have any questions about this, check with your doctor.

For patients using *cromolyn oral inhalation* regularly (for example, every day):
- *In order for cromolyn to work properly, it must be inhaled every day in regularly spaced doses as ordered by your doctor.* Up to 4 weeks may pass before you feel the full effects of the medicine.

Dosing—The dose of cromolyn will be different for different patients. *Follow your doctor's orders or the directions on the label.* The following information includes only the average doses of cromolyn inhalation. *If your dose is different, do not change it* unless your doctor tells you to do so.

The number of doses you take each day, the time allowed between doses, and the length of time you take the medicine depend on the medical problem for which you are taking cromolyn inhalation.

- For *inhalation aerosol* dosage form:

  —For prevention of asthma symptoms:
  - Adults and children 5 years of age or older—2 inhalations (puffs) taken four times a day with doses spaced four to six hours apart.
  - Children up to 5 years of age—Dose must be determined by your doctor.

  —For prevention of bronchospasm caused by exercise or a condition or substance:
  - Adults and children 5 years of age or older—2 inhalations (puffs) taken at least ten to fifteen (but not more than sixty) minutes before exercise or exposure to any condition or substance that may cause an attack.
  - Children up to 5 years of age—Dose must be determined by your doctor.
- For *capsule for inhalation* dosage form:

  —For prevention of asthma symptoms:
  - Adults and children 2 years of age or older—20 mg (contents of 1 capsule) taken four times a day with doses spaced four to six hours apart.
  - Children up to 2 years of age—Dose must be determined by your doctor.

  —For prevention of bronchospasm caused by exercise or a condition or substance:
  - Adults and children 2 years of age or older—20 mg (contents of 1 capsule) taken at least ten to fifteen (but not more than sixty) minutes before exercise or exposure to any condition or substance that may cause an attack.
  - Children up to 2 years of age—Dose must be determined by your doctor.
- For *inhalation solution* dosage form:

  —For prevention of asthma symptoms:
  - Adults and children 2 years of age or older—20 mg (contents of 1 ampul) used in a nebulizer. This medicine should be used four times a day with doses spaced four to six hours apart. Use a new ampul of solution for each dose.
  - Children up to 2 years of age—Dose must be determined by your doctor.

  —For prevention of bronchospasm caused by exercise or a condition or substance:
  - Adults and children 2 years of age or older—20 mg (contents of 1 ampul) used in a nebulizer. This medicine should be used at least ten to fifteen (but not more than sixty) minutes before exercise or exposure to any condition or substance that may cause an attack. Use a new ampul of solution for each dose.
  - Children up to 2 years of age—Dose must be determined by your doctor.

Missed dose—If you are using cromolyn regularly and you miss a dose, use it as soon as possible. Then use any remaining doses for that day at regularly spaced times.

Storage—To store this medicine:
- Keep out of the reach of children.
- Store the aerosol or solution form of this medicine at room temperature away from heat or cold. Keep this medicine from freezing.
- Store the capsule or solution form of this medicine away from direct light. Store the aerosol form of this medicine away from direct sunlight.
- Do not store the capsule form of this medicine in the bathroom, near the kitchen sink, or in other damp places. Heat or moisture may cause the medicine to break down.
- Do not puncture, break, or burn the aerosol container, even if it is empty.
- Do not keep outdated medicine or medicine no longer needed. Be sure that any discarded medicine is out of the reach of children.

Precautions While Using This Medicine

If your symptoms do not improve within 4 weeks or if your condition becomes worse after you begin using cromolyn, check with your doctor.

If you are also taking a corticosteroid or a bronchodilator for your asthma along with this medicine, do not stop taking the corticosteroid or bronchodilator even if your asthma seems better, unless you are told to do so by your doctor.

Dryness of the mouth or throat or throat irritation may occur after you use this medicine. Gargling and rinsing your mouth or taking a drink of water after each dose may help prevent these effects.

Side Effects of This Medicine

Along with its needed effects, a medicine may cause some unwanted effects. Although not all of these side effects may occur, if they do occur they may need medical attention.

Check with your doctor as soon as possible if any of the following side effects occur:

Rare

Difficulty in swallowing; hives; increased wheezing or difficulty in breathing; itching of skin; swelling of face, lips, or eyelids

Other side effects may occur that usually do not need medical attention. These side effects may go away during treatment as your body adjusts to the medicine. However, check with your doctor if any of the following side effects continue or are bothersome:

More common

Throat irritation or dryness

If you are using the cromolyn inhalation aerosol, you may notice an unpleasant taste. This may be expected and will go away when you stop using the medicine.

Other side effects not listed above may also occur in some patients. If you notice any other effects, check with your doctor.

Revised: 04/23/96

CROMOLYN Nasal

Some commonly used brand names are:

In the U.S.—

Nasalcrom

In Canada—

Rynacrom

Another commonly used name is sodium cromoglycate.

Description

Cromolyn (KROE-moe-lin) nasal solution is used to help prevent or treat the symptoms (sneezing, wheezing, runny nose, itching) of seasonal (short-term) or chronic (long-term) allergic rhinitis. Cromolyn powder for nasal inhalation is used to help prevent seasonal (short-term) allergic rhinitis.

This medicine works by acting on certain cells in the body, called mast cells, to prevent them from releasing substances that cause the allergic reaction.

When cromolyn is used to treat chronic (long-term) allergic rhinitis, an antihistamine and/or a nasal decongestant may be used with this medicine, especially during the first few weeks of treatment.

Nasal cromolyn is available only with your doctor's prescription, in the following dosage forms:

Nasal
- Nasal insufflation (powder for nasal inhalation) (Canada)
- Nasal solution (U.S. and Canada)

Before Using This Medicine

In deciding to use a medicine, the risks of using the medicine must be weighed against the good it will do. This is a decision you and your doctor will make. For nasal cromolyn, the following should be considered:

Allergies—Tell your doctor if you have ever had any unusual or allergic reaction to cromolyn. Also tell your health care professional if you are allergic to any other substances, such as foods, preservatives, or dyes.

Pregnancy—Nasal cromolyn has not been shown to cause birth defects in humans. However, studies in animals have shown that cromolyn, when given by injection in very large amounts, causes a decrease in successful pregnancies and a decrease in the weight of the animal fetus. Before using this medicine, make sure your doctor knows if you are pregnant or if you may become pregnant.

Breast-feeding—It is not known whether cromolyn passes into the breast milk. Although most medicines pass into breast milk in small amounts, many of them may be used safely while breast-feeding. Mothers who are using this medicine and who wish to breast-feed should discuss this with their doctor.

Children—Studies on this medicine have been done only in adult patients, and there is no specific information comparing use of nasal cromolyn in children up to 6 years of age (in Canada, up to 5 years of age) with use in other age groups. In older children, this medicine is not expected to cause different side effects or problems than it does in adults.

Older adults—Many medicines have not been studied specifically in older people. Therefore, it may not be known whether they work exactly the same way they do in younger adults. Although there is no specific information comparing use of nasal cromolyn in the elderly with use in other age groups, this medicine is not expected to cause different side effects or problems in older people than it does in younger adults.

Other medical problems—The presence of other medical problems may affect the use of nasal cromolyn. Make sure you tell your doctor if you have any other medical problems, especially:

- Polyps or growths inside the nose—Cromolyn may not work if nasal passages are blocked

Proper Use of This Medicine

This medicine usually comes with patient directions. Read them carefully before using the medicine.

Before using this medicine, clear the nasal passages by blowing your nose.

For patients using *cromolyn nasal solution:*

- Cromolyn nasal solution is used with a special spray device.
- To keep clean, wipe the nosepiece with a clean tissue and replace the dust cap after use.

For patients using *cromolyn powder for nasal inhalation:*

- This medicine is used with a special inhaler. Be sure you understand exactly how to use it.
- To keep clean, wipe the nosepiece with a clean tissue and replace the dust cap after use. Only the nosepiece may be washed in warm water, but must be dried thoroughly. *The bulb unit should not be washed or dampened inside.*

Use this medicine only as directed. Do not use more of it and do not use it more often than your doctor ordered. To do so may increase the chance of side effects.

In order for this medicine to work properly, it must be used every day in regularly spaced doses as ordered by your doctor:

- For patients using cromolyn for *seasonal (short-term) allergic rhinitis,* up to 1 week may pass before you begin to feel better.
- For patients using cromolyn for *chronic (long-term) allergic rhinitis,* up to 4 weeks may pass before you feel the full effects of this medicine, although you may begin to feel better after 1 week.

Dosing—The dose of nasal cromolyn will be different for different patients. *Follow your doctor's orders or the directions on the label.* The following information includes only the average doses of nasal cromolyn. *If your dose is different, do not change it* unless your doctor tells you to do so.

- For *nasal solution* dosage form:
  - —For allergic rhinitis:
    - Adults and children 6 years of age (in Canada, 5 years of age) and older—One spray into each nostril three to six times a day.
    - Children up to 6 years of age (in Canada, up to 5 years of age)—Use and dose must be determined by your doctor.
- For *powder for nasal inhalation* dosage form:
  - —For allergic rhinitis:
    - Adults and children 5 years of age and older—One inhalation into each nostril four times a day until condition is better; then, one inhalation into each nostril two or three times a day.
    - Children up to 5 years of age—Use and dose must be determined by your doctor.

Missed dose—If you miss a dose of this medicine, use it as soon as possible. Then use any remaining doses for that day at regularly spaced intervals. Do not double doses.

Storage—To store this medicine:

- Keep out of the reach of children.
- Store away from heat and direct light.
- Store the powder form of this medicine in a dry place. Do not store it in the bathroom, near the kitchen sink, or in other damp places. Heat or moisture may cause the medicine to break down.
- Keep the solution form of this medicine from freezing.
- Do not keep outdated medicine or medicine no longer needed. Be sure that any discarded medicine is out of the reach of children.

Precautions While Using This Medicine

If your symptoms do not improve or if your condition becomes worse, check with your doctor.

Side Effects of This Medicine

Along with its needed effects, a medicine may cause some unwanted effects. Although not all of these side effects may occur, if they do occur they may need medical attention.

Check with your doctor as soon as possible if any of the following side effects occur:

Rare

Allergic reaction (coughing; difficulty in swallowing; hives or itching; swelling of face, lips, or eyelids; wheezing or difficulty in breathing); nosebleeds; skin rash

Other side effects may occur that usually do not need medical attention. These side effects may go away during

treatment as your body adjusts to the medicine. However, check with your doctor if any of the following side effects continue or are bothersome:

More common
Burning, stinging, or irritation inside of nose; increase in sneezing

Less common
Cough; headache; postnasal drip; unpleasant taste

Other side effects not listed above may also occur in some patients. If you notice any other effects, check with your doctor.

Revised: 04/20/94

CROMOLYN Ophthalmic

Some commonly used brand names are:

In the U.S.—
Crolom

In Canada—
Opticrom
Vistacrom

Other commonly used names are cromoglicic acid, cromoglycic acid, and sodium cromoglycate.

Description

Cromolyn (KROE-moe-lin) ophthalmic solution is used in the eye to treat certain disorders of the eye caused by allergies. It works by acting on certain cells, called mast cells, to prevent them from releasing substances that cause the allergic reaction.

Cromolyn is available only with your doctor's prescription, in the following dosage form:

Ophthalmic
- Ophthalmic solution (eye drops) (U.S. and Canada)

Before Using This Medicine

In deciding to use a medicine, the risks of using the medicine must be weighed against the good it will do. This is a decision you and your doctor will make. For ophthalmic cromolyn, the following should be considered:

Allergies—Tell your doctor if you have ever had any unusual or allergic reaction to cromolyn. Also tell your health care professional if you are allergic to any other substances, such as foods, preservatives, or dyes.

Pregnancy—Cromolyn has not been studied in pregnant women. Studies in animals have shown that cromolyn causes a decrease in successful pregnancies and a decrease in the weight of the animal fetus when given by injection in very large amounts. However, it is unlikely that ophthalmic cromolyn will cause problems in humans when used in the eye as directed.

Breast-feeding—It is not known whether cromolyn passes into the breast milk. Although most medicines pass into breast milk in small amounts, many of them may be used safely while breast-feeding. Mothers who are taking this medicine and who wish to breast-feed should discuss this with their doctor.

Children—Studies on this medicine have been done only in adult patients, and there is no specific information comparing use of cromolyn in children up to 4 years of age with use in other age groups. For older children, this medicine is not expected to cause different side effects or problems than it does in adults.

Older adults—Many medicines have not been studied specifically in older people. Therefore, it may not be known whether they work exactly the same way they do in younger adults. Although there is no specific information comparing use of ophthalmic cromolyn in the elderly with use in other age groups, this medicine is not expected to cause different side effects or problems in older people than it does in younger adults.

Proper Use of This Medicine

To use the *eye drops:*
- First, wash your hands. Tilt the head back and, pressing your finger gently on the skin just beneath the lower eyelid, pull the lower eyelid away from the eye to make a space. Drop the medicine into this space. Let go of the eyelid and gently close the eyes. Do not blink. Keep the eyes closed for 1 or 2 minutes to allow the medicine to be absorbed by the eye.
- If you think you did not get the drop of medicine into your eye properly, use another drop.
- To keep the medicine as germ-free as possible, do not touch the applicator tip to any surface (including the eye). Also, keep the container tightly closed.

Use cromolyn eye drops only as directed. Do not use more of this medicine and do not use it more often than your doctor ordered. To do so may increase the chance of side effects.

In order for this medicine to work properly, it must be used every day in regularly spaced doses as ordered by your doctor. A few days may pass before you begin to feel better. However, in some conditions, it may take several weeks before you begin to feel better.

Dosing—The dose of ophthalmic cromolyn will be different for different patients. *Follow your doctor's orders or the directions on the label.* The following information includes only the average doses of ophthalmic cromolyn. *If your dose is different, do not change it* unless your doctor tells you to do so.

- For *ophthalmic solution (eye drops)* dosage form:
  —For eye allergies:
    - Adults and children 4 years of age and older—Use one drop four to six times a day in regularly spaced doses.
    - Children up to 4 years of age—Use and dose must be determined by your doctor.

Missed dose—If you miss a dose of this medicine, use it as soon as possible. Then go back to your regular dosing schedule.

Storage—To store this medicine:
- Keep out of the reach of children.
- Store away from heat and direct light.
- Keep the medicine from freezing.
- Do not keep outdated medicine or medicine no longer needed. Be sure that any discarded medicine is out of the reach of children.

Precautions While Using This Medicine

If your symptoms do not improve or if your condition becomes worse, check with your doctor.

Side Effects of This Medicine

Along with its needed effects, a medicine may cause some unwanted effects. Although not all of these side effects may occur, if they do occur they may need medical attention.

Check with your doctor as soon as possible if any of the following side effects occur:

Rare

Rash or redness around the eyes; swelling of the membrane covering the white part of the eye, redness of the white part of the eye, styes, or other eye irritation not present before therapy

Other side effects may occur that usually do not need medical attention. These side effects may go away during treatment as your body adjusts to the medicine. However, check with your doctor if any of the following side effects continue or are bothersome:

More common

Burning or stinging of eye (mild and temporary)

Less common or rare

Dryness or puffiness around the eye; watering or itching of eye (increased)

Other side effects not listed above may also occur in some patients. If you notice any other effects, check with your doctor.

Revised: 04/19/94
Interim revision: 07/10/95

CROMOLYN Oral

Some commonly used brand names are:

In the U.S.—
Gastrocrom

In Canada—
Nalcrom

Another commonly used name is sodium cromoglycate.

Description

Cromolyn (KROE-moe-lin) is used to treat the symptoms of mastocytosis. Mastocytosis is a rare condition caused by too many mast cells in the body. These mast cells release substances that cause the symptoms of the disease, such as abdominal pain, nausea, vomiting, diarrhea, headache, flushing or itching of skin, or hives.

Cromolyn works by acting on the mast cells in the body to prevent them from releasing substances that cause the symptoms of mastocytosis.

Cromolyn is available only with your doctor's prescription, in the following dosage form:

Oral
- Capsules (U.S. and Canada)

Before Using This Medicine

In deciding to use a medicine, the risks of taking the medicine must be weighed against the good it will do. This is a decision you and your doctor will make. For oral cromolyn, the following should be considered:

Allergies—Tell your doctor if you have ever had any unusual or allergic reaction to cromolyn. Also tell your health care professional if you are allergic to any other substances, such as foods, preservatives, or dyes.

Diet—Make certain your health care professional knows if you are on any special diet, such as a low-sodium diet. This medicine contains sodium.

Pregnancy—Cromolyn has not been studied in pregnant women. However, studies in animals have shown that cromolyn, when given by injection in very large amounts, causes a decrease in successful pregnancies and a decrease in the weight of the animal fetus. Before using this medicine, make sure your doctor knows if you are pregnant or if you may become pregnant.

Breast-feeding—It is not known whether cromolyn passes into the breast milk. Although most medicines pass into breast milk in small amounts, many of them may be used safely while breast-feeding. Mothers who are taking this medicine and who wish to breast-feed should discuss this with their doctor.

Children—Although there is no specific information comparing use of oral cromolyn in children with use in other age groups, this medicine is not expected to cause different side effects or problems in children than it does in adults.

Older adults—Many medicines have not been studied specifically in older people. Therefore, it may not be known whether they work exactly the same way they do in younger adults. Although there is no specific information comparing use of oral cromolyn in the elderly with use in other age groups, this medicine is not expected to cause different side effects or problems in older people than it does in younger adults.

Other medicines—Although certain medicines should not be used together at all, in other cases two different med-

icines may be used together even if an interaction might occur. In these cases, your doctor may want to change the dose, or other precautions may be necessary. Tell your health care professional if you are taking any other prescription or nonprescription (over-the-counter [OTC]) medicine.

Other medical problems—The presence of other medical problems may affect the use of oral cromolyn. Make sure you tell your doctor if you have any other medical problems, especially:

- Kidney disease or
- Liver disease—The effects of cromolyn may be increased, which may increase the chance of side effects

Proper Use of This Medicine

Unless otherwise directed by your doctor, it is best to take oral cromolyn as follows:

- Open the cromolyn capsule(s) and pour all of the powder into one-half glass (4 ounces) of hot water. Stir the solution until the powder is completely dissolved and the solution is clear. Then add an equal amount (one-half glass) of cold water to the solution while stirring.
- Be sure to drink all of the liquid to get the full dose of medicine.
- Do not mix this medicine with fruit juice, milk, or food because they may keep the medicine from working properly.

Take cromolyn only as directed. Do not take more of it and do not take it more often than your doctor ordered. To do so may increase the chance of side effects.

Dosing—The dose of cromolyn will be different for different patients. *Follow your doctor's orders or the directions on the label.* The following information includes only the average doses of cromolyn. *If your dose is different, do not change it* unless your doctor tells you to do so.

- For *oral* dosage form (capsules):
  - —For symptoms of mastocytosis:
    - Adults—200 milligrams (mg) dissolved in water and taken four times a day, thirty minutes before meals and at bedtime.
    - Children 2 to 12 years of age—100 mg dissolved in water and taken four times a day, thirty minutes before meals and at bedtime. Your doctor may increase the dose if your symptoms are not under control within two to three weeks after you begin taking this medicine.
    - Infants and children up to 2 years of age—Dose is based on body weight and must be determined by your doctor. The dose is usually 20 mg per kilogram (kg) (9.1 mg per pound) of body weight a day. This dose is divided into four doses. Your doctor may increase the dose if your symptoms are not under control within two to three weeks after you begin taking this medicine.
    - Premature infants—Use is not recommended.

Missed dose—If you miss a dose of this medicine, take it as soon as possible. Then take any remaining doses for that day at regularly spaced times.

Storage—To store this medicine:

- Keep out of the reach of children.
- Store away from heat, in a tightly closed container.
- Do not store the capsule form of this medicine in the bathroom, near the kitchen sink, or in other damp places. Heat or moisture may cause the medicine to break down.
- Do not keep outdated medicine or medicine no longer needed. Be sure that any discarded medicine is out of the reach of children.

Precautions While Using This Medicine

If your symptoms do not improve or if your condition becomes worse, check with your doctor.

Side Effects of This Medicine

Along with its needed effects, a medicine may cause some unwanted effects. Although not all of these side effects may occur, if they do occur they may need medical attention.

Check with your doctor immediately if any of the following side effects occur:

Rare
Coughing; difficulty in swallowing; hives or itching of skin; swelling of face, lips, or eyelids; wheezing or difficulty in breathing

Also, check with your doctor as soon as possible if the following side effect occurs:

Less common
Skin rash

Other side effects may occur that usually do not need medical attention. These side effects may go away during treatment as your body adjusts to the medicine. However, check with your doctor if any of the following side effects continue or are bothersome:

More common
Diarrhea; headache

Less common
Abdominal pain; irritability; joint pain; nausea; trouble in sleeping

Note: If the above side effects occur in patients with mastocytosis, they are usually only temporary and could be symptoms of the disease.

Other side effects not listed above may also occur in some patients. If you notice any other effects, check with your doctor.

Revised: 09/06/94

CROTAMITON Topical

Some commonly used brand names are:

In the U.S.—
- Eurax Cream
- Eurax Lotion

In Canada—
- Eurax Cream

Description

Crotamiton (kroe-TAM-i-tonn) is used to treat scabies infection. It is also used to relieve the itching of certain skin conditions.

This medicine is available only with your doctor's prescription, in the following dosage forms:

Topical
- Cream (U.S. and Canada)
- Lotion (U.S.)

Before Using This Medicine

In deciding to use a medicine, the risks of using the medicine must be weighed against the good it will do. This is a decision you and your doctor will make. For crotamiton, the following should be considered:

Allergies—Tell your doctor if you have ever had any unusual or allergic reaction to crotamiton. Also tell your health care professional if you are allergic to any other substances, such as preservatives or dyes.

Pregnancy—Studies on effects in pregnancy have not been done in either humans or animals.

Breast-feeding—Topical crotamiton has not been reported to cause problems in nursing babies.

Children—Studies on this medicine have been done only in adult patients, and there is no specific information comparing use of this medicine in children with use in other age groups.

Older adults—Many medicines have not been studied specifically in older people. Therefore, it may not be known whether they work exactly the same way they do in younger adults or if they cause different side effects or problems in older people. There is no specific information comparing use of crotamiton in the elderly with use in other age groups.

Other medicines—Although certain medicines should not be used together at all, in other cases two different medicines may be used together even if an interaction might occur. In these cases, your doctor may want to change the dose, or other precautions may be necessary. Tell your health care professional if you are using any other topical prescription or nonprescription (over-the-counter [OTC]) medicine that is to be applied to the same area of the skin.

Other medical problems—The presence of other medical problems may affect the use of crotamiton. Make sure you tell your doctor if you have any other medical problems, especially:

- Severely inflamed skin or raw oozing areas of the skin—Use of crotamiton on these areas may make the condition worse

Proper Use of This Medicine

Keep crotamiton away from the mouth. It may be harmful if swallowed.

Use this medicine only as directed. Do not use it more often than your doctor ordered. To do so may increase the chance of side effects.

Keep crotamiton away from the eyes and other mucous membranes, such as the inside of the nose. It may cause irritation. If you should accidentally get some in your eyes, flush them thoroughly with water at once.

This medicine usually comes with patient directions. Read them carefully before using.

If you take a bath or shower before using this medicine, dry the skin well before applying crotamiton.

For patients using this medicine *for scabies:*
- Apply enough medicine to cover the entire skin surface from the chin down, and rub in well. This applies especially to folds and creases in the skin and to the hands, feet (including the soles), between fingers and toes, and moist areas (such as underarms and groin).
- Do not wash off the first coat of this medicine.
- Apply a second coat of this medicine 24 hours after the first one.
- The next day, put on freshly washed or dry-cleaned clothing and change bedding in order to prevent reinfection.
- Then, 48 hours after the second application of this medicine, take a cleansing bath to remove the medicine.
- Your sexual partners, especially, and all members of your household may need to be treated also, since the infection may spread to persons in close contact. If these persons are not being treated or if you have any questions about this, check with your doctor.

Dosing—The dose of crotamiton will be different for different patients. *Follow your doctor's orders or the directions on the label.* The following information includes only the average doses of crotamiton. *If your dose is different, do not change it* unless your doctor tells you to do so.

- For *topical* dosage forms (cream and lotion):
  - —For scabies:
    - Adults—Use two times. Apply one time the first day, and one time the second day. For severe cases, treatment may be repeated one time after one week.
    - Children—Use and dose must be determined by your doctor.
  - —For pruritus:
    - Adults—Use when necessary according to the directions on the label or your doctor's instructions.

- Children—Use and dose must be determined by your doctor.

Storage—To store this medicine:
- Keep out of the reach of children.
- Store away from heat and direct light.
- Keep the medicine from freezing.
- Do not keep outdated medicine or medicine no longer needed. Be sure that any discarded medicine is out of the reach of children.

Precautions While Using This Medicine

If your condition does not improve or if it becomes worse, check with your doctor.

For patients using this medicine *for scabies:*
- To prevent reinfection or spreading of the infection to other people, good health habits are also required. These include machine washing all underwear, pajamas, sheets, pillowcases, towels, and washcloths in very hot water and drying them using the hot cycle of a dryer. Clothing or bedding that cannot be washed in this way should be dry cleaned.

Side Effects of This Medicine

Along with its needed effects, a medicine may cause some unwanted effects. Although not all of these side effects may occur, if they do occur they may need medical attention.

Check with your doctor as soon as possible if either of the following side effects occur:

Rare

Skin irritation or rash not present before use of this medicine

Other side effects not listed above may also occur in some patients. If you notice any other effects, check with your doctor.

Revised: 04/22/94

CYCLANDELATE Systemic*

A commonly used brand name is Cyclospasmol.

*Not commercially available in the U.S.

Description

Cyclandelate (sye-KLAN-de-late) belongs to the group of medicines commonly called vasodilators. These medicines increase the size of blood vessels. Cyclandelate is used to treat problems resulting from poor blood circulation.

Cyclandelate is available in the following dosage form:

Oral
- Tablets (Canada)

Before Using This Medicine

In deciding to use a medicine, the risks of taking the medicine must be weighed against the good it will do. This is a decision you and your doctor will make. For cyclandelate, the following should be considered:

Allergies—Tell your doctor if you have ever had any unusual or allergic reaction to cyclandelate. Also tell your health care professional if you are allergic to any other substances, such as foods, preservatives, or dyes.

Pregnancy—Studies on effects in pregnancy have not been done in either humans or animals.

Breast-feeding—It is not known whether cyclandelate passes into breast milk. However, cyclandelate has not been reported to cause problems in nursing babies.

Children—Studies on this medicine have been done only in adult patients, and there is no specific information comparing use of cyclandelate in children with use in other age groups.

Older adults—Many medicines have not been studied specifically in older people. Therefore, it may not be known whether they work exactly the same way they do in younger adults. Although there is no specific information comparing use of cyclandelate in the elderly with use in other age groups, this medicine is not expected to cause different side effects or problems in older people than in younger adults.

Other medicines—Although certain medicines should not be used together at all, in other cases two different medicines may be used together even if an interaction might occur. In these cases, your doctor may want to change the dose, or other precautions may be necessary. Tell your health care professional if you are taking any other prescription or nonprescription (over-the-counter [OTC]) medicine, or if you smoke.

Other medical problems—The presence of other medical problems may affect the use of cyclandelate. Make sure you tell your doctor if you have any other medical problems, especially:
- Angina (chest pain) or
- Bleeding problems or
- Glaucoma or
- Hardening of the arteries or
- Heart attack (recent) or
- Stroke (recent)—The chance of unwanted effects may be increased

Proper Use of This Medicine

If this medicine upsets your stomach, it may be taken with meals, milk, or antacids.

Dosing—The dose of cyclandelate will be different for different patients. *Follow your doctor's orders or the directions on the label.* The following information includes only the average doses of cyclandelate. *If your dose is different, do not change it* unless your doctor tells you to do so.

The number of tablets that you take depends on the strength of the medicine.

- For *oral* dosage form (tablets):
  —For treating poor circulation:
    - Adults—At first, 1.2 to 1.6 grams a day. This is taken in divided doses before meals and at bedtime. Then, your doctor will gradually lower your dose to 400 to 800 milligrams (mg) a day. This is divided into two to four doses.
    - Children—Use and dose must be determined by your doctor.

Missed dose—If you miss a dose of this medicine, take it as soon as you remember. Then go back to your regular dosing schedule. However, if it is almost time for your next dose, skip the missed dose and go back to your regular dosing schedule. Do not double doses.

Storage—To store this medicine:

- Keep out of the reach of children.
- Store away from heat and direct light.
- Do not store in the bathroom, near the kitchen sink, or in other damp places. Heat or moisture may cause the medicine to break down.
- Do not keep outdated medicine or medicine no longer needed. Be sure that any discarded medicine is out of the reach of children.

Precautions While Using This Medicine

It may take some time for this medicine to work. If you feel that the medicine is not working, do not stop taking it on your own. Instead, check with your doctor.

The helpful effects of this medicine may be decreased if you smoke.

Dizziness may occur, especially when you get up from a lying or sitting position or climb stairs. Getting up slowly may help. If this problem continues or gets worse, check with your doctor.

Side Effects of This Medicine

Along with its needed effects, a medicine may cause some unwanted effects. The following side effects may go away during treatment as your body adjusts to the medicine. However, check with your doctor if any of these effects continue or are bothersome:

Less common
: Belching, heartburn, nausea, or stomach pain; dizziness; fast heartbeat; flushing of face; headache; sweating; tingling sensation in face, fingers, or toes; weakness

Other side effects not listed above may also occur in some patients. If you notice any other effects, check with your doctor.

Revised: 10/15/92
Interim revision: 04/14/94; 08/18/97

CYCLOBENZAPRINE Systemic

Some commonly used brand names are:

In the U.S.—
Cycoflex   Flexeril
Generic name product may also be available.

In Canada—
Flexeril

Description

Cyclobenzaprine (sye-kloe-BEN-za-preen) is used to help relax certain muscles in your body. It helps relieve the pain, stiffness, and discomfort caused by strains, sprains, or injuries to your muscles. However, this medicine does not take the place of rest, exercise or physical therapy, or other treatment that your doctor may recommend for your medical problem. Cyclobenzaprine acts on the central nervous system (CNS) to produce its muscle relaxant effects. Its actions on the CNS may also cause some of this medicine's side effects.

Cyclobenzaprine may also be used for other conditions as determined by your doctor.

Cyclobenzaprine is available only with your doctor's prescription, in the following dosage form:

Oral
- Tablets (U.S. and Canada)

Before Using This Medicine

In deciding to use a medicine, the risks of taking the medicine must be weighed against the good it will do. This is a decision you and your doctor will make. For cyclobenzaprine, the following should be considered:

Allergies—Tell your doctor if you have ever had any unusual or allergic reaction to cyclobenzaprine. Also tell your health care professional if you are allergic to any other substances, such as foods, preservatives, or dyes.

Pregnancy—Studies on birth defects with cyclobenzaprine have not been done in humans. However, cyclobenzaprine has not been shown to cause birth defects or other problems in animal studies.

Breast-feeding—It is not known whether cyclobenzaprine passes into breast milk. Although most medicines pass into the breast milk in small amounts, many of them may be used safely while breast-feeding. Mothers who are taking this medicine and who wish to breast-feed should discuss this with their doctor.

Children—Studies on this medicine have been done only in adult patients, and there is no specific information comparing use of cyclobenzaprine in children with use in other age groups.

Teenagers—Studies on this medicine have been done only in adult patients, and there is no specific information comparing use of cyclobenzaprine in teenagers up to 15 years of age with use in other age groups.

Older adults—Many medicines have not been studied specifically in older people. Therefore, it may not be known whether they work exactly the same way they do in younger adults or if they cause different side effects or problems in older people. There is no specific information comparing use of cyclobenzaprine in the elderly with use in other age groups.

Other medicines—Although certain medicines should not be used together at all, in other cases two different medicines may be used together even if an interaction might occur. In these cases, your doctor may want to change the dose, or other precautions may be necessary. When you are taking cyclobenzaprine, it is especially important that your health care professional know if you are taking any of the following:

- Alcohol or
- Central nervous system (CNS) depressants or
- Tricyclic antidepressants (amitriptyline [e.g., Elavil], amoxapine [e.g., Asendin], clomipramine [e.g., Anafranil], desipramine [e.g., Pertofrane], doxepin [e.g., Sinequan], imipramine [e.g., Tofranil], nortriptyline [e.g., Aventyl], protriptyline [e.g., Vivactil], trimipramine [e.g., Surmontil])—The chance of side effects may be increased
- Monoamine oxidase (MAO) inhibitors (furazolidone [e.g., Furoxone], isocarboxazid [e.g., Marplan], phenelzine [e.g., Nardil], procarbazine [e.g., Matulane], selegiline (e.g., Eldepryl), tranylcypromine [e.g., Parnate])—Taking cyclobenzaprine while you are taking or within 2 weeks of taking monoamine oxidase (MAO) inhibitors may increase the chance of side effects

Other medical problems—The presence of other medical problems may affect the use of cyclobenzaprine. Make sure you tell your doctor if you have any other medical problems, especially:

- Glaucoma or
- Problems with urination—Cyclobenzaprine can make your condition worse
- Heart or blood vessel disease or
- Overactive thyroid—The chance of side effects may be increased

Proper Use of This Medicine

Take this medicine only as directed by your doctor. Do not take more of it and do not take it more often than your doctor ordered. To do so may increase the chance of serious side effects.

Dosing—The dose of cyclobenzaprine will be different for different people. *Follow your doctor's orders or the directions on the label.* The following information includes only the average doses of cyclobenzaprine. *If your dose is different, do not change it* unless your doctor tells you to do so.

- For the *oral* dosage form (tablets):
  - —For relaxing stiff muscles:
    - Adults and teenagers 15 years of age and older—The usual dose is 10 milligrams (mg) three times a day. The largest amount should be no more than 60 mg (six 10-mg tablets) a day.
    - Children and teenagers up to 15 years of age—Dose must be determined by your doctor.

Missed dose—If you miss a dose of this medicine and remember within an hour or so of the missed dose, take it right away. Then go back to your regular dosing schedule. But if you do not remember until later, skip the missed dose and go back to your regular dosing schedule. Do not double doses.

Storage—To store this medicine:

- Keep out of the reach of children.
- Store away from heat and direct light.
- Do not store this medicine in the bathroom, near the kitchen sink, or in other damp places. Heat or moisture may cause the medicine to break down.
- Do not keep outdated medicine or medicine no longer needed. Be sure that any discarded medicine is out of the reach of children.

Precautions While Using This Medicine

This medicine will add to the effects of alcohol and other CNS depressants (medicines that slow down the nervous system, possibly causing drowsiness). Some examples of CNS depressants are antihistamines or medicine for hay fever, other allergies, or colds; sedatives, tranquilizers, or sleeping medicine; prescription pain medicine or narcotics; barbiturates; medicine for seizures; other muscle relaxants; or anesthetics, including some dental anesthetics. *Check with your doctor before taking any of the above while you are using this medicine.*

This medicine may cause some people to have blurred vision or to become drowsy, dizzy, or less alert than they are normally. *Make sure you know how you react to this medicine before you drive, use machines, or do anything else that could be dangerous if you are dizzy or are not alert and able to see well.*

Cyclobenzaprine may cause dryness of the mouth. For temporary relief, use sugarless candy or gum, melt bits of ice in your mouth, or use a saliva substitute. However, if your mouth continues to feel dry for more than 2 weeks, check with your medical doctor or dentist. Continuing dryness of the mouth may increase the chance of dental disease, including tooth decay, gum disease, and fungus infections.

Side Effects of This Medicine

Along with its needed effects, a medicine may cause some unwanted effects. Although not all of these side effects may occur, if they do occur they may need medical attention.

The following side effects may mean that you are having a serious allergic reaction to the medicine. *Get emergency help right away if any of them occurs:*

Rare

Changes in the skin color of the face; fast or irregular breathing; large swellings that look like hives on the face, eyelids, mouth, lips, and/or tongue; puffiness or swelling of the eyelids or the area around the eyes; shortness of breath, troubled breathing, tightness in chest, and/or wheezing; skin rash, hives, or itching

Also, check with your doctor immediately if any of the following side effects occur:

Rare

Fainting

Symptoms of overdose

Convulsions (seizures); drowsiness (severe); dry, hot, flushed skin; fast or irregular heartbeat; hallucinations (seeing, hearing, or feeling things that are not there); increase or decrease in body temperature; troubled breathing; unexplained muscle stiffness; unusual nervousness or restlessness (severe); vomiting (occurring together with other symptoms of overdose)

Also, check with your doctor as soon as possible if any of the following side effects occur:

Rare

Clumsiness or unsteadiness; confusion; mental depression or other mood or mental changes; problems in urinating; ringing or buzzing in the ears; skin rash, hives, or itching occurring without other symptoms of an allergic reaction listed above; unusual thoughts or dreams; yellow eyes or skin

Other side effects may occur that usually do not need medical attention. These side effects may go away during treatment as your body adjusts to the medicine. However, check with your doctor if any of the following side effects continue or are bothersome:

More common

Dizziness or lightheadedness; drowsiness; dryness of mouth

Less common or rare

Bloated feeling or gas, indigestion, nausea or vomiting, or stomach cramps or pain; blurred vision; constipation; decrease in blood pressure; diarrhea; excitement or nervousness; frequent urination; general feeling of discomfort or illness; headache; muscle twitching; numbness, tingling, pain, or weakness in hands or feet; pounding heartbeat; problems in speaking; trembling; trouble in sleeping; unpleasant taste or other taste changes; unusual muscle weakness; unusual tiredness

Other side effects not listed above may also occur in some patients. If you notice any other effects, check with your doctor.

Additional Information

Once a medicine has been approved for marketing for a certain use, experience may show that it is also useful for other medical problems. Although this use is not included in product labeling, cyclobenzaprine is used in certain patients with fibromyalgia syndrome (also called fibrositis or fibrositis syndrome).

There is no additional information relating to proper use, precautions, or side effects for this use of cyclobenzaprine.

Revised: 07/28/94

CYCLOPENTOLATE Ophthalmic

Some commonly used brand names are:

In the U.S.—

Ak-Pentolate
Cyclogyl
I-Pentolate
Ocu-Pentolate
Pentolair
Spectro-Pentolate

Generic name product may also be available.

In Canada

Ak-Pentolate
Cyclogyl
Minims Cyclopentolate

Description

Cyclopentolate (sye-kloe-PEN-toe-late) is used to dilate (enlarge) the pupil. It is used before eye examinations (such as cycloplegic refraction or ophthalmoscopy), before or after certain eye surgery, and to treat certain eye conditions.

This medicine is available only with your doctor's prescription, in the following dosage form:

Ophthalmic

- Ophthalmic solution (eye drops) (U.S. and Canada)

Before Using This Medicine

In deciding to use a medicine, the risks of using the medicine must be weighed against the good it will do. This is a decision you and your doctor will make. For cyclopentolate, the following should be considered:

Allergies—Tell your doctor if you have ever had any unusual or allergic reaction to cyclopentolate. Also tell your health care professional if you are allergic to any other substances, such as preservatives.

Pregnancy—Cyclopentolate may be absorbed into the body. However, studies on effects in pregnancy have not been done in either humans or animals.

Breast-feeding—Cyclopentolate may be absorbed into the mother's body. It is not known whether cyclopentolate passes into the breast milk. However, cyclopentolate has not been reported to cause problems in nursing babies.

Children—Infants and young children and children with blond hair or blue eyes may be especially sensitive to the effects of cyclopentolate. This may increase the chance of side effects during treatment.

Older adults—Elderly people are especially sensitive to the effects of cyclopentolate. This may increase the chance of side effects during treatment.

Other medicines—Although certain medicines should not be used together at all, in other cases two different medicines may be used together even if an interaction might occur. In these cases, your doctor may want to change the dose, or other precautions may be necessary. Tell your health care professional if you are using any other prescription or nonprescription (over-the-counter [OTC]) medicine.

Other medical problems—The presence of other medical problems may affect the use of cyclopentolate. Make sure

you tell your doctor if you have any other medical problems, especially:

- Brain damage (in children) or
- Down's syndrome (mongolism) (in children and adults) or
- Glaucoma or
- Spastic paralysis (in children)—Cyclopentolate may make the condition worse

Proper Use of This Medicine

To use:

- First, wash your hands. Tilt the head back and with the index finger of one hand, press gently on the skin just beneath the lower eyelid and pull the lower eyelid away from the eye to make a space. Drop the medicine into this space. Let go of the eyelid and gently close the eyes. Do not blink. Keep the eyes closed and apply pressure to the inner corner of the eye with your finger for 2 or 3 minutes, to allow the medicine to be absorbed. *This is especially important in infants.*
- Immediately after using the eye drops, wash your hands to remove any medicine that may be on them. If you are using the eye drops for an infant or child, be sure to wash the infant's or child's hands also, and do not let any of the medicine get in the infant's or child's mouth.
- To keep the medicine as germ-free as possible, do not touch the applicator tip to any surface (including the eye). Also, keep the container tightly closed.

Use this medicine only as directed. Do not use more of it and do not use it more often than your doctor ordered. To do so may increase the chance of too much medicine being absorbed into the body and the chance of side effects.

Dosing—The dose of cyclopentolate will be different for different patients. *Follow your doctor's orders or the directions on the label.* The following information includes only the average doses of cyclopentolate. *If your dose is different, do not change it unless your doctor tells you to do so.*

- For *ophthalmic solution (eye drops)* dosage form:
  - —For eye examinations:
    - Adults—One drop 40 to 50 minutes before the exam. Dose may be repeated in five to ten minutes.
    - Children—One drop 40 to 50 minutes before the exam. After five to ten minutes, another drop may be used.
    - Babies—One drop of 0.5% solution.

Missed dose—If you miss a dose of this medicine, apply it as soon as possible. However, if it is almost time for your next dose, skip the missed dose and go back to your regular dosing schedule. Do not double doses.

Storage—To store this medicine:

- Keep out of the reach of children. Overdose of this medicine is very dangerous for infants and children.
- Store away from heat and direct light.
- Keep the medicine from freezing.
- Do not keep outdated medicine or medicine no longer needed. Be sure that any discarded medicine is out of the reach of children.

Precautions While Using This Medicine

After you apply this medicine to your eyes:

- Your pupils will become unusually large and you will have blurring of vision, especially for close objects. *Make sure your vision is clear before you drive, use machines, or do anything else that could be dangerous if you are not able to see well.*
- Your eyes will become more sensitive to light than they are normally. When you go out during the daylight hours, even on cloudy days, *wear sunglasses that block ultraviolet (UV) light to protect your eyes from sunlight and other bright lights.* Ordinary sunglasses may not protect your eyes. If you have any questions about the kind of sunglasses to wear, check with your doctor.

If these side effects continue for longer than 36 hours after you have stopped using this medicine, check with your doctor.

Side Effects of This Medicine

Along with its needed effects, a medicine may cause some unwanted effects. Although not all of these side effects may occur, if they do occur they may need medical attention.

Check with your doctor as soon as possible if any of the following side effects occur:

Symptoms of too much medicine being absorbed into the body

Clumsiness or unsteadiness; confusion; fast or irregular heartbeat; fever; flushing or redness of face; hallucinations (seeing, hearing, or feeling things that are not there); skin rash; slurred speech; swollen stomach in infants; thirst or dryness of mouth; unusual behavior, especially in children; unusual drowsiness, tiredness, or weakness

Other side effects may occur that usually do not need medical attention. These side effects may go away during treatment as your body adjusts to the medicine. However, check with your doctor if any of the following side effects continue or are bothersome:

Blurred vision; burning of eye; eye irritation not present before therapy; increased sensitivity of eyes to light

Other side effects not listed above may also occur in some patients. If you notice any other effects, check with your doctor.

Additional Information

Once a medicine has been approved for marketing for a certain use, experience may show that it is also useful for

other medical problems. Although this use is not included in product labeling, cyclopentolate is used in certain patients with the following medical conditions:

- Posterior synechiae
- Uveitis

Other than the above information, there is no additional information relating to proper use, precautions, or side effects for these uses.

Revised: 03/04/92
Interim revision: 08/30/93

CYCLOPHOSPHAMIDE Systemic

Some commonly used brand names are:

In the U.S.—

Cytoxan	Neosar

Generic name product may also be available.

In Canada—

Cytoxan	Procytox

Description

Cyclophosphamide (sye-kloe-FOSS-fa-mide) belongs to the group of medicines called alkylating agents. It is used to treat some kinds of cancer.

Cyclophosphamide interferes with the growth of cancer cells, which are eventually destroyed. Since the growth of normal body cells may also be affected by cyclophosphamide, other effects will also occur. Some of these may be serious and must be reported to your doctor. Other effects, like hair loss, may not be serious but may cause concern. Some effects may not occur for months or years after the medicine is used.

Cyclophosphamide is also used for treatment of some kinds of kidney disease.

Cyclophosphamide may also be used for other conditions as determined by your doctor.

Before you begin treatment with cyclophosphamide, you and your doctor should talk about the good this medicine will do as well as the risks of using it.

Cyclophosphamide is available only with your doctor's prescription, in the following dosage forms:

Oral
- Oral solution (U.S. and Canada)
- Tablets (U.S. and Canada)

Parenteral
- Injection (U.S. and Canada)

Before Using This Medicine

In deciding to use a medicine, the risks of taking the medicine must be weighed against the good it will do. This is a decision you and your doctor will make. For cyclophosphamide, the following should be considered:

Allergies—Tell your doctor if you have ever had any unusual or allergic reaction to cyclophosphamide.

Pregnancy—This medicine may cause several different birth defects if either the male or female is taking it at the time of conception or if it is taken during pregnancy. In addition, many cancer medicines may cause sterility. Although sterility occurs commonly with cyclophosphamide, it is usually only temporary.

Be sure that you have discussed this with your doctor before taking this medicine. It is best to use some kind of birth control while you are taking cyclophosphamide. Tell your doctor right away if you think you have become pregnant while taking cyclophosphamide.

Breast-feeding—Cyclophosphamide passes into the breast milk. Because this medicine may cause serious side effects, breast-feeding is generally not recommended while you are taking it.

Children—This medicine has been tested in children and has not been shown to cause different side effects or problems than it does in adults.

Older adults—Many medicines have not been studied specifically in older people. Therefore, it may not be known whether they work exactly the same way they do in younger adults. Although there is no specific information comparing use of cyclophosphamide in the elderly with use in other age groups, it is not expected to cause different side effects or problems in older people than it does in younger adults.

Other medicines—Although certain medicines should not be used together at all, in other cases two different medicines may be used together even if an interaction might occur. In these cases, your doctor may want to change the dose, or other precautions may be necessary. When you are taking or receiving cyclophosphamide, it is especially important that your health care professional know if you are taking any of the following:

- Amphotericin B by injection (e.g., Fungizone) or
- Antithyroid agents (medicine for overactive thyroid) or
- Chloramphenicol (e.g., Chloromycetin) or
- Colchicine or
- Flucytosine (e.g., Ancobon) or
- Ganciclovir (e.g., Cytovene) or
- Interferon (e.g., Intron A, Roferon-A) or
- Plicamycin (e.g., Mithracin) or
- Zidovudine (e.g., AZT, Retrovir) or
- If you have ever been treated with radiation or cancer medicines—Cyclophosphamide may increase the effects of these medicines or radiation therapy on the blood
- Azathioprine (e.g., Imuran) or
- Chlorambucil (e.g., Leukeran) or
- Corticosteroids (cortisone-like medicine) or
- Cyclosporine (e.g., Sandimmune) or
- Mercaptopurine (e.g., Purinethol) or
- Muromonab-CD3 (monoclonal antibody) (e.g., Orthoclone OKT3)—There may be an increased risk of infection and development of cancer because cyclophosphamide reduces the body's ability to fight them
- Probenecid (e.g., Benemid) or

- Sulfinpyrazone (e.g., Anturane)—Cyclophosphamide may increase the amount of uric acid in the blood. Since these medicines are used to lower uric acid levels, they may not work as well in patients taking cyclophosphamide

Other medical problems—The presence of other medical problems may affect the use of cyclophosphamide. Make sure you tell your doctor if you have any other medical problems, especially:

- Chickenpox (including recent exposure) or
- Herpes zoster (shingles)—Risk of severe disease affecting other parts of the body
- Gout (history of) or
- Kidney stones—(history of)—Cyclophosphamide may increase levels of uric acid in the body, which can cause gout or kidney stones
- Infection—Cyclophosphamide can decrease your body's ability to fight infection
- Kidney disease—Effects of cyclophosphamide may be increased because of slower removal from the body
- Liver disease—The effect of cyclophosphamide may be decreased

Proper Use of This Medicine

Take this medicine only as directed by your doctor. Do not take more or less of it, and do not take it more often than your doctor ordered. The exact amount of medicine you need has been carefully worked out. Taking too much may increase the chance of side effects, while taking too little may not improve your condition.

Cyclophosphamide is sometimes given together with certain other medicines. If you are using a combination of medicines, make sure that you take each one at the proper time and do not mix them. Ask your health care professional to help you plan a way to remember to take your medicines at the right times.

While you are using cyclophosphamide, it is important that you drink extra fluids so that you will pass more urine. Also, empty your bladder frequently, including at least once during the night. This will help prevent kidney and bladder problems and keep your kidneys working well. Cyclophosphamide passes from the body in the urine. If too much of it appears in the urine or if the urine stays in the bladder too long, it can cause dangerous irritation. *Follow your doctor's instructions carefully about how much fluid to drink every day.* Some patients may have to drink up to 7 to 12 cups (3 quarts) of fluid a day.

Usually it is best to take cyclophosphamide first thing in the morning, to reduce the risk of bladder problems. However, your doctor may want you to take it with food in smaller doses over the day, to lessen stomach upset or help the medicine work better. Follow your doctor's instructions carefully about when to take cyclophosphamide.

Cyclophosphamide often causes nausea, vomiting, and loss of appetite. However, it is very important that you continue to use the medicine even if you begin to feel ill. *Do not stop taking this medicine without first checking with your doctor.* Ask your health care professional for ways to lessen these effects.

If you vomit shortly after taking a dose of cyclophosphamide, check with your doctor. You will be told whether to take the dose again or to wait until the next scheduled dose.

Dosing—The dose of cyclophosphamide will be different for different patients. The dose that is used may depend on a number of things, including what the medicine is being used for, the patient's weight, whether the medicine is being given by mouth or by injection, and whether or not other medicines are also being taken. *If you are taking or receiving cyclophosphamide at home, follow your doctor's orders or the directions on the label.* If you have any questions about the proper dose of cyclophosphamide, ask your doctor.

Missed dose—If you miss a dose of this medicine, do not take the missed dose at all and do not double the next one. Instead, go back to your regular dosing schedule and check with your doctor.

Storage—To store this medicine:

- Keep out of the reach of children.
- Store away from heat and direct light.
- Do not store in the bathroom, near the kitchen sink, or in other damp places. Heat or moisture may cause the medicine to break down.
- Store the oral solution form of this medicine in the refrigerator. Keep it from freezing.
- Do not keep outdated medicine or medicine no longer needed. Be sure that any discarded medicine is out of the reach of children.

Precautions While Using This Medicine

It is very important that your doctor check your progress at regular visits to make sure that this medicine is working properly and to check for unwanted effects.

While you are being treated with cyclophosphamide, and after you stop treatment with it, *do not have any immunizations (vaccinations) without your doctor's approval.* Cyclophosphamide may lower your body's resistance and there is a chance you might get the infection the immunization is meant to prevent. In addition, other persons living in your house should not take oral polio vaccine since there is a chance they could pass the polio virus on to you. Also, avoid persons who have recently taken oral polio vaccine. Do not get close to them, and do not stay in the same room with them for very long. If you cannot take these precautions, you should consider wearing a protective face mask that covers the nose and mouth.

Before having any kind of surgery, including dental surgery, or emergency treatment, make sure the medical doctor or dentist in charge knows that you are taking this medicine, especially if you have taken it within the last 10 days.

Cyclophosphamide can temporarily lower the number of white blood cells in your blood, increasing the chance of getting an infection. It can also lower the number of platelets, which are necessary for proper blood clotting. If this occurs, there are certain precautions you can take, especially when your blood count is low, to reduce the risk of infection or bleeding:

- If you can, avoid people with infections. *Check with your doctor immediately* if you think you are getting an infection or if you get a fever or chills, cough or hoarseness, lower back or side pain, or painful or difficult urination.
- *Check with your doctor immediately* if you notice any unusual bleeding or bruising; black, tarry stools; blood in urine or stools; or pinpoint red spots on your skin.
- Be careful when using a regular toothbrush, dental floss, or toothpick. Your medical doctor, dentist, or nurse may recommend other ways to clean your teeth and gums. Check with your medical doctor before having any dental work done.
- Do not touch your eyes or the inside of your nose unless you have just washed your hands and have not touched anything else in the meantime.
- Be careful not to cut yourself when you are using sharp objects such as a safety razor or fingernail or toenail cutters.
- Avoid contact sports or other situations where bruising or injury could occur.

Before you have any medical tests, tell the medical doctor in charge that you are taking this medicine. The results of some tests may be affected by this medicine.

Side Effects of This Medicine

Along with its needed effects, a medicine may cause some unwanted effects. Although not all of these side effects may occur, if they do occur they may need medical attention.

Also, because of the way these medicines act on the body, there is a chance that they might cause other unwanted effects that may not occur until months or years after the medicine is used. These may include certain types of cancer, such as leukemia or bladder cancer. Discuss these possible effects with your doctor.

Stop taking this medicine and check with your doctor immediately if the following side effects occur:

With high doses and/or long-term treatment

Blood in urine; painful urination

Check with your doctor or nurse immediately if any of the following side effects occur:

Less common

Cough or hoarseness; fever or chills; lower back or side pain; painful or difficult urination

Rare

Black, tarry stools; blood in urine or stools; pinpoint red spots on skin; shortness of breath (sudden); unusual bleeding or bruising

Check with your doctor as soon as possible if any of the following side effects occur:

More common

Dizziness, confusion, or agitation; missing menstrual periods; unusual tiredness or weakness

Less common

Fast heartbeat; joint pain; shortness of breath; swelling of feet or lower legs

Rare

Frequent urination; redness, swelling, or pain at place of injection; sores in mouth and on lips; unusual thirst; yellow eyes or skin

Other side effects may occur that usually do not need medical attention. These side effects may go away during treatment as your body adjusts to the medicine. Also, your health care professional may be able to tell you about ways to prevent or reduce some of these side effects. Check with your health care professional if any of the following side effects continue or are bothersome or if you have any questions about them:

More common

Darkening of skin and fingernails; loss of appetite; nausea or vomiting

Less common

Diarrhea or stomach pain; flushing or redness of face; headache; increased sweating; skin rash, hives, or itching; swollen lips

Cyclophosphamide may cause a temporary loss of hair in some people. After treatment has ended, normal hair growth should return, although the new hair may be a slightly different color or texture.

After you stop using cyclophosphamide, it may still produce some side effects that need attention. During this period of time, *check with your doctor immediately* if you notice the following side effect:

Blood in urine

Other side effects not listed above may also occur in some patients. If you notice any other effects, check with your doctor.

Additional Information

Once a medicine has been approved for marketing for a certain use, experience may show that it is also useful for other medical problems. Although these uses are not included in product labeling, cyclophosphamide is used in certain patients with the following medical conditions:

- Organ transplant rejection (prevention)
- Rheumatoid arthritis
- Wegener's granulomatosis
- Systemic lupus erythematosus
- Systemic dermatomyositis or
- Multiple sclerosis

Other than the above information, there is no additional information relating to proper use, precautions, or side effects for these uses.

Revised: 07/11/94

CYCLOSERINE Systemic†

A commonly used brand name is Seromycin.

†Not commercially available in Canada.

Description

Cycloserine (sye-kloe-SER-een) belongs to the family of medicines called antibiotics. It is used to treat tuberculosis (TB). When cycloserine is used for TB, it is given with other medicines for TB. Cycloserine may also be used for other conditions as determined by your doctor.

To help clear up your tuberculosis (TB) completely, you must keep taking this medicine for the full time of treatment, even if you begin to feel better. This is very important. It is also important that you do not miss any doses.

Cycloserine is available only with your doctor's prescription, in the following dosage form:

Oral

- Capsules (U.S.)

Before Using This Medicine

In deciding to use a medicine, the risks of taking the medicine must be weighed against the good it will do. This is a decision you and your doctor will make. For cycloserine, the following should be considered:

Allergies—Tell your doctor if you have ever had any unusual or allergic reaction to cycloserine. Also, tell your health care professional if you are allergic to any other substances, such as foods, preservatives, or dyes.

Pregnancy—Cycloserine has not been shown to cause birth defects or other problems in humans.

Breast-feeding—Cycloserine passes into the breast milk. However, cycloserine has not been reported to cause problems in nursing babies.

Children—Although there is no specific information comparing use of cycloserine in children with use in other age groups, this medicine is not expected to cause different side effects or problems in children than it does in adults.

Older adults—Many medicines have not been studied specifically in older people. Therefore, it may not be known whether they work exactly the same way they do in younger adults. Although there is no specific information comparing use of cycloserine in the elderly with use in other age groups, this medicine is not expected to cause different side effects or problems in older people than it does in younger adults.

Other medicines—Although certain medicines should not be used together at all, in other cases two different medicines may be used together even if an interaction might occur. In these cases, your doctor may want to change the dose, or other precautions may be necessary. When you are taking cycloserine, it is especially important that your health care professional know if you are taking the following:

- Ethionamide (e.g., Trecator-SC)—Ethionamide may increase the risk of nervous system side effects, especially seizures

Other medical problems—The presence of other medical problems may affect the use of cycloserine. Make sure you tell your doctor if you have any other medical problems, especially:

- Alcohol abuse (or history of) or
- Convulsive disorders such as seizures or epilepsy—Cycloserine may increase the risk of seizures in patients who drink alcohol or have a history of seizures
- Kidney disease—Cycloserine is removed from the body through the kidneys, and patients with kidney disease may need an adjustment in dose or the medicine may need to be discontinued
- Mental disorders such as mental depression, psychosis, or severe anxiety—Cycloserine may cause anxiety, mental depression, or psychosis

Proper Use of This Medicine

Cycloserine may be taken after meals if it upsets your stomach.

To help clear up your infection completely, *it is very important that you keep taking this medicine for the full time of treatment,* even if you begin to feel better after a few weeks. If you are taking this medicine for TB, you may have to take it every day for as long as 1 to 2 years or more. If you stop taking this medicine too soon, your symptoms may return.

This medicine works best when there is a constant amount in the blood or urine. *To help keep the amount constant, do not miss any doses. Also, it is best to take the doses at evenly spaced times day and night.* For example, if you are to take 2 doses a day, the doses should be spaced about 12 hours apart. If this interferes with your sleep or other daily activities, or if you need help in planning the best times to take your medicine, check with your health care professional.

Dosing—The dose of cycloserine will be different for different patients. *Follow your doctor's orders or the directions on the label.* The following information includes only the average doses of cycloserine. *If your dose is different, do not change it* unless your doctor tells you to do so.

- For the *oral* dosage form (capsules):
  - —For treatment of tuberculosis:
    - Adults and teenagers—250 milligrams (mg) two times a day to start. Your doctor may slowly increase your dose up to 250 mg three or four times a day. This medicine must be taken along with other medicines to treat tuberculosis.
    - Children—Use and dose must be determined by your doctor. Doses of 10 to 20 mg per kilogram (4.5 to 9.1 mg per pound) of body weight per day have been used. This medicine must be taken along with other medicines to treat tuberculosis.

Missed dose—If you do miss a dose of this medicine, take it as soon as possible. This will help to keep a constant amount of medicine in the blood or urine. However, if it is almost time for your next dose, skip the missed dose and go back to your regular dosing schedule. Do not double doses.

Storage—To store this medicine:
- Keep out of the reach of children.
- Store away from heat and direct light.
- Do not store in the bathroom, near the kitchen sink, or in other damp places. Heat or moisture may cause the medicine to break down.
- Do not keep outdated medicine or medicine no longer needed. Be sure that any discarded medicine is out of the reach of children.

Precautions While Using This Medicine

It is very important that your doctor check your progress at regular visits.

If your symptoms do not improve within 2 to 3 weeks, or if they become worse, check with your doctor.

If cycloserine causes you to feel very depressed or to have thoughts of suicide, check with your doctor immediately. Your doctor will probably want to change your medicine.

This medicine may cause some people to become dizzy, drowsy, or less alert than they are normally. *Make sure you know how you react to this medicine before you drive, use machines, or do anything else that could be dangerous if you are dizzy or are not alert.* If these reactions are especially bothersome, check with your doctor.

Some of cycloserine's side effects (for example, convulsions [seizures]) may be more likely to occur if you drink alcoholic beverages regularly while you are taking this medicine. Therefore, *you should not drink alcoholic beverages while you are taking this medicine.*

Side Effects of This Medicine

Along with its needed effects, a medicine may cause some unwanted effects. Although not all of these side effects may occur, if they do occur they may need medical attention.

Check with your doctor immediately if any of the following side effects occur:

More common
: Anxiety; confusion; dizziness; drowsiness; increased irritability; increased restlessness; mental depression; muscle twitching or trembling; nervousness; nightmares; other mood or mental changes; speech problems; thoughts of suicide

Less common
: Convulsions (seizures); numbness, tingling, burning pain, or weakness in the hands or feet; skin rash

Other side effects may occur that usually do not need medical attention. These side effects may go away during treatment as your body adjusts to the medicine. However, check with your doctor if the following side effect continues or is bothersome:

More common
: Headache

Other side effects not listed above may also occur in some patients. If you notice any other effects, check with your doctor.

Additional Information

Once a medicine has been approved for marketing for a certain use, experience may show that it is also useful for other medical problems. Although this use is not included in product labeling, ethambutol is used in certain patients with the following medical condition:
- Atypical mycobacterial infections, such as *Mycobacterium avium* complex (MAC)

Other than the above information, there is no additional information relating to proper use, precautions, or side effects for this use.

Revised: 05/02/94

CYCLOSPORINE Systemic

A commonly used brand name in the U.S. and Canada is Sandimmune. Some other commonly used names are ciclosporin and cyclosporin A.

Description

Cyclosporine (SYE-kloe-spor-een) belongs to the group of medicines known as immunosuppressive agents. It is used to reduce the body's natural immunity in patients who receive organ (for example, kidney, liver, and heart) transplants.

When a patient receives an organ transplant, the body's white blood cells will try to get rid of (reject) the transplanted organ. Cyclosporine works by preventing the white blood cells from doing this.

Cyclosporine may also be used for other conditions, as determined by your doctor.

Cyclosporine is a very strong medicine. It may cause side effects that could be very serious, such as high blood pressure and kidney and liver problems. It may also reduce the body's ability to fight infections. You and your doctor should talk about the good this medicine will do as well as the risks of using it.

Cyclosporine is available only with your doctor's prescription, in the following dosage forms:

Oral
- Capsules (U.S. and Canada)
- Oral solution (U.S. and Canada)

Parenteral
- Injection (U.S. and Canada)

Before Using This Medicine

In deciding to use a medicine, the risks of taking the medicine must be weighed against the good it will do. This is

a decision you and your doctor will make. For cyclosporine, the following should be considered:

Allergies—Tell your doctor if you have ever had any unusual or allergic reaction to cyclosporine.

Pregnancy—Studies have not been done in humans. However, studies in rats and rabbits have shown that cyclosporine at toxic doses (2 to 5 times the human dose) causes birth defects or death of the fetus.

Breast-feeding—Cyclosporine passes into breast milk. There is a chance that it could cause the same side effects in the baby that it does in people taking it. It may be necessary for you to stop breast-feeding during treatment. Be sure you have discussed the risks and benefits of the medicine with your doctor.

Children—This medicine has been tested in children and, in effective doses, has not been shown to cause different side effects or problems than it does in adults.

Older adults—Many medicines have not been studied specifically in older people. Therefore, it may not be known whether they work exactly the same way they do in younger adults. Although there is no specific information comparing use of cyclosporine in the elderly with use in other age groups, this medicine is not expected to cause different side effects or problems in older people than it does in younger adults.

Other medicines—Although certain medicines should not be used together at all, in other cases two different medicines may be used together even if an interaction might occur. In these cases, your doctor may want to change the dose, or other precautions may be necessary. When you are taking cyclosporine, it is especially important that your health care professional knows if you are taking any of the following:

- Amiloride or
- Spironolactone (e.g., Aldactone) or
- Triamterene (e.g., Dyrenium)—Since both cyclosporine and these medicines increase the amount of potassium in the body, potassium levels could become too high
- Androgens (male hormones) or
- Cimetidine (e.g., Tagamet) or
- Danazol (e.g., Danocrine) or
- Diltiazem (e.g., Cardizem) or
- Erythromycins (medicine for infection) or
- Estrogens (female hormones) or
- Ketoconazole (e.g., Nizoral)—May increase effects of cyclosporine by increasing the amount of this medicine in the body
- Azathioprine (e.g., Imuran) or
- Chlorambucil (e.g., Leukeran) or
- Corticosteroids (cortisone-like medicine) or
- Cyclophosphamide (e.g., Cytoxan) or
- Mercaptopurine (e.g., Purinethol) or
- Muromonab-CD3 (monoclonal antibody) (e.g., Orthoclone OKT3)—There may be an increased risk of infection and cancer because both cyclosporine and these medicines decrease the body's ability to fight them
- Lovastatin (e.g., Mevacor)—May increase the risk of kidney problems

Other medical problems—The presence of other medical problems may affect the use of cyclosporine. Make sure you tell your doctor if you have any other medical problems, especially:

- Chickenpox (including recent exposure) or
- Herpes zoster (shingles)—Risk of severe disease affecting other parts of the body
- Infection—Cyclosporine decreases the body's ability to fight infection
- Intestine problems—Effects may be decreased because cyclosporine cannot be absorbed into the body
- Kidney disease—Cyclosporine can have harmful effects on the kidney when it is taken for long periods of time
- Liver disease—Effects of cyclosporine may be increased because of slower removal from the body

Proper Use of This Medicine

Take this medicine only as directed by your doctor. Do not take more or less of it and do not take it more often than your doctor ordered. The exact amount of medicine you need has been carefully worked out. Taking too much may increase the chance of side effects, while taking too little may not improve your condition.

To help you remember to take your medicine, try to get into the habit of taking it at the same time each day. This will also help cyclosporine work better by keeping a constant amount in the blood.

This medicine is to be taken by mouth even if it comes in a dropper bottle. The amount you should take is to be measured only with the specially marked dropper provided with your prescription. The dropper should be wiped with a clean towel after it is used, and stored in its container. If the dropper needs to be cleaned, make sure it is completely dry before using it again.

To make cyclosporine taste better, mix it in a glass container with milk, chocolate milk, or orange juice (preferably at room temperature). Do not use a wax-lined or plastic disposable container. Stir it well, then drink it immediately. After drinking all the liquid containing the medicine, rinse the glass with a little more liquid and drink that also, to make sure you get all the medicine. Dry the dropper used to measure the cyclosporine, but do not rinse it with water.

If this medicine upsets your stomach, your doctor may recommend that you take it with meals. However, check with your doctor before you decide to do this on your own.

Do not stop taking this medicine without first checking with your doctor. You may have to take medicine for the rest of your life to prevent your body from rejecting the transplant.

Dosing—The dose of cyclosporine will be different for different patients. *Follow your doctor's orders or the directions on the label.* The following information includes only the average doses of cyclosporine. *If your dose is different, do not change it* unless your doctor tells you to do so.

The number of capsules or teaspoonfuls of oral solution that you take depends on the strength of the medicine. Also, *the number of doses you take each day, the time allowed between doses, and the length of time you take the medicine depend on the medical problem for which you are taking cyclosporine.*

- For *oral* dosage forms (capsules, oral solution):
  - —For transplant rejection:
    - Adults, teenagers, or children: Dose is based on body weight. The usual dose in the beginning is 12 to 15 milligrams (mg) per kilogram (kg) (5.5 to 6.8 mg per pound) a day. After a period of time, the dose may be decreased to 5 to 10 mg per kg (2.3 to 4.5 mg per pound) a day.
- For *injection* dosage form:
  - —For transplant rejection:
    - Adults, teenagers, or children: Dose is based on body weight. The usual dose is 2 to 6 mg per kg (0.9 to 2.7 mg per pound) a day.

Missed dose—If you miss a dose of cyclosporine and remember it within 12 hours, take the missed dose as soon as you remember. However, if it is almost time for the next dose, skip the missed dose, go back to your regular dosing schedule, and check with your doctor. Do not double doses.

Storage—To store this medicine:

- Keep out of the reach of children.
- Store away from heat and direct light.
- Do not store in the bathroom, near the kitchen sink, or in other damp places. Heat or moisture may cause the medicine to break down.
- Do not store the oral solution in the refrigerator.
- Do not keep outdated medicine or medicine no longer needed. Be sure that any discarded medicine is out of the reach of children.

Precautions While Using This Medicine

It is very important that your doctor check your progress at regular visits. Your doctor will want to do laboratory tests to make sure that cyclosporine is working properly and to check for unwanted effects.

While you are being treated with cyclosporine, and after you stop treatment with it, *do not have any immunizations (vaccinations) without your doctor's approval.* Cyclosporine lowers your body's resistance and there is a chance you might get the infection the immunization is meant to prevent. In addition, other persons living in your house should not take oral polio vaccine since there is a chance they could pass the polio virus on to you. Also, avoid persons who have recently taken oral polio vaccine. Do not get close to them, and do not stay in the same room with them for very long. If you cannot take these precautions, you should consider wearing a protective face mask that covers the nose and mouth.

In some patients (usually younger patients), tenderness, swelling, or bleeding of the gums may appear soon after treatment with cyclosporine is started. Brushing and flossing your teeth carefully and regularly and massaging your gums may help prevent this. *See your dentist regularly to have your teeth cleaned. Check with your medical doctor or dentist if you have any questions about how to take care of your teeth and gums, or if you notice any tenderness, swelling, or bleeding of your gums.*

Side Effects of This Medicine

Along with its needed effects, a medicine may cause some unwanted effects. Some side effects will have signs or symptoms that you can see or feel. Your doctor will watch for others by doing certain tests.

Also, because of the way that cyclosporine acts on the body, there is a chance that it may cause effects that may not occur until years after the medicine is used. These delayed effects may include certain types of cancer, such as lymphomas or skin cancers. You and your doctor should discuss the good this medicine will do as well as the risks of using it.

Check with your doctor or nurse immediately if any of the following side effects occur:

Less common

Fever or chills; frequent urge to urinate

Rare

Blood in urine; flushing of face and neck (for injection only); wheezing or shortness of breath (for injection only)

Check with your doctor as soon as possible if any of the following side effects occur:

More common

Bleeding, tender, or enlarged gums

Less common

Convulsions (seizures)

Rare

Confusion; irregular heartbeat; numbness or tingling in hands, feet, or lips; shortness of breath or difficult breathing; stomach pain (severe) with nausea and vomiting; unexplained nervousness; unusual tiredness or weakness; weakness or heaviness of legs

This medicine may also cause the following side effects that your doctor will watch for:

More common

High blood pressure; kidney problems

Less common

Liver problems

Other side effects may occur that usually do not need medical attention. These side effects may go away during treatment as your body adjusts to the medicine. However, check with your doctor if any of the following side effects continue or are bothersome:

More common

Increase in hair growth; trembling and shaking of hands

Less common

Acne or oily skin; headache; leg cramps; nausea or vomiting

Other side effects not listed above may also occur in some patients. If you notice any other effects, check with your doctor.

Revised: 06/09/93
Interim revision: 05/12/94

CYSTEAMINE Systemic†

A commonly used brand name in the U.S. is Cystagon.

†Not commercially available in Canada.

Description

Cysteamine (SIS-tee-a-meen) is used to prevent damage that may be caused by the buildup of cystine crystals in organs such as the kidneys. This medicine works by removing the extra cystine from the cells of the body.

Oral

- Capsules (U.S.)

Before Using This Medicine

In deciding to use a medicine, the risks of taking the medicine must be weighed against the good it will do. This is a decision you and your doctor will make. For cysteamine, the following should be considered:

Allergies—Tell your health care professional if you have ever had any unusual or allergic reaction to cysteamine or penicillamine. Also tell your health care professional if you are allergic to any other substances, such as foods, preservatives, or dyes.

Pregnancy—Cysteamine has not been studied in pregnant women. However, studies in animals have shown that cysteamine causes a decrease in fertility and a decrease in survival of their offspring. Before taking this medicine, make sure your health care professional knows if you are pregnant or if you may become pregnant.

Breast-feeding—It is not known whether cysteamine passes into breast milk. Since cysteamine has been reported to cause problems in nursing animals, it may be necessary for you to stop taking this medicine or to stop breast-feeding during treatment.

Children—This medicine has been tested in children and, in effective doses, has not been shown to cause different side effects or problems than it does in adults.

Older adults—Many medicines have not been studied specifically in older people. Therefore, it may not be known whether they work exactly the same way they do in younger adults or if they cause different side effects or problems in older people. There is no specific information comparing use of cysteamine in the elderly with use in other age groups.

Other medical problems—The presence of other medical problems may affect the use of cysteamine. Make sure you tell your doctor if you have any other medical problems, especially:

- Blood problems (or a history of) or
- Convulsions (seizures) or
- Liver disease—Cysteamine may make these conditions worse

Proper Use of This Medicine

If you vomit your dose of cysteamine within 20 minutes of taking it, take the dose again. However, if you vomit the dose a second time, do not repeat the dose but wait and take your next dose as scheduled. Also, if vomiting occurs more than 20 minutes after you take your dose, do not repeat the dose.

It is important that you follow any special instructions from your doctor, such as taking dietary supplements. These supplements will replace minerals lost through the kidneys.

For children under 6 years of age, the capsule may be opened and the contents of the capsule sprinkled on food or mixed in formula.

Dosing—The dose of cysteamine will be different for different patients. *Follow your health care professional's orders or the directions on the label.* The following information includes only the average doses of cysteamine. *If your dose is different, do not change it* unless your health care professional tells you to do so.

- For *oral* dosage form (capsules):
  - —To prevent buildup of cystine crystals in the kidney:
    - Adults and teenagers—The starting dose must be determined by your doctor. Your doctor may gradually increase your dose.
    - Children—The starting dose is based on body size and must be determined by your doctor. Your doctor may gradually increase your dose.

Missed dose—If you miss a dose of this medicine, take it as soon as possible. However, if it is almost time for your next dose, skip the missed dose and go back to your regular dosing schedule. Do not double doses.

Storage—To store this medicine:

- Keep out of the reach of children.
- Store away from heat and direct light.
- Do not store in the bathroom, near the kitchen sink, or in other damp places. Heat or moisture may cause the medicine to break down.
- Keep the medicine from freezing. Do not refrigerate.
- Do not keep outdated medicine or medicine no longer needed. Be sure that any discarded medicine is out of the reach of children.

Precautions While Using This Medicine

Your doctor should check your progress at regular visits to make sure that this medicine is working properly and does not cause unwanted effects.

This medicine may cause some people to become dizzy or drowsy. Make sure you know how you react to this medicine before you drive, use machines, or do anything else that could be dangerous if you are dizzy or are not alert.

Side Effects of This Medicine

Along with its needed effects, a medicine may cause some unwanted effects. Although not all of these side effects may occur, if they do occur they may need medical attention.

Check with your doctor as soon as possible if any of the following side effects occur:

More common
Abdominal pain, diarrhea, drowsiness, fever, loss of appetite, nausea or vomiting, skin rash

Less common
Confusion, dizziness, headache, mental depression, sore throat, trembling

Rare
Convulsions (seizures), increased thirst, unusual tiredness or weakness

Other side effects may occur that usually do not need medical attention. These side effects may go away during treatment as your body adjusts to the medicine. However, check with your doctor if any of the following side effects continue or are bothersome:

Less common
Breath odor, constipation

Other side effects not listed above may also occur in some patients. If you notice any other effects, check with your doctor.

Developed: 01/31/96

CYTARABINE Systemic

Some commonly used brand names are:

In the U.S.
Cytosar-U

Generic name product may also be available.

In Canada
Cytosar

Other commonly used names are ara-C and cytosine arabinoside.

Description

Cytarabine (sye-TARE-a-been) belongs to the group of medicines called antimetabolites. It is used to treat some kinds of cancer.

Cytarabine interferes with the growth of cancer cells, which are eventually destroyed. Since the growth of normal body cells may also be affected by cytarabine, other effects will also occur. Some of these may be serious and must be reported to your doctor. Other effects, like hair loss, may not be serious but may cause concern. Some effects may not occur for months or years after the medicine is used.

Before you begin treatment with cytarabine, you and your doctor should talk about the good this medicine will do as well as the risks of using it.

Cytarabine is to be administered only by or under the immediate supervision of your doctor. It is available in the following dosage form:

Parenteral
- Injection (U.S. and Canada)

Before Using This Medicine

In deciding to use a medicine, the risks of taking the medicine must be weighed against the good it will do. This is a decision you and your doctor will make. For cytarabine, the following should be considered:

Allergies—Tell your doctor if you have ever had any unusual or allergic reaction to cytarabine.

Pregnancy—This medicine may cause birth defects (such as defects of the arms, legs, or ears, which occurred in two babies) if either the male or female is taking it at the time of conception or if it is taken during pregnancy. In addition, many cancer medicines may cause sterility. Although sterility has been reported with this medicine, it is usually only temporary.

Be sure that you have discussed this with your doctor before taking this medicine. It is best to use some kind of birth control while you are receiving cytarabine. Tell your doctor right away if you think you have become pregnant while receiving cytarabine.

Breast-feeding—Because cytarabine may cause serious side effects, breast-feeding is generally not recommended while you are receiving it.

Children—Although there is no specific information comparing use of cytarabine in children with use in other age groups, this medicine is not expected to cause different side effects or problems in children than it does in adults.

Older adults—Many medicines have not been studied specifically in older people. Therefore, it may not be known whether they work exactly the same way they do in younger adults. Although there is no specific information comparing use of cytarabine in the elderly with use in other age groups, this medicine is not expected to cause different side effects or problems in older people than it does in younger adults.

Other medicines—Although certain medicines should not be used together at all, in other cases two different medicines may be used together even if an interaction might occur. In these cases, your doctor may want to change the dose, or other precautions may be necessary. When you are receiving cytarabine, it is especially important that your health care professional know if you are taking any of the following:

- Amphotericin B by injection (e.g., Fungizone) or
- Antithyroid agents (medicine for overactive thyroid) or
- Azathioprine (e.g., Imuran) or
- Chloramphenicol (e.g., Chloromycetin) or
- Colchicine or
- Flucytosine (e.g., Ancobon) or
- Ganciclovir (e.g., Cytovene) or
- Interferon (e.g., Intron A, Roferon-A) or
- Plicamycin (e.g., Mithracin) or
- Zidovudine (e.g., AZT, Retrovir) or

- If you have ever been treated with radiation or cancer medicines—Cytarabine may increase the effects of these medicines or radiation therapy on the blood
- Azathioprine (e.g., Imuran) or
- Chlorambucil (e.g., Leukeran) or
- Corticosteroids (cortisone-like medicine) or
- Cyclosporine (e.g., Sandimmune) or
- Mercaptopurine (e.g., Purinethol) or
- Muromonab-CD3 (monoclonal antibody) (e.g., Orthoclone OKT3) or
- Tacrolimus (e.g., Prograf)—There may be an increased risk of infection because cytarabine decreases your body's ability to fight it
- Probenecid (e.g., Benemid) or
- Sulfinpyrazone (e.g., Anturane)—Cytarabine may raise the concentration of uric acid in the blood. Since these medicines are used to lower uric acid levels, they may not work as well in patients receiving cytarabine

Other medical problems—The presence of other medical problems may affect the use of cytarabine. Make sure you tell your doctor if you have any other medical problems, especially:

- Chickenpox (including recent exposure) or
- Herpes zoster (shingles)—Risk of severe disease affecting other parts of the body
- Gout (history of) or
- Kidney stones (history of)—Cytarabine may increase levels of uric acid in the body, which can cause gout or kidney stones
- Infection—Cytarabine can decrease your body's ability to fight infection
- Kidney disease or
- Liver disease—Effects of cytarabine may be increased because of slower removal from the body

Proper Use of This Medicine

This medicine is sometimes given together with certain other medicines. If you are using a combination of medicines, it is important that you receive each one at the proper time. If you are taking some of these medicines by mouth, ask your health care professional to help you plan a way to take them at the right times.

While you are receiving this medicine, your doctor may want you to drink extra fluids so that you will pass more urine. This will help prevent kidney problems and keep your kidneys working well.

This medicine often causes nausea and vomiting. However, it is very important that you continue to receive the medicine even if you begin to feel ill. Ask your health care professional for ways to lessen these effects.

Dosing—The dose of cytarabine will be different for different patients. The dose that is used may depend on a number of things, including what the medicine is being used for, the patient's weight, and whether or not other medicines are also being taken. *If you are receiving cytarabine at home, follow your doctor's orders or the directions on the label.* If you have any questions about the proper dose of cytarabine, ask your doctor.

Precautions While Using This Medicine

It is very important that your doctor check your progress at regular visits to make sure that this medicine is working properly and to check for unwanted effects.

While you are being treated with cytarabine, and after you stop treatment with it, *do not have any immunizations (vaccinations) without your doctor's approval.* Cytarabine may lower your body's resistance and there is a chance you might get the infection the immunization is meant to prevent. In addition, other persons living in your household should not take oral polio vaccine since there is a chance they could pass the polio virus on to you. Also, avoid persons who have taken oral polio vaccine. Do not get close to them and do not stay in the same room with them for very long. If you cannot take these precautions, you should consider wearing a protective face mask that covers the nose and mouth.

Cytarabine can temporarily lower the number of white blood cells in your blood, increasing the chance of getting an infection. It can also lower the number of platelets, which are necessary for proper blood clotting. If this occurs, there are certain precautions you can take, especially when your blood count is low, to reduce the risk of infection or bleeding:

- If you can, avoid people with infections. *Check with your doctor immediately* if you think you are getting an infection or if you get a fever or chills, cough or hoarseness, lower back or side pain, or painful or difficult urination.
- *Check with your doctor immediately* if you notice any unusual bleeding or bruising; black, tarry stools; blood in urine or stools; or pinpoint red spots on your skin.
- Be careful when using a regular toothbrush, dental floss, or toothpick. Your medical doctor, dentist, or nurse may recommend other ways to clean your teeth and gums. Check with your medical doctor before having any dental work done.
- Do not touch your eyes or the inside of your nose unless you have just washed your hands and have not touched anything else in the meantime.
- Be careful not to cut yourself when you are using sharp objects such as a safety razor or fingernail or toenail cutters.
- Avoid contact sports or other situations where bruising or injury could occur.

Side Effects of This Medicine

Along with its needed effects, a medicine may cause some unwanted effects. Although not all of these side effects may occur, if they do occur they may need medical attention.

Also, because of the way these medicines act on the body, there is a chance that they might cause other unwanted effects that may not occur until months or years after the medicine is used. These delayed effects may include certain types of cancer, such as leukemia. Discuss these possible effects with your doctor.

Check with your doctor or nurse immediately if any of the following side effects occur:

Less common

Black, tarry stools; blood in urine; cough or hoarseness; fever or chills; lower back or side pain; painful or difficult urination; pinpoint red spots on skin; unusual bleeding or bruising

Check with your health care professional as soon as possible if any of the following side effects occur:

More common
Sores in mouth and on lips

Less common
Joint pain; numbness or tingling in fingers, toes, or face; swelling of feet or lower legs; unusual tiredness

Rare
Bone or muscle pain; chest pain; decrease in urination; difficulty in swallowing; fainting spells; general feeling of discomfort or illness or weakness; heartburn; irregular heartbeat; pain at place of injection; reddened eyes; shortness of breath; skin rash; weakness; yellow eyes or skin

Other side effects may occur that usually do not need medical attention. These side effects may go away during treatment as your body adjusts to the medicine. Also, your health care professional may be able to tell you about ways to prevent or reduce some of these side effects. Check with your health care professional if any of the following side effects continue or are bothersome or if you have any questions about them:

More common
Loss of appetite; nausea and vomiting

Less common or rare
Diarrhea; dizziness; headache; itching of skin; skin freckling

This medicine may cause a temporary loss of hair in some people. After treatment with cytarabine has ended, normal hair growth should return.

After you stop receiving cytarabine, it may still produce some side effects that need attention. During this period of time check with your doctor if you notice any of the following:

Black, tarry stools; blood in urine or stools; cough or hoarseness; fever or chills; lower back or side pain; painful or difficult urination; pinpoint red spots on skin; unusual bleeding or bruising

Other side effects not listed above may also occur in some patients. If you notice any other effects, check with your doctor.

Revised: 07/15/94

DACARBAZINE Systemic

Some commonly used brand names are:

In the U.S.—
DTIC-Dome

Generic name product may also be available.

In Canada—
DTIC

Description

Dacarbazine (da-KAR-ba-zeen) belongs to the group of medicines called alkylating agents. It is used to treat some kinds of cancer.

Dacarbazine interferes with the growth of cancer cells, which are eventually destroyed. Since the growth of normal body cells may also be affected by dacarbazine, other effects will also occur. Some of these may be serious and must be reported to your doctor. Other effects, like hair loss, may not be serious but may cause concern. Some effects may not occur for months or years after the medicine is used.

Before you begin treatment with dacarbazine, you and your doctor should talk about the good this medicine will do as well as the risks of using it.

Dacarbazine is to be administered only by or under the immediate supervision of your doctor. It is available in the following dosage form:

Parenteral
- Injection (U.S. and Canada)

Before Using This Medicine

In deciding to use a medicine, the risks of taking the medicine must be weighed against the good it will do. This is a decision you and your doctor will make. For dacarbazine, the following should be considered:

Allergies—Tell your doctor if you have ever had any unusual or allergic reaction to dacarbazine.

Pregnancy—There is a chance that this medicine may cause birth defects if either the male or female is taking it at the time of conception or if it is taken during pregnancy. In addition, many cancer medicines may cause sterility, which could be permanent. Although sterility has not been reported with this medicine, the possibility should be kept in mind. Dacarbazine has caused birth defects and a decrease in successful pregnancies in animal studies involving rats and rabbits given doses several times the usual human adult dose.

Be sure that you have discussed this with your doctor before taking this medicine. It is best to use some kind of birth control while you are receiving dacarbazine. Tell your doctor right away if you think you have become pregnant while receiving dacarbazine.

Breast-feeding—It is not known whether dacarbazine passes into breast milk. However, because this medicine may cause serious side effects, breast-feeding is generally not recommended while you are receiving it.

Children—Studies on this medicine have been done only in adult patients and there is no specific information comparing use of dacarbazine in children with use in other age groups.

Older adults—Many medicines have not been studied specifically in older people. Therefore, it may not be known whether they work exactly the same way they do in younger adults or if they cause different side effects or problems in older people. There is no specific information about the use of dacarbazine in the elderly.

Other medicines—Although certain medicines should not be used together at all, in other cases two different medicines may be used together even if an interaction might occur. In these cases, your doctor may want to change the dose, or other precautions may be necessary. When receiving dacarbazine it is especially important that your health care professional know if you are taking any of the following:

- Amphotericin B by injection (e.g., Fungizone) or
- Antithyroid agents (medicine for overactive thyroid) or
- Azathioprine (e.g., Imuran) or
- Chloramphenicol (e.g., Chloromycetin) or
- Colchicine or
- Flucytosine (e.g., Ancobon) or
- Ganciclovir (e.g., Cytovene) or
- Interferon (e.g., Intron A, Roferon-A) or
- Plicamycin (e.g., Mithracin) or
- Zidovudine (e.g., AZT, Retrovir) or
- If you have ever been treated with radiation or cancer medicines—Dacarbazine may increase the effects of these medicines or radiation therapy on the blood

Other medical problems—The presence of other medical problems may affect the use of dacarbazine. Make sure you tell your doctor if you have any other medical problems, especially:

- Chickenpox (including recent exposure) or
- Herpes zoster (shingles)—Risk of severe disease affecting other parts of the body
- Infection—Dacarbazine can decrease your body's ability to fight infection
- Kidney disease or
- Liver disease—Effects of dacarbazine may be increased because of slower removal from the body

Proper Use of This Medicine

Dacarbazine is sometimes given together with certain other medicines. If you are using a combination of medicines, it is important that you receive each one at the proper time. If you are taking some of these medicines by mouth, ask your health care professional to help you plan a way to remember to take them at the right times.

This medicine often causes nausea, vomiting, and loss of appetite. The injection may also cause a feeling of burning or pain. However, it is very important that you continue to receive the medicine, even if you have discomfort or begin to feel ill. After 1 or 2 days, your stomach upset should lessen. Ask your health care professional for ways to lessen these effects.

Dosing—The dose of dacarbazine will be different for different patients. The dose that is used may depend on a number of things, including what the medicine is being used for, the patient's weight, and whether or not other medicines are also being taken. *If you are receiving dacarbazine at home, follow your doctor's orders or the directions on the label.* If you have any questions about the proper dose of dacarbazine, ask your doctor.

Precautions While Using This Medicine

It is very important that your doctor check your progress at regular visits to make sure that this medicine is working properly and to check for unwanted effects.

While you are being treated with dacarbazine, and after you stop treatment with it, *do not have any immunizations (vaccinations) without your doctor's approval.* Dacarbazine may lower your body's resistance and there is a chance you might get the infection the immunization is meant to prevent. In addition, other persons living in your household should not take oral polio vaccine since there is a chance they could pass the polio virus on to you. Also, avoid persons who have taken oral polio vaccine. Do not get close to them, and do not stay in the same room with them for very long. If you cannot take these precautions, you should consider wearing a protective face mask that covers the nose and mouth.

Dacarbazine can temporarily lower the number of white blood cells in your blood, increasing the chance of getting an infection. It can also lower the number of platelets, which are necessary for proper blood clotting. If this occurs, there are certain precautions you can take, especially when your blood count is low, to reduce the risk of infection or bleeding:

- If you can, avoid people with infections. *Check with your doctor immediately* if you think you are getting an infection or if you get a fever or chills, cough or hoarseness, lower back or side pain, or painful or difficult urination.
- *Check with your doctor immediately* if you notice any unusual bleeding or bruising; black, tarry stools; blood in urine or stools; or pinpoint red spots on your skin.
- Be careful when using a regular toothbrush, dental floss, or toothpick. Your medical doctor, dentist, or nurse may recommend other ways to clean your teeth and gums. Check with your medical doctor before having any dental work done.
- Do not touch your eyes or the inside of your nose unless you have just washed your hands and have not touched anything else in the meantime.
- Be careful not to cut yourself when you are using sharp objects such as a safety razor or fingernail or toenail cutters.
- Avoid contact sports or other situations where bruising or injury could occur.

If dacarbazine accidentally seeps out of the vein into which it is injected, it may damage some tissues and cause scarring. *Tell the doctor or nurse right away if you notice redness, pain, or swelling at the place of injection.*

Side Effects of This Medicine

Along with its needed effects, a medicine may cause some unwanted effects. Although not all of these side effects may occur, if they do occur they may need medical attention.

Also, because of the way these medicines act on the body, there is a chance that they might cause other unwanted effects that may not occur until months or years after the medicine is used. These delayed effects may include certain types of cancer, such as leukemia. Discuss these possible effects with your doctor.

Check with your doctor or nurse immediately if any of the following side effects occur:

More common

Redness, pain, or swelling at place of injection

Less common

Black, tarry stools; blood in urine or stools; cough or hoarseness; fever or chills; lower back or side pain; painful or difficult urination; pinpoint red spots on skin; unusual bleeding or bruising

Rare

Shortness of breath; stomach pain; swelling of face; yellow eyes or skin

Check with your health care professional as soon as possible if the following side effect occurs:

Rare

Sores in mouth and on lips

Other side effects may occur that usually do not need medical attention. These side effects may go away during treatment as your body adjusts to the medicine. Also, your health care professional may be able to tell you about ways to prevent or reduce some of these side effects. Check with your health care professional if any of the following side effects continue or are bothersome or if you have any questions about them:

More common

Loss of appetite; nausea or vomiting (should lessen after 1 or 2 days)

Less common

Feelings of uneasiness; flushing of face; muscle pain; numbness of face

This medicine may cause a temporary loss of hair in some people. After treatment with dacarbazine has ended, normal hair growth should return.

After you stop receiving dacarbazine, it may still produce some side effects that need attention. During this period of time check with your doctor if you notice any of the following:

Black, tarry stools; blood in urine or stools; cough or hoarseness; fever or chills; lower back or side pain; painful or difficult urination; pinpoint red spots on skin; unusual bleeding or bruising

Other side effects not listed above may also occur in some patients. If you notice any other effects, check with your doctor.

Revised: 07/11/94

DACTINOMYCIN Systemic

A commonly used brand name in the U.S. and Canada is Cosmegen. Another commonly used name is actinomycin-D.

Description

Dactinomycin (dak-ti-noe-MYE-sin) belongs to the group of medicines known as antineoplastics. It is used to treat some kinds of cancer.

Dactinomycin interferes with the growth of cancer cells, which are eventually destroyed. Since the growth of normal body cells may also be affected by dactinomycin, other effects will also occur. Some of these may be serious and must be reported to your doctor. Other effects, like hair loss, may not be serious but may cause concern. Some effects may not occur for months or years after the medicine is used.

Before you begin treatment with dactinomycin, you and your doctor should talk about the good this medicine will do as well as the risks of using it.

Dactinomycin is to be administered only by or under the immediate supervision of your doctor. It is available in the following dosage form:

Parenteral

- Injection (U.S. and Canada)

Before Using This Medicine

In deciding to use a medicine, the risks of taking the medicine must be weighed against the good it will do. This is a decision you and your doctor will make. For dactinomycin, the following should be considered:

Allergies—Tell your doctor if you have ever had any unusual or allergic reaction to dactinomycin.

Pregnancy—There is a chance that this medicine may cause birth defects if either the male or female is receiving it at the time of conception or if it is taken during pregnancy. Studies have shown that dactinomycin causes birth defects in animals. In addition, many cancer medicines may cause sterility which could be permanent. Although sterility has not been reported with this medicine, the possibility should be kept in mind.

Be sure that you have discussed this with your doctor before receiving this medicine. It is best to use some kind of birth control while you are receiving dactinomycin. Tell your doctor right away if you think you have become pregnant while receiving dactinomycin.

Breast-feeding—It is not known whether dactinomycin passes into breast milk. However, because this medicine may cause serious side effects, breast-feeding is generally not recommended while you are receiving it.

Children—Because of increased toxicity, use of dactinomycin in infants less than 6 to 12 months of age is not recommended.

Older adults—Many medicines have not been studied specifically in older people. Therefore, it may not be known whether they work exactly the same way they do in younger adults or if they cause different side effects or problems in older people. There is no specific information about the use of dactinomycin in the elderly.

Other medicines—Although certain medicines should not be used together at all, in other cases two different medicines may be used together even if an interaction might occur. In these cases, your doctor may want to change the dose, or other precautions may be necessary. When receiving dactinomycin it is especially important that your health care professional know if you are taking any of the following:

- Amphotericin B by injection (e.g., Fungizone) or
- Antithyroid agents (medicine for overactive thyroid) or
- Azathioprine (e.g., Imuran) or
- Chloramphenicol (e.g., Chloromycetin) or
- Flucytosine (e.g., Ancobon) or
- Ganciclovir (e.g., Cytovene) or
- Interferon (e.g., Intron A, Roferon-A) or
- Plicamycin (e.g., Mithramycin) or
- Zidovudine (e.g., AZT, Retrovir) or
- If you have ever been treated with radiation or cancer medicine—Dactinomycin may increase the effects of these medicines or radiation therapy on the blood
- Probenecid (e.g., Benemid) or
- Sulfinpyrazone (e.g., Anturane)—Dactinomycin may increase concentrations of uric acid in the blood. Since these medicines are used to lower uric acid levels, they may not be as effective in patients receiving dactinomycin

Other medical problems—The presence of other medical problems may affect the use of dactinomycin. Make sure you tell your doctor if you have any other medical problems, especially:

- Chickenpox (including recent exposure) or
- Herpes zoster (shingles)—Risk of severe disease affecting other parts of the body
- Gout (or history of) or
- Kidney stones—Dactinomycin may increase levels of uric acid in the body, which can cause gout or kidney stones
- Infection—Dactinomycin can decrease your body's ability to fight infection
- Liver disease—Effects of dactinomycin may be increased

Proper Use of This Medicine

Dactinomycin is sometimes given together with certain other medicines. If you are receiving a combination of medicines, it is important that you receive each one at the proper time. If you are taking some of these medicines by mouth, ask your health care professional to help you plan a way to remember to take them at the right times.

This medicine often causes nausea and vomiting. However, it is very important that you continue to receive the medicine, even if you begin to feel ill. Ask your health care professional for ways to lessen these effects.

Dosing—The dose of dactinomycin will be different for different patients. The dose that is used may depend on a number of things, including what the medicine is being used for, the patient's weight, and whether or not other medicines are also being taken. *If you are receiving dactinomycin at home, follow your doctor's orders or the di-*

rections on the label. If you have any questions about the proper dose of dactinomycin, ask your doctor.

Precautions While Using This Medicine

It is very important that your doctor check your progress at regular visits to make sure that this medicine is working properly and to check for unwanted effects.

While you are being treated with dactinomycin, and after you stop treatment with it, *do not have any immunizations (vaccinations) without your doctor's approval.* Dactinomycin may lower your body's resistance, and there is a chance you might get the infection the immunization is meant to prevent. In addition, other persons living in your household should not take oral polio vaccine since there is a chance they could pass the polio virus on to you. Also, avoid persons who have taken oral polio vaccine. Do not get close to them, and do not stay in the same room with them for very long. If you cannot take these precautions, you should consider wearing a protective face mask that covers the nose and mouth.

Dactinomycin can temporarily lower the number of white blood cells in your blood increasing the chance of getting an infection. It can also lower the number of platelets, which are necessary for proper blood clotting. If this occurs, there are certain precautions you can take, especially when your blood count is low, to reduce the risk of infection or bleeding:

- If you can, avoid people with infections. *Check with your doctor immediately* if you think you are getting an infection or if you get a fever or chills, cough or hoarseness, lower back or side pain, or painful or difficult urination.
- *Check with your doctor immediately* if you notice any unusual bleeding or bruising; black, tarry stools; blood in urine or stools; or pinpoint red spots on your skin.
- Be careful when using a regular toothbrush, dental floss, or toothpick. Your medical doctor, dentist, or nurse may recommend other ways to clean your teeth and gums. Check with your medical doctor before having any dental work done.
- Do not touch your eyes or the inside of your nose unless you have just washed your hands and have not touched anything else in the meantime.
- Be careful not to cut yourself when you are using sharp objects such as a safety razor or fingernail or toenail cutters.
- Avoid contact sports or other situations where bruising or injury could occur.

If dactinomycin accidentally seeps out of the vein into which it is injected, it may severely damage some tissues and cause scarring. *Tell your health care professional right away if you notice redness, pain, or swelling at the place of injection.*

Side Effects of This Medicine

Along with its needed effects, a medicine may cause some unwanted effects. Although not all of these side effects may occur, if they do occur they may need medical attention.

Also, because of the way these medicines act on the body, there is a chance that they might cause other unwanted effects that may not occur until months or years after the medicine is used. These delayed effects may include certain types of cancer, such as leukemia. Discuss these possible effects with your doctor.

Check with your doctor or nurse immediately if any of the following side effects occur:

Less common

Black, tarry stools; blood in urine or stools; cough or hoarseness; fever or chills; lower back or side pain; painful or difficult urination; pinpoint red spots on skin; unusual bleeding or bruising

Rare

Pain at place of injection; wheezing

Check with your health care professional as soon as possible if any of the following side effects occur:

More common

Diarrhea (continuing); difficulty in swallowing; heartburn; sores in mouth and on lips; stomach pain (continuing)

Rare

Joint pain; swelling of feet or lower legs; yellow eyes or skin

Other side effects may occur that usually do not need medical attention. These side effects may go away during treatment as your body adjusts to the medicine. Also, your health care professional may be able to tell you about ways to prevent or reduce some of these side effects. Check with your health care professional if any of the following side effects continue or are bothersome or if you have any questions about them:

More common

Darkening of skin; nausea and vomiting; redness of skin; skin rash or acne; unusual tiredness

This medicine often causes a temporary loss of hair, sometimes including the eyebrows. After treatment with dactinomycin has ended, normal hair growth should return.

After you stop receiving dactinomycin, it may still produce some side effects that need attention. During this period of time check with your doctor if you notice any of the following:

Black, tarry stools; blood in urine or stools; cough or hoarseness; diarrhea; fever or chills; lower back or side pain; painful or difficult urination; pinpoint red spots on skin; sores in mouth and on lips; stomach pain; unusual bleeding or bruising; yellow eyes or skin

Other side effects not listed above may also occur in some patients. If you notice any other effects, check with your doctor.

Revised: 07/11/94

DALTEPARIN Systemic

A commonly used brand name in the U.S. and Canada is Fragmin.

Description

Dalteparin (dal-TE-pa-rin) is used to prevent deep venous thrombosis, a condition in which harmful blood clots form in the blood vessels of the legs. These blood clots can travel to the lungs and can become lodged in the blood vessels of the lungs, causing a condition called pulmonary embolism. Dalteparin is used for several days after abdominal surgery, while you are unable to walk. It is during this time that blood clots are most likely to form. Dalteparin also may be used for other conditions as determined by your doctor.

Dalteparin is available only with your doctor's prescription, in the following dosage form:

Parenteral

- Injection (U.S. and Canada)

Before Using This Medicine

In deciding to use a medicine, the risks of taking the medicine must be weighed against the good it will do. This is a decision you and your doctor will make. For dalteparin, the following should be considered:

Allergies—Tell your doctor if you have ever had any unusual or allergic reaction to dalteparin or heparin. Also tell your health care professional if you are allergic to any other substances, such as foods, especially pork or pork products, preservatives, or dyes.

Pregnancy—Dalteparin has not been studied in pregnant women. However, it has not been shown to cause birth defects or other problems in animals.

Breast-feeding—It is not known whether this medicine passes into breast milk. Although most medicines pass into breast milk in small amounts, many of them may be used safely while breast-feeding. Mothers who are using this medicine and who wish to breast-feed should discuss this with their doctor.

Children—Studies on this medicine have been done only in adult patients, and there is no specific information comparing use of dalteparin in children with use in other age groups.

Older adults—This medicine has been tested and has not been shown to cause different side effects or problems in older people than it does in younger adults.

Other medicines—Although certain medicines should not be used together at all, in other cases two different medicines may be used together even if an interaction might occur. In these cases, your doctor may want to change the dose, or other precautions may be necessary. When you are using dalteparin, it is especially important that your health care professional know if you are taking any of the following:

- Aspirin or
- Inflammation or pain medicine, except narcotics, or
- Ticlopidine—Using any of these medicines together with dalteparin may increase the risk of bleeding

Other medical problems—The presence of other medical problems may affect the use of dalteparin. Make sure you tell your doctor if you have any other medical problems, especially:

- Bleeding problems or
- Eye problems caused by diabetes or high blood pressure or
- Heart infection or
- High blood pressure (hypertension) or
- Kidney disease or
- Liver disease or
- Stomach or intestinal ulcer (active) or
- Stroke—The risk of bleeding may be increased

Also, tell your doctor if you have received dalteparin or heparin before and had a reaction to either of them called thrombocytopenia (a low platelet count in the blood), or if new blood clots formed while you were receiving the medicine.

In addition, *tell your doctor if you have recently had medical surgery.* This may increase the risk of serious bleeding when you are taking dalteparin.

Proper Use of This Medicine

If you are using dalteparin at home, your health care professional will teach you how to inject yourself with the medicine. *Be sure to follow the directions carefully. Check with your health care professional if you have any problems using the medicine.*

Put used syringes in a puncture-resistant, disposable container, or dispose of them as directed by your health care professional.

Dosing—The dose of dalteparin will be different for different patients. *Follow your doctor's orders or the directions on the label.* The following information includes only the average doses of dalteparin. *If your dose is different, do not change it* unless your doctor tells you to do so.

- For *injection* dosage form:
  - —For prevention of deep venous thrombosis (leg clots) and pulmonary embolism (lung clots):
    - Adults—2500 International Units (IU) once a day for five to ten days after surgery.
    - Children—Use and dose must be determined by your doctor.

Missed dose—If you miss a dose of this medicine, use it as soon as possible. However, if it is almost time for your next dose, skip the missed dose and go back to your regular dosing schedule. Do not double doses.

Storage—To store this medicine:

- Keep out of the reach of children.
- Store away from heat and direct light.
- Keep the medicine from freezing. Do not refrigerate.
- Do not keep outdated medicine or medicine no longer needed. Be sure that any discarded medicine is out of the reach of children.

Precautions While Using This Medicine

Tell all your medical doctors and dentists that you are using this medicine.

Side Effects of This Medicine

Along with its needed effects, a medicine may cause some unwanted effects. Although not all of these side effects may occur, if they do occur they may need medical attention.

Stop using this medicine and check with your doctor immediately if any of the following side effects occur:

More common

Deep, dark purple bruise, pain, or swelling at place of injection

Less common

Bleeding of gums; coughing up blood; difficulty in breathing or swallowing; dizziness; headache; increased menstrual flow or vaginal bleeding; nosebleeds; paralysis; prolonged bleeding from cuts; red or dark brown urine; red or black, tarry stools; shortness of breath; unexplained pain, swelling, or discomfort, especially in the chest, abdomen, joints, or muscles; unusual bruising; vomiting of blood or coffee ground–like material; weakness

Rare

Bleeding from mucous membranes; bluish or black discoloration, flushing, or redness of skin; coughing; feeling faint; fever; skin rash (which may consist of pinpoint, purple-red spots), hives, or itching; sloughing of skin at place of injection; swelling of eyelids, face, or lips; tightness in chest or wheezing

Other side effects not listed above may also occur in some patients. If you notice any other effects, check with your doctor.

Developed: 1/6/96

DANAZOL Systemic

Some commonly used brand names are:

In the U.S.—

Danocrine

Generic name product may also be available.

In Canada—

Cyclomen

Description

Danazol (DA-na-zole) may be used for a number of different medical problems. These include treatment of:

- pain and/or infertility due to endometriosis;
- a tendency for females to develop cysts in the breasts (fibrocystic breast disease); or
- hereditary angioedema, which causes swelling of the face, arms, legs, throat, windpipe, bowels, or sexual organs.

Danazol may also be used for other conditions as determined by your doctor.

This medicine is available only with your doctor's prescription, in the following dosage form:

Oral

- Capsules (U.S. and Canada)

Before Using This Medicine

In deciding to use a medicine, the risks of taking the medicine must be weighed against the good it will do. This is a decision you and your doctor will make. For danazol, the following should be considered:

Allergies—Tell your doctor if you have ever had any unusual or allergic reaction to danazol, androgens (male hormones), or anabolic steroids. Also tell your health care professional if you are allergic to any other substances, such as foods, preservatives, or dyes.

Pregnancy—Danazol is not recommended for use during pregnancy, since it may cause a female baby to develop certain male characteristics.

Breast-feeding—Breast-feeding is not recommended while you are taking this medicine because it may cause unwanted effects in the baby.

Children—Danazol may cause male-like changes in female children and cause premature sexual development in male children. It may also slow or stop growth in any child.

Older adults—Many medicines have not been studied specifically in older people. Therefore, it may not be known whether they work exactly the same way they do in younger adults. Although there is no specific information comparing use of danazol in the elderly with use in other age groups, danazol has effects similar to androgens (male hormones). Androgens used in older males may increase the risk of developing prostate enlargement or cancer.

Other medicines—Although certain medicines should not be used together at all, in other cases two different medicines may be used together even if an interaction might occur. In these cases, your doctor may want to change the dose, or other precautions may be necessary. When you are taking danazol, it is especially important that your health care professional know if you are taking any of the following:

- Anticoagulants (blood thinners)—Danazol may increase the effects of these medicines and possibly increase the risk of severe bleeding

Other medical problems—The presence of other medical problems may affect the use of danazol. Make sure you tell your doctor if you have any other medical problems, especially:

- Diabetes mellitus (sugar diabetes)—Danazol may increase blood glucose levels

- Epilepsy or
- Heart disease or
- Kidney disease or
- Migraine headaches—These conditions can be made worse by the fluid retention (keeping too much body water) that can be caused by danazol
- Liver disease

Proper Use of This Medicine

In order for danazol to help you, *it must be taken regularly for the full time of treatment* as ordered by your doctor.

Dosing—The dose of danazol will be different for different patients. *Follow your doctor's orders or the directions on the label.* The following information includes only the average doses of danazol. *If your dose is different, do not change it* unless your doctor tells you to do so.

The number of capsules that you take depends on the strength of the medicine. Also, *the number of doses you take each day, the time allowed between doses, and the length of time you take the medicine depend on the medical problems for which you are taking danazol.*

- For *capsules* dosage forms:
  —Adults:
    - For treatment of endometriosis: 100 to 400 milligrams two times a day.
    - For treatment of fibrocystic breast disease: 50 to 200 milligrams two times a day.
    - For prevention of attacks of hereditary angioedema: 200 milligrams two or three times a day. The dose may be lowered, depending upon your condition.

Missed dose—If you miss a dose of this medicine, take it as soon as possible. However, if it is almost time for your next dose, skip the missed dose and go back to your regular dosing schedule. Do not double doses.

Storage—To store this medicine:

- Keep out of the reach of children.
- Store away from heat and direct light.
- Do not store in the bathroom, near the kitchen sink, or in other damp places. Heat or moisture may cause the medicine to break down.
- Do not keep outdated medicine or medicine no longer needed. Be sure that any discarded medicine is out of the reach of children.

Precautions While Using This Medicine

Your doctor should check your progress at regular visits to make sure that this medicine does not cause unwanted effects.

For diabetic patients:

- This medicine may affect blood glucose levels. If you notice a change in the results of your blood or urine glucose test or if you have any questions about this, check with your doctor.

If you are taking danazol for *endometriosis* or *fibrocystic breast disease:*

- During the time you are taking danazol, your menstrual period may not be regular or you may not have a menstrual period at all. This is to be expected when you are taking this medicine. If regular menstruation does not begin within 60 to 90 days after you stop taking this medicine, check with your doctor.
- During the time you are taking danazol, you should use birth control methods that do not contain hormones. If you have any questions about this, check with your health care professional.
- *If you suspect that you may have become pregnant, stop taking this medicine and check with your doctor.* Continued use of danazol during pregnancy may cause male-like changes in female babies.

Danazol may cause your skin to be more sensitive to sunlight than it is normally. Exposure to sunlight, even for brief periods of time, may cause a skin rash, itching, redness, or other discoloration of the skin, or a severe sunburn. When you begin taking this medicine:

- Stay out of direct sunlight, especially between the hours of 10:00 a.m. and 3:00 p.m., if possible.
- Wear protective clothing, including a hat. Also, wear sunglasses.
- Apply a sun block product that has a skin protection factor (SPF) of a least 15. Some patients may require a product with a higher SPF number, especially if they have a fair complexion. If you have questions about this, check with your health care professional.
- Apply a sun block lipstick that has an SPF of at least 15 to protect your lips.
- Do not use a sunlamp or tanning bed or booth.

If you have a severe reaction from the sun, check with your doctor.

Side Effects of This Medicine

Along with its needed effects, a medicine may cause some unwanted effects. Although not all of these side effects may occur, if they do occur they may need medical attention.

Check with your doctor as soon as possible if any of the following side effects occur:

For both females and males

Less common

Acne or increased oiliness of skin or hair; muscle cramps or spasms; swelling of feet or lower legs; unusual tiredness or weakness; weight gain (rapid)

Rare

Bleeding gums; bloating, pain or tenderness of abdomen or stomach; blood in urine; changes in vision; chest pain; chills; cough; dark-colored urine; diarrhea; discharge from nipple; eye pain; fast heartbeat; fever; headache; hives or other skin rashes; joint pain; light-colored stools; loss of appetite (continuing); more frequent nosebleeds; muscle aches; nausea; pain, numbness, tingling, or burning in all fingers except the smallest finger; purple- or red-colored, or other spots on body or inside the mouth or nose; sore throat; tingling, numbness, or weakness in legs, which may move upward to arms, trunk, or face; unusual bruising or bleeding; unusual tiredness, weakness, or general feeling of illness; vomiting; yellow eyes or skin

For females only

More common

Decrease in breast size; irregular menstrual periods; weight gain

Rare

Enlarged clitoris; hoarseness or deepening of voice; unnatural hair growth

For males only

Rare

Decrease in size of testicles

Other side effects may occur that usually do not need medical attention. These side effects may go away during treatment as your body adjusts to the medicine. However, check with your doctor if any of the following side effects continue or are bothersome:

For both females and males

Less common

Flushing or redness of skin; mood or mental changes; nervousness; sweating

Rare

Increased sensitivity of skin to sunlight

For females only

Less common

Burning, dryness, or itching of vagina or vaginal bleeding

Other side effects not listed above may also occur in some patients. If you notice any other effects, check with your doctor.

Additional Information

Once a medicine has been approved for marketing for a certain use, experience may show that it is also useful for other medical problems. Although these uses are not included in product labeling, danazol is used in certain patients with the following medical conditions:

- Gynecomastia (excess breast development in males)
- Menorrhagia (excessively long menstrual periods)
- Precocious puberty in females (premature sexual development)

Other than the above information, there is no additional information relating to proper use, precautions, or side effects for these uses.

Revised: 02/19/93

DANTROLENE Systemic

Some commonly used brand names in the U.S. and Canada are Dantrium and Dantrium Intravenous.

Description

Dantrolene (DAN-troe-leen) is used to help relax certain muscles in your body. It relieves the spasms, cramping, and tightness of muscles caused by certain medical problems such as multiple sclerosis (MS), cerebral palsy, stroke, or injury to the spine. Dantrolene does not cure these problems, but it may allow other treatment, such as physical therapy, to be more helpful in improving your condition. Dantrolene acts directly on the muscles to produce its relaxant effects.

Dantrolene is also used to prevent or treat a medical problem called malignant hyperthermia that may occur in some people during or following surgery or anesthesia. Malignant hyperthermia consists of a group of symptoms including very high fever, fast and irregular heartbeat, and breathing problems. It is believed that the tendency to develop malignant hyperthermia is inherited.

Dantrolene has been shown to cause cancer and noncancerous tumors in some animals (but not in others) when given in large doses for a long time. It is not known whether long-term use of dantrolene causes cancer or tumors in humans. Before taking this medicine, be sure that you have discussed this with your doctor.

This medicine is available only with your doctor's prescription, in the following dosage forms:

Oral

- Capsules (U.S. and Canada)

Parenteral

- Injection (U.S. and Canada)

Before Using This Medicine

In deciding to use a medicine, the risks of taking the medicine must be weighed against the good it will do. This is a decision you and your doctor will make. For dantrolene, the following should be considered:

Allergies—Tell your doctor if you have ever had any unusual or allergic reaction to dantrolene. Also tell your health care professional if you are allergic to any other substances, such as foods, preservatives, or dyes.

Pregnancy—Dantrolene has not been shown to cause birth defects or other problems in humans.

Breast-feeding—Use of dantrolene is not recommended during breast-feeding.

Children—This medicine has been tested in children 5 years of age and older and has not been shown to cause different side effects or problems than it does in adults.

Older adults—Many medicines have not been studied specifically in older people. Therefore, it may not be known whether they work exactly the same way they do in younger adults or if they cause different side effects or problems in older people. There is no specific information comparing use of dantrolene in the elderly with use in other age groups.

Other medicines—Although certain medicines should not be used together at all, in other cases two different medicines may be used together even if an interaction might occur. In these cases, your doctor may want to change the

dose, or other precautions may be necessary. When you are taking dantrolene, it is especially important that your health care professional know if you are taking any of the following:

- Acetaminophen (e.g., Tylenol) (with long-term, high-dose use) or
- Amiodarone (e.g., Cordarone) or
- Anabolic steroids (dromostanolone [e.g., Drolban], ethylestrenol [e.g., Maxibolin], nandrolone [e.g., Anabolin], oxandrolone [e.g., Anavar], oxymetholone [e.g., Anadrol], stanozolol [e.g., Winstrol]) or
- Androgens (male hormones) or
- Anti-infectives by mouth or by injection (medicine for infection) or
- Antithyroid agents (medicine for overactive thyroid) or
- Carbamazepine (e.g., Tegretol) or
- Carmustine (e.g., BiCNU) or
- Central nervous system (CNS) depressants (medicine that causes drowsiness) or
- Chloroquine (e.g., Aralen) or
- Daunorubicin (e.g., Cerubidine) or
- Disulfiram (e.g., Antabuse) or
- Divalproex (e.g., Depakote) or
- Estrogens (female hormones) or
- Etretinate (e.g., Tegison) or
- Gold salts (medicine for arthritis) or
- Hydroxychloroquine (e.g., Plaquenil) or
- Mercaptopurine (e.g., Purinethol) or
- Methotrexate (e.g., Mexate) or
- Methyldopa (e.g., Aldomet) or
- Naltrexone (e.g., Trexan) (with long-term, high-dose use) or
- Oral contraceptives (birth control pills) containing estrogen or
- Phenothiazines (acetophenazine [e.g., Tindal], chlorpromazine [e.g., Thorazine], fluphenazine [e.g., Prolixin], mesoridazine [e.g., Serentil], perphenazine [e.g., Trilafon], prochlorperazine [e.g., Compazine], promazine [e.g., Sparine], promethazine [e.g., Phenergan], thioridazine [e.g., Mellaril], trifluoperazine [e.g., Stelazine], triflupromazine [e.g., Vesprin], trimeprazine [e.g., Temaril]) or
- Phenytoin (e.g., Dilantin) or
- Plicamycin (e.g., Mithracin) or
- Tricyclic antidepressants (medicine for depression) (amitriptyline [e.g., Elavil], amoxapine [e.g., Asendin], clomipramine [e.g., Anafranil], desipramine [e.g., Pertofrane], doxepin [e.g., Sinequan], imipramine [e.g., Tofranil], nortriptyline [e.g., Aventyl], protriptyline [e.g., Vivactil], trimipramine [e.g., Surmontil]) or
- Valproic acid (e.g., Depakene)—The chance of side effects may be increased

Other medical problems—The presence of other medical problems may affect the use of dantrolene. Make sure you tell your doctor if you have any other medical problems, especially:

- Emphysema, asthma, bronchitis, or other chronic lung disease or
- Heart disease or
- Liver disease, such as hepatitis or cirrhosis (or history of)—The chance of serious side effects may be increased

Proper Use of This Medicine

If you are unable to swallow the capsules, you may empty the number of capsules needed for one dose into a small amount of fruit juice or other liquid. Stir gently to mix the powder with the liquid before drinking. Drink the medicine right away. Rinse the glass with a little more liquid and drink that also to make sure that you have taken all of the medicine.

Dantrolene may be taken with or without food or on a full or empty stomach. However, if your doctor tells you to take the medicine a certain way, take it exactly as directed.

Take this medicine only as directed by your doctor. Do not take more of it and do not take it more often than your doctor ordered. Dantrolene may cause liver damage or other unwanted effects if too much is taken.

Dosing—The dose of dantrolene will be different for different patients. *Follow your doctor's orders or the directions on the label.* The following information includes only the average doses of dantrolene. *If your dose is different, do not change it* unless your doctor tells you to do so:

The number of capsules that you take depends on the strength of the medicine. Also, the number of doses you take each day, the time allowed between doses, and the length of time you take the medicine depend on the medical problem for which you are taking dantrolene.

- For *oral* dosage form (capsules):
  - —For prevention or treatment of a malignant hyperthermic crisis:
    - Adults—Dose is based on body weight and must be determined by your doctor. The usual dose is 4 to 8 milligrams (mg) per kilogram (kg) (1.8 to 3.6 mg per pound) of body weight. The doctor will instruct you exactly when and how often to take your medicine.
  - —To relieve spasms:
    - Adults—To start, 25 mg once a day. The doctor may increase your dose as needed and tolerated. However, the dose is usually not more than 100 mg four times a day.
    - Children—Dose is based on body weight and must be determined by your doctor. To start, the dose is usually 0.5 mg per kg (0.23 mg per pound) of body weight twice a day. The doctor may increase the dose as needed and tolerated. However, the dose is usually not more than 3 mg per kg or 100 mg four times a day.
- For *injection* dosage form:
  - —For prevention or treatment of a malignant hyperthermia crisis:
    - Adults, teenagers, and children—Dose is based on body weight and must be determined by your doctor.

Missed dose—If you miss a dose of this medicine and remember within an hour or so of the missed dose, take it right away. Then go back to your regular dosing schedule. But if you do not remember until later, skip the missed dose and go back to your regular dosing schedule. Do not double doses.

Storage—To store this medicine:

- Keep out of the reach of children.
- Store away from heat and direct light.

- Do not store this medicine in the bathroom, near the kitchen sink, or in other damp places. Heat or moisture may cause the medicine to break down.
- Do not keep outdated medicine or medicine no longer needed. Be sure that any discarded medicine is out of the reach of children.

Precautions While Using This Medicine

If you will be taking dantrolene for a long time (for example, for several months at a time), your doctor should check your progress at regular visits. It may be necessary to have certain blood tests to check for unwanted effects while you are taking dantrolene.

This medicine will add to the effects of alcohol and other CNS depressants (medicines that slow down the nervous system, possibly causing drowsiness). Some examples of CNS depressants are antihistamines or medicine for hay fever, other allergies, or colds; sedatives, tranquilizers, or sleeping medicine; prescription pain medicine or narcotics; barbiturates; medicine for seizures; other muscle relaxants; or anesthetics, including some dental anesthetics. Therefore, *do not drink alcoholic beverages, and check with your doctor before taking any of the medicines listed above, while you are using this medicine.*

This medicine may cause drowsiness, dizziness or lightheadedness, vision problems, or muscle weakness in some people. *Make sure you know how you react to this medicine before you drive, use machines, or do anything else that could be dangerous if you are dizzy or are not alert, well-coordinated, and able to see well.*

Side Effects of This Medicine

Along with its needed effects, a medicine may cause some unwanted effects. Although not all of these side effects may occur, if they do occur they may need medical attention. Serious side effects are very rare when dantrolene is taken for a short time (for example, when it is used for a few days before, during, or after surgery or anesthesia to prevent or treat malignant hyperthermia). However, serious side effects may occur, especially when the medicine is taken for a long time.

Check with your doctor immediately if any of the following side effects occur:

Less common

Convulsions (seizures); pain, tenderness, changes in skin color, or swelling of foot or leg; shortness of breath or slow or troubled breathing

Also, check with your doctor as soon as possible if any of the following side effects occur:

Less common

Bloody or dark urine; chest pain; confusion; constipation (severe); diarrhea (severe); difficult urination; mental depression; skin rash, hives, or itching; yellow eyes or skin

Other side effects may occur that usually do not need medical attention. These side effects may go away during treatment as your body adjusts to the medicine. However, check with your doctor if any of the following side effects continue or are bothersome:

More common

Diarrhea (mild); dizziness or lightheadedness; drowsiness; general feeling of discomfort or illness; muscle weakness; nausea or vomiting; unusual tiredness

Less common

Abdominal or stomach cramps or discomfort; blurred or double vision or any change in vision; chills and fever; constipation (mild); difficulty in swallowing; frequent urge to urinate or uncontrolled urination; headache; loss of appetite; slurring of speech or other speech problems; sudden decrease in amount of urine; trouble in sleeping; unusual nervousness

Other side effects not listed above may also occur in some patients. If you notice any other effects, check with your doctor.

Revised: 05/10/93

DAPIPRAZOLE Ophthalmic

A commonly used brand name in the U.S. and Canada is Rev-Eyes.

Description

Dapiprazole (da-PI-pray-zole) is used in the eye to reduce the size of the pupil after certain kinds of eye examinations.

Some eye examinations are best done when your pupil (the black center of the colored part of your eye) is very large, so the doctor can see into your eye better. This medicine helps to reduce the size of your pupil back to its normal size after the eye examination.

Dapiprazole is available in the following dosage form:

Ophthalmic

- Ophthalmic solution (eye drops) (U.S. and Canada)

Before Using This Medicine

In deciding to use a medicine, the risks of using the medicine must be weighed against the good it will do. This is a decision you and your doctor will make. For dapiprazole, the following should be considered:

Allergies—Tell your doctor if you have ever had any unusual or allergic reaction to dapiprazole. Also tell your health care professional if you are allergic to any other substances, such as foods, preservatives, or dyes.

Pregnancy—Dapiprazole has not been studied in pregnant women. However, dapiprazole has not been shown to cause birth defects or other problems in animal studies.

Breast-feeding—It is not known whether dapiprazole passes into the breast milk. However, this medicine has not been reported to cause problems in nursing babies.

Children—Studies on this medicine have been done only in adult patients, and there is no specific information comparing use of dapiprazole in children with use in other age groups.

Older adults—Many medicines have not been studied specifically in older people. Therefore, it may not be known whether they work exactly the same way they do in younger adults. Although there is no specific information comparing use of dapiprazole in the elderly with use in other age groups, this medicine is not expected to cause different side effects or problems in older people than it does in younger adults.

Other medicines—Although certain medicines should not be used together at all, in other cases two different medicines may be used together even if an interaction might occur. In these cases, your doctor may want to change the dose, or other precautions may be necessary. Tell your health care professional if you are using any other ophthalmic (eye) prescription or nonprescription (over-the-counter [OTC]) medicine.

Other medical problems—The presence of other medical problems may affect the use of dapiprazole. Make sure you tell your doctor if you have any other medical problems, especially:

- Eye problems, other—Use of dapiprazole may make the condition worse

Proper Use of This Medicine

Dosing—The dose of dapiprazole will be different for different patients. *Follow your doctor's orders or the directions on the label.* The following information includes only the average doses of dapiprazole. *If your dose is different, do not change it* unless your doctor tells you to do so.

- For *ophthalmic solution (eye drops)* dosage form:
  - —For reduction of size of pupil of eye:
    - Adults—One drop, then one drop in five minutes, following eye examination.
    - Children—Use and dose must be determined by your doctor.

Precautions While Using This Medicine

Even after using this medicine, you may have blurred vision or other vision problems. If any of these occur, *do not drive, use machines, or do anything else that could be dangerous if you are not able to see well.*

This medicine may cause your eyes to become more sensitive to light than they are normally. Wearing sunglasses and avoiding too much exposure to bright light may help lessen the discomfort.

Side Effects of This Medicine

Along with its needed effects, a medicine may cause some unwanted effects. Although not all of these side effects may occur, if they do occur they may need medical attention.

Check with your doctor as soon as possible if any of the following side effects occur:

Less common

Irritation (severe) or swelling of the clear part of the eye

Other side effects may occur that usually do not need medical attention. These side effects may go away during treatment as your body adjusts to the medicine. However, check with your doctor if any of the following side effects continue or are bothersome:

More common

Burning of eye when medicine is applied; redness of the white part of the eye

Less common

Blurring of vision; browache; drooping of upper eyelid; dryness of eye; headache; increased sensitivity of eye to light; itching of eye; redness of eyelid; swelling of eyelid; swelling of the membrane covering the white part of the eye; tearing of eye

Other side effects not listed above may also occur in some patients. If you notice any other effects, check with your doctor.

Revised: 04/13/92
Interim revision: 08/16/93

DAPSONE Systemic

A commonly used brand name in Canada is Avlosulfon.

Another commonly used name is DDS.

Description

Dapsone (DAP-sone), a sulfone, belongs to the family of medicines called anti-infectives.

Dapsone is used to treat leprosy (Hansen's disease) and to help control dermatitis herpetiformis, a skin problem. When it is used to treat leprosy, dapsone may be given with one or more other medicines. Dapsone may also be used for other conditions as determined by your doctor.

Dapsone is available only with your doctor's prescription, in the following dosage form:

Oral

- Tablets (U.S. and Canada)

Before Using This Medicine

In deciding to use a medicine, the risks of taking the medicine must be weighed against the good it will do. This is a decision you and your doctor will make. For dapsone, the following should be considered:

Allergies—Tell your doctor if you have ever had any unusual or allergic reaction to dapsone or sulfonamides. Also tell your health care professional if you are allergic to any other substances, such as foods, preservatives, or dyes.

Pregnancy—Studies have not been done in humans or animals. However, reports on the use of dapsone in humans have not shown that this medicine causes birth defects or other problems.

Breast-feeding—Dapsone passes into the breast milk. Dapsone may cause blood problems in nursing babies with glucose-6-phosphate dehydrogenase (G6PD) deficiency. Breast-feeding may need to be stopped because of the risks to the baby.

Children—Although there is no specific information comparing use of dapsone in children with use in other age groups, this medicine is not expected to cause different side effects or problems in children than it does in adults.

Older adults—Many medicines have not been studied specifically in older people. Therefore, it may not be known whether they work exactly the same way they do in younger adults or if they cause different side effects or problems in older people. There is no specific information comparing use of dapsone in the elderly with use in other age groups.

Other medicines—Although certain medicines should not be used together at all, in other cases two different medicines may be used together even if an interaction might occur. In these cases, your doctor may want to change the dose, or other precautions may be necessary. When you are taking dapsone, it is especially important that your health care professional knows if you are taking any of the following:

- Acetohydroxamic acid (e.g., Lithostat) or
- Antidiabetics, oral (diabetes medicine you take by mouth) or
- Furazolidone (e.g., Furoxone) or
- Methyldopa (e.g., Aldomet) or
- Nitrofurantoin (e.g., Furadantin) or
- Primaquine or
- Procainamide (e.g., Pronestyl) or
- Quinidine (e.g., Quinidex) or
- Quinine (e.g., Quinamm) or
- Sulfonamides (sulfa medicine) or
- Vitamin K (e.g., AquaMEPHYTON, Synkayvite)—Use of dapsone with these medicines may increase the chance of side effects affecting the blood
- Dideoxyinosine (e.g., ddI, Videx)—Use of dideoxyinosine with dapsone may decrease the effectiveness of dapsone

Other medical problems—The presence of other medical problems may affect the use of dapsone. Make sure you tell your doctor if you have any other medical problems, especially:

- Anemia (severe) or
- Glucose-6-phosphate dehydrogenase (G6PD) deficiency or
- Methemoglobin reductase deficiency—There is an increased risk of severe blood disorders and a decrease in red blood cell survival
- Liver disease—Dapsone may on rare occasion cause liver damage

Proper Use of This Medicine

For patients taking dapsone for leprosy:

- To help clear up your leprosy completely or to keep it from coming back, *it is very important that you keep taking this medicine for the full time of treatment,* even if you begin to feel better after a few weeks or months. You may have to take it every day for as long as 3 years or more, or for life. If you stop taking this medicine too soon, your symptoms may return.
- This medicine works best when there is a constant amount in the blood. *To help keep the amount constant, do not miss any doses. Also, it is best to take each dose at the same time every day.* If you need help in planning the best time to take your medicine, check with your health care professional.

For patients taking dapsone for dermatitis herpetiformis:

- Your doctor may want you to follow a gluten-free diet. If you have any questions about this, check with your doctor.

Dosing—The dose of dapsone will be different for different patients. *Follow your doctor's orders or the directions on the label.* The following information includes only the average doses of dapsone. *If your dose is different, do not change it* unless your doctor tells you to do so.

The number of tablets that you take depends on the strength of the medicine. Also, *the number of doses you take each day, the time allowed between doses, and the length of time you take the medicine depend on the medical problem for which you are taking dapsone.*

- *For oral* dosage form (tablets):
  - —For Hansen's disease (leprosy):
    - Adults and teenagers—50 to 100 milligrams (mg) once a day; or 1.4 mg per kilogram (kg) (0.6 mg per pound) of body weight once a day. Dapsone should be taken with other medicines to treat Hansen's disease.
    - Children—Dose is based on body weight. The usual dose is 1.4 mg per kg (0.6 mg per pound) of body weight once a day. Dapsone should be taken with other medicines to treat Hansen's disease.
  - —For dermatitis herpetiformis:
    - Adults and teenagers—50 mg once a day to start. Your doctor will increase your dose, up to 300 mg once a day, until your symptoms are controlled. Then your dose will be decreased to the lowest dose that will still control your symptoms.
    - Children—Dose is based on body weight. The usual dose is 2 mg per kg (0.9 mg per pound) of body weight once a day to start. Your doctor will increase your dose until your symptoms are controlled. Then your dose will be decreased to the lowest dose that will still control your symptoms.

Missed dose—You may skip a missed dose if it does not make your symptoms come back or get worse. If your symptoms do come back or get worse, take the missed dose as soon as possible. Then go back to your regular dosing schedule.

Storage—To store this medicine:

- Keep out of the reach of children.
- Store away from heat and direct light.

- Do not store in the bathroom, near the kitchen sink, or in other damp places. Heat or moisture may cause the medicine to break down.
- Do not keep outdated medicine or medicine no longer needed. Be sure that any discarded medicine is out of the reach of children.

Precautions While Using This Medicine

It is very important that your doctor check your progress at regular visits.

If your symptoms do not improve within 2 to 3 months (for leprosy), or within a few days (for dermatitis herpetiformis), or if they become worse, check with your doctor.

Side Effects of This Medicine

Along with its needed effects, a medicine may cause some unwanted effects. Although not all of these side effects may occur, if they do occur they may need medical attention.

Check with your doctor immediately if any of the following side effects occur:

More common

Back, leg, or stomach pains; bluish fingernails, lips, or skin; difficult breathing; fever; loss of appetite; pale skin; skin rash; unusual tiredness or weakness

Rare

Itching, dryness, redness, scaling, or peeling of the skin, or loss of hair; mood or other mental changes; numbness, tingling, pain, burning, or weakness in hands or feet; sore throat; unusual bleeding or bruising; yellow eyes or skin

Other side effects may occur that usually do not need medical attention. These side effects may go away during treatment as your body adjusts to the medicine. However, check with your doctor if any of the following side effects continue or are bothersome:

Rare

Headache; loss of appetite; nausea or vomiting; nervousness; trouble in sleeping

Other side effects not listed above may also occur in some patients. If you notice any other effects, check with your doctor.

Additional Information

Once a medicine has been approved for marketing for a certain use, experience may show that it is also useful for other medical problems. Although these uses are not specifically included in product labeling, dapsone is used in certain patients with the following medical conditions:

- Actinomycotic mycetoma
- Granuloma annulare
- Malaria (prevention of)
- Pemphigoid
- *Pneumocystis carinii* pneumonia
- Pyoderma gangrenosum
- Relapsing polychondritis
- Subcorneal pustular dermatosis
- Systemic lupus erythematosus

For patients taking this medicine for *Pneumocystis carinii* pneumonia (PCP):

- To help clear up PCP completely or to keep it from coming back, *it is very important that you keep taking this medicine for the full time of treatment.*
- If you miss a dose of this medicine, take it as soon as possible. This will help keep a constant amount of medicine in the blood. However, if it is almost time for your next dose, skip the missed dose and go back to your regular dosing schedule. Do not double doses.
- If your symptoms do not improve within 1 week, or if they become worse, check with your doctor.

Other than the above information, there is no additional information relating to proper use, precautions, or side effects for these uses.

Revised: 06/26/92
Interim revision: 03/17/94

DAUNORUBICIN Systemic

A commonly used brand name in the U.S. and Canada is Cerubidine.

Description

Daunorubicin (daw-noe-ROO-bi-sin) belongs to the general group of medicines known as antineoplastics. It is used to treat some kinds of cancer.

Daunorubicin seems to interfere with the growth of cancer cells, which are eventually destroyed. Since the growth of normal body cells may also be affected by daunorubicin, other effects will also occur. Some of these may be serious and must be reported to your doctor. Other effects, like hair loss, may not be serious but may cause concern. Some effects may not occur for months or years after the medicine is used.

Before you begin treatment with daunorubicin, you and your doctor should talk about the good this medicine will do as well as the risks of using it.

Daunorubicin is to be administered only by or under the immediate supervision of your doctor. It is available in the following dosage form:

Parenteral

- Injection (U.S. and Canada)

Before Using This Medicine

In deciding to use a medicine, the risks of taking the medicine must be weighed against the good it will do. This is a decision you and your doctor will make. For daunorubicin, the following should be considered:

Allergies—Tell your doctor if you have ever had any unusual or allergic reaction to daunorubicin.

Pregnancy—This medicine may cause birth defects if either the male or female is receiving it at the time of conception or if it is taken during pregnancy. In addition, many cancer medicines may cause sterility which could be permanent. Although sterility has been reported only in male dogs with this medicine, the possibility of an effect in human males should be kept in mind.

Be sure that you have discussed this with your doctor before receiving this medicine. It is best to use some kind of birth control while you are receiving daunorubicin. Tell your doctor right away if you think you have become pregnant while receiving daunorubicin.

Breast-feeding—Because daunorubicin may cause serious side effects, breast-feeding is generally not recommended while you are receiving it.

Children—Although daunorubicin is used in children, there is no specific information comparing use in children with use in other age groups.

Older adults—Heart problems are more likely to occur in the elderly, who are usually more sensitive to the effects of daunorubicin. The elderly may also be more likely to have blood problems.

Other medicines—Although certain medicines should not be used together at all, in other cases two different medicines may be used together even if an interaction might occur. In these cases, your doctor may want to change the dose, or other precautions may be necessary. When receiving daunorubicin it is especially important that your health care professional know if you are taking any of the following:

- Amphotericin B by injection (e.g., Fungizone) or
- Antithyroid agents (medicine for overactive thyroid) or
- Azathioprine (e.g., Imuran) or
- Chloramphenicol (e.g., Chloromycetin) or
- Colchicine or
- Flucytosine (e.g., Ancobon) or
- Ganciclovir (e.g., Cytovene) or
- Interferon (e.g., Intron A, Roferon-A) or
- Plicamycin (e.g., Mithracin) or
- Zidovudine (e.g., AZT, Retrovir) or
- If you have ever been treated with radiation or cancer medicines—Daunorubicin may increase the effects of these medicines or radiation therapy on the blood
- Probenecid (e.g., Benemid) or
- Sulfinpyrazone (e.g., Anturane)—Daunorubicin may raise the concentration of uric acid in the blood. Since these medicines are used to lower uric acid levels, they may not be as effective in patients receiving daunorubicin

Other medical problems—The presence of other medical problems may affect the use of daunorubicin. Make sure you tell your doctor if you have any other medical problems, especially:

- Chickenpox (including recent exposure) or
- Herpes zoster (shingles)—Risk of severe disease affecting other parts of the body
- Gout (history of) or
- Kidney stones—Daunorubicin may increase uric acid in the body, which can cause gout or kidney stones
- Heart disease—Risk of heart problems caused by daunorubicin may be increased
- Infection—Daunorubicin can decrease your body's ability to fight infection
- Kidney disease or
- Liver disease—Effects of daunorubicin may be increased because of slower removal from the body

Proper Use of This Medicine

Daunorubicin is sometimes given together with certain other medicines. If you are using a combination of medicines, it is important that you receive each one at the proper time. If you are taking some of these medicines by mouth, ask your health care professional to help you plan a way to take them at the right times.

While you are receiving daunorubicin, your doctor may want you to drink extra fluids so that you will pass more urine. This will help prevent kidney problems and keep your kidneys working well.

This medicine often causes nausea and vomiting. However, it is very important that you continue to receive it, even if you begin to feel ill. Ask your health care professional for ways to lessen these effects.

Dosing—The dose of daunorubicin will be different for different patients. The dose that is used may depend on a number of things, including what the medicine is being used for, the patient's size, and whether or not other medicines are also being taken. *If you are receiving daunorubicin at home, follow your doctor's orders or the directions on the label.* If you have any questions about the proper dose of daunorubicin, ask your doctor.

Precautions While Using This Medicine

It is very important that your doctor check your progress at regular visits to make sure that this medicine is working properly and to check for unwanted effects.

While you are being treated with daunorubicin, and after you stop treatment with it, *do not have any immunizations (vaccinations) without your doctor's approval.* Daunorubicin may lower your body's resistance and there is a chance you might get the infection the immunization is meant to prevent. In addition, other persons living in your household should not take oral polio vaccine since there is a chance they could pass the polio virus on to you. Also, avoid persons who have taken oral polio vaccine. Do not get close to them, and do not stay in the same room with them for very long. If you cannot take these precautions, you should consider wearing a protective face mask that covers the nose and mouth.

Daunorubicin can temporarily lower the number of white blood cells in your blood, increasing the chance of getting an infection. It can also lower the number of platelets, which are necessary for proper blood clotting. If this occurs, there are certain precautions you can take, especially when your blood count is low, to reduce the risk of infection or bleeding:

- If you can, avoid people with infections. *Check with your doctor immediately* if you think you are getting an infection or if you get a fever or chills, cough or hoarseness, lower back or side pain, or painful or difficult urination.
- *Check with your doctor immediately* if you notice any unusual bleeding or bruising; black, tarry stools; blood in urine or stools; or pinpoint red spots on your skin.

- Be careful when using a regular toothbrush, dental floss, or toothpick. Your medical doctor, dentist, or nurse may recommend other ways to clean your teeth and gums. Check with your medical doctor before having any dental work done.
- Do not touch your eyes or the inside of your nose unless you have just washed your hands and have not touched anything else in the meantime.
- Be careful not to cut yourself when you are using sharp objects such as a safety razor or fingernail or toenail cutters.
- Avoid contact sports or other situations where bruising or injury could occur.

If daunorubicin accidentally seeps out of the vein into which it is injected, it may damage some tissues and cause scarring. *Tell the doctor or nurse right away if you notice redness, pain, or swelling at the place of injection.*

Side Effects of This Medicine

Along with its needed effects, a medicine may cause some unwanted effects. Although not all of these side effects may occur, if they do occur they may need medical attention.

Also, because of the way these medicines act on the body, there is a chance that they might cause other unwanted effects that may not occur until months or years after the medicine is used. These delayed effects may include certain types of cancer, such as leukemia. Discuss these possible effects with your doctor.

Check with your doctor or nurse immediately if any of the following side effects occur:

Less common

Cough or hoarseness; fever or chills; irregular heartbeat; lower back or side pain; pain at place of injection; painful or difficult urination; shortness of breath; swelling of feet and lower legs

Rare

Black, tarry stools; blood in urine or stools; pinpoint red spots on skin; unusual bleeding or bruising

Check with your health care professional as soon as possible if any of the following side effects occur:

More common

Sores in mouth and on lips

Less common

Joint pain

Rare

Skin rash or itching

Other side effects may occur that usually do not need medical attention. These side effects may go away during treatment as your body adjusts to the medicine. Also, your health care professional may be able to tell you about ways to prevent or reduce some of these side effects. Check with your health care professional if any of the following side effects continue or are bothersome or if you have any questions about them:

More common

Nausea and vomiting

Less common or rare

Darkening or redness of skin; diarrhea

Daunorubicin causes the urine to turn reddish in color, which may stain clothes. This is not blood. It is perfectly normal and lasts for only 1 or 2 days after each dose is given.

This medicine often causes a temporary and total loss of hair. After treatment with daunorubicin has ended, normal hair growth should return.

After you stop receiving daunorubicin, it may still produce some side effects that need attention. During this period of time *check with your doctor immediately* if you notice any of the following side effects:

Irregular heartbeat; shortness of breath; swelling of feet and lower legs

Other side effects not listed above may also occur in some patients. If you notice any other effects, check with your health care professional.

Revised: 07/11/94

DECONGESTANTS AND ANALGESICS Systemic

Some commonly used brand names are:

In the U.S.—

Actifed Sinus Daytime[8]
Actifed Sinus Daytime Caplets[8]
Advil Cold and Sinus[10]
Advil Cold and Sinus Caplets[10]
Alka-Seltzer Plus Sinus Medicine[7]
Allerest No-Drowsiness Caplets[8]
Aspirin-Free Bayer Select Sinus Pain Relief Caplets[8]
BC Cold Powder Non-Drowsy Formula[7]
Coldrine[8]
Contac Allergy/Sinus Day Caplets[8]
Contac Non-Drowsy Formula Sinus Caplets[8]
Dimetapp Sinus Caplets[10]
Dristan Cold Caplets[8]
Dristan Sinus Caplets[8]
Dynafed Maximum Strength[8]
Motrin IB Sinus[10]
Motrin IB Sinus Caplets[10]
Ornex Maximum Strength Caplets[8]
Ornex No Drowsiness Caplets[8]
PhenAPAP Without Drowsiness[8]
Rhinocaps[4]
Saleto D Caplets[6]
Sinarest No-Drowsiness Caplets[8]
Sine-Aid IB Caplets[10]
Sine-Aid Maximum Strength[8]
Sine-Aid Maximum Strength Caplets[8]
Sine-Aid Maximum Strength Gelcaps[8]
Sine-Off Maximum Strength No Drowsiness Formula Caplets[8]
Sinus Excedrin Extra Strength[8]
Sinus Excedrin Extra Strength Caplets[8]
Sinus-Relief[8]
Sinutab Sinus Maximum Strength Without Drowsiness[8]
Sinutab Sinus Maximum Strength Without Drowsiness Caplets[8]
Sinutrol 500 Caplets[8]
Sudafed Sinus Maximum Strength Without Drowsiness[8]
Sudafed Sinus Maximum Strength Without Drowsiness Caplets[8]
TheraFlu Sinus Maximum Strength Caplets[8]
Tylenol Sinus Maximum Strength[8]
Tylenol Sinus Maximum Strength Caplets[8]
Tylenol Sinus Maximum Strength Gelcaps[8]
Tylenol Sinus Maximum Strength Geltabs[8]
Ursinus Inlay[9]
Vicks DayQuil Sinus Pressure & Pain Relief Caplets[10]

In Canada—

- Coricidin Non-Drowsy Sinus Formula[7]
- Dilotab[3]
- Dimetapp-A Sinus[2]
- Dristan N.D. Caplets[8]
- Dristan N.D. Extra Strength Caplets[8]
- Emertabs[5]
- Neo Citran Extra Strength Sinus[1]
- Sinutab No Drowsiness Caplets[8]
- Sinutab No Drowsiness Extra Strength Caplets[8]
- Sudafed Head Cold and Sinus Extra Strength Caplets[8]
- Tylenol Sinus Medication Regular Strength Caplets[8]
- Tylenol Sinus Medication Extra Strength Caplets[8]

Note: For quick reference, the following decongestants and analogs are numbered to match the corresponding brand names.

This information applies to the following medicines:

1. Phenylephrine (fen-ill-EF-rin) and Acetaminophen (a-seat-a-MIN-oh-fen)*
2. Phenylephrine, Phenylpropanolamine (fen-ill-proe-pa-NOLE-a-meen), and Acetaminophen*
3. Phenylpropanolamine and Acetaminophen
4. Phenylpropanolamine, Acetaminophen, and Aspirin (AS-pir-in)†
5. Phenylpropanolamine, Acetaminophen, and Caffeine (kaf-EEN)*
6. Phenylpropanolamine, Acetaminophen, Salicylamide (sal-i-SILL-a-mide), and Caffeine†
7. Phenylpropanolamine and Aspirin
8. Pseudoephedrine (soo-doe-e-FED-rin) and Acetaminophen
9. Pseudoephedrine and Aspirin†
10. Pseudoephedrine and Ibuprofen (eye-byoo-PRO-fen)

†Not commercially available in Canada.
*Not commercially available in the U.S.

Description

Decongestant and analgesic combinations are taken by mouth to relieve sinus and nasal congestion (stuffy nose) and headache of colds, allergy, and hay fever.

Decongestants, such as phenylephrine, phenylpropanolamine (also known as PPA), and pseudoephedrine produce a narrowing of blood vessels. This leads to clearing of nasal congestion, but it may also cause an increase in blood pressure in patients who have high blood pressure.

Analgesics, such as acetaminophen, ibuprofen, and salicylates (e.g., aspirin, salicylamide), are used in these combination medicines to help relieve headache and sinus pain.

Acetaminophen and salicylates may cause kidney damage or cancer of the kidney or urinary bladder if large amounts of both medicines are taken together for a long time. However, taking the recommended amounts of combination medicines that contain both acetaminophen and a salicylate for short periods of time has not been shown to cause these unwanted effects.

These medicines are available without a prescription. However, your doctor may have special instructions on the proper dose of these medicines for your medical condition. They are available in the following dosage forms:

Oral

- Phenylephrine and Acetaminophen
  - For oral solution (Canada)
- Phenylephrine, Phenylpropanolamine, and Acetaminophen
  - Tablets (Canada)
- Phenylpropanolamine and Acetaminophen
  - Oral solution (U.S.)
  - Tablets (Canada)
- Phenylpropanolamine, Acetaminophen, and Aspirin
  - Capsules (U.S.)
- Phenylpropanolamine, Acetaminophen, and Caffeine
  - Tablets (Canada)
- Phenylpropanolamine, Acetaminophen, Salicylamide, and Caffeine
  - Tablets (U.S.)
- Phenylpropanolamine and Aspirin
  - For oral solution (U.S.)
  - Effervescent tablets (U.S.)
  - Tablets (Canada)
- Pseudoephedrine and Acetaminophen
  - Capsules (U.S.)
  - Tablets (U.S. and Canada)
- Pseudoephedrine and Aspirin
  - Tablets (U.S.)
- Pseudoephedrine and Ibuprofen
  - Tablets (U.S. and Canada)

Before Using This Medicine

If you are taking this medicine without a prescription, carefully read and follow any precautions on the label. For decongestant and analgesic combinations, the following should be considered:

Allergies—Tell your doctor if you have ever had any unusual or allergic reaction to any of the ingredients contained in this medicine.

If this medicine contains *aspirin, salicylamide,* or *ibuprofen,* before taking it check with your doctor if you have ever had any unusual or allergic reaction to any of the following medicines:

- Aspirin or other salicylates
- Diclofenac (e.g., Voltaren)
- Diflunisal (e.g., Dolobid)
- Etodolac (e.g., Lodine)
- Fenoprofen (e.g., Nalfon)
- Floctafenine (e.g., Idarac)
- Flurbiprofen, by mouth (e.g., Ansaid)
- Ibuprofen (e.g., Motrin)
- Indomethacin (e.g., Indocin)
- Ketoprofen (e.g., Orudis)
- Ketorolac (e.g., Toradol)
- Meclofenamate (e.g., Meclomen)
- Mefenamic acid (e.g., Ponstel)
- Methyl salicylate (oil of wintergreen)
- Nabumetone (e.g., Relafen)
- Naproxen (e.g., Naprosyn)
- Oxaprozin (e.g., Daypro)
- Oxyphenbutazone (e.g., Tandearil)
- Phenylbutazone (e.g., Butazolidin)
- Piroxicam (e.g., Feldene)
- Sulindac (e.g., Clinoril)
- Suprofen (e.g., Suprol)
- Tenoxicam (e.g., Mobiflex)
- Tiaprofenic acid (e.g., Surgam)
- Tolmetin (e.g., Tolectin)
- Zomepirac (e.g., Zomax)

Also tell your health care professional if you are allergic to any other substances, such as foods, preservatives, or dyes.

Pregnancy—The occasional use of decongestant and analgesic combinations at the doses recommended on the label is not likely to cause problems in the fetus or in the newborn baby. However, for the individual ingredients of these combinations, the following information applies:

- *Alcohol*—Some of these combination medicines contain large amounts of alcohol. Too much use of alcohol during pregnancy may cause birth defects.
- *Caffeine*—Studies in humans have not shown that caffeine causes birth defects. However, studies in animals have shown that caffeine causes birth defects when given in very large doses (amounts equal to the amount of caffeine contained in 12 to 24 cups of coffee a day).
- *Ibuprofen*—Studies on birth defects have not been done in humans. However, there is a chance that ibuprofen may cause unwanted effects on the heart or blood flow of the fetus or newborn baby if it is taken regularly during the last few months of pregnancy.
- *Phenylephrine*—Studies on birth defects have not been done in either humans or animals with phenylephrine.
- *Phenylpropanolamine*—Studies on birth defects have not been done in either humans or animals with phenylpropanolamine. However, it seems that women who take phenylpropanolamine in the weeks following delivery are more likely to suffer mental or mood changes.
- *Pseudoephedrine*—Studies on birth defects with pseudoephedrine have not been done in humans. In animal studies pseudoephedrine did not cause birth defects. However, when given to animals in high doses, pseudoephedrine did cause a decrease in average weight, length, and rate of bone formation in the animal fetus.
- *Salicylates (e.g., aspirin)*—Studies on birth defects in humans have been done with aspirin, but not with salicylamide. Although salicylates have been shown to cause birth defects in animals, they have not been shown to cause birth defects in humans.

  Regular use of salicylates late in pregnancy may cause unwanted effects on the heart or blood flow in the fetus or newborn baby. Use of salicylates during the last 2 weeks of pregnancy may cause bleeding problems in the fetus before or during delivery, or in the newborn baby. Also, too much use of salicylates during the last 3 months of pregnancy may increase the length of pregnancy, prolong labor and cause other problems during delivery, or cause severe bleeding in the mother before, during, or after delivery. *Do not take aspirin during the last 3 months of pregnancy unless it has been ordered by your doctor.*

Breast-feeding—If you are breast-feeding the chance that problems might occur depends on the ingredients of the combination. For the individual ingredients of these combinations, the following apply:

- *Acetaminophen*—Acetaminophen passes into the breast milk. However, it has not been reported to cause problems in nursing babies.
- *Alcohol*—Alcohol passes into the breast milk. However, the amount of alcohol in recommended doses of this medicine does not usually cause problems in nursing babies.
- *Caffeine*—Small amounts of caffeine pass into the breast milk and may build up in the nursing baby. However, the amount of caffeine in recommended doses of this medicine does not usually cause problems in nursing babies.
- *Decongestants (e.g., phenylephrine, phenylpropanolamine, pseudoephedrine)*—Decongestants may pass into the breast milk and may cause unwanted effects in nursing babies of mothers taking this medicine.
- *Salicylates (e.g., aspirin, salicylamide)*—Salicylates pass into the breast milk. Although salicylates have not been reported to cause problems in nursing babies, it is possible that problems may occur if large amounts are taken regularly.

Children—Very young children are usually more sensitive to the effects of this medicine. *Before giving any of these combination medicines to a child, check the package label very carefully. Some of these medicines are too strong for use in children.* If you are not certain whether a specific product can be given to a child, or if you have any questions about the amount to give, check with your health care professional, especially if it contains:

- *Decongestants (e.g., phenylephrine, phenylpropanolamine, pseudoephedrine)*—Increases in blood pressure may be more likely to occur in children taking decongestants. Also, mental changes may be more likely to occur in young children taking phenylpropanolamine-containing combinations.
- *Salicylates (e.g., aspirin)—Do not give aspirin or other salicylates to a child with a fever or other symptoms of a virus infection, especially flu or chickenpox, without first discussing its use with your child's doctor.* This is very important because salicylates may cause a serious illness called Reye's syndrome in these children. Also, children may be more sensitive to the aspirin or other salicylates contained in some of these medicines, especially if they have a fever or have lost large amounts of body fluid because of vomiting, diarrhea, or sweating.

Teenagers—*Do not give aspirin or other salicylates to a teenager with a fever or other symptoms of a virus infection, especially flu or chickenpox, without first discussing its use with your child's doctor.* This is very important because salicylates may cause a serious illness called Reye's syndrome in these individuals.

Older adults—The elderly are usually more sensitive to the effects of this medicine.

Other medicines—Although certain medicines should not be used together at all, in other cases two different medicines may be used together even if an interaction might occur. In these cases, your doctor may want to change the dose, or other precautions may be necessary. Tell your health care professional if you are taking *any* other prescription or nonprescription (over-the-counter [OTC]) medicine, for example, aspirin or other medicine for allergies. Some medicines may change the way this medicine affects your body. Also, the effect of other medicines may be increased or reduced by some of the ingredients in this medicine. Check with your health care professional about which medicines you should not take together with this medicine.

Other medical problems—The presence of other medical problems may affect the use of decongestant and analgesic combinations. Make sure you tell your doctor if you have any other medical problems, especially:

- Alcohol abuse—Acetaminophen-containing medicine increases the chance of liver damage
- Anemia—Taking aspirin-, salicylamide-, or ibuprofen-containing medicine may make the anemia worse
- Asthma, allergies, and nasal polyps, history of—Taking salicylate- or ibuprofen-containing medicine may cause an allergic reaction in which breathing becomes difficult
- Diabetes mellitus (sugar diabetes)—The decongestant in this medicine may put the patient with diabetes at a greater risk of having heart or blood vessel disease
- Gout—Aspirin-containing medicine may make the gout worse and reduce the benefit of the medicines used for gout
- Hepatitis or other liver disease—Liver disease increases the chance of side effects because the medicine is not broken down and may build up in the body; also, if liver disease is severe there is a greater chance that aspirin-containing medicine may cause bleeding, and that ibuprofen-containing medicine may cause serious kidney damage
- Heart or blood vessel disease or
- High blood pressure—The decongestant in this medicine may cause the blood pressure to increase and may also speed up the heart rate; also, caffeine-containing medicine if taken in large amounts may increase the heart rate; ibuprofen-containing medicine may cause the blood pressure to increase
- Hemophilia or other bleeding problems—Aspirin- or ibuprofen-containing medicine increases the chance of bleeding
- Kidney disease—The kidneys may be affected, especially if too much of this medicine is taken for a long time
- Mental illness (history of)—The decongestant in this medicine may increase the chance of mental side effects
- Overactive thyroid—If an overactive thyroid has caused a fast heart rate, the decongestant in this medicine may cause the heart rate to speed up further
- Stomach ulcer or other stomach problems—Salicylate- or ibuprofen-containing medicine may make the ulcer worse or cause bleeding of the stomach
- Systemic lupus erythematosus (SLE)—Ibuprofen-containing medicine may put the patient with SLE at a greater risk of having unwanted effects on the central nervous system and/or kidneys
- Ulcers, sores, or white spots in the mouth—This may be a sign of a serious side effect of ibuprofen-containing medicine; if you already have ulcers or sores in the mouth you and your doctor may not be able to tell when this side effect occurs

Proper Use of This Medicine

Take this medicine only as directed. Do not take more of it and do not take it more often than recommended on the label, unless otherwise directed by your doctor. To do so may increase the chance of side effects.

For *aspirin- or salicylamide-containing medicines:*

- If this medicine irritates your stomach, you may take it with food or a glass of water or milk to lessen the irritation.
- *If a combination medicine containing aspirin has a strong vinegar-like odor, do not use it.* This odor means the medicine is breaking down. If you have any questions about this, check with your pharmacist.

For *ibuprofen-containing medicines:*

- To lessen stomach upset, these medicines may be taken with food or an antacid.
- Take with a full glass (8 ounces) of water. Also, do not lie down for about 15 to 30 minutes after taking the medicine. Doing so may cause irritation that may lead to trouble in swallowing.

Dosing—The dose of these combination medicines will be different for different products. *Follow the directions on the box if you are buying this medicine without a prescription. Or, follow your doctor's orders if this medicine was prescribed.* The following information includes only the average doses for these combinations.

The number of capsules or tablets or teaspoonfuls of liquid that you take depends on the strengths of the medicines.

There is a large variety of decongestant and analgesic combination products on the market. Some products are for use in adults only, while others may be used in children. If you have any questions about this, check with your health care professional.

- For *oral* dosage forms (capsules, liquid, or tablets):
  - —For sinus pain and congestion:
    - Adults and children 12 years of age and older: 1 to 2 capsules or tablets every four to six hours.
    - Children up to 6 years of age: Use and dose must be determined by your doctor.
    - Children 6 to 12 years of age: 1 tablet, 4 to 6 chewable tablets, or 1 to 2 teaspoonfuls of liquid every four hours.

Missed dose—If you must take this medicine regularly and you miss a dose, take it as soon as possible. However, if it is almost time for your next dose, skip the missed dose and go back to your regular dosing schedule. Do not double doses.

Storage—To store this medicine:

- Keep this medicine out of the reach of children. Overdose is very dangerous in young children.
- Store away from heat and direct light.
- Do not store the capsule or tablet form of this medicine in the bathroom, near the kitchen sink, or in other damp places. Heat or moisture may cause the medicine to break down.
- Keep the liquid form of this medicine from freezing.
- Do not keep outdated medicine or medicine no longer needed. Be sure that any discarded medicine is out of the reach of children.

Precautions While Using This Medicine

Check with your doctor if your symptoms do not improve or become worse, or if you have a high fever.

This medicine may add to the central nervous system (CNS) stimulant and other effects of phenylpropanolamine (PPA)-containing diet aids. *Do not use medicines for diet or appetite control while taking this medicine unless you have checked with your doctor.*

This medicine may cause some people to become nervous or restless or to have trouble in sleeping. If you have trouble in sleeping, *take the last dose of this medicine for each day a few hours before bedtime.* If you have any questions about this, check with your doctor.

Before having any kind of surgery (including dental surgery) or emergency treatment, tell the medical doctor or dentist in charge that you are taking this medicine.

Check the label of all over-the-counter (OTC), nonprescription, and prescription medicines you now take. If any of them contain acetaminophen, aspirin, other salicylates such as bismuth subsalicylate (e.g., Pepto Bismol) or magnesium salicylate (e.g., Nuprin Backache Caplets), or salicylic acid (present in some shampoos and skin products), *check with your health care professional. Using any of them together with this medicine may cause an overdose.*

Do not drink alcoholic beverages while taking this medicine. Stomach problems may be more likely to occur if you drink alcoholic beverages while you are taking aspirin or ibuprofen. Also, liver damage may be more likely to occur if you drink large amounts of alcoholic beverages while you are taking acetaminophen.

If you think that you or anyone else may have taken an overdose of this medicine, get emergency help at once. Taking an overdose of a salicylate may cause unconsciousness or death. The first sign of an aspirin overdose may be ringing or buzzing in the ears. Other signs include convulsions (seizures), hearing loss, confusion, severe drowsiness or tiredness, severe excitement or nervousness, and unusually fast or deep breathing. Signs of severe acetaminophen overdose may not appear until 2 to 4 days after the overdose is taken, but treatment to prevent liver damage or death must be started within 24 hours or less after the overdose is taken.

For patients *taking aspirin-containing medicine:*

- Do not take aspirin-containing medicine for 5 days before any surgery, including dental surgery, unless otherwise directed by your medical doctor or dentist. Taking aspirin during this time may cause bleeding problems.

For diabetic patients *taking salicylate-containing medicine:*

- False urine sugar test results may occur if you take 8 or more 325-mg (5-grain) doses of aspirin every day for several days in a row. Smaller doses or occasional use of aspirin usually will not affect urine sugar tests. If you have any questions about this, check with your health care professional, especially if your diabetes is not well controlled.

For patients *taking ibuprofen-containing medicine:*

- This medicine may cause some people to become confused, drowsy, dizzy, lightheaded, or less alert than they are normally. It may also cause blurred vision or other vision problems in some people. *Make sure you know how you react to this medicine before you drive, use machines, or do anything else that could be dangerous if you are dizzy or are not alert and able to see well.*

Side Effects of This Medicine

Along with its needed effects, a medicine may cause some unwanted effects. Although serious side effects occur rarely when this medicine is taken as recommended, they may be more likely to occur if:

- too much medicine is taken.
- it is taken in large doses.
- it is taken for a long period of time.

Get emergency help immediately if any of the following symptoms of overdose occur:

For all combinations

Convulsions (seizures); dizziness or lightheadedness (severe); fast, slow, or irregular heartbeat; hallucinations (seeing, hearing, or feeling things that are not there); headache (continuing and severe); increased sweating; mood or mental changes; nausea or vomiting (severe or continuing); nervousness or restlessness (severe); shortness of breath or troubled breathing; stomach cramps or pain (severe or continuing); swelling or tenderness in the upper abdomen or stomach area; trouble in sleeping

For acetaminophen-containing only

Diarrhea; loss of appetite

For aspirin- or salicylamide-containing only

Any loss of hearing; changes in behavior (in children); confusion; diarrhea (severe or continuing); drowsiness or tiredness (severe, especially in children); fast or deep breathing (especially in children); ringing or buzzing in ears (continuing); uncontrollable flapping movements of the hands, (especially in elderly patients); unexplained fever; unusual thirst; vision problems

Also, check with your doctor as soon as possible if any of the following side effects occur:

More common

Nausea, vomiting, or stomach pain (mild—for combinations containing aspirin or ibuprofen)

Less common or rare

Bloody or black, tarry stools; bloody or cloudy urine; blurred vision or any changes in vision or eyes; changes in facial skin color; changes in hearing; changes or problems with urination; difficult or painful urination; fever; headache, severe, with fever and stiff neck; increased blood pressure; muscle cramps or pain; skin rash, hives, or itching; sores, ulcers, or white spots on lips or in mouth; swelling of face, fingers, feet, or lower legs; swollen and/or painful glands; unexplained sore throat and fever; unusual bleeding or bruising; unusual tiredness or weakness; vomiting of blood or material that looks like coffee grounds; weight gain (unusual); yellow eyes or skin

Other side effects may occur that usually do not need medical attention. These side effects may go away during treatment as your body adjusts to the medicine. However, check with your doctor if any of the following side effects continue or are bothersome:

More common

Heartburn or indigestion (for medicines containing salicylate or ibuprofen); nervousness or restlessness

Less common

Drowsiness (for medicines containing salicylamide)

Not all of the side effects listed above have been reported for each of these medicines, but they have been reported for at least one of them. There are some similarities among these combination medicines, so many of the above side effects may occur with any of these medicines.

Other side effects not listed above may also occur in some patients. If you notice any other effects, check with your doctor.

Revised: 09/07/94
Interim revision: 07/18/95; 08/28/96

DEFEROXAMINE Systemic

A commonly used brand name in the U.S. and Canada is Desferal. Another commonly used name is desferrioxamine.

Description

Deferoxamine (dee-fer-OX-a-meen) is used to remove excess iron from the body. This may be necessary in certain patients with anemia who must receive many blood transfusions. It is also used to treat acute iron poisoning, especially in small children.

Deferoxamine combines with iron in the bloodstream. The combination of iron and deferoxamine is then removed from the body by the kidneys. By removing the excess iron, the medicine lessens damage to various organs and tissues of the body. This medicine may be used for other conditions as determined by your doctor.

Deferoxamine is to be administered only by or under the immediate supervision of your doctor. It is available in the following dosage form:

Parenteral

- Injection (U.S. and Canada)

Before Receiving This Medicine

In deciding to use a medicine, the risks of taking the medicine must be weighed against the good it will do. This is a decision you and your doctor will make. For deferoxamine, the following should be considered:

Allergies—Tell your doctor if you have ever had any unusual or allergic reaction to deferoxamine. Also tell your health care professional if you are allergic to any other substances, such as foods, preservatives, or dyes.

Pregnancy—Deferoxamine has not been shown to cause birth defects or other problems in humans. However, in animal studies this medicine caused birth defects when given in doses just above the recommended human dose. In general, deferoxamine is not recommended for women who may become pregnant or for use during early pregnancy, unless the woman's life is in danger from too much iron.

Breast-feeding—It is not known whether deferoxamine passes into breast milk. Although most medicines pass into breast milk in small amounts, many of them may be used safely while breast-feeding. Mothers who are taking this medicine and who wish to breast-feed should discuss this with their doctor.

Children—Deferoxamine is not used for long-term treatment of children up to 3 years of age. Also, younger patients are more likely to develop hearing and vision problems with the use of deferoxamine in high doses for a long time.

Older adults—The combination of deferoxamine and vitamin C should be used with caution in older patients, since this combination may be more likely to cause heart problems in these patients than in younger adults.

Other medicines—Although certain medicines should not be used together at all, in other cases two different medicines may be used together even if an interaction might occur. In these cases, your doctor may want to change the dose, or other precautions may be necessary. When you are receiving deferoxamine, it is especially important that your health care professional know if you are taking the following:

- Ascorbic acid (vitamin C)—Use with deferoxamine may be harmful to body tissues, especially in the elderly

Other medical problems—The presence of other medical problems may affect the use of deferoxamine. Make sure you tell your doctor if you have any other medical problems, especially:

- Kidney disease—Patients with kidney disease may be more likely to have side effects

Proper Use of This Medicine

Deferoxamine may sometimes be given at home to patients who do not need to be in the hospital. If you are receiving this medicine at home, *make sure you clearly understand and carefully follow your doctor's instructions.*

Dosing—The dose of deferoxamine will be different for different patients. *Follow your doctor's orders or the directions on the label.* The following information includes only the average doses of deferoxamine. *If your dose is different, do not change it* unless your doctor tells you to do so.

- For *injection* dosage form:
  - —For acute iron toxicity:
    - Adults and children over 3 years of age—Dose is based on body weight and must be determined

by your doctor. The usual dose is 90 milligrams (mg) per kilogram (kg) (41 mg per pound) of body weight, followed by 45 mg per kg (20 mg per pound) of body weight, injected into a muscle every four to twelve hours. If it is injected into a vein, the usual dose is 15 mg per kg (7 mg per pound) of body weight per hour every eight hours.

• Children up to 3 years of age—The usual dose is 15 mg per kg (7 mg per pound) of body weight per hour, injected into a vein.

—For chronic iron toxicity:

• Adults and children over 3 years of age—The usual dose is 500 mg to 1 gram a day, injected into a muscle. Or, the medicine may be injected under the skin by an infusion pump. The usual dose is 1 to 2 grams (20 to 40 mg per kg [9 to 18 mg per pound] of body weight) a day, injected under the skin, over a period of eight to twenty-four hours. If you are receiving blood transfusions, the usual dose is 500 mg to 1 gram a day, injected into a muscle. An extra 2 grams of the medicine is injected into a vein with each unit of blood at a rate of 15 mg per kg of body weight per hour.

• Children up to 3 years of age—Use and dose must be determined by your doctor. The usual dose is 10 mg per kg (5 mg per pound) of body weight a day, injected under the skin.

Storage—To store this medicine:

- Keep out of the reach of children.
- Store away from heat and direct light.
- Store the mixed medicine at room temperature for no longer than recommended by your doctor or the manufacturer. Do not refrigerate.
- Do not keep outdated medicine or medicine that is no longer needed. Be sure any discarded medicine is out of the reach of children.

Precautions While Receiving This Medicine

It is important that your doctor check your progress at regular visits to make sure that this medicine is working properly and to prevent unwanted effects. Certain blood and urine tests must be done regularly to check for the need for dosage changes.

Deferoxamine may cause some people, especially younger patients, to have hearing and vision problems within a few weeks after they start taking it. *If you notice any problems with your vision, such as blurred vision, difficulty in seeing at night, or difficulty in seeing colors, or difficulty with your hearing, check with your doctor as soon as possible.* The dose of deferoxamine may need to be adjusted.

Do not take vitamin C unless your doctor has told you to do so.

Side Effects of This Medicine

Along with its needed effects, a medicine may cause some unwanted effects. Although not all of these side effects may occur, if they do occur they may need medical attention.

Check with your doctor as soon as possible if any of the following side effects occur:

More common

Bluish fingernails, lips, or skin; blurred vision or other problems with vision; convulsions (seizures); difficulty in breathing (wheezing), or fast breathing; fast heartbeat; hearing problems; pain or swelling at place of injection; redness or flushing of skin; skin rash, hives, or itching

Less common

Diarrhea; difficult urination; fever; leg cramps; stomach and muscle cramps; stomach discomfort; unusual bleeding or bruising

Hearing and vision problems are more likely to occur in younger patients taking high doses and on long-term treatment.

Deferoxamine may cause the urine to turn orange-rose in color. This is to be expected while you are using this medicine.

Other side effects not listed above may also occur in some patients. If you notice any other effects, check with your doctor.

Additional Information

Once a medicine has been approved for marketing for a certain use, experience may show that it is also useful for other medical problems. Although this use is not included in product labeling, deferoxamine is used in certain patients with the following medical condition:

- Aluminum toxicity (too much aluminum in the body)

Other than the above information, there is no additional information relating to proper use, precautions, or side effects for this use.

Revised: 05/27/94

DESFLURANE Inhalation-Systemic†

A commonly used brand name in the U.S. is Suprane.

†Not commercially available in Canada.

Description

Desflurane (DES-flure-ane) belongs to the group of medicines known as general anesthetics (an-ess-THET-iks). Desflurane is used to cause general anesthesia (loss of consciousness) before and during surgery. It is breathed in (inhaled). Although desflurane can be used by itself, combinations of anesthetics are often used together. This helps produce more effective anesthesia in some patients.

General anesthetics are given only by or under the immediate supervision of a medical doctor trained to use them. If you will be receiving a general anesthetic during surgery, your doctor will give you the medicine and closely follow your progress.

Desflurane is available in the following dosage form:

- Inhalation (U.S.)

Before Receiving This Medicine

In deciding to use a medicine, the risks of using the medicine must be weighed against the good it will do. For desflurane, the following should be considered:

Allergies—Tell your doctor if you have ever had any unusual or allergic reaction to an anesthetic. Also tell your doctor if you are allergic to any other substances, such as foods, preservatives, or dyes.

Pregnancy—Desflurane has not been studied in pregnant women. It did not cause birth defects in animal studies. However, desflurane caused other unwanted effects in the animal fetus when given for many days in a row in amounts that were large enough to cause harmful effects in the mother.

Breast-feeding—Small amounts of desflurane may pass into the breast milk. Your doctor may want you to stop breast-feeding for about 24 hours after receiving the medicine.

Children—Desflurane has been tested in children. It is not used to start anesthesia in children who are awake because it causes irritation and other unwanted effects. However, when it is used to continue general anesthesia that has been started with another anesthetic, desflurane does not cause different side effects or problems in children than it does in adults.

Older adults—Desflurane has been tested and has not been shown to cause different side effects or problems in older people than it does in younger adults. However, older people usually need smaller amounts of an anesthetic than younger people. Your doctor will take your age into account when deciding on the right amount of desflurane for you.

Other medicines—Although certain medicines should not be used together at all, in other cases 2 different medicines may be used together even if an interaction might occur. In these cases, your doctor may want to change the dose, or other precautions may be necessary. When you are receiving a general anesthetic, it is especially important that your doctor know if you are taking **any** other prescription or nonprescription (over-the-counter [OTC]) medicine or any of the following:

- "Street" drugs, such as amphetamines ("uppers"), barbiturates ("downers"), cocaine, marijuana, phencyclidine (PCP or "angel dust"), and heroin or other narcotics—Serious, possibly fatal, side effects may occur if your doctor gives you an anesthetic without knowing that you have taken another medicine

Other medical problems—The presence of other medical problems may affect the use of desflurane. Make sure you tell your doctor if you have **any** other medical problems, especially:

- Diseases that can cause muscle weakness, such as familial periodic paralysis, muscular dystrophy, myasthenia gravis, or Eaton-Lambert syndrome, or
- Heart or blood vessel disease—The chance of side effects may be increased, but serious problems can be prevented if your doctor knows that these conditions are present before giving you an anesthetic
- Malignant hyperthermia, during or shortly after receiving an anesthetic (history of, or family history of). Signs of malignant hyperthermia include very high fever, fast and irregular heartbeat, muscle spasms or tightness, and breathing problems—This side effect may occur again

Proper Use of This Medicine

Dosing—The dose of desflurane will be different for different patients. Your doctor will decide on the right amount for you, depending on:

- Your age.
- Your general physical condition.
- The kind of surgery being performed.
- Other medicines you are taking or will receive before and during surgery.

Precautions After Receiving This Medicine

For patients going home within 24 hours after receiving a general anesthetic:

- General anesthetics may cause some people to feel drowsy, tired, or weak for a while after they have been given. They may also cause problems with coordination and one's ability to think. Therefore, for about 24 hours (or longer if necessary) after receiving a general anesthetic, *do not drive, use machines, or do anything else that could be dangerous if you are not alert.*
- Unless otherwise directed by your doctor or dentist, *do not drink alcoholic beverages or take other CNS depressants (medicines that slow down the nervous system, possibly causing drowsiness) for about 24 hours after you have received a general anesthetic.* To do so may add to the effects of the anesthetic. Some examples of CNS depressants are antihistamines or medicine for hay fever, other allergies, or colds; other sedatives, tranquilizers, or sleeping medicine; prescription pain medicine or narcotics; barbiturates; medicine for seizures; and muscle relaxants.

Side Effects of This Medicine

Along with its needed effects, a medicine may cause some unwanted effects. Although not all of these side effects may occur, if they do occur they may need medical attention. While you are receiving and recovering from a general anesthetic, your health care professional will closely follow its effects. However, some effects may not be noticed until later.

The following side effects should go away as the effects of the anesthetic wear off. However, check with your doctor if any of them continue or are bothersome:

More common

Coughing; nausea or vomiting

Less common or rare

Dizziness; headache; irritated or red eyes; nervousness and restlessness; sore throat

Other side effects not listed above may also occur in some patients. If you notice any other effects, check with your doctor.

Developed: 12/21/93

DESMOPRESSIN Systemic

Some commonly used brand names are:

In the U.S.—

DDAVP
DDAVP Nasal Spray
DDAVP Rhinal Tube
Stimate
Stimate Nasal Spray

Generic name product may also be available.

In Canada—

DDAVP
DDAVP Spray
DDAVP Rhinyle Nasal Solution
Octostim

Description

Desmopressin (des-moe-PRESS-in) is a hormone taken through the nose or given by injection to prevent or control the frequent urination, increased thirst, and loss of water associated with diabetes insipidus (water diabetes). It is used also to control frequent urination and increased thirst associated with certain types of brain injuries or brain surgery or bed-wetting. Desmopressin works by acting on the kidneys to reduce the flow of urine.

Desmopressin is also given by injection to treat some patients with certain bleeding problems such as hemophilia or von Willebrand's disease.

Desmopressin is available only with your doctor's prescription, in the following dosage forms:

Nasal

- Nasal solution (U.S. and Canada)

Parenteral

- Injection (U.S. and Canada)

Before Using This Medicine

In deciding to use a medicine, the risks of taking the medicine must be weighed against the good it will do. This is a decision you and your doctor will make. For desmopressin, the following should be considered:

Allergies—Tell your doctor if you have ever had any unusual or allergic reaction to desmopressin. Also tell your health care professional if you are allergic to any other substances, such as foods, preservatives, or dyes.

Pregnancy—Studies have not been done in pregnant women. Desmopressin has been used before and during pregnancy to treat diabetes insipidus and has not been shown to cause birth defects.

Breast-feeding—Desmopressin passes into breast milk in very small amounts. However, it has not been reported to cause problems in nursing babies.

Children—Infants may be more sensitive to the effects of this medicine.

Older adults—Some side effects (confusion, drowsiness, continuing headache, problem with urination, weight gain) may be especially likely to occur in elderly patients, who are usually more sensitive than younger adults to the effects of desmopressin.

Other medicines—Although certain medicines should not be used together at all, in other cases two different medicines may be used together even if an interaction might occur. In these cases, your doctor may want to change the dose, or other precautions may be necessary. Tell your health care professional if you are taking any other prescription or nonprescription (over-the-counter [OTC]) medicine.

Other medical problems—The presence of other medical problems may affect the use of desmopressin. Make sure you tell your doctor if you have any other medical problems, especially:

- Cystic fibrosis—Excess water retention and serious side effects may be more likely to occur in patients with this condition
- Heart or blood vessel disease or
- High blood pressure—Large doses of desmopressin can cause an increase in blood pressure
- Stuffy nose caused by cold or allergy—May prevent nasal desmopressin from being absorbed through the lining of the nose into the bloodstream

Proper Use of This Medicine

For patients using the *nasal solution form* of this medicine:

- *Use this medicine only as directed.* Do not use more of it and do not use it more often than your doctor ordered. To do so may increase the chance of side effects.
- This medicine usually comes with patient directions. Read them carefully before using this medicine.

Dosing—When you are using desmopressin, it is very important that you get the exact amount of medicine that you need. The dose of desmopressin will be different for different patients. Your doctor will determine the proper dose of desmopressin for you.

The number of doses you use each day, the time allowed between doses, and the length of time you use the medicine depend on the medical problem for which you are using desmopressin.

- For *nasal* dosage form (nasal solution):
  - —For preventing or controlling diabetes insipidus (water diabetes):
    - Adults and teenagers—At first, 10 micrograms (mcg) inhaled in a nostril at bedtime. Your doctor may increase the dose gradually each night if needed. Then, your doctor may want you to use 10 to 40 mcg. The dose may be used as a single dose or it may be divided into two or three doses a day.
    - Children up to 3 months of age—Dose must be determined by your doctor.
    - Children 3 months to 12 years of age—At first, 5 mcg (0.05 mL) inhaled in a nostril at bedtime. Your doctor may increase the dose gradually each night if needed. Then, your doctor may change the dose based on your body weight. The usual dose is 2 to 4 mcg per kilogram (kg) (0.91 to 1.82 mcg per pound) of body weight a day. The dose may be used as a single dose or it may be divided into two doses a day.
  - —For controlling bed-wetting:
    - Adults, teenagers, and children over 6 years of age—At first, 10 mcg inhaled into each nostril at bedtime. Then, your doctor may change the dose to 10 to 40 mcg a day.
    - Children up to 6 years of age—Dose must be determined by your doctor.
- For *parenteral* dosage form (injection):
  - —For preventing or controlling frequent urination:
    - Adults and teenagers—2 to 4 mcg injected into a vein or under the skin a day. This dose is usually divided into two doses.
  - —For treating some bleeding problems such as hemophilia or von Willebrand's disease:
    - Adults and teenagers—0.3 mcg per kg (0.14 mcg per pound) of body weight mixed in fifty mL of 0.9% sodium chloride. This solution is injected into a vein slowly over fifteen to thirty minutes. Your doctor may repeat this treatment if needed.
    - Children up to 3 months of age—Use is not recommended.
    - Children 3 months of age or older—The dose is based on body weight and must be determined by your doctor:
      - —For children weighing 10 kg (22 pounds) or less—0.3 mcg per kg (0.135 mcg per pound) of body weight mixed in ten mL of 0.9% sodium chloride and injected over fifteen or thirty minutes into a vein by your doctor. Your doctor may repeat this treatment if needed.
      - —For children weighing more than 10 kg (22 pounds)—0.3 mcg per kg (0.14 mcg per pound) of body weight mixed in fifty mL of 0.9% sodium chloride and injected into a vein slowly over fifteen to thirty minutes by your doctor. Your doctor may repeat this treatment if needed.

Missed dose—*For nasal solution form of this medicine:* If you miss a dose of this medicine and your dosing schedule is—

- One dose a day—Use the missed dose as soon as possible. Then go back to your regular dosing schedule. However, if you do not remember the missed dose until the next day, skip the missed dose and go back to your regular dosing schedule. Do not double doses.
- More than one dose a day—Use the missed dose as soon as possible. Then go back to your regular dosing schedule. However, if it is almost time for your next dose, skip the missed dose and go back to your regular dosing schedule. Do not double doses.

Storage—To store this medicine:

- Keep out of the reach of children.
- Store in the refrigerator. However, keep the medicine from freezing.
- Do not keep outdated medicine or medicine no longer needed. Be sure that any discarded medicine is out of the reach of children.

Side Effects of This Medicine

Along with its needed effects, a medicine may cause some unwanted effects. Although not all of these effects may occur, if they do occur they may need medical attention.

Check with your doctor immediately if any of the following side effects occur:

Confusion; convulsions (seizures); drowsiness; headache (continuing); decreased urination; weight gain (rapid)

Other side effects may occur that usually do not need medical attention. These side effects may go away during treatment as your body adjusts to the medicine. However, check with your doctor if any of the following side effects continue or are bothersome:

Less common or rare

Abdominal or stomach cramps; flushing or redness of skin; headache; nausea; pain in the vulva (genital area outside of the vagina)

With intranasal (through the nose) use

Runny or stuffy nose

With intravenous use

Pain, redness, or swelling at place of injection

Other side effects not listed above may also occur in some patients. If you notice any other effects, check with your doctor.

Revised: 10/26/92
Interim revision: 06/02/94; 07/19/96

DEXTROMETHORPHAN Systemic

Some commonly used brand names are:

In the U.S.—

Benylin Adult
Benylin Pediatric
Children's Hold
Cough-X
Creo-Terpin
Delsym
Drixoral Cough Liquid Caps
Hold
Mediquell
Pertussin Cough Suppressant
Pertussin CS
Pertussin ES
Robitussin Cough Calmers
Robitussin Maximum Strength Cough Suppressant
Robitussin Pediatric
St. Joseph Cough Suppressant for Children
Sucrets Cough Control Formula
Trocal
Vicks Formula 44 Pediatric Formula

In Canada—

Balminil D.M.
Broncho-Grippol-DM
Calmylin #1
Delsym
DM Syrup
Koffex
Neo-DM
Ornex•DM 15
Ornex•DM 30
Robidex
Robitussin Pediatric
Sedatuss

Description

Dextromethorphan (dex-troe-meth-OR-fan) is used to relieve coughs due to colds or influenza (flu). It should not be used for chronic cough that occurs with smoking, asthma, or emphysema or when there is an unusually large amount of mucus or phlegm (flem) with the cough.

Dextromethorphan relieves cough by acting directly on the cough center in the brain.

This medicine is available without a prescription; however, your doctor may have special instructions on the proper use of this medicine for your medical condition. It is available in the following dosage forms:

Oral

- Capsules (U.S. and Canada)
- Lozenges (U.S.)
- Extended-release oral suspension (U.S. and Canada)
- Syrup (U.S. and Canada)
- Chewable tablets (U.S.)

Before Using this Medicine

If you are taking this medicine without a prescription, carefully read and follow any precautions on the label. For dextromethorphan, the following should be considered:

Allergies—Tell your doctor if you have ever had any unusual or allergic reaction to dextromethorphan. Also tell your health care professional if you are allergic to any other substances, such as foods, preservatives, or dyes.

Diet—Make certain your health care professional knows if you are on a low-sodium, low-sugar, or any other special diet. Most medicines contain more than their active ingredient, and many liquid medicines contain alcohol.

Pregnancy—Dextromethorphan has not been shown to cause birth defects or other problems in humans.

Breast-feeding—Dextromethorphan has not been reported to cause problems in nursing babies.

Children—Although there is no specific information comparing use of dextromethorphan in children with use in other age groups, this medicine is not expected to cause different side effects or problems in children than it does in adults.

Older adults—Many medicines have not been studied specifically in older people. Therefore, it may not be known whether they work exactly the same way they do in younger adults or if they cause different side effects or problems in older people. There is no specific information comparing use of dextromethorphan in the elderly with use in other age groups.

Other medicines—Although certain medicines should not be used together at all, in other cases 2 different medicines may be used together even if an interaction might occur. In these cases, your doctor may want to change the dose, or other precautions may be necessary. When you are taking dextromethorphan it is especially important that your health care professional know if you are taking any of the following:

- Central nervous system (CNS) depressants (medicines that cause drowsiness)—The CNS depressant effects of either these medicines or dextromethorphan may be increased
- Monoamine oxidase (MAO) inhibitors (furazolidone [e.g., Furoxone], isocarboxazid [e.g., Marplan], phenelzine [e.g., Nardil], procarbazine [e.g., Matulane], tranylcypromine [e.g., Parnate])—Taking dextromethorphan if you are taking MAO inhibitors or have taken them within the past 2 weeks may cause coma, dizziness, excited or unusual behavior, fever, high blood pressure, nausea, sluggishness, spasms, and tremors

Other medical problems—The presence of other medical problems may affect the use of dextromethorphan. Make sure you tell your doctor if you have any other medical problems, especially:

- Asthma—Since dextromethorphan decreases coughing, it makes it difficult to get rid of the mucus that collects in the lungs and airways during asthma
- Liver disease—Dextromethorphan may build up in the body and cause unwanted effects
- Mucus or phlegm with cough—Since dextromethorphan decreases coughing, it makes it difficult to get rid of the mucus that may collect in the lungs and airways with some diseases

Proper Use of This Medicine

Use this medicine only as directed by your doctor or the directions on the label. Do not use more of it, do not use it more often, and do not use it for a longer time than your doctor or the label says. Although this effect has happened only rarely, dextromethorphan has become habit-forming (causing mental or physical dependence) in some persons who used too much for a long time.

Dosing—The dose of dextromethorphan will be different for different patients. *Follow your doctor's orders or the directions on the label.* The following information includes only the average doses of dextromethorphan. *If your dose is different, do not change it* unless your doctor tells you to do so.

The number of capsules or tablets or teaspoonfuls of suspension or syrup that you take depends on the strength of the medicine.

- For *regular (short-acting) oral* dosage form (capsules, lozenges, syrup, or tablets):
  - —For cough:
    - Adults—10 to 20 milligrams (mg) every four hours or 30 mg every six to eight hours, as needed.
    - Children younger than 2 years of age—Use and dose must be determined by your doctor.
    - Children 2 to 6 years of age—2.5 to 5 mg every four hours or 7.5 mg every six to eight hours, as needed.
    - Children 6 to 12 years of age—5 to 10 mg every four hours or 15 mg every six to eight hours, as needed.
- For *long-acting oral* dosage form (extended-release oral suspension):
  - —For cough:
    - Adults—60 mg every twelve hours, as needed.
    - Children younger than 2 years of age—Use and dose must be determined by your doctor.
    - Children 2 to 6 years of age—15 mg every twelve hours, as needed.
    - Children 6 to 12 years of age—30 mg every twelve hours, as needed.

Missed dose—If you must take this medicine regularly and you miss a dose, take it as soon as possible. However, if it is almost time for your next dose, skip the missed dose and go back to your regular dosing schedule. Do not double doses.

Storage—To store this medicine:

- Store away from heat and direct light.
- Keep out of the reach of children.
- Do not store the tablet form of this medicine in the bathroom, near the kitchen sink, or in other damp places. Heat or moisture may cause the medicine to break down.
- Keep the liquid form of this medicine from freezing.
- Do not keep outdated medicine or medicine no longer needed. Be sure that any discarded medicine is out of the reach of children.

Precautions While Using This Medicine

If your cough has not improved after 7 days or if you have a high fever, skin rash, or continuing headache with the cough, check with your doctor. These signs may mean that you have other medical problems.

Side Effects of This Medicine

Along with its needed effects, a medicine may cause some unwanted effects. Although not all of these side effects may occur, if they do occur they may need medical attention.

Check with your doctor as soon as possible if any of the following side effects occur:

Symptoms of overdose

Confusion; drowsiness or dizziness; nausea or vomiting (severe); unusual excitement, nervousness, restlessness, or irritability (severe)

Other side effects may occur that usually do not need medical attention. These side effects may go away during treatment as your body adjusts to the medicine. However, check with your health care professional if any of the following side effects continue or are bothersome:

Less common or rare

Dizziness (mild); drowsiness (mild); nausea or vomiting; stomach pain

Other side effects not listed above may also occur in some patients. If you notice any other effects, check with your doctor.

Revised: 06/23/94
Interim revision: 06/13/95

DEXTROTHYROXINE Systemic

Some commonly used brand names are:

In the U.S.—
Choloxin

In Canada—
Choloxin

Other—

Biotirmone	Dynothel
Debetrol	Eulipos
Dethyrona	Lisolipin
Dethyrone	Nadrothyron-D

Description

Dextrothyroxine (dex-troe-thye-ROX-een) is used to lower high cholesterol levels in the blood. However, it has generally been replaced by safer medicines for the treatment of high cholesterol.

Dextrothyroxine is available only with your doctor's prescription, in the following dosage form:

Oral

- Tablets (U.S. and Canada)

Before Using This Medicine

In deciding to use a medicine, the risks of taking the medicine must be weighed against the good it will do. This is a decision you and your doctor will make. For dextrothyroxine, the following should be considered:

Allergies—Tell your doctor if you have ever had any unusual or allergic reaction to dextrothyroxine. Also tell your health care professional if you are allergic to any other substances, such as foods, preservatives, or dyes.

Diet—Before prescribing medicine for your condition, your doctor will probably try to control your condition by prescribing a personal diet for you. Such a diet may be low in fats, sugars, and/or cholesterol. Many people are able to control their condition by carefully following their doctor's orders for proper diet and exercise. *Medicine is prescribed only when additional help is needed* and is effective only when a schedule of diet and exercise is properly followed.

Also, this medicine is less effective if you are greatly overweight. It may be very important for you to go on a reducing diet. However, check with your doctor before going on any diet.

Make certain your health care professional knows if you are on any special diet, such as a low-sodium or low-sugar diet.

Pregnancy—Dextrothyroxine has not been studied in pregnant women. However, studies in animals have not shown that dextrothyroxine causes birth defects or other problems. Before taking this medicine, make sure your doctor knows if you are pregnant or if you may become pregnant.

Breast-feeding—It is not known whether dextrothyroxine passes into breast milk. Although most medicines pass into breast milk in small amounts, many of them may be used safely while breast-feeding. Mothers who are taking this medicine and who wish to breast-feed should discuss this with their doctor.

Children—There is no specific information comparing use of dextrothyroxine in children to use in other age groups. However, use is not recommended in children under 2 years of age since cholesterol is needed for normal development.

Older adults—Side effects are more likely to occur in the elderly, who are usually more sensitive to the effects of dextrothyroxine.

Other medicines—Although certain medicines should not be used together at all, in other cases two different medicines may be used together even if an interaction might occur. In these cases, your doctor may want to change the dose, or other precautions may be necessary. When you are taking dextrothyroxine, it is especially important that your health care professional know if you are taking any of the following:

- Anticoagulants (blood thinners)—The effects of the anticoagulant may be altered; a change in dosage of the anticoagulant may be necessary
- Cholestyramine (e.g., Questran) or
- Colestipol (e.g., Colestid)—The effects of dextrothyroxine may decrease; these two medicines should be taken at least 4 to 5 hours before or after dextrothyroxine

Other medical problems—The presence of other medical problems may affect the use of dextrothyroxine. Make sure you tell your doctor if you have any other medical problems, especially:

- Diabetes mellitus (sugar diabetes)—Blood sugar levels may be increased
- Heart or blood vessel disease or
- High blood pressure or
- Overactive thyroid—Dextrothyroxine may make these conditions worse
- Kidney disease—Higher blood levels of dextrothyroxine may result and increase the chance of side effects
- Liver disease—May lead to an increase in cholesterol blood levels
- Underactive thyroid—There may be an increased sensitivity to the effects of dextrothyroxine

Proper Use of This Medicine

Take this medicine exactly as directed by your doctor. Try not to miss any doses and do not take more medicine than your doctor ordered.

Remember that this medicine will not cure your cholesterol problem but it does help control it. Therefore, you must continue to take it as directed if you expect to lower your cholesterol level.

Follow carefully the special diet your doctor gave you. This is the most important part of controlling your condition, and is necessary if the medicine is to work properly.

Dosing—The dose of dextrothyroxine will be different for different patients. *Follow your doctor's orders or the directions on the label.* The following information includes only the average doses of dextrothyroxine. *If your dose is different, do not change it* unless your doctor tells you to do so.

The number of tablets that you take depends on the strength of the medicine.

- For *tablets* dosage form:
  - —For treatment of high cholesterol:
    - Adults—1 to 8 milligrams (mg) a day.
    - Children up to two years of age—Use is not recommended.
    - Children two years of age and older—50 to 100 micrograms (0.05 to 0.1 mg) per kilogram of body weight a day.

Missed dose—If you miss a dose of this medicine, take it as soon as possible. However, if it is almost time for your next dose, skip the missed dose and go back to your regular dosing schedule. Do not double doses.

Storage—To store this medicine:

- Keep out of the reach of children.
- Store away from heat and direct light.
- Do not store in the bathroom, near the kitchen sink, or in other damp places. Heat or moisture may cause the medicine to break down.
- Do not keep outdated medicine or medicine no longer needed. Be sure that any discarded medicine is out of the reach of children.

Precautions While Using This Medicine

It is very important that your doctor check your progress at regular visits. This will allow your doctor to see if the medicine is working properly to lower your cholesterol levels and if you should continue to take it.

Do not stop taking this medicine without first checking with your doctor. When you stop taking this medicine, your blood cholesterol levels may increase again. Your doctor may want you to follow a special diet to help prevent this from happening.

Before having any kind of surgery (including dental surgery) or emergency treatment, *tell the medical doctor or dentist in charge that you are taking this medicine.*

Side Effects of This Medicine

Along with its needed effects, a medicine may cause some unwanted effects. Although not all of these side effects may occur, if they do occur they may need medical attention.

Check with your doctor immediately if any of the following side effects occur:

Rare

Chest pain; fast or irregular heartbeat; stomach pain (severe) with nausea and vomiting

Check with your doctor as soon as possible if the following side effects occur, since they may indicate too much medicine is being taken:

Rare

Changes in appetite; changes in menstrual periods; diarrhea; fast or irregular heartbeat; fever; hand tremors; headache; increase in urination; irritability, nervousness, or trouble in sleeping; leg cramps; shortness of breath; skin rash or itching; sweating, flushing, or increased sensitivity to heat; unusual weight loss; vomiting

Other side effects not listed above may also occur in some patients. If you notice any other effects, check with your doctor.

Revised: 04/22/93

DEZOCINE Systemic†

A commonly used brand name in the U.S. is Dalgan.

†Not commercially available in Canada.

Description

Dezocine (DEZ-oh-seen) belongs to the group of medicines known as narcotic analgesics (nar-KOT-ik an-al-JEE-zicks). Narcotic analgesics act in the central nervous system (CNS) to relieve pain. Some of their side effects are also caused by actions in the CNS.

Dezocine is available only with your doctor's prescription. It is available in the following dosage form:

Parenteral

- Injection (U.S.)

Before Using This Medicine

In deciding to use a medicine, the risks of using the medicine must be weighed against the good it will do. This is a decision you and your doctor will make. For dezocine, the following should be considered:

Allergies—Tell your doctor if you have ever had any unusual or allergic reaction to dezocine. Also tell your health care professional if you are allergic to any other substances, such as foods, preservatives, or dyes.

Pregnancy—Studies on birth defects with dezocine have not been done in pregnant women. Dezocine did not cause birth defects in animal studies. However, the birth weights of the newborn animals were lower than normal, probably because the pregnant animals ate less than usual.

Too much use of a narcotic during pregnancy may cause the baby to become dependent on the medicine. This may lead to withdrawal side effects after birth. Also, narcotics may cause breathing problems in the newborn infant if taken just before delivery.

Breast-feeding—It is not known whether dezocine passes into the breast milk. However, it has not been reported to cause problems in nursing babies.

Children—Studies on this medicine have been done only in adult patients, and there is no specific information comparing use of dezocine in patients up to 18 years of age with use in other age groups.

Older adults—Elderly people are especially sensitive to the effects of narcotic analgesics such as dezocine. This may increase the chance of side effects, especially breathing problems, during treatment.

Other medicines—Although certain medicines should not be used together at all, in other cases two different medicines may be used together even if an interaction might occur. In these cases, your doctor may want to change the dose, or other precautions may be necessary. When you are using dezocine, it is especially important that your health care professional know if you are taking any of the following:

- Central nervous system (CNS) depressants, including other narcotics, or
- Tricyclic antidepressants (amitriptyline [e.g., Elavil], amoxapine [e.g., Asendin], clomipramine [e.g., Anafranil], desipramine [e.g., Pertofrane], doxepin [e.g., Sinequan], imipramine [e.g., Tofranil], nortriptyline [e.g., Aventyl], protriptyline [e.g., Vivactil], trimipramine [e.g., Surmontil])—The chance of side effects may be increased
- Naltrexone (e.g., Trexan)—Dezocine may not be effective in people taking naltrexone

Other medical problems—The presence of other medical problems may affect the use of dezocine. Make sure you tell your doctor if you have any other medical problems, especially:

- Alcohol abuse, or history of, or
- Drug dependence, especially narcotic abuse, or history of, or

- Emotional problems—The chance of side effects may be increased; also, withdrawal symptoms may occur if a narcotic you are dependent on is replaced by dezocine
- Brain disease or head injury or
- Colitis or other intestinal disease or
- Diarrhea or
- Emphysema, asthma, or other chronic lung disease or
- Enlarged prostate or problems with urination—Some of the side effects of narcotic analgesics can be dangerous if these conditions are present
- Heart or blood vessel disease, severe, or
- Gallbladder disease or gallstones or
- Kidney disease or
- Liver disease or
- Underactive thyroid—The chance of side effects may be increased

Proper Use of This Medicine

Some narcotic analgesics given by injection may be used at home by patients who do not need to be in the hospital. If you are using dezocine at home, *make sure you clearly understand and carefully follow your doctor's directions.*

Take this medicine only as directed by your doctor. Do not use more of it, do not use it more often, and do not use it for a longer time than your doctor ordered. This is especially important for elderly patients, who are more sensitive than younger adults to the effects of narcotic analgesics. If too much is taken, the medicine may become habit-forming (causing mental or physical dependence) or lead to medical problems because of an overdose.

Dosing—The dose of dezocine will be different for different patients. *Follow your doctor's orders or the directions on the label.* The following information includes only the average doses of dezocine. *If your dose is different, do not change it* unless your doctor tells you to do so.

The number of milliliters (mL) of injection that you use for each dose depends on the strength of the medicine.

- For *parenteral* dosage form (injection):
  - —For pain:
    - Adults—The usual dose is 10 milligrams (mg), injected into a muscle every three to six hours as needed. Some people may need only 5 mg and others may need 15 or 20 mg. The medicine may also be injected into a vein in a dose of 2.5 to 10 mg every two to four hours as needed. The total amount used in twenty-four hours should not be more than 120 mg. Elderly people, people who are very ill, and people with breathing problems may have to use lower doses than other adults.
    - Children and teenagers up to 18 years of age—Use and dose must be determined by your doctor.

Missed dose—If your doctor has ordered you to use dezocine according to a regular schedule and you miss a dose, use it as soon as you remember. However, if it is almost time for your next dose, skip the missed dose and go back to your regular dosing schedule. *Do not double doses.*

Storage—To store this medicine:
- Keep out of the reach of children. Overdose is very dangerous in young children.
- Store away from heat and direct light.
- Keep the medicine from freezing.
- Do not keep outdated medicine or medicine no longer needed. Be sure that any discarded medicine is out of the reach of children.

Precautions While Using This Medicine

Dezocine will add to the effects of alcohol and other CNS depressants (medicines that slow down the nervous system, possibly causing drowsiness). Some examples of CNS depressants are antihistamines or medicine for hay fever, other allergies, or colds; sedatives, tranquilizers, or sleeping medicine; other prescription pain medicines including other narcotics; barbiturates; medicine for seizures; muscle relaxants; or anesthetics, including some dental anesthetics. *Do not drink alcoholic beverages, and check with your doctor before taking any of the medicines listed above, while you are using this medicine.*

This medicine may cause some people to become drowsy, dizzy, or lightheaded. *Make sure you know how you react to this medicine before you drive, use machines, or do anything else that could be dangerous if you are dizzy or are not alert.*

Dizziness, lightheadedness, or fainting may occur, especially when you get up suddenly from a lying or sitting position. Getting up slowly may help lessen this problem. Also, lying down for a while may help relieve these effects.

Nausea or vomiting may occur, especially after the first couple of doses. This effect may go away if you lie down for a while. However, if nausea or vomiting continues, check with your doctor.

Before having any kind of surgery (including dental surgery) or emergency treatment, tell the health care professional in charge that you are taking this medicine. Serious side effects may occur if your health care professional gives you certain medicines without knowing that you are using dezocine.

If you think you or someone else may have taken an overdose, get emergency help at once. Taking an overdose of this medicine or taking alcohol or CNS depressants with it may lead to unconsciousness or death. Signs of overdose of narcotic analgesics include convulsions (seizures), confusion, severe nervousness or restlessness, severe dizziness, severe drowsiness, slow or troubled breathing, and severe weakness.

Side Effects of This Medicine

Along with its needed effects, a medicine may cause some unwanted effects. Although not all of these side effects may occur, if they do occur they may need medical attention.

Get emergency help immediately if any of the following symptoms of overdose occur:

Cold, clammy skin; confusion, nervousness, or restlessness (severe); convulsions (seizures); dizziness (severe); drowsiness (severe); low blood pressure; pinpoint pupils of eyes; slow heartbeat; slow or troubled breathing; weakness (severe)

Also, check with your doctor as soon as possible if any of the following side effects occur:

Rare

Chest pain; coughing occurring together with breathing problems; difficult, decreased, or frequent urination; difficult, slow, or shallow breathing; increase or decrease in blood pressure; irregular heartbeat; mental depression or other mood or mental changes; skin rash or itching; swelling of face, fingers, lower legs, or feet; weight gain

Other side effects may occur that usually do not need medical attention. These side effects may go away during treatment as your body adjusts to the medicine. However, check with your doctor if any of the following side effects continue or are bothersome:

More common

Drowsiness; nausea or vomiting

Less common or rare

Abdominal or stomach pain; anxiety or crying; blurred or double vision; confusion; constipation; diarrhea; dizziness or lightheadedness; flushing or redness of skin; slurred speech

After you stop using this medicine, your body may need time to adjust. The length of time this takes depends on the amount of medicine you were using and how long you used it. During this period of time check with your doctor if you notice any of the following side effects:

Body aches; diarrhea; fast heartbeat; fever, runny nose, or sneezing; gooseflesh; increased sweating; increased yawning; loss of appetite; nausea or vomiting; nervousness, restlessness, or irritability; shivering or trembling; stomach cramps; trouble in sleeping; unusually large pupils of eyes; weakness

Other side effects not listed above may also occur in some patients. If you notice any other effects, check with your doctor.

Revised: 08/29/94

DIAZOXIDE Oral

A commonly used brand name in the U.S. and Canada is Proglycem.

Description

Diazoxide (dye-az-OX-ide) when taken by mouth is used in the treatment of hypoglycemia (low blood sugar). It works by preventing release of insulin from the pancreas.

Diazoxide is available only with your doctor's prescription, in the following dosage forms:

Oral

- Capsules (U.S. and Canada)
- Suspension (U.S. and Canada)

Before Using This Medicine

In deciding to use a medicine, the risks of taking the medicine must be weighed against the good it will do. This is a decision you and your doctor will make. For diazoxide, the following should be considered:

Allergies—Tell your doctor if you have ever had any unusual or allergic reaction to diazoxide, sulfonamides (sulfa medicine), or thiazide diuretics (certain types of water pills). Also tell your health care professional if you are allergic to any other substances, such as foods, preservatives, or dyes.

Pregnancy—Studies have not been done in pregnant women. However, too much use of diazoxide during pregnancy may cause unwanted effects (high blood sugar, loss of hair or increased hair growth, blood problems) in the baby. Studies in animals have shown that diazoxide causes some birth defects (in the skeleton, heart, and pancreas) and other problems (delayed birth, decrease in successful pregnancies).

Breast-feeding—It is not known whether diazoxide passes into breast milk. However, this medicine has not been reported to cause problems in nursing babies.

Children—Infants are more likely to retain (keep) body water because of diazoxide. In some infants, this may lead to certain types of heart problems. Also, a few children who received diazoxide for prolonged periods (longer than 4 years) developed changes in their facial structure.

Older adults—Many medicines have not been tested in older people. Therefore, it may not be known whether they work exactly the same way they do in younger adults or if they cause different side effects or problems in older people. There is no specific information comparing use of oral diazoxide in the elderly with use in other age groups.

Other medicines—Although certain medicines should not be used together at all, in other cases two different medicines may be used together even if an interaction might occur. In these cases, your doctor may want to change the dose, or other precautions may be necessary. When you are taking diazoxide, it is especially important that your health care professional know if you are taking any of the following:

- Amantadine (e.g., Symmetrel) or
- Antidepressants (medicine for depression) or
- Antihypertensives (high blood pressure medicine) or
- Antipsychotics (medicines for mental illness) or
- Bromocriptine (e.g., Parlodel) or
- Cyclandelate (e.g., Cyclospasmol) or
- Deferoxamine (e.g., Desferal) or
- Diuretics (water pills) or
- Hydralazine (e.g., Apresoline) or
- Isoxsuprine (e.g., Vasodilan) or

- Levobunolol (e.g., Betagan) (use in the eye) or
- Levodopa (e.g., Dopar) or
- Medicine for heart disease or
- Metipranolol (e.g., OptiPranolol) or
- Nabilone (e.g., Cesamet) (with high doses) or
- Narcotic pain medicine or
- Nicotinyl alcohol (e.g., Roniacol) or
- Nimodipine (e.g., Nimotop) or
- Nylidrin (e.g., Arlidin) or
- Papaverine (e.g., Pavabid) or
- Pentamidine (e.g., Pentam) or
- Pimozide (e.g., Orap) or
- Promethazine (e.g., Phenergan) or
- Timolol (e.g., Timoptic) (use in the eye) or
- Trimeprazine (e.g., Temaril)—Use of any of these medicines with diazoxide may cause low blood pressure
- Ethotoin (e.g., Peganone) or
- Mephenytoin (e.g., Mesantoin) or
- Phenytoin (e.g., Dilantin)—Any of these medicines and diazoxide may be less effective is they are taken at the same time

Other medical problems—The presence of other medical problems may affect the use of diazoxide. Make sure you tell your doctor if you have any other medical problems, especially:

- Angina (chest pain)
- Gout—Diazoxide may make this condition worse
- Heart attack (recent)
- Heart or blood vessel disease
- Kidney disease—The effects of diazoxide may last longer because the kidney may not be able to get the medicine out of the bloodstream as it normally would
- Liver disease
- Stroke (recent)

Proper Use of This Medicine

Take this medicine only as directed by your doctor. Do not take more or less of it than your doctor ordered, and take it at the same time each day.

Follow carefully the special diet your doctor gave you. This is an important part of controlling your condition, and is necessary if the medicine is to work properly.

Test for sugar in your urine or blood with a diabetic urine or blood test kit as directed by your doctor. This is a convenient way to make sure your condition is being controlled, and it provides an early warning when it is not. Your doctor may also want you to test your urine for acetone.

Dosing—The dose of diazoxide will be different for different patients. *Follow your doctor's orders or the directions on the label.* The following information includes only the average doses of diazoxide. *If your dose is different, do not change it* unless your doctor tells you to do so.

The number of capsules that you take depends on the strength of the medicine.

- For *oral* dosage forms (capsules or suspension):
  - —For treating hypoglycemia (low blood sugar):
    - Adults, teenagers, and children—Dose is based on body weight and must be determined by your doctor. At first, the usual dose is 1 milligram (mg) per kilogram (kg) (0.45 mg per pound) of body weight every eight hours. Then, your doctor may increase your dose to 3 to 8 mg per kg (1.4 to 3.6 mg per pound) of body weight a day. This dose may be divided into two or three doses.
    - Newborn babies and infants—Dose is based on body weight and must be determined by your doctor. At first, the usual dose is 3.3 mg per kg (1.5 mg per pound) of body weight every eight hours. Then, your doctor may increase the dose to 8 to 15 mg per kg (3.6 to 6.8 mg per pound) of body weight a day. This dose may be divided into two or three doses.

Missed dose—If you miss a dose of this medicine, take it as soon as possible. However, if it is almost time for your next dose, skip the missed dose and go back to your regular dosing schedule. Do not double doses.

Storage—To store this medicine:

- Keep out of the reach of children.
- Store away from heat and direct light.
- Do not store in the bathroom, near the kitchen sink, or in other damp places. Heat or moisture may cause the medicine to break down.
- Keep the oral liquid form of this medicine from freezing.
- Do not keep outdated medicine or medicine no longer needed. Be sure that any discarded medicine is out of the reach of children.

Precautions While Using This Medicine

It is very important that your doctor check your progress at regular visits, especially during the first few weeks of treatment, to make sure that this medicine is working properly.

Before you have any kind of surgery, dental treatment, or emergency treatment, *tell the medical doctor or dentist in charge that you are using this medicine.*

Do not take any other medicine, unless prescribed or approved by your doctor, since some may interfere with this medicine's effects. This especially includes over-the-counter (OTC) or nonprescription medicine such as that for colds, cough, asthma, hay fever, or appetite control.

Check with your doctor right away if symptoms of high blood sugar (hyperglycemia) occur. These symptoms usually include:

Drowsiness
Flushed, dry skin
Fruit-like breath odor
Increased urination
Loss of appetite (continuing)
Unusual thirst

These symptoms may occur if the dose of the medicine is too high, or if you have a fever or infection or are experiencing unusual stress.

Check with your doctor as soon as possible also if these symptoms of low blood sugar (hypoglycemia) occur:
- Anxiety
- Chills
- Cold sweats
- Cool pale skin
- Drowsiness
- Excessive hunger
- Fast pulse
- Headache
- Nausea
- Nervousness
- Shakiness
- Unusual tiredness or weakness

Symptoms of both low blood sugar and high blood sugar must be corrected before they progress to a more serious condition. In either situation, you should check with your doctor immediately.

Side Effects of This Medicine

Along with its needed effects, a medicine may cause some unwanted effects. Although not all of these side effects may occur, if they do occur they may need medical attention.

Stop taking this medicine and get emergency help immediately if any of the following side effects occur:

Rare
Chest pain caused by exercise or activity; confusion; numbness of the hands; shortness of breath (unexplained)

Check with your doctor as soon as possible if any of the following side effects occur:

More common
Decreased urination; swelling of feet or lower legs; weight gain (rapid)

Less common
Fast heartbeat

Rare
Fever; skin rash; stiffness of arms or legs; trembling and shaking of hands and fingers; unusual bleeding or bruising

Other side effects may occur that usually do not need medical attention. These side effects may go away during treatment as your body adjusts to the medicine. However, check with your doctor if any of the following side effects continue or are bothersome:

Less common
Changes in ability to taste; constipation; increased hair growth on forehead, back, arms, and legs; loss of appetite; nausea and vomiting; stomach pain

This medicine may cause a temporary increase in hair growth in some people when it is used for a long time. After treatment with diazoxide has ended, normal hair growth should return.

Other side effects not listed above may also occur in some patients. If you notice any other effects, check with your doctor.

Revised: 12/15/92
Interim revision: 05/24/94

DIDANOSINE Systemic

A commonly used brand name in the U.S. and Canada is Videx. Another commonly used name is ddI.

Description

Didanosine (di-DAN-oe-seen) (also known as ddI) is used in the treatment of the infection caused by the human immunodeficiency virus (HIV). HIV is the virus responsible for acquired immune deficiency syndrome (AIDS).

Didanosine (ddI) will not cure or prevent HIV infection or AIDS; however, it helps keep HIV from reproducing and appears to slow down the destruction of the immune system. This may help delay the development of problems usually related to AIDS or HIV disease. Didanosine will not keep you from spreading HIV to other people. People who receive this medicine may continue to have the problems usually related to AIDS or HIV disease.

Didanosine may cause some serious side effects, including pancreatitis (inflammation of the pancreas). Symptoms of pancreatitis include stomach pain, and nausea and vomiting. Didanosine may also cause peripheral neuropathy. Symptoms of peripheral neuropathy include tingling, burning, numbness, and pain in the hands or feet. *Check with your doctor if any new health problems or symptoms occur while you are taking didanosine.*

Didanosine is available only with your doctor's prescription, in the following dosage forms:

Oral
- Oral solution (U.S.)
- Oral suspension (U.S. and Canada)
- Tablets (U.S. and Canada)

Before Using This Medicine

In deciding to use a medicine, the risks of taking the medicine must be weighed against the good it will do. This is a decision you and your doctor will make. For didanosine, the following should be considered:

Allergies—Tell your doctor if you have ever had any unusual or allergic reaction to didanosine. Also tell your health care professional if you are allergic to any other substances, such as foods, preservatives, or dyes.

Diet—Make certain your health care professional knows if you are on any special diet, such as a low-sodium (low-salt) diet. Didanosine chewable tablets and the oral solution packets contain a large amount of sodium. Also, didanosine tablets contain phenylalanine, which must be restricted in patients with phenylketonuria.

Pregnancy—Didanosine crosses the placenta. Studies in pregnant women have not been done. However, didanosine has not been shown to cause birth defects or other problems in animal studies. Also, it is not known whether didanosine reduces the chances that a baby born to an HIV-infected mother will also be infected.

Breast-feeding—It is not known whether didanosine passes into the breast milk. However, if your baby does not already have the AIDS virus, there is a chance that you could pass it to your baby by breast-feeding. Talk to your doctor first if you are thinking about breast-feeding your baby.

Children—Didanosine can cause serious side effects in any patient. Therefore, it is especially important that you discuss with your child's doctor the good that this medicine may do as well as the risks of using it. Your child must be carefully followed, and frequently seen, by the doctor while taking didanosine.

Older adults—Many medicines have not been studied specifically in older people. Therefore, it may not be known whether they work exactly the same way they do in younger adults or if they cause different side effects or problems in older people. There is no specific information comparing use of didanosine in the elderly with use in other age groups.

Other medicines—Although certain medicines should not be used together at all, in other cases 2 different medicines may be used together even if an interaction might occur. In these cases, your doctor may want to change the dose, or other precautions may be necessary. When you are taking didanosine, it is especially important that your health care professional know if you are taking any of the following:

- Alcohol or
- Asparaginase (e.g., Elspar) or
- Azathioprine (e.g., Imuran) or
- Estrogens (female hormones) or
- Furosemide (e.g., Lasix) or
- Methyldopa (e.g., Aldomet) or
- Pentamidine (e.g., Pentam, Pentacarinat) or
- Sulfonamides (e.g., Bactrim, Septra) or
- Sulindac (e.g., Clinoril) or
- Thiazide diuretics (e.g., Diuril, Hydrodiuril) or
- Valproic acid (e.g., Depakote)—Use of these medicines with didanosine may increase the chance of pancreatitis (inflammation of the pancreas)
- Chloramphenicol (e.g., Chloromycetin) or
- Cisplatin (e.g., Platinol) or
- Ethambutol (e.g., Myambutol) or
- Ethionamide (e.g., Trecator-SC) or
- Hydralazine (e.g., Apresoline) or
- Isoniazid (e.g., Nydrazid) or
- Lithium (e.g., Eskalith, Lithobid) or
- Metronidazole (e.g., Flagyl) or
- Nitrous oxide or
- Phenytoin (e.g., Dilantin) or
- Stavudine (e.g., D4T) or
- Vincristine (e.g., Oncovin) or
- Zalcitabine (e.g., HIVID)—Use of these medicines with didanosine may increase the chance of peripheral neuropathy (tingling, burning, numbness, or pain in your hands or feet)
- Ciprofloxacin (e.g., Cipro) or
- Enoxacin (e.g., Penetrex) or
- Itraconazole (e.g., Sporanox) or
- Ketoconazole (e.g., Nizoral) or
- Lomefloxacin (e.g., Maxaquin) or
- Norfloxacin (e.g., Noroxin) or
- Ofloxacin (e.g., Floxin) or
- Trimethoprim (e.g., Proloprim, Trimpex)—Use of these medicines with didanosine may keep these medicines from working properly; these medicines should be taken at least 2 hours before or 2 hours after taking didanosine
- Dapsone (e.g., Avlosulfon)—Use of dapsone with didanosine may increase the chance of peripheral neuropathy (tingling, burning, numbness, or pain in your hands or feet); it may also keep dapsone from working properly; dapsone should be taken at least 2 hours before or 2 hours after taking didanosine
- Nitrofurantoin (e.g., Macrodantin)—Use of nitrofurantoin with didanosine may increase the chance of pancreatitis (inflammation of the pancreas) and peripheral neuropathy (tingling, burning, numbness, or pain in your hands or feet)
- Tetracyclines (e.g., Achromycin, Minocin)—Use of tetracyclines with didanosine may increase the chance of pancreatitis (inflammation of the pancreas); it may also keep the tetracycline from working properly; tetracyclines should be taken at least 2 hours before or 2 hours after taking didanosine

Other medical problems—The presence of other medical problems may affect the use of didanosine. Make sure you tell your doctor if you have any other medical problems, especially:

- Alcoholism, active, or
- Increased blood triglycerides (substance formed in the body from fats in foods) or
- Pancreatitis (or a history of)—Patients with these medical problems may be at increased risk of pancreatitis (inflammation of the pancreas)
- Edema or
- Heart disease or
- High blood pressure or
- Kidney disease or
- Liver disease or
- Toxemia of pregnancy—The salt contained in the didanosine tablets and the oral solution packets may make these conditions worse
- Gouty arthritis—Didanosine may cause an attack or worsen gout
- Peripheral neuropathy—Didanosine may make this condition worse
- Phenylketonuria (PKU)—Didanosine tablets contain phenylalanine, which must be restricted in patients with PKU

Proper Use of This Medicine

Take this medicine exactly as directed by your doctor. Do not take more of it, do not take it more often, and do not take it for a longer time than your doctor ordered. Also, do not stop taking this medicine without checking with your doctor first. However, stop taking didanosine and call your doctor right away if you get severe nausea, vomiting, and stomach pain.

Otherwise, keep taking didanosine for the full time of treatment, even if you begin to feel better.

For patients taking *didanosine pediatric oral suspension:*

- Use a specially marked measuring spoon or other device to measure each dose accurately. The average household teaspoon may not hold the right amount of liquid.

For patients taking *didanosine for oral solution:*

- Open the foil packet and pour its contents into approximately 1/2 glass (4 ounces) of water. *Do not mix with fruit juice* or other acid-containing drinks.
- Stir for approximately 2 to 3 minutes until the powder is dissolved.
- Drink at once.

For patients taking *didanosine tablets:*

- Tablets should be thoroughly chewed or crushed or mixed in at least 1 ounce of water before swallowing. The tablets are hard and some people may find them difficult to chew. If the tablets are mixed in water, stir well until a uniform suspension is formed and take at once.
- *Two tablets must be taken together by patients over 1 year of age.* These tablets contain a special buffer to keep didanosine from being destroyed in the stomach. In order to get the correct amount of buffer, 2 tablets always need to be taken together. Infants from 6 to 12 months of age will get enough buffer from just 1 tablet.

Didanosine should be taken on an empty stomach since food may decrease the absorption in the stomach and keep it from working properly. Didanosine should be taken at least 2 hours before or 2 hours after you eat.

This medicine works best when there is a constant amount in the blood. *To help keep the amount constant, do not miss any doses.* If you need help in planning the best times to take your medicine, check with your health care professional.

Dosing—The dose of didanosine will be different for different patients. *Follow your doctor's orders or the directions on the label.* The following information includes only the average doses of didanosine. *If your dose is different, do not change it* unless your doctor tells you to do so.

The number of tablets or teaspoonfuls of solution or suspension that you take depends on the strength of the medicine.

- For the treatment of advanced HIV infection or AIDS:
  - —For *oral* dosage form (solution):
    - Adults and teenagers—Dose is based on body weight.
      - —For patients weighing less than 60 kilograms (kg) (132 pounds): 167 milligrams (mg) every twelve hours.
      - —For patients weighing 60 kg (132 pounds) or more: 250 mg every twelve hours.
    - Children—The oral solution is usually not used for small children.
  - —For *oral* dosage form (pediatric suspension):
    - Adults and teenagers—The pediatric oral suspension is usually not used in adults and teenagers.
    - Children—Dose is based on body size and must be determined by your doctor. The dose usually ranges from 31 to 125 mg every eight to twelve hours.
  - —For *oral* dosage form (tablets):
    - Adults and teenagers—Dose is based on body weight.
      - —For patients weighing less than 60 kg (132 pounds): 125 mg every twelve hours.
      - —For patients weighing 60 kg (132 pounds) or more: 200 mg every twelve hours.
    - Children—Dose is based on body size and must be determined by your doctor. The dose usually ranges from 25 to 100 mg every eight to twelve hours.

Missed dose—If you do miss a dose of this medicine, take it as soon as possible. However, if it is almost time for your next dose, skip the missed dose and go back to your regular dosing schedule. Do not double doses.

Only take medicine that your doctor has prescribed specifically for you. Do not share your medicine with others.

Storage—To store this medicine:

- Keep out of the reach of children.
- Store away from heat and direct light.
- Do not store in the bathroom, near the kitchen sink, or in other damp places. Heat or moisture may cause the medicine to break down.
- Do not keep outdated medicine or medicine no longer needed. Be sure that any discarded medicine is out of the reach of children.

Precautions While Using This Medicine

It is very important that your doctor check your progress at regular visits.

Do not take any other medicines without checking with your doctor first. To do so may increase the chance of side effects from didanosine.

HIV may be acquired from or spread to other people through infected body fluids, including blood, vaginal fluid, or semen. *If you are infected, it is best to avoid any sexual activity involving an exchange of body fluids with other people. If you do have sex, always wear (or have your partner wear) a condom (''rubber'').* Only use condoms made of latex, and *use them every time you have vaginal, anal, or oral sex.* The use of a spermicide (such as nonoxynol-9) may also help prevent transmission of HIV if it is not irritating to the vagina, rectum, or mouth. Spermicides have been shown to kill HIV in lab tests. Do not use oil-based jelly, cold cream, baby oil, or shortening as a lubricant—these products can cause the condom to break. Lubricants without oil, such as *K-Y jelly*, are recommended. Women may wish to carry their own condoms. Birth control pills and diaphragms will help protect against pregnancy, but they will not prevent someone from giving or getting the AIDS virus. *If you inject drugs*, get help to stop. *Do not share needles or equipment with anyone.* In some cities, more than half of the drug users are infected and sharing even 1 needle or syringe can spread the virus. If you have any questions about this, check with your health care professional.

Side Effects of This Medicine

Along with its needed effects, a medicine may cause some unwanted effects. Although not all of these side effects may occur, if they do occur they may need medical attention.

Check with your doctor immediately if any of the following side effects occur:

Less common

Nausea and vomiting; stomach pain; tingling, burning, numbness, and pain in the hands or feet

Rare

Convulsions (seizures); fever and chills; shortness of breath; skin rash and itching; sore throat; swelling of feet or lower legs; unusual bleeding and bruising; unusual tiredness and weakness; yellow skin and eyes

Other side effects may occur that usually do not need medical attention. These side effects may go away during treatment as your body adjusts to the medicine. However, check with your doctor if any of the following side effects continue or are bothersome:

More common

Anxiety; diarrhea; difficulty in sleeping; dryness of mouth; headache; irritability; restlessness

Other side effects not listed above may also occur in some patients. If you notice any other effects, check with your doctor.

Revised: 06/22/94
Interim revision: 01/11/95

DIETHYLCARBAMAZINE Systemic

A commonly used brand name in the U.S. and Canada is Hetrazan.

Generic name product may be available in the U.S.

Description

Diethylcarbamazine (dye-eth-il-kar-BAM-a-zeen) is used in the treatment of certain worm infections. This medicine works by killing the worms. It is used to treat:

- Bancroft's filariasis;
- Eosinophilic lung (tropical pulmonary eosinophilia; tropical eosinophilia);
- Loiasis; and
- River blindness (onchocerciasis).

It will not work for other kinds of worm infections (for example, pinworms or tapeworms).

Diethylcarbamazine is available only with your doctor's prescription, in the following dosage form:

Oral

- Tablets (U.S. and Canada)

Before Using This Medicine

In deciding to use a medicine, the risks of taking the medicine must be weighed against the good it will do. This is a decision you and your doctor will make. For diethylcarbamazine, the following should be considered:

Allergies—Tell your doctor if you have ever had any unusual or allergic reaction to diethylcarbamazine. Also tell your health care professional if you are allergic to any other substances, such as foods, preservatives, or dyes.

Pregnancy—Treatment of pregnant patients with diethylcarbamazine should be delayed until after delivery. However, diethylcarbamazine has not been shown to cause birth defects or other problems in humans.

Breast-feeding—It is not known whether diethylcarbamazine passes into breast milk. Although most medicines pass into breast milk in small amounts, many of them may be used safely while breast-feeding. Mothers who are taking this medicine and who wish to breast-feed should discuss this with their doctor.

Children—Although there is no specific information comparing use of diethylcarbamazine in children with use in other age groups, this medicine is not expected to cause different side effects or problems in children than it does in adults.

Older adults—Many medicines have not been studied specifically in older people. Therefore, it may not be known whether they work exactly the same way they do in younger adults or if they cause different side effects or problems in older people. There is no specific information comparing use of diethylcarbamazine in the elderly with use in other age groups.

Other medicines—Although certain medicines should not be used together at all, in other cases two different medicines may be used together even if an interaction might occur. In these cases, your doctor may want to change the dose, or other precautions may be necessary. Tell your health care professional if you are taking any other prescription or nonprescription (over-the-counter [OTC]) medicine.

Proper Use of This Medicine

Diethylcarbamazine should be taken immediately after meals.

To help clear up your infection completely, *keep taking this medicine for the full time of treatment,* even if your symptoms begin to clear up after a few days. In some patients, a second course of this medicine may be required to clear up the infection completely. If you stop taking this medicine too soon, your infection may return. *Do not miss any doses.*

Dosing—The dose of diethylcarbamazine will be different for different patients. *Follow your doctor's orders or the directions on the label.* The following information includes only the average doses of diethylcarbamazine. *If your dose is different, do not change it* unless your doctor tells you to do so.

The number of tablets that you take depends on the strength of the medicine. Also, *the number of doses you take each day, the time allowed between doses, and the length of time you take the medicine depend on the medical problem for which you are taking diethylcarbamazine.*

- For *oral* dosage form (tablets):
  - —For Bancroft's filariasis, loiasis, and river blindness:
    - Adults—Dose is based on body weight and must be determined by your doctor. The usual dose is 2 to 3 milligrams (mg) per kilogram (kg) (0.9 to 1.3 mg per pound) of body weight three times a day.
    - Children—Use and dose must be determined by your doctor.
  - —For eosinophilic lung:
    - Adults—Dose is based on body weight and must be determined by your doctor. The usual dose is 6 mg per kg (2.7 mg per pound) of body weight a day. This is taken for four to seven days.
    - Children—Use and dose must be determined by your doctor.

Missed dose—If you miss a dose of this medicine, take it as soon as possible. However, if it is almost time for your next dose, skip the missed dose and go back to your regular dosing schedule. Do not double doses.

Storage—To store this medicine:

- Keep out of the reach of children.
- Store away from heat and direct light.
- Do not store in the bathroom, near the kitchen sink, or in other damp places. Heat or moisture may cause the medicine to break down.
- Do not keep outdated medicine or medicine no longer needed. Be sure that any discarded medicine is out of the reach of children.

Precautions While Using This Medicine

If your symptoms do not improve within a few days, or if they become worse, check with your doctor.

For patients taking diethylcarbamazine *for river blindness:*

- It is important that your doctor check your progress at regular visits. This is to help make sure that the infection is cleared up completely. Also, your doctor may want you to have your eyes checked by an ophthalmologist (eye doctor).
- Diethylcarbamazine may cause loss of vision, night blindness, or tunnel vision with prolonged use. This medicine may also cause some people to become dizzy. *Make sure you know how you react to this medicine before you drive, use machines, or do anything else that could be dangerous if you are dizzy or are not alert or able to see well.* If these reactions are especially bothersome, check with your doctor.
- Doctors may also prescribe a corticosteroid (a cortisone-like medicine) for certain patients with river blindness, especially those with severe symptoms. This is to help reduce the inflammation caused by the death of the worms. If your doctor prescribes these two medicines together, it is important to take the corticosteroid along with diethylcarbamazine. Take them exactly as directed by your doctor. Do not miss any doses.

Side Effects of This Medicine

Along with its needed effects, a medicine may cause some unwanted effects. Although not all of these side effects may occur, if they do occur they may need medical attention.

Check with your doctor immediately if any of the following side effects occur:

More common

Itching and swelling of face, especially eyes

Less common

Fever; painful and tender glands in neck, armpits, or groin; skin rash

Additional side effects may occur if you use this medicine for a long time in the treatment of river blindness. Check with your doctor as soon as possible if any of the following side effects occur:

Loss of vision; night blindness; tunnel vision

Other side effects may occur that usually do not need medical attention. These side effects may go away during treatment as your body adjusts to the medicine. However, check with your doctor if any of the following side effects continue or are bothersome:

More common

Headache; joint pain; unusual tiredness or weakness

Less common

Dizziness; nausea or vomiting

Other side effects not listed above may also occur in some patients. If you notice any other effects, check with your doctor.

Revised: 8/11/95

DIETHYLTOLUAMIDE Topical

Some commonly used brand names are:

In the U.S.—

Backwoods Cutter
Cutter Pleasant Protection
Deep Woods OFF!
Deep Woods OFF! For Sportsmen
Muskol
OFF!
OFF! For Maximum Protection
OFF! Skintastic
OFF! Skintastic For Children
OFF! Skintastic For Kids
Ultra Muskol

In Canada—

Deep Woods OFF!
Muskol
OFF!
OFF! For Maximum Protection
OFF! Skintastic

Other commonly used names are DEET and m-DET.

Description

Diethyltoluamide (dye-eth-il-toe-LOO-a-mide) is an insect repellent used to keep insects away. This product is effective against mosquitoes, biting flies (gnats, sandflies, deer flies, stable flies, black flies), ticks, harvest mites, and fleas.

Diethyltoluamide is available without a prescription in the following dosage forms:

Topical

- Liquid (U.S. and Canada)
- Lotion (U.S. and Canada)
- Topical aerosol (U.S. and Canada)
- Topical spray solution (U.S. and Canada)
- Towelettes (U.S.)

Before Using This Product

If you are using this product without a prescription, carefully read and follow any precautions on the label. For diethyltoluamide, the following should be considered:

Allergies—Tell your doctor if you have ever had any unusual or allergic reaction to diethyltoluamide. Also tell your health care professional if you are allergic to any other substances, such as foods, preservatives, or dyes.

Pregnancy—Diethyltoluamide has not been studied in pregnant women. However, studies in animals have shown that diethyltoluamide is passed on to the offspring. One animal study has shown diethyltoluamide to cause death of the fetus. Before using diethyltoluamide, make sure your doctor knows if you are pregnant or if you may become pregnant.

Breast-feeding—Diethyltoluamide has not been reported to cause problems in nursing babies.

Children—Children may be at increased risk of side effects because of increased absorption of diethyltoluamide through their skin. Use only products that have low amounts of diethyltoluamide and apply it sparingly to the exposed skin of children.

Other medicines—Although certain medicines and products should not be used together at all, in other cases two different products may be used together even if an interaction might occur. In these cases, your doctor may want to change the dose, or other precautions may be necessary. Tell your health care professional if you are using any other prescription or nonprescription (over-the-counter [OTC]) medicine.

Proper Use of This Product

Diethyltoluamide is *for external use only.*

For safe and effective use, read the directions on the label before using any diethyltoluamide-containing preparations.

Use a product that contains *low amounts (less than 30%) of diethyltoluamide and apply it sparingly.* Use just enough to cover the exposed area(s) of the skin. One application using a product that contains low amounts of diethyltoluamide will last about 4 to 8 hours.

If you are applying this product on your face, *keep it away from your eyes, lips, or the inside of your nose.* If you accidentally get some in your eyes or onto your lips or the inside of your nose, immediately rinse these areas with plenty of water. Check with your doctor if irritation, especially of your eyes, continues. If you are using an aerosol or spray form, do not spray it directly on your face. Instead, spray the palm of your hand and rub the repellent on, spreading it carefully on your face.

Do not apply this product to wounds or irritated or broken skin. To do so may increase the chance of absorption through the skin and the chance of unwanted effects. Apply sparingly onto skin folds because increased irritation is more likely to occur in these areas.

Wear long sleeves and long pants when possible and apply the repellent to clothing (shirts, pants, socks, and hats) instead of your skin to lessen exposure of your skin to diethyltoluamide. Do not apply it under clothing. (Diethyltoluamide will not damage clothing materials, such as cotton, wool, or nylon. However, it may damage acetate, rayon, spandex, or some other synthetic materials.) Wash treated clothing after use or when protection is no longer needed.

Read the label very carefully to see if the product contains alcohol. Alcohol is flammable and can catch on fire. *Do not use any product containing alcohol near a fire or open flame, or while smoking. Also, do not smoke after applying one of these products and do not expose your treated skin to fire or open flame until the diethyltoluamide on your skin has completely dried.* In addition, keep your treated clothing away from fire, open flame, or smoke.

Do not keep the repellent on your skin any longer than necessary. Once it is not needed, or after you return indoors, wash treated skin with soap and water.

Do not use the product on or near furniture, plastics, watch crystals, leather, or painted or varnished surfaces, including automobiles, because diethyltoluamide may damage these materials.

To use the *liquid* or *lotion forms* of diethyltoluamide:

- Apply enough repellent to cover the exposed area(s) of skin, rub in gently, and allow it to dry.

To use the *topical aerosol* or *topical spray forms* of diethyltoluamide:

- Hold container 6 to 8 inches from skin or clothing. Spray in a slow, sweeping motion just enough repellent to cover exposed skin. Then spread evenly with hands to moisten all exposed skin and allow it to dry.

To use the *towelette form* of diethyltoluamide:

- Wipe the towelette over the exposed skin and allow to dry.

Dosing—*Follow your doctor's orders or the directions on the label.* The following information includes only the average dose of diethyltoluamide.

- For *topical* dosage forms (lotion, topical aerosol, topical spray solution, and towelettes):
  - —To keep away insects, ticks, or mites:
    - Adults and children—Apply a small amount to exposed area(s) of skin. Reapply when needed.

Storage—To store this product:

- Keep out of the reach of children.
- Store away from heat and direct light.
- Keep the product from freezing. Do not refrigerate.
- Do not keep outdated repellent or repellent no longer needed. Be sure that any discarded repellent is out of the reach of children.

Precautions While Using This Product

Avoid breathing in diethyltoluamide.

Do not apply this product to the hands of young children. After applying this product to the skin of children, *watch the children carefully to make sure that they do not get any of the repellent into their eyes or mouth.* Do not apply the product under the diapers. Discourage children from licking the area of application. Diethyltoluamide can cause serious side effects, especially in children, if it gets into the mouth or is swallowed.

If you think that a side effect has occurred after application of this product, *wash the treated skin and check with your doctor.* Take the container of diethyltoluamide with you for the doctor to see.

Side Effects of This Product

Along with its needed effects, diethyltoluamide may cause some unwanted effects. Although not all of these side effects may occur, if they do occur they may need medical attention.

Check with your doctor as soon as possible if any of the following side effects occur:

Rare

Changes in facial skin color; clumsiness or unsteadiness; confusion; convulsions (seizures); fast or irregular breathing; loss of consciousness; mood or mental changes; muscle cramping; puffiness or swelling of the eyelids or around the eyes; reddening of skin; shortness of breath, troubled breathing, tightness in chest, and/or wheezing; skin blisters; skin rash, hives, and/or itching; slow heartbeat; slurred speech; tremors; trouble in sleeping; uncontrolled jerking movement; unusual tiredness or weakness

Other side effects not listed above may also occur in some patients. If you notice any other effects, check with your doctor.

Developed: 06/23/95

DIFENOXIN AND ATROPINE Systemic†

A commonly used brand name in the U.S. is Motofen.

†Not commercially available in Canada.

Description

Difenoxin (dye-fen-OX-in) and atropine (A-troe-peen) combination medicine is used along with other measures to treat severe diarrhea in adults. Difenoxin helps stop diarrhea by slowing down the movements of the intestines.

Since difenoxin is chemically related to some narcotics, it may be habit-forming if taken in doses that are larger than prescribed. To help prevent possible abuse, atropine (an anticholinergic) has been added. If higher-than-normal doses of the combination are taken, the atropine will cause unpleasant effects, making it unlikely that such doses will be taken again.

Difenoxin and atropine combination medicine should not be used in children. Children with diarrhea should be given solutions of carbohydrates (sugars) and electrolytes (important salts) to replace the water and important salts that are lost from the body during diarrhea.

This medicine is available only with your doctor's prescription, in the following dosage form:

Oral

- Tablets (U.S.)

Before Using This Medicine

In deciding to use a medicine, the risks of taking the medicine must be weighed against the good it will do. This is a decision you and your doctor will make. For difenoxin and atropine, the following should be considered:

Allergies—Tell your doctor if you have ever had any unusual or allergic reaction to difenoxin or atropine. Also tell your health care professional if you are allergic to any other substances, such as foods, preservatives, or dyes.

Pregnancy—Difenoxin and atropine combination has not been studied in pregnant women. However, studies in rats have shown that difenoxin and atropine combination, when given in doses many times the human dose, increases the delivery time and the chance of death of the newborn.

Breast-feeding—Both difenoxin and atropine pass into the breast milk. Although it is not known how much of these drugs pass into the breast milk, difenoxin and atropine combination could cause serious effects in the nursing baby. Be sure you have discussed the risks and benefits of this medicine with your doctor.

Children—This medicine should not be used in children. Children, especially very young children, are very sensitive to the effects of difenoxin and atropine. This may increase the chance of side effects during treatment. Also, the fluid loss caused by diarrhea may result in a severe condition. For this reason, it is very important that a sufficient amount of liquids be given to replace the fluid lost by the body. If you have any questions about this, check with your health care professional.

Older adults—Shortness of breath or difficulty in breathing may be more likely to occur in elderly patients, who are usually more sensitive than younger adults to the effects of difenoxin. Also, the fluid loss caused by diarrhea may result in a severe condition. For this reason, elderly persons should not take this medicine without first checking with their doctor. It is also very important that a sufficient amount of liquids be taken to replace the fluid lost by the body. If you have any questions about this, check with your health care professional.

Other medicines—Although certain medicines should not be used together at all, in other cases two different medicines may be used together even if an interaction might occur. In these cases, your doctor may want to change the dose, or other precautions may be necessary. When you are taking difenoxin and atropine, it is especially important that your health care professional know if you are taking any of the following:

- Antibiotics, such as cephalosporins (e.g., Ceftin, Keflex), clindamycin (e.g., Cleocin), erythromycins (e.g., E.E.S., PCE), tetracyclines (e.g., Achromycin, Doryx)—These antibiotics may cause diarrhea. Difenoxin and atropine may make the diarrhea caused by antibiotics worse or make it last longer
- Central nervous system (CNS) depressants (medicines that cause drowsiness)—Effects, such as drowsiness, of CNS depressants or of difenoxin and atropine may become greater
- Monoamine oxidase (MAO) inhibitors (furazolidone [e.g., Furoxone], isocarboxazid [e.g., Marplan], phenelzine [e.g., Nardil], procarbazine [e.g., Matulane], tranylcypromine [e.g., Parnate])—Taking difenoxin and atropine while you are taking or within 2 weeks of taking MAO inhibitors may cause severe side effects; these medicines should not be used together
- Naltrexone (e.g., Trexan)—Withdrawal side effects may occur in patients who have become addicted to the difenoxin in this combination medicine; also, naltrexone will make this medicine less effective against diarrhea
- Other anticholinergics (medicine to help reduce stomach acid and abdominal or stomach spasms or cramps)—Use of other anticholinergics with this combination medicine may increase the effects of the atropine in this combination; however, this is not likely to happen with the usual doses of difenoxin and atropine

Other medical problems—The presence of other medical problems may affect the use of difenoxin and atropine. Make sure you tell your doctor if you have any other medical problems, especially:

- Alcohol abuse (or history of) or
- Drug abuse (history of)—There is a greater chance that this medicine may become habit-forming
- Colitis (severe)—A more serious problem of the colon may develop if you use this medicine
- Down's syndrome (mongolism)—Side effects may be more likely and severe in these patients
- Dysentery—This condition may get worse; a different kind of treatment may be needed
- Emphysema, asthma, bronchitis, or other chronic lung disease—There is a greater chance that this medicine may cause breathing problems in patients who have any of these conditions
- Enlarged prostate or
- Urinary tract blockage or difficult urination—Problems with urination may develop with the use of this medicine
- Gallbladder disease or gallstones—Use of this medicine may cause spasms of the biliary tract and make the condition worse
- Glaucoma—Severe pain in the eye may occur with the use of this medicine; however, the chance of this happening is low
- Heart disease—This medicine may have some effects on the heart, which may make the condition worse
- Hiatal hernia—The atropine in this medicine may make this condition worse; however, the chance of this happening is low
- High blood pressure (hypertension)—The atropine in this medicine may cause an increase in blood pressure; however, the chance of this happening is low
- Intestinal blockage—This medicine may make the condition worse
- Kidney disease—The atropine in this medicine may build up in the body and cause side effects
- Liver disease—The chance of central nervous system (CNS) side effects, including coma, may be greater in patients who have this condition
- Myasthenia gravis—This medicine may make the condition worse
- Overactive or underactive thyroid—Unwanted effects on breathing and heart rate may occur
- Overflow incontinence—This medicine may make the condition worse

Proper Use of This Medicine

If this medicine upsets your stomach, your doctor may want you to take it with food.

Take this medicine only as directed by your doctor. Do not take more of it, do not take it more often, and do not take it for a longer time than your doctor ordered. If too much is taken, it may become habit-forming.

Importance of diet and fluids while treating diarrhea:

- *In addition to using medicine for diarrhea, it is very important that you replace the fluid lost by the body and follow a proper diet.* For the first 24 hours you should eat gelatin and drink plenty of caffeine-free clear liquids, such as ginger ale, decaffeinated cola, decaffeinated tea, and broth. During the next 24 hours you may eat bland foods, such as cooked cereals, bread, crackers, and applesauce. Fruits, vegetables, fried or spicy foods, bran, candy, caffeine, and alcoholic beverages may make the condition worse.

- If too much fluid has been lost by the body due to the diarrhea a serious condition may develop. Check with your doctor as soon as possible if any of the following symptoms of too much fluid loss occur:

  Decreased urination
  Dizziness and lightheadedness
  Dryness of mouth
  Increased thirst
  Wrinkled skin

Dosing—The dose of difenoxin and atropine combination medicine will be different for different patients. *Follow your doctor's orders or the directions on the label.* The following information includes only the average doses of difenoxin and atropine combination. *If your dose is different, do not change it* unless your doctor tells you to do so.

- For *oral* dosage form (tablets):
  —For severe diarrhea:
    - Adults and teenagers—The first dose is usually 2 milligrams (mg). After that, the dose is 1 mg taken after each loose stool or every three or four hours as needed. *Do not take more than 8 mg in any twenty-four-hour period.*
    - Children—Use is not recommended.

Missed dose—If you are taking this medicine on a regular schedule and you miss a dose, take it as soon as possible. However, if it is almost time for your next dose, skip the missed dose and go back to your regular dosing schedule. Do not double doses.

Storage—To store this medicine:

- Keep out of the reach of children. Overdose is especially dangerous in children, and even part of an adult's pill can cause serious problems in children.
- Store away from heat and direct light.
- Do not store in the bathroom, near the kitchen sink, or in other damp places. Heat or moisture may cause the medicine to break down.
- Do not keep outdated medicine or medicine no longer needed. Be sure that any discarded medicine is out of the reach of children.

Precautions While Using This Medicine

Your doctor should check your progress at regular visits if you will be taking this medicine regularly for a long time.

Check with your doctor if your diarrhea does not stop after 2 days or if you develop a fever.

This medicine will add to the effects of alcohol and other CNS depressants (medicines that slow down the nervous system, possibly causing drowsiness). Some examples of CNS depressants are antihistamines or medicine for hay fever, other allergies, or colds; sedatives, tranquilizers, or sleeping medicine; prescription pain medicine or narcotics; barbiturates; medicine for seizures; muscle relaxants; or anesthetics, including some dental anesthetics. *Check with your doctor before taking any of the above while you are taking this medicine.*

If you think you or someone else in your home may have taken an overdose of this medicine, get emergency help at once. Taking an overdose of this medicine may lead to unconsciousness and possibly death. Symptoms of overdose include severe drowsiness; fast heartbeat; shortness of breath or troubled breathing; and unusual warmth, dryness, and flushing of skin.

Before having any kind of surgery (including dental surgery) or emergency treatment, tell the medical doctor or dentist in charge that you are using this medicine.

This medicine may cause some people to become dizzy, drowsy, or less alert than they are normally. Even if taken at bedtime, it may cause some people to feel drowsy or less alert on arising. *Make sure you know how you react to this medicine before you drive, use machines, or do anything else that could be dangerous if you are dizzy or are not alert.*

Side Effects of This Medicine

Along with its needed effects, a medicine may cause some unwanted effects. Although not all of these side effects may occur, if they do occur they may need medical attention.

When this medicine is used for short periods of time at low doses, side effects usually are rare. However, check with your doctor immediately if any of the following side effects are severe and occur suddenly, since they may be signs of a more severe and dangerous problem with your bowels:

Bloating; constipation; loss of appetite; stomach pain (severe) with nausea and vomiting

Check with your doctor also if any of the following effects occur, since they may be signs of an overdose of this medicine:

Blurred vision (continuing) or changes in near vision; drowsiness (severe); dryness of mouth, nose, and throat (severe); fast heartbeat; shortness of breath or troubled breathing (severe); unusual excitement, nervousness, restlessness, or irritability; unusual warmth, dryness, and flushing of skin

Other side effects may occur that usually do not need medical attention. These side effects may go away during treatment as your body adjusts to the medicine. However, check with your doctor if any of the following side effects continue, worsen, or are bothersome:

Less common or rare

Blurred vision; confusion; difficult urination; dizziness or lightheadedness; drowsiness; dryness of skin and mouth; fever; headache; trouble in sleeping; unusual tiredness or weakness

After you stop using this medicine, your body may need time to adjust. The length of time this takes depends on the amount of medicine you were using and how long you used it. During this period of time check with your doctor if you notice any of the following side effects:

Increased sweating; muscle cramps; nausea or vomiting; shivering or trembling; stomach cramps

Other side effects not listed above may also occur in some patients. If you notice any other effects, check with your doctor.

Revised: 07/15/94

DIGITALIS MEDICINES Systemic

Some commonly used brand names are:

In the U.S.—

Crystodigin[1]
Lanoxicaps[2]
Lanoxin[2]

In Canada—

Digitaline[1]
Lanoxin[2]
Novodigoxin[2]

Note: For quick reference, the following digitalis medicines are numbered to match the corresponding brand names.

This information applies to the following medicines:

1. Digitoxin (di-ji-TOX-in)‡
2. Digoxin (di-JOX-in)‡

‡Generic name product may also be available in the U.S.

Description

Digitalis medicines are used to improve the strength and efficiency of the heart, or to control the rate and rhythm of the heartbeat. This leads to better blood circulation and reduced swelling of hands and ankles in patients with heart problems.

Although digitalis has been prescribed to help some patients lose weight, it should *never* be used in this way. When used improperly, digitalis can cause serious problems.

Digitalis medicines are available only with your doctor's prescription, in the following dosage forms:

Oral

Digitoxin
- Tablets (U.S. and Canada)

Digoxin
- Capsules (U.S.)
- Elixir (U.S. and Canada)
- Tablets (U.S. and Canada)

Parenteral

Digoxin
- Injection (U.S. and Canada)

Before Using This Medicine

In deciding to use a medicine, the risks of taking the medicine must be weighed against the good it will do. This is a decision you and your doctor will make. For digitalis medicines, the following should be considered:

Allergies—Tell your doctor if you have ever had any unusual or allergic reaction to digitalis medicines. Also tell your health care professional if you are allergic to any other substances, such as foods, preservatives, or dyes.

Pregnancy—Digitalis medicines pass from the mother to the fetus. However, studies on effects in pregnancy have not been done in either humans or animals. Make sure your doctor knows if you are pregnant or if you may become pregnant before taking digitalis medicines.

Breast-feeding—Although small amounts of digitalis medicines pass into breast milk, they have not been reported to cause problems in nursing babies.

Children—This medicine has been tested in children and, in effective doses, has not been shown to cause different side effects or problems than it does in adults. However, the dose is very different for babies and children, and it is important to follow your doctor's instructions exactly.

Older adults—Signs and symptoms of overdose may be especially likely to occur in elderly patients, who are usually more sensitive than younger adults to the effects of digitalis medicines.

Other medicines—Although certain medicines should not be used together at all, in other cases 2 different medicines may be used together even if an interaction might occur. In these cases, your doctor may want to change the dose, or other precautions may be necessary. When you are taking or receiving digitalis medicines it is especially important that your health care professional know if you are taking any of the following:

- Amiodarone (e.g., Cordarone)—May cause levels of digitalis medicines in the body to be higher than usual, which could lead to signs or symptoms of overdose
- Amphetamines or
- Appetite suppressants (diet pills) or
- Digitalis medicines (other) or other heart medicine or
- Medicine for asthma or other breathing problems or
- Medicine for colds, sinus problems, or hay fever or other allergies (including nose drops or sprays)—May increase the risk of heart rhythm problems
- Calcium channel blocking agents (bepridil [e.g., Bepadin, Vascor], diltiazem [e.g., Cardizem, Cardizem CD, Cardizem SR], felodipine [e.g., Plendil], flunarizine [e.g., Sibelium], isradipine [e.g., DynaCirc], nicardipine [e.g., Cardene], nifedipine [e.g., Adalat, Procardia, Procardia XL], nimodipine [e.g., Nimotop], verapamil [e.g., Calan, Calan SR, Isoptin, Isoptin SR, Verelan]) or
- Propafenone—May cause levels of digitalis medicines in the body to be higher than usual, which could lead to signs or symptoms of overdose
- Cholestyramine (e.g., Questran) or
- Colestipol (e.g., Colestid) or
- Diarrhea medicine or
- Sucralfate or
- If your diet contains large amounts of fiber, such as bran—May decrease effects of digitalis medicines by keeping them from being absorbed into the body; digitalis medicines should be taken several hours apart from these
- Diuretics (water pills) or
- Other medicines that decrease the amount of potassium in the body (corticosteroids [cortisone-like medicines], alcohol, capreomycin, corticotropin, insulin, laxatives, salic-

ylates [aspirin], vitamin B_{12}, vitamin D [high doses])—These medicines can cause hypokalemia (low levels of potassium in the body), which can increase the unwanted effects of digitalis medicines

- Potassium-containing medicines or supplements—If levels of potassium in the body become too high, there is a serious risk of heart rhythm problems being caused by digitalis medicines
- Quinidine (e.g., Quinidex)—May cause levels of digitalis medicines in the body to be higher than usual, which could lead to signs or symptoms of overdose

Other medical problems—The presence of other medical problems may affect the use of digitalis medicines. Make sure you tell your doctor if you have any other medical problems, especially:

- Heart disease or
- Lung disease (severe)—The heart may be more sensitive to the effects of digitalis medicines
- Heart rhythm problems—Digitalis glycosides may make certain heart rhythm problems worse
- Kidney disease or
- Liver disease—Effects may be increased because of slower removal of digitalis medicines from the body
- Thyroid disease—Patients with low or high thyroid gland activity may be more or less sensitive to the effects of digitalis glycosides

Proper Use of This Medicine

To keep your heart working properly, *take this medicine exactly as directed even though you may feel well.* Do not take more of it than your doctor ordered and do not miss any doses.

For patients taking the *liquid form of digoxin:*

- This medicine is to be taken by mouth even if it comes in a dropper bottle. The amount you should take is to be measured only with the specially marked dropper.

To help you remember to take your dose of medicine, try to take it at the same time every day.

Ask your doctor about checking your pulse rate. Then, while you are taking this medicine, check your pulse regularly. If it is much slower, or faster, than your usual rate (or less than 60 beats per minute), or if it changes in rhythm or force, check with your doctor. Such changes may mean that side effects are developing.

Dosing—When you are taking digitalis medicines, it is very important that you get the exact amount of medicine that you need. The dose of digitalis medicine will be different for different patients. Your doctor will determine the proper dose of digitalis medicine for you. *Follow your doctor's orders or the directions on the label.*

After you begin taking digitalis medicines, your doctor may sometimes check your blood level of digitalis medicine to find out if your dose needs to be changed. *Do not change your dose of digitalis medicine* unless your doctor tells you to do so.

The number of capsules, tablets, drops, or dropperfuls of solution that you take depends on the strength of the medicine.

Missed dose—If you miss a dose of this medicine, and you remember it within 12 hours, take it as soon as you remember. However, if you do not remember until later, do not take the missed dose at all and do not double the next one. Instead, go back to your regular dosing schedule. If you have any questions about this or if you miss doses for 2 or more days in a row, check with your doctor.

Storage—To store this medicine:

- Keep out of the reach of children.
- Store away from heat and direct light.
- Do not store in the bathroom, near the kitchen sink, or in other damp places. Heat or moisture may cause the medicine to break down.
- Keep the oral liquid form of this medicine from freezing.
- Do not keep outdated medicine or medicine no longer needed. Be sure that any discarded medicine is out of the reach of children.

Precautions While Using This Medicine

It is important that your doctor check your progress at regular visits to make sure the medicine is working properly. This will allow your doctor to make any changes in directions for taking it, if necessary.

Do not stop taking this medicine without first checking with your doctor. Stopping suddenly may cause a serious change in heart function.

Keep this medicine out of the reach of children. Digitalis medicines are a major cause of accidental poisoning in children.

Watch for signs and symptoms of overdose while you are taking digitalis medicine. Follow your doctor's directions carefully. The amount of this medicine needed to help most people is very close to the amount that could cause serious problems from overdose. Some early warning signs of overdose are loss of appetite, nausea, vomiting, diarrhea, or extremely slow heartbeat. In infants and small children, the earliest signs of overdose are changes in the rate and rhythm of the heartbeat. Children may not show the other symptoms as soon as adults.

Before having any kind of surgery (including dental surgery) or emergency treatment, tell the medical doctor or dentist in charge that you are using this medicine.

Your doctor may want you to carry a medical identification card or bracelet stating that you are taking this medicine.

Do not take any other medicine unless ordered by your doctor. Many over-the-counter (OTC) or nonprescription medicines contain ingredients that interfere with digitalis medicines or that may make your condition worse. These medicines include antacids; laxatives; asthma remedies; cold, cough, or sinus preparations; medicine for diarrhea; and reducing or diet medicines.

For patients taking the *tablet or capsule* form of this medicine:

- This medicine may look like other tablets or capsules you now take. It is very important that you do not get the medicines mixed up since this may have serious results. Ask your pharmacist for ways to avoid mix-ups with medicines that look alike.

Side Effects of This Medicine

Along with its needed effects, a medicine may cause some unwanted effects. Although not all of these side effects may occur, if they do occur they may need medical attention.

Check with your doctor as soon as possible if any of the following side effects or symptoms of overdose occur:

Rare

Skin rash or hives

Signs and symptoms of overdose (in the order in which they may occur)

Loss of appetite; nausea or vomiting; lower stomach pain; diarrhea; unusual tiredness or weakness (extreme); slow or irregular heartbeat (may be fast heartbeat in children); blurred vision or "yellow, green, or white vision" (yellow, green, or white halo seen around objects); drowsiness; confusion or mental depression; headache; fainting

Note: Overdose symptoms in infants and small children may occur at first only as changes in the heartbeat rate or rhythm, while in adults and older children the first symptoms may be mostly stomach upset, stomach pain, loss of appetite, or unusually slow heartbeat.

Other side effects not listed above may also occur in some patients. If you notice any other effects, check with your doctor.

Revised: 03/10/93
Interim revision: 04/24/95; 03/31/97; 05/15/97; 08/19/97

DIMETHYL SULFOXIDE Mucosal

A commonly used brand name in the U.S. and Canada is Rimso-50.
Another commonly used name is DMSO.
Generic name product may also be available in the U.S.

Description

Dimethyl sulfoxide (dye-METH-il sul-FOX-ide) is a purified preparation used in the bladder to relieve the symptoms of the bladder condition called interstitial cystitis. A catheter (tube) or syringe is used to put the solution into the bladder where it is allowed to remain for about 15 minutes. Then, the solution is expelled by urinating.

Interstitial cystitis is the only human use for dimethyl sulfoxide that is approved by the U.S. Food and Drug Administration (FDA).

Claims that dimethyl sulfoxide is effective for treating various types of arthritis, ulcers in scleroderma, muscle sprains and strains, bruises, infections of the skin, burns, wounds, and mental conditions have not been proven.

Although other preparations of dimethyl sulfoxide are available for industrial and veterinary (animal) use, they must not be used by humans, because of their unknown purity. Impurities in these preparations may cause serious unwanted effects in humans. Even if dimethyl sulfoxide is applied to the skin, it is absorbed into the body through the skin and mucous membranes.

This medicine is available only with your doctor's prescription, in the following dosage form:

Topical

- Bladder irrigation (U.S. and Canada)

Before Using This Medicine

In deciding to use a medicine, the risks of taking the medicine must be weighed against the good it will do. This is a decision you and your doctor will make. For dimethyl sulfoxide, the following should be considered:

Allergies—Tell your doctor if you have ever had any unusual or allergic reaction to dimethyl sulfoxide. Also tell your health care professional if you are allergic to any other substances, such as preservatives.

Pregnancy—Dimethyl sulfoxide has not been studied in pregnant women. However, some studies in animals have shown that dimethyl sulfoxide causes birth defects when used on the skin and when given in high doses by injection. Before using this medicine, make sure your doctor knows if you are pregnant or if you may become pregnant.

Breast-feeding—Dimethyl sulfoxide is absorbed into the body. It is not known whether dimethyl sulfoxide passes into the breast milk. However, this medicine has not been reported to cause problems in nursing babies.

Children—Studies on this medicine have been done only in adult patients, and there is no specific information comparing use of this medicine in children with use in other age groups.

Older adults—Many medicines have not been studied specifically in older people. Therefore, it may not be known whether they work exactly the same way they do in younger adults or if they cause different side effects or problems in older people. There is no specific information comparing use of this medicine in the elderly with use in other age groups.

Other medicines—Although certain medicines should not be used together at all, in other cases two different medicines may be used together even if an interaction might occur. In these cases, your doctor may want to change the dose, or other precautions may be necessary. Tell your health care professional if you are using any other prescription or nonprescription (over-the-counter [OTC]) medicine.

Proper Use of This Medicine

Dosing—The dose of dimethyl sulfoxide will be different for different patients. The following information includes only the average doses of dimethyl sulfoxide. *Your dose may be different.*

- For *bladder irrigation* dosage form:
  - —For interstitial cystitis of bladder:
    - Adults—50 mL (milliliters) of a 50% solution is instilled into the bladder and left there for fifteen minutes. The treatment is repeated every two weeks until relief is obtained; then the treatment is repeated less often.
    - Children—Use and dose must be determined by your doctor.

Side Effects of This Medicine

Along with its needed effects, a medicine may cause some unwanted effects. Although not all of these side effects may occur, if they do occur they may need medical attention.

Check with your doctor immediately if any of the following side effects occur:

Nasal congestion; shortness of breath or troubled breathing; skin rash, hives, or itching; swelling of face

Some patients may have some discomfort during the time this medicine is being put into the bladder. However, the discomfort usually becomes less each time the medicine is used.

Dimethyl sulfoxide may cause you to have a garlic-like taste within a few minutes after the medicine is put into the bladder. This effect may last for several hours. It may also cause your breath and skin to have a garlic-like odor, which may last up to 72 hours.

Other side effects not listed above may also occur in some patients. If you notice any other effects, check with your doctor.

Revised: 03/04/92
Interim revision: 03/28/94

DINOPROST Intra-amniotic*

A commonly used brand name in Canada is Prostin F_2 Alpha.

*Not commercially available in the U.S.

Description

Dinoprost (DYE-noe-prost) is used to cause abortion during the second trimester of pregnancy. It may also be used for other purposes as determined by your doctor.

Dinoprost is to be administered only by or under the immediate care of your doctor. It is available in the following dosage form:

Parenteral

- Injection (Canada)

Before Receiving This Medicine

In deciding to use a medicine, the risks of taking the medicine must be weighed against the good it will do. This is a decision you and your doctor will make. For dinoprost, the following should be considered:

Allergies—Tell your doctor if you have ever had any unusual or allergic reaction to dinoprost or other oxytocics (medicines that stimulate the uterus to contract). Also tell your health care professional if you are allergic to any other substances, such as foods, preservatives, or dyes.

Other medicines—Although certain medicines should not be used together at all, in other cases two different medicines may be used together even if an interaction might occur. In these cases, your doctor may want to change the dose, or other precautions may be necessary. Tell your doctor if you are taking any prescription or nonprescription (over-the-counter [OTC]) medicine.

Other medical problems—The presence of other medical problems may affect the use of dinoprost. Make sure you tell your doctor if you have any other medical problems, especially:

- Anemia (history of)—In some patients, abortion with dinoprost may result in loss of blood that may require a transfusion
- Asthma (or history of) or
- Lung disease—Dinoprost may cause narrowing of the blood vessels in the lungs or narrowing of the lung passages
- Diabetes mellitus (sugar diabetes) (history of)
- Epilepsy (or history of)—Rarely, dinoprost has been reported to cause seizures in patients who have epilepsy
- Fibroid tumors of the uterus or
- Uterus surgery (history of)—There is an increased risk of rupture of the uterus
- Glaucoma—Rarely the pressure within the eye has increased and constriction of the pupils has occurred during the use of dinoprost
- Heart or blood vessel disease (or history of) or
- High blood pressure (history of) or
- Low blood pressure (history of)—Dinoprost may cause changes in heart function or blood pressure changes
- Jaundice (history of)
- Kidney disease (or history of)
- Liver disease (or history of)—The body may not get dinoprost out of the bloodstream at the usual rate, which may make the medicine work longer or cause toxic effects

Proper Use of This Medicine

Dosing—The dose of dinoprost will be different for different patients. Your doctor will give you the dose of this medicine and follow your care in a hospital or another health care setting.

- For *injection* dosage form:
  - —For aborting a pregnancy:
    - Adults—Your doctor will slowly inject 40 milligrams (mg) into the amniotic sac (bag that surrounds the fetus). If needed, your doctor may give you another dose in twenty–four hours to complete the abortion.

—For inducing labor:
- Adults—Your doctor will slowly inject 1 to 4 mg a day into a vein.

Side Effects of This Medicine

Along with its needed effects, a medicine may cause some unwanted effects. Although not all of these side effects may occur, if they do occur they may need medical attention.

Tell the health care professional immediately if any of the following side effects occur:

Less common or rare

Chest pain; coughing (sudden); cramping of the uterus (continuing and severe); fast heartbeat; hives; numbness in legs or other body parts; pale, cool, or blotchy skin on arms or legs; pressing or painful feeling in chest; redness and itching of skin; shortness of breath; slow or irregular heartbeat; swelling of eyelids, face, or inside of nose; tightness in chest; trouble in breathing; weak or absent pulse in arms or legs; wheezing

Also, check with the health care professional as soon as possible if any of the following side effects occur:

Less common or rare

Abdominal or stomach pain (severe or continuing); blood in urine; constipation; decreased frequency of urination; difficult or painful urination; double vision or burning eyes; pain in legs, back, or shoulder; tender or mildly bloated abdomen

Other side effects may occur that usually do not need medical attention. These side effects usually go away after the medicine is stopped. However, let the health care professional know if any of the following side effects continue or are bothersome:

More common

Diarrhea; nausea; stomach cramps or pain; vomiting

Less common

Anxiety; breast fullness or tenderness; burning feeling in breasts; chills or shivering; cough (continuing); dizziness; drowsiness; fever (temporary); flushing or redness of face; headache; hiccups; increased sweating; inflammation and pain at place of injection; unusual thirst

After the procedure has been completed, this procedure may still produce some side effects that need medical attention. Check with your doctor if you notice any of the following side effects:

Chills or shivering (continuing); fever (continuing); foul-smelling vaginal discharge; pain in lower abdomen; unusual increase in uterus bleeding

Other side effects not listed above may also occur in some patients. If you notice any other effects, check with your health care professional.

Additional Information

Once a medicine has been approved for marketing for a certain use, experience may show that it is also useful for other medical problems. Although these uses are not specifically included in product labeling, dinoprost is used in certain patients for the following medical procedures:
- Angiography (x-ray pictures of the blood vessels)
- Inducing labor

Other than the above information, there is no additional information relating to proper use, precautions, or side effects for these uses.

Revised: 10/26/92
Interim revision: 05/16/94

DINOPROSTONE Cervical/Vaginal

Some commonly used brand names are:

In the U.S.—
Cervidil
Prepidil
Prostin E_2

In Canada—
Prepidil
Prostin E_2

Other commonly used names are prostaglandin E_2 or PGE_2.

Description

Dinoprostone (dye-noe-PROST-one) works by causing the cervix to thin and dilate (open) and the uterus to contract (cramp) the way it does during labor.

Dinoprostone may also be used for other purposes as determined by your doctor.

Dinoprostone is to be administered only by or under the immediate care of your doctor. It is available in the following dosage forms:

Cervical
- Gel (U.S. and Canada)

Vaginal
- Gel (Canada)
- Suppositories (U.S.)
- System (U.S.)

Before Receiving This Medicine

In deciding to use a medicine, the risks of taking the medicine must be weighed against the good it will do. This is a decision you and your doctor will make. For dinoprostone, the following should be considered:

Allergies—Tell your doctor if you have ever had any unusual or allergic reaction to dinoprostone, misoprostol, oxytocin or other medicines that stimulate the uterus to contract.

Other medicines—Although certain medicines should not be used together at all, in other cases two different medicines may be used together even if an interaction might occur. In these cases, your doctor may want to change the dose, or other precautions may be necessary. When you are receiving dinoprostone, it is especially important that your doctor knows if you are using any other vaginal prescription or nonprescription (over-the-counter [OTC]) medicine.

Other medical problems—The presence of other medical problems may affect the use of dinoprostone. Make sure you tell your doctor if you have any other medical problems, especially:

- Anemia (or history of)—Dinoprostone, when used in doses that stimulate the uterus to contact, may result in loss of blood in some patients that may require a blood transfusion
- Asthma (or history of, including childhood asthma) or
- Lung disease—Dinoprostone may cause narrowing of the blood vessels in the lungs or narrowing of the lung passages, especially when it is used in doses that stimulate the uterus to contract
- Epilepsy (or history of)—Rarely, seizures have occurred with dinoprostone when it is used in doses that stimulate the uterus to contract
- Glaucoma—Rarely, the pressure within the eye has increased and constriction of the pupils has occurred during the use of medicines like dinoprostone; this may also be a problem with dinoprostone when it is used in doses that stimulate the uterus to contract
- Heart or blood vessel disease (or history of) or
- High blood pressure (or history of) or
- Low blood pressure (history of)—Dinoprostone may cause changes in heart function or blood pressure changes; two patients with a history of heart disease had heart attacks when dinoprostone was used in doses that stimulated the uterus to contract
- Kidney disease (or history of) or
- Liver disease (or history of)—The body may not remove dinoprostone from the blood stream at the usual rate, which may make the dinoprostone work longer or cause an increased chance of side effects, especially when dinoprostone is used in doses that stimulate the uterus to contract
- Problems during delivery, history of or
- Surgery of uterus (history of) or
- Unusual vaginal bleeding—There is an increased risk of problems occurring with dinoprostone when it is used in doses that stimulate the uterus to contract

Proper Use of This Medicine

After dinoprostone is given, you will need to lie down for 10 minutes to 2 hours so that the medicine can be absorbed. The length of time you must remain lying down will depend on what form of the medicine you are using.

Dosing—The dose of dinoprostone will be different for different patients. The following information includes only the average doses for dinoprostone. Your doctor will give you the dose of this medicine and follow your care in a hospital or other health care setting.

- For *cervical* dosage form (gel):
  - —To thin and widen the opening of the cervix just before labor:
    - Adults and teenagers—Your doctor will insert 0.5 milligram (mg) (one application) of dinoprostone into the canal of your cervix. You should remain lying on your back for at least ten to thirty minutes after it has been applied.
- For *vaginal* dosage form (gel):
  - —To cause the uterus to contract for labor:
    - Adults and teenagers—Your doctor will insert 1 milligram (mg) (one applicatorful) of dinoprostone into your vagina. You should remain lying on your back for at least thirty minutes after it has been applied. You may need another dose of 1 to 2 mg six hours after the first dose.
- For *vaginal* dosage form (suppositories):
  - —To cause the uterus to contract to abort a pregnancy:
    - Adults and teenagers—Your doctor will insert 20 milligrams (mg) (one suppository) into your vagina every three to five hours as needed. You should remain lying on your back for at least ten minutes after it has been inserted.
- For *vaginal* dosage form (system):
  - —To thin and widen the opening of the cervix just before labor:
    - Adults and teenagers—Your doctor will insert 10 milligrams (mg) (one system) into your vagina. You should remain lying on your back for at least two hours after it has been inserted.

Side Effects of This Medicine

Along with its needed effects, a medicine may cause some unwanted effects. Although not all of these side effects may occur, if they do occur they may need medical attention.

Tell the health care professional immediately if any of the following side effects occur:

Less common or rare

Fast or slow heartbeat; hives; increased pain of the uterus; pale, cool, blotchy skin on arms or legs; pressing or painful feeling in chest; shortness of breath; swelling of face, inside the nose, and eyelids; tightness in chest; trouble in breathing; weak or absent pulse in arms or legs; wheezing

Other side effects may occur that usually do not need medical attention. These side effects usually go away after the medicine is stopped. However, let the health care professional know if any of the following side effects continue or are bothersome:

More common

Abdominal or stomach cramps; diarrhea; fever; nausea; vomiting

Less common or rare

Chills or shivering; constipation; flushing; headache; swelling of the genital area (vulva); tender or mildly bloated abdomen or stomach

This procedure may still result in some effects, which occur after the procedure is completed, that need medical attention. Check with your doctor if any of the following side effects occur:

Chills or shivering (continuing); fever (continuing); foul-smelling vaginal discharge; pain in lower abdomen; unusual increase in bleeding of the uterus

Other side effects not listed above may also occur in some patients. If you notice any other effects, check with your health care professional.

Additional Information

Once a medicine has been approved for marketing for a certain use, experience may show that it is also useful for other medical problems. Although these uses are not included in product labeling, dinoprostone is used in certain patients with the following medical condition:

- Unusual increase in bleeding of the uterus after delivery (postpartum hemorrhage)

Other than the above information, there is no additional information relating to proper use, precautions, or side effects for this use.

Revised: 08/20/97

DIPHENIDOL Systemic†

A commonly used brand name in the U.S. is Vontrol.

Another commonly used name is difenidol.

†Not commercially available in Canada.

Description

Diphenidol (dye-FEN-i-dole) is used to relieve or prevent nausea, vomiting, and dizziness caused by certain medical problems.

Diphenidol is available only with your doctor's prescription in the following dosage form:

Oral
- Tablets (U.S.)

Before Using This Medicine

In deciding to use a medicine, the risks of taking the medicine must be weighed against the good it will do. This is a decision you and your doctor will make. For diphenidol, the following should be considered:

Allergies—Tell your doctor if you have ever had any unusual or allergic reaction to diphenidol. Also tell your health care professional if you are allergic to any other substances, such as foods, preservatives, or dyes.

Pregnancy—Diphenidol has not been shown to cause birth defects or other problems in human or animal studies.

Breast-feeding—Diphenidol has not been reported to cause problems in nursing babies.

Children—There is no specific information comparing use of diphenidol for dizziness in children with use in other age groups. Also, there is no specific information about the use of diphenidol for nausea and vomiting in children who weigh less than 22.8 kg (50 lbs).

Older adults—Many medicines have not been studied specifically in older people. Therefore, it may not be known whether they work exactly the same way they do in younger adults or if they cause different side effects or problems in older people. There is no specific information comparing use of diphenidol in the elderly with use in other age groups.

Other medicines—Although certain medicines should not be used together at all, in other cases 2 different medicines may be used together even if an interaction might occur. In these cases, your doctor may want to change the dose, or other precautions may be necessary. When you are taking diphenidol, it is especially important that your health care professional know if you are taking any of the following:

- Central nervous system (CNS) depressants (medicine that causes drowsiness) or
- Tricyclic antidepressants (medicine for depression)—Using these medicines with diphenidol may increase the CNS depressant effects

Other medical problems—The presence of other medical problems may affect the use of diphenidol. Make sure you tell your doctor if you have any other medical problems, especially:

- Enlarged prostate or
- Glaucoma or
- Intestinal blockage or
- Low blood pressure or
- Stomach ulcer—Diphenidol may make the condition worse
- Kidney disease or
- Urinary tract blockage—Higher blood levels of diphenidol may occur, increasing the chance of side effects

Proper Use of This Medicine

If you are taking diphenidol to prevent nausea and vomiting, it may be taken with food or a glass of water or milk to lessen stomach irritation, unless otherwise directed by your doctor. However, if you are already suffering from nausea and vomiting, it is best to keep the stomach empty, and this medicine should be taken only with a small amount of water.

Take this medicine only as directed. Do not take more of it and do not take it more often than directed by your doctor. To do so may increase the chance of side effects.

Dosing—The dose of diphenidol will be different for different patients. *Follow your doctor's orders or the directions on the label.* The following information includes only the average doses of diphenidol. *If your dose is different, do not change it* unless your doctor tells you to do so.

The number of tablets that you take depends on the strength of the medicine. Also, *the number of doses you take each day, the time allowed between doses, and the length of time you take the medicine depend on the medical problem for which you are taking diphenidol.*

- For *tablets* dosage form:
  - —Adults: 25 to 50 milligrams (mg) every four hours as needed.
  - —Children: The dose is based on body weight and must be determined by the doctor.

Missed dose—If your doctor has ordered you to take this medicine on a regular schedule and you miss a dose, take it as soon as possible. However, if it is almost time for your next dose, skip the missed dose and go back to your regular dosing schedule. Do not double doses.

Storage—To store this medicine:
- Keep out of the reach of children.
- Store away from heat and direct light.
- Do not store the tablet form of this medicine in the bathroom, near the kitchen sink, or in other damp places. Heat or moisture may cause the medicine to break down.
- Do not keep outdated medicine or medicine no longer needed. Be sure that any discarded medicine is out of the reach of children.

Precautions While Using This Medicine

This medicine will add to the effects of alcohol and other CNS depressants (medicines that slow down the nervous system, possibly causing drowsiness). Some examples of CNS depressants are antihistamines or medicine for hay fever, other allergies, or colds; sedatives, tranquilizers, or sleeping medicine; prescription pain medicine or narcotics; barbiturates; medicine for seizures; muscle relaxants; or anesthetics, including some dental anesthetics. *Check with your doctor before taking any of the above while you are using this medicine.*

This medicine may cause some people to have blurred vision or to become dizzy, drowsy or less alert than they are normally. *Make sure you know how you react to this medicine before you drive, use machines, or do anything else that could be dangerous if you are dizzy or are not alert or able to see well.*

Side Effects of This Medicine

Along with its needed effects, a medicine may cause some unwanted effects. Although not all of these side effects may occur, if they do occur they may need medical attention.

Check with your doctor as soon as possible if any of the following side effects occur:

Rare

Confusion; hallucinations (seeing, hearing, or feeling things that are not there)

Symptoms of overdose

Drowsiness (severe); shortness of breath or troubled breathing; unusual tiredness or weakness (severe)

Other side effects may occur that usually do not need medical attention. These side effects may go away during treatment as your body adjusts to the medicine. However, check with your doctor if any of the following side effects continue or are bothersome:

More common

Drowsiness

Less common or rare

Blurred vision; dizziness; dryness of mouth; headache; heartburn; nervousness, restlessness, or trouble in sleeping; skin rash; stomach upset or pain; unusual tiredness or weakness

Other side effects not listed above may also occur in some patients. If you notice any other effects, check with your doctor.

Revised: 04/16/93

DIPHENOXYLATE AND ATROPINE Systemic

Some commonly used brand names are:

In the U.S.—

Lofene	Lomotil
Logen	Lonox
Lomocot	Vi-Atro

Generic name product may also be available.

In Canada—

Lomotil

Description

Diphenoxylate (dye-fen-OX-i-late) and atropine (A-troe-peen) is a combination medicine used along with other measures to treat severe diarrhea in adults. Diphenoxylate helps stop diarrhea by slowing down the movements of the intestines.

Since diphenoxylate is chemically related to some narcotics, it may be habit-forming if taken in doses that are larger than prescribed. To help prevent possible abuse, atropine (an anticholinergic) has been added. If higher than normal doses of the combination are taken, the atropine will cause unpleasant effects, making it unlikely that such doses will be taken again.

Diphenoxylate and atropine combination medicine should not be used in children. Children with diarrhea should be given solutions of carbohydrates (sugars) and important salts (electrolytes) to replace the water, sugars, and important salts that are lost from the body during diarrhea. For more information on these solutions, see the *Carbohydrates and Electrolytes (Systemic)* monograph.

This medicine is available only with your doctor's prescription in the following dosage forms:

Oral
- Oral solution (U.S.)
- Tablets (U.S. and Canada)

Before Using This Medicine

In deciding to use a medicine, the risks of taking the medicine must be weighed against the good it will do. This is

a decision you and your doctor will make. For diphenoxylate and atropine, the following should be considered:

Allergies—Tell your doctor if you have ever had any unusual or allergic reaction to diphenoxylate or atropine. Also tell your health care professional if you are allergic to any other substances, such as foods, preservatives, or dyes.

Pregnancy—Studies have not been done in humans. In animal studies this medicine given in larger doses than the usual human dose has not been shown to cause birth defects. However, some studies in rats have shown that this medicine reduces the weight gain of the pregnant rat and lessens the chance of conceiving or becoming pregnant when given in doses many times the usual human dose.

Breast-feeding—Although both diphenoxylate and atropine pass into the breast milk, this medicine has not been shown to cause problems in nursing babies.

Children—This medicine should not be used in children. Children, especially very young children, are very sensitive to the effects of diphenoxylate and atropine. This may increase the chance of side effects during treatment. Also, the fluid loss caused by diarrhea may result in a severe condition. For this reason, it is very important that a sufficient amount of liquids be given to replace the fluid lost by the body. If you have any questions about this, check with your health care professional.

Older adults—Shortness of breath or difficulty in breathing may be especially likely to occur in elderly patients, who are usually more sensitive than younger adults to the effects of diphenoxylate. Also, the fluid loss caused by diarrhea may result in a severe condition. For this reason, elderly persons should not take this medicine without first checking with their doctor. It is also very important that a sufficient amount of liquids be taken to replace the fluid lost by the body. If you have any questions about this, check with your health care professional.

Other medicines—Although certain medicines should not be used together at all, in other cases two different medicines may be used together even if an interaction might occur. In these cases, your doctor may want to change the dose, or other precautions may be necessary. When you are taking diphenoxylate and atropine, it is especially important that your health care professional know if you are taking any of the following:

- Antibiotics, such as cephalosporins (e.g., Ceftin, Keflex), clindamycin (e.g., Cleocin), erythromycins (e.g., E.E.S., PCE), tetracyclines (e.g., Achromycin, Doryx)—These antibiotics may cause diarrhea. Diphenoxylate and atropine may make the diarrhea caused by antibiotics worse or make it last longer
- Central nervous system (CNS) depressants (medicines that cause drowsiness)—Effects, such as drowsiness, of CNS depressants or of diphenoxylate and atropine may become greater
- Monoamine oxidase (MAO) inhibitors (furazolidone [e.g., Furoxone], isocarboxazid [e.g., Marplan], phenelzine [e.g., Nardil], procarbazine [e.g., Matulane], selegiline [e.g., Eldepryl], tranylcypromine [e.g., Parnate])—Taking diphenoxylate and atropine while you are taking or within 2 weeks of taking MAO inhibitors may cause severe side effects; these medicines should not be used together
- Naltrexone (e.g., Trexan)—Withdrawal side effects may occur in patients who have become addicted to the diphenoxylate in this combination medicine; also, naltrexone will make this medicine less effective against diarrhea
- Other anticholinergics (medicine to help reduce stomach acid and abdominal or stomach spasms or cramps)—Use of other anticholinergics with this combination medicine may increase the effects of the atropine in this combination; however, this is not likely to happen with the usual doses of diphenoxylate and atropine

Other medical problems—The presence of other medical problems may affect the use of diphenoxylate and atropine. Make sure you tell your doctor if you have any other medical problems, especially:

- Alcohol abuse (or history of) or
- Drug abuse (history of)—There is a greater chance that this medicine will become habit-forming
- Colitis (severe)—A more serious problem of the colon may develop if you use this medicine
- Down's syndrome (mongolism)—Side effects may be more likely and severe in these patients
- Dysentery—This condition may get worse; a different kind of treatment may be needed
- Emphysema, asthma, bronchitis, or other chronic lung disease—There is a greater chance that this medicine may cause serious breathing problems in patients who have any of these conditions
- Enlarged prostate or
- Urinary tract blockage or difficult urination—Severe problems with urination may develop with the use of this medicine
- Gallbladder disease or gallstones—Use of this medicine may cause spasms of the biliary tract and make the condition worse
- Glaucoma—Severe pain in the eye may occur with the use of this medicine; however, the chance of this happening is small
- Heart disease—This medicine may have some effects on the heart, which may make the condition worse
- Hiatal hernia—The atropine in this medicine may make this condition worse; however, the chance of this happening is small
- High blood pressure (hypertension)—The atropine in this medicine may cause an increase in blood pressure; however, the chance of this happening is small
- Intestinal blockage—This medicine may make the condition worse
- Kidney disease—The atropine in this medicine may build up in the body and cause side effects
- Liver disease—The chance of central nervous system (CNS) side effects, including coma, may be greater in patients who have this condition
- Myasthenia gravis—This medicine may make the condition worse
- Overactive or underactive thyroid—Unwanted effects on breathing and heart rate may occur
- Overflow incontinence—This medicine may make the condition worse

Proper Use of This Medicine

If this medicine upsets your stomach, your doctor may want you to take it with food.

Take this medicine only as directed by your doctor. Do not take more of it, do not take it more often, and do not take it for a longer time than your doctor ordered. If too much is taken, it may become habit-forming.

For patients taking the liquid form of this medicine:

- This medicine is to be taken by mouth even if it comes in a dropper bottle. The amount to be taken is to be measured with the specially marked dropper.

Importance of diet and fluids while treating diarrhea:

- *In addition to using medicine for diarrhea, it is very important that you replace the fluid lost by the body and follow a proper diet.* For the first 24 hours you should eat gelatin and drink plenty of caffeine-free clear liquids, such as ginger ale, decaffeinated cola, decaffeinated tea, and broth. During the next 24 hours you may eat bland foods, such as cooked cereals, bread, crackers, and applesauce. Fruits, vegetables, fried or spicy foods, bran, candy, caffeine, and alcoholic beverages may make the condition worse.
- If too much fluid has been lost by the body due to the diarrhea a serious condition may develop. Check with your doctor as soon as possible if any of the following signs or symptoms of too much fluid loss occur:

  Decreased urination
  Dizziness and lightheadedness
  Dryness of mouth
  Increased thirst
  Wrinkled skin

Dosing—The dose of diphenoxylate and atropine combination medicine will be different for different patients. *Follow your doctor's orders or the directions on the label.* The following information includes only the average doses of diphenoxylate and atropine combination. *If your dose is different, do not change it* unless your doctor tells you to do so.

- For severe diarrhea:
  - —For *oral* dosage form (oral solution):
    - Adults and teenagers—At first, the dose is 5 milligrams (mg) (2 teaspoonfuls) three or four times a day. Then, the dose is usually 5 mg (2 teaspoonfuls) once a day, as needed.
    - Children up to 12 years of age—Use is not recommended.
  - —For *oral* dosage form (tablets):
    - Adults and teenagers—At first, the dose is 5 mg (2 tablets) three or four times a day. Then, the dose is usually 5 mg (2 tablets) once a day, as needed.
    - Children up to 12 years of age—Use is not recommended.

Missed dose—If you are taking this medicine on a regular schedule and you miss a dose, take it as soon as possible. However, if it is almost time for your next dose, skip the missed dose and go back to your regular dosing schedule. Do not double doses.

Storage—To store this medicine:

- Keep out of the reach of children since overdose is especially dangerous in children.
- Store away from heat and direct light.
- Do not store the tablet form of this medicine in the bathroom, near the kitchen sink, or in other damp places. Heat or moisture may cause the medicine to break down.
- Keep the liquid form of this medicine from freezing.
- Do not keep outdated medicine or medicine no longer needed. Be sure that any discarded medicine is out of the reach of children.

Precautions While Using This Medicine

Your doctor should check your progress at regular visits if you will be taking this medicine regularly for a long time.

Check with your doctor if your diarrhea does not stop after two days or if you develop a fever.

This medicine will add to the effects of alcohol and other CNS depressants (medicines that slow down the nervous system, possibly causing drowsiness). Some examples of CNS depressants are antihistamines or medicine for hay fever, other allergies, or colds; sedatives, tranquilizers, or sleeping medicine; prescription pain medicine or narcotics; barbiturates; medicine for seizures; muscle relaxants; or anesthetics, including some dental anesthetics. *Check with your doctor before taking any of the above while you are taking this medicine.*

If you think you or anyone else may have taken an overdose, get emergency help at once. Taking an overdose of this medicine may lead to unconsciousness and possibly death. Signs or symptoms of overdose include severe drowsiness; shortness of breath or troubled breathing; fast heartbeat; and unusual warmth, dryness, and flushing of the skin.

Before having any kind of surgery (including dental surgery) or emergency treatment, tell the medical doctor or dentist in charge that you are taking this medicine.

This medicine may cause some people to become dizzy, drowsy, or less alert than they are normally. Even if taken at bedtime, it may cause some people to feel drowsy or less alert on arising. *Make sure you know how you react to this medicine before you drive, use machines, or do anything else that could be dangerous if you are dizzy or are not alert.*

Side Effects of This Medicine

Along with its needed effects, a medicine may cause some unwanted effects. Although not all of these side effects may occur, if they do occur they may need medical attention.

When this medicine is used for short periods of time at low doses, side effects usually are rare. However, check with your doctor immediately if any of the following side effects are severe and occur suddenly, since they may be signs of a more severe and dangerous problem with your bowels:

Bloating; constipation; loss of appetite; stomach pain (severe) with nausea and vomiting

Check with your doctor immediately also if the following effects occur, since they may be signs of an overdose of this medicine:

Blurred vision (continuing) or changes in near vision; drowsiness (severe); dryness of mouth, nose, and throat (severe); fast heartbeat; shortness of breath or troubled breathing (severe); unusual excitement, nervousness, restlessness, or irritability; unusual warmth, dryness, and flushing of the skin

Other side effects may occur that usually do not need medical attention. These side effects may go away during treatment as your body adjusts to the medicine. However, check with your doctor if any of the following side effects continue, worsen, or are bothersome:

Less common or rare

Blurred vision; confusion; difficult urination; dizziness or lightheadedness; drowsiness; dryness of skin and mouth; fever; headache; mental depression; numbness of hands or feet; skin rash or itching; swelling of the gums

After you stop using this medicine, your body may need time to adjust. The length of time this takes depends on the amount of medicine you were using and how long you used it. During this time check with your doctor if you notice any of the following side effects:

Rare

Increased sweating; muscle cramps; nausea or vomiting; shivering or trembling; stomach cramps

Other side effects not listed above may also occur in some patients. If you notice any other effects, check with your doctor.

Revised: 08/22/94

DIPHTHERIA AND TETANUS TOXOIDS Systemic

A commonly used name for diphtheria and tetanus toxoids for pediatric use is DT.

A commonly used name for tetanus and diphtheria toxoids for adult use is Td.

This information applies to the following medicines:

1. Diphtheria and Tetanus Toxoids for Pediatric Use (dif-THEE-ree-a and TET-n-us)
2. Tetanus and Diphtheria Toxoids for Adult Use (TET-n-us and dif-THEE-ree-a)

Description

Diphtheria and Tetanus Toxoids (also known as DT and Td) is a combination immunizing agent given by injection to prevent diphtheria and tetanus.

Diphtheria is a serious illness that can cause breathing difficulties, heart problems, nerve damage, pneumonia, and possibly death. The risk of serious complications and death is greatest in very young children and in the elderly.

Tetanus (also known as lockjaw) is a serious illness that causes convulsions (seizures) and severe muscle spasms that can be strong enough to cause bone fractures of the spine. Tetanus causes death in 30 to 40 percent of cases.

Immunization with diphtheria and tetanus toxoids for pediatric use (DT) is recommended for infants and children from 6 weeks of age (8 weeks in Canada) up until their 7th birthday.

Children 7 years of age and older and adults should be immunized with tetanus and diphtheria toxoids for adult use (Td). In addition, these children and adults should receive booster doses of Td every 10 years for the rest of their lives.

Diphtheria and tetanus are serious diseases that can cause life-threatening illnesses. Although some serious side effects can occur after a dose of DT or Td, these are rare. The chance of your child catching one of these diseases and being permanently injured or dying as a result is much greater than the chance of your child getting a serious side effect from the DT or Td vaccine.

DT and Td are available in the following dosage form:

Parenteral

- Injection (U.S. and Canada)

Before Receiving This Vaccine

In deciding to use a vaccine, the risks of using the vaccine must be weighed against the good it will do. This is a decision you and your doctor will make. For DT and Td, the following should be considered:

Allergies—Tell your doctor if you have ever had any unusual or allergic reaction to diphtheria toxoid, tetanus toxoid, DT, or Td. Also tell your health care professional if you are allergic to any other substances, such as preservatives.

Pregnancy—This vaccine has not been shown to cause birth defects or other problems in humans. Immunization of a pregnant woman can prevent her newborn baby from getting tetanus at birth.

Breast-feeding—This vaccine has not been shown to cause problems in nursing babies.

Children—For infants up to 6 weeks of age, use of DT or Td is not recommended.

For infants and children 6 weeks up to 7 years of age, Td is not recommended. DT is used instead.

For children 7 years of age and older, DT is not recommended. Td is used instead.

Older adults—DT is not recommended. Td is used instead. Td is not expected to cause different side effects or problems in older people than it does in younger adults. However, Td may be slightly less effective in older people than in younger adults.

Other medical problems—The presence of other medical problems may affect the use of DT or Td. Make sure you tell your doctor if you have any other medical problems, especially:

- Fever or
- Infection or illness (severe)—Use of DT or Td may make the condition worse or may increase the chance of side effects

Proper Use of This Vaccine

Dosing—The doses of DT and Td will be different for different patients. The following information includes only the average doses of DT and Td.

For DT

- For *injection* dosage form:
  - —For prevention of diphtheria and tetanus:
    - Children up to 6 weeks of age—Use is not recommended.
    - Children 6 weeks to 1 year of age—One dose is given every four to eight weeks for a total of three doses. A fourth dose is given six to twelve months after the third dose. A booster (fifth) dose is given when the child is four to six years of age. The booster (fifth) dose is given only if the fourth dose was given before the child's fourth birthday. The doses are injected into a muscle.
    - Children 1 to 7 years of age—One dose is given at the first visit to the doctor, followed by a second dose four to eight weeks later. A third dose is given six to twelve months after the second dose. A booster (fourth) dose is given when the child is four to six years of age. The booster (fourth dose) is given only if the third dose was given before the child's fourth birthday. The doses are injected into a muscle.
    - Adults and children 7 years of age and over—Use is not recommended. Td should be used instead.

For Td

- For *injection* dosage form:
  - —For prevention of diphtheria and tetanus:
    - Children up to 7 years of age—Use is not recommended. DT should be used instead.
    - Adults and children 7 years of age and over—One dose is given at the first visit to the doctor, followed by a second dose four to eight weeks later. A third dose is given six to twelve months after the second dose. You should receive a booster dose every ten years. In addition, if you get a wound that is unclean or hard to clean, you may need an emergency booster injection if it has been more than five years since your last booster dose. The doses are injected into a muscle.

Side Effects of This Medicine

Along with its needed effects, a medicine may cause some unwanted effects. Although not all of these side effects may occur, if they do occur they may need medical attention. *It is very important that you tell your doctor about any side effect that occurs after a dose of DT or Td,* even if the side effect has gone away without treatment. Some types of side effects may mean that you should not receive any more doses of DT or Td.

Get emergency help immediately if any of the following side effects occur:

Rare—Symptoms of allergic reaction

Difficulty in breathing or swallowing; hives; itching, especially of feet or hands; reddening of skin, especially around ears; swelling of eyes, face, or inside of nose; unusual tiredness or weakness (sudden and severe)

Check with your doctor as soon as possible if any of the following side effects occur:

Rare

Confusion; convulsions (seizures); excessive sleepiness; fever over 39.4 °C (103 °F); headache or vomiting (severe or continuing); hives; itching; joint aches or pain; skin rash; swelling, blistering, pain, or other severe reaction at the place of injection (generally starts within 2 to 8 hours after the injection); unusual irritability

Other side effects may occur that usually do not need medical attention. However, check with your doctor if any of the following side effects continue or are bothersome:

More common—For DT and Td

Redness or hard lump at the place of injection (this may last for a few days; however, less often, the hard lump may last for a few weeks)

More common—For DT only

Fever under 39.4 °C (103 °F); swelling, pain, or tenderness at the place of injection (this may last for a few days)

Less common—For DT and Td

Dent or indentation at the place of injection

Less common—For DT only

Crying (continuing); drowsiness; fretfulness; loss of appetite; vomiting

Less common—For Td only

Chills; fast heartbeat; fever under 39.4 °C (103 °F); general feeling of discomfort or illness; headache; muscle aches; swelling of glands in armpit; unusual tiredness or weakness

Other side effects not listed above may also occur in some patients. If you notice any other effects, check with your doctor.

Developed: 04/26/95

DIPHTHERIA AND TETANUS TOXOIDS AND PERTUSSIS VACCINE ADSORBED Systemic

Some commonly used brand names in the U.S. are Acel-Imune, Tri-Immunol, and Tripedia.

Other commonly used names are acellular DTP, DTaP, DTP, DTwP, and whole-cell DTP.

Generic name product may also be available in the U.S. and Canada.

Description

Diphtheria (dif-THEER-ee-a) and Tetanus (TET-n-us) Toxoids and Pertussis (per-TUSS-iss) Vaccine (also known as DTP) is a combination immunizing agent given by injection to prevent diphtheria, tetanus, and pertussis.

Diphtheria is a serious illness that can cause breathing difficulties, heart problems, nerve damage, pneumonia, and possibly death. The risk of serious complications and death is greater in very young children and in the elderly.

Tetanus (also known as lockjaw) is a serious illness that causes convulsions (seizures) and severe muscle spasms that can be strong enough to cause bone fractures of the spine. Tetanus causes death in 30 to 40 percent of cases.

Pertussis (also known as whooping cough) is a serious disease that causes severe spells of coughing that can interfere with breathing. Pertussis can also cause pneumonia, long-lasting bronchitis, seizures, brain damage, and death.

Immunization against diphtheria, tetanus, and pertussis is recommended for all infants and children from 6 or 8 weeks of age up until their 7th birthday. Children 7 years of age and older and adults should receive immunizing agents that contain only diphtheria and tetanus toxoids and not pertussis vaccine. Persons should receive the diphtheria and tetanus injections every 10 years for the rest of their lives.

Diphtheria, tetanus, and pertussis are serious diseases that can cause life-threatening illnesses. Although some serious side effects can occur after a dose of DTP (usually from the pertussis vaccine in DTP), this rarely happens. The chance of your child catching one of these diseases and being permanently injured or dying as a result is much greater than the chance of your child getting a serious side effect from the DTP vaccine.

DTP is available in the following dosage form:

Parenteral

- Injection (U.S. and Canada)

Before Receiving This Vaccine

In deciding to use a medicine, the risks of taking the medicine must be weighed against the good it will do. This is a decision you and your doctor will make. For DTP, the following should be considered:

Allergies—Tell your doctor if your child has ever had any unusual or allergic reaction to diphtheria toxoid, tetanus toxoid, pertussis vaccine, or DTP. Also tell your health care professional if your child is allergic to any other substances, such as preservatives.

Other medical problems—The presence of other medical problems may affect the use of DTP. Make sure you tell your doctor if your child has any other medical problems, especially:

- Brain disease or
- Central nervous system (CNS) disease or
- Epilepsy or
- Fever or
- Spasms or
- Seizures (convulsions)—Use of DTP may make the condition worse or may increase the chance of side effects

Proper Use of This Vaccine

Dosing—The dose of DTP will be different for different patients. The following information includes only the average doses of DTP.

- For *injection* dosage form:
  - —For prevention of diphtheria, tetanus, and pertussis:
    - Adults and children 7 years of age and older—Use is not recommended.
    - Children 2 months to 7 years of age—One dose every four to eight weeks for a total of three doses, then a fourth dose six to twelve months after the third dose. A booster dose should be given at four to six years of age. (The booster dose is given only if the fourth dose was given before the child's fourth birthday.)

Precautions After Receiving This Vaccine

At the time of the DTP injection, your doctor may give your child a dose of acetaminophen (or another medicine that helps prevent fever). This is to help prevent some of the side effects of DTP. Your doctor may also want your child to take this medicine every 4 hours for 24 hours after your child receives the DTP injection. Check with your doctor if you have any questions.

Side Effects of This Vaccine

Along with its needed effects, a vaccine may cause some unwanted effects. Although not all of these side effects may occur, if they do occur they may need medical attention. *It is very important that you tell your doctor about any side effect that occurs after a dose of DTP*, even though the side effect may have gone away without treatment. Some types of side effects may mean that your child should not receive any more doses of DTP.

Get emergency help immediately if any of the following side effects occur:

Rare

Collapse; confusion; convulsions (seizures); crying for three or more hours; difficulty in breathing or swallowing; fever of 40.5 °C (105 °F) or more; headache (severe or continuing); hives; irritability (unusual); itching, especially of feet or hands; periods of unconsciousness or lack of awareness; reddening of skin, especially around ears; sleepiness (unusual and continuing); swelling of eyes, face, or inside of nose; unusual tiredness, weakness, or limpness (sudden and severe); vomiting (severe or continuing)

Other side effects may occur that usually do not need medical attention. These side effects may go away as your child's body adjusts to the vaccine. However, check with your doctor if any of the following side effects continue or are bothersome:

More common

Fever between 38 and 39 °C (100.4 and 102.2 °F) (may occur with fretfulness, drowsiness, vomiting, and loss of appetite); lump at place of injection (may be present for a few weeks after injection); redness, swelling, tenderness, or pain at place of injection

Less common

Fever between 39 and 40 °C (102.2 and 104 °F) (may occur with fretfulness, drowsiness, vomiting, and loss of appetite)

Rare

Fever between 40 and 40.5 °C (104 and 105 °F) (may occur with fretfulness, drowsiness, vomiting, and loss of appetite); skin rash; swollen glands on side of neck (following DTP injection into arm)

Other side effects not listed above may also occur in some patients. If you notice any other effects, check with your doctor.

Revised: 06/09/93
Interim revision: 03/29/94

DIPHTHERIA AND TETANUS TOXOIDS AND PERTUSSIS VACCINE ADSORBED AND HAEMOPHILUS B CONJUGATE VACCINE Systemic

Some commonly used brand names are:

In the U.S.—
Tetramune

In Canada—
DPT-Hib
Tetramune

Other commonly used names are DTP-HbOC, DTP-Hib, and DTP-PRP-D.

Description

Diphtheria (dif-THEER-ee-a) and tetanus (TET-n-us) toxoids and pertussis (per-TUSS-iss) vaccine (also known as DTP vaccine) combined with Haemophilus b conjugate (hem-OFF-fil-us BEE KON-ja-gat) vaccine (also known as Hib vaccine) is a combination immunizing agent used to prevent illness caused by diphtheria, tetanus, pertussis, and *Haemophilus influenzae* type b (Hib) bacteria. The vaccine works by causing the body to produce its own protection (antibodies) against these diseases. This combination vaccine is also known as DTP-Hib vaccine.

Diphtheria is a serious illness that can cause breathing difficulties, heart problems, nerve damage, pneumonia, and possibly death. The risk of serious complications and death is greater in very young children and in the elderly.

Tetanus (also known as lockjaw) is a serious illness that causes convulsions (seizures) and severe muscle spasms that can be strong enough to cause bone fractures of the spine. Tetanus causes death in 30 to 40 percent of cases.

Pertussis (also known as whooping cough) is a serious disease that causes severe spells of coughing that can interfere with breathing. Pertussis can also cause pneumonia, long-lasting bronchitis, seizures, brain damage, and death.

Infection by *Haemophilus influenzae* type b (Hib) bacteria can cause life-threatening illnesses, such as meningitis, which affects the brain; epiglottitis, which can cause death by suffocation; pericarditis, which affects the heart; pneumonia, which affects the lungs; and septic arthritis, which affects the bones and joints. Hib meningitis causes death in 5 to 10% of children who are infected. Also, approximately 30% of children who survive Hib meningitis are left with some type of serious permanent damage, such as mental retardation, deafness, epilepsy, or partial blindness.

DTP-Hib vaccine is available in the following dosage form:

Parenteral

- Injection (U.S. and Canada)

Before Receiving This Vaccine

In deciding to use a vaccine, the risks of receiving the vaccine must be weighed against the good it will do. This is a decision you and your doctor will make. For DTP-Hib vaccine, the following should be considered:

Allergies—Tell your doctor if your child has ever had any unusual or allergic reaction to diphtheria toxoid, tetanus toxoid, pertussis vaccine, DTP vaccine, Haemophilus b conjugate vaccine, Hib vaccine, or Haemophilus b polysaccharide vaccine. Also tell your health care professional if your child is allergic to any other substances, such as thimerosal or other preservatives.

Children—This vaccine is not recommended for children younger than 2 months of age or older than 7 years of age.

Other medical problems—The presence of other medical problems may affect the use of DTP-Hib vaccine. Make sure you tell your doctor if your child has any other medical problems, especially:

- Brain disease or
- Central nervous system (CNS) disease or family history of or
- Convulsions (seizures) or family history of—Use of the vaccine may make the condition worse or may increase the chance of side effects
- Fever or
- Serious illness—The symptoms of the condition may be confused with some of the possible side effects of the vaccine

Proper Use of This Vaccine

Dosing—The number of doses of DTP-Hib vaccine will be different for different patients. The following information includes only the average doses of DTP-Hib vaccine.

- For *injection* dosage form:
  - —For prevention of diphtheria, tetanus, pertussis, and *Haemophilus influenzae* type b illnesses:
    - Children up to 2 months of age—Use is not recommended.
    - Children 2 to 6 months of age at the first dose—Three doses, at least two months apart. Then a fourth dose at 12 to 18 months of age after at least 6 months have passed since the third dose. The doses are injected into a muscle.
    - Children 7 to 11 months of age at the first dose—Two doses, at least two months apart, followed by additional doses of either this vaccine, DTP vaccine, or Hib vaccine, depending on the immunization schedule. The doses are injected into a muscle.
    - Children 12 to 14 months of age at the first dose—One dose, followed by additional doses of either this vaccine, DTP vaccine, or Hib vaccine, depending on the immunization schedule. The doses are injected into a muscle.
    - Children 15 to 59 months of age at the first dose—One dose, followed by additional doses of DTP vaccine to complete the immunization schedule for DTP. The doses are injected into a muscle.
    - Adults and children 7 years of age and older—Use is not recommended.

After Receiving This Vaccine

At the time of the DTP-Hib vaccine injection, your doctor may give your child a dose of acetaminophen (or another medicine that helps prevent fever). This is to help prevent some of the side effects of this vaccine. Your doctor may also want your child to take this medicine every 4 hours for 24 hours after your child receives this vaccine. Check with your doctor if you have any questions.

This vaccine may interfere with laboratory tests that check for Hib disease. Make sure your doctor knows that your child has received DTP-Hib vaccine if your child is treated for a severe infection during the 2 weeks after your child receives this vaccine.

Side Effects of This Vaccine

Along with its needed effects, a vaccine may cause some unwanted effects. Although not all of these side effects may occur, if they do occur they may need medical attention. *It is very important that you tell your doctor about any side effect that occurs after a dose of DTP-Hib vaccine*, even if the side effect goes away without treatment. Some types of side effects may mean that your child should not receive any more doses of DTP-Hib vaccine.

Get emergency help immediately if any of the following side effects occur:

Rare

Collapse; confusion; convulsions (seizures); crying for three or more hours; fever of 40.5 °C (105 °F) or more; headache (severe or continuing); irritability (unusual and continuing); periods of unconsciousness or lack of awareness; sleepiness (unusual and continuing); vomiting (severe or continuing)

Check with your doctor immediately if any of the following side effects occur:

Rare

Symptoms of allergic reactions—Difficulty in breathing or swallowing; hives; itching (especially of feet or hands); reddening of skin (especially around ears); swelling of eyes, face, or inside of nose; unusual tiredness or weakness (sudden and severe)

Other side effects may occur that usually do not need medical attention. These side effects may go away as your child's body adjusts to the vaccine. However, check with your doctor if any of the following side effects continue or are bothersome:

More common

Drowsiness; fever of up to 102.2 °F (39 °C) (usually lasts less than 48 hours and may occur with fretfulness, drowsiness, vomiting, and loss of appetite); fretfulness; irritability; lump at place of injection (may be present for a few weeks after injection); redness, warm feeling, swelling, tenderness, or pain at place of injection

Less common

Diarrhea; fever between 102.2 and 104 °F (39 and 40 °C) (usually lasts less than 48 hours and may occur with fretfulness, drowsiness, vomiting, and loss of appetite); hard lump at place of injection (may be present for a few days after injection); loss of appetite; vomiting

Rare

Fever between 104 and 104.8 °F (40 and 40.4 °C) (usually lasts less than 48 hours and may occur with fretfulness, drowsiness, vomiting, and loss of appetite); lack of interest; reduced physical activity; skin rash

Other side effects not listed above may also occur in some patients. If you notice any other effects, check with your doctor.

Developed: 11/27/96

DIPIVEFRIN Ophthalmic

Some commonly used brand names are:

In the U.S.—

Propine C Cap B.I.D.

Generic name product may also be available.

In Canada—

Ophtho-Dipivefrin

Propine C Cap B.I.D.

Generic name product may also be available.

Another commonly used name is dipivefrine.

Description

Dipivefrin (dye-PI-ve-frin) is used to treat certain types of glaucoma.

This medicine is available only with your doctor's prescription, in the following dosage form:

Ophthalmic

- Ophthalmic solution (eye drops) (U.S. and Canada)

Before Using This Medicine

In deciding to use a medicine, the risks of taking the medicine must be weighed against the good it will do. This is a decision you and your doctor will make. For dipivefrin, the following should be considered:

Allergies—Tell your doctor if you have ever had any unusual or allergic reaction to dipivefrin or epinephrine. Also tell your health care professional if you are allergic to any other substances, such as preservatives.

Pregnancy—Dipivefrin has not been studied in pregnant women. However, this medication has not been shown to cause birth defects or other problems in animal studies.

Breast-feeding—Dipivefrin may be absorbed into the body, but it is not known whether dipivefrin passes into the breast milk.

Children—Although there is no specific information comparing use of this medicine in children with use in other age groups, this medicine is not expected to cause different side effects or problems in children than it does in adults.

Older adults—Many medicines have not been studied specifically in older people. Therefore, it may not be known whether they work exactly the same way they do in younger adults. Although there is no specific information comparing use of this medicine in the elderly with use in other age groups, this medicine is not expected to cause different side effects or problems in older people than it does in younger adults.

Other medicines—Although certain medicines should not be used together at all, in other cases two different medicines may be used together even if an interaction might occur. In these cases, your doctor may want to change the dose, or other precautions may be necessary. Tell your health care professional if you are using any other prescription or nonprescription (over-the-counter [OTC]) medicine.

Other medical problems—The presence of other medical problems may affect the use of dipivefrin. Make sure you tell your doctor if you have any other medical problems, especially:

- Eye disease or problems (other)—Dipivefrin may make the condition worse

Proper Use of This Medicine

Use this medicine only as directed. Do not use more of it and do not use it more often than your doctor ordered. To do so may increase the chance of too much medicine being absorbed into the body and the chance of side effects.

To use:

- First, wash your hands. Tilt the head back and, pressing your finger gently on the skin just beneath the lower eyelid, pull the lower eyelid away from the eye to make a space. Drop the medicine into this space. Let go of the eyelid and gently close the eyes. Do not blink. Keep the eyes closed and apply pressure to the inner corner of the eye with your finger for 1 or 2 minutes to allow the medicine to be absorbed by the eye.
- Immediately after using the eye drops, wash your hands to remove any medicine that may be on them.
- To keep the medicine as germ-free as possible, do not touch the applicator tip to any surface (including the eye). Also, keep the container tightly closed.
- If you are using the medicine with the compliance cap (C Cap):

  —Before using the eye drops for the first time, make sure the number 1 or the correct day of the week appears in the window on the cap.

  —Remove the cap and use the eye drops as directed.

  —Replace the cap. Holding the cap between your thumb and forefinger, rotate the bottle until the cap clicks to the next station. This will tell you your next dose.

  —After every dose, rotate the bottle until the cap clicks to the position that tells you your next dose.

Dosing—The dose of dipivefrin will be different for different patients. *Follow your doctor's orders or the directions on the label.* The following information includes only the average doses of dipivefrin. *If your dose is different, do not change it* unless your doctor tells you to do so.

- For *ophthalmic solution* (eye drops) dosage form:

  —For glaucoma:

  - Adults and children—One drop every twelve hours.

Missed dose—If you miss a dose of this medicine, apply the missed dose as soon as possible. However, if it is almost time for your next dose, skip the missed dose and go back to your regular dosing schedule. Do not double doses.

Storage—To store this medicine:

- Keep out of the reach of children.
- Store away from heat and direct light.

- Keep the medicine from freezing.
- Do not keep outdated medicine or medicine no longer needed. Be sure that any discarded medicine is out of the reach of children.

Precautions While Using This Medicine

Your doctor should check your eye pressure at regular visits.

Side Effects of This Medicine

Along with its needed effects, a medicine may cause some unwanted effects. Although not all of these side effects may occur, if they do occur they may need medical attention.

Check with your doctor as soon as possible if either of the following side effects occurs:

Rare—Signs and symptoms of too much medicine being absorbed into the body

Fast or irregular heartbeat; increase in blood pressure

Other side effects may occur that usually do not need medical attention. These side effects may go away during treatment as your body adjusts to the medicine. However, check with your doctor if any of the following side effects continue or are bothersome:

Less common

Burning, stinging, or other eye irritation; increased sensitivity of eyes to light

Other side effects not listed above may also occur in some patients. If you notice any other effects, check with your doctor.

Revised: 05/14/92
Interim revision: 08/16/93; 10/19/93; 12/14/93

DIPYRIDAMOLE—Diagnostic Systemic

Some commonly used brand names are:

In the U.S.—

Dipridacot
I.V. Persantine
Persantine

Generic name product may also be available.

In Canada—

Apo-Dipyridamole
Novodipiradol
Persantine

Description

Dipyridamole (dye-peer-ID-a-mole) is used as part of a medical test that shows how well blood is flowing to your heart. The test can show your doctor whether any of the blood vessels that bring blood to the heart are blocked or in danger of becoming blocked. Your doctor can then decide on the best treatment for you. Exercise (for example, walking on a treadmill) is usually used to give your doctor this information. Dipyridamole is used instead of exercise for people who are not able to exercise at all, or cannot exercise hard enough.

The dose of dipyridamole that is used to test how well blood is flowing to your heart will be different for different patients and depends on your body weight.

For information on other uses of dipyridamole, see Dipyridamole—Therapeutic (Systemic).

Dipyridamole is available only with your doctor's prescription, in the following dosage forms:

Oral

- Tablets (U.S. and Canada)

Parenteral

- Injection (U.S. and Canada)

Before Having This Test

In deciding to use a diagnostic test, any risks of the test must be weighed against the good it will do. This is a decision you and your doctor will make. Also, test results may be affected by other things. For dipyridamole, the following should be considered:

Allergies—Tell your doctor if you have ever had any unusual or allergic reaction to dipyridamole. Also tell your health care professional if you are allergic to any other substances, such as foods, preservatives, or dyes.

Pregnancy—Although studies have not been done in pregnant women, dipyridamole has not been reported to cause birth defects or other problems. Also, dipyridamole has not been shown to cause birth defects or other problems in mice, rats, or rabbits given many times the maximum human dose.

Breast-feeding—Although dipyridamole passes into breast milk, it has not been reported to cause problems in nursing babies.

Children—This medicine has been tested only in adults, and there is no specific information comparing use of dipyridamole in children with use in other age groups.

Older adults—Dipyridamole for diagnostic use has been tested in older people. It has not been shown to cause different side effects or problems in older people than it does in younger adults.

Other medicines—Although certain medicines should not be used together at all, in other cases two different medicines may be used together even if an interaction might occur. In these cases, your doctor may want to change the dose, or other precautions may be necessary. Before you receive dipyridamole, it is especially important that your doctor knows if you are taking any of the following:

- Aminophylline (e.g., Somophyllin) or
- Caffeine (e.g., NoDoz) or
- Dyphylline (e.g., Lufyllin) or
- Oxtriphylline (e.g., Choledyl) or
- Theophylline (e.g., Somophyllin-T)—These medicines will interfere with the results of this test. Caffeine should not

be taken for 8 to 12 hours before the test. It is present in many medicines (for example, stay-awake products, pain relievers, and medicines for relieving migraine headaches) and foods or beverages (for example, coffee, tea, colas or other soft drinks, cocoa, and chocolate). If you are not sure whether any medicine you are taking contains caffeine, check with your pharmacist

The other medicines listed here are used to treat asthma or other lung or breathing problems. They should not be taken for about 36 hours before the test. However, *do not stop taking the medicine on your own.* Instead, at least 3 or 4 days before the test, tell the doctor in charge of giving the test that you are taking the medicine. He or she can call the doctor who ordered the medicine for you, and together they will decide whether you should stop taking the medicine for a while

- Anticoagulants (blood thinners) or
- Aspirin or
- Carbenicillin by injection (e.g., Geopen) or
- Cefamandole (e.g., Mandol) or
- Cefoperazone (e.g., Cefobid) or
- Cefotetan (e.g., Cefotan) or
- Divalproex (e.g., Depakote) or
- Heparin or
- Inflammation or pain medicine, except narcotics, or
- Pentoxifylline (e.g., Trental) or
- Plicamycin (e.g., Mithracin) or
- Sulfinpyrazone (e.g., Anturane) or
- Ticarcillin (e.g., Ticar) or
- Ticlopidine (e.g., Ticlid) or
- Valproic acid (e.g., Depakene)—The chance of bleeding may be increased

Other medical problems—The presence of other medical problems may affect the use of dipyridamole. Make sure you tell your doctor if you have any other medical problems, especially:

- Asthma or history of or
- Chest pain—The chance of side effects may be increased
- Low blood pressure—Large amounts of dipyridamole can make your condition worse

Side Effects of This Medicine

Along with its needed effects, a medicine may cause some unwanted effects. Although not all of these side effects may occur, if they do occur they may need medical attention.

While you are receiving dipyridamole, and for a while after you have received it, your doctor will closely follow its effects. If necessary, your doctor can give you a medicine that will stop any unwanted effects. *Tell your doctor right away if you notice any of the following side effects:*

More common

Chest pain

Less common or rare

Headache (severe and throbbing); shortness of breath, troubled breathing, tightness in chest, or wheezing

Other side effects may occur that usually do not need medical attention. These side effects may go away in a little while. However, check with your doctor if they continue or are bothersome:

More common

Dizziness or lightheadedness; headache

Less common

Flushing; nausea or vomiting

Other side effects not listed above may also occur in some patients. If you notice any other effects, check with your doctor.

Revised: 01/30/92
Interim revision: 08/17/94; 01/18/95

DIPYRIDAMOLE—Therapeutic Systemic

Some commonly used brand names are:

In the U.S.—

Dipridacot — Persantine

Generic name product may also be available.

In Canada—

Apo-Dipyridamole — Persantine
Novodipiradol

Description

Dipyridamole (dye-peer-ID-a-mole) is used to lessen the chance of stroke or other serious medical problems that may occur when a blood vessel is blocked by blood clots. It is given only when there is a larger-than-usual chance that these problems may occur. For example, it is given to people who have had diseased heart valves replaced by mechanical valves, because dangerous blood clots are especially likely to occur in these patients. Dipyridamole works by helping to prevent dangerous blood clots from forming.

Dipyridamole may also be used for other heart and blood conditions as determined by your doctor.

Dipyridamole is also sometimes used as part of a medical test that shows how well blood is flowing to your heart. For information on this use of dipyridamole, see Dipyridamole—Diagnostic (Systemic).

Dipyridamole is available only with your doctor's prescription, in the following dosage forms:

Oral

- Tablets (U.S. and Canada)

Parenteral

- Injection (Canada)

Before Using This Medicine

In deciding to use a medicine, the risks of taking the medicine must be weighed against the good it will do. This is a decision you and your doctor will make. For dipyridamole, the following should be considered:

Allergies—Tell your doctor if you have ever had any unusual or allergic reaction to dipyridamole. Also tell your health care professional if you are allergic to any other substances, such as foods, preservatives, or dyes.

Pregnancy—Although studies have not been done in pregnant women, dipyridamole has not been reported to cause birth defects or other problems. Also, dipyridamole has not been shown to cause birth defects or other problems in mice, rats, or rabbits given many times the maximum human dose.

Breast-feeding—Although dipyridamole passes into breast milk, it has not been reported to cause problems in nursing babies.

Children—This medicine has been tested only in adults, and there is no specific information comparing use of dipyridamole in children with use in other age groups.

Older adults—Dipyridamole has not been studied specifically in older people taking the medicine regularly to prevent blood clots from forming. Although there is no specific information comparing this use of dipyridamole in the elderly with use in other age groups, it is not expected to cause different side effects or problems in older people than it does in younger adults.

Other medicines—Although certain medicines should not be used together at all, in other cases two different medicines may be used together even if an interaction might occur. In these cases, your doctor may want to change the dose, or other precautions may be necessary. When you are taking dipyridamole, it is especially important that your health care professional know if you are taking any of the following:

- Anticoagulants (blood thinners) or Aspirin or
- Carbenicillin by injection (e.g., Geopen) or
- Cefamandole (e.g., Mandol) or
- Cefoperazone (e.g., Cefobid) or
- Cefotetan (e.g., Cefotan) or
- Divalproex (e.g., Depakote) or
- Heparin or
- Inflammation or pain medicine, except narcotics, or
- Pentoxifylline (e.g., Trental) or
- Plicamycin (e.g., Mithracin) or
- Sulfinpyrazone (e.g., Anturane) or
- Ticarcillin (e.g., Ticar) or
- Ticlopidine (e.g., Ticlid) or
- Valproic acid (e.g., Depakene)—The chance of bleeding may be increased

Other medical problems—The presence of other medical problems may affect the use of dipyridamole. Make sure you tell your doctor if you have any other medical problems, especially:

- Chest pain—The chance of side effects may be increased
- Low blood pressure—Large amounts of dipyridamole can make your condition worse

Proper Use of This Medicine

This medicine works best when there is a constant amount in the blood. To help keep the amount constant, *dipyridamole must be taken in regularly spaced doses*, as ordered by your doctor.

This medicine works best when taken with a full glass (8 ounces) of water at least 1 hour before or 2 hours after meals. However, to lessen stomach upset, your doctor may want you to take the medicine with food or milk.

Dosing—The dose of dipyridamole will be different for different patients. *Follow your doctor's orders or the directions on the label.* The following information includes only the average doses of dipyridamole. *If your dose is different, do not change it* unless your doctor tells you to do so.

- For preventing blood clots:
  - —For *oral* dosage form (tablets):
    - Adults—The usual dose is 75 to 100 milligrams (mg) four times a day taken together with an anticoagulant (blood-thinning) medicine.
    - Children—Use and dose must be determined by your doctor.

Missed dose—If you miss a dose of this medicine, take it as soon as possble. However, if it is within 4 hours of your next scheduled dose, skip the missed dose and go back to your regular dosing schedule. Do not double doses.

Storage—To store this medicine:

- Keep out of the reach of children.
- Store away from heat and direct light.
- Do not store in the bathroom, near the kitchen sink, or in other damp places. Heat or moisture may cause the medicine to break down.
- Do not keep outdated medicine or medicine no longer needed. Be sure that any discarded medicine is out of the reach of children.

Precautions While Using This Medicine

Dipyridamole is sometimes used together with an anticoagulant (blood thinner) or aspirin. The combination of medicines may provide better protection against the formation of blood clots than any of the medicines used alone. However, the risk of bleeding may also be increased. To reduce the risk of bleeding:

- *Do not take aspirin, or any combination medicine containing aspirin, unless the same doctor who directed you to take dipyridamole also directs you to take aspirin.* This is especially important if you are taking an anticoagulant together with dipyridamole.
- If you have been directed to take aspirin together with dipyridamole, *take only the amount of aspirin ordered by your doctor.* If you need a medicine to relieve pain or a fever, your doctor may not want you to take extra aspirin. It is a good idea to discuss this with your doctor, so that you will know ahead of time what medicine to take.
- Your doctor should check your progress at regular visits.

Tell all medical doctors and dentists you go to that you are taking dipyridamole, and whether or not you are taking an anticoagulant (blood thinner) or aspirin together with it.

Dizziness, lightheadedness, or fainting may occur, especially when you get up from a lying or sitting position. Getting up slowly may help. If this problem continues or gets worse, check with your doctor.

Side Effects of This Medicine

Along with its needed effects, a medicine may cause some unwanted effects. Although not all of these side effects may occur, if they do occur they may need medical attention.

Check with your doctor as soon as possible if the following side effect occurs shortly after you start taking this medicine:

Less common
Skin rash or itching

Rare
Chest pain or tightness in chest

Other side effects may occur that usually do not need medical attention. These side effects may go away during treatment as your body adjusts to the medicine. However, check with your doctor if they continue or are bothersome:

More common
Dizziness

Less common
Flushing; headache; nausea or vomiting; stomach cramping; weakness

Other side effects not listed above may also occur in some patients. If you notice any other effects, check with your doctor.

Revised: 01/30/92
Interim revision: 08/17/94; 01/24/95

DIRITHROMYCIN Systemic†

A commonly used brand name in the U.S. is Dynabac.

†Not commercially available in Canada.

Description

Dirithromycin (dye-RITH-roe-mye-sin) is used to treat bacterial infections in many different parts of the body. It works by killing bacteria or preventing their growth. However, this medicine will not work for colds, flu, or other virus infections.

Dirithromycin is available only with your doctor's prescription, in the following dosage form:

Oral
- Tablets (U.S.)

Before Using This Medicine

In deciding to use a medicine, the risks of taking the medicine must be weighed against the good it will do. This is a decision you and your doctor will make. For dirithromycin, the following should be considered:

Allergies—Tell your doctor if you have ever had any unusual or allergic reaction to dirithromycin or to any related medicines, such as erythromycin. Also tell your health care professional if you are allergic to any other substances, such as foods, preservatives, or dyes.

Pregnancy—Dirithromycin has not been studied in pregnant women. However, studies in animals have shown that dirithromycin causes birth defects and other problems at high doses. Before taking this medicine, make sure your doctor knows if you are pregnant or if you may become pregnant.

Breast-feeding—It is not known whether dirithromycin passes into breast milk. Although most medicines pass into breast milk in small amounts, many of them may be used safely while breast-feeding. Mothers who are taking this medicine and who wish to breast-feed should discuss this with their doctor.

Children—Studies on this medicine have been only in adult patients, and there is no specific information comparing use of dirithromycin in children with use in other age groups.

Older adults—This medicine has been tested in a limited number of elderly patients and has not been shown to cause different side effects or problems in older people than it does in younger adults.

Other medicines—Although certain medicines should not be used together at all, in other cases two different medicines may be used together even if an interaction might occur. In these cases, your doctor may want to change the dose, or other precautions may be necessary. Tell your health care professional if you are taking any other prescription or nonprescription (over-the-counter [OTC]) medicine.

Other medical problems—The presence of other medical problems may affect the use of dirithromycin. Make sure you tell your doctor if you have any other medical problems, especially:

- Liver disease—Patients with moderate to severe liver disease may have an increased chance of side effects

Proper Use of This Medicine

Dirithromycin should be taken with food or within 1 hour after eating.

To help clear up your infection completely, *keep taking dirithromycin for the full time of treatment,* even if you begin to feel better after a few days. If you stop taking this medicine too soon, your symptoms may return.

Do not cut, crush, or chew dirithromycin tablets.

Dosing—The dose of dirithromycin will be different for different patients. *Follow your doctor's orders or the directions on the label.* The following information includes only the average doses of dirithromycin. *If your dose is different, do not change it* unless your doctor tells you to do so.

- For *oral* dosage form (tablets):
  - —For bacterial infections:
    - Adults and teenagers—500 milligrams (mg) once a day for seven to fourteen days.

• Children up to 12 years of age—Use and dose must be determined by your doctor.

Missed dose—If you miss a dose of this medicine, take it as soon as possible. However, if it is almost time for your next dose, skip the missed dose and go back to your regular dosing schedule. Do not double doses.

Storage—To store this medicine:

- Keep out of the reach of children.
- Store away from heat and direct light.
- Do not store in the bathroom, near the kitchen sink, or in other damp places. Heat or moisture may cause the medicine to break down.
- Do not keep outdated medicine or medicine no longer needed. Be sure that any discarded medicine is out of the reach of children.

Precautions While Using This Medicine

If your symptoms do not improve within a few days, or if they become worse, check with your doctor.

Side Effects of This Medicine

Along with its needed effects, a medicine may cause some unwanted effects. Although not all of these side effects may occur, if they do occur they may need medical attention.

Check with your doctor as soon as possible if any of the following side effects occur:

Rare

Abdominal tenderness; fever; severe abdominal or stomach cramps and pain; watery and severe diarrhea, which may also be bloody

Other side effects may occur that usually do not need medical attention. These side effects may go away during treatment as your body adjusts to the medicine. However, check with your doctor if any of the following side effects continue or are bothersome:

Less common

Diarrhea; dizziness; headache; nausea; vomiting; weakness

Other side effects not listed above may also occur in some patients. If you notice any other effects, check with your doctor.

Developed: 06/24/96

DISOPYRAMIDE Systemic

Some commonly used brand names are:

In the U.S.—

Norpace
Norpace CR

Generic name product may also be available.

In Canada—

Norpace	Rythmodan
Norpace CR	Rythmodan-LA

Description

Disopyramide (dye-soe-PEER-a-mide) is used to correct irregular heartbeats to a normal rhythm and to slow an overactive heart. This allows the heart to work more efficiently.

Disopyramide is available only with your doctor's prescription, in the following dosage forms:

Oral

- Capsules (U.S. and Canada)
- Extended-release capsules (U.S.)
- Extended-release tablets (Canada)

Parenteral

- Injection (Canada)

Before Using This Medicine

In deciding to use a medicine, the risks of taking the medicine must be weighed against the good it will do. This is a decision you and your doctor will make. For disopyramide, the following should be considered:

Allergies—Tell your doctor if you have ever had any unusual or allergic reaction to disopyramide. Also tell your health care professional if you are allergic to any other substance, such as foods, preservatives, or dyes.

Pregnancy—Disopyramide has not been studied in pregnant women. However, use of disopyramide in a small number of pregnant women seems to show that this medicine may cause contractions of the uterus. Studies in animals have shown that disopyramide increases the risk of miscarriages. Before taking this medicine, make sure your doctor knows if you are pregnant or if you may become pregnant.

Breast-feeding—Disopyramide passes into breast milk.

Children—This medicine has been tested in children and has not been shown to cause different side effects or problems than it does in adults.

Older adults—Some side effects, such as difficult urination and dry mouth, may be especially likely to occur in elderly patients, who are usually more sensitive than younger adults to the effects of disopyramide.

Other medicines—Although certain medicines should not be used together at all, in other cases two different medicines may be used together even if an interaction might occur. In these cases, your doctor may want to change the dose, or other precautions may be necessary. When you are taking disopyramide, it is especially important that your health care professional know if you are taking any of the following:

- Other heart medicine—Effects on the heart may be increased
- Pimozide (e.g., Orap)—Risk of heart rhythm problems may be increased

Other medical problems—The presence of other medical problems may affect the use of disopyramide. Make sure

you tell your doctor if you have any other medical problems, especially:

- Diabetes mellitus (sugar diabetes)—Disopyramide may cause low blood sugar
- Difficult urination or
- Enlarged prostate—Disopyramide may cause difficult urination
- Glaucoma (history of) or
- Myasthenia gravis—Disopyramide may make these conditions worse
- Kidney disease or
- Liver disease—Effects may be increased because of slower removal of disopyramide from the body

Proper Use of This Medicine

Take disopyramide exactly as directed by your doctor even though you may feel well. Do not take more medicine than ordered.

For patients taking the *extended-release capsules:*

- Swallow the capsule whole without breaking, crushing, or chewing.

For patients taking the *extended-release tablets:*

- Do not crush or chew the tablet.

This medicine works best when there is a constant amount in the blood. *To help keep the amount constant, do not miss any doses. Also, it is best to take the doses at evenly spaced times day and night.* For example, if you are to take 4 doses a day, the doses should be spaced about 6 hours apart. If this interferes with your sleep or other daily activities, or if you need help in planning the best times to take your medicine, check with your health care professional.

Dosing—The dose of disopyramide will be different for different patients. *Follow your doctor's orders or the directions on the label.* The following information includes only the average doses of disopyramide. *If your dose is different, do not change it* unless your doctor tells you to do so.

The number of tablets or capsules that you take depends on the strength of the medicine.

- For *treatment* of arrhythmias:
  - —For *short-acting oral* dosage forms (capsules):
    - Adults—300 milligrams (mg) for the first dose. Then 100 to 150 mg taken every six to eight hours.
    - Children—Dose is based on body weight and age. It must be determined by your doctor. The dose is usually 6 to 30 mg per kilogram (kg) of body weight (2.73 to 13.64 mg per pound) per day. This dose is evenly divided and taken every six hours.
  - —For *long-acting oral* dosage forms (extended-release capsules or tablets):
    - Adults—200 or 300 mg every twelve hours.
    - Children—Use is not recommended.
  - —For *injection* dosage form:
    - Adults—
      - —*First few doses:* Dose is based on body weight and must be determined by your doctor. It is usually 2 mg per kg of body weight (0.91 mg per pound) injected in three divided doses, or, 2 mg per kg of body weight (0.91 mg per pound) infused over fifteen minutes.
      - —*Dose following first few doses:* Dose is based on body weight and must be determined by your doctor. It is usually 0.4 mg per kg of body weight (0.18 mg per pound) per hour given for up to twenty-four hours.
    - Children—Use is not recommended.

Missed dose—*If you miss a dose of this medicine, take it as soon as possible unless the next scheduled dose is in less than 4 hours.* If you do not remember until later, skip the missed dose and go back to your regular dosing schedule. Do not double doses.

Storage—To store this medicine:

- Keep out of the reach of children.
- Store away from heat and direct light.
- Do not store in the bathroom, near the kitchen sink, or in other damp places. Heat or moisture may cause the medicine to break down.
- Do not keep outdated medicine or medicine no longer needed. Be sure that any discarded medicine is out of the reach of children.

Precautions While Using This Medicine

Your doctor should check your progress at regular visits to make sure the medicine is working properly.

Do not stop taking this medicine without first checking with your doctor. Stopping suddenly may cause a serious change in heart function.

Dizziness, lightheadedness, or fainting may occur, especially when you get up from a lying or sitting position. This is due to lowered blood pressure. Getting up slowly may help. This effect does not occur often at doses of disopyramide usually used; however, *make sure you know how you react to this medicine before you drive, use machines, or do anything else that could be dangerous if you are not alert.* If the problem continues or gets worse, check with your doctor.

Avoid alcoholic beverages until you have discussed their use with your doctor. Alcohol may make the low blood sugar effect worse and/or increase the possibility of dizziness or fainting.

Disopyramide may cause hypoglycemia (low blood sugar) in some people. Patients with congestive heart disease or diabetes especially should be aware of the signs of hypoglycemia. (See *Side Effects of This Medicine.*) *If these signs appear, eat or drink a food containing sugar and call your doctor right away.*

This medicine may cause blurred vision or other vision problems. If any of these occur, *do not drive, use ma-*

chines, or do anything else that could be dangerous if you are not able to see well.

Disopyramide may cause dryness of the mouth, nose, and throat. For temporary relief of mouth dryness, use sugarless candy or gum, melt bits of ice in your mouth, or use a saliva substitute. However, if dry mouth continues for more than 2 weeks, check with your medical doctor or dentist. Continuing dryness of the mouth may increase the chance of dental disease, including tooth decay, gum disease, and fungus infections.

This medicine will often make you sweat less, allowing your body temperature to increase. *Use extra care not to become overheated during exercise or hot weather while you are taking this medicine*, since overheating could possibly result in heat stroke.

Side Effects of This Medicine

Along with its needed effects, a medicine may cause some unwanted effects. Although not all of these side effects may occur, if they do occur they may need medical attention.

Check with your doctor as soon as possible if any of the following side effects occur:

More common
Difficult urination

Less common
Chest pains; dizziness, lightheadedness, or fainting; fast or slow heartbeat; muscle weakness; shortness of breath (unexplained); swelling of feet or lower legs; weight gain (rapid)

Rare
Eye pain; mental depression; sore throat and fever; yellow eyes or skin

Signs and symptoms of hypoglycemia (low blood sugar)
Anxious feeling; chills; cold sweats; confusion; cool, pale skin; drowsiness; fast heartbeat; headache; hunger (excessive); nausea; nervousness; shakiness; unsteady walk; unusual tiredness or weakness

Other side effects may occur that usually do not need medical attention. These side effects may go away during treatment as your body adjusts to the medicine. However, check with your health care professional if any of the following side effects continue or are bothersome:

More common
Dryness of mouth and throat

Less common
Bloating or stomach pain; blurred vision; constipation; decreased sexual ability; dry eyes and nose; frequent urge to urinate; loss of appetite

Other side effects not listed above may also occur in some patients. If you notice any other effects, check with your doctor.

Revised: 05/14/93

DISULFIRAM Systemic

A commonly used brand name in the U.S. and Canada is Antabuse.

Generic name product may also be available in the U.S.

Description

Disulfiram (dye-SUL-fi-ram) is used to help overcome your drinking problem. It is not a cure for alcoholism, but rather will discourage you from drinking.

Disulfiram is available only with your doctor's prescription, in the following dosage form:

Oral
- Tablets (U.S. and Canada)

Before Using This Medicine

In deciding to use a medicine, the risks of taking the medicine must be weighed against the good it will do. This is a decision you and your doctor will make. For disulfiram, the following should be considered:

Allergies—Tell your doctor if you have had any unusual or allergic reactions to disulfiram, rubber, pesticides, or fungicides.

Diet—In addition to beverages, alcohol is found in many other products. Reading the list of ingredients on foods and other products before using them will help you to avoid alcohol. Do not use alcohol-containing foods such as sauces and vinegars.

Pregnancy—Disulfiram has not been studied in pregnant women. However, there have been a few reports of birth defects in infants whose mothers took disulfiram during pregnancy. Before taking this medicine, make sure your doctor knows if you are pregnant or if you may become pregnant.

Breast-feeding—Disulfiram has not been reported to cause problems in nursing babies.

Children—Studies on this medicine have been done only in adult patients, and there is no specific information comparing use of disulfiram in children with use in other age groups.

Older adults—Many medicines have not been studied specifically in older people. Therefore, it may not be known whether they work exactly the same way they do in younger adults or if they cause different side effects or problems in older people. There is no specific information comparing use of disulfiram in the elderly with use in other age groups.

Other medicines—Although certain medicines should not be used together at all, in other cases 2 different medicines may be used together even if an interaction might occur. In these cases, your doctor may want to change the dose, or other precautions may be necessary. When you are taking disulfiram, it is especially important that your health care professional know if you are taking any of the following:

- Anticoagulants (blood thinners)—Taking disulfiram may increase the effects of anticoagulants, changing the amount you need to take
- Ethotoin (e.g., Peganone) or
- Mephenytoin (e.g., Mesantoin) or
- Phenytoin (e.g., Dilantin)—Taking these medicines with disulfiram may change the amount of anticonvulsant medicine you need to take
- Isoniazid (e.g., INH, Nydrazid)—Disulfiram may increase central nervous system (CNS) effects, such as dizziness, clumsiness, irritability, or trouble in sleeping
- Metronidazole (e.g., Flagyl) or
- Paraldehyde (e.g., Paral)—These medicines should not be taken with or within several days of disulfiram because serious side effects may occur

Ethylene dibromide or organic solvents (such as chemicals which may contain alcohol, acetaldehyde, paraldehyde, or other related chemicals used in factories and in hobbies [e.g., paint thinner])—Make sure you tell your doctor if you will come in contact with or breathe the fumes of ethylene dibromide or organic solvents while you are taking disulfiram.

Other medical problems—The presence of other medical problems may affect the use of disulfiram. Make sure you tell your doctor if you have any other medical problems, especially:

- Asthma or other lung disease, severe, or
- Diabetes mellitus (sugar diabetes) or
- Epilepsy or other seizure disorder or
- Heart or blood vessel disease or
- Kidney disease or
- Liver disease or cirrhosis of the liver or
- Underactive thyroid—A disulfiram-alcohol reaction may make the condition worse
- Depression or
- Severe mental illness—Disulfiram may make the condition worse
- Skin allergy—Disulfiram may cause an allergic reaction

Proper Use of This Medicine

Before you take the first dose of this medicine, *make sure you have not taken any alcoholic beverage or alcohol-containing product or medicine* (for example, tonics, elixirs, and cough syrups) *during the past 12 hours.* If you are not sure about the alcohol content of medicines you may have taken, check with your health care professional.

Take this medicine every day as directed by your doctor. The medicine is usually taken each morning. However, if it makes you drowsy, ask your doctor if you may take it at bedtime instead.

Dosing—The dose of disulfiram will be different for different patients. *Follow your doctor's orders or the directions on the label.* The following information includes only the average doses of disulfiram. *If your dose is different, do not change it* unless your doctor tells you to do so.

- For *oral* dosage form (tablets):
  - —To help overcome drinking problems:
    - Adults and teenagers—At first, the dose is 500 milligrams (mg) or less, once a day for one or two weeks. Then, your doctor may lower your dose to 125 to 500 mg (usually to 250 mg) once a day.
    - Children—Use and dose must be determined by your doctor.

Storage—To store this medicine:

- Keep out of the reach of children.
- Store away from heat and direct light.
- Do not store in the bathroom, near the kitchen sink, or in other damp places. Heat or moisture may cause the medicine to break down.
- Do not keep outdated medicine or medicine no longer needed. Be sure that any discarded medicine is out of the reach of children.

Precautions While Using This Medicine

Do not drink any alcohol, even small amounts, while you are taking this medicine and for 14 days after you stop taking it, because the alcohol may make you very sick. In addition to beverages, alcohol is found in many other products. Reading the list of ingredients on foods and other products before using them will help you to avoid alcohol. You can also avoid alcohol if you:

- Do not use alcohol-containing foods, products, or medicines, such as elixirs, tonics, sauces, vinegars, cough syrups, mouth washes, or gargles.
- *Do not come in contact with or breathe in the fumes of chemicals that may contain alcohol, acetaldehyde, paraldehyde, or other related chemicals,* such as paint thinner, paint, varnish, or shellac.
- *Use caution when using alcohol-containing products that are applied to the skin,* such as some transdermal (stick-on patch) medicines or rubbing alcohol, back rubs, after-shave lotions, colognes, perfumes, toilet waters, or after-bath preparations. Using such products while you are taking disulfiram may cause headache, nausea, or local redness or itching because the alcohol in these products may be absorbed into your body. Before using alcohol-containing products on your skin, first test the product by applying some to a small area of your skin. Allow the product to remain on your skin for 1 or 2 hours. If no redness, itching, or other unwanted effects occur, you should be able to use the product.
- *Do not use any alcohol-containing products on raw skin or open wounds.*

Check with your doctor if you have any questions.

Some of the symptoms you may experience if you use any alcohol while taking this medicine are:

Blurred vision
Chest pain
Confusion
Dizziness or fainting
Fast or pounding heartbeat
Flushing or redness of face

Increased sweating
Nausea and vomiting
Throbbing headache
Troubled breathing
Weakness

These symptoms will last as long as there is any alcohol left in your system, from 30 minutes to several hours. On rare occasions, if you have a severe reaction or have taken a large enough amount of alcohol, a heart attack, unconsciousness, convulsions (seizures), and death may occur.

Your doctor may want you to carry an identification card stating that you are using this medicine. This card should list the symptoms most likely to occur if alcohol is taken, and the doctor, clinic, or hospital to be contacted in case of an emergency. These cards may be available from the manufacturer. Ask your health care professional if you have any questions about this.

If you will be taking this medicine for a long period of time (for example, for several months at a time), your doctor should check your progress at regular visits.

Before buying or using any liquid prescription or nonprescription medicine, check with your pharmacist to see if it contains any alcohol.

This medicine may cause some people to become drowsy or less alert than they are normally. If this occurs, *do not drive, use machines, or do anything else that could be dangerous if you are not alert.*

Disulfiram will add to the effects of other CNS depressants (medicines that slow down the nervous system, possibly causing drowsiness). Some examples of CNS depressants are antihistamines or medicine for hay fever, other allergies, or colds; sedatives, tranquilizers, or sleeping medicine; prescription pain medicine or narcotics; barbiturates; medicine for seizures; muscle relaxants; or anesthetics, including some dental anesthetics. *Check with your doctor before taking any of the above while you are using this medicine.*

Side Effects of This Medicine

Along with its needed effects, a medicine may cause some unwanted effects. Although not all of these side effects may occur, if they do occur they may need medical attention.

Check with your doctor as soon as possible if any of the following side effects occur:

Less common

Eye pain or tenderness or any change in vision; mood or mental changes; numbness, tingling, pain, or weakness in hands or feet

Rare

Darkening of urine; light gray–colored stools; severe stomach pain; yellow eyes or skin

Other side effects may occur that usually do not need medical attention. These side effects may go away during treatment as your body adjusts to the medicine. However, check with your doctor if any of the following side effects continue or are bothersome:

More common

Drowsiness

Less common or rare

Decreased sexual ability in males; headache; metallic or garlic-like taste in mouth; skin rash; unusual tiredness

Other side effects not listed above may also occur in some patients. If you notice any other effects, check with your doctor.

Revised: 01/27/92
Interim revision: 07/20/94

DIURETICS, LOOP Systemic

Some commonly used brand names are:

In the U.S.—

Bumex[1]
Edecrin[2]
Lasix[3]
Myrosemide[3]

In Canada—

Apo-Furosemide[3]
Edecrin[2]
Furoside[3]
Lasix[3]
Lasix Special[3]
Novosemide[3]
Uritol[3]

Note: For quick reference, the following loop diuretics are numbered to match the corresponding brand names.

This information applies to the following medicines:

1. Bumetanide (byoo-MET-a-nide)†‡
2. Ethacrynic Acid (eth-a-KRIN-ik AS-id)
3. Furosemide (fur-OH-se-mide)‡§

†Not commercially available in Canada.
‡Generic name product may also be available in the U.S.
§Generic name product may also be available in Canada.

Description

Loop diuretics are given to help reduce the amount of water in the body. They work by acting on the kidneys to increase the flow of urine.

Furosemide is also used to treat high blood pressure (hypertension) in those patients who are not helped by other medicines or in those patients who have kidney problems.

High blood pressure adds to the work load of the heart and arteries. If it continues for a long time, the heart and arteries may not function properly. This can damage the blood vessels of the brain, heart, and kidneys, resulting in a stroke, heart failure, or kidney failure. High blood pressure may also increase the risk of heart attacks. These problems may be less likely to occur if blood pressure is controlled.

Loop diuretics may also be used for other conditions as determined by your doctor.

This medicine is available only with your doctor's prescription, in the following dosage forms:

Oral

Bumetanide
- Tablets (U.S.)

Ethacrynic Acid
- Oral solution (U.S. and Canada)
- Tablets (U.S. and Canada)

Furosemide
- Oral solution (U.S. and Canada)
- Tablets (U.S. and Canada)

Parenteral

Bumetanide
- Injection (U.S.)

Ethacrynic Acid
- Injection (U.S. and Canada)

Furosemide
- Injection (U.S. and Canada)

Before Using This Medicine

In deciding to use a medicine, the risks of taking the medicine must be weighed against the good it will do. This is a decision you and your doctor will make. For loop diuretics, the following should be considered:

Allergies—Tell your doctor if you have ever had any unusual or allergic reaction to bumetanide, ethacrynic acid, furosemide, sulfonamides (sulfa drugs), or thiazide diuretics (water pills). Also tell your health care professional if you are allergic to any other substances, such as foods, preservatives, or dyes.

Pregnancy—Studies have not been done in pregnant women. However, studies in animals have shown this medicine to cause harmful effects.

In general, diuretics are not useful for normal swelling of feet and hands that occurs during pregnancy. Diuretics should not be taken during pregnancy unless recommended by your doctor.

Breast-feeding—These medicines have not been reported to cause problems in nursing babies. Furosemide passes into breast milk; it is not known whether bumetanide or ethacrynic acid passes into breast milk.

Children—Although there is no specific information comparing the use of loop diuretics in children with use in any other age group, these medicines are not expected to cause different side effects in children than they do in adults.

Older adults—Dizziness, lightheadedness, or signs of too much potassium loss may be more likely to occur in the elderly, who are more sensitive to the effects of this medicine. Elderly patients may also be more likely to develop blood clots.

Other medicines—Although certain medicines should not be used together at all, in other cases two different medicines may be used together even if an interaction might occur. In these cases, your doctor may want to change the dose, or other precautions may be necessary. When you are taking loop diuretics, it is especially important that your health care professional know if you are taking *any* other medicines.

Other medical problems—The presence of other medical problems may affect the use of loop diuretics. Make sure you tell your doctor if you have any other medical problems, especially:

- Diabetes mellitus (sugar diabetes)—Loop diuretics may increase the amount of sugar in the blood
- Gout or
- Hearing problems or
- Pancreatitis (inflammation of the pancreas)—Loop diuretics may make these conditions worse
- Heart attack, recent—Use of loop diuretics after a recent heart attack may increase the chance of side effects
- Kidney disease (severe) or
- Liver disease—Higher blood levels of the loop diuretic may occur, which may increase the chance of side effects
- Lupus erythematosus (history of)—Ethacrynic acid and furosemide may make this condition worse

Proper Use of This Medicine

This medicine may cause you to have an unusual feeling of tiredness when you begin to take it. You may also notice an increase in the amount of urine or in your frequency of urination. After you have taken the medicine for a while, these effects should lessen. In general, to keep the increase in urine from affecting your sleep:

- If you are to take a single dose a day, take it in the morning after breakfast.
- If you are to take more than one dose a day, take the last dose no later than 6 p.m., unless otherwise directed by your doctor.

However, it is best to plan your dose or doses according to a schedule that will least affect your personal activities and sleep. Ask your health care professional to help you plan the best time to take this medicine.

To help you remember to take your medicine, try to get into the habit of taking it at the same time each day.

For patients taking the *oral liquid form* of furosemide:
- This medicine is to be taken by mouth even if it comes in a dropper bottle. If this medicine does not come in a dropper bottle, use a specially marked measuring spoon or other device to measure each dose accurately, since the average household teaspoon may not hold the right amount of liquid.

For patients taking this medicine for *high blood pressure:*
- In addition to the use of the medicine your doctor has prescribed, appropriate treatment for your high blood pressure may include weight control and care in the types of foods you eat, especially foods high in sodium. Your doctor will tell you which factors are most important for you. You should check with your doctor before changing your diet.
- Many patients who have high blood pressure will not notice any signs of the problem. In fact, many may feel normal. It is very important that you *take your medicine exactly as directed* and that you keep your appointments with your doctor even if you feel well.
- Remember that this medicine will not cure your high blood pressure but it does help control it. Therefore, you must continue to take it as directed if you expect to lower your blood pressure and keep it down. *You may have to take high blood pressure medicine for*

the rest of your life. If high blood pressure is not treated, it can cause serious problems such as heart failure, blood vessel disease, stroke, or kidney disease.

If this medicine upsets your stomach, it may be taken with meals or milk. If stomach upset (nausea, vomiting, or stomach pain) continues or gets worse, or if you suddenly get severe diarrhea, check with your doctor.

Dosing—The dose of loop diuretics will be different for different patients. *Follow your doctor's orders or the directions on the label.* The following information includes only the average doses of loop diuretics. *If your dose is different, do not change it* unless your doctor tells you to do so.

The number of tablets or teaspoonfuls of solution that you take depends on the strength of the medicine. Also, *the number of doses you take each day, the time allowed between doses, and the length of time you take the medicine depend on the medical problem for which you are taking loop diuretics.*

For bumetanide

- For *oral* dosage form (tablets):
  - —To lower the amount of water in the body:
    - Adults—0.5 to 2 milligrams (mg) once a day. Your doctor may increase your dose if needed.
    - Children—Dose must be determined by your doctor.
- For *injection* dosage form:
  - —To lower the amount of water in the body:
    - Adults—0.5 to 1 mg injected into a muscle or a vein every two to three hours as needed.
    - Children—Dose must be determined by your doctor.

For ethacrynic acid

- For *oral* dosage form (oral solution or tablets):
  - —To lower the amount of water in the body:
    - Adults—50 to 200 milligrams (mg) a day. This may be taken as a single dose or divided into smaller doses.
    - Children—At first, 25 mg a day. Your doctor may increase your dose as needed.
- For *injection* dosage form:
  - —To lower the amount of water in the body:
    - Adults—50 mg injected into a vein every two to six hours as needed.
    - Children—Dose is based on body weight and must be determined by your doctor. The usual dose is 1 mg per kilogram (kg) (0.45 mg per pound) of body weight injected into a vein.

For furosemide

- For *oral* dosage form (oral solution or tablets):
  - —To lower the amount of water in the body:
    - Adults—At first, 20 to 80 milligrams (mg) once a day. Then, your doctor may increase your dose as needed. Your doctor may tell you to take a dose once a day, two or three times a day, or every other day.
    - Children—Dose is based on body weight and must be determined by your doctor. The usual dose is 2 mg per kilogram (kg) (0.91 mg per pound) of body weight for one dose. Then, your doctor may increase your dose every six to eight hours as needed.
  - —For high blood pressure:
    - Adults—40 mg two times a day. Your doctor may increase your dose.
- For *injection* dosage form:
  - —To lower the amount of water in the body:
    - Adults—At first, 20 to 40 mg injected into a muscle or a vein for one dose. Then, your doctor may increase your dose every two hours as needed. Once the medicine is working, the dose is injected into a muscle or a vein one or two times a day.
    - Children—Dose is based on body weight and must be determined by your doctor. The usual dose is 1 mg per kg (0.45 mg per pound) of body weight injected into a muscle or a vein for one dose. Your doctor may increase your dose every two hours as needed.
  - —For very high blood pressure:
    - Adults—40 to 200 mg injected into a vein.

Missed dose—If you miss a dose of this medicine, take it as soon as possible. However, if it is almost time for your next dose, skip the missed dose and go back to your regular dosing schedule. Do not double doses.

Storage—To store this medicine:

- Keep out of the reach of children.
- Store away from heat and direct light.
- Do not store in the bathroom, near the kitchen sink, or in other damp places. Heat or moisture may cause the medicine to break down.
- Keep the oral liquid form of this medicine from freezing.
- Do not keep outdated medicine or medicine no longer needed. Be sure that any discarded medicine is out of the reach of children.

Precautions While Using This Medicine

It is important that your doctor check your progress at regular visits to make sure that this medicine is working properly.

This medicine may cause a loss of potassium from your body:

- To help prevent this, your doctor may want you to:
  - —eat or drink foods that have a high potassium content (for example, orange or other citrus fruit juices), or
  - —take a potassium supplement, or
  - —take another medicine to help prevent the loss of the potassium in the first place.

- It is very important to follow these directions. Also, it is important not to change your diet on your own. This is more important if you are already on a special diet (as for diabetes), or if you are taking a potassium supplement or a medicine to reduce potassium loss. Extra potassium may not be necessary and, in some cases, too much potassium could be harmful.

To prevent the loss of too much water and potassium, tell your doctor if you become sick, especially with severe or continuing nausea and vomiting or diarrhea.

Before having any kind of surgery (including dental surgery) or emergency treatment, make sure the medical doctor or dentist in charge knows that you are taking this medicine.

Dizziness, lightheadedness, or fainting may occur, especially when you get up from a lying or sitting position. This is more likely to occur in the morning. *Getting up slowly may help.* When you get up from lying down, sit on the edge of the bed with your feet dangling for 1 or 2 minutes. Then stand up slowly. If the problem continues or gets worse, check with your doctor.

The dizziness, lightheadedness, or fainting is also more likely to occur if you drink alcohol, stand for long periods of time, exercise, or if the weather is hot. *While you are taking this medicine, be careful to limit the amount of alcohol you drink. Also, use extra care during exercise or hot weather or if you must stand for long periods of time.*

For *diabetic patients:*
- This medicine may affect blood sugar levels. While you are using this medicine, be especially careful in testing for sugar in your blood or urine.

For patients taking this medicine for *high blood pressure:*
- *Do not take other medicines unless they have been discussed with your doctor.* This especially includes over-the-counter (nonprescription) medicines for appetite control, asthma, colds, cough, hay fever, or sinus problems, since they may tend to increase your blood pressure.

For patients taking *furosemide:*
- Furosemide may cause your skin to be more sensitive to sunlight than it is normally. Exposure to sunlight, even for brief periods of time, may cause a skin rash, itching, redness or other discoloration of the skin, or a severe sunburn. When you begin taking this medicine:

  —Stay out of direct sunlight, especially between the hours of 10:00 a.m. and 3:00 p.m., if possible.

  —Wear protective clothing, including a hat. Also, wear sunglasses.

  —Apply a sun block product that has a skin protection factor (SPF) of at least 15. Some patients may require a product with a higher SPF number, especially if they have a fair complexion. If you have any questions about this, check with your health care professional.

  —Apply a sun block lipstick that has an SPF of at least 15 to protect your lips.

  —Do not use a sunlamp or tanning bed or booth.

  If you have a severe reaction from the sun, check with your doctor.

Side Effects of This Medicine

Along with its needed effects, a medicine may cause some unwanted effects. Although not all of these side effects may occur, if they do occur they may need medical attention.

Check with your doctor as soon as possible if any of the following side effects occur:

Rare

Black, tarry stools; blood in urine or stools; cough or hoarseness; fever or chills; joint pain; lower back or side pain; painful or difficult urination; pinpoint red spots on skin; ringing or buzzing in ears or any loss of hearing—more common with ethacrynic acid; skin rash or hives; stomach pain (severe) with nausea and vomiting; unusual bleeding or bruising; yellow eyes or skin; yellow vision—for furosemide only

Signs and symptoms of too much potassium loss

Dryness of mouth; increased thirst; irregular heartbeat; mood or mental changes; muscle cramps or pain; nausea or vomiting; unusual tiredness or weakness; weak pulse

Other side effects may occur that usually do not need medical attention. These side effects may go away during treatment as your body adjusts to the medicine. However, check with your doctor if any of the following side effects continue or are bothersome:

More common

Dizziness or lightheadedness when getting up from a lying or sitting position

Less common or rare

Blurred vision; chest pain—with bumetanide only; confusion—with ethacrynic acid only; diarrhea—more common with ethacrynic acid; headache; increased sensitivity of skin to sunlight—with furosemide only; loss of appetite—more common with ethacrynic acid; nervousness—with ethacrynic acid only; premature ejaculation or difficulty in keeping an erection—with bumetanide only; redness or pain at place of injection; stomach cramps or pain

Other side effects not listed above may also occur in some patients. If you notice any other effects, check with your doctor.

Additional Information

Once a medicine has been approved for marketing for a certain use, experience may show that it is also useful for other medical problems. Although these uses are not included in product labeling, loop diuretics are used in certain patients with the following medical conditions:
- Hypercalcemia (too much calcium in the blood)
- Diagnostic aid for kidney disease

Other than the above information, there is no additional information relating to proper use, precautions, or side effects for these uses.

Revised: 08/02/94
Interim revision: 04/24/95

DIURETICS, POTASSIUM-SPARING Systemic

Some commonly used brand names are:

In the U.S.—
Aldactone[2]
Dyrenium[3]
Midamor[1]

In Canada—
Aldactone[2]
Dyrenium[3]
Midamor[1]
Novospiroton[2]

Note: For quick reference, the following potassium-sparing diuretics are numbered to match the corresponding brand names.

This information applies to the following medicines:
1. Amiloride (a-MILL-oh-ride)‡
2. Spironolactone (speer-on-oh-LAK-tone)‡
3. Triamterene (trye-AM-ter-een)

‡Generic name product may also be available in the U.S.

Description

Potassium-sparing diuretics are commonly used to help reduce the amount of water in the body. Unlike some other diuretics, these medicines do not cause your body to lose potassium.

Amiloride and spironolactone are also used to treat high blood pressure (hypertension). High blood pressure adds to the workload of the heart and arteries. If the condition continues for a long time, the heart and arteries may not function properly. This can damage the blood vessels of the brain, heart, and kidneys, resulting in a stroke, heart failure, or kidney failure. High blood pressure may also increase the risk of heart attacks. These problems may be less likely to occur if blood pressure is controlled.

Spironolactone is also used to help increase the amount of potassium in the body when it is getting too low.

Potassium-sparing diuretics help to reduce the amount of water in the body by acting on the kidneys to increase the flow of urine. This also helps to lower blood pressure.

These medicines can also be used for other conditions as determined by your doctor.

Potassium-sparing diuretics are available only with your doctor's prescription, in the following dosage forms:

Oral
- Amiloride
  - Tablets (U.S. and Canada)
- Spironolactone
  - Tablets (U.S. and Canada)
- Triamterene
  - Capsules (U.S.)
  - Tablets (Canada)

Before Using This Medicine

In deciding to use a medicine, the risks of taking the medicine must be weighed against the good it will do. This is a decision you and your doctor will make. For potassium-sparing diuretics, the following should be considered:

Allergies—Tell your doctor if you have ever had any unusual or allergic reaction to amiloride, spironolactone, or triamterene. Also tell your health care professional if you are allergic to any other substances, such as foods, preservatives, or dyes.

Pregnancy—Studies have not been done in pregnant women. However, this medicine has not been shown to cause birth defects or other problems in animals.

In general, diuretics are not useful for normal swelling of feet and hands that occurs during pregnancy. Diuretics should not be taken during pregnancy unless recommended by your doctor.

Breast-feeding—Although amiloride, spironolactone, and triamterene may pass into breast milk, these medicines have not been reported to cause problems in nursing babies.

Children—This medicine has been tested in children and, in effective doses, has not been shown to cause different side effects or problems in children than it does in adults.

Older adults—Signs and symptoms of too much potassium are more likely to occur in the elderly, who are more sensitive than younger adults to the effects of this medicine.

Other medicines—Although certain medicines should not be used together at all, in other cases two different medicines may be used together even if an interaction might occur. In these cases, your doctor may want to change the dose, or other precautions may be necessary. When you are taking potassium-sparing diuretics, it is especially important that your health care professional know if you are taking any of the following:
- Angiotensin-converting enzyme (ACE) inhibitors (benazepril [e.g., Lotensin], captopril [e.g., Capoten], enalapril [e.g., Vasotec], fosinopril [e.g., Monopril], lisinopril [e.g., Prinivil, Zestril], quinapril [e.g., Accupril], ramipril [e.g., Altace]) or

- Cyclosporine (e.g., Sandimmune) or
- Potassium-containing medicines or supplements—Use with potassium-sparing diuretics may cause high blood levels of potassium, which may increase the chance of side effects
- Digoxin—Use with spironolactone may cause high blood levels of digoxin, which may increase the chance of side effects
- Lithium (e.g., Lithane)—Use with potassium-sparing diuretics may cause high blood levels of lithium, which may increase the chance of side effects

Other medical problems—The presence of other medical problems may affect the use of potassium-sparing diuretics. Make sure you tell your doctor if you have any other medical problems, especially:

- Diabetes mellitus (sugar diabetes) or
- Kidney disease or
- Liver disease—Higher blood levels of potassium may occur, which may increase the chance of side effects
- Gout or
- Kidney stones (history of)—Triamterene may make these conditions worse
- Menstrual problems or breast enlargement—Spironolactone may make these conditions worse

Proper Use of This Medicine

This medicine may cause you to have an unusual feeling of tiredness when you begin to take it. You may also notice an increase in the amount of urine or in your frequency of urination. After you have taken the medicine for a while, these effects should lessen. In general, to keep the increase in urine from affecting your sleep:

- If you are to take a single dose a day, take it in the morning after breakfast.
- If you are to take more than one dose a day, take the last dose no later than 6 p.m., unless otherwise directed by your doctor.

However, it is best to plan your dose or doses according to a schedule that will least affect your personal activities and sleep. Ask your health care professional to help you plan the best time to take this medicine.

To help you remember to take your medicine, try to get into the habit of taking it at the same time each day.

If this medicine upsets your stomach, it may be taken with meals or milk. If stomach upset (nausea, vomiting, stomach pain or cramps) continues, check with your doctor.

For patients taking this medicine for *high blood pressure:*

- In addition to the use of the medicine your doctor has prescribed, treatment for your high blood pressure may include weight control and care in the types of foods you eat, especially foods high in sodium. Your doctor will tell you which of these are most important for you. You should check with your doctor before changing your diet.
- Many patients who have high blood pressure will not notice any signs of the problem. In fact, many may feel normal. It is very important that you *take your medicine exactly as directed* and that you keep your appointments with your doctor even if you feel well.
- Remember that this medicine will not cure your high blood pressure but it does help control it. Therefore, you must continue to take it as directed if you expect to lower your blood pressure and keep it down. *You may have to take high blood pressure medicine for the rest of your life.* If high blood pressure is not treated, it can cause serious problems such as heart failure, blood vessel disease, stroke, or kidney disease.

Dosing—The dose of potassium-sparing diuretics will be different for different patients. *Follow your doctor's orders or the directions on the label.* The following information includes only the average doses of potassium-sparing diuretics. *If your dose is different, do not change it* unless your doctor tells you to do so.

The number of capsules or tablets that you take depends on the strength of the medicine. Also, *the number of doses you take each day, the time allowed between doses, and the length of time you take the medicine depend on the medical problem for which you are taking potassium-sparing diuretics.*

For amiloride

- For *oral* dosage form (tablets):
  - —For high blood pressure or to lower the amount of water in the body:
    - Adults—5 to 10 milligrams (mg) once a day.
    - Children—Dose must be determined by your doctor.

For spironolactone

- For *oral* dosage form (tablets):
  - —To lower the amount of water in the body:
    - Adults—At first, 25 to 200 milligrams (mg) a day. This is divided into two to four doses. Your doctor may increase your dose to 75 to 400 mg a day.
    - Children—Dose is based on body weight and must be determined by your doctor. The usual dose is 1 to 3 mg per kilogram (kg) (0.45 to 1.36 mg per pound) of body weight a day. The dose may be taken as a single dose or divided into two to four doses. Your doctor may increase your dose as needed.
  - —For high blood pressure:
    - Adults—At first, 50 to 100 milligrams (mg) a day. This may be taken as a single dose or divided into two to four doses. Your doctor may gradually increase your dose up to 200 mg a day.
    - Children—Dose is based on body weight and must be determined by your doctor. The usual dose is 1 to 3 mg per kg (0.45 to 1.36 mg per pound) of body weight a day. The dose may be taken as a single dose or divided into two to four doses. Your doctor may increase your dose as needed.
  - —To treat high aldosterone levels in the body:
    - Adults—100 to 400 mg a day. This is divided into two to four doses and taken until you have

surgery. If you are not having surgery, your doses may be smaller.

—For detecting high aldosterone levels in the body:

- Adults—400 mg a day, taken in two to four divided doses. Your doctor may want you to take this dose for as little as four days or as long as three to four weeks. Follow your doctor's instructions.

—To treat low potassium levels in the blood:

- Adults—25 to 100 mg a day. This may be taken as a single dose or divided into two to four doses.

For triamterene

- For *oral* dosage form (capsules or tablets):

—To lower the amount of water in the body:

- Adults—25 to 100 milligrams (mg) a day. Your doctor may gradually increase your dose.
- Children—Dose is based on body weight and must be determined by your doctor. To start, the usual dose is 2 to 4 mg per kilogram (kg) (0.9 to 1.82 mg per pound) of body weight a day or every other day. This is divided into smaller doses. Your doctor may increase your dose as needed.

Missed dose—If you miss a dose of this medicine, take it as soon as possible. However, if it is almost time for your next dose, skip the missed dose and go back to your regular dosing schedule. Do not double doses.

Storage—To store this medicine:

- Keep out of the reach of children.
- Store away from heat and direct light.
- Do not store in the bathroom, near the kitchen sink, or in other damp places. Heat or moisture may cause the medicine to break down.
- Do not keep outdated medicine or medicine no longer needed. Be sure that any discarded medicine is out of the reach of children.

Precautions While Using This Medicine

It is important that your doctor check your progress at regular visits to make sure that this medicine is working properly.

This medicine does not cause a loss of potassium from your body as some other diuretics (water pills) do. Therefore, it is not necessary for you to get extra potassium in your diet, and too much potassium could even be harmful. Since salt substitutes and low-sodium milk may contain potassium, do not use them unless told to do so by your doctor.

Check with your doctor if you become sick and have severe or continuing nausea, vomiting, or diarrhea. These problems may cause you to lose additional water, which could be harmful, or to lose potassium, which could lessen the medicine's helpful effects.

Before having any kind of surgery (including dental surgery) or emergency treatment, tell the medical doctor or dentist in charge that you are taking this medicine.

Before you have any medical tests, tell the doctor in charge that you are taking this medicine. The results of some tests may be affected by this medicine.

For patients taking this medicine for *high blood pressure:*

- *Do not take other medicines unless they have been discussed with your doctor.* This especially includes over-the-counter (nonprescription) medicines for appetite control, asthma, colds, cough, hay fever, or sinus problems, since these medicines may tend to increase your blood pressure.

For patients taking *triamterene:*

- This medicine may cause your skin to be more sensitive to sunlight than it is normally. Exposure to sunlight, even for brief periods of time, may cause a skin rash, itching, redness or other discoloration of the skin, or a severe sunburn. When you begin taking this medicine:

—Stay out of direct sunlight, especially between the hours of 10:00 a.m. and 3:00 p.m., if possible.

—Wear protective clothing, including a hat. Also, wear sunglasses.

—Apply a sun block product that has a skin protection factor (SPF) of at least 15. Some patients may require a product with a higher SPF number, especially if they have a fair complexion. If you have any questions about this, check with your health care professional.

—Apply a sun block lipstick that has an SPF of at least 15 to protect your lips.

—Do not use a sunlamp or tanning bed or booth.

—If you have a severe reaction from the sun, check with your doctor.

Side Effects of This Medicine

In rats, spironolactone has been found to increase the risk of tumors. It is not known if spironolactone increases the chance of tumors in humans.

Along with its needed effects, a medicine may cause some unwanted effects. Although not all of these side effects may occur, if they do occur they may need medical attention.

Check with your doctor as soon as possible if any of the following side effects occur:

Rare

For amiloride, spironolactone, and triamterene

Skin rash or itching; shortness of breath

For spironolactone and triamterene only (in addition to effects listed above)

Cough or hoarseness; fever or chills; lower back or side pain; painful or difficult urination

For triamterene only (in addition to effects listed above)

Black, tarry stools; blood in urine or stools; bright red tongue; burning, inflamed feeling in tongue; cracked corners of mouth; lower back pain (severe); pinpoint red spots on skin; unusual bleeding or bruising; weakness

Signs and symptoms of too much potassium
Confusion; irregular heartbeat; nervousness; numbness or tingling in hands, feet, or lips; shortness of breath or difficult breathing; unusual tiredness or weakness; weakness or heaviness of legs

Other side effects may occur that usually do not need medical attention. These side effects may go away during treatment as your body adjusts to the medicine. However, check with your doctor if any of the following side effects continue or are bothersome:

More common (less common with amiloride and triamterene)
Nausea and vomiting; stomach cramps and diarrhea

Less common

For amiloride, spironolactone, and triamterene
Dizziness; headache

For amiloride and spironolactone only (in addition to effects listed above)
Decreased sexual ability

For amiloride only (in addition to effects listed above)
Constipation; muscle cramps

For spironolactone only (in addition to effects listed above for spironolactone)
Breast tenderness in females; clumsiness; deepening of voice in females; enlargement of breasts in males; inability to have or keep an erection; increased hair growth in females; irregular menstrual periods; sweating

For triamterene only (in addition to effects listed above for triamterene)
Increased sensitivity of skin to sunlight

Signs and symptoms of too little sodium
Drowsiness; dryness of mouth; increased thirst; lack of energy

For *male patients:*
- Spironolactone sometimes causes enlarged breasts in males, especially when they take large doses of it for a long time. Breasts usually decrease in size gradually over several months after this medicine is stopped. If you have any questions about this, check with your doctor.

Other side effects not listed above may also occur in some patients. If you notice any other effects, check with your doctor.

Additional Information

Once a medicine has been approved for marketing for a certain use, experience may show that it is also useful for other medical problems. Although these uses are not included in product labeling, spironolactone is used in certain patients with the following medical conditions:
- Polycystic ovary syndrome
- Hirsutism, female (increased hair growth)

Other than the above information, there is no additional information relating to proper use, precautions, or side effects for these uses.

Revised: 10/15/92
Interim revision: 05/18/94

DIURETICS, POTASSIUM-SPARING, AND HYDROCHLOROTHIAZIDE Systemic

Some commonly used brand names are:

In the U.S.—
Aldactazide[2]
Dyazide[3]
Maxzide[3]
Moduretic[1]
Spirozide[2]

Generic name product may also be available.

In Canada—
Aldactazide[2]
Apo-Triazide[3]
Dyazide[3]
Moduret[1]
Novo-Spirozine[2]
Novo-Triamzide[3]

Note: For quick reference, the following medicines are numbered to match the corresponding brand names.

This information applies to the following medicines:
1. Amiloride (a-MILL-oh-ride) and Hydrochlorothiazide (hye-droe-klor-oh-THYE-a-zide)‡
2. Spironolactone (speer-on-oh-LAK-tone) and Hydrochlorothiazide‡
3. Triamterene (trye-AM-ter-een) and Hydrochlorothiazide‡

‡Generic name product may also be available in the U.S.

Description

This medicine is a combination of two diuretics (water pills). It is commonly used to help reduce the amount of water in the body.

This combination is also used to treat high blood pressure (hypertension). High blood pressure adds to the work load of the heart and arteries. If it continues for a long time, the heart and arteries may not function properly. This can damage the blood vessels of the brain, heart, and kidneys, resulting in a stroke, heart failure, or kidney failure. High blood pressure may also increase the risk of heart attacks. These problems may be less likely to occur if blood pressure is controlled.

Diuretics help to reduce the amount of water in the body by acting on the kidneys to increase the flow of urine. This also helps to lower blood pressure.

This combination is also used to treat problems caused by too little potassium in the body.

This medicine is available only with your doctor's prescription, in the following dosage forms:

Oral
Amiloride and Hydrochlorothiazide
- Tablets (U.S. and Canada)

Spironolactone and Hydrochlorothiazide
- Tablets (U.S. and Canada)

Triamterene and Hydrochlorothiazide
- Capsules (U.S.)
- Tablets (U.S. and Canada)

Before Using This Medicine

In deciding to use a medicine, the risks of taking the medicine must be weighed against the good it will do. This is a decision you and your doctor will make. For potassium-sparing diuretics and hydrochlorothiazide, the following should be considered:

Allergies—Tell your doctor if you have ever had any unusual or allergic reaction to amiloride, spironolactone, triamterene, sulfonamides (sulfa drugs), bumetanide, furosemide, acetazolamide, dichlorphenamide, methazolamide, or to hydrochlorothiazide or any of the other thiazide diuretics. Also tell your health care professional if you are allergic to any other substances, such as foods, preservatives, or dyes.

Pregnancy—In general, diuretics are not useful for normal swelling of feet and hands that occurs during pregnancy. They should not be taken during pregnancy unless recommended by your doctor.

Breast-feeding—Hydrochlorothiazide and spironolactone pass into breast milk. It is not known whether amiloride or triamterene passes into breast milk. Hydrochlorothiazide may also decrease the flow of breast milk. Therefore, you should avoid use of potassium-sparing diuretic and hydrochlorothiazide combinations during the first month of breast-feeding.

Children—Studies on this combination medicine have been done only in adult patients, and there is no specific information comparing use of potassium-sparing diuretic and hydrochlorothiazide combinations in children with use in other age groups.

Older adults—Dizziness or lightheadedness and signs and symptoms of too much potassium in the body or too little potassium in the body may be more likely to occur in the elderly, who are more sensitive than younger adults to the effects of this medicine.

Other medicines—Although certain medicines should not be used together at all, in other cases two different medicines may be used together even if an interaction might occur. In these cases, your doctor may want to change the dose, or other precautions may be necessary. When you are taking potassium-sparing diuretics and hydrochlorothiazide, it is especially important that your health care professional know if you are taking any of the following:

- Angiotensin-converting enzyme (ACE) inhibitors (benazepril [e.g., Lotensin], captopril [e.g., Capoten], enalapril [e.g., Vasotec], fosinopril [e.g., Monopril], lisinopril [e.g., Prinivil, Zestril], quinapril [e.g., Accupril], ramipril [e.g., Altace]) or
- Cyclosporine (e.g., Sandimmune) or
- Potassium-containing medicines or supplements—Use with potassium-sparing diuretic and hydrochlorothiazide combinations may cause high blood levels of potassium, which may increase the chance of side effects
- Cholestyramine or
- Colestipol—Use with potassium-sparing diuretic and hydrochlorothiazide combinations may prevent the diuretic from working properly; take the diuretic at least 1 hour before or 4 hours after cholestyramine or colestipol
- Digitalis glycosides (heart medicine)—Use with diuretics may cause high blood levels of digoxin, which may increase the chance of side effects
- Lithium (e.g., Lithane)—Use with diuretics may cause high blood levels of lithium, which may increase the chance of side effects

Other medical problems—The presence of other medical problems may affect the use of potassium-sparing diuretics and hydrochlorothiazde. Make sure you tell your doctor if you have any other medical problems, especially:

- Diabetes mellitus (sugar diabetes) or
- Kidney disease or
- Liver disease—Higher blood levels of potassium may occur, which may increase the chance of side effects
- Gout (history of) or
- Kidney stones (history of)—Triamterene and hydrochlorothiazide combination may make these conditions worse
- Heart or blood vessel disease—These medicines may cause high cholesterol levels or high triglyceride levels
- Lupus erythematosus (history of) or
- Pancreatitis (inflammation of pancreas)—Potassium-sparing diuretic and hydrochlorothiazide combinations may make these conditions worse
- Menstrual problems in women or breast enlargement in men—Spironolactone and hydrochlorothiazide combination may make these conditions worse

Proper Use of This Medicine

This medicine may cause you to have an unusual feeling of tiredness when you begin to take it. You may also notice an increase in the amount of urine or in your frequency of urination. After you have taken the medicine for a while, these effects should lessen. In general, to keep the increase in urine from affecting your sleep:

- If you are to take a single dose a day, take it in the morning after breakfast.
- If you are to take more than one dose a day, take the last dose no later than 6 p.m., unless otherwise directed by your doctor.

However, it is best to plan your dose or doses according to a schedule that will least affect your personal activities and sleep. Ask your health care professional to help you plan the best time to take this medicine.

To help you remember to take your medicine, try to get into the habit of taking it at the same time each day.

If this medicine upsets your stomach, it may be taken with meals or milk. If stomach upset (nausea, vomiting, stomach pain, or cramps) continues, check with your doctor.

For patients taking this medicine for *high blood pressure:*

- In addition to the use of the medicine your doctor has prescribed, treatment for your high blood pressure may include weight control and care in the types of foods you eat, especially foods high in sodium. Your doctor will tell you which of these are most important for you. You should check with your doctor before changing your diet.
- Many patients who have high blood pressure will not notice any signs of the problem. In fact, many may feel normal. It is very important that you *take your medicine exactly as directed* and that you keep your appointments with your doctor even if you feel well.

- Remember that this medicine will not cure your high blood pressure but it does help control it. Therefore, you must continue to take it as directed if you expect to lower your blood pressure and keep it down. *You may have to take high blood pressure medicine for the rest of your life.* If high blood pressure is not treated, it can cause serious problems such as heart failure, blood vessel disease, stroke, or kidney disease.

Dosing—The dose of potassium-sparing diuretic and hydrochlorothiazide combinations will be different for different patients. *Follow your doctor's orders or the directions on the label.* The following information includes only the average doses of potassium-sparing diuretic and hydrochlorothiazide combinations. *If your dose is different, do not change it* unless your doctor tells you to do so.

The number of capsules or tablets that you take depends on the strength of the medicine. Also, *the number of doses you take each day depends on the strength of the medicine and the medical problem for which you are taking potassium-sparing diuretic and hydrochlorothiazide combinations.*

For amiloride and hydrochlorothiazide combination

- For *oral* dosage form (tablets):
  —For high blood pressure or lowering the amount of water in the body:
  - Adults—1 or 2 tablets a day.
  - Children—Dose must be determined by your doctor.

For spironolactone and hydrochlorothiazide combination

- For *oral* dosage form (tablets):
  —For high blood pressure or lowering the amount of water in the body:
  - Adults—1 to 4 tablets a day.
  - Children—Dose is based on body weight and must be determined by your doctor.

For triamterene and hydrochlorothiazide combination

- For *oral* dosage form (capsules):
  —For high blood pressure or lowering the amount of water in the body:
  - Adults—1 or 2 capsules once a day.
  - Children—Dose must be determined by your doctor.
- For *oral* dosage form (tablets):
  —For high blood pressure or lowering the amount of water in the body:
  - Adults—1 to 4 tablets a day, depending on the strength of your tablet.
  - Children—Dose must be determined by your doctor.

Missed dose—If you miss a dose of this medicine, take it as soon as possible. However, if it is almost time for your next dose, skip the missed dose and go back to your regular dosing schedule. Do not double doses.

Storage—To store this medicine:

- Keep out of the reach of children.
- Store away from heat and direct light.
- Do not store in the bathroom, near the kitchen sink, or in other damp places. Heat or moisture may cause the medicine to break down.
- Do not keep outdated medicine or medicine no longer needed. Be sure that any discarded medicine is out of the reach of children.

Precautions While Using This Medicine

It is important that your doctor check your progress at regular visits to make sure that this medicine is working properly.

This medicine may cause a loss or increase of potassium in your body. Your doctor may have special instructions about whether or not you need to eat or drink foods or beverages that have a high potassium content (for example, orange or other citrus fruit juices), taking a potassium supplement, or using salt substitutes. Since too much potassium can be harmful, it is important not to change your diet on your own. Tell your doctor if you are already on a special diet (as for diabetes). Since salt substitutes and low-sodium milk may contain potassium, do not use them unless told to do so by your doctor. Check with your health care professional if you need a list of foods that are high in potassium or if you have any questions.

Check with your doctor if you become sick and have severe or continuing vomiting or diarrhea. These problems may cause you to lose additional water and potassium and lead to low blood pressure.

For *diabetic patients:*

- Hydrochlorothiazide (contained in this combination medicine) may raise blood sugar levels. While you are taking this medicine, be especially careful in testing for sugar in your blood or urine.

Potassium-sparing diuretics and hydrochlorothiazide may cause your skin to be more sensitive to sunlight than it is normally. Exposure to sunlight, even for brief periods of time, may cause a skin rash, itching, redness or other discoloration of the skin, or a severe sunburn. When you begin taking this medicine:

- Stay out of direct sunlight, especially between the hours of 10:00 a.m. and 3:00 p.m., if possible.
- Wear protective clothing, including a hat. Also, wear sunglasses.
- Apply a sun block product that has a skin protection factor (SPF) of at least 15. Some patients may require a product with a higher SPF number, especially if they have a fair complexion. If you have any questions about this, check with your health care professional.
- Apply a sun block lipstick that has an SPF of at least 15 to protect your lips.
- Do not use a sunlamp or tanning bed or booth.

If you have a severe reaction from the sun, check with your doctor.

Before having any kind of surgery (including dental surgery) or emergency treatment, tell the medical doctor or dentist in charge that you are taking this medicine.

For patients taking *triamterene and hydrochlorothiazide combination:*

- Do not change brands of triamterene and hydrochlorothiazide without first checking with your doctor. Different products may not work the same way. If you refill your medicine and it looks different, check with your pharmacist.

For patients taking this medicine for *high blood pressure:*

- *Do not take other medicines unless they have been discussed with your doctor.* This especially includes over-the-counter (nonprescription) medicines for appetite control, asthma, colds, cough, hay fever, or sinus problems, since they may tend to increase your blood pressure.

Tell the doctor in charge that you are taking this medicine before you have any medical tests. The results of some tests may be affected by this medicine.

Side Effects of This Medicine

In rats, spironolactone has been found to increase the risk of development of tumors. However, the doses given were many times the dose of spironolactone given to humans. It is not known whether spironolactone causes tumors in humans.

Along with its needed effects, a medicine may cause some unwanted effects. Although not all of these side effects may occur, if they do occur they may need medical attention.

Check with your doctor as soon as possible if any of the following side effects occur:

Rare

Black, tarry stools; blood in urine or stools; cough or hoarseness; fever or chills; joint pain; lower back or side pain; painful or difficult urination; pinpoint red spots on skin; skin rash or hives; stomach pain (severe) with nausea and vomiting; unusual bleeding or bruising; yellow eyes or skin

Signs and symptoms of changes in potassium

Confusion; dryness of mouth; increased thirst; irregular heartbeat; mood or mental changes; muscle cramps or pain; numbness or tingling in hands, feet, or lips; shortness of breath or difficulty breathing; unusual tiredness or weakness; weak pulse; weakness or heaviness of legs

Reported for triamterene only (rare)

Bright red tongue; burning, inflamed feeling in tongue; cracked corners of mouth

Other side effects may occur that usually do not need medical attention. These side effects may go away during treatment as your body adjusts to the medicine. However, check with your doctor if any of the following side effects continue or are bothersome:

More common (less common with triamterene)

Loss of appetite; nausea and vomiting; stomach cramps and diarrhea; upset stomach

Less common

Decreased sexual ability; dizziness or lightheadedness when getting up from a lying or sitting position; headache; increased sensitivity of skin to sunlight

Reported for amiloride only (less common)

Constipation

Reported for spironolactone only (less common)

Breast tenderness in females; deepening of voice in females; enlargement of breasts in males; increased hair growth in females; irregular menstrual periods; sweating

Spironolactone sometimes causes enlarged breasts in males, especially when they take large doses of it for a long time. Breasts usually decrease in size gradually over several months after this medicine is stopped. If you have any questions about this, check with your doctor.

Other side effects not listed above may also occur in some patients. If you notice any other effects, check with your doctor.

Revised: 08/03/94

DIURETICS, THIAZIDE Systemic

Some commonly used brand names are:

In the U.S.—

Anhydron[5]
Aquatensen[8]
Diucardin[7]
Diulo[9]
Diuril[3]
Enduron[8]
Esidrix[6]
Exna[2]
Hydrex[2]
Hydro-chlor[6]
Hydro-D[6]
HydroDIURIL[6]
Hydromox[11]
Hygroton[4]
Metahydrin[12]
Mykrox[9]
Naqua[12]
Naturetin[1]
Oretic[6]
Renese[10]
Saluron[7]
Thalitone[4]
Trichlorex[12]
Zaroxolyn[9]

In Canada—

Apo-Chlorthalidone[4]
Apo-Hydro[6]
Diuchlor H[6]
Duretic[8]
HydroDIURIL[6]
Hygroton[4]
Naturetin[1]
Neo-Codema[6]
Novo-Hydrazide[6]
Novo-Thalidone[4]
Uridon[4]
Urozide[6]
Zaroxolyn[9]

Note: For quick reference, the following thiazide diuretics are numbered to match the corresponding brand names.

This information applies to the following medicines:

1. Bendroflumethiazide (ben-droe-floo-meth-EYE-a-zide)
2. Benzthiazide (benz-THYE-a-zide)†‡
3. Chlorothiazide (klor-oh-THYE-a-zide)†‡
4. Chlorthalidone (klor-THAL-i-doan)‡§
5. Cyclothiazide (sye-kloe-THYE-a-zide)†

6. Hydrochlorothiazide (hye-droe-klor-oh-THYE-a-zide)‡§
7. Hydroflumethiazide (hye-droe-floo-meth-EYE-a-zide)†‡
8. Methyclothiazide (meth-ee-kloe-THYE-a-zide)‡
9. Metolazone (me-TOLE-a-zone)
10. Polythiazide (pol-i-THYE-a-zide)†
11. Quinethazone (kwin-ETH-a-zone)†
12. Trichlormethiazide (trye-klor-meth-EYE-a-zide)†‡

†Not commercially available in Canada.
‡Generic name product may also be available in the U.S.
§Generic name product may also be available in Canada.

Description

Thiazide or thiazide-like diuretics are commonly used to treat high blood pressure (hypertension). High blood pressure adds to the workload of the heart and arteries. If it continues for a long time, the heart and arteries may not function properly. This can damage the blood vessels of the brain, heart, and kidneys, resulting in a stroke, heart failure, or kidney failure. High blood pressure may also increase the risk of heart attacks. These problems may be less likely to occur if blood pressure is controlled.

Thiazide diuretics are also used to help reduce the amount of water in the body by increasing the flow of urine. They may also be used for other conditions as determined by your doctor.

Thiazide diuretics are available only with your doctor's prescription, in the following dosage forms:

Oral
- Bendroflumethiazide
  - Tablets (U.S. and Canada)
- Benzthiazide
  - Tablets (U.S.)
- Chlorothiazide
  - Oral suspension (U.S.)
  - Tablets (U.S.)
- Chlorthalidone
  - Tablets (U.S. and Canada)
- Cyclothiazide
  - Tablets (U.S.)
- Hydrochlorothiazide
  - Oral solution (U.S.)
  - Tablets (U.S. and Canada)
- Hydroflumethiazide
  - Tablets (U.S.)
- Methyclothiazide
  - Tablets (U.S. and Canada)
- Metolazone
  - Tablets (U.S. and Canada)
- Polythiazide
  - Tablets (U.S.)
- Quinethazone
  - Tablets (U.S.)
- Trichlormethiazide
  - Tablets (U.S.)

Parenteral
- Chlorothiazide
  - Injection (U.S.)

Before Using This Medicine

In deciding to use a medicine, the risks of taking the medicine must be weighed against the good it will do. This is a decision you and your doctor will make. For thiazide diuretics, the following should be considered:

Allergies—Tell your doctor if you have ever had any unusual or allergic reaction to sulfonamides (sulfa drugs), bumetanide, furosemide, acetazolamide, dichlorphenamide, methazolamide, or to any of the thiazide diuretics. Also tell your health care professional if you are allergic to any other substances, such as foods, preservatives, or dyes.

Pregnancy—When this medicine is used during pregnancy, it may cause side effects including jaundice, blood problems, and low potassium in the newborn infant. In addition, although this medicine has not been shown to cause birth defects or other problems in animals, studies have not been done in humans.

In general, diuretics are not useful for normal swelling of feet and hands that occurs during pregnancy. They should not be taken during pregnancy unless recommended by your doctor.

Breast-feeding—Thiazide diuretics pass into breast milk. These medicines also may decrease the flow of breast milk. Therefore, you should avoid use of thiazide diuretics during the first month of breast-feeding.

Children—Although there is no specific information comparing the use of thiazide diuretics in children with use in other age groups, these medicines are not expected to cause different side effects or problems in children than they do in adults. However, extra caution may be necessary in infants with jaundice, because these medicines can make the condition worse.

Older adults—Dizziness or lightheadedness and signs of too much potassium loss may be more likely to occur in the elderly, who are more sensitive than younger adults to the effects of thiazide diuretics.

Other medicines—Although certain medicines should not be used together at all, in other cases two different medicines may be used together even if an interaction might occur. In these cases, your doctor may want to change the dose, or other precautions may be necessary. When you are taking thiazide diuretics, it is especially important that your health care professional know if you are taking any of the following:

- Cholestyramine or
- Colestipol—Use with thiazide diuretics may prevent the diuretic from working properly; take the diuretic at least 1 hour before or 4 hours after cholestyramine or colestipol
- Digitalis glycosides (heart medicine)—Use with thiazide diuretics may cause high blood levels of digoxin, which may increase the chance of side effects
- Lithium (e.g., Lithane)—Use with thiazide diuretics may cause high blood levels of lithium, which may increase the chance of side effects

Other medical problems—The presence of other medical problems may affect the use of thiazide diuretics. Make sure you tell your doctor if you have any other medical problems, especially:

- Diabetes mellitus (sugar diabetes)—Thiazide diuretics may increase the amount of sugar in the blood
- Gout (history of) or
- Lupus erythematosus (history of) or
- Pancreatitis (inflammation of the pancreas)—Thiazide diuretics may make these conditions worse
- Heart or blood vessel disease—Thiazide diuretics may cause high cholesterol levels or high triglyceride levels

- Liver disease or
- Kidney disease (severe)—Higher blood levels of the thiazide diuretic may occur, which may prevent the thiazide diuretic from working properly

Proper Use of This Medicine

This medicine may cause you to have an unusual feeling of tiredness when you begin to take it. You may also notice an increase in the amount of urine or in your frequency of urination. After you have taken the medicine for a while, these effects should lessen. In general, to keep the increase in urine from affecting your sleep:

- If you are to take a single dose a day, take it in the morning after breakfast.
- If you are to take more than one dose a day, take the last dose no later than 6 p.m., unless otherwise directed by your doctor.

However, it is best to plan your dose or doses according to a schedule that will least affect your personal activities and sleep. Ask your health care professional to help you plan the best time to take this medicine.

To help you remember to take your medicine, try to get into the habit of taking it at the same time each day.

For patients taking this medicine for *high blood pressure:*

- In addition to the use of the medicine your doctor has prescribed, appropriate treatment for your high blood pressure may include weight control and care in the types of foods you eat, especially foods high in sodium. Your doctor will tell you which factors are most important for you. You should check with your doctor before changing your diet.
- Many patients who have high blood pressure will not notice any signs of the problem. In fact, many may feel normal. It is very important that you *take your medicine exactly as directed* and that you keep your appointments with your doctor even if you feel well.
- Remember that this medicine will not cure your high blood pressure but it does help control it. Therefore, you must continue to take it as directed if you expect to lower your blood pressure and keep it down. *You may have to take high blood pressure medicine for the rest of your life.* If high blood pressure is not treated, it can cause serious problems such as heart failure, blood vessel disease, stroke, or kidney disease.

For patients taking the *oral liquid form of hydrochlorothiazide,* which comes in a dropper bottle:

- This medicine is to be taken by mouth. The amount you should take is to be measured only with the specially marked dropper.

Dosing—The dose of these medicines will be different for different patients. *Follow your doctor's orders or the directions on the label.* The following information includes only the average doses of these medicines. *If your dose is different, do not change it* unless your doctor tells you to do so.

The number of tablets or teaspoonfuls of solution or suspension that you take depends on the strength of the medicine. Also, *the number of doses you take each day, the time allowed between doses, and the length of time you take the medicine depend on the medical problem for which you are taking thiazide diuretics.*

For bendroflumethiazide

- For *oral* dosage form (tablets):
  - —To lower the amount of water in the body:
    - Adults—At first, 2.5 to 10 milligrams (mg) one or two times a day. Then, your doctor may lower your dose to 2.5 to 5 mg once a day. Or, your doctor may want you to take this dose once every other day or once a day for only three to five days out of the week.
    - Children—Dose is based on body weight and must be determined by your doctor. The usual dose is 50 to 100 micrograms (mcg) per kilogram (kg) (22.7 to 45.4 mcg per pound) of body weight once a day.
  - —For high blood pressure:
    - Adults—2.5 to 20 mg a day. This may be taken as a single dose or divided into two doses.
    - Children—Dose is based on body weight and must be determined by your doctor. The usual dose is 50 to 400 mcg per kg (22.7 to 181.8 mcg per pound) of body weight a day. This may be taken as a single dose or divided into two doses.

For benzthiazide

- For *oral* dosage form (tablets):
  - —To lower the amount of water in the body:
    - Adults—25 to 100 milligrams (mg) two times a day. Or, your doctor may want you to take this dose once every other day or once a day for only three to five days out of the week.
    - Children—Dose is based on body weight and must be determined by your doctor.
  - —For high blood pressure:
    - Adults—50 to 100 mg a day. This may be taken as a single dose or divided into two doses.
    - Children—Dose is based on body weight and must be determined by your doctor.

For chlorothiazide

- For *oral* dosage forms (oral suspension or tablets):
  - —To lower the amount of water in the body:
    - Adults—250 milligrams (mg) every six to twelve hours.
    - Children—Dose is based on body weight and must be determined by your doctor.
  - —For high blood pressure:
    - Adults—250 to 1000 mg a day. This may be taken as a single dose or divided into smaller doses.
    - Children—Dose is based on body weight and must be determined by your doctor.
- For *injection* dosage form:
  - —To lower the amount of water in the body:
    - Adults—250 mg injected into a vein every six to twelve hours.

- Children—Use and dose must be determined by your doctor.

—For high blood pressure:

- Adults—500 to 1000 mg a day, injected into a vein. This dose may be given as a single dose or divided into two doses.
- Children—Use and dose must be determined by your doctor.

For chlorthalidone

- For *oral* dosage form (tablets):

—To lower the amount of water in the body:

- Adults—25 to 100 milligrams (mg) once a day. Or, 100 to 200 mg taken once every other day or once a day for three days out of the week.
- Children—Dose is based on body weight and must be determined by your doctor.

—For high blood pressure:

- Adults—25 to 100 mg once a day.
- Children—Dose is based on body weight and must be determined by your doctor.

For cyclothiazide

- For *oral* dosage form (tablets):

—To lower the amount of water in the body:

- Adults—1 to 2 milligrams (mg) once a day. Or, your doctor may want you to take this dose once every other day or once a day for only two or three days out of the week.
- Children—Dose is based on body weight and must be determined by your doctor.

—For high blood pressure:

- Adults—2 mg once a day.
- Children—Dose is based on body weight and must be determined by your doctor.

For hydrochlorothiazide

- For *oral* dosage forms (oral solution or tablets):

—To lower the amount of water in the body:

- Adults—25 to 100 milligrams (mg) one or two times a day. Or, your doctor may want you to take this dose once every other day or once a day for three to five days out of the week.
- Children—Dose is based on body weight and must be determined by your doctor.

—For high blood pressure:

- Adults—25 to 100 mg a day. This may be taken as a single dose or divided into two doses.
- Children—Dose is based on body weight and must be determined by your doctor.

For hydroflumethiazide

- For *oral* dosage form (tablets):

—To lower the amount of water in the body:

- Adults—25 to 100 milligrams (mg) one or two times a day. Or, your doctor may want you to take this dose once every other day or once a day for three to five days out of the week.
- Children—Dose is based on body weight and must be determined by your doctor.

—For high blood pressure:

- Adults—50 to 100 mg a day. This may be taken as a single dose or divided into two doses.
- Children—Dose is based on body weight and must be determined by your doctor.

For methyclothiazide

- For *oral* dosage form (tablets):

—To lower the amount of water in the body:

- Adults—2.5 to 10 milligrams (mg) once a day. Or, your doctor may want you to take this dose once every other day or once a day for three to five days out of the week.
- Children—Dose is based on body weight and must be determined by your doctor.

—For high blood pressure:

- Adults—2.5 to 5 mg once a day.
- Children—Dose is based on body weight and must be determined by your doctor.

For metolazone

- For *oral* dosage form (*extended* metolazone tablets):

—To lower the amount of water in the body:

- Adults—5 to 20 milligrams (mg) once a day.
- Children—Dose must be determined by your doctor.

—For high blood pressure:

- Adults—2.5 to 5 mg once a day.
- Children—Dose must be determined by your doctor.

- For *oral* dosage form (*prompt* metolazone tablets):

—For high blood pressure:

- Adults—At first, 500 micrograms (mcg) once a day. Then, 500 to 1000 mcg once a day.
- Children—Dose must be determined by your doctor.

For polythiazide

- For *oral* dosage form (tablets):

—To lower the amount of water in the body:

- Adults—1 to 4 milligrams (mg) once a day. Or, your doctor may want you to take this dose once every other day or once a day for three to five days out of the week.
- Children—Dose is based on body weight and must be determined by your doctor.

—For high blood pressure:

- Adults—2 to 4 mg once a day.
- Children—Dose is based on body weight and must be determined by your doctor.

For quinethazone

- For *oral* dosage form (tablets):

—To lower the amount of water in the body or for high blood pressure:

- Adults—50 to 200 milligrams (mg) a day. This may be taken as a single dose or divided into two doses.

• Children—Dose must be determined by your doctor.

For trichlormethiazide

• For *oral* dosage form (tablets):

—To lower the amount of water in the body:

• Adults—1 to 4 milligrams (mg) once a day. Or, your doctor may want you to take this dose once every other day or once a day for three to five days out of the week.

• Children—Dose is based on body weight and must be determined by your doctor.

—For high blood pressure:

• Adults—2 to 4 mg once a day.

• Children—Dose is based on body weight and must be determined by your doctor.

Missed dose—If you miss a dose of this medicine, take it as soon as possible. However, if it is almost time for your next dose, skip the missed dose and go back to your regular dosing schedule. Do not double doses.

Storage—To store this medicine:

- Keep out of the reach of children.
- Store away from heat and direct light.
- Do not store in the bathroom, near the kitchen sink, or in other damp places. Heat or moisture may cause the medicine to break down.
- Keep the oral liquid form of this medicine from freezing.
- Do not keep outdated medicine or medicine no longer needed. Be sure that any discarded medicine is out of the reach of children.

Precautions While Using This Medicine

It is important that your doctor check your progress at regular visits to make sure that this medicine is working properly.

This medicine may cause a loss of potassium from your body:

- To help prevent this, your doctor may want you to:
  —eat or drink foods that have a high potassium content (for example, orange or other citrus fruit juices), or
  —take a potassium supplement, or
  —take another medicine to help prevent the loss of the potassium in the first place.
- It is very important to follow these directions. Also, it is important not to change your diet on your own. This is more important if you are already on a special diet (as for diabetes), or if you are taking a potassium supplement or a medicine to reduce potassium loss. Extra potassium may not be necessary and, in some cases, too much potassium could be harmful.

Check with your doctor if you become sick and have severe or continuing vomiting or diarrhea. These problems may cause you to lose additional water and potassium.

For *diabetic patients:*

- Thiazide diuretics may raise blood sugar levels. While you are using this medicine, be especially careful in testing for sugar in your blood or urine.

Thiazide diuretics may cause your skin to be more sensitive to sunlight than it is normally. Exposure to sunlight, even for brief periods of time, may cause a skin rash, itching, redness or other discoloration of the skin, or a severe sunburn. When you begin taking this medicine:

- Stay out of direct sunlight, especially between the hours of 10:00 a.m. and 3:00 p.m., if possible.
- Wear protective clothing, including a hat. Also, wear sunglasses.
- Apply a sun block product that has a skin protection factor (SPF) of at least 15. Some patients may require a product with a higher SPF number, especially if they have a fair complexion. If you have any questions about this, check with your health care professional.
- Apply a sun block lipstick that has an SPF of at least 15 to protect your lips.
- Do not use a sunlamp or tanning bed or booth.

If you have a severe reaction from the sun, check with your doctor.

For patients taking this medicine for *high blood pressure:*

- *Do not take other medicines unless they have been discussed with your doctor.* This especially includes over-the-counter (nonprescription) medicines for appetite control, asthma, colds, cough, hay fever, or sinus problems, since they may tend to increase your blood pressure.

Side Effects of This Medicine

Along with its needed effects, a medicine may cause some unwanted effects. Although not all of these side effects may occur, if they do occur they may need medical attention.

Check with your doctor as soon as possible if any of the following side effects occur:

Rare

Black, tarry stools; blood in urine or stools; cough or hoarseness; fever or chills; joint pain; lower back or side pain; painful or difficult urination; pinpoint red spots on skin; skin rash or hives; stomach pain (severe) with nausea and vomiting; unusual bleeding or bruising; yellow eyes or skin

Signs and symptoms of too much potassium loss

Dryness of mouth; increased thirst; irregular heartbeat; mood or mental changes; muscle cramps or pain; nausea or vomiting; unusual tiredness or weakness; weak pulse

Signs and symptoms of too much sodium loss

Confusion; convulsions; decreased mental activity; irritability; muscle cramps; unusual tiredness or weakness

Other side effects may occur that usually do not need medical attention. These side effects may go away during treatment as your body adjusts to the medicine. However,

check with your doctor if any of the following side effects continue or are bothersome:

Less common

Decreased sexual ability; diarrhea; dizziness or lightheadedness when getting up from a lying or sitting position; increased sensitivity of skin to sunlight; loss of appetite; upset stomach

Other side effects not listed above may also occur in some patients. If you notice any other effects, check with your doctor.

Additional Information

Once a medicine has been approved for marketing for a certain use, experience may show that it is also useful for other medical problems. Although these uses are not specifically included in product labeling, thiazide diuretics are used in certain patients with the following medical conditions:

- Diabetes insipidus (water diabetes)
- Kidney stones (calcium-containing)

For patients taking this medicine for *diabetes insipidus (water diabetes):*

- Some thiazide diuretics are used in the treatment of diabetes insipidus (water diabetes). In patients with water diabetes, this medicine causes a decrease in the flow of urine and helps the body hold water. Thus, the information given above about increased urine flow will not apply to you.

Other than the above information, there is no additional information relating to proper use, precautions, or side effects for these uses.

Revised: 06/07/92
Interim revision: 06/30/94

DORNASE ALFA Inhalation

A commonly used brand name in the U.S. and Canada is Pulmozyme. Other commonly used names are: rhDNase and DNase I.

Description

Dornase alfa (DOR-nayse AL-fa) is used in the management of cystic fibrosis. It is used every day with other cystic fibrosis medicines, especially antibiotics, bronchodilators (medicines that open up narrowed breathing passages), and corticosteroids (cortisone-like medicines).

Cystic fibrosis is a condition in which thick mucus is formed in the lungs and breathing passages. The mucus blocks the airways and increases the chance of lung infections. The infections then cause the mucus to become even thicker, making it more difficult to breathe.

Dornase alfa will not cure cystic fibrosis. However, when it is used every day, it helps make breathing easier and reduces the number of serious lung infections that require treatment with antibiotics.

Dornase alfa is available only with your doctor's prescription, in the following dosage form:

Inhalation

- Inhalation solution (U.S. and Canada)

Before Using This Medicine

In deciding to use a medicine, the risks of taking the medicine must be weighed against the good it will do. This is a decision you and your doctor will make. For dornase alfa, the following should be considered:

Allergies—Tell your doctor if you have ever had any unusual or allergic reaction to dornase alfa. Also tell your health care professional if you are allergic to any other substances, such as foods, preservatives, or dyes.

Pregnancy—Dornase alfa has not been studied in pregnant women. However, this medicine has not been shown to cause birth defects or other problems in animals.

Breast-feeding—It is not known whether dornase alfa passes into human breast milk. Although most medicines pass into breast milk in small amounts, many of them may be used safely while breast-feeding. Mothers who are using this medicine and who wish to breast-feed should discuss this with their doctor.

Children—Although there is no specific information comparing use of dornase alfa in children up to 5 years of age with use in other age groups, the medicine is not expected to cause different side effects or problems in children than it does in adults.

Older adults—Many medicines have not been studied specifically in older people. Therefore, it may not be known whether they work exactly the same way they do in younger adults. Although there is no specific information comparing use of dornase alfa in the elderly with use in other age groups, this medicine is not expected to cause different side effects or problems in older people than it does in younger adults.

Other medicines—Although certain medicines should not be used together at all, in other cases two different medicines may be used together even if an interaction might occur. In these cases, your doctor may want to change the dose, or other precautions may be necessary. Tell your health care professional if you are taking any other prescription or nonprescription (over-the-counter [OTC]) medicine.

Proper Use of This Medicine

Dornase alfa usually comes with patient instructions. Read them carefully before using this medicine.

Dornase alfa is packaged in small plastic containers called ampuls. Each ampul contains one full dose of dornase alfa. *Do not use an ampul that has already been opened. Also, do not use an ampul of this medicine after the expiration date printed on the package.*

Do not use dornase alfa solution if it is cloudy or discolored.

Dornase alfa must be used in a nebulizer with a compressor. Only the following nebulizers and compressors should be used with this medicine:

- Hudson T Up-draft II disposable jet nebulizer used with the Pulmo-Aide compressor
- Marquest Acorn II disposable jet nebulizer used with the Pulmo-Aide compressor
- Reusable PARI LC Jet+ nebulizer used with the PARI PRONEB compressor

Your health care professional will help you decide which nebulizer and compressor to use.

It is very important that you *use dornase alfa only as directed.* Use the mouthpiece provided with the nebulizer. Do not use a face mask with the nebulizer because less medicine will get into your lungs. *Make sure you understand exactly how to use this medicine in the nebulizer.*

In order to receive the full effects of this medicine, *you must use it every day as ordered by your doctor.* If possible, dornase alfa should be used at about the same time each day. You may notice some improvement in your condition within the first week of treatment. However, some patients may not feel the full effects of this medicine for weeks or months.

If you are taking any other medicines for cystic fibrosis, keep taking them as you did before you started using dornase alfa, unless otherwise directed by your doctor. However, *do not put any other inhaled medicine in the nebulizer at the same time that you use dornase alfa.* Other inhaled medicines may be used in a clean nebulizer before or after your treatment with dornase alfa.

To prepare the nebulizer for use:

- Wash your hands well with soap and water before putting the nebulizer together and preparing the medicine. This will help prevent infection.
- Put the nebulizer together only on a clean surface. If dirt or germs get on the nebulizer or in the medicine, they may cause infection.
- After you put the nebulizer together, test the compressor (following the manufacturer's directions) to make sure it works properly. If you have any questions about this, ask your health care professional.

To prepare the medicine for use in the nebulizer:

- Remove one ampul of dornase alfa from the refrigerator. Hold the tab at the base of the ampul firmly. Twist off the top of the ampul, but do not squeeze the body of the ampul while doing so.
- Take the cap off the nebulizer cup. Turn the opened ampul upside down over the cup. Squeeze the ampul gently until all the contents are emptied into the cup. *It is very important that you use the full dose of this medicine.*
- Replace the cap on the nebulizer cup. Connect the nebulizer and compressor, following the manufacturer's directions.
- Turn on the compressor. Make sure there is mist coming from the nebulizer.

To use the medicine in the nebulizer:

- Place the mouthpiece between your teeth and on top of your tongue. Close your lips around the mouthpiece. Be sure that you do not block the airflow with your tongue or teeth.
- Breathe normally, in and out, through your mouth. *Do not breathe through your nose.* If you have trouble breathing only through your mouth, use a nose clip.
- During treatment, moisture may collect in the long connecting tube of the nebulizer. This should be expected. However, if you notice a leak or feel moisture coming from the nebulizer during the treatment, turn off the compressor. Then check to make sure the nebulizer cap is sealed correctly before you continue the treatment.
- When the nebulizer begins ''spitting,'' gently tap the nebulizer cup. Continue breathing until the cup is empty or no more mist comes from the nebulizer.
- If you have to stop the treatment for some reason or if you start coughing during the treatment, turn off the compressor. To begin the treatment again, turn on the compressor and continue as before.
- The complete treatment usually takes 10 to 15 minutes. *Be sure to inhale the full dose of dornase alfa.*

After using dornase alfa:

- Turn off the compressor. Then take apart the nebulizer system.
- Follow the manufacturer's directions for care and cleaning of your nebulizer and compressor.

Dosing—The dose of dornase alfa will be different for different patients. *Follow your doctor's orders or the directions on the label.* The following information includes only the average doses of dornase alfa. *If your dose is different, do not change it* unless your doctor tells you to do so.

- For *inhalation* dosage form (inhalation solution):
  - —For cystic fibrosis:
    - Adults and children 5 years of age and older—The usual dose is 2.5 milligrams (mg) (one ampul), used in a nebulizer once a day for about 10 to 15 minutes. However, your doctor may want you to use this medicine two times a day at regularly spaced times.
    - Children up to 5 years of age—Use and dose must be determined by your doctor.

Missed dose—If you miss a dose of this medicine, use it as soon as possible. However, if it is almost time for your next dose, skip the missed dose and go back to your regular dosing schedule.

Storage—To store this medicine:
- Keep out of the reach of children
- Store away from heat and light.
- Store the medicine in the refrigerator in the foil pouches. However, keep the medicine from freezing. Do not leave this medicine out of the refrigerator for longer than 24 hours. If an ampul of medicine is left out for longer than this, it should be thrown away and a new ampul should be used.
- Do not keep outdated medicine or medicine no longer needed. Be sure that any discarded medicine is out of the reach of children.

Precautions While Using This Medicine

If your condition becomes worse while you are using this medicine, check with your doctor.

Side Effects of This Medicine

Along with its needed effects, a medicine may cause some unwanted effects. The following side effects may go away during treatment as your body adjusts to the medicine. However, check with your doctor if any of the following side effects continue or are bothersome:

More common
Chest pain or discomfort; hoarseness; sore throat

Less common
Difficulty breathing; fever; redness, itching, pain, swelling, or other irritation of eyes; runny nose; skin rash; upset stomach

Other side effects not listed above may also occur in some patients. If you notice any other effects, check with your doctor.

Revised: 07/24/97

DORZOLAMIDE Ophthalmic†

A commonly used brand name in the U.S. is Trusopt.

†Not commercially available in Canada.

Description

Dorzolamide (dor-ZOLE-a-mide) is a carbonic anhydrase inhibitor that is used in the eye. It is used to treat increased pressure in the eye caused by open-angle glaucoma. It is also used to treat a condition called hypertension of the eye.

Dorzolamide is available only with your doctor's prescription, in the following dosage form:

Ophthalmic
- Ophthalmic solution (eye drops) (U.S.)

Before Using This Medicine

In deciding to use a medicine, the risks of using the medicine must be weighed against the good it will do. This is a decision you and your doctor will make. For ophthalmic dorzolamide, the following should be considered:

Allergies—Tell your doctor if you have ever had any unusual or allergic reaction to ophthalmic dorzolamide or to any of the sulfonamides (sulfa medicines); furosemide (e.g., Lasix) or thiazide diuretics (water pills); oral antidiabetics (diabetes medicine you take by mouth); or the carbonic anhydrase inhibitor-type glaucoma medicine you take by mouth (for example, acetazolamide [e.g., Diamox], dichlorphenamide [e.g., Daranide], or methazolamide [e.g., Neptazane]). Also tell your health care professional if you are allergic to any other substances, such as benzalkonium chloride or other preservatives.

Pregnancy—Ophthalmic dorzolamide has not been studied in pregnant women. However, one animal study has shown that this medicine, when given in very high doses, causes toxicity in the mother and birth defects in the fetus. Before using this medicine, make sure your doctor knows if you are pregnant or if you may become pregnant.

Breast-feeding—It is not known whether ophthalmic dorzolamide passes into breast milk. However, other carbonic anhydrase inhibitors may pass into breast milk. These medicines are not recommended during breast-feeding, because they may cause unwanted effects in nursing babies. It may be necessary for you to use another medicine or to stop breast-feeding during treatment. Be sure you have discussed this with your doctor.

Children—Studies on this medicine have been done only in adult patients and there is no specific information comparing use of ophthalmic dorzolamide in children with use in other age groups.

Older adults—This medicine has been tested in a limited number of patients 65 years of age or older and has not been shown to cause different side effects or problems in older people than it does in younger adults.

Other medicines—Although certain medicines should not be used together at all, in other cases two different medicines may be used together even if an interaction might occur. In these cases, your doctor may want to change the dose, or other precautions may be necessary. When you are using ophthalmic dorzolamide, it is especially important that your health care professional know if you are using any of the following:
- Silver preparations for the eye, such as silver nitrate—Ophthalmic dorzolamide should not be used with ophthalmic silver preparations, since a chemical reaction may occur

Other medical problems—The presence of other medical problems may affect the use of ophthalmic dorzolamide. Make sure you tell your doctor if you have any other medical problems, especially:
- Kidney disease, severe, or
- Liver disease—Use of ophthalmic dorzolamide may lead to increased side effects from the medication
- Kidney stones—Use of ophthalmic dorzolamide may make this condition worse

Proper Use of This Medicine

To use: First, wash your hands. Tilt the head back and, pressing your finger gently on the skin just beneath the lower eyelid, pull the lower eyelid away from the eye to make a space. Drop the medicine into this space. Let go of the eyelid and gently close the eyes. Do not blink. Keep the eyes closed and apply pressure to the inner corner of the eye with your finger for 1 or 2 minutes to allow the medicine to be absorbed by the eye.

Use this medicine only as directed. Do not use more of it and do not use it more often than your doctor ordered. To do so may increase the chance of too much medicine being absorbed into the body and the chance of side effects.

If your doctor ordered two different eye drops to be used together, wait at least 10 minutes between the times you apply the medicines. This will help to keep the second medicine from ''washing out'' the first one.

Dosing—The dose of ophthalmic dorzolamide will be different for different patients. *Follow your doctor's orders or the directions on the label.* The following information includes only the average doses of ophthalmic dorzolamide. *If your dose is different, do not change it* unless your doctor tells you to do so.

- For *ophthalmic* dosage form (eye drops):
  - —For glaucoma or hypertension of the eye:
    - Adults and teenagers—Use one drop in the eye three times a day.
    - Children—Use and dose must be determined by your doctor.

Missed dose—If you miss a dose of this medicine, use it as soon as possible. However, if it is almost time for your next dose, skip the missed dose and go back to your regular dosing schedule. Do not double doses.

Storage—To store this medicine:

- Keep out of the reach of children.
- Store away from heat and direct light.
- Keep the medicine from freezing. Do not refrigerate.
- Do not keep outdated medicine or medicine no longer needed. Be sure that any discarded medicine is out of the reach of children.

Precautions While Using This Medicine

It is important that your doctor check your progress at regular visits. Your doctor may want to do certain tests to see if the medicine is working properly or to see if certain side effects may be occurring without your knowing it.

If itching, redness, swelling, or other signs of eye or eyelid irritation occur, check with your doctor. These signs may mean that you are allergic to ophthalmic dorzolamide.

This medicine may cause some people to have blurred vision for a short time. *Make sure you know how you react to this medicine before you drive, use machines, or do anything else that could be dangerous if you cannot see properly.* Also, since blurred vision may be a sign of a side effect that needs medical attention, check with your doctor if it continues.

Ophthalmic dorzolamide may cause your eyes to become more sensitive to light than they are normally. Wearing sunglasses and avoiding too much exposure to bright light may help lessen the discomfort. If the discomfort continues, check with your doctor.

Side Effects of This Medicine

Along with its needed effects, a medicine may cause some unwanted effects. Although not all of these side effects may occur, if they do occur they may need medical attention.

Check with your doctor as soon as possible if any of the following side effects occur:

More common

Itching, redness, swelling, or other sign of eye or eyelid irritation

Rare

Blurred vision, eye pain, tearing, skin rash, symptoms of kidney stone (blood in urine, nausea or vomiting, or pain in side, back, or abdomen)

Other side effects may occur that usually do not need medical attention. These side effects may go away during treatment as your body adjusts to the medicine. However, check with your doctor if any of the following side effects continue or are bothersome:

More common

Bitter taste; burning, stinging, or discomfort when medicine is applied; feeling of something in eye; sensitivity of eyes to light

Less common

Dryness of eyes, headache, nausea, unusual tiredness or weakness

Other side effects not listed above may also occur in some patients. If you notice any other effects, check with your doctor.

Developed: 01/31/96

DOXAZOSIN Systemic

A commonly used brand name in the U.S. and Canada is Cardura.

Description

Doxazosin (dox-AY-zoe-sin) belongs to the general class of medicines called antihypertensives. It is used to treat high blood pressure (hypertension).

High blood pressure adds to the workload of the heart and arteries. If it continues for a long time, the heart and arteries may not function properly. This can damage the blood vessels of the brain, heart, and kidneys, resulting in a stroke, heart failure, or kidney failure. High blood pressure may also increase the risk of heart attacks. These

problems may be less likely to occur if blood pressure is controlled.

Doxazosin works by relaxing blood vessels so that blood passes through them more easily. This helps to lower blood pressure.

Doxazosin is also used to treat benign (noncancerous) enlargement of the prostate (benign prostatic hyperplasia [BPH]). Benign enlargement of the prostate is a problem that can occur in men as they get older. The prostate gland is located below the bladder. As the prostate gland enlarges, certain muscles in the gland may become tight and get in the way of the tube that drains urine from the bladder. This can cause problems in urinating, such as a need to urinate often, a weak stream when urinating, or a feeling of not being able to empty the bladder completely.

Doxazosin helps relax the muscles in the prostate and the opening of the bladder. This may help increase the flow of urine and/or decrease the symptoms. However, doxazosin will not shrink the prostate. The prostate may continue to get larger. This may cause the symptoms to become worse over time. Therefore, even though doxazosin may lessen the problems caused by enlarged prostate now, surgery still may be needed in the future.

Doxazosin is available only with your doctor's prescription, in the following dosage form:

Oral
- Tablets (U.S. and Canada)

Before Using This Medicine

In deciding to use a medicine, the risks of taking the medicine must be weighed against the good it will do. This is a decision you and your doctor will make. For doxazosin, the following should be considered:

Allergies—Tell your doctor if you have ever had any unusual or allergic reaction to doxazosin, prazosin, or terazosin. Also tell your health care professional if you are allergic to any other substances, such as foods, preservatives, or dyes.

Pregnancy—Doxazosin has not been studied in pregnant women. However, studies in rabbits have shown that doxazosin given at very high doses may cause death of the fetus. Before taking this medicine, make sure your doctor knows if you are pregnant or if you may become pregnant.

Breast-feeding—It is not known whether doxazosin passes into breast milk. However, doxazosin passes into the milk of rats. Although most medicines pass into breast milk in small amounts, many of them may be used safely while breast-feeding. Mothers who are taking this medicine and who wish to breast-feed should discuss this with their doctor.

Children—Studies on this medicine have been done only in adult patients, and there is no specific information comparing use of doxazosin in children with use in other age groups.

Older adults—Dizziness, lightheadedness, or fainting may be especially likely to occur in elderly patients with high blood pressure, because these patients are usually more sensitive than younger adults to the effects of doxazosin.

Other medicines—Although certain medicines should not be used together at all, in other cases two different medicines may be used together even if an interaction might occur. In these cases, your doctor may want to change the dose, or other precautions may be necessary. Tell your health care professional if you are using any other prescription or nonprescription (over-the-counter [OTC]) medicine.

Other medical problems—The presence of other medical problems may affect the use of doxazosin. Make sure you tell your doctor if you have any other medical problems, especially:
- Kidney disease—Possible increased sensitivity to the effects of doxazosin
- Liver disease—The effects of doxazosin may be increased, which may increase the chance of side effects

Proper Use of This Medicine

For patients *taking this medicine for high blood pressure:*
- In addition to the use of the medicine your doctor has prescribed, treatment for your high blood pressure may include weight control and care in the types of foods you eat, especially foods high in sodium. Your doctor will tell you which of these are most important for you. You should check with your doctor before changing your diet.
- Many patients who have high blood pressure will not notice any signs of the problem. In fact, many may feel normal. It is very important that you *take your medicine exactly as directed* and that you keep your appointments with your doctor even if you feel well.
- Remember that doxazosin will not cure your high blood pressure but it does help control it. Therefore, you must continue to take it as directed if you expect to lower your blood pressure and keep it down. *You may have to take high blood pressure medicine for the rest of your life.* If high blood pressure is not treated, it can cause serious problems such as heart failure, blood vessel disease, stroke, or kidney disease.

For patients *taking this medicine for benign enlargement of the prostate:*
- Remember that doxazosin will not shrink the size of your prostate but it does help to relieve the symptoms of this condition. You may still need to have surgery later.
- It may take up to 2 weeks before your symptoms improve.

To help you remember to take your medicine, try to get into the habit of taking it at the same time each day.

Dosing—The dose of doxazosin will be different for different patients. *Follow your doctor's orders or the directions on the label.* The following information includes only the average doses of doxazosin. *If your dose is different, do not change it* unless your doctor tells you to do so.

The number of tablets that you take depends on the strength of the medicine.

- For *oral* dosage form (tablets):
  - —For benign enlargement of the prostate:
    - Adults—At first, 1 milligram (mg) taken at bedtime. Your doctor may increase your dose up to 8 mg once a day.
  - —For high blood pressure:
    - Adults—1 mg once a day to start. Your doctor may increase your dose slowly to as much as 16 mg once a day.
    - Children—Use and dose must be determined by your doctor.

Missed dose—If you miss a dose of this medicine, take it as soon as possible. However, if it is almost time for your next dose, skip the missed dose and go back to your regular dosing schedule. Do not double doses.

Storage—To store this medicine:

- Keep out of the reach of children.
- Store away from heat and direct light.
- Do not store in the bathroom, near the kitchen sink, or in other damp places. Heat or moisture may cause the medicine to break down.
- Do not keep outdated medicine or medicine no longer needed. Be sure that any discarded medicine is out of the reach of children.

Precautions While Using This Medicine

It is important that your doctor check your progress at regular visits to make sure that this medicine is working properly. This is especially important for elderly patients, who may be more sensitive to the effects of this medicine.

For patients *taking this medicine for high blood pressure:*

- *Do not take other medicines unless they have been discussed with your doctor.* This especially includes over-the-counter (nonprescription) medicines for appetite control, asthma, colds, cough, hay fever, or sinus problems, since they may tend to increase your blood pressure.

Dizziness, lightheadedness, or sudden fainting may occur after you take this medicine, especially when you get up from a lying or sitting position. These effects are more likely to occur when you take the first dose of this medicine. Taking the first dose at bedtime may prevent problems. However, *be especially careful if you need to get up during the night.* These effects may also occur with any doses you take after the first dose. Getting up slowly may help lessen this problem. *If you feel dizzy, lie down so that you do not faint.* Then sit for a few moments before standing to prevent the dizziness from returning.

The dizziness, lightheadedness, or sudden fainting is more likely to occur if you drink alcohol, stand for a long time, exercise, or if the weather is hot. *While you are taking this medicine, be careful to limit the amount of alcohol you drink. Also, use extra care during exercise or hot weather or if you must stand for a long time.*

Doxazosin may cause some people to become drowsy or less alert than they are normally. *Make sure you know how you react to this medicine before you drive, use machines, or do anything else that could be dangerous if you are dizzy, drowsy, or are not alert.* After you have taken several doses of this medicine, these effects should lessen.

Side Effects of This Medicine

Along with its needed effects, a medicine may cause some unwanted effects. Although not all of these side effects may occur, if they do occur they may need medical attention.

Check with your doctor as soon as possible if any of the following side effects occur:

More common

Dizziness or lightheadedness

Less common

Dizziness or lightheadedness when getting up from a lying or sitting position; fainting (sudden); fast and pounding heartbeat; irregular heartbeat; shortness of breath; swelling of feet or lower legs

Other side effects may occur that usually do not need medical attention. These side effects may go away during treatment as your body adjusts to the medicine. However, check with your doctor if any of the following side effects continue or are bothersome:

More common

Headache; unusual tiredness

Less common

Nausea; nervousness, restlessness, unusual irritability; runny nose; sleepiness or drowsiness

Other side effects not listed above may also occur in some patients. If you notice any other effects, check with your doctor.

Revised: 08/02/94
Interim revision: 05/12/95

DOXEPIN Topical

A commonly used brand name in the U.S. and Canada is Zonalon.

Description

Topical doxepin (DOX-e-pin) is used to relieve itching in patients with certain types of eczema. It appears to work by preventing the effects of histamine, which is a substance produced by the body that causes itching.

Doxepin is available only with your doctor's prescription in the following dosage form:

Topical

- Cream (U.S. and Canada)

Before Using This Medicine

In deciding to use a medicine, the risks of using the medicine must be weighed against the good it will do. This is a decision you and your doctor will make. For topical doxepin, the following should be considered:

Allergies—Tell your doctor if you have ever had any unusual or allergic reaction to doxepin. Also tell your health care professional if you are allergic to any other substances, such as foods, preservatives, or dyes.

Pregnancy—Doxepin has not been studied in pregnant women. However, doxepin has not been shown to cause birth defects or other problems in animal studies.

Breast-feeding—Doxepin passes into the breast milk. Oral doxepin has been shown to cause unwanted effects in the breast-fed baby. Therefore, it may be necessary for you to use another medicine or to stop breast-feeding during treatment with topical doxepin. Be sure you have discussed the risk and benefits of the medicine with your doctor.

Children—Studies on this medicine have been done only in adult patients, and there is no specific information comparing use of doxepin in children with use in other age groups.

Older adults—Many medicines have not been studied specifically in older people. Therefore, it may not be known whether they work exactly the same way they do in younger adults. Although there is no specific information comparing use of doxepin in the elderly with use in other age groups, this medicine is not expected to cause different side effects or problems in older people than it does in younger adults.

Other medicines—Although certain medicines should not be used together at all, in other cases two different medicines may be used together even if an interaction might occur. In these cases, your doctor may want to change the dose, or other precautions may be necessary. When you are using topical doxepin, it is especially important that your health care professional know if you are taking any of the following:

- Alcohol or
- Central nervous system (CNS) depressants (medicines that cause drowsiness) or
- Tricyclic antidepressants (medicines for depression)—Drinking alcohol or using these medicines with topical doxepin may cause increased CNS depressant effects such as drowsiness
- Cimetidine (e.g., Tagamet)
- Debrisoquine (e.g., Declinax)
- Dextromethorphan (e.g., Benylin DM)
- Medicines that correct heart rhythm problems, (encainide [e.g., Enkaid], flecainide [e.g., Tambocor], propafenone [e.g., Rythmol], quinidine [e.g., Cardioquin])—Using these medicines with topical doxepin may increase the chance of side effects
- Monoamine oxidase (MAO) inhibitors (furazolidone [e.g., Furoxone], isocarboxazid [e.g., Marplan], phenelzine [e.g., Nardil], procarbazine [e.g., Matulane], selegiline [e.g., Eldepryl], tranylcypromine [e.g., Parnate])—Using topical doxepin while you are taking or within 2 weeks of taking MAO inhibitors may cause sudden high body temperature, excitability, severe convulsions, and even death; however, sometimes some of these medicines may be used together under close supervision by your doctor

Other medical problems—The presence of other medical problems may affect the use of topical doxepin. Make sure you tell your doctor if you have any other medical problems, especially:

- Glaucoma or
- Urinary tract blockage or difficult urination—Using topical doxepin may make these conditions worse

Proper Use of This Medicine

Topical doxepin is *for external use only.* Do not use this medicine orally, do not use it on the eyes, or inside of the vagina.

Use this medicine exactly as directed. Do not use more of it, do not use it more often, and do not use it for more than 8 days. Also, do not apply it to an area of skin larger than recommended by your doctor. To do so may increase the chance of side effects.

Apply a thin layer of doxepin cream to only the affected area(s) of the skin and rub in gently.

To help clear up your skin problem it is very important that you keep using topical doxepin for the full time of treatment. Do not miss any doses.

Do not cover with a bandage or otherwise wrap the area of skin being treated. This may increase the amount of medicine that gets into the bloodstream, thereby increasing the chance of side effects.

Dosing—The dose of topical doxepin will be different for different patients. *Follow your doctor's orders or the directions on the label.* The following information includes only the average dose of topical doxepin. *If your dose is different, do not change it* unless your doctor tells you to do so.

The number of doses you apply each day, the time allowed between doses, and the length of time you use the medicine depend on the severity of the medical problem for which you are using topical doxepin.

- For *topical* dosage form (cream):
  —For itching due to eczema:
    - Adults—Apply a thin layer to the affected area(s) of the skin four times a day. Space the doses or applications at least three or four hours apart. Treatment may be continued for up to eight days.
    - Children—Use and dose must be determined by your doctor.

Missed dose—If you miss a dose of this medicine, apply it as soon as possible. However, if it is almost time for your next dose, skip the missed dose and go back to your regular dosing schedule. Do not double doses.

Storage—To store this medicine:

- Keep out of the reach of children.
- Store away from heat and direct light.
- Keep the medicine from freezing. Do not refrigerate.

• Do not keep outdated medicine or medicine no longer needed. Be sure that any discarded medicine is out of the reach of children.

Precautions While Using This Medicine

If your skin problem does not improve after 8 days or if it becomes worse, check with your doctor.

This medicine will add to the effects of alcohol (alcoholic beverages or other alcohol-containing preparations [e.g., elixirs, cough syrups, tonics]) and other CNS depressants (medicines that slow down the nervous system, possibly causing drowsiness). Some examples of CNS depressants are antihistamines or medicine for hay fever, other allergies, or colds; sedatives, tranquilizers, or sleeping medicine; prescription pain medicine or narcotics; barbiturates; medicine for seizures; muscle relaxants; or anesthetics, including some dental anesthetics. *Check with your doctor before taking any of the above while you are using this medicine.*

Topical doxepin may cause some people to become drowsy. Make sure you know how to react to this medicine before you drive, use machines, or do other jobs that require you to be alert. If too much drowsiness occurs, it may be necessary to use less medicine, use it less often, or stop using it completely. However, check with your doctor first before lessening your dose or stopping use of this medicine.

This medicine may cause dryness of the mouth. For temporary relief, use sugarless gum or candy, or melt bits of ice in your mouth, or use a saliva substitute. However, if your mouth continues to feel dry for more than 2 weeks, check with your medical doctor or dentist. Continuing dryness of the mouth may increase the chance of dental disease, including tooth decay, gum disease, and fungus infections.

Side Effects of This Medicine

Along with its needed effects, a medicine may cause some unwanted effects. Although not all of these side effects may occur, if they do occur they may need medical attention.

Check with your doctor as soon as possible if any of the following side effects occur:

More common

Burning, crawling, or tingling sensation of the skin; swelling at the site of application; worsening of eczema and itching

Rare

Fever

Symptoms of overdose

Abdominal pain and swelling; blurring of vision; convulsions (seizures); decreased awareness or responsiveness; difficulty in breathing; difficulty in passing urine; dizziness, fainting, or lightheadedness; drowsiness; enlarged pupils; excessive dryness of mouth; extremely high fever or body temperature; extremely low body temperature; fast heartbeat; increased or excessive unconscious or jerking movements; incurable constipation; irregular heartbeat; unconsciousness; vomiting; weak pulse

Other side effects may occur that usually do not need medical attention. These side effects may go away during treatment as your body adjusts to the medicine. However, check with your doctor if any of the following side effects continue or are bothersome:

More common

Burning and/or stinging at the site of application; changes in taste; dizziness; drowsiness; dryness and tightness of skin; dryness of mouth and/or lips; emotional changes; headache; thirst; unusual tiredness or weakness

Less common

Anxiety; irritation, tingling, scaling, and cracking of skin; nausea

Other side effects not listed above may also occur in some patients. If you notice any other effects, check with your doctor.

Developed: 05/26/95

DOXORUBICIN Systemic

Some commonly used brand names are:

In the U.S.—

Adriamycin PFS
Adriamycin RDF
Rubex

Generic name product may also be available.

In Canada—

Adriamycin PFS
Adriamycin RDF

Description

Doxorubicin (dox-oh-ROO-bi-sin) belongs to the general group of medicines known as antineoplastics. It is used to treat some kinds of cancer.

Doxorubicin seems to interfere with the growth of cancer cells, which are eventually destroyed. Since the growth of normal body cells may also be affected by doxorubicin, other effects will also occur. Some of these may be serious and must be reported to your doctor. Other effects, like hair loss, may not be serious but may cause concern. Some effects may not occur for months or years after the medicine is used.

Before you begin treatment with doxorubicin, you and your doctor should talk about the good this medicine will do as well as the risks of using it.

Doxorubicin is to be administered only by or under the supervision of your doctor. It is available in the following dosage form:

Parenteral

• Injection (U.S. and Canada)

Before Using This Medicine

In deciding to use a medicine, the risks of taking the medicine must be weighed against the good it will do. This is a decision you and your doctor will make. For doxorubicin, the following should be considered:

Allergies—Tell your doctor if you have ever had any unusual or allergic reaction to doxorubicin or lincomycin.

Pregnancy—There is a chance that this medicine may cause birth defects if either the male or female is receiving it at the time of conception or if it is taken during pregnancy. Studies in rats and rabbits have shown that doxorubicin causes birth defects in the fetus and other problems (including miscarriage). In addition, many cancer medicines may cause sterility which could be permanent. Although sterility has been reported in animals and humans with this medicine, the effect is weaker in humans than in animals.

Be sure that you have discussed these possible effects with your doctor before receiving this medicine. It is best to use some kind of birth control while you are receiving doxorubicin. Tell your doctor right away if you think you have become pregnant while receiving doxorubicin. Before receiving doxorubicin make sure your doctor knows if you are pregnant or if you may become pregnant.

Breast-feeding—Because doxorubicin may cause serious side effects, breast-feeding is generally not recommended while you are receiving it.

Children—Heart problems are more likely to occur in children under 2 years of age, who are usually more sensitive to the effects of doxorubicin.

Older adults—Heart problems are more likely to occur in the elderly, who are usually more sensitive to the effects of doxorubicin. The elderly may also be more likely to have blood problems.

Other medicines—Although certain medicines should not be used together at all, in other cases two different medicines may be used together even if an interaction might occur. In these cases, your doctor may want to change the dose, or other precautions may be necessary. When receiving doxorubicin it is especially important that your health care professional know if you are taking any of the following:

- Amphotericin B by injection (e.g., Fungizone) or
- Antithyroid agents (medicine for overactive thyroid) or
- Azathioprine (e.g., Imuran) or
- Chloramphenicol (e.g., Chloromycetin) or
- Colchicine or
- Flucytosine (e.g., Ancobon) or
- Ganciclovir (e.g., Cytovene) or
- Interferon (e.g., Intron A, Roferon-A) or
- Plicamycin (e.g., Mithracin) or
- Zidovudine (e.g., AZT, Retrovir) or
- If you have ever been treated with radiation or cancer medicines—Doxorubicin may increase the effects of these medicines or radiation therapy on the blood
- Probenecid (e.g., Benemid) or
- Sulfinpyrazone (e.g., Anturane)—Doxorubicin may raise the concentration of uric acid in the blood. Since these medicines are used to lower uric acid levels, they may not work as well in patients receiving doxorubicin

Other medical problems—The presence of other medical problems may affect the use of doxorubicin. Make sure you tell your doctor if you have any other medical problems, especially:

- Chickenpox (including recent exposure) or
- Herpes zoster (shingles)—Risk of severe disease affecting other parts of the body
- Gout or
- Kidney stones—Doxorubicin may increase levels of uric acid in the body, which can cause gout or kidney stones
- Heart disease—Risk of heart problems caused by doxorubicin may be increased
- Liver disease—Effects of doxorubicin may be increased because of slower removal from the body

Proper Use of This Medicine

Doxorubicin is sometimes given together with certain other medicines. If you are receiving a combination of medicines, it is important that you receive each one at the proper time. If you are taking some of these medicines by mouth, ask your health care professional to help you plan a way to take them at the right times.

While you are using this medicine, your doctor may want you to drink extra fluids so that you will pass more urine. This will help prevent kidney problems and keep your kidneys working well.

Doxorubicin often causes nausea and vomiting. However, it is very important that you continue to receive it, even if you begin to feel ill. Ask your health care professional for ways to lessen these effects.

Dosing—The dose of doxorubicin will be different for different patients. The dose that is used may depend on a number of things, including what the medicine is being used for, the patient's body size, and whether or not other medicines are also being taken. *If you are receiving doxorubicin at home, follow your doctor's orders or the directions on the label.* If you have any questions about the proper dose of doxorubicin, ask your doctor.

Precautions While Using This Medicine

It is very important that your doctor check your progress at regular visits to make sure that this medicine is working properly and to check for unwanted effects.

While you are being treated with doxorubicin, and after you stop treatment with it, *do not have any immunizations (vaccinations) without your doctor's approval.* Doxorubicin may lower your body's resistance, and there is a chance you might get the infection the immunization is meant to prevent. In addition, other persons living in your household should not take oral polio vaccine since there is a chance they could pass the polio virus on to you. Also, avoid persons who have taken oral polio vaccine. Do not get close to them, and do not stay in the same room with them for very long. If you cannot take these precautions, you should consider wearing a protective face mask that covers the nose and mouth.

Doxorubicin can temporarily lower the number of white blood cells in your blood, increasing the chance of getting an infection. It can also lower the number of platelets,

which are necessary for proper blood clotting. If this occurs, there are certain precautions you can take, especially when your blood count is low, to reduce the risk of infection or bleeding:

- If you can, avoid people with infections. *Check with your doctor immediately* if you think you are getting an infection or if you get a fever or chills, cough or hoarseness, lower back or side pain, or painful or difficult urination.
- *Check with your doctor immediately* if you notice any unusual bleeding or bruising; black, tarry stools; blood in urine or stools; or pinpoint red spots on your skin.
- Be careful when using a regular toothbrush, dental floss, or toothpick. Your medical doctor, dentist, or nurse may recommend other ways to clean your teeth and gums. Check with your medical doctor before having any dental work done.
- Do not touch your eyes or the inside of your nose unless you have just washed your hands and have not touched anything else in the meantime.
- Be careful not to cut yourself when you are using sharp objects such as a safety razor or fingernail or toenail cutters.
- Avoid contact sports or other situations where bruising or injury could occur.

If doxorubicin accidentally seeps out of the vein into which it is injected, it may damage some tissues and cause scarring. *Tell the doctor or nurse right away if you notice redness, pain, or swelling at the place of injection.*

Side Effects of This Medicine

Along with its needed effects, a medicine may cause some unwanted effects. Although not all of these side effects may occur, if they do occur they may need medical attention.

Also, because of the way these medicines act on the body, there is a chance that they might cause other unwanted effects that may not occur until months or years after the medicine is used. These delayed effects may include certain types of cancer, such as leukemia. Discuss these possible effects with your doctor.

Check with your doctor or nurse immediately if any of the following side effects occur:

Less common

Cough or hoarseness; fast or irregular heartbeat; fever or chills; lower back or side pain; pain at place of injection; painful or difficult urination; shortness of breath; swelling of feet and lower legs

Rare

Black, tarry stools; blood in urine; pinpoint red spots on skin; unusual bleeding or bruising; wheezing

Check with your health care professional as soon as possible if any of the following side effects occur:

More common

Sores in mouth and on lips

Less common

Darkening or redness of skin (after x-ray treatment); joint pain; red streaks along injected vein

Rare

Skin rash or itching

Other side effects may occur that usually do not need medical attention. These side effects may go away during treatment as your body adjusts to the medicine. Also, your health care professional may be able to tell you about ways to prevent or reduce some of these side effects. Check with your health care professional if any of the following side effects continue or are bothersome or if you have any questions about them:

More common

Nausea and vomiting

Less common

Darkening of soles, palms, or nails; diarrhea

Doxorubicin causes the urine to turn reddish in color, which may stain clothes. This is not blood. It is to be expected and only lasts for 1 or 2 days after each dose is given.

This medicine often causes a temporary and total loss of hair. After treatment with doxorubicin has ended, normal hair growth should return.

After you stop receiving doxorubicin, it may still produce some side effects that need attention. During this period of time, *check with your doctor or nurse immediately* if you notice any of the following side effects:

Fast or irregular heartbeat; shortness of breath; swelling of feet and lower legs

Other side effects not listed above may also occur in some patients. If you notice any other effects, check with your health care professional.

Revised: 07/11/94
Interim revision: 01/19/95

DRONABINOL Systemic

A commonly used brand name in the U.S. and Canada is Marinol. Another commonly used name is delta-9-tetrahydrocannabinol (THC).

Description

Dronabinol (droe-NAB-i-nol) is used to prevent the nausea and vomiting that may occur after treatment with cancer medicines. It is used only when other kinds of medicine for nausea and vomiting do not work. Dronabinol is also used to increase appetite in patients with acquired immunodeficiency syndrome (AIDS).

Dronabinol is available only with your doctor's prescription. Prescriptions cannot be refilled, and you must obtain a new prescription from your doctor each time you need this medicine. It is available in the following dosage form:

Oral

- Capsules (U.S. and Canada)

Before Using This Medicine

In deciding to use a medicine, the risks of taking the medicine must be weighed against the good it will do. This is a decision you and your doctor will make. For dronabinol, the following should be considered:

Allergies—Tell your doctor if you have ever had any unusual or allergic reaction to dronabinol, marijuana products, or sesame oil. Also tell your health care professional if you are allergic to any other substances, such as foods, preservatives, or dyes.

Pregnancy—Studies have not been done in pregnant women. However, studies in animals have shown that dronabinol, given in doses many times the usual human dose, increases the risk of death of the fetus and decreases the number of live babies born.

Breast-feeding—Dronabinol passes into the breast milk. There is a possibility that the baby may become dependent on this medicine.

Children—Although there is no specific information comparing use of dronabinol in children with use in other age groups, the effects that this medicine may have on the mind may be of special concern in children. Children should be watched closely while they are taking this medicine.

Older adults—This medicine has been tested in a limited number of patients up to 82 years of age and has not been shown to cause different side effects or problems in older people than it does in younger adults. However, the effects this medicine may have on the mind may be of special concern in the elderly. Therefore, older people should be watched closely while they are taking this medicine.

Other medicines—Although certain medicines should not be used together at all, in other cases 2 different medicines may be used together even if an interaction might occur. In these cases, your doctor may want to change the dose, or other precautions may be necessary. When you are taking dronabinol, it is especially important that your health care professional know if you are taking any of the following:

- Central nervous system (CNS) depressants (medicine that causes drowsiness) or
- Tricyclic antidepressants (medicine for depression)—Taking these medicines with dronabinol may increase the CNS depressant effects

Other medical problems—The presence of other medical problems may affect the use of dronabinol. Make sure you tell your doctor if you have any other medical problems, especially:

- Alcohol abuse (or history of) or
- Drug abuse or dependence (or history of)—Dependence on dronabinol may develop

- Heart disease or
- High blood pressure (hypertension) or
- Manic depression or
- Schizophrenia—Dronabinol may make the condition worse

Proper Use of This Medicine

Take this medicine only as directed by your physician. Do not take more of it, do not take it more often, and do not take it for a longer time than your doctor ordered. If too much is taken, it may lead to medical problems because of an overdose.

Dosing—The dose of dronabinol will be different for different patients. *Follow your doctor's orders or the directions on the label.* The following information includes only the average doses of dronabinol. *If your dose is different, do not change it* unless your doctor tells you to do so.

The number of capsules that you take depends on the strength of the medicine. Also, *the number of doses you take each day, the time allowed between doses, and the length of time you take the medicine depend on the medical problem for which you are taking dronabinol.*

- For *oral* dosage form (capsules):
  - —For nausea and vomiting caused by cancer medicines:
    - Adults and teenagers—Dose is based on body surface area. Your doctor will tell you how much medicine to take and when to take it.
    - Children—Use and dose must be determined by your doctor.
  - —For increasing appetite in patients with AIDS:
    - Adults and teenagers—To start, 2.5 milligrams (mg) two times a day, taken before lunch and supper. Your doctor may change your dose depending on your condition. However, the dose is usually not more than 20 mg a day.
    - Children—Use and dose must be determined by your doctor.

Missed dose—If you miss a dose of this medicine, take it as soon as you remember. However, if it is almost time for your next dose, skip the missed dose and go back to your regular dosing schedule. *Do not double doses.*

Storage—To store this medicine:

- Keep out of the reach of children. Overdose is very dangerous in young children.
- Store away from heat and direct light.
- Do not store this medicine in the bathroom, near the kitchen sink, or in other damp places. Heat or moisture may cause the medicine to break down.
- Keep this medicine in the refrigerator but keep it from freezing.
- Do not keep outdated medicine or medicine no longer needed. Be sure that any discarded medicine is out of the reach of children.

Precautions While Using This Medicine

Dronabinol will add to the effects of alcohol and other CNS depressants (medicines that slow down the nervous system, possibly causing drowsiness). Some examples of CNS depressants are antihistamines or medicine for hay fever, other allergies, or colds; sedatives, tranquilizers, or sleeping medicine; prescription pain medicines including other narcotics; barbiturates; medicine for seizures; muscle relaxants; or anesthetics, including some dental anesthetics. *Check with your doctor before taking any of the above while you are taking this medicine.*

This medicine may cause some people to become drowsy, dizzy, or lightheaded, or to feel a false sense of well-being. *Make sure you know how you react to this medicine before you drive, use machines, or do anything else that could be dangerous if you are dizzy or are not alert and clearheaded.*

Dizziness, lightheadedness, or fainting may occur, especially when you get up suddenly from a lying or sitting position. Getting up slowly may help lessen this problem.

If you think you or someone else may have taken an overdose of dronabinol, get emergency help at once. Taking an overdose of this medicine or taking alcohol or CNS depressants with this medicine may lead to severe mental effects. Signs of overdose include changes in mood, confusion, hallucinations, mental depression, nervousness or anxiety, and fast or pounding heartbeat.

Side Effects of This Medicine

Along with its needed effects, a medicine may cause some unwanted effects. Although not all of these side effects may occur, if they do occur they may need medical attention.

Check with your health care professional immediately if any of the following side effects occur:

Less common (may also be signs of overdose)

Changes in mood; confusion; fast or pounding heartbeat; hallucinations (seeing, hearing, or feeling things that are not there); mental depression; nervousness or anxiety

Symptoms of overdose

Being forgetful; change in your sense of smell, taste, sight, sound, or touch; change in how fast you think time is passing; constipation; problems in urinating; redness of eyes; slurred speech

Other side effects may occur that usually do not need medical attention. These side effects may go away during treatment as your body adjusts to the medicine. However, check with your doctor if any of the following side effects continue or are bothersome:

More common

Clumsiness or unsteadiness; dizziness; drowsiness; trouble thinking

Less common or rare

Blurred vision or any changes in vision; dryness of mouth; feeling faint or lightheaded; restlessness; unusual tiredness or weakness

Other side effects not listed above may also occur in some patients. If you notice any other effects, check with your doctor.

Revised: 06/07/93

DYPHYLLINE Systemic†

Some commonly used brand names are:

In the U.S.—

Dilor
Dilor-400
Lufyllin
Lufyllin-400

Generic name product may be available.

†Not commercially available in Canada.

Description

Dyphylline (DYE-fi-lin) is used to treat and/or prevent the symptoms of bronchial asthma, chronic bronchitis, and emphysema. It works by opening up the bronchial tubes (air passages of the lungs) and increasing the flow of air through them.

This medicine is available only with your doctor's prescription, in the following dosage forms:

Oral
- Elixir (U.S.)
- Tablets (U.S.)

Parenteral
- Injection (U.S.)

Before Using This Medicine

In deciding to use a medicine, the risks of taking the medicine must be weighed against the good it will do. This is a decision you and your doctor will make. For dyphylline, the following should be considered:

Allergies—Tell your doctor if you have ever had any unusual or allergic reaction to aminophylline, caffeine, dyphylline, oxtriphylline, theobromine, or theophylline. Also tell your health care professional if you are allergic to any other substances, such as foods, preservatives, or dyes.

Pregnancy—Dyphylline has not been studied in pregnant women. Before taking this medicine, make sure your doctor knows if you are pregnant or if you may become pregnant.

Breast-feeding—Dyphylline passes into breast milk. However, this medicine has not been reported to cause problems in nursing babies.

Children—Use of other bronchodilator medicines is preferred.

Older adults—As in younger patients, use of other bronchodilator medicines is preferred. Also, older patients with kidney disease may require a lower dose of dyphylline than do older adults without kidney disease.

Other medicines—Although certain medicines should not be used together at all, in other cases two different medicines may be used together even if an interaction might occur. In these cases, your doctor may want to change the dose, or other precautions may be necessary. When you are taking dyphylline, it is especially important that your health care provider know if you are taking any of the following:

- Beta-blockers including ophthalmics (acebutolol [e.g., Sectral], atenolol [e.g., Tenormin], betaxolol [e.g., Betoptic, Kerlone], bisoprolol [e.g., Zebeta], carteolol [e.g., Cartrol], labetalol [e.g., Normodyne], levobunolol [e.g., Betagan], metipranolol [e.g., OptiPranolol], metoprolol [e.g., Lopressor], nadolol [e.g., Corgard], oxprenolol [e.g., Trasicor], penbutolol [e.g., Levatol], pindolol [e.g., Visken], propranolol [e.g., Inderal], sotalol [e.g., Sotacor], timolol [e.g., Blocadren, Timoptic])—These medicines may prevent dyphylline from working properly

- Probenecid (e.g., Benemid)—This medicine may increase the effects of dyphylline
- Xanthine-derivatives (aminophylline [e.g., Somophyllin], caffeine [e.g., NoDoz], Oxtriphylline [e.g., Choledyl], theophylline [e.g., Somophyllin-T])—The chance of side effects may be increased

Other medical problems—The presence of other medical problems may affect the use of dyphylline. Make sure you tell your doctor if you have any other medical problems, especially:

- Heart or blood vessel disease or
- Stomach ulcer (or history of) or other stomach problems—Dyphylline may make these conditions worse
- Heart failure or
- Kidney disease—The effects of dyphylline may be increased

Proper Use of This Medicine

For patients *taking this medicine by mouth:*

This medicine works best when there is a constant amount in the blood. To help keep the amount constant, dyphylline must be taken at regularly spaced times, as ordered by your doctor. Do not miss any doses.

This medicine also works best when taken with a glass of water on an empty stomach (either 30 minutes to 1 hour before meals or 2 hours after meals). However, in some cases your doctor may want you to take this medicine with meals or right after meals to lessen stomach upset.

Dosing—The dose of dyphylline will be different for different patients. *Follow your doctor's orders or the directions on the label.* The following information includes only the average doses of dyphylline. *If your dose is different, do not change it* unless your doctor tells you to do so.

The number of tablets or teaspoonfuls of elixir that you take depends on the strength of the medicine. Also, *the number of doses you take each day, the time allowed between doses, and the length of time you take the medicine depend on the medical problem for which you are taking dyphylline.*

- *For oral* dosage forms (elixir or tablets):
  - —For asthma, bronchitis, or emphysema:
    - Adults—Dose is based on body weight. The usual dose is 15 milligrams (mg) per kilogram (6.8 mg per pound) of body weight up to four times a day (about six hours apart).
    - Children—Dose must be determined by your doctor.

Missed dose—If you miss a dose of this medicine, take it as soon as possible. However, if it is almost time for your next dose, skip the missed dose and go back to your regular dosing schedule. Do not double doses.

Storage—To store this medicine:

- Keep out of the reach of children.
- Store away from heat and direct light.
- Do not store tablets in the bathroom, near the kitchen sink, or in other damp places. Heat or moisture may cause the medicine to break down.
- Keep the liquid form of this medicine from freezing. Do not refrigerate.
- Do not keep outdated medicine or medicine no longer needed. Be sure that any discarded medicine is out of the reach of children.

Precautions While Using This Medicine

Your doctor should check your progress at regular visits, especially during the first few weeks of your treatment with this medicine.

This medicine may add to the central nervous system (CNS) stimulant effects of caffeine-containing foods or beverages such as chocolate, cocoa, tea, coffee, and cola drinks. *Avoid eating or drinking large amounts of these foods or beverages while using this medicine.* If you have questions about this, check with your doctor.

Before you have any kind of surgery that requires general anesthesia, tell the medical doctor in charge that you are using this medicine.

Side Effects of This Medicine

Along with its needed effects, a medicine may cause some unwanted effects. Although not all of these side effects may occur, if they do occur they may need medical attention.

Check with your doctor as soon as possible if any of the following side effects occur:

Less common

Heartburn; vomiting

Symptoms of overdose

Abdominal pain (continuing or severe); confusion or change in behavior; convulsions (seizures); dark or bloody vomit; diarrhea; fast and irregular heartbeat; fast heartbeat (continuing); nervousness or restlessness (continuing); trembling (continuing)

Other side effects may occur that usually do not need medical attention. These side effects may go away during treatment as your body adjusts to the medicine. However, check with your doctor if any of the following side effects continue or are bothersome:

Less common

Fast heartbeat; headache; increased urination; nausea; nervousness; trembling; trouble in sleeping

Other side effects not listed above may also occur in some patients. If you notice any other effects, check with your doctor.

Developed: 07/10/95

ECONAZOLE Topical

Some commonly used brand names are:

In the U.S.—
Spectazole

In Canada—
Ecostatin

Description

Econazole (e-KONE-a-zole) belongs to the family of medicines called antifungals, which are used to treat infections caused by a fungus. They work by killing the fungus or preventing its growth.

Econazole cream is applied to the skin to treat fungus infections. These include:

- ringworm of the body (tinea corporis);
- ringworm of the foot (tinea pedis; athlete's foot);
- ringworm of the groin (tinea cruris; jock itch);
- tinea versicolor (sometimes called "sun fungus"); and
- certain other fungus infections, such as Candida (Monilia) infections.

Econazole is available only with your doctor's prescription, in the following dosage form:

Topical
- Cream (U.S. and Canada)

Before Using This Medicine

In deciding to use a medicine, the risks of using the medicine must be weighed against the good it will do. This is a decision you and your doctor will make. For topical econazole, the following should be considered:

Allergies—Tell your doctor if you have ever had any unusual or allergic reaction to econazole. Also tell your health care professional if you are allergic to any other substances, such as preservatives or dyes.

Pregnancy—Topical econazole has not been studied in pregnant women. Oral econazole has not been shown to cause birth defects in animal studies; however, it has been shown to cause other problems. Before using this medicine, make sure your doctor knows if you are pregnant or if you may become pregnant.

Breast-feeding—It is not known whether topical econazole passes into the breast milk. This medicine has not been reported to cause problems in nursing babies. However, econazole, when given by mouth, does pass into the milk of rats and has caused problems in the young.

Children—Although there is no specific information comparing use of this medicine in children with use in other age groups, this medicine is not expected to cause different side effects or problems in children than it does in adults.

Older adults—Many medicines have not been studied specifically in older people. Therefore, it may not be known whether they work exactly the same way they do in younger adults. Although there is no specific information comparing use of econazole in the elderly with use in other age groups, this medicine is not expected to cause different side effects or problems in older people than it does in younger adults.

Proper Use of This Medicine

Apply enough econazole to cover the affected and surrounding skin areas, and rub in gently.

Keep this medicine away from the eyes.

When econazole is used to treat certain types of fungus infections of the skin, an occlusive dressing (airtight covering, such as kitchen plastic wrap) should *not* be applied over the medicine. To do so may cause irritation of the skin. *Do not apply an airtight covering over this medicine unless you have been directed to do so by your doctor.*

To help clear up your infection completely, *it is very important that you keep using econazole for the full time of treatment,* even if your symptoms begin to clear up after a few days. Since fungus infections may be very slow to clear up, you may have to continue using this medicine every day for several weeks or more. If you stop using this medicine too soon, your symptoms may return. *Do not miss any doses.*

Dosing—The dose of topical econazole will be different for different patients. *Follow your doctor's orders or the directions on the label.* The following information includes only the average dose of topical econazole. *If your dose is different, do not change it* unless your doctor tells you to do so.

- For *topical* dosage form (cream):
  —For fungus infections:
    - Adults and children—Apply to the affected area(s) of the skin one or two times a day. If you have to use the cream two times a day, apply it in the morning and evening.

Missed dose—If you miss a dose of this medicine, apply it as soon as possible. However, if it is almost time for your next dose, skip the missed dose and go back to your regular dosing schedule.

Storage—To store this medicine:
- Keep out of the reach of children.
- Store away from heat and direct light.
- Keep the medicine from freezing.
- Do not keep outdated medicine or medicine no longer needed. Be sure that any discarded medicine is out of the reach of children.

Precautions While Using This Medicine

If your skin problem does not improve within 2 weeks or more, or if it becomes worse, check with your doctor.

To help clear up your infection completely and to help make sure it does not return, good health habits are also required.

- For patients using econazole for ringworm of the groin (tinea cruris; jock itch):
  —Avoid wearing underwear that is tight-fitting or made from synthetic materials (for example, rayon or nylon). Instead, wear loose-fitting, cotton underwear.
  —Use a bland, absorbent powder (for example, talcum powder) or an antifungal powder (for example, tolnaftate) on the skin. It is best not to use econazole cream or any other antifungal cream at the same time that you use the powder.

These measures will help reduce chafing and irritation and will also help keep the groin area cool and dry.

- For patients using econazole for ringworm of the foot (tinea pedis; athlete's foot):
  —Carefully dry the feet, especially between the toes, after bathing.
  —Avoid wearing socks made from wool or synthetic materials (for example, rayon or nylon). Instead, wear clean, cotton socks and change them daily or more often if the feet sweat freely.
  —Wear well-ventilated shoes (for example, shoes with holes) or sandals.
  —Use a bland, absorbent powder (for example, talcum powder) or an antifungal powder (for example, tolnaftate) between the toes, on the feet, and in socks and shoes freely once or twice a day. It is best not to use econazole cream or any other antifungal cream at the same time that you use the powder.

  These measures will help keep the feet cool and dry.

If you have any questions about this, check with your health care professional.

Side Effects of This Medicine

Along with its needed effects, a medicine may cause some unwanted effects. Although not all of these side effects may occur, if they do occur they may need medical attention.

Check with your doctor as soon as possible if any of the following side effects occur:

Less common

Burning, itching, stinging, redness, or other sign of irritation not present before use of this medicine

Other side effects not listed above may also occur in some patients. If you notice any other effects, check with your doctor.

Revised: 04/14/92
Interim revision: 06/06/94

ENCAINIDE Systemic*†

A commonly used brand name is Enkaid.

*Not commercially available in the U.S.
†Not commercially available in Canada.

Description

Encainide (en-KAY-nide) belongs to the group of medicines known as antiarrhythmics. It is used to correct irregular heartbeats to a normal rhythm.

Encainide produces its helpful effects by slowing nerve impulses in the heart and making the heart tissue less sensitive.

There is a chance that encainide may cause new heart rhythm problems when it is used. Since it has been shown to cause severe problems in some patients, it is only used to treat serious heart rhythm problems. Discuss this possible effect with your doctor.

This medicine is available only from your doctor in the following dosage form:

Oral
- Capsules

Before Using This Medicine

In deciding to use a medicine, the risks of taking the medicine must be weighed against the good it will do. This is a decision you and your doctor will make. For encainide, the following should be considered:

Allergies—Tell your doctor if you have ever had any unusual or allergic reaction to encainide. Also tell your health care professional if you are allergic to any other substances, such as foods, preservatives, or dyes.

Pregnancy—Encainide has not been studied in pregnant women. However, this medicine has not been shown to cause birth defects or other problems in animal studies, but has been shown to reduce fertility in rats. Before taking encainide, make sure your doctor knows if you are pregnant or if you may become pregnant.

Breast-feeding—Encainide passes into the milk of some animals and may also pass into the milk of humans. However, this medicine has not been reported to cause problems in nursing babies.

Children—Studies on this medicine have been done only in adult patients. Therefore, be sure to discuss with your doctor the use of this medicine in children.

Older adults—Many medicines have not been tested in older people. Therefore, it may not be known whether they work exactly the same way they do in younger adults or if they cause different side effects or problems in older people. There is no specific information about the use of encainide in the elderly.

Other medical problems—The presence of other medical problems may affect the use of encainide. Make sure you

tell your doctor if you have any other medical problems, especially:

- Diabetes mellitus—Encainide may raise blood sugar levels
- Kidney disease—Effects of encainide may be increased because of slower removal from the body
- Liver disease—Effects of encainide may be changed
- Recent heart attack—Risk of irregular heartbeats may be increased
- If you have a pacemaker—Encainide may interfere with the pacemaker and require more careful follow-up by the doctor

Proper Use of This Medicine

Take encainide exactly as directed by your doctor, even though you may feel well. Do not take more or less of it than your doctor ordered.

This medicine works best when there is a constant amount in the blood. *To help keep the amount constant, do not miss any doses. Also, it is best to take each dose at evenly spaced times day and night.* For example, if you are to take 3 doses a day, doses should be spaced about 8 hours apart. If you need help in planning the best times to take your medicine, check with your health care professional.

Dosing—The dose of encainide will be different for different patients. *Follow your doctor's orders or the directions on the label.* The following information includes only the average doses of encainide. *If your dose is different, do not change it* unless your doctor tells you to do so.

- For *oral* dosage form (capsules):
  - —For irregular heartbeat:
    - Adults—25 to 50 milligrams (mg) every eight hours.
    - Children—Use and dose must be determined by your doctor.

Missed dose—If you miss a dose of encainide and remember within 4 hours, take it as soon as possible. However, if you do not remember until later, skip the missed dose and go back to your regular dosing schedule. Do not double doses.

Storage—To store this medicine:

- Keep out of the reach of children.
- Store away from heat and direct light.
- Do not store in the bathroom, near the kitchen sink, or in other damp places. Heat or moisture may cause the medicine to break down.
- Do not keep outdated medicine or medicine no longer needed. Be sure that any discarded medicine is out of the reach of children.

Precautions While Using This Medicine

It is important that your doctor check your progress at regular visits to make sure the medicine is working properly. This will allow changes to be made in the amount of medicine you are taking, if necessary.

Your doctor may want you to carry a medical identification card or bracelet stating that you are using this medicine.

Before having any kind of surgery (including dental surgery) or emergency treatment, tell the medical doctor or dentist in charge that you are taking this medicine.

Encainide may cause some people to become dizzy or lightheaded. Make sure you know how you react to this medicine before you drive, use machines, or do anything else that could be dangerous if you are dizzy.

Side Effects of This Medicine

Along with its needed effects, a medicine may cause some unwanted effects. Although not all of these side effects may occur, if they do occur they may need medical attention.

Check with your doctor as soon as possible if any of the following side effects occur:

More common

Chest pain; fast or irregular heartbeat

Rare

Shortness of breath; swelling of feet or lower legs; trembling or shaking

Other side effects may occur that usually do not need medical attention. These side effects may go away during treatment as your body adjusts to the medicine. However, check with your doctor if any of the following side effects continue or are bothersome:

Less common

Blurred or double vision; dizziness; headache; nausea; pain in arms or legs; skin rash; unusual tiredness or weakness

Other side effects not listed above may also occur in some patients. If you notice any other effects, check with your doctor.

Revised: 06/08/93
Interim revision: 01/26/95

ENOXAPARIN Systemic

A commonly used brand name in the U.S. and Canada is Lovenox.

Description

Enoxaparin (e-nox-a-PA-rin) is used to prevent deep venous thrombosis, a condition in which harmful blood clots form in the blood vessels of the legs. This medicine is used for several days after hip or knee replacement surgery, while you are unable to walk. It is during this time that blood clots are most likely to form. Enoxaparin also may be used for other conditions as determined by your doctor.

Enoxaparin is available only with your doctor's prescription, in the following dosage form:

Parenteral

- Injection (U.S. and Canada)

Before Using This Medicine

In deciding to use a medicine, the risks of taking the medicine must be weighed against the good it will do. This is a decision you and your doctor will make. For enoxaparin, the following should be considered:

Allergies—Tell your doctor if you have ever had any unusual or allergic reaction to enoxaparin or to heparin. Also tell your health care professional if you are allergic to any other substances, such as foods, especially pork or pork products, preservatives, or dyes.

Pregnancy—Enoxaparin has not been studied in pregnant women. However, it has not been shown to cause birth defects or other problems in animal studies.

Breast-feeding—It is not known whether this medicine passes into breast milk. Although most medicines pass into breast milk in small amounts, many of them may be used safely while breast-feeding. Mothers who are using this medicine and who wish to breast-feed should discuss this with their doctor.

Children—Studies on this medicine have been done only in adult patients, and there is no specific information comparing use of enoxaparin in children with use in other age groups.

Older adults—This medicine has been tested and has not been shown to cause different side effects or problems in older people than it does in younger adults.

Other medicines—Although certain medicines should not be used together at all, in other cases two different medicines may be used together even if an interaction might occur. In these cases, your doctor may want to change the dose, or other precautions may be necessary. When you are using enoxaparin, it is especially important that your health care professional know if you are taking any of the following:

- Aspirin or
- Divalproex (e.g., Depakote) or
- Inflammation or pain medicine, except narcotics, or
- Plicamycin (e.g., Mithracin) or
- Sulfinpyrazone (e.g., Anturane) or
- Thrombolytic agents or
- Ticlopidine (e.g., Ticlid) or
- Valproic acid (e.g., Depakene)—Using any of these medicines together with enoxaparin may increase the risk of bleeding

Other medical problems—The presence of other medical problems may affect the use of enoxaparin. Make sure you tell your doctor if you have any other medical problems, especially:

- Blood disease or bleeding problems or
- Blood vessel problems or
- Heart infection or
- High blood pressure (hypertension) or
- Kidney disease or
- Liver disease or
- Stomach ulcer (active) or
- Threatened miscarriage—The risk of bleeding may be increased

Also, tell your doctor if you have received enoxaparin or heparin before and had a reaction to either of them called thrombocytopenia, or if new blood clots formed while you were receiving the medicine.

In addition, *tell your doctor if you have recently given birth, fallen or suffered a blow to the body or head, or had medical or dental surgery.* These events may increase the risk of serious bleeding when you are taking enoxaparin.

Proper Use of This Medicine

If you are using enoxaparin at home, your health care professional will teach you how to inject yourself with the medicine. *Be sure to follow the directions carefully. Check with your health care professional if you have any problems using the medicine.*

Put used syringes in a puncture-resistant, disposable container, or dispose of them as directed by your health care professional.

Dosing—The dose of enoxaparin will be different for different patients. *Follow your doctor's orders or the directions on the label.* The following information includes only the average doses of enoxaparin. *If your dose is different, do not change it* unless your doctor tells you to do so.

- For *injection* dosage form:
  - —For prevention of deep venous thrombosis:
    - Adults—30 milligrams (mg) every twelve hours for seven to ten days.
    - Children—Use and dose must be determined by your doctor.

Missed dose—If you miss a dose of this medicine, use it as soon as possible. However, if it is almost time for your next dose, skip the missed dose and go back to your regular dosing schedule. Do not double doses.

Storage—To store this medicine:

- Keep out of the reach of children.
- Store away from heat and direct light.
- Keep the medicine from freezing. Do not refrigerate.
- Do not keep outdated medicine or medicine no longer needed. Be sure that any discarded medicine is out of the reach of children.

Precautions While Using This Medicine

Tell all your medical doctors and dentists that you are using this medicine.

Side Effects of This Medicine

Along with its needed effects, a medicine may cause some unwanted effects. Although not all of these side effects may occur, if they do occur they may need medical attention.

Stop using this medicine and check with your doctor immediately if any of the following side effects occur:

Less common

Blood in urine; bloody or black, tarry stools; bruising; chest discomfort; collection of blood under the skin;

confusion; continuing bleeding or oozing from the nose and/or mouth, or surgical wound; convulsions; coughing up blood; fever; headache; irritability; lightheadedness; moderate to severe pain or numbness in the arms, legs, hands, feet; nosebleed; shortness of breath; swelling of hands and/or feet; unusual bleeding; unusual tiredness or weakness; vomiting of blood or material that looks like coffee grounds

Rare

Chest pain; dizziness or lightheadedness when getting up from a lying or sitting position; fast or irregular heartbeat; skin rash or hives; sudden fainting; swelling of the face, genitals, mouth, or tongue

Other side effects may occur that usually do not need medical attention. These side effects may go away during treatment as your body adjusts to the medicine. However, check with your doctor if any of the following side effects continue or are bothersome:

Less common

Increased menstrual bleeding; irritation, pain, or redness at place of injection; nausea; vomiting

Other side effects not listed above may also occur in some patients. If you notice any other effects, check with your doctor.

Developed: 11/22/93

ENTERAL NUTRITION FORMULAS Systemic

Some commonly used brand names are:

In the U.S.—

Acupep HPF[6]
Advera[2]
Alitraq[6]
Amin-Aid[2]
Attain[7]
Carnation Instant Breakfast[4]
Carnation Instant Breakfast No Sugar Added[4]
Casec[5]
CitriSource[7]
Citrotein[7]
Compleat Modified[1]
Compleat Regular[1]
Comply[7]
Criticare HN[6]
Crucial[2]
Deliver 2.0[7]
DiabetiSource[2]
Elementra[5]
Ensure[7]
Ensure with Fiber[3]
Ensure High Protein[7]
Ensure HN[7]
Ensure Plus[7]
Ensure Plus HN[7]
Entrition Half-Strength[7]
Entrition HN[7]
Fiberlan[3]
Fibersource[3]
Fibersource HN[3]
Glucerna[2]
Glytrol[2,3]
Great Shake[4]
Great Shake Jr.[4]
Hepatic-Aid II[2]
Immun-Aid[2]
Impact[2]
Impact with Fiber[2,3]
Introlan[7]
Introlite[7]
Isocal[7]
Isocal HN[7]
Isolan[7]
Isosource[7]
Isosource HN[7]
IsoSource VHN[3]
Isotein HN[7]
Jevity[3]
Kindercal[3]
Lipisorb[2]
Magnacal[2,7]
MCT Oil[5]
Menu Magic Instant Breakfast[4]
Menu Magic Milk Shake[4]
Meritene[4]
Microlipid[5]
Moducal[5]
Nepro[2]
NuBasics[7]
NuBasics with Fiber[3]
NuBasics Plus[7]
NuBasics VHP[7]
Nutren 1.0[7]
Nutren 1.5[7]
Nutren 2.0[2,7]
Nutren 1.0 with Fiber[3]
NutriHep[2]
Nutrilan[7]
NutriVent[2]
Osmolite[7]
Osmolite HN[7]
Pediasure[7]
Pediasure with Fiber[3]
Peptamen[2,6]
Peptamen Junior[2,6]
Peptamen VHP[2,6]
Perative[2]
Polycose[5]
Pre-Attain[7]
ProBalance[3]
Profiber[3]
ProMod[5]
Promote[7]
Promote with Fiber[3]
Propac Plus[5]
Protain XL[2]
Pulmocare[2]
Reabilan[6]
Reabilan HN[6]
Replete[7]
Replete with Fiber[3]
Resource[7]
Resource Plus[7]
Respalor[2]
SandoSource Peptide[6]
206 Shake[4]
Sumacal[5]
Suplena[2]
Sustacal[7]
Sustacal Basic[7]
Sustacal with Fiber[3]
Sustacal Plus[7]
Sustagen[4]
Tasty Shake[4]
Tolerex[6]
TraumaCal[2]
Traum-Aid HBC[2]
Travasorb HN[6]
Travasorb Renal Diet[2]
Travasorb STD[6]
TwoCal HN[7]
Ultracal[3]
Ultralan[7]
Vital High Nitrogen[6]
Vitaneed[1]
Vivonex Pediatric[6]
Vivonex Plus[6]
Vivonex T.E.N.[6]

In Canada—

CitriSource[7]
Citrotein[2]
Compleat Modified[1]
Enercal[7]
Ensure[7]
Ensure with Fiber[3]
Ensure High Protein[7]
Ensure Plus[7]
Glucerna[2]
Great Shake Jr.[4]
Impact[2]
Isosource[7]
Isosource HN[7]
Jevity[3]
MCT Oil[5]
Meritene[4]
Nepro[2]
NutriSource[3]
NutriSource HN[3]
Osmolite HN[7]
Pediasure[7]
Polycose[5]
ProMod[5]
Pulmocare[2]
Resource[7]
Resource Plus[7]
SandoSource Peptide[6]
Suplena[2]
Sustagen[4]
Tolerex[6]
Vital High Nitrogen[6]
Vivonex Pediatric[6]
Vivonex Plus[6]
Vivonex T.E.N.[6]

Note: For quick reference, the following enteral nutrition formulas are numbered to match the corresponding brand names.

This information applies to the following enteral nutrition formulas:

1. Enteral nutrition formulas, blenderized
2. Enteral nutrition formulas, disease-specific
3. Enteral nutrition formulas, fiber-containing
4. Enteral nutrition formulas, milk-based
5. Enteral nutrition formulas, modular
6. Enteral nutrition formulas, monomeric (elemental)
7. Enteral nutrition formulas, polymeric

Description

Enteral nutrition formulas are used as nutritional replacements for patients who are unable to get enough nutrients in their diet. These formulas are taken by mouth or through a feeding tube and are used by the body for energy and to form substances needed for normal body functions.

Patients with the following conditions may be more likely to need enteral feedings:

- Acquired immunodeficiency syndrome (AIDS)
- Burns
- Cancer
- Infections, prolonged
- Kidney problems
- Liver problems
- Lung problems
- Pancreas problems
- Stomach problems
- Surgery
- Trauma
- Vomiting, prolonged

Enteral nutrition formulas are available without a prescription. However, they should only be used under medical supervision.

The benefits of enteral formulas in healthy people have not been proven.

Enteral nutrition formulas are available in the following dosage forms:

Oral

Blenderized Enteral Nutrition
- Oral solution (U.S. and Canada)

Disease-specific Enteral Nutrition
- Oral solution (U.S. and Canada)
- Powder for solution (U.S. and Canada)

Fiber-containing Enteral Nutrition
- Oral solution (U.S. and Canada)

Milk-based Enteral Nutrition
- Oral solution (U.S. and Canada)
- Powder for solution (U.S. and Canada)

Modular Enteral Nutrition
- Oral solution (U.S. and Canada)
- Oral powder (U.S. and Canada)

Monomeric Enteral Nutrition
- Oral solution (U.S. and Canada)
- Powder for solution (U.S.)

Polymeric Enteral Nutrition
- Oral solution (U.S. and Canada)
- Powder for solution (U.S.)

Before Using This Enteral Nutrition Formula

If you are taking any of these enteral nutrition formulas without a prescription, carefully read and follow any precautions on the label. For enteral nutrition formulas, the following should be considered:

Allergies—Tell your doctor if you have ever had any unusual or allergic reaction to any of the ingredients listed for your enteral nutrition formula. Also tell your health care professional if you are allergic to any other substances, such as foods, preservatives, or dyes.

Pregnancy—Studies on effects in pregnancy have not been done in either humans or animals.

Breast-feeding—This enteral nutrition formula has not been reported to cause problems in nursing babies.

Children—Caution should be used when giving enteral feedings to children less than one year of age. Very young children may not be able to eliminate the feeding from the body. Although there is no specific information about the use of enteral feedings in older children, it is not expected to cause different side effects or problems in these children than it does in adults.

Older adults—Older adults may be at risk of developing problems related to the use of a nasogastric tube (tube going through the nose into the stomach), such as aspiration (sucking fluid into the lungs) or removing the nasogastric tube. The enteral feeding itself has not been shown to cause different side effects or problems in older people than it does in younger adults.

Medicines—Although certain medications and enteral nutrition formulas should not be used together at all, in other cases they may be used together even if an interaction might occur. In these cases, your doctor may want to change the dose, or other precautions may be necessary. Tell your health care professional if you are taking any prescription or nonprescription (over-the-counter [OTC]) medicine.

Other medical problems—The presence of other medical problems may affect the use of enteral feedings. Make sure you tell your doctor if you have any other medical problems, especially:

- Breathing problems or
- Dehydration or
- Diabetes mellitus (sugar diabetes) or
- Diarrhea or
- Heart problems or
- Hyperglycemia (high levels of sugar in the blood) or
- Hyperlipidemia or
- Lactose intolerance or
- Liver problems or
- Pancreas problems—Enteral feedings may make these conditions worse; your doctor may recommend a special formula for your condition
- Intestine problems or
- Stomach problems—These problems may prevent enteral formulas from being absorbed properly
- Kidney problems—Higher blood levels of certain ingredients of the enteral feeding may result, and a smaller amount of enteral feeding may be needed.
- Malnutrition, severe—Heart and nerve problems have been reported when feeding a patient who is severely malnourished; enteral formula may need to be used in smaller amounts

Proper Use of This Enteral Nutrition Formula

Your enteral feeding may be given by mouth or by a feeding tube. Use the amount recommended by your doctor.

For patients taking the *oral liquid* form of enteral nutrition:

- This preparation is in ready-to-use form. No dilution is needed unless directed by your physician.
- Shake the preparation well before opening. Refrigerate after opening, out of the reach of children. Most formulas can be kept in the refrigerator for 1 to 2 days. Check the label of your product.

For patients using the *powder* form of this preparation:
- For mixing or other use, follow carefully the instructions on the package.
- Any unused solution should be kept in the refrigerator, out of the reach of children. Most formulas can be kept in the refrigerator for 1 to 2 days. Check the label of your product.

Storage—To store the unopened container:
- Keep out of the reach of children.
- Store away from heat and direct light.
- Do not store in the bathroom, near the kitchen sink, or in other damp places. Heat or moisture may cause the enteral nutrition formula to break down.
- Keep the enteral nutrition formula from freezing. Do not refrigerate, unless the product has been opened or mixed.
- Do not keep outdated enteral nutrition formulas or those no longer needed. Be sure that any discarded enteral nutrition formula is out of the reach of children.

Precautions While Using This Enteral Nutrition Formula

Enteral feedings must be handled properly to protect them from bacteria. Enteral feedings should be used for no more than 12 hours at room temperature and then should be discarded.

If you are taking your enteral feeding through a tube, enteral formulas that are too thick may clog the feeding tube. If this happens, check with your doctor, nurse, dietitian, or pharmacist.

Side Effects of This Enteral Nutrition Formula

Some problems may result from improper use of an enteral formula or use of the incorrect formula in your condition. Check with your doctor if any of the following problems occur:

More common

Confusion; convulsions (seizures); decrease in urine volume; dryness of mouth; frequent urination; increased thirst; irregular heartbeat; mood or mental changes; muscle cramps or pain; numbness or tingling in hands, feet, or lips; respiratory distress, shortness of breath or difficulty breathing; unexplained nervousness; unusual tiredness or weakness; weakness or heaviness of legs; weak pulse

Other problems may occur that usually do not need medical attention. They may go away during treatment as your body adjusts to the enteral nutrition formula. However, check with your doctor if any of the following side effects continue or are bothersome:

More common

Constipation; diarrhea; nausea or vomiting

Other side effects not listed above may also occur in some patients. If you notice any other effects, check with your doctor.

Developed: 08/31/93
Interim revision: 08/03/95

EPINEPHRINE Ophthalmic

Some commonly used brand names are:

In the U.S.—

Epifrin[1] Eppy/N[2]
Epinal[2] Glaucon[1]

In Canada—

Epifrin[1]

Note: For quick reference, the following medicines are numbered to match the corresponding brand names.

This information applies to the following medicines:

1. Epinephrine (ep-i-NEF-rin)‡
2. Epinephryl Borate (ep-i-NEF-rill BOR-ate)

‡Generic name product may also be available in the U.S.

Description

Ophthalmic epinephrine is used to treat certain types of glaucoma. It may also be used in eye surgery.

This medicine is available only with your doctor's prescription, in the following dosage forms:

Ophthalmic

Epinephrine
- Ophthalmic solution (eye drops) (U.S. and Canada)

Epinephryl Borate
- Ophthalmic solution (eye drops) (U.S.)

Before Using This Medicine

In deciding to use a medicine, the risks of taking the medicine must be weighed against the good it will do. This is a decision you and your doctor will make. For epinephrine, the following should be considered:

Allergies—Tell your doctor if you have ever had any unusual or allergic reaction to epinephrine. Also tell your health care professional if you are allergic to any other substances, such as sulfites or other preservatives.

Pregnancy—Ophthalmic epinephrine may be absorbed into the body. However, studies on effects in pregnancy have not been done in either humans or animals.

Breast-feeding—Ophthalmic epinephrine may be absorbed into the body. However, it is not known whether epinephrine passes into the breast milk.

Children—Studies on this medicine have been done only in adult patients, and there is no specific information comparing use of this medicine in children with use in other age groups.

Older adults—Many medicines have not been studied specifically in older people. Therefore, it may not be known whether they work exactly the same way they do in younger adults. Although there is no specific information comparing use of this medicine in the elderly with use in other age groups, this medicine is not expected to cause different side effects or problems in older people than it does in younger adults.

Other medicines—Although certain medicines should not be used together at all, in other cases two different medicines may be used together even if an interaction might occur. In these cases, your doctor may want to change the dose, or other precautions may be necessary. Tell your health care professional if you are using any other prescription or nonprescription (over-the-counter [OTC]) medicine.

Other medical problems—The presence of other medical problems may affect the use of epinephrine. Make sure you tell your doctor if you have any other medical problems, especially:

- Bronchial asthma or
- Diabetes mellitus (sugar diabetes) or
- Eye disease (other) or
- Heart or blood vessel disease or
- High blood pressure or
- Overactive thyroid—Epinephrine may make the condition worse
- Dental surgery on gums—Dental surgery may include the use of epinephrine in topical or injection form. Use of ophthalmic epinephrine during this time may increase blood levels of the medicine and increase the chance of side effects

Proper Use of This Medicine

Use this medicine only as directed. Do not use more of it and do not use it more often than your doctor ordered. To do so may increase the chance of too much medicine being absorbed into the body and the chance of side effects.

To use:

- First, wash your hands. Tilt the head back and, pressing your finger gently on the skin just beneath the lower eyelid, pull the lower eyelid away from the eye to make a space. Drop the medicine into this space. Let go of the eyelid and gently close the eyes. Do not blink. Keep the eyes closed and apply pressure to the inner corner of the eye with your finger for 1 or 2 minutes to allow the medicine to be absorbed by the eye.
- Immediately after using the eye drops, wash your hands to remove any medicine that may be on them.
- To keep the medicine as germ-free as possible, do not touch the applicator tip to any surface (including the eye). Also, keep the container tightly closed.

For patients using *epinephrine ophthalmic solution:*

- Do not use if the solution turns pinkish or brownish in color, or if it becomes cloudy.

For patients using *epinephryl borate ophthalmic solution:*

- The color of this solution may vary from colorless to amber yellow. Do not use if the solution turns dark brown or becomes cloudy.

Dosing—The dose of ophthalmic epinephrine will be different for different patients. *Follow your doctor's orders or the directions on the label.* The following information includes only the average doses of ophthalmic epinephrine. *If your dose is different, do not change it* unless your doctor tells you to do so.

For epinephrine and epinephryl borate

- For *ophthalmic solution (eye drops)* dosage forms:
  —For glaucoma:
    - Adults and teenagers—One drop one or two times a day.
    - Children—Use and dose must be determined by your doctor.

Missed dose—If you miss a dose of this medicine, apply the missed dose as soon as possible. However, if it is almost time for your next dose, skip the missed dose and go back to your regular dosing schedule. Do not double doses.

Storage—To store this medicine:

- Keep out of the reach of children.
- Store away from heat and direct light.
- Keep the medicine from freezing.
- Do not keep outdated medicine or medicine no longer needed. Be sure that any discarded medicine is out of the reach of children.

Precautions While Using This Medicine

Your doctor should check your eye pressure at regular visits.

This medicine may cause blurred vision or other vision problems for a short time after it is applied. If any of these occur, *do not drive, use machines, or do anything else that could be dangerous if you are not able to see well.*

Side Effects of This Medicine

Along with its needed effects, a medicine may cause some unwanted effects. Although not all of these side effects may occur, if they do occur they may need medical attention.

Check with your doctor as soon as possible if any of the following side effects occur:

Less common

Blurred or decreased vision

Symptoms of too much medicine being absorbed into the body

Fast, irregular, or pounding heartbeat; feeling faint; increased sweating; paleness; trembling

Other side effects may occur that usually do not need medical attention. These side effects may go away during treatment as your body adjusts to the medicine. However, check with your doctor if any of the following side effects continue or are bothersome:

More common

Headache or browache; stinging, burning, redness, or other eye irritation; watering of eyes

Less common
Eye pain or ache

Other side effects not listed above may also occur in some patients. If you notice any other effects, check with your doctor.

Revised: 11/28/94

EPOETIN Systemic

Some commonly used brand names are:

In the U.S.—
Epogen
Procrit

In Canada—
Eprex

Other commonly used names are human erythropoietin, recombinant; EPO; and r-HuEPO.

Description

Epoetin (eh-POH-ee-tin) is a man-made version of human erythropoietin (EPO). EPO is produced naturally in the body, mostly by the kidneys. It stimulates the bone marrow to produce red blood cells. If the body does not produce enough EPO, severe anemia can occur. This often occurs in people whose kidneys are not working properly. Epoetin is used to treat severe anemia in these people.

Epoetin may also be used to prevent or treat anemia caused by other conditions, as determined by your doctor.

Epoetin is given by injection. It is available only with your doctor's prescription and is available in the following dosage form:

Parenteral
- Injection (U.S. and Canada)

Before Using This Medicine

In deciding to use a medicine, the risks of taking the medicine must be weighed against the good it will do. This is a decision you and your doctor will make. For epoetin, the following should be considered:

Allergies—Tell your doctor if you have ever had any unusual or allergic reaction to epoetin or to human albumin. Also tell your health care professional if you are allergic to any other substances, such as foods, preservatives, or dyes.

Pregnancy—Epoetin has not been reported to cause birth defects or other problems in humans. However, it did cause problems, including unwanted effects on the bones and spine, in some animal studies.

Breast-feeding—It is not known whether epoetin passes into the breast milk. However, it has not been reported to cause problems in nursing babies.

Children—There is no specific information about the use of epoetin in children up to 12 years of age.

Older adults—Epoetin has been given to elderly people. However, there is no specific information about whether epoetin works the same way it does in younger adults or whether it causes different side effects or problems in older people.

Other medicines—Although certain medicines should not be used together at all, in other cases two different medicines may be used together even if an interaction might occur. In these cases, your doctor may want to change the dose, or other precautions may be necessary. When you are taking epoetin, it is important that your health care professional know if you are taking any other prescription or nonprescription (over-the-counter [OTC]) medicine.

Other medical problems—The presence of other medical problems may affect the use of epoetin. Make sure you tell your doctor if you have any other medical problems, especially:

- Blood clots (history of) or other problems with the blood or
- Heart or blood vessel disease or
- High blood pressure—The chance of side effects may be increased
- Bone problems or
- Sickle cell anemia—Epoetin may not work properly
- Seizures (history of)—The chance of seizures may be increased

Proper Use of This Medicine

Epoetin is usually given by a health care professional after a dialysis treatment. However, medicines given by injection are sometimes used at home. If you will be using epoetin at home, your health care professional will teach you how the injections are to be given. You will also have a chance to practice giving them. *Be certain that you understand exactly how the medicine is to be injected.*

Dosing—The dose of epoetin will be different for different patients. *Follow your doctor's orders or the directions on the label.* The following information includes only the average doses of epoetin. *If your dose is different, do not change it* unless your doctor tells you to do so.

- For *injection* dosage form:
  - —For severe anemia:
    - Adults and teenagers—Dose is based on body weight and must be determined by your doctor. The usual dose is 50 to 100 Units per kilogram (kg) (23 to 45 Units per pound) of body weight three times a week, injected into a vein or under the skin. Your doctor may then gradually decrease the dose by 25 Units per kg (11 Units per pound) of body weight every four weeks or more until the lowest effective dose is reached.
    - Children up to 12 years of age—Dose must be determined by your doctor.

Missed dose—If you miss a dose of this medicine, use it as soon as possible. However, if it is almost time for your next dose, skip the missed dose and go back to your regular dosing schedule. Do not double doses.

Storage—To store this medicine:
- Keep out of the reach of children.
- Store in the refrigerator. However, keep the medicine from freezing.
- Do not keep outdated medicine or medicine no longer needed. Be sure that any discarded medicine is out of the reach of children.

Precautions While Using This Medicine

Epoetin sometimes causes convulsions (seizures), especially during the first 90 days of treatment. During this time, it is best to avoid driving, operating heavy machinery, or other activities that could cause a serious injury if a seizure occurs while you are performing them.

People with severe anemia usually feel very tired and sick. When epoetin begins to work, usually in about 6 weeks, most people start to feel better. Some people are able to be more active. However, epoetin only corrects anemia. It has no effect on kidney disease or any other medical problem that needs regular medical attention. Therefore, even if you are feeling much better, *it is very important that you do not miss any appointments with your doctor or any dialysis treatments.*

Many people with kidney problems need to be on a special diet. Also, people with high blood pressure (which may be caused by kidney disease or by epoetin treatment) may need to be on a special diet and/or to take medicine to keep their blood pressure under control. After their anemia has been corrected, some people feel so much better that they want to eat more than before. To keep your kidney disease or your high blood pressure from getting worse, *it is very important that you follow your special diet and take your medicines regularly,* even if you are feeling better.

In addition to epoetin, your body needs iron to make red blood cells. Your doctor may direct you to take iron supplements. He or she may also direct you to take certain vitamins that help the iron work better. *Be sure to follow your doctor's orders carefully,* because epoetin will not work properly if there is not enough iron in your body.

Side Effects of This Medicine

Along with its needed effects, a medicine may cause some unwanted effects. Although not all of these side effects may occur, if they do occur they may need medical attention.

Check with your doctor immediately if any of the following side effects occur:

More common
Chest pain

Less common
Convulsions (seizures); shortness of breath

Also, check with your doctor as soon as possible if any of the following side effects occur:

More common
Fast heartbeat; headache; increased blood pressure; swelling of face, fingers, ankles, feet, or lower legs; vision problems; weight gain

Rare
Skin rash or hives

Other side effects may occur that usually do not need medical attention. These side effects may go away during treatment as your body adjusts to the medicine. Epoetin sometimes causes an influenza-like reaction, with symptoms such as muscle aches, bone pain, chills, shivering, and sweating, occurring about 1 or 2 hours after an injection. These symptoms usually go away within 12 hours. However, check with your doctor if this influenza-like reaction or any of the following side effects continue or are bothersome:

More common
Bone pain; diarrhea; muscle weakness (severe); nausea or vomiting; tiredness

Other side effects not listed above may also occur in some patients. If you notice any other effects, check with your doctor.

Additional Information

For patients receiving epoetin who do not have anemia caused by kidney disease:
- The information about the importance of keeping dialysis appointments and following a special diet for people with kidney problems does not apply to you. However, your doctor may have other special directions for you to follow. Be sure to follow these directions carefully, even if you feel much better after receiving epoetin for a while.

Revised: 07/07/92
Interim revision: 05/02/94

ERGOLOID MESYLATES Systemic

Some commonly used brand names are:

In the U.S.—
Gerimal
Hydergine LC
Hydergine
Generic name product may also be available.

In Canada—
Hydergine
Another commonly used name is dihydrogenated ergot alkaloids.

Description

Ergoloid mesylates (ER-goe-loid MESS-i-lates) belongs to the group of medicines known as ergot alkaloids. It is used to treat some mood, behavior, or other problems that may be due to changes in the brain from Alzheimer's disease or multiple small strokes.

This medicine is different from other ergot alkaloids such as ergotamine and methysergide. It is not useful for treating migraine headache. The exact way ergoloid mesylates acts on the body is not known.

This medicine is available only with your doctor's prescription, in the following dosage forms:

Oral
- Capsules (U.S.)
- Oral solution (U.S.)
- Tablets (U.S. and Canada)

Sublingual (under-the-tongue)
- Tablets (U.S.)

Before Using This Medicine

In deciding to use a medicine, the risks of taking the medicine must be weighed against the good it will do. This is a decision you and your doctor will make. For ergoloid mesylates, the following should be considered:

Allergies—Tell your doctor if you have ever had any unusual or allergic reaction to ergot alkaloids. Also tell your health care professional if you are allergic to any other substances, such as foods, preservatives, or dyes.

Other medicines—Although certain medicines should not be used together at all, in other cases 2 different medicines may be used together even if an interaction might occur. In these cases, your doctor may want to change the dose, or other precautions may be necessary. Tell your health care professional if you are taking any other prescription or nonprescription (over-the-counter [OTC]) medicine.

Other medical problems—The presence of other medical problems may affect the use of ergoloid mesylates. Make sure you tell your doctor if you have any other medical problems, especially:
- Liver disease—Higher blood levels of ergoloid mesylates may occur, increasing the chance of side effects
- Low blood pressure or
- Other mental problems or
- Slow heartbeat—Ergoloid mesylates may make the condition worse

Proper Use of This Medicine

Take this medicine only as directed by your doctor. Do not take more or less of it, and do not take it more often or for a longer period of time than your doctor ordered. To do so may increase the chance of unwanted effects.

For patients taking the *sublingual (under-the-tongue) tablets:*
- Dissolve the tablet under your tongue. The sublingual tablet should not be chewed or swallowed, since it works much faster when absorbed through the lining of the mouth. Do not eat, drink, or smoke while a tablet is dissolving.

Dosing—The dose of ergoloid mesylates will be different for different patients. *Follow your doctor's orders or the directions on the label.* The following information includes only the average doses of ergoloid mesylates. *If your dose is different, do not change it* unless your doctor tells you to do so.

The number of tablets or milliliters of oral solution that you take depends on the strength of the medicine. Also, *the number of doses you take each day, the time allowed between doses, and the length of time you take the medicine depend on the medical problem for which you are taking ergoloid mesylates.*
- For *oral* dosage forms (capsules, tablets, sublingual tablets, or oral solution):
  —Adults: 1 to 2 milligrams (mg) three times a day.

Missed dose—If you miss a dose of this medicine, skip the missed dose and go back to your regular dosing schedule. Do not double doses. If you have any questions about this, or if you miss two or more doses in a row, check with your doctor.

Storage—To store this medicine:
- Keep out of the reach of children.
- Store away from heat and direct light.
- Do not store in the bathroom, near the kitchen sink, or in other damp places. Heat or moisture may cause the medicine to break down.
- Keep the oral solution from freezing.
- Do not keep outdated medicine or medicine no longer needed. Be sure that any discarded medicine is out of the reach of children.

Precautions While Using This Medicine

It is important that your doctor check your progress at regular visits to make sure this medicine is working and to check for unwanted effects.

It may take several weeks for this medicine to work. *However, do not stop taking this medicine without first checking with your doctor.*

Side Effects of This Medicine

Along with its needed effects, a medicine may cause some unwanted effects. Although not all of these side effects may occur, if they do occur they may need medical attention.

Check with your doctor as soon as possible if any of the following side effects occur:

Less common or rare

Dizziness or lightheadedness when getting up from a lying or sitting position; drowsiness; skin rash; slow pulse

Signs and symptoms of overdose

Blurred vision; dizziness; fainting; flushing; headache; loss of appetite; nausea or vomiting; stomach cramps; stuffy nose

Other side effects may occur that usually do not need medical attention. These side effects may go away during treatment as your body adjusts to the medicine. However,

check with your doctor if any of the following side effects continue or are bothersome:

Less common or rare

Soreness under tongue (with sublingual use)

Other side effects not listed above may also occur in some patients. If you notice any other effects, check with your doctor.

Revised: 04/16/93

ERGONOVINE/METHYLERGONOVINE Systemic

Some commonly used brand names are:

In the U.S.—

Ergotrate[1]
Methergine[2]

In Canada—

Ergotrate Maleate[1]

Other commonly used names are:

Ergometrine[1] Methylergometrine[2]

Note: For quick reference, the following medicines are numbered to match the corresponding brand names.

This information applies to the following medicines:

1. Ergonovine (er-goe-NOE-veen)§
2. Methylergonovine (meth-ill-er-goe-NOE-veen)†

†Not commercially available in Canada.
§Generic name product may also be available in Canada.

Description

Ergonovine and methylergonovine belong to the group of medicines known as ergot alkaloids. These medicines are usually given to stop excessive bleeding that sometimes occurs after abortion or a baby is delivered. They work by causing the muscle of the uterus to contract.

Ergonovine and methylergonovine may also be used for other conditions as determined by your doctor.

These medicines are available only on prescription and are to be administered only by or under the supervision of your doctor. They are available in the following dosage forms:

Oral

Ergonovine
- Tablets (U.S. and Canada)

Methylergonovine
- Tablets (U.S.)

Parenteral

Ergonovine
- Injection (U.S. and Canada)

Methylergonovine
- Injection (U.S.)

Before Using This Medicine

In deciding to use a medicine, the risks of taking the medicine must be weighed against the good it will do. This is a decision you and your doctor will make. For ergonovine and methylergonovine, the following should be considered:

Allergies—Tell your doctor if you have ever had any unusual or allergic reaction to ergonovine, methylergonovine, or other ergot medicines. Also tell your health care professional if you are allergic to any other substances, such as foods, preservatives, or dyes.

Breast-feeding—This medicine passes into the breast milk and may cause unwanted effects, such as vomiting; decreased circulation in the hands, lower legs, and feet; diarrhea; weak pulse; unstable blood pressure; or convulsions (seizures) in infants of mothers taking large doses.

Children—Although there is no specific information comparing use of ergonovine or methylergonovine in children with use in other age groups, these medicines are not expected to cause different problems in children than they do in adults.

Older adults—Many medicines have not been studied specifically in older people. Therefore, it may not be known whether they work exactly the same way they do in younger adults or if they cause different side effects or problems in older people. There is no specific information comparing use of ergonovine or methylergonovine in the elderly with use in other age groups.

Other medicines—Although certain medicines should not be used together at all, in other cases two different medicines may be used together even if an interaction might occur. In these cases, your doctor may want to change the dose, or other precautions may be necessary. When you are taking ergonovine or methylergonovine it is especially important that your health care professional know if you are taking any of the following:

- Bromocriptine (e.g., Parlodel) or
- Other ergot alkaloids (dihydroergotamine [e.g., D.H.E. 45], ergoloid mesylates [e.g., Hydergine], ergotamine [e.g., Gynergen], methysergide [e.g., Sansert])—Use of these medicines with ergonovine or methylergonovine may increase the chance of side effects of these medicines.
- Nitrates or
- Other medicines for angina—Use of these medicines with ergonovine or methylergonovine may keep these medicines from working properly

Other medical problems—The presence of other medical problems may affect the use of ergonovine or methylergonovine. Make sure you tell your doctor if you have any other medical problems, especially:

- Angina (chest pain) or other heart problems or
- Blood vessel disease or
- High blood pressure (or history of) or
- Stroke (history of)—These medicines may cause changes in how the heart works or blood pressure changes
- Infection—Infections may cause an increased sensitivity to the effect of these medicines
- Kidney disease
- Liver disease—The body may not remove these medicines from the bloodstream at the usual rate, which may make the medicine work longer or increase the chance for side effects

- Raynaud's phenomenon—Use of these medicines may cause worsening of the blood vessel narrowing that occurs with this disease

Proper Use of This Medicine

Take this medicine only as directed by your doctor. Do not take more of it, do not take it more often, and do not take it for a longer time than your doctor ordered. If too much is taken or if it is taken for a longer time than your doctor ordered, it may cause serious effects.

Dosing—The dose of ergonovine or methylergonovine will be different for different patients. *Follow your doctor's orders or the directions on the label.* The following information includes only the average doses of ergonovine and methylergonovine. *If your dose is different, do not change it* unless your doctor tells you to do so.

For ergonovine
- For *oral* dosage forms (tablets):
  —For treatment of excessive uterine bleeding:
    - Adults—0.2 to 0.4 milligram, swallowed or placed under the tongue every six to twelve hours. Usually this medicine is taken for forty-eight hours or less.
- For *injection* dosage form:
  —For treatment of excessive uterine bleeding:
    - Adults—0.2 milligram, injected into a muscle or vein. This dose can be repeated up to five times if needed, with a two- to four-hour wait between doses.

For methylergonovine
- For *oral* dosage forms (tablets):
  —For treatment of excessive uterine bleeding:
    - Adults—0.2 to 0.4 milligram, taken every six to twelve hours. Usually this medicine is taken for forty-eight hours or less.
- For *injection* dosage form:
  —For treatment of excessive uterine bleeding:
    - Adults—0.2 milligram, injected into a muscle or vein. This dose can be repeated up to five times if needed, with a two- to four-hour wait between doses.

Missed dose—If you miss a dose of this medicine, do not take the missed dose at all and do not double the next one. Instead, go back to your regular dosing schedule. If you have any questions about this, check with your doctor.

Storage—To store this medicine:
- Keep out of the reach of children.
- Store away from heat and direct light.
- Do not store in the bathroom, near the kitchen sink, or in other damp places. Heat or moisture may cause the medicine to break down.
- Do not keep outdated medicine or medicine no longer needed. Be sure that any discarded medicine is out of the reach of children.

Precautions While Using This Medicine

If you have an infection or illness of any kind, check with your doctor before taking this medicine, since you may be more sensitive to its effects.

Side Effects of This Medicine

Along with its needed effects, a medicine may cause some unwanted effects. Although not all of these side effects may occur, if they do occur they may need medical attention.

Check with the health care professional immediately if any of the following side effects occur:

Less common
Chest pain

Rare
Blurred vision; convulsions (seizures); crushing chest pain; headache (sudden and severe); irregular heartbeat; unexplained shortness of breath

Check with your doctor as soon as possible if any of the following side effects occur:

Less common
Slow heartbeat

Rare
Itching of skin; pain in arms, legs, or lower back; pale or cold hands or feet; weakness in legs

Symptoms of overdose
Bluish color of skin or inside of nose or mouth; chest pain; cool, pale, or numb arms or legs; confusion; cramping of the uterus (severe); decreased breathing rate; drowsiness; heartbeat changes; muscle pain; small pupils; tingling, itching, and cool skin; trouble in breathing; unconsciousness; unusual thirst; weak or absent pulse in arms or legs; weak pulse

With long-term use
Dry, shriveled-looking skin on hands, lower legs, or feet; false feeling of insects crawling on the skin; pain and redness in an arm or leg; paralysis of one side of the body

Other side effects may occur that usually do not need medical attention. These side effects may go away during treatment as your body adjusts to the medicine. However, check with your doctor if any of the following side effects continue or are bothersome:

More common
Cramping of the uterus; nausea; vomiting

Less common
Abdominal or stomach pain; diarrhea; dizziness; headache (mild and temporary); ringing in the ears; stuffy nose; sweating; unpleasant taste

Other side effects not listed above may also occur in some patients. If you notice any other effects, check with your doctor.

Revised: 06/07/93

ERGOTAMINE, BELLADONNA ALKALOIDS, AND PHENOBARBITAL Systemic

Some commonly used brand names are:

In the U.S.—
Bellergal-S

In Canada—
Bellergal
Bellergal Spacetabs

Description

Ergotamine (er-GOT-a-meen), belladonna alkaloids (bell-a-DON-a AL-ka-loids), and phenobarbital (feen-oh-BAR-bi-tal) combination is used to treat some symptoms of menopause (such as hot flashes, sweating, restlessness, and trouble in sleeping). However, it is not effective against other problems that may occur after menopause, such as osteoporosis. This medicine is also used to prevent migraine or cluster headaches in people who get these headaches often. It is not used to treat a headache that has already started. This combination medicine may also be used for other problems as determined by your doctor.

The phenobarbital in this combination medicine belongs to the group of medicines known as barbiturates.

This medicine is available only with your doctor's prescription, in the following dosage forms:

Oral
- Tablets (Canada)
- Extended-release tablets (U.S. and Canada)

Before Using This Medicine

In deciding to use a medicine, the risks of taking the medicine must be weighed against the good it will do. This is a decision you and your doctor will make. For ergotamine, belladonna alkaloids, and phenobarbital combination, the following should be considered:

Allergies—Tell your doctor if you have ever had any unusual or allergic reaction to ergotamine or other ergot medicines, atropine, belladonna, or barbiturates. Also tell your health care professional if you are allergic to any other substances, such as foods, preservatives, or dyes.

Pregnancy—
- *For ergotamine*—Ergotamine is not recommended for use during pregnancy since it has been shown to increase the chance of early labor, which could result in a miscarriage.
- *For belladonna alkaloids*—Belladonna alkaloids have not been shown to cause problems in humans.
- *For phenobarbital*—Barbiturates such as phenobarbital have been shown to increase the chance of birth defects. Also, when taken during pregnancy, barbiturates may cause bleeding problems in the newborn baby. Be sure that you have discussed these problems with your doctor before taking this medicine.

Breast-feeding—
- *For ergotamine*—Ergotamine passes into the breast milk and may cause unwanted effects, such as vomiting, diarrhea, weak pulse, unstable blood pressure, or convulsions (seizures), in nursing babies whose mothers take large amounts of the medicine. Large amounts of ergotamine may also decrease the flow of breast milk.
- *For belladonna alkaloids*—Although belladonna alkaloids pass into the breast milk, the amount of belladonna alkaloids in this combination medicine has not been shown to cause problems in nursing babies. However, because the belladonna alkaloids tend to decrease the secretions of the body, it is possible that the flow of breast milk may be reduced in some patients.
- *For phenobarbital*—Phenobarbital passes into the breast milk. Taking this combination medicine two or three times a day is not likely to cause problems in nursing babies. However, larger amounts of the medicine may cause drowsiness, unusually slow heartbeat, shortness of breath, or troubled breathing in nursing babies.

Be sure that you discuss these possible problems with your doctor before taking this medicine.

Children—Children may be especially sensitive to the effects of the belladonna alkaloids and the phenobarbital in this combination medicine. This may increase the chance of side effects during treatment. Although there is no specific information about the use of ergotamine in children, it is not expected to cause different side effects or problems in children than it does in adults.

Older adults—Elderly people are especially sensitive to the effects of ergotamine, belladonna alkaloids, and barbiturates such as phenobarbital. This may increase the chance of side effects during treatment.

Other medicines—Although certain medicines should not be used together at all, in other cases two different medicines may be used together even if an interaction might occur. In these cases, your doctor may want to change the dose, or other precautions may be necessary. When you are taking this combination medicine, it is especially important that your health care professional know if you are taking any of the following:

- Antacids or
- Diarrhea medicine containing kaolin or attapulgite—These medicines may decrease the effects of the belladonna alkaloids and the phenobarbital in this combination medicine; to prevent this, take the 2 medicines at least 1 hour apart
- Anticoagulants (blood thinners)—The phenobarbital in this combination medicine may decrease the effects of anticoagulants; a change in the dose of anticoagulant may be needed
- Anticholinergics (medicine for abdominal or stomach spasms or cramps) or
- Carbamazepine (e.g., Tegretol) or
- Central nervous system (CNS) depressants (medicine that causes drowsiness) or
- Cocaine or

- Contraceptives, oral, (birth control pills) containing estrogens or progestins or
- Digitalis glycosides (heart medicine) or
- Monoamine oxidase (MAO) inhibitors (furazolidone [e.g., Furoxone], isocarboxazid [e.g., Marplan], phenelzine [e.g., Nardil], procarbazine [e.g., Matulane], selegiline [e.g., Eldepryl], tranylcypromine [e.g., Parnate] (taken currently or within the past 2 weeks) or
- Other ergot medicines (dihydroergotamine [e.g., D.H.E. 45], ergoloid mesylates [e.g., Hydergine], ergonovine [e.g., Ergotrate], methylergonovine [e.g., Methergine], methysergide [e.g., Sansert]) or
- Other medicines for migraine that contain ergotamine in combination with other ingredients, such as ergotamine and caffeine (e.g., Cafergot), or
- Potassium chloride (e.g., Kay Ciel) or
- Tricyclic antidepressants (amitriptyline [e.g., Elavil], amoxapine [e.g., Asendin], clomipramine [e.g., Anafranil], desipramine [e.g., Pertofrane], doxepin [e.g., Sinequan], imipramine [e.g., Tofranil], nortriptyline [e.g., Aventyl], protriptyline [e.g., Vivactil], trimipramine [e.g., Surmontil])—The chance of serious side effects may be increased
- Ketoconazole (e.g., Nizoral)—The belladonna alkaloids in this combination medicine may reduce the effects of ketoconazole; to prevent this, take the ergotamine, belladonna alkaloids, and phenobarbital combination at least 2 hours after taking ketoconazole

Other medical problems—The presence of other medical problems may affect the use of this combination medicine. Make sure you tell your doctor if you have any other medical problems, especially:

- Asthma (or history of), emphysema, or other chronic lung disease or
- Brain damage (in children) or
- Difficult urination or
- Down's syndrome (mongolism) or
- Dry mouth (severe and continuing) or
- Enlarged prostate or
- Heart or blood vessel disease or
- High blood pressure (severe) or
- Hyperactivity (in children) or
- Infection or
- Intestinal blockage or other intestinal problems or
- Itching (severe) or
- Kidney disease or
- Liver disease or
- Overactive thyroid or
- Porphyria or
- Spastic paralysis (in children) or
- Urinary tract blockage—The chance of side effects may be increased
- Glaucoma—The belladonna alkaloids in this combination medicine may make your condition worse

Also tell your doctor if you have recently had an angioplasty (a procedure done to improve the flow of blood in a blocked blood vessel) or surgery on a blood vessel, because the chance of side effects caused by the ergotamine in this combination medicine may be increased.

Proper Use of This Medicine

Take this medicine only as directed by your doctor. If the amount you are to take does not seem to work, do not take more than your doctor ordered. Instead, check with your doctor. Taking too much of this medicine or taking it too often may cause serious effects such as nausea and vomiting; cold, painful hands or feet; or even gangrene. Also, if too much is used, it may become habit-forming.

To take the *extended-release tablet* form of this medicine:

- Swallow the tablet whole.
- Do not crush, break, or chew the tablet before swallowing it.

Dosing—The dose of this combination medicine will be different for different patients. *Follow your doctor's orders or the directions on the label.* The following information includes only the average doses of this medicine. *If your dose is different, do not change it* unless your doctor tells you to do so.

- For *oral tablet* dosage form:
  - —For relieving symptoms of menopause and for preventing headaches:
    - Adults—One tablet in the morning, one tablet at noon, and two tablets at bedtime.
    - Children—Use and dose must be determined by your doctor.
- For *oral extended-release tablet* dosage form:
  - —For relieving symptoms of menopause and for preventing headaches:
    - Adults—One tablet in the morning and one tablet in the evening.
    - Children—Use and dose must be determined by your doctor.

Missed dose—If you miss a dose of this medicine, skip the missed dose and go back to your regular dosing schedule. Do not double doses.

Storage—To store this medicine:

- Keep out of the reach of children since overdose is especially dangerous in children.
- Store away from heat and direct light.
- Do not store in the bathroom, near the kitchen sink, or in other damp places. Heat and moisture may cause the medicine to break down.
- Do not keep outdated medicine or medicine no longer needed. Be sure that any discarded medicine is out of the reach of children.

Precautions While Using This Medicine

If you have been taking this medicine regularly, *do not stop taking it without first checking with your doctor.* Your doctor may want you to reduce gradually the amount you are using before stopping completely.

Do not take antacids or medicine for diarrhea within 1 hour of taking this medicine. Taking them too close together will make the belladonna alkaloids less effective.

This medicine will add to the effects of alcohol and other CNS depressants (medicines that slow down the nervous system, possibly causing drowsiness). Some examples of CNS depressants are antihistamines or medicine for hay fever, other allergies, or colds; sedatives, tranquilizers, or sleeping medicine; prescription pain medicine or narcotics; other barbiturates; medicine for seizures; muscle relaxants; or anesthetics, including some dental anesthetics. *Check with your doctor before taking any of the above while you are taking this medicine.* Also, alcohol may make headaches worse, so it is best to avoid alcoholic beverages if you are taking this medicine to prevent headaches.

This medicine may cause some people to have blurred vision or to become drowsy, dizzy, lightheaded, or less alert than they are normally. *Make sure you know how you react to this medicine before you drive, use machines, or do anything else that could be dangerous if you are dizzy or are not alert and able to see well.*

Since smoking may increase some of the harmful effects of this medicine, it is best to avoid smoking while you are using it. If you have any questions about this, check with your doctor.

This medicine may make you more sensitive to cold temperatures, especially if you have blood circulation problems. It tends to decrease blood circulation in the skin, fingers, and toes. Dress warmly during cold weather and be careful during prolonged exposure to cold, such as in winter sports. This is especially important for elderly people, who are more likely than younger adults to already have problems with their circulation.

Belladonna alkaloids (contained in this combination medicine) will often make you sweat less, causing your body temperature to increase. *Use extra care not to become overheated during exercise or hot weather while you are taking this medicine,* as overheating may result in a heat stroke. Also, hot baths or saunas may make you feel dizzy or faint while you are taking this medicine. This is especially important in children taking this medicine.

This medicine may cause your eyes to become more sensitive to light than they are normally. Wearing sunglasses may help lessen the discomfort from bright light.

If you have a serious infection or illness of any kind, check with your doctor before taking this medicine, since you may be more sensitive to its effects.

This medicine may cause dryness of the mouth, nose and throat. For temporary relief of mouth dryness, use sugarless candy or gum, melt bits of ice in your mouth, or use a saliva substitute. However, if dry mouth continues for more than 2 weeks, check with your medical doctor or dentist. Continuing dryness of the mouth may increase the chance of dental disease, including tooth decay, gum disease, and fungus infections.

Side Effects of This Medicine

Along with its needed effects, a medicine may cause some unwanted effects. Although not all of these side effects may occur, if they do occur they may need medical attention.

Check with your doctor immediately if the following side effects occur, because they may mean that you are developing a problem with blood circulation:

Less common or rare

Anxiety or confusion (severe); change in vision; chest pain; increase in blood pressure; pain in arms, legs, or lower back, especially if pain occurs in your calves or heels while you are walking; pale, bluish-colored, or cold hands or feet (not caused by cold temperatures and occurring together with other side effects listed in this section); red or violet-colored blisters on the skin of the hands or feet

Also check with your doctor immediately if any of the following side effects occur since they may be symptoms of an overdose:

Convulsions (seizures); diarrhea, nausea, vomiting, or stomach pain or bloating (severe) occurring together with other signs of overdose or of problems with blood circulation; dizziness, drowsiness, or weakness (severe), occurring together with other signs of overdose or of problems with blood circulation; fast or slow heartbeat; shortness of breath; unusual excitement

Also check with your doctor as soon as possible if any of the following side effects occur:

More common

Swelling of face, fingers, feet, and/or lower legs

Less common or rare

Skin rash, hives, or itching; sore throat and fever; unusual bleeding or bruising; weakness in legs; yellow eyes or skin

Other side effects may occur that usually do not need medical attention. These side effects may go away during treatment as your body adjusts to the medicine. However, check with your doctor if any of the following side effects continue or are bothersome:

More common

Constipation; decreased sweating; dizziness or lightheadedness; drowsiness; dryness of mouth, nose, throat, or skin

Less common or rare

Blurred vision, diarrhea, nausea, or vomiting (occurring without other signs of overdose or blood circulation problems); difficult urination (especially in older men); difficulty in swallowing; increased sensitivity of eyes to sunlight; loss of memory; reduced sweating; unusual excitement (especially in older adults); unusual tiredness or weakness

After you stop taking this medicine, your body may need time to adjust. The length of time this takes depends on the amount of medicine you were taking and how long you took it. During this time check with your doctor if your headaches or other symptoms begin again or worsen.

Other side effects not listed above may also occur in some patients. If you notice any other effects, check with your doctor.

Revised: 08/30/94

ERYTHROMYCIN Ophthalmic

A commonly used brand name in the U.S. and Canada is Ilotycin. Generic name product may also be available.

Description

Erythromycin (eh-rith-roe-MYE-sin) belongs to the family of medicines called antibiotics. Erythromycin ophthalmic preparations are used to treat infections of the eye. They also may be used to prevent certain eye infections of newborn babies, such as neonatal conjunctivitis and ophthalmia neonatorum. They may be used with other medicines for some eye infections.

Erythromycin is available only with your doctor's prescription, in the following dosage form:

Ophthalmic
- Ophthalmic ointment (U.S. and Canada)

Before Using This Medicine

In deciding to use a medicine, the risks of taking the medicine must be weighed against the good it will do. This is a decision you and your doctor will make. For ophthalmic erythromycin, the following should be considered:

Allergies—Tell your doctor if you have ever had any unusual or allergic reaction to this or any of the other erythromycins. Also tell your health care professional if you are allergic to any other substances, such as preservatives.

Pregnancy—Ophthalmic erythromycin has not been shown to cause birth defects or other problems in humans.

Breast-feeding—Ophthalmic erythromycin has not been reported to cause problems in nursing babies.

Children—Studies on this medicine have been done only in adult patients, and there is no specific information comparing use of this medicine in children with use in other age groups.

Older adults—Many medicines have not been studied specifically in older people. Therefore, it may not be known whether they work exactly the same way they do in younger adults or if they cause different side effects or problems in older people. There is no specific information comparing use of this medicine in the elderly with use in other age groups.

Proper Use of This Medicine

To use:

- First, wash your hands. Tilt the head back and, pressing your finger gently on the skin just beneath the lower eyelid, pull the lower eyelid away from the eye to make a space. Squeeze a thin strip of ointment into this space. A 1-cm (approximately 1/3-inch) strip of ointment is usually enough, unless you have been told by your doctor to use a different amount. Let go of the eyelid and gently close the eyes. Keep the eyes closed for 1 or 2 minutes to allow the medicine to come into contact with the infection.
- To keep the medicine as germ-free as possible, do not touch the applicator tip to any surface (including the eye). After using erythromycin eye ointment, wipe the tip of the ointment tube with a clean tissue and keep the tube tightly closed.

To help clear up your infection completely, *keep using this medicine for the full time of treatment,* even if your symptoms begin to clear up after a few days. If you stop using this medicine too soon, your symptoms may return. *Do not miss any doses.*

Dosing—The dose of ophthalmic erythromycin will be different for different patients. *Follow your doctor's orders or the directions on the label.* The following information includes only the average doses of ophthalmic erythromycin. *If your dose is different, do not change it* unless your doctor tells you to do so.

- For *ophthalmic ointment* dosage form:
  - —For treatment of eye infections:
    - Adults and children—Use in the eyes up to six times a day as directed by your doctor.
  - —For prevention of neonatal conjunctivitis and ophthalmia neonatorum:
    - Newborn babies—Use in the eyes once at birth.

Missed dose—If you do miss a dose of this medicine, apply it as soon as possible. However, if it is almost time for your next dose, skip the missed dose and go back to your regular dosing schedule.

Storage—To store this medicine:
- Keep out of the reach of children.
- Store away from heat and direct light.
- Keep the medicine from freezing.
- Do not keep outdated medicine or medicine no longer needed. Be sure that any discarded medicine is out of the reach of children.

Precautions While Using This Medicine

If your symptoms do not improve within a few days, or if they become worse, check with your doctor.

After application, eye ointments usually cause your vision to blur for a few minutes.

Side Effects of This Medicine

Along with its needed effects, a medicine may cause some unwanted effects.

Check with your doctor as soon as possible if the following side effect occurs:

Rare
Eye irritation not present before therapy

Other side effects not listed above may also occur in some patients. If you notice any other effects, check with your doctor.

Revised: 11/28/94

ERYTHROMYCIN Topical

Some commonly used brand names are:

In the U.S.—

Akne-Mycin	Erymax
A/T/S	Ery-Sol
Erycette	ETS
EryDerm	Staticin
Erygel	T-Stat

Generic name product may also be available.

In Canada—

Sans-Acne
Staticin

Description

Erythromycin (eh-rith-roe-MYE-sin) belongs to the family of medicines called antibiotics. Erythromycin topical preparations are used on the skin to help control acne. They may be used alone or with one or more other medicines that are applied to the skin or taken by mouth for acne. They may also be used for other problems, such as skin infections, as determined by your doctor.

Erythromycin is available only with your doctor's prescription, in the following dosage forms:

Topical
- Gel (U.S.)
- Ointment (U.S.)
- Pledgets (U.S.)
- Solution (U.S. and Canada)

Before Using This Medicine

In deciding to use a medicine, the risks of taking the medicine must be weighed against the good it will do. This is a decision you and your doctor will make. For topical erythromycin, the following should be considered:

Allergies—Tell your doctor if you have ever had any unusual or allergic reaction to this or any of the other erythromycins. Also tell your health care professional if you are allergic to any other substances, such as preservatives or dyes.

Pregnancy—Topical erythromycin has not been studied in pregnant women. However, this medication has not been shown to cause birth defects or other problems in animal studies.

Breast-feeding—It is not known whether topical erythromycin passes into the breast milk. Erythromycin, given by mouth or by injection, does pass into the breast milk. However, erythromycin topical preparations have not been reported to cause problems in nursing babies.

Children—Erythromycin topical solution has been tested in children 12 years of age and older and, in effective doses, has not been shown to cause different side effects or problems than it does in adults.

Older adults—Many medicines have not been studied specifically in older people. Therefore, it may not be known whether they work exactly the same way they do in younger adults. Although there is no specific information comparing use of topical erythromycin in the elderly with use in other age groups, this medicine is not expected to cause different side effects or problems in older people than it does in younger adults.

Other medicines—Although certain medicines should not be used together at all, in other cases two different medicines may be used together even if an interaction might occur. In these cases, your doctor may want to change the dose, or other precautions may be necessary. Tell your health care professional if you are using any other topical prescription or nonprescription (over-the-counter [OTC]) medicine that is to be applied to the same area of the skin.

Proper Use of This Medicine

Before applying this medicine, thoroughly wash the affected area with warm water and soap, rinse well, and pat dry. After washing or shaving, it is best to wait 30 minutes before applying the pledget (swab), topical gel, or topical liquid form. The alcohol in them may irritate freshly washed or shaved skin.

This medicine will not cure your acne. However, to help keep your acne under control, *keep using this medicine for the full time of treatment,* even if your symptoms begin to clear up after a few days. You may have to continue using this medicine every day for months or even longer in some cases. If you stop using this medicine too soon, your symptoms may return. *It is important that you do not miss any doses.*

Dosing—The dose of topical erythromycin will be different for different patients. *Follow your doctor's orders or the directions on the label.* The following information includes only the average doses of topical erythromycin. *If your dose is different, do not change it unless* your doctor tells you to do so.

- For acne:
  - —For *gel* dosage form:
    - Adults—Apply to the affected area(s) of the skin two times a day, morning and evening.
    - Children—Dose must be determined by your doctor.
  - —For *ointment* dosage form:
    - Adults, teenagers, and children—Apply to the affected area(s) of the skin two times a day, morning and evening.
  - —For *pledgets* dosage form:
    - Adults, teenagers, and children—Apply to the affected area(s) of the skin two times a day.
  - —For *topical solution* dosage form:
    - Adults, teenagers, and children 12 years of age and over—Apply to the affected area(s) of the skin two times a day, morning and evening.
    - Children up to 12 years of age—Dose must be determined by your doctor.

Missed dose—If you miss a dose of this medicine, apply it as soon as possible. However, if it is almost time for your next dose, skip the missed dose and go back to your regular dosing schedule.

For patients using the pledget (swab), topical gel, or topical liquid form of erythromycin:

- These forms contain alcohol and are flammable. *Do not use near heat, near open flame, or while smoking.*
- It is important that you do not use this medicine more often than your doctor ordered. It may cause your skin to become too dry or irritated.
- Also, you should avoid washing the acne-affected areas too often. This may dry your skin and make your acne worse. Washing with a mild, bland soap 2 or 3 times a day should be enough, unless you have oily skin. If you have any questions about this, check with your doctor.
- To use:

  —The topical liquid form of this medicine may come in a bottle with an applicator tip, which may be used to apply the medicine directly to the skin. Use the applicator with a dabbing motion instead of a rolling motion (not like a roll-on deodorant, for example). If the medicine does not come in an applicator bottle, you may moisten a pad with the medicine and then rub the pad over the whole affected area. Or you may also apply this medicine with your fingertips. Be sure to wash the medicine off your hands afterward.

  —Apply a thin film of medicine, using enough to cover the affected area lightly. *You should apply the medicine to the whole area usually affected by acne, not just to the pimples themselves.* This will help keep new pimples from breaking out.

  —The pledget (swab) form should be rubbed over the whole affected area. You may use extra pledgets (swabs), if needed, to cover larger areas.

  —Since these medicines contain alcohol, they may sting or burn. Therefore, *do not get these medicines in the eyes, nose, mouth, or on other mucous membranes.* Spread the medicine away from these areas when applying. If these medicines do get in the eyes, wash them out immediately, but carefully, with large amounts of cool tap water. If your eyes still burn or are painful, check with your doctor.

Storage—To store this medicine:

- Keep out of the reach of children.
- Store away from heat and direct light.
- Keep the medicine from freezing.
- Do not keep outdated medicine or medicine no longer needed. Be sure that any discarded medicine is out of the reach of children.

Precautions While Using This Medicine

If your acne does not improve within 3 to 4 weeks, or if it becomes worse, check with your health care professional. However, treatment of acne may take up to 8 to 12 weeks before you see full improvement.

For patients using the pledget (swab), topical gel, or topical liquid form of erythromycin:

- If your doctor has ordered another medicine to be applied to the skin along with this medicine, it is best to wait at least 1 hour before you apply the second medicine. This may help keep your skin from becoming too irritated. Also, if the medicines are used too close together, they may not work properly.
- After application of this medicine to the skin, mild stinging or burning may be expected and may last up to a few minutes or more.
- This medicine may also cause the skin to become unusually dry, even with normal use. If this occurs, check with your doctor.
- You may continue to use cosmetics (make-up) while you are using this medicine for acne. However, it is best to use only "water-base" cosmetics. Also, it is best not to use cosmetics too heavily or too often. They may make your acne worse. If you have any questions about this, check with your doctor.

Side Effects of This Medicine

Along with its needed effects, a medicine may cause some unwanted effects. The following side effects may go away during treatment as your body adjusts to the medicine. However, check with your doctor if any of the following side effects continue or are bothersome:

For erythromycin ointment

Less common

Peeling; redness

For erythromycin pledget (swab), topical gel, or topical liquid form

More common

Dry or scaly skin; irritation; itching; stinging or burning feeling

Less common

Peeling; redness

Other side effects not listed above may also occur in some patients. If you notice any other effects, check with your doctor.

Revised: 06/23/92
Interim revision: 06/07/94

ERYTHROMYCIN AND BENZOYL PEROXIDE Topical†

A commonly used brand name in the U.S. is Benzamycin.

†Not commercially available in Canada.

Description

Erythromycin (eh-rith-roe-MYE-sin) and benzoyl peroxide (BEN-zoe-ill per-OX-ide) combination is used to help control acne.

This medicine is applied to the skin. It may be used alone or with other medicines that are applied to the skin or taken by mouth for acne.

Erythromycin and benzoyl peroxide combination is available only with your doctor's prescription, in the following dosage form:

Topical
- Topical gel (U.S.)

Before Using This Medicine

In deciding to use a medicine, the risks of using the medicine must be weighed against the good it will do. This is a decision you and your doctor will make. For erythromycin and benzoyl peroxide combination, the following should be considered:

Allergies—Tell your doctor if you have ever had any unusual or allergic reaction to this medicine, to any of the other erythromycins, or to benzoyl peroxide (e.g., Pan-Oxyl). Also tell your health care professional if you are allergic to any other substances, such as preservatives or dyes.

Pregnancy—Studies on effects in pregnancy have not been done in either humans or animals. However, the benzoyl peroxide in this medicine may be absorbed into the body. Before using this medicine, make sure your doctor knows if you are pregnant or if you may become pregnant.

Breast-feeding—It is not known whether topical erythromycin or topical benzoyl peroxide passes into the breast milk. Erythromycin (e.g., E-Mycin), given by mouth or by injection, does pass into the breast milk. In addition, the benzoyl peroxide in this medicine may be absorbed into the mother's body. However, erythromycin and benzoyl peroxide combination has not been reported to cause problems in nursing babies.

Children—Studies on this medicine have been done only in adult patients, and there is no specific information comparing use of this medicine in children up to 12 years of age with use in other age groups.

Older adults—Many medicines have not been studied specifically in older people. Therefore, it may not be known whether they work exactly the same way they do in younger adults or if they cause different side effects or problems in older people. There is no specific information comparing use of this medicine in the elderly with use in other age groups.

Other medicines—Although certain medicines should not be used together at all, in other cases two different medicines may be used together even if an interaction might occur. In these cases, your doctor may want to change the dose, or other precautions may be necessary. Tell your health care professional if you are using any other topical prescription or nonprescription (over-the-counter [OTC]) medicine that is to be applied to the same area of the skin.

Proper Use of This Medicine

Do not use this medicine on raw or irritated skin.

Before applying this medicine, thoroughly wash the affected area(s) with warm water and soap, rinse well, and gently pat dry. After washing or shaving, it is best to wait 30 minutes before applying the medicine. The alcohol in it may irritate freshly washed or shaved skin.

Avoid washing the acne-affected area(s) too often. This may dry your skin and make your acne worse. Washing with a mild, bland soap 2 or 3 times a day should be enough, unless you have oily skin. If you have any questions about this, check with your doctor.

To use:
- *Use this medicine only as directed.* Do not use more of it and do not use it more often than your doctor ordered. To do so may cause your skin to become too dry or irritated.
- After washing the affected area(s), you may apply this medicine with your fingertips. However, be sure to wash the medicine off your hands afterward.
- Apply and rub in a thin film of medicine, using enough to cover the affected area(s) lightly. *You should apply the medicine to the whole area usually affected by acne, not just to the pimples themselves.*
- Since this medicine contains alcohol, it may sting or burn. Therefore, *do not get this medicine in or around your eyes, nose, or mouth, or on other mucous membranes.* Spread the medicine away from these areas when applying. If this medicine does get in your eyes, wash them out immediately, but carefully, with large amounts of cool tap water. If your eyes still burn or are painful, check with your doctor.

Do not use this medicine after the expiration date on the label. The medicine may not work properly. Get a fresh supply from your pharmacist. Check with your pharmacist if you have any questions about this.

To help keep your acne under control, *keep using this medicine for the full time of treatment.* You may have to continue using this medicine every day for months or even longer in some cases.

Dosing—The dose of erythromycin and benzoyl peroxide combination will be different for different patients. *Follow your doctor's orders or the directions on the label.* The following information includes only the average dose of erythromycin and benzoyl peroxide combination. *If your dose is different, do not change it unless your doctor tells you to do so.*

- For *gel* dosage form:
  - —For acne:
    - Adults and children 12 years of age and over—Apply to the affected area(s) of the skin two times a day, morning and evening, or as directed by your doctor.
    - Children up to 12 years of age—Dose must be determined by your doctor.

Missed dose—If you miss a dose of this medicine, apply it as soon as possible. However, if it is almost time for your next dose, skip the missed dose and go back to your regular dosing schedule.

Storage—To store this medicine:
- Keep out of the reach of children.
- Store in the refrigerator. Heat will cause this medicine to break down. However, keep the medicine from freezing. Follow the directions on the label.

- Do not keep outdated medicine or medicine no longer needed. Be sure that any discarded medicine is out of the reach of children.

Precautions While Using This Medicine

If your acne does not improve within 3 to 4 weeks, or if it becomes worse, check with your health care professional. However, treatment of acne may take up to 8 to 12 weeks before you see full improvement.

If your doctor has ordered another medicine to be applied to the skin along with this medicine, it is best to apply the second medicine at least 1 hour after you apply the first medicine. This may help keep your skin from becoming too irritated. Also, if the medicines are used too close together, they may not work properly.

Mild stinging or burning of the skin may be expected after this medicine is applied. These effects may last up to a few minutes or more. If irritation continues, check with your doctor. You may have to use the medicine less often. Follow your doctor's directions.

This medicine may also cause the skin to become unusually dry, even with normal use. If this occurs, check with your doctor.

This medicine may bleach hair or colored fabrics.

You may continue to use cosmetics (make-up) while you are using this medicine for acne. However, it is best to use only ''oil-free'' cosmetics. Also, it is best not to use cosmetics too heavily or too often. They may make your acne worse. If you have any questions about this, check with your doctor.

Side Effects of This Medicine

Along with its needed effects, a medicine may cause some unwanted effects. Although not all of these side effects may occur, if they do occur they may need medical attention.

Check with your doctor as soon as possible if any of the following side effects occur:

Less common or rare

Burning, blistering, crusting, itching, severe redness, or swelling of the skin; painful irritation of the skin; skin rash

Symptoms of topical overdose

Burning, itching, scaling, redness, or swelling of the skin (severe)

Other side effects may occur that usually do not need medical attention. These side effects may go away during treatment as your body adjusts to the medicine. However, check with your doctor if any of the following side effects continue or are bothersome:

Less common

Dryness or peeling of the skin; feeling of warmth, mild stinging, or redness of the skin

Other side effects not listed above may also occur in some patients. If you notice any other effects, check with your doctor.

Revised: 06/26/92
Interim revision: 07/06/94

ERYTHROMYCINS Systemic

Some commonly used brand names are:

In the U.S.—

E-Base[1]
E-Mycin[1]
ERYC[1]
Ery-Tab
E.E.S.[3]
EryPed[3]
Erythro[3]
Erythrocin[5, 6]
Erythrocot[6]
Ilotycin[1, 4]
Ilosone[2]
My-E[6]
PCE[1]
Wintrocin[6]

In Canada—

Apo-Erythro[1]
Apo-Erythro E-C[1]
Apo-Erythro-ES[3]
Apo-Erythro-S[6]
E-Mycin[1]
E.E.S.[3]
Erybid[1]
EryPed[3]
ERYC-250[1]
ERYC-333[1]
Erythrocin[5, 6]
Erythromid[1]
Ilosone[2]
Ilotycin[4]
Novo-rythro[2, 6]
Novo-rythro Encap[1]
PCE[1]

Note: For quick reference, the following erythromycins are numbered to match the corresponding brand names.

This information applies to the following medicines:

1. Erythromycin Base (er-ith-roe-MYE-sin)‡§
2. Erythromycin Estolate (ESS-toe-layt)‡
3. Erythromycin Ethylsuccinate (eth-ill-SUK-sin-ayt)‡
4. Erythromycin Gluceptate (gloo-SEP-tayt)
5. Erythromycin Lactobionate (lak-toe-BYE-oh-nayt)‡
6. Erythromycin Stearate (STEER-ate)‡

‡Generic name product may also be available in the U.S.
§Generic name product may also be available in Canada.

Description

Erythromycins (eh-rith-roe-MYE-sins) are used to treat many kinds of infections. Erythromycins are also used to prevent ''strep'' infections in patients with a history of rheumatic heart disease who may be allergic to penicillin.

These medicines may also be used to treat Legionnaires' disease and for other problems as determined by your doctor. They will not work for colds, flu, or other virus infections.

Erythromycins are available only with your doctor's prescription, in the following dosage forms:

Oral

Erythromycin Base
- Delayed-release capsules (U.S. and Canada)
- Delayed-release tablets (U.S. and Canada)
- Tablets (U.S. and Canada)

Erythromycin Estolate
- Capsules (U.S. and Canada)
- Oral suspension (U.S. and Canada)
- Tablets (U.S. and Canada)

Erythromycin Ethylsuccinate
- Chewable tablets (U.S. and Canada)
- Oral suspension (U.S. and Canada)
- Tablets (U.S. and Canada)

Erythromycin Stearate
- Oral suspension (Canada)
- Tablets (U.S. and Canada)

Parenteral

Erythromycin Gluceptate
- Injection (U.S. and Canada)

Erythromycin Lactobionate
- Injection (U.S. and Canada)

Before Using This Medicine

In deciding to use a medicine, the risks of taking the medicine must be weighed against the good it will do. This is a decision you and your doctor will make. For erythromycins, the following should be considered:

Allergies—Tell your doctor if you have ever had any unusual or allergic reaction to erythromycins, or any related medicines, such as azithromycin or clarithromycin. Also tell your health care professional if you are allergic to any other substances, such as foods, preservatives, or dyes.

Pregnancy—Erythromycin estolate has caused side effects involving the liver in some pregnant women. However, none of the erythromycins has been shown to cause birth defects or other problems in human babies.

Breast-feeding—Erythromycins pass into the breast milk. However, erythromycins have not been shown to cause problems in nursing babies.

Children—This medicine has been tested in children and, in effective doses, has not been shown to cause different side effects or problems in children than it does in adults.

Older adults—This medicine has been tested and has not been shown to cause different side effects or problems in older people than it does in younger adults. However, older adults may be at increased risk of hearing loss, especially if they are taking high doses of erythromycin and/or have kidney or liver disease.

Other medicines—Although certain medicines should not be used together at all, in other cases two different medicines may be used together even if an interaction might occur. In these cases, your doctor may want to change the dose, or other precautions may be necessary. When you are taking or receiving erythromycins, it is especially important that your health care professional know if you are taking any of the following:

- Acetaminophen (e.g., Tylenol) (with long-term, high-dose use) or
- Amiodarone (e.g., Cordarone) or
- Anabolic steroids (nandrolone [e.g., Anabolin], oxandrolone [e.g., Anavar], oxymetholone [e.g., Anadrol], stanozolol [e.g., Winstrol]) or
- Androgens (male hormones) or
- Antithyroid agents (medicine for overactive thyroid) or
- Carmustine (e.g., BiCNU) or
- Chloroquine (e.g., Aralen) or
- Dantrolene (e.g., Dantrium) or
- Daunorubicin (e.g., Cerubidine) or
- Disulfiram (e.g., Antabuse) or
- Divalproex (e.g., Depakote) or
- Estrogens (female hormones) or
- Etretinate (e.g., Tegison) or
- Gold salts (medicine for arthritis) or
- Hydroxychloroquine (e.g., Plaquenil) or
- Mercaptopurine (e.g., Purinethol) or
- Methotrexate (e.g., Mexate) or
- Methyldopa (e.g., Aldomet) or
- Naltrexone (e.g., Trexan) (with long-term, high-dose use) or
- Oral contraceptives (birth control pills) containing estrogen or
- Other anti-infectives by mouth or by injection (medicine for infection) or
- Phenothiazines (acetophenazine [e.g., Tindal], chlorpromazine [e.g., Thorazine], fluphenazine [e.g., Prolixin], mesoridazine [e.g., Serentil], perphenazine [e.g., Trilafon], prochlorperazine [e.g., Compazine], promazine [e.g., Sparine], promethazine [e.g., Phenergan], thioridazine [e.g., Mellaril], trifluoperazine [e.g., Stelazine], triflupromazine [e.g., Vesprin], trimeprazine [e.g., Temaril]) or
- Phenytoin (e.g., Dilantin) or
- Plicamycin (e.g., Mithracin) or
- Valproic acid (e.g., Depakene)—Use of these medicines with erythromycins, especially erythromycin estolate, may increase the chance of liver problems

- Aminophylline (e.g., Somophyllin) or
- Caffeine (e.g., NoDoz) or
- Oxtriphylline (e.g., Choledyl) or
- Theophylline (e.g., Somophyllin-T, Theo-Dur)—Use of these medicines with erythromycins may increase the chance of side effects from aminophylline, caffeine, oxtriphylline, or theophylline
- Astemizole (e.g., Hismanal) or
- Terfenadine (e.g., Seldane)—Use of astemizole or terfenadine with erythromycins may cause heart problems, such as an irregular heartbeat; these medicines should not be used together

- Carbamazepine (e.g., Tegretol)—Use of carbamazepine with erythromycin may increase the side effects of carbamazepine or increase the chance of liver problems

- Chloramphenicol (e.g., Chloromycetin) or
- Clindamycin (e.g., Cleocin) or
- Lincomycin (e.g., Lincocin)—Use of these medicines with erythromycins may decrease the effectiveness of these other antibiotics

- Cyclosporine (e.g., Sandimmune) or
- Warfarin (e.g., Coumadin)—Use of any of these medicines with erythromycins may increase the side effects of these medicines

Other medical problems—The presence of other medical problems may affect the use of erythromycins. Make sure you tell your doctor if you have any other medical problems, especially:

- Heart disease—High doses of erythromycin may increase the chance of side effects in patients with a history of an irregular heartbeat
- Liver disease—Erythromycins, especially erythromycin estolate, may increase the chance of side effects involving the liver
- Loss of hearing—High doses of erythromycins may, on rare occasion, cause hearing loss, especially if you have kidney or liver disease

Proper Use of This Medicine

Generally, erythromycins are best taken with a full glass (8 ounces) of water on an empty stomach (at least 1 hour before or 2 hours after meals). If stomach upset occurs, these medicines may be taken with food. If you have questions about the erythromycin medicine you are taking, check with your health care professional.

For patients taking the *oral liquid form* of this medicine:

- This medicine is to be taken by mouth even if it comes in a dropper bottle. If this medicine does not come in a dropper bottle, use a specially marked measuring spoon or other device to measure each dose accurately. The average household teaspoon may not hold the right amount of liquid.
- Do not use after the expiration date on the label. The medicine may not work properly after that date. Check with your pharmacist if you have any questions about this.

For patients taking the *chewable tablet form* of this medicine:

- Tablets must be chewed or crushed before they are swallowed.

For patients taking the *delayed-release capsule form (with enteric-coated pellets) or the delayed-release tablet form* of this medicine:

- Swallow capsules or tablets whole. Do not break or crush. If you are not sure about which type of capsule or tablet you are taking, check with your pharmacist.

To help clear up your infection completely, *keep taking this medicine for the full time of treatment,* even if you begin to feel better after a few days. *If you have a "strep" infection, you should keep taking this medicine for at least 10 days. This is especially important in "strep" infections. Serious heart problems could develop later* if your infection is not cleared up completely. Also, if you stop taking this medicine too soon, your symptoms may return.

This medicine works best when there is a constant amount in the blood. *To help keep the amount constant, do not miss any doses. Also, it is best to take the doses at evenly spaced times day and night.* For example, if you are to take 4 doses a day, the doses should be spaced about 6 hours apart. If this interferes with your sleep or other daily activities, or if you need help in planning the best times to take your medicine, check with your health care professional.

Dosing—The dose of erythromycin will be different for different patients. *Follow your doctor's orders or the directions on the label.* The following information includes only the average doses of erythromycin. *If your dose is different, do not change it* unless your doctor tells you to do so.

The number of capsules or tablets or teaspoonfuls of suspension that you take depends on the strength of the medicine. Also, *the number of doses you take each day, the time allowed between doses, and the length of time you take the medicine depend on the medical problem for which you are taking erythromycin.*

For erythromycin base

- For *oral* dosage forms (capsules, tablets):
  —For treatment of infections:
    - Adults and teenagers—250 to 500 milligrams (mg) two to four times a day.
    - Children—Dose is based on body weight. The usual dose is 7.5 to 12.5 mg per kilogram (kg) (3.4 to 5.6 mg per pound) of body weight four times a day, or 15 to 25 mg per kg (6.8 to 11.4 mg per pound) of body weight two times a day.
  —For prevention of heart infections:
    - Adults and teenagers—Take 1 gram two hours before your dental appointment or surgery, then 500 mg six hours after taking the first dose.
    - Children—Dose is based on body weight. The usual dose is 20 mg per kg (9.1 mg per pound) of body weight two hours before the dental appointment or surgery, then 10 mg per kg (4.5 mg per pound) of body weight six hours after taking the first dose.

For erythromycin estolate

- For *oral* dosage forms (capsules, oral suspension, tablets):
  —For treatment of infections:
    - Adults and teenagers—250 to 500 milligrams (mg) two to four times a day.
    - Children—Dose is based on body weight. The usual dose is 7.5 to 12.5 mg per kilogram (kg) (3.4 to 5.6 mg per pound) of body weight four times a day, or 15 to 25 mg per kg (6.8 to 11.4 mg per pound) of body weight two times a day.
  —For prevention of heart infections:
    - Adults and teenagers—Take 1 gram two hours before your dental appointment or surgery, then 500 mg six hours after taking the first dose.
    - Children—Dose is based on body weight. The usual dose is 20 mg per kg (9.1 mg per pound) of body weight two hours before the dental appointment or surgery, then 10 mg per kg (4.5 mg per pound) of body weight six hours after taking the first dose.

For erythromycin ethylsuccinate

- For *oral* dosage forms (oral suspension, tablets):
  —For treatment of infections:
    - Adults and teenagers—400 to 800 milligrams (mg) two to four times a day.
    - Children—Dose is based on body weight. The usual dose is 7.5 to 12.5 mg per kilogram (kg) (3.4 to 5.6 mg per pound) of body weight four times a day, or 15 to 25 mg per kg (6.8 to 11.4 mg per pound) of body weight two times a day.
  —For prevention of heart infections:
    - Adults and teenagers—Take 1.6 grams two hours before your dental appointment or surgery, then 800 mg six hours after taking the first dose.
    - Children—Dose is based on body weight. The usual dose is 20 mg per kg (9.1 mg per pound)

of body weight two hours before the dental appointment or surgery, then 10 mg per kg (4.5 mg per pound) of body weight six hours after taking the first dose.

For erythromycin gluceptate

- For *injection* dosage forms:
  - —For treatment of infections:
    - Adults and teenagers—250 to 500 milligrams (mg) injected into a vein every six hours; or 3.75 to 5 mg per kilogram (kg) (1.7 to 2.3 mg per pound) of body weight injected into a vein every six hours.
    - Children—Dose is based on body weight. The usual dose is 3.75 to 5 mg per kg (1.7 to 2.3 mg per pound) of body weight injected into a vein every six hours.

For erythromycin lactobionate

- For *injection* dosage forms:
  - —For treatment of infections:
    - Adults and teenagers—250 to 500 milligrams (mg) injected into a vein every six hours; or 3.75 to 5 mg per kilogram (kg) (1.7 to 2.3 mg per pound) of body weight injected into a vein every six hours.
    - Children—Dose is based on body weight. The usual dose is 3.75 to 5 mg per kg (1.7 to 2.3 mg per pound) of body weight injected into a vein every six hours.

For erythromycin stearate

- For *oral* dosage forms (oral suspension, tablets):
  - —For treatment of infections:
    - Adults and teenagers—250 to 500 milligrams (mg) two to four times a day.
    - Children—Dose is based on body weight. The usual dose is 7.5 to 12.5 mg per kilogram (kg) (3.4 to 5.6 mg per pound) of body weight four times a day; or 15 to 25 mg per kg (6.8 to 11.4 mg per pound) of body weight two times a day.
  - —For prevention of heart infections:
    - Adults and teenagers—Take 1 gram two hours before your dental appointment or surgery, then 500 mg six hours after taking the first dose.
    - Children—Dose is based on body weight. The usual dose is 20 mg per kg (9.1 mg per pound) of body weight two hours before the dental appointment or surgery, then 10 mg per kg (4.5 mg per pound) of body weight six hours after taking the first dose.

Missed dose—If you miss a dose of this medicine, take it as soon as possible. This will help to keep a constant amount of medicine in the blood. However, if it is almost time for your next dose, skip the missed dose and go back to your regular dosing schedule. Do not double doses.

Storage—To store this medicine:

- Keep out of the reach of children.
- Store away from heat and direct light.
- Do not store the capsule or tablet form of erythromycins in the bathroom, near the kitchen sink, or in other damp places. Heat or moisture may cause the medicine to break down.
- Store the oral liquid form of some erythromycins in the refrigerator because heat will cause this medicine to break down. However, keep the medicine from freezing. Follow the directions on the label.
- Do not keep outdated medicine or medicine no longer needed. Be sure that any discarded medicine is out of the reach of children.

Precautions While Using This Medicine

If your symptoms do not improve within a few days, or if they become worse, check with your doctor.

Side Effects of This Medicine

Along with its needed effects, a medicine may cause some unwanted effects. Although not all of these side effects may occur, if they do occur they may need medical attention.

Check with your doctor immediately if any of the following side effects occur:

Less common

Fever; nausea; skin rash, redness, or itching; stomach pain (severe); unusual tiredness or weakness; vomiting; yellow eyes or skin–with erythromycin estolate (rare with other erythromycins)

Less common–with erythromycin injection only

Pain, swelling, or redness at place of injection

Rare

Fainting (repeated); irregular or slow heartbeat; loss of hearing (temporary)

Other side effects may occur that usually do not need medical attention. These side effects may go away during treatment as your body adjusts to the medicine. However, check with your doctor if any of the following side effects continue or are bothersome:

More common

Abdominal or stomach cramping and discomfort; diarrhea; nausea or vomiting

Less common

Sore mouth or tongue; vaginal itching and discharge

Other side effects not listed above may also occur in some patients. If you notice any other effects, check with your doctor.

Additional Information

Once a medicine has been approved for marketing for a certain use, experience may show that it is also useful for

other medical problems. Although these uses are not included in product labeling, erythromycins are used in certain patients with the following medical conditions:

- Acne
- Actinomycosis
- Anthrax
- Chancroid
- Gastroparesis
- Lyme disease
- Lymphogranuloma venereum
- Relapsing fever

Other than the above information, there is no additional information relating to proper use, precautions, or side effects for these uses.

Revised: 07/22/94

ERYTHROMYCIN AND SULFISOXAZOLE Systemic

Some commonly used brand names are:

In the U.S.—

Eryzole
Pediazole
Sulfimycin

Generic name product may also be available.

In Canada—

Pediazole

Description

Erythromycin (eh-rith-roe-MYE-sin) and sulfisoxazole (sul-fi-SOX-a-zole) is a combination antibiotic used to treat ear infections in children. It may also be used for other problems as determined by your doctor. It will not work for colds, flu, or other virus infections.

Erythromycin and sulfisoxazole combination is available only with your doctor's prescription, in the following dosage form:

Oral

- Suspension (U.S. and Canada)

Before Using This Medicine

In deciding to use a medicine, the risks of taking the medicine must be weighed against the good it will do. This is a decision you and your doctor will make. For erythromycin and sulfisoxazole, the following should be considered:

Allergies—Tell your doctor if you have ever had any unusual or allergic reaction to the erythromycins or sulfa medicines, furosemide (e.g., Lasix) or thiazide diuretics (water pills), oral antidiabetics (diabetes medicine you take by mouth), or glaucoma medicine you take by mouth (for example, acetazolamide [e.g., Diamox], dichlorphenamide [e.g., Daranide], methazolamide [e.g., Neptazane]). Also tell your health care professional if you are allergic to any other substances, such as foods, preservatives, or dyes.

Pregnancy—Studies have not been done in humans with either erythromycins or sulfa medicines. In addition, erythromycins have not been shown to cause birth defects or other problems in humans. However, studies in mice, rats, and rabbits have shown that some sulfa medicines cause birth defects, including cleft palate and bone problems.

Breast-feeding—Erythromycins and sulfa medicines pass into the breast milk. This medicine is not recommended for use during breast-feeding. It may cause liver problems, anemia, and other unwanted effects in nursing babies, especially those with glucose-6-phosphate dehydrogenase (G6PD) deficiency.

Children—This medicine has been tested in children over the age of 2 months and has not been shown to cause different side effects or problems than it does in adults.

Older adults—This medicine is intended for use in children and is not generally used in adult patients.

Other medicines—Although certain medicines should not be used together at all, in other cases two different medicines may be used together even if an interaction might occur. In these cases, your doctor may want to change the dose, or other precautions may be necessary. When you are taking erythromycin and sulfisoxazole, it is especially important that your health care professional know if you are taking any of the following:

- Acetaminophen (e.g., Tylenol) (with long-term, high-dose use) or
- Amiodarone (e.g., Cordarone) or
- Anabolic steroids (nandrolone [e.g., Anabolin], oxandrolone [e.g., Anavar], oxymetholone [e.g., Anadrol], stanozolol [e.g., Winstrol]) or
- Androgens (male hormones) or
- Antithyroid agents (medicine for overactive thyroid) or
- Carbamazepine (e.g., Tegretol) or
- Carmustine (e.g., BiCNU) or
- Chloroquine (e.g., Aralen) or
- Dantrolene (e.g., Dantrium) or
- Daunorubicin (e.g., Cerubidine) or
- Disulfiram (e.g., Antabuse) or
- Divalproex (e.g., Depakote) or
- Estrogens (female hormones) or
- Etretinate (e.g., Tegison) or
- Gold salts (medicine for arthritis) or
- Hydroxychloroquine (e.g., Plaquenil) or
- Mercaptopurine (e.g., Purinethol) or
- Methotrexate (e.g., Mexate) or
- Methyldopa (e.g., Aldomet) or
- Naltrexone (e.g., Trexan) (with long-term, high-dose use) or
- Oral contraceptives (birth control pills) containing estrogen or
- Other anti-infectives by mouth or by injection (medicine for infection) or
- Phenothiazines (acetophenazine [e.g., Tindal], chlorpromazine [e.g., Thorazine], fluphenazine [e.g., Prolixin], mesoridazine [e.g., Serentil], perphenazine [e.g., Trilafon], prochlorperazine [e.g., Compazine], promazine [e.g., Sparine], promethazine [e.g., Phenergan], thioridazine

[e.g. Mellaril], trifluoperazine [e.g., Stelazine], triflupromazine [e.g., Vesprin], trimeprazine [e.g., Temaril]) or
- Phenytoin (e.g., Dilantin) or
- Plicamycin (e.g., Mithracin) or
- Valproic acid (e.g., Depakene)—Use of erythromycin and sulfisoxazole with any of these medicines may increase the chance of side effects affecting the liver
- Acetohydroxamic acid (e.g., Lithostat) or
- Dapsone or
- Furazolidone (e.g., Furoxone) or
- Nitrofurantion (e.g., Furadantin) or
- Primaquine or
- Procainamide (e.g., Pronestyl) or
- Quinidine (e.g., Quinidex) or
- Quinine (e.g., Quinamm) or
- Sulfoxone (e.g., Diasone)—Use of erythromycin and sulfisoxazole with these medicines may increase the chance of side effects
- Alfentanil—Long-term use of erythromycin and sulfisoxazole may increase the action of alfentanil and increase the chance of side effects
- Aminophylline (e.g., Somophyllin) or
- Caffeine (e.g., NoDoz) or
- Oxtriphylline (e.g., Choledyl) or
- Theophylline (e.g., Slo-Phyllin, Somophyllin-T, Theo-dur)—Use of erythromycin and sulfisoxazole with these medicines may increase the side effects of these medicines
- Anticoagulants (blood thinners) or
- Antidiabetics, oral (diabetes medicine you take by mouth) or
- Ethotoin (e.g., Peganone) or
- Mephenytoin (e.g., Mesantoin)—Use of erythromycin and sulfisoxazole with these medicines may increase the effects of these medicines, thereby increasing the chance of side effects
- Chloramphenicol or
- Lincomycins—Use of erythromycin and sulfisoxazole with these medicines may decrease the effectiveness of these medicines
- Methenamine (e.g., Mandelamine)—Use of erythromycin and sulfisoxazole with this medicine may, on rare occasion, increase the chance of side effects affecting the kidneys
- Oral contraceptives (birth control pills) containing estrogen—Use of erythromycin and sulfisoxazole with oral contraceptives may decrease the effectiveness of oral contraceptives, increasing the chance of breakthrough bleeding and pregnancy
- Vitamin K (e.g., AquaMEPHYTON, Synkayvite)—Patients taking erythromycin and sulfisoxazole may have an increased need for vitamin K

Other medical problems—The presence of other medical problems may affect the use of erythromycin and sulfisoxazole. Make sure you tell your doctor if you have any other medical problems, especially:
- Anemia or other blood problems or
- Glucose-6-phosphate dehydrogenase (G6PD) deficiency—Erythromycin and sulfisoxazole may increase the chance of blood problems
- Kidney disease or
- Liver disease—Patients with liver or kidney disease may have an increased chance of side effects
- Loss of hearing—High doses of erythromycin and sulfisoxazole may increase the chance for hearing loss in some patients
- Porphyria—Erythromycin and sulfisoxazole may increase the chance of a porphyria attack

Proper Use of This Medicine

Erythromycin and sulfisoxazole combination is best taken with extra amounts of water and may be taken with food. *Additional amounts of water should be taken several times every day,* unless otherwise directed by your doctor. Drinking extra water will help to prevent some unwanted effects (e.g., kidney stones) of sulfa medicines.

Do not give this medicine to infants under 2 months of age, unless otherwise directed by your doctor. Sulfa medicines may cause liver problems in these infants.

Use a specially marked measuring spoon or other device to measure each dose accurately. The average household teaspoon may not hold the right amount of liquid.

Do not use after the expiration date on the label. The medicine may not work properly after that date. Check with your pharmacist if you have any questions about this.

To help clear up your infection completely, *keep taking this medicine for the full time of treatment,* even if you begin to feel better after a few days. If you stop taking this medicine too soon, your symptoms may return.

This medicine works best when there is a constant amount in the blood. *To help keep the amount constant, do not miss any doses. Also, it is best to take the doses at evenly spaced times day and night.* For example, if you are to take 4 doses a day, the doses should be spaced about 6 hours apart. If this interferes with your sleep or other daily activities, or if you need help in planning the best times to take your medicine, check with your health care professional.

Dosing—The dose of erythromycin and sulfisoxazole combination will be different for different patients. *Follow your doctor's orders or the directions on the label.* The following information includes only the average doses of erythromycin and sulfisoxazole combination. *If your dose is different, do not change it* unless your doctor tells you to do so.

- For *oral* dosage form (suspension):
  - —For infections caused by bacteria:
    - Adults and teenagers—This medicine is used only in children.
    - Children—This medicine is usually not used in children younger than 2 months of age. For children 2 months of age and older, the dose is based on body weight:
      - —Children weighing less than 8 kilograms (kg) (under 18 pounds): Dose must be determined by your doctor.
      - —Children weighing 8 to 16 kg (18 to 35 pounds): 1/2 teaspoonful (2.5 milliliter [mL]) every six hours for ten days.
      - —Children weighing 16 to 24 kg (35 to 53 pounds): 1 teaspoonful (5 mL) every six hours for ten days.

—Children weighing 24 to 45 kg (53 to 100 pounds): 1 1/2 teaspoonfuls (7.5 mL) every six hours for ten days.

—Children weighing more than 45 kg (over 100 pounds): 2 teaspoonfuls (10 mL) every six hours for ten days.

Missed dose—If you miss a dose of this medicine, take it as soon as possible. This will help to keep a constant amount of medicine in the blood. However, if it is almost time for your next dose, skip the missed dose and go back to your regular dosing schedule. Do not double the dose.

Storage—To store this medicine:

- Keep out of the reach of children.
- Store away from heat and direct light.
- Store in the refrigerator because heat will cause this medicine to break down. However, keep the medicine from freezing. Follow the directions on the label.
- Do not keep outdated medicine or medicine no longer needed. Be sure that any discarded medicine is out of the reach of children.

Precautions While Using This Medicine

It is very important that your doctor check you at regular visits for any blood problems that may be caused by this medicine, especially if you will be taking this medicine for a long time.

If your symptoms do not improve within a few days, or if they become worse, check with your doctor.

Erythromycin and sulfisoxazole may cause your skin to be more sensitive to sunlight than it is normally. Exposure to sunlight, even for brief periods of time, may cause a skin rash, itching, redness or other discoloration of the skin, or a severe sunburn. When you begin taking this medicine:

- Stay out of direct sunlight, especially between the hours of 10:00 a.m. and 3:00 p.m., if possible.
- Wear protective clothing, including a hat. Also, wear sunglasses.
- Apply a sun block product that has a skin protection factor (SPF) of at least 15. Some patients may require a product with a higher SPF number, especially if they have a fair complexion. If you have any questions about this, check with your health care professional.
- Apply a sun block lipstick that has an SPF of at least 15 to protect your lips.
- Do not use a sunlamp or tanning bed or booth.

If you have a severe reaction from the sun, check with your doctor.

Erythromycin and sulfisoxazole combination may cause blood problems. These problems may result in a greater chance of infection, slow healing, and bleeding of the gums. Therefore, you should be careful when using regular toothbrushes, dental floss, and toothpicks. Dental work should be delayed until your blood counts have returned to normal. Check with your medical docto[r or den]tist if you have any questions about proper oral hygie[ne] (mouth care) during treatment.

Side Effects of This Medicine

Along with its needed effects, a medicine may cause some unwanted effects. Although not all of these side effects may occur, if they do occur they may need medical attention.

Check with your doctor immediately if any of the following side effects occur:

More common

Itching; skin rash

Less common

Aching of joints and muscles; difficulty in swallowing; pale skin; redness, blistering, peeling, or loosening of skin; sore throat and fever; unusual bleeding or bruising; unusual tiredness or weakness; yellow eyes or skin

Rare

Blood in urine; dark or amber urine; temporary loss of hearing (with kidney disease and high doses); lower back pain; pain or burning while urinating; pale stools; severe stomach pain; swelling of front part of neck

In addition to the side effects listed above, check with your doctor as soon as possible if the following side effect occurs:

More common

Increased sensitivity to sunlight

Other side effects may occur that usually do not need medical attention. These side effects may go away during treatment as your body adjusts to the medicine. However, check with your doctor if any of the following side effects continue or are bothersome:

More common

Abdominal or stomach cramping and discomfort; diarrhea; headache; loss of appetite; nausea or vomiting

Less common

Sore mouth or tongue

Other side effects not listed above may also occur in some patients. If you notice any other effects, check with your doctor.

Additional Information

Once a medicine has been approved for marketing for a certain use, experience may show that it is also useful for other medical problems. Although this use is not specifically included in product labeling, erythromycin and sulfisoxazole combination is used in certain patients with the following medical condition:

- Sinusitis (sinus infection)

Other than the above information, there is no additional information relating to proper use, precautions, or side effects for this use.

Revised: 08/27/92
Interim revision: 03/18/94

ESTRAMUSTINE Systemic

Some commonly used brand names are:

In the U.S.—
Emcyt

In Canada—
Emcyt

Other—
Estracyt

Description

Estramustine (ess-tra-MUSS-teen) belongs to the general group of medicines called antineoplastics. It is used to treat some cases of prostate cancer.

Estramustine is a combination of two medicines, an estrogen and mechlorethamine. The way that estramustine works against cancer is not completely understood. However, it seems to interfere with the growth of cancer cells, which are eventually destroyed.

Estramustine is available only with your doctor's prescription, in the following dosage form:

Oral
- Capsules (U.S. and Canada)

Before Using This Medicine

In deciding to use a medicine, the risks of taking the medicine must be weighed against the good it will do. This is a decision you and your doctor will make. For estramustine, the following should be considered:

Allergies—Tell your doctor if you have ever had any unusual or allergic reaction to estramustine, estrogens, or mechlorethamine.

Pregnancy—There is a chance that this medicine may cause birth defects if the male is taking it at the time of conception. It may also cause permanent sterility after it has been taken for a while. Be sure that you have discussed this with your doctor before taking this medicine. Before taking estramustine, make sure your doctor knows if you intend to have children.

Older adults—Many medicines have not been studied specifically in older people. Therefore, it may not be known whether they work exactly the same way they do in younger adults or if they cause different side effects or problems in older people. There is no specific information comparing use of estramustine in the elderly with use in other age groups.

Other medicines—Although certain medicines should not be used together at all, in other cases two different medicines may be used together even if an interaction might occur. In these cases, your doctor may want to change the dose, or other precautions may be necessary. When you are taking estramustine, it is especially important that your health care professional know if you are taking any of the following:

- Acetaminophen (e.g., Tylenol) (with long-term, high-dose use) or
- Amiodarone (e.g., Cordarone) or
- Anabolic steroids (nandrolone [e.g., Anabolin], oxandrolone [e.g., Anavar], oxymetholone [e.g., Anadrol], stanozolol [e.g., Winstrol]) or
- Androgens (male hormones) or
- Anti-infectives by mouth or by injection (medicine for infection) or
- Antithyroid agents (medicine for overactive thyroid) or
- Carbamazepine (e.g., Tegretol) or
- Carmustine (e.g., BiCNU) or
- Chloroquine (e.g., Aralen) or
- Dantrolene (e.g., Dantrium) or
- Disulfiram (e.g., Antabuse) or
- Divalproex (e.g., Depakote) or
- Estrogens (female hormones) or
- Etretinate (e.g., Tegison) or
- Gold salts (medicine for arthritis) or
- Hydroxychloroquine (e.g., Plaquenil) or
- Mercaptopurine (e.g., Purinethol) or
- Methotrexate (e.g., Mexate) or
- Methyldopa (e.g., Aldomet) or
- Naltrexone (e.g., Trexan) (with long-term, high-dose use) or
- Oral contraceptives (birth control pills) containing estrogen or
- Phenothiazines (acetophenazine [e.g., Tindal], chlorpromazine [e.g., Thorazine], fluphenazine [e.g., Prolixin], mesoridazine [e.g., Serentil], perphenazine [e.g., Trilafon], prochlorperazine [e.g., Compazine], promazine [e.g., Sparine], promethazine [e.g., Phenergan], thioridazine [e.g., Mellaril], trifluoperazine [e.g., Stelazine], triflupromazine [e.g., Vesprin], trimeprazine [e.g., Temaril]) or
- Phenytoin (e.g., Dilantin) or
- Plicamycin (e.g., Mithracin) or
- Valproic acid (e.g., Depakene)—May increase the risk of liver problems

Other medical problems—The presence of other medical problems may affect the use of estramustine. Make sure you tell your doctor if you have any other medical problems, especially:

- Asthma or
- Epilepsy or
- Mental depression (or history of) or
- Migraine headaches or
- Kidney disease—Fluid retention sometimes caused by estramustine may worsen these conditions

- Blood clots (or history of) or
- Stroke (or history of) or
- Recent heart attack or stroke—May be worsened because of blood vessel problems caused by estramustine

- Chickenpox (including recent exposure) or
- Herpes zoster (shingles)—Risk of severe disease affecting other parts of the body

- Diabetes mellitus (sugar diabetes)—Estramustine may change the amount of antidiabetic medicine needed

- Gallbladder disease (or history of)—May be worsened by estramustine

- Heart or blood vessel disease—Estramustine can cause circulation problems

- Jaundice or hepatitis (or history of) or other liver disease—Effects, including liver problems, may be increased

- Stomach ulcer—May be aggravated by estramustine

Smoking—Because smoking causes narrowing of blood vessels, it can increase the risk of serious circulation problems, which can lead to stroke or heart attack.

Proper Use of This Medicine

Use this medicine only as directed by your doctor. Do not use more or less of it, and do not use it more often than your doctor ordered. The exact amount of medicine you need has been carefully worked out. Taking too much may increase the chance of side effects, while taking too little may not improve your condition.

Do not take estramustine within 1 hour before or 2 hours after meals or after the time you take milk, milk formulas, or other dairy products, since they may keep the medicine from working properly.

This medicine commonly causes nausea and sometimes causes vomiting. However, it may have to be taken for several weeks to months to be effective. Even if you begin to feel ill, *do not stop using this medicine without first checking with your doctor.* Ask your health care professional for ways to lessen these effects.

If you vomit shortly after taking a dose of estramustine, check with your doctor. You will be told whether to take the dose again or to wait until the next scheduled dose.

Dosing—The dose of estramustine will be different for different patients. The dose that is used may depend on a number of things, including what the medicine is being used for, the patient's size, and whether or not other medicines are also being taken. *If you are taking estramustine at home, follow your doctor's orders or the directions on the label.* If you have any questions about the proper dose of estramustine, ask your doctor.

Missed dose—If you miss a dose of this medicine, skip the missed dose and go back to your regular dosing schedule. Do not double doses.

Storage—To store this medicine:

- Keep out of the reach of children.
- Store in the refrigerator, away from direct light.
- Do not store in the bathroom, near the kitchen sink, or in other damp places. Heat or moisture may cause the medicine to break down.
- Do not keep outdated medicine or medicine no longer needed. Be sure that any discarded medicine is out of the reach of children.

Precautions While Using This Medicine

It is very important that your doctor check your progress at regular visits to make sure that the medicine is working properly and does not cause unwanted effects.

While you are being treated with estramustine, and after you stop treatment with it, *do not have any immunizations (vaccinations) without your doctor's approval.* Estramustine may lower your body's resistance and there is a chance you might get the infection the immunization is meant to prevent. In addition, other persons living in your household should not take oral polio vaccine since there is a chance they could pass the polio virus on to you. Also, avoid persons who have recently taken oral polio vaccine. Do not get close to them and do not stay in the same room with them for very long. If you cannot take these precautions, you should consider wearing a protective face mask that covers the nose and mouth.

Side Effects of This Medicine

Along with its needed effects, a medicine may cause some unwanted effects. Although not all of these side effects may occur, if they do occur they may need medical attention.

Check with your doctor immediately if any of the following side effects occur. If your doctor is not available, go to the nearest hospital emergency room.

Rare

Black, tarry stools; blood in urine or stools; cough or hoarseness; fever or chills; headaches (severe or sudden); loss of coordination (sudden); lower back or side pain; painful or difficult urination; pains in chest, groin, or leg (especially calf of leg); pinpoint red spots on skin; shortness of breath (sudden, for no apparent reason); slurred speech (sudden); unusual bleeding or bruising; vision changes (sudden); weakness or numbness in arm or leg

Check with your doctor as soon as possible if any of the following side effects occur:

More common

Swelling of feet or lower legs

Rare

Skin rash or fever; unusual tiredness or weakness

Other side effects may occur that usually do not need medical attention. These side effects may go away during treatment as your body adjusts to the medicine. However, check with your doctor if any of the following side effects continue or are bothersome or if you have any questions about them:

More common

Breast tenderness or enlargement; decreased interest in sex; diarrhea; nausea

Less common

Trouble in sleeping; vomiting

Other side effects not listed above may also occur in some patients. If you notice any other effects, check with your doctor.

Revised: 07/11/94

ESTROGENS Systemic

Some commonly used brand names are:

In the U.S.—

Aquest[5]
Climara[4]
Clinagen LA 40[4]
Delestrogen[4]
depGynogen[4]
Depo-Estradiol[4]
Depogen[4]
Dioval 40[4]
Dioval XX[4]
Dura-Estrin[4]
Duragen-20[4]
E-Cypionate[4]
Estinyl[7]
Estrace[4]
Estraderm[4]
Estragyn 5[5]
Estragyn LA 5[4]
Estra-L 40[4]
Estratab[3]
Estro-A[5]
Estro-Cyp[4]
Estrofem[4]
Estro-L.A.[4]
Estrone '5'[5]
Estro-Span[4]
Gynogen L.A. 20[4]
Gynogen L.A. 40[4]
Kestrone-5[5]
Menaval-20[4]
Menest[3]
Ogen .625[6]
Ogen 1.25[6]
Ogen 2.5[6]
Ortho-Est .625[6]
Ortho-Est 1.25[6]
Premarin[1]
Premarin Intravenous[1]
Stilphostrol[2]
Valergen-10[4]
Valergen-20[4]
Valergen-40[4]
Vivelle[4]
Wehgen[5]

In Canada—

C.E.S.[1]
Congest[1]
Delestrogen[4]
Estinyl[7]
Estrace[4]
Estraderm[4]
Femogex[4]
Honvol[2]
Neo-Estrone[3]
Ogen[6]
Premarin[1]
Premarin Intravenous[1]
Stilbestrol[2]
Vivelle[4]

Other commonly used names are:

DES[2]
Fosfestrol[2]
Oestradiol[4]
Oestrone[5]
Piperazine Estrone Sulfate[6]
Stilboestrol[2]

Note: For quick reference, the following estrogens are numbered to match the corresponding brand names.

This information applies to the following medicines:

1. Conjugated Estrogens (CON-ju-gate-ed-ES-troe-jenz)§
2. Diethylstilbestrol (dye-eth-il-stil-BES-trole)
3. Esterified Estrogens (es-TAIR-i-fyed Es-troe-jenz)
4. Estradiol (es-tra-DYE-ole)‡
5. Estrone (ES-trone)†‡
6. Estropipate (es-troe-PIH-pate)‡
7. Ethinyl Estradiol (ETH-in-il es-tra-DYE-ole)

†Not commercially available in Canada.
‡Generic name product may also be available in the U.S.
§Generic name product may also be available in Canada.

Description

Estrogens (ES-troe-jenz) are female hormones. They are produced by the body and are necessary for the normal sexual development of the female and for the regulation of the menstrual cycle during the childbearing years.

The ovaries begin to produce less estrogen after menopause (the change of life). This medicine is prescribed to make up for the lower amount of estrogen. Estrogens help relieve signs of menopause, such as hot flashes and unusual sweating, chills, faintness, or dizziness.

Estrogens are prescribed for several reasons:

- to provide additional hormone when the body does not produce enough of its own, such as during menopause or when female puberty (development of female sexual organs) does not occur on time. Other conditions include a genital skin condition (vulvar atrophy), inflammation of the vagina (atrophic vaginitis), or ovary problems (female hypogonadism or failure or removal of both ovaries).
- to help prevent weakening of bones (osteoporosis) in women past menopause.
- in the treatment of selected cases of breast cancer in men and women.
- in the treatment of men with cancer of the prostate.

Estrogens may also be used for other conditions as determined by your doctor.

There is *no* medical evidence to support the belief that the use of estrogens will keep the patient feeling young, keep the skin soft, or delay the appearance of wrinkles. Nor has it been proven that the use of estrogens during menopause will relieve emotional and nervous symptoms, unless these symptoms are caused by other menopausal symptoms, such as hot flashes or hot flushes.

Estrogens are available only with your doctor's prescription, in the following dosage forms:

Oral

Conjugated Estrogens
- Tablets (U.S. and Canada)

Diethylstilbestrol
- Tablets (U.S. and Canada)

Esterified Estrogens
- Tablets (U.S. and Canada)

Estradiol
- Tablets (U.S. and Canada)

Estropipate
- Tablets (U.S. and Canada)

Ethinyl Estradiol
- Tablets (U.S. and Canada)

Parenteral

Conjugated Estrogens
- Injection (U.S. and Canada)

Diethylstilbestrol
- Injection (U.S. and Canada)

Estradiol
- Injection (U.S. and Canada)

Estrone
- Injection (U.S.)

Topical

Estradiol
- Transdermal system (skin patch) (U.S. and Canada)

Before Using This Medicine

In deciding to use a medicine, the risks of taking the medicine must be weighed against the good it will do. This is a decision you and your doctor will make. For estrogens, the following should be considered:

Allergies—Tell your doctor if you have ever had any unusual or allergic reaction to estrogens. Also tell your health care professional if you are allergic to any other substances, such as foods, preservatives, or dyes.

Pregnancy—Estrogens are not recommended for use during pregnancy or right after giving birth. Becoming pregnant or maintaining a pregnancy is not likely to occur around the time of menopause.

Certain estrogens have been shown to cause serious birth defects in humans and animals. Some daughters of women who took diethylstilbestrol (DES) during pregnancy have developed reproductive (genital) tract problems and, rarely, cancer of the vagina or cervix (opening to the uterus) when they reached childbearing age. Some sons of women who took DES during pregnancy have developed urinary-genital tract problems.

Breast-feeding—Use of this medicine is not recommended in nursing mothers. Estrogens pass into the breast milk and their possible effect on the baby is not known.

Older adults—This medicine has been tested and has not been shown to cause different side effects or problems in older women than it does in younger women.

Other medicines—Although certain medicines should not be used together at all, in other cases two different medicines may be used together even if an interaction might occur. In these cases, your doctor may want to change the dose, or other precautions may be necessary. When you are taking estrogens, it is especially important that your health care professional know if you are taking any of the following:

- Acetaminophen (e.g., Tylenol) (with long-term, high-dose use) or
- Amiodarone (e.g., Cordarone) or
- Anabolic steroids (nandrolone [e.g., Anabolin], oxandrolone [e.g., Anavar], oxymetholone [e.g., Anadrol], stanozolol [e.g., Winstrol]) or
- Androgens (male hormones) or
- Anti-infectives by mouth or by injection (medicine for infection) or
- Antithyroid agents (medicine for overactive thyroid) or
- Carbamazepine (e.g., Tegretol) or
- Carmustine (e.g., BiCNU) or
- Chloroquine (e.g., Aralen) or
- Dantrolene (e.g., Dantrium) or
- Daunorubicin (e.g., Cerubidine) or
- Disulfiram (e.g., Antabuse) or
- Divalproex (e.g., Depakote) or
- Etretinate (e.g., Tegison) or
- Gold salts (medicine for arthritis) or
- Hydroxychloroquine (e.g., Plaquenil) or
- Isoniazid or
- Mercaptopurine (e.g., Purinethol) or
- Methotrexate (e.g., Mexate) or
- Methyldopa (e.g., Aldomet) or
- Naltrexone (e.g., Trexan) (with long-term, high-dose use) or
- Oral contraceptives (birth control pills) containing estrogen or
- Phenothiazines (acetophenazine [e.g., Tindal], chlorpromazine [e.g., Thorazine], fluphenazine [e.g., Prolixin], mesoridazine [e.g., Serentil], perphenazine [e.g., Trilafon], prochlorperazine [e.g., Compazine], promazine [e.g., Sparine], promethazine [e.g., Phenergan], thioridazine [e.g., Mellaril], trifluoperazine [e.g., Stelazine], triflupromazine [e.g., Vesprin], trimeprazine [e.g., Temaril]) or
- Phenytoin (e.g., Dilantin) or
- Plicamycin (e.g., Mithracin) or
- Valproic acid (e.g., Depakene)—Use of these medicines with estrogens may increase the chance of problems occurring that affect the liver
- Cyclosporine (e.g., Sandimmune)—Estrogens can prevent cyclosporine's removal from the body; this can lead to cyclosporine causing kidney or liver problems
- Protease inhibitors, such as ritonavir (e.g., Norvir)—May decrease the effect of estrogens

Other medical problems—The presence of other medical problems may affect the use of estrogens. Make sure you tell your doctor if you have any other medical problems, especially:

For all patients

- Blood clotting problems (or history of during previous estrogen therapy)—Estrogens usually are not used until blood clotting problems stop; using estrogens is not a problem for most patients without a history of blood clotting problems due to estrogen use
- Bone cancer or
- Breast cancer or
- Cancer of the uterus or
- Fibroid tumors of the uterus—Estrogens may interfere with the treatment of breast or bone cancer or worsen cancer of the uterus when these conditions are present
- Changes in genital or vaginal bleeding of unknown causes—Use of estrogens may delay diagnosis or worsen condition. The reason for the bleeding should be determined before estrogens are used
- Endometriosis or
- Gallbladder disease or gallstones (or history of) or
- High cholesterol or triglycerides (or history of) or
- Liver disease (or history of) or
- Pancreatitis (inflammation of pancreas)—Estrogens may worsen these conditions. Although estrogens can improve blood cholesterol, they can worsen blood triglycerides for some people

For males treated for breast or prostate cancer

- Blood clots or
- Heart or circulation disease or
- Stroke—Males with these medical problems may be more likely to have clotting problems while taking estrogens; the high doses of estrogens used to treat male breast or prostate cancer have been shown to increase the chances of heart attack, phlebitis (inflamed veins) caused by a blood clot, or blood clots in the lungs

Proper Use of This Medicine

Estrogens usually come with patient information or directions. Read them carefully before taking this medicine.

Take this medicine only as directed by your doctor. Do not take more of it and do not take or use it for a longer time than your doctor ordered. For patients taking any of the estrogens by mouth, try to take the medicine at the same time each day to reduce the possibility of side effects and to allow it to work better.

For patients taking any of the estrogens by mouth or by injection:

- Nausea may occur during the first few weeks after you start taking estrogens. This effect usually disappears with continued use. If the nausea is bothersome, it can usually be prevented or reduced by taking each dose with food or immediately after food.

For patients using the transdermal (skin patch) form of estradiol:
- Wash and dry your hands thoroughly before and after handling the patch.
- Apply the patch to a clean, dry, nonoily skin area of your abdomen (stomach) or buttocks that has little or no hair and is free of cuts or irritation.
- *Do not apply to the breasts.* Also, do not apply to the waistline or anywhere else where tight clothes may rub the patch loose.
- Press the patch firmly in place with the palm of your hand for about 10 seconds. Make sure there is good contact, especially around the edges.
- If a patch becomes loose or falls off, you may reapply it or discard it and apply a new patch.
- Each dose is best applied to a different area of skin on your abdomen so that at least 1 week goes by before the same area is used again. This will help prevent skin irritation.

Dosing—The dose of these medicines will be different for different patients. *Follow your doctor's orders or the directions on the label.* The following information includes only the average doses of these medicines. *If your dose is different, do not change it* unless your doctor tells you to do so.

The number of capsules or tablets that you take or the amount of injection you use depends on the strength of the medicine. Also, *the number of doses you take or use each day or patches you apply each week, the time allowed between doses, and the length of time you take or use the medicine depend on the medical problem for which you are taking, using, or applying estrogen.*

For conjugated estrogens
- For *oral* dosage form (tablets):
  - —For treating breast cancer in women after menopause and in men:
    - Adults—10 milligrams (mg) three times a day for at least three months.
  - —For treating a genital skin condition (vulvar atrophy), inflammation of the vagina (atrophic vaginitis), or symptoms of menopause:
    - Adults—0.3 to 1.25 mg a day. Your doctor may want you to take the medicine each day or only on certain days of the month.
  - —To prevent loss of bone (osteoporosis):
    - Adults—0.625 mg a day. Your doctor may want you to take the medicine each day or only on certain days of the month.
  - —For treating ovary problems (female hypogonadism or for starting puberty):
    - Adults—2.5 to 7.5 mg a day. This dose is divided up and taken in smaller doses. Your doctor may want you to take the medicine only on certain days of the month.
  - —For treating ovary problems (failure or removal of both ovaries):
    - Adults—1.25 mg a day. Your doctor may want you to take the medicine each day or only on certain days of the month.
  - —For treating prostate cancer:
    - Adults—1.25 to 2.5 mg three times a day.
- For *injection* dosage form:
  - —For controlling abnormal bleeding of the uterus:
    - Adults—25 mg injected into a muscle or vein. This may be repeated in six to twelve hours if needed.

For diethylstilbestrol
- For *oral* dosage forms (tablets):
  - —For treating prostate cancer:
    - Adults—At first, 1 to 3 milligrams (mg) a day. Later, your doctor may decrease your dose to 1 mg a day.

For diethylstilbestrol diphosphate
- For *oral* dosage form (tablets):
  - —For treating prostate cancer:
    - Adults—50 to 200 milligrams (mg) three times a day.
- For *injection* dosage form:
  - —For treating prostate cancer:
    - Adults—At first, 500 mg mixed in solution with sodium chloride or dextrose injection and injected slowly into a vein. Your doctor may increase your dose to 1 gram a day for five or more straight days as needed. Then, your doctor may lower your dose to 250 to 500 mg one or two times a week.

For esterified estrogens
- For *oral* dosage form (tablets):
  - —For treating breast cancer in women after menopause and in men:
    - Adults—10 milligrams (mg) three times a day for at least three months.
  - —For treating a genital skin condition (vulvar atrophy) or inflammation of the vagina (atrophic vaginitis):
    - Adults—0.3 to 1.25 mg a day. Your doctor may want you to take the medicine each day or only on certain days of the month.
  - —For treating ovary problems (failure or removal of both ovaries):
    - Adults—1.25 mg a day. Your doctor may want you to take the medicine each day or only on certain days of the month.
  - —For treating ovary problems (female hypogonadism):
    - Adults—2.5 to 7.5 mg a day. This dose may be divided up and taken in smaller doses. Your doctor may want you to take the medicine each day or only on certain days of the month.
  - —For treating symptoms of menopause:
    - Adults—0.625 to 1.25 mg a day. Your doctor may want you to take the medicine each day or only on certain days of the month.
  - —For treating prostate cancer:
    - Adults—1.25 to 2.5 mg three times a day.

For estradiol

- For *oral* dosage form (tablets):
  - —For treating breast cancer in women after menopause and in men:
    - Adults—10 milligrams (mg) three times a day for at least three months.
  - —For treating a genital skin condition (vulvar atrophy), inflammation of the vagina (atrophic vaginitis), ovary problems (female hypogonadism or failure or removal of both ovaries), or symptoms of menopause:
    - Adults—0.5 to 2 mg a day. Your doctor may want you to take the medicine each day or only on certain days of the month.
  - —For treating prostate cancer:
    - Adults—1 to 2 mg three times a day.
  - —To prevent loss of bone (osteoporosis):
    - Adults—0.5 mg a day. Your doctor may want you to take the medicine each day or only on certain days of the month.
- For *transdermal* dosage form (skin patches):
  - —For treating a genital skin condition (vulvar atrophy), inflammation of the vagina (atrophic vaginitis), symptoms of menopause, ovary problems (female hypogonadism or failure or removal of both ovaries), or to prevent loss of bone (osteoporosis):

    For the Climara patches
    - Adults—0.05 or 0.1 milligram (mg) (one patch) applied to the skin and worn for one week. Then, remove that patch and apply a new one. A new patch should be applied once a week for three weeks. During the fourth week, you may or may not wear a patch. Your health care professional will tell you what you should do for this fourth week. After the fourth week, you will repeat the cycle.

    For the Estraderm or Vivelle patches
    - Adults—0.025 to 0.1 mg (one patch) applied to the skin and worn for one half of a week. Then, remove that patch and apply and wear a new patch for the rest of the week. A new patch should be applied two times a week for three weeks. During the fourth week, you may or may not apply new patches. Your health care professional will tell you what you should do for this fourth week. After the fourth week, you will repeat the cycle.

For estradiol cypionate

- For *injection* dosage form:
  - —For treating ovary problems (female hypogonadism):
    - Adults—1.5 to 2 milligrams (mg) injected into a muscle once a month.
  - —For treating symptoms of menopause:
    - Adults—1 to 5 mg injected into a muscle every three to four weeks.

For estradiol valerate

- For *injection* dosage form:
  - —For treating a genital skin condition (vulvar atrophy), inflammation of the vagina (atrophic vaginitis), symptoms of menopause, or ovary problems (female hypogonadism or failure or removal of both ovaries):
    - Adults—10 to 20 milligrams (mg) injected into a muscle every four weeks as needed.
  - —For treating prostate cancer:
    - Adults—30 mg injected into a muscle every one or two weeks.

For estrone

- For *injection* dosage form:
  - —For controlling abnormal bleeding of the uterus:
    - Adults—2 to 5 milligrams (mg) a day, injected into a muscle for several days.
  - —For treating a genital skin condition (vulvar atrophy), inflammation of the vagina (atrophic vaginitis), or symptoms of menopause:
    - Adults—0.1 to 0.5 mg injected into a muscle two or three times a week. Your doctor may want you to receive the medicine each week or only during certain weeks of the month.
  - —For treating ovary problems (female hypogonadism or failure or removal of both ovaries):
    - Adults—0.1 to 1 mg a week. This is injected into a muscle as a single dose or divided into more than one dose. Your doctor may want you to receive the medicine each week or only during certain weeks of the month.
  - —For treating prostate cancer:
    - Adults—2 to 4 mg injected into a muscle two or three times a week.

For estropipate

- For oral dosage form (tablets):
  - —For treating a genital skin condition (vulvar atrophy), inflammation of the vagina (atrophic vaginitis), or symptoms of menopause:
    - Adults—0.75 to 6 milligrams (mg) a day. Your doctor may want you to take the medicine each day or only on certain days of the month.
  - —For treating ovary problems (female hypogonadism, failure or removal of both ovaries):
    - Adults—1.5 to 9 mg a day. Your doctor may want you to take the medicine each day or only on certain days of the month.
  - —To prevent loss of bone (osteoporosis):
    - Adults—0.75 mg a day. Your doctor may want you to take the medicine each day for twenty-five days of a thirty-one-day cycle.

For ethinyl estradiol

- For *oral* dosage form (tablets):
  - —For treating breast cancer in women after menopause:
    - Adults—1 milligram (mg) three times a day.

—For treating ovary problems (female hypogonadism or failure or removal of both ovaries):

- Adults—0.05 mg one to three times a day for three to six months. Your doctor may want you to take the medicine each day or only on certain days of the month.

—For treating prostate cancer:

- Adults—0.15 to 3 mg a day.

—For treating symptoms of menopause:

- Adults—0.02 to 0.05 mg a day. Your doctor may want you to take the medicine each day or only on certain days of the month.

Missed dose—

- For patients taking any of the estrogens by mouth: If you miss a dose of this medicine, take it as soon as possible. However, if it is almost time for your next dose, skip the missed dose and go back to your regular dosing schedule. Do not double doses.
- For patients using the transdermal (skin patch) form of estradiol: If you forget to apply a new patch when you are supposed to, apply it as soon as possible. However, if it is almost time for the next patch, skip the missed one and go back to your regular schedule. Always remove the old patch before applying a new one. Do not apply more than one patch at a time.

Storage—To store this medicine:

- Keep out of the reach of children.
- Store away from heat and direct light.
- Do not store in the bathroom medicine cabinet because the heat or moisture may cause the medicine to break down.
- Keep the injection form of this medicine from freezing.
- Do not keep outdated medicine or medicine no longer needed. Be sure that any discarded medicine is out of the reach of children.

Precautions While Using This Medicine

It is very important that your doctor check your progress at regular visits to make sure this medicine does not cause unwanted effects. These visits will usually be every year, but some doctors require them more often.

In some patients using estrogens, tenderness, swelling, or bleeding of the gums may occur. Brushing and flossing your teeth carefully and regularly and massaging your gums may help prevent this. See your dentist regularly to have your teeth cleaned. Check with your medical doctor or dentist if you have any questions about how to take care of your teeth and gums, or if you notice any tenderness, swelling, or bleeding of your gums.

It is not yet known whether the use of estrogens increases the risk of breast cancer in women. Therefore, it is very important that you regularly check your breasts for any unusual lumps or discharge. Report any problems to your doctor. You should also have a mammogram (x-ray pictures of the breasts) done if your doctor recommends it. Because breast cancer has occurred in men taking estrogens, regular breast self-exams and exams by your doctor for any unusual lumps or discharge should be done.

If your menstrual periods have stopped, they may start again. This effect will continue for as long as the medicine is taken. However, if taking the continuous treatment (0.625 mg conjugated estrogens and 2.5 mg medroxyprogestone once a day), monthly bleeding usually stops by 10 months.

Also, vaginal bleeding between your regular menstrual periods may occur during the first 3 months of use. Do not stop taking your medicine. *Check with your doctor if bleeding continues for an unusually long time, if your period has not started within 45 days of your last period, or if you think you are pregnant.*

Tell the doctor in charge that you are taking this medicine before having any laboratory test because some results may be affected.

Side Effects of This Medicine

Women rarely have a severe side effect from taking estrogens to replace estrogen. Discuss these possible effects with your doctor:

- The prolonged use of estrogens has been reported to increase the risk of endometrial cancer (cancer of the lining of the uterus) in women after the menopause. This risk seems to increase as the dose and the length of use increase. When estrogens are used in low doses for less than 1 year, there is less risk. The risk is also reduced if a progestin (another female hormone) is added to, or replaces part of, your estrogen dose. If the uterus has been removed by surgery (total hysterectomy), there is no risk of endometrial cancer.
- It is not yet known whether the use of estrogens increases the risk of breast cancer in women. Although some large studies show an increased risk, most studies and information gathered to date do not support this idea. Breast cancer has been reported in men taking estrogens.

The following side effects may be caused by blood clots, which could lead to stroke, heart attack, or death. These side effects rarely occur, and, when they do occur, they occur in men treated for cancer using high doses of estrogens. *Get emergency help immediately* if any of the following side effects occur:

Rare—for males being treated for breast or prostate cancer only

Headache (sudden or severe); loss of coordination (sudden); loss of vision or change of vision (sudden); pains in chest, groin, or leg, especially in calf of leg; shortness of breath (sudden and unexplained); slurring of speech (sudden); weakness or numbness in arm or leg

Also, check with your doctor as soon as possible if any of the following side effects occur:

More common

Breast pain (in females and males); increased breast size (in females and males); swelling of feet and lower legs; weight gain (rapid)

Less common or rare

Changes in vaginal bleeding (spotting, breakthrough bleeding, prolonged or heavier bleeding, or complete stoppage of bleeding); lumps in, or discharge from, breast (in females and males); pains in stomach, side, or abdomen; yellow eyes or skin

Other side effects may occur that usually do not need medical attention. These side effects may go away during treatment as your body adjusts to the medicine. However, check with your doctor if any of the following side effects continue or are bothersome:

More common

Bloating of stomach; cramps of lower stomach; loss of appetite; nausea; skin irritation or redness where skin patch was worn

Less common

Diarrhea (mild); dizziness (mild); headaches (mild); migraine headaches; problems in wearing contact lenses; unusual decrease in sexual desire (in males); unusual increase in sexual desire (in females); vomiting (usually with high doses)

Also, many women who are taking estrogens with a progestin (another female hormone) will start having monthly vaginal bleeding, similar to menstrual periods, again. This effect will continue for as long as the medicine is taken. However, monthly bleeding will not occur in women who have had the uterus removed by surgery (total hysterectomy).

Other side effects not listed above may also occur in some patients. If you notice any other effects, check with your doctor.

Additional Information

Once a medicine has been approved for marketing for a certain use, experience may show that it is also useful for other medical problems. Although these uses are not included in product labeling, estrogen is used in certain patients with the following medical conditions:

- Atherosclerotic disease (hardening of the arteries)
- Osteoporosis caused by lack of estrogen before menopause
- Turner's syndrome (a genetic disorder)

Other than the above information, there is no additional information relating to proper use, precautions, or side effects for these uses.

Revised: 08/24/97

ESTROGENS Vaginal

Some commonly used brand names are:

In the U.S.—

Estrace[3]
Estring[3]
Ogen[5]
Ortho Dienestrol[2]
Premarin[1]

In Canada—

Estring[3]
Oestrilin[4]
Ortho Dienestrol[2]
Premarin[1]

Other commonly used names are dienoestrol[2], oestradiol[3], and piperazine estrone sulfate[5].

Note: For quick reference, the following estrogens are numbered to match the corresponding brand names.

This information applies to the following medicines:

1. Conjugated Estrogens (CON-ju-gate-ed ES-troe-jenz)
2. Dienestrol (dye-en-ES-trole)
3. Estradiol (es-tra-DYE-ole)
4. Estrone (ES-trone)*
5. Estropipate (es-troe-PIH-pate)†

*Not commercially available in the U.S.
†Not commercially available in Canada.

Description

Estrogens (ES-troe-jenz) are hormones produced by the body. Among other things, estrogens help develop and maintain female organs.

When your body is in short supply of this hormone, replacing it can ease uncomfortable changes that occur in the vagina, vulva (female genitals), and urethra (part of the urinary system). Conditions that are treated with vaginal estrogens include a genital skin condition (vulvar atrophy), inflammation of the vagina (atrophic vaginitis), and inflammation of the urethra (atrophic urethritis).

Estrogens work partly by increasing a normal clear discharge from the vagina and making the vulva and urethra healthy. Using or applying an estrogen relieves or lessens:

- Dryness and soreness in the vagina
- Itching, redness, or soreness of the vulva
- Feeling an urge to urinate more often than is needed or experiencing pain while urinating
- Pain during sexual intercourse

When used vaginally or on the skin, most estrogens are absorbed into the bloodstream and cause some, but not all, of the same effects as when they are taken by mouth. Estrogens used vaginally at very low doses for treating local problems of the genitals and urinary system will not protect against osteoporosis, or stop the hot flushes caused by menopause.

Estrogens for vaginal use are available only with your doctor's prescription, in the following dosage forms:

Vaginal

Conjugated Estrogens
- Cream (U.S. and Canada)

Dienestrol
- Cream (U.S. and Canada)

Estradiol
- Cream (U.S.)
- Insert (or ring) (U.S. and Canada)

Estrone
- Cream (Canada)
- Suppositories (Canada)

Estropipate
- Cream (U.S.)

Before Using This Medicine

In deciding to use a medicine, the risks of using the medicine must be weighed against the good it will do. This is a decision you and your doctor will make. For vaginal estrogens, the following should be considered:

Allergies—Tell your doctor if you have ever had any unusual or allergic reaction to estrogens or to parabens. Also tell your health care professional if you are allergic to any other substances, such as foods, preservatives, or dyes.

Pregnancy—Estrogens are not recommended for use during pregnancy, since an estrogen called diethylstilbestrol (DES) that is no longer taken for hormone replacement has caused serious birth defects in humans and animals.

Breast-feeding—Use of this medicine is not recommended in nursing mothers. Estrogens pass into the breast milk.

Older adults—This medicine has been tested and has not been shown to cause different side effects or problems in older people than it does in younger adults.

Other medicines—Although certain medicines should not be used together at all, in other cases two different medicines may be used together even if an interaction might occur. In these cases, your doctor may want to change the dose, or other precautions may be necessary. Tell your health care professional if you are taking or using any other prescription or nonprescription (over-the-counter [OTC]) medicine.

Other medical problems—The presence of other medical problems may affect the use of estrogens. Make sure you tell your doctor if you have any other medical problems, especially:

- Blood clotting problems—Although worsening of a blood clotting condition is unlikely, some doctors do not prescribe vaginal estrogens for patients with blood clotting problems or a history of these problems
- Certain cancers, including cancers of the breast, bone, or uterus (active or suspected)—Estrogens may interfere with the treatment of breast or bone cancer or worsen cancer of the uterus when these conditions are present
- Endometriosis or
- Fibroid tumors of the uterus—Estrogens may worsen endometriosis or increase the size of fibroid tumors
- Irritation or infection of the vagina—Usually estrogens decrease infections or irritation of the vagina, but sometimes these conditions may become worse
- Liver disease, severe—Estrogens may worsen the condition in some cases; however, many doctors recommend vaginal use of estrogen because it has less effect on the liver than when estrogens are taken by mouth
- Physical problems within the vagina, such as narrow vagina, vaginal stenosis, or vaginal prolapse—Estradiol vaginal insert may be more likely to slip out of place or cause problems, such as irritation of the vagina
- Unusual genital or vaginal bleeding of unknown causes—Use of estrogens may delay diagnosis or worsen the condition. The reason for the bleeding should be determined before estrogens are used

Proper Use of This Medicine

Vaginal estrogen products usually come with patient directions. *Read them carefully before using this medicine.* Wash your hands before and after using this medicine. Also, keep the medicine out of your eyes. If this medicine does get into your eyes, wash them out immediately, but carefully, with large amounts of tap water. If your eyes still burn or are painful, check with your doctor.

Use this medicine only as directed. Do not use more of it and do not use it for a longer time than your doctor ordered. It can take up to 4 months to see the full effect of the estrogens. Your doctor may reconsider continuing your estrogen treatment or may lower your dose several times within the first one to two months, and every 3 to 6 months after that. Sometimes a switch to oral estrogens may be required for added benefits or for higher doses. When using the estradiol vaginal insert, you will need to replace it every 3 months or remove it after 3 months.

For vaginal creams or suppositories—

Vaginal creams and some vaginal suppositories are inserted with a plastic applicator. Directions for using the applicator are supplied with your medicine. If you do not see your dose marked on the applicator, ask your health care professional for more information.

- *To fill the applicator for cream dosage forms:*
  - —Break the metal seal at the opening of the tube by using the point on the top of the cap.
  - —Screw the applicator onto the tube.
  - —Squeeze the medicine into the applicator slowly until it is measured properly.
  - —Remove the applicator from the tube. Replace the cap on the tube.
- *To fill the applicator for suppository dosage form*
  - —Place the suppository into the applicator.
- *To place the dose using the applicator for cream and suppository dosage forms:*
  - —Relax while lying on your back with your knees bent or stand with one foot on a chair.
  - —Hold the full applicator in one hand. Slide the applicator slowly into the vagina. Stop before it becomes uncomfortable.
  - —Slowly press the plunger until it stops.
  - —Withdraw the applicator. The medicine will be left behind in the vagina.
- *To care for the applicator for cream and suppository dosage forms:*
  - —Clean the applicator after use by pulling the plunger out of the applicator and washing both parts completely in warm, soapy water. *Do not use hot or boiling water.*
  - —Rinse well.
  - —After drying the applicator, replace the plunger.

For vaginal insert dosage form

- *To place the vaginal insert*
  - —Relax while lying on your back with your knees bent or stand with one foot on a chair.
  - —Pinch or press the sides of the vaginal insert together, between your forefinger and middle finger.

—With one hand, part the folds of skin around your vagina.

—Slide the vaginal insert slowly into the upper third of your vagina. Stop before it becomes uncomfortable. The exact location is not too important but it should be comfortable.

—If it seems uncomfortable, then carefully push the vaginal insert higher into the vagina.

- *To remove the vaginal insert*

—Stand with one foot on a chair.

—Slide one finger into the vagina and hook it around the closest part of the vaginal insert.

—Slowly pull the vaginal insert out.

—Dispose of the vaginal insert by wrapping it up and throwing it into the trash. *Do not flush it down the toilet.*

Dosing—The dose of vaginal estrogens will be different for different women. *Follow your doctor's orders or the directions on the label.* The following information includes only the average doses of these medicines. *If your dose is different, do not change it* unless your doctor tells you to do so.

For conjugated estrogens

- For *vaginal* dosage form (cream):

—For treating a genital skin condition (vulvar atrophy) and inflammation of the vagina (atrophic vaginitis):

• Adults: 0.3 to 1.25 milligrams (mg) of conjugated estrogens (one half to two grams of cream) inserted into the vagina once a day or as directed by your doctor to achieve the lowest dose possible. Usually your doctor will want you to use this medicine for only three weeks of each month (three weeks on and one week off).

For dienestrol

- For *vaginal* dosage form (cream):

—For treating a genital skin condition (vulvar atrophy) and inflammation of the vagina (atrophic vaginitis):

• Adults: At first, one applicatorful of 0.01% cream inserted into the vagina one or two times a day for one to two weeks, decreasing the dose by one half over two and four weeks. After four weeks, your doctor will probably ask you to use the medicine less often, such as one applicatorful one to three times a *week* and for only three weeks of each month (three weeks on and one week off).

For estradiol

- For *vaginal* dosage form (cream):

—For treating a genital skin condition (vulvar atrophy) and inflammation of the vagina (atrophic vaginitis):

• Adults: 200 to 400 micrograms (mcg) of estradiol (two to four grams of cream) inserted into the vagina once a day for one to two weeks, decreasing the dose by one half over two and four weeks. After four weeks, your doctor will probably ask you to use the medicine less often, such as 100 mcg (one gram of cream) one to three times a *week* and for only three weeks of each month (three weeks on and one week off).

- For *vaginal* dosage form (insert):

—For treating a genital skin condition (vulvar atrophy), inflammation of the vagina (atrophic vaginitis) in postmenopausal women, and inflammation of the urethra (urethritis) in postmenopausal women:

• Adults: 2 milligrams (mg) of estradiol (7.5 mcg released every twenty-four hours with continuous use) and replaced every three months.

For estrone

- For *vaginal* dosage form (cream):

—For treating a genital skin condition (vulvar atrophy) and inflammation of the vagina (atrophic vaginitis) in postmenopausal women:

• Adults: 2 to 4 milligrams of estrone (two to four grams of cream) inserted into the vagina once a day or as directed by your doctor.

- For *vaginal* dosage form (suppository):

—For treating a genital skin condition (vulvar atrophy) and inflammation of the vagina (atrophic vaginitis) in postmenopausal women:

• Adults: 250 to 500 micrograms (mcg) inserted into the vagina once a day or as directed by your doctor.

For estropipate

- For *vaginal* dosage form (cream):

—For treating a genital skin condition (vulvar atrophy) and inflammation of the vagina (atrophic vaginitis):

• Adults: 3 to 6 milligrams (mg) of estropipate (two to four grams of cream) inserted into the vagina once a day. Your doctor will probably ask you to use the medicine for only three weeks of each month (three weeks on and one week off).

Missed dose—When using the suppository or cream several times a week: If you miss a dose of this medicine and remember it within 1 or 2 days of the missed dose, use the missed dose as soon as possible. However, if it is almost time for your next dose, skip the missed dose and go back to your regular dosing schedule. Do not double doses.

When using the cream or suppositories more than several times a week: If you miss a dose of the medicine, use it as soon as possible if remembered within 12 hours of the missed dose. However, if it is almost time for your next dose, skip the missed dose and go back to your regular dosing schedule. Do not double doses.

Storage—To store this medicine:

- Keep out of the reach of children.
- Store away from heat and direct light.
- Keep the medicine from freezing.

- Do not keep outdated medicine or medicine no longer needed. Be sure that any discarded medicine is out of the reach of children.

Precautions While Using This Medicine

It is very important that your doctor check your progress at regular visits to make sure this medicine does not cause unwanted effects. Plan on going to see your doctor every year, but some doctors require visits more often.

It is not yet known whether the use of vaginal estrogens increases the risk of breast cancer in women. Therefore, it is very important that you regularly check your breasts for any unusual lumps or discharge. Report any problems to your doctor. You should also have a mammogram (x-ray pictures of the breasts) done if your doctor recommends it.

If you think that you may be pregnant, stop using the medicine immediately and check with your doctor.

Tell the doctor in charge that you are using this medicine before having any laboratory test, because some test results may be affected.

For vaginal creams

- Avoid using latex condoms, diaphragms, or cervical caps for up to 72 hours after using estrogen vaginal creams. Certain estrogen products may contain oils in the creams that can weaken latex (rubber) products and cause condoms to break or leak, or cervical caps or diaphragms to wear out sooner. Check with your health care professional to make sure the vaginal estrogen product you are using can be used with latex devices.
- This medicine is often used at bedtime to increase effectiveness through better absorption.
- Vaginal creams of suppositories will melt and leak out of the vagina. A minipad or sanitary napkin will protect your clothing. *Do not use tampons* (like those used for menstrual periods) since they may soak up the medicine and make the medicine less effective.
- Avoid exposing your male sexual partner to your vaginal estrogen cream or suppository by not having sexual intercourse right after using these medicines. Your male partner might absorb the medicine through his penis if it comes in contact with the medicine.

For estradiol vaginal insert

- It is not necessary to remove the vaginal insert for sexual intercourse unless desired.
- If you do take it out or if it accidentally slips or comes out of the vagina, you can replace the vaginal insert in the vagina after washing it with lukewarm water. *Never use hot or boiling water.*
- If it slips down, gently push it upwards back into place.
- Replace the vaginal insert every 3 months.

Side Effects of This Medicine

The risk of any serious adverse effect is unlikely for most women using low doses of estrogens vaginally. Even women with special risks have used vaginal estrogens without problems.

Check with your doctor as soon as possible if any of the following side effects occur:

Less common

Breast pain; enlarged breasts; itching of the vagina or genitals; headache; nausea; stinging or redness of the genital area; thick, white vaginal discharge without odor or with a mild odor

Rare

Feeling of vaginal pressure (with use of estradiol vaginal insert); vaginal burning or pain (with use of estradiol vaginal insert); unusual or unexpected uterine bleeding or spotting

Other side effects may occur that usually do not need medical attention. These side effects may go away during treatment as your body adjusts to the medicine. However, check with your doctor if any of the following side effects continue or are bothersome:

Less common

Abdominal or back pain; clear vaginal discharge (usually means the medicine is working)

Also, many women who are using estrogens with a progestin (another female hormone) will start having monthly vaginal bleeding, similar to menstrual periods, again. This effect will continue for as long as the medicine is taken. However, monthly bleeding will not occur in women who have had the uterus removed by surgery (total hysterectomy).

Other side effects not listed above may also occur in some patients. If you notice any other effects, check with your doctor.

Revised: 08/24/97

ESTROGENS AND PROGESTINS Oral Contraceptives Systemic

Some commonly used brand names are:

In the U.S.—

Alesse[3]
Brevicon[5]
Demulen 1/35[2]
Demulen 1/50[2]
Desogen[1]
Estrostep[4]
Estrostep Fe[4]
Genora 0.5/35[5]
Genora 1/35[5]
Genora 1/50[6]
Intercon 0.5/35[5]
Intercon 1/35[5]
Intercon 1/50[6]
Jenest[5]
Levlen[3]
Levora 0.15/30[3]
Loestrin 1/20[4]
Loestrin Fe 1/20[4]
Loestrin 1.5/30[4]
Loestrin Fe 1.5/30[4]
Lo/Ovral[8]
ModiCon[5]
Necon 0.5/35[5]
Necon 1/35[5]
Necon 1/50[6]
Necon 10/11[5]
N.E.E. 1/35[5]
N.E.E. 1/50[5]
Nelova 0.5/35E[5]
Nelova 1/35E[5]
Nelova 1/50M[6]

Nelova 10/11[5]	Ortho-Novum 10/11[5]
Nordette[3]	Ortho Tri-Cyclen[7]
Norethin 1/35E[5]	Ovcon-35[5]
Norethin 1/50M[6]	Ovcon-50[5]
Norinyl 1+35[5]	Ovral[8]
Norinyl 1+50[6]	Tri-Levlen[3]
Ortho-Cept[1]	Tri-Norinyl[5]
Ortho-Cyclen[7]	Triphasil[3]
Ortho-Novum 1/35[5]	Zovia 1/35E[2]
Ortho-Novum 1/50[6]	Zovia 1/50E[2]
Ortho-Novum 7/7/7[5]	

In Canada—

Brevicon 0.5/35[5]	Ortho 1/35[5]
Brevicon 1/35[5]	Ortho 7/7/7[5]
Cyclen[7]	Ortho 10/11[5]
Demulen 30[2]	Ortho-Cept[1]
Demulen 50[2]	Ortho-Novum 1/50[6]
Loestrin 1.5/30[4]	Ovral[8]
Marvelon[1]	Synphasic[5]
Minestrin 1/20[4]	Tri-Cyclen[7]
Min-Ovral[3]	Triphasil[3]
Norinyl 1/50[6]	Triquilar[3]
Ortho 0.5/35[5]	

Other commonly used names are:

Ethinylestradiol [Ethinyl estradiol]	Etynodiol [Ethynodiol diacetate]
Ethinyloestradiol [Ethinyl estradiol]	Etynodiol acetate [Ethynodiol diacetate]
Ethynodiol [Ethynodiol diacetate]	Norethindrone [Norethisterone]

Note: For quick reference, the following estrogens and progestins are numbered to match the corresponding brand names.

This information applies to the following medicines:

1. Desogestrel and Ethinyl Estradiol (des-oh-JES-trel and ETH-in-il es-tra-DYE-ole)
2. Ethynodiol Diacetate and Ethinyl Estradiol (e-thye-noe-DYE-ole dye-AS-e-tate and ETH-in-il es-tra-DYE-ole)
3. Levonorgestrel and Ethinyl Estradiol (LEE-voh-nor-jes-trel and ETH-in-il es-tra-DYE-ole)
4. Norethindrone Acetate and Ethinyl Estradiol (nor-eth-IN-drone AS-e-tate and ETH-in-il es-tra-DYE-ole)
5. Norethindrone and Ethinyl Estradiol (nor-eth-IN-drone and ETH-in-il es-tra-DYE-ole)
6. Norethindrone and Mestranol (nor-eth-IN-drone and MES-tra-nole)
7. Norgestimate and Ethinyl Estradiol (nor-JES-ti-mate and ETH-in-il es-tra-DYE-ole)
8. Norgestrel and Ethinyl Estradiol (nor-JES-trel and ETH-in-il es-tra-DYE-ole)

For information about norethindrone (e.g., Micronor) or norgestrel (e.g., Ovrette) when used as single-ingredient oral contraceptives, see *Progestins—For Contraceptive Use (Systemic)*.

Description

Oral contraceptives are known also as the Pill, OCs, BCs, BC tablets, or birth control pills. This medicine usually contains two types of hormones, estrogens (ES-troh-jenz) and progestins (proh-JES-tins) and, when taken properly, prevents pregnancy. It works by stopping a woman's egg from fully developing each month. The egg can no longer accept a sperm and fertilization is prevented. Although oral contraceptives have other effects that help prevent a pregnancy from occurring, this is the main action.

Sometimes a woman's egg can still develop even though the medication is taken once each day, especially when more than 24 hours pass between two doses. In almost all cases when the medicine was taken properly and an egg develops, fertilization can still be stopped by oral contraceptives. This is because oral contraceptives also thicken cervical mucus at the opening of the uterus. This makes it hard for the partner's sperm to reach the egg. In addition, oral contraceptives change the uterus lining just enough so that an egg will not stop in the uterus to develop. All of these effects make it difficult to become pregnant when properly taking an oral contraceptive.

No contraceptive method is 100 percent effective. *Studies show that fewer than one of each one hundred women correctly using oral contraceptives becomes pregnant during the first year of use.* Birth control methods such as having surgery to become sterile or not having sex are more effective. Using condoms, diaphragms, progestin-only oral contraceptives, or spermicides is not as effective as using oral contraceptives containing estrogens and progestins. Discuss with your health care professional your options for birth control.

The triphasic cycle product of norgestimate and ethinyl estradiol (the brand name *Ortho Tri-Cyclen)* can improve acne in females who also need contraception.

Sometimes these preparations can be used for other conditions as determined by your doctor.

Oral contraceptives are available only with your doctor's prescription, in the following dosage forms:

Oral

Desogestrel and Ethinyl Estradiol
- Tablets (U.S. and Canada)

Ethynodiol Diacetate and Ethinyl Estradiol
- Tablets (U.S. and Canada)

Levonorgestrel and Ethinyl Estradiol
- Tablets (U.S. and Canada)

Norethindrone Acetate and Ethinyl Estradiol
- Tablets (U.S. and Canada)

Norethindrone and Ethinyl Estradiol
- Tablets (U.S. and Canada)

Norethindrone and Mestranol
- Tablets (U.S. and Canada)

Norgestimate and Ethinyl Estradiol
- Tablets (U.S. and Canada)

Norgestrel and Ethinyl Estradiol
- Tablets (U.S. and Canada)

Before Using This Medicine

In deciding to use a medicine, the risks of taking the medicine must be weighed against the good it will do. If you are using oral contraceptives for contraception you should understand how their benefits and risks compare to those of other birth control methods. This is a decision you, your sexual partner, and your doctor will make. For oral contraceptives, the following should be considered:

Allergies—Tell your doctor if you have ever had any unusual or allergic reaction to estrogens or progestins. Also tell your health care professional if you are allergic to any other substances, such as foods, preservatives, or dyes.

Diet—Make certain your health care professional knows if you are on any special diet, such as a low-sodium or low-sugar diet.

Pregnancy—Oral contraceptives are not recommended for use during pregnancy and should be discontinued if you become pregnant or think you are pregnant. In rare cases when oral contraceptives have been taken early in a pregnancy, problems in the fetus have not occurred.

Women who are not breast-feeding may begin to take oral contraceptives two weeks after having a baby.

Breast-feeding—Oral contraceptives pass into the breast milk and can change the content or lower the amount of breast milk. Also, they may shorten a woman's ability to breast-feed by about 1 month, especially when the mother is only partially breast-feeding. Because the amount of hormones is so small in low-dose contraceptives, your doctor may allow you to begin using an oral contraceptive after you have been breast-feeding for a while. However, it may be necessary for you to use another method of birth control or to stop breast-feeding while taking oral contraceptives.

Teenagers—This medicine is frequently used for birth control in teenage females and has not been shown to cause different side effects or problems than it does in adults. Some teenagers may need extra information on the importance of taking this medication exactly as prescribed.

Other medicines—Although certain medicines should not be used together at all, in other cases two different medicines may be used together even if an interaction might occur. In these cases, your doctor may want to change the dose, or other precautions may be necessary. When you are taking oral contraceptives, it is especially important that your health care professional know if you are taking any of the following:

- Amiodarone (e.g., Cordarone) or
- Anabolic steroids (nandrolone [e.g., Anabolin], oxandrolone [e.g., Anavar], oxymetholone [e.g., Anadrol], stanozolol [e.g., Winstrol]) or
- Androgens (male hormones) or
- Anti-infectives by mouth or by injection (medicine for infection) or
- Barbiturates or
- Carbamazepine (e.g., Tegretol) or
- Carmustine (e.g., BiCNU) or
- Dantrolene (e.g., Dantrium) or
- Daunorubicin (e.g., Cerubidine) or
- Disulfiram (e.g., Antabuse) or
- Divalproex (e.g., Depakote) or
- Estrogens (female hormones) or
- Etretinate (e.g., Tegison) or
- Gold salts (medicine for arthritis) or
- Griseofulvin (e.g., Fulvicin) or
- Hydroxychloroquine (e.g., Plaquenil) or
- Mercaptopurine (e.g., Purinethol) or
- Methotrexate (e.g., Mexate) or
- Methyldopa (e.g., Aldomet) or
- Naltrexone (e.g., Trexan) (with long-term, high-dose use) or
- Phenothiazines (acetophenazine [e.g., Tindal], chlorpromazine [e.g., Thorazine], fluphenazine [e.g., Prolixin], mesoridazine [e.g., Serentil], perphenazine [e.g., Trilafon], prochlorperazine [e.g., Compazine], promazine [e.g., Sparine], promethazine [e.g., Phenergan], thioridazine [e.g., Mellaril], trifluoperazine [e.g., Stelazine], triflupromazine [e.g., Vesprin], trimeprazine [e.g., Temaril]) or
- Phenylbutazone (e.g., Butazolidin) or
- Phenytoin (e.g., Dilantin) or
- Plicamycin (e.g., Mithracin) or
- Primidone (e.g., Mysoline) or
- Rifabutin (e.g., Mycobutin) or
- Rifampin (e.g., Rifadin) or
- Troleandomycin (e.g., TAO)—These medicines may increase the chance of liver problems if taken with oral contraceptives; also, these medicines may decrease the effect of oral contraceptives and increase your chance of pregnancy. Use of an additional form of birth control is recommended unless directed otherwise by your health care professional
- Corticosteroids (cortisone-like medicine) or
- Theophylline—Oral contraceptives may increase the effects of these medicines and increase the chance of problems occurring
- Cyclosporine—Oral contraceptives increase the effect of cyclosporine and increase the chance of problems occurring
- Ritonavir (e.g., Norvir) or
- Troglitazone (e.g., Resulin)—These medicines may decrease the effect of oral contraceptives and increase your chance of pregnancy. Use of an additional form of birth control is recommended unless directed otherwise by your health care professional
- Smoking, tobacco—Smoking may decrease the effect of oral contraceptives and increase the chance of causing serious blood clot, vein, or heart problems

Other medical problems—The presence of other medical problems may affect the use of oral contraceptives. Make sure you tell your doctor if you have any other medical problems, especially:

- Abnormal changes in menstrual or uterine bleeding or
- Endometriosis or
- Fibroid tumors of the uterus—Oral contraceptives usually improve these female conditions but sometimes they can make them worse or make the diagnosis of these problems more difficult
- Blood clots (or history of) or
- Heart or circulation disease or
- Stroke (or history of)—If these conditions are already present, oral contraceptives may have a greater chance of causing blood clots or circulation problems, especially in women who smoke tobacco. Otherwise, oral contraceptives may help prevent circulation and heart disease if you are healthy and do not smoke
- Breast disease (not involving cancer)—Oral contraceptives usually protect against certain breast diseases, such as breast cysts or breast lumps; however, your doctor may want to follow your condition more closely
- Cancer, including breast cancer (or history of or family history of)—Oral contraceptives may worsen some cancers, especially when breast, cervical, or uterine cancers already exist. Use of oral contraceptives is not recommended if you have any of these conditions. If you have a family history of breast disease, oral contraceptives may still be a good choice but you may need to be tested more often
- Chorea gravidarum or
- Gallbladder disease or gallstones (or history of) or
- High blood cholesterol or
- Liver disease (or history of, including jaundice during pregnancy) or
- Mental depression (or history of)—Oral contraceptives may make these conditions worse or, rarely, cause them to occur again. Oral contraceptives may still be a good choice but you may need to be tested more often
- Diabetes mellitus (sugar diabetes)—Use of oral contraceptives may cause an increase, usually only a small increase, in your blood sugar and usually does not affect the amount of diabetes medicine that you take. You or your doctor

will want to test for any changes in your blood sugar for 12 to 24 months after starting to take oral contraceptives in case the dose of your diabetes medicine needs to be changed
- Epilepsy (seizures) (or history of) or
- Heart or circulation problems or
- High blood pressure (hypertension) or
- Migraine headaches—Oral contraceptives may cause fluid build-up and may cause these conditions to become worse; however, some people have fewer migraine headaches when they use oral contraceptives

Proper Use of This Medicine

To make using oral contraceptives as safe and reliable as possible, you should understand how and when to take them and what effects may be expected.

A paper with information for the patient will be given to you with your filled prescription, and will provide many details concerning the use of oral contraceptives. Read this paper carefully and ask your health care professional if you need additional information or explanation.

Take this medicine with food to help prevent nausea that might occur during the first few weeks. Nausea usually disappears with continued use or if the medicine is taken at bedtime.

When you begin to use oral contraceptives, your body will require at least 7 days to adjust before a pregnancy will be prevented. You will need to use an additional birth control method for at least 7 days. Some doctors recommend using an additional method of birth control for the first cycle (or 3 weeks) to ensure full protection. Follow the advice of your doctor or other health care professional.

Try to take the doses no more than 24 hours apart to reduce the possibility of side effects and to prevent pregnancy. Since one of the most important factors in the proper use of oral contraceptives is taking every dose exactly on schedule, you should never let your tablet supply run out. When possible, try to keep an extra month's supply of tablets on hand and replace it monthly.

It is very important that you keep the tablets in their original container and take the tablets in the same order that they appear in the container. The containers help you keep track of which tablets to take next. Different colored tablets in the same package contain different amounts of hormones or are placebos (tablets that do not contain hormones). *The effectiveness of the medicine is reduced if the tablets are taken out of order.*

- *Monophasic (one-phase) cycle* dosing schedule: Most available dosing schedules are monophasic. If you are taking tablets of one strength (color) for 21 days, you are using a monophasic schedule. For the 28-day monophasic cycle you will also take an additional 7 inactive tablets, which are another color.
- *Biphasic (two-phase) cycle* dosing schedule: If you are using a biphasic twenty-one–day schedule, you are taking tablets of one strength (color) for either seven or ten days, depending on the medication prescribed (the first phase). You then take tablets of a second strength (color) for the next eleven or fourteen days, depending on the medication prescribed (the second phase). At this point, you will have taken a total of twenty-one tablets. For the twenty-eight–day biphasic cycle you will also take an additional seven inactive tablets, which are a third color.
- *Triphasic (three-phase) cycle* dosing schedule: If you are using a triphasic twenty-one–day schedule, you are taking tablets of one strength (color) for five, six or seven days, depending on the medicine prescribed (the first phase). You then take tablets of a second strength (color) for the next five, seven, or nine days, depending on the medicine prescribed (the second phase). After that, you take tablets of a third strength (color) for the next five, seven, nine, or ten days, depending on the medicine prescribed (the third phase). At this point, you will have taken a total of twenty-one tablets. For the twenty-eight-day triphasic cycle you will also take an additional seven inactive tablets, which are a fourth color.

If you are taking one of the brand name products *Estrostep Fe* or *Loestrin Fe* each of the last seven tablets that you will take on Days 21 through 28 of your cycle contains iron. These tablets are also a different color from the other tablets in your package. They help ro replace some of the iron you lose when you have a menstrual period.

Dosing—Your health care professional may begin your dose on the first day of your menstrual period (called Day-1 start) or on Sunday (called Sunday start). *When you begin on a certain day it is important that you follow that schedule, even when you miss a dose. Do not change your schedule on your own.* If the schedule that you have been put on is not convenient, check with your health care professional about changing schedules.

- For *oral* dosage forms (monophasic, biphasic, or triphasic tablets):
  - —For contraception:
    - Adults and teenagers—
      - —For the twenty-one–day cycle: Take 1 tablet a day for twenty-one days. Skip seven days. Then repeat the cycle.
      - —For the twenty-eight–day cycle: Take 1 tablet a day for twenty-eight days. Then repeat the cycle.
- For *oral* dosage forms (norgestimate and ethinyl estradiol triphasic tablets):
  - —To treat acne:
    - Adults and teenagers 15 years of age and over
      - —For the twenty-one-day cycle: Take 1 tablet a day for twenty-one days. Skip seven days. Then repeat the cycle.
      - —For the twenty-eight-day cycle: Take 1 tablet a day for twenty-eight days. Then repeat the cycle.
    - Teenagers up to 15 years of age—Use and dose must be determined by your doctor.

Missed dose—*Follow your doctor's orders or the directions on the label* if you miss a dose of this medicine. The following information includes only some of the ways to handle missed doses. Your health care professional may want you to stop taking the medicine and use other birth control methods for the rest of the month until you have your menstrual period. Then your health care professional can tell you how to begin taking your medicine again.

For monophasic, biphasic, or triphasic cycles:

- If you miss the first tablet of a new cycle—Take the missed tablet as soon as you remember and take the next tablet at the usual time. You may take 2 tablets in one day. Then continue your regular dosing schedule. Also, use another birth control method until you have taken seven days of your tablets after the last missed dose.
- If you miss 1 tablet during the cycle—Take the missed tablet as soon as you remember. Take the next tablet at the usual time. You may take 2 tablets in one day. Then continue your regular dosing schedule.
- If you miss 2 tablets in a row in the first or second week—Take 2 tablets on the day that you remember and 2 tablets the next day. Continue taking 1 tablet a day. Also use another birth control method until you begin a new cycle.
- If you miss 2 tablets in a row in the third week; or
- If you miss 3 or more tablets in a row at any time during the cycle—

  Using a Day-1 start: Throw out your current cycle and begin taking a new cycle. Also, use another birth control method until you have taken seven days of your tablets after the last missed dose. You may not have a menstrual period this month. But if you miss two menstrual periods in a row, call your health care professional.

  Using a Sunday start: Keep taking one tablet a day from your current pack until Sunday. Then, on Sunday, throw out your old pack and begin a new pack. Also use another birth control method until you have taken seven days of your tablets after the last missed dose. You may not have a menstrual period this month. But if you miss two menstrual periods in a row, call your health care professional.

If you miss any of the last seven (inactive) tablets of a twenty-eight–day cycle, there is no danger of pregnancy. However, the first tablet (active) of the next month's cycle must be taken on the regularly scheduled day, in spite of any missed doses, if pregnancy is to be avoided. The active and inactive tablets are colored differently for your convenience.

Storage—To store this medicine:

- Keep out of the reach of children.
- Store away from heat and direct light.
- Do not store in the bathroom, near the kitchen sink, or in other damp places. Heat and moisture may cause the medicine to break down.
- Do not keep outdated medicine or medicine no longer needed. Be sure that any discarded medicine is out of the reach of children.

Precautions While Using This Medicine

It is very important that your doctor check your progress at regular visits to make sure this medicine does not cause unwanted effects. These visits will usually be every 6 to 12 months, but some doctors require them more often.

Tell the medical doctor or dentist in charge that you are taking this medicine before any kind of surgery (including dental surgery) or emergency treatment. Your doctor will decide whether you should continue taking this medicine.

The following medicines may reduce the effectiveness of oral contraceptives. *You should use an additional method of birth control during each cycle in which any of the following medicines are used:*

Ampicillin
Barbiturates
Carbamazepine (e.g., Tegretol)
Griseofulvin (e.g., Fulvicin)
Penicillin V
Phenytoin (e.g., Dilantin)
Primidone (e.g., Mysoline)
Rifampin (e.g., Rifadin)
Ritonavir (e.g., Norvir)
Tetracyclines (medicine for infection)
Troglitazone (e.g., Rezulin)

Check with your doctor if you have any questions about this.

Vaginal bleeding of various amounts may occur between your regular menstrual periods during the first 3 months of use. This is sometimes called spotting when slight, or breakthrough bleeding when heavier. If this should occur:

- Continue on your regular dosing schedule.
- The bleeding usually stops within 1 week.
- Check with your doctor if the bleeding continues for more than 1 week.
- After you have been taking oral contraceptives on schedule and for more than 3 months and bleeding continues, check with your doctor.

Missed menstrual periods may occur:

- If you have not taken the medicine exactly as scheduled. Pregnancy must be considered a possibility.
- If the medicine is not the right strength or type for your needs.
- If you stop taking oral contraceptives, especially if you have taken oral contraceptives for 2 or more years.

Check with your doctor if you miss any menstrual periods so that the cause may be determined.

In some patients using estrogen-containing oral contraceptives, tenderness, swelling, or bleeding of the gums may occur. Brushing and flossing your teeth carefully and regularly and massaging your gums may help prevent this. See your dentist regularly to have your teeth cleaned. Check with your medical doctor or dentist if you have any questions about how to take care of your teeth and gums, or if you notice any tenderness, swelling, or bleeding of your gums. Also, it has been shown that estrogen-containing oral contraceptives may cause a healing problem called dry socket after a tooth has been removed. If you are going to have a tooth removed, tell your dentist or oral surgeon that you are taking oral contraceptives.

Some people who take oral contraceptives may become more sensitive to sunlight than they are normally. When you begin taking this medicine, avoid too much sun and do not use a sunlamp until you see how you react to the sun, especially if you tend to burn easily. If you have a severe reaction, check with your doctor. Some people may develop brown, blotchy spots on exposed areas. These spots usually disappear gradually when the medicine is stopped.

If you suspect that you may have become pregnant, stop taking this medicine immediately and check with your doctor.

If you are scheduled for any laboratory tests, tell your doctor that you are taking birth control pills.

Check with your doctor before refilling an old prescription, especially after a pregnancy. You will need another physical examination and your doctor may change your prescription.

Side Effects of This Medicine

Healthy women who do not smoke cigarettes have almost no chance of having a severe side effect from taking oral contraceptives. For most women, more problems occur because of pregnancy than will occur from taking oral contraceptives. But for some women who have special health problems, oral contraceptives can cause some unwanted effects. Some of these unwanted effects include benign (not cancerous) liver tumors, liver cancer, or blood clots or related problems, such as a stroke. Although these effects are very rare, they can be serious enough to cause death. You may want to discuss these effects with your doctor.

Smoking cigarettes during the use of oral contraceptives has been found to greatly increase the chances of these serious side effects occurring. *To reduce the risk of serious side effects, do not smoke cigarettes while you are taking oral contraceptives.*

The following side effects may be caused by blood clots. *Get emergency help immediately* if any of the following side effects occur:

Rare

Abdominal or stomach pain (sudden, severe, or continuing); coughing up blood; headache (severe or sudden); loss of coordination (sudden); loss of vision or change in vision (sudden); pains in chest, groin, or leg (especially in calf of leg); shortness of breath (sudden or unexplained); slurring of speech (sudden); weakness, numbness, or pain in arm or leg (unexplained)

Check with your doctor as soon as possible if any of the following side effects occur:

More common—usually less common after the first 3 months of oral contraceptive use

Changes in the uterine bleeding pattern at menses or between menses, such as decreased bleeding at menses, breakthrough bleeding or spotting between periods, prolonged bleeding at menses, complete stopping of menstrual bleeding that occurs over several months in a row, or stopping of menstrual bleeding that only occurs sometimes

Less common

Headaches or migraines (although headaches may lessen in many users, in others, they may increase in number or become worse); increased blood pressure; vaginal infection with vaginal itching or irritation, or thick, white, or curd-like discharge

For women with diabetes mellitus

Mild increase of blood sugar—Faintness, nausea, pale skin, or sweating

Rare

Mental depression; swelling, pain, or tenderness in upper abdominal area

For women who smoke tobacco

Pains in stomach, side, or abdomen; yellow eyes or skin

For women with a history of breast disease

Lumps in breast

Other side effects may occur that usually do not need medical attention. These side effects may go away during treatment as your body adjusts to the medicine. However, check with your doctor if any of the following side effects continue or are bothersome:

More common

Abdominal cramping or bloating; acne (usually less common after first 3 months and may improve if acne already exists); breast pain, tenderness, or swelling; dizziness; nausea; swelling of ankles and feet; unusual tiredness or weakness; vomiting

Less common

Brown, blotchy spots on exposed skin; gain or loss of body or facial hair; increased or decreased interest in sexual intercourse; increased sensitivity of skin to sunlight; weight gain or loss

Other side effects not listed above may also occur in some patients. If you notice any other effects, check with your doctor.

Additional Information

Once a medicine has been approved for marketing for a certain use, experience may show that it is also useful for other medical problems. Although these uses are not included in product labeling, oral contraceptives are used in certain patients with the following medical conditions:

- Amenorrhea (stopping of menses for several consecutive months)
- Dysfunctional uterine bleeding (abnormal uterine bleeding)
- Dysmenorrhea (painful menstrual bleeding)
- Hypermenorrhea (excessive menstrual bleeding)
- Emergency contraception within 72 hours of unprotected intercourse
- Endometriosis (painful bleeding from uterine-like tissue that can grow in different parts of the female body)
- Hirsutism in females (male-like hair growth)
- Hyperandrogenism, ovarian (excessive production of male hormones)
- Polycystic ovary syndrome (many problems that include amenorrhea, hirsutism, infertility, and many tiny cysts or sacs usually in both ovaries)

For patients taking this medicine for *emergency contraception:*

- Must be taken with food within 72 hours of unprotected sexual intercourse. One single course (2 doses 12 hours apart) is a one-time emergency protection.

Using more than one course in a month will reduce the effectiveness.
- Because the hormones are strong, watch for danger signs. Call your doctor if you experience any severe pains in leg, stomach, or chest; any vision or breathing changes; yellowing of skin; headaches; numbness; or trouble in speaking.
- You may experience nausea so take it with food and call your doctor if you vomit the medicine.
- Your menstrual period may start earlier than usual. If it doesn't start, call your doctor.

For patients taking this medicine for *hirsutism:*
- You may need to use oral contraceptives for 6 to 12 months before you see less new hair growth.

For patients taking this medicine for *endometriosis:*
- Sometimes instead of following the directions on the oral contraceptive's package, your doctor may ask you to follow different directions, such as taking the active tablets in the package each day without stopping for 6 to 9 months. This means that after 21 days you will start a new package of pills. If you are not sure about how to take this medicine, discuss any questions with your health care professional.
- Also, your symptoms of endometriosis may worsen at first but with continued use of the oral contraceptives your symptoms should lessen and your condition improve.

Other than the above information, there is no additional information relating to proper use, precautions, or side effects for these uses.

Revised: 06/28/96
Interim revision: 08/24/97

ETHAMBUTOL Systemic

Some commonly used brand names are:

In the U.S.—
Myambutol

In Canada—
Etibi
Myambutol

Description

Ethambutol (e-THAM-byoo-tole) is used to treat tuberculosis (TB). It is used with other medicines for TB. This medicine may also be used for other problems as determined by your doctor.

To help clear up your tuberculosis (TB) infection completely, you must keep taking this medicine for the full time of treatment, even if you begin to feel better. This is very important. It is also important that you do not miss any doses.

Ethambutol is available only with your doctor's prescription, in the following dosage form:

Oral
- Tablets (U.S. and Canada)

Before Using This Medicine

In deciding to use a medicine, the risks of taking the medicine must be weighed against the good it will do. This is a decision you and your doctor will make. For ethambutol, the following should be considered:

Allergies—Tell your doctor if you have ever had any unusual or allergic reaction to ethambutol. Also tell your health care professional if you are allergic to any other substances, such as foods, preservatives, or dyes.

Pregnancy—Pregnant women with tuberculosis (TB) should be treated with TB medicines, including ethambutol. Ethambutol has not been shown to cause birth defects or other problems in humans. However, studies in animals have shown that ethambutol causes cleft palate, skull and spine defects, absence of one eye, and hare lip.

Breast-feeding—Ethambutol passes into breast milk. However, ethambutol has not been shown to cause problems in nursing babies.

Children—This medicine has been tested in children 13 years of age or older and has not been shown to cause different side effects or problems than it does in adults. Ethambutol may be used for children with TB when other medicines cannot be used. However, ethambutol is usually not used in children up to 6 years of age because it may be hard to tell if they are having side effects affecting their eyes.

Older adults—Many medicines have not been studied specifically in older people. Therefore, it may not be known whether they work exactly the same way they do in younger adults. Although there is no specific information comparing use of ethambutol in the elderly with its use in other age groups, this medicine is not expected to cause different side effects or problems in older people than it does in younger adults.

Other medicines—Although certain medicines should not be used together at all, in other cases two different medicines may be used together even if an interaction might occur. In these cases, your doctor may want to change the dose, or other precautions may be necessary. Tell your health care professional if you are taking any other prescription or nonprescription (over-the-counter [OTC]) medicine.

Other medical problems—The presence of other medical problems may affect the use of ethambutol. Make sure you tell your doctor if you have any other medical problems, especially:
- Gouty arthritis—Ethambutol may cause or worsen attacks of gout
- Kidney disease—Patients with kidney disease may be more likely to have side effects
- Optic neuritis (eye nerve damage)—Ethambutol may cause or worsen eye disease

Proper Use of This Medicine

Ethambutol may be taken with food if this medicine upsets your stomach.

To help clear up your tuberculosis (TB) completely, *it is very important that you keep taking this medicine for the full time of treatment,* even if you begin to feel better after a few weeks. You may have to take it every day for as long as 1 to 2 years or more. *It is important that you do not miss any doses.*

Dosing—The dose of ethambutol will be different for different patients. *Follow your doctor's orders or the directions on the label.* The following information includes only the average doses of ethambutol. *If your dose is different, do not change it* unless your doctor tells you to do so.

The number of tablets that you take depends on the strength of the medicine.

- For *oral* dosage form (tablets):
  - —For the treatment of tuberculosis (TB):
    - Adults and children 13 years of age and older—15 to 25 milligrams (mg) per kilogram (kg) (6.8 to 11.4 mg per pound) of body weight once a day. Instead, your doctor may tell you to take 50 mg per kg (22.8 mg per pound) of body weight, up to a total of 2.5 grams, two times a week. Another dose that your doctor may tell you to take is 25 to 30 mg per kg (11.4 to 13.6 mg per pound) of body weight, up to a total of 2.5 grams, three times a week. Ethambutol must be taken with other medicines to treat tuberculosis.
    - Infants and children up to 13 years of age—Use and dose must be determined by your doctor.

Missed dose—If you miss a dose of this medicine, take it as soon as possible. However, if it is almost time for your next dose, skip the missed dose and go back to your regular dosing schedule. Do not double doses.

Storage—To store this medicine:
- Keep out of the reach of children.
- Store away from heat and direct light.
- Do not store in the bathroom, near the kitchen sink, or in other damp places. Heat or moisture may cause the medicine to break down.
- Do not keep outdated medicine or medicine no longer needed. Be sure that any discarded medicine is out of the reach of children.

Precautions While Using This Medicine

If your symptoms do not improve within 2 to 3 weeks, or if they become worse, check with your doctor.

It is very important that your doctor check your progress at regular visits.

Check with your doctor immediately if blurred vision, eye pain, red-green color blindness, or loss of vision occurs during treatment. Your doctor may want you to have your eyes checked by an ophthalmologist (eye doctor). *Also, make sure you know how you react to this medicine before you drive, use machines, or do anything else that could be dangerous if you are not alert or able to see well.*

Side Effects of This Medicine

Along with its needed effects, a medicine may cause some unwanted effects. Although not all of these side effects may occur, if they do occur they may need medical attention.

Check with your doctor immediately if any of the following side effects occur:

Less common

Chills; pain and swelling of joints, especially big toe, ankle, or knee; tense, hot skin over affected joints

Rare

Blurred vision, eye pain, red-green color blindness, or any loss of vision (more common with high doses); fever; joint pain; numbness, tingling, burning pain, or weakness in hands or feet; skin rash

Other side effects may occur that usually do not need medical attention. These side effects may go away during treatment as your body adjusts to the medicine. However, check with your doctor if any of the following side effects continue or are bothersome:

Less common

Abdominal pain; confusion; headache; loss of appetite; nausea and vomiting

Other side effects not listed above may also occur in some patients. If you notice any other effects, check with your doctor.

Additional Information

Once a medicine has been approved for marketing for a certain use, experience may show that it is also useful for other medical problems. Although this use is not included in product labeling, ethambutol is used in certain patients with the following medical condition:

- Atypical mycobacterial infections, such as *Mycobacterium avium* complex (MAC)

Other than the above information, there is no additional information relating to proper use, precautions, or side effects for this use.

Revised: 08/15/97

ETHCHLORVYNOL Systemic

A commonly used brand name in the U.S. and Canada is Placidyl. Generic name product may also be available in the U.S.

Description

Ethchlorvynol (eth-klor-VI-nole) is used to treat insomnia (trouble in sleeping). However, it has generally been replaced by other medicines for the treatment of insomnia. If ethchlorvynol is used regularly (for example, every day) to help produce sleep, it is usually not effective for more than 1 week.

This medicine is available only with your doctor's prescription, in the following dosage form:

Oral
- Capsules (U.S. and Canada)

Before Using This Medicine

In deciding to use a medicine, the risks of taking the medicine must be weighed against the good it will do. This is a decision you and your doctor will make. For ethchlorvynol, the following should be considered:

Allergies—Tell your doctor if you have ever had any unusual or allergic reaction to ethchlorvynol. Also tell your health care professional if you are allergic to any other substances, such as foods, preservatives, or dyes.

Pregnancy—Ethchlorvynol has not been studied in pregnant women. However, use of ethchlorvynol during the first 6 months of pregnancy is not recommended because studies in animals have shown that high doses of ethchlorvynol increase the chance of stillbirths and decrease the chance of the newborn surviving. Taking ethchlorvynol during the last 3 months of pregnancy may cause slow heartbeat, shortness of breath, troubled breathing, or withdrawal side effects in the newborn baby.

Breast-feeding—It is not known whether ethchlorvynol passes into the breast milk.

Children—Studies on this medicine have been done only in adult patients and there is no specific information comparing use of ethchlorvynol in children with use in other age groups.

Older adults—Elderly people may be especially sensitive to the effects of ethchlorvynol. This may increase the chance of side effects during treatment.

Other medicines—Although certain medicines should not be used together at all, in other cases 2 different medicines may be used together even if an interaction might occur. In these cases, your doctor may want to change the dose, or other precautions may be necessary. When you are taking ethchlorvynol, it is especially important that your health care professional know if you are taking any of the following:

- Anticoagulants (blood thinners)—Ethchlorvynol may change the amount of anticoagulant you need to take
- Central nervous system (CNS) depressants (medicine that causes drowsiness) or
- Tricyclic antidepressants (medicine for depression)—Using these medicines together with ethchlorvynol may increase the CNS and other depressant effects

Other medical problems—The presence of other medical problems may affect the use of ethchlorvynol. Make sure you tell your doctor if you have any other medical problems, especially:

- Alcohol abuse (or history of) or
- Drug abuse or dependence (or history of)—Dependence on ethchlorvynol may develop
- Kidney disease or
- Liver disease—Higher blood levels of ethchlorvynol may result and increase the chance of side effects
- Mental depression or
- Porphyria—Ethchlorvynol may make the condition worse

Proper Use of This Medicine

Ethchlorvynol is best taken with food or a glass of milk to lessen the possibility of dizziness, clumsiness, or unsteadiness, which may occur shortly after you take this medicine.

Take this medicine only as directed by your doctor. Do not take more of it, do not take it more often, and do not take it for a longer time than your doctor ordered. If too much is taken, it may become habit-forming.

Dosing—The dose of ethchlorvynol will be different for different patients. *Follow your doctor's orders or the directions on the label.* The following information includes only the average doses of ethchlorvynol. *If your dose is different, do not change it* unless your doctor tells you to do so.

- For *oral* dosage forms (capsules):
  - —Adults: 500 to 1000 milligrams at bedtime.
  - —Children: Dose must be determined by the doctor.

Storage—To store this medicine:

- Keep out of the reach of children. Overdose of ethchlorvynol is especially dangerous in children.
- Store away from heat and direct light.
- Do not store in the bathroom, near the kitchen sink, or in other damp places. Heat or moisture may cause the medicine to break down.
- Do not keep outdated medicine or medicine no longer needed. Be sure that any discarded medicine is out of the reach of children.

Precautions While Using This Medicine

If you will be taking this medicine regularly for a long time:

- Your doctor should check your progress at regular visits.
- Do not stop taking it without first checking with your doctor. Your doctor may want you to reduce gradually the amount you are taking before stopping completely.

This medicine will add to the effects of alcohol and other CNS depressants (medicines that slow down the nervous system, possibly causing drowsiness). Some examples of CNS depressants are antihistamines or medicine for hay fever, other allergies, or colds; sedatives, tranquilizers, or sleeping medicine; prescription pain medicine or narcotics; barbiturates; medicine for seizures; muscle relaxants; or anesthetics, including some dental anesthetics. *Check with your doctor before taking any of the above while you are taking this medicine.*

If you think you or someone else may have taken an overdose of this medicine, get emergency help at once. Taking an overdose of ethchlorvynol or taking alcohol or other CNS depressants with ethchlorvynol may lead to unconsciousness and possibly death. Some signs of an overdose are continuing confusion, severe weakness, shortness of breath or slow or troubled breathing, slurred speech, staggering, and slow heartbeat.

This medicine may cause some people to become dizzy, lightheaded, drowsy, or less alert than they are normally. Even if taken at bedtime, it may cause some people to feel drowsy or less alert on arising. *Make sure you know how you react to this medicine before you drive, use machines, or do anything else that could be dangerous if you are dizzy or are not alert.*

Side Effects of This Medicine

Along with its needed effects, a medicine may cause some unwanted effects. Although not all of these side effects may occur, if they do occur they may need medical attention.

Check with your doctor as soon as possible if any of the following side effects occur:

Less common

Skin rash or hives; unusual bleeding or bruising; unusual excitement, nervousness, or restlessness

Rare

Darkening of urine; itching; pale stools; yellow eyes or skin

Symptoms of overdose

Confusion (continuing); double vision; low body temperature; numbness, tingling, pain, or weakness in hands or feet; shortness of breath or slow or troubled breathing; slow heartbeat; slurred speech; staggering; trembling; unusual movements of the eyes; weakness (severe)

Other side effects may occur that usually do not need medical attention. These side effects may go away during treatment as your body adjusts to the medicine. However, check with your doctor if any of the following side effects continue or are bothersome:

More common

Blurred vision; dizziness or lightheadedness; indigestion; nausea or vomiting; numbness of face; stomach pain; unpleasant aftertaste; unusual tiredness or weakness

Less common

Clumsiness or unsteadiness; confusion; drowsiness (daytime)

After you stop using this medicine, your body may need time to adjust. If you took this medicine in high doses or for a long time, this may take up to 2 weeks. During this period of time check with your doctor if you notice any of the following side effects:

Convulsions (seizures); hallucinations (seeing, hearing, or feeling things that are not there); muscle twitching; nausea or vomiting; restlessness, nervousness, or irritability; sweating; trembling; trouble in sleeping; weakness

Other side effects not listed above may also occur in some patients. If you notice any other effects, check with your doctor.

Revised: 03/09/90

ETHIONAMIDE Systemic†

A commonly used brand name in the U.S. is Trecator-SC.

†Not commercially available in Canada.

Description

Ethionamide (e-thye-ON-am-ide) is used with other medicines to treat tuberculosis (TB). Ethionamide may also be used for other problems as determined by your doctor.

To help clear up your tuberculosis (TB) completely, you must keep taking this medicine for the full time of treatment, even if you begin to feel better. This is very important. It is also important that you do not miss any doses.

Ethionamide is available only with your doctor's prescription, in the following dosage form:

Oral

- Tablets (U.S.)

Before Using This Medicine

In deciding to use a medicine, the risks of taking the medicine must be weighed against the good it will do. This is a decision you and your doctor will make. For ethionamide, the following should be considered:

Allergies—Tell your doctor if you have ever had any unusual or allergic reaction to ethionamide, isoniazid (e.g., INH; Nydrazid), pyrazinamide, or niacin (e.g., Nicobid; nicotinic acid). Also tell your health care professional if you are allergic to any other substances, such as foods, preservatives, or dyes.

Pregnancy—Ethionamide causes birth defects in rats and rabbits given doses greater than the usual human dose. However, women with tuberculosis (TB) should be treated with medicines to treat TB. If you have any concerns, talk to your doctor.

Breast-feeding—It is not known whether ethionamide passes into breast milk. Although most medicines pass into breast milk in small amounts, many of them may be used safely while breast-feeding. Mothers who are taking this medicine and who wish to breast-feed should discuss this with their doctor.

Children—Although there is no specific information comparing use of ethionamide in children with use in other age groups, this medicine is not expected to cause different side effects or problems in children than it does in adults.

Older adults—Many medicines have not been studied specifically in older people. Therefore, it may not be known whether they work exactly the same way they do in younger adults or if they cause different side effects or problems in older people. There is no specific information comparing use of ethionamide in the elderly with use in other age groups.

Other medicines—Although certain medicines should not be used together at all, in other cases two different medicines may be used together even if an interaction might occur. In these cases, your doctor may want to change the dose, or other precautions may be necessary. When you are taking ethionamide, it is especially important that your health care professional know if you are taking any of the following:

- Cycloserine—Use of ethionamide with cycloserine may increase the chance for nervous system side effects, such as convulsions (seizures)

Other medical problems—The presence of other medical problems may affect the use of ethionamide. Make sure you tell your doctor if you have any other medical problems, especially:

- Diabetes mellitus (sugar diabetes)—Diabetes may be harder to control in patients taking ethionamide
- Liver disease (severe)—Patients with severe liver disease may have an increased chance of side effects

Proper Use of This Medicine

Ethionamide may be taken with or after meals if it upsets your stomach.

To help clear up your tuberculosis (TB) completely, *it is very important that you keep taking this medicine for the full time of treatment,* even if you begin to feel better after a few weeks. You may have to take it every day for 1 to 2 years or more. *It is important that you do not miss any doses.*

Your doctor may also want you to take pyridoxine (e.g., Hexa-Betalin; vitamin B_6) every day to help prevent or lessen some of the side effects of ethionamide. If so, *it is very important to take pyridoxine every day along with this medicine. Do not miss any doses.*

Dosing—The dose of ethionamide will be different for different patients. *Follow your doctor's orders or the directions on the label.* The following information includes only the average doses of ethionamide. *If your dose is different, do not change it* unless your doctor tells you to do so.

- For *oral* dosage form (tablets):
  - —For the treatment of tuberculosis (TB):
    - Adults and teenagers—250 milligrams (mg) every eight to twelve hours. Ethionamide must be taken with other medicines to treat tuberculosis.
    - Children—Dose is based on body weight. The usual dose is 4 to 5 mg per kilogram of body weight every eight hours. Ethionamide must be taken with other medicines to treat tuberculosis.

Missed dose—If you do miss a dose of either of these medicines, take it as soon as possible. However, if it is almost time for your next dose, skip the missed dose and go back to your regular dosing schedule. Do not double doses.

Storage—To store this medicine:

- Keep out of the reach of children.
- Store away from heat and direct light.
- Do not store in the bathroom, near the kitchen sink, or in other damp places. Heat or moisture may cause the medicine to break down.
- Do not keep outdated medicine or medicine no longer needed. Be sure that any discarded medicine is out of the reach of children.

Precautions While Using This Medicine

If your symptoms do not improve within 2 to 3 weeks, or if they become worse, check with your doctor.

It is very important that your doctor check your progress at regular visits. Also, *check with your doctor immediately if blurred vision or any loss of vision, with or without eye pain, occurs during treatment.* Your doctor may want you to have your eyes checked by an ophthalmologist (eye doctor).

Since this medicine may cause blurred vision or loss of vision, *make sure you know how you react to this medicine before you drive, use machines, or do anything else that could be dangerous if you are not able to see well.*

If this medicine causes clumsiness; unsteadiness; or numbness, tingling, burning, or pain in the hands and feet, check with your doctor immediately. These may be early warning symptoms of more serious nerve problems that could develop later.

Side Effects of This Medicine

Along with its needed effects, a medicine may cause some unwanted effects. Although not all of these side effects may occur, if they do occur they may need medical attention.

Check with your doctor immediately if any of the following side effects occur:

Less common

Clumsiness or unsteadiness; confusion; mental depression; mood or other mental changes; numbness, tingling, burning, or pain in hands and feet; yellow eyes or skin

Rare

Blurred vision or loss of vision, with or without eye pain; changes in menstrual periods; coldness; decreased sexual ability (in males); difficulty in concentrating; dry, puffy skin; faster heartbeat; increased hunger; nervousness; shakiness; skin rash; swelling of front part of neck; weight gain

Other side effects may occur that usually do not need medical attention. These side effects may go away during treatment as your body adjusts to the medicine. However,

check with your doctor if any of the following side effects continue or are bothersome:

More common

Dizziness (especially when getting up from a lying or sitting position); loss of appetite; metallic taste; nausea or vomiting; sore mouth

Less common or rare

Enlargement of the breasts (in males)

Other side effects not listed above may also occur in some patients. If you notice any other effects, check with your doctor.

Additional Information

Once a medicine has been approved for marketing for a certain use, experience may show that it is also useful for other medical problems. Although these uses are not included in product labeling, ethionamide is used in certain patients with the following medical conditions:

- Atypical mycobacterial infections, such as *Mycobacterium avium* complex (MAC)
- Leprosy (Hansen's disease)

Other than the above information, there is no additional information relating to proper use, precautions, or side effects for these uses.

Revised: 06/22/94

ETIDRONATE Systemic

A commonly used brand name in the U.S. and Canada is Didronel. Another commonly used name is EHDP.

Description

Etidronate (eh-tih-DROE-nate) is used to treat Paget's disease of bone. It may also be used to treat or prevent a certain type of bone problem that may occur after hip replacement surgery or spinal injury.

Etidronate is also used to treat hypercalcemia (too much calcium in the blood) that may occur with some types of cancer.

This medicine is available only with your doctor's prescription, in the following dosage forms:

Oral

- Tablets (U.S. and Canada)

Parenteral

- Injection (U.S.)

Before Using This Medicine

In deciding to use a medicine, the risks of taking the medicine must be weighed against the good it will do. This is a decision you and your doctor will make. For etidronate, the following should be considered:

Allergies—Tell your doctor if you have ever had any unusual or allergic reaction to etidronate. Also tell your health care professional if you are allergic to any other substances, such as foods, preservatives, or dyes.

Diet—Make certain your health care professional knows if your diet includes large amounts of calcium, such as milk or other dairy products, or if you are on any special diet, such as a low-sodium or low-sugar diet. Calcium in the diet may prevent the absorption of oral etidronate.

Pregnancy—Studies have not been done in humans. However, studies in rats injected with large doses of etidronate have shown that etidronate causes deformed bones in the fetus.

Breast-feeding—It is not known if etidronate passes into breast milk. However, this medicine has not been reported to cause problems in nursing babies.

Children—Some changes in bone growth may occur in children, but will usually go away when the medicine is stopped.

Older adults—When etidronate is given by injection along with a large amount of fluids, older people tend to retain (keep) the excess fluid.

Other medicines—Although certain medicines should not be used together at all, in other cases two different medicines may be used together even if an interaction might occur. In these cases, your doctor may want to change the dose, or other precautions may be necessary. When you are taking etidronate, it is especially important that your health care professional know if you are taking any of the following:

- Antacids containing calcium, magnesium, or aluminum or
- Mineral supplements or other medicines containing calcium, iron, magnesium, or aluminum—These medicines may decrease the effects of etidronate, and should be taken at least 2 hours before or after taking etidronate

Other medical problems—The presence of other medical problems may affect the use of etidronate. Make sure you tell your doctor if you have any other medical problems, especially:

- Bone fracture, especially of arm or leg—Etidronate may increase the risk of bone fractures
- Intestinal or bowel disease—Etidronate may increase the risk of diarrhea
- Kidney disease—High blood levels of etidronate may result causing serious side effects

Proper Use of This Medicine

Take etidronate with water on an empty stomach at least 2 hours before or after food (midmorning is best) or at bedtime. Food may decrease the amount of etidronate absorbed by your body.

Take etidronate only as directed. Do not take more of it, do not take it more often, and do not take it for a longer time than your doctor ordered. To do so may increase the chance of side effects.

In some patients, etidronate takes up to 3 months to work. If you feel that the medicine is not working, do not stop taking it on your own. Instead, check with your doctor.

It is important that you eat a well-balanced diet with an adequate amount of calcium and vitamin D (found in milk or other dairy products). Too much or too little of either may increase the chance of side effects while you are taking etidronate. Your doctor can help you choose the meal plan that is best for you. *However, do not take any food, especially milk, milk formulas, or other dairy products, or antacids, mineral supplements, or other medicines that are high in calcium or iron (high amounts of these minerals may also be in some vitamin preparations), magnesium, or aluminum* within 2 hours of taking etidronate. To do so may keep this medicine from working properly.

Dosing—The dose of etidronate will be different for different patients. *Follow your doctor's order or the directions on the label.* The following information includes only the average doses of etidronate. *If your dose is different, do not change it* unless your doctor tells you to do so.

- For *oral* dosage form (tablets):
  - —For treating Paget's disease of bone:
    - Adults—Dose is based on body weight and must be determined by your doctor. The dose to start is 5 milligrams (mg) per kilogram (kg) (2.3 mg per pound) of body weight a day, usually as a single dose, for not more than six months. Some people may need 6 to 10 mg per kg (2.7 to 4.6 mg per pound) of body weight a day for not more than six months. Others may need 11 to 20 mg per kg (5 to 9.1 mg per pound) of body weight a day for not more than three months. Your doctor may change your dose depending on your response to treatment.
    - Children—Dose must be determined by your doctor.
  - —For treating or preventing a certain type of bone problem that may occur after hip replacement:
    - Adults—Dose is based on body weight and must be determined by your doctor. The usual dose is 20 mg per kg (9.1 mg per pound) of body weight a day for one month before surgery, and for three months after surgery.
    - Children—Dose must be determined by your doctor.
  - —For treating or preventing a certain type of bone problem that may occur after spinal injury:
    - Adults—Dose is based on body weight and must be determined by your doctor. The usual dose is 20 mg per kg (9.1 mg per pound) of body weight a day for two weeks, beginning as soon as possible after your injury. Your doctor may then decrease your dose to 10 mg per kg (4.5 mg per pound) of body weight for an additional ten weeks.
    - Children—Dose must be determined by your doctor.
  - —For treating hypercalcemia (too much calcium in the blood):
    - Adults—Dose is based on body weight and must be determined by your doctor. The usual dose is 20 mg per kg (9.1 mg per pound) of body weight a day for thirty days. Treatment usually does not continue beyond ninety days.
    - Children—Dose must be determined by your doctor.
- For *injection* dosage form:
  - —For treating hypercalcemia (too much calcium in the blood):
    - Adults—Dose is based on body weight and must be determined by your doctor. The usual dose is 7.5 mg per kg (3.4 mg per pound) of body weight, injected slowly into your vein over 2 hours. This dose is repeated for two more days. Your doctor may repeat the treatment after at least seven days.
    - Children—Dose must be determined by your doctor.

Missed dose—If you miss a dose of this medicine, take it as soon as possible. However, if it is almost time for your next dose, skip the missed dose and go back to your regular dosing schedule. Do not double doses.

Storage—To store this medicine:

- Keep out of the reach of children.
- Store away from heat and direct light.
- Do not store in the bathroom, near the kitchen sink, or in other damp places. Heat or moisture may cause the medicine to break down.
- Do not keep outdated medicine or medicine no longer needed. Be sure that any discarded medicine is out of the reach of children.

Precautions While Using This Medicine

It is important that your doctor check your progress at regular visits even if you are between treatments and are not taking this medicine. If your condition has improved and your doctor has told you to stop taking etidronate, your progress must still be checked. The results of laboratory tests or the occurrence of certain symptoms will tell your doctor if more medicine must be taken. Your doctor may want you to begin another course of treatment after you have been off the medicine for at least 3 months.

If this medicine causes you to have nausea or diarrhea and it continues, check with your doctor. The dose may need to be changed.

If bone pain occurs or worsens during treatment, check with your doctor.

Side Effects of This Medicine

Along with its needed effects, a medicine may cause some unwanted effects. Although not all of these side effects may occur, if they do occur they may need medical attention.

Check with your doctor as soon as possible if any of the following side effects occur:

More common

Bone pain or tenderness (increased, continuing, or returning—in patients with Paget's disease)

Less common

Bone fractures, especially of the thigh bone

Rare

Hives; skin rash or itching; swelling of the arms, legs, face, lips, tongue, and/or throat

Other side effects may occur that usually do not need medical attention. These side effects may go away during treatment as your body adjusts to the medicine. However, check with your doctor if any of the following side effects continue or are bothersome:

More common—at higher doses

Diarrhea; nausea

Less common—with injection

Loss of taste or metallic or altered taste

Other side effects not listed above may also occur in some patients. If you notice any other effects, check with your doctor.

Revised: 08/19/92
Interim revision: 08/10/94

ETOPOSIDE Systemic

A commonly used brand name is:

In the U.S.—
VePesid

In Canada—
VePesid

Generic name product may also be available.

Another commonly used name is VP-16.

Description

Etoposide (e-TOE-poe-side) belongs to the group of medicines known as antineoplastic agents. It is used to treat cancer of the testicles and certain types of lung cancer. It is also sometimes used to treat some other kinds of cancer in both males and females.

The exact way that etoposide acts against cancer is not known. However, it seems to interfere with the growth of the cancer cells, which are eventually destroyed. Since the growth of normal body cells may also be affected by etoposide, other effects will also occur. Some of these may be serious and must be reported to your doctor. Other effects, like hair loss, may not be serious but may cause concern. Some effects may not occur for months or years after the medicine is used.

Before you begin treatment with etoposide, you and your doctor should talk about the good this medicine will do as well as the risks of using it.

This medicine is available only with your doctor's prescription, in the following dosage forms:

Oral

- Capsules (U.S. and Canada)

Parenteral

- Injection (U.S. and Canada)

Before Using This Medicine

In deciding to use a medicine, the risks of taking the medicine must be weighed against the good it will do. This is a decision you and your doctor will make. For etoposide, the following should be considered:

Allergies—Tell your doctor if you have ever had any unusual or allergic reaction to etoposide.

Pregnancy—There is a good chance that this medicine will cause birth defects if it is being used at the time of conception or during pregnancy. In addition, many cancer medicines may cause sterility which could be permanent. Although sterility has not been reported with etoposide, the possibility should be kept in mind.

Be sure that you have discussed this with your doctor before receiving this medicine. It is best to use some kind of birth control while you are taking etoposide. Tell your doctor right away if you think you have become pregnant while taking etoposide. Before taking etoposide make sure your doctor knows if you are pregnant or if you may become pregnant.

Breast-feeding—Because etoposide may cause serious side effects, breast-feeding is generally not recommended while you are receiving it.

Children—Although this medicine has been used in children, there is no specific information comparing use of etoposide in children with use in other age groups.

Older adults—Many medicines have not been studied specifically in older people. Therefore, it may not be known whether they work exactly the same way they do in younger adults or if they cause different side effects or problems in older people. There is no specific information comparing use of etoposide in the elderly with use in other age groups.

Other medicines—Although certain medicines should not be used together at all, in other cases two different medicines may be used together even if an interaction might occur. In these cases, your doctor may want to change the dose, or other precautions may be necessary. When you are taking or receiving etoposide, it is especially important that your health care professional know if you are taking any of the following:

- Amphotericin B by injection (e.g., Fungizone) or
- Antithyroid agents (medicine for overactive thyroid) or
- Azathioprine (e.g., Imuran) or
- Chloramphenicol (e.g., Chloromycetin) or
- Colchicine or
- Flucytosine (e.g., Ancobon) or
- Ganciclovir (e.g., Cytovene) or

- Interferon (e.g., Intron A, Roferon-A) or
- Plicamycin (e.g., Mithracin) or
- Zidovudine (e.g., AZT, Retrovir)
- If you have ever been treated with radiation or cancer medicines—Etoposide may increase the effects of these medicines or radiation therapy on the blood

Other medical problems—The presence of other medical problems may affect the use of etoposide. Make sure you tell your doctor if you have any other medical problems, especially:

- Chickenpox (including recent exposure) or
- Herpes zoster (shingles)—Risk of severe disease affecting other parts of the body
- Infection—Etoposide can decrease your body's ability to fight infection
- Kidney disease or
- Liver disease—Effects of etoposide may be increased because of slower removal from the body

Proper Use of This Medicine

Take etoposide only as directed by your doctor. Do not use more or less of it, and do not use it more often than your doctor ordered. The exact amount of medicine you need has been carefully worked out. Taking too much may increase the chance of side effects, while taking too little may not improve your condition.

Etoposide is sometimes given together with certain other medicines. If you are using a combination of medicines, make sure that you take each one at the proper time and do not mix them. If you are taking some of these medicines by mouth, ask your health care professional to help you plan a way to remember to take your medicines at the right times.

Etoposide often causes nausea, vomiting, and loss of appetite, which may be severe. However, it is very important that you continue to receive the medicine, even if you begin to feel ill. Ask your health care professional for ways to lessen these effects.

If you vomit shortly after taking a dose of etoposide, check with your doctor. You will be told whether to take the dose again or to wait until the next dose.

Dosing—The dose of etoposide will be different for different patients. The dose that is used may depend on a number of things, including what the medicine is being used for, the patient's size, whether the medicine is being given by mouth or by injection, and whether or not other medicines are also being taken. *If you are taking or receiving etoposide at home, follow your doctor's orders or the directions on the label.* If you have any questions about the proper dose of etoposide, ask your doctor.

Missed dose—If you miss a dose of this medicine, do not take the missed dose at all and do not double the next one. Instead, go back to your regular dosing schedule and check with your doctor.

Storage—To store this medicine:

- Keep out of the reach of children.
- Store in the refrigerator.
- Do not store in the bathroom, near the kitchen sink, or in other damp places. Heat or moisture may cause the medicine to break down.
- Do not keep outdated medicine or medicine no longer needed. Be sure that any discarded medicine is out of the reach of children.

Precautions While Using This Medicine

It is very important that your doctor check your progress at regular visits to make sure that etoposide is working properly and to check for unwanted effects.

While you are being treated with etoposide, and after you stop treatment with it, *do not have any immunizations (vaccinations) without your doctor's approval.* Etoposide may lower your body's resistance and there is a chance you might get the infection the immunization is meant to prevent. In addition, other persons living in your household should not take oral polio vaccine since there is a chance they could pass the polio virus on to you. Also, avoid persons who have recently taken oral polio vaccine. Do not get close to them and do not stay in the same room with them for very long. If you cannot take these precautions, you should consider wearing a protective face mask that covers the nose and mouth.

Etoposide can temporarily lower the number of white blood cells in your blood, increasing the chance of getting an infection. It can also lower the number of platelets, which are necessary for proper blood clotting. If this occurs, there are certain precautions you can take, especially when your blood count is low, to reduce the risk of infection or bleeding:

- If you can, avoid people with infections. *Check with your doctor immediately* if you think you are getting an infection or if you get a fever or chills, cough or hoarseness, lower back or side pain, or painful or difficult urination.
- *Check with your doctor immediately* if you notice any unusual bleeding or bruising; black, tarry stools; blood in urine or stools; or pinpoint red spots on your skin.
- Be careful when using a regular toothbrush, dental floss, or toothpick. Your medical doctor, dentist, or nurse may recommend other ways to clean your teeth and gums. Check with your medical doctor before having any dental work done.
- Do not touch your eyes or the inside of your nose unless you have just washed your hands and have not touched anything else in the meantime.
- Be careful not to cut yourself when you are using sharp objects such as a safety razor or fingernail or toenail cutters.
- Avoid contact sports or other situations where bruising or injury could occur.

Side Effects of This Medicine

Along with its needed effects, a medicine may cause some unwanted effects. Although not all of these side effects may occur, if they do occur they may need medical attention.

Also, because of the way these medicines act on the body, there is a chance that they might cause other unwanted effects that may not occur until months or years after the medicine is used. These delayed effects may include certain types of cancer, such as leukemia. Discuss these possible effects with your doctor.

Check with your doctor or nurse immediately if any of the following side effects occur:

Less common

Black, tarry stools; blood in urine or stools; cough or hoarseness; fever or chills; lower back or side pain; painful or difficult urination; pinpoint red spots on skin; unusual bleeding or bruising

Check with your health care professional as soon as possible if any of the following side effects occur:

Less common

Fast heartbeat; shortness of breath or wheezing; sores in mouth or on lips

Rare

Back pain; difficulty in walking; numbness or tingling in fingers and toes; pain at place of injection; skin rash or itching; sweating; swelling of face or tongue; tightness in throat; weakness

Other side effects may occur that usually do not need medical attention. These side effects may go away during treatment as your body adjusts to the medicine. Also, your health care professional may be able to tell you about ways to prevent or reduce some of these side effects. Check with your health care professional if any of the following side effects continue or are bothersome or if you have any questions about them:

More common

Loss of appetite; nausea and vomiting

Less common

Diarrhea; unusual tiredness

This medicine often causes a temporary loss of hair. After treatment with etoposide has ended, normal hair growth should return.

Other side effects not listed above may also occur in some patients. If you notice any other effects, check with your doctor or nurse.

Revised: 08/09/92
Interim revision: 08/08/94

ETRETINATE Systemic

A commonly used brand name in the U.S. and Canada is Tegison.

Description

Etretinate (e-TRET-i-nate) is used to treat severe psoriasis. It is usually used only after other medicines have been tried and have failed to help the psoriasis.

Etretinate must not be used to treat women who are able to bear children unless other forms of treatment have been tried first and have failed. Etretinate must not be taken during pregnancy, because it causes birth defects in humans. In addition, if you take etretinate, you must plan on never having children in the future. If you are able to bear children, it is very important that you read, understand, and follow the pregnancy warnings for etretinate.

It is also recommended that etretinate not be used to treat children unless all other forms of treatment have been tried first and have failed. Etretinate may interfere with bone growth. In addition, children may be more sensitive to the side effects of the medicine.

This medicine is available only with your doctor's prescription, in the following dosage form:

Oral

- Capsules (U.S. and Canada)

Before Using This Medicine

In deciding to use a medicine, the risks of taking the medicine must be weighed against the good it will do. This is a decision you and your doctor will make. For etretinate, the following should be considered:

Allergies—Tell your doctor if you have ever had any unusual or allergic reaction to etretinate, isotretinoin, tretinoin, or vitamin A–like preparations. Also tell your health care professional if you are allergic to any other substances, such as foods, preservatives, or dyes.

Pregnancy—*Etretinate must not be taken during pregnancy, because it causes birth defects in humans. In addition, since it is not known how long pregnancy should be avoided after treatment stops, you must plan on never having children if you are treated with etretinate.* If you are able to bear children, you must have a pregnancy test within 2 weeks before beginning treatment with etretinate to make sure you are not pregnant. Therapy with etretinate will then be started on the second or third day of your next normal menstrual period. *Also, etretinate must not be taken unless an effective form of contraception (birth control) is used for at least 1 month before beginning treatment. Contraception must be continued during treatment and for as long as you are able to become pregnant after etretinate is stopped. Be sure you have discussed this information with your doctor.*

Breast-feeding—It is not known whether etretinate passes into the breast milk. However, etretinate is not recommended during breast-feeding or if you plan to breast-feed in the future, because it may cause unwanted effects in nursing babies.

Children—It is recommended that etretinate not be used to treat children, unless all other forms of treatment have been tried first and have failed. Etretinate may interfere with bone growth. In addition, children may be more sensitive to the side effects of the medicine.

Older adults—Many medicines have not been studied specifically in older people. Therefore, it may not be

known whether they work exactly the same way they do in younger adults or if they cause different side effects or problems in older people. There is no specific information comparing use of etretinate in the elderly with use in other age groups.

Other medicines—Although certain medicines should not be used together at all, in other cases two different medicines may be used together even if an interaction might occur. In these cases, your doctor may want to change the dose, or other precautions may be necessary. When you are using etretinate, it is especially important that your health care professional know if you are using any of the following:

- Abrasive or medicated soaps or cleansers or
- Cosmetics or soaps that dry the skin or
- Medicated cosmetics or ''cover-ups'' or
- Topical acne preparation or preparation containing a peeling agent, such as benzoyl peroxide, resorcinol, salicylic acid, sulfur, or tretinoin (vitamin A acid), or
- Topical alcohol-containing preparation, such as after-shave lotion, astringent, cologne, perfume, or shaving cream or lotion, or
- Topical medicine for the skin, other—Use of etretinate with these products will increase the chance of dryness and other irritation of the skin
- Isotretinoin (e.g., Accutane) or
- Methotrexate (e.g., Mexate) or
- Tretinoin (vitamin A acid) (e.g., Retin-A) or
- Vitamin A or any preparation containing vitamin A (e.g., Alphalin)—Use of etretinate with these products will cause an increase in side effects
- Tetracyclines (medicine for infection)—Use of etretinate may increase the chance of the side effect called pseudotumor cerebri, which is a swelling of the brain

Other medical problems—The presence of other medical problems may affect the use of etretinate. Make sure you tell your doctor if you have any other medical problems, especially:

- Alcoholism or excess use of alcohol (or history of) or
- Diabetes mellitus (sugar diabetes) (or a family history of) or
- Heart or blood vessel disease (or history of increased risk of or family history of) or
- High triglyceride (a fat-like substance) levels in the blood (history of or a family history of) or
- Severe weight problems—Use of etretinate may increase blood levels of triglyceride (a fat-like substance), which may increase the chance of heart or blood vessel problems in patients who have a family history of high triglycerides, are greatly overweight, are diabetic, or use a lot of alcohol. For persons with diabetes mellitus, use of etretinate may also change blood sugar levels
- Liver disease (or history of or family history of)—Use of etretinate may make the condition worse

Proper Use of This Medicine

Take each dose of etretinate with milk or a fatty food. This is important because taking fats with etretinate will help your body absorb the medicine better. *However, you should follow a low-fat diet during the rest of the day* because eating a high-fat diet while you are taking this medicine may cause high triglyceride (fat-like substance) levels in the blood. This may increase the chance of heart and blood vessel disease.

It is very important that you take etretinate only as directed. Do not take more of it, do not take it more often, and do not take it for a longer period of time than your doctor ordered. To do so may increase the chance of side effects.

Dosing—The dose of etretinate will be different for different patients. *Follow your doctor's orders or the directions on the label.* The following information includes only the average doses of etretinate. *If your dose is different, do not change it* unless your doctor tells you to do so.

The number of capsules that you take depends on the strength of the medicine. Also, *the number of doses you take each day, the time allowed between doses, and the length of time you take the medicine depend on the medical problem for which you are taking etretinate.*

- For *oral* dosage form (capsules):
  - —For psoriasis:
    - Adults and teenagers—Dose is based on body weight and must be determined by your doctor. The usual dose is 0.75 to 1 milligram (mg) per kilogram (kg) (0.34 to 0.45 mg per pound) of body weight a day, divided into several doses.
    - Children—Use is usually not recommended.

Missed dose—If you miss a dose of this medicine, take it as soon as possible with milk or a fatty food. However, if it is almost time for your next dose, skip the missed dose and go back to your regular dosing schedule. Do not double doses.

Storage—To store this medicine:

- Keep out of the reach of children.
- Store away from heat and direct light.
- Do not store in the bathroom, near the kitchen sink, or in other damp places. Heat or moisture may cause the medicine to break down.
- Do not keep outdated medicine or medicine no longer needed. Be sure that any discarded medicine is out of the reach of children.

Precautions While Using This Medicine

Your doctor should check your progress at regular visits to make sure this medicine does not cause unwanted effects.

Etretinate causes birth defects in humans if taken during pregnancy. In addition, it is not known how long pregnancy should be avoided after treatment stops, to prevent birth defects. Therefore, you must plan on never having children if you are treated with etretinate. For as long as you are able to become pregnant, you must use a reliable form of birth control. In addition, you must not change your birth control method unless you have checked with your doctor first. If you suspect that you may have become pregnant while taking etretinate, stop taking the medicine immediately and check with your doctor. Also, if you become pregnant at any time after you have stopped taking this medicine, check with your doctor as soon as possible.

In either case, you should talk to your doctor about the risks of continuing the pregnancy.

It is not known how long etretinate stays in the blood. *Therefore, to prevent the possibility of a pregnant patient receiving your blood, you must plan on never donating blood to a blood bank if you are being treated with etretinate or if you have ever been treated with etretinate.*

Do not take vitamin A or any vitamin supplement containing vitamin A while you are taking this medicine. To do so may increase the chance of side effects.

Drinking too much alcohol while you are taking this medicine may cause high triglyceride (fat-like substance) levels in the blood. This may increase the chance of heart and blood vessel disease. Therefore, *while taking this medicine, do not drink alcoholic beverages or, at least, reduce the amount you usually drink.* If you have any questions about this, check with your doctor.

For *diabetic patients*:

- This medicine may affect blood sugar levels. If you notice a change in the results of your blood or urine sugar tests or if you have any questions, check with your doctor.

In some patients, etretinate may cause a decrease in night vision. This decrease may occur suddenly. If it does occur, *do not drive, use machines, or do anything else that could be dangerous if you are not able to see well.* Also, check with your doctor.

Etretinate may cause dryness of the eyes. Therefore, if you wear contact lenses, your eyes may be more sensitive to them while you are taking etretinate and for several weeks or longer after you stop taking it. To help relieve dryness of the eyes, check with your doctor about using an eye lubricating solution, such as artificial tears. If your eyes become inflamed, check with your doctor.

Some people who take this medicine may become more sensitive to sunlight than they are normally. When you begin taking this medicine:

- Stay out of direct sunlight, especially between the hours of 10:00 a.m. and 3:00 p.m., if possible.
- Wear protective clothing, including a hat and sunglasses.
- Apply a sun block product that has a skin protection factor (SPF) of at least 15. Some patients may require a product with a higher SPF number, especially if they have a fair complexion. If you have any questions about this, check with your health care professional.
- Do not use a sunlamp or tanning bed or booth.

If you have a severe reaction, check with your doctor.

This medicine may cause dryness of the mouth and nose. For temporary relief of mouth dryness, use sugarless candy or gum, melt bits of ice in your mouth, or use a saliva substitute. However, if dry mouth continues for more than 2 weeks, check with your medical doctor or dentist. Continuing dryness of the mouth may increase the chance of dental disease, including tooth decay, gum disease, and fungus infections.

During the first month of treatment with etretinate, your psoriasis may seem to get worse before it gets better. There may be more redness or itching, but this usually goes away during treatment. It may take 2 or 3 months before the full effects of etretinate are seen. If irritation or other symptoms of your condition become severe, check with your doctor.

Side Effects of This Medicine

Along with its needed effects, a medicine may cause some unwanted effects. Although not all of these side effects may occur, if they do occur they may need medical attention.

Stop taking this medicine and check with your doctor immediately if any of the following side effects occur:

Less common

Blurred or double vision or other changes in vision; dark-colored urine; flu-like symptoms; yellow eyes or skin

Rare

Headache (severe or continuing); nausea and vomiting

Check with your doctor as soon as possible if any of the following side effects occur:

More common

Bone or joint pain, tenderness, or stiffness; burning, redness, itching, feeling of dryness, pain, tenderness, excessive tearing (continuing), or other sign of inflammation or irritation of eyes; cramps or pain in upper abdomen or stomach area; muscle cramps; unusual bruising

Less common

Change in hearing, earache or pain in ear, or drainage from ear

Rare

Bleeding or inflammation of gums; confusion; mental depression; mood or mental changes

Other side effects may occur that usually do not need medical attention. These side effects may go away during treatment as your body adjusts to the medicine. However, check with your doctor if any of the following side effects continue or are bothersome:

More common

Changes in appetite; chapped lips; dryness of nose or nosebleeds; dryness, redness, scaling, itching, rash, or other sign of inflammation or irritation of the skin; headache (mild); increased sensitivity to contact lenses (may occur during and after treatment); increased sensitivity of skin to sunlight; peeling of skin on fingertips, palms of hands, or soles of feet; thinning of hair; unusual thirst; unusual tiredness

Less common
Dizziness; dryness of mouth; fever; nausea (mild); redness or soreness around fingernails; loosening of the fingernails; soreness of tongue; soreness, cracking, swelling, or unusual redness of lips

Other side effects not listed above may also occur in some patients. If you notice any other effects, check with your doctor.

Revised: June 1990
Interim revision: 06/17/94

FACTOR IX Systemic

Some commonly used brand names are:

In the U.S.—

AlphaNine SD	Mononine
Bebulin VH	Profilnine SD
BeneFix	Proplex T
Konӯne 80	

In Canada—

AlphaNine SD	BeneFix
Bebulin VH	Immunine VH

Other commonly used names are Christmas factor, plasma thromboplastin component (PTC), and prothrombin complex concentrate (PCC).

Description

Factor IX is a protein produced naturally in the body. It helps the blood form clots to stop bleeding. Injections of factor IX are used to treat hemophilia B, which is sometimes called Christmas disease. This is a condition in which the body does not make enough factor IX. If you do not have enough factor IX and you become injured, your blood will not form clots as it should, and you may bleed into and damage your muscles and joints.

Injections of one form of factor IX, called factor IX complex, also are used to treat certain people with hemophilia A. In hemophilia A, sometimes called classical hemophilia, the body does not make enough factor VIII, and, just as in hemophilia B, the blood cannot form clots as it should. Injections of factor IX complex may be used in patients in whom the medicine used to treat hemophilia A is no longer effective. Injections of factor IX complex also may be used for other conditions as determined by your doctor.

The factor IX product that your doctor will give you is obtained naturally from human blood, or artificially by a man-made process. Factor IX obtained from human blood has been treated and is not likely to contain harmful viruses such as hepatitis B virus, hepatitis C (non-A, non-B) virus, or human immunodeficiency virus (HIV), the virus that causes acquired immunodeficiency syndrome (AIDS). The man-made factor IX product does not contain these viruses.

Factor IX is available only with your doctor's prescription, in the following dosage form:

Parenteral

- Injection (U.S. and Canada)

Before Using This Medicine

In deciding to use a medicine, the risks of using the medicine must be weighed against the good it will do. This is a decision you and your doctor will make. For factor IX, the following should be considered:

Allergies—Tell your doctor if you have ever had any unusual or allergic reaction to injections of factor IX, hamster protein, or mouse protein. Also tell your health care professional if you are allergic to any other substances, such as foods, preservatives, or dyes.

Pregnancy—Studies on effects in pregnancy have not been done in either humans or animals.

Breast-feeding—It is not known whether the ingredients in factor IX products pass into breast milk. Although most medicines pass into breast milk in small amounts, many of them may be used safely while breast-feeding. Mothers who are using this medicine and who wish to breast-feed should discuss this with their doctor.

Children—Blood clots may be especially likely to occur in premature and newborn babies, who are usually more sensitive than adults to the effects of injections of factor IX.

Older adults—This medicine has been tested and has not been shown to cause different side effects or problems in older people than it does in younger adults.

Other medicines—Although certain medicines should not be used together at all, in other cases two different medicines may be used together even if an interaction might occur. In these cases, your doctor may want to change the dose, or other precautions may be necessary. Tell your health care professional if you are using any other prescription or nonprescription (over-the-counter [OTC]) medicine.

Other medical problems—The presence of other medical problems may affect the use of factor IX products. Make sure you tell your doctor if you have any other medical problems, especially:

- Blood clots or a history of medical problems caused by blood clots or
- Liver disease—Risk of bleeding or developing blood clots may be increased

Proper Use of This Medicine

Some medicines given by injection may sometimes be given at home to patients who do not need to be in the hospital. If you are using this medicine at home, your health care professional will teach you how to prepare and inject the medicine. You will have a chance to practice preparing and injecting it. *Be sure that you understand exactly how the medicine is to be prepared and injected.*

To prepare this medicine:

- Take the dry medicine and the liquid (diluent) out of the refrigerator and *bring them to room temperature*, as directed by your doctor.
- When injecting the liquid (diluent) into the dry medicine, *aim the stream of liquid (diluent) against the wall of the container of dry medicine* to prevent foaming.
- *Swirl the container gently to dissolve the medicine. Do not shake the container.*

Use this medicine right away. It should not be kept longer than 3 hours after it has been prepared.

A plastic disposable syringe and filter needle must be used with this medicine. The medicine may stick to the inside of a glass syringe, and you may not receive a full dose.

Do not reuse syringes and needles. Put used syringes and needles in a puncture-resistant disposable container, or dispose of them as directed by your health care professional.

Dosing—The dose of factor IX will be different for different patients. The dose you receive will be based on:

- The condition for which you are using this medicine.
- Your body weight.
- The amount of factor IX your body is able to make.
- How much, how often, and where in your body you are bleeding.
- Whether or not your body has built up a defense (antibody) against this medicine.

Your dose of this medicine may even be different at different times. It is important that you *follow your doctor's orders.*

Missed dose—If you miss a dose of this medicine, check with your doctor as soon as possible for instructions.

Storage—To store this medicine:

- Keep out of the reach of children.
- Some factor IX products must be stored in the refrigerator, and some may be kept at room temperature for short periods of time. Store this medicine as directed by your doctor or the manufacturer.
- Do not keep outdated medicine or medicine no longer needed. Be sure that any discarded medicine is out of the reach of children.

Precautions While Using This Medicine

If you were recently diagnosed with hemophilia B, you should receive hepatitis A and hepatitis B vaccines to reduce even further your risk of getting hepatitis A or hepatitis B from factor IX products.

After a while, your body may build up a defense (antibody) against this medicine. *Tell your doctor if this medicine seems to be less effective than usual.*

It is recommended that you carry identification stating that you have hemophilia A or hemophilia B. If you have any questions about what kind of identification to carry, check with your health care professional.

Side Effects of This Medicine

Along with its needed effects, a medicine may cause some unwanted effects. Although not all of these side effects may occur, if they do occur they may need medical attention.

Check with your doctor immediately if any of the following side effects occur, because they may mean that you are having a serious allergic reaction to the medicine:

Less common or rare

Changes in facial skin color; fast or irregular breathing; puffiness or swelling of the eyelids or around the eyes; shortness of breath, troubled breathing, tightness in chest, and/or wheezing; skin rash, hives, and/or itching

Also, check with your doctor immediately if any of the following side effects occur, because they may mean that you are developing a problem with blood clotting:

More common

Bluish coloring (especially of the hands and feet); convulsions; dizziness or lightheadedness when getting up from a lying or sitting position; increased heart rate; large blue or purplish patches in the skin (at places of injection); nausea or vomiting; pains in chest, groin, or legs (especially calves); persistent bleeding from puncture sites, gums, inner linings of the nose and/or mouth, or blood in the stool or urine; severe pain or pressure in the chest and/or the neck, back, or left arm; severe, sudden headache; shortness of breath or fast breathing; sudden loss of coordination; sudden and unexplained slurred speech, vision changes, and/or weakness or numbness in arm or leg

Also, check with your doctor immediately if any of the following side effects occur, because they may mean that your medicine is being given too fast:

Less common

Burning or stinging at place of injection; changes in blood pressure or pulse rate; chills; drowsiness; fever; headache; nausea or vomiting; redness of face; shortness of breath

Other side effects not listed above may also occur in some patients. If you notice any other effects, check with your doctor.

Revised: 08/15/97

FAMCICLOVIR Systemic†

A commonly used brand name in the U.S. is Famvir.

†Not commercially available in Canada.

Description

Famciclovir (fam-SYE-kloe-veer) is used to treat the symptoms of herpes zoster (also known as shingles), a herpes virus infection of the skin. Although famciclovir will not cure herpes zoster, it does help relieve the pain and discomfort and helps the sores heal faster.

Famciclovir is available only with your doctor's prescription, in the following dosage form:

Oral

- Tablets (U.S.)

Before Using This Medicine

In deciding to use a medicine, the risks of taking the medicine must be weighed against the good it will do. This is a decision you and your doctor will make. For famciclovir, the following should be considered:

Allergies—Tell your doctor if you have ever had any unusual or allergic reaction to famciclovir. Also tell your health care professional if you are allergic to any other substances, such as foods, sulfites or other preservatives, or dyes.

Pregnancy—Famciclovir has not been studied in pregnant women. However, famciclovir has not been shown to cause birth defects or other problems in animal studies.

Breast-feeding—It is not known whether famciclovir passes into the breast milk of humans; however, it does pass into the milk of rats. Famciclovir is not recommended during breast-feeding because it may cause unwanted effects in nursing babies.

Children—Studies on this medicine have been done only in adult patients, and there is no specific information comparing use of famciclovir in children with use in other age groups.

Older adults—Famciclovir has been used in the elderly and has not been shown to cause different side effects or problems in older people than it does in younger adults.

Other medicines—Although certain medicines should not be used together at all, in other cases two different medicines may be used together even if an interaction might occur. In these cases, your doctor may want to change your dose or other precautions may be necessary. Tell your health care professional if you are taking any other prescription or nonprescription (over-the-counter [OTC]) medicine.

Other medical problems—The presence of other medical problems may affect the use of famciclovir. Make sure you tell your doctor if you have any other medical problems, especially:

- Kidney disease—Kidney disease may increase blood levels of this medicine, increasing the chance of side effects

Proper Use of This Medicine

Famciclovir is best used within 48 hours after the symptoms of shingles (for example, pain, burning, blisters) begin to appear.

Famciclovir may be taken with meals.

To help clear up your herpes infection, *keep taking famciclovir for the full time of treatment,* even if your symptoms begin to clear up after a few days. *Do not miss any doses.* However, *do not use this medicine more often or for a longer time than your doctor ordered.*

Dosing—The dose of famciclovir will be different for different patients. *Follow your doctor's orders or the directions on the label.* The following information includes only the average doses of famciclovir. Your dose may be different if you have kidney disease. *If your dose is different, do not change it* unless your doctor tells you to do so.

- For *oral* dosage form (tablets):
  - —For treatment of shingles:
    - Adults—500 milligrams (mg) every eight hours for seven days.
    - Children—Use and dose must be determined by your doctor.

Missed dose—If you miss a dose of this medicine, take it as soon as possible. However, if it is almost time for your next dose, skip the missed dose and go back to your regular dosing schedule. Do not double doses.

Storage—To store this medicine:

- Keep out of the reach of children.
- Store away from heat and direct light.
- Do not store the tablets in the bathroom, near the kitchen sink, or in other damp places. Heat or moisture may cause the medicine to break down.
- Do not keep outdated medicine or medicine no longer needed. Be sure that any discarded medicine is out of the reach of children.

Precautions While Using This Medicine

If your symptoms do not improve within a few days, or if they become worse, check with your doctor.

The areas affected by herpes should be kept as clean and dry as possible. Also, wear loose-fitting clothing to avoid irritating the sores (blisters).

Side Effects of This Medicine

Along with its needed effects, a medicine may cause some unwanted effects. Although not all of these side effects may occur, if they do occur they may need medical attention.

Side effects may occur that usually do not need medical attention. These side effects may go away during treatment as your body adjusts to the medicine. However, check with your doctor if any of the following side effects continue or are bothersome:

More common
Headache

Less common
Diarrhea; dizziness; nausea; unusual tiredness or weakness; vomiting

Other side effects not listed above may also occur in some patients. If you notice any other effects, check with your doctor.

Developed: 11/28/94

FAT EMULSIONS Systemic

Some commonly used brand names are:

In the U.S.—
Intralipid
Liposyn II
Liposyn III

In Canada—
Intralipid
Liposyn II

Description

Fat emulsions are used as dietary supplements for patients who are unable to get enough fat in their diet, usually because of certain illnesses or recent surgery. Fats are used by the body for energy and to form substances needed for normal body functions.

Fat emulsions are available by injection only with your doctor's prescription, in the following dosage form:

Parenteral
- Injection (U.S. and Canada)

Before Using This Medicine

In deciding to use a medicine, the risks of using the medicine must be weighed against the good it will do. This is a decision you and your doctor will make. For fat emulsions, the following should be considered:

Allergies—Tell your doctor if you have ever had any unusual or allergic reaction to eggs, soybeans, beans, peas, or fat emulsions. Also tell your health care professional if you are allergic to any other substances, such as foods, preservatives, or dyes.

Pregnancy—Studies on effects in pregnancy have not been done in either animals or humans.

Breast-feeding—It is not known whether fat emulsions pass into the breast milk. However, this medicine has not been reported to cause problems in nursing babies.

Children—Fat emulsions may cause or worsen lung problems or jaundice if given to premature infants. Although there is no specific information comparing use of fat emulsions in older children with use in other age groups, it is not expected to cause different side effects or problems in older children than it does in adults.

Older adults—Many medicines have not been studied specifically in older people. Therefore, it may not be known whether they work exactly the same way they do in younger adults or if they cause different side effects or problems in older people. Although there is no specific information comparing use of fat emulsions in the elderly with use in other age groups, this medicine is not expected to cause different side effects or problems in older people than it does in younger adults.

Other medicines—Although certain medicines should not be used together at all, in other cases two different medicines may be used together even if an interaction might occur. In these cases, your doctor may want to change the dose, or other precautions may be necessary. Tell your health care professional if you are using any other prescription or nonprescription (over-the-counter [OTC]) medicine.

Other medical problems—The presence of other medical problems may affect the use of fat emulsions. Make sure you tell your doctor if you have any other medical problems, especially:

- Blood problems or
- Diabetes mellitus (sugar diabetes) or
- High cholesterol levels or
- Infection or
- Jaundice or
- Kidney disease or
- Liver disease or
- Lung disease or
- Pancreas disease—Fat emulsions may make these conditions worse

Proper Use of This Medicine

Dosing—The amount of fat emulsions to be used will be different for different patients. *Follow your doctor's orders or the directions on the label.* The following information includes only the average dose of fat emulsions. *If your dose is different, do not change it* unless your doctor tells you to do so.

The amount of fat emulsions that is infused into your vein depends on the strength of the fat emulsions used.

- For *injection* dosage form:
  - —For nutritional supplement:
    - Adults and teenagers—At first, the dose is 0.5 to 1 milliliter (mL) per minute injected slowly into a vein over a period of fifteen to thirty minutes. Your doctor may increase the rate of the injection until up to 250 to 500 mL have been injected over four to six hours.
    - Children—At first, the dose is 0.1 mL per minute injected slowly into a vein over a period of fifteen minutes. Your doctor may increase the rate of the injection up to 50 to 100 mL per hour.

Storage—To store this medicine:

- Keep out of the reach of children.
- Store away from heat and direct light.
- Do not store in the bathroom, near the kitchen sink, or in other damp places. Heat or moisture may cause the medicine to break down.
- Keep the medicine from freezing. Do not refrigerate.
- Do not keep outdated medicine or medicine no longer needed. Be sure that any discarded medicine is out of the reach of children.

Precautions While Using This Medicine

It is very important that your doctor check your progress weekly while you are receiving fat emulsions to make sure that this medicine does not cause unwanted effects.

Fat emulsions can lower your ability to fight infection. If you think you are getting an infection, check with your doctor.

Side Effects of This Medicine

Along with its needed effects, a medicine may cause some unwanted effects. Although not all of these side effects may occur, if they do occur they may need medical attention.

Check with your doctor as soon as possible if any of the following side effects occur:

More common

Chills; fever; sore throat

Rare

Bluish color of skin; chest or back pain; difficulty in breathing; headache; hives; unusual bleeding or bruising; unusual irritability; unusual tiredness or weakness; yellow eyes or skin

Other side effects may occur that usually do not need medical attention. These side effects may go away during treatment as your body adjusts to the medicine. However, check with your doctor if any of the following side effects continue or are bothersome:

More common

Redness, swelling, or pain at place of injection

Less common

Diarrhea; dizziness; flushing; nausea and vomiting

Other side effects not listed above may also occur in some patients. If you notice any other effects, check with your doctor.

Revised: 05/12/93
Interim revision: 06/27/94

FELBAMATE Systemic†

A commonly used brand name in the U.S. is Felbatol.
Another commonly used name is FBM.

†Not commercially available in Canada.

Description

Felbamate (FEL-ba-mate) is used to control some types of seizures in the treatment of epilepsy. Felbamate acts on the central nervous system (CNS) to make it more difficult for seizures to start or to continue. This medicine cannot cure epilepsy and will only work to control seizures for as long as you continue to use it.

Felbamate is available only with your doctor's prescription, in the following dosage forms:

Oral

- Suspension (U.S.)
- Tablets (U.S.)

Before Using This Medicine

In deciding to use a medicine, the risks of taking the medicine must be weighed against the good it will do. This is a decision you and your doctor will make. For felbamate, the following should be considered:

Allergies—Tell your doctor if you have ever had any unusual or allergic reaction to felbamate or to medicines like felbamate such as carbromal, carisoprodol (Soma, Rela), mebutamate, meprobamate (Equanil, Miltown), or tybamate (Tybatran). Also tell your health care professional if you are allergic to any other substances, such as foods, preservatives, or dyes.

Pregnancy—Felbamate has not been studied in pregnant women. However, studies in pregnant animals have shown that felbamate may cause lowered birth weight and lowered survival of offspring when given to the mother in doses more than one and one-half times the usual human dose. Before taking this medicine, make sure your doctor knows if you are pregnant or if you may become pregnant.

Breast-feeding—Felbamate passes into breast milk. However, it is not known whether this medicine causes problems in nursing babies.

Children—This medicine has some very serious unwanted effects. Children may not be able to tell their parent or guardian or their doctor if they have symptoms of these effects, such as chills or stomach pain. Felbamate should be used in children only if other medicines have not controlled their seizures.

Older adults—Many medicines have not been studied specifically in older people. Therefore, it may not be known whether they work exactly the same way they do in younger adults or if they cause different side effects or problems in older people. There is no specific information comparing use of felbamate in the elderly with use in other age groups. However, older people are more likely to have other illnesses and to use other medicines that may affect the way felbamate works. Your doctor may start with a lower felbamate dose or may increase the dose more slowly.

Other medicines—Although certain medicines should not be used together at all, in other cases two different medicines may be used together even if an interaction might occur. In these cases, your doctor may want to change the dose, or other precautions may be necessary. When you are taking felbamate, it is especially important that your health care professional know if you are taking any of the following:

- Carbamazepine (e.g., Tegretol) or
- Phenytoin (e.g., Dilantin) or
- Valproic acid (e.g., Depakene)—Higher or lower blood levels of these medicines or felbamate may occur, which may increase the chance of unwanted effects; your doctor may need to change the dose of either these medicines or felbamate

Other medical problems—The presence of other medical problems may affect the use of felbamate. Make sure you tell your doctor if you have any other medical problems, especially:

- Anemia or other blood problems (or history of) or
- Liver problems (or history of)—Felbamate may make the condition worse

Proper Use of This Medicine

Take this medicine only as directed by your doctor, to benefit your condition as much as possible. Do not take more of it, do not take it more often, and do not take it for a longer time than your doctor ordered.

For patients taking the *oral liquid form* of this medicine:

- Shake the bottle well before measuring the dose.
- Use a specially marked measuring spoon, a plastic syringe, or a small marked measuring cup to measure each dose accurately. The average household teaspoon may not hold the right amount of liquid.

To lessen stomach upset, felbamate may be taken with food, unless your doctor has told you to take it on an empty stomach.

Dosing—The dose of felbamate will be different for different patients. *Follow your doctor's orders or the directions on the label.* The following information includes only the average doses of felbamate. *If your dose is different, do not change it* unless your doctor tells you to do so.

The number of tablets or teaspoonfuls of suspension that you take depends on the strength of the medicine.

- For *oral* dosage forms (suspension or tablets):
  - —For epilepsy:
    - Adults and teenagers 14 years of age and older—At first, usually 1200 milligrams (mg) a day, divided into three or four smaller doses. Your doctor may increase the dose gradually over several weeks if needed. However, the dose is usually not more than 3600 mg a day.
    - Children 2 to 14 years of age—At first, usually 15 mg per kilogram (kg) [6.8 mg per pound] of body weight per day, divided into smaller doses that are given three or four times during the day. Your doctor may increase the dose gradually over a few weeks if needed. However, the dose is usually not more than 45 mg per kg [20.5 mg per pound] or 3600 mg per day, whichever is less.

Missed dose—If you miss a dose of this medicine, take it as soon as possible. However, if it is almost time for your next dose, skip the missed dose and go back to your regular dosing schedule. Do not double doses.

Storage—To store this medicine:

- Keep out of the reach of children.
- Store away from heat and direct sunlight.
- Do not store in the bathroom, near the kitchen sink, or in other damp places. Heat or moisture may cause the medicine to break down.
- Do not keep outdated medicine or medicine no longer needed. Be sure that any discarded medicine is out of the reach of children.

Precautions While Using This Medicine

It is important that your doctor check your progress at regular visits. This is necessary to allow dose adjustments and to test for serious unwanted effects.

Do not stop taking felbamate without first checking with your doctor. Your doctor may want you to gradually reduce the amount you are taking before stopping completely. Stopping the medicine suddenly may cause your seizures to return or to occur more often.

Felbamate may cause blurred vision, double vision, or other changes in vision. It may also cause some people to become dizzy or drowsy. *Make sure you know how you react to this medicine before you drive, use machines, or do anything else that could be dangerous if you are not alert or able to see well.* If these reactions are especially bothersome, check with your doctor.

Side Effects of This Medicine

Felbamate may cause some serious side effects, including blood problems and liver problems. *You and your doctor should discuss the good this medicine will do as well as the risks of receiving it.*

Along with its needed effects, a medicine may cause some unwanted effects. Some side effects will have signs or symptoms that you can see or feel. Your doctor may watch for others by doing certain tests. Although not all of these side effects may occur, if they do occur they may need medical attention.

Check with your doctor immediately if any of the following side effects occur:

More common

Fever; purple or red spots on skin

Rare

Black or tarry stools; blood in urine or stools; chills; continuing headache; continuing stomach pain; continuing vomiting; dark-colored urine; general feeling of tiredness or weakness; light-colored stools; nosebleeds or other unusual bruising or bleeding; shortness of breath, trouble in breathing, wheezing, or tightness in chest; sore throat; sores, ulcers, or white spots on lips or in mouth; swelling of face; swollen or painful glands; yellow eyes or skin

Check with your doctor as soon as possible if any of the following side effects occur:

More common

Walking in unusual manner

Less common

Agitation, aggression, or other mood or mental changes; clumsiness or unsteadiness; skin rash; trembling or shaking

Rare

Chest pain; hives or itching; muscle cramps; nasal congestion; pain; sensitivity of skin to sunlight; swollen lymph nodes

Other side effects may occur that usually do not need medical attention. These side effects may go away during treatment as your body adjusts to the medicine. However, check with your doctor if any of the following side effects continue or are bothersome:

More common

Change in your sense of taste; constipation; difficulty in sleeping; dizziness; headache; indigestion; loss of appetite; nausea; stomach pain; vomiting

Less common

Blurred or double vision; coughing; diarrhea; drowsiness; ear congestion or pain; runny nose; sneezing; weight loss

This medicine may also cause the following side effects that your doctor will watch for:

Rare

Blood problems

Other side effects not listed above may also occur in some patients. If you notice any other effects, check with your doctor.

Developed: 08/30/94
Interim revision: 10/06/94; 03/28/95

FENFLURAMINE Systemic

Some commonly used brand names are:

In the U.S.—

Pondimin

In Canada—

Ponderal
Ponderal Pacaps
Pondimin

Description

Fenfluramine (fen-FLURE-a-meen) has been used as an appetite suppressant in the short-term treatment of obesity. However, this medicine may cause very serious heart valve problems. These heart valve problems may not have any symptoms at first. However, doctors can do special tests to see if any heart valve damage has been done, even in patients who do not have symptoms. Fenfluramine may also cause a very serious lung problem called primary pulmonary hypertension. Symptoms that may develop in patients with heart valve damage or primary pulmonary hypertension include a decrease in the ability to exercise, swelling of the feet or lower legs, trouble in breathing, fainting, or chest pain.

Because of the serious side effects described above, fenfluramine was taken off the market in September of 1997.

If you have been taking fenfluramine, contact your doctor for advice. Since some patients may still have this medicine at home the following information is made available.

Before Using This Medicine

In deciding to use a medicine, the risks of taking the medicine must be weighed against the good it will do. This is a decision you and your doctor will make. For fenfluramine, the following should be considered:

Allergies—Tell your doctor if you have ever had any unusual or allergic reaction to this medicine or amphetamine, dextroamphetamine, ephedrine, epinephrine, isoproterenol, metaproterenol, methamphetamine, norepinephrine, phenylephrine, phenylpropanolamine, pseudoephedrine, terbutaline, or other appetite suppressants. Also tell your health care professional if you are allergic to any other substances, such as foods, preservatives, or dyes.

Pregnancy—Studies have not been done in pregnant women. However, animal studies have shown that fenfluramine, when given at many times the human dose, reduces fertility and may have toxic or harmful effects on the fetus.

Breast-feeding—It is not known if fenfluramine passes into breast milk. However, this medicine has not been reported to cause problems in nursing babies.

Children—Fenfluramine should not be used as an appetite suppressant by children under 12 years of age.

Older adults—Many medicines have not been studied specifically in older people. Therefore, it may not be known whether they work exactly the same way they do in younger adults or if they cause different side effects or problems in older people. There is no specific information comparing use of fenfluramine in the elderly to use in other age groups.

Other medicines—Although certain medicines should not be used together at all, in other cases two different medicines may be used together even if an interaction might occur. In these cases, your doctor may want to change the dose, or other precautions may be necessary. When you are taking fenfluramine, it is especially important that your health care professional know if you are taking any of the following:

- Amphetamines (amphetamine, dextroamphetamine [e.g., Dexedrine], methamphetamine [e.g., Desoxyn]) or
- Appetite suppressants, other (benzphetamine [e.g., Didrex], diethylpropion [e.g., Tenuate], mazindol [e.g., Sanorex], phendimetrazine [e.g., Adipost], phentermine [e.g., Ionamin])—Serious unwanted effects on the heart valves have occurred in patients using fenfluramine with another appetite suppressant. Use of fenfluramine with another appetite suppressant is not recommended.
- Central nervous system (CNS) depressants (medicine that causes drowsiness) or
- Tricyclic antidepressants (medicine for depression)—Using these medicines with fenfluramine may increase the CNS depressant effects
- Monoamine oxidase (MAO) inhibitors (furazolidone [e.g., Furoxone], isocarboxazid [e.g., Marplan], phenelzine [e.g., Nardil], procarbazine [e.g., Matulane], selegiline [e.g., Eldepryl], tranylcypromine [e.g., Parnate])—Taking fenfluramine while you are taking or within 2 weeks of taking monoamine oxidase (MAO) inhibitors may cause sudden extremely high blood pressure; at least 14 days should be allowed between stopping treatment with one medicine and starting treatment with the other

Other medical problems—The presence of other medical problems may affect the use of appetite suppressants. Make sure you tell your doctor if you have any other medical problems, especially:

- Alcohol abuse (or history of) or
- Drug abuse or dependence (or history of)—Dependence on fenfluramine may develop
- Diabetes mellitus (sugar diabetes)—The amount of insulin or oral antidiabetic medicine that you need to take may change
- Glaucoma or
- Heart or blood vessel disease or
- High blood pressure or
- Mental depression or
- Mental illness (severe)—Fenfluramine may make the condition worse

Proper Use of This Medicine

Take fenfluramine only as directed by your doctor. Do not take more of it, do not take it more often, and do not take it for a longer time than your doctor ordered. If too much is taken, it may become habit-forming.

If you think this medicine is not working properly after you have taken it for a few weeks, *do not increase the dose.* Instead, check with your doctor.

For patients taking the *long-acting form* of this medicine:
- These capsules or tablets are to be swallowed whole. Do not break, crush, or chew before swallowing.

Dosing—The dose of fenfluramine will be different for different patients. *Follow your doctor's orders or the directions on the label.* The following information includes only the average doses of fenfluramine. *If your dose is different, do not change it* unless your doctor tells you to do so.
- For *oral extended-release capsule* dosage form:
  —For appetite suppression:
    - Adults—At first, 60 milligrams (mg) once a day. Your doctor may need to adjust your dose.
    - Children—Use is not recommended.
- For *oral tablet* dosage form:
  —For appetite suppression:
    - Adults—At first, 20 mg three times a day, taken thirty to sixty minutes before meals. Your doctor may need to adjust your dose.
    - Children—Use is not recommended.

Storage—To store this medicine:
- Keep out of the reach of children.
- Store away from heat and direct light.
- Do not store in the bathroom, near the kitchen sink, or in other damp places. Heat or moisture may cause the medicine to break down.
- Do not keep outdated medicine or medicine no longer needed. Be sure that any discarded medicine is out of the reach of children.

Precautions While Using This Medicine

Your doctor should check your progress at regular visits in order to make sure that this medicine does not cause unwanted effects.

Fenfluramine will add to the effects of alcohol and other CNS depressants (medicines that cause drowsiness). Some examples of CNS depressants are antihistamines or medicine for hay fever, other allergies, or colds; sedatives, tranquilizers, or sleeping medicine; prescription pain medicine or narcotics; barbiturates; medicine for seizures; muscle relaxants; or anesthetics, including some dental anesthetics. *Check with your medical doctor or dentist before taking any such depressants while you are using this medicine.*

This medicine may cause some people to have a false sense of well-being or to become dizzy, lightheaded, drowsy, or less alert than they are normally. *Make sure you know how you react to this medicine before you drive, use machines, or do anything else that could be dangerous if you are dizzy or are not alert.*

Before having any kind of surgery, dental treatment, or emergency treatment, tell the medical doctor or dentist in charge that you are using this medicine. Taking fenfluramine together with medicines that are used during surgery or dental or emergency treatments may increase the CNS depressant effects.

Check with your doctor immediately if you notice a decrease in your ability to exercise, if you faint, or if you have chest pain, swelling of your feet or lower legs, or trouble in breathing. These may be symptoms of very serious heart or lung problems.

If you have been taking fenfluramine for a long time or in large doses and *you think you may have become mentally or physically dependent on it, check with your doctor.*
- Some signs of dependence on fenfluramine are:
  —a strong desire or need to continue taking the medicine.
  —a need to increase the dose to receive the effects of the medicine.
  —withdrawal side effects (for example, mental depression, trouble in sleeping, or nightmares when you stop taking the medicine).

For *diabetic patients:*
- This medicine may affect blood sugar levels. If you notice a change in the results of your urine or blood sugar test or if you have any questions, check with your doctor.

If you have been taking fenfluramine in large doses for a long time, *do not stop taking it without first checking with your doctor.* Your doctor may want you to reduce gradually the amount you are taking before stopping completely.

Side Effects of This Medicine

Fenfluramine may cause some very serious side effects, including heart valve disease and lung problems (primary pulmonary hypertension). *Because of these side effects, fenfluramine has been taken off the market and its use is not recommended.* If you have been taking fenfluramine, contact your doctor for advice.

Along with its needed effects, a medicine may cause some unwanted effects. Although not all of these side effects may occur, if they do occur they may need medical attention.

Check with your doctor immediately if any of the following side effects occur:

Symptoms of primary pulmonary hypertension or heart valve disease
Chest pain; decreased ability to exercise; fainting; swelling of feet or lower legs; trouble in breathing

Check with your doctor as soon as possible if any of the following side effects occur:

Less common
Confusion or mental depression; skin rash or hives

Rare
Increased blood pressure

Symptoms of overdose
Abdominal or stomach cramps; fast breathing; fever; nausea or vomiting (severe); tremor

Other side effects may occur that usually do not need medical attention. These side effects may go away during treatment as your body adjusts to the medicine. However,

check with your doctor if any of the following side effects continue or are bothersome:

More common

Diarrhea; drowsiness; dryness of mouth

Less common

Blurred vision; changes in sexual desire or decreased sexual ability; clumsiness or unsteadiness; constipation; difficult or painful urination; difficulty in talking; dizziness or lightheadedness; false sense of well-being; frequent urge to urinate or increased urination; headache; increased sweating; irritability; nausea or vomiting; nervousness or restlessness; pounding heartbeat; stomach cramps or pain; trouble in sleeping or nightmares; unpleasant taste; unusual tiredness or weakness

After you stop using this medicine, your body may need time to adjust. The length of time this takes depends on the amount of medicine you were using and how long you used it. During this time check with your doctor if you notice any of the following side effects:

Mental depression; trouble in sleeping or nightmares

Other side effects not listed above may also occur in some patients. If you notice any other effects, check with your doctor.

Revised: 08/29/94; 08/15/97; 9/23/97

FENTANYL Transdermal-Systemic

A commonly used brand name in the U.S. and Canada is Duragesic.

Description

Fentanyl (FEN-ta-nil) belongs to the group of medicines called narcotic analgesics (nar-KOT-ik an-al-GEE-ziks). Narcotic analgesics are used to relieve pain. The transdermal system (skin patch) form of fentanyl is used to treat chronic pain (pain that continues for a long time).

Fentanyl acts in the central nervous system (CNS) to relieve pain. Some of its side effects are also caused by actions in the CNS.

When a narcotic is used for a long time, it may become habit-forming (causing mental or physical dependence). However, *people who have continuing pain should not let the fear of dependence keep them from using narcotics to relieve their pain.* Mental dependence (addiction) is not likely to occur when narcotics are used for this purpose. Physical dependence may lead to withdrawal side effects if treatment is stopped suddenly. However, severe withdrawal side effects can usually be prevented by reducing the dose gradually over a period of time before treatment is stopped completely.

This medicine is available only with your doctor's prescription. Prescriptions for transdermal fentanyl cannot be refilled. You will need to obtain a new prescription from your doctor each time you need the medicine. This medicine is available in the following dosage form:

Transdermal

- Transdermal system (stick-on skin patch) (U.S. and Canada)

Before Using This Medicine

In deciding to use a medicine, the risks of using the medicine must be weighed against the good it will do. This is a decision you and your health care professional will make. For fentanyl, the following should be considered:

Allergies—Tell your health care professional if you have ever had any unusual or allergic reaction to fentanyl, alfentanil (e.g., Alfenta), or sufentanil (e.g., Sufenta). Also tell your health care professional if you are allergic to any other substances, including the adhesives that keep stick-on bandages in place.

Pregnancy—Although studies on birth defects with fentanyl have not been done in pregnant women, it has not been reported to cause birth defects. However, using any narcotic regularly during pregnancy may cause physical dependence in the fetus. This may lead to withdrawal side effects after birth. Also, use of this medicine near the end of pregnancy may cause drowsiness and breathing problems in newborn babies.

Breast-feeding—Fentanyl passes into the breast milk. Nursing babies whose mothers are using this medicine regularly may receive enough of it to cause unwanted effects such as drowsiness, breathing problems, and physical dependence. Similar effects may also occur with some other narcotics if they are taken regularly in large amounts. A mother who wishes to breast-feed and who needs treatment for continuing pain should discuss the risks and benefits of different pain treatments with her health care professional.

Children—Studies with the fentanyl skin patch have been done only in adult patients, and there is no specific information comparing the use of this medicine in children with use in other age groups.

Teenagers—Studies with the fentanyl skin patch have been done only in patients 18 years of age and older. There is no specific information comparing the use of this medicine in teenagers with use in other age groups.

Older adults—Elderly people are especially sensitive to the effects of narcotic analgesics. This may increase the chance of side effects, especially breathing problems, during treatment. Your health care professional will take this into consideration when deciding on the amount of transdermal fentanyl you should receive.

Other medicines—Although certain medicines should not be used together at all, in other cases two different medicines may be used together even if an interaction might occur. In these cases, your health care professional may want to change the dose, or other precautions may be necessary. When you are using fentanyl, it is especially important that your health care professional know if you are taking any of the following:

- Buprenorphine (e.g., Buprenex) or
- Dezocine (e.g., Dalgan) or
- Nalbuphine (e.g., Nubain) or
- Pentazocine (e.g., Talwin)—Like all narcotic analgesics, these medicines may add to the effects of fentanyl, which may increase the chance of side effects or overdose. However, buprenorphine, dezocine, nalbuphine, and pentazocine sometimes decrease the effects of fentanyl, so that fentanyl might be less effective in relieving pain. Also, these medicines can cause withdrawal side effects if they are given to someone who is physically dependent on fentanyl
- Central nervous system (CNS) depressants (medicines that cause drowsiness), including other narcotics, or
- Tricyclic antidepressants—These medicines may add to the effects of fentanyl. This may increase the chance of serious side effects
- Naltrexone (e.g., Trexan)—Fentanyl will not be effective in people taking naltrexone

Other medical problems—The presence of other medical problems may affect the use of fentanyl. Make sure you tell your health care professional if you have any other medical problems, especially:

- Alcohol abuse, or history of, or
- Drug dependence, especially narcotic abuse or dependence, or history of, or
- Emotional problems or
- Kidney disease or
- Liver disease or
- Underactive thyroid—The chance of side effects may be increased
- Brain tumor or
- Diarrhea caused by antibiotic treatment or poisoning or
- Emphysema, asthma, or other chronic lung disease or
- Enlarged prostate or problems with urination or
- Gallbladder disease or gallstones or
- Intestinal problems such as colitis or Crohn's disease—Some of the side effects of fentanyl can cause serious problems in people who have these medical problems
- Slow heartbeat—Fentanyl can make this condition worse

Proper Use of This Medicine

Transdermal fentanyl comes with patient instructions. Read them carefully before using the product. If you do not receive any printed instructions with the medicine, check with your pharmacist.

To use:

- *Use this medicine exactly as directed by your doctor.* It will work only if it has been applied correctly.
- Fentanyl skin patches are packaged in sealed pouches. *Do not remove the patch from the sealed pouch until you are ready to apply it.*
- When handling the skin patch, *be careful not to touch the adhesive (sticky) surface with your hand.* The adhesive part of the system contains some fentanyl, which can be absorbed into your body too fast through the skin of your hand. If any of the medicine does get on your hand, *rinse the area right away with a lot of clear water. Do not use soap or other cleansers.*
- *Be careful not to tear the patch or make any holes in it.* Damage to a patch may allow fentanyl to pass into your skin too quickly. This can cause an overdose.
- Apply the patch to a dry, flat skin area on your upper arm, chest, or back. *Choose a place where the skin is not very oily and is free of scars, cuts, burns, or any other skin irritations. Also, do not apply this medicine to areas that have received radiation (x-ray) treatment.*
- The patch will stay in place better if it is applied to an area with little or no hair. If you need to apply the patch to a hairy area, you may first clip the hair with scissors, *but do not shave it off.*
- If you need to clean the area before applying the medicine, *use only plain water. Do not use soaps, other cleansers, lotions, or anything that contains oils or alcohol.* Be sure that the skin is completely dry before applying the medicine.
- Remove the liner covering the sticky side of the skin patch. Then press the patch firmly in place, using the palm of your hand, for about 30 seconds. Make sure that the entire adhesive surface is attached to your skin, especially around the edges.
- If you need to apply more than 1 patch at a time, *place the patches far enough apart so that the edges do not touch or overlap each other.*
- Wash your hands with a lot of clear water after applying the medicine. Do not use soap or other cleansers.
- Remove the patch after 72 hours (3 days). *Choose a different place on your skin to apply the next patch.* If possible, use a place on the other side of your body. *Wait at least 3 days before using the first area again.*

After a patch is applied, the fentanyl it contains passes into the skin a little at a time. A certain amount of the medicine must build up in the skin before it is absorbed into the body. Therefore, up to a day may pass before the first dose begins to work. Your health care professional may need to change the dose during the first several applications (each kept in place for 3 days) before finding the amount that works best for you. Even if you feel that the medicine is not working, *do not increase the amount of transdermal fentanyl that you apply.* Instead, check with your health care professional.

You will probably need to take a faster-acting narcotic to relieve pain during the first few days of transdermal fentanyl treatment. You may continue to need another narcotic while your dose of fentanyl is being adjusted, and also to relieve any ''break through'' pain that occurs later on. *Be sure that you do not take more of the other narcotic, and do not take it more often, than directed. Taking other narcotics together with fentanyl can increase the chance of an overdose.*

Dosing—The dose of transdermal fentanyl will be different for different patients. *Follow your doctor's orders or the directions on the label.* The following information includes only the average doses of this medicine. *If your* *dose is different, do not change it* unless your doctor tells you to do so.

- For *transdermal* dosage form (stick-on patch):
  - —For relief of severe, continuing pain:
    - Adults—If you have not already been using other narcotics regularly, your first dose will probably be one patch that releases 25 micrograms (mcg) of fentanyl every hour. If you have already been using other narcotics regularly, your first dose will depend on the amount of other narcotic you have been taking every day. If necessary, your health care professional will change the dose after 3 days, when the first patch is replaced. The size of the new dose will depend on how well the medicine is working and on whether you had any side effects during the first 3-day application. Other changes in dose may be needed later on. Some people may need to use more than one patch at a time.
    - Children—Use and dose must be determined by the doctor.

Missed dose—If you miss a dose of this medicine, apply it as soon as possible. Remove the new patch 3 days after applying it.

Storage—To store this medicine:
- Keep out of the reach of children.
- Store away from heat and direct light.
- Do not keep outdated medicine or medicine no longer needed. To dispose of this medicine, first fold the patch in half, with the sticky side inside. If the patch has not been used, take it out of the pouch and remove the liner that covers the sticky side of the patch before folding it in half. Then flush it down the toilet right away.

Precautions While Using This Medicine

Check with your health care professional at regular times while using fentanyl. Be sure to report any side effects.

After you have been using this medicine for a while, ''break through'' pain may occur more often than usual, and it may not be relieved by your regular dose of medicine. If this occurs, *do not increase the amount of transdermal fentanyl or other narcotic that you are taking without first checking with your health care professional.*

This medicine will add to the effects of alcohol and other CNS depressants (medicines that can make you drowsy or less alert). Some examples of CNS depressants are antihistamines or medicine for hay fever, other allergies, or colds; sedatives, tranquilizers, or sleeping medicine; other prescription pain medicine or narcotics; barbiturates; medicine for seizures; muscle relaxants; or anesthetics, including some dental anesthetics. You will probably be directed to take other pain relievers if you still have pain while using transdermal fentanyl. However, *check with your health care professional before taking any of the other medicines listed above while you are using this medicine.*

Fentanyl may cause some people to become drowsy, dizzy, or lightheaded, or to feel a false sense of well-being. *Make sure you know how you react to this medicine before you drive, use machines, or do anything else that could be dangerous if you are dizzy or not alert and clearheaded.* These effects usually go away after a few days of treatment, when your body gets used to the medicine. However, *check with your health care professional if drowsiness that is severe enough to interfere with your activities continues for more than a few days.*

Dizziness, lightheadedness, or even fainting may occur when you get up suddenly from a lying or sitting position. *Getting up slowly may help lessen this problem.* Also, lying down for a while may relieve dizziness or lightheadedness.

Nausea or vomiting may occur, especially during the first several days of treatment. Lying down for a while may relieve these effects. However, if they are especially bothersome or if they continue for more than a few days, check with your health care professional. You may be able to take another medicine to help prevent these problems.

Using narcotics for a long time can cause severe constipation. To prevent this, your health care professional may direct you to take laxatives, drink a lot of fluids, or increase the amount of fiber in your diet. *Be sure to follow the directions carefully,* because continuing constipation can lead to more serious problems.

Heat can cause the fentanyl in the patch to be absorbed into your body faster. This may increase the chance of serious side effects or an overdose. While you are using this medicine, *do not use a heating pad, a sunlamp, or a heated water bed, and do not take sunbaths or long baths or showers in hot water.* Also, *check with your health care professional if you get a fever.*

Before having any kind of surgery (including dental surgery) or emergency treatment, tell the medical doctor or dentist in charge that you are using this medicine. Serious side effects can occur if your medical doctor or dentist gives you certain other medicines without knowing that you are using fentanyl.

You may bathe, shower, or swim while wearing a fentanyl skin patch. However, be careful to wash and dry the area around the patch gently. Rubbing may cause the patch to get loose or come off. If this does occur, throw away the patch and apply a new one in a different place. Make sure the area is completely dry before applying the new patch.

If you have been using this medicine regularly for several weeks or more, *do not suddenly stop using it without first checking with your health care professional.* You may be directed to reduce gradually the amount you are using before stopping treatment completely, or to take another narcotic for a while, to lessen the chance of withdrawal side effects.

Using too much transdermal fentanyl, or taking too much of another narcotic while using transdermal fentanyl, may cause an overdose. If this occurs, get emergency help right away. An overdose can cause severe breathing problems (breathing may even stop), unconsciousness, and death. Serious signs of an overdose include very slow breathing

Side Effects of This Medicine

Along with its needed effects, a medicine may cause some unwanted effects. Although not all of these side effects may occur, if they do occur they may need medical attention.

Get emergency help immediately if the following signs of overdose occur:

Cold, clammy skin; convulsions (seizures); drowsiness that is so severe that you are not able to answer when spoken to or, if asleep, cannot be awakened; low blood pressure; pinpoint pupils of eyes; slow heartbeat; very slow (fewer than 8 breaths a minute) or troubled breathing

Also, check with your doctor as soon as possible if any of the following side effects occur:

More common

Decrease in amount of urine or in the frequency of urination; hallucinations (seeing, hearing, or feeling things that are not there)

Less common

Chest pain; difficulty in speaking; fainting; irregular heartbeat; mood or mental changes; problems with walking; redness, swelling, itching, or bumps on the skin at place of application; spitting blood

Rare

Any change in vision; bladder pain; difficulty in speaking; fever with or without chills; fluid-filled blisters on skin; frequent urge to urinate; noisy breathing, shortness of breath, tightness in chest, or wheezing; red, thickened, or scaly skin; swelling of abdomen or stomach area; swollen and/or painful glands; unusual bruising

Other side effects may occur that usually do not need medical attention. These side effects may go away during treatment as your body adjusts to the medicine. However, check with your doctor if any of the following side effects continue or are bothersome:

More common

Abdominal or stomach pain that was not present before treatment; confusion; constipation; diarrhea; dizziness, drowsiness, or lightheadedness; false sense of well-being; feeling anxious; headache; indigestion; loss of appetite; nausea or vomiting; nervousness; sweating; weakness

Less common

Bloated feeling or gas; feeling anxious and restless at the same time; feeling of crawling, tingling, or burning of the skin; memory loss; unusual dreams

After you stop using this medicine, your body may need time to adjust. The length of time this takes depends on the amount of medicine you were using and how long you used it. During this period of time check with your doctor if you notice any of the following side effects:

Body aches; diarrhea; fast heartbeat; fever, runny nose, or sneezing; gooseflesh; increased sweating; increased yawning; loss of appetite; nausea or vomiting; nervousness, restlessness, or irritability; shivering or trembling; stomach cramps; trouble in sleeping; unusually large pupils of eyes; weakness

Other side effects not listed above may also occur in some patients. If you notice any other effects, check with your doctor.

Developed: 07/27/94

FINASTERIDE Systemic

A commonly used brand name in the U.S. and Canada is Proscar.

Description

Finasteride (fin-AS-tur-ide) belongs to the group of medicines called enzyme inhibitors. It is used to treat urinary problems caused by enlargement of the prostate (benign prostatic hyperplasia or BPH). In men with very enlarged prostates and mild to moderate symptoms (difficulty urinating, decreased flow of urination, hesitation at the beginning of urination, getting up at night to urinate), finasteride may decrease the severity of symptoms.

Finasteride blocks an enzyme called 5-alpha-reductase, which is necessary to change testosterone to another hormone that causes the prostate to grow. As a result, the size of the prostate is decreased. The effect of finasteride on the prostate lasts only as long as the medicine is taken. If it is stopped, the prostate begins to grow again.

Finasteride is available only with your doctor's prescription, in the following dosage form:

Oral

- Tablets (U.S. and Canada)

Before Using This Medicine

In deciding to use a medicine, the risks of taking the medicine must be weighed against the good it will do. This is a decision you and your doctor will make. For finasteride, the following should be considered:

Allergies—Tell your doctor if you have ever had any unusual or allergic reaction to finasteride. Also tell your health care professional if you are allergic to any other substances, such as foods, preservatives, or dyes.

Pregnancy—Women who are or may become pregnant should not take finasteride or should not be exposed to crushed finasteride tablets, because it can cause changes in the genitals (sex organs) of male fetuses.

Older adults—This medicine has been tested and has not been shown to cause different side effects or problems in older people than it does in younger adults.

Other medicines—Although certain medicines should not be used together at all, in other cases two different medicines may be used together even if an interaction might occur. In these cases, your doctor may want to change the dose, or other precautions may be necessary. Tell your health care professional if you are taking any other prescription or nonprescription (over-the-counter) [OTC]) medicine.

Proper Use of This Medicine

To help you remember to take your medicine, try to get into the habit of taking it at the same time each day.

Remember that this medicine does not cure BPH but it does help reduce the size of the prostate. Therefore, you must continue to take it if you expect to keep the size of your prostate down. *You may have to take this medicine for at least 6 months to see the full effect. You may have to take this medicine for the rest of your life.* Do not stop taking this medicine without first discussing it with your doctor.

Finasteride tablets may be crushed to make them easier to swallow. However, women who are or may become pregnant should not handle crushed finasteride tablets.

This medicine helps to reduce urinary problems in men with BPH. In general, it is best to avoid drinking fluids, especially coffee or alcohol, in the evening. Then your sleep will not be disturbed by your need to urinate during the night.

Dosing—The dose of finasteride will be different for different patients. *Follow your doctor's orders or the directions on the label.* The following information includes only the average dose of finasteride. *If your dose is different, do not change it* unless your doctor tells you to do so:

- For *oral* dosage form (tablets):
  - —For treatment of benign prostatic hyperplasia (BPH):
    - Adults—5 milligrams (mg) once a day.

Missed dose—If you miss a dose of this medicine, take it as soon as possible. However, if it is almost time for your next dose, skip the missed dose and go back to your regular dosing schedule. Do not double doses.

Storage—To store this medicine:

- Keep out of the reach of children.
- Store away from heat and direct light.
- Do not store in the bathroom, near the kitchen sink, or in other damp places. Heat or moisture may cause the medicine to break down.
- Do not keep outdated medicine or medicine no longer needed. Be sure that any discarded medicine is out of the reach of children.

Precautions While Using This Medicine

Women who are or who may become pregnant should not handle crushed finasteride tablets. There is a risk that the medicine could get into the pregnant woman's body and cause birth defects in a male fetus.

Side Effects of This Medicine

Along with its needed effects, a medicine may cause some unwanted effects. Although not all of these side effects may occur, if they do occur they may need medical attention.

Check with your doctor as soon as possible if any of the following side effects occur:

Less common

Breast enlargement and tenderness; skin rash; swelling of lips

Other side effects may occur that usually do not need medical attention. The following side effects may go away during treatment as your body adjusts to the medicine. However, check with your doctor if any of the following side effects continue or are bothersome:

Less common or rare

Abdominal pain; back pain; decreased libido (decreased interest in sex); decreased volume of ejaculate (amount of semen); diarrhea; dizziness; headache; impotence (inability to have or keep an erection)

Note: A decrease in the amount of semen during ejaculation should not affect your sexual performance and is not a sign of any change in fertility.

Other side effects not listed above may also occur in some patients. If you notice any other effects, check with your doctor.

Revised: 05/23/97

FLAVOXATE Systemic

A commonly used brand name in the U.S. and Canada is Urispas.

Description

Flavoxate (fla-VOX-ate) belongs to the group of medicines called antispasmodics. It is taken by mouth to help decrease muscle spasms of the bladder and relieve difficult urination.

Flavoxate is available only with your doctor's prescription, in the following dosage form:

Oral

- Tablets (U.S. and Canada)

Before Using This Medicine

In deciding to use a medicine, the risks of taking the medicine must be weighed against the good it will do. This is a decision you and your doctor will make. For flavoxate, the following should be considered:

Allergies—Tell your doctor if you have ever had any unusual or allergic reaction to flavoxate. Also tell your health care professional if you are allergic to any other substances, such as foods, preservatives, or dyes.

Pregnancy—Flavoxate has not been studied in pregnant women. However, flavoxate has not been shown to cause birth defects or other problems in animal studies.

Breast-feeding—Flavoxate has not been reported to cause problems in nursing babies.

Children—Although there is no specific information comparing the use of flavoxate in children with use in other age groups, this medicine is not expected to cause different side effects or problems in children than it does in adults.

Older adults—Confusion may be especially likely to occur in elderly patients, who are usually more sensitive than younger adults to the effects of flavoxate.

Other medicines—Although certain medicines should not be used together at all in other cases two different medicines may be used together even if an interaction might occur. In these cases, your doctor may want to change the dose, or other precautions may be necessary. Tell your health care professional if you are taking any other prescription or nonprescription (over-the-counter [OTC]) medicine.

Other medical problems—The presence of other medical problems may affect the use of flavoxate. Make sure you tell your doctor if you have any other medical problems, especially:

- Bleeding (severe) or
- Glaucoma or
- Intestinal blockage or other intestinal or stomach problems or
- Urinary tract blockage—Use of flavoxate may make these conditions worse
- Enlarged prostate—Use of flavoxate may cause difficult urination

Proper Use of This Medicine

This medicine is usually taken with water on an empty stomach. However, your doctor may want you to take it with food or milk to lessen stomach upset.

Take this medicine only as directed. Do not take more of it, do not take it more often, and do not take it for a longer time than your doctor ordered. To do so may increase the chance of side effects.

Dosing—The dose of flavoxate will be different for different patients. *Follow your doctor's orders or the directions on the label.* The following information includes only the average dose of flavoxate. *If your dose is different, do not change it* unless your doctor tells you to do so. The number of tablets that you take depends on the strength of the medicine.

- Adults and children 12 years of age and older: 100 to 200 milligrams three or four times a day.
- Children up to 12 years of age: Dose must be determined by the doctor.

Missed dose—If you miss a dose of this medicine, take it as soon as possible. However, if it is almost time for your next dose, skip the missed dose and go back to your regular dosing schedule. Do not double doses.

Storage—To store this medicine:

- Keep out of the reach of children.
- Store away from heat and direct light.
- Do not store in the bathroom, near the kitchen sink, or in other damp places. Heat or moisture may cause the medicine to break down.
- Do not keep outdated medicine or medicine no longer needed. Be sure that any discarded medicine is out of the reach of children.

Precautions While Using This Medicine

This medicine may cause your eyes to become more sensitive to light than they are normally. Wearing sunglasses may help lessen the discomfort from bright light.

This medicine may cause some people to become drowsy or have blurred vision. *Make sure you know how you react to this medicine before you drive, use machines, or do anything else that could be dangerous if you are not alert or able to see well.*

Flavoxate may make you sweat less, causing your body temperature to increase. *Use extra care not to become overheated during exercise or hot weather while you are taking this medicine,* since overheating may result in heat stroke. Also, hot baths or saunas may make you feel dizzy or faint while you are taking this medicine.

Your mouth and throat may feel very dry while you are taking this medicine. For temporary relief of mouth dryness, use sugarless candy or gum, melt bits of ice in your mouth, or use a saliva substitute. However, if your mouth continues to feel dry for more than 2 weeks, check with your medical doctor or dentist. Continuing dryness of the mouth may increase the chance of dental disease, including tooth decay, gum disease, and fungus infections.

Side Effects of This Medicine

Along with its needed effects, a medicine may cause some unwanted effects. Although not all of these side effects may occur, if they do occur they may need medical attention.

Check with your doctor as soon as possible if any of the following side effects occur:

Rare

Confusion; eye pain; skin rash or hives; sore throat and fever

Symptoms of overdose

Clumsiness or unsteadiness; dizziness (severe); drowsiness (severe); fever; flushing or redness of face; hallucinations (seeing, hearing, or feeling things that are not there); shortness of breath or troubled breathing; unusual excitement, nervousness, restlessness, or irritability

Other side effects may occur that usually do not need medical attention. These side effects may go away during treatment as your body adjusts to the medicine. However, check with your doctor if any of the following side effects continue or are bothersome:

More common

Drowsiness; dryness of mouth and throat

Less common or rare
Blurred vision; constipation; difficult urination; difficulty concentrating; dizziness; fast heartbeat; headache; increased sensitivity of eyes to light; increased sweating; nausea or vomiting; nervousness; stomach pain

Other side effects not listed above may also occur in some patients. If you notice any other effects, check with your doctor.

Revised: 01/18/93

FLECAINIDE Systemic

A commonly used brand name in the U.S. and Canada is Tambocor. Generic name product may be available in the U.S.

Description

Flecainide (FLEK-a-nide) belongs to the group of medicines known as antiarrhythmics. It is used to correct irregular heartbeats to a normal rhythm.

Flecainide produces its helpful effects by slowing nerve impulses in the heart and making the heart tissue less sensitive.

There is a chance that flecainide may cause new or make worse existing heart rhythm problems when it is used. Since it has been shown to cause severe problems in some patients, it is only used to treat serious heart rhythm problems. Discuss this possible effect with your doctor.

This medicine is available only with your doctor's prescription, in the following dosage form:

Oral
- Tablets (U.S. and Canada)

Before Using This Medicine

In deciding to use a medicine, the risks of taking the medicine must be weighed against the good it will do. This is a decision you and your doctor will make. For flecainide, the following should be considered:

Allergies—Tell your doctor if you have ever had any unusual or allergic reaction to flecainide, lidocaine, tocainide, or anesthetics. Also tell your health care professional if you are allergic to any other substances, such as foods, preservatives, or dyes.

Pregnancy—Flecainide has not been studied in pregnant women. However, studies in one kind of rabbit given about 4 times the usual human dose have shown that flecainide causes birth defects. Before taking flecainide, make sure your doctor knows if you are pregnant or if you may become pregnant.

Breast-feeding—Flecainide passes into breast milk. However, this medicine has not been shown to cause problems in nursing babies.

Children—Studies on this medicine have been done only in adult patients, and there is no specific information comparing use of flecainide in children with use in other age groups.

Older adults—Elderly people are especially sensitive to the effects of flecainide. Flecainide may be more likely to cause irregular heartbeat in the elderly.

Other medicines—Although certain medicines should not be used together at all, in other cases two different medicines may be used together even if an interaction might occur. In these cases, your doctor may want to change the dose, or other precautions may be necessary. When you are taking flecainide it is especially important that your health care professional knows if you are taking any of the following:

- Other medicine for heart rhythm problems—Both wanted and unwanted effects on the heart may increase

Other medical problems—The presence of other medical problems may affect the use of flecainide. Make sure you tell your doctor if you have any other medical problems, especially:

- Congestive heart failure—Flecainide may make this condition worse
- Kidney disease or
- Liver disease—Effects of flecainide may be increased because of slower removal from the body
- Recent heart attack—Risk of irregular heartbeats may be increased
- If you have a pacemaker—Flecainide may interfere with the pacemaker and require more careful follow-up by the doctor

Proper Use of This Medicine

Take flecainide exactly as directed by your doctor, even though you may feel well. Do not take more medicine than ordered.

This medicine works best when there is a constant amount in the blood. *To help keep this amount constant, do not miss any doses. Also, it is best to take the doses 12 hours apart, in the morning and at night*, unless otherwise directed by your doctor. If you need help in planning the best times to take your medicine, check with your health care professional.

Dosing—The dose of flecainide will be different for different patients. *Follow your doctor's orders or the directions on the label.* The following information includes only the average doses of flecainide. *If your dose is different, do not change it* unless your doctor tells you to do so.

The number of tablets that you take depends on the strength of the medicine.

- For *oral* dosage form (tablets):
  - —For correcting irregular heartbeat:
    - Adults—50 to 150 milligrams (mg) every twelve hours.
    - Children—Use and dose must be determined by your doctor.

Missed dose—If you miss a dose of flecainide and remember within 6 hours, take it as soon as possible. However, if you do not remember until later, skip the missed dose and go back to your regular dosing schedule. Do not double doses.

Storage—To store this medicine:
- Keep out of the reach of children.
- Store away from heat and direct light.
- Do not store in the bathroom, near the kitchen sink, or in other damp places. Heat or moisture may cause the medicine to break down.
- Do not keep outdated medicine or medicine no longer needed. Be sure that any discarded medicine is out of the reach of children.

Precautions While Using This Medicine

It is important that your doctor check your progress at regular visits to make sure the medicine is working properly. This will allow for changes to be made in the amount of medicine you are taking, if necessary.

Your doctor may want you to carry a medical identification card or bracelet stating that you are using this medicine.

Before having any kind of surgery (including dental surgery) or emergency treatment, tell the medical doctor or dentist in charge that you are taking this medicine.

Flecainide may cause some people to become dizzy, lightheaded, or less alert than they are normally. *Make sure you know how you react to this medicine before you drive, use machines, or do anything else that could be dangerous if you are dizzy or are not alert.*

If you have been using this medicine regularly for several weeks, do not suddenly stop using it. Check with your doctor for the best way to reduce gradually the amount you are taking before stopping completely.

Side Effects of This Medicine

Along with its needed effects, a medicine may cause some unwanted effects. Although not all of these side effects may occur, if they do occur they may need medical attention.

Check with your doctor as soon as possible if any of the following side effects occur:

Less common

Chest pain; irregular heartbeat; shortness of breath; swelling of feet or lower legs; trembling or shaking

Rare

Yellow eyes or skin

Other side effects may occur that usually do not need medical attention. These side effects may go away during treatment as your body adjusts to the medicine. However, check with your doctor if any of the following side effects continue or are bothersome:

More common

Blurred vision or seeing spots; dizziness or lightheadedness

Less common

Anxiety or mental depression; constipation; headache; nausea or vomiting; skin rash; stomach pain or loss of appetite; unusual tiredness or weakness

Other side effects not listed above may also occur in some patients. If you notice any other effects, check with your doctor.

Revised: 09/24/92
Interim revision: 04/29/94; 08/15/97

FLOXURIDINE Systemic†

A commonly used brand name in the U.S. is FUDR.
Generic name product may also be available in the U.S.

†Not commercially available in Canada.

Description

Floxuridine (flox-YOOR-i-deen) belongs to the group of medicines known as antimetabolites. It is used to treat some kinds of cancer.

Floxuridine interferes with the growth of cancer cells, which are eventually destroyed. Since the growth of normal body cells may also be affected by floxuridine, other effects will also occur. Some of these may be serious and must be reported to your doctor. Other effects, like hair loss, may not be serious but may cause concern. Some effects may not occur for months or years after the medicine is used.

Before you begin treatment with floxuridine, you and your doctor should talk about the good this medicine will do as well as the risks of using it.

Floxuridine is to be administered only by or under the immediate supervision of your doctor. It is available in the following dosage form:

Parenteral
- Injection (U.S.)

Before Using This Medicine

In deciding to use a medicine, the risks of taking the medicine must be weighed against the good it will do. This is a decision you and your doctor will make. For floxuridine, the following should be considered:

Allergies—Tell your doctor if you have ever had any unusual or allergic reaction to floxuridine.

Pregnancy—There is a chance that this medicine may cause birth defects if either the male or female is receiving it at the time of conception or if it is taken during pregnancy. Floxuridine has been shown to cause birth defects in mice and rats. In addition, many cancer medicines may cause sterility which could be permanent. Although sterility has not been reported with this medicine, the possibility should be kept in mind.

Be sure that you have discussed this with your doctor before receiving this medicine. It is best to use some kind of birth control while you are receiving floxuridine. Tell your doctor right away if you think you have become pregnant while receiving floxuridine.

Breast-feeding—Tell your doctor if you are breast-feeding or if you intend to breast-feed during treatment with this medicine. Because floxuridine may cause serious side effects, breast-feeding is generally not recommended while you are receiving it.

Children—There is no specific information comparing use of floxuridine in children with use in other age groups.

Older adults—Many medicines have not been studied specifically in older people. Therefore, it may not be known whether they work exactly the same way they do in younger adults or if they cause different side effects or problems in older people. Although there is no specific information comparing use of floxuridine in the elderly with use in other age groups, this medicine is not expected to cause different side effects or problems in older people than it does in younger adults.

Other medicines—Although certain medicines should not be used together at all, in other cases two different medicines may be used together even if an interaction might occur. In these cases, your doctor may want to change the dose, or other precautions may be necessary. When you are receiving floxuridine, it is especially important that your health care professional know if you are taking any of the following:

- Amphotericin B by injection (e.g., Fungizone) or
- Antithyroid agents (medicine for overactive thyroid) or
- Azathioprine (e.g., Imuran) or
- Chloramphenicol (e.g., Chloromycetin) or
- Colchicine or
- Flucytosine (e.g., Ancobon) or
- Ganciclovir (e.g., Cytovene) or
- Interferon (Intron A, Roferon-A) or
- Plicamycin (e.g., Mithracin) or
- Zidovudine (e.g., AZT, Retrovir) or
- If you have ever been treated with radiation or cancer medicines—Floxuridine may increase the effects of these medicines or radiation on the blood

Other medical problems—The presence of other medical problems may affect the use of floxuridine. Make sure you tell your doctor if you have any other medical problems, especially:

- Chickenpox (including recent exposure) or
- Herpes zoster (shingles)—Risk of severe disease affecting other parts of the body
- Hepatitis (history of)—Increased risk of hepatitis
- Kidney disease or
- Liver disease (other)—Effects of floxuridine may be increased because of slower removal from the body
- Infection—Floxuridine can decrease your body's ability to fight infection

Proper Use of This Medicine

Floxuridine sometimes causes nausea and vomiting. *Tell your doctor if this occurs, especially if you have stomach pain.*

Dosing—The dose of floxuridine will be different for different patients. The dose that is used may depend on a number of things, including what the medicine is being used for, the patient's weight, and whether or not other medicines are also being taken. *If you are receiving floxuridine at home, follow your doctor's orders or the directions on the label.* If you have any questions about the proper dose of floxuridine, ask your doctor.

Precautions While Using This Medicine

It is very important that your doctor check your progress at regular visits to make sure that this medicine is working properly and to check for unwanted effects.

While you are being treated with floxuridine, and after you stop treatment with it, *do not have any immunizations (vaccinations) without your doctor's approval.* Floxuridine may lower your body's resistance and there is a chance you might get the infection the immunization is meant to prevent. In addition, other persons living in your household should not take oral polio vaccine since there is a chance they could pass the polio virus on to you. Also, avoid persons who have recently taken oral polio vaccine. Do not get close to them and do not stay in the same room with them for very long. If you cannot take these precautions, you should consider wearing a protective face mask that covers the nose and mouth.

Side Effects of This Medicine

Along with its needed effects, a medicine may cause some unwanted effects. Although not all of these side effects may occur, if they do occur they may need medical attention.

Also, because of the way these medicines act on the body, there is a chance that they might cause other unwanted effects that may not occur until months or years after the medicine is used. These delayed effects may include certain types of cancer, such as leukemia. Discuss these possible effects with your doctor.

Check with your doctor or nurse immediately if any of the following side effects occur:

More common

Diarrhea; sores in mouth and on lips; stomach pain or cramps

Less common

Black, tarry stools; heartburn; nausea and vomiting; scaling or redness of hands or feet; swelling or soreness of the tongue

Rare

Blood in urine or stools; cough or hoarseness; fever or chills; lower back or side pain; painful or difficult urination; pinpoint red spots on skin; trouble in walking; unusual bleeding or bruising; yellow eyes or skin

Other side effects may occur that usually do not need medical attention. These side effects may go away during treatment as your body adjusts to the medicine. Also, your health care professional may be able to tell you about ways to prevent or reduce some of these side effects. Check with your health care professional if any of the

following side effects continue or are bothersome or if you have any questions about them:

Less common or rare

Loss of appetite; skin rash or itching

This medicine sometimes causes temporary thinning of hair. After treatment with floxuridine has ended, normal hair growth should return.

Other side effects not listed above may also occur in some patients. If you notice any other effects, check with your health care professional.

Revised: 07/26/94

FLUCYTOSINE Systemic

Some commonly used brand names are:

In the U.S.—

Ancobon

In Canada

Ancotil

Other commonly used names are 5-fluorocytosine and 5-FC.

Description

Flucytosine (floo-SYE-toe-seen) belongs to the group of medicines called antifungals. It is used to treat certain fungus infections.

Flucytosine is available only with your doctor's prescription, in the following dosage form:

Oral

- Capsules (U.S. and Canada)

Before Using This Medicine

In deciding to use a medicine, the risks of taking the medicine must be weighed against the good it will do. This is a decision you and your doctor will make. For flucytosine, the following should be considered:

Allergies—Tell your doctor if you have ever had any unusual or allergic reaction to flucytosine. Also tell your health care professional if you are allergic to any other substances, such as foods, preservatives, or dyes.

Pregnancy—Flucytosine has not been reported to cause birth defects or other problems in humans. However, studies in rats have shown that flucytosine causes birth defects.

Breast-feeding—Flucytosine has not been reported to cause problems in nursing babies.

Children—Although there is no specific information comparing use of flucytosine in children with use in other age groups, this medicine is not expected to cause different side effects or problems in children than it does in adults.

Older adults—Many medicines have not been studied specifically in older people. Therefore, it may not be known whether they work exactly the same way they do in younger adults. Although there is no specific information comparing use of flucytosine in the elderly with use in other age groups, this medicine is not expected to cause different side effects or problems in older people than it does in younger adults.

Other medicines—Although certain medicines should not be used together at all, in other cases two different medicines may be used together even if an interaction might occur. In these cases, your doctor may want to change the dose, or other precautions may be necessary. When you are taking flucytosine, it is especially important that your health care professional knows if you are taking any of the following:

- Amphotericin B by injection (e.g., Fungizone) or
- Antineoplastics (cancer medicine) or
- Antithyroid agents (medicine for overactive thyroid) or
- Azathioprine (e.g., Imuran) or
- Chloramphenicol (e.g., Chloromycetin) or
- Colchicine or
- Cyclophosphamide (e.g., Cytoxan) or
- Ganciclovir (e.g., Cytovene) or
- Interferon (e.g., Intron A, Roferon-A) or
- Mercaptopurine (e.g., Purinethol) or
- Methotrexate (e.g., Mexate) or
- Plicamycin (e.g., Mithracin) or
- Zidovudine (e.g., AZT, Retrovir) or
- X-ray treatment—Use of flucytosine with any of these medicines may increase the chance for side effects of the blood

Other medical problems—The presence of other medical problems may affect the use of flucytosine. Make sure you tell your doctor if you have any other medical problems, especially:

- Blood disease—Flucytosine may cause blood problems
- Kidney disease—Patients with kidney disease may have an increased chance of side effects
- Liver disease—Flucytosine may cause liver side effects

Proper Use of This Medicine

In some patients this medicine may cause nausea or vomiting. If you are taking more than 1 capsule for each dose, you may space them out over a period of 15 minutes to help lessen the nausea or vomiting. If this does not help or if you have any questions, check with your doctor.

To help clear up your infection completely, *keep taking this medicine for the full time of treatment,* even if you begin to feel better after a few days. *Do not miss any doses.*

Dosing—The dose of flucytosine will be different for different patients. *Follow your doctor's orders or the directions on the label.* The following information includes only the average doses of flucytosine. *If your dose is different, do not change it* unless your doctor tells you to do so.

- For *oral* dosage form (capsules):
  - —For fungus infections:
    - Adults and children—Dose is based on body weight. The usual dose is 12.5 to 37.5 milligrams

(mg) per kilogram (kg) (5.7 to 17 mg per pound) of body weight every six hours.

Missed dose—If you miss a dose of this medicine, take it as soon as possible. However, if it is almost time for your next dose, skip the missed dose and go back to your regular dosing schedule. Do not double doses.

Storage—To store this medicine:

- Keep out of the reach of children.
- Store away from heat and direct light.
- Do not store in the bathroom, near the kitchen sink, or in other damp places. Heat or moisture may cause the medicine to break down.
- Do not keep outdated medicine or medicine no longer needed. Be sure that any discarded medicine is out of the reach of children.

Precautions While Using This Medicine

Your doctor should check your progress at regular visits to make sure that this medicine does not cause unwanted effects.

Flucytosine may cause blood problems. These problems may result in a greater chance of infection, slow healing, and bleeding of the gums. Therefore, you should be careful when using regular toothbrushes, dental floss, and toothpicks. Dental work, whenever possible, should be done before you begin taking this medicine or delayed until your blood counts have returned to normal. Check with your medical doctor or dentist if you have any questions about proper oral hygiene (mouth care) during treatment.

Flucytosine may cause your skin to be more sensitive to sunlight than it is normally. Exposure to sunlight, even for brief periods of time, may cause skin rash, itching, redness, or other discoloration of the skin, or a severe sunburn. When you begin taking this medicine:

- Stay out of direct sunlight, especially between the hours of 10:00 a.m. and 3:00 p.m., if possible.
- Wear protective clothing, including a hat. Also, wear sunglasses.
- Apply a sun block product that has a skin protection factor (SPF) of at least 15. Some patients may require a product with a higher SPF number, especially if they have a fair complexion. If you have any questions about this, check with your health care professional.
- Apply a sun block lipstick that has an SPF of at least 15 to protect your lips.
- Do not use a sunlamp or tanning bed or booth.

If you have a severe reaction from the sun, check with your doctor.

This medicine may also cause some people to become dizzy, lightheaded, drowsy, or less alert than they are normally. *Make sure you know how you react to this medicine before you drive, use machines, or do anything else that could be dangerous if you are dizzy or are not alert.* If these reactions are especially bothersome, check with your doctor.

Side Effects of This Medicine

Along with its needed effects, a medicine may cause some unwanted effects. Although not all of these side effects may occur, if they do occur they may need medical attention.

Check with your doctor immediately if any of the following side effects occur:

More common

Skin rash, redness, or itching; sore throat and fever; unusual bleeding or bruising; unusual tiredness or weakness; yellow eyes or skin

Less common

Confusion; hallucinations (seeing, hearing, or feeling things that are not there); increased sensitivity of skin to sunlight

Other side effects may occur that usually do not need medical attention. These side effects may go away during treatment as your body adjusts to the medicine. However, check with your doctor if any of the following side effects continue or are bothersome:

More common

Abdominal pain; diarrhea; loss of appetite; nausea or vomiting

Less common

Dizziness or lightheadedness; drowsiness; headache

Other side effects not listed above may also occur in some patients. If you notice any other effects, check with your doctor.

Revised: 07/24/92
Interim revision: 03/17/94

FLUDARABINE Systemic

A commonly used brand name in the U.S. and Canada is Fludara.

Description

Fludarabine (floo-DARE-a-been) belongs to the group of medicines called antimetabolites. It is used to treat chronic lymphocytic leukemia (CLL), a type of cancer.

Fludarabine interferes with the growth of cancer cells, which are eventually destroyed. Since the growth of normal body cells may also be affected by fludarabine, other effects will also occur. Some of these may be serious and must be reported to your doctor. Other effects may not be serious but may cause concern. Some effects may not occur for months or years after the medicine is used.

Before you begin treatment with fludarabine, you and your doctor should talk about the good this medicine will do as well as the risks of using it.

Fludarabine is to be administered only by or under the immediate supervision of your doctor. It is available in the following dosage form:

Parenteral

- Injection (U.S. and Canada)

Before Using This Medicine

In deciding to use a medicine, the risks of taking the medicine must be weighed against the good it will do. This is a decision you and your doctor will make. For fludarabine, the following should be considered:

Allergies—Tell your doctor if you have ever had any unusual or allergic reaction to fludarabine.

Pregnancy—There is a chance that this medicine may cause birth defects if either the male or female is taking it at the time of conception or if it is taken during pregnancy. Fludarabine has been shown to cause birth defects in rats and rabbits. In addition, many cancer medicines may cause sterility which could be permanent. Although sterility has not been reported with this medicine, it does occur in animals and the possibility should be kept in mind.

Be sure that you have discussed this with your doctor before taking this medicine. It is best to use some kind of birth control while you are receiving fludarabine. Tell your doctor right away if you think you have become pregnant while receiving fludarabine.

Breast-feeding—It is not known whether fludarabine passes into breast milk. However, because this medicine may cause serious side effects, breast-feeding is generally not recommended while you are receiving it.

Children—There is no specific information comparing use of fludarabine in children with use in other age groups.

Older adults—Many medicines have not been studied specifically in older people. Therefore, it may not be known whether they work exactly the same way they do in younger adults. Although there is no specific information comparing use of fludarabine in the elderly with use in other age groups, it is not expected to cause different side effects or problems in older people than it does in younger adults.

Other medicines—Although certain medicines should not be used together at all, in other cases two different medicines may be used together even if an interaction might occur. In these cases, your doctor may want to change the dose, or other precautions may be necessary. When receiving fludarabine it is especially important that your health care professional know if you are taking any of the following:

- Amphotericin B by injection (e.g., Fungizone) or
- Antithyroid agents (medicine for overactive thyroid) or
- Azathioprine (e.g., Imuran) or
- Chloramphenicol (e.g., Chloromycetin) or
- Colchicine or
- Flucytosine (e.g., Ancobon) or
- Ganciclovir (e.g., Cytovene) or
- Interferon (e.g., Intron A, Roferon-A) or
- Plicamycin (e.g., Mithracin) or
- Zidovudine (e.g., AZT, Retrovir) or
- If you have ever been treated with radiation or cancer medicines—Fludarabine may increase the effects of these medicines or radiation therapy on the blood
- Probenecid (e.g., Benemid) or
- Sulfinpyrazone (e.g., Anturane)—Fludarabine may raise the amount of uric acid in the blood. Since these medicines are used to lower uric acid levels, they may not be as effective in patients receiving fludarabine

Other medical problems—The presence of other medical problems may affect the use of fludarabine. Make sure you tell your doctor if you have any other medical problems, especially:

- Chickenpox (including recent exposure) or
- Herpes zoster (shingles)—Risk of severe disease affecting other parts of the body
- Gout (history of) or
- Kidney stones (history of)—Fludarabine may increase levels of uric acid in the body, which can cause gout or kidney stones
- Infection—Fludarabine may decrease your body's ability to fight infection
- Kidney disease—Effects of fludarabine may be increased because of slower removal from the body

Proper Use of This Medicine

This medicine may cause nausea and vomiting. However, it is very important that you continue to receive the medicine even if you begin to feel ill. Ask your health care professional for ways to lessen these effects.

Dosing—The dose of fludarabine will be different for different patients. The dose that is used may depend on a number of things, including what the medicine is being used for, the patient's size, and whether or not other medicines are also being taken. *If you are receiving fludarabine at home, follow your doctor's orders or the directions on the label.* If you have any questions about the proper dose of fludarabine, ask your doctor.

Precautions While Using This Medicine

It is very important that your doctor check your progress at regular visits to make sure that this medicine is working properly and to check for unwanted effects.

While you are being treated with fludarabine, and after you stop treatment with it, *do not have any immunizations (vaccinations) without your doctor's approval.* Fludarabine may lower your body's resistance and there is a chance you might get the infection the immunization is meant to prevent. In addition, other persons living in your household should not take oral polio vaccine since there is a chance they could pass the polio virus on to you. Also, avoid persons who have recently taken oral polio vaccine. Do not get close to them and do not stay in the same room with them for very long. If you cannot take these precautions, you should consider wearing a protective face mask that covers the nose and mouth.

Fludarabine can temporarily lower the number of white blood cells in your blood, increasing the chance of getting an infection. It can also lower the number of platelets,

which are necessary for proper blood clotting. If this occurs, there are certain precautions you can take, especially when your blood count is low, to reduce the risk of infection or bleeding:

- If you can, avoid people with infections. *Check with your doctor immediately* if you think you are getting an infection or if you get a fever or chills, cough or hoarseness, lower back or side pain, or painful or difficult urination.
- *Check with your doctor immediately* if you notice any unusual bleeding or bruising; black, tarry stools; blood in urine or stools; or pinpoint red spots on your skin.
- Be careful when using a regular toothbrush, dental floss, or toothpick. Your medical doctor, dentist, or nurse may recommend other ways to clean your teeth and gums. Check with your medical doctor before having any dental work done.
- Do not touch your eyes or the inside of your nose unless you have just washed your hands and have not touched anything else in the meantime.
- Be careful not to cut yourself when you are using sharp objects such as a safety razor or fingernail or toenail cutters.
- Avoid contact sports or other situations where bruising or injury could occur.

Side Effects of This Medicine

Along with its needed effects, a medicine may cause some unwanted effects. Although not all of these side effects may occur, if they do occur they may need medical attention.

Also, because of the way cancer medicines act on the body, there is a chance that they might cause other unwanted effects that may not occur until months or years after the medicine is used. These delayed effects may include certain types of cancer. Discuss these possible effects with your doctor.

Check with your doctor or nurse immediately if any of the following side effects occur:

More common
Cough or hoarseness; fever or chills; lower back or side pain; painful or difficult urination; shortness of breath

Less common
Black, tarry stools; blood in urine; pinpoint red spots on skin; unusual bleeding or bruising

Check with your health care professional as soon as possible if any of the following side effects occur:

More common
Pain

Less common
Agitation or confusion; blurred vision; loss of hearing; numbness or tingling in fingers, toes, or face; sores in mouth and on lips; swelling of feet or lower legs; unusual tiredness or weakness

Other side effects may occur that usually do not need medical attention. These side effects may go away during treatment as your body adjusts to the medicine. Also, your health care professional may be able to tell you about ways to prevent or reduce some of these side effects. Check with your health care professional if any of the following side effects continue or are bothersome or if you have any questions about them:

More common
Diarrhea; nausea or vomiting; skin rash

Less common
Aching muscles; general feeling of discomfort or illness; headache; loss of appetite

This medicine may rarely cause a temporary loss of hair in some people. After treatment with fludarabine has ended, normal hair growth should return.

After you stop treatment with fludarabine, it may still produce some side effects that need attention. During this period of time, check with your doctor if you notice the following:

Rare
Cough or hoarseness; fever or chills; loss of vision; lower back or side pain; painful or difficult urination

Other side effects not listed above may also occur in some patients. If you notice any other effects, check with your doctor.

Revised: 08/02/94

FLUDROCORTISONE Systemic

A commonly used brand name in the U.S. and Canada is Florinef.

Description

Fludrocortisone (floo-droe-KOR-tis-sone) is a corticosteroid (kor-ti-koe-STE-roid) (cortisone-like medicine). It belongs to the family of medicines called steroids. Your body naturally produces similar corticosteroids, which are necessary to maintain the balance of certain minerals and water for good health. If your body does not produce enough corticosteroids, your doctor may have prescribed this medicine to help make up the difference.

Fludrocortisone may also be used to treat other medical conditions as determined by your doctor.

Fludrocortisone is available only with your doctor's prescription, in the following dosage form:

Oral
- Tablets (U.S. and Canada)

Before Using This Medicine

In deciding to use a medicine, the risks of taking the medicine must be weighed against the good it will do. This is

a decision you and your doctor will make. For fludrocortisone, the following should be considered:

Allergies—Tell your doctor if you have ever had any unusual or allergic reaction to fludrocortisone. Also tell your health care professional if you are allergic to any other substances, such as foods, preservatives, or dyes.

Diet—Your doctor may want you to control the amount of sodium in your diet. When fludrocortisone is used to treat certain types of kidney diseases, too much sodium may cause high blood sodium, high blood pressure, and excess body water.

Pregnancy—Studies on birth defects in humans or animals have not been done with fludrocortisone. However, it is possible that too much use of this medicine during pregnancy may cause the baby to have an underactive adrenal gland after birth.

Breast-feeding—Fludrocortisone passes into the breast milk and may cause problems with growth or other unwanted effects in the nursing baby.

Children—Fludrocortisone may slow or stop growth in children or growing adolescents when used for a long time. The natural production of corticosteroids by the body may also be decreased by the use of this medicine. Before this medicine is given to a child or adolescent, you and your child's doctor should talk about the good this medicine will do as well as the risks of using it. Follow the doctor's directions very carefully to lessen the chance that these unwanted effects will occur.

Older adults—Many medicines have not been studied specifically in older people. Therefore, it may not be known whether they work exactly the same way they do in younger adults or if they cause different side effects or problems in older people. There is no specific information comparing the use of fludrocortisone in the elderly with its use in other age groups.

Other medicines—Although certain medicines should not be used together at all, in other cases two different medicines may be used together even if an interaction might occur. In these cases, your doctor may want to change the dose, or other precautions may be necessary. When you are taking fludrocortisone, it is especially important that your health care professional know if you are taking any of the following:

- Acetazolamide (e.g., Diamox) or
- Amphotericin B by injection (e.g., Fungizone) or
- Azlocillin (e.g., Azlin) or
- Capreomycin (e.g., Capastat) or
- Carbenicillin by injection (e.g., Geopen) or
- Corticotropin (ACTH) or
- Dichlorphenamide (e.g., Daranide) or
- Diuretics (water pills) or
- Insulin or
- Laxatives (with overdose or chronic misuse) or
- Methazolamide (e.g., Neptazane) or
- Mezlocillin (e.g., Mezlin) or
- Piperacillin (e.g., Pipracil) or
- Salicylates or
- Sodium bicarbonate (e.g., baking soda) or
- Ticarcillin (e.g., Ticar) or
- Ticarcillin and clavulanate (e.g., Timentin) or
- Vitamin B_{12} (e.g., AlphaRedisol, Rubramin-PC) (when used in megaloblastic anemia) or
- Vitamin D—Fludrocortisone and these medicines decrease the amount of potassium in the blood, which may increase the chance of severe low blood potassium
- Alcohol—Alcohol and fludrocortisone decrease the amount of potassium in the blood, which may increase the chance of severe low blood potassium; alcohol may also make fludrocortisone less effective by causing the body to get rid of it faster
- Barbiturates or
- Carbamazepine (e.g., Tegretol) or
- Griseofulvin (e.g., Fulvicin) or
- Phenylbutazone (e.g., Butazolidin) or
- Phenytoin (e.g., Dilantin) or
- Primidone (e.g., Mysoline) or
- Rifampin (e.g., Rifadin)—Using these medicines may make fludrocortisone less effective because they cause the body to get rid of it faster
- Digitalis glycosides (heart medicine)—Fludrocortisone decreases the amount of potassium in the blood, which may increase the chance of irregular heartbeat
- Other corticosteroids (cortisone-like medicine)—Using any corticosteroid medicine with fludrocortisone will cause the body to get rid of both medicines faster. This may make either or both medicines less effective. Also, fludrocortisone and other corticosteroids decrease the amount of potassium in the blood, which may increase the chance of severe low blood potassium
- Sodium-containing medicine—When using fludrocortisone to treat certain types of kidney diseases, too much sodium may cause high blood sodium, high blood pressure, and excess body water

Other medical problems—The presence of other medical problems may affect the use of fludrocortisone. Make sure you tell your doctor if you have any other medical problems, especially:

- Bone disease—Fludrocortisone may make bone disease worse because it causes more calcium to pass into the urine
- Edema (swelling of feet or lower legs) or
- Heart disease or
- High blood pressure or
- Kidney disease—Fludrocortisone causes the body to retain (keep) more salt and water. These conditions may be made worse by this extra body water
- Liver disease or
- Thyroid disease—The body may not get fludrocortisone out of the bloodstream at the usual rate, which may increase the effect of fludrocortisone or cause more side effects

Proper Use of This Medicine

Take this medicine only as directed by your doctor. Do not take more or less of it, do not take it more often, and do not take it for a longer time than your doctor ordered. To do so may increase the chance of side effects.

Dosing—The dose of fludrocortisone will be different for different patients. *Follow your doctor's orders or the directions on the label.* The following information includes only the average doses of fludrocortisone. *If your dose is different, do not change it* unless your doctor tells you to do so.

- For *oral* dosage forms (tablets):
  —Adults
  - For adrenal gland deficiency: 50 to 200 micrograms a day.
  - For adrenogenital syndrome: 100 to 200 micrograms a day.

  —Children: For adrenal gland deficiency: 50 to 100 micrograms a day.

Missed dose—If you miss a dose of this medicine, take it as soon as you remember. However, if it is almost time for your next dose, skip the missed dose and go back to your regular dosing schedule. Do not double doses.

Storage—To store this medicine:
- Keep out of the reach of children.
- Store away from heat and direct light.
- Do not store in the bathroom, near the kitchen sink, or in other damp places. Heat or moisture may cause the medicine to break down.
- Do not keep outdated medicine or medicine no longer needed. Be sure that any discarded medicine is out of the reach of children.

Precautions While Using This Medicine

Your doctor should check your progress at regular visits to make sure this medicine does not cause unwanted effects.

If you will be using this medicine for a long time, your doctor may want you to carry a medical identification card stating that you are using this medicine.

While you are taking fludrocortisone, be careful to limit the amount of alcohol you drink.

Side Effects of This Medicine

Along with its needed effects, a medicine may cause some unwanted effects. Although not all of these side effects may occur, if they do occur they may need medical attention.

Check with your doctor immediately if any of the following side effects occur:

Less common or rare

Cough; difficulty swallowing; hives; irregular breathing or shortness of breath; irregular heartbeat; redness and itching of skin; redness of eyes; swelling of nasal passages, face, or eyelids; swollen neck veins; unusual tiredness or weakness

Check with your doctor as soon as possible if any of the following side effects occur:

Less common or rare

Dizziness; headache (severe or continuing); loss of appetite; muscle cramps or pain; nausea; swelling of feet or lower legs; weakness in arms, legs, or trunk (severe); weight gain (rapid); vomiting

Other side effects not listed above may also occur in some patients. If you notice any other effects, check with your doctor.

Additional Information

Once a medicine has been approved for marketing for a certain use, experience may show that it is also useful for other medical problems. Although these uses are not included in product labeling, fludrocortisone is used in certain patients with the following medical conditions:
- Idiopathic orthostatic hypotension (a certain type of low blood pressure)
- Too much acid in the blood, caused by kidney disease

Other than the above information, there is no additional information relating to proper use, precautions, or side effects for these uses.

Revised: 06/15/93

FLUOROQUINOLONES Systemic

Some commonly used brand names are:

In the U.S.—

Cipro[1]
Cipro IV[1]
Floxin[5]
Floxin IV[5]
Maxaquin[3]
Noroxin[4]
Penetrex[2]

In Canada—

Cipro[1]
Floxin[5]
Maxaquin[3]
Penetrex[2]

Note: For quick reference, the following fluoroquinolones are numbered to match the corresponding brand names.

This information applies to the following medicines:

1. Ciprofloxacin (sip-roe-FLOX-a-sin)
2. Enoxacin (en-OX-a-sin)
3. Lomefloxacin (loe-me-FLOX-a-sin)
4. Norfloxacin (nor-FLOX-a-sin)
5. Ofloxacin (oe-FLOX-a-sin)

Description

Fluoroquinolones (flu-roe-KWIN-a-lones) are used to treat bacterial infections in many different parts of the body. They work by killing bacteria or preventing their growth. However, these medicines will not work for colds, flu, or other virus infections. Fluoroquinolones may be used for other problems as determined by your doctor.

Fluoroquinolones are available only with your doctor's prescription, in the following dosage forms:

Oral

Ciprofloxacin
- Tablets (U.S. and Canada)

Enoxacin
- Tablets (U.S. and Canada)

Lomefloxacin
- Tablets (U.S. and Canada)

Norfloxacin
- Tablets (U.S. and Canada)

Ofloxacin
- Tablets (U.S. and Canada)

Parenteral
Ciprofloxacin
- Injection (U.S. and Canada)

Ofloxacin
- Injection (U.S.)

Before Using This Medicine

In deciding to use a medicine, the risks of taking the medicine must be weighed against the good it will do. This is a decision you and your doctor will make. For the fluoroquinolones, the following should be considered:

Allergies—Tell your doctor if you have ever had any unusual or allergic reaction to any of the fluoroquinolones or to any related medicines such as cinoxacin (e.g., Cinobac) or nalidixic acid (e.g., NegGram). Also tell your health care professional if you are allergic to any other substances, such as foods, preservatives, or dyes.

Pregnancy—Studies have not been done in humans. However, use is not recommended during pregnancy since fluoroquinolones have been reported to cause bone development problems in young animals.

Breast-feeding—Some of the fluoroquinolones are known to pass into human breast milk. Since fluoroquinolones have been reported to cause bone development problems in young animals, breast-feeding is not recommended during treatment with these medicines.

Children—Use is not recommended for infants or children since fluoroquinolones have been shown to cause bone development problems in young animals. However, your doctor may choose to use one of these medicines if other medicines cannot be used.

Teenagers—Use is not recommended for teenagers up to 18 years of age since fluoroquinolones have been shown to cause bone development problems in young animals. However, your doctor may choose to use one of these medicines if other medicines cannot be used.

Older adults—These medicines have been tested and, in effective doses, have not been shown to cause different side effects or problems in older people than they do in younger adults.

Other medicines—Although certain medicines should not be used together at all, in other cases two different medicines may be used together even if an interaction might occur. In these cases, your doctor may want to change the dose, or other precautions may be necessary. When you are taking a fluoroquinolone, it is especially important that your health care professional know if you are taking any of the following:

- Aminophylline or
- Oxtriphylline (e.g., Choledyl) or
- Theophylline (e.g., Somophyllin-T, Theodur, Elixophyllin)—Enoxacin, ciprofloxacin, and norfloxacin may increase the chance of side effects of aminophylline, oxtriphylline, or theophylline
- Antacids, aluminum-, calcium-, or magnesium-containing, or
- Iron supplements or
- Sucralfate—Antacids, iron, or sucralfate may keep any of the fluoroquinolones from working properly
- Caffeine—Enoxacin, ciprofloxacin, and norfloxacin may increase the chance of side effects of caffeine
- Didanosine (e.g., Videx, ddI)—Didanosine may keep any of the fluoroquinolones from working properly
- Warfarin (e.g., Coumadin)—Enoxacin, ciprofloxacin, and norfloxacin may increase the effect of warfarin, increasing the chance of bleeding

Other medical problems—The presence of other medical problems may affect the use of fluoroquinolones. Make sure you tell your doctor if you have any other medical problems, especially:

- Brain or spinal cord disease, including hardening of the arteries in the brain or epilepsy or other seizures—Fluoroquinolones may cause nervous system side effects
- Kidney disease or
- Kidney disease and liver disease—Patients with kidney disease (alone) or kidney disease and liver disease (together) may have an increased chance of side effects

Proper Use of This Medicine

Do not take fluoroquinolones if you are pregnant. Do not give fluoroquinolones to infants, children, or teenagers unless otherwise directed by your doctor. These medicines have been shown to cause bone development problems in young animals.

Fluoroquinolones are best taken with a full glass (8 ounces) of water. Several additional glasses of water should be taken every day, unless you are otherwise directed by your doctor. Drinking extra water will help to prevent some unwanted effects of ciprofloxacin and norfloxacin.

Ciprofloxacin and lomefloxacin may be taken with meals or on an empty stomach.

Enoxacin, norfloxacin, and ofloxacin should be taken on an empty stomach.

To help clear up your infection completely, *keep taking your medicine for the full time of treatment,* even if you begin to feel better after a few days. If you stop taking this medicine too soon, your symptoms may return.

This medicine works best when there is a constant amount in the blood or urine. *To help keep the amount constant, do not miss any doses. Also, it is best to take the doses at evenly spaced times, day and night.* For example, if you are to take 2 doses a day, the doses should be spaced about 12 hours apart. If this interferes with your sleep or other daily activities, or if you need help in planning the best times to take your medicine, check with your health care professional.

Dosing—The dose of fluoroquinolones will be different for different patients. *Follow your doctor's orders or the directions on the label.* The following information includes only the average doses of fluoroquinolones. Your dose may be different if you have kidney disease. *If your dose is different, do not change it* unless your doctor tells you to do so.

The number of tablets that you take depends on the strength of the medicine. Also, *the number of doses you take each day, the time allowed between doses, and the length of time you take the medicine depend on the medical problem for which you are using a fluoroquinolone.*

For ciprofloxacin

- For *oral* dosage form (tablets):
  - —Adults: 250 to 750 milligrams (mg) every twelve hours for five to fourteen days, depending on the medical problem being treated. Gonorrhea is usually treated with a single oral dose of 250 mg.
  - —Children up to 18 years of age: This medicine is not recommended in infants, children, or teenagers.
- For *injection* dosage form:
  - —Adults: 200 to 400 mg every twelve hours.
  - —Children up to 18 years of age: This medicine is not recommended in infants, children, or teenagers.

For enoxacin

- For *oral* dosage form (tablets):
  - —Adults: 200 to 400 mg every twelve hours for seven to fourteen days, depending on the medical problem being treated. Gonorrhea is usually treated with a single, oral dose of 400 mg.
  - —Children up to 18 years of age: This medicine is not recommended in infants, children, or teenagers.

For lomefloxacin

- For *oral* dosage form (tablets):
  - —Adults: 400 mg once a day for ten to fourteen days, depending on the medical problem being treated.
  - —Children up to 18 years of age: This medicine is not recommended in infants, children, or teenagers.

For norfloxacin

- For *oral* dosage form (tablets):
  - —Adults: 400 mg every twelve hours for three to twenty-one days, depending on the medical problem being treated. Gonorrhea is usually treated with a single, oral dose of 800 mg.
  - —Children up to 18 years of age: This medicine is not recommended in infants, children, or teenagers.

For ofloxacin

- For *oral* dosage form (tablets):
  - —Adults: 200 to 400 mg every twelve hours for three to ten days, depending on the medical problem being treated. Gonorrhea is usually treated with a single, oral dose of 400 mg.
  - —Children up to 18 years of age: This medicine is not recommended in infants, children, or teenagers.
- For *injection* dosage form:
  - —Adults: 200 to 400 mg every twelve hours for three to ten days, depending on the medical problem being treated. Gonorrhea is usually treated with a single, oral dose of 400 mg.
  - —Children up to 18 years of age: This medicine is not recommended in infants, children, or teenagers.

Missed dose—If you miss a dose of this medicine, take it as soon as possible. This will help to keep a constant amount of medicine in the blood or urine. However, if it is almost time for your next dose, skip the missed dose and go back to your regular dosing schedule. Do not double doses.

Storage—To store this medicine:

- Keep out of the reach of children.
- Store away from heat and direct light.
- Do not store in the bathroom, near the kitchen sink, or in other damp places. Heat or moisture may cause the medicine to break down.
- Do not keep outdated medicine or medicine no longer needed. Be sure that any discarded medicine is out of the reach of children.

Precautions While Using This Medicine

If your symptoms do not improve within a few days, or if they become worse, check with your doctor.

If you are taking aluminum- or magnesium-containing antacids, or sucralfate, do not take them at the same time that you take this medicine. It is best to take these medicines at least 2 hours before or 2 hours after taking norfloxacin or ofloxacin, at least 4 hours before or 2 hours after taking ciprofloxacin or lomefloxacin, and at least 8 hours before or 2 hours after taking enoxacin. These medicines may keep fluoroquinolones from working properly.

Some people who take fluoroquinolones may become more sensitive to sunlight than they are normally. Exposure to sunlight, even for brief periods of time, may cause severe sunburn; skin rash, redness, itching, or discoloration; or vision changes. When you begin taking this medicine:

- Stay out of direct sunlight, especially between the hours of 10:00 a.m. and 3:00 p.m., if possible.
- Wear protective clothing, including a hat and sunglasses.
- Apply a sun block product that has a skin protection factor (SPF) of at least 15. Some patients may require a product with a higher SPF number, especially if they have a fair complexion. If you have any questions about this, check with your health care professional.
- Do not use a sunlamp or tanning bed or booth.

If you have a severe reaction from the sun, check with your doctor.

Fluoroquinolones may also cause some people to become dizzy, lightheaded, drowsy, or less alert than they are normally. *Make sure you know how you react to this medicine before you drive, use machines, or do anything else that could be dangerous if you are dizzy or are not alert.* If these reactions are especially bothersome, check with your doctor.

Side Effects of This Medicine

Along with its needed effects, a medicine may cause some unwanted effects. Although not all of these side effects may occur, if they do occur they may need medical attention.

Check with your doctor immediately if any of the following side effects occur:

Rare

Agitation; confusion; fever; hallucinations (seeing, hearing, or feeling things that are not there); pain at site of injection; pain in calves, radiating to heels; peeling of the skin; shakiness or tremors; shortness of breath; skin rash, itching, or redness; swelling of face or neck; swelling of calves or lower legs

Other side effects may occur that usually do not need medical attention. These side effects may go away during treatment as your body adjusts to the medicine. However, check with your doctor if any of the following side effects continue or are bothersome:

More common

Abdominal or stomach pain or discomfort; diarrhea; dizziness; drowsiness; headache; lightheadedness; nausea or vomiting; nervousness; trouble in sleeping

Less frequent or rare

Increased sensitivity of skin to sunlight

Other side effects not listed above may also occur in some patients. If you notice any other effects, check with your doctor.

Revised: 05/20/93
Interim revision: 07/29/95; 08/31/96

FLUOROURACIL Systemic

A commonly used brand name in the U.S. and Canada is Adrucil. Generic name product may also be available in the U.S. and Canada. Another commonly used name is 5-FU.

Description

Fluorouracil (flure-oh-YOOR-a-sill) belongs to the group of medicines known as antimetabolites. It is used to treat some kinds of cancer.

Fluorouracil interferes with the growth of cancer cells, which are eventually destroyed. Since the growth of normal body cells may also be affected by fluorouracil, other effects will also occur. Some of these may be serious and must be reported to your doctor. Other effects, like hair loss, may not be serious but may cause concern. Some effects may not occur for months or years after the medicine is used.

Before you begin treatment with fluorouracil, you and your doctor should talk about the good this medicine will do as well as the risks of using it.

Fluorouracil is to be administered only by or under the immediate supervision of your doctor. It is available in the following dosage form:

Parenteral

- Injection (U.S. and Canada)

Before Using This Medicine

In deciding to use a medicine, the risks of taking the medicine must be weighed against the good it will do. This is a decision you and your doctor will make. For fluorouracil, the following should be considered:

Allergies—Tell your doctor if you have ever had any unusual or allergic reaction to fluorouracil.

Pregnancy—Tell your doctor if you are pregnant or if you intend to have children. There is a chance that this medicine may cause birth defects if either the male or female is receiving it at the time of conception or if it is taken during pregnancy. Fluorouracil has been reported to cause birth defects in mice given doses slightly higher than the human dose. Also, there has been one case of a baby born with several birth defects after the mother received fluorouracil. In addition, many cancer medicines may cause sterility. Although sterility has been reported with this medicine, it is usually only temporary; the possibility should be kept in mind.

Be sure that you have discussed this with your doctor before receiving this medicine. It is best to use some kind of birth control while you are receiving fluorouracil. Tell your doctor right away if you think you have become pregnant while receiving fluorouracil.

Breast-feeding—Tell your doctor if you are breast-feeding or if you intend to breast-feed during treatment with this medicine. It is not known whether fluorouracil passes into breast milk. However, because fluorouracil may cause serious side effects, breast-feeding is generally not recommended while you are receiving it.

Children—Although there is no specific information comparing use of fluorouracil in children with use in other age groups, it is not expected to cause different side effects or problems in children than it does in adults.

Older adults—Many medicines have not been studied specifically in older people. Therefore, it may not be known whether they work exactly the same way they do in younger adults. Although there is no specific information comparing use of fluorouracil in the elderly with use in other age groups, it is not expected to cause different side effects or problems in older people than it does in younger adults.

Other medicines—Although certain medicines should not be used together at all, in other cases two different medicines may be used together even if an interaction might occur. In these cases, your doctor may want to change the dose, or other precautions may be necessary. When you are receiving fluorouracil, it is especially important that your health care professional know if you are taking any of the following:

- Amphotericin B by injection (e.g., Fungizone) or
- Antithyroid agents (medicine for overactive thyroid) or
- Azathioprine (e.g., Imuran) or
- Chloramphenicol (e.g., Chloromycetin) or

- Colchicine or
- Flucytosine (e.g., Ancobon) or
- Ganciclovir (e.g., Cytovene) or
- Interferon (e.g., Intron A, Roferon-A) or
- Plicamycin (e.g., Mithracin) or
- Zidovudine (e.g., AZT, Retrovir) or
- If you have ever been treated with radiation or cancer medicines—Fluorouracil may increase the effects of these medicines or radiation on the blood

Other medical problems—The presence of other medical problems may affect the use of fluorouracil. Make sure you tell your doctor if you have any other medical problems, especially:

- Chickenpox (including recent exposure) or
- Herpes zoster (shingles)—Risk of severe disease affecting other parts of the body
- Infection—Fluorouracil can decrease your body's ability to fight infection
- Kidney disease or
- Liver disease—Effects of fluorouracil may be increased because of slower removal from the body

Proper Use of This Medicine

This medicine is sometimes given together with certain other medicines. If you are using a combination of medicines, it is important that you receive each one at the proper time. If you are taking some of these medicines by mouth, ask your health care professional to help you plan a way to remember to take them at the right times.

Fluorouracil often causes nausea and vomiting. However, it is very important that you continue to receive the medicine, even if your stomach is upset. Ask your health care professional for ways to lessen these effects.

Dosing—The dosing of fluorouracil will be different for different patients. The dose that is used may depend on a number of things, including what the medicine is being used for, the patient's weight, and whether or not other medicines are also being taken. *If you are receiving fluorouracil at home, follow your doctor's orders or the directions on the label.* If you have any questions about the proper dose of fluorouracil, ask your doctor.

Precautions While Using This Medicine

It is very important that your doctor check your progress at regular visits to make sure that this medicine is working properly and to check for unwanted effects.

While you are being treated with fluorouracil, and after you stop treatment with it, *do not have any immunizations (vaccinations) without your doctor's approval.* Fluorouracil may lower your body's resistance and there is a chance you might get the infection the immunization is meant to prevent. In addition, other persons living in your household should not take oral polio vaccine since there is a chance they could pass the polio virus on to you. Also, avoid persons who have recently taken oral polio vaccine. Do not get close to them and do not stay in the same room with them for very long. If you cannot take these precautions, you should consider wearing a protective face mask that covers the nose and mouth.

Fluorouracil can temporarily lower the number of white blood cells in your blood, increasing the chance of getting an infection. It can also lower the number of platelets, which are necessary for proper blood clotting. If this occurs, there are certain precautions you can take, especially when your blood count is low, to reduce the risk of infection or bleeding:

- If you can, avoid people with infections. *Check with your doctor immediately* if you think you are getting an infection or if you get a fever or chills, cough or hoarseness, lower back or side pain, or painful or difficult urination.
- *Check with your doctor immediately* if you notice any unusual bleeding or bruising; black, tarry stools; blood in urine or stools; or pinpoint red spots on your skin.
- Be careful when using a regular toothbrush, dental floss, or toothpick. Your medical doctor, dentist, or nurse may recommend other ways to clean your teeth and gums. Check with your medical doctor before having any dental work done.
- Do not touch your eyes or the inside of your nose unless you have just washed your hands and have not touched anything else in the meantime.
- Be careful not to cut yourself when you are using sharp objects such as a safety razor or fingernail or toenail cutters.
- Avoid contact sports or other situations where bruising or injury could occur.

Side Effects of This Medicine

Along with its needed effects, a medicine may cause some unwanted effects. Although not all of these side effects may occur, if they do occur they may need medical attention.

Also, because of the way these medicines act on the body, there is a chance that they might cause other unwanted effects that may not occur until months or years after the medicine is used. These delayed effects may include certain types of cancer, such as leukemia. Discuss these possible effects with your doctor.

Check with your doctor or nurse immediately if any of the following side effects occur:

More common
Diarrhea; heartburn; sores in mouth and on lips

Less common
Black, tarry stools; cough or hoarseness; fever or chills; lower back or side pain; nausea and vomiting (severe); painful or difficult urination; stomach cramps

Rare
Blood in urine or stools; pinpoint red spots on skin; unusual bleeding or bruising

Check with your health care professional as soon as possible if any of the following side effects occur:

Rare
Chest pain; shortness of breath; tingling of hands and feet, followed by pain, redness, and swelling; trouble with balance

Other side effects may occur that usually do not need medical attention. These side effects may go away during treatment as your body adjusts to the medicine. Also, your health care professional may be able to tell you about ways to prevent or reduce some of these side effects. Check with your health care professional if any of the following side effects continue or are bothersome or if you have any questions about them:

More common

Loss of appetite; nausea and vomiting; skin rash and itching; weakness

Less common

Dry or cracked skin

This medicine often causes a temporary loss of hair. After treatment with fluorouracil has ended, normal hair growth should return.

After you stop receiving fluorouracil, it may still produce some side effects that need attention. During this period of time, *check with your doctor or nurse immediately* if you notice any of the following:

Black, tarry stools; blood in urine or stools; cough or hoarseness; fever or chills; lower back or side pain; painful or difficult urination; pinpoint red spots on skin; unusual bleeding or bruising

Other side effects not listed above may also occur in some patients. If you notice any other effects, check with your health care professional.

Revised: 07/26/94

FLUOROURACIL Topical

Some commonly used brand names are:

In the U.S.—

Efudex

Fluoroplex

In Canada—

Efudex

Fluoroplex

Another commonly used name is 5-FU.

Description

Fluorouracil (flure-oh-YOOR-a-sill) belongs to the group of medicines known as antimetabolites. When applied to the skin, it is used to treat certain skin problems, including cancer or conditions that could become cancerous if not treated.

Fluorouracil interferes with the growth of abnormal cells, which are eventually destroyed.

Fluorouracil is available only with your doctor's prescription, in the following dosage forms:

Topical

- Cream (U.S. and Canada)
- Topical solution (U.S. and Canada)

Before Using This Medicine

In deciding to use a medicine, the risks of using the medicine must be weighed against the good it will do. This is a decision you and your doctor will make. For topical fluorouracil, the following should be considered:

Allergies—Tell your doctor if you have ever had any unusual or allergic reaction to fluorouracil.

Pregnancy—Tell your doctor if you are pregnant or if you intend to become pregnant. Although fluorouracil applied to the skin has not been shown to cause problems in humans, some of it is absorbed through the skin and there is a chance that it could cause birth defects. Be sure that you have discussed this with your doctor before using this medicine.

Breast-feeding—Although fluorouracil applied to the skin has not been shown to cause problems in nursing babies, some of it is absorbed through the skin.

Children—There is no specific information comparing use of fluorouracil on the skin in children with use in other age groups.

Older adults—Many medicines have not been studied specifically in older people. Therefore, it may not be known whether they work exactly the same way they do in younger adults or if they cause different side effects or problems in older people. Although there is no specific information comparing use of fluorouracil on the skin in the elderly with use in other age groups, this medicine is not expected to cause different side effects or problems in older people than it does in younger adults.

Other medical problems—The presence of other medical problems may affect the use of fluorouracil on the skin. Make sure you tell your doctor if you have any other medical problems, especially:

- Other skin problems—May be aggravated

Proper Use of This Medicine

Keep using this medicine for the full time of treatment. However, *do not use this medicine more often or for a longer time than your doctor ordered.* Apply enough medicine each time to cover the entire affected area with a thin layer.

After washing the area with soap and water and drying carefully, use a cotton-tipped applicator or your fingertips to apply the medicine in a thin layer to your skin.

If you apply this medicine with your fingertips, make sure you *wash your hands immediately afterwards,* to prevent any of the medicine from accidentally getting in your eyes or mouth.

Fluorouracil may cause redness, soreness, scaling, and peeling of affected skin after 1 or 2 weeks of use. This effect may last for several weeks after you stop using the medicine and is to be expected. Sometimes a pink, smooth area is left when the skin treated with this medicine heals. This area will usually fade after 1 to 2 months. Do not stop using this medicine without first checking with your doctor. If the reaction is very uncomfortable, check with your doctor.

Dosing—The dose of fluorouracil will be different for different patients. *Follow your doctor's orders or the directions on the label.* The following information includes only the average doses of fluorouracil. *If your dose is different, do not change it* unless your doctor tells you to do so.

- For *cream* dosage form:
  - —For precancerous skin condition caused by the sun:
    - Adults—Use the 1% cream on the affected areas of skin one or two times a day. The 5% cream is sometimes used on the hands.
    - Children—Use and dose must be determined by your doctor.
  - —For skin cancer:
    - Adults—Use the 5% cream on the affected areas of skin two times a day. Treatment may continue for several weeks.
    - Children—Use and dose must be determined by your doctor.
- For *topical solution* dosage form:
  - —For precancerous skin condition caused by the sun:
    - Adults—Use the 1% solution on the affected areas of skin one or two times a day. The 2% or 5% solution is sometimes used on the hands.
    - Children—Use and dose must be determined by your doctor.
  - —For skin cancer:
    - Adults—Use the 5% solution on the affected areas of skin two times a day. Treatment may continue for several weeks.
    - Children—Use and dose must be determined by your doctor.

Missed dose—If you miss a dose of this medicine, apply it as soon as you remember. However, if more than a few hours have passed, skip the missed dose and go back to your regular dosing schedule. If you miss more than one dose, check with your doctor.

Storage—To store this medicine:

- Keep out of the reach of children.
- Store away from heat and direct light.
- Do not store in the bathroom, near the kitchen sink, or in other damp places. Heat or moisture may cause the medicine to break down.
- Protect the solution from freezing.
- Do not keep outdated medicine or medicine no longer needed. Be sure that any discarded medicine is out of the reach of children.

Precautions While Using This Medicine

It is very important that your doctor check your progress at regular visits to make sure that this medicine is working properly and to check for unwanted effects.

Apply this medicine very carefully when using it on your face. Avoid getting any in your eyes, nose, or mouth.

While using this medicine, and for 1 or 2 months after you stop using it, your skin may become more sensitive to sunlight than usual and too much sunlight may increase the effect of the drug. *During this period of time:*

- Stay out of direct sunlight, especially between the hours of 10:00 a.m. and 3:00 p.m., if possible.
- Wear protective clothing, including a hat and sunglasses.
- Apply a sun block product that has a skin protection factor (SPF) of at least 15. Some patients may require a product with a higher SPF number, especially if they have a fair complexion. If you have any questions about this, check with your health care professional.
- Do not use a sunlamp or tanning bed or booth.

If you have a severe reaction from the sun, check with your doctor.

Side Effects of This Medicine

Along with its needed effects, a medicine may cause some unwanted effects. Although not all of these side effects may occur, if they do occur they may need medical attention.

Check with your doctor immediately if the following side effects occur:

Redness and swelling of normal skin

Other side effects may occur that usually do not need medical attention. These side effects may go away during treatment as your body adjusts to the medicine. However, check with your doctor if any of the following side effects continue, worsen, or are bothersome:

More common

Burning feeling where medicine is applied; increased sensitivity of skin to sunlight; itching; oozing; skin rash; soreness or tenderness of skin

Less common or rare

Darkening of skin; scaling; watery eyes

Other side effects not listed above may also occur in some patients. If you notice any other effects, check with your doctor.

Revised: 06/09/93
Interim revision: 05/02/94

FLUOXETINE Systemic

A commonly used brand name in the U.S. and Canada is Prozac.

Description

Fluoxetine (floo-OX-uh-teen) is used to treat mental depression. It is also used to treat obsessive-compulsive disorder.

This medicine is available only with your doctor's prescription, in the following dosage form:

Oral
- Capsules (U.S. and Canada)
- Oral Solution (U.S. and Canada)

Before Using This Medicine

There have been recent suggestions that the use of fluoxetine may be related to increased thoughts about suicide in a very small number of patients. More study is needed to determine if the medicine caused this effect. Be sure you discuss this, and any possible precautions you should take, with your doctor before taking fluoxetine.

In deciding to use a medicine, the risks of taking the medicine must be weighed against the good it will do. This is a decision you and your doctor will make. For fluoxetine, the following should be considered:

Allergies—Tell your doctor if you have ever had any unusual or allergic reaction to fluoxetine. Also tell your health care professional if you are allergic to any other substances, such as foods, preservatives, or dyes.

Pregnancy—Studies have not been done in pregnant women. However, fluoxetine has not been shown to cause birth defects or other problems in animal studies.

Breast-feeding—Fluoxetine passes into breast milk and may cause unwanted effects, such as vomiting, watery stools, crying, and sleep problems in nursing babies. It may be necessary for you to take another medicine or to stop breast-feeding during treatment. Be sure you have discussed the risks and benefits of the medicine with your doctor.

Children—Studies on this medicine have been done only in adult patients, and there is no specific information comparing use of fluoxetine in children with use in other age groups.

Older adults—Many medicines have not been tested in older people. Therefore, it may not be known whether they work exactly the same way they do in younger adults or if they cause different side effects or problems in older people. In studies done to date that included elderly people, fluoxetine did not cause different side effects or problems in older people than it did in younger adults.

Other medicines—Although certain medicines should not be used together at all, in other cases two different medicines may be used together even if an interaction might occur. In these cases, your doctor may want to change the dose, or other precautions may be necessary. When you are taking fluoxetine, it is especially important that your health care professional know if you are taking any of the following:

- Anticoagulants (blood thinners) or
- Digitalis glycosides (heart medicine)—Higher or lower blood levels of these medicines or fluoxetine may occur; your doctor may need to change the dose of either medicine
- Central nervous system (CNS) depressants (medicines that cause drowsiness)—The CNS depressant effects may be increased
- Monoamine oxidase (MAO) inhibitors (furazolidone [e.g., Furoxone], isocarboxazid [e.g., Marplan], pargyline [e.g., Eutonyl], phenelzine [e.g., Nardil], procarbazine [e.g., Matulane], tranylcypromine [e.g., Parnate])—Taking fluoxetine while you are taking or within 2 weeks of taking MAO inhibitors may cause confusion, agitation, restlessness, stomach or intestinal symptoms, sudden high body temperature, extremely high blood pressure, and severe convulsions; at least 14 days should be allowed between stopping treatment with an MAO inhibitor and starting treatment with fluoxetine; if you have been taking fluoxetine, at least 5 weeks should be allowed before starting treatment with an MAO inhibitor
- Phenytoin—Taking this medicine with fluoxetine may result in higher blood levels of phenytoin, which increases the chance of serious side effects.
- Tryptophan—Taking this medicine with fluoxetine may result in increased agitation or restlessness, and stomach or intestinal problems

Other medical problems—The presence of other medical problems may affect the use of fluoxetine. Make sure you tell your doctor if you have any other medical problems, especially:

- Diabetes—The amount of insulin or oral antidiabetic medicine that you need to take may change
- Kidney disease or
- Liver disease—Higher blood levels of fluoxetine may occur, increasing the chance of side effects
- Seizure disorders (history of)—The risk of seizures may be increased

Proper Use of This Medicine

Take this medicine only as directed by your doctor, to benefit your condition as much as possible. Do not take more of it, do not take it more often, and do not take it for a longer time than your doctor ordered.

If this medicine upsets your stomach, it may be taken with food.

Sometimes fluoxetine must be taken for up to 4 weeks or longer before you begin to feel better. Your doctor should check your progress at regular visits during this time.

Dosing—The dose of fluoxetine will be different for different patients. *Follow your doctor's orders or the directions on the label.* The following information includes only the average doses of fluoxetine. *If your dose is different, do not change it* unless your doctor tells you to do so:

The number of capsules or teaspoonfuls of solution that you take depends on the strength of the medicine. Also, *the number of doses you take each day, the time allowed between doses, and the length of time you take the medicine depend on the medical problem for which you are taking fluoxetine.*

- For *oral* dosage forms (capsules or solution):
  - —For depression or obsessive-compulsive disorder:
    - Adults—At first, usually 20 milligrams (mg) a day, taken as a single dose in the morning.
    - Children—Use and dose must be determined by your doctor.

Missed dose—If you miss a dose of this medicine, it is not necessary to make up the missed dose. Skip the missed dose and continue with your next scheduled dose. Do not double doses.

Storage—To store this medicine:

- Keep out of the reach of children.
- Store away from heat and direct light.
- Do not store in the bathroom, near the kitchen sink, or in other damp places. Heat or moisture may cause the medicine to break down.
- Do not keep outdated medicine or medicine no longer needed. Be sure that any discarded medicine is out of the reach of children.

Precautions While Using This Medicine

It is important that your doctor check your progress at regular visits, to allow dosage adjustments and help reduce any side effects.

This medicine will add to the effects of alcohol and other CNS depressants (medicines that slow down the nervous system, possibly causing drowsiness). Some examples of CNS depressants are antihistamines or medicine for hay fever, other allergies, or colds; sedatives, tranquilizers, or sleeping medicine; prescription pain medicine or narcotics; barbiturates; medicine for seizures; muscle relaxants; or anesthetics, including some dental anesthetics. *Check with your doctor before taking any of the above while you are using this medicine.*

If you develop a skin rash or hives, stop taking fluoxetine and check with your doctor as soon as possible.

For diabetic patients:

- This medicine may affect blood sugar levels. If you notice a change in the results of your blood or urine sugar tests or if you have any questions, check with your doctor.

This medicine may cause some people to become drowsy. *Make sure you know how you react to fluoxetine before you drive, use machines, or do anything else that could be dangerous if you are not alert.*

Dizziness, lightheadedness, or fainting may occur, especially when you get up from a lying or sitting position. Getting up slowly may help. If this problem continues or gets worse, check with your doctor.

This medicine may cause dryness of the mouth. For temporary relief, use sugarless gum or candy, melt bits of ice in your mouth, or use a saliva substitute. However, if your mouth continues to feel dry for more than 2 weeks, check with your medical doctor or dentist. Continuing dryness of the mouth may increase the chance of dental disease, including tooth decay, gum disease, and fungus infections.

Side Effects of This Medicine

Along with its needed effects, a medicine may cause some unwanted effects. Although not all of these side effects may occur, if they do occur they may need medical attention.

Check with your doctor as soon as possible if any of the following side effects occur:

Less common

Chills or fever; joint or muscle pain; skin rash, hives, or itching; trouble in breathing

Rare

Convulsions (seizures); signs of hypoglycemia (low blood sugar); including anxiety or nervousness, chills, cold sweats, confusion, cool, pale skin, difficulty in concentration, drowsiness, excessive hunger, fast heartbeat, headache, shakiness or unsteady walk, or unusual tiredness or weakness; skin rash or hives that may occur with burning or tingling in fingers, hands, or arms, chills or fever, joint or muscle pain, swelling of feet or lower legs, swollen glands, or trouble in breathing

Symptoms of overdose

Agitation and restlessness; convulsions (seizures); nausea and vomiting (severe); unusual excitement

Other side effects may occur that usually do not need medical attention. These side effects may go away during treatment as your body adjusts to the medicine. However, check with your doctor if any of the following side effects continue or are bothersome:

More common

Anxiety and nervousness; diarrhea; drowsiness; headache; increased sweating; nausea; trouble in sleeping

Less common

Abnormal dreams; change in taste; changes in vision; chest pain; constipation; cough; decreased appetite or weight loss; decreased sexual drive or ability; decrease in concentration; dizziness or lightheadedness; dryness of mouth; fast or irregular heartbeat; feeling of warmth or heat; flushing or redness of skin, especially on face and neck; frequent urination; increased appetite; menstrual pain; stomach cramps, gas, or pain; stuffy nose; tiredness or weakness; tremor; vomiting

Other side effects not listed above may also occur in some patients. If you notice any other effects, check with your doctor.

Revised: 08/04/92
Interim revision: 04/29/94

FLUTAMIDE Systemic

Some commonly used brand names are:

In the U.S.—
Eulexin

In Canada—
Euflex

Description

Flutamide (FLOO-ta-mide) is used to treat cancer of the prostate gland.

Flutamide belongs to the group of medicines known as antiandrogens. It blocks the effect of testosterone in the body. Giving flutamide with another medicine that decreases testosterone levels is one way of treating cancer of the prostate.

Flutamide is available only with your doctor's prescription, in the following dosage forms:

Oral
- Capsules (U.S.)
- Tablets (Canada)

Before Using This Medicine

In deciding to use a medicine, the risks of taking the medicine must be weighed against the good it will do. This is a decision you and your doctor will make. For flutamide, the following should be considered:

Allergies—Tell your doctor if you have ever had any unusual or allergic reaction to flutamide.

Pregnancy—This medicine causes low sperm count and the medicine it is used with causes sterility which may be permanent. If you intend to have children, be sure that you have discussed this with your doctor before taking this medicine.

Older adults—Many medicines have not been studied specifically in older people. Therefore, it may not be known whether they work exactly the same way they do in younger adults or if they cause different side effects or problems in older people. The effects of a dose of flutamide may last a little longer in elderly patients. However, the dose that is prescribed has that taken into account. Flutamide is not expected to cause different side effects or problems in older people than in younger adults.

Proper Use of This Medicine

Take this medicine exactly as directed by your doctor. Do not use more or less of it, and do not use it more often than your doctor ordered. The exact amount of medicine you need has been carefully worked out. Taking too much may increase the chance of side effects, while taking too little may not improve your condition.

Flutamide is usually taken with another medicine. *It is very important that the two medicines be used as directed. Follow your doctor's instructions very carefully about when to use these medicines.*

Flutamide in combination therapy sometimes causes unwanted effects such as hot flashes or decreased sexual ability. It may also cause difficulty in urinating when you begin to take it. However, it is very important that you continue to take the medicine, even after you begin to feel better. *Do not stop taking this medicine without first checking with your doctor.*

If you vomit shortly after taking a dose of flutamide, check with your doctor. You will be told whether to take the dose again or to wait until the next scheduled dose.

Dosing—The dose of flutamide may be different for different patients. *Follow your doctor's orders or the directions on the label.* The following information includes only the average doses of flutamide. *If your dose is different, do not change it* unless your doctor tells you to do so.

- For *oral* dosage forms (capsules or tablets):
  - —For prostate cancer:
    - Adults—250 milligrams (mg) every eight hours. This is usually taken in combination with another medicine that decreases testosterone levels.

Missed dose—If you miss a dose of this medicine, take it as soon as possible. However, if it is almost time for your next dose, skip the missed dose and go back to your regular dosing schedule. Do not double doses.

Storage—To store this medicine:
- Keep out of the reach of children.
- Store away from heat and direct light.
- Do not store in the bathroom, near the kitchen sink, or in other damp places. Heat or moisture may cause the medicine to break down.
- Do not keep outdated medicine or medicine no longer needed. Be sure that any discarded medicine is out of the reach of children.

Precautions While Using This Medicine

It is very important that your doctor check your progress at regular visits to make sure that this medicine is working properly and to check for unwanted effects.

Side Effects of This Medicine

Along with its needed effects, a medicine may cause some unwanted effects. Although not all of these side effects may occur, if they do occur they may need medical attention.

Check with your doctor immediately if any of the following side effects occur:

Rare

Bluish-colored lips, fingernails, or palms of hands; dark urine; dizziness (extreme) or fainting; feeling of extreme pressure in head; itching; loss of appetite; nausea or vomiting; pain in right side; shortness of breath; weak and fast heartbeat; yellow eyes or skin

This medicine may also cause the following side effects that your doctor will watch out for:

Rare

High blood pressure; liver problems; methemoglobinemia (a blood problem)

Other side effects may occur that usually do not need medical attention. The side effects listed below are for flutamide used together with the medicine that decreases testosterone. These side effects may go away during treatment as your body adjusts to the medicine. However, check with your health care professional if any of the following side effects continue or are bothersome:

More common

Diarrhea; impotence or decrease in sexual desire; sweating and feelings of warmth (sudden)

Less common

Loss of appetite; numbness or tingling of hands or feet; swelling and increased tenderness of breasts; swelling of feet or lower legs

Other side effects not listed above may also occur in some patients. If you notice any other effects, check with your doctor.

Revised: 08/03/94

FOLIC ACID (Vitamin B_9) Systemic

Some commonly used brand names are:

In the U.S.—

Folvite

Generic name product may also be available.

In Canada—

Apo-Folic

Folvite

Novo-Folacid

Generic name product may also be available.

Another commonly used name is Vitamin B_9.

Description

Vitamins (VYE-ta-mins) are compounds that you *must* have for growth and health. They are needed in small amounts only and are usually available in the foods that you eat. Folic (FOE-lik) acid (vitamin B_9) is necessary for strong blood.

Lack of folic acid may lead to anemia (weak blood). Your health care professional may treat this by prescribing folic acid for you.

Some conditions may increase your need for folic acid. These include:

- Alcoholism
- Anemia, hemolytic
- Diarrhea (continuing)
- Fever (prolonged)
- Hemodialysis
- Illness (prolonged)
- Intestinal diseases
- Liver disease
- Stress (continuing)
- Surgical removal of stomach

In addition, infants smaller than normal, breast-fed infants, or those receiving unfortified formulas (such as evaporated milk or goat's milk) may need additional folic acid.

Increased need for folic acid should be determined by your health care professional.

Some studies have found that folic acid taken by women before they become pregnant and during early pregnancy may reduce the chances of certain birth defects (neural tube defects).

Claims that folic acid and other B vitamins are effective for preventing mental problems have not been proven. Many of these treatments involve large and expensive amounts of vitamins.

Injectable folic acid is given by or under the direction of your health care professional. Another form of folic acid is available without a prescription.

Folic acid is available in the following dosage forms:

Oral

- Tablets (U.S. and Canada)

Parenteral

- Injection (U.S. and Canada)

Importance of Diet

For good health, it is important that you eat a balanced and varied diet. Follow carefully any diet program your health care professional may recommend. For your specific dietary vitamin and/or mineral needs, ask your health care professional for a list of appropriate foods. If you think that you are not getting enough vitamins and/or minerals in your diet, you may choose to take a dietary supplement.

Folic acid is found in various foods, including vegetables, especially green vegetables; potatoes; cereal and cereal products; fruits; and organ meats (for example, liver or kidney). It is best to eat fresh fruits and vegetables whenever possible since they contain the most vitamins. Food processing may destroy some of the vitamins. For example, heat may reduce the amount of folic acid in foods.

Vitamins alone will not take the place of a good diet and will not provide energy. Your body also needs other substances found in food such as protein, minerals, carbohydrates, and fat. Vitamins themselves often cannot work without the presence of other foods.

The daily amount of folic acid needed is defined in several different ways.

For U.S.—

- Recommended Dietary Allowances (RDAs) are the amount of vitamins and minerals needed to provide for adequate nutrition in most healthy persons. RDAs for a given nutrient may vary depending on a person's age, sex, and physical condition (e.g., pregnancy).

- Daily Values (DVs) are used on food and dietary supplement labels to indicate the percent of the recommended daily amount of each nutrient that a serving provides. DV replaces the previous designation of United States Recommended Daily Allowances (USRDAs).

For Canada—

- Recommended Nutrient Intakes (RNIs) are used to determine the amounts of vitamins, minerals, and protein needed to provide adequate nutrition and lessen the risk of chronic disease.

Normal daily recommended intakes in micrograms (mcg) for folic acid are generally defined as follows:

Persons	U.S. (mcg)	Canada (mcg)
Infants and children		
Birth to 3 years of age	25–50	50–80
4 to 6 years of age	75	90
7 to 10 years of age	100	125–180
Adolescent and adult males	150–200	150–220
Adolescent and adult females	150–180	145–190
Pregnant females	400	445–475
Breast-feeding females	260–280	245–275

Before Using This Dietary Supplement

In deciding to use folic acid, the risks of taking it must be weighed against the good it will do. This is a decision you and your health care professional will make. For folic acid, the following should be considered:

Allergies—Tell your health care professional if you have ever had any unusual or allergic reaction to folic acid. Also tell your health care professional if you are allergic to any other substances, such as foods, preservatives, or dyes.

Pregnancy—It is especially important that you are receiving enough vitamins when you become pregnant and that you continue to receive the right amount of vitamins, especially folic acid, throughout your pregnancy. The healthy growth and development of the fetus depend on a steady supply of nutrients from the mother. However, taking large amounts of a dietary supplement in pregnancy may be harmful to the mother and/or fetus and should be avoided.

Your health care professional may recommend that you take folic acid alone or as part of a multivitamin supplement before you become pregnant and during early pregnancy. Folic acid may reduce the chances of your baby being born with a certain type of birth defect (neural tube defects).

Breast-feeding—It is especially important that you receive the right amounts of vitamins so that your baby will also get the vitamins needed to grow properly. However, taking large amounts of a dietary supplement while breast-feeding may be harmful to the mother and/or baby and should be avoided.

Children—Problems in children have not been reported with intake of normal daily recommended amounts.

Older adults—Problems in older adults have not been reported with intake of normal daily recommended amounts.

Medicines or other dietary supplements—Although certain medicines or dietary supplements should not be used together at all, in other cases they may be used together even if an interaction might occur. In these cases, your health care professional may want to change the dose, or other precautions may be necessary. Tell your health care professional if you are taking any other dietary supplement or any prescription or nonprescription (over-the-counter [OTC]) medicine.

Other medical problems—The presence of other medical problems may affect the use of folic acid. Make sure you tell your health care professional if you have any other medical problems, especially:

- Pernicious anemia (a type of blood problem)—Taking folic acid while you have pernicious anemia may cause serious side effects. You should be sure that you do not have pernicious anemia before beginning folic acid supplementation

Proper Use of This Dietary Supplement

Dosing—The amount of folic acid needed to meet normal daily recommended intakes will be different for different individuals. The following information includes only the average amounts of folic acid.

- For *oral* dosage form (tablets):
  - —To prevent deficiency, the amount taken by mouth is based on normal daily recommended intakes:

    For the U.S.

    - Adult and teenage males—150 to 200 micrograms (mcg) per day.
    - Adult and teenage females—150 to 180 mcg per day.
    - Pregnant females—400 mcg per day.
    - Breast-feeding females—260 to 280 mcg per day.
    - Children 7 to 10 years of age—100 mcg per day.
    - Children 4 to 6 years of age—75 mcg per day.
    - Children birth to 3 years of age—25 to 50 mcg per day.

    For Canada

    - Adult and teenage males—150 to 220 mcg per day.
    - Adult and teenage females—145 to 190 mcg per day.
    - Pregnant females—445 to 475 mcg per day.
    - Breast-feeding females—245 to 275 mcg per day.
    - Children 7 to 10 years of age—125 to 180 mcg per day.
    - Children 4 to 6 years of age—90 mcg per day.
    - Children birth to 3 years of age—50 to 80 mcg per day.

—To treat deficiency:

- Adults, teenagers, and children—Treatment dose is determined by prescriber for each individual based on the severity of deficiency.

Missed dose—If you miss taking a vitamin for one or more days there is no cause for concern, since it takes some time for your body to become seriously low in vitamins. However, if your health care professional has recommended that you take this vitamin, try to remember to take it as directed every day.

Storage—To store this dietary supplement:

- Keep out of the reach of children.
- Store away from heat and direct light.
- Do not store in the bathroom, near the kitchen sink, or in other damp places. Heat or moisture may cause the dietary supplement to break down.
- Do not keep outdated dietary supplements or those no longer needed. Be sure that any discarded dietary supplement is out of the reach of children.

Side Effects of This Dietary Supplement

Along with its needed effects, a dietary supplement may cause some unwanted effects. Although folic acid does not usually cause any side effects, check with your health care professional as soon as possible if any of the following side effects occur:

Rare

Fever; reddened skin; shortness of breath; skin rash or itching; tightness in chest; troubled breathing; wheezing

Other side effects not listed above may also occur in some individuals. If you notice any other effects, check with your health care professional.

Revised: 05/20/92

Interim revision: 08/17/94; 05/01/95

FOSCARNET Systemic†

A commonly used brand name in the U.S. is Foscavir.

Other commonly used names are phosphonoformic acid and PFA.

†Not commercially available in Canada.

Description

Foscarnet (foss-KAR-net) is used to treat the symptoms of cytomegalovirus (CMV) infection of the eyes in patients with acquired immune deficiency syndrome (AIDS). Foscarnet will not cure this eye infection, but it may help to control worsening of the symptoms. Foscarnet may also be used for other serious viral infections as determined by your doctor. However, it does not work in treating certain viruses, such as the common cold or the flu.

Foscarnet is administered only by or under the supervision of your doctor. It is available in the following dosage form:

Parenteral

- Injection (U.S.)

Before Receiving This Medicine

In deciding to use a medicine, the risks of taking the medicine must be weighed against the good it will do. This is a decision you and your doctor will make. For foscarnet, the following should be considered:

Allergies—Tell your doctor if you have ever had any unusual or allergic reaction to foscarnet. Also tell your health care professional if you are allergic to any other substances, such as foods, preservatives, or dyes.

Pregnancy—Foscarnet has not been studied in pregnant women. However, studies in animals have shown that foscarnet causes birth defects. Before taking this medicine, make sure your doctor knows if you are pregnant or if you may become pregnant.

Breast-feeding—It is not known whether foscarnet passes into the breast milk. Although most medicines pass into breast milk in small amounts, many of them may be used safely while breast-feeding. Mothers who are taking this medicine and who wish to breast-feed should discuss this with their doctor.

Children—There is no specific information comparing use of foscarnet in children with use in other age groups. Foscarnet can cause serious side effects in any patient. Therefore, it is especially important that you discuss with the child's doctor the good that this medicine may do as well as the risks of using it.

Older adults—Many medicines have not been studied specifically in older people. Therefore, it may not be known whether they work exactly the same way they do in younger adults or if they cause different side effects or problems in older people. There is no specific information comparing use of foscarnet in the elderly with use in other age groups.

Other medicines—Although certain medicines should not be used together at all, in other cases 2 different medicines may be used together even if an interaction might occur. In these cases, your doctor may want to change the dose, or other precautions may be necessary. When you are taking foscarnet, it is especially important that your health care professional know if you are taking any of the following:

- Carmustine (e.g., BiCNU) or
- Cisplatin (e.g., Platinol) or
- Combination pain medicine containing acetaminophen and aspirin (e.g., Excedrin) or other salicylates (with large amounts taken regularly) or
- Cyclosporine (e.g., Sandimmune) or
- Deferoxamine (e.g., Desferal) (with long-term use) or
- Gold salts (medicine for arthritis) or
- Inflammation or pain medicine, except narcotics, or
- Lithium (e.g., Lithane) or
- Methotrexate (e.g., Mexate) or
- Other anti-infectives (e.g., amphotericin B) or

- Penicillamine (e.g., Cupramine) or
- Plicamycin (e.g., Mithracin) or
- Streptozocin (e.g., Zanosar) or
- Tiopronin (e.g., Thiola)—Use of these medicines may increase the chance of side effects affecting the kidneys
- Pentamidine (e.g., Pentam)—Use of pentamidine injection with foscarnet may lower the level of important minerals (calcium and magnesium) in the blood; it may also increase the chance of side effects affecting the kidneys

Other medical problems—The presence of other medical problems may affect the use of foscarnet. Make sure you tell your doctor if you have any other medical problems, especially:

- Anemia—Foscarnet may cause or worsen anemia
- Dehydration or
- Kidney disease—Patients who are dehydrated or have kidney disease may have an increased chance of side effects

Proper Use of This Medicine

To ensure the best response, foscarnet must be given for the full time of treatment. Also, this medicine works best when there is a constant amount in the blood. To help keep the amount constant, foscarnet must be given on a regular schedule.

Several glasses of water should be taken every day, unless otherwise directed by your doctor. Drinking extra water will help to prevent some unwanted effects foscarnet has on the kidneys.

This medicine may cause sores on the genitals (sex organs). Washing your genitals after urination may decrease the chance of your developing this problem.

Dosing—The dose of foscarnet will be different for different patients. *Follow your doctor's orders or the directions on the label.* The following information includes only the average doses of foscarnet. *If your dose is different, do not change it* unless your doctor tells you to do so.

- For *injection* dosage form:
  - —For cytomegalovirus (CMV) retinitis induction (first stage of dosing):
    - Adults and children—The usual dose is 60 milligrams (mg) per kilogram (kg) (27.3 mg per pound) of body weight every eight hours for fourteen to twenty-one days. Each dose is injected slowly into a vein by an infusion pump over at least one hour.
  - —For CMV retinitis maintenance (second stage of dosing):
    - Adults and children—The usual dose is 90 to 120 mg per kg (41 to 54.5 mg per pound) of body weight once a day. This dose is injected slowly into a vein by an infusion pump over at least two hours.

Precautions After Receiving This Medicine

It is very important that your doctor check your progress at regular visits. This will allow your doctor to check for possible unwanted effects.

It is also *very important that your ophthalmologist (eye doctor) check your eyes* at regular visits since you may have some loss of eyesight due to retinitis even while you are receiving foscarnet.

Side Effects of This Medicine

Along with their needed effects, medicines like foscarnet can sometimes cause serious side effects such as kidney problems; these are described below. Foscarnet may also decrease the amount of calcium in your blood, causing you to have a tingling sensation around your mouth, and pain or numbness in your hands and feet. If this occurs, especially while you are receiving the medicine, notify your health care professional immediately.

Along with its needed effects, a medicine may cause some unwanted effects. Although not all of these side effects may occur, if they do occur they may need medical attention.

Check with your doctor immediately if any of the following side effects occur:

More common

Increased or decreased frequency of urination or amount of urine; increased thirst

Less common

Convulsions (seizures); fever, chills, and sore throat; muscle twitching; pain at place of injection; pain or numbness in hands or feet; tingling sensation around mouth; tremor; unusual tiredness and weakness

Rare

Sores or ulcers on the mouth or throat, penis, or vulva

Other side effects may occur that usually do not need medical attention. These side effects may go away during treatment as your body adjusts to the medicine. However, check with your doctor if any of the following side effects continue or are bothersome:

More common

Abdominal or stomach pain; anxious feeling; confusion; dizziness; headache; loss of appetite; nausea and vomiting; unusual tiredness or weakness

Other side effects not listed above may also occur in some patients. If you notice any other effects, check with your doctor.

Additional Information

Once a medicine has been approved for marketing for a certain use, experience may show that it is also useful for other medical problems. Although these uses are not included in product labeling, foscarnet is used in certain patients with the following medical conditions:

- Cytomegalovirus infections in places other than the eyes, such as the lungs, esophagus, or intestines
- Herpes simplex infections of the lips and mouth that do not respond to treatment with acyclovir in patients with HIV infection
- Varicella-zoster infection (shingles) that does not respond to treatment with acyclovir in patients with HIV infection

Other than the above information, there is no additional information relating to proper use, precautions, or side effects for these uses.

Revised: 07/22/94

FRUCTOSE, DEXTROSE, AND PHOSPHORIC ACID Oral

A commonly used brand name in the U.S. and Canada is Emetrol.

Description

Fructose (FRUK-tose), dextrose (DEX-trose), and phosphoric (fos-FOR-ik) acid combination is used to treat nausea and vomiting. However, this combination has not been proven to be effective.

This medicine is available without a prescription; however, your doctor may have special instructions on the proper use and dose for your medical problem. Fructose, dextrose, and phosphoric acid combination is available in the following dosage form:

Oral

- Oral solution (U.S. and Canada)

Before Using This Medicine

If you are taking this medicine without a prescription, carefully read and follow any precautions on the label. For fructose, dextrose, and phosphoric acid combination, the following should be considered:

Allergies—Tell your doctor if you have ever had any unusual or allergic reaction to fructose, dextrose, or phosphoric acid.

Pregnancy—Studies on effects in pregnancy have not been done in either humans or animals.

Breast-feeding—This medicine has not been reported to cause problems in nursing babies.

Children—The fluid loss caused by vomiting may result in a severe condition, especially in children under 3 years of age. Do not give medicine for vomiting to children without first checking with their doctor.

Older adults—The fluid loss caused by vomiting may result in a severe condition. Elderly persons should not take any medicine for vomiting without first checking with their doctor.

Other medical problems—The presence of other medical problems may affect the use of fructose, dextrose, and phosphoric acid. Make sure you tell your doctor if you have any other medical problems, especially:

- Appendicitis, symptoms of, or
- Inflamed bowel, symptoms of—Make sure nausea and vomiting are not due to appendicitis or inflamed bowel before using this product. These conditions may become more severe if they are not treated by your doctor
- Diabetes mellitus—The sugars contained in this medicine may cause problems in diabetics
- Fructose intolerance, hereditary—The fructose in this medicine may cause severe side effects in patients with this condition

Proper Use of This Medicine

For safe use of this medicine:

- Follow your doctor's instructions if this medicine was prescribed.
- Follow the manufacturer's package directions if you are treating yourself.

Do not dilute this medicine with other liquids. Also, do not drink any other liquids immediately before or after taking this medicine. To do so may keep this medicine from working properly.

Dosing—The dose of this combination product will be different for different patients. *Follow your doctor's orders or the directions on the label.* The following information includes only the average doses. *If your dose is different, do not change it* unless your doctor tells you to do so.

- For *oral* dosage form (oral solution):
  - —For morning sickness:
    - Pregnant women: One or two tablespoonfuls upon arising and every three hours as needed.
  - —For nausea:
    - Adults: One or two tablespoonfuls. Dose may be repeated every fifteen minutes until nausea stops. You should not take this product for more than one hour (5 doses) without checking with your doctor.
    - Children over 3 years of age: One or two teaspoonfuls. Dose may be repeated every fifteen minutes until nausea stops. This product should not be taken for more than one hour (5 doses) without checking with your doctor.
    - Children under 3 years of age: Use is not recommended.

Storage—To store this medicine:

- Keep out of the reach of children.
- Store away from heat and direct light.
- Keep the medicine from freezing.
- Do not keep outdated medicine or medicine no longer needed. Be sure that any discarded medicine is out of the reach of children.

Precautions While Using This Medicine

Check with your doctor if your nausea and vomiting continue or become worse after you have taken this medicine.

Do not take this medicine if you have any signs of appendicitis or inflamed bowel (such as stomach or lower abdominal pain, cramping, bloating, soreness, or continuing or severe nausea or vomiting). Instead, check with your doctor as soon as possible.

Side Effects of This Medicine

Along with its needed effects, a medicine may cause some unwanted effects. Although not all of these side effects may occur, if they do occur they may need medical attention.

Stop using this medicine and check with your doctor as soon as possible if any of the following side effects occur:

Signs of fructose intolerance

Fainting; swelling of face, arms, and legs; unusual bleeding; vomiting; weight loss; yellow eyes or skin

Other side effects may occur that usually do not need medical attention. These side effects may go away during treatment as your body adjusts to the medicine. However, check with your doctor if any of the following side effects continue or are bothersome:

Less common—more common with large doses
Diarrhea; stomach or abdominal pain

Other side effects not listed above may also occur in some patients. If you notice any other effects, check with your doctor.

Revised: 05/12/93

FURAZOLIDONE Oral†

Some commonly used brand names in the U.S. are Furoxone and Furoxone Liquid.

†Not commercially available in Canada.

Description

Furazolidone (fyoor-a-ZOE-li-done) is used to treat bacterial and protozoal (proe-toe-ZOE-al) infections. It works by killing bacteria and protozoa (tiny, one-celled animals). Some protozoa are parasites that can cause many different kinds of infections in the body.

Furazolidone is taken by mouth. It works inside the intestinal tract to treat cholera, colitis, and/or diarrhea caused by bacteria, and giardiasis (jee-ar-DYE-a-siss). This medicine is sometimes given with other medicines for bacterial infections.

Furazolidone may cause some serious side effects when taken with certain foods, beverages, or other medicines. Check with your health care professional for a list of products that should be avoided.

Furazolidone is available only with your doctor's prescription, in the following dosage forms:

Oral
- Oral suspension (U.S.)
- Tablets (U.S.)

Before Using This Medicine

In deciding to use a medicine, the risks of taking the medicine must be weighed against the good it will do. This is a decision you and your doctor will make. For furazolidone, the following should be considered:

Allergies—Tell your doctor if you have ever had any unusual or allergic reaction to furazolidone or to any related medicines such as nitrofurantoin (e.g., Furadantin) or nitrofurazone (e.g., Furacin). Also tell your health care professional if you are allergic to any other substances, such as foods, preservatives, or dyes.

Pregnancy—Studies have not been done in humans. However, furazolidone has not been shown to cause birth defects or other problems in humans or in animals given high doses for a long time.

Breast-feeding—It is not known whether furazolidone passes into breast milk. However, breast-feeding is not recommended for nursing babies up to 1 month of age because furazolidone may cause anemia.

Children—Because furazolidone may cause anemia, use in infants up to 1 month of age is not recommended.

Older adults—Many medicines have not been studied specifically in older people. Therefore, it may not be known whether they work exactly the same way they do in younger adults or if they cause different side effects or problems in older people. There is no specific information comparing use of furazolidone in the elderly with use in other age groups.

Other medicines—Although certain medicines should not be used together at all, in other cases two different medicines may be used together even if an interaction might occur. In these cases, your doctor may want to change the dose, or other precautions may be necessary. When you are taking furazolidone, it is especially important that your health care professional know if you are taking any of the following:

- Amphetamines or
- Appetite suppressants (diet pills) or
- Ephedrine (e.g., Primatene) or
- Isocarboxazid (e.g., Marplan) or
- Phenelzine (e.g., Nardil) or
- Phenylephrine (e.g., Neo-Synephrine) or
- Phenylpropanolamine (e.g., Dexatrim) or
- Procarbazine (e.g., Matulane) or
- Pseudoephedrine (e.g., Sudafed) or
- Selegiline (e.g., Eldepryl) or
- Tranylcypromine (e.g., Parnate) or
- Tricyclic antidepressants (amitriptyline [e.g., Elavil], amoxapine [e.g., Asendin], clomipramine [e.g., Anafranil], desipramine [e.g., Pertofrane], doxepin [e.g., Sinequan], imipramine [e.g., Tofranil], nortriptyline [e.g., Aventyl], protriptyline [e.g., Vivactil], trimipramine [e.g., Surmontil])—The use of furazolidone with any of these medicines may result in a severe increase in blood pressure

Other medical problems—The presence of other medical problems may affect the use of furazolidone. Make sure you tell your doctor if you have any other medical problems, especially:

- Glucose-6-phosphate dehydrogenase deficiency (lack of G6PD enzyme)—Patients with G6PD-deficiency may develop mild anemia while taking furazolidone

Proper Use of This Medicine

Do not give furazolidone to infants up to 1 month of age, unless otherwise directed by your doctor. This medicine may cause anemia in these patients.

Furazolidone may be taken with food to lessen the chance of an upset stomach.

To use the *oral suspension:*
- Use a specially marked measuring spoon or other device to measure each dose accurately. The average household teaspoon may not hold the right amount of liquid.

To help clear up your infection completely, *keep taking furazolidone for the full time of treatment,* even if you begin to feel better after a few days. If you stop taking this medicine too soon, your symptoms may return. *Do not miss any doses.*

Dosing—The dose of furazolidone will be different for different patients. *Follow your doctor's orders or the directions on the label.* The following information includes only the average doses of furazolidone. *If your dose is different, do not change it* unless your doctor tells you to do so.

The number of tablets or teaspoonfuls of suspension that you take depends on the strength of the medicine. Also, *the number of doses you take each day, the time allowed between doses, and the length of time you take the medicine depend on the medical problem for which you are taking furazolidone.*

- For *oral* dosage forms (oral suspension or tablets):
  —For cholera or diarrhea caused by bacteria:
    - Adults—100 milligrams (mg) taken four times a day for five to seven days.
    - Children up to 1 month of age—Use is not recommended.
    - Children 1 month of age and over—Dose is based on body weight and must be determined by your doctor. The usual dose is 1.25 mg per kilogram (kg) (0.56 mg per pound) of body weight taken four times a day for five to seven days.

  —For giardiasis:
    - Adults—100 mg taken four times a day for seven to ten days.
    - Children up to 1 month of age—Use is not recommended.
    - Children 1 month of age and over—Dose is based on body weight and must be determined by your doctor. The usual dose is 1.25 mg to 2 mg per kg (0.56 to 0.90 mg per pound) of body weight taken four times a day for seven to ten days.

Missed dose—If you miss a dose of this medicine, take it as soon as possible. However, if it is almost time for your next dose, skip the missed dose and go back to your regular dosing schedule. Do not double doses.

Storage—To store this medicine:
- Keep out of the reach of children.
- Store away from heat and direct light.
- Do not store the tablet form of this medicine in the bathroom, near the kitchen sink, or in other damp places. Heat or moisture may cause the medicine to break down.
- Keep the oral suspension form of this medicine from freezing.
- Do not keep outdated medicine or medicine no longer needed. Be sure that any discarded medicine is out of the reach of children.

Precautions While Using This Medicine

It is important that your doctor check your progress at regular visits. This is to check whether or not the infection is cleared up completely.

If your symptoms do not improve within a week, or if they become worse, check with your doctor.

Drinking alcoholic beverages or taking other alcohol-containing preparations (for example, elixirs, cough syrups, tonics, or injections of alcohol) while taking furazolidone may rarely cause problems. These problems include increased side effects such as redness of the face, difficult breathing, fainting, and a feeling of tightness in the chest. These side effects usually go away within 24 hours without treatment. However, these effects may occur if you drink alcoholic beverages for up to 4 days after you stop taking furazolidone. Therefore, *you should not drink alcoholic beverages or take other alcohol-containing preparations while you are taking furazolidone and for 4 days after stopping it.*

Certain foods, drinks, or other medicines may cause very dangerous reactions, such as severe high blood pressure, when taken with furazolidone. Aged or fermented foods and drinks commonly contain tyramine or other substances that increase blood pressure. To avoid such reactions, the following measures are recommended:
- *Do not eat foods that have a high tyramine content (most common in foods that are aged or fermented to increase their flavor), such as cheeses; yeast or meat extracts; fava or broad bean pods; smoked or pickled meat, poultry, or fish; fermented sausage (bologna, pepperoni, salami, summer sausage) or other fermented meat; or any overripe fruit. If a list of these foods is not given to you, ask your health care professional to provide one.*
- *Do not drink alcoholic beverages or alcohol-free or reduced-alcohol beer and wine.*
- Do not eat or drink large amounts of caffeine-containing food or beverages such as chocolate, coffee, tea, or cola.
- *Do not take any other medicines unless approved or prescribed by your doctor.* This includes nonprescription (over-the-counter [OTC]) appetite suppressants (diet pills) or medicine for colds, sinus problems, or hay fever or other allergies.
- *Do not take any of the above-listed foods, drinks, or medicine for at least 2 weeks after you stop taking furazolidone.* They may continue to react with this medicine during that time.
- Other foods may also contain tyramine or other substances that increase blood pressure. However, these products generally do not cause serious problems when taken with furazolidone, especially if eaten when fresh and in small amounts. These include yogurt, sour cream, cream cheese, cottage cheese, chocolate, and soy sauce. If you have any questions about

this, ask your health care professional. Also ask for a list of foods, beverages, or medicines that may cause serious problems when taken with furazolidone.

Side Effects of This Medicine

Along with its needed effects, a medicine may cause some unwanted effects. Although not all of these side effects may occur, if they do occur they may need medical attention.

Check with your doctor immediately if any of the following side effects occur:

Rare

Fever; itching; joint pain; skin rash or redness; sore throat

Other side effects may occur that usually do not need medical attention. These side effects may go away during treatment as your body adjusts to the medicine. However, check with your doctor if any of the following side effects continue or are bothersome:

Less common

Abdominal or stomach pain; diarrhea; headache; nausea or vomiting

This medicine commonly causes dark yellow to brown discoloration of urine. This side effect does not usually need medical attention.

Other side effects not listed above may also occur in some patients. If you notice any other effects, check with your doctor.

Revised: 08/11/95

GABAPENTIN Systemic

A commonly used brand name in the U.S. and Canada is Neurontin. Another commonly used name is GBP.

Description

Gabapentin (GA-ba-pen-tin) is used to help control some types of seizures in the treatment of epilepsy. This medicine cannot cure epilepsy and will only work to control seizures for as long as you continue to take it.

Gabapentin is available only with your doctor's prescription, in the following dosage form:

Oral
- Capsules (U.S. and Canada)

Before Using This Medicine

In deciding to use a medicine, the risks of taking the medicine must be weighed against the good it will do. This is a decision you and your doctor will make. For gabapentin, the following should be considered:

Allergies—Tell your doctor if you have ever had any unusual or allergic reaction to gabapentin. Also tell your health care professional if you are allergic to any other substances, such as foods, preservatives, or dyes.

Pregnancy—Gabapentin has not been studied in pregnant women. However, studies in pregnant animals have shown that gabapentin may cause bone or kidney problems in offspring when given to the mother in doses as large as the largest human dose. Before taking this medicine, make sure your doctor knows if you are pregnant or if you may become pregnant.

Breast-feeding—It is not known whether gabapentin passes into breast milk. Although most medicines pass into breast milk in small amounts, many of them may be used safely while breast-feeding. Mothers who are taking this medicine and who wish to breast-feed should discuss this with their doctor.

Children—This medicine has not been studied in children younger than 12 years of age, and there is no specific information comparing use of gabapentin in children with use in other age groups.

Teenagers—This medicine has been tested in a small number of patients 12 to 18 years of age. In effective doses, gabapentin has not been shown to cause different side effects or problems than it does in adults.

Older adults—Gabapentin is removed from the body more slowly in elderly people than in younger people. Higher blood levels may occur, which may increase the chance of unwanted effects. Your doctor may give you a different gabapentin dose than a younger person would receive.

Other medicines—Although certain medicines should not be used together at all, in other cases two different medicines may be used together even if an interaction might occur. In these cases, your doctor may want to change the dose, or other precautions may be necessary. When you are taking gabapentin, it is especially important that your health care professional know if you are taking any of the following:

- Antacids (e.g., Maalox)—Lower blood levels of gabapentin may occur, so gabapentin may not work properly; gabapentin should be taken at least 2 hours after any antacid is taken.

Other medical problems—The presence of other medical problems may affect the use of gabapentin. Make sure you tell your doctor if you have any other medical problems, especially:

- Kidney disease—Higher blood levels of gabapentin may occur, which may increase the chance of unwanted effects; your doctor may need to change your dose

Proper Use of This Medicine

Take this medicine only as directed by your doctor, to help your condition as much as possible. Do not take more or less of it, and do not take it more or less often than your doctor ordered.

Gabapentin may be taken with or without food or on a full or empty stomach. However, if your doctor tells you to take the medicine a certain way, take it exactly as directed.

When taking gabapentin 3 times a day, do not allow more than 12 hours to pass between any 2 doses.

If you have trouble swallowing capsules, you may open the gabapentin capsule and mix the medicine with applesauce or juice. Mix only one dose at a time just before taking it. *Do not mix any doses to save for later,* because the medicine may change over time and may not work properly.

Dosing—The dose of gabapentin will be different for different patients. *Follow your doctor's orders or the directions on the label.* The following information includes only the average doses of gabapentin. *If your dose is different, do not change it* unless your doctor tells you to do so.

The number of capsules that you take depends on the strength of the medicine.

- For *oral* dosage form (capsules):
  - —For epilepsy:
    - Adults and teenagers 12 years of age and older—300 milligrams (mg) at bedtime the first day, a total of 600 mg divided into two smaller doses the second day, then a total of 900 mg divided into three smaller doses each day. Your doctor may increase the dose gradually if needed. However, the dose is usually not more than 3600 mg a day.
    - Children up to 12 years of age—Use and dose must be determined by the doctor.

Missed dose—If you miss a dose of this medicine, take it as soon as possible. However, if it is less than 2 hours until your next dose, take the missed dose right away, and take the next dose 1 to 2 hours later. Then go back to your regular dosing schedule. Do not double doses.

Storage—To store this medicine:
- Keep out of the reach of children.
- Store away from heat and direct light.
- Do not store in the bathroom, near the kitchen sink, or in other damp places. Heat or moisture may cause the medicine to break down.
- Do not keep outdated medicine or medicine no longer needed. Be sure that any discarded medicine is out of the reach of children.

Precautions While Using This Medicine

It is important that your doctor check your progress at regular visits, especially for the first few months you take gabapentin. This is necessary to allow dose adjustments and to reduce any unwanted effects.

This medicine will add to the effects of alcohol and other CNS depressants (medicines that slow down the nervous system, possibly causing drowsiness). Some examples of CNS depressants are antihistamines or medicine for hay fever, other allergies, or colds; sedatives, tranquilizers, or sleeping medicine; prescription pain medicine or narcotics; barbiturates; other medicines for seizures; muscle relaxants; or anesthetics, including some dental anesthetics. *Check with your medical doctor or dentist before taking any of the above while you are taking gabapentin.*

Gabapentin may cause blurred vision, double vision, clumsiness, unsteadiness, dizziness, drowsiness, or trouble in thinking. *Make sure you know how you react to this medicine before you drive, use machines, or do anything else that could be dangerous if you are not alert, well-coordinated, or able to think or see well.* If these reactions are especially bothersome, check with your doctor.

Before you have any medical tests, tell the doctor in charge that you are taking gabapentin. The results of dipstick tests for protein in the urine may be affected by this medicine.

Do not stop taking gabapentin without first checking with your doctor. Stopping the medicine suddenly may cause your seizures to return or to occur more often. Your doctor may want you to gradually reduce the amount you are taking before stopping completely.

Side Effects of This Medicine

Along with its needed effects, a medicine may cause some unwanted effects. Although not all of these side effects may occur, if they do occur they may need medical attention.

Check with your doctor as soon as possible if any of the following side effects occur:

More common

Clumsiness or unsteadiness; continuous, uncontrolled back and forth and/or rolling eye movements

Less common

Depression, irritability, or other mood or mental changes; loss of memory

Rare

Fever or chills, cough or hoarseness, lower back or side pain, painful or difficult urination

Symptoms of overdose

Double vision; severe diarrhea; severe dizziness; severe drowsiness; severe slurred speech; sluggishness

Other side effects may occur that usually do not need medical attention. These side effects may go away during treatment as your body adjusts to the medicine. However, check with your doctor if any of the following side effects continue or are bothersome:

More common

Blurred or double vision; dizziness; drowsiness; muscle ache or pain; swelling of hands, feet, or lower legs; trembling or shaking; unusual tiredness or weakness

Less common

Diarrhea; dryness of mouth or throat; frequent urination; headache; indigestion; low blood pressure; nausea; noise in ears; runny nose; slurred speech; trouble in thinking; trouble in sleeping; vomiting; weakness or loss of strength; weight gain

Other side effects not listed above may also occur in some patients. If you notice any other effects, check with your doctor.

Developed: 02/28/95

GALLIUM NITRATE Systemic†

A commonly used brand name in the U.S. is Ganite.

†Not commercially available in Canada; however it is available by emergency drug release from the Health Protection Branch.

Description

Gallium nitrate (GAL-ee-um NYE-trate) is used to treat hypercalcemia (too much calcium in the blood) that may occur with some types of cancer.

This medicine is available only with your doctor's prescription in the following dosage form:

Parenteral
- Injection (U.S.)

Before Receiving This Medicine

In deciding to use a medicine, the risks of taking the medicine must be weighed against the good it will do. This is a decision you and your doctor will make. For gallium nitrate the following should be considered:

Allergies—Tell your health care professional if you are allergic to any other substances, such as foods, preservatives, or dyes.

Diet—Make certain your health care professional knows if your diet includes large amounts of calcium-containing foods and/or vitamin D, such as milk or other dairy products. Also let your health care professional know if you are on any special diet, such as a low-sodium or a low-sugar diet.

Pregnancy—Studies on effects in pregnancy have not been done in either humans or animals.

Breast-feeding—It is not known whether gallium nitrate passes into breast milk. However, this medicine is not recommended for use during breast-feeding, because it may cause unwanted effects in nursing babies.

Children—Studies on this medicine have been done only in adult patients, and there is no specific information comparing use of gallium nitrate in children with use in other age groups.

Older adults—Many medicines have not been studied specifically in older people. Therefore, it may not be known whether they work exactly the same way they do in younger adults. Although there is no specific information comparing use of gallium nitrate in the elderly with use in other age groups, this medicine is not expected to cause different side effects or problems in older people than it does in younger adults.

Other medicines—Although certain medicines should not be used together at all, in other cases two different medicines may be used together even if an interaction might occur. In these cases, your doctor may want to change the dose, or other precautions may be necessary. When you are taking gallium nitrate, it is especially important that your health care professional know if you are taking any of the following:

- Anti-infectives by mouth or by injection (medicine for infection) or
- Cisplatin (e.g., Platinol) or
- Combination pain medicine containing acetaminophen and aspirin (e.g., Excedrin) or other salicylates (with large amounts taken regularly) or
- Cyclosporine (e.g., Sandimmune) or
- Deferoxamine (e.g., Desferal) (with long-term use) or
- Gold salts (medicine for arthritis) or
- Lithium (e.g., Lithane) or
- Methotrexate (e.g., Mexate) or
- Penicillamine (e.g., Cuprimine)—Use with gallium nitrate may cause or worsen kidney problems

Other medical problems—The presence of other medical problems may affect the use of gallium nitrate. Make sure you tell your doctor if you have any other medical problems, especially:

- Kidney disease—Gallium nitrate may make this condition worse

Proper Use of This Medicine

Dosing—The dose of gallium nitrate will be different for different patients. *Follow your doctor's orders.*

- For *injection* dosage form:
  - —For treatment of too much calcium in the blood:
    - Adults and teenagers—The dose is based on body size and must be determined by your doctor. Gallium nitrate is injected slowly into a vein over 24 hours, for five days. The dose may be repeated in two to four weeks.
    - Children up to 12 years of age—Use and dose must be determined by your doctor.

Storage—To store this medicine:

- Keep out of the reach of children.
- Store away from heat and direct light.
- Do not store in the bathroom, near the kitchen sink, or in other damp places. Heat or moisture may cause the medicine to break down.
- Keep the medicine from freezing. Do not refrigerate.
- Do not keep outdated medicine or medicine no longer needed. Be sure that any discarded medicine is out of the reach of children.

Precautions While Receiving This Medicine

It is important that your doctor check your progress at regular visits while you are receiving this medicine. If your condition has improved and you are no longer receiving gallium nitrate, your progress must still be checked. The results of laboratory tests or the occurrence of certain symptoms will tell your doctor if your condition is coming back.

Side Effects of This Medicine

Along with its needed effects, a medicine may cause some unwanted effects. Although not all of these side effects may occur, if they do occur they may need medical attention.

More common

Blood in urine; bone pain; greatly increased or decreased frequency of urination or amount of urine; increased thirst; loss of appetite; muscle weakness; nausea or vomiting

Less common

Abdominal cramps; confusion; muscle spasms

Rare

Unusual tiredness or weakness

Other side effects may occur that usually do not need medical attention. These side effects may go away during treatment as your body adjusts to the medicine. However, check with your doctor if any of the following side effects continue or are bothersome:

More common

Diarrhea; metallic taste

Other side effects not listed above may also occur in some patients. If you notice any other effects, check with your doctor.

Revised: 06/28/96

GANCICLOVIR Systemic

Some commonly used brand names are:

In the U.S.—
Cytovene
Cytovene-IV

In Canada—
Cytovene

Another commonly used name is DHPG.

Description

Ganciclovir (gan-SYE-kloe-vir) is an antiviral. It is used to treat infections caused by viruses.

Ganciclovir is used to treat the symptoms of cytomegalovirus (CMV) infection of the eyes in people whose immune system is not working fully. This includes patients with acquired immune deficiency syndrome (AIDS). Ganciclovir will not cure this eye infection, but it may help to keep the symptoms from becoming worse. It is also used to help prevent CMV infection in patients who receive organ or bone marrow transplants. Ganciclovir may be used for other serious CMV infections as determined by your doctor. However, it does not work in treating certain viruses, such as the common cold or the flu.

This medicine may cause some serious side effects, including anemia and other blood problems. Before you begin treatment with ganciclovir, you and your doctor should talk about the good this medicine will do as well as the risks of using it.

Ganciclovir is to be administered only by or under the supervision of your doctor. It is available in the following dosage forms:

Oral
- Capsules (U.S.)

Parenteral
- Injection (U.S. and Canada)

Before Receiving This Medicine

In deciding to use a medicine, the risks of taking the medicine must be weighed against the good it will do. This is a decision you and your doctor will make. For ganciclovir, the following should be considered:

Allergies—Tell your doctor if you have ever had any unusual or allergic reaction to acyclovir or ganciclovir. Also tell your health care professional if you are allergic to any other substances, such as foods, preservatives, or dyes.

Pregnancy—Use of ganciclovir during pregnancy should be avoided whenever possible since ganciclovir has caused cancer and birth defects in animal studies. The use of birth control is recommended during ganciclovir therapy. Men should use a condom while receiving ganciclovir, and for at least 90 days following treatment. Also, animal studies have shown that ganciclovir causes a decrease in fertility.

Breast-feeding—Breast-feeding should be stopped during treatment with this medicine because ganciclovir may cause serious unwanted effects in nursing babies.

Children—Ganciclovir can cause serious side effects in any patient. Therefore, it is especially important that you discuss with the child's doctor the good that this medicine may do as well as the risks of using it.

Older adults—Many medicines have not been studied specifically in older people. Therefore, it may not be known whether they work exactly the same way they do in younger adults or if they cause different side effects or problems in older people. There is no specific information comparing use of ganciclovir in the elderly with use in other age groups.

Other medicines—Although certain medicines should not be used together at all, in other cases 2 different medicines may be used together even if an interaction might occur. In these cases, your doctor may want to change the dose, or other precautions may be necessary. When you are taking ganciclovir, it is especially important that your health care professional know if you are taking any of the following:

- Amphotericin B by injection (e.g., Fungizone) or
- Antineoplastics (cancer medicine) or
- Antithyroid agents (medicine for overactive thyroid) or
- Azathioprine (e.g., Imuran) or
- Chloramphenicol (e.g., Chloromycetin) or
- Colchicine or
- Cyclophosphamide (e.g., Cytoxan) or
- Flucytosine (e.g., Ancobon) or
- Interferon (e.g., Intron A, Roferon-A) or
- Mercaptopurine (e.g., Purinethol) or
- Zidovudine (e.g., AZT, Retrovir)—Caution should be used if these medicines and ganciclovir are used together; receiving ganciclovir while you are using these medicines may make anemia and other blood problems worse
- Carmustine (e.g., BiCNU) or
- Cisplatin (e.g., Platinol) or
- Combination pain medicine containing acetaminophen and aspirin (e.g., Excedrin) or other salicylates (with large amounts taken regularly) or
- Cyclosporine (e.g., Sandimmune) or
- Deferoxamine (e.g., Desferal) (with long-term use) or
- Gold salts (medicine for arthritis) or
- Inflammation or pain medicine, except narcotics, or
- Lithium (e.g., Lithane) or
- Other anti-infectives (e.g., amphotericin B) or
- Penicillamine (e.g., Cupramine) or
- Streptozocin (e.g., Zanosar) or
- Tiopronin (e.g., Thiola)—Use of these medicines may increase the chance of side effects affecting the kidneys
- Methotrexate (e.g., Mexate) or
- Plicamycin (e.g., Mithracin)—These medicines may increase the chance of side effects affecting the blood and the kidneys

Other medical problems—The presence of other medical problems may affect the use of ganciclovir. Make sure you tell your doctor if you have any other medical problems, especially:

- Kidney disease—Ganciclovir may build up in the blood in patients with kidney disease, increasing the chance of side effects
- Low platelet count or
- Low white blood cell count—Ganciclovir may make these blood diseases that you have worse

Proper Use of This Medicine

It is *important that you take ganciclovir capsules with food.* This is to make sure the medicine is fully absorbed into the body and will work properly.

To get the best results, *ganciclovir must be given for the full time of treatment.* Also, this medicine works best when there is a constant amount in the blood. To help keep the amount constant, ganciclovir must be given on a regular schedule.

Dosing—The dose of ganciclovir will be different for different patients. *Follow your doctor's orders or the directions on the label.* The following information includes only the average doses of ganciclovir. *If your dose is different, do not change it* unless your doctor tells you to do so.

- For *oral* dosage form (capsules):
  - —For treatment of CMV retinitis after you have received ganciclovir injection for at least fourteen to twenty-one days:
    - Adults and teenagers—1000 milligrams (mg) three times a day with food; or 500 mg six times a day, every three hours with food, during waking hours.
    - Children—Use and dose must be determined by your doctor.
- For *injection* dosage form:
  - —For treatment of CMV retinitis:
    - Adults and teenagers—Dose is based on body weight and must be determined by your doctor. At first, 5 mg per kilogram (2.3 mg per pound) of body weight is injected into a vein every twelve hours for fourteen to twenty-one days. Then, 5 mg per kilogram (2.3 mg per pound) of body weight is injected into a vein once a day for seven days of the week; or 6 mg per kilogram (2.7 mg per pound) of body weight is injected into a vein once a day for five days of the week.
    - Children—Use and dose must be determined by your doctor.
  - —For prevention of CMV in transplant patients:
    - Adults and teenagers—Dose is based on body weight and must be determined by your doctor. At first, 5 mg per kilogram (2.3 mg per pound) of body weight is injected into a vein every twelve hours for seven to fourteen days. Then the dose is reduced to 5 mg per kilogram (2.3 mg per pound) of body weight once a day for seven days of the week; or 6 mg per kilogram (2.7 mg per pound) of body weight is injected into a vein once a day for five days of the week.
    - Children—Use and dose must be determined by your doctor.

Precautions After Receiving This Medicine

Ganciclovir can lower the number of white blood cells in your blood, increasing the chance of getting an infection. It can also lower the number of platelets, which are necessary for proper blood clotting. If this occurs, there are certain precautions you can take to reduce the risk of infection or bleeding:

- *Check with your doctor immediately* if you think you are getting an infection or if you get a fever or chills.
- *Check with your doctor immediately* if you notice any unusual bleeding or bruising; black, tarry stools; blood in urine or stools; or pinpoint red spots on your skin.
- Be careful when using a regular toothbrush, dental floss, or toothpick. Your medical doctor, dentist, or nurse may recommend other ways to clean your teeth and gums. Check with your medical doctor before having any dental work done.
- Be careful not to cut yourself when you are using sharp objects such as a safety razor or fingernail or toenail cutters.

The *use of birth control is recommended for both men and women.* Women should use effective birth control methods while receiving this medicine. Men should use a condom during treatment with this medicine and for at least 90 days after treatment has been completed.

It is very important that your doctor check you at regular visits for any blood problems that may be caused by this medicine.

If you have CMV retinitis: It is also very important that your ophthalmologist (eye doctor) check your eyes at regular visits since it is still possible that you may have some loss of eyesight during ganciclovir treatment.

Side Effects of This Medicine

Along with its needed effects, a medicine may cause some unwanted effects. Although not all of these side effects may occur, if they do occur they may need medical attention.

Medicines like ganciclovir can sometimes cause serious side effects such as blood problems; these are described below. Discuss these possible effects with your doctor.

Check with your doctor immediately if any of the following side effects occur:

More common

For oral capsules and injection into the vein only

Sore throat and fever; unusual bleeding or bruising

Less common

For oral capsules and injection into the vein only

Mood or other mental changes; nervousness; pain at place of injection; skin rash; tremor; unusual tiredness and weakness

For injection into the eye only

Decreased vision or any change in vision

Other side effects may occur that usually do not need medical attention. These side effects may go away during treatment as your body adjusts to the medicine. However,

check with your doctor if any of the following side effects continue or are bothersome:

Less common
Abdominal or stomach pain; loss of appetite; nausea and vomiting

Other side effects not listed above may also occur in some patients. If you notice any other effects, check with your doctor.

Revised: 08/08/95

GEMCITABINE Systemic

A commonly used brand name in the U.S. and Canada is Gemzar.

Description

Gemcitabine (jem-SITE-a-been) belongs to the group of medicines called antimetabolites. It is used to treat cancer of the pancreas. It may also be used to treat other kinds of cancer, as determined by your doctor.

Gemcitabine interferes with the growth of cancer cells, which are eventually destroyed. Since the growth of normal cells may also be affected by the medicine, other effects will also occur. Some of these may be serious and must be reported to your doctor. Other effects, like hair loss, may not be serious but may cause concern. Some effects may occur after treatment with gemcitabine has been stopped.

This medicine is available only with your doctor's prescription, in the following dosage form:

Parenteral
- Injection (U.S. and Canada)

Before Using This Medicine

In deciding to use a medicine, the risks of taking the medicine must be weighed against the good it will do. This is a decision you and your doctor will make. For gemcitabine, the following should be considered:

Allergies—Tell your doctor if you have ever had any unusual or allergic reaction to gemcitabine.

Pregnancy—Tell your doctor if you are pregnant. Studies in mice and rabbits have shown that gemcitabine causes birth defects and death of the fetus, as well as problems in the mother. Be sure that you have discussed this with your doctor before starting treatment with this medicine. It is best to use birth control while you are receiving gemcitabine. Also, tell your doctor right away if you think you have become pregnant during treatment.

Breast-feeding—It is not known whether gemcitabine passes into breast milk. However, because this medicine may cause serious side effects, breast-feeding is generally not recommended while you are receiving it.

Children—There is no specific information comparing use of gemcitabine in children with use in other age groups.

Older adults—Gemcitabine has been tested in elderly patients and has not been shown to cause different side effects or problems in older people than it does in younger adults. However, seriously low blood counts tend to occur more often in elderly patients.

Other medicines—Although certain medicines should not be used together at all, in other cases two different medicines may be used together even if an interaction might occur. In these cases, your doctor may want to change the dose, or other precautions may be necessary. When you are taking gemcitabine, it is especially important that your health care professional know if you are taking any of the following:

- Amphotericin B by injection (e.g., Fungizone) or
- Antithyroid agents (medicine for overactive thyroid) or
- Azathioprine (e.g., Imuran) or
- Chloramphenicol (e.g., Chloromycetin) or
- Colchicine or
- Flucytosine (e.g., Ancobon) or
- Ganciclovir (e.g., Cytovene) or
- Interferon (e.g., Intron A, Roferon-A) or
- Plicamycin (e.g., Mithracin) or
- Zidovudine (e.g., AZT, Retrovir) or
- If you have ever been treated with radiation or other cancer medicines—The risk of developing seriously low blood counts may be increased. Also, gemcitabine can cause problems, sometimes serious, in areas treated by radiation
- Azathioprine (e.g., Imuran) or
- Chlorambucil (e.g., Leukeran) or
- Corticosteroids (cortisone-like medicine) or
- Cyclosporine (e.g., Purinethol) or
- Muromonab-CD3 (monoclonal antibody) (e.g., Orthoclone OKT3) or
- Tacrolimus (e.g., Prograf)—There may be an increased risk of infection because gemcitabine decreases your body's ability to fight it

Other medical problems—The presence of other medical problems may affect the use of gemcitabine. Make sure you tell your doctor if you have any other medical problems, especially:

- Chickenpox (including recent exposure) or
- Herpes zoster (shingles)—Risk of severe disease spreading to other parts of the body
- Infection—Gemcitabine can decrease your body's ability to fight infection
- Kidney disease or
- Liver disease, severe—These conditions sometimes increase the effects of medicines by causing them to be removed from the body more slowly

Proper Use of This Medicine

Gemcitabine often causes nausea and vomiting. It can also cause flu-like symptoms such as chills, fever, general feeling of illness, headache, muscle pain, and weakness. It is very important that you continue to receive the medicine even if it makes you feel ill. Ask your health care professional for ways to lessen these effects.

Dosing—The dose of gemcitabine will be different for different patients. The dose that is used may depend on a number of things, including the type of cancer being treated, the patient's size, and whether or not other treatments are also being given. *If you are receiving gemcitabine at home, follow your doctor's orders or the directions on the label.* If you have any questions about the proper dose of gemcitabine, ask your doctor.

Precautions While Using This Medicine

It is very important that your doctor check your progress at regular visits to make sure that this medicine is working properly. Blood tests will be needed to check for unwanted effects.

While you are being treated with gemcitabine, and after you stop treatment with it, *do not have any immunizations (vaccinations) without your doctor's approval.* Gemcitabine may lower your body's resistance, and there is a chance you might get the infection that the immunization is meant to prevent. In addition, other persons living in your household should not take oral polio vaccine, since there is a chance they could pass the polio virus on to you. Also, avoid persons who have taken oral polio vaccine. Do not get close to them and do not stay in the same room with them for very long. If you cannot take these precautions, you should consider wearing a protective face mask that covers the nose and mouth.

Check with your doctor immediately if shortness of breath occurs or worsens while you are being treated with gemcitabine.

Gemcitabine can temporarily lower the number of white blood cells in your blood, increasing the chance of getting an infection. It can also lower the number of platelets, which are needed for proper blood clotting. If this occurs, there are certain precautions you can take, especially when your blood count is low, to reduce the risk of infection or bleeding:

- If you can, avoid people with infections. *Check with your doctor immediately* if you think you are getting an infection or if you get a fever or chills, cough or hoarseness, lower back or side pain, or painful or difficult urination.
- *Check with your doctor immediately* if you notice any unusual bleeding or bruising; black, tarry stools; blood in urine or stools; or pinpoint red spots on your skin.
- Be careful when using a regular toothbrush, dental floss, or toothpick. Your medical doctor, dentist, or nurse may recommend other ways to clean your teeth and gums. Also, check with your medical doctor before having any dental work done.
- Do not touch your eyes or the inside of your nose unless you have just washed your hands and have not touched anything else in the meantime.
- Be careful not to cut yourself when you are using sharp objects such as a safety razor or fingernail or toenail cutters.
- Avoid contact sports or other situations where bruising or injury could occur.

Side Effects of This Medicine

Along with its needed effects, a medicine may cause some unwanted effects. Although not all of these side effects may occur, if they do occur they may need medical attention.

Check with your doctor immediately if any of the following side effects occur:

More common

Shortness of breath

Less common

Cough or hoarseness; fever or chills; headache (sudden and severe); lower back or side pain; painful or difficult urination; pain in chest, arm, or back; pressure or squeezing in chest; slurred speech or inability to speak; troubled breathing, tightness in chest, and/or wheezing; weakness in arm and/or leg on one side of the body (sudden and severe)

Rare

Coughing; noisy or rattling breathing

The following side effects may mean that you are having a serious allergic reaction to this medicine, especially if they occur together with breathing problems. *Check with your doctor immediately* if any of them occur:

Rare

Change in skin color of the face; skin rash, hives, and/or itching; swelling or puffiness of the face, especially the eyelids or area around the eyes

Also, check with your doctor as soon as possible if any of the following side effects occur:

More common

Black, tarry stools; blood in urine or stools; cloudy urine; fever; pinpoint red spots on skin; skin rash, with or without itching; swelling of fingers, feet, or lower legs; unusual bleeding or bruising; unusual tiredness or weakness

Less common

Fast or irregular heartbeat; high blood pressure

Rare

Increased or decreased urination; yellow eyes or skin

Some of the above side effects may occur, or continue to occur, after treatment with gemcitabine has ended. Check with your doctor if you notice any of them after you stop receiving the medicine.

Other side effects may occur that usually do not need medical attention. These side effects may go away during treatment as your body adjusts to the medicine. However, check with your doctor if any of the following side effects continue or are bothersome:

More common

Constipation; diarrhea; general feeling of illness; loss of appetite; muscle pain; nausea and vomiting; runny nose; sweating; trouble in sleeping

Less common

Drowsiness (severe); irritation, pain, or redness at place of injection; numbness or tingling of hands or feet; sores, ulcers, or white spots on lips and in mouth

Gemcitabine may also cause a temporary loss of hair in some people. After treatment with gemcitabine has ended, normal hair growth should return.

Other side effects not listed above may also occur in some patients. If you notice any other effects, check with your doctor.

Developed: 08/15/97

GEMFIBROZIL Systemic

A commonly used brand name in the U.S. and Canada is Lopid.

Description

Gemfibrozil (gem-FI-broe-zil) is used to lower cholesterol and triglyceride (fat-like substances) levels in the blood. This may help prevent medical problems caused by such substances clogging the blood vessels.

Gemfibrozil is available only with your doctor's prescription, in the following dosage forms:

Oral
- Capsules (Canada)
- Tablets (U.S. and Canada)

Before Using This Medicine

In addition to its helpful effects in treating your medical problem, this type of medicine may have some harmful effects.

Results of a large study using gemfibrozil seem to show that it may cause a higher rate of some cancers in humans. In addition, the action of gemfibrozil is similar to that of another medicine called clofibrate. Studies with clofibrate have suggested that it may increase the patient's risk of cancer, liver disease, pancreatitis (inflammation of the pancreas), gallstones and problems from gallbladder surgery, although it may also decrease the risk of heart attacks. Other studies have not found all of these effects.

Studies with gemfibrozil in rats found an increased risk of liver tumors when doses up to 10 times the human dose were given for a long time.

Be sure you have discussed this with your doctor before taking this medicine.

In deciding to use a medicine, the risks of taking the medicine must be weighed against the good it will do. This is a decision you and your doctor will make. For gemfibrozil, the following should be considered:

Allergies—Tell your doctor if you have ever had any unusual or allergic reaction to gemfibrozil. Also tell your health care professional if you are allergic to any other substances, such as foods, preservatives, or dyes.

Diet—Before prescribing medicine for your condition, your doctor will probably try to control your condition by prescribing a personal diet for you. Such a diet may be low in fats, sugars, and/or cholesterol. Many people are able to control their condition by carefully following their doctor's orders for proper diet and exercise. *Medicine is prescribed only when additional help is needed* and is effective only when a schedule of diet and exercise is properly followed.

Also, this medicine is less effective if you are greatly overweight. It may be very important for you to go on a reducing diet. However, check with your doctor before going on any diet.

Make certain your health care professional knows if you are on a low-sodium, low-sugar, or any other special diet. Most medicines contain more than their active ingredient.

Pregnancy—Gemfibrozil has not been studied in pregnant women. However, studies in animals have shown that high doses of gemfibrozil may increase the number of fetal deaths, decrease birth weight, or cause some skeletal defects. Before taking this medicine, make sure your doctor knows if you are pregnant or if you may become pregnant.

Breast-feeding—It is not known whether gemfibrozil passes into breast milk. However, studies in animals have shown that high doses of gemfibrozil may increase the risk of some kinds of tumors. Therefore, you should consider this when deciding whether to breast-feed your baby while taking this medicine.

Children—There is no specific information about the use of gemfibrozil in children. However, use is not recommended in children under 2 years of age since cholesterol is needed for normal development.

Older adults—Many medicines have not been studied specifically in older people. Therefore, it may not be known whether they work exactly the same way they do in younger adults or if they cause different side effects or problems in older people. There is no specific information comparing use of gemfibrozil in the elderly with use in other age groups.

Other medicines—Although certain medicines should not be used together at all, in other cases two different medicines may be used together even if an interaction might occur. In these cases, your doctor may want to change the dose, or other precautions may be necessary. When you are taking gemfibrozil it is especially important that your health care professional know if you are taking any of the following:

- Anticoagulants (blood thinners)—Use with gemfibrozil may increase the effect of the anticoagulant
- Lovastatin—Use with gemfibrozil may cause muscle or kidney problems or make them worse

Other medical problems—The presence of other medical problems may affect the use of gemfibrozil. Make sure you tell your doctor if you have any other medical problems, especially:

- Gallbladder disease or
- Gallstones—Gemfibrozil may make these conditions worse
- Kidney disease or

• Liver disease—Higher blood levels of gemfibrozil may result, which may increase the chance of side effects; a decrease in the dose of gemfibrozil may be needed

Proper Use of This Medicine

Use this medicine only as directed by your doctor. Do not use more or less of it, and do not use it more often or for a longer time than your doctor ordered.

This medicine is usually taken twice a day. If you are taking 2 doses a day, it is best to take the medicine 30 minutes before your breakfast and evening meal.

Follow carefully the special diet your doctor gave you. This is the most important part of controlling your condition and is necessary if the medicine is to work properly.

Dosing—The dose of gemfibrozil will be different for different patients. *Follow your doctor's orders or the directions on the label.* The following information includes only the average doses of gemfibrozil. *If your dose is different, do not change it* unless your doctor tells you to do so:

- For *oral* dosage forms (tablets):
  —Adults: 600 milligrams two times a day to be taken thirty minutes before the morning and evening meals.

Missed dose—If you miss a dose of this medicine, take it as soon as possible. However, if it is almost time for your next dose, skip the missed dose and go back to your regular dosing schedule. Do not double doses.

Storage—To store this medicine:

- Keep out of the reach of children.
- Store away from heat and direct light.
- Do not store in the bathroom, near the kitchen sink, or in other damp places. Heat or moisture may cause the medicine to break down.
- Do not keep outdated medicine or medicine no longer needed. Be sure that any discarded medicine is out of the reach of children.

Precautions While Using This Medicine

It is very important that your doctor check your progress at regular visits. This will allow your doctor to see if the medicine is working properly to lower your cholesterol and triglyceride levels and to decide if you should continue to take it.

Do not stop taking this medication without first checking with your doctor. When you stop taking this medicine, your blood cholesterol levels may increase again. Your doctor may want you to follow a special diet to help prevent this from happening.

Side Effects of This Medicine

Along with its needed effects, a medicine may cause some unwanted effects. Although not all of these side effects may occur, if they do occur they may need medical attention.

Check with your doctor immediately if any of the following side effects occur:

Rare
Cough or hoarseness; fever or chills; lower back or side pain; painful or difficult urination; stomach pain (severe) with nausea and vomiting

Check with your doctor as soon as possible if either of the following side effects occurs:

Rare
Muscle pain; unusual tiredness or weakness

Other side effects may occur that usually do not need medical attention. These side effects may go away during treatment as your body adjusts to the medicine. However, check with your doctor if any of the following side effects continue or are bothersome:

More common
Stomach pain, gas, or heartburn

Less common
Diarrhea; nausea or vomiting; skin rash

Other side effects not listed above may also occur in some patients. If you notice any other effects, check with your doctor.

Revised: 05/24/93
Interim revision: 06/28/95

GENTAMICIN Ophthalmic

Some commonly used brand names are:

In the U.S.—

Garamycin
Genoptic Liquifilm
Genoptic S.O.P.
Gentacidin
Gentafair
Gentak
Gentrasul
Ocu-Mycin
Spectro-Genta

Generic name product may also be available.

In Canada—

Alcomicin
Garamycin
Gentrasul

Another commonly used name is gentamycin.

Description

Gentamicin (jen-ta-MYE-sin) belongs to the family of medicines called antibiotics. Gentamicin ophthalmic preparations are used to treat infections of the eye.

Gentamicin is available only with your doctor's prescription, in the following dosage forms:

Ophthalmic
- Ophthalmic ointment (U.S. and Canada)
- Ophthalmic solution (eye drops) (U.S. and Canada)

Before Using This Medicine

In deciding to use a medicine, the risks of using the medicine must be weighed against the good it will do. This is a decision you and your doctor will make. For ophthalmic gentamicin, the following should be considered:

Allergies—Tell your doctor if you have ever had any unusual or allergic reaction to this medicine or to any related antibiotic, such as amikacin (e.g., Amikin), gentamicin by injection (e.g., Garamycin), kanamycin (e.g., Kantrex), neomycin (e.g., Mycifradin), netilmicin (e.g., Netromycin), streptomycin, or tobramycin (e.g., Nebcin). Also tell your health care professional if you are allergic to any other substances, such as preservatives.

Pregnancy—Gentamicin ophthalmic preparations have not been shown to cause birth defects or other problems in humans.

Breast-feeding—Gentamicin ophthalmic preparations have not been reported to cause problems in nursing babies.

Children—Studies on this medicine have been done only in adult patients, and there is no specific information comparing use of this medicine in children with use in other age groups.

Older adults—Many medicines have not been studied specifically in older people. Therefore, it may not be known whether they work exactly the same way they do in younger adults or if they cause different side effects or problems in older people. There is no specific information comparing use of this medicine in the elderly with use in other age groups.

Proper Use of This Medicine

For patients using the *eye drop form* of this medicine:

- The bottle is only partially full to provide proper drop control.
- To use:
  —First, wash your hands. Tilt the head back and with the index finger of one hand, press gently on the skin just beneath the lower eyelid and pull the lower eyelid away from the eye to make a space. Drop the medicine into this space. Let go of the eyelid and gently close the eyes. Do not blink. Keep the eyes closed for 1 or 2 minutes, to allow the medicine to come into contact with the infection.
- If you think you did not get the drop of medicine into your eye properly, use another drop.
- To keep the medicine as germ-free as possible, do not touch the applicator tip to any surface (including the eye). Also, keep the container tightly closed.

For patients using the *eye ointment form* of this medicine:

- First, wash your hands. Tilt the head back and with the index finger of one hand, press gently on the skin just beneath the lower eyelid and pull the lower eyelid away from the eye to make a space. Squeeze a thin strip of ointment into this space. A 1-cm (approximately 1/3-inch) strip of ointment is usually enough unless otherwise directed by your doctor. Let go of the eyelid and gently close the eyes and keep them closed for 1 or 2 minutes, to allow the medicine to come into contact with the infection.
- To keep the medicine as germ-free as possible, do not touch the applicator tip to any surface (including the eye). After using gentamicin eye ointment, wipe the tip of the ointment tube with a clean tissue and keep the tube tightly closed.

To help clear up your infection completely, *keep using this medicine for the full time of treatment,* even if your symptoms have disappeared. *Do not miss any doses.*

Dosing—The dose of ophthalmic gentamicin will be different for different patients. *Follow your doctor's orders or the directions on the label.* The following information includes only the average doses of ophthalmic gentamicin. *If your dose is different, do not change it* unless your doctor tells you to do so.

- For *ophthalmic ointment* dosage form:
  —For eye infections:
  - Adults and children—Use every eight to twelve hours.
- For *ophthalmic solution (eye drops)* dosage form:
  —For mild to moderate eye infections:
  - Adults and children—One drop every four hours.

  —For severe eye infections:
  - Adults and children—One drop every hour.

Missed dose—If you do miss a dose of this medicine, apply it as soon as possible. However, if it is almost time for your next dose, skip the missed dose and go back to your regular dosing schedule.

Storage—To store this medicine:

- Keep out of the reach of children.
- Store away from heat and direct light.
- Keep the medicine from freezing.
- Do not keep outdated medicine or medicine no longer needed. Be sure that any discarded medicine is out of the reach of children.

Precautions While Using This Medicine

If your symptoms do not improve within a few days, or if they become worse, check with your doctor.

Side Effects of This Medicine

Along with its needed effects, a medicine may cause some unwanted effects. Although not all of these side effects may occur, if they do occur they may need medical attention.

Check with your doctor immediately if any of the following side effects occur:

Less common

Itching, redness, swelling, or other sign of irritation not present before use of this medicine

Other side effects may occur that usually do not need medical attention. These side effects may go away during treatment as your body adjusts to the medicine. However,

check with your doctor if either of the following side effects continues or is bothersome:

Less common

Burning or stinging

After application, eye ointments usually cause your vision to blur for a few minutes.

Other side effects not listed above may also occur in some patients. If you notice any other effects, check with your doctor.

Revised: 6/23/92
Interim revision: 8/30/93

GENTAMICIN Otic*

A commonly used brand name in Canada is Garamycin Otic Solution*.

*Not commercially available in the U.S.

Description

Gentamicin (jen-ta-MYE-sin) belongs to the family of medicines called antibiotics. Gentamicin otic preparations are used to treat infections of the ear canal.

Gentamicin is available only with your doctor's prescription, in the following dosage form:

Otic

- Solution (Canada)

Before Using This Medicine

In deciding to use a medicine, the risks of using the medicine must be weighed against the good it will do. This is a decision you and your doctor will make. For gentamicin otic preparations, the following should be considered:

Allergies—Tell your doctor if you have ever had any unusual or allergic reaction to this medicine or to any related antibiotics such as amikacin (e.g., Amikin), gentamicin by injection (e.g., Garamycin), kanamycin (e.g., Kantrex), neomycin (e.g., Mycifradin), netilmicin (e.g., Netromycin), streptomycin, or tobramycin (e.g., Nebcin). Also tell your health care professional if you are allergic to any other substances, such as preservatives.

Pregnancy—Gentamicin otic preparations have not been shown to cause birth defects or other problems in humans.

Breast-feeding—Gentamicin otic preparations have not been reported to cause problems in nursing babies.

Children—Although there is no specific information comparing use of this medicine in children with use in other age groups, this medicine is not expected to cause different side effects or problems in children than it does in adults.

Older adults—Many medicines have not been studied specifically in older people. Therefore, it may not be known whether they work exactly the same way they do in younger adults. Although there is no specific information comparing use of this medicine in the elderly with use in other age groups, this medicine is not expected to cause different side effects or problems in older people than it does in younger adults.

Other medical problems—The presence of other medical problems may affect the use of gentamicin otic preparations. Make sure you tell your doctor if you have any other medical problems, especially:

- Any other ear infection or problem (including punctured eardrum)—Use of gentamicin otic preparations in persons with this condition may lead to systemic absorption, and increase the chance of side effects

Proper Use of This Medicine

To use:

- Lie down or tilt the head so that the infected ear faces up. Gently pull the earlobe up and back for adults (down and back for children) to straighten the ear canal. Drop the medicine into the ear canal. Keep the ear facing up for about 1 or 2 minutes to allow the medicine to come into contact with the infection. A sterile cotton plug may be gently inserted into the ear opening to prevent the medicine from leaking out.
- To keep the medicine as germ-free as possible, do not touch the applicator tip to any surface (including the ear). Also, keep the container tightly closed.

To help clear up your infection completely, *keep using this medicine for the full time of treatment,* even if your symptoms have disappeared. *Do not miss any doses.*

Dosing—The dose of gentamicin otic will be different for different patients. *Follow your doctor's orders or the directions on the label.* The following information includes only the average doses of gentamicin otic. *If your dose is different, do not change it* unless your doctor tells you to do so.

- For *ear drops* dosage form:
  - —For ear infections:
    - Adults and children—Place three or four drops in the ear three times a day.

Missed dose—If you miss a dose of this medicine, apply it as soon as possible. However, if it is almost time for your next dose, skip the missed dose and go back to your regular dosing schedule.

Storage—To store this medicine:

- Keep out of the reach of children.
- Store away from heat and direct light.
- Keep the medicine from freezing.
- Do not keep outdated medicine or medicine no longer needed. Be sure that any discarded medicine is out of the reach of children.

Precautions While Using This Medicine

If your symptoms do not improve within a few days, or if they become worse, check with your doctor.

Side Effects of This Medicine

Along with its needed effects, a medicine may cause some unwanted effects. Although not all of these side effects may occur, if they do occur they may need medical attention.

Check with your doctor immediately if any of the following side effects occur:

Less common

Itching, redness, swelling, or other sign of irritation not present before use of this medicine

Other side effects may occur that usually do not need medical attention. These side effects may go away during treatment as your body adjusts to the medicine. However, check with your doctor if either of the following side effects continues or is bothersome:

Less common

Burning or stinging

Other side effects not listed above may also occur in some patients. If you notice any other effects, check with your doctor.

Revised: 08/12/92
Interim revision: 04/11/94

GENTAMICIN Topical

Some commonly used brand names are:

In the U.S.—

Garamycin
G-Myticin
Gentamar

Generic name product may also be available.

In Canada—

Garamycin

Description

Gentamicin (jen-ta-MYE-sin) belongs to the family of medicines called antibiotics. Gentamicin topical preparations are used to treat infections of the skin.

Gentamicin is available only with your doctor's prescription, in the following dosage forms:

Topical

- Cream (U.S. and Canada)
- Ointment (U.S. and Canada)

Before Using This Medicine

In deciding to use a medicine, the risks of using the medicine must be weighed against the good it will do. This is a decision you and your doctor will make. For topical gentamicin, the following should be considered:

Allergies—Tell your doctor if you have ever had any unusual or allergic reaction to this medicine or any related antibiotics, such as amikacin (e.g., Amikin), gentamicin by injection (e.g., Garamycin), kanamycin (e.g., Kantrex), neomycin (e.g., Mycifradin), netilmicin (e.g., Netromycin), streptomycin, or tobramycin (e.g., Nebcin). Also tell your health care professional if you are allergic to any other substances, such as preservatives or dyes.

Pregnancy—Gentamicin topical preparations have not been shown to cause birth defects or other problems in humans.

Breast-feeding—Gentamicin topical preparations have not been reported to cause problems in nursing babies.

Children—This medicine has been tested in children over 1 year of age and, in effective doses, has not been shown to cause different side effects or problems than it does in adults.

Older adults—Many medicine have not been studied specifically in older people. Therefore, it may not be known whether they work exactly the same way they do in younger adults. Although there is no specific information comparing use of this medicine in the elderly with use in other age groups, this medicine is not expected to cause different side effects or problems in older people than it does in younger adults.

Other medicines—Although certain medicines should not be used together at all, in other cases two different medicines may be used together even if an interaction might occur. In these cases, your doctor may want to change the dose, or other precautions may be necessary. Tell your health care professional if you are using any other topical prescription or nonprescription (over-the-counter [OTC]) medicine that is to be applied to the same area of the skin.

Proper Use of This Medicine

Before applying this medicine, wash the affected area with soap and water, and dry thoroughly. Apply a small amount to the affected area and rub in gently.

After this medicine is applied, the treated area may be covered with a gauze dressing if desired.

To help clear up your infection completely, *keep using this medicine for the full time of treatment,* even though your symptoms may have disappeared. *Do not miss any doses.*

Dosing—The dose of topical gentamicin will be different for different patients. *Follow your doctor's orders or the directions on the label.* The following information includes only the average dose of topical gentamicin. *If your dose is different, do not change it* unless your doctor tells you to do so.

- For *topical* dosage forms (cream or ointment):
  - —For bacterial infections:
    - Adults and children 1 year of age and over—Apply to affected area(s) of the skin three or four times a day.

Missed dose—If you miss a dose of this medicine, apply it as soon as possible. However, if it is almost time for your next dose, skip the missed dose and go back to your regular dosing schedule.

Storage—To store this medicine:

- Keep out of the reach of children.
- Store away from heat and direct light.
- Keep the medicine from freezing.
- Do not keep outdated medicine or medicine no longer needed. Be sure that any discarded medicine is out of the reach of children.

Precautions While Using This Medicine

If your skin problem does not improve within 1 week, or if it becomes worse, check with your doctor.

Side Effects of This Medicine

Along with its needed effects, a medicine may cause some unwanted effects. Although not all of these side effects may occur, if they do occur they may need medical attention.

Check with your doctor immediately if any of the following side effects occur:

Less common

Itching, redness, swelling, or other sign of irritation not present before use of this medicine

Other side effects not listed above may also occur in some patients. If you notice any other effects, check with your doctor.

Revised: 06/23/92
Interim revision: 06/08/94

GLUCAGON Systemic

A commonly used brand name in the U.S. and Canada is Glucagon Emergency Kit.

Description

Glucagon (GLOO-ka-gon) belongs to the group of medicines called hormones. It is an emergency medicine used to treat severe hypoglycemia (low blood sugar) in patients with diabetes who have passed out or cannot take some form of sugar by mouth.

Glucagon is also used during x-ray tests of the stomach and bowels. Glucagon helps to improve test results by relaxing the muscles of the stomach and bowels. This also makes the testing more comfortable for the patient.

Glucagon may also be used for other conditions as determined by your doctor.

Glucagon is available only with your doctor's prescription, in the following dosage form:

Parenteral

- Injection (U.S. and Canada)

Before Using This Medicine

In deciding to use a medicine, the risks of taking the medicine must be weighed against the good it will do. This is a decision you and your doctor will make. For glucagon, the following should be considered:

Allergies—Tell your doctor if you have ever had any unusual or allergic reaction to glucagon or other proteins. Also, tell your health care professional if you are allergic to any other substances, such as foods, preservatives, or dyes.

Pregnancy—Glucagon has not been studied in pregnant women. However, glucagon has not been shown to cause birth defects or other problems in animal studies.

Breast-feeding—It is not known whether glucagon passes into breast milk. However, this medicine has not been reported to cause problems in nursing babies.

Children—This medicine has been tested in children and, in effective doses, has not been shown to cause different side effects or problems than it does in adults.

Older adults—Many medicines have not been studied specifically in older people. Therefore, it may not be known whether they work exactly the same way they do in younger adults. Although there is no specific information comparing use of glucagon in the elderly with use in other age groups, it is not expected to cause different side effects or problems in older people than it does in younger adults.

Other medicines—Although certain medicines should not be used together at all, in other cases two different medicines may be used together even if an interaction might occur. In these cases, your doctor may want to change the doses or other precautions may be necessary. Tell your health care professional if you are using any other prescription or nonprescription (over-the-counter [OTC]) medicine.

Other medical problems—The presence of other medical problems may affect the use of glucagon. Make sure you tell your doctor if you have any other medical problems, especially:

- Diabetes mellitus—When glucagon is used for test or x-ray procedures in diabetes that is well-controlled, too high blood sugar may occur; otherwise, glucagon is an important part of the management of diabetes because it is used to treat hypoglycemia (low blood sugar)
- Insulinoma (tumors of the pancreas gland that make too much insulin) (or history of)—Blood sugar concentrations may decrease
- Pheochromocytoma—Glucagon can cause high blood pressure

Proper Use of This Medicine

Dosing—The dose of glucagon will be different for different patients. *Follow your doctor's orders or the directions on the label.* The following information includes only the average doses of glucagon. *If your dose is different, do not change it* unless your doctor tells you to do so.

- As an *emergency treatment for hypoglycemia:*
  —Adults and adolescents: 0.5 to 1 milligram. The dose may be repeated in 20 minutes if necessary.
  —Children: Dose is based on body weight (25 micrograms of glucagon per kilogram [11.4 micrograms per pound] of body weight). The dose may be repeated in 20 minutes if necessary.

Glucagon is an emergency medicine and must be used only as directed by your doctor. *Make sure that you and your family or a friend understand exactly when and how to use this medicine before it must be used.*

Some brands of glucagon come in a kit of 2 vials (one powder containing the medicine and one liquid to mix the medicine with). The contents of these 2 vials must be mixed before use. Other brands of glucagon are packaged in a kit with a vial of powder containing the medicine and a syringe filled with liquid to mix the medicine with. *Directions for mixing and injecting are in the package. Read them carefully* and ask your health care professional for additional explanation, if necessary.

If your glucagon kit does not already have a syringe in it, your doctor may want you to inject glucagon with the type of syringe you normally use to inject your insulin. Other patients may be told to use a different type of syringe that will allow a deeper injection. If you have any questions about the type of syringe you should be using, check with your health care professional. Also, you should *regularly check to see if you have a sterile syringe and needles always available* to be used for the glucagon. It is a good idea to keep a sterile syringe taped to the glucagon carton.

Glucagon is usually mixed when an emergency occurs. However, it may be mixed ahead of time and kept in the refrigerator, ready for use. The date of mixing should then be written on the package. Mixed glucagon kept more than 48 hours (2 full days) (even if it is refrigerated) should be discarded and replaced by a fresh preparation.

Glucagon should not be mixed after the expiration date printed on the kit and on one vial. *Check the date regularly and replace the medicine before it expires.* The printed expiration date does not apply after mixing.

Storage—To store this medicine:

- Keep out of the reach of children.
- Store away from heat and direct light.
- Store the unmixed medication at room temperature.
- Do not store the unmixed or mixed medication in the bathroom, near the kitchen sink, or in other damp places. Heat or moisture may cause the medicine to break down.
- Store the mixed solution in the refrigerator for no longer than 48 hours. Do not allow it to freeze.
- Do not keep outdated medicine or medicine no longer needed. Be sure that any discarded medicine is out of the reach of children.

Precautions While Using This Medicine

Diabetic patients should be aware of the symptoms of hypoglycemia (low blood sugar). These symptoms may develop in a very short time and may result from:

- using too much insulin (''insulin reaction'') or as a side effect from oral antidiabetes medicines.
- delaying or missing a scheduled snack or meal.
- sickness (especially with vomiting).
- exercising more than usual.

Unless corrected, hypoglycemia will lead to unconsciousness, convulsions (seizures), and possibly death. Early symptoms of hypoglycemia include:

Abdominal or stomach pain (mild)
Anxious feeling
Chills (continuing)
Cold sweats
Confusion
Cool pale skin
Difficulty in concentrating
Drowsiness
Excessive hunger
Fast heartbeat
Headache (continuing)
Nausea or vomiting (continuing)
Nervousness
Shakiness
Unsteady walk
Unusual tiredness or weakness
Vision changes

- Symptoms of hypoglycemia can differ from person to person. It is important that you learn your own signs of low blood sugar so that you can treat it quickly. It is a good idea also to check your blood sugar to confirm that it is low.
- *Eat or drink something containing sugar and check with your doctor right away if mild symptoms of low blood sugar (hypoglycemia) appear.* Doing this when symptoms of hypoglycemia first appear will usually prevent them from getting worse, and will probably make the use of glucagon unnecessary. Good sources of sugar include glucose tablets or gel, fruit juice, corn syrup, honey, nondiet soft drinks, or sugar cubes or table sugar (dissolved in water).
- *Tell someone to take you to your doctor or to a hospital right away if the symptoms do not improve after eating or drinking a sweet food. Do not try to drive yourself.*
- Even if you correct these symptoms by eating sugar, it is very important to call your doctor or hospital emergency service right away. Then, eat some food (such as crackers and cheese, half a sandwich, or milk) to keep your blood sugar from going down again.
- Check your blood sugar again to make sure it is not still too low.
- *If severe symptoms such as convulsions (seizures) or unconsciousness occur, diabetics should not eat or drink anything.* There is a chance that they could choke from not swallowing correctly. Emergency medical help should be obtained immediately.

If it becomes necessary to inject glucagon in an unconscious patient, a family member or friend should know the following:

- *After injection, turn the unconscious patient on his or her side.* Glucagon may cause some patients to vomit and this position will reduce the possibility of choking.
- *Call the patient's doctor at once.*
- The patient should become conscious in less than 15 minutes after glucagon is injected into the muscle, but if not, a second dose may be given. *Get the patient to a doctor or to hospital emergency care as soon as possible,* since being unconscious too long can be harmful.
- *When the patient is conscious and can swallow, give some form of sugar.* Glucagon is not effective for much longer than 1½ hours and is *used only until the patient is able to swallow.* Fruit juice, corn syrup, honey, and sugar cubes or table sugar (dissolved in water) all work quickly. Then, if a snack or meal is not scheduled for an hour or more, the patient should also eat some crackers and cheese or half a sandwich, or drink a glass of milk. This will prevent hypoglycemia from occurring again before the next meal or snack.
- The patient or care-giver should continue to monitor the patient's blood sugar. For about 3 to 4 hours after the patient is conscious, check his or her blood sugar every hour.
- *If nausea prevents a patient from swallowing some form of sugar for an hour after glucagon is given, medical help should be obtained.*

Keep your doctor informed of any hypoglycemic episodes or use of glucagon even if the symptoms are successfully controlled and there seem to be no continuing problems. Complete information is necessary to provide the best possible treatment of any condition.

Replace your supply of glucagon as soon as possible, in case another hypoglycemic episode occurs.

You should wear a medical I.D. bracelet or chain at all times. In addition, you should carry an identification card that lists your medical conditions and medications.

Side Effects of This Medicine

Along with its needed effects, a medicine may cause some unwanted effects. Although not all of these side effects may occur, if they do occur they may need medical attention.

Get emergency help immediately if any of the following side effects occur:

Less common

Dizziness; lightheadedness; trouble in breathing

Symptoms of overdose

Irregular heartbeat; loss of appetite; muscle cramps or pain; nausea (continuing); vomiting (continuing); weakness of arms, legs, and trunk (severe)

Check with your doctor as soon as possible if any of the following side effects occur:

Less common

Skin rash or hives

Other side effects may occur that usually do not need medical attention. These side effects may go away during treatment as your body adjusts to the medicine. However, check with your doctor if any of the following side effects continue or are bothersome:

Nausea; vomiting

Other side effects not listed above may also occur in some patients. If you notice any other effects, check with your doctor.

Additional Information

Once a medicine has been approved for marketing for a certain use, experience may show that it is also useful for other medical problems. Although these uses are not included in product labeling, glucagon is used in certain patients with the following medical conditions or undergoing certain medical procedures:

- Overdose of beta-blocker medicines
- Overdose of calcium channel blockers
- Removing food or an object stuck in the esophagus
- Hysterosalpingography (x-ray examination of the uterus and fallopian tubes)

Other than the above information, there is no additional information relating to proper use, precautions, or side effects for these uses.

Revised: 01/13/93

GLYCERIN Systemic

Some commonly used brand names in the U.S. are Glyrol and Osmoglyn.

Generic name product may also be available in the U.S.

Description

Glycerin (GLI-ser-in), when taken by mouth, is used to treat certain conditions in which there is increased eye pressure, such as glaucoma. It may also be used before eye surgery to reduce pressure in the eye.

Glycerin may also be used for other conditions as determined by your doctor.

This medicine is available only with your doctor's prescription, in the following dosage form:

Oral

- Oral solution (U.S.)

Before Using This Medicine

In deciding to use a medicine, the risks of taking the medicine must be weighed against the good it will do. This is a decision you and your doctor will make. For glycerin, the following should be considered:

Allergies—Tell your doctor if you have ever had any unusual or allergic reaction to glycerin. Also tell your health care professional if you are allergic to any other substances, such as foods, preservatives, or dyes.

Pregnancy—Studies on effects in pregnancy have not been done in either humans or animals.

Breast-feeding—It is not known whether glycerin passes into breast milk. This medicine has not been reported to cause problems in nursing babies.

Children—Although there is no specific information comparing use of glycerin in children with use in other age groups, this medicine is not expected to cause different side effects or problems in children than it does in adults.

Older adults—Glycerin reduces water in the body, and there may be an increased risk that elderly patients taking it could become dehydrated.

Other medicines—Although certain medicines should not be used together at all, in other cases two different medicines may be used together even if an interaction might occur. In these cases, your doctor may want to change the dose, or other precautions may be necessary. Tell your health care professional if you are taking any other prescription or nonprescription (over-the-counter [OTC]) medicine.

Other medical problems—The presence of other medical problems may affect the use of glycerin. Make sure you tell your doctor if you have any other medical problems, especially:

- Diabetes mellitus (sugar diabetes)—Use of glycerin may increase the chance of dehydration (loss of too much body water)
- Confused mental states or
- Heart disease or
- Kidney disease—Glycerin may make these conditions worse

Proper Use of This Medicine

It is very important that you take this medicine only as directed. Do not take more of it and do not take it more often than your doctor ordered.

To improve the taste of this medicine, mix it with a small amount of unsweetened lemon, lime, or orange juice, pour over cracked ice, and sip through a straw.

Dosing—The dose of glycerin will be different for different patients. *Follow your doctor's orders or the directions on the label.* The following information includes only the average doses of glycerin. *If your dose is different, do not change it* unless your doctor tells you to do so.

- For *oral* dosage form (oral solution):
  —To lower pressure in the eye:
    - Adults—Dose is based on body weight and must be determined by your doctor. The usual dose is 1 to 2 grams per kilogram (kg) (0.45 to 0.91 grams per pound) of body weight taken one time. Then, additional doses of 500 milligrams (mg) per kg (227 mg per pound) of body weight every six hours may be taken if needed.
    - Children—Dose is based on body weight and must be determined by your doctor. The usual dose is 1 to 1.5 grams per kg (0.45 to 0.68 grams per pound) of body weight taken one time. The dose may be repeated in four to eight hours if needed.

Missed dose—If you miss a dose of this medicine, take it as soon as possible. However, if it is almost time for your next dose, skip the missed dose and go back to your regular dosing schedule. Do not double doses.

Storage—To store this medicine:

- Keep out of the reach of children.
- Store away from heat and direct light.
- Do not store in the bathroom, near the kitchen sink, or in other damp places. Heat or moisture may cause the medicine to break down.
- Keep the medicine from freezing.
- Do not keep outdated medicine or medicine no longer needed. Be sure that any discarded medicine is out of the reach of children.

Precautions While Using This Medicine

Your doctor should check your progress at regular visits to make sure that this medicine is working properly.

In some patients, headaches may occur when this medicine is taken. To help prevent or relieve the headache, lie down while you are taking this medicine and for a short time after taking it. If headaches become severe or continue, check with your doctor.

Side Effects of This Medicine

Along with its needed effects, a medicine may cause some unwanted effects. Although not all of these side effects may occur, if they do occur they may need medical attention.

Check with your doctor as soon as possible if either of the following side effects occurs:

Less common
Confusion

Rare
Irregular heartbeat

Other side effects may occur that usually do not need medical attention. These side effects may go away during treatment as your body adjusts to the medicine. However, check with your doctor if any of the following side effects continue or are bothersome:

More common
Headache; nausea or vomiting

Less common
Diarrhea; dizziness; dryness of mouth or increased thirst

Other side effects not listed above may also occur in some patients. If you notice any other effects, check with your doctor.

Additional Information

Once a medicine has been approved for marketing for a certain use, experience may show that it is also useful for other medical problems. Although this use is not included in product labeling, glycerin is used in certain patients with the following medical conditions:

- Cerebral edema (swelling of the brain)

Other than the above information, there is no additional information relating to proper use, precautions, or side effects for these uses.

Revised: 08/03/94

GOLD COMPOUNDS Systemic

Some commonly used brand names are:

In the U.S.—

Myochrysine[3] Solganal[2]
Ridaura[1]

In Canada—

Myochrysine[3] Ridaura[1]

Note: For quick reference, the following gold compounds are numbered to match the corresponding brand names.

This information applies to the following medicines:

1. Auranofin (au-RANE-oh-fin)
2. Aurothioglucose (aur-oh-thye-oh-GLOO-kose)
3. Gold Sodium Thiomalate (gold SO-dee-um thye-oh-MAH-late)‡

‡Generic name product may also be available in the U.S.

Description

The gold compounds are used in the treatment of rheumatoid arthritis. They may also be used for other conditions as determined by your doctor.

In addition to the helpful effects of this medicine in treating your medical problem, it has side effects that can be very serious. Before you take this medicine, you should discuss with your doctor the good that this medicine will do as well as the risks of using it.

Auranofin is available only with your doctor's prescription. The other gold compounds are given by your health care professional.

These medicines are available in the following dosage forms:

Oral

Auranofin

- Capsules (U.S. and Canada)

Parenteral

Aurothioglucose

- Injection (U.S.)

Gold sodium thiomalate

- Injection (U.S. and Canada)

Before Using This Medicine

In deciding to use a medicine, the risks of taking the medicine must be weighed against the good it will do. This is a decision you and your doctor will make. For gold compounds, the following should be considered:

Allergies—Tell your doctor if you have ever had any unusual or allergic reaction to gold or other metals, if you have received a gold compound before and developed serious side effects from it, or if any medicine you have taken has caused an allergy or a reaction that affected your blood. Also tell your health care professional if you are allergic to any other substances, such as foods, preservatives, or dyes.

Pregnancy—Studies on birth defects with gold compounds have not been done in humans. However, studies in animals have shown that gold compounds may cause birth defects.

Breast-feeding—Aurothioglucose and gold sodium thiomalate pass into the breast milk and may cause unwanted effects in nursing babies. It is not known whether auranofin passes into the breast milk.

Children—Auranofin has been tested only in adult patients and there is no specific information about its use in children. However, aurothioglucose and gold sodium thiomalate have been tested in children and have not been shown to cause different side effects or problems than they do in adults.

Older adults—These medicines have been tested and have not been shown to cause different side effects or problems in older people than they do in younger adults.

Other medicines—Although certain medicines should not be used together at all, in other cases two different medicines may be used together even if an interaction might occur. In these cases, your doctor may want to change the dose, or other precautions may be necessary. When you are taking a gold compound, it is important that your health care professional know if you are taking *any* other prescription or nonprescription (over-the-counter [OTC]) medicine, especially:

- Penicillamine (e.g., Cuprimine)—The chance of side effects may be increased.

Other medical problems—The presence of other medical problems may affect the use of gold compounds. Make sure you tell your doctor if you have any other medical problems, especially:

- Blood or blood vessel disease or
- Colitis or
- Kidney disease (or history of) or
- Lupus erythematosus or
- Sjögren's syndrome or
- Skin disease—The chance of unwanted effects may be increased

Proper Use of This Medicine

In order for this medicine to work, it must be taken regularly as ordered by your doctor. Continue receiving the injections or taking auranofin even if you think the medicine is not working. You may not notice the effects of this medicine until after three to six months of regular use.

For patients taking *auranofin:*

- *Do not take more of this medicine than ordered by your doctor.* Taking too much auranofin may increase the chance of serious unwanted effects.

If you have any questions about this, check with your doctor.

Dosing—The dose of these medicines will be different for different patients. *Follow your doctor's orders or the directions on the label.* The following information includes only the average doses of these medicines. *If your dose is different, do not change it* unless your doctor tells you to do so.

For auranofin

- For *oral* dosage form (capsules):
  - —For arthritis:
    - Adults—6 milligrams (mg) once a day or 3 mg twice a day. After six months, your doctor may increase the dose to 3 mg three times a day.
    - Children—Dose must be determined by your doctor.

For aurothioglucose

- For *injection* dosage form:
  - —For arthritis:
    - Adults and teenagers—10 milligrams (mg) for the first dose, then 25 mg once a week for the next two weeks, then 25 or 50 mg once a week. The medicine is injected into a muscle. After several months, the injections may be given less often (25 or 50 mg every two weeks for a while, then every three or four weeks).
    - Children 6 to 12 years of age—2.5 mg for the first dose, then 6.25 mg once a week for the next two weeks, then 12.5 mg once a week. The medicine is injected into a muscle. After several months, the injections may be given less often (6.25 or 12.5 mg every three or four weeks).
    - Children younger than 6 years of age—Dose must be determined by your doctor.

For gold sodium thiomalate

- For *injection* dosage form:
  - —For arthritis:
    - Adults and teenagers—10 milligrams (mg) for the first dose, then 25 mg a week later, then 25 or 50 mg once a week. The medicine is injected into a muscle. After several months, the injections may be given less often (25 or 50 mg every two weeks for a while, then every three or four weeks).
    - Children—10 mg for the first dose, then 1 mg per kilogram (about 0.45 mg per pound) of body weight, but not more than a total of 50 mg, once a week. The medicine is injected into a muscle. After several months, the same dose may be given less often (every two weeks for a while, then every three or four weeks).

Missed dose—For patients taking *auranofin:* If you miss a dose of this medicine, and your dosing schedule is—

- One dose a day—Take the missed dose as soon as possible. However, if you do not remember until the next day, skip the missed dose and go back to your regular dosing schedule. Do not double doses.
- More than one dose a day—Take the missed dose as soon as possible. However, if it is almost time for your next dose, skip the missed dose and go back to your regular dosing schedule. Do not double doses.

Storage—To store this medicine:

- Keep out of the reach of children.
- Store away from heat and direct light.
- Do not store this medicine in the bathroom, near the kitchen sink, or in other damp places. Heat or moisture may cause the medicine to break down.
- Do not keep outdated medicine or medicine no longer needed. Be sure that any discarded medicine is out of the reach of children.

Precautions While Using This Medicine

Gold compounds may cause some people to become more sensitive to sunlight than they are normally. These people may break out in a rash after being in the sun, or a skin rash that is already present may become worse. To protect yourself, it is best to:

- Stay out of direct sunlight, especially between the hours of 10:00 a.m. and 3:00 p.m., if possible.
- Wear protective clothing.
- Ask your doctor if you may apply a sun block product. Products that have a skin protection factor (SPF) of at least 15 work best, but some patients may require a product with a higher SPF number, especially if they have a fair complexion.
- Do not use a sunlamp or tanning bed or booth.

If you have a severe reaction from the sun, check with your doctor.

For patients taking *auranofin:*

- Your doctor should check your progress at regular visits. Blood and urine tests may be needed to make certain that this medicine is not causing unwanted effects.

For patients receiving *gold injections:*

- Immediately following an injection of this medicine, side effects such as dizziness, feeling faint, flushing or redness of the face, nausea or vomiting, increased sweating, or unusual weakness may occur. These will usually go away after you lie down for a few minutes. If any of these effects continue or become worse, or if you notice any other effects within 10 minutes or so after receiving an injection, tell your health care professional right away.
- Joint pain may occur for 1 or 2 days after you receive an injection of this medicine. This effect usually disappears after the first few injections. However, if this continues or is bothersome, check with your doctor.

Side Effects of This Medicine

Gold compounds have been shown to cause tumors and cancer of the kidney when given to animals in large amounts for a long time. However, these effects have not been reported in humans receiving gold compounds for arthritis. If you have any questions about this, check with your doctor.

Along with its needed effects, a medicine may cause some unwanted effects. Although not all of these side effects may occur, side effects may occur at any time during treatment with this medicine *and up to many months after treatment has ended,* and they may need medical attention.

Check with your doctor as soon as possible if any of the following side effects occur:

More common

Irritation or soreness of tongue—less common with auranofin; metallic taste—less common with auranofin; skin rash or itching; redness, soreness, swelling, or bleeding of gums—rare with auranofin; ulcers, sores, or white spots on lips or in mouth or throat

Less common

Bloody or cloudy urine; hives

Rare

Abdominal or stomach pain, cramping, or burning (severe); bloody or black, tarry stools; confusion; convulsions (seizures); coughing, hoarseness, difficulty in breathing, shortness of breath, tightness in chest, or wheezing; dark urine; decreased urination; decreased vision; difficulty in swallowing; feeling of something in the eye; fever; hair loss; hallucinations (hearing, seeing, or feeling things that are not there); irritation of nose, throat, or upper chest area, possibly with hoarseness or coughing; irritation of vagina; nausea, vomiting, or heartburn (severe and/or continuing); numbness, tingling, pain, or weakness, especially in the face, hands, arms, or feet; pale stools; painful or difficult urination; pain in lower back, side, or lower abdomen (stomach) area; pain, redness, itching, or tearing of eyes; pinpoint red spots on skin; problems with muscle coordination; red, thickened, or scaly skin; sore throat and fever with or without chills; swelling of face, fingers, ankles, lower legs, or feet; swellings (large) on face, eyelids, mouth, lips, and/or tongue; swollen and/or painful glands; unusual bleeding or bruising; unusual tiredness or weakness; vomiting of blood or material that looks like coffee grounds; yellow eyes or skin

Other side effects may occur that usually do not need medical attention. These side effects may go away during treatment as your body adjusts to the medicine. However, check with your doctor if the following side effects continue or are bothersome:

More common with auranofin; rare with injections

Abdominal or stomach cramps or pain (mild or moderate); bloated feeling, gas, or indigestion (mild or moderate); decrease or loss of appetite; diarrhea or loose stools; nausea or vomiting (mild or moderate)

Less common

Constipation—with auranofin; joint pain—with injections

Some patients receiving auranofin have noticed changes in the taste of certain foods. If you notice a metallic taste while receiving any gold compound, check with your doctor as soon as possible. If you notice any other taste changes while you are taking auranofin, it is not necessary to check with your doctor unless you find this effect especially bothersome.

Other side effects not listed above may also occur in some patients. If you notice any other effects, check with your doctor.

Revised: June 1990
Interim revision: 08/22/94

GONADORELIN Systemic

A commonly used brand name in the U.S. and Canada is Factrel.

Other commonly used names are gonadotropin-releasing hormone, GnRH, and LHRH.

Description

Gonadorelin (goe-nad-oh-RELL-in) is a medicine that is the same as gonadotropin-releasing hormone (GnRH) that is naturally released from the hypothalamus gland. GnRH causes the pituitary gland to release other hormones (luteinizing hormone [LH] and follicle-stimulating hormone [FSH]). These other hormones control development in children and fertility in adults.

Gonadorelin is used to test how well the hypothalamus and the pituitary glands are working. It is also used to cause ovulation (release of an egg from the ovary) in women who do not have regular ovulation and menstrual periods because the hypothalamus gland does not release enough GnRH.

Gonadorelin may also be used for other conditions as determined by your doctor.

Gonadorelin is available in the following dosage form:

Parenteral

- Injection (U.S. and Canada)

Before Using This Medicine

In deciding to use a medicine, the risks of using the medicine must be weighed against the good it will do. This is a decision you and your doctor will make. For gonadorelin, the following should be considered:

Allergies—Tell your doctor if you have ever had any unusual or allergic reaction to gonadorelin. Also tell your health care professional if you are allergic to any other substances, such as foods, preservatives, or dyes.

Pregnancy—Gonadorelin has not been studied in pregnant women. However, it has not been shown to cause birth defects or other problems in animal studies.

Breast-feeding—Gonadorelin has not been reported to cause problems in nursing babies.

Children—This medicine has been tested and used in children and, in effective doses, has not been shown to cause different side effects or problems in children than it does in adults.

Other medicines—Although certain medicines should not be used together at all, in other cases two different medicines may be used together even if an interaction might occur. In these cases, your doctor may want to change the dose, or other precautions may be necessary. When you are using gonadorelin, it is especially important that your health care professional know if you are taking any other prescription or nonprescription (over-the-counter [OTC]) medicine.

Proper Use of This Medicine

If you are having a test done with gonadorelin, one or more samples of your blood will be taken. Then gonadorelin is given by an intravenous (into a vein) or a subcutaneous (under the skin) injection. At regular times after it is given, more blood samples will be taken. Then the results of the test will be studied.

Dosing—The dose of gonadorelin will be different for different patients. *Follow your doctor's orders.* The following information includes only the average doses of gonadorelin.

- For *injectable* dosage form:
  - —For testing the hypothalamus and pituitary glands:
    - Adults—0.1 milligram (mg) injected once under the skin or into a vein.
    - Children 12 years of age and older—0.1 mg injected once under the skin or into a vein.

Side Effects of This Medicine

Along with its needed effects, a medicine may cause some unwanted effects. Although the following side effects usually occur rarely with the use of repeated injections, they require immediate medical attention. *Get emergency help immediately* if any of the following side effects occur:

Difficulty in breathing; flushing (continuing)

Check with your doctor as soon as possible if any of the following side effects occur:

With repeated doses

Hardening of skin around place of injection; hives; skin rash (at place of injection or over entire body)

Other side effects may occur that usually do not need medical attention. These side effects may go away during treatment as your body adjusts to the medicine. However, check with your doctor if any of the following side effects continue or are bothersome:

Less common

Abdominal or stomach discomfort; flushing (lasting only a short time); headaches; itching, pain, or swelling at place of injection; lightheadedness; nausea

Other side effects not listed above may also occur in some patients. If you notice any other effects, check with your doctor.

Additional Information

Once a medicine has been approved for marketing for a certain use, experience may show that it is also useful for other medical problems. Although not specifically included in product labeling, gonadorelin is used in certain patients with the following medical conditions:

- Delayed puberty
- Infertility in males

Other than the above information, there is no additional information relating to proper use, precautions, or side effects for these uses.

Revised: August 1990
Interim revision: 05/16/94

GOSERELIN Systemic

A commonly used brand name in the U.S. and Canada is Zoladex.

Description

Goserelin (GOE-se-rel-in) is used to treat cancer of the prostate gland. It is usually given once a month.

Goserelin is similar to a hormone normally released from the hypothalamus gland. When given regularly, it decreases testosterone levels. Reducing the amount of testosterone in the body is one way of treating cancer of the prostate.

Goserelin is to be given only by or under the supervision of your doctor. It is injected under the skin and is available in the following dosage form:

Parenteral

- Implants (U.S. and Canada)

Before Using This Medicine

In deciding to use a medicine, the risks of taking the medicine must be weighed against the good it will do. This is a decision you and your doctor will make. For goserelin, the following should be considered:

Allergies—Tell your doctor if you have ever had any unusual or allergic reaction to goserelin.

Fertility—Goserelin causes sterility which may be permanent. If you intend to have children, discuss this with your doctor before receiving this medicine.

Older adults—Many medicines have not been tested in older people. Therefore, it may not be known whether they work exactly the same way they do in younger adults. Although there is no specific information comparing use of goserelin in the elderly to use in other age groups, it has been used mostly in elderly patients and is not expected to cause different side effects or problems in older people than it does in younger adults.

Proper Use of This Medicine

Goserelin sometimes causes unwanted effects such as hot flashes or decreased sexual ability. It may also cause a temporary increase in pain, numbness or tingling of hands or feet, trouble in urinating, or weakness in your legs when you begin treatment with it. However, it is very important that you continue to receive the medicine, even after you begin to feel better. *Do not stop treatment with this medicine without first checking with your doctor.*

Dosing—The dose of goserelin may be different for different patients. Goserelin implants are usually given by a doctor in the office or hospital. The following information includes only the average dose of goserelin:

- For *implant* dosage form:
  - —For prostate cancer:
    - Adults—3.6 milligrams (mg) (one implant) injected under the skin every twenty-eight days.

Missed dose—If you miss getting a dose of this medicine, get it as soon as possible.

Precautions While Using This Medicine

It is very important that your doctor check your progress at regular visits to make sure that this medicine is working properly and to check for unwanted effects.

Side Effects of This Medicine

Along with its needed effects, a medicine may cause some unwanted effects. Although not all of these side effects may occur, if they do occur they may need medical attention.

The following side effects are symptoms of a flareup of your condition that may occur during the first few days of treatment. After a few days, these symptoms should lessen. However, they may need medical attention. Check with your doctor if any of the following side effects occur or get worse:

Bone pain; numbness or tingling of hands or feet; trouble in urinating; weakness in legs

Also check with your doctor as soon as possible if any of the following side effects occur:

Less common

Chest pain; irregular heartbeat; joint pain; painful or cold hands or feet; shortness of breath; skin rash; weakness (sudden)

Other side effects may occur that usually do not need medical attention. These side effects may go away during treatment as your body adjusts to the medicine. However, check with your doctor if any of the following side effects continue or are bothersome:

More common

Decrease in sexual desire; impotence; sudden sweating and feelings of warmth (''hot flashes'')

Less common

Anxiety or mental depression; constipation; diarrhea; dizziness; headache; loss of appetite; nausea or vomiting; swelling and increased tenderness of breasts; swelling of feet or lower legs; trouble in sleeping; unusual tiredness or weakness; weight gain

Other side effects not listed above may also occur in some patients. If you notice any other effects, check with your doctor.

Revised: 07/90
Interim revision: 07/08/94

GRANISETRON Systemic†

A commonly used brand name in the U.S. is Kytril.

†Not commercially available in Canada.

Description

Granisetron (gra-NI-se-tron) is used to prevent the nausea and vomiting that may occur after treatment with anti-cancer medicines (chemotherapy).

Granisetron is to be given only by or under the immediate supervision of your doctor. It is available in the following dosage forms:

Oral

- Tablets (U.S.)

Parenteral

- Injection (U.S.)

Before Receiving This Medicine

In deciding to use a medicine, the risks of taking the medicine must be weighed against the good it will do. This is a decision you and your doctor will make. For granisetron, the following should be considered:

Allergies—Tell your doctor if you have ever had any unusual or allergic reaction to granisetron or ondansetron. Also tell your health care professional if you are allergic to any other substances, such as foods, preservatives, or dyes.

Pregnancy—Granisetron has not been studied in pregnant women. However, granisetron has not been shown to cause birth defects or other problems in animal studies.

Breast-feeding—It is not known whether granisetron passes into breast milk. Although most medicines pass into breast milk in small amounts, many of them may be used safely while breast-feeding. Mothers who are taking this medicine and who wish to breast-feed should discuss this with their doctor.

Children—This medicine has been tested in children 2 years of age and older and, in effective doses, has not been shown to cause different side effects or problems than it does in adults.

Older adults—This medicine has been tested in a limited number of patients 65 years of age or older and has not been shown to cause different side effects or problems in older people than it does in younger adults.

Other medicines—Although certain medicines should not be used together at all, in other cases two different medicines may be used together even if an interaction might occur. In these cases, your doctor may want to change the dose, or other precautions may be necessary. Tell your health care professional if you are taking any other prescription or nonprescription (over-the-counter [OTC]) medicine.

Other medical problems—The presence of other medical problems may affect the use of granisetron. Make sure you tell your doctor if you have any other medical problems.

Proper Use of This Medicine

Dosing—The dose of granisetron will be different for different patients. The following information includes only the average doses of granisetron.

- For prevention of nausea and vomiting caused by anticancer medicine:
  - —For *oral* dosage form (tablets):
    - Adults and teenagers—Dose is usually 1 milligram (mg) taken up to one hour before the anticancer medicine. The 1-mg dose is taken again twelve hours after the first dose.
    - Children—Dose must be determined by your doctor.
  - —For *injection* dosage form:
    - Adults and children 2 years of age or older—Dose is based on body weight and must be determined by your doctor. It is usually 10 micrograms (mcg) per kilogram (kg) (4.5 mcg per pound) of body weight. It is injected into a vein over a period of five minutes, beginning within thirty minutes before the anticancer medicine is given.
    - Children up to 2 years of age—Dose must be determined by your doctor.

Precautions While Receiving This Medicine

Check with your doctor if severe nausea and vomiting occur after receiving the anticancer medicine.

Side Effects of This Medicine

Along with its needed effects, a medicine may cause some unwanted effects. Although not all of these side effects may occur, if they do occur they may need medical attention.

Check with your doctor as soon as possible if any of the following side effects occur:

Less common
Fever

Rare
Chest pain; fainting; irregular heartbeat; shortness of breath; skin rash, hives, and itching

Other side effects may occur that usually do not need medical attention. These side effects may go away during treatment as your body adjusts to the medicine. However, check with your doctor if any of the following side effects continue or are bothersome:

More common
Abdominal pain; constipation; diarrhea; headache; unusual tiredness or weakness

Less common
Agitation; dizziness; drowsiness; trouble in sleeping; unusual taste in mouth

Additional Information

Once a medicine has been approved for marketing for a certain use, experience may show that it is also useful for other medical problems. Although this use is not included in product labeling, granisetron injection is used in certain patients to prevent the nausea and vomiting that may occur after cancer radiation treatment in patients undergoing bone marrow transplantation.

Other than the above information, there is no additional information relating to proper use, precautions, or side effects for this use.

Developed: 12/16/94
Interim revision: 08/02/95

GRISEOFULVIN Systemic

Some commonly used brand names are:

In the U.S.—

Fulvicin P/G	Grisactin
Fulvicin-U/F	Grisactin Ultra
Grifulvin V	Gris-PEG

Generic name product may also be available.

In Canada—

Fulvicin P/G	Grisovin-FP
Fulvicin U/F	

Description

Griseofulvin (gri-see-oh-FUL-vin) belongs to the group of medicines called antifungals. It is used to treat fungus infections of the skin, hair, fingernails, and toenails. This medicine may be taken alone or used along with medicines that are applied to the skin for fungus infections.

Griseofulvin is available only with your doctor's prescription, in the following dosage forms:

Oral
- Capsules (U.S.)
- Suspension (U.S.)
- Tablets (U.S. and Canada)

Before Using This Medicine

In deciding to use a medicine, the risks of taking the medicine must be weighed against the good it will do. This is

a decision you and your doctor will make. For griseofulvin, the following should be considered:

Allergies—Tell your doctor if you have ever had any unusual or allergic reaction to penicillins, penicillamine (e.g., Cuprimine), or griseofulvin. Also tell your health care professional if you are allergic to any other substances, such as foods, preservatives, or dyes.

Diet—Griseofulvin is absorbed best when it is taken with a high fat meal, such as a cheeseburger, whole milk, or ice cream. Tell your doctor if you are on a low-fat diet.

Pregnancy—Griseofulvin should not be used during pregnancy. The birth of twins that were joined together has been reported, although rarely, in women who took griseofulvin during the first 3 months of pregnancy. In addition, studies in rats and dogs have shown that griseofulvin causes birth defects and other problems.

Breast-feeding—It is not known if griseofulvin is excreted in breast milk. However, griseofulvin has not been reported to cause problems in nursing babies.

Children—This medicine has been tested in a limited number of children 2 years of age or older. In effective doses, the medicine has not been shown to cause different side effects or problems than it does in adults.

Older adults—Many medicines have not been studied specifically in older people. Therefore, it may not be known whether they work exactly the same way they do in younger adults. Although there is no specific information comparing use of griseofulvin in the elderly with use in other age groups, this medicine is not expected to cause different side effects or problems in older people than it does in younger adults.

Other medicines—Although certain medicines should not be used together at all, in other cases two different medicines may be used together even if an interaction might occur. In these cases, your doctor may want to change the dose, or other precautions may be necessary. When you are taking griseofulvin, it is especially important that your health care professional knows if you are taking any of the following:

- Anticoagulants (blood thinners)—Griseofulvin may decrease the effectiveness of anticoagulants in some patients
- Oral contraceptives (birth control pills) containing estrogen—Griseofulvin may decrease the effectiveness of birth control pills, which may result in breakthrough bleeding and unwanted pregnancies

Other medical problems—The presence of other medical problems may affect the use of griseofulvin. Make sure you tell your doctor if you have any other medical problems, especially:

- Liver disease—Griseofulvin may on rare occasion cause side effects affecting the liver
- Lupus erythematosus or lupus-like diseases—Griseofulvin may worsen lupus symptoms in patients who have lupus erythematosus or lupus-like diseases
- Porphyria—Griseofulvin may increase attacks of porphyria in patients with acute intermittent porphyria

Proper Use of This Medicine

Griseofulvin is best taken with or after meals, especially fatty ones (for example, whole milk or ice cream). This lessens possible stomach upset and helps to clear up the infection by helping your body absorb the medicine better. *However, if you are on a low-fat diet, check with your doctor.*

For patients taking the *oral liquid form of griseofulvin:*

- Use a specially marked measuring spoon or other device to measure each dose accurately. The average household teaspoon may not hold the right amount of liquid.

To help clear up your infection completely, *keep taking this medicine for the full time of treatment,* even if you begin to feel better after a few days. *Do not miss any doses.*

Dosing—The dose of griseofulvin will be different for different patients. *Follow your doctor's orders or the directions on the label.* The following information includes only the average doses of griseofulvin. *If your dose is different, do not change it* unless your doctor tells you to do so.

The number of capsules or tablets or teaspoonfuls of suspension that you take depends on the strength of the medicine. Also, *the number of doses you take each day, the time allowed between doses, and the length of time you take the medicine depend on the medical problem for which you are taking griseofulvin.*

- For microsize capsules, tablets, and suspension:
  - —Adults and teenagers:
    - Treatment of fungus infections of the feet and nails—500 milligrams (mg) every twelve hours.
    - Treatment of fungus infections of the scalp, skin, and groin—250 mg every twelve hours; or 500 mg once a day.
  - —Children:
    - Treatment of fungus infections—Dose is based on body weight. The usual dose is 5 mg per kilogram (kg) (2.3 mg per pound) of body weight every twelve hours; or 10 mg per kg (4.6 mg per pound) of body weight once a day.
- For ultramicrosize tablets:
  - —Adults and teenagers:
    - Treatment of fungus infections of the feet and nails—250 to 375 mg every twelve hours.
    - Treatment of fungus infections of the scalp, skin, and groin—125 to 187.5 mg every twelve hours; or 250 to 375 mg once a day.
  - —Infants and children up to 2 years of age:
    - Treatment of fungus infections—Use and dose must be determined by your doctor.
  - —Children 2 years of age and over:
    - Treatment of fungus infections—Dose is based on body weight. The usual dose is 2.75 to 3.65 mg per kg (1.25 to 1.7 mg per pound) of body weight every twelve hours; or 5.5 to 7.3 mg per kg (2.5 to 3.3 mg per pound) of body weight once a day.

Missed dose—If you miss a dose of this medicine, take it as soon as possible. However, if it is almost time for your next dose, skip the missed dose and go back to your regular dosing schedule. Do not double doses.

Storage—To store this medicine:
- Keep out of the reach of children.
- Store away from heat and direct light.
- Do not store the capsule or tablet form of this medicine in the bathroom, near the kitchen sink, or in other damp places. Heat or moisture may cause the medicine to break down.
- Keep the oral liquid form of this medicine from freezing.
- Do not keep outdated medicine or medicine no longer needed. Be sure that any discarded medicine is out of the reach of children.

Precautions While Using This Medicine

Your doctor should check your progress at regular visits to make sure that griseofulvin does not cause unwanted effects.

Oral contraceptives (birth control pills) containing estrogen may not work properly if you take them while you are taking griseofulvin. Unplanned pregnancies may occur. You should use a different or additional means of birth control while you are taking griseofulvin and for one month after stopping griseofulvin. If you have any questions about this, check with your health care professional.

Griseofulvin may increase the effects of alcohol. If taken with alcohol it may also cause fast heartbeat, flushing, increased sweating, or redness of the face. Therefore, if you have this reaction, do not drink alcoholic beverages while you are taking this medicine, unless you have first checked with your doctor.

This medicine may cause some people to become dizzy or less alert than they are normally. *Make sure you know how you react to this medicine before you drive, use machines, or do other things that could be dangerous if you are dizzy or are not alert.* If these reactions are especially bothersome, check with your doctor.

Griseofulvin may cause your skin to be more sensitive to sunlight than it is normally. Exposure to sunlight, even for brief periods of time, may cause a skin rash, itching, redness or other discoloration of the skin, or a severe sunburn. When you begin taking this medicine:
- Stay out of direct sunlight, especially between the hours of 10:00 a.m. and 3:00 p.m., if possible.
- Wear protective clothing, including a hat. Also, wear sunglasses.
- Apply a sun block product that has a skin protection factor (SPF) of at least 15. Some patients may require a product with a higher SPF number, especially if they have a fair complexion. If you have any questions about this, check with your health care professional.
- Apply a sun block lipstick that has an SPF of at least 15 to protect your lips.
- Do not use a sunlamp or tanning bed or booth.

If you have a severe reaction from the sun, check with your doctor.

Side Effects of This Medicine

Griseofulvin has been shown to cause liver and thyroid tumors in some animals. *You and your doctor should discuss the good this medicine will do, as well as the risks of taking it.*

Along with its needed effects, a medicine may cause some unwanted effects. Although not all of these side effects may occur, if they do occur they may need medical attention.

Check with your doctor as soon as possible if any of the following side effects occur:

Less common
Confusion; increased sensitivity of skin to sunlight; skin rash, hives, or itching; soreness or irritation of mouth or tongue

Rare
Numbness, tingling, pain, or weakness in hands or feet; sore throat and fever; yellow eyes or skin

Other side effects may occur that usually do not need medical attention. These side effects may go away during treatment as your body adjusts to the medicine. However, check with your doctor if any of the following side effects continue or are bothersome:

More common
Headache

Less common
Diarrhea; dizziness; nausea or vomiting; stomach pain; trouble in sleeping; unusual tiredness

Other side effects not listed above may also occur in some patients. If you notice any other effects, check with your doctor.

Revised: 09/06/92
Interim revision: 03/17/94; 04/24/95

GROWTH HORMONE Systemic

Some commonly used brand names are:

In the U.S.—
Humatrope[2]
Nutropin[2]
Protropin[1]

In Canada—
Humatrope[2]
Protropin[1]

Note: For quick reference, the following growth hormones are numbered to match the corresponding brand names.

This information applies to the following medicines:

1. Somatrem (SOE-ma-trem)
2. Somatropin, Recombinant (soe-ma-TROE-pin, re-KOM-bi-nant)

Other commonly used names are GH and human growth hormone (hGH).

Description

Somatrem and somatropin are man-made versions of human growth hormone. Growth hormone is naturally produced by the pituitary gland and is necessary to stimulate growth in children. If a child fails to grow normally because his or her body is not producing enough growth hormone, this medicine may be used to stimulate growth.

This medicine is available only with your doctor's prescription, in the following dosage forms:

Parenteral

Somatrem
- Injection (U.S. and Canada)

Somatropin, Recombinant
- Injection (U.S. and Canada)

Before Using This Medicine

In deciding to use a medicine, the risks of taking the medicine must be weighed against the good it will do. This is a decision you and your doctor will make. For growth hormone, the following should be considered:

Allergies—Tell your doctor if you have ever had any unusual or allergic reaction to growth hormone. Also tell your health care professional if you are allergic to any other substances, such as foods, preservatives, or dyes.

Other medicines—Although certain medicines should not be used together at all, in other cases two different medicines may be used together even if an interaction might occur. In these cases, your doctor may want to change the dose, or other precautions may be necessary. When you are taking growth hormone, it is especially important that your health care professional know if you are taking any of the following:

- Corticosteroids (cortisone-like medicines)—These medicines can interfere with the effects of growth hormone

Other medical problems—The presence of other medical problems may affect the use of growth hormone. Make sure you tell your doctor if you have any other medical problems, especially:

- Underactive thyroid—This condition can interfere with the effects of growth hormone

Proper Use of This Medicine

Dosing—The dose of these medicines will be different for different patients. *Follow your doctor's orders or the directions on the label.* The following information includes only the average doses of these medicines. *If your dose is different, do not change it* unless your doctor tells you to do so.

For somatrem

- For *injection* dosage form:
  - —For stimulating growth:
    - Children—Dose is based on body weight and must be determined by your doctor. The usual total weekly dose is 0.3 milligram (mg) per kilogram (kg) (0.136 mg per pound) of body weight. This is divided into smaller doses and usually is injected under the skin, but may be injected into a muscle as determined by your doctor.

For somatropin

- For *injection* dosage form:
  - —For stimulating growth:
    - Children—Dose is based on body weight and must be determined by your doctor. The usual total weekly dose is 0.18 to 0.3 milligram (mg) per kilogram (kg) (0.082 to 0.136 mg per pound) of body weight. This is divided into smaller doses and usually is injected under the skin, but may be injected into a muscle as determined by your doctor.

Precautions While Using This Medicine

It is important that your doctor check your progress at regular visits.

Side Effects of This Medicine

Leukemia has been reported in a few patients after treatment with growth hormone. However, it is not definitely known whether the leukemia was caused by the growth hormone. Leukemia has also been reported in patients whose bodies do not make enough growth hormone and who have not yet been treated with man-made growth hormone. However, discuss this possible effect with your doctor.

If growth hormone is given to children or adults with normal growth, who do not need growth hormone, serious unwanted effects may occur because levels in the body become too high. These effects include the development of diabetes, abnormal growth of bones and internal organs such as the heart, kidneys, and liver, atherosclerosis (hardening of the arteries), and hypertension (high blood pressure).

Along with its needed effects, a medicine may cause some unwanted effects. Although not all of these side effects may occur, if they do occur they may need medical attention. When growth hormone is used to promote growth in children who have a lack of naturally produced human growth hormone, serious side effects do not usually occur. However, check with your doctor as soon as possible if any of the following side effects occur:

Rare

Limp; pain and swelling at place of injection; pain in hip or knee; skin rash or itching

Other side effects not listed above may also occur in some patients. If you notice any other effects, check with your doctor.

Revised: 11/18/92
Interim revision: 06/30/94; 08/15/95

GUAIFENESIN Systemic

Some commonly used brand names are:

In the U.S.—

Anti-Tuss	Humibid Sprinkle
Breonesin	Hytuss
Diabetic Tussin EX	Hytuss-2X
Fenesin	Naldecon Senior EX
Gee-Gee	Organidin NR
Genatuss	Pneumomist
GG-CEN	Robitussin
Glycotuss	Scot-tussin Expectorant
Glytuss	Sinumist-SR
Guiatuss	Touro EX
Halotussin	Uni-tussin
Humibid L.A.	

Generic name product may also be available.

In Canada—

Balminil Expectorant	Resyl
Benylin-E	Robitussin
Calmylin Expectorant	

Another commonly used name is glyceryl guaiacolate.

Description

Guaifenesin (gwye-FEN-e-sin) is used to help coughs caused by colds or similar illnesses clear mucus or phlegm (pronounced flem) from the chest. It works by thinning the mucus or phlegm in the lungs.

Some guaifenesin preparations are available only with your doctor's prescription. Others are available without a prescription; however, your doctor may have special instructions on the proper dose of guaifenesin for your medical condition. Guaifenesin is available in the following dosage forms:

Oral
- Capsules (U.S.)
- Extended-release capsules (U.S.)
- Oral solution (U.S.)
- Syrup (U.S. and Canada)
- Tablets (U.S. and Canada)
- Extended-release tablets (U.S.)

Before Using This Medicine

If you are taking this medicine without a prescription, carefully read and follow any precautions on the label. For guaifenesin, the following should be considered:

Allergies—Tell your doctor if you have ever had any unusual or allergic reaction to guaifenesin. Also tell your health care professional if you are allergic to any other substances, such as foods, preservatives, or dyes.

Pregnancy—Several groups of women taking guaifenesin during pregnancy have been studied. In one group, when guaifenesin was taken during the first 3 months of pregnancy, the babies had more inguinal hernias than expected. However, more birth defects than expected did not occur in the babies of other groups of women taking guaifenesin during pregnancy. Studies have not been done in animals.

Breast-feeding—It is not known whether guaifenesin passes into breast milk. However, guaifenesin has not been reported to cause problems in nursing babies.

Children—Although there is no specific information comparing use of guaifenesin in children with use in other age groups, this medicine is not expected to cause different side effects or problems in children than it does in adults. However, check with your doctor before using this medicine in children who have a chronic cough, such as occurs with asthma, or who have an unusually large amount of mucus or phlegm with the cough. Children with these conditions may need a different kind of medicine. Also, guaifenesin should not be given to children younger than 2 years of age unless you are directed to do so by your doctor.

Older adults—Many medicines have not been studied specifically in older people. Therefore, it may not be known whether they work exactly the same way they do in younger adults. Although there is no specific information comparing use of guaifenesin in the elderly with use in other age groups, this medicine is not expected to cause different side effects or problems in older people than it does in younger adults.

Proper Use of This Medicine

Drinking plenty of water while taking guaifenesin may help loosen mucus or phlegm in the lungs.

For patients taking the *extended-release capsule* form of this medicine:
- Swallow the capsule whole, or open the capsule and sprinkle the contents on soft food such as applesauce, jelly, or pudding and swallow without crushing or chewing.

For patients taking the *extended-release tablet* form of this medicine:
- If the tablet has a groove in it, you may carefully break it into two pieces along the groove. Then swallow the pieces whole, without crushing or chewing them.
- If the tablet does not have a groove in it, it must be swallowed whole. Do not break, crush, or chew it before swallowing.

Dosing—The dose of guaifenesin will be different for different patients. *Follow your doctor's orders or the directions on the label.* The following information includes only the average doses of guaifenesin. *If your dose is different, do not change it* unless your doctor tells you to do so.

- For *regular (short-acting) oral* dosage forms (capsules, oral solution, syrup, or tablets):
  —For cough:
  - Adults—200 to 400 milligrams (mg) every four hours.
  - Children younger than 2 years of age—Use and dose must be determined by your doctor.
  - Children 2 to 6 years of age—50 to 100 mg every four hours.
  - Children 6 to 12 years of age—100 to 200 mg every four hours.

• For *long-acting oral* dosage forms (extended-release capsules or tablets):

—For cough:

• Adults—600 to 1200 mg every twelve hours.

• Children younger than 2 years of age—Use is not recommended.

• Children 2 to 6 years of age—300 mg every twelve hours.

• Children 6 to 12 years of age—600 mg every twelve hours.

Missed dose—If you must take this medicine regularly and you miss a dose, take it as soon as possible. However, if it is almost time for your next dose, skip the missed dose and go back to your regular dosing schedule. Do not double doses.

Storage—To store this medicine:
- Keep out of the reach of children.
- Store away from heat and direct light.
- Do not store the capsule or tablet form of this medicine in the bathroom, near the kitchen sink, or in other damp places. Heat or moisture may cause the medicine to break down.
- Do not refrigerate the syrup form of this medicine.
- Do not keep outdated medicine or medicine no longer needed. Be sure that any discarded medicine is out of the reach of children.

Precautions While Using This Medicine

If your cough has not improved after 7 days or if you have a fever, skin rash, continuing headache, or sore throat with the cough, check with your doctor. These signs may mean that you have other medical problems.

Side Effects of This Medicine

Along with its needed effects, a medicine may cause some unwanted effects. Although not all of these side effects may occur, if they do occur they may need medical attention. Some side effects may occur that usually do not need medical attention. These side effects may go away during treatment as your body adjusts to the medicine. However, check with your doctor if any of the following side effects continue or are bothersome:

Less common or rare

Diarrhea; dizziness; headache; hives; nausea or vomiting; skin rash; stomach pain

Other side effects not listed above may also occur in some patients. If you notice any other effects, check with your doctor.

Revised: 08/14/95

GUANABENZ Systemic†

A commonly used brand name in the U.S. is Wytensin.

†Not commercially available in Canada.

Description

Guanabenz (GWAHN-a-benz) belongs to the general class of medicines called antihypertensives. It is used to treat high blood pressure (hypertension).

High blood pressure adds to the work load of the heart and arteries. If it continues for a long time, the heart and arteries may not function properly. This can damage the blood vessels of the brain, heart, and kidneys, resulting in a stroke, heart failure, or kidney failure. High blood pressure may also increase the risk of heart attacks. These problems may be less likely to occur if blood pressure is controlled.

Guanabenz works by controlling nerve impulses along certain nerve pathways. As a result, it relaxes blood vessels so that blood passes through them more easily. This helps to lower blood pressure.

Guanabenz is available only with your doctor's prescription, in the following dosage form:

Oral
- Tablets (U.S.)

Before Using This Medicine

In deciding to use a medicine, the risks of taking the medicine must be weighed against the good it will do. This is a decision you and your doctor will make. For guanabenz, the following should be considered:

Allergies—Tell your doctor if you have ever had any unusual or allergic reaction to guanabenz. Also tell your health care professional if you are allergic to any other substance, such as foods, preservatives, or dyes.

Pregnancy—Guanabenz has not been studied in pregnant women. However, studies in rats have shown that guanabenz given in doses 9 to 10 times the maximum human dose caused a decrease in fertility. In addition, 3 to 6 times the maximum human dose caused birth defects (in the skeleton) in mice, and 6 to 9 times the maximum human dose caused death of the fetus in rats. Before taking this medicine, make sure your doctor knows if you are pregnant or if you may become pregnant.

Breast-feeding—It is not known whether guanabenz passes into the breast milk. However, this medicine has not been reported to cause problems in nursing babies.

Children—Studies on this medicine have been done only in adult patients, and there is no specific information comparing use of guanabenz in children with use in other age groups.

Older adults—Many medicines have not been studied specifically in older people. Therefore, it may not be known whether they work exactly the same way they do in younger adults or if they cause different side effects or problems in older people. There is no specific information

comparing use of guanabenz in the elderly with use in other age groups. However, dizziness, faintness, or drowsiness may be more likely to occur in the elderly, who are usually more sensitive to the effects of guanabenz.

Other medicines—Although certain medicines should not be used together at all, in other cases two different medicines may be used together even if an interaction might occur. In these cases, your doctor may want to change the dose, or other precautions may be necessary. When you are taking guanabenz, it is especially important that your health care professional know if you are taking any of the following:

- Beta-blockers (acebutolol [e.g., Sectral], atenolol [e.g., Tenormin], betaxolol [Kerlone], bisoprolol [e.g., Zebeta], carteolol [e.g., Cartrol], labetalol [e.g., Normodyne], metoprolol [e.g., Lopressor], nadolol [e.g., Corgard], oxprenolol [e.g., Trasicor], penbutolol [e.g., Levatol], pindolol [e.g., Visken], propranolol [e.g., Inderal], sotalol [e.g., Sotacor], timolol [e.g., Blocadren])—Effects on blood pressure may be increased. Also, the risk of unwanted effects when guanabenz treatment is stopped suddenly may be increased

Other medical problems—The presence of other medical problems may affect the use of guanabenz. Make sure you tell your doctor if you have any other medical problems, especially:

- Heart or blood vessel disease—Lowering blood pressure may make some conditions worse
- Kidney disease or
- Liver disease—Effects of guanabenz may be increased because of slower removal of guanabenz from the body

Proper Use of This Medicine

In addition to the use of the medicine your doctor has prescribed, treatment for your high blood pressure may include weight control and care in the types of foods you eat, especially foods high in sodium. Your doctor will tell you which of these are most important for you. You should check with your doctor before changing your diet.

Many patients who have high blood pressure will not notice any signs of the problem. In fact, many may feel normal. It is very important that you *take your medicine exactly as directed* and that you keep your appointments with your doctor even if you feel well.

Remember that this medicine will not cure your high blood pressure but it does help control it. Therefore, you must continue to take it as directed if you expect to lower your blood pressure and keep it down. *You may have to take high blood pressure medicine for the rest of your life.* If high blood pressure is not treated, it can cause serious problems such as heart failure, blood vessel disease, stroke, or kidney disease.

To help you remember to take your medicine, try to get into the habit of taking it at the same time each day.

Dosing—The dose of guanabenz will be different for different patients. *Follow your doctor's orders or the directions on the label.* The following information includes only the average doses of guanabenz. *If your dose is different, do not change it* unless your doctor tells you to do so.

The number of tablets that you take depends on the strength of the medicine.

- For *oral* dosage form (tablets):
  - —For high blood pressure:
    - Adults—At first, 4 milligrams (mg) two times a day. Then, your doctor may gradually increase your dose.
    - Children—Use and dose must be determined by your doctor.

Missed dose—

- If you miss a dose of this medicine, take it as soon as possible. However, if it is almost time for your next dose, skip the missed dose and go back to your regular dosing schedule. Do not double doses.
- If you miss two or more doses in a row, check with your doctor. If your body suddenly goes without this medicine, some unpleasant effects may occur. If you have any questions about this, check with your doctor.

Storage—To store this medicine:

- Keep out of the reach of children.
- Store away from heat and direct light.
- Do not store in the bathroom, near the kitchen sink, or in other damp places. Heat or moisture may cause the medicine to break down.
- Do not keep outdated medicine or medicine no longer needed. Be sure that any discarded medicine is out of the reach of children.

Precautions While Using This Medicine

It is important that your doctor check your progress at regular visits to make sure that this medicine is working properly.

Check with your doctor before you stop taking guanabenz. Your doctor may want you to reduce gradually the amount you are taking before stopping completely.

Before having any kind of surgery (including dental surgery) or emergency treatment, tell the medical doctor or dentist in charge that you are using this medicine.

Do not take other medicines unless they have been discussed with your doctor. This especially includes over-the-counter (nonprescription) medicines for appetite control, asthma, colds, cough, hay fever, or sinus problems, since they may tend to increase your blood pressure.

Guanabenz will add to the effects of alcohol and other CNS depressants (medicines that slow down the nervous system, possibly causing drowsiness). Some examples of CNS depressants are antihistamines or medicine for hay fever, other allergies, or colds; sedatives, tranquilizers, or sleeping medicine; prescription pain medicine or narcotics; barbiturates; medicine for seizures; muscle relaxants; or anesthetics, including some dental anesthetics. *Check with your doctor before taking any of the above while you are using this medicine.*

Guanabenz may cause some people to become dizzy, drowsy, or less alert than they are normally. *Make sure you know how you react to this medicine before you drive, use machines, or do anything else that could be dangerous if you are dizzy or are not alert.*

Guanabenz may cause dryness of the mouth, nose, and throat. For temporary relief of mouth dryness, use sugarless candy or gum, melt bits of ice in your mouth, or use a saliva substitute. However, if your mouth continues to feel dry for more than 2 weeks, check with your medical doctor or dentist. Continuing dryness of the mouth may increase the chance of dental disease, including tooth decay, gum disease, and fungus infections.

Side Effects of This Medicine

Along with its needed effects, a medicine may cause some unwanted effects. Although not all of these side effects may occur, if they do occur they may need medical attention.

Check with your doctor as soon as possible if any of the following side effects occur:

Signs and symptoms of overdose

Dizziness (severe); irritability; nervousness; pinpoint pupils; slow heartbeat; unusual tiredness or weakness

Other side effects may occur that usually do not need medical attention. These side effects may go away during treatment as your body adjusts to the medicine. However, check with your doctor if any of the following side effects continue or are bothersome:

More common

Dizziness; drowsiness; dryness of mouth; weakness

Less common or rare

Decreased sexual ability; headache; nausea

After you have been using this medicine for a while, unpleasant effects may occur if you stop taking it too suddenly. After you stop taking this medicine, check with your doctor if any of the following effects occur:

Anxiety or tenseness; chest pain; fast or irregular heartbeat; headache; increased salivation; increase in sweating; nausea or vomiting; nervousness or restlessness; shaking or trembling of hands or fingers; stomach cramps; trouble in sleeping

Other side effects not listed above may also occur in some patients. If you notice any other effects, check with your doctor.

Revised: 06/28/96

GUANADREL Systemic†

A commonly used brand name in the U.S. is Hylorel.

†Not commercially available in Canada.

Description

Guanadrel (GWAHN-a-drel) belongs to the general class of medicines called antihypertensives. It is used to treat high blood pressure (hypertension).

High blood pressure adds to the work load of the heart and arteries. If it continues for a long time, the heart and arteries may not function properly. This can damage the blood vessels of the brain, heart, and kidneys resulting in a stroke, heart failure, or kidney failure. High blood pressure may also increase the risk of heart attacks. These problems may be less likely to occur if blood pressure is controlled.

Guanadrel works by controlling nerve impulses along certain nerve pathways. As a result, it relaxes the blood vessels so that blood passes through them more easily. This helps to lower blood pressure.

Guanadrel is available only with your doctor's prescription, in the following dosage form:

Oral

- Tablets (U.S.)

Before Using This Medicine

In deciding to use a medicine, the risks of taking the medicine must be weighed against the good it will do. This is a decision you and your doctor will make. For guanadrel, the following should be considered:

Allergies—Tell your doctor if you have ever had any unusual or allergic reaction to guanadrel. Also tell your health care professional if you are allergic to any other substances, such as foods, preservatives, or dyes.

Pregnancy—Guanadrel has not been studied in pregnant women. However, guanadrel has not been shown to cause birth defects or other problems in animal studies.

Breast-feeding—It is not known whether guanadrel passes into breast milk. However, it has not been reported to cause problems in nursing babies.

Children—Studies on this medicine have been done only in adult patients, and there is no specific information comparing use of guanadrel in children with use in other age groups.

Older adults—Dizziness or faintness may be more likely to occur in the elderly, who are usually more sensitive to the effects of guanadrel.

Other medicines—Although certain medicines should not be used together at all, in other cases two different medicines may be used together even if an interaction might occur. In these cases, your doctor may want to change the dose, or other precautions may be necessary. When you are taking guanadrel, it is especially important that your health care professional know if you are taking any of the following:

- Chlorprothixene (e.g., Taractan) or
- Loxapine (e.g., Loxitane) or
- Thiothixene (e.g., Navane) or

- Tricyclic antidepressants (amitriptyline [e.g., Elavil], amoxapine [e.g., Asendin], clomipramine [e.g., Anafranil], desipramine [e.g., Pertofrane], doxepin [e.g., Sinequan], imipramine [e.g., Tofranil], nortriptyline [e.g., Aventyl], protriptyline [e.g., Vivactil], trimipramine [e.g., Surmontil]) or
- Trimeprazine (e.g., Temaril)—May decrease the effects of guanadrel on blood pressure
- Monoamine oxidase (MAO) inhibitors (furazolidone [e.g., Furoxone], isocarboxazid [e.g., Marplan], phenelzine [e.g., Nardil], procarbazine [e.g., Matulane], selegiline [e.g., Eldepryl], tranylcypromine [e.g., Parnate])—Taking guanadrel while you are taking or within 1 week of taking MAO inhibitors may cause a severe increase in blood pressure

Other medical problems—The presence of other medical problems may affect the use of guanadrel. Make sure you tell your doctor if you have any other medical problems, especially:

- Asthma (history of) or
- Diarrhea or
- Pheochromocytoma or
- Stomach ulcer (history of)—Guanadrel may worsen these conditions
- Fever—Effects of guanadrel may be increased
- Heart attack or stroke (recent) or
- Heart or blood vessel disease—Lowering blood pressure may make problems resulting from these conditions worse

Proper Use of This Medicine

In addition to the use of the medicine your doctor has prescribed, treatment for your high blood pressure may include weight control and care in the types of foods you eat, especially foods high in sodium. Your doctor will tell you which of these are most important for you. You should check with your doctor before changing your diet.

Many patients who have high blood pressure will not notice any signs of the problem. In fact, many may feel normal. It is very important that you *take your medicine exactly as directed* and that you keep your appointments with your doctor even if you feel well.

Remember that guanadrel will not cure your high blood pressure but it does help control it. Therefore, you must continue to take it as directed if you expect to lower your blood pressure and keep it down. *You may have to take high blood pressure medicine for the rest of your life.* If high blood pressure is not treated, it can cause serious problems such as heart failure, blood vessel disease, stroke, or kidney disease.

To help you remember to take your medicine, try to get into the habit of taking it at the same time each day.

Dosing—The dose of guanadrel will be different for different patients. *Follow your doctor's orders or the directions on the label.* The following information includes only the average doses of guanadrel. *If your dose is different, do not change it* unless your doctor tells you to do so.

The number of tablets that you take depends on the strength of the medicine.

- For *oral* dosage form (tablets):
  - —For high blood pressure:
    - Adults—At first, 5 milligrams (mg) two times a day. Then, your doctor may increase your dose to 20 to 75 mg a day, divided into two to four doses.
    - Children—Use and dose must be determined by your doctor.

Missed dose—If you miss a dose of guanadrel, take it as soon as possible. However, if it is almost time for your next dose, skip the missed dose and go back to your regular dosing schedule. Do not double doses.

Storage—To store this medicine:

- Keep out of the reach of children.
- Store away from heat and direct light.
- Do not store in the bathroom, near the kitchen sink, or in other damp places. Heat or moisture may cause the medicine to break down.
- Do not keep outdated medicine or medicine no longer needed. Be sure that any discarded medicine is out of the reach of children.

Precautions While Using This Medicine

It is important that your doctor check your progress at regular visits to make sure that this medicine is working properly.

Dizziness, lightheadedness, or fainting may occur, especially when you get up from a lying or sitting position. This may be more likely to occur in the morning. *Getting up slowly may help.* If you feel dizzy, sit or lie down. When you get up from lying down, sit on the edge of the bed with your feet dangling for 1 or 2 minutes. Then stand up slowly. If the problem continues or gets worse, check with your doctor.

The dizziness, lightheadedness, or fainting is also more likely to occur if you drink alcohol, stand for long periods of time, exercise, or if the weather is hot. *While you are taking guanadrel, be careful to limit the amount of alcohol you drink. Also, use extra care during exercise or hot weather or if you must stand for long periods of time.*

Do not take other medicines unless they have been discussed with your doctor. This especially includes over-the-counter (nonprescription) medicines for appetite control, asthma, colds, cough, hay fever, or sinus problems, since they may tend to increase your blood pressure.

Before having any kind of surgery (including dental surgery) or emergency treatment, tell the medical doctor or dentist in charge that you are taking guanadrel.

Tell your doctor if you get a fever since that may change the amount of medicine you have to take.

Side Effects of This Medicine

Along with its needed effects, a medicine may cause some unwanted effects. Although not all of these side effects may occur, if they do occur they may need medical attention.

Check with your doctor immediately if either of the following side effects occurs since they may be symptoms of an overdose:

Rare

Blurred vision; dizziness or faintness (severe)

Check with your doctor as soon as possible if any of the following side effects occur:

More common

Swelling of feet or lower legs

Less common or rare

Chest pain; shortness of breath

Other side effects may occur that usually do not need medical attention. These side effects may go away during treatment as your body adjusts to the medicine. However, check with your doctor if any of the following side effects continue or are bothersome:

More common

Difficulty in ejaculating; dizziness, lightheadedness, or fainting, especially when getting up from a lying or sitting position; drowsiness; unusual tiredness or weakness; weight gain or loss (excessive)

Less common or rare

Diarrhea or increase in bowel movements; dryness of mouth; headache; muscle pain or tremors; nighttime urination

Other side effects not listed above may also occur in some patients. If you notice any other effects, check with your doctor.

Revised: 01/03/96

GUANETHIDINE Systemic

Some commonly used brand names are:

In the U.S.—

Ismelin

Generic name product may also be available.

In Canada—

Apo-Guanethidine
Ismelin

Description

Guanethidine (gwahn-ETH-i-deen) belongs to the general class of medicines called antihypertensives. It is used to treat high blood pressure (hypertension).

High blood pressure adds to the work load of the heart and arteries. If it continues for a long time, the heart and arteries may not function properly. This can damage the blood vessels of the brain, heart, and kidneys, resulting in a stroke, heart failure, or kidney failure. High blood pressure may also increase the risk of heart attacks. These problems may be less likely to occur if blood pressure is controlled.

Guanethidine works by controlling nerve impulses along certain nerve pathways. As a result, it relaxes the blood vessels so that blood passes through them more easily. This helps to lower blood pressure.

Guanethidine is available only with your doctor's prescription, in the following dosage form:

Oral

- Tablets (U.S. and Canada)

Before Using This Medicine

In deciding to use a medicine, the risks of taking the medicine must be weighed against the good it will do. This is a decision you and your doctor will make. For guanethidine, the following should be considered:

Allergies—Tell your doctor if you have ever had any unusual or allergic reaction to guanethidine. Also tell your health care professional if you are allergic to any other substances, such as foods, preservatives, or dyes.

Pregnancy—Studies on effects in pregnancy have not been done in either humans or animals.

Breast-feeding—Small amounts of guanethidine pass into breast milk. However, this medicine has not been reported to cause problems in nursing babies.

Children—Although there is no specific information comparing use of guanethidine in children with use in other age groups, this medicine is not expected to cause different side effects or problems in children than it does in adults.

Older adults—Many medicines have not been studied specifically in older people. Therefore, it may not be known whether they work exactly the same way they do in younger adults. Although there is no specific information comparing use of guanethidine in the elderly with use in other age groups, dizziness, lightheadedness, or fainting may be more likely to occur in the elderly, who are more sensitive to the effects of guanethidine.

Other medicines—Although certain medicines should not be used together at all, in other cases two different medicines may be used together even if an interaction might occur. In these cases, your doctor may want to change the dose, or other precautions may be necessary. When you are taking guanethidine, it is especially important that your health care professional knows if you are taking any of the following:

- Antidiabetics, oral (diabetes medicine you take by mouth)—Effects may be increased by guanethidine
- Loxapine (e.g., Loxitane) or
- Thioxanthenes (chlorprothixene [e.g., Taractan], thiothixene [e.g., Navane]) or
- Tricyclic antidepressants (amitriptyline [e.g., Elavil], amoxapine [e.g., Asendin], clomipramine [e.g., Anafranil], desipramine [e.g., Pertofrane], doxepin [e.g., Sinequan], imipramine [e.g., Tofranil], nortriptyline [e.g., Aventyl], protriptyline [e.g., Vivactil], trimipramine [e.g., Surmontil]) or

- Trimeprazine (e.g., Temaril)—May decrease the effects of guanethidine on blood pressure
- Minoxidil (e.g., Loniten)—Effects on blood pressure may be greatly increased
- Monoamine oxidase (MAO) inhibitors (furazolidone [e.g., Furoxone], isocarboxazid [e.g., Marplan], phenelzine [e.g., Nardil], procarbazine [e.g., Matulane], selegiline [e.g., Eldepryl], tranylcypromine [e.g., Parnate])—Taking guanethidine while you are taking or within 1 week of taking MAO inhibitors may cause a severe increase in blood pressure

Other medical problems—The presence of other medical problems may affect the use of guanethidine. Make sure you tell your doctor if you have any other medical problems, especially:

- Asthma (history of) or
- Diarrhea or
- Pheochromocytoma or
- Stomach ulcer (history of)—Guanethidine may worsen these conditions
- Diabetes mellitus (sugar diabetes)—Effects of medicine used to treat this condition may be increased by guanethidine
- Fever—Effects of guanethidine may be increased
- Heart attack or stroke (recent) or
- Heart or blood vessel disease—Lowering blood pressure may make problems resulting from these conditions worse
- Kidney disease—Guanethidine may worsen this condition. Also, effects of guanethidine may be increased because of slower removal of this medicine from the body
- Liver disease—Effects of guanethidine may be increased because of slower removal from the body

Proper Use of This Medicine

In addition to the use of the medicine your doctor has prescribed, treatment for your high blood pressure may include weight control and care in the types of foods you eat, especially foods high in sodium. Your doctor will tell you which of these are most important for you. You should check with your doctor before changing your diet.

Many patients who have high blood pressure will not notice any signs of the problem. In fact, many may feel normal. It is very important that you *take your medicine exactly as directed* and that you keep your appointments with your doctor even if you feel well.

Remember that guanethidine will not cure your high blood pressure but it does help control it. Therefore, you must continue to take it as directed if you expect to lower your blood pressure and keep it down. *You may have to take high blood pressure medicine for the rest of your life.* If high blood pressure is not treated, it can cause serious problems such as heart failure, blood vessel disease, stroke, or kidney disease.

To help you remember to take your medicine, try to get into the habit of taking it at the same time each day.

Dosing—The dose of guanethidine will be different for different patients. *Follow your doctor's orders or the directions on the label.* The following information includes only the average doses of guanethidine. *If your dose is different, do not change it* unless your doctor tells you to do so.

The number of tablets that you take depends on the strength of the medicine.

- For *oral* dosage form (tablets):
  - —For high blood pressure:
    - Adults—At first, 10 or 12.5 milligrams (mg) once a day. Then, your doctor may increase your dose to 25 to 50 mg once a day.
    - Children—The dose is based on body weight and must be determined by your doctor. The usual dose is 200 micrograms (mcg) per kilogram (kg) (90.9 mcg per pound) of body weight a day. Then, your doctor may increase your dose as needed.

Missed dose—If you miss a dose of guanethidine, take it as soon as possible. However, if it is almost time for your next dose, skip the missed dose and go back to your regular dosing schedule. Do not double doses.

Storage—To store this medicine:

- Keep out of the reach of children.
- Store away from heat and direct light.
- Do not store in the bathroom, near the kitchen sink, or in other damp places. Heat or moisture may cause the medicine to break down.
- Do not keep outdated medicine or medicine no longer needed. Be sure that any discarded medicine is out of the reach of children.

Precautions While Using This Medicine

It is important that your doctor check your progress at regular visits to make sure that this medicine is working properly.

Dizziness, lightheadedness, or fainting may occur, especially when you get up from a lying or sitting position. This is more likely to occur in the morning. *Getting up slowly may help.* When you get up from lying down, sit on the edge of the bed with your feet dangling for 1 or 2 minutes. Then stand up slowly. If the problem continues or gets worse, check with your doctor.

The dizziness, lightheadedness, or fainting is also more likely to occur if you drink alcohol, stand for long periods of time, exercise, or if the weather is hot. *While you are taking this medicine, be careful in the amount of alcohol you drink. Also, use extra care during exercise or hot weather or if you must stand for long periods of time.*

Do not take other medicines unless they have been discussed with your doctor. This especially includes over-the-counter (nonprescription) medicines for appetite control, asthma, colds, cough, hay fever, or sinus problems, since they may tend to increase your blood pressure.

Before having any kind of surgery (including dental surgery) or emergency treatment, tell the medical doctor or dentist in charge that you are taking this medicine.

Tell your doctor if you get a fever since that may change the amount of medicine you have to take.

Male patients: This medicine may interfere with ejaculation.

Side Effects of This Medicine

Along with its needed effects, a medicine may cause some unwanted effects. Although not all of these side effects may occur, if they do occur they may need medical attention.

Check with your doctor as soon as possible if any of the following side effects occur:

More common

Swelling of feet or lower legs

Less common or rare

Chest pain; shortness of breath

Other side effects may occur that usually do not need medical attention. These side effects may go away during treatment as your body adjusts to the medicine. However, check with your doctor if any of the following side effects continue or are bothersome:

More common

Diarrhea or increase in bowel movements; dizziness, lightheadedness, or fainting, especially when getting up from a lying or sitting position; sexual problems in males; slow heartbeat; stuffy nose; unusual tiredness or weakness

Less common or rare

Blurred vision; drooping eyelids; dryness of mouth; headache; loss of hair on scalp; muscle pain or tremors; nausea or vomiting; nighttime urination; skin rash

Other side effects not listed above may also occur in some patients. If you notice any other effects, check with your doctor.

Revised: 01/03/96

GUANETHIDINE AND HYDROCHLOROTHIAZIDE Systemic

Some commonly used brand names are:

In the U.S.—
Esimil

In Canada—
Ismelin-Esidrix

Description

Guanethidine (gwahn-ETH-i-deen) and hydrochlorothiazide (hye-droe-klor-oh-THYE-a-zide) combination is used to treat high blood pressure (hypertension).

High blood pressure adds to the work load of the heart and arteries. If it continues for a long time, the heart and arteries may not function properly. This can damage the blood vessels of the brain, heart, and kidneys, resulting in a stroke, heart failure, or kidney failure. High blood pressure may also increase the risk of heart attacks. These problems may be less likely to occur if blood pressure is controlled.

Guanethidine works by controlling nerve impulses along certain nerve pathways. As a result, it relaxes the blood vessels so that blood passes through them more easily. The hydrochlorothiazide in this combination is a thiazide diuretic (water pill) that helps reduce the amount of water in the body by increasing the flow of urine.

Guanethidine and hydrochlorothiazide combination is available only with your doctor's prescription, in the following dosage form:

Oral

- Tablets (U.S. and Canada)

Before Using This Medicine

In deciding to use a medicine, the risks of taking the medicine must be weighed against the good it will do. This is a decision you and your doctor will make. For guanethidine and hydrochlorothiazide, the following should be considered:

Allergies—Tell your doctor if you have ever had any unusual or allergic reaction to guanethidine, sulfonamides (sulfa drugs), hydrochlorothiazide, bumetanide, furosemide, acetazolamide, dichlorphenamide, methazolamide, or to other thiazide diuretics (water pills). Also tell your health care professional if you are allergic to any other substance, such as foods, preservatives, or dyes.

Pregnancy—When hydrochlorothiazide is used during pregnancy, it may cause side effects including jaundice, blood problems, and low potassium in the newborn infant. However, this medicine has not been shown to cause birth defects.

Breast-feeding—Guanethidine and hydrochlorothiazide pass into breast milk. However, this medicine has not been reported to cause problems in nursing babies.

Children—Although there is no specific information about the use of this medicine in children, it is not expected to cause different side effects or problems in children than it does in adults. However, extra caution may be necessary in infants with jaundice, because thiazide diuretics can make the condition worse.

Older adults—Dizziness, lightheadedness, fainting, or signs and symptoms of too much potassium loss may be more likely to occur in the elderly, who are more sensitive to the effects of guanethidine and hydrochlorothiazide.

Other medicines—Although certain medicines should not be used together at all, in other cases two different medicines may be used together even if an interaction might occur. In these cases, your doctor may want to change the dose, or other precautions may be necessary. When you are taking guanethidine and hydrochlorothiazide, it is especially important that your health care professional know if you are taking any of the following:

- Antidiabetics, oral (diabetes medicine you take by mouth)—Effects may be increased by guanethidine

- Cholestyramine or
- Colestipol—Use with thiazide diuretics may prevent the diuretic from working properly; take the diuretic at least 1 hour before or 4 hours after cholestyramine or colestipol
- Digitalis glycosides (heart medicine)—Hydrochlorothiazide may cause low potassium in the blood, which can lead to symptoms of digitalis toxicity
- Lithium (e.g., Lithane)—Risk of lithium overdose, even at usual doses, may be increased
- Loxapine (e.g., Loxitane) or
- Thioxanthenes (chlorprothixene [e.g., Taractan], thiothixene [e.g., Navane]) or
- Tricyclic antidepressants (amitriptyline [e.g., Elavil], amoxapine [e.g., Asendin], clomipramine [e.g., Anafranil], desipramine [e.g., Pertofrane], doxepin [e.g., Sinequan], imipramine [e.g., Tofranil], nortriptyline [e.g., Aventyl], protriptyline [e.g., Vivactil], trimipramine [e.g., Surmontil]) or
- Trimeprazine (e.g., Temaril)—May decrease the effects of guanethidine on blood pressure
- Monoamine oxidase (MAO) inhibitors (furazolidone [e.g., Furoxone], isocarboxazid [e.g., Marplan], phenelzine [e.g., Nardil], procarbazine [e.g., Matulane], selegiline [e.g., Eldepryl], tranylcypromine [e.g., Parnate])—Taking guanethidine while you are taking or within 2 weeks of taking MAO inhibitors may cause a severe increase in blood pressure

Other medical problems—The presence of other medical problems may affect the use of guanethidine and hydrochlorothiazide. Make sure you tell your doctor if you have any other medical problems, especially:

- Asthma (history of) or
- Diarrhea or
- Pheochromocytoma or
- Stomach ulcer (history of)—May be worsened by guanethidine
- Diabetes mellitus (sugar diabetes)—Effects of medicine used to treat this may be increased by guanethidine. Hydrochlorothiazide may change the amount of diabetes medicine needed
- Fever—Effects of guanethidine may be increased
- Gout (history of)—Hydrochlorothiazide may increase the amount of uric acid in the blood, which can lead to gout
- Heart or blood vessel disease or
- Heart attack or stroke (recent)—Lowering blood pressure may make problems resulting from these conditions worse
- Kidney disease—May be worsened. Also, effects may be increased because of slower removal of guanethidine from the body
- Liver disease—Effects may be increased because of slower removal of guanethidine from the body
- Lupus erythematosus (history of)—Hydrochlorothiazide may worsen the condition
- Pancreatitis (inflammation of the pancreas)

Proper Use of This Medicine

This medicine may cause you to have an unusual feeling of tiredness when you begin to take it. You may also notice an increase in the amount of urine or in your frequency of urination. After taking the medicine for a while, these effects should lessen. In general, in order to keep the increase in urine from affecting your sleep:

- If you are to take a single dose a day, take it in the morning after breakfast.
- If you are to take more than one dose a day, take the last dose no later than 6 p.m., unless otherwise directed by your doctor.

However, it is best to plan your dose or doses according to a schedule that will least affect your personal activities and sleep. Ask your health care professional to help you plan the best time to take this medicine.

In addition to the use of the medicine your doctor has prescribed, treatment for your high blood pressure may include weight control and care in the types of foods you eat, especially foods high in sodium. Your doctor will tell you which of these are most important for you. You should check with your doctor before changing your diet.

Many patients who have high blood pressure will not notice any signs of the problem. In fact, many may feel normal. It is very important that you *take your medicine exactly as directed* and that you keep your appointments with your doctor even if you feel well.

Remember that this medicine will not cure your high blood pressure but it does help control it. Therefore, you must continue to take it as directed if you expect to lower your blood pressure and keep it down. *You may have to take high blood pressure medicine for the rest of your life.* If high blood pressure is not treated, it can cause serious problems such as heart failure, blood vessel disease, stroke, or kidney disease.

To help you remember to take your medicine, try to get into the habit of taking it at the same time each day.

Dosing—The dose of guanethidine and hydrochlorothiazide combination will be different for different patients. *Follow your doctor's orders or the directions on the label.* The following information includes only the average dose of guanethidine and hydrochlorothiazide combination. *If your dose is different, do not change it* unless your doctor tells you to do so.

- For *oral* dosage form (tablets):
  - For high blood pressure:
    - Adults—2 tablets a day.
    - Children—Dose must be determined by your doctor.

Missed dose—If you miss a dose of this medicine, take it as soon as possible. However, if it is almost time for your next dose, skip the missed dose and go back to your regular dosing schedule. Do not double doses.

Storage—To store this medicine:

- Keep out of the reach of children.
- Store away from heat and direct light.
- Do not store in the bathroom, near the kitchen sink, or in other damp places. Heat or moisture may cause the medicine to break down.
- Do not keep outdated medicine or medicine no longer needed. Be sure that any discarded medicine is out of the reach of children.

Precautions While Using This Medicine

It is important that your doctor check your progress at regular visits to make sure that this medicine is working properly.

Do not take other medicines unless they have been discussed with your doctor. This especially includes over-the-counter (nonprescription) medicines for appetite control, asthma, colds, cough, hay fever, or sinus problems, since they may tend to increase your blood pressure.

This medicine may cause a loss of potassium from your body.

- To help prevent this, your doctor may want you to:
  - —eat or drink foods that have a high potassium content (for example, orange or other citrus fruit juices), or
  - —take a potassium supplement, or
  - —take another medicine to help prevent the loss of the potassium in the first place.
- It is very important to follow these directions. Also, it is important not to change your diet on your own. This is more important if you are already on a special diet (as for diabetes), or if you are taking a potassium supplement or a medicine to reduce potassium loss. Extra potassium may not be necessary and, in some cases, too much potassium could be harmful.

Check with your doctor if you become sick and have severe or continuing vomiting or diarrhea. These problems may cause you to lose additional water and potassium.

Dizziness, lightheadedness, or fainting may occur, especially when you get up from a lying or sitting position. This is more likely to occur in the morning. *Getting up slowly* may help. When you get up from lying down, sit on the edge of the bed with your feet dangling for 1 or 2 minutes. Then stand up slowly. If the problem continues or gets worse, check with your doctor.

The dizziness, lightheadedness, or fainting is also more likely to occur if you drink alcohol, stand for long periods of time or exercise, or if the weather is hot. *While you are taking this medicine, be careful in the amount of alcohol you drink. Also, use extra care during exercise or hot weather or if you must stand for long periods of time.*

For *diabetic patients*:

- This medicine may raise blood sugar levels. While you are using this medicine, be especially careful in testing for sugar in your blood or urine. If you have any questions about this, check with your doctor.

Some people who take this medicine may become more sensitive to sunlight than they are normally. Exposure to sunlight, even for brief periods of time, may cause severe sunburn; skin rash, redness, itching, or discoloration; or vision changes. When you begin taking this medicine:

- Stay out of direct sunlight, especially between the hours of 10:00 a.m. and 3:00 p.m., if possible.
- Wear protective clothing, including a hat and sunglasses.
- Apply a sun block product that has a skin protection factor (SPF) of at least 15. Some patients may require a product with a higher SPF number, especially if they have a fair complexion. If you have any questions about this, check with your health care professional.
- Do not use a sunlamp or tanning bed or booth.

If you have a severe reaction from the sun, check with your doctor.

Tell your doctor if you get a fever since that may change the amount of medicine you have to take.

Before having any kind of surgery (including dental surgery) or emergency treatment, tell the medical doctor or dentist in charge that you are taking this medicine.

Side Effects of This Medicine

Along with its needed effects, a medicine may cause some unwanted effects. Although not all of these side effects may occur, if they do occur they may need medical attention.

Check with your doctor as soon as possible if any of the following side effects occur, especially since some of them may mean that your body is losing too much potassium:

Signs and symptoms of too much potassium loss

Dryness of mouth; increased thirst; irregular heartbeats; mood or mental changes; muscle cramps or pain; nausea or vomiting; unusual tiredness or weakness; weak pulse

Signs and symptoms of too much sodium loss

Confusion; convulsions; decreased mental activity; irritability; muscle cramps; unusual tiredness or weakness

Less common

Chest pain

Rare

Black, tarry stools; blood in urine or stools; cough or hoarseness; fever or chills; joint pain; lower back or side pain; painful or difficult urination; pinpoint red spots on skin; skin rash or hives; sore throat and fever; stomach pain (severe) with nausea and vomiting; unusual bleeding or bruising; yellow eyes or skin

Other side effects may occur that usually do not need medical attention. These side effects may go away during treatment as your body adjusts to the medicine. However, check with your doctor if any of the following side effects continue or are bothersome:

More common

Diarrhea or increase in bowel movements; dizziness, lightheadedness, or fainting, especially when getting up from a lying or sitting position; sexual problems in males; slow heartbeat; stuffy nose

Less common or rare

Blurred vision; drooping eyelids; headache; increased sensitivity of skin to sunlight; loss of appetite; loss of hair; nighttime urination

Other side effects not listed above may also occur in some patients. If you notice any other effects, check with your doctor.

Revised: 07/14/92
Interim revision: 04/29/94

GUANFACINE Systemic†

A commonly used brand name in the U.S. is Tenex.

†Not commercially available in Canada.

Description

Guanfacine (GWAHN-fa-seen) belongs to the general class of medicines called antihypertensives. It is used to treat high blood pressure (hypertension).

High blood pressure adds to the workload of the heart and arteries. If it continues for a long time, the heart and arteries may not function properly. This can damage the blood vessels of the brain, heart, and kidneys, resulting in a stroke, heart failure, or kidney failure. High blood pressure may also increase the risk of heart attacks. These problems may be less likely to occur if blood pressure is controlled.

Guanfacine works by controlling nerve impulses along certain nerve pathways. As a result, it relaxes blood vessels so that blood passes through them more easily. This helps to lower blood pressure.

Guanfacine is available only with your doctor's prescription, in the following dosage form:

Oral
- Tablets (U.S.)

Before Using This Medicine

In deciding to use a medicine, the risks of taking the medicine must be weighed against the good it will do. This is a decision you and your doctor will make. For guanfacine, the following should be considered:

Allergies—Tell your doctor if you have ever had any unusual or allergic reaction to guanfacine. Also tell your health care professional if you are allergic to any other substance, such as foods, preservatives, or dyes.

Pregnancy—Guanfacine has not been studied in pregnant women. However, guanfacine has not been shown to cause birth defects or other problems in rats or rabbits given many times the human dose. In rats and rabbits given extremely high doses (up to 200 times the human dose), there was an increase in deaths of the animal fetus.

Breast-feeding—It is not known whether guanfacine passes into breast milk. However, this medicine has not been reported to cause problems in nursing babies.

Children—Studies on this medicine have been done only in adult patients, and there is no specific information comparing use of guanfacine in children with use in other age groups.

Older adults—Dizziness, drowsiness, or faintness may be more likely to occur in the elderly, who are more sensitive to the effects of guanfacine.

Other medicines—Although certain medicines should not be used together at all, in other cases two different medicines may be used together even if an interaction might occur. In these cases, your doctor may want to change the dose, or other precautions may be necessary. Tell your health care professional if you are taking any other prescription or nonprescription (over-the-counter [OTC]) medicine.

Other medical problems—The presence of other medical problems may affect the use of guanfacine. Make sure you tell your doctor if you have any other medical problems, especially:
- Heart disease or
- Heart attack or stroke (recent)—Lowering blood pressure may make problems resulting from these conditions worse
- Liver disease—Effects may be increased because of slower removal of guanfacine from the body
- Mental depression—Guanfacine may cause mental depression

Proper Use of This Medicine

In addition to the use of the medicine your doctor has prescribed, treatment for your high blood pressure may include weight control and care in the types of foods you eat, especially foods high in sodium. Your doctor will tell you which of these are most important for you. You should check with your doctor before changing your diet.

Many patients who have high blood pressure will not notice any signs of the problem. In fact, many may feel normal. It is very important that you *take your medicine exactly as directed* and that you keep your appointments with your doctor even if you feel well.

Remember that this medicine will not cure your high blood pressure but it does help control it. Therefore, you must continue to use it as directed if you expect to lower your blood pressure and keep it down. *You may have to take high blood pressure medicine for the rest of your life.* If high blood pressure is not treated, it can cause serious problems such as heart failure, blood vessel disease, stroke, or kidney disease.

Take your daily dose of guanfacine at bedtime. (If you are taking more than one dose a day, take your last dose at bedtime.) Taking it this way will help lessen daytime drowsiness.

Dosing—The dose of guanfacine will be different for different patients. *Follow your doctor's orders or the directions on the label.* The following information includes only the average doses of guanfacine. *If your dose is different, do not change it* unless your doctor tells you to do so.

The number of tablets that you take depends on the strength of the medicine.

- For *oral* dosage form (tablets):
  —For high blood pressure:
  - Adults—At first, 1 milligram (mg) once a day at bedtime. Then, your doctor may gradually increase your dose up to 3 mg a day, if needed.
  - Children—Dose must be determined by your doctor.

Missed dose—If you miss a dose of this medicine, take it as soon as possible. However, if it is almost time for your next dose, skip the missed dose and go back to your regular dosing schedule. Do not double doses. *If you miss taking guanfacine for two or more days in a row, check with your doctor.* If your body suddenly goes without this medicine, some unwanted effects may occur. If you have any questions about this, check with your doctor.

Storage—To store this medicine:
- Keep out of the reach of children.
- Store away from heat and direct light.
- Do not store in the bathroom, near the kitchen sink, or in other damp places. Heat or moisture may cause the medicine to break down.
- Do not keep outdated medicine or medicine no longer needed. Be sure any discarded medicine is out of the reach of children.

Precautions While Using This Medicine

It is important that your doctor check your progress at regular visits to make sure this medicine is working properly.

Check with your doctor before you stop taking guanfacine. Your doctor may want you to reduce gradually the amount you are taking before stopping completely.

Make sure that you have enough guanfacine on hand to last through weekends, holidays, and vacations. You should not miss any doses. You may want to ask your doctor for another written prescription for guanfacine to carry in your wallet or purse. You can then have it filled if you run out when you are away from home.

Before having any kind of surgery (including dental surgery) or emergency treatment, tell the medical doctor or dentist in charge that you are using this medicine.

Do not take other medicines unless they have been discussed with your doctor. This especially includes over-the-counter (nonprescription) medicines for appetite control, asthma, colds, cough, hay fever, or sinus problems, since they may tend to increase your blood pressure.

Guanfacine will add to the effects of alcohol and other CNS depressants (medicines that slow down the nervous system, possibly causing drowsiness). Some examples of CNS depressants are antihistamines or medicine for hay fever, other allergies, or colds; sedatives, tranquilizers, or sleeping medicine; prescription pain medicine or narcotics; barbiturates; medicine for seizures; muscle relaxants; or anesthetics, including some dental anesthetics. *Check with your doctor before taking any of the above while you are using this medicine.*

Guanfacine may cause some people to become dizzy, drowsy, or less alert than they are normally. *Make sure you know how you react to this medicine before you drive, use machines, or do anything else that could be dangerous if you are dizzy or are not alert.*

Guanfacine may cause dryness of the mouth, nose, and throat. For temporary relief of mouth dryness, use sugarless candy or gum, melt bits of ice in your mouth, or use a saliva substitute. However, if dry mouth continues for more than 2 weeks, check with your physician or dentist. Continuing dryness of the mouth may increase the chance of dental disease, including tooth decay, gum disease, and fungus infections.

Side Effects of This Medicine

Along with its needed effects, a medicine may cause some unwanted effects. Although not all of these side effects may occur, if they do occur they may need medical attention.

Check with your doctor as soon as possible if any of the following side effects occur:

Less common

Confusion; mental depression

Signs and symptoms of overdose

Difficulty in breathing; dizziness (extreme) or faintness; slow heartbeat; unusual tiredness or weakness (severe)

Other side effects may occur that usually do not need medical attention. These side effects may go away during treatment as your body adjusts to the medicine. However, check with your doctor if any of the following side effects continue or are bothersome:

More common

Constipation; dizziness; drowsiness; dryness of mouth

Less common

Decreased sexual ability; dry, itching, or burning eyes; headache; nausea or vomiting; trouble in sleeping; unusual tiredness or weakness

After you have been using this medicine for a while, unwanted effects may occur if you stop taking it too suddenly. After you stop taking this medicine, check with your doctor if any of the following side effects occur:

Anxiety or tenseness; chest pain; fast or irregular heartbeat; headache; increased salivation; nausea or vomiting; nervousness or restlessness; shaking or trembling of hands and fingers; stomach cramps; sweating; trouble in sleeping

Other side effects not listed above may also occur in some patients. If you notice any other effects, check with your doctor.

Revised: 10/21/92
Interim revision: 07/05/94

HAEMOPHILUS B CONJUGATE VACCINE Systemic

Some commonly used brand names are:

In the U.S.—

Act-Hib
Hibtiter
Pedvaxhib
Prohibit

In Canada—

Act-Hib
Hibtiter
Pedvaxhib
Prohibit

Other commonly used names are: HbOC, PRP-D, PRP-OMP, and PRP-T.

Description

Haemophilus b conjugate (hem-OFF-fil-us BEE KON-ja-gat) vaccine is an active immunizing agent used to prevent infection by *Haemophilus influenzae* type b (Hib) bacteria. The vaccine works by causing your body to produce its own protection (antibodies) against the disease.

Haemophilus b conjugate vaccine is an haemophilus b vaccine that has been prepared by adding a diphtheria-, meningococcal-, or tetanus-related substance. However, this vaccine does *not* take the place of the regular diphtheria or tetanus toxoid injections (for example, DTP, DT, or T) that children should receive, the regular tetanus toxoid or diphtheria and tetanus toxoid injections (for example T or Td) that adults should receive, or the meningococcal vaccine injection that some children and adults should receive.

Infection by *Haemophilus influenzae* type b (Hib) bacteria can cause life-threatening illnesses, such as meningitis, which affects the brain; epiglottitis, which can cause death by suffocation; pericarditis, which affects the heart; pneumonia, which affects the lungs; and septic arthritis, which affects the bones and joints. Hib meningitis causes death in 5 to 10% of children who are infected. Also, approximately 30% of children who survive Hib meningitis are left with some type of serious permanent damage, such as mental retardation, deafness, epilepsy, or partial blindness.

Immunization against Hib is recommended for all children 2 months up to 5 years of age (i.e., up to the 5th birthday).

Immunization against Hib may also be recommended for adults and children over 5 years of age with certain medical problems.

This vaccine is to be administered only by or under the supervision of your doctor or other authorized health care professional. It is available in the following dosage form:

Parenteral

- Injection (U.S. and Canada)

Before Receiving This Vaccine

In deciding to use a medicine, the risks of taking the medicine must be weighed against the good it will do. This is a decision you and your doctor will make. For haemophilus b conjugate vaccine, the following should be considered:

Allergies—Tell your doctor if you have ever had any unusual or allergic reaction to haemophilus b conjugate vaccine, haemophilus b polysaccharide vaccine, diphtheria or tetanus toxoid, or meningococcal vaccine. Also tell your health care professional if you are allergic to any other substances, such as preservatives.

Pregnancy—Studies on effects in pregnancy have not been done in either humans or animals.

Breast-feeding—This vaccine has not been reported to cause problems in nursing babies.

Children—This vaccine is not recommended for children less than 2 months of age.

Older adults—Many medicines have not been studied specifically in older people. Therefore, it may not be known whether they work exactly the same way they do in younger adults. Although there is no specific information comparing use of this vaccine in the elderly with use in other age groups, this vaccine is not expected to cause different side effects or problems in older people than it does in younger adults.

Other medicines—Although certain medicines should not be used together at all, in other cases two different medicines may be used together even if an interaction might occur. In these cases, your doctor may want to change the dose, or other precautions may be necessary. Tell your health care professional if you are using any other prescription or nonprescription (over-the-counter [OTC]) medicine.

Other medical problems—The presence of other medical problems may affect the use of haemophilus b conjugate vaccine. Make sure you tell your doctor if you have any other medical problems, especially:

- Fever or
- Serious illness—The symptoms of the condition may be confused with some of the possible side effects of the vaccine

Proper Use of This Vaccine

Dosing—Haemophilus b conjugate vaccine is an haemophilus b vaccine that has been prepared by adding a diphtheria-, meningococcal-, or tetanus-related substance to it. If the vaccine was prepared using a diphtheria-related substance, it is called either HbOC or PRP-D. If the vaccine was prepared using a meningococcal-related substance, it is called PRP-OMP. If the vaccine was prepared using a tetanus-related substance, it is called PRP-T. *All of these subtypes of haemophilus b conjugate vaccine work the same way,* but may be given at different ages or times.

The dose of haemophilus b conjugate vaccine will be different for different patients. The following information includes only the average doses of haemophilus b conjugate vaccine.

- For prevention of *Haemophilus influenzae* type b infection:
  - —For *HbOC or PRP-T injection* dosage form:
    - Adults and children 5 years of age and older—Use and dose must be determined by your doctor.

• Infants 2 to 6 months of age at the first dose—Three doses, two months apart, then a booster dose at fifteen months of age. The doses are injected into a muscle.

• Children 7 to 11 months of age at the first dose—Two doses, two months apart, then a booster dose at fifteen months of age. The doses are injected into a muscle.

• Children 12 to 14 months of age at the first dose—One dose, then a booster dose at fifteen months of age. The doses are injected into a muscle.

• Children 15 to 59 months of age at the first dose—One dose injected into a muscle.

—For *PRP-D injection* dosage form:

• Adults and children 5 years of age and older—Use and dose must be determined by your doctor.

• Infants and children up to 15 months of age—Use is not recommended.

• Children 15 to 59 months of age at the first dose—One dose injected into a muscle.

—For *PRP-OMP injection* dosage form:

• Adults and children 5 years of age and older—Use and dose must be determined by your doctor.

• Infants 2 to 6 months of age at the first dose—Two doses, two months apart, then a booster dose at twelve months of age. The doses are injected into a muscle.

• Children 7 to 11 months of age at the first dose—Two doses, two months apart, then a booster dose at fifteen months of age. The doses are injected into a muscle.

• Children 12 to 14 months of age at the first dose—One dose, then a booster dose at fifteen months of age. The doses are injected into a muscle.

• Children 15 to 59 months of age at the first dose—One dose injected into a muscle.

After Receiving This Vaccine

This vaccine may interfere with laboratory tests that check for Hib disease. Make sure your doctor knows that you have received Hib vaccine if you are treated for a severe infection during the 2 weeks after you receive this vaccine.

Side Effects of This Vaccine

Along with its needed effects, a vaccine may cause some unwanted effects. Although not all of these side effects may occur, if they do occur they may need medical attention.

Get emergency help immediately if any of the following side effects occur:

Symptoms of allergic reactions

Difficulty in breathing or swallowing; hives; itching (especially of feet or hands); reddening of skin (especially around ears); swelling of eyes, face, or inside of nose; unusual tiredness or weakness (sudden and severe)

Check with your doctor immediately if the following side effect occurs:

Rare

Convulsions (seizures)

Other side effects may occur that usually do not need medical attention. However, check with your doctor if any of the following side effects continue or are bothersome:

More common

Fever of up to 102 °F (39 °C) (usually lasts less than 48 hours); irritability; loss of appetite; lack of interest; redness at place of injection; reduced physical activity; tenderness at place of injection; tiredness

Less common

Diarrhea; fever over 102 °F (39 °C) (usually lasts less than 48 hours); hard lump, swelling, or warm feeling at place of injection; skin rash; vomiting

Other side effects not listed above may also occur in some patients. If you notice any other effects, check with your doctor.

Revised: 06/21/93
Interim revision: 03/29/94

HAEMOPHILUS B POLYSACCHARIDE VACCINE Systemic*†

Commonly used names are:

Haemophilus influenzae type b polysaccharide vaccine	Hib CPS
HbPV	Hib polysaccharide vaccine
	PRP

*Not commercially available in the U.S.
†Not commercially available in Canada.

Description

Haemophilus b polysaccharide (hem-OFF-fil-us BEE pol-i-SAK-ka-ryd) vaccine is an active immunizing agent used to prevent infection by *Haemophilus influenzae* type b (Hib) bacteria. The vaccine works by causing your body to produce its own protection (antibodies) against the disease.

The following information applies only to the Haemophilus b polysaccharide vaccine.

Infection by *Haemophilus influenzae* type b (Hib) bacteria can cause life-threatening illnesses, such as meningitis, which affects the brain; epiglottitis, which can cause death by suffocation; pericarditis, which affects the heart; pneumonia, which affects the lungs; and septic arthritis, which affects the bones and joints. Hib meningitis causes death in 5 to 10% of children who are infected. Also, approximately 30% of children who survive Hib meningitis are left with some type of serious permanent damage, such as mental retardation, deafness, epilepsy, or partial blindness.

Immunization against Hib is recommended for all children 24 months up to 5 years of age (i.e., up to the 5th birthday). In addition, immunization is recommended for children 18 to 24 months of age, especially:

- Children attending day-care facilities.
- Children with chronic illnesses associated with increased risk of Hib disease. These illnesses include asplenia, sickle cell disease, antibody deficiency syndromes, immunosuppression, and Hodgkin's disease.
- Children 18 to 24 months of age who have already had Hib disease. These children may get the disease again if they are not immunized. Children who developed Hib disease when 24 months of age or older do not need to be immunized, since most children in this age group will develop antibodies against the disease.
- Children with human immunodeficiency virus (HIV) infection or acquired immunodeficiency syndrome (AIDS).
- Children of certain racial groups, such as American Indian and Alaskan Eskimo. Children in these groups seem to be at increased risk of Hib disease.
- Children living close together with groups of other persons. Close living conditions increase a child's risk of being exposed to persons who have Hib infection or who carry the bacteria.

It is recommended that children immunized when they were 18 to 24 months of age receive a second dose of vaccine, since these children may not produce enough antibodies to fully protect them from Hib disease. Children who were first immunized when they were 24 months of age or older do not need to be reimmunized.

This vaccine is available only from your doctor or other authorized health care professional, in the following dosage form:

Parenteral
- Injection

Before Receiving This Vaccine

In deciding to use a medicine, the risks of taking the medicine must be weighed against the good it will do. This is a decision you and your doctor will make. For haemophilus b polysaccharide vaccine, the following should be considered:

Allergies—Tell your doctor if you have ever had any unusual or allergic reaction to haemophilus b polysaccharide vaccine or haemophilus b conjugate vaccine. Also tell your health care professional if you are allergic to any other substances, such as preservatives.

Children—This vaccine is not recommended for children less than 18 months of age.

Other medicines—Although certain medicines should not be used together at all, in other cases two different medicines may be used together even if an interaction might occur. In these cases, your doctor may want to change the dose, or other precautions may be necessary. Tell your health care professional if you are using any other prescription or nonprescription (over-the-counter [OTC]) medicine.

Other medical problems—The presence of other medical problems may affect the use of haemophilus b polysaccharide vaccine. Make sure you tell your doctor if you have any other medical problems, especially:

- Fever or
- Serious illness—The symptoms of the condition may be confused with the possible side effects of the vaccine

Proper Use of This Vaccine

Dosing—The dose of haemophilus b polysaccharide vaccine will be different for different patients. The following information includes only the average doses of haemophilus b polysaccharide vaccine.

- For *injection* dosage form:
  - —For prevention of *Haemophilus influenzae* type b infection:
    - Adults and children 5 years of age and older—Use is not recommended.
    - Children up to 18 months of age—Use is not recommended.
    - Children 18 to 24 months of age—Use and dose must be determined by your doctor.
    - Children 24 months to 5 years of age—One dose injected under the skin or into a muscle.

Side Effects of This Vaccine

Along with its needed effects, a vaccine may cause some unwanted effects. Although not all of these side effects may occur, if they do occur they may need medical attention.

Get emergency help immediately if any of the following side effects occur:

Symptoms of allergic reaction
Difficulty in breathing or swallowing; hives; itching (especially of feet or hands); reddening of skin (especially around ears); swelling of eyes, face, or inside of nose; unusual tiredness or weakness (sudden and severe)

Check with your doctor immediately if the following side effect occurs:

Rare
Convulsions (seizures)

Other side effects may occur that usually do not need medical attention. However, check with your doctor if any of the following side effects continue or are bothersome:

More common
Diarrhea; fever up to 102 °F (39 °C) (usually lasts less than 48 hours); irritability; lack of appetite; lack of interest; redness at place of injection; reduced physical activity; tenderness at place of injection

Less common
Fever over 102 °F (39 °C) (usually lasts less than 48 hours); hard lump at place of injection; itching; joint aches or pains; skin rash; swelling at place of injection; trouble in sleeping; vomiting

Other side effects not listed above may also occur in some patients. If you notice any other effects, check with your doctor.

Revised: 06/21/93
Interim revision: 03/29/94

HALOFANTRINE Systemic*†

A commonly used brand name is Halfan.

*Not commercially available in the U.S.
†Not commercially available in Canada.

Description

Halofantrine (ha-loe-FAN-trin) is used to treat certain types of malaria infection. It works by killing the malaria parasites (tiny one-celled animals).

Halofantrine is available only with your doctor's prescription, in the following dosage forms:

Oral
- Oral suspension (United Kingdom)
- Tablets (United Kingdom)

Before Using This Medicine

In deciding to use a medicine, the risks of taking the medicine must be weighed against the good it will do. This is a decision you and your doctor will make. For halofantrine, the following should be considered:

Allergies—Tell your doctor if you have ever had any unusual or allergic reaction to halofantrine. Also tell your health care professional if you are allergic to any other substances, such as foods, preservatives, or dyes.

Pregnancy—Halofantrine has not been studied in pregnant women. However, it has been found to cause unwanted effects, including death of the fetus, in animals. Before taking this medicine, make sure your doctor knows if you are pregnant or if you may become pregnant.

Breast-feeding—Halofantrine may pass into breast milk and cause unwanted effects in nursing babies. It may be necessary for you to take another medicine or to stop breast-feeding while taking halofantrine. Be sure you have discussed the risks and benefits of the medicine with your doctor.

Children—Although there is no specific information comparing use of halofantrine in children with use in other age groups, this medicine is not expected to cause different side effects or problems in children than it does in adults.

Older adults—Many medicines have not been studied specifically in older people. Therefore, it may not be known whether they work exactly the same way they do in younger adults or if they cause different side effects or problems in older people. There is no specific information comparing use of halofantrine in the elderly with use in other age groups.

Other medicines—Although certain medicines should not be used together at all, in other cases two different medicines may be used together even if an interaction might occur. In these cases, your doctor may want to change the dose, or other precautions may be necessary. When you are taking halofantrine, it is especially important that your health care professional know if you are taking any of the following:

- Mefloquine (e.g., Lariam)—Recent use of mefloquine or use of mefloquine with halofantrine may cause fast and irregular heartbeat

Other medical problems—The presence of other medical problems may affect the use of halofantrine. Make sure you tell your doctor if you have any other medical problems, especially:

- Heart problems especially abnormal heartbeat or
- Thiamine deficiency or
- Unexplained sudden fainting—These conditions increase the chance of side effects affecting the heart, including fast irregular heartbeat

Proper Use of This Medicine

Halofantrine is best taken on an empty stomach to decrease the chance of side effects.

To help clear up your infection completely, *take this medicine exactly as directed by your doctor for the full time of treatment.* Your symptoms may come back if you stop your treatment too early. Your doctor may also instruct you to take a second course of treatment after one week.

Dosing—The dose of halofantrine will be different for different patients. *Follow your doctor's orders or the directions on the label.* The following information includes only the average doses of halofantrine. *If your dose is different, do not change it* unless your doctor tells you to do so.

The number of tablets or teaspoonfuls of suspension that you take depends on the strength of the medicine. Also, *the number of doses you take each day, the time allowed between doses, and the length of time you take the medicine depend on the medical problem for which you are taking halofantrine.*

- For malaria:
  - —For *oral* dosage form (oral suspension):
    - Adults and children over 12 years of age—500 milligrams (mg), taken on an empty stomach every six hours three times a day for one day. Treatment may need to be repeated after one week.
    - Children—Dose is based on age and/or body weight. Treatment may need to be repeated after one week.
      - —1 to 2 years of age: 100 mg, taken on an empty stomach every six hours three times a day for one day.
      - —2 to 5 years of age: 150 mg, taken on an empty stomach every six hours three times a day for one day.
      - —5 to 8 years of age: 200 mg, taken on an empty stomach every six hours three times a day for one day.
      - —8 to 10 years of age: 250 mg, taken on an empty stomach every six hours three times a day for one day.
      - —10 to 12 years of age: 300 mg, taken on an empty stomach every six hours three times a day for one day.

—For *oral* dosage form (tablets):

- Adults and children over 37 kilograms (81.4 pounds) of body weight—500 mg, taken on an empty stomach every six hours three times a day for one day. Treatment may need to be repeated after one week.
- Children—Dose is based on body weight and must be determined by your doctor. Treatment may need to be repeated after one week.
  —Up to 23 kilograms (50.6 pounds) of body weight: Dosage has not been established.
  —23 to 31 kilograms (50.6 to 68.2 pounds) of body weight: 250 mg, taken on an empty stomach every six hours three times a day for one day.
  —32 to 37 kilograms (70.4 to 81.4 pounds) of body weight: 375 mg, taken on an empty stomach every six hours three times a day for one day.

Missed dose—If you miss a dose of this medicine, take it as soon as possible. However, if it is almost time for your next dose, skip the missed dose and go back to your regular dosing schedule. Do not double doses.

Storage—To store this medicine:

- Keep out of the reach of children.
- Store away from heat and direct light.
- Do not store in the bathroom, near the kitchen sink, or in other damp places. Heat or moisture may cause the medicine to break down.
- Keep the liquid form of this medicine from freezing.
- Do not keep outdated medicine or medicine no longer needed. Be sure that any discarded medicine is out of the reach of children.

Precautions While Using This Medicine

It is important that your doctor check your progress after treatment. This is to make sure that the infection is cleared up completely, and to allow your doctor to check for any unwanted effects.

If your symptoms do not improve after you have taken this medicine for the full course of treatment, or if they become worse, check with your doctor.

Malaria is spread by the bites of certain kinds of infected female mosquitoes. If you are living in, or will be traveling to, an area where there is a chance of getting malaria, the following mosquito-control measures will help to prevent infection:

- If possible, avoid going out between dusk and dawn because it is at these times when mosquitoes most commonly bite.
- Wear long-sleeved shirts and long trousers to protect your arms and legs, especially from dusk through dawn when mosquitoes are out.
- Apply insect repellant, preferably one containing DEET, to uncovered areas of the skin from dusk through dawn when mosquitoes are out.
- If possible, sleep in a screened or air-conditioned room or under mosquito netting sprayed with insecticide to avoid being bitten by malaria-carrying mosquitoes.
- Use mosquito coils or sprays to kill mosquitoes in living and sleeping quarters during evening and night-time hours.

Side Effects of This Medicine

Along with its needed effects, a medicine may cause some unwanted effects. Although not all of these side effects may occur, if they do occur they may need medical attention.

Check with your doctor immediately if any of the following side effects occur:

Rare

Anxiety; black or decreased amount of urine; chest or lower back pain; fast and irregular heartbeat; feeling restless; flushing of the whole body; rapid breathing

Other side effects may occur that usually do not need medical attention. These side effects may go away during treatment as your body adjusts to the medicine. However, check with your doctor if any of the following side effects continue or are bothersome:

Less common

Abdominal or stomach pain; diarrhea; nausea; skin itching or rash; vomiting

Other side effects not listed above may also occur in some patients. If you notice any other effects, check with your doctor.

Revised: 8/31/93

HALOPERIDOL Systemic

Some commonly used brand names are:

In the U.S.—

Haldol
Haldol Decanoate

Generic name product may also be available.

In Canada—

Apo-Haloperidol
Haldol
Haldol LA
Novo-Peridol
Peridol
PMS Haloperidol

Generic name product may also be available.

Description

Haloperidol (ha-loe-PER-i-dole) is used to treat nervous, mental, and emotional conditions. It is also used to control the symptoms of Tourette's disorder. Haloperidol may also be used for other conditions as determined by your doctor.

Haloperidol is available only with your doctor's prescription, in the following dosage forms:

Oral

- Solution (U.S. and Canada)
- Tablets (U.S. and Canada)

Parenteral

- Injection (U.S. and Canada)

Before Using This Medicine

In deciding to use a medicine, the risks of taking the medicine must be weighed against the good it will do. This is a decision you and your doctor will make. For haloperidol, the following should be considered:

Allergies—Tell your doctor if you have ever had any unusual or allergic reaction to haloperidol. Also tell your health care professional if you are allergic to any other substances, such as foods, preservatives, or dyes.

Pregnancy—Haloperidol has not been studied in pregnant women. However, studies in animals given 2 to 20 times the usual maximum human dose of haloperidol have shown reduced fertility, delayed delivery, cleft palate, and an increase in the number of stillbirths and newborn deaths.

Breast-feeding—Haloperidol passes into breast milk. Animal studies have shown that haloperidol in breast milk causes drowsiness and unusual muscle movements in the nursing offspring. Breast-feeding is not recommended during treatment with haloperidol.

Children—Side effects, especially muscle spasms of the neck and back, twisting movements of the body, trembling of fingers and hands, and inability to move the eyes are more likely to occur in children, who usually are more sensitive than adults to the effects of haloperidol.

Older adults—Constipation, dizziness or fainting, drowsiness, dryness of mouth, trembling of the hands and fingers, and symptoms of tardive dyskinesia (such as rapid, worm-like movements of the tongue or any other uncontrolled movements of the mouth, tongue, or jaw, and/or arms and legs) are especially likely to occur in elderly patients, who are usually more sensitive than younger adults to the effects of haloperidol.

Other medicines—Although certain medicines should not be used together at all, in other cases 2 different medicines may be used together even if an interaction might occur. In these cases, your doctor may want to change the dose, or other precautions may be necessary. When you are taking haloperidol, it is especially important that your health care professional know if you are taking any of the following:

- Amoxapine (e.g., Asendin) or
- Metoclopramide (e.g., Reglan) or
- Metyrosine (e.g., Demser) or
- Other antipsychotics (medicine for mental illness) or
- Pemoline (e.g., Cylert) or
- Pimozide (e.g., Orap) or
- Promethazine (e.g., Phenergan) or
- Rauwolfia alkaloids (alseroxylon [e.g., Rauwiloid], deserpidine [e.g., Harmonyl], rauwolfia serpentina [e.g., Raudixin], reserpine [e.g., Serpasil]) or
- Trimeprazine (e.g., Temaril)—Taking these medicines with haloperidol may increase the frequency and severity of certain side effects
- Central nervous system (CNS) depressants (medicine that causes drowsiness) or
- Tricyclic antidepressants (medicine for depression)—Taking these medicines with haloperidol may result in increased CNS and other depressant effects, and in an increased chance of low blood pressure (hypotension)
- Epinephrine (e.g., Adrenalin)—Severe low blood pressure or irregular heartbeat may occur
- Levodopa (e.g., Dopar, Larodopa)—Haloperidol may interfere with the effects of this medicine
- Lithium (e.g., Eskalith, Lithane)—Although lithium and haloperidol are sometimes used together, their use must be closely monitored by your doctor, who may change the amount of medicine you need to take

Other medical problems—The presence of other medical problems may affect the use of haloperidol. Make sure you tell your doctor if you have any other medical problems, especially:

- Alcohol abuse—The risk of heat stroke may be increased
- Difficult urination or
- Glaucoma or
- Heart or blood vessel disease or
- Lung disease or
- Parkinson's disease—Haloperidol may make the condition worse
- Epilepsy—The risk of seizures may be increased
- Kidney disease or
- Liver disease—Higher blood levels of haloperidol may occur, increasing the chance of side effects
- Overactive thyroid—Serious unwanted effects may occur

Proper Use of This Medicine

If this medicine upsets your stomach, it may be taken with food or milk to lessen stomach irritation.

For patients taking the *liquid form of this medicine*:

- This medicine is to be taken by mouth even if it comes in a dropper bottle. Each dose is to be measured with the specially marked dropper provided with your prescription. Do not use other droppers since they may not deliver the correct amount of medicine.
- This medicine should be mixed with water or a beverage such as orange juice, apple juice, tomato juice, or cola and taken immediately after mixing. Haloperidol should not be mixed with tea or coffee, since they cause the medicine to separate out of solution.

Take this medicine only as directed by your doctor. Do not take more of it, do not take it more often, and do not take it for a longer time than your doctor ordered. This is particularly important for children or elderly patients, since they may react very strongly to this medicine.

Continue taking this medicine for the full time of treatment. *Sometimes haloperidol must be taken for several days to several weeks before its full effect is reached.*

Dosing—The dose of haloperidol will be different for different patients. *Follow your doctor's orders or the directions on the label.* The following information includes only the average doses of haloperidol. *If your dose is different, do not change it* unless your doctor tells you to do so.

The number of tablets or dropperfuls of solution that you take or injections that you receive depends on the strength of the medicine. Also, *the number of doses you take each day, the time allowed between doses, and the length of time you take the medicine depend on the medical problem for which you are using haloperidol.*

- For *oral* dosage forms (solution and tablets):
  —Adults and adolescents: To start, 500 micrograms to 5 milligrams two or three times a day. Your doctor may increase your dose if needed. However, the dose is usually not more than 100 milligrams a day.
  —Children 3 to 12 years of age or weighing 15 to 40 kilograms (33 to 88 pounds): Dose is based on body weight. The usual dose is 25 to 150 micrograms per kilogram (11 to 68 micrograms per pound) a day, taken in smaller doses two or three times a day.
  —Children up to 3 years of age: Dose must be determined by the doctor.
  —Older adults: To start, 500 micrograms to 2 milligrams two or three times a day. The doctor may increase your dose if needed.
- For *short-acting injection* dosage form:
  —Adults and adolescents: To start, 2 to 5 milligrams, usually injected into a muscle. The dose may be repeated every one to eight hours, depending on your condition.
  —Children: Dose must be determined by the doctor.
- For *long-acting or depot injection* dosage form:
  —Adults and adolescents: To start, the dose is usually 10 to 15 times the daily oral dose you were taking, injected into a muscle once a month. The doctor may adjust how much of this medicine you need and how often you will need it, depending on your condition.
  —Children: Dose must be determined by the doctor.

Missed dose—If you miss a dose of this medicine, take it as soon as possible. Then take any remaining doses for that day at regularly spaced intervals. Do not double doses.

Storage—To store this medicine:

- Keep out of the reach of children.
- Store away from heat and direct light.
- Do not store the tablet form of this medicine in the bathroom, near the kitchen sink, or in other damp places. Heat or moisture may cause the medicine to break down.
- Keep the liquid form of this medicine from freezing.
- Do not keep outdated medicine or medicine no longer needed. Be sure that any discarded medicine is out of the reach of children.

Precautions While Using This Medicine

Your doctor should check your progress at regular visits, especially during the first few months of treatment with this medicine. The amount of haloperidol you take may be changed often to meet the needs of your condition. This also helps prevent side effects.

Do not stop taking this medicine without first checking with your doctor. Your doctor may want you to reduce gradually the amount you are taking before stopping completely. This will allow your body time to adjust and help avoid a worsening of your medical condition.

This medicine will add to the effects of alcohol and other CNS depressants (medicines that slow down the nervous system, possibly causing drowsiness). Some examples of CNS depressants are antihistamines or medicine for hay fever, other allergies, or colds; sedatives, tranquilizers, or sleeping medicine; prescription pain medicine or narcotics; barbiturates; medicine for seizures; muscle relaxants; or anesthetics, including some dental anesthetics. *Check with your doctor before taking any of the above while you are taking this medicine.*

This medicine may cause some people to become dizzy, drowsy, or less alert than they are normally, especially as the amount of medicine is increased. Even if you take haloperidol at bedtime, you may feel drowsy or less alert on arising. *Make sure you know how you react to this medicine before you drive, use machines, or do anything else that could be dangerous if you are dizzy or are not alert.*

Although not a problem for many patients, dizziness, lightheadedness, or fainting may occur, especially when you get up from a lying or sitting position. Getting up slowly may help. However, if the problem continues or gets worse, check with your doctor.

This medicine will often make you sweat less, causing your body temperature to increase. *Use extra care not to become overheated during exercise or hot weather while you are taking this medicine, since overheating may result in heat stroke.* Also, hot baths or saunas may make you feel dizzy or faint while you are taking this medicine.

Before using any prescription or over-the-counter (OTC) medicine for colds or allergies, check with your doctor. These medicines may increase the chance of heat stroke or other unwanted effects, such as dizziness, dry mouth, blurred vision, and constipation, while you are taking haloperidol.

Before having any kind of surgery, dental treatment, or emergency treatment, tell the medical doctor or dentist in charge that you are using this medicine. Taking haloperidol together with medicines that are used during surgery or dental or emergency treatments may increase the CNS depressant effects.

Haloperidol may cause your skin to be more sensitive to sunlight than it is normally. Exposure to sunlight, even for brief periods of time, may cause a skin rash, itching, redness or other discoloration of the skin, or a severe sunburn. When you begin taking this medicine:

- Stay out of direct sunlight, especially between the hours of 10:00 a.m. and 3:00 p.m., if possible.
- Wear protective clothing, including a hat. Also, wear sunglasses.

- Apply a sun block product that has a skin protection factor (SPF) of at least 15. Some patients may require a product with a higher SPF number, especially if they have a fair complexion. If you have any questions about this, check with your health care professional.
- Apply a sun block lipstick that has an SPF of at least 15 to protect your lips.
- Do not use a sunlamp or tanning bed or booth.

If you have a severe reaction from the sun, check with your doctor.

Haloperidol may cause dryness of the mouth. For temporary relief, use sugarless candy or gum, melt bits of ice in your mouth, or use a saliva substitute. However, if your mouth continues to feel dry for more than 2 weeks, check with your medical doctor or dentist. Continuing dryness of the mouth may increase the chance of dental disease, including tooth decay, gum disease, and fungus infections.

If you are taking the liquid form of this medicine, avoid getting it on your skin because it may cause a skin rash or other irritation.

If you are *receiving this medicine by injection:*

- The effects of the long-acting injection form of this medicine may last for up to 6 weeks. *The precautions and side effects information for this medicine applies during this time.*

Side Effects of This Medicine

Along with its needed effects, haloperidol can sometimes cause serious side effects. Tardive dyskinesia (a movement disorder) may occur and may not go away after you stop using the medicine. Signs of tardive dyskinesia include fine, worm-like movements of the tongue, or other uncontrolled movements of the mouth, tongue, cheeks, jaw, or arms and legs. Other serious but rare side effects may also occur. These include severe muscle stiffness, fever, unusual tiredness or weakness, fast heartbeat, difficult breathing, increased sweating, loss of bladder control, and seizures (neuroleptic malignant syndrome). *You and your doctor should discuss the good this medicine will do as well as the risks of taking it.*

Stop taking haloperidol and get emergency help immediately if any of the following side effects occur:

Rare

Convulsions (seizures); difficult or fast breathing; fast heartbeat or irregular pulse; fever (high); high or low blood pressure; increased sweating; loss of bladder control; muscle stiffness (severe); unusually pale skin; unusual tiredness or weakness

Check with your doctor as soon as possible if any of the following side effects occur:

More common

Difficulty in speaking or swallowing; inability to move eyes; loss of balance control; mask-like face; muscle spasms, especially of the neck and back; restlessness or need to keep moving (severe); shuffling walk; stiffness of arms and legs; trembling and shaking of fingers and hands; twisting movements of body; weakness of arms and legs

Less common

Decreased thirst; difficulty in urination; dizziness, lightheadedness, or fainting; hallucinations (seeing or hearing things that are not there); lip smacking or puckering; puffing of cheeks; rapid or worm-like movements of tongue; skin rash; uncontrolled chewing movements; uncontrolled movements of arms and legs

Rare

Confusion; hot, dry skin, or lack of sweating; increased blinking or spasms of eyelid; muscle weakness; sore throat and fever; uncontrolled twisting movements of neck, trunk, arms, or legs; unusual bleeding or bruising; unusual facial expressions or body positions; yellow eyes or skin

Symptoms of overdose

Difficulty in breathing (severe); dizziness (severe); drowsiness (severe); muscle trembling, jerking, stiffness, or uncontrolled movements (severe); unusual tiredness or weakness (severe)

Other side effects may occur that usually do not need medical attention. These side effects may go away during treatment as your body adjusts to the medicine. However, check with your doctor if any of the following side effects continue or are bothersome:

More common

Blurred vision; changes in menstrual period; constipation; dryness of mouth; swelling or pain in breasts (in females); unusual secretion of milk; weight gain

Less common

Decreased sexual ability; drowsiness; increased sensitivity of skin to sun (skin rash, itching, redness or other discoloration of skin, or severe sunburn); nausea or vomiting

Some side effects, such as trembling of fingers and hands, or uncontrolled movements of the mouth, tongue, and jaw, may occur after you have stopped taking this medicine. If you notice any of these effects, check with your doctor as soon as possible.

Other side effects not listed above may also occur in some patients. If you notice any other effects, check with your doctor.

Additional Information

Once a medicine has been approved for marketing for a certain use, experience may show that it is also useful for other medical problems. Although these uses are not included in product labeling, haloperidol is used in certain patients with the following medical conditions:

- Huntington's chorea (an hereditary movement disorder)
- Infantile autism
- Nausea and vomiting caused by cancer chemotherapy

Other than the above information, there is no additional information relating to proper use, precautions, or side effects for these uses.

Revised: 03/19/93
Interim revision: 08/04/95

HALOPROGIN Topical

A commonly used brand name in the U.S. and Canada is Halotex.

Description

Haloprogin (ha-loe-PROE-jin) belongs to the group of medicines called antifungals. It is used to treat some types of fungus infections.

Haloprogin is available only with your doctor's prescription, in the following dosage forms:

Topical
- Cream (U.S. and Canada)
- Solution (U.S. and Canada)

Before Using This Medicine

In deciding to use a medicine, the risks of using the medicine must be weighed against the good it will do. This is a decision you and your doctor will make. For haloprogin, the following should be considered:

Allergies—Tell your doctor if you have ever had any unusual or allergic reaction to haloprogin. Also tell your health care professional if you are allergic to any other substances, such as preservatives or dyes.

Pregnancy—Haloprogin has not been studied in pregnant women. However, this medicine has not been shown to cause birth defects or other problems in animal studies.

Breast-feeding—It is not known whether topical haloprogin is absorbed into the body and passes into the breast milk. Although most medicines pass into breast milk in small amounts, many of them may be used safely while breast-feeding. Mothers who are using this medicine and who wish to breast-feed should discuss this with their doctor.

Children—Studies on this medicine have been done only in adult patients, and there is no specific information comparing use of haloprogin in children with use in other age groups.

Older adults—Many medicines have not been studied specifically in older people. Therefore, it may not be known whether they work exactly the same way they do in younger adults. Although there is no specific information comparing use of this medicine in the elderly with use in other age groups, this medicine is not expected to cause different side effects or problems in older people than it does in younger adults.

Proper Use of This Medicine

Apply enough haloprogin to cover the affected area, and rub in gently.

Keep this medicine away from the eyes.

To help clear up your infection completely, *keep using this medicine for the full time of treatment,* even if your condition has improved. *Do not miss any doses.*

Dosing—The dose of topical haloprogin will be different for different patients. *Follow your doctor's orders or the directions on the label.* The following information includes only the average doses of topical haloprogin. *If your dose is different, do not change it* unless your doctor tells you to do so.

The number of doses you use each day, the time allowed between doses, and the length of time you use the medicine depend on the medical problem for which you are using topical haloprogin.

- For *cream* or *topical solution* dosage forms:
  - —For treatment of fungus infections:
    - Adults—Use 2 times a day for 2 to 4 weeks.
    - Children—Use and dose must be determined by your doctor.

Missed dose—If you miss a dose of this medicine, apply it as soon as possible. However, if it is almost time for your next dose, skip the missed dose and go back to your regular dosing schedule.

Storage—To store this medicine:
- Keep out of the reach of children.
- Store away from heat and direct light.
- Keep the medicine from freezing.
- Do not keep outdated medicine or medicine no longer needed. Be sure that any discarded medicine is out of the reach of children.

Precautions While Using This Medicine

If your skin problem does not improve within 4 weeks, or if it becomes worse, check with your doctor.

Side Effects of This Medicine

Along with its needed effects, a medicine may cause some unwanted effects. Although not all of these side effects may occur, if they do occur they may need medical attention.

Check with your doctor as soon as possible if any of the following side effects occur:

Blistering, burning, itching, or other sign of skin irritation not present before use of this medicine

When you apply the solution form of this medicine, a mild temporary stinging may be expected.

Other side effects not listed above may also occur in some patients. If you notice any other effects, check with your doctor.

Revised: 06/21/93

HEADACHE MEDICINES, ERGOT DERIVATIVE–CONTAINING Systemic

Some commonly used brand names are:

In the U.S.—

Cafergot[3]	Ergomar[2]
Cafertine[3]	Ergostat[2]
Cafetrate[3]	Gotamine[3]
D.H.E. 45[1]	Migergot[3]
Ercaf[3]	Wigraine[3]
Ergo-Caff[3]	

In Canada—

Cafergot[3]	Gravergol[7]
Cafergot-PB[5]	Gynergen[2]
Dihydroergotamine-Sandoz[1]	Medihaler Ergotamine[2]
Ergodryl[8]	Megral[6]
Ergomar[2]	Wigraine[4]

Note: For quick reference, the following ergot derivative–containing headache medicines are numbered to match the corresponding brand names.

This information applies to the following medicines:

1. Dihydroergotamine (dye-hye-droe-er-GOT-a-meen)
2. Ergotamine (er-GOT-a-meen)
3. Ergotamine and Caffeine (kaf-EEN)‡
4. Ergotamine, Caffeine, and Belladonna Alkaloids (bell-a-DON-a AL-ka-loids)*
5. Ergotamine, Caffeine, Belladonna Alkaloids, and Pentobarbital (pen-toe-BAR-bi-tal)*
6. Ergotamine, Caffeine, and Cyclizine (SYE-kli-zeen)*
7. Ergotamine, Caffeine, and Dimenhydrinate (dye-men-HYE-dri-nate)*
8. Ergotamine, Caffeine, and Diphenhydramine (dye-fen-HYE-dra-mine)*

*Not commercially available in the U.S.
‡Generic name product may also be available in the U.S.

Description

Dihydroergotamine and ergotamine belong to the group of medicines known as ergot alkaloids. They are used to treat severe, throbbing headaches, such as migraine and cluster headaches. Dihydroergotamine and ergotamine are not ordinary pain relievers. They will not relieve any kind of pain other than throbbing headaches. Because these medicines can cause serious side effects, they are usually used for patients whose headaches are not relieved by acetaminophen, aspirin, or other pain relievers.

Dihydroergotamine and ergotamine may cause blood vessels in the body to constrict (become narrower). This effect can lead to serious side effects that are caused by a decrease in the flow of blood (blood circulation) to many parts of the body.

The caffeine present in many ergotamine-containing combinations helps ergotamine work better and faster by causing more of it to be quickly absorbed into the body. The belladonna alkaloids, cyclizine, dimenhydrinate, and diphenhydramine in some combinations help to relieve nausea and vomiting, which often occur together with the headaches. Cyclizine, dimenhydinate, diphenhydramine, and pentobarbital also help the patient relax and even sleep. This also helps relieve headaches.

Dihydroergotamine is also used for other conditions, as determined by your doctor.

These medicines are available only with your doctor's prescription, in the following dosage forms:

Oral

- Ergotamine
  - Inhalation aerosol (Canada)
  - Sublingual tablets (U.S. and Canada)
  - Tablets (Canada)
- Ergotamine and Caffeine
  - Tablets (U.S. and Canada)
- Ergotamine, Caffeine, and Belladonna Alkaloids
  - Tablets (Canada)
- Ergotamine, Caffeine, Belladonna Alkaloids, and Pentobarbital
  - Tablets (Canada)
- Ergotamine, Caffeine, and Cyclizine
  - Tablets (Canada)
- Ergotamine, Caffeine, and Dimenhydrinate
  - Capsules (Canada)
- Ergotamine, Caffeine, and Diphenhydramine
  - Capsules (Canada)

Parenteral

- Dihydroergotamine
  - Injection (U.S. and Canada)

Rectal

- Ergotamine and Caffeine
  - Suppositories (U.S. and Canada)
- Ergotamine, Caffeine, and Belladonna Alkaloids
  - Suppositories (Canada)
- Ergotamine, Caffeine, Belladonna Alkaloids, and Pentobarbital
  - Suppositories (Canada)

Before Using This Medicine

In deciding to use a medicine, the risks of taking the medicine must be weighed against the good it will do. This is a decision you and your doctor will make. For these headache medicines, the following should be considered:

Allergies—Tell your doctor if you have ever had any unusual or allergic reaction to atropine, belladonna, pentobarbital or other barbiturates, caffeine, cyclizine, dimenhydrinate, diphenhydramine, or an ergot medicine. Also tell your health care professional if you are allergic to any other substances, such as foods, preservatives, or dyes.

Pregnancy—Use of dihydroergotamine or ergotamine by pregnant women may cause serious harm, including death of the fetus and miscarriage. Therefore, *these medicines should not be used during pregnancy.*

Breast-feeding—

- *For dihydroergotamine and ergotamine:* These medicines pass into the breast milk and may cause unwanted effects, such as vomiting, diarrhea, weak pulse, changes in blood pressure, or convulsions (seizures) in nursing babies. Large amounts of these medicines may also decrease the flow of breast milk.
- *For caffeine:* Caffeine passes into the breast milk. Large amounts of it may cause the baby to appear jittery or to have trouble in sleeping.

- *For belladonna alkaloids, cyclizine, dimenhydrinate, and diphenhydramine:* These medicines have drying effects. Therefore, it is possible that they may reduce the amount of breast milk in some people. Dimenhydrinate passes into the breast milk. Cylizine may also pass into the breast milk.
- *For pentobarbital:* Pentobarbital passes into the breast milk. Large amounts of it may cause unwanted effects such as drowsiness in nursing babies.

Be sure that you discuss these possible problems with your doctor before taking any of these medicines.

Children—

- *For dihydroergotamine and ergotamine:* These medicines are used to relieve severe, throbbing headaches in children 6 years of age or older. They have not been shown to cause different side effects or problems in children than they do in adults. However, these medicines can cause serious side effects in any patient. Therefore, it is especially important that you discuss with the child's doctor the good that this medicine may do as well as the risks of using it.
- *For belladonna alkaloids:* Young children, especially children with spastic paralysis or brain damage, may be especially sensitive to the effects of belladonna alkaloids. This may increase the chance of side effects during treatment.
- *For cyclizine, dimenhydrinate, diphenhydramine, and pentobarbital:* Although these medicines often cause drowsiness, some children become excited after taking them.

Older adults—

- *For dihydroergotamine and ergotamine:* The chance of serious side effects caused by decreases in blood flow is increased in elderly people receiving these medicines.
- *For belladonna alkaloids, cyclizine, dimenhydrinate, diphenhydramine, and pentobarbital:* Elderly people are more sensitive than younger adults to the effects of these medicines. This may increase the chance of side effects such as excitement, depression, dizziness, drowsiness, and confusion.

Other medicines—Although certain medicines should not be used together at all, in other cases two different medicines may be used together even if an interaction might occur. In these cases, your doctor may want to change the dose, or other precautions may be necessary. Many medicines can add to or decrease the effects of the belladonna alkaloids, caffeine, cyclizine, dimenhydrinate, diphenhydramine, or pentobarbital present in some of these headache medicines. Therefore, you should tell your health care professional if you are taking *any* other prescription or nonprescription (over-the-counter [OTC]) medicine. This is especially important if any medicine you take causes excitement, trouble in sleeping, dryness of the mouth, dizziness, or drowsiness.

When you are taking dihydroergotamine or ergotamine, it is especially important that your health care professional know if you are taking any of the following:

- Cocaine or
- Epinephrine by injection [e.g., Epi-Pen] or
- Other ergot medicines (ergoloid mesylates [e.g., Hydergine], ergonovine [e.g., Ergotrate], methylergonovine [e.g., Methergine], methysergide [e.g., Sansert])—The chance of serious side effects caused by dihydroergotamine or ergotamine may be increased

Other medical problems—The presence of other medical problems may affect the use of these headache medicines. Make sure you tell your doctor if you have any other medical problems, especially:

- Agoraphobia (fear of open or public places) or
- Panic attacks or
- Stomach ulcer or
- Trouble in sleeping (insomnia)—Caffeine can make your condition worse
- Diarrhea—Rectal dosage forms (suppositories) will not be effective if you have diarrhea
- Difficult urination or
- Enlarged prostate or
- Glaucoma (not well controlled) or
- Heart or blood vessel disease or
- High blood pressure (not well controlled) or
- Infection or
- Intestinal blockage or other intestinal problems or
- Itching (severe) or
- Kidney disease or
- Liver disease or
- Mental depression or
- Overactive thyroid or
- Urinary tract blockage—The chance of side effects may be increased

Also, tell your doctor if you need, or if you have recently had, an angioplasty (a procedure done to improve the flow of blood in a blocked blood vessel) or surgery on a blood vessel. The chance of serious side effects caused by dihydroergotamine or ergotamine may be increased.

Proper Use of This Medicine

Use this medicine only as directed by your doctor. Do not use more of it, and do not use it more often, than directed. If the amount you are to use does not relieve your headache, check with your doctor. Taking too much dihydroergotamine or ergotamine, or taking it too often, may cause serious effects, especially in elderly patients. Also, if a headache medicine (especially ergotamine) is used too often for migraines, it may lose its effectiveness or even cause a type of physical dependence. If this occurs, your headaches may actually get worse.

This medicine works best if you:

- *Use it at the first sign of headache or migraine attack. If you get warning signals of a coming migraine, take it before the headache actually starts.*
- *Lie down in a quiet, dark room until you are feeling better.*

Your doctor may direct you to take another medicine to help prevent headaches. *It is important that you follow your doctor's directions, even if your headaches continue to occur.* Headache-preventing medicines may take several weeks to start working. Even after they do start working, your headaches may not go away completely. However, your headaches should occur less often, and they should be less severe and easier to relieve. This can reduce the amount of dihydroergotamine, ergotamine, or pain relievers that you need. If you do not notice any improvement after several weeks of headache-preventing treatment, check with your doctor.

For patients using *dihydroergotamine:*

- Dihydroergotamine is given only by injection. Your health care professional will teach you how to inject yourself with the medicine. Be sure to follow the directions carefully. Check with your health care professional if you have any problems using the medicine.

For patients using *ergotamine inhalation* [e.g., Medihaler Ergotamine]:

- This medicine comes with patient directions. Read them carefully before using the medicine, and check with your health care professional if you have any questions.
- To use the inhaler—Remove the cap, then shake the container well. After breathing out, place the mouthpiece of the inhaler in your mouth. Aim it at the back of the throat. Breathe in; at the same time, press the vial down into the adapter. After inhaling the medicine, hold your breath as long as you can.

For patients using the *sublingual (under-the-tongue) tablets of ergotamine:*

- To use—Place the tablet under your tongue and let it remain there until it disappears. The sublingual tablet should not be chewed or swallowed, because it works faster when it is absorbed into the body through the lining of the mouth. Do not eat, drink, or smoke while the tablet is under your tongue.

For patients using *rectal suppository forms of a headache medicine:*

- If the suppository is too soft to use, chill it in the refrigerator for 30 minutes or run cold water over it before removing the foil wrapper.
- If you have been directed to use part of a suppository, you should divide the suppository into pieces that all contain the same amount of medicine. To do this, use a sharp knife and carefully cut the suppository lengthwise (from top to bottom) into pieces that are the same size. The suppository will be easier to cut if it has been kept in the refrigerator.
- To insert the suppository—First remove the foil wrapper and moisten the suppository with cold water. Lie down on your side and use your finger to push the suppository well up into the rectum.

Dosing—The dose of these headache medicines will be different for different patients. *Follow your doctor's orders or the directions on the label.* The following information includes only the average doses of these medicines. *If your dose is different, do not change it* unless your doctor tells you to do so.

For dihydroergotamine

- Adults: For relieving a migraine or cluster headache—1 mg. If your headache is not better, and no side effects are occurring, a second 1-mg dose may be used at least one hour later.
- Children 6 years of age and older: For relieving a migraine headache—It is not likely that a child will be receiving dihydrogergotamine at home. If a child needs the medicine, the dose will have to be determined by the doctor.

For ergotamine

- Some headache medicines contain only ergotamine. Some of them contain other medicines along with the ergotamine. The number of tablets, capsules, or suppositories that you need for each dose depends on the amount of ergotamine in them. The size of each dose, and the number of doses that you take, also depends on the reason you are taking the medicine and on how you react to the medicine.
- For *oral* (capsule or tablet) and *sublingual* (under-the-tongue tablet) dosage forms:
  —Adults:
  - For relieving a migraine or cluster headache—1 or 2 mg of ergotamine. If your headache is not better, and no side effects are occurring, a second dose and even a third dose may be taken; however the doses should be taken at least 30 minutes apart. People who usually need more than one dose of the medicine, and who do not get side effects from it, may be able to take a larger first dose of not more than 3 mg of ergotamine. This may provide better relief of the headache with only one dose. *The medicine should not be taken more often than 2 times a week, at least five days apart.*
  - For preventing cluster headaches—The dose of ergotamine, and the number of doses you need every day, will depend on how many headaches you usually get each day. For some people, 1 or 2 mg of ergotamine once a day may be enough. Other people may need to take 1 or 2 mg of ergotamine 2 or 3 times a day.
  - For all uses—*Do not take more than 6 mg of ergotamine a day in the form of capsules or tablets.*

  —Children 6 years of age and older: For relieving migraine headaches—1 mg of ergotamine. If the headache is not better, and no side effects are occurring, a second dose and even a third dose may be taken; however, the doses should be taken at least 30 minutes apart. *Children should not take more than 3 mg of ergotamine a day in the form of capsules or tablets. Also, this medicine should not be taken more often than 2 times a week, at least five days apart.*
- For *rectal suppository* dosage forms:
  —Adults: For relieving migraine or cluster headaches—Usually 1 mg of ergotamine, but the dose may range from half of this amount to up to 2 mg. If your headache is not better, and no side effects are occurring, a second dose and even a third dose may be used; however the doses should be taken at

least 30 minutes apart. People who usually need more than one dose of the medicine, and who do not get side effects from it, may be able to use a larger first dose of not more than 3 mg. This may provide better relief of the headache with only one dose. *Adults should not use more than 4 mg of ergotamine a day in suppository form. Also, this medicine should not be used more often than 2 times a week, at least five days apart.*

—Children 6 years of age and older: For relieving migraine headaches—One-half or 1 mg of ergotamine. *Children should not receive more than 1 mg a day of ergotamine in suppository form. Also, this medicine should not be used more often than 2 times a week, at least five days apart.*

- For the *oral inhalation* dosage form:

—Adults: For relieving a migraine or cluster headache—1 spray (1 inhalation). Another inhalation may be used at least 5 minutes later, if needed. Up to a total of 6 inhalations a day may be used, at least 5 minutes apart. *This medicine should not be used more often than 2 times a week, at least five days apart.*

—Children: To be determined by the doctor.

Storage—To store this medicine:
- Keep out of the reach of children since overdose is especially dangerous in children.
- Store away from heat and direct light.
- Do not store in the bathroom, near the kitchen sink, or in other damp places. Heat or moisture may cause the medicine to break down.
- Suppositories should be stored in a cool place, but not allowed to freeze. Some manufacturers recommend keeping them in a refrigerator; others do not. Follow the directions on the package. However, cutting the suppository into smaller pieces, if you need to do so, will be easier if the suppository is kept in the refrigerator.
- Do not puncture, break, or burn the ergotamine inhalation aerosol container, even after it is empty.
- Do not keep outdated medicine or medicine no longer needed. Be sure that any discarded medicine is out of the reach of children.

Precautions While Using This Medicine

Check with your doctor:
- If your migraine headaches are worse than they were before you started using this medicine, or your headache medicine stops working as well as it did when you first started using it. This may mean that you are in danger of becoming dependent on the headache medicine. *Do not try to get better relief by increasing the dose.*
- If your migraine headaches are occurring more often than they did before you started using this medicine. This is especially important if a new headache occurs within 1 day after you took your last dose of headache medicine, or if you are having headaches every day. This may mean that you are dependent on the headache medicine. *Continuing to take this medicine will cause even more headaches later on.* Your doctor can give you advice on how to relieve the headaches.

Drinking alcoholic beverages can make headaches worse or cause new headaches to occur. People who suffer from severe headaches should probably avoid alcoholic beverages, especially during a headache.

Smoking may increase some of the harmful effects of dihydroergotamine or ergotamine. It is best to avoid smoking for several hours after taking these medicines.

Dihydroergotamine and ergotamine may make you more sensitive to cold temperatures, especially if you have blood circulation problems. They tend to decrease blood flow in the skin, fingers, and toes. Dress warmly during cold weather and be careful during prolonged exposure to cold temperatures. This is especially important for older patients, who are more likely than younger adults to already have problems with their circulation.

If you have a serious infection or illness of any kind, check with your doctor before using this medicine, since you may be more sensitive to its effects.

For patients using *ergotamine inhalation* [e.g., Medihaler Ergotamine]:
- Cough, hoarseness, or throat irritation may occur. Gargling and rinsing your mouth after each dose may help prevent the hoarseness and irritation. However, check with your doctor if these or any other side effects continue or are bothersome.

For patients taking one of the combination medicines that contains *caffeine:*
- Caffeine may interfere with the results of a test that uses dipyridamole (e.g., Persantine) to help find out how well your blood is flowing through certain blood vessels. You should not have any caffeine for at least 12 hours before the test.
- Caffeine may also interfere with some other laboratory tests. Before having any other laboratory tests, tell the person in charge if you have taken a medicine that contains caffeine.

For patients taking one of the combination medicines that contains *belladonna alkaloids, cyclizine, dimenhydrinate, diphenhydramine, or pentobarbital:*
- These medicines may cause some people to have blurred vision or to become drowsy, dizzy, lightheaded, or less alert than they are normally. These effects may be especially severe if you also take CNS depressants (medicines that slow down the nervous system, possibly causing drowsiness) together with one of these combination medicines. Some examples of CNS depressants are antihistamines or medicine for hay fever, other allergies, or colds; sedatives, tranquilizers, or sleeping medicine; prescription pain medicine or narcotics; barbiturates; medicine for seizures; muscle relaxants; and antiemetics (medicines that prevent or relieve nausea or vomiting). If you are not able to lie down for a while, *make sure you know how you react to this medicine or combination of medicines before you drive, use machines, or do any-*

thing else that could be dangerous if you are dizzy or are not alert and able to see well.

- Belladonna alkaloids, cyclizine, dimenhydrinate, and diphenhydramine may cause dryness of the mouth, nose, and throat. For temporary relief of mouth dryness, use sugarless candy or gum, melt bits of ice in your mouth, or use a saliva substitute.
- Belladonna alkaloids may interfere with certain laboratory tests that check the amount of acid in your stomach. They should not be taken for 24 hours before the test.
- Cyclizine, dimenhydrinate, and diphenhydramine may interfere with skin tests that show whether you are allergic to certain substances. They should not be taken for 3 days before the test.

Side Effects of This Medicine

Along with its needed effects, a medicine may cause some unwanted effects. Although not all of these side effects may occur, if they do occur they may need medical attention.

Check with your doctor immediately if the following side effects occur, because they may mean that you are developing a problem with blood circulation:

Less common or rare

Anxiety or confusion (severe); change in vision; chest pain; increase in blood pressure; pain in arms, legs, or lower back, especially if pain occurs in your calves or heels while you are walking; pale, bluish-colored, or cold hands or feet (not caused by cold temperatures and occurring together with other side effects listed in this section); red or violet-colored blisters on the skin of the hands or feet

Also check with your doctor immediately if any of the following side effects occur, because they may mean that you have taken an overdose of the medicine:

Less common or rare

Convulsions (seizures); diarrhea, nausea, vomiting, or stomach pain or bloating (severe) occurring together with other signs of overdose or of problems with blood circulation; dizziness, drowsiness, or weakness (severe), occurring together with other signs of overdose or of problems with blood circulation; fast or slow heartbeat; diarrhea; headaches, more often and/or more severe than before; problems with moving bowels, occurring together with pain or discomfort in the rectum (with rectal suppositories only); shortness of breath; unusual excitement

The following side effects may go away after a little while. *Do not take any more medicine while they are present.* If any of them occur together with other signs of problems with blood circulation, *check with your doctor right away.* Even if any of the following side effects occur without other signs of problems with blood circulation, *check with your doctor if any of them continue for more than one hour:*

More common

Itching of skin; coldness, numbness, or tingling in fingers, toes, or face; weakness in legs

Also, check with your doctor as soon as possible if you notice any of the following side effects:

More common

Swelling of face, fingers, feet, or lower legs

Other side effects may occur that usually do not need medical attention. These side effects may go away after a little while. However, check with your doctor if any of the following side effects continue or are bothersome:

More common

Diarrhea, nausea, or vomiting (occurring without other signs of overdose or problems with blood circulation); dizziness or drowsiness (occurring without other signs of overdose or problems with blood circulation, especially with combinations containing cyclizine, dimenhydrinate, diphenhydramine, or pentobarbital); nervousness or restlessness; dryness of mouth (especially with combinations containing belladonna alkaloids, cyclizine, dimenhydrinate, or diphenhydramine)

After you stop taking this medicine, your body may need time to adjust. The length of time this takes depends on the amount of medicine you were taking and how long you took it. During this time check with your doctor if your headaches begin again or worsen.

Other side effects not listed above may also occur in some patients. If you notice any other effects, check with your doctor.

Additional Information

Once a medicine has been approved for marketing for a certain use, experience may show that it is also useful for other medical problems. Although this use is not specifically included in product labeling, dihydroergotamine is sometimes used together with another medicine (heparin) to help prevent blood clots that may occur after certain kinds of surgery. It is also used to prevent or treat low blood pressure in some patients.

For patients receiving this medicine for *preventing blood clots:*

- You may need to receive this medicine two or three times a day for several days in a row. This may increase the chance of problems caused by decreased blood flow. Your health care professional will be following your progress, to make sure that this medicine is not causing problems with blood circulation.

For patients using this medicine to *prevent or treat low blood pressure:*

- Take this medicine every day as directed by your doctor.
- The dose of dihydroergotamine will depend on whether the medicine is going to be injected under the skin or into a muscle, and, sometimes, on the weight of the patient. For these reasons, the dose will have to be determined by your doctor.
- Your doctor will need to check your progress at regular visits, to make sure that the medicine is working properly without causing side effects.

- This medicine is less likely to cause problems with blood circulation in patients with low blood pressure than it is in patients with normal or high blood pressure.
- In patients being treated for low blood pressure, an increase in blood pressure is the wanted effect, not a side effect that may need medical attention.

Other than the above information, there is no additional information relating to proper use, precautions, or side effects for these uses.

Revised: 09/08/92

HEPARIN Systemic

Some commonly used brand names are:

In the U.S.—

Calciparine
Liquaemin

Generic name product may also be available.

In Canada—

Calcilean
Calciparine
Hepalean
Heparin Leo

Generic name product may also be available.

Description

Heparin (HEP-a-rin) is an anticoagulant. It is used to decrease the clotting ability of the blood and help prevent harmful clots from forming in the blood vessels. This medicine is sometimes called a blood thinner, although it does not actually thin the blood. Heparin will not dissolve blood clots that have already formed, but it may prevent the clots from becoming larger and causing more serious problems.

Heparin is often used as a treatment for certain blood vessel, heart, and lung conditions. Heparin is also used to prevent blood clotting during open-heart surgery, bypass surgery, and dialysis. It is also used in low doses to prevent the formation of blood clots in certain patients, especially those who must have certain types of surgery or who must remain in bed for a long time.

Heparin is available only with your doctor's prescription, in the following dosage form:

Parenteral
- Injection (U.S. and Canada)

Before Using This Medicine

In deciding to use a medicine, the risks of taking the medicine must be weighed against the good it will do. This is a decision you and your doctor will make. For heparin, the following should be considered:

Allergies—Tell your doctor if you have ever had any unusual or allergic reaction to heparin, to beef, or to pork. Also tell your health care professional if you are allergic to any other substances, such as foods, preservatives, or dyes.

Pregnancy—Heparin has not been shown to cause birth defects or bleeding problems in the baby. However, use during the last 3 months of pregnancy or during the month following the baby's delivery may cause bleeding problems in the mother.

Breast-feeding—Heparin does not pass into the breast milk. However, heparin can rarely cause bone problems in the nursing mother. This effect has been reported to occur when heparin is used for 2 weeks or more. Be sure to discuss this with your doctor.

Children—Heparin has been tested in children and, in effective doses, has not been shown to cause different side effects or problems than it does in adults.

Older adults—Bleeding problems may be more likely to occur in elderly patients, especially women, who are usually more sensitive than younger adults to the effects of heparin.

Other medicines—Although certain medicines should not be used together at all, in other cases two different medicines may be used together even if an interaction might occur. In these cases, your doctor may want to change the dose, or other precautions may be necessary. When you are taking heparin, it is especially important that your health care professional know if you are taking any of the following:

- Aspirin or
- Carbenicillin by injection (e.g., Geopen) or
- Cefamandole (e.g., Mandol) or
- Cefoperazone (e.g., Cefobid) or
- Cefotetan (e.g., Cefotan) or
- Dipyridamole (e.g., Persantine) or
- Divalproex (e.g., Depakote) or
- Medicine for inflammation or pain, except narcotics, or
- Medicine for overactive thyroid or
- Pentoxifylline (e.g., Trental) or
- Plicamycin (e.g., Mithracin) or
- Probenecid (e.g., Benemid) or
- Sulfinpyrazone (e.g., Anturane) or
- Ticarcillin (e.g., Ticar) or
- Valproic acid (e.g., Depakene)—Using any of these medicines together with heparin may increase the risk of bleeding

Also, tell your doctor if you are now receiving any kind of medicine by intramuscular (IM) injection.

Other medical problems—The presence of other medical problems may affect the use of heparin. Make sure you tell your doctor if you have any other medical problems, especially:

- Allergies or asthma (history of)—The risk of an allergic reaction to heparin may be increased
- Blood disease or bleeding problems or
- Colitis or stomach ulcer (or history of) or
- Diabetes mellitus (sugar diabetes) (severe) or
- High blood pressure (hypertension) or
- Kidney disease or
- Liver disease or

- Tuberculosis (active)—The risk of bleeding may be increased

Also, tell your doctor if you have received heparin before and had a reaction to it called thrombocytopenia, or if new blood clots formed while you were receiving the medicine.

In addition, it is important that you tell your doctor if you have recently had any of the following conditions or medical procedures:

- Childbirth or
- Falls or blows to the body or head or
- Heavy or unusual menstrual bleeding or
- Insertion of intrauterine device (IUD) or
- Medical or dental surgery or
- Spinal anesthesia or
- X-ray (radiation) treatment—The risk of serious bleeding may be increased

Proper Use of This Medicine

If you are using these injections at home, make sure your doctor has explained exactly how this medicine is to be given.

To obtain the best results without causing serious bleeding, *use this medicine exactly as directed by your doctor. Be certain that you are using the right amount of heparin, and that you use it according to schedule.* Be especially careful that you do not use more of it, do not use it more often, and do not use it for a longer time than your doctor ordered.

Your doctor should check your progress at regular visits. A blood test must be taken regularly to see how fast your blood is clotting so that your doctor can decide on the proper amount of heparin you should be receiving each day.

Dosing—The dose of heparin will be different for different patients and must be determined by your doctor. The dose you receive will be based on the type of heparin you receive, the condition for which you are receiving heparin, and your body weight.

Missed dose—If you miss a dose of this medicine, use it as soon as possible. However, if it is almost time for your next dose, do not use the missed dose at all and do not double the next one. *Doubling the dose may cause bleeding.* Instead, go back to your regular dosing schedule. It is best to keep a record of each dose as you use it to avoid mistakes. Be sure to give your doctor a record of any doses you miss. If you have any questions about this, check with your doctor.

Storage—To store this medicine:

- Keep out of the reach of children.
- Store away from heat and direct light.
- Keep the medicine from freezing.
- Do not keep outdated medicine or medicine no longer needed. Be sure that any discarded medicine is out of the reach of children.

Precautions While Using This Medicine

Do not take aspirin while using this medicine. Many nonprescription (over-the-counter [OTC]) medicines and some prescription medicines contain aspirin. Check the labels of all medicines you take. Also, do not take ibuprofen unless it has been ordered by your doctor. In addition, there are many other medicines that may change the way heparin works or increase the chance of bleeding if they are used together with heparin. It is best to check with your health care professional before taking any other medicine while you are using heparin.

Tell all medical doctors and dentists you visit that you are using this medicine.

It is recommended that you carry identification stating that you are using heparin. If you have any questions about what kind of identification to carry, check with your health care professional.

While you are using this medicine, it is very important that you avoid sports and other activities that may cause you to be injured. Report to your doctor any falls, blows to the body or head, or other injuries, since serious bleeding inside the body may occur without your knowing about it.

Take special care in brushing your teeth and in shaving. Use a soft toothbrush and floss gently. Also, it is best to use an electric shaver rather than a blade.

Side Effects of This Medicine

Since many things can affect the way your body reacts to this medicine, you should always watch for signs of unusual bleeding. Unusual bleeding may mean that your body is getting more heparin than it needs.

Along with its needed effects, a medicine may cause some unwanted effects. Although not all of these side effects may occur, if they do occur they may need medical attention.

Check with your doctor immediately if any of the following signs and symptoms of bleeding inside the body occur:

Abdominal or stomach pain or swelling; back pain or backaches; blood in urine; bloody or black, tarry stools; constipation; coughing up blood; dizziness; headaches (severe or continuing); joint pain, stiffness, or swelling; vomiting of blood or material that looks like coffee grounds

Also, *check with your doctor immediately* if any of the following side effects occur, since they may mean that you are having a serious allergic reaction to the medicine:

Changes in the skin color of the face; fast or irregular breathing; puffiness or swelling of the eyelids or around the eyes; shortness of breath, troubled breathing, tightness in chest, and/or wheezing; skin rash, hives, and/or itching

Also, check with your doctor as soon as possible if any of the following occur:

Bleeding from gums when brushing teeth; heavy bleeding or oozing from cuts or wounds; unexplained bruising or purplish areas on skin; unexplained nosebleeds; unusually heavy or unexpected menstrual bleeding

Other side effects that may need medical attention may occur while you are using this medicine. Check with your doctor as soon as possible if any of the following side effects occur:

Less common or rare

Back or rib pain (with long-term use only); change in skin color, especially near the place of injection or in the fingers, toes, arms, or legs; chest pain; chills and/or fever; collection of blood under skin (blood blister) at place of injection; decrease in height (with long-term use only); frequent or persistent erection; irritation, pain, redness, or ulcers at place of injection; itching and burning feeling, especially on the bottom of the feet; nausea and/or vomiting; numbness or tingling in hands or feet; pain, coldness, or blue color of skin of arms or legs; peeling of skin; runny nose; tearing of eyes; unusual hair loss (with long-term use only)

Other side effects not listed above may also occur in some patients. If you notice any other effects, check with your doctor.

Revised: August 1990
Interim revision: 08/23/94

HEPATITIS A VACCINE INACTIVATED Systemic

Some commonly used brand names are:

In the U.S.—
Havrix
Vaqta

In Canada—
Havrix

Description

Hepatitis (hep-ah-TY-tiss) A is a serious disease of the liver that can cause death. It is caused by the hepatitis A virus (HAV), and is spread most often through infected food or water. Hepatitis A may also be spread by close person-to-person contact with infected persons (such as between persons living in the same household). Although some infected persons do not appear to be sick, they are still able to spread the virus to others.

Hepatitis A is less common in the U.S. and other areas of the world that have a higher level of sanitation and good water and sewage (waste) systems. However, it is a significant health problem in parts of the world that do not have such systems. If you are traveling to certain countries or remote (out-of-the-way) areas, hepatitis A vaccine will help protect you from hepatitis A disease.

It is recommended that persons 2 years of age and older be vaccinated with hepatitis A vaccine when traveling to the following parts of the world:

- Africa.
- Asia (except Japan).
- parts of the Caribbean.
- Central and South America.
- eastern Europe.
- the Mediterranean basin.
- the Middle East.
- Mexico.

Hepatitis A vaccine is also recommended for all persons 2 years of age and older who live in areas that have frequent outbreaks of hepatitis A disease or who may be at increased risk of infection from hepatitis A virus. These persons include:

- Military personnel.
- Persons living in or moving to areas that have a high rate of HAV infection.
- Persons who may be exposed to the hepatitis A virus repeatedly due to a high rate of hepatitis A disease, such as Alaskan Eskimos and Native Americans.
- Persons engaging in high-risk sexual activity, such as homosexual males.
- Persons who use illegal injectable drugs.
- Persons living in a community experiencing an outbreak of hepatitis A.
- Persons working in facilities for the mentally retarded.
- Employees of and children in day-care centers.
- Persons who work with hepatitis A virus in the laboratory.
- Persons who handle primate animals.
- Food handlers.
- Persons with chronic liver disease.

Hepatitis A vaccine is to be used only by or under the supervision of a doctor. It is available in the following dosage form:

Parenteral

- Injection (U.S. and Canada)

Before Receiving This Vaccine

In deciding to use a medicine, the risks of taking the medicine must be weighed against the good it will do. This is a decision you and your doctor will make. For hepatitis A vaccine, the following should be considered:

Allergies—Tell your doctor if you have ever had any unusual or allergic reaction to hepatitis A vaccine. Also tell your health care professional if you are allergic to any other substances, such as preservatives.

Pregnancy—Studies on effects in pregnancy have not been done in either humans or animals.

Breast-feeding—This vaccine has not been reported to cause problems in nursing babies.

Children—Hepatitis A vaccine is not recommended for infants and children younger than 2 years of age. For children 2 years of age and older, this vaccine is not expected to cause different side effects or problems than it does in adults.

Older adults—Many medicines have not been studied specifically in older people. Therefore, it may not be known whether they work exactly the same way they do in younger adults. Although there is no specific information comparing use of hepatitis A vaccine in the elderly with use in other age groups, this vaccine is not expected to cause different side effects or problems in older people than it does in younger adults.

Other medicines—Although certain medicines should not be used together at all, in other cases two different medicines may be used together even if an interaction might occur. In these cases, your doctor may want to change the dose, or other precautions may be necessary. Tell your health care professional if you are taking any other prescription or nonprescription (over-the-counter [OTC]) medicine.

Other medical problems—The presence of other medical problems may affect the use of hepatitis A vaccine. Make sure you tell your doctor if you have any other medical problems.

Proper Use of This Vaccine

Dosing—The dose of hepatitis A vaccine will be different for different patients. *Follow your doctor's orders.* The following information includes only the average doses of hepatitis A vaccine.

- For *injection* dosage form:
  - —For prevention of hepatitis A disease:
    - Adults—One adult dose injected into a muscle. A booster (repeat) dose may be needed six to twelve months after the first dose.
    - Children 2 to 18 years of age—One or two pediatric doses injected into a muscle. A booster (repeat) dose may be needed six to twelve months after the first dose.
    - Children up to 2 years of age—Use is not recommended.

Side Effects of This Vaccine

Along with its needed effects, a vaccine may cause some unwanted effects. Although not all of these side effects may occur, if they do occur they may need medical attention. *It is very important that you tell your doctor about any side effects that occur after a dose of hepatitis A vaccine,* even though the side effect may have gone away without treatment. Some types of side effects may mean that you should not receive any more doses of hepatitis A vaccine.

Get emergency help immediately if any of the following side effects occur:

Rare

Difficulty in breathing or swallowing; hives; itching, especially of feet or hands; reddening of skin, especially around ears; swelling of eyes, face, or inside of nose; unusual tiredness or weakness (sudden and severe)

Other side effects may occur that usually do not need medical attention. However, check with your doctor if any of the following side effects continue or are bothersome:

More common

Soreness at place of injection

Less common

Fever of 100 °F (37.7 °C) or higher, general feeling of discomfort or illness, headache, lack of appetite, nausea, tenderness or warmth at injection site

Rare

Aches or pain in joints or muscles, diarrhea or stomach cramps or pain, itching, swelling of glands in armpits or neck, vomiting, welts

Other side effects not listed above may also occur in some patients. If you notice any other effects, check with your doctor.

Developed: 02/06/97

HEPATITIS B VACCINE RECOMBINANT Systemic

Some commonly used brand names are:

In the U.S.—

Engerix-B
Recombivax HB
Recombivax HB Dialysis Formulation

In Canada—

Engerix-B
Recombivax HB
Recombivax HB Dialysis Formulation

Another commonly used name is HB vaccine.

Description

Hepatitis (hep-ah-TY-tiss) B vaccine recombinant is used to prevent infection by the hepatitis B virus. The vaccine works by causing your body to produce its own protection (antibodies) against the disease.

Hepatitis B vaccine recombinant is made without any human blood or blood products or any other substances of human origin and cannot give you the hepatitis B virus (HBV) or the human immunodeficiency virus (HIV).

HBV infection is a major cause of serious liver diseases, such as virus hepatitis and cirrhosis, and a type of liver cancer called primary hepatocellular carcinoma.

Pregnant women who have hepatitis B infection or are carriers of hepatitis B virus can give the disease to their babies when they are born. These babies often suffer serious long-term illnesses from the disease.

Immunization against hepatitis B disease is recommended for all newborn babies, infants, children, and adolescents up to 19 years old. It is also recommended for adults who live in areas that have a high rate of hepatitis B disease or who may be at increased risk of infection from hepatitis B virus. These adults include:

- Sexually active homosexual and bisexual males, including those with HIV infection.
- Sexually active heterosexual persons with multiple partners.
- Persons who may be exposed to the virus by means of blood, blood products, or human bites, such as health care workers, employees in medical facilities, patients and staff of live-in facilities and day-care programs for the developmentally disabled, morticians and embalmers, police and fire department personnel, and military personnel.
- Persons who have kidney disease or who undergo blood dialysis for kidney disease.
- Persons with blood clotting disorders who receive transfusions of clotting-factor concentrates.
- Household and sexual contacts of HBV carriers.
- Persons in areas with high risk of HBV infection [in the population], such as Alaskan Eskimos, Pacific Islanders, Haitian and Indochinese immigrants, and refugees from areas that have a high rate of hepatitis B disease; persons accepting orphans or adoptees from these areas; and travelers to these areas.
- Persons who use illegal injection drugs.
- Prisoners.

This vaccine is available only from your doctor or other authorized health care professional, in the following dosage form:

Parenteral

- Injection (U.S. and Canada)

Before Receiving This Vaccine

In deciding to use a medicine, the risks of using the medicine must be weighed against the good it will do. This is a decision you and your doctor will make. For hepatitis B recombinant vaccine, the following should be considered:

Allergies—Tell your doctor if you have ever had any unusual or allergic reaction to this vaccine or to the hepatitis B vaccine made from human plasma. Also tell your health care professional if you are allergic to any other substances, such as foods (especially yeast). The vaccine is made by using yeast; persons allergic to yeast may also be allergic to the vaccine.

Pregnancy—Studies on effects in pregnancy have not been done in either humans or animals. However, the vaccine is not expected to cause problems during pregnancy.

Breast-feeding—It is not known whether hepatitis B vaccine passes into the breast milk. However, the vaccine is not expected to cause problems in nursing babies.

Children—Hepatitis B vaccine has been tested in newborns, infants, and children and, in effective doses, has not been shown to cause different side effects or problems than it does in adults. The vaccine strength for use in dialysis patients has been studied only in adult patients, and there is no specific information about its use in children receiving dialysis.

Teenagers—Hepatitis B vaccine is very effective when administered to adolescents and young adults. It is recommended that all adolescents who have not previously received three doses of hepatitis B vaccine should start or complete the vaccine series at 11 to 12 years of age. Hepatitis B vaccine has not been shown to cause different side effects or problems in adolescents and young adults than it does in other age groups.

Older adults—This vaccine is not expected to cause different side effects or problems in older people than it does in younger adults. However, persons over 50 years of age may not become as immune to the virus as do younger adults.

Other medicines—Although certain medicines should not be used together at all, in other cases two different medicines may be used together even if an interaction might occur. In these cases, your doctor may want to change the dose, or other precautions may be necessary. Tell your health care professional if you are using any other prescription or nonprescription (over-the-counter [OTC]) medicine.

Other medical problems—The presence of other medical problems may affect the use of hepatitis B vaccine. Make sure you tell your doctor if you have any other medical problems, especially:

- Allergic reaction to hepatitis B vaccine, history of—Use of hepatitis B vaccine is not recommended

Proper Use of This Vaccine

Dosing—The dose of hepatitis B vaccine will be different for different patients. *Follow your doctor's orders.* The following information includes only the average doses of hepatitis B vaccine.

- For *injection* dosage form:
  - —For prevention of hepatitis B infection:
    - Adults, adolescents, and older children—2.5 to 20 micrograms (mcg) injected into the arm muscle during the first office visit, then one month and six months after the first dose, for a total of three doses.
    - Adults who also receive or will receive blood dialysis—40 mcg injected into the arm muscle during the first office visit, then one month and six months after the first dose, for a total of three doses; or 40 mcg injected into the arm muscle during the first office visit, then one month, two months, and six months after the first dose, for a total of four doses.
    - Infants and young children—2.5 to 20 mcg injected into the thigh muscle during the first office visit, then one month and six months after the first dose, for a total of three doses.
    - Newborn babies—2.5 to 20 mcg injected into the thigh muscle at birth or within seven days of birth, then one month and six months after the first dose, for a total of three doses; or 10 or 20 mcg injected into the thigh muscle at birth or

within seven days of birth, then one month, two months, and twelve months after the first dose, for a total of four doses.

Side Effects of This Vaccine

Along with its needed effects, a vaccine may cause some unwanted effects. Although not all of these side effects may occur, if they do occur they may need medical attention.

Get emergency help immediately if any of the following side effects occur:

Symptoms of allergic reaction—rare

Difficulty in breathing or swallowing; hives; itching, especially of feet or hands; reddening of skin, especially around ears; swelling of eyes, face, or inside of nose; unusual tiredness or weakness (sudden and severe)

Check with your doctor as soon as possible if any of the following side effects occur:

Rare

Aches or pain in joints, fever, or skin rash or welts (may occur days or weeks after receiving the vaccine); blurred vision or other vision changes; muscle weakness or numbness or tingling of arms and legs

Other side effects may occur that usually do not need medical attention. However, check with your doctor if any of the following side effects continue or are bothersome:

More common

Soreness at the place of injection

Less common

Dizziness; fever of 37.7 °C (100 °F) or higher; hard lump, redness, swelling, pain, itching, purple spot, tenderness, or warmth at place of injection; headache; unusual tiredness or weakness

Rare

Aches or pain in muscles; back pain or stiffness or pain in neck or shoulder; chills; diarrhea or stomach cramps or pain; general feeling of discomfort or illness; increased sweating; headache (mild), sore throat, runny nose, or fever (mild); itching; lack of appetite or decreased appetite; nausea or vomiting; sudden redness of skin; swelling of glands in armpit or neck; trouble in sleeping; welts

Other side effects not listed above may also occur in some patients. If you notice any other effects, check with your doctor.

Revised: 06/20/97

HISTAMINE H_2-RECEPTOR ANTAGONISTS Systemic

Some commonly used brand names are:

In the U.S.—

Axid[3]
Axid AR[3]
Pepcid[2]
Pepcid I.V.[2]
Pepcid AC[2]
Tagamet[1]
Tagamet HB[1]
Zantac[4]
Zantac EFFERdose Granules[4]
Zantac EFFERdose Tablets[4]
Zantac 75[4]
Zantac 150 GELdose[4]
Zantac 300 GELdose[4]

In Canada—

Apo-Cimetidine[1]
Apo-Ranitidine[4]
Axid[3]
Novocimetine[1]
Pepcid[2]
Pepcid I.V.[2]
Peptol[1]
Tagamet[1]
Zantac[4]
Zantac-C[4]

Note: For quick reference, the following histamine H_2-receptor antagonists are numbered to match the corresponding brand names.

This information applies to the following medicines:

1. Cimetidine (sye-MET-i-deen)‡
2. Famotidine (fa-MOE-ti-deen)
3. Nizatidine (ni-ZA-ti-deen)
4. Ranitidine (ra-NIT-ti-deen)

‡Generic name product may also be available in the U.S.

Description

Histamine H_2-receptor antagonists, also known as H_2-blockers, are used to treat duodenal ulcers and prevent their return. They are also used to treat gastric ulcers and for some conditions, such as Zollinger-Ellison disease, in which the stomach produces too much acid. In over-the-counter (OTC) strengths, these medicines are used to relieve and/or prevent heartburn, acid indigestion, and sour stomach. H_2-blockers may also be used for other conditions as determined by your doctor.

H_2-blockers work by decreasing the amount of acid produced by the stomach.

They are available in the following dosage forms:

Oral

Cimetidine
- Oral solution (U.S. and Canada)
- Tablets (U.S. and Canada)

Famotidine
- Oral suspension (U.S.)
- Tablets (U.S. and Canada)

Nizatidine
- Capsules (U.S. and Canada)
- Tablets (U.S.)

Ranitidine
- Capsules (U.S. and Canada)
- Effervescent granules (U.S.)
- Syrup (U.S. and Canada)
- Tablets (U.S. and Canada)
- Effervescent tablets (U.S.)

Parenteral

Cimetidine
- Injection (U.S. and Canada)

Famotidine
- Injection (U.S. and Canada)

Ranitidine
- Injection (U.S. and Canada)

Before Using This Medicine

In deciding to use a medicine, the risks of taking the medicine must be weighed against the good it will do. This is

a decision you and your doctor will make. For H_2-blockers, the following should be considered:

Allergies—Tell your doctor if you have ever had any unusual or allergic reaction to cimetidine, famotidine, nizatidine, or ranitidine.

Pregnancy—H_2-blockers have not been studied in pregnant women. In animal studies, famotidine and ranitidine have not been shown to cause birth defects or other problems. However, one study in rats suggested that cimetidine may affect male sexual development. More studies are needed to confirm this. Also, studies in rabbits with very high doses have shown that nizatidine causes miscarriages and low birth weights. Make sure your doctor knows if you are pregnant or if you may become pregnant before taking H_2-blockers.

Breast-feeding—Cimetidine, famotidine, nizatidine, and ranitidine pass into the breast milk and may cause unwanted effects, such as decreased amount of stomach acid and increased excitement, in the nursing baby. It may be necessary for you to take another medicine or to stop breast-feeding during treatment. Be sure you have discussed the risks and benefits of the medicine with your doctor.

Children—This medicine has been tested in children and, in effective doses, has not been shown to cause different side effects or problems than it does in adults when used for short periods of time.

Older adults—Confusion and dizziness may be especially likely to occur in elderly patients, who are usually more sensitive than younger adults to the effects of H_2-blockers.

Other medicines—Although certain medicines should not be used together at all, in other cases two different medicines may be used together even if an interaction might occur. In these cases, your doctor may want to change the dose, or other precautions may be necessary. When you are taking or receiving H_2-blockers it is especially important that your health care professional know if you are taking any of the following:

- Aminophylline (e.g., Somophyllin) or
- Anticoagulants (blood thinners) or
- Caffeine (e.g., NoDoz) or
- Metoprolol (e.g., Lopressor) or
- Oxtriphylline (e.g., Choledyl) or
- Phenytoin (e.g., Dilantin) or
- Propranolol (e.g., Inderal) or
- Theophylline (e.g., Somophyllin-T) or
- Tricyclic antidepressants (amitriptyline [e.g., Elavil], amoxapine [e.g., Asendin], clomipramine [e.g., Anafranil], desipramine [e.g., Pertofrane], doxepin [e.g., Sinequan], imipramine [e.g., Tofranil], nortriptyline [e.g., Aventyl], protriptyline [e.g., Vivactil], trimipramine [e.g., Surmontil])—Use of these medicines with cimetidine has been shown to increase the effects of cimetidine. This is less of a problem with ranitidine and has not been reported for famotidine or nizatidine. However, all of the H_2-blockers are similar, so drug interactions may occur with any of them
- Itraconazole (e.g., Sporanox) or
- Ketoconazole (e.g., Nizoral)—H_2-blockers may decrease the effects of itraconazole or ketoconazole; H_2-blockers should be taken at least 2 hours after these medicines

Other medical problems—The presence of other medical problems may affect the use of H_2-blockers. Make sure you tell your doctor if you have any other medical problems, especially:

- Kidney disease or
- Liver disease—The H_2-blocker may build up in the bloodstream, which may increase the risk of side effects
- Weakened immune system (difficulty fighting infection)—Decrease in stomach acid caused by H_2-blockers may increase the possibility of a certain type of infection

Proper Use of This Medicine

For patients taking the *nonprescription strengths* of these medicines for heartburn, acid indigestion, and sour stomach:

- Do not take the maximum daily dosage continuously for more than 2 weeks, unless directed to do so by your doctor.
- If you have trouble in swallowing, or persistent abdominal pain, see your doctor promptly. These may be signs of a serious condition that may need different treatment.

For patients taking the *prescription strengths* of these medicines for more serious problems:

- One dose a day—Take it at bedtime, unless otherwise directed.
- Two doses a day—Take one in the morning and one at bedtime.
- Several doses a day—Take them with meals and at bedtime for best results.

It may take several days before this medicine begins to relieve stomach pain. To help relieve this pain, antacids may be taken with the H_2-blocker, unless your doctor has told you not to use them. However, you should wait one-half to one hour between taking the antacid and the H_2-blocker.

Take this medicine for the full time of treatment, even if you begin to feel better. Also, it is important that you keep your appointments with your doctor for check-ups so that your doctor will be better able to tell you when to stop taking this medicine.

For patients taking *ranitidine effervescent granules or tablets:*

- Remove the foil wrapping and dissolve the dose in 6 to 8 ounces of water before drinking.

Dosing—The dose of histamine H_2-receptor antagonists (also called H_2-blockers) will be different for different patients. *Follow your doctor's orders or the directions on the label.* The following information includes only the average doses of these medicines. *If your dose is different, do not change it unless your doctor tells you to do so.*

The number of capsules or tablets or teaspoonfuls of solution, suspension, or syrup that you take depends on the strength of the medicine. Also, *the number of doses you take each day, the time allowed between doses, and the length of time you take the medicine depend on the medical problem for which you are taking the H_2-receptor antagonist.*

For cimetidine

- For *oral* dosage forms (solution and tablets):
  - —To treat duodenal or gastric ulcers:
    - Older adults, adults, and teenagers—300 milligrams (mg) four times a day, with meals and at bedtime. Some people may take 400 or 600 mg two times a day, on waking up and at bedtime. Others may take 800 mg at bedtime.
    - Children—20 to 40 mg per kilogram (kg) (9.1 to 18.2 mg per pound) of body weight a day, divided into four doses, taken with meals and at bedtime.
  - —To prevent duodenal ulcers:
    - Older adults, adults, and teenagers—300 mg two times a day, on waking up and at bedtime. Instead some people may take 400 mg at bedtime.
    - Children—Dose must be determined by your doctor.
  - —To treat heartburn, acid indigestion, and sour stomach:
    - Adults and teenagers—200 mg with water when symptoms start. The dose may be repeated once in twenty-four hours. Do not take more than 400 mg in twenty-four hours.
    - Children—Dose must be determined by your doctor.
  - —To treat conditions in which the stomach produces too much acid:
    - Adults—300 mg four times a day, with meals and at bedtime. Your doctor may change the dose if needed.
    - Children—Dose must be determined by your doctor.
  - —To treat gastroesophageal reflux disease:
    - Adults—800 to 1600 mg a day, divided into smaller doses. Treatment usually lasts for 12 weeks.
    - Children—Dose must be determined by your doctor.
- For *injectable* dosage form:
  - —To treat duodenal ulcers, gastric ulcers or conditions in which the stomach produces too much acid:
    - Older adults, adults, and teenagers—300 mg injected into muscle, every six to eight hours. Or, 300 mg injected slowly into a vein every six to eight hours. Instead, 900 mg may be injected slowly into a vein around the clock at the rate of 37.5 mg per hour. Some people may need 150 mg at first, before beginning the around-the-clock treatment.
    - Children—5 to 10 mg per kg (2.3 to 4.5 mg per pound) of body weight injected into a vein or muscle, every six to eight hours.
  - —To prevent stress-related bleeding:
    - Older adults, adults, and teenagers—50 mg per hour injected slowly into a vein around the clock for up to 7 days.
    - Children—Dose must be determined by your doctor.

For famotidine

- For *oral* dosage forms (suspension and tablets):
  - —To treat duodenal ulcers:
    - Older adults, adults, and teenagers—40 milligrams (mg) once a day at bedtime. Some people may take 20 mg two times day.
    - Children—Dose must be determined by your doctor.
  - —To prevent duodenal ulcers:
    - Older adults, adults, and teenagers—20 mg once a day at bedtime.
    - Children—Dose must be determined by your doctor.
  - —To treat gastric ulcers:
    - Older adults, adults, and teenagers—40 mg once a day at bedtime.
    - Children—Dose must be determined by your doctor.
  - —To treat heartburn, acid indigestion, and sour stomach:
    - Adults and teenagers—10 mg with water when symptoms start. The dose may be repeated once in twenty-four hours. Do not take more than 20 mg in twenty-four hours.
    - Children—Dose must be determined by your doctor.
  - —To prevent heartburn, acid indigestion, and sour stomach:
    - Adults and teenagers—10 mg taken one hour before eating a meal you expect to cause symptoms. The dose may be repeated once in twenty-four hours. Do not take more than 20 mg in twenty-four hours.
    - Children—Dose must be determined by your doctor.
  - —To treat conditions in which the stomach produces too much acid:
    - Older adults, adults, and children—20 mg every six hours. Your doctor may change the dose if needed.
    - Children—Dose must be determined by your doctor.
  - —To treat gastroesophageal reflux disease:
    - Older adults, adults, and teenagers—20 mg two times a day, usually for up to 6 weeks.
    - Children weighing more than 10 kg (22 pounds): 1 to 2 mg per kilogram (kg) (0.5 to 0.9 mg per pound) of body weight a day divided into two doses.
    - Children weighing less than 10 kg (22 pounds): 1 to 2 mg per kg (0.5 to 0.9 mg per pound) of body weight a day, divided into three doses.
- For *injectable* dosage form:
  - —To treat duodenal ulcers, gastric ulcers, or conditions in which the stomach produces too much acid:
    - Older adults, adults, and teenagers—20 mg injected into a vein, every twelve hours.

• Children—Dose must be determined by your doctor.

For nizatidine

• For *oral* dosage forms (capsules and tablets):

—To treat duodenal or gastric ulcers:

• Older adults, adults, and teenagers—300 milligrams (mg) once a day at bedtime. Some people may take 150 mg two times a day.

• Children—Dose must be determined by your doctor.

—To prevent duodenal ulcers:

• Adults and teenagers—150 mg once a day at bedtime.

• Children—Dose must be determined by your doctor.

—To prevent heartburn, acid indigestion, and sour stomach:

• Adults and teenagers—75 mg taken thirty to sixty minutes before eating a meal you expect to cause symptoms. The dose may be repeated once in twenty-four hours.

• Children—Dose must be determined by your doctor.

—To treat gastroesophageal reflux disease:

• Adults and teenagers—150 mg two times a day.

• Children—Dose must be determined by your doctor.

For ranitidine

• For *oral* dosage forms (capsules, effervescent granules, syrup, tablets, effervescent tablets):

—To treat duodenal ulcers:

• Older adults, adults, and teenagers—150 milligrams (mg) two times a day. Some people may take 300 mg once a day at bedtime.

• Children—2 to 4 mg per kilogram (kg) (1 to 2 mg per pound) of body weight two times a day. However, your dose will not be more than 300 mg a day.

—To prevent duodenal ulcers:

• Older adults, adults, and teenagers—150 mg at bedtime.

• Children—Dose must be determined by your doctor.

—To treat gastric ulcers:

• Older adults, adults, and teenagers—150 mg two times a day.

• Children—2 to 4 mg per kg (1 to 2 mg per pound) of body weight two times a day. However, your dose will not be more than 300 mg a day.

—To treat heartburn, acid indigestion, and sour stomach:

• Adults and teenagers—75 mg with water when symptoms start. The dose may be repeated once in twenty-four hours. Do not take more than 150 mg in twenty-four hours.

• Children—Dose must be determined by your doctor.

—To treat some conditions in which the stomach produces too much acid:

• Older adults, adults, and teenagers—150 mg two times a day. Your doctor may change the dose if needed.

• Children—Dose must be determined by your doctor.

—To treat gastroesophageal reflux disease:

• Older adults, adults, and teenagers—150 mg two times a day. Your dose may be increased if needed.

• Children—2 to 8 mg per kg (1 to 3.6 mg per pound) of body weight a day, three times a day. However, most children usually will not take more than 300 mg a day.

• For *injectable* dosage form:

—To treat duodenal ulcers, gastric ulcers, or conditions in which the stomach produces too much acid:

• Older adults, adults, and teenagers—50 mg injected into a muscle every six to eight hours. Or, 50 mg injected slowly into a vein every six to eight hours. Instead, you may receive 6.25 mg per hour injected slowly into a vein around the clock. However, most people will usually not need more than 400 mg a day.

—To treat duodenal or gastric ulcers:

• Children—2 to 4 mg per kg (1 to 2 mg per pound) of body weight a day, injected slowly into a vein.

Missed dose—If you miss a dose of this medicine, take it as soon as possible. However, if it is almost time for your next dose, skip the missed dose and go back to your regular dosing schedule. Do not double doses.

Storage—To store this medicine:

- Keep out of the reach of children.
- Store away from heat and direct light.
- Do not store the capsule or tablet form of this medicine in the bathroom, near the kitchen sink, or in other damp places. Heat or moisture may cause the medicine to break down.
- Keep the liquid form of this medicine from freezing.
- Do not keep outdated medicine or medicine no longer needed. Be sure that any discarded medicine is out of the reach of children.

Precautions While Using This Medicine

Some tests may be affected by this medicine. Tell the doctor in charge that you are taking this medicine before:

- You have any skin tests for allergies.
- You have any tests to determine how much acid your stomach produces.

Remember that certain medicines, such as aspirin, and certain foods and drinks (e.g., citrus products, carbonated drinks, etc.) irritate the stomach and may make your problem worse.

Cigarette smoking tends to decrease the effect of H_2-blockers by increasing the amount of acid produced by the stomach. This is more likely to affect the stomach's nighttime production of acid. While taking H_2-blockers, stop smoking completely, or at least do not smoke after taking the last dose of the day.

Drinking alcoholic beverages while taking an H_2-receptor antagonist has been reported to increase the blood levels of alcohol. You should consult your health care professional for guidance.

Check with your doctor if your ulcer pain continues or gets worse.

Side Effects of This Medicine

Along with its needed effects, a medicine may cause some unwanted effects. Although not all of these side effects may occur, if they do occur they may need medical attention.

Check with your doctor as soon as possible if any of the following side effects occur:

Rare

Burning, redness, skin rash, or swelling; confusion; fast, pounding, or irregular heartbeat; fever; slow heartbeat; sore throat; tightness in chest; unusual bleeding or bruising; unusual tiredness or weakness

Other side effects may occur that usually do not need medical attention. These side effects may go away during treatment as your body adjusts to the medicine. However, check with your doctor if any of the following side effects continue or are bothersome:

Less common or rare

Blurred vision; constipation; decreased sexual ability (especially in patients with Zollinger-Ellison disease who have received high doses of cimetidine for at least 1 year); decrease in sexual desire; diarrhea; dizziness; drowsiness; dryness of mouth or skin; headache; increased sweating; joint or muscle pain; loss of appetite; loss of hair (temporary); nausea or vomiting; ringing or buzzing in ears; skin rash; swelling of breasts or breast soreness in females and males

Not all of the side effects listed above have been reported for each of these medicines, but they have been reported for at least one of them. All of the H_2-blockers are similar, so any of the above side effects may occur with any of these medicines.

Other side effects not listed above may also occur in some patients. If you notice any other effects, check with your doctor.

Additional Information

Once a medicine has been approved for marketing for a certain use, experience may show that it is also useful for other medical problems. Although these uses are not included in product labeling, H_2-blockers are used in certain patients with the following medical conditions:

- Damage to the stomach and/or intestines due to stress or trauma
- Hives
- Pancreatic problems
- Stomach or intestinal ulcers (sores) resulting from damage caused by medication used to treat rheumatoid arthritis

Other than the above information, there is no additional information relating to proper use, precautions, or side effects for these uses.

Revised: 08/08/96
Interim revision: 08/08/97

HMG-CoA REDUCTASE INHIBITORS Systemic

Some commonly used brand names are:

In the U.S.—

Lescol[1]	Pravachol[3]
Mevacor[2]	Zocor[4]

In Canada—

Mevacor[2]	Zocor[4]
Pravachol[3]	

Other commonly used names are:

Epistatin[4]	Mevinolin[2]
Eptastatin[3]	Synvinolin[4]

Note: For quick reference, the following HMG-CoA reductase inhibitors are numbered to match the corresponding brand names.

This information applies to the following medicines:

1. Fluvastatin (FLOO-va-sta-tin)†
2. Lovastatin (LOE-va-sta-tin)
3. Pravastatin (PRA-va-stat-in)
4. Simvastatin (SIM-va-stat-in)

†Not commercially available in Canada.

Description

Fluvastatin, lovastatin, pravastatin, and simvastatin are used to lower levels of cholesterol and other fats in the blood. This may help prevent medical problems caused by cholesterol clogging the blood vessels.

These medicines belong to the group of medicines called 3-hydroxy-3-methylglutaryl coenzyme A (HMG-CoA) reductase inhibitors. They work by blocking an enzyme that is needed by the body to make cholesterol. Thus, less cholesterol is made.

HMG-CoA reductase inhibitors are available only with your doctor's prescription, in the following dosage forms:

Oral

Fluvastatin
- Capsules (U.S.)

Lovastatin
- Tablets (U.S. and Canada)

Pravastatin
- Tablets (U.S. and Canada)

Simvastatin
- Tablets (U.S and Canada)

Before Using This Medicine

In deciding to use a medicine, the risks of taking the medicine must be weighed against the good it will do. This is

a decision you and your doctor will make. For HMG-CoA reductase inhibitors, the following should be considered:

Allergies—Tell your doctor if you have ever had any unusual or allergic reaction to HMG-CoA reductase inhibitors. Also tell your health care professional if you are allergic to any other substances, such as foods, preservatives, or dyes.

Diet—Before prescribing medicines to lower your cholesterol, your doctor will probably try to control your condition by prescribing a personal diet for you. Such a diet will be lower in total fat, particularly saturated fat, and dietary cholesterol. Many people are able to control their condition by carefully following their doctor's orders for proper diet and exercise. *Medicine is prescribed only when additional help is needed* and is effective only when a schedule of diet and exercise is properly followed.

Also, this medicine is less effective if you are greatly overweight. It may be very important for you to go on a reducing diet. However, check with your doctor before going on any diet.

Pregnancy—HMG-CoA reductase inhibitors should not be used during pregnancy or by women who plan to become pregnant in the near future. These medicines block formation of cholesterol, which is necessary for the fetus to develop properly. HMG-CoA reductase inhibitors may cause birth defects or other problems in the baby if taken during pregnancy. An effective form of birth control should be used during treatment with these medicines. *Check with your doctor immediately if you think you have become pregnant while taking this medicine.* Be sure you have discussed this with your doctor.

Breast-feeding—These medicines are not recommended for use during breast-feeding because they may cause unwanted effects in nursing babies.

Children—Studies on this medicine have been done only in adult patients, and there is no specific information comparing use of HMG-CoA reductase inhibitors in children with use in other age groups. However, lovastatin and simvastatin have been used in a limited number of children under 18 years of age. Early information seems to show that these medicines may be effective in children, but their long-term safety has not been studied.

Older adults—This medicine has been tested in a limited number of patients 65 years of age or older and has not been shown to cause different side effects or problems in older people than it does in younger adults.

Other medicines—Although certain medicines should not be used together at all, in other cases two different medicines may be used together even if an interaction might occur. In these cases, your doctor may want to change the dose, or other precautions may be necessary. When you are taking HMG-CoA reductase inhibitors, it is especially important that your health care professional know if you are taking any of the following:

- Cyclosporine (e.g., Sandimmune) or
- Gemfibrozil (e.g., Lopid) or
- Niacin—Use of these medicines with an HMG-CoA reductase inhibitor may increase the risk of developing muscle problems and kidney failure

Other medical problems—The presence of other medical problems may affect the use of HMG-CoA reductase inhibitors. Make sure you tell your doctor if you have any other medical problems, especially:

- Alcohol abuse (or history of) or
- Liver disease—Use of this medicine may make liver problems worse
- Convulsions (seizures), not well-controlled, or
- Organ transplant with therapy to prevent transplant rejection or
- If you have recently had major surgery—Patients with these conditions may be at risk of developing problems that may lead to kidney failure

Proper Use of This Medicine

Use this medicine only as directed by your doctor. Do not use more or less of it, and do not use it more often or for a longer time than your doctor ordered.

Remember that this medicine will not cure your condition but it does help control it. Therefore, you must continue to take it as directed if you expect to keep your cholesterol levels down.

Follow carefully the special diet your doctor gave you. This is the most important part of controlling your condition, and is necessary if the medicine is to work properly.

For patients taking *lovastatin:*

- This medicine works better when it is taken with food. If you are taking this medicine once a day, take it with the evening meal. If you are taking more than one dose a day, take each dose with a meal or snack.

Dosing—The dose of these medicines will be different for different patients. *Follow your doctor's orders or the directions on the label.* The following information includes only the average doses of these medicines. *If your dose is different, do not change it* unless your doctor tells you to do so.

The number of capsules or tablets that you take depends on the strength of the medicine.

For fluvastatin

- For *oral* dosage form (capsules):
  - —For high cholesterol:
    - Adults—20 to 40 milligrams (mg) once a day in the evening.
    - Children—Use and dose must be determined by your doctor.

For lovastatin

- For *oral* dosage form (tablets):
  - —For high cholesterol:
    - Adults—20 to 80 milligrams (mg) a day taken as a single dose or divided into smaller doses. Take with meals.
    - Children—Use and dose must be determined by your doctor.

For pravastatin
- For *oral* dosage form (tablets):
  - —For high cholesterol:
    - Adults—10 to 40 mg once a day at bedtime.
    - Children—Use and dose must be determined by your doctor.

For simvastatin
- For *oral* dosage form (tablets):
  - —For high cholesterol:
    - Adults—5 to 40 mg once a day in the evening.
    - Children—Use and dose must be determined by your doctor.

Missed dose—If you miss a dose of this medicine, take it as soon as possible. However, if it is almost time for your next dose, skip the missed dose and go back to your regular dosing schedule. Do not double doses.

Storage—To store this medicine:
- Keep out of the reach of children.
- Store away from heat and direct light.
- Do not store in the bathroom, near the kitchen sink, or in other damp places. Heat or moisture may cause the medicine to break down.
- Keep the medicine from freezing. Do not refrigerate.
- Do not keep outdated medicine or medicine no longer needed. Be sure that any discarded medicine is out of the reach of children.

Precautions While Using This Medicine

It is very important that your doctor check your progress at regular visits. This will allow your doctor to see if the medicine is working properly to lower your cholesterol levels and that it does not cause unwanted effects.

Check with your doctor immediately if you think that you may be pregnant. HMG-CoA reductase inhibitors may cause birth defects or other problems in the baby if taken during pregnancy.

Do not stop taking this medicine without first checking with your doctor. When you stop taking this medicine, your blood cholesterol levels may increase again. Your doctor may want you to follow a special diet to help prevent this from happening.

Before having any kind of surgery (including dental surgery) or emergency treatment, tell the medical doctor or dentist in charge that you are taking this medicine.

Side Effects of This Medicine

Along with its needed effects, a medicine may cause some unwanted effects. Although not all of these side effects may occur, if they do occur they may need medical attention.

Check with your doctor as soon as possible if any of the following side effects occur:

Less common or rare

Fever; muscle aches or cramps; severe stomach pain; unusual tiredness or weakness

Other side effects may occur that usually do not need medical attention. These side effects may go away during treatment as your body adjusts to the medicine. However, check with your doctor if any of the following side effects continue or are bothersome:

More common

Constipation; diarrhea; dizziness; gas; headache; heartburn; nausea; skin rash; stomach pain

Rare

Decreased sexual ability; trouble in sleeping

Other side effects not listed above may also occur in some patients. If you notice any other effects, check with your doctor.

Revised: 03/06/95

HYDRALAZINE Systemic

Some commonly used brand names are:

In the U.S.—

Apresoline

Generic name product may also be available.

In Canada—

Apresoline

Novo-Hylazin

Description

Hydralazine (hye-DRAL-a-zeen) belongs to the general class of medicines called antihypertensives. It is used to treat high blood pressure (hypertension). It is also used to control high blood pressure in the mother during pregnancy (pre-eclampsia or eclampsia) or in emergency situations when blood pressure is extremely high (hypertensive crisis).

High blood pressure adds to the work load of the heart and arteries. If it continues for a long time, the heart and arteries may not function properly. This can damage the blood vessels of the brain, heart, and kidneys, resulting in a stroke, heart failure, or kidney failure. High blood pressure may also increase the risk of heart attacks. These problems may be less likely to occur if blood pressure is controlled.

Hydralazine works by relaxing blood vessels and increasing the supply of blood and oxygen to the heart while reducing its work load.

Hydralazine may also be used for other conditions as determined by your doctor.

Hydralazine is available only with your doctor's prescription, in the following dosage forms:

Oral
- Tablets (U.S. and Canada)

Parenteral
- Injection (U.S.)

Before Using This Medicine

In deciding to use a medicine, the risks of taking the medicine must be weighed against the good it will do. This is a decision you and your doctor will make. For hydralazine, the following should be considered:

Allergies—Tell your doctor if you have ever had any unusual or allergic reaction to hydralazine. Also tell your health care professional if you are allergic to any other substance, such as foods, preservatives, or dyes.

Pregnancy—Hydralazine has not been studied in pregnant women. However, blood problems and other problems have been reported in infants of mothers who took hydralazine during pregnancy. In addition, studies in mice have shown that hydralazine causes birth defects (cleft palate, defects in head and face bones). These birth defects may also occur in rabbits, but do not occur in rats. Before taking this medicine, make sure your doctor knows if you are pregnant or if you may become pregnant.

Breast-feeding—It is not known whether hydralazine passes into breast milk. Although most medicines pass into breast milk in small amounts, many of them may be used safely while breast-feeding. Mothers who are taking this medicine and who wish to breast-feed should discuss this with their doctor.

Children—Although there is no specific information comparing use of hydralazine in children with use in other age groups, this medicine is not expected to cause different side effects or problems in children than it does in adults.

Older adults—Many medicines have not been studied specifically in older people. Therefore, it may not be known whether they work exactly the same way they do in younger adults. Although there is no specific information comparing use of hydralazine in the elderly with use in other age groups, this medicine is not expected to cause different side effects or problems in older people than it does in younger adults. However, dizziness or lightheadedness may be more likely to occur in the elderly, who are more sensitive to the effects of hydralazine.

Other medicines—Although certain medicines should not be used together at all, in other cases two different medicines may be used together even if an interaction might occur. In these cases, your doctor may want to change the dose, or other precautions may be necessary. When you are taking hydralazine, it is especially important that your health care professional know if you are taking the following:

- Diazoxide (e.g., Proglycem)—Effect on blood pressure may be increased

Other medical problems—The presence of other medical problems may affect the use of hydralazine. Make sure you tell your doctor if you have any other medical problems, especially:

- Heart or blood vessel disease or
- Stroke—Lowering blood pressure may make problems resulting from these conditions worse
- Kidney disease—Effects may be increased because of slower removal of hydralazine from the body

Proper Use of This Medicine

For patients taking this medicine *for high blood pressure:*

- In addition to the use of the medicine your doctor has prescribed, treatment for your high blood pressure may include weight control and care in the types of foods you eat, especially foods high in sodium. Your doctor will tell you which of these are most important for you. You should check with your doctor before changing your diet.
- Many patients who have high blood pressure will not notice any signs of the problem. In fact, many may feel normal. It is very important that you *take your medicine exactly as directed* and that you keep your appointments with your doctor even if you feel well.
- Remember that hydralazine will not cure your high blood pressure but it does help control it. Therefore, you must continue to take it as directed if you expect to lower your blood pressure and keep it down. *You may have to take high blood pressure medicine for the rest of your life.* If high blood pressure is not treated, it can cause serious problems such as heart failure, blood vessel disease, stroke, or kidney disease.

To help you remember to take your medicine, try to get into the habit of taking it at the same time each day.

Dosing—The dose of hydralazine will be different for different patients. *Follow your doctor's orders or the directions on the label.* The following information includes only the average doses of hydralazine. *If your dose is different, do not change it* unless your doctor tells you to do so.

The number of tablets that you take depends on the strength of the medicine.

- For *oral* dosage form (tablets):
  —For high blood pressure:
  - Adults—10 to 50 milligrams (mg) four times a day.
  - Children—Dose is based on body weight. The usual dose is 0.75 to 7.5 mg per kilogram (kg) (0.34 to 3.4 mg per pound) of body weight a day. This is divided into four doses.
- For *injection* dosage form:
  —For high blood pressure:
  - Adults—5 to 40 mg injected into a muscle or a vein. Your doctor may repeat the dose as needed.
  - Children—Dose is based on body weight. The usual dose is 1.7 to 3.5 mg per kg (0.77 to 1.6 mg per pound) of body weight a day. This is divided into four to six doses and injected into a muscle or a vein.

  —For high blood pressure during pregnancy:
  - Adults—5 mg injected into a vein every fifteen to thirty minutes.

Missed dose—If you miss a dose of this medicine, take it as soon as possible. However, if it is almost time for your next dose, skip the missed dose and go back to your regular dosing schedule. Do not double doses.

Storage—To store this medicine:

- Keep out of the reach of children.
- Store away from heat and direct light.
- Do not store in the bathroom, near the kitchen sink, or in other damp places. Heat or moisture may cause the medicine to break down.
- Do not keep outdated medicine or medicine no longer needed. Be sure that any discarded medicine is out of the reach of children.

Precautions While Using This Medicine

It is important that your doctor check your progress at regular visits to make sure that this medicine is working properly.

Hydralazine may cause some people to have headaches or to feel dizzy. *Make sure you know how you react to this medicine before you drive, use machines, or do anything else that could be dangerous if you are dizzy or are not alert.*

For patients taking this medicine *for high blood pressure:*

- *Do not take other medicines unless they have been discussed with your doctor.* This especially includes over-the-counter (nonprescription) medicines for appetite control, asthma, colds, cough, hay fever, or sinus problems, since they may tend to increase your blood pressure.

Side Effects of This Medicine

Along with its needed effects, a medicine may cause some unwanted effects. Although not all of these side effects may occur, if they do occur they may need medical attention.

In general, side effects with hydralazine are rare at lower doses. However, check with your doctor as soon as possible if any of the following occur:

Less common

Blisters on skin; chest pain; general feeling of discomfort or illness or weakness; muscle pain; joint pain; numbness, tingling, pain, or weakness in hands or feet; skin rash or itching; sore throat and fever; swelling of feet or lower legs; swelling of lymph glands

Rare

Fever; general feeling of discomfort or illness; sore throat; weakness

Other side effects may occur that usually do not need medical attention. These side effects may go away during treatment as your body adjusts to the medicine. However, check with your doctor if any of the following side effects continue or are bothersome:

More common

Diarrhea; fast or irregular heartbeat; headache; loss of appetite; nausea or vomiting; pounding heartbeat

Less common

Constipation; dizziness or lightheadedness; redness or flushing of face; shortness of breath; stuffy nose; watering or irritated eyes

Other side effects not listed above may also occur in some patients. If you notice any other effects, check with your doctor.

Additional Information

Once a medicine has been approved for marketing for a certain use, experience may show that it is also useful for other medical problems. Although this use is not specifically included in product labeling, hydralazine is used in certain patients with the following medical condition:

- Congestive heart failure

Other than the above information, there is no additional information relating to proper use, precautions, or side effects for this use.

Revised: 08/08/96

HYDRALAZINE AND HYDROCHLOROTHIAZIDE Systemic†

Some commonly used brand names are:

In the U.S.—

Apresazide	Aprozide
Apresoline-Esidrix	Hydra-zide

Generic name product may also be available.

†Not commercially available in Canada.

Description

Hydralazine (hye-DRAL-a-zeen) and hydrochlorothiazide (hye-droe-klor-oh-THYE-a-zide) combination is used to treat high blood pressure (hypertension).

High blood pressure adds to the work load of the heart and arteries. If it continues for a long time, the heart and arteries may not function properly. This can damage the blood vessels of the brain, heart, and kidneys, resulting in a stroke, heart failure, or kidney failure. High blood pressure may also increase the risk of heart attacks. These problems may be less likely to occur if blood pressure is controlled.

Hydralazine works by relaxing blood vessels and increasing the supply of blood and oxygen to the heart while reducing its work load. The hydrochlorothiazide in this combination helps reduce the amount of water in the body by acting on the kidneys to increase the flow of urine.

This medicine is available only with your doctor's prescription, in the following dosage forms:

Oral

- Capsules (U.S.)
- Tablets (U.S.)

Before Using This Medicine

In deciding to use a medicine, the risks of taking the medicine must be weighed against the good it will do. This is a decision you and your doctor will make. For hydralazine and hydrochlorothiazide, the following should be considered:

Allergies—Tell your doctor if you have ever had any unusual or allergic reaction to hydralazine, sulfonamides (sulfa drugs), indapamide, or any of the thiazide diuretics (water pills). Also tell your health care professional if you are allergic to any other substance, such as foods, preservatives, or dyes.

Pregnancy—When hydrochlorothiazide is used during pregnancy, it may cause side effects including jaundice, blood problems, and low potassium in the newborn infant.

Studies with hydralazine have not been done in humans. However, blood problems have been reported in infants of mothers who took hydralazine during pregnancy. In addition, studies in mice have shown that hydralazine causes birth defects (cleft palate, defects in head and face bones); these birth defects may also occur in rabbits, but do not occur in rats.

Breast-feeding—Hydrochlorothiazide passes into breast milk. However, neither hydralazine nor hydrochlorothiazide has been reported to cause problems in nursing babies.

Children—Although there is no specific information comparing use of this medicine in children with use in other age groups, this medicine is not expected to cause different side effects or problems in children than it does in adults. However, extra caution may be necessary in infants with jaundice, because thiazide diuretics can make this condition worse.

Older adults—Many medicines have not been studied specifically in older people. Therefore, it may not be known whether they work exactly the same way they do in younger adults. Although there is no specific information comparing use of hydralazine and hydrochlorothiazide combination in the elderly with use in other age groups, this medicine is not expected to cause different side effects or problems in older people than it does in younger adults. However, dizziness or lightheadedness or symptoms of too much potassium loss may be more likely to occur in the elderly, who are usually more sensitive to the effects of this medicine. Also, this medicine may reduce tolerance to cold temperatures in elderly patients.

Other medicines—Although certain medicines should not be used together at all, in other cases two different medicines may be used together even if an interaction might occur. In these cases, your doctor may want to change the dose, or other precautions may be necessary. When you are taking hydralazine and hydrochlorothiazide, it is especially important that your health care professional know if you are taking any of the following:

- Cholestyramine or
- Colestipol—Use with thiazide diuretics may prevent the diuretic from working properly; take the diuretic at least 1 hour before or 4 hours after cholestyramine or colestipol
- Diazoxide (e.g., Proglycem)—Effect on blood pressure may be increased
- Digitalis glycosides (heart medicine)—Hydrochlorothiazide may cause low potassium in the blood, which can lead to symptoms of digitalis toxicity
- Lithium (e.g., Lithane)—Risk of lithium overdose, even at usual doses, may be increased

Other medical problems—The presence of other medical problems may affect the use of hydralazine and hydrochlorothiazide. Make sure you tell your doctor if you have any other medical problems, especially:

- Diabetes mellitus (sugar diabetes)—Hydrochlorothiazide may change the amount of diabetes medicine needed
- Gout (history of)—Hydrochlorothiazide may increase the amount of uric acid in the blood, which can lead to gout
- Heart or blood vessel disease or
- Stroke (recent)—Lowering blood pressure may make problems resulting from these conditions worse
- Kidney disease—Hydrochlorothiazide may worsen this condition. Also, the blood pressure lowering effects may be increased because of slower removal of hydralazine from the body
- Liver disease—If hydrochlorothiazide causes loss of too much water from the body, liver disease can become much worse
- Lupus erythematosus (history of)—Hydrochlorothiazide may worsen the condition
- Pancreatitis (inflammation of the pancreas)

Proper Use of This Medicine

This medicine may cause you to have an unusual feeling of tiredness when you begin to take it. You may also notice an increase in the amount of urine or in your frequency of urination. After taking the medicine for a while, these effects should lessen. To keep the increase in urine from affecting your sleep:

- If you are to take a single dose a day, take it in the morning after breakfast.
- If you are to take more than one dose a day, take the last dose no later than 6 p.m., unless otherwise directed by your doctor.

However, it is best to plan your dose or doses according to a schedule that will least affect your personal activities and sleep. Ask your health care professional to help you plan the best time to take this medicine.

In addition to the use of the medicine your doctor has prescribed, treatment for your high blood pressure may include weight control and care in the types of foods you eat, especially foods high in sodium. Your doctor will tell you which of these are most important for you. You should check with your doctor before changing your diet.

Many patients who have high blood pressure will not notice any signs of the problem. In fact, many may feel normal. It is very important that you *take your medicine exactly as directed* and that you keep your appointments with your doctor even if you feel well.

Remember that this medicine will not cure your high blood pressure but it does help control it. Therefore, you must continue to take it as directed if you expect to lower your blood pressure and keep it down. *You may have to take high blood pressure medicine for the rest of your life.* If high blood pressure is not treated, it can cause serious problems such as heart failure, blood vessel disease, stroke, or kidney disease.

To help you remember to take your medicine, try to get into the habit of taking it at the same time each day.

Dosing—The dose of hydralazine and hydrochlorothiazide combination will be different for different patients. *Follow your doctor's orders or the directions on the label.* The following information includes only the average dose of hydralazine and hydrochlorothiazide combination. *If your dose is different, do not change it* unless your doctor tells you to do so.

The number of capsules or tablets that you take depends on the strength of the medicine.

- For *oral* dosage forms (capsules or tablets):
  - —For high blood pressure:
    - Adults—1 capsule or tablet two times a day.
    - Children—Dose must be determined by your doctor.

Missed dose—If you miss a dose of this medicine, take it as soon as possible. However, if it is almost time for your next dose, skip the missed dose and go back to your regular dosing schedule. Do not double doses.

Storage—To store this medicine:

- Keep out of the reach of children.
- Store away from heat and direct light.
- Do not store in the bathroom, near the kitchen sink, or in other damp places. Heat or moisture may cause the medicine to break down.
- Do not keep outdated medicine or medicine no longer needed. Be sure that any discarded medicine is out of the reach of children.

Precautions While Using This Medicine

It is important that your doctor check your progress at regular visits to make sure that this medicine is working properly.

Do not take other medicines unless they have been discussed with your doctor. This especially includes over-the-counter (nonprescription) medicines for appetite control, asthma, colds, cough, hay fever, or sinus problems, since they may tend to increase your blood pressure.

This medicine may cause some people to have headaches or to feel dizzy. *Make sure you know how you react to this medicine before you drive, use machines, or do anything else that could be dangerous if you are dizzy or are not alert.*

Dizziness, lightheadedness, or fainting may occur, especially when you get up from a lying or sitting position. This is more likely to occur in the morning. *Getting up slowly may help.* When you get up from lying down, sit on the edge of the bed with your feet dangling for 1 or 2 minutes. Then stand up slowly. If the problem continues or gets worse, check with your doctor.

The dizziness, lightheadedness, or fainting is also more likely to occur if you drink alcohol, stand for a long time, exercise, or if the weather is hot. *While you are taking this medicine, be careful in the amount of alcohol you drink. Also, use extra care during exercise or hot weather or if you must stand for a long time.*

This medicine may cause a loss of potassium from your body.

- To help prevent this, your doctor may want you to:
  - —eat or drink foods that have a high potassium content (for example, orange or other citrus fruit juices), or
  - —take a potassium supplement, or
  - —take another medicine to help prevent the loss of the potassium in the first place.
- It is very important to follow these directions. Also, it is important not to change your diet on your own. This is more important if you are already on a special diet (as for diabetes), or if you are taking a potassium supplement or a medicine to reduce potassium loss. Extra potassium may not be necessary and, in some cases, too much potassium could be harmful.

Check with your doctor if you become sick and have severe or continuing nausea, vomiting, or diarrhea. These problems may cause you to lose additional water and potassium.

For *diabetic patients*:

- Thiazide diuretics may raise blood sugar levels. While you are using this medicine, be especially careful in testing for sugar in your blood or urine. If you have any questions about this, check with your doctor.

Some people who take this medicine may become more sensitive to sunlight than they are normally. Exposure to sunlight, even for brief periods of time, may cause severe sunburn; skin rash, redness, itching, or discoloration; or vision changes. When you begin taking this medicine:

- Stay out of direct sunlight, especially between the hours of 10:00 a.m. and 3:00 p.m., if possible.
- Wear protective clothing, including a hat and sunglasses.
- Apply a sun block product that has a skin protection factor (SPF) of at least 15. Some patients may require a product with a higher SPF number, especially if they have a fair complexion. If you have any questions about this, check with your health care professional.
- Do not use a sunlamp or tanning bed or booth.

If you have a severe reaction from the sun, check with your doctor.

Side Effects of This Medicine

Along with its needed effects, a medicine may cause some unwanted effects. Although not all of these side effects may occur, if they do occur they may need medical attention.

Check with your doctor as soon as possible if any of the following side effects occur:

Signs and symptoms of too much potassium loss

Dryness of mouth; increased thirst; irregular heartbeats; mood or mental changes; muscle cramps or pain; weak pulse

Signs and symptoms of too much sodium loss
Confusion; convulsions; decreased mental activity; irritability; muscle cramps; unusual tiredness or weakness

Less common
Blisters on skin; chest pain; general feeling of discomfort or illness or weakness; joint pain; numbness, tingling, pain, or weakness in hands or feet; skin rash or itching; sore throat and fever; swelling of the lymph glands

Rare
Lower back or side pain; severe stomach pain with nausea and vomiting; unusual bleeding or bruising; yellow eyes or skin

Other side effects may occur that usually do not need medical attention. These side effects may go away during treatment as your body adjusts to the medicine. However, check with your doctor if any of the following side effects continue or are bothersome:

More common
Diarrhea; fast or irregular heartbeat; headache; loss of appetite; nausea or vomiting

Less common
Constipation; decreased sexual ability; dizziness or lightheadedness, especially when getting up from a lying or sitting position; increased sensitivity of skin to sunlight; redness or flushing of face; shortness of breath with exercise or work; stuffy nose; watering or irritated eyes

Other side effects not listed above may also occur in some patients. If you notice any other effects, check with your doctor.

Revised: 08/24/92
Interim revision: 04/29/94

HYDROCORTISONE Rectal

Some commonly used brand names are:

In the U.S.—

Anucort-HC
Anusol-HC
Cort-Dome High Potency
Corticaine
Hemril-HC
Proctocort

Generic name product may also be available.

In Canada

Cortiment-10
Cortiment-40
Rectocort

Another commonly used name is cortisol.

Description

Rectal hydrocortisone (hye-droe-KOR-ti-sone) is used to help relieve swelling, itching, and discomfort of some rectal problems. Rectal hydrocortisone may also be applied to the area around the anus or rectum to relieve itching and discomfort. Hydrocortisone is a corticosteroid (kor-ti-ko-STER-oyd), which is a cortisone-like medicine. Hydrocortisone belongs to the general family of medicines called steroids.

Some hydrocortisone products for rectal use are available without a prescription; however, your doctor may have special instructions on the proper dose for your medical condition. Other hydrocortisone products for rectal use are available only with your doctor's prescription.

Rectal hydrocortisone is available in the following dosage forms:

Rectal
- Cream (U.S.)
- Ointment (Canada)
- Suppositories (U.S. and Canada)

Before Using This Medicine

In deciding to use rectal hydrocortisone, the risks of using it must be weighed against the good it will do. This is a decision you and possibly your doctor will make. The following information may help you in making your decision:

Allergies—If you have ever had any unusual or allergic reaction to hydrocortisone or other corticosteroids, it is best to check with your doctor before using rectal hydrocortisone.

Pregnancy—When used properly, this medicine has not been shown to cause problems in humans. Studies on birth defects with rectal hydrocortisone have not been done in humans. However, studies in animals have shown that topical corticosteroids, such as the hydrocortisone contained in this medicine, when used in large amounts or for a long time, may be absorbed through the skin and could cause birth defects.

Breast-feeding—When used properly, rectal hydrocortisone has not been reported to cause problems in nursing babies.

Children—Children and teenagers who must use this medicine should be checked often by their doctor. Hydrocortisone may be absorbed through the lining of the rectum and, rarely, may affect growth, especially if used in large amounts or for a long time. Before using this medicine in children, you should discuss its use with your child's doctor.

Older adults—Although there is no specific information comparing use of rectal hydrocortisone in the elderly with use in other age groups, this medicine is not expected to cause different side effects or problems in older people than it does in younger adults.

Other medical problems—The presence of other medical problems may affect the use of rectal hydrocortisone. Since in some cases rectal hydrocortisone should not be used, check with your doctor if you have any of the following:

- Diabetes mellitus (sugar diabetes)—Too much use of hydrocortisone may cause a loss of control of diabetes by increasing blood and urine glucose. However, this is not

likely to happen when hydrocortisone is used for a short period of time
- Infection or sores at the place of treatment or
- Tuberculosis—Corticosteroids may make existing infections worse or cause new infections
- Skin conditions that cause thinning of skin with easy bruising—Corticosteroids may make thinning of the skin worse

Proper Use of This Medicine

For patients using *hydrocortisone rectal cream or ointment:*
- If you are applying this medicine to the outer rectal area, first bathe and dry the rectal area. Then apply a small amount and rub it in gently.
- If you have been directed to insert this medicine into the rectum, first attach the plastic applicator tip onto the opened tube. Insert the applicator tip into the rectum and gently squeeze the tube to deliver the medicine. Remove the applicator tip from the tube and wash it with hot, soapy water. Replace the cap of the tube after use.

For patients using *hydrocortisone suppositories:*
- If the suppository is too soft to insert, chill it in the refrigerator for 30 minutes or run cold water over it before removing the foil wrapper.
- To insert suppository: First remove the foil wrapper and moisten the suppository with cold water. Lie down on your side and use your finger to push the suppository well up into the rectum.

Do not use rectal hydrocortisone in larger amounts, more often, or for a longer time than your doctor ordered or the package label directs. To do so may increase the chance of absorption through the lining of the rectum and the chance of side effects.

If this medicine was ordered by your doctor, do not use any leftover medicine for future rectal problems without first checking with your doctor. Also, if you are treating yourself, check with your doctor before using rectal hydrocortisone for problems other than those stated on the package, or if you suspect that an infection may be present. The medicine should not be used if many kinds of bacterial, virus, or fungus infections are present.

Missed dose—If your doctor has ordered you to use this medicine according to a regular schedule and you miss a dose, use it as soon as you remember. However, if it is almost time for your next dose, skip the missed dose and go back to your regular dosing schedule. Do not double doses.

Storage—To store this medicine:
- Keep out of the reach of children.
- Store away from heat and direct light.
- Do not store hydrocortisone suppositories in the bathroom medicine cabinet because the heat or moisture may cause the medicine to break down.
- Keep the medicine from freezing.
- Do not keep outdated medicine or medicine no longer needed. Be sure that any discarded medicine is out of the reach of children.

Precautions While Using This Medicine

Avoid using tight-fitting diapers or plastic pants on children using this medicine. Plastic pants and tight-fitting diapers may increase the chance of absorption of the medicine through the skin and the chance of side effects.

Side Effects of This Medicine

Along with its needed effects, a medicine may cause some unwanted effects. Although not all of these side effects may occur, if they do occur they may need medical attention.

Check with your doctor as soon as possible if any of the following side effects occur:

Signs of irritation or infection such as rectal bleeding, pain, burning, itching, or blistering not present before use of this medicine

Additional side effects may occur if you use this medicine for a long time. Check with your doctor as soon as possible if any of the following side effects occur:

Reddish-purple lines (stretch marks) on treated areas; thinning of skin with easy bruising

Other side effects not listed above may also occur in some patients. If you notice any other effects, check with your doctor.

Revised: 11/18/92

HYDROXYCHLOROQUINE Systemic

A commonly used brand name in the U.S. and Canada is Plaquenil.

Description

Hydroxychloroquine (hye-drox-ee-KLOR-oh-kwin) belongs to the family of medicines called antiprotozoals. Protozoa are tiny, one-celled animals. Some are parasites that can cause many different kinds of infections in the body.

This medicine is used to prevent and to treat malaria and to treat some conditions such as liver disease caused by protozoa. It is also used in the treatment of arthritis to help relieve inflammation, swelling, stiffness, and joint pain and to help control the symptoms of lupus erythematosus (lupus; SLE).

This medicine may be given alone or with one or more other medicines. It may also be used for other conditions as determined by your doctor.

Hydroxychloroquine is available only with your doctor's prescription, in the following dosage form:

Oral

- Tablets (U.S. and Canada)

Before Using This Medicine

In deciding to use a medicine, the risks of taking the medicine must be weighed against the good it will do. This is a decision you and your doctor will make. For hydroxychloroquine, the following should be considered:

Allergies—Tell your doctor if you have ever had any unusual or allergic reaction to hydroxychloroquine or chloroquine. Also tell your health care professional if you are allergic to any other substances, such as foods, preservatives, or dyes.

Pregnancy—Unless you are taking it for malaria or liver disease caused by protozoa, use of this medicine is not recommended during pregnancy. In animal studies, hydroxychloroquine has been shown to cause damage to the central nervous system (brain and spinal cord) of the fetus, including damage to hearing and sense of balance, bleeding inside the eyes, and other eye problems. However, when given in low doses (once a week) to prevent malaria, this medicine has not been shown to cause birth defects or other problems in pregnant women.

Breast-feeding—A very small amount of hydroxychloroquine passes into the breast milk. It has not been reported to cause problems in nursing babies to date. However, babies and children are especially sensitive to the effects of hydroxychloroquine.

Children—Children are especially sensitive to the effects of hydroxychloroquine. This may increase the chance of side effects during treatment. Overdose is especially dangerous in children. Taking as few as 3 or 4 tablets (250-milligrams [mg] strength) of chloroquine has resulted in death in small children. Because hydroxychloroquine is so similar to chloroquine, it is probably just as toxic.

Older adults—Many medicines have not been studied specifically in older people. Therefore, it may not be known whether they work exactly the same way they do in younger adults or if they cause different side effects or problems in older people. There is no specific information comparing use of hydroxychloroquine in the elderly with use in other age groups.

Other medicines—Although certain medicines should not be used together at all, in other cases 2 different medicines may be used together even if an interaction might occur. In these cases, your doctor may want to change the dose, or other precautions may be necessary. Tell your health care professional if you are taking any other prescription or nonprescription (over-the-counter [OTC]) medicine.

Other medical problems—The presence of other medical problems may affect the use of hydroxychloroquine. Make sure you tell your doctor if you have any other medical problems, especially:

- Blood disease (severe)—Hydroxychloroquine may cause blood disorders
- Eye or vision problems—Hydroxychloroquine may cause serious eye side effects, especially in high doses
- Glucose-6-phosphate dehydrogenase (G6PD) deficiency—Hydroxychloroquine may cause serious blood side effects in patients with this deficiency
- Liver disease—May decrease the removal of hydroxychloroquine from the blood, increasing the chance of side effects
- Nerve or brain disease (severe), including convulsions (seizures)—Hydroxychloroquine may cause muscle weakness and, in high doses, seizures
- Porphyria—Hydroxychloroquine may worsen the symptoms of porphyria
- Psoriasis—Hydroxychloroquine may bring on severe attacks of psoriasis
- Stomach or intestinal disease (severe)—Hydroxychloroquine may cause stomach irritation

Proper Use of This Medicine

Take this medicine with meals or milk to lessen possible stomach upset, unless otherwise directed by your doctor.

Keep this medicine out of the reach of children. Children are especially sensitive to the effects of hydroxychloroquine and overdose is especially dangerous in children. Taking as few as 3 or 4 tablets (250-mg strength) of chloroquine has resulted in death in small children. Hydroxychloroquine is probably just as dangerous.

It is very important that you *take this medicine only as directed.* Do not take more of it, do not take it more often, and do not take it for a longer time than your doctor ordered. To do so may increase the chance of serious side effects.

If you are taking this medicine to help keep you from getting malaria, *keep taking it for the full time of treatment.* If you already have malaria, you should still keep taking this medicine for the full time of treatment even if you begin to feel better after a few days. This will help to clear up your infection completely. If you stop taking this medicine too soon, your symptoms may return.

Hydroxychloroquine works best when you take it on a regular schedule. For example, if you are to take it once a week to prevent malaria, it is best to take it on the same day each week. Or if you are to take 2 doses a day, 1 dose may be taken with breakfast and the other with the evening meal. *Make sure that you do not miss any doses.* If you have any questions about this, check with your health care professional.

Dosing—The dose of hydroxychloroquine will be different for different patients. *Follow your doctor's orders or the directions on the label.* The following information includes only the average doses of hydroxychloroquine. *If your dose is different, do not change it* unless your doctor tells you to do so.

The number of doses you take each day, the time allowed between doses, and the length of time you take the medicine depend on the medical problem for which you are taking hydroxychloroquine.

- For *tablets* dosage form:
  —For prevention of malaria:
    - Adults—400 milligrams (mg) once every seven days.
    - Children—Dose is based on body weight and must be determined by your doctor. The usual dose is 6.4 mg per kilogram (kg) (2.9 mg per pound) of body weight once every seven days.

  —For treatment of malaria:
    - Adults—800 mg as a single dose. This may sometimes be followed by a dose of 400 mg six to eight hours after the first dose, then 400 mg once a day on the second and third days.
    - Children—Dose is based on body weight and must be determined by your doctor. The usual dose is 32 mg per kg (14.5 mg per pound) of body weight taken over a period of three days.

  —For treatment of arthritis:
    - Adults—Dose is based on body weight and must be determined by your doctor. The usual dose is 6.5 mg per kg (2.9 mg per pound) of body weight per day.

Missed dose—If you miss a dose of this medicine, take it as soon as possible. However, if it is almost time for your next dose, skip the missed dose and go back to your regular dosing schedule. Do not double doses.

For patients taking hydroxychloroquine *to prevent malaria:*

- Your doctor may want you to start taking this medicine 1 to 2 weeks before you travel to an area where there is a chance of getting malaria. This will help you to see how you react to the medicine. Also, it will allow time for your doctor to change to another medicine if you have a reaction to this medicine.
- Also, you should keep taking this medicine while you are in the area and for 4 to 6 weeks after you leave the area. No medicine will protect you completely from malaria. However, to protect you as completely as possible, *it is important to keep taking this medicine for the full time your doctor ordered.* Also, if fever develops during your travels or within 2 months after you leave the area, *check with your doctor immediately.*

For patients taking hydroxychloroquine *for arthritis or lupus:*

- This medicine must be taken regularly as ordered by your doctor in order for it to help you. It may take up to several weeks before you begin to feel better. It may take up to 6 months before you feel the full benefit of this medicine.

For patients *unable to swallow hydroxychloroquine tablets:*

- Your pharmacist can crush the tablets and put each dose in a capsule. Contents of the capsules may then be mixed with a teaspoonful of jam, jelly, or jello. Be sure you take all the food in order to get the full dose of medicine.

Storage—To store this medicine:

- Keep out of the reach of children. Overdose of hydroxychloroquine is very dangerous in children.
- Store away from heat and direct light.
- Do not store in the bathroom, near the kitchen sink, or in other damp places. Heat or moisture may cause the medicine to break down.
- Do not keep outdated medicine or medicine no longer needed. Be sure that any discarded medicine is out of the reach of children.

Precautions While Using This Medicine

If you will be taking this medicine for a long time, *it is very important that your doctor check you at regular visits* for any blood problems or muscle weakness that may be caused by this medicine. In addition, *check with your doctor immediately if blurred vision, difficulty in reading, or any other change in vision occurs during or after treatment.* Your doctor may want you to have your eyes checked by an ophthalmologist (eye doctor).

If your symptoms do not improve within a few days (or a few weeks or months for arthritis), or if they become worse, check with your doctor.

Hydroxychloroquine may cause blurred vision, difficulty in reading, or other change in vision. It may also cause some people to become dizzy or lightheaded. *Make sure you know how you react to this medicine before you drive, use machines, or do anything else that could be dangerous if you are dizzy or are not alert or able to see well.* If these reactions are especially bothersome, check with your doctor.

Malaria is spread by mosquitoes. If you are living in, or will be traveling to, an area where there is a chance of getting malaria, the following mosquito-control measures will help to prevent infection:

- If possible, sleep under mosquito netting to avoid being bitten by malaria-carrying mosquitoes.
- Wear long-sleeved shirts or blouses and long trousers to protect your arms and legs, especially from dusk through dawn when mosquitoes are out.
- Apply mosquito repellent to uncovered areas of the skin from dusk through dawn when mosquitoes are out.

Side Effects of This Medicine

Along with its needed effects, a medicine may cause some unwanted effects. Although not all of these side effects may occur, if they do occur they may need medical attention. When this medicine is used for short periods of time, side effects usually are rare. However, when it is used for a long time and/or in high doses, side effects are more likely to occur and may be serious.

Check with your doctor immediately if any of the following side effects occur:

Less common

Blurred vision or any other change in vision—this side effect may also occur or get worse after you stop taking this medicine

Rare

Convulsions (seizures); increased muscle weakness; mood or other mental changes; ringing or buzzing in ears or any loss of hearing; sore throat and fever; unusual bleeding or bruising; unusual tiredness; weakness

Symptoms of overdose

Drowsiness; headache; increased excitability

Other side effects may occur that usually do not need medical attention. These side effects may go away during treatment as your body adjusts to the medicine. However, check with your doctor if any of the following side effects continue or are bothersome:

More common

Diarrhea; difficulty in seeing to read; headache; itching (more common in black patients); loss of appetite; nausea or vomiting; stomach cramps or pain

Less common

Bleaching of hair or increased hair loss; blue-black discoloration of skin, fingernails, or inside of mouth; dizziness or lightheadedness; nervousness or restlessness; skin rash

Other side effects not listed above may also occur in some patients. If you notice any other effects, check with your doctor.

Additional Information

Once a medicine has been approved for marketing for a certain use, experience may show that it is also useful for other medical problems. Although these uses are not included in product labeling, hydroxychloroquine is used in certain patients with the following medical conditions:

- Arthritis, juvenile
- Hypercalcemia, sarcoid-associated
- Polymorphous light eruption
- Porphyria cutanea tarda
- Urticaria, solar
- Vasculitis, chronic cutaneous

Other than the above information, there is no additional information relating to proper use, precautions, or side effects for these uses.

Revised: 12/30/94

HYDROXYPROPYL CELLULOSE Ophthalmic

A commonly used brand name in the U.S. and Canada is Lacrisert.

Description

Hydroxypropyl cellulose (hye-drox-ee-PROE-pil SELL-yoo-lose) belongs to the group of medicines known as artificial tears. It is inserted in the eye to relieve dryness and irritation caused by reduced tear flow that occurs in certain eye diseases.

This medicine is available only with your doctor's prescription, in the following dosage form:

Ophthalmic

- Ocular system (eye system) (U.S. and Canada)

Before Using This Medicine

In deciding to use a medicine, the risks of using the medicine must be weighed against the good it will do. This is a decision you and your doctor will make. For hydroxypropyl cellulose, the following should be considered:

Allergies—Tell your doctor if you have ever had any unusual or allergic reaction to hydroxypropyl cellulose. Also tell your health care professional if you are allergic to any other substances, such as preservatives.

Pregnancy—Hydroxypropyl cellulose has not been shown to cause birth defects or other problems in humans.

Breast-feeding—Hydroxypropyl cellulose has not been reported to cause problems in nursing babies.

Children—Although there is no specific information comparing use of this medicine in children with use in other age groups, this medicine is not expected to cause different side effects or problems in children than it does in adults.

Older adults—Many medicines have not been studied specifically in older people. Therefore, it may not be known whether they work exactly the same way they do in younger adults. Although there is no specific information comparing use of this medicine in the elderly with use in other age groups, this medicine is not expected to cause different side effects or problems in older people than it does in younger adults.

Proper Use of This Medicine

To use:

- This medicine usually comes with patient directions. Read them carefully before using this medicine. It is very important that you understand how to insert this eye system properly. If you have any questions about this, check with your doctor.
- Before opening the package containing this medicine, wash your hands thoroughly with soap and water.
- If the eye system accidentally comes out of your eye, as sometimes occurs when the eye is rubbed, do not put it back in the eye, since it may be contaminated. Instead, insert another eye system if needed.
- You may have to use this medicine for several weeks before your eye symptoms get better.

Dosing—The dose of hydroxypropyl cellulose will be different for different patients. *Follow your doctor's orders or the directions on the label.* The following information includes only the average doses of hydroxypropyl cellulose. *If your dose is different, do not change it* unless your doctor tells you to do so.

The number of doses you use, the time allowed between doses, and the length of time you use the medicine depend on the medical problem for which you are using hydroxypropyl cellulose.

- For *eye system* dosage form:
  - —For dry eyes or eye irritation:
    - Adults and children—Place one insert in the eye each day.

Missed dose—If you forget to insert an eye system at the proper time, insert it as soon as possible. Then go back to your regular dosing schedule.

Storage—To store this medicine:
- Keep out of the reach of children.
- Store away from heat and direct light.
- Do not keep outdated medicine or medicine no longer needed. Be sure that any discarded medicine is out of the reach of children.

Precautions While Using This Medicine

This medicine may cause blurred vision for a short time after each dose is applied. *Make sure your vision is clear before you drive, use machines, or do anything else that could be dangerous if you are not able to see well.*

This medicine may also cause your eyes to become more sensitive to light than they are normally. Wearing sunglasses and avoiding too much exposure to bright light may help lessen the discomfort.

If your eye symptoms get worse or if you get new eye symptoms, remove the eye system and check with your doctor as soon as possible.

Side Effects of This Medicine

Along with its needed effects, a medicine may cause some unwanted effects. The following side effects may go away during treatment as your body adjusts to the medicine. However, check with your doctor if any of these effects continue or are bothersome:

Less common

Blurred vision; eye redness or discomfort or other irritation not present before use of this medicine; increased sensitivity of eyes to light; matting or stickiness of eyelashes; swelling of eyelids; watering of eyes

Other side effects not listed above may also occur in some patients. If you notice any other effects, check with your doctor.

Revised: 06/21/93

HYDROXYPROPYL METHYLCELLULOSE Ophthalmic

Some commonly used brand names are:

In the U.S.—

Artificial Tears	Moisture Drops
Bion Tears	Nature's Tears
Gonak	Ocucoat
Goniosoft	Ocucoat PF
Goniosol	Tearisol
Isopto Alkaline	Tears Naturale
Isopto Plain	Tears Naturale II
Isopto Tears	Tears Naturale Free
Just Tears	Tears Renewed
Lacril	Ultra Tears

In Canada—

Eyelube	Ocutears
Isopto Tears	Tears Naturale
Methocel	Tears Naturale II
Moisture Drops	Tears Naturale Free

Another commonly used name is hypromellose.

Description

Hydroxypropyl methylcellulose (hye-drox-ee-PROE-pil meth-ill-SELL-yoo-lose) belongs to the group of medicines known as artificial tears. It is used to relieve dryness and irritation caused by reduced tear flow. It helps prevent damage to the eye in certain eye diseases. Hydroxypropyl methylcellulose may also be used to moisten hard contact lenses and artificial eyes. In addition, it may be used in certain eye examinations.

Some of these preparations are available only with your doctor's prescription. Others are available without a prescription; however, your doctor may have special instructions on the proper use of this medicine for your medical problem.

Hydroxypropyl methylcellulose is available in the following dosage form:

Ophthalmic
- Ophthalmic solution (eye drops) (U.S. and Canada)

Before Using This Medicine

If you are using this medicine without a prescription, carefully read and follow any precautions on the label. For hydroxypropyl methylcellulose, the following should be considered:

Allergies—Tell your doctor if you have ever had any unusual or allergic reaction to hydroxypropyl methylcellulose. Also tell your health care professional if you are allergic to any other substances, such as preservatives.

Pregnancy—Hydroxypropyl methylcellulose has not been shown to cause birth defects or other problems in humans.

Breast-feeding—Hydroxypropyl methylcellulose has not been reported to cause problems in nursing babies.

Children—Although there is no specific information comparing use of hydroxypropyl methylcellulose in children with use in other age groups, this medicine is not expected to cause different side effects or problems in children than it does in adults.

Older adults—Many medicine have not been studied specifically in older people. Therefore, it may not be known whether they work exactly the same way they do in younger adults. Although there is no specific information comparing use of hydroxypropyl methylcellulose in the elderly with use in other age groups, this medicine is not expected to cause different side effects or problems in older people than it does in younger adults.

Proper Use of This Medicine

To use:

- First, wash your hands. Then tilt the head back and pull the lower eyelid away from the eye to form a pouch. Drop the medicine into the pouch and gently close the eyes. Do not blink. Keep the eyes closed for 1 or 2 minutes to allow the medicine to be absorbed.
- To keep the medicine as germ-free as possible, do not touch the applicator tip to any surface (including the eye). Also, keep the container tightly closed.

For patients *wearing hard contact lenses:*

- Take care not to float the lens from your eye when applying this medicine. If you have any questions about this, check with your health care professional.

Dosing—The dose of hydroxypropyl methylcellulose will be different for different patients. *Follow your doctor's orders or the directions on the label.* The following information includes only the average doses of hydroxypropyl methylcellulose. *If your dose is different, do not change it* unless your doctor tells you to do so.

The number of doses you use each day, the time allowed between doses, and the length of time you use the medicine depend on the medical problem for which you are using hydroxypropyl methylcellulose.

- For dry eyes:
  - —For *ophthalmic solution (eye drops)* dosage form:
    - Adults and children—Use 1 drop three or four times a day.

Storage—To store this medicine:

- Keep out of the reach of children.
- Store away from heat and direct light.
- Keep the medicine from freezing.
- Do not keep outdated medicine or medicine no longer needed. Be sure that any discarded medicine is out of the reach of children.

Precautions While Using This Medicine

If you experience eye pain, changes in vision, continued redness or irritation of the eye, or if your symptoms continue for more than 3 days or become worse, check with your doctor.

Side Effects of This Medicine

Along with its needed effects, a medicine may cause some unwanted effects. Although not all of these side effects may occur, if they do occur they may need medical attention.

Check with your doctor as soon as possible if the following side effect occurs:

Eye irritation not present before use of this medicine

Other side effects may occur that usually do not need medical attention. These side effects may go away during treatment as your body adjusts to the medicine. However, check with your health care professional if any of the following side effects continue or are bothersome:

Less common—more common with 1% solution

Blurred vision; matting or stickiness of eyelashes

Other side effects not listed above may also occur in some patients. If you notice any other effects, check with your health care professional.

Revised: 08/14/95

HYDROXYUREA Systemic

A commonly used brand name in the U.S. and Canada is Hydrea.

Description

Hydroxyurea (hye-DROX-ee-yoo-REE-ah) belongs to the group of medicines called antimetabolites. It is used to treat some kinds of cancer.

Hydroxyurea seems to interfere with the growth of cancer cells, which are eventually destroyed. Since the growth of normal body cells may also be affected by hydroxyurea, other effects will also occur. Some of these may be serious and must be reported to your doctor. Other effects may not be serious but may cause concern. Some effects may not occur for months or years after the medicine is used.

Before you begin treatment with hydroxyurea, you and your doctor should talk about the good this medicine will do as well as the risks of using it.

Hydroxyurea is available only with your doctor's prescription, in the following dosage form:

Oral

- Capsules (U.S. and Canada)

Before Using This Medicine

In deciding to use a medicine, the risks of taking the medicine must be weighed against the good it will do. This is a decision you and your doctor will make. For hydroxyurea, the following should be considered:

Allergies—Tell your doctor if you have ever had any unusual or allergic reaction to hydroxyurea.

Pregnancy—Tell your doctor if you are pregnant or if you intend to have children. There is a chance that this medicine may cause birth defects if either the male or female is taking it at the time of conception or if it is taken during pregnancy. Studies have shown that hydroxyurea causes birth defects in animals. In addition, many cancer medicines may cause sterility. Although sterility seems to be only temporary with this medicine, the possibility should be kept in mind.

Be sure that you have discussed this with your doctor before taking this medicine. It is best to use some kind of birth control while you are taking hydroxyurea. Tell your doctor right away if you think you have become pregnant while taking hydroxyurea.

Breast-feeding—Tell your doctor if you are breast-feeding or if you intend to breast-feed during treatment with this medicine. Because hydroxyurea may cause serious side effects, breast-feeding is generally not recommended while you are taking it.

Children—Side effects may be likely to occur in children, who may be more sensitive to the effects of hydroxyurea.

Older adults—Side effects may be more likely to occur in the elderly, who may be more sensitive to the effects of hydroxyurea.

Other medicines—Although certain medicines should not be used together at all, in other cases two different medicines may be used together even if an interaction might occur. In these cases, your doctor may want to change the dose, or other precautions may be necessary. When you are taking hydroxyurea, it is especially important that your health care professional know if you are taking any of the following:

- Amphotericin B by injection (e.g., Fungizone) or
- Antithyroid agents (medicine for overactive thyroid) or
- Azathioprine (e.g., Imuran) or
- Chloramphenicol (e.g., Chloromycetin) or
- Colchicine or
- Flucytosine (e.g., Ancobon) or
- Ganciclovir (e.g., Cytovene) or
- Interferon (e.g., Intron A, Roferon-A) or
- Plicamycin (e.g., Mithracin) or
- Zidovudine (e.g., AZT, Retrovir) or
- If you have ever been treated with x-rays or cancer medicines—Hydroxyurea may increase the effects of these medicines or radiation therapy on the blood
- Probenecid (e.g., Benemid) or
- Sulfinpyrazone (e.g., Anturane)—Hydroxyurea may increase the amount of uric acid in the blood. Since these medicines are used to lower uric acid levels, they may not be as effective in patients taking hydroxyurea

Other medical problems—The presence of other medical problems may affect the use of hydroxyurea. Make sure you tell your doctor if you have any other medical problems, especially:

- Anemia—May be worsened
- Chickenpox (including recent exposure) or
- Herpes zoster (shingles)—Risk of severe disease affecting other parts of the body
- Gout or
- Kidney stones—Hydroxyurea may increase levels of uric acid in the body, which can cause gout or kidney stones
- Infection—Hydroxyurea may decrease your body's ability to fight infection
- Kidney disease—Effects may be increased because of slower removal of hydroxyurea from the body

Proper Use of This Medicine

Take hydroxyurea only as directed by your doctor. Do not use more or less of it, and do not use it more often than your doctor ordered. The exact amount of medicine you need has been carefully worked out. Taking too much may increase the chance of side effects, while taking too little may not improve your condition.

For patients who *cannot swallow the capsules:*

- The contents of the capsule may be emptied into a glass of water and then taken immediately. Some powder may float on the surface of the water, but that is just filler from the capsule.

This medicine is sometimes given together with certain other medicines. If you are using a combination of medicines, make sure that you take each one at the right time and do not mix them. Ask your health care professional to help you plan a way to take your medicine at the right times.

While you are using this medicine, your doctor may want you to drink extra fluids so that you will pass more urine. This will help prevent kidney problems and keep your kidneys working well.

This medicine commonly causes nausea, vomiting, and diarrhea. However, it is very important that you continue to use the medicine, even if you begin to feel ill. Ask your health care professional for ways to lessen these effects.

If you vomit shortly after taking a dose of hydroxyurea, check with your doctor. You will be told whether to take the dose again or to wait until the next scheduled dose.

Dosing—The dose of hydroxyurea will be different for different patients. The dose that is used may depend on a number of things, including what the medicine is being used for, the patient's weight, and whether or not other medicines are also being taken. *If you are taking hydroxyurea at home, follow your doctor's orders or the directions on the label.* If you have any questions about the proper dose of hydroxyurea, ask your doctor.

Missed dose—If you miss a dose of this medicine, do not take the missed dose at all and do not double the next one. Instead, go back to your regular dosing schedule and check with your doctor.

Storage—To store this medicine:

- Keep out of the reach of children.
- Store away from heat and direct light.
- Do not store in the bathroom, near the kitchen sink, or in other damp places. Heat or moisture may cause the medicine to break down.
- Do not keep outdated medicine or medicine no longer needed. Be sure that any discarded medicine is out of the reach of children.

Precautions While Using This Medicine

It is very important that your doctor check your progress at regular visits to make sure that this medicine is working properly and to check for unwanted effects.

While you are being treated with hydroxyurea, and after you stop treatment with it, *do not have any immunizations (vaccinations) without your doctor's approval.* Hydroxyurea may lower your body's resistance and there is a chance you might get the infection the immunization is meant to prevent. In addition, other persons living in your household should not take oral polio vaccine since there is a chance they could pass the polio virus on to you. Also, avoid persons who have recently taken oral polio vaccine. Do not get close to them and do not stay in the same room with them for very long. If you cannot take these precautions, you should consider wearing a protective face mask that covers the nose and mouth.

Hydroxyurea can temporarily lower the number of white blood cells in your blood, increasing the chance of getting an infection. It can also lower the number of platelets, which are necessary for proper blood clotting. If this occurs, there are certain precautions you can take, especially when your blood count is low, to reduce the risk of infection or bleeding:

- If you can, avoid people with infections. *Check with your doctor immediately* if you think you are getting an infection or if you get a fever or chills, cough or hoarseness, lower back or side pain, or painful or difficult urination.
- *Check with your doctor immediately* if you notice any unusual bleeding or bruising; black, tarry stools; blood in urine or stools; or pinpoint red spots on your skin.
- Be careful when using a regular toothbrush, dental floss, or toothpick. Your medical doctor, dentist, or nurse may recommend other ways to clean your teeth and gums. Check with your medical doctor before having any dental work done.
- Do not touch your eyes or the inside of your nose unless you have just washed your hands and have not touched anything else in the meantime.
- Be careful not to cut yourself when you are using sharp objects such as a safety razor or fingernail or toenail cutters.
- Avoid contact sports or other situations where bruising or injury could occur.

Side Effects of This Medicine

Along with their needed effects, medicines like hydroxyurea can sometimes cause unwanted effects such as blood problems and other side effects. These and others are described below. Also, because of the way these medicines act on the body, there is a chance that they might cause other unwanted effects that may not occur until months or years after the medicine is used. These delayed effects may include certain types of cancer, such as leukemia. Ask your health care professional for ways to lessen these effects.

Although not all of these side effects may occur, if they do occur they may need medical attention.

Check with your doctor or nurse immediately if any of the following side effects occur:

Less common

Cough or hoarseness; fever or chills; lower back or side pain; painful or difficult urination

Rare

Black, tarry stools; blood in urine or stools; pinpoint red spots on skin; unusual bleeding or bruising

Check with your doctor as soon as possible if any of the following side effects occur:

Less common

Sores in mouth and on lips

Rare

Confusion; convulsions (seizures); dizziness; hallucinations (seeing, hearing, or feeling things that are not there); headache; joint pain; swelling of feet or lower legs

Other side effects may occur that usually do not need medical attention. These side effects may go away during treatment as your body adjusts to the medicine. Also, your health care professional may be able to tell you about ways to prevent or reduce some of these side effects. Check with your health care professional if any of the following side effects continue or are bothersome or if you have any questions about them:

More common

Diarrhea; drowsiness; loss of appetite; nausea or vomiting

Less common

Constipation; redness of skin; skin rash and itching

After you stop taking hydroxyurea, your body may need time to adjust. The length of time this takes depends on the amount of medicine you were using and how long you used it. During this period of time check with your doctor if you notice any of the following side effects:

Black, tarry stools; blood in urine or stools; cough or hoarseness; fever or chills; lower back or side pain; painful or difficult urination; pinpoint red spots on skin; unusual bleeding or bruising

Other side effects not listed above may also occur in some patients. If you notice any other effects, check with your doctor.

Revised: 06/16/92
Interim revision: 06/21/94

IDARUBICIN Systemic

A commonly used brand name in the U.S. and Canada is Idamycin.

Description

Idarubicin (eye-da-RUE-bi-sin) belongs to the general group of medicines known as antineoplastics. It is used to treat some kinds of cancer, including leukemia.

Idarubicin seems to interfere with the growth of cancer cells, which are eventually destroyed. Since the growth of normal body cells may also be affected by idarubicin, other effects will also occur. Some of these may be serious and must be reported to your doctor. Other effects, like hair loss, may not be serious but may cause concern. Some effects may not occur for months or years after the medicine is used.

Before you begin treatment with idarubicin, you and your doctor should talk about the good this medicine will do as well as the risks of using it.

Idarubicin is to be administered only by or under the supervision of your doctor. It is available in the following dosage form:

Parenteral
- Injection (U.S. and Canada)

Before Using This Medicine

In deciding to use a medicine, the risks of taking the medicine must be weighed against the good it will do. This is a decision you and your doctor will make. For idarubicin, the following should be considered:

Allergies—Tell your doctor if you have ever had any unusual or allergic reaction to idarubicin.

Pregnancy—There is a chance that this medicine may cause birth defects if either the male or female is receiving it at the time of conception or if it is taken during pregnancy. Studies in rats and rabbits have shown that idarubicin causes birth defects in the fetus and other problems (including miscarriage). In addition, many cancer medicines may cause sterility which could be permanent. Although sterility has been reported only in male dogs with this medicine, the possibility of an effect in human males should be kept in mind.

Be sure that you have discussed these possible effects with your doctor before receiving this medicine. It is best to use some kind of birth control while you are receiving idarubicin. Tell your doctor right away if you think you have become pregnant while receiving idarubicin. Before receiving idarubicin make sure your doctor knows if you are pregnant or if you may become pregnant.

Breast-feeding—Because idarubicin may cause serious side effects, breast-feeding is generally not recommended while you are receiving it.

Children—There is no specific information comparing use of idarubicin in children with use in other age groups.

Older adults—Heart problems are more likely to occur in the elderly, who are usually more sensitive to the effects of idarubicin.

Other medicines—Although certain medicines should not be used together at all, in other cases two different medicines may be used together even if an interaction might occur. In these cases, your doctor may want to change the dose, or other precautions may be necessary. When you are receiving idarubicin, it is especially important that your health care professional know if you have ever been treated with x-rays or cancer medicines or if you are taking any of the following:

- Amphotericin B by injection (e.g., Fungizone) or
- Antithyroid agents (medicine for overactive thyroid) or
- Azathioprine (e.g., Imuran) or
- Chloramphenicol (e.g., Chloromycetin) or
- Colchicine or
- Flucytosine (e.g., Ancobon) or
- Ganciclovir (e.g., Cytovene) or
- Interferon (e.g., Intron A, Roferon-A) or
- Plicamycin (e.g., Mithracin) or
- Zidovudine (e.g., AZT, Retrovir)—Idarubicin may increase the effects of these medicines or radiation therapy on the blood
- Probenecid (e.g., Benemid) or
- Sulfinpyrazone (e.g., Anturane)—Idarubicin may raise the concentration of uric acid in the blood, which these medicines are used to lower

Other medical problems—The presence of other medical problems may affect the use of idarubicin. Make sure you tell your doctor if you have any other medical problems, especially:

- Chickenpox (including recent exposure) or
- Herpes zoster (shingles)—Risk of severe disease affecting other parts of the body
- Gout or
- Kidney stones—Idarubicin may increase levels of a chemical called uric acid in the body, which can cause gout or kidney stones
- Heart disease—Risk of heart problems caused by idarubicin may be increased
- Kidney disease or
- Liver disease—Effects may be increased because of slower removal of idarubicin from the body

Proper Use of This Medicine

Idarubicin is sometimes given together with certain other medicines. If you are receiving a combination of medicines, it is important that you receive each one at the proper time. If you are taking some of these medicines by mouth, ask your health care professional to help you plan a way to take them at the right times.

While you are receiving this medicine, your doctor may want you to drink extra fluids so that you will pass more urine. This will help prevent kidney problems and keep your kidneys working well.

Idarubicin often causes nausea and vomiting. However, it is very important that you continue to receive it, even if you begin to feel ill. Ask your health care professional for ways to lessen these effects.

Dosing—The dose of idarubicin will be different for different patients. The dose that is used may depend on a number of things, including what the medicine is being used for, the patient's size, and whether or not other medicines are also being taken. *If you are receiving idarubicin at home, follow your doctor's orders or the directions on the label.* If you have any questions about the proper dose of idarubicin, ask your doctor.

Precautions While Using This Medicine

It is very important that your doctor check your progress at regular visits to make sure that this medicine is working properly and to check for unwanted effects.

While you are being treated with idarubicin, and after you stop treatment with it, *do not have any immunizations (vaccinations) without your doctor's approval.* Idarubicin may lower your body's resistance, and there is a chance you might get the infection the immunization is meant to prevent. In addition, other persons living in your household should not take oral polio vaccine since there is a chance they could pass the polio virus on to you. Also, avoid persons who have taken oral polio vaccine. Do not get close to them, and do not stay in the same room with them for very long. If you cannot take these precautions, you should consider wearing a protective face mask that covers the nose and mouth.

Idarubicin can temporarily lower the number of white blood cells in your blood, increasing the chance of getting an infection. It can also lower the number of platelets, which are necessary for proper blood clotting. If this occurs, there are certain precautions you can take, especially when your blood count is low, to reduce the risk of infection or bleeding:

- If you can, avoid people with infections. *Check with your doctor immediately* if you think you are getting an infection or if you get a fever or chills, cough or hoarseness, lower back or side pain, or painful or difficult urination.
- *Check with your doctor immediately* if you notice any unusual bleeding or bruising; black, tarry stools; blood in urine or stools; or pinpoint red spots on your skin.
- Be careful when using a regular toothbrush, dental floss, or toothpick. Your medical doctor, dentist, or nurse may recommend other ways to clean your teeth and gums. Check with your medical doctor before having any dental work done.
- Do not touch your eyes or the inside of your nose unless you have just washed your hands and have not touched anything else in the meantime.
- Be careful not to cut yourself when you are using sharp objects such as a safety razor or fingernail or toenail cutters.
- Avoid contact sports or other situations where bruising or injury could occur.

If idarubicin accidentally seeps out of the vein into which it is injected, it may damage some tissues and cause scarring. *Tell the health care professional right away if you notice redness, pain, or swelling at the place of injection.*

Side Effects of This Medicine

Along with its needed effects, a medicine may cause some unwanted effects. Although not all of these side effects may occur, if they do occur they may need medical attention.

Also, because of the way cancer medicines act on the body, there is a chance that they might cause other unwanted effects that may not occur until months or years after the medicine is used. These delayed effects may include certain types of cancer. Discuss these possible effects with your doctor.

Check with your health care professional immediately if any of the following side effects occur:

More common

Black, tarry stools; blood in urine or stools; cough or hoarseness; fever or chills; lower back or side pain; painful or difficult urination; pinpoint red spots on skin; unusual bleeding or bruising

Less common

Fast or irregular heartbeat; pain at place of injection; shortness of breath; swelling of feet and lower legs

Rare

Stomach pain (severe)

Check with your health care professional as soon as possible if any of the following side effects occur:

More common

Sores in mouth and on lips

Less common

Joint pain

Rare

Skin rash or hives

Other side effects may occur that usually do not need medical attention. These side effects may go away during treatment as your body adjusts to the medicine. Also, your health care professional may be able to tell you about ways to prevent or reduce some of these side effects. Check with your health care professional if any of the following side effects continue or are bothersome or if you have any questions about them:

More common

Diarrhea or stomach cramps; headache; nausea and vomiting

Less common

Darkening or redness of skin (after x-ray treatment); numbness or tingling of fingers, toes, or face

Idarubicin causes the urine to turn reddish in color, which may stain clothes. This is not blood. It is perfectly normal and lasts for only a day or two after each dose is given.

This medicine often causes a temporary and total loss of hair. After treatment with idarubicin has ended, normal hair growth should return.

After you stop receiving idarubicin, it may still produce some side effects that need attention. During this period of time, *check with your health care professional immediately* if you notice any of the following side effects:

Fast or irregular heartbeat; shortness of breath; swelling of feet and lower legs

Other side effects not listed above may also occur in some patients. If you notice any other effects, check with your health care professional.

Revised: 06/18/93
Interim revision: 11/22/93; 06/21/94

IDOXURIDINE Ophthalmic

Some commonly used brand names in the U.S. and Canada are Herplex Liquifilm and Stoxil.

Description

Idoxuridine (eye-dox-YOOR-i-deen) belongs to the family of medicines called antivirals. Idoxuridine is used to treat virus infections of the eye.

Idoxuridine is available only with your doctor's prescription, in the following dosage forms:

Ophthalmic
- Ophthalmic ointment (U.S. and Canada)
- Ophthalmic solution (eye drops) (U.S. and Canada)

Before Using This Medicine

In deciding to use a medicine, the risks of using the medicine must be weighed against the good it will do. This is a decision you and your doctor will make. For idoxuridine, the following should be considered:

Allergies—Tell your doctor if you have ever had any unusual or allergic reaction to idoxuridine or to iodine or iodine-containing preparations. Also tell your health care professional if you are allergic to any other substances, such as preservatives.

Pregnancy—Idoxuridine ophthalmic preparations have not been shown to cause birth defects or other problems in humans. However, studies in animals have shown that idoxuridine causes protruding eyes (eyes that stick out too far) and deformed front legs in rabbits. Before using this medicine, make sure your doctor knows if you are pregnant or if you may become pregnant.

Breast-feeding—It is not known whether idoxuridine passes into the breast milk. Although most medicines pass into breast milk in small amounts, many of them may be used safely while breast-feeding. Mothers who are using this medicine and who wish to breast-feed should discuss this with their doctor.

Children—Studies on this medicine have been done only in adult patients, and there is no specific information comparing use of this medicine in children with use in other age groups.

Older adults—Many medicines have not been studied specifically in older people. Therefore, it may not be known whether they work exactly the same way they do in younger adults or if they cause different side effects or problems in older people. There is no specific information comparing use of idoxuridine in the elderly with use in other age groups.

Other medicines—Although certain medicines should not be used together at all, in other cases two different medicines may be used together even if an interaction might occur. In these cases, your doctor may want to change the dose, or other precautions may be necessary. When you are using idoxuridine, it is especially important that your health care professional know if you are using the following:

- Eye product containing boric acid—Boric acid may interact with the idoxuridine preparation causing a gritty substance to form or may interact with the preservative in the idoxuridine preparation causing a toxic effect in the eye

Proper Use of This Medicine

For patients using the *eye drop form* of idoxuridine:
- The bottle is only partially full to provide proper drop control.
- To use:

  —First, wash your hands. Then tilt the head back and pull the lower eyelid away from the eye to form a pouch. Drop the medicine into the pouch and gently close the eyes. Do not blink. Keep the eyes closed for 1 or 2 minutes to allow the medicine to come into contact with the infection.

  —If you think you did not get the drop of medicine into your eye properly, use another drop.

  —To keep the medicine as germ-free as possible, do not touch the applicator tip to any surface (including the eye). Also, keep the container tightly closed.

For patients using the *eye ointment form* of idoxuridine:
- To use:

  —First, wash your hands. Then pull the lower eyelid away from the eye to form a pouch. Squeeze a thin strip of ointment into the pouch. A 1-cm (approximately 1/3-inch) strip of ointment is usually enough unless otherwise directed by your doctor. Gently close the eyes and keep them closed for 1 or 2 minutes to allow the medicine to come into contact with the infection.

  —To keep the medicine as germ-free as possible, do not touch the applicator tip to any surface (including the eye). After using idoxuridine eye ointment, wipe the tip of the ointment tube with a clean tissue and keep the tube tightly closed.

Do not use this medicine more often or for a longer time than your doctor ordered. To do so may cause problems in the eyes. If you have any questions about this, check with your doctor.

To help clear up your infection completely, *keep using this medicine for the full time of treatment,* even though your symptoms may have disappeared. *Do not miss any doses.*

Dosing—The dose of idoxuridine will be different for different patients. *Follow your doctor's orders or the directions on the label.* The following information includes only the average doses of idoxuridine. *If your dose is different, do not change it* unless your doctor tells you to do so.

The number of doses you use each day, the time allowed between doses, and the length of time you use the medicine depend on the medical problem for which you are using idoxuridine.

- For virus infections of the eye:
  - —For *eye ointment* dosage form:
    - Adults and children—Use every four hours during the day (five times a day).
  - —For *eye solution (eye drops)* dosage form:
    - Adults and children—Use every hour during the day and every two hours during the night. After the eye condition gets better, use every two hours during the day and every four hours during the night.

Missed dose—If you miss a dose of this medicine, apply it as soon as possible. However, if it is almost time for your next dose, skip the missed dose and go back to your regular dosing schedule.

Storage—To store this medicine:
- Keep out of the reach of children.
- Store in the refrigerator or in a cool place because heat will cause this medicine to break down. However, keep the medicine from freezing. Follow the directions on the label.
- Do not keep outdated medicine or medicine no longer needed. Be sure that any discarded medicine is out of the reach of children.

Precautions While Using This Medicine

It is very important that your doctor check your progress at regular visits.

If your symptoms do not improve within a week, or if they become worse, check with your doctor.

This medicine may cause your eyes to become more sensitive to light than they are normally. Wearing sunglasses and avoiding too much exposure to bright light may help lessen the discomfort.

Side Effects of This Medicine

Along with its needed effects, a medicine may cause some unwanted effects. Although not all of these side effects may occur, if they do occur they may need medical attention.

Check with your doctor as soon as possible if any of the following side effects occur:

Less common

Increased sensitivity of eyes to light; itching, redness, swelling, pain, or other sign of irritation not present before use of this medicine

Rare

Blurring, dimming, or haziness of vision

Other side effects may occur that usually do not need medical attention. These side effects may go away during treatment as your body adjusts to the medicine. However, check with your doctor if the following side effect continues or is bothersome:

Less common

Excess flow of tears

After application, eye ointments usually cause your vision to blur for a few minutes.

Other side effects not listed above may also occur in some patients. If you notice any other effects, check with your doctor.

Revised: 06/21/93

IFOSFAMIDE Systemic

A commonly used brand name in the U.S. and Canada is IFEX.

Description

Ifosfamide (eye-FOSS-fa-mide) belongs to the group of medicines called alkylating agents. It is used to treat cancer of the testicles as well as some other kinds of cancer. Another medicine, called mesna, is usually given along with ifosfamide to prevent bladder problems that can be caused by ifosfamide.

Ifosfamide interferes with the growth of cancer cells, which are eventually destroyed. Since the growth of normal body cells may also be affected by ifosfamide, other effects will also occur. Some of these may be serious and must be reported to your doctor. Other effects, like hair loss, may not be serious but may cause concern. Some effects may not occur for months or years after the medicine is used.

Before you begin treatment with ifosfamide, you and your doctor should talk about the good this medicine will do as well as the risks of using it.

Ifosfamide is to be administered only by or under the immediate supervision of your doctor. It is available in the following dosage form:

Parenteral

Injection (U.S. and Canada)

Before Using This Medicine

In deciding to use a medicine, the risks of taking the medicine must be weighed against the good it will do. This is a decision you and your doctor will make. For ifosfamide, the following should be considered:

Allergies—Tell your doctor if you have ever had any unusual or allergic reaction to ifosfamide.

Pregnancy—Tell your doctor if you are pregnant or if you intend to have children. There is a chance that this medicine may cause birth defects if either the male or female is taking it at the time of conception or if it is taken during pregnancy. Ifosfamide causes birth defects in animals. In addition, many cancer medicines may cause sterility which could be permanent. Although sterility has not been reported with this medicine, the possibility should be kept in mind.

Be sure that you have discussed this with your doctor before taking this medicine. It is best to use some kind of birth control while you are receiving ifosfamide. Tell your doctor right away if you think you have become pregnant while receiving ifosfamide.

Breast-feeding—Tell your doctor if you are breast-feeding or if you intend to breast-feed during treatment with this medicine. Because ifosfamide may cause serious side effects, breast-feeding is generally not recommended while you are receiving it.

Children—Although there is no specific information comparing use of ifosfamide in children with use in other age groups, this medicine is not expected to cause different side effects or problems in children than it does in adults.

Older adults—Many medicines have not been studied specifically in older people. Therefore, it may not be known whether they work exactly the same way they do in younger adults or if they cause different side effects or problems in older people. There is no specific information comparing use of ifosfamide in the elderly with use in other age groups.

Other medicines—Although certain medicines should not be used together at all, in other cases two different medicines may be used together even if an interaction might occur. In these cases, your doctor may want to change the dose, or other precautions may be necessary. When you are taking ifosfamide, it is especially important that your health care professional know if you are taking any of the following:

- Amphotericin B by injection (e.g., Fungizone) or
- Antithyroid agents (medicine for overactive thyroid) or
- Azathioprine (e.g., Imuran) or
- Chloramphenicol (e.g., Chloromycetin) or
- Colchicine or
- Flucytosine (e.g., Ancobon) or
- Ganciclovir (e.g., Cytovene) or
- Interferon (e.g., Intron A, Roferon-A) or
- Plicamycin (e.g., Mithracin) or
- Zidovudine (e.g., AZT, Retrovir) or
- If you have ever been treated with x-rays or cancer medicines—Ifosfamide may increase the effects of these medicines or radiation therapy on the blood

Other medical problems—The presence of other medical problems may affect the use of ifosfamide. Make sure you tell your doctor if you have any other medical problems, especially:

- Chickenpox (including recent exposure) or
- Herpes zoster (shingles)—Risk of severe disease affecting other parts of the body
- Infection—Ifosfamide can decrease your body's ability to fight infection
- Kidney disease—Effects may be increased because of slower removal of ifosamide from the body
- Liver disease—Effects may be increased or decreased because the liver both makes ifosfamide work and removes it from the body

Proper Use of This Medicine

Ifosfamide is sometimes given together with certain other medicines. If you are using a combination of medicines, make sure that you take each one at the proper time and do not mix them. Ask your health care professional to help you plan a way to remember to take your medicines at the right times.

While you are receiving ifosfamide, it is important that you drink extra fluids so that you will pass more urine. Also, empty your bladder frequently, including at least once during the night. This will help prevent kidney and bladder problems and keep your kidneys working well. Ifosfamide passes from the body in the urine. If too much of it appears in the urine or if the urine stays in the bladder too long, it can cause dangerous irritation. Follow your doctor's instructions carefully about how much fluid to drink every day. Some patients may have to drink up to 7 to 12 cups (3 quarts) of fluid a day.

Ifosfamide often causes nausea and vomiting. However, it is very important that you continue to receive the medicine even if you begin to feel ill. Ask your health care professional for ways to lessen these effects.

Dosing—The dose of ifosfamide will be different for different patients. The dose that is used may depend on a number of things, including what the medicine is being used for, the patient's size, and whether or not other medicines are also being taken. *If you are receiving ifosfamide at home, follow your doctor's orders or the directions on the label.* If you have any questions about the proper dose of ifosfamide, ask your doctor.

Precautions While Using This Medicine

It is very important that your doctor check your progress at regular visits to make sure that this medicine is working properly and to check for unwanted effects.

While you are being treated with ifosfamide, and after you stop treatment with it, *do not have any immunizations (vaccinations) without your doctor's approval.* Ifosfamide may lower your body's resistance and there is a chance you might get the infection the immunization is meant to prevent. In addition, other persons living in your house should not take oral polio vaccine since there is a chance they could pass the polio virus on to you. Also, avoid persons who have recently taken oral polio vaccine. Do not get close to them, and do not stay in the same room with them for very long. If you cannot take these precautions, you should consider wearing a protective face mask that covers the nose and mouth.

Ifosfamide can temporarily lower the number of white blood cells in your blood, increasing the chance of getting an infection. It can also lower the number of platelets, which are necessary for proper blood clotting. If this occurs, there are certain precautions you can take to reduce the risk of infection or bleeding:

- If you can, avoid people with infections. *Check with your doctor immediately* if you think you are getting an infection or if you get a fever or chills, cough or hoarseness, lower back or side pain, or painful or difficult urination.
- *Check with your doctor immediately* if you notice any unusual bleeding or bruising; black, tarry stools; blood in urine or stools; or pinpoint red spots on your skin.
- Be careful when using a regular toothbrush, dental floss, or toothpick. Your medical doctor, dentist, or nurse may recommend other ways to clean your teeth and gums. Check with your medical doctor before having any dental work done.
- Do not touch your eyes or the inside of your nose unless you have just washed your hands and have not touched anything else in the meantime.
- Be careful not to cut yourself when you are using sharp objects such as a safety razor or fingernail or toenail cutters.
- Avoid contact sports or other situations where bruising or injury could occur.

Side Effects of This Medicine

Along with their needed effects, medicines like ifosfamide can sometimes cause unwanted effects such as blood problems, loss of hair, and problems with the bladder. These and others are described below. Also, because of the way these medicines act on the body, there is a chance that they might cause other unwanted effects that may not occur until months or years after the medicine is used. These may include certain types of cancer, such as leukemia. Discuss these possible effects with your doctor.

Although not all of these side effects may occur, if they do occur they may need medical attention.

Check with your doctor immediately if any of the following side effects occur:

More common

Blood in urine; frequent urination; painful urination

Less common

Cough or hoarseness; fever or chills; lower back or side pain

Rare

Black, tarry stools; blood in stools; pinpoint red spots on skin; unusual bleeding or bruising

Check with your doctor as soon as possible if any of the following side effects occur:

More common

Agitation; confusion; hallucinations (seeing, hearing, or feeling things that are not there); unusual tiredness

Less common

Dizziness; redness, swelling, or pain at place of injection

Rare

Cough or shortness of breath; convulsions (seizures); sores in mouth and on lips

Other side effects may occur that usually do not need medical attention. These side effects may go away during treatment as your body adjusts to the medicine. Also, your health care professional may be able to tell you about ways to prevent or reduce some of these side effects. Check with your doctor if any of the following side effects continue or are bothersome or if you have any questions about them:

More common

Nausea and vomiting

Ifosfamide often causes a temporary loss of hair. After treatment has ended, normal hair growth should return.

After you stop receiving ifosfamide, it may still produce some side effects that need attention. During this period of time, *check with your doctor immediately* if you notice the following side effect:

Blood in urine

Other side effects not listed above may also occur in some patients. If you notice any other effects, check with your doctor.

Revised: 09/09/92
Interim revision: 06/21/94

IMIGLUCERASE Systemic†

A commonly used brand name in the U.S. is Cerezyme.

†Not commercially available in Canada.

Description

Imiglucerase (im-i-GLOO-ser-ase) is used to treat Gaucher's disease caused by the lack of a certain enzyme, glucocerebrosidase, in the body. This enzyme is necessary for your body to use fats.

Imiglucerase is available only from your doctor in the following dosage form:

Parenteral

- Injection (U.S.)

Before Using This Medicine

In deciding to use a medicine, the risks of taking the medicine must be weighed against the good it will do. This is

a decision you and your doctor will make. For imiglucerase, the following should be considered:

Allergies—Tell your doctor if you have ever had any unusual or allergic reaction to alglucerase or imiglucerase. Also tell your health care professional if you are allergic to any other substances, such as foods, preservatives, or dyes.

Pregnancy—Studies on effects in pregnancy have not been done in either humans or animals.

Breast-feeding—It is not known whether imiglucerase passes into human breast milk. Although most medicines pass into breast milk in small amounts, many of them may be used safely while breast-feeding. Mothers who are taking this medicine and who wish to breast-feed should discuss this with their doctor.

Children—Although there is no specific information comparing use of imiglucerase in children with use in other age groups, this medicine is not expected to cause different side effects or problems in children than it does in adults.

Older adults—Many medicines have not been studied specifically in older people. Therefore, it may not be known whether they work exactly the same way they do in younger adults or if they cause different side effects or problems in older people. There is no specific information comparing use of imiglucerase in the elderly with use in other age groups.

Other medicines—Although certain medicines should not be used together at all, in other cases two different medicines may be used together even if an interaction might occur. In these cases, your doctor may want to change the dose, or other precautions may be necessary. Tell your health care professional if you are taking any other prescription or nonprescription (over-the-counter [OTC]) medicines.

Proper Use of This Medicine

This medicine helps control and reverse problems caused by Gaucher's disease. Therefore, you must continue to receive it if you expect to keep your condition under control. You may have to receive imiglucerase for the rest of your life. If Gaucher's disease is not treated, it can cause serious blood, liver, skeletal, or spleen problems.

Dosing—The dose of imiglucerase will be different for different patients. *Follow your doctor's orders.* The following information includes only the average doses of imiglucerase:

- For Gaucher's disease:
  - —For *injection* dosage form:
    - Adults and children—The dose is based on body weight and must be determined by your doctor. The usual dose is 15 to 60 Units per kilogram (kg) (6.8 to 27 Units per pound) of body weight injected into a vein over one to two hours. The dose may be repeated several times a week to once every 2 weeks, depending on your condition. Later your doctor may lower your dose.

Precautions While Using This Medicine

It is important that your doctor check your progress while you are receiving imiglucerase to make sure that the dosage is correct for you.

Side Effects of This Medicine

Along with its needed effects, a medicine may cause some unwanted effects. Although not all of these side effects may occur, if they do occur they may need medical attention.

The following side effects may go away during treatment as your body adjusts to the medicine. However, check with your doctor if any of the following side effects continue or are bothersome:

Less common

Abdominal discomfort; decrease in blood pressure, decrease in frequency of urination; dizziness; headache; itching; nausea; rash

Other side effects not listed above may also occur in some patients. If you notice any other effects, check with your doctor.

Developed: 06/16/95

IMIPENEM AND CILASTATIN Systemic

Some commonly used brand names are:

In the U.S.—
Primaxin IM
Primaxin IV

In Canada—
Primaxin

Description

Imipenem (i-mi-PEN-em) and cilastatin (sye-la-STAT-in) combination is used in the treatment of infections caused by bacteria. It works by killing bacteria or preventing their growth. This medicine will not work for colds, flu, or other virus infections.

Imipenem and cilastatin combination is used to treat infections in many different parts of the body. It is sometimes given with other antibiotics.

This medicine is available only with your doctor's prescription, in the following dosage form:

Parenteral

- Injection (U.S. and Canada)

Before Receiving This Medicine

In deciding to use a medicine, the risks of taking the medicine must be weighed against the good it will do. This is

a decision you and your doctor will make. For imipenem and cilastatin, the following should be considered:

Allergies—Tell your doctor if you have ever had any unusual or allergic reaction to imipenem and cilastatin, penicillins or cephalosporins. Also tell your health care professional if you are allergic to any other substances, such as foods, preservatives, or dyes.

Pregnancy—Studies have not been done in humans. However, imipenem and cilastatin combination has not been reported to cause birth defects or other problems in animal studies.

Breast-feeding—It is not known whether imipenem or cilastatin passes into the breast milk. However, this medicine has not been reported to cause problems in nursing babies.

Children—This medicine has been tested in a limited number of children 12 years of age and older and, in effective doses, has not been reported to cause different side effects or problems in children than it does in adults.

Older adults—Many medicines have not been studied specifically in older people. Therefore, it may not be known whether they work exactly the same way they do in younger adults. Although there is no specific information comparing use of imipenem and cilastatin in the elderly with use in other age groups, this medicine is not expected to cause different side effects or problems in older people than it does in younger adults.

Other medicines—Although certain medicines should not be used together at all, in other cases two different medicines may be used together even if an interaction might occur. In these cases, your doctor may want to change the dose, or other precautions may be necessary. Tell your health care professional if you are taking any other prescription or nonprescription (over-the-counter [OTC]) medicine.

Other medical problems—The presence of other medical problems may affect the use of imipenem and cilastatin. Make sure you tell your doctor if you have any other medical problems, especially:

- Central nervous system (CNS) disorders (for example, brain disease or history of seizures)—Patients with nervous system disorders, including seizures, may be more likely to have side effects
- Kidney disease—Patients with kidney disease may be more likely to have side effects

Proper Use of This Medicine

To help clear up your infection completely, *imipenem and cilastatin combination must be given for the full time of treatment,* even if you begin to feel better after a few days. Also, this medicine works best when there is a constant amount in the blood or urine. To help keep the amount constant, it must be given on a regular schedule.

Dosing—The dose of imipenem and cilastatin combination will be different for different patients. *Follow your doctor's orders or the directions on the label.* The following information includes only the average doses of imipenem and cilastatin combination. *If your dose is different, do not change it* unless your doctor tells you to do so.

- For *injection* dosage form:
  - —For bacterial infections:
    - Adults and children 12 years of age and over—250 milligrams (mg) to 1 gram injected into a vein every six to eight hours; or 500 to 750 mg injected into a muscle every twelve hours, depending on how severe your infection is.
    - Children up to 12 years of age—Use and dose must be determined by your doctor.

Precautions While Using This Medicine

Some patients may develop tremors or seizures while receiving this medicine. If you already have a history of seizures and you are taking anticonvulsants, you should continue to take them unless otherwise directed by your doctor.

In some patients, imipenem and cilastatin combination may cause diarrhea.

- Severe diarrhea may be a sign of a serious side effect. *Do not take any diarrhea medicine without first checking with your doctor.* Diarrhea medicines may make your diarrhea worse or make it last longer.
- For mild diarrhea, diarrhea medicine containing kaolin (e.g., Kaopectate liquid) or attapulgite (e.g., Kaopectate tablets, Diasorb) may be taken. However, other kinds of diarrhea medicine should not be taken. They may make your diarrhea worse or make it last longer.
- If you have any questions about this or if mild diarrhea continues or gets worse, check with your health care professional.

Side Effects of This Medicine

Along with its needed effects, a medicine may cause some unwanted effects. Although not all of these side effects may occur, if they do occur they may need medical attention.

Check with your health care professional immediately if any of the following side effects occur:

More common

Confusion; convulsions (seizures); dizziness; pain at place of injection; skin rash, hives, itching, fever, or wheezing; tremors

Less common

Dizziness; increased sweating; nausea or vomiting; unusual tiredness or weakness

Rare

Fever; severe abdominal or stomach cramps and pain; watery and severe diarrhea, which may also be bloody (these side effects may also occur up to several weeks after you stop receiving this medicine)

Other side effects may occur that usually do not need medical attention. These side effects may go away during

treatment as your body adjusts to the medicine. However, check with your doctor if the following side effects continue or are bothersome:

More common
Diarrhea; nausea and vomiting

Other side effects not listed above may also occur in some patients. If you notice any other effects, check with your doctor.

Revised: 09/08/92
Interim revision: 04/01/94; 01/11/95

IMMUNE GLOBULIN INTRAVENOUS (HUMAN) Systemic

Some commonly used brand names are:

In the U.S.—
Gamimune N
Gammagard
Gammar–IV
Iveegam
Polygam
Sandoglobulin
Venoglobulin–I

In Canada—
Gamimune N
Iveegam

Other commonly used names are IGIV and IVIG.

Description

Immune globulin intravenous (IGIV) belongs to a group of medicines known as immunizing agents. IGIV is used to prevent or treat some illnesses that can occur when your body does not produce enough of its own immunity to prevent those diseases.

IGIV is manufactured from plasma that comes from blood that has been donated by many people. The immunity to diseases that is in the donated blood is used by your own body to increase your immunity.

IGIV is also used to treat a disorder known as idiopathic thrombocytopenic purpura (ITP). When a person has ITP, there is an increase in the breakdown of a part of the blood known as platelets. Low platelet levels in the blood increase a person's chance of bleeding or hemorrhaging. IGIV is used to increase the number of platelets in the blood to prevent this bleeding.

IGIV does not contain harmful products of hepatitis B virus, human immunodeficiency virus (HIV), acquired immunodeficiency syndrome (AIDS), or AIDS-related complex (ARC).

IGIV is available in the following dosage form:

Parenteral
- Injection (U.S. and Canada)

Before Using This Medicine

In deciding to use a medicine, the risks of taking the medicine must be weighed against the good it will do. This is a decision you and your doctor will make. For immune globulin intravenous (IGIV), the following should be considered:

Allergies—Tell your doctor if you have ever had any unusual or allergic reaction to intramuscular or intravenous immune globulins. Also tell your health care professional if you are allergic to any other substances, such as foods, preservatives, or dyes.

Diet—Make certain your health care professional knows if you are on any special diet, such as a low-sodium or low-sugar diet.

Pregnancy—Studies on effects in pregnancy have not been done in either humans or animals.

Breast-feeding—It is not known whether IGIV passes into the breast milk. Although most medicines pass into breast milk in small amounts, many of them may be used safely while breast-feeding. Mothers who are using this medicine and who wish to breast-feed should discuss this with their doctor.

Children—Although there is no specific information comparing use of IGIV in children with use in other age groups, this medicine is not expected to cause different side effects or problems in children than it does in adults.

Older adults—Many medicines have not been studied specifically in older people. Therefore, it may not be known whether they work exactly the same way they do in younger adults. Although there is no specific information comparing use of IGIV in the elderly with use in other age groups, this medicine is not expected to cause different side effects or problems in older people than it does in younger adults.

Other medicines—Although certain medicines should not be used together at all, in other cases two different medicines may be used together even if an interaction might occur. In these cases, your doctor may want to change the dose, or other precautions may be necessary. Tell your health care professional if you are using any other prescription or nonprescription (over-the-counter [OTC]) medicine.

Other medical problems—The presence of other medical problems may affect the use of IGIV. Make sure you tell your doctor if you have any other medical problems, especially:

- Agammaglobulinemia or
- Hypogammaglobulinemia—Patients with these conditions who have never received immune globulin substitution therapy or who were last treated more than 8 weeks ago may have more side effects to IGIV
- Heart problems or
- Immunoglobulin A (IgA) deficiencies—IGIV may make the conditions worse

Proper Use of This Medicine

Dosing—The dose of IGIV will be different for different patients. Doses are based on body weight and the condition for which you are being treated. The following information includes only the average doses of IGIV. *If your dose is different, do not change it* unless your doctor tells you to do so.

- For *injection* dosage form:
  - —For immunodeficiency:
    - Adults and children—200 to 800 milligrams per kilogram (mg/kg) (90 to 360 milligrams per pound) of body weight per month, injected into a vein.
  - —For idiopathic thrombocytopenic purpura (ITP):
    - Adults and children—Either 400 milligrams per kilogram (mg/kg) (180 milligrams per pound) of body weight per day for 2 to 5 days or 1 gram per kilogram (450 milligrams per pound) of body weight per day for 1 or 2 days, injected into a vein. Doses are usually repeated every 10 to 21 days.
  - —For bacterial infection secondary to B-cell chronic lymphocytic leukemia (CLL):
    - Adults and children—400 milligrams per kilogram (mg/kg) (180 milligrams per pound) of body weight, given once every 3 or 4 weeks, injected into a vein.
  - —For any other condition: The dose will be determined by your doctor.

Side Effects of This Medicine

Along with its needed effects, a medicine may cause some unwanted effects. Although not all of these side effects may occur, if they do occur they may need medical attention.

Check with your doctor immediately if any of the following side effects occur:

Symptoms of overdose

Chest tightness; chills; dizziness; fever; nausea; redness of face; sweating; unusual tiredness or weakness; vomiting

Check with your doctor as soon as possible if any of the following side effects occur:

More common

Fast or pounding heartbeat; troubled breathing

Less common

Bluish coloring of lips or nailbeds; burning sensation in head; faintness or lightheadedness; unusual tiredness or weakness; wheezing

Other side effects may occur that usually do not need medical attention. These side effects may go away during treatment as your body adjusts to the medicine. However, check with your doctor if any of the following side effects continue or are bothersome:

More common

Backache; general feeling of discomfort or illness; headache; joint pain; muscle pain

Less common

Chest, back, or hip pain; hives; leg cramps; redness, rash, or pain at place of injection

Other side effects not listed above may also occur in some patients. If you notice any other effects, check with your doctor.

Revised: 06/21/93
Interim revision: 02/23/94

INDAPAMIDE Systemic

Some commonly used brand names are:

In the U.S.—
Lozol

In Canada—
Lozide

Description

Indapamide (in-DAP-a-mide) belongs to the group of medicines known as diuretics. It is commonly used to treat high blood pressure (hypertension).

High blood pressure adds to the workload of the heart and arteries. If it continues for a long time, the heart and arteries may not function properly. This can damage the blood vessels of the brain, heart, and kidneys resulting in a stroke, heart failure, or kidney failure. High blood pressure may also increase the risk of heart attacks. These problems may be less likely to occur if blood pressure is controlled.

Indapamide is also used to help reduce the amount of water in the body by increasing the flow of urine.

Indapamide is available only with your doctor's prescription, in the following dosage form:

Oral

- Tablets (U.S. and Canada)

Before Using This Medicine

In deciding to use a medicine, the risks of taking the medicine must be weighed against the good it will do. This is a decision you and your doctor will make. For indapamide, the following should be considered:

Allergies—Tell your doctor if you have ever had any unusual or allergic reaction to indapamide or other sulfonamide-type medicines. Also tell your health care professional if you are allergic to any other substances, such as foods, preservatives, or dyes.

Pregnancy—Indapamide has not been studied in pregnant women. However, indapamide has not been shown to cause birth defects or other problems in animal studies.

In general, diuretics are not useful for normal swelling of feet and hands that occurs during pregnancy. Diuretics should not be taken during pregnancy unless recommended by your doctor.

Breast-feeding—It is not known whether indapamide passes into breast milk. However, this medicine has not been reported to cause problems in nursing babies.

Children—Studies on this medicine have been done only in adult patients, and there is no specific information comparing use of indapamide in children with use in other age groups.

Older adults—Dizziness or lightheadedness and signs and symptoms of too much potassium loss are more likely to occur in the elderly, who are usually more sensitive than younger adults to the effects of indapamide.

Other medicines—Although certain medicines should not be used together at all, in other cases two different medicines may be used together even if an interaction might occur. In these cases, your doctor may want to change the dose, or other precautions may be necessary. When you are taking indapamide, it is especially important that your health care professional know if you are taking any of the following:

- Digitalis glycosides (heart medicine)—Use with indapamide may increase the chance of side effects of digitalis glycosides
- Lithium (e.g., Lithane)—Use with indapamide may cause high blood levels of lithium, which may increase the chance of side effects

Other medical problems—The presence of other medical problems may affect the use of indapamide. Make sure you tell your doctor if you have any other medical problems, especially:

- Diabetes mellitus (sugar diabetes) or
- Gout (history of)—Indapamide may make these conditions worse
- Kidney disease—May prevent indapamide from working properly
- Liver disease—Higher blood levels of indapamide may occur, which may increase the chance of side effects

Proper Use of This Medicine

Indapamide may cause you to have an unusual feeling of tiredness when you begin to take it. You may also notice an increase in the amount of urine or in your frequency of urination. After taking the medicine for a while, these effects should lessen. In general, to keep the increase in urine from affecting your sleep:

- If you are to take a single dose a day, take it in the morning after breakfast.
- If you are to take more than one dose a day, take the last dose no later than 6 p.m., unless otherwise directed by your doctor.

However, it is best to plan your dose or doses according to a schedule that will least affect your personal activities and sleep. Ask your health care professional to help you plan the best time to take this medicine.

To help you remember to take indapamide, try to get into the habit of taking it at the same time each day.

For patients taking indapamide for *high blood pressure:*

- In addition to the use of the medicine your doctor has prescribed, treatment for your high blood pressure may include weight control and care in the types of foods you eat, especially foods high in sodium. Your doctor will tell you which of these are most important for you. You should check with your doctor before changing your diet.
- Many patients who have high blood pressure will not notice any signs of the problem. In fact, many may feel normal. It is very important that you *take your medicine exactly as directed* and that you keep your appointments with your doctor even if you feel well.
- Remember that this medicine will not cure your high blood pressure but it does help control it. Therefore, you must continue to take it as directed if you expect to lower your blood pressure and keep it down. *You may have to take high blood pressure medicine for the rest of your life.* If high blood pressure is not treated, it can cause serious problems such as heart failure, blood vessel disease, stroke, or kidney disease.

Dosing—The dose of indapamide will be different for different patients. *Follow your doctor's orders or the directions on the label.* The following information includes only the average doses of indapamide. *If your dose is different, do not change it* unless your doctor tells you to do so:

- For *oral* dosage forms (tablets):
  —Adults: 2.5 to 5 milligrams once a day.

Missed dose—If you miss a dose of this medicine, take it as soon as possible. However, if it is almost time for your next dose, skip the missed dose and go back to your regular dosing schedule. Do not double doses.

Storage—To store this medicine:

- Keep out of the reach of children.
- Store away from heat and direct light.
- Do not store in the bathroom, near the kitchen sink, or in other damp places. Heat or moisture may cause the medicine to break down.
- Do not keep outdated medicine or medicine no longer needed. Be sure that any discarded medicine is out of the reach of children.

Precautions While Using This Medicine

It is important that your doctor check your progress at regular visits to make sure that indapamide is working properly.

This medicine may cause a loss of potassium from your body:

- To help prevent this, your doctor may want you to:
  —eat or drink foods that have a high potassium content (for example, orange or other citrus fruit juices), or
  —take a potassium supplement, or
  —take another medication to help prevent the loss of the potassium in the first place.
- It is very important to follow these directions. Also, it is important not to change your diet on your own. This is more important if you are already on a special diet (as for diabetes), or if you are taking a potassium supplement or a medicine to reduce potassium loss.

Extra potassium may not be necessary and, in some cases, too much potassium could be harmful.

Check with your doctor if you become sick and have severe or continuing vomiting or diarrhea. These problems may cause you to lose additional water and potassium.

For patients taking this medicine for *high blood pressure:*

- *Do not take other medicines unless they have been discussed with your doctor.* This especially includes over-the-counter (nonprescription) medicines for appetite control, asthma, colds, hay fever, or sinus problems, since they may tend to increase your blood pressure.

Side Effects of This Medicine

Along with its needed effects, a medicine may cause some unwanted effects. Although not all of these side effects may occur, if they do occur they may need medical attention.

Check with your doctor as soon as possible if any of the following side effects occur:

Dryness of mouth; increased thirst; irregular heartbeat; mood or mental changes; muscle cramps or pain; nausea or vomiting; unusual tiredness or weakness; weak pulse

Rare

Skin rash, itching, or hives

Other side effects may occur that usually do not need medical attention. These side effects may go away during treatment as your body adjusts to the medicine. However, check with your doctor if any of the following side effects continue or are bothersome:

Less common or rare

Diarrhea; dizziness or lightheadedness, especially when getting up from a lying or sitting position; headache; loss of appetite; trouble in sleeping; stomach upset

Other side effects not listed above may also occur in some patients. If you notice any other effects, check with your doctor.

Revised: 01/20/93

INFANT FORMULAS Systemic

Some commonly used brand names are:

In the U.S.—

Alimentum[1]
Alsoy[3]
Carnation Follow-Up Formula[2]
Carnation Good Start[2]
Enfamil[2]
Enfamil Human Milk Fortifier[2]
Enfamil with Iron[2]
Enfamil Premature Formula[2]
Enfamil Premature Formula with Iron[2]
Gerber Baby Formula with Iron[2]
Gerber Soy Formula[3]
Isomil[3]
Isomil SF[3]
Lactofree[2]
Nursoy[3]
Nutramigen[1]
Preemie SMA 20[2]
Preemie SMA 24[2]
Pregestimil[1]
ProSobee[3]
RCF[3]
Similac 13[2]
Similac 20[2]
Similac 24[2]
Similac 27[2]
Similac with Iron 20[2]
Similac with Iron 24[2]
Similac Natural Care Human Milk Fortifier[2]
Similac PM 60/40[2]
Similac Special Care 20[2]
Similac Special Care 24[2]
Similac Special Care with Iron 24[2]
SMA 13[2]
SMA 20[2]
SMA 24[2]
SMA 27[2]
SMA Lo-Iron 13[2]
SMA Lo-Iron 20[2]
SMA Lo-Iron 24[2]
Soyalac[3]

In Canada—

Alimentum[1]
Isomil[3]
Nursoy[3]
Nutramigen[1]
Preemie SMA 20[2]
Preemie SMA 24[2]
Pregestimil[1]
ProSobee[3]
RCF[3]
Similac 13[2]
Similac 20[2]
Similac 24[2]
Similac 27[2]
Similac PM 60/40[2]
Similac Special Care 20[2]
Similac Special Care 24[2]
SMA 13[2]
SMA 20[2]
SMA 24[2]
SMA 27[2]
SMA Lo-Iron 13[2]
SMA Lo-Iron 20[2]
SMA Lo-Iron 24[2]

Note: For quick reference, the following infant formulas are numbered to match the corresponding brand names.

This monograph includes information on the following:

1. Infant Formulas, Hypoallergenic
2. Infant Formulas, Milk-based
3. Infant Formulas, Soy-based

Description

Infant formulas are used to supply all or part of the nutrients infants need for growth and development. These formulas are used by the body for energy and to form substances for normal body functions.

The amount and type of nutrients contained in infant formulas are regulated by the Food and Drug Administration (FDA). The FDA also regulates the manufacturing process, labeling, and recall procedure for infant formulas.

Infant formulas are available without a prescription. However, they should only be used under medical supervision. They are available in the following forms:

Oral

Infant Formulas, Hypoallergenic (for infants allergic to milk)

- Oral concentrate (U.S.)
- Oral solution (U.S. and Canada)
- Powder for oral solution (U.S. and Canada)

Infant Formulas, Milk-based (for infants not allergic to milk)

- Oral concentrate (U.S.)
- Oral powder (U.S.)
- Oral solution (U.S. and Canada)
- Powder for oral solution (U.S. and Canada)

Infant Formulas, Soy-based (for infants allergic to milk but not to soy)

- Oral concentrate (U.S. and Canada)
- Oral solution (U.S. and Canada)
- Powder for oral solution (U.S. and Canada)

Before Using This Infant Formula

If you are giving your infant this infant formula, carefully read and follow any precautions on the label. For infant formulas, the following should be considered:

Allergies—Tell your doctor if your infant has ever had any unusual or allergic reaction to infant formulas. Also tell your health care professional if your infant is allergic to any other substances, such as foods, preservatives, or dyes.

Children—Problems may occur if the infant formula is not mixed properly or is not used under medical care.

Medicines, dietary supplements, or infant formulas—Although certain medicines, dietary supplements, or infant formulas should not be used together at all, in other cases they may be used together even if an interaction might occur. In these cases, your doctor may want to change the feeding schedule, or other precautions may be necessary. When you are giving your infant an infant formula, it is especially important that your health care professional know if you are giving your infant any dietary supplements or any prescription or nonprescription (over-the-counter [OTC]) medicine.

Other medical problems—The presence of other medical problems may affect the use of infant formulas. Make sure you tell your doctor if your infant has any medical problems, especially:

- Breathing problems or
- Dehydration or
- Diabetes mellitus (sugar diabetes) or
- Diarrhea or
- Heart problems or
- Hyperglycemia (high levels of sugar in the blood) or
- Liver problems or
- Pancreas problems—Infant formulas may make these conditions worse
- Intestine problems or
- Stomach problems—These problems may prevent infant formulas from being absorbed properly
- Kidney problems—Higher blood levels of certain ingredients of the infant formula may result, and a smaller amount of infant formula may be needed
- Phenylketonuria—Infant formulas contain phenylalanine, which may make the condition worse

Proper Use of This Infant Formula

Infant formulas may be given by mouth or, in some cases, by a tube feeding. Use the amount of infant formula and the feeding schedule recommended by your doctor.

For infants receiving the *concentrate or powder for oral solution* form of this preparation:

- For mixing or other use, follow carefully the instructions on the package.
- Any unused solution should be kept in the refrigerator. Most formulas can be kept in the refrigerator for 1 to 2 days. Check the label of your product.

For infants receiving the *oral liquid* form of this preparation:

- This preparation is in ready-to-use form. No dilution is needed unless directed by your doctor.
- Shake the preparation well before opening. Refrigerate after opening. Most formulas can be kept in the refrigerator for 1 to 2 days. Check the label of your product.

For infants receiving *Enfamil Human Milk Fortifier:*

- This powder should be added to mother's breast milk. For mixing or other use, follow carefully the instructions on the package.
- Any unused solution should be kept in the refrigerator for up to 1 day.

For infants receiving *Similac Natural Care:*

- This liquid should be added to the mother's breast milk. It may also be fed alternating with breast milk to low-birth-weight infants as directed by the infant's doctor. For mixing or other use, follow carefully the instructions on the package.
- Any unused solution should be kept in the refrigerator for up to 1 day.

Feeding—The amount of an infant formula to be given will be different for different infants. *Follow your doctor's orders.*

Storage—To store the unopened container:

- Keep out of the reach of children.
- Store away from heat and direct light.
- Do not store in the bathroom, near the kitchen sink, or in other damp places. Heat or moisture may cause the infant formula to break down.
- Keep the infant formula from freezing. Do not refrigerate until after the product has been opened or mixed.
- Do not keep outdated infant formulas or those no longer needed. Be sure that any discarded infant formula is out of the reach of children.

Side Effects of This Infant Formula

Along with its needed effects, an infant formula may cause some unwanted effects. Although not all of these side effects may occur, if they do occur they may need medical attention.

More common

Diarrhea; unusual thirst; unusual tiredness or weakness

Note: Diarrhea can lead to severe fluid loss in your infant very quickly. Diarrhea can be caused by improper infant formula preparation. Make sure that you are following the directions for mixing on the container of your product.

Less common

Signs of milk allergy (hives, wheezing); signs of milk intolerance (abdominal bloating, diarrhea, stomach cramps, vomiting)

Developed: 09/23/93
Interim revision: 08/03/95

INFLUENZA VIRUS VACCINE Systemic

Some commonly used brand names are:

In the U.S.—
- FluShield
- Fluvirin
- Fluzone

Generic name product may also be available.

In Canada—
- Fluviral
- Fluviral S/F
- Fluzone

Another commonly used name is flu vaccine.

Description

Influenza (in-floo-EN-za) virus vaccine is used to prevent infection by the influenza viruses. The vaccine works by causing your body to produce its own protection (antibodies) against the disease. It is also known as a "flu shot."

There are many kinds of influenza viruses, but not all will cause problems in any given year. Therefore, before the influenza vaccine for each year is produced, the World Health Organization (WHO) and the U.S. and Canadian Public Health Services decide which influenza viruses will be most likely to cause influenza infection that year. Then they include the antigens (substances that cause protective antibodies to be formed) to these viruses in the influenza vaccine made available. Usually, the U.S. and Canada use the same influenza vaccine; however, they are not required to do so.

It is necessary to receive an influenza vaccine injection each year, since influenza infections are usually caused by different kinds of influenza viruses each year and because the protection gained by the vaccine lasts less than a year.

Influenza is a virus infection of the throat, bronchial tubes, and lungs. Influenza infection causes fever, chills, cough, headache, and muscle aches and pains in your back, arms, and legs. In addition, adults and children weakened by other diseases or medical conditions and persons 65 years of age and over, even if they are healthy, may get a much more serious illness and may have to be treated in a hospital. Each year thousands of people die as a result of an influenza infection.

The best way to help prevent influenza infection is to get an influenza vaccination each year, usually in early November. Immunization (administration of vaccine) against influenza is approved for infants 6 months of age and over, all children, and all adults.

This vaccine is to be administered only by or under the supervision of your doctor or other health care professional. It is available in the following dosage form:

Parenteral
- Injection (U.S. and Canada)

Before Receiving This Vaccine

In deciding to use a medicine, the risks of taking the medicine must be weighed against the good it will do. This is a decision you and your doctor will make. For influenza vaccine, the following should be considered:

Allergies—Tell your doctor if you have ever had any unusual or allergic reaction to influenza vaccine or to antibiotics, such as gentamicin, streptomycin, or other aminoglycosides. Influenza vaccine available in the U.S. or Canada may contain these antibiotics in very small amounts. Also tell your health care professional if you are allergic to any other substances, such as foods (especially eggs) or preservatives (especially sodium bisulfite or thimerosal). Influenza vaccine is grown in the fluids of chick embryos.

Pregnancy—Influenza vaccine has not been shown to cause birth defects or other problems in humans.

Breast-feeding—Influenza vaccine has not been reported to cause problems in nursing babies.

Children—*Use is not recommended for infants up to 6 months of age.* In addition, only a split-virus influenza vaccine should be given to children 6 months to 12 years of age. Some side effects of the vaccine, such as fever, unusual tiredness or weakness, or aches or pains in muscles, are more likely to occur in infants and children, who are usually more sensitive than adults to the effects of influenza vaccine.

Older adults—This vaccine is not expected to cause different side effects or problems in older persons than it does in younger adults. However, elderly persons may not become as immune to head and upper chest influenza infections as younger adults, although the vaccine may still be effective in preventing lower chest influenza infections and other complications of influenza.

Other medicines—Although certain medicines should not be used together at all, in other cases two different medicines may be used together even if an interaction might occur. In these cases, your doctor may want to change the dose, or other precautions may be necessary. Tell your health care professional if you are using any other prescription or nonprescription (over-the-counter [OTC]) medicine.

Other medical problems—The presence of other medical problems may affect the use of influenza vaccine. Make sure you tell your doctor if you have any other medical problems, especially:
- Bronchitis, pneumonia, or other illness involving lungs or bronchial tubes—Use of influenza vaccine may make the condition worse
- Severe illness with fever—The symptoms of the condition may be confused with the possible side effects of the vaccine

Proper Use of This Vaccine

Dosing—The dose of influenza vaccine will be different for different patients. *Follow your doctor's orders.* The following information includes only the average dose of influenza vaccine.

• For *injection* dosage form:
—To help prevent influenza infection:
• Adults and children 9 years of age and older—One injection each year.
• Children 6 months to 9 years of age—One or two injections, depending on whether the child has received influenza vaccine in the past. The dose is given each year. If two doses are needed, they should be spaced 4 weeks apart.

Side Effects of This Vaccine

In 1976, a number of persons who received the ''swine flu'' influenza vaccine developed Guillain-Barré syndrome (GBS). Most of these persons were over 25 years of age. Although only 10 out of one million persons receiving the vaccine actually developed GBS, this number was 6 times more than would normally have been expected. Most of the persons who got GBS recovered completely from the paralysis it caused.

It is assumed that the ''swine flu'' virus included in the 1976 vaccine caused the problem, but this has not been proven. Since that time, the ''swine flu'' virus has not been used in influenza vaccines, and there has been no recurrence of GBS associated with influenza vaccinations.

Along with its needed effects, a vaccine may cause some unwanted effects. Although not all of these side effects may occur, if they do occur they may need medical attention.

Get emergency help immediately if any of the following side effects occur:

Symptoms of allergic reaction
Difficulty in breathing or swallowing; hives; itching, especially of feet or hands; reddening of skin, especially around ears; swelling of eyes, face, or inside of nose; unusual tiredness or weakness (sudden and severe)

Other side effects may occur that usually do not need medical attention. These side effects generally do not last for more than 1 or 2 days. However, check with your doctor if any of the following side effects continue or are bothersome:

More common
Tenderness, redness, or hard lump at place of injection

Less common
Fever, general feeling of discomfort or illness, or aches or pains in muscles

Other side effects not listed above may also occur in some patients. If you notice any other effects, check with your doctor.

Revised: 07/25/97

INSULIN Systemic

Some commonly used brand names are:

In the U.S.—

Humulin 50/50[10]
Humulin 70/30[10]
Humulin L[7]
Humulin N[9]
Humulin R[5]
Humulin U Ultralente[3]
Lente Iletin I[6]
Lente Iletin II[6]
Lente L[6]
Novolin 70/30[10]
Novolin L[7]
Novolin N[9]
Novolin N PenFill[9]
Novolin N Prefilled[9]
Novolin 70/30 PenFill[10]
Novolin 70/30 Prefilled[10]
Novolin R[5]
Novolin R PenFill[5]
Novolin R Prefilled[5]
NPH Iletin I[8]
NPH Iletin II[8]
NPH-N[8]
Regular (Concentrated) Iletin II, U-500[4]
Regular Iletin I[4]
Regular Iletin II[4]
Regular Insulin[4]
Velosulin BR[1]

In Canada—

Humulin 10/90[10]
Humulin 20/80[10]
Humulin 30/70[10]
Humulin 40/60[10]
Humulin 50/50[10]
Humulin-L[7]
Humulin-N[9]
Humulin-R[5]
Humulin-U[3]
Insulin-Toronto[4]
Lente Iletin[6]
Lente Iletin II[6]
Lente Insulin[6]
Novolin ge 30/70[10]
Novolin ge Lente[7]
Novolin ge NPH[9]
Novolin ge NPH Penfill[9]
Novolin ge 10/90 Penfill[10]
Novolin ge 20/80 Penfill[10]
Novolin ge 30/70 Penfill[10]
Novolin ge 40/60 Penfill[10]
Novolin ge 50/50 Penfill[10]
Novolin ge Toronto[5]
Novolin ge Toronto Penfill[5]
Novolin ge Ultralente[3]
NPH Iletin[8]
NPH Iletin II[8]
NPH Insulin[8]
Regular Iletin[4]
Regular Iletin II[4]
Semilente Insulin[11]
Ultralente Insulin[2]
Velosulin Human[1]

Other commonly used names are:
lente insulin, L[6, 7]
NPH insulin, NPH[8, 9]
regular insulin, R[1, 4, 5]
semilente insulin, S[11]
ultralente insulin, U[2, 3]

Note: For quick reference, the following insulins are numbered to match the corresponding brand names.

This information applies to the following medicines:

1. Buffered Insulin (IN-su-lin) Human, (R)
2. Extended Insulin Zinc, (U)*
3. Extended Insulin Zinc, Human, (U)
4. Insulin, (R)
5. Insulin Human, (R)
6. Insulin Zinc, (L)
7. Insulin Zinc, Human, (L)
8. Isophane (EYE-so-fayn) Insulin, (NPH)
9. Isophane Insulin, Human, (NPH)
10. Isophane Insulin, Human, and Insulin Human, (NPH and R)
11. Prompt Insulin Zinc, (S)*

*Not commercially available in the U.S.

Description

Insulin (IN-su-lin) is one of many hormones that help the body turn the food we eat into energy. Also, insulin helps us store energy that we can use later. After we eat, insulin works by causing sugar to go from the blood into our body's cells to make fat, sugar, and protein. When we need more energy between meals, insulin will help us use the fat, sugar, and protein that we have stored. This occurs whether we make our own insulin in the pancreas gland or take it by injection.

Diabetes mellitus (sugar diabetes) is a condition in which the body does not make enough insulin to meet its needs or does not properly use the insulin it makes. Without insulin, glucose cannot get into the body's cells. Without glucose, the cells will not work properly.

To work properly, the amount of insulin you use must be balanced against the amount and type of food you eat and the amount of exercise you do. If you change your diet, your exercise, or both without changing your insulin dose, your blood glucose level can drop too low or rise too high. A prescription is not necessary to purchase most insulin. However, your doctor must first determine your insulin needs and provide you with special instructions for control of your diabetes.

Insulin can be obtained from beef or pork pancreas glands. Another type of insulin that you may use is called human insulin. It is just like the insulin made by humans but it is made by methods called semi-synthetic or recombinant DNA. All types of insulin must be injected because, if taken by mouth, insulin is destroyed in the stomach.

Insulin is available in the following dosage forms:

Parenteral

- Buffered Insulin Human (a regular insulin)
  - Injection (U.S. and Canada)
- Extended Insulin Zinc (an ultralente insulin)
  - Injection (Canada)
- Extended Insulin Zinc, Human (an ultralente insulin)
  - Injection (U.S. and Canada)
- Insulin (a regular insulin)
  - Injection (U.S. and Canada)
- Insulin Human (a regular insulin)
  - Injection (U.S. and Canada)
- Insulin Zinc (a lente insulin)
  - Injection (U.S. and Canada)
- Insulin Zinc, Human (a lente insulin)
  - Injection (U.S. and Canada)
- Isophane Insulin (an NPH insulin)
  - Injection (U.S. and Canada)
- Isophane Insulin, Human (an NPH insulin)
  - Injection (U.S. and Canada)
- Isophane Insulin, Human, and Insulin Human (an NPH and regular insulins)
  - Injection (U.S. and Canada)
- Prompt Insulin Zinc (a semilente insulin)
  - Injection (Canada)

Before Using This Medicine

In deciding to use a medicine, the risks of taking the medicine must be weighed against the good it will do. This is a decision you and your doctor will make. For insulin, the following should be considered:

Allergies—Tell your doctor if you have ever had any reactions to insulin, especially in the skin area where you injected the insulin. Also, tell your health care professional if you are allergic to any other substances, such as foods, preservatives, or dyes.

Pregnancy—The amount of insulin you need changes during and after pregnancy. It is especially important for your health and your baby's health that your blood sugar be closely controlled. Close control of your blood sugar can reduce the chance of your baby gaining too much weight, having birth defects, or having high or low blood sugar. Be sure to tell your doctor if you plan to become pregnant or if you think you are pregnant.

Breast-feeding—Insulin does not pass into breast milk and will not affect the nursing infant. However, most women need less insulin while breast-feeding than they needed before. You will need to test your blood sugar often for several months in case your insulin dose needs to be changed.

Children—Children are especially sensitive to the effects of insulin before puberty (the time when sexual changes occur). Therefore, low blood sugar may be especially likely to occur.

Teenagers—Use in teenagers is similar to use in older age groups. The insulin need may be higher during puberty and lower after puberty.

Older adults—Use in older adults is similar to use in other age groups. However, sometimes the first signs of low or high blood sugar are missing or not easily seen in older patients. This may increase the chance of low blood sugar during treatment. Also, some older people may have vision problems or other medical problems that make it harder for them to measure and inject the medicine. Special training and equipment may be needed.

Other medicines—Although certain medicines should not be used together at all, in other cases two different medicines may be used together even if an interaction might occur. *Do not take any other medicine, unless prescribed or approved by your doctor.* In these cases, your doctor may want to change the dose, or other precautions may be necessary. When you are using insulin, it is especially important that your health care professional know if you are taking any of the following:

- Alcohol—Small amounts of alcohol taken with meals do not usually cause a problem; however, more than small amounts of alcohol taken for a long time or in one sitting without food can increase the effect of insulin to lower blood sugar. This can keep the blood sugar low for a longer period of time than normal
- Beta-blockers (acebutolol [e.g., Sectral], atenolol [e.g., Tenormin], carteolol [e.g., Cartrol], labetalol [e.g., Normodyne], metoprolol [e.g., Lopressor], nadolol [e.g., Corgard], oxprenolol [e.g., Trasicor], penbutolol [e.g., Levatol], pindolol [e.g., Visken], propranolol [e.g., Inderal], sotalol [e.g., Sotacor], timolol [e.g., Blocadren])—Beta-blockers may increase the chance of developing either high or low blood sugar levels. Also, they can cover up symptoms of low blood sugar (such as fast heartbeat). Because of this, a person with diabetes might not recognize that he or she has low blood sugar and might not take immediate steps to treat it. Beta-blockers can also cause a low blood sugar level to last longer than normal
- Corticosteroids (e.g., prednisone or other cortisone-like medicines)—Corticosteroids taken over several weeks, applied to the skin over a long period of time, or injected into a joint may increase the amount of blood sugar. Higher doses of insulin may be needed during corticosteroid treatment and for a period of time after corticosteroid treatment ends
- Pentamidine (e.g., NebuPent)—Your dose of pentamidine or insulin or both may need to be adjusted if your pancreas

can still make some insulin, because pentamidine may cause your pancreas to release its insulin too fast. This effect at first lowers the blood sugar but then causes high blood sugar

Other medical problems—The presence of other medical problems may affect the dose of insulin you need. Be sure to tell your doctor if you have any other medical problems, especially:

- Changes in female hormones for some women (e.g., during puberty, pregnancy, or menstruation) or
- High fever or
- Infection, severe, or
- Psychological stress or
- Other conditions that cause high blood sugar—These conditions increase blood sugar and may increase the amount of insulin you need to take, make it necessary to change the time when you inject the insulin dose, and increase the need to take blood sugar tests
- Adrenal gland, low activity, not properly controlled, or,
- Pituitary gland, low activity, not properly controlled, or
- Other conditions that cause low blood sugar—These conditions lower blood sugar and may lower the amount of insulin you need, make it necessary for you to change the time when you inject the insulin dose, and increase the need to take blood sugar tests
- Diarrhea or
- Gastroparesis (slow stomach emptying) or
- Intestinal blockage or
- Vomiting or
- Other conditions that delay food absorption or stomach emptying—These conditions may slow the time it takes to breakdown and absorb your meal from your stomach or intestines, which may change the amount of insulin you need, make it necessary to change the time when you inject the insulin dose, and increase the need to take blood sugar tests
- Injury or
- Surgery—Effects of insulin may be increased or decreased. The amount and type of insulin you need may change rapidly
- Kidney disease—Effects of insulin may be increased or decreased, partly because of slower removal of insulin from the body; this may change the amount of insulin you need
- Liver disease—Effects of insulin may be increased or decreased, partly because of slower removal of insulin from the body; this may change the amount of insulin you need
- Overactive thyroid, not properly controlled—Effects of insulin may be increased or decreased, partly because of faster removal of insulin from the body. Until your thyroid condition is controlled, the amount of insulin you need may change, make it necessary to change the time when you inject the insulin dose, and increase the need to take blood sugar tests

Proper Use of This Medicine

Make sure you have the type (beef and pork, pork, or human) and the strength of insulin that your doctor ordered for you. You may find that keeping an insulin label with you is helpful when buying insulin supplies.

The concentration (strength) of insulin is measured in USP Insulin Units and USP Insulin Human Units and is usually expressed in terms such as U-100 insulin.

Insulin doses are measured and injected with specially marked insulin syringes. Your insulin syringe will allow you to measure the insulin dose in USP Insulin Units and USP Insulin Human Units. The appropriate syringe is chosen based on your insulin dose to make measuring the dose easy to read. This helps you measure your dose accurately. These syringes come in 3 sizes: 3/10 cubic centimeters (cc) measuring up to 30 USP Units of insulin, 1/2 cc measuring up to 50 USP Units of insulin, and 1 cc measuring up to 100 USP Units of insulin.

Ask your health care professional where on your body you should inject the insulin.

If you are mixing more than one type of insulin in the same syringe, you will prepare your insulin dose differently than will someone who is injecting only one type of insulin in a syringe at a time. Also, there is more than one way to do the following steps. If you have been instructed differently, discuss this with your health care professional.

There are several important steps that will help you successfully prepare your insulin injection. To draw the insulin up into the syringe correctly, you need to follow these steps:

- Wash your hands with soap and water.
- If your insulin contains zinc or isophane (normally cloudy), be sure that it is completely mixed. Mix the insulin by slowly rolling the bottle between your hands or gently tipping the bottle over a few times.
- Never shake the bottle vigorously (hard).
- Do not use the insulin if it looks lumpy or grainy, seems unusually thick, sticks to the bottle, or seems to be even a little discolored. Do not use the insulin if it contains crystals or if the bottle looks frosted. Regular insulin (short-acting) should be used only if it is clear and colorless.
- Remove the colored protective cap on the bottle. Do *not* remove the rubber stopper.
- Wipe the top of the bottle with an alcohol swab.
- Remove the needle cover from the insulin syringe.

How to prepare your insulin dose if you are using 1 type of insulin:

- Draw air into the syringe by pulling back on the plunger. The amount of air should be equal to your insulin dose.
- Gently push the needle through the top of the rubber stopper with the bottle standing upright.
- Push plunger in all the way to inject air into the bottle.
- Turn the bottle with syringe upside down in one hand. Be sure the tip of the needle is covered by the insulin. With your other hand, draw the plunger back slowly to draw the correct dose of insulin into the syringe.
- Check your dose. Hold the syringe with the scale at eye level to see that the proper dose is withdrawn and to check for air bubbles. To remove air bubbles, tap gently on the measuring scale of the syringe to move any bubbles to the top of the syringe near the needle.

Then, push the insulin slowly back into the bottle and draw up your dose again.

- If your dose measures too low in the syringe, withdraw more solution from the bottle. If there is too much insulin in the syringe, put some back into the bottle. Then check your dose again.
- Remove the needle from the bottle and re-cover the needle.

How to prepare your insulin dose if you are using 2 types of insulin:

- When you mix regular insulin with another type of insulin, *always* draw the regular insulin into the syringe first. When you mix 2 types of insulins other than regular insulin, it does not matter in what order you draw them into the syringe.
- After you decide on a certain order for drawing up your insulin, you should use the same order each time.
- Some mixtures of insulins have to be injected immediately. Others may be stable for longer periods of time, which means that you can wait before you inject the mixture. Check with your health care professional to find out which type you have.
- Draw air into the syringe by pulling back on the plunger. The amount of air in the syringe should be equal to the part of the dose that you will be taking from the first bottle. Inject the air into the first bottle. *Do not draw the insulin yet.* Next, draw into the syringe an amount of air equal to the part of the dose that you will be taking from the *second* bottle. Inject the air into the second bottle.
- Return to the first bottle of the combination. With the plunger at zero, draw the first insulin dose of the combination (usually regular insulin) into the syringe.
- Check your dose. Hold the syringe with the scale at eye level to help you see that the proper dose is withdrawn and to check for air bubbles. To remove air bubbles, tap gently on the measuring scale of the syringe to move any bubbles to the top of the syringe near the needle.
- At this point, if the first part of the dose measures too low in the syringe, you can withdraw more solution from the bottle. If there is too much insulin in your syringe, put some back into the bottle. Then check your dose again.
- Then, without moving the plunger, insert the needle into the second bottle of insulin and withdraw the dose. Sometimes withdrawing a little bit more insulin from the second bottle than needed will help you correct the second dose more easily when you remove for air bubbles.
- Again, check that the proper dose is withdrawn. The syringe will now contain 2 types of insulin. It is important *not* to squirt *any* extra solution from the syringe back into the bottle. Doing so might change the insulin in the bottle. Throw away any extra insulin in the syringe.
- *If you are not sure that you have done this correctly,* throw away the dose into the sink and begin the steps again. *Do not place any of the solutions back into either bottle.* You can use the same syringe to begin the procedure again.
- If you prepared your mixture ahead of time, gently turn the filled syringe back and forth to remix the insulins before you inject them. Do not shake the syringe.

How to inject your insulin dose:

- After you have prepared your syringe and chosen the area of your body to inject, you are ready to inject the insulin into the fatty skin.
  —Clean the area where the injection is to be given with an alcohol swab or with soap and water. Let the area dry.
  —Pinch up a large area of skin and hold it firmly. With your other hand, hold the syringe like a pencil. Push the needle straight into the pinched-up skin at a 90-degree angle for an adult or at a 45-degree angle for a child. Be sure the needle is all the way in. It is not necessary to draw back on the syringe each time to check for blood (also called routine aspiration).
  —Push the plunger all the way down, using less than 5 seconds to inject the dose. Let go of the skin. Hold an alcohol swab near the needle and pull the needle straight out of the skin.
  —Press the swab against the injection area for several seconds. Do not rub.
  —If you are either thin or greatly overweight, you may be given special instructions for giving yourself insulin injections.

How to use special injection devices:

- It is important to follow the information that comes with your insulin and with the device you use for injecting your insulin. This will ensure proper use and proper insulin dosing. If you need more information about this, ask your health care professional.
- Laws in some states require that used insulin syringes and needles be destroyed. Be careful when you recap, bend, or break a needle, because these actions increase the chances of a needle-stick injury. It is best to put used syringes and needles in a disposable container that is puncture-resistant (such as an empty plastic liquid laundry detergent or bleach bottle) or to use a needle-clipping device. The chance of a syringe being reused by someone else is lower if the plunger is taken out of the barrel and broken in half when you dispose of a syringe.

For patients using an *automatic injector* (with a disposable syringe):

- After the dose is drawn, the disposable syringe is placed inside the automatic injector. Pressing a button on the device quickly plunges the needle into the skin, releasing the insulin dose.

For patients using *a continuous subcutaneous infusion insulin pump:*

- Buffered regular human insulin, when available, is the recommended insulin for insulin pumps. Otherwise non-buffered regular insulin can be used.

- The pump consists of a tube, with a needle on the end of it that is taped to the abdomen, and a computerized device that is worn at the waist. Insulin is received continuously from the pump. A button is pressed at mealtime to release an extra insulin dose.
- It is important to follow the pump manufacturer's directions on how to load the syringe and/or pump reservoir. If you do not load the syringe and/or pump properly, you may not get the correct insulin dose.
- Check the infusion tubing and infusion-site dressing often to make sure the pump is working properly as your health care professional recommends.

For patients using *disposable syringes:*

- Manufacturers of disposable syringes recommend that they be used only once, because the sterility of a reused syringe cannot be guaranteed. However, some patients prefer to reuse a syringe until its needle becomes dull. Most insulins have chemicals added that keep them from growing the bacteria that are usually found on the skin. However, the syringe should be thrown away when the needle becomes dull, has been bent, or has come into contact with any surface other than the cleaned and swabbed area of skin. Do not wipe the needle with alcohol. Also, if you plan to reuse a syringe, the needle must be recapped after each use. Check with your health care professional to find out the best way to reuse syringes.

For patients using an *insulin pen device* (cartridge and disposable needles):

- Change the dose by rotating the head of the pen. Put the pen next to your skin and press the plunger to inject the medicine. Some pen devices can only inject certain doses of insulin with each injection. Injection amounts can be different for different pen devices. To receive the right dose, you might have to count the number of times you press the plunger. Also, these devices use special cartridges of isophane insulin (NPH), regular insulin (R), or a mixture of these 2 types.

For patients using *nondisposable syringes* (glass syringe and metal needle):

- These types of syringes and needles may be used repeatedly if they are sterilized after each use. You should get an instruction sheet that tells you how to do this. If you need more information about this, ask your health care professional.

For patients using *a spray injector* (device without needles):

- The dose is measured by rotating part of the device. Insulin is drawn up into the spray device from an insulin bottle. Pressing a button forcefully sprays the insulin dose into the skin. This involves a wider area of skin than an injection would.

Use this medicine only as directed. Do not use more insulin than recommended by your doctor. To do so may increase the chance of serious side effects.

Your doctor will give you instructions about diet, exercise, how to test your blood sugar levels, and how to adjust your dose when you are sick.

- Diet—The daily number of calories in the meal plan should be adjusted by your doctor or a registered dietitian to help you reach and maintain a healthy body weight. In addition, regular meals and snacks are arranged to meet the energy needs of your body at different times of the day. *It is very important that you carefully follow your meal plan.*
- Exercise—Ask your doctor what kind of exercise to do, the best time to do it, and how much you should do each day.
- Blood tests—This is the best way to tell whether your diabetes is being controlled properly. Blood sugar testing helps you and your health care team adjust your insulin dose, meal plan, and exercise schedule.
- Changes in dose—Your doctor may change the first dose of the day. A change in the first dose of the day might change your blood sugar later in the day or change the amount of insulin you should use in other doses later that day. *That is why your doctor should know any time your dose changes, even temporarily, unless you have been told otherwise.*
- On sick days—When you become sick with a cold, fever, or the flu, you need to take your usual insulin dose, even if you feel too ill to eat. This is especially true if you have nausea, vomiting, or diarrhea. Infection usually increases your need for insulin. Call your doctor for specific instructions.

  Continue taking your insulin and try to stay on your regular meal plan. However, if you have trouble eating solid food, drink fruit juices, non-diet soft drinks, or clear soups, or eat small amounts of bland foods. A dietitian or your doctor can give you a list of foods and the amounts to use for sick days.

  Test your blood sugar level at least every 4 hours while you are awake and check your urine for ketones. If ketones are present, call your doctor at once. If you have severe or prolonged vomiting, check with your doctor. Even when you start feeling better, let your doctor know how you are doing.

Dosing—The dose of these medicines will be different for different patients. *Follow your doctor's orders or the directions on the label.* The following information applies to the average doses of these medicines. *If your dose is different, do not change it* unless your doctor tells you to do so.

The number of injections that you receive each day depends on the strength or type of the medicine. Also, *the number of doses you receive each day, the time allowed between doses, and the length of time you receive the medicine depend on the amount of sugar in your blood or urine.*

For regular insulin (R)—crystalline zinc, human buffered, and human regular insulins

- For *injection* dosage form:
  —For treating sugar diabetes (diabetes mellitus):
    - Adults and teenagers—The dose is based on your blood sugar and must be determined by your

doctor. The medicine is injected under the skin fifteen or thirty minutes before meals and/or a bedtime snack. Also, your doctor may want you to use one or more type of insulin.

- Children—Dose is based on your blood sugar and body weight and must be determined by your doctor.

For isophane insulin (NPH)—isophane and human isophane insulins

- For *injection* dosage form:
  - —For treating sugar diabetes (diabetes mellitus):
    - Adults and teenagers—The dose is based on your blood sugar and must be determined by your doctor. The medicine is injected under the skin thirty to sixty minutes before a meal and/or a bedtime snack. Also, your doctor may want you to use one or more type of insulin.
    - Children—Dose is based on your blood sugar and body weight and must be determined by your doctor.

For isophane insulin, human/insulin, human (NPH/R)—human isophane/human regular insulin

- For *injection* dosage form:
  - —For treating sugar diabetes (diabetes mellitus):
    - Adults and teenagers—The dose is based on your blood sugar and must be determined by your doctor. The medicine is injected under the skin fifteen to thirty minutes before breakfast. You may need a dose before another meal or at bedtime. Also, your doctor may want you to use one or more type of insulin.
    - Children—Dose is based on your blood sugar and body weight and must be determined by your doctor.

For insulin zinc (L)—lente and human lente insulins

- For *injection* dosage form:
  - —For treating sugar diabetes (diabetes mellitus):
    - Adults and teenagers—The dose is based on your blood sugar and must be determined by your doctor. The medicine is injected under the skin thirty minutes before breakfast. You may need a dose before another meal and/or a bedtime snack. Also, your doctor may want you to use one or more type of insulin.
    - Children—Dose is based on your blood sugar and body weight and must be determined by your doctor.

For insulin zinc extended (U)—ultralente and human ultralente insulins

- For *injection* dosage form:
  - —For treating sugar diabetes (diabetes mellitus):
    - Adults and teenagers—The dose is based on your blood sugar and must be determined by your doctor. The medicine is injected under the skin thirty to sixty minutes before a meal and/or a bedtime snack. Your doctor may want you to use one or more type of insulin.
    - Children—Dose is based on your blood sugar and body weight and must be determined by your doctor.

For prompt insulin zinc (S)—semilente and human semilente insulins

- For *injection* dosage form:
  - —For treating sugar diabetes (diabetes mellitus):
    - Adults and teenagers—The dose is based on your blood sugar and must be determined by your doctor. The medicine is injected under the skin thirty to sixty minutes before breakfast. You may need a dose thirty minutes before another meal and/or a bedtime snack. Your doctor may want you to use one or more type of insulin.
    - Children—Dose is based on your blood sugar and body weight and must be determined by your doctor.

Storage—To store this medicine:

- Unopened bottles of insulin should be refrigerated until needed and may be used until the printed expiration date on the label. Insulin should never be frozen. Remove the insulin from the refrigerator and allow it to reach room temperature before injecting it.
- An insulin bottle in use may be kept at room temperature for up to 1 month. Insulin that has been kept at room temperature for longer than a month should be thrown away.
- Storing prefilled syringes in the refrigerator with the needle pointed up reduces problems that can occur, such as crystals forming in the needle and blocking it up.
- Do not expose insulin to extremely hot temperatures or to sunlight. Extreme heat will cause insulin to become less effective much more quickly.

Precautions While Using This Medicine

It is very important that your doctor check your progress at regular visits, especially during the first few weeks of insulin treatment.

It is very important to follow carefully any instructions from your health care team about:

- Alcohol—Drinking alcohol may cause severe low blood sugar. Discuss this with your health care team.
- Tobacco—If you have been smoking for a long time and suddenly stop, your dosage of insulin may need to be reduced. If you decide to quit, tell your doctor first.
- Other medicines—Do not take other medicines unless they have been discussed with your doctor. This especially includes nonprescription medicines such as aspirin, and medicines for appetite control, asthma, colds, cough, hay fever, or sinus problems.
- Counseling—Other family members need to learn how to prevent side effects or help with side effects if they occur. Also, diabetics, especially teenagers, may need special counseling about insulin dosing changes that might occur because of lifestyle changes, such as changes in exercise and diet. Fur-

thermore, counseling on contraception and pregnancy may be needed because of the problems that can occur in diabetics during pregnancy.
- Travel—Keep a recent prescription and your medical history with you. Be prepared for an emergency as you would normally. Make allowances for changing time zones, keep your meal times as close as possible to your usual meal times, and store insulin properly.

In case of emergency—There may be a time when you need emergency help for a problem caused by your diabetes. You need to be prepared for these emergencies. It is a good idea to:
- Wear a medical identification (I.D.) bracelet or neck chain at all times. Also, carry an I.D. card in your wallet or purse that says that you have diabetes and lists all of your medicines.
- Keep an extra supply of insulin and syringes with needles on hand in case high blood sugar occurs.
- Have a glucagon kit and a syringe and needle available in case severe low blood sugar occurs. Check and replace any expired kits regularly.
- Keep some kind of quick-acting sugar handy to treat low blood sugar.

Too much insulin can cause low blood sugar (also called hypoglycemia or insulin reaction). *Symptoms of low blood sugar must be treated before they lead to unconsciousness (passing out).* Different people may feel different symptoms of low blood sugar. *It is important that you learn what symptoms of low blood sugar you usually have so that you can treat it quickly.*
- Symptoms of low blood sugar can include: Anxious feeling, behavior change similar to being drunk, blurred vision, cold sweats, confusion, cool pale skin, difficulty in concentrating, drowsiness, excessive hunger, headache, nausea, nervousness, rapid heartbeat, shakiness, unusual tiredness or weakness.
- The symptoms of low blood sugar may develop quickly and may result from:
  —delaying or missing a scheduled meal or snack.
  —exercising more than usual.
  —drinking a significant amount of alcohol.
  —taking certain medicines.
  —using too much insulin.
  —sickness (especially with vomiting or diarrhea).
- Know what to do if symptoms of low blood sugar occur. Eating some form of quick-acting sugar when symptoms of low blood sugar first appear will usually prevent them from getting worse.
  —Good sources of sugar include:
  - Glucagon is used in emergency situations such as unconsciousness. Have a glucagon kit available, along with a syringe and needle, and know how to prepare and use it. Members of your household also should know how and when to use it.
  - Glucose tablets or gel, fruit juice or non-diet soft drink (4 to 6 ounces [one-half cup]), corn syrup or honey (1 tablespoon), sugar cubes (6 one-half-inch sized), or table sugar (dissolved in water).

  —Do not use chocolate because its fat slows down the sugar entering into the bloodstream.

  —If a snack is not scheduled for an hour or more you should also eat a light snack, such as cheese and crackers, half a sandwich, or drink an 8-ounce glass of milk.

High blood sugar (hyperglycemia) is another problem related to uncontrolled diabetes. *If you have any symptoms of high blood sugar, contact your health care team right away.* If high blood sugar is not treated, severe hyperglycemia can occur, leading to ketoacidosis (diabetic coma) and death.
- The symptoms of mild high blood sugar appear more slowly than those of low blood sugar. Symptoms can include: Blurred vision, drowsiness, dry mouth, flushed and dry skin, fruit-like breath odor, increased urination, loss of appetite, nausea or vomiting, sleepiness, stomachache, tiredness, troubled breathing (rapid and deep), unusual thirst.
- Symptoms of severe high blood sugar (called ketoacidosis or diabetic coma) that need immediate hospitalization include: Flushed dry skin, fruit-like breath odor, ketones in urine, passing out, troubled breathing (rapid and deep).
- High blood sugar symptoms may occur if you:
  —have a fever or an infection.
  —do not take enough insulin.
  —skip a dose of insulin.
  —do not exercise as much as usual.
  —overeat or do not follow your meal plan.
- Know what to do if high blood sugar occurs. Your doctor may recommend changes in your insulin dose or meal plan to avoid high blood sugar. Symptoms of high blood sugar must be corrected before they progress to more serious conditions. Check with your doctor often to make sure you are controlling your blood sugar. Your doctor might discuss the following with you:

  —Decreasing your dose for a short time for special needs, such as when you can't exercise as you normally do.

  —Increasing your insulin dose when you plan to eat an unusually large dinner, such as on holidays. This type of increase is called an anticipatory dose.

  —Delaying a meal if your blood glucose is over 200 mg/dL to allow time for your blood sugar to go down. An extra insulin dose may be needed if your blood sugar does not come down shortly.

  —Not exercising if your blood glucose is over 240 mg/dL and reporting this to your doctor immediately.

  —Being hospitalized if ketoacidosis or diabetic coma occurs.

Side Effects of This Medicine

Along with its needed effects, a medicine may cause some unwanted effects. Although not all of these side effects

may occur, if they do occur they may need medical attention.

Check with your doctor immediately if any of the following side effects occur:

More common

Convulsions (seizures), fainting or unconsciousness

Also, check with your doctor as soon as possible if any of the following side effects occur:

More common

Low blood sugar (mild), including anxious feeling, behavior change similar to being drunk, blurred vision, cold sweats, confusion, cool pale skin, difficulty in concentrating, drowsiness, excessive hunger, fast heartbeat, headache, nausea, nervousness, nightmares, restless sleep, shakiness, slurred speech, unusual tiredness or weakness; or weight gain

Rare

Depressed skin at the place of injection; swelling of face, fingers, feet, or ankles; thickening of the skin layers at the place of injection

Not all of the side effects listed above have been reported for each of these medicines, but they have been reported for at least one of them. All of the insulins are similar, so any of the above side effects may occur with any of these medicines.

Other side effects not listed above may also occur in some patients. If you notice any other effects, check with your doctor.

Additional Information

Once a medicine has been approved for marketing for a certain use, experience may show that it is also useful for other medical problems. Although this use is not included in product labeling, regular insulin is used in certain patients to test for growth hormone deficiency.

Other than the above information, there is no additional information relating to proper use, precautions, or side effects for this use.

Revised: 07/26/95

INTERFERON, GAMMA Systemic†

A commonly used brand name in the U.S. is Actimmune.

†Not commercially available in Canada.

Description

Gamma interferon (in-ter-FEER-on) is a synthetic (man-made) version of a substance naturally produced by cells in the body to help fight infections and tumors. Gamma interferon is used to treat chronic granulomatous disease.

Gamma interferon is available only with your doctor's prescription, in the following dosage form:

Parenteral

- Injection (U.S.)

Before Using This Medicine

In deciding to use a medicine, the risks of taking the medicine must be weighed against the good it will do. This is a decision you and your doctor will make. For gamma interferon, the following should be considered:

Allergies—Tell your doctor if you have ever had any unusual or allergic reaction to gamma interferon.

Pregnancy—Gamma interferon has not been studied in pregnant women. However, in monkeys given 100 times the human dose of gamma interferon and in mice, there was an increase in deaths of the fetus. Also, in mice, toxic doses of gamma interferon caused bleeding of the uterus.

Breast-feeding—It is not known whether gamma interferon passes into the breast milk. However, because this medicine may cause serious side effects, breast-feeding may not be recommended while you are receiving it. Discuss with your doctor whether or not you should breast-feed while you are receiving gamma interferon.

Children—Studies on this medicine have been done mostly in children and it is not expected to cause different side effects or problems than it does in adults.

Older adults—Many medicines have not been studied specifically in older people. Therefore, it may not be known whether they work exactly the same way they do in younger adults or if they cause different side effects or problems in older people. There is no specific information comparing use of gamma interferon in the elderly with use in other age groups.

Other medicines—Although certain medicines should not be used together at all, in other cases two different medicines may be used together even if an interaction might occur. In these cases, your doctor may want to change the dose, or other precautions may be necessary. Tell your health care professional if you are taking any other prescription or nonprescription (over-the-counter [OTC]) medicine.

Other medical problems—The presence of other medical problems may affect the use of gamma interferon. Make sure you tell your doctor if you have any other medical problems, especially:

- Convulsions (seizures) or
- Mental problems (or history of)—Risk of problems affecting the central nervous system may be increased
- Heart disease or
- Multiple sclerosis or
- Systemic lupus erythematosus—May be worsened by gamma interferon

Proper Use of This Medicine

If you are injecting this medicine yourself, *use it exactly as directed by your doctor*. Do not use more or less of it, and do not use it more often than your doctor ordered.

The exact amount of medicine you need has been carefully worked out. Using too much will increase the risk of side effects, while using too little may not improve your condition.

Each package of gamma interferon contains a patient instruction sheet. Read this sheet carefully and make sure you understand:

- How to prepare the injection.
- Proper use of disposable syringes.
- How to give the injection.
- How long the injection is stable.

If you have any questions about any of this, check with your health care professional.

While you are using gamma interferon, your doctor may want you to drink extra fluids. This will help prevent low blood pressure due to loss of too much water.

Gamma interferon often causes flu-like symptoms, which can be severe. This effect is less likely to cause problems if you inject your gamma interferon at bedtime.

Dosing—The dose of gamma interferon will be different for different patients. The dose that is used may depend on a number of things, including the patient's body size. *If you are receiving gamma interferon at home, follow your doctor's orders or the directions on the label.* If you have any questions about the proper dose of gamma interferon, ask your doctor.

Missed dose—If you miss a dose of this medicine, do not give the missed dose at all and do not double the next one. Check with your doctor for further instructions.

Storage—To store this medicine:

- Keep out of the reach of children.
- Store in the refrigerator.
- Keep the medicine from freezing.
- Do not keep outdated medicine or medicine no longer needed. Ask your health care professional how you should dispose of any medicine you do not use. Be sure that any discarded medicine is out of the reach of children.

Precautions While Using This Medicine

It is very important that your doctor check your progress at regular visits to make sure that this medicine is working properly and to check for unwanted effects.

This medicine commonly causes a flu-like reaction, with aching muscles, fever and chills, and headache. To prevent problems from your temperature going too high, your doctor may ask you to take acetaminophen before each dose of gamma interferon. You may also need to take it after a dose to bring your temperature down. *Follow your doctor's instructions carefully about taking your temperature, and how much and when to take the acetaminophen.*

Side Effects of This Medicine

Along with its needed effects, a medicine may cause some unwanted effects. Although not all of these side effects may occur, if they do occur they may need medical attention.

Check with your doctor as soon as possible if any of the following side effects occur:

Rare

Black, tarry stools; blood in urine or stools; confusion; cough or hoarseness; loss of balance control; lower back or side pain; mask-like face; painful or difficult urination; pinpoint red spots on skin; shuffling walk; stiffness of arms or legs; trembling and shaking of hands and fingers; trouble in speaking or swallowing; trouble in thinking or concentrating; trouble in walking; unusual bleeding or bruising

Other side effects may occur that usually do not need medical attention. These side effects may go away during treatment as your body adjusts to the medicine. However, check with your doctor if any of the following side effects continue or are bothersome:

More common

Aching muscles; diarrhea; fever and chills; general feeling of discomfort or illness; headache; nausea or vomiting; skin rash; unusual tiredness

Less common

Back pain; dizziness; joint pain; loss of appetite; weight loss

Other side effects not listed above may also occur in some patients. If you notice any other effects, check with your doctor.

Revised: 06/04/92
Interim revision: 07/05/94

INTERFERONS, ALPHA Systemic

Some commonly used brand names are:

In the U.S.—

Alferon N[4]
Intron A[2]
Roferon-A[1]

In Canada—

Roferon-A
Wellferon[3]
Intron A[2]

Note: For quick reference, the following alpha interferons are numbered to match the corresponding brand names.

This information applies to the following medicines:

1. Interferon Alfa-2a, Recombinant
2. Interferon Alfa-2b, Recombinant
3. Interferon Alfa-n1 (Ins)*
4. Interferon Alfa-n3†

*Not commercially available in the U.S.
†Not commercially available in Canada.

Description

Interferons (in-ter-FEER-ons) are substances naturally produced by cells in the body to help fight infections and tumors. They may also be synthetic (man-made) versions of these substances. Alpha interferons are used to treat hairy cell leukemia and AIDS-related Kaposi's sarcoma. They are also used to treat laryngeal papillomatosis (growths in the respiratory tract) in children, genital warts, and some kinds of hepatitis.

Alpha interferons may also be used for other conditions as determined by your doctor.

Alpha interferons are available only with your doctor's prescription, in the following dosage form:

Parenteral

- Interferon Alfa-2a, Recombinant
  - Injection (U.S. and Canada)
- Interferon Alfa-2b, Recombinant
  - Injection (U.S. and Canada)
- Interferon Alfa-n1 (lns)
  - Injection (Canada)
- Interferon Alfa-n3
  - Injection (U.S.)

Before Using This Medicine

In deciding to use a medicine, the risks of taking the medicine must be weighed against the good it will do. This is a decision you and your doctor will make. For interferons, the following should be considered:

Allergies—Tell your doctor if you have ever had any unusual or allergic reaction to alpha interferon.

Pregnancy—Alpha interferons have not been shown to cause birth defects or other problems in humans. However, in monkeys given 20 to 500 times the human dose of recombinant interferon alfa-2a or 90 to 180 times the usual dose of recombinant interferon alfa-2b there was an increase in deaths of the fetus.

Breast-feeding—It is not known whether alpha interferons pass into the breast milk. However, because this medicine may cause serious side effects, breast-feeding may not be recommended while you are receiving it. Discuss with your doctor whether or not you should breast-feed while you are are receiving alpha interferon.

Children—There is no specific information comparing use of alpha interferon for cancer or genital warts in children with use in other age groups.

Teenagers—Alpha interferons may cause changes in the menstrual cycle. Discuss this possible effect with your doctor.

Older adults—Some side effects of alpha interferons (chest pain, irregular heartbeat, unusual tiredness, confusion, mental depression, trouble in thinking or concentrating) may be more likely to occur in the elderly, who are usually more sensitive to the effects of alpha interferons.

Other medicines—Although certain medicines should not be used together at all, in other cases two different medicines may be used together even if an interaction might occur. In these cases, your doctor may want to change the dose, or other precautions may be necessary. Tell your health care professional if you are taking any other prescription or nonprescription (over-the-counter [OTC]) medicine.

Other medical problems—The presence of other medical problems may affect the use of alpha interferons. Make sure you tell your doctor if you have any other medical problems, especially:

- Bleeding problems—May be worsened by recombinant interferon alfa-2b
- Chickenpox (including recent exposure) or
- Herpes zoster (shingles)—Risk of severe disease affecting other parts of the body
- Convulsions (seizures) or
- Mental problems (or history of)—Risk of problems affecting the central nervous system may be increased
- Diabetes mellitus (sugar diabetes) or
- Heart attack (recent) or
- Heart disease or
- Kidney disease or
- Liver disease or
- Lung disease—May be worsened by alpha interferons
- Problems with overactive immune system—Alpha interferons make the immune system even more active
- Thyroid disease—Recombinant interferon alfa-2b can cause thyroid problems when it is used to treat hepatitis

Proper Use of This Medicine

If you are injecting this medicine yourself, *use it exactly as directed by your doctor.* Do not use more or less of it, and do not use it more often than your doctor ordered. The exact amount of medicine you need has been carefully worked out. Using too much will increase the risk of side effects, while using too little may not improve your condition.

Each package of alpha interferon contains a patient instruction sheet. Read this sheet carefully and make sure you understand:

- How to prepare the injection.
- Proper use of disposable syringes.
- How to give the injection.
- How long the injection is stable.

If you have any questions about any of this, check with your health care professional.

While you are using alpha interferon, your doctor may want you to drink extra fluids. This will help prevent low blood pressure due to loss of too much water.

Alpha interferons often cause unusual tiredness, which can be severe. This effect is less likely to cause problems if you inject your interferon at bedtime.

Dosing—The dose of alpha interferons will be different for different patients. The dose that is used may depend on a number of things, including what the medicine is being used for, the patient's size, and whether or not other medicines are also being taken. *If you are receiving alpha interferons at home, follow your doctor's orders or the directions on the label.* If you have any questions about the proper dose of alpha interferons, ask your doctor.

Missed dose—If you miss a dose of this medicine, do not give the missed dose at all and do not double the next one. Check with your doctor for further instructions.

Storage—To store this medicine:

- Keep out of the reach of children.
- Store in the refrigerator.
- Keep the medicine from freezing.

- Do not keep outdated medicine or medicine no longer needed. Ask your health care professional how you should dispose of any medicine you do not use. Be sure that any discarded medicine is out of the reach of children.

Precautions While Using This Medicine

It is very important that your doctor check your progress at regular visits to make sure that this medicine is working properly and to check for unwanted effects.

Do not change to another brand of alpha interferon without checking with your physician. Different kinds of alpha interferon have different doses. If you refill your medicine and it looks different, check with your pharmacist.

This medicine will add to the effects of alcohol and other CNS depressants (medicines that slow down the nervous system, possibly causing drowsiness). Some examples of CNS depressants are antihistamines or medicine for hay fever, other allergies, or colds; sedatives, tranquilizers, or sleeping medicine; prescription pain medicine or narcotics; barbiturates; medicine for seizures; muscle relaxants; or anesthetics, including some dental anesthetics. *Check with your doctor before taking any of the above while you are using this medicine.*

Alpha interferon may cause some people to become unusually tired or dizzy, or less alert than they are normally. *Make sure you know how you react to this medicine before you drive, use machines, or do anything else that could be dangerous if you are dizzy or if you are not alert.*

This medicine commonly causes a flu-like reaction, with aching muscles, fever and chills, and headache. To prevent problems from your temperature going too high, your doctor may ask you to take acetaminophen before each dose of interferon. You may also need to take it after a dose to bring your temperature down. *Follow your doctor's instructions carefully about taking your temperature, and how much and when to take the acetaminophen.*

Alpha interferon can lower the number of white blood cells in your blood temporarily, increasing the chance of getting an infection. It can also lower the number of platelets, which are necessary for proper blood clotting. If this occurs, there are certain precautions you can take, especially when your blood count is low, to reduce the risk of infection or bleeding:

- If you can, avoid people with infections. *Check with your doctor immediately* if you think you are getting an infection or if you get a fever or chills, cough or hoarseness, lower back or side pain, or painful or difficult urination.
- *Check with your doctor immediately* if you notice any unusual bleeding or bruising; black, tarry stools; blood in urine or stools; or pinpoint red spots on your skin.
- Be careful when using a regular toothbrush, dental floss, or toothpick. Your medical doctor, dentist, or nurse may recommend other ways to clean your teeth and gums. Check with your medical doctor before having any dental work done.
- Do not touch your eyes or the inside of your nose unless you have just washed your hands and have not touched anything else in the meantime.
- Be careful not to cut yourself when you are using sharp objects such as a safety razor or fingernail or toenail cutters.
- Avoid contact sports or other situations where bruising or injury could occur.

Side Effects of This Medicine

Along with its needed effects, a medicine may cause some unwanted effects. Although not all of these side effects may occur, if they do occur they may need medical attention.

Because this medicine is used for many different conditions and in many different doses, the actual frequency of side effects may vary. In general, side effects are less common with low doses than with high doses. Also, when alpha interferon is used for genital warts, very little of it gets into the rest of the body, so side effects are generally less common than in other conditions.

Check with your doctor as soon as possible if any of the following side effects occur:

Less common

Confusion; mental depression; nervousness; numbness or tingling of fingers, toes, and face; trouble in sleeping; trouble in thinking or concentrating

Rare

Black, tarry stools; blood in urine or stools; chest pain; cough or hoarseness; fever or chills (beginning after 3 weeks of treatment); irregular heartbeat; lower back or side pain; painful or difficult urination; pinpoint red spots on skin; unusual bleeding or bruising

Other side effects may occur that usually do not need medical attention. These side effects may go away during treatment as your body adjusts to the medicine. However, check with your doctor if any of the following side effects continue or are bothersome:

More common

Aching muscles; change in taste or metallic taste; fever and chills (should lessen after the first 1 or 2 weeks of treatment); general feeling of discomfort or illness; headache; loss of appetite; nausea and vomiting; skin rash; unusual tiredness

Less common or rare

Back pain; blurred vision; diarrhea; dizziness; dryness of mouth; dry skin or itching; increased sweating; joint pain; leg cramps; sores in mouth and on lips; weight loss

Alpha interferon may cause a temporary loss of some hair. After treatment has ended, normal hair growth should return.

Other side effects not listed above may also occur in some patients. If you notice any other effects, check with your doctor.

Additional Information

Once a medicine has been approved for marketing for a certain use, experience may show that it is also useful for other medical problems. Although these uses are not in-

cluded in product labeling, alpha interferons are used in certain patients with the following medical conditions:

- Bladder cancer
- Cervical cancer
- Chronic myelocytic leukemia
- Kidney cancer
- Laryngeal papillomatosis (growths on larynx)
- Lymphomas, non-Hodgkin's
- Malignant melanoma
- Multiple myeloma
- Mycosis fungoides

Other than the above information, there is no additional information relating to proper use, precautions, or side effects for these uses.

Revised: 01/16/92
Interim revision: 04/17/93; 07/05/94

IOBENGUANE, RADIOIODINATED Therapeutic*†

A commonly used name for iobenguane is meta-iodobenzylguanidine or mIBG.

*Not commercially available in the U.S.
†Not commercially available in Canada.

Description

Radioiodinated iobenguane is a radiopharmaceutical (ray-dee-oh-far-ma-SOO-ti-kal). Radiopharmaceuticals are radioactive agents, which may be used to find and treat certain diseases or to study the function of the body's organs.

Radioiodinated iobenguane is used to treat certain kinds of cancer of the adrenal glands.

When very small doses of radioiodinated iobenguane are given, the radioactivity taken up by the adrenal gland helps find tumors of the adrenal glands. An image of the gland on film or on a computer screen can be provided to help with the diagnosis.

The information that follows applies only to the use of radioiodinated iobenguane in treating cancer of the adrenal gland.

Radioiodinated iobenguane is to be given only by or under the direct supervision of a doctor with specialized training in nuclear medicine. Radioiodinated iobenguane is available in the following dosage form:

Parenteral
- Injection

Before Using This Medicine

In deciding to use a medicine, the risks of taking the medicine must be weighed against the good it will do. This is a decision you and your doctor will make. For radioiodinated iobenguane, the following should be considered:

Pregnancy—This radiopharmaceutical is not recommended for use during pregnancy. This is to avoid exposing the fetus to harmful levels of radiation.

Breast-feeding—Some radiopharmaceuticals pass into the breast milk and may expose the baby to radiation. If you must receive radioiodinated iobenguane, it may be necessary for you to stop breast-feeding after receiving it. Be sure you have discussed this with your doctor.

Children and adolescents—Children and adolescents are especially sensitive to the effects of radiation. This may increase the chance of side effects during and after treatment. Be sure you have discussed this with your doctor.

Older adults—Radioiodinated iobenguane has been used in older people and has not been shown to cause different side effects or problems in older people than it does in younger adults.

Other medicines—Although certain medicines should not be used together at all, in other cases two different medicines may be used together even if an interaction might occur. In these cases, your doctor may want to change the dose, or other precautions may be necessary. When you are receiving radioiodinated iobenguane, it is especially important that your doctor knows if you are taking any of the following:

- Amphetamines or
- Appetite suppressants (diet pills) or
- Calcium channel blocking agents (diltiazem [e.g., Cardizem], nicardipine [e.g., Cardene], nifedipine [e.g., Procardia], verapamil [e.g., Calan]) or
- Cocaine or
- Guanethidine (e.g., Ismelin) or
- Haloperidol (e.g., Haldol) or
- Labetalol (e.g., Normodyne) or
- Loxapine (e.g., Loxitane) or
- Medicines for colds, sinus problems, or hay fever or other allergies (including nose drops or sprays) or
- Phenothiazines (acetophenazine [e.g., Tindal], chlorpromazine [e.g., Thorazine], fluphenazine [e.g., Prolixin], mesoridazine [e.g., Serentil], perphenazine [e.g., Trilafon], prochlorperazine [e.g., Compazine], promazine [e.g., Sparine], promethazine [e.g., Phenergan], thioridazine [e.g., Mellaril], trifluoperazine [e.g., Stelazine], triflupromazine [e.g., Vesprin], trimeprazine [e.g., Temaril]) or
- Reserpine (e.g., Serpasil) or
- Thiothixene (e.g., Navane) or
- Tricyclic antidepressants (amitriptyline [e.g., Elavil], amoxapine [e.g., Asendin], clomipramine [e.g., Anafranil], desipramine [e.g., Pertofrane], doxepin [e.g., Sinequan], imipramine [e.g., Tofranil], nortriptyline [e.g., Aventyl], protriptyline [e.g., Vivactil], trimipramine [e.g., Surmontil])—These medicines may keep the affected organ or tissue from getting the amount of radioiodinated iobenguane it needs to fight the disease

Other medical problems—The presence of other medical problems may affect the use of radioiodinated iobenguane. Make sure you tell your doctor if you have any other medical problems.

Preparation for This Treatment

Your doctor may have special instructions for you in preparation for your treatment. If you have not received such instructions or you do not understand them, check with your doctor in advance.

This radiopharmaceutical contains radioactive iodine, which may be taken up in your thyroid. To protect your thyroid, your doctor will prescribe a medicine (e.g., potassium iodide or SSKI) that contains non-radioactive iodine. You must take this medicine before starting treatment with radioiodinated iobenguane and continue taking it after treatment for as long as your doctor tells you.

Side Effects of This Medicine

Along with its needed effects, a medicine may cause some unwanted effects. Although not all of these side effects may occur, if they do occur they may need medical attention.

Check with your doctor as soon as possible if any of the following side effects occur after treatment for tumors of the adrenal gland:

Rare

Pale skin; sore throat and fever; unusual bleeding or bruising; unusual tiredness or weakness

Other side effects may occur that usually do not need medical attention. These side effects may go away during treatment as your body adjusts to the medicine. However, check with your doctor if the following side effects continue or are bothersome:

Less common or rare

Flushing of skin; nausea; slight and temporary increase in blood pressure

Other side effects not listed above may also occur in some patients. If you notice any other effects, check with your doctor.

Revised: 05/05/93

IODINE Topical†

Generic name product is available in the U.S.

†Not commercially available in Canada.

Description

Topical iodine (EYE -oh-din) is used to prevent and treat infections that may occur in minor scrapes and cuts. It works by killing bacteria that can cause infections.

This medicine is available in the following dosage form:

Topical

- Tincture (U.S.)

Before Using This Medicine

If you are using this medicine without a prescription, carefully read and follow any precautions on the label. For topical iodine, the following should be considered:

Allergies—Tell your doctor if you have ever had any unusual or allergic reaction to iodine. Also tell your health care professional if you are allergic to any other substances, such as foods, preservatives, or dyes.

Pregnancy—Use of topical iodine is not recommended during pregnancy because it has been shown to cause thyroid problems in the newborn infant. Before using this medicine, make sure your doctor knows if you are pregnant or you may become pregnant.

Breast-feeding—Topical iodine passes into the breast milk and has been shown to cause unwanted effects, such as thyroid problems in nursing babies. It may be necessary for you to use another medicine or to stop breast-feeding during treatment. Be sure you have discussed the risks and benefits of the medicine with your doctor.

Children—Use of topical iodine is not recommended for newborn infants because it may cause skin and thyroid problems.

Older adults—Many medicines have not been studied specifically in older people. Therefore, it may not be known whether they work exactly the same way they do in younger adults. Although there is no specific information comparing use of topical iodine in the elderly with use in other age groups, this medicine is not expected to cause different side effects or problems in older people than it does in younger adults.

Other medicines—Although certain medicines should not be used together at all, in other cases two different medicines may be used together even if an interaction might occur. In these cases, your doctor may want to change the dose, or other precautions may be necessary. Tell your health care professional if you are using any other topical prescription or nonprescription (over-the-counter [OTC]) medicine that is to be applied to the same area of the skin.

Other medical problems—The presence of other medical problems may affect the use of topical iodine. Make sure you tell your doctor if you have any other medical problems, especially:

- Animal bites or
- Deep wounds or
- Serious burns—The chance of side effects may be increased

Proper Use of This Medicine

Use this medicine only as directed.

This medicine is for external use only. Do not swallow it.

Keep this medicine away from the eyes because it may cause irritation. If you should accidentally get some in your eyes, wash it away with water immediately.

Do not use topical iodine on deep, puncture wounds, animal bites, or serious burns. To do so may increase the chance of side effects.

Do not cover the wound to which you have applied topical iodine with a tight dressing or bandage since this may increase the chance of side effects.

Dosing—*Follow your doctor's orders or the directions on the label before using this medicine.* The following information includes only the average doses of iodine. *If your dose is different, do not change it* unless your doctor tells you to do so.

- For *topical* dosage form (tincture):
  - —For minor bacterial skin infections:
    - Adults and children 1 month of age and over—Use when necessary, according to the directions on the label or your doctor's instructions. Do not use for more than ten days.
    - Infants and children under 1 month of age—Use is not recommended.

To help clear up your infection completely, it *is very important that you keep using topical iodine for the full time of treatment. Do not miss any doses.*

Missed dose—If you miss a dose of this medicine, apply it as soon as possible. However, if it is almost time for your next dose, skip the missed dose and go back to your regular dosing schedule.

Storage—To store this medicine:
- Keep out of the reach of children.
- Store away from heat and direct light.
- Keep the medicine from freezing. Do not refrigerate.
- Do not keep outdated medicine or medicine no longer needed. Be sure that any discarded medicine is out of the reach of children.

Precautions While Using This Medicine

Check with your doctor if the skin problem for which you are using topical iodine becomes worse, or if you develop a constant irritation such as itching or burning that was not present before you started using this medicine.

This medicine can stain your skin and clothing. Alcohol may be used to remove iodine stain on the skin. Stains on clothing can be removed by washing and rinsing them in ammonia diluted with water. Stains on starched linens can be removed by washing them in soap and water.

Side Effects of This Medicine

Along with its needed effects, a medicine may cause some unwanted effects. Although not all of these side effects may occur, if they do occur they may need medical attention.

Check with your doctor as soon as possible if any of the following side effects occur:

Rare
Blistering, crusting, irritation, itching, or reddening of skin

Symptoms of overdose (when swallowed)
Abdominal or stomach pain; diarrhea; fever; nausea; not being able to pass urine; thirst, severe; vomiting

Other side effects not listed above may also occur in some patients. If you notice any other effects, check with your doctor.

Developed: 02/22/94

IODINE, STRONG Systemic

Another commonly used name in the U.S. and Canada is Lugol's solution.

Description

Strong iodine (EYE-oh-dine) is used to treat overactive thyroid, iodine deficiency, and to protect the thyroid gland from the effects of radiation from radioactive forms of iodine. It may be used before and after administration of a radioactive medicine containing radioactive iodine or after accidental exposure to radiation (for example, from nuclear power plant accidents). It may also be used for other conditions as determined by your doctor.

Strong iodine is available only with your doctor's prescription, in the following dosage form:

Oral
- Oral solution (U.S. and Canada)

Before Using This Medicine

In deciding to use a medicine, the risks of taking the medicine must be weighed against the good it will do. This is a decision you and your doctor will make. For strong iodine, the following should be considered:

Allergies—Tell your doctor if you have ever had any unusual or allergic reaction to iodine or potassium iodide. Also tell your health care professional if you are allergic to any substances, such as foods, preservatives, or dyes.

Pregnancy—Taking strong iodine during pregnancy may cause thyroid problems or goiter in the newborn infant.

Breast-feeding—Strong iodine may cause skin rash and thyroid problems in nursing babies.

Children—Strong iodine may cause skin rash and thyroid problems in infants.

Older adults—Many medicines have not been studied specifically in older people. Therefore, it may not be known whether they work exactly the same way they do in younger adults. Although there is no specific information comparing use of strong iodine in the elderly with use in other age groups, this medicine is not expected to cause different side effects or problems in older people than it does in younger adults.

Other medicines—Although certain medicines should not be used together at all, in other cases two different medicines may be used together even if an interaction might occur. In these cases, your doctor may want to change the dose, or other precautions may be necessary. When you are taking strong iodine, it is especially important that your health care professional know if you are taking any of the following:

- Amiloride (e.g., Midamor) or
- Spironolactone (e.g., Aldactone) or
- Triamterene (e.g., Dyrenium)—Use of these medicines with strong iodine may increase the amount of potassium in the blood and increase the chance of side effects
- Antithyroid agents (medicine for overactive thyroid) or
- Lithium (e.g., Lithane)—Use of these medicines with strong iodine may increase the chance of side effects

Other medical problems—The presence of other medical problems may affect the use of strong iodine. Make sure you tell your doctor if you have any other medical problems, especially:

- Bronchitis or
- Other lung conditions—Use of strong iodine may make this condition worse
- Hyperkalemia (too much potassium in the blood) or
- Kidney disease—Use of strong iodine may increase the amount of potassium in the blood and increase the chance of side effects

Proper Use of This Medicine

For patients taking this medicine for *radiation exposure:*

- Take this medicine only when directed to do so by state or local public health authorities.
- Take this medicine once a day for 10 days, unless otherwise directed by public health authorities. *Do not take more of it and do not take it more often than directed.* Taking more of the medicine will not protect you better and may result in a greater chance of side effects.

If strong iodine upsets your stomach, *take it after meals or with food or milk* unless otherwise directed by your doctor. If stomach upset (nausea, vomiting, stomach pain, or diarrhea) continues, check with your doctor.

This medicine is to be taken by mouth even if it comes in a dropper bottle.

Do not use this solution if it turns brownish yellow.

Take strong iodine in a full glass (8 ounces) of water or in fruit juice, milk, or broth to improve the taste and lessen stomach upset. Be sure to drink all of the liquid to get the full dose of medicine.

If crystals form in strong iodine solution, they may be dissolved by warming the closed container of solution in warm water and then gently shaking the container.

Dosing—The dose of strong iodine will be different for different patients. *Follow your doctor's orders or the directions on the label.* The following information includes only the average doses of strong iodine. *If your dose is different, do not change it* unless your doctor tells you to do so.

- For *oral* dosage form (solution):
  - —To treat overactive thyroid (hyperthyroid):
    - Adults and teenagers—One milliliter (mL) three times a day. The first dose is taken at least one hour after the first dose of your antithyroid medicine.
    - Children—Use and dose must be determined by your doctor.
  - —To prepare for surgery to remove thyroid gland:
    - Adults, teenagers, and children—3 to 5 drops (approximately 0.1 to 0.3 mL) three times a day for ten days before surgery. This medicine is usually given along with your antithyroid medicine.
  - —To protect the thyroid gland against radiation exposure:
    - Adults and teenagers—130 mg once a day for ten days.
    - Children—65 mg once a day for ten days.
  - —To treat iodine deficiency:
    - Adults and teenagers—0.3 to 1 mL three to four times a day.
    - Children—Use and dose must be determined by your doctor.

Missed dose—If you miss a dose of this medicine, take it as soon as possible. However, if it is almost time for your next dose, skip the missed dose and go back to your regular dosing schedule. Do not double doses.

Storage—To store this medicine:

- Keep out of the reach of children.
- Store away from heat and direct light.
- Do not store in the bathroom, near the kitchen sink, or in other damp places.
- Keep the medicine from freezing. Do not refrigerate.
- Do not keep outdated medicine or medicine no longer needed. Be sure that any discarded medicine is out of the reach of children.

Precautions While Using This Medicine

Your doctor should check your progress at regular visits to make sure that this medicine does not cause unwanted effects.

For patients on a low-potassium diet:

- *This medicine contains potassium.* Check with your health care professional before you take this medicine.

Side Effects of This Medicine

Along with its needed effects, a medicine may cause some unwanted effects. Although not all of these side effects may occur, if they do occur they may need medical attention. When this medicine is used for a short time at low doses, side effects usually are rare.

Check with your doctor as soon as possible if any of the following side effects occur:

Less common

Hives; joint pain; swelling of the arms, face, legs, lips, tongue, and/or throat; swelling of the lymph glands

With long-term use

Burning of mouth or throat; confusion; headache (severe); increased watering of mouth; irregular heartbeat; metallic taste; numbness, tingling, pain, or weakness in hands or feet; soreness of teeth and gums; stomach upset; symptoms of head cold; unusual tiredness; weakness or heaviness of legs

Other side effects may occur that usually do not need medical attention. These side effects may go away during treatment as your body adjusts to the medicine. However, check with your doctor if any of the following side effects continue or are bothersome:

Less common

Diarrhea; nausea or vomiting; stomach pain

Other side effects not listed above may also occur in some patients. If you notice any other effects, check with your doctor.

Revised: 04/15/92
Interim revision: 08/10/94

IODOQUINOL Oral

Some commonly used brand names are:

In the U.S.—

Diquinol
Yodoquinol
Yodoxin

Generic name product may also be available.

In Canada—

Diodoquin

Other commonly used names are diiodohydroxyquin and diiodohydroxyquinoline.

Description

Iodoquinol (eye-oh-doe-KWIN-ole) belongs to the group of medicines called antiprotozoals. These medicines are used to treat infections caused by protozoa (tiny, one-celled animals). Iodoquinol is used most often in the treatment of an intestinal infection called amebiasis. However, it may be used to treat other types of infection as determined by your doctor.

Iodoquinol is available only with your doctor's prescription, in the following dosage form:

Oral

- Tablets (U.S. and Canada)

Before Using This Medicine

In deciding to use a medicine, the risks of taking the medicine must be weighed against the good it will do. This is a decision you and your doctor will make. For iodoquinol, the following should be considered:

Allergies—Tell your doctor if you have ever had any unusual or allergic reaction to iodoquinol, chloroxine (e.g., Capitrol), clioquinol (e.g., Vioform), iodine, pamaquine, pentaquine, or primaquine. Also tell your health care professional if you are allergic to any other substances, such as foods, preservatives, or dyes.

Pregnancy—Iodoquinol has not been reported to cause birth defects or other problems in humans.

Breast-feeding—It is not known whether iodoquinol passes into breast milk. Although most medicines pass into breast milk in small amounts, many of them may be used safely while breast-feeding. Mothers who are taking this medicine and who wish to breast-feed should discuss this with their doctor.

Children—Children may be more likely to develop certain side effects, especially if given high doses for a long time.

Older adults—Many medicines have not been studied specifically in older people. Therefore, it may not be known whether they work exactly the same way they do in younger adults or if they cause different side effects or problems in older people. There is no specific information comparing use of iodoquinol in the elderly with use in other age groups.

Other medicines—Although certain medicines should not be used together at all, in other cases two different medicines may be used together even if an interaction might occur. In these cases, your doctor may want to change the dose, or other precautions may be necessary. Tell your health care professional if you are taking any other prescription or nonprescription (over-the-counter [OTC]) medicine.

Other medical problems—The presence of other medical problems may affect the use of iodoquinol. Make sure you tell your doctor if you have any other medical problems, especially:

- Eye disease—Iodoquinol may cause side effects affecting the eye or make eye disease worse
- Kidney disease or
- Liver disease or
- Thyroid disease—Patients with kidney disease, liver disease, or thyroid disease may have an increased chance of side effects

Proper Use of This Medicine

Take this medicine after meals to lessen possible stomach upset, unless otherwise directed by your doctor.

If the tablets are too large to swallow whole, they may be crushed and mixed with a small amount of applesauce or chocolate syrup.

To help clear up your infection completely, *keep taking this medicine for the full time of treatment,* even if you begin to feel better after a few days. *Do not miss any doses.*

Dosing—The dose of iodoquinol will be different for different patients. *Follow your doctor's orders or the directions on the label.* The following information includes only the average doses of iodoquinol. *If your dose is different, do not change it* unless your doctor tells you to do so.

The number of tablets that you take depends on the strength of the medicine.

- For *oral* dosage form (tablets):
  - —For amebiasis:
    - Adults—630 or 650 milligrams (mg) three times a day for twenty days.
    - Children—Dose is based on body weight and must be determined by your doctor. The usual dose is 10 to 13.3 mg per kilogram (kg) (4.5 to 6 mg per pound) of body weight three times a day for twenty days.

Missed dose—If you miss a dose of this medicine, take it as soon as possible. However, if it is almost time for your next dose, skip the missed dose and go back to your regular dosing schedule. Do not double doses.

Storage—To store this medicine:
- Keep out of the reach of children.
- Store away from heat and direct light.
- Do not store in the bathroom, near the kitchen sink, or in other damp places. Heat or moisture may cause the medicine to break down.
- Do not keep outdated medicine or medicine no longer needed. Be sure that any discarded medicine is out of the reach of children.

Precautions While Using This Medicine

This medicine may cause blurred vision or loss of vision. *Make sure you know how you react to this medicine before you drive, use machines, or do anything else that could be dangerous if you are not able to see well.* If these reactions are especially bothersome, check with your doctor.

If you must have thyroid function tests, make sure the doctor knows that you are taking this medicine or have taken it within the past 6 months.

Side Effects of This Medicine

Along with its needed effects, a medicine may cause some unwanted effects. Although not all of these side effects may occur, if they do occur they may need medical attention.

Check with your doctor immediately if any of the following side effects occur:

Less common
Fever or chills; skin rash, hives, or itching; swelling of neck

With long-term use of high doses—especially in children
Blurred vision or any change in vision; clumsiness or unsteadiness; decreased vision or eye pain; increased weakness; muscle pain; numbness, tingling, pain, or weakness in hands or feet

Other side effects may occur that usually do not need medical attention. These side effects may go away during treatment as your body adjusts to the medicine. However, check with your doctor if any of the following side effects continue or are bothersome:

More common
Diarrhea; nausea or vomiting; stomach pain

Less common
Headache; itching of the rectal area

Other side effects not listed above may also occur in some patients. If you notice any other effects, check with your doctor.

Additional Information

Once a medicine has been approved for marketing for a certain use, experience may show that it is also useful for other medical problems. Although these uses are not included in product labeling, iodoquinol is used in certain patients with the following parasite infections:
- Amebiasis, extraintestinal or invasive (amebiasis infection occurring outside the intestine)
- Balantidiasis (an infection caused by protozoa)

For patients taking this medicine for *extraintestinal* or *invasive amebiasis infection*:
- You should take iodoquinol along with metronidazole, which is another medicine that your doctor has prescribed, for treating your amebiasis infection.

Other than the above information, there is no additional information relating to proper use, precautions, or side effects for these uses.

Revised: 03/25/96

IPECAC Oral

Available in the U.S. and Canada as generic name product.

Description

Ipecac (IP-e-kak) is used in the emergency treatment of certain kinds of poisoning. It is used to cause vomiting of the poison.

Only the syrup form of ipecac should be used. A bottle of ipecac labeled as being Ipecac Fluidextract or Ipecac Tincture should not be used. These dosage forms are too strong and may cause serious side effects or death. Only ipecac syrup contains the proper strength of ipecac for treating poisonings.

Ordinarily, this medicine should not be used if strychnine, corrosives such as alkalies (lye) and strong acids, or petroleum distillates such as kerosene, gasoline, coal oil, fuel oil, paint thinner, or cleaning fluid have been swallowed. It may cause seizures, additional injury to the throat, or pneumonia.

Ipecac should not be used to cause vomiting as a means of losing weight. If used regularly for this purpose, serious heart problems or even death may occur.

This medicine in amounts of more than 1 ounce is available only with your doctor's prescription. It is available in $^{1}/_{2}$- and 1-ounce bottles without a prescription. However, before using ipecac syrup, call a poison control center, your doctor, or an emergency room for advice.

Oral
- Syrup (U.S. and Canada)

Before Using This Medicine

Before using this medicine to cause vomiting in poisoning, call a poison control center, your doctor, or an emergency room for advice. It is a good idea to have these telephone numbers readily available. In addition, before you use ipecac, the following should be considered:

Pregnancy—Studies on effects in pregnancy have not been done in either humans or animals.

Children—Infants and very young children are at a greater risk of choking with their own vomit (or getting vomit in their lungs). Therefore, it is especially important to call a poison control center, your doctor, or an emergency room for instructions before giving ipecac to an infant or young child.

Older adults—This medicine has been tested and has not been shown to cause different side effects or problems in older people than it does in younger adults.

Other medical problems—The presence of other medical problems may affect the use of ipecac. Make sure you tell your doctor or the person you talk to at the poison control center or the emergency room if you have any other medical problems, especially:
- Heart disease—There is an increased risk of heart problems, such as unusually fast heartbeat, if the ipecac is not vomited

Proper Use of This Medicine

It is very important that you take this medicine only as directed. Do not take more of it and do not take it more often than recommended on the label, unless otherwise directed. When too much ipecac is used, it can cause damage to the heart and other muscles, and may even cause death.

Do not give this medicine to unconscious or very drowsy persons, since the vomited material may enter the lungs and cause pneumonia.

To help this medicine cause vomiting of the poison, adults should drink 1 full glass (8 ounces) of water and children should drink $^{1}/_{2}$ to 1 full glass (4 to 8 ounces) of water immediately after taking this medicine. Water may be given first in the case of a small or scared child.

Do not take this medicine with milk, milk products, or with carbonated beverages. Milk or milk products may prevent this medicine from working properly, and carbonated beverages may cause swelling of the stomach.

If vomiting does not occur within 20 to 30 minutes after you have taken the first dose of this medicine, take a second dose. If vomiting does not occur after you have taken the second dose, you must immediately see your doctor or go to an emergency room.

If you have been told to take both this medicine and activated charcoal to treat the poisoning, *do not take the activated charcoal until after you have taken this medicine to cause vomiting and vomiting has stopped. This takes usually about 30 minutes.*

Dosing—The dose of ipecac will be different for different patients. *Follow your doctor's orders or the directions on the label.* The following information includes only the average doses of ipecac. *If your dose is different, do not change it* unless your doctor tells you to do so.
- For *oral* dosage form (syrup):
  - —For treatment of poisoning:
    - Adults and teenagers—The usual dose is 15 to 30 milliliters (mL) (1 to 2 tablespoonfuls), followed immediately by one full glass (240 mL) of water. The dose may be repeated one time after twenty to thirty minutes if vomiting does not occur.
    - Children 1 to 12 years of age—The usual dose is 15 mL (1 tablespoonful). One-half to one full glass (120 to 240 mL) of water should be taken right before or right after the dose. The dose may be repeated one time after twenty to thirty minutes if vomiting does not occur.
    - Children 6 months to 1 year of age—The usual dose is 5 to 10 mL (1 to 2 teaspoonfuls). One-half to one full glass (120 to 240 mL) of water should be taken right before or right after the dose. The dose may be repeated one time after twenty to thirty minutes if vomiting does not occur.
    - Children up to 6 months of age—Ipecac must be given only under the direction of your doctor.

Storage—To store this medicine:
- Keep out of the reach of children since overdose is very dangerous in children.
- Store away from heat and direct light.
- Keep the syrup from freezing.
- Do not keep outdated medicine or medicine no longer needed. Be sure that any discarded medicine is out of the reach of children.
- Do not keep a bottle of ipecac that has been opened. Ipecac may evaporate over a period of time. It is best to replace it with a new one.

Side Effects of This Medicine

Along with its needed effects, a medicine may cause some unwanted effects. Although side effects usually do not occur with recommended doses of ipecac, if they do occur they may need medical attention.

Check with your doctor as soon as possible if any of the following side effects occur:

Symptoms of overdose (may also occur if ipecac is taken regularly)

Diarrhea; fast or irregular heartbeat; nausea or vomiting (continuing more than 30 minutes); stomach cramps or pain; troubled breathing; unusual tiredness or weakness; weakness, aching, and stiffness of muscles, especially those of the neck, arms, and legs

Other side effects not listed above may also occur in some patients. If you notice any other effects, check with your doctor.

Revised: 08/04/94

IPRATROPIUM Inhalation

Some commonly used brand names are:

In the U.S.—
Atrovent

In Canada—
Apo-Ipravent
Atrovent
Kendral-Ipratropium

Description

Ipratropium (I-pra-TROE-pee-um) is a bronchodilator (medicine that opens up narrowed breathing passages). It is taken by inhalation to help control the symptoms of lung diseases, such as asthma, chronic bronchitis, and emphysema. Ipratropium helps decrease coughing, wheezing, shortness of breath, and troubled breathing by increasing the flow of air into the lungs.

When ipratropium inhalation is used to treat acute, severe attacks of asthma, bronchitis, or emphysema, it is used only in combination with other bronchodilators.

Ipratropium is available only with your doctor's prescription, in the following dosage forms:

Inhalation

- Inhalation aerosol (U.S. and Canada)
- Inhalation solution (U.S. and Canada)

Before Using This Medicine

In deciding to use a medicine, the risks of using the medicine must be weighed against the good it will do. This is a decision you and your doctor will make. For ipratropium, the following should be considered:

Allergies—Tell your doctor if you have ever had any unusual or allergic reaction to ipratropium, atropine, belladonna, hyoscyamine, or scopolamine, or to other inhalation aerosol medicines. Also tell your health care professional if you are allergic to soya lecithin or related food substances such as soybeans and peanuts.

Pregnancy—Ipratropium has not been studied in pregnant women. However, it has not been shown to cause birth defects or other problems in animal studies.

Breast-feeding—It is not known whether ipratropium passes into the breast milk. Although most medicines pass into breast milk in small amounts, many of them may be used safely while breast-feeding. Mothers who are using this medicine and who wish to breast-feed should discuss this with their doctor.

Children—This medicine has been tested in children and, in effective doses, has not been shown to cause different side effects or problems in children than it does in adults.

Older adults—Ipratropium inhalation has been tested in patients 65 years of age or older. This medicine is not expected to cause different side effects or problems in older people than it does in younger adults.

Other medicines—Although certain medicines should not be used together at all, in other cases two different medicines may be used together even if an interaction might occur. In these cases, your doctor may want to change the dose, or other precautions may be necessary. When you are taking ipratropium, it is especially important that your health care professional know if you are taking any other prescription or nonprescription (over-the-counter [OTC]) medicine.

Other medical problems—The presence of other medical problems may affect the use of ipratropium. Make sure you tell your doctor if you have any other medical problem, especially:

- Difficult urination—Ipratropium may make the condition worse
- Glaucoma—Ipratropium may make the condition worse if it gets into the eyes

Proper Use of This Medicine

Ipratropium is used to help control the symptoms of lung diseases, such as chronic bronchitis, emphysema, and asthma. However, for treatment of bronchospasm or asthma attacks that have already started, ipratropium is used only in combination with other bronchodilators.

It is very important that you use ipratropium only as directed. Do not use more of it and do not use it more often than your doctor ordered. To do so may increase the chance of side effects.

Keep the spray or solution away from the eyes because this medicine may cause irritation or blurred vision. Closing your eyes while you are inhaling ipratropium may keep the medicine from getting into your eyes. Rinsing your eyes with cool water may help if any medicine does get into your eyes.

Ipratropium usually comes with patient directions. Read them carefully before using this medicine.

If you are taking this medicine every day to help control your symptoms, it must be taken at regularly spaced times as ordered by your doctor.

Dosing—The dose of ipratropium will be different for different patients. *Follow your doctor's orders or the directions on the label.* The following information includes only the average doses of ipratropium. *If your dose is different, do not change it* unless your doctor tells you to do so.

- For symptoms of chronic obstructive pulmonary disease, such as chronic bronchitis or emphysema:
  - —For *inhalation aerosol* dosage form:
    - Adults and children 12 years of age and older—2 to 4 inhalations (puffs) three or four times a day, at regularly spaced times. Some patients may need up to 6 to 8 puffs three times a day.
  - —For *inhalation solution* dosage form:
    - Adults and children 12 years of age and older—250 to 500 mcg used in a nebulizer three or four times a day, every six to eight hours.
- For symptoms of asthma:
  - —For *inhalation aerosol* dosage form:
    - Adults and children 12 years of age and older—1 to 4 inhalations (puffs) four times a day, at regularly spaced times, as needed.
    - Children up to 12 years of age—1 or 2 inhalations (puffs) three or four times a day, at regularly spaced times, as needed.
  - —For *inhalation solution* dosage form:
    - Adults and children 12 years of age and older—500 mcg used in a nebulizer three or four times a day, every six to eight hours, as needed.
    - Children 5 to 12 years of age—125 to 250 mcg used in a nebulizer three or four times a day, every four to six hours as needed.
    - Children up to 5 years of age—Use and dose must be determined by your doctor.

Missed dose—If you use ipratropium inhalation regularly and you miss a dose of this medicine, use it as soon as possible. Then use any remaining doses for that day at regularly spaced times.

Storage—To store this medicine:

- Keep out of the reach of children.
- Store away from heat.
- Store the solution form of this medicine away from direct light. Store the aerosol form of this medicine away from direct sunlight.
- Keep the medicine from freezing.
- Store any opened bottles of the solution form of this medicine in the refrigerator.
- Do not puncture, break, or burn the aerosol container, even if it is empty.
- Do not keep outdated medicine or medicine no longer needed. Be sure that any discarded medicine is out of the reach of children.

For patients using *ipratropium inhalation aerosol:*

- If you do not understand the directions or you are not sure how to use the inhaler, ask your health care professional to show you how to use it. Also, ask your health care professional to check regularly how you use the inhaler to make sure you are using it properly.
- When you use the inhaler for the first time, or if you have not used it for a while, the inhaler may not give the right amount of medicine with the first puff. Therefore, before using the inhaler, test or prime it.
- *To test or prime the inhaler:*

  —Insert the canister firmly into the clean mouthpiece according to the manufacturer's instructions. Check to make sure it is placed properly into the mouthpiece.

  —Take the cap off the mouthpiece and shake the inhaler three or four times.

  —Hold the inhaler away from you at arm's length and press the top of the canister, spraying the medicine once into the air. The inhaler will now be ready to give the right amount of medicine when you use it.
- *To use the inhaler:*

  —Using your thumb and one or two fingers, hold the inhaler upright, with the mouthpiece end down and pointing toward you.

  —Take the cap off the mouthpiece. Check the mouthpiece to make sure it is clear. Then, gently shake the inhaler three or four times.

  —Breathe out slowly to the end of a normal breath.

  —Use the inhalation method recommended by your doctor:
    - Open-mouth method—Place the mouthpiece about 1 or 2 inches (2 fingerwidths) in front of your widely opened mouth. Make sure the inhaler is aimed into your mouth so the spray does not hit the roof of your mouth or your tongue.
    - Closed-mouth method—Place the mouthpiece in your mouth between your teeth and over your tongue with your lips closed tightly around it. Make sure your tongue or teeth are not blocking the opening.

  —Start to breathe in slowly and deeply through your mouth. At the same time, press the top of the canister once to get one puff of medicine. Continue to breathe in slowly for 5 to 10 seconds. Count the seconds while breathing in. It is important to press the canister and breathe in slowly at the same time so the medicine gets into your lungs. This step may be difficult at first. If you are using the closed-mouth method and you see a fine mist coming from your mouth or nose, the inhaler is not being used correctly.

  —Hold your breath as long as you can up to 10 seconds. This gives the medicine time to settle into your airways and lungs.

  —Take the mouthpiece away from your mouth and breathe out slowly.

—If your doctor has told you to inhale more than one puff of medicine at each dose, gently shake the inhaler again, and take the second puff following exactly the same steps you used for the first puff. Press the canister one time for each puff of medicine.

—When you are finished, wipe off the mouthpiece and replace the cap.

- Your doctor may want you to use a spacer device or holding chamber with the inhaler. A spacer helps get the medicine into the lungs and reduces the amount of medicine that stays in your mouth and throat.

  —*To use a spacer device with the inhaler:*

  - Attach the spacer to the inhaler according to the manufacturer's directions. There are different types of spacers available, but the method of breathing remains the same with most spacers.
  - Gently shake the inhaler and spacer three or four times.
  - Hold the mouthpiece of the spacer away from your mouth and breathe out slowly to the end of a normal breath.
  - Place the mouthpiece into your mouth between your teeth and over your tongue with your lips closed around it.
  - Press the top of the canister once to release one puff of medicine into the spacer. Within 1 or 2 seconds, start to breathe in slowly and deeply through your mouth for 5 to 10 seconds. Count the seconds while inhaling. Do not breathe in through your nose.
  - Hold your breath as long as you can up to 10 seconds.
  - Take the mouthpiece away from your mouth and breathe out slowly.
  - If your doctor has told you to take more than one puff of medicine at each dose, gently shake the inhaler and spacer again and take the next puff, following exactly the same steps you used for the first puff. Do not put more than one puff of medicine into the spacer at a time.
  - When you are finished, remove the spacer device from the inhaler and replace the cap.

- Clean the inhaler, mouthpiece, and spacer at least twice a week.

  —*To clean the inhaler:*

  - Remove the canister from the inhaler and set aside.
  - Wash the mouthpiece, cap, and the spacer with warm, soapy water. Then, rinse well with warm, running water.
  - Shake off the excess water and let the inhaler parts air dry completely before putting the inhaler back together.

- The ipratropium canister provides about 200 inhalations. You should keep a record of the number of inhalations you use so you will know when the canister is almost empty. This canister, unlike other aerosol canisters, cannot be floated in water to test its fullness.

For patients using *ipratropium inhalation solution:*

- Use this medicine only in a power-operated nebulizer with an adequate flow rate and equipped with a face mask or mouthpiece. Your doctor will tell you which nebulizer to use. Make sure you understand exactly how to use it. If you have any questions about this, check with your doctor.
- *To prepare the medicine for use in the nebulizer:*

  —*If you are using the single-dose vial of ipratropium:*

  - Break away one vial by pulling it firmly from the strip.
  - Twist off the top to open the vial. Use the contents of the vial as soon as possible after opening it.
  - Squeeze the contents of the vial into the cup of the nebulizer. If your doctor has told you to use less than a full vial of solution, use a syringe to withdraw the correct amount of solution from the vial and add it to the nebulizer cup. Be sure to throw away the syringe after one use.

  —*If you are using the multiple-dose bottle of ipratropium:*

  - Use a syringe to withdraw the correct amount of solution from the bottle and add it to the nebulizer cup. Do not use the same syringe more than once.

- If you have been told to dilute the ipratropium inhalation solution in the nebulizer cup with the sodium chloride solution provided, use a new syringe to add the sodium chloride solution to the cup as directed by your health care professional.
- If your doctor told you to use another inhalation solution with the ipratropium inhalation solution, add that solution also to the nebulizer cup.
- *To use the nebulizer:*

  —Gently shake the nebulizer cup to mix the solutions well.

  —Connect the nebulizer tube to the air or oxygen pump and begin the treatment. Adjust the mask, if you are using one, to prevent mist from getting into your eyes.

  —Use the method of breathing your doctor told you to use to take the treatment. One way is to breathe slowly and deeply through the mask or mouthpiece. Another way is to breathe in and out normally with the mouthpiece in your mouth, taking a deep breath every 1 or 2 minutes. Continue to breathe in the medicine as instructed until no more mist is formed in the nebulizer cup or until you hear a sputtering (spitting or popping) sound.

  —When you have finished, replace the caps on the solutions. Store the bottles of solution in the refrigerator until the next treatment.

  —Clean the nebulizer according to the manufacturer's directions.

Precautions While Using This Medicine

Check with your doctor at once if your symptoms do not improve within 30 minutes after using a dose of this medicine or if your condition gets worse.

For patients using *ipratropium inhalation solution:*

- *If you are also using cromolyn inhalation solution, do not mix that solution with the ipratropium inhalation solution containing the preservative benzalkonium chloride for use in a nebulizer.* To do so will cause the solution to become cloudy. However, if your condition requires you to use cromolyn inhalation solution with ipratropium inhalation solution, it may be mixed with ipratropium inhalation solution that is preservative-free.

Side Effects of This Medicine

Along with its needed effects, a medicine may cause some unwanted effects. Although not all of these side effects may occur, if they do occur they may require medical attention.

Check with your doctor as soon as possible if any of the following side effects occur:

Rare

Constipation (continuing) or lower abdominal pain or bloating; increased wheezing, tightness in chest, or difficulty in breathing; severe eye pain; skin rash or hives; swelling of face, lips, or eyelids

Other side effects may occur that usually do not need medical attention. These side effects may go away during treatment as your body adjusts to the medicine. However, check with your doctor if any of the following side effects continue or are bothersome:

More common

Cough; dryness of mouth; unpleasant taste

Less common or rare

Blurred vision or other changes in vision; burning eyes; difficult urination; dizziness; headache; nausea; nervousness; pounding heartbeat; sweating; trembling

Other side effects not listed above may also occur in some patients. If you notice any other effects, check with your doctor.

Revised: 06/21/96

IPRATROPIUM Nasal*

A commonly used brand name in Canada is Atrovent.

*Not commercially available in the U.S.

Description

Ipratropium (i-pra-TROE-pee-um) nasal aerosol is used to relieve runny nose caused by continuing nasal inflammation.

When this medicine is sprayed into your nose, it works by preventing the glands in your nose from producing large amounts of fluid.

Ipratropium is available only with your doctor's prescription, in the following dosage form:

Nasal

- Nasal aerosol (Canada)

Before Using This Medicine

In deciding to use a medicine, the risks of using the medicine must be weighed against the good it will do. This is a decision you and your doctor will make. For ipratropium nasal aerosol, the following should be considered:

Allergies—Tell your doctor if you have ever had any unusual or allergic reaction to ipratropium, atropine, belladonna, hyoscyamine, or scopolamine, or to other nasal aerosol medicines.

Pregnancy—Ipratropium has not been studied in pregnant women. However, it has not been shown to cause birth defects in animal studies.

Breast-feeding—It is not known whether ipratropium nasal aerosol passes into the breast milk. Although most medicines pass into breast milk in small amounts, many of them may be used safely while breast-feeding. Mothers who are using this medicine and who wish to breast-feed should discuss this with their doctor.

Children—Although there is no specific information comparing the use of ipratropium nasal aerosol in children with use in other age groups, this medicine is not expected to cause different side effects or problems in children than it does in adults.

Older adults—Many medicines have not been studied specifically in older people. Therefore, it may not be known whether they work exactly the same way they do in younger adults. Although there is no specific information comparing the use of ipratropium nasal aerosol in the elderly with use in other age groups, this medicine is not expected to cause different side effects in older people than it does in younger adults.

Other medicines—Although certain medicines should not be used together at all, in other cases two different medicines may be used together even if an interaction might occur. In these cases, your doctor may want to change the dose, or other precautions may be necessary. Tell your health care professional if you are taking any other prescription or nonprescription (over-the-counter [OTC]) medicine.

Other medical problems—The presence of other medical problems may affect the use of ipratropium nasal aerosol. Make sure you tell your doctor if you have any other medical problem, especially:

- Glaucoma—If ipratropium nasal aerosol is sprayed into the eyes, it may make the condition worse

Proper Use of This Medicine

It is very important that you use ipratropium nasal aerosol only as directed. Do not use more of it and do not use it more often than your doctor ordered. To do so may increase the chance of side effects.

Keep the aerosol spray away from the eyes. If the spray accidently gets in your eyes, it may cause irritation and blurred vision. Rinsing your eyes with cool water may help if any medicine does get into your eyes.

Ipratropium nasal aerosol usually comes with patient directions. Read them carefully before using this medicine.

If you do not understand the directions or if you are not sure how to use the ipratropium nasal aerosol, ask your health care professional to show you how to use it.

When you use the nasal aerosol for the first time or if you have not used it for a while, the spray device may not deliver the right amount of medicine with the first spray. Therefore, before using the aerosol, test the device to make sure it works properly.

To test the aerosol spray device:
- Insert the canister firmly into the clean nosepiece according to the manufacturer's instructions. Check to make sure it is placed properly into the nosepiece.
- Take the cover off the nosepiece and shake the aerosol container well.
- Hold the aerosol container against a light background and press the top of the canister once or twice, spraying the medicine away from yourself, into the air. If you see a fine mist of medicine, you will know that the spray device is working properly and that you will get the right amount of medicine when you use it.

To use the nasal aerosol:
- Gently blow your nose, making sure your nostrils are clear.
- Hold the aerosol container upright between your thumb and forefinger, with the nosepiece down and pointing toward you.
- Take off the nosepiece cover and gently shake the aerosol container well.
- Insert the nosepiece into one nostril. Point it slightly toward the outside nostril wall. Hold your other nostril closed with one finger.
- Tilt your head back a little. Press down on the top of the canister to release one spray. Do not breathe in at the same time you are spraying the medicine. If the spray tends to drip out, you may sniff gently to keep the spray in your nose.
- If your doctor has told you to use more than one spray in the same nostril, slightly change the direction of the nosepiece in your nostril and spray again.
- Remove the nosepiece from your nostril.
- Gently shake the container well. Place the nosepiece into the second nostril.
- Repeat the same steps for spraying the medicine into the second nostril that you used for the first nostril.
- Remove the nosepiece from your nostril.
- When you have finished, replace the cover on the nosepiece to keep it clean.
- Do not blow your nose for the next 15 minutes.

Clean the aerosol spray device often to prevent the medicine from building up and blocking the nosepiece.

To clean the aerosol spray device:
- After each use—Wipe off the nosepiece.
- At least once a week:
  - —Remove the canister from the nosepiece.
  - —Wash the nosepiece well in lukewarm water.
  - —If you use soap or detergent, rinse the nosepiece well in clear water.
  - —Shake off the excess water and let the nosepiece air dry completely.
  - —The canister stem may get dirty or blocked. While the canister is out of the nosepiece, check the two small holes in the stem of the canister.
  - —If the holes seem blocked, rinse them with clear, lukewarm water.
  - —Let the canister air dry completely before you put it back into the dry nosepiece.
  - —Replace the cover to keep the nosepiece clean.

Dosing—The dose of ipratropium nasal aerosol will be different for different patients. *Follow your doctor's orders or the directions on the label.* The following information includes only the average doses of ipratropium nasal aerosol. *If your dose is different, do not change it* unless your doctor tells you to do so:
- For *nasal* aerosol:
  - —For runny nose:
    - Adults and children 12 years of age and older—40 micrograms (mcg) (2 sprays) into each nostril two to four times a day. Do not use more often than every 6 hours. Do not use more than 16 sprays in twenty-four hours.
    - Children up to 12 years of age—Use is not recommended.

Missed dose—If you are using ipratropium nasal aerosol regularly and you miss a dose of this medicine, use it as soon as possible. Then use any remaining doses for that day at regularly spaced times.

Storage—To store this medicine:
- Keep out of the reach of children.
- Store away from heat and direct sunlight.
- Keep the medicine from freezing.
- Do not puncture, break, or burn the container, even if it is empty.
- Do not keep outdated medicine or medicine no longer needed. Be sure that any discarded medicine is out of the reach of children.

Precautions While Using This Medicine

If your symptoms do not improve within one or two weeks or if your condition becomes worse, check with your doctor.

Ipratropium nasal aerosol may cause dryness of the mouth or throat. For temporary relief, use sugarless candy or gum, melt bits of ice in your mouth, or use a saliva substitute. However, if your mouth continues to feel dry for more than 2 weeks, check with your medical doctor or dentist. Continuing dryness of the mouth may increase the chance of dental disease, including tooth decay, gum disease, and fungus infections.

Side Effects of This Medicine

Along with its needed effects, a medicine may cause some unwanted effects. Although not all of these side effects may occur, if they do occur they may require medical attention.

Check with your doctor as soon as possible if any of the following side effects occur:

Rare

Blurred vision or other changes in vision; difficult or painful urination; difficulty in swallowing; eye pain; fast or irregular heartbeat; skin rash or hives; swelling of tongue or lips; sores in mouth and on lips; wheezing, tightness in chest, or difficulty in breathing

Other side effects may occur that usually do not need medical attention. These side effects may go away during treatment as your body adjusts to the medicine. However, check with your doctor if any of the following side effects continue or are bothersome:

More common

Dryness of nose or mouth; headache; irritation and crusting in nose

Less common or rare

Bleeding or burning in nose; diarrhea or constipation; dryness of throat; nausea; nervousness; stomach pain; stuffy nose

Other side effects not listed above may occur in some patients. If you notice any other effects, check with your doctor.

Developed: 08/09/94

IRON SUPPLEMENTS Systemic

Some commonly used brand names are:

In the U.S.—

DexFerrum
Femiron[1]
Feosol[3]
Feostat[1]
Feostat Drops[1]
Feratab[3]
Fer-gen-sol[3]
Fergon[2]
Fer-In-Sol Capsules[3]
Fer-In-Sol Drops[3]
Fer-In-Sol Syrup[3]
Fer-Iron Drops[3]
Fero-Gradumet[3]
Ferospace[3]
Ferralet[2]
Ferralet Slow Release[2]
Ferralyn Lanacaps[3]
Ferra-TD[3]
Ferretts
Fumasorb[1]
Fumerin[1]
Hemocyte[1]
Hytinic[5]
InFeD[4]
Ircon[1]
Mol-Iron[3]
Nephro-Fer[1]
Niferex[5]
Niferex-150[5]
Nu-Iron[5]
Nu-Iron 150[5]
Simron[2]
Slow Fe[3]
Span-FF[1]

In Canada—

Apo-Ferrous Gluconate[2]
Apo-Ferrous Sulfate[3]
DexIron[4]
Fer-In-Sol Drops[3]
Fer-In-Sol Syrup[3]
Fero-Grad[3]
Fertinic[2]
Jectofer[6]
Neo-Fer[1]
Novoferrogluc[2]
Novoferrosulfa[3]
Novofumar[1]
Palafer[1]
PMS-Ferrous Sulfate[3]
Slow Fe[3]

Note: For quick reference, the following iron supplements are numbered to match the corresponding brand names.

This information applies to the following:

1. Ferrous Fumarate (FER-us FYOO-ma-rate)‡
2. Ferrous Gluconate (FER-us GLOO-koe-nate)‡§
3. Ferrous Sulfate (FER-us SUL-fate)‡§
4. Iron Dextran (DEX-tran)
5. Iron-Polysaccharide (pol-i-SAK-a-ride)†
6. Iron Sorbitol (SOR-bi-tole)*

*Not commercially available in the U.S.
†Not commercially available in Canada.
‡Generic name product may also be available in the U.S.
§Generic name product may also be available in Canada.

Description

Iron is a mineral that the body needs to produce red blood cells. When the body does not get enough iron, it cannot produce the number of normal red blood cells needed to keep you in good health. This condition is called iron deficiency (iron shortage) or iron deficiency anemia.

Although many people in the U.S. get enough iron from their diet, some must take additional amounts to meet their needs. For example, iron is sometimes lost with slow or small amounts of bleeding in the body that you would not be aware of and which can only be detected by your doctor. Your doctor can determine if you have an iron deficiency, what is causing the deficiency, and if an iron supplement is necessary.

Lack of iron may lead to unusual tiredness, shortness of breath, a decrease in physical performance, and learning problems in children and adults, and may increase your chance of getting an infection.

Some conditions may increase your need for iron. These include:

- Bleeding problems
- Burns
- Hemodialysis
- Intestinal diseases
- Stomach problems
- Stomach removal

In addition, infants, especially those receiving breast milk or low-iron formulas, may need additional iron.

Increased need for iron supplements should be determined by your health care professional.

Injectable iron is administered only by or under the supervision of your health care professional. Other forms of iron are available without a prescription; however, your health care professional may have special instructions on the proper use and dose for your condition.

Iron supplements are available in the following dosage forms:

Oral

- Ferrous Fumarate
  - Capsules (Canada)
  - Extended-release capsules (U.S.)
  - Solution (U.S.)
  - Suspension (U.S. and Canada)
  - Tablets (U.S. and Canada)
  - Chewable tablets (U.S.)
- Ferrous Gluconate
  - Capsules (U.S.)
  - Elixir (U.S.)
  - Syrup (Canada)
  - Tablets (U.S. and Canada)
  - Extended-release tablets (U.S.)
- Ferrous Sulfate
  - Capsules (U.S.)
  - Extended-release capsules (U.S.)
  - Elixir (U.S.)
  - Solution (U.S. and Canada)
  - Tablets (U.S. and Canada)
  - Enteric-coated tablets (U.S. and Canada)
  - Extended-release tablets (U.S. and Canada)
- Iron-Polysaccharide
  - Capsules (U.S.)
  - Elixir (U.S.)
  - Tablets (U.S.)

Parenteral

- Iron Dextran
  - Injection (U.S. and Canada)
- Iron Sorbitol
  - Injection (Canada)

Importance of Diet

For good health, it is important that you eat a balanced and varied diet. Follow carefully any diet program your health care professional may recommend. For your specific dietary vitamin and/or mineral needs, ask your health care professional for a list of appropriate foods. If you think that you are not getting enough vitamins and/or minerals in your diet, you may choose to take a dietary supplement.

Iron is found in the diet in two forms—heme iron, which is well absorbed, and nonheme iron, which is poorly absorbed. The best dietary source of absorbable (heme) iron is lean red meat. Chicken, turkey, and fish are also sources of iron, but they contain less than red meat. Cereals, beans, and some vegetables contain poorly absorbed (nonheme) iron. Foods rich in vitamin C (e.g., citrus fruits and fresh vegetables), eaten with small amounts of heme iron–containing foods, such as meat, may increase the amount of nonheme iron absorbed from cereals, beans, and other vegetables. Some foods (e.g., milk, eggs, spinach, fiber-containing, coffee, tea) may decrease the amount of nonheme iron absorbed from foods. Additional iron may be added to food from cooking in iron pots.

The daily amount of iron needed is defined in several different ways.

For U.S.—

- Recommended Dietary Allowances (RDAs) are the amount of vitamins and minerals needed to provide for adequate nutrition in most healthy persons. RDAs for a given nutrient may vary depending on a person's age, sex, and physical condition (e.g., pregnancy).
- Daily Values (DVs) are used on food and dietary supplement labels to indicate the percent of the recommended daily amount of each nutrient that a serving provides. DV replaces the previous designation of United States Recommended Daily Allowances (USRDAs).

For Canada—

- Recommended Nutrient Intakes (RNIs) are used to determine the amounts of vitamins, minerals, and protein needed to provide adequate nutrition and lessen the risk of chronic disease.

Normal daily recommended intakes in milligrams (mg) for iron are generally defined as follows (Note that the RDA and RNI are expressed as an actual amount of iron, which is referred to as ''elemental'' iron. The product form [e.g., ferrous fumarate, ferrous gluconate, ferrous sulfate] has a different strength):

Persons	U.S. (mg)	Canada (mg)
Infants and children		
Birth to 3 years of age	6–10	0.3–6
4 to 6 years of age	10	8
7 to 10 years of age	10	8–10
Adolescent and adult males	10	8–10
Adolescent and adult females	10–15	8–13
Pregnant females	30	17–22
Breast-feeding females	15	8–13

Before Using This Dietary Supplement

If you are taking this dietary supplement without a prescription, carefully read and follow any precautions on the label. For iron supplements, the following should be considered:

Allergies—Tell your health care professional if you have ever had any unusual or allergic reaction to iron medicine. Also tell your health care professional if you are allergic to any other substances, such as foods, preservatives, or dyes.

Pregnancy—It is especially important that you are receiving enough vitamins and minerals when you become pregnant and that you continue to receive the right amount of vitamins and minerals throughout your pregnancy. Healthy fetal growth and development depend on a steady supply of nutrients from mother to fetus. During the first 3 months of pregnancy, a proper diet usually provides enough iron. However, during the last 6 months, in order to meet the increased needs of the developing baby, an iron supplement may be recommended by your health care professional.

However, taking large amounts of a dietary supplement in pregnancy may be harmful to the mother and/or fetus and should be avoided.

Breast-feeding—It is especially important that you receive the right amounts of vitamins and minerals so that your baby will also get the vitamins and minerals needed to grow properly. Iron normally is present in breast milk in small amounts. When prescribed by a health care professional, iron preparations are not known to cause problems during breast-feeding. However, nursing mothers are advised to check with their health care professional before taking iron supplements or any other medication. Taking large amounts of a dietary supplement while breast-feeding may be harmful to the mother and/or infant and should be avoided.

Children—Problems in children have not been reported with intake of normal daily recommended amounts. Iron supplements, when prescribed by your health care professional, are not expected to cause different side effects in children than they do in adults. However, it is important to follow the directions carefully, since iron overdose in children is especially dangerous.

Older adults—Problems in older adults have not been reported with intake of normal daily recommended amounts. Elderly people sometimes do not absorb iron as easily as younger adults and may need a larger dose. If you think you need to take an iron supplement, check with your health care professional first. Only your health care professional can decide if you need an iron supplement and how much you should take.

Medicines or other dietary supplements—Although certain medicines or dietary supplements should not be used together at all, in other cases they may be used together even if an interaction might occur. In these cases, your health care professional may want to change the dose, or other precautions may be necessary. When you are taking iron supplements, it is especially important that your health care professional know if you are taking any of the following:

- Acetohydroxamic acid (e.g., Lithostat)—Use with iron supplements may cause either medicine to be less effective
- Antacids—Use with iron supplements may make the iron supplements less effective; iron supplements should be taken 1 or 2 hours before or after antacids
- Dimercaprol—Iron supplements and dimercaprol may combine in the body to form a harmful chemical
- Etidronate or
- Fluoroquinolones (e.g., ciprofloxacin, enoxacin, lomefloxacin, norfloxacin, ofloxacin) or
- Tetracyclines (taken by mouth) (medicine for infection)—Use with iron supplements may make these medicines less effective; iron supplements should be taken 2 hours before or after these medicines

Other medical problems—The presence of other medical problems may affect the use of iron supplements. Make sure you tell your health care professional if you have any other medical problems, especially:

- Alcohol abuse (or history of) or
- Kidney infection or
- Liver disease or
- Prophyria cutaneous tarda—Higher blood levels of the iron supplement may occur, which may increase the chance of side effects
- Arthritis (rheumatoid) or
- Asthma or allergies or
- Heart disease—The injected form of iron may make these conditions worse
- Colitis or other intestinal problems or
- Iron overload conditions (e.g., hemochromatosis, hemosiderosis) or
- Stomach ulcer—Iron supplements may make these conditions worse

Proper Use of This Dietary Supplement

Dosing—The amount of iron needed to meet normal daily recommended intakes will be different for different individuals. The following information includes only the average amounts of iron.

- For *oral* dosage forms (capsules, tablets, oral solution):
  - —To prevent deficiency, the amount taken by mouth is based on normal daily recommended intakes:

    For the U.S.
    - Adult and teenage males—10 milligrams (mg) per day.
    - Adult and teenage females—10 to 15 mg per day.
    - Pregnant females—30 mg per day.
    - Breast-feeding females—15 mg per day.
    - Children 7 to 10 years of age—10 mg per day.
    - Children 4 to 6 years of age—10 mg per day.
    - Children birth to 3 years of age—6 to 10 mg per day.

    For Canada
    - Adult and teenage males—8 to 10 mg per day.
    - Adult and teenage females—8 to 13 mg per day.
    - Pregnant females—17 to 22 mg per day.
    - Breast-feeding females—8 to 13 mg per day.
    - Children 7 to 10 years of age—8 to 10 mg per day.
    - Children 4 to 6 years of age—8 mg per day.
    - Children birth to 3 years of age—0.3 to 6 mg per day.
  - —To treat deficiency:
    - Adults, teenagers, and children—Treatment dose is determined by prescriber for each individual based on the severity of deficiency.

After you start using this dietary supplement, continue to return to your health care professional to see if you are benefiting from the iron. Some blood tests may be necessary for this.

Iron is best absorbed when taken on an empty stomach, with water or fruit juice (adults: full glass or 8 ounces; children: 1/2 glass or 4 ounces), about 1 hour before or 2 hours after meals. However, to lessen the possibility of stomach upset, iron may be taken with food or immediately after meals.

For safe and effective use of iron supplements:
- Follow your health care professional's instructions if this dietary supplement was prescribed.
- Follow the manufacturer's package directions if you are treating yourself. If you think you still need iron after taking it for 1 or 2 months, check with your health care professional.

Liquid forms of iron supplement tend to stain the teeth. To prevent, reduce, or remove these stains:
- Mix each dose in water, fruit juice, or tomato juice. You may use a drinking tube or straw to help keep the iron supplement from getting on the teeth.
- When doses of liquid iron supplement are to be given by dropper, the dose may be placed well back on the tongue and followed with water or juice.
- Iron stains on teeth can usually be removed by brushing with baking soda (sodium bicarbonate) or medicinal peroxide (hydrogen peroxide 3%).

Missed dose—If you miss a dose of this dietary supplement, skip the missed dose and go back to your regular dosing schedule. Do not double doses.

Storage—To store this dietary supplement:
- Keep out of the reach of children because iron overdose is especially dangerous in children. As few as 3 or 4 adult iron tablets can cause serious poisoning in small children. Vitamin-iron products for use during pregnancy and flavored vitamins with iron often cause iron overdose in small children.
- Store away from heat and direct light.
- Do not store in the bathroom, near the kitchen sink, or in other damp places. Heat or moisture may cause the dietary supplement to break down.
- Keep the liquid form of this dietary supplement from freezing.
- Do not keep outdated dietary supplements or those no longer needed. Be sure that any discarded dietary supplement is out of the reach of children.

Precautions While Using This Dietary Supplement

When iron is combined with certain foods it may lose much of its value. If you are taking iron, the following foods should be avoided, or only taken in very small amounts, for at least 1 hour before or 2 hours after you take iron:

Cheese and yogurt
Eggs
Milk
Spinach
Tea or coffee
Whole-grain breads and cereals and bran

Do not take iron supplements and antacids or calcium supplements at the same time. It is best to space doses of these 2 products 1 to 2 hours apart, to get the full benefit from each medicine or dietary supplement.

If you are taking iron supplements *without a prescription:*
- Do not take iron supplements by mouth if you are receiving iron injections. To do so may result in iron poisoning.
- Do not regularly take large amounts of iron for longer than 6 months without checking with your health care professional. People differ in their need for iron, and those with certain medical conditions can gradually become poisoned by taking too much iron over a period of time. Also, unabsorbed iron can mask the presence of blood in the stool, which may delay discovery of a serious condition.

If you have been taking a long-acting or coated iron tablet and your stools have *not* become black, check with your health care professional. The tablets may not be breaking down properly in your stomach, and you may not be receiving enough iron.

It is important to keep iron preparations out of the reach of children. Keep a 1-ounce bottle of *syrup* of ipecac available at home to be taken in case of an iron overdose emergency when a doctor, poison control center, or emergency room orders its use.

If you think you or anyone else has taken an overdose of iron medicine:
- *Immediate medical attention is very important.*
- *Call your doctor, a poison control center, or the nearest hospital emergency room at once.* Always keep these phone numbers readily available.
- *Follow any instructions given to you.* If syrup of ipecac has been ordered and given, do not delay going to the emergency room while waiting for the ipecac syrup to empty the stomach, since it may require 20 to 30 minutes to show results.
- *Go to the emergency room without delay.*
- *Take the container of iron with you.*

Early signs of iron overdose may not appear for up to 60 minutes or more. Do not delay going to the emergency room while waiting for signs to appear.

Side Effects of This Dietary Supplement

Along with its needed effects, a dietary supplement may cause some unwanted effects. Although not all of these effects may occur, if they do occur they may need medical attention.

Check with your health care professional if any of the following side effects occur:

More common—with the injection only

Backache or muscle pain; chest pain; chills; dizziness; fainting; fast heartbeat; fever with increased sweating; flushing; headache; metallic taste; nausea or vomiting; numbness, pain, or tingling of hands or feet; pain or redness at injection site; redness of skin; skin rash or hives; troubled breathing

More common—when taken by mouth only

Abdominal or stomach pain, cramping, or soreness (continuing)

Less common or rare—when taken by mouth only
Chest or throat pain, especially when swallowing; stools with signs of blood (red or black color)

Early symptoms of iron overdose
Diarrhea (may contain blood); nausea; stomach pain or cramping (sharp); vomiting, severe (may contain blood)

Note: Symptoms of iron overdose may not occur for up to 60 minutes or more after the overdose was taken. By this time you should have had emergency room treatment. Do not delay going to emergency room while waiting for signs to appear.

Late symptoms of iron overdose
Bluish-colored lips, fingernails, and palms of hands; convulsions (seizures); drowsiness; pale, clammy skin; unusual tiredness or weakness; weak and fast heartbeat

Other side effects may occur that usually do not need medical attention. These side effects may go away during treatment as your body adjusts to the dietary supplement. However, check with your health care professional if any of the following side effects continue or are bothersome:

More common
Constipation; diarrhea; nausea; vomiting

Less common
Darkened urine; heartburn

Stools commonly become dark green or black when iron preparations are taken by mouth. This is caused by unabsorbed iron and is harmless. However, in rare cases, black stools of a sticky consistency may occur along with other side effects such as red streaks in the stool, cramping, soreness, or sharp pains in the stomach or abdominal area. Check with your health care professional immediately if these side effects appear.

If you have been receiving injections of iron, you may notice a brown discoloration of your skin. This color usually fades within several weeks or months.

Other side effects not listed above may also occur in some individuals. If you notice any other effects, check with your health care professional.

Revised: 04/16/92
Interim revision: 06/29/92; 06/19/95; 07/11/97

ISOMETHEPTENE, DICHLORALPHENAZONE, AND ACETAMINOPHEN Systemic

Some commonly used brand names are:

In the U.S.—

Amidrine
I.D.A.
Iso-Acetazone
Isocom
Midchlor
Midrin
Migrapap
Migquin
Migratine
Migrazone
Migrend
Migrex
Mitride

Description

Isometheptene (eye-soe-meth-EP-teen), dichloralphenazone (dye-klor-al-FEN-a-zone), and acetaminophen (a-seat-a-MIN-oh-fen) combination is used to treat certain kinds of headaches, such as "tension" headaches and migraine headaches. This combination is not used regularly (for example, every day) to prevent headaches. It should be taken only after headache pain begins, or after a warning sign that a migraine is coming appears. Isometheptene helps to relieve throbbing headaches, but it is not an ordinary pain reliever. Dichloralphenazone helps you to relax, and acetaminophen relieves pain.

This medicine is available only with your doctor's prescription, in the following dosage form:

Oral
- Capsules (U.S.)

Before Using This Medicine

In deciding to use a medicine, the risks of taking the medicine must be weighed against the good it will do. This is a decision you and your doctor will make. For this combination medicine, the following should be considered:

Allergies—Tell your doctor if you have ever had any unusual or allergic reaction to acetaminophen or to this combination medicine. Also tell your health care professional if you are allergic to any other substances, such as foods, preservatives, or dyes.

Pregnancy—Studies with this combination medicine have not been done in either humans or animals.

Breast-feeding—Acetaminophen passes into the breast milk in small amounts. However, this medicine has not been shown to cause problems in nursing babies.

Children—Studies with this medicine have been done only in adult patients, and there is no specific information about its use in children.

Older adults—Many medicines have not been tested in older people. Therefore, it may not be known whether they work exactly the same way they do in younger adults or if they cause different side effects or problems in older people. There is no specific information comparing use of this combination medicine in the elderly with use in other age groups.

Other medicines—Although certain medicines should not be used together at all, in other cases two different medicines may be used together even if an interaction might occur. In these cases, your doctor may want to change the dose, or other precautions may be necessary. When you are taking this combination medicine, it is especially important that your health care professional know if you are taking any of the following:

- Monoamine oxidase (MAO) inhibitors (furazolidone [e.g., Furoxone], isocarboxazid [e.g., Marplan], phenelzine [e.g., Nardil], procarbazine [e.g., Matulane], selegiline [e.g., Eldepryl], tranylcypromine [e.g., Parnate])—Taking this combination medicine while you are taking or within 2 weeks of taking a monoamine oxidase (MAO) inhibitor may increase the chance of side effects

Other medical problems—The presence of other medical problems may affect the use of this medicine. Make sure you tell your doctor if you have any other medical problems, especially:

- Alcohol abuse or
- Heart attack (recent) or
- Heart or blood vessel disease or
- Kidney disease or
- Liver disease or
- Stroke (recent) or
- Virus infection of the liver (viral hepatitis)—The chance of side effects may be increased
- Glaucoma, not well controlled, or
- High blood pressure (hypertension), not well controlled—The isometheptene in this combination medicine may make these conditions worse

Proper Use of This Medicine

Take this medicine only as directed by your doctor. Do not take more of it, do not take it more often than directed, and do not take it every day for several days in a row. If the amount you are to take does not relieve your headache, check with your doctor. If a headache medicine is used too often, it may lose its effectiveness or even cause a type of physical dependence. If this occurs, your headaches may actually get worse. Also, taking too much acetaminophen can cause liver damage.

This medicine works best if you:

- *Take it as soon as the headache begins.* If you get warning signals of a migraine, take this medicine as soon as you are sure that the migraine is coming. This may even stop the headache pain from occurring.
- *Lie down in a quiet, dark room until you are feeling better.*

People who get a lot of headaches may need to take a different medicine to help prevent headaches. *It is important that you follow your doctor's directions, even if your headaches continue to occur.* Headache-preventing medicines may take several weeks to start working. Even after they do start working, your headaches may not go away completely. However, your headaches should occur less often, and they should be less severe and easier to relieve, than before. This will reduce the amount of headache relievers that you need. If you do not notice any improvement after several weeks of headache-preventing treatment, check with your doctor.

Dosing—The dose of this combination medicine will be different for different patients. *Follow your doctor's orders or the directions on the label.* The following information includes only the average doses of this medicine. *If your dose is different, do not change it unless your doctor tells you to do so.*

- *For "tension" headaches:*
  —Adults: 1 or 2 capsules every 4 hours, as needed. Not more than 8 capsules a day.
  —Children: Dose must be determined by the doctor.
- *For migraine headaches:*
  —Adults: 2 capsules for the first dose, then 1 capsule every hour, as needed. Not more than 5 capsules in 12 hours.
  —Children: Dose must be determined by the doctor.

Storage—To store this medicine:

- Keep out of the reach of children.
- Store away from heat and direct light.
- Do not store in the bathroom, near the kitchen sink, or in other damp places. Heat and moisture may cause the medicine to break down.
- Do not keep outdated medicine or medicine no longer needed. Be sure that any discarded medicine is out of the reach of children.

Precautions While Using This Medicine

Check with your doctor:

- *If the medicine stops working as well as it did when you first started using it.* This may mean that you are in danger of becoming dependent on the medicine. *Do not try to get better relief by increasing the dose.*
- *If you are having headaches more often than you did before you started using this medicine.* This is especially important if a new headache occurs within 1 day after you took your last dose of headache medicine, headaches begin to occur every day, or a headache continues for several days in a row. This may mean that you are dependent on the medicine. *Continuing to take this medicine will cause even more headaches later on.* Your doctor can give you advice on how to relieve the headaches.

Check the labels of all nonprescription (over-the-counter [OTC]) and prescription medicines you now take. Taking other medicines that contain acetaminophen together with this medicine may lead to an overdose. If you have any questions about this, check with your health care professional.

This medicine may cause some people to become drowsy, dizzy, or less alert than they are normally. These effects may be especially severe if you also take CNS depressants (medicines that slow down the nervous system, possibly causing drowsiness) together with this medicine. Some examples of CNS depressants are antihistamines or medicine for hay fever, other allergies, or colds; sedatives, tranquilizers, or sleeping medicine; prescription pain medicine or narcotics; barbiturates; medicine for seizures; muscle relaxants; antiemetics (medicines that prevent or relieve nausea or vomiting), and anesthetics. If you are not able to lie down for a while, *make sure you know how you react to this medicine or combination of medicines before you drive, use machines, or do anything else that could be dangerous if you are drowsy or dizzy or are not alert.*

Do not drink alcoholic beverages while taking this medicine. To do so may increase the chance of liver damage caused by acetaminophen, especially if you drink large amounts of alcoholic beverages regularly. Also, because drinking alcoholic beverages may make your headaches worse or cause new headaches to occur, people who often get headaches should probably avoid alcohol.

Side Effects of This Medicine

Along with its needed effects, a medicine may cause some unwanted effects. Although not all of these side effects

may occur, if they do occur they may need medical attention.

Check with your doctor as soon as possible if any of the following side effects occur:

Less common
Unusual tiredness or weakness

Rare
Black, tarry stools; blood in urine or stools; pinpoint red spots on skin; skin rash, hives, or itching; sore throat and fever; unusual bleeding or bruising; yellow eyes or skin

Symptoms of dependence on this medicine
Headaches, more severe and/or more frequent than before

Symptoms of acetaminophen overdose
Diarrhea; increased sweating; loss of appetite; nausea or vomiting; pain, tenderness, and/or swelling in the upper abdominal (stomach) area; stomach cramps or pain

Other side effects may occur that usually do not need medical attention. These side effects may go away during treatment as your body adjusts to the medicine. However, check with your doctor if any of the following side effects continue or are bothersome:

More common
Drowsiness

Rare
Dizziness; fast or irregular heartbeat

Other side effects not listed above may also occur in some patients. If you notice any other effects, check with your doctor.

Revised: 08/18/92

ISONIAZID Systemic

Some commonly used brand names are:

In the U.S.—
Laniazid
Nydrazid
Generic name product may also be available.

In Canada—
Isotamine
PMS Isoniazid

Another commonly used name is INH.

Description

Isoniazid (eye-soe-NYE-a-zid) is used to prevent or treat tuberculosis (TB). It may be given alone to prevent, or, in combination with other medicines, to treat TB. This medicine may also be used for other problems as determined by your doctor.

This medicine may cause some serious side effects, including damage to the liver. Liver damage is more likely to occur in patients over 50 years of age. You and your doctor should talk about the good this medicine will do, as well as the risks of taking it.

If you are being treated for active tuberculosis (TB): To help clear up your TB completely, you must keep taking this medicine for the full time of treatment, even if you begin to feel better. This is very important. It is also important that you do not miss any doses.

Isoniazid is available only with your doctor's prescription, in the following dosage forms:

Oral
- Syrup (U.S. and Canada)
- Tablets (U.S. and Canada)

Parenteral
- Injection (U.S.)

Before Using This Medicine

In deciding to use a medicine, the risks of taking the medicine must be weighed against the good it will do. This is a decision you and your doctor will make. For isoniazid, the following should be considered:

Allergies—Tell your doctor if you have ever had any unusual or allergic reaction to isoniazid, ethionamide (e.g., Trecator-SC), pyrazinamide, or niacin (e.g., Nicobid, nicotinic acid). Also tell your health care professional if you are allergic to any other substances, such as foods, preservatives, or dyes.

Diet—Make certain your health care professional knows if you are on a low-sodium, low-sugar, or any other special diet. Most medicines contain more than just the active ingredient, and many liquid medicines contain alcohol.

Pregnancy—Isoniazid has not been shown to cause birth defects or other problems in humans or animals. Studies in rats and rabbits have shown that isoniazid may increase the risk of fetal death. However, tuberculosis is a very serious disease and many women have been treated with isoniazid during pregnancy with no problems to their babies.

Breast-feeding—Isoniazid passes into the breast milk. However, isoniazid has not been reported to cause problems in nursing babies. Also, there is not enough isoniazid in breast milk to protect or treat babies that have been exposed to tuberculosis.

Children—Isoniazid can cause serious side effects in any patient. Therefore, it is especially important that you discuss with the child's doctor the good that this medicine may do as well as the risks of using it.

Older adults—Hepatitis may be especially likely to occur in older patients, who are usually more sensitive than younger adults to the effects of isoniazid.

Other medicines—Although certain medicines should not be used together at all, in other cases two different medicines may be used together even if an interaction might occur. In these cases, your doctor may want to change the dose, or other precautions may be necessary. When you are taking or receiving isoniazid it is especially important that your health care professional know if you are taking any of the following:

- Acetaminophen (e.g., Tylenol) (with long-term, high-dose use) or
- Alfentanil (e.g., Cordarone) or
- Amiodarone (e.g., Cordarone) or
- Anabolic steroids (nandrolone [e.g., Anabolin], oxandrolone [e.g., Anavar], oxymetholone [e.g., Anadrol], stanozolol [e.g., Winstrol]) or
- Androgens (male hormones) or
- Antithyroid agents (medicine for overactive thyroid) or
- Carmustine (e.g., BiCNU) or
- Chloroquine (e.g., Aralen) or
- Dantrolene (e.g., Dantrium) or
- Daunorubicin (e.g., Cerubidine) or
- Disulfiram (e.g., Antabuse) or
- Divalproex (e.g., Depakote) or
- Estrogens (female hormones) or
- Etretinate (e.g., Tegison) or
- Gold salts (medicine for arthritis) or
- Hydroxychloroquine (e.g., Plaquenil) or
- Mercaptopurine (e.g., Purinethol) or
- Methotrexate (e.g., Mexate) or
- Methyldopa (e.g., Aldomet) or
- Naltrexone (e.g., Trexan) (with long-term, high-dose use) or
- Oral contraceptives (birth control pills) containing estrogen or
- Phenothiazines (acetophenazine [e.g., Tindal], chlorpromazine [e.g., Thorazine], fluphenazine [e.g., Prolixin], mesoridazine [e.g., Serentil], perphenazine [e.g., Trilafon], prochlorperazine [e.g., Compazine], promazine [e.g., Sparine], promethazine [e.g., Phenergan], thioridazine [e.g., Mellaril], trifluoperazine [e.g., Stelazine], triflupromazine [e.g., Vesprin], trimeprazine [e.g., Temaril]) or
- Plicamycin (e.g., Mithracin) or
- Valproic acid (e.g., Depakene)—These medicines may increase the chance of liver damage if taken with isoniazid
- Carbamazepine (e.g., Tegretol) or
- Phenytoin (e.g., Dilantin)—These medicines may increase the chance of liver damage if taken with isoniazid. There may also be an increased chance of side effects of carbamazepine and phenytoin
- Disulfiram (e.g., Antabuse)—This medicine may increase the chance of liver damage and side effects, such as dizziness, lack of coordination, irritability, and trouble in sleeping
- Ketoconazole (e.g., Nizoral) or
- Rifampin (e.g., Rifadin)—Use of these medicines with isoniazid can lower the blood levels of ketoconazole or rifampin, decreasing their effects

Other medical problems—The presence of other medical problems may affect the use of isoniazid. Make sure you tell your doctor if you have any other medical problems, especially:

- Alcohol abuse (or history of) or
- Liver disease—There may be an increased chance of hepatitis with daily drinking of alcohol or in patients with liver disease
- Kidney disease (severe)—There may be an increased chance of side effects in patients with severe kidney disease
- Seizure disorders such as epilepsy—There may be an increased chance of seizures (convulsions) in some patients

Proper Use of This Medicine

If you are taking isoniazid by mouth and it upsets your stomach, take it with food. Antacids may also help. However, do not take aluminum-containing antacids within 1 hour of taking isoniazid. They may keep this medicine from working properly.

For patients taking the *oral liquid form* of isoniazid:

- Use a specially marked measuring spoon or other device to measure each dose accurately. The average household teaspoon may not hold the right amount of liquid.

To help clear up your tuberculosis (TB) completely, *it is very important that you keep taking this medicine for the full time of treatment,* even if you begin to feel better after a few weeks. You may have to take it every day for as long as 6 months to 2 years. *It is important that you do not miss any doses.*

Your doctor may also want you to take pyridoxine (e.g., Hexa-Betalin, vitamin B_6) every day to help prevent or lessen some of the side effects of isoniazid. This is not usually needed in children, who receive enough pyridoxine in their diet. If it is needed, *it is very important to take pyridoxine every day along with this medicine. Do not miss any doses.*

Dosing—The dose of isoniazid will be different for different patients. *Follow your doctor's orders or the directions on the label.* The following information includes only the average doses of isoniazid. *If your dose is different, do not change it* unless your doctor tells you to do so.

The number of tablets or teaspoonfuls of syrup that you take depends on the strength of the medicine.

- For *oral* dosage forms (tablets, syrup):
  - —For prevention of tuberculosis:
    - Adults and teenagers—300 milligrams (mg) once a day.
    - Children—Dose is based on body weight. The usual dose is 10 mg per kilogram (kg) (4.5 mg per pound) of body weight, up to 300 mg, once a day.
  - —For treatment of tuberculosis:
    - Adults and teenagers—300 mg once a day; or 15 mg per kg (6.8 mg per pound) of body weight, up to 900 mg, two times a week or three times a week, depending on the schedule your doctor chooses for you.
    - Children—Dose is based on body weight. The usual dose is 10 to 20 mg per kg (4.5 to 9.1 mg per pound) of body weight, up to 300 mg, once a day; or 20 to 40 mg per kg (9.1 to 18.2 mg per pound) of body weight, up to 900 mg, two times a week or three times a week, depending on the schedule your doctor chooses for you.
- For *injection* dosage form:
  - —For prevention of tuberculosis:
    - Adults and teenagers—300 mg once a day.

- Children—Dose is based on body weight. The usual dose is 10 mg per kg (4.5 mg per pound) of body weight, up to 300 mg, once a day.

—For treatment of tuberculosis:

- Adults and teenagers—300 mg once a day; or 15 mg per kg (6.8 mg per pound) of body weight, up to 900 mg, two times a week or three times a week, depending on the schedule your doctor chooses for you.
- Children—Dose is based on body weight. The usual dose is 10 to 20 mg per kg (4.5 to 9.1 mg per pound) of body weight, up to 300 mg, once a day; or 20 to 40 mg per kg (9.1 to 18.2 mg per pound) of body weight, up to 900 mg, two times a week or three times a week, depending on the schedule your doctor chooses for you.

Missed dose—If you miss a dose of this medicine, take it as soon as possible. However, if it is almost time for your next dose, skip the missed dose and go back to your regular dosing schedule. Do not double doses.

Storage—To store this medicine:

- Keep out of the reach of children.
- Store away from heat and direct light.
- Do not store the tablet form of this medicine in the bathroom, near the kitchen sink, or in other damp places. Heat or moisture may cause the medicine to break down.
- Keep the oral liquid form of this medicine from freezing.
- Do not keep outdated medicine or medicine no longer needed. Be sure that any discarded medicine is out of the reach of children.

Precautions While Using This Medicine

It is very important that your doctor check your progress at regular visits. Also, check with your doctor immediately if blurred vision or loss of vision, with or without eye pain, occurs during treatment. Your doctor may want you to have your eyes checked by an ophthalmologist (eye doctor).

If your symptoms do not improve within 2 to 3 weeks, or if they become worse, check with your doctor.

Certain foods such as cheese (Swiss or Cheshire) or fish (tuna, skipjack, or Sardinella) may rarely cause reactions in some patients taking isoniazid. Check with your doctor if redness or itching of the skin, hot feeling, fast or pounding heartbeat, sweating, chills or clammy feeling, headache, or lightheadedness occurs while you are taking this medicine.

Liver problems may be more likely to occur if you drink alcoholic beverages regularly while you are taking this medicine. Also, the regular use of alcohol may keep this medicine from working properly. Therefore, *you should strictly limit the amount of alcoholic beverages you drink while you are taking this medicine.*

If this medicine causes you to feel very tired or very weak; or causes clumsiness; unsteadiness; a loss of appetite; nausea; numbness, tingling, burning, or pain in the hands and feet; or vomiting, check with your doctor immediately. These may be early warning signs of more serious liver or nerve problems that could develop later.

For diabetic patients:

- *This medicine may cause false test results with some urine sugar tests.* Check with your doctor before changing your diet or the dosage of your diabetes medicine.

Side Effects of This Medicine

Along with its needed effects, a medicine may cause some unwanted effects. Although not all of these side effects may occur, if they do occur they may need medical attention.

Check with your doctor immediately if any of the following side effects occur:

More common

Clumsiness or unsteadiness; dark urine; loss of appetite; nausea or vomiting; numbness, tingling, burning, or pain in hands and feet; unusual tiredness or weakness; yellow eyes or skin

Rare

Blurred vision or loss of vision, with or without eye pain; convulsions (seizures); fever and sore throat; joint pain; mental depression; mood or other mental changes; skin rash; unusual bleeding or bruising

Other side effects may occur that usually do not need medical attention. These side effects may go away during treatment as your body adjusts to the medicine. However, check with your doctor if any of the following side effects continue or are bothersome:

More common

Diarrhea; stomach pain

For injection form

Irritation at the place of injection

Dark urine and yellowing of the eyes or skin (signs of liver problems) are more likely to occur in patients over 50 years of age.

Other side effects not listed above may also occur in some patients. If you notice any other effects, check with your doctor.

Revised: 08/15/97

ISOPROTERENOL AND PHENYLEPHRINE Inhalation†

A commonly used brand name in the U.S. is Duo-Medihaler.

†Not commercially available in Canada.

Description

Isoproterenol (eye-soe-proe-TER-e-nole) and phenylephrine (fen-ill-EF-rin) combination medicine is used to treat asthma, bronchitis, or emphysema. It is used by oral inhalation (breathed in through the mouth) to open up the bronchial tubes (air passages) of the lungs.

This medicine is available only with your doctor's prescription, in the following dosage form:

Inhalation
- Inhalation aerosol (U.S.)

Before Using This Medicine

In deciding to use a medicine, the risks of taking the medicine must be weighed against the good it will do. This is a decision you and your doctor will make. For isoproterenol and phenylephrine combination, the following should be considered:

Allergies—Tell your doctor if you have ever had any unusual or allergic reaction to isoproterenol and phenylephrine or to medicines like them, such as amphetamines, ephedrine, epinephrine, metaproterenol, norepinephrine, phenylpropanolamine, pseudoephedrine, or terbutaline, or to other inhalation aerosol medicines.

Pregnancy—Studies on effects in pregnancy with isoproterenol and phenylephrine have not been done in humans. However, use of phenylephrine during late pregnancy or during labor may cause a lack of oxygen and slow heartbeat in the fetus. Use of phenylephrine should be avoided during pregnancy.

Breast-feeding—It is not known whether isoproterenol and phenylephrine pass into the breast milk. Although most medicines pass into breast milk in small amounts, many of them may be used safely while breast-feeding. Mothers who are using this medicine and who wish to breast-feed should discuss this with their doctor.

Children—Studies on isoproterenol and phenylephrine combination have been done only in adult patients, and there is no specific information comparing use of isoproterenol and phenylephrine combination in children with use in other age groups. Use of this medicine in children up to 12 years of age is not recommended.

Older adults—Many medicines have not been studied specifically in older people. Therefore, it may not be known whether they work exactly the same way they do in younger adults or if they cause different side effects or problems in older people. There is no specific information comparing use of isoproterenol and phenylephrine combination in the elderly with use in other age groups.

Other medicines—Although certain medicines should not be used together at all, in other cases two different medicines may be used together even if an interaction might occur. In these cases, your doctor may want to change the dose, or other precautions may be necessary. When you are taking isoproterenol and phenylephrine combination, it is especially important that your health care professional know if you are taking any of the following:

- Beta-blockers, including those used in the eyes (acebutolol [e.g., Sectral], atenolol [e.g., Tenormin], betaxolol [e.g., Betoptic, Kerlone], bisoprolol [e.g., Zebeta], carteolol [e.g., Cartrol], labetalol [e.g., Normodyne], levobunolol [e.g., Betagan], metipranolol [e.g., OptiPranolol], metoprolol [e.g., Lopressor], nadolol [e.g., Corgard], oxprenolol [e.g., Trasicor], penbutolol [e.g., Levatol], pindolol [e.g., Visken], propranolol [e.g., Inderal], sotalol [e.g., Sotacor], timolol [e.g., Blocadren, Timoptic])—Taking these medicines with isoproterenol and phenylephrine combination may prevent either medicine from working properly

Other medical problems—The presence of other medical problems may affect the use of isoproterenol and phenylephrine combination. Make sure you tell your doctor if you have any other medical problems, especially:

- Heart disease or
- High blood pressure—Isoproterenol and phenylephrine combination may make these conditions worse
- Overactive thyroid—The chance of side effects may be increased in patients with this condition

Proper Use of This Medicine

This medicine usually comes with patient directions. Read them carefully before using this medicine.

Keep spray away from the eyes.

Shake well before use.

Use 1 inhalation (puff) of this medicine, unless otherwise directed by your doctor. Wait 2 to 5 minutes after the first inhalation to see if you need to use a second inhalation.

Save your applicator. Refill units of this medicine may be available.

Use this medicine only as directed. Do not use more of it and do not use it more often than your doctor ordered. Using the medicine more often may increase the chance of serious side effects.

Dosing—The dose of isoproterenol and phenylephrine combination will be different for different patients. *Follow your doctor's orders or the directions on the label.* The following information includes only the average doses of isoproterenol and phenylephrine combination. *If your dose is different, do not change it* unless your doctor tells you to do so.

- For *inhalation aerosol* dosage form:
  - —For symptoms of asthma, bronchitis, or emphysema:
    - Adults and children 12 years of age and older—One inhalation, repeated after two to five minutes if necessary, four to six times a day.
    - Children up to 12 years of age—Use is not recommended.

Storage—To store this medicine:
- Keep out of the reach of children.
- Store away from heat and direct sunlight.
- Do not puncture, break, or burn container, even if it is empty.
- Do not keep outdated medicine or medicine no longer needed. Be sure that any discarded medicine is out of the reach of children.

Precautions While Using This Medicine

If you still have trouble breathing after using this medicine, or if your condition becomes worse, check with your doctor at once.

Side Effects of This Medicine

Along with its needed effects, a medicine may cause some unwanted effects. Although not all of these side effects may occur, if they do occur they may need medical attention.

Check with your doctor as soon as possible if any of the following side effects occur:

Rare
Chest pain; irregular heartbeat

Symptoms of overdose
Chest pain (continuing); dizziness or lightheadedness (continuing); fast, slow, or pounding heartbeat (continuing); headache (continuing); irregular heartbeat (continuing); nausea or vomiting (continuing); unusual restlessness; weakness (severe)

Other side effects may occur that usually do not need medical attention. These side effects may go away during treatment as your body adjusts to the medicine. However, check with your doctor if any of the following side effects continue or are bothersome:

More common
Nervousness; restlessness; trouble in sleeping

Less common
Dizziness or lightheadedness; fast or pounding heartbeat; flushing or redness of face or skin; headache; increased sweating; nausea or vomiting; trembling; weakness

This medicine may cause the saliva to turn pinkish to red in color. This is to be expected while you are using this medicine.

Other side effects not listed above may also occur in some patients. If you notice any other effects, check with your doctor.

Revised: 02/18/97
Interim revision: 04/08/97

ISOTRETINOIN Systemic

Some commonly used brand names are:

In the U.S.—
Accutane

In Canada—
Accutane Roche

Description

Isotretinoin (eye-soe-TRET-i-noyn) is used to treat severe, disfiguring nodular acne. It should be used only after other acne medicines have been tried and have failed to help the acne. Isotretinoin may also be used to treat other skin diseases as determined by your doctor.

Isotretinoin must not be used to treat women who are able to bear children unless other forms of treatment have been tried first and have failed. Isotretinoin must not be taken during pregnancy, because it causes birth defects in humans. If you are able to bear children, it is very important that you read, understand, and follow the pregnancy warnings for isotretinoin.

This medicine is available only with your doctor's prescription and should be prescribed only by a doctor who has special knowledge in the diagnosis and treatment of severe, uncontrollable cystic acne.

Isotretinoin is available in the following dosage form:

Oral
- Capsules (U.S. and Canada)

Before Using This Medicine

Isotretinoin comes with patient information. It is very important that you read and understand this information. Be sure to ask your doctor about anything you do not understand.

In deciding to use a medicine, the risks of taking the medicine must be weighed against the good it will do. This is a decision you and your doctor will make. For isotretinoin, the following should be considered:

Allergies—Tell your doctor if you have ever had any unusual or allergic reaction to isotretinoin, etretinate, tretinoin, or vitamin A preparations. Also tell your health care professional if you are allergic to any other substances, such as foods, preservatives, or dyes.

Pregnancy—*Isotretinoin must not be taken during pregnancy, because it causes birth defects in humans. In addition, isotretinoin must not be taken if there is a chance that you may become pregnant during treatment or within one month following treatment.* Women who are able to have children must have a pregnancy blood test within 2 weeks before beginning treatment with isotretinoin to make sure they are not pregnant. Treatment with isotretinoin will then be started on the second or third day of the woman's next normal menstrual period. In addition, you must have a pregnancy blood test each month while you are taking this medicine and one month after treatment is completed. Also, *isotretinoin must not be taken unless* *an effective form of contraception (birth control) has been used for at least 1 month before the beginning of treatment. Contraception must be continued during the period of treatment, which is up to 20 weeks, and for 1 month after isotretinoin is stopped. Be sure you have discussed this information with your doctor. In addition, you will be asked to sign an informed consent form stating that you understand the above information.*

Breast-feeding—It is not known whether isotretinoin passes into the breast milk. However, isotretinoin is not recommended during breast-feeding, because it may cause unwanted effects in nursing babies.

Children—Children may be especially sensitive to the effects of isotretinoin. This may increase the chance of side effects during treatment.

Older adults—Many medicines have not been studied specifically in older people. Therefore, it may not be known whether they work exactly the same way they do in younger adults or if they cause different side effects or problems in older people. There is no specific information comparing use of isotretinoin in the elderly with use in other age groups.

Other medicines—Although certain medicines should not be used together at all, in other cases two different medicines may be used together even if an interaction might occur. In these cases, your doctor may want to change the dose, or other precautions may be necessary. When you are using isotretinoin, it is especially important that your health care professional know if you are using any of the following:

- Etretinate (e.g., Tegison) or
- Tretinoin (vitamin A acid) (e.g., Retin-A) or
- Vitamin A or any preparation containing vitamin A—Use of isotretinoin with these medicines will result in an increase in side effects
- Tetracyclines (medicine for infection)—Use of isotretinoin with these medicines may increase the chance of a side effect called pseudotumor cerebri, which is a swelling of the brain

Other medical problems—The presence of other medical problems may affect the use of isotretinoin. Make sure you tell your doctor if you have any other medical problems, especially:

- Alcoholism or excess use of alcohol (or history of) or
- Diabetes mellitus (sugar diabetes) (or a family history of) or
- Family history of high triglyceride (a fat-like substance) levels in the blood or
- Severe weight problems—Use of isotretinoin may increase blood levels of triglyceride (a fat-like substance), which may increase the chance of heart or blood vessel problems in patients who have a family history of high triglycerides, are greatly overweight, are diabetic, or use a lot of alcohol. For persons with diabetes mellitus, use of isotretinoin may also change blood sugar levels

Proper Use of This Medicine

It is very important that you take isotretinoin only as directed. Do not take more of it, do not take it more often, and do not take it for a longer time than your doctor ordered. To do so may increase the chance of side effects.

Dosing—The dose of isotretinoin will be different for different patients. *Follow your doctor's orders or the directions on the label.* The following information includes only the average doses of isotretinoin. *If your dose is different, do not change it* unless your doctor tells you to do so.

The number of capsules that you take depends on the strength of the medicine. Also, *the number of doses you take each day, the time allowed between doses, and the length of time you take the medicine depend on the medical problem for which you are taking isotretinoin.*

- For *oral* dosage form (capsules):
  - —For acne:
    - Adults and teenagers—Dose is based on body weight and must be determined by your doctor. The usual dose is 0.5 to 1 milligram (mg) per kilogram (kg) (0.23 to 0.45 mg per pound) of body weight a day, divided into two doses.
    - Children—Use is usually not recommended.

Missed dose—If you miss a dose of this medicine, take it as soon as possible. However, if it is almost time for your next dose, skip the missed dose and go back to your regular dosing schedule. Do not double doses.

Storage—To store this medicine:

- Keep out of the reach of children.
- Store away from heat and direct light.
- Do not store in the bathroom, near the kitchen sink, or in other damp places. Heat or moisture may cause the medicine to break down.
- Do not keep outdated medicine or medicine no longer needed. Be sure that any discarded medicine is out of the reach of children.

Precautions While Using This Medicine

Your doctor should check your progress at regular visits to make sure this medicine does not cause unwanted effects.

Isotretinoin causes birth defects in humans if taken during pregnancy. Therefore, if you suspect that you may have become pregnant, stop taking this medicine immediately and check with your doctor.

Do not donate blood to a blood bank while you are taking isotretinoin or for 30 days after you stop taking it. This is to prevent the possibility of a pregnant patient receiving the blood.

Do not take vitamin A or any vitamin supplement containing vitamin A while taking this medicine, unless otherwise directed by your doctor. To do so may increase the chance of side effects.

Drinking too much alcohol while taking this medicine may cause high triglyceride (fat-like substance) levels in the blood and possibly increase the chance of unwanted effects on the heart and blood vessels. Therefore, *while taking this medicine, it is best that you do not drink alcoholic beverages or that you at least reduce the amount you usually drink.* If you have any questions about this, check with your doctor.

For diabetic patients:
- This medicine may affect blood sugar levels. If you notice a change in the results of your blood or urine sugar tests or if you have any questions, check with your doctor.

In some patients, isotretinoin may cause a decrease in night vision. This decrease may occur suddenly. If it does occur, *do not drive, use machines, or do anything else that could be dangerous if you are not able to see well.* Also, check with your doctor.

Isotretinoin may cause dryness of the eyes. Therefore, if you wear contact lenses, your eyes may be more sensitive to them during the time you are taking isotretinoin and for up to about 2 weeks after you stop taking it. To help relieve dryness of the eyes, check with your doctor about using an eye lubricating solution, such as artificial tears. If eye inflammation occurs, check with your doctor.

Some people who take this medicine may become more sensitive to sunlight than they are normally. When you first begin taking this medicine, avoid too much sun and do not use a sunlamp until you see how you react to the sun, especially if you tend to burn easily. If you have a severe reaction, check with your doctor.

Isotretinoin may cause dryness of the mouth and nose. For temporary relief of mouth dryness, use sugarless candy or gum, melt bits of ice in your mouth, or use a saliva substitute. However, if dry mouth continues for more than 2 weeks, check with your medical doctor or dentist. Continuing dryness of the mouth may increase the chance of dental disease, including tooth decay, gum disease, and fungus infections.

For patients taking isotretinoin for acne:
- When you begin taking isotretinoin, your acne may seem to get worse before it gets better. If irritation or other symptoms of your condition become severe, check with your doctor.

Side Effects of This Medicine

Along with its needed effects, a medicine may cause some unwanted effects. Although not all of these side effects may occur, if they do occur they may need medical attention.

Check with your doctor as soon as possible if any of the following side effects occur:

More common

Burning, redness, itching, or other sign of eye inflammation; nosebleeds; scaling, redness, burning, pain, or other sign of inflammation of lips

Less common

Mental depression; skin infection or rash

Rare

Abdominal or stomach pain (severe); bleeding or inflammation of gums; blurred vision or other changes in vision; diarrhea (severe); headache (severe or continuing); mood changes; nausea and vomiting; pain or tenderness of eyes; rectal bleeding; yellow eyes or skin

Other side effects may occur that usually do not need medical attention. These side effects may go away during treatment as your body adjusts to the medicine. However, check with your doctor if any of the following side effects continue or are bothersome:

More common

Dryness of mouth or nose; dryness or itching of skin

Less common

Dryness of eyes; headache (mild); increased sensitivity of skin to sunlight; pain, tenderness, or stiffness in muscles, bones, or joints; peeling of skin on palms of hands or soles of feet; stomach upset; thinning of hair; unusual tiredness

Other side effects not listed above may also occur in some patients. If you notice any other effects, check with your doctor.

Revised: June 1990
Interim revision: 07/14/94

ISOXSUPRINE Systemic

A commonly used brand name in the U.S. and Canada is Vasodilan.

Generic name product may also be available in the U.S.

Description

Isoxsuprine (eye-SOX-syoo-preen) belongs to the group of medicines called vasodilators. Vasodilators increase the size of blood vessels. Isoxsuprine is used to treat problems resulting from poor blood circulation.

It may also be used for other conditions as determined by your doctor.

Isoxsuprine is available only with your doctor's prescription, in the following dosage forms:

Oral
- Tablets (U.S. and Canada)

Parenteral
- Injection (Canada)

Before Using This Medicine

In deciding to use a medicine, the risks of taking the medicine must be weighed against the good it will do. This is a decision you and your doctor will make. For isoxsuprine, the following should be considered:

Allergies—Tell your doctor if you have ever had any unusual or allergic reaction to isoxsuprine. Also tell your health care professional if you are allergic to any other substances, such as foods, preservatives, or dyes.

Pregnancy—Isoxsuprine has not been shown to cause birth defects in humans. However, isoxsuprine given shortly before delivery may cause fast heartbeat and other problems (low blood sugar, bowel problems, low blood pressure) in the newborn.

Breast-feeding—Isoxsuprine has not been reported to cause problems in nursing babies.

Older adults—Many medicines have not been studied specifically in older people. Therefore, it may not be known whether they work exactly the same way they do in younger adults or if they cause different side effects or problems in older people. There is no specific information comparing use of isoxsuprine in the elderly with use in other age groups. However, isoxsuprine may reduce tolerance to cold temperatures in elderly patients.

Other medicines—Although certain medicines should not be used together at all, in other cases two different medicines may be used together even if an interaction might occur. In these cases, your doctor may want to change the dose, or other precautions may be necessary. Tell your health care professional if you are taking any other prescription or nonprescription (over-the-counter [OTC]) medicine, or if you smoke.

Other medical problems—The presence of other medical problems may affect the use of isoxsuprine. Make sure you tell your doctor if you have any other medical problems, especially:

- Angina (chest pain) or
- Bleeding problems or
- Glaucoma or
- Hardening of the arteries or
- Heart attack (recent) or
- Stroke (recent)—The chance of side effects may be increased

Proper Use of This Medicine

If this medicine upsets your stomach, it may be taken with meals, milk, or antacids.

Dosing—The dose of isoxsuprine will be different for different patients. *Follow your doctor's orders or the directions on the label.* The following information includes only the average doses of isoxsuprine. *If your dose is different, do not change it* unless your doctor tells you to do so.

The number of tablets that you take depends on the strength of the medicine.

- For *oral* dosage form (tablets):
  - —For poor blood circulation:
    - Adults—10 to 20 milligrams (mg) three or four times a day.

Missed dose—If you miss a dose of this medicine, take it as soon as possible. However, if it is almost time for your next dose, skip the missed dose and go back to your regular dosing schedule. Do not double doses.

Storage—To store this medicine:

- Keep out of the reach of children.
- Store away from heat and direct light.
- Do not store in the bathroom, near the kitchen sink, or in other damp places. Heat or moisture may cause the medicine to break down.
- Do not keep outdated medicine or medicine no longer needed. Be sure that any discarded medicine is out of the reach of children.

Precautions While Using This Medicine

It may take some time for this medicine to work. If you feel that the medicine is not working, do not stop taking it on your own. Instead, check with your doctor.

The helpful effects of this medicine may be decreased if you smoke. If you have any questions about this, check with your doctor.

Dizziness may occur, especially when you get up from a lying or sitting position or climb stairs. Getting up slowly may help. If this problem continues or gets worse, check with your doctor.

Side Effects of This Medicine

Along with its needed effects, a medicine may cause some unwanted effects. Although not all of these side effects may occur, if they do occur they may need medical attention.

Check with your doctor as soon as possible if any of the following side effects occur:

Rare

Chest pain; dizziness or faintness (more common for injection); fast heartbeat (more common for injection); shortness of breath; skin rash

Other side effects may occur that usually do not need medical attention. These side effects may go away during treatment as your body adjusts to the medicine. However, check with your doctor if the following side effects continue or are bothersome:

Less common

Nausea or vomiting (more common for injection)

Other side effects not listed above may also occur in some patients. If you notice any other effects, check with your doctor.

Additional Information

Although this use is not included in U.S. product labeling, isoxsuprine is used in certain women to stop premature labor.

In addition to the above information, the following information applies when this medicine is used to stop premature labor:

- Before you begin treatment with this medicine, tell your doctor if you have any of the following medical problems:
  Asthma
  Diabetes mellitus (sugar diabetes)
  Heart disease
  High blood pressure
  Overactive thyroid
- *Check with your doctor immediately:*
  —if your contractions begin again or your water breaks.
  —if you notice chest pain or shortness of breath while taking isoxsuprine.

Revised: 07/06/92
Interim revision: 07/15/94

JAPANESE ENCEPHALITIS VIRUS VACCINE Systemic

A commonly used brand name in the U.S. and Canada is Je-Vax.

Description

Japanese encephalitis (in-cef-a-LY-tis) virus vaccine is an immunizing agent used to help prevent infection by the Japanese encephalitis virus. Japanese encephalitis is caused by the bite of a mosquito that lives in certain parts of Asia. The vaccine works by causing your body to produce its own protection (antibodies) against the virus.

This vaccine is available only from your doctor or other authorized health care professional, in the following dosage form:

Parenteral
- Injection (U.S. and Canada)

Before Receiving This Vaccine

In deciding to use a medicine, the risks of receiving the medicine must be weighed against the good it will do. This is a decision you and your doctor will make. For Japanese encephalitis virus vaccine, the following should be considered:

Allergies—Tell your doctor if you have ever had any unusual or allergic reaction to thimerosal, formaldehyde, gelatin, or rodent protein or brain products. Also tell your health care professional if you are allergic to any other substances, such as foods, preservatives, or dyes.

Pregnancy—Studies on effects in pregnancy have not been done in either humans or animals.

Breast-feeding—It is not known whether this vaccine passes into breast milk. Although most medicines pass into breast milk in small amounts, many of them may be used safely while breast-feeding. Mothers who are receiving this vaccine and who wish to breast-feed should discuss this with their doctor.

Children—Studies on this vaccine have been done only in adults and children 1 year of age and older. There is no specific information comparing use of this vaccine in infants under 1 year of age with use in other age groups.

Older adults—Many medicines have not been studied specifically in older people. Therefore, it may not be known whether they work exactly the same way they do in younger adults. Although there is no specific information comparing use of Japanese encephalitis virus vaccine in the elderly with use in other age groups, this vaccine is not expected to cause different side effects or problems in older people than it does in younger adults. In addition, immunization may be especially useful for the elderly, since older persons may have a higher risk of illness following infection with the Japanese encephalitis virus.

Other medical problems—The presence of other medical problems may affect the use of this vaccine. Make sure you tell your doctor if you have any other medical problems, especially:

- Hives (history of)—May increase the chance of side effects of the vaccine

Proper Use of This Vaccine

It is important that you receive 3 doses of the vaccine. If there is not enough time for you to get all 3 doses, you may get 2 doses of the vaccine. However, *2 doses of the vaccine will not protect you as well as 3 doses.*

It is important that you receive all 3 doses of the vaccine at least 10 days before you plan on traveling out of the country. There is a chance of side effects that do not show up right away, and, if they do occur, they may need medical attention. In addition, the 10 days will give your body time to produce antibodies against the Japanese encephalitis virus.

Dosing—The number of doses you receive and the time allowed between doses of Japanese encephalitis virus vaccine will be different for different patients.

- For help preventing Japanese encephalitis:
  —For *injection* dosage form:
    - Adults and children 1 year of age and older—One dose injected under the skin on days zero, seven, and thirty, for a total of three doses.
    - Children up to 1 year of age—Use and dose must be determined by your doctor.

Precautions After Receiving This Vaccine

Since the vaccine may not protect everyone completely, *it is very important that you still use precautions to reduce your chance of mosquito bites.* These include using insect repellents and mosquito netting, wearing protective clothing, and staying indoors during twilight and after dark.

Side Effects of This Vaccine

Along with its needed effects, a medicine may cause some unwanted effects. Although not all of these side effects may occur, if they do occur they may need medical attention. *It is very important that you tell your doctor about any side effect that occurs after a dose of the vaccine,* even if the side effect goes away without treatment. Some types of side effects may mean that you should not receive any more doses of the vaccine.

Get emergency help immediately if the following side effect occurs:

Rare
Swelling of face, lips, eyelids, throat, tongue, hands, or feet

Check with your doctor immediately if any of the following side effects occur:

Rare
Hives; tiredness or weakness (severe or unusual); wheezing or troubled breathing

Although the following side effects usually do not need medical attention and may go away on their own, *their presence may also mean that more serious side effects are about to occur*. Therefore, check with your doctor as soon as possible if any of the following side effects occur:

More common

Tenderness, soreness, redness, or swelling at place of injection

Less common

Abdominal pain; aches or pains in muscles; chills or fever; dizziness; general feeling of discomfort or illness; headache; itching or skin rash; nausea or vomiting

Rare

Joint swelling

Other side effects not listed above may also occur in some patients. If you notice any other effects, check with your doctor.

Revised: 06/21/93
Interim revision: 06/27/95

KANAMYCIN Oral†

A commonly used brand name in the U.S. is Kantrex.

†Not commercially available in Canada.

Description

Oral kanamycin (kan-a-MYE-sin) belongs to the family of medicines called antibiotics. It is used before surgery affecting the bowel to help prevent infection during surgery.

Kanamycin is available only with your doctor's prescription, in the following dosage form:

Oral

- Capsules (U.S.)

Before Using This Medicine

In deciding to use a medicine, the risks of taking the medicine must be weighed against the good it will do. This is a decision you and your doctor will make. For oral kanamycin, the following should be considered:

Allergies—Tell your doctor if you have ever had any unusual or allergic reaction to oral kanamycin or to any related antibiotics such as amikacin (e.g., Amikin), gentamicin (e.g., Garamycin), kanamycin by injection (e.g., Kantrex), neomycin (e.g., Mycifradin), netilmicin (e.g., Netromycin), streptomycin, or tobramycin (e.g., Nebcin). Also tell your health care professional if you are allergic to any other substances, such as foods, preservatives, or dyes.

Pregnancy—Oral kanamycin has not been reported to cause birth defects or other problems in humans.

Breast-feeding—Oral kanamycin has not been reported to cause problems in nursing babies.

Children—Although there is no specific information comparing use of oral kanamycin in children with use in other age groups, this medicine is not expected to cause different side effects or problems in children than it does in adults.

Older adults—Many medicines have not been studied specifically in older people. Therefore, it may not be known whether they work exactly the same way they do in younger adults or if they cause different side effects or problems in older people. There is no specific information comparing use of oral kanamycin in the elderly with use in other age groups.

Other medicines—Although certain medicines should not be used together at all, in other cases two different medicines may be used together even if an interaction might occur. In these cases, your doctor may want to change the dose, or other precautions may be necessary. Tell your health care professional if you are taking any other prescription or nonprescription (over-the-counter [OTC]) medicine.

Other medical problems—The presence of other medical problems may affect the use of oral kanamycin. Make sure you tell your doctor if you have any other medical problems, especially:

- Blockage of the bowel—Oral kanamycin should never be used in patients who have a blockage of the bowel
- Eighth-cranial-nerve disease (loss of hearing and/or balance)—Use of oral kanamycin may increase problems related to hearing and/or balance
- Kidney disease or
- Ulcers of the bowel—Use of kanamycin in patients with either condition may cause an increase in side effects

Proper Use of This Medicine

This medicine may be taken on a full or empty stomach.

Keep taking this medicine for the full time of treatment. Do not miss any doses.

Dosing—The dose of oral kanamycin will be different for different patients. *Follow your doctor's orders or the directions on the label.* The following information includes only the average doses of oral kanamycin. *If your dose is different, do not change it* unless your doctor tells you to do so.

- For *oral* dosage form (capsule):
  - —For patients in a coma from liver disease:
    - Adults and children—2 to 3 grams every six hours.
  - —For cleaning the bowel before surgery:
    - Adults and children—1 gram every hour for four hours; then, 1 gram every six hours for thirty-six to seventy-two hours.

Missed dose—For patients taking *oral kanamycin before any surgery affecting the bowel:*

- If you miss a dose of this medicine, take it as soon as possible. However, if it is almost time for your next dose, skip the missed dose and go back to your regular dosing schedule. Do not double doses.

Storage—To store this medicine:

- Keep out of the reach of children.
- Store away from heat and direct light.
- Do not store in the bathroom, near the kitchen sink, or in other damp places. Heat and moisture may cause the medicine to break down.
- Do not keep outdated medicine or medicine no longer needed. Be sure that any discarded medicine is out of the reach of children.

Side Effects of This Medicine

Along with its needed effects, a medicine may cause some unwanted effects. Although not all of these side effects may occur, if they do occur they may need medical attention.

Check with your doctor immediately if any of the following side effects occur:

Rare—with long-term use and high doses

Any loss of hearing; clumsiness; dizziness; greatly decreased frequency of urination or amount of urine; increased thirst; ringing or buzzing or a feeling of fullness in the ears; unsteadiness

Other side effects may occur that usually do not need medical attention. These side effects may go away during treatment as your body adjusts to the medicine. However, check with your doctor if any of the following side effects continue or are bothersome:

More common

Diarrhea; nausea or vomiting

Rare—with prolonged treatment

Increased amount of gas; light-colored, frothy, fatty-appearing stools

Other side effects not listed above may also occur in some patients. If you notice any other effects, check with your doctor.

Revised: 09/08/92
Interim revision: 03/17/94

KAOLIN AND PECTIN Oral

Some commonly used brand names are:

In the U.S.—

Kao-Spen
Kapectolin
K-P

Generic product may also be available.

In Canada—

Donnagel-MB

Description

Kaolin (KAY-oh-lin) and pectin (PEK-tin) combination medicine is used to treat diarrhea.

Kaolin is a clay-like powder believed to work by attracting and holding onto the bacteria or germ that may be causing the diarrhea.

This medicine is available without a prescription; however, the product's directions and warnings should be carefully followed. In addition, your doctor may have special instructions on the proper dose or use of kaolin and pectin combination medicine for your medical condition. Kaolin and pectin combination is available in the following dosage form:

Oral

- Oral suspension (U.S. and Canada)

Before Using This Medicine

If you are taking this medicine without a prescription, carefully read and follow any precautions on the label. For kaolin and pectin combination, the following should be considered:

Pregnancy—This medicine is not absorbed into the body and is not likely to cause problems.

Breast-feeding—This medicine is not absorbed into the body and is not likely to cause problems.

Children—The fluid loss caused by diarrhea may result in a severe condition. For this reason, antidiarrheals must not be given to young children (under 3 years of age) without first checking with their doctor. In older children with diarrhea, antidiarrheals may be used, but it is also very important that a sufficient amount of liquids be given to replace the fluid lost by the body. If you have any questions about this, check with your health care professional.

Older adults—The fluid loss caused by diarrhea may result in a severe condition. For this reason, elderly persons with diarrhea, in addition to using an antidiarrheal, must receive a sufficient amount of liquids to replace the fluid lost by the body. If you have any questions about this, check with your health care professional.

Other medicines—Although certain medicines should not be used together at all, in other cases two different medicines may be used together even if an interaction might occur. In these cases, your doctor may want to change the dose, or other precautions may be necessary. Tell your health care professional if you are taking any other prescription or nonprescription (over-the-counter [OTC]) medicine.

Other medical problems—The presence of other medical problems may affect the use of kaolin and pectin. Make sure you tell your doctor if you have any other medical problems, especially:

- Dysentery—This condition may get worse; a different kind of treatment may be needed

Proper Use of This Medicine

Do not use kaolin and pectin combination to treat your diarrhea if you have a fever or if there is blood or mucus in your stools. Contact your doctor.

Take this medicine, following the directions in the product package, after each loose bowel movement until the diarrhea is controlled, unless otherwise directed by your doctor.

Importance of diet and fluid intake while treating diarrhea:

- *In addition to using medicine for diarrhea, it is very important that you replace the fluid lost by the body and follow a proper diet.* For the first 24 hours you should eat gelatin and drink plenty of clear liquids, such as ginger ale, decaffeinated cola, decaffeinated tea, and broth. During the next 24 hours you may eat bland foods, such as cooked cereals, bread, crackers, and applesauce. Fruits, vegetables, fried or spicy foods, bran, candy, and caffeine and alcoholic beverages may make the condition worse.
- If too much fluid has been lost by the body due to the diarrhea, a serious condition may develop. Check

with your doctor as soon as possible if any of the following signs or symptoms of too much fluid loss occur:

Decreased urination
Dizziness and lightheadedness
Dryness of mouth
Increased thirst
Wrinkled skin

Dosing—The dose of kaolin and pectin combination will be different for different patients. *Follow your doctor's orders or the directions on the label.* The following information includes only the average doses of kaolin and pectin.

The number of tablespoonfuls of suspension that you take depends on the strength of the medicine.

- For diarrhea:
  - —For *oral* dosage form (suspension):
    - Adults—The usual dose is 4 to 8 tablespoonfuls (60 to 120 milliliters [mL]) taken after each loose bowel movement.
    - Children 12 years of age and over—The usual dose is 3 to 4 tablespoonfuls (45 to 60 mL) taken after each loose bowel movement.
    - Children 6 to 12 years of age—The usual dose is 2 to 4 tablespoonfuls (30 to 60 mL) taken after each loose bowel movement.
    - Children 3 to 6 years of age—The usual dose is 1 to 2 tablespoonfuls (15 to 30 mL) taken after each loose bowel movement.
    - Children up to 3 years of age—Use and dose must be determined by your doctor.

Storage—To store this medicine:

- Keep out of the reach of children.
- Store away from heat and direct light.
- Keep this medicine from freezing.
- Do not keep outdated medicine or medicine no longer needed. Be sure that any discarded medicine is out of the reach of children.

Precautions While Using This Medicine

Check with your doctor if your diarrhea does not stop after 1 or 2 days or if you develop a fever.

If you are taking any other medicine, do not take it within 2 to 3 hours of taking kaolin and pectin. Taking the medicines together may prevent the other medicine from being absorbed by your body. If you have any questions about this, check with your health care professional.

Side Effects of This Medicine

Along with its needed effects, a medicine may cause some unwanted effects. No serious side effects have been reported for this medicine. However, this medicine may cause constipation in some patients, especially if they take a lot of it. Check with your doctor as soon as possible if constipation continues or is bothersome.

Other side effects not listed above may also occur in some patients. If you notice any other effects, check with your doctor.

Revised: 08/04/94

KAOLIN, PECTIN, AND BELLADONNA ALKALOIDS Systemic*

A commonly used brand name in Canada is Donnagel.

*Not commercially available in the U.S.

Description

Kaolin (KAY-oh-lin), pectin (PEK-tin), and belladonna alkaloids (bell-a-DON-a AL-ka-loyds) combination medicine is used to treat diarrhea. However, it has generally been replaced by safer medicines for the treatment of diarrhea.

Kaolin, pectin, and belladonna alkaloids combination medicine is available only with your doctor's prescription, in the following dosage form:

Oral

- Oral suspension (Canada)

Before Using This Medicine

In deciding to use a medicine, the risks of taking the medicine must be weighed against the good it will do. This is a decision you and your doctor will make. For kaolin, pectin, and belladonna alkaloids combination medicine, the following should be considered:

Allergies—Tell your doctor if you have ever had any unusual or allergic reaction to any of the belladonna alkaloids (atropine, hyoscyamine, scopolamine) or to any related products. Also, tell your health care professional if you are allergic to any other substances, such as foods, preservatives, or dyes.

Pregnancy—This medicine has not been shown to cause birth defects or other problems in humans.

Breast-feeding—Although the belladonna alkaloids in this medicine pass into breast milk, this medicine has not been reported to cause problems in nursing babies.

Children—Children are especially sensitive to the effects of belladonna alkaloids. This may increase the chance of side effects during treatment. Also, the fluid loss caused by the diarrhea may result in a serious condition (dehydration), which may be hidden by the use of this medicine. For these reasons, do not give this medicine for diarrhea to young children (under 6 years of age) without first checking with their doctor. In older children with diarrhea, medicine for diarrhea may be used, but it is also very important that enough liquids be given to replace the fluid lost by the body. If you have any questions about this, check with your health care professional.

Older adults—Elderly people are especially sensitive to the effects of belladonna alkaloids. This may increase the chance of side effects during treatment. Also, the fluid loss caused by the diarrhea may result in a serious condition (dehydration), which may be hidden by the use of this medicine. For this reason, elderly persons should not take this medicine without first checking with their doctor. It is also very important that enough liquids be taken to replace the fluid lost by the body. If you have any questions about this, check with your health care professional.

Other medicines—Although certain medicines should not be used together at all, in other cases two different medicines may be used together even if an interaction might occur. In these cases, your doctor may want to change the dose, or other precautions may be necessary. When you are taking belladonna alkaloids (contained in this combination medicine), it is especially important that your health care professional know if you are taking any of the following:

- Central nervous system (CNS) depressants (medicine that causes drowsiness) or
- Tricyclic antidepressants (medicines for depression)—Effects of CNS depressants or of belladonna alkaloids, such as drowsiness, may become greater
- Ketoconazole [e.g., Nizoral]—Use of this medicine with ketoconazole may decrease the effectiveness of ketoconazole
- Monoamine oxidase (MAO) inhibitors (furazolidone [e.g., Furoxone], isocarboxazid [e.g., Marplan], phenelzine [e.g., Nardil], procarbazine [e.g., Matulane], selegiline [e.g., Eldepryl], tranylcypromine [e.g., Parnate])—Taking belladonna alkaloids while you are taking or within 2 weeks of taking MAO inhibitors may cause an increase in the effects of belladonna alkaloids
- Potassium chloride (e.g., Kay Ciel)—Use with belladonna alkaloids may worsen stomach and intestinal problems caused by potassium

Other medical problems—The presence of other medical problems may affect the use of this medicine. Make sure you tell your doctor if you have any other medical problems, especially:

- Brain damage (children) or
- Down's syndrome (mongolism) or
- Spastic paralysis (children)—The effects of belladonna alkaloids may be increased
- Colitis or other intestinal disease—A more serious condition may develop with the use of this medicine
- Difficult urination or
- Dryness of the mouth (severe and continuing) or
- Emphysema, asthma, bronchitis, or other chronic lung disease or
- Enlarged prostate or
- Glaucoma or
- Heart disease or
- Hiatal hernia—The belladonna alkaloids contained in this medicine may make these conditions worse
- Dysentery—This condition may get worse; a different kind of treatment may be needed
- Kidney disease or
- Liver disease—Higher blood levels of the belladonna alkaloids may result, increasing the chance of side effects

Proper Use of This Medicine

If this medicine upsets your stomach, you may take it with food.

Take this medicine only as directed on the label or as ordered by your doctor. Do not take more of it and do not take it for a longer time than directed. To do so may increase the chance of unwanted effects. This is especially important for children and elderly patients, who may be more sensitive to the effects of this medicine.

Use a specially marked measuring spoon or other device to measure each dose accurately. The average household teaspoon may not hold the right amount of liquid.

Importance of diet and fluids while treating diarrhea:

- *In addition to using medicine for diarrhea, it is very important that you replace the fluid lost by the body and follow a proper diet.* For the first 24 hours you should eat gelatin and drink plenty of caffeine-free clear liquids, such as ginger ale, decaffeinated cola, decaffeinated tea, and broth. During the next 24 hours you may eat bland foods, such as cooked cereals, bread, crackers, and applesauce. Fruits, vegetables, fried or spicy foods, bran, candy, caffeine, and alcoholic beverages may make the condition worse.
- If too much fluid has been lost by the body due to the diarrhea, a serious condition (dehydration) may develop. This condition may be hidden by the use of this medicine. Check with your doctor as soon as possible if any of the following signs of too much fluid loss occur:

  Decreased urination
  Dizziness and lightheadedness
  Dryness of mouth
  Increased thirst
  Wrinkled skin

Dosing—The dose of kaolin, pectin, and belladonna alkaloids combination medicine will be different for different patients. *Follow your doctor's orders or the directions on the label.* The following information includes only the average doses of kaolin, pectin, and belladonna alkaloids combination medicine. *If your dose is different, do not change it* unless your doctor tells you to do so.

- For *oral* dosage form (suspension):
  - —For diarrhea:
    - Adults and teenagers—Dose is usually 2 tablespoonfuls (30 milliliters [mL]) every three hours as needed. No more than four doses should be taken in twenty-four hours.
    - Children over 6 years of age—Dose is usually 1 or 2 teaspoonfuls (5 or 10 mL) every three hours as needed. No more than four doses should be taken in twenty-four hours.
    - Children up to 6 years of age—Use and dose must be determined by your doctor.

Storage—To store this medicine:
- Keep out of the reach of children since overdose is especially dangerous in children.
- Store away from heat and direct light.
- Keep this medicine from freezing.
- Do not keep outdated medicine or medicine no longer needed. Be sure that any discarded medicine is out of the reach of children.

Precautions While Using This Medicine

Check with your doctor if your diarrhea does not stop after 1 or 2 days or if you develop a fever.

Before you have any medical tests, tell the doctor in charge that you are taking this medicine. The results of some tests may be affected by this medicine.

This medicine will add to the effects of alcohol and other CNS depressants (medicines that make you drowsy or less alert). Some examples of CNS depressants are antihistamines or medicine for hay fever, other allergies, or colds; sedatives, tranquilizers, or sleeping medicine; prescription pain medicine or narcotics; barbiturates; medicine for seizures; muscle relaxants; or anesthetics, including some dental anesthetics. *Check with your doctor before taking any of the above while you are taking this medicine.*

This medicine may cause some people to become dizzy, drowsy, or less alert than they are normally. Even if taken at bedtime, it may cause some people to feel drowsy or less alert on arising. *Make sure you know how you react to this medicine before you drive, use machines, or do anything else that could be dangerous if you are dizzy or are not alert.*

This medicine may cause your eyes to become more sensitive to light than they are normally. Wearing sunglasses and avoiding too much exposure to bright light may help lessen the discomfort.

This medicine may make you sweat less, causing your body temperature to increase. *Use extra care not to become overheated during exercise or hot weather while you are taking this medicine,* since overheating may result in heatstroke. Also, hot baths or saunas may make you feel dizzy or faint while you are taking this medicine.

This medicine may cause dryness of the mouth, nose, and throat. For temporary relief, use sugarless candy or gum, melt bits of ice in your mouth, or use a saliva substitute. However, if your mouth continues to feel dry for more than 2 weeks, check with your medical doctor or dentist. Continuing dryness of the mouth may increase the chance of dental disease, including tooth decay, gum disease, and fungus infections.

Side Effects of This Medicine

Along with its needed effects, a medicine may cause some unwanted effects. Although not all of these side effects appear very often, when they do occur they may need medical attention.

Check with your doctor immediately if any of the following side effects are severe and occur suddenly since they may be signs of a more severe and dangerous problem with your bowels:

Rare

Bloating; constipation; loss of appetite; stomach pain (severe) with nausea and vomiting

Also, check with your doctor as soon as possible if the following effects occur:

Rare

Eye pain; hallucinations (seeing, hearing, or feeling things that are not there); shortness of breath; skin rash or itching; slow heartbeat; troubled breathing

Other side effects may occur that usually do not need medical attention. These side effects may go away during treatment as your body adjusts to the medicine. However, check with your doctor if any of the following side effects continue or are bothersome:

More common with large doses

Confusion; constipation; decreased sweating; difficult urination; dizziness; drowsiness; dryness of mouth, nose, throat, or skin; faintness; fast heartbeat; flushing or redness of face; headache; increased sweating; lightheadedness; loss of memory (especially in the elderly with continued use)

Less common

Blurred vision; decreased sexual ability; increased sensitivity of eyes to sunlight; nervousness; reduced sense of taste

Other side effects not listed above may also occur in some patients. If you notice any other effects, check with your doctor.

Revised: 04/27/95

KAOLIN, PECTIN, AND PAREGORIC Systemic*

A commonly used brand name in Canada is Donnagel-PG.

*Not commercially available in the U.S.

Description

Kaolin (KAY-oh-lin), pectin (PEK-tin), and paregoric (par-e-GOR-ik) combination medicine is used to treat diarrhea. However, it has generally been replaced by safer medicines for the treatment of diarrhea.

Kaolin, pectin, and paregoric combination medicine is available only with your doctor's prescription, in the following dosage form:

Oral
- Oral suspension (Canada)

Before Using This Medicine

In deciding to use a medicine, the risks of taking the medicine must be weighed against the good it will do. This is

a decision you and your doctor will make. For kaolin, pectin, and paregoric combination medicine, the following should be considered:

Allergies—Tell your doctor if you have ever had an unusual or allergic reaction to paregoric or any other narcotic medicine. Also, tell your health care professional if you are allergic to any other substances, such as foods, preservatives, or dyes.

Pregnancy—This medicine has not been shown to cause birth defects or other problems in humans. However, too much use of opium preparations such as paregoric (contained in this combination medicine) late in pregnancy may cause the baby to become dependent on the medicine. This may lead to withdrawal side effects after birth.

Breast-feeding—Although the paregoric in this medicine passes into breast milk, it has not been reported to cause problems in nursing babies.

Children—Children are especially sensitive to the effects of paregoric (contained in this combination medicine). This may increase the chance of side effects during treatment. Also, the fluid loss caused by the diarrhea may result in a severe condition (dehydration), which may be hidden by this medicine. For this reason, antidiarrheals must not be given to young children without first checking with their doctor. In older children with diarrhea, antidiarrheals may be used, but it is also very important that a sufficient amount of liquids be given to replace the fluid lost by the body. If you have any questions about this, check with your health care professional.

Older adults—Elderly people are especially sensitive to the effects of paregoric (contained in this combination medicine). This may increase the chance of side effects during treatment. Also, the fluid loss caused by the diarrhea may result in a severe condition (dehydration), which may be hidden by this medicine. For this reason, elderly persons should not take this medicine without first checking with their doctor. It is also very important that a sufficient amount of liquids be taken to replace the fluid lost by the body. If you have any questions about this, check with your health care professional.

Other medicines—Although certain medicines should not be used together at all, in other cases two different medicines may be used together even if an interaction might occur. In these cases, your doctor may want to change the dose, or other precautions may be necessary. When you are taking this medicine, it is especially important that your health care professional know if you are taking any of the following:

- Central nervous system (CNS) depressants—Effects of CNS depressants or of paregoric, such as drowsiness, may become greater
- Naloxone (e.g., Narcan) or
- Naltrexone (e.g., ReVia)—These medicines block the effect of paregoric and make it less effective in treating diarrhea
- Other diarrhea medicine—The chance of severe constipation may be increased

Other medical problems—The presence of other medical problems may affect the use of this medicine. Make sure you tell your doctor if you have any other medical problems, especially:

- Alcohol or drug abuse or dependence (history of)—There is a greater chance that this medicine may become habit-forming
- Brain disease or head injury or
- Emphysema, asthma, bronchitis, or other chronic lung disease or
- Enlarged prostate or problems with urination or
- Gallbladder disease or gallstones or
- Heart disease or
- Irregular heartbeat or
- Overflow incontinence or
- Seizures (convulsions) (history of)—The paregoric contained in this medicine may make these conditions worse
- Colitis or other intestinal disease—A more serious condition may develop with the use of this medicine
- Diarrhea caused by antibiotics—This medicine may make the diarrhea caused by antibiotics worse or make it last longer
- Dysentery—This condition may get worse; a different kind of treatment may be needed
- Kidney disease or
- Liver disease—In patients with kidney or liver disease, paregoric may build up in the body; smaller doses of this medicine may be needed
- Underactive thyroid—This medicine may cause central nervous system (CNS) depression and breathing problems in patients with this condition

Proper Use of This Medicine

If this medicine upsets your stomach, you may take it with food.

Take this medicine only as directed on the label or as ordered by your doctor. Do not take more of it, do not take it more often, and do not take it for a long time. If too much is taken, it may become habit-forming.

Use a specially marked measuring spoon or other device to measure each dose accurately. The average household teaspoon may not hold the right amount of liquid.

Importance of diet and fluid intake while treating diarrhea:

- *In addition to using medicine for diarrhea, it is very important that you replace the fluid lost by the body and follow a proper diet.* For the first 24 hours you should eat gelatin and drink plenty of clear liquids, such as ginger ale, decaffeinated cola, decaffeinated tea, and broth. During the next 24 hours you may eat bland foods, such as cooked cereals, bread, crackers, and applesauce. Fruits, vegetables, fried or spicy foods, bran, candy, and caffeine and alcoholic beverages may make the condition worse.
- If too much fluid has been lost by the body due to the diarrhea a serious condition (dehydration) may develop. This condition may be hidden by use of this

medicine. Check with your doctor as soon as possible if any of the following signs of too much fluid loss occur:

Decreased urination
Dizziness and lightheadedness
Dryness of mouth
Increased thirst
Wrinkled skin

Dosing—The dose of kaolin, pectin, and paregoric combination medicine will be different for different patients. *Follow your doctor's orders or the directions on the label.* The following information includes only the average doses of kaolin, pectin, and paregoric combination medicine. *If your dose is different, do not change it* unless your doctor tells you to do so.

- For *oral* dosage form (suspension):
  - —For diarrhea:
    - Adults and teenagers—The usual dose is 2 tablespoonfuls (30 milliliters [mL]) after each loose bowel movement. No more than 4 doses should be taken in twelve hours.
    - Children 2 years of age and over weighing 13.5 kilograms (kg) (29.7 pounds) or more—The usual dose is 1 to 2 teaspoonfuls (5 to 10 mL) after each loose bowel movement. No more than 4 doses should be taken in twelve hours.
    - Children 2 years of age and over weighing 9 to 13.5 kg (19.8 to 29.7 pounds)—The usual dose is 1 teaspoonful (5 mL) after each loose bowel movement. No more than 4 doses should be taken in twelve hours.
    - Children 2 years of age and over weighing 4.5 to 9 kg (9.9 to 19.8 pounds)—The usual dose is 1/2 teaspoonful (2.5 mL) after each loose bowel movement. No more than 4 doses should be taken in twelve hours.
    - Children 2 years of age and over weighing less than 4.5 kg (9.9 pounds)—Dose must be determined by your doctor.
    - Children up to 2 years of age—Use is not recommended.

Storage—To store this medicine:

- Keep out of the reach of children since overdose is especially dangerous in children.
- Store away from heat and direct light.
- Do not store this medicine in the refrigerator. If it does get cold and you notice any solid particles in it, throw it away.
- Keep this medicine from freezing.
- Keep the container for this medicine tightly closed to prevent the alcohol from evaporating and the medicine from becoming stronger.
- Do not keep outdated medicine or medicine no longer needed. Be sure that any discarded medicine is out of the reach of children.

Precautions While Using This Medicine

Check with your doctor if your diarrhea does not stop after 1 or 2 days or if you develop a fever.

This medicine will add to the effects of alcohol and other CNS depressants (medicines that make you drowsy or less alert). Some examples of CNS depressants are antihistamines or medicine for hay fever, other allergies, or colds; sedatives, tranquilizers, or sleeping medicine; prescription pain medicine or narcotics; barbiturates; medicine for seizures; muscle relaxants; or anesthetics, including some dental anesthetics. *Check with your doctor before taking any of the above while you are taking this medicine.*

This medicine may cause some people to become dizzy, drowsy, or less alert than they are normally. Even if taken at bedtime, it may cause some people to feel drowsy or less alert on arising. *Make sure you know how you react to this medicine before you drive, use machines, or do anything else that could be dangerous if you are dizzy or are not alert.*

Side Effects of This Medicine

Along with its needed effects, a medicine may cause some unwanted effects. Although not all of these side effects appear very often, when they do occur they may require medical attention. *Check with your doctor immediately* if any of the following side effects are severe and occur suddenly since they may indicate a more severe and dangerous problem with your bowels:

Rare

Bloating; constipation (severe); loss of appetite; nausea or vomiting; stomach pain (severe)

Also, check with your doctor as soon as possible if the following effects occur:

Rare

Decreased blood pressure; fast heartbeat; hives, itching, or skin rash; increased sweating; mental depression; redness or flushing of face; shortness of breath, troubled breathing, or wheezing

Other side effects may occur that usually do not need medical attention. These side effects may go away during treatment as your body adjusts to the medicine. However, check with your doctor if any of the following side effects continue or are bothersome:

More common with large doses

Constipation (mild); decreased, difficult, or painful urination or frequent urge to urinate; dizziness, feeling faint, lightheadedness, unusual tiredness or weakness; drowsiness; nervousness or restlessness

Other side effects not listed above may also occur in some patients. If you notice any other effects, check with your doctor.

Revised: 04/26/95

KETOCONAZOLE Topical

Some commonly used brand names in the U.S. and Canada are Nizoral Cream and Nizoral Shampoo.

Description

Ketoconazole (kee-toe-KOE-na-zole) is used to treat infections caused by a fungus or yeast. It works by killing the fungus or yeast or preventing its growth.

Ketoconazole cream is used to treat:

- Athlete's foot (tinea pedis; ringworm of the foot);
- Ringworm of the body (tinea corporis);
- Ringworm of the groin (tinea cruris; jock itch);
- Seborrheic dermatitis;
- ''Sun fungus'' (tinea versicolor; pityriasis versicolor); and
- Yeast infection of the skin (cutaneous candidiasis).

Ketoconazole shampoo is used to treat dandruff.

This medicine may also be used for other fungus infections of the skin as determined by your doctor.

Ketoconazole is available only with your doctor's prescription, in the following dosage forms:

Topical

- Cream (U.S. and Canada)
- Shampoo (U.S. and Canada)

Before Using This Medicine

In deciding to use a medicine, the risks of using the medicine must be weighed against the good it will do. This is a decision you and your doctor will make. For topical ketoconazole, the following should be considered:

Allergies—Tell your doctor if you have ever had any unusual or allergic reaction to ketoconazole, miconazole or other imidazoles, or sulfites. The cream form of ketoconazole contains sulfites. Also tell your health care professional if you are allergic to any other substances, such as preservatives or dyes.

Pregnancy—Ketoconazole has not been studied in pregnant women. However, studies in animals have shown that ketoconazole causes birth defects or other problems. Before using this medicine, make sure your doctor knows if you are pregnant or if you may become pregnant.

Breast-feeding—It is not known whether topical ketoconazole, used on a regular basis, is absorbed into the mother's body enough to pass into the breast milk. However, this medicine was not absorbed through the skin after a single dose. Therefore, it is unlikely to cause problems in nursing babies.

Children—Studies on this medicine have been done only in adult patients, and there is no specific information comparing use of this medicine in children with use in other age groups.

Older adults—Many medicines have not been studied specifically in older people. Therefore, it may not be known whether they work exactly the same way they do in younger adults or if they cause different side effects or problems in older people. There is no specific information comparing use of topical ketoconazole in the elderly with use in other age groups.

Other medicines—Although certain medicines should not be used together at all, in other cases two different medicines may be used together even if an interaction might occur. In these cases, your doctor may want to change the dose, or other precautions may be necessary. Tell your health care professional if you are using any other prescription or nonprescription (over-the-counter [OTC]) medicine.

Proper Use of This Medicine

Keep this medicine away from the eyes.

For patients using the *cream form* of this medicine:

- Apply enough ketoconazole cream to cover the affected and surrounding skin areas, and rub in gently.
- To help clear up your infection completely, *it is very important that you keep using ketoconazole cream for the full time of treatment,* even if your symptoms begin to clear up after a few days. Since fungus or yeast infections may be very slow to clear up, you may have to continue using this medicine every day for up to several weeks. If you stop using this medicine too soon, your symptoms may return. *Do not miss any doses.*

For patients using the *shampoo form* of this medicine:

- Wet your hair and scalp well with water.
- Apply enough shampoo to work up a good lather and gently massage it over your entire scalp for about 1 minute.
- Rinse your hair and scalp with warm water.
- Repeat application, then leave the shampoo on your scalp for 3 minutes more.
- Rinse your hair and scalp well with warm water, and dry your hair.

Dosing—The dose of topical ketoconazole will be different for different patients. *Follow your doctor's orders or the directions on the label.* The following information includes only the average doses of topical ketoconazole. *If your dose is different, do not change it* unless your doctor tells you to do so.

The number of doses you use each day, the time allowed between doses, and the length of time you use the medicine depend on the medical problem for which you are using topical ketoconazole.

- For *cream* dosage form:
  - —For cutaneous candidiasis, tinea corporis, tinea cruris, tinea pedis, or pityriasis versicolor:
    - Adults—Apply once a day to the affected skin and surrounding area.
    - Children—Use and dose must be determined by your doctor.

—For seborrheic dermatitis:

• Adults—Apply two times a day to the affected skin and surrounding area.

• Children—Use and dose must be determined by your doctor.

• For *shampoo* dosage form:

—For dandruff:

• Adults—Use every 4 days for 4 weeks. Then use once every 1 or 2 weeks to keep dandruff under control.

• Children—Use and dose must be determined by your doctor.

Missed dose—If you miss a dose of this medicine, apply it as soon as possible. However, if it is almost time for your next dose, skip the missed dose and go back to your regular dosing schedule.

Storage—To store this medicine:

- Keep out of the reach of children.
- Store away from heat and direct light.
- Keep the medicine from freezing.
- Do not keep outdated medicine or medicine no longer needed. Be sure that any discarded medicine is out of the reach of children.

Precautions While Using This Medicine

For patients using the *cream form* of this medicine:

- If your skin problem does not improve within 2 to 4 weeks, or if it becomes worse, check with your doctor.
- *To help clear up your infection completely and to help make sure it does not return, good health habits are also required.*
- For patients using ketoconazole cream for *athlete's foot* (tinea pedis; ringworm of the foot), the following instructions will help keep the feet cool and dry.

  —Avoid wearing socks made from wool or synthetic materials (for example, rayon or nylon). Instead, wear clean, cotton socks and change them daily or more often if your feet sweat a lot.

  —Wear sandals or well-ventilated shoes (for examples, shoes with holes).

  —Use a bland, absorbent powder (for example, talcum powder) or an antifungal powder between the toes, on the feet, and in socks and shoes one or two times a day. It is best to use the powder between the times you use ketoconazole cream.

  If you have any questions about these instructions, check with your health care professional.

- For patients using ketoconazole cream for *ringworm of the groin* (tinea cruris; jock itch), the following instructions will help reduce chafing and irritation and will also help keep the groin area cool and dry.

  —Avoid wearing underwear that is tight-fitting or made from synthetic materials (for example, rayon or nylon). Instead, wear loose-fitting, cotton underwear.

  —Use a bland, absorbent powder (for example, talcum powder) or an antifungal powder on the skin. It is best to use the powder between the times you use ketoconazole cream.

  If you have any questions about these instructions, check with your health care professional.

Side Effects of This Medicine

Along with its needed effects, a medicine may cause some unwanted effects. Although not all of these side effects may occur, if they do occur they may need medical attention.

Check with your doctor as soon as possible if any of the following side effects occur:

More common

Itching, stinging, or irritation not present before use of this medicine

Other side effects not listed above may also occur in some patients. If you notice any other effects, check with your doctor.

Revised: 06/21/93

KETOROLAC Ophthalmic

A commonly used brand name in the U.S. and Canada is Acular.

Description

Ophthalmic ketorolac (kee-toe-ROLE-ak) is an anti-inflammatory medicine. It is used in the eye to treat itching caused by seasonal allergic conjunctivitis (an allergy that occurs at only certain times of the year).

This medicine may also be used to prevent or treat other conditions, as determined by your ophthalmologist (eye doctor).

Ophthalmic

- Ophthalmic solution (eye drops) (U.S. and Canada)

Before Using This Medicine

In deciding to use a medicine, the risks of using the medicine must be weighed against the good it will do. This is a decision you and your doctor will make. For ophthalmic ketorolac, the following should be considered:

Allergies—Tell your doctor if you have ever had any unusual or allergic reaction to aspirin or other salicylates, ophthalmic ketorolac, systemic ketorolac (e.g., Toradol), diclofenac (e.g., Voltaren), or any of the other ophthalmic or systemic anti-inflammatory medicines.

Also tell your health care professional if you are allergic to any other substances, such as preservatives.

Pregnancy—Ophthalmic ketorolac has not been studied in pregnant women. However, studies in some animals have shown that ophthalmic ketorolac causes birth defects. Before using this medicine, make sure your doctor knows if you are pregnant or if you may become pregnant.

Breast-feeding—Ophthalmic ketorolac has not been reported to cause problems in nursing babies.

Children—Studies on this medicine have been done only in adult patients, and there is no specific information comparing use of ophthalmic ketorolac in children with use in other age groups.

Older adults—Many medicines have not been studied specifically in older people. Therefore, it may not be known whether they work exactly the same way they do in younger adults. Although there is no specific information comparing use of ophthalmic ketorolac in the elderly with use in other age groups, this medicine is not expected to cause different side effects or problems in older people than it does in younger adults.

Other medicines—Although certain medicines should not be used together at all, in other cases two different medicines may be used together even if an interaction might occur. In these cases, your doctor may want to change the dose, or other precautions may be necessary. Tell your health care professional if you are using any other ophthalmic prescription or non-prescription (over-the-counter [OTC]) medicine.

Proper Use of This Medicine

To use:

- First, wash your hands. Tilt the head back and, pressing your finger gently on the skin just beneath the lower eyelid, pull the lower eyelid away from the eye to make a space. Drop the medicine into this space. Let go of the eyelid and gently close the eyes. Do not blink. Keep the eyes closed for 1 or 2 minutes to allow the medicine to be absorbed by the eye.
- If you think you did not get the drop of medicine into your eye properly, use another drop.
- To keep the medicine as germ-free as possible, do not touch the applicator tip to any surface (including the eye). Also, keep the container tightly closed.

Dosing—The dose of ophthalmic ketorolac will be different for different patients. *Follow your doctor's orders or the directions on the label.* The following information includes only the average dose of ophthalmic ketorolac. *If your dose is different, do not change it* unless your doctor tells you to do so.

- For *ophthalmic solution (eye drops)* dosage form:
  - —For itching of the eye
    - Adults—Use one drop in each eye four times a day for up to one week or as directed by your doctor.
    - Children—Use and dose must be determined by your doctor.

Missed dose—If you miss a dose of this medicine, use it as soon as possible. However, if it is almost time for your next dose, skip the missed dose and go back to your regular dosing schedule. Do not double doses.

Storage—To store this medicine:

- Keep out of the reach of children.
- Store away from heat and direct light.
- Keep the medicine from freezing. Do not refrigerate.
- Do not keep outdated medicine or medicine no longer needed. Be sure that any discarded medicine is out of the reach of children.

Precautions While Using This Medicine

If your symptoms do not improve within a few days, or if they become worse, check with your doctor.

While applying this medicine, your eyes will probably sting or burn for a short time. This is to be expected.

Side Effects of This Medicine

Along with its needed effects, a medicine may cause some unwanted effects. Although not all of these side effects may occur, if they do occur they may need medical attention.

Check with your doctor as soon as possible if any of the following side effects occur:

Less common or rare

Burning, itching, redness, swelling, tearing, or other sign of eye irritation not present before therapy or becoming worse during therapy; skin rash around eye

Other side effects may occur that usually do not need medical attention. These side effects may go away during treatment as your body adjusts to the medicine. However, check with your doctor if any of the following side effects continue or are bothersome:

More common

Stinging or burning of eye when medicine is applied

Other side effects not listed above may also occur in some patients. If you notice any other effects, check with your doctor.

Additional Information

Once a medicine has been approved for marketing for a certain use, experience may show that it is also useful for other medical problems. Although this use is not included in product labeling, ophthalmic ketorolac is used in certain patients with the following medical condition:

- Inflammation, ocular (redness of the eye that occurs after eye surgery in patients having cataracts removed from their eyes)

For patients using this medicine for *ocular inflammation after eye surgery:*

- Make sure you tell your doctor if you have hemophilia or other bleeding problems, since the possibility of bleeding may be increased during eye surgery.

Other than the above information, there is no additional information relating to proper use, precautions, or side effects for this use.

Developed: 08/11/94

KETOROLAC Systemic

A commonly used brand name in the U.S. and Canada is Toradol.

Description

Ketorolac (kee-TOE-role-ak) is used to relieve moderately severe pain, usually pain that occurs after an operation or other painful procedure. It belongs to the group of medicines called nonsteroidal anti-inflammatory drugs (NSAIDs). Ketorolac is not a narcotic and is not habit-forming. It will not cause physical or mental dependence, as narcotics can. However, ketorolac is sometimes used together with a narcotic to provide better pain relief than either medicine used alone.

Ketorolac has side effects that can be very dangerous. The risk of having a serious side effect increases with the dose of ketorolac and with the length of treatment. Therefore, ketorolac should not be used for more than 5 days. Before using this medicine, you should discuss with your doctor the good that this medicine can do as well as the risks of using it.

Ketorolac is available only with your doctor's prescription, in the following dosage forms:

Oral
- Tablets (U.S. and Canada)

Parenteral
- Injection (U.S. and Canada)

Before Using This Medicine

In deciding to use a medicine, the risks of taking the medicine must be weighed against the good it will do. This is a decision you and your doctor will make. For ketorolac, the following should be considered:

Allergies—Tell your doctor if you have ever had any unusual or allergic reaction to ketorolac or to any of the following medicines:

Aspirin or other salicylates
Diclofenac (e.g., Voltaren)
Diflunisal (e.g., Dolobid)
Etodolac (e.g., Lodine)
Fenoprofen (e.g., Nalfon)
Floctafenine (e.g., Idarac)
Flurbiprofen, oral (e.g., Ansaid)
Ibuprofen (e.g., Motrin)
Indomethacin (e.g., Indocin)
Ketoprofen (e.g., Orudis)
Meclofenamate (e.g., Meclomen)
Mefenamic acid (e.g., Ponstel)
Nabumetone (e.g., Relafen)
Naproxen (e.g., Naprosyn)
Oxaprozin (e.g., Daypro)
Oxyphenbutazone (e.g., Tandearil)
Phenylbutazone (e.g., Butazolidin)
Piroxicam (e.g., Feldene)
Sulindac (e.g., Clinoril)
Suprofen (e.g., Suprol)
Tenoxicam (e.g., Mobiflex)
Tiaprofenic acid (e.g., Surgam)
Tolmetin (e.g., Tolectin)
Zomepirac (e.g., Zomax)

Also tell your health care professional if you are allergic to any other substances, such as foods, preservatives, or dyes.

Pregnancy—Studies on birth defects with ketorolac have not been done in pregnant women. However, it crosses the placenta. There is a chance that regular use of ketorolac during the last few months of pregnancy may cause unwanted effects on the heart or blood flow of the fetus or newborn baby. Ketorolac has not been shown to cause birth defects in animal studies. However, animal studies have shown that, if taken late in pregnancy, ketorolac may increase the length of pregnancy, prolong labor, or cause other problems during delivery.

Breast-feeding—Ketorolac passes into the breast milk and may cause unwanted effects in nursing babies. It may be necessary for you to use another pain reliever or to stop breast-feeding during treatment. Be sure that you have discussed the use of this medicine with your doctor.

Children—Studies on this medicine have been done only in adult patients, and there is no specific information comparing use of ketorolac in children up to 16 years of age with use in other age groups.

Older adults—Stomach or intestinal problems, swelling of the face, feet, or lower legs, or sudden decrease in the amount of urine may be especially likely to occur in elderly patients, who are usually more sensitive than younger adults to the effects of ketorolac. Also, elderly people are more likely than younger adults to get very sick if the medicine causes stomach problems. Studies in older adults have shown that ketorolac stays in the body longer than it does in younger people. Your doctor will consider this when deciding on how much ketorolac should be given for each dose and how often it should be given.

Other medicines—Although certain medicines should not be used together at all, in other cases two different medicines may be used together even if an interaction might occur. In these cases, your doctor may want to change the dose, or other precautions may be necessary. When you are using ketorolac, it is especially important that your health care professional know if you are taking any of the following:

- Anticoagulants (blood thinners) or
- Cefamandole (e.g., Mandol) or
- Cefoperazone (e.g., Cefobid) or
- Cefotetan (e.g., Cefotan) or
- Heparin or
- Plicamycin (e.g., Mithracin) or
- Valproic acid (e.g., Depakene)—Use of any of these medicines together with ketorolac may increase the chance of bleeding
- Aspirin or other salicylates or
- Other medicine for inflammation or pain, except narcotics—The chance of serious side effects may be increased
- Lithium (e.g., Lithane) or
- Methotrexate (e.g., Mexate)—Higher blood levels of lithium or methotrexate and an increased chance of side effects may occur

- Probenecid (e.g., Benemid)—Higher blood levels of ketorolac and an increased chance of side effects may occur

Other medical problems—The presence of other medical problems may affect the use of ketorolac. Make sure you tell your doctor if you smoke tobacco or if you have any other medical problems, especially:
- Alcohol abuse or
- Diabetes mellitus (sugar diabetes) or
- Edema (swelling of face, fingers, feet or lower legs caused by too much fluid in the body) or
- Kidney disease or
- Liver disease (severe) or
- Systemic lupus erythematosus (SLE)—The chance of serious side effects may be increased
- Asthma or
- Heart disease or
- High blood pressure—Ketorolac may make your condition worse.
- Bleeding in the brain (history of) or
- Hemophilia or other bleeding problems—Ketorolac may increase the chance of serious bleeding
- Bleeding from the stomach or intestines (history of) or
- Colitis, stomach ulcer, or other stomach or intestinal problems (or history of)—Ketorolac may make stomach or intestinal problems worse. Also, bleeding from the stomach or intestines is more likely to occur during ketorolac treatment in people with these conditions

Proper Use of This Medicine

For patients taking *ketorolac tablets:*
- To lessen stomach upset, ketorolac tablets should be taken with food (a meal or a snack) or with an antacid.
- Take this medicine with a full glass of water. Also, do not lie down for about 15 to 30 minutes after taking it. This helps to prevent irritation that may lead to trouble in swallowing.

For patients using *ketorolac injection:*
- Medicines given by injection are sometimes used at home. If you will be using ketorolac at home, your health care professional will teach you how the injections are to be given. You will also have a chance to practice giving injections. Be certain that you understand exactly how the medicine is to be injected.

For safe and effective use of this medicine, do not use more of it, do not use it more often, and do not use it for more than 5 days. Using too much of this medicine increases the chance of unwanted effects, especially in elderly patients.

Ketorolac should be used only when it is ordered by your doctor for treating certain kinds of pain. Because of the risk of serious side effects, *do not save any left over ketorolac for use in the future, and do not share it with other people.*

Dosing—The dose of ketorolac will be different for different patients. *Follow your doctor's orders or the directions on the label.* The following information includes only the average doses of ketorolac. *If your dose is different, do not change it* unless your doctor tells you to do so.

- For *oral* dosage form (tablets):
  - —For pain:
    - Adults (patients 16 years of age and older)—One 10-milligram (mg) tablet four times a day, four to six hours apart. Some people may be directed to take two tablets for the first dose only.
    - Children up to 16 years of age—Use and dose must be determined by your doctor.
- For *injection* dosage form:
  - —For pain:
    - Adults (patients 16 years of age and older)—15 or 30 mg, injected into a muscle or a vein four times a day, at least 4 to 6 hours apart. This amount of medicine may be contained in 1 mL or in one-half (0.5) mL of the injection, depending on the strength. Some people who do not need more than one injection may receive one dose of 60 mg, injected into a muscle.
    - Children up to 16 years of age—Use and dose must be determined by your doctor.

Missed dose—If you have been directed to use this medicine according to a regular schedule, and you miss a dose, use it as soon as possible. However, if it is almost time for your next dose, skip the missed dose and go back to your regular dosing schedule. Do not double doses.

Storage—To store this medicine:
- Keep out of the reach of children.
- Store away from heat and direct light.
- Do not store ketorolac tablets in the bathroom, near the kitchen sink, or in other damp places. Heat or moisture may cause the medicine to break down.
- Keep the injection form of ketorolac from freezing. Do not store it in the refrigerator.
- Do not keep outdated medicine or medicine no longer needed. Be sure that any discarded medicine is out of the reach of children.

Precautions While Using This Medicine

Taking certain other medicines together with ketorolac may increase the chance of unwanted effects. The risk will depend on how much of each medicine you take every day, and on how long you take the medicines together. Therefore, do not take acetaminophen (e.g., Tylenol) together with ketorolac for more than a few days, unless otherwise directed by your medical doctor or dentist. Also, *do not take any of the following medicines together with ketorolac, unless your medical doctor or dentist has directed you to do so and is following your progress*:

Aspirin or other salicylates
Diclofenac (e.g., Voltaren)
Diflunisal (e.g., Dolobid)
Etodolac (e.g., Lodine)
Fenoprofen (e.g., Nalfon)
Floctafenine (e.g., Idarac)
Flurbiprofen, oral (e.g., Ansaid)
Ibuprofen (e.g., Motrin)
Indomethacin (e.g., Indocin)
Ketoprofen (e.g., Orudis)
Meclofenamate (e.g., Meclomen)
Mefenamic acid (e.g., Ponstel)

Nabumetone (e.g., Relafen)
Naproxen (e.g., Naprosyn)
Oxaprozin (e.g., Daypro)
Phenylbutazone (e.g., Butazolidin)
Piroxicam (e.g., Feldene)
Sulindac (e.g., Clinoril)
Tenoxicam (e.g., Mobiflex)
Tiaprofenic acid (e.g., Surgam)
Tolmetin (e.g., Tolectin)

Ketorolac may cause some people to become dizzy or drowsy. If either of these side effects occurs, *do not drive, use machines, or do anything else that could be dangerous if you are not alert.*

Side Effects of This Medicine

Along with its needed effects, a medicine may cause some unwanted effects. Although not all of these side effects may occur, if they do occur they may need medical attention.

Stop using this medicine and check with your doctor immediately if any of the following side effects occur:

Rare

Bleeding from the rectum or bloody or black, tarry stools; bleeding or crusting sores on lips; blue lips and fingernails; chest pain; convulsions; fainting; shortness of breath, fast, irregular, noisy, or troubled breathing, tightness in chest, and/or wheezing; vomiting of blood or material that looks like coffee grounds

Also, check with your doctor as soon as possible if any of the following side effects occur:

More common

Swelling of face, fingers, lower legs, ankles, and/or feet; weight gain (unusual)

Less common

Bruising (not at place of injection); high blood pressure; skin rash or itching; small, red spots on skin; sores, ulcers, or white spots on lips or in mouth

Rare

Abdominal or stomach pain, cramping, or burning (severe); bloody or cloudy urine; blurred vision of other vision change; burning, red, tender, thick, scaly, or peeling skin; cough or hoarseness; dark urine; decrease in amount of urine (sudden); fever with severe headache, drowsiness, confusion, and stiff neck or back; fever with or without chills or sore throat; general feeling of illness; hallucinations (seeing, hearing, or feeling things that are not there); hearing loss; hives; increase in amount of urine or urinating often; light-colored stools; low blood pressure; mood changes or unusual behavior; muscle cramps or pain; nausea, heartburn, and/or indigestion (severe and continuing); nosebleeds; pain in lower back and/or side; pain, tenderness, and/or swelling in the upper abdominal area; painful or difficult urination; puffiness or swelling of the eyelids or around the eyes; ringing or buzzing in ears; runny nose; severe restlessness; skin rash; swollen and/or painful glands; swollen tongue; thirst (continuing); unusual tiredness or weakness; yellow eyes or skin

Other side effects may occur that usually do not need medical attention. These side effects may go away during treatment as your body adjusts to the medicine. However, check with your doctor if any of the following side effects continue or are bothersome:

More common

Abdominal or stomach pain (mild or moderate); bruising at place of injection; diarrhea; dizziness; drowsiness; headache; indigestion; nausea

Less common or rare

Bloating or gas; burning or pain at place of injection; constipation; feeling of fullness in abdominal or stomach area; increased sweating; vomiting

Other side effects not listed above may also occur in some patients. If you notice any other effects, check with your doctor.

Revised: 07/24/95

LAMIVUDINE Systemic

Some commonly used brand names are:

In the U.S.—
Epivir

In Canada—
3TC

Description

Lamivudine (la-MI-vyoo-deen) is used in the treatment of the infection caused by the human immunodeficiency virus (HIV). HIV is the virus that causes acquired immune deficiency syndrome (AIDS). Lamivudine is taken together with zidovudine (AZT).

Lamivudine will not cure or prevent HIV infection or AIDS; however, it helps keep HIV from reproducing and appears to slow down the destruction of the immune system. This may help delay the development of problems usually related to AIDS or HIV disease. Lamivudine will not keep you from spreading HIV to other people. People who receive this medicine may continue to have other problems usually related to AIDS or HIV disease.

Lamivudine is available only with your doctor's prescription, in the following dosage form:

Oral
- Oral solution (U.S. and Canada)
- Tablets (U.S. and Canada)

Before Using This Medicine

In deciding to use a medicine, the risks of taking the medicine must be weighed against the good it will do. This is a decision you and your doctor will make. For lamivudine, the following should be considered:

Allergies—Tell your doctor if you have ever had any unusual or allergic reaction to lamivudine. Also tell your health care professional if you are allergic to any other substances, such as foods, preservatives, or dyes.

Pregnancy—Lamivudine has not been studied in pregnant women. However, studies in animals have shown that lamivudine causes birth defects when given in very high doses. Before taking this medicine, make sure your doctor knows if you are pregnant or if you may become pregnant.

Breast-feeding—It is not known whether lamivudine passes into the breast milk. However, if your baby does not already have the AIDS virus, there is a chance that you could pass it to your baby by breast-feeding. Talk to your doctor first if you are thinking about breast-feeding your baby.

Children—Lamivudine can cause serious side effects. In one study, children with advanced AIDS were more likely than children who were less ill to develop pancreatitis (inflammation of the pancreas) and peripheral neuropathy (a problem involving the nerves). Therefore, it is especially important that you discuss with your child's doctor the good that this medicine may do as well as the risks of using it. Your child must be seen frequently and your child's progress carefully followed by the doctor while the child is taking lamivudine.

Older adults—Lamivudine has not been studied specifically in older people. Therefore, it is not known whether it causes different side effects or problems in the elderly than it does in younger adults.

Other medicines—Although certain medicines should not be used together at all, in other cases two different medicines may be used together even if an interaction might occur. In these cases, your doctor may want to change the dose, or other precautions may be necessary. Tell your health care professional if you are taking any other prescription or nonprescription (over-the-counter [OTC]) medicine.

Other medical problems—The presence of other medical problems may affect the use of lamivudine. Make sure you tell your doctor if you have any other medical problems, especially:

- Kidney disease—Patients with kidney disease may have an increased chance of side effects

Proper Use of This Medicine

Take this medicine exactly as directed by your doctor. Do not take more of it, do not take it more often, and do not take it for a longer time than your doctor ordered. Also, do not stop taking lamivudine or zidovudine without checking with your doctor first.

Keep taking lamivudine for the full time of treatment, even if you begin to feel better.

This medicine works best when there is a constant amount in the blood. *To help keep the amount constant, do not miss any doses.* If you need help in planning the best times to take your medicine, check with your health care professional.

If you are using *lamivudine oral suspension,* use a specially marked measuring spoon or other device to measure each dose accurately. The average household teaspoon may not hold the right amount of liquid.

Only take medicine that your doctor has prescribed specifically for you. Do not share your medicine with others.

Dosing—The dose of lamivudine will be different for different patients. *Follow your doctor's orders or the directions on the label.* The following information includes only the average doses of lamivudine. Your dose may be different if you have kidney disease. *If your dose is different, do not change it* unless your doctor tells you to do so:

- For *oral* dosage forms (oral solution and tablets):
  - —For treatment of HIV infection or AIDS:
    - Adults and teenagers 12 years of age and older weighing 50 kilograms (kg) (110 pounds) or more—150 milligrams (mg) twice a day together with zidovudine.
    - Adults weighing less than 50 kg (110 pounds)—2 mg per kg of body weight twice a day together with zidovudine.

- Children 3 months to 12 years of age—4 mg per kg of body weight, up to 150 mg per dose, twice a day together with zidovudine.

Missed dose—If you miss a dose of this medicine, take it as soon as possible. However, if it is almost time for your next dose, skip the missed dose and go back to your regular dosing schedule. Do not double doses.

Storage—To store this medicine:
- Keep out of the reach of children.
- Store away from heat and direct light.
- Do not store in the bathroom, near the kitchen sink, or in other damp places. Heat or moisture may cause the medicine to break down.
- Do not keep outdated medicine or medicine no longer needed. Be sure that any discarded medicine is out of the reach of children.

Precautions While Using This Medicine

It is very important that your doctor check your progress at regular visits.

Do not take any other medicines without checking with your doctor first. To do so may increase the chance of side effects from lamivudine.

Side Effects of This Medicine

Along with its needed effects, a medicine may cause some unwanted effects. Although not all of these side effects may occur, if they do occur they may need medical attention.

Check with your doctor immediately if any of the following side effects occur:

Less common—More common in children
Abdominal or stomach pain (severe); nausea; tingling, burning, numbness, or pain in the hands, arms, feet, or legs; vomiting

Rare
Fever, chills, or sore throat; skin rash; unusual tiredness or weakness

Other side effects may occur that usually do not need medical attention. These side effects may go away during treatment as your body adjusts to the medicine. However, check with your doctor if any of the following side effects continue or are bothersome:

Less common
Abdominal or stomach pain; cough; diarrhea; dizziness; headache; nausea; trouble in sleeping; unusual tiredness or weakness; vomiting

Rare
Hair loss

Other side effects not listed above may also occur in some patients. If you notice any other effects, check with your doctor.

Additional Information

Once a medicine has been approved for marketing for a certain use, experience may show that it is also useful for other medical problems. Although this use is not included in product labeling, lamivudine is used in certain patients with the following medical condition:
- Human immunodeficiency virus (HIV) infection due to occupational exposure (possible prevention of)

Other than the above information, there is no additional information relating to proper use, precautions, or side effects for this use.

Developed: 08/08/96

LAMOTRIGINE Systemic

A commonly used brand name in the U.S. and Canada is Lamictal. Another commonly used name is LTG.

Description

Lamotrigine (la-MOE-tri-jeen) is used to help control some types of seizures in the treatment of epilepsy. This medicine cannot cure epilepsy and will only work to control seizures for as long as you continue to take it.

Lamotrigine is available only with your doctor's prescription, in the following dosage form:

Oral
- Tablets (U.S. and Canada)

Before Using This Medicine

In deciding to use a medicine, the risks of taking the medicine must be weighed against the good it will do. This is a decision you and your doctor will make. For lamotrigine, the following should be considered:

Allergies—Tell your doctor if you have ever had any unusual or allergic reaction to lamotrigine. Also tell your health care professional if you are allergic to any other substances, such as foods, preservatives, or dyes.

Pregnancy—Lamotrigine has not been studied in pregnant women. However, if you might become pregnant while taking lamotrigine, your doctor may want you to take folic acid supplements. Studies in animals have shown that lamotrigine, even when given to the mother in doses smaller than the largest human dose, may cause some offspring to die. Before taking this medicine, make sure your doctor knows if you are pregnant or if you may become pregnant.

Breast-feeding—Lamotrigine passes into breast milk. However, it is not known whether this medicine causes problems in nursing babies. Mothers who are taking lamotrigine and who wish to breast-feed should discuss this with their doctor.

Children—This medicine has been tested in a small number of children 2 to 16 years of age. In effective doses, lamotrigine has not been shown to cause different side effects or problems than it does in adults. Lamotrigine may be removed from the body more quickly in children than in adults, and a child may need a different dose or a different number of doses a day than an adult would receive. However, more testing is needed to be sure lamotrigine is safe and works well in children.

Older adults—Lamotrigine is removed from the body more slowly in elderly people than in younger people. Higher blood levels of the medicine may occur, which may increase the chance of unwanted effects. Your doctor may give you a different lamotrigine dose than a younger person would receive.

Other medicines—Although certain medicines should not be used together at all, in other cases two different medicines may be used together even if an interaction might occur. In these cases, your doctor may want to change the dose, or other precautions may be necessary. When you are taking lamotrigine, it is especially important that your health care professional know if you are taking any of the following:

- Carbamazepine (e.g., Tegretol) or
- Phenobarbital (e.g., Luminal) or
- Phenytoin (e.g., Dilantin) or
- Primidone (e.g., Mysoline) or
- Valproic acid (e.g., Depakote)—These medicines may increase or decrease the blood levels of lamotrigine, which may increase the chance of unwanted effects; your doctor may need to change the dose of either these medicines or lamotrigine

Other medical problems—The presence of other medical problems may affect the use of lamotrigine. Make sure you tell your doctor if you have any other medical problems, especially:

- Heart disease
- Kidney disease or
- Liver disease—Higher blood levels of lamotrigine may occur, which may increase the chance of unwanted effects; your doctor may need to change your dose
- Thalassemia—Lamotrigine may cause your body to stop making or to make fewer red blood cells

Proper Use of This Medicine

Take lamotrigine only as directed by your doctor to help your condition as much as possible and to decrease the chance of unwanted effects. Do not take more or less of this medicine, and do not take it more or less often than your doctor ordered.

Lamotrigine may be taken with or without food or on a full or empty stomach. However, if your doctor tells you to take the medicine a certain way, take it exactly as directed.

Dosing—The dose of lamotrigine will be different for different patients, and depends on what other medicines you are taking. *Follow your doctor's orders or the directions on the label.* The following information includes only the average doses of lamotrigine. *If your dose is different, do not change it* unless your doctor tells you to do so.

The number of tablets that you take depends on the strength of the medicine.

- For *oral* dosage form (tablets):
  - —For treatment of epilepsy:
    - Adults *not* taking valproic acid (e.g., Depakote) but taking carbamazepine (e.g., Tegretol), phenobarbital (e.g., Luminal), phenytoin (e.g., Dilantin), and/or primidone (e.g., Mysoline)—At first, 50 milligrams (mg) of lamotrigine once a day for two weeks, then a total of 100 mg divided into two smaller doses each day for two weeks. After this, your doctor may increase the dose gradually if needed. However, the dose is usually not more than 500 mg a day.
    - Adults taking valproic acid (e.g., Depakote) and also taking carbamazepine (e.g., Tegretol), phenobarbital (e.g., Luminal), phenytoin (e.g., Dilantin), and/or primidone (e.g., Mysoline)—At first, 25 mg of lamotrigine once every other day for two weeks, then 25 mg once every day for two weeks. After this, your doctor may increase the dose gradually if needed. However, the dose is usually not more than 200 mg a day.
    - Children—Use and dose must be determined by your doctor.

Missed dose—If you miss a dose of this medicine, take it as soon as possible. However, if it is almost time for your next dose, skip the missed dose and go back to your regular dosing schedule. Do not double doses.

Storage—To store this medicine:

- Keep out of the reach of children.
- Store away from heat and direct light.
- Do not store in the bathroom, near the kitchen sink, or in other damp places. Heat or moisture may cause the medicine to break down.
- Do not keep outdated medicine or medicine no longer needed. Be sure that any discarded medicine is out of the reach of children.

Precautions While Using This Medicine

It is important that your doctor check your progress at regular visits, especially during the first few months of your treatment with lamotrigine. This will allow your doctor to change your dose, if necessary, and will help reduce any unwanted effects.

This medicine may increase the effects of alcohol and other CNS depressants (medicines that slow down the nervous system, possibly causing drowsiness). Some examples of CNS depressants are antihistamines or medicine for hay fever, other allergies, or colds; sedatives, tranquilizers, or sleeping medicine; prescription pain medicine or narcotics; barbiturates; medicine for seizures; muscle relaxants; or anesthetics, including some dental anesthetics. *Check with your doctor before taking any of the above while you are using this medicine.*

Lamotrigine may cause blurred vision, double vision, clumsiness, unsteadiness, dizziness, or drowsiness. *Make sure you know how you react to this medicine before you drive, use machines, or do anything else that could be dangerous if you are not alert, well-coordinated, or able to see well.* If these reactions are especially bothersome, check with your doctor.

Skin rash may be a sign of a serious unwanted effect. *Check with your doctor immediately if you develop a rash or if your seizures increase.*

Do not stop taking lamotrigine without first checking with your doctor. Stopping this medicine suddenly may cause your seizures to return or to occur more often. Your doctor may want you to gradually reduce the amount you are taking before stopping completely.

Side Effects of This Medicine

Along with its needed effects, a medicine may cause some unwanted effects. Although not all of these side effects may occur, if they do occur they may need medical attention.

Check with your doctor immediately if any of the following side effects occur:

More common

Skin rash

Less common

Increase in seizures

Rare

Blistering, peeling, or loosening of skin; dark-colored urine; fever, chills, and/or sore throat; flu-like symptoms; itching; muscle cramps, pain, or weakness; red or irritated eyes; small red or purple spots on skin; sores, ulcers, or white spots on lips or in mouth; swelling of face, mouth, hands, or feet; swollen lymph nodes; trouble in breathing; unusual bleeding or bruising; unusual tiredness or weakness; yellow eyes or skin

Symptoms of overdose

Clumsiness or unsteadiness (severe); coma; continuous, uncontrolled back and forth and/or rolling eye movements (severe); dizziness (severe); drowsiness (severe); dryness of mouth; increased heart rate; slurred speech (severe)

Check with your doctor as soon as possible if any of the following side effects occur:

More common

Blurred or double vision or other changes in vision; clumsiness or unsteadiness

Less common

Anxiety, confusion, depression, irritability, or other mood or mental changes; continuous, uncontrolled back and forth and/or rolling eye movements

Other side effects may occur that usually do not need medical attention. These side effects may go away during treatment as your body adjusts to the medicine. However, check with your doctor if any of the following side effects continue or are bothersome:

More common

Dizziness (more common in women); drowsiness; headache; nausea; vomiting

Less common

Indigestion; loss of strength; runny nose; slurred speech; trembling or shaking; trouble in sleeping

Other side effects not listed above may also occur in some patients. If you notice any other effects, check with your doctor.

Developed: 05/23/96

LANSOPRAZOLE Systemic

A commonly used brand name in the U.S. and Canada is Prevacid.

Description

Lansoprazole (lan-SOE-pra-zole) is used to treat certain conditions in which there is too much acid in the stomach. It is used to treat duodenal ulcers and gastroesophageal reflux disease (GERD), a condition in which the acid in the stomach washes back up into the esophagus. Lansoprazole is also used to treat Zollinger-Ellison disease, a condition in which the stomach produces too much acid. It may also be used for other conditions as determined by your doctor.

Lansoprazole works by decreasing the amount of acid produced by the stomach.

This medicine is available only with your doctor's prescription.

Oral

- Delayed-release capsules (U.S. and Canada)

Before Using This Medicine

In deciding to use a medicine, the risks of taking the medicine must be weighed against the good it will do. This is a decision you and your doctor will make. For lansoprazole, the following should be considered:

Allergies—Tell your doctor if you have ever had any unusual or allergic reaction to lansoprazole. Also tell your health care professional if you are allergic to any other substances, such as foods, preservatives, or dyes.

Pregnancy—Studies have not been done in humans. However, studies in animals have not shown that lansoprazole causes harm to the fetus.

Breast-feeding—Lansoprazole may pass into the breast milk. Since this medicine has been shown to cause unwanted effects such as tumors in animals, it may be necessary for you to take another medicine or to stop breast-feeding during treatment. Be sure you have discussed the risks and benefits of the medicine with your doctor.

Children—There is no specific information comparing the use of lansoprazole in children with use in other age groups.

Older adults—In studies done to date that have included older adults, lansoprazole did not cause different side effects or problems than it did in younger adults.

Other medicines—Although certain medicines should not be used together at all, in other cases two different medicines may be used together even if an interaction might occur. In these cases, your doctor may want to change the dose, or other precautions may be necessary. When you are taking lansoprazole, it is especially important that your health care professional know if you are taking any of the following:

- Sucralfate (e.g., Carafate)—Lansoprazole should be taken at least 30 minutes before sucralfate so that lansoprazole will be properly absorbed

Proper Use of This Medicine

Take lansoprazole before a meal, preferably in the morning.

Swallow the capsule whole. Do not crush, break, or chew the capsule. If you cannot swallow the capsule whole, you may open it and sprinkle the granules contained in the capsule on one tablespoonful of applesauce and swallow it immediately; do not chew or crush the granules.

Take this medicine for the full time of treatment, even if you begin to feel better. Also, keep your appointments with your doctor for check-ups so that your doctor will be better able to tell you when to stop taking this medicine.

Dosing—The dose of lansoprazole will be different for different patients. *Follow your doctor's orders or the directions on the label.* The following information includes only the average doses of lansoprazole. *If your dose is different, do not change it* unless your doctor tells you to do so.

The number of doses you take each day and the length of time you take the medicine depend on the medical problem for which you are taking lansoprazole.

- For *oral* dosage form (delayed-release capsule):
  - —To treat duodenal ulcers:
    - Adults—At first, 15 milligrams (mg) once a day, preferably taken in the morning before a meal. Your doctor may increase your dose if needed.
    - Children up to 18 years of age—Use and dose must be determined by your doctor.
  - —To treat gastroesophageal reflux disease (GERD):
    - Adults—30 mg once a day, preferably taken in the morning before a meal.
    - Children up to 18 years of age—Use and dose must be determined by your doctor.
  - —To treat conditions in which the stomach produces too much acid:
    - Adults—At first, 60 mg once a day, preferably taken in the morning before a meal. Your doctor may increase your dose if needed.
    - Children up to 18 years of age—Use and dose must be determined by your doctor.

Missed dose—If you miss a dose of this medicine, take it as soon as possible. However, if it is almost time for your next dose, skip the missed dose and go back to your regular dosing schedule. Do not double doses.

Storage—To store this medicine:

- Keep out of the reach of children.
- Store away from heat and direct light.
- Do not store in the bathroom, near the kitchen sink, or in other damp places. Heat or moisture may cause the medicine to break down.
- Do not keep outdated medicine or medicine no longer needed. Be sure that any discarded medicine is out of the reach of children.

Precautions While Using This Medicine

It is important that your doctor check your progress at regular intervals. If your condition does not improve, or if it becomes worse, discuss this with your doctor.

Side Effects of This Medicine

Along with its needed effects, a medicine may cause some unwanted effects. Although not all of these side effects may occur, if they do occur they may need medical attention.

Check with your doctor as soon as possible if any of the following side effects occur:

More common

Diarrhea; skin rash or itching

Less common

Abdominal or stomach pain; increased or decreased appetite; nausea

Rare

Anxiety; cold or flu-like symptoms; constipation; increased cough; mental depression; muscle pain; rectal bleeding; unusual bleeding or bruising

Other side effects may occur that usually do not need medical attention. These side effects may go away during treatment as your body adjusts to the medicine. However, check with your doctor if any of the following side effects continue or are bothersome:

More common

Dizziness; headache

Other side effects not listed above may also occur in some patients. If you notice any other effects, check with your doctor.

Additional Information

Once a medicine has been approved for marketing for a certain use, experience may show that it is also useful for other medical problems. Although this use is not included in product labeling, lansoprazole is used in certain patients with the following medical condition:

- Gastric ulcer

Other than the above information, there is no additional information relating to proper use, precautions, or side effects for this use.

Developed: 05/29/96

LAXATIVES Oral

Some commonly used brand names and other names are:

In the U.S.—

Afko-Lube[43]
Afko-Lube Lax[37]
Agoral Marshmallow[24]
Agoral Raspberry[24]
Alaxin[44]
Alophen[33]
Alphamul[31]
Alramucil Orange[6]
Alramucil Regular[6]
Bilagog[17]
Bilax[39]
Bisac-Evac[26]
Black-Draught[27]
Black-Draught Lax-Senna[34]
Carter's Little Pills[26]
Cholac[13]
Chronulac[13]
Cillium[5]
Citroma[14]
Citrucel Orange Flavor[3]
Citrucel Sugar-Free Orange Flavor[3]
Colace[43]
Colax[41]
Cologel[3]
Constilac[13]
Constulose[13]
Correctol[26]
Correctol Caplets[26]
Correctol Herbal Tea[34]
Correctol Stool Softener Soft Gels[43]
Dacodyl[26]
DC Softgels[43]
Decholin[32]
Deficol[26]
Dialose[43]
Dialose Plus[41]
Diocto[43]
Diocto-C[37]
Diocto-K[43]
Diocto-K Plus[37]
Dioctolose Plus[37]
Dioeze[43]
Diosuccin[43]
Di-Sosul[43]
Di-Sosul Forte[37]
Docucal-P[41]
Docu-K Plus[37]
DOK[43]
DOK Softgels[43]
D.O.S. Softgels[43]
Dosaflex[34]
Doxidan Liqui-Gels[37]
Dr. Caldwell Senna Laxative[34]
DSMC Plus[37]
D-S-S[43]
D-S-S plus[37]
Dulcolax[26]
Duosol[43]
Duphalac[13]
Effer-syllium[6]
Emulsoil[31]
Enulose[13]
Epsom salts[17]
Equalactin[4]
Evac-U-Gen[33]
Evac-U-Lax[33]
Evalose[13]
Ex-Lax[33]
Ex-Lax Gentle Nature Pills[35]
Ex-Lax Maximum Relief Formula[33]
Ex-Lax Pills[33]
Extra Gentle Ex-Lax[41]
FemiLax[41]
Fiberall[6]
Fibercon Caplets[4]
Fiber-Lax[4]
FiberNorm[4]
Fleet Laxative[26]
Fleet Mineral Oil[22]
Fleet Phospho-Soda[18]
Fleet Soflax Gelcaps[43]
Fleet Soflax Overnight Gelcaps[37]
Fletcher's Castoria[34]
Genasoft Plus Softgels[37]
Gentle Laxative[26]
Haley's M-O[19]
Hepahydrin[32]
Heptalac[13]
Herbal Laxative[35]
Hydrocil Instant[6]
Kasof[43]
Kellogg's Castor Oil[31]
Kondremul Plain[22]
Konsyl[4, 5]
Konsyl-D[6]
Konsyl-Orange[6]
Konsyl-Orange Sugar Free[6]
Laxinate 100[43]
Lax-Pills[33]
Liqui-Doss[22]
Mag-Ox 400[16]
Maltsupex[1]
Maox 420[16]
Medilax[33]
Metamucil[6]
Metamucil Apple Crisp Fiber Wafers[6]
Metamucil Cinnamon Spice Fiber Wafers[6]
Metamucil Orange Flavor[6]
Metamucil Smooth, Citrus Flavor[6]
Metamucil Smooth, Orange Flavor[6]
Metamucil Smooth Sugar-Free, Citrus Flavor[6]
Metamucil Smooth Sugar-Free, Orange Flavor[6]
Metamucil Smooth Sugar-Free, Regular Flavor[6]
Metamucil Sugar-Free, Lemon-Lime Flavor[6]
Metamucil Orange Flavor[6]
Metamucil Sugar-Free, Orange Flavor[6]
Milkinol[22]
Mitrolan[4]
Modane[33]
Modane Bulk[6]
Modane Plus[41]
Modane Soft[43]
Molatoc[43]
Molatoc-CST[37]
Mylanta Natural Fiber Supplement[6]
Mylanta Sugar Free Natural Fiber Supplement[6]
Naturacil[5]
Nature's Remedy[29]
Neolax[39]
Neoloid[31]
Nytilax[35]
Perdiem[8]
Perdiem Fiber[5]
Peri-Colace[37]
Peri-Dos Softgels[37]
Petrogalar Plain[22]
Phenolphthalein Petrogalar[24]
Phillips' Chewable[15]
Phillips' Concentrated[15]
Phillips' Gelcaps[41]
Phillips' LaxCaps[41]
Phillips' Milk of Magnesia[15]
Portalac[13]
Pro-Cal-Sof[43]
Pro-Lax[6]
Prompt[10]
Pro-Sof[43]
Pro-Sof Plus[37]
Prulet[33]
Purge[31]
Regulace[37]
Regulax SS[43]
Reguloid Natural[6]
Reguloid Natural Sugar Free[6]
Reguloid Orange[6]
Reguloid Orange Sugar Free[6]
Senexon[34]
Senna-Gen[34]
Senokot[34]
Senokot Children's Syrup[35]
Senokot-S[42]
SenokotXTRA[35]
Senolax[34]
Serutan[6]
Serutan Toasted Granules[7]
Silace[43]
Silace-C[37]
Stulex[43]
Sulfolax[43]
Surfak[43]
Syllact[5]
Syllamalt[2]
Trilax[40]
Unilax[41]
Veracolate[30]
V-Lax[6]
X-Prep Liquid[34]
Zymenol[22]

In Canada—

Acilac[13]
Agarol Plain[19a]
Agarol Strawberry[20]
Agarol Vanilla[20]
Albert Docusate[43]
Apo-Bisacodyl[26]
Bicholate Lilas[30]
Bisacolax[26]
Caroid[30]
Carter's Little Pills[33]
Chronulac[13]
Citro-Mag[14]
Colace[43]
Correctol[26]
Correctol Stool Softener Soft Gels[43]
Doss[38]
Doxidan[41]
Dulcodos[36]
Dulcolax[26]
Ex-Lax[33]
Ex-Lax Light Formula[41]
Ex-Lax Pills[33]
Feen-a-Mint Pills[26]
Fibrepur[6]
Fletcher's Castoria[35]
Glysennid[35]
Herbal Laxative[34]
Karacil[6]
Kondremul[22]
Lactulax[13]
Lansoÿl[22]
Lansoÿl Sugar Free[22]
Laxavite[30]
Laxilose[13]
Laxit[26]
Magnolax[19]
Metamucil[6]
Metamucil Orange Flavor[6]
Metamucil Sugar Free[6]
Metamucil Sugar-Free, Orange Flavor[6]
Mitrolan[4]
Mucinum[33a]
Natural Source Fibre Laxative[6]
Nature's Remedy[29]
Nujol[22]
Peri-Colace[37]
Phillips' Magnesia Tablets[15]
Phillips' Milk of Magnesia[15]
PMS-Bisacodyl[26]
PMS-Docusate Calcium[43]
PMS-Docusate Sodium[43]
PMS-Lactulose[13]
PMS-Phosphates[18]
PMS-Sennosides[35]
Prodiem Plain[6]
Prodiem Plus[9]
Regulex[43]
Regulex-D[38]
Senokot[34]
Senokot-S[42]
SenoKot XTRA[35]
Silace[43]
Soflax[43]
Surfak[43]
Vitalax Super Smooth Sugar Free Orange Flavor[6]
Vitalax Unflavored[6]

Note: For quick reference the following laxatives are numbered to match the corresponding brand names.

Bulk-forming laxatives—

1. Malt Soup Extract†
2. Malt Soup Extract and Psyllium (SILL-i-yum)†
3. Methylcellulose (meth-ill-SELL-yoo-lose)†‡
4. Polycarbophil (pol-i-KAR-boe-fil)
5. Psyllium†
6. Psyllium Hydrophilic Mucilloid (hye-droe-FILL-ik MYOO-sill-oid)
7. Psyllium Hydrophilic Mucilloid and Carboxymethylcellulose (kar-box-ee-meth-ill-SELL-yoo-lose)†

Bulk-forming and stimulant combinations—

8. Psyllium and Senna†
9. Psyllium Hydrophilic Mucilloid and Senna*
10. Psyllium Hydrophilic Mucilloid and Sennosides†

Bulk-forming, stimulant, and stool softener (emollient) combinations—

11. Product not available

Bulk-forming and stool softener (emollient) combinations—

12. Product not available

Hyperosmotic laxatives—Lactulose:

13. Lactulose‡§

Hyperosmotic laxatives—Saline:

14. Magnesium Citrate (mag-NEE-zhum SI-trate)‡§
15. Magnesium Hydroxide‡§
16. Magnesium Oxide†
17. Magnesium Sulfate (SUL-fate)†‡
18. Sodium Phosphate (SOE-dee-um FOS-fate)†‡

Hyperosmotic and lubricant combinations—
19. Milk of Magnesia and Mineral Oil†
19a. Mineral Oil and Glycerin*

Hyperosmotic, lubricant, and stimulant combinations—
20. Mineral Oil, Glycerin, and Phenolphthalein (fee-nole-THAY-leen)*

Hyperosmotic and stimulant combinations—
21. Milk of Magnesia and Cascara Sagrada (kas-KAR-a sa-GRA-da)†‡

Lubricant laxatives—
22. Mineral Oil‡§

Lubricant and stimulant combinations—
24. Mineral Oil and Phenolphthalein†
25. Product not available

Stimulant laxatives—
26. Bisacodyl (bis-a-KOE-dill)‡
27. Casanthranol†
28. Cascara Sagrada‡§
29. Cascara Sagrada and Aloe
30. Cascara Sagrada and Phenolphthalein
31. Castor (KAS-tor) Oil‡§
32. Dehydrocholic (dee-hye-droe-KOE-lik) Acid†‡
33. Phenolphthalein
33a. Phenolphthalein and Senna*
34. Senna
35. Sennosides§

Stimulant and stool softener (emollient) combinations—
36. Bisacodyl and Docusate*
37. Casanthranol and Docusate‡
38. Danthron and Docusate*
39. Dehydrocholic Acid and Docusate†
40. Dehydrocholic Acid, Docusate, and Phenolphthalein†
41. Phenolphthalein and Docusate
42. Sennosides and Docusate

Stool softener (emollient) laxatives—
43. Docusate‡§
44. Poloxamer 188 (pol-OX-a-mer)†

*Not commercially available in the U.S.
†Not commercially available in Canada.
‡Generic name product may be available in the U.S.
§Generic name product may be available in Canada.

Description

Oral laxatives are medicines taken by mouth to encourage bowel movements to relieve constipation.

There are several different types of oral laxatives and they work in different ways. Since directions for use are different for each type, it is important to know which one you are taking. The different types of oral laxatives include:

Bulk-formers—Bulk-forming laxatives are not digested but absorb liquid in the intestines and swell to form a soft, bulky stool. The bowel is then stimulated normally by the presence of the bulky mass. Some bulk-forming laxatives, like psyllium and polycarbophil, may be prescribed by your doctor to treat diarrhea.

Hyperosmotics—Hyperosmotic laxatives encourage bowel movements by drawing water into the bowel from surrounding body tissues. This provides a soft stool mass and increased bowel action.

There are two types of hyperosmotic laxatives taken by mouth—the saline and the lactulose types. The *saline type* is often called ''salts.'' They are used for rapid emptying of the lower intestine and bowel. They are not used for long-term or repeated correction of constipation. With smaller doses than those used for the laxative effect, some saline laxatives are used as antacids. The information that follows applies only to their use as laxatives. Sodium phosphate may also be prescribed for other conditions as determined by your doctor.

The *lactulose type* is a special sugar-like laxative that works the same way as the saline type. However, it produces results much more slowly and is often used for long-term treatment of chronic constipation. Lactulose may sometimes be used in the treatment of certain medical conditions to reduce the amount of ammonia in the blood. It is available only with your doctor's prescription.

Lubricants—Lubricant laxatives, such as mineral oil, taken by mouth encourage bowel movements by coating the bowel and the stool mass with a waterproof film. This keeps moisture in the stool. The stool remains soft and its passage is made easier.

Stimulants—Stimulant laxatives, also known as contact laxatives, encourage bowel movements by acting on the intestinal wall. They increase the muscle contractions that move along the stool mass. Stimulant laxatives are a popular type of laxative for self-treatment. However, they also are more likely to cause side effects. One of the stimulant laxatives, dehydrocholic acid, may also be used for treating certain conditions of the biliary tract.

Stool softeners (emollients)—Stool softeners encourage bowel movements by helping liquids mix into the stool and prevent dry, hard stool masses. This type of laxative has been said not to *cause* a bowel movement but instead *allows* the patient to have a bowel movement without straining.

Combinations—There are many products that you can buy for constipation that contain more than one type of laxative. For example, a product may contain both a stool softener and a stimulant laxative. In general, combination products may be more likely to cause side effects because of the multiple ingredients. In addition, they may not offer any advantage over products containing only one type of laxative. *If you are taking a combination laxative, make certain you know the proper use and precautions for each of the different ingredients.*

Most laxatives (except saline laxatives) may be used to provide relief:

- during pregnancy.
- for a few days after giving birth.
- during preparation for examination or surgery.
- for constipation of bedfast patients.
- for constipation caused by other medicines.
- following surgery when straining should be avoided.
- following a period of poor eating habits or a lack of physical exercise in order to develop normal bowel function (bulk-forming laxatives only).

- for some medical conditions that may be made worse by straining, for example:
  Heart disease
  Hemorrhoids
  Hernia (rupture)
  High blood pressure (hypertension)
  History of stroke

Saline laxatives have more limited uses and may be used to provide rapid results:

- during preparation for examination or surgery.
- for elimination of food or drugs from the body in cases of poisoning or overdose.
- for simple constipation that happens on occasion (although another type of laxative may be preferred).
- in supplying a fresh stool sample for diagnosis.

Most laxatives are available without a prescription; however, your doctor may have special instructions for the proper use and dose for your medical condition. They are available in the following dosage forms:

Oral

Bulk-forming laxatives—

Malt Soup Extract
- Powder (U.S.)
- Oral solution (U.S.)
- Tablets (U.S.)

Malt Soup Extract and Psyllium
- Powder (U.S.)

Methylcellulose
- Capsules (U.S.)
- Granules (U.S.)
- Powder (U.S.)
- Oral solution (U.S.)
- Tablets (U.S.)

Polycarbophil
- Tablets (U.S.)
- Chewable tablets (U.S. and Canada)

Psyllium
- Caramels (U.S.)
- Granules (U.S.)
- Powder (U.S.)

Psyllium Hydrophilic Mucilloid
- Granules (U.S. and Canada)
- Powder (U.S. and Canada)
- Effervescent powder (U.S.)
- For oral suspension (Canada)
- Wafers (U.S.)

Psyllium Hydrophilic Mucilloid and Carboxymethylcellulose
- Granules (U.S.)

Bulk-forming and stimulant combinations—

Psyllium and Senna
- Granules (U.S.)

Psyllium Hydrophilic Mucilloid and Senna
- Granules (Canada)

Psyllium Hydrophilic Mucilloid and Sennosides
- Powder (U.S.)

Hyperosmotic laxative—Lactulose:

Lactulose
- Solution (U.S. and Canada)

Hyperosmotic laxatives—Saline:

Magnesium Citrate
- Oral solution (U.S. and Canada)

Magnesium Hydroxide
- Milk of magnesia (U.S. and Canada)
- Tablets (U.S. and Canada)

Magnesium Oxide
- Tablets (U.S.)

Magnesium Sulfate
- Crystals (U.S and Canada)
- Tablets (U.S.)

Sodium Phosphate
- Effervescent powder (U.S.)
- Oral solution (U.S. and Canada)

Hyperosmotic and lubricant combinations—

Milk of Magnesia and Mineral Oil
- Emulsion (U.S. and Canada)

Mineral Oil and Glycerin
- Emulsion (Canada)

Hyperosmotic, lubricant, and stimulant combination—

Mineral Oil, Glycerin, and Phenolphthalein
- Emulsion (Canada)

Hyperosmotic and stimulant combination—

Milk of Magnesia and Cascara Sagrada
- Oral Suspension (U.S.)

Lubricant laxatives—

Mineral Oil
- Oil (U.S. and Canada)
- Emulsion (U.S. and Canada)
- Gel (Canada)
- Oral suspension (U.S.)

Lubricant and stimulant combinations—

Mineral Oil and Phenolphthalein
- Emulsion (U.S.)
- Oral suspension (U.S.)

Stimulant laxatives—

Bisacodyl
- Tablets (U.S. and Canada)

Casanthranol
- Syrup (U.S.)

Cascara Sagrada
- Fluidextract (U.S. and Canada)
- Tablets (U.S. and Canada)

Cascara Sagrada and Aloe
- Tablets (U.S. and Canada)

Cascara Sagrada and Phenolphthalein
- Tablets (U.S. and Canada)

Castor Oil
- Oil (U.S. and Canada)
- Emulsion (U.S.)

Dehydrocholic Acid
- Tablets (U.S.)

Phenolphthalein
- Tablets (U.S. and Canada)
- Chewable tablets (U.S. and Canada)

Phenolphthalein and Senna
- Tablets (Canada)

Senna
- Granules (U.S.)
- Oral solution (U.S and Canada)
- For oral solution (U.S.)
- Syrup (U.S.)
- Tablets (U.S. and Canada)

Sennosides
- Granules (U.S. and Canada)
- Oral solution (Canada)
- Syrup (U.S. and Canada)
- Tablets (U.S. and Canada)

Stimulant and stool softener (emollient) combinations—

Bisacodyl and Docusate
- Tablets (Canada)

Casanthranol and Docusate
- Capsules (U.S. and Canada)
- Syrup (U.S.)
- Tablets (U.S.)

Danthron and Docusate
- Capsules (Canada)
- Tablets (Canada)

Dehydrocholic Acid and Docusate
- Capsules (U.S.)
- Tablets (U.S.)

Dehydrocholic Acid, Docusate, and Phenolphthalein
- Capsules (U.S.)

Phenolphthalein and Docusate
- Capsules (U.S. and Canada)
- Tablets (U.S. and Canada)

Sennosides and Docusate
- Tablets (U.S. and Canada)

Stool softener (emollient) laxatives—

Docusate
- Capsules (U.S. and Canada)
- Oral solution (U.S. and Canada)
- Syrup (U.S. and Canada)
- Tablets (U.S.)

Poloxamer 188
- Capsules (U.S.)

Before Using This Medicine

Importance of diet, fluids, and exercise to prevent constipation—Laxatives are to be used to provide short-term relief only, unless otherwise directed by a doctor. A proper diet containing roughage (whole grain breads and cereals, bran, fruit, and green, leafy vegetables), with 6 to 8 full glasses (8 ounces each) of liquids each day, and daily exercise are most important in maintaining healthy bowel function. Also, for individuals who have problems with constipation, foods such as pastries, puddings, sugar, candy, cake, and cheese may make the constipation worse.

If you are taking this medicine without a prescription, carefully read and follow any precautions on the label. For oral laxatives, the following should be considered:

Allergies—Tell your doctor if you have ever had any unusual or allergic reaction to laxatives. Also tell your health care professional if you are allergic to any other substances, such as foods, preservatives, or dyes.

Diet—Make certain your health care professional knows if you are on any special diet, such as a low-sodium or low-sugar diet. Some laxatives have large amonts of sodium or sugars in them.

Pregnancy—Although laxatives are often used during pregnancy, some types are better than others. Stool softeners (emollient) laxatives and bulk-forming laxatives are probably used most often. If you are using a laxative during pregnancy, remember that:

- Some laxatives (in particular, the bulk-formers) contain a large amount of sodium or sugars, which may have possible unwanted effects such as increasing blood pressure or causing water to be held in the body.
- Saline laxatives containing magnesium, potassium, or phosphates may have to be avoided if your kidney function is not normal.
- Mineral oil is usually not used during pregnancy because of possible unwanted effects on the mother or infant. Mineral oil may interfere with the absorption of nutrients and vitamins in the mother. Also, if taken for a long time during pregnancy, mineral oil may cause severe bleeding in the newborn infant.
- Stimulant laxatives may cause unwanted effects in the expectant mother if improperly used. Castor oil in particular should not be used as it may cause contractions of the womb.

Breast-feeding—Laxatives containing cascara, danthron, and phenolphthalein may pass into the breast milk. Although the amount of laxative in the milk is generally thought to be too small to cause problems in the baby, your doctor should be told if you plan to use such laxatives. Some reports claim that diarrhea has been caused in the infant.

Children—*Laxatives should not be given to young children (up to 6 years of age) unless prescribed by their doctor.* Since children usually cannot describe their symptoms very well, they should be checked by a doctor before being given a laxative. The child may have a condition that needs other treatment. If so, laxatives will not help, and may even cause unwanted effects or make the condition worse.

Mineral oil should not be given to young children (up to 6 years of age) because a form of pneumonia may be caused by the inhalation of oil droplets into the lungs.

Also, bisacodyl tablets should not be given to children up to 6 years of age because if chewed they may cause stomach irritation.

Older adults—Mineral oil should not be taken by bedridden elderly persons because a form of pneumonia may be caused by the inhalation of oil droplets into the lungs. Also, stimulant laxatives (e.g., bisacodyl, casanthranol, or phenolphthalein), if taken too often, may worsen weakness, lack of coordination, or dizziness and lightheadedness.

Other medicines—Although certain medicines should not be used together at all, in other cases two different medicines may be used together even if an interaction might occur. In these cases, your doctor may want to change the dose, or other precautions may be necessary. When you are taking oral laxatives, it is especially important that your health care professional know if you are taking any of the following:

- Anticoagulants, oral (blood thinners you take by mouth) or
- Digitalis glycosides (heart medicine)—The use of magnesium-containing laxatives may reduce the effects of these medicines
- Ciprofloxacin (e.g., Cipro) or
- Etidronate (e.g., Didronel) or
- Sodium polysterene sulfonate—Use of magnesium-containing laxatives will keep these medicines from working
- Tetracyclines taken by mouth (medicine for infection)—Use of bulk-forming or magnesium-containing laxatives will keep the tetracycline medicine from working

Other medical problems—The presence of other medical problems may affect the use of oral laxatives. Make sure

you tell your doctor if you have any other medical problems, especially:

- Appendicitis (or signs of) or
- Rectal bleeding of unknown cause—These conditions need immediate attention by a doctor
- Colostomy or
- Intestinal blockage or
- Ileostomy—The use of laxatives may create other problems if these conditions are present
- Diabetes mellitus (sugar diabetes)—Diabetic patients should be careful since some laxatives contain large amounts of sugars, such as dextrose, galactose, and/or sucrose
- Heart disease or
- High blood pressure—Some laxatives contain large amounts of sodium, which may make these conditions worse
- Kidney disease—Magnesium and potassium (contained in some laxatives) may build up in the body if kidney disease is present; a serious condition may develop
- Swallowing difficulty—Mineral oil should not be used since it may get into the lungs by accident and cause pneumonia; also, bulk-forming laxatives may get lodged in the esophagus of patients who have difficulty in swallowing

Proper Use of This Medicine

For safe and effective use of your laxative:

- Follow your doctor's instructions if this laxative was prescribed.
- Follow the manufacturer's package directions if you are treating yourself.

With all kinds of laxatives, at least 6 to 8 glasses (8 ounces each) of liquids should be taken each day. This will help make the stool softer.

For *patients taking laxatives containing a bulk-forming ingredient:*

- Do not try to swallow in the dry form. Take with liquid.
- To allow bulk-forming laxatives to work properly and to prevent intestinal blockage, it is necessary to drink plenty of fluids during their use. Each dose should be taken in or with a full glass (8 ounces) or more of cold water or fruit juice. This will provide enough liquid for the laxative to work properly. A second glass of water or juice by itself is often recommended with each dose for best effect and to avoid side effects.
- When taking a product that contains only a bulk-forming ingredient, results often may be obtained in 12 hours. However, this may not occur for some individuals until after 2 or 3 days.

For *patients taking laxatives containing a stool softener (emollient):*

- Liquid forms may be taken in milk or fruit juice to improve flavor.
- When taking a product that contains only a stool softener, results usually occur 1 to 2 days after the first dose. However, this may not occur for some individuals until after 3 to 5 days.

For *patients taking laxatives containing a hyperosmotic ingredient:*

- Each dose should be taken in or with a full glass (8 ounces) or more of cold water or fruit juice. This will provide enough liquid for the laxative to work properly. A second glass of water or juice by itself is often recommended with each dose for best effect and, in the case of saline laxatives, to prevent you from becoming dehydrated.
- The unpleasant taste produced by some hyperosmotic laxatives may be improved by following each dose with citrus fruit juice or citrus-flavored carbonated beverage.
- Lactulose may not produce laxative results for 24 to 48 hours.
- Saline laxatives usually produce results within 1/2 to 3 hours following a dose. When a larger dose is taken on an empty stomach, the results are quicker. When a smaller dose is taken with food, the results are delayed. Therefore, large doses of saline laxatives are usually not taken late in the day on an empty stomach.

For *patients taking laxatives containing mineral oil:*

- Mineral oil should not be taken within 2 hours of meals because of possible interference with food digestion and absorption of nutrients and vitamins.
- Mineral oil is usually taken at bedtime (but not while lying down) for convenience and because it requires about 6 to 8 hours to produce results.

For *patients taking laxatives containing a stimulant ingredient:*

- Stimulant laxatives are usually taken on an empty stomach for rapid effect. Results are slowed if taken with food.
- Many stimulant laxatives (but not castor oil) are often taken at bedtime to produce results the next morning (although some may require 24 hours or more).
- *Castor oil* is not usually taken late in the day because its results occur within 2 to 6 hours.
- The unpleasant taste of *castor oil* may be improved by chilling in the refrigerator for at least an hour and then stirring the dose into a full glass of cold orange juice just before it is taken. Also, flavored preparations of castor oil are available.
- *Bisacodyl tablets* are specially coated to allow them to work properly without causing irritation and/or nausea. To protect this coating, do not chew, crush, or take the tablets within an hour of milk or antacids.
- Because of the way *phenolphthalein* works in the body, a single dose may cause a laxative effect in some people for up to 3 days.

Dosing—There are a large number of laxative products on the market. The dose of laxatives will be different for different products. The number of capsules or tablets or teaspoonfuls of crystals, gel, granules, liquid, or powder that you use; the number of caramels or wafers that you eat; or the number of pieces of gum that you chew depends on the strength of the medicine. *Follow your doctor's orders if this medicine was prescribed, or follow the direc-*

tions on the box if you are buying this medicine without a prescription.

Storage—To store this medicine:
- Keep out of the reach of children.
- Store away from heat and direct light.
- Do not store the capsule, tablet, granules, or powder form of this medicine in the bathroom, near the kitchen sink, or in other damp places. Heat or moisture may cause the medicine to break down.
- Keep the liquid form of this medicine from freezing.
- Do not keep outdated medicine or medicine no longer needed. Be sure that any discarded medicine is out of the reach of children.

Precautions While Using This Medicine

Do not take any type of laxative:
- *if you have signs of appendicitis or inflamed bowel* (such as stomach or lower abdominal pain, cramping, bloating, soreness, nausea, or vomiting). Instead, check with your doctor as soon as possible.
- *for more than 1 week* unless your doctor has prescribed or ordered a special schedule for you. This is true even when you have had no results from the laxative.
- *within 2 hours of taking other medicine* because the desired effect of the other medicine may be reduced.
- *if you do not need it,* as for the common cold, ''to clean out your system,'' or as a ''tonic to make you feel better.''
- *if you miss a bowel movement for a day or two.*
- *if you develop a skin rash* while taking a laxative or if you had a rash the last time you took it. Instead, check with your doctor.

If you notice a sudden change in bowel habits or function that lasts longer than 2 weeks, or that keeps returning off and on, check with your doctor before using a laxative. This will allow the cause of your problem to be determined before it may become more serious.

The ''laxative habit''—Laxative products are overused by many people. Such a practice often leads to dependence on the laxative action to produce a bowel movement. In severe cases, overuse of some laxatives has caused damage to the nerves, muscles, and tissues of the intestines and bowel. If you have any questions about the use of laxatives, check with your health care professional.

Many laxatives often contain large amounts of sugars, carbohydrates, and sodium. If you are on a low-sugar, low-caloric, or low-sodium diet, check with your health care professional before using a laxative.

For *patients taking laxatives containing mineral oil:*
- Mineral oil should not be taken often or for long periods of time because:

  —gradual build-up in body tissues may create additional problems.

  —the use of mineral oil may interfere with the body's ability to absorb certain food nutrients and vitamins A, D, E, and K.
- Large doses of mineral oil may cause some leakage from the rectum. The use of absorbent pads or a decrease in dose may be necessary to prevent the soiling of clothing.
- Do not take mineral oil within 2 hours of a stool softener (emollient laxative). The stool softener may increase the amount of mineral oil absorbed.

For *patients taking laxatives containing a stimulant ingredient:*
- Stimulant laxatives are most often associated with:

  —overuse and the laxative habit.

  —skin rashes.

  —intestinal cramping after dosing (especially if taken on an empty stomach).

  —potassium loss.

Side Effects of This Medicine

Along with its needed effects, a medicine may cause some unwanted effects. Although not all of these side effects may occur, if they do occur they may need medical attention.

Check with your doctor as soon as possible if any of the following side effects occur:

For bulk-forming–containing
: Difficulty in breathing; intestinal blockage; skin rash or itching; swallowing difficulty (feeling of lump in throat)

For hyperosmotic-containing
: Confusion; dizziness or lightheadedness; irregular heartbeat; muscle cramps; unusual tiredness or weakness

For stimulant-containing
: Confusion; irregular heartbeat; muscle cramps; pink to red coloration of alkaline urine and stools (for phenolphthalein only); pink to red, red to violet, or red to brown coloration of alkaline urine (for cascara, danthron, and/or senna only); skin rash; unusual tiredness or weakness; yellow to brown coloration of acid urine (for cascara, phenolphthalein, and/or senna only)

For stool softener (emollient)–containing
: Skin rash

Other side effects may occur that usually do not need medical attention. These side effects are less common and may go away during treatment as your body adjusts to the medicine. However, check with your doctor if any of the following side effects continue or are bothersome:

For hyperosmotic-containing
: Cramping; diarrhea; gas; increased thirst

For lubricant-containing
: Skin irritation surrounding rectal area

For stimulant-containing
: Belching; cramping; diarrhea; nausea

For stool softener (emollient)-containing
: Stomach and/or intestinal cramping; throat irritation (liquid forms only)

Other side effects not listed above may also occur in some patients. If you notice any other effects, check with your doctor.

Additional Information

Once a medicine has been approved for marketing for a certain use, experience may show that it is also useful for other medical problems. Although this use is not included in product labeling, psyllium hydrophilic mucilloid is used in certain patients with high cholesterol (hypercholesterolemia).

For patients taking psyllium hydrophilic mucilloid for *high cholesterol*:

- Importance of diet—Before prescribing medicine for your condition, your doctor will probably try to control your condition by prescribing a personal diet for you. Such a diet may be low in fats, sugars, and/or cholesterol. Many people are able to control their condition by carefully following their doctor's orders for proper diet and exercise. Medicine is prescribed only when additional help is needed. *Follow carefully the special diet your doctor gave you,* since the medicine is effective only when a schedule of diet and exercise is properly followed.
- Do not try to swallow the powder form of this medicine in the dry form. Mix with liquid following the directions in the package.
- Remember that this medicine will not cure your cholesterol problem but it will help control it. Therefore, you must continue to take it as directed by your doctor if you expect to lower your cholesterol level.

Other than the above information, there is no additional information relating to proper use, precautions, or side effects for this use.

Revised: 06/25/93
Interim revision: 08/01/95; 07/31/96

LAXATIVES Rectal

Some commonly used brand names are:

In the U.S.—

Bisco-Lax[1]
Ceo-Two[5]
Dacodyl[1]
Deficol[1]
Dulcolax[1]
Fleet Babylax[3]
Fleet Bisacodyl[1]
Fleet Enema[7]
Fleet Enema for Children[7]
Fleet Enema Mineral Oil[4]
Fleet Glycerin Laxative[3]
Fleet Laxative[1]
Sani-Supp[3]
Senokot[6]
Theralax[1]
Therevac Plus[2]
Therevac-SB[2]

In Canada—

Apo-Bisacodyl[1]
Bisacolax[1]
Dulcolax[1]
Enemol[7]
Fleet Enema[7]
Fleet Enema Mineral Oil[4]
Fleet Pediatric Enema[7]
Gent-L-Tip[7]
Laxit[1]
PMS-Bisacodyl[1]
Senokot[6]

Note: For quick reference, the following laxatives are numbered to match the corresponding brand names.

This information applies to the following medicines:

1. Bisacodyl (bis-a-KOE-dill)‡§
2. Docusate (DOK-yoo-sate)†
3. Glycerin (GLI-ser-in)‡§
4. Mineral Oil
5. Potassium Bitartrate and Sodium Bicarbonate (SOE-dee-um Bye-KAR-boe-nate)†
6. Senna
7. Sodium Phosphates (SOE-dee-um FOS-fates)

†Not commercially available in Canada.
‡Generic name product may be available in the U.S.
§Generic name product may be available in Canada.

Description

Rectal laxatives are used as enemas or suppositories to produce bowel movements in a short time.

There are several different types of rectal laxatives and they work in different ways. Since directions for use are different for each type, it is important to know which one you are taking. The different types of rectal laxatives include:

Carbon dioxide–releasing—Carbon dioxide–releasing laxatives (e.g., potassium bitartrate and sodium bicarbonate) are suppositories that encourage bowel movements by forming carbon dioxide, a gas. This gas pushes against the intestinal wall, causing contractions that move along the stool mass.

Hyperosmotic—Hyperosmotic laxatives (e.g., glycerin; sodium phosphates) draw water into the bowel from surrounding body tissues. This provides a soft stool mass and increased bowel action.

Lubricant—Mineral oil coats the bowel and the stool mass with a waterproof film. This keeps moisture in the stool. The stool remains soft and its passage is made easier.

Stimulants—Stimulant laxatives (e.g., bisacodyl; senna), also known as contact laxatives, act on the intestinal wall. They increase the muscle contractions that move along the stool mass.

Stool softeners (emollients)—Stool softeners (emollient laxatives—e.g., docusate) encourage bowel movements by helping liquids mix into the stool and prevent dry, hard stool masses. This type of laxative has been said not to *cause* a bowel movement but instead *allows* the patient to have a bowel movement without straining.

Rectal laxatives may provide relief in a number of situations such as:

- before giving birth.
- for a few days after giving birth.
- preparation for examination or surgery.
- to aid in developing normal bowel function following a period of poor eating habits or a lack of physical exercise (glycerin suppositories only).
- following surgery when straining should be avoided.
- constipation caused by other medicines.

Some of these laxatives are available only with your doctor's prescription. Others are available without a prescription; however, your doctor may have special instructions for the proper use and dose for your medical condition. They are available in the following dosage forms:

Rectal

Bisacodyl
- Rectal solution (U.S. and Canada)
- Suppositories (U.S. and Canada)

Docusate
- Rectal solution (U.S.)

Glycerin
- Rectal solution (U.S.)
- Suppositories (U.S. and Canada)

Mineral Oil
- Enema (U.S. and Canada)

Potassium Bitartrate and Sodium Bicarbonate
- Suppositories (U.S.)

Senna
- Suppositories (U.S. and Canada)

Sodium Phosphates
- Enema (U.S. and Canada)

Before Using This Medicine

Importance of diet, fluids, and exercise to prevent constipation—Laxatives are to be used to provide short-term relief only, unless otherwise directed by your doctor. A proper diet containing roughage (whole grain breads and cereals, bran, fruit, and green, leafy vegetables), with 6 to 8 full glasses (8 ounces each) of liquids each day, and daily exercise are most important in maintaining healthy bowel function. Also, for individuals who have problems with constipation, foods such as pastries, puddings, sugar, candy, cake, and cheese may make the constipation worse.

If you are using this medicine without a prescription, carefully read and follow any precautions on the label. For rectal laxatives, the following should be considered:

Allergies—Tell your doctor if you have ever had any unusual or allergic reaction to rectal laxatives. Also tell your health care professional if you are allergic to any other substances, such as preservatives or dyes.

Children—*Laxatives should not be given to young children (up to 6 years of age) unless prescribed by their doctor.* Since children cannot usually describe their symptoms very well, they should be checked by a doctor before being given a laxative. The child may have a condition that needs other treatment. If so, laxatives will not help and may even cause unwanted effects or make the condition worse.

Also, weakness, increased sweating, and convulsions (seizures) may be especially likely to occur in children receiving enemas or rectal solutions, since they may be more sensitive than adults to their effects.

Older adults—Weakness, increased sweating, and convulsions (seizures) may be especially likely to occur in elderly patients, since they may be more sensitive than younger adults to the effects of rectal laxatives.

Other medical problems—The presence of other medical problems may affect the use of rectal laxatives. Make sure you tell your doctor if you have any other medical problems, especially:

- Appendicitis (or signs of) or
- Rectal bleeding of unknown cause—These conditions need immediate attention by a doctor
- Intestinal blockage—The use of laxatives may create other problems if this condition is present

Proper Use of This Medicine

For safe and effective use of laxatives:
- Follow your doctor's orders if this laxative was prescribed.
- Follow the manufacturer's package directions if you are treating yourself.

For patients using *the enema or rectal solution form* of this medicine:
- This medicine usually comes with patient directions. Read them carefully before using this medicine.
- Lubricate anus with petroleum jelly before inserting the enema applicator.
- Gently insert the rectal tip of the enema applicator to prevent damage to the rectal wall.
- Results often may be obtained with:
  —bisacodyl enema in 15 minutes to 1 hour.
  —docusate enema in 2 to 15 minutes.
  —glycerin enema in 15 minutes to 1 hour.
  —mineral oil enema in 2 to 15 minutes.
  —senna enema in 30 minutes, but may not occur for some individuals for up to 2 hours.
  —sodium phosphates enema in 2 to 5 minutes.

For patients using *the suppository form* of this medicine:
- If the suppository is too soft to insert, chill the suppository in the refrigerator for 30 minutes or run cold water over it, before removing the foil wrapper.
- To insert suppository: First remove the foil wrapper and moisten the suppository with cold water. Lie down on your side and use your finger to push the suppository well up into the rectum.
- Results often may be obtained with:
  —bisacodyl suppositories in 15 minutes to 1 hour.
  —carbon dioxide–releasing suppositories in 5 to 30 minutes.
  —glycerin suppositories in 15 minutes to 1 hour.
  —senna suppositories in 30 minutes, but may not occur for some individuals for up to 2 hours.

Dosing—There are a large number of laxative products on the market. The dose of laxatives will be different for different products. The amount of enema or the number of suppositories that you use depends on the strength of the medicine. *Follow your doctor's orders if this medicine was prescribed, or follow the directions on the box if you are buying this medicine without a prescription.*

Storage—To store this medicine:
- Keep out of the reach of children.
- Store away from heat and direct light.
- Do not store in the bathroom, near the kitchen sink, or in other damp places. Heat or moisture may cause the medicine to break down.
- Do not keep outdated medicine or medicine no longer needed. Be sure that any discarded medicine is out of the reach of children.

Precautions While Using This Medicine

Do not use any type of laxative:

- *if you have signs of appendicitis or inflamed bowel* (such as stomach or lower abdominal pain, cramping, bloating, soreness, nausea, or vomiting). Instead, check with your doctor as soon as possible.
- *more often than your doctor prescribed. This is true even when you have had no results from the laxative.*
- *if you do not need it,* as for the common cold, "to clean out your system," or as a "tonic to make you feel better."
- *if you miss a bowel movement for a day or two.*

If you notice a sudden change in bowel habits or function that lasts longer than 2 weeks, or keeps returning off and on, check with your doctor before using a laxative. This will allow the cause of your problem to be determined before it becomes more serious.

The "laxative habit"—Laxative products are overused by many people. Such a practice often leads to dependence on the laxative action to produce a bowel movement. In severe cases, overuse of some laxatives has caused damage to the nerves, muscles, and tissues of the intestines and bowel. If you have any questions about the use of laxatives, check with your health care professional.

For patients using *the enema or rectal solution form* of this medicine:

- *Check with your doctor if you notice rectal bleeding, blistering, pain, burning, itching, or other sign of irritation not present before you started using this medicine.*

For patients using *the suppository form* of this medicine:

- Do not lubricate the suppository with mineral oil or petroleum jelly before inserting into the rectum. To do so may affect the way the suppository works. Moisten only with water.

Side Effects of This Medicine

Along with its needed effects, a medicine may cause some unwanted effects. Although not all of these side effects may occur, if they do occur they may need medical attention.

Check with your doctor as soon as possible if any of the following side effects occur:

Less common

Rectal bleeding, blistering, burning, itching, or pain (with enemas only)

Other side effects may occur that usually do not need medical attention. These side effects may go away during treatment as your body adjusts to the medicine. However, check with your doctor if the following side effect continues or is bothersome:

Less common

Skin irritation surrounding rectal area

Other side effects not listed above may also occur in some patients. If you notice any other effects, check with your doctor.

Revised: 06/25/93
Interim revision: 08/01/95; 07/31/96

LEUCOVORIN Systemic

A commonly used brand name in the U.S. is Wellcovorin.
Generic name product may also be available in the U.S. and Canada.
Other commonly used names are citrovorum factor and folinic acid.

Description

Leucovorin (loo-koe-VOR-in) is used as an antidote to the harmful effects of methotrexate (a cancer medicine) that is given in high doses. It is used also to prevent or treat certain kinds of anemia. Leucovorin acts the same way in the body as folic acid, which may be low in these patients.

Leucovorin is also used along with fluorouracil (a cancer medicine) to treat cancer of the colon (bowel).

Leucovorin is available only with a prescription and is to be given only by or under the supervision of your doctor. It is available in the following dosage forms:

Oral

- Tablets (U.S. and Canada)

Parenteral

- Injection (U.S. and Canada)

Before Using This Medicine

In deciding to use a medicine, the risks of taking the medicine must be weighed against the good it will do. This is a decision you and your doctor will make. For leucovorin, the following should be considered:

Allergies—Tell your doctor if you have ever had any unusual or allergic reaction to leucovorin. Also tell your health care professional if you are allergic to any other substance, such as foods, sulfites or other preservatives, or dyes.

Pregnancy—Studies on effects in pregnancy have not been done in either humans or animals.

Breast-feeding—It is not known whether leucovorin passes into the breast milk. However, it has not been reported to cause problems in nursing babies.

Children—In children with seizures, leucovorin may increase the number of seizures that occur.

Older adults—Many medicines have not been studied specifically in older people. Therefore, it may not be known whether they work exactly the same way they do in younger adults or if they cause different side effects or problems in older people. There is no specific information comparing use of leucovorin in the elderly with use in other age groups.

Other medicines—Although certain medicines should not be used together at all, in other cases two different medicines may be used together even if an interaction might occur. In these cases, your doctor may want to change the dose, or other precautions may be necessary. Tell your health care professional if you are taking any other prescription or nonprescription (over-the-counter [OTC]) medicine.

Other medical problems—The presence of other medical problems may affect the use of leucovorin. If you are taking leucovorin as an antidote to methotrexate, make sure you tell your doctor if you have any other medical problems, especially:

- Kidney disease—Levels of methotrexate may be increased because of its slower removal from the body, so the dose of leucovorin may not be enough to block the unwanted effects of methotrexate
- Nausea and vomiting—Not enough leucovorin may be absorbed into the body to block the unwanted effects of methotrexate

Proper Use of This Medicine

It is very important that you *take leucovorin exactly as directed,* especially when it is being taken to counteract the harmful effects of cancer medicine. *Do not miss any doses. Also, it is best to take the doses at evenly spaced times day and night.* For example, if you are to take 4 doses a day, the doses should be spaced about 6 hours apart. If this interferes with your sleep or other daily activities, or if you need help in planning the best times to take your medicine, check with your health care professional.

Do not stop taking leucovorin without checking with your doctor. It is very important that you get exactly the right amount.

Dosing—The dose of leucovorin will be different for different patients. *Follow your doctor's orders or the directions on the label.* The following information includes only the average doses of leucovorin. *If your dose is different, do not change it* unless your doctor tells you to do so.

The number of tablets or doses of injection that you take depends on the strength of the medicine. Also, *the number of doses you take each day, the time allowed between doses, and the length of time you take the medicine depend on the medical problem for which you are taking leucovorin.*

- For use as an antidote to methotrexate:
  - —For *oral* (tablets) or *injection* dosage forms:
    - Adults, teenagers, and children—Dose is based on body size and must be determined by your doctor.
- For use as an antidote to other medicines:
  - —For *oral* (tablets) or *injection* dosage forms:
    - Adults, teenagers, and children—Dose may range from 0.4 milligrams (mg) to 15 mg a day and must be determined by your doctor.
- For certain kinds of anemia:
  - —For *oral* (tablets) or *injection* dosage forms:
    - Adults, teenagers, and children—Up to 1 mg a day.
- For colon cancer:
  - —For *injection* dosage forms:
    - Adults and teenagers—Dose is based on body size and must be determined by your doctor.
    - Children—Dose must be determined by your doctor.

Missed dose—If you miss a dose of leucovorin or if you vomit shortly after taking a dose, *check with your doctor right away.* Your doctor may want you to take extra leucovorin to make up for what you missed. Do not take more medicine on your own, however, since it is very important that you receive just the right dose at the right time.

Storage—To store this medicine:

- Keep out of the reach of children.
- Store away from heat and direct light.
- Do not store in the bathroom, near the kitchen sink, or in other damp places. Heat or moisture may cause the medicine to break down.
- Do not keep outdated medicine or medicine no longer needed. Be sure that any discarded medicine is out of the reach of children.

Side Effects of This Medicine

Along with its needed effects, a medicine may cause some unwanted effects. Leucovorin usually does not cause any side effects. However, *check with your doctor immediately* if any of the following side effects occur shortly after you receive this medicine:

Rare
Skin rash, hives, or itching; wheezing

Check with your doctor as soon as possible if the following side effect occurs:

Rare—reported with use in treatment of cancer
Convulsions (seizures)

Other side effects not listed above may also occur in some patients. If you notice any other effects, check with your doctor.

Revised: 07/23/92
Interim revision: 07/05/94; 04/11/95

LEUPROLIDE Systemic

Some commonly used brand names in the U.S. and Canada are Lupron and Lupron Depot.

Another commonly used name is leuprorelin.

Description

Leuprolide (loo-PROE-lide) may be used for a number of different medical problems. These include treatment of:

- cancer of the prostate gland in men;
- pain and/or infertility due to endometriosis in women.

Leuprolide is similar to a hormone normally released from the hypothalamus gland.

When given regularly to men, leuprolide decreases testosterone levels. Reducing the amount of testosterone in the body is one way of treating cancer of the prostate.

When given regularly to women, leuprolide decreases estrogen levels. Reducing the amount of estrogen in the body is one way of treating endometriosis.

Leuprolide is available only with your doctor's prescription, in the following dosage form:

Parenteral

- Injection (U.S. and Canada)

Before Using This Medicine

In deciding to use a medicine, the risks of taking the medicine must be weighed against the good it will do. This is a decision you and your doctor will make. For leuprolide, the following should be considered:

Allergies—Tell your doctor if you have ever had any unusual or allergic reaction to leuprolide, buserelin, gonadorelin, histrelin, or nafarelin.

Pregnancy—Tell your doctor if you intend to have children.

- For men: Leuprolide may cause sterility which probably is only temporary. Be sure that you have discussed this with your doctor before receiving this medicine.
- For women: There is a chance that leuprolide may cause birth defects if it is taken after you become pregnant. It could also cause a miscarriage if taken during pregnancy. *Stop using this medicine and tell your doctor immediately if you think you have become pregnant* while receiving this medicine.

Older adults—Many medicines have not been studied specifically in older people. Therefore, it may not be known whether they work exactly the same way they do in younger adults. Although there is no specific information comparing use of leuprolide in the elderly to use in other age groups, it is not expected to cause different side effects or problems in older people than it does in younger adults.

Other medical problems—The presence of other medical problems may affect the use of leuprolide. Make sure you tell your doctor if you have any other medical problems, especially:

- Bleeding from the vagina with unknown cause (for use in endometriosis)
- Problems in passing urine (for use for cancer of the prostate)—May get worse for a short time after leuprolide treatment is started

Proper Use of This Medicine

Leuprolide comes with patient directions. Read these instructions carefully.

Use the syringes provided in the kit. Other syringes may not provide the correct dose. These disposable syringes and needles are already sterilized and designed to be used one time only and then discarded. If you have any questions about the use of disposable syringes, check with your health care professional.

Use this medicine only as directed by your doctor. Do not use more or less of it, and do not use it more often than your doctor ordered. The exact amount of medicine you need has been carefully worked out. Using too much may increase the chance of side effects, while using too little may not improve your condition.

For patients receiving leuprolide for *endometriosis*:

- Leuprolide sometimes causes unwanted effects such as hot flashes or decreased interest in sex. It may also cause a temporary increase in pain when you first begin to use it. However, it is very important that you continue to use the medicine, even after you begin to feel better. *Do not stop using this medicine without first checking with your doctor.*

For patients receiving leuprolide for *cancer of the prostate:*

- Leuprolide sometimes causes unwanted effects such as hot flashes or decreased sexual ability. It may also cause a temporary increase in pain or difficulty in urinating, as well as temporary numbness or tingling of hands or feet or weakness when you first begin to use it. However, it is very important that you continue to use the medicine, even after you begin to feel better. *Do not stop using this medicine without first checking with your doctor.*

Dosing—The dose of leuprolide will be different for different patients. *Follow your doctor's orders or the directions on the label.* The following information includes only the average doses of leuprolide. *If your dose is different, do not change it* unless your doctor tells you to do so:

- For injection dosage form:
  - For *endometriosis:*
    - Adults—3.75 milligrams (mg) injected into the muscle once a month.

—For *cancer of the prostate:*
- Adults—
  1 mg injected under the skin once a day or 7.5 mg injected into the muscle once a month.

Missed dose—If you are using this medicine every day and you miss a dose, give it as soon as possible. However, if you do not remember until the next day, skip the missed dose and go back to your regular dosing schedule. Do not double doses.

Storage—To store this medicine:
- Keep out of the reach of children.
- Store away from heat and direct light.
- Keep the medicine from freezing.
- Do not keep outdated medicine or medicine no longer needed. Dispose of used syringes properly in the container provided. Be sure that any discarded medicine is out of the reach of children.

Precautions While Using This Medicine

It is very important that your doctor check your progress at regular visits to make sure that this medicine is working properly and to check for unwanted effects.

For patients receiving leuprolide for *endometriosis:*
- During the time you are receiving leuprolide, your menstrual period may not be regular or you may not have a menstrual period at all. This is to be expected when being treated with this medicine. If regular menstruation does not begin within 60 to 90 days after you stop receiving this medicine, check with your doctor.
- During the time you are receiving leuprolide, you should use birth control methods which do not contain hormones. If you have any questions about this, check with your health care professional.
- *If you suspect you may have become pregnant, stop using this medicine and check with your doctor.* There is a chance that continued use of leuprolide during pregnancy could cause birth defects or a miscarriage.

Side Effects of This Medicine

Along with its needed effects, a medicine may cause some unwanted effects. Some side effects will have signs or symptoms that you can see or feel. Your doctor may watch for others by doing certain tests.

The following side effects may be caused by blood clots but occur only rarely. However, they require immediate medical attention. *Get emergency help immediately* if any of the following side effects occur:

For males only
Rare
Pains in groin or legs (especially in calves of legs); shortness of breath (sudden)

Check with your doctor as soon as possible if any of the following side effects occur:

For both females and males
Less common
Fast or irregular heartbeat

For females only
Less common
Deepening of voice; increased hair growth

For males only
Less common
Chest pain

Other side effects may occur that usually do not need medical attention. These side effects may go away during treatment as your body adjusts to the medicine. However, check with your doctor if any of the following side effects continue or are bothersome:

For both females and males
More common
Sudden sweating and feelings of warmth (''hot flashes'')

Less common
Blurred vision; burning, itching, redness, or swelling at place of injection; dizziness; headache; nausea or vomiting; numbness or tingling of hands or feet; swelling of feet or lower legs; trouble in sleeping; weight gain

For females only
More common
Light, irregular vaginal bleeding; stopping of menstrual periods

Less common
Burning, dryness, or itching of vagina; decreased interest in sex; increased tenderness of breasts; mood changes; pelvic pain

For males only
Less common
Bone pain; constipation; decreased size of testicles; impotence or decreased interest in sex; loss of appetite; swelling and increased tenderness of breasts

Other side effects not listed above may also occur in some patients. If you notice any other effects, check with your doctor.

Revised: 06/25/93

LEVAMISOLE Systemic

A commonly used brand name in the U.S. and Canada is Ergamisol.

Description

Levamisole (lee-VAM-i-sole) is used with another cancer medicine (fluorouracil) to help make it work better against cancer of the colon.

Levamisole is available only with your doctor's prescription in the following dosage form:

Oral

- Tablets (U.S. and Canada)

Before Using This Medicine

In deciding to use a medicine, the risks of taking the medicine must be weighed against the good it will do. This is a decision you and your doctor will make. For levamisole, the following should be considered:

Allergies—Tell your doctor if you have ever had any unusual or allergic reaction to levamisole or to any other medicines.

Pregnancy—Levamisole has not been studied in pregnant women. However, studies in rats and rabbits have not shown that levamisole causes birth defects or other problems.

Breast-feeding—It is not known whether levamisole passes into the breast milk in humans, although it passes into cows' milk. However, this medicine has not been reported to cause problems in nursing babies.

Children—Studies on this medicine have been done only in adult patients, and there is no specific information comparing use of levamisole in children with use in other age groups.

Older adults—Many medicines have not been studied specifically in older people. Therefore, it may not be known whether they work exactly the same way they do in younger adults or if they cause different side effects or problems in older people. Although there is no specific information comparing use of levamisole in the elderly with use in other age groups, this medicine has been used in elderly patients and is not expected to cause different side effects or problems in older people than it does in younger adults.

Other medicines—Although certain medicines should not be used together at all, in other cases two different medicines may be used together even if an interaction might occur. In these cases, your doctor may want to change the dose, or other precautions may be necessary. Tell your health care professional if you are taking any other prescription or nonprescription (over-the-counter [OTC]) medicine.

Other medical problems—The presence of other medical problems may affect the use of levamisole. Make sure you tell your doctor if you have any other medical problems, especially:

- Infection—Levamisole may decrease your body's ability to fight infection

Proper Use of This Medicine

Take this medicine only as directed by your doctor. Do not take more or less of it, and do not take it more often than your doctor ordered. The exact amount of medicine you need has been carefully worked out. Taking too much may increase the chance of side effects, while taking too little may not improve your condition.

If you vomit shortly after taking a dose of levamisole, check with your doctor. You will be told whether to take the dose again or to wait until the next scheduled dose.

Dosing—The dose of levamisole will be different for different patients. The dose that is used may depend on a number of things, including what the medicine is being used for and whether or not other medicines are also being taken. *If you are taking levamisole at home, follow your doctor's orders or the directions on the label.* If you have any questions about the proper dose of levamisole, ask your doctor.

Missed dose—If you miss a dose of this medicine, do not take the missed dose at all and do not double the next one. Instead, go back to your regular dosing schedule and check with your doctor.

Storage—To store this medicine:

- Keep out of the reach of children.
- Store away from heat and direct light.
- Do not store in the bathroom, near the kitchen sink, or in other damp places. Heat or moisture may cause the medicine to break down.
- Do not keep outdated medicine or medicine no longer needed. Be sure that any discarded medicine is out of the reach of children.

Precautions While Using This Medicine

It is very important that your doctor check your progress at regular visits to make sure that this medicine is working properly and to check for unwanted effects.

Side Effects of This Medicine

Along with its needed effects, a medicine may cause some unwanted effects. Although not all of these side effects may occur, if they do occur they may need medical attention.

Check with your doctor immediately if any of the following side effects occur:

Less common

Fever or chills; unusual feeling of discomfort or weakness

Rare

Black, tarry stools; blood in urine or stools; cough or hoarseness; lower back or side pain; painful or difficult urination; pinpoint red spots on skin; unusual bleeding or bruising

Check with your doctor as soon as possible if the following side effects occur:

Less common

Sores in mouth and on lips

Rare
Blurred vision; confusion; convulsions (seizures); lip smacking or puffing; numbness, tingling, or pain in face, hands, or feet; paranoia (feelings of persecution); puffing of cheeks; rapid or worm-like movements of tongue; trembling or shaking; trouble in walking; uncontrolled movements of arms and legs

Other side effects may occur that usually do not need medical attention. These side effects may go away during treatment as your body adjusts to the medicine. Also, your health care professional may be able to tell you about ways to prevent or reduce some of these side effects. However, check with your doctor if any of the following side effects continue or are bothersome:

More common
Diarrhea; metallic taste; nausea

Less common
Anxiety or nervousness; dizziness; headache; mental depression; nightmares; pain in joints or muscles; skin rash or itching; trouble in sleeping; unusual tiredness or sleepiness; vomiting

Levamisole may cause a temporary loss of hair in some people. After treatment has ended, normal hair growth should return.

Other side effects not listed above may also occur in some patients. If you notice any other effects, check with your doctor.

Revised: 08/12/92
Interim revision: 07/08/94

LEVOCABASTINE Ophthalmic

A commonly used brand name in the U.S. and Canada is Livostin.

Description

Levocabastine (lee-voe-KAB-as-teen) is used to treat certain disorders of the eye caused by allergies. It works by preventing the effects of a substance called histamine, which is produced in certain cells in your eyes and which causes the allergic reaction.

Levocabastine is available only with your doctor's prescription, in the following dosage form:

Ophthalmic
- Ophthalmic suspension (eye drops) (U.S. and Canada)

Before Using This Medicine

In deciding to use a medicine, the risks of using the medicine must be weighed against the good it will do. This is a decision you and your doctor will make. For levocabastine, the following should be considered:

Allergies—Tell your doctor if you have ever had any unusual or allergic reaction to levocabastine. Also tell your health care professional if you are allergic to any other substances, such as preservatives.

Pregnancy—Levocabastine has not been studied in pregnant women. However, studies in animals have shown that levocabastine, when given in very high doses, causes birth defects. Before using this medicine, make sure your doctor knows if you are pregnant or if you may become pregnant.

Breast-feeding—Although levocabastine passes into the breast milk, it has not been reported to cause problems in nursing babies. However, be sure you have discussed the risks and benefits of the medicine with your doctor.

Children—Studies on this medicine have been done only in adult patients and there is no specific information comparing use of levocabastine in children up to 12 years of age with use in other age groups.

Older adults—Many medicines have not been studied specifically in older people. Therefore, it may not be known whether they work exactly the same way they do in younger adults or if they cause different side effects or problems in older people. There is no specific information comparing use of levocabastine in the elderly with use in other age groups.

Other medicines—Although certain medicines should not be used together at all, in other cases two different medicines may be used together even if an interaction might occur. In these cases, your doctor may want to change the dose, or other precautions may be necessary. Tell your health care professional if you are using any other prescription or nonprescription (over the-counter [OTC]) medicine.

Proper Use of This Medicine

To use the *eye drops:*
- First, wash your hands. Tilt the head back and, pressing your finger gently on the skin just beneath the lower eyelid, pull the lower eyelid away from the eye to make a space. Drop the medicine into this space. Let go of the eyelid and gently close the eyes. Do not blink. Keep the eyes closed for 1 or 2 minutes to allow the medicine to be absorbed by the eye.
- If you think you did not get the drop of medicine into your eye properly, use another drop.
- To keep the medicine as germ-free as possible, do not touch the applicator tip to any surface (including the eye). Also, keep the container tightly closed.

In order for this medicine to work properly, it must be used every day in regularly spaced doses as ordered by your doctor. A few days may pass before you begin to feel better.

Dosing—The dose of levocabastine will be different for different patients. *Follow your doctor's orders or the directions on the label.* The following information includes only the average dose of levocabastine. *If your dose is different, do not change it* unless your doctor tells you to do so.

- For *ophthalmic suspension (eye drops)* dosage form:
  - —For eye allergy:
    - Adults and children over 12 years of age—Use one drop in each eye four times a day for up to two weeks.
    - Children up to 12 years of age—Use and dose must be determined by your doctor.

Missed dose—If you miss a dose of this medicine, use it as soon as possible. Then go back to your regular dosing schedule.

Storage—To store this medicine:
- Keep out of the reach of children.
- Store away from heat and direct light.
- Keep the medicine from freezing. Do not refrigerate.
- Do not keep outdated medicine or medicine no longer needed. Be sure that any discarded medicine is out of the reach of children.

Precautions While Using This Medicine

If your symptoms do not improve within 3 days or if your condition becomes worse, check with your doctor.

After application of this medicine to the eye, occasional stinging or burning may occur.

Side Effects of This Medicine

Along with its needed effects, a medicine may cause some unwanted effects. Although not all of these side effects may occur, if they do occur they may need medical attention.

Check with your doctor as soon as possible if any of the following side effects occur:

Less common
Headache

Rare
Change in vision or trouble in seeing; cough; eye pain; nausea; redness, tearing, discharge, or other eye irritation not present before therapy or becoming worse during therapy; skin rash; sore throat; swelling of eyelids; troubled breathing; unusual tiredness or weakness

Other side effects may occur that usually do not need medical attention. These side effects may go away during treatment as your body adjusts to the medicine. However, check with your doctor if any of the following side effects continue or are bothersome:

More common
Burning or stinging when medicine is applied

Less common
Dry eyes; dry mouth; feeling sleepy

Other side effects not listed above may also occur in some patients. If you notice any other effects, check with your doctor.

Developed: 08/11/94

LEVOCARNITINE Systemic

A commonly used brand name in the U.S. and Canada is Carnitor.
Another commonly used name is L-carnitine.

Description

Levocarnitine (lee-voe-KAR-ni-teen) is used to treat a lack of carnitine. It is given to people whose body cannot properly use carnitine from their diet. Lack of carnitine can lead to liver, heart, and muscle problems. Your doctor may treat lack of carnitine by prescribing levocarnitine for you.

Carnitine comes in two forms. Levocarnitine (L-carnitine) should not be confused with the D,L-carnitine form (labeled as ''vitamin B_T''). Only the L-form of carnitine is used by the body to treat serious carnitine deficiency. The D,L-form does not help the body use fat and can actually interfere with and cause a lack of levocarnitine.

Certain levocarnitine products have been specifically approved by the U.S. Food and Drug Administration for medical use and are available only with your doctor's prescription. Other levocarnitine products are sold without a prescription as food supplements and should not be used to treat serious levocarnitine deficiency.

Levocarnitine is available by prescription in the following dosage forms:

Oral
- Solution (U.S. and Canada)
- Tablets (U.S. and Canada)

Parenteral
- Injection (U.S. and Canada)

Before Using This Medicine

In deciding to use a medicine, the risks of taking the medicine must be weighed against the good it will do. This is a decision you and your doctor will make. For levocarnitine, the following should be considered:

Allergies—Tell your health care professional if you are allergic to any substances, such as foods, preservatives, or dyes.

Pregnancy—Studies have not been done in humans. However, levocarnitine has not been shown to cause birth defects or other problems in animal studies.

Breast-feeding—It is not known whether levocarnitine passes into the breast milk. Carnitine normally is present in breast milk, even in women not taking supplements of it, because it is obtained from the diet.

Children—Although there is no specific information comparing use of levocarnitine in children with use in other age groups, this dietary supplement is not expected to cause different side effects or problems in children than it does in adults.

Older adults—There is no specific information comparing use of levocarnitine in the elderly with use in other age groups; however, this medicine is not expected to cause different side effects or problems in older people than it does in younger adults.

Other medicines—Although certain medicines should not be used together at all, in other cases they may be used together even if an interaction might occur. In these cases, your doctor may want to change the dose, or other precautions may be necessary. Tell your health care professional if you are taking any other prescription or nonprescription (over-the-counter [OTC]) medicine.

Proper Use of This Medicine

Take levocarnitine with or just after meals. Also, if you are taking it in liquid form, drink it slowly. It will be less likely to upset your stomach if you take it this way.

This medicine is also less likely to cause unwanted effects when there is a constant amount in the blood. If you are taking more than one dose a day, take the doses at evenly spaced times throughout the day. Doses should be spaced at least 3 to 4 hours apart. If you need help in planning the best times to take your medicine, check with your health care professional.

Dosing—The dose of levocarnitine will be different for different patients. *Follow your doctor's orders or the directions on the label.* The following information includes only the average doses of levocarnitine. *If your dose is different, do not change it* unless your doctor tells you to do so.

The number of tablets or of teaspoonfuls of solution that you take or the number of injections you receive depends on the strength of the medicine. Also, *the number of doses you take each day, the time allowed between doses, and the length of time you take the medicine depend on the medical problem for which you are taking levocarnitine.*

Do NOT change brands or dosage forms of levocarnitine without first checking with your doctor. Different products may not work in the same way. If you refill your medicine and it looks different, check with your pharmacist.

- For *oral* dosage form (solution):
  - —To prevent or treat carnitine deficiency:
    - Adults and teenagers—At first, 1 gram taken once a day with food. Your doctor may change the dose if needed.
    - Children—The dose is based on body weight and must be determined by your doctor. The usual dose at first is 50 mg per kg (22.7 mg per pound) of body weight a day, divided into smaller amounts with meals. Your doctor may change the dose if needed.
- For *oral* dosage form (tablets):
  - —To prevent or treat carnitine deficiency:
    - Adults and teenagers—1 gram taken two or three times a day with meals.
    - Children—The dose is based on body weight and must be determined by your doctor. The usual dose at first is 50 mg per kg (22.7 mg per pound) of body weight a day, divided into smaller amounts with meals. Your doctor may change the dose if needed.
- For *injection* dosage form:
  - —To treat carnitine deficiency:
    - Adults and children—The dose is based on body weight and must be determined by your doctor. The usual dose is 50 mg per kg (22.7 mg per pound) of body weight a day injected into a vein. Your doctor may change the dose if needed.

Missed dose—If you miss a dose of this medicine, skip the missed dose and go back to your regular dosing schedule. Do not double doses. Taking doses too close together may increase stomach upset.

Storage—To store this medicine:
- Keep out of the reach of children.
- Store away from heat and direct light.
- Do not store in the bathroom, near the kitchen sink, or in other damp places. Heat or moisture may cause the medicine to break down.
- Keep the oral solution form of this medicine from freezing. Do not refrigerate.
- Do not keep outdated medicines or those no longer needed. Be sure that any discarded medicine is out of the reach of children.

Precautions While Using This Medicine

Do *not* change brands or dosage forms of levocarnitine without first checking with your doctor. Different products may not work in the same way. If you refill your medicine and it looks different, check with your pharmacist.

Side Effects of This Medicine

Along with its needed effects, a medicine may cause some unwanted effects. The following side effects may go away during treatment as your body adjusts to the medicine. However, check with your doctor if any of these effects continue or are bothersome:

More common

Body odor; diarrhea or stomach cramps; nausea or vomiting

Other side effects not listed above may also occur in some patients. If you notice any other effects, check with your doctor.

Additional Information

Once a medicine has been approved for marketing for a certain use, experience may show that it is also useful for other medical problems. Although this use is not included in product labeling, levocarnitine is used in certain patients with the following medical condition:
- Carnitine deficiency that results from treatment with valproic acid

Other than the above information, there is no additional information relating to proper use, precautions, or side effects for this use.

Revised: 03/04/92
Interim revision: 08/10/92; 08/29/94; 08/07/95

LEVODOPA Systemic

Some commonly used brand names are:

In the U.S.—

Dopar[2]
Larodopa[2]
Sinemet[1]
Sinemet CR[1]

In Canada—

Larodopa[2]
Sinemet[1]
Sinemet CR[1]

Note: For quick reference, the following medicines are numbered to match the corresponding brand names.

This information applies to the following medicines:

1. Carbidopa and Levodopa (KAR-bi-doe-pa and LEE-voe-doe-pa)
2. Levodopa

Description

Levodopa is used alone or in combination with carbidopa to treat Parkinson's disease, sometimes referred to as shaking palsy or paralysis agitans. Some patients require the combination of medicine, while others benefit from levodopa alone. By improving muscle control, this medicine allows more normal movements of the body.

Levodopa alone or in combination is available only with your doctor's prescription. It is available in the following dosage forms:

Oral

Carbidopa and Levodopa
- Tablets (U.S. and Canada)
- Extended-release tablets (U.S. and Canada)

Levodopa
- Capsules (U.S.)
- Tablets (U.S. and Canada)

Before Using This Medicine

In deciding to use a medicine, the risks of taking the medicine must be weighed against the good it will do. This is a decision you and your doctor will make. For levodopa and for carbidopa and levodopa combination, the following should be considered:

Allergies—Tell your doctor if you have ever had any unusual or allergic reaction to levodopa alone or in combination with carbidopa. Also tell your health care professional if you are allergic to any other substances, such as foods, preservatives, or dyes.

Diet—Since protein may interfere with the body's response to levodopa, high protein diets should be avoided. Intake of normal amounts of protein should be spaced equally throughout the day.

For patients taking levodopa by itself:

- Pyridoxine (vitamin B_6) has been found to reduce the effects of levodopa when levodopa is taken by itself. This does not happen with the combination of carbidopa and levodopa. *If you are taking levodopa by itself, do not take vitamin products containing vitamin B_6 during treatment, unless prescribed by your doctor.*
- Large amounts of pyridoxine are also contained in some foods such as avocado, bacon, beans, beef liver, dry skim milk, oatmeal, peas, pork, sweet potato, tuna, and certain health foods. Check with your doctor about how much of these foods you may have in your diet while you are taking levodopa. Also, ask your health care professional for help when selecting vitamin products.

Pregnancy—Studies have not been done in pregnant women. However, studies in animals have shown that levodopa affects the baby's growth both before and after birth if given during pregnancy in doses many times the human dose. Also, studies in rabbits have shown that levodopa, alone or in combination with carbidopa, causes birth defects.

Breast-feeding—Levodopa and carbidopa pass into the breast milk and may cause unwanted side effects in the nursing baby. Also, levodopa may reduce the flow of breast milk.

Children—Studies on this medicine have been done only in adult patients, and there is no specific information comparing use of levodopa or carbidopa in children with use in other age groups.

Older adults—Elderly people are especially sensitive to the effects of levodopa. This may increase the chance of side effects during treatment.

Other medicines—Although certain medicines should not be used together at all, in other cases 2 different medicines may be used together even if an interaction might occur. In these cases, your doctor may want to change the dose, or other precautions may be necessary. When you are taking levodopa or carbidopa and levodopa combination, it is especially important that your health care professional know if you are taking any of the following:

- Cocaine—Cocaine use by individuals taking levodopa, alone or in combination with carbidopa, may cause an irregular heartbeat

- Ethotoin (e.g., Peganone) or
- Haloperidol (e.g., Haldol) or
- Mephenytoin (e.g., Mesantoin) or
- Phenothiazines (acetophenazine [e.g., Tindal], chlorpromazine [e.g., Thorazine], fluphenazine [e.g., Prolixin], mesoridazine [e.g., Serentil], perphenazine [e.g., Trilafon], prochlorperazine [e.g., Compazine], promazine [e.g., Sparine], promethazine [e.g., Phenergan], thioridazine [e.g., Mellaril], trifluoperazine [e.g., Stelazine], triflupromazine [e.g., Vesprin], trimeprazine [e.g., Temaril]) or
- Phenytoin (e.g., Dilantin)—Taking these medicines with levodopa may lessen the effects of levodopa
- Monoamine oxidase (MAO) inhibitors (furazolidone [e.g., Furoxone], isocarboxazid [e.g., Marplan], phenelzine [e.g., Nardil], procarbazine [e.g., Matulane], tranylcypromine [e.g., Parnate])—Taking levodopa while you are taking or within 2 weeks of taking monoamine oxidase (MAO) inhibitors may cause sudden extremely high blood pressure; at least 14 days should be allowed between stopping treatment with one medicine and starting treatment with the other medicine

- Pyridoxine (vitamin B_6, e.g., Hexa-Betalin), present in some foods and vitamin formulas (for levodopa used alone)—Pyridoxine reverses the effects of levodopa

- Selegiline—Dosage of levodopa or carbidopa and levodopa combination may need to be decreased

Other medical problems—The presence of other medical problems may affect the use of levodopa. Make sure you tell your doctor if you have any other medical problems, especially:

- Diabetes mellitus (sugar diabetes)—The amount of insulin or antidiabetic medicine that you need to take may change
- Emphysema, asthma, bronchitis, or other chronic lung disease or
- Glaucoma or
- Heart or blood vessel disease or
- Hormone problems or
- Melanoma (a type of skin cancer) (or history of) or
- Mental illness—Levodopa may make the condition worse
- Kidney disease or
- Liver disease—Higher blood levels of levodopa may occur, increasing the chance of side effects
- Seizure disorders, such as epilepsy (history of)—The risk of seizures may be increased
- Stomach ulcer (history of)—The ulcer may occur again

Proper Use of This Medicine

It is best not to take this medicine with or after food, especially high-protein food, since food may decrease levodopa's effect. However, *to lessen possible stomach upset, your doctor may want you to take food shortly after taking this medicine (about 15 minutes after).* If stomach upset is severe or continues, check with your doctor.

Take this medicine only as directed. Do not take more or less of it, and do not take it more often than your doctor ordered.

For patients taking *carbidopa and levodopa extended-release tablets*:

- Swallow the tablet whole without crushing or chewing, unless your doctor tells you not to. If your doctor tells you to, you may break the tablet in half.

Some people must take this medicine for several weeks or months before full benefit is received. *Do not stop taking it even if you do not think it is working.* Instead, check with your doctor.

Dosing—The dose of levodopa or carbidopa and levodopa combination will be different for different patients. *Follow your doctor's orders or the directions on the label.* The following information includes only the average doses of levodopa or carbidopa and levodopa combination. *If your dose is different, do not change it* unless your doctor tells you to do so.

The number of capsules or tablets that you take depends on the strength of the medicine. Also, *the number of doses you take each day, the time allowed between doses, and the length of time you take the medicine depend on your special needs.*

For levodopa

- For Parkinson's disease:
  - —For *oral* dosage form (capsules and tablets):
    - Adults and teenagers—At first, 250 milligrams (mg) two to four times a day. Your doctor may increase your dose if needed. However, the dose is usually not more than 8000 mg a day.
    - Children up to 12 years of age—Use and dose must be determined by your doctor.

For levodopa and carbidopa combination

- For Parkinson's disease:
  - —For *oral tablet* dosage form:
    - Adults—At first, 1 tablet three or four times a day. Your doctor may need to change your dose, depending on how you respond to this combination medicine.
    - Children and teenagers—Use and dose must be determined by your doctor.
  - —For *oral extended-release tablet* dosage form:
    - Adults—At first, 1 tablet two times a day. However, you may need to take more than this. Your doctor will decide the right dose for you, depending on your condition and the other medicines you may be taking for Parkinson's disease.
    - Children and teenagers—Use and dose must be determined by your doctor.

Missed dose—If you miss a dose of this medicine, take it as soon as possible. However, if your next scheduled dose is within 2 hours, skip the missed dose and go back to your regular dosing schedule. Do not double doses.

Storage—To store this medicine:

- Keep out of the reach of children.
- Store away from heat and direct light.
- Do not store in the bathroom, near the kitchen sink, or in other damp places. Heat or moisture may cause the medicine to break down.
- Do not keep outdated medicine or medicine no longer needed. Be sure that any discarded medicine is out of the reach of children.

Precautions While Using This Medicine

Before having any kind of surgery (including dental surgery) or emergency treatment, tell the medical doctor or dentist in charge that you are taking this medicine.

For *diabetic patients*:

- This medicine may cause test results for urine sugar or ketones to be wrong. Check with your doctor before depending on home tests using the paper-strip or tablet method.

This medicine may cause some people to become drowsy or less alert than they are normally. *Make sure you know how you react to this medicine before you drive, use machines, or do anything else that could be dangerous if you are not alert.*

Dizziness, lightheadedness, or fainting may occur, especially when you get up from a lying or sitting position. Getting up slowly may help. If the problem continues or gets worse, check with your doctor.

For patients taking levodopa by itself:

- Pyridoxine (vitamin B_6) has been found to reduce the effects of levodopa when levodopa is taken by itself.

This does not happen with the combination of carbidopa and levodopa. *If you are taking levodopa by itself, do not take vitamin products containing vitamin B_6 during treatment, unless prescribed by your doctor.*

- Large amounts of pyridoxine are also contained in some foods such as avocado, bacon, beans, beef liver, dry skim milk, oatmeal, peas, pork, sweet potato, tuna, and certain health foods. Check with your doctor about how much of these foods you may have in your diet while you are taking levodopa. Also, ask your health care professional for help when selecting vitamin products.

As your condition improves and your body movements become easier, *be careful not to overdo physical activities. Injuries resulting from falls may occur.* Physical activities must be increased gradually to allow your body to adjust to changing balance, circulation, and coordination. *This is especially important in the elderly.*

After taking this medicine for long periods of time, such as a year or more, some patients suddenly lose the ability to move. Their muscles do not seem to work. This loss of movement may last from a few minutes to several hours. The patient then is able to move as before. This condition may unexpectedly occur again and again. If you should have this problem, sometimes called the ''on-off'' effect, check with your doctor.

Side Effects of This Medicine

Along with its needed effects, a medicine may cause some unwanted effects. Although not all of these side effects may occur, if they do occur they may need medical attention.

Check with your doctor as soon as possible if any of the following side effects occur:

More common

Mental depression; mood or mental changes (such as aggressive behavior); unusual and uncontrolled movements of the body

Less common—more common when levodopa is used alone

Difficult urination; dizziness or lightheadedness when getting up from a lying or sitting position; irregular heartbeat; nausea or vomiting (severe or continuing); spasm or closing of eyelids (not more common when levodopa is used alone)

Rare

High blood pressure; stomach pain; unusual tiredness or weakness

Other side effects may occur that usually do not need medical attention. These side effects may go away during treatment as your body adjusts to the medicine. However, check with your doctor if any of the following side effects continue or are bothersome:

More common

Anxiety, confusion, or nervousness (especially in elderly patients receiving other medicine for Parkinson's disease)

Less common

Constipation (more common when levodopa is used alone); diarrhea; dryness of mouth; flushing of skin; headache; loss of appetite; muscle twitching; nightmares (more common when levodopa is used alone); trouble in sleeping

This medicine may sometimes cause the urine and sweat to be darker in color than usual. The urine may at first be reddish, then turn to nearly black after being exposed to air. Some bathroom cleaning products will produce a similar effect when in contact with urine containing this medicine. This is to be expected during treatment with this medicine.

Other side effects not listed above may also occur in some patients. If you notice any other effects, check with your doctor.

Revised: 08/18/92
Interim revision: 08/17/94

LEVOMETHADYL Systemic†

A commonly used brand name in the U.S. is Orlaam.

Other commonly used names are LAAM, LAM, levacetylmethadol, levo-alpha-acetylmethadol, levomethadyl acetate, and MK790.

†Not commercially available in Canada.

Description

Levomethadyl (lee-voe-METH-a-dil) belongs to the group of medicines known as narcotic analgesics (nar-KOT-ik an-al-GEE-zicks). It is used as a substitute for illegal narcotics in addiction treatment programs. This medicine is not a cure for addiction. It is used as part of an overall program that may include counseling, attending support group meetings, and other treatment recommended by your doctor.

Levomethadyl helps prevent the withdrawal symptoms that may occur when an addict stops using other narcotics. In detoxification programs, the amount of levomethadyl used is slowly decreased until an addict becomes drug-free. In maintenance programs, it is used on a long-term basis to help narcotic addicts stay away from street drugs. With long-term use, levomethadyl may decrease an addict's craving for other narcotics.

Another narcotic, methadone, is also used in detoxification and maintenance programs. Methadone begins to work faster than levomethadyl does when treatment is started, but it has to be taken every day. Levomethadyl starts to work slowly, but it does not have to be taken every day. Therefore, some people may start treatment with methadone and then change over to levomethadyl after several weeks. Other people may receive only one medicine or the other during the entire time of treatment. Your doctor and your counselor at the clinic will decide on the best treatment plan for you.

In the U.S., levomethadyl is available only in government-approved treatment clinics, in the following dosage form:

Oral

- Oral solution (U.S.)

Before Using This Medicine

In deciding to use a medicine, the risks of taking the medicine must be weighed against the good it will do. This is a decision you and your doctor will make. For levomethadyl, the following should be considered:

Allergies—Tell your doctor if you have ever had any unusual or allergic reaction to levomethadyl. Also tell your health care professional if you are allergic to any other substances, such as foods, preservatives, or dyes.

Pregnancy—Methadone is the best medicine for treating pregnant narcotic addicts. Although there may be rare exceptions, levomethadyl is not recommended for use by pregnant women. Breathing problems and withdrawal symptoms are likely to occur in babies born to mothers who use levomethadyl during pregnancy. Also, although levomethadyl did not cause birth defects, it caused early deliveries and stillbirths in animal studies. In the U.S., the law requires that women who may become pregnant must be given pregnancy tests before levomethadyl treatment is started and once a month during treatment.

Breast-feeding—It is not known whether levomethadyl passes into the breast milk in amounts that may cause dependence or other side effects in nursing babies. Breast-feeding mothers who wish to use levomethadyl should discuss this with their doctor.

Children—In the U.S., the law does not allow levomethadyl to be used for treating addicts younger than 18 years of age.

Older adults—Many medicines have not been studied specifically in older people. Therefore, it may not be known whether they work exactly the same way they do in younger adults or if they cause different side effects or problems in older people. There is no specific information comparing use of levomethadyl in the elderly with use in other age groups.

Other medicines—Although certain medicines should not be used together at all, in other cases two different medicines may be used together even if an interaction might occur. In these cases, your doctor may want to change the dose, or other precautions may be necessary. When you are taking levomethadyl, it is especially important that your health care professional know if you are taking any of the following:

- Alcohol or
- Barbiturates or
- Carbamazepine (e.g., Tegretol) or
- Chloramphenicol (e.g., Chloromycetin) or
- Cimetidine (e.g., Tagamet) or
- Corticosteroids (cortisone-like medicines) or
- Diltiazem (e.g., Cardizem) or
- Disulfiram (e.g., Antabuse) or
- Divalproex (e.g., Depakote) or
- Erythromycins (medicine for infection) or
- Griseofulvin (e.g., Fulvicin) or
- Isoniazid (e.g., INH, Nydrazid) or
- Oral contraceptives (birth control pills) containing estrogen or
- Phenylbutazone (e.g., Butazolidin) or
- Phenytoin (e.g., Dilantin) or
- Primidone (e.g., Mysoline) or
- Quinine (e.g., Quinamm) or
- Rifampin (e.g., Rifadin)
- Ranitidine (e.g., Zantac) or
- Valproic acid (e.g., Depakene) or
- Verapamil (e.g., Calan)—These medicines may change the way levomethadyl works in your body. Some of them may cause levomethadyl to start working more quickly, but to keep working for a shorter time, than usual. Others may cause levomethadyl to start working more slowly, but to keep working for a longer time, than usual
- Buprenorphine (e.g., Buprenex) or
- Butorphanol or (e.g., Stadol) or
- Dezocine (e.g., Dalgan) or
- Nalbuphine (e.g., Nubain) or
- Pentazocine (e.g., Talwin)—Like levomethadyl, these medicines are narcotics. However, they may cause withdrawal symptoms if they are taken during levomethadyl treatment
- Central nervous system (CNS) depressants (medicine that causes drowsiness) or
- Other narcotics or
- Tricyclic antidepressants (medicine for depression)—The chance of serious side effects is increased; deaths have occurred when people continued to use CNS depressant ''street'' drugs, including other narcotics, while taking levomethadyl
- Naltrexone (e.g., ReVia)—Naltrexone blocks the effects of levomethadyl and will cause withdrawal symptoms if taken during levomethadyl treatment

Other medical problems—The presence of other medical problems may affect the use of levomethadyl. Make sure you tell your doctor if you have any other medical problems, especially:

- Asthma, emphysema, or other chronic lung disease, or
- Brain disease or head injury or
- Colitis or
- Crohn's disease or
- Enlarged prostate or problems with urination or
- Gallbladder disease or gallstones or
- Heart disease or
- High blood pressure—Levomethadyl has side effects that could be dangerous to people with these conditions
- Kidney disease or
- Liver disease or
- Underactive thyroid—The chance of side effects may be increased

Proper Use of This Medicine

Each dose of levomethadyl must be taken at the clinic. In the U.S., the law does not allow the medicine to be taken home. Most people will have to go to the clinic 3 times a week.

Dosing—The dose of levomethadyl will be different for different patients. The following information includes only the average doses of levomethadyl.

- For *oral* dosage form (oral solution):
  - —For treating narcotic addiction:
    - Adults—The first dose of levomethadyl for patients who have not started treatment with

methadone is between 20 and 40 milligrams (mg). The first dose for patients who have been receiving methadone will be a little higher than the amount of methadone that was being taken every day, but not more than 120 mg. Your doctor will then adjust your dose, depending on whether you experience withdrawal symptoms or side effects after the first dose. More than one change in the dose may be needed, until the right dose for you has been found.

Most people will receive levomethadyl 3 times a week, either on Monday, Wednesday, and Friday or on Tuesday, Thursday, and Saturday. Some people need a larger dose on Friday or Saturday, so that the medicine will last until the next visit. In detoxification programs, the dose of levomethadyl will gradually be decreased until the patient is able to stop taking it. In maintenance programs, treatment may be continued as long as needed.

- Children—In the U.S., levomethadyl cannot be used for patients younger than 18 years of age.

Precautions While Using This Medicine

Taking levomethadyl is only part of your treatment. Your doctor and your counselor at the clinic will make a treatment plan for you to follow. This plan may include seeing your counselor at the clinic regularly, attending support group meetings, and making changes in your lifestyle that will help you stay away from illegal drugs. *The success of your treatment will depend on how carefully you follow your treatment plan.*

This medicine will add to the effects of alcohol and other CNS depressants (medicines that slow down the nervous system, possibly causing drowsiness). Some examples of CNS depressants are antihistamines or medicine for hay fever, other allergies, or colds; sedatives, tranquilizers, or sleeping medicine; prescription pain medicine or other narcotics; barbiturates; medicine for seizures; muscle relaxants; or anesthetics, including some dental anesthetics. *It is very important that you do not drink alcoholic beverages or take any CNS depressants during levomethadyl treatment unless you have been directed to do so by a doctor who knows that you are taking levomethadyl.* Even if you continue to have some withdrawal symptoms and to crave narcotics for a while after levomethadyl treatment has been started, *do not use illegal narcotics or other CNS depressant "street" drugs. Taking "street" drugs together with levomethadyl has caused some people to die from an overdose.*

Levomethadyl may cause some people to become drowsy, especially when treatment is started or the dose is increased. *Make sure you know how you react to this medicine before you drive, use machines, or do anything else that could be dangerous if you are drowsy or are not alert and clearheaded.* This effect usually goes away after a few days, when your body gets used to the medicine. However, *tell your counselor at your next visit to the clinic if any dose causes drowsiness that is severe enough to interfere with your activities.*

Dizziness, lightheadedness, or even fainting may occur when you get up suddenly from a lying or sitting position. *Getting up slowly may help lessen this problem.* Also, lying down for a while may relieve dizziness or lightheadedness.

Tell all health care professionals you go to that you are taking levomethadyl. This is especially important if any kind of surgery or emergency treatment is needed. Serious side effects can occur if your health care professional gives you certain other medicines without knowing that you are taking levomethadyl.

Using narcotics such as levomethadyl for a long time can cause severe constipation. To prevent this, your counselor may direct you to take laxatives, drink a lot of fluids, or increase the amount of fiber in your diet. Be sure to follow the directions carefully, because continuing constipation can lead to more serious problems.

Levomethadyl may cause dryness of the mouth. For temporary relief, use sugarless candy or gum, melt bits of ice in your mouth, or use a saliva substitute. However, if dry mouth continues for more than 2 weeks, check with your dentist. Continuing dryness of the mouth may increase the chance of dental disease, including tooth decay, gum disease, and fungus infections.

For *women* only:

- *Although there may be rare exceptions, levomethadyl is not recommended for use by pregnant women.* Pregnancy tests will be given once a month during treatment. *If you miss any of these tests you may not be able to continue receiving levomethadyl.*
- *Women who may become pregnant should use effective birth control during levomethadyl treatment.* If you are not sure what method of birth control will work best for you, check with your counselor at the clinic.
- If you plan to become pregnant, you should first discuss your plans with your doctor or your counselor. They can arrange for you to receive methadone instead of levomethadyl.
- If you think you have become pregnant during treatment, *tell your counselor right away.*

Some people may be transferred to methadone after receiving levomethadyl for a while. If you are given any take-home doses of methadone, *do not take the first dose of methadone for at least 48 hours (2 days) after your last dose of levomethadyl.* Taking the 2 medicines too close together may cause an overdose.

If you think you may have taken an overdose of narcotics, get emergency help right away. Taking an overdose of narcotics, or taking alcohol or CNS depressants with narcotics, may lead to unconsciousness or death. Signs of overdose include convulsions (seizures); confusion; severe dizziness, drowsiness, nervousness, restlessness, or weakness; and very slow or troubled breathing. *It is very important that the emergency room doctor knows that you are physically dependent on a narcotic called levomethadyl, that using naloxone to treat your overdose is very likely to cause withdrawal symptoms, and that you will need to be watched for a long time because levomethadyl's effects last for several days.* However, you may not be able to give this information to the doctor yourself. Therefore, *you should direct friends and family members to give this information to the doctor, if necessary.*

Side Effects of This Medicine

Along with its needed effects, a medicine may cause some unwanted effects. Although not all of these side effects may occur, if they do occur they may need medical attention.

Get emergency help immediately if any of the following side effects occur:

Signs and symptoms of overdose

Cold, clammy skin; confusion; convulsions (seizures); dizziness (severe); drowsiness (severe); low blood pressure; nervousness or restlessness (severe); pinpoint pupils of eyes; slow heartbeat; slow or troubled breathing; weakness (severe)

Also, tell your counselor at the clinic as soon as possible if any of the following side effects occur:

Less common

Mental depression; skin rash; swelling of face, fingers, feet, and/or lower legs; weight gain

At each visit to the clinic, be sure to tell your counselor if any of the following side effects occurred after your last dose of levomethadyl:

Signs of too much levomethadyl

Drowsiness (severe); feeling ''wired''

Signs of not enough levomethadyl (withdrawal symptoms)

Body aches, diarrhea; fast heartbeat; gooseflesh; increased sweating; loss of appetite; nausea or vomiting; nervousness, restlessness, or irritability; runny nose; shivering or trembling; sneezing; stomach cramps; trouble in sleeping; unexplained fever; unusually large pupils of eyes; weakness; yawning

The withdrawal side effects listed above may also occur after levomethadyl treatment has been stopped or during a changeover from levomethadyl to methadone. *Always check with your counselor at the clinic if withdrawal side effects occur after you stop taking levomethadyl.*

Other side effects may occur that usually do not need medical attention. These side effects may go away during treatment as your body adjusts to the medicine. However, check with your counselor at the clinic if any of the following side effects continue or are bothersome:

More common

Abdominal or stomach pain; constipation; general feeling of discomfort or illness; joint pain; sexual problems in males

Less common or rare

Anxiety; back pain; blurred vision; chills; coughing; decreased desire for sex; dizziness, lightheadedness, or feeling faint when rising from a lying or sitting position; drowsiness; dry mouth; false sense of well-being; flu-like symptoms; headache; hot flashes; muscle pain; unusual dreams; watery eyes

Other side effects not listed above may also occur in some patients. If you notice any other effects, check with your doctor.

Developed: 08/11/95

LIDOCAINE AND PRILOCAINE Topical

A commonly used brand name in the U.S. and Canada is EMLA.

Another commonly used name for lidocaine is lignocaine.

Description

This medicine contains a mixture of 2 local anesthetics (an-ess-THET-iks), lidocaine (LYE-doe-kane) and prilocaine (PRIL-oh-kane). It is used to produce numbness or loss of feeling before certain painful procedures, such as injections, drawing blood from a vein, or removing small growths (warts, for example) from the skin.

This medicine deadens the nerve endings in the skin. It does not cause unconsciousness as general anesthetics used for surgery do.

In the U.S., this medicine is available only with your doctor's prescription. In Canada, it is available without a prescription. However, your doctor may have special instructions on the proper use and dose, depending on the reason you are using this medicine.

Topical

- Cream (U.S. and Canada)

Before Using This Medicine

In deciding to use a medicine, the risks of using the medicine must be weighed against the good it will do. This is a decision you and your doctor will make. For this medicine, the following should be considered:

Allergies—Tell your doctor if you have ever had any unusual or allergic reaction to lidocaine, prilocaine, or other local anesthetics given by injection or applied to any part of the body as a liquid, cream, ointment, or spray. Also tell your health care professional if you are allergic to any other substances, such as foods, preservatives, or dyes.

Pregnancy—This mixture of lidocaine and prilocaine has not been studied in pregnant women. However, lidocaine and prilocaine (separately) have been given to pregnant women and have not been reported to cause birth defects or other problems.

Breast-feeding—Small amounts of lidocaine, and probably of prilocaine also, pass into breast milk. Many medicines that pass into breast milk in small amounts may be used safely while breast-feeding. Mothers who are breast-feeding and who wish to use this medicine should discuss this with their doctor.

Children—This medicine has been tested in children. Very young children (less than 1 year of age) may be especially sensitive to the effects of lidocaine and prilocaine. This may increase the chance of side effects. However, in effective doses, this medicine has not been shown to cause different side effects or problems in children older than 1 year of age than it does in adults.

Young children are often frightened when they receive injections or have other painful procedures done. This medicine helps prevent pain, but it will not calm a frightened child. Parents can help by staying calm and by comforting and reassuring the child.

Older adults—This medicine has not been studied specifically in older people. However, it is possible that the chance of some side effects may be increased in elderly people. Experience with local anesthetics given by injection or applied to other areas of the body (for example, the throat or the inside of the mouth) has shown that elderly people are usually more sensitive than younger adults to the effects of local anesthetics.

Other medicines—Although certain medicines should not be used together at all, in other cases two different medicines may be used together even if an interaction might occur. In these cases, your doctor may want to change the dose, or other precautions may be necessary. Before using this medicine, tell your health care professional if you are taking any other prescription or nonprescription (over-the-counter [OTC]) medicine, especially:

- Sulfonamides (sulfa medicine)—The chance of a side effect (methemoglobinemia) may be increased, especially in infants.

Other medical problems—The presence of other medical problems may affect the use of this medicine. Make sure you tell your doctor if you have any other medical problems, especially:

- Broken or inflamed skin, burns, or open wounds at place of application or
- Atopic dermatitis or
- Eczema—More of this medicine can be absorbed into the body quickly, which increases the chance of side effects
- Glucose-6-phosphate dehydrogenase (G6PD) deficiency—A possible side effect of this medicine (methemoglobinemia) may be more likely to occur
- Liver disease (severe)—The chance of side effects may be increased if large amounts of this medicine are absorbed into the body quickly
- Methemoglobinemia—This medicine may make your condition worse

Proper Use of This Medicine

For safe and effective use of this medicine:

- Use this medicine only when directed to do so by your health care professional. *Do not use it for any other reason without first checking with your doctor.* This medicine may be more likely than other topical anesthetics to cause unwanted effects if it is used too much, because more of it is absorbed into the body through the skin.
- Unless otherwise directed by your health care professional, *do not apply this medicine to open wounds, burns, or broken or inflamed skin.*
- *Be careful not to get any of this medicine in your eyes,* because it can cause severe eye irritation. If any of the medicine does get into your eye, *do not rub or wipe the eye, even if it hurts. Instead, check with your doctor right away.*
- Be careful not to get any of this medicine on your lips or in your mouth.
- *Follow carefully any directions given to you by your health care professional about how this medicine should be used.* If you have not received other instructions about how to apply this medicine, *follow the patient directions that come with the medicine.*
- *Check with your health care professional if you have any questions* about how to apply this medicine, where to apply it, or what time to apply it.

To use:

- Apply a thick layer of medicine to the area or areas where local anesthesia (numbness or loss of feeling) is needed. *Do not spread out the medicine.*
- This medicine is used together with a special bandage (called an occlusive dressing). *Check with your health care professional if you did not receive any bandages with the medicine.* Cover the medicine with the bandage. *Seal the edges of the bandage tightly, making sure that none of the medicine leaks out.* Do not lift the bandage or otherwise disturb it. Keeping the medicine tightly covered helps it work properly.
- If your health care professional has directed you to remove the bandage and wipe off the medicine after a certain amount of time, follow the directions carefully. Then clean the area with the antiseptic solution recommended by your health care professional. *If your health care professional has not directed you to remove the bandage and the medicine, keep them in place until your health care professional removes them.*

Dosing—The dose of this medicine will be different for different patients. *Follow your doctor's orders or the directions that come with the medicine.* The following information includes only the average doses of this medicine. *If your dose is different, do not change it* unless your doctor tells you to do so.

- For *topical* dosage form (cream):
  - —For preventing pain caused by injections or drawing blood from a vein:
    - Adults and children—Apply 2.5 grams of cream (one-half of the amount in a 5-gram tube) in a thick layer to an area about two inches by two inches (twenty to twenty-five square centimeters) in size. Your health care professional may direct you to apply the medicine in two places. The medicine should remain in place, covered by the bandage that comes with it, for at least one hour.

—For preventing pain caused by certain procedures:
- Adults—The size of the area to be covered by a thick layer of this medicine and the amount of time that the medicine must be kept in place depend on the procedure that is being done. The medicine sometimes needs to be kept in place, covered with the bandage, for two hours or more.
- Children—The size of the area to be covered by a thick layer of this medicine and the amount of time that the medicine must be kept in place depend on the procedure that is being done. However, the largest area that may be covered by this medicine depends on the child's weight and must be determined by your doctor. The medicine sometimes needs to be kept in place, covered with the bandage, for two hours or more.

Storage—To store this medicine:
- Keep out of the reach of children.
- Store away from heat and direct light.
- Keep the medicine from freezing.
- Do not keep outdated medicine or medicine no longer needed. Be sure that any discarded medicine is out of the reach of children.

Precautions After Using This Medicine

After applying this medicine to the skin of a child, *watch the child carefully to make sure that he or she does not loosen or remove the bandage. Also, keep the child from getting any of the medicine into his or her mouth.* This medicine can cause serious side effects, especially in children, if any of it gets into the mouth or is swallowed.

During the time that the area to which the medicine was applied feels numb, serious injury can occur without your knowing about it. *Be especially careful to avoid injury until the anesthetic wears off or feeling returns to the area.* For example, do not scratch or rub the area or allow very hot or very cold objects to touch it.

Side Effects of This Medicine

Along with its needed effects, a medicine may cause some unwanted effects. Although not all of these side effects may occur, if they do occur they may need medical attention.

The following side effects may mean that a serious allergic reaction is occurring. Check with your doctor or get emergency help immediately if they occur, especially if several of them occur at the same time.

Rare
Coughing, shortness of breath, troubled breathing, tightness in chest, or wheezing; difficulty in swallowing; large, hive-like swellings on eyelids, face, lips, or tongue; severe dizziness or feeling faint; skin rash, itching, or hives; stuffy nose

Also check with your health care professional, or get emergency help right away, if any of the following side effects occur:

Signs of too much medicine being absorbed into the body
Blue or blue-purple color of lips, fingernails, or skin; blurred or double vision; dark urine; dizziness or drowsiness; feeling hot, cold, or numb; headache; irregular or fast heartbeat; muscle twitching or trembling; nausea or vomiting; ringing or buzzing in the ears; shortness of breath or troubled breathing; unusual excitement, nervousness, or restlessness; unusual tiredness or weakness

Note: The above side effects are not likely to occur when usual amounts of this medicine are used properly. However, they may occur if the medicine is used too often, applied to broken skin (for example, cuts or scrapes), applied to very large areas, or kept on the skin too long.

Other side effects may occur that usually do not need medical attention. However, check with your doctor if any of the following side effects continue or are bothersome:

More common
Burning feeling, swelling, itching, or skin rash at place of application (without other signs of an allergic reaction listed above); white or red skin at place of application

Other side effects not listed above may also occur in some patients. If you notice any other effects, check with your doctor.

Additional Information

Once a medicine has been approved for marketing for a certain use, experience may show that it is also useful for other uses. Although this use is not included in product labeling, this medicine is used to produce loss of feeling in the genital area of adults before certain kinds of procedures are done. When used for this purpose, the medicine will be applied and removed by your doctor.

Other than the above information, there is no additional information relating to precautions or side effects for this use.

Revised: 08/18/93

LINCOMYCIN Systemic

A commonly used brand name is:

In the U.S.—
Lincocin
Lincorex

In Canada—
Lincocin

Description

Lincomycin belongs to the family of medicines called antibiotics. These medicines are used to treat infections. They will not work for colds, flu, or other virus infections.

Lincomycin is available only with your doctor's prescription, in the following dosage forms:

Oral
- Capsules (U.S. and Canada)

Parenteral
- Injection (U.S. and Canada)

Before Using This Medicine

In deciding to use a medicine, the risks of taking the medicine must be weighed against the good it will do. This is a decision you and your doctor will make. For lincomycin, the following should be considered:

Allergies—Tell your doctor if you have ever had any unusual or allergic reaction to lincomycin, clindamycin, or doxorubicin. Also tell your health care professional if you are allergic to any other substances, such as foods, preservatives, or dyes.

Pregnancy—Lincomycin has not been reported to cause birth defects or other problems in humans.

Breast-feeding—Lincomycin passes into the breast milk. However, lincomycin has not been reported to cause problems in nursing babies.

Children—Lincomycin has been used in children 1 month of age or older and has not been reported to cause different side effects or problems than it does in adults.

Older adults—Many medicines have not been studied specifically in older people. Therefore, it may not be known whether they work exactly the same way they do in younger adults or if they cause different side effects or problems in older people. There is no specific information comparing use of lincomycin in the elderly with use in other age groups.

Other medicines—Although certain medicines should not be used together at all, in other cases two different medicines may be used together even if an interaction might occur. In these cases, your doctor may want to change the dose, or other precautions may be necessary. When you are taking lincomycin, it is especially important that your health care professional know if you are taking any of the following:

- Chloramphenicol (e.g., Chloromycetin) or
- Diarrhea medicine containing kaolin or attapulgite or
- Erythromycins (medicine for infection)—Taking these medicines along with lincomycin may decrease the effects of lincomycin
- Diarrhea medicine, such as loperamide (Imodium A-D)—Patients who take diarrhea medicine, such as loperamide (Imodium A-D) or diphenyoxylate and atropine (Lomotil), may worsen diarrhea that is a side effect of lincomycin

Other medical problems—The presence of other medical problems may affect the use of lincomycin. Make sure you tell your doctor if you have any other medical problems, especially:

- Kidney disease (severe) or
- Liver disease (severe)—Severe kidney or liver disease may increase blood levels of this medicine, increasing the chance of side effects
- Stomach or intestinal disease, history of (especially colitis, including colitis caused by antibiotics, or enteritis)—Patients with a history of stomach or intestinal disease may have an increased chance of side effects

Proper Use of This Medicine

Lincomycin is best taken with a full glass (8 ounces) of water on an empty stomach (either 1 hour before or 2 hours after meals), unless otherwise directed by your doctor.

To help clear up your infection completely, *keep taking this medicine for the full time of treatment,* even if you begin to feel better after a few days. *If you have a "strep" infection, you should keep taking this medicine for at least 10 days. This is especially important in "strep" infections. Serious heart problems could develop later* if your infection is not cleared up completely. Also, if you stop taking this medicine too soon, your symptoms may return.

This medicine works best when there is a constant amount in the blood. *To help keep the amount constant, do not miss any doses. Also, it is best to take each dose at evenly spaced times day and night.* For example, if you are to take 4 doses a day, doses should be spaced about 6 hours apart. If this interferes with your sleep or other daily activities, or if you need help in planning the best times to take your medicine, check with your health care professional.

Dosing—The dose of lincomycin will be different for different patients. *Follow your doctor's orders or the directions on the label.* The following information includes only the average doses of lincomycin. *If your dose is different, do not change it* unless your doctor tells you to do so.

- For infections caused by bacteria:
  - —For *oral* dosage form (capsules):
    - Adults and teenagers—500 milligrams (mg) every six to eight hours.
    - Infants up to 1 month of age—Use and dose must be determined by your doctor.
    - Children 1 month of age and older—Dose is based on body weight. The usual dose is 7.5 to 15 mg per kilogram (kg) (3.4 to 6.8 mg per pound) of body weight every six hours; or 10 to 20 mg per kg (4.5 to 9.1 mg per pound) of body weight every eight hours.
  - —For *injection* dosage form:
    - Adults and teenagers—600 mg to 1 gram injected into a vein over at least one hour, every eight to twelve hours; or 600 mg injected into a muscle every twelve to twenty-four hours.
    - Infants up to 1 month of age—Use and dose must be determined by your doctor.
    - Children 1 month of age and older—Dose is based on body weight. The usual dose is 10 mg per kg (4.5 mg per pound) of body weight injected into a muscle every twelve to twenty-four hours; or 3.3 to 6.7 mg per kg (1.5 to 3 mg per pound) of body weight injected into a vein every eight hours; or 5 to 10 mg per kg (2.3 to 4.5 mg per pound) of body weight injected into a vein every twelve hours.

Missed dose—If you miss a dose of this medicine, take it as soon as possible. This will help to keep a constant amount of medicine in the blood. However, if it is almost time for your next dose, skip the missed dose and go back to your regular dosing schedule. Do not double doses.

Storage—To store this medicine:
- Keep out of the reach of children.
- Store away from heat and direct light.
- Do not store the capsule form of this medicine in the bathroom, near the kitchen sink, or in other damp places. Heat or moisture may cause the medicine to break down.
- Do not keep outdated medicine or medicine no longer needed. Be sure that any discarded medicine is out of the reach of children.

Precautions While Using This Medicine

It is important that your doctor check your progress at regular visits.

If your symptoms do not improve within a few days, or if they become worse, check with your doctor.

In some patients, lincomycin may cause diarrhea.
- Severe diarrhea may be a sign of a serious side effect. *Do not take any diarrhea medicine without first checking with your doctor.* Diarrhea medicines may make your diarrhea worse or make it last longer.
- For mild diarrhea, diarrhea medicine containing attapulgite (e.g., Kaopectate tablets, Diasorb) may be taken. However, kaolin or attapulgite may keep lincomycin from being absorbed into the body. Therefore, these diarrhea medicines should be taken at least 2 hours before or 3 to 4 hours after you take lincomycin by mouth. Other kinds of diarrhea medicine should not be taken. They may make your diarrhea worse or make it last longer.
- If you have any questions about this or if mild diarrhea continues or gets worse, check with your health care professional.

Before having surgery (including dental surgery) with a general anesthetic, tell the medical doctor or dentist in charge that you are taking lincomycin.

Side Effects of This Medicine

Along with its needed effects, a medicine may cause some unwanted effects. Although not all of these side effects may occur, if they do occur they may need medical attention.

Check with your doctor immediately if any of the following side effects occur:

More common

Abdominal or stomach cramps and pain (severe); abdominal tenderness; diarrhea (watery and severe), which may also be bloody; fever

Note: The above side effects may also occur up to several weeks after you stop taking this medicine.

Less common

Skin rash, redness, and itching; sore throat and fever; unusual bleeding and bruising

Other side effects may occur that usually do not need medical attention. These side effects may go away during treatment as your body adjusts to the medicine. However, check with your doctor if any of the following side effects continue or are bothersome:

More common

Diarrhea (mild); nausea and vomiting; stomach pain

Less common

Itching of rectal or genital (sex organ) areas

Other side effects not listed above may also occur in some patients. If you notice any other effects, check with your doctor.

Revised: 10/06/92
Interim revision: 03/24/94

LINDANE Topical

Some commonly used brand names are:

In the U.S.—

Bio-Well	Kwell
GBH	Kwildane
G-well	Scabene
Kildane	Thionex

Generic name product may also be available.

In Canada—

GBH	Kwellada
Hexit	PMS Lindane

Generic name product may also be available.

Another commonly used name for lindane is gamma benzene hexachloride.

Description

Lindane (LIN-dane), formerly known as gamma benzene hexachloride, is an insecticide and is used to treat scabies and lice infestations.

Lindane cream and lotion are usually used to treat only scabies infestation. Lindane shampoo is used to treat only lice infestations.

Lindane is available only with your doctor's prescription, in the following dosage forms:

Topical
- Cream (U.S. and Canada)
- Lotion (U.S. and Canada)
- Shampoo (U.S. and Canada)

Before Using This Medicine

In deciding to use a medicine, the risks of using the medicine must be weighed against the good it will do. This is a decision you and your doctor will make. For lindane, the following should be considered:

Allergies—Tell your doctor if you have ever had any unusual or allergic reaction to lindane. Also tell your health care professional if you are allergic to any other substances, such as preservatives or dyes.

Pregnancy—Lindane is absorbed through the skin and could possibly cause toxic effects in the central nervous system (CNS) of the unborn baby. *Use lindane only as directed by your doctor. Do not use more of it, do not use it more often, and do not use it for a longer time than your doctor ordered. In addition, you should not be treated with lindane more than twice during your pregnancy.*

Breast-feeding—Lindane is absorbed through the mother's skin and is present in breast milk. Even though lindane has not been reported to cause problems in nursing babies, you should use another method of feeding your baby for 2 days after you use lindane. Be sure you have discussed this with your doctor.

Children—Infants and children are especially sensitive to the effects of lindane. This may increase the chance of side effects during treatment. In addition, use of lindane is not recommended in premature infants.

Older adults—Absorption of lindane may be increased in the elderly. This may increase the chance of problems during treatment with this medicine.

Other medicines—Although certain medicines should not be used together at all, in other cases two different medicines may be used together even if an interaction might occur. In these cases, your doctor may want to change the dose, or other precautions may be necessary. When you are using lindane, it is especially important that your health care professional know if you are using any other prescription or nonprescription (over-the-counter [OTC]) medicine.

Other medical problems—The presence of other medical problems may affect the use of lindane. Make sure you tell your doctor if you have any other medical problems, especially:

- Seizure disorder—Use of lindane may make the condition worse
- Skin rash or raw or broken skin—Condition may increase the absorption of lindane and the chance of side effects

Proper Use of This Medicine

Lindane is poisonous. Keep it away from the mouth because it is harmful and may be fatal if swallowed.

Use lindane only as directed by your doctor. Do not use more of it, do not use it more often, and do not use it for a longer time than your doctor ordered. To do so may increase the chance of absorption through the skin and the chance of lindane poisoning.

Keep lindane away from the eyes. If you should accidentally get some in your eyes, flush them thoroughly with water at once and contact your doctor.

Do not use lindane on open wounds, such as cuts or sores on the skin or scalp. To do so may increase the chance of lindane poisoning.

When applying lindane to another person, you should wear plastic disposable or rubber gloves, especially if you are pregnant or are breast-feeding. This will prevent lindane from being absorbed through your skin. If you have any questions about this, check with your doctor.

Lindane usually comes with patient directions. Read them carefully before using lindane.

Your sexual partner or partners, especially, and all members of your household may need to be treated also, since the infestation may spread to persons in close contact. If these persons have not been checked for an infestation or if you have any questions about this, check with your doctor.

To use the *cream or lotion form of lindane for scabies:*

- If your skin has any cream, lotion, ointment, or oil on it, wash, rinse, and dry your skin well before applying lindane.
- If you take a warm bath or shower before using lindane, dry the skin well before applying it.
- Apply enough lindane to your dry skin to cover the entire skin surface from the neck down, including the soles of your feet, and rub in well.
- Leave lindane on for no more than 8 hours, then remove by washing thoroughly.

To use the *shampoo form of lindane for lice:*

- If your hair has any cream, lotion, ointment, or oil-based product on it, shampoo, rinse, and dry your hair and scalp well before applying lindane.
- If you apply this shampoo in the shower or in the bathtub, make sure the shampoo is not allowed to run down on other parts of your body. Also, do not apply this shampoo in a bathtub where the shampoo may run into the bath water in which you are sitting. To do so may increase the chance of absorption through the skin. When you rinse out the shampoo, be sure to thoroughly rinse your entire body also to remove any shampoo that may have gotten on it.
- Apply enough shampoo to your dry hair (1 ounce or less for short hair, $1^1/_2$ ounces for medium length hair, and 2 ounces or less for long hair) to thoroughly wet the hair and skin or scalp of the affected and surrounding hairy areas.
- Thoroughly rub the shampoo into the hair and skin or scalp and allow to remain in place for 4 minutes. Then, use just enough water to work up a good lather.
- Rinse thoroughly and dry with a clean towel.
- When the hair is dry, comb with a fine-toothed comb to remove any remaining nits (eggs) or nit shells.
- *Do not use as a regular shampoo.*

Dosing—*Follow your doctor's orders or the directions on the label.* The following information includes only the average doses of lindane. *If your dose is different, do not change it* unless your doctor tells you to do so.

- For cream and lotion dosage forms:
  - —For scabies:
    - Adults and children—Apply to the affected area(s) of the skin one time.
    - Premature infants—Use is not recommended.

• For shampoo dosage form:
  —For lice:
    • Adults and children—Apply to the scalp or the affected area(s) of the skin one time. Treatment may be repeated after seven days if necessary.
    • Premature infants—Use is not recommended.

Storage—To store this medicine:
- Keep out of the reach of children.
- Store away from heat and direct light.
- Keep lindane from freezing.
- Do not keep outdated lindane or lindane no longer needed. Be sure that any discarded lindane is out of the reach of children.

Precautions While Using This Medicine

To help prevent reinfestation or spreading of the infestation to other persons:
- For scabies—All recently worn underwear and pajamas and used sheets, pillowcases, and towels should be washed in very hot water or dry-cleaned.
- For lice—All recently worn clothing and used bed linens and towels should be washed in very hot water or dry-cleaned.

Side Effects of This Medicine

In infants and children, the risk of lindane being absorbed through the skin and causing unwanted side effects is greater than in adults. In premature newborn infants, use of lindane is not recommended, because lindane may be more likely to be absorbed through their skin than through the skin of older infants. You should discuss these possible effects with your doctor.

Along with its needed effects, a medicine may cause some unwanted effects. Although not all of these side effects may occur, if they do occur they may need medical attention.

Check with your doctor as soon as possible if any of the following side effects occur:

Rare
  Skin irritation not present before use of lindane; skin rash

Symptoms of lindane poisoning
  Convulsions (seizures); dizziness, clumsiness, or unsteadiness; fast heartbeat; muscle cramps; nervousness, restlessness, or irritability; vomiting

After you stop using lindane, itching may occur and continue for 1 to several weeks. If this continues longer or is bothersome, check with your doctor.

Other side effects not listed above may also occur in some patients. If you notice any other effects, check with your doctor.

Revised: 08/15/94

LITHIUM Systemic

Some commonly used brand names are:

In the U.S.—

Cibalith-S	Lithobid
Eskalith	Lithonate
Eskalith CR	Lithotabs
Lithane	

Generic name product may also be available.

In Canada—

Carbolith	Lithane
Duralith	Lithizine

Description

Lithium (LITH-ee-um) is used to treat the manic stage of bipolar disorder (manic-depressive illness). Manic-depressive patients experience severe mood changes, ranging from an excited or manic state (for example, unusual anger or irritability or a false sense of well-being) to depression or sadness. Lithium is used to reduce the frequency and severity of manic states. Lithium may also reduce the frequency and severity of depression in bipolar disorder.

It is not known how lithium works to stabilize a person's mood. However, it does act on the central nervous system. It helps you to have more control over your emotions and helps you cope better with the problems of living.

It is important that you and your family understand all the effects of lithium. These effects depend on your individual condition and response and the amount of lithium you use. You also must know when to contact your doctor if there are problems with the medicine's use. Lithium may also be used for other conditions as determined by your doctor.

This medicine is available only with your doctor's prescription, in the following dosage forms:

Oral
- Capsules (U.S. and Canada)
- Slow-release capsules (Canada)
- Syrup (U.S.)
- Tablets (U.S. and Canada)
- Extended-release tablets (U.S. and Canada)

Before Using This Medicine

In deciding to use a medicine, the risks of taking the medicine must be weighed against the good it will do. This is a decision you and your doctor will make. For lithium, the following should be considered:

Allergies—Tell your doctor if you have ever had any unusual or allergic reaction to lithium. Also tell your health care professional if you are allergic to any other substances, such as foods, preservatives, or dyes.

Diet—Make certain your health care professional knows if you are on a low-sodium or low-salt diet. Too little salt in your diet could lead to serious side effects.

Pregnancy—Lithium is not recommended for use during pregnancy, especially during the first 3 months. Studies have shown that lithium may rarely cause thyroid problems and heart or blood vessel defects in the baby. It has also been shown to cause muscle weakness and severe drowsiness in newborn babies of mothers taking lithium near time of delivery.

Breast-feeding—Lithium passes into the breast milk. It has been reported to cause unwanted effects such as muscle weakness, lowered body temperature, and heart problems in nursing babies. Before taking this medicine, be sure you have discussed with your doctor the risks and benefits of breast-feeding.

Children—Lithium may cause weakened bones in children during treatment.

Older adults—Unusual thirst, an increase in amount of urine, diarrhea, drowsiness, loss of appetite, muscle weakness, trembling, slurred speech, nausea or vomiting, goiter, or symptoms of underactive thyroid are especially likely to occur in elderly patients, who are often more sensitive than younger adults to the effects of lithium.

Other medicines—Although certain medicines should not be used together at all, in other cases 2 different medicines may be used together even if an interaction might occur. In these cases, your doctor may want to change the dose, or other precautions may be necessary. When you are taking lithium, it is especially important that your health care professional know if you are taking any of the following:

- Antipsychotics (medicine for mental illness)—Blood levels of both medicines may change, increasing the chance of serious side effects
- Diuretics (water pills) or
- Inflammation or pain medicine, except narcotics—Higher blood levels of lithium may occur, increasing the chance of serious side effects
- Medicine for asthma, bronchitis, emphysema, sinusitis, or cystic fibrosis that contains the following:
  Calcium iodide or
  Iodinated glycerol or
  Potassium iodide—Unwanted effects on the thyroid gland may occur

Other medical problems—The presence of other medical problems may affect the use of lithium. Make sure you tell your doctor if you have any other medical problems, especially:

- Brain disease or
- Schizophrenia—You may be especially sensitive to lithium, and mental effects (such as increased confusion) may occur
- Diabetes mellitus (sugar diabetes)—Lithium may increase the blood levels of insulin; the dose of insulin you need to take may change
- Difficult urination or
- Infection (severe, occurring with fever, prolonged sweating, diarrhea, or vomiting) or
- Kidney disease—Higher blood levels of lithium may occur, increasing the chance of serious side effects
- Epilepsy or
- Goiter or other thyroid disease, or
- Heart disease or
- Parkinson's disease or
- Psoriasis—Lithium may make the condition worse
- Leukemia (history of)—Lithium may cause the leukemia to occur again

Proper Use of This Medicine

Take this medicine after a meal or snack. Doing so will reduce stomach upset, tremors, or weakness and may also prevent a laxative effect.

For patients taking the *long-acting or slow-release form* of lithium:

- Swallow the tablet or capsule whole.
- Do not break, crush, or chew before swallowing.

For patients taking the *syrup form* of lithium:

- Dilute the syrup in fruit juice or another flavored beverage before taking.

During treatment with lithium, drink 2 or 3 quarts of water or other fluids each day, and use a normal amount of salt in your food, unless otherwise directed by your doctor.

Take this medicine exactly as directed. Do not take more or less of it, do not take it more or less often, and do not take it for a longer time than your doctor ordered. To do so may increase the chance of unwanted effects.

Sometimes lithium must be taken for 1 to several weeks before you begin to feel better.

In order for lithium to work properly, it must be taken every day in regularly spaced doses as ordered by your doctor. This is necessary to keep a constant amount of lithium in your blood. To help keep the amount constant, do not miss any doses and *do not stop taking the medicine even if you feel better.*

Dosing—The dose of lithium will be different for different patients. *Follow your doctor's orders or the directions on the label.* The following information includes only the average doses of lithium. *If your dose is different, do not change it* unless your doctor tells you to do so.

The number of capsules or tablets or teaspoonfuls of syrup that you take depends on the strength of the medicine. Also, *the number of doses you take each day, the time allowed between doses, and the length of time you take the medicine depend on the medical problem for which you are using lithium.*

- For *short-acting oral* dosage forms (capsules, tablets, syrup):
  —Adults and adolescents: To start, 300 to 600 milligrams three times a day.
  —Children up to 12 years of age: The dose is based on body weight. To start, the usual dose is 15 to 20 milligrams per kilogram of body weight (6.8 to 9 milligrams per pound) a day, given in smaller doses two or three times during the day.
- For *long-acting oral* dosage forms (slow-release capsules, extended-release tablets):
  —Adults and adolescents: 300 to 600 milligrams three times a day, or 450 to 900 milligrams two times a day.
  —Children up to 12 years of age: Dose must be determined by the doctor.

Missed dose—If you miss a dose of this medicine, take it as soon as possible. However, if it is within 4 hours (about 6 hours for extended-release tablets or slow-release capsules) of your next dose, skip the missed dose and go back to your regular dosing schedule. Do not double doses.

Storage—To store this medicine:
- Keep out of the reach of children.
- Store away from heat and direct light.
- Do not store in the bathroom, near the kitchen sink, or in other damp places. Heat or moisture may cause the medicine to break down.
- Keep the syrup form of this medicine from freezing.
- Do not keep outdated medicine or medicine no longer needed. Be sure that any discarded medicine is out of the reach of children.

Precautions While Using This Medicine

Your doctor should check your progress at regular visits to make sure that the medicine is working properly and that possible side effects are avoided. Laboratory tests may be necessary.

Lithium may not work properly if you drink large amounts of caffeine-containing coffee, tea, or colas.

This medicine may cause some people to become dizzy, drowsy, or less alert than they are normally. *Make sure you know how you react to this medicine before you drive, use machines, or do anything else that could be dangerous if you are dizzy or are not alert.*

Use extra care in hot weather and during activities that cause you to sweat heavily, such as hot baths, saunas, or exercising. The loss of too much water and salt from your body could lead to serious side effects from this medicine.

If you have an infection or illness that causes heavy sweating, vomiting, or diarrhea, check with your doctor. The loss of too much water and salt from your body could lead to serious side effects from lithium.

Do not go on a diet to lose weight and do not make a major change in your diet without first checking with your doctor. Improper dieting could cause the loss of too much water and salt from your body and could lead to serious side effects from this medicine.

For patients taking the *slow-release capsules or the extended-release tablets:*
- Do not use this medicine interchangeably with other lithium products.

It is important that you and your family know the early symptoms of lithium overdose or toxicity and when to call the doctor.

Side Effects of This Medicine

Along with its needed effects, a medicine may cause some unwanted effects. Although not all of these side effects may occur, if they do occur they may need medical attention.

Check with your doctor immediately if any of the following side effects occur:

Early symptoms of overdose or toxicity

Diarrhea; drowsiness; loss of appetite; muscle weakness; nausea or vomiting; slurred speech; trembling

Late symptoms of overdose or toxicity

Blurred vision; clumsiness or unsteadiness; confusion; convulsions (seizures); dizziness; increase in amount of urine; trembling (severe)

Check with your doctor as soon as possible if any of the following side effects occur:

Less common

Fainting; fast or slow heartbeat; irregular pulse; troubled breathing (especially during hard work or exercise); unusual tiredness or weakness; weight gain

Rare

Blue color and pain in fingers and toes; coldness of arms and legs; dizziness; eye pain; headache; noises in the ears; vision problems

Signs of low thyroid function

Dry, rough skin; hair loss; hoarseness; mental depression; sensitivity to cold; swelling of feet or lower legs; swelling of neck; unusual excitement

Other side effects may occur that usually do not need medical attention. These side effects may go away during treatment as your body adjusts to the medicine. However, check with your doctor if any of the following side effects continue or are bothersome:

More common

Increased frequency of urination or loss of bladder control—more common in women than in men, usually beginning 2 to 7 years after start of treatment; increased thirst; nausea (mild); trembling of hands (slight)

Less common

Acne or skin rash; bloated feeling or pressure in the stomach; muscle twitching (slight)

Other side effects not listed above may also occur in some patients. If you notice any other effects, check with your doctor.

Additional Information

Once a medicine has been approved for marketing for a certain use, experience may show that it is also useful for other medical problems. Although these uses are not included in product labeling, lithium is used in certain patients with the following medical conditions:
- Cluster headaches
- Mental depression
- Neutropenia (a blood condition in which there is a decreased number of a certain type of white blood cells)

Other than the above information, there is no additional information relating to proper use, precautions, or side effects for these uses.

Revised: 03/09/93

LODOXAMIDE Ophthalmic†

A commonly used brand name in the U.S. is Alomide.
Another commonly used name is lodoxamide trometamol.

†Not commercially available in Canada.

Description

Lodoxamide (loe-DOX-a-mide) ophthalmic solution is used in the eye to treat certain disorders of the eye caused by allergies. It works by acting on certain cells, called mast cells, to prevent them from releasing substances that cause the allergic reaction.

Lodoxamide is available only with your doctor's prescription, in the following dosage form:

Ophthalmic
- Ophthalmic solution (eye drops) (U.S.)

Before Using This Medicine

In deciding to use a medicine, the risks of using the medicine must be weighed against the good it will do. This is a decision you and your doctor will make. For lodoxamide, the following should be considered:

Allergies—Tell your doctor if you have ever had any unusual or allergic reaction to lodoxamide. Also tell your health care professional if you are allergic to any other substances, such as foods, preservatives, or dyes.

Pregnancy—Lodoxamide has not been studied in pregnant women. However, lodoxamide has not been shown to cause birth defects or other problems in animal studies.

Breast-feeding—It is not known whether lodoxamide passes into the breast milk. Although most medicines pass into breast milk in small amounts, many of them may be used safely while breast-feeding. Mothers who are using this medicine and who wish to breast-feed should discuss this with their doctor.

Children—Studies on this medicine have been done only in adult patients, and there is no specific information comparing use of lodoxamide in children up to 2 years of age with use in other age groups. For older children, this medicine is not expected to cause different side effects or problems than it does in adults.

Older adults—Many medicines have not been studied specifically in older people. Therefore, it may not be known whether they work exactly the same way they do in younger adults or if they cause different side effects or problems in older people. There is no specific information comparing use of lodoxamide in the elderly with use in other age groups.

Proper Use of This Medicine

To use the *eye drops:*
- First, wash your hands. Tilt the head back and, pressing your finger gently on the skin just beneath the lower eyelid, pull the lower eyelid away from the eye to make a space. Drop the medicine into this space. Let go of the eyelid and gently close the eyes. Do not blink. Keep the eyes closed for 1 or 2 minutes to allow the medicine to be absorbed by the eye.
- If you think you did not get the drop of medicine into your eye properly, use another drop.
- To keep the medicine as germ-free as possible, do not touch the applicator tip to any surface (including the eye). Also, keep the container tightly closed.

In order for this medicine to work properly, it should be used every day in regularly spaced doses as ordered by your doctor.

Dosing—The dose of ophthalmic lodoxamide will be different for different patients. *Follow your doctor's orders or the directions on the label.* The following information includes only the average doses of ophthalmic lodoxamide. *If your dose is different, do not change it* unless your doctor tells you to do so.

- For *ophthalmic solution (eye drops)* dosage form:
  - —For eye allergies:
    - Adults and children 2 years of age and older—Use one drop four times a day at regularly spaced times for up to three months.
    - Children up to 2 years of age—Use and dose must be determined by your doctor.

Missed dose—If you miss a dose of this medicine, use it as soon as possible. Then go back to your regular dosing schedule.

Storage—To store this medicine:
- Keep out of the reach of children.
- Store away from heat and direct light.
- Keep the medicine from freezing.
- Do not keep outdated medicine or medicine no longer needed. Be sure that any discarded medicine is out of the reach of children.

Precautions While Using This Medicine

If your symptoms do not improve or if your condition becomes worse, check with your doctor.

Side Effects of This Medicine

Along with its needed effects, a medicine may cause some unwanted effects. Although not all of these side effects may occur, if they do occur they may need medical attention.

Check with your doctor as soon as possible if any of the following side effects occur:

Less common

Blurred vision; feeling of something in eye, itching, discomfort, redness, tearing or discharge, or other eye or eyelid irritation (not present before you started using this medicine or becoming worse while you are using this medicine)

Rare

Dizziness; mucus from eye, eye pain, or swelling of eye or eyelid (not present before you started using this medicine or becoming worse while you are using this medicine); headache; sensitivity of eyes to light; skin rash

Other side effects may occur that usually do not need medical attention. These side effects may go away during treatment as your body adjusts to the medicine. However, check with your doctor if any of the following side effects continue or are bothersome:

More common

Burning or stinging (when medicine is applied)

Less common or rare

Aching eyes; crusting in corner of eye or on eyelid; drowsiness or sleepiness; dryness of nose or eyes; feeling of heat in eye; heat sensation on body; nausea or stomach discomfort; scales on eyelid or eyelash; sneezing; sticky feeling of eyes; tired eyes

Other side effects not listed above may also occur in some patients. If you notice any other effects, check with your doctor.

Developed: 03/29/94

LOMUSTINE Systemic

A commonly used brand name in the U.S. and Canada is CeeNU. Another commonly used name is CCNU.

Description

Lomustine (loe-MUS-teen) belongs to the group of medicines known as alkylating agents. It is used to treat some kinds of cancer.

Lomustine interferes with the growth of cancer cells, which are eventually destroyed. Since the growth of normal body cells may also be affected by lomustine, other effects will also occur. Some of these may be serious and must be reported to your doctor. Other effects, like hair loss, may not be serious but may cause concern. Some effects may not occur for months or years after the medicine is used.

Before you begin treatment with lomustine, you and your doctor should talk about the good this medicine will do as well as the risks of using it.

Lomustine is available only with your doctor's prescription, in the following dosage form:

Oral

- Capsules (U.S. and Canada)

Before Using This Medicine

In deciding to use a medicine, the risks of taking the medicine must be weighed against the good it will do. This is a decision you and your doctor will make. For lomustine, the following should be considered:

Allergies—Tell your doctor if you have ever had any unusual or allergic reaction to lomustine.

Pregnancy—Tell your doctor if you are pregnant or if you intend to have children. There is a chance that this medicine may cause birth defects if either the male or female is taking it at the time of conception or if it is taken during pregnancy. Lomustine causes birth defects in rats and causes toxic or harmful effects in the fetus of rats and rabbits at doses about the same as the human dose. In addition, many cancer medicines may cause sterility which could be permanent. Sterility has been reported in animals and humans with this medicine.

Be sure that you have discussed this with your doctor before taking this medicine. It is best to use some kind of birth control while you are taking lomustine. Tell your doctor right away if you think you have become pregnant while taking lomustine.

Breast-feeding—Tell your doctor if you are breast-feeding or if you intend to breast-feed during treatment with this medicine. Because lomustine may cause serious side effects, breast-feeding is generally not recommended while you are receiving it.

Children—Although there is no specific information comparing use of lomustine in children with use in other age groups, this medicine is not expected to cause different side effects or problems in children than it does in adults.

Older adults—Many medicines have not been studied specifically in older people. Therefore, it may not be known whether they work exactly the same way they do in younger adults or if they cause different side effects or problems in older people. There is no specific information comparing use of lomustine in the elderly with use in other age groups.

Other medicines—Although certain medicines should not be used together at all, in other cases two different medicines may be used together even if an interaction might occur. In these cases, your doctor may want to change the dose, or other precautions may be necessary. When you are taking lomustine, it is especially important that your health care professional know if you have ever been treated with x-rays or cancer medicines or if you are taking any of the following:

- Amphotericin B by injection (e.g., Fungizone) or
- Antithyroid agents (medicine for overactive thyroid) or
- Azathioprine (e.g., Imuran) or
- Chloramphenicol (e.g., Chloromycetin) or
- Colchicine or
- Flucytosine (e.g., Ancobon) or
- Ganciclovir (e.g., Cytovene) or
- Interferon (e.g., Intron A, Roferon-A) or
- Plicamycin (e.g., Mithracin) or
- Zidovudine (e.g., AZT, Retrovir)—Lomustine may increase the effects of these medicines or radiation therapy on the blood

Other medical problems—The presence of other medical problems may affect the use of lomustine. Make sure you tell your doctor if you have any other medical problems, especially:

- Chickenpox (including recent exposure) or

- Herpes zoster (shingles)—Risk of severe disease affecting other parts of the body
- Infection—Lomustine can decrease your body's ability to fight infection
- Kidney disease—Effects of lomustine may be increased because of slower removal from the body
- Lung disease—Risk of lung problems caused by lomustine may be increased

Proper Use of This Medicine

Take this medicine only as directed by your doctor. Do not take more or less of it than your doctor ordered. The exact amount of medicine you need has been carefully worked out. Taking too much may increase the chance of side effects, while taking too little may not improve your condition.

In order that you receive the proper dose of lomustine, there may be two or more different types of capsules in the container. This is not an error. It is important that you take all of the capsules in the container as one dose so that you receive the right dose of the medicine.

This medicine is sometimes given together with certain other medicines. If you are using a combination of medicines, make sure that you take each one at the right time and do not mix them. Ask your health care professional to help you plan a way to remember to take your medicines at the right times.

Nausea and vomiting occur often after lomustine is taken, but usually last less than 24 hours. Loss of appetite may last for several days. This medicine is best taken on an empty stomach at bedtime so that it will cause less stomach upset. Ask your health care professional for other ways to lessen these effects.

If you vomit shortly after taking a dose of lomustine, check with your doctor. You may be told to take the dose again.

Dosing—The dose of lomustine will be different for different patients. The dose that is used may depend on a number of things, including what the medicine is being used for, the patient's size, and whether or not other medicines are also being taken. *If you are taking lomustine at home, follow your doctor's orders or the directions on the label.* If you have any questions about the proper dose of lomustine, ask your doctor.

Precautions While Using This Medicine

It is important that your doctor check your progress at regular visits to make sure that this medicine is working properly and to check for unwanted effects.

While you are being treated with lomustine, and after you stop treatment with it, *do not have any immunizations (vaccinations) without your doctor's approval.* Lomustine may lower your body's resistance and there is a chance you might get the infection the immunization is meant to prevent. In addition, other persons living in your household should not take oral polio vaccine since there is a chance they could pass the polio virus on to you. Also, avoid persons who have recently taken oral polio vaccine. Do not get close to them, and do not stay in the same room with them for very long. If you cannot take these precautions, you should consider wearing a protective face mask that covers the nose and mouth.

Lomustine can temporarily lower the number of white blood cells in your blood, increasing the chance of getting an infection. It can also lower the number of platelets, which are necessary for proper blood clotting. If this occurs, there are certain precautions you can take, especially when your blood count is low, to reduce the risk of infection or bleeding:

- If you can, avoid people with infections. *Check with your doctor immediately* if you think you are getting an infection or if you get a fever or chills, cough or hoarseness, lower back or side pain, or painful or difficult urination.
- *Check with your doctor immediately* if you notice any unusual bleeding or bruising; black, tarry stools; blood in urine or stools; or pinpoint red spots on your skin.
- Be careful when using a regular toothbrush, dental floss, or toothpick. Your medical doctor, dentist, or nurse may recommend other ways to clean your teeth and gums. Check with your medical doctor before having any dental work done.
- Do not touch your eyes or the inside of your nose unless you have just washed your hands and have not touched anything else in the meantime.
- Be careful not to cut yourself when you are using sharp objects such as a safety razor or fingernail or toenail cutters.
- Avoid contact sports or other situations where bruising or injury could occur.

Side Effects of This Medicine

Along with their needed effects, medicines like lomustine can sometimes cause unwanted effects such as blood problems, loss of hair, and other side effects; these are described below. Also, because of the way these medicines act on the body, there is a chance that they might cause other unwanted effects that may not occur until months or years after the medicine is used. These delayed effects may include certain types of cancer, such as leukemia. Discuss these possible effects with your doctor.

Although not all of these side effects may occur, if they do occur they may need medical attention.

Check with your doctor or nurse immediately if any of the following side effects occur:

Less common

Black, tarry stools; blood in urine or stools; cough or hoarseness; fever or chills; lower back or side pain; painful or difficult urination; pinpoint red spots on skin; unusual bleeding or bruising

Check with your doctor as soon as possible if any of the following side effects occur:

Less common

Awkwardness; confusion; decrease in urination; slurred speech; sores in mouth and on lips; swelling of feet or lower legs; unusual tiredness or weakness

Rare
Cough; shortness of breath

Other side effects may occur that usually do not need medical attention. These side effects may go away during treatment as your body adjusts to the medicine. Also, your health care professional may be able to tell you about ways to prevent or reduce some of these side effects. Check with your health care professional if any of the following side effects continue or are bothersome or if you have any questions about them:

More common
Loss of appetite
Nausea and vomiting (usually last less than 24 hours)

Less common
Darkening of skin; diarrhea; skin rash and itching

This medicine may cause a temporary loss of hair in some people. After treatment with lomustine has ended, normal hair growth should return.

After you stop using this medicine, it may still produce some side effects that need attention. During this period of time, check with your doctor if you notice any of the following side effects:

Black, tarry stools; blood in urine or stools; cough or hoarseness; fever or chills; lower back or side pain; painful or difficult urination; pinpoint red spots on skin; unusual bleeding or bruising

Other side effects not listed above may also occur in some patients. If you notice any other effects, check with your doctor.

Revised: 08/09/92
Interim revision: 06/21/94

LOPERAMIDE Oral

Some commonly used brand names are:

In the U.S.

Imodium
Imodium A-D
Imodium A-D Caplets
Kaopectate II
Maalox Anti-Diarrheal
Pepto Diarrhea Control

Generic name product may also be available.

In Canada

Imodium
PMS-Loperamide Hydrochloride

Generic name product may also be available.

Description

Loperamide (loe-PER-a-mide) is a medicine used along with other measures to treat diarrhea. Loperamide helps stop diarrhea by slowing down the movements of the intestines.

In the U.S., loperamide capsules are available only with your doctor's prescription, while the liquid form and the tablet form are available without a prescription. In Canada, all the dosage forms are available without a prescription.

Loperamide is available in the following dosage forms:

Oral
- Capsules (U.S. and Canada)
- Oral solution (U.S. and Canada)
- Tablets (U.S. and Canada)

Before Using This Medicine

If you are taking this medicine without a prescription, carefully read and follow any precautions on the label. For loperamide, the following should be considered:

Allergies—Tell your doctor if you have ever had any unusual or allergic reaction to loperamide. Also tell your health care professional if you are allergic to any other substances, such as foods, preservatives, or dyes.

Pregnancy—Studies have not been done in humans. However, studies in animals have not shown that loperamide causes cancer or birth defects or lessens the chances of becoming pregnant even when given in doses many times the human dose.

Breast-feeding—It is not known whether loperamide passes into breast milk. Although most medicines pass into breast milk in small amounts, many of them may be used safely while breast-feeding. Mothers who are taking this medicine and who wish to breast-feed should discuss this with their doctor.

Children—This medicine should not be used in children under 6 years of age unless directed by a doctor. Children, especially very young children, are very sensitive to the effects of loperamide. This may increase the chance of side effects during treatment. Also, the fluid loss caused by diarrhea may result in a serious health problem (dehydration). Loperamide may hide the symptoms of dehydration. For these reasons, do not give medicine for diarrhea to children without first checking with their doctor. If you have any questions about this, check with your health care professional.

Older adults—The fluid loss caused by diarrhea may result in a serious health problem (dehydration). Loperamide may hide the symptoms of dehydration. For this reason, elderly persons with diarrhea, in addition to using medicine for diarrhea, must receive a sufficient amount of liquids to replace the fluid lost by the body. If you have any questions about this, check with your health care professional.

Other medicines—Although certain medicines should not be used together at all, in other cases two different medicines may be used together even if an interaction might occur. In these cases, your doctor may want to change the dose, or other precautions may be necessary. When you are taking loperamide, it is especially important that your health care professional know if you are taking any of the following:

- Antibiotics such as cephalosporins (e.g., Ceftin, Keflex), clindamycin (e.g., Cleocin), erythromycins (e.g., E.E.S.,

PCE), tetracyclines (e.g., Achromycin, Doryx)—These antibiotics may cause diarrhea; loperamide may make the diarrhea caused by antibiotics worse or make it last longer

- Narcotic pain medicine—There is a greater chance that severe constipation may occur if loperamide is used together with narcotic pain medicine

Other medical problems—The presence of other medical problems may affect the use of loperamide. Make sure you tell your doctor if you have any other medical problems, especially:

- Colitis (severe)—A more serious problem of the colon may develop if you use loperamide
- Dysentery—This condition may get worse; a different kind of treatment may be needed
- Liver disease—The chance of severe central nervous system (CNS) side effects may be greater in patients with liver disease

Proper Use of This Medicine

Do not use loperamide to treat your diarrhea if you have a fever or if there is blood or mucus in your stools. Contact your doctor.

For safe and effective use of this medicine:

- *Follow your doctor's instructions if this medicine was prescribed.*
- Follow the manufacturer's package directions if you are treating yourself.

Use a specially marked measuring spoon or other device to measure each dose accurately. The average household teaspoon may not hold the right amount of liquid.

Importance of diet and fluid intake while treating diarrhea:

- *In addition to using medicine for diarrhea, it is very important that you replace the fluid lost by the body and follow a proper diet.* For the first 24 hours, you should eat gelatin, and drink plenty of caffeine-free clear liquids, such as ginger ale, decaffeinated cola, decaffeinated tea, and broth. During the next 24 hours you may eat bland foods, such as cooked cereals, bread, crackers, and applesauce. Fruits, vegetables, fried or spicy foods, bran, candy, caffeine, and alcoholic beverages may make the condition worse.
- If too much fluid has been lost by the body due to the diarrhea, a serious condition (dehydration) may develop. Check with your doctor as soon as possible if any of the following signs or symptoms of too much fluid loss occur:

  Decreased urination
  Dizziness and lightheadedness
  Dryness of mouth
  Increased thirst
  Wrinkled skin

Dosing—The dose of loperamide will be different for different patients. *Follow your doctor's orders or the directions on the label.* The following information includes only the average doses of loperamide. *If your dose is different, do not change it* unless your doctor tells you to do so.

- For diarrhea:
  - —For *oral* dosage form (capsules):
    - Adults and teenagers—The usual dose is 4 milligrams (mg) (2 capsules) after the first loose bowel movement, and 2 mg (1 capsule) after each loose bowel movement after the first dose has been taken. No more than 16 mg (8 capsules) should be taken in any twenty-four-hour period.
    - Children 8 to 12 years of age—The usual dose is 2 mg (1 capsule) three times a day.
    - Children 6 to 8 years of age—The usual dose is 2 mg (1 capsule) two times a day.
    - Children up to 6 years of age—Use is not recommended unless directed by your doctor.
  - —For *oral* dosage form (oral solution):
    - Adults and teenagers—The usual dose is 4 teaspoonfuls (4 mg) after the first loose bowel movement, and 2 teaspoonfuls (2 mg) after each loose bowel movement after the first dose has been taken. No more than 8 teaspoonfuls (8 mg) should be taken in any twenty-four-hour period.
    - Children 9 to 11 years of age—The usual dose is 2 teaspoonfuls (2 mg) after the first loose bowel movement, and 1 teaspoonful (1 mg) after each loose bowel movement after the first dose has been taken. No more than 6 teaspoonfuls (6 mg) should be taken in any twenty-four-hour period.
    - Children 6 to 8 years of age—The usual dose is 2 teaspoonfuls (2 mg) after the first loose bowel movement, and 1 teaspoonful (1 mg) after each loose bowel movement after the first dose has been taken. No more than 4 teaspoonfuls (4 mg) should be taken in any twenty-four-hour period.
    - Children up to 6 years of age—Use is not recommended unless directed by your doctor.
  - —For *oral* dosage form (tablets):
    - Adults and teenagers—The usual dose is 4 mg (2 tablets) after the first loose bowel movement, and 1 mg (1/2 tablet) after each loose bowel movement after the first dose has been taken. No more than 8 mg (4 tablets) should be taken in any twenty-four-hour period.
    - Children 9 to 11 years of age—The usual dose is 2 mg (1 tablet) after the first loose bowel movement, and 1 mg (1/2 tablet) after each loose bowel movement after the first dose has been taken. No more than 6 mg (3 tablets) should be taken in any twenty-four-hour period.
    - Children 6 to 8 years of age—The usual dose is 2 mg (1 tablet) after the first loose bowel movement, and 1 mg (1/2 tablet) after each loose bowel movement after the first dose has been taken. No more than 4 mg (2 tablets) should be taken in any twenty-four-hour period.
    - Children up to 6 years of age—Use is not recommended unless directed by your doctor.

Missed dose—If you must take this medicine regularly and you miss a dose, skip the missed dose and go back to your regular dosing schedule. Do not double doses.

Storage—To store this medicine:
- Keep out of the reach of children.
- Store away from heat and direct light.
- Do not store the capsule or tablet form of this medicine in the bathroom, near the kitchen sink, or in other damp places. Heat or moisture may cause the medicine to break down.
- Keep the liquid form of this medicine from freezing.
- Do not keep outdated medicine or medicine no longer needed. Be sure that any discarded medicine is out of the reach of children.

Precautions While Using This Medicine

Loperamide should not be used for more than 2 days, unless directed by your doctor. If you will be taking this medicine regularly for a long time, your doctor should check your progress at regular visits.

Check with your doctor if your diarrhea does not stop after two days or if you develop a fever.

Side Effects of This Medicine

Along with its needed effects, a medicine may cause some unwanted effects. *When this medicine is used for short periods of time at low doses, side effects usually are rare.*

However, check with your doctor immediately if any of the following side effects are severe and occur suddenly since they may be signs of a more severe and dangerous problem with your bowels:

Rare

Bloating; constipation; loss of appetite; stomach pain (severe) with nausea and vomiting

Also, check with your doctor as soon as possible if the following side effect occurs:

Rare

Skin rash

Other side effects may occur that usually do not need medical attention. These side effects may go away during treatment as your body adjusts to the medicine. However, check with your doctor if any of the following side effects continue or are bothersome:

Rare

Dizziness or drowsiness; dryness of mouth

Other side effects not listed above may also occur in some patients. If you notice any other effects, check with your doctor.

Revised: 01/25/95

LORACARBEF Systemic†

A commonly used brand name in the U.S. is Lorabid.

†Not commercially available in Canada.

Description

Loracarbef (loe-ra-KAR-bef) is used to treat bacterial infections in many different parts of the body. It works by killing bacteria or preventing their growth. This medicine will not work for colds, flu, or other virus infections.

Loracarbef is available only with your doctor's prescription, in the following dosage forms:

Oral
- Capsules (U.S.)
- Oral suspension (U.S.)

Before Using This Medicine

In deciding to use a medicine, the risks of taking the medicine must be weighed against the good it will do. This is a decision you and your doctor will make. For loracarbef, the following should be considered:

Allergies—Tell your doctor if you have ever had any unusual or allergic reaction to loracarbef or to any related medicines such as penicillins or cephalosporins. Also tell your health care professional if you are allergic to any other substances, such as foods, preservatives, or dyes.

Pregnancy—Loracarbef has not been studied in pregnant women. However, loracarbef has not been shown to cause birth defects or other problems in animal studies.

Breast-feeding—It is not known whether loracarbef passes into breast milk.

Children—This medicine has been tested in a limited number of children 6 months of age and older. In effective doses, the medicine has not been shown to cause different side effects or problems than it does in adults.

Older adults—This medicine has been tested in a limited number of elderly patients and has not been shown to cause different side effects or problems in older people than it does in younger adults.

Other medicines—Although certain medicines should not be used together at all, in other cases two different medicines may be used together even if an interaction might occur. In these cases, your doctor may want to change the dose, or other precautions may be necessary. When you are taking loracarbef, it is especially important that your health care professional know if you are taking any of the following:
- Probenicid (e.g., Benemid)—Probenecid increases the blood level of loracarbef, increasing the chance of side effects

Other medical problems—The presence of other medical problems may affect the use of loracarbef. Make sure you tell your doctor if you have any other medical problems, especially:
- Kidney disease—Kidney disease may increase the blood level of loracarbef, increasing the chance of side effects

Proper Use of This Medicine

Loracarbef should be taken at least 1 hour before or at least 2 hours after meals.

To help clear up your infection completely, *keep taking loracarbef for the full time of treatment,* even if you begin to feel better after a few days. *If you have a ''strep'' infection, you should keep taking this medicine for at least 10 days. This is especially important in ''strep'' infections. Serious heart problems could develop later* if your infection is not cleared up completely. Also, if you stop taking this medicine too soon, your symptoms may return.

This medicine works best when there is a constant amount in the blood or urine. *To help keep the amount constant, do not miss any doses. Also, it is best to take the doses at evenly spaced times, day and night.* If this interferes with your sleep or other daily activities, or if you need help in planning the best times to take your medicine, check with your health care professional.

Dosing—The dose of loracarbef will be different for different patients. *Follow your doctor's orders or the directions on the label.* The following information includes only the average doses of loracarbef. Your dose may be different if you have kidney disease. *If your dose is different, do not change it* unless your doctor tells you to do so.

The number of capsules or teaspoonfuls of suspension that you take depends on the strength of the medicine. Also, *the number of doses you take each day, the time allowed between doses, and the length of time you take the medicine depend on the medical problem for which you are taking loracarbef.*

- For *oral* dosage forms (capsules or oral suspension):
  - —For bronchitis:
    - Adults and children 13 years of age and older—200 to 400 milligrams (mg) every twelve hours for seven days.
    - Children 6 months to 12 years of age—Use and dose to be determined by your doctor.
  - —For otitis media (ear infection):
    - Children 6 months to 12 years of age—Dose is based on body weight and must be determined by your doctor.
  - —For pneumonia:
    - Adults and children 13 years of age and older—400 mg every twelve hours for fourteen days.
    - Children 6 months to 12 years of age—Use and dose to be determined by your doctor.
  - —For sinusitis:
    - Adults and children 13 years of age and older—400 mg every twelve hours for ten days.
    - Children 6 months to 12 years of age—Use and dose to be determined by your doctor.
  - —For skin and soft tissue infections:
    - Adults and children 13 years of age and older—200 mg every twelve hours for seven days.
    - Children 6 months to 12 years of age—Dose is based on body weight and must be determined by your doctor.
  - —For streptococcal pharyngitis (''strep throat''):
    - Adults and children 13 years of age and older—200 mg every twelve hours for ten days.
    - Children 6 months to 12 years of age—Dose is based on body weight and must be determined by your doctor.
  - —For urinary tract infections:
    - Adults and children 13 years of age and older—200 to 400 mg every twelve to twenty-four hours for seven to fourteen days.
    - Children 6 months to 12 years of age—Use and dose to be determined by your doctor.

Missed dose—If you do miss a dose of this medicine, take it as soon as possible. This will help to keep a constant amount of medicine in the blood or urine. However, if it is almost time for your next dose, skip the missed dose and go back to your regular dosing schedule. Do not double doses.

Storage—To store this medicine:
- Keep out of the reach of children.
- Store away from heat and direct light.
- Do not store the capsule form of this medicine in the bathroom, near the kitchen sink, or in other damp places. Heat or moisture may cause the medicine to break down.
- Do not keep outdated medicine or medicine no longer needed. Be sure that any discarded medicine is out of the reach of children.

Precautions While Using This Medicine

If your symptoms do not improve within a few days, or if they become worse, check with your doctor.

In some patients, loracarbef may cause diarrhea.
- Severe diarrhea may be a sign of a serious side effect. *Do not take any diarrhea medicine without first checking with your doctor.* Diarrhea medicines may make your diarrhea worse or last longer.
- For mild diarrhea, diarrhea medicine containing kaolin or attapulgite (e.g., Kaopectate tablets, Diasorb) may be taken. However, other kinds of diarrhea medicine should not be taken. They may make your diarrhea worse or last longer.
- If you have any questions about this or if mild diarrhea continues or gets worse, check with your health care professional.

Side Effects of This Medicine

Along with its needed effects, a medicine may cause some unwanted effects. Although not all of these side effects may occur, if they do occur they may need medical attention.

Check with your doctor as soon as possible if any of the following side effects occur:

More common

Itching; skin rash

Other side effects may occur that usually do not need medical attention. These side effects may go away during

treatment as your body adjusts to the medicine. However, check with your doctor if any of the following side effects continue or are bothersome:

More common

Diarrhea; loss of appetite; nausea and vomiting; stomach pain

Rare

Dizziness; drowsiness; headache; itching or discharge from the vagina; nervousness; trouble in sleeping

Other side effects not listed above may also occur in some patients. If you notice any other effects, check with your doctor.

Revised: 08/18/93
Interim revision: 06/20/95

LOSARTAN Systemic†

A commonly used brand name in the U.S. is Cozaar.

†Not commercially available in Canada.

Description

Losartan (loe-SAR-tan) is used to treat high blood pressure (hypertension). High blood pressure adds to the work load of the heart and arteries. If it continues for a long time, the heart and arteries may not function properly. This can damage the blood vessels of the brain, heart, and kidneys, resulting in a stroke, heart failure, or kidney failure. High blood pressure may also increase the risk of heart attacks. These problems may be less likely to occur if blood pressure is controlled.

Losartan works by blocking the action of a substance in the body that causes blood vessels to tighten. As a result, losartan relaxes blood vessels. This lowers blood pressure.

Losartan is available only with your doctor's prescription, in the following dosage form:

Oral

- Tablets (U.S.)

Before Using This Medicine

In deciding to use a medicine, the risks of taking the medicine must be weighed against the good it will do. This is a decision you and your doctor will make. For losartan, the following should be considered:

Allergies—Tell your doctor if you have ever had any unusual or allergic reaction to losartan. Also tell your health care professional if you are allergic to any other substances, such as foods, preservatives, or dyes.

Diet—Make certain your health care professional knows if you are on any special diet, such as a low-sodium diet.

Pregnancy—Use of losartan during pregnancy, especially during the second and third trimesters (after the first three months) can cause low blood pressure, severe kidney failure, or even death in the newborn. *Therefore, it is important that you check with your doctor immediately if you think that you may be pregnant.* Be sure that you have discussed this with your doctor before taking this medicine.

Breast-feeding—It is not known whether losartan passes into breast milk. However, losartan passes into the milk of lactating rats.

Children—Studies on this medicine have been done only in adult patients, and there is no specific information comparing use of losartan in children with use in other age groups.

Older adults—This medicine has been tested in a limited number of patients 65 years of age or older and has not been shown to cause different side effects or problems in older people than it does in younger adults.

Other medicines—Although certain medicines should not be used together at all, in other cases two different medicines may be used together even if an interaction might occur. In these cases, your doctor may want to change the dose, or other precautions may be necessary. When you are taking losartan, it is especially important that your health care professional know if you are taking any of the following:

- Diuretics (water pills)—Effects on blood pressure may be increased. In addition, some diuretics make the increase in potassium in the blood caused by losartan even greater

Other medical problems—The presence of other medical problems may affect the use of losartan. Make sure you tell your doctor if you have any other medical problems, especially:

- Kidney disease or
- Liver disease—Effects may be increased because of slower removal of losartan from the body

Proper Use of This Medicine

To help you remember to take your medicine, try to get into the habit of taking it at the same time each day.

In addition to the use of the medicine your doctor has prescribed, treatment for your high blood pressure may include weight control and care in the types of foods you eat, especially foods high in sodium. Your doctor will tell you which of these are most important for you. You should check with your doctor before changing your diet.

Many patients who have high blood pressure will not notice any signs of the problem. In fact, many may feel normal. It is very important that you *take your medicine exactly as directed* and that you keep your appointments with your doctor even if you feel well.

Remember that this medicine will not cure your high blood pressure but it does help control it. Therefore, you must continue to take it as directed if you expect to lower your blood pressure and keep it down. *You may have to take high blood pressure medicine for the rest of your life.* If high blood pressure is not treated, it can cause serious problems such as heart failure, blood vessel disease, stroke, or kidney disease.

This medicine may be taken with or without food.

Dosing—The dose of losartan will be different for different patients. *Follow your doctor's orders or the directions on the label.* The following information includes only the average doses of losartan. *If your dose is different, do not change it* unless your doctor tells you to do so.

The number of tablets that you take depends on the strength of the medicine.

- For *oral* dosage form (tablets):
  - —For high blood pressure:
    - Adults—25 to 100 milligrams (mg) a day. The dose may be taken once a day or divided into two doses.
    - Children—Use and dose must be determined by your doctor.

Missed dose—If you miss a dose of this medicine, take it as soon as possible. However, if it is almost time for your next dose, skip the missed dose and go back to your regular dosing schedule. Do not double doses.

Storage—To store this medicine:

- Keep out of the reach of children.
- Store away from heat and direct light.
- Do not store in the bathroom, near the kitchen sink, or in other damp places. Heat or moisture may cause the medicine to break down.
- Keep the medicine from freezing. Do not refrigerate.
- Do not keep outdated medicine or medicine no longer needed. Be sure that any discarded medicine is out of the reach of children.

Precautions While Using This Medicine

Check with your doctor immediately if you think that you may be pregnant. Losartan may cause birth defects or other problems in the baby if taken during pregnancy.

It is important that your doctor check your progress at regular visits to make sure that this medicine is working properly and to check for unwanted effects.

Do not take other medicines unless they have been discussed with your doctor. This especially includes over-the-counter (nonprescription) medicines for appetite control, asthma, colds, cough, hay fever, or sinus problems, since they may tend to increase your blood pressure.

Dizziness or lightheadedness may occur after the first dose of this medicine, especially if you have been taking a diuretic (water pill). Make sure you know how you react to this medicine before you drive, use machines, or do anything else that could be dangerous if you are dizzy.

Check with your doctor right away if you become sick while taking this medicine, especially with severe or continuing nausea and vomiting or diarrhea. These conditions may cause you to lose too much water and lead to low blood pressure.

Dizziness, lightheadedness, or fainting may also occur if you exercise or if the weather is hot. Heavy sweating can cause loss of too much water and result in low blood pressure. Use extra care during exercise or hot weather.

Avoid alcoholic beverages until you have discussed their use with your doctor. Alcohol may make the low blood pressure effect worse and/or increase the possibility of dizziness or fainting.

Side Effects of This Medicine

Along with its needed effects, a medicine may cause some unwanted effects. Although not all of these side effects may occur, if they do occur they may need medical attention.

Check with your doctor immediately if any of the following side effects occur:

Rare

Hoarseness; swelling of face, mouth, hands, or feet; trouble in swallowing or breathing (sudden)

Check with your doctor as soon as possible if any of the following side effects occur:

Less common

Cough, fever or sore throat; dizziness

Other side effects may occur that usually do not need medical attention. These side effects may go away during treatment as your body adjusts to the medicine. However, check with your doctor if any of the following side effects continue or are bothersome:

More common

Headache

Less common

Back pain; diarrhea; fatigue; nasal congestion

Rare

Cough, dry; leg pain; muscle cramps or pain; sinus problems; trouble in sleeping

Other side effects not listed above may also occur in some patients. If you notice any other effects, check with your doctor.

Developed: 08/15/95
Interim revision: 09/21/95

LOXAPINE Systemic

Some commonly used brand names are:

In the U.S.—

Loxitane
Loxitane IM
Loxitane C

Generic name product may also be available.

In Canada—

Loxapac

Description

Loxapine (LOX-a-peen) is used to treat nervous, mental, and emotional conditions.

Loxapine is available only with your doctor's prescription, in the following dosage forms:

Oral

- Solution (U.S. and Canada)
- Capsules (U.S.)
- Tablets (Canada)

Parenteral

- Injection (U.S. and Canada)

Before Using This Medicine

In deciding to use a medicine, the risks of taking the medicine must be weighed against the good it will do. This is a decision you and your doctor will make. For loxapine, the following should be considered:

Allergies—Tell your doctor if you have ever had any unusual or allergic reaction to loxapine or amoxapine. Also tell your health care professional if you are allergic to any other substances, such as foods, preservatives, or dyes.

Pregnancy—Loxapine has not been shown to cause birth defects or other problems in humans. However, animal studies have shown unwanted effects in the fetus.

Breast-feeding—It is not known if loxapine passes into breast milk.

Children—Studies on this medicine have been done only in adult patients, and there is no specific information comparing use of loxapine in children with use in other age groups.

Older adults—Elderly patients are usually more sensitive than younger adults to the effects of loxapine. Constipation, dizziness or fainting, drowsiness, dry mouth, trembling of the hands and fingers, and symptoms of tardive dyskinesia (such as rapid, worm-like movements of the tongue or any other uncontrolled movements of the mouth, tongue, or jaw, and/or arms and legs) are especially likely to occur in elderly patients.

Other medicines—Although certain medicines should not be used together at all, in other cases 2 different medicines may be used together even if an interaction might occur. In these cases, your doctor may want to change the dose, or other precautions may be necessary. When you are taking loxapine, it is especially important that your health care professional know if you are taking any of the following:

- Amoxapine (e.g., Asendin) or
- Methyldopa (e.g., Aldomet) or
- Metoclopramide (e.g., Reglan) or
- Metyrosine (e.g., Demser) or
- Other antipsychotics (medicine for mental illness) or
- Pemoline (e.g., Cylert) or
- Pimozide (e.g., Orap) or
- Promethazine (e.g., Phenergan) or
- Rauwolfia alkaloids (alseroxylon [e.g., Rauwiloid], deserpidine [e.g., Harmonyl], rauwolfia serpentina [e.g., Raudixin], reserpine [e.g., Serpasil]) or
- Trimeprazine (e.g., Temaril)—Taking these medicines with loxapine may increase the chance and seriousness of some side effects
- Central nervous system (CNS) depressants (medicine that causes drowsiness) or
- Tricyclic antidepressants (medicine for depression)—Taking these medicines with loxapine may increase the CNS depressant effects
- Guanadrel (e.g., Hylorel) or
- Guanethidine (e.g., Ismelin)—Loxapine may decrease the effects of these medicines

Other medical problems—The presence of other medical problems may affect the use of loxapine. Make sure you tell your doctor if you have any other medical problems, especially:

- Alcohol abuse—CNS depressant effects may be increased
- Difficult urination or
- Enlarged prostate or
- Glaucoma (or predisposition to) or
- Parkinson's disease—Loxapine may make the condition worse
- Heart or blood vessel disease—An increased risk of low blood pressure (hypotension) or changes in the rhythm of your heart may occur
- Liver disease—Higher blood levels of loxapine may occur, increasing the chance of side effects
- Seizure disorders—Loxapine may increase the risk of seizures

Proper Use of This Medicine

This medicine may be taken with food or a full glass (8 ounces) of water or milk to reduce stomach irritation.

For patients taking the *oral solution*:

- Measure the solution only with the dropper provided by the manufacturer. This will give a more accurate dose.

The liquid medicine must be mixed with orange juice or grapefruit juice just before you take it to make it easier to take.

Do not take more of this medicine, do not take it more often, and do not take it for a longer time than your doctor ordered. To do so may increase the chance of unwanted effects.

Dosing—The dose of loxapine will be different for different patients. *Follow your doctor's orders or the directions on the label.* The following information includes only the average doses of loxapine. *If your dose is different, do not change it* unless your doctor tells you to do so.

The number of capsules or tablets or amount of solution that you take depends on the strength of the medicine. Also, *the number of doses you take each day, the time allowed between doses, and the length of time you take the medicine depend on the medical problem for which you are taking loxapine.*

- For *oral* dosage forms (capsules, oral solution, or tablets):
  - —Adults: To start, 10 milligrams taken two times a day. Your doctor may increase your dose if needed.
  - —Children up to 16 years of age: The dose must be determined by the doctor.
- For *injection* dosage form:
  - —Adults: 12.5 to 50 milligrams every four to six hours, injected into a muscle.
  - —Children up to 16 years of age: The dose must be determined by the doctor.

Missed dose—If you miss a dose of this medicine, take it as soon as possible. However, if it is within one hour of your next dose, skip the missed dose and go back to your regular dosing schedule. Do not double doses.

Storage—To store this medicine:

- Keep out of the reach of children.
- Store away from heat and direct light.
- Do not store the capsule or tablet form of this medicine in the bathroom, near the kitchen sink, or in other damp places. Heat or moisture may cause the medicine to break down.
- Keep the liquid form of this medicine from freezing.
- Do not keep outdated medicine or medicine no longer needed. Be sure that any discarded medicine is out of the reach of children.

Precautions While Using This Medicine

Your doctor should check your progress at regular visits, especially during the first few months of treatment with this medicine. The amount of loxapine you take may be changed often to meet the needs of your condition and to help avoid side effects.

Do not stop taking this medicine without first checking with your doctor. Your doctor may want you to reduce gradually the amount you are taking before stopping completely. This will allow your body time to adjust and to keep your condition from becoming worse.

This medicine will add to the effects of alcohol and other CNS depressants (medicines that slow down the nervous system, possibly causing drowsiness). Some examples of CNS depressants are antihistamines or medicine for hay fever, other allergies, or colds; sedatives, tranquilizers, or sleeping medicine; prescription pain medicine or narcotics; barbiturates; medicine for seizures; or anesthetics, including some dental anesthetics. *Check with your doctor before taking any of the above while you are taking this medicine.*

Do not take this medicine within two hours of taking antacids or medicine for diarrhea. Taking loxapine and antacids or medicine for diarrhea too close together may make this medicine less effective.

This medicine may cause some people to become drowsy or less alert than they are normally, especially as the amount of medicine is increased. Even if you take this medicine at bedtime, you may feel drowsy or less alert on arising. *Make sure you know how you react to this medicine before you drive, use machines, or do anything else that could be dangerous if you are not alert.*

Although it is not a problem for most patients, dizziness, lightheadedness, or fainting may occur, especially when you get up from a lying or sitting position. Getting up slowly may help. However, if the problem continues or gets worse, check with your doctor.

Loxapine may cause your skin to be more sensitive to sunlight than it is normally. Exposure to sunlight, even for brief periods of time, may cause a skin rash, itching, redness or other discoloration of the skin, or a severe sunburn. When you begin taking this medicine:

- Stay out of direct sunlight, especially between the hours of 10:00 a.m. and 3:00 p.m., if possible.
- Wear protective clothing, including a hat. Also, wear sunglasses.
- Apply a sun block product that has a skin protection factor (SPF) of at least 15. Some patients may require a product with a higher SPF number, especially if they have a fair complexion. If you have any questions about this, check with your health care professional.
- Apply a sun block lipstick that has an SPF of at least 15 to protect your lips.
- Do not use a sunlamp or tanning bed or booth.

If you have a severe reaction from the sun, check with your doctor.

Loxapine may cause dryness of the mouth. For temporary relief, use sugarless candy or gum, melt bits of ice in your mouth, or use a saliva substitute. However, if your mouth continues to feel dry for more than 2 weeks, check with your medical doctor or dentist. Continuing dryness of the mouth may increase the chance of dental disease, including tooth decay, gum disease, and fungus infections.

Before having any kind of surgery, dental treatment, or emergency treatment, tell the medical doctor or dentist in charge that you are taking this medicine. Taking loxapine together with medicines that are used during surgery or dental or emergency treatments may increase the CNS depressant effects.

Side Effects of This Medicine

Along with its needed effects, loxapine can sometimes cause serious side effects. Tardive dyskinesia (a movement disorder) may occur and may not go away after you stop using the medicine. Signs of tardive dyskinesia include fine, worm-like movements of the tongue, or other uncontrolled movements of the mouth, tongue, cheeks, jaw, or arms and legs. Other serious but rare side effects may also occur. These include severe muscle stiffness, fever, unusual tiredness or weakness, fast heartbeat, difficult breathing, increased sweating, loss of bladder control, and seizures (neuroleptic malignant syndrome). *You and your doctor should discuss the good this medicine will do as well as the risks of taking it.*

Stop taking loxapine and get emergency help immediately if any of the following side effects occur:

Rare

Convulsions (seizures); difficult or fast breathing; fast heartbeat or irregular pulse; fever (high); high or low blood pressure; increased sweating; loss of bladder control; muscle stiffness (severe); unusually pale skin; unusual tiredness or weakness

Check with your doctor immediately if any of the following side effects occur:

More common

Lip smacking or puckering; puffing of cheeks; rapid or fine, worm-like movements of tongue; uncontrolled chewing movements; uncontrolled movements of arms or legs

Also, check with your doctor as soon as possible if any of the following side effects occur:

More common (occurring with increase of dosage)

Difficulty in speaking or swallowing; loss of balance control; mask-like face; restlessness or desire to keep moving; shuffling walk; slowed movements; stiffness of arms and legs; trembling and shaking of fingers and hands

Less common

Constipation (severe); difficult urination; inability to move eyes; muscle spasms, especially of the neck and back; skin rash; twisting movements of the body

Rare

Sore throat and fever; increased blinking or spasms of eyelid; uncontrolled twisting movements of neck, trunk, arms, or legs; unusual bleeding or bruising; unusual facial expressions or body positions; yellow eyes or skin

Symptoms of overdose

Dizziness (severe); drowsiness (severe); muscle trembling, jerking, stiffness, or uncontrolled movements (severe); troubled breathing (severe); unusual tiredness or weakness (severe)

Other side effects may occur that usually do not need medical attention. These side effects may go away during treatment as your body adjusts to the medicine. However, check with your doctor if any of the following side effects continue or are bothersome:

More common

Blurred vision; confusion; dizziness, lightheadedness, or fainting; drowsiness; dryness of mouth

Less common

Constipation (mild); decreased sexual ability; enlargement of breasts (males and females); headache; increased sensitivity of skin to sun; missing menstrual periods; nausea or vomiting; trouble in sleeping; unusual secretion of milk; weight gain

Certain side effects of this medicine may occur after you have stopped taking it. Check with your doctor as soon as possible if you notice any of the following effects after you have stopped taking loxapine:

Dizziness; nausea and vomiting; rapid or worm-like movements of the tongue; stomach upset or pain; trembling of fingers and hands; uncontrolled chewing movements

Other side effects not listed above may also occur in some patients. If you notice any other effects, check with your doctor.

Additional Information

Once a medicine has been approved for marketing for a certain use, experience may show that it is also useful for other medical problems. Although this use is not included in product labeling, loxapine is used in certain patients with the following medical condition:

- Anxiety associated with mental depression

Other than the above information, there is no additional information relating to proper use, precautions, or side effects for this use.

Revised: 01/29/93

LYPRESSIN Systemic

A commonly used brand name in the U.S. is Diapid.

Description

Lypressin (lye-PRESS-in) is a hormone used to prevent or control the frequent urination, increased thirst, and loss of water associated with diabetes insipidus (water diabetes).

Lypressin is available only with your doctor's prescription, in the following dosage form:

Nasal

- Nasal spray (U.S.)

Before Using This Medicine

In deciding to use a medicine, the risks of taking the medicine must be weighed against the good it will do. This is a decision you and your doctor will make. For lypressin, the following should be considered:

Allergies—Tell your doctor if you have ever had any unusual or allergic reaction to lypressin or vasopressin. Also tell your health care professional if you are allergic to any other substances, such as foods, preservatives, or dyes.

Pregnancy—Studies on the effects in pregnancy have not been done in either humans or animals.

Breast-feeding—It is not known whether lypressin passes into breast milk. However, this medicine has not been reported to cause problems in nursing babies.

Children—Although there is no specific information comparing use of lypressin in children with use in other age groups, this medicine is not expected to cause different side effects or problems in children than it does in adults.

Older adults—Many medicines have not been studied specifically in older people. Therefore, it may not be known whether they work exactly the same way they do in younger adults or if they cause different side effects or problems in older people. There is no specific information

comparing use of lypressin in the elderly with use in other age groups.

Other medicines—Although certain medicines should not be used together at all, in other cases two different medicines may be used together even if an interaction might occur. In these cases, your doctor may want to change the dose, or other precautions may be necessary. Tell your health care professional if you are taking any other prescription or nonprescription (over-the-counter [OTC]) medicine.

Other medical problems—The presence of other medical problems may affect the use of lypressin. Make sure you tell your doctor if you have any other medical problems, especially:

- Hay fever or other allergies or
- Infection of ears, lungs, nose, or throat or
- Stuffy nose—May prevent nasal lypressin from being absorbed into the bloodstream, through the lining of the nose
- High blood pressure—Lypressin may increase blood pressure

Proper Use of This Medicine

Use this medicine only as directed. Do not use more of it and do not use it more often than your doctor ordered. To do so may increase the chance of unwanted effects.

To use:

- Blow nose gently. Hold the bottle in an upright position. With head upright, spray the medicine into each nostril by squeezing the bottle quickly and firmly. Do not lie down when spraying this medicine.

Rinse the tip of the bottle with hot water, taking care not to suck water into the bottle, and dry with a clean tissue. Replace the cap right after use.

Dosing—The dose of lypressin will be different for different patients. *Follow your doctor's orders or the directions on the label.* The following information includes only the average doses of lypressin. *If your dose is different, do not change it* unless your doctor tells you to do so.

- For *nasal* dosage forms:
  —Adults: One or two sprays in each nostril four times a day.
  —Children six weeks of age and older: One or two sprays in each nostril four times a day.
  —Children less than six weeks of age: Use is generally not recommended.

Missed dose—If you miss a dose of this medicine, use it as soon as possible. However, if it is almost time for your next dose, skip the missed dose and go back to your regular dosing schedule. Do not double doses.

Storage—To store this medicine:

- Keep out of the reach of children.
- Store away from heat and direct light.
- Do not store in the bathroom, near the kitchen sink, or in other damp places. Heat or moisture may cause the medicine to break down.
- Keep the medicine from freezing.
- Do not keep outdated medicine or medicine no longer needed. Be sure that any discarded medicine is out of the reach of children.

Side Effects of This Medicine

Along with its needed effects, a medicine may cause some unwanted effects. Although not all of these effects may occur, if they do occur they may need medical attention.

Check with your doctor immediately if any of the following side effects occur since they may be signs or symptoms of too much fluid in the body or overdose:

Coma; confusion; convulsions (seizures); drowsiness; headache (continuing); problems with urination; weight gain

Check with your doctor as soon as possible if any of the following side effects occur:

Rare

Cough (continuing); feeling of tightness in chest; shortness of breath or troubled breathing

Other side effects may occur that usually do not need medical attention. These side effects may go away during treatment as your body adjusts to the medicine. However, check with your doctor if any of the following side effects continue or are bothersome:

Less common or rare

Abdominal or stomach cramps; headache; heartburn; increased bowel movements; irritation or pain in the eye; itching, irritation, or sores inside nose; runny or stuffy nose

Other side effects not listed above may also occur in some patients. If you notice any other effects, check with your doctor.

Revised: 07/01/93

MAFENIDE Topical†

A commonly used brand name in the U.S. is Sulfamylon.

†Not commercially available in Canada.

Description

Mafenide (MA-fe-nide), a sulfa medicine, is used to prevent and treat bacterial or fungus infections. It works by preventing growth of the fungus or bacteria.

Mafenide cream is applied to the skin and/or burned area(s) to prevent and treat bacterial or fungus infections that may occur in burns.

Other medicines are used along with this medicine for burns. Patients with severe burns or burns over a large area of the body must be treated in a hospital.

This medicine is available only with your doctor's prescription, in the following dosage form:

Topical

- Cream (U.S.)

Before Using This Medicine

In deciding to use a medicine, the risks of taking the medicine must be weighed against the good it will do. This is a decision you and your doctor will make. For mafenide, the following should be considered:

Allergies—Tell your doctor if you have ever had any unusual or allergic reaction to mafenide, acetazolamide (e.g., Diamox), oral antidiabetics (diabetes medicine you take by mouth), dichlorphenamide (e.g., Daranide), furosemide (e.g., Lasix), methazolamide (e.g., Neptazane), other sulfa medicines, or thiazide diuretics (water pills). Also tell your health care professional if you are allergic to any other substances, such as preservatives or dyes.

Pregnancy—Studies on effects in pregnancy have not been done in either humans or animals. However, use is not recommended in women during their child-bearing years unless the burn area covers more than 20% of the total body surface. In addition, sulfa medicines may increase the chance of liver problems in newborn infants and should not be used near the due date of the pregnancy.

Breast-feeding—Mafenide, when used on skin and/or burns, is absorbed into the mother's body. It is not known whether this medicine passes into breast milk. Sulfa medicines given by mouth do pass into the breast milk, and may cause liver problems, anemia (iron-poor blood), and other unwanted effects in nursing babies, especially those with glucose-6-phosphate dehydrogenase deficiency (lack of G6PD enzyme). Be sure you have discussed the risks and benefits of mafenide with your doctor.

Children—Use of mafenide is not recommended in premature or newborn infants up to 2 months of age. Sulfa medicines may cause liver problems in these infants.

Older adults—Many medicines have not been tested in older people. Therefore, it may not be known whether they work exactly the same way they do in younger adults or if they cause different side effects or problems in older people. There is no specific information comparing use of mafenide in the elderly with use in other age groups.

Other medicines—Although certain medicines should not be used together at all, in other cases two different medicines may be used together even if an interaction might occur. In these cases, your doctor may want to change the dose, or other precautions may be necessary. Tell your health care professional if you are using any other prescription or nonprescription (over-the-counter [OTC]) medicine.

Other medical problems—The presence of other medical problems may affect the use of mafenide. Make sure you tell your doctor if you have any other medical problems, especially:

- Blood problems—Use of mafenide may make the condition worse
- Glucose-6-phosphate dehydrogenase deficiency (lack of G6PD enzyme)—Use of mafenide in persons with this condition may result in hemolytic anemia
- Kidney problems or
- Lung problems or
- Metabolic acidosis—Use of mafenide in persons with any of these conditions may increase the risk of a side effect called metabolic acidosis

Proper Use of This Medicine

To use:

- Before applying this medicine, cleanse the affected area(s). Remove dead or burned skin and other debris.
- Wear a sterile glove to apply this medicine. Apply a thin layer (about 1/16 inch) of mafenide to the affected area(s). Keep the affected area(s) covered with the medicine at all times.
- If this medicine is rubbed off the affected area(s) by moving around or if it is washed off during bathing, showering, or the use of a whirlpool bath, reapply the medicine.
- After this medicine has been applied, the treated area(s) may be covered with a dressing or left uncovered as desired.

To help clear up your skin and/or burn infection completely, *keep using mafenide for the full time of treatment.* You should keep using this medicine until the burn area has healed or is ready for skin grafting. *Do not miss any doses.*

Dosing—The dose of topical mafenide will be different for different patients. *Follow your doctor's orders or the directions on the label.* The following information includes only the average doses of topical mafenide. *If your dose is different, do not change it* unless your doctor tells you to do so.

- For *topical* dosage form (cream):
  - —For bacterial or fungus infection:
    - Adults and children 2 months of age and over—Use one or two times a day.

- Infants and children up to 2 months of age—Use is not recommended.

Missed dose—If you miss a dose of this medicine, apply it as soon as possible. However, if it is almost time for your next dose, skip the missed dose and go back to your regular dosing schedule.

Storage—To store this medicine:
- Keep out of the reach of children.
- Store away from heat and direct light.
- Keep the medicine from freezing.
- Do not keep outdated medicine or medicine no longer needed. Be sure that any discarded medicine is out of the reach of children.

Precautions While Using This Medicine

It is important that your doctor check your progress at regular visits.

If your skin infection or burn does not improve within a few days or if your more serious burns or burns over larger areas do not improve within a few weeks, or if they become worse, check with your doctor.

Side Effects of This Medicine

Along with its needed effects, a medicine may cause some unwanted effects. Although not all of these side effects may occur, if they do occur they may need medical attention.

Check with your doctor immediately if any of the following side effects occur:

Less common
Itching; skin rash or redness; swelling of face or skin; wheezing or troubled breathing

Rare
Bleeding or oozing of skin; drowsiness; fast, deep breathing; nausea

Other side effects may occur that usually do not need medical attention. These side effects may go away during treatment as your body adjusts to the medicine. However, check with your doctor if any of the following side effects continue or are bothersome:

More common
Pain or burning feeling on treated area(s)

Other side effects not listed above may also occur in some patients. If you notice any other effects, check with your doctor.

Revised: 04/22/94

MAGNESIUM SUPPLEMENTS Systemic

Some commonly used brand names are:

In the U.S.—

Almora[4]	Mag-Ox 400[7]
Chloromag[1]	Mag-Tab SR[6]
Citroma[2]	Magtrate[4]
Concentrated Phillips' Milk of Magnesia[5]	Maox[7]
Mag-200[7]	MGP[4]
Mag-L-100[1]	Phillips' Chewable Tablets[5]
Magonate[4]	Phillips' Milk of Magnesia[5]
	Slow-Mag[1]
	Uro-Mag[7]

In Canada—

Citro-Mag[2]	Magnesium-Rougier[3]
Mag 2[8]	Phillips' Magnesia Tablets[5]
Maglucate[4]	Phillips' Milk of Magnesia[5]

Note: For quick reference, the following magnesium supplements are numbered to match the corresponding brand names.

This information applies to the following:

1. Magnesium Chloride (mag-NEE-zhum KLOR-ide)†‡
2. Magnesium Citrate (SIH-trayt)‡#
3. Magnesium Gluceptate (gloo-SEP-tate)*
4. Magnesium Gluconate (GLOO-ko-nate)‡
5. Magnesium Hydroxide (hye-DROX-ide)‡#††
6. Magnesium Lactate (LAK-tate)†
7. Magnesium Oxide (OX-ide)‡§#
8. Magnesium Pidolate (PID-o-late)*
9. Magnesium Sulfate (SUL-fate)‡§#**

*Not commercially available in the U.S.
†Not commercially available in Canada.
‡Generic name product may be available in the U.S.
§Generic name product may be available in Canada.
#See *Laxatives (Oral)* for laxative use of magnesium citrate, magnesium hydroxide, magnesium oxide, and magnesium sulfate.
**See *Magnesium Sulfate (Systemic)* for use in seizures and uterine tetany.
††See *Antacids* (Oral) for antacid use of magnesium hydroxide and magnesium oxide.

Description

Magnesium is used as a dietary supplement for individuals who are deficient in magnesium. Although a balanced diet usually supplies all the magnesium a person needs, magnesium supplements may be needed by patients who have lost magnesium because of illness or treatment with certain medicines.

Lack of magnesium may lead to irritability, muscle weakness, and irregular heartbeat.

Injectable magnesium is given only by or under the supervision of a health care professional. Some oral magnesium preparations are available only with a prescription. Others are available without a prescription.

Magnesium supplements are available in the following dosage forms:

Oral
Magnesium Chloride
- Tablets (U.S.)
- Enteric-coated tablets (U.S.)
- Extended-release tablets (U.S.)

Magnesium Citrate
- Oral solution (U.S. and Canada)

Magnesium Gluceptate
- Oral solution (Canada)

Magnesium Gluconate
- Oral solution (U.S.)
- Tablets (U.S. and Canada)

Magnesium Hydroxide
- Tablets (U.S.)
- Chewable tablets (U.S. and Canada)
- Oral solution (U.S. and Canada)

Magnesium Lactate
- Extended-release tablets (U.S.)

Magnesium Oxide
- Capsules (U.S.)
- Tablets (U.S. and Canada)

Magnesium Pidolate
- Powder for oral solution (Canada)

Magnesium Sulfate
- Crystals (U.S.)

Parenteral

Magnesium Chloride
- Injection (U.S.)

Magnesium Sulfate
- Injection (U.S. and Canada)

Importance of Diet

For good health, it is important that you eat a balanced and varied diet. Follow carefully any diet program your health care professional may recommend. For your specific dietary vitamin and/or mineral needs, ask your health care professional for a list of appropriate foods. If you think that you are not getting enough vitamins and/or minerals in your diet, you may choose to take a dietary supplement.

The best dietary sources of magnesium include green leafy vegetables, nuts, peas, beans, and cereal grains in which the germ or outer layers have not been removed. Hard water has been found to contain more magnesium than soft water. A diet high in fat may cause less magnesium to be absorbed. Cooking may decrease the magnesium content of food.

The daily amount of magnesium needed is defined in several different ways.

For U.S.—

- Recommended Dietary Allowances (RDAs) are the amount of vitamins and minerals needed to provide for adequate nutrition in most healthy persons. RDAs for a given nutrient may vary depending on a person's age, sex, and physical condition (e.g., pregnancy).
- Daily Values (DVs) are used on food and dietary supplement labels to indicate the percent of the recommended daily amount of each nutrient that a serving provides. DV replaces the previous designation of United States Recommended Daily Allowances (USRDAs).

For Canada—

- Recommended Nutrient Intakes (RNIs) are used to determine the amounts of vitamins, minerals, and protein needed to provide adequate nutrition and lessen the risk of chronic disease.

Normal daily recommended intakes in milligrams (mg) for magnesium are generally defined as follows:

Persons	U.S. (mg)	Canada (mg)
Infants and children		
Birth to 3 years of age	40–80	20–50
4 to 6 years of age	120	65
7 to 10 years of age	170	100–135
Adolescent and adult males	270–400	130–250
Adolescent and adult females	280–300	135–210
Pregnant females	320	195–245
Breast-feeding females	340–355	245–265

Before Using This Dietary Supplement

If you are taking this dietary supplement without a prescription, carefully read and follow any precautions on the label. For magnesium supplements, the following should be considered:

Allergies—Tell your health care professional if you have ever had any unusual or allergic reaction to magnesium. Also tell your health care professional if you are allergic to any other substances, such as foods, preservatives, or dyes.

Pregnancy—It is especially important that you are receiving enough vitamins and minerals when you become pregnant and that you continue to receive the right amount of vitamins and minerals throughout your pregnancy. The healthy growth and development of the fetus depend on a steady supply of nutrients from the mother. However, taking large amounts of dietary supplements during pregnancy may be harmful to the mother and/or fetus and should be avoided.

Breast-feeding—It is especially important that you receive the right amount of vitamins and minerals so that your baby will also get the vitamins and minerals needed to grow properly. However, taking large amounts of a dietary supplement while breast-feeding may be harmful to the mother and/or baby and should be avoided.

Children—Problems in children have not been reported with intake of normal daily recommended amounts.

Older adults—Problems in older adults have not been reported with intake of normal daily recommended amounts.

Studies have shown that older adults may have lower blood levels of magnesium than younger adults. Your health care professional may recommend that you take a magnesium supplement.

Medicines or other dietary supplements—Although certain medicines or other dietary supplements should not be used together at all, in other cases they may be used together even if an interaction might occur. In these cases, your health care professional may want to change the dose, or other precautions may be necessary. When you are taking magnesium, it is especially important that your health care professional know if you are taking any of the following:

- Cellulose sodium phosphate—Use with magnesium supplements may prevent cellulose sodium phosphate from working properly; magnesium supplements should be taken at least 1 hour before or after cellulose sodium phosphate
- Magnesium-containing preparations, other, including magnesium enemas—Use with magnesium supplements may cause high blood levels of magnesium, which may increase the chance of side effects
- Sodium polystyrene sulfonate—Use with magnesium supplements may cause the magnesium supplement to be less effective
- Tetracyclines, oral—Use with magnesium supplements may prevent the tetracycline from working properly; magnesium supplements should be taken at least 1 to 3 hours before or after oral tetracycline

Other medical problems—The presence of other medical problems may affect the use of magnesium. Make sure you tell your health care professional if you have any other medical problems, especially:

- Heart disease—Magnesium supplements may make this condition worse
- Kidney problems—Magnesium supplements may increase the risk of hypermagnesemia (too much magnesium in the blood), which could cause serious side effects; your health care professional may need to change your dose

Proper Use of This Dietary Supplement

Dosing—The amount of magnesium needed to meet normal daily recommended intakes will be different for different patients. The following information includes only the average amounts of magnesium.

- For *oral* dosage form (capsules, chewable tablets, crystals for oral solution, extended-release tablets, enteric-coated tablets, powder for oral solution, tablets, oral solution):
  —To prevent deficiency, the amount taken by mouth is based on normal daily recommended intakes (Note that the normal daily recommended intakes are expressed as an actual amount of magnesium. The salt form [e.g., magnesium chloride, magnesium gluconate, etc.] has a different strength.):

  For the U.S.

  - Adult and teenage males—270 to 400 milligrams (mg) per day.
  - Adult and teenage females—280 to 300 mg per day.
  - Pregnant females—320 mg per day.
  - Breast-feeding females—340 to 355 mg per day.
  - Children 7 to 10 years of age—170 mg per day.
  - Children 4 to 6 years of age—120 mg per day.
  - Children birth to 3 years of age—40 to 80 mg per day.

  For Canada

  - Adult and teenage males—130 to 250 mg per day.
  - Adult and teenage females—135 to 210 mg per day.
  - Pregnant females—195 to 245 mg per day.
  - Breast-feeding females—245 to 265 mg per day.
  - Children 7 to 10 years of age—100 to 135 mg per day.
  - Children 4 to 6 years of age—65 mg per day.
  - Children birth to 3 years of age—20 to 50 mg per day.

  —To treat deficiency:

  - Adults, teenagers, and children—Treatment dose is determined by prescriber for each individual based on severity of deficiency.

Magnesium supplements should be taken with meals. Taking magnesium supplements on an empty stomach may cause diarrhea.

For individuals taking the *extended-release form* of this dietary supplement:

- Swallow the tablets whole. Do not chew or suck on the tablet.
- Some tablets may be broken or crushed and sprinkled on applesauce or other soft food. However, check with your health care professional first, since this should not be done for most tablets.

For individuals taking the *powder form* of this dietary supplement:

- Pour powder into a glass.
- Add water and stir.

Missed dose—If you miss taking your magnesium supplement for one or more days there is no cause for concern, since it takes some time for your body to become seriously low in magnesium. However, if your health care professional has recommended that you take magnesium, try to remember to take it as directed every day.

Storage—To store this dietary supplement:

- Keep out of the reach of children.
- Store away from heat and direct light.
- Do not store in the bathroom, near the kitchen sink, or in other damp places. Heat or moisture may cause the dietary supplement to break down.
- Keep the dietary supplement from freezing. Do not refrigerate.
- Do not keep dietary supplements that are outdated or are no longer needed. Be sure that any discarded dietary supplement is out of the reach of children.

Side Effects of This Dietary Supplement

Along with its needed effects, a dietary supplement may cause some unwanted effects. Although not all of these side effects may occur, if they do occur they may need medical attention.

Check with your health care professional immediately if any of the following side effects occur:

Rare (with injectable magnesium only)
Dizziness or fainting; flushing; irritation and pain at injection site—for intramuscular administration only; muscle paralysis; troubled breathing

Symptoms of overdose (rare in individuals with normal kidney function)
Blurred or double vision; coma; dizziness or fainting; drowsiness (severe); increased or decreased urination; slow heartbeat; troubled breathing

Other side effects may occur that usually do not need medical attention. These side effects may go away during treatment as your body adjusts to the medicine. However, check with your health care professional if the following side effect continues or is bothersome:

Less common (with oral magnesium)
Diarrhea

Other side effects not listed above may also occur in some individuals. If you notice any other effects, check with your health care professional.

Revised: 12/03/92
Interim revision: 03/28/93; 08/23/94; 07/11/95

MALATHION Topical

Some commonly used brand names are:

In the U.S.—
Ovide

Other—
Derbac-M
Suleo-M

Description

Malathion (mal-a-THYE-on) belongs to the group of medicines known as pediculicides (medicines that kill lice). Malathion is applied to the hair and scalp to treat head lice infections. It acts by killing both the lice and their eggs.

This medicine is available only with your doctor's prescription, in the following dosage form:

Topical
- Lotion (U.S.)

Before Using This Medicine

In deciding to use a medicine, the risks of taking the medicine must be weighed against the good it will do. This is a decision you and your doctor will make. For malathion, the following should be considered:

Allergies—Tell your doctor if you have ever had any unusual or allergic reaction to malathion. Also tell your health care professional if you are allergic to any other substances, such as preservatives or dyes.

Pregnancy—Malathion may be absorbed through the skin. Although it has not been studied in pregnant women, malathion has not been shown to cause birth defects or other problems in animal studies.

Breast-feeding—Malathion may be absorbed through the mother's skin. It is not known whether malathion passes into the breast milk. Although most medicines pass into breast milk in small amounts, many of them may be used safely while breast-feeding. Mothers who are using this medicine and who wish to breast-feed should discuss this with their doctor.

Children—This medicine has been tested in children 2 years of age and older and, in effective doses, has not been shown to cause different side effects or problems than it does in adults. There is no specific information comparing use of malathion in children less than 2 years of age with use in other age groups.

Older adults—Many medicines have not been studied specifically in older people. Therefore, it may not be known whether they work exactly the same way they do in younger adults or if they cause different side effects or problems in older people. There is no specific information comparing use of malathion in the elderly with use in other age groups.

Other medicines—Although certain medicines should not be used together at all, in other cases two different medicines may be used together even if an interaction might occur. In these cases, your doctor may want to change the dose, or other precautions may be necessary. When you are using malathion, it is especially important that your health care professional know if you are using any of the following:

- Antimyasthenics (ambenonium, neostigmine, pyridostigmine) or
- Demecarium, echothiophate, or isoflurophate eye medicine—Use of malathion with these medicines may increase the chance of side effects

Other medical problems—The presence of other medical problems may affect the use of malathion. Make sure you tell your doctor if you have any other medical problems, especially:

- Anemia (severe) or
- Brain surgery, recent, or
- Liver disease or
- Malnutrition—These conditions may increase the chance of some side effects of malathion

- Asthma or
- Epilepsy or other seizure disorders or
- Heart disease or
- Myasthenia gravis or other nerve/muscle disease or
- Parkinson's disease or
- Stomach ulcer or other stomach or intestinal problems—Use of malathion may make the condition worse

Proper Use of This Medicine

Malathion is a poison. Keep it away from the mouth because it is harmful if swallowed.

Use this medicine only as directed by your doctor. Do not use more of it, do not use it more often, and do not use it for a longer time than your doctor ordered. To do so may increase the chance of absorption through the skin and the chance of malathion poisoning.

To use:
- Apply malathion by sprinkling on dry hair and rubbing in until the hair and scalp are thoroughly moistened.
- Immediately after using this medicine, wash your hands to remove any medicine that may be on them.
- Allow the hair to dry naturally. Use no heat (as from a hair dryer) and leave the hair uncovered.
- After the medicine has been allowed to remain on the hair and scalp for 8 to 12 hours, *wash the hair with a nonmedicated shampoo and then rinse thoroughly.*
- After rinsing, use a fine-toothed comb to remove the dead lice and eggs from the hair.

Keep this medicine away from the eyes. If you should accidentally get some in your eyes, flush them thoroughly with water at once.

This medicine is flammable. Do not use near heat, near open flame, or while smoking.

Head lice can be easily transferred from one person to another by direct contact with clothing, hats, scarves, bedding, towels, washcloths, hairbrushes and combs, or hairs from infected persons. Therefore, *all household members of your family should be examined for head lice and receive treatment if they are found to be infected.* If you have any questions about this, check with your doctor.

Dosing—The dose of malathion will be different for different patients. *Follow your doctor's orders or the directions on the label.* The following information includes only the average doses of malathion. *If your dose is different, do not change it* unless your doctor tells your to do so.

- For *lotion* dosage form:
  - —For head lice infestations:
    - Adults and children 2 years of age and older—Apply to the hair and scalp one time. Treatment may be repeated after seven to nine days if necessary.
    - Children up to 2 years of age—Use and dose must be determined by your doctor.

Storage—To store this medicine:
- Keep out of the reach of children.
- Store away from heat and direct light.
- Keep the medicine from freezing.
- Do not keep outdated medicine or medicine no longer needed. Be sure that any discarded medicine is out of the reach of children.

Precautions While Using This Medicine

To prevent reinfection or the spreading of the infection to other people, good health habits are also required. These include the following:
- Wash all clothing, bedding, towels, and washcloths in very hot water or dry-clean them.
- Wash all hairbrushes and combs in very hot soapy water and do not share them with other people.
- Clean the house or room by thorough vacuuming.

If you have any questions about this, check with your doctor.

Breathing in even small amounts of carbamate- or organophosphate-type insecticides or pesticides (for example, carbaryl [Sevin], demeton [Systox], diazinon, malathion, parathion, ronnel [Trolene]) may add to the effects of this medicine. Farmers, gardeners, residents of communities undergoing insecticide or pesticide spraying or dusting, workers in plants manufacturing such products, or other persons exposed to such poisons should protect themselves by wearing a mask over the nose and mouth, changing clothes frequently, and washing hands often while using this medicine.

Side Effects of This Medicine

Along with its needed effects, a medicine may cause some unwanted effects. Although not all of these side effects may occur, if they do occur they may need medical attention.

Check with your doctor as soon as possible if any of the following side effects occur:

Rare

Skin rash

When malathion is applied to the skin in recommended doses, symptoms of poisoning have not been reported. However, the chance may exist, especially if the skin is broken. *Symptoms of malathion poisoning* include:

Abdominal or stomach cramps; anxiety or restlessness; clumsiness or unsteadiness; confusion or mental depression; convulsions (seizures); diarrhea; difficult or labored breathing; dizziness; drowsiness; increased sweating; increased watering of mouth or eyes; loss of bowel or bladder control; muscle twitching of eyelids, face, and neck; pinpoint pupils; slow heartbeat; trembling; unusual weakness

Other side effects may occur that usually do not need medical attention. These side effects may go away during treatment as your body adjusts to the medicine. However, check with your doctor if either of the following side effects continues or is bothersome:

Less common or rare

Stinging or irritation of scalp

Other side effects not listed above may also occur in some patients. If you notice any other effects, check with your doctor.

Revised: 07/25/94

MANGANESE SUPPLEMENTS Systemic

This information applies to the following:
1. Manganese Chloride (MAN-ga-nees KLOR-ide)†‡
2. Manganese Sulfate (SUL-fate)†

†Not commercially available in Canada.
‡Generic name product may be available in the U.S.

Description

Manganese supplements are used to prevent or treat manganese deficiency.

The body needs manganese for normal growth and health. For patients who are unable to get enough manganese in their regular diet or who have a need for more manganese, manganese supplements may be necessary. Manganese helps your body break down fats, carbohydrates, and proteins. It does so as part of several enzymes.

Manganese deficiency has not been reported in humans. Lack of manganese in animals has been found to cause improper formation of bone and cartilage, may decrease the body's ability to use sugar properly, and may cause growth problems.

Injectable manganese supplements are given by or under the supervision of a health care professional.

Manganese supplements are available in the following dosage forms:

Oral

Manganese is available orally as part of a multivitamin/mineral combination.

Parenteral

Manganese Chloride
- Injection (U.S.)

Manganese Sulfate
- Injection (U.S.)

Importance of Diet

For good health, it is important that you eat a balanced and varied diet. Follow carefully any diet program your health care professional may recommend. For your specific dietary vitamin and/or mineral needs, ask your health care professional for a list of appropriate foods. If you think that you are not getting enough vitamins and/or minerals in your diet, you may choose to take a dietary supplement.

Manganese is found in whole grains, cereal products, lettuce, dry beans, and peas.

The daily amount of manganese needed is defined in several different ways.

For U.S.—
- Recommended Dietary Allowances (RDAs) are the amount of vitamins and minerals needed to provide for adequate nutrition in most healthy persons. RDAs for a given nutrient may vary depending on a person's age, sex, and physical condition (e.g., pregnancy).
- Daily Values (DVs) are used on food and dietary supplement labels to indicate the percent of the recommended daily amount of each nutrient that a serving provides. DV replaces the previous designation of United States Recommended Daily Allowances (USRDAs).

For Canada—
- Recommended Nutrient Intakes (RNIs) are used to determine the amounts of vitamins, minerals, and protein needed to provide adequate nutrition and lessen the risk of chronic disease.

Because a lack of manganese is rare, there is no RDA or RNI for it. The following daily intakes are thought to be plenty for most individuals:
- Infants and children—
  - Birth to 3 years of age: 0.3 to 1.5 milligrams (mg).
  - 4 to 6 years of age: 1.5 to 2 mg.
  - 7 to 10 years of age: 2 to 3 mg.
- Adolescents and adults—2 to 5 mg.

Before Using This Dietary Supplement

If you are taking this dietary supplement without a prescription, carefully read and follow any precautions on the label. For manganese, the following should be considered:

Allergies—Tell your health care professional if you have ever had any unusual or allergic reaction to manganese. Also tell your health care professional if you are allergic to any other substances, such as foods, preservatives, or dyes.

Pregnancy—It is especially important that you are receiving enough vitamins and minerals when you become pregnant and that you continue to receive the right amount of vitamins and minerals throughout your pregnancy. The healthy growth and development of the fetus depend on a steady supply of nutrients from the mother. However, taking large amounts of a dietary supplement in pregnancy may be harmful to the mother and/or fetus and should be avoided.

Breast-feeding—It is important that you receive the right amounts of vitamins and minerals so that your baby will also get the vitamins and minerals needed to grow properly. However, taking large amounts of a dietary supplement while breast-feeding may be harmful to the mother and/or baby and should be avoided.

Children—Problems in children have not been reported with intake of normal daily recommended amounts.

Older adults—Problems in older adults have not been reported with intake of normal daily recommended amounts.

Medicines or other dietary supplements—Although certain medicines or dietary supplements should not be used together at all, in other cases they may be used together even if an interaction might occur. In these cases, your health care professional may want to change the dose, or other precautions may be necessary. Tell your health care professional if you are taking any other dietary supplement or any prescription or nonprescription (over-the-counter [OTC]) medicines.

Other medical problems—The presence of other medical problems may affect the use of manganese. Make sure you tell your health care professional if you have any other medical problems, especially:

- Biliary disease or
- Liver disease—Taking manganese supplements may cause high blood levels of manganese, and dosage of manganese may have to be changed

Proper Use of This Dietary Supplement

Dosing—The amount of manganese needed to meet normal daily recommended intakes will be different for different individuals. The following information includes only the average amounts of manganese.

- For *oral* dosage form (as part of a multivitamin/mineral supplement):
  - —To prevent deficiency, the amount taken by mouth is based on normal daily recommended intakes:
    - Adults and teenagers—2 to 5 milligrams (mg) per day.
    - Children 7 to 10 years of age—2 to 3 mg per day.
    - Children 4 to 6 years of age—1.5 to 2 mg per day.
    - Children birth to 3 years of age—0.3 to 1.5 mg per day.
  - —To treat deficiency:
    - Adults, teenagers, and children—Treatment dose is determined by prescriber for each individual based on severity of deficiency.

Missed dose—If you miss taking manganese supplements for one or more days there is no cause for concern, since it takes some time for your body to become seriously low in manganese. However, if your health care professional has recommended that you take manganese, try to remember to take it as directed every day.

Storage—To store this dietary supplement:

- Keep out of the reach of children.
- Store away from heat and direct light.
- Do not store in the bathroom, near the kitchen sink, or in other damp places. Heat or moisture may cause the dietary supplement to break down.
- Keep the dietary supplement from freezing. Do not refrigerate.
- Do not keep outdated dietary supplements or those no longer needed. Be sure that any discarded dietary supplement is out of the reach of children.

Side Effects of This Dietary Supplement

No side effects or toxic effects have been reported for manganese. However, check with your health care professional if you notice any unusual effects while you are taking it.

Revised: 02/01/92
Interim revision: 08/07/92; 08/15/94; 04/25/95

MAPROTILINE Systemic

A commonly used brand name in the U.S. and Canada is Ludiomil.

Generic name product may also be available in the U.S.

Description

Maprotiline (ma-PROE-ti-leen) is used to relieve mental depression, including anxiety that sometimes occurs with depression.

Maprotiline is available only with your doctor's prescription, in the following dosage form:

Oral

- Tablets (U.S. and Canada)

Before Using This Medicine

In deciding to use a medicine, the risks of taking the medicine must be weighed against the good it will do. This is a decision you and your doctor will make. For maprotiline, the following should be considered:

Allergies—Tell your doctor if you have ever had any unusual or allergic reaction to maprotiline or tricyclic antidepressants. Also tell your health care professional if you are allergic to any other substances, such as foods, preservatives, or dyes.

Pregnancy—Maprotiline has not been studied in pregnant women. However, this medicine has not been shown to cause birth defects or other problems in animal studies.

Breast-feeding—Maprotiline passes into the breast milk. However, this medicine has not been reported to cause problems in nursing babies.

Children—Studies on this medicine have been done only in adult patients, and there is no specific information comparing use of maprotiline in children with use in other age groups.

Older adults—Drowsiness, dizziness or lightheadedness; confusion; vision problems; dryness of mouth; constipation; and difficulty in urinating may be especially likely to occur in elderly patients, who are usually more sensitive than younger adults to the effects of maprotiline.

Other medicines—Although certain medicines should not be used together at all, in other cases two different medicines may be used together even if an interaction might occur. In these cases, your doctor may want to change the dose, or other precautions may be necessary. When you are taking maprotiline, it is especially important that your

health care professional know if you are taking any of the following:

- Amphetamines or
- Appetite suppressants (diet pills) or
- Medicine for asthma or other breathing problems or
- Medicine for colds, sinus problems, or hay fever or other allergies (including nose drops or sprays)—Using these medicines with maprotiline may cause serious unwanted effects on your heart and blood pressure
- Central nervous system (CNS) depressants (medicines that cause drowsiness)—Taking these medicines with maprotiline may increase the CNS depressant effects
- Monoamine oxidase (MAO) inhibitors (furazolidone [e.g., Furoxone], isocarboxazid [e.g., Marplan], phenelzine [e.g., Nardil], procarbazine [e.g., Matulane], selegiline [e.g., Eldepryl], tranylcypromine [e.g., Parnate])—Taking maprotiline while you are taking or within 2 weeks of taking monoamine oxidase (MAO) inhibitors may cause very serious side effects, such as sudden high body temperature, extremely high blood pressure, and severe convulsions; at least 14 days should be allowed between stopping treatment with one medicine and starting treatment with the other

Other medical problems—The presence of other medical problems may affect the use of maprotiline. Make sure you tell your doctor if you have any other medical problems, especially:

- Alcohol abuse or
- Seizure disorders (including epilepsy)—The risk of seizures may be increased
- Asthma or
- Difficult urination or
- Enlarged prostate or
- Glaucoma or
- Mental illness (severe) or
- Stomach or intestinal problems—Maprotiline may make the condition worse
- Heart or blood vessel disease or
- Overactive thyroid—Serious effects on your heart may occur
- Liver disease—Higher blood levels of maprotiline may occur, increasing the chance of side effects

Proper Use of This Medicine

Take this medicine only as directed by your doctor to benefit your condition as much as possible. Do not take more of it, do not take it more often, and do not take it for a longer time than your doctor ordered.

Sometimes this medicine must be taken for up to two or three weeks before you begin to feel better. Your doctor should check your progress at regular visits.

Dosing—The dose of maprotiline will be different for different patients. *Follow your doctor's orders or the directions on the label.* The following information includes only the average doses of maprotiline. *If your dose is different, do not change it* unless your doctor tells you to do so.

The number of tablets that you take depends on the strength of the medicine. Also, *the number of doses you take each day, the time allowed between doses, and the length of time you take the medicine depend on the medical problem for which you are taking maprotiline.*

- For *oral* dosage form (tablets):
  - For depression:
    - Adults—At first, 25 milligrams (mg) taken one to three times a day. Your doctor may increase your dose as needed. However, the dose is usually not more than 150 mg a day, unless you are in the hospital. Some hospitalized patients may need higher doses.
    - Children—Use and dose must be determined by your doctor.

Missed dose—If you miss a dose of this medicine and your dosing schedule is:

- One dose a day at bedtime—Do not take the missed dose in the morning since it may cause disturbing side effects during waking hours. Instead, check with your doctor.
- More than one dose a day—Take the missed dose as soon as possible. Then go back to your regular dosing schedule. However, if it is almost time for your next dose, skip the missed dose and go back to your regular dosing schedule. Do not double doses. If you have any questions about this, check with your doctor.

Storage—To store this medicine:

- Keep out of the reach of children.
- Store away from heat and direct light.
- Do not store in the bathroom, near the kitchen sink, or in other damp places. Heat or moisture may cause the medicine to break down.
- Do not keep outdated medicine or medicine no longer needed. Be sure that any discarded medicine is out of the reach of children.

Precautions While Using This Medicine

It is very important that your doctor check your progress at regular visits. This will allow your dosage to be changed if necessary and will help to reduce side effects.

This medicine will add to the effects of alcohol and other CNS depressants (medicines that slow down the nervous system, possibly causing drowsiness). Some examples of CNS depressants are antihistamines or medicine for hay fever, other allergies, or colds; sedatives, tranquilizers, or sleeping medicine; prescription pain medicine or narcotics; barbiturates; medicine for seizures; or anesthetics, including some dental anesthetics. *Check with your doctor before taking any of the above while you are using this medicine.*

This medicine may cause blurred vision, especially during the first few weeks of treatment. It may also cause some people to become drowsy or less alert than they are normally. *If these effects occur, do not drive, use machines, or do anything else that could be dangerous if you are not alert or able to see well.*

Dizziness, lightheadedness, or fainting may occur, especially when you get up from a lying or sitting position. Getting up slowly may help. If this problem continues or gets worse, check with your doctor.

Maprotiline may cause dryness of the mouth. For temporary relief, use sugarless gum or candy, melt bits of ice in your mouth, or use a saliva substitute. However, if your mouth continues to feel dry for more than 2 weeks, check with your medical doctor or dentist. Continuing dryness of the mouth may increase the chance of dental disease, including tooth decay, gum disease, and fungus infections.

Before having any kind of surgery, dental treatment, or emergency treatment, tell the medical doctor or dentist in charge that you are using this medicine. Taking maprotiline together with medicines that are used during surgery or dental or emergency treatments may increase the CNS depressant effects.

Do not stop taking this medicine without first checking with your doctor. Your doctor may want you to reduce gradually the amount you are taking before stopping completely. This will allow your body to adjust properly and will reduce the possibility of unwanted effects.

Side Effects of This Medicine

Along with its needed effects, a medicine may cause some unwanted effects. Although not all of these side effects may occur, if they do occur they may need medical attention.

Check with your doctor as soon as possible if any of the following side effects occur:

More common

Skin rash, redness, swelling, or itching

Less common

Constipation (severe); nausea or vomiting; shakiness or trembling; seizures (convulsions); unusual excitement; weight loss

Rare

Breast enlargement—in males and females; confusion (especially in the elderly); difficulty in urinating; fainting; hallucinations (seeing, hearing, or feeling things that are not there); inappropriate secretion of milk—in females; irregular heartbeat (pounding, racing, skipping); sore throat and fever; swelling of testicles; yellow eyes or skin

Symptoms of overdose

Convulsions (seizures); dizziness (severe); drowsiness (severe); fast or irregular heartbeat; fever; muscle stiffness or weakness (severe); restlessness or agitation; trouble in breathing; vomiting

Other side effects may occur that usually do not need medical attention. These side effects may go away during treatment as your body adjusts to the medicine. However, check with your doctor if any of the following side effects continue or are bothersome:

More common

Blurred vision; decreased sexual ability; dizziness or lightheadedness (especially in the elderly); drowsiness; dryness of mouth; headache; increased or decreased sexual drive; tiredness or weakness

Less common

Constipation (mild); diarrhea; heartburn; increased appetite and weight gain; increased sensitivity of skin to sunlight; increased sweating; trouble in sleeping; weight loss

After you stop taking this medicine, your body will need time to adjust. This usually takes about 3 to 10 days. Continue to follow the precautions listed above during this period of time.

Other side effects not listed above may also occur in some patients. If you notice any other effects, check with your doctor.

Additional Information

Once a medicine has been approved for marketing for a certain use, experience may show that it is also useful for other medical problems. Although this use in not included in product labeling, maprotiline is used in certain patients with the following medical condition:

- Chronic neurogenic pain (a certain type of pain that is continuing)

Other than the above information, there is no additional information relating to proper use, precautions, or side effects for these uses.

Revised: 08/29/94

MASOPROCOL Topical†

A commonly used brand name in the U.S. is Actinex.

†Not commercially available in Canada.

Description

Masoprocol (ma-SOE-pro-kole) is applied to the skin to treat a condition called actinic keratoses, which can become cancerous if not treated.

Masoprocol is available only with your doctor's prescription, in the following dosage form:

Topical

- Cream (U.S.)

Before Using This Medicine

In deciding to use a medicine, the risks of using the medicine must be weighed against the good it will do. This is a decision you and your doctor will make. For topical masoprocol, the following should be considered:

Allergies—Tell your doctor if you have ever had any unusual or allergic reaction to masoprocol. Also tell your health care professional if you are allergic to any other substances, such as sulfites or other preservatives or dyes. Masoprocol for use on the skin contains sulfites.

Pregnancy—Tell your doctor if you are pregnant or if you intend to become pregnant. Although masoprocol applied to the skin has not been shown to cause problems in humans, some of it is absorbed through the skin. Be sure that you have discussed this with your doctor before using this medicine.

Breast-feeding—Although masoprocol applied to the skin has not been shown to cause problems in nursing babies, some of it is absorbed through the skin.

Children—There is no specific information comparing use of masoprocol on the skin in children with use in other age groups.

Older adults—Many medicines have not been studied specifically in older people. Therefore, it may not be known whether they work exactly the same way they do in younger adults or if they cause different side effects or problems in older people. Although there is no specific information comparing use of masoprocol on the skin in the elderly with use in other age groups, this medicine is not expected to cause different side effects or problems in older people than it does in younger adults.

Proper Use of This Medicine

Keep using this medicine for the full time of treatment. However, *do not use this medicine more often or for a longer time than your doctor ordered.* Apply enough medicine each time to cover the entire affected area with a thin layer.

After washing the area with mild soap and water and drying carefully, use your fingertips to apply the medicine in a thin layer to your skin and rub it in gently.

Make sure you *wash your hands immediately after applying the cream,* to prevent any of the medicine from accidentally getting in your eyes or mouth.

Masoprocol commonly causes redness, soreness, swelling, itching, dryness, and flaking of affected skin. This effect will go away about 2 weeks after you stop using the medicine. However, do not stop using this medicine without first checking with your doctor. If this reaction occurs, check with your doctor.

Dosing—The dose of masoprocol will be different for different patients. *Follow your doctor's orders or the directions on the label.* The following information includes only the average dose of masoprocol. *If your dose is different, do not change it* unless your doctor tells you to do so.

- Adults—Use the 10% cream on the affected areas of skin two times a day.
- Children—Use and dose must be determined by your doctor.

Missed dose—If you miss a dose of this medicine, apply it as soon as possible. However, if more than a few hours have passed, skip the missed dose and go back to your regular dosing schedule. If you miss more than one dose, check with your doctor.

Storage—To store this medicine:

- Keep out of the reach of children.
- Store away from heat and direct light.
- Do not store in the bathroom, near the kitchen sink, or in other damp places. Heat or moisture may cause the medicine to break down.
- Do not keep outdated medicine or medicine no longer needed. Be sure that any discarded medicine is out of the reach of children.

Precautions While Using This Medicine

It is very important that your doctor check your progress at regular visits to make sure that this medicine is working properly and to check for unwanted effects.

Apply this medicine very carefully when using it on your face. Avoid getting any in your eyes, nose, or mouth.

This preparation contains sulfites as a preservative. Sulfites may cause an allergic reaction in some people. Signs of an allergic reaction to sulfites include bluish discoloration of skin, severe dizziness or feeling faint, or wheezing or trouble in breathing. *If any of these signs occur, check with your doctor immediately.*

Side Effects of This Medicine

Along with its needed effects, a medicine may cause some unwanted effects. Although not all of these side effects may occur, if they do occur they may need medical attention.

Stop using this medicine and check with your doctor immediately if the following side effects occur:

More common

Redness and swelling of normal skin

Check with your doctor immediately if the following side effect occurs:

Less common

Blistering or oozing where medicine is applied

Signs and symptoms of allergic reaction to sulfites

Bluish discoloration of skin; dizziness (severe) or feeling faint; wheezing or trouble in breathing

Check with your doctor as soon as possible if the following side effects occur:

More common

Redness, soreness, swelling, itching, dryness, and flaking of skin where medicine is applied

Other side effects may occur that usually do not need medical attention. These side effects may go away during treatment as your body adjusts to the medicine. However, check with your doctor if any of the following side effects continue, worsen, or are bothersome:

More common

Burning feeling where medicine is applied

Less common

Leathery feeling to skin; skin roughness; wrinkles

Other side effects not listed above may also occur in some patients. If you notice any other effects, check with your doctor.

Developed: 07/31/95

MEASLES, MUMPS, AND RUBELLA VIRUS VACCINE LIVE Systemic

A commonly used brand name in the U.S. and Canada is M-M-R II.

Description

Measles (MEE-zills), mumps, and rubella (rue-BELL-a) virus vaccine live is an active immunizing agent used to prevent infection by the measles, mumps, and rubella viruses. It works by causing your body to produce its own protection (antibodies) against the virus.

Measles (also known as coughing measles, hard measles, morbilli, red measles, rubeola, and 10-day measles) is an infection that is easily spread from one person to another. Infection with measles can cause serious problems, such as stomach problems, pneumonia, ear infections, sinus problems, convulsions (seizures), brain damage, and possibly death. The risk of serious complications and death is greater for adults and infants than for children and teenagers.

Mumps is an infection that can cause serious problems, such as encephalitis and meningitis, which affect the brain. In addition, adolescent boys and men are very susceptible to a condition called orchitis, which causes pain and swelling in the testicles and scrotum and, in rare cases, sterility. Also, mumps infection can cause spontaneous abortion in women during the first 3 months of pregnancy.

Rubella (also known as German measles) is a serious infection that causes miscarriages, stillbirths, or birth defects in unborn babies when pregnant women get the disease.

While immunization against measles, mumps, and rubella is recommended for all persons 12 months of age and older, it is especially important for women of child-bearing age and persons traveling outside the U.S.

If measles, mumps, and rubella vaccine is to be given to a child, the child should be at least 12 months of age. This is to make sure the measles vaccine is effective. In a younger child, antibodies from the mother may interfere with the effectiveness of the vaccine.

This vaccine should be administered only by or under the supervision of your doctor or other health care professional. It is available in the following dosage form:

Parenteral
- Injection (U.S. and Canada)

Before Receiving This Vaccine

In deciding to use a medicine, the risks of taking the medicine must be weighed against the good it will do. This is a decision you and your doctor will make. For measles, mumps, and rubella vaccine, the following should be considered:

Allergies—Tell your doctor if you have ever had any unusual or allergic reaction to measles, mumps, and rubella vaccine, to the antibiotic neomycin, to gelatin or to eggs. Also tell your health care professional if you are allergic to any other substances, such as preservatives.

Pregnancy—Tell your doctor if you are pregnant or if you may become pregnant within 3 months after receiving this vaccine. Although adequate studies have not been done in either humans or animals and problems have not been shown to occur, use of measles, mumps, and rubella vaccine during pregnancy, or becoming pregnant within 3 months after receiving the measles, mumps, and rubella vaccine, is not recommended. Because the natural measles infection has been shown to increase the chance of birth defects and other problems, it is thought that the live virus vaccine may cause similar problems. Mumps vaccine may infect the placenta, although the vaccine has not been shown to infect the fetus or to cause birth defects. Rubella vaccine crosses the placenta. However, the Centers for Disease Control observed more than 200 women who received the vaccine within 3 months before or after becoming pregnant and those women gave birth to normal babies.

Breast-feeding—Mothers who are receiving measles, mumps, and rubella vaccine and who wish to breast-feed should discuss this with their doctors, because rubella vaccine virus may pass into the breast milk and may cause mild rubella infection in nursing babies. However, studies have not shown that this infection causes any serious problems.

Children—Use is not recommended for infants younger than 12 months of age, unless the risk of measles infection is high. Waiting until children are at least 12 months of age is important because antibodies that infants receive from their mothers before birth may interfere with the effectiveness of the vaccine. In addition, there may be special reasons why children between 6 months and 12 months of age also may require measles vaccination.

Other medicines—Although certain medicines should not be used together at all, in other cases two different medicines may be used together even if an interaction might occur. In these cases, your doctor may want to change the dose, or other precautions may be necessary. Before you receive measles, mumps, and rubella vaccine, it is especially important that your health care professional know if you have received any of the following:

- Cancer medicines or
- Radiation therapy—May reduce the useful effect of the vaccine

Other medical problems—The presence of other medical problems may affect the use of measles, mumps, and rubella vaccine. Make sure you tell your doctor if you have any other medical problems, especially:

- Immune deficiency condition (or family history of)—Condition may increase the chance and severity of side effects of the vaccine and/or may decrease the useful effects of the vaccine
- Severe illness with fever—The symptoms of the condition may be confused with the possible side effects of the vaccine

Proper Use of This Vaccine

Dosing—The dose of measles, mumps, and rubella vaccine will be different for different patients. The following information includes only the average dose of measles, mumps, and rubella vaccine.

- For *injection* dosage form:
  - —For prevention of measles, mumps, and rubella:
    - Adults and children 12 months of age and older—One dose injected under the skin.
    - Children up to 12 months of age—Use is not recommended.

Precautions After Receiving This Vaccine

Do not become pregnant for 3 months after receiving measles, mumps, and rubella vaccine without first checking with your doctor. There is a chance that this vaccine may cause birth defects.

Tell your doctor that you have received this vaccine:

- If you are to receive a tuberculin skin test within 8 weeks after receiving this vaccine. The results of the test may be affected by this vaccine.
- If you are to receive any other live virus vaccines within 1 month after receiving this vaccine.
- If you are to receive blood transfusions or other blood products within 2 weeks after receiving this vaccine.
- If you are to receive gamma globulin or other globulins within 2 weeks after receiving this vaccine.

Side Effects of This Vaccine

Along with its needed effects, a vaccine may cause some unwanted effects. Although not all of these side effects may occur, if they do occur they may need medical attention.

Get emergency help immediately if any of the following side effects occur:

Symptoms of allergic reaction

Difficulty in breathing or swallowing; hives; itching, especially of feet or hands; reddening of skin, especially around ears; swelling of eyes, face, or inside of nose; unusual tiredness or weakness (sudden and severe)

Check with your doctor as soon as possible if any of the following side effects occur:

More common

Fever higher than 103 °F (39.4 °C)

Less common

Pain or tenderness of eyes

Rare

Bruising or purple spots on skin; confusion; convulsions (seizures); double vision; headache (severe or continuing); irritability; pain, numbness, or tingling of hands, arms, legs, or feet; pain, tenderness, or swelling in testicles and scrotum; stiff neck; vomiting

Other side effects may occur that usually do not need medical attention. However, check with your doctor if any of the following side effects continue or are bothersome:

More common

Burning or stinging at place of injection; fever between 100 and 103 °F (37.7 and 39.4 °C); skin rash; swelling of glands in neck

Less common

Aches or pain in joints; headache (mild); itching, swelling, redness, tenderness, or hard lump at place of injection; nausea; runny nose; sore throat; vague feeling of bodily discomfort

The above side effects (especially aches or pain in joints) are more likely to occur in adults, particularly women.

Other side effects not listed above also may occur in some patients. If you notice any other effects, check with your doctor.

Developed: 1/27/97

MEASLES AND RUBELLA VIRUS VACCINE LIVE Systemic†

A commonly used brand name in the U.S. is M-R-VAX II.

†Not commercially available in Canada.

Description

Measles (MEE-zills) and rubella (rue-BELL-a) virus vaccine live is an active immunizing agent used to prevent infection by the measles and rubella viruses. It works by causing your body to produce its own protection (antibodies) against the viruses.

Measles (also known as coughing measles, hard measles, morbilli, red measles, rubeola, and 10-day measles) is an infection that is easily spread from one person to another. Infection with measles can cause serious problems, such as pneumonia, ear infections, sinus problems, convulsions (seizures), brain damage, and possibly death. The risk of serious complications and death is greater for adults and infants than for children and teenagers.

Rubella (also known as German measles) is a serious infection that causes miscarriages, stillbirths, or birth defects in unborn babies when pregnant women get the disease.

While immunization against measles and rubella is recommended for all persons 12 months of age and older, it is especially important for women of childbearing age and persons traveling outside the U.S.

If measles and rubella vaccine is to be given to a child, the child should be at least 12 months of age. This is to make sure the measles vaccine is effective. In a younger child, antibodies from the mother may prevent the vaccine from working.

This vaccine should be administered only by or under the supervision of your doctor or other health care professional. It is available in the following dosage form:

Parenteral

- Injection (U.S.)

Before Receiving This Vaccine

In deciding to use a medicine, the risks of taking the medicine must be weighed against the good it will do. This is a decision you and your doctor will make. For measles and rubella vaccine, the following should be considered:

Allergies—Tell your doctor if you have ever had any unusual or allergic reaction to measles and rubella vaccine, to the antibiotic neomycin, or to gelatin. Also tell your health care professional if you are allergic to any other substances, such as preservatives.

Pregnancy—Tell your doctor if you are pregnant or if you may become pregnant within 3 months after receiving this vaccine. Although adequate studies have not been done in either humans or animals, and problems have not been shown to occur, use of measles and rubella vaccine during pregnancy, or becoming pregnant within 3 months after receiving the measles and rubella vaccine, is not recommended. Because the natural measles infection has been shown to increase the chance of birth defects and other problems, it is thought that the live virus vaccine might cause similar problems. Rubella vaccine crosses the placenta. However, the Centers for Disease Control and Prevention monitored over 200 women who received the vaccine within 3 months before or after becoming pregnant, and those women gave birth to normal babies.

Breast-feeding—Rubella vaccine virus passes into breast milk. However, this vaccine has not been reported to cause problems in nursing babies.

Children—Use of this vaccine is not recommended for infants younger than 12 months of age, unless the risk of measles infection is high. Waiting until children are at least 12 months of age is important because antibodies that infants receive from their mothers before birth may interfere with the effectiveness of the vaccine. In addition, there may be special reasons why children between 6 months and 12 months of age also may require measles vaccination.

Other medicines—Although certain medicines should not be used together at all, in other cases two different medicines may be used together even if an interaction might occur. In these cases, your doctor may want to change the dose, or other precautions may be necessary. Before you receive measles and rubella vaccine, it is especially important that your health care professional know if you have received any of the following:

- Cancer medicines or
- X-ray treatment—May reduce the useful effect of the vaccine

Other medical problems—The presence of other medical problems may affect the use of measles and rubella vaccine. Make sure you tell your doctor if you have any other medical problems, especially:

- Immune deficiency condition (or family history of)—Condition may increase the chance and severity of side effects of the vaccine and/or may decrease the useful effects of the vaccine
- Severe illness with fever—The symptoms of the condition may be confused with the possible side effects of the vaccine

Proper Use of This Vaccine

Dosing—The following information includes only the average dose of measles and rubella vaccine.

- For *injection* dosage form:
  - —For prevention of measles and rubella:
    - Adults and children 12 months of age and older—One dose injected under the skin.
    - Children up to 12 months of age—Use is not recommended.

Precautions After Receiving This Vaccine

Do not become pregnant for 3 months after receiving measles and rubella vaccine without first checking with your doctor. There may be a chance that this vaccine can cause birth defects.

Tell your doctor that you have received this vaccine:

- If you are to receive a tuberculin skin test within 4 to 6 weeks after receiving this vaccine. The results of the test may be affected by this vaccine.
- If you are to receive blood products or immune globulins within 14 days of receiving this vaccine.
- If you are to receive this vaccine within 3 to 11 months of receiving blood products or immune globulins

Side Effects of This Vaccine

Along with its needed effects, a vaccine may cause some unwanted effects. Although not all of these side effects may occur, if they do occur they may need medical attention.

Get emergency help immediately if any of the following side effects occur:

Symptoms of allergic reaction—rare

Difficulty in breathing or swallowing; hives; itching, especially of feet or hands; reddening of skin, especially around ears; swelling of eyes, face, or inside of nose; unusual tiredness or weakness (sudden and severe)

Check with your doctor as soon as possible if any of the following side effects occur:

More common

Fever over 103 °F (39.4 °C)

Less common

Pain or tenderness of eyes

Rare

Bruising or purple spots on skin; confusion; convulsions (seizures); double vision; headache (severe or continuing); irritability; pain, numbness, or tingling of hands, arms, legs, or feet; stiff neck; vomiting

Other side effects may occur that usually do not need medical attention. However, check with your doctor if any of the following side effects continue or are bothersome:

More common

Burning or stinging at place of injection; fever between 100 and 103 °F (37.7 and 39.4 °C); skin rash; swelling of glands in neck

Less common

Aches or pain in joints; headache (mild); itching, swelling, redness, tenderness, or hard lump at place of injection; nausea; runny nose; sore throat; vague feeling of bodily discomfort

The above side effects (especially aches or pain in joints) are more likely to occur in adults, particularly women.

Other side effects not listed above may also occur in some patients. If you notice any other effects, check with your doctor.

Developed: 04/29/97

MEASLES VIRUS VACCINE LIVE Systemic

A commonly used brand name in the U.S. is Attenuvax.
Generic name product may be available in Canada.

Description

Measles (MEE-zills) Virus Vaccine Live is an immunizing agent used to prevent infection by the measles virus. It works by causing your body to produce its own protection (antibodies) against the virus. This vaccine does not protect you against German measles (Rubella). A separate immunization is needed for that type of measles.

Measles (also known as coughing measles, hard measles, morbilli, red measles, rubeola, and ten-day measles) is an infection that is easily spread from one person to another. Infection with measles can lead to serious problems, such as pneumonia, ear infections, sinus problems, convulsions (seizures), brain damage, and possibly death. The risk of serious complications and death is greater for adults and infants than for children and teenagers.

Immunization against measles is recommended for everyone 12 to 15 months of age and older. In addition, there may be special reasons why children from 6 months of age up to 12 months of age may also require measles vaccine.

Immunization against measles is usually not recommended for infants up to 12 months of age, unless the risk of their getting a measles infection is high. This is because antibodies they received from their mothers before birth may interfere with the effectiveness of the vaccine. Children who were immunized against measles before 12 months of age should be immunized twice again.

You can be considered to be immune to measles only if you received two doses of measles vaccine starting on or after your first birthday and have the medical record to prove it, if you have a doctor's diagnosis of a previous measles infection, or if you have had a blood test showing immunity to measles.

This vaccine is to be administered only by or under the supervision of your doctor or other health care professional. It is available in the following dosage form:

Parenteral

- Injection (U.S. and Canada)

Before Receiving This Vaccine

In deciding to use a medicine, the risks of taking the medicine must be weighed against the good it will do. This is a decision you and your doctor will make. For measles vaccine, the following should be considered:

Allergies—Tell your doctor if you have ever had any unusual or allergic reaction to measles vaccine or to any form of the antibiotic neomycin. Also, tell your health care professional if you are allergic to any other substances, such as gelatin.

Pregnancy—Although studies on effects in pregnancy have not been done in humans and problems have not been shown to occur, use of measles vaccine during pregnancy, or becoming pregnant within 3 months after receiving measles vaccine, is not recommended.

Breast-feeding—Measles vaccine virus may pass into breast milk. However, this vaccine has not been reported to cause problems in nursing babies.

Children—Measles vaccine usually is not recommended for infants up to 12 months of age. In special cases, such as children traveling outside the U.S. or children living in high-risk areas, measles vaccine may be given to children as young as 6 months of age.

Other medicines—Although certain medicines should not be used together at all, in other cases two different medicines may be used together even if an interaction might occur. In these cases, your doctor may want to change the dose, or other precautions may be necessary. Before you receive measles vaccine, it is especially important that your health care professional knows if you have received any of the following:

- Treatment with x-rays or cancer medicines—Treatment may increase the action of the vaccine, causing an increase in vaccine side effects, or treatment may interfere with the useful effect of the vaccine

Other medical problems—The presence of other medical problems may affect the use of measles vaccine. Make sure you tell your doctor if you have any other medical problems, especially:

- Immune deficiency condition (or family history of)—Condition may increase the chance and severity of side effects of the vaccine and/or may decrease the useful effects of the vaccine
- Severe illness with fever—The symptoms of the condition may be confused with the possible side effects of the vaccine

Proper Use of This Vaccine

Dosing—The dose of measles vaccine will be different for different patients. The following information includes only the average doses of measles vaccine.

- For *injection* dosage form:
  - —For prevention of measles:
    - Adults and children 12 months of age and older—One dose injected under the skin, followed by a second dose at least one month later.

Precautions After Receiving This Vaccine

Do not become pregnant for 3 months after receiving measles vaccine without first checking with your doctor.

Tell your doctor that you have received this vaccine:

- If you are to receive a tuberculin skin test within 4 to 6 weeks after receiving this vaccine. The results of the test may be affected by this vaccine.
- If you are to receive this vaccine within 2 weeks before or 3 to 11 months after receiving blood transfusions or other blood products.
- If you are to receive this vaccine 2 weeks before or 3 to 11 months after receiving gamma globulin or other immune globulins.

Side Effects of This Vaccine

Along with its needed effects, a vaccine may cause some unwanted effects. Although not all of these side effects may occur, if they do occur they may need medical attention.

Get emergency help immediately if any of the following side effects occur:

Symptoms of allergic reaction

Difficulty in breathing or swallowing; hives; itching, especially of feet or hands; reddening of skin, especially around ears; swelling of eyes, face, or inside of nose; unusual tiredness or weakness (sudden and severe)

Check with your doctor as soon as possible if any of the following side effects occur:

More common

Fever over 103 °F (39.4 °C)

Rare

Bruising or purple spots on skin; confusion; double vision; headache (severe or continuing); irritability; stiff neck; swelling, blistering or pain at place of injection; swelling of glands in neck; vomiting

Other side effects may occur that usually do not need medical attention. However, check with your doctor if any of the following side effects continue or are bothersome:

More common

Burning or stinging at place of injection; fever of 100 °F (37.7 °C) or less

Less common

Fever between 100 and 103 °F (37.7 and 39.4 °C); itching, swelling, redness, tenderness, or hard lump at place of injection; skin rash

Fever or skin rash may occur from 5 to 12 days after vaccination and usually lasts several days.

Other side effects not listed above may also occur in some patients. If you notice any other effects, check with your doctor.

Revised: 07/23/97

MEBENDAZOLE Systemic

A commonly used brand name in the U.S. and Canada is Vermox. Generic name product may be available in the U.S.

Description

Mebendazole (me-BEN-da-zole) belongs to the family of medicines called anthelmintics (ant-hel-MIN-tiks). Anthelmintics are medicines used in the treatment of worm infections.

Mebendazole is used to treat:

- Common roundworms (ascariasis);
- Hookworm infections (uncinariasis);
- Pinworms (enterobiasis; oxyuriasis);
- Whipworms (trichuriasis); and
- More than one worm infection at a time.

This medicine may also be used for other worm infections as determined by your doctor.

Mebendazole works by keeping the worm from absorbing sugar (glucose). This gradually causes loss of energy and death of the worm.

Mebendazole is available only with your doctor's prescription, in the following dosage form:

Oral

- Chewable tablets (U.S. and Canada)

Before Using This Medicine

In deciding to use a medicine, the risks of taking the medicine must be weighed against the good it will do. This is a decision you and your doctor will make. For mebendazole, the following should be considered:

Allergies—Tell your doctor if you have ever had any unusual or allergic reaction to mebendazole. Also tell your health care professional if you are allergic to any other substances, such as foods, preservatives, or dyes.

Pregnancy—Mebendazole is not recommended for use during pregnancy. It has been shown to cause birth defects and other problems in rats given a single dose, which was several times the usual human dose. However, mebendazole did not cause birth defects or other problems in women who took this medicine during the first 3 months of pregnancy. Be sure you have discussed this with your doctor.

Breast-feeding—It is not known whether mebendazole passes into the breast milk. Although most medicines pass into breast milk in small amounts, many of them may be used safely while breast-feeding. Mothers who are taking this medicine and who wish to breast-feed should discuss this with their doctor.

Children—This medicine has been tested in a limited number of children 2 years of age or older and, in effective doses, has not been shown to cause different side effects or problems in children than it does in adults.

Older adults—Many medicines have not been studied specifically in older people. Therefore, it may not be known whether they work exactly the same way they do in younger adults or if they cause different side effects or problems in older people. There is no specific information comparing use of mebendazole in the elderly with use in other age groups.

Other medicines—Although certain medicines should not be used together at all, in other cases two different medicines may be used together even if an interaction might occur. In these cases, your doctor may want to change the dose, or other precautions may be necessary. Tell your health care professional if you are taking any prescription or nonprescription (over-the-counter [OTC]) medicine.

Other medical problems—The presence of other medical problems may affect the use of mebendazole. Make sure you tell your doctor if you have any other medical problems, especially:

- Crohn's disease or
- Liver disease or
- Ulcerative colitis—Patients with these diseases may have an increased chance of side effects from mebendazole

Proper Use of This Medicine

Mebendazole usually comes with patient directions. Read them carefully before using this medicine.

No special preparations or other steps (for example, special diets, fasting, other medicines, laxatives, or enemas) are necessary before, during, or immediately after taking mebendazole.

Mebendazole tablets may be chewed, swallowed whole, or crushed and mixed with food.

For patients taking *mebendazole for hookworms, roundworms, or whipworms:*

- To help clear up your infection completely, *take this medicine exactly as directed by your doctor for the full time of treatment.* In some patients a second course of this medicine may be required to clear up the infection completely. *Do not miss any doses.*

For patients taking *mebendazole for pinworms:*

- To help clear up your infection completely, *take this medicine exactly as directed by your doctor.* A second course of this medicine is usually required to clear up the infection completely.
- Pinworms may be easily passed from one person to another, especially in a household. Therefore, all household members may have to be treated at the same time. This helps to prevent infection or reinfection of other household members. Also, all household members may have to be treated again in 2 to 3 weeks to clear up the infection completely.

For patients taking mebendazole for infections in which *high doses* are needed:

- *Mebendazole is best taken with meals, especially fatty ones (for example, meals that include whole milk or ice cream).* This helps to clear up the infection by helping your body absorb the medicine better. *However, if you are on a low-fat diet, check with your doctor.*

Dosing—The dose of mebendazole will be different for different patients. *Follow your doctor's orders or the directions on the label.* The following information includes only the average doses of mebendazole. *If your dose is different, do not change it* unless your doctor tells you to do so.

The number of doses you take each day, the time allowed between doses, and the length of time you take the medicine depend on the medical problem for which you are taking mebendazole.

- For *oral* dosage form (chewable tablets):
  - —For common roundworms, hookworms, and whipworms:
    - Adults and children 2 years of age and over—100 milligrams (mg) two times a day, morning and evening, for three days. Treatment may need to be repeated in two to three weeks.
    - Children up to 2 years of age—Use and dose must be determined by your doctor.
  - —For pinworms:
    - Adults and children 2 years of age and over—100 mg once a day for one day. Treatment may need to be repeated in two to three weeks.
    - Children up to 2 years of age—Use and dose must be determined by your doctor.
  - —For more than one worm infection at a time:
    - Adults and children 2 years of age and over—100 mg two times a day, morning and evening, for three days.
    - Children up to 2 years of age—Use and dose must be determined by your doctor.

Missed dose—If you miss a dose of this medicine, take it as soon as possible. However, if it is almost time for your next dose, skip the missed dose and go back to your regular dosing schedule. Do not double doses.

Storage—To store this medicine:

- Keep out of the reach of children.
- Store away from heat and direct light.
- Do not store in the bathroom, near the kitchen sink, or in other damp places. Heat or moisture may cause the medicine to break down.
- Do not keep outdated medicine or medicine no longer needed. Be sure that any discarded medicine is out of the reach of children.

Precautions While Using This Medicine

It is important that your doctor check your progress at regular visits, especially in infections in which high doses are needed. This is to make sure that the infection is cleared up completely and to allow your doctor to check for any unwanted effects.

If your symptoms do not improve within a few days, or if they become worse, check with your doctor.

For patients taking *mebendazole for pinworms:*

- In some patients, pinworms may return after treatment with mebendazole. Washing (not shaking) all bedding and nightclothes (pajamas) after treatment may help to prevent this.
- Some doctors may also recommend other measures to help keep your infection from returning. If you have any questions about this, check with your doctor.

For patients taking *mebendazole for hookworms or whipworms:*

- In hookworm and whipworm infections anemia may occur. Therefore, your doctor may want you to take iron supplements to help clear up the anemia. If so, it is important to take iron every day while you are being treated for hookworms or whipworms; do not miss any doses. Your doctor may also want you to keep taking iron supplements for up to 6 months after you stop taking mebendazole. If you have any questions about this, check with your doctor.

Side Effects of This Medicine

Along with its needed effects, a medicine may cause some unwanted effects. Although not all of these side effects may occur, if they do occur they may need medical attention.

Check with your doctor as soon as possible if any of the following side effects occur:

Rare

Fever; skin rash or itching; sore throat and fever; unusual tiredness and weakness

Other side effects may occur that usually do not need medical attention. These side effects may go away during treatment as your body adjusts to the medicine. However, check with your doctor if any of the following side effects continue or are bothersome:

Less common

Abdominal or stomach pain or upset; diarrhea; nausea or vomiting

Rare

Dizziness; hair loss; headache

Other side effects not listed above may also occur in some patients. If you notice any other effects, check with your doctor.

Revised: 08/01/95

MECAMYLAMINE Systemic†

A commonly used brand name in the U.S. is Inversine.

†Not commercially available in Canada.

Description

Mecamylamine (mek-a-MILL-a-meen) belongs to the general class of medicines called antihypertensives. It is used to treat high blood pressure (hypertension).

High blood pressure adds to the workload of the heart and arteries. If it continues for a long time, the heart and arteries may not function properly. This can damage the blood vessels of the brain, heart, and kidneys, resulting in a stroke, heart failure, or kidney failure. High blood pressure may also increase the risk of heart attacks. These problems may be less likely to occur if blood pressure is controlled.

Mecamylamine works by controlling impulses along certain nerve pathways. As a result, it relaxes blood vessels so that blood passes through them more easily. This helps to lower blood pressure.

Mecamylamine is available only with your doctor's prescription, in the following dosage form:

Oral

- Tablets (U.S.)

Before Using This Medicine

In deciding to use a medicine, the risks of taking the medicine must be weighed against the good it will do. This is a decision you and your doctor will make. For mecamylamine, the following should be considered:

Allergies—Tell your doctor if you have ever had any unusual or allergic reaction to mecamylamine. Also tell your health care professional if you are allergic to any other substances, such as foods, preservatives, or dyes.

Pregnancy—Studies on effects in pregnancy have not been done in either humans or animals. However, in general, use of this medicine during pregnancy is not recommended because pregnant women may be more sensitive to its effects. In addition, mecamylamine may cause bowel problems in the unborn baby.

Breast-feeding—It is not known whether mecamylamine passes into breast milk. However, this medicine has not been reported to cause problems in nursing babies.

Children—Studies on this medicine have been done only in adult patients, and there is no specific information comparing use of mecamylamine in children with use in other age groups.

Older adults—Dizziness or lightheadedness may be more likely to occur in the elderly, who are more sensitive to the effects of mecamylamine.

Other medicines—Although certain medicines should not be used together at all, in many cases two different medicines may be used together even if an interaction might occur. In these cases, changes in dose or other precautions may be necessary. When taking mecamylamine it is especially important that your health care professional know if you are taking any of the following:

- Antibiotics or
- Sulfonamides (sulfa medicine)—Patients with chronic pyelonephritis being treated with these medications should not be treated with mecamylamine
- Antimyasthenics (ambenonium [e.g., Mytelase], neostigmine [e.g., Prostigmin], pyridostigmine [e.g., Mestinon])—Effects of these medicines may be decreased by mecamylamine
- Urinary alkalizers (medicine that makes the urine less acid, such as acetazolamide [e.g., Diamox], calcium- and/or magnesium-containing antacids, dichlorphenamide [e.g., Daranide], methazolamide [e.g., Neptazane], potassium or sodium citrate and/or citric acid, sodium bicarbonate [baking soda])—Effects of mecamylamine may be increased because these medicines cause it to be removed more slowly from the body

Other medical problems—The presence of other medical problems may affect the use of mecamylamine. Make sure you tell your doctor if you have any other medical problems, especially:

- Bladder or prostate problems—Mecamylamine may interfere with urination
- Bowel problems—Patients with bowel problems who take mecamylamine may be at inceased risk for serious bowel side effects of mecamylamine
- Diarrhea or
- Fever or infection or
- Nausea or vomiting—Effects of mecamylamine on blood pressure may be increased
- Glaucoma—Mecamylamine may make this condition worse
- Heart or blood vessel disease or
- Heart attack or stroke (recent)—Lowering of blood pressure by mecamylamine may make problems resulting from these conditions worse
- Kidney disease—Effects of mecamylamine may be increased because of slower removal of mecamylamine from the body

Proper Use of This Medicine

In addition to the use of the medicine your doctor has prescribed, treatment for your high blood pressure may include weight control and care in the types of foods you eat, especially foods high in sodium. Your doctor will tell you which of these are most important for you. You should check with your doctor before changing your diet.

Many patients who have high blood pressure will not notice any signs of the problem. In fact, many may feel normal. *It is very important that you take your medicine exactly as directed and that you keep your appointments with your doctor* even if you feel well.

Remember that this medicine will not cure your high blood pressure but it does help control it. Therefore, you must continue to take it as directed if you expect to lower your blood pressure and keep it down. *You may have to take high blood pressure medicine for the rest of your life.* If high blood pressure is not treated, it can cause serious problems such as heart failure, blood vessel disease, stroke, or kidney disease.

To help you remember to take your medicine, try to get into the habit of taking it at the same time each day.

Dosing—The dose of mecamylamine will be different for different patients. *Follow your doctor's orders or the directions on the label.* The following information includes only the average doses of mecamylamine. *If your dose is different, do not change it* unless your doctor tells you to do so:

- For *oral* dosage forms (tablets):
  —Adults: 2.5 milligrams two times a day to 25 milligrams three times a day.

Missed dose—If you miss a dose of this medicine, take it as soon as possible. Then go back to your regular dosing schedule. *If you miss two or more doses in a row, check with your doctor right away.* If your body goes without this medicine for too long, your blood pressure may go up to a dangerously high level.

Storage—To store this medicine:

- Keep out of the reach of children.
- Store away from heat and direct light.
- Do not store in the bathroom, near the kitchen sink, or in other damp places. Heat or moisture may cause the medicine to break down.
- Do not keep outdated medicine or medicine no longer needed. Be sure that any discarded medicine is out of the reach of children.

Precautions While Using This Medicine

It is important that your doctor check your progress at regular visits to make sure that this medicine is working properly.

Check with your doctor before you stop taking this medicine. Your doctor may want you to reduce gradually the amount you are taking before stopping completely.

Make sure that you have enough medicine on hand to last through weekends, holidays, or vacations. You should not miss taking any doses. You may want to ask your doctor for another written prescription for mecamylamine to carry in your wallet or purse. You can then have it filled if you run out of medicine when you are away from home.

Do not take other medicines unless they have been discussed with your doctor. This especially includes over-the-counter (nonprescription) medicines for appetite control, asthma, colds, cough, hay fever, or sinus problems, since they may tend to increase your blood pressure.

Dizziness, lightheadedness, or fainting may occur, especially when you get up from a lying or sitting position. This is more likely to occur in the morning. *Getting up slowly may help.* When you get up from lying down, sit on the edge of the bed with your feet dangling for one or two minutes. Then stand up slowly. If you feel dizzy, sit or lie down. If the problem continues or gets worse, check with your doctor.

The dizziness, lightheadedness, or fainting is also more likely to occur if you drink alcohol, stand for a long time, exercise, or if the weather is hot. *While you are taking this medicine, be careful to limit the amount of alcohol you drink. Also, use extra care during exercise or hot weather or if you must stand for a long time.*

Sodium bicarbonate (commonly known as baking soda) may cause you to get a greater than normal effect from this medicine. To prevent problems, check with your health care professional before using an antacid or medicine for heartburn since some of these contain sodium bicarbonate.

Tell your doctor if you get a fever or infection since that may change the amount of medicine you have to take.

Mecamylamine may cause dryness of the mouth, nose, and throat. For temporary relief of mouth dryness, use sugarless candy or gum, melt bits of ice in your mouth, or use a saliva substitute. However, if your mouth continues to feel dry for more than 2 weeks, check with your medical doctor or dentist. Continuing dryness of the mouth may increase the chance of dental disease, including tooth decay, gum disease, and fungus infections.

Before having any kind of surgery (including dental surgery) or emergency treatment, tell the medical doctor or dentist in charge that you are taking this medicine.

Side Effects of This Medicine

Along with its needed effects, a medicine may cause some unwanted effects. Although not all of these side effects may occur, if they do occur they may need medical attention.

Check with your doctor as soon as possible if any of the following side effects occur:

More common

Dizziness or lightheadedness, especially when getting up from a lying or sitting position

Less common

Difficult urination

Rare

Bloating and frequent loose stools; confusion or excitement; constipation (severe); convulsions (seizures); mental depression; shortness of breath; trembling; uncontrolled movements of face, hands, arms, or legs

Other side effects may occur that usually do not need medical attention. These side effects may go away during treatment as your body adjusts to the medicine. However, check with your doctor if any of the following side effects continue or are bothersome:

More common

Constipation; drowsiness; unusual tiredness

Less common or rare

Blurred vision; decreased sexual ability or interest in sex; dryness of mouth; enlarged pupils; loss of appetite; nausea and vomiting; weakness

Other side effects not listed above may also occur in some patients. If you notice any other effects, check with your doctor.

Revised: 01/20/93

MECHLORETHAMINE Systemic

A commonly used brand name in the U.S. and Canada is Mustargen.
Other commonly used names are chlormethine and nitrogen mustard.

Description

Mechlorethamine (me-klor-ETH-a-meen) belongs to the group of medicines called alkylating agents. It is used to treat some kinds of cancer as well as some noncancerous conditions.

Mechlorethamine interferes with the growth of cancer cells, which are eventually destroyed. Since the growth of normal body cells may also be affected by mechlorethamine, other effects will also occur. Some of these may be serious and must be reported to your doctor. Other effects, like hair loss, may not be serious but may cause concern. Some effects may not occur for months or years after the medicine is used.

Before you begin treatment with mechlorethamine, you and your doctor should talk about the good this medicine will do as well as the risks of using it.

Mechlorethamine is to be administered only by or under the immediate supervision of your doctor. It is available in the following dosage form:

Parenteral

- Injection (U.S. and Canada)

Before Using This Medicine

In deciding to use a medicine, the risks of taking the medicine must be weighed against the good it will do. This is a decision you and your doctor will make. For mechlorethamine, the following should be considered:

Allergies—Tell your doctor if you have ever had any unusual or allergic reaction to mechlorethamine, including a reaction if it was applied to the skin.

Pregnancy—Tell your doctor if you are pregnant or if you intend to have children. This medicine may cause birth defects if either the male or female is receiving it at the time of conception or if it is used during pregnancy. In addition, many cancer medicines may cause sterility which could be permanent. Sterility has been reported with mechlorethamine and the possibility should be kept in mind.

Be sure that you have discussed this with your doctor before receiving this medicine. It is best to use some kind of birth control while you are receiving mechlorethamine. Tell your doctor right away if you think you have become pregnant while receiving mechlorethamine.

Breast-feeding—Tell your doctor if you are breast-feeding or if you intend to breast-feed during treatment with this medicine. Because mechlorethamine may cause serious side effects, breast-feeding is generally not recommended while you are receiving it.

Children—Although there is no specific information comparing use of mechlorethamine in children with use in other age groups, it is not expected to cause different side effects or problems in children than it does in adults.

Older adults—Many medicines have not been studied specifically in older people. Therefore, it may not be known whether they work exactly the same way they do in younger adults or if they cause different side effects or problems in older people. There is no specific information comparing use of mechlorethamine in the elderly with use in other age groups.

Other medicines—Although certain medicines should not be used together at all, in other cases two different medicines may be used together even if an interaction might occur. In these cases, your doctor may want to change the dose, or other precautions may be necessary. When you are receiving mechlorethamine, it is especially important that your health care professional know if you are taking any of the following:

- Amphotericin B by injection (e.g., Fungizone) or
- Antithyroid agents (medicine for overactive thyroid) or
- Azathioprine (e.g., Imuran) or
- Chloramphenicol (e.g., Chloromycetin) or
- Colchicine or
- Flucytosine (e.g., Ancobon) or
- Ganciclovir (e.g., Cytovene) or
- Interferon (e.g., Intron A, Roferon-A) or
- Plicamycin (e.g., Mithracin) or
- Zidovudine (e.g., AZT, Retrovir) or
- If you have ever been treated with radiation or cancer medicines—Mechlorethamine may increase the effects of these medicines or radiation therapy on the blood
- Probenecid (e.g., Benemid) or
- Sulfinpyrazone (e.g., Anturane)—Mechlorethamine may raise the concentration of uric acid in the blood. Since these medicines are used to lower uric acid levels, they may not be as effective in patients receiving mechlorethamine

Other medical problems—The presence of other medical problems may affect the use of mechlorethamine. Make sure you tell your doctor if you have any other medical problems, especially:

- Chickenpox (including recent exposure) or
- Herpes zoster (shingles)—Risk of severe disease affecting other parts of the body
- Gout or
- Kidney stones—Mechlorethamine may increase levels of uric acid in the body, which can cause gout and kidney stones
- Infection—Mechlorethamine may decrease your body's ability to fight infection

Proper Use of This Medicine

Mechlorethamine is sometimes given together with certain other medicines. If you are using a combination of medicines, it is important that you receive each one at the proper time. If you are taking some of these medicines by mouth, ask your health care professional to help you plan a way to take them at the right times.

While you are using this medicine, your doctor may want you to drink extra fluids so that you will pass more urine. This will help prevent kidney problems and keep your kidneys working well.

Mechlorethamine often causes nausea and vomiting, which usually last only 8 to 24 hours. It is very important that you continue to receive the medicine, even if you begin to feel ill. Ask your health care professional for ways to lessen these effects.

Dosing—The dose of mechlorethamine will be different for different patients. The dose that is used may depend on a number of things, including what the medicine is being used for, the patient's weight, and whether or not other medicines are also being taken. *If you are receiving mechlorethamine at home, follow your doctor's orders or the directions on the label.* If you have any questions about the proper dose of mechlorethamine, ask your doctor.

Precautions While Using This Medicine

It is very important that your doctor check your progress at regular visits to make sure that this medicine is working properly and to check for unwanted effects.

While you are being treated with mechlorethamine, and after you stop treatment with it, *do not have any immunizations (vaccinations) without your doctor's approval.* Mechlorethamine may lower your body's resistance and there is a chance you might get the infection the immunization is meant to prevent. In addition, other persons living in your household should not take oral polio vaccine since there is a chance they could pass the polio virus on to you. Also, avoid persons who have taken oral polio vaccine. Do not get close to them, and do not stay in the same room with them for very long. If you cannot take these precautions, you should consider wearing a protective face mask that covers the nose and mouth.

Mechlorethamine can temporarily lower the number of white blood cells in your blood, increasing the chance of getting an infection. It can also lower the number of platelets, which are necessary for proper blood clotting. If this occurs, there are certain precautions you can take, especially when your blood count is low, to reduce the risk of infection or bleeding:

- If you can, avoid people with infections. *Check with your doctor immediately* if you think you are getting an infection or if you get a fever or chills, cough or hoarseness, lower back or side pain, or painful or difficult urination.
- *Check with your doctor immediately* if you notice any unusual bleeding or bruising; black, tarry stools; blood in urine or stools; or pinpoint red spots on your skin.
- Be careful when using a regular toothbrush, dental floss, or toothpick. Your medical doctor, dentist, or nurse may recommend other ways to clean your teeth and gums. Check with your medical doctor before having any dental work done.
- Do not touch your eyes or the inside of your nose unless you have just washed your hands and have not touched anything else in the meantime.

- Be careful not to cut yourself when you are using sharp objects such as a safety razor or fingernail or toenail cutters.
- Avoid contact sports or other situations where bruising or injury could occur.

If mechlorethamine accidentally seeps out of the vein into which it is injected, it may damage some tissues and cause scarring. *Tell the health care professional right away if you notice redness, pain, or swelling at the place of injection.*

Side Effects of This Medicine

Along with its needed effects, a medicine may cause some unwanted effects. Although not all of these side effects may occur, if they do occur they may need medical attention.

Also, because of the way cancer medicines act on the body, there is a chance that they might cause other effects that may not occur until months or years after these medicines are used. These delayed effects may include certain types of cancer. Discuss these possible effects with your doctor.

Check with your doctor or nurse immediately if any of the following side effects occur:

Less common

Black, tarry stools; blood in urine or stools; cough or hoarseness; fever or chills; lower back or side pain; pain or redness at place of injection; painful or difficult urination; pinpoint red spots on skin; unusual bleeding or bruising

Rare

Shortness of breath, itching, or wheezing

Check with your health care professional as soon as possible if any of the following side effects occur:

More common

Missing menstrual periods; painful rash

Less common

Dizziness; joint pain; loss of hearing; ringing in ears; swelling of feet or lower legs

Rare

Numbness, tingling, or burning of fingers, toes, or face; sores in mouth and on lips; yellow eyes or skin

Other side effects may occur that usually do not need medical attention. These side effects may go away during treatment as your body adjusts to the medicine. Also, your health care professional may be able to tell you about ways to prevent or reduce some of these side effects. Check with your health care professional if any of the following side effects continue or are bothersome or if you have any questions about them:

More common

Nausea and vomiting (usually lasts only 8 to 24 hours)

Less common

Confusion; diarrhea; drowsiness; headache; loss of appetite; metallic taste; weakness

This medicine may cause a temporary loss of hair in some people. After treatment with mechlorethamine has ended, normal hair growth should return.

After you stop receiving mechlorethamine, it may still produce some side effects that need attention. During this period of time, check with your doctor if you notice any of the following side effects:

Black, tarry stools; blood in urine or stools; cough or hoarseness; fever or chills; lower back or side pain; painful or difficult urination; pinpoint red spots on skin; unusual bleeding or bruising

Other side effects not listed above may also occur in some patients. If you notice any other effects, check with your doctor.

Revised: 8/90
Interim revision: 07/29/93; 12/15/93; 06/21/94

MECLIZINE/BUCLIZINE/CYCLIZINE Systemic

Some commonly used brand names are:

In the U.S.—

Antivert[3]
Antivert/25[3]
Antivert/50[3]
Bonine[3]
Dramamine II[3]
D-Vert 15[3]
D-Vert 30[3]
Marezine[2]
Meni-D[3]

In Canada—

Bonamine[3]
Marzine[2]

Note: For quick reference, the following medicines are numbered to match the corresponding brand names.

This information applies to the following medicines:
1. Buclizine (BYOO-kli-zeen)*†
2. Cyclizine (SYE-kli-zeen)
3. Meclizine (MEK-li-zeen)‡

*Not commercially available in the U.S.
†Not commercially available in Canada.
‡Generic name product may be available in the U.S.

Description

Buclizine (BYOO-kli-zeen), cyclizine (SYE-kli-zeen), and meclizine (MEK-li-zeen) are used to prevent and treat nausea, vomiting, and dizziness associated with motion sickness, and vertigo (dizziness caused by other medical problems).

Some of these preparations are available only with your doctor's prescription. Others are available without a prescription; however, your doctor may have special instructions on the proper dose of the medicine for your medical condition. They are available in the following dosage forms:

Oral

Buclizine
- Chewable tablets

Cyclizine
- Tablets (U.S.)

Meclizine
- Capsules (U.S.)
- Tablets (U.S.)
- Chewable tablets (U.S. and Canada)

Parenteral

Cyclizine
- Injection (Canada)

Before Using This Medicine

If you are taking this medicine without a prescription, carefully read and follow any precautions on the label. For buclizine, cyclizine, and meclizine, the following should be considered:

Allergies—Tell your doctor if you have ever had any unusual or allergic reaction to buclizine, cyclizine, or meclizine. Also tell your health care professional if you are allergic to any other substances, such as foods, preservatives, or dyes.

Pregnancy—These medicines have not been shown to cause birth defects or other problems in humans. However, studies in animals have shown that buclizine, cyclizine, and meclizine given in doses many times the usual human dose cause birth defects, such as cleft palate.

Breast-feeding—Although these medicines may pass into the breast milk, they have not been reported to cause problems in nursing babies. However, since these medicines tend to decrease the secretions of the body, it is possible that the flow of breast milk may be reduced in some patients.

Children—There is no specific information comparing use of buclizine, cyclizine, and meclizine in children with use in other age groups. However, children may be especially sensitive to the anticholinergic effects (e.g., dryness of mouth, nose, and throat) of these medicines.

Older adults—There is no specific information comparing use of buclizine, cyclizine, and meclizine in the elderly with use in other age groups. Many medicines have not been studied specifically in older people. Therefore, it may not be known whether they work exactly the same way they do in younger adults. However, older people may be especially sensitive to the anticholinergic effects (e.g., constipation; difficult urination; dryness of mouth, nose, and throat) of these medicines.

Other medicines—Although certain medicines should not be used together at all, in other cases two different medicines may be used together even if an interaction might occur. In these cases, your doctor may want to change the dose, or other precautions may be necessary. When you are taking buclizine, cyclizine, or meclizine, it is especially important that your health care professional know if you are taking the following:

- Central nervous system (CNS) depressants, other (medicines that make you drowsy or less alert)—Use with buclizine, cyclizine, or meclizine may increase the side effects of either medicine

Other medical problems—The presence of other medical problems may affect the use of buclizine, cyclizine, or meclizine. Make sure you tell your doctor if you have any other medical problems, especially:

- Asthma, bronchitis, emphysema, or other chronic lung disease—Cyclizine or meclizine may cause serious breathing problems in patients who have any of these conditions
- Enlarged prostate or
- Glaucoma or
- Intestinal blockage or
- Urinary tract blockage—Buclizine, cyclizine, or meclizine may make these conditions worse
- Heart failure—Cyclizine may make the condition worse

Proper Use of This Medicine

This medicine is used to relieve or prevent the symptoms of motion sickness or vertigo (dizziness caused by other medical problems). Take it only as directed. Do not take more of it or take it more often than stated on the label or ordered by your doctor. To do so may increase the chance of side effects.

Dosing—The dose of buclizine, cyclizine, or meclizine will be different for different patients. *Follow your doctor's orders or the directions on the label.* The following information includes only the average doses of buclizine, cyclizine, or meclizine. *If your dose is different, do not change it* unless your doctor tells you to do so.

For buclizine

- For *oral* dosage form (chewable tablets):
  - —To prevent motion sickness:
    - Adults and teenagers—The usual dose is 50 milligrams (mg) thirty minutes before travel. The dose may be repeated every four to six hours if needed. Not more than 150 mg should be taken in one day.
    - Children—Dose must be determined by your doctor.

For cyclizine

- For *oral* dosage form (tablets):
  - —To prevent and treat motion sickness:
    - Adults and teenagers—The usual dose is 50 milligrams (mg) thirty minutes before travel. The dose may be repeated every four to six hours if needed. Not more than 200 mg should be taken in one day.
    - Children 6 to 12 years of age—The usual dose is 25 mg thirty minutes before travel. The dose may be repeated every six to eight hours if needed. Not more than 75 mg should be taken in one day.
    - Children up to 6 years of age—Use and dose must be determined by your doctor.
- For *injection* dosage form:
  - —To prevent and treat motion sickness:
    - Adults and teenagers—The usual dose is 50 mg injected into a muscle every four to six hours as needed.
    - Children—Dose is based on body weight and must be determined by your doctor. The usual dose is 1 mg per kilogram (0.45 mg per pound) of body weight injected into a muscle three times a day as needed.

For meclizine

- For *oral* dosage forms (capsules, tablets, chewable tablets):
  - —To prevent and treat motion sickness:
    - Adults and children 12 years of age or older—The usual dose is 25 to 50 milligrams (mg) one hour before travel. The dose may be repeated every twenty-four hours as needed.
    - Children up to 12 years of age—Use and dose must be determined by your doctor.
  - —To prevent and treat vertigo (dizziness):
    - Adults and children 12 years of age or older—The usual dose is 25 to 100 mg a day as needed, divided into smaller doses.
    - Children up to 12 years of age—Use and dose must be determined by your doctor.

Missed dose—If you must take this medicine regularly and you miss a dose, take the missed dose as soon as possible. However, if it is almost time for your next dose, skip the missed dose and go back to your regular dosing schedule. Do not double doses.

Storage—To store this medicine:

- Keep out of the reach of children.
- Store away from heat and direct light.
- Do not store the capsules or tablets in the bathroom, near the kitchen sink, or in other damp places. Heat or moisture may cause the medicine to break down.
- Do not keep outdated medicine or medicine no longer needed. Be sure that any discarded medicine is out of the reach of children.

Precautions While Using This Medicine

Tell the doctor in charge that you are taking this medicine before you have any skin tests for allergies. The results of the test may be affected by this medicine.

Buclizine, cyclizine, or meclizine will add to the effects of alcohol and other CNS depressants (medicines that make you drowsy or less alert). Some examples of CNS depressants are antihistamines or medicine for hay fever, other allergies, or colds; sedatives, tranquilizers, or sleeping medicine; prescription pain medicine or narcotics; barbiturates; medicine for seizures; muscle relaxants; or anesthetics, including some dental anesthetics. *Check with your doctor before taking any of the above while you are using this medicine.*

This medicine may cause some people to become drowsy or less alert than they are normally. *Make sure you know how you react to this medicine before you drive, use machines, or do anything else that could be dangerous if you are not alert.*

Buclizine, cyclizine, and meclizine may cause dryness of the mouth. For temporary relief use sugarless candy or gum, melt bits of ice in your mouth, or use a saliva substitute. However, if your mouth continues to feel dry for more than 2 weeks, check with your medical doctor or dentist. Continuing dryness of the mouth may increase the chance of dental disease, including tooth decay, gum disease, and fungus infections.

Side Effects of This Medicine

Along with its needed effects, a medicine may cause some unwanted effects. The following side effects may go away during treatment as your body adjusts to the medicine; however, check with your doctor if they continue or are bothersome:

More common

Drowsiness

Less common or rare

Blurred or double vision; constipation; diarrhea; difficult or painful urination; dizziness; dryness of mouth, nose, and throat; fast heartbeat; headache; loss of appetite; nervousness, restlessness, or trouble in sleeping; skin rash; upset stomach

Not all of the side effects listed above have been reported for each of these medicines, but they have been reported for at least one of them. Buclizine, cyclizine, and meclizine are similar, so any of the above side effects may occur with any of these medicines.

Other side effects not listed above may also occur in some patients. If you notice any other effects, check with your doctor.

Additional Information

Once a medicine has been approved for marketing for a certain use, experience may show that it is also useful for other medical problems. Although these uses are not included in product labeling, some of these medicines are used in certain patients to prevent the following medical conditions:

- Nausea and vomiting following surgery
- Nausea and vomiting following cancer radiation treatment

Other than the above information, there is no additional information relating to proper use, precautions, or side effects for these uses.

Revised: 01/03/96

MEFLOQUINE Systemic†

A commonly used brand name in the U.S. is Lariam.

†Not commercially available in Canada.

Description

Mefloquine (ME-floe-kwin) is used to prevent or treat malaria. It works by killing malaria parasites (tiny, one-celled animals) or preventing their growth.

Mefloquine will not actually prevent you from becoming infected with malaria. However, it will prevent the development of symptoms of malaria in people who are living in, or will be traveling to, an area where there is a chance of getting malaria. This medicine may also be used to treat malaria in patients who have already developed symptoms of malaria. Mefloquine may be taken alone or with other medicines for malaria.

This medicine may cause some serious side effects. Therefore, it is usually used only to prevent the symptoms of malaria or to treat serious malaria infections in areas where it is known that other medicines may not work.

Mefloquine is available only with your doctor's prescription, in the following dosage form:

Oral

- Tablets (U.S.)

Before Using This Medicine

In deciding to use a medicine, the risks of taking the medicine must be weighed against the good it will do. This is a decision you and your doctor will make. For mefloquine, the following should be considered:

Allergies—Tell your doctor if you have ever had any unusual or allergic reaction to mefloquine, quinidine (e.g., Quinidex), quinine (e.g., Quinamm), or any related medicines. Also tell your health care professional if you are allergic to any other substances, such as foods, preservatives, or dyes.

Pregnancy—Mefloquine has not been studied in pregnant women, and its use is not recommended during pregnancy. Studies in animals have shown that mefloquine may cause birth defects and other problems.

However, mefloquine has been used in some women in the second and third trimesters of pregnancy. It is important to prevent malaria since if a pregnant woman gets malaria, there is an increased chance of premature births, stillbirths, and abortion.

It is best if pregnant women can avoid traveling to areas where there is a chance of getting malaria. However, if travel is necessary and mefloquine is used, women who may become pregnant should use effective birth control measures while taking this medicine and for 2 months after taking the last dose.

Breast-feeding—Mefloquine passes into the breast milk in small amounts.

Children—Studies on mefloquine use in children have shown that this medicine causes side effects in children like those seen in adults, e.g., nausea, vomiting, and dizziness. Its use is not recommended in infants and children up to 2 years of age or those weighing up to 15 kg (33 pounds).

Older adults—Many medicines have not been studied specifically in older people. Therefore, it may not be known whether they work exactly the same way they do in younger adults or if they cause different side effects or problems in older people. There is no specific information comparing use of mefloquine in the elderly with use in other age groups.

Other medicines—Although certain medicines should not be used together at all, in other cases two different medicines may be used together even if an interaction might occur. In these cases, your doctor may want to change the dose, or other precautions may be necessary. When you are taking mefloquine, it is especially important that your health care professional know if you are taking any of the following:

- Bepridil (e.g., Vascor) or
- Beta-adrenergic blocking agents (acebutolol [e.g., Sectral], atenolol [e.g., Tenormin], betaxolol [e.g., Kerlone], carteolol [e.g., Cartrol], labetalol [e.g., Normodyne], metoprolol [e.g., Lopressor], nadolol [e.g., Corgard], oxprenolol [e.g., Trasicor], penbutolol [e.g., Levatol], pindolol [e.g., Visken], propranolol [e.g., Inderal], sotalol [e.g., Sotacor], timolol [e.g., Blocadren]) or
- Diltiazem (e.g., Cardizem) or
- Flunarizine (e.g., Sibelium) or
- Isradipine (e.g., DynaCirc) or
- Nicardipine (e.g., Cardene) or
- Nifedipine (e.g., Procardia) or
- Nimodipine (e.g., Nimotop) or
- Quinidine (e.g., Quinidex) or
- Quinine (e.g., Quinamm) or
- Verapamil (e.g., Calan)—Use of these medicines together with mefloquine may result in slow heartbeat and other heart problems; also, an increased chance of convulsions (seizures) may occur when quinine is taken together with mefloquine
- Chloroquine (e.g., Aralen)—Use of chloroquine with mefloquine may increase the chance of convulsions (seizures)
- Divalproex (e.g., Depakote) or
- Valproic acid (e.g., Depakene)—Use of these medicines together with mefloquine may result in low blood levels of valproic acid and an increased chance of convulsions (seizures)
- Typhoid vaccine, oral (e.g., Vivotif Vaccine)—Use of the oral typhoid vaccine with mefloquine may keep the vaccine from working properly

Other medical problems—The presence of other medical problems may affect the use of mefloquine. Make sure you tell your doctor if you have any other medical problems, especially:

- Convulsions (seizures) or
- Epilepsy or
- Heart block or
- Psychiatric (mental) disorders, history of—Mefloquine may make these conditions worse

Proper Use of This Medicine

Do not give this medicine to infants and children up to 2 years of age or to those weighing less than 15 kg (33 pounds).

Mefloquine is best taken with a full glass (8 ounces) of water and with food, unless otherwise directed by your doctor.

For patients taking *mefloquine* to *prevent the symptoms of malaria:*

- Your doctor will want you to start taking this medicine 1 week before you travel to an area where there is a chance of getting malaria. This will help you to see how you react to the medicine. Also, it will allow time for your doctor to prescribe another medicine for you if you have a reaction to this medicine.

- Also, you should keep taking this medicine while you are in the area and for 4 weeks after you leave the area. No medicine will protect you completely from malaria. However, to protect you as completely as possible, *it is important that you keep taking this medicine for the full time your doctor ordered.* Also, if fever or "flu-like" symptoms develop during your travels or within 2 to 3 months after you leave the area, *check with your doctor immediately.*
- This medicine works best when you take it on a regular schedule. For example, if you are to take it once a week, it is best to take it on the same day each week. *Do not miss any doses.* If you have any questions about this, check with your health care professional.

For patients taking *mefloquine* to *treat malaria:*

- To help clear up your infection completely, *take this medicine exactly as directed by your doctor.*

Dosing—The dose of mefloquine will be different for different patients. *Follow your doctor's orders or the directions on the label.* The following information includes only the average doses of mefloquine. *If your dose is different, do not change it* unless your doctor tells you to do so.

The number of doses you take each day, the time allowed between doses, and the length of time you take the medicine depend on whether you are using mefloquine to prevent or to treat malaria.

- For *oral* dosage form (tablets):
  - —For prevention of malaria:
    - Adults and children weighing over 45 kilograms (kg) (99 pounds)—250 milligrams (mg) (1 tablet) one week before traveling to an area where malaria occurs. Then 250 mg once a week while staying in the area and every week for four weeks after leaving the area.
    - Children—Dose is based on body weight and must be determined by your doctor.
      - —Children weighing up to 15 kg (33 pounds): Use is not recommended.
      - —Children weighing 15 to 19 kg (33 to 41.8 pounds): 62.5 mg (1/4 tablet) one week before traveling to an area where malaria occurs. Then 62.5 mg once a week while staying in the area and every week for four weeks after leaving the area.
      - —Children weighing 20 to 30 kg (44 to 66 pounds): 125 mg (1/2 tablet) one week before traveling to an area where malaria occurs. Then 125 mg once a week while staying in the area and every week for four weeks after leaving the area.
      - —Children weighing 31 to 45 kg (68.2 to 99 pounds): 187.5 mg (3/4 tablet) one week before traveling to an area where malaria occurs. Then 187.5 mg once a week while staying in the area and every week for four weeks after leaving the area.
  - —For treatment of malaria:
    - Adults—1250 mg as a single dose.
    - Children—Dose is based on body weight and must be determined by your doctor. The usual dose is 16.5 mg per kg (7 mg per pound) of body weight as a single dose.

Missed dose—If you miss a dose of this medicine, take it as soon as possible. This will help to keep you taking your medicine on a regular schedule. However, if it is almost time for your next dose, skip the missed dose and go back to your regular dosing schedule. Do not double doses.

Storage—To store this medicine:

- Keep out of the reach of children.
- Store away from heat and direct light.
- Do not store in the bathroom, near the kitchen sink, or in other damp places. Heat or moisture may cause the medicine to break down.
- Do not keep outdated medicine or medicine no longer needed. Be sure that any discarded medicine is out of the reach of children.

Precautions While Using This Medicine

Mefloquine may cause vision problems. It may also cause some people to become dizzy or lightheaded or to have hallucinations (seeing, hearing, or feeling things that are not there). *Make sure you know how you react to this medicine before you drive, use machines, or do anything else that could be dangerous if you are dizzy or are not alert or able to see well.* This is especially important for people whose jobs require fine coordination. If these reactions are especially bothersome, check with your doctor.

Malaria is spread by the bite of certain kinds of infected female mosquitoes. If you are living in, or will be traveling to, an area where there is a chance of getting malaria, the following mosquito-control measures will help to prevent infection:

- If possible, sleep under mosquito netting to avoid being bitten by malaria-carrying mosquitoes.
- Wear long-sleeved shirts or blouses and long trousers to protect your arms and legs, especially from dusk through dawn when mosquitoes are out.
- Apply mosquito repellant, preferably one containing DEET, to uncovered areas of the skin from dusk through dawn when mosquitoes are out.
- Using a pyrethrum-containing flying insect spray to kill mosquitoes in living and sleeping quarters during evening and nighttime hours.

If you are taking quinidine (e.g., Quinidex) or quinine (e.g., Quinamm) talk to your doctor before you take mefloquine. While you are taking mefloquine, take mefloquine at least 12 hours after the last dose of quinidine or quinine. Taking mefloquine and either of these medicines at the same time may result in a greater chance of serious side effects.

For patients taking *mefloquine* to *treat malaria:*
- If your symptoms do not improve within a few days, or if they become worse, check with your doctor.

Side Effects of This Medicine

Along with its needed effects, a medicine may cause some unwanted effects. Although not all of these side effects may occur, if they do occur they may need medical attention.

Check with your doctor immediately if any of the following side effects occur:

Rare

Anxiety; confusion; convulsions (seizures); hallucinations (seeing, hearing, or feeling things that are not there); mental depression; mood or mental changes; restlessness; slow heartbeat

Other side effects may occur that usually do not need medical attention. These side effects may go away during treatment as your body adjusts to the medicine. However, check with your doctor if any of the following side effects continue or are bothersome:

More common

Abdominal or stomach pain; diarrhea; difficulty concentrating; dizziness; headache; lightheadedness; loss of appetite; nausea or vomiting; trouble in sleeping; visual changes

Other side effects not listed above may also occur in some patients. If you notice any other effects, check with your doctor.

Revised: 10/06/92
Interim revision: 08/26/94

MELPHALAN Systemic

A commonly used brand name in the U.S. and Canada is Alkeran. Other commonly used names are L-PAM and phenylalanine mustard.

Description

Melphalan (MEL-fa-lan) belongs to the group of medicines called alkylating agents. It is used to treat some kinds of cancer.

Melphalan interferes with the growth of cancer cells, which are eventually destroyed. Since the growth of normal body cells may also be affected by melphalan, other effects will also occur. Some of these may be serious and must be reported to your doctor. Other effects may not be serious but may cause concern. Some effects may not occur for months or years after the medicine is used.

Before you begin treatment with melphalan, you and your doctor should talk about the good this medicine will do as well as the risks of using it.

Melphalan is available only with your doctor's prescription, in the following dosage form:

Oral
- Tablets (U.S. and Canada)

Before Using This Medicine

In deciding to use a medicine, the risks of taking the medicine must be weighed against the good it will do. This is a decision you and your doctor will make. For melphalan, the following should be considered:

Allergies—Tell your doctor if you have ever had any unusual or allergic reaction to melphalan or chlorambucil.

Pregnancy—Tell your doctor if you are pregnant or if you intend to have children. There is a chance that this medicine may cause birth defects if either the male or female is taking it at the time of conception or if it is taken during pregnancy. In addition, many cancer medicines may cause sterility which could be permanent. Sterility has been reported with melphalan and the possibility should be kept in mind.

Be sure that you have discussed this with your doctor before taking this medicine. It is best to use some kind of birth control while you are taking melphalan. Tell your doctor right away if you think you have become pregnant while taking melphalan.

Breast-feeding—Tell your doctor if you are breast-feeding or if you intend to breast-feed during treatment with this medicine. Because melphalan may cause serious side effects, breast-feeding is generally not recommended while you are taking it.

Children—There is no specific information about the use of melphalan in children.

Older adults—Many medicines have not been tested in older people. Therefore, it may not be known whether they work exactly the same way they do in younger adults or if they cause different side effects or problems in older people. There is no specific information about the use of melphalan in the elderly.

Other medicines—Although certain medicines should not be used together at all, in other cases two different medicines may be used together even if an interaction might occur. In these cases, your doctor may want to change the dose, or other precautions may be necessary. When you are taking melphalan, it is especially important that your health care professional know if you are taking any of the following:
- Amphotericin B by injection (e.g., Fungizone) or
- Antithyroid agents (medicine for overactive thyroid) or
- Azathioprine (e.g., Imuran) or
- Chloramphenicol (e.g., Chloromycetin) or
- Colchicine or
- Flucytosine (e.g., Ancobon) or
- Interferon (e.g., Intron A, Roferon-A) or
- Plicamycin (e.g., Mithracin) or
- Zidovudine (e.g., Retrovir) or
- If you have ever been treated with x-rays or cancer medicines—Melphalan may increase the effects of these medicines or radiation therapy on the blood
- Probenecid (e.g., Benemid) or

- Sulfinpyrazone (e.g., Anturane)—Melphalan may raise the concentration of uric acid in the blood, which these medicines are used to lower

Other medical problems—The presence of other medical problems may affect the use of melphalan. Make sure you tell your doctor if you have any other medical problems, especially:
- Chickenpox (including recent exposure) or
- Herpes zoster (shingles)—Risk of severe disease affecting other parts of the body
- Gout (history of) or
- Kidney stones (history of)—Melphalan may increase levels of a chemical called uric acid in the body, which can cause gout or kidney stones
- Infection—Melphalan can reduce immunity to infection
- Kidney disease

Proper Use of This Medicine

Take melphalan only as directed by your doctor. Do not take more or less of it, do not take it more often, and do not take it for a longer time than your doctor ordered. The exact amount of medicine you need has been carefully worked out. Taking too much may increase the chance of side effects, while taking too little may not improve your condition.

This medicine is sometimes given together with certain other medicines. If you are using a combination of medicines, make sure that you take each one at the proper time and do not mix them. Ask your health care professional to help you plan a way to remember to take your medicine at the right times.

While you are using melphalan, your doctor may want you to drink extra fluids so that you will pass more urine. This will help prevent kidney problems and keep your kidneys working well.

This medicine often causes nausea, vomiting, and loss of appetite. However, it may have to be taken for several months to be effective. Even if you begin to feel ill, *do not stop using this medicine without first checking with your doctor.* Ask your health care professional for ways to lessen these effects.

If you vomit shortly after taking a dose of melphalan, check with your doctor. You will be told whether to take the dose again or to wait until the next scheduled dose.

Dosing—The dose of melphalan will be different for different patients. The dose that is used may depend on a number of things, including what the medicine is being used for, the patient's weight, whether the medicine is being given by mouth or by injection, and whether or not other medicines are also being taken. *If you are taking or receiving melphalan at home, follow your doctor's orders or the directions on the label.* If you have any questions about the proper dose of melphalan, ask your doctor.

Missed dose—If you miss a dose of this medicine, do not take the missed dose at all and do not double the next one. Instead, go back to your regular dosing schedule and check with your doctor.

Storage—To store this medicine:
- Keep out of the reach of children.
- Store in the original glass container away from heat and direct light.
- Do not store in the bathroom, near the kitchen sink, or in other damp places. Heat or moisture may cause the medicine to break down.
- Do not keep outdated medicine or medicine no longer needed. Be sure that any discarded medicine is out of the reach of children.

Precautions While Using This Medicine

It is very important that your doctor check your progress at regular visits to make sure that this medicine is working properly and to check for unwanted effects.

While you are being treated with melphalan, and after you stop treatment with it, *do not have any immunizations (vaccinations) without your doctor's approval.* Melphalan may lower your body's resistance and there is a chance you might get the infection the immunization is meant to prevent. In addition, other persons living in your household should not take or should not have recently taken oral polio vaccine since there is a chance they could pass the polio virus on to you. Also, avoid other persons who have taken oral polio vaccine. Do not get close to them and do not stay in the same room with them for very long. If you cannot take these precautions, you should consider wearing a protective face mask that covers the nose and mouth.

Melphalan can lower the number of white blood cells in your blood temporarily, increasing the chance of getting an infection. It can also lower the number of platelets, which are necessary for proper blood clotting. If this occurs, there are certain precautions you can take, especially when your blood count is low, to reduce the risk of infection or bleeding:
- If you can, avoid people with infections. *Check with your doctor immediately* if you think you are getting an infection or if you get a fever or chills, cough or hoarseness, lower back or side pain, or painful or difficult urination.
- *Check with your doctor immediately* if you notice any unusual bleeding or bruising; black, tarry stools; blood in urine or stools; or pinpoint red spots on your skin.
- Be careful when using a regular toothbrush, dental floss, or toothpick. Your medical doctor, dentist, or nurse may recommend other ways to clean your teeth and gums. Check with your medical doctor before having any dental work done.
- Do not touch your eyes or the inside of your nose unless you have just washed your hands and have not touched anything else in the meantime.
- Be careful not to cut yourself when you are using sharp objects such as a safety razor or fingernail or toenail cutters.
- Avoid contact sports or other situations where bruising or injury could occur.

Side Effects of This Medicine

Along with their needed effects, medicines like melphalan can sometimes cause unwanted effects such as blood problems and other side effects. These and others are described below. Also, because of the way these medicines act on the body, there is a chance that they might cause other unwanted effects that may not occur until months or years after the medicine is used. These delayed effects may include certain types of cancer, such as leukemia. Discuss these possible effects with your doctor.

Although not all of these side effects may occur, if they do occur they may need medical attention.

Check with your doctor immediately if any of the following side effects occur:

Less common

Black, tarry stools; blood in urine or stools; cough or hoarseness; fever or chills; lower back or side pain; painful or difficult urination; pinpoint red spots on skin; skin rash or itching (sudden); unusual bleeding or bruising

Check with your doctor as soon as possible if any of the following side effects occur:

Less common or rare

Joint pain; sores in mouth and on lips; swelling of feet or lower legs

Other side effects may occur that usually do not need medical attention. These side effects may go away during treatment as your body adjusts to the medicine. Also, your health care professional may be able to tell you about ways to prevent or reduce some of these side effects. Check with your health care professional if the following side effects continue or are bothersome or if you have any questions about them:

Less common

Nausea and vomiting

After you stop taking melphalan, it may still produce some side effects that need attention. During this period of time, check with your doctor if you notice any of the following side effects:

Black, tarry stools; blood in urine or stools; cough or hoarseness; fever or chills; lower back or side pain; painful or difficult urination; pinpoint red spots on skin; unusual bleeding or bruising

Other side effects not listed above may also occur in some patients. If you notice any other effects, check with your doctor.

Revised: 08/90
Interim revision: 07/29/93; 07/11/94

MENINGOCOCCAL POLYSACCHARIDE VACCINE Systemic

A commonly used brand name in the U.S. and Canada is Menomune.

Description

Meningococcal polysaccharide (ma-nin-ja-KOK-kal pol-i-SAK-ka-ryd) vaccine is an active immunizing agent used to prevent infection by certain groups of meningococcal bacteria. The vaccine works by causing your body to produce its own protection (antibodies) against the disease.

The following information applies only to the meningococcal vaccine used for meningococcal bacteria Groups A, C, Y, and W-135. These groups cause approximately 50% of meningococcal meningitis cases in the U.S. The vaccine will not protect against infection caused by other meningococcal bacteria groups, such as Group B.

Meningococcal infection can cause life-threatening illnesses, such as meningococcal meningitis, which affects the brain, and meningococcemia, which affects the blood. Approximately 10% of persons with meningococcal meningitis and 30% of persons with meningococcemia die. These diseases are more likely to occur in young children and in persons with certain diseases or conditions that make them more susceptible to a meningococcal infection or more likely to develop serious problems from a meningococcal infection.

Immunization against meningococcal disease is recommended for persons 2 years of age or older who are at risk of getting the disease because:

- they have certain diseases or conditions that make them more susceptible to a meningococcal infection or more likely to develop serious problems from a meningococcal infection.
- they are living in, working in, or visiting an area where there is a high possibility of getting meningococcal disease.

Usually a person needs to receive meningococcal vaccine only once. However, additional injections may be needed for young children who remain at high risk of meningococcal disease.

Meningococcal polysaccharide vaccine is to be administered only by or under the supervision of your doctor or other health care professional. It is available in the following dosage form:

Parenteral

- Injection (U.S. and Canada)

Before Receiving This Vaccine

In deciding to use a medicine, the risks of taking the medicine must be weighed against the good it will do. This is a decision you and your doctor will make. For meningococcal vaccine, the following should be considered:

Allergies—Tell your doctor if you have ever had any unusual or allergic reaction to meningococcal vaccine. Also tell your health care professional if you are allergic to any other substances, such as food (especially lactose) or preservatives (especially thimerosal). This vaccine contains lactose and thimerosal.

Pregnancy—Meningococcal vaccine has not been shown to cause birth defects or other problems in humans.

Breast-feeding—Meningococcal vaccine has not been reported to cause problems in nursing babies.

Children—Use of meningococcal vaccine is not recommended in infants and children younger than 2 years of age. This vaccine has been tested in older children and, in effective doses, has not been shown to cause different side effects or problems than it does in adults.

Older adults—Many medicines have not been studied specifically in older people. Therefore, it may not be known whether they work exactly the same way they do in younger adults. Although there is no specific information comparing use of this vaccine in the elderly with use in other age groups, this vaccine is not expected to cause different side effects or problems in older people than it does in younger adults.

Other medicines—Although certain medicines should not be used together at all, in other cases two different medicines may be used together even if an interaction might occur. In these cases, your doctor may want to change the dose, or other precautions may be necessary. Before you receive meningococcal vaccine, it is especially important that your health care professional know if you have received any of the following:

- Cancer medicines or
- Corticosteroids (e.g., cortisone-like medicines) or
- Radiation therapy—May reduce the useful effect of the vaccine

Other medical problems—The presence of other medical problems may affect the use of meningococcal vaccine. Make sure you tell your doctor if you have any other medical problems, especially:

- Severe illness with fever—The symptoms of the condition may be confused with the possible side effects of the vaccine

Proper Use of This Vaccine

Dosing—The dose of meningococcal vaccine will be different for different patients. The following information includes only the average doses of meningococcal vaccine.

- For *injection* dosage form:
  - —For prevention of meningococcal meningitis:
    - Adults and children 2 years of age and older—One dose injected under the skin.
    - Children up to 2 years of age—Use is not recommended.

Side Effects of This Vaccine

Along with its needed effects, a vaccine may cause some unwanted effects. Although not all of these side effects may occur, if they do occur they may need medical attention.

Get emergency help immediately if any of the following side effects occur:

Symptoms of allergic reactions

Difficulty in breathing or swallowing; hives; itching, especially of feet or hands; reddening of skin, especially around ears; swelling of eyes, face, or inside of nose; unusual tiredness or weakness (sudden and severe)

Other side effects may occur that usually do not need medical attention. However, check with your doctor if any of the following side effects continue or are bothersome:

More common

Redness at place of injection—may last 1 or 2 days; tenderness, soreness, or pain at place of injection

Less common

Chills; fever over 100 °F (37.8 °C); general feeling of discomfort or illness; hard lump at place of injection; headache; tiredness or weakness

Other side effects not listed above may also occur in some patients. If you notice any other effects, check with your doctor.

Revised: 07/12/94

MENOTROPINS Systemic

A commonly used brand name in the U.S. and Canada is Pergonal.

Another commonly used name is human menopausal gonadotropins (HMG).

Description

Menotropins (men-oh-TROE-pins) are a mixture of follicle-stimulating hormone (FSH) and luteinizing hormone (LH) that are naturally produced by the pituitary gland.

Use in females:

FSH is primarily responsible for stimulating growth of the ovarian follicle, which includes the developing egg, the cells surrounding the egg that produce the hormones needed to support a pregnancy, and the fluid around the egg. As the follicle grows, an increasing amount of the hormone estrogen is produced by the cells in the follicle and released into the bloodstream. Estrogen causes the endometrium (lining of the uterus) to thicken before ovulation occurs. The higher blood levels of estrogen will also tell the hypothalamus and pituitary gland to slow the production and release of FSH.

LH also helps to increase the amount of estrogen produced by the follicle cells. However, its main function is to cause ovulation. The sharp rise in the blood level of LH that triggers ovulation is called the LH surge. After ovulation, the group of hormone-producing follicle cells become the corpus luteum, which will produce estrogen and large amounts of another hormone, progesterone. Progesterone causes the endometrium to mature so that it can support implantation of the fertilized egg or embryo. If implantation of a fertilized egg does not occur, the levels of estrogen and progesterone decrease, the endometrium sloughs off, and menstruation occurs.

Menotropins are usually given in combination with human chorionic gonadotropin (hCG). The actions of hCG are almost the same as those of LH. It is given to simulate the natural LH surge. This results in ovulation at an expected time.

Many women choosing treatment with menotropins have already tried clomiphene (e.g., Serophene) and have not been able to conceive yet. Menotropins may also be used to cause the ovary to produce several follicles, which can then be harvested for use in gamete intrafallopian transfer (GIFT) or *in vitro* fertilization (IVF).

Use in males:

Menotropins are used to stimulate the production of sperm in some forms of male infertility.

Menotropins are to be given only by or under the supervision of your doctor. It is available in the following dosage form:

Parenteral

- Injection (U.S. and Canada)

Before Using This Medicine

In deciding to use a medicine, the risks of taking the medicine must be weighed against the good it will do. This is a decision you and your doctor will make. For menotropins, the following should be considered:

Allergies—Tell your doctor if you have ever had any unusual or allergic reaction to menotropins. Also tell your health care professional if you are allergic to any other substances, such as foods, preservatives, or dyes.

Pregnancy—If you become pregnant as a result of using this medicine, there is an increased chance of a multiple pregnancy.

Other medicines—Although certain medicines should not be used together at all, in other cases two different medicines may be used together even if an interaction might occur. In these cases, your doctor may want to change the dose, or other precautions may be necessary. Tell your health care professional if you are taking any other prescription or nonprescription (over-the-counter [OTC]) medicine.

Other medical problems—The presence of other medical problems may affect the use of menotropins. Make sure you tell your doctor if you have any other medical problems, especially:

- Cyst on ovary—Menotropins can cause further growth of cysts on the ovary
- Unusual vaginal bleeding—Some irregular vaginal bleeding is a sign that the endometrium is growing too rapidly, possibly of endometrial cancer, or some hormone imbalances; the increases in estrogen production caused by menotropins can make these problems worse. If a hormonal imbalance is present, it should be treated before the beginning of menotropins therapy

Proper Use of This Medicine

Dosing—The dose of menotropins will be different for different patients. *Follow your doctor's orders or the directions on the label.* The following information includes only the average doses of menotropins. *If your dose is different, do not change it* unless your doctor tells you to do so.

- For *injection* dosage form:
  - —For causing ovulation to help in becoming pregnant:
    - Adults—75 Units of FSH and 75 Units of LH injected into a muscle once a day for seven or more days. Usually your doctor will give you another medicine called chorionic gonadotropin (hCG) the day after the last dose of menotropins.
  - —For help in becoming pregnant while using other pregnancy methods (assisted reproductive technology [ART]):
    - Adults—150 Units of FSH and 150 Units of LH injected into a muscle once a day for seven or more days. Usually your doctor will give you another medicine called chorionic gonadotropin (hCG) the day after the last dose of menotropins.
  - —For producing sperm:
    - Adults—75 Units of FSH and 75 Units of LH injected into a muscle three times a week for four or more months. Usually your doctor will give you another medicine called chorionic gonadotropin before and during treatment with menotropins. If needed, your doctor may increase your dose to 150 Units of FSH and 150 Units of LH three times a week after four months.

Precautions While Using This Medicine

It is very important that your doctor check your progress at regular visits to make sure that the medicine is working properly and to check for unwanted effects. Your doctor will likely want to watch the development of the ovarian follicle(s) by measuring the amount of estrogen in your bloodstream and by checking the size of the follicle(s) with ultrasound examinations.

For females only:

- If your doctor has asked you to record your basal body temperatures (BBTs) daily, make sure that you do this every day. It is important that intercourse take place around the time of ovulation to give you the best chance of becoming pregnant. *Follow your doctor's instructions carefully.*

Side Effects of This Medicine

Along with its needed effects, a medicine may cause some unwanted effects. Although not all of these side effects may occur, if they do occur they may need medical attention.

Check with your doctor as soon as possible if any of the following side effects occur:

For females only

More common

Bloating (mild); pain, swelling, or irritation at place of injection; rash at place of injection or on body; stomach or pelvic pain

Less common or rare
Abdominal or stomach pain (severe); bloating (moderate to severe); decreased amount of urine; feeling of indigestion; nausea, vomiting, or diarrhea (continuing or severe); pelvic pain (severe); shortness of breath; swelling of the lower legs; weight gain (rapid)

For males only

More common
Dizziness; fainting; headache; irregular heartbeat; loss of appetite; more frequent nosebleeds; shortness of breath

Other side effects may occur that usually do not need medical attention. These side effects may go away during treatment as your body adjusts to the medicine. However, check with your doctor if the following side effect continues or is bothersome:

For males only

Less common
Enlargement of breasts

After you stop using this medicine, your body may need time to adjust. The length of time this takes depends on the amount of medicine you were using and how long you used it. During this period of time check with your doctor if you notice any of the following side effects:

For females only
Abdominal or stomach pain (severe); bloating (moderate to severe); decreased amount of urine; feeling of indigestion; nausea, vomiting, or diarrhea (continuing or severe); pelvic pain (severe); shortness of breath; weight gain (rapid)

Other side effects not listed above may also occur in some patients. If you notice any other effects, check with your doctor.

Revised: 07/07/92
Interim revision: 06/30/94

MEPROBAMATE Systemic

Some commonly used brand names are:

In the U.S.—

Equanil	'Miltown'-400
Meprospan 200	'Miltown'-600
Meprospan 400	Probate
'Miltown'-200	Trancot

Generic name product may also be available.

In Canada—

Apo-Meprobamate	Meprospan-400
Equanil	Miltown

Description

Meprobamate (me-proe-BA-mate) is used to relieve nervousness or tension. This medicine should not be used for nervousness or tension caused by the stress of everyday life.

Meprobamate is available only with your doctor's prescription, in the following dosage forms:

Oral
- Extended-release capsules (U.S. and Canada)
- Tablets (U.S. and Canada)

Before Using This Medicine

In deciding to use a medicine, the risks of taking the medicine must be weighed against the good it will do. This is a decision you and your doctor will make. For meprobamate, the following should be considered:

Allergies—Tell your doctor if you have ever had any unusual or allergic reaction to meprobamate or to medicines like meprobamate such as carbromal, carisoprodol, mebutamate, or tybamate. Also tell your health care professional if you are allergic to any other substances, such as foods, preservatives, or dyes.

Pregnancy—Meprobamate has been reported to increase the chance of birth defects if taken during the first 3 months of pregnancy.

Breast-feeding—Meprobamate passes into the breast milk and may cause drowsiness in babies of mothers taking this medicine.

Children—Studies on this medicine have been done only in adult patients, and there is no specific information comparing use of meprobamate in children with use in other age groups.

Older adults—Elderly people may be especially sensitive to the effects of meprobamate. This may increase the chance of side effects during treatment.

Other medicines—Although certain medicines should not be used together at all, in other cases two different medicines may be used together even if an interaction might occur. In these cases, your doctor may want to change the dose, or other precautions may be necessary. When you are taking meprobamate, it is especially important that your health care professional know if you are taking any of the following:
- Central nervous system (CNS) depressants (medicines that cause drowsiness) or
- Tricyclic antidepressants (medicine for depression)—Taking these medicines with meprobamate may increase the CNS depressant effects

Other medical problems—The presence of other medical problems may affect the use of meprobamate. Make sure you tell your doctor if you have any other medical problems, especially:
- Alcohol abuse (or history of) or
- Drug abuse or dependence (or history of)—Dependence on meprobamate may develop
- Epilepsy—The risk of seizures may be increased
- Kidney disease or
- Liver disease—Higher blood levels of meprobamate may occur, increasing the chance of side effects
- Porphyria—Meprobamate may make the condition worse

Proper Use of This Medicine

Take this medicine only as directed by your doctor. Do not take more of it, do not take it more often, and do not take it for a longer time than your doctor ordered. If too much is taken, it may become habit-forming.

Dosing—The dose of meprobamate will be different for different patients. *Follow your doctor's orders or the directions on the label.* The following information includes only the average doses of meprobamate. *If your dose is different, do not change it* unless your doctor tells you to do so:

- For *regular (short-acting)* tablets:
  - —Adults and children 12 years of age and older: 400 milligrams three or four times a day, or 600 milligrams two times a day.
  - —Children 6 to 12 years of age: 100 to 200 milligrams two or three times a day.
  - —Children up to 6 years of age: Dose must be determined by the doctor.
- For *long-acting* dosage forms (extended-release tablets):
  - —Adults and children 12 years of age or older: 400 to 800 milligrams two times a day, in the morning and at bedtime.
  - —Children 6 to 12 years of age: 200 milligrams two times a day, in the morning and at bedtime.
  - —Children up to 6 years of age: Dose must be determined by the doctor.

Missed dose—If you miss a dose of this medicine and remember within an hour or so of the missed dose, take it right away. However, if you do not remember until later, skip the missed dose and go back to your regular dosing schedule. Do not double doses.

Storage—To store this medicine:

- Keep out of the reach of children. Overdose of meprobamate is very dangerous in children.
- Store away from heat and direct light.
- Do not store in the bathroom, near the kitchen sink, or in other damp places. Heat or moisture may cause the medicine to break down.
- Do not keep outdated medicine or medicine no longer needed. Be sure that any discarded medicine is out of the reach of children.

Precautions While Using This Medicine

If you will be taking this medicine regularly for a long time:

- Your doctor should check your progress at regular visits.
- Check with your doctor at least every 4 months to make sure you need to continue taking this medicine.

If you will be taking this medicine in large doses or for a long time, do not stop taking it without first checking with your doctor. Your doctor may want you to reduce gradually the amount you are taking before stopping completely.

This medicine will add to the effects of alcohol and other CNS depressants (medicines that slow down the nervous system, possibly causing drowsiness). Some examples of CNS depressants are antihistamines or medicine for hay fever, other allergies, or colds; sedatives, tranquilizers, or sleeping medicine; prescription pain medicine or narcotics; barbiturates; medicine for seizures; muscle relaxants; or anesthetics, including some dental anesthetics. *Check with your doctor before taking any of the above while you are taking this medicine.*

Before you have any medical tests, tell the medical doctor in charge that you are taking this medicine. The results of some tests, such as the metyrapone test and the phentolamine test, may be affected by this medicine.

If you think you or someone else may have taken an overdose of this medicine, get emergency help at once. Taking an overdose of meprobamate or taking alcohol or other CNS depressants with meprobamate may lead to unconsciousness and possibly death. Some signs of an overdose are severe confusion, drowsiness, or weakness; shortness of breath or slow or troubled breathing; slurred speech; staggering; and slow heartbeat.

This medicine may cause some people to become dizzy, lightheaded, drowsy, or less alert than they are normally. Even if taken at bedtime, it may cause some people to feel drowsy or less alert on arising. *Make sure you know how you react to this medicine before you drive, use machines, or do anything else that could be dangerous if you are dizzy or are not alert.*

Meprobamate may cause dryness of the mouth. For temporary relief, use sugarless candy or gum, melt bits of ice in your mouth, or use a saliva substitute. However, if your mouth continues to feel dry for more than 2 weeks, check with your medical doctor or dentist. Continuing dryness of the mouth may increase the chance of dental disease, including tooth decay, gum disease, and fungus infections.

Side Effects of This Medicine

Along with its needed effects, a medicine may cause some unwanted effects. Although not all of these side effects may occur, if they do occur they may need medical attention.

Check with your doctor as soon as possible if any of the following side effects occur:

Less common

Skin rash, hives, or itching

Rare

Confusion; fast, pounding, or irregular heartbeat; sore throat and fever; unusual bleeding or bruising; unusual excitement; wheezing, shortness of breath, or troubled breathing

Symptoms of overdose

Confusion (severe); dizziness or lightheadedness (continuing); drowsiness (severe); shortness of breath or slow or troubled breathing; slow heartbeat; slurred speech; staggering; weakness (severe)

Other side effects may occur that usually do not need medical attention. These side effects may go away during treatment as your body adjusts to the medicine. However,

check with your doctor if any of the following side effects continue or are bothersome:

More common

Clumsiness or unsteadiness; drowsiness

Less common

Blurred vision or change in near or distant vision; diarrhea; dizziness or lightheadedness; false sense of well-being; headache; nausea or vomiting; unusual tiredness or weakness

After you stop using this medicine, your body may need time to adjust. If you took this medicine in high doses or for a long time, this may take about 2 days. During this period of time check with your doctor if you notice any of the following side effects:

Clumsiness or unsteadiness; confusion; convulsions (seizures); hallucinations (seeing, hearing, or feeling things that are not there); increased dreaming; muscle twitching; nausea or vomiting; nervousness or restlessness; nightmares; trembling; trouble in sleeping

Other side effects not listed above may also occur in some patients. If you notice any other effects, check with your doctor.

Revised: 01/13/93

MEPROBAMATE AND ASPIRIN Systemic

Some commonly used brand names are:

In the U.S.—

Epromate-M
Equagesic
Heptogesic
Meprogesic
Meprogesic Q
Micrainin

Generic name product may also be available.

In Canada—

Equagesic‡

‡In Canada, Equagesic also contains ethoheptazine citrate.

Description

Meprobamate (me-proe-BA-mate) and aspirin (AS-pir-in) combination is used to relieve pain, anxiety, and tension in certain disorders or diseases.

This medicine is available only with your doctor's prescription, in the following dosage form:

Oral

- Tablets (U.S. and Canada)

Before Using This Medicine

In deciding to use a medicine, the risks of taking the medicine must be weighed against the good it will do. This is a decision you and your doctor will make. For meprobamate and aspirin combination, the following should be considered:

Allergies—Tell your doctor if you have ever had any unusual or allergic reaction to meprobamate or to medicines like meprobamate such as carbromal, carisoprodol, mebutamate, or tybamate, or to aspirin or other salicylates, including methyl salicylate (oil of wintergreen), or to any of the following medicines:

Diclofenac (e.g., Voltaren)
Diflunisal (e.g., Dolobid)
Etodolac (e.g., Lodine)
Fenoprofen (e.g., Nalfon)
Floctafenine (e.g., Idarac)
Flurbiprofen, oral (e.g., Ansaid)
Ibuprofen (e.g., Motrin)
Indomethacin (e.g., Indocin)
Ketoprofen (e.g., Orudis)
Ketorolac (e.g., Toradol)
Meclofenamate (e.g., Meclomen)
Mefenamic acid (e.g., Ponstel)
Naproxen (e.g., Naprosyn)
Oxyphenbutazone (e.g., Tandearil)
Phenylbutazone (e.g., Butazolidin)
Piroxicam (e.g., Feldene)
Sulindac (e.g., Clinoril)
Suprofen (e.g., Suprol)
Tiaprofenic acid (e.g., Surgam)
Tolmetin (e.g., Tolectin)
Zomepirac (e.g., Zomax)

Also tell your health care professional if you are allergic to any other substances, such as foods, preservatives, or dyes.

Pregnancy—Meprobamate (contained in this combination medicine) has been reported to increase the chance of birth defects if taken during the first 3 months of pregnancy.

Studies in humans have not shown that aspirin (contained in this combination medicine) causes birth defects. However, studies in animals have shown that aspirin causes birth defects. Some reports have suggested that too much use of aspirin late in pregnancy may cause a decrease in the newborn's weight and possible death of the fetus or newborn infant. However, the mothers in these reports had been taking much larger amounts of aspirin than are usually recommended. Studies of mothers taking aspirin in the doses that are usually recommended did not show these unwanted effects. However, regular use of aspirin late in pregnancy may cause unwanted effects on the heart or blood flow in the fetus or in the newborn infant. Also, use of aspirin during the last 2 weeks of pregnancy may cause bleeding problems in the fetus before or during delivery or in the newborn infant. In addition, too much use of aspirin during the last 3 months of pregnancy may increase the length of pregnancy, prolong labor, cause other problems during delivery, or cause severe bleeding in the mother before, during, or after delivery.

Breast-feeding—Meprobamate (contained in this combination medicine) passes into the breast milk and may cause drowsiness in babies of mothers taking this medicine. Although aspirin (contained in this combination medicine) passes into the breast milk, it has not been shown to cause problems in nursing babies.

Children—*Do not give a medicine containing aspirin to a child with a fever or other symptoms of a virus infection, especially flu or chickenpox, without first discussing this with your child's doctor.* This is very important because aspirin may cause a serious illness called Reye's syndrome in children with fever caused by a virus infection, especially flu or chickenpox. Children who do not have a virus infection may also be more sensitive to the effects of aspirin (contained in this combination medicine), especially if they have a fever or have lost large amounts of body fluid because of vomiting, diarrhea, or sweating. This may increase the chance of side effects during treatment.

Teenagers—*Teenagers with fever or other symptoms of a virus infection, especially flu or chickenpox, should check with a doctor before taking this medicine.* The aspirin in this combination medicine may cause a serious illness called Reye's syndrome in teenagers with fever caused by a virus infection, especially flu or chickenpox.

Older adults—Elderly people may be especially sensitive to the effects of meprobamate and aspirin. This may increase the chance of side effects during treatment.

Other medicines—Although certain medicines should not be used together at all, in other cases two different medicines may be used together even if an interaction might occur. In these cases, your doctor may want to change the dose, or other precautions may be necessary. When you are taking meprobamate and aspirin combination, it is especially important that your health care professional know if you are taking any of the following:

- Anticoagulants (blood thinners) or
- Carbenicillin by injection (e.g., Geopen) or
- Cefamandole (e.g., Mandol) or
- Cefoperazone (e.g., Cefobid) or
- Cefotetan (e.g., Cefotan) or
- Dipyridamole (e.g., Persantine) or
- Divalproex (e.g., Depakote) or
- Heparin or
- Inflammation or pain medicine, except narcotics, or
- Moxalactam (e.g., Moxam) or
- Pentoxifylline (e.g., Trental) or
- Plicamycin (e.g., Mithracin) or
- Ticarcillin (e.g., Ticar) or
- Valproic acid (e.g., Depakene)—Taking these medicines together with aspirin may increase the chance of bleeding
- Antidiabetics, oral (diabetes medicine you take by mouth)—Aspirin may increase the effects of the antidiabetic medicine; a change in dose may be needed if meprobamate and aspirin combination is taken regularly
- Central nervous system (CNS) depressants (medicine that causes drowsiness) or
- Tricyclic antidepressants (medicine for depression)—Taking these medicines with meprobamate and aspirin combination may increase the CNS depressant effects
- Methotrexate (e.g., Mexate)—The chance of serious side effects may be increased
- Probenecid (e.g., Benemid)—Aspirin may keep probenecid from working properly in the treatment of gout
- Sulfinpyrazone (e.g., Anturane)—Aspirin may keep sulfinpyrazone from working properly in the treatment of gout; also, there may be an increased chance of bleeding
- Urinary alkalizers (medicine that makes the urine less acid, such as acetazolamide [e.g., Diamox], calcium- and/or magnesium-containing antacids, dichlorphenamide [e.g., Daranide], methazolamide [e.g., Neptazane], potassium or sodium citrate and/or citric acid, sodium bicarbonate [baking soda])—These medicines may make aspirin less effective by causing it to be removed from the body more quickly
- Vancomycin (e.g., Vancocin)—Hearing loss may occur and may lead to deafness

Other medical problems—The presence of other medical problems may affect the use of meprobamate and aspirin combination. Make sure you tell your doctor if you have any other medical problems, especially:

- Alcohol abuse (or history of) or
- Drug abuse or dependence (or history of)—Dependence on meprobamate may develop
- Anemia or
- Stomach ulcer or other stomach problems—Aspirin may make your condition worse
- Asthma, allergies, and nasal polyps (history of) or
- Kidney disease or
- Liver disease—The chance of side effects may be increased.
- Epilepsy—The risk of seizures may be increased
- Gout—Aspirin may make this condition worse and may also lessen the effects of some medicines used to treat gout
- Hemophilia or other bleeding problems—The chance of bleeding may be increased by aspirin
- Porphyria—Meprobamate may make the condition worse

Proper Use of This Medicine

Take this medicine with food or a full glass (8 ounces) of water to lessen stomach irritation.

If this combination medicine containing aspirin has a strong vinegar-like odor, do not use it. This odor means the medicine is breaking down. If you have any questions about this, check with your pharmacist.

Take this medicine only as directed by your doctor. Do not take more of it, do not take it more often, and do not take it for a longer time than your doctor ordered. If too much meprobamate is taken, it may become habit-forming. Also, taking too much aspirin may cause stomach problems or lead to medical problems because of an overdose.

Dosing—The dose of meprobamate and aspirin combination will be different for different patients. *Follow your doctor's orders or the directions on the label.* The following information includes only the average doses of meprobamate and aspirin combination. *If your dose is different, do not change it* unless your doctor tells you to do so:

- Adults—Oral, 1 or 2 tablets three or four times a day, as needed.
- Children up to 12 years of age: Use is not recommended.

Storage—To store this medicine:

- Keep this medicine out of the reach of children. Overdose of meprobamate is very dangerous in children.
- Store away from heat and direct light.

- Do not store in the bathroom, near the kitchen sink, or in other damp places. Heat or moisture may cause the medicine to break down.
- Do not keep outdated medicine or medicine no longer needed. Be sure that any discarded medicine is out of the reach of children.

Precautions While Using This Medicine

If you will be taking this medicine regularly for a long time:

- Your doctor should check your progress at regular visits.
- Check with your doctor at least every 4 months to make sure you need to continue taking this medicine.

If you will be taking this medicine in large doses or for a long time, do not stop taking it without first checking with your doctor. Your doctor may want you to reduce gradually the amount you are taking before stopping completely.

Check the labels of all nonprescription (over-the-counter [OTC]) and prescription medicines you now take. If any contain aspirin or other salicylates (including bismuth subsalicylate [e.g., Pepto-Bismol]), be especially careful. Taking or using any of these medicines while taking this combination medicine containing aspirin may lead to overdose. If you have any questions about this, check with your health care professional.

This medicine will add to the effects of alcohol and other CNS depressants (medicines that slow down the nervous system, possibly causing drowsiness). Some examples of CNS depressants are antihistamines or medicine for hay fever, other allergies, or colds; sedatives, tranquilizers, or sleeping medicine; prescription pain medicine or narcotics; barbiturates; medicine for seizures; muscle relaxants; or anesthetics, including some dental anesthetics. *Check with your doctor before taking any of the above while you are taking this medicine.*

Stomach problems may be more likely to occur if you drink alcoholic beverages while being treated with this medicine, especially if you are taking the medicine in high doses or for a long time. Check with your doctor if you have any questions about this.

Too much use of this medicine together with certain other medicines may increase the chance of stomach problems. Therefore, do not regularly take this medicine together with any of the following medicines, unless directed to do so by your medical doctor or dentist:

Acetaminophen (e.g., Tylenol)
Diclofenac (e.g., Voltaren)
Diflunisal (e.g., Dolobid)
Etodolac (e.g., Lodine)
Fenoprofen (e.g., Nalfon)
Floctafenine (e.g., Idarac)
Flurbiprofen (oral) (e.g., Ansaid)
Ibuprofen (e.g., Motrin)
Indomethacin (e.g., Indocin)
Ketoprofen (e.g., Orudis)
Ketorolac (e.g., Toradol)
Meclofenamate (e.g., Meclomen)
Mefenamic acid (e.g., Ponstel)
Naproxen (e.g., Naprosyn)
Phenylbutazone (e.g., Butazolidin)
Piroxicam (e.g., Feldene)
Sulindac (e.g., Clinoril)
Tiaprofenic acid (e.g., Surgam)
Tolmetin (e.g., Tolectin)

If you are taking a laxative containing cellulose, do not take it within 2 hours of taking this medicine. Taking these medicines close together may make this medicine less effective by preventing the aspirin (contained in this combination medicine) from being absorbed by your body.

For diabetic patients:

- False urine sugar test results may occur if you take 8 or more 325-mg (5-grain) doses of aspirin (contained in this combination medicine) every day for several days in a row. Smaller doses or occasional use of aspirin usually will not affect urine sugar tests. If you have any questions about this, check with your doctor, especially if your diabetes is not well controlled.

Before you have any medical tests, tell the medical doctor in charge that you are taking this medicine. The results of some tests, such as the metyrapone test and the phentolamine test, may be affected by this medicine.

If you plan to have surgery, including dental surgery, do not take aspirin (contained in this combination medicine) for 5 days before the surgery, unless otherwise directed by your medical doctor or dentist. Taking aspirin during this time may cause bleeding problems.

If you think you or someone else may have taken an overdose of this medicine, get emergency help at once. Taking an overdose of this medicine or taking alcohol or other CNS depressants with it may lead to unconsciousness and possibly death. Some signs of an overdose are continuing ringing or buzzing in ears; any hearing loss; severe confusion, drowsiness, or weakness; shortness of breath or slow or troubled breathing; staggering; and slow heartbeat.

This medicine may cause some people to become dizzy, lightheaded, drowsy, or less alert than they are normally. *Make sure you know how you react to this medicine before you drive, use machines, or do anything else that could be dangerous if you are dizzy or are not alert.*

Meprobamate (contained in this combination medicine) may cause dryness of the mouth. For temporary relief, use sugarless candy or gum, melt bits of ice in your mouth, or use a saliva substitute. However, if your mouth continues to feel dry for more than 2 weeks, check with your medical doctor or dentist. Continuing dryness of the mouth may increase the chance of dental disease, including tooth decay, gum disease, and fungus infections.

Side Effects of This Medicine

Along with its needed effects, a medicine may cause some unwanted effects. Although not all of these side effects may occur, if they do occur they may need medical attention.

Check with your doctor immediately if any of the following side effects occur:

Rare

Wheezing, shortness of breath, troubled breathing, or tightness in chest

Symptoms of overdose

Any loss of hearing; bloody urine; confusion (severe); convulsions (seizures); diarrhea (severe or continuing); dizziness or lightheadedness (continuing); drowsiness (severe); fast or deep breathing; hallucinations (seeing, hearing, or feeling things that are not there); headache (severe or continuing); increased sweating; nausea or vomiting (continuing); nervousness or excitement (severe); ringing or buzzing in ears (continuing); slow heartbeat; slurred speech; staggering; stomach pain (severe or continuing); unexplained fever; unusual or uncontrolled flapping movements of the hands, especially in elderly patients; unusual thirst; vision problems; weakness (severe)

Symptoms of overdose in children

Changes in behavior; drowsiness or tiredness (severe); fast or deep breathing

Also, check with your doctor as soon as possible if any of the following side effects occur:

Rare

Bloody or black, tarry stools; confusion; skin rash, hives, or itching; sore throat and fever; unusual bleeding or bruising; unusual excitement; unusual tiredness or weakness; vomiting of blood or material that looks like coffee grounds

Other side effects may occur that usually do not need medical attention. These side effects may go away during treatment as your body adjusts to the medicine. However, check with your doctor if any of the following side effects continue or are bothersome:

More common

Drowsiness; heartburn or indigestion; nausea with or without vomiting; stomach pain (mild)

Less common

Blurred vision or change in near or distant vision; dizziness or lightheadedness; headache

After you stop using this medicine, your body may need time to adjust. The length of time this takes depends on the amount of medicine you were using and how long you used it. During this period of time check with your doctor if you notice any of the following side effects:

Clumsiness or unsteadiness; confusion; convulsions (seizures); hallucinations (seeing, hearing, or feeling things that are not there); increased dreaming; muscle twitching; nausea or vomiting; nervousness or restlessness; nightmares; trembling; trouble in sleeping

Other side effects not listed above may also occur in some patients. If you notice any other effects, check with your doctor.

Revised: 01/13/93

MERCAPTOPURINE Systemic

A commonly used brand name in the U.S. and Canada is Purinethol. Another commonly used name is 6-MP.

Description

Mercaptopurine (mer-kap-toe-PYOOR-een) belongs to the group of medicines known as antimetabolites. It is used to treat some kinds of cancer.

Mercaptopurine interferes with the growth of cancer cells, which are eventually destroyed. Since the growth of normal body cells may also be affected by mercaptopurine, other effects will also occur. Some of these may be serious and must be reported to your doctor. Other effects may not be serious but may cause concern. Some effects may not occur for months or years after the medicine is used.

Before you begin treatment with mercaptopurine, you and your doctor should talk about the good this medicine will do as well as the risks of using it.

Mercaptopurine may also be used for other conditions as determined by your doctor.

Mercaptopurine is available only with your doctor's prescription, in the following dosage form:

Oral

- Tablets (U.S. and Canada)

Before Using This Medicine

In deciding to use a medicine, the risks of taking the medicine must be weighed against the good it will do. This is a decision you and your doctor will make. For mercaptopurine, the following should be considered:

Allergies—Tell your doctor if you have ever had any unusual or allergic reaction to mercaptopurine.

Pregnancy—Tell your doctor if you are pregnant or if you intend to have children. There is a chance that this medicine may cause birth defects if either the male or female is taking it at the time of conception or if it is taken during pregnancy. However, studies have not been done in humans. Mercaptopurine has been shown to cause damage to the fetus in rats and increases the risk of miscarriage or premature births in humans. In addition, many cancer medicines may cause sterility which could be permanent. Although this has not been reported with this medicine, the possibility should be kept in mind.

Be sure that you have discussed this with your doctor before taking this medicine. It is best to use some kind of birth control while you are taking mercaptopurine. Tell your doctor right away if you think you have become pregnant while taking mercaptopurine.

Breast-feeding—Tell your doctor if you are breast-feeding or if you intend to breast-feed during treatment with this medicine. Because mercaptopurine may cause serious side effects, breast-feeding is generally not recommended while you are taking it.

Children—Although there is no specific information comparing use of mercaptopurine in children with use in other age groups, it is not expected to cause different side effects or problems in children than it does in adults.

Older adults—Many medicines have not been studied specifically in older people. Therefore, it may not be known whether they work exactly the same way they do in younger adults or if they cause different side effects or problems in older people. There is no specific information comparing use of mercaptopurine in the elderly with use in other age groups.

Other medicines—Although certain medicines should not be used together at all, in other cases two different medicines may be used together even if an interaction might occur. In these cases, your doctor may want to change the dose, or other precautions may be necessary. When you are taking mercaptopurine, it is especially important that your health care professional know if you are taking any of the following:

- Acetaminophen (e.g., Tylenol) (with long-term, high-dose use) or
- Amiodarone (e.g., Cordarone) or
- Anabolic steroids (nandrolone [e.g., Anabolin], oxandrolone [e.g., Anavar], oxymetholone [e.g., Anadrol], stanozolol [e.g., Winstrol]) or
- Androgens (male hormones) or
- Anti-infectives by mouth or by injection (medicine for infection) or
- Antithyroid agents (medicine for overactive thyroid) or
- Carbamazepine (e.g., Tegretol) or
- Chloroquine (e.g., Aralen) or
- Dantrolene (e.g., Dantrium) or
- Disulfiram (e.g., Antabuse) or
- Divalproex (e.g., Depakote) or
- Estrogens (female hormones) or
- Etretinate (e.g., Tegison) or
- Gold salts (medicine for arthritis) or
- Hydroxychloroquine (e.g., Plaquenil) or
- Methyldopa (e.g., Aldomet) or
- Naltrexone (e.g., Trexan) (with long-term, high-dose use) or
- Oral contraceptives (birth control pills) containing estrogen or
- Phenothiazines (acetophenazine [e.g., Tindal], chlorpromazine [e.g., Thorazine], fluphenazine [e.g., Prolixin], mesoridazine [e.g., Serentil], perphenazine [e.g., Trilafon], prochlorperazine [e.g., Compazine], promazine [e.g., Sparine], promethazine [e.g., Phenergan], thioridazine [e.g., Mellaril], trifluoperazine [e.g., Stelazine], triflupromazine [e.g., Vesprin], trimeprazine [e.g., Temaril]) or
- Phenytoin (e.g., Dilantin) or
- Plicamycin (e.g., Mithracin) or
- Valproic acid (e.g., Depakene)—Risk of unwanted effects on the liver may be increased
- Azathioprine (e.g., Imuran) or
- Corticosteroids (cortisone-like medicine) or
- Cyclosporine (e.g., Sandimmune) or
- Muromonab-CD3 (monoclonal antibody) (e.g., Orthoclone OKT3)—There may be an increased risk of infection and development of cancer because mercaptopurine reduces the body's immunity
- Allopurinol (e.g., Zyloprim)—Effects of mercaptopurine may be increased because allopurinol blocks its removal from the body
- Amphotericin B by injection (e.g., Fungizone) or
- Antithyroid agents (medicine for overactive thyroid) or
- Azathioprine (e.g., Imuran) or
- Chloramphenicol (e.g., Chloromycetin) or
- Colchicine or
- Flucytosine (e.g., Ancobon) or
- Ganciclovir (e.g., Cytovene) or
- Interferon (e.g., Intron A, Roferon-A) or
- Plicamycin (e.g., Mithracin) or
- Zidovudine (e.g., AZT, Retrovir) or
- If you have ever been treated with radiation or cancer medicines—Mercaptopurine may increase the effects of these medicines or radiation therapy on the blood
- Probenecid (e.g., Benemid) or
- Sulfinpyrazone (e.g., Anturane)—Mercaptopurine may raise the concentration of uric acid in the blood. Since these medicines are used to lower uric acid levels, they may not be as effective in patients taking mercaptopurine

Other medical problems—The presence of other medical problems may affect the use of mercaptopurine. Make sure you tell your doctor if you have any other medical problems, especially:

- Chickenpox (including recent exposure) or
- Herpes zoster (shingles)—Risk of severe disease affecting other parts of the body
- Gout (history of) or
- Kidney stones (history of)—Mercaptopurine may increase levels of uric acid in the body, which can cause gout or kidney stones
- Infection—Mercaptopurine may decrease your body's ability to fight infection
- Kidney disease or
- Liver disease—Effects of mercaptopurine may be increased because of slower removal from the body

Proper Use of This Medicine

Use this medicine only as directed by your doctor. Do not use more or less of it, and do not use it more often than your doctor ordered. The exact amount of medicine you need has been carefully worked out. Taking too much may increase the chance of side effects, while taking too little may not improve your condition.

Mercaptopurine is often given together with certain other medicines. If you are using a combination of medicines, make sure that you take each one at the right time and do not mix them. Ask your health care professional to help you plan a way to remember to take your medicines at the right times.

While you are using mercaptopurine, your doctor may want you to drink extra fluids so that you will pass more urine. This will help prevent kidney problems and keep your kidneys working well.

If you vomit shortly after taking a dose of mercaptopurine, check with your doctor. You will be told whether to take the dose again or to wait until the next scheduled dose.

Dosing—The dose of mercaptopurine will be different for different patients. The dose that is used may depend on a number of things, including what the medicine is being used for, the patient's weight, and whether or not other medicines are also being taken. *If you are taking mercaptopurine at home, follow your doctor's orders or the directions on the label.* If you have any questions about the proper dose of mercaptopurine, ask your doctor.

Missed dose—If you miss a dose of this medicine, do not take the missed dose at all and do not double the next one. Instead, go back to your regular dosing schedule and check with your doctor.

Storage—To store this medicine:

- Keep out of the reach of children.
- Store away from heat and direct light.
- Do not store in the bathroom, near the kitchen sink, or in other damp places. Heat or moisture may cause the medicine to break down.
- Do not keep outdated medicine or medicine no longer needed. Be sure that any discarded medicine is out of the reach of children.

Precautions While Using This Medicine

It is very important that your doctor check your progress at regular visits to make sure that this medicine is working properly and to check for unwanted effects.

Avoid alcoholic beverages until you have discussed their use with your doctor. Alcohol may increase the harmful effects of this medicine.

While you are being treated with mercaptopurine, and after you stop treatment with it, *do not have any immunizations (vaccinations) without your doctor's approval.* Mercaptopurine may lower your body's resistance and there is a chance you might get the infection the immunization is meant to prevent. In addition, other persons living in your household should not take oral polio vaccine since there is a chance they could pass the polio virus on to you. Also, avoid persons who have taken oral polio vaccine. Do not get close to them and do not stay in the same room with them for very long. If you cannot take these precautions, you should consider wearing a protective face mask that covers the nose and mouth.

Mercaptopurine can temporarily lower the number of white blood cells in your blood, increasing the chance of getting an infection. It can also lower the number of platelets, which are necessary for proper blood clotting. If this occurs, there are certain precautions you can take, especially when your blood count is low, to reduce the risk of infection or bleeding:

- If you can, avoid people with infections. *Check with your doctor immediately* if you think you are getting an infection or if you get a fever or chills, cough or hoarseness, lower back or side pain, or painful or difficult urination.
- *Check with your doctor immediately* if you notice any unusual bleeding or bruising; black, tarry stools; blood in urine or stools; or pinpoint red spots on your skin.
- Be careful when using a regular toothbrush, dental floss, or toothpick. Your medical doctor, dentist, or nurse may recommend other ways to clean your teeth and gums. Check with your medical doctor before having any dental work done.
- Do not touch your eyes or the inside of your nose unless you have just washed your hands and have not touched anything else in the meantime.
- Be careful not to cut yourself when you are using sharp objects such as a safety razor or fingernail or toenail cutters.
- Avoid contact sports or other situations where bruising or injury could occur.

Tell the doctor in charge that you are taking this medicine before you have any medical tests. The results of tests for the amount of sugar or uric acid in the blood measured by a machine called a sequential multiple analyzer (SMA) may be affected by this medicine.

Side Effects of This Medicine

Along with its needed effects, a medicine may cause some unwanted effects. Although not all of these side effects may occur, if they do occur they may need medical attention.

Also, because of the way cancer medicines act on the body, there is a chance that they might cause other unwanted effects that may not occur until months or years after the medicine is used. These delayed effects may include certain types of cancer. Discuss these possible effects with your doctor.

Check with your doctor immediately if any of the following side effects occur:

Less common

Black, tarry stools; blood in urine or stools; cough or hoarseness; fever or chills; lower back or side pain; painful or difficult urination; pinpoint red spots on skin; unusual bleeding or bruising

Check with your doctor as soon as possible if any of the following side effects occur:

More common

Unusual tiredness or weakness; yellow eyes or skin

Less common

Joint pain; loss of appetite; nausea and vomiting; swelling of feet or lower legs

Rare

Sores in mouth and on lips

Other side effects may occur that usually do not need medical attention. These side effects may go away during treatment as your body adjusts to the medicine. Also, your health care professional may be able to tell you about ways to prevent or reduce some of these side effects. Check with your health care professional if any of the following side effects continue or are bothersome or if you have any questions about them:

Less common

Darkening of skin; diarrhea; headache; skin rash and itching; weakness

After you stop taking mercaptopurine, it may still produce some side effects that need attention. During this period of time, check with your doctor if you notice any of the following side effects:

Black, tarry stools; blood in urine or stools; cough or hoarseness; fever or chills; lower back or side pain; painful or difficult urination; pinpoint red spots on skin; unusual bleeding or bruising; yellow eyes or skin

Other side effects not listed above may also occur in some patients. If you notice any other effects, check with your doctor.

Revised: August 1990
Interim revision: 07/29/93; 12/10/93; 06/21/94

MESALAMINE Oral

Some commonly used brand names are:

In the U.S.—

Asacol
Pentasa

In Canada—

Asacol
Mesasal
Pentasa
Salofalk

Other commonly used names are: 5-aminosalicylic acid, 5-ASA, and mesalazine.

Description

Mesalamine (me-SAL-a-meen) is used to treat inflammatory bowel disease, such as ulcerative colitis. It works inside the bowel by helping to reduce the inflammation and other symptoms of the disease.

Mesalamine is available only with your doctor's prescription. It is available in the following dosage forms:

Oral

- Extended-release capsules (U.S. and Canada)
- Delayed-release tablets (U.S. and Canada)
- Extended-release tablets (Canada)

Before Using This Medicine

In deciding to use a medicine, the risks of taking the medicine must be weighed against the good it will do. This is a decision you and your doctor will make. For mesalamine, the following should be considered:

Allergies—Tell your doctor if you have ever had any unusual or allergic reaction to mesalamine, olsalazine, sulfasalazine, or any salicylates (for example, aspirin). Also tell your health care professional if you are allergic to any other substances, such as foods, preservatives, or dyes.

Pregnancy—Mesalamine has not been studied in pregnant women. However, mesalamine has not been shown to cause birth defects or other problems in animal studies.

Breast-feeding—Mesalamine may pass into the breast milk. However, this medicine has not been reported to cause problems in nursing babies.

Children—Studies on this medicine have been done only in adult patients, and there is no specific information comparing use of mesalamine in children with use in other age groups.

Older adults—Many medicines have not been studied specifically in older people. Therefore, it may not be known whether they work exactly the same way they do in younger adults or if they cause different side effects or problems in older people. There is no information comparing use of mesalamine in the elderly with use in other age groups.

Other medicines—Although certain medicines should not be used together at all, in other cases two different medicines may be used together even if an interaction might occur. In these cases, your doctor may want to change the dose, or other precautions may be necessary. Tell your health care professional if you are using any other prescription or nonprescription (over-the-counter [OTC]) medicine.

Other medical problems—The presence of other medical problems may affect the use of mesalamine. Make sure you tell your doctor if you have any other medical problems, especially:

- Kidney disease—The use of mesalamine may cause further damage to the kidneys
- Narrowing of the tube where food passes out of the stomach—May delay release of mesalamine into the body

Proper Use of This Medicine

Swallow the capsule or tablet whole. Do not break, crush, or chew it before swallowing.

Take this medicine before meals and at bedtime with a full glass (8 ounces) of water, unless otherwise directed by your doctor.

Keep taking this medicine for the full time of treatment, even if you begin to feel better after a few days. *Do not miss any doses.*

Do not change to another brand without checking with your doctor. The doses are different for different brands. If you refill your medicine and it looks different, check with your pharmacist.

Dosing—The dose of mesalamine will be different for different patients. *Follow your doctor's orders or the directions on the label.* The following information includes only the average doses of mesalamine. *If your dose is different, do not change it* unless your doctor tells you to do so.

The number of capsules or tablets that you take depends on the brand and strength of the medicine.

- For inflammatory bowel disease:
  - —For *long-acting oral* dosage form (extended-release capsules or tablets):
    - Adults—1 gram four times a day for up to eight weeks.
    - Children—Use and dose must be determined by your doctor.

—For *long-acting oral* dosage form (delayed-release tablets):

- Adults—
  —For *Asacol:* 800 milligrams (mg) three times a day for six weeks.
  —For *Mesasal:* A total of 1.5 to 3 grams a day, divided into smaller doses that are taken at separate times.
  —For *Salofalk:* 1 gram three or four times a day.
- Children—Use and dose must be determined by your doctor.

Missed dose—If you miss a dose of this medicine, take it as soon as possible. However, if it is almost time for your next dose, skip the missed dose and go back to your regular dosing schedule. Do not double doses.

Storage—To store this medicine:

- Keep out of the reach of children.
- Store away from heat and direct light.
- Do not store in the bathroom, near the kitchen sink, or in other damp places. Heat or moisture may cause the medicine to break down.
- Keep the medicine from freezing. Do not refrigerate.
- Do not keep outdated medicine or medicine no longer needed. Be sure that any discarded medicine is out of the reach of children.

Precautions While Using This Medicine

It is important that your doctor check your progress at regular visits.

For patients taking the capsule form of this medicine:

- You may sometimes notice what looks like small beads in your stool. These are just the empty shells that are left after the medicine has been absorbed into your body.

For patients taking the tablet form of this medicine:

- You may sometimes notice what looks like a tablet in your stool. This is just the empty shell that is left after the medicine has been absorbed into your body.

Side Effects of This Medicine

Along with its needed effects, a medicine may cause some unwanted effects. Although not all of these side effects may occur, if they do occur they may need medical attention.

Stop taking this medicine and check with your doctor immediately if any of the following side effects occur:

Less common
Abdominal or stomach cramps or pain (severe); bloody diarrhea; fever; headache (severe); skin rash and itching

Rare
Anxiety; back or stomach pain (severe); blue or pale skin; chest pain, possibly moving to the left arm, neck, or shoulder; chills; fast heartbeat; nausea or vomiting; shortness of breath; swelling of the stomach; unusual tiredness or weakness; yellow eyes or skin

Symptoms of overdose
Confusion; diarrhea (severe or continuing); dizziness or lightheadedness; drowsiness (severe); fast or deep breathing; headache (severe or continuing); hearing loss or ringing or buzzing in ears (continuing); nausea or vomiting (continuing)

Other side effects may occur that usually do not need medical attention. These side effects may go away during treatment as your body adjusts to the medicine. However, check with your doctor if any of the following side effects continue or are bothersome:

More common
Abdominal or stomach cramps or pain (mild); diarrhea (mild); dizziness; headache (mild); runny or stuffy nose or sneezing

Less common
Acne; back or joint pain; gas or flatulence; indigestion; loss of appetite; loss of hair

Other side effects not listed above may also occur in some patients. If you notice any other effects, check with your doctor.

Additional Information

Once a medicine has been approved for marketing for a certain use, experience may show that it is also useful for other medical problems. Although this use is not included in product labeling, mesalamine may be used to treat mild or moderate Crohn's disease and help prevent it from occurring again.

Other than the above information, there is no additional information relating to proper use, precautions, or side effects for this use.

Developed: 03/17/95

MESALAMINE Rectal

Some commonly used brand names are:

In the U.S.—
Rowasa

In Canada—
Salofalk

Other commonly used names are 5-aminosalicylic acid, 5-ASA, and mesalazine.

Description

Mesalamine (me-SAL-a-meen) is used to treat inflammatory bowel disease, such as ulcerative colitis. This medicine works inside the bowel by helping to reduce inflammation and other symptoms.

Mesalamine is available only with your doctor's prescription in the following dosage forms:

Rectal
- Enema (U.S. and Canada)
- Suppositories (U.S. and Canada)

Before Using This Medicine

In deciding to use a medicine, the risks of using the medicine must be weighed against the good it will do. This is a decision you and your doctor will make. For mesalamine, the following should be considered:

Allergies—Tell your doctor if you have ever had any unusual or allergic reaction to mesalamine, olsalazine, sulfasalazine, or salicylates (e.g., aspirin). Also tell your health care professional if you are allergic to any other substances, such as foods, preservatives, or dyes.

Pregnancy—Mesalamine has not been studied in pregnant women. However, mesalamine has not been shown to cause birth defects or other problems in animal studies.

Breast-feeding—It is not known whether mesalamine passes into the breast milk. Although most medicines pass into breast milk in small amounts, many of them may be used safely while breast-feeding. Mothers who are taking this medicine and who wish to breast-feed should discuss this with their doctor.

Children—Studies on this medicine have been done only in adult patients, and there is no specific information comparing use of mesalamine in children with use in other age groups.

Older adults—Many medicines have not been studied specifically in older people. Therefore, it may not be known whether they work exactly the same way they do in younger adults or if they cause different side effects or problems in older people. There is no specific information comparing use of mesalamine in the elderly with use in other age groups.

Other medicines—Although certain medicines should not be used together at all, in other cases two different medicines may be used together even if an interaction might occur. In these cases, your doctor may want to change the dose, or other precautions may be necessary. Tell your health care professional if you are taking any other medicines.

Other medical problems—The presence of other medical problems may affect the use of mesalamine. Make sure you tell your doctor if you have any other medical problems, especially:
- Kidney disease—The use of mesalamine may make this condition worse

Proper Use of This Medicine

For best results, empty your bowel just before using the rectal enema or suppository.

Keep using this medicine for the full time of treatment even if you begin to feel better after a few days. *Do not miss any doses.*

For patients using *the enema form* of this medicine:
- This medicine usually comes with patient directions. Read them carefully before using this medicine.
- Remove the bottles from the protective foil pouch, being careful not to squeeze or puncture them. The enema is an off-white to tan color. Contents of the enemas removed from the foil pouch may darken with time. Slight darkening will not affect the potency of the contents. However, enemas with dark brown contents should be discarded.
- Shake the bottle well to make sure that the medication is thoroughly mixed. Remove the protective cover from the applicator tip. Hold bottle at the neck so that no medicine spills out.
- Lie on your left side with your left leg straight and your right knee bent in front of you for balance. You can also lie in the knee-chest position, on your knees with your chest touching the bed.
- Gently insert the rectal tip of the enema applicator pointed slightly toward your naval to prevent damage to the rectal wall. Tilt the nozzle slightly toward the back and squeeze slowly to cause the enema to flow into your rectum. Steady pressure will discharge most of the medicine. After administering, withdraw and discard the bottle.
- Remain in position for at least 30 minutes to allow the medicine to distribute thoroughly. Retain the medicine all night if possible.

For patients using *the suppository form* of this medicine:
- This medicine usually comes with patient directions. Read them carefully before using this medicine.
- Detach one suppository from strip of suppositories. Hold suppository upright and carefully remove the foil wrapper.
- Avoid excessive handling of the suppository, which is designed to melt at body temperature.
- Insert suppository (pointed end first) completely into rectum with gentle pressure. Retain the suppository for 3 hours or longer, if possible, to achieve the best result.

Dosing—The dose of mesalamine may be different for different patients. *Follow your doctor's orders or the directions on the label.* The following information includes only the average doses of mesalamine. *If your dose is different, do not change it* unless your doctor tells you to do so.
- For inflammatory bowel disease:
  - —For *enema* dosage form:
    - Adults and teenagers—4 grams (1 unit), used as directed, every night for three to six weeks.
    - Children—Use and dose must be determined by your doctor.
  - —For *suppository* dosage form:
    - Adults and teenagers—500 milligrams (mg), inserted into your rectum, two or three times a day for three to six weeks.
    - Children—Use and dose must be determined by your doctor.

Missed dose—If you miss a dose of mesalamine enema, use it as soon as possible if you remember it that same night. However, if you do not remember it until the next morning, skip the missed dose and go back to your regular dosing schedule. If you miss a dose of mesalamine suppository, use it as soon as possible unless it is almost time for your next dose. Do not double doses.

Storage—To store this medicine:
- Keep out of the reach of children.
- Store away from heat and direct light.
- Keep the enema from freezing.
- Keep the suppositories at room temperature.
- Do not keep outdated medicine or medicine no longer needed. Be sure that any discarded medicine is out of the reach of children.

Precautions While Using This Medicine

It is important that your doctor check your progress at regular visits.

Check with your doctor if you notice rectal bleeding, blistering, pain, burning, itching, or other sign of irritation not present before you started using this medicine.

Mesalamine rectal enema may stain clothing, fabrics, painted surfaces, marble, granite, vinyl, or other surfaces it touches.

Side Effects of This Medicine

Along with its needed effects, a medicine may cause some unwanted effects. Although not all of these side effects may occur, if they do occur they may need medical attention.

Stop using this medicine and check with your doctor immediately if any of the following side effects occur:

Rare

Abdominal or stomach cramps or pain (severe); anxiety; back pain (severe); bloody diarrhea; blue or pale skin; chest pain, possibly moving to the left arm, neck, or shoulder; chills; fast heartbeat; fever; headache (severe); nausea or vomiting; shortness of breath; skin rash; swelling of the stomach; unusual tiredness or weakness; yellow eyes or skin

Also, check with your doctor as soon as possible if the following side effect occurs:

Rare

Rectal irritation

Other side effects may occur that usually do not need medical attention. These side effects may go away during treatment as your body adjusts to the medicine. However, check with your doctor if the following side effects continue or are bothersome:

More common

Abdominal or stomach cramps or pain (mild); gas or flatulence; headache (mild); nausea

Less common or rare

Loss of hair

Other side effects not listed above may also occur in some patients. If you notice any other effects, check with your doctor.

Additional Information

Once a medicine has been approved for marketing for a certain use, experience may show that it is also useful for other medical problems. Although this use is not included in product labeling, mesalamine may be used in patients who have had ulcerative colitis to prevent the condition from occurring again.

Other than the above information, there is no additional information relating to proper use, precautions, or side effects for this use.

Revised: 01/30/96

MESNA Systemic

Some commonly used brand names are:

In the U.S.—
MESNEX

In Canada—
Uromitexan

Description

Mesna is used to reduce the harmful effects of some cancer medicines on the bladder.

Mesna is to be given only by or under the immediate supervision of your doctor. It is available in the following dosage form:

Parenteral
- Injection (U.S. and Canada)

Before Using This Medicine

In deciding to use a medicine, the risks of taking the medicine must be weighed against the good it will do. This is a decision you and your doctor will make. For mesna, the following should be considered:

Allergies—Tell your doctor if you have ever had any unusual or allergic reaction to mesna.

Pregnancy—Mesna has not been shown to cause birth defects or other problems in humans.

Breast-feeding—It is not known whether mesna passes into the breast milk. However, this medicine has not been reported to cause problems in nursing babies.

Children—Although there is no specific information comparing use of mesna in children with use in other age groups, this medicine is not expected to cause different side effects or problems in children than it does in adults.

Older adults—Many medicines have not been studied specifically in older people. Therefore, it may not be known whether they work exactly the same way they do in younger adults or if they cause different side effects or problems in older people. There is no specific information

comparing use of mesna in the elderly with use in other age groups.

Proper Use of This Medicine

Dosing—The dose of mesna will be different for different patients and must be determined by your doctor. Mesna is usually given by a doctor or nurse in the hospital. If you have any questions about the proper dose of mesna, ask your doctor.

Side Effects of This Medicine

Along with its needed effects, a medicine may cause some unwanted effects. Although not all of these side effects may occur, if they do occur they may need medical attention.

Check with your doctor as soon as possible if either of the following side effects occur:

Rare
Skin rash or itching

Other side effects may occur that usually do not need medical attention. These side effects may go away during treatment as your body adjusts to the medicine. However, check with your doctor if any of the following side effects continue or are bothersome:

Less common
Diarrhea; nausea or vomiting; unpleasant taste

Other side effects not listed above may also occur in some patients. If you notice any other effects, check with your doctor.

Revised: 08/09/92
Interim revision: 07/06/94

METFORMIN Systemic

Some commonly used brand names are:

In the U.S.—
Glucophage

In Canada—
Glucophage
Novo-Metformin

Description

Metformin (met-FOR-min) is used to treat a type of diabetes mellitus (sugar diabetes) called non–insulin-dependent, or Type II, diabetes mellitus (NIDDM). With this type of diabetes, insulin produced by the pancreas is not able to get sugar into the cells of the body where it can work properly. Using metformin will help to lower blood sugar when it is too high and help restore the way you use food to make energy.

Many people can control NIDDM with diet alone or diet and exercise. Following a specially planned diet and exercising will always be important when you have diabetes, even when you are taking medicines. To work properly, the amount of metformin you take must be balanced against the amount and type of food you eat and the amount of exercise you do. If you change your diet, your exercise, or both, you will want to test your blood sugar to find out if it is too low. Your health care professional will teach you what to do if this happens.

At some point, this medicine may stop working as well and your blood glucose will increase. You will need to know if this happens and what to do. Instead of taking more of this medicine, your doctor may want you to change to another antidiabetic medicine. If that doesn't lower your blood sugar, your doctor may have you stop taking the medicine and begin receiving insulin injections instead.

Metformin does not help diabetic patients who have insulin-dependent or Type I diabetes mellitus (IDDM) because these patients cannot produce insulin from their pancreas gland. Their blood glucose is best controlled by insulin injections.

Metformin is available only with your doctor's prescription, in the following dosage form:

Oral
- Tablets (U.S. and Canada)

Before Using This Medicine

In deciding to use a medicine, the risks of taking the medicine must be weighed against the good it will do. This is a decision you and your doctor will make. For metformin, the following should be considered:

Allergies—Tell your doctor if you have ever had any unusual or allergic reaction to metformin. Also tell your health care provider if you are allergic to any other substances, such as foods, preservatives, or dyes.

Pregnancy—Metformin has not been shown to cause birth defects or other problems in humans. However, metformin is not used during pregnancy. Instead, your doctor may want to control your blood sugar by diet or by a combination of diet and insulin. It is especially important for your health and your baby's health that your blood sugar be closely controlled. Close control of your blood sugar can reduce the chance of your baby gaining too much weight, having birth defects, or having high or low blood sugar. Be sure to tell your doctor if you plan to become pregnant or if you think you are pregnant.

Breast-feeding—Metformin passes into breast milk. It has not been shown to cause problems in nursing babies.

Children—Studies of this medicine have been done only in adult patients, and there is no specific information comparing use of metformin in children with use in other age groups.

Teenagers—Studies of this medicine have been done only in adult patients, and there is no specific information comparing use of metformin in teenagers with use in other age groups.

Older adults—Use in older adults is similar to use in adults of younger age. However, if you have blood vessel disorders or kidney problems, your health care provider may adjust your dose or tell you to stop taking this medicine, if necessary.

Other medicines—Although certain medicines should not be used together at all, in other cases two different medicines may be used together even if an interaction might occur. *Do not take any other medicine unless prescribed or approved by your doctor.* In these cases, your doctor may want to change the dose, or other precautions may be necessary. When you are taking metformin, it is especially important that your health care provider know if you are taking any of the following:

- Alcohol—Small amounts of alcohol taken with meals do not usually cause a problem; however, larger amounts of alcohol taken either for a long time or a large amount of alcohol taken in one sitting without food can increase the effect of metformin. This can keep the blood sugar low for a longer period of time than normal
- Amiloride (e.g., Midamor) or
- Calcium channel blockers (amlodipine [e.g., Norvasc], bepridil [e.g., Bepadin], diltiazem [e.g., Cardizem], felodipine [e.g., Plendil], flunarizine [e.g., Sibelium], isradipine [e.g., DynaCirc], nicardipine [e.g., Cardene], nifedipine [e.g., Procardia], nimodipine [e.g., Nimotop], verapamil [e.g., Calan]) or
- Cimetidine (e.g., Tagamet) or
- Digoxin (heart medicine) or
- Furosemide (e.g., Lasix) or
- Morphine (e.g., Demerol) or
- Procainamide (e.g., Pronestyl) or
- Quinidine (e.g., Quinidex) or
- Quinine (e.g., Quinamm) or
- Ranitidine (e.g., Zantac) or
- Triamterene (e.g., Dyrenium) or
- Trimethoprim (e.g., Proloprim) or
- Vancomycin (e.g., Vancocin)—Use with metformin may cause high blood levels of metformin, which may increase the chance of low blood sugar or side effects

Other medical problems—The presence of other medical problems may affect the use of metformin. Make sure you tell your doctor if you have any other medical problems, especially:

- Acid in the blood (ketoacidosis or lactic acidosis) or
- Burns (severe) or
- Dehydration or
- Diabetic coma or
- Diarrhea (severe) or
- Female hormone changes for some women (e.g., during puberty, pregnancy, or menstruation) or
- High fever or
- Infection (severe) or
- Injury (severe) or
- Ketones in the urine or
- Mental stress (severe) or
- Overactive adrenal gland (not properly controlled) or
- Problems with intestines (severe) or
- Slow stomach emptying or
- Surgery (major) or
- Vomiting or
- Any other condition that causes problems with eating or absorbing food or
- Any other condition in which blood sugar changes rapidly—Metformin in many cases will be replaced by your doctor with insulin, possibly only for a short time. Use of insulin is best to help control diabetes mellitus in patients with these conditions that cause quick changes in the blood sugar without warning.
- Heart or blood vessel disorders or
- Kidney disease or kidney problems or
- Liver disease (or history of)—Lactic acidosis can occur in these conditions and chances of it occurring are even greater with use of metformin
- Kidney, heart, or other problems that require medical tests or examinations that use certain medicines called contrast agents, with x-rays—Metformin should be stopped 2 days before medical exams or diagnostic tests that might cause less urine output than usual. Passing unusually low amounts of urine may increase the chance of a build-up of metformin and unwanted effects
- Overactive thyroid (not properly controlled) or
- Underactive thyroid (not properly controlled)—Until the thyroid condition is controlled, it may change the amount or type of antidiabetic medicine you need
- Underactive adrenal gland (not properly controlled) or
- Underactive pituitary gland (not properly controlled) or
- Undernourished condition or
- Weakened physical condition or
- Any other condition that causes low blood sugar—Patients who have any of these conditions may be more likely to develop low blood sugar, which can affect the dose of metformin you need and increase the need for blood sugar testing

Proper Use of This Medicine

Use this medicine as directed even if you feel well and do not notice any signs of high blood sugar. Do not take more of this medicine and do not take it more often than your doctor ordered. To do so may increase the chance of serious side effects.

Remember that this medicine will not cure your diabetes but it does help control it. Therefore, you must continue to take it as directed if you expect to lower your blood sugar and keep it low. *You may have to take an antidiabetic medicine for the rest of your life.* If high blood sugar is not treated, it can cause serious problems, such as heart failure, blood vessel disease, eye disease, or kidney disease.

Your doctor will give you instructions about diet, exercise, how to test your blood sugar, and how to adjust your dose when you are sick.

- Blood sugar tests—Testing for blood sugar is the best way to tell whether your diabetes is being controlled properly. Blood sugar testing helps you and your health care team adjust your antidiabetic medicine dose, meal plan, and exercise schedule.
- Diet—The daily number of calories in your meal plan should be adjusted by your doctor or a registered dietitian to help you reach and maintain a healthy body weight. In addition, regular meals and snacks are arranged to meet the energy needs of your body at dif-

ferent times of the day. *It is very important that you carefully follow your meal plan.*

- Exercise—Ask your doctor what kind of exercise to do, the best time to do it, and how much you should do each day.
- Fluid (water) replacement—It is important to replace the water or fluid that your body uses. Tell your doctor if you have less urine output than usual or severe diarrhea that lasts for more than one day.
- On sick days—When you become sick with a cold, fever, or the flu, you need to take your usual dose of metformin, even if you feel too ill to eat. This is especially true if you have nausea, vomiting, or diarrhea. Infection usually increases your need to produce more insulin. Sometimes you may need to be switched from metformin to insulin for a short period of time while you are sick to properly control blood glucose. *Call your doctor for specific instructions, especially if severe or prolonged vomiting occurs.*

  Continue taking your metformin and try to stay on your regular meal plan. If you have trouble eating solid food, drink fruit juices, non-diet soft drinks, or clear soups, or eat small amounts of bland foods. A dietitian or your health care professional can give you a list of foods and the amounts to use for sick days.

  Test your blood sugar and check your urine for ketones. If ketones are present, call your doctor at once. Even when you start feeling better, let your doctor know how you are doing.

Dosing—The dose of metformin will be different for different patients. *Follow your doctor's orders or the directions on the label.* The following information includes only the average doses of metformin. *If your dose is different, do not change it* unless your doctor tells you to do so.

The number of tablets that you take depends on the strength of the medicine. Also, *the number of doses you take each day, the time allowed between doses, and the length of time you take the medicine depend on the amount of sugar in your blood or urine.*

- For *oral* dosage form (tablets):
  - —For non–insulin-dependent diabetes mellitus (NIDDM or Type II):
    - Adults—At first, 500 milligrams (mg) two times a day taken with the morning and evening meals. Or, 850 mg a day taken with the morning meal. Then, your doctor may increase your dose a little at a time every week or every other week if needed. Later, your doctor may want you to take 500 to 850 mg two to three times a day with meals.
    - Children—The type of diabetes treated with this medicine is rare in children.

Missed dose—If you miss a dose of this medicine, take it as soon as possible. However, if it is almost time for your next dose, skip the missed dose and go back to your regular dosing schedule. Do not double doses.

Storage—To store this medicine:

- Keep out of the reach of children.
- Store away from heat and direct light.
- Keep the medicine from freezing. Do not refrigerate.
- Do not keep outdated medicine or medicine no longer needed. Be sure that any discarded medicine is out of the reach of children.

Precautions While Using This Medicine

Your doctor will want to check your progress at regular visits, especially during the first few weeks that you take this medicine.

It is very important to follow carefully any instructions from your health care team about:

- Alcohol—Drinking alcohol may cause very low blood sugar. Discuss this with your health care team.
- Other medicines—Do not take other medicines unless they have been discussed with your doctor. This especially includes nonprescription medicines such as aspirin, and medicines for appetite control, asthma, colds, cough, hay fever, or sinus problems.
- Counseling—Other family members need to learn how to prevent side effects or help with side effects if they occur. Counseling on birth control and pregnancy may be needed because of the problems that can occur in pregnancy for diabetics.
- Travel—Carry a recent prescription and your medical history. Be prepared for an emergency as you would normally. Make allowances for changing time zones, but keep your meal times as close as possible to your usual meal times.

In case of emergency—There may be a time when you need emergency help for a problem caused by your diabetes. You need to be prepared for these emergencies. It is a good idea to:

- Wear a medical identification (I.D.) bracelet or neck chain at all times. Also, carry an I.D. card in your wallet or purse that says that you have diabetes and a list of all of your medicines.
- Have a glucagon kit and a syringe and needle available in case severe low blood sugar occurs. Check and replace any expired kits regularly.
- Keep some kind of quick-acting sugar handy to treat low blood sugar.

Also, too much metformin, under certain conditions, can cause low blood sugar (also called hypoglycemia) or lactic acidosis. *Symptoms of low blood sugar or lactic acidosis must be treated before they lead to unconsciousness (passing out).*

Symptoms of lactic acidosis are severe and quick to appear and usually occur when other health problems not related to the medicine are present and are very severe, such as a heart attack or kidney failure. Symptoms include diarrhea, fast and shallow breathing, severe muscle pain or cramping, sleepiness, or unusual tiredness or weakness. *Get immediate emergency medical help if these symptoms occur.*

Also, *tell your doctor if severe vomiting occurs.*

Different people may feel different symptoms of low blood sugar. *It is important that you learn which symptoms of low blood sugar you usually have so that you can treat it quickly and call someone on your health care team right away when you need advice.*

- Symptoms of low blood sugar can include anxious feeling, behavior change similar to being drunk, blurred vision, cold sweats, confusion, cool pale skin, difficulty in concentrating, drowsiness, excessive hunger, headache, nausea, nervousness, rapid heartbeat, shakiness, unusual tiredness or weakness.
- The symptoms of low blood sugar may develop quickly and may result from:

  —delaying or missing a scheduled meal or snack.

  —exercising more than usual.

  —drinking a large amount of alcohol.

  —taking certain medicines.

  —if also using insulin or a sulfonylurea, using too much of these medicines.

  —sickness (especially with vomiting or diarrhea).
- Know what to do if symptoms of low blood sugar occur. Eating some form of quick-acting sugar when symptoms of low blood sugar first appear will usually prevent them from getting worse.

  Good ways to increase your blood sugar include:

  —Glucagon injections are used in emergency situations such as unconsciousness. Have a glucagon kit available, along with a syringe and needle, and know how to prepare and use it. Members of your household also should know how and when to use it.

  —Eating glucose tablets or gel or sugar cubes (6 one-half-inch sized). Or, drinking fruit juice or non-diet soft drink (4 to 6 ounces [one-half cup]), corn syrup or honey (1 tablespoon), or table sugar (dissolved in water).

  - Do not use chocolate. The sugar in chocolate may not enter into your bloodstream fast enough. This is because the fat in chocolate slows down the sugar entering into the bloodstream.
  - If a meal is not scheduled for an hour or more you should also eat a light snack, such as crackers or half a sandwich.

High blood sugar (hyperglycemia) is another problem related to uncontrolled diabetes. Symptoms of mild high blood sugar appear more slowly than those of low blood sugar.

- *Check with your health care team as soon as possible if you notice any of the following symptoms:* Blurred vision, drowsiness, dry mouth, increased urination, loss of appetite, nausea or vomiting, sleepiness, stomachache, tiredness, unusual thirst.
- *Get emergency help right away if you notice any of the following symptoms:* Flushed dry skin, fruit-like breath odor, ketones in urine, passing out, troubled breathing (rapid and deep). If high blood sugar is not treated, severe hyperglycemia can occur, leading to ketoacidosis (diabetic coma) and death.
- It is important to recognize what can cause the loss of blood glucose control. Calling your doctor early may be important to prevent problems from developing when the following occur. High blood sugar symptoms may occur if you:

  —have a fever or an infection.

  —are using insulin, sulfonylurea, or metformin, do not take enough of these medicines or skip a dose.

  —do not exercise as much as usual.

  —take certain nondiabetic medicines that change the amount of sugar in your blood.

  —overeat or do not follow your meal plan.
- Know what to do if high blood sugar occurs. Your doctor may recommend changes in your antidiabetic medicine dose(s) or meal plan to avoid high blood sugar. Symptoms of high blood sugar must be corrected before they progress to more serious conditions. Check with your doctor often to make sure you are controlling your blood sugar, *but do not change your dose without checking with your doctor*. Your doctor might discuss the following with you:

  —Delaying a meal if your blood glucose is over 200 mg/dL to allow time for your blood sugar to go down. An extra dose or an injection of insulin may be needed if your blood sugar does not come down shortly.

  —Not exercising if your blood glucose is over 240 mg/dL and reporting this to your doctor immediately.

  —Being hospitalized if ketoacidosis or diabetic coma occurs.

Side Effects of This Medicine

Along with its needed effects, a medicine may cause some unwanted effects. Although not all of these side effects may occur, if they do occur they may need medical attention.

Check with your doctor as soon as possible if any of the following side effects occur:

Rare

Lactic acidosis (quick and severe), including diarrhea, fast shallow breathing, muscle pain or cramping, tiredness or weakness, unusual sleepiness

Also, check with your doctor as soon as possible if any of the following side effects occur:

More common

Low blood sugar (mild), including anxious feeling, behavior change similar to being drunk, blurred vision, cold sweats, confusion, cool pale skin, difficulty in concentrating, drowsiness, excessive hunger, fast heartbeat, headache, nausea, nervousness, shakiness,

Rare

Unusual tiredness or weakness (continuing)

Other side effects may occur that usually do not need medical attention. These side effects may go away during treatment as your body adjusts to the medicine. However,

check with your doctor if any of the following side effects continue or are bothersome:

More common

Changes in taste; gas; headache; loss of appetite; nausea; stomach pain, fullness, or discomfort; vomiting; weight loss

Other side effects not listed above may also occur in some patients. If you notice any other effects, check with your doctor.

Developed: 07/26/95

METHACHOLINE Inhalation†

A commonly used brand name in the U.S. is Provocholine.

†Not commercially available in Canada.

Description

Methacholine (METH-a-koe-leen) is used to help find out whether a patient has asthma.

Before the test with methacholine inhalation is given, another test will be done to find out how well your lungs are working.

How test is done: Although there are 5 different strengths of methacholine solution that may be used in this test, not all of them may be necessary. It depends on how you react to each increasing strength of solution during the test. The weakest strength solution is used first. It is placed in a nebulizer and 5 inhalations are taken by mouth. After 3 to 5 minutes, a test will be done to determine what effect the medicine had on your lungs. Each time the test dose is repeated, a stronger solution will be used. During this test, wheezing and difficulty in breathing may occur. If these effects do occur, your doctor may give you a bronchodilator (medicine that opens up the bronchial tubes [air passages] of the lungs) by inhalation to relieve the discomfort.

Methacholine is to be used only by or under the immediate supervision of a doctor. It is available in the following dosage form:

Inhalation

- Inhalation solution (U.S.)

Before Having This Test

In deciding to use a diagnostic test, any risks of the test must be weighed against the good it will do. This is a decision you and your doctor will make. Also, test results may be affected by other things. For methacholine, the following should be considered:

Allergies—Tell your doctor if you have ever had any unusual or allergic reaction to methacholine or to similar medicines, such as ambenonium, bethanechol, neostigmine, and pyridostigmine. Also tell your health care professional if you are allergic to any other substances, such as foods, preservatives, or dyes.

Pregnancy—Studies on birth defects have not been done in either humans or animals. However, if the test is necessary, women who are able to bear children should be given the test within 10 days after the beginning of the last menstrual period or within 2 weeks after a pregnancy test has shown they are not pregnant.

Breast-feeding—It is not known whether methacholine passes into the breast milk. Although most medicines pass into breast milk in small amounts, many of them may be used safely while breast-feeding. Mothers who are receiving the methacholine test and who wish to breast-feed should discuss this with their doctor.

Children—Although there is no specific information comparing use of methacholine in children less than 5 years old with use in other age groups, this medicine is not expected to cause different side effects or problems in these children than it does in adults.

Older adults—Many medicines have not been studied specifically in older people. Therefore, it may not be known whether they work exactly the same way they do in younger adults or if they cause different side effects or problems in older people. There is no specific information comparing use of methacholine in the elderly with use in other age groups.

Other medicines—Although certain medicines should not be used together at all, in other cases two different medicines may be used together even if an interaction might occur. In these cases, your doctor may want to change the dose, or other precautions may be necessary. When you are receiving the methacholine test, it is especially important that your health care professional know if you are taking or using any of the following:

- Anticholinergics (medicine for abdominal or stomach spasms or cramps) or
- Corticosteroids (cortisone-like medicines) or
- Cromolyn (e.g., Intal) or
- Medicine for breathing problems, colds, sinus problems, or hay fever or other allergies (including nose drops or sprays) or
- Smoking tobacco—These medicines or smoking tobacco may affect the results of this test
- Beta-blockers (acebutolol [e.g., Sectral], atenolol [e.g., Tenormin], betaxolol [e.g., Kerlone], bisoprolol [e.g., Zebeta], carteolol [e.g., Cartrol], labetalol [e.g., Normodyne], metoprolol [e.g., Lopressor], nadolol [e.g., Corgard], oxprenolol [e.g., Trasicor], penbutolol [e.g., Levatol], pindolol [e.g., Visken], propranolol [e.g., Inderal], sotalol [e.g., Sotacor], timolol [e.g., Blocadren])—These medicines may increase the reaction to the methacholine test

Other medical problems—The presence of other medical problems may affect the use of methacholine . Make sure you tell your doctor if you have any other medical problems, especially:

- Asthma (or if any member of your family has asthma), hay fever, allergic rhinitis, wheezing, chronic lung disease, or

respiratory virus illness—Methacholine may cause severe difficulty in breathing
- Epilepsy or
- Heart or blood vessel disease or
- Stomach ulcer or
- Thyroid disease or
- Urinary tract blockage—Use of methacholine may make the condition worse

Preparation for This Test

Unless otherwise directed by your doctor:
- *For 24 hours before the test, do not take any extended-release capsule or tablet form of aminophylline, oxtriphylline, or theophylline. For 12 hours before the test, do not use any other medicine,* especially anticholinergics (medicine for abdominal or stomach spasms or cramps) or medicine for breathing problems, sinus problems, or hay fever or other allergies (including nose drops or sprays). To do so may affect the results of this test.

Side Effects of This Medicine

Along with its needed effects, a medicine may cause some unwanted effects. Although not all of these side effects may occur, if they do occur they may need medical attention.

Check with your health care professional immediately if any of the following side effects occur:

Wheezing, tightness in chest, or difficulty in breathing (continuing or severe)

Other side effects may occur that usually do not need medical attention. These side effects should go away as the effects of the medicine wear off. However, check with your doctor if any of the following side effects continue or are bothersome:

Less common or rare

Headache or lightheadedness; irritation of throat; itching

Other side effects not listed above may also occur in some patients. If you notice any other effects, check with your doctor.

Revised: 08/09/94

METHENAMINE Systemic

Some commonly used brand names are:

In the U.S.—

Hiprex
Urex
Mandelamine

Generic name product may also be available.

In Canada

Hip-Rex
Mandelamine

Description

Methenamine (meth-EN-a-meen) belongs to the family of medicines called anti-infectives. It is used to help prevent and treat infections of the urinary tract. Methenamine is available only with your doctor's prescription, in the following dosage forms:

Oral
- Enteric-coated tablets (U.S.)
- Granules for oral solution (U.S.)
- Oral suspension (U.S.)
- Tablets (U.S. and Canada)

Before Using This Medicine

In deciding to use a medicine, the risks of taking the medicine must be weighed against the good it will do. This is a decision you and your doctor will make. For methenamine, the following should be considered:

Allergies—Tell your doctor if you have ever had any unusual or allergic reaction to methenamine. Also tell your health care professional if you are allergic to any other substances, such as foods, preservatives, or dyes.

Pregnancy—Methenamine has not been studied in either humans or animals. However, individual case reports on the use of methenamine during pregnancy have not shown that this medicine causes birth defects or other problems in humans.

Breast-feeding—Methenamine passes into the breast milk. However, methenamine has not been reported to cause problems in nursing babies.

Children—Although there is no special information comparing use of methenamine in children with use in other age groups, this medicine is not expected to cause different side effects or problems in children than it does in adults.

Older adults—Many medicines have not been studied specifically in older people. Therefore, it may not be known whether they work exactly the same way they do in younger adults or if they cause different side effects or problems in older people. There is no specific information comparing use of methenamine in the elderly with use in other age groups.

Other medicines—Although certain medicines should not be used together at all, in other cases two different medicines may be used together even if an interaction might occur. In these cases, your doctor may want to change the dose, or other precautions may be necessary. When you are taking methenamine, it is especially important that your health care professional knows if you are taking any of the following:
- Thiazide diuretics (water pills) or
- Urinary alkalizers (medicine that makes the urine less acid, such as acetazolamide [e.g., Diamox], calcium- and/or magnesium-containing antacids, dichlorphenamide [e.g., Daranide], methazolamide [e.g., Neptazane], potassium or sodium citrate and/or citric acid, sodium bicarbonate [bak-

ing soda])—Use of methenamine with any of these medicines may decrease the effectiveness of methenamine

Other medical problems—The presence of other medical problems may affect the use of methenamine. Make sure you tell your doctor if you have any other medical problems, especially:

- Dehydration (severe) or
- Kidney disease (severe)—Patients with severe kidney disease who take methenamine may have an increase in side effects that affect the kidneys
- Liver disease (severe)—Patients with severe liver disease who take methenamine may have an increase in symptoms of their liver disease

Proper Use of This Medicine

Before you start taking this medicine, check your urine with phenaphthazine paper or another test to see if it is acid. *Your urine must be acidic (pH 5.5 or below) for this medicine to work properly.* If you have any questions about this, check with your health care professional.

The following changes in your diet may help make your urine more acid; however, check with your doctor first if you are on a special diet (for example, for diabetes). Avoid most fruits (especially citrus fruits and juices), milk and other dairy products, and other foods that make the urine less acid. Also, avoid antacids unless otherwise directed by your doctor. Eating more protein and foods such as cranberries (especially cranberry juice with vitamin C added), plums, or prunes may also help. If your urine is still not acid enough, check with your doctor.

If this medicine causes nausea or upset stomach, it may be taken after meals and at bedtime.

For patients taking the *dry granule form of this medicine:*

- Dissolve the contents of each packet in 2 to 4 ounces of cold water immediately before taking. Stir well. Be sure to drink all the liquid to get the full dose of medicine.

For patients taking the *oral liquid form of this medicine:*

- Use a specially marked measuring spoon or other device to measure each dose accurately. The average household teaspoon may not hold the right amount of liquid.

For patients taking the *enteric-coated tablet form of this medicine:*

- Swallow tablets whole. Do not break, crush, or take if chipped.

To help clear up your infection completely, *keep taking this medicine for the full time of treatment,* even if you begin to feel better after a few days. *Do not miss any doses.*

Dosing—The dose of methenamine will be different for different patients. *Follow your doctor's orders or the directions on the label.* The following information includes only the average doses of methenamine. *If your dose is different, do not change it* unless your doctor tells you to do so.

The number of tablets or teaspoonfuls of solution or suspension that you take depends on the strength of the medicine.

- For the treatment of urinary tract infections:
  - —For *oral* dosage form (methenamine hippurate tablets):
    - Adults and children 12 years of age and over—1 gram two times a day. Take in the morning and the evening.
    - Children up to 6 years of age—Use and dose must be determined by your doctor.
    - Children 6 to 12 years of age—500 milligrams (mg) to 1 gram two times a day. Take in the morning and the evening.
  - —For *oral* dosage form (methenamine mandelate enteric-coated tablets, regular tablets, solution, and suspension):
    - Adults and children 12 years of age and over—1 gram four times a day. Take after meals and at bedtime.
    - Children up to 6 years of age—Dose is based on body weight. The usual dose is 18.3 mg per kilogram (kg) (8.3 mg per pound) of body weight four times a day. Take after meals and at bedtime.
    - Children 6 to 12 years of age—500 mg four times a day. Take after meals and at bedtime.

Missed dose—If you miss a dose of this medicine, take it as soon as possible. However, if it is almost time for your next dose, skip the missed dose and go back to your regular dosing schedule. Do not double doses.

Storage—To store this medicine:

- Keep out of the reach of children.
- Store away from heat and direct light.
- Do not store the dry granule or tablet form of this medicine in the bathroom, near the kitchen sink, or in other damp places. Heat or moisture may cause the medicine to break down.
- Keep the oral liquid form of this medicine from freezing.
- Do not keep outdated medicine or medicine no longer needed. Be sure that any discarded medicine is out of the reach of children.

Precautions While Using This Medicine

If your symptoms do not improve within a few days, or if they become worse, check with your doctor.

Side Effects of This Medicine

Along with its needed effects, a medicine may cause some unwanted effects. Although not all of these side effects may occur, if they do occur they may need medical attention.

Check with your doctor immediately if any of the following side effects occur:

Less common
Skin rash

Rare
Blood in urine; lower back pain; pain or burning while urinating

Other side effects may occur that usually do not need medical attention. These side effects may go away during treatment as your body adjusts to the medicine. However, check with your doctor if any of the following side effects continue or are bothersome:

Less common

Nausea and vomiting

Other side effects not listed above may also occur in some patients. If you notice any other effects, check with your doctor.

Revised: 10/20/92
Interim revision: 03/17/94

METHOTREXATE—For Cancer Systemic

Some commonly used brand names are:

In the U.S.—

Folex
Folex PFS
Mexate
Mexate-AQ

Generic name product may also be available in the U.S. and Canada.

Another commonly used name is amethopterin.

Description

Methotrexate (meth-o-TREX-ate) belongs to the group of medicines known as antimetabolites. It is used to treat some kinds of cancer.

Methotrexate blocks an enzyme needed by the cell to live. This interferes with the growth of cancer cells, which are eventually destroyed. Since the growth of normal body cells may also be affected by methotrexate, other effects will also occur. Some of these may be serious and must be reported to your doctor. Other effects, like hair loss, may not be serious but may cause concern. Some effects may not occur for months or years after the medicine is used.

Before you begin treatment with methotrexate, you and your doctor should talk about the good this medicine will do as well as the risks of using it.

Methotrexate is available only with your doctor's prescription, in the following dosage forms:

Oral

- Tablets (U.S. and Canada)

Parenteral

- Injection (U.S. and Canada)

Before Using This Medicine

In deciding to use a medicine, the risks of taking the medicine must be weighed against the good it will do. This is a decision you and your doctor will make. For methotrexate, the following should be considered:

Allergies—Tell your doctor if you have ever had any unusual or allergic reaction to methotrexate.

Pregnancy—Tell your doctor if you are pregnant or if you intend to have children. There is a good chance that this medicine may cause birth defects if either the male or female is taking it at the time of conception or if it is taken during pregnancy. Methotrexate may cause harm or even death of the fetus. In addition, many cancer medicines may cause sterility which could be permanent. Although sterility is probably rare with this medicine, the possibility should be kept in mind.

Be sure that you have discussed this with your doctor before taking this medicine. It is best to use some kind of birth control while you are taking methotrexate. Tell your doctor right away if you think you have become pregnant while taking methotrexate.

Breast-feeding—Tell your doctor if you are breast-feeding or if you intend to breast-feed during treatment with this medicine. Because methotrexate may cause serious side effects, breast-feeding is generally not recommended while you are taking it.

Children—Newborns and other infants may be more sensitive to the effects of methotrexate. However, in other children it is not expected to cause different side effects or problems than it does in adults.

Older adults—Side effects may be more likely to occur in the elderly, who are usually more sensitive to the effects of methotrexate.

Other medicines—Although certain medicines should not be used together at all, in other cases two different medicines may be used together even if an interaction might occur. In these cases, your doctor may want to change the dose, or other precautions may be necessary. When you are taking methotrexate, it is especially important that your health care professional know if you are taking any other prescription or nonprescription (over-the-counter [OTC]) medicine. They should also be told if you have ever been treated with x-rays or cancer medicines or if you drink alcohol.

Other medical problems—The presence of other medical problems may affect the use of methotrexate. Make sure you tell your doctor if you have any other medical problems, especially:

- Alcohol abuse (or history of)—Increased risk of unwanted effects on the liver
- Chickenpox (including recent exposure) or
- Herpes zoster (shingles)—Risk of severe disease affecting other parts of the body
- Colitis
- Disease of the immune system
- Gout (history of) or
- Kidney stones (or history of)—Methotrexate may increase levels of a chemical called uric acid in the body, which can cause gout or kidney stones
- Infection—Methotrexate can reduce immunity to infection
- Intestine blockage or
- Kidney disease or
- Liver disease—Effects may be increased because of slower removal of methotrexate from the body

- Mouth sores or inflammation or
- Stomach ulcer—May be worsened

Proper Use of This Medicine

Take this medicine only as directed by your doctor. Do not take more or less of it, and do not take it more often than your doctor ordered. The exact amount of medicine you need has been carefully worked out. Taking too much may increase the chance of side effects, while taking too little may not improve your condition.

Methotrexate is often given together with certain other medicines. If you are using a combination of medicines, make sure that you take each one at the proper time and do not mix them. Ask your health care professional to help you plan a way to remember to take your medicines at the right times.

While you are using methotrexate, your doctor may want you to drink extra fluids so that you will pass more urine. This will help the drug to pass from the body, and will prevent kidney problems and keep your kidneys working well.

Methotrexate commonly causes nausea and vomiting. Even if you begin to feel ill, *do not stop using this medicine without first checking with your doctor.* Ask your health care professional for ways to lessen these effects.

If you vomit shortly after taking a dose of methotrexate, check with your doctor. You will be told whether to take the dose again or to wait until the next scheduled dose.

Dosing—The dose of methotrexate will be different for different patients. The dose that is used may depend on a number of things, including what the medicine is being used for, the patient's size, whether the medicine is being given by mouth or by injection, and whether or not other medicines are also being taken. *If you are taking or receiving methotrexate at home, follow your doctor's orders or the directions on the label.* If you have any questions about the proper dose of methotrexate, ask your doctor.

Missed dose—If you miss a dose of this medicine, do not take the missed dose at all and do not double the next one. Instead, go back to your regular dosing schedule and check with your doctor.

Storage—To store this medicine:
- Keep out of the reach of children.
- Store away from heat and direct light.
- Do not store in the bathroom, near the kitchen sink, or in other damp places. Heat or moisture may cause the medicine to break down.
- Do not keep outdated medicine or medicine no longer needed. Be sure that any discarded medicine is out of the reach of children.

Precautions While Using This Medicine

It is very important that your doctor check your progress at regular visits to make sure that this medicine is working properly and to check for unwanted effects.

Do not drink alcohol while using this medicine. Alcohol can increase the chance of liver problems.

Some patients who take methotrexate may become more sensitive to sunlight than they are normally. When you first begin taking methotrexate, avoid too much sun and do not use a sunlamp until you see how you react to the sun, especially if you tend to burn easily. In case of a severe burn, check with your doctor.

Do not take medicine for inflammation or pain (aspirin or other salicylates, diclofenac, diflunisal, fenoprofen, ibuprofen, indomethacin, ketoprofen, meclofenamate, mefenamic acid, naproxen, phenylbutazone, piroxicam, sulindac, suprofen, tolmetin) without first checking with your doctor. These medicines may increase the effects of methotrexate, which could be harmful.

While you are being treated with methotrexate, and after you stop treatment with it, *do not have any immunizations (vaccinations) without your doctor's approval.* Methotrexate may lower your body's resistance and there is a chance you might get the infection the immunization is meant to prevent. In addition, other persons living in your household should not take or should not have recently taken oral polio vaccine since there is a chance they could pass the polio virus on to you. Also, avoid other persons who have taken oral polio vaccine. Do not get close to them, and do not stay in the same room with them for very long. If you cannot take these precautions, you should consider wearing a protective face mask that covers the nose and mouth.

Methotrexate can lower the number of white blood cells in your blood temporarily, increasing the chance of getting an infection. It can also lower the number of platelets, which are necessary for proper blood clotting. If this occurs, there are certain precautions you can take, especially when your blood count is low, to reduce the risk of infection or bleeding:
- If you can, avoid people with infections. *Check with your doctor immediately* if you think you are getting an infection or if you get a fever or chills, cough or hoarseness, lower back or side pain, or painful or difficult urination.
- *Check with your doctor immediately* if you notice any unusual bleeding or bruising; black, tarry stools; blood in urine or stools; or pinpoint red spots on your skin.
- Be careful when using a regular toothbrush, dental floss, or toothpick. Your medical doctor, dentist, or nurse may recommend other ways to clean your teeth and gums. Check with your medical doctor before having any dental work done.
- Do not touch your eyes or the inside of your nose unless you have just washed your hands and have not touched anything else in the meantime.
- Be careful not to cut yourself when you are using sharp objects such as a safety razor or fingernail or toenail cutters.
- Avoid contact sports or other situations where bruising or injury could occur.

Side Effects of This Medicine

Along with their needed effects, medicines like methotrexate can sometimes cause unwanted effects such as blood problems, kidney problems, stomach or liver problems, loss of hair, and other side effects. These and others are described below. Also, because of the way these medicines act on the body, there is a chance that they might cause other unwanted effects that may not occur until months or years after the medicine is used. These delayed effects may include certain types of cancer, such as leukemia. Discuss these possible effects with your doctor.

Although not all of these side effects may occur, if they do occur they may need medical attention.

Check with your doctor immediately if any of the following side effects occur:

More common

Black, tarry stools; bloody vomit; diarrhea; reddening of skin; sores in mouth and on lips; stomach pain

Less common

Blood in urine or stools; blurred vision; confusion; convulsions (seizures); cough or hoarseness; fever or chills; lower back or side pain; painful or difficult urination; pinpoint red spots on skin; shortness of breath; swelling of feet or lower legs; unusual bleeding or bruising

Check with your doctor as soon as possible if any of the following side effects occur:

Less common

Back pain; dark urine; dizziness; drowsiness; headache; joint pain; unusual tiredness or weakness; yellow eyes or skin

Other side effects may occur that usually do not need medical attention. These side effects may go away during treatment as your body adjusts to the medicine. Also, your health care professional may be able to tell you about ways to prevent or reduce some of these side effects. Check with your health care professional if any of the following side effects continue or are bothersome or if you have any questions about them:

More common

Loss of appetite; nausea or vomiting

Less common

Acne; boils; pale skin; skin rash or itching

This medicine may cause a temporary loss of hair in some people. After treatment with methotrexate has ended, normal hair growth should return.

After you stop using methotrexate, it may still produce some side effects that need attention. During this period of time, check with your doctor as soon as possible if you notice any of the following side effects:

Back pain; blurred vision; confusion; convulsions (seizures); dizziness; drowsiness; fever; headache; unusual tiredness or weakness

Other side effects not listed above may also occur in some patients. If you notice any other effects, check with your doctor.

Revised: 8/90
Interim revision: 06/21/94

METHOTREXATE—For Noncancerous Conditions Systemic

Some commonly used brand names are:

In the U.S.—

Folex
Folex PFS
Mexate
Mexate-AQ
Rheumatrex

In Canada—

Rheumatrex

Generic name product may also be available in the U.S. and Canada.

Another commonly used name is amethopterin.

Description

Methotrexate (meth-o-TREX-ate) belongs to the group of medicines known as antimetabolites. It is used to treat psoriasis and rheumatoid arthritis. It may also be used for other conditions as determined by your doctor.

Methotrexate blocks an enzyme needed by the cell to live. This interferes with the growth of certain cells, such as skin cells in psoriasis that are growing rapidly. Since the growth of normal body cells may also be affected by methotrexate, other effects will also occur. Some of these may be serious and must be reported to your doctor. Other effects, like hair loss, may not be serious but may cause concern. Some effects may not occur for months or years after the medicine is used.

Before you begin treatment with methotrexate, you and your doctor should talk about the good this medicine will do as well as the risks of using it.

Methotrexate is available only with your doctor's prescription, in the following dosage forms:

Oral

- Tablets (U.S. and Canada)

Parenteral

- Injection (U.S. and Canada)

Before Using This Medicine

In deciding to use a medicine, the risks of taking the medicine must be weighed against the good it will do. This is a decision you and your doctor will make. For methotrexate, the following should be considered:

Allergies—Tell your doctor if you have ever had any unusual or allergic reaction to methotrexate.

Pregnancy—There is a good chance that this medicine may cause birth defects if either the male or female is taking it at the time of conception or if it is taken during pregnancy. Methotrexate may cause harm or even death of the fetus. In addition, this medicine may rarely cause temporary sterility.

Methotrexate is not recommended during pregnancy. Be sure that you have discussed this with your doctor before taking this medicine. It is best to use some kind of birth control while you are taking methotrexate. Tell your doctor right away if you think you have become pregnant while taking methotrexate.

Breast-feeding—Tell your doctor if you are breast-feeding or if you intend to breast-feed during treatment with this medicine. Because methotrexate may cause serious side effects, breast-feeding is generally not recommended while you are taking it.

Children—Newborns and other infants may be more sensitive to the effects of methotrexate. However, in other children it is not expected to cause different side effects or problems than it does in adults.

Older adults—Side effects may be more likely to occur in the elderly, who are usually more sensitive to the effects of methotrexate.

Other medicines—Although certain medicines should not be used together at all, in other cases two different medicines may be used together even if an interaction might occur. In these cases, your doctor may want to change the dose, or other precautions may be necessary. When you are taking methotrexate, it is especially important that your health care professional know if you are taking any other prescription or nonprescription (over-the-counter [OTC]) medicine. They should also be told if you have ever been treated with x-rays or cancer medicines or if you drink alcohol.

Other medical problems—The presence of other medical problems may affect the use of methotrexate. Make sure you tell your doctor if you have any other medical problems, especially:

- Alcohol abuse (or history of)—Increased risk of unwanted effects on the liver
- Chickenpox (including recent exposure) or
- Herpes zoster (shingles)—Risk of severe disease affecting other parts of the body
- Colitis
- Disease of the immune system
- Infection—Methotrexate can reduce immunity to infection
- Intestine blockage or
- Kidney disease or
- Liver disease—Effects may be increased because of slower removal of methotrexate from the body
- Mouth sores or inflammation or
- Stomach ulcer—May be worsened

Proper Use of This Medicine

Take this medicine only as directed by your doctor. Do not take more or less of it, and do not take it more often than your doctor ordered. The exact amount of medicine you need has been carefully worked out. Taking too much may increase the chance of side effects, while taking too little may not improve your condition.

Methotrexate may cause nausea. Even if you begin to feel ill, *do not stop using this medicine without first checking with your doctor.* Ask your health care professional for ways to lessen these effects. If you begin vomiting, check with your doctor.

If you vomit shortly after taking a dose of methotrexate, check with your doctor. You will be told whether to take the dose again or to wait until the next scheduled dose.

Dosing—The dose of methotrexate will be different for different patients. *Follow your doctor's orders or the directions on the label.* The following information includes only the average doses of methotrexate. *If your dose is different, do not change it* unless your doctor tells you to do so.

The number of tablets that you take or doses of injection that you use depends on the strength of the medicine. Also, *the number of doses you take each day, the time allowed between doses, and the length of time you take the medicine depend on the medical problem for which you are taking methotrexate.*

- For *oral* dosage form (tablets):
  - —For psoriasis or rheumatoid arthritis:
    - Adults—2.5 to 5 milligrams (mg) every twelve hours for three doses once a week, or 10 mg once a week. Your doctor may increase the dose as needed.
    - Children—Dose must be determined by your doctor.
- For *injection* dosage form:
  - —For psoriasis:
    - Adults—To start, 10 mg injected into a muscle or vein once a week. Your doctor may increase the dose as needed.
    - Children—Dose must be determined by your doctor.

Missed dose—If you miss a dose of this medicine, do not take the missed dose at all and do not double the next one. Instead, go back to your regular dosing schedule and check with your doctor.

Storage—To store this medicine:

- Keep out of the reach of children.
- Store away from heat and direct light.
- Do not store in the bathroom, near the kitchen sink, or in other damp places. Heat or moisture may cause the medicine to break down.
- Do not keep outdated medicine or medicine no longer needed. Be sure that any discarded medicine is out of the reach of children.

Precautions While Using This Medicine

It is very important that your doctor check your progress at regular visits to make sure that this medicine is working properly and to check for unwanted effects.

Do not drink alcohol while using this medicine. Alcohol can increase the chance of liver problems.

Some patients who take methotrexate may become more sensitive to sunlight than they are normally. When you first begin taking methotrexate, avoid too much sun and do not use a sunlamp until you see how you react to the sun, especially if you tend to burn easily. In case of a severe burn, check with your doctor. This is especially important if you are taking this medicine for psoriasis because sunlight can make the psoriasis worse.

Do not take medicine for inflammation or pain (aspirin or other salicylates, diclofenac, diflunisal, fenoprofen, ibuprofen, indomethacin, ketoprofen, meclofenamate, mefenamic acid, naproxen, phenylbutazone, piroxicam, sulindac, suprofen, tolmetin) without first checking with your doctor. These medicines may increase the effects of methotrexate, which could be harmful.

While you are being treated with methotrexate, and after you stop treatment with it, *do not have any immunizations (vaccinations) without your doctor's approval.* Methotrexate may lower your body's resistance and there is a chance you might get the infection the immunization is meant to prevent. In addition, other persons living in your household should not take or should not have recently taken oral polio vaccine since there is a chance they could pass the polio virus on to you. Also, avoid other persons who have taken oral polio vaccine. Do not get close to them, and do not stay in the same room with them for very long. If you cannot take these precautions, you should consider wearing a protective face mask that covers the nose and mouth.

Methotrexate can lower the number of white blood cells in your blood temporarily, increasing the chance of getting an infection. It can also lower the number of platelets, which are necessary for proper blood clotting. If this occurs, there are certain precautions you can take, especially when your blood count is low, to reduce the risk of infection or bleeding:

- If you can, avoid people with infections. *Check with your doctor immediately* if you think you are getting an infection or if you get a fever or chills, cough or hoarseness, lower back or side pain, or painful or difficult urination.
- *Check with your doctor immediately* if you notice any unusual bleeding or bruising; black, tarry stools; blood in urine or stools; or pinpoint red spots on your skin.
- Be careful when using a regular toothbrush, dental floss, or toothpick. Your medical doctor, dentist, or nurse may recommend other ways to clean your teeth and gums. Check with your medical doctor before having any dental work done.
- Do not touch your eyes or the inside of your nose unless you have just washed your hands and have not touched anything else in the meantime.
- Be careful not to cut yourself when you are using sharp objects such as a safety razor or fingernail or toenail cutters.
- Avoid contact sports or other situations where bruising or injury could occur.

Side Effects of This Medicine

Along with their needed effects, medicines like methotrexate can sometimes cause unwanted effects such as blood problems, kidney problems, stomach or liver problems, loss of hair, and other side effects. These and others are described below. Also, because of the way these medicines act on the body, there is a chance that they might cause other unwanted effects that may not occur until months or years after the medicine is used. These delayed effects may include certain types of cancer, such as leukemia. Discuss these possible effects with your doctor.

Although not all of these side effects may occur, if they do occur they may need medical attention.

Check with your doctor immediately if any of the following side effects occur:

Less common

Diarrhea; reddening of skin; sores in mouth and on lips; stomach pain

Rare

Black, tarry stools; blood in urine or stools; blurred vision; convulsions (seizures); cough or hoarseness; fever or chills; lower back or side pain; painful or difficult urination; pinpoint red spots on skin; shortness of breath; unusual bleeding or bruising

Check with your doctor as soon as possible if any of the following side effects occur:

Rare

Back pain; dark urine; dizziness; drowsiness; headache; unusual tiredness or weakness; yellow eyes or skin

Other side effects may occur that usually do not need medical attention. These side effects may go away during treatment as your body adjusts to the medicine. Also, your health care professional may be able to tell you about ways to prevent or reduce some of these side effects. Check with your health care professional if any of the following side effects continue or are bothersome or if you have any questions about them:

Less common or rare

Acne; boils; loss of appetite; nausea or vomiting; pale skin; skin rash or itching

This medicine may cause a temporary loss of hair in some people. After treatment with methotrexate has ended, normal hair growth should return.

Other side effects not listed above may also occur in some patients. If you notice any other effects, check with your doctor.

Additional Information

Once a medicine has been approved for marketing for a certain use, experience may show that it is also useful for other medical problems. Although these uses are not included in product labeling, methotrexate is used in certain patients with the following medical conditions:

- Psoriatic arthritis
- Systemic dermatomyositis

Other than the above information, there is no additional information relating to proper use, precautions, or side effects for these uses.

Revised: 08/90
Interim revision: 07/08/93; 07/05/94

METHOXSALEN Systemic

Some commonly used brand names are:

In the U.S.—

8-MOP
Oxsoralen-Ultra

In Canada—

Oxsoralen
Ultra MOP

Description

Methoxsalen (meth-OX-a-len) belongs to the group of medicines called psoralens. It is used along with ultraviolet light (found in sunlight and some special lamps) in a treatment called PUVA to treat vitiligo, a disease in which skin color is lost, and psoriasis, a skin condition associated with red and scaly patches.

Methoxsalen is also used with ultraviolet light in the treatment of white blood cells. This treatment is called photopheresis and is used to treat the skin problems associated with mycosis fungoides, which is a type of lymphoma.

Methoxsalen may also be used for other conditions as determined by your doctor.

This medicine is available only with your doctor's prescription, in the following dosage forms:

Oral

- Hard gelatin capsules (U.S. and Canada)
- Soft gelatin capsules (U.S. and Canada)

Before Using This Medicine

Methoxsalen is a very strong medicine that increases the skin's sensitivity to sunlight. In addition to causing serious sunburns if not properly used, it has been reported to increase the chance of skin cancer and cataracts. Also, like too much sunlight, PUVA can cause premature aging of the skin. Therefore, methoxsalen should be used only as directed and it should *not* be used simply for suntanning. Before using this medicine, be sure that you have discussed its use with your doctor.

In deciding to use a medicine, the risks of using the medicine must be weighed against the good it will do. This is a decision you and your doctor will make. For methoxsalen, the following should be considered:

Allergies—Tell your doctor if you have ever had any unusual or allergic reaction to methoxsalen. Also tell your health care professional if you are allergic to any other substances, such as foods, preservatives, or dyes.

Diet—Eating certain foods while you are taking methoxsalen may increase your skin's sensitivity to sunlight. To help prevent this, avoid eating limes, figs, parsley, parsnips, mustard, carrots, and celery while you are being treated with this medicine.

Pregnancy—Studies on effects in pregnancy have not been done in either humans or animals.

Breast-feeding—It is not known whether methoxsalen passes into breast milk. Although most medicines pass into breast milk in small amounts, many of them may be used safely while breast-feeding. Mothers who are using this medicine and who wish to breast-feed should discuss this with their doctor.

Children—Some of the side effects are more likely to occur in children up to 12 years of age, since these children may be more sensitive to the effects of methoxsalen.

Older adults—Many medicines have not been studied specifically in older people. Therefore, it may not be known whether they work exactly the same way they do in younger adults or if they cause different side effects or problems in older people. There is no specific information comparing use of methoxsalen in the elderly with use in other age groups.

Other medicines—Although certain medicines should not be used together at all, in other cases two different medicines may be used together even if an interaction might occur. In these cases, your doctor may want to change the dose, or other precautions may be necessary. When you are using methoxsalen, it is especially important that your health care professional know if you are using the following:

- Arsenicals or recent treatment with x-rays, or cancer medicines or plans to have x-rays in the near future—Arsenicals, x-rays and cancer medicines increase the chance of side effects from treatment with PUVA

Other medical problems—The presence of other medical problems may affect the use of methoxsalen. Make sure you tell your doctor if you have any other medical problems, especially:

- Allergy to sunlight (or family history of) or
- Infection or
- Lupus erythematosus or
- Porphyria or
- Skin cancer (history of) or
- Skin conditions (other) or
- Stomach problems—Use of PUVA may make the condition worse
- Eye problems, such as cataracts or loss of the lens of the eye—The light treatment may make the condition worse or may cause damage to the eye
- Heart or blood vessel disease (severe)—The heat or prolonged standing associated with each light treatment may make the condition worse
- Liver disease—Condition may cause increased blood levels of the medicine and cause an increase in side effects

Proper Use of This Medicine

Methoxsalen usually comes with patient directions. Read them carefully before using this medicine.

This medicine may take 6 to 8 weeks to really help your condition. *Do not increase the amount of methoxsalen you are taking or spend extra time in the sunlight or under an ultraviolet lamp.* This will not make the medicine act any more quickly and may result in a serious burn.

If this medicine upsets your stomach:

- Patients taking the hard gelatin capsules may take them with food or milk.

- Patients taking the soft gelatin capsules may take them with low fat food or low fat milk.

Dosing—The dose of methoxsalen will be different for different patients. *Follow your doctor's orders or the directions on the label.* The following information includes only the average doses of methoxsalen. *If your dose is different, do not change it* unless your doctor tells you to do so.

The number of capsules that you take depends on the strength of the medicine. Also, *the number of doses you take each day, the time allowed between doses, and the length of time you take the medicine depend on the medical problem for which you are taking methoxsalen.*

- For *oral* dosage form (hard gelatin capsule):
  - —For vitiligo:
    - Adults and children 12 years of age and over—20 milligrams (mg) per day taken two to four hours before ultraviolet light A (UVA) exposure. This treatment (methoxsalen and UVA) is given two or three times a week with the treatment spaced at least forty-eight hours apart.
    - Children up to 12 years of age—Use and dose must be determined by your doctor.
  - —For psoriasis:
    - Adults and children 12 years of age and over—Dose is based on body weight and must be determined by your doctor. However, the usual dose is 0.6 mg per kilogram (kg) (0.27 mg per pound) of body weight taken two hours before UVA exposure. This treatment (methoxsalen and UVA) is given two or three times a week with the treatment spaced at least forty-eight hours apart.
    - Children up to 12 years of age—Use and dose must be determined by your doctor.
- For *oral* dosage form (soft gelatin capsule):
  - —For psoriasis:
    - Adults and children 12 years of age and over—Dose is based on body weight and must be determined by your doctor. The usual dose is 0.4 mg per kg (0.18 mg per pound) of body weight taken one and one-half to two hours before UVA exposure. This treatment (methoxsalen and UVA) is given two or three times a week, with the treatment spaced at least forty-eight hours apart.
    - Children up to 12 years of age—Use and dose must be determined by your doctor.

Missed dose—If you are late in taking, or miss taking, a dose of this medicine, notify your doctor so your light treatment can be rescheduled. Remember that exposure to sunlight or ultraviolet light must take place a certain number of hours *after* you take the medicine or it will not work. For patients taking the hard gelatin capsules, this is 2 to 4 hours. For patients taking the soft gelatin capsules, this is 1½ to 2 hours. If you have any questions about this, check with your doctor.

Storage—To store this medicine:

- Keep out of the reach of children.
- Store away from heat and direct light.
- Do not store in the bathroom, near the kitchen sink, or in other damp places. Heat or moisture may cause the medicine to break down.
- Do not keep outdated medicine or medicine no longer needed. Be sure that any discarded medicine is out of the reach of children.

Precautions While Using This Medicine

Your doctor should check your progress at regular visits to make sure this medicine is working and that it does not cause unwanted effects. Eye examinations should be included.

This medicine increases the sensitivity of your skin and lips to sunlight. Therefore, *exposure to the sun, even through window glass or on a cloudy day, could cause a serious burn.* If you must go out during the daylight hours:

- *Before each treatment, cover your skin for at least 24 hours* by wearing protective clothing, such as long-sleeved shirts, full-length slacks, wide-brimmed hat, and gloves. In addition, *protect your lips with a special sun block lipstick that has a skin protection factor (SPF) of at least 15.* Check with your doctor before using sun block products on other parts of your body before a treatment, since sun block products should not be used on the areas of your skin that are to be treated.
- *After each treatment, cover your skin for at least 8 hours* by wearing protective clothing. In addition, use a sun block product that has a skin protection factor (SPF) of at least 15 on your lips and on those areas of your body that cannot be covered.

If you have any questions about this, check with your health care professional.

Your skin may continue to be sensitive to sunlight for some time after treatment with this medicine. Use extra caution for at least 48 hours following each treatment if you plan to spend any time in the sun. In addition, do not sunbathe anytime during your course of treatment with methoxsalen.

For 24 hours after you take each dose of methoxsalen, your eyes should be protected during daylight hours with special wraparound sunglasses that totally block or absorb ultraviolet light (ordinary sunglasses are not adequate). This is to prevent cataracts. Your doctor will tell you what kind of sunglasses to use. These glasses should be worn even in indirect light, such as light coming through window glass or on a cloudy day.

This medicine may cause your skin to become dry or itchy. *However, check with your doctor before applying anything to your skin to treat this problem.*

Side Effects of This Medicine

Along with its needed effects, a medicine may cause some unwanted effects. Although not all of these side effects

may occur, if they do occur they may need medical attention.

Check with your doctor immediately if you think you have taken an overdose or if any of the following side effects occur, since they may indicate a serious burn:

Blistering and peeling of skin; reddened, sore skin; swelling (especially of feet or lower legs)

Other side effects may occur that usually do not need medical attention. These side effects may go away during treatment as your body adjusts to the medicine. However, check with your doctor if any of the following side effects continue for more than 48 hours or are bothersome:

More common

Itching of skin; nausea

Less common

Dizziness; headache; mental depression; nervousness; trouble in sleeping

Treatment with this medicine usually causes a slight reddening of your skin 24 to 48 hours after the treatment. This is an expected effect and is no cause for concern. However, check with your doctor right away if your skin becomes sore and red or blistered.

There is an increased risk of developing skin cancer after use of methoxsalen. You should check your body regularly and show your doctor any skin sores that do not heal, new skin growths, and skin growths that have changed in the way they look or feel.

Premature aging of the skin may occur as a result of prolonged methoxsalen therapy. This effect is permanent and is similar to what happens when a person sunbathes for long periods of time.

Other side effects not listed above may also occur in some patients. If you notice any other effects, check with your doctor.

Revised: 06/24/94

METHOXSALEN Topical

Some commonly used brand names are:

In the U.S.—

Oxsoralen Lotion

In Canada—

Oxsoralen Lotion
UltraMOP Lotion

Description

Methoxsalen (meth-OX-a-len) belongs to the group of medicines called psoralens. It is used along with ultraviolet light (found in sunlight and some special lamps) in a treatment called psoralen plus ultraviolet light A (PUVA) to treat vitiligo, a disease in which skin color is lost. Methoxsalen may also be used for other conditions as determined by your doctor.

Methoxsalen is available only with a prescription and is to be administered by or under the direct supervision of your doctor, in the following dosage form:

Topical

- Topical solution (U.S. and Canada)

Before Using This Medicine

Methoxsalen is a very strong medicine that increases the skin's sensitivity to sunlight. In addition to causing serious sunburns if not properly used, it has been reported to increase the chance of skin cancer. Also, like too much sunlight, PUVA can cause premature aging of the skin. Therefore, methoxsalen should be used only as directed and should *not* be used simply for suntanning. Before using this medicine, be sure that you have discussed its use with your doctor.

In deciding to use a medicine, the risks of using the medicine must be weighed against the good it will do. This is a decision you and your doctor will make. For topical methoxsalen, the following should be considered:

Allergies—Tell your doctor if you have ever had any unusual or allergic reaction to methoxsalen. Also tell your health care professional if you are allergic to any other substances, such as foods, preservatives, or dyes.

Diet—Eating certain foods while you are using methoxsalen may increase your skin's sensitivity to sunlight. To help prevent this, avoid eating limes, figs, parsley, parsnips, mustard, carrots, and celery while you are being treated with this medicine.

Pregnancy—Studies on effects in pregnancy have not been done in either humans or animals.

Breast-feeding—It is not known whether methoxsalen passes into breast milk. Although most medicines pass into breast milk in small amounts, many of them may be used safely while breast-feeding. Mothers who are taking this medicine and who wish to breast-feed should discuss this with their doctor.

Children—Studies on this medicine have been done only in adult patients, and there is no specific information comparing use of methoxsalen in children up to 12 years of age with use in other age groups.

Older adults—Many medicines have not been studied specifically in older people. Therefore, it may not be known whether they work exactly the same way they do in younger adults or if they cause different side effects or problems in older people. There is no specific information comparing use of topical methoxsalen in the elderly with use in other age groups.

Other medicines—Although certain medicines should not be used together at all, in other cases two different med-

icines may be used together even if an interaction might occur. In these cases, your doctor may want to change the dose, or other precautions may be necessary. When you are using topical methoxsalen, it is especially important that your health care professional know if you are receiving the following:

- Recent treatment with x-rays or cancer medicines or plans to have x-rays in the near future—Increases the chance of side effects from treatment with PUVA

Other medical problems—The presence of other medical problems may affect the use of topical methoxsalen. Make sure you tell your doctor if you have any other medical problems, especially:

- Allergy to sunlight (or family history of) or
- Infection or
- Lupus erythematosus or
- Porphyria or
- Skin cancer (history of) or
- Skin conditions (other)—Use of PUVA may make the condition worse
- Heart or blood vessel disease (severe)—The heat or prolonged standing associated with each light treatment may make the condition worse

Proper Use of This Medicine

Use this medicine only under the direct supervision of your doctor.

After UVA exposure, wash the treated area of skin with soap and water. Then use a sunscreen or wear protective clothing to protect the area.

Dosing—Follow your doctor's directions in using this medicine. The following information includes only the average doses of methoxsalen. *If your dose is different, do not change it* unless your doctor tells you to do so.

- For *topical solution* dosage form:
  - For vitiligo:
    - Adults and children 12 years of age and over—Apply to the affected area of the skin and allow to dry for one to two minutes, then apply again within two to two and one-half hours before UVA exposure.
    - Children under 12 years of age—Use and dose must be determined by your doctor.

Precautions While Using This Medicine

It is important that you visit your doctor as directed for treatments and to have your progress checked.

This medicine increases the sensitivity of the treated areas of your skin to sunlight. Therefore, *exposure to the sun, even through window glass or on a cloudy day, could cause a serious burn.* After each light treatment, thoroughly wash the treated areas of your skin. Also, if you must go out during daylight hours, cover the treated areas of your skin for at least 12 to 48 hours following treatment by wearing protective clothing or a sun block product that has a skin protection factor (SPF) of at least 15. Some patients may require a product with a higher SPF number, especially if they have a fair complexion. If you have any questions about this, check with your health care professional.

The treated areas of your skin may continue to be sensitive to sunlight for some time after treatment with this medicine. Use extra caution for at least 72 hours following each treatment if you plan to spend any time in the sun. In addition, do not sunbathe anytime during your course of treatment with methoxsalen.

This medicine may cause your skin to become dry or itchy. *However, check with your doctor before applying anything to your skin to treat this problem.*

Side Effects of This Medicine

Along with its needed effects, a medicine may cause some unwanted effects. Although not all of these side effects may occur, if they do occur they may need medical attention.

Check with your doctor immediately if any of the following side effects occur, since they may indicate a serious burn:

Blistering and peeling of skin; reddened, sore skin; swelling, especially of the feet or lower legs

There is an increased risk of developing skin cancer after use of methoxsalen. You should check the treated areas of your body regularly and show your doctor any skin sores that do not heal, new skin growths, and skin growths that have changed in the way they look or feel.

Premature aging of the skin may occur as a result of prolonged methoxsalen therapy. This effect is permanent and is similar to the result of sunbathing for long periods of time.

Other side effects not listed above may also occur in some patients. If you notice any other effects, check with your doctor.

Additional Information

Once a medicine has been approved for marketing for a certain use, experience may show that it is also useful for other medical problems. Although these uses are not included in product labeling, topical methoxsalen is used in certain patients with the following medical conditions:

- Alopecia areata
- Eczema
- Inflammatory dermatoses
- Lichen planus
- Mycosis fungoides
- Need to increase tolerance of skin to sunlight
- Psoriasis

Other than the above information, there is no additional information relating to proper use, precautions, or side effects for these uses.

Revised: 05/26/94

METHYLDOPA Systemic

Some commonly used brand names are:

In the U.S.—

Aldomet

Generic name product may also be available.

In Canada—

Aldomet
Apo-Methyldopa
Nu-Medopa
Dopamet
Novomedopa

Description

Methyldopa (meth-ill-DOE-pa) belongs to the general class of medicines called antihypertensives. It is used to treat high blood pressure (hypertension).

High blood pressure adds to the work load of the heart and arteries. If it continues for a long time, the heart and arteries may not function properly. This can damage the blood vessels of the brain, heart, and kidneys, resulting in a stroke, heart failure, or kidney failure. High blood pressure may also increase the risk of heart attacks. These problems may be less likely to occur if blood pressure is controlled.

Methyldopa works by controlling impulses along certain nerve pathways. As a result, it relaxes blood vessels so that blood passes through them more easily. This helps to lower blood pressure.

Methyldopa is available only with your doctor's prescription, in the following dosage forms:

Oral
- Oral suspension (U.S.)
- Tablets (U.S. and Canada)

Parenteral
- Injection (U.S. and Canada)

Before Using This Medicine

In deciding to use a medicine, the risks of taking the medicine must be weighed against the good it will do. This is a decision you and your doctor will make. For methyldopa, the following should be considered:

Allergies—Tell your doctor if you have ever had any unusual or allergic reaction to methyldopa. Also tell your health care professional if you are allergic to any other substances, such as foods, sulfites or other preservatives, or dyes. Some methyldopa products may contain sulfites. Your health care professional can help you avoid products that may cause a problem.

Pregnancy—Methyldopa has not been studied in pregnant women in the first and second trimesters (the first 6 months of pregnancy). However, studies in pregnant women during the third trimester (the last 3 months of pregnancy) have not shown that methyldopa causes birth defects or other problems.

Breast-feeding—Although methyldopa passes into breast milk, it has not been reported to cause problems in nursing babies.

Children—Although there is no specific information comparing use of methyldopa in children with use in other age groups, this medicine is not expected to cause different side effects or problems in children than it does in adults.

Older adults—Dizziness or lightheadedness and drowsiness may be more likely to occur in the elderly, who are more sensitive to the effects of methyldopa.

Other medicines—Although certain medicines should not be used together at all, in other cases two different medicines may be used together even if an interaction might occur. In these cases, your doctor may want to change the dose, or other precautions may be necessary. When you are taking methyldopa, it is especially important that your health care professional know if you are taking any of the following:

- Monoamine oxidase (MAO) inhibitors (furazolidone [e.g., Furoxone], isocarboxazid [e.g., Marplan], phenelzine [e.g., Nardil], procarbazine [e.g., Matulane], selegiline [e.g., Eldepryl], tranylcypromine [e.g., Parnate])—Taking methyldopa while you are taking or within 2 weeks of taking MAO inhibitors may cause nervousness in patients receiving MAO inhibitors; headache, severe high blood pressure, and hallucinations have been reported

Other medical problems—The presence of other medical problems may affect the use of methyldopa. Make sure you tell your doctor if you have any other medical problems, especially:

- Angina (chest pain) or
- Parkinson's disease—Methyldopa may make these conditions worse
- Kidney disease or
- Liver disease—Effects of methyldopa may be increased because of slower removal from the body
- Mental depression (history of)—Methyldopa can cause mental depression
- Pheochromocytoma—Methyldopa may interfere with tests for the condition; in addition, there have been reports of increased blood pressure
- If you have taken methyldopa in the past and developed liver problems

Proper Use of This Medicine

In addition to the use of the medicine your doctor has prescribed, treatment for your high blood pressure may include weight control and care in the types of foods you eat, especially foods high in sodium. Your doctor will tell you which of these are most important for you. You should check with your doctor before changing your diet.

Many patients who have high blood pressure will not notice any signs of the problem. In fact, many may feel normal. It is very important that you *take your medicine exactly as directed* and that you keep your appointments with your doctor even if you feel well.

Remember that methyldopa will not cure your high blood pressure but it does help control it. Therefore, you must continue to take it as directed if you expect to lower your blood pressure and keep it down. *You may have to take high blood pressure medicine for the rest of your life.* If high blood pressure is not treated, it can cause serious problems such as heart failure, blood vessel disease, stroke, or kidney disease.

To help you remember to take your medicine, try to get into the habit of taking it at the same time each day.

Dosing—The dose of methyldopa will be different for different patients. *Follow your doctor's orders or the directions on the label.* The following information includes only the average doses of methyldopa. *If your dose is different, do not change it* unless your doctor tells you to do so.

The number of tablets or teaspoonfuls of suspension that you take depends on the strength of the medicine.

- For *oral* dosage form (suspension or tablets):
  - —For high blood pressure:
    - Adults—250 milligrams (mg) to 2 grams a day. This is divided into two to four doses.
    - Children—Dose is based on body weight or size and must be determined by your doctor. The usual dose is 10 mg per kilogram (kg) (4.5 mg per pound) of body weight a day. This is divided into two to four doses. Your doctor may increase the dose as needed.
- For *injection* dosage form:
  - —For high blood pressure:
    - Adults—250 to 500 mg mixed in 100 milliliters (mL) of solution (5% dextrose) and slowly injected into a vein every six hours as needed.
    - Children—Dose is based on body weight and must be determined by your doctor. The usual dose is 20 to 40 mg per kg (9.1 to 18.2 mg per pound) of body weight. This is mixed in a solution (5% dextrose) and slowly injected into a vein every six hours as needed.

Missed dose—If you miss a dose of this medicine, take it as soon as possible. However, if it is almost time for your next dose, skip the missed dose and go back to your regular dosing schedule. Do not double doses.

Storage—To store this medicine:

- Keep out of the reach of children.
- Store away from heat and direct light.
- Do not store in the bathroom, near the kitchen sink, or in other damp places. Heat or moisture may cause the medicine to break down.
- Keep the oral liquid form of this medicine from freezing.
- Do not keep outdated medicine or medicine no longer needed. Be sure that any discarded medicine is out of the reach of children.

Precautions While Using This Medicine

It is important that your doctor check your progress at regular visits to make sure that this medicine is working properly.

Do not take other medicines unless they have been discussed with your doctor. This especially includes over-the-counter (nonprescription) medicines for appetite control, asthma, colds, cough, hay fever, or sinus problems, since they may tend to increase your blood pressure.

If you have a fever and there seems to be no reason for it, check with your doctor. This is especially important during the first few weeks you take methyldopa, since fever may be a sign of a serious reaction to this medicine.

Before having any kind of surgery (including dental surgery) or emergency treatment, make sure the medical doctor or dentist in charge knows that you are taking this medicine.

Methyldopa may cause some people to become drowsy or less alert than they are normally. This is more likely to happen when you begin to take it or when you increase the amount of medicine you are taking. *Make sure you know how you react to this medicine before you drive, use machines, or do anything else that could be dangerous if you are not alert.*

Dizziness, lightheadedness, or fainting may occur, especially when you get up from a lying or sitting position. Getting up slowly may help, but if the problem continues or gets worse, check with your doctor.

Methyldopa may cause dryness of the mouth. For temporary relief, use sugarless candy or gum, melt bits of ice in your mouth, or use a saliva substitute. However, if your mouth continues to feel dry for more than 2 weeks, check with your medical doctor or dentist. Continuing dryness of the mouth may increase the chance of dental disease, including tooth decay, gum disease, and fungus infections.

Tell the doctor in charge that you are taking this medicine before you have any medical tests. The results of some tests may be affected by this medicine.

Side Effects of This Medicine

Along with its needed effects, a medicine may cause some unwanted effects. Although not all of these side effects may occur, if they do occur they may need medical attention.

Check with your doctor immediately if the following side effect occurs:

Less common

Fever, shortly after starting to take this medicine

Check with your doctor as soon as possible if any of the following side effects occur:

More common

Swelling of feet or lower legs

Less common

Mental depression or anxiety; nightmares or unusually vivid dreams

Rare

Dark or amber urine; diarrhea or stomach cramps (severe or continuing); fever, chills, troubled breathing, and fast heartbeat; general feeling of discomfort or illness or weakness; joint pain; pale stools; skin rash or itching; stomach pain (severe) with nausea and vomiting; tiredness or weakness after having taken this medicine for several weeks (continuing); yellow eyes or skin

Other side effects may occur that usually do not need medical attention. These side effects may go away during treatment as your body adjusts to the medicine. However, check with your doctor if any of the following side effects continue or are bothersome:

More common

Drowsiness; dryness of mouth; headache

Less common

Decreased sexual ability or interest in sex; diarrhea; dizziness or lightheadedness when getting up from a lying or sitting position; nausea or vomiting; numbness, tingling, pain, or weakness in hands or feet; slow heartbeat; stuffy nose; swelling of breasts or unusual milk production

Other side effects not listed above may also occur in some patients. If you notice any other effects, check with your doctor.

Revised: 07/22/96

METHYLDOPA AND THIAZIDE DIURETICS Systemic

Some commonly used brand names are:

In the U.S.—

Aldoclor[1]
Aldoril[2]

In Canada—

Aldoril[2]
Novodoparil[2]
PMS Dopazide[2]
Supres[1]

Note: For quick reference, the following medicines are numbered to match the corresponding brand names.

This information applies to the following medicines:

1. Methyldopa (meth-ill-DOE-pa) and Chlorothiazide (klor-oh-THYE-a-zide)‡
2. Methyldopa and Hydrochlorothiazide (hye-droe-klor-oh-THYE-a-zide)‡

‡Generic name product may also be available in the U.S.

Description

Combinations of methyldopa and a thiazide diuretic (chlorothiazide or hydrochlorothiazide) are used to treat high blood pressure (hypertension).

High blood pressure adds to the workload of the heart and arteries. If it continues for a long time, the heart and arteries may not function properly. This can damage the blood vessels of the brain, heart, and kidneys, resulting in a stroke, heart failure, or kidney failure. High blood pressure may also increase the risk of heart attacks. These problems may be less likely to occur if blood pressure is controlled.

Methyldopa works by controlling nerve impulses along certain nerve pathways. As a result, it relaxes blood vessels so that blood passes through them more easily. Thiazide diuretics help reduce the amount of water in the body by increasing the flow of urine. These actions help to lower blood pressure.

This medicine is available only with your doctor's prescription, in the following dosage forms:

Oral

Methyldopa and Chlorothiazide
- Tablets (U.S. and Canada)

Methyldopa and Hydrochlorothiazide
- Tablets (U.S. and Canada)

Before Using This Medicine

In deciding to use a medicine, the risks of taking the medicine must be weighed against the good it will do. This is a decision you and your doctor will make. For methyldopa and thiazide diuretics, the following should be considered:

Allergies—Tell your doctor if you have ever had any unusual or allergic reaction to methyldopa, sulfonamides (sulfa drugs), bumetanide, furosemide, indapamide, acetazolamide, dichlorphenamide, methazolamide, or thiazide diuretics (water pills). Also tell your health care professional if you are allergic to any other substances, such as foods, sulfites or other preservatives, or dyes.

Pregnancy—Studies in humans have not shown that methyldopa causes birth defects or other problems. However, when thiazide diuretics are used during pregnancy, they may cause side effects including jaundice, blood problems, and low potassium in the newborn infant. Thiazide diuretics have not been shown to cause birth defects.

Breast-feeding—This medicine passes into breast milk. Thiazide diuretics may decrease the flow of breast milk. Therefore, you should avoid use of thiazide diuretics during the first month of breast-feeding.

Children—Although there is no specific information comparing use of this medicine in children with use in other age groups, it is not expected to cause different side effects or problems in children than it does in adults.

Older adults—Dizziness or lightheadedness, drowsiness, or signs of too much potassium loss may be more likely to occur in the elderly, who are more sensitive to the effects of methyldopa and thiazide diuretics.

Other medicines—Although certain medicines should not be used together at all, in other cases two different medicines may be used together even if an interaction might occur. In these cases, your doctor may want to change the dose, or other precautions may be necessary. When you are taking methyldopa and thiazide diuretics, it is especially important that your health care professional know if you are taking any of the following:

- Digitalis glycosides (heart medicine)—Thiazide diuretics may cause low potassium in the blood, which can lead to symptoms of digitalis toxicity
- Lithium (e.g., Lithane)—Risk of lithium overdose, even at usual doses, may be increased
- Monoamine oxidase (MAO) inhibitors (furazolidone [e.g., Furoxone], isocarboxazid [e.g., Marplan], phenelzine [e.g., Nardil], procarbazine [e.g., Matulane], selegiline [e.g., Eldepryl], tranylcypromine [e.g., Parnate])—Taking methyldopa while you are taking or within 2 weeks of

taking MAO inhibitors may cause nervousness; headache, severe high blood pressure, and hallucinations have been reported

Other medical problems—The presence of other medical problems may affect the use of methyldopa and thiazide diuretics. Make sure you tell your doctor if you have any other medical problems, especially:

- Angina (chest pain)—Methyldopa may worsen the condition
- Diabetes mellitus (sugar diabetes)—Thiazide diuretics may change the amount of diabetes medicine needed
- Gout (history of)—Thiazide diuretics may increase the amount of uric acid in the blood, which can lead to gout
- High cholesterol—Thiazide diuretics may raise cholesterol levels
- Kidney disease—Effects of methyldopa and thiazide diuretics may be increased because of slower removal from the body. If severe, thiazide diuretics may not work
- Liver disease—Effects of methyldopa may be increased because of slower removal from the body. If thiazide diuretics cause loss of too much water from the body, liver disease can become much worse
- Lupus erythematosus (history of)—Thiazide diuretics may worsen the condition
- Mental depression (history of)—Methyldopa can cause mental depression
- Pancreatitis (inflammation of the pancreas)
- Parkinson's disease—Methyldopa may worsen the condition
- Pheochromocytoma—Methyldopa may interfere with tests for the condition; in addition, there have been reports of increased blood pressure
- If you have taken methyldopa in the past and developed liver problems

Proper Use of This Medicine

In addition to the use of the medicine your doctor has prescribed, appropriate treatment for your high blood pressure may include weight control and care in the types of foods you eat, especially foods high in sodium. Your doctor will tell you which factors are most important for you. You should check with your doctor before changing your diet.

Many patients who have high blood pressure will not notice any signs of the problem. In fact, many may feel normal. It is very important *that you take your medicine exactly as directed* and that you keep your appointments with your doctor even if you feel well.

Remember that this medicine will not cure your high blood pressure but it does help control it. Therefore, you must continue to take it as directed if you expect to lower your blood pressure and keep it down. *You may have to take high blood pressure medicine for the rest of your life.* If high blood pressure is not treated, it can cause serious problems such as heart failure, blood vessel disease, stroke, or kidney disease.

This medicine may cause you to have an unusual feeling of tiredness when you begin to take it. You may also notice an increase in the amount of urine or in your frequency of urination. After taking the medicine for a while, these effects should lessen. In general, to keep the increase in urine from affecting your sleep:

- If you are to take a single dose a day, take it in the morning after breakfast.
- If you are to take more than one dose a day, take the last dose no later than 6 p.m., unless otherwise directed by your doctor.

However, it is best to plan your dose or doses according to a schedule that will least affect your personal activities and sleep. Ask your health care professional to help you plan the best time to take this medicine.

To help you remember to take your medicine, try to get into the habit of taking it at the same time each day.

Dosing—The dose of methyldopa and thiazide diuretic combinations will be different for different patients. *Follow your doctor's orders or the directions on the label.* The following information includes only the average doses of methyldopa and thiazide diuretic combinations. *If your dose is different, do not change it* unless your doctor tells you to do so:

For methyldopa and chlorothiazide

- For *oral* dosage form (tablets):
  —Adults: Two to four tablets a day, taken as a single dose or in divided doses.
  —Children: Dose must be determined by your doctor.

For methyldopa and hydrochlorothiazide

- For *oral* dosage form (tablets):
  —Adults: Two to four tablets a day, taken as a single dose or in divided doses.
  —Children: Dose must be determined by your doctor.

Missed dose—If you miss a dose of this medicine, take it as soon as possible. However, if it is almost time for your next dose, skip the missed dose and go back to your regular dosing schedule. Do not double doses.

Storage—To store this medicine:

- Keep out of the reach of children.
- Store away from heat and direct light.
- Do not store in the bathroom, near the kitchen sink, or in other damp places. Heat or moisture may cause the medicine to break down.
- Do not keep outdated medicine or medicine no longer needed. Be sure that any discarded medicine is out of the reach of children.

Precautions While Using This Medicine

It is important that your doctor check your progress at regular visits to make sure that this medicine is working properly.

Do not take other medicines unless they have been discussed with your doctor. This especially includes over-the-counter (nonprescription) medicines for appetite control, asthma, colds, cough, hay fever, or sinus problems, since they may tend to increase your blood pressure.

This medicine may cause a loss of potassium from your body:

- To help prevent this, your doctor may want you to:
  - —eat or drink foods that have a high potassium content (for example, orange or other citrus fruit juices), or
  - —take a potassium supplement, or
  - —take another medicine to help prevent the loss of the potassium in the first place.
- It is very important to follow these directions. Also, it is important not to change your diet on your own. This is more important if you are already on a special diet (as for diabetes), or if you are taking a potassium supplement or a medicine to reduce potassium loss. Extra potassium may not be necessary and, in some cases, too much potassium could be harmful.

Check with your doctor if you become sick and have severe or continuing vomiting or diarrhea. These problems may cause you to lose additional water and potassium.

Before having any kind of surgery (including dental surgery) or emergency treatment, tell the medical doctor or dentist in charge that you are taking this medicine.

If you have a fever and there seems to be no reason for it, check with your doctor. This is especially important during the first few weeks you take this medicine since fever may be a sign of a serious reaction to methyldopa.

This medicine may cause some people to become drowsy or less alert than they are normally. This is more likely to happen when you begin to take it or when you increase the amount of medicine you are taking. *Make sure you know how you react to this medicine before you drive, use machines, or do anything else that could be dangerous if you are not alert.*

Dizziness, lightheadedness, or fainting may occur, especially when you get up from a lying or sitting position. Getting up slowly may help, but if the problem continues or gets worse, check with your doctor.

The dizziness, lightheadedness, or fainting is also more likely to occur if you drink alcohol, stand for long periods of time, exercise, or if the weather is hot. Drinking alcoholic beverages may also make the drowsiness worse. *While you are taking this medicine, be careful in the amount of alcohol you drink.* Also, use extra care during exercise or hot weather or if you must stand for long periods of time.

For *diabetic patients*:

- This medicine may raise blood sugar levels. While you are using this medicine, be especially careful in testing for sugar in your urine. If you have any questions about this, check with your doctor.

This medicine may cause dryness of the mouth. For temporary relief, use sugarless candy or gum, melt bits of ice in your mouth, or use a saliva substitute. However, if your mouth continues to feel dry for more than 2 weeks, check with your medical doctor or dentist. Continuing dryness of the mouth may increase the chance of dental disease, including tooth decay, gum disease, and fungus infections.

Thiazide diuretics may cause your skin to be more sensitive to sunlight than it is normally. Exposure to sunlight, even for brief periods of time, may cause a skin rash, itching, redness or other discoloration of the skin, or a severe sunburn. When you begin taking this medicine:

- Stay out of direct sunlight, especially between the hours of 10:00 a.m. and 3:00 p.m., if possible.
- Wear protective clothing, including a hat. Also, wear sunglasses.
- Apply a sun block product that has a skin protection factor (SPF) of at least 15. Some patients may require a product with a higher SPF number, especially if they have a fair complexion. If you have any questions about this, check with your health care professional.
- Apply a sun block lipstick that has an SPF of at least 15 to protect your lips.
- Do not use a sunlamp or tanning bed or booth.

If you have a severe reaction from the sun, check with your doctor.

Before you have any medical tests, tell the doctor in charge that you are taking this medicine. The results of some tests may be affected by this medicine.

Side Effects of This Medicine

Along with its needed effects, a medicine may cause some unwanted effects. Although not all of these side effects may occur, if they do occur they may need medical attention.

Check with your doctor immediately if the following side effect occurs:

Rare

Unexplained fever shortly after starting to take this medicine

Check with your doctor as soon as possible if any of the following side effects occur, especially since some of them may mean that your body is losing too much potassium:

Signs and symptoms of too much potassium loss

Dry mouth; increased thirst; irregular heartbeats; muscle cramps or pain; nausea or vomiting; unusual tiredness or weakness; weak pulse

Less common

Mental depression or anxiety; nightmares or unusually vivid dreams

Rare

Cough or hoarseness; dark or amber urine; diarrhea or stomach cramps (severe or continuing); fever, chills, troubled breathing, and fast heartbeat; general feeling of discomfort or illness or weakness; joint pain; lower back or side pain; painful or difficult urination; pale stools; skin rash, hives, or itching; stomach pain (severe) with nausea and vomiting; tiredness or weakness after having taken this medicine for several weeks (continuing); yellow eyes or skin

Other side effects may occur that usually do not need medical attention. These side effects may go away during treatment as your body adjusts to the medicine. However,

check with your doctor if any of the following side effects continue or are bothersome:

More common

Dizziness or lightheadedness when getting up from a lying or sitting position; drowsiness; dryness of mouth; headache

Less common

Decreased sexual ability or interest in sex; diarrhea; increased sensitivity of skin to sunlight (skin rash, itching, redness or other discoloration of skin or severe sunburn after exposure to sunlight); loss of appetite; numbness, tingling, pain, or weakness in hands or feet; slow heartbeat; stuffy nose; swelling of breasts or unusual milk production

Other side effects not listed above may also occur in some patients. If you notice any other effects, check with your doctor.

Revised: 04/13/93

METHYLPHENIDATE Systemic

Some commonly used brand names are:

In the U.S.—

Ritalin
Ritalin-SR

Generic name product may also be available.

In Canada—

PMS-Methylphenidate
Ritalin
Ritalin SR

Description

Methylphenidate (meth-ill-FEN-i-date) belongs to the group of medicines called central stimulants. It is used to treat attention-deficit hyperactivity disorder (ADHD).

Methylphenidate works by increasing attention and decreasing restlessness in children and adults who are overactive, cannot concentrate for very long or are easily distracted, and are impulsive. This medicine is used as part of a total treatment program that also includes social, educational, and psychological treatment.

Methylphenidate is also used in the treatment of narcolepsy (uncontrollable desire for sleep or sudden attacks of deep sleep).

This medicine is available only with a doctor's prescription. Prescriptions cannot be refilled. A new written prescription must be obtained from your doctor each time you or your child needs this medicine.

Methylphenidate is available in the following dosage forms:

Oral

- Tablets (U.S. and Canada)
- Extended-release tablets (U.S. and Canada)

Before Using This Medicine

In deciding to use a medicine, the risks of taking the medicine must be weighed against the good it will do. This is a decision you and your doctor will make. For methylphenidate, the following should be considered:

Allergies—Tell your doctor if you have ever had any unusual or allergic reaction to methylphenidate. Also tell your health care professional if you are allergic to any other substances, such as foods, preservatives, or dyes.

Pregnancy—Studies on effects in pregnancy have not been done in either humans or animals.

Breast-feeding—It is not known whether methylphenidate passes into breast milk.

Children—Loss of appetite, trouble in sleeping, stomach pain, and weight loss, may be especially likely to occur in children, who are usually more sensitive than adults to the effects of methylphenidate. Also, there have been reports of children's growth rate being slowed when methylphenidate was used for a long time. Some doctors recommend drug-free periods during treatment with methylphenidate.

Older adults—Many medicines have not been studied specifically in older people. Therefore, it may not be known whether they work exactly the same way they do in younger adults or if they cause different side effects or problems in older people. There is no specific information comparing use of methylphenidate in the elderly with use in other age groups.

Other medicines—Although certain medicines should not be used together at all, in other cases two different medicines may be used together even if an interaction might occur. In these cases, your doctor may want to change the dose, or other precautions may be necessary. When you are taking methylphenidate, it is especially important that your health care professional know if you are taking any of the following:

- Amantadine (e.g., Symmetrel) or
- Amphetamines or
- Appetite suppressants (diet pills), except fenfluramine (e.g., Pondimin) or
- Caffeine (e.g., NoDoz) or
- Chlophedianol (e.g., Ulone) or
- Cocaine or
- Medicine for asthma or other breathing problems or
- Medicine for colds, sinus problems, hay fever or other allergies (including nose drops or sprays) or
- Nabilone (e.g., Cesamet) or
- Pemoline (e.g., Cylert)—Using these medicines with methylphenidate may cause severe nervousness, irritability, trouble in sleeping, or possibly irregular heartbeat or seizures
- Monoamine oxidase (MAO) inhibitors (furazolidone [e.g., Furoxone], isocarboxazid [e.g., Marplan], phenelzine [e.g., Nardil], procarbazine [e.g., Matulane], selegiline [e.g., Eldepryl], tranylcypromine [e.g., Parnate])—Taking methylphenidate while you are taking or within 2 weeks of taking MAO inhibitors may cause sudden extremely

high blood pressure and severe convulsions; at least 14 days should be allowed between stopping treatment with one medicine and starting treatment with the other
- Pimozide (e.g., Orap)—The cause of tics may be masked

Other medical problems—The presence of other medical problems may affect the use of methylphenidate. Make sure you tell your doctor if you have any other medical problems, especially:
- Alcohol abuse (or history of) or
- Drug abuse or dependence (or history of)—Dependence on methylphenidate may develop
- Epilepsy or other seizure disorders—The risk of convulsions (seizures) may be increased
- Gilles de la Tourette's disorder (or history of) or
- Glaucoma or
- High blood pressure or
- Psychosis or
- Severe anxiety, agitation, tension, or depression or
- Tics (other than Tourette's disorder)—Methylphenidate may make the condition worse

Proper Use of This Medicine

Take this medicine only as directed by your doctor. Do not take more of it, do not take it more often, and do not take it for a longer time than your doctor ordered. If too much is taken, it may become habit-forming.

Take this medicine with or after meals or a snack.

To help prevent trouble in sleeping, take the last dose of the short-acting tablets before 6 p.m., unless otherwise directed by your doctor.

If you think this medicine is not working properly after you have taken it for several weeks, *do not increase the dose.* Instead, check with your doctor.

If you are taking the long-acting form of this medicine:
- These tablets are to be swallowed whole. Do not break, crush, or chew before swallowing.

Dosing—The dose of methylphenidate will be different for different patients. *Follow your doctor's orders or the directions on the label.* The following information includes only the average doses of methylphenidate. *If your dose is different, do not change it* unless your doctor tells you to do so.

The number of tablets that you take depends on the strength of the medicine. Also, *the number of doses you take each day, the time allowed between doses, and the length of time you take the medicine depend on the medical problem for which you are using methylphenidate.*

- For attention-deficit hyperactivity disorder:
  —For *short-acting oral* dosage form (tablets):
    - Adults and teenagers—5 to 20 milligrams (mg) two or three times a day, taken with or after meals.
    - Children 6 years of age and over—To start, 5 mg two times a day, taken with or after breakfast and lunch. Your doctor may increase the dose if needed by 5 to 10 mg a week until symptoms improve or a maximum dose is reached.
    - Children up to 6 years of age—The dose must be determined by the doctor.

  —For *long-acting oral* dosage form (extended-release tablets):
    - Adults and teenagers—20 mg one to three times a day, spaced eight hours apart.
    - Children 6 years of age and over—20 mg one to three times a day, spaced eight hours apart.
    - Children up to 6 years of age—The dose must be determined by the doctor.
- For narcolepsy:
  —For *short-acting oral* dosage form (tablets):
    - Adults and teenagers—5 to 20 mg two or three times a day, taken with or after meals.

  —For *long-acting oral* dosage form (extended-release tablets):
    - Adults and teenagers—20 mg one to three times a day, spaced eight hours apart.

Missed dose—If you miss a dose of this medicine, take it as soon as possible. Then take any remaining doses for that day at regularly spaced intervals. Do not double doses.

Storage—To store this medicine:
- Keep out of the reach of children.
- Store away from heat and direct light.
- Do not store in the bathroom, near the kitchen sink, or in other damp places. Heat or moisture may cause the medicine to break down.
- Do not keep outdated medicine or medicine no longer needed. Be sure that any discarded medicine is out of the reach of children.

Precautions While Using This Medicine

Your doctor should check your progress at regular visits to make sure that this medicine does not cause unwanted effects.

If you will be taking this medicine in large doses for a long time, *do not stop taking it without first checking with your doctor.* Your doctor may want you to reduce gradually the amount you are taking before stopping completely.

If you have been using this medicine for a long time and you think you may have become mentally or physically dependent on it, check with your doctor. Some signs of dependence on methylphenidate are:
- A strong desire or need to continue taking the medicine.
- A need to increase the dose to receive the effects of the medicine.
- Withdrawal side effects (for example, mental depression, unusual behavior, or unusual tiredness or weakness) occurring after the medicine is stopped.

Side Effects of This Medicine

Along with its needed effects, a medicine may cause some unwanted effects. Although not all of these side effects

may occur, if they do occur they may need medical attention.

Check with your doctor as soon as possible if any of the following side effects occur:

More common

Fast heartbeat; increased blood pressure

Less common

Black, tarry stools; blood in urine or stools; chest pain; fever; joint pain; pinpoint red spots on skin; skin rash or hives; uncontrolled movements of the body; unusual bleeding or bruising

Rare

Blurred vision or any change in vision; uncontrolled vocal outbursts and tics (uncontrolled and repeated body movements)

With long-term use or at high doses

Mood or mental changes; weight loss

Symptoms of overdose

Agitation; confusion (severe); convulsions (seizures); dryness of mouth or mucous membranes; false sense of well-being; fast, pounding, or irregular heartbeat; fever; headache (severe); increased blood pressure; increased sweating; large pupils; muscle twitching; overactive reflexes; seeing, hearing, or feeling things that are not there; trembling or tremors; vomiting

Other side effects may occur that usually do not need medical attention. These side effects may go away during treatment as your body adjusts to the medicine. However, check with your doctor if any of the following side effects continue or are bothersome:

More common

Loss of appetite; nervousness; trouble in sleeping

Less common

Dizziness; drowsiness; headache; nausea; stomach pain

After you stop using this medicine, your body may need time to adjust. The length of time this takes depends on the amount of medicine you were using and how long you used it. During this period of time check with your doctor if you notice any of the following side effects:

Mental depression (severe); unusual behavior; unusual tiredness or weakness

Other side effects not listed above may also occur in some patients. If you notice any other effects, check with your doctor.

Revised: 08/15/95

METHYSERGIDE Systemic

A commonly used brand name in the U.S. and Canada is Sansert.

Description

Methysergide (meth-i-SER-jide) belongs to the group of medicines known as ergot alkaloids. It is used to prevent migraine headaches and some kinds of throbbing headaches. It is not used to treat an attack once it has started. The exact way methysergide acts on the body is not known.

This medicine is available only with your doctor's prescription, in the following dosage form:

Oral

- Tablets (U.S. and Canada)

Before Using This Medicine

In deciding to use a medicine, the risks of taking the medicine must be weighed against the good it will do. This is a decision you and your doctor will make. For methysergide, the following should be considered:

Allergies—Tell your doctor if you have ever had any unusual or allergic reaction to methysergide or to other ergot medicines. Also tell your health care professional if you are allergic to any other substances, such as foods, preservatives, or dyes.

Pregnancy—Studies with methysergide have not been done in either humans or animals.

Breast-feeding—This medicine passes into the breast milk and may cause unwanted effects such as vomiting, diarrhea, weak pulse, unstable blood pressure, and convulsions (seizures) in nursing babies.

Children—Methysergide can cause serious side effects in any patient. Therefore, it is especially important that you discuss with the child's doctor the good that this medicine may do as well as the risks of using it.

Older adults—Elderly people are especially sensitive to the effects of methysergide. This may increase the chance of side effects during treatment.

Other medicines—Although certain medicines should not be used together at all, in other cases two different medicines may be used together even if an interaction might occur. In these cases, your doctor may want to change the dose, or other precautions may be necessary. When you are taking methysergide, it is important that your health care professional know if you are using any other prescription or nonprescription (over-the-counter [OTC]) medicine, or if you smoke.

Other medical problems—The presence of other medical problems may affect the use of methysergide. Make sure you tell your doctor if you have any other medical problems, especially:

- Arthritis or
- Heart or blood vessel disease or
- Infection or
- Itching (severe) or
- Kidney disease or
- Liver disease or
- Lung disease—The chance of serious side effects may be increased
- High blood pressure or
- Stomach ulcer—Methysergide can make your condition worse

Proper Use of This Medicine

Take this medicine only as directed by your doctor. If the amount you are to take does not prevent your headaches from occurring as often as before, do not take more than your doctor ordered. Instead, check with your doctor. Taking too much of this medicine or taking it too frequently may cause serious effects such as nausea and vomiting; cold, painful hands or feet; or even gangrene.

If this medicine upsets your stomach, it may be taken with meals or milk. If stomach upset continues or is severe, check with your doctor.

Dosing—The dose of methysergide will be different for different patients. *Follow your doctor's orders or the directions on the label.* The following information includes only the average doses of methysergide. *If your dose is different, do not change it* unless your doctor tells you to do so.

- For *oral* dosage form (tablets:)
  - —For preventing migraine and other throbbing headaches:
    - Adults—2 milligrams (mg) (one tablet) two or three times a day.
    - Children—Use is not recommended.

Missed dose—If you miss a dose of this medicine, skip the missed dose and go back to your regular dosing schedule. Do not double doses.

Storage—To store this medicine:

- Keep out of the reach of children.
- Store away from heat and direct light.
- Do not store in the bathroom, near the kitchen sink, or in other damp places. Heat or moisture may cause the medicine to break down.
- Do not keep outdated medicine or medicine no longer needed. Be sure that any discarded medicine is out of the reach of children.

Precautions While Using This Medicine

If you have been taking this medicine regularly, *do not stop taking it without first checking with your doctor.* Your doctor may want you to reduce gradually the amount you are using before stopping completely. If you stop taking it suddenly, your headaches may return or worsen.

Your doctor will tell you how long you should take this medicine. Usually it is not taken for longer than 6 months at a time. *If the doctor tells you to stop taking the medicine for a while, do not continue to take it.* If your body does not get a rest from the medicine, it can have harmful effects.

This medicine may cause some people to become dizzy, lightheaded, drowsy, or less alert than they are normally. Even if taken at bedtime, it may cause some people to feel drowsy or less alert on arising. *Make sure you know how you react to this medicine before you drive, use machines, or do anything else that could be dangerous if you are dizzy or are not alert.*

If dizziness occurs, get up slowly after lying or sitting down. If the problem continues or gets worse, check with your doctor.

Since drinking alcoholic beverages may make headaches worse, it is best to avoid alcohol while you are suffering from them. If you have any questions about this, check with your doctor.

Since smoking may increase some of the harmful effects of this medicine, it is best to avoid smoking while you are using it. If you have any questions about this, check with your doctor.

This medicine may make you more sensitive to cold temperatures, especially if you have blood circulation problems. It tends to decrease blood circulation in the skin, fingers, and toes. Dress warmly during cold weather and be careful during prolonged exposure to cold, such as in winter sports. This is especially important for elderly people, who are more likely than younger adults to already have problems with their circulation.

Check with your doctor if a serious infection or illness of any kind occurs while you are taking methysergide, since an infection may make you more sensitive to the medicine's effects.

Side Effects of This Medicine

Along with its needed effects, a medicine may cause some unwanted effects. Although not all of these side effects may occur, if they do occur they may need medical attention.

Check with your doctor immediately if any of the following side effects occur:

Chest pain or tightness in chest; difficult or painful urination; dizziness (severe); fever or chills; increase or decrease (large) in the amount of urine; leg cramps; pain in arms, legs, groin, lower back, or side; pale or cold hands or feet; shortness of breath or difficult breathing; swelling of hands, ankles, feet, or lower legs

Check with your doctor as soon as possible if the following side effects occur:

More common

Abdominal or stomach pain; itching; numbness and tingling of fingers, toes, or face; weakness in the legs

Less common or rare

Changes in vision; clumsiness or unsteadiness; cough or hoarseness; excitement or difficulty in thinking; fast or slow heartbeat; feeling of being outside the body; hallucinations (seeing, hearing, or feeling things that are not there); loss of appetite or weight loss; mental depression; nightmares; raised red spots on skin; redness or flushing of face; skin rash

Other side effects may occur that usually do not need medical attention. These side effects may go away during treatment as your body adjusts to the medicine. However, check with your doctor if any of the following side effects continue or are bothersome:

More common

Diarrhea; dizziness or lightheadedness, especially when you get up from a lying or sitting position; drowsiness; nausea or vomiting

Less common or rare
Constipation; heartburn; trouble in sleeping

After you stop using this medicine, your body may need time to adjust. The length of time this takes depends on the amount of medicine you were using and how long you used it. During this time check with your doctor if your headaches begin again or worsen.

Other side effects not listed above may also occur in some patients. If you notice any other effects, check with your doctor.

Revised: July 1990
Interim revision: 08/17/94

METOCLOPRAMIDE Systemic

Some commonly used brand names are:

In the U.S.—

Clopra
Octamide
Octamide PFS
Reclomide
Reglan

Generic name product may also be available.

In Canada—

Apo-Metoclop
Emex
Maxeran
Reglan

Description

Metoclopramide (met-oh-KLOE-pra-mide) is a medicine that increases the movements or contractions of the stomach and intestines. When given by injection it is used to help diagnose certain problems of the stomach and/or intestines. It is also used by injection to prevent the nausea and vomiting that may occur after treatment with anticancer medicines. Another medicine may be used with metoclopramide to prevent side effects that may occur when metoclopramide is used with anticancer medicines.

When taken by mouth, metoclopramide is used to treat the symptoms of a certain type of stomach problem called diabetic gastroparesis. It relieves symptoms such as nausea, vomiting, continued feeling of fullness after meals, and loss of appetite. Metoclopramide is also used, for a short time, to treat symptoms such as heartburn in patients who suffer esophageal injury from a backward flow of gastric acid into the esophagus.

Metoclopramide may also be used for other conditions as determined by your doctor.

Metoclopramide is available only with your doctor's prescription. It is available in the following dosage forms:

Oral
- Tablets (U.S. and Canada)
- Syrup (U.S. and Canada)

Parenteral
- Injection (U.S. and Canada)

Before Using This Medicine

In deciding to use a medicine, the risks of taking the medicine must be weighed against the good it will do. This is a decision you and your doctor will make. For metoclopramide, the following should be considered:

Allergies—Tell your doctor if you have ever had any unusual or allergic reaction to metoclopramide, procaine, or procainamide. Also tell your health care professional if you are allergic to any other substances, such as foods, preservatives, or dyes.

Pregnancy—Not enough studies have been done in humans to determine metoclopramide's safety during pregnancy. However, metoclopramide has not been shown to cause birth defects or other problems in animal studies.

Breast-feeding—Although metoclopramide passes into the breast milk, it has not been shown to cause problems in nursing babies.

Children—Muscle spasms, especially of jaw, neck, and back, and tic-like (jerky) movements of head and face may be especially likely to occur in children, who are usually more sensitive than adults to the effects of metoclopramide. Premature and full-term infants may develop blood problems if given high doses of metoclopramide.

Older adults—Shuffling walk and trembling and shaking of hands may be especially likely to occur in elderly patients after they have taken metoclopramide over a long time.

Other medicines—Although certain medicines should not be used together at all, in other cases 2 different medicines may be used together even if an interaction might occur. In these cases, your doctor may want to change the dose, or other precautions may be necessary. When you are taking metoclopramide, it is especially important that your health care professional know if you are taking the following:

- Central nervous system (CNS) depressants (medicine that causes drowsiness)—Use with metoclopramide may cause severe drowsiness

Other medical problems—The presence of other medical problems may affect the use of metoclopramide. Make sure you tell your doctor if you have any other medical problems, especially:

- Abdominal or stomach bleeding or
- Asthma or
- High blood pressure or
- Intestinal blockage or
- Parkinson's disease—Metoclopramide may make these conditions worse
- Epilepsy—Metoclopramide may increase the risk of having a seizure
- Kidney disease (severe) or
- Liver disease (severe)—Higher blood levels of metoclopramide may result, possibly increasing the chance of side effects

Proper Use of This Medicine

Take this medicine 30 minutes before meals and at bedtime, unless otherwise directed by your doctor.

Take metoclopramide only as directed. Do not take more of it, do not take it more often, and do not take it for a longer time than your doctor ordered. To do so may increase the chance of side effects.

Dosing—The dose of metoclopramide will be different for different patients. *Follow your doctor's orders or the directions on the label.* The following information includes only the average doses of metoclopramide. *If your dose is different, do not change it* unless your doctor tells you to do so.

The number of tablets or teaspoonfuls of syrup that you take depends on the strength of the medicine. Also, *the number of doses you take each day, the time allowed between doses, and the length of time you take the medicine depend on the medical problem for which you are taking metoclopramide.*

- For *oral* dosage forms (syrup or tablets):
  - —To treat the symptoms of a stomach problem called diabetic gastroparesis:
    - Adults and teenagers—10 milligrams (mg) thirty minutes before symptoms are likely to begin or before each meal and at bedtime. The dose may be taken up to four times a day. However, most people usually will not take more than 500 micrograms (mcg) per kilogram (kg) (227 mcg per pound) of body weight a day.
    - Children—Dose must be determined by your doctor.
  - —For heartburn:
    - Adults and teenagers—10 to 15 mg thirty minutes before symptoms are likely to begin or before each meal and at bedtime. The dose may be taken up to four times a day. However, most people usually will not take more than 500 mcg per kg (227 mcg per pound) of body weight a day.
    - Children—Dose must be determined by your doctor.
  - —To increase movements or contractions of the stomach and intestines:
    - Children 5 to 14 years of age—2.5 to 5 mg three times a day, thirty minutes before meals. Some children may receive 100 to 200 mcg per kg (45.5 to 90.9 mcg per pound) of body weight, thirty minutes before meals and at bedtime.
- For *injection* dosage form:
  - —To increase movements or contractions of the stomach and intestine:
    - Adults and teenagers—10 mg injected into a vein.
    - Children—Dose is based on body weight and must be determined by your doctor. The usual dose is 1 mg per kilogram (kg) (0.45 mg per pound) of body weight injected into a vein. Your doctor may repeat this dose after sixty minutes if needed.
  - —To prevent nausea and vomiting caused by anticancer medicines:
    - Adults and teenagers—Dose is based on body weight and must be determined by your doctor. The usual dose is 1 to 2 mg per kg (0.45 to 0.9 mg per pound) of body weight, injected slowly into a vein, thirty minutes before you take your anticancer medicine. Your doctor may repeat this dose every two or three hours if needed. Some people may need a larger dose to start.
    - Children—1 mg per kg (0.45 mg per pound) of body weight injected into a vein. Your doctor may repeat this dose after sixty minutes if needed.
  - —To prevent vomiting after surgery:
    - Adults and teenagers—10 to 20 mg injected into a muscle near the end of surgery.
    - Children—Dose must be determined by your doctor.

Missed dose—If you miss a dose of this medicine, take it as soon as possible. However, if it is almost time for your next dose, skip the missed dose and go back to your regular dosing schedule. Do not double doses.

Storage—To store this medicine:
- Keep out of the reach of children.
- Store away from heat and direct light.
- Do not store the tablet form of this medicine in the bathroom, near the kitchen sink, or in other damp places. Heat or moisture may cause the medicine to break down.
- Keep the syrup form of this medicine from freezing.
- Do not keep outdated medicine or medicine no longer needed. Be sure that any discarded medicine is out of the reach of children.

Precautions While Using This Medicine

This medicine will add to the effects of alcohol and other CNS depressants (medicines that slow down the nervous system, possibly causing drowsiness). Some examples of CNS depressants are antihistamines or medicine for hay fever, other allergies, or colds; sedatives, tranquilizers, or sleeping medicine; prescription pain medicine or narcotics; barbiturates; medicine for seizures; muscle relaxants; or anesthetics, including some dental anesthetics. *Check with your doctor before taking any of the above while you are using this medicine.*

This medicine may cause some people to become dizzy, lightheaded, drowsy, or less alert than they are normally. *Make sure you know how you react to this medicine before you drive, use machines, or do anything else that could be dangerous if you are dizzy or are not alert.*

Side Effects of This Medicine

Along with its needed effects, a medicine may cause some unwanted effects. Although not all of these side effects may occur, if they do occur they may need medical attention.

Check with your doctor as soon as possible if any of the following side effects occur:

Rare

Chills; difficulty in speaking or swallowing; dizziness or fainting; fast or irregular heartbeat; fever; general feeling of tiredness or weakness; headache (severe or continuing); increase in blood pressure; lip smacking or puckering; loss of balance control; mask-like face; rapid or worm-like movements of tongue; shuffling walk; sore throat; stiffness of arms or legs; trembling and shaking of hands and fingers; uncontrolled chewing movements; uncontrolled movements of arms and legs

With high doses—may occur within minutes of receiving a dose of metoclopramide and last for 2 to 24 hours

Aching or discomfort in lower legs; panic-like sensation; sensation of crawling in legs; unusual nervousness, restlessness, or irritability

Symptoms of overdose—may also occur rarely with usual doses, especially in children and young adults, and with high doses used to treat the nausea and vomiting caused by anticancer medicines

Confusion; drowsiness (severe)

Other side effects may occur that usually do not need medical attention. These side effects may go away during treatment as your body adjusts to the medicine. However, check with your doctor if any of the following side effects continue or are bothersome:

More common

Diarrhea—with high doses; drowsiness; restlessness

Less common or rare

Breast tenderness and swelling; changes in menstruation; constipation; depression; increased flow of breast milk; nausea; skin rash; trouble in sleeping; unusual dryness of mouth; unusual irritability

Other side effects not listed above may also occur in some patients. If you notice any other effects, check with your doctor.

Additional Information

Once a medicine has been approved for marketing for a certain use, experience may show that it is also useful for other medical problems. Although these uses are not included in product labeling, metoclopramide is used in certain patients with the following medical conditions:

- Failure of the stomach to empty its contents
- Nausea and vomiting caused by other medicines
- Persistent hiccups
- Prevention of aspirating fluid into the lungs during surgery
- Vascular headaches

Other than the above information, there is no additional information relating to proper use, precautions, or side effects for these uses.

Revised: 05/20/92
Interim revision: 08/16/94

METRONIDAZOLE Systemic

Some commonly used brand names are:

In the U.S.—

Flagyl	Metric 21
Flagyl I.V.	Metro I.V.
Flagyl I.V. RTU	Protostat

Generic name product may also be available.

In Canada—

Apo-Metronidazole	Novonidazol
Flagyl	Trikacide

Generic name product may also be available.

Description

Metronidazole (me-troe-NI-da-zole) is used to treat infections. It may also be used for other problems as determined by your doctor. It will not work for colds, flu, or other virus infections.

Metronidazole is available only with your doctor's prescription, in the following dosage forms:

Oral

- Capsules (Canada)
- Tablets (U.S. and Canada)

Parenteral

- Injection (U.S. and Canada)

Before Using This Medicine

In deciding to use a medicine, the risks of taking the medicine must be weighed against the good it will do. This is a decision you and your doctor will make. For metronidazole, the following should be considered:

Allergies—Tell your doctor if you have ever had any unusual or allergic reaction to metronidazole. Also tell your health care professional if you are allergic to any other substances, such as foods, preservatives, or dyes.

Pregnancy—Studies have not been done in humans. Metronidazole has not been shown to cause birth defects in animal studies; however, use is not recommended during the first trimester of pregnancy.

Breast-feeding—Use is not recommended in nursing mothers since metronidazole passes into the breast milk and may cause unwanted effects in the baby. However, in some infections your doctor may want you to stop breast-feeding and take this medicine for a short time. During this time the breast milk should be squeezed out or sucked out with a breast pump and thrown away. One or two days after you finish taking this medicine, you may go back to breast-feeding.

Children—Metronidazole has been used in children and, in effective doses, has not been shown to cause different side effects or problems in children than it does in adults.

Older adults—Many medicines have not been studied specifically in older people. Therefore, it may not be known whether they work exactly the same way they do in younger adults or if they cause different side effects or problems in older people. There is no specific information comparing use of metronidazole in the elderly with use in other age groups.

Other medicines—Although certain medicines should not be used together at all, in other cases two different medicines may be used together even if an interaction might occur. In these cases, your doctor may want to change the dose, or other precautions may be necessary. When you are taking metronidazole, it is especially important that your health care professional knows if you are taking any of the following:

- Anticoagulants (blood thinners)—Patients taking anticoagulants with metronidazole may have an increased chance of bleeding
- Disulfiram (e.g., Antabuse)—Patients taking disulfiram with metronidazole may have an increase in side effects affecting the central nervous system

Other medical problems—The presence of other medical problems may affect the use of metronidazole. Make sure you tell your doctor if you have any other medical problems, especially:

- Blood disease or a history of blood disease—Metronidazole may make the condition worse
- Central nervous system (CNS) disease, including epilepsy—Metronidazole may increase the chance of seizures (convulsions) or other CNS side effects
- Heart disease—Metronidazole by injection may make heart disease worse
- Liver disease, severe—Patients with severe liver disease may have an increase in side effects

Proper Use of This Medicine

If this medicine upsets your stomach, it may be taken with meals or a snack. If stomach upset (nausea, vomiting, stomach pain, or diarrhea) continues, check with your doctor.

To help clear up your infection completely, *keep taking this medicine for the full time of treatment,* even if you begin to feel better after a few days. If you stop taking this medicine too soon, your symptoms may return.

In some kinds of infections, this medicine works best when there is a constant amount in the blood. *To help keep the amount constant, do not miss any doses. Also, it is best to take the doses at evenly spaced times, day and night.* For example, if you are to take 4 doses a day, the doses should be spaced about 6 hours apart. If this interferes with your sleep or other daily activities, or if you need help in planning the best times to take your medicine, check with your health care professional.

Dosing—The dose of metronidazole will be different for different patients. *Follow your doctor's orders or the directions on the label.* The following information includes only the average doses of metronidazole. *If your dose is different, do not change it* unless your doctor tells you to do so.

The number of capsules or tablets that you take depends on the strength of the medicine. Also, *the number of doses you take each day, the time allowed between doses, and the length of time you take the medicine depend on the medical problem for which you are taking metronidazole.*

- For *oral* dosage forms (capsules, tablets):
  - —For bacterial infections:
    - Adults and teenagers—Dose is based on body weight. The usual dose is 7.5 milligrams (mg) per kilogram (kg) (3.4 mg per pound) of body weight, up to a maximum dose of 1 gram, every six hours for at least seven days.
    - Children—Dose is based on body weight. The usual dose is 7.5 mg per kg (3.4 mg per pound) of body weight every six hours; or 10 mg per kg (4.5 mg per pound) every eight hours.
  - —For amebiasis infections:
    - Adults and teenagers—500 to 750 mg three times a day for five to ten days.
    - Children—Dose is based on body weight. The usual dose is 11.6 to 16.7 mg per kg (5.3 to 7.6 mg per pound) of body weight three times a day for ten days.
  - —For trichomoniasis infections:
    - Adults and teenagers—A single dose of 2 grams; or 1 gram two times a day for one day; or 250 mg three times a day for seven days.
    - Children—Dose is based on body weight. The usual dose is 5 mg per kg (2.3 mg per pound) of body weight three times a day for seven days.
- For *injection* dosage form:
  - —For bacterial infections:
    - Adults and children over 1 week of age—Dose is based on body weight. The usual dose is 15 mg per kg (6.8 mg per pound) of body weight one time to start, then 7.5 mg per kg (3.4 mg per pound) of body weight injected into a vein every six hours for at least seven days.
    - Preterm infants—Dose is based on body weight. The usual dose is 15 mg per kg (6.8 mg per pound) of body weight one time to start, then 7.5 mg per kg (3.4 mg per pound) of body weight, injected into a vein, every twelve hours starting forty-eight hours after the first dose.
    - Full-term infants—Dose is based on body weight. The usual dose is 15 mg per kg (6.8 mg per pound) of body weight one time to start, then 7.5 mg per kg (3.4 mg per pound) of body weight, injected into a vein, every twelve hours starting twenty-four hours after the first dose.
  - —For treatment before and during bowel surgery:
    - Adults and teenagers—Dose is based on body weight. The usual dose is 15 mg per kg (6.8 mg per pound), injected into a vein, one hour before surgery, then 7.5 mg per kg (3.4 mg per pound) of body weight, injected into a vein, six hours and twelve hours after the first dose.
    - Children—Use and dose must be determined by your doctor.

Missed dose—If you miss a dose of this medicine, take it as soon as possible. This will help to keep a constant amount of medicine in the blood. However, if it is almost time for your next dose, skip the missed dose and go back to your regular dosing schedule. Do not double doses.

Storage—To store this medicine:

- Keep out of the reach of children.
- Store away from heat and direct light.
- Do not store the capsule or tablet form of this medicine in the bathroom, near the kitchen sink, or in other damp places. Heat or moisture may cause the medicine to break down.
- Do not keep outdated medicine or medicine no longer needed. Be sure that any discarded medicine is out of the reach of children.

Precautions While Using This Medicine

If your symptoms do not improve within a few days, or if they become worse, check with your doctor.

Drinking alcoholic beverages while taking this medicine may cause stomach pain, nausea, vomiting, headache, or flushing or redness of the face. Other alcohol-containing preparations (for example, elixirs, cough syrups, tonics) may also cause problems. These problems may last for at least a day after you stop taking metronidazole. Also, this medicine may cause alcoholic beverages to taste different. Therefore, *you should not drink alcoholic beverages or take other alcohol-containing preparations while you are taking this medicine and for at least a day after stopping it.*

Metronidazole may cause dryness of the mouth, an unpleasant or sharp metallic taste, and a change in taste sensation. For temporary relief of dry mouth, use sugarless candy or gum, melt bits of ice in your mouth, or use a saliva substitute. However, if your mouth continues to feel dry for more than 2 weeks, check with your medical doctor or dentist. Continuing dryness of the mouth may increase the chance of dental disease, including tooth decay, gum disease, and fungus infections.

This medicine may also cause some people to become dizzy or lightheaded. *Make sure you know how you react to this medicine before you drive, use machines, or do anything else that could be dangerous if you are dizzy or are not alert.* If these reactions are especially bothersome, check with your doctor.

If you are taking this medicine for trichomoniasis (an infection of the sex organs in males and females), your doctor may want to treat your sexual partner at the same time you are being treated, even if he or she has no symptoms. Also, it may be desirable to use a condom (prophylactic) during intercourse. These measures will help keep you from getting the infection back again from your partner. If you have any questions about this, check with your doctor.

Side Effects of This Medicine

Along with its needed effects, a medicine may cause some unwanted effects. Although not all of these side effects may occur, if they do occur they may need medical attention.

Check with your doctor immediately if any of the following side effects occur:

Less common

Numbness, tingling, pain, or weakness in hands or feet

Rare

Convulsions (seizures)

Also, check with your doctor as soon as possible if any of the following side effects occur:

Less common

Any vaginal irritation, discharge, or dryness not present before use of this medicine; clumsiness or unsteadiness; mood or other mental changes; skin rash, hives, redness, or itching; sore throat and fever; stomach and back pain (severe)

For injection form

Pain, tenderness, redness, or swelling over vein in which the medicine is given

Other side effects may occur that usually do not need medical attention. These side effects may go away during treatment as your body adjusts to the medicine. However, check with your doctor if any of the following side effects continue or are bothersome:

More common

Diarrhea; dizziness or lightheadedness; headache; loss of appetite; nausea or vomiting; stomach pain or cramps

Less common or rare

Change in taste sensation; dryness of mouth; unpleasant or sharp metallic taste

In some patients metronidazole may cause dark urine. This is only temporary and will go away when you stop taking this medicine.

Other side effects not listed above may also occur in some patients. If you notice any other effects, check with your doctor.

Additional Information

Once a medicine has been approved for marketing for a certain use, experience may show that it is also useful for other medical problems. Although these uses are not included in product labeling, metronidazole is used in certain patients with the following medical conditions:

- Antibiotic-associated colitis
- Bacterial vaginosis
- Balantidiasis
- Dental infections
- Gastritis or ulcer due to *Helicobacter pylori*
- Giardiasis
- Inflammatory bowel disease

For patients taking this medicine for *giardiasis*:

- After treatment, it is important that your doctor check whether or not the infection in your intestinal tract has been cleared up completely.

Other than the above information, there is no additional information relating to proper use, precautions, or side effects for this use.

Revised: 10/20/92
Interim revision: 03/24/94

METRONIDAZOLE Topical

A commonly used brand name in the U.S. and Canada is MetroGel.

Description

Topical metronidazole (me-troe-NI-da-zole) is applied to the skin in adults to help control rosacea (roe-ZAY-she-ah), also known as acne rosacea and ''adult acne.'' This medicine helps to reduce the redness of the skin and the number of pimples, usually found on the face, in patients with rosacea.

Topical metronidazole is available only with your doctor's prescription, in the following dosage form:

Topical
- Gel (U.S. and Canada)

Before Using This Medicine

In deciding to use a medicine, the risks of taking the medicine must be weighed against the good it will do. This is a decision you and your doctor will make. For topical metronidazole, the following should be considered:

Allergies—Tell your doctor if you have ever had any unusual or allergic reaction to metronidazole. Also tell your health care professional if you are allergic to any other substances, such as preservatives or dyes.

Pregnancy—Topical metronidazole has not been studied in pregnant women. However, metronidazole given by mouth (e.g., Flagyl) has not been shown to cause birth defects or other problems in animal studies.

Breast-feeding—Topical metronidazole is absorbed into the mother's body only in small amounts. The small amounts of this medicine that are absorbed are unlikely to cause serious problems in nursing babies.

Children—Rosacea is usually considered an adult disease. Therefore, topical metronidazole is not generally used in children.

Older adults—Many medicines have not been studied specifically in older people. Therefore, it may not be known whether they work exactly the same way they do in younger adults or if they cause different side effects or problems in older people. There is no specific information comparing use of topical metronidazole in the elderly with use in other age groups.

Other medicines—Although certain medicines should not be used together at all, in other cases two different medicines may be used together even if an interaction might occur. In these cases, your doctor may want to change the dose, or other precautions may be necessary. Tell your health care professional if you are using any other topical prescription or nonprescription (over-the-counter [OTC]) medicine that is to be applied to the same area of the skin.

Proper Use of This Medicine

Do not use this medicine in or near the eyes. Watering of the eyes may occur when the medicine is used too close to the eyes.

If this medicine does get into your eyes, wash them out immediately, but carefully, with large amounts of cool tap water. If your eyes still burn or are painful, check with your doctor.

Before applying this medicine, thoroughly wash the affected area(s) with a mild, nonirritating cleanser, rinse well, and gently pat dry.

To use:
- After washing the affected area(s), apply this medicine with your fingertips.
- Apply and rub in a thin film of medicine, using enough to cover the affected area(s) lightly. *You should apply the medicine to the whole area usually affected by rosacea, not just to the pimples themselves.*
- Wash the medicine off your hands.

To help keep your rosacea under control, *keep using this medicine for the full time of treatment.* You may have to continue using this medicine every day for 9 weeks or longer. *Do not miss any doses.*

Dosing—The dose of topical metronidazole will be different for different patients. *Follow your doctor's orders or the directions on the label.* The following information includes only the average doses of topical metronidazole. *If your dose is different, do not change it* unless your doctor tells you to do so.

- For *topical* dosage form (gel):
  - —For rosacea:
    - Adults—Apply to the affected area(s) of skin two times a day, morning and evening, for nine weeks.
    - Children—Use and dose must be determined by your doctor.

Missed dose—If you miss a dose of this medicine, apply it as soon as possible. However, if it is almost time for your next dose, skip the missed dose and go back to your regular dosing schedule.

Storage—To store this medicine:
- Keep out of the reach of children.
- Store away from heat and direct light.
- Keep the medicine from freezing.
- Do not keep outdated medicine or medicine no longer needed. Be sure that any discarded medicine is out of the reach of children.

Precautions While Using This Medicine

If your rosacea does not improve within 3 weeks, or if it becomes worse, check with your doctor. However, treatment of rosacea may take up to 9 weeks or longer before you see full improvement.

Stinging or burning of the skin may be expected after this medicine is applied. These effects may last up to a few minutes or more. If irritation continues, check with your doctor. You may have to use the medicine less often or stop using it altogether. Follow your doctor's directions.

You may continue to use cosmetics (make-up) while you are using this medicine for rosacea. However, it is best to use only ''oil-free'' cosmetics. Also, it is best not to use cosmetics too heavily or too often. They may make your rosacea worse. If you have any questions about this, check with your doctor.

Side Effects of This Medicine

Along with its needed effects, a medicine may cause some unwanted effects. The following side effects may go away during treatment as your body adjusts to the medicine. However, check with your doctor if any of these effects continue or are bothersome:

Less common

Dry skin; redness or other signs of skin irritation not present before use of this medicine; stinging or burning of the skin; watering of eyes

Other side effects not listed above may also occur in some patients. If you notice any other effects, check with your doctor.

Revised: 06/24/94

METRONIDAZOLE Vaginal

Some commonly used brand names are:

In the U.S.—
MetroGel-Vaginal

In Canada—
Flagyl Nidagel

Description

Metronidazole (me-troe-NI-da-zole) is used to treat certain vaginal infections. It works by killing bacteria. This medicine will not work for vaginal fungus or yeast infections.

Metronidazole is available only with your doctor's prescription, in the following dosage forms:

Vaginal
- Cream (Canada)
- Gel (U.S. and Canada)
- Tablets (Canada)

Before Using This Medicine

In deciding whether to use a medicine, the risks of using the medicine must be weighed against the good it will do. This is a decision you and your doctor will make. For vaginal metronidazole, the following should be considered:

Allergies—Tell your doctor if you have ever had any unusual or allergic reaction to metronidazole. Also tell your health care professional if you are allergic to any other substances, such as foods, preservatives, or dyes.

Pregnancy—Vaginal metronidazole has not been studied in pregnant women. Metronidazole given by mouth (e.g., Flagyl) has not been shown to cause birth defects. Before taking this medicine, make sure your doctor knows if you are pregnant or if you may become pregnant.

Breast-feeding—Use is not recommended in nursing mothers since metronidazole passes into breast milk and may cause unwanted effects in the baby. In addition, metronidazole may change the taste of your breast milk. Your doctor may want you to stop breast-feeding and use this medicine for a short time. During this time the breast milk should be pumped or drawn out with a breast pump and thrown away. Two days after you finish using this medicine, you may go back to breast-feeding.

Children—Studies on these medicines have been done only in adult patients, and there is no specific information comparing use of vaginal metronidazole in children with use in other age groups.

Older adults—Many medicines have not been studied specifically in older people. Therefore, it may not be known whether they work exactly the same way they do in younger adults or if they cause different side effects or problems in older people. There is no specific information comparing use of metronidazole in the elderly with use in other age groups.

Other medicines—Although certain medicines should not be used together at all, in other cases two different medicines may be used together even if an interaction might occur. In these cases, your doctor may want to change the dose, or other precautions may be necessary. When you are using vaginal metronidazole it is especially important that your health care professional know if you are taking any of the following:

- Alcohol or alcohol-containing medicines (e.g., NyQuil, Geritol)—Metronidazole can cause serious side effects such as abdominal cramping, flushing, headache, nausea, or vomiting when it is used with alcohol
- Anticoagulants (blood thinners)—Taking metronidazole may increase the effects of anticoagulants, changing the amount you need to take
- Disulfiram (e.g., Antabuse)—Severe confusion or mental problems can occur if metronidazole is used together with disulfiram or if it is used up to 2 weeks after disulfiram treatment has been stopped

Other medical problems—The presence of other medical problems may affect the use of vaginal metronidazole. Make sure you tell your doctor if you have any other medical problems, especially:

- Central nervous system (CNS) disease, including epilepsy—Metronidazole may increase the chance of seizures (convulsions) or other side effects
- Liver disease, severe—Patients with severe liver disease may have an increase in side effects
- Low white blood cell count (or history of)—Metronidazole may make the condition worse

Proper Use of This Medicine

Wash your hands before and after using the medicine. Also, keep the medicine out of your eyes.

If this medicine does get into your eyes, wash them out immediately, but carefully, with large amounts of tap water. If your eyes still burn or are painful, check with your doctor.

Vaginal metronidazole products usually come with patient directions. Read them carefully before using this medicine.

Use vaginal metronidazole exactly as directed by your doctor.

- *To fill the applicator*
  - —For cream or gel dosage forms:
    - Break the metal seal at the opening of the tube by using the point on the top of the cap.
    - Screw the applicator onto the tube.
    - Squeeze the medicine into the applicator slowly until it is full.
    - Remove the applicator from the tube. Replace the cap on the tube.
  - —For vaginal tablet dosage form:
    - Place the vaginal tablet into the applicator. Wet the vaginal tablet with water for a few seconds.
- *To insert vaginal metronidazole using the applicator*
  - —For all dosage forms:
    - Relax while lying on your back with your knees bent.
    - Hold the full applicator in one hand. Insert it slowly into the vagina. Stop before it becomes uncomfortable.
    - Slowly press the plunger until it stops.
    - Withdraw the applicator. The medicine will be left behind in the vagina.
- *To care for the applicator*
  - —For all dosage forms:
    - Clean the applicator after use by pulling the plunger out of the applicator and washing both parts completely in warm soapy water.
    - Rinse well.
    - After drying the applicator, replace the plunger.

To help clear up your infection completely, *it is very important that you keep using this medicine for the full time of treatment,* even if your symptoms begin to clear up after a few days. If you stop using this medicine too soon, your symptoms may return. *Do not miss any doses.* Also, *continue using this medicine even if your menstrual period starts during the time of treatment.*

Dosing—The dose of vaginal metronidazole will be different for different patients. The following information includes only the average doses of vaginal metronidazole. *If your dose is different, do not change it* unless your doctor tells you to do so.

- *For vaginal cream* dosage form:
  - —For bacterial vaginosis or trichomoniasis:
    - Adults and teenagers—One applicatorful (500 milligrams [mg]), inserted into the vagina. Use the medicine one or two times a day for ten or twenty days.
    - Children—Use and dose must be determined by your doctor.
- *For vaginal gel* dosage form:
  - —For bacterial vaginosis:
    - Adults and teenagers—One applicatorful (37.5 mg), inserted into the vagina one or two times a day for five days.
    - Children—Use and dose must be determined by your doctor.
- *For vaginal tablets* dosage form:
  - —For bacterial vaginosis or trichomoniasis:
    - Adults and teenagers—One 500-mg tablet, inserted high into the vagina. Use the medicine once a day in the evening for ten or twenty days.
    - Children—Use and dose must be determined by your doctor.

Missed dose—If you miss a dose of this medicine, use it as soon as possible. However, if it is almost time for your next dose, skip the missed dose and go back to your regular dosing schedule.

Storage—To store this medicine:
- Keep out of the reach of children.
- Store away from heat and direct light.
- Do not store the vaginal tablets in the bathroom, near the kitchen sink, or in other damp places. Heat or moisture may cause the medicine to break down.
- Keep this medicine from freezing.
- Do not keep outdated medicine or medicine no longer needed. Be sure that any discarded medicine is out of the reach of children.

Precautions While Using This Medicine

If your symptoms do not improve within a few days, or if they become worse, check with your doctor.

It is important that you visit your doctor after you have used all your medicine to make sure that the infection is gone.

Drinking alcoholic beverages while using this medicine may cause stomach pain, nausea, vomiting, headache, or flushing or redness of the face. Alcohol-containing medicines (for example, elixirs, cough syrups, tonics) may also cause problems. The chance of these problems occurring may continue for at least a day after you stop using metronidazole. Therefore, *you should not drink alcoholic beverages or take other alcohol-containing medicines while you are using this medicine and for at least a day after stopping it.*

This medicine may cause some people to become dizzy or lightheaded. *Make sure you know how you react to this medicine before you drive, use machines, or do anything else that could be dangerous if you are dizzy or are not alert.* If these reactions are especially bothersome, check with your doctor.

Vaginal medicines usually leak out of the vagina during treatment. To keep the medicine from getting on your clothing, wear a minipad or sanitary napkin. *Do not use tampons* (like those used for menstrual periods) since they may soak up the medicine.

To help clear up your infection completely and to help make sure it does not return, good health habits are also required.

- Wear cotton panties (or panties or pantyhose with cotton crotches) instead of synthetic (for example, nylon or rayon) panties.
- Wear only freshly washed panties daily.

Do not have sexual intercourse while you are using this medicine. Having sexual intercourse may reduce the strength of the medicine. This may cause the medicine to not work as well. Also, oils in the cream and vaginal tablets (but not the vaginal gel) may damage latex (rubber) contraceptive devices, such as cervical caps, condoms, or diaphragms, causing them to leak, wear out sooner, or not work properly.

Many vaginal infections (for example, trichomoniasis) are spread by having sexual intercourse. You can give the infection to your sexual partner, and he can give the infection back to you later. Your partner may also need to be treated for some infections. *Until you are sure that the infection is completely cleared up after your treatment with this medicine, your partner should wear a condom during sexual intercourse.* If you have any questions about this, check with your health care professional.

Side Effects of This Medicine

Along with its needed effects, a medicine may cause some unwanted effects. Although not all of these side effects may occur, if they do occur they may need medical attention.

Check with your doctor as soon as possible if any of the following side effects occur:

More common

Itching in the vagina; pain during sexual intercourse; thick, white vaginal discharge with no odor or with a mild odor

Less common

Abdominal or stomach cramping or pain; burning or irritation of penis of sexual partner; burning on urination or need to urinate more often; itching, stinging or redness of the genital area

Other side effects may occur that usually do not need medical attention. These side effects may go away during treatment as your body adjusts to the medicine. However, check with your doctor if any of the following side effects continue or are bothersome:

Less common

Diarrhea; dizziness or lightheadedness; dryness of mouth; headache; feeling of a furry tongue; loss of appetite; metallic taste or other change in taste sensation; nausea; vomiting

Metronidazole may cause your urine to become dark. This is harmless and will go away when you stop using this medicine.

After you stop using this medicine, your body may need time to adjust. The length of time this takes depends on the amount of medicine you were using and how long you used it. During this period of time check with your doctor if you notice any of the following side effects:

Any vaginal or genital irritation or itching; pain during sexual intercouse; thick, white vaginal discharge not present before treatment, with no odor or with a mild odor

Other side effects not listed above may also occur in some patients. If you notice any other effects, check with your doctor.

Developed: 05/16/94
Interim revision: 08/19/97

METYROSINE Systemic†

A commonly used brand name in the U.S. is Demser.

†Not commercially available in Canada.

Description

Metyrosine (me-TYE-roe-seen) belongs to the general class of medicines called antihypertensives. It is used to treat high blood pressure (hypertension) caused by a disease called pheochromocytoma (a noncancerous tumor of the adrenal gland).

Metyrosine reduces the amount of certain chemicals in the body. When these chemicals are present in large amounts, they cause high blood pressure.

Metyrosine is available only with your doctor's prescription, in the following dosage form:

Oral

- Capsules (U.S.)

Before Using This Medicine

In deciding to use a medicine, the risks of taking the medicine must be weighed against the good it will do. This is a decision you and your doctor will make. For metyrosine, the following should be considered:

Allergies—Tell your doctor if you have ever had any unusual or allergic reaction to metyrosine. Also tell your health care professional if you are allergic to any other substances, such as foods, sulfites or other preservatives, or dyes.

Pregnancy—Studies on effects in pregnancy have not been done in either humans or animals.

Breast-feeding—It is not known whether metyrosine passes into breast milk. However, this medicine has not been reported to cause problems in nursing babies.

Children—Studies on this medicine have been done only in adult patients, and there is no specific information comparing use of metyrosine in children with use in other age groups.

Older adults—Many medicines have not been studied specifically in older people. Therefore, it may not be known whether they work exactly the same way they do in younger adults or if they cause different side effects or problems in older people. There is no specific information comparing use of metyrosine in the elderly with use in other age groups.

Other medicines—Although certain medicines should not be used together at all, in other cases two different medicines may be used together even if an interaction might occur. In these cases, your doctor may want to change the dose, or other precautions may be necessary. Tell your health care professional if you are taking any other prescription or nonprescription (over-the-counter [OTC]) medicine.

Other medical problems—The presence of other medical problems may affect the use of metyrosine. Make sure you tell your doctor if you have any other medical problems, especially:

- Kidney disease or
- Liver disease—Effects of metyrosine may be increased because of slower removal from the body
- Mental depression (or history of) or
- Parkinson's disease—Metyrosine may make these conditions worse

Proper Use of This Medicine

Take this medicine only as directed by your doctor. Do not take more or less of it than your doctor ordered.

To help you remember to take your medicine, try to get into the habit of taking it at the same times each day.

Dosing—The dose of metyrosine will be different for different patients. *Follow your doctor's orders or the directions on the label.* The following information includes only the average doses of metyrosine. *If your dose is different, do not change it* unless your doctor tells you to do so:

- For *oral* dosage forms (capsules):
  —Adults and children 12 years of age and older: 1000 milligrams to 3000 milligrams (1 to 3 grams) a day, divided into four doses.

Missed dose—If you miss a dose of this medicine, take it as soon as possible. However, if it is almost time for your next dose, skip the missed dose and go back to your regular dosing schedule. Do not double doses.

Storage—To store this medicine:

- Keep out of the reach of children.
- Store away from heat and direct light.
- Do not store in the bathroom, near the kitchen sink, or in other damp places. Heat or moisture may cause the medicine to break down.
- Do not keep outdated medicine or medicine no longer needed. Be sure that any discarded medicine is out of the reach of children.

Precautions While Using This Medicine

It is important that your doctor check your progress at regular visits to make sure that this medicine is working properly and to check for unwanted effects.

While taking this medicine, it is important that you drink plenty of fluids and urinate often. This will help prevent kidney problems and keep your kidneys working well. If you have any questions about how much you should drink, check with your doctor.

This medicine will add to the effects of alcohol and other CNS depressants (medicines that slow down the nervous system, possibly causing drowsiness). Some examples of CNS depressants are antihistamines or medicine for hay fever, other allergies, or colds; sedatives, tranquilizers, or sleeping medicine; prescription pain medicine or narcotics; barbiturates; medicine for seizures; tricyclic antidepressants (medicine for depression); muscle relaxants; or anesthetics, including some dental anesthetics. *Check with your doctor before taking any of the above while you are taking this medicine.*

Before having any kind of surgery (including dental surgery), tell the medical doctor or dentist in charge that you are taking this medicine.

This medicine may cause most people to become drowsy or less alert than they are normally. *Make sure you know how you react to this medicine before you drive, use machines, or do anything else that could be dangerous if you are not alert.*

Side Effects of This Medicine

Along with its needed effects, a medicine may cause some unwanted effects. Although not all of these side effects may occur, if they do occur they may need medical attention.

Check with your doctor as soon as possible if any of the following side effects occur:

More common

Diarrhea; drooling; trembling and shaking of hands and fingers; trouble in speaking

Less common

Anxiety; confusion; hallucinations (seeing, hearing, or feeling things that are not there); mental depression

Rare

Black, tarry stools; blood in urine or stools; unusual bleeding or bruising; muscle spasms, especially of neck and back; painful urination; pinpoint red spots on skin; restlessness; shortness of breath; shuffling walk; skin rash and itching; swelling of feet or lower legs; tic-like (jerky) movements of head, face, mouth, and neck; unusual tiredness or weakness

Other side effects may occur that usually do not need medical attention. These side effects may go away during treatment as your body adjusts to the medicine. However, check with your doctor if any of the following side effects continue or are bothersome:

More common

Drowsiness

Less common

Decreased sexual ability in men; dryness of mouth; nausea, vomiting, or stomach pain; stuffy nose; swelling of breasts or unusual milk production

After you stop taking this medicine, it may still produce some side effects that need attention. During this period of time check with your doctor if you notice the following side effect:

Diarrhea

Also, after you stop taking this medicine, you may have feelings of increased energy or you may have trouble sleeping. However, these effects should last only for two or three days.

Other side effects not listed above may also occur in some patients. If you notice any other effects, check with your doctor.

Revised: 01/20/93

MEXILETINE Systemic

A commonly used brand name in the U.S. and Canada is Mexitil.

Description

Mexiletine (MEX-i-le-teen) belongs to the group of medicines known as antiarrhythmics. It is used to correct irregular heartbeats to a normal rhythm.

Mexiletine produces its helpful effects by slowing nerve impulses in the heart and making the heart tissue less sensitive.

Mexiletine is available only with your doctor's prescription, in the following dosage form:

Oral

- Capsules (U.S. and Canada)

Before Using This Medicine

In deciding to use a medicine, the risks of taking the medicine must be weighed against the good it will do. This is a decision you and your doctor will make. For mexiletine, the following should be considered:

Allergies—Tell your doctor if you have ever had any unusual or allergic reaction to mexiletine, lidocaine, or tocainide. Also tell your health care professional if you are allergic to any other substance, such as foods, preservatives, or dyes.

Pregnancy—Mexiletine has not been studied in pregnant women. However, studies in animals have shown that mexiletine causes a decrease in successful pregnancies but no birth defects. Before taking this medicine, make sure your doctor knows if you are pregnant or if you may become pregnant.

Breast-feeding—Mexiletine passes into breast milk. Because this medicine may cause serious side effects, breast-feeding is generally not recommended while you are receiving it. Be sure you have discussed this with your doctor before taking mexiletine.

Children—Studies on this medicine have been done only in adult patients, and there is no specific information comparing use of mexiletine in children with use in other age groups.

Older adults—Many medicines have not been studied specifically in older people. Therefore, it may not be known whether they work exactly the same way they do in younger adults or if they cause different side effects or problems in older people. There is no specific information comparing use of mexiletine in the elderly with use in other age groups.

Other medicines—Although certain medicines should not be used together at all, in other cases two different medicines may be used together even if an interaction might occur. In these cases, your doctor may want to change the dose, or other precautions may be necessary. Tell your health care professional if you are taking any other prescription or nonprescription (over-the-counter [OTC]) medicine.

Smoking—Smoking may decrease the effects of mexiletine.

Other medical problems—The presence of other medical problems may affect the use of mexiletine. Make sure you tell your doctor if you have any other medical problems, especially:

- Congestive heart failure or
- Low blood pressure—Mexiletine may make these conditions worse
- Heart attack (severe) or
- Liver disease—Effects may last longer because of slower removal of mexiletine from the body
- Seizures (history of)—Mexiletine can cause seizures

Proper Use of This Medicine

Take mexiletine exactly as directed by your doctor, even though you may feel well. Do not take more medicine than ordered.

To lessen the possibility of stomach upset, mexiletine should be taken with food or immediately after meals or with milk or an antacid.

This medicine works best when there is a constant amount in the blood. *To help keep this amount constant, do not miss any doses. Also it is best to take the doses at evenly spaced times day and night.* For example, if you are to take 3 doses a day, the doses should be spaced about 8 hours apart. If this interferes with your sleep or other daily activities, or if you need help in planning the best times to take your medicine, check with your health care professional.

Dosing—The dose of mexiletine will be different for different patients. *Follow your doctor's orders or the directions on the label.* The following information includes only the average dose of mexiletine. *If your dose is dif-*

ferent, do not change it unless your doctor tells you to do so.

The number of capsules that you take depends on the strength of the medicine.

- For *oral* dosage form (capsules):
  —For irregular heartbeat (arrhythmias):
    - Adults—At first, 200 milligrams (mg) every eight hours. Then, your doctor may raise or lower your dose as needed.
    - Children—Use and dose must be determined by your doctor.

Missed dose—If you miss a dose of this medicine and remember within 4 hours, take it as soon as possible. Then go back to your regular dosing schedule. However, if you do not remember until later, skip the missed dose and go back to your regular dosing schedule. Do not double doses.

Storage—To store this medicine:
- Keep out of the reach of children.
- Store away from heat and direct light.
- Do not store in the bathroom, near the kitchen sink, or in other damp places. Heat or moisture may cause the medicine to break down.
- Do not keep outdated medicine or medicine no longer needed. Be sure that any discarded medicine is out of the reach of children.

Precautions While Using This Medicine

It is important that your doctor check your progress at regular visits to make sure the medicine is working properly. This will allow for changes to be made in the amount of medicine you are taking, if necessary.

Your doctor may want you to carry a medical identification card or bracelet stating that you are using this medicine.

Before having any kind of surgery (including dental surgery) or emergency treatment, tell the medical doctor or dentist in charge that you are taking this medicine.

Mexiletine may cause some people to become dizzy, lightheaded, or less alert than they are normally. *Make sure you know how you react to this medicine before you drive, use machines, or do anything else that could be dangerous if you are dizzy or are not alert.*

Side Effects of This Medicine

Along with its needed effects, a medicine may cause some unwanted effects. Although not all of these side effects may occur, if they do occur they may need medical attention.

Check with your doctor as soon as possible if any of the following side effects occur:

Less common
Chest pain; fast or irregular heartbeat; shortness of breath

Rare
Convulsions (seizures); fever or chills; unusual bleeding or bruising

Other side effects may occur that usually do not need medical attention. These side effects may go away during treatment as your body adjusts to the medicine. However, check with your doctor if any of the following side effects continue or are bothersome:

More common
Dizziness or lightheadedness; heartburn; nausea and vomiting; nervousness; trembling or shaking of the hands; unsteadiness or difficulty in walking

Less common
Blurred vision; confusion; constipation or diarrhea; headache; numbness or tingling of fingers and toes; ringing in the ears; skin rash; slurred speech; trouble in sleeping; unusual tiredness or weakness

Other side effects not listed above may also occur in some patients. If you notice any other effects, check with your doctor.

Revised: 10/06/92
Interim revision: 07/14/94

MICONAZOLE Topical

Some commonly used brand names are:

In the U.S.—
Micatin
Monistat-Derm
Zeasorb-AF
Generic name product may also be available.

In Canada—
Micatin
Monistat-Derm

Description

Miconazole (mi-KON-a-zole) belongs to the group of medicines called antifungals. Topical miconazole is used to treat some types of fungus infections.

Some of these preparations may be available without a prescription; however, your doctor may have special instructions on the proper use of these medicines for your medical problem. Others are available only with your doctor's prescription.

Topical miconazole is available in the following dosage forms:

Topical
- Aerosol powder (U.S.)
- Aerosol solution (U.S.)
- Cream (U.S. and Canada)
- Lotion (U.S. and Canada)
- Powder (U.S.)

Before Using This Medicine

If you are using this medicine without a prescription, carefully read and follow any precautions on the label. For miconazole, the following should be considered:

Allergies—Tell your doctor if you have ever had any unusual or allergic reaction to miconazole. Also, tell your health care professional if you are allergic to any other substances, such as preservatives or dyes.

Pregnancy—Miconazole topical preparations have not been shown to cause birth defects or other problems in humans.

Breast-feeding—Miconazole topical preparations have not been reported to cause problems in nursing babies.

Children—Although there is no specific information comparing use of topical miconazole in children with use in other age groups, this medicine is not expected to cause different side effects or problems in children than it does in adults.

Older adults—Many medicines have not been studied specifically in older people. Therefore, it may not be known whether they work exactly the same way they do in younger adults. Although there is no specific information comparing use of topical miconazole in the elderly with use in other age groups, this medicine is not expected to cause different side effects or problems in older people than it does in younger adults.

Other medicines—Although certain medicines should not be used together at all, in other cases two different medicines may be used together even if an interaction might occur. In these cases, your doctor may want to change the dose, or other precautions may be necessary. Tell your health care professional if you are using any other topical prescription or nonprescription (over-the-counter [OTC]) medicine that is to be applied to the same area of the skin.

Proper Use of This Medicine

Keep this medicine away from the eyes.

Apply enough miconazole to cover the affected area, and rub in gently.

To use the *aerosol powder form* of miconazole:

- Shake well before using.
- From a distance of 6 to 10 inches, spray the powder on the affected areas. If it is used on the feet, spray it between the toes, on the feet, and in the socks and shoes.
- Do not inhale the powder.
- Do not use near heat, near open flame, or while smoking.

To use the *aerosol solution form* of miconazole:

- Shake well before using.
- From a distance of 4 to 6 inches, spray the solution on the affected areas. If it is used on the feet, spray it between the toes and on the feet.
- Do not inhale the vapors from the spray.
- Do not use near heat, near open flame, or while smoking.

To use the *powder form* of miconazole:

- If the powder is used on the feet, sprinkle it between the toes, on the feet, and in the socks and shoes.

When miconazole is used to treat certain types of fungus infections of the skin, an occlusive dressing (airtight covering, such as kitchen plastic wrap) should *not* be applied over this medicine. To do so may cause irritation of the skin. *Do not apply an occlusive dressing over this medicine unless you have been directed to do so by your doctor.*

To help clear up your infection completely, *keep using this medicine for the full time of treatment,* even if your condition has improved. *Do not miss any doses.*

Dosing—The dose of topical miconazole will be different for different patients. *Follow your doctor's orders or the directions on the label.* The following information includes only the average doses of topical miconazole. *If your dose is different, do not change it* unless your doctor tells you to do so.

- For *aerosol powder, aerosol solution, cream,* and *powder* dosage forms:
  - —For fungus infections:
    - Adults and children—Apply to the affected area(s) of the skin two times a day, morning and evening.
- For *cream* and *lotion* dosage forms:
  - —For sun fungus:
    - Adults and children—Apply to the affected area(s) of the skin once a day.

Missed dose—If you miss a dose of this medicine, apply it as soon as possible. However, if it is almost time for your next dose, skip the missed dose and go back to your regular dosing schedule.

Storage—To store this medicine:

- Keep out of the reach of children.
- Store away from heat and direct light.
- Do not store the powder form of this medicine in the bathroom, near the kitchen sink, or in other damp places. Heat or moisture may cause the medicine to break down.
- Keep the cream, lotion, and aerosol solution forms of this medicine from freezing.
- Do not puncture, break, or burn the aerosol powder or aerosol solution container.
- Do not keep outdated medicine or medicine no longer needed. Be sure that any discarded medicine is out of the reach of children.

Precautions While Using This Medicine

If your skin problem does not improve within 4 weeks, or if it becomes worse, check with your health care professional.

Side Effects of This Medicine

Along with its needed effects, a medicine may cause some unwanted effects. Although not all of these side effects may occur, if they do occur they may need medical attention.

Check with your doctor as soon as possible if any of the following side effects occur:

Blistering, burning, redness, skin rash, or other sign of skin irritation not present before use of this medicine

Other side effects not listed above may also occur in some patients. If you notice any other effects, check with your doctor.

Revised: 07/25/94

MIDAZOLAM Systemic

A commonly used brand name in the U.S. and Canada is Versed.

Description

Midazolam (mid-AY-zoe-lam) is used to produce sleepiness or drowsiness and to relieve anxiety before surgery or certain procedures. It is also used to produce loss of consciousness before and during surgery.

Midazolam is given only by or under the immediate supervision of a doctor trained to use this medicine. If you will be receiving midazolam during surgery, your doctor or anesthesiologist will give you the medicine and closely follow your progress.

Midazolam is available in the following dosage form:

Parenteral

- Injection (U.S. and Canada)

Before Receiving This Medicine

In deciding to use a medicine, the risks of taking the medicine must be weighed against the good it will do. This is a decision you and your doctor will make. For midazolam, the following should be considered:

Allergies—Tell your doctor if you have ever had any unusual or allergic reaction to midazolam or other benzodiazepines (such as alprazolam [e.g., Xanax], bromazepam [e.g., Lectopam], chlordiazepoxide [e.g., Librium], clonazepam [e.g., Klonopin], diazepam [e.g., Valium], estazolam [e.g., ProSom], flurazepam [e.g., Dalmane], halazepam [e.g., Paxipam], ketazolam [e.g., Loftran], lorazepam [e.g., Ativan], nitrazepam [e.g., Mogadon], oxazepam [e.g., Serax], prazepam [e.g., Centrax], quazepam [e.g., Doral], temazepam [e.g., Restoril], triazolam [e.g., Halcion]). Also, tell your health care professional if you are allergic to any other substances, such as foods, preservatives, or dyes.

Pregnancy—Midazolam is not recommended for use during pregnancy because it may cause birth defects. Other benzodiazepines, such as chlordiazepoxide (e.g., Librium) and diazepam (e.g., Valium) that are related chemically and in action to midazolam, have been reported to increase the chance of birth defects when used during the first 3 months of pregnancy. Also, use of midazolam during pregnancy, especially during the last few days, may cause drowsiness, slow heartbeat, shortness of breath, or troubled breathing in the newborn infant. In addition, receiving midazolam just before or during labor may cause weakness in the newborn infant.

Breast-feeding—It is not known whether midazolam passes into the breast milk. However, this medicine has not been reported to cause problems in nursing babies.

Children—Although there is no specific information comparing use of midazolam in children with use in other age groups, this medicine is not expected to cause different side effects or problems in children than it does in adults.

Older Adults—Elderly people are especially sensitive to the effects of midazolam. This may increase the chance of side effects during the use of this medicine. Also, time to complete recovery after midazolam is given may be slower in the elderly than in younger adults.

Other medicines—Although certain medicines should not be used together at all, in other cases 2 different medicines may be used together even if an interaction might occur. In these cases, your doctor may want to change the dose, or other precautions may be necessary. When you are receiving midazolam, it is especially important that your health care professional know if you are taking any of the following:

- Central nervous system (CNS) depressants (medicine that causes drowsiness)—The CNS depressant and other effects of either these medicines or midazolam may be increased; also, the effects of midazolam may be prolonged

Other medical problems—The presence of other medical problems may affect the use of midazolam. Make sure you tell your doctor if you have any other medical problems, especially:

- Heart disease or
- Kidney disease or
- Liver disease or
- Obesity (overweight)—The effects of midazolam may be prolonged
- Lung disease or
- Myasthenia gravis or other muscle and nerve disease—Midazolam may make the condition worse

Proper Use of This Medicine

Dosing—The dose of midazolam will be different for different patients. Your doctor will decide on the right amount for you. The dose will depend on:

- Your age;
- Your weight;
- Your general physical condition;
- The kind of surgery or other procedure you are having; and
- Other medicines you are taking or will receive before and during the procedure.

Precautions After Receiving This Medicine

For patients going home within 24 hours after receiving midazolam:

- Midazolam may cause some people to feel drowsy, tired, or weak for one or two days after it has been given. It may also cause problems with coordination and one's ability to think. Therefore, *do not drive, use machines, or do anything else that could be dangerous if you are not alert* until the effects of the medicine have disappeared or until the day after you receive midazolam, whichever period of time is longer.

- *Do not drink alcoholic beverages or take other CNS depressants (medicines that slow down the nervous system, possibly causing drowsiness) for about 24 hours after you have received midazolam, unless otherwise directed by your doctor.* To do so may add to the effects of the medicine. Some examples of CNS depressants are antihistamines or medicine for hay fever, other allergies, or colds; other sedatives, tranquilizers, or sleeping medicine; prescription pain medicine or narcotics; medicine for seizures; and muscle relaxants.

Side Effects of This Medicine

Some side effects may occur that usually do not need medical attention. The following side effects may go away as the effects of midazolam wear off. However, check with your doctor if any of the following side effects continue or are bothersome:

Less common or rare

Blurred vision or other changes in vision; coughing; dizziness, lightheadedness, or feeling faint; drowsiness (prolonged); headache; hiccups; nausea or vomiting; numbness, tingling, pain, or weakness in hands or feet; redness, pain, lump or hardness, or muscle stiffness at place of injection

Other side effects not listed above may also occur in some patients. If you notice any other effects, check with your doctor.

Revised: 11/11/91
Interim revision: 08/17/94

MINOXIDIL Systemic

A commonly used brand name in the U.S. and Canada is Loniten. Generic name product may also be available in the U.S.

Description

Minoxidil (mi-NOX-i-dill) belongs to the general class of medicines called antihypertensives. It is used to treat high blood pressure (hypertension).

High blood pressure adds to the workload of the heart and arteries. If it continues for a long time, the heart and arteries may not function properly. This can damage the blood vessels of the brain, heart, and kidneys, resulting in a stroke, heart failure, or kidney failure. High blood pressure may also increase the risk of heart attacks. These problems may be less likely to occur if blood pressure is controlled.

Minoxidil works by relaxing blood vessels so that blood passes through them more easily. This helps to lower blood pressure.

Minoxidil has other effects that could be bothersome for some patients. These include increased hair growth, weight gain, fast heartbeat, and chest pain. Before you take this medicine, be sure that you have discussed the use of it with your doctor.

Minoxidil is being applied to the scalp in liquid form by some balding men to stimulate hair growth. However, improper use of liquids made from minoxidil tablets can result in minoxidil being absorbed into the body, where it may cause unwanted effects on the heart and blood vessels.

Minoxidil is available only with your doctor's prescription, in the following dosage form:

Oral

- Tablets (U.S. and Canada)

Before Using This Medicine

In deciding to use a medicine, the risks of taking the medicine must be weighed against the good it will do. This is a decision you and your doctor will make. For minoxidil, the following should be considered:

Allergies—Tell your doctor if you have ever had any unusual or allergic reaction to minoxidil. Also tell your health care professional if you are allergic to any other substances, such as foods, preservatives, or dyes.

Pregnancy—Minoxidil has not been studied in pregnant women. However, there have been reports of babies born with extra thick or dark hair on their bodies after the mothers took minoxidil during pregnancy. Discuss this possible effect with your doctor.

Studies in rats found a decreased rate of conception, and studies in rabbits at 5 times the human dose have shown a decrease in successful pregnancies. Minoxidil did not cause birth defects in rats or rabbits.

Breast-feeding—Although minoxidil passes into breast milk, it has not been reported to cause problems in nursing babies.

Children—Although there is no specific information comparing use of minoxidil in children with use in other age groups, this medicine is not expected to cause different side effects or problems in children than it does in adults.

Older adults—Elderly patients may be more sensitive to the effects of minoxidil. In addition, minoxidil may reduce tolerance to cold temperatures in elderly patients.

Other medicines—Although certain medicines should not be used together at all, in other cases two different medicines may be used together even if an interaction might occur. In these cases, your doctor may want to change the dose, or other precautions may be necessary. When taking minoxidil it is especially important that your health care professional know if you are taking any of the following:

- Guanethidine (e.g., Ismelin) or
- Nitrates (medicine for angina)—Severe lowered blood pressure may occur

Other medical problems—The presence of other medical problems may affect the use of minoxidil. Make sure you tell your doctor if you have any other medical problems, especially:

- Angina (chest pain)—Minoxidil may make this condition worse
- Heart attack or stroke (recent)—Lowering blood pressure may make problems resulting from heart attack or stroke worse
- Heart or blood vessel disease—Minoxidil can cause fluid buildup, which can cause problems
- Kidney disease—Effects may be increased because of slower removal of minoxidil from the body
- Pheochromocytoma—Minoxidil may cause the tumor to be more active

Proper Use of This Medicine

In addition to the use of the medicine your doctor has prescribed, treatment for your high blood pressure may include weight control and care in the types of foods you eat, especially foods high in sodium. Your doctor will tell you which of these are most important for you. You should check with your doctor before changing your diet.

Many patients who have high blood pressure will not notice any signs of the problem. In fact, many may feel normal. It is very important that you *take your medicine exactly as directed* and that you keep your appointments with your doctor even if you feel well.

Remember that minoxidil will not cure your high blood pressure but it does help control it. Therefore, you must continue to take it as directed if you expect to lower your blood pressure and keep it down. *You may have to take high blood pressure medicine for the rest of your life.* If high blood pressure is not treated, it can cause serious problems such as heart failure, blood vessel disease, stroke, or kidney disease.

To help you remember to take your medicine, try to get into the habit of taking it at the same time each day.

This medicine is usually given together with certain other medicines. If you are using a combination of drugs, make sure that you take each medicine at the proper time and do not mix them. Ask your health care professional to help you plan a way to remember to take your medicines at the right time.

Dosing—The dose of minoxidil will be different for different patients. *Follow your doctor's orders or the directions on the label.* The following information includes only the average doses of minoxidil. *If your dose is different, do not change it* unless your doctor tells you to do so:

- For *oral* dosage forms (tablets):
  —Adults and children over 12 years of age: 5 to 40 milligrams taken as a single dose or in divided doses.
  —Children up to 12 years of age: 200 micrograms to 1 milligram per kilogram of body weight a day to be taken as a single dose or in divided doses.

Missed dose—If you miss a dose of this medicine and remember it within a few hours, take it when you remember. However, if you do not remember until the next day, skip the missed dose and go back to your regular dosing schedule. Do not double doses.

Storage—To store this medicine:

- Keep out of the reach of children.
- Store away from heat and direct light.
- Do not store in the bathroom, near the kitchen sink, or in other damp places. Heat or moisture may cause the medicine to break down.
- Do not keep outdated medicine or medicine no longer needed. Be sure that any discarded medicine is out of the reach of children.

Precautions While Using This Medicine

It is important that your doctor check your progress at regular visits to make sure that this medicine is working properly.

Ask your doctor about checking your pulse rate before and after taking minoxidil. Then, while you are taking this medicine, *check your pulse regularly while you are resting*. If it increases by 20 beats or more a minute, check with your doctor right away.

While you are taking minoxidil, *weigh yourself every day*. A weight gain of 2 to 3 pounds (about 1 kg) in an adult is normal and should be lost with continued treatment. However, if you suddenly gain 5 pounds (2 kg) or more (for a child, 2 pounds [1 kg] or more) or if you notice swelling of your feet or lower legs, check with your doctor right away.

Do not take other medicines unless they have been discussed with your doctor. This especially includes over-the-counter (nonprescription) medicines for appetite control, asthma, colds, cough, hay fever, or sinus problems, since they may tend to increase your blood pressure.

Side Effects of This Medicine

Along with its needed effects, a medicine may cause some unwanted effects. Although not all of these side effects may occur, if they do occur they may need medical attention.

Check with your doctor immediately if any of the following side effects occur:

More common
Fast or irregular heartbeat; weight gain (rapid) of more than 5 pounds (2 pounds in children)

Less common
Chest pain; shortness of breath

Check with your doctor as soon as possible if any of the following side effects occur:

More common
Bloating; flushing or redness of skin; swelling of feet or lower legs

Less common
Numbness or tingling of hands, feet, or face
Rare
Skin rash and itching

Other side effects may occur that usually do not need medical attention. These side effects may go away during treatment as your body adjusts to the medicine. However, check with your doctor if any of the following side effects continue or are bothersome:

More common
Increase in hair growth, usually on face, arms, and back
Less common or rare
Breast tenderness in males and females; headache

This medicine causes a temporary increase in hair growth in most people. Hair may grow longer and darker in both men and women. This may first be noticed on the face several weeks after you start taking minoxidil. Later, new hair growth may be noticed on the back, arms, legs, and scalp. Talk to your doctor about shaving or using a hair remover during this time. After treatment with minoxidil has ended, the hair will stop growing, although it may take several months for the new hair growth to go away.

Other side effects not listed above may also occur in some patients. If you notice any other effects, check with your doctor.

Revised: 05/26/93

MINOXIDIL Topical

Some commonly used brand names are:

In the U.S.—
Rogaine for Men
Rogaine for Women

Generic name product may also be available.

In Canada—
Apo-Gain
Gen-Minoxidil
Minoxigaine
Rogaine

Description

Minoxidil (mi-NOX-i-dill) applied to the scalp is used to stimulate hair growth in men and women with a certain type of baldness. The exact way that it works is not known.

If hair growth is going to occur with the use of minoxidil, it usually occurs after the medicine has been used for about 4 months and lasts only as long as the medicine continues to be used. The new hair will be lost within a few months after minoxidil treatment is stopped.

In the U.S., this medicine is available without a prescription. In Canada, this medicine is available only with your doctor's prescription. It is available in the following dosage form:

Topical
- Topical solution (U.S. and Canada)

Before Using This Medicine

In deciding to use a medicine, the risks of using the medicine must be weighed against the good it will do. This is a decision you and your doctor will make. For topical minoxidil, the following should be considered:

Allergies—Tell your doctor if you have ever had any unusual or allergic reaction to minoxidil. Also tell your health care professional if you are allergic to any other substances, such as preservatives or dyes.

Pregnancy—Topical minoxidil has not been studied in pregnant women. However, some studies in animals have shown that minoxidil, when given by mouth, causes problems during pregnancy, although the studies have not shown that the medicine causes birth defects. Before using this medicine, make sure your doctor knows if you are pregnant or if you may become pregnant.

Breast-feeding—It is not known whether topical minoxidil passes into breast milk. However, minoxidil, taken by mouth, does pass into breast milk. Minoxidil is not recommended during breast-feeding, because it may cause problems in nursing babies.

Older adults—Many medicines have not been studied specifically in older people. Therefore, it may not be known whether they work exactly the same way they do in younger adults or if they cause different side effects or problems in older people. There is no specific information comparing use of minoxidil on the scalp in the elderly with use in other age groups.

Other medicines—Although certain medicines should not be used together at all, in other cases two different medicines may be used together even if an interaction might occur. In these cases, your doctor may want to change the dose, or other precautions may be necessary. When you are using topical minoxidil, it is especially important that your health care professional know if you are taking any other prescription or nonprescription (over-the-counter [OTC]) medicine or if you are using any of the following on your scalp:

- Corticosteroids (cortisone-like medicine) or
- Petrolatum (e.g., Vaseline) or
- Tretinoin (e.g., Retin A)—Use of these products on your scalp may cause too much topical minoxidil to be absorbed into the body and may increase the chance of side effects
- Minoxidil, systemic (e.g., Loniten)—Use of topical minoxidil with minoxidil taken by mouth for high blood pressure may increase the chance of side effects

Other medical problems—The presence of other medical problems may affect the use of topical minoxidil. Make sure you tell your doctor if you have any other medical problems, especially:

- Any other skin problems or an irritation or a sunburn on the scalp—The condition may cause too much topical mi-

noxidil to be absorbed into the body and may increase the chance of side effects
- Heart disease or
- Hypertension (high blood pressure)—The condition may get worse if too much medicine is absorbed into the body

Proper Use of This Medicine

This medicine usually comes with patient instructions. It is important that you read the instructions carefully.

It is very important that you use this medicine only as directed. Do not use more of it and do not use it more often than your doctor ordered. To do so may increase the chance of it being absorbed through the skin. For the same reason, do not apply minoxidil to other parts of your body. Absorption into the body may affect the heart and blood vessels and cause unwanted effects.

Do not use any other skin products on the same skin area on which you use minoxidil.

To apply minoxidil solution:
- Shampoo your hair each morning before applying minoxidil. Make sure your hair and scalp are completely dry before applying this medicine.
- Apply the amount prescribed to the area of the scalp being treated, beginning in the center of the area. Follow your doctor's instructions on how to apply the solution, using the applicator provided.
- Immediately after using this medicine, wash your hands to remove any medicine that may be on them.
- Do not use a hairdryer to dry the scalp after you apply minoxidil solution. Blowing with a hairdryer on the scalp may make the treatment less effective.
- If you are using this medicine at bedtime, do not go to bed until at least 30 minutes after you use it. That way, less of the medicine will rub off on the pillowcase.

If your scalp becomes abraded, irritated, or sunburned, check with your doctor before applying minoxidil.

Keep this medicine away from the eyes, nose, and mouth. If you should accidentally get some in your eyes, nose, or mouth, flush the area thoroughly with cool tap water. If you are using the pump spray, be careful not to breathe the spray in.

Dosing—The dose of topical minoxidil will be different for different patients. *Follow your doctor's orders or the directions on the label.* The following information includes only the average dose of topical minoxidil. *If your dose is different, do not change it* unless your doctor tells you to do so.

- For *topical solution* dosage form:
  - For hair growth:
    - Adults—Apply 1 milliliter to the scalp two times a day.

Missed dose—If you miss a dose of this medicine, go back to your regular dosing schedule. Do not double doses.

Storage—To store this medicine:
- Keep out of the reach of children.
- Store away from heat and direct light.
- Keep the medicine from freezing.
- Do not keep outdated medicine or medicine no longer needed. Be sure that any discarded medicine is out of the reach of children.

Precautions While Using This Medicine

It is important that your doctor check your progress at regular visits to make sure that this medicine is working properly and to check for unwanted effects.

Tell your doctor if you notice itching, redness, or burning of your scalp after you apply minoxidil. If the itching, redness, or burning is severe, wash the medicine off and check with your doctor before using it again.

Side Effects of This Medicine

Along with its needed effects, a medicine may cause some unwanted effects. Although not all of these side effects may occur, if they do occur they may need medical attention.

Check with your doctor as soon as possible if any of the following side effects occur:

Less common

Itching or skin rash

Rare

Blurred vision or other change in vision; burning of scalp; decrease of sexual ability or desire; dizziness; increased hair loss; lightheadedness; soreness at root of hair; swelling of face

Signs and symptoms of too much medicine being absorbed into the body—Rare

Chest pain; fast or irregular heartbeat; flushing; headache; numbness or tingling of hands, feet, or face; swelling of face, hands, feet, or lower legs; weight gain (rapid)

Other side effects may occur that usually do not need medical attention. These side effects may go away during treatment as your body adjusts to the medicine. However, check with your doctor if either of the following side effects continues or is bothersome:

Less common

Dry or flaking skin; reddened skin

Other side effects not listed above may also occur in some patients. If you notice any other effects, check with your doctor.

Revised: 04/14/92
Interim revision: 07/14/94; 07/15/96

MISOPROSTOL Systemic

A commonly used brand name in the U.S. and Canada is Cytotec.

Description

Misoprostol (mye-soe-PROST-ole) is taken to prevent stomach ulcers in patients taking anti-inflammatory drugs, including aspirin. Misoprostol may also be used for other conditions as determined by your doctor.

Misoprostol helps the stomach protect itself against acid damage. It also decreases the amount of acid produced by the stomach.

This medicine is available only with your doctor's prescription, in the following dosage form:

Oral

- Tablets (U.S. and Canada)

Before Using This Medicine

In deciding to use a medicine, the risks of taking the medicine must be weighed against the good it will do. This is a decision you and your doctor will make. For misoprostol, the following should be considered:

Allergies—Tell your doctor if you have ever had any unusual or allergic reaction to misoprostol. Also tell your health care professional if you are allergic to any other substances, such as foods, preservatives, or dyes.

Pregnancy—*Misoprostol must not be used during pregnancy.* It has been shown to cause contractions and bleeding of the uterus. Misoprostol may also cause miscarriage.

Before starting to take this medicine you must have had a negative pregnancy test within the previous 2 weeks. Also, you must start taking misoprostol only on the second or third day of your next normal menstrual period. In addition, it will be necessary that you use an effective form of birth control while taking this medicine. Be sure that you have discussed this with your doctor before taking this medicine.

Breast-feeding—It is not known whether misoprostol passes into breast milk. However, misoprostol is not recommended for use during breast-feeding because it may cause diarrhea in nursing babies.

Children—Studies on this medicine have been done only in adult patients, and there is no specific information comparing use of misoprostol in children with use in other age groups.

Older adults—This medicine has been tested and has not been shown to cause different side effects or problems in older people than it does in younger adults.

Other medicines—Although certain medicines should not be used together at all, in other cases two different medicines may be used together even if an interaction might occur. In these cases, your doctor may want to change the dose, or other precautions may be necessary. Tell your health care professional if you are taking any other prescription or nonprescription (over-the-counter [OTC]) medicine.

Other medical problems—The presence of other medical problems may affect the use of misoprostol. Make sure you tell your doctor if you have any other medical problems, especially:

- Blood vessel disease—Medicines similar to misoprostol have been shown to make this condition worse
- Epilepsy (uncontrolled)—Medicines similar to misoprostol have been shown to cause convulsions (seizures)

Proper Use of This Medicine

Misoprostol is best taken with or after meals and at bedtime, unless otherwise directed by your doctor.

Dosing—The dose of misoprostol will be different for different patients. *Follow your doctor's orders or the directions on the label.* The following information includes only the average doses of misoprostol. *If your dose is different, do not change it* unless your doctor tells you to do so.

- To prevent stomach ulcers in patients taking anti-inflammatory medicines including aspirin:
  - —For *oral* dosage form (tablets):
    - Adults—200 micrograms (mcg) four times a day, with or after meals and at bedtime. Or, your dose may be 400 mcg two times day with the last dose taken at bedtime. Your doctor may reduce the dose to 100 mcg if you are sensitive to high doses.
    - Children and teenagers—Dose must be determined by your doctor.

Missed dose—If you miss a dose of this medicine, take it as soon as possible. However, if it is almost time for your next dose, skip the missed dose and go back to your regular dosing schedule. Do not double doses.

Storage—To store this medicine:

- Keep out of the reach of children.
- Store away from heat and direct light.
- Do not store in the bathroom, near the kitchen sink, or in other damp places. Heat or moisture may cause the medicine to break down.
- Do not keep outdated medicine or medicine no longer needed. Be sure that any discarded medicine is out of the reach of children.

Precautions While Using This Medicine

Misoprostol may cause miscarriage if taken during pregnancy. Therefore, if you suspect that you may have become pregnant, stop taking this medicine immediately and check with your doctor.

This medicine may cause diarrhea in some people. The diarrhea will usually disappear within a few days as your body adjusts to the medicine. However, check with your doctor if the diarrhea is severe and/or does not stop after a week. Your doctor may have to lower the dose of misoprostol you are taking.

Side Effects of This Medicine

Along with its needed effects, a medicine may cause some unwanted effects. Some side effects may occur that usually do not need medical attention. These side effects may go away during treatment as your body adjusts to the medicine. However, check with your doctor if any of the following side effects continue or are bothersome:

More common

Abdominal or stomach pain (mild); diarrhea

Less common or rare

Bleeding from vagina; constipation; cramps in lower abdomen or stomach area; gas; headache; nausea and/or vomiting

Other side effects not listed above may also occur in some patients. If you notice any other effects, check with your doctor.

Additional Information

Once a medicine has been approved for marketing for a certain use, experience may show that it is also useful for other medical problems. Although this use is not included in product labeling, misoprostol is used in certain patients with the following medical condition:

- Duodenal ulcers

For patients taking this medicine for *duodenal ulcers*:

- Antacids may be taken with misoprostol, if needed, to help relieve stomach pain, unless you are otherwise directed by your doctor. However, do not take magnesium-containing antacids, since they may cause diarrhea or worsen the diarrhea that is sometimes caused by misoprostol.
- Take this medicine for the full time of treatment, even if you begin to feel better. Also, it is important that you keep your appointments with your doctor so that your doctor will be better able to tell you when to stop taking this medicine.
- *Misoprostol is not normally taken for more than 4 weeks when used to treat duodenal ulcers.* However, your doctor may order treatment for a second 4-week period if needed.

Other than the above information, there is no additional information relating to proper use, precautions, or side effects for these uses.

Revised: 04/14/92
Interim revision: 08/10/94

MITOMYCIN Systemic

A commonly used brand name in the U.S. and Canada is Mutamycin.

Description

Mitomycin (mye-toe-MYE-sin) belongs to the group of medicines known as antineoplastics. It is used to treat some kinds of cancer.

Mitomycin interferes with the growth of cancer cells, which are eventually destroyed. Since the growth of normal body cells may also be affected by mitomycin, other effects will also occur. Some of these may be serious and must be reported to your doctor. Other effects, like hair loss, may not be serious but may cause concern. Some effects may not occur for months or years after the medicine is used.

Before you begin treatment with mitomycin, you and your doctor should talk about the good this medicine will do as well as the risks of using it.

Mitomycin is to be administered only by or under the immediate supervision of your doctor. It is available in the following dosage form:

Parenteral

- Injection (U.S. and Canada)

Before Using This Medicine

In deciding to use a medicine, the risks of taking the medicine must be weighed against the good it will do. This is a decision you and your doctor will make. For mitomycin, the following should be considered:

Allergies—Tell your doctor if you have ever had any unusual or allergic reaction to mitomycin.

Pregnancy—Tell your doctor if you are pregnant or if you intend to have children. There is a chance that this medicine may cause birth defects if either the male or female is taking it at the time of conception or if it is taken during pregnancy. Studies have shown that mitomycin causes birth defects in animals. In addition, many cancer medicines may cause sterility which could be permanent. Although sterility has not been reported with this medicine, the possibility should be kept in mind.

Be sure that you have discussed this with your doctor before taking this medicine. It is best to use some kind of birth control while you are receiving mitomycin. Tell your doctor right away if you think you have become pregnant while receiving mitomycin.

Breast-feeding—Tell your doctor if you are breast-feeding or if you intend to breast-feed during treatment with this medicine. Because mitomycin may cause serious side effects, breast-feeding is generally not recommended while you are receiving it.

Children—Although there is no specific information comparing use of mitomycin in children with use in other age groups, it is not expected to cause different side effects or problems in children than it does in adults.

Older adults—Many medicines have not been studied specifically older people. Therefore, it may not be known whether they work exactly the same way they do in younger adults or if they cause different side effects or problems in older people. There is no specific information comparing use of mitomycin in the elderly with use in other age groups.

Other medicines—Although certain medicines should not be used together at all, in other cases two different medicines may be used together even if an interaction might occur. In these cases, your doctor may want to change the dose, or other precautions may be necessary. When you are receiving mitomycin, it is especially important that your health care professional know if you are taking any of the following:

- Amphotericin B by injection (e.g., Fungizone) or
- Antithyroid agents (medicine for overactive thyroid) or
- Azathioprine (e.g., Imuran) or
- Chloramphenicol (e.g., Chloromycetin) or
- Colchicine or
- Flucytosine (e.g., Ancobon) or
- Ganciclovir (e.g., Cytovene) or
- Interferon (e.g., Intron A, Roferon-A) or
- Plicamycin (e.g., Mithracin) or
- Zidovudine (e.g., AZT, Retrovir) or
- If you have ever been treated with radiation or cancer medicines—Mitomycin may increase the effects of these medicines or radiation therapy on the blood

Other medical problems—The presence of other medical problems may affect the use of mitomycin. Make sure you tell your doctor if you have any other medical problems, especially:

- Bleeding problems
- Chickenpox (including recent exposure) or
- Herpes zoster (shingles)—Risk of severe disease affecting other parts of the body
- Infection—Mitomycin may decrease your body's ability to fight infection
- Kidney disease—May be worsened

Proper Use of This Medicine

Mitomycin is usually given together with certain other medicines. If you are using a combination of medicines, it is important that you receive each one at the proper time. If you are taking some of these medicines by mouth, ask your health care professional to help you plan a way to remember to take them at the right times.

This medicine often causes nausea, vomiting, and loss of appetite. However, it is very important that you continue to receive the medicine, even if you begin to feel ill. Ask your health care professional for ways to lessen these effects.

Dosing—The dose of mitomycin will be different for different patients. The dose that is used may depend on a number of things, including what the medicine is being used for, the patient's size, and whether or not other medicines are also being taken. *If you are receiving mitomycin at home, follow your doctor's orders or the directions on the label.* If you have any questions about the proper dose of mitomycin, ask your doctor.

Precautions While Using This Medicine

It is very important that your doctor check your progress at regular visits to make sure that this medicine is working properly and to check for unwanted effects.

While you are being treated with mitomycin, and after you stop treatment with it, *do not have any immunizations (vaccinations) without your doctor's approval.* Mitomycin may lower your body's resistance and there is a chance you might get the infection the immunization is meant to prevent. In addition, other persons living in your household should not take oral polio vaccine since there is a chance they could pass the polio virus on to you. Also, avoid persons who have taken oral polio vaccine. Do not get close to them, and do not stay in the same room with them for very long. If you cannot take these precautions, you should consider wearing a protective face mask that covers the nose and mouth.

Mitomycin can temporarily lower the number of white blood cells in your blood, increasing the chance of getting an infection. It can also lower the number of platelets, which are necessary for proper blood clotting. If this occurs, there are certain precautions you can take, especially when your blood count is low, to reduce the risk of infection or bleeding:

- If you can, avoid people with infections. *Check with your doctor immediately* if you think you are getting an infection or if you get a fever or chills, cough or hoarseness, lower back or side pain, or painful or difficult urination.
- *Check with your doctor immediately* if you notice any unusual bleeding or bruising; black, tarry stools; blood in urine or stools; or pinpoint red spots on your skin.
- Be careful when using a regular toothbrush, dental floss, or toothpick. Your medical doctor, dentist, or nurse may recommend other ways to clean your teeth and gums. Check with your medical doctor before having any dental work done.
- Do not touch your eyes or the inside of your nose unless you have just washed your hands and have not touched anything else in the meantime.
- Be careful not to cut yourself when you are using sharp objects such as a safety razor or fingernail or toenail cutters.
- Avoid contact sports or other situations where bruising or injury could occur.

If mitomycin accidentally seeps out of the vein into which it is injected, it may damage the skin and cause scarring. In some patients, this may occur weeks or even months after this medicine is given. *Tell the doctor or nurse right away if you notice redness, pain, or swelling at the place of injection or anywhere else on your skin.*

Side Effects of This Medicine

Along with its needed effects, a medicine may cause some unwanted effects. Although not all of these side effects may occur, if they do occur they may need medical attention.

Also, because of the way cancer medicines act on the body, there is a chance that they might cause other unwanted effects that may not occur until months or years after the medicine is used. These delayed effects may include certain types of cancer. Discuss these possible effects with your doctor.

Check with your doctor or nurse immediately if any of the following side effects occur:

Less common

Black, tarry stools; blood in urine or stools; cough or hoarseness; fever or chills; lower back or side pain; painful or difficult urination; pinpoint red spots on skin; unusual bleeding or bruising

Rare

Redness or pain, especially at place of injection

Check with your doctor as soon as possible if any of the following side effects occur:

Less common

Cough; decreased urination; shortness of breath; sores in mouth and on lips; swelling of feet or lower legs

Rare

Bloody vomit

Other side effects may occur that usually do not need medical attention. These side effects may go away during treatment as your body adjusts to the medicine. Also, your health care professional may be able to tell you about ways to prevent or reduce some of these side effects. Check with your doctor if any of the following side effects continue or are bothersome or if you have any questions about them:

More common

Loss of appetite; nausea and vomiting

Less common

Numbness or tingling in fingers and toes; purple-colored bands on nails; skin rash; unusual tiredness or weakness

Mitomycin sometimes causes a temporary loss of hair. After treatment has ended, normal hair growth should return.

After you stop receiving mitomycin, it may still produce some side effects that need attention. During this period of time, *check with your doctor immediately* if you notice the following:

Blood in urine

Also, check with your doctor if you notice any of the following:

Black, tarry stools; blood in stools; cough or hoarseness; decreased urination; fever or chills; lower back or side pain; painful or difficult urination; pinpoint red spots on skin; red or painful skin; shortness of breath; swelling of feet or lower legs; unusual bleeding or bruising

Other side effects not listed above may also occur in some patients. If you notice any other effects, check with your doctor.

Revised: 06/90
Interim revision: 07/30/93; 12/13/93; 07/05/94

MITOTANE Systemic

A commonly used brand name in the U.S. and Canada is Lysodren.

Description

Mitotane (MYE-toe-tane) is a medicine that acts on a part of the body called the adrenal cortex. It is used to treat some kinds of cancer that affect the adrenal cortex. Also, it is sometimes used when the adrenal cortex is overactive without being cancerous.

Mitotane reduces the amounts of adrenocorticoids (cortisone-like hormones) produced by the adrenal cortex. These steroids are important for various functions of the body, including growth. However, too much of these steroids can cause problems.

Mitotane is available only with your doctor's prescription, in the following dosage form:

Oral

- Tablets (U.S. and Canada)

Before Using This Medicine

In deciding to use a medicine, the risks of taking the medicine must be weighed against the good it will do. This is a decision you and your doctor will make. For mitotane, the following should be considered:

Allergies—Tell your doctor if you have ever had any unusual or allergic reaction to mitotane. Also tell your health care professional if you are allergic to any other substance, such as foods, preservatives, or dyes.

Pregnancy—Mitotane has not been shown to cause problems in humans.

Breast-feeding—Although it is not known whether mitotane passes into the breast milk, it has not been reported to cause problems in nursing babies.

Children—Although there is no specific information about the use of mitotane in children, it is not expected to cause different side effects or problems in children than it does in adults.

Older adults—Many medicines have not been tested in older people. Therefore, it may not be known whether they work exactly the same way they do in younger adults or if they cause different side effects or problems in older people. There is no specific information about the use of mitotane in the elderly.

Other medicines—Although certain medicines should not be used together at all, in other cases two different medicines may be used together even if an interaction might occur. In these cases, your doctor may want to change the dose, or other precautions may be necessary. When you are taking mitotane, it is especially important that your health care professional know if you are taking any of the following:

- Central nervous system (CNS) depressants—CNS depressant effects may be increased

Other medical problems—The presence of other medical problems may affect the use of mitotane. Make sure you tell your doctor if you have any other medical problems, especially:

- Infection

- Liver disease—Effects may be increased because of slower removal of mitotane from the body

Proper Use of This Medicine

Take mitotane only as directed by your doctor. Do not take more or less of it, and do not take it more often than your doctor ordered.

Do not stop taking this medicine without first checking with your doctor. To do so may increase the chance of unwanted effects.

Dosing—The dose of mitotane will be different for different patients. The dose that is used may depend on a number of things, including what the medicine is being used for and whether or not other medicines are also being taken. *If you are taking mitotane at home, follow your doctor's orders or the directions on the label.* If you have any questions about the proper dose of mitotane, ask your doctor.

Missed dose—If you miss a dose of this medicine, take the missed dose as soon as you remember it. However, if it is almost time for the next dose, skip the missed dose and do not double the next one. Instead, go back to your regular dosing schedule and check with your doctor.

Storage—To store this medicine:

- Keep out of the reach of children.
- Store away from heat and direct light.
- Do not store in the bathroom, near the kitchen sink, or in other damp places. Heat or moisture may cause the medicine to break down.
- Do not keep outdated medicine or medicine no longer needed. Be sure that any discarded medicine is out of the reach of children.

Precautions While Using This Medicine

It is very important that your doctor check your progress at regular visits to make sure this medicine is working properly and to check for unwanted effects.

Your doctor may want you to carry an identification card stating that you are taking this medicine.

This medicine will add to the effects of alcohol and other CNS depressants (medicines that slow down the nervous system, possibly causing drowsiness). Some examples of CNS depressants are antihistamines or medicine for hay fever, other allergies, or colds; sedatives, tranquilizers, or sleeping medicine; prescription pain medicine or narcotics; barbiturates; medicine for seizures; tricyclic antidepressants (medicine for depression); muscle relaxants; or anesthetics, including some dental anesthetics. *Check with your doctor before taking any of the above while you are using this medicine.*

This medicine may cause some people to become dizzy, drowsy, or less alert than they are normally. *Make sure you know how you react to this medicine before you drive, use machines, or do anything else that could be dangerous if you are dizzy or are not alert.*

Check with your doctor right away if you get an injury, infection, or illness of any kind. This medicine may weaken your body's defenses against infection or inflammation.

Side Effects of This Medicine

Along with its needed effects, a medicine may cause some unwanted effects. Although not all of these side effects may occur, if they do occur they may need medical attention.

Check with your doctor as soon as possible if any of the following side effects occur:

More common

Darkening of skin; diarrhea; dizziness; drowsiness; loss of appetite; mental depression; nausea and vomiting; skin rash; unusual tiredness

Less common

Blood in urine; blurred vision; double vision

Rare

Shortness of breath; wheezing

Other side effects may occur that usually do not need medical attention. These side effects may go away during treatment as your body adjusts to the medicine. However, check with your health care professional if any of the following side effects continue or are bothersome:

Less common

Aching muscles; dizziness or lightheadedness when getting up from a lying or sitting position; fever; flushing or redness of skin; muscle twitching

Other side effects not listed above may also occur in some patients. If you notice any other effects, check with your doctor.

Revised: 08/90
Interim revision: 06/30/94

MITOXANTRONE Systemic

A commonly used brand name in the U.S. and Canada is Novantrone.

Description

Mitoxantrone (mye-toe-ZAN-trone) belongs to the general group of medicines known as antineoplastics. It is used to treat some kinds of cancer.

Mitoxantrone seems to interfere with the growth of cancer cells, which are eventually destroyed. Since the growth of normal body cells may also be affected by mitoxantrone, other effects will also occur. Some of these may be serious and must be reported to your doctor. Other effects, like hair loss, may not be serious but may cause concern. Some effects may not occur for months or years after the medicine is used.

Before you begin treatment with mitoxantrone, you and your doctor should talk about the good this medicine will do as well as the risks of using it.

Mitoxantrone is to be administered only by or under the immediate supervision of your doctor. It is available in the following dosage form:

Parenteral
- Injection (U.S. and Canada)

Before Using This Medicine

In deciding to use a medicine, the risks of taking the medicine must be weighed against the good it will do. This is a decision you and your doctor will make. For mitoxantrone, the following should be considered:

Allergies—Tell your doctor if you have ever had any unusual or allergic reaction to mitoxantrone.

Pregnancy—Tell your doctor if you are pregnant or if you intend to have children. There is a chance that this medicine may cause birth defects if either the male or female is receiving it at the time of conception or if it is taken during pregnancy. Mitoxantrone has been reported to cause low birth weight and slow growth of the kidney in rats and premature birth in rabbits. In addition, many cancer medicines may cause sterility, which could be permanent. Although sterility has not been reported with this medicine, the possibility should be kept in mind.

Be sure that you have discussed this with your doctor before receiving this medicine. It is best to use some kind of birth control while you are receiving mitoxantrone. Tell your doctor right away if you think you have become pregnant while receiving mitoxantrone.

Breast-feeding—Tell your doctor if you are breast-feeding or if you intend to breast-feed during treatment with this medicine. It is not known whether mitoxantrone passes into breast milk. However, because mitoxantrone may cause serious side effects, breast-feeding is generally not recommended while you are receiving it.

Children—There is no specific information comparing use of mitoxantrone in children with use in other age groups.

Older adults—Many medicines have not been studied specifically in older people. Therefore, it may not be known whether they work exactly the same way they do in younger adults or if they cause different side effects or problems in older people. There is no specific information comparing use of mitoxantrone in the elderly with use in other age groups.

Other medicines—Although certain medicines should not be used together at all, in other cases two different medicines may be used together even if an interaction might occur. In these cases, your doctor may want to change the dose, or other precautions may be necessary. When you are receiving mitoxantrone, it is especially important that your health care professional know if you are taking any of the following:

- Amphotericin B by injection (e.g., Fungizone) or
- Antithyroid agents (medicine for overactive thyroid) or
- Azathioprine (e.g., Imuran) or
- Chloramphenicol (e.g., Chloromycetin) or
- Colchicine or
- Flucytosine (e.g., Ancobon) or
- Ganciclovir (e.g., Cytovene) or
- Interferon (e.g., Intron A, Roferon-A) or
- Plicamycin (e.g., Mithracin) or
- Zidovudine (e.g., AZT, Retrovir) or
- If you have been treated with radiation or cancer medicines—Mitoxantrone may increase the effects of these medicines or radiation on the blood
- Probenecid (e.g., Benemid) or
- Sulfinpyrazone (e.g., Anturane)—Mitoxantrone may increase the concentration of uric acid in the blood. Since these medicines are used to lower uric acid levels, they may not work as well in patients receiving mitoxantrone

Other medical problems—The presence of other medical problems may affect the use of mitoxantrone. Make sure you tell your doctor if you have any other medical problems, especially:

- Chickenpox (including recent exposure) or
- Herpes zoster (shingles)—Risk of severe disease affecting other parts of the body
- Gout (history of) or
- Kidney stones—Mitoxantrone may increase levels of uric acid in the body, which can cause gout or kidney stones
- Heart disease—Risk of heart problems caused by mitoxantrone may be increased
- Infection—Mitoxantrone may decrease your body's ability to fight infection
- Liver disease—Effects of mitoxantrone may be increased because of slower removal from the body

Proper Use of This Medicine

Mitoxantrone is sometimes given together with certain other medicines. If you are using a combination of medicines, it is important that you receive each one at the proper time. If you are taking some of these medicines by mouth, ask your health care professional to help you plan a way to take them at the right times.

While you are receiving mitoxantrone, your doctor may want you to drink extra fluids so that you will pass more urine. This will help prevent kidney problems and keep your kidneys working well.

Mitoxantrone often causes nausea and vomiting. However, it is very important that you continue to receive the medicine, even if your stomach is upset. Ask your health care professional for ways to lessen these effects.

Dosing—The dose of mitoxantrone will be different for different patients. The dose that is used may depend on a number of things, including what the medicine is being used for, the patient's size, and whether or not other medicines are also being taken. *If you are receiving mitoxantrone at home, follow your doctor's orders or the directions on the label.* If you have any questions about the proper dose of mitoxantrone, ask your doctor.

Precautions While Using This Medicine

It is very important that your doctor check your progress at regular visits to make sure that this medicine is working properly and to check for unwanted effects.

While you are being treated with mitoxantrone, and after you stop treatment with it, *do not have any immunizations* (vaccinations) without your doctor's approval. Mitoxantrone may lower your body's resistance and there is a chance you might get the infection the immunization is meant to prevent. In addition, other persons living in your household should not take oral polio vaccine since there is a chance they could pass the polio virus on to you. Also, avoid persons who have taken oral polio vaccine. Do not get close to them and do not stay in the same room with them for very long. If you cannot take these precautions, you should consider wearing a protective face mask that covers the nose and mouth.

Mitoxantrone can temporarily lower the number of white blood cells in your blood, increasing the chance of getting an infection. It can also lower the number of platelets, which are necessary for proper blood clotting. If this occurs, there are certain precautions you can take, especially when your blood count is low, to reduce the risk of infection or bleeding:

- If you can, avoid people with infections. *Check with your doctor immediately* if you think you are getting an infection or if you get a fever or chills, cough or hoarseness, lower back or side pain, or painful or difficult urination.
- *Check with your doctor immediately* if you notice any unusual bleeding or bruising; black, tarry stools; blood in urine or stools; or pinpoint red spots on your skin.
- Be careful when using a regular toothbrush, dental floss, or toothpick. Your medical doctor, dentist, or nurse may recommend other ways to clean your teeth and gums. Check with your medical doctor before having any dental work done.
- Do not touch your eyes or the inside of your nose unless you have just washed your hands and have not touched anything else in the meantime.
- Be careful not to cut yourself when you are using sharp objects such as a safety razor or fingernail or toenail cutters.
- Avoid contact sports or other situations where bruising or injury could occur.

Side Effects of This Medicine

Along with its needed effects, a medicine may cause some unwanted effects. Although not all of these side effects may occur, if they do occur they may need medical attention.

Also, because of the way cancer medicines act on the body, there is a chance that they might cause other unwanted effects that may not occur until months or years after the medicine is used. These delayed effects may include certain types of cancer, such as leukemia. Discuss these possible effects with your doctor.

Check with your doctor or nurse immediately if any of the following side effects occur:

More common

Black, tarry stools; cough or shortness of breath

Less common

Blood in urine or stools; fast or irregular heartbeat; fever or chills; lower back or side pain; painful or difficult urination; pinpoint red spots on skin; swelling of feet and lower legs; unusual bleeding or bruising

Check with your health care professional as soon as possible if any of the following side effects occur:

More common

Sores in mouth and on lips; stomach pain

Less common

Decrease in urination; seizures; sore, red eyes; yellow eyes or skin

Rare

Blue skin at place of injection; pain or redness at place of injection; skin rash

Other side effects may occur that usually do not need medical attention. These side effects may go away during treatment as your body adjusts to the medicine. Also, your health care professional may be able to tell you about ways to prevent or reduce some of these side effects. Check with your health care professional if any of the following side effects continue or are bothersome:

More common

Diarrhea; headache; nausea and vomiting

Mitoxantrone may cause the urine to turn a blue-green color. It may also cause the whites of the eyes to turn a blue color. These effects are normal and last for only 1 or 2 days after each dose is given.

This medicine often causes a temporary loss of hair. After treatment with mitoxantrone has ended, normal hair growth should return.

Other side effects not listed above may also occur in some patients. If you notice any other effects, check with your health care professional.

Revised: 03/16/95

MOEXIPRIL Systemic†

A commonly used brand name in the U.S. is Univasc.

†Not commercially available in Canada.

Description

Moexipril (moe-EX-i-pril) belongs to the class of medicines called angiotensin-converting enzyme (ACE) inhibitors. It is used to treat high blood pressure (hypertension).

High blood pressure adds to the work load of the heart and arteries. If it continues for a long time, the heart and arteries may not function properly. This can damage the blood vessels of the brain, heart, and kidneys, resulting in a stroke, heart failure, or kidney failure. High blood pressure may also increase the risk of heart attacks. These

problems may be less likely to occur if blood pressure is controlled.

The exact way that moexipril works is not completely known. It blocks an enzyme in the body that is necessary to produce angiotensin II, a substance that causes blood vessels to tighten. As a result, moexipril relaxes blood vessels. This lowers blood pressure and increases the supply of blood and oxygen to the heart.

Moexipril is available only with your doctor's prescription, in the following dosage form:

Oral
- Tablets (U.S.)

Before Using This Medicine

In deciding to use a medicine, the risks of taking the medicine must be weighed against the good it will do. This is a decision you and your doctor will make. For moexipril, the following should be considered:

Allergies—Tell your doctor if you have ever had any unusual or allergic reaction to moexipril or other ACE inhibitors (benazepril, captopril, enalapril, fosinopril, lisinopril, quinapril, ramipril, or trandolapril). Also tell your health care professional if you are allergic to any other substances, such as foods, preservatives, or dyes.

Pregnancy—Use of moexipril during pregnancy, especially in the second and third trimesters (after the first three months) can cause low blood pressure, severe kidney failure, or even death in the fetus or newborn. *Therefore, it is important that you check with your doctor immediately if you think that you may be pregnant.* Be sure that you have discussed this with your doctor before taking this medicine.

Breast-feeding—It is not known whether moexipril passes into the breast milk. However, this medicine has not been reported to cause problems in nursing babies.

Children—Studies on this medicine have been done only in adult patients and there is no specific information comparing use of moexipril in children with use in other age groups.

Older adults—This medicine has been tested in a limited number of patients 65 years of age or older and has not been shown to cause different side effects or problems in older people than it does in younger adults.

Other medicines—Although certain medicines should not be used together at all, in other cases two different medicines may be used together even if an interaction might occur. In these cases, your doctor may want to change the dose, or other precautions may be necessary. When you are taking moexipril, it is especially important that your health care professional know if you are taking any of the following:

- Diuretics (water pills)—Effects on blood pressure may be increased. In addition, some diuretics make the increase in potassium in the blood caused by moexipril even greater
- Potassium-containing medicines or supplements or
- Salt substitutes that contain potassium—Use of these substances with moexipril may result in an unusually high potassium level in the blood, which can lead to irregular heart rhythm and other problems

Other medical problems—The presence of other medical problems may affect the use of moexipril. Make sure you tell your doctor if you have any other medical problems, especially:

- Bee sting allergy or dialysis treatments—Increased risk of serious allergic reaction occurring
- Dehydration—Lowering effects on blood pressure may be increased
- Diabetes mellitus (sugar diabetes)—Increased risk of potassium levels in the body becoming too high; your body may also be more sensitive to insulin or more tolerant of glucose
- Heart attack or stroke (recent) or
- Heart or blood vessel disease—Lowering blood pressure may make problems resulting from these conditions worse
- Kidney disease or
- Liver disease—Effects of this medicine may be increased because of slower removal of medicine from the body
- Previous reaction to any ACE inhibitor involving hoarseness; swelling of the face, mouth, hands, or feet; or sudden trouble in swallowing or breathing—Reaction is more likely to occur again
- Systemic lupus erythematosus (SLE) or scleroderma—Increased risk of blood problems caused by moexipril

Proper Use of This Medicine

To maintain the blood pressure lowering effect of moexipril, try to make a habit of taking it at the same time each day.

Moexipril should be taken 1 hour before a meal.

In addition to the use of the medicine your doctor has prescribed, treatment for your high blood pressure may include weight control and care in the types of foods you eat, especially foods high in sodium. Your doctor will tell you which of these are most important for you. You should check with your doctor before changing your diet.

Many patients who have high blood pressure will not notice any signs of the problem. In fact, many may feel normal. It is very important that you *take your medicine exactly as directed* and that you keep your appointments with your doctor even if you feel well.

Remember that this medicine will not cure your high blood pressure but it does help control it. Therefore, you must continue to take it as directed if you expect to lower your blood pressure and keep it down. *You may have to take high blood pressure medicine for the rest of your life.* If high blood pressure is not treated, it can cause serious problems such as heart failure, blood vessel disease, stroke, or kidney disease.

Dosing—The dose of moexipril will be different for different patients. *Follow your doctor's orders or the directions on the label.* The following information includes only the average doses of moexipril. *If your dose is different, do not change it* unless your doctor tells you to do so.

The number of tablets that you take depends on the strength of the medicine.

- *For oral* dosage form (tablets):
  —For high blood pressure:
  - Adults—At first, 7.5 milligrams (mg) once a day. Then, your doctor may increase your dose up to 30 mg a day as a single dose or divided into two doses. Each dose should be taken one hour before a meal.
  - Children—Use and dose must be determined by your doctor.

Missed dose—If you miss a dose of this medicine, take it as soon as possible. However, if it is almost time for your next dose, skip the missed dose and go back to your regular dosing schedule. Do not double doses.

Storage—To store this medicine:

- Keep out of the reach of children.
- Store at room temperature, away from heat and direct light.
- Do not store in the bathroom, near the kitchen sink, or in other damp places. Heat or moisture may cause the medicine to break down.
- Do not keep outdated medicine or medicine no longer needed. Be sure that any discarded medicine is out of the reach of children.

Precautions While Using This Medicine

It is important that your doctor check your progress at regular visits to make sure that this medicine is working properly and to check for unwanted effects.

Do not take other medicines unless they have been discussed with your doctor. This especially includes over-the-counter (nonprescription) medicines for appetite control, asthma, colds, cough, hay fever, or sinus problems, since they may tend to increase your blood pressure. Because moexipril can increase potassium in the blood, you also should not take potassium supplements and salt substitutes that contain potassium without first discussing them with your doctor.

Dizziness or lightheadness may occur, especially after the first dose of this medicine or if you have been taking a diuretic (water pill). Make sure you know how you react to this medicine before you drive, use machines, or do anything else that could be dangerous if you are dizzy.

Check with your doctor right away if you have signs of an infection, such as a fever, sore throat, or chills.

Check with your doctor right away if you notice hoarseness; swelling of the face, mouth, hands, or feet; and/or sudden difficulty in swallowing or breathing.

Check with your doctor right away if you become sick while taking this medicine, especially with severe or continuing nausea and vomiting or diarrhea. These conditions may cause you to lose too much water and may lead to low blood pressure.

Dizziness, lightheadedness, or fainting may also occur if you exercise or if the weather is hot. Heavy sweating can cause loss of too much water and low blood pressure. Use extra care during exercise or hot weather.

Avoid alcoholic beverages until you have discussed their use with your doctor. Alcohol may make the low blood pressure effect worse and/or increase the possibility of dizziness or fainting.

Before having any kind of surgery (including dental surgery) or emergency treatment, tell the medical doctor or dentist in charge that you are taking this medicine.

Side Effects of This Medicine

Along with its needed effects, a medicine may cause some unwanted effects. Although not all of these side effects may occur, if they do occur, they may need medical attention.

Check with your doctor immediately if any of the following side effects occur:

Rare
Fever, chills, or sore throat; hoarseness; sudden trouble in swallowing or breathing; swelling of face, mouth, hands, or feet; yellow eyes or skin

Check with your doctor as soon as possible if any of the following side effects occur:

Less common
Lightheadedness, or fainting; skin rash

Rare
Bleeding gums, nosebleeds, or pale skin; bloating or pain of the stomach; fever; nausea, or vomiting; chest pain; swelling of ankles, feet, or legs

Signs and symptoms of too much potassium in the body
Confusion; irregular heartbeat; nervousness; numbness or tingling in hands, feet, or lips; shortness of breath or troubled breathing; weakness or heaviness of legs

Other side effects may occur that usually do not need medical attention. These side effects may go away during treatment as your body adjusts to the medicine. However, check with your doctor if any of the following side effects continue or are bothersome:

More common
Cough (dry, persistent); dizziness; flushing

Less common
Diarrhea; dry mouth; headache; increased sensitivity to the sun; itching; loss of taste; muscle pain; nausea; unusual sweating; unusual tiredness

Other side effects not listed above may also occur in some patients. If you notice any other effects, check with your doctor.

Developed: 08/19/97

MOLINDONE Systemic†

Some commonly used brand names in the U.S. are Moban and Moban Concentrate.

†Not commercially available in Canada.

Description

Molindone (moe-LIN-done) is used to treat nervous, mental, and emotional conditions.

Molindone is available only with your doctor's prescription, in the following dosage forms:

Oral

- Solution (U.S.)
- Tablets (U.S.)

Before Using This Medicine

In deciding to use a medicine, the risks of taking the medicine must be weighed against the good it will do. This is a decision you and your doctor will make. For molindone, the following should be considered:

Allergies—Tell your doctor if you have ever had any unusual or allergic reaction to molindone, phenothiazines, thioxanthenes, haloperidol, or loxapine. Also tell your health care professional if you are allergic to any other substances, such as foods, preservatives, or dyes.

Pregnancy—Molindone has not been shown to cause birth defects or other problems in humans. However, studies in mice have shown a slight decrease in successful pregnancies.

Breast-feeding—It is not known if molindone passes into breast milk.

Children—Studies on this medicine have been done only in adult patients, and there is no specific information comparing use of molindone in children with use in other age groups.

Older adults—Elderly patients are usually more sensitive than younger adults to the effects of molindone. Constipation, dizziness or lightheadedness, drowsiness, dryness of mouth, trembling of the hands and fingers, and symptoms of tardive dyskinesia (such as rapid, worm-like movements of the tongue or any other uncontrolled movements of the mouth, tongue, or jaw, and/or arms and legs) are especially likely to occur in elderly patients.

Other medicines—Although certain medicines should not be used together at all, in other cases 2 different medicines may be used together even if an interaction might occur. In these cases, your doctor may want to change the dose, or other precautions may be necessary. When you are taking molindone, it is especially important that your health care professional know if you are taking any of the following:

- Amoxapine (e.g., Asendin) or
- Methyldopa (e.g., Aldomet) or
- Metoclopramide (e.g., Reglan) or
- Metyrosine (e.g., Demser) or
- Other antipsychotics (medicine for mental illness) or
- Pemoline (e.g., Cylert) or
- Pimozide (e.g., Orap) or
- Promethazine (e.g., Phenergan) or
- Rauwolfia alkaloids (alseroxylon [e.g., Rauwiloid], deserpidine [e.g., Harmonyl], rauwolfia serpentina [e.g., Raudixin], reserpine [e.g., Serpasil]) or
- Trimeprazine (e.g., Temaril)—Taking these medicines with molindone may increase the chance and seriousness of some side effects
- Central nervous system (CNS) depressants (medicine that causes drowsiness) or
- Tricyclic antidepressants (medicine for depression)—Taking these medicines with molindone may increase the CNS depressant effects
- Lithium (e.g., Eskalith, Lithane)—The chance of serious side effects may be increased

Other medical problems—The presence of other medical problems may affect the use of molindone. Make sure you tell your doctor if you have any other medical problems, especially:

- Brain tumor or
- Intestinal blockage—Molindone may interfere with the diagnosis of these conditions
- Difficult urination or
- Enlarged prostate or
- Glaucoma or
- Liver disease or
- Parkinson's disease—Molindone may make the condition worse

Proper Use of This Medicine

Molindone should be taken with food or a full glass (8 ounces) of water or milk to reduce stomach irritation.

The liquid form of molindone may be taken undiluted or mixed with milk, water, fruit juice, or carbonated beverages.

Take this medicine only as directed by your doctor. Do not take more of it, do not take it more often, and do not take it for a longer time than your doctor ordered. To do so may increase the chance of side effects.

Sometimes this medicine must be taken for several weeks before its full effect is reached in the treatment of certain mental and emotional conditions.

Dosing—The dose of molindone will be different for different patients. *Follow your doctor's orders or the directions on the label.* The following information includes only the average doses of molindone. *If your dose is different, do not change it* unless your doctor tells you to do so.

The number of tablets or amount of solution that you take depends on the strength of the medicine. Also, *the number of doses you take each day, the time allowed between doses, and the length of time you take the medicine depend on the medical problem for which you are using molindone.*

- For *oral* dosage forms (solution or tablets):
  —Adults: To start, 50 to 75 milligrams a day, taken in smaller doses three or four times during the day.

For maintenance, the dose you take will depend on your condition and may be from 15 to 225 milligrams a day, taken in smaller doses three or four times during the day.

—Children up to 12 years of age: The dose must be determined by the doctor.

Missed dose—If you miss a dose of this medicine, take it as soon as possible. However, if it is within 2 hours of your next dose, skip the missed dose and go back to your regular dosing schedule. Do not double doses.

Storage—To store this medicine:

- Keep out of the reach of children.
- Store away from heat and direct light.
- Do not store the tablets in the bathroom, near the kitchen sink, or in other damp places. Heat or moisture may cause the medicine to break down.
- Keep the liquid form of this medicine from freezing
- Do not keep outdated medicine or medicine no longer needed. Be sure that any discarded medicine is out of the reach of children.

Precautions While Using This Medicine

Your doctor should check your progress at regular visits. This will allow the dosage of the medicine to be adjusted when necessary and also will reduce the possibility of side effects.

Do not stop taking this medicine without first checking with your doctor. Your doctor may want you to reduce gradually the amount you are taking before stopping completely.

Do not take molindone within 1 or 2 hours of taking antacids or medicine for diarrhea. Taking them too close together may make molindone less effective.

This medicine will add to the effects of alcohol and other CNS depressants (medicines that slow down the nervous system, possibly causing drowsiness). Some examples of CNS depressants are antihistamines or medicine for hay fever, other allergies, or colds; sedatives, tranquilizers, or sleeping medicine; prescription pain medicine or narcotics; barbiturates; medicine for seizures; muscle relaxants; or anesthetics, including some dental anesthetics. *Check with your doctor before taking any of the above while you are using this medicine.*

Molindone may cause some people to become drowsy or less alert than they are normally, especially during the first few weeks the medicine is being taken. Even if you take this medicine only at bedtime, you may feel drowsy or less alert on arising. *Make sure you know how you react to this medicine before you drive, use machines, or do anything else that could be dangerous if you are not alert.*

Dizziness or lightheadedness may occur, especially when you get up from a lying or sitting position. Getting up slowly may help. If the problem continues or gets worse, check with your doctor.

These medicines may make you sweat less, causing your body temperature to increase. *Use extra care not to become overheated during exercise or hot weather while you are taking this medicine, since overheating may result in heat stroke.* Also, hot baths or saunas may make you feel dizzy or faint while you are taking this medicine.

Molindone may cause dryness of the mouth. For temporary relief, use sugarless candy or gum, melt bits of ice in your mouth, or use a saliva substitute. However, if your mouth continues to feel dry for more than 2 weeks, check with your medical doctor or dentist. Continuing dryness of the mouth may increase the chance of dental disease, including tooth decay, gum disease, and fungus infection.

Side Effects of This Medicine

Along with its needed effects, molindone can sometimes cause serious side effects. Tardive dyskinesia (a movement disorder) may occur and may not go away after you stop using the medicine. Symptoms of tardive dyskinesia include fine, worm-like movements of the tongue, or other uncontrolled movements of the mouth, tongue, cheeks, jaw, or arms and legs. Other serious but rare side effects may also occur. These include severe muscle stiffness, fever, unusual tiredness or weakness, fast heartbeat, difficult breathing, increased sweating, loss of bladder control, and seizures (neuroleptic malignant syndrome). *You and your doctor should discuss the good this medicine will do as well as the risks of taking it.*

Stop taking molindone and get emergency help immediately if any of the following side effects occur:

Rare

Convulsions (seizures); difficult or fast breathing; fast heartbeat or irregular pulse; fever (high); high or low (irregular) blood pressure; increased sweating; loss of bladder control; muscle stiffness (severe); unusually pale skin; unusual tiredness or weakness

Also, check with your doctor as soon as possible if any of the following side effects occur:

More common

Difficulty in talking or swallowing; inability to move eyes; lip smacking or puckering; loss of balance control; mask-like face; muscle spasms, especially of the neck and back; puffing of cheeks; rapid or worm-like movements of tongue; restlessness or need to keep moving (severe); shuffling walk; stiffness of arms and legs; trembling and shaking of hands; twisting movements of body; uncontrolled movements of arms and legs; unusual chewing movements

Less common

Mental depression

Rare

Confusion; hot, dry skin, or lack of sweating; muscle weakness; skin rash; yellow eyes or skin

Other side effects may occur that usually do not need medical attention. These side effects may go away during treatment as your body adjusts to the medicine. However, check with your doctor if any of the following side effects continue or are bothersome:

More common

Blurred vision; constipation; decreased sweating; difficult urination; dizziness or lightheadedness, especially when getting up suddenly from a lying or sitting position; drowsiness; dryness of mouth; headache; nausea; stuffy nose

Less common
Changes in menstrual periods; decreased sexual ability; false sense of well-being; swelling of breasts; unusual secretion of milk

Some side effects may occur after you have stopped taking this medicine. Check with your doctor as soon as possible if you notice any of the following effects:
Lip smacking or puckering; puffing of cheeks; rapid or worm-like movements of tongue; uncontrolled chewing movements; uncontrolled movements of arms and legs

Other side effects not listed above may also occur in some patients. If you notice any other effects, check with your doctor.

Revised: 03/19/93

MOLYBDENUM SUPPLEMENTS Systemic†

A commonly used brand name in the U.S. is Molypen.
Generic name product may also be available.

†Not commercially available in Canada.

Description

The body needs molybdenum (moh-LIB-den-um) for normal growth and health. For patients who are unable to get enough molybdenum in their regular diet or who have a need for more molybdenum, molybdenum supplements may be necessary. They are generally taken by mouth in multivitamin/mineral products but some patients may have to receive them by injection. Molybdenum is part of certain enzymes that are important for several body functions.

A deficiency of molybdenum is rare. However, if the body does not get enough molybdenum, certain enzymes needed by the body are affected. This may lead to a build up of unwanted substances in some people.

Injectable molybdenum is administered only by or under the supervision of your health care professional. Molybdenum is available in the following dosage forms:

Oral
Molybdenum is available orally as part of a multivitamin/mineral combination.

Parenteral
- Injection (U.S.)

Importance of Diet

For good health, it is important that you eat a balanced and varied diet. Follow carefully any diet program your health care professional may recommend. For your specific dietary vitamin and/or mineral needs, ask your health care professional for a list of appropriate foods. If you think that you are not getting enough vitamins and/or minerals in your diet, you may choose to take a dietary supplement.

The amount of molybdenum in foods depends on the soil in which the food is grown. Some soils have more molybdenum than others. Peas, beans, cereal products, leafy vegetables, and low-fat milk are good sources of molybdenum.

The daily amount of molybdenum needed is defined in several different ways.

For U.S.—
- Recommended Dietary Allowances (RDAs) are the amount of vitamins and minerals needed to provide for adequate nutrition in most healthy persons. RDAs for a given nutrient may vary depending on a person's age, sex, and physical condition (e.g., pregnancy).
- Daily Values (DVs) are used on food and dietary supplement labels to indicate the percent of the recommended daily amount of each nutrient that a serving provides. DV replaces the previous designation of United States Recommended Daily Allowances (USRDAs).

For Canada—
- Recommended Nutrient Intakes (RNIs) are used to determine the amounts of vitamins, minerals, and protein needed to provide adequate nutrition and lessen the risk of chronic disease.

Because a lack of molybdenum is rare, there is no RDA or RNI for it. The following daily intakes are thought to be plenty for most individuals:
- Infants and children—
  Birth to 3 years of age: 15 to 50 micrograms (mcg).
  4 to 6 years of age: 30 to 75 mcg.
  7 to 10 years of age: 50 to 150 mcg.
- Adolescents and adults—75 to 250 mcg.

Before Using This Dietary Supplement

If you are taking this dietary supplement without a prescription, carefully read and follow any precautions on the label. For molybdenum, the following should be considered:

Allergies—Tell your health care professional if you have ever had any unusual or allergic reaction to molybdenum. Also tell your health care professional if you are allergic to any other substances, such as foods, preservatives, or dyes.

Pregnancy—It is especially important that you are receiving enough vitamins and minerals when you become pregnant and that you continue to receive the right amount of vitamins and minerals throughout your pregnancy. The healthy growth and development of the fetus depend on a steady supply of nutrients from the mother. However, taking large amounts of a dietary supplement in pregnancy may be harmful to the mother and/or fetus and should be avoided.

Breast-feeding—It is important that you receive the right amounts of vitamins and minerals so that your baby will also get the vitamins and minerals needed to grow properly. However, taking large amounts of a dietary supplement while breast-feeding may be harmful to the mother and/or baby and should be avoided.

Children—Problems in children have not been reported with intake of normal daily recommended amounts.

Older adults—Problems in older adults have not been reported with intake of normal daily recommended amounts.

Medicines or other dietary supplements—Although certain medicines or dietary supplements should not be used together at all, in other cases they may be used together even if an interaction might occur. In these cases, your health care professional may want to change the dose, or other precautions may be necessary. Tell your health care professional if you are taking any other dietary supplement or any prescription or nonprescription (over-the-counter [OTC]) medicine.

Other medical problems—The presence of other medical problems may affect the use of molybdenum. Make sure you tell your health care professional if you have any other medical problems, especially:

- Copper deficiency—Molybdenum may make this condition worse
- Kidney diease or
- Liver disease—These conditions may cause higher blood levels of molybdenum, which may increase the chance of unwanted effects

Proper Use of This Dietary Supplement

Molybdenum is available orally only as part of a multivitamin/mineral product.

Dosing—The amount of molybdenum needed to meet normal daily recommended intakes will be different for different individuals. The following information includes only the average amounts of molybdenum.

- For *oral* dosage form (as part of a multivitamin/mineral supplement):
  - —To prevent deficiency, the amount taken by mouth is based on normal daily recommended intakes:
    - Adults and teenagers—75 to 250 micrograms (mcg) per day.
    - Children 7 to 10 years of age—50 to 150 mcg per day.
    - Children 4 to 6 years of age—30 to 75 mcg per day.
    - Children birth to 3 years of age—15 to 150 mcg per day.
  - —To treat deficiency:
    - Adults, teenagers, and children—Treatment dose is determined by prescriber for each individual based on severity of deficiency.

Missed dose—If you miss taking your multivitamin containing molybdenum for one or more days there is no cause for concern, since it takes some time for your body to become seriously low in molybdenum. However, if your health care professional has recommended that you take molybdenum, try to remember to take it as directed every day.

Storage—To store this dietary supplement:

- Keep out of the reach of children.
- Store away from heat and direct light.
- Do not store in the bathroom, near the kitchen sink, or in other damp places. Heat or moisture may cause the dietary supplement to break down.
- Keep the dietary supplement from freezing. Do not refrigerate.
- Do not keep outdated dietary supplements or those no longer needed. Be sure that any discarded dietary supplement is out of the reach of children.

Precautions While Using This Dietary Supplement

Large amounts of molybdenum may cause your body to lose copper. Your health care professional may recommend that you take a copper supplement while on molybdenum therapy.

Side Effects of This Dietary Supplement

Along with its needed effects, a dietary supplement may cause some unwanted effects. Although oral molybdenum supplements have not been reported to cause any side effects, *check with your health care professional immediately* if any of the following side effects occur:

Symptoms of overdose

Joint pain; side, lower back, or stomach pain; swelling of feet or lower legs

Note: Reported rarely in individuals consuming foods grown in soil containing a high content of molybdenum.

Other side effects not listed above may also occur in some individuals. If you notice any other effects, check with your health care professional.

Revised: 03/02/92
Interim revision: 07/31/92; 08/10/94; 04/25/95

MONOCTANOIN Local†

A commonly used brand name in the U.S. is Moctanin.
Another commonly used name is monooctanoin.

†Not commercially available in Canada.

Description

Monoctanoin (mon-OCK-ta-noyn) is used to dissolve cholesterol gallstones. Gallstones, which are found in the gallbladder or bile duct, sometimes remain in the bile duct even after the gallbladder has been removed by surgery. These stones may be too large to pass out of the body on their own. A catheter or tube is used to put the solution of monoctanoin into the bile duct where it will come in contact with the gallstone or gallstones and dissolve them. This process continues for 2 to 10 days.

Monoctanoin is administered only by or under the supervision of your doctor. It is available in the following dosage form:

Local

- Irrigation (U.S.)

Before Using This Medicine

In deciding to use a medicine, the risks of taking the medicine must be weighed against the good it will do. This is a decision you and your doctor will make. For monoctanoin, the following should be considered:

Allergies—Tell your doctor if you have ever had any unusual or allergic reaction to monoctanoin or any vegetable oils. Also, tell your doctor if you are allergic to any other substances, such as foods, preservatives, or dyes.

Pregnancy—Studies on effects in pregnancy have not been done in either humans or animals.

Breast-feeding—It is not known whether monoctanoin passes into the breast milk. However, this medicine has not been reported to cause problems in nursing babies.

Children—Studies on this medicine have been done only in adult patients, and there is no specific information comparing use of monoctanoin in children with use in other age groups.

Older adults—Many medicines have not been studied specifically in older people. Therefore, it may not be known whether they work exactly the same way they do in younger adults or if they cause different side effects or problems in older people. There is no specific information comparing use of monoctanoin in the elderly with use in other age groups.

Other medical problems—The presence of other medical problems may affect the use of monoctanoin. Make sure you tell your doctor if you have any other medical problems, especially:

- Bile duct blockage—The chance of serious side effects may be increased
- Biliary tract problems (other) or
- Jaundice or
- Pancreatitis (inflammation of the pancreas)—Monoctanoin may make these conditions worse
- Duodenal ulcer (recent) or
- Intestinal problems—Monoctanoin may make these conditions worse and may increase the chance of bleeding
- Liver disease (severe)—Unwanted effects may occur if the liver is not working properly

Proper Use of This Medicine

Dosing—The dose of monoctanoin will be different for different patients. The following information includes only the average doses of monoctanoin.

- For *irrigation* dosage form:
  - —For gallstone disease:
    - Adults and teenagers—The usual dose is 3 to 5 milliliters (mL) per hour given through a catheter or tube. The dose is given over a period of 2 to 10 days.
    - Children—Use and dose must be determined by your doctor.

Side Effects of This Medicine

Along with its needed effects, a medicine may cause some unwanted effects. Although not all of these side effects appear very often, when they do occur they may require medical attention.

Check with your doctor as soon as possible if any of the following side effects occur:

Less common or rare

Abdominal or stomach pain (severe); back pain (severe); chills, fever, or sore throat; drowsiness (severe); nausea (continuing); shortness of breath (severe)

Other side effects may occur that usually do not need medical attention. These side effects may go away during treatment as your body adjusts to the medicine. However, check with your doctor if any of the following side effects continue or are bothersome:

More common

Abdominal or stomach pain (mild) or burning sensation

Less common or rare

Back pain (mild); diarrhea; flushing or redness of face; loss of appetite; metallic taste; nausea or vomiting

Other side effects not listed above may also occur in some patients. If you notice any other effects, check with your doctor.

Revised: 07/20/95

MORICIZINE Systemic†

A commonly used brand name in the U.S. is Ethmozine.

†Not commercially available in Canada.

Description

Moricizine (mor-IH-siz-een) belongs to the group of medicines known as antiarrhythmics. It is used to correct irregular or rapid heartbeats to a normal rhythm by making the heart tissue less sensitive.

There is a chance that moricizine may cause new or make worse existing heart rhythm problems when it is used. Since other antiarrhythmic medicines have been shown to cause severe problems in some patients, moricizine is only used to treat serious heart rhythm problems. Discuss this possible effect with your doctor.

This medicine is available only with your doctor's prescription, in the following dosage form:

Oral

- Tablets (U.S.)

Before Using This Medicine

In deciding to use a medicine, the risks of taking the medicine must be weighed against the good it will do. This is a decision you and your doctor will make. For moricizine, the following should be considered:

Allergies—Tell your doctor if you have ever had any unusual or allergic reaction to moricizine. Also tell your health care professional if you are allergic to any other substances, such as foods, preservatives, or dyes.

Pregnancy—Moricizine has not been studied in pregnant women. However, this medicine has not been shown to cause birth defects or other problems in animal studies, although it affected weight gain in some animals. Before taking moricizine, make sure your doctor knows if you are pregnant or if you may become pregnant.

Breast-feeding—Moricizine passes into the milk of some animals and may also pass into the milk of humans. However, this medicine has not been reported to cause problems in nursing babies.

Children—Studies on this medicine have been done only in adult patients, and there is no specific information comparing use of moricizine in children with use in other age groups.

Older adults—Many medicines have not been studied specifically in older people. Therefore, it may not be known whether they work exactly the same way they do in younger adults or if they cause different side effects or problems in older people. There is no specific information comparing use of moricizine in the elderly with use in other age groups, although the risk of some unwanted effects may be increased.

Other medicines—Although certain medicines should not be used together at all, in other cases two different medicines may be used together even if an interaction might occur. In these cases, your doctor may want to change the dose, or other precautions may be necessary. Tell your health care professional if you are taking any other prescription or nonprescription (over-the-counter [OTC]) medicine.

Other medical problems—The presence of other medical problems may affect the use of moricizine. Make sure you tell your doctor if you have any other medical problems, especially:

- Kidney disease or
- Liver disease—Effects may be increased because of slower removal of moricizine from the body
- Heart disease or
- Recent heart attack or
- If you have a pacemaker—Risk of irregular heartbeats may be increased

Proper Use of This Medicine

Take moricizine exactly as directed by your doctor, even though you may feel well. Do not take more or less of it than your doctor ordered.

This medicine works best when there is a constant amount in the blood. *To help keep the amount constant, do not miss any doses. Also, it is best to take each dose at evenly spaced times day and night.* For example, if you are to take 3 doses a day, doses should be spaced about 8 hours apart. If you need help in planning the best times to take your medicine, check with your health care professional.

Dosing—The dose of moricizine will be different for different patients. *Follow your doctor's orders or the directions on the label.* The following information includes only the average doses of moricizine. *If your dose is different, do not change it* unless your doctor tells you to do so.

The number of tablets that you take depends on the strength of the medicine.

- For *oral* dosage form (tablets):
  - —For irregular heartbeat (arrhythmias):
    - Adults—600 to 900 milligrams (mg) a day. This is divided into three doses and taken every eight hours.
    - Children—Use and dose must be determined by your doctor.

Missed dose—If you miss a dose of moricizine and remember within 4 hours, take it as soon as possible. However, if you do not remember until later, skip the missed dose and go back to your regular dosing schedule. Do not double doses.

Storage—To store this medicine:

- Keep out of the reach of children.
- Store away from heat and direct light.
- Do not store in the bathroom, near the kitchen sink, or in other damp places. Heat or moisture may cause the medicine to break down.
- Do not keep outdated medicine or medicine no longer needed. Be sure that any discarded medicine is out of the reach of children.

Precautions While Using This Medicine

It is important that your doctor check your progress at regular visits to make sure the medicine is working properly. This will allow changes to be made in the amount of medicine you are taking, if necessary.

Your doctor may want you to carry a medical identification card or bracelet stating that you are using this medicine.

Before having any kind of surgery (including dental surgery) or emergency treatment, tell the medical doctor or dentist in charge that you are taking this medicine.

Moricizine may cause some people to become dizzy or lightheaded. Make sure you know how you react to this medicine before you drive, use machines, or do anything else that could be dangerous if you are dizzy.

Side Effects of This Medicine

Along with its needed effects, a medicine may cause some unwanted effects. Although not all of these side effects may occur, if they do occur they may need medical attention.

Check with your doctor as soon as possible if any of the following side effects occur:

Less common
Chest pain; fast or irregular heartbeat; shortness of breath; swelling of feet or lower legs

Rare
Fever (sudden, high)

Other side effects may occur that usually do not need medical attention. These side effects may go away during treatment as your body adjusts to the medicine. However, check with your doctor if any of the following side effects continue or are bothersome:

More common
Dizziness

Less common
Blurred vision; diarrhea; dryness of mouth; headache; nausea or vomiting; nervousness; numbness or tingling in arms or legs or around mouth; pain in arms or legs; stomach pain; trouble in sleeping; unusual tiredness or weakness

Other side effects not listed above may also occur in some patients. If you notice any other effects, check with your doctor.

Revised: 09/27/92
Interim revision: 06/30/94

MRI CONTRAST AGENTS Diagnostic

This information applies to the following medicines:
1. Gadodiamide (gad-oh-DYE-a-mide)
2. Gadopentetate (gad-o-PEN-te-tate)†
3. Gadoteridol (gad-oh-TER-i-dol)†

†Not commercially available in Canada.

Description

MRI (magnetic resonance imaging) contrast agents (also called paramagnetic agents) are used to help provide a clear picture during MRI. MRI is a special kind of diagnostic procedure. It uses magnets and computers to create images or ''pictures'' of certain areas inside the body. Unlike x-rays, it does not involve ionizing radiation.

MRI contrast agents are given by injection before or during MRI to help diagnose problems or diseases of the brain or the spine. In addition, gadopentetate is used to help diagnose problems in other parts of the body, such as the bones and joints, breast, liver, soft tissues, and uterus.

MRI contrast agents may also be used to diagnose other conditions as determined by your doctor.

MRI contrast agents are injected into a vein. The doses of these agents will be different for different patients depending on the weight of the person.

These agents are to be used only by or under the supervision of a doctor.

Before Having This Test

In deciding to use a diagnostic test, any risks of the test must be weighed against the good it will do. This is a decision you and your doctor will make. Also, test results may be affected by other things. For MRI contrast agents, the following should be considered:

Allergies—Tell your doctor if you have ever had any unusual or allergic reaction to contrast agents such as gadodiamide, gadopentetate, or gadoteridol. Also, tell your doctor if you are allergic to any other substances, such as foods, preservatives, or dyes.

Pregnancy—Studies have not been done in pregnant women. However, in animal studies, MRI contrast agents caused a delay in development of the animal fetus, increased the risk of losing the fetus, and caused birth defects and other side effects in the offspring when these agents were given to the mother in doses many times the human dose. Also, it is not known yet what effect the magnetic field used in MRI might have on the development of the fetus. Be sure you have discussed this with your doctor.

Breast-feeding—It is not known what amount of MRI contrast agents passes into the breast milk. However, your doctor may want you to stop breast-feeding for some time after you receive an MRI contrast agent. Be sure you have discussed this with your doctor.

Children—Although there is no specific information comparing use of MRI contrast agents in children with use in other age groups, these agents are not expected to cause different side effects or problems in children than they do in adults.

Older adults—These contrast agents have been tested and have not been shown to cause different side effects or problems in older people than they do in younger adults.

Other medical problems—The presence of other medical problems may affect the use of MRI contrast agents. Make sure you tell your doctor if you have any other medical problems, especially:

- Allergies or asthma (history of)—If you have a history of allergies or asthma, you may be at greater risk of having an allergic reaction to the contrast agent
- Anemia or
- Low blood pressure—MRI contrast agents may make these conditions worse
- Epilepsy—There may be an increased chance of seizures

- Kidney disease (severe)—Kidney disease can cause the MRI agent to stay in the body longer than usual, which may increase the chance of side effects
- Sickle cell disease—There may be a greater risk of blockage of the blood vessels in patients with this condition

Preparation for This Test

Your doctor may have special instructions for you to get ready for your test, depending on the type of test you are having. If you do not understand the instructions you receive or if you have not received any instructions, check with your doctor ahead of time.

Side Effects of This Medicine

Along with their needed effects, MRI contrast agents may cause some unwanted effects. Although not all of these side effects may occur, if they do occur they may need medical attention.

Less common or rare

Convulsions (seizures); fast or irregular heartbeat; itching, watery eyes; skin rash or hives; swelling of face; thickening of tongue; unusual tiredness or weakness (severe); wheezing, tightness in chest, or troubled breathing

Other side effects may occur that usually do not need medical attention. These side effects may go away as your body adjusts to this agent. However, check with your doctor if any of the following side effects continue or are bothersome:

More common

Coldness at the place of injection; dizziness; headache; nausea

Less common or rare

Agitation; anxiety; changes in taste; chest pains; confusion; diarrhea; dryness of mouth; fever; increased watering of mouth; pain and/or burning sensation at place of injection; ringing or buzzing in ears; stomach pain; unusual warmth and flushing of skin; vomiting; weakness or tiredness

Not all of the side effects listed above have been reported for each of these agents, but they have been reported for at least one of them. There are some similarities among these agents, so many of the above side effects may occur with any of them.

Other side effects not listed above may also occur in some patients. If you notice any other effects, check with your doctor.

Revised: 08/19/94

MUMPS VIRUS VACCINE LIVE Systemic

A commonly used brand name in the U.S. and Canada is Mumpsvax.

Description

Mumps virus vaccine live is an active immunizing agent used to prevent infection by the mumps virus. It works by causing your body to produce its own protection (antibodies) against the virus infection.

Mumps is an infection that can cause serious problems, such as encephalitis and meningitis, which affect the brain. In addition, adolescent boys and men are very susceptible to a condition called orchitis, which causes pain and swelling in the testicles and scrotum and, in rare cases, sterility. Also, mumps infection can cause spontaneous abortion in women during the first 3 months of pregnancy.

Immunization against mumps is recommended for all persons 12 months of age or older.

Immunization against mumps is not recommended for infants less than 12 months of age, because antibodies they received from their mothers before birth may interfere with the effectiveness of the vaccine. Children who were immunized against mumps before 12 months of age should be immunized again.

You can be considered to be immune to mumps only if you:

- received mumps vaccine on or after your first birthday and have the medical record to prove it, or
- have a doctor's diagnosis of a previous mumps infection, or
- have had a laboratory test that shows that you are immune to mumps.

This vaccine is to be administered only by or under the supervision of your doctor or other health care professional. It is available in the following dosage form:

Parenteral

- Injection (U.S. and Canada)

Before Receiving This Vaccine

In deciding to use a medicine, the risks of taking the medicine must be weighed against the good it will do. This is a decision you and your doctor will make. For mumps vaccine, the following should be considered:

Allergies—Tell your doctor if you have ever had any unusual or allergic reaction to mumps vaccine or to any form of the antibiotic neomycin. Also tell your health care professional if you are allergic to any other substances, such as gelatin.

Pregnancy—Tell your doctor if you are now pregnant or if you may become pregnant within 30 days after receiving this vaccine. Studies on effects in pregnancy have not been done in either humans or animals. However, use during pregnancy is not recommended, because mumps vaccine may infect the placenta, although the vaccine has not been shown to cause birth defects.

Breast-feeding—Mumps vaccine virus may pass into breast milk. However, this vaccine has not been reported to cause problems in nursing babies.

Children—Use is not recommended for infants up to 12 months of age. Children who received the vaccine when less than 12 months of age should receive another dose of the vaccine at 12 months of age.

Other medicines—Although certain medicines should not be used together at all, in other cases two different medicines may be used together even if an interaction might occur. In these cases, your doctor may want to change the dose, or other precautions may be necessary. Before receiving mumps vaccine, it is especially important that your health care professional know if you have received any of the following:

- Cancer medicines or
- Corticosteroids (i.e., cortisone-like medicines) or
- Radiation therapy—May decrease the useful effect of mumps vaccine

Other medical problems—The presence of other medical problems may affect the use of mumps vaccine. Make sure you tell your doctor if you have any other medical problems, especially:

- Immune deficiency condition (or family history of)—The condition may decrease the useful effect of the vaccine or may increase the risk and severity of side effects
- Serious illness with fever—The symptoms of the illness may be confused with the possible side effects of the vaccine

Proper Use of This Vaccine

Dosing—The dose of mumps vaccine will be different for different patients. The following information includes only the average doses of mumps vaccine.

- For *injection* dosage form:
  - —For prevention of mumps:
    - Adults and children 12 months of age and older—One dose injected under the skin.
    - Children up to 12 months of age—Use is not recommended.

Precautions After Receiving This Vaccine

Do not become pregnant for 30 days after receiving mumps virus vaccine live without first checking with your doctor. There is a chance that this vaccine may cause problems during pregnancy.

Tell your doctor that you have received this vaccine:

- if you are to receive blood products or immune globulins within 14 days of receiving this vaccine
- if you are to receive this vaccine within 3 months of receiving blood products or immune globulins
- if you are to receive a tuberculin skin test within 4 to 6 weeks after receiving this vaccine. The results of the test may be affected by this vaccine.

Side Effects of This Vaccine

Along with its needed effects, a medicine may cause some unwanted effects. Although not all of these side effects may occur, if they do occur they may need medical attention.

Get emergency help immediately if any of the following side effects occur:

Symptoms of allergic reaction

Difficulty in breathing or swallowing; hives; itching, especially of feet or hands; reddening of skin, especially around ears; swelling of eyes, face, or inside of nose; unusual tiredness or weakness (sudden and severe)

Check with your doctor as soon as possible if any of the following side effects occur:

Rare

Bruising or purple spots on skin; confusion; fever over 103 °F (39.4 °C); headache (severe or continuing); irritability; pain, tenderness, or swelling in testicles and scrotum (in adolescent boys and men); stiff neck; vomiting

Other side effects may occur that usually do not need medical attention. However, check with your doctor if any of the following side effects continue or are bothersome:

More common

Burning or stinging at place of injection

Less common or rare

Fever of 100 °F (37.7 °C) or less; itching, swelling, redness, tenderness, or hard lump at place of injection; skin rash; swollen glands on side of face or neck

Other side effects not listed above may also occur in some patients. If you notice any other effects, check with your doctor.

Revised: 07/23/97

MUPIROCIN Topical

A commonly used brand name in the U.S. and Canada is Bactroban. Another commonly used name is pseudomonic acid.

Description

Mupirocin (myoo-PEER-oh-sin) is used to treat bacterial infections. It works by killing bacteria or preventing their growth.

Mupirocin ointment is applied to the skin to treat impetigo. It may also be used for other bacterial skin infections as determined by your doctor.

Mupirocin is available in the U.S. only with your doctor's prescription. It is available in Canada without a prescription; however, your doctor may have special instructions on the proper use of this medicine for your medical problem. Mupirocin is available in the following dosage form:

Topical

- Ointment (U.S. and Canada)

Before Using This Medicine

In deciding to use a medicine, the risks of taking the medicine must be weighed against the good it will do. This is

a decision you and your doctor will make. For topical mupirocin, the following should be considered:

Allergies—Tell your doctor if you have ever had any unusual or allergic reaction to mupirocin. Also tell your health care professional if you are allergic to any other substances, such as preservatives or dyes.

Pregnancy—Topical mupirocin has not been studied in pregnant women. However, this medication has not been shown to cause birth defects or other problems in animal studies.

Breast-feeding—It is not known whether topical mupirocin passes into the breast milk. However, this medicine is unlikely to pass into the breast milk in large amounts, since very little mupirocin is absorbed into the mother's body when applied to the skin.

Children—Studies on this medicine have been done only in adult patients, and there is no specific information comparing use of mupirocin in children with use in other age groups.

Older adults—Many medicines have not been studied specifically in older people. Therefore, it may not be known whether they work exactly the same way they do in younger adults or if they cause different side effects or problems in older people. There is no specific information comparing use of mupirocin in the elderly with use in other age groups.

Other medicines—Although certain medicines should not be used together at all, in other cases two different medicines may be used together even if an interaction might occur. In these cases, your doctor may want to change the dose, or other precautions may be necessary. Tell your health care professional if you are using any other prescription or nonprescription (over-the-counter [OTC]) medicine that is to be applied to the same area of skin.

Proper Use of This Medicine

Do not use this medicine in the eyes.

To use:

- Before applying this medicine, wash the affected area(s) with soap and water, and dry thoroughly. Then apply a small amount to the affected area(s) and rub in gently.
- After applying this medicine, the treated area(s) may be covered with a gauze dressing if desired.

To help clear up your skin infection completely, keep using mupirocin for the full time of treatment, even if your symptoms have disappeared. *Do not miss any doses.*

Dosing—*Follow your doctor's orders or the directions on the label.* The following information includes only the average dose of mupirocin. *If your dose is different, do not change it* unless your doctor tells you to do so.

- For *ointment* dosage form:
  - —Impetigo:
    - Adults and children—Apply three times a day.

Missed dose—If you miss a dose of this medicine, apply it as soon as possible. However, if it is almost time for your next dose, skip the missed dose and go back to your regular dosing schedule.

Storage—To store this medicine:

- Keep out of the reach of children.
- Store away from heat and direct light.
- Keep the medicine from freezing.
- Do not keep outdated medicine or medicine no longer needed. Be sure that any discarded medicine is out of the reach of children.

Precautions While Using This Medicine

If your skin infection does not improve within 3 to 5 days, or if it becomes worse, check with your health care professional.

Side Effects of This Medicine

Along with its needed effects, a medicine may cause some unwanted effects. The following side effects may go away during treatment as your body adjusts to the medicine. However, check with your doctor if any of these effects continue or are bothersome:

Less common

Dry skin; skin burning, itching, pain, rash, redness, stinging, or swelling

Other side effects not listed above may also occur in some patients. If you notice any other effects, check with your doctor.

Revised: 06/24/94

MUROMONAB-CD3 Systemic

A commonly used brand name in the U.S. and Canada is Orthoclone OKT3.

Description

Muromonab (myoor-oh-MON-ab)-CD3 is a monoclonal antibody. It is used to reduce the body's natural immunity in patients who receive organ (for example, kidney) transplants.

When a patient receives an organ transplant, the body's white blood cells will try to get rid of (reject) the transplanted organ. Muromonab-CD3 works by preventing the white blood cells from doing this.

The effect of muromonab-CD3 on the white blood cells may also reduce the body's ability to fight infections. Before you begin treatment, you and your doctor should talk about the good this medicine will do as well as the risks of using it.

Muromonab-CD3 is to be administered only by or under the immediate supervision of your doctor. It is available in the following dosage form:

Parenteral
- Injection (U.S. and Canada)

Before Using This Medicine

In deciding to use a medicine, the risks of taking the medicine must be weighed against the good it will do. This is a decision you and your doctor will make. For muromonab-CD3, the following should be considered:

Allergies—Tell your doctor if you have ever had any unusual or allergic reaction to muromonab-CD3 or to rodents (such as mice or rats). Muromonab-CD3 is grown in a mouse cell culture. Also tell your health care professional if you are allergic to any other substance, such as preservatives.

Pregnancy—Studies have not been done in either humans or animals. Muromonab-CD3 may cross the placenta, but it is not known whether it causes harmful effects on the fetus. Before receiving this medicine, make sure your doctor knows if you are pregnant or if you may become pregnant.

Breast-feeding—It is not known whether muromonab-CD3 passes into breast milk. Muromonab-CD3 has not been reported to cause problems in nursing babies. However, it may be necessary for you to stop breast-feeding during treatment. Be sure you have discussed the risks and benefits of the medicine with your doctor.

Children—There is no specific information comparing use of muromonab-CD3 in children with use in other age groups. However, children are more likely to get dehydrated from the diarrhea and vomiting that may be caused by this medicine.

Older adults—Many medicines have not been studied specifically in older people. Therefore, it may not be known whether they work exactly the same way they do in younger adults or if they cause different side effects or problems in older people. There is no specific information comparing use of muromonab-CD3 in the elderly with use in other age groups.

Other medicines—Although certain medicines should not be used together at all, in other cases two different medicines may be used together even if an interaction might occur. In these cases, your doctor may want to change the dose, or other precautions may be necessary. When you are receiving muromonab-CD3, it is especially important that your health care professional know if you are taking any of the following:

- Azathioprine (e.g., Imuran) or
- Chlorambucil (e.g., Leukeran) or
- Corticosteroids (cortisone-like medicine) or
- Cyclophosphamide (e.g., Cytoxan) or
- Cyclosporine (e.g., Sandimmune) or
- Cytarabine (e.g., Cytosar-U) or
- Mercaptopurine (e.g., Purinethol)—There may be an increased risk of infection and development of cancer because muromonab-CD3 reduces the body's ability to fight them

Other medical problems—The presence of other medical problems may affect the use of muromonab-CD3. Make sure you tell your doctor if you have any other medical problems, especially:

- Angina (chest pain) or
- Circulation problems or
- Convulsions (seizures) or
- Heart attack (recent) or
- Heart problems, other, or
- Kidney problems or
- Lung problems or
- Nervous system problems—Increased risk of serious unwanted effects from muromonab-CD3
- Blood clots (history of)—Risk of blood clots in transplanted organ or blood vessels
- Chickenpox (including recent exposure) or
- Herpes zoster (shingles)—Risk of severe disease affecting other parts of the body
- Infection—Muromonab-CD3 decreases your body's ability to fight infection

Proper Use of This Medicine

Dosing—The dose of muromonab-CD3 may be different for different patients. Muromonab-CD3 is usually given by a doctor or nurse in the hospital. The following information includes only the average doses of muromonab-CD3:

- For *injection* dosage form:
  - —To prevent organ transplant rejection:
    - Adults—5 milligrams (mg) injected into a vein once a day.
    - Children less than 12 years of age—Dose is based on body weight and must be determined by your doctor.

Precautions While Using This Medicine

It is very important that your doctor check your progress at regular visits to make sure that this medicine is working properly and to check for unwanted effects.

While you are being treated with muromonab-CD3 and after you stop treatment with it, *do not have any immunizations (vaccinations) without your doctor's approval.* Muromonab-CD3 may lower your body's resistance and there is a chance you might get the infection the immunization is meant to prevent. In addition, other persons living in your house should not take oral polio vaccine since there is a chance they could pass the polio virus on to you. Also, avoid persons who have recently taken oral polio vaccine. Do not get close to them and do not stay in the same room with them for very long. If you cannot take these precautions, you should consider wearing a protective face mask that covers the nose and mouth.

Treatment with muromonab-CD3 may also increase the chance of getting other infections. If you can, avoid people with colds or other infections. If you think you are getting a cold or other infection, check with your doctor.

This medicine commonly causes chest pain, dizziness, fever and chills, shortness of breath, stomach upset, and trembling within a few hours after the first dose. These effects should be less after the second dose. However, *check with your doctor or nurse immediately* if you have chest pain, rapid or irregular heartbeat, shortness of breath or wheezing, or swelling of the face or throat after any dose.

Side Effects of This Medicine

Along with its needed effects, a medicine may cause some unwanted effects. Because of the way that muromonab-CD3 acts on the body, there is a chance that it may cause effects that may not occur until years after the medicine is used. These delayed effects may include certain types of cancer, such as lymphomas and skin cancers. Discuss these possible effects with your doctor.

Although not all of the following side effects may occur, if they do occur, they may need medical attention.

Check with your doctor or nurse immediately if the following side effects occur:

Less common

Chest pain; rapid or irregular heartbeat; shortness of breath or wheezing; swelling of face or throat

Check with your doctor as soon as possible if any of the following side effects occur:

More common

Diarrhea; dizziness or faintness; fever and chills; general feeling of discomfort or illness; headache; muscle or joint pain; nausea and vomiting

Less common

Confusion; hallucinations (seeing, hearing, or feeling things that are not there); itching or tingling; skin rash; stiff neck; trembling and shaking of hands; unusual sensitivity of eyes to light; unusual tiredness; weakness

Rare

Convulsions (seizures)

After you stop using this medicine, it may still produce some side effects that need medical attention. During this period of time check with your doctor if you notice the following side effects:

Fever and chills

Other side effects not listed above may also occur in some patients. If you notice any other effects, check with your doctor.

Revised: 08/08/95

NABILONE Systemic*

A commonly used brand name in Canada is Cesamet.

*Not commercially available in the U.S.

Description

Nabilone (NAB-i-lone) is chemically related to marijuana. It is used to prevent the nausea and vomiting that may occur after treatment with cancer medicines. It is used only when other kinds of medicine for nausea and vomiting do not work.

Nabilone is available only with your doctor's prescription. Prescriptions cannot be refilled and you must obtain a new prescription from your doctor each time you need this medicine. Nabilone is available in the following dosage form:

Oral
- Capsules (Canada)

Before Using This Medicine

In deciding to use a medicine, the risks of taking the medicine must be weighed against the good it will do. This is a decision you and your doctor will make. For nabilone, the following should be considered:

Allergies—Tell your doctor if you have ever had any unusual or allergic reaction to nabilone or marijuana products. Also tell your health care professional if you are allergic to any other substances, such as foods, preservatives, or dyes.

Pregnancy—Studies have not been done in pregnant women. However, studies in animals have shown a decrease in successful pregnancies and a decrease in the number of live babies born, when nabilone was given in doses many times the usual human dose.

Breast-feeding—It is not known whether nabilone passes into the breast milk. However, nabilone is not recommended during breast-feeding because other medicines similar to nabilone that pass into the breast milk have been shown to cause unwanted effects in the nursing baby.

Children—Studies on this medicine have been done only in adult patients, and there is no specific information comparing use of nabilone in children with use in other age groups.

Older adults—Fast or pounding heartbeat, feeling faint or lightheaded, and unusual tiredness or weakness may be especially likely to occur in elderly patients, who are usually more sensitive than younger adults to the effects of nabilone. Also, the effects this medicine may have on the mind may be of special concern in the elderly. Therefore, older people should be watched closely while taking this medicine.

Other medicines—Although certain medicines should not be used together at all, in other cases 2 different medicines may be used together even if an interaction might occur. In these cases, your doctor may want to change the dose, or other precautions may be necessary. When you are taking nabilone, it is especially important that your health care professional know if you are taking any of the following:

- Central nervous system (CNS) depressants (medicine that causes drowsiness) or
- Tricyclic antidepressants (medicine for depression)—Taking these medicines with nabilone may increase the CNS depressant effects

Other medical problems—The presence of other medical problems may affect the use of nabilone. Make sure you tell your doctor if you have any other medical problems, especially:

- Alcohol abuse (or history of) or
- Drug abuse or dependence (or history of)—Dependence on nabilone may develop
- Heart disease or
- High blood pressure or
- Low blood pressure or
- Manic depression or
- Schizophrenia—Nabilone may make the condition worse
- Liver disease (severe)—Higher blood levels of nabilone may occur, increasing the chance of side effects

Proper Use of This Medicine

Take this medicine only as directed by your doctor. Do not take more of it, do not take it more often, and do not take it for a longer time than your doctor ordered. If too much is taken, it may lead to other medical problems because of an overdose.

Dosing—The dose of nabilone will be different for different patients. *Follow your doctor's orders or the directions on the label.* The following information includes only the average doses of nabilone. *If your dose is different, do not change it* unless your doctor tells you to do so.

- For *oral* dosage forms (capsules):
  - —For nausea and vomiting caused by cancer medicines:
    - Adults and teenagers—Usually 1 or 2 milligrams (mg) twice a day. Your doctor will tell you how and when to take this medicine while you are taking your cancer medicine.
    - Children—Use and dose must be determined by your doctor.

Missed dose—If you miss a dose of this medicine, take it as soon as you remember. However, if it is almost time for your next dose, skip the missed dose and go back to your regular dosing schedule. *Do not double doses.*

Storage—To store this medicine:
- Keep out of the reach of children.
- Store away from heat and direct light.
- Do not store this medicine in the bathroom, near the kitchen sink, or in other damp places. Heat or moisture may cause the medicine to break down.
- Do not keep outdated medicine or medicine no longer needed. Be sure that any discarded medicine is out of the reach of children.

Precautions While Using This Medicine

Nabilone will add to the effects of alcohol and other central nervous system (CNS) depressants (medicines that slow down the nervous system, possibly causing drowsiness). Some examples of CNS depressants are antihistamines or medicine for hay fever, other allergies, or colds; sedatives, tranquilizers, or sleeping medicine; prescription pain medicines including other narcotics; barbiturates; medicine for seizures; muscle relaxants; or anesthetics, including some dental anesthetics. *Check with your doctor before taking any of the above while you are taking this medicine.*

If you think you or someone else may have taken an overdose, get emergency help at once. Taking an overdose of this medicine or taking alcohol or CNS depressants with this medicine may cause severe mental effects. Symptoms of overdose include changes in mood; confusion; difficulty in breathing; dizziness (severe) or fainting; hallucinations (seeing, hearing, or feeling things that are not there); increase in blood pressure; mental depression; nervousness or anxiety; fast, slow, irregular, or pounding heartbeat; and unusual tiredness or weakness (severe).

This medicine may cause some people to become drowsy, dizzy, or lightheaded, or to feel a false sense of well-being. *Make sure you know how you react to this medicine before you drive, use machines, or do anything else that could be dangerous if you are dizzy or are not alert and clearheaded.*

Dizziness, lightheadedness, or fainting may occur, especially when you get up suddenly from a lying or sitting position. Getting up slowly may help lessen this problem.

Nabilone may cause dryness of the mouth. For temporary relief, use sugarless candy or gum, melt bits of ice in your mouth, or use a saliva substitute. However, if your mouth continues to feel dry for more than 2 weeks, check with your medical doctor or dentist. Continuing dryness of the mouth may increase the chance of dental disease, including tooth decay, gum disease, and fungus infections.

Side Effects of This Medicine

Along with its needed effects, a medicine may cause some unwanted effects. Although not all of these side effects may occur, if they do occur they may need medical attention.

Check with your health care professional immediately if any of the following side effects occur:

Symptoms of overdose

Changes in mood; confusion; difficulty in breathing; dizziness (severe) or fainting; fast, slow, irregular, or pounding heartbeat; hallucinations (seeing, hearing, or feeling things that are not there); increase in blood pressure; mental depression; nervousness or anxiety; unusual tiredness or weakness (severe)

Other side effects may occur that usually do not need medical attention. These side effects may go away during treatment as your body adjusts to the medicine. However, check with your doctor if any of the following side effects continue or are bothersome:

More common

Clumsiness or unsteadiness; difficulty concentrating; dizziness; drowsiness; dryness of mouth; false sense of well-being; headache

Less common or rare

Blurred vision or any changes in vision; dizziness or lightheadedness, especially when getting up from a lying or sitting position—more common with high doses; loss of appetite; muscle pain or weakness

Other side effects not listed above may also occur in some patients. If you notice any other effects, check with your doctor.

Revised: 06/17/93

NAFARELIN Systemic

A commonly used brand name in the U.S. and Canada is Synarel.

Description

Nafarelin (NAF-a-re-lin) is used to treat endometriosis. Endometriosis is a condition in which tissue similar to the lining of the uterus implants in other places in a woman's pelvis area. These growths increase in response to estrogen. Nafarelin works by stopping the production of estrogen by the ovaries.

Nafarelin is usually only used in those women who cannot or do not want to take danazol (e.g., Danocrine), oral contraceptives (birth control pills), or a progestin (another type of female hormone) or choose not to undergo surgery. Danazol and nafarelin work equally well for pain caused by endometriosis, but each has different types of side effects. Danazol is similar to testosterone. Because of this, it causes side effects such as acne, oily skin or hair, rapid weight gain, decreased breast size, enlarged clitoris, hoarseness or deepening of the voice, and unnatural hair growth. Most of the side effects of nafarelin are related to the lower amount of estrogen in the bloodstream. This includes a temporary thinning of the bones that occurs with a continued shortage of estrogen. Because it is not yet known if repeating therapy with nafarelin can increase a woman's risk of osteoporosis (brittle bones) and an increased risk of broken bones in later life, nafarelin therapy is usually only used for short periods of time (a few months) and is generally not repeated.

Nasal

- Spray solution (U.S. and Canada)

Before Using This Medicine

In deciding to use a medicine, the risks of taking the medicine must be weighed against the good it will do. This is

a decision you and your doctor will make. For nafarelin, the following should be considered:

Allergies—Tell your doctor if you have ever had any unusual or allergic reaction to nafarelin. Also tell your health care professional if you are allergic to any other substances, such as foods, preservatives, or dyes.

Pregnancy—Nafarelin is not recommended during pregnancy. Nafarelin has not been studied in pregnant women. Some animal studies showed an increase in stillbirths and decreases in fetal weight, which would be expected from the changes in hormones caused by nafarelin. Because of this, you and your partner should use a birth control method that does not contain hormones, such as condoms, a diaphragm, or a cervical cap, with a spermicide. If you suspect that you may have become pregnant, stop taking this medicine and check with your doctor.

Breast-feeding—It is not known whether nafarelin passes into the breast milk.

Other medicines—Although certain medicines should not be used together at all, in other cases two different medicines may be used together even if an interaction might occur. In these cases, your doctor may want to change the dose, or other precautions may be necessary. When you are taking nafarelin, it is especially important that your health care professional know if you are taking the following:

- Nasal decongestant sprays—It is not known whether nasal decongestant sprays can decrease the amount of nafarelin that enters the bloodstream through the lining of the nose. For this reason, you should allow at least 30 minutes to pass before you use a nasal decongestant spray after using nafarelin

Other medical problems—The presence of other medical problems may affect the use of nafarelin. Make sure you tell your doctor if you have any other medical problems, especially:

- Other conditions that increase the chances for osteoporosis (brittle bones)—Since nafarelin causes a temporary thinning of the bones, it is important that your doctor know if you already have an increased risk of osteoporosis. Some things that can increase your risk for having osteoporosis include cigarette smoking, alcohol abuse, taking or drinking a lot of caffeine, and a family history of osteoporosis or easily broken bones. Some medicines, such as adrenocorticoids (cortisone-like medicines) or anticonvulsants (seizure medicine), can also cause thinning of the bones

Proper Use of This Medicine

You will be given a fact sheet with your prescription for nafarelin that explains how to use the pump spray bottle. If you have any questions about using the pump spray, ask your health care professional.

To use *nafarelin spray:*

- Before you use each new bottle of nafarelin, the spray pump needs to be started. To do this, point the bottle away from you and pump the bottle firmly about 7 times. A spray should come out by the seventh time you pump the spray bottle. *This only needs to be done once for each new bottle of nafarelin.* Be careful not to breathe in this spray. You could inhale extra doses of nafarelin, since the medicine is dissolved in the spray.
- Before you take your daily doses of nafarelin, blow your nose gently. Hold your head forward a little. Put the spray tip into one nostril. Aim the tip toward the back and outside of your nostril. You do not need to put the tip too far into your nose.
- Close your other nostril off by pressing on the outside of your nose with a finger. Then, sniff in the spray as you pump the bottle once.
- Take the spray bottle out of your nose. Tilt your head back for a few seconds, to let the spray get onto the back of your nose.
- Repeat these steps for each dose of medicine.
- Each time you use the spray bottle, wipe off the tip with a clean tissue or cloth. Keep the blue safety clip and plastic cap on the bottle when you are not using it.
- Every 3 or 4 days you should clean the tip of the spray bottle. To do this, hold the bottle sideways. Rinse the tip with warm water, while wiping the tip with your finger or soft cloth for about 15 seconds. Dry the tip with a soft cloth or tissue. Replace the cap right after use. Be careful not to get water into the bottle, since this could dilute the medicine.

Dosing—The dose of nafarelin will be different for different patients. *Follow your doctor's orders or the directions on the label.* The following information includes only the average dose of nafarelin. *If your dose is different, do not change it* unless your doctor tells you to do so.

- For *nasal solution* dosage form:
  - —For treating endometriosis:
    - Adults and teenagers—200 micrograms (mcg) (one spray) inhaled into one nostril in the morning and one spray inhaled into the other nostril in the evening, for six months. Begin your treatment on Day 2, 3, or 4 of your menstrual period.

Missed dose—If you miss a dose of this medicine, take it as soon as possible. However, if it is almost time for your next dose, skip the missed dose and go back to your regular dosing schedule. Do not double doses.

Storage—To store this medicine:

- Keep out of the reach of children.
- The bottle should be stored standing upright, with the tip up.
- Store away from heat and direct light.
- Keep the medicine from freezing. Do not refrigerate.
- Do not keep outdated medicine or medicine no longer needed. Be sure that any discarded medicine is out of the reach of children.

Precautions While Using This Medicine

Your doctor should check your progress at regular visits to make sure that this medicine is working properly and to check for unwanted effects.

Using nafarelin can cause dryness of the vagina. If this is uncomfortable, especially during sex, there are several water-based vaginal lubricant products that you can use. Using a lubricant may also help to prevent soreness or damage to the vagina from sex. If you decide to use a lubricant during sex and you are using condoms, a cervical cap, or a diaphragm, make sure the lubricant you choose will not damage the birth control device. Some products contain oils, which can break down latex rubber and cause any of these types of birth control devices to rip or tear.

Side Effects of This Medicine

In some animal studies, nafarelin was shown to increase the chance of certain types of tumors. The doses given were higher and were used longer than those used in humans. These effects have not been found in humans using recommended doses.

Along with its needed effects, a medicine may cause some unwanted effects. Although not all of these side effects may occur, if they do occur they may need medical attention.

Check with your doctor as soon as possible if any of the following side effects occur:

More common

Light vaginal bleeding between regular menstrual periods, which does not need the use of a pad or tampon (''spotting''); longer or heavier menstrual periods; vaginal bleeding between regular menstrual periods, which may need the use of a pad or tampon (''breakthrough bleeding'')

Rare

Allergic reaction (shortness of breath, chest pain, hives); joint pain; pelvic or lower abdomen bloating or tenderness (mild); unexpected or excess flow of milk

Other side effects may occur that usually do not need medical attention. Some of these side effects may go away during treatment as your body adjusts to the medicine. However, check with your doctor if any of the following side effects continue or are bothersome:

More common

Lower estrogen in the bloodstream (acne, decreased sex drive, dryness of the vagina, hot flashes, pain during sex, decreased breast size, palpitations, oily skin); stopping of menstrual periods

Less common or rare

Breast pain; headache (mild and transient); irritated or runny nose; mental depression (mild and transient); mood swings; skin rash; weight changes

Other side effects not listed above may also occur in some patients. If you notice any other effects, check with your doctor.

Revised: 10/26/92
Interim revision: 07/05/94

NAFTIFINE Topical

A commonly used brand name in the U.S. and Canada is Naftin.

Description

Naftifine (NAF-ti-feen) is used to treat fungus infections. It works by killing the fungus or preventing its growth.

Naftifine is applied to the skin to treat:

- athlete's foot (ringworm of the foot; tinea pedis);
- jock itch (ringworm of the groin; tinea cruris); and
- ringworm of the body (tinea corporis).

This medicine may also be used for other fungus infections of the skin as determined by your doctor.

Naftifine is available with or without your doctor's prescription, in the following dosage forms:

Topical

- Cream (U.S. and Canada)
- Gel (U.S. and Canada)

Before Using This Medicine

In deciding to use a medicine, the risks of taking the medicine must be weighed against the good it will do. This is a decision you and your doctor will make. For topical naftifine, the following should be considered:

Allergies—Tell your doctor if you have ever had any unusual or allergic reaction to naftifine. Also tell your health care professional if you are allergic to any other substances, such as preservatives or dyes.

Pregnancy—Topical naftifine has not been studied in pregnant women. However, naftifine, when given by mouth, has not been shown to cause birth defects or other problems in animal studies.

Breast-feeding—Topical naftifine is absorbed into the body. However, it is not known whether naftifine passes into the breast milk. In addition, this medicine has not been reported to cause problems in nursing babies. Mothers who are using this medicine and who wish to breast-feed should discuss this with their doctor.

Children—Studies on this medicine have been done only in adult patients, and there is no specific information comparing use of naftifine in children with use in other age groups.

Older adults—Many medicines have not been studied specifically in older people. Therefore, it may not be known whether they work exactly the same way they do in younger adults or if they cause different side effects or problems in older people. There is no specific information comparing use of naftifine in the elderly with use in other age groups.

Other medicines—Although certain medicines should not be used together at all, in other cases two different medicines may be used together even if an interaction might occur. In these cases, your doctor may want to change the dose, or other precautions may be necessary. Tell your

health care professional if you are using any other prescription or non-prescription (over-the-counter [OTC]) medicine.

Proper Use of This Medicine

Keep this medicine away from the eyes and mucous membranes such as the inside of the nose, mouth, or vagina.

The area to which you have applied naftifine should not be covered with an occlusive dressing (airtight covering such as plastic wrap or bandage) unless otherwise directed by your doctor.

To use:

- Apply enough naftifine to cover the affected skin and surrounding areas, and rub in gently.
- After applying naftifine, wash your hands to remove any medicine that may be on them.

To help clear up your skin infection completely, *keep using naftifine for the full time of treatment.* You should keep using this medicine for 1 to 2 weeks after your symptoms have disappeared. If you stop using this medicine too soon, your symptoms may return. *Do not miss any doses.*

Dosing—The dose of naftifine will be different for different patients. *Follow your doctor's orders or the directions on the label.* The following information includes only the average doses of naftifine. *If your dose is different, do not change it* unless your doctor tells you to do so.

- For fungus infections:
  - —For *cream* dosage form:
    - Adults—Apply to the affected area(s) of the skin once a day.
    - Children—Use and dose must be determined by your doctor.
  - —For *gel* dosage form:
    - Adults—Apply to the affected area(s) of the skin two times a day, morning and evening.
    - Children—Use and dose must be determined by your doctor.

Missed dose—If you miss a dose of this medicine, apply it as soon as possible. However, if it is almost time for your next dose, skip the missed dose and go back to your regular dosing schedule.

Storage—To store this medicine:

- Keep out of the reach of children.
- Store away from heat and direct light.
- Keep the medicine from freezing.
- Do not keep outdated medicine or medicine no longer needed. Be sure that any discarded medicine is out of the reach of children.

Precautions While Using This Medicine

If your skin infection does not improve within 4 weeks, or if it becomes worse, check with your doctor.

To help clear up your skin infection completely and to help make sure it does not return, the following good health habits are important:

- *For patients using naftifine for athlete's foot*, these measures will help keep the feet cool and dry:
  - —Carefully dry the feet, especially between the toes, after bathing.
  - —Avoid wearing socks made from wool or synthetic materials (for example, rayon or nylon). Instead, wear clean, cotton socks and change them daily or more often if your feet sweat very much.
  - —Wear well-ventilated shoes (for example, shoes with holes on top or on the side) or sandals.
  - —Use a bland, absorbent powder (for example, talcum powder) or an antifungal powder freely between the toes, on the feet, and in socks and shoes once or twice a day. Be sure to use the powder after naftifine has been applied and has disappeared into the skin. Do not use the powder as the only treatment for your fungus infection.
- *For patients using naftifine for jock itch*, these measures will help reduce chafing and irritation and will also help keep the groin area cool and dry:
  - —Carefully dry the groin area after bathing.
  - —Avoid wearing underwear that is tight-fitting or made from synthetic materials (for example, rayon or nylon). Instead, wear loose-fitting, cotton underwear.
  - —Use a bland, absorbent powder (for example, talcum powder) or an antifungal powder freely once or twice a day. Be sure to use the powder after naftifine has been applied and has disappeared into the skin. Do not use the powder as the only treatment for your fungus infection.
- *For patients using naftifine for ringworm of the body*, these measures will help keep the affected areas cool and dry:
  - —Carefully dry yourself after bathing.
  - —Avoid too much heat and humidity if possible. Try to keep moisture from building up on affected areas of the body.
  - —Wear well-ventilated clothing.
  - —Use a bland, absorbent powder (for example, talcum powder) or an antifungal powder freely once or twice a day. Be sure to use the powder after naftifine has been applied and has disappeared into the skin. Do not use the powder as the only treatment for your fungus infection.

If you have any questions about this, check with your health care professional.

Side Effects of This Medicine

Along with its needed effects, a medicine may cause some unwanted effects. The following side effects may go away during treatment as your body adjusts to the medicine.

However, check with your doctor if any of these effects continue or are bothersome:

More common

Burning or stinging feeling on treated area(s)

Less common

Dry skin; itching, redness, or other sign of skin irritation not present before use of this medicine

Other side effects not listed above may also occur in some patients. If you notice any other effects, check with your doctor.

Revised: 07/25/94

NALIDIXIC ACID Systemic

A commonly used brand name in the U.S. and Canada is NegGram.

Description

Nalidixic (nal-i-DIX-ik) acid is used to treat infections of the urinary tract. It may be used for other problems as determined by your doctor.

Nalidixic acid is available only with your doctor's prescription, in the following dosage forms:

Oral

- Suspension (U.S.)
- Tablets (U.S. and Canada)

Before Using This Medicine

In deciding to use a medicine, the risks of taking the medicine must be weighed against the good it will do. This is a decision you and your doctor will make. For nalidixic acid, the following should be considered:

Allergies—Tell your doctor if you have ever had any unusual or allergic reaction to nalidixic acid, or to any related medicines such as cinoxacin (e.g., Cinobac), ciprofloxacin (e.g., Cipro), enoxacin (e.g. Penetrex), lomefloxacin (e.g., Maxaquin), norfloxacin (e.g., Noroxin), or ofloxacin (e.g., Floxin). Also tell your health care professional if you are allergic to any other substances, such as foods, preservatives, or dyes.

Pregnancy—Studies have not been done in humans. However, use is not recommended during pregnancy since nalidixic acid has been shown to cause bone development problems in young animals.

Breast-feeding—Nalidixic acid passes into the breast milk. This medicine may cause blood problems in nursing babies with glucose-6-phosphate dehydrogenase (G6PD) deficiency. However, problems in other nursing babies have not been reported.

Children—This medicine is not recommended for use in infants up to 3 months of age since nalidixic acid has been shown to cause bone problems in young animals.

Older adults—This medicine has been studied in a limited number of elderly patients and has not been shown to cause different side effects or problems in older people than it does in younger adults.

Other medicines—Although certain medicines should not be used together at all, in other cases two different medicines may be used together even if an interaction might occur. In these cases, your doctor may want to change the dose, or other precautions may be necessary. When you are taking nalidixic acid, it is especially important that your health care professional know if you are taking any of the following:

- Anticoagulants (blood thinners)—Patients taking nalidixic acid with anticoagulants may have an increased chance of bleeding

Other medical problems—The presence of other medical problems may affect the use of nalidixic acid. Make sure you tell your doctor if you have any other medical problems, especially:

- Convulsive disorders, history of (seizures, epilepsy) or
- Hardening of the arteries in the brain (severe)—Patients with these medical problems may have an increased chance of side effects affecting the nervous system
- Glucose-6-phosphate dehydrogenase (G6PD) deficiency—Patients with G6PD deficiency may have an increased chance of side effects affecting the blood
- Kidney disease (severe) or
- Liver disease—Patients with liver disease or severe kidney disease may have an increase in side effects

Proper Use of This Medicine

Do not give this medicine to infants or children unless otherwise directed by your doctor. It has been shown to cause bone problems in young animals and may cause these problems in children.

Nalidixic acid is best taken with a full glass (8 ounces) of water on an empty stomach (either 1 hour before or 2 hours after meals). However, if this medicine causes nausea or upset stomach, it may be taken with food or milk.

For patients taking the *oral liquid form* of this medicine:

- Use a specially marked measuring spoon or other device to measure each dose accurately. The average household teaspoon may not hold the right amount of liquid.

To help clear up your infection completely, *keep taking this medicine for the full time of treatment,* even if you begin to feel better after a few days. *Do not miss any doses.*

Dosing—The dose of nalidixic acid will be different for different patients. *Follow your doctor's orders or the directions on the label.* The following information includes only the average doses of nalidixic acid. *If your dose is different, do not change it* unless your doctor tells you to do so.

The number of tablets or teaspoonfuls of suspension that you take depends on the strength of the medicine. Also, *the number of doses you take each day, the time allowed between doses, and the length of time you take the medicine depend on the medical problem for which you are taking nalidixic acid.*

- For *oral* dosage forms (oral suspension or tablets):
  —Adults and children 12 years of age and older: 1 gram (g) every six hours for one to two weeks to start; then, 500 milligrams (mg) every six hours.
  —Children 3 months to 12 years of age: The dose is based on body weight and must be determined by the doctor.
  —Infants up to 3 months of age: This medicine is not recommended in infants up to 3 months of age since nalidixic acid has been shown to cause bone problems in young animals.

Missed dose—If you do miss a dose of this medicine, take it as soon as possible. However, if it is almost time for your next dose, skip the missed dose and go back to your regular dosing schedule. Do not double doses.

Storage—To store this medicine:
- Keep out of the reach of children.
- Store away from heat and direct light.
- Do not store the tablet form of this medicine in the bathroom, near the kitchen sink, or in other damp places. Heat or moisture may cause the medicine to break down.
- Keep the oral liquid form of this medicine from freezing.
- Do not keep outdated medicine or medicine no longer needed. Be sure that any discarded medicine is out of the reach of children.

Precautions While Using This Medicine

If you will be taking this medicine for more than 2 weeks, your doctor should check your progress at regular visits.

If your symptoms do not improve within 2 days, or if they become worse, check with your doctor.

This medicine may cause blurred vision or other vision problems. It may also cause some people to become dizzy, drowsy, or less alert than they are normally. *Make sure you know how you react to this medicine before you drive, use machines, or do anything else that could be dangerous if you are dizzy or are not alert or able to see well.* If these reactions are especially bothersome, check with your doctor.

Nalidixic acid may cause your skin to be more sensitive to sunlight than it is normally. Exposure to sunlight, even for brief periods of time, may cause a skin rash, itching, redness or other discoloration of the skin, or a severe sunburn. When you begin taking this medicine:
- Stay out of direct sunlight, especially between the hours of 10:00 a.m. and 3:00 p.m., if possible.
- Wear protective clothing, including a hat. Also, wear sunglasses.
- Apply a sun block product that has a skin protection factor (SPF) of at least 15. Some patients may require a product with a higher SPF number, especially if they have a fair complexion. If you have any questions about this, check with your health care professional.
- Apply a sun block lipstick that has an SPF of at least 15 to protect your lips.
- Do not use a sunlamp or tanning bed or booth.

If you have a severe reaction from the sun, check with your doctor.

For diabetic patients:
- *This medicine may cause false test results with some urine glucose (sugar) tests.* Check with your doctor before changing your diet or the dosage of your diabetes medicine.

Side Effects of This Medicine

Along with its needed effects, a medicine may cause some unwanted effects. Although not all of these side effects may occur, if they do occur they may need medical attention.

Check with your doctor immediately if any of the following side effects occur:

More common

Blurred or decreased vision; change in color vision; double vision; halos around lights; overbright appearance of lights

Rare

Bulging of fontanel (soft spot) on top of head of an infant; convulsions (seizures); dark or amber urine; hallucinations (seeing, hearing, or feeling things that are not there); headache (severe); mood or other mental changes; pale skin; pale stools; skin rash and itching; sore throat and fever; stomach pain (severe); unusual bleeding or bruising; unusual tiredness or weakness; yellow eyes or skin

Other side effects may occur that usually do not need medical attention. These side effects may go away during treatment as your body adjusts to the medicine. However, check with your doctor if any of the following side effects continue or are bothersome:

More common

Diarrhea; dizziness; drowsiness; headache; nausea or vomiting; stomach pain

Less common

Increased sensitivity of skin to sunlight

Other side effects not listed above may also occur in some patients. If you notice any other effects, check with your doctor.

Revised: 05/14/93

NALTREXONE Systemic

A commonly used brand name in the U.S. and Canada is ReVia.

Description

Naltrexone (nal-TREK-zone) is used to help narcotic addicts who have stopped taking narcotics to stay drug-free. It is also used to help alcoholics stay alcohol-free. The medicine is not a cure for addiction. It is used as part of an overall program that may include counseling, attending support group meetings, and other treatment recommended by your doctor.

Naltrexone is not a narcotic. It works by blocking the effects of narcotics, especially the "high" feeling that makes you want to use them. It also may block the "high" feeling that may make you want to use alcohol. It will not produce any narcotic-like effects or cause mental or physical dependence. It will not prevent you from becoming impaired while drinking alcohol.

Naltrexone will cause withdrawal symptoms in people who are physically dependent on narcotics. Therefore, naltrexone treatment is started after you are no longer dependent on narcotics. The length of time this takes may depend on which narcotic you took, the amount you took, and how long you took it. Before you start taking this medicine, be sure to tell your doctor if you think you are still having withdrawal symptoms.

Naltrexone is available only with your doctor's prescription, in the following dosage form:

Oral

- Tablets (U.S. and Canada)

Before Using This Medicine

In deciding to use a medicine, the risks of taking the medicine must be weighed against the good it will do. This is a decision you and your doctor will make. For naltrexone, the following should be considered:

Allergies—Tell your doctor if you have ever had any unusual or allergic reaction to naltrexone. Also tell your health care professional if you are allergic to any other substances, such as foods, preservatives, or dyes.

Pregnancy—Naltrexone has not been studied in pregnant women. However, studies in animals have shown that naltrexone causes unwanted effects when given in very large doses. Before taking this medicine, make sure your doctor knows if you are pregnant or if you may become pregnant.

Breast-feeding—It is not known whether naltrexone passes into the breast milk. However, this medicine has not been reported to cause problems in nursing babies.

Children—Naltrexone has been tested only in adult patients and there is no specific information about its use in patients up to 18 years of age.

Older adults—Many medicines have not been studied specifically in older people. Therefore, it may not be known whether they work exactly the same way they do in younger adults or if they cause different side effects or problems in older people. There is no specific information comparing the use of naltrexone in the elderly with use in other age groups.

Other medicines—Although certain medicines should not be used together at all, in other cases two different medicines may be used together even if an interaction might occur. In these cases, your doctor may want to change the dose, or other precautions may be necessary. When you are taking naltrexone, it is especially important that your health care professionals know if you are taking any of the following:

- Opioid (Narcotic) analgesics (e.g., butorphanol [e.g., Stadol], codeine, hydrocodone [e.g., Hycodan], hydromorphone [e.g., Dilaudid], levorphanol [e.g., Levo-Dromoran], meperidine [e.g., Demerol], methadone [e.g., Dolophine], morphine [e.g., MSIR], nalbuphine [e.g., Nubain], oxycodone [e.g., Roxicodone], propoxyphene [e.g., Darvon]) or
- Opioid-containing medications, other—The effects of these medications may be blocked by naltrexone. Alternative medications for relief of pain should be used in patients receiving naltrexone. Naltrexone may cause withdrawal in patients dependent on narcotics.

Other medical problems—The presence of other medical problems may affect the use of naltrexone. Make sure you tell your doctor if you have any other medical problems, especially:

- Hepatitis or other liver disease—The chance of side effects may be increased

Proper Use of This Medicine

Take naltrexone regularly as ordered by your doctor. It may be helpful to have someone else, such as a family member, doctor, or nurse, give you each dose as scheduled.

Dosing—The dose of naltrexone will be different for different patients. *Follow your doctor's orders or the directions on the label.* The following information includes only the average doses of naltrexone. *If your dose is different, do not change it* unless your doctor tells you to do so.

- For *oral* dosage form (tablets):
  - —For treating narcotic addiction:
    - Adults—25 milligrams (mg) (one-half tablet) for the first dose, then another 25 mg one hour later. After that, the dose is 350 mg a week. Your doctor will direct you to divide up this weekly dose and take naltrexone according to one of the following schedules:

      50 mg (one tablet) every day; or

      50 mg a day during the week and 100 mg (two tablets) on Saturday; or

      100 mg every other day; or

      100 mg on Mondays and Wednesdays, and 150 mg (three tablets) on Fridays; or

      150 mg every three days.

• Children and teenagers up to 18 years of age—Use and dose must be determined by your doctor.

—For treating alcoholism:

• Adults—The first dose may be 25 milligrams (mg) (one-half tablet). After that, the dose is 50 mg (one tablet) every day.

• Children and teenagers up to 18 years of age—Use and dose must be determined by your doctor.

Missed dose—If you miss a dose of this medicine, and your regular dosing schedule is:

• One tablet every day:

—Take the missed dose as soon as possible. However, if you do not remember until the next day, skip the missed dose and go back to your regular dosing schedule. Do not double the next day's dose.

• One tablet every weekday and two tablets on Saturday:

—If you miss a weekday dose, follow the directions for one tablet every day.

—If you miss the Saturday dose, take it as soon as possible. However, if you do not remember until Sunday, take one tablet on Sunday. Then go back to your regular dosing schedule on Monday.

• Two tablets every other day:

—Take two tablets as soon as you remember, then skip a day, then go back to taking the medicine every other day; or

—Take two tablets as soon as possible if you remember the same day. However, if you do not remember until the next day, take one tablet the next day. Then go back to your regular dosing schedule.

• Two tablets on Monday and Wednesday and three tablets on Friday:

—If you miss one of the Monday or Wednesday doses, take it as soon as possible. However, if you do not remember until the next day, take one tablet the next day. Then go back to your regular dosing schedule.

—If you miss the Friday dose, take it as soon as possible if you remember the same day. However, if you do not remember until Saturday, take two tablets on Saturday. If you do not remember until Sunday, take one tablet on Sunday. Then go back to your regular dosing schedule on Monday.

• Three tablets every three days:

—Take three tablets as soon you remember, then skip two days, then go back to taking the medicine every three days; or

—Take three tablets as soon as possible if you remember the same day. However, if you do not remember until the next day, take two tablets, then skip a day and go back to your regular dosing schedule. If you do not remember until the second day, take one tablet. Then go back to your regular dosing schedule.

Storage—To store this medicine:

• Keep out of the reach of children.
• Store away from heat and direct light.
• Do not store this medicine in the bathroom, near the kitchen sink, or in other damp places. Heat or moisture may cause the medicine to break down.
• Do not keep outdated medicine.

Precautions While Using This Medicine

It is very important that your doctor check your progress at regular visits. Your doctor may want to do certain blood tests to see if the medicine is causing unwanted effects.

Remember that use of naltrexone is only part of your treatment. *Be sure that you follow all of your doctor's orders, including seeing your therapist and/or attending support group meetings on a regular basis.*

Do not try to overcome the effects of naltrexone by taking narcotics. To do so may cause coma or death. You may be more sensitive to the effects of narcotics than you were before beginning naltrexone therapy.

Naltrexone also blocks the useful effects of narcotics. *Always use a non-narcotic medicine to treat pain, diarrhea, or cough.* If you have any questions about the proper medicine to use, check with your health care professional.

Naltrexone will not prevent you from becoming impaired when you drink alcohol. *Do not take naltrexone in order to drive or perform other activities while under the influence of alcohol.*

Never share this medicine with anyone else, especially someone who is using narcotics. Naltrexone causes withdrawal symptoms in people who are using narcotics.

Tell all medical doctors, dentists, and pharmacists you go to that you are taking naltrexone.

It is recommended that you carry identification stating that you are taking naltrexone. Identification cards may be available from your doctor.

Side Effects of This Medicine

Along with its needed effects, a medicine may cause some unwanted effects. Although not all of these side effects may occur, if they do occur they may need medical attention.

Check with your doctor as soon as possible if any of the following side effects occur:

Less common
Skin rash

Rare
Abdominal or stomach pain (severe); blurred vision or aching, burning, or swollen eyes; chest pain; confusion; discomfort while urinating and/or frequent urination; fever; hallucinations (seeing, hearing, or feeling things that are not there); itching; mental depression or other mood or mental changes; ringing or buzzing in ears; shortness of breath; swelling of face, feet, or lower legs; weight gain

Other side effects may occur that usually do not need medical attention. These side effects may go away during treatment as your body adjusts to the medicine. However, check with your doctor if any of the following side effects continue or are bothersome:

More common

Abdominal or stomach cramping or pain (mild or moderate); anxiety, nervousness, restlessness, and/or trouble in sleeping; headache; joint or muscle pain; nausea or vomiting; unusual tiredness

Less common or rare

Chills; constipation; cough, hoarseness, runny or stuffy nose, sinus problems, sneezing, and/or sore throat; diarrhea; dizziness; fast or pounding heartbeat; increased thirst; irritability; loss of appetite; sexual problems in males

Other side effects not listed above, possibly including withdrawal symptoms, may also occur in some patients. If you notice any other effects, check with your doctor.

Revised: 08/13/97

NAPHAZOLINE Ophthalmic

Some commonly used brand names are:

In the U.S.—

Ak-Con
Albalon
Allerest
Allergy Drops
Clear Eyes Lubricating Eye Redness Reliever
Comfort Eye Drops
Degest 2
Estivin II
I-Naphline
Muro's Opcon
Nafazair
Naphcon
Naphcon Forte
Ocu-Zoline Sterile Ophthalmic Solution
VasoClear
VasoClear A
Vasocon Regular

Generic name product may also be available.

In Canada—

Ak-Con
Albalon Liquifilm
Naphcon Forte
Vasocon

Description

Naphazoline (naf-AZ-oh-leen) is used to relieve redness due to minor eye irritations, such as those caused by colds, dust, wind, smog, pollen, swimming, or wearing contact lenses.

Some of these preparations are available only with your doctor's prescription. Others are available without a prescription; however, your doctor may have special instructions on the proper use of this medicine for your medical problem.

Naphazoline is available in the following dosage form:

Ophthalmic

- Ophthalmic solution (eye drops) (U.S. and Canada)

Before Using This Medicine

If you are using this medicine without a prescription, carefully read and follow any precautions on the label. For ophthalmic naphazoline, the following should be considered:

Allergies—Tell your doctor if you have ever had any unusual or allergic reaction to naphazoline. Also tell your health care professional if you are allergic to any other substances, such as preservatives.

Pregnancy—This medicine may be absorbed into the body. However, studies on effects in pregnancy have not been done in either humans or animals.

Breast-feeding—Naphazoline may be absorbed into the mother's body. However, this medicine has not been reported to cause problems in nursing babies.

Children—Use by infants and children is not recommended, since they are especially sensitive to the effects of naphazoline.

Older adults—Many medicines have not been studied specifically in older people. Therefore, it may not be known whether they work exactly the same way they do in younger adults or if they cause different side effects or problems in older people. There is no specific information comparing use of naphazoline in the elderly with use in other age groups.

Other medicines—Although certain medicines should not be used together at all, in other cases two different medicines may be used together even if an interaction might occur. In these cases, your doctor may want to change the dose, or other precautions may be necessary. Tell your health care professional if you are using any other prescription or nonprescription (over-the-counter [OTC]) medicine.

Other medical problems—The presence of other medical problems may affect the use of ophthalmic naphazoline. Make sure you tell your doctor if you have any other medical problems, especially:

- Diabetes mellitus (sugar diabetes) or
- Heart disease or
- High blood pressure or
- Overactive thyroid—Use of ophthalmic naphazoline may make the condition worse
- Eye disease, infection, or injury—The symptoms of the condition may be confused with possible side effects of ophthalmic naphazoline

Proper Use of This Medicine

Do not use naphazoline ophthalmic solution if it becomes cloudy or changes color.

Naphazoline should not be used in infants and children. It may cause severe slowing down of the central nervous system (CNS), which may lead to unconsciousness. It may also cause a severe decrease in body temperature.

Use this medicine only as directed. Do not use more of it, do not use it more often, and do not use it for more than 72 hours, unless otherwise directed by your doctor. To do so may make your eye redness and irritation worse and may also increase the chance of side effects.

To use:

- First, wash your hands. With the middle finger, apply pressure to the inside corner of the eye (and continue to apply pressure for 1 or 2 minutes after the medicine has been placed in the eye). Tilt the head back and with the index finger of the same hand, pull the lower eyelid away from the eye to form a pouch. Drop the medicine into the pouch and gently close the eyes. Do not blink. Keep the eyes closed for 1 or 2 minutes to allow the medicine to be absorbed.
- To keep the medicine as germ-free as possible, do not touch the applicator tip to any surface (including the eye). Also, keep the container tightly closed.

Dosing—The dose of ophthalmic naphazoline will be different for different patients. *Follow your doctor's orders or the directions on the label.* The following information includes only the average doses of ophthalmic naphazoline. *If your dose is different, do not change it* unless your doctor tells you to do so.

- For *ophthalmic solution (eye drop)* dosage form:
  - —For eye redness:
    - Adults—Use one drop not more often than every four hours.
    - Children—Use is not recommended.

Storage—To store this medicine:

- Keep out of the reach of children.
- Store away from heat and direct light.
- Keep the medicine from freezing.
- Do not keep outdated medicine or medicine no longer needed. Be sure that any discarded medicine is out of the reach of children.

Precautions While Using This Medicine

If eye pain or change in vision occurs or if redness or irritation of the eye continues, gets worse, or lasts for more than 72 hours, stop using the medicine and check with your doctor.

Side Effects of This Medicine

Along with its needed effects, a medicine may cause some unwanted effects. Although not all of these side effects may occur, if they do occur they may need medical attention.

When this medicine is used for short periods of time at recommended doses, side effects usually are rare. However, check with your doctor as soon as possible if any of the following occur:

With overuse or long-term use
Increase in eye irritation

Symptoms of too much medicine being absorbed into the body
Dizziness; headache; increased sweating; nausea; nervousness; weakness

Symptoms of overdose
Decrease in body temperature; drowsiness; slow heartbeat; weakness (severe)

Other side effects may occur that usually do not need medical attention. These side effects may go away during treatment as your body adjusts to the medicine. However, check with your health care professional if either of the following side effects continues or is bothersome:

Less common or rare
Blurred vision; large pupils

Other side effects not listed above may also occur in some patients. If you notice any other effects, check with your health care professional.

Revised: 05/14/92
Interim revision: 02/24/94

NARCOTIC ANALGESICS—For Pain Relief Systemic

Some commonly used brand names are:

In the U.S.—

Astramorph PF[9]
Buprenex[1]
Cotanal-65[15]
Darvon[15]
Darvon-N[15]
Demerol[7]
Dilaudid[5]
Dilaudid-5[5]
Dilaudid-HP[5]
Dolophine[8]
Duramorph[9]
Hydrostat IR[5]
Levo-Dromoran[6]
Methadose[8]
M S Contin[9]
MSIR[9]
MS/L[9]
MS/L Concentrate[9]
MS/S[9]
Nubain[10]
Numorphan[13]
OMS Concentrate[9]
Oramorph SR[9]
PP-Cap[15]
Rescudose[9]
RMS Uniserts[9]
Roxanol[9]
Roxanol 100[9]
Roxanol UD[9]
Roxicodone[12]
Roxicodone Intensol[12]
Stadol[2]
Talwin[14]
Talwin-Nx[14]

In Canada—

Darvon-N[15]
Demerol[7]
Dilaudid[5]
Dilaudid-HP[5]
Epimorph[9]
Hycodan[4]#
Levo-Dromoran[6]
M-Eslon[9]
Morphine Extra-Forte[9]
Morphine Forte[9]
Morphine H.P.[9]
Morphitec[9]
M.O.S.[9]
M.O.S.-S.R.[9]
M S Contin[9]
MS•IR[9]
Nubain[10]
Numorphan[13]
Oramorph SR[9]
Pantopon[11]
Paveral[3]
PMS-Hydromorphone[5]
PMS-Hydromorphone Syrup[5]
Robidone[4]
642[15]
Statex[9]
Statex Drops[9]
Supeudol[12]
Talwin[14]

Other commonly used names are:

dextropropoxyphene[15]
dihydromorphinone[5]
levorphan[6]
papaveretum[11]
pethidine[7]

Note: For quick reference, the following narcotic analgesics are numbered to match the corresponding brand names.

This information applies to the following medicines:

1. Buprenorphine (byoo-pre-NOR-feen)
2. Butorphanol (byoo-TOR-fa-nole)†
3. Codeine (KOE-deen)‡§
4. Hydrocodone (hye-droe-KOE-done)*
5. Hydromorphone (hye-droe-MOR-fone)‡
6. Levorphanol (lee-VOR-fa-nole)‡
7. Meperidine (me-PER-i-deen)‡§
8. Methadone (METH-a-done)‡**
9. Morphine (MOR-feen)‡§
10. Nalbuphine (NAL-byoo-feen)‡
11. Opium Injection (OH-pee-um)*
12. Oxycodone (ox-i-KOE-done)
13. Oxymorphone (ox-i-MOR-fone)
14. Pentazocine (pen-TAZ-oh-seen)
15. Propoxyphene (proe-POX-i-feen)‡

This information does *not* apply to Opium Tincture or Paregoric.

*Not commercially available in the U.S.
†Not commercially available in Canada.
‡Generic name product may be available in the U.S.
§Generic name product may be available in Canada.
#For Canadian product only. In the U.S., *Hycodan* also contains homatropine; in Canada, *Hycodan* contains only hydrocodone.
**In Canada, methadone is available only through doctors who have received special approval to prescribe it for treating drug addicts.

Description

Narcotic (nar-KOT-ik) analgesics (an-al-JEE-zicks) are used to relieve pain. Some of these medicines are also used just before or during an operation to help the anesthetic work better. Codeine and hydrocodone are also used to relieve coughing. Methadone is also used to help some people control their dependence on heroin or other narcotics. Narcotic analgesics may also be used for other conditions as determined by your doctor.

Narcotic analgesics act in the central nervous system (CNS) to relieve pain. Some of their side effects are also caused by actions in the CNS.

If a narcotic is used for a long time, it may become habit-forming (causing mental or physical dependence). Physical dependence may lead to withdrawal side effects when you stop taking the medicine.

These medicines are available only with your medical doctor's or dentist's prescription. For some of them, prescriptions cannot be refilled and you must obtain a new prescription from your medical doctor or dentist each time you need the medicine. In addition, other rules and regulations may apply when methadone is used to treat narcotic dependence.

These medicines are available in the following dosage forms:

Oral

Codeine
- Oral solution (U.S. and Canada)
- Tablets (U.S. and Canada)

Hydrocodone
- Syrup (Canada)
- Tablets (Canada)

Hydromorphone
- Oral solution (U.S. and Canada)
- Tablets (U.S. and Canada)

Levorphanol
- Tablets (U.S. and Canada)

Meperidine
- Syrup (U.S.)
- Tablets (U.S. and Canada)

Methadone
- Oral concentrate (U.S.)
- Oral solution (U.S.)
- Tablets (U.S.)
- Dispersible tablets (U.S.)

Morphine
- Capsules (U.S.)
- Extended-release capsules (Canada)
- Oral solution (U.S. and Canada)
- Syrup (Canada)
- Tablets (U.S. and Canada)
- Extended-release tablets (U.S. and Canada)

Oxycodone
- Oral solution (U.S.)
- Tablets (U.S. and Canada)

Pentazocine
- Tablets (Canada)

Pentazocine and Naloxone
- Tablets (U.S.)

Propoxyphene
- Capsules (U.S. and Canada)
- Oral suspension (U.S.)
- Tablets (U.S. and Canada)

Parenteral

Buprenorphine
- Injection (U.S.)

Butorphanol
- Injection (U.S.)

Codeine
- Injection (U.S. and Canada)

Hydromorphone
- Injection (U.S. and Canada)

Levorphanol
- Injection (U.S. and Canada)

Meperidine
- Injection (U.S. and Canada)

Methadone
- Injection (U.S.)

Morphine
- Injection (U.S. and Canada)

Nalbuphine
- Injection (U.S. and Canada)

Opium
- Injection (Canada)

Oxymorphone
- Injection (U.S. and Canada)

Pentazocine
- Injection (U.S. and Canada)

Rectal

Hydromorphone
- Suppositories (U.S. and Canada)

Morphine
- Suppositories (U.S. and Canada)

Oxycodone
- Suppositories (Canada)

Oxymorphone
- Suppositories (U.S. and Canada)

Before Using This Medicine

In deciding to use a medicine, the risks of taking the medicine must be weighed against the good it will do. This is

a decision you and your doctor will make. For narcotic analgesics, the following should be considered:

Allergies—Tell your doctor if you have ever had any unusual or allergic reaction to any of the narcotic analgesics. Also tell your health care professional if you are allergic to any other substances, such as foods, preservatives, or dyes.

Pregnancy—Although studies on birth defects with narcotic analgesics have not been done in pregnant women, these medicines have not been reported to cause birth defects. However, hydrocodone, hydromorphone, and morphine caused birth defects in animals when given in very large doses. Buprenorphine and codeine did not cause birth defects in animal studies, but they caused other unwanted effects. Butorphanol, nalbuphine, pentazocine, and propoxyphene did not cause birth defects in animals. There is no information about whether other narcotic analgesics cause birth defects in animals.

Too much use of a narcotic during pregnancy may cause the baby to become dependent on the medicine. This may lead to withdrawal side effects after birth. Also, some of these medicines may cause breathing problems in the newborn infant if taken just before delivery.

Breast-feeding—Most narcotic analgesics have not been reported to cause problems in nursing babies. However, when the mother is taking large amounts of methadone (in a methadone maintenance program), the nursing baby may become dependent on the medicine. Also, butorphanol, codeine, meperidine, morphine, opium, and propoxyphene pass into the breast milk.

Children—Breathing problems may be especially likely to occur in children younger than 2 years of age. These children are usually more sensitive than adults to the effects of narcotic analgesics. Also, unusual excitement or restlessness may be more likely to occur in children receiving these medicines.

Older adults—Elderly people are especially sensitive to the effects of narcotic analgesics. This may increase the chance of side effects, especially breathing problems, during treatment.

Other medicines—Although certain medicines should not be used together at all, in other cases two different medicines may be used together even if an interaction might occur. In these cases, your doctor may want to change the dose, or other precautions may be necessary. When you are taking a narcotic analgesic, it is especially important that your health care professional know if you are taking any of the following:

- Carbamazepine (e.g., Tegretol)—Propoxyphene may increase the blood levels of carbamazepine, which increases the chance of serious side effects
- Central nervous system (CNS) depressants or
- Monoamine oxidase (MAO) inhibitors (furazolidone [e.g., Furoxone], isocarboxazid [e.g., Marplan], pargyline [e.g., Eutonyl], phenelzine [e.g., Nardil], procarbazine [e.g., Matulane], tranylcypromine [e.g., Parnate] (taken currently or within the past 2 weeks) or
- Tricyclic antidepressants (amitriptyline [e.g., Elavil], amoxapine [e.g., Asendin], clomipramine [e.g., Anafranil], desipramine [e.g., Pertofrane], doxepin [e.g., Sinequan], imipramine [e.g., Tofranil], nortriptyline [e.g., Aventyl], protriptyline [e.g., Vivactil], trimipramine [e.g., Surmontil])—The chance of side effects may be increased; the combination of meperidine (e.g., Demerol) and MAO inhibitors is especially dangerous
- Naltrexone (e.g., Trexan)—Narcotics will not be effective in people taking naltrexone
- Rifampin (e.g., Rifadin)—Rifampin decreases the effects of methadone and may cause withdrawal symptoms in people who are dependent on methadone
- Zidovudine (e.g., AZT, Retrovir)—Morphine may increase the blood levels of zidovudine and increase the chance of serious side effects

Other medical problems—The presence of other medical problems may affect the use of narcotic analgesics. Make sure you tell your doctor if you have any other medical problems, especially:

- Alcohol abuse, or history of, or
- Drug dependence, especially narcotic abuse, or history of, or
- Emotional problems—The chance of side effects may be increased; also, withdrawal symptoms may occur if a narcotic you are dependent on is replaced by buprenorphine, butorphanol, nalbuphine, or pentazocine
- Brain disease or head injury or
- Emphysema, asthma, or other chronic lung disease or
- Enlarged prostate or problems with urination or
- Gallbladder disease or gallstones—Some of the side effects of narcotic analgesics can be dangerous if these conditions are present
- Colitis or
- Heart disease or
- Kidney disease or
- Liver disease or
- Underactive thyroid—The chance of side effects may be increased
- Convulsions (seizures), history of—Some of the narcotic analgesics can cause convulsions

Proper Use of This Medicine

Some narcotic analgesics given by injection may be given at home to patients who do not need to be in the hospital. If you are using an injection form of this medicine at home, *make sure you clearly understand and carefully follow your doctor's instructions.*

To take the *syrup form of meperidine:*

- Unless otherwise directed by your medical doctor or dentist, *take this medicine mixed with a half glass (4 ounces) of water* to lessen the numbing effect of the medicine on your mouth and throat.

To take the *oral liquid forms of methadone:*

- *This medicine may have to be mixed with water or another liquid before you take it.* Read the label carefully for directions. If you have any questions about this, check with your health care professional.

To take the *dispersible tablet form of methadone:*

- *These tablets must be stirred into water or fruit juice just before each dose is taken. Read the label carefully for directions.* If you have any questions about this, check with your health care professional.

To take *oral liquid forms of morphine:*

- This medicine may be mixed with a glass of fruit juice just before you take it, if desired, to improve the taste.

To take *long-acting morphine tablets:*

- *These tablets must be swallowed whole.* Do not break, crush, or chew them before swallowing.

To use *suppositories:*

- If the suppository is too soft to insert, chill it in the refrigerator for 30 minutes or run cold water over it before removing the foil wrapper.
- To insert the suppository: First remove the foil wrapper and moisten the suppository with cold water. Lie down on your side and use your finger to push the suppository well up into the rectum.

Take this medicine only as directed by your medical doctor or dentist. Do not take more of it, do not take it more often, and do not take it for a longer time than your medical doctor or dentist ordered. This is especially important for young children and elderly patients, who are especially sensitive to the effects of narcotic analgesics. If too much is taken, the medicine may become habit-forming (causing mental or physical dependence) or lead to medical problems because of an overdose.

If you think this medicine is not working properly after you have been taking it for a few weeks, *do not increase the dose.* Instead, check with your doctor.

Dosing—The dose of these medicines will be different for different patients. *Follow your doctor's orders or the directions on the label.* The following information includes only the average doses of these medicines. *If your dose is different, do not change it* unless your doctor tells you to do so.

The number of capsules or tablets or teaspoonfuls of oral solution or syrup that you take, or the amount of injection that you are directed to use, depends on the strength of the medicine. Also, *the number of doses you take each day, the time allowed between doses, and the length of time you take the medicine depend on the narcotic you are taking, whether or not you are taking a long-acting form of the medicine, and the reason you are taking the medicine.*

For buprenorphine

- For *injection* dosage form:
  - —For pain:
    - Adults and teenagers—0.3 milligrams (mg), injected into a muscle or a vein every six hours as needed.
    - Children up to 2 years of age—Dose must be determined by your doctor.
    - Children 2 to 12 years of age—0.002 to 0.006 mg per kilogram (kg) (0.0008 to 0.0024 mg per pound) of body weight, injected into a muscle or a vein every four to six hours as needed.

For butorphanol

- For *injection* dosage form:
  - —For pain:
    - Adults—1 to 4 milligrams (mg) (usually 2 mg), injected into a muscle every three or four hours as needed. Some people may receive 0.5 to 2 mg (usually 1 mg) injected into a vein every three or four hours as needed.
    - Children and teenagers—Dose must be determined by your doctor.

For codeine

- For *oral* dosage forms (oral solution or tablets):
  - —For pain:
    - Adults—15 to 60 milligrams (mg) (usually 30 mg) every three to six hours as needed.
    - Children—0.5 mg per kilogram (kg) (0.2 mg per pound) of body weight every four to six hours as needed. Young children will probably take the oral solution, rather than tablets. Small doses may need to be measured by a special dropper instead of a teaspoon.
  - —For cough:
    - Adults—10 to 20 mg every four to six hours.
    - Children up to 2 years of age—Use is not recommended.
    - Children 2 years of age—3 mg every four to six hours, up to a maximum of 12 mg a day. Children this young will probably take the oral solution, rather than tablets. Small doses may need to be measured by a special dropper instead of a teaspoon.
    - Children 3 years of age—3.5 mg every four to six hours, up to a maximum of 14 mg a day. Children this young will probably take the oral solution, rather than tablets. Small doses may need to be measured by a special dropper instead of a teaspoon.
    - Children 4 years of age—4 mg every four to six hours, up to a maximum of 16 mg a day. Children this young will probably take the oral solution, rather than tablets. Small doses may need to be measured by a special dropper instead of a teaspoon.
    - Children 5 years of age—4.5 mg every four to six hours, up to a maximum of 18 mg a day. Children this young will probably take the oral solution, rather than tablets. Small doses may need to be measured by a special dropper instead of a teaspoon.
    - Children 6 to 12 years of age—5 to 10 mg every four to six hours, up to a maximum of 60 mg a day.
- For *injection* dosage form:
  - —For pain:
    - Adults—15 to 60 mg (usually 30 mg), injected into a muscle or a vein or under the skin every four to six hours as needed.

• Children—0.5 mg per kg (0.2 mg per pound) of body weight, injected into a muscle or under the skin every four to six hours as needed.

For hydrocodone

• For *oral* dosage form (syrup or tablets):

—For pain:

• Adults—5 to 10 milligrams (mg) every four to six hours as needed.

• Children—0.15 mg per kilogram (kg) (0.06 mg per pound) of body weight every six hours as needed.

—For cough:

• Adults—5 mg every four to six hours as needed.

• Children—Dose must be determined by your doctor.

For hydromorphone

• For *oral* dosage form (oral solution or tablets):

—For pain:

• Adults—2 or 2.5 milligrams (mg) every three to six hours as needed.

• Children—Dose must be determined by your doctor.

• For *injection* dosage form:

—For pain:

• Adults—1 or 2 mg, injected into a muscle or under the skin every three to six hours as needed. Some people may receive 0.5 mg, injected slowly into a vein every three hours as needed.

• Children—Dose must be determined by your doctor.

• For *rectal suppository* dosage form:

—For pain:

• Adults—3 mg every four to eight hours as needed.

• Children—Dose must be determined by your doctor.

For levorphanol

• For *oral* dosage form (tablets):

—For pain:

• Adults—2 milligrams (mg). Some people with severe pain may need 3 or 4 mg.

• Children—Dose must be determined by your doctor.

• For *injection* dosage form:

—For pain:

• Adults—2 mg, injected under the skin or into a vein. Some people may need 3 mg.

• Children—Dose must be determined by your doctor.

For meperidine

• For *oral* dosage form (syrup or tablets):

—For pain:

• Adults—50 to 150 milligrams (mg) (usually 100 mg) every three or four hours as needed.

• Children—1.1 to 1.76 mg per kilogram (kg) (0.44 to 0.7 mg per pound) of body weight, up to a maximum of 100 mg, every three or four hours as needed. Young children will probably take the syrup, rather than tablets. Small doses may need to be measured by a special dropper instead of a teaspoon.

• For *injection* dosage form:

—For pain:

• Adults—50 to 150 milligrams (mg) (usually 100 mg), injected into a muscle or under the skin every three or four hours as needed. The medicine may also be injected continuously into a vein at a rate of 15 to 35 mg an hour.

• Children—1.1 to 1.76 mg per kg (0.44 to 0.7 mg per pound) of body weight, up to a maximum of 100 mg, injected into a muscle or under the skin every three or four hours as needed.

For methadone

• For *oral solution* dosage form:

—For pain:

• Adults—5 to 20 mg every four to eight hours.

• Children—Dose must be determined by your doctor.

—For narcotic addiction:

• Adults 18 years of age or older—

—For detoxification: At first, 15 to 40 mg once a day. Your doctor will gradually decrease the dose you take every day until you do not need the medicine any more.

—For maintenance: Dose must be determined by the needs of the individual patient, up to a maximum of 120 mg a day.

• Children up to 18 years of age—Special conditions must be met before methadone can be used for narcotic addiction in patients younger than 18 years of age. Use and dose must be determined by your doctor.

• For *oral tablet* dosage form:

—For pain:

• Adults—2.5 to 10 mg every three or four hours as needed.

• Children—Dose must be determined by your doctor.

—For narcotic addiction:

• Adults 18 years of age or older—

—For detoxification: At first, 15 to 40 mg once a day. Your doctor will gradually decrease the dose you take every day until you do not need the medicine any more.

—For maintenance: Dose must be determined by the needs of the individual patient, up to a maximum of 120 mg a day.

• Children up to 18 years of age—Special conditions must be met before methadone can be used for narcotic addiction in patients younger than 18 years of age. Use and dose must be determined by your doctor.

- For *injection* dosage form:
  - —For pain:
    - Adults—2.5 to 10 mg, injected into a muscle or under the skin, every three or four hours as needed.
    - Children—Dose must be determined by your doctor.
  - —For narcotic addiction:
    - Adults 18 years of age and older—For detoxification only, in patients unable to take medicine by mouth: At first, 15 to 40 mg a day. Your doctor will gradually decrease the dose you receive every day until you do not need the medicine any more.
    - Children younger than 18 years of age—Use and dose must be determined by your doctor.

For morphine

- For *short-acting oral* dosage forms (capsules, oral solution, syrup, or tablets):
  - —For severe, chronic pain (severe pain that lasts a long time):
    - Adults—At first, 10 to 30 milligrams (mg) every four hours. Your doctor will then adjust the dose according to your individual needs. If you have already been taking other narcotics to relieve severe, chronic pain, your starting dose will depend on the amount of other narcotic you were taking every day.
    - Children—Dose must be determined by your doctor.
- For *long-acting oral* dosage forms (extended-release capsules or tablets):
  - —For severe, chronic pain (severe pain that lasts a long time):
    - Adults—Long-acting forms of morphine are usually used for patients who have already been receiving narcotics to relieve pain. The starting dose will depend on the amount of narcotic you have been receiving every day. Your doctor will then adjust the dose according to your individual needs. To be helpful, these medicines need to be taken two times a day at regularly scheduled times. Some people may need to take a short-acting form of morphine if breakthrough pain occurs between doses of the long-acting medicine.
    - Children—Dose must be determined by your doctor.
- For *injection* dosage form:
  - —For pain:
    - Adults—5 to 20 mg (usually 10 mg), injected into a muscle or under the skin every four hours as needed. Some people may receive 4 to 10 mg, injected slowly into a vein. Morphine may also be injected continuously into a vein or under the skin at a rate that depends on the needs of the patient. This medicine may also be injected into the spinal area. The dose will depend on where and how the medicine is injected into the spinal area and on the needs of the patient.
    - Children—0.1 to 0.2 mg per kg (0.04 or 0.08 mg per pound) of body weight, up to a maximum of 15 mg, injected under the skin every four hours as needed. Some patients may receive 0.05 to 0.1 mg per kg (0.02 to 0.04 mg per pound) of body weight, injected slowly into a vein.
- For *rectal suppository* dosage form:
  - —For pain:
    - Adults—10 to 30 mg every four to six hours as needed.
    - Children—Dose must be determined by your doctor.

For nalbuphine

- For *injection* dosage form:
  - —For pain:
    - Adults—10 milligrams (mg) every three to six hours as needed, injected into a muscle or a vein or under the skin.
    - Children—Dose must be determined by your doctor.

For opium

- For *injection* dosage form:
  - —For pain:
    - Adults—5 to 20 milligrams (mg), injected into a muscle or under the skin every four to five hours as needed.
    - Children—Dose must be determined by your doctor.

For oxycodone

- For *oral* dosage form (oral solution or tablets):
  - —For pain:
    - Adults—5 milligrams (mg) every three to six hours or 10 mg three or four times a day as needed.
    - Children—Dose must be determined by your doctor. Children up to 6 years of age will probably take the oral solution, rather than tablets. Small doses may need to be measured by a special dropper instead of a teaspoon.
- For *rectal suppository* dosage form:
  - —For pain:
    - Adults—10 to 40 mg three or four times a day.
    - Children—Dose must be determined by your doctor.

For oxymorphone

- For *injection* dosage form:
  - —For pain:
    - Adults—1 to 1.5 milligrams (mg), injected into a muscle or under the skin every three to six hours as needed. Some patients may receive 0.5 mg, injected into a vein.
    - Children—Dose must be determined by your doctor.

- For *rectal suppository* dosage form:
  - —For pain:
    - Adults—5 mg every four to six hours as needed.
    - Children—Dose must be determined by your doctor.

For pentazocine

- For *oral* dosage form (tablets):
  - —For pain:
    - Adults—50 mg every three to four hours as needed. Some patients may need 100 mg every three to four hours. The usual maximum dose is 600 mg a day.
    - Children—Dose must be determined by your doctor.
- For *injection* dosage form:
  - —For pain:
    - Adults—30 mg, injected into a muscle or a vein or under the skin every three to four hours as needed.
    - Children—Dose must be determined by your doctor.

For propoxyphene

- For *oral* dosage form (capsules, oral suspension, or tablets):
  - —For pain:
    - Adults—Propoxyphene comes in two different forms, propoxyphene hydrochloride and propoxyphene napsylate. 100 mg of propoxyphene napsylate provides the same amount of pain relief as 65 mg of propoxyphene hydrochloride. The dose of propoxyphene hydrochloride is 65 milligrams (mg) every four hours as needed, up to a maximum of 390 mg a day. The dose of propoxyphene napsylate is 100 mg every four hours as needed, up to a maximum of 600 mg a day.
    - Children—Dose must be determined by your doctor.

Missed dose—If your medical doctor or dentist has ordered you to take this medicine according to a regular schedule and you miss a dose, take it as soon as you remember. However, if it is almost time for your next dose, skip the missed dose and go back to your regular dosing schedule. *Do not double doses.*

Storage—To store this medicine:

- Keep out of the reach of children. Overdose is very dangerous in young children.
- Store away from heat and direct light.
- Do not store tablets or capsules in the bathroom, near the kitchen sink, or in other damp places. Heat or moisture may cause the medicine to break down.
- Store hydromorphone, oxycodone, or oxymorphone suppositories in the refrigerator.
- Keep liquid (including injections) and suppository forms of the medicine from freezing.
- Do not keep outdated medicine or medicine no longer needed. Be sure that any discarded medicine is out of the reach of children.

Precautions While Using This Medicine

If you will be taking this medicine for a long time (for example, for several months at a time), your doctor should check your progress at regular visits.

Narcotic analgesics will add to the effects of alcohol and other CNS depressants (medicines that slow down the nervous system, possibly causing drowsiness). Some examples of CNS depressants are antihistamines or medicine for hay fever, other allergies, or colds; sedatives, tranquilizers, or sleeping medicine; other prescription pain medicines including other narcotics; barbiturates; medicine for seizures; muscle relaxants; or anesthetics, including some dental anesthetics. *Do not drink alcoholic beverages, and check with your medical doctor or dentist before taking any of the medicines listed above, while you are using this medicine.*

This medicine may cause some people to become drowsy, dizzy, or lightheaded, or to feel a false sense of well-being. *Make sure you know how you react to this medicine before you drive, use machines, or do anything else that could be dangerous if you are dizzy or are not alert and clearheaded.*

Dizziness, lightheadedness, or fainting may occur, especially when you get up suddenly from a lying or sitting position. Getting up slowly may help lessen this problem.

Nausea or vomiting may occur, especially after the first couple of doses. This effect may go away if you lie down for a while. However, if nausea or vomiting continues, check with your medical doctor or dentist. Lying down for a while may also help relieve some other side effects, such as dizziness or lightheadedness, that may occur.

Before having any kind of surgery (including dental surgery) or emergency treatment, tell the medical doctor or dentist in charge that you are taking this medicine.

Narcotic analgesics may cause dryness of the mouth. For temporary relief, use sugarless candy or gum, melt bits of ice in your mouth, or use a saliva substitute. However, if dry mouth continues for more than 2 weeks, check with your dentist. Continuing dryness of the mouth may increase the chance of dental disease, including tooth decay, gum disease, and fungus infections.

If you have been taking this medicine regularly for several weeks or more, *do not suddenly stop using it without first checking with your doctor.* Your doctor may want you to reduce gradually the amount you are taking before stopping completely, in order to lessen the chance of withdrawal side effects.

If you think you or someone else may have taken an overdose, get emergency help at once. Taking an overdose of this medicine or taking alcohol or CNS depressants with this medicine may lead to unconsciousness or death. Signs of overdose include convulsions (seizures), confusion, severe nervousness or restlessness, severe dizziness, severe drowsiness, slow or troubled breathing, and severe weakness.

Side Effects of This Medicine

Along with its needed effects, a medicine may cause some unwanted effects. Although not all of these side effects may occur, if they do occur they may need medical attention.

Get emergency help immediately if any of the following symptoms of overdose occur:

Cold, clammy skin; confusion; convulsions (seizures); dizziness (severe); drowsiness (severe); low blood pressure; nervousness or restlessness (severe); pinpoint pupils of eyes; slow heartbeat; slow or troubled breathing; weakness (severe)

Also, check with your doctor as soon as possible if any of the following side effects occur:

Less common or rare

Dark urine (for propoxyphene only); fast, slow, or pounding heartbeat; feelings of unreality; hallucinations (seeing, hearing, or feeling things that are not there); hives, itching, or skin rash; increased sweating (more common with hydrocodone, meperidine, and methadone); irregular breathing; mental depression or other mood or mental changes; pale stools (for propoxyphene only); redness or flushing of face (more common with hydrocodone, meperidine, and methadone); ringing or buzzing in the ears; shortness of breath, wheezing, or troubled breathing; swelling of face; trembling or uncontrolled muscle movements; unusual excitement or restlessness (especially in children); yellow eyes or skin (for propoxyphene only)

Other side effects may occur that usually do not need medical attention. These side effects may go away during treatment as your body adjusts to the medicine. However, check with your doctor if any of the following side effects continue or are bothersome:

More common

Dizziness, lightheadedness, or feeling faint; drowsiness; nausea or vomiting

Less common or rare

Blurred or double vision or other changes in vision; constipation (more common with long-term use and with codeine); decrease in amount of urine; difficult or painful urination; dry mouth; false sense of well-being; frequent urge to urinate; general feeling of discomfort or illness; headache; loss of appetite; nervousness or restlessness; nightmares or unusual dreams; redness, swelling, pain, or burning at place of injection; stomach cramps or pain; trouble in sleeping; unusual tiredness or weakness

After you stop using this medicine, your body may need time to adjust. The length of time this takes depends on the amount of medicine you were using and how long you used it. During this period of time check with your doctor if you notice any of the following side effects:

Body aches; diarrhea; fast heartbeat; fever, runny nose, or sneezing; gooseflesh; increased sweating; increased yawning; loss of appetite; nausea or vomiting; nervousness, restlessness, or irritability; shivering or trembling; stomach cramps; trouble in sleeping; unusually large pupils of eyes; weakness

Other side effects not listed above may also occur in some patients. If you notice any other effects, check with your doctor.

Revised: July 1990
Interim revision: 06/28/95

NARCOTIC ANALGESICS—For Surgery and Obstetrics Systemic

Some commonly used brand names are:

In the U.S.—

Alfenta[1]
Astramorph[6]
Astramorph PF[6]
Buprenex[2]
Demerol[5]
Duramorph[6]
Nubain[7]
Stadol[3]
Sublimaze[4]
Sufenta[9]
Ultiva[8]

In Canada—

Alfenta[1]
Demerol[5]
Epimorph[6]
Nubain[7]
Stadol[3]
Sublimaze[4]
Sufenta[9]
Ultiva[8]

Another commonly used name for meperidine is pethidine.

Note: For quick reference, the following narcotic analgesics are numbered to match the corresponding brand names.

This information applies to the following medicines:

1. Alfentanil (al-FEN-ta-nil)
2. Buprenorphine (byoo-pre-NOR-feen)
3. Butorphanol (byoo-TOR-fa-nole)†
4. Fentanyl (FEN-ta-nil)‡
5. Meperidine (me-PER-i-deen)‡§
6. Morphine (MOR-feen)‡§
7. Nalbuphine (NAL-byoo-feen)‡
8. Remifentanil (rem-i-FEN-ta-nil)
9. Sufentanil (soo-FEN-ta-nil)‡

†Not commercially available in Canada.
‡Generic name product may also be available in the U.S.
§Generic name product may also be available in Canada.

Description

Narcotic analgesics (nar-KOT-ik an-al-JEE-zicks) are given to relieve pain before and during surgery (including dental surgery) or during labor and delivery. These medicines may also be given before or together with an anesthetic (either a general anesthetic or a local anesthetic), even when the patient is not in pain, to help the anesthetic work better.

When a narcotic analgesic is used for surgery or obstetrics (labor and delivery), it will be given by or under the immediate supervision of a medical doctor or dentist, or by a specially trained nurse, in the doctor's office or in a hospital.

The following information applies only to these special uses of narcotic analgesics. If you are taking or receiving a narcotic analgesic to relieve pain after surgery, or for any other reason, ask your health care professional for additional information about the medicine and its use.

These medicines are available in the following dosage forms:

Parenteral

Alfentanil
- Injection (U.S. and Canada)

Buprenorphine
- Injection (U.S.)

Butorphanol
- Injection (U.S.)

Fentanyl
- Injection (U.S. and Canada)

Meperidine
- Injection (U.S. and Canada)

Morphine
- Injection (U.S. and Canada)

Nalbuphine
- Injection (U.S. and Canada)

Remifentanil
- Injection (U.S. and Canada)

Sufentanil
- Injection (U.S. and Canada)

Before Receiving This Medicine

In deciding to use a medicine, the risks of using the medicine must be weighed against the good it will do. This is a decision you and your doctor will make. For narcotic analgesics, the following should be considered:

Allergies—Tell your doctor if you have ever had any unusual or allergic reaction to a narcotic analgesic. Also tell your health care professional if you are allergic to any other substances, such as foods, preservatives, or dyes.

Pregnancy—Although studies on birth defects have not been done in pregnant women, these medicines have not been reported to cause birth defects. However, in animal studies, many narcotics have caused birth defects or other unwanted effects when they were given for a long time in amounts that were large enough to cause harmful effects in the mother.

Use of a narcotic during labor and delivery sometimes causes drowsiness or breathing problems in the newborn baby. If this happens, your health care professional can give the baby another medicine that will overcome these effects. Narcotics are usually not used during the delivery of a premature baby.

Breast-feeding—Some narcotics have been shown to pass into the breast milk. However, these medicines have not been reported to cause problems in nursing babies.

Children—Children younger than 2 years of age may be especially sensitive to the effects of narcotic analgesics. This may increase the chance of side effects.

Older adults—Elderly people are especially sensitive to the effects of narcotic analgesics. This may increase the chance of side effects.

Other medicines—Although certain medicines should not be used together at all, in other cases two different medicines may be used together even if an interaction might occur. In these cases, it may be necessary to change the dose, or other precautions may be necessary. It is very important that you tell the person in charge if you are taking:

- Any other medicine, prescription or nonprescription (over-the-counter [OTC]), or
- ''Street'' drugs, such as amphetamines (''uppers''), barbiturates (''downers''), cocaine (including ''crack''), marijuana, phencyclidine (PCP, ''angel dust''), and heroin or other narcotics—Serious side effects may occur if anyone gives you an anesthetic without knowing that you have taken another medicine

Other medical problems—The presence of other medical problems may affect the use of narcotic analgesics. Make sure you tell your doctor if you have *any* other medical problems.

Proper Use of This Medicine

Dosing—The dose of narcotic analgesic will be different for different patients. Your health care professional will decide on the right amount for you, depending on:

- Your age;
- Your general physical condition;
- The reason you are receiving the narcotic analgesic; and
- Other medicines you are taking or will receive before or after the narcotic analgesic is given.

Precautions After Receiving This Medicine

For patients going home within a few hours after surgery:

- Narcotic analgesics and other medicines that may be given with them during surgery may cause some people to feel drowsy, tired, or weak for up to a few days after they have been given. Therefore, for at least 24 hours (or longer if necessary) after receiving this medicine, *do not drive, use machines, or do anything else that could be dangerous if you are dizzy or are not alert.*
- Unless otherwise directed by your medical doctor or dentist, *do not drink alcoholic beverages or take other CNS depressants (medicines that slow down the nervous system, possibly causing drowsiness) for about 24 hours after you have received this medicine.* To do so may add to the effects of the narcotic analgesic. Some examples of CNS depressants are antihistamines or medicine for hay fever, other allergies, or colds; sedatives, tranquilizers, or sleeping medicine; prescription pain medicine or narcotics; barbiturates; medicine for seizures; and muscle relaxants.

Side Effects of This Medicine

Along with its needed effects, a medicine may cause some unwanted effects. Before you leave the hospital or doctor's office, your health care professional will closely follow the effects of this medicine. However, some effects may continue, or may not be noticed until later.

The following side effects usually do not need medical attention. They will gradually go away as the effects of the medicine wear off. However, check with your medical doctor or dentist if any of the following side effects continue or are bothersome:

More common

Dizziness, lightheadedness, or feeling faint; drowsiness; nausea or vomiting; unusual tiredness or weakness

Less common or rare

Blurred or double vision or other vision problems; confusion; constipation; difficult or painful urination; dryness of mouth; general feeling of discomfort or illness; headache; mental depression or other mood or mental changes; nightmares or unusual dreams

Other side effects not listed above may also occur in some patients. If you notice any other effects, check with your doctor.

Revised: July 1990
Interim revision: 06/28/95; 08/13/97

NARCOTIC ANALGESICS AND ACETAMINOPHEN Systemic

Some commonly used brand names are:

In the U.S.—

- Allay[4]
- Anexsia 5/500[4]
- Anexsia 7.5/650[4]
- Anolor DH 5[4]
- Bancap-HC[4]
- Capital with Codeine[1]
- Co-Gesic[4]
- Darvocet-N 50[7]
- Darvocet-N 100[7]
- DHCplus[3]
- Dolacet[4]
- Dolagesic[4]
- Duocet[4]
- E-Lor[7]
- Endocet[5]
- EZ III[1]
- Hycomed[4]
- Hyco-Pap[4]
- Hydrocet[4]
- Hydrogesic[4]
- HY-PHEN[4]
- Lorcet 10/650[4]
- Lorcet-HD[4]
- Lorcet Plus[4]
- Lortab[4]
- Lortab 2.5/500[4]
- Lortab 5/500[4]
- Lortab 7.5/500[4]
- Margesic #3[1]
- Margesic-H[4]
- Oncet[4]
- Panacet 5/500[4]
- Panlor[4]
- Percocet[5]
- Phenaphen with Codeine No.3[1]#
- Phenaphen with Codeine No.4[1]#
- Polygesic[4]
- Propacet 100[7]
- Pyregesic-C[1]
- Roxicet[5]
- Roxicet 5/500[5]
- Roxilox[5]
- Stagesic[4]
- Talacen[6]
- T-Gesic[4]
- Tylenol with Codeine Elixir[1]
- Tylenol with Codeine No.2[1]
- Tylenol with Codeine No.3[1]
- Tylenol with Codeine No.4[1]
- Tylox[5]
- Ugesic[4]
- Vanacet[4]
- Vendone[4]
- Vicodin[4]
- Vicodin ES[4]
- Wygesic[7]
- Zydone[4]

In Canada—

- Acet-2[2]
- Acet-3[2]
- Acet Codeine 30[1]
- Acet Codeine 60[1]
- Atasol-8[2]
- Atasol-15[2]
- Atasol-30[2]
- Cetaphen with Codeine[2]
- Cetaphen Extra-Strength with Codeine[2]
- Cotabs[2]
- Empracet-30[1]
- Empracet-60[1]
- Emtec-30[1]
- Endocet[5]
- Exdol-8[2]
- Lenoltec with Codeine No.1[2]
- Lenoltec with Codeine No.2[2]
- Lenoltec with Codeine No.3[2]
- Lenoltec with Codeine No.4[1]
- Novo-Gesic C8[2]
- Novo-Gesic C15[2]
- Novo-Gesic C30[2]
- Oxycocet[5]
- Percocet[5]
- Percocet-Demi[5]
- PMS-Acetaminophen with Codeine[1]
- Roxicet[5]
- Triatec-8[2]
- Triatec-30[1]
- Triatec-8 Strong[2]
- Tylenol with Codeine Elixir[1]
- Tylenol with Codeine No.1[2]
- Tylenol with Codeine No.2[2]
- Tylenol with Codeine No.3[2]
- Tylenol with Codeine No.4[1]
- Tylenol with Codeine No.1 Forte[2]

Other commonly used names are:

- APAP with codeine[1]
- Co-codAPAP[1]
- Co-hycodAPAP[4]
- Co-oxycodAPAP[5]
- Co-proxAPAP[7]
- drocode, acetaminophen, and caffeine[3]
- hydrocodone with APAP[4]
- oxycodone with APAP[5]
- propoxyphene with APAP[7]

Note: For quick reference, the following narcotic analgesics and acetaminophen combinations are numbered to match the corresponding brand names.

This information applies to the following medicines:

1. Acetaminophen (a-seat-a-MIN-oh-fen) and Codeine (KOE-deen)‡§
2. Acetaminophen, Codeine, and Caffeine (kaf-EEN)*§
3. Dihydrocodeine (dye-hye-droe-KOE-deen), Acetaminophen, and Caffeine†
4. Hydrocodone (hye-droe-KOE-done) and Acetaminophen†‡
5. Oxycodone (ox-i-KOE-done) and Acetaminophen‡
6. Pentazocine (pen-TAZ-oh-seen) and Acetaminophen†
7. Propoxyphene (proe-POX-i-feen) and Acetaminophen†‡

*Not commercially available in the U.S.
†Not commercially available in Canada.
‡Generic name product may be available in the U.S.
§Generic name product may be available in Canada.
#In Canada, *Phenaphen with Codeine* is different from the product with that name in the U.S. The Canadian product contains phenobarbital, ASA, and codeine.

Description

Combination medicines containing narcotic (nar-KOT-ik) analgesics (an-al-JEE-zicks) and acetaminophen are used to relieve pain. A narcotic analgesic and acetaminophen used together may provide better pain relief than either medicine used alone. In some cases, relief of pain may come at lower doses of each medicine.

Narcotic analgesics act in the central nervous system (CNS) to relieve pain. Many of their side effects are also caused by actions in the CNS. When narcotics are used for a long time, your body may get used to them so that larger amounts are needed to relieve pain. This is called tolerance to the medicine. Also, when narcotics are used for a long time or in large doses, they may become habit-forming (causing mental or physical dependence). Physical dependence may lead to withdrawal symptoms when you stop taking the medicine.

Acetaminophen does not become habit-forming when taken for a long time or in large doses, but it may cause other unwanted effects, including liver damage, if too much is taken.

In the U.S., these medicines are available only with your medical doctor's or dentist's prescription. In Canada, some acetaminophen, codeine, and caffeine combinations are available without a prescription.

These medicines are available in the following dosage forms:

Oral

Acetaminophen and Codeine
- Capsules (U.S.)
- Oral solution (U.S. and Canada)
- Oral suspension (U.S.)
- Tablets (U.S. and Canada)

Acetaminophen, Codeine, and Caffeine
- Tablets (Canada)

Dihydrocodeine, Acetaminophen, and Caffeine
- Capsules (U.S.)

Hydrocodone and Acetaminophen
- Capsules (U.S.)
- Oral solution (U.S.)
- Tablets (U.S.)

Oxycodone and Acetaminophen
- Capsules (U.S.)
- Oral solution (U.S.)
- Tablets (U.S. and Canada)

Pentazocine and Acetaminophen
- Tablets (U.S.)

Propoxyphene and Acetaminophen
- Tablets (U.S.)

Before Using This Medicine

In deciding to use a medicine, the risks of taking the medicine must be weighed against the good it will do. This is a decision you and your doctor will make. For narcotic analgesic and acetaminophen combinations, the following should be considered:

Allergies—Tell your doctor if you have ever had any unusual or allergic reaction to acetaminophen or to a narcotic analgesic. Also tell your health care professional if you are allergic to any other substances, such as foods, preservatives, or dyes.

Pregnancy—
- *For acetaminophen:* Although studies on birth defects with acetaminophen have not been done in pregnant women, it has not been reported to cause birth defects or other problems.
- *For narcotic analgesics:* Although studies on birth defects with narcotic analgesics have not been done in pregnant women, they have not been reported to cause birth defects. However, hydrocodone caused birth defects in animal studies when very large doses were used. Codeine did not cause birth defects in animals, but it caused slower development of bones and other toxic or harmful effects in the fetus. Pentazocine and propoxyphene did not cause birth defects in animals. There is no information about whether dihydrocodeine or oxycodone causes birth defects in animals.

Too much use of a narcotic during pregnancy may cause the fetus to become dependent on the medicine. This may lead to withdrawal side effects in the newborn baby. Also, some of these medicines may cause breathing problems in the newborn baby if taken just before or during delivery.

- *For caffeine:* Studies in humans have not shown that caffeine (contained in some of these combination medicines) causes birth defects. However, studies in animals have shown that caffeine causes birth defects when given in very large doses (amounts equal to those present in 12 to 24 cups of coffee a day).

Breast-feeding—Acetaminophen, codeine, and propoxyphene pass into the breast milk. It is not known whether other narcotic analgesics pass into the breast milk. However, these medicines have not been reported to cause problems in nursing babies.

Children—Breathing problems may be especially likely to occur when narcotic analgesics are given to children younger than 2 years of age. These children are usually more sensitive than adults to the effects of narcotic analgesics. Also, unusual excitement or restlessness may be more likely to occur in children receiving these medicines.

Acetaminophen has been tested in children and has not been shown to cause different side effects or problems in children than it does in adults.

Older adults—Elderly people are especially sensitive to the effects of narcotic analgesics. This may increase the chance of side effects, especially breathing problems, during treatment.

Acetaminophen has been tested and has not been shown to cause different side effects or problems in older people than it does in younger adults.

Other medicines—Although certain medicines should not be used together at all, in other cases two different medicines may be used together even if an interaction might occur. In these cases, your doctor may want to change the dose, or other precautions may be necessary. When you are taking a narcotic analgesic and acetaminophen combination, it is especially important that your health care professional know if you are taking any of the following:

- Carbamazepine (e.g., Tegretol)—Propoxyphene may increase the blood levels of carbamazepine, which increases the chance of serious side effects
- Central nervous system (CNS) depressants or
- Monoamine oxidase (MAO) inhibitors (furazolidone [e.g., Furoxone], isocarboxazid [e.g., Marplan], pargyline [e.g., Eutonyl], phenelzine [e.g., Nardil], procarbazine [e.g., Matulane], tranylcypromine [e.g., Parnate]) (taken currently or within the past 2 weeks) or
- Tricyclic antidepressants (amitriptyline [e.g., Elavil], amoxapine [e.g., Asendin], clomipramine [e.g., Anafranil], desipramine [e.g., Pertofrane], doxepin [e.g., Sinequan], imipramine [e.g., Tofranil], nortriptyline [e.g., Aventyl], protriptyline [e.g., Vivactil], trimipramine [e.g., Surmontil])—Taking these medicines together with a narcotic analgesic may increase the chance of serious side effects
- Naltrexone (e.g., Trexan)—Naltrexone keeps narcotic analgesics from working to relieve pain; people taking naltrexone should take pain relievers that do not contain a narcotic
- Zidovudine (e.g., AZT, Retrovir)—Acetaminophen may increase the blood levels of zidovudine, which increases the chance of serious side effects

Other medical problems—The presence of other medical problems may affect the use of narcotic analgesic and acetaminophen combinations. Make sure you tell your doctor if you have any other medical problems, especially:

- Alcohol and/or other drug abuse, or history of, or
- Brain disease or head injury or
- Colitis or
- Convulsions (seizures), history of, or
- Emotional problems or mental illness or
- Emphysema, asthma, or other chronic lung disease or
- Hepatitis or other liver disease or
- Kidney disease or
- Underactive thyroid—The chance of serious side effects may be increased
- Enlarged prostate or problems with urination or
- Gallbladder disease or gallstones—Some of the effects of narcotic analgesics may be especially serious in people with these medical problems
- Heart disease—Caffeine (present in some of these combination medicines) can make some kinds of heart disease worse

Proper Use of This Medicine

Take this medicine only as directed by your medical doctor or dentist. Do not take more of it, do not take it more often, and do not take it for a longer time than your medical doctor or dentist ordered. This is especially important for young children and elderly patients, who may be more sensitive than other people to the effects of narcotic analgesics. If too much of a narcotic analgesic is taken, it may become habit-forming (causing mental or physical dependence) or lead to medical problems because of an overdose. Taking too much acetaminophen may cause liver damage.

If you think that this medicine is not working properly after you have been taking it for a few weeks, *do not increase the dose.* Instead, check with your medical doctor or dentist.

Dosing—The dose of these medicines will be different for different patients. *Follow your doctor's orders or the directions on the label.* The following information includes only the average doses of these medicines. *If your dose is different, do not change it* unless your doctor tells you to do so.

The number of capsules or tablets or teaspoonfuls of solution or suspension that you take depends on the strength of the medicine.

For acetaminophen and codeine

- For *oral capsule or tablet* dosage form:
  - —For pain:
    - Adults—1 or 2 capsules or tablets containing acetaminophen with 15 or 30 milligrams (mg) of codeine, or 1 capsule or tablet containing acetaminophen with 60 mg of codeine, every four hours as needed.
    - Children—Dose must be determined by the doctor, depending on the age of the child. Most young children will receive the oral solution or suspension, rather than tablets or capsules.
- For *oral solution or suspension* dosage form:
  - —For pain:
    - Adults—1 tablespoonful (3 teaspoonfuls) every four hours as needed.
    - Children younger than 3 years of age—Dose must be determined by your doctor.
    - Children 3 to 7 years of age—1 teaspoonful three or four times a day as needed.
    - Children 7 to 12 years of age—2 teaspoonfuls three or four times a day as needed.

For acetaminophen, codeine, and caffeine

- For *oral tablet* dosage form:
  - —For pain:
    - Adults—1 or 2 tablets every four hours as needed.
    - Children—Dose must be determined by your doctor.

For dihydrocodeine, acetaminophen, and caffeine

- For *oral capsule* dosage form:
  - —For pain:
    - Adults—2 capsules every four hours.
    - Children—Dose must be determined by your doctor.

For hydrocodone and acetaminophen

- For *oral capsule* dosage form:
  - —For pain:
    - Adults—1 capsule every four to six hours as needed.
    - Children—Dose must be determined by your doctor.
- For *oral solution* dosage form:
  - —For pain:
    - Adults—1 to 3 teaspoonfuls every four to six hours as needed.
    - Children—Dose must be determined by your doctor.
- For *oral tablet* dosage form:
  - —For pain:
    - Adults—1 or 2 tablets containing acetaminophen with 2.5 milligrams (mg) of hydrocodone, or 1 tablet containing acetaminophen with 5, 7.5, or 10 mg of hydrocodone, every four to six hours as needed.
    - Children—Dose must be determined by your doctor.

For oxycodone and acetaminophen

- For *oral capsule or tablet* dosage form:
  - —For pain:
    - Adults—1 capsule or tablet every four to six hours as needed.
    - Children—Dose must be determined by your doctor.

- For *oral solution* dosage form:
  - —For pain:
    - Adults—1 teaspoonful every four to six hours as needed.
    - Children—Dose must be determined by your doctor.

For pentazocine and acetaminophen

- For *oral tablet* dosage form:
  - —For pain:
    - Adults—1 tablet every four hours.
    - Children—Dose must be determined by your doctor.

For propoxyphene and acetaminophen

- For *oral tablet* dosage form:
  - —For pain:
    - Adults—1 or 2 tablets, depending on the strength, every four hours as needed.
    - Children—Dose must be determined by your doctor.

Missed dose—If your medical doctor or dentist has ordered you to take this medicine according to a regular schedule and you miss a dose, take it as soon as you remember. However, if it is almost time for your next dose, skip the missed dose and go back to your regular dosing schedule. *Do not double doses.*

Storage—To store this medicine:

- Keep out of the reach of children. Overdose is very dangerous in young children.
- Store away from heat and direct light.
- Do not store tablets or capsules in the bathroom, near the kitchen sink, or in other damp places. Heat or moisture may cause the medicine to break down.
- Keep the liquid forms of this medicine from freezing.
- Do not keep outdated medicine or medicine no longer needed. Be sure that any discarded medicine is out of the reach of children.

Precautions While Using This Medicine

If you will be taking this medicine for a long time (for example, for several months at a time), or in high doses, your doctor should check your progress at regular visits.

Check the labels of all nonprescription (over-the-counter [OTC]) and prescription medicines you now take. If any contain acetaminophen or a narcotic be especially careful, since taking them while taking this medicine may lead to overdose. If you have any questions about this, check with your medical doctor, dentist, or pharmacist.

The narcotic analgesic in this medicine will add to the effects of alcohol and other CNS depressants (medicines that slow down the nervous system, possibly causing drowsiness). Some examples of CNS depressants are antihistamines or medicine for hay fever, other allergies, or colds; sedatives, tranquilizers, or sleeping medicine; other prescription pain medicine or narcotics; barbiturates; medicine for seizures; muscle relaxants; or anesthetics, including some dental anesthetics. Also, there may be a greater risk of liver damage if large amounts of alcoholic beverages are used while you are taking acetaminophen. *Do not drink alcoholic beverages, and check with your medical doctor or dentist before taking any of the medicines listed above, while you are using this medicine.*

Too much use of the acetaminophen in this combination medicine together with certain other medicines may increase the chance of unwanted effects. The risk will depend on how much of each medicine you take every day, and on how long you take the medicines together. If your doctor directs you to take these medicines together on a regular basis, follow his or her directions carefully. However, do not take this medicine together with any of the following medicines for more than a few days, unless your doctor has directed you to do so and is following your progress:

Aspirin or other salicylates
Diclofenac (e.g., Voltaren)
Diflunisal (e.g., Dolobid)
Etodolac (e.g., Lodine)
Fenoprofen (e.g., Nalfon)
Floctafenine (e.g., Idarac)
Flurbiprofen, oral (e.g., Ansaid)
Ibuprofen (e.g., Motrin)
Indomethacin (e.g., Indocin)
Ketoprofen (e.g., Orudis)
Ketorolac (e.g., Toradol)
Meclofenamate (e.g., Meclomen)
Mefenamic acid (e.g., Ponstel)
Nabumetone (e.g., Relafen)
Naproxen (e.g., Naprosyn)
Oxaprozin (e.g., Daypro)
Phenylbutazone (e.g., Butazolidin)
Piroxicam (e.g., Feldene)
Sulindac (e.g., Clinoril)
Tenoxicam (e.g., Mobiflex)
Tiaprofenic acid (e.g., Surgam)
Tolmetin (e.g., Tolectin)

This medicine may cause some people to become drowsy, dizzy, or lightheaded, or to feel a false sense of well-being. *Make sure you know how you react to this medicine before you drive, use machines, or do anything else that could be dangerous if you are dizzy or are not alert and clearheaded.*

Dizziness, lightheadedness, or fainting may occur, especially when you get up suddenly from a lying or sitting position. Getting up slowly may help lessen this problem.

Nausea or vomiting may occur, especially after the first couple of doses. This effect may go away if you lie down for a while. However, if nausea or vomiting continues, check with your medical doctor or dentist. Lying down for a while may also help relieve some other side effects, such as dizziness or lightheadedness, that may occur.

Before having any kind of surgery (including dental surgery) or emergency treatment, tell the medical doctor or dentist in charge that you are taking this medicine.

Narcotic analgesics may cause dryness of the mouth. For temporary relief, use sugarless candy or gum, melt bits of ice in your mouth, or use a saliva substitute. However, if dry mouth continues for more than 2 weeks, check with your dentist. Continuing dryness of the mouth may increase the chance of dental disease, including tooth decay, gum disease, and fungus infections.

If you have been taking this medicine regularly for several weeks or more, *do not suddenly stop taking it without first checking with your doctor.* Your doctor may want you to reduce gradually the amount you are taking before stopping completely, to lessen the chance of withdrawal side effects. This will depend on which of these medicines you have been taking, and the amount you have been taking every day.

If you think you or someone else may have taken an overdose of this medicine, get emergency help at once. Taking an overdose of this medicine or taking alcohol or CNS depressants with this medicine may lead to unconsciousness or death. Signs of overdose of narcotics include convulsions (seizures), confusion, severe nervousness or restlessness, severe dizziness, severe drowsiness, shortness of breath or troubled breathing, and severe weakness. Signs of severe acetaminophen overdose may not occur until several days after the overdose is taken.

Side Effects of This Medicine

Along with its needed effects, a medicine may cause some unwanted effects. Although not all of these side effects may occur, if they do occur they may need medical attention.

Get emergency help immediately if any of the following symptoms of overdose occur:

Cold, clammy skin; confusion (severe); convulsions (seizures); diarrhea; dizziness (severe); drowsiness (severe); increased sweating; low blood pressure; nausea or vomiting (continuing); nervousness or restlessness (severe); pinpoint pupils of eyes; shortness of breath or unusually slow or troubled breathing; slow heartbeat; stomach cramps or pain; weakness (severe)

Also, check with your doctor as soon as possible if any of the following side effects occur:

Less common or rare

Black, tarry stools; bloody or cloudy urine; confusion; dark urine; difficult or painful urination; fast, slow, or pounding heartbeat; frequent urge to urinate; hallucinations (seeing, hearing, or feeling things that are not there); increased sweating; irregular breathing or wheezing; mental depression; pain in lower back and/or side (severe and/or sharp); pale stools; pinpoint red spots on skin; redness or flushing of face; ringing or buzzing in ears; skin rash, hives, or itching; sore throat and fever; sudden decrease in amount of urine; swelling of face; trembling or uncontrolled muscle movements; unusual bleeding or bruising; unusual excitement (especially in children); yellow eyes or skin

Other side effects may occur that usually do not need medical attention. These side effects may go away during treatment as your body adjusts to the medicine. However, check with your medical doctor or dentist if any of the following side effects continue or are bothersome:

More common

Dizziness, lightheadedness, or feeling faint; drowsiness; nausea or vomiting; unusual tiredness or weakness

Less common or rare

Blurred or double vision or other changes in vision; constipation (more common with long-term use and with codeine or meperidine); dry mouth; false sense of well-being; general feeling of discomfort or illness; headache; loss of appetite; nervousness or restlessness; nightmares or unusual dreams; trouble in sleeping

Although not all of the side effects listed above have been reported for all of these combination medicines, they have been reported for at least one of them. However, since all of the narcotic analgesics are very similar, any of the above side effects may occur with any of these medicines.

After you stop using this medicine, your body may need time to adjust. The length of time this takes depends on which of these medicines you were taking, the amount of medicine you were using, and how long you used it. During this time check with your doctor if you notice any of the following side effects:

Body aches; diarrhea; fast heartbeat; fever, runny nose, or sneezing; gooseflesh; increased sweating; increased yawning; loss of appetite; nausea or vomiting; nervousness, restlessness, or irritability; shivering or trembling; stomach cramps; trouble in sleeping; weakness

Other side effects not listed above may also occur in some patients. If you notice any other effects, check with your doctor.

Revised: July 1990
Interim revision: 07/11/95

NARCOTIC ANALGESICS AND ASPIRIN Systemic

Some commonly used brand names are:

In the U.S.—

Azdone[5]
Damason-P[5]
Darvon Compound-65[9]
Empirin with Codeine No.3[2]
Empirin with Codeine No.4[2]
Endodan[6]
Lortab ASA[5]
Panasal 5/500[5]
PC-Cap[9]
Percodan[6]
Percodan-Demi[6]
Propoxyphene Compound-65[9]
Roxiprin[6]
Synalgos-DC[1]
Talwin Compound[7]

In Canada—

Anacin with Codeine[3]
C2 Buffered with Codeine[4]
C2 with Codeine[3]
Darvon-N Compound[9]
Darvon-N with A.S.A.[8]
Endodan[6]
Novo-AC and C[3]
Oxycodan[6]
Percodan[6]
Percodan-Demi[6]
692[9]
222[3]
282[3]
292[3]

Other commonly used names are:

A.C.&C[3]
AC and C[3]
Co-codaprin[2]
dihydrocodeine compound[1]
drocode and aspirin[1]
propoxyphene hydrochloride compound[9]

Note: For quick reference, the following narcotic analgesics and aspirin combinations are numbered to match the corresponding brand names.

This information applies to the following medicines:

1. Aspirin, Caffeine, and Dihydrocodeine (dye-hye-droe-KOE-deen)†
2. Aspirin (AS-pir-in) and Codeine (KOE-deen)†‡
3. Aspirin, Codeine, and Caffeine (kaf-EEN)*§#
4. Aspirin, Codeine, and Caffeine, Buffered*#
5. Hydrocodone (hye-droe-KOE-done) and Aspirin†
6. Oxycodone (ox-i-KOE-done) and Aspirin‡#
7. Pentazocine (pen-TAZ-oh-seen) and Aspirin†
8. Propoxyphene (proe-POX-i-feen) and Aspirin*#
9. Propoxyphene, Aspirin, and Caffeine‡#

*Not commercially available in the U.S.
†Not commercially available in Canada.
‡Generic name product may be available in the U.S.
§Generic name product may be available in Canada.
#In Canada, *Aspirin* is a brand name. Acetylsalicylic acid is the generic name in Canada. ASA, a synonym for acetylsalicylic acid, is the term that commonly appears on Canadian product labels.

Description

Combination medicines containing narcotic (nar-KOT-ik) analgesics (an-al-JEE-zicks) and aspirin are used to relieve pain. A narcotic analgesic and aspirin used together may provide better pain relief than either medicine used alone. In some cases, relief of pain may come at lower doses of each medicine.

Narcotic analgesics act in the central nervous system (CNS) to relieve pain. Many of their side effects are also caused by actions in the CNS. When narcotics are used for a long time, your body may get used to them so that larger amounts are needed to relieve pain. This is called tolerance to the medicine. Also, when narcotics are used for a long time or in large doses, they may become habit-forming (causing mental or physical dependence). Physical dependence may lead to withdrawal symptoms when you stop taking the medicine.

Aspirin does not become habit-forming when taken for a long time or in large doses, but it may cause other unwanted effects if too much is taken.

In the U.S., these medicines are available only with your medical doctor's or dentist's prescription. In Canada, some strengths of aspirin, codeine, and caffeine combination are available without a prescription.

These medicines are available in the following dosage forms:

Oral

- Aspirin, Caffeine, and Dihydrocodeine
  - Capsules (U.S.)
- Aspirin and Codeine
  - Tablets (U.S.)
- Aspirin, Codeine, and Caffeine
  - Tablets (Canada)
- Aspirin, Codeine, and Caffeine, Buffered
  - Tablets (Canada)
- Hydrocodone and Aspirin
  - Tablets (U.S.)
- Oxycodone and Aspirin
  - Tablets (U.S. and Canada)
- Pentazocine and Aspirin
  - Tablets (U.S.)
- Propoxyphene and Aspirin
  - Capsules (Canada)
- Propoxyphene, Aspirin, and Caffeine
  - Capsules (U.S. and Canada)
  - Tablets (Canada)

Before Using This Medicine

In deciding to use a medicine, the risks of taking the medicine must be weighed against the good it will do. This is a decision you and your doctor will make. For narcotic analgesic and aspirin combinations, the following should be considered:

Allergies—Tell your doctor if you have ever had any unusual or allergic reaction to a narcotic analgesic, aspirin or other salicylates, including methyl salicylate (oil of wintergreen), or any of the following medicines:

Diclofenac (e.g., Voltaren)
Diflunisal (e.g., Dolobid)
Etodolac (e.g., Lodine)
Fenoprofen (e.g., Nalfon)
Floctafenine (e.g., Idarac)
Flurbiprofen, oral (e.g., Ansaid)
Ibuprofen (e.g., Motrin)
Indomethacin (e.g., Indocin)
Ketoprofen (e.g., Orudis)
Ketorolac (e.g., Toradol)
Meclofenamate (e.g., Meclomen)
Mefenamic acid (e.g., Ponstel)
Nabumetone (e.g., Relafen)
Naproxen (e.g., Naprosyn)
Oxaprozin (e.g., Daypro)
Oxyphenbutazone (e.g., Tandearil)
Phenylbutazone (e.g., Butazolidin)
Piroxicam (e.g., Feldene)
Sulindac (e.g., Clinoril)
Suprofen (e.g., Suprol)
Tenoxicam (e.g., Mobiflex)
Tiaprofenic acid (e.g., Surgam)
Tolmetin (e.g., Tolectin)
Zomepirac (e.g., Zomax)

Also tell your health care professional if you are allergic to any other substances, such as foods, preservatives, or dyes.

Pregnancy—

- *For aspirin:* Studies in humans have not shown that aspirin causes birth defects. However, studies in animals have shown that aspirin causes birth defects.

  Some reports have suggested that too much use of aspirin late in pregnancy may cause a decrease in the newborn's weight and possible death of the fetus or newborn baby. However, the mothers in these reports had been taking much larger amounts of aspirin than are usually recommended. Studies of mothers taking aspirin in the doses that are usually recommended did not show these effects. However, regular use of aspirin late in pregnancy may cause unwanted effects on the heart or blood flow in the fetus or in the newborn baby. Also, use of aspirin during the last 2 weeks of pregnancy may cause bleeding problems in the fetus before or during delivery or in the newborn baby.

Too much use of aspirin during the last 3 months of pregnancy may increase the length of pregnancy, prolong labor, cause other problems during delivery, or cause severe bleeding in the mother before, during, or after delivery. *Do not take aspirin during the last 3 months of pregnancy unless it has been ordered by your doctor.*

- *For narcotic analgesics:* Although studies on birth defects with narcotic analgesics have not been done in pregnant women, they have not been reported to cause birth defects. However, hydrocodone caused birth defects in animal studies when given in very large doses. Codeine did not cause birth defects in animals, but it caused slower development of bones and other toxic or harmful effects on the fetus. Pentazocine and propoxyphene did not cause birth defects in animals. There is no information about whether dihydrocodeine or oxycodone causes birth defects in animals.

  Too much use of a narcotic during pregnancy may cause the fetus to become dependent on the medicine. This may lead to withdrawal side effects in the newborn baby. Also, some of these medicines may cause breathing problems in the newborn baby if taken just before or during delivery.
- *For caffeine:* Studies in humans have not shown that caffeine (contained in some of these combination medicines) causes birth defects. However, studies in animals have shown that caffeine causes birth defects when given in very large doses (amounts equal to those present in 12 to 24 cups of coffee a day).

Breast-feeding—These combination medicines have not been reported to cause problems in nursing babies. However, aspirin, caffeine, codeine, and propoxyphene pass into the breast milk. It is not known whether dihydrocodeine, hydrocodone, oxycodone, or pentazocine passes into the breast milk.

Children—*Do not give a medicine containing aspirin to a child or a teenager with a fever or other symptoms of a virus infection, especially flu or chickenpox, without first discussing its use with your child's doctor.* This is very important because aspirin may cause a serious illness called Reye's syndrome in children with fever caused by a virus infection, especially flu or chickenpox. Children who do not have a virus infection may also be more sensitive to the effects of aspirin, especially if they have a fever or have lost large amounts of body fluid because of vomiting, diarrhea, or sweating. This may increase the chance of side effects during treatment.

The narcotic analgesic in this combination medicine can cause breathing problems, especially in children younger than 2 years of age. These children are usually more sensitive than adults to the effects of narcotic analgesics. Also, unusual excitement or restlessness may be more likely to occur in children receiving these medicines.

Older adults—Elderly people are especially sensitive to the effects of aspirin and of narcotic analgesics. This may increase the chance of side effects, especially breathing problems caused by narcotic analgesics, during treatment.

Other medicines—Although certain medicines should not be used together at all, in other cases two different medicines may be used together even if an interaction might occur. In these cases, your doctor may want to change the dose, or other precautions may be necessary. When you are taking a narcotic analgesic and aspirin combination, it is especially important that your health care professional know if you are taking any of the following:

- Anticoagulants (blood thinners) or
- Carbenicillin by injection (e.g., Geopen) or
- Cefamandole (e.g., Mandol) or
- Cefoperazone (e.g., Cefobid) or
- Cefotetan (e.g., Cefotan) or
- Dipyridamole (e.g., Persantine) or
- Divalproex (e.g., Depakote) or
- Heparin or
- Medicine for inflammation or pain, except narcotics, or
- Pentoxifylline (e.g., Trental) or
- Plicamycin (e.g., Mithracin) or
- Ticarcillin (e.g., Ticar) or
- Valproic acid (e.g., Depakene)—Taking these medicines together with aspirin may increase the chance of bleeding
- Antidiabetics, oral (diabetes medicine you take by mouth)—Aspirin may increase the effects of the antidiabetic medicine; a change in the dose of the antidiabetic medicine may be needed if aspirin is taken regularly
- Carbamazepine (e.g., Tegretol)—Propoxyphene can increase the blood levels of carbamazepine, which increases the chance of serious side effects
- Central nervous system (CNS) depressants or
- Diarrhea medicine or
- Methotrexate (e.g., Mexate) or
- Tricyclic antidepressants (amitriptyline [e.g., Elavil], amoxapine [e.g., Asendin], clomipramine [e.g., Anafranil], desipramine [e.g., Pertofrane], doxepin [e.g., Sinequan], imipramine [e.g., Tofranil], nortriptyline [e.g., Aventyl], protriptyline [e.g., Vivactil], trimipramine [e.g., Surmontil]) or
- Vancomycin (e.g., Vancocin)—The chance of side effects may be increased
- Naltrexone (e.g., Trexan)—Naltrexone keeps narcotic analgesics from working to relieve pain; people taking naltrexone should use pain relievers that do not contain a narcotic
- Probenecid (e.g., Benemid) or
- Sulfinpyrazone (e.g., Anturane)—Aspirin can keep these medicines from working as well for treating gout; also, use of sulfinpyrazone and aspirin together may increase the chance of bleeding
- Urinary alkalizers (medicine that makes the urine less acid, such as acetazolamide [e.g., Diamox], calcium- and/or magnesium-containing antacids, dichlorphenamide [e.g., Daranide], methazolamide [e.g., Neptazane], potassium or sodium citrate and/or citric acid, sodium bicarbonate [baking soda])—These medicines may make aspirin less effective by causing it to be removed from the body more quickly
- Zidovudine (e.g., AZT, Retrovir)—Higher blood levels of zidovudine and an increased chance of serious side effects may occur

Other medical problems—The presence of other medical problems may affect the use of narcotic analgesic and aspirin combinations. Make sure you tell your doctor if you have any other medical problems, especially:

- Alcohol and/or other drug abuse, or history of, or
- Asthma, allergies, and nasal polyps (history of) or
- Brain disease or head injury or
- Colitis or
- Convulsions (seizures), history of, or
- Emotional problems or mental illness or
- Emphysema or other chronic lung disease or
- Kidney disease or
- Liver disease or
- Underactive thyroid—The chance of serious side effects may be increased
- Anemia or
- Overactive thyroid or
- Stomach ulcer or other stomach problems—Aspirin may make these conditions worse
- Enlarged prostate or problems with urination or
- Gallbladder disease or gallstones—Narcotic analgesics have side effects that may be dangerous if these medical problems are present
- Gout—Aspirin can make this condition worse and can also lessen the effects of some medicines used to treat gout
- Heart disease—Large amounts of aspirin and caffeine (present in some of these combination medicines) can make some kinds of heart disease worse
- Hemophilia or other bleeding problems or
- Vitamin K deficiency—Aspirin increases the chance of serious bleeding

Proper Use of This Medicine

Take this medicine with food or a full glass (8 ounces) of water to lessen stomach irritation.

Do not take this medicine if it has a strong vinegar-like odor. This odor means the aspirin in it is breaking down. If you have any questions about this, check with your health care professional.

Take this medicine only as directed by your medical doctor or dentist. Do not take more of it, do not take it more often, and do not take it for a longer time than your medical doctor or dentist ordered. This is especially important for children and elderly patients, who are usually more sensitive to the effects of these medicines. If too much of a narcotic analgesic is taken, it may become habit-forming (causing mental or physical dependence) or lead to medical problems because of an overdose. Also, taking too much aspirin may cause stomach problems or lead to medical problems because of an overdose.

If you think that this medicine is not working as well after you have been taking it for a few weeks, *do not increase the dose.* Instead, check with your medical doctor or dentist.

Dosing—The dose of these medicines will be different for different patients. *Follow your doctor's orders or the directions on the label.* The following information includes only the average doses of these medicines. *If your dose is different, do not change it* unless your doctor tells you to do so.

The number of capsules or tablets that you take depends on the strength of the medicine and on the amount of pain you are having.

For aspirin, caffeine, and dihydrocodeine

- For *oral* dosage form (capsules):
  - —For pain:
    - Adults—2 capsules every four hours as needed.
    - Children—Dose must be determined by your doctor.

For aspirin and codeine

- For *oral* dosage form (tablets):
  - —For pain:
    - Adults—1 or 2 tablets every four hours as needed.
    - Children—Dose must be determined by your doctor.

For aspirin, codeine, and caffeine

- For *oral* dosage form (tablets):
  - —For pain:
    - Adults—1 or 2 tablets every four hours as needed.
    - Children—Dose must be determined by your doctor.

For buffered aspirin, codeine, and caffeine

- For *oral* dosage form (tablets):
  - —For pain:
    - Adults—1 or 2 tablets every four hours as needed.
    - Children—Dose must be determined by your doctor.

For hydrocodone and aspirin

- For *oral* dosage form (tablets):
  - —For pain:
    - Adults—1 or 2 tablets every four to six hours as needed.
    - Children—Dose must be determined by your doctor.

For oxycodone and aspirin

- For *oral* dosage form (tablets):
  - —For pain:
    - Adults—1 or 2 half-strength tablets, or 1 full-strength tablet, every four to six hours as needed.
    - Children up to 6 years of age—Use is not recommended.
    - Children 6 to 12 years of age—One-quarter of a half-strength tablet every six hours as needed.
    - Children 12 years of age and older—One-half of a half-strength tablet every six hours as needed.

For pentazocine and aspirin

- For *oral* dosage form (tablets):
  - —For pain:
    - Adults—2 tablets three or four times a day as needed.

- Children—Dose must be determined by your doctor.

For propoxyphene and aspirin

- For *oral* dosage form (capsules):
  - —For pain:
    - Adults—1 capsule every four hours as needed.
    - Children—Dose must be determined by your doctor.

For propoxyphene, aspirin, and caffeine

- For *oral* dosage form (capsules or tablets):
  - —For pain:
    - Adults—1 capsule or tablet every four hours as needed.
    - Children—Dose must be determined by your doctor.

Missed dose—If your medical doctor or dentist has ordered you to take this medicine according to a regular schedule and you miss a dose, take it as soon as you remember. However, if it is almost time for your next dose, skip the missed dose and go back to your regular dosing schedule. *Do not double doses.*

Storage—To store this medicine:

- Keep out of the reach of children. Overdose is very dangerous in young children.
- Store away from heat and direct light.
- Do not store this medicine in the bathroom, near the kitchen sink, or in other damp places. Heat or moisture may cause the medicine to break down.
- Do not keep outdated medicine or medicine no longer needed. Be sure that any discarded medicine is out of the reach of children.

Precautions While Using This Medicine

If you will be taking this medicine for a long time (for example, for several months at a time), your doctor should check your progress at regular visits.

Check the labels of all nonprescription (over-the-counter [OTC]) and prescription medicines you now take. If any contain a narcotic, aspirin, or other salicylates, check with your health care professional. Taking them together with this medicine may cause an overdose.

This medicine will add to the effects of alcohol and other CNS depressants (medicines that slow down the nervous system, possibly causing drowsiness). Some examples of CNS depressants are antihistamines or medicine for hay fever, other allergies, or colds; sedatives, tranquilizers, or sleeping medicine; other prescription pain medicine or narcotics; barbiturates; medicine for seizures; muscle relaxants; or anesthetics, including some dental anesthetics. Also, stomach problems may be more likely to occur if you drink alcoholic beverages while you are taking aspirin. *Do not drink alcoholic beverages, and check with your medical doctor or dentist before taking any of the medicines listed above, while you are using this medicine.*

Taking acetaminophen or certain other medicines together with the aspirin in this combination medicine may increase the chance of unwanted effects. The risk will depend on how much of each medicine you take every day, and on how long you take the medicines together. If your medical doctor or dentist directs you to take these medicines together on a regular basis, follow his or her directions carefully. However, do not take acetaminophen or any of the following medicines together with this combination medicine for more than a few days, unless your medical doctor or dentist has directed you to do so and is following your progress:

Diclofenac (e.g., Voltaren)
Diflunisal (e.g., Dolobid)
Etodolac (e.g., Lodine)
Fenoprofen (e.g., Nalfon)
Floctafenine (e.g., Idarac)
Flurbiprofen, oral (e.g., Ansaid)
Ibuprofen (e.g., Motrin)
Indomethacin (e.g., Indocin)
Ketoprofen (e.g., Orudis)
Ketorolac (e.g., Toradol)
Meclofenamate (e.g., Meclomen)
Mefenamic acid (e.g., Ponstel)
Nabumetone (e.g., Relafen)
Naproxen (e.g., Naprosyn)
Oxaprozin (e.g., Daypro)
Phenylbutazone (e.g., Butazolidin)
Piroxicam (e.g., Feldene)
Sulindac (e.g., Clinoril)
Tenoxicam (e.g., Mobiflex)
Tiaprofenic acid (e.g., Surgam)
Tolmetin (e.g., Tolectin)

This medicine may cause some people to become drowsy, dizzy, or lightheaded, or to feel a false sense of well-being. *Make sure you know how you react to this medicine before you drive, use machines, or do anything else that could be dangerous if you are dizzy or are not alert and clearheaded.*

Dizziness, lightheadedness, or fainting may occur, especially when you get up suddenly from a lying or sitting position. Getting up slowly may help lessen this problem.

Nausea or vomiting may occur, especially after the first couple of doses. This effect may go away if you lie down for a while. However, if nausea or vomiting continues, check with your doctor. Lying down for a while may also help some other side effects, such as dizziness or lightheadedness.

Before having any kind of surgery (including dental surgery) or emergency treatment, tell the medical doctor or dentist in charge that you are taking this medicine.

Do not take this medicine for 5 days before any surgery, including dental surgery, unless otherwise directed by your medical doctor or dentist. Taking aspirin during this time may cause bleeding problems.

For patients taking the *buffered aspirin, codeine, and caffeine* combination (C2 Buffered with Codeine):

- This product contains antacids that can keep many other medicines, especially some medicines used to treat infections, from working properly. This problem can be prevented by not taking the 2 medicines too close together. Ask your pharmacist how long you should wait between taking any other medicine and the buffered aspirin, codeine, and caffeine combination.

For *diabetic patients:*

- False urine sugar test results may occur if you are regularly taking 8 or more 325-mg (5-grain) or 5 or more 500-mg doses of aspirin a day. Smaller amounts or occasional use of aspirin usually will not affect urine sugar tests. If you have any questions about this, check with your health care professional, especially if your diabetes is not well controlled.

Narcotic analgesics may cause dryness of the mouth. For temporary relief, use sugarless candy or gum, melt bits of ice in your mouth, or use a saliva substitute. However, if dry mouth continues for more than 2 weeks, check with your dentist. Continuing dryness of the mouth may increase the chance of dental disease, including tooth decay, gum disease, and fungus infections.

If you have been taking this medicine regularly for several weeks or more, *do not suddenly stop using it without first checking with your doctor.* Depending on which of these medicines you have been taking, and the amount you have been taking every day, your doctor may want you to reduce gradually the amount you are taking before stopping completely, to lessen the chance of withdrawal side effects.

If you think you or someone else may have taken an overdose of this medicine, get emergency help at once. Taking an overdose of this medicine or taking alcohol or CNS depressants with this medicine may lead to unconsciousness or death. Signs of overdose of this medicine include convulsions (seizures); hearing loss; confusion; ringing or buzzing in the ears; severe excitement, nervousness, or restlessness; severe dizziness, severe drowsiness, shortness of breath or troubled breathing, and severe weakness.

Side Effects of This Medicine

Along with its needed effects, a medicine may cause some unwanted effects. Although not all of these side effects may occur, if they do occur they may need medical attention.

Get emergency help immediately if any of the following symptoms of overdose occur:

Any loss of hearing; bloody urine; cold, clammy skin; confusion (severe); convulsions (seizures); diarrhea (severe or continuing); dizziness or lightheadedness (severe); drowsiness (severe); excitement, nervousness, or restlessness (severe); fever; hallucinations (seeing, hearing, or feeling things that are not there); headache (severe or continuing); increased sweating; increased thirst; low blood pressure; nausea or vomiting (severe or continuing); pinpoint pupils of eyes; ringing or buzzing in the ears; shortness of breath or unusually slow or troubled breathing; slow heartbeat; stomach pain (severe or continuing); uncontrollable flapping movements of the hands (especially in elderly patients); vision problems; weakness (severe)

Also, check with your doctor as soon as possible if any of the following side effects occur:

Less common or rare

Bloody or black, tarry stools; confusion; dark urine; fast, slow, or pounding heartbeat; increased sweating (more common with hydrocodone); irregular breathing; mental depression; pale stools; redness or flushing of face (more common with hydrocodone); skin rash, hives, or itching; stomach pain (severe); swelling of face; tightness in chest or wheezing; trembling or uncontrolled muscle movements; unusual excitement (especially in children); unusual tiredness or weakness; vomiting of blood or material that looks like coffee grounds; yellow eyes or skin

Other side effects may occur that usually do not need medical attention. These side effects may go away during treatment as your body adjusts to the medicine. However, check with your doctor if any of the following side effects continue or are bothersome:

More common

Dizziness, lightheadedness, or feeling faint; drowsiness; heartburn or indigestion; nausea or vomiting; stomach pain (mild)

Less common or rare

Blurred or double vision or other changes in vision; constipation (more common with long-term use and with codeine); difficult, painful, or decreased urination; dryness of mouth; false sense of well-being; frequent urge to urinate; general feeling of discomfort or illness; headache; loss of appetite; nervousness or restlessness; nightmares or unusual dreams; trouble in sleeping; unusual tiredness; unusual weakness

Although not all of the side effects listed above have been reported for all of these medicines, they have been reported for at least one of them. However, since all of the narcotic analgesics are very similar, any of the above side effects may occur with any of these medicines.

After you stop using this medicine, your body may need time to adjust. The length of time this takes depends on which of these medicines you were taking, the amount of medicine you were using, and how long you used it. During this period of time check with your doctor if you notice any of the following side effects:

Body aches; diarrhea; fever, runny nose, or sneezing; gooseflesh; increased sweating; increased yawning; loss of appetite; nausea or vomiting; nervousness, restlessness, or irritability; shivering or trembling; stomach cramps; trouble in sleeping; weakness

Other side effects not listed above may also occur in some patients. If you notice any other effects, check with your medical doctor or dentist.

Revised: July 1990
Interim revision: 07/05/95

NATAMYCIN Ophthalmic†

A commonly used brand name in the U.S. is Natacyn.
Another commonly used name is pimaricin.

†Not commercially available in Canada.

Description

Natamycin (na-ta-MYE-sin) belongs to the group of medicines called antifungals. It is used to treat some types of fungus infections of the eye.

Natamycin is available only with your doctor's prescription, in the following dosage form:

Ophthalmic

- Ophthalmic suspension (eye drops) (U.S.)

Before Using This Medicine

In deciding to use a medicine, the risks of taking the medicine must be weighed against the good it will do. This is a decision you and your doctor will make. For ophthalmic natamycin, the following should be considered:

Allergies—Tell your doctor if you have ever had any unusual or allergic reaction to natamycin. Also tell your health care professional if you are allergic to any other substances, such as preservatives.

Pregnancy—Studies on effects in pregnancy have not been done in either humans or animals.

Breast-feeding—It is not known whether natamycin passes into breast milk. Although most medicines pass into breast milk in small amounts, many of them may be used safely while breast-feeding. Mothers who are using this medicine and who wish to breast-feed should discuss this with their doctor.

Children—Studies on this medicine have been done only in adult patients, and there is no specific information comparing use of natamycin in children with use in other age groups.

Older adults—Many medicines have not been studied specifically in older people. Therefore, it may not be known whether they work exactly the same way they do in younger adults. Although there is no specific information comparing use of natamycin in the elderly with use in other age groups, this medicine is not expected to cause different side effects or problems in older people than it does in younger adults.

Proper Use of This Medicine

The bottle is only partially full to provide proper drop control.

To use:

- First, wash your hands. Tilt the head back and, pressing your finger gently on the skin just beneath the lower eyelid, pull the lower eyelid away from the eye to make a space. Drop the medicine into this space. Let go of the eyelid and gently close the eyes. Do not blink. Keep the eyes closed for 1 or 2 minutes to allow the medicine to come into contact with the infection.
- If you think you did not get the drop of medicine into your eye properly, use another drop.
- To keep the medicine as germ-free as possible, do not touch the applicator tip to any surface (including the eye). Also, keep the container tightly closed.

To help clear up your eye infection completely, *keep using this medicine for the full time of treatment,* even if your condition has improved. *Do not miss any doses.*

Dosing—The dose of ophthalmic natamycin will be different for different patients. *Follow your doctor's orders or the directions on the label.* The following information includes only the average doses of ophthalmic natamycin. *If your dose is different, do not change it* unless your doctor tells you to do so.

- For fungus infection of the eye:
  —For *eye drops* dosage form:
    - Adults—Use one drop in the eye every four to six hours. For more serious infections, your doctor may tell you to use one drop in the eye every one or two hours for three or four days, then one drop six to eight times a day thereafter.
    - Children—Use and dose must be determined by your doctor.

Missed dose—If you miss a dose of this medicine, apply it as soon as possible. Then go back to your regular dosing schedule.

Storage—To store this medicine:

- Keep out of the reach of children.
- Store away from heat and direct light.
- Keep the medicine from freezing.
- Do not keep outdated medicine or medicine no longer needed. Be sure that any discarded medicine is out of the reach of children.

Precautions While Using This Medicine

Your doctor should check your progress at regular visits. For some eye infections, these visits may be as often as several times a week.

If your symptoms do not improve within 7 to 10 days, or if they become worse, check with your doctor.

Side Effects of This Medicine

Along with its needed effects, a medicine may cause some unwanted effects. Although not all of these side effects may occur, if they do occur they may need medical attention.

Check with your doctor as soon as possible if any of the following side effects occur:

Eye irritation, redness, or swelling not present before use of this medicine

Other side effects not listed above may also occur in some patients. If you notice any other effects, check with your doctor.

Revised: 05/16/94

NEDOCROMIL Inhalation

A commonly used brand name in the U.S. and Canada is Tilade.

Description

Nedocromil (ne-DOK-roe-mil) is used to prevent the symptoms of asthma. When it is used regularly, nedocromil lessens the number and severity of asthma attacks by reducing inflammation in the lungs. Nedocromil is also used just before exposure to conditions or substances (for example, allergens, chemicals, cold air, or air pollutants) that cause reactions, to prevent bronchospasm (wheezing or difficulty in breathing). In addition, nedocromil is used to prevent bronchospasm following exercise. This medicine will not help an asthma or bronchospasm attack that has already started.

Nedocromil may be used alone or with other asthma medicines, such as bronchodilators (medicines that open up narrowed breathing passages) and corticosteroids (cortisone-like medicines).

Nedocromil works by acting on certain inflammatory cells in the lungs to prevent them from releasing substances that cause asthma symptoms and/or bronchospasm.

This medicine is available only with your doctor's prescription, in the following dosage form:

Inhalation
- Inhalation aerosol (U.S. and Canada)

Before Using This Medicine

In deciding to use a medicine, the risks of using the medicine must be weighed against the good it will do. This is a decision you and your doctor will make. For nedocromil, the following should be considered:

Allergies—Tell your doctor if you have ever had any unusual or allergic reaction to nedocromil or to any other inhalation aerosol medicine.

Pregnancy—Nedocromil has not been studied in pregnant women. However, nedocromil has not been shown to cause birth defects or other problems in animal studies.

Breast-feeding—It is not known whether nedocromil passes into breast milk. Although most medicines pass into breast milk in small amounts, many of them may be used safely while breast-feeding. Mothers who are using this medicine and who wish to breast-feed should discuss this with their doctor.

Children—Nedocromil has been tested in a limited number of children 6 years of age and older. In effective doses, it is not expected to cause different side effects or problems in children than it does in adults.

Older adults—Many medicines have not been studied specifically in older people. Therefore, it may not be known whether they work the same way they do in younger adults. Although there is no specific information comparing use of nedocromil in the elderly with use in other age groups, it is not expected to cause different side effects or problems in older people than it does in younger adults.

Proper Use of This Medicine

Nedocromil is used to help prevent symptoms of asthma or bronchospasm (wheezing or difficulty in breathing). When this medicine is used regularly, it decreases the number and severity of asthma attacks. Nedocromil will not relieve an asthma or bronchospasm attack that has already started.

Nedocromil inhalation aerosol usually comes with patient directions. Read them carefully before using this medicine. If you do not understand the directions or if you are not sure how to use the inhaler, ask your health care professional to show you what to do. Also, ask your health care professional to check regularly how you use the inhaler to make sure you are using it properly.

The nedocromil aerosol canister provides about 56 or 112 inhalations, depending on the size of the canister your doctor ordered. You should keep a record of the number of inhalations you use so you will know when the canister is almost empty. This canister, unlike other aerosol canisters, cannot be floated in water to test its fullness.

When you use the inhaler for the first time, or if you have not used it for several days, the inhaler may not deliver the right amount of medicine with the first puff. Therefore, before using the inhaler, test it to make sure it works properly.

To test the inhaler:
- Insert the metal canister firmly into the clean mouthpiece according to the manufacturer's instructions. Check to make sure the canister is placed properly into the mouthpiece.
- Take the cover off the mouthpiece and shake the inhaler well.
- Hold the canister well away from you against a light background, and press the top of the canister, spraying the medicine one time into the air. If you see a fine mist, you will know the inhaler is working properly to provide the right amount of medicine when you use it. If you do not see a fine mist, try a second time.

To use the inhaler:
- Using your thumb and one or two fingers, hold the inhaler upright with the mouthpiece end down and pointing toward you.
- Take the cover off the mouthpiece. Check the mouthpiece for any foreign objects. Do not use the inhaler with any other mouthpieces.
- Gently shake the inhaler three or four times.
- Hold the mouthpiece away from your mouth and breathe out slowly and completely to the end of a normal breath.
- Use the inhalation method recommended by your doctor.
  —Open-mouth method: Place the mouthpiece about 1 to 2 inches (2 fingerwidths) in front of your widely

opened mouth. Make sure the inhaler is aimed into your mouth so the spray does not hit the roof of your mouth or your tongue. Close your eyes just before spraying to keep the spray out of your eyes.

—Closed-mouth method: Place the mouthpiece in your mouth between your teeth and over your tongue with your lips closed tightly around it. Make sure your tongue or teeth are not blocking the opening.

- Tilt your head back a little. Start to breathe in slowly and deeply through your mouth and, at the same time, press the top of the canister once to get one puff of medicine. Continue to breathe in slowly for 3 to 4 seconds until you have taken a full breath. It is important to press down on the canister and breathe in slowly at the same time so the medicine is pulled into your lungs. This step may be difficult at first. If you are using the closed-mouth method and you see a fine mist coming from your mouth or nose, the inhaler is not being used correctly.
- Hold your breath as long as you can for up to 10 seconds (count slowly to 10). This gives the medicine time to get into your airways and lungs.
- Take the mouthpiece away from your mouth and breathe out slowly.
- If your doctor has told you to inhale more than one puff of medicine at each dose, wait 1 minute between puffs. Then, gently shake the inhaler again, and take the second puff following exactly the same steps you used for the first puff. Breathe in only one puff at a time.
- If your doctor has told you to use an inhaled bronchodilator before using nedocromil, you should wait at least 2 minutes after using the bronchodilator before using nedocromil. This allows the nedocromil to get deeper into your lungs.
- When you are finished, wipe off the mouthpiece and replace the cover to keep the mouthpiece clean and free of foreign objects.

Your doctor may want you to use a spacer device with the inhaler. A spacer makes the inhaler easier to use. It allows more of the medicine to reach your lungs and helps make sure that less of it stays in your mouth and throat.

To use a spacer device with the inhaler:

- Attach the spacer to the inhaler according to the manufacturer's directions. There are different types of spacers available, but the method of breathing remains the same with most spacers.
- Gently shake the inhaler and spacer three or four times.
- Hold the mouthpiece of the spacer away from your mouth and breathe out slowly to the end of a normal breath.
- Place the mouthpiece into your mouth between your teeth and over your tongue with your lips closed around it.
- Press down on the canister top once to release one puff of medicine into the spacer. Then, within one or two seconds, begin to breathe in slowly and deeply through your mouth for 5 to 10 seconds. Count the seconds while inhaling. Do not breathe in through your nose.
- Hold your breath as long as you can for up to 10 seconds (count slowly to ten).
- Breathe out slowly. Do not remove the mouthpiece from your mouth. Breathe in and out slowly two or three times to make sure the spacer device is emptied.
- If your doctor has told you to take more than one puff of medicine at each dose, wait a minute between puffs. Then, gently shake the inhaler and spacer again and take the second puff, following exactly the same steps you used for the first puff.
- When you have finished, remove the spacer device from the inhaler and replace the cover of the mouthpiece.

To clean the inhaler:

- Clean the inhaler often to prevent build-up of medicine and blocking of the mouthpiece. The mouthpiece can be washed every day and should be washed at least twice a week.
- Remove the metal canister from the inhaler and set it aside. Do not get the canister wet.
- Wash the mouthpiece in hot water.
- Shake off the excess water and let the mouthpiece air dry completely before replacing the metal canister and cover.

For patients using nedocromil regularly (for example, every day):

- *In order for nedocromil to work properly, it must be inhaled every day in regularly spaced doses as ordered by your doctor.*
- Usually about 2 to 4 weeks may pass before you begin to feel the full effects of this medicine.

Missed dose—If you are using nedocromil regularly and you miss a dose of this medicine, take it as soon as possible. Then take any remaining doses for that day at regularly spaced times.

Dosing—The dose of nedocromil will be different for different patients. *Follow your doctor's orders or the directions on the label.* The following information includes only the average doses of nedocromil. *If your dose is different, do not change it* unless your doctor tells you to do so:

- For *inhalation* dosage form (inhalation aerosol):
  - —For prevention of asthma symptoms:
    - Adults and children 12 years of age or older—3.5 or 4 milligrams (mg) (2 puffs) two to four times a day at regularly spaced times.
    - Children up to 12 years of age—Use and dose must be determined by the doctor.
  - —For prevention of bronchospasm caused by exercise or a substance:
    - Adults and children 12 years of age or older—4 mg (2 puffs) as a single dose up to thirty minutes before exercise or exposure to any condition or substance that may cause an attack.

- Children up to 12 years of age—Use and dose must be determined by the doctor.

Storage—To store this medicine:
- Keep out of the reach of children.
- Store away from heat and direct sunlight.
- Keep the medicine from freezing.
- Do not puncture, break, or burn the aerosol container, even if it is empty.
- Do not keep outdated medicine or medicine no longer needed. Be sure that any discarded medicine is out of the reach of children.
- Always keep the dust cover on the mouthpiece when the inhaler is not in use.

Precautions While Using This Medicine

If your symptoms do not improve within 2 to 4 weeks, check with your doctor. Also, check with your doctor if your condition becomes worse.

You may also be taking a corticosteroid or a bronchodilator for asthma along with this medicine. *Do not stop taking the corticosteroid or bronchodilator even if your asthma seems better, unless you are told to do so by your doctor.*

Throat irritation and/or an unpleasant taste may occur after you use this medicine. Gargling and rinsing the mouth after each dose may help prevent these effects.

Side Effects of This Medicine

Along with its needed effects, a medicine may cause some unwanted effects. Although not all of these side effects may occur, if they do occur they may need medical attention.

Check with your doctor as soon as possible if any of the following side effects occur:

Less common

Increased wheezing, tightness in chest, or difficulty in breathing

Other side effects may occur that usually do not need medical attention. These side effects may go away during treatment as your body adjusts to the medicine. However, check with your doctor if any of the following side effects continue or are bothersome:

Less common

Cough; headache; nausea; runny or stuffy nose; throat irritation

After you use nedocromil inhalation aerosol, you may notice an unpleasant taste. This may be expected and will usually go away after a while.

Other side effects not listed above may also occur in some patients. If you notice any other effects, check with your doctor.

Revised: 08/09/94

NEOMYCIN Ophthalmic*†

*Not commercially available in the U.S.
†Not commercially available in Canada.

Description

Neomycin (nee-oh-MYE-sin) belongs to the family of medicines called antibiotics. Neomycin ophthalmic preparations are used to treat infections of the eye.

Neomycin is available only with your doctor's prescription, in the following dosage form:

Ophthalmic
- Ophthalmic ointment

Before Using This Medicine

In deciding to use a medicine, the risks of taking the medicine must be weighed against the good it will do. This is a decision you and your doctor will make. For neomycin ophthalmic preparations, the following should be considered:

Allergies—Tell your doctor if you have ever had any unusual or allergic reaction to this medicine or to any related antibiotic, such as amikacin (e.g., Amikin), gentamicin (e.g., Garamycin), kanamycin (e.g., Kantrex), netilmicin (e.g., Netromycin), streptomycin, or tobramycin (e.g., Nebcin). Also tell your health care professional if you are allergic to any other substances, such as preservatives.

Pregnancy—Neomycin ophthalmic preparations have not been shown to cause birth defects or other problems in humans.

Breast-feeding—Neomycin ophthalmic preparations have not been reported to cause problems in nursing babies.

Children—Studies on this medicine have been done only in adult patients, and there is no specific information comparing use of neomycin in children with use in other age groups.

Older adults—Many medicines have not been studied specifically in older people. Therefore, it may not be known whether they work exactly the same way they do in younger adults or if they cause different side effects or problems in older people. There is no specific information comparing use of neomycin in the elderly with use in other age groups.

Proper Use of This Medicine

To use:
- First, wash your hands. Tilt the head back and, pressing your finger gently on the skin just beneath the lower eyelid, pull the lower eyelid away from the eye to make a space. Squeeze a thin strip of ointment into this space. A 1-cm (approximately 1/3-inch) strip of ointment is usually enough, unless you have been told by your doctor to use a different amount. Let go of

the eyelid and gently close the eyes. Keep the eyes closed for 1 or 2 minutes to allow the medicine to come into contact with the infection.

- To keep the medicine as germ-free as possible, do not touch the applicator tip to any surface (including the eye). After using neomycin eye ointment, wipe the tip of the ointment tube with a clean tissue and keep the tube tightly closed.

To help clear up your infection completely, *keep using this medicine for the full time of treatment,* even if your symptoms have disappeared. *Do not miss any doses.*

Dosing—The dose of ophthalmic neomycin will be different for different patients. *Follow your doctor's orders or the directions on the label.* The following information includes only the average doses of ophthalmic neomycin. *If your dose is different, do not change it* unless your doctor tells you to do so.

- For eye infection:
  —For *eye ointment* dosage form:
    - Adults and children—Use in the eye every eight to twenty-four hours.

Missed dose—If you miss a dose of this medicine, apply it as soon as possible. However, if it is almost time for your next dose, skip the missed dose and go back to your regular dosing schedule.

Storage—To store this medicine:

- Keep out of the reach of children.
- Store away from heat and direct light.
- Keep the medicine from freezing.
- Do not keep outdated medicine or medicine no longer needed. Be sure that any discarded medicine is out of the reach of children.

Precautions While Using This Medicine

If your symptoms do not improve within a few days, or if they become worse, check with your doctor.

Side Effects of This Medicine

Along with its needed effects, a medicine may cause some unwanted effects. Although not all of these side effects may occur, if they do occur they may need medical attention.

Check with your doctor immediately if any of the following side effects occur:

More common

Itching, rash, redness, swelling, or other sign of irritation not present before use of this medicine

Other side effects may occur that usually do not need medical attention. These side effects may go away during treatment as your body adjusts to the medicine. However, check with your doctor if either of the following side effects continues or is bothersome:

Less common

Burning or stinging

After application, eye ointments may be expected to cause your vision to blur for a few minutes.

Other side effects not listed above may also occur in some patients. If you notice any other effects, check with your doctor.

Revised: 05/16/94

NEOMYCIN Oral

A commonly used brand name in the U.S. and Canada is Mycifradin. Generic name product may also be available in the U.S.

Description

Oral neomycin (nee-oh-MYE-sin) is used to help lessen the symptoms of hepatic coma, a complication of liver disease. In addition, it may be used with another medicine before any surgery affecting the bowels to help prevent infection during surgery.

Neomycin is available only with your doctor's prescription, in the following dosage forms:

Oral

- Solution (U.S. and Canada)
- Tablets (U.S. and Canada)

Before Using This Medicine

In deciding to use a medicine, the risks of taking the medicine must be weighed against the good it will do. This is a decision you and your doctor will make. For oral neomycin, the following should be considered:

Allergies—Tell your doctor if you have ever had any unusual or allergic reaction to oral neomycin, or to any related antibiotics such as amikacin (e.g., Amikin), gentamicin (e.g., Garamycin), kanamycin (e.g., Kantrex), neomycin by injection (e.g., Mycifradin), netilmicin (e.g., Netromycin), streptomycin, or tobramycin (e.g., Nebcin). Also tell your health care professional if you are allergic to any other substances, such as foods, preservatives, or dyes.

Pregnancy—Studies have shown that neomycin may damage the infant's kidneys. In addition, some reports have shown that related medicines, especially streptomycin and tobramycin (e.g., Nebcin), may damage the infant's hearing and sense of balance. Be sure you have discussed this with your doctor.

Breast-feeding—It is not known whether neomycin passes into the breast milk. However, neomycin has not been reported to cause problems in nursing babies.

Children—Damage to hearing, sense of balance, and kidneys is more likely to occur in premature infants and neonates, who are more sensitive than adults to the effects of neomycin.

Older adults—Serious side effects, such as damage to hearing, sense of balance, and kidneys may occur in elderly patients, who are usually more sensitive than younger adults to the effects of neomycin.

Other medicines—Although certain medicines should not be used together at all, in other cases two different medicines may be used together even if an interaction might occur. In these cases, your doctor may want to change the dose, or other precautions may be necessary. Tell your health care professional if you are taking any other prescription or nonprescription (over-the-counter [OTC]) medicine.

Other medical problems—The presence of other medical problems may affect the use of oral neomycin. Make sure you tell your doctor if you have any other medical problems, especially:

- Blockage of the bowel
- Eighth-cranial-nerve disease (loss of hearing and/or balance)—Oral neomycin may increase the chance of hearing loss and/or balance problems
- Kidney disease—Patients with kidney disease may have an increased chance of side effects
- Myasthenia gravis or
- Parkinson's disease—Patients with myasthenia gravis or Parkinson's disease may have an increased chance of developing muscular weakness
- Ulcers of the bowel—Patients with ulcers of the bowel may have an increased chance of side effects since more neomycin may be absorbed by the body

Proper Use of This Medicine

This medicine may be taken on a full or empty stomach.

For patients taking the *oral liquid form* of neomycin:

- Use a specially marked measuring spoon or other device to measure each dose accurately. The average household teaspoon may not hold the right amount of liquid.

Keep taking this medicine for the full time of treatment. Do not miss any doses.

Dosing—The dose of oral neomycin will be different for different patients. *Follow your doctor's orders or the directions on the label.* The following information includes only the average doses of oral neomycin. *If your dose is different, do not change it* unless your doctor tells you to do so.

- For *oral* dosage forms (solution, tablets):
  - —For patients in a coma from liver disease:
    - Adults and teenagers—1 to 3 grams every six hours for five or six days.
    - Children—Dose is based on body size (not weight) and must be determined by your doctor. That dose is given every six hours for five or six days.
  - —For cleaning the bowel before surgery:
    - Adults and teenagers—1 gram every hour for four hours, then 1 gram every four hours for the rest of a twenty-four hour period; or 1 gram nineteen hours before surgery, 1 gram eighteen hours before surgery, and 1 gram nine hours before surgery.
    - Children—Dose is based on body weight. The usual dose is 14.7 milligrams (mg) per kilogram (kg) (6.7 mg per pound) of body weight every four hours for three days.

Missed dose—If you miss a dose of this medicine, take it as soon as possible. However, if it is almost time for your next dose, skip the missed dose and go back to your regular dosing schedule. Do not double doses.

Storage—To store this medicine:

- Keep out of the reach of children.
- Store away from heat and direct light.
- Do not store the tablet form of this medicine in the bathroom, near the kitchen sink, or in other damp places. Heat or moisture may cause the medicine to break down.
- Keep the oral liquid form of this medicine from freezing.
- Do not keep outdated medicine or medicine no longer needed. Be sure that any discarded medicine is out of the reach of children.

Side Effects of This Medicine

Along with its needed effects, a medicine may cause some unwanted effects. Although not all of these side effects may occur, if they do occur they may need medical attention.

Check with your doctor immediately if any of the following side effects occur:

Rare

Any loss of hearing; clumsiness; diarrhea; difficulty in breathing; dizziness; drowsiness; greatly decreased frequency of urination or amount of urine; increased amount of gas; increased thirst; light-colored, frothy, fatty-appearing stools; ringing or buzzing or a feeling of fullness in the ears; skin rash; unsteadiness; weakness

Other side effects may occur that usually do not need medical attention. These side effects may go away during treatment as your body adjusts to the medicine. However, check with your doctor if any of the following side effects continue or are bothersome:

More common

Irritation or soreness of the mouth or rectal area; nausea or vomiting

Other side effects not listed above may also occur in some patients. If you notice any other effects, check with your doctor.

Revised: 10/20/92
Interim revision: 03/17/94

NEOMYCIN Topical

A commonly used brand name in the U.S. and Canada is Myciguent. Generic name product may also be available in the U.S.

Description

Neomycin (nee-oh-MYE-sin) belongs to the family of medicines called antibiotics. Neomycin topical preparations are used to help prevent infections of the skin. This medicine may be used for other problems as determined by your doctor.

Neomycin topical preparations are available without a prescription; however, your doctor may have special instructions on the proper use of topical neomycin for your medical problem.

Topical neomycin is available in the following dosage forms:

Topical
- Cream (U.S.)
- Ointment (U.S. and Canada)

Before Using This Medicine

In deciding to use a medicine, the risks of using the medicine must be weighed against the good it will do. This is a decision you and your doctor will make. For topical neomycin, the following should be considered:

Allergies—Tell your doctor if you have ever had any unusual or allergic reaction to this medicine or to any related antibiotic, such as amikacin (e.g., Amikin), gentamicin (e.g., Garamycin), kanamycin (e.g., Kantrex), neomycin by mouth or by injection (e.g., Mycifradin), netilmicin (e.g., Netromycin), streptomycin, or tobramycin (e.g., Nebcin). Also tell your health care professional if you are allergic to any other substances, such as preservatives or dyes.

Pregnancy—Neomycin topical preparations have not been shown to cause birth defects or other problems in humans.

Breast-feeding—Neomycin topical preparations have not been reported to cause problems in nursing babies.

Children—Studies on this medicine have been done only in adult patients, and there is no specific information comparing use of topical neomycin in children with use in other age groups.

Older adults—Many medicines have not been studied specifically in older people. Therefore, it may not be known whether they work exactly the same way they do in younger adults or if they cause different side effects or problems in older people. There is no specific information comparing use of topical neomycin in the elderly with use in other age groups.

Other medicines—Although certain medicines should not be used together at all, in other cases two different medicines may be used together even if an interaction might occur. In these cases, your doctor may want to change the dose, or other precautions may be necessary. Tell your health care professional if you are using any other topical prescription or nonprescription (over-the-counter [OTC]) medicine that is to be applied to the same area of the skin.

Proper Use of This Medicine

If you are using this medicine without a prescription, do not use it to treat deep wounds, puncture wounds, serious burns, or raw areas without first checking with your health care professional.

Do not use this medicine in the eyes.

Before applying this medicine, wash the affected area with soap and water, and dry thoroughly.

For patients using the *cream form* of this medicine:
- Apply a generous amount of cream to the affected area, and rub in gently until the cream disappears.

For patients using the *ointment form* of this medicine:
- Apply a generous amount of ointment to the affected area, and rub in gently.

After this medicine is applied, the treated area may be covered with a gauze dressing if desired.

To help clear up your infection completely, *keep using this medicine for the full time of treatment,* even if your symptoms have disappeared. *Do not miss any doses.*

Dosing—The dose of topical neomycin will be different for different patients. *Follow your doctor's orders or the directions on the label.* The following information includes only the average dose of topical neomycin. *If your dose is different, do not change it* unless your doctor tells you to do so.

- For *topical* dosage forms (cream or ointment):
  —For minor bacterial skin infections:
  - Adults and children—Apply to the affected area(s) of the skin one to three times a day.

Missed dose—If you miss a dose of this medicine, apply it as soon as possible. However, if it is almost time for your next dose, skip the missed dose and go back to your regular dosing schedule.

Storage—To store this medicine:
- Keep out of the reach of children.
- Store away from heat and direct light.
- Keep the medicine from freezing.
- Do not keep outdated medicine or medicine no longer needed. Be sure that any discarded medicine is out of the reach of children.

Precautions While Using This Medicine

If your skin problem does not improve within 1 week, or if it becomes worse, check with your health care professional.

Side Effects of This Medicine

Along with its needed effects, a medicine may cause some unwanted effects. Although not all of these side effects

may occur, if they do occur they may need medical attention.

Check with your doctor immediately if any of the following side effects occur:

More common

Itching, rash, redness, swelling, or other sign of skin irritation not present before use of this medicine

Rare

Any loss of hearing

Other side effects not listed above may also occur in some patients. If you notice any other effects, check with your doctor.

Revised: 08/15/94

NEOMYCIN AND POLYMYXIN B Topical†

A commonly used brand name in the U.S. is Neosporin Cream‡.

†Not commercially available in Canada.
‡In Canada, Neosporin cream also contains gramicidin.

Description

Neomycin (nee-oh-MYE-sin) and polymyxin (pol-i-MIX-in) B combination is used to prevent bacterial infections. It works by killing bacteria.

Neomycin and polymyxin B cream is applied to the skin to prevent minor bacterial skin infections. It may also be used for other problems as determined by your doctor.

This medicine is available without a prescription; however, your doctor may have special instructions on the proper use of this medicine for your medical problem.

Neomycin and polymyxin B combination is available in the following dosage form:

Topical

- Cream (U.S.)

Before Using This Medicine

If you are using this medicine without a prescription, carefully read and follow any precautions on the label. For neomycin and polymyxin B topical preparations, the following should be considered:

Allergies—Tell your doctor if you have ever had any unusual or allergic reaction to neomycin and polymyxin B combination or to any related antibiotic: Amikacin (e.g., Amikin), colistimethate (e.g., Coly-Mycin M), colistin (e.g., Coly-Mycin S), gentamicin (e.g., Garamycin), kanamycin (e.g., Kantrex), neomycin by mouth or by injection (e.g., Mycifradin), netilmicin (e.g., Netromycin), paromomycin (e.g., Humatin), polymyxin B by injection (e.g., Aerosporin), streptomycin, or tobramycin (e.g., Nebcin). Also, tell your health care professional if you are allergic to any other substances, such as preservatives or dyes.

Pregnancy—Neomycin and polymyxin B topical preparations have not been shown to cause birth defects or other problems in humans.

Breast-feeding—Neomycin and polymyxin B topical preparations have not been reported to cause problems in nursing babies.

Children—Although there is no specific information comparing use of neomycin and polymyxin B combination in children with use in other age groups, this medicine is not expected to cause different side effects or problems in children than it does in adults.

Older adults—Many medicines have not been studied specifically in older people. Therefore, it may not be known whether they work exactly the same way they do in younger adults or if they cause different side effects or problems in older people. There is no specific information comparing use of neomycin and polymyxin B combination in the elderly with use in other age groups.

Other medicines—Although certain medicines should not be used together at all, in other cases two different medicines may be used together even if an interaction might occur. In these cases, your doctor may want to change the dose, or other precautions may be necessary. Tell your health care professional if you are using any other topical prescription or nonprescription (over-the-counter [OTC]) medicine that is to be applied to the same area of the skin.

Proper Use of This Medicine

If you are using this medicine without a prescription, *do not use it to treat deep wounds, puncture wounds, animal bites, serious burns, or raw areas* without first checking with your health care professional.

Do not use this medicine in the eyes.

To use:

- Before applying this medicine, wash the affected area(s) with soap and water, and dry thoroughly.
- Apply a small amount of this medicine to the affected area(s) and rub in gently.
- After applying this medicine, the treated area(s) may be covered with a gauze dressing if desired.

Do not use this medicine for longer than 1 week or on large areas of the skin, unless otherwise directed by your doctor. To do so may increase the chance of side effects.

To help clear up your skin infection completely, *keep using this medicine for the full time of treatment,* even if your symptoms have disappeared. *Do not miss any doses.*

Dosing—The dose of neomycin and polymyxin B combination will be different for different patients. *Follow your doctor's orders or the directions on the label.* The following information includes only the average dose of neomycin and polymyxin B combination. *If your dose is different, do not change it* unless your doctor tells you to do so.

- For *topical* dosage form (cream):
  —For prevention of minor bacterial infections:
    - Adults and children 2 years of age and older—Apply to the affected area(s) of the skin one to three times a day.
    - Children up to 2 years of age—Use and dose must be determined by your doctor.

Missed dose—If you miss a dose of this medicine, apply it as soon as possible. However, if it is almost time for your next dose, skip the missed dose and go back to your regular dosing schedule.

Storage—To store this medicine:
- Keep out of the reach of children.
- Store away from heat and direct light.
- Keep the medicine from freezing.
- Do not keep outdated medicine or medicine no longer needed. Be sure that any discarded medicine is out of the reach of children.

Precautions While Using This Medicine

If your skin infection does not improve within 1 week, or if it becomes worse, check with your health care professional.

Side Effects of This Medicine

Along with its needed effects, a medicine may cause some unwanted effects. Although not all of these side effects may occur, if they do occur they may need medical attention.

Check with your doctor immediately if any of the following side effects occur:

More common
Itching, pain, skin rash, swelling, redness, or other sign of skin irritation not present before use of this medicine

Rare
Loss of hearing

Other side effects not listed above may also occur in some patients. If you notice any other effects, check with your doctor.

Revised: 06/09/94

NEOMYCIN, POLYMYXIN B, AND BACITRACIN Ophthalmic

Some commonly used brand names are:

In the U.S.—

Ak-Spore Ophthalmic Ointment
Neocidin Ophthalmic Ointment
Neosporin Ophthalmic Ointment
Neotal
Ocu-Spor-B
Ocusporin
Ocutricin Ophthalmic Ointment Ophthalmic
Spectro-Sporin
Triple Antibiotic

Generic name product may be available.

In Canada—

Neosporin Ophthalmic Ointment

Description

Neomycin (nee-oh-MYE-sin), polymyxin (pol-i-MIX-in) B, and bacitracin (bass-i-TRAY-sin) combination antibiotic medicine is used to treat infections of the eye.

Neomycin, polymyxin B, and bacitracin combination is available only with your doctor's prescription, in the following dosage form:

Ophthalmic
- Ophthalmic ointment (U.S. and Canada)

Before Using This Medicine

In deciding to use a medicine, the risks of using the medicine must be weighed against the good it will do. This is a decision you and your doctor will make. For neomycin, polymyxin B, and bacitracin ophthalmic combination, the following should be considered:

Allergies—Tell your doctor if you have ever had any unusual or allergic reaction to this medicine or to any related antibiotic, such as amikacin (e.g., Amikin), colistimethate (e.g., Coly-Mycin M), colistin (e.g., Coly-Mycin S), gentamicin (e.g., Garamycin), kanamycin (e.g., Kantrex), netilmicin (e.g., Netromycin), paromomycin (e.g., Humatin), streptomycin, or tobramycin (e.g., Nebcin). Also tell your health care professional if you are allergic to any other substances, such as preservatives or dyes.

Pregnancy—Neomycin, polymyxin B, and bacitracin ophthalmic combination has not been shown to cause birth defects or other problems in humans.

Breast-feeding—Neomycin, polymyxin B, and bacitracin ophthalmic combination has not been reported to cause problems in nursing babies.

Children—Studies on this medicine have been done only in adult patients, and there is no specific information comparing use of neomycin, polymyxin B, and bacitracin combination in children with use in other age groups.

Older adults—Many medicines have not been studied specifically in older people. Therefore, it may not be known whether they work exactly the same way they do in younger adults or if they cause different side effects or problems in older people. There is no specific information comparing use of neomycin, polymyxin B, and bacitracin combination in the elderly with use in other age groups.

Proper Use of This Medicine

To use:
- First, wash your hands. Tilt the head back and, pressing your finger gently on the skin just beneath the lower eyelid, pull the lower eyelid away from the eye to make a space. Squeeze a thin strip of ointment into this space. A 1-cm (approximately 1/3-inch) strip of ointment is usually enough, unless you have been told by your doctor to use a different amount. Let go of

the eyelid and gently close the eyes. Keep the eyes closed for 1 or 2 minutes to allow the medicine to come into contact with the infection.
- To keep the medicine as germ-free as possible, do not touch the applicator tip to any surface (including the eye). After using neomycin, polymyxin B, and bacitracin eye ointment, wipe the tip of the ointment tube with a clean tissue and keep the tube tightly closed.

To help clear up your infection completely, *keep using this medicine for the full time of treatment,* even if your symptoms have disappeared. *Do not miss any doses.*

Dosing—The dose of neomycin, polymyxin B, and bacitracin ophthalmic combination will be different for different patients. *Follow your doctor's orders or the directions on the label.* The following information includes only the average dose of neomycin, polymyxin B, and bacitracin ophthalmic combination. *If your dose is different, do not change it* unless your doctor tells you to do so.

- For eye infections:
  - —For *eye ointment* dosage forms:
    - Adults and children—Use a thin strip of ointment in the eyes every three or four hours for seven to ten days.

Missed dose—If you miss a dose of this medicine, apply it as soon as possible. However, if it is almost time for your next dose, skip the missed dose and go back to your regular dosing schedule.

Storage—To store this medicine:
- Keep out of the reach of children.
- Store away from heat and direct light.
- Keep the medicine from freezing.
- Do not keep outdated medicine or medicine no longer needed. Be sure that any discarded medicine is out of the reach of children.

Precautions While Using This Medicine

If your symptoms do not improve within a few days, or if they become worse, check with your doctor.

Side Effects of This Medicine

Along with its needed effects, a medicine may cause some unwanted effects. Although not all of these side effects may occur, if they do occur they may need medical attention.

Check with your doctor immediately if any of the following side effects occur:

More common

Itching, rash, redness, swelling, or other sign of irritation not present before use of this medicine

After application, eye ointments usually cause your vision to blur for a few minutes.

Other side effects not listed above may also occur in some patients. If you notice any other effects, check with your doctor.

Revised: 05/16/94
Interim revision: 05/24/95

NEOMYCIN, POLYMYXIN B, AND BACITRACIN Topical

Some commonly used brand names are:

In the U.S.—

Bactine First Aid Antibiotic
Foille
Mycitracin
Neosporin Maximum Strength Ointment
Neosporin Ointment
Topisporin

Generic name product may also be available in the U.S. and Canada.

Description

Neomycin (nee-oh-MYE-sin), polymyxin (pol-i-MIX-in) B, and bacitracin (bass-i-TRAY-sin) is a combination antibiotic medicine used to help prevent infections of the skin.

Neomycin, polymyxin B, and bacitracin combination is available without a prescription; however, your doctor may have special instructions on the proper use of this medicine for your medical problem.

Topical neomycin, polymyxin B, and bacitracin combination is available in the following dosage form:

Topical
- Ointment (U.S. and Canada)

Before Using This Medicine

If you are using this medicine without a prescription, carefully read and follow any precautions on the label. For topical neomycin, polymyxin B, and bacitracin combination, the following should be considered:

Allergies—Tell your doctor if you have ever had any unusual or allergic reaction to this medicine or to any related antibiotic, such as amikacin (e.g., Amikin), colistimethate (e.g., Coly-Mycin M), colistin (e.g., Coly-Mycin S), gentamicin (e.g., Garamycin), kanamycin (e.g., Kantrex), neomycin by mouth or by injection (e.g., Mycifradin), netilmicin (e.g., Netromycin), paromomycin (e.g., Humatin), polymyxin B by injection (e.g., Aerosporin), streptomycin, or tobramycin (e.g., Nebcin). Also tell your health care professional if you are allergic to any other substances, such as preservatives or dyes.

Pregnancy—Neomycin, polymyxin B, and bacitracin topical preparations have not been studied in pregnant women. However, this medicine has not been shown to cause birth defects or other problems in humans.

Breast-feeding—It is not known whether topical neomycin, polymyxin B, and bacitracin combination passes into breast milk. However, this medicine has not been reported to cause problems in nursing babies.

Children—Studies on this medicine have been done only in adult patients, and there is no specific information comparing use of topical neomycin, polymyxin B, and bacitracin combination in children with use in other age groups.

Older adults—Many medicines have not been studied specifically in older people. Therefore, it may not be known whether they work exactly the same way they do in younger adults or if they cause different side effects or problems in older people. There is no specific information comparing use of topical neomycin, polymyxin B, and bacitracin combination in the elderly with use in other age groups.

Other medicines—Although certain medicines should not be used together at all, in other cases two different medicines may be used together even if an interaction might occur. In these cases, your doctor may want to change the dose, or other precautions may be necessary. Tell your health care professional if you are using any other prescription or nonprescription (over-the-counter [OTC]) medicine.

Proper Use of This Medicine

If you are using this medicine without a prescription, do not use it to treat deep wounds, puncture wounds, serious burns, or raw areas without first checking with your health care professional.

Do not use this medicine in the eyes.

Before applying this medicine, wash the affected area with soap and water, and dry thoroughly.

After applying this medicine, the treated area may be covered with a gauze dressing if desired.

To help clear up your infection completely, *keep using this medicine for the full time of treatment,* even if your symptoms have disappeared. *Do not miss any doses.*

Dosing—The dose of topical neomycin, polymyxin B, and bacitracin combination will be different for different patients. *Follow your doctor's orders or the directions on the label.* The following information includes only the average doses of topical neomycin, polymyxin B, and bacitracin combination. *If your dose is different, do not change it* unless your doctor tells you to do so.

- For *topical* dosage form (ointment):
  - —For prevention of minor bacterial infections:
    - Adults and children—Apply to the affected area(s) of the skin two to five times a day.

Missed dose—If you miss a dose of this medicine, apply it as soon as possible. However, if it is almost time for your next dose, skip the missed dose and go back to your regular dosing schedule.

Storage—To store this medicine:
- Keep out of the reach of children.
- Store away from heat and direct light.
- Keep the medicine from freezing.
- Do not keep outdated medicine or medicine no longer needed. Be sure that any discarded medicine is out of the reach of children.

Precautions While Using This Medicine

If your skin problem does not improve within 1 week, or if it becomes worse, check with your health care professional.

Side Effects of This Medicine

Along with its needed effects, a medicine may cause some unwanted effects. Although not all of these side effects may occur, if they do occur they may need medical attention.

Check with your doctor immediately if any of the following side effects occur:

More common
Itching, skin rash, redness, swelling, or other sign of irritation not present before use of this medicine

Rare
Any loss of hearing

Other side effects not listed above may also occur in some patients. If you notice any other effects, check with your doctor.

Revised: 07/25/94

NEOMYCIN, POLYMYXIN B, AND GRAMICIDIN Ophthalmic

Some commonly used brand names are:

In the U.S.—
Ak-Spore Ophthalmic Solution
Neocidin Ophthalmic Solution
Neosporin Ophthalmic Solution
Ocu-Spor-G
Ocutricin Ophthalmic Solution
P.N. Ophthalmic
Tribiotic
Tri-Ophthalmic

Generic name product may also be available.

In Canada—
Neosporin Ophthalmic Solution

Description

Neomycin (nee-oh-MYE-sin), polymyxin (pol-i-MIX-in) B, and gramicidin (gram-i-SYE-din) is a combination antibiotic medicine used to treat infections of the eye.

Neomycin, polymyxin B, and gramicidin combination is available only with your doctor's prescription, in the following dosage form:

Ophthalmic
- Ophthalmic solution (eye drops) (U.S. and Canada)

Before Using This Medicine

In deciding to use a medicine, the risks of taking the medicine must be weighed against the good it will do. This is a decision you and your doctor will make. For neomycin, polymyxin B, and gramicidin ophthalmic drops, the following should be considered:

Allergies—Tell your doctor if you have ever had any unusual or allergic reaction to this medicine or to any related antibiotic, such as amikacin (e.g., Amikin), colistimethate (e.g., Coly-Mycin M), colistin (e.g., Coly-Mycin S), gentamicin (e.g., Garamycin), kanamycin (e.g., Kantrex), netilmicin (e.g., Netromycin), paromomycin (e.g., Humatin), streptomycin, or tobramycin (e.g., Nebcin). Also tell your health care professional if you are allergic to any other substances, such as preservatives.

Pregnancy—Neomycin, polymyxin B, and gramicidin combination has not been shown to cause birth defects or other problems in humans.

Breast-feeding—Neomycin, polymyxin B, and gramicidin combination has not been reported to cause problems in nursing babies.

Children—Studies on this medicine have been done only in adult patients, and there is no specific information comparing use of this combination in children with use in other age groups.

Older adults—Many medicines have not been studied specifically in older people. Therefore, it may not be known whether they work exactly the same way they do in younger adults or if they cause different side effects or problems in older people. There is no specific information comparing use of neomycin, polymyxin B, and gramicidin combination in the elderly with use in other age groups.

Proper Use of This Medicine

The bottle is only partially full to provide proper drop control.

To use:

- First, wash your hands. Tilt the head back and, pressing your finger gently on the skin just beneath the lower eyelid, pull the lower eyelid away from the eye to make a space. Drop the medicine into this space. Let go of the eyelid and gently close the eyes. Do not blink. Keep the eyes closed for 1 or 2 minutes to allow the medicine to come into contact with the infection.
- If you think you did not get the drop of medicine into your eye properly, use another drop.
- To keep the medicine as germ-free as possible, do not touch the applicator tip or dropper to any surface (including the eye). Also, keep the container tightly closed.

To help clear up your infection completely, *keep using this medicine for the full time of treatment*, even if your symptoms have disappeared. *Do not miss any doses.*

Dosing—The dose of neomycin, polymyxin B, and gramicidin ophthalmic combination will be different for different patients. *Follow your doctor's orders or the directions on the label.* The following information includes only the average doses of neomycin, polymyxin B, and gramicidin ophthalmic combination. *If your dose is different, do not change it* unless your doctor tells you to do so.

- For eye infections:
  - —For *eye drops* dosage form:
    - Adults and children—Use one drop in the eye two to four times a day for seven to ten days. If you have a more serious infection, your doctor may want you to use one drop in the eye every fifteen to thirty minutes at first. Then your doctor may have you use the medicine less often.

Missed dose—If you miss a dose of this medicine, apply it as soon as possible. However, if it is almost time for your next dose, skip the missed dose and go back to your regular dosing schedule.

Storage—To store this medicine:

- Keep out of the reach of children.
- Store away from heat and direct light.
- Keep the medicine from freezing.
- Do not keep outdated medicine or medicine no longer needed. Be sure that any discarded medicine is out of the reach of children.

Precautions While Using This Medicine

If your symptoms do not improve within a few days, or if they become worse, check with your doctor.

Side Effects of This Medicine

Along with its needed effects, a medicine may cause some unwanted effects. Although not all of these side effects may occur, if they do occur they may need medical attention.

Check with your doctor immediately if any of the following side effects occur:

More common

Itching, rash, redness, swelling, or other sign of irritation in or around the eye not present before use of this medicine

Other side effects may occur that usually do not need medical attention. These side effects may go away during treatment as your body adjusts to the medicine. However, check with your doctor if either of the following side effects continues or is bothersome:

Less common

Burning or stinging of the eye

Other side effects not listed above may also occur in some patients. If you notice any other effects, check with your doctor.

Revised: 06/21/94

NEOMYCIN, POLYMYXIN B, AND HYDROCORTISONE Ophthalmic

Some commonly used brand names are:

In the U.S.—

- Ak-Spore H.C.
- Bacticort
- Cobiron
- Cortisporin Ophthalmic Suspension
- Cortomycin
- Hydromycin
- I-Neocort
- Ocutricin HC
- Triple-Gen

Generic name product may also be available.

In Canada—

- Cortisporin Ophthalmic Suspension

Description

Neomycin (nee-oh-MYE-sin), polymyxin (pol-i-MIX-in) B, and hydrocortisone (hye-droe-KOR-ti-sone) is a combination antibiotic and cortisone-like medicine. It is used to treat infections of the eye and to help provide relief from redness, irritation, and discomfort of certain eye problems.

Neomycin, polymyxin B, and hydrocortisone combination is available only with your doctor's prescription, in the following dosage form:

Ophthalmic

- Ophthalmic suspension (eye drops) (U.S. and Canada)

Before Using This Medicine

In deciding to use a medicine, the risks of using the medicine must be weighed against the good it will do. This is a decision you and your doctor will make. For neomycin, polymyxin B, and hydrocortisone ophthalmic drops, the following should be considered:

Allergies—Tell your doctor if you have ever had any unusual or allergic reaction to this medicine or to any related antibiotic, such as amikacin (e.g., Amikin), colistimethate (e.g., Coly-Mycin M), colistin (e.g., Coly-Mycin S), gentamicin (e.g., Garamycin), kanamycin (e.g., Kantrex), netilmicin (e.g., Netromycin), paromomycin (e.g., Humatin), streptomycin, or tobramycin (e.g., Nebcin). Also tell your health care professional if you are allergic to any other substances, such as preservatives.

Pregnancy—Neomycin, polymyxin B, and hydrocortisone ophthalmic preparations have not been studied in pregnant women. However, studies in animals have shown that topical corticosteroids cause birth defects. Before using this medicine, make sure your doctor knows if you are pregnant or if you may become pregnant.

Breast-feeding—Neomycin, polymyxin B, and hydrocortisone ophthalmic drops have not been reported to cause problems in nursing babies.

Children—Studies on this medicine have been done only in adult patients, and there is no specific information comparing use in children with use in other age groups.

Older adults—Many medicines have not been studied specifically in older people. Therefore, it may not be known whether they work exactly the same way they do in younger adults or if they cause different side effects or problems in older people. There is no specific information comparing use of ophthalmic neomycin, polymyxin B, and hydrocortisone combination in the elderly with use in other age groups.

Other medical problems—The presence of other medical problems may affect the use of neomycin, polymyxin B, and hydrocortisone ophthalmic drops. Make sure you tell your doctor if you have any other medical problems, especially:

- Any other eye infection or condition—Use of neomycin, polymyxin B, and hydrocortisone ophthalmic drops may make the condition worse

Proper Use of This Medicine

The bottle is only partially full to provide proper drop control.

To use:

- First, wash your hands. Then tilt the head back and pull the lower eyelid away from the eye to form a pouch. Drop the medicine into the pouch and gently close the eyes. Do not blink. Keep the eyes closed for 1 or 2 minutes to allow the medicine to come into contact with the infection.
- If you think you did not get the drop of medicine into your eye properly, use another drop.
- To keep the medicine as germ-free as possible, do not touch the applicator tip to any surface (including the eye). Also, keep the container tightly closed.

To help clear up your infection completely, *keep using this medicine for the full time of treatment,* even if your symptoms have disappeared. *Do not miss any doses.*

Dosing—The dose of ophthalmic neomycin, polymyxin B, and hyrdocortisone combination will be different for different patients. *Follow your doctor's orders or the directions on the label.* The following information includes only the average doses of ophthalmic neomycin, polymyxin B, and hydrocortisone combination. *If your dose is different, do not change it* unless your doctor tells you to do so.

The number of doses you use each day, the time allowed between doses, and the length of time you use the medicine depend on the medical problem for which you are using ophthalmic neomycin, polymyxin B, and hydrocortisone combination.

- For eye infection:
  - —For *ophthalmic suspension* dosage forms:
    - Adults and children—One drop every three to four hours.

Missed dose—If you miss a dose of this medicine, apply it as soon as possible. However, if it is almost time for your next dose, skip the missed dose and go back to your regular dosing schedule.

Do not use any leftover medicine for future eye problems without checking with your doctor first. This medicine should not be used on many different kinds of infection.

Storage—To store this medicine:
- Keep out of the reach of children.
- Store away from heat and direct light.
- Keep the medicine from freezing.
- Do not keep outdated medicine or medicine no longer needed. Be sure that any discarded medicine is out of the reach of children.

Precautions While Using This Medicine

If you will be using this medicine for a long time (for example, longer than 6 weeks), your doctor should check your eyes at regular visits.

If your symptoms do not improve within a few days, or if they become worse, check with your doctor.

Side Effects of This Medicine

Along with its needed effects, a medicine may cause some unwanted effects. Although not all of these side effects may occur, if they do occur they may need medical attention.

Check with your doctor immediately if any of the following side effects occur:

More common
Itching, rash, redness, swelling, or other sign of irritation not present before use of this medicine

Other side effects may occur that usually do not need medical attention. These side effects may go away during treatment as your body adjusts to the medicine. However, check with your doctor if either of the following side effects continues or is bothersome:

Less common
Burning or stinging

Other side effects not listed above may also occur in some patients. If you notice any other effects, check with your doctor.

Revised: 07/01/93

NEOMYCIN, POLYMYXIN B, AND HYDROCORTISONE Otic

Some commonly used brand names are:

In the U.S.—
- AK-Spore HC Otic
- Antibiotic Ear
- Cortatrigen Ear
- Cortatrigen Modified Ear Drops
- Cort-Biotic
- Cortisporin
- Cortomycin
- Drotic
- Ear-Eze
- LazerSporin-C
- Masporin Otic
- Octicair
- Octigen
- Otic-Care
- Otic-Care Ear
- Otimar
- Otisan
- Otocidin
- Otocort
- Pediotic
- UAD Otic

Generic name product may be available.

In Canada—
- Cortisporin

Description

Neomycin (nee-oh-MYE-sin), polymyxin (pol-i-MIX-in) B, and hydrocortisone (hye-droe-KOR-ti-sone) is a combination antibiotic and cortisone-like medicine. It is used to treat infections of the ear canal and to help provide relief from redness, irritation, and discomfort of certain ear problems.

Neomycin, polymyxin B, and hydrocortisone preparation is available only with your doctor's prescription, in the following dosage forms:

Otic
- Solution (U.S. and Canada)
- Suspension (U.S. and Canada)

Before Using This Medicine

In deciding to use a medicine, the risks of using the medicine must be weighed against the good it will do. This is a decision you and your doctor will make. For neomycin, polymyxin B, and hydrocortisone otic preparations, the following should be considered:

Allergies—Tell your doctor if you have ever had any unusual or allergic reaction to this medicine or to any related antibiotic, such as amikacin (e.g., Amikin), colistimethate (e.g., Coly-Mycin M), colistin (e.g., Coly-Mycin S), gentamicin (e.g., Garamycin), kanamycin (e.g., Kantrex), neomycin by mouth or by injection (e.g., Mycifradin), netilmicin (e.g., Netromycin), paromomycin (e.g., Humatin), polymyxin B by injection (e.g., Aerosporin), streptomycin, or tobramycin (e.g., Nebcin). Also tell your health care professional if you are allergic to any other substances, such as preservatives or dyes.

Pregnancy—Neomycin, polymyxin B, and hydrocortisone otic preparations have not been studied in pregnant women. However, studies in animals have shown that topical corticosteroids (such as hydrocortisone) cause birth defects. Before using this medicine, make sure your doctor knows if you are pregnant or if you may become pregnant.

Breast-feeding—Neomycin, polymyxin B, and hydrocortisone otic preparations have not been reported to cause problems in nursing babies.

Children—Although there is no specific information comparing use of otic neomycin, polymyxin B, and hydrocortisone preparation in children with use in other age groups, this preparation is not expected to cause different side effects or problems in children than it does in adults.

Older adults—Many medicines have not been studied specifically in older people. Therefore, it may not be known whether they work exactly the same way they do in younger adults. Although there is no specific information comparing use of otic neomycin, polymyxin B, and hydrocortisone preparation in the elderly with use in other age groups, this preparation is not expected to cause different side effects or problems in older people than it does in younger adults.

Other medicines—Although certain medicines should not be used together at all, in other cases two different medicines may be used together even if an interaction might occur. In these cases, your doctor may want to change the dose, or other precautions may be necessary. Tell your health care professional if you are using any other otic (for the ear) prescription or nonprescription (over-the-counter [OTC] medicine).

Other medical problems—The presence of other medical problems may affect the use of neomycin, polymyxin B, and hydrocortisone otic preparations. Make sure you tell your doctor if you have any other medical problems, especially:

- Any other ear infection or condition (including punctured eardrum)—Use of neomycin, polymyxin B, and hydrocortisone otic preparations may make the condition worse

Proper Use of This Medicine

You may warm the ear drops to body temperature (37 °C or 98.6 °F), but no higher, by holding the bottle in your hand for a few minutes before using the medicine. If the medicine gets too warm, it may break down and not work at all.

To use:

- Lie down or tilt the head so that the infected ear faces up. Gently pull the earlobe up and back for adults (down and back for children) to straighten the ear canal. Drop the medicine into the ear canal. Keep the ear facing up for about 5 minutes to allow the medicine to coat the ear canal. (For young children and other patients who cannot stay still for 5 minutes, try to keep the ear facing up for at least 1 or 2 minutes.) Your doctor may have inserted a gauze or cotton wick into your ear and may want you to keep the wick moistened with this medicine. Your doctor also may have other directions for you, such as how long you should keep the wick in your ear or when you should return to your doctor to have the wick replaced. If you have any questions about this, check with your doctor.
- To keep the medicine as germ-free as possible, do not touch the dropper to any surface (including the ear). Also, keep the container tightly closed.

To help clear up your infection completely, *keep using this medicine for the full time of treatment,* even if your symptoms have disappeared. *Do not miss any doses.*

Dosing—The dose of neomycin, polymyxin B, and hydrocortisone otic preparation will be different for different patients. *Follow your doctor's orders or the directions on the label.* The following information includes only the average doses of neomycin, polymyxin B, and hydrocortisone otic preparation. *If your dose is different, do not change it* unless your doctor tells you to do so.

- For *otic (ear drops)* dosage forms:
  —For ear canal infection:
    - Adults—Use four drops in the ear three or four times a day.
    - Children—Use three drops in the ear three or four times a day.

  —For mastoid cavity infection:
    - Adults—Use four to ten drops in the ear every six to eight hours.
    - Children—Use four or five drops in the ear every six to eight hours.

Missed dose—If you miss a dose of this medicine, apply it as soon as possible. However, if it is almost time for your next dose, skip the missed dose and go back to your regular dosing schedule.

Do not use this medicine for more than 10 days unless otherwise directed by your doctor.

Storage—To store this medicine:

- Keep out of the reach of children.
- Store away from heat and direct light.
- Keep the medicine from freezing.
- Do not keep outdated medicine or medicine no longer needed. Be sure that any discarded medicine is out of the reach of children.

Precautions While Using This Medicine

If your symptoms do not improve within 1 week, or if they become worse, check with your doctor.

Side Effects of This Medicine

Along with its needed effects, a medicine may cause some unwanted effects. Although not all of these side effects may occur, if they do occur they may need medical attention.

Check with your doctor immediately if any of the following side effects occur:

More common

Itching, skin rash, redness, swelling, or other sign of irritation in or around the ear not present before use of this medicine

Other side effects not listed above may also occur in some patients. If you notice any other effects, check with your doctor.

Revised: 06/21/94
Interim revision: 06/02/95

NIACIN—For High Cholesterol Systemic

Some commonly used brand names are:

In the U.S.—

Endur-Acin	Nico-400
Nia-Bid	Nicobid Tempules
Niac	Nicolar
Niacels	Nicotinex Elixir
Niacor	Slo-Niacin

Generic name product may also be available.

In Canada—

Novo-Niacin

Generic name product may also be available.

Other commonly used names are nicotinic acid or vitamin B_3.

Description

Niacin (NYE-a-sin) is used to help lower high cholesterol and fat levels in the blood. This may help prevent medical problems caused by cholesterol and fat clogging the blood vessels.

Some strengths of niacin are available only with your doctor's prescription. Others are available without a prescription, since niacin is also a vitamin. However, it is best to take it only under your doctor's direction so that you can be sure you are taking the correct dose.

Niacin for use in the treatment of high cholesterol is available in the following dosage forms:

Oral

- Extended-release capsules (U.S.)
- Solution (U.S.)
- Tablets (U.S. and Canada)
- Extended-release tablets (U.S. and Canada)

Before Using This Medicine

If you are taking this medicine without a prescription, carefully read and follow any precautions on the label. For niacin, the following should be considered:

Allergies—Tell your doctor if you have ever had any unusual or allergic reaction to niacin. Also tell your health care professional if you are allergic to any other substances, such as foods, preservatives, or dyes.

Diet—Before prescribing medicine for your condition, your doctor will probably try to control your condition by prescribing a personal diet for you. Such a diet may be low in fats, sugars, and/or cholesterol. Many people are able to control their condition by carefully following their doctor's orders for proper diet and exercise. *Medicine is prescribed only when additional help is needed* and is effective only when a schedule of diet and exercise is properly followed.

Also, this medicine is less effective if you are greatly overweight. It may be very important for you to go on a reducing diet. However, check with your doctor before going on any diet.

Make certain your health care professional knows if you are on any special diet, such as a low-sodium or low-sugar diet.

Pregnancy—Studies have not been done in either humans or animals.

Breast-feeding—Niacin has not been reported to cause problems in nursing babies.

Children—There is no specific information comparing the use of niacin for high cholesterol in children with use in other age groups. However, use is not recommended in children under 2 years of age since cholesterol is needed for normal development.

Older adults—Many medicines have not been studied specifically in older people. Therefore, it may not be known whether they work exactly the same way they do in younger adults or if they cause different side effects or problems in older people. Although there is no specific information comparing the use of niacin for high cholesterol in the elderly with use in other age groups, it is not expected to cause different side effects or problems in older people than in younger adults.

Other medicines—Although certain medicines should not be used together at all, in other cases two different medicines may be used together even if an interaction might occur. In these cases, your doctor may want to change the dose, or other precautions may be necessary. Tell your health care professional if you are using any other prescription or nonprescription (over-the-counter [OTC]) medicine.

Other medical problems—The presence of other medical problems may affect the use of niacin. Make sure you tell your doctor if you have any other medical problems, especially:

- Bleeding problems or
- Diabetes mellitus (sugar diabetes) or
- Glaucoma or
- Gout or
- Liver disease or
- Low blood pressure or
- Stomach ulcer—Niacin may make these conditions worse

Proper Use of This Medicine

Use this medicine only as directed by your doctor. Do not use more or less of it, do not use it more often, and do not use it for a longer time than your doctor ordered. To do so may increase the chance of unwanted effects.

Remember that niacin will not cure your condition but it does help control it. Therefore, you must continue to take it as directed if you expect to keep your cholesterol levels down.

Follow carefully the special diet your doctor gave you. This is the most important part of controlling your condition, and is necessary if the medicine is to work properly.

If this medicine upsets your stomach, it may be taken with meals or milk. If stomach upset (nausea or diarrhea) continues, check with your doctor.

For patients taking the *extended-release capsule form* of this medicine:

- Swallow the capsule whole. Do not crush, break, or chew before swallowing. However, if the capsule is too large to swallow, you may mix the contents of the capsule with jam or jelly and swallow without chewing.

For patients taking the *extended-release tablet form* of this medicine:

- Swallow the tablet whole. If the tablet is scored, it may be broken, but not crushed or chewed, before being swallowed.

Dosing—The dose of niacin will be different for different patients. *Follow your doctor's orders or the directions on the label.* The following information includes only the average doses of niacin. *If your dose is different, do not change it* unless your doctor tells you to do so.

The number of capsules or tablets or teaspoonfuls of solution that you take depends on the strength of the medicine.

- For *oral* dosage form (extended-release capsules, extended-release tablets, oral solution, or regular tablets):
  - —For treatment of high cholesterol:
    - Adults and teenagers—1 to 2 grams three times a day.
    - Children—Use and dose must be determined by your doctor.

Missed dose—If you miss a dose of this medicine, take it as soon as possible. However, if it is almost time for your next dose, skip the missed dose and go back to your regular dosing schedule. Do not double doses.

Storage—To store this medicine:

- Keep out of the reach of children.
- Store away from heat and direct light.
- Do not store in the bathroom, near the kitchen sink, or in other damp places. Heat or moisture may cause the medicine to break down.
- Keep the liquid form of this medicine from freezing.
- Do not keep outdated medicine or medicine no longer needed. Be sure that any discarded medicine is out of the reach of children.

Precautions While Using This Medicine

It is very important that your doctor check your progress at regular visits. This will allow your doctor to see if the medicine is working properly to lower your cholesterol and triglyceride (fat) levels and if you should continue to take it.

Do not stop taking niacin without first checking with your doctor. When you stop taking this medicine, your blood cholesterol levels may increase again. Your doctor may want you to follow a special diet to help prevent this from happening.

This medicine may cause you to feel dizzy or faint, especially when you get up from a lying or sitting position. Getting up slowly may help. This effect should lessen after a week or two as your body gets used to the medicine. However, if the problem continues or gets worse, check with your doctor.

Side Effects of This Medicine

Along with its needed effects, a medicine may cause some unwanted effects. Although not all of these side effects may occur, if they do occur they may need medical attention. *Check with your doctor immediately* if any of the following side effects occur:

Less common

With prolonged use of extended-release niacin

Darkening of urine; light gray-colored stools; loss of appetite; severe stomach pain; yellow eyes or skin

Other side effects may occur that usually do not need medical attention. These side effects may go away during treatment as your body adjusts to the medicine. However, check with your doctor if any of the following side effects continue or are bothersome:

Less common

Feeling of warmth; flushing or redness of skin, especially on face and neck; headache

With high doses

Diarrhea; dizziness or faintness; dryness of skin; fever; frequent urination; itching of skin; joint pain; muscle aching or cramping; nausea or vomiting; side, lower back, or stomach pain; swelling of feet or lower legs; unusual thirst; unusual tiredness or weakness; unusually fast, slow, or irregular heartbeat

Other side effects not listed above may also occur in some patients. If you notice any other effects, check with your health care professional.

Revised: 11/09/91
Interim revision: 08/10/94

NIACIN (Vitamin B_3) Systemic

Some commonly used brand names are:

In the U.S.—

Endur-Acin[1]
Nia-Bid[1]
Niac[1]
Niacels[1]
Niacor[1]
Nico-400[1]
Nicobid Tempules[1]
Nicolar[1]
Nicotinex Elixir[1]
Slo-Niacin[1]

In Canada—

Novo-Niacin[1]

Other commonly used names are:

Nicotinamide[2]
Nicotinic acid[1]
Vitamin B_3[1,2]

Note: For quick reference, the following products are numbered to match the corresponding brand names.

This information applies to the following products:

1. Niacin (nye-a-SIN)‡§
2. Niacinamide (nye-a-SIN-a-mide)‡§

‡Generic name product may also be available in the U.S.
§Generic name product may also be available in Canada.

Description

Vitamins (VYE-ta-mins) are compounds that you *must* have for growth and health. They are needed in small amounts only and are usually available in the foods that you eat. Niacin and niacinamide are necessary for many normal functions of the body, including normal tissue metabolism. They may have other effects as well.

Lack of niacin may lead to a condition called pellagra. Pellagra causes diarrhea, stomach problems, skin problems, sores in the mouth, anemia (weak blood), and mental problems. Your health care professional may treat this by prescribing niacin for you.

Some conditions may increase your need for niacin. These include:

- Cancer
- Diabetes mellitus (sugar diabetes)
- Diarrhea (prolonged)
- Fever (prolonged)
- Hartnup disease
- Infection (prolonged)
- Intestinal problems
- Liver disease
- Mouth or throat sores
- Overactive thyroid
- Pancreas disease
- Stomach ulcer
- Stress (prolonged)
- Surgical removal of stomach

Increased need for niacin should be determined by your health care professional.

Claims that niacin is effective for treatment of acne, alcoholism, unwanted effects of drug abuse, leprosy, motion sickness, muscle problems, poor circulation, and mental problems, and for prevention of heart attacks, have not been proven. Many of these treatments involve large and expensive amounts of vitamins.

Injectable niacin and niacinamide are given by or under the supervision of a health care professional. Other forms of niacin and niacinamide are available without a prescription.

Niacin and niacinamide are available in the following dosage forms:

Oral

Niacin
- Extended-release capsules (U.S.)
- Solution (U.S.)
- Tablets (U.S. and Canada)
- Extended-release tablets (U.S. and Canada)

Niacinamide
- Tablets (U.S. and Canada)

Parenteral

Niacin
- Injection (U.S.)

Niacinamide
- Injection (U.S.)

Importance of Diet

For good health, it is important that you eat a balanced and varied diet. Follow carefully any diet program your health care professional may recommend. For your specific dietary vitamin and/or mineral needs, ask your health care professional for a list of appropriate foods. If you think that you are not getting enough vitamins and/or minerals in your diet, you may choose to take a dietary supplement.

Niacin is found in meats, eggs, and milk and dairy products. Little niacin is lost from foods during ordinary cooking.

Vitamins alone will not take the place of a good diet and will not provide energy. Your body also needs other substances found in food such as protein, minerals, carbohydrates, and fat. Vitamins themselves often cannot work without the presence of other foods.

The daily amount of niacin needed is defined in several different ways.

For U.S.—
- Recommended Dietary Allowances (RDAs) are the amount of vitamins and minerals needed to provide for adequate nutrition in most healthy persons. RDAs for a given nutrient may vary depending on a person's age, sex, and physical condition (e.g., pregnancy).
- Daily Values (DVs) are used on food and dietary supplement labels to indicate the percent of the recommended daily amount of each nutrient that a serving provides. DV replaces the previous designation of United States Recommended Daily Allowances (USRDAs).

For Canada—
- Recommended Nutrient Intakes (RNIs) are used to determine the amounts of vitamins, minerals, and protein needed to provide adequate nutrition and lessen the risk of chronic disease.

Normal daily recommended intakes in milligrams (mg) for niacin are generally defined as follows:

Persons	U.S. (mg)	Canada (mg)
Infants and children		
Birth to 3 years of age	5–9	4–9
4 to 6 years of age	12	13
7 to 10 years of age	13	14–18
Adolescent and adult males	15–20	14–23
Adolescent and adult females	13–15	14–16
Pregnant females	17	14–16
Breast-feeding females	20	14–16

Before Using This Dietary Supplement

If you are taking this dietary supplement without a prescription, carefully read and follow any precautions on the label. For niacin or niacinamide, the following should be considered:

Allergies—Tell your health care professional if you have ever had any unusual or allergic reaction to niacin or niacinamide. Also tell your health care professional if you are allergic to any other substances, such as foods, preservatives, or dyes.

Pregnancy—It is especially important that you are receiving enough vitamins when you become pregnant and that you continue to receive the right amount of vitamins throughout your pregnancy. The healthy growth and development of the fetus depend on a steady supply of nutrients from the mother. However, taking large amounts of a dietary supplement in pregnancy may be harmful to the mother and/or fetus and should be avoided.

Breast-feeding—It is especially important that you receive the right amounts of vitamins so that your baby will also get the vitamins needed to grow properly. However, taking large amounts of a dietary supplement while breast-feeding may be harmful to the mother and/or baby and should be avoided.

Children—Problems in children have not been reported with intake of normal daily recommended amounts.

Older adults—Problems in older adults have not been reported with intake of normal daily recommended amounts.

Medicines or other dietary supplements—Although certain medicines or dietary supplements should not be used together at all, in other cases they may be used together even if an interaction might occur. In these cases, your health care professional may want to change the dose, or other precautions may be necessary. Tell your health care professional if you are using any other dietary supplement or any prescription or nonprescription (over-the-counter [OTC]) medicine.

Other medical problems—The presence of other medical problems may affect the use of niacin or niacinamide. Make sure you tell your health care professional if you have any other medical problems, especially:

- Bleeding problems or
- Diabetes mellitus (sugar diabetes) or
- Glaucoma or
- Gout or
- Liver disease or
- Low blood pressure or
- Stomach ulcer—Niacin or niacinamide may make these conditions worse

Proper Use of This Dietary Supplement

Dosing—The amount of niacin and niacinamide needed to meet normal daily recommended intakes will be different for different individuals. The following information includes only the average amounts of niacin and niacinamide.

For niacin

- For *oral* dosage form (capsules, extended-release capsules and tablets, tablets, oral solution):
  —To prevent deficiency, the amount taken by mouth is based on normal daily recommended intakes:
  For the U.S.
  - Adult and teenage males—15 to 20 milligrams (mg) per day.
  - Adult and teenage females—13 to 15 mg per day.
  - Pregnant females—17 mg per day.
  - Breast-feeding females—20 mg per day.
  - Children 7 to 10 years of age—13 mg per day.
  - Children 4 to 6 years of age—12 mg per day.
  - Children birth to 3 years of age—5 to 9 mg per day.

  For Canada
  - Adult and teenage males—14 to 23 mg per day.
  - Adult and teenage females—14 to 16 mg per day.
  - Pregnant females—14 to 16 mg per day.
  - Breast-feeding females—14 to 16 mg per day.
  - Children 7 to 10 years of age—14 to 18 mg per day.
  - Children 4 to 6 years of age—13 mg per day.
  - Children birth to 3 years of age—4 to 9 mg per day.

  —To treat deficiency:
  - Adults, teenagers, and children—Treatment dose is determined by prescriber for each individual based on the severity of deficiency.

For niacinamide

- For *oral* dosage form (tablets):
  —To prevent deficiency, the amount taken by mouth is based on normal daily recommended intakes:
  For the U.S.
  - Adult and teenage males—15 to 20 milligrams (mg) per day.
  - Adult and teenage females—13 to 15 mg per day.
  - Pregnant females—17 mg per day.
  - Breast-feeding females—20 mg per day.
  - Children 7 to 10 years of age—13 mg per day.
  - Children 4 to 6 years of age—12 mg per day.
  - Children birth to 3 years of age—5 to 9 mg per day.

  For Canada
  - Adult and teenage males—14 to 23 mg per day.
  - Adult and teenage females—14 to 16 mg per day.

- Pregnant females—14 to 16 mg per day.
- Breast-feeding females—14 to 16 mg per day.
- Children 7 to 10 years of age—14 to 18 mg per day.
- Children 4 to 6 years of age—13 mg per day.
- Children birth to 3 years of age—4 to 9 mg per day.

—To treat deficiency:

- Adults, teenagers, and children—Treatment dose is determined by prescriber for each individual based on the severity of deficiency.

If this dietary supplement upsets your stomach, it may be taken with meals or milk. If stomach upset (nausea or diarrhea) continues, check with your health care professional.

For individuals taking the *extended-release capsule form* of this dietary supplement:

- Swallow the capsule whole. Do not crush, break, or chew before swallowing. However, if the capsule is too large to swallow, you may mix the contents of the capsule with jam or jelly and swallow without chewing.

For individuals taking the *extended-release tablet form* of this dietary supplement:

- Swallow the tablet whole. If the tablet is scored, it may be broken, but not crushed or chewed, before being swallowed.

Missed dose—If you miss taking a vitamin for one or more days there is no cause for concern, since it takes some time for your body to become seriously low in vitamins. However, if your health care professional has recommended that you take this vitamin, try to remember to take it as directed every day.

Storage—To store this dietary supplement:

- Keep out of the reach of children.
- Store away from heat and direct light.
- Do not store in the bathroom, near the kitchen sink, or in other damp places. Heat or moisture may cause the dietary supplement to break down.
- Keep the liquid form of this dietary supplement from freezing.
- Do not keep outdated dietary supplements or those no longer needed. Be sure that any discarded dietary supplement is out of the reach of children.

Precautions While Using This Dietary Supplement

This dietary supplement may cause you to feel dizzy or faint, especially when you get up from a lying or sitting position. Getting up slowly may help. This effect should lessen after a week or two as your body gets used to the dietary supplement. However, if the problem continues or gets worse, check with your health care professional.

Side Effects of This Dietary Supplement

Along with its needed effects, a dietary supplement may cause some unwanted effects. Although not all of these side effects may occur, if they do occur they may need medical attention.

Check with your health care professional immediately if any of the following side effects occur:

With injection only
Skin rash or itching; wheezing

With prolonged use of extended-release niacin
Darkening of urine; light gray-colored stools; loss of appetite; severe stomach pain; yellow eyes or skin

Other side effects may occur that usually do not need medical attention. These side effects may go away during treatment as your body adjusts to the dietary supplement. However, check with your health care professional if any of the following side effects continue or are bothersome:

Less common—with niacin only
Feeling of warmth; flushing or redness of skin, especially on face and neck; headache

With high doses
Diarrhea; dizziness or faintness; dryness of skin; fever; frequent urination; itching of skin; joint pain; muscle aching or cramping; nausea or vomiting; side, lower back, or stomach pain; swelling of feet or lower legs; unusual thirst; unusual tiredness or weakness; unusually fast, slow, or irregular heartbeat

Other side effects not listed above may also occur in some individuals. If you notice any other effects, check with your health care professional.

Revised: 11/09/91
Interim revision: 08/10/94; 05/26/95

NICLOSAMIDE Oral†

A commonly used brand name in the U.S. is Niclocide.

†Not commercially available in Canada.

Description

Niclosamide (ni-KLOE-sa-mide) belongs to the family of medicines called anthelmintics (ant-hel-MIN-tiks). Anthelmintics are medicines used in the treatment of worm infections.

Niclosamide is used to treat broad or fish tapeworm, dwarf tapeworm, and beef tapeworm infections. Niclosamide may also be used for other tapeworm infections as determined by your doctor. It will not work for other types of worm infections (for example, pinworms or roundworms).

Niclosamide works by killing tapeworms on contact. The killed worms are then passed in the stool. However, you may not notice them since they are sometimes destroyed in the intestine.

Niclosamide is available only with your doctor's prescription, in the following dosage form:

Oral

- Chewable tablets (U.S.)

Before Using This Medicine

In deciding to use a medicine, the risks of taking the medicine must be weighed against the good it will do. This is a decision you and your doctor will make. For niclosamide, the following should be considered:

Allergies—Tell your doctor if you have ever had any unusual or allergic reaction to niclosamide. Also tell your health care professional if you are allergic to any other substances, such as foods, preservatives, or dyes.

Pregnancy—Niclosamide has not been studied in pregnant women. However, it has not been shown to cause birth defects or other problems in animal studies.

Breast-feeding—It is not known whether niclosamide passes into breast milk. Although most medicines pass into breast milk in small amounts, many of them may be used safely while breast-feeding. Mothers who are taking this medicine should discuss this with their doctor.

Children—This medicine has been tested in a limited number of children 2 years of age or older and, in effective doses, has not been reported to cause different side effects or problems in children than it does in adults.

Older adults—Many medicines have not been studied specifically in older people. Therefore, it may not be known whether they work exactly the same way they do in younger adults or if they cause different side effects or problems in older people. There is no specific information comparing use of niclosamide in the elderly with use in other age groups.

Other medicines—Although certain medicines should not be used together at all, in other cases two different medicines may be used together even if an interaction might occur. In these cases, your doctor may want to change the dose, or other precautions may be necessary. Tell your health care professional if you are taking any other prescription or nonprescription (over-the-counter [OTC]) medicine.

Proper Use of This Medicine

No special preparations or additional steps (for example, special diets, fasting, other medicines, laxatives, or enemas) are necessary before, during, or immediately after taking niclosamide.

Niclosamide may be taken on an empty stomach (either 1 hour before or 2 hours after a meal). However, to prevent stomach upset, it is best taken after a light meal (for example, breakfast).

Niclosamide tablets should be thoroughly chewed or crushed and then swallowed with a small amount of water. If this medicine is being given to a young child, the tablets should be crushed to a fine powder and mixed with a small amount of water to form a paste.

For patients taking this medicine for *beef tapeworms or broad or fish tapeworms:*

- To help clear up your infection completely, *take this medicine exactly as directed by your doctor.* Usually one dose is enough. However, in some patients a second dose of this medicine may be required to clear up the infection completely.

For patients taking this medicine for *dwarf tapeworms:*

- To help clear up your infection completely, *keep taking this medicine for the full time of treatment (usually 7 days),* even if your symptoms begin to clear up after a few days. In some patients, a second course of this medicine may be required to clear up the infection completely. If you stop taking this medicine too soon, your infection may return. *Do not miss any doses.* Some patients with tapeworm infections may not notice any symptoms or may have only mild symptoms.

Dosing—The dose of niclosamide will be different for different patients. *Follow your doctor's orders or the directions on the label.* The following information includes only the average doses of niclosamide. *If your dose is different, do not change it* unless your doctor tells you to do so.

The number of doses you take each day, the time allowed between doses, and the length of time you take the medicine depend on the medical problem for which you are taking niclosamide.

- For *oral* dosage form (tablets):
  - —For fish tapeworm or beef tapeworm:
    - Adults—2 grams as a single dose. Treatment may be repeated in seven days if needed.
    - Children—Dose is based on body weight and must be determined by your doctor.
      - —For children weighing 11 to 34 kilograms (kg) (24.2 to 74.8 pounds): 1 gram as a single dose. Treatment may be repeated in seven days if needed.
      - —For children weighing over 34 kg (74.8 pounds): 1.5 grams as a single dose. Treatment may be repeated in seven days if needed.
  - —For dwarf tapeworm:
    - Adults—2 grams a day for seven days. Treatment may be repeated in seven to fourteen days if needed.
    - Children—Dose is based on body weight and must be determined by your doctor.
      - —For children weighing 11 to 34 kg (24.2 to 74.8 pounds): 1 gram on the first day. Then 500 milligrams (mg) once a day for the next six days. Treatment may be repeated in seven to fourteen days if needed.
      - —For children weighing over 34 kg (74.8 pounds): 1.5 grams on the first day. Then 1 gram once a day for the next six days. Treatment may be repeated in seven to fourteen days if needed.

Missed dose—If you miss a dose of this medicine, take it as soon as possible. However, if it is almost time for your next dose, skip the missed dose and go back to your regular dosing schedule. Do not double doses.

Storage—To store this medicine:

- Keep out of the reach of children.
- Store away from heat and direct light.
- Do not store in the bathroom, near the kitchen sink, or in other damp places. Heat or moisture may cause the medicine to break down.
- Do not keep outdated medicine or medicine no longer needed. Be sure that any discarded medicine is out of the reach of children.

Precautions While Using This Medicine

It is important that your doctor check your progress at regular visits. This is to make sure that the infection is cleared up completely.

If your symptoms do not improve within a few days, or if they become worse, check with your doctor.

Side Effects of This Medicine

Along with its needed effects, a medicine may cause some unwanted effects. The following side effects may go away during treatment as your body adjusts to the medicine. However, check with your doctor if any of the following side effects continue or are bothersome:

Less common

Abdominal or stomach cramps or pain; diarrhea; loss of appetite; nausea or vomiting

Rare

Dizziness or lightheadedness; drowsiness; itching of the rectal area; skin rash; unpleasant taste

Other side effects not listed above may also occur in some patients. If you notice any other effects, check with your doctor.

Revised: 06/23/95

NICOTINE Systemic

Some commonly used brand names are:

In the U.S.—

Habitrol
Nicoderm
Nicorette
Nicotrol
ProStep

In Canada—

Habitrol
Nicoderm
Nicorette
Nicorette Plus
Nicotrol
ProStep

Description

Nicotine (NIK-o-teen), in a flavored chewing gum or a skin patch, is used to help you stop smoking. It is used for up to 12 to 20 weeks as part of a supervised stop-smoking program. These programs may include education, counseling, and psychological support. Using nicotine replacement products without taking part in a supervised stop-smoking program has not been shown to be effective.

- As you chew nicotine gum, nicotine passes through the lining of your mouth and into your body.
- When you wear a nicotine patch, nicotine passes through your skin into your bloodstream.

This nicotine takes the place of nicotine that you would otherwise get from smoking. In this way, the withdrawal effects of not smoking are less severe. Then, as your body adjusts to not smoking, the use of the nicotine gum is decreased gradually, or the strength of the patches is decreased over a few weeks. Finally, use is stopped altogether.

Children, pregnant women, and nonsmokers should not use nicotine gum or patches because of unwanted effects.

Nicotine gum is available without a prescription. Nicotine patches are available only with your doctor's prescription. Nicotine is available in the following dosage forms:

Oral

- Chewing gum (U.S. and Canada)

Topical

- Transdermal (stick-on) skin patch (U.S. and Canada)

Before Using This Medicine

In deciding to use a medicine, the risks of taking the medicine must be weighed against the good it will do. This is a decision you and your doctor will make. For nicotine gum, the following should be considered:

Allergies—Tell your doctor if you have ever had any unusual or allergic reaction to nicotine. Also tell your health care professional if you are allergic to any other substances, such as foods, preservatives, or dyes. If you plan to use the nicotine patches, tell your doctor if you have ever had a rash or irritation from adhesive tape or bandages.

Pregnancy—Nicotine, whether from smoking or from the gum or patches, is not recommended during pregnancy. Studies in humans show that miscarriages have occurred in pregnant women using nicotine replacement products. In addition, studies in animals have shown that nicotine can cause harmful effects in the fetus.

Breast-feeding—Nicotine passes into breast milk and may cause unwanted effects in the baby. It may be necessary for you to stop breast-feeding during treatment.

Children—Small amounts of nicotine can cause serious harm in children. Even used nicotine patches contain enough nicotine to cause problems in children.

Older adults—Nicotine gum and patches have been used in a limited number of patients 60 years of age or older, and have not been shown to cause different side effects or problems in older people than in younger adults.

Other medicines—Although certain medicines should not be used together at all, in other cases 2 different medicines may be used together even if an interaction might occur.

In these cases, your doctor may want to change the dose, or other precautions may be necessary. When you are using nicotine gum or patches, it is especially important that your health care professional know if you are taking any of the following:

- Aminophylline (e.g., Somophyllin) or
- Insulin or
- Oxtriphylline (e.g., Choledyl) or
- Propoxyphene (e.g., Darvon) or
- Propranolol (e.g., Inderal) or
- Theophylline (e.g., Somophyllin-T)—Stopping smoking may increase the effects of these medicines; the amount of medicine you need to take may change

Other medical problems—The presence of other medical problems may affect the use of nicotine gum or patches. Make sure you tell your doctor if you have any other medical problems, especially:

- Dental problems (with gum only) or
- Diabetes mellitus (sugar diabetes) or
- Heart or blood vessel disease or
- High blood pressure or
- Inflammation of mouth or throat (with gum only) or
- Irritated skin (with patches only) or
- Overactive thyroid or
- Pheochromocytoma (PCC) or
- Stomach ulcer or
- Temporomandibular (jaw) joint disorder (TMJ) (with gum only)—Nicotine gum or patches may make the condition worse

Proper Use of This Medicine

For patients using the *chewing gum:*

- Nicotine gum usually comes with patient directions. *Read the directions carefully before using this medicine.*
- *When you feel the urge to smoke, chew one piece of gum very slowly* until you taste it or feel a slight tingling in your mouth. Stop chewing, and place (''park'') the chewing gum between your cheek and gum until the taste or tingling is almost gone. Then chew slowly until you taste it again. Continue chewing and stopping (''parking'') in this way for about 30 minutes in order to get the full dose of nicotine.
- *Do not chew too fast*, do not chew more than one piece at a time, and do not chew a piece of gum too soon after another. To do so may cause unwanted side effects or an overdose. Also, slower chewing will reduce the possibility of belching.
- *Use nicotine gum exactly as directed on the label or by your doctor.* Remember that it is also important to participate in a stop-smoking program during treatment. This may make it easier for you to stop smoking.
- As your urge to smoke becomes less frequent, *gradually reduce the number of pieces of gum you chew each day* until you are chewing one or two pieces a day. This may be possible within 2 to 3 months.
- *Remember to carry nicotine gum with you at all times* in case you feel the sudden urge to smoke. One cigarette may be enough to start you on the smoking habit again.
- Using hard sugarless candy between doses of gum may help to relieve the discomfort in your mouth.

For patients using the *transdermal system (skin patch):*

- *Use this medicine exactly as directed by your doctor.* It will work only if applied correctly. *This medicine usually comes with patient instructions. Read them carefully before using this product.* Remember that it is also important to participate in a stop-smoking program during treatment. This may make it easier for you to stop smoking.
- Do not remove the patch from its sealed pouch until you are ready to put it on your skin. The patch may not work as well if it is unwrapped too soon.
- Do not try to trim or cut the adhesive patch to adjust the dosage. Check with your doctor if you think the medicine is not working as it should.
- Apply the patch to a clean, dry area of skin on your upper arm, chest, or back. Choose an area that is not very oily, has little or no hair, and is free of scars, cuts, burns, or any other skin irritations.
- Press the patch firmly in place with the palm of your hand for about 10 seconds. Make sure there is good contact with your skin, especially around the edges of the patch.
- The patch should stay in place even when you are showering, bathing, or swimming. Apply a new patch if one falls off.
- Rinse your hands with plain water after you have finished applying the patch to your skin. Nicotine on your hands could get into your eyes and nose and cause stinging, redness, or more serious problems. Using soap to wash your hands will increase the amount of nicotine that passes through your skin.
- After 16 or 24 hours, depending on which product you are using, remove the patch. Choose a different place on your skin to apply the next patch. Do not put a new patch in the same place for at least one week. Do not leave the patch on for more than 24 hours. It will not work as well after that time and it may irritate your skin.
- After removing a used patch, fold the patch in half with the sticky sides together. Place the folded, used patch in its protective pouch or in aluminum foil. Make sure to dispose of it out of the reach of children and pets.
- Try to change the patch at the same time each day. If you want to change the time when you put on your patch, just remove the patch you are wearing and put on a new patch. After that, apply a fresh patch at the new time each day.

Dosing—The dose of nicotine will be different for different patients. *Follow your doctor's orders or the directions on the label.* The following information includes only the average doses of nicotine. *If your dose is different, do not change it* unless your doctor tells you to do so.

- For the *oral* dosage form (chewing gum):
  —To help you stop smoking:
    - Adults and older children—The usual dose is 20 to 24 milligrams (mg) a day. However, the

number of pieces of nicotine gum you chew each day depends on how often you have the urge to smoke, how fast you chew, and the strength of the gum. You should not chew more than 24 pieces of gum a day.

• Children up to 12 years of age—Use and dose must be determined by your doctor.

• For the *transdermal* (stick-on) skin patch:

—To help you stop smoking:

• Adults—The dose you receive will be based on your body weight, how often you have the urge to smoke, and the strength of the patch you use. This dose will be determined by your doctor.

• Children—Use and dose must be determined by your doctor.

Storage—To store this medicine:

- Keep out of the reach of children because even small doses of nicotine can cause serious harm in children.
- Store away from heat and direct light.
- Do not store in the bathroom, near the kitchen sink, or in other damp places. Heat or moisture may cause the medicine to break down.
- Do not keep outdated medicine or medicine no longer needed. Be sure that any discarded medicine is out of the reach of children and pets.

Precautions While Using This Medicine

Your doctor should check your progress at regular visits to make sure that the nicotine patches are working properly and that possible side effects are avoided.

Do not smoke during treatment with nicotine gum or patches because of the risk of nicotine overdose.

Nicotine should not be used in pregnancy. If there is a possibility you might become pregnant, you may want to use some type of birth control. If you think you may have become pregnant, stop taking this medicine immediately and check with your doctor.

Nicotine products must be kept out of the reach of children and pets. Even used nicotine patches contain enough nicotine to cause problems in children. If a child chews or swallows one or more pieces of nicotine gum, contact your doctor or poison control center at once. If a child puts on a nicotine patch or plays with a patch that is out of the sealed pouch, take it away from the child and contact your doctor or poison control center at once.

For patients using the *chewing gum:*

- *Do not chew more than 24 pieces of gum a day.* Chewing too many pieces may be harmful because of the risk of overdose.
- *Do not use nicotine gum for longer than 6 months.* To do so may result in physical dependence on the nicotine.
- *If the gum sticks to your dental work, stop using it and check with your medical doctor or dentist.* Dentures or other dental work may be damaged because nicotine gum is stickier and harder to chew than ordinary gum.

For patients using the *transdermal system (skin patch):*

- Mild itching, burning, or tingling may occur when the patch is first applied, and should go away within an hour. After a patch is removed, the skin underneath it may be somewhat red. It should not remain red for more than a day. *If you get a skin rash from the patch, or if the skin becomes swollen or very red, call your doctor.* Do not put on a new patch. If you become allergic to the nicotine in the patch, you could get sick from using cigarettes or other products that contain nicotine.
- *Do not use nicotine patches for longer than 12 to 20 weeks* (depending on the product) if you have stopped smoking because continuing use of nicotine in any form can be harmful and addictive.

Side Effects of This Medicine

Along with its needed effects, a medicine may cause some unwanted effects. Although not all of these side effects may occur, if they do occur they may need medical attention.

Check with your doctor as soon as possible if any of the following side effects occur:

More common

Injury to mouth, teeth, or dental work—with chewing gum only

Rare

Hives, itching, rash, redness, or swelling; irregular heartbeat

Symptoms of overdose (may occur in the following order)

Nausea and/or vomiting; increased watering of mouth (severe); abdominal or stomach pain (severe); diarrhea (severe); cold sweat; headache (severe); dizziness (severe); drooling; disturbed hearing and vision; confusion; weakness (severe); fainting; low blood pressure; difficulty in breathing (severe); fast, weak, or irregular heartbeat; convulsions (seizures)

Other side effects may occur that usually do not need medical attention. These side effects may go away during treatment as your body adjusts to the medicine. However, check with your doctor if any of the following side effects continue or are bothersome:

More common

Belching—with chewing gum only; fast heartbeat; headache (mild); increased appetite; increased watering of mouth (mild)—with chewing gum only; jaw muscle ache—with chewing gum only; redness, itching, and/or burning at site of application of patch—usually stops within an hour; sore mouth or throat—with chewing gum only

Less common or rare
Constipation; coughing (increased); diarrhea; dizziness or lightheadedness (mild); drowsiness; dryness of mouth; hiccups—with chewing gum only; hoarseness—with chewing gum only; irritability or nervousness; loss of appetite; menstrual pain; muscle or joint pain; stomach upset or indigestion (mild); sweating (increased); trouble in sleeping or unusual dreams

Other side effects not listed above may also occur in some patients. If you notice any other effects, check with your doctor.

Revised: 09/08/92
Interim revision: 05/19/94; 07/11/96

NICOTINYL ALCOHOL Systemic*

A commonly used brand name in Canada is Roniacol.

*Not commercially available in the U.S.

Description

Nicotinyl (nik-oh-TIN-ill) alcohol belongs to the group of medicines called vasodilators. Vasodilators increase the size of blood vessels and are used to treat problems resulting from poor blood circulation.

Nicotinyl alcohol is available without a prescription, in the following dosage form:

Oral
- Extended-release tablets (Canada)

Before Using This Medicine

If you are taking this medicine without a prescription, carefully read and follow any precautions on the label. For nicotinyl alcohol, the following should be considered:

Allergies—Tell your doctor if you have ever had any unusual or allergic reaction to nicotinyl alcohol. Also tell your health care professional if you are allergic to any other substances, such as foods, preservatives, or dyes.

Pregnancy—Studies on effects in pregnancy have not been done in either humans or animals.

Breast-feeding—It is not known whether nicotinyl alcohol passes into breast milk. However, this medicine has not been reported to cause problems in nursing babies.

Older adults—Many medicines have not been studied specifically in older people. Therefore, it may not be known whether they work exactly the same way they do in younger adults or if they cause different side effects or problems in older people. There is no specific information comparing use of nicotinyl alcohol in the elderly with use in other age groups. However, nicotinyl alcohol may reduce tolerance to cold temperatures in elderly patients.

Other medicines—Although certain medicines should not be used together at all, in other cases two different medicines may be used together even if an interaction might occur. In these cases, your doctor may want to change the dose, or other precautions may be necessary. Tell your health care professional if you are taking any other prescription or nonprescription (over-the-counter [OTC]) medicine, or if you smoke.

Other medical problems—The presence of other medical problems may affect the use of nicotinyl alcohol. Make sure you tell your doctor if you have any other medical problems, especially:
- Angina (chest pain) or
- Diabetes mellitus (sugar diabetes) or
- Heart attack (recent) or
- Stomach ulcer or
- Stroke (recent)—Nicotinyl alcohol can make your condition worse
- Glaucoma or
- High cholesterol levels—The chance of side effects may be increased

Proper Use of This Medicine

Nicotinyl alcohol tablets should be swallowed whole. Do not break, crush, or chew the tablets before swallowing them.

Dosing—The dose of nicotinyl alcohol will be different for different patients. *Follow your doctor's orders or the directions on the label.* The following information includes only the average doses of nicotinyl alcohol. *If your dose is different, do not change it* unless your doctor tells you to do so:
- For *oral* dosage forms (tablets):
  —Adults: 150 to 300 milligrams two times a day, taken in the morning and evening.

Missed dose—If you miss a dose of this medicine, take it as soon as you remember. However, if it is almost time for your next dose, skip the missed dose and go back to your regular dosing schedule. Do not double doses.

Storage—To store this medicine:
- Keep out of the reach of children.
- Store away from heat and direct light.
- Do not store in the bathroom, near the kitchen sink, or in other damp places. Heat or moisture may cause the medicine to break down.
- Do not keep outdated medicine or medicine no longer needed. Be sure that any discarded medicine is out of the reach of children.

Precautions While Using This Medicine

It may take some time for this medicine to work. If you feel that the medicine is not working, do not stop taking it on your own. Instead, check with your doctor.

The helpful effects of this medicine may be decreased if you smoke.

Side Effects of This Medicine

Along with its needed effects, a medicine may cause some unwanted effects. Although not all of these side effects may occur, if they do occur they may need medical attention.

Check with your doctor as soon as possible if any of the following side effects occur:

Rare

Swelling of feet or lower legs; yellow eyes or skin

Other side effects may occur that usually do not need medical attention. These side effects may go away during treatment as your body adjusts to the medicine. However, check with your doctor if any of the following side effects continue or are bothersome:

More common

Flushing; warmth or tingling

Less common or rare

Diarrhea; dizziness or faintness; increased hair loss; nausea and vomiting; skin rash

Other side effects not listed above may also occur in some patients. If you notice any other effects, check with your doctor.

Revised: 04/06/93

NITRATES—Lingual Aerosol Systemic

This information applies to nitroglycerin oral spray.

A commonly used brand name in the U.S. and Canada is Nitrolingual.

Another commonly used name is glyceryl trinitrate.

Description

Nitrates (NYE-trates) are used to treat the symptoms of angina (chest pain). Depending on the type of dosage form and how it is taken, nitrates are used to treat angina in three ways:

- to relieve an attack that is occurring by using the medicine when the attack begins;
- to prevent attacks from occurring by using the medicine just before an attack is expected to occur; or
- to reduce the number of attacks that occur by using the medicine regularly on a long-term basis.

When used as a lingual (in the mouth) spray, nitroglycerin is used either to relieve the pain of angina attacks or to prevent an expected angina attack.

Nitroglycerin works by relaxing blood vessels and increasing the supply of blood and oxygen to the heart while reducing its work load.

Nitroglycerin as discussed here is available only with your doctor's prescription, in the following dosage form:

Oral

- Lingual aerosol (U.S. and Canada)

Before Using This Medicine

In deciding to use a medicine, the risks of taking the medicine must be weighed against the good it will do. This is a decision you and your doctor will make. For nitroglycerin lingual aerosol, the following should be considered:

Allergies—Tell your doctor if you have ever had any unusual or allergic reaction to nitrates or nitrites. Also tell your health care professional if you are allergic to any other substances, such as certain foods, preservatives, or dyes.

Pregnancy—Studies on effects in pregnancy have not been done in either humans or animals.

Breast-feeding—It is not known whether this medicine passes into breast milk. Although most medicines pass into breast milk in small amounts, many of them may be used safely while breast-feeding. Mothers who are taking this medicine and who wish to breast-feed should discuss this with their doctor.

Children—Studies on this medicine have been done only in adult patients, and there is no specific information comparing use of nitroglycerin in children with use in other age groups.

Older adults—Dizziness or lightheadedness may be more likely to occur in the elderly, who may be more sensitive to the effects of nitrates.

Other medicines—Although certain medicines should not be used together at all, in other cases two different medicines may be used together even if an interaction might occur. In these cases, your doctor may want to change the dose, or other precautions may be necessary. When you are taking nitroglycerin, it is especially important that your health care professional know if you are taking any of the following:

- Antihypertensives (high blood pressure medicine) or
- Other heart medicine—May increase the effects of nitroglycerin on blood pressure

Other medical problems—The presence of other medical problems may affect the use of nitroglycerin. Make sure you tell your doctor if you have any other medical problems, especially:

- Anemia (severe)
- Glaucoma—May be worsened by nitroglycerin
- Head injury (recent) or
- Stroke (recent)—Nitroglycerin may increase pressure in the brain, which can make problems worse
- Heart attack (recent)—Nitroglycerin may lower blood pressure, which can aggravate problems associated with heart attack
- Kidney disease or
- Liver disease—Effects may be increased because of slower removal of nitroglycerin from the body
- Overactive thyroid

Proper Use of This Medicine

Use nitroglycerin spray exactly as directed by your doctor. It will work only if used correctly.

This medicine usually comes with patient instructions. Read them carefully before you actually need to use it. Then, if you need the medicine quickly, you will know how to use it.

To use nitroglycerin lingual spray:

- Remove the plastic cover. *Do not shake the container.*
- Hold the container upright. With the container held close to your mouth, press the button to spray onto or under your tongue. *Do not inhale the spray.*
- Release the button and close your mouth. Avoid swallowing immediately after using the spray.

For patients using nitroglycerin oral spray *to relieve the pain of an angina attack*:

- *When you begin to feel an attack of angina starting (chest pains or a tightness or squeezing in the chest), sit down. Then use 1 or 2 sprays as directed by your doctor.* This medicine works best when you are standing or sitting. However, since you may become dizzy, lightheaded, or faint soon after using a spray, it is safer to sit rather than stand while the medicine is working. If you become dizzy or faint while sitting, take several deep breaths and bend forward with your head between your knees.
- Remain calm and you should feel better in a few minutes.
- *This medicine usually gives relief in less than 5 minutes.* However, if the pain is not relieved, use a second spray. If the pain continues for another 5 minutes, a third spray may be used. *If you still have the chest pains after a total of 3 sprays in a 15-minute period, contact your doctor or go to a hospital emergency room immediately.*

For patients using nitroglycerin oral spray *to prevent an expected angina attack*:

- You may prevent anginal chest pains for up to 1 hour by using a spray 5 to 10 minutes before expected emotional stress or physical exertion that in the past seemed to bring on an attack.

Dosing—The dose of nitroglycerin lingual spray will be different for different patients. *Follow your doctor's orders or the directions on the label.* The following information includes only the average doses of nitroglycerin lingual spray. *If your dose is different, do not change it* unless your doctor tells you to do so.

- For *oral* dosage form (lingual spray):
  - —For chest pain:
    - Adults—One or two sprays on or under the tongue. The dose may be repeated every five minutes as needed. If the chest pain is not relieved after a total of three sprays in a fifteen-minute period, call your doctor or go to the emergency room right away.

Storage—To store this medicine:

- Keep out of the reach of children.
- Store away from heat and direct light.
- Keep the medicine from freezing.
- Do not puncture, break, or burn the aerosol container, even after it is empty.
- Do not keep outdated medicine or medicine no longer needed. Be sure that any discarded medicine is out of the reach of children.

Precautions While Using This Medicine

If you have been using this medicine regularly for several weeks, do not suddenly stop using it. Stopping suddenly may bring on attacks of angina. Check with your doctor for the best way to reduce gradually the amount you are using before stopping completely.

Dizziness, lightheadedness, or faintness may occur, especially when you get up quickly from a lying or sitting position. Getting up slowly may help. If you feel dizzy, sit or lie down.

The dizziness, lightheadedness, or fainting is also more likely to occur if you drink alcohol, stand for long periods of time, exercise, or if the weather is hot. *While you are taking this medicine, be careful to limit the amount of alcohol you drink. Also, use extra care during exercise or hot weather or if you must stand for long periods of time.*

After using a dose of this medicine you may get a headache that lasts for a short time. This is a common side effect, which should become less noticeable after you have used the medicine for a while. If this effect continues or if the headaches are severe, check with your doctor.

Side Effects of This Medicine

Along with its needed effects, a medicine may cause some unwanted effects. Although not all of these side effects may occur, if they do occur they may need medical attention.

Check with your doctor as soon as possible if any of the following side effects occur:

Rare

Blurred vision; dryness of mouth; headache (severe or prolonged); skin rash

Signs and symptoms of overdose (in the order in which they may occur)

Bluish-colored lips, fingernails, or palms of hands; dizziness (extreme) or fainting; feeling of extreme pressure in head; shortness of breath; unusual tiredness or weakness; weak and fast heartbeat; fever; convulsions (seizures)

Other side effects may occur that usually do not need medical attention. These side effects may go away during treatment as your body adjusts to the medicine. However,

check with your doctor if any of the following side effects continue or are bothersome:

More common

Dizziness or lightheadedness, especially when getting up from a lying or sitting position; fast pulse; flushing of face and neck; headache; nausea or vomiting; restlessness

Other side effects not listed above may also occur in some patients. If you notice any other effects, check with your doctor.

Revised: 10/06/93

NITRATES—Oral Systemic

Some commonly used brand names are:

In the U.S.—

Cardilate[1]
Dilatrate-SR[2]
Duotrate[5]
IMDUR[3]
ISMO[3]
Iso-Bid[2]
Isonate[2]
Isorbid[2]
Isordil[2]
Isotrate[2]
Klavikordal[4]
Monoket[3]
Niong[4]
Nitrocap[4]
Nitrocap T.D.[4]
Nitroglyn[4]
Nitrolin[4]
Nitronet[4]
Nitrong [4]
Nitrospan[4]
Pentylan[5]
Peritrate[5]
Peritrate SA[5]
Sorbitrate[2]
Sorbitrate SA[2]

In Canada—

Apo-ISDN[2]
Cardilate[1]
Cedocard-SR[2]
Coronex[2]
Isordil[2]
Nitrong SR[4]
Novosorbide[2]
Peritrate[5]
Peritrate Forte[5]
Peritrate SA[5]

Other commonly used names are:

Eritrityl tetranitrate[1]
Erythritol tetranitrate[1]
Glyceryl trinitrate[4]
Pentaerithrityl tetranitrate[5]
P.E.T.N.[5]

Note: For quick reference, the following nitrates are numbered to match the corresponding brand names.

This information applies to the following medicines:

1. Erythrityl Tetranitrate (e-RI-thri-till tet-ra-NYE-trate)
2. Isosorbide Dinitrate (eye-soe-SOR-bide dye-NYE-trate)‡
3. Isosorbide Mononitrate (eye-soe-SOR-bide mon-oh-NYE-trate)†
4. Nitroglycerin (nye-troe-GLI-ser-in)‡
5. Pentaerythritol Tetranitrate (pen-ta-er-ITH-ri-tole tet-ra-NYE-trate)‡

Note: This information does *not* apply to amyl nitrite or mannitol hexanitrate.

†Not commercially available in Canada.
‡Generic name product may also be available in the U.S.

Description

Nitrates (NYE-trates) are used to treat the symptoms of angina (chest pain). Depending on the type of dosage form and how it is taken, nitrates are used to treat angina in three ways:

- to relieve an attack that is occurring by using the medicine when the attack begins;
- to prevent attacks from occurring by using the medicine just before an attack is expected to occur; or
- to reduce the number of attacks that occur by using the medicine regularly on a long-term basis.

When taken orally and swallowed, nitrates are used to reduce the number of angina attacks that occur. They do not act fast enough to relieve the pain of an angina attack.

Nitrates work by relaxing blood vessels and increasing the supply of blood and oxygen to the heart while reducing its work load.

Nitrates may also be used for other conditions as determined by your doctor.

The nitrates discussed here are available only with your doctor's prescription, in the following dosage forms:

Oral

Erythrityl tetranitrate
- Tablets (U.S. and Canada)

Isosorbide dinitrate
- Capsules (U.S.)
- Extended-release capsules (U.S.)
- Tablets (U.S. and Canada)
- Chewable tablets (U.S.)
- Extended-release tablets (U.S. and Canada)

Isosorbide mononitrate
- Extended-release tablets (U.S.)
- Tablets (U.S.)

Nitroglycerin
- Extended-release capsules (U.S.)
- Extended-release tablets (U.S. and Canada)

Pentaerythritol tetranitrate
- Extended-release capsules (U.S.)
- Tablets (U.S. and Canada)
- Extended-release tablets (U.S. and Canada)

Before Using This Medicine

In deciding to use a medicine, the risks of taking the medicine must be weighed against the good it will do. This is a decision you and your doctor will make. For nitrates, the following should be considered:

Allergies—Tell your doctor if you have ever had any unusual or allergic reaction to nitrates or nitrites. Also tell your health care professional if you are allergic to any other substances, such as certain foods, preservatives, or dyes.

Pregnancy—Nitrates have not been studied in pregnant women. However, studies in rabbits given large doses of isosorbide dinitrate have shown adverse effects on the fetus. Before taking these medicines, make sure your doctor knows if you are pregnant or if you may become pregnant.

Breast-feeding—It is not known whether these medicines pass into breast milk. Although most medicines pass into breast milk in small amounts, many of them may be used safely while breast-feeding. Mothers who are taking these medicines and who wish to breast-feed should discuss this with their doctor.

Children—Studies on these medicines have been done only in adult patients, and there is no specific information comparing use of nitrates in children with use in other age groups.

Older adults—Dizziness or lightheadedness may be more likely to occur in the elderly, who may be more sensitive to the effects of nitrates.

Other medicines—Although certain medicines should not be used together at all, in other cases two different medicines may be used together even if an interaction might occur. In these cases, your doctor may want to change the dose, or other precautions may be necessary. When you are taking nitrates, it is especially important that your health care professional know if you are taking any of the following:

- Antihypertensives (high blood pressure medicine) or
- Other heart medicine—May increase the effects of nitrates on blood pressure

Other medical problems—The presence of other medical problems may affect the use of nitrates. Make sure you tell your doctor if you have any other medical problems, especially:

- Anemia (severe)
- Glaucoma—May be worsened by nitrates
- Head injury (recent) or
- Stroke (recent)—Nitrates may increase pressure in the brain, which can make problems worse
- Heart attack (recent)—Nitrates may lower blood pressure, which can aggravate problems associated with heart attack
- Kidney disease or
- Liver disease—Effects may be increased because of slower removal of nitroglycerin from the body
- Overactive thyroid

Proper Use of This Medicine

Take this medicine exactly as directed by your doctor. It will work only if taken correctly.

This form of nitrate is used to reduce the number of angina attacks. In most cases, it will not relieve an attack that has already started, because it works too slowly (the extended-release form releases medicine gradually over a 6-hour period to provide its effect for 8 to 10 hours). Check with your doctor if you need a fast-acting medicine to relieve the pain of an angina attack.

Take this medicine with a full glass (8 ounces) of water on an empty stomach. If taken either 1 hour before or 2 hours after meals, it will start working sooner.

Extended-release capsules and tablets are not to be broken, crushed, or chewed before they are swallowed. If broken up, they will not release the medicine properly.

Dosing—The dose of nitrates will be different for different patients. *Follow your doctor's orders or the directions on the label.* The following information includes only the average doses of nitrates. *If your dose is different, do not change it* unless your doctor tells you to do so.

The number of capsules or tablets that you take depends on the strength of the medicine. Also, *the number of doses you take each day, the time allowed between doses, and the length of time you take the medicine depend on the medical problem for which you are taking nitrates.*

For erythrityl tetranitrate

- For angina (chest pain):
  - —For *oral* dosage form (tablets):
    - Adults—5 to 10 milligrams (mg) three or four times a day.
    - Children—Dose must be determined by your doctor.

For isosorbide dinitrate

- For angina (chest pain):
  - —For *regular (short-acting) oral* dosage forms (capsules or tablets):
    - Adults—5 to 40 mg four times a day.
    - Children—Dose must be determined by your doctor.
  - —For *long-acting oral* dosage forms (extended-release capsules or tablets):
    - Adults—20 to 80 mg every eight to twelve hours.
    - Children—Dose must be determined by your doctor.

For isosorbide mononitrate

- For angina (chest pain):
  - —For *regular (short-acting) oral* dosage form (tablets):
    - Adults—20 mg two times a day. The two doses should be taken seven hours apart.
    - Children—Use and dose must be determined by your doctor.
  - —For *long-acting oral* dosage forms (extended-release tablets):
    - Adults—30 to 240 mg once a day.
    - Children—Use and dose must be determined by your doctor.

For nitroglycerin

- For angina (chest pain):
  - —For *long-acting oral* dosage forms (capsules or tablets):
    - Adults—1.3 to 9.0 mg every eight to twelve hours.
    - Children—Dose must be determined by your doctor.

For pentaerythritol tetranitrate

- For angina (chest pain):
  - —For *regular (short-acting) oral* dosage forms (tablets):
    - Adults—10 to 20 mg four times a day.
    - Children—Dose must be determined by your doctor.
  - —For *long-acting oral* dosage forms (capsules or tablets):
    - Adults—30 to 80 mg two times a day.
    - Children—Dose must be determined by your doctor.

Missed dose—If you are taking this medicine regularly and you miss a dose, take it as soon as possible. However, if the next scheduled dose is within 2 hours (or within 6 hours for extended-release capsules or tablets), skip the missed dose and go back to your regular dosing schedule. Do not double doses.

Storage—To store this medicine:
- Keep out of the reach of children.
- Store away from heat and direct light.
- Do not store in the bathroom, near the kitchen sink, or in other damp places. Heat or moisture may cause the medicine to break down.
- Do not keep outdated medicine or medicine no longer needed. Be sure that any discarded medicine is out of the reach of children.

Precautions While Using This Medicine

If you have been taking this medicine regularly for several weeks or more, do not suddenly stop using it. Stopping suddenly may bring on attacks of angina. Check with your doctor for the best way to reduce gradually the amount you are taking before stopping completely.

Dizziness, lightheadedness, or faintness may occur, especially when you get up quickly from a lying or sitting position. Getting up slowly may help. If you feel dizzy, sit or lie down.

The dizziness, lightheadedness, or fainting is also more likely to occur if you drink alcohol, stand for long periods of time, exercise, or if the weather is hot. *While you are taking this medicine, be careful to limit the amount of alcohol you drink. Also, use extra care during exercise or hot weather or if you must stand for long periods of time.*

After taking a dose of this medicine you may get a headache that lasts for a short time. This is a common side effect, which should become less noticeable after you have taken the medicine for a while. If this effect continues, or if the headaches are severe, check with your doctor.

For patients taking the *extended-release dosage forms of isosorbide dinitrate or pentaerythritol tetranitrate*:
- Partially dissolved tablets have been found in the stools of a few patients taking the extended-release tablets. Be alert to this possibility, especially if you have frequent bowel movements, diarrhea, or digestive problems. Notify your doctor if any such tablets are discovered. The tablets must be properly digested to provide the correct dose of medicine.

Side Effects of This Medicine

Along with its needed effects, a medicine may cause some unwanted effects. Although not all of these side effects may occur, if they do occur they may need medical attention.

Check with your doctor as soon as possible if any of the following side effects occur:

Rare

Blurred vision; dryness of mouth; headache (severe or prolonged); skin rash

Signs and symptoms of overdose (in the order in which they may occur)

Bluish-colored lips, fingernails, or palms of hands; dizziness (extreme) or fainting; feeling of extreme pressure in head; shortness of breath; unusual tiredness or weakness; weak and fast heartbeat; fever; convulsions (seizures)

Other side effects may occur that usually do not need medical attention. These side effects may go away during treatment as your body adjusts to the medicine. However, check with your doctor if any of the following side effects continue or are bothersome:

More common

Dizziness or lightheadedness, especially when getting up from a lying or sitting position; fast pulse; flushing of face and neck; headache; nausea or vomiting; restlessness

Other side effects not listed above may also occur in some patients. If you notice any other effects, check with your doctor.

Revised: 10/06/93
Interim revision: 02/22/94

NITRATES—Sublingual, Chewable, or Buccal Systemic

Some commonly used brand names are:

In the U.S.—

Cardilate[1]
Isonate[2]
Isorbid[2]
Isordil[2]
Nitrogard[3]
Nitrostat[3]
Sorbitrate[2]

In Canada—

Apo-ISDN[2]
Cardilate[1]
Coronex[2]
Isordil[2]
Nitrogard SR[3]
Nitrostat[3]

Other commonly used names are:

Eritrityl tetranitrate[1]
Erythritol tetranitrate[1]
Glyceryl trinitrate[3]

Note: For quick reference, the following nitrates are numbered to match the corresponding brand names.

This information applies to the following medicines:
1. Erythrityl Tetranitrate (e-RI-thri-till tet-ra-NYE-trate)
2. Isosorbide Dinitrate (eye-soe-SOR-bide dye-NYE-trate)‡
3. Nitroglycerin (nye-troe-GLI-ser-in)‡§

Note: This information doses *not* apply to amyl nitrite or pentaerythritol tetranitrate.

‡Generic name product may also be available in the U.S.
§Generic name product may also be available in Canada.

Description

Nitrates (NYE-trates) are used to treat the symptoms of angina (chest pain). Depending on the type of dosage form and how it is taken, nitrates are used to treat angina in three ways:

- to relieve an attack that is occurring by using the medicine when the attack begins;
- to prevent attacks from occurring by using the medicine just before an attack is expected to occur; or
- to reduce the number of attacks that occur by using the medicine regularly on a long-term basis.

Nitrates are available in different forms. Sublingual nitrates are generally placed under the tongue where they dissolve and are absorbed through the lining of the mouth. Some can also be used buccally, being placed under the lip or in the cheek. The chewable dosage forms, after being chewed and held in the mouth before swallowing, are absorbed in the same way. *It is important to remember that each dosage form is different and that the specific directions for each type must be followed if the medicine is to work properly.*

Nitrates that are used *to relieve the pain* of an angina attack include:

- sublingual nitroglycerin;
- buccal nitroglycerin;
- sublingual isosorbide dinitrate; and
- chewable isosorbide dinitrate.

Those that can be used *to prevent expected attacks* of angina include:

- sublingual nitroglycerin;
- buccal nitroglycerin;
- sublingual erythrityl tetranitrate;
- sublingual isosorbide dinitrate; and
- chewable isosorbide dinitrate.

Products that are used regularly on a long-term basis *to reduce the number of attacks* that occur include:

- buccal nitroglycerin;
- oral/sublingual erythrityl tetranitrate;
- chewable isosorbide dinitrate; and
- sublingual isosorbide dinitrate.

Nitrates work by relaxing blood vessels and increasing the supply of blood and oxygen to the heart while reducing its work load.

Nitrates may also be used for other conditions as determined by your doctor.

The nitrates discussed here are available only with your doctor's prescription, in the following dosage forms:

Buccal
Nitroglycerin
- Extended-release tablets (U.S. and Canada)

Chewable
Isosorbide dinitrate
- Tablets (U.S.)

Sublingual
Erythrityl tetranitrate
- Tablets (U.S. and Canada)

Isosorbide dinitrate
- Tablets (U.S. and Canada)

Nitroglycerin
- Tablets (U.S. and Canada)

Before Using This Medicine

In deciding to use a medicine, the risks of taking the medicine must be weighed against the good it will do. This is a decision you and your doctor will make. For nitrates, the following should be considered:

Allergies—Tell your doctor if you have ever had any unusual or allergic reaction to nitrates or nitrites. Also tell your health care professional if you are allergic to any other substances, such as certain foods, preservatives, or dyes.

Pregnancy—Nitrates have not been studied in pregnant women. However, studies in rabbits given large doses of isosorbide dinitrate have shown adverse effects on the fetus. Before taking these medicines, make sure your doctor knows if you are pregnant or if you may become pregnant.

Breast-feeding—It is not known whether these medicines pass into breast milk. Although most medicines pass into breast milk in small amounts, many of them may be used safely while breast-feeding. Mothers who are taking these medicines and who wish to breast-feed should discuss this with their doctor.

Children—Studies on these medicines have been done only in adult patients, and there is no specific information comparing use of nitrates in children with use in other age groups.

Older adults—Dizziness or lightheadedness may be more likely to occur in the elderly, who may be more sensitive to the effects of nitrates.

Other medicines—Although certain medicines should not be used together at all, in other cases two different medicines may be used together even if an interaction might occur. In these cases, your doctor may want to change the dose, or other precautions may be necessary. When you are taking nitrates, it is especially important that your health care professional know if you are taking any of the following:

- Antihypertensives (high blood pressure medicine) or
- Other heart medicine—May increase the effects of nitrates on blood pressure

Other medical problems—The presence of other medical problems may affect the use of nitrates. Make sure you tell your doctor if you have any other medical problems, especially:

- Anemia (severe)
- Glaucoma—May be worsened by nitrates
- Head injury (recent) or
- Stroke (recent)—Nitrates may increase pressure in the brain, which can make problems worse
- Heart attack (recent)—Nitrates may lower blood pressure, which can aggravate problems associated with heart attack
- Kidney disease or
- Liver disease—Effects may be increased because of slower removal of nitroglycerin from the body
- Overactive thyroid

Proper Use of This Medicine

Take this medicine exactly as directed by your doctor. It will work only if taken correctly.

Sublingual tablets should not be chewed, crushed, or swallowed. They work much faster when absorbed through the lining of the mouth. Place the tablet under the tongue, between the lip and gum, or between the cheek and gum and let it dissolve there. Do not eat, drink, smoke, or use chewing tobacco while a tablet is dissolving.

Buccal extended-release tablets should not be chewed, crushed, or swallowed. They are designed to release a dose of nitroglycerin over a period of hours, not all at once.

- Allow the tablet to dissolve slowly in place between the upper lip and gum (above the front teeth), or between the cheek and upper gum. If food or drink is to be taken during the 3 to 5 hours when the tablet is dissolving, place the tablet between the *upper* lip and gum, above the front teeth. If you have dentures, you may place the tablet anywhere between the cheek and gum.
- Touching the tablet with your tongue or drinking hot liquids may cause the tablet to dissolve faster.
- Do not go to sleep while a tablet is dissolving because it could slip down your throat and cause choking.
- If you accidentally swallow the tablet, replace it with another one.
- Do not use chewing tobacco while a tablet is in place.

Chewable tablets must be chewed well and held in the mouth for about 2 minutes before you swallow them. This will allow the medicine to be absorbed through the lining of the mouth.

For patients using *nitroglycerin or isosorbide dinitrate to relieve the pain of an angina attack*:

- *When you begin to feel an attack of angina starting (chest pains or a tightness or squeezing in the chest), sit down. Then place a tablet in your mouth, either sublingually or buccally, or chew a chewable tablet.* This medicine works best when you are standing or sitting. However, since you may become dizzy, lightheaded, or faint soon after using a tablet, it is safer to sit rather than stand while the medicine is working. If you become dizzy or faint while sitting, take several deep breaths and bend forward with your head between your knees.
- Remain calm and you should feel better in a few minutes.
- *This medicine usually gives relief in 1 to 5 minutes.* However, if the pain is not relieved, and you are using:

  —Sublingual tablets, either sublingually or buccally: Use a second tablet. If the pain continues for another 5 minutes, a third tablet may be used. *If you still have the chest pains after a total of 3 tablets in a 15-minute period, contact your doctor or go to a hospital emergency room immediately.*

  —Buccal extended-release tablets: *Use a sublingual (under the tongue) nitroglycerin tablet and check with your doctor.* Do not use another buccal tablet since the effects of a buccal tablet last for several hours.

For patients using *nitroglycerin, erythrityl tetranitrate, or isosorbide dinitrate to prevent an expected angina attack:*

- You may prevent anginal chest pains for up to 1 hour (6 hours for the extended-release nitroglycerin tablet) by using a buccal or sublingual tablet or chewing a chewable tablet 5 to 10 minutes before expected emotional stress or physical exertion that in the past seemed to bring on an attack.

For patients using *isosorbide dinitrate or extended-release buccal nitroglycerin regularly on a long-term basis to reduce the number of angina attacks that occur*:

- Chewable or sublingual isosorbide dinitrate and buccal extended-release nitroglycerin tablets can be used either to prevent angina attacks or to help relieve an attack that has already started.

Dosing—The dose of nitrates will be different for different patients. *Follow your doctor's orders or the directions on the label.* The following information includes only the average doses of nitrates. *If your dose is different, do not change it* unless your doctor tells you to do so.

For erythrityl tetranitrate

- For angina (chest pain):
  - —For *buccal or sublingual* dosage form (tablets):
    - Adults—5 to 10 milligrams (mg) three or four times a day.
    - Children—Dose must be determined by your doctor.

For isosorbide dinitrate

- For angina (chest pain):
  - —For *chewable* dosage form (tablets):
    - Adults—5 mg every two to three hours, chewed well and held in mouth for one or two minutes.
    - Children—Dose must be determined by your doctor.
  - —For *buccal or sublingual* dosage form (tablets):
    - Adults—2.5 to 5 mg every two to three hours.
    - Children—Dose must be determined by your doctor.

For nitroglycerin

- For angina (chest pain):
  - —For *buccal* dosage form (extended-release tablets):
    - Adults—1 mg every five hours while awake. Your doctor may increase your dose.
    - Children—Dose must be determined by your doctor.
  - —For *sublingual* dosage form (tablets):
    - Adults—150 to 600 micrograms (mcg) (0.15 to 0.6 mg) every five minutes. If you still have chest pain after a total of three tablets in fifteen minutes, call your doctor or go to the emergency room right away.
    - Children—Dose must be determined by your doctor.

Missed dose—For patients using isosorbide dinitrate or extended-release buccal nitroglycerin regularly on a long-term basis to reduce the number of angina attacks that occur:

- If you miss a dose of this medicine, use it as soon as possible. However, if the next scheduled dose is within 2 hours, skip the missed dose and go back to your regular dosing schedule. Do not double doses.

Stability and proper storage—

For sublingual nitroglycerin

- Sublingual nitroglycerin tablets may lose some of their strength if they are exposed to air, heat, or moisture for long periods of time. However, if you screw the cap on tightly after each use and you properly store the bottle, the tablets should retain their strength until the expiration date on the bottle.
- Some people think they should test the strength of their sublingual nitroglycerin tablets by looking for a tingling or burning sensation, a feeling of warmth or flushing, or a headache after a tablet has been dissolved under the tongue. This kind of testing is not completely reliable since some patients may be unable to detect these effects. In addition, newer, stabilized sublingual nitroglycerin tablets are less likely to produce these detectable effects.
- To help keep the nitroglycerin tablets at full strength:

  —keep the medicine in the original glass, screw-cap bottle. For patients who wish to carry a small number of tablets with them for emergency use, a specially designed container is available. However, only containers specifically labeled as suitable for use with nitroglycerin sublingual tablets should be used.

  —remove the cotton plug that comes in the bottle and *do not* put it back.

  —*put the cap on the bottle quickly and tightly after each use.*

  —to select a tablet for use, pour several into the bottle cap, take one, and pour the others back into the bottle. Try not to hold them in the palm of your hand because they may pick up moisture and crumble.

  —do not keep other medicines in the same bottle with the nitroglycerin since they will weaken the nitroglycerin effect.

  —keep the medicine handy at all times but try not to carry the bottle close to the body. Medicine may lose strength because of body warmth. Instead, carry the tightly closed bottle in your purse or the pocket of a jacket or other loose-fitting clothing whenever possible.

  —store the bottle of nitroglycerin tablets in a cool, dry place. Storage at average room temperature away from direct heat or direct sunlight is best. Do not store in the refrigerator or in a bathroom medicine cabinet because the moisture usually present in these areas may cause the tablets to crumble if the container is not tightly closed. Do not keep the tablets in your automobile glove compartment.

- Keep out of the reach of children.
- Do not keep outdated medicine or medicine no longer needed. Be sure that any discarded medicine is out of the reach of children.

For erythrityl tetranitrate, isosorbide dinitrate, and buccal extended-release nitroglycerin

- These forms of nitrates are more stable than sublingual nitroglycerin.
- Keep out of the reach of children.
- Store away from heat and direct light.
- Do not store in the bathroom, near the kitchen sink, or in other damp places. Heat or moisture may cause the medicine to break down.
- Do not keep outdated medicine or medicine no longer needed. Be sure that any discarded medicine is out of the reach of children.

Precautions While Using This Medicine

If you have been taking this medicine regularly for several weeks, do not suddenly stop using it. Stopping suddenly may bring on attacks of angina. Check with your doctor for the best way to reduce gradually the amount you are taking before stopping completely.

Dizziness, lightheadedness, or faintness may occur, especially when you get up quickly from a lying or sitting position. Getting up slowly may help. If you feel dizzy, sit or lie down.

The dizziness, lightheadedness, or fainting is also more likely to occur if you drink alcohol, stand for long periods of time, exercise, or if the weather is hot. *While you are taking this medicine, be careful to limit the amount of alcohol you drink. Also, use extra care during exercise or hot weather or if you must stand for long periods of time.*

After taking a dose of this medicine you may get a headache that lasts for a short time. This is a common side effect, which should become less noticeable after you have taken the medicine for a while. If this effect continues or if the headaches are severe, check with your doctor.

Side Effects of This Medicine

Along with its needed effects, a medicine may cause some unwanted effects. Although not all of these side effects may occur, if they do occur they may need medical attention.

Check with your doctor as soon as possible if any of the following side effects occur:

Rare

Blurred vision; dryness of mouth; headache (severe or prolonged); skin rash

Signs and symptoms of overdose (in the order in which they may occur)

Bluish-colored lips, fingernails, or palms of hands; dizziness (extreme) or fainting; feeling of extreme pressure in head; shortness of breath; unusual tiredness or weakness; weak and fast heartbeat; fever; convulsions (seizures)

Other side effects may occur that usually do not need medical attention. These side effects may go away during treatment as your body adjusts to the medicine. However,

check with your doctor if any of the following side effects continue or are bothersome:

More common

Dizziness or lightheadedness, especially when getting up from a lying or sitting position; fast pulse; flushing of face and neck; headache; nausea or vomiting; restlessness

Other side effects not listed above may also occur in some patients. If you notice any other effects, check with your doctor.

Revised: 10/06/93

NITRATES—Topical Systemic

Some commonly used brand names are:

In the U.S.—

Deponit[2]
Minitran[2]
Nitro-Bid[1]
Nitrodisc[2]
Nitro-Dur[2]
Nitrol[1]
Nitrong[1]
Nitrostat[1]
Transderm-Nitro[2]

In Canada—

Minitran[2]
Nitro-Bid[1]
Nitro-Dur[2]
Nitrol[1]
Nitrong[1]
Transderm-Nitro[2]

Another commonly used name for nitroglycerin is glyceryl trinitrate.

Note: For quick reference, the following nitrates are numbered to match the corresponding brand names.

This information applies to the following medicines:

1. Nitroglycerin Ointment
2. Nitroglycerin Transdermal Patches

Description

Nitrates (NYE-trates) are used to treat the symptoms of angina (chest pain). Depending on the type of dosage form and how it is taken, nitrates are used to treat angina in three ways:

- to relieve an attack that is occurring by using the medicine when the attack begins;
- to prevent attacks from occurring by using the medicine just before an attack is expected to occur; or
- to reduce the number of attacks that occur by using the medicine regularly on a long-term basis.

When applied to the skin, nitrates are used to reduce the number of angina attacks that occur. The only nitrate available for this purpose is topical nitroglycerin (nye-troe-GLI-ser-in).

Topical nitroglycerin is absorbed through the skin. It works by relaxing blood vessels and increasing the supply of blood and oxygen to the heart while reducing its work load. This helps prevent future angina attacks from occurring.

Topical nitroglycerin may also be used for other conditions as determined by your doctor.

Nitroglycerin as discussed here is available only with your doctor's prescription, in the following dosage forms:

Topical

- Ointment (U.S. and Canada)
- Transdermal (stick-on) patch (U.S. and Canada)

Before Using This Medicine

In deciding to use a medicine, the risks of taking the medicine must be weighed against the good it will do. This is a decision you and your doctor will make. For nitroglycerin applied to the skin, the following should be considered:

Allergies—Tell your doctor if you have ever had any unusual or allergic reaction to nitrates or nitrites. Also tell your health care professional if you are allergic to any other substances, such as certain foods, preservatives, or dyes.

Pregnancy—Nitrates have not been studied in pregnant women. Before taking these medicines, make sure your doctor knows if you are pregnant or if you may become pregnant.

Breast-feeding—It is not known whether this medicine passes into breast milk. Although most medicines pass into breast milk in small amounts, many of them may be used safely while breast-feeding. Mothers who are taking these medicines and who wish to breast-feed should discuss this with their doctor.

Children—Studies on these medicines have been done only in adult patients, and there is no specific information comparing use of nitrates in children with use in other age groups.

Older adults—Dizziness or lightheadedness may be more likely to occur in the elderly, who may be more sensitive to the effects of nitrates.

Other medicines—Although certain medicines should not be used together at all, in other cases two different medicines may be used together even if an interaction might occur. In these cases, your doctor may want to change the dose, or other precautions may be necessary. When you are using nitroglycerin, it is especially important that your health care professional know if you are taking any of the following:

- Antihypertensives (high blood pressure medicine) or
- Other heart medicine—May increase the effects of nitroglycerin on blood pressure

Other medical problems—The presence of other medical problems may affect the use of nitroglycerin. Make sure you tell your doctor if you have any other medical problems, especially:

- Anemia (severe)
- Glaucoma—May be worsened by nitroglycerin
- Head injury (recent) or

- Stroke (recent)—Nitroglycerin may increase pressure in the brain, which can make problems worse
- Heart attack (recent)—Nitroglycerin may lower blood pressure, which can aggravate problems associated with heart attack
- Kidney disease or
- Liver disease—Effects may be increased because of slower removal of nitroglycerin from the body
- Overactive thyroid

Proper Use of This Medicine

Use nitroglycerin exactly as directed by your doctor. It will work only if applied correctly.

The ointment and transdermal forms of nitroglycerin are used to reduce the number of angina attacks. They will not relieve an attack that has already started because they work too slowly. Check with your doctor if you need a fast-acting medicine to relieve the pain of an angina attack.

This medicine usually comes with patient instructions. Read them carefully before using.

For patients using the *ointment* form of this medicine:

- Before applying a new dose of ointment, remove any ointment remaining on the skin from a previous dose. This will allow the fresh ointment to release the nitroglycerin properly.
- This medicine comes with dose-measuring papers. Use them to measure the length of ointment squeezed from the tube and to apply the ointment to the skin. *Do not rub or massage the ointment into the skin; just spread in a thin, even layer, covering an area of the same size each time it is applied.*
- Apply the ointment to skin that has little or no hair.
- Apply each dose of ointment to a different area of skin to prevent irritation or other skin problems.
- If your doctor has ordered an occlusive dressing (airtight covering, such as kitchen plastic wrap) to be applied over this medicine, make sure you know how to apply it. Since occlusive dressings increase the amount of medicine absorbed through the skin and the possibility of side effects, use them only as directed. If you have any questions about this, check with your health care professional.

For patients using the *transdermal (stick-on patch) system:*

- Do not try to trim or cut the adhesive patch to adjust the dosage. Check with your doctor if you think the medicine is not working as it should.
- Apply the patch to a clean, dry skin area with little or no hair and free of scars, cuts, or irritation. Remove the previous patch before applying a new one.
- Apply a new patch if the first one becomes loose or falls off.
- Apply each dose to a different area of skin to prevent skin irritation or other problems.

Dosing—The dose of nitroglycerin will be different for different patients. *Follow your doctor's orders or the directions on the label.* The following information includes only the average doses of nitrates. *If your dose is different, do not change it* unless your doctor tells you to do so.

For nitroglycerin

- For angina (chest pain):
  - —For *ointment* dosage form:
    - Adults—15 to 30 milligrams (mg) (about one to two inches of ointment squeezed from tube) every six to eight hours.
    - Children—Use and dose must be determined by your doctor.
  - —For *transdermal system (skin patch)* dosage form:
    - Adults—Apply one transdermal dosage system (skin patch) to intact skin once a day. The patch is usually left on for 12 to 14 hours a day and then taken off. Follow your doctor's instructions for when to put on and take off the skin patch.
    - Children—Use and dose must be determined by your doctor.

Missed dose—

- For patients using the *ointment* form of this medicine: If you miss a dose of this medicine, apply it as soon as possible unless the next scheduled dose is within 2 hours. Then go back to your regular dosing schedule. Do not increase the amount used.
- For patients using the *transdermal (stick-on patch) system*: If you miss a dose of this medicine, apply it as soon as possible. Then go back to your regular dosing schedule.

Storage—

- To store the *ointment* form of this medicine:
  - —Keep out of the reach of children.
  - —Store the tube of nitroglycerin ointment in a cool place and keep it tightly closed.
  - —Do not keep outdated medicine or medicine no longer needed. Be sure that any discarded medicine is out of the reach of children.
- To store the *transdermal (stick-on patch) system*:
  - —Keep out of the reach of children.
  - —Store away from heat and direct light.
  - —Do not store in the bathroom, near the kitchen sink, or in other damp places. Heat or moisture may cause the medicine to break down.
  - —Do not keep outdated medicine or medicine no longer needed. Be sure that any discarded medicine is out of the reach of children.

Precautions While Using This Medicine

If you have been using nitroglycerin regularly for several weeks or more, do not suddenly stop using it. Stopping suddenly may bring on attacks of angina. Check with your doctor for the best way to reduce gradually the amount you are using before stopping completely.

Dizziness, lightheadedness, or faintness may occur, especially when you get up quickly from a lying or sitting position. Getting up slowly may help. If you feel dizzy, sit or lie down.

The dizziness, lightheadedness, or fainting is also more likely to occur if you drink alcohol, stand for long periods of time, exercise, or if the weather is hot. *While you are taking this medicine, be careful to limit the amount of alcohol you drink. Also, use extra care during exercise or hot weather or if you must stand for long periods of time.*

After using a dose of this medicine you may get a headache that lasts for a short time. This is a common side effect, which should become less noticeable after you have used the medicine for a while. If this effect continues, or if the headaches are severe, check with your doctor.

Side Effects of This Medicine

Along with its needed effects, a medicine may cause some unwanted effects. Although not all of these side effects may occur, if they do occur they may need medical attention.

Check with your doctor as soon as possible if any of the following side effects occur:

Rare

Blurred vision; dryness of mouth; headache (severe or prolonged)

Signs and symptoms of overdose (in the order in which they may occur)

Bluish-colored lips, fingernails, or palms of hands; dizziness (extreme) or fainting; feeling of extreme pressure in head; shortness of breath; unusual tiredness or weakness; weak and fast heartbeat; fever; convulsions (seizures)

Other side effects may occur that usually do not need medical attention. These side effects may go away during treatment as your body adjusts to the medicine. However, check with your doctor if any of the following side effects continue or are bothersome:

More common

Dizziness or lightheadedness, especially when getting up from a lying or sitting position; fast pulse; flushing of face and neck; headache; nausea or vomiting; restlessness

Less common

Sore, reddened skin

Other side effects not listed above may also occur in some patients. If you notice any other effects, check with your doctor.

Revised: 10/06/93
Interim revision: 08/19/97

NITROFURANTOIN Systemic

Some commonly used brand names are:

In the U.S.—

Furadantin, Furalan, Furatoin, Macrobid, Macrodantin, Nitrofuracot

Generic name product may also be available.

In Canada—

Apo-Nitrofurantoin, Macrodantin

Description

Nitrofurantoin (nye-troe-fyoor-AN-toyn) belongs to the family of medicines called anti-infectives. It is used to treat infections of the urinary tract. It may also be used for other conditions as determined by your doctor.

Nitrofurantoin is available only with your doctor's prescription, in the following dosage forms:

Oral

- Capsules (U.S. and Canada)
- Extended-release Capsules (U.S.)
- Oral Suspension (U.S.)
- Tablets (U.S. and Canada)

Before Using This Medicine

In deciding to use a medicine, the risks of taking the medicine must be weighed against the good it will do. This is a decision you and your doctor will make. For nitrofurantoin, the following should be considered:

Allergies—Tell your doctor if you have ever had any unusual or allergic reaction to nitrofurantoin or to any related medicines such as furazolidone (e.g., Furoxone) or nitrofurazone (e.g., Furacin). Also tell your health care professional if you are allergic to any other substances, such as foods, preservatives, or dyes.

Pregnancy—Nitrofurantoin should not be used if you are within a week or 2 of your delivery date or during labor and delivery. It may cause problems in the infant.

Breast-feeding—Nitrofurantoin passes into the breast milk in small amounts and may cause problems in nursing babies, especially those with glucose-6-phosphate dehydrogenase (G6PD) deficiency.

Children—Infants up to 1 month of age should not be given this medicine because they are especially sensitive to the effects of nitrofurantoin.

Older adults—Elderly people may be more sensitive to the effects of nitrofurantoin. This may increase the chance of side effects during treatment.

Other medicines—Although certain medicines should not be used together at all, in other cases two different medicines may be used together even if an interaction might occur. In these cases, your doctor may want to change the dose, or other precautions may be necessary. When you are taking nitrofurantoin, it is especially important that your health care professional know if you are taking any of the following:

- Acetohydroxamic acid (e.g., Lithostat) or
- Antidiabetics, oral (diabetes medicine you take by mouth) or
- Dapsone or
- Furazolidone (e.g., Furoxone) or
- Methyldopa (e.g., Aldomet) or

- Primaquine or
- Procainamide (e.g., Pronestyl) or
- Quinidine (e.g., Quinidex) or
- Sulfonamides (sulfa medicine) or
- Sulfoxone (e.g., Diasone) or
- Vitamin K (e.g., AquaMEPHYTON, Synkayvite)—Patients who take nitrofurantoin with any of these medicines may have an increase in side effects affecting the blood
- Carbamazepine (e.g., Tegretol) or
- Chloroquine (e.g., Aralen) or
- Cisplatin (e.g., Platinol) or
- Cytarabine (e.g., Cytosar-U) or
- Diphtheria, tetanus, and pertussis (DTP) vaccine or
- Disulfiram (e.g., Antabuse) or
- Ethotoin (e.g., Peganone) or
- Hydroxychloroquine (e.g., Plaquenil) or
- Lindane, topical (e.g., Kwell) or
- Lithium (e.g., Lithane) or
- Mephenytoin (e.g., Mesantoin) or
- Mexiletine (e.g., Mexitil) or
- Other anti-infectives by mouth or by injection (medicine for infection) or
- Pemoline (e.g., Cylert) or
- Phenytoin (e.g., Dilantin) or
- Pyridoxine (e.g., Hexa-Betalin) (with long-term, high-dose use) or
- Vincristine (e.g., Oncovin)—Patients who take nitrofurantoin with any of these medicines, or who have received a DTP vaccine within the last 30 days or are going to receive a DTP may have an increase in side effects affecting the nervous system
- Probenecid (e.g., Benemid) or
- Sulfinpyrazone (e.g., Anturane)—Patients who take nitrofurantoin with any of these medicines may have an increase in side effects
- Quinine (e.g., Quinamm)—Patients who take nitrofurantoin with quinine may have an increase in side effects affecting the blood and the nervous system

Other medical problems—The presence of other medical problems may affect the use of nitrofurantoin. Make sure you tell your doctor if you have any other medical problems, especially:

- Glucose-6-phosphate dehydrogenase (G6PD) deficiency—Nitrofurantoin may cause anemia in patients with G6PD deficiency
- Kidney disease (other than infection)—The chance of side effects of this medicine may be increased and the medicine may be less effective in patients with kidney disease
- Lung disease or
- Nerve damage—Patients with lung disease or nerve damage may have an increase in side effects when they take nitrofurantoin

Proper Use of This Medicine

Do not give this medicine to infants up to 1 month of age.

Nitrofurantoin is best taken with food or milk. This may lessen stomach upset and help your body absorb the medicine better.

For patients taking the *oral liquid form of this medicine:*

- Shake the oral liquid forcefully before each dose to help make it pour more smoothly and to be sure the medicine is evenly mixed.
- Use a specially marked measuring spoon or other device to measure each dose accurately. The average household teaspoon may not hold the right amount of liquid.
- Nitrofurantoin may be mixed with water, milk, fruit juices, or infants' formulas. If it is mixed with other liquids, take the medicine immediately after mixing. Be sure to drink all the liquid in order to get the full dose of medicine.

For patients taking the *extended-release capsule* form of this medicine:

- Swallow the capsules whole.
- Do not open, crush, or chew the capsules before swallowing them.

To help clear up your infection completely, *keep taking this medicine for the full time of treatment,* even if you begin to feel better after a few days. *Do not miss any doses.*

Dosing—The dose of nitrofurantoin will be different for different patients. *Follow your doctor's orders or the directions on the label.* The following information includes only the average doses of nitrofurantoin. *If your dose is different, do not change it* unless your doctor tells you to do so.

- For the *capsule, oral suspension, and tablet* dosage forms:
  —Adults and adolescents: 50 to 100 mg every six hours.

  —Children 1 month of age and older: Dose is based on body weight and will be determined by your doctor.

  —Children up to 1 month of age: Use is not recommended.
- For the *extended-release capsule* dosage form:
  —Adults and children 12 years of age and older: 100 mg every twelve hours for seven days.

  —Children up to 12 years of age: Dose must be determined by the doctor.

Missed dose—If you do miss a dose of this medicine, take it as soon as possible. However, if it is almost time for your next dose, skip the next dose and go back to your regular dosing schedule. Do not double doses.

Storage—To store this medicine:

- Keep out of the reach of children.
- Store away from heat and direct light.
- Do not store the capsule or tablet form of this medicine in the bathroom, near the kitchen sink, or in other damp places. Heat or moisture may cause the medicine to break down.
- Keep the oral liquid form of this medicine from freezing.
- Do not keep outdated medicine or medicine no longer needed. Be sure that any discarded medicine is out of the reach of children.

Precautions While Using This Medicine

It is important that your doctor check your progress at regular visits if you will be taking this medicine for a long time.

If your symptoms do not improve within a few days, or if they become worse, check with your doctor.

For *diabetic patients:*

- *This medicine may cause false test results with some urine sugar tests.* Check with your doctor before changing your diet or the dosage of your diabetes medicine.

Side Effects of This Medicine

Along with its needed effects, a medicine may cause some unwanted effects. Although not all of these side effects may occur, if they do occur they may need medical attention.

Check with your doctor immediately if any of the following side effects occur:

More common
Chest pain; chills; cough; fever; troubled breathing

Less common
Dizziness; drowsiness; headache; numbness, tingling, or burning of face or mouth; sore throat and fever; unusual muscle weakness; unusual tiredness or weakness

Rare
Itching; joint pain; pale skin; skin rash; yellow eyes or skin

Other side effects may occur that usually do not need medical attention. These side effects may go away during treatment as your body adjusts to the medicine. However, check with your doctor if any of the following side effects continue or are bothersome:

More common
Abdominal or stomach pain or upset; diarrhea; loss of appetite; nausea or vomiting

This medicine may cause the urine to become rust-yellow to brown. This side effect does not require medical attention.

Other side effects not listed above may also occur in some patients. If you notice any other effects, check with your doctor.

Revised: 01/19/93

NORFLOXACIN Ophthalmic

Some commonly used brand names are:

In the U.S.—
Chibroxin

In Canada—
Noroxin

Description

Norfloxacin (nor-FLOX-a-sin) is an antibiotic. The ophthalmic preparation is used to treat infections of the eye.

Norfloxacin is available only with your doctor's prescription, in the following dosage form:

Ophthalmic
- Ophthalmic solution (eye drops) (U.S. and Canada)

Before Using This Medicine

In deciding to use a medicine, the risks of taking the medicine must be weighed against the good it will do. This is a decision you and your doctor will make. For ophthalmic norfloxacin, the following should be considered:

Allergies—Tell your doctor if you have ever had any unusual or allergic reaction to norfloxacin or to any related medicines, such as cinoxacin (e.g., Cinobac), ciprofloxacin (e.g., Cipro or Ciloxan), enoxacin (e.g., Penetrax), lomefloxacin (e.g., Maxaquin), nalidixic acid (e.g., NegGram), or ofloxacin (e.g., Floxin or Ocuflox). Also tell your health care professional if you are allergic to any other substances, such as foods, preservatives, or dyes.

Pregnancy—Studies have not been done in humans. However, norfloxacin taken by mouth can cause bone problems in young animals. Since it is not known whether ophthalmic norfloxacin can cause bone problems in infants, use is not recommended during pregnancy.

Breast-feeding—It is not known whether ophthalmic norfloxacin passes into the breast milk. Low doses of norfloxacin taken by mouth do not pass into breast milk, but other related medicines do. Also, norfloxacin taken by mouth can cause bone problems in young animals. Since it is not known whether ophthalmic norfloxacin can cause bone problems in infants, use is not recommended in nursing mothers.

Children—Use is not recommended in infants and children up to 1 year of age. Norfloxacin taken by mouth has been shown to cause bone problems in young animals. It is not known whether ophthalmic norfloxacin can cause bone problems in infants. In children 1 year of age and older, this medicine is not expected to cause different side effects or problems than it does in adults.

Older adults—Many medicines have not been studied specifically in older people. Therefore, it may not be known whether they work exactly the same way they do in younger adults. Although there is no specific information comparing use of ophthalmic norfloxacin in the elderly with use in other age groups, this medicine is not expected to cause different side effects or problems in older people than it does in younger adults.

Other medicines—Although certain medicines should not be used together at all, in other cases two different medicines may be used together even if an interaction might occur. In these cases, your doctor may want to change the dose, or other precautions may be necessary. Tell your

health care professional if you are taking or using any prescription or nonprescription (over -the-counter [OTC]) medicine.

Proper Use of This Medicine

To use:

- First, wash your hands. Tilt the head back and with the index finger of one hand, press gently on the skin just beneath the lower eyelid and pull the lower eyelid away from the eye to make a space. Drop the medicine into this space. Let go of the eyelid and gently close the eyes. Do not blink. Keep the eyes closed for 1 or 2 minutes, to allow the medicine to come into contact with the infection.
- If you think you did not get the drop of medicine into your eye properly, use another drop.
- To keep the medicine as germ-free as possible, do not touch the applicator tip to any surface (including the eye). Also, keep the container tightly closed.

Dosing—The dose of ophthalmic norfloxacin will be different for different patients. *Follow your doctor's orders or the directions on the label.* The following information includes only the average doses of ophthalmic norfloxacin. *If your dose is different, do not change it* unless your doctor tells you to do so:

- For infants and children up to 1 year of age: Use is not recommended.
- For adults and children 1 year of age and over: Place 1 drop in each eye four times a day for 7 days.

To help clear up your infection completely, *keep using this medicine for the full time of treatment,* even if your symptoms begin to clear up after a few days. If you stop using this medicine too soon, your symptoms may return. *Do not miss any doses.*

Missed dose—If you do miss a dose of this medicine, apply it as soon as possible. However, if it is almost time for your next dose, skip the missed dose and go back to your regular dosing schedule.

Storage—To store this medicine:

- Keep out of the reach of children.
- Store away from heat and direct light.
- Keep the medicine from freezing.
- Do not keep outdated medicine or medicine no longer needed. Be sure that any discarded medicine is out of the reach of children.

Precautions While Using This Medicine

If your symptoms do not improve within a few days, or if they become worse, check with your doctor.

This medicine may cause your eyes to become more sensitive to light than they are normally. Wearing sunglasses and avoiding too much exposure to bright light may help lessen the discomfort.

Side Effects of This Medicine

Along with its needed effects, a medicine may cause some unwanted effects. Although not all of these side effects may occur, if they do occur they may need medical attention.

Check with your doctor immediately if any of the following side effects occur:

Rare

Skin rash or other sign of allergic reaction

Other side effects may occur that usually do not need medical attention. These side effects may go away during treatment as your body adjusts to the medicine. However, check with your doctor if any of the following side effects continue or are bothersome:

More common

Burning or other eye discomfort

Less common

Bitter taste following use in the eye; increased sensitivity of eye to light; redness of the lining of the eyelids; swelling of the membrane covering the white part of the eye

Other side effects not listed above may also occur in some patients. If you notice any other effects, check with your doctor.

Revised: 12/22/93

NYSTATIN Oral

Some commonly used brand names are:

In the U.S.—

Mycostatin
Nilstat
Nystex

Generic name product may also be available.

In Canada—

Mycostatin
Nadostine
Nilstat
PMS Nystatin

Description

Nystatin (nye-STAT-in) belongs to the group of medicines called antifungals. The dry powder, lozenge (pastille), and liquid forms of this medicine are used to treat fungus infections in the mouth.

Nystatin is available only with your doctor's prescription, in the following dosage forms:

Oral

- Lozenges (Pastilles) (U.S.)
- Oral suspension (U.S. and Canada)
- Powder for oral suspension (U.S. and Canada)
- Tablets (U.S. and Canada)

Before Using This Medicine

In deciding to use a medicine, the risks of taking the medicine must be weighed against the good it will do. This is

a decision you and your doctor will make. For nystatin, the following should be considered:

Allergies—Tell your doctor if you have ever had any unusual or allergic reaction to nystatin. Also tell your health care professional if you are allergic to any other substances, such as foods, preservatives, or dyes.

Pregnancy—Studies in humans have not shown that oral nystatin causes birth defects or other problems.

Breast-feeding—Oral nystatin has not been reported to cause problems in nursing babies.

Children—This medicine has been tested in children and has not been reported to cause different side effects or problems in children than it does in adults. However, since children up to 5 years of age may be too young to use the lozenges (pastilles) or tablets safely, the oral suspension dosage form is best for this age group.

Older adults—Many medicines have not been studied specifically in older people. Therefore, it may not be known whether they work exactly the same way they do in younger adults or if they cause different side effects or problems in older people. There is no specific information comparing use of oral nystatin in the elderly with use in other age groups.

Proper Use of This Medicine

For patients taking the *dry powder form of nystatin:*

- Add about 1/8 teaspoonful of dry powder to about 4 ounces of water immediately before taking. Stir well.
- After it is mixed, take this medicine by dividing the whole amount (4 ounces) into several portions. Hold each portion of the medicine in your mouth or swish it around in your mouth for as long as possible, gargle, and swallow. Be sure to use all the liquid to get the full dose of medicine.

For patients taking the *lozenge (pastille) form of nystatin:*

- Nystatin lozenges (pastilles) should be held in the mouth and allowed to dissolve slowly and completely. This may take 15 to 30 minutes. Also, the saliva should be swallowed during this time. *Do not chew or swallow the lozenges whole.*
- *Do not give nystatin lozenges (pastilles) to infants or children up to 5 years of age.* They may be too young to use the lozenges safely.

For patients taking the *oral liquid form of nystatin:*

- This medicine is to be taken by mouth even if it comes in a dropper bottle. If it does come in a dropper bottle, use the specially marked dropper to measure each dose accurately.
- Take this medicine by placing one-half of the dose in each side of your mouth. Hold the medicine in your mouth or swish it around in your mouth for as long as possible, then gargle and swallow.

Patients with full or partial dentures may need to soak their dentures nightly in nystatin for oral suspension to eliminate the fungus from the dentures. In rare cases when this does not eliminate the fungus, it may be necessary to have new dentures made.

To help clear up your infection completely, *keep taking this medicine for the full time of treatment,* even if your condition has improved. *Do not miss any doses.*

Dosing—The dose of nystatin will be different for different patients. *Follow your doctor's orders or the directions on the label.* The following information includes only the average doses of nystatin. *If your dose is different, do not change it* unless your doctor tells you to do so.

The number of lozenges, tablets, or milliliters (mL) of suspension that you take depends on the strength of the medicine. Also, *the number of doses you take each day, the time allowed between doses, and the length of time you take the medicine depend on the medical problem for which you are taking nystatin.*

- For the *lozenge (pastille) and tablet* dosage forms:
  - —Adults and children 5 years of age and older: 1 or 2 lozenges or tablets three to five times a day for up to fourteen days.
  - —Children up to 5 years of age: Children this young may not be able to use the lozenges or tablets safely. The oral suspension is better for this age group.
- For the *suspension* dosage form:
  - —Adults and children 5 years of age and older: 4 to 6 milliliters (mL) (about 1 teaspoonful) four times a day.
  - —For older infants: 2 mL four times a day.
  - —For premature and low-birth-weight infants: 1 mL four times a day.

Missed dose—If you do miss a dose of this medicine, take it as soon as possible. However, if it is almost time for your next dose, skip the missed dose and go back to your regular dosing schedule. Do not double doses.

Storage—To store this medicine:

- Keep out of the reach of children.
- Store away from heat and direct light.
- Do not store the tablet or dry powder form of this medicine in the bathroom, near the kitchen sink, or in other damp places. Heat or moisture may cause the medicine to break down.
- Store the lozenge (pastille) form in the refrigerator. Heat will cause this medicine to break down.
- Keep the oral liquid form of this medicine from freezing.
- Do not keep outdated medicine or medicine no longer needed. Be sure that any discarded medicine is out of the reach of children.

Side Effects of This Medicine

Along with its needed effects, a medicine may cause some unwanted effects. The following side effects may go away during treatment as your body adjusts to the medicine. However, check with your doctor if any of the following side effects continue or are bothersome:

Less common

Diarrhea; nausea or vomiting; stomach pain

Other side effects not listed above may also occur in some patients. If you notice any other effects, check with your doctor.

Additional Information

Once a medicine has been approved for marketing for a certain use, experience may show that it is also useful for other medical problems. Although this use is not included in product labeling, nystatin is used in certain patients with the following medical condition:

- Candidiasis, oral (fungus infection of the mouth) (prevention)

Other than the above information, there is no additional information relating to proper use, precautions, or side effects for this use.

Revised: 01/19/93

NYSTATIN Topical

Some commonly used brand names are:

In the U.S.—

Mycostatin
Nilstat
Nystex

Generic name product may also be available.

In Canada—

Mycostatin
Nadostine
Nilstat
Nyaderm

Description

Nystatin (nye-STAT-in) belongs to the group of medicines called antifungals. Topical nystatin is used to treat some types of fungus infections.

Nystatin is available only with your doctor's prescription, in the following dosage forms:

Topical

- Cream (U.S. and Canada)
- Ointment (U.S. and Canada)
- Topical powder (U.S. and Canada)

Before Using This Medicine

In deciding to use a medicine, the risks of using the medicine must be weighed against the good it will do. This is a decision you and your doctor will make. For nystatin, the following should be considered:

Allergies—Tell your doctor if you have ever had any unusual or allergic reaction to nystatin. Also tell your health care professional if you are allergic to any other substances, such as preservatives or dyes.

Pregnancy—Nystatin topical preparations have not been shown to cause birth defects or other problems in humans.

Breast-feeding—It is not known whether nystatin passes into the breast milk. Although most medicines pass into breast milk in small amounts, many of them may be used safely while breast-feeding. Mothers who are using this medicine and who wish to breast-feed should discuss this with their doctor.

Children—Although there is no specific information comparing use of topical nystatin in children with use in other age groups, this medicine is not expected to cause different side effects or problems in children than it does in adults.

Older adults—Many medicines have not been studied specifically in older people. Therefore, it may not be known whether they work exactly the same way they do in younger adults or if they cause different side effects or problems in older people. There is no specific information comparing use of topical nystatin in the elderly with use in other age groups.

Other medicines—Although certain medicines should not be used together at all, in other cases two different medicines may be used together even if an interaction might occur. In these cases, your doctor may want to change the dose, or other precautions may be necessary. Tell your health care professional if you are using any other topical prescription or nonprescription (over-the-counter [OTC]) medicine that is to be applied to the same area of the skin.

Proper Use of This Medicine

Topical nystatin should not be used in the eyes.

Apply enough nystatin to cover the affected area.

For patients using the *powder form* of this medicine on the feet:

- Sprinkle the powder between the toes, on the feet, and in socks and shoes.

The use of any kind of occlusive dressing (airtight covering, such as kitchen plastic wrap) over this medicine may increase the chance of irritation. Therefore, *do not bandage, wrap, or apply any occlusive dressing over this medicine* unless directed to do so by your doctor. When using this medicine on the diaper area of children, *avoid tight-fitting diapers and plastic pants.*

To help clear up your infection completely, *keep using this medicine for the full time of treatment,* even if your condition has improved. *Do not miss any doses.*

Dosing—The dose of topical nystatin will be different for different patients. *Follow your doctor's orders or the directions on the label.* The following information includes only the average dose of topical nystatin. *If your dose is different, do not change it* unless your doctor tells you to do so.

- For *topical* dosage forms (cream, ointment, or powder):
  —For fungus infections:
    - Adults and children—Apply to the affected area(s) of the skin two or three times a day.

Missed dose—If you miss a dose of this medicine, apply it as soon as possible. Then go back to your regular dosing schedule.

Storage—To store this medicine:

- Keep out of the reach of children.

- Store away from heat and direct light.
- Do not store the powder form of this medicine in the bathroom, near the kitchen sink, or in other damp places. Heat or moisture may cause the medicine to break down.
- Keep the cream and ointment forms of this medicine from freezing.
- Do not keep outdated medicine or medicine no longer needed. Be sure that any discarded medicine is out of the reach of children.

Side Effects of This Medicine

Along with its needed effects, a medicine may cause some unwanted effects. Although not all of these side effects may occur, if they do occur they may need medical attention.

Check with your doctor as soon as possible if the following side effect occurs:

Skin irritation not present before use of this medicine

Other side effects not listed above may also occur in some patients. If you notice any other effects, check with your doctor.

Revised: 07/25/94

NYSTATIN Vaginal

Some commonly used brand names are:

In the U.S.—

Mycostatin
Nilstat

Generic name product may also be available.

In Canada—

Mycostatin
Nadostine
Nilstat
Nyaderm

Description

Nystatin (nye-STAT-in) belongs to the group of medicines called antifungals. Vaginal nystatin is used to treat fungus infections of the vagina. Nystatin vaginal cream or tablets may also be used for other problems as determined by your doctor.

Nystatin is available only with your doctor's prescription, in the following dosage forms:

Vaginal
- Cream (Canada)
- Tablets (U.S. and Canada)

Before Using This Medicine

In deciding to use a medicine, the risks of taking the medicine must be weighed against the good it will do. This is a decision you and your doctor will make. For nystatin, the following should be considered:

Allergies—Tell your doctor if you have ever had any unusual or allergic reaction to nystatin. Also tell your health care professional if you are allergic to any other substances, such as foods, preservatives, or dyes.

Pregnancy—Studies have not been done in animals. However, nystatin vaginal tablets have not been shown to cause birth defects or other problems in humans.

Breast-feeding—It is not known whether nystatin passes into breast milk. However, this medicine has not been reported to cause problems in nursing babies.

Children—Studies on this medicine have been done only in adults, and there is no specific information comparing use of vaginal nystatin in children with use in other age groups.

Older adults—Many medicines have not been studied specifically in older people. Therefore, it may not be known whether they work exactly the same way they do in younger adults or if they cause different side effects or problems in older people. There is no specific information comparing the use of vaginal nystatin in the elderly with use in other age groups.

Other medicines—Although certain medicines should not be used together at all, in other cases two different medicines may be used together even if an interaction might occur. In these cases, your doctor may want to change the dose, or other precautions may be necessary. Tell your health care professional if you are using any other vaginal prescription or nonprescription (over-the-counter [OTC]) medicine.

Proper Use of This Medicine

Nystatin usually comes with patient directions. Read them carefully before using this medicine.

This medicine is usually inserted into the vagina with an applicator. However, if you are pregnant, check with your doctor before using the applicator to insert the vaginal tablet.

To help clear up your infection completely, *keep using this medicine for the full time of treatment,* even if your condition has improved. Also, keep using this medicine even if you begin to menstruate during the time of treatment. *Do not miss any doses.*

Dosing—The dose of nystatin will be different for different patients. *Follow your doctor's orders or the directions on the label.* The following information includes only the average doses of nystatin. *If your dose is different, do not change it* unless your doctor tells you to do so.

- For treating fungus (yeast) infections:
  - —For *vaginal cream* dosage form:
    - Adults and teenagers—One 100,000-Unit applicatorful inserted into the vagina one or two times a day for two weeks. Or, your doctor may want you to insert one 500,000-Unit applicatorful into the vagina once a day.

• Children—Dose must be determined by your doctor.

—For *vaginal tablet* dosage form:

• Adults and teenagers—One 100,000-unit tablet inserted into the vagina one or two times a day for two weeks.

• Children—Dose must be determined by your doctor.

Missed dose—If you do miss a dose of this medicine, insert it as soon as possible. However, if it is almost time for your next dose, skip the missed dose and go back to your regular dosing schedule.

Storage—To store this medicine:

- Keep out of the reach of children.
- Store away from heat and direct light.
- Do not store in the bathroom, near the kitchen sink, or in other damp places. Heat or moisture may cause the medicine to break down.
- Do not keep outdated medicine or medicine no longer needed. Be sure that any discarded medicine is out of the reach of children.

Precautions While Using This Medicine

To help cure the infection and to help prevent reinfection, good health habits are required.

- Wear cotton panties (or panties or pantyhose with cotton crotches) instead of synthetic (for example, nylon, rayon) underclothes.
- Wear freshly laundered underclothes.

If you have any questions about this, check with your health care professional.

If you have any questions about douching or intercourse during the time of treatment with nystatin, check with your doctor.

Since there may be some vaginal drainage while you are using this medicine, a sanitary napkin may be worn to protect your clothing.

Side Effects of This Medicine

Along with its needed effects, a medicine may cause some unwanted effects. Although not all of these side effects may occur, if they do occur they may need medical attention.

Check with your doctor as soon as possible if the following side effect occurs:

Rare

Vaginal irritation not present before use of this medicine

Other side effects not listed above may also occur in some patients. If you notice any other effects, check with your doctor.

Revised: 09/08/92
Interim revision: 06/30/94

NYSTATIN AND TRIAMCINOLONE Topical†

Some commonly used brand names are:

In the U.S.—

Dermacomb	Myco-Triacet II
Myco II	Mykacet
Mycobiotic II	Mykacet II
Mycogen II	Mytrex
Mycolog II	Tristatin II

Generic name product may also be available.

†Not commercially available in Canada.

Description

Nystatin (nye-STAT-in) and triamcinolone (trye-am-SIN-oh-lone) combination contains an antifungal and a corticosteroid (kor-ti-co-STI-roid) (cortisone-like medicine).

Antifungals are used to treat infections caused by a fungus. They work by killing the fungus or preventing its growth. This medicine will not work for other kinds of infections. Corticosteroids belong to the family of medicines called steroids. They are used to help relieve redness, swelling, itching, and other discomfort of many skin problems.

This medicine is used to treat certain fungus infections, such as Candida (Monilia), and to help relieve the discomfort of the infection.

Topical corticosteroids may rarely cause some serious side effects. Some of the side effects may be more likely to occur in children. *Before using this medicine in children, be sure to talk to your doctor about these problems, as well as the good this medicine may do.*

Nystatin and triamcinolone combination is available only with your doctor's prescription, in the following dosage forms:

Topical

- Cream (U.S.)
- Ointment (U.S.)

Before Using This Medicine

In deciding to use a medicine, the risks of using the medicine must be weighed against the good it will do. This is a decision you and your doctor will make. For nystatin and triamcinolone combination, the following should be considered:

Allergies—Tell your doctor if you have ever had any unusual or allergic reaction to nystatin or triamcinolone. Also tell your health care professional if you are allergic to any other substances, such as preservatives or dyes.

Pregnancy—Nystatin and triamcinolone combination has not been studied in pregnant women. However, studies in animals have shown that corticosteroids given by mouth or by injection may cause birth defects, even at low doses. Also, some of the stronger corticosteroids have been shown to cause birth defects when applied to the skin of animals. Therefore, this medicine should not be used on large areas of skin, in large amounts, or for a long time in pregnant patients. Before using this medicine, make sure your doctor knows if you are pregnant or if you may become pregnant.

Breast-feeding—It is not known whether nystatin or triamcinolone passes into the breast milk. Although this combination medicine has not been reported to cause problems in humans, topical corticosteroids may be absorbed into the body. Corticosteroids that are given by mouth or by injection do pass into the breast milk and may cause unwanted effects, such as interfering with nursing babies' growth.

Children—Children may be especially sensitive to the effects of topical nystatin and triamcinolone combination. This may increase the chance of side effects during treatment. Therefore, it is especially important that you discuss with your child's doctor the good that this medicine may do as well as the risks of using it.

Older adults—Many medicines have not been studied specifically in older people. Therefore, it may not be known whether they work exactly the same way they do in younger adults. Although there is no specific information comparing use of topical nystatin and triamcinolone combination in the elderly with use in other age groups, this medicine is not expected to cause different side effects or problems in older people than it does in younger adults.

Other medicines—Although certain medicines should not be used together at all, in other cases two different medicines may be used together even if an interaction might occur. In these cases, your doctor may want to change the dose, or other precautions may be necessary. When you are using nystatin and triamcinolone combination, it is especially important that your health care professional know if you are using any other prescription or nonprescription (over-the-counter [OTC]) medicine.

Other medical problems—The presence of other medical problems may affect the use of nystatin and triamcinolone combination. Make sure you tell your doctor if you have any other medical problems, especially:

- Herpes
- Vaccinia (cowpox)
- Varicella (chickenpox)
- Other virus infections of the skin—Triamcinolone may speed up the spread of virus infections
- Tuberculosis (TB) of the skin—Triamcinolone may make a TB infection worse

Proper Use of This Medicine

Do not use this medicine in or around the eyes.

Check with your doctor before using this medicine on any other skin problems. It should not be used on bacterial or virus infections. Also, it should only be used on certain fungus infections of the skin.

Apply a thin layer of this medicine to the affected area and rub in gently and thoroughly.

The use of any kind of airtight covering over this medicine may increase absorption of the medicine and the chance of irritation and other side effects. Therefore, *do not bandage, wrap, or apply any airtight covering or other occlusive dressing (for example, kitchen plastic wrap) over this medicine* unless directed to do so by your doctor. Also, wear loose-fitting clothing when using this medicine on the groin area. When using this medicine on the diaper area of children, *avoid tight-fitting diapers and plastic pants.*

To help clear up your infection completely, *keep using this medicine for the full time of treatment,* even if your symptoms have disappeared. *Do not miss any doses.* However, *do not use this medicine more often or for a longer time than your doctor ordered.* To do so may increase absorption through your skin and the chance of side effects. In addition, too much use, especially on thin skin areas (for example, face, armpits, groin), may result in thinning of the skin and stretch marks.

Dosing—The dose of topical nystatin and triamcinolone combination will be different for different patients. *Follow your doctor's orders or the directions on the label.* The following information includes only the average doses of topical nystatin and triamcinolone combination. *If your dose is different, do not change it* unless your doctor tells you to do so.

- For fungus infections:
  - —For cream dosage form:
    - Adults and children—Apply to the affected area(s) of the skin two times a day, morning and evening
  - —For ointment dosage form:
    - Adults and children—Apply to the affected area(s) of the skin two or three times a day.

Missed dose—If you miss a dose of this medicine, apply it as soon as possible. However, if it is almost time for your next dose, skip the missed dose and go back to your regular dosing schedule.

Storage—To store this medicine:

- Keep out of the reach of children.
- Store away from heat and direct light.
- Keep the medicine from freezing.
- Do not keep outdated medicine or medicine no longer needed. Be sure that any discarded medicine is out of the reach of children.

Precautions While Using This Medicine

To help clear up your infection completely and to help make sure it does not return, good health habits are also required. Keep the affected area as cool and dry as possible.

If your skin problem does not improve within 2 or 3 weeks, or if it becomes worse, check with your doctor.

The corticosteroid in this medicine may be absorbed through the skin and may be more likely to cause side effects in children. Long-term use may affect growth and development as well. *Children who must use this medicine should be followed closely by their doctor.*

For diabetic patients:

- *Although rare, the corticosteroid in this medicine may cause higher blood and urine sugar levels, especially if you have severe diabetes and are using large amounts of this medicine.* Check with your doctor before changing your diet or the dosage of your diabetes medicine.

Side Effects of This Medicine

Along with its needed effects, a medicine may cause some unwanted effects. Although not all of these side effects may occur, if they do occur they may need medical attention.

Check with your doctor immediately if any of the following side effects occur:

Rare

Blistering, burning, dryness, itching, peeling, or other sign of irritation not present before use of this medicine

Additional side effects may occur if you use this medicine for a long time. Check with your doctor as soon as possible if any of the following side effects occur:

Acne or oily skin; increased hair growth, especially on the face; increased loss of hair, especially on the scalp; reddish purple lines on arms, face, legs, trunk, or groin; thinning of skin with easy bruising

Many of the above side effects are more likely to occur in children, who may absorb greater amounts of this medicine.

Other side effects not listed above may also occur in some patients. If you notice any other effects, check with your doctor.

Revised: 08/15/94

OCTREOTIDE Systemic

A commonly used brand name in the U.S. and Canada is Sandostatin.

Description

Octreotide (oak-TREE-oh-tide) is used to treat the severe diarrhea and other symptoms that occur with certain intestinal tumors. It does not cure the tumor but it helps the patient live a more normal life.

Also, this medicine is used to treat a condition called acromegaly, which is caused by too much growth hormone in the body. Too much growth hormone produced in adults causes the hands, feet, and parts of the face to become large, thick, and bulky. Other problems such as arthritis also can develop. Octreotide works by lowering the amount of of growth hormone that the body produces and helps to stop this process from continuing.

Octreotide may also be used for other medical conditions as determined by your doctor.

Octreotide is available only with your doctor's prescription, in the following dosage form:

Parenteral
- Injection (U.S. and Canada)

Before Using This Medicine

In deciding to use a medicine, the risks of using the medicine must be weighed against the good it will do. This is a decision you and your doctor will make. For octreotide, the following should be considered:

Allergies—Tell your doctor if you have ever had any unusual or allergic reaction to octreotide. Also tell your health care professional if you are allergic to any other substances, such as foods, preservatives, or dyes.

Pregnancy—Studies have not been done in humans. However, studies in rats and rabbits have not shown that octreotide causes birth defects or other problems, even when given in doses many times the human dose.

Breast-feeding—It is not known whether octreotide passes into the breast milk. However, octreotide has not been reported to cause problems in nursing babies.

Children—This medicine has been tested in a limited number of children as young as 1 month of age and has not been shown to cause different side effects or problems than it does in adults.

Older adults—This medicine has been used in persons up to 83 years of age and has not been shown to cause different side effects or problems in older people than it does in younger adults.

Other medicines—Although certain medicines should not be used together at all, in other cases two different medicines may be used together even if an interaction might occur. In these cases, your doctor may want to change the dose, or other precautions may be necessary. When you are taking octreotide, it is especially important that your health care professional know if you are taking any of the following:

- Antidiabetics, oral (diabetes medicine you take by mouth) or
- Glucagon or
- Insulin—Octreotide may cause high or low blood sugar; your doctor may need to change the dose of your diabetes medicine
- Growth hormone—Octreotide may cause high or low blood sugar; your doctor may need to change the dose of this medicine

Other medical problems—The presence of other medical problems may affect the use of octreotide. Make sure you tell your doctor if you have any other medical problems, especially:

- Diabetes mellitus (sugar diabetes)—Octreotide may cause high or low blood sugar; your doctor may need to change the dose of your diabetes medicine
- Gallbladder disease or gallstones (or history of)—This medicine may increase the chance of having gallstones
- Kidney disease (severe)—If you have this condition, octreotide may remain longer in the body; your doctor may need to change the dose of your medicine

Proper Use Of This Medicine

To control the symptoms of your medical problem, this medicine must be taken daily in evenly spaced doses as ordered by your doctor. He or she will tell you how much octreotide you need to take each day and how to divide the doses through the day. *Make sure that you understand exactly how to use this medicine.*

Octreotide is packaged in a kit containing an ampule opener, alcohol swabs, and ampules of the medicine. *Directions on how to use the medicine are in the package. Read them carefully* and ask your health care professional for additional explanation, if necessary.

Dosing—The dose of octreotide will be different for different patients. *Follow your doctor's orders or the directions on the label.* The following information includes only the average doses of octreotide. *If your dose is different, do not change it* unless your doctor tells you to do so.

- For *injection* dosage form:
  - —For treating acromegaly:
    - Adults—At first, 0.05 milligrams (mg) injected under or into the skin, two or three times a day. Then, the dose is slowly increased to 0.1 mg three times a day. Higher doses may be needed, as determined by your doctor.
  - —For treating the severe diarrhea that occurs with intestinal tumors:
    - Adults and teenagers—At first, 0.05 mg injected under the skin, one or two times a day. Then, the dose is slowly increased. Some people may need doses as high as 0.1 to 0.6 mg a day for the first two weeks. However, the dose is usually not more than 0.75 mg a day.

• Children—The dose is based on body weight and must be determined by your doctor. The usual dose is 0.001 to 0.01 mg per kilogram (kg) (0.0005 to 0.005 mg per pound) of body weight a day, injected under the skin.

Missed dose—If you miss a dose of this medicine, use it as soon as you remember it. However, if it is almost time for the next dose, skip the missed dose and go back to your regular dosing schedule. Do not double doses. Although you will not be harmed by forgetting a dose, the symptoms that you are trying to control (for example, diarrhea) may reappear. To be able to control your symptoms, your doses should be evenly spaced over a period of 24 hours. If you have any questions about this, check with your health care professional.

Storage—To store this medicine:

- Keep out of the reach of children.
- Store the ampules of octreotide in the refrigerator until they are to be used. Remove the ampule that is going to be used from the refrigerator and allow it to reach room temperature before using it. Using octreotide at room temperature will help lessen the burning sensation that some people feel when injecting octreotide. Do not use heat to warm the solution faster. Ampules may be kept at room temperature for for 14 days when they are protected from light. If the ampules are not protected from light, problems with the solution can develop much sooner.
- Do not keep outdated medicine or medicine no longer needed. Be sure that any discarded medicine and syringes are out of the reach of children.

Precautions While Using This Medicine

It is very important that your doctor check your progress at regular visits to make sure that this medicine is working properly and to check for unwanted effects.

It is very important to follow any instructions from your doctor about the careful selection and rotation of injection sites on your body. This will help prevent skin problems, such as irritation.

Side Effects of This Medicine

Along with its needed effects, a medicine may cause some unwanted effects. Although these problems are rare, patients using octreotide may develop symptoms of high blood sugar (hyperglycemia) or low blood sugar (hypoglycemia). *If any of the following symptoms of hyperglycemia or hypoglycemia occur, stop using octreotide and check with your doctor right away:*

Symptoms of hyperglycemia usually include:

Drowsiness; dry mouth; flushed, dry skin; fruit-like breath odor; increased urination; loss of appetite; stomachache, nausea, or vomiting; troubled breathing (rapid and deep); unusual thirst; unusual tiredness; weight loss (rapid)

Early symptoms of hypoglycemia include:

Anxious feeling; chills; cool pale skin; difficulty in concentrating; headache; hunger; nausea; nervousness; shakiness; sweating; unusual tiredness; weakness

Other side effects may occur that usually do not need medical attention. These side effects may go away during treatment as your body adjusts to the medicine. However, check with your doctor if any of the following side effects continue or are bothersome:

More common

Abdominal or stomach pain or discomfort; diarrhea; nausea and vomiting; pain, stinging, tingling, or burning sensation at place of injection, with redness and swelling

Less common or rare

Dizziness or lightheadedness; unusual tiredness or weakness; headache; redness or flushing of face; swelling of feet and lower legs

Other side effects not listed above may also occur in some patients. If you notice any other effects, check with your doctor.

Additional Information

Once a medicine has been approved for marketing for a certain use, experience may show that it is also useful for other medical problems. Although this use is not included in product labeling, octreotide is used in certain patients with the following medical conditions:

- Acquired immune deficiency syndrome (AIDS)–related diarrhea
- Insulin-producing tumors of the pancreas

Other than the above information, there is no additional information relating to proper use, precautions, or side effects for these uses.

Revised: 12/15/92
Interim revision: 06/30/94; 08/08/95

OFLOXACIN Ophthalmic†

A commonly used brand name in the U.S. is Ocuflox.

†Not commercially available in Canada.

Description

Ofloxacin (oh-FLOKS-a-sin) is an antibiotic used to treat bacterial infections of the eye.

Ofloxacin is available only with your doctor's prescription, in the following dosage form:

Ophthalmic

- Ophthalmic solution (eye drops) (U.S.)

Before Using This Medicine

In deciding to use a medicine, the risks of using the medicine must be weighed against the good it will do. This is

a decision you and your doctor will make. For ophthalmic ofloxacin, the following should be considered:

Allergies—Tell your doctor if you have ever had any unusual or allergic reaction to ophthalmic or systemic ofloxacin (e.g., Floxin) or any related medicines, such as cinoxacin (e.g., Cinobac), ciprofloxacin (e.g., Ciloxan or Cipro), enoxacin (e.g., Penetrax), lomefloxacin (e.g., Maxaquin), nalidixic acid (e.g., NegGram), or norfloxacin (e.g., Chibroxin or Noroxin). Also tell your health care professional if you are allergic to any other substances, such as foods, preservatives, or dyes.

Pregnancy—Ophthalmic ofloxacin has not been studied in pregnant women. However, studies in animals that were given very high doses of ofloxacin by mouth have shown that ofloxacin can cause birth defects or other problems. Before taking this medicine, make sure your doctor knows if you are pregnant or if you may become pregnant.

Breast-feeding—It is not known whether ophthalmic ofloxacin passes into breast milk. However, ofloxacin given by mouth does pass into breast milk. Although most medicines pass into breast milk in small amounts, many of them may be used safely while breast-feeding. Mothers who are using this medicine and who wish to breast-feed should discuss this with their doctor.

Children—Use is not recommended in infants up to 1 year of age. In children 1 year of age and older, this medicine is not expected to cause different side effects or problems than it does in adults.

Older adults—Many medicines have not been studied specifically in older people. Therefore, it may not be known whether they work exactly the same way they do in younger adults or if they cause different side effects or problems in older people. There is no specific information comparing use of ophthalmic ofloxacin in the elderly with use in other age groups.

Other medicines—Although certain medicines should not be used together at all, in other cases two different medicines may be used together even if an interaction might occur. In these cases, your doctor may want to change the dose, or other precautions may be necessary. Tell your health care professional if you're using any other prescription or nonprescription (over-the-counter [OTC]) medicine that is to be used in the eye.

Proper Use of This Medicine

To use:

- First, wash your hands. Tilt the head back and with the index finger of one hand, press gently on the skin just beneath the lower eyelid and pull the lower eyelid away from the eye to make a space. Drop the medicine into this space. Let go of the eyelid and gently close the eyes. Do not blink. Keep the eyes closed for 1 to 2 minutes, to allow the medicine to come into contact with the infection.
- If you think you did not get the drop of medicine into your eyes properly, use another drop.
- To keep the medicine as germ-free as possible, do not touch the applicator tip to any surface (including the eye). Also, keep the container tightly closed.

To help clear up your eye infection completely, *keep using ophthalmic ofloxacin for the full time of treatment,* even if your symptoms have disappeared. *Do not miss any doses.*

Dosing—The dose of ophthalmic ofloxacin will be different for different patients. *Follow your doctor's orders or the directions on the label.* The following information includes only the average doses of ophthalmic ofloxacin. *If your dose is different, do not change it* unless your doctor tells you to do so.

- For *ophthalmic (eye drops)* dosage form:
  - —For eye infection:
    - Adults and children 1 year of age and older—Use 1 drop in each eye every two to four hours, while you are awake, for two days. Then, use 1 drop in each eye four times a day for up to five more days.
    - Infants up to 1 year of age—Use and dose must be determined by your doctor.

Missed dose—If you miss a dose of this medicine, use it as soon as possible. However, if it is almost time for your next dose, skip the missed dose and go back to your regular dosing schedule.

Storage—To store this medicine:

- Keep out of the reach of children.
- Store away from heat and direct light.
- Keep the medicine from freezing. Do not refrigerate.
- Do not keep outdated medicine or medicine no longer needed. Be sure that any discarded medicine is out of the reach of children.

Precautions While Using This Medicine

If your eye infection does not improve within 7 days, or if it becomes worse, check with your doctor.

This medicine may cause your eyes to become more sensitive to light than they are normally. Wearing sunglasses and avoiding too much exposure to bright light may help lessen the discomfort.

Side Effects of This Medicine

Along with its needed effects, a medicine may cause some unwanted effects. Although not all of these side effects may occur, if they do occur they may need medical attention.

Check with your doctor as soon as possible if the following side effect occurs:

Rare
Dizziness

Other side effects may occur that usually do not need medical attention. These side effects may go away during treatment as your body adjusts to the medicine. However, check with your doctor if any of the following side effects continue or are bothersome:

More common
Burning of eye

Less common
Increased sensitivity of eye to light; stinging, redness, itching, tearing, or dryness of eye

Other side effects not listed above may also occur in some patients. If you notice any other effects, check with your doctor.

Developed: 12/21/93

OLSALAZINE Oral

A commonly used brand name in the U.S. and Canada is Dipentum.

Other commonly used names are azodisal sodium and sodium azodisalicylate.

Description

Olsalazine (ole-SAL-a-zeen) is used in patients who have had ulcerative colitis to prevent the condition from occurring again. It works inside the bowel by helping to reduce inflammation and other symptoms of the disease.

Olsalazine is available only with your doctor's prescription, in the following dosage form:

Oral
- Capsules (U.S. and Canada)

Before Using This Medicine

In deciding to use a medicine, the risks of taking the medicine must be weighed against the good it will do. This is a decision you and your doctor will make. For olsalazine, the following should be considered:

Allergies—Tell your doctor if you have ever had any unusual or allergic reaction to olsalazine, mesalamine, sulfasalazine, or any salicylates (for example, aspirin). Also tell your health care professional if you are allergic to any other substances, such as foods, preservatives, or dyes.

Pregnancy—Olsalazine has not been studied in pregnant women. However, studies in rats have shown that olsalazine causes birth defects and other problems at doses 5 to 20 times the human dose. Before taking this medicine, make sure your doctor knows if you are pregnant or if you may become pregnant.

Breast-feeding—It is not known whether olsalazine passes into human breast milk. However, olsalazine has been shown to cause unwanted effects, such as slowed growth, in the pups of rats given olsalazine while nursing. It may be necessary for you to take another medicine or to stop breast-feeding during treatment. Be sure you have discussed the risks and benefits of the medicine with your doctor.

Children—Studies on this medicine have been done only in adult patients, and there is no specific information comparing use of olsalazine in children with use in other age groups.

Older adults—Many medicines have not been studied specifically in older people. Therefore, it may not be known whether they work exactly the same way they do in younger adults. Although there is no specific information comparing use of olsalazine in the elderly with use in other age groups, this medicine is not expected to cause different side effects or problems in older people than it does in younger adults.

Other medicines—Although certain medicines should not be used together at all, in other cases two different medicines may be used together even if an interaction might occur. In these cases, your doctor may want to change the dose, or other precautions may be necessary. Tell your health care professional if you are using any other prescription or nonprescription (over-the-counter [OTC]) medicine.

Other medical problems—The presence of other medical problems may affect the use of olsalazine. Make sure you tell your doctor if you have any other medical problems, especially:

- Kidney disease—The use of olsalazine may cause further damage to the kidneys

Proper Use of This Medicine

Olsalazine is best taken with food, to lessen stomach upset. If stomach or intestinal problems continue or are bothersome, check with your doctor.

Keep taking this medicine for the full time of treatment, even if you begin to feel better after a few days. *Do not miss any doses.*

Dosing—The dose of olsalazine will be different for different patients. *Follow your doctor's orders or the directions on the label.* The following information includes only the average doses of olsalazine. *If your dose is different, do not change it* unless your doctor tells you to do so.

- For *oral* dosage form (capsules):
  - —To prevent ulcerative colitis from occurring again:
    - Adults and teenagers—500 milligrams (mg) two times a day.
    - Children—Use and dose must be determined by your doctor.

Missed dose—If you miss a dose of this medicine, take it as soon as possible. However, if it is almost time for your next dose, skip the missed dose and go back to your regular dosing schedule. Do not double doses.

Storage—To store this medicine:
- Keep out of the reach of children.
- Store away from heat and direct light.
- Do not store this medicine in the bathroom, near the kitchen sink, or in other damp places. Heat or moisture may cause the medicine to break down.

- Do not keep outdated medicine or medicine no longer needed. Be sure that any discarded medicine is out of the reach of children.

Precautions While Using This Medicine

It is very important that your doctor check your progress at regular visits, especially if you will be taking olsalazine for a long time.

Side Effects of This Medicine

Along with its needed effects, a medicine may cause some unwanted effects. Although not all of these side effects may occur, if they do occur they may need medical attention.

Check with your doctor as soon as possible if any of the following side effects occur:

Rare

Back or stomach pain (severe); bloody diarrhea; fast heartbeat; fever; nausea or vomiting; skin rash; swelling of the stomach; yellow eyes or skin

Other side effects may occur that usually do not need medical attention. These side effects may go away during treatment as your body adjusts to the medicine. However, check with your doctor if any of the following side effects continue or are bothersome:

More common

Abdominal or stomach pain or upset; diarrhea; loss of appetite

Less common

Aching joints and muscles; acne; anxiety or depression; dizziness or drowsiness; headache; trouble in sleeping

Other side effects not listed above may also occur in some patients. If you notice any other effects, check with your doctor.

Additional Information

Once a medicine has been approved for marketing for a certain use, experience may show that it is also useful for other medical problems. Although this use is not included in product labeling, olsalazine may be used in certain patients to treat mild or moderate ulcerative colitis.

Other than the above information, there is no additional information relating to proper use, precautions, or side effects for this use.

Revised: 03/15/95

OMEPRAZOLE Systemic

Some commonly used brand names are:

In the U.S.—
Prilosec

In Canada—
Losec

Description

Omeprazole (o-MEP-ra-zole) is used to treat certain conditions in which there is too much acid in the stomach. It is used to treat gastric and duodenal ulcers and gastroesophageal reflux disease, a condition in which the acid in the stomach washes back up into the esophagus.

Omeprazole is also used to treat Zollinger-Ellison disease, a condition in which the stomach produces too much acid.

Omeprazole works by decreasing the amount of acid produced by the stomach.

This medicine is available only with your doctor's prescription.

Oral

- Delayed-release capsules (U.S.)
- Delayed-release tablets (Canada)

Before Using This Medicine

In deciding to use a medicine, the risks of taking the medicine must be weighed against the good it will do. This is a decision you and your doctor will make. For omeprazole, the following should be considered:

Allergies—Tell your doctor if you have ever had any unusual or allergic reaction to omeprazole. Also tell your health care professional if you are allergic to any other substances, such as foods, preservatives, or dyes.

Pregnancy—Studies have not been done in humans. However, studies in animals have shown that omeprazole may cause harm to the fetus.

Breast-feeding—Omeprazole may pass into the breast milk. Since this medicine has been shown to cause unwanted effects, such as tumors and cancer in animals, it may be necessary for you to take another medicine or to stop breast-feeding during treatment. Be sure you have discussed the risks and benefits of the medicine with your doctor.

Children—There is no specific information comparing the use of omeprazole in children with use in other age groups.

Older adults—Many medicines have not been studied specifically in older people. Therefore, it may not be known whether they work exactly the same way they do in younger adults or if they cause different side effects or problems in older people. There is no specific information comparing use of omeprazole in the elderly with use in other age groups.

Other medicines—Although certain medicines should not be used together at all, in other cases two different medicines may be used together even if an interaction might occur. In these cases, your doctor may want to change the dose, or other precautions may be necessary. When you are taking omeprazole, it is especially important that your

health care professional know if you are taking any of the following:

- Anticoagulants (blood thinners) or
- Diazepam (e.g., Valium) or
- Phenytoin (e.g., Dilantin)—Use with omeprazole may cause high blood levels of these medicines, which may increase the chance of side effects

Other medical problems—The presence of other medical problems may affect the use of omeprazole. Make sure you tell your doctor if you have any other medical problems, especially:

- Liver disease or a history of liver disease—This condition may cause omeprazole to build up in the body

Proper Use of This Medicine

Take omeprazole *capsules* immediately before a meal, preferably in the morning. Omeprazole *tablets* may be taken with food or on an empty stomach.

It may take several days before this medicine begins to relieve stomach pain. To help relieve this pain, antacids may be taken with omeprazole, unless your doctor has told you not to use them.

Swallow the *capsule* form of omeprazole whole. Do not crush, break, chew, or open the capsule.

Take this medicine for the full time of treatment, even if you begin to feel better. Also, keep your appointments with your doctor for check-ups so that your doctor will be better able to tell you when to stop taking this medicine.

Dosing—The dose of omeprazole will be different for different patients. *Follow your doctor's orders or the directions on the label.* The following information includes only the average doses of omeprazole. *If your dose is different, do not change it* unless your doctor tells you to do so.

- For *oral* dosage forms (capsules, tablets):
  - —To treat gastroesophageal reflux disease:
    - Adults—20 milligrams (mg) taken once a day for four to eight weeks. Or, your doctor may tell you to take 40 mg a day for certain conditions. Also, your doctor may want you to take omeprazole for more than eight weeks for certain conditions.
    - Children—Dose must be determined by your doctor.
  - —To treat conditions in which the stomach produces too much acid:
    - Adults—60 mg taken once a day. Your doctor may change the dose as needed. Your treatment may be continued for as long as it is needed.
    - Children—Dose must be determined by your doctor.
  - —To treat duodenal ulcers:
    - Adults—20 mg taken once a day. Or, your doctor may tell you to take 40 mg a day for certain conditions.
    - Children—Dose must be determined by your doctor.
  - —To treat gastric ulcers:
    - Adults—40 mg taken once a day for four to eight weeks.
    - Children—Dose must be determined by your doctor.

Missed dose—If you miss a dose of this medicine, take it as soon as possible. However, if it is almost time for your next dose, skip the missed dose and go back to your regular dosing schedule. Do not double doses.

Storage—To store this medicine:

- Keep out of the reach of children.
- Store away from heat and direct light.
- Do not store in the bathroom, near the kitchen sink, or in other damp places. Heat or moisture may cause the medicine to break down.
- Do not keep outdated medicine or medicine no longer needed. Be sure that any discarded medicine is out of the reach of children.

Precautions While Using This Medicine

If your condition does not improve, or if it becomes worse, check with your doctor.

Side Effects of This Medicine

Along with its needed effects, a medicine may cause some unwanted effects. Although not all of these side effects may occur, if they do occur they may need medical attention.

Check with your doctor as soon as possible if any of the following side effects occur:

Rare

Bloody or cloudy urine; continuing ulcers or sores in mouth; difficult, burning, or painful urination; frequent urge to urinate; sore throat and fever; unusual bleeding or bruising; unusual tiredness or weakness

Other side effects may occur that usually do not need medical attention. These side effects may go away during treatment as your body adjusts to the medicine. However, check with your doctor if any of the following side effects continue or are bothersome:

More common

Abdominal or stomach pain

Less common

Chest pain; constipation; diarrhea or loose stools; dizziness; gas; headache; heartburn; muscle pain; nausea and vomiting; skin rash or itching; unusual drowsiness; unusual tiredness

Other side effects not listed above may also occur in some patients. If you notice any other effects, check with your doctor.

Revised: 08/05/96

ONDANSETRON Systemic

A commonly used brand name in the U.S. and Canada is Zofran.

Description

Ondansetron (on-DAN-se-tron) is used to prevent the nausea and vomiting that may occur after treatment with anticancer medicines (chemotherapy) or radiation, or after surgery.

Ondansetron is available only with your doctor's prescription, in the following dosage forms:

Oral
- Tablets (U.S. and Canada)

Parenteral
- Injection (U.S. and Canada)

Before Using This Medicine

In deciding to use a medicine, the risks of taking the medicine must be weighed against the good it will do. This is a decision you and your doctor will make. For ondansetron, the following should be considered:

Allergies—Tell your doctor if you have ever had any unusual or allergic reaction to ondansetron or granisetron. Also tell your health care professional if you are allergic to any other substances, such as foods, preservatives, or dyes.

Pregnancy—Ondansetron has not been studied in pregnant women. However, this medicine has not been shown to cause birth defects or other problems in animal studies.

Breast-feeding—It is not known whether ondansetron passes into the breast milk. Although most medicines pass into breast milk in small amounts, many of them may be used safely while breast-feeding. Mothers who are taking this medicine and who wish to breast-feed should discuss this with their doctor.

Children—This medicine has been tested in a limited number of children with cancer 4 years of age or older. In effective doses, the medicine has not been shown to cause different side effects or problems than it does in adults.

Older adults—This medicine has been tested in a limited number of cancer patients 65 years of age or older and has not been shown to cause different side effects or problems in older people than it does in younger adults.

Other medicines—Although certain medicines should not be used together at all, in other cases two different medicines may be used together even if an interaction might occur. In these cases, your doctor may want to change the dose, or other precautions may be necessary. Tell your health care professional if you are taking any other prescription or nonprescription (over-the-counter [OTC]) medicine.

Other medical problems—The presence of other medical problems may affect the use of ondansetron. Make sure you tell your doctor if you have any other medical problems, especially:

- Abdominal surgery—Use of ondansetron may cover up stomach problems
- Liver disease—Patients with liver disease may have an increased chance of side effects

Proper Use of This Medicine

If you vomit within 30 minutes after taking this medicine, take the same amount of medicine again. If vomiting continues, check with your doctor.

Dosing—The dose of ondansetron will be different for different patients. *Follow your doctor's orders or the directions on the label.* The following information includes only average doses of ondansetron. *If your dose is different, do not change it* unless your doctor tells you to do so.

- For *oral* dosage form (tablets):
  —For prevention of nausea and vomiting after anticancer medicine:
    - Adults and children 12 years of age and older—At first, the dose is 8 milligrams (mg) taken thirty minutes before the anticancer medicine is given. The 8-mg dose is taken again eight hours after the first dose. Then, the dose is 8 mg every twelve hours for one to two days.
    - Children 4 to 12 years of age—At first, the dose is 4 mg taken thirty minutes before the anticancer medicine is given. The 4-mg dose is taken again four and eight hours after the first dose. Then, the dose is 4 mg every eight hours for one to two days.
    - Children up to 4 years of age—Dose must be determined by your doctor.

  —For prevention of nausea and vomiting after surgery:
    - Adults—Dose is usually 16 mg one hour before anesthesia (medicine to put you to sleep before surgery).
    - Children—Dose must be determined by your doctor.

  —For prevention of nausea and vomiting after radiation treatment:
    - Adults—At first, the dose is 8 mg taken one to two hours before radiation treatment. Then, the dose is 8 mg every eight hours each day radiation treatment is given.
    - Children—Dose must be determined by your doctor.
- For *injection* dosage form:
  —For prevention of nausea and vomiting after anticancer medicine:
    - Adults—Dose is usually 32 mg injected into a vein, over a period of fifteen minutes, beginning thirty minutes before the anticancer medicine is given. Or, if the dose is based on body weight, it is usually 150 micrograms (mcg) per kilogram (kg) (68 mcg per pound) of body weight. This dose is injected into a vein over a period of fifteen

minutes, beginning thirty minutes before the anticancer medicine is given. It is injected again four and eight hours after the first dose.

• Children 4 to 18 years of age—Dose is based on body weight and must be determined by your doctor. It is usually 150 mcg per kg (68 mcg per pound) of body weight, injected into a vein over a period of fifteen minutes, beginning thirty minutes before the anticancer medicine is given. The dose is given again four and eight hours after the first dose.

• Children up to 4 years of age—Dose must be determined by your doctor.

—For prevention of nausea and vomiting after surgery:

• Adults—Dose is usually 4 mg injected into a vein over a period of thirty seconds to five minutes. It is given just before anesthesia (medicine to put you to sleep before surgery).

• Children—Dose must be determined by your doctor.

Missed dose—If you miss a dose of this medicine, and you do not feel nauseous, skip the missed dose and go back to your regular dosing schedule. If you miss a dose of this medicine, and you feel nauseous or you vomit, take the missed dose as soon as possible.

Storage—To store this medicine:

- Keep out of the reach of children.
- Store away from heat and direct light.
- Do not store in the bathroom, near the kitchen sink, or in other damp places. Heat or moisture may cause the medicine to break down.
- Keep the medicine from freezing.
- Do not keep outdated medicine or medicine no longer needed. Be sure that any discarded medicine is out of the reach of children.

Side Effects of This Medicine

Along with its needed effects, a medicine may cause some unwanted effects. Although not all of these side effects may occur, if they do occur they may need medical attention.

Check with your doctor immediately if any of the following side effects occur:

Rare

Chest pain; shortness of breath; skin rash, hives, and/or itching; tightness in chest; troubled breathing; wheezing

Other side effects may occur that usually do not need medical attention. These side effects may go away during treatment as your body adjusts to the medicine. However, check with your doctor if any of the following side effects continue or are bothersome:

More common

Constipation; diarrhea; fever; headache

Less common

Abdominal pain or stomach cramps; dizziness or lightheadedness; drowsiness; dryness of mouth; unusual tiredness or weakness

Other side effects not listed above may also occur in some patients. If you notice any other effects, check with your doctor.

Revised: 01/19/95
Interim revision: 08/15/95; 07/29/96

OPIUM PREPARATIONS Systemic

Some commonly used names are:

In the U.S.—

Camphorated Opium Tincture[2]
Laudanum[1]

In Canada—

Camphorated Opium Tincture[2]
Laudanum[1]

Note: For quick reference, the following opium preparations are numbered to match the corresponding brand names.

This information applies to the following medicines:

1. Opium Tincture (OH-pee-um)
2. Paregoric (par-e-GOR-ik)

Description

Opium preparations are used along with other measures to treat severe diarrhea. These medicines belong to the group of medicines called narcotics. If too much of a narcotic is taken, it may become habit-forming, causing mental or physical dependence. Physical dependence may lead to withdrawal side effects when you stop taking the medicine.

Opium preparations are available only with your doctor's prescription, in the following dosage forms:

Oral

Opium Tincture
- Oral liquid (U.S. and Canada)

Paregoric
- Oral liquid (U.S. and Canada)

Before Using This Medicine

In deciding to use a medicine, the risks of taking the medicine must be weighed against the good it will do. This is a decision you and your doctor will make. For opium preparations, the following should be considered:

Allergies—Tell your doctor if you have ever had any unusual or allergic reaction to morphine, codeine, or papaverine. Also tell your health care professional if you are allergic to any other substances, such as foods, preservatives, or dyes.

Pregnancy—Opium preparations have not been studied in pregnant women. However, morphine (contained in these medicines) has caused birth defects in animals when given in very large doses.

Regular use of opium preparations during pregnancy may cause the fetus to become dependent on the medicine. This may lead to withdrawal side effects in the newborn baby. Also, these medicines may cause breathing problems in the newborn baby, especially if they are taken just before delivery.

Breast-feeding—Opium preparations have not been reported to cause problems in nursing babies.

Children—Breathing problems may be especially likely to occur in children up to 2 years of age, who are usually more sensitive than adults to the effects of opium preparations.

Older adults—Breathing problems may be especially likely to occur in elderly patients, who are usually more sensitive than younger adults to the effects of opium preparations.

Other medicines—Although certain medicines should not be used together at all, in other cases two different medicines may be used together even if an interaction might occur. In these cases, your doctor may want to change the dose, or other precautions may be necessary. When you are taking an opium preparation, it is especially important that your health care professional know if you are taking any of the following:

- Anticholinergics (medicine for abdominal or stomach spasms or cramps) or
- Central nervous system (CNS) depressants, especially other narcotics, or
- Other diarrhea medicine or
- Tricyclic antidepressants (amitriptyline [e.g., Elavil], amoxapine [e.g., Asendin], clomipramine [e.g., Anafranil], desipramine [e.g., Pertofrane], doxepin [e.g., Sinequan], imipramine [e.g., Tofranil], nortriptyline [e.g., Aventyl], protriptyline [e.g., Vivactil], trimipramine [e.g., Surmontil])—The chance of side effects is increased
- Naltrexone (e.g., Trexan)—Naltrexone blocks the effects of opium preparations and makes them less effective in treating diarrhea

Other medical problems—The presence of other medical problems may affect the use of opium preparations. Make sure you tell your doctor if you have any other medical problems, especially:

- Alcohol or other drug abuse (or history of) or
- Colitis or
- Heart disease or
- Kidney disease or
- Liver disease or
- Underactive thyroid—The chance of side effects may be increased
- Brain disease or head injury or
- Emphysema, asthma, bronchitis, or other chronic lung disease or
- Enlarged prostate or problems with urination or
- Gallbladder disease or gallstones—Some of the side effects of opium preparations can be dangerous if these conditions are present
- Convulsions (seizures), history of—Opium can rarely cause convulsions

Proper Use of This Medicine

This medicine is to be taken by mouth even if it comes in a dropper bottle. The amount you should take is to be measured with the special dropper provided with your prescription and diluted with water just before you take each dose. This will cause the medicine to turn milky in color, but it will still work.

If your prescription does not come in a dropper bottle and the directions on the bottle say to take it by the teaspoonful, it is not necessary to dilute it before using.

If this medicine upsets your stomach, your doctor may want you to take it with food.

Take this medicine only as directed by your doctor. Do not take more of it, do not take it more often, and do not take it for a longer time than your doctor ordered. This is especially important for young children and for elderly patients, who are especially sensitive to the effects of opium preparations. If too much is taken, this medicine may become habit-forming (causing mental or physical dependence) or lead to problems because of an overdose.

Dosing—The dose of these medicines will be different for different patients. *Follow your doctor's orders or the directions on the label.* The following information includes only the average doses of these medicines. *If your dose is different, do not change it* unless your doctor tells you to do so.

For opium tincture (laudanum)

- For *oral liquid* dosage form (drops):
  - —For diarrhea:
    - Adults—5 to 16 drops of liquid, measured with the dropper in the bottle and mixed with a little water, four times a day until diarrhea is controlled.
    - Children—Dose must be determined by your doctor.

For paregoric

- For *oral liquid* dosage form:
  - —For diarrhea:
    - Adults—1 or 2 teaspoonfuls one to four times a day until diarrhea is controlled. Use a measuring spoon to measure the dose. An ordinary household teaspoon that is used at the table may not hold the right amount of medicine.
    - Children 2 years of age and older—0.25 to 0.5 milliliters (mL) (4 to 8 drops), mixed with a little water, one to four times a day until diarrhea is controlled. This amount of medicine must be measured with a dropper or a special measuring device that can be used for very small amounts of liquid. If you did not receive a dropper or measuring device with the medicine, check with your pharmacist.

Missed dose—If you miss a dose of this medicine, take it as soon as you remember. However, if it is almost time for your next dose, skip the missed dose and go back to your regular dosing schedule. *Do not double doses.*

Storage—To store this medicine:

- Keep out of the reach of children. Overdose is very dangerous in young children.
- Store away from heat and direct light.

- Keep the container for this medicine tightly closed to prevent the alcohol from evaporating and the medicine from becoming stronger.
- Do not store this medicine in the refrigerator or allow the medicine to freeze. If it does get cold and you notice any solid particles in it, throw it away.
- Do not keep outdated medicine or medicine no longer needed. Be sure that any discarded medicine is out of the reach of children.

Precautions While Using This Medicine

Check with your doctor if your diarrhea does not stop after 1 or 2 days or if you develop a fever.

This medicine will add to the effects of alcohol and other CNS depressants (medicines that slow down the nervous system, possibly causing drowsiness). Some examples of CNS depressants are antihistamines or medicine for hay fever, other allergies, or colds; sedatives, tranquilizers, or sleeping medicine; prescription pain medicine or other narcotics; barbiturates; medicine for seizures; muscle relaxants; or anesthetics, including some dental anesthetics. *Do not drink alcoholic beverages, and check with your doctor before taking any of the medicines listed above, while you are taking this medicine.*

This medicine may cause some people to become drowsy, dizzy, lightheaded, or less alert than they are normally. Even if taken at bedtime, it may cause some people to feel drowsy or less alert on arising. *Make sure you know how you react to this medicine before you drive, use machines, or do anything else that could be dangerous if you are dizzy or are not alert.*

Dizziness, lightheadedness, or fainting may be especially likely to occur when you get up suddenly from a lying or sitting position. Getting up slowly may help lessen this problem. If you feel very dizzy, lightheaded, or faint after taking this medicine, lying down for a while may help.

If you have been taking this medicine regularly for several weeks or more, *do not stop using it without first checking with your doctor.* Your doctor may want you to reduce gradually the amount you are using before stopping completely, to lessen the chance of withdrawal side effects.

If you think you or someone else may have taken an overdose, get emergency help at once. Taking an overdose of this medicine or taking alcohol or other CNS depressants with this medicine may lead to unconsciousness and possibly death. Signs of overdose include convulsions (seizures), confusion, severe nervousness or restlessness, severe dizziness, severe drowsiness, slow or irregular breathing, and severe weakness.

Side Effects of This Medicine

Along with its needed effects, a medicine may cause some unwanted effects. Although not all of these side effects may occur, if they do occur they may need medical attention.

Get emergency help immediately if any of the following symptoms of overdose occur:

Cold, clammy skin; confusion; convulsions (seizures); dizziness (severe); drowsiness (severe); low blood pressure; nervousness or restlessness (severe); pinpoint pupils of eyes; slow heartbeat; slow or irregular breathing; weakness (severe)

Also, *check with your doctor immediately* if any of the following side effects are severe and occur suddenly since they may indicate a more severe and dangerous problem with your bowels:

Rare

Bloating; constipation; loss of appetite; nausea or vomiting; stomach cramps or pain

In addition, check with your doctor as soon as possible if any of the following side effects occur:

Rare

Fast heartbeat; increased sweating; mental depression; redness or flushing of face; shortness of breath, wheezing, or troubled breathing; skin rash, hives, or itching; slow heartbeat

Other side effects may occur that usually do not need medical attention. These side effects may go away during treatment as your body adjusts to the medicine. However, check with your doctor if any of the following side effects continue or are bothersome:

More common with large doses

Difficult or painful urination; dizziness, lightheadedness, or feeling faint; drowsiness; frequent urge to urinate; nervousness or restlessness; unusual decrease in amount of urine; unusual tiredness or weakness

After you stop using this medicine, your body may need time to adjust. The length of time this takes depends on the amount of medicine you were using and how long you used it. During this period of time check with your doctor if you notice any of the following side effects:

Body aches; diarrhea; fever, runny nose, or sneezing; gooseflesh; increased sweating; increased yawning; loss of appetite; nausea or vomiting; nervousness, restlessness, or irritability; shivering or trembling; stomach cramps; trouble in sleeping; unusually large pupils of eyes; weakness (severe)

Other side effects not listed above may also occur in some patients. If you notice any other effects, check with your doctor.

Revised: 10/05/92
Interim revision: 09/08/94

ORPHENADRINE Systemic

Some commonly used brand names are:

In the U.S.—

Antiflex
Banflex
Flexoject
Mio-Rel
Myolin
Myotrol
Norflex
Orfro
Orphenate

Generic name product may also be available.

In Canada—

Disipal
Norflex

Description

Orphenadrine (or-FEN-a-dreen) is used to help relax certain muscles in your body and relieve the stiffness, pain, and discomfort caused by strains, sprains, or other injury to your muscles. One form of orphenadrine is also used to relieve trembling caused by Parkinson's disease. However, this medicine does not take the place of rest, exercise or physical therapy, or other treatment that your doctor may recommend for your medical problem.

Orphenadrine acts in the central nervous system (CNS) to produce its muscle relaxant effects. Orphenadrine also has other actions (anticholinergic) that produce its helpful effects in Parkinson's disease. Orphenadrine's CNS and anticholinergic actions may also be responsible for some of its side effects.

In the U.S., this medicine is available only with your doctor's prescription. In Canada, it may be available without a prescription. It is available in the following dosage forms:

Oral

- Tablets (Canada)
- Extended-release tablets (U.S. and Canada)

Parenteral

- Injection (U.S. and Canada)

Before Using This Medicine

In deciding to use a medicine, the risks of taking the medicine must be weighed against the good it will do. This is a decision you and your doctor will make. For orphenadrine, the following should be considered:

Allergies—Tell your doctor if you have ever had any unusual or allergic reaction to orphenadrine. Also tell your health care professional if you are allergic to any other substances, such as foods, preservatives, or dyes.

Pregnancy—Orphenadrine has not been reported to cause birth defects or other problems in humans.

Breast-feeding—It is not known whether orphenadrine passes into the breast milk. However, orphenadrine has not been reported to cause problems in nursing babies.

Children—Studies on this medicine have been done only in adult patients, and there is no specific information comparing use of orphenadrine in children with use in other age groups.

Older adults—Many medicines have not been tested in older people. Therefore, it may not be known whether they work exactly the same way they do in younger adults or if they cause different side effects or problems in older people. There is no specific information about the use of orphenadrine in the elderly.

Other medicines—Although certain medicines should not be used together at all, in other cases two different medicines may be used together even if an interaction might occur. In these cases, your doctor may want to change the dose, or other precautions may be necessary. When you are taking orphenadrine, it is especially important that your health care professional knows if you are taking any of the following:

- Alcohol or
- Central nervous system (CNS) depressants or
- Tricyclic antidepressants (amitriptyline [e.g., Elavil], amoxapine [e.g., Asendin], clomipramine [e.g., Anafranil], desipramine [e.g., Pertofrane], doxepin [e.g., Sinequan], imipramine [e.g., Tofranil], nortriptyline [e.g., Aventyl], protriptyline [e.g., Vivactil], trimipramine [e.g., Surmontil])—The chance of side effects may be increased

Other medical problems—The presence of other medical problems may affect the use of orphenadrine. Make sure you tell your doctor if you have any other medical problems, especially:

- Disease of the digestive tract, especially esophagus disease, stomach ulcer, or intestinal blockage, or
- Enlarged prostate or
- Fast or irregular heartbeat or
- Glaucoma or
- Myasthenia gravis or
- Urinary tract blockage—Orphenadrine has side effects that may be harmful to people with these conditions
- Heart disease or
- Kidney disease or
- Liver disease—The chance of side effects may be increased

Proper Use of This Medicine

Dosing—The dose of orphenadrine will be different for different patients. *Follow your doctor's orders or the directions on the label.* The following information includes only the average doses of orphenadrine. *If your dose is different, do not change it* unless your doctor tells you to do so.

- For *extended-release tablet* dosage form:
  —For relaxing stiff, sore muscles:
    - Adults and teenagers—100 milligrams (mg) two times a day, in the morning and evening.
    - Children—Use and dose must be determined by your doctor.
- For *oral tablet* dosage form:
  —For relaxing stiff, sore muscles and for Parkinson's disease:
    - Adults—50 mg three times a day.
    - Children—Dose must be determined by your doctor.

• For *injection* dosage form:
—For relaxing stiff, sore muscles:
• Adults—60 mg, injected into a muscle or a vein, every twelve hours as needed.
• Children—Use and dose must be determined by your doctor.

Missed dose—If you miss a dose of this medicine and remember within an hour or so of the missed dose, take it right away. But if you do not remember until later, skip the missed dose and go back to your regular dosing schedule. Do not double doses.

Storage—To store this medicine:
- Keep out of the reach of children.
- Store away from heat and direct light.
- Do not store this medicine in the bathroom, near the kitchen sink, or in other damp places. Heat or moisture may cause the medicine to break down.
- Do not keep outdated medicine or medicine no longer needed. Be sure that any discarded medicine is out of the reach of children.

Precautions While Using This Medicine

If you will be taking this medicine for a long time (for example, more than a few weeks), your doctor should check your progress at regular visits.

This medicine may add to the effects of alcohol and other CNS depressants (medicines that slow down the nervous system, possibly causing drowsiness). Some examples of CNS depressants are antihistamines or medicine for hay fever, other allergies, or colds; sedatives, tranquilizers, or sleeping medicine; prescription pain medicine or narcotics; barbiturates; medicine for seizures; other muscle relaxants; or anesthetics, including some dental anesthetics. *Do not drink alcoholic beverages, and check with your doctor before taking any of the medicines listed above, while you are using this medicine.*

This medicine may cause some people to have blurred vision or to become drowsy, dizzy, lightheaded, faint, or less alert than they are normally. It may also cause muscle weakness in some people. *Make sure you know how you react to this medicine before you drive, use machines, or do anything else that could be dangerous if you are dizzy or are not alert and able to see well.*

Orphenadrine may cause dryness of the mouth. For temporary relief, use sugarless candy or gum, melt bits of ice in your mouth, or use a saliva substitute. However, if dry mouth continues for more than 2 weeks, check with your dentist. Continuing dryness of the mouth may increase the chance of dental disease, including tooth decay, gum disease, and fungus infections.

Side Effects of This Medicine

Along with its needed effects, a medicine may cause some unwanted effects. Although not all of these side effects may occur, if they do occur they may need medical attention.

Check with your doctor as soon as possible if any of the following side effects occur:

Less common
Decreased urination; eye pain; fainting; fast or pounding heartbeat

Rare
Hallucinations (seeing, hearing, or feeling things that are not there); shortness of breath, troubled breathing, tightness in chest, and/or wheezing; skin rash, hives, itching, or redness; sores, ulcers, or white spots on lips or in mouth; swollen and/or painful glands; unusual bruising or bleeding; unusual tiredness or weakness

Other side effects may occur that usually do not need medical attention. These side effects may go away during treatment as your body adjusts to the medicine. However, check with your doctor if any of the following side effects continue or are bothersome:

More common
Dryness of mouth

Less common or rare
Abdominal or stomach cramps or pain; blurred or double vision or other vision problems; confusion; constipation; difficult urination; dizziness or lightheadedness; drowsiness; excitement, irritability, nervousness, or restlessness; headache; muscle weakness; nausea or vomiting; trembling; unusually large pupils of eyes

Other side effects not listed above may also occur in some patients. If you notice any other effects, check with your doctor.

Revised: 08/11/95

ORPHENADRINE AND ASPIRIN Systemic

Some commonly used brand names are:

In the U.S.—

Norgesic	N3 Gesic
Norgesic Forte	N3 Gesic Forte
Norphadrine	Orphenagesic
Norphadrine Forte	Orphenagesic Forte

In Canada—‡

Norgesic	Norgesic Forte

‡In Canada, *Aspirin* is a brand name. Acetylsalicylic acid is the generic name in Canada. ASA, a synonym for acetylsalicylic acid, is the term that commonly appears on Canadian product labels.

Description

Orphenadrine (or-FEN-a-dreen) and aspirin (AS-pir-in) combination is used to help relax certain muscles in your body and relieve the pain and discomfort caused by strains, sprains, or other injury to your muscles. However, this medicine does not take the place of rest, exercise, or other treatment that your doctor may recommend for your medical problem.

Orphenadrine acts in the central nervous system (CNS) to produce its muscle relaxant effects. Actions in the CNS may also be responsible for some of its side effects. Orphenadrine also has other actions (antimuscarinic) that may be responsible for some of its side effects.

This combination medicine also contains caffeine (kaf-EEN).

In the U.S., this combination medicine is available only with your doctor's prescription. In Canada, it is available without a prescription.

These medicines are available in the following dosage forms:

Oral

- Tablets (U.S. and Canada)

Before Using This Medicine

In deciding to use a medicine, the risks of taking the medicine must be weighed against the good it will do. This is a decision you and your doctor will make. For orphenadrine and aspirin combination, the following should be considered:

Allergies—Tell your doctor if you have ever had any unusual or allergic reaction to orphenadrine, caffeine, aspirin or other salicylates including methyl salicylate (oil of wintergreen), or to any of the following medicines:

Diclofenac (e.g., Voltaren)
Diflunisal (e.g., Dolobid)
Etodolac (e.g., Lodine)
Fenoprofen (e.g., Nalfon)
Floctafenine (e.g., Idarac)
Flurbiprofen, oral (e.g., Ansaid)
Ibuprofen (e.g., Motrin)
Indomethacin (e.g., Indocin)
Ketoprofen (e.g., Orudis)
Ketorolac (e.g., Toradol)
Meclofenamate (e.g., Meclomen)
Mefenamic acid (e.g., Ponstel)
Nabumetone (e.g., Relafen)
Naproxen (e.g., Naprosyn)
Oxaprozin (e.g., Daypro)
Oxyphenbutazone (e.g., Tandearil)
Phenylbutazone (e.g., Butazolidin)
Piroxicam (e.g., Feldene)
Sulindac (e.g., Clinoril)
Suprofen (e.g., Suprol)
Tenoxicam (e.g., Mobiflex)
Tiaprofenic acid (e.g., Surgam)
Tolmetin (e.g., Tolectin)
Zomepirac (e.g., Zomax)

Also tell your health care professional if you are allergic to any other substances, such as foods, preservatives, or dyes.

Pregnancy—

- *For aspirin:* Studies in humans have not shown that aspirin causes birth defects. However, aspirin has caused birth defects in animal studies.

  Some reports have suggested that too much use of aspirin late in pregnancy may cause a decrease in the newborn's weight and possible death of the fetus or newborn baby. However, the mothers in these reports had been taking much larger amounts of aspirin than are usually recommended. Studies of mothers taking aspirin in the doses that are usually recommended did not show these unwanted effects.

  Regular use of aspirin late in pregnancy may cause unwanted effects on the heart or blood flow in the fetus or in the newborn baby. Also, use of aspirin during the last 2 weeks of pregnancy may cause bleeding problems in the fetus before or during delivery or in the newborn baby. In addition, too much use of aspirin during the last 3 months of pregnancy may increase the length of pregnancy, prolong labor, cause other problems during delivery, or cause severe bleeding in the mother before, during, or after delivery. *Do not take aspirin during the last 3 months of pregnancy unless it has been ordered by your doctor.*
- *For orphenadrine:* Orphenadrine has not been reported to cause birth defects or other problems in humans.

Breast-feeding—This medicine has not been shown to cause problems in nursing babies. However, aspirin passes into the breast milk. Also, caffeine passes into the breast milk in small amounts. It is not known whether orphenadrine passes into the breast milk.

Children—*Do not give a medicine containing aspirin to a child or a teenager with a fever or other symptoms of a virus infection, especially flu or chickenpox, without first discussing its use with your child's doctor.* This is very important because aspirin may cause a serious illness called Reye's syndrome in children with fever caused by a virus infection, especially flu or chickenpox. Children who do not have a virus infection may also be more sensitive to the effects of aspirin, especially if they have a fever or have lost large amounts of body fluid because of vomiting, diarrhea, or sweating. This may increase the chance of side effects during treatment.

There is no specific information about the use of orphenadrine in children.

Older adults—Elderly people are especially sensitive to the effects of aspirin. This may increase the chance of side effects during treatment.

There is no specific information about the use of orphenadrine in the elderly.

Other medicines—Although certain medicines should not be used together at all, in other cases two different medicines may be used together even if an interaction might occur. In these cases, your doctor may want to change the dose, or other precautions may be necessary. When you

are taking orphenadrine and aspirin combination, it is especially important that your health care professional know if you are taking any of the following:

- Anticoagulants (blood thinners) or
- Carbenicillin by injection (e.g., Geopen) or
- Cefamandole (e.g., Mandol) or
- Cefoperazone (e.g., Cefobid) or
- Cefotetan (e.g., Cefotan) or
- Dipyridamole (e.g., Persantine) or
- Divalproex (e.g., Depakote) or
- Heparin or
- Medicine for inflammation or pain, except narcotics, or
- Moxalactam (e.g., Moxam) or
- Pentoxifylline (e.g., Trental) or
- Plicamycin (e.g., Mithracin) or
- Ticarcillin (e.g., Ticar) or
- Valproic acid (e.g., Depakene)—Taking these medicines together with aspirin may increase the chance of bleeding
- Anticholinergics (medicine for abdominal or stomach spasms or cramps) or
- Central nervous system (CNS) depressants or
- Methotrexate (e.g., Mexate) or
- Tricyclic antidepressants (amitriptyline [e.g., Elavil], amoxapine [e.g., Asendin], clomipramine [e.g., Anafranil], desipramine [e.g., Pertofrane], doxepin [e.g., Sinequan], imipramine [e.g., Tofranil], nortriptyline [e.g., Aventyl], protriptyline [e.g., Vivactil], trimipramine [e.g., Surmontil]) or
- Vancomycin (e.g., Vancocin)—The chance of side effects may be increased
- Antidiabetics, oral (diabetes medicine you take by mouth)—Aspirin may increase the effects of the antidiabetic medicine; a change in dose may be needed if aspirin is taken regularly
- Probenecid (e.g., Benemid) or
- Sulfinpyrazone (e.g., Anturane)—Aspirin can keep these medicines from working properly for treating gout; also, taking aspirin together with sulfinpyrazone may increase the chance of bleeding
- Urinary alkalizers (medicine that makes the urine less acid, such as acetazolamide [e.g., Diamox], dichlorphenamide [e.g., Daranide], methazolamide [e.g., Neptazane], potassium or sodium citrate and/or citric acid)—These medicines may make aspirin less effective by causing it to be removed from the body more quickly
- Zidovudine (e.g., AZT; Retrovir)—Aspirin may increase the blood levels of zidovudine, which increases the chance of serious side effects

Other medical problems—The presence of other medical problems may affect the use of orphenadrine and aspirin combination. Make sure you tell your doctor if you have any other medical problems, especially:

- Anemia or
- Overactive thyroid or
- Stomach ulcer or other stomach problems—Aspirin may make your condition worse
- Asthma, allergies, and nasal polyps, history of or
- Glucose-6-phosphate dehydrogenase (G6PD) deficiency or
- Kidney disease or
- Liver disease—The chance of side effects may be increased
- Disease of the digestive tract, especially esophagus disease or intestinal blockage, or
- Enlarged prostate or
- Fast or irregular heartbeat or
- Glaucoma or
- Myasthenia gravis or
- Urinary tract blockage—Orphenadrine has side effects that may be harmful to people with these conditions
- Gout—Aspirin can make this condition worse and can also lessen the effects of some medicines used to treat gout
- Heart disease—The chance of some side effects may be increased. Also, the caffeine present in this combination medicine can make your condition worse
- Hemophilia or other bleeding problems or
- Vitamin K deficiency—Aspirin may increase the chance of bleeding

Proper Use of This Medicine

Take this medicine with food or a full glass (8 ounces) of water to lessen stomach irritation.

Do not take this medicine if it has a strong vinegar-like odor. This odor means the aspirin in it is breaking down. If you have any questions about this, check with your health care professional.

Do not take more of this medicine than your doctor ordered to lessen the chance of side effects or overdose.

Dosing—The dose of orphenadrine and aspirin combination medicine will be different for different people. *Follow your doctor's orders or the directions on the label.* The following information includes only the average doses of the combination medicine. *If your dose is different, do not change it* unless your doctor tells you to do so.

- For *oral* dosage forms (tablets):
  —For muscle pain and stiffness:
    - Adults and teenagers—One or two tablets containing 25 milligrams (mg) of orphenadrine and 385 mg of aspirin, or one-half or one tablet containing 50 mg of orphenadrine and 770 mg of aspirin, three or four times a day.
    - Children—Dose must be determined by your doctor.

Missed dose—If you miss a dose of this medicine and remember within an hour or so of the missed dose, take it right away. But if you do not remember until later, skip the missed dose and go back to your regular dosing schedule. Do not double doses.

Storage—To store this medicine:

- Keep out of the reach of children. Overdose of aspirin is especially dangerous in young children.
- Store away from heat and direct light.
- Do not store this medicine in the bathroom, near the kitchen sink, or in other damp places. Heat or moisture may cause the medicine to break down.
- Do not keep outdated medicine or medicine no longer needed. Be sure that any discarded medicine is out of the reach of children.

Precautions While Using This Medicine

If you will be taking this medicine for a long time (for example, more than a few weeks), your doctor should check your progress at regular visits.

Check the labels of all nonprescription (over-the-counter [OTC]) and prescription medicines you now take. If any contain orphenadrine or aspirin or other salicylates be especially careful, since taking them while taking this medicine may lead to overdose. If you have any questions about this, check with your health care professional.

Too much use of acetaminophen or certain other medicines together with the aspirin in this combination medicine may increase the chance of unwanted effects. The risk depends on how much of each medicine you take every day, and on how long you take the medicines together. If your doctor directs you to take these medicines together on a regular basis, follow his or her directions carefully. However, do not take acetaminophen or any of the following medicines together with this combination medicine for more than a few days, unless your doctor has directed you to do so and is following your progress:

Diclofenac (e.g., Voltaren)
Diflunisal (e.g., Dolobid)
Etodolac (e.g., Lodine)
Fenoprofen (e.g., Nalfon)
Floctafenine (e.g., Idarac)
Flurbiprofen, oral (e.g., Ansaid)
Ibuprofen (e.g., Motrin)
Indomethacin (e.g., Indocin)
Ketoprofen (e.g., Orudis)
Ketorolac (e.g., Toradol)
Meclofenamate (e.g., Meclomen)
Mefenamic acid (e.g., Ponstel)
Nabumetone (e.g., Relafen)
Naproxen (e.g., Naprosyn)
Oxaprozin (e.g., Daypro)
Phenylbutazone (e.g., Butazolidin)
Piroxicam (e.g., Feldene)
Sulindac (e.g., Clinoril)
Tenoxicam (e.g., Mobiflex)
Tiaprofenic acid (e.g., Surgam)
Tolmetin (e.g., Tolectin)

For *diabetic patients:*

- The aspirin in this combination medicine may cause false urine sugar test results if you are regularly taking 6 or more of the regular-strength tablets or 3 or more of the double-strength tablets of this medicine a day. Smaller doses or occasional use of aspirin usually will not affect urine sugar tests. If you have any questions about this, check with your health care professional especially if your diabetes is not well controlled.

Do not take this medicine for 5 days before any surgery, including dental surgery, unless otherwise directed by your medical doctor or dentist. Taking aspirin during this time may cause bleeding problems.

The orphenadrine in this combination medicine may add to the effects of alcohol and other CNS depressants (medicines that slow down the nervous system, possibly causing drowsiness). Some examples of CNS depressants are antihistamines or medicine for hay fever, other allergies, or colds; sedatives, tranquilizers, or sleeping medicine; prescription pain medicine or narcotics; barbiturates; medicine for seizures; other muscle relaxants; or anesthetics, including some dental anesthetics. Also, stomach problems may be more likely to occur if you drink alcoholic beverages while you are taking aspirin. *Do not drink alcoholic beverages, and check with your doctor before taking any of the medicines listed above, while you are using this medicine.*

This medicine may cause some people to have blurred vision or to become drowsy, dizzy, lightheaded, faint, or less alert than they are normally. *Make sure you know how you react to this medicine before you drive, use machines, or do anything else that could be dangerous if you are dizzy or are not alert.*

Dryness of the mouth may occur while you are taking this medicine. For temporary relief, use sugarless candy or gum, melt bits of ice in your mouth, or use a saliva substitute. However, if dry mouth continues for more than 2 weeks, check with your dentist. Continuing dryness of the mouth may increase the chance of dental disease, including tooth decay, gum disease, and fungus infections.

If you think that you or someone else may have taken an overdose of this medicine, get emergency help at once. Taking an overdose of this medicine may cause unconsciousness or death. Signs of overdose include convulsions (seizures), hearing loss, confusion, ringing or buzzing in the ears, severe drowsiness or tiredness, severe excitement or nervousness, and fast or deep breathing.

Side Effects of This Medicine

Along with its needed effects, a medicine may cause some unwanted effects. Although not all of these side effects may occur, if they do occur they may need medical attention.

Get emergency help immediately if any of the following symptoms of overdose occur:

Any loss of hearing; bloody urine; confusion; convulsions (seizures); diarrhea; dizziness or lightheadedness (severe); drowsiness (severe); excitement or nervousness (severe); fast or deep breathing; hallucinations (seeing, hearing, or feeling things that are not there); headache (severe or continuing); increased sweating; nausea or vomiting (severe or continuing); ringing or buzzing in the ears (continuing); uncontrollable flapping movements of the hands, especially in elderly patients; unexplained fever; unusual thirst; vision problems

Symptoms of overdose in children

Changes in behavior; drowsiness or tiredness (severe); fast or deep breathing

Also, check with your doctor as soon as possible if any of the following side effects occur:

Less common or rare

Abdominal or stomach pain, cramping, or burning (severe); bloody or black, tarry stools; decreased urination; eye pain; fainting; fast or pounding heartbeat; shortness of breath, troubled breathing, tightness in chest, or wheezing; skin rash, hives, itching, or redness; sores, ulcers, or white spots on lips or in mouth; swollen and/or painful glands; unusual bleeding or bruising; unusual tiredness or weakness; vomiting of blood or material that looks like coffee grounds

Other side effects may occur that usually do not need medical attention. These side effects may go away during treatment as your body adjusts to the medicine. However,

check with your doctor if any of the following side effects continue or are bothersome:

More common

Abdominal or stomach cramps, pain, or discomfort (mild to moderate); dryness of mouth; heartburn or indigestion; nausea or vomiting (mild)

Less common

Blurred or double vision or other vision problems; confusion; constipation; difficult urination; dizziness or lightheadedness; drowsiness; excitement, nervousness, or restlessness; headache; muscle weakness; trembling; unusually large pupils of eyes

Other side effects not listed above may also occur in some patients. If you notice any other effects, check with your doctor.

Revised: July 1990
Interim revision: 08/11/94

OXAMNIQUINE Systemic†

A commonly used brand name in the U.S. is Vansil.

†Not commercially available in Canada.

Description

Oxamniquine (ox-AM-ni-kwin) is used to treat a certain kind of worm infection (blood fluke), also known as snail fever, Manson's schistosomiasis (shis-toe-soe-MYE-a-siss), or bilharziasis (bil-har-ZYE-a-siss). It will not work for other kinds of worm infections (for example, pinworms or roundworms).

Oxamniquine is available only with your doctor's prescription, in the following dosage form:

Oral

- Capsules (U.S.)

Before Using This Medicine

In deciding to use a medicine, the risks of taking the medicine must be weighed against the good it will do. This is a decision you and your doctor will make. For oxamniquine, the following should be considered:

Allergies—Tell your doctor if you have ever had any unusual or allergic reaction to oxamniquine. Also tell your health care professional if you are allergic to any other substances, such as foods, preservatives, or dyes.

Pregnancy—Studies have not been done in humans. Studies in animals have shown that oxamniquine may harm the unborn animal when it is given in high doses. However, there have been no reports of problems with the pregnancies or babies of pregnant women who took oxamniquine.

Breast-feeding—It is not known whether oxamniquine passes into the breast milk. However, this medicine has not been reported to cause problems in nursing babies.

Children—This medicine has been used in children, and, in effective doses, has not been shown to cause different side effects or problems in children than it does in adults.

Older adults—Many medicines have not been studied specifically in older people. Therefore, it may not be known whether they work exactly the same way they do in younger adults or if they cause different side effects or problems in older people. There is no specific information comparing use of oxamniquine in the elderly with use in other age groups.

Other medicines—Although certain medicines should not be used together at all, in other cases two different medicines may be used together even if an interaction might occur. In these cases, your doctor may want to change the dose, or other precautions may be necessary. Tell your health care professional if you are taking any other prescription or nonprescription (over-the-counter [OTC]) medicine.

Other medical problems—The presence of other medical problems may affect the use of oxamniquine. Make sure you tell your doctor if you have any other medical problems, especially:

- History of epilepsy or other medical problems that cause convulsions—Patients with a history of epilepsy may be more likely to have side effects

Proper Use of This Medicine

No special preparations (for example, special diets, fasting, other medicines, laxatives, or enemas) are necessary before, during, or immediately after taking oxamniquine.

Take this medicine after meals to lessen the chance of side effects such as stomach upset, drowsiness, or dizziness, unless otherwise directed by your doctor.

To help clear up your infection completely, *take this medicine exactly as directed by your doctor for the full time of treatment. Do not miss any doses.*

Dosing—The dose of oxamniquine will be different for different patients. *Follow your doctor's orders or the directions on the label.* The following information includes only the average doses of oxamniquine. *If your dose is different, do not change it* unless your doctor tells you to do so.

- For *oral* dosage form (capsules):
  - —For East, North, or South African snail fever:
    - Adults and children—Dose is based on body weight and must be determined by your doctor. The usual dose is 15 milligrams (mg) per kilogram (kg) (6.8 mg per pound) of body weight two times a day for one, two, or three days.
  - —For West African and Western Hemisphere snail fever:
    - Adults and children weighing 30 kg (66 pounds) and over—Dose is based on body weight and must be determined by your doctor. The

usual dose is 15 mg per kg (6.8 mg per pound) of body weight as a single dose.

• Children weighing up to 30 kg (66 pounds)—Dose is based on body weight and must be determined by your doctor. The usual dose is 10 mg per kg (4.5 mg per pound) of body weight taken twice a day, two to eight hours apart.

Missed dose—If you miss a dose of this medicine, take it as soon as possible. However, if it is almost time for your next dose, skip the missed dose and go back to your regular dosing schedule. Do not double doses.

Storage—To store this medicine:

- Keep out of the reach of children.
- Store away from heat and direct light.
- Do not store in the bathroom, near the kitchen sink, or in other damp places. Heat or moisture may cause the medicine to break down.
- Do not keep outdated medicine or medicine no longer needed. Be sure that any discarded medicine is out of the reach of children.

Precautions While Using This Medicine

It is important that your doctor check your progress at regular visits.

If your symptoms do not improve after you take this medicine for the full time of treatment, or if they become worse, check with your doctor.

This medicine may cause some people to become dizzy, drowsy, or less alert than they are normally. *Make sure you know how you react to this medicine before you drive, use machines, or do anything else that could be dangerous if you are dizzy or are not alert.* If these reactions are especially bothersome, check with your doctor.

Side Effects of This Medicine

Along with its needed effects, a medicine may cause some unwanted effects. Although not all of these side effects may occur, if they do occur they may need medical attention.

Check with your doctor immediately if any of the following side effects occur:

Rare

Convulsions (seizures); fever; hallucinations (seeing, hearing, or feeling things that are not there); skin rash or hives

Other side effects may occur that usually do not need medical attention. These side effects may go away during treatment as your body adjusts to the medicine. However, check with your doctor if any of the following side effects continue or are bothersome:

More common

Dizziness; drowsiness; headache

Less common

Abdominal or stomach pain; diarrhea; loss of appetite; nausea or vomiting

This medicine may cause the urine to turn reddish orange. This side effect does not require medical attention.

Other side effects not listed above may also occur in some patients. If you notice any other effects, check with your doctor.

Revised: 01/19/93
Interim revision: 07/21/94

OXICONAZOLE Topical†

A commonly used brand name in the U.S. is Oxistat.

†Not commercially available in Canada.

Description

Oxiconazole (ox-i-KON-a-zole) is used to treat infections caused by a fungus. It works by killing the fungus or preventing its growth.

Oxiconazole is applied to the skin to treat:

- ringworm of the body (tinea corporis);
- ringworm of the foot (tinea pedis; athlete's foot); and
- ringworm of the groin (tinea cruris; jock itch).

Oxiconazole is available only with your doctor's prescription, in the following dosage forms:

Topical

- Cream (U.S.)
- Lotion (U.S.)

Before Using This Medicine

In deciding to use a medicine, the risks of using the medicine must be weighed against the good it will do. This is a decision you and your doctor will make. For oxiconazole, the following should be considered:

Allergies—Tell your doctor if you have ever had any unusual or allergic reaction to oxiconazole. Also tell your health care professional if you are allergic to any other substances, such as foods, preservatives, or dyes.

Pregnancy—Oxiconazole has not been studied in pregnant women. However, this medication has not been shown to cause birth defects or other problems in animal studies.

Breast-feeding—Topical oxiconazole passes into breast milk. Mothers who are using this medicine and who wish to breast-feed should discuss this with their doctor.

Children—Although there is no specific information comparing use of topical oxiconazole in children with use in other age groups, this medicine is not expected to cause different side effects or problems in children than it does in adults.

Older adults—Many medicines have not been studied specifically in older people. Therefore, it may not be known whether they work exactly the same way they do in younger adults. Although there is no specific information comparing use of topical oxiconazole in the elderly with use in other age groups, this medicine is not expected to cause different side effects or problems in older people than it does in younger adults.

Other medicines—Although certain medicines should not be used together at all, in other cases two different medicines may be used together even if an interaction might occur. In these cases, your doctor may want to change the dose, or other precautions may be necessary. Tell your health care professional if you are using any other topical prescription or nonprescription (over-the-counter [OTC]) medicine that is to be applied to the same area of the skin.

Proper Use of This Medicine

Apply enough oxiconazole to cover the affected and surrounding skin areas and rub in gently.

Keep this medicine away from the eyes. Also, do not use it in the vagina.

To help clear up your infection completely, *it is very important that you keep using oxiconazole for the full time of treatment,* even if your symptoms begin to clear up after a few days. Since fungus infections may be very slow to clear up, you may have to continue using this medicine every day for several weeks or more. If you stop using this medicine too soon, your symptoms may return. *Do not miss any doses.*

Dosing—The dose of topical oxiconazole will be different for different patients. *Follow your doctor's orders or the directions on the label.* The following information includes only the average doses of topical oxiconazole. *If your dose is different, do not change it* unless your doctor tells you to do so.

The number of doses you use each day, the time allowed between doses, and the length of time you use the medicine depend on the medical problem for which you are using topical oxiconazole.

- For *cream* or *lotion* dosage form:
  - —For ringworm of the body or groin:
    - Adults and children—Use 1 or 2 times a day for at least 2 weeks.
  - —For athlete's foot:
    - Adults and children—Use 1 or 2 times a day for at least 4 weeks.

Missed dose—If you miss a dose of this medicine, use it as soon as possible. However, if it is almost time for your next dose, skip the missed dose and go back to your regular dosing schedule.

Storage—To store this medicine:
- Keep out of the reach of children.
- Store away from heat and direct light.
- Keep the medicine from freezing. Do not refrigerate.
- Do not keep outdated medicine or medicine no longer needed. Be sure that any discarded medicine is out of the reach of children.

Precautions While Using This Medicine

If your skin problem does not improve within 2 to 4 weeks, or if it becomes worse, check with your doctor.

To help clear up your infection completely and to help make sure it does not return, good health habits are also required. The following measures will help reduce chafing and irritation and will also help keep the area cool and dry.

- *For patient using oxiconazole for ringworm of the groin:*

  —Avoid wearing underwear that is tight-fitting or made from synthetic materials (for example, rayon or nylon). Instead, wear loose-fitting, cotton underwear.

  —Use a bland, absorbent powder (for example, talcum powder) or an antifungal powder on the skin. It is best to use the powder between the times you use oxiconazole.
- *For patients using oxiconazole for ringworm of the foot:*

  —Carefully dry the feet, especially between the toes, after bathing.

  —Avoid wearing socks made from wool or synthetic materials (for example, rayon or nylon). Instead, wear clean, cotton socks and change them daily or more often if the feet sweat a lot.

  —Wear sandals or other well-ventilated shoes.

  —Use a bland, absorbent powder (for example, talcum powder) or an antifungal powder between the toes, on the feet, and in socks and shoes 1 or 2 times a day. It is best to use the powder between the times you use oxiconazole.

If you have any questions about these measures, check with your health care professional.

Side Effects of This Medicine

Along with its needed effects, a medicine may cause some unwanted effects. Although not all of these side effects may occur, if they do occur they may need medical attention.

Check with your doctor as soon as possible if the following side effect occurs:

Rare

Rash

Other side effects may occur that usually do not need medical attention. These side effects may go away during treatment as your body adjusts to the medicine. However, check with your doctor if any of the following side effects continue or are bothersome:

Less common

Burning, stinging, itching, redness, or other sign of irritation not present before use of this medicine

Other side effects not listed above may also occur in some patients. If you notice any other effects, check with your doctor.

Revised: 07/06/93

OXTRIPHYLLINE AND GUAIFENESIN Systemic

Some commonly used brand names are:

In the U.S.—

Brondelate

Generic name product may also be available.

In Canada—

Choledyl Expectorant

Description

Oxtriphylline (ox-TRYE-fi-lin) and guaifenesin (gwye-FEN-e-sin) combination is used to treat or prevent the symptoms of asthma or to treat chronic bronchitis and emphysema. This medicine relieves cough, wheezing, shortness of breath, and troubled breathing. It works by opening up the bronchial tubes (air passages of the lungs) and increasing the flow of air through them.

This medicine is available only with your doctor's prescription, in the following dosage form:

Oral

- Elixir (U.S. and Canada)

Before Using This Medicine

In deciding to use a medicine, the risks of taking the medicine must be weighed against the good it will do. This is a decision you and your doctor will make. For oxtriphylline and guaifenesin combination, the following should be considered:

Allergies—Tell your doctor if you have ever had any unusual or allergic reaction to aminophylline, guaifenesin, oxtriphylline, or theophylline.

Diet—Make certain your health care professional knows if you are on any special diet, such as a high-protein, low-carbohydrate or low-protein, high-carbohydrate diet.

Pregnancy—Oxtriphylline is used to treat asthma in pregnant women. Although there are no studies on birth defects in humans, problems have not been reported. Some studies in animals have shown that oxtriphylline can cause birth defects when given in doses many times the human dose.

Because your ability to clear oxtriphylline from your body may decrease later in pregnancy, your doctor may want to take blood samples during your pregnancy to measure the amount of medicine in the blood. This will help your doctor decide whether the dose of this medicine should be changed.

Oxtriphylline crosses the placenta. Use of this medicine during pregnancy may cause unwanted effects such as fast heartbeat, irritability, jitteriness, or vomiting in the newborn infant if the amount of medicine in your blood is too high.

Several groups of women taking guaifenesin during pregnancy have been studied. In one group, when guaifenesin was taken during the first 3 months of pregnancy, the babies had more inguinal hernias than expected. However, more birth defects than expected did not occur in the babies of other groups of women taking guaifenesin during pregnancy. Studies with guaifenesin have not been done in animals.

Breast-feeding—Theophylline passes into the breast milk and may cause irritability in nursing babies. Guaifenesin has not been reported to cause problems in nursing babies.

Children—Use of this medicine is not recommended because of high alcohol content.

Although there is no specific information about the use of guaifenesin in children, it is not expected to cause different side effects or problems in children than it does in adults.

Older adults—Patients older than 60 years of age are likely to require a lower dose than younger adults. If the amount of oxtriphylline is too high, side effects are more likely to occur. Your doctor may want to take blood samples to determine whether a dose change is needed.

Although there is no specific information about the use of guaifenesin in the elderly, it is not expected to cause different side effects or problems in older people than it does in younger adults.

Other medicines—Although certain medicines should not be used together at all, in other cases two different medicines may be used together even if an interaction might occur. In these cases, your doctor may want to change the dose, or other precautions may be necessary. When you are taking oxtriphylline and guaifenesin combination, it is especially important that your health care professional know if you are taking any of the following:

- Beta-adrenergic blocking agents including those used in the eyes (acebutolol [e.g., Sectral], atenolol [e.g., Tenormin], betaxolol [e.g., Betoptic, Kerlone], bisoprolol [e.g., Zebeta], carteolol [e.g., Cartrol], labetalol [e.g., Normodyne], levobunolol [e.g., Betagan], metipranolol [e.g., OptiPranolol], metoprolol [e.g., Lopressor], nadolol [e.g., Corgard], oxprenolol [e.g., Trasicor], penbutolol [e.g., Levatol], pindolol [e.g., Visken], propranolol [e.g., Inderal], sotalol [e.g., Sotacor], timolol [e.g., Blocadren, Timoptic])—These medicines may prevent oxtriphylline from working properly
- Cimetidine (e.g., Tagamet) or
- Ciprofloxacin (e.g., Cipro) or
- Clarithromycin (e.g., Biaxin) or
- Enoxacin (e.g., Penetrex) or
- Erythromycin (e.g., E-Mycin) or
- Fluvoxamine (e.g., Luvox) or
- Mexiletine (e.g., Mexitil) or
- Pentoxifylline (e.g., Trental) or
- Tacrine (e.g., Cognex) or
- Thiabendazole or
- Ticlopidine (e.g., Ticlid) or
- Troleandomycin (e.g., TAO)—These medicines may increase the effects of oxtriphylline
- Moricizine (e.g., Ethmozine) or
- Phenytoin (e.g., Dilantin) or
- Rifampin (e.g., Rifadin)—These medicines may decrease the effects of oxtriphylline
- Smoking tobacco or marijuana—Starting or stopping smoking may change the effectiveness of this medicine

Other medical problems—The presence of other medical problems may affect the use of oxtriphylline and guaifenesin combination. Make sure you tell your doctor if you have any other medical problems, especially:

- Convulsions (seizures)—Oxtriphylline may make this condition worse
- Heart failure or
- Liver disease or
- Underactive thyroid—The effects of oxtriphylline may be increased

Proper Use of This Medicine

This medicine works best when taken with a glass of water on an empty stomach (either 30 minutes to 1 hour before meals or 2 hours after meals) since that way it will get into the blood sooner. However, in some cases your doctor may want you to take this medicine with meals or right after meals to lessen stomach upset. If you have any questions about how you should be taking this medicine, check with your doctor.

Take this medicine only as directed by your doctor. Do not take more of it, do not take it more often, and do not take it for a longer time than your doctor ordered. To do so may increase the chance of serious side effects.

In order for this medicine to help your medical problem, it must be taken every day in regularly spaced doses as ordered by your doctor. This is necessary to keep a constant amount of the medicine in the blood. To help keep the amount constant, do not miss any doses.

Dosing—When you are taking oxtriphylline and guaifenesin combination, it is very important that you get the exact amount of medicine that you need. The dose of this medicine will be different for different patients. Your doctor will determine the proper dose of the oxtriphylline and guaifenesin combination for you. *Follow your doctor's orders or the directions on the label.*

After you begin taking oxtriphylline and guaifenesin combination, it is very important that your doctor check your blood level of theophylline at regular intervals to find out if your dose of oxtriphylline and guaifenesin combination needs to be changed. *Do not change your dose of this medicine unless your doctor tells you to do so.*

Missed dose—If you miss a dose of this medicine, take it as soon as possible. However, if it is almost time for your next dose, skip the missed dose and go back to your regular dosing schedule. Do not double doses.

Storage—To store this medicine:

- Keep out of the reach of children.
- Store away from heat and direct light.
- Keep this medicine from freezing.
- Do not keep outdated medicine or medicine no longer needed. Be sure that any discarded medicine is out of the reach of children.

Precautions While Using This Medicine

Your doctor should check your progress at regular visits, especially for the first few weeks after you begin using this medicine. A blood test may be taken to help your doctor decide whether the dose of this medicine should be changed.

The oxtriphylline in this medicine may add to the central nervous system stimulant effects of caffeine-containing foods or beverages such as chocolate, cocoa, tea, coffee, and cola drinks. *Avoid eating or drinking large amounts of these foods or beverages while taking this medicine.* If you have any questions about this, check with your doctor.

A change in your usual behavior or physical well-being may affect the way this medicine works in your body. *Check with your doctor if you:*

- have a fever of 102 °F or higher for at least 24 hours or higher than 100 °F for longer than 24 hours.
- start or stop smoking.
- start or stop taking another medicine.
- change your diet for a long time.

Before you have myocardial perfusion studies (a medical test that shows how well blood is flowing to your heart), tell the medical doctor in charge that you are taking this medicine. The results of the test may be affected by this medicine.

Side Effects of This Medicine

Along with its needed effects, a medicine may cause some unwanted effects. Although not all of these side effects may occur, if they do occur they may need medical attention.

Check with your doctor as soon as possible if any of the following side effects occur:

Less common or rare

Heartburn and/or vomiting

Symptoms of toxicity

Abdominal pain, continuing or severe; confusion or change in behavior; convulsions (seizures); dark or bloody vomit; diarrhea; dizziness or lightheadedness; fast and/or irregular heartbeat, continuing; nervousness or restlessness, continuing; trembling, continuing

Other side effects may occur that usually do not need medical attention. These side effects may go away during treatment as your body adjusts to the medicine. However, check with your doctor if any of the following side effects continue or are bothersome:

Less common

Headache; fast heartbeat; increased urination; nausea; nervousness; trembling; trouble in sleeping

Other side effects not listed above may also occur in some patients. If you notice any other effects, check with your doctor.

Revised: 06/21/96

OXYBUTYNIN Systemic

A commonly used brand name in the U.S. and Canada is Ditropan. Generic name product may also be available in the U.S.

Description

Oxybutynin (ox-i-BYOO-ti-nin) belongs to the group of medicines called antispasmodics. It helps decrease muscle spasms of the bladder and the frequent urge to urinate caused by these spasms.

Oxybutynin is available only with your doctor's prescription, in the following dosage forms:

Oral
- Syrup (U.S. and Canada)
- Tablets (U.S. and Canada)

Before Using This Medicine

In deciding to use a medicine, the risks of taking the medicine must be weighed against the good it will do. This is a decision you and your doctor will make. For oxybutynin, the following should be considered:

Allergies—Tell your doctor if you have ever had any unusual or allergic reaction to oxybutynin. Also tell your health care professional if you are allergic to any other substances, such as foods, preservatives, or dyes.

Pregnancy—Oxybutynin has not been studied in pregnant women. However, it has not been shown to cause birth defects or other problems in animal studies.

Breast-feeding—Oxybutynin has not been reported to cause problems in nursing babies. However, since this medicine tends to decrease the secretions of the body, it is possible that the flow of breast milk may be reduced in some patients.

Children—There is no specific information about the use of oxybutynin in children under 5 years of age. In older children, oxybutynin is not expected to cause different side effects or problems than it does in adults.

Older adults—Elderly people are especially sensitive to the effects of oxybutynin. This may increase the chance of side effects during treatment.

Other medicines—Although certain medicines should not be used together at all, in other cases two different medicines may be used together even if an interaction might occur. In these cases, your doctor may want to change the dose, or other precautions may be necessary. When you are taking oxybutynin, it is especially important that your health care professional know if you are taking any of the following:
- Amantadine (e.g., Symmetrel) or
- Anticholinergics (medicine for abdominal or stomach spasms or cramps) or
- Antidepressants (medicine for depression) or
- Antidyskinetics (medicine for Parkinson's disease or other conditions affecting control of muscles) or
- Antihistamines or
- Antipsychotics (medicine for mental illness) or
- Buclizine (e.g., Bucladin) or
- Carbamazepine (e.g., Tegretol) or
- Cyclizine (e.g., Marezine) or
- Cyclobenzaprine (e.g., Flexeril) or
- Disopyramide (e.g., Norpace) or
- Flavoxate (e.g., Urispas) or
- Ipratropium (e.g., Atrovent) or
- Meclizine (e.g., Antivert) or
- Methylphenidate (e.g., Ritalin) or
- Orphenadrine (e.g., Norflex) or
- Procainamide (e.g., Pronestyl) or
- Promethazine (e.g., Phenergan) or
- Quinidine (e.g., Quinidex) or
- Trimeprazine (e.g., Temaril)—Taking oxybutynin with these medicines may increase the effects of either medicine

Other medical problems—The presence of other medical problems may affect the use of oxybutynin. Make sure you tell your doctor if you have any other medical problems, especially:
- Bleeding (severe)—Oxybutynin may increase heart rate, which may make this condition worse
- Colitis (severe) or
- Dryness of mouth (severe and continuing) or
- Enlarged prostate or
- Glaucoma or
- Heart disease or
- Hiatal hernia or
- High blood pressure (hypertension) or
- Intestinal blockage or other intestinal or stomach problems or
- Myasthenia gravis or
- Toxemia of pregnancy or
- Urinary tract blockage or problems with urination—Oxybutynin may make these conditions worse
- Kidney disease or
- Liver disease—Higher blood levels of oxybutynin may occur, which increases the chance of side effects
- Overactive thyroid—Oxybutynin may further increase heart rate

Proper Use of This Medicine

This medicine is usually taken with water on an empty stomach. However, your doctor may want you to take it with food or milk to lessen stomach upset.

Take this medicine only as directed. Do not take more of it, do not take it more often, and do not take it for a longer time than your doctor ordered. To do so may increase the chance of side effects.

Dosing—The dose of oxybutynin will be different for different patients. *Follow your doctor's orders or the directions on the label.* The following information includes only the average doses of oxybutynin. *If your dose is different, do not change it* unless your doctor tells you to do so.

- For *oral* dosage forms (syrup or tablets):
  - —For treatment of bladder problems:
    - Adults and children 12 years of age and over—5 milligrams (mg) two or three times a day.
    - Children up to 5 years of age—Use and dose have not been determined.

- Children 5 to 12 years of age—5 mg two or three times a day. The dose is usually not more than 15 mg a day.

Missed dose—If you miss a dose of this medicine, take it as soon as possible. However, if it is almost time for your next dose, skip the missed dose and go back to your regular dosing schedule. Do not double doses.

Storage—To store this medicine:

- Keep out of the reach of children.
- Store away from heat and direct light.
- Do not store the tablet form of this medicine in the bathroom, near the kitchen sink, or in other damp places. Heat or moisture may cause the medicine to break down.
- Keep the syrup form of this medicine from freezing.
- Do not keep outdated medicine or medicine no longer needed. Be sure that any discarded medicine is out of the reach of children.

Precautions While Using This Medicine

This medicine will add to the effects of alcohol and other CNS depressants (medicines that slow down the nervous system, possibly causing drowsiness). Some examples of CNS depressants are antihistamines or medicine for hay fever, other allergies, or colds; sedatives, tranquilizers, or sleeping medicine; prescription pain medicine or narcotics; barbiturates; medicine for seizures; muscle relaxants; or anesthetics, including some dental anesthetics. *Check with your doctor before taking any of the above while you are using this medicine.*

This medicine may cause your eyes to become more sensitive to light than they are normally. Wearing sunglasses and avoiding too much exposure to bright light may help lessen the discomfort.

This medicine may cause some people to become drowsy or have blurred vision. *Make sure you know how you react to this medicine before you drive, use machines, or do anything else that could be dangerous if you are not alert or able to see well.*

Oxybutynin may make you sweat less, causing your body temperature to increase. *Use extra care not to become overheated during exercise or hot weather while you are taking this medicine,* since overheating may result in heat stroke. Also, hot baths or saunas may make you feel dizzy or faint while you are taking this medicine.

Your mouth, nose, and throat may feel very dry while you are taking this medicine. For temporary relief of mouth dryness, use sugarless candy or gum, melt bits of ice in your mouth, or use a saliva substitute. However, if your mouth continues to feel dry for more than 2 weeks, check with your medical doctor or dentist. Continuing dryness of the mouth may increase the chance of dental disease, including tooth decay, gum disease, and fungus infections.

Side Effects of This Medicine

Along with its needed effects, a medicine may cause some unwanted effects. Although not all of these side effects may occur, if they do occur they may need medical attention.

Check with your doctor as soon as possible if any of the following side effects occur:

Rare

Eye pain; skin rash or hives

Symptoms of overdose

Clumsiness or unsteadiness; confusion; dizziness; drowsiness (severe); fast heartbeat; fever; flushing or redness of face; hallucinations (seeing, hearing, or feeling things that are not there); shortness of breath or troubled breathing; unusual excitement, nervousness, restlessness, or irritability

Other side effects may occur that usually do not need medical attention. These side effects may go away during treatment as your body adjusts to the medicine. However, check with your doctor if any of the following side effects continue or are bothersome:

More common

Constipation; decreased sweating; drowsiness; dryness of mouth, nose, and throat

Less common or rare

Blurred vision; decreased flow of breast milk; decreased sexual ability; difficult urination; difficulty in swallowing; headache; increased sensitivity of eyes to light; nausea or vomiting; trouble in sleeping; unusual tiredness or weakness

Other side effects not listed above may also occur in some patients. If you notice any other effects, check with your doctor.

Revised: 06/16/93

OXYMETAZOLINE Nasal

Some commonly used brand names are:

In the U.S.—

Afrin Cherry Scented Nasal Spray
Afrin Children's Strength Nose Drops
Afrin Extra Moisturizing Nasal Decongestant Spray
Afrin Menthol Nasal Spray
Afrin Nasal Spray
Afrin Nose Drops
Afrin Sinus Spray
Afrin Spray Pump
Allerest 12 Hour Nasal Spray
Cheracol Nasal Spray
Cheracol Nasal Spray Pump Cherry Scented
Dristan 12-Hr Nasal Spray
Duramist Plus Up To 12 Hours Decongestant Nasal Spray
Duration 12 Hour Nasal Spray
Duration 12 Hour Nasal Spray Pump
Nasal-12 Hour
Nasal Relief
Nasal Spray 12-Hour
Nasal Spray Long Acting
Neo-Synephrine 12 Hour Nasal Spray
Neo-Synephrine 12 Hour Nasal Spray Pump
Nostrilla Long-Acting Nasal Decongestant
NTZ Long Acting Decongestant Nasal Spray

NTZ Long Acting Decongestant Nose Drops
Sinarest 12 Hour Nasal Spray
Vicks Sinex Long-Acting 12-Hour Formula Decongestant Nasal Spray
Vicks Sinex Long-Acting 12-Hour Formula Decongestant Ultra Fine Mist
4-Way Long Lasting Nasal Spray

Generic name product may be available.

In Canada—
Dristan
Dristan Mentholated
Drixoral

Description

Oxymetazoline (ox-i-met-AZ-oh-leen) is used for the temporary relief of nasal (of the nose) congestion or stuffiness caused by hay fever or other allergies, colds, or sinus trouble.

This medicine may also be used for other conditions as determined by your doctor.

This medicine is available without a prescription; however, your doctor may have special instructions on the proper use or dose for your medical condition.

Oxymetazoline is available in the following dosage forms:
Nasal
- Nasal drops (U.S.)
- Nasal spray (U.S. and Canada)

Before Using This Medicine

If you are using this medicine without a prescription, carefully read and follow any precautions on the label. For oxymetazoline, the following should be considered:

Allergies—Tell your doctor if you have ever had any unusual or allergic reaction to oxymetazoline or any other nasal decongestant. Also tell your health care professional if you are allergic to any other substances, such as foods, preservatives, or dyes.

Pregnancy—The medication may be absorbed into the body. However, oxymetazoline has not been shown to cause birth defects or other problems in humans.

Breast-feeding—Oxymetazoline may be absorbed into the body. However, oxymetazoline has not been reported to cause problems in nursing babies.

Children—Children may be especially sensitive to the effects of oxymetazoline. This may increase the chance of side effects during treatment.

Older adults—Many medicines have not been tested in older people. Therefore, it may not be known whether they work exactly the same way they do in younger adults or if they cause different side effects or problems in older people. There is no specific information about the use of oxymetazoline in the elderly.

Other medicines—Although certain medicines should not be used together at all, in other cases two different medicines may be used together even if an interaction might occur. In these cases, your doctor may want to change the dose, or other precautions may be necessary. When you are using oxymetazoline, it is especially important that your health care professional know if you are taking any other prescription or nonprescription (over-the-counter [OTC]) medicine.

Other medical problems—The presence of other medical problems may affect the use of oxymetazoline. Make sure you tell your doctor if you have any other medical problems, especially:
- Diabetes mellitus (sugar diabetes)
- Heart or blood vessel disease or
- High blood pressure—Oxymetazoline may make the condition worse
- Overactive thyroid

Proper Use of This Medicine

To use the *nose drops:*
- Blow your nose gently. Tilt the head back while standing or sitting up, or lie down on a bed and hang the head over the side. Place the drops into each nostril and keep the head tilted back for a few minutes to allow the medicine to spread throughout the nose.
- Rinse the dropper with hot water and dry with a clean tissue. Replace the cap right after use.
- To avoid spreading the infection, do not use the container for more than one person.

To use the *nose spray:*
- Blow your nose gently. With the head upright, spray the medicine into each nostril. Sniff briskly while squeezing the bottle quickly and firmly. For best results, spray once into each nostril, wait 3 to 5 minutes to allow the medicine to work, then blow the nose gently and thoroughly. Repeat until the complete dose is used.
- Rinse the tip of the spray bottle with hot water, taking care not to suck water into the bottle, and dry with a clean tissue. Replace the cap right after use.
- To avoid spreading the infection, do not use the container for more than one person.

Use this medicine only as directed. Do not use more of it, do not use it more often, and do not use it for longer than 3 days without first checking with your doctor. To do so may make your runny or stuffy nose worse and may also increase the chance of side effects.

Dosing—The dose of oxymetazoline will be different for different patients. *Follow your doctor's orders or the directions on the label.* The following information includes only the average doses of oxymetazoline. *If your dose is different, do not change it* unless your doctor tells you to do so.

- For *nasal* dosage form (nose drops or spray):
  —For nasal congestion or stuffiness:
    - Adults and children 6 years of age and older—Use 2 or 3 drops or sprays of 0.05% solution in each nostril two times a day, morning and evening.
    - Children 2 to 6 years of age—Use 2 or 3 drops of 0.025% solution in each nostril two times a day, morning and evening.
    - Children up to 2 years of age—Use and dose must be determined by your doctor.

Missed dose—If you are using this medicine on a regular schedule and you miss a dose, use it right away if you remember within an hour or so of the missed dose. However, if you do not remember until later, skip the missed dose and go back to your regular dosing schedule. Do not double doses.

Storage—To store this medicine:

- Keep out of the reach of children.
- Store away from heat and direct light.
- Keep the medicine from freezing.
- Do not keep outdated medicine or medicine no longer needed. Be sure that any discarded medicine is out of the reach of children.

Side Effects of This Medicine

Along with its needed effects, a medicine may cause some unwanted effects. Although not all of these side effects may occur, if they do occur they may need medical attention.

When this medicine is used for short periods of time at low doses, side effects usually are rare. However, check with your doctor as soon as possible if any of the following occur:

Increase in runny or stuffy nose

Symptoms of too much medicine being absorbed into the body

Fast, irregular, or pounding heartbeat; headache or lightheadedness; nervousness; trembling; trouble in sleeping

The above side effects are more likely to occur in children because there is a greater chance in children that too much of this medicine may be absorbed into the body.

Other side effects may occur that usually do not need medical attention. These side effects may go away during treatment as your body adjusts to the medicine. However, check with your health care professional if any of the following side effects continue or are bothersome:

Burning, dryness, or stinging inside of nose; sneezing

Other side effects not listed above may also occur in some patients. If you notice any other effects, check with your health care professional.

Revised: 04/19/94
Interim revision: 03/28/95; 05/24/95

OXYMETAZOLINE Ophthalmic

Some commonly used brand names are:

In the U.S.—
OcuClear
Visine L.R.

In Canada—
OcuClear

Description

Oxymetazoline (ox-i-met-AZ-oh-leen) is used to relieve redness due to minor eye irritations, such as those caused by colds, dust, wind, smog, pollen, swimming, or wearing contact lenses.

Oxymetazoline is available without a prescription; however, your doctor may have special instructions on the proper use of this medicine for your medical condition.

Oxymetazoline is available in the following dosage form:

Ophthalmic

- Ophthalmic solution (eye drops) (U.S. and Canada)

Before Using This Medicine

If you are taking this medicine without a prescription, carefully read and follow any precautions on the label. For ophthalmic oxymetazoline, the following should be considered:

Allergies—Tell your doctor if you have ever had any unusual or allergic reaction to oxymetazoline or to any other decongestant used in the eye. Also tell your health care provider if you are allergic to any other substances, such as preservatives.

Pregnancy—Studies in humans have not shown that oxymetazoline causes birth defects or other problems in humans.

Breast-feeding—Oxymetazoline may be absorbed into the body. However, oxymetazoline has not been shown to cause problems in nursing babies.

Children—Check with your doctor before using oxymetazoline eye drops in children up to 6 years of age. Eye redness in children can occur with illnesses, such as allergies, fevers, colds, and measles, that may require medical attention.

Older adults—Many medicines have not been studied specifically in older people. Therefore, it may not be known whether they work exactly the same way they do in younger adults or if they cause different side effects or problems in older people. There is no specific information comparing use of oxymetazoline in the elderly with use in other age groups.

Other medicines—Although certain medicines should not be used together at all, in other cases two different medicines may be used together even if an interaction might occur. In these cases, your doctor may want to change the dose, or other precautions may be necessary. Tell your health care provider if you are using any other prescription or nonprescription (over-the-counter [OTC]) medicine.

Other medical problems—The presence of other medical problems may affect the use of ophthalmic oxymetazoline. Make sure you tell your doctor if you have any other medical problems, especially:

- Eye disease, infection, or injury—This medicine may mask the symptoms of these conditions

- Heart or blood vessel disease or
- High blood pressure or
- Overactive thyroid—If absorbed into the body, this medicine may cause side effects that may make the medical problem worse
- Use of soft contact lenses—Because of the preservative in this medicine, some eye conditions may get worse if this medicine is used on top of soft contact lenses

Proper Use of This Medicine

Do not use oxymetazoline ophthalmic solution if it becomes cloudy or changes color.

To use:

- First, wash your hands. With the middle finger, apply pressure to the inside corner of the eye (and continue to apply pressure for 1 or 2 minutes after the medicine has been placed in the eye). Tilt the head back and with the index finger of the same hand, pull the lower eyelid away from the eye to form a pouch. Drop the medicine into the pouch and gently close the eyes. Do not blink. Keep the eyes closed for 1 or 2 minutes to allow the medicine to be absorbed.
- To keep the medicine as germ-free as possible, do not touch the applicator tip to any surface (including the eye). Also, keep the container tightly closed.

Use this medicine only as directed. Do not use more of it, do not use it more often, and do not use it for more than 72 hours, unless otherwise directed by your doctor. To do so may make your eye irritation worse and may also increase the chance of side effects.

Dosing—The dose of ophthalmic oxymetazoline will be different for different patients. *Follow your doctor's orders or the directions on the label.* The following information includes only the average doses of ophthalmic oxymetazoline. *If your dose is different, do not change it* unless your doctor tells you to do so.

- For *ophthalmic solution (eye drops)* dosage form:
  - —For eye redness:
    - Adults and children 6 years of age and older—Use one drop in the eye every six hours.
    - Children up to 6 years of age—Use and dose must be determined by your doctor.

Storage—To store this medicine:

- Keep out of the reach of children.
- Store away from heat and direct light.
- Keep the medicine from freezing.
- Do not keep outdated medicine or medicine no longer needed. Be sure that any discarded medicine is out of the reach of children.

Precautions While Using This Medicine

If eye pain or change in vision occurs or if redness or irritation of the eye continues, gets worse, or lasts for more than 72 hours, stop using the medicine and check with your doctor.

Side Effects of This Medicine

Along with its needed effects, a medicine may cause some unwanted effects. Although not all of these side effects may occur, if they do occur they may need medical attention.

When this medicine is used for short periods of time at low doses, side effects usually are rare.

Check with your doctor as soon as possible if any of the following side effects occur:

With overuse or long-term use
Increase in irritation or redness of eyes

Symptoms of too much medicine being absorbed into the body
Fast, irregular, or pounding heartbeat; headache or lightheadedness; nervousness; trembling; trouble in sleeping

Other side effects not listed above may also occur in some patients. If you notice any other effects, check with your doctor.

Revised: 04/29/92
Interim revision: 02/17/94

OXYTOCIN Systemic

Some commonly used brand names are:

In the U.S.—
Pitocin
Syntocinon

Generic name product may also be available.

In Canada—
Syntocinon

Description

Oxytocin (ox-i-TOE-sin) is a hormone used to help start or continue labor and to control bleeding after delivery. It is also sometimes used to help milk secretion in breast-feeding.

Oxytocin may also be used for other conditions as determined by your doctor.

In general, oxytocin should not be used to start labor unless there are specific medical reasons. Be sure you have discussed this with your doctor before receiving this medicine.

Oxytocin is available only with your doctor's prescription, in the following dosage forms:

Nasal
- Solution (U.S. and Canada)

Parenteral
- Injection (U.S. and Canada)

Before Using This Medicine

In deciding to use a medicine, the risks of taking the medicine must be weighed against the good it will do. This is

a decision you and your doctor will make. For oxytocin, the following should be considered:

Allergies—Tell your doctor if you have ever had any unusual or allergic reaction to oxytocin. Also tell your health care professional if you are allergic to any other substances, such as foods, preservatives, or dyes.

Breast-feeding—Although very small amounts of this medicine pass into breast milk, it has not been reported to cause problems in nursing babies.

Other medicines—Although certain medicines should not be used together at all, in other cases two different medicines may be used together even if an interaction might occur. In these cases, your doctor may want to change the dose, or other precautions may be necessary. Tell your health care professional if you are taking any other prescription or nonprescription (over-the-counter [OTC]) medicine.

Other medical problems—The presence of other medical problems may affect the use of oxytocin. Make sure you tell your doctor if you have any other medical problems, especially:

- Heart disease
- Hypertension
- Kidney disease

Proper Use of This Medicine

For patients using the *nasal spray* form of this medicine:

- This medicine usually comes with directions for use. Read them carefully before using.

Dosing—The dose of oxytocin will be different for different patients. *Follow your doctor's orders.* The following information includes only the average doses of oxytocin.

- For *nasal* dosage form:
  —For increasing milk production in breast feeding:
    - Adults—One spray into one or both nostrils two or three minutes before nursing or pumping milk from breasts.
- For *injection* dosage form:
  —For helping to start or continue labor:
    - Adults—At first, 0.5 to 2 milliunits per minute slowly injected into a vein. Then, your doctor may increase the dose every fifteen to sixty minutes as needed.

  —For treating incomplete abortion, causing abortion, or controlling bleeding after an abortion:
    - Adults—10 units injected slowly into a vein.

  —For helping to control bleeding after delivery:
    - Adults—10 units injected into a muscle or slowly into a vein.

Storage—To store this medicine:

- Keep out of the reach of children.
- Store away from heat and direct light.
- Protect the medicine from freezing.
- Do not keep outdated medicine or medicine no longer needed. Be sure that any discarded medicine is out of the reach of children.

Precautions While Using This Medicine

Oxytocin nasal spray may not help milk secretion in some breast-feeding women. Call your doctor if this medicine is not working.

Side Effects of This Medicine

Oxytocin can be very useful for helping labor. However, there are certain risks with using it. Oxytocin causes contractions of the uterus. In women who are unusually sensitive to its effects, these contractions may become too strong. In rare cases, this may lead to tearing of the uterus. Also, if contractions are too strong, the supply of blood and oxygen to the fetus may be decreased.

Oxytocin has been reported to cause irregular heartbeat and increase bleeding after delivery in some women. It has also been reported to cause jaundice in some newborn infants.

Along with its needed effects, a medicine may cause some unwanted effects. Although not all of these side effects may occur, if they do occur they may need medical attention:

Rare (with use of injection)

Confusion; convulsions (seizures); difficulty in breathing; dizziness; fast or irregular heartbeat; headache (continuing or severe); hives; pelvic or abdominal pain (severe); skin rash or itching; vaginal bleeding (increased or continuing); weakness; weight gain (rapid)

Rare (with use of nasal spray)

Convulsions (seizures); mental disturbances; unexpected bleeding or contractions of the uterus

Other side effects may occur that usually do not need medical attention. However, check with your doctor if any of the following side effects continue or are bothersome:

Rare (with use of injection)

Nausea; vomiting

Rare (with use of nasal spray)

Nasal irritation; runny nose; tearing of the eyes

Other side effects not listed above may also occur in some patients. If you notice any other effects, check with your doctor.

Additional information

Once a medicine has been approved for marketing for a certain use, experience may show that it is also useful for other medical problems. Although this use is not included in product labeling, oxytocin is used in certain patients for the following:

- Testing the ability of the placenta to support a pregnancy

Other than the above information, there is no additional information relating to proper use, precautions, or side effects for this use.

Revised: 07/14/93
Interim revision: 06/30/94

PACLITAXEL Systemic

A commonly used brand name in the U.S. and Canada is Taxol.

Description

Paclitaxel (pak-li-TAX-el) belongs to the group of medicines called antineoplastics. It is used to treat cancer of the ovary.

Paclitaxel interferes with the growth of cancer cells, which are eventually destroyed. Since the growth of normal body cells may also be affected by paclitaxel, other effects will also occur. Some of these may be serious and must be reported to your doctor. Other effects may not be serious but may cause concern. Some effects may not occur for months or years after the medicine is used.

Paclitaxel may also be used to treat other conditions as determined by your doctor.

Before you begin treatment with paclitaxel, you and your doctor should talk about the good this medicine will do as well as the risks of using it.

Paclitaxel is to be administered only by or under the immediate supervision of your doctor. It is available in the following dosage form:

Parenteral
- Injection (U.S. and Canada)

Before Using This Medicine

In deciding to use a medicine, the risks of taking the medicine must be weighed against the good it will do. This is a decision you and your doctor will make. For paclitaxel, the following should be considered:

Allergies—Tell your doctor if you have ever had any unusual or allergic reaction to paclitaxel.

Pregnancy—Tell your doctor if you are pregnant or if you intend to become pregnant. Studies in rats and rabbits have shown that paclitaxel causes miscarriages and deaths of the fetus, as well as problems in the mother.

Be sure that you have discussed this with your doctor before taking this medicine. It is best to use some kind of birth control while you are receiving paclitaxel. Tell your doctor right away if you think you have become pregnant while receiving paclitaxel.

Breast-feeding—It is not known whether paclitaxel passes into breast milk. However, because this medicine may cause serious side effects, breast-feeding is generally not recommended while you are receiving it.

Children—There is no specific information comparing use of paclitaxel in children with use in other age groups.

Older adults—This medicine has been tested in a limited number of patients and has not been shown to cause different side effects or problems in older people than it does in younger adults.

Other medicines—Although certain medicines should not be used together at all, in other cases two different medicines may be used together even if an interaction might occur. In these cases, your doctor may want to change the dose, or other precautions may be necessary. When you are receiving paclitaxel, it is especially important that your health care professional know if you are taking any of the following:

- Amphotericin B by injection (e.g., Fungizone) or
- Antithyroid agents (medicine for overactive thyroid) or
- Azathioprine (e.g., Imuran) or
- Chloramphenicol (e.g., Chloromycetin) or
- Colchicine or
- Flucytosine (e.g., Ancobon) or
- Ganciclovir (e.g., Cytovene) or
- Interferon (e.g., Intron A, Roferon-A) or
- Plicamycin (e.g., Mithracin) or
- Zidovudine (e.g., AZT, Retrovir) or
- If you have ever been treated with x-rays or cancer medicines—Paclitaxel may increase the effects of these medicines or radiation therapy on the blood

Other medical problems—The presence of other medical problems may affect the use of paclitaxel. Make sure you tell your doctor if you have any other medical problems, especially:

- Chickenpox (including recent exposure) or
- Herpes zoster (shingles)—Risk of severe disease affecting other parts of the body
- Heart rhythm problems—May be made worse by paclitaxel
- Infection—Paclitaxel may decrease your body's ability to fight infection

Proper Use of This Medicine

This medicine often causes nausea and vomiting, which is usually mild. However, it is very important that you continue to receive the medicine even if you begin to feel ill. Ask your health care professional for ways to lessen these effects.

Dosing—The dose of paclitaxel will be different for different patients. The dose that is used may depend on a number of things, including what the medicine is being used for, the patient's size, and whether or not other medicines are also being taken. *If you are receiving paclitaxel at home, follow your doctor's orders or the directions on the label.* If you have any questions about the proper dose of paclitaxel, ask your doctor.

Precautions While Using This Medicine

It is very important that your doctor check your progress at regular visits to make sure that this medicine is working properly and to check for unwanted effects.

While you are being treated with paclitaxel, and after you stop treatment with it, *do not have any immunizations (vaccinations) without your doctor's approval.* Paclitaxel may lower your body's resistance and there is a chance you might get the infection the immunization is meant to prevent. In addition, other persons living in your household should not take oral polio vaccine since there is a chance they could pass the polio virus on to you. Also, avoid persons who have taken oral polio vaccine. Do not get close to them and do not stay in the same room with them for very long. If you cannot take these precautions, you should consider wearing a protective face mask that covers the nose and mouth.

Paclitaxel can temporarily lower the number of white blood cells in your blood, increasing the chance of getting an infection. It can also lower the number of platelets, which are necessary for proper blood clotting. If this occurs, there are certain precautions you can take, especially when your blood count is low, to reduce the risk of infection or bleeding:

- If you can, avoid people with infections. *Check with your doctor immediately* if you think you are getting an infection or if you get a fever or chills, cough or hoarseness, lower back or side pain, or painful or difficult urination.
- *Check with your doctor immediately* if you notice any unusual bleeding or bruising; black, tarry stools; blood in urine or stools; or pinpoint red spots on your skin.
- Be careful when using a regular toothbrush, dental floss, or toothpick. Your medical doctor, dentist, or nurse may recommend other ways to clean your teeth and gums. Check with your medical doctor before having any dental work done.
- Do not touch your eyes or the inside of your nose unless you have just washed your hands and have not touched anything else in the meantime.
- Be careful not to cut yourself when you are using sharp objects such as a safety razor or fingernail or toenail cutters.
- Avoid contact sports or other situations where bruising or injury could occur.

Side Effects of This Medicine

Along with its needed effects, a medicine may cause some unwanted effects. Some side effects will have signs or symptoms that you can see or feel. Your doctor may watch for others by doing certain tests.

Also, because of the way these medicines act on the body, there is a chance that they might cause other unwanted effects that may not occur until months or years after the medicine is used. These delayed effects may include certain types of cancer. Discuss these possible effects with your doctor.

Check with your doctor immediately if any of the following side effects occur:

More common
Cough or hoarseness; fever or chills; lower back or side pain; painful or difficult urination

Less common
Black, tarry stools; blood in urine or stools; pinpoint red spots on skin; unusual bleeding or bruising

Rare
Shortness of breath (severe); skin reaction (severe)

Check with your doctor as soon as possible if any of the following side effects occur:

More common
Flushing of face; shortness of breath; skin rash or itching

Rare
Pain or redness at place of injection; sores in mouth and on lips (usually get better within 7 days after treatment)

This medicine may also cause the following side effects that your doctor will watch out for:

More common
Anemia; low white blood cell count; low platelet count in blood

Less common
Low blood pressure; slow heartbeat; effects on liver

Other side effects may occur that usually do not need medical attention. These side effects may go away during treatment as your body adjusts to the medicine. Also, your health care professional may be able to tell you about ways to prevent or reduce some of these side effects. Check with your health care professional if any of the following side effects continue or are bothersome or if you have any questions about them:

More common
Diarrhea; nausea and vomiting; numbness, burning, or tingling in hands or feet; pain in joints or muscles, especially in arms or legs (begins 2 to 3 days after treatment and may last up to 5 days)

This medicine usually causes a temporary and total loss of hair (including eyebrows, eyelashes, and pubic hair) about 2 to 3 weeks after treatment begins. After treatment with paclitaxel has ended, normal hair growth should return.

Other side effects not listed above may also occur in some patients. If you notice any other effects, check with your doctor.

Revised: 09/15/93
Interim revision: 07/05/94

PAMIDRONATE Systemic

A commonly used brand name in the U.S. and Canada is Aredia. Another commonly used name is APD.

Description

Pamidronate (pa-mi-DROE-nate) is used to treat hypercalcemia (too much calcium in the blood) that may occur with some types of cancer. It is also used to treat Paget's disease of bone and to treat bone metastases (spread of cancer).

This medicine is to be administered only by or under the supervision of your doctor. It is available in the following dosage form:

Parenteral
- Injection (U.S. and Canada)

Before Receiving This Medicine

In deciding to use a medicine, the risks of receiving the medicine must be weighed against the good it will do. This is a decision you and your doctor will make. For pamidronate, the following should be considered:

Allergies—Tell your doctor if you have ever had any unusual or allergic reaction to pamidronate or etidronate. Also tell your health care professional if you are allergic to any other substances, such as foods, preservatives, or dyes.

Pregnancy—Studies have not been done in humans. However, studies in rats given higher doses of oral pamidronate have shown that the medicine may decrease fertility, increase the length of pregnancy, and cause death of the baby rat.

Breast-feeding—It is not known if pamidronate passes into breast milk.

Children—Studies on this medicine have been done only in adult patients, and there is no specific information comparing use of pamidronate in children with use in other age groups.

Older adults—When pamidronate is given along with a large amount of fluids, older people tend to retain (keep) the excess fluid.

Other medicines—Although certain medicines should not be used together at all, in other cases two different medicines may be used together even if an interaction might occur. In these cases, your doctor may want to change the dose, or other precautions may be necessary. When you are receiving pamidronate, it is especially important that your health care professional know if you are taking any of the following:

- Calcium-containing preparations or
- Vitamin D–containing preparations—Use with pamidronate may keep pamidronate from working properly

Other medical problems—The presence of other medical problems may affect the use of pamidronate. Make sure you tell your doctor if you have any other medical problems, especially:

- Heart problems—The increased amount of fluid may make this condition worse
- Kidney problems—Pamidronate may build up in the bloodstream, which may increase the chance of unwanted effects

Proper Use of This Medicine

Dosing—The dose of pamidronate will be different for different patients. *Follow your doctor's orders.* The following information includes only the average doses of pamidronate.

- For *injection* dosage form:
  - —For treating hypercalcemia (too much calcium in the blood):
    - Adults: 30 to 90 milligrams (mg) in a solution to be injected over 4 to 24 hours into a vein.
    - Children: Use and dose must be determined by your doctor.
  - —For treating Paget's disease of bone:
    - Adults: Dose and frequency must be determined by your doctor. The usual dose range is 90 to 180 mg in a solution injected into a vein. Your doctor may repeat this dose.
    - Children: Use and dose must be determined by your doctor.
  - —For treating bone metastases:
    - Adults—90 mg in a solution to be injected over 2 to 4 hours into a vein. Your dose may be given every three to four weeks or once a month.
    - Children—Use and dose must be determined by your doctor.

Precautions While Receiving This Medicine

It is important that your doctor check your progress at regular visits after you have received pamidronate. If your condition has improved, your progress must still be checked. The results of laboratory tests or the occurrence of certain symptoms will tell your doctor if your condition is coming back and a second treatment is needed.

For patients using this medicine for *hypercalcemia (too much calcium in the blood):*

- Your doctor may want you to follow a low-calcium diet. If you have any questions about this, check with your doctor.

Side Effects of This Medicine

Along with its needed effects, a medicine may cause some unwanted effects. Although not all of these side effects may occur, if they do occur they may need medical attention.

Check with your doctor as soon as possible if any of the following side effects occur:

More common

Abdominal cramps; chills; confusion; fever; muscle spasms; sore throat

Note: Abdominal cramps, confusion, and muscle spasms are less common when pamidronate is given in doses of 60 mg or less.

Other side effects may occur that usually do not need medical attention. These side effects may go away during treatment as your body adjusts to the medicine. However, check with your doctor if any of the following side effects continue or are bothersome:

More common—at higher doses

Nausea; pain and swelling at place of injection

Less common

Muscle stiffness

Other side effects not listed above may also occur in some patients. If you notice any other effects, check with your doctor.

Developed: 06/02/93
Interim revision: 08/07/95; 06/07/96; 03/18/97

PANCRELIPASE Systemic

Some commonly used brand names are:

In the U.S.—

Cotazym	Pancrease MT 16
Cotazym-S	Pancrease MT 20
Enzymase-16	Panokase
Ilozyme	Protilase
Ku-Zyme HP	Ultrase MT 12
Pancoate	Ultrase MT 20
Pancrease	Viokase
Pancrease MT 4	Zymase
Pancrease MT 10	

Generic name product may be available.

In Canada—

Cotazym	Pancrease
Cotazym-65 B	Pancrease MT 4
Cotazym E.C.S. 8	Pancrease MT 10
Cotazym E.C.S. 20	Pancrease MT 16

Another commonly used name is lipancreatin.

Description

Pancrelipase (pan-kre-LI-pase) is used to help digestion in certain conditions in which the pancreas is not working properly. It may also be used for other conditions as determined by your doctor.

Pancrelipase contains the enzymes needed for the digestion of proteins, starches, and fats.

Pancrelipase is available only with your doctor's prescription, in the following dosage forms:

Oral

- Capsules (U.S. and Canada)
- Delayed-release capsules (U.S. and Canada)
- Powder (U.S.)
- Tablets (U.S.)

Before Using This Medicine

In deciding to use a medicine, the risks of taking the medicine must be weighed against the good it will do. This is a decision you and your doctor will make. For pancrelipase, the following should be considered:

Allergies—Tell your doctor if you have ever had any unusual or allergic reaction to pancrelipase, pancreatin, or pork products. Also tell your health care professional if you are allergic to any other substances, such as foods, preservatives, or dyes.

Pregnancy—Studies have not been done in either humans or animals.

Breast-feeding—Pancrelipase has not been reported to cause problems in nursing babies.

Children—This medicine has been tested in children 6 months of age or older and has not been shown to cause different side effects or problems than it does in adults.

Older adults—Many medicines have not been studied specifically in older people. Therefore, it may not be known whether they work exactly the same way they do in younger adults. Although there is no specific information comparing use of pancrelipase in the elderly with use in other age groups, this medicine is not expected to cause different side effects or problems in older people than it does in younger adults.

Other medicines—Although certain medicines should not be used together at all, in other cases two different medicines may be used together even if an interaction might occur. In these cases, your doctor may want to change the dose, or other precautions may be necessary. Tell your health care professional if you are taking any other prescription or nonprescription (over-the-counter [OTC]) medicine.

Other medical problems—The presence of other medical problems may affect the use of pancrelipase. Make sure you tell your doctor if you have any other medical problems, especially:

- Pancreatitis (sudden, severe inflammation of the pancreas)—Pancrelipase may make this condition worse

Proper Use of This Medicine

Take this medicine before or with meals and snacks, unless otherwise directed by your doctor.

When prescribing this medicine for your condition, your doctor may also prescribe a personal diet for you. Follow carefully the special diet your doctor gave you. This is most important and necessary for the medicine to work properly and to avoid indigestion.

For patients taking the *tablet form* of this medicine:

- *Swallow the tablets quickly with some liquid, without chewing*, to avoid mouth irritation.

For patients taking the *capsules containing the enteric-coated spheres:*

- Swallow the capsule whole.
- Do not crush, break, or chew before swallowing.
- When given to children, the capsule may be opened and sprinkled on a small amount of liquid or soft food that can be swallowed without chewing, such as applesauce or gelatin. However, it should not be mixed with alkaline foods, such as milk and ice cream, which may reduce its effect.

Dosing—The dose of pancrelipase will be different for different patients. *Follow your doctor's orders or the directions on the label.* The following information includes only the average doses of pancrelipase. *If your dose is different, do not change it* unless your doctor tells you to do so.

- To help digestion:
  - —For *oral* dosage form (capsules):
    - Older adults, adults, and teenagers—One to three capsules before or with meals and snacks. Your doctor may change your dose if needed.
    - Children—The contents of one to three capsules sprinkled on food at each meal. Your doctor may change your dose if needed.
  - —For *oral* dosage form (delayed-release capsules):
    - Olders adults, adults, and teenagers—One to two capsules before or with meals and snacks. Your doctor may change your dose if needed.

• Children—The contents of one to two capsules with meals. Your doctor may change your dose if needed. You should take the contents of the capsules with a liquid or a small amount of a soft food that you do not have to chew.

—For *oral* dosage form (powder):

• Older adults, adults, and teenagers—1/4 teaspoonful (0.7 gram) with meals and snacks. Your doctor may change your dose if needed.

• Children—1/4 teaspoonful with meals. Your doctor may change your dose if needed.

—For *oral* dosage form (tablets):

• Older adults, adults, and teenagers—One to three tablets before or with meals and snacks. Your doctor may change your dose if needed.

• Children—One to two tablets with meals.

Missed dose—If you miss a dose of this medicine, take it as soon as possible. However, if it is almost time for your next dose, skip the missed dose and go back to your regular dosing schedule. Do not double doses.

Storage—To store this medicine:
- Keep out of the reach of children.
- Store away from heat and direct light.
- Do not store the capsule, powder, or tablet form of this medicine in the bathroom, near the kitchen sink, or in other damp places. Heat or moisture may cause the medicine to break down.
- Do not keep outdated medicine or medicine no longer needed. Be sure that any discarded medicine is out of the reach of children.

Precautions While Using This Medicine

Your doctor may recommend that you take pancrelipase with another medicine, such as certain antacids or anti-ulcer medicines. However, antacids that contain calcium carbonate and/or magnesium hydroxate may not let the pancrelipase work properly and should be avoided.

Do not change brands or dosage forms of pancrelipase without first checking with your doctor. Different products may not work in the same way. If you refill your medicine and it looks different, check with your pharmacist.

For patients taking the *capsules containing the powder:*
- If the capsules are opened to mix with food, be careful not to breathe in the powder. To do so may cause harmful effects such as stuffy nose, shortness of breath, troubled breathing, wheezing, or tightness in chest.

For patients taking the *powder form* of this medicine:
- Avoid breathing in the powder. To do so may cause harmful effects such as stuffy nose, shortness of breath, troubled breathing, wheezing, or tightness in chest.

Side Effects of This Medicine

Along with its needed effects, a medicine may cause some unwanted effects. Although not all of these side effects may occur, if they do occur they may need medical attention.

Check with your doctor as soon as possible if any of the following side effects occur:

Rare

Skin rash or hives

With high doses

Diarrhea; intestinal blockage; nausea; stomach cramps or pain

With very high doses

Blood in urine; joint pain; swelling of feet or lower legs

With powder dosage form or powder from opened capsules—if breathed in

Shortness of breath; stuffy nose; tightness in chest; troubled breathing; wheezing

With tablets—if held in mouth

Irritation of the mouth

Other side effects not listed above may also occur in some patients. If you notice any other effects, check with your doctor.

Revised: 02/13/92
Interim revision: 08/01/94; 08/01/95

PANTOTHENIC ACID (Vitamin B_5) Systemic†

Other commonly used names are vitamin B_5 and calcium pantothenate. Generic name product may also be available in the U.S.

†Not commercially available in Canada.

Description

Vitamins (VYE-ta-mins) are compounds that you *must* have for growth and health. They are needed in only small amounts and are usually available in the foods that you eat. Pantothenic acid (pan-toh-THEN-ik AS-id) (vitamin B_5) is needed for the breakdown of carbohydrates, proteins, and fats.

No problems have been found that are due to a lack of pantothenic acid alone. However, a lack of one B vitamin usually goes along with a lack of others, so pantothenic acid is often included in B complex products.

Claims that pantothenic acid is effective for treatment of nerve damage, breathing problems, itching and other skin problems, and poisoning with some other drugs; for getting rid of or preventing gray hair; for preventing arthritis, allergies, and birth defects; or for improving mental ability have not been proven.

This vitamin is available without a prescription in the following dosage forms:

Oral

Calcium pantothenate
- Tablets (U.S.)

Pantothenic acid
- Capsules (U.S.)
- Oral solution (U.S.)
- Tablets (U.S.)
- Extended-release tablets (U.S.)

Importance of Diet

For good health, it is important that you eat a balanced and varied diet. Follow carefully any diet program your health care professional may recommend. For your specific dietary vitamin and/or mineral needs, ask your health care professional for a list of appropriate foods. If you think that you are not getting enough vitamins and/or minerals in your diet, you may choose to take a dietary supplement.

Pantothenic acid is found in various foods including peas and beans (except green beans), lean meat, poultry, fish, and whole-grain cereals. Little pantothenic acid is lost from foods with ordinary cooking.

Vitamins alone will not take the place of a good diet and will not provide energy. Your body also needs other substances found in food—protein, minerals, carbohydrates, and fat.

The daily amount of pantothenic acid needed is defined in several different ways.

For U.S.—
- Recommended Dietary Allowances (RDAs) are the amount of vitamins and minerals needed to provide for adequate nutrition in most healthy persons. RDAs for a given nutrient may vary depending on a person's age, sex, and physical condition (e.g., pregnancy).
- Daily Values (DVs) for nutrients are used on food and dietary supplement labels to indicate the percent of the recommended daily amount of each nutrient that a serving provides. DVs replace the previous designation of United States Recommended Daily Allowances (USRDAs).

For Canada—
- Recommended Nutrient Intakes (RNIs) are used to determine the amounts of vitamins, minerals, and protein needed to provide adequate nutrition and lessen the risk of chronic disease.

Because lack of pantothenic acid is so rare, there is no RDA or RNI for this vitamin. The following daily intakes are thought to be plenty for most individuals:
- Infants and children—
  Birth to 3 years of age: 2 to 3 milligrams (mg).
  4 to 6 years of age: 3 to 4 mg.
  7 to 10 years of age: 4 to 5 mg.
- Adolescents and adults—4 to 7 mg.

Before Using This Dietary Supplement

If you are taking this dietary supplement without a prescription, carefully read and follow any precautions on the label. For pantothenic acid, the following should be considered:

Allergies—Tell your health care professional if you are allergic to any substances, such as foods, preservatives, or dyes.

Pregnancy—It is especially important that you are receiving enough vitamins when you become pregnant and that you continue to receive the right amount of vitamins throughout your pregnancy. The healthy growth and development of the fetus depend on a steady supply of nutrients from the mother. However, taking large amounts of a nutritional supplement during pregnancy may be harmful to the mother and/or fetus and should be avoided.

Breast-feeding—It is especially important that you receive the right amounts of vitamins so that your baby will also get the vitamins needed to grow properly. However, taking large amounts of a nutritional supplement while breast-feeding may be harmful to the mother and/or baby and should be avoided.

Children—Problems in children have not been reported with intake of normal daily recommended amounts.

Older adults—Problems in older adults have not been reported with intake of normal daily recommended amounts.

Other medicines or dietary supplements—Although certain medicines or dietary supplements should not be used together at all, in other cases two different medicines or dietary supplements may be used together even if an interaction might occur. In these cases, your health care professional may want to change the dose, or other precautions may be necessary. Tell your health care professional if you are taking any other prescription, nonprescription (over-the-counter [OTC]) medicine, or dietary supplements.

Proper Use of This Dietary Supplement

Dosing—The amount of pantothenic acid needed to meet normal daily recommended intakes will be different for different individuals. The following information includes only the average amounts of pantothenic acid.
- For *oral* dosage forms (capsules, tablets, oral solution):
  —To prevent deficiency, the amount taken by mouth is based on normal daily recommended intakes:
  - Adults and teenagers—4 to 7 milligrams (mg) per day.
  - Children 7 to 10 years of age—4 to 5 mg per day.
  - Children 4 to 6 years of age—3 to 4 mg per day.
  - Children birth to 3 years of age—2 to 3 mg per day.

  —To treat deficiency:
  - Adults, teenagers, and children—Treatment dose is determined by prescriber for each individual based on severity of deficiency.

Missed dose—If you miss taking a vitamin for one or more days there is no cause for concern, since it takes some time for your body to become seriously low in vitamins. However, if your health care professional has recommended that you take this vitamin, try to remember to take it as directed every day.

Storage—To store this dietary supplement:
- Keep out of the reach of children.
- Store away from heat and direct light.
- Do not store in the bathroom, near the kitchen sink, or in other damp places. Heat or moisture may cause the dietary supplement to break down.
- Do not keep outdated dietary supplements or those no longer needed. Be sure that any discarded dietary supplement is out of the reach of children.

Side Effects of This Dietary Supplement

Along with its needed effects, a dietary supplement may cause some unwanted effects. Although pantothenic acid does not usually cause any side effects, check with your health care professional if you notice any unusual effects while you are taking it.

Revised: 07/16/92
Interim revision: 08/15/94

PAPAVERINE Intracavernosal

Generic name product available in the U.S. and Canada.

Description

Papaverine (pa-PAV-er-een) belongs to the group of medicines called vasodilators. Vasodilators cause blood vessels to expand, thereby increasing blood flow. Papaverine is used to produce erections in some impotent men. When papaverine is injected into the penis (intracavernosal), it increases blood flow to the penis, which results in an erection.

Papaverine injection should not be used as a sexual aid by men who are not impotent. If the medicine is not used properly, permanent damage to the penis and loss of the ability to have erections could result.

Papaverine is available only with your doctor's prescription, in the following dosage form:

Parenteral
- Injection (U.S. and Canada)

Before Using This Medicine

In deciding to use a medicine, the risks of taking the medicine must be weighed against the good it will do. This is a decision you and your doctor will make. For papaverine, the following should be considered:

Allergies—Tell your doctor if you have ever had any unusual or allergic reaction to papaverine. Also tell your health care professional if you are allergic to any other substances, such as foods, preservatives, or dyes.

Older adults—Many medicines have not been studied specifically in older people. Therefore, it may not be known whether they work exactly the same way they do in younger adults or if they cause different side effects or problems in older people. Although there is no specific information comparing the use of papaverine for impotence in the elderly with use in other age groups, this medicine is not expected to cause different side effects or problems in older people than it does in younger adults.

Other medicines—Although certain medicines should not be used together at all, in other cases two different medicines may be used together even if an interaction might occur. In these cases, your doctor may want to change the dose, or other precautions may be necessary. Tell your health care professional if you are taking any other prescription or nonprescription (over-the-counter [OTC]) medicine.

Other medical problems—The presence of other medical problems may affect the use of papaverine. Make sure you tell your doctor if you have any other medical problems, especially:
- Bleeding problems—These conditions increase the risk of bleeding at the place of injection
- Liver disease—Papaverine can cause liver damage when it is given in ways that allow it to get into the bloodstream (by mouth or by injection into a muscle, a vein, or an artery); when papaverine is given by intracavernosal injection, liver damage is much less likely because the medicine enters the bloodstream very slowly
- Priapism (history of) or
- Sickle cell disease—Patients with these conditions have an increased risk of priapism (erection lasting longer than 4 hours) while using papaverine

Proper Use of This Medicine

To give papaverine injection:
- Cleanse the injection site with alcohol. Using a sterile needle, *inject the medicine slowly and directly into the base of the penis as instructed by your doctor. Papaverine should not be injected just under the skin.* The injection is usually not painful, although you may feel some tingling in the tip of your penis. If the injection is very painful or you notice bruising or swelling at the place of injection, that means you have been injecting the medicine under the skin. Stop, withdraw the needle, and reposition it properly before continuing with the injection.
- After you have completed the injection, put pressure on the place of injection to prevent bruising. Then massage your penis as instructed by your doctor. This helps the medicine spread to all parts of the penis, so that it will work better.

This medicine usually begins to work in about 10 minutes. You should attempt intercourse within 2 hours after injecting the medicine.

Dosing—The dose of papaverine will be different for different patients. *Follow your doctor's orders or the directions on the label.* The following information includes only the average doses of papaverine. *If your dose is different, do not change it* unless your doctor tells you to do so.

- For *injection* dosage form:
  - —For the treatment of impotence:
    - Adults—30 to 60 milligrams (mg) injected very slowly into the area of your penis as directed by your doctor. Allow one or two minutes to completely inject the dose. Do not inject more than one dose in a day. Also, do not use this medicine more than two days in a row or more than three times a week.

Storage—To store this medicine:

- Keep out of the reach of children.
- Store away from heat and direct light.
- Keep the medicine from freezing.

Precautions While Using This Medicine

Use papaverine injection exactly as directed by your doctor. Do not use more of it and do not use it more often than ordered. If too much is used, the erection may become so strong that it lasts too long and does not reverse when it should. This condition is called priapism, and it can be very dangerous. If the effect is not reversed, the blood supply to the penis may be cut off and permanent damage may occur.

Contact your doctor immediately if the erection lasts for longer than 4 hours or if it becomes painful. This may be a sign of priapism and must be treated right away to prevent permanent damage.

If you notice bleeding at the site when you inject papaverine, put pressure on the spot until the bleeding stops. If it doesn't stop, check with your doctor.

It is important for you to examine your penis regularly. Check with your doctor if you find a lump where the medicine has been injected or if you notice that your penis is becoming curved. These may be signs that unwanted tissue is growing (called fibrosis), which should be seen by your doctor.

Side Effects of This Medicine

Along with its needed effects, a medicine may cause some unwanted effects. Although not all of these side effects may occur, if they do occur they may need medical attention.

Check with your doctor immediately if the following side effect occurs:

Rare

Erection continuing for more than 4 hours, or painful erection

Check with your doctor as soon as possible if the following side effects occur:

Rare

Dizziness; lumps in the penis

Other side effects may occur that usually do not need medical attention. These side effects may go away during treatment as your body adjusts to the medicine. However, check with your doctor if any of the following side effects continue or are bothersome:

Less common or rare

Bruising or bleeding at place of injection; burning (mild) along penis; difficulty in ejaculating; swelling at place of injection

Papaverine injected into the penis may cause tingling at the tip of the penis. This is no cause for concern.

Other side effects not listed above may also occur in some patients. If you notice any other effects, check with your doctor.

Revised: 08/06/92
Interim revision: 06/07/94

PAPAVERINE Systemic

Some commonly used brand names are:

In the U.S.—

Cerespan	Pavagen
Genabid	Pavarine
Pavabid	Pavased
Pavabid HP	Pavatine
Pavacels	Pavatym
Pavacot	Paverolan

Generic name product may also be available in the U.S. and Canada.

Description

Papaverine (pa-PAV-er-een) belongs to the group of medicines called vasodilators. Vasodilators cause blood vessels to expand, thereby increasing blood flow. This medicine is used to treat problems resulting from poor blood circulation.

Papaverine is available only with your doctor's prescription, in the following dosage forms:

Oral

- Extended-release capsules (U.S.)
- Tablets (U.S. and Canada)

Parenteral

- Injection (U.S. and Canada)

Before Using This Medicine

In deciding to use a medicine, the risks of taking the medicine must be weighed against the good it will do. This is a decision you and your doctor will make. For papaverine, the following should be considered:

Allergies—Tell your doctor if you have ever had any unusual or allergic reaction to papaverine. Also tell your

health care professional if you are allergic to any other substances, such as foods, preservatives, or dyes.

Pregnancy—Studies on effects in pregnancy have not been done in either humans or animals.

Breast-feeding—It is not known whether papaverine passes into the breast milk. However, this medicine has not been reported to cause problems in nursing babies.

Children—Although there is no specific information comparing use of papaverine in children with use in other age groups, this medicine is not expected to cause different side effects or problems in children than it does in adults.

Older adults—Papaverine may reduce tolerance to cold temperatures in elderly patients.

Other medicines—Although certain medicines should not be used together at all, in other cases two different medicines may be used together even if an interaction might occur. In these cases, your doctor may want to change the dose, or other precautions may be necessary. Tell your health care professional if you are taking any other prescription or nonprescription (over-the-counter [OTC]) medicine, or if you smoke.

Other medical problems—The presence of other medical problems may affect the use of papaverine. Make sure you tell your doctor if you have any other medical problems, especially:

- Angina (chest pain) or
- Glaucoma or
- Heart disease or
- Myocardial infarction (''heart attack''), recent, or
- Stroke, recent—The chance of unwanted effects may be increased

Proper Use of This Medicine

If this medicine upsets your stomach, it may be taken with meals, milk, or antacids.

For patients taking the *extended-release capsule* form of this medicine:

- Swallow the capsules whole. Do not crush, break, or chew before swallowing. However, if the capsule is too large to swallow, you may mix the contents with jam or jelly and swallow without chewing.

Dosing—The dose of papaverine will be different for different patients. *Follow your doctor's orders or the directions on the label.* The following information includes only the average doses of papaverine. *If your dose is different, do not change it* unless your doctor tells you to do so:

- For *oral* dosage form (extended-release capsules):
  —Adults: 150 milligrams (mg) every twelve hours. The dose may be increased to 150 mg every eight hours or 300 mg every twelve hours.
- For *oral* dosage form (tablets):
  —Adults: 100 to 300 mg three to five times a day.
- For *injection* dosage form:
  —Adults: 30 to 120 mg every three hours injected slowly into the muscle or vein.
  —Children: 1.5 mg per kilogram (0.68 mg per pound) of body weight four times a day injected into the muscle or vein.

Missed dose—If you miss a dose of this medicine, take it as soon as you remember. However, if it is almost time for the next dose, skip the missed dose and go back to your regular dosing schedule. Do not double doses.

Storage—To store this medicine:

- Keep out of the reach of children.
- Store away from heat and direct light.
- Do not store in the bathroom, near the kitchen sink, or in other damp places. Heat or moisture may cause the medicine to break down.
- Do not keep outdated medicine or medicine no longer needed. Be sure that any discarded medicine is out of the reach of children.

Precautions While Using This Medicine

It may take some time for this medicine to work. If you feel that the medicine is not working, do not stop taking it on your own. Instead, check with your doctor.

The helpful effects of this medicine may be decreased if you smoke. If you have any questions about this, check with your doctor.

Dizziness may occur, especially when you get up from a lying or sitting position or climb stairs. Getting up slowly may help. If this problem continues or gets worse, check with your doctor.

Side Effects of This Medicine

Along with its needed effects, a medicine may cause some unwanted effects. Although not all of these side effects may occur, if they do occur they may need medical attention.

Check with your doctor as soon as possible if any of the following side effects occur:

Symptoms of overdose
Blurred or double vision; drowsiness; weakness

Rare
Yellow eyes or skin

Other side effects may occur after papaverine is given by injection. Check with your doctor if you notice any redness, swelling, or pain at the place of injection.

Other side effects that usually do not need medical attention may occur soon after an injection of this medicine. They usually go away after a little while. However, check with your doctor if any of the following side effects continue or are bothersome:

Deep breathing; dizziness; fast heartbeat; flushing of face

Other side effects not listed above may also occur in some patients. If you notice any other effects, check with your doctor.

Revised: 04/13/93

PAROXETINE Systemic

A commonly used brand name in the U.S. and Canada is Paxil.

Description

Paroxetine (pa-ROX-uh-teen) is used to treat mental depression, obsessive-compulsive disorder, and panic disorder.

Paroxetine belongs to a group of medicines known as selective serotonin reuptake inhibitors (SSRIs). These medicines are thought to work by increasing the activity of a certain chemical, called serotonin, in the brain.

This medicine is available only with your doctor's prescription, in the following dosage form:

Oral

- Tablets (U.S. and Canada)

Before Using This Medicine

In deciding to use a medicine, the risks of taking the medicine must be weighed against the good it will do. This is a decision you and your doctor will make. For paroxetine, the following should be considered:

Allergies—Tell your doctor if you have ever had any unusual or allergic reaction to paroxetine. Also tell your health care professional if you are allergic to any other substances, such as foods, preservatives, or dyes.

Pregnancy—Studies have not been done in pregnant women. However, studies in animals have shown that paroxetine may cause decreased survival rates of offspring when given in doses lower than the maximum human dose. Before taking this medicine, make sure your doctor knows if you are pregnant or if you may become pregnant.

Breast-feeding—Paroxetine passes into the breast milk. However, the effects of this medicine in nursing babies are not known.

Children—Studies on this medicine have been done only in adult patients, and there is no specific information comparing use of paroxetine in children with use in other age groups.

Older adults—In studies that have included elderly people, paroxetine did not cause different side effects or problems in older people than it did in younger adults. However, paroxetine may be removed from the body more slowly in elderly people. An older adult may need a lower dose than a younger adult.

Other medicines—Although certain medicines should not be used together at all, in other cases two different medicines may be used together even if an interaction might occur. In these cases, your doctor may want to change the dose, or other precautions may be necessary. When you are taking paroxetine, it is especially important that your health care professional know if you are taking any of the following:

- Monoamine oxidase (MAO) inhibitors (furazolidone) [e.g., Furoxone], isocarboxazid [e.g., Marplan], phenelzine [e.g., Nardil], procarbazine [e.g., Matulane], selegiline [e.g., Eldepryl], tranylcypromine [e.g., Parnate]—*Do not take paroxetine while you are taking or within 2 weeks of taking MAO inhibitors,* or you may develop confusion, agitation, restlessness, stomach or intestinal symptoms, sudden high body temperature, extremely high blood pressure, and severe convulsions; at least 14 days should be allowed between stopping treatment with one medicine and starting treatment with the other
- Tricyclic antidepressants (amitriptyline [e.g., Elavil], amoxapine [e.g., Asendin], clomipramine [e.g., Anafranil], desipramine [e.g., Pertofrane], doxepin [e.g., Sinequan], imipramine [e.g.,Tofranil], nortriptyline [e.g., Aventyl], protriptyline [e.g., Vivactil], trimipramine [e.g., Surmontil])—Taking a tricyclic antidepressant together with paroxetine may increase the risk of side effects; your doctor may need to adjust the dose of either medicine or check blood levels of the tricyclic antidepressant
- Tryptophan—Taking this medicine while you are taking paroxetine may increase the risk of serious side effects; taking tryptophan while you are taking paroxetine is not recommended
- Warfarin (e.g., Coumadin)—Taking this medicine together with paroxetine may cause bleeding problems; your doctor may need to adjust the dosage of either medicine

Other medical problems—The presence of other medical problems may affect the use of paroxetine. Make sure you tell your doctor if you have any other medical problems, especially:

- Brain disease or damage, or mental retardation or
- Seizures (history of)—The risk of seizures may be increased
- Kidney disease, severe, or
- Liver disease, severe—Higher blood levels of paroxetine may occur, increasing the chance of side effects

Proper Use of This Medicine

Take this medicine only as directed by your doctor to benefit your condition as much as possible. Do not take more of it, do not take it more often, and do not take it for a longer time than your doctor ordered.

Paroxetine may be taken with or without food or on a full or empty stomach. However, if your doctor tells you to take the medicine a certain way, take it exactly as directed.

You may have to take paroxetine for several weeks before you begin to feel better. Your doctor should check your progress at regular visits during this time.

Dosing—The dose of paroxetine will be different for different patients. *Follow your doctor's orders or the directions on the label.* The following information includes only the average doses of paroxetine. *If your dose is different, do not change it* unless your doctor tells you to do so.

- For *oral* dosage form (tablets):
  - —For treatment of depression:
    - Adults—At first, 20 milligrams (mg) once a day, usually taken in the morning. Your doctor may increase your dose if needed. However, the dose usually is not more than 50 mg a day.

• Children—Use and dose must be determined by your doctor.

• Older adults—At first, 10 mg once a day, usually taken in the morning. Your doctor may increase your dose if needed. However, the dose usually is not more than 40 mg a day.

—For treatment of obsessive-compulsive disorder:

• Adults—At first, 20 milligrams (mg) once a day, usually taken in the morning. Your doctor may increase your dose if needed. However, the dose usually is not more than 60 mg a day.

• Children—Use and dose must be determined by your doctor.

• Older adults—At first, 10 mg once a day, usually taken in the morning. Your doctor may increase your dose if needed. However, the dose usually is not more than 40 mg a day.

—For treatment of panic disorder:

• Adults—At first, 10 milligrams (mg) once a day, usually taken in the morning. Your doctor may increase your dose if needed. However, the dose usually is not more than 60 mg a day.

• Children—Use and dose must be determined by your doctor.

• Older adults—At first, 10 mg once a day, usually taken in the morning. Your doctor may increase your dose if needed. However, the dose usually is not more than 40 mg a day.

Missed dose—If you miss a dose of this medicine, take it as soon as possible. However, if it is almost time for your next dose, skip the missed dose and go back to your regular dosing schedule. Do not double doses.

Storage—To store this medicine:

- Keep out of the reach of children.
- Store away from heat and direct light.
- Do not store in the bathroom, near the kitchen sink, or in other damp places. Heat or moisture may cause the medicine to break down.
- Do not keep outdated medicine or medicine no longer needed. Be sure that any discarded medicine is out of the reach of children.

Precautions While Using This Medicine

It is important that your doctor check your progress at regular visits, to allow for changes in your dose and to help reduce any side effects.

Do not stop taking this medicine without first checking with your doctor. Your doctor may want you to gradually reduce the amount you are taking before stopping completely. This is to decrease the chance of side effects.

Do not take paroxetine if you have taken a monoamine oxidase (MAO) inhibitor in the past 2 weeks. Do not start taking an MAO inhibitor within 2 weeks of stopping paroxetine. If you do, you may develop confusion, agitation, restlessness, stomach or intestinal symptoms, sudden high body temperature, extremely high blood pressure, and severe convulsions.

This medicine could possibly add to the effects of alcohol and other CNS depressants (medicines that cause drowsiness). Some examples of CNS depressants are antihistamines or medicine for hay fever, other allergies, or colds; sedatives, tranquilizers, or sleeping medicine; prescription pain medicine or narcotics; barbiturates; medicine for seizures; muscle relaxants; or anesthetics, including some dental anesthetics. *Check with your doctor before taking any of the above while you are using this medicine.*

Paroxetine may cause some people to become drowsy or have blurred vision. *Make sure you know how you react to this medicine before you drive, use machines, or do anything else that could be dangerous if you are not alert or able to see clearly.*

This medicine may cause dryness of the mouth. For temporary relief, use sugarless gum or candy, melt bits of ice in your mouth, or use a saliva substitute. However, if your mouth continues to feel dry for more than 2 weeks, check with your medical doctor or dentist. Continuing dryness of the mouth may increase the chance of dental disease, including tooth decay, gum disease, and fungus infections.

Side Effects of This Medicine

Along with its needed effects, a medicine may cause some unwanted effects. One rare but serious unwanted effect that may occur with paroxetine use is the serotonin syndrome. The serotonin syndrome is more likely to occur shortly after the dose of paroxetine is increased.

Although not all of these side effects may occur, if they do occur they may need medical attention.

Check with your doctor as soon as possible if any of the following side effects occur:

Less common

Agitation; muscle pain or weakness; skin rash

Rare

Absence of or decrease in body movements; difficulty in speaking; inability to move eyes; incomplete, sudden, or unusual body or facial movements; red or purple patches on skin; talking, feeling, and acting with excitement and activity you cannot control

Rare—Symptoms of low blood sodium (usually two or more occur together)

Confusion; drowsiness; dryness of mouth; increased thirst; lack of energy; convulsions (seizures)

Rare—Symptoms of serotonin syndrome (usually two or more occur together)

Diarrhea; fever; increased sweating; mood or behavior changes; overactive reflexes; racing heartbeat; restlessness; shivering or shaking

Symptoms of overdose

Drowsiness (severe); dryness of mouth (severe); irritability; large pupils; nausea (severe); racing heartbeat; trembling or shaking (severe); vomiting (severe)

Other side effects may occur that usually do not need medical attention. These side effects may go away during treatment as your body adjusts to the medicine. However, check with your doctor if any of the following side effects continue or are bothersome:

More common

Constipation; decreased sexual ability; diarrhea; dizziness; drowsiness; dryness of mouth; headache; increased sweating; nausea; problems in urinating; trembling or shaking; trouble in sleeping; unusual tiredness or weakness; vomiting

Less common

Anxiety or nervousness; blurred vision; change in your sense of taste; decreased or increased appetite; decreased sexual desire; feeling of fast or irregular heartbeat; tingling, burning, or prickling sensations; weight loss or gain

After you stop using this medicine, your body may need time to adjust. The length of time this takes depends on the amount of medicine you were using and how long you used it. During this period of time check with your doctor if you notice any of the following side effects:

Agitation, confusion, or restlessness; diarrhea; dizziness or lightheadedness; headache; increased sweating; muscle pain; nausea or vomiting; runny nose; trembling or shaking; trouble in sleeping; unusual tiredness or weakness; vision changes

Other side effects not listed above may also occur in some patients. If you notice any other effects, check with your doctor.

Developed: 08/22/94
Revised: 08/04/97

PEMOLINE Systemic

Some commonly used brand names are:

In the U.S.—
Cylert
Cylert Chewable

In Canada—
Cylert

Description

Pemoline (PEM-oh-leen) belongs to the group of medicines called central nervous system (CNS) stimulants. It is used to treat children with attention-deficit hyperactivity disorder (ADHD).

Pemoline increases attention and decreases restlessness in children who are overactive, cannot concentrate for very long or are easily distracted, and are emotionally unstable. This medicine is used as part of a total treatment program that also includes social, educational, and psychological treatment.

Pemoline is available only with your doctor's prescription, in the following dosage forms:

Oral
- Tablets (U.S. and Canada)
- Chewable tablets (U.S.)

Before Using This Medicine

In deciding to use a medicine, the risks of taking the medicine must be weighed against the good it will do. This is a decision you and your doctor will make. For pemoline, the following should be considered:

Allergies—Tell your doctor if you have ever had any unusual or allergic reaction to pemoline. Also tell your health care professional if you are allergic to any other substances, such as foods, preservatives, or dyes.

Pregnancy—Pemoline has not been shown to cause birth defects or other problems in humans. However, studies in animals given large doses of pemoline have shown that pemoline causes an increase in stillbirths and decreased survival of the offspring after birth.

Breast-feeding—It is not known if pemoline is excreted in breast milk.

Children—Slowed growth rate in children who received pemoline for a long period of time have been reported. Some doctors recommend drug-free periods during treatment with pemoline.

Other medicines—Although certain medicines should not be used together at all, in other cases 2 different medicines may be used together even if an interaction might occur. In these cases, your doctor may want to change the dose, or other precautions may be necessary. Tell your health care professional if you are taking any other prescription or nonprescription (over-the-counter [OTC]) medicine.

Other medical problems—The presence of other medical problems may affect the use of pemoline. Make sure you tell your doctor if you have any other medical problems, especially:

- Gilles de la Tourette's disorder or other tics or
- Mental illness (severe) or
- Liver disease—Pemoline may make the condition worse
- Kidney disease—Higher blood levels of pemoline may occur, increasing the chance of side effects

Proper Use of This Medicine

For patients taking the *chewable tablet form* of this medicine:

- These tablets must be chewed before swallowing. Do not swallow whole.

Sometimes this medicine must be taken for 3 to 4 weeks before improvement is noticed.

Take pemoline only as directed by your doctor. Do not take more of it, do not take it more often, and do not take it for a longer time than your doctor ordered. If too much is taken, it may become habit-forming.

Dosing—The dose of pemoline will be different for different patients. *Follow your doctor's orders or the directions on the label.* The following information includes only the average doses of pemoline. *If your dose is different, do not change it* unless your doctor tells you to do so.

The number of tablets that you take depends on the strength of the medicine. Also, *the number of doses you take each day, the time allowed between doses, and the length of time you take the medicine depend on the medical problem for which you are taking pemoline.*

- For *oral* or *chewable* dosage forms (tablets):
  —Children 6 years of age and over: To start, 37.5 milligrams (mg) every morning. Your doctor may increase your dose if needed. However, the dose is usually not more than 112.5 mg a day.
  —Children up to 6 years of age: Dose must be determined by the doctor.

Missed dose—If you miss a dose of this medicine, take it as soon as possible. Then go back to your regular dosing schedule. But if you do not remember the missed dose until the next day, skip it and go back to your regular dosing schedule. Do not double doses.

Storage—To store this medicine:
- Keep out of the reach of children.
- Store away from heat and direct light.
- Do not store in the bathroom, near the kitchen sink, or in other damp places. Heat or moisture may cause the medicine to break down.
- Do not keep outdated medicine or medicine no longer needed. Be sure that any discarded medicine is out of the reach of children.

Precautions While Using This Medicine

Your doctor should check your progress at regular visits to make sure that this medicine does not cause unwanted effects.

If you will be taking this medicine in large doses for a long time, do not stop taking it without first checking with your doctor. Your doctor may want you to reduce gradually the amount you are taking before stopping completely.

This medicine may cause some people to become dizzy or less alert than they are normally. *Make sure you know how you react to this medicine before you ride a bicycle or do anything else that could be dangerous if you are dizzy or are not alert.*

If you have been using this medicine for a long time and you think you may have become mentally or physically dependent on it, check with your doctor. Some signs of dependence on pemoline are:
- a strong desire or need to continue taking the medicine.
- a need to increase the dose to receive the effects of the medicine.
- withdrawal side effects (for example, mental depression, unusual behavior, or unusual tiredness or weakness) occurring after the medicine is stopped.

Side Effects of This Medicine

Along with their needed effects, medicines like pemoline, when used for a long time, have been reported to slow the growth rate of children. Some doctors recommend drug-free periods during treatment with pemoline. Pemoline may also cause unwanted effects on behavior in children with severe emotional problems.

Although not all of these side effects may occur, if they do occur they may need medical attention.

Check with your doctor as soon as possible if any of the following side effects occur:

Rare

Yellow eyes or skin

Symptoms of overdose

Agitation; confusion; convulsions (seizures); false sense of well-being; fast heartbeat; hallucinations (seeing, hearing, or feeling things that are not there); headache (severe); high blood pressure; high fever with sweating; large pupils; muscle trembling or twitching; nervousness or restlessness; uncontrolled movements of the eyes or other parts of the body; vomiting

Other side effects may occur that usually do not need medical attention. These side effects may go away during treatment as your body adjusts to the medicine. However, check with your doctor if any of the following side effects continue or are bothersome:

More common

Loss of appetite; trouble in sleeping; weight loss

Less common

Dizziness; drowsiness; increased irritability; mental depression; nausea; skin rash; stomach ache

After you stop using this medicine, your body may need time to adjust. The length of time this takes depends on the amount of medicine you were using and how long you used it. During this period of time check with your doctor if you notice any of the following side effects:

Mental depression (severe); unusual behavior; unusual tiredness or weakness

Other side effects not listed above may also occur in some patients. If you notice any other effects, check with your doctor.

Revised: 04/16/93

PENICILLAMINE Systemic

Some commonly used brand names in the U.S. and Canada are Cuprimine and Depen.

Description

Penicillamine (pen-i-SILL-a-meen) is used in the treatment of medical problems such as Wilson's disease (too much copper in the body) and rheumatoid arthritis. Also, it is used to prevent kidney stones. Penicillamine may also be used for other conditions as determined by your doctor.

In addition to the helpful effects of this medicine, it has side effects that can be very serious. Before you take penicillamine, be sure that you have discussed the use of it with your doctor.

This medicine is available only with your doctor's prescription, in the following dosage forms:

Oral

- Capsules (U.S. and Canada)
- Tablets (U.S. and Canada)

Before Using This Medicine

In deciding to use a medicine, the risks of taking the medicine must be weighed against the good it will do. This is a decision you and your doctor will make. For penicillamine, the following should be considered:

Allergies—Tell your doctor if you have ever had any unusual or allergic reaction to penicillin or to penicillamine. Also tell your health care professional if you are allergic to any other substances, such as foods, preservatives, or dyes.

Pregnancy—Penicillamine may cause birth defects if taken during pregnancy.

Breast-feeding—It is not known whether penicillamine passes into breast milk.

Children—Although there is no specific information about the use of penicillamine in children, it is not expected to cause different side effects or problems in children than it does in adults.

Older adults—Sore throat and fever, with or without chills; sores, ulcers, or white spots on the lips or in the mouth; shortness of breath, troubled breathing, tightness in the chest, and/or wheezing; swollen and/or painful glands; black, tarry stools; blood in urine or stools; pinpoint red spots on skin; cough or hoarseness; lower back or side pain; painful or difficult urination; unusual bleeding or bruising; and unusual tiredness or weakness may be especially likely to occur in elderly patients, who are usually more sensitive than younger adults to some of the effects of penicillamine.

Other medicines—Although certain medicines should not be used together at all, in other cases two different medicines may be used together even if an interaction might occur. In these cases, your doctor may want to change the dose, or other precautions may be necessary. When you are taking penicillamine, it is important that your health care professional know if you are taking *any* other prescription or nonprescription (over-the-counter [OTC]) medicine, especially:

- Gold compounds (e.g., Ridaura) or
- Phenylbutazone (e.g., Cotylbutazone)—The chance of serious side effects may be increased

Other medical problems—The presence of other medical problems may affect the use of penicillamine. Make sure you tell your doctor if you have any other medical problems, especially:

- Blood disease caused by penicillamine treatment, history of, or
- Kidney disease or history of (only for patients with rheumatoid arthritis)—The chance of side effects may be increased

Proper Use of This Medicine

Since penicillamine is taken in different ways for different medical problems, it is very important that you understand exactly why you are taking this medicine and how to take it. See below for information on specific medical problems. If you have any questions about this, check with your doctor.

For patients taking this medicine to *prevent kidney stones:*

- You should drink 2 full glasses (8 ounces each) of water at bedtime and another 2 full glasses (8 ounces each) during the night.
- It is very important that you follow any special instructions from your doctor, such as following a low-methionine diet. If you have any questions about this, check with your doctor.

For patients taking this medicine for *rheumatoid arthritis:*

- Take this medicine on an empty stomach (at least 1 hour before meals or 2 hours after meals) and at least 1 hour before or after any other food, milk, or medicine.
- After you begin taking this medicine, 2 to 3 months may pass before you feel its effects. It is very important that you keep taking the medicine, even if you do not feel better, in order to give it time to work.

For patients taking this medicine for *Wilson's disease:*

- Take this medicine on an empty stomach (at least 1/2 to 1 hour before meals or 2 hours after meals).
- It is very important that you follow any special instructions from your doctor, such as following a low-copper diet. If you have any questions about this, check with your doctor.
- After you begin taking this medicine, 1 to 3 months may pass before you notice any improvement in your condition.

For patients taking this medicine for *lead poisoning:*

- Take this medicine on an empty stomach (2 hours before meals or at least 3 hours after meals).

For *all patients:*

- *Take this medicine regularly as directed. Do not stop taking it without first checking with your doctor,* since stopping the medicine and then restarting it may increase the possibility of side effects.

Dosing—The dose of penicillamine will be different for different patients. *Follow your doctor's orders or the directions on the label.* The following information includes only the average doses of penicillamine. *If your dose is different, do not change it* unless your doctor tells you to do so.

- For *oral* dosage form (capsules or tablets):
  - —For Wilson's disease (too much copper in the body):
    - Adults and teenagers—At first, 250 milligrams (mg) four times a day. After a while, your doctor may need to increase the dose, depending on the amount of copper in your urine. Most people do

not need more than 2000 mg a day (two 250-mg capsules or tablets four times a day).
- Children—At first, 250 mg a day. After a while, your doctor may need to increase the dose, depending on the amount of copper in your urine. Older children may need the same dose as adults.

—For rheumatoid arthritis:
- Adults—At first, 125 or 250 mg once a day. Your doctor may increase the dose after a few months, depending on how well the medicine is working and whether it causes any side effects. The largest dose is not more than 1500 mg a day (two 250-mg capsules or tablets three times a day).
- Children—Use and dose must be determined by your doctor.

—For preventing kidney stones:
- Adults—At first, 500 mg (two 250-mg capsules or tablets) four times a day. After a while, your doctor may need to change the dose, depending on the results of your urine tests. Some people may need as much as 4000 mg a day (four 250-mg capsules or tablets four times a day).
- Children—The dose is based on body weight and must be determined by your doctor. At first, 7.5 mg per kilogram (kg) (about 3.5 mg per pound) of body weight four times a day. After a while, your doctor may need to change the dose, depending on the results of your urine tests.

Missed dose—If you miss a dose of this medicine and your dosing schedule is:
- One dose a day—Take the missed dose as soon as possible. But if you do not remember the missed dose until the next day, skip the missed dose and go back to your regular dosing schedule. Do not double the next day's dose.
- Two doses a day—Take the missed dose as soon as possible. However, if it is almost time for your next dose, skip the missed dose and go back to your regular dosing schedule. Do not double doses.
- More than two doses a day—If you remember within an hour or so of the missed dose, take it right away. But if you do not remember until later, skip the missed dose and go back to your regular dosing schedule. Do not double doses.

If you have any questions about this, check with your doctor.

Storage—To store this medicine:
- Keep out of the reach of children.
- Store away from heat and direct light.
- Do not store this medicine in the bathroom, near the kitchen sink, or in other damp places. Heat or moisture may cause the medicine to break down.
- Do not keep outdated medicine or medicine no longer needed. Be sure that any discarded medicine is out of the reach of children.

Precautions While Using This Medicine

Your doctor should check your progress at regular visits to make sure that this medicine does not cause unwanted effects.

Before having any kind of surgery (including dental surgery), tell the medical doctor or dentist in charge that you are taking this medicine.

If you are taking iron preparations, or vitamin preparations containing iron, do not take them within 2 hours of the time you take this medicine. Taking the 2 medicines too close together may keep the penicillamine from working properly.

Side Effects of This Medicine

Along with its needed effects, a medicine may cause some unwanted effects. Although not all of these side effects may occur, if they do occur they may need medical attention.

Check with your doctor as soon as possible if any of the following side effects occur:

More common

Fever; joint pain; skin rash, hives, or itching; swollen and/or painful glands; ulcers, sores, or white spots on lips or in mouth

Less common

Bloody or cloudy urine; shortness of breath, troubled breathing, tightness in chest, or wheezing; sore throat and fever with or without chills; swelling of face, feet, or lower legs; unusual bleeding or bruising; unusual tiredness or weakness; weight gain

Rare

Abdominal or stomach pain (severe); blisters on skin; bloody or black, tarry stools; chest pain; coughing or hoarseness; dark urine; difficulty in breathing, chewing, talking, or swallowing; eye pain, blurred or double vision, or any change in vision; general feeling of discomfort or illness or weakness; lower back or side pain; muscle weakness; painful or difficult urination; pale stools; pinpoint red spots on skin; redness, tenderness, itching, burning, or peeling of skin; red or irritated eyes; red, thick, or scaly skin; ringing or buzzing in the ears; spitting blood; yellow eyes or skin

Other side effects may occur that usually do not need medical attention. These side effects may go away during treatment as your body adjusts to the medicine. However, check with your doctor if any of the following side effects continue or are bothersome:

More common

Diarrhea; lessening or loss of taste sense; loss of appetite; nausea or vomiting; stomach pain (mild)

Other side effects not listed above may also occur in some patients. If you notice any other effects, check with your doctor.

Revised: July 1990
Interim revision: 09/01/94

PENICILLINS Systemic

Some commonly used brand names are:

In the U.S.—

Amoxil[1]
Bactocill[11]
Beepen-VK[13]
Betapen-VK[13]
Bicillin L-A[12]
Cloxapen[5]
Crysticillin 300 A.S.[12]
Dynapen[6]
Dycill[6]
Geocillin[4]
Geopen[4]
Ledercillin VK[13]
Mezlin[9]
Nafcil[10]
Nallpen[10]
Omnipen[2]
Omnipen-N[2]
Pathocil[6]
Pentids[12]
Pen Vee K[13]
Permapen[12]
Pfizerpen[12]
Pfizerpen-AS[12]
Pipracil[14]
Polycillin[2]
Polycillin-N[2]
Polymox[1]
Principen[2]
Prostaphlin[11]
Spectrobid[3]
Staphcillin[8]
Tegopen[5]
Ticar[17]
Totacillin[2]
Totacillin-N[2]
Trimox[1]
Unipen[10]
V-Cillin K[13]
Veetids[13]
Wycillin[12]
Wymox[1]

In Canada—

Amoxil[1]
Ampicin[2]
Apo-Amoxi[1]
Apo-Ampi[2]
Apo-Cloxi[5]
Apo-Pen VK[13]
Ayercillin[12]
Bicillin L-A[12]
Fluclox[7]
Geopen Oral[4]
Ledercillin VK[13]
Megacillin[12]
Nadopen-V[13]
Nadopen-V 200[13]
Nadopen-V 400[13]
Novamoxin[1]
Novo-Ampicillin[2]
Novo-Cloxin[5]
Novo-Pen-VK[13]
Nu-Amoxi[1]
Nu-Ampi[2]
Nu-Cloxi[5]
Nu-Pen-VK[13]
Orbenin[5]
Penbritin[2]
Penglobe[3]
Pen-Vee[13]
Pipracil[14]
Pondocillin[15]
PVF[13]
PVF K[13]
Pyopen[4]
Selexid[16]
Tegopen[5]
Ticar[17]
Unipen[10]
V-Cillin K[13]
Wycillin[12]

Note: For quick reference, the following penicillins are numbered to match the corresponding brand names.

This information applies to the following medicines:

1. Amoxicillin (a-mox-i-SILL-in)‡
2. Ampicillin (am-pi-SILL-in)‡
3. Bacampicillin (ba-kam-pi-SILL-in)
4. Carbenicillin (kar-ben-i-SILL-in)
5. Cloxacillin (klox-a-SILL-in)‡
6. Dicloxacillin (dye-klox-a-SILL-in)†‡
7. Flucloxacillin (floo-klox-a-SILL-in)*
8. Methicillin (meth-i-SILL-in)†
9. Mezlocillin (mez-loe-SILL-in)†
10. Nafcillin (naf-SILL-in)‡
11. Oxacillin (ox-a-SILL-in)†‡
12. Penicillin G (pen-i-SILL-in)§
13. Penicillin V‡
14. Piperacillin (pi-PER-a-sill-in)
15. Pivampicillin (piv-am-pi-SILL-in)*
16. Pivmecillinam (piv-me-SILL-in-am)*
17. Ticarcillin (tye-kar-SILL-in)

*Not commercially available in the U.S.
†Not commercially available in Canada.
‡Generic name product may also be available in the U.S.
§Generic name product may also be available in Canada.

Description

Penicillins are used to treat infections caused by bacteria. They work by killing the bacteria or preventing their growth.

There are several different kinds of penicillins. Each is used to treat different kinds of infections. One kind of penicillin usually may not be used in place of another. In addition, penicillins are used to treat bacterial infections in many different parts of the body. They are sometimes given with other antibacterial medicines (antibiotics). Some of the penicillins may also be used for other problems as determined by your doctor. However, none of the penicillins will work for colds, flu, or other virus infections.

Penicillins are available only with your doctor's prescription, in the following dosage forms:

Oral

Amoxicillin
- Capsules (U.S. and Canada)
- Oral suspension (U.S. and Canada)
- Chewable tablets (U.S. and Canada)

Ampicillin
- Capsules (U.S. and Canada)
- Oral suspension (U.S. and Canada)

Bacampicillin
- Oral suspension (U.S.)
- Tablets (U.S. and Canada)

Carbenicillin
- Tablets (U.S. and Canada)

Cloxacillin
- Capsules (U.S. and Canada)
- Oral solution (U.S. and Canada)

Dicloxacillin
- Capsules (U.S.)
- Oral suspension (U.S.)

Flucloxacillin
- Capsules (Canada)
- Oral suspension (Canada)

Nafcillin
- Capsules (U.S.)
- Tablets (U.S.)

Oxacillin
- Capsules (U.S.)
- Oral solution (U.S.)

Penicillin G Benzathine
- Oral suspension (Canada)

Penicillin G Potassium
- Oral solution (U.S.)
- Tablets (U.S. and Canada)

Penicillin V Benzathine
- Oral suspension (Canada)

Penicillin V Potassium
- Oral solution (U.S. and Canada)
- Tablets (U.S. and Canada)

Pivampicillin
- Oral suspension (Canada)
- Tablets (Canada)

Pivmecillinam
- Tablets (Canada)

Parenteral

Ampicillin
- Injection (U.S. and Canada)

Carbenicillin
- Injection (U.S. and Canada)

Cloxacillin
- Injection (Canada)

Methicillin
- Injection (U.S.)

Mezlocillin
- Injection (U.S.)

Nafcillin
- Injection (U.S. and Canada)

Oxacillin
- Injection (U.S.)

Penicillin G Benzathine
- Injection (U.S. and Canada)

Penicillin G Potassium
- Injection (U.S. and Canada)

Penicillin G Procaine
- Injection (U.S. and Canada)

Penicillin G Sodium
- Injection (U.S. and Canada)

Piperacillin
- Injection (U.S. and Canada)

Ticarcillin
- Injection (U.S. and Canada)

Before Using This Medicine

In deciding to use a medicine, the risks of taking the medicine must be weighed against the good it will do. This is a decision you and your doctor will make. For penicillins, the following should be considered:

Allergies—Tell your doctor if you have ever had any unusual or allergic reaction to any of the penicillins or cephalosporins. Also tell your health care professional if you are allergic to any other substances, such as foods, preservatives, or dyes, or procaine (e.g., Novocain) or other ester-type anesthetics (medicines that cause numbing) if you are receiving penicillin G procaine.

Diet—Make certain your health care professional knows if you are on a low-sodium (low-salt) diet. Some of these medicines contain enough sodium to cause problems in some people.

Pregnancy—Penicillins have not been studied in pregnant women. However, penicillins have been widely used in pregnant women and have not been shown to cause birth defects or other problems in animal studies.

Breast-feeding—Penicillins pass into the breast milk. Even though only small amounts may pass into breast milk, allergic reactions, diarrhea, fungus infections, and skin rash may occur in nursing babies.

Children—Many penicillins have been used in children and, in effective doses, are not expected to cause different side effects or problems in children than they do in adults.

Older adults—Penicillins have been used in the elderly and have not been shown to cause different side effects or problems in older people than they do in younger adults.

Other medicines—Although certain medicines should not be used together at all, in other cases two different medicines may be used together even if an interaction might occur. In these cases, your doctor may want to change the dose, or other precautions may be necessary. When you are taking a penicillin, it is especially important that your health care professional know if you are taking any of the following:

- Acetaminophen (e.g., Tylenol) (with long-term, high-dose use) or
- Amiodarone (e.g., Cordarone) or
- Anabolic steroids (nandrolone [e.g., Anabolin], oxandrolone [e.g., Anavar], oxymetholone [e.g., Anadrol], stanozolol [e.g., Winstrol]) or
- Androgens (male hormones) or
- Antithyroid agents (medicine for overactive thyroid) or
- Carmustine (e.g., BiCNU) or
- Chloroquine (e.g., Aralen) or
- Dantrolene (e.g., Dantrium) or
- Daunorubicin (e.g., Cerubidine) or
- Disulfiram (e.g., Antabuse) or
- Divalproex (e.g., Depakote) or
- Estrogens (female hormones) or
- Etretinate (e.g., Tegison) or
- Gold salts (medicine for arthritis) or
- Hydroxychloroquine (e.g., Plaquenil) or
- Mercaptopurine (e.g., Purinethol) or
- Methotrexate (e.g., Mexate) or
- Methyldopa (e.g., Aldomet) or
- Naltrexone (e.g., Trexan) (with long-term, high-dose use) or
- Oral contraceptives (birth control pills) containing estrogen or
- Other anti-infectives by mouth or by injection (medicine for infection) or
- Phenothiazines (acetophenazine [e.g., Tindal], chlorpromazine [e.g., Thorazine], fluphenazine [e.g., Prolixin], mesoridazine [e.g., Serentil], perphenazine [e.g., Trilafon], prochlorperazine [e.g., Compazine], promazine [e.g., Sparine], promethazine [e.g., Phenergan], thioridazine [e.g., Mellaril], trifluoperazine [e.g., Stelazine], triflupromazine [e.g., Vesprin], trimeprazine [e.g., Temaril]) or
- Plicamycin (e.g., Mithracin) or
- Valproic acid (e.g., Depakene)—These medicines may increase the chance of liver damage if taken with cloxacillin, dicloxacillin, flucloxacillin, mezlocillin, nafcillin, oxacillin, or piperacillin

- Amiloride (e.g., Midamor) or
- Benazepril (e.g., Lotensin) or
- Captopril (e.g., Capoten) or
- Enalapril (e.g., Vasotec) or
- Fosinopril (e.g., Monopril) or
- Lisinopril (e.g., Prinivil, Zestril) or
- Potassium-containing medicine or
- Quinapril (e.g., Accupril) or
- Ramipril (e.g., Altace) or
- Spironolactone (e.g., Aldactone) or
- Triamterene (e.g., Dyrenium)—Use of these medicines with penicillin G by injection may cause an increase in side effects

- Anticoagulants (blood thinners) or
- Dipyridamole (e.g., Persantine) or
- Divalproex (e.g., Depakote) or
- Heparin (e.g., Panheprin) or
- Inflammation or pain medicine (except narcotics) or
- Pentoxifylline (e.g., Trental) or
- Plicamycin (e.g., Mithracin) or
- Sulfinpyrazone (e.g., Anturane) or

- Valproic acid (e.g., Depakene)—Use of these medicines with high doses of carbenicillin, piperacillin, or ticarcillin may increase the chance of bleeding
- Cloramphenicol (e.g., Chloromycetin) or
- Erythromycins (e.g., E.E.S., E-Mycin, ERYC) or
- Sulfonamides (e.g., Gantanol, Gantrisin) or
- Tetracyclines (e.g., Achromycin, Minocin, Vibramycin)—Use of these medicines with penicillins may prevent the penicillin from working properly
- Cholestyramine (e.g., Questran) or
- Colestipol (e.g., Colestid)—Use of these medicines with oral penicillin G may prevent penicillin G from working properly
- Oral contraceptives (birth control pills) containing estrogen—Use of ampicillin, amoxicillin, or penicillin V with estrogen-containing oral contraceptives may prevent oral contraceptives from working properly, increasing the chance of pregnancy
- Methotrexate (e.g., Mexate)—Use of methotrexate with penicillins may increase the chance of side effects of methotrexate
- Probenecid (e.g., Benemid)—Probenecid causes penicillins to build up in the blood. This may increase the chance of side effects. However, your doctor may want to give you probenecid with a penicillin to treat some infections

Other medical problems—The presence of other medical problems may affect the use of penicillins. Make sure you tell your doctor if you have any other medical problems, especially:

- Allergy, general (such as asthma, eczema, hay fever, hives), history of—Patients with a history of general allergies may be more likely to have a severe reaction to penicillins
- Bleeding problems, history of—Patients with a history of bleeding problems may be more likely to have bleeding when receiving carbenicillin, piperacillin, or ticarcillin
- Congestive heart failure (CHF) or
- High blood pressure—Large doses of carbenicillin or ticarcillin may make these conditions worse, because these medicines contains a large amount of salt
- Cystic fibrosis—Patients with cystic fibrosis may have an increased chance of fever and skin rash when receiving piperacillin
- Kidney disease—Patients with kidney disease may have an increased chance of side effects
- Mononucleosis (''mono'')—Patients with mononucleosis may have an increased chance of skin rash when receiving ampicillin, bacampicillin, or pivampicillin
- Stomach or intestinal disease, history of (especially colitis, including colitis caused by antibiotics)—Patients with a history of stomach or intestinal disease may be more likely to develop colitis while taking penicillins

Proper Use of This Medicine

Penicillins (except bacampicillin tablets, amoxicillin, penicillin V, pivampicillin, and pivmecillinam) are best taken with a full glass (8 ounces) of water on an empty stomach (either 1 hour before or 2 hours after meals) unless otherwise directed by your doctor.

For patients taking *amoxicillin, penicillin V, pivampicillin, and pivmecillinam:*

- Amoxicillin, penicillin V, pivampicillin, and pivmecillinam may be taken on a full or empty stomach.
- The *liquid form of amoxicillin* may also be taken by itself or mixed with formulas, milk, fruit juice, water, ginger ale, or other cold drinks. If mixed with other liquids, take immediately after mixing. Be sure to drink all the liquid to get the full dose of medicine.

For patients taking *bacampicillin:*

- The liquid form of this medicine is best taken with a full glass (8 ounces) of water on an empty stomach (either 1 hour before or 2 hours after meals) unless otherwise directed by your doctor.
- The tablet form of this medicine may be taken on a full or empty stomach.

For patients taking *penicillin G by mouth:*

- Do not drink acidic fruit juices (for example, orange or grapefruit juice) or other acidic beverages within 1 hour of taking penicillin G since this may keep the medicine from working properly.

For patients taking the *oral liquid form of penicillins:*

- This medicine is to be taken by mouth even if it comes in a dropper bottle. If this medicine does not come in a dropper bottle, use a specially marked measuring spoon or other device to measure each dose accurately. The average household teaspoon may not hold the right amount of liquid.
- Do not use after the expiration date on the label. The medicine may not work properly after that date. If you have any questions about this, check with your pharmacist.

For patients taking the *chewable tablet form of amoxicillin:*

- Tablets should be chewed or crushed before they are swallowed.

To help clear up your infection completely, *keep taking this medicine for the full time of treatment*, even if you begin to feel better after a few days. *If you have a ''strep'' infection, you should keep taking this medicine for at least 10 days. This is especially important in ''strep'' infections. Serious heart problems could develop later* if your infection is not cleared up completely. Also, if you stop taking this medicine too soon, your symptoms may return.

This medicine works best when there is a constant amount in the blood or urine. *To help keep the amount constant, do not miss any doses. Also, it is best to take the doses at evenly spaced times, day and night.* For example, if you are to take 4 doses a day, the doses should be spaced about 6 hours apart. If this interferes with your sleep or other daily activities, or if you need help in planning the best times to take your medicine, check with your health care professional.

Dosing—The dose of these medicines will be different for different patients. *Follow your doctor's orders or the directions on the label.* The following information includes only the average doses of these medicines. *If your dose is different, do not change it* unless your doctor tells you to do so.

The number of tablets or teaspoonfuls of suspension that you take depends on the strength of the medicine. Also, *the number of doses you take each day, the time allowed between doses, and the length of time you take the medicine depend on the medical problem for which you are taking a penicillin.*

For amoxicillin

- For bacterial infections:
  - —For *oral* dosage forms (capsules, chewable tablets, and oral suspension):
    - Adults, teenagers, and children weighing more than 20 kilograms (kg) (44 pounds)—250 to 500 milligrams (mg) every eight hours.
    - Infants and children weighing 8 to 20 kg (17 to 44 pounds): Dose is based on body weight and must be determined by your doctor. The usual dose is 6.7 to 13.3 mg per kg (3 to 6 mg per pound) of body weight every eight hours.
    - Infants weighing 6 to 8 kg (13 to 17 pounds): 50 to 100 mg every eight hours.
    - Infants weighing up to 6 kg (13 pounds): 25 to 50 mg every eight hours.

For ampicillin

- For bacterial infections:
  - —For *oral* dosage forms (capsules and oral suspension):
    - Adults, teenagers, and children weighing more than 20 kilograms (kg) (44 pounds)—250 to 500 milligrams (mg) every six hours.
    - Infants and children weighing up to 20 kg (44 pounds)—Dose is based on body weight and must be determined by your doctor. The usual dose is 12.5 to 25 mg per kg (5.7 to 11.4 mg per pound) of body weight every six hours; or 16.7 to 33.3 mg per kg (7.6 to 15 mg per pound) of body weight every eight hours.
  - —For *injection* dosage form:
    - Adults, teenagers, and children weighing more than 20 kg (44 pounds)—250 to 500 mg, injected into a vein or muscle every three to six hours.
    - Infants and children weighing up to 20 kg (44 pounds)—Dose is based on body weight and must be determined by your doctor. The usual dose is 12.5 mg per kg (5.7 mg per pound) of body weight, injected into a vein or muscle every six hours.

For bacampicillin

- For bacterial infections:
  - —For *oral* dosage forms (oral suspension and tablets):
    - Adults, teenagers, and children weighing more than 25 kilograms (kg) (55 pounds)—400 to 800 milligrams (mg) every twelve hours.
    - Children weighing up to 25 kg (55 pounds)—Bacampicillin tablets are not recommended for use in children weighing up to 25 kg (55 pounds). The dose of the oral suspension is based on body weight and must be determined by your doctor. The usual dose is 12.5 to 25 mg per kg (5.7 to 11.4 mg per pound) of body weight every twelve hours.

For carbenicillin

- For bacterial infections:
  - —For *oral* dosage form (tablets):
    - Adults and teenagers—500 milligrams (mg) to 1 gram every six hours.
    - Children—Dose must be determined by your doctor.
  - —For *injection* dosage form:
    - Adults and teenagers—Dose is based on body weight and must be determined by your doctor. The usual dose is 50 to 83.3 mg per kilogram (kg) (22.8 to 37.9 mg per pound) of body weight, injected into a vein or muscle every four hours.
    - Older infants and children—Dose is based on body weight and must be determined by your doctor. The usual dose 16.7 to 75 mg per kg (7.6 to 34 mg per pound) of body weight, injected into a vein or muscle every four to six hours.

For cloxacillin

- For bacterial infections:
  - —For *oral* dosage form (capsules and oral solution):
    - Adults, teenagers, and children weighing more than 20 kilograms (kg) (44 pounds)—250 to 500 milligrams (mg) every six hours.
    - Infants and children weighing up to 20 kg (44 pounds)—Dose is based on body weight and must be determined by your doctor. The usual dose is 6.25 to 12.5 mg per kg (2.8 to 5.7 mg per pound) of body weight every six hours.
  - —For *injection* dosage form:
    - Adults, teenagers, and children weighing more than 20 kg—250 to 500 mg, injected into a vein every six hours.
    - Infants and children weighing up to 20 kg (44 pounds)—Dose is based on body weight and must be determined by your doctor. The usual dose is 6.25 to 12.5 mg per kg (2.8 to 5.7 mg per pound) of body weight, injected into a vein every six hours.

For dicloxacillin

- For bacterial infections:
  - —For *oral* dosage form (capsules and oral suspension):
    - Adults, teenagers, and children weighing more than 40 kilograms (kg) (88 pounds)—125 to 250 milligrams (mg) every six hours.
    - Infants and children weighing up to 40 kg (88 pounds)—Dose is based on body weight and must be determined by your doctor. The usual dose is 3.1 to 6.2 mg per kg (1.4 to 2.8 mg per pound) of body weight every six hours.

For flucloxacillin

- For bacterial infections:
  - —For *oral* dosage form (capsules and oral suspension):
    - Adults, teenagers, and children more than 12 years of age and weighing more than 40 kilograms (kg) (88 pounds)—250 to 500 milligrams (mg) every six hours.
    - Children less than 12 years of age and weighing up to 40 kg (88 pounds)—125 to 250 mg every six hours; or 6.25 to 12.5 mg per kg (2.8 to 5.7 mg per pound) of body weight every six hours.
    - Infants up to 6 months of age—Dose is based on body weight and must be determined by your doctor. The usual dose is 6.25 mg per kg (2.8 mg per pound) of body weight every six hours.

For methicillin

- For bacterial infections:
  - —For *injection* dosage form:
    - Adults, teenagers, and children weighing more than 40 kilograms (kg) (88 pounds)—1 gram injected into a muscle every four to six hours; or 1 gram injected into a vein every six hours.
    - Children weighing up to 40 kg (88 pounds)—Dose is based on body weight and must be determined by your doctor. The usual dose is 25 milligrams (mg) per kg (11.4 mg per pound) of body weight, injected into a vein or muscle every six hours.

For mezlocillin

- For bacterial infections:
  - —For *injection* dosage form:
    - Adults and teenagers—Dose is based on body weight and must be determined by your doctor. The usual dose 33.3 to 87.5 milligrams (mg) per kilogram (kg) (15.1 to 39.8 mg per pound) of body weight, injected into a vein or muscle every four to six hours; or 3 to 4 grams every four to six hours.
    - Infants over 1 month of age and children up to 12 years of age—Dose is based on body weight and must be determined by your doctor. The usual dose is 50 mg per kg (22.7 mg per pound) of body weight, injected into a vein or muscle every four hours.

For nafcillin

- For bacterial infections:
  - —For *oral* dosage form (capsules and tablets):
    - Adults and teenagers—250 milligrams (mg) to 1 gram every four to six hours.
    - Older infants and children—Dose is based on body weight and must be determined by your doctor. The usual dose is 6.25 to 12.5 mg per kilogram (kg) (2.8 to 5.7 mg per pound) of body weight every six hours.
    - Newborns—Dose is based on body weight and must be determined by your doctor. The usual dose is 10 mg per kg (4.5 mg per pound) of body weight every six to eight hours.
  - —For *injection* dosage form:
    - Adults and teenagers—500 mg to 2 grams injected into a vein or muscle every four to six hours.
    - Infants and children—Dose is based on body weight and must be determined by your doctor. The usual dose is 10 to 25 mg per kg (4.5 to 11.4 mg per pound) of body weight, injected into a muscle every twelve hours; or 10 to 40 mg per kg (4.5 to 18.2 mg per pound) of body weight, injected into a vein every four to eight hours.

For oxacillin

- For bacterial infections:
  - —For *oral* dosage form (capsules and oral solution):
    - Adults, teenagers, and children weighing more than 40 kilograms (kg) (88 pounds)—500 milligrams (mg) to 1 gram every four to six hours.
    - Children weighing up to 40 kg (88 pounds)—Dose is based on body weight and must be determined by your doctor. The usual dose is 12.5 to 25 mg per kg (5.7 to 11.4 mg per pound) of body weight every six hours.
  - —For *injection* dosage form:
    - Adults, teenagers, and children weighing more than 40 kg (88 pounds)—250 mg to 1 gram injected into a vein or muscle every four to six hours.
    - Children weighing up to 40 kg (88 pounds)—Dose is based on body weight and must be determined by your doctor. The usual dose is 12.5 to 25 mg per kg (5.7 to 11.4 mg per pound) of body weight, injected into a vein or muscle every four to six hours.
    - Premature infants and newborns—Dose is based on body weight and must be determined by your doctor. The usual dose is 6.25 mg per kg (2.8 mg per pound) of body weight, injected into a vein or muscle every six hours.

For penicillin G

- For bacterial infections:
  - —For *oral* dosage form (oral solution, oral suspension, and tablets):
    - Adults and teenagers—200,000 to 500,000 Units (125 to 312 milligrams [mg]) every four to six hours.
    - Infants and children less than 12 years of age—Dose is based on body weight and must be determined by your doctor. The usual dose is 4167 to 30,000 Units per kilogram (kg) (189 to 13,636 Units per pound) of body weight every four to eight hours.
  - —For *benzathine injection* dosage form:
    - Adults and teenagers—1,200,000 to 2,400,000 Units injected into a muscle as a single dose.
    - Infants and children—300,000 to 1,200,000 Units injected into a muscle as a single dose; or

50,000 Units per kg (22,727 Units per pound) of body weight injected into a muscle as a single dose.

—For *injection* dosage forms (potassium and sodium salts):

• Adults and teenagers—1,000,000 to 5,000,000 Units, injected into a vein or muscle every four to six hours.

• Older infants and children—Dose is based on body weight and must be determined by your doctor. The usual dose is 8333 to 25,000 Units per kg (3788 to 11,363 Units per pound) of body weight, injected into a vein or muscle every four to six hours.

• Premature infants and newborns—Dose is based on body weight and must be determined by your doctor. The usual dose is 30,000 Units per kg (13,636 Units per pound) of body weight, injected into a vein or muscle every twelve hours.

—For *procaine injection* dosage form:

• Adults and teenagers—600,000 to 1,200,000 Units injected into a muscle once a day.

• Children—Dose is based on body weight and must be determined by your doctor. The usual dose is 50,000 Units per kg (22,727 Units per pound) of body weight, injected into a muscle once a day.

For penicillin V

• For bacterial infections:

—For the *benzathine salt oral* dosage form (oral solution):

• Adults and teenagers—200,000 to 500,000 Units every six to eight hours.

• Children—100,000 to 250,000 Units every six to eight hours.

—For the *potassium salt oral* dosage forms (oral solution, oral suspension, and tablets):

• Adults and teenagers—125 to 500 milligrams (mg) every six to eight hours.

• Children—Dose is based on body weight and must be determined by your doctor. The usual dose is 2.5 to 16.7 mg per kilogram (kg) (1.1 to 7.6 mg per pound) of body weight every four to eight hours.

For piperacillin

• For bacterial infections:

—For *injection* dosage form:

• Adults and teenagers—3 to 4 grams, injected into a vein or muscle every four to six hours.

• Infants and children—Dose must be determined by your doctor.

For pivampicillin

• For bacterial infections:

—For *oral* dosage form (oral suspension):

• Adults, teenagers, and children 10 years of age and older—525 to 1050 milligrams (mg) two times a day.

• Children 7 to 10 years of age—350 mg two times a day.

• Children 4 to 6 years of age—262.5 mg two times a day.

• Children 1 to 3 years of age—175 mg two times a day.

• Infants 3 to 12 months of age—Dose is based on body weight and must be determined by your doctor. The usual dose is 20 to 30 mg per kilogram (kg) (9.1 to 13.6 mg per pound) of body weight two times a day.

—For *oral* dosage form (tablets):

• Adults, teenagers, and children 10 years of age and older—500 mg to 1 gram two times a day.

• Children up to 10 years of age—Dose must be determined by your doctor.

For pivmecillinam

• For bacterial infections:

—For *oral* dosage form (tablets):

• Adults, teenagers, and children weighing more than 40 kilograms (kg) (88 pounds)—200 milligrams (mg) two to four times a day for three days.

• Children up to 40 kg (88 pounds)—Dose must be determined by your doctor.

For ticarcillin

• For bacterial infections:

—For *injection* dosage form:

• Adults, teenagers, and children weighing more than 40 kilograms (kg) (88 pounds)—3 grams injected into a vein every four hours; or 4 grams injected into a vein every six hours.

• Children up to 40 kg (88 pounds)—Dose is based on body weight and must be determined by your doctor. The usual dose is 33.3 to 75 milligrams (mg) per kg (15 to 34 mg per pound) of body weight, injected into a vein every four to six hours.

Missed dose—If you miss a dose of this medicine, take it as soon as possible. This will help to keep a constant amount of medicine in the blood or urine. However, if it is almost time for your next dose, skip the missed dose and go back to your regular dosing schedule. Do not double doses.

Storage—To store this medicine:

• Keep out of the reach of children.
• Store away from heat and direct light.
• Do not store the capsule or tablet form of penicillins in the bathroom, near the kitchen sink, or in other damp places. Heat or moisture may cause the medicine to break down.
• Store the oral liquid form of penicillins in the refrigerator because heat will cause this medicine to break down. However, keep the medicine from freezing. Follow the directions on the label.

• Do not keep outdated medicine or medicine no longer needed. Be sure that any discarded medicine is out of the reach of children.

Precautions While Using This Medicine

If your symptoms do not improve within a few days, or if they become worse, check with your doctor.

Penicillins may cause diarrhea in some patients.

- *Check with your doctor if severe diarrhea occurs.* Severe diarrhea may be a sign of a serious side effect. *Do not take any diarrhea medicine without first checking with your doctor.* Diarrhea medicines may make your diarrhea worse or make it last longer.
- For mild diarrhea, diarrhea medicine containing kaolin or attapulgite (e.g., Kaopectate tablets, Diasorb) may be taken. However, other kinds of diarrhea medicine should not be taken. They may make your diarrhea worse or make it last longer.
- If you have any questions about this or if mild diarrhea continues or gets worse, check with your health care professional.

Oral contraceptives (birth control pills) containing estrogen may not work properly if you take them while you are taking ampicillin, amoxicillin, or penicillin V. Unplanned pregnancies may occur. You should use a different or additional means of birth control while you are taking any of these penicillins. If you have any questions about this, check with your health care professional.

For *diabetic patients:*

- *Penicillins may cause false test results with some urine sugar tests.* Check with your doctor before changing your diet or the dosage of your diabetes medicine.

Before you have any medical tests, tell the doctor in charge that you are taking this medicine. The results of some tests may be affected by this medicine.

Side Effects of This Medicine

Along with its needed effects, a medicine may cause some unwanted effects. Although not all of these side effects may occur, if they do occur they may need medical attention.

Stop taking this medicine and get emergency help immediately if any of the following side effects occur:

Less common

Fast or irregular breathing; fever; joint pain; lightheadedness or fainting (sudden); puffiness or swelling around the face; red, scaly skin; shortness of breath; skin rash, hives, itching

In addition to the side effects mentioned above, *check with your doctor immediately* if any of the following side effects occur:

Rare

Abdominal or stomach cramps and pain (severe); abdominal tenderness; convulsions (seizures); decreased amount of urine; diarrhea (watery and severe), which may also be bloody; mental depression; nausea and vomiting; pain at place of injection; sore throat and fever; unusual bleeding or bruising; yellow eyes or skin

Note: Some of the above side effects (severe abdominal or stomach cramps and pain, and watery and severe diarrhea, which may also be bloody) may also occur up to several weeks after you stop taking any of these medicines.

Rare—For penicillin G procaine only

Agitation or combativeness; anxiety; confusion; fear of impending death; feeling, hearing, or seeing things that are not real

Other side effects may occur that usually do not need medical attention. These side effects may go away during treatment as your body adjusts to the medicine. However, check with your doctor if any of the following side effects continue or are bothersome:

More common

Diarrhea (mild); headache; sore mouth or tongue; vaginal itching and discharge; white patches in the mouth and/or on the tongue

Other side effects not listed above may also occur in some patients. If you notice any other effects, check with your doctor.

Additional Information

Once a medicine has been approved for marketing for a certain use, experience may show that it is also useful for other medical problems. Although these uses are not included in product labeling, penicillins are used in certain patients with the following medical conditions:

- Chlamydia infections in pregnant women—Amoxicillin and ampicillin
- Gas gangrene—Penicillin G
- *Helicobacter pylori*-associated gastritis or peptic ulcer disease—Amoxicillin
- Leptospirosis—Ampicillin and penicillin G
- Lyme disease—Amoxicillin and penicillin V
- Typhoid fever—Amoxicillin and ampicillin

Other than the above information, there is no additional information relating to proper use, precautions, or side effects for these uses.

Revised: 08/25/94
Interim revision: 04/26/95

PENICILLINS AND BETA-LACTAMASE INHIBITORS Systemic

Some commonly used brand names are:

In the U.S.—

Augmentin[1]
Timentin[4]
Unasyn[2]
Zosyn[3]

In Canada—

Clavulin-250[1]
Clavulin-125F[1]
Clavulin-250F[1]
Clavulin-500F[1]
Tazocin[3]
Timentin[4]

Note: For quick reference, the following penicillins and beta-lactamase inhibitors are numbered to match the corresponding brand names.

This information applies to the following medicines:

1. Amoxicillin and Clavulanate (a-mox-i-SILL-in and klav-yoo-LAN-ate)
2. Ampicillin and Sulbactam (am-pi-SILL-in and sul-BAK-tam)†
3. Piperacillin and Tazobactam (pi-PER-a-sill-in and ta-zoe-BAK-tam)
4. Ticarcillin and Clavulanate (tye-kar-SILL-in and klav-yoo-LAN-ate)

†Not commercially available in Canada.

Description

Penicillins and beta-lactamase inhibitors are used to treat infections caused by bacteria. They work by killing the bacteria or preventing their growth. The beta-lactamase inhibitor is added to the penicillin to protect the penicillin from certain substances (enzymes) that will destroy the penicillin before it can kill the bacteria.

There are several different kinds of penicillins. Each is used to treat different kinds of infections. One kind of penicillin usually may not be used in place of another. In addition, penicillins are used to treat bacterial infections in many different parts of the body. They are sometimes given with other antibacterial medicines. Some of the penicillins may also be used for other problems as determined by your doctor. However, none of the penicillins will work for colds, flu, or other virus infections.

Penicillins are available only with your doctor's prescription, in the following dosage forms:

Oral

Amoxicillin and Clavulanate
- Oral suspension (U.S. and Canada)
- Tablets (U.S. and Canada)
- Chewable tablets (U.S.)

Parenteral

Ampicillin and Sulbactam
- Injection (U.S.)

Piperacillin and Tazobactam
- Injection (U.S.)

Ticarcillin and Clavulanate
- Injection (U.S. and Canada)

Before Using This Medicine

In deciding to use a medicine, the risks of taking the medicine must be weighed against the good it will do. This is a decision you and your doctor will make. For penicillins, the following should be considered:

Allergies—Tell your doctor if you have ever had any unusual or allergic reaction to any of the penicillins, cephalosporins, or beta-lactamase inhibitors. Also tell your health care professional if you are allergic to any other substances, such as foods, preservatives, or dyes.

Diet—Tell your doctor if you are on a low-sodium (low-salt) diet. Some of these medicines contain enough sodium to cause problems in some people.

Pregnancy—Penicillins and beta-lactamase inhibitors have not been studied in pregnant women. However, penicillins have not been shown to cause birth defects or other problems in animal studies.

Breast-feeding—Penicillins and sulbactam, a beta-lactamase inhibitor, pass into the breast milk. Even though only small amounts may pass into breast milk, allergic reactions, diarrhea, fungus infections, and skin rash may occur in nursing babies.

Children—Penicillins and beta-lactamase inhibitors have been used in children and, in effective doses, are not expected to cause different side effects or problems in children than they do in adults.

Older adults—Penicillins and beta-lactamase inhibitors have been used in the elderly and have not been shown to cause different side effects or problems in older people than they do in younger adults.

Other medicines—Although certain medicines should not be used together at all, in other cases two different medicines may be used together even if an interaction might occur. In these cases, your doctor may want to change the dose, or other precautions may be necessary. When you are taking a penicillin and beta-lactamase inhibitor combination, it is especially important that your health care professional know if you are taking any of the following:

- Anticoagulants (blood thinners) or
- Dipyridamole (e.g., Persantine) or
- Divalproex (e.g., Depakote) or
- Heparin (e.g., Panheprin) or
- Inflammation or pain medicine (except narcotics) or
- Pentoxifylline (e.g., Trental) or
- Plicamycin (e.g., Mithracin) or
- Sulfinpyrazone (e.g., Anturane) or
- Valproic acid (e.g., Depakene)—Use of these medicines with piperacillin and tazobactam combination or with ticarcillin and clavulanate combination may increase the chance of bleeding
- Probenecid (e.g., Benemid)—Probenecid causes penicillins, sulbactam, and tazobactam to build up in the blood. This may increase the chance of side effects. However, your doctor may want to give you probenecid with a penicillin and beta-lactamase inhibitor combination to treat some infections

Other medical problems—The presence of other medical problems may affect the use of penicillin and beta-lactamase inhibitor combinations. Make sure you tell your doctor if you have any other medical problems, especially:

- Allergies or a history of allergies, such as asthma, eczema, hay fever, or hives—Patients with a history of allergies may be more likely to have a severe allergic reaction to a penicillin and beta-lactamase inhibitor combination
- Bleeding problems, history of—Patients with a history of bleeding problems may be more likely to have bleeding when receiving piperacillin and tazobactam combination or ticarcillin and clavulanate combination
- Congestive heart failure (CHF) or
- High blood pressure—Large doses of ticarcillin and clavulanate combination may make these conditions worse, because this medicine contains a large amount of salt
- Cystic fibrosis—Patients with cystic fibrosis may have an increased chance of fever and skin rash when receiving piperacillin and tazobactam combination
- Kidney disease—Patients with kidney disease may have an increased chance of side effects
- Mononucleosis (''mono'')—Patients with mononucleosis may have an increased chance of skin rash when receiving ampicillin and sulbactam combination
- Stomach or intestinal disease, history of (especially colitis, including colitis caused by antibiotics)—Patients with a

history of stomach or intestinal disease may be more likely to develop colitis while taking penicillins and beta-lactamase inhibitors

Proper Use of This Medicine

Amoxicillin and clavulanate combination may be taken on a full or empty stomach. Taking amoxicillin and clavulanate combination with food may decrease the chance of diarrhea, nausea, and vomiting.

For patients taking the *oral liquid form of amoxicillin and clavulanate combination:*

- Use a specially marked measuring spoon or other device to measure each dose accurately. The average household teaspoon may not hold the right amount of liquid.
- Do not use after the expiration date on the label. The medicine may not work properly after that date. If you have any questions about this, check with your pharmacist.

For patients taking the *chewable tablet form of amoxicillin and clavulanate combination:*

- Tablets should be chewed or crushed before they are swallowed.

To help clear up your infection completely, *keep taking this medicine for the full time of treatment*, even if you begin to feel better after a few days.

This medicine works best when there is a constant amount in the blood or urine. *To help keep the amount constant, do not miss any doses. Also, it is best to take the doses at evenly spaced times, day and night.* For example, if you are to take 4 doses a day, the doses should be spaced about 6 hours apart. If this interferes with your sleep or other daily activities, or if you need help in planning the best times to take your medicine, check with your health care professional.

Dosing—The dose of these medicines will be different for different patients. *Follow your doctor's orders or the directions on the label.* The following information includes only the average doses of these medicines. *If your dose is different, do not change it* unless your doctor tells you to do so.

The number of tablets or teaspoonfuls of suspension that you take depends on the strength of the medicine. Also, *the number of doses you take each day, the time allowed between doses, and the length of time you take the medicine depend on the medical problem for which you are taking a penicillin and beta-lactamase inhibitor combination.*

For amoxicillin and clavulanate combination

- For bacterial infections:
  - —For *oral* dosage forms (chewable tablets and suspension):
    - Adults, teenagers, and children weighing more than 40 kilograms (kg) (88 pounds)—250 to 500 milligrams (mg) of amoxicillin, in combination with 62.5 to 125 mg of clavulanate, every eight hours for seven to ten days.
    - Infants and children weighing up to 40 kg (88 pounds)—6.7 to 13.3 mg of amoxicillin per kg (3 to 6 mg per pound) of body weight, in combination with 1.7 to 3.3 mg of clavulanate per kg (0.8 to 1.5 mg per pound) of body weight, every eight hours for seven to ten days.
  - —For *oral* dosage form (tablets):
    - Adults, teenagers, and children weighing more than 40 kg (88 pounds)—250 to 500 mg of amoxicillin, in combination with 125 mg of clavulanate, every eight hours for seven to ten days.
    - Infants and children weighing up to 40 kg (88 pounds)—6.7 to 13.3 mg of amoxicillin per kg (3 to 6 mg per pound) of body weight, in combination with 1.7 to 3.3 mg of clavulanate per kg (0.8 to 1.5 mg per pound) of body weight, every eight hours for seven to ten days.

For ampicillin and sulbactam combination

- For bacterial infections:
  - —For *injection* dosage form:
    - Adults and teenagers—1 to 2 grams of ampicillin, in combination with 500 milligrams (mg) to 1 gram of sulbactam, injected into a vein or a muscle every six hours.
    - Children up to 12 years of age—Use and dose must be determined by your doctor.

For piperacillin and tazobactam combination

- For bacterial infections:
  - —For *injection* dosage form:
    - Adults and teenagers—3 to 4 grams of piperacillin, in combination with 0.375 to 0.5 grams of tazobactam, injected into a vein every six to eight hours for seven to ten days.
    - Children up to 12 years of age—Use and dose must be determined by your doctor.

For ticarcillin and clavulanate combination

- For bacterial infections:
  - —For *injection* dosage form:
    - Adults and teenagers weighing 60 kilograms (kg) (132 pounds) or more—3 grams of ticarcillin, in combination with 100 milligrams (mg) of clavulanate, injected into a vein every four to six hours.
    - Adults and teenagers weighing less than 60 kg (132 pounds)—33.3 to 75 mg of ticarcillin per kg (15 to 34.1 mg per pound) of body weight, in combination with 1.1 to 2.5 mg of clavulanate per kg (0.5 to 1.1 mg per pound) of body weight, injected into a vein every four to six hours.
    - Infants and children 1 month to 12 years of age—50 mg of ticarcillin per kg (22.7 mg per pound) of body weight, in combination with 1.7 mg of clavulanate per kg (0.8 mg per pound) of body weight, injected into a vein every four to six hours.

Missed dose—If you miss a dose of this medicine, take it as soon as possible. This will help to keep a constant amount of medicine in the blood or urine. However, if it is almost time for your next dose, skip the missed dose and go back to your regular dosing schedule. Do not double doses.

Storage—To store this medicine:

- Keep out of the reach of children.
- Store away from heat and direct light.
- Do not store capsules or tablets in the bathroom, near the kitchen sink, or in other damp places. Heat or moisture may cause the medicine to break down.
- Store the oral liquid form of penicillins in the refrigerator because heat will cause this medicine to break down. However, keep the medicine from freezing. Follow the directions on the label.
- Do not keep outdated medicine or medicine no longer needed. Be sure that any discarded medicine is out of the reach of children.

Precautions While Using This Medicine

If your symptoms do not improve within a few days, or if they become worse, check with your doctor.

Penicillins may cause diarrhea in some patients.

- *Check with your doctor if severe diarrhea occurs.* Severe diarrhea may be a sign of a serious side effect. *Do not take any diarrhea medicine.* Diarrhea medicines may make your diarrhea worse or make it last longer.
- For mild diarrhea, diarrhea medicine containing kaolin or attapulgite (e.g., Kaopectate tablets, Diasorb) may be taken. However, other kinds of diarrhea medicine should not be taken. They may make your diarrhea worse or make it last longer.
- If you have any questions about this or if mild diarrhea continues or gets worse, check with your health care professional.

For *diabetic patients:*

- *Penicillin and beta-lactamase inhibitor combinations may cause false test results with some urine sugar tests.* Check with your doctor before changing your diet or the dosage of your diabetes medicine.

Before you have any medical tests, tell the doctor in charge that you are taking this medicine. The results of some tests may be affected by this medicine.

Side Effects of This Medicine

Along with its needed effects, a medicine may cause some unwanted effects. Although not all of these side effects may occur, if they do occur they may need medical attention.

Stop taking this medicine and get emergency help immediately if any of the following side effects occur:

Less common

Fast or irregular breathing; fever; joint pain; lightheadedness or fainting (sudden); puffiness or swelling around the face; shortness of breath; skin rash, hives, itching

In addition to the side effects mentioned above, *check with your doctor immediately* if any of the following side effects occur:

Rare

Abdominal or stomach cramps and pain (severe); convulsions (seizures); diarrhea (watery and severe), which may also be bloody; pain at place of injection; sore throat and fever; unusual bleeding or bruising

Note: Some of the above side effects (severe abdominal or stomach cramps and pain, and watery and severe diarrhea, which may also be bloody) may also occur up to several weeks after you stop taking any of these medicines.

Other side effects may occur that usually do not need medical attention. These side effects may go away during treatment as your body adjusts to the medicine. However, check with your doctor if any of the following side effects continue or are bothersome:

More common

Diarrhea (mild); headache; nausea or vomiting; sore mouth or tongue; stomach pain; vaginal itching and discharge; white patches in the mouth and/or on the tongue

Other side effects not listed above may also occur in some patients. If you notice any other effects, check with your doctor.

Developed: 07/29/94
Revised: 04/19/95

PENTAMIDINE Inhalation

Some commonly used brand names are:

In the U.S.—
NebuPent

In Canada—
Pentacarinat
Pneumopent

Description

Pentamidine (pen-TAM-i-deen) is used to try to prevent *Pneumocystis* (noo-moe-SISS-tis) *carinii* pneumonia (PCP), a very serious type of pneumonia. This type of pneumonia occurs commonly in patients whose immune systems are not working normally, such as patients with acquired immune deficiency syndrome (AIDS). Inhaled pentamidine does not prevent illness in parts of the body outside the lungs. This medicine may also be used for other conditions as determined by your doctor.

Pentamidine is available only with your doctor's prescription, in the following dosage form:

Inhalation

- Inhalation solution (U.S. and Canada)

Before Using This Medicine

In deciding to use a medicine, the risks of taking the medicine must be weighed against the good it will do. This is a decision you and your doctor will make. For pentamidine inhalation, the following should be considered:

Allergies—Tell your doctor if you have ever had any unusual or allergic reaction to pentamidine inhalation. Also tell your health care professional if you are allergic to any other substances, such as foods, preservatives, or dyes.

Pregnancy—Studies on birth defects have not been done in humans. However, studies in rabbits, given doses by injection much larger than humans would absorb into their bloodstream through the lungs, have shown an increase in miscarriages and bone defects in the fetus.

Breast-feeding—It is not known whether pentamidine passes into breast milk. However, pentamidine has not been reported to cause problems in nursing babies.

Children—Studies on this medicine have been done only in adult patients, and there is no specific information comparing use of pentamidine inhalation in children with use in other age groups. However, pentamidine inhalation is recommended in children 5 years of age and older who cannot tolerate other medicines.

Older adults—Many medicines have not been studied specifically in older people. Therefore, it may not be known whether they work exactly the same way they do in younger adults or if they cause different side effects or problems in older people. There is no specific information comparing use of pentamidine inhalation in the elderly with use in other age groups.

Other medicines—Although certain medicines should not be used together at all, in other cases two different medicines may be used together even if an interaction might occur. In these cases, your doctor may want to change the dose, or other precautions may be necessary. Tell your health care professional if you are taking any other prescription or nonprescription (over-the-counter [OTC]) medicine.

Other medical problems—The presence of other medical problems may affect the use of pentamidine inhalation. Make sure you tell your doctor if you have any other medical problems, especially:

- Asthma—Patients with asthma may have an increase in coughing or difficulty in breathing while receiving pentamidine inhalation

Proper Use of This Medicine

To help prevent the development or return of pneumocystis pneumonia, you must receive pentamidine inhalation on a regular basis, even if you are feeling well.

Dosing—The dose of pentamidine inhalation will be different for different patients. *Follow your doctor's orders or the directions on the label.* The following information includes only the average doses of pentamidine inhalation. *If your dose is different, do not change it* unless your doctor tells you to do so.

- For the *inhalation* dosage form:
  - —For the prevention of *Pneumocystis carinii* pneumonia (PCP):
    - Adults and children 5 years of age and older—300 milligrams (mg) by oral inhalation once every four weeks.
    - Children younger than 5 years of age—Use and dose must be determined by your doctor.

Missed dose—If you miss a dose of this medicine, receive your treatment as soon as possible.

Precautions While Using This Medicine

If you are also using the inhalation form of a bronchodilator (medicine used to help relieve breathing problems), use the pentamidine inhalation at least 5 to 10 minutes after the bronchodilator, unless otherwise directed by your doctor. This will help to reduce the possibility of side effects. Do not use the bronchodilator or any medicine other than pentamidine in the nebulizer.

A bitter or metallic taste may occur during use of this medicine. Sucking on a hard candy after each treatment can help reduce this problem.

Cigarette smoking can increase the chance of coughing and difficulty in breathing during pentamidine inhalation therapy.

Side Effects of This Medicine

On rare occasions, pneumocystis infections have occurred in parts of the body outside the lungs in patients receiving pentamidine inhalation therapy. You should discuss this possible problem with your doctor.

Along with its needed effects, a medicine may cause some unwanted effects. Although not all of these side effects may occur, if they do occur they may need medical attention.

Check with your health care professional immediately if any of the following side effects occur:

More common

Burning pain, dryness, or sensation of lump in throat; chest pain or congestion; coughing; difficulty in breathing; difficulty in swallowing; skin rash; wheezing

Rare

Nausea and vomiting; pain in upper abdomen, possibly radiating to the back; pain in side of chest (severe); shortness of breath (sudden and severe)

Rare—with daily treatment doses only

Anxiety; chills; cold sweats; cool, pale skin; decreased urination; headache; increased hunger; loss of appetite; nausea and vomiting; nervousness; shakiness; stomach pain; unusual tiredness

Other side effects not listed above may also occur in some patients. If you notice any other effects, check with your doctor.

Revised: 03/03/92
Interim revision: 03/28/94

PENTAMIDINE Systemic

Some commonly used brand names are:

In the U.S.—
Pentam 300
Generic name product may also be available.

In Canada—
Pentacarinat
Generic name product may also be available.

Description

Pentamidine (pen-TAM-i-deen) is used to treat *Pneumocystis* (noo-moe-SISS-tis) *carinii* pneumonia (PCP), a very serious kind of pneumonia. This kind of pneumonia occurs commonly in patients whose immune system is not working normally, such as cancer patients, transplant patients, and patients with acquired immune deficiency syndrome (AIDS). In addition, your doctor may prescribe pentamidine for some other medical problems caused by protozoa. This medicine may also be used for other conditions as determined by your doctor.

Pentamidine may cause some serious side effects. Before you begin treatment with pentamidine, you and your doctor should talk about the good this medicine will do as well as the risks of using it.

Pentamidine is to be administered only by or under the immediate supervision of your doctor. It is available in the following dosage form:

Parenteral
- Injection (U.S. and Canada)

Before Receiving This Medicine

In deciding to use a medicine, the risks of taking the medicine must be weighed against the good it will do. This is a decision you and your doctor will make. For pentamidine, the following should be considered:

Allergies—Tell your doctor if you have ever had any unusual or allergic reaction to pentamidine. Also tell your health care professional if you are allergic to any other substances, such as foods, preservatives, or dyes.

Diet—Make certain your health care professional knows if you are on a low-sodium, low-sugar, or any other special diet. Since most medicines contain more than their active ingredient, some products may have to be avoided.

Pregnancy—Pentamidine has not been studied in pregnant women. However, studies in rabbits have shown an increase in miscarriages and bone defects in the fetus.

Breast-feeding—It is not known whether pentamidine passes into breast milk. However, because of the risk of side effects in the newborn, breast-feeding is not recommended during treatment with this medicine.

Children—Although pentamidine has not been widely used in children, this medicine is not expected to cause different side effects or problems in children than it does in adults.

Older adults—Many medicines have not been studied specifically in older people. Therefore, it may not be known whether they work exactly the same way they do in younger adults or if they cause different side effects or problems in older people. There is no specific information comparing use of pentamidine in the elderly with use in other age groups.

Other medicines—Although certain medicines should not be used together at all, in other cases two different medicines may be used together even if an interaction might occur. In these cases, your doctor may want to change the dose, or other precautions may be necessary. When you are receiving pentamidine, it is especially important that your health care professional know if you are taking any of the following:

- Amphotericin B by injection (e.g., Fungizone) or
- Antithyroid agents (medicine for overactive thyroid) or
- Azathioprine (e.g., Imuran) or
- Chloramphenicol (e.g., Chloromycetin) or
- Colchicine or
- Cyclophosphamide (e.g., Cytoxan) or
- Flucytosine (e.g., Ancobon) or
- Ganciclovir (e.g., Cytovene) or
- Interferon (e.g., Intron A, Roferon-A) or
- Mercaptopurine (e.g., Purinethol) or
- X-ray treatment or
- Zidovudine (e.g., AZT, Retrovir) or
- If you have ever been treated with x-rays or cancer medicine—When taken with pentamidine, these medicines may increase the chance of damage to your blood cells
- Carmustine (e.g., BiCNU) or
- Cisplatin (e.g., Platinol) or
- Combination pain medicine containing acetaminophen and aspirin (e.g., Excedrin) or other salicylates (with large amounts taken regularly) or
- Cyclosporine (e.g., Sandimmune) or
- Deferoxamine (e.g., Desferal) (with long-term use) or
- Foscarnet (e.g., Foscavir) or
- Gold salts (medicine for arthritis) or
- Inflammation or pain medicine (except narcotics) or
- Lithium (e.g., Lithane) or
- Other anti-infectives by mouth or by injection (medicine for infection) or
- Penicillamine (e.g., Cuprimine) or
- Streptozocin (e.g., Zanosar) or
- Tiopronin (e.g., Thiola)—When taken with pentamidine, these medicines may increase the chance of kidney damage
- Didanosine (e.g., ddI, Videx)—When taken with pentamidine, didanosine may increase the chance of pancreatitis (inflammation of the pancreas)
- Methotrexate (e.g., Mexate) or
- Plicamycin (e.g., Mithracin)—When taken with pentamidine, these medicines may increase the chance of damage to your blood cells and your kidneys

Other medical problems—The presence of other medical problems may affect the use of pentamidine. Make sure you tell your doctor if you have any other medical problems, especially:

- Anemia or
- Bleeding disorders (history of) or
- Heart disease or
- Hypotension (low blood pressure) or
- Kidney disease or

- Liver disease—Pentamidine may make these conditions worse
- Diabetes mellitus (sugar diabetes) or
- Hypoglycemia (low blood sugar)—Pentamidine may increase or decrease blood sugar levels and may disturb control of sugar diabetes

Proper Use of This Medicine

To help clear up your infection completely, *pentamidine must be given for the full time of treatment,* even if you begin to feel better after a few days. Also, this medicine works best when there is a constant amount in the blood. To help keep the amount constant, pentamidine must be given on a regular schedule.

Dosing—The dose of pentamidine will be different for different patients. *Follow your doctor's orders or the directions on the label.* The following information includes only the average doses of pentamidine. *If your dose is different, do not change it* unless your doctor tells you to do so.

- For *injection* dosage form:
  - —For *Pneumocystis carinii* pneumonia (PCP):
    - Adults and children—Dose is based on body weight and must be determined by your doctor. The usual dose is 4 milligrams (mg) per kilogram (kg) (1.8 mg per pound) of body weight given once a day for fourteen to twenty-one days. This dose is injected slowly into a vein over a one- to two-hour period of time.

Precautions While Using This Medicine

Some patients may develop sudden, severe low blood pressure after a dose of pentamidine. Therefore, you should be lying down while you are receiving this medicine. Also, your doctor may want to check your blood pressure while you are receiving a pentamidine injection and several times after the dose has been given until your blood pressure is stable.

Pentamidine can lower the number of white blood cells in your blood, increasing the chance of your getting certain infections. It can also lower the number of platelets, which are necessary for proper blood clotting. If these problems occur, there are certain precautions you can take to reduce the risk of infection or bleeding:

- *Check with your doctor immediately* if you think you are getting a cold or any other infection.
- *Check with your doctor immediately* if you notice any unusual bleeding or bruising.
- Be careful when using regular toothbrushes, dental floss, or toothpicks. Your medical doctor, dentist, or nurse may recommend other ways to clean your teeth and gums. Check with your health care professional before having any dental work done.
- Avoid using a safety razor. Use an electric shaver instead. Also, be careful when using fingernail or toenail cutters.

Side Effects of This Medicine

Pentamidine may cause some serious side effects, including heart problems, low blood pressure, low or high blood sugar, and other blood problems. *You and your doctor should discuss the good this medicine will do as well as the risks of receiving it.*

Along with its needed effects, a medicine may cause some unwanted effects. Although not all of these side effects may occur, if they do occur they may need medical attention.

Check with your health care professional immediately if any of the following side effects occur:

More common

Decrease in urination; sore throat and fever; unusual bleeding or bruising

Signs of diabetes mellitus or high blood sugar

Drowsiness; flushed, dry skin; fruit-like breath odor; increased thirst; increased urination; loss of appetite

Signs of low blood sugar

Anxiety; chills; cold sweats; cool, pale skin; headache; increased hunger; nausea; nervousness; shakiness

Signs of low blood pressure

Blurred vision; confusion; dizziness; fainting or lightheadedness; unusual tiredness or weakness

Note: *Signs of diabetes mellitus or high blood sugar, or signs of low blood sugar* may also occur up to several months after you stop receiving this medicine.

Less common

Fast or irregular pulse; fever; nausea and vomiting; pain in upper abdomen; pain, redness, and/or hardness at place of injection; skin rash, redness, or itching

Other side effects may occur that usually do not need medical attention. These side effects may go away during treatment as your body adjusts to the medicine. However, check with your doctor if any of the following side effects continue or are bothersome:

More common

Diarrhea; loss of appetite; nausea and vomiting

Stomach problems, such as nausea and vomiting, or loss of appetite, are common minor side effects seen in pentamidine treatment. However, if you have these problems, and at the same time have sharp pain in the upper abdomen, or an unusual decrease in the amount of urine, check with your doctor immediately.

Pentamidine may also cause an unpleasant metallic taste. This side effect is to be expected and does not require medical attention.

Other side effects not listed above may also occur in some patients. If you notice any other effects, check with your doctor.

Additional Information

Once a medicine has been approved for marketing for a certain use, experience may show that it is also useful for other medical problems. Although these uses are not included in product labeling, pentamidine is used in certain patients with the following medical conditions:

- Leishmaniasis, cutaneous
- Leishmaniasis, visceral (kala-azar)
- Trypanosomiasis, African (African sleeping sickness)

If you are living in or will be traveling to an area where there is a chance of getting kala-azar or African sleeping sickness, the following measures will help to prevent reinfection with either disease:

- If possible, sleep under fine-mesh netting to avoid being bitten by sandflies (which carry kala-azar) or tsetse flies (which carry African sleeping sickness).
- Wear long-sleeved shirts or blouses and long trousers to protect your arms and legs, especially at dusk or during evening hours when sandflies are out. Since tsetse flies can bite through thin clothing, it is best to wear clothing made from fairly heavy material to protect arms and legs.
- Apply insect repellant to uncovered areas of the skin when sandflies or tsetse flies are out.

Other than the above information, there is no additional information relating to proper use, precautions, or side effects for these uses.

Revised: 05/27/94
Interim revision: 04/24/95

PENTOSTATIN Systemic

A commonly used brand name in the U.S. and Canada is Nipent. Other commonly used names are 2′-deoxycoformycin and 2′DCF.

Description

Pentostatin (PEN-toe-stat-in) belongs to the group of medicines called antimetabolites. It is used to treat hairy cell leukemia.

Pentostatin interferes with the growth of cancer cells, which are eventually destroyed. Since the growth of normal body cells may also be affected by pentostatin, other effects will also occur. Some of these may be serious and must be reported to your doctor. Other effects may not be serious but may cause concern. Some effects may not occur for months or years after the medicine is used.

Before you begin treatment with pentostatin, you and your doctor should talk about the good this medicine will do as well as the risks of using it.

Pentostatin is to be administered only by or under the immediate supervision of your doctor. It is available in the following dosage form:

Parenteral
- Injection (U.S. and Canada)

Before Using This Medicine

In deciding to use a medicine, the risks of taking the medicine must be weighed against the good it will do. This is a decision you and your doctor will make. For pentostatin, the following should be considered:

Allergies—Tell your doctor if you have ever had any unusual or allergic reaction to pentostatin.

Pregnancy—There is a chance that this medicine may cause birth defects if either the male or female is taking it at the time of conception or if it is taken during pregnancy. Pentostatin has been shown to cause birth defects in rats and mice. In addition, many cancer medicines may cause sterility which could be permanent. Although sterility has not been reported with this medicine, it does occur in animals and the possibility should be kept in mind.

Be sure that you have discussed this with your doctor before taking this medicine. It is best to use some kind of birth control while you are receiving pentostatin. Tell your doctor right away if you think you have become pregnant while receiving pentostatin.

Breast-feeding—It is not known whether pentostatin passes into breast milk. However, because this medicine may cause serious side effects, breast-feeding is generally not recommended while you are receiving it.

Children—There is no specific information comparing use of pentostatin in children with use in other age groups.

Older adults—Many medicines have not been studied specifically in older people. Therefore, it may not be known whether they work exactly the same way they do in younger adults. Although there is no specific information comparing use of pentostatin in the elderly with use in other adults, this medicine is not expected to cause different side effects or problems in older people than it does in younger adults.

Other medicines—Although certain medicines should not be used together at all, in other cases two different medicines may be used together even if an interaction might occur. In these cases, your doctor may want to change the dose, or other precautions may be necessary. When you are receiving pentostatin, it is especially important that your health care professional know if you are taking any of the following:

- Amphotericin B by injection (e.g., Fungizone) or
- Antithyroid agents (medicine for overactive thyroid) or
- Azathioprine (e.g., Imuran) or
- Chloramphenicol (e.g., Chloromycetin) or
- Colchicine or
- Flucytosine (e.g., Ancobon) or
- Ganciclovir (e.g., Cytovene) or
- Interferon (e.g., Intron A, Roferon-A) or
- Plicamycin (e.g., Mithracin) or
- Zidovudine (e.g., AZT, Retrovir) or
- If you have ever been treated with x-rays or cancer medicines—Pentostatin may increase the effects of these medicines or radiation therapy on the blood
- Probenecid (e.g., Benemid) or
- Sulfinpyrazone (e.g., Anturane)—Pentostatin may raise the amount of uric acid in the blood. Since these medicines are used to lower uric acid levels, they may not be as effective in patients receiving pentostatin

Other medical problems—The presence of other medical problems may affect the use of pentostatin. Make sure you

tell your doctor if you have any other medical problems, especially:

- Chickenpox (including recent exposure) or
- Herpes zoster (shingles)—Risk of severe disease affecting other parts of the body
- Gout (history of) or
- Kidney stones (history of)—Pentostatin may increase levels of uric acid in the body, which can cause gout or kidney stones
- Infection—Pentostatin may decrease your body's ability to fight infection
- Kidney disease—Effects of pentostatin may be increased because of slower removal from the body

Proper Use of This Medicine

This medicine often causes nausea and vomiting. However, it is very important that you continue to receive the medicine even if you begin to feel ill. Ask your health care professional for ways to lessen these effects.

Dosing—The dose of pentostatin will be different for different patients. The dose that is used may depend on a number of things, including what the medicine is being used for, the patient's size, and whether or not other medicines are also being taken. *If you are receiving pentostatin at home, follow your doctor's orders or the directions on the label.* If you have any questions about the proper dose of pentostatin, ask your doctor.

Precautions While Using This Medicine

It is very important that your doctor check your progress at regular visits to make sure that this medicine is working properly and to check for unwanted effects.

While you are being treated with pentostatin, and after you stop treatment with it, *do not have any immunizations (vaccinations) without your doctor's approval*. Pentostatin may lower your body's resistance and there is a chance you might get the infection the immunization is meant to prevent. In addition, other persons living in your household should not take oral polio vaccine since there is a chance they could pass the polio virus on to you. Also, avoid persons who have taken oral polio vaccine. Do not get close to them and do not stay in the same room with them for very long. If you cannot take these precautions, you should consider wearing a protective face mask that covers the nose and mouth.

Pentostatin can lower the number of white blood cells in your blood temporarily, increasing the chance of getting an infection. It can also lower the number of platelets, which are necessary for proper blood clotting. If this occurs, there are certain precautions you can take, especially when your blood count is low, to reduce the risk of infection or bleeding:

- If you can, avoid people with infections. *Check with your doctor immediately* if you think you are getting an infection or if you get a fever or chills, cough or hoarseness, lower back or side pain, or painful or difficult urination.
- *Check with your doctor immediately* if you notice any unusual bleeding or bruising; black, tarry stools; blood in urine or stools; or pinpoint red spots on your skin.
- Be careful when using a regular toothbrush, dental floss, or toothpick. Your medical doctor, dentist, or nurse may recommend other ways to clean your teeth and gums. Check with your medical doctor before having any dental work done.
- Do not touch your eyes or the inside of your nose unless you have just washed your hands and have not touched anything else in the meantime.
- Be careful not to cut yourself when you are using sharp objects such as a safety razor or fingernail or toenail cutters.
- Avoid contact sports or other situations where bruising or injury could occur.

Side Effects of This Medicine

Along with its needed effects, a medicine may cause some unwanted effects. Some side effects will have signs or symptoms that you can see or feel. Your doctor may watch for others by doing certain tests.

Also, because of the way these medicines act on the body, there is a chance that they might cause other unwanted effects that may not occur until months or years after the medicine is used. These delayed effects may include certain types of cancer. Discuss these possible effects with your doctor.

Check with your doctor or nurse immediately if any of the following side effects occur:

More common
Cough or hoarseness; fever or chills; lower back or side pain; painful or difficult urination

Less common
Black, tarry stools; blood in urine or stools; chest pain; pinpoint red spots on skin; unusual bleeding or bruising

Check with your health care professional as soon as possible if any of the following side effects occur:

More common
Pain; skin rash or itching (sudden); unusual tiredness

Less common
Anxiety or nervousness; changes in vision; confusion; cramps in lower legs; mental depression; nosebleed; numbness or tingling of hands or feet; shortness of breath; sleepiness; sore, red eyes; sores in mouth or on lips; stomach pain; swelling of feet or lower legs; trouble in sleeping

This medicine may also cause the following side effects that your doctor will watch for:

More common
Anemia; liver problems; low platelet counts

Less common
Kidney problems

Other side effects may occur that usually do not need medical attention. These side effects may go away during treatment as your body adjusts to the medicine. Also, your health care professional may be able to tell you about ways to prevent or reduce some of these side effects. Check with your health care professional if any of the

following side effects continue or are bothersome or if you have any questions about them:

More common

Diarrhea; headache; loss of appetite; muscle pain; nausea and vomiting; skin rash

Less common

Back pain; bloating or gas; constipation; dry skin; general feeling of discomfort or illness; itching; joint pain; weakness; weight loss

Other side effects not listed above may also occur in some patients. If you notice any other effects, check with your doctor.

Revised: 05/06/93
Interim revision: 06/30/94

PENTOXIFYLLINE Systemic

A commonly used brand name in the U.S. and Canada is Trental.

Generic name product may be available.

Another commonly used name is oxypentifylline.

Description

Pentoxifylline (pen-tox-IF-i-lin) improves the flow of blood through blood vessels. It is used to reduce leg pain caused by poor blood circulation. Pentoxifylline makes it possible to walk farther before having to rest because of leg cramps.

Pentoxifylline is available only with your doctor's prescription, in the following dosage form:

Oral

- Extended-release tablets (U.S. and Canada)

Before Using This Medicine

In deciding to use a medicine, the risks of taking the medicine must be weighed against the good it will do. This is a decision you and your doctor will make. For pentoxifylline, the following should be considered:

Allergies—Tell your doctor if you have ever had any unusual or allergic reaction to pentoxifylline or to other xanthines such as aminophylline, caffeine, dyphylline, ethylenediamine (contained in aminophylline), oxtriphylline, theobromine, or theophylline. Also tell your health care professional if you are allergic to any other substances, such as foods, preservatives, or dyes.

Pregnancy—Pentoxifylline has not been studied in pregnant women. Studies in animals have not shown that it causes birth defects. However, at very high doses it has caused other harmful effects. Before taking this medicine, make sure your doctor knows if you are pregnant or if you may become pregnant.

Breast-feeding—Pentoxifylline passes into breast milk. The medicine has not been reported to cause problems in nursing babies. However, pentoxifylline has caused noncancerous tumors in animals when given for a long time in doses much larger than those used in humans. Therefore, your doctor may not want you to breast-feed while taking it. Be sure that you discuss the risks and benefits of this medicine with your doctor.

Children—Studies on this medicine have been done only in adult patients, and there is no specific information comparing use of pentoxifylline in children with use in other age groups.

Older adults—Side effects may be more likely to occur in the elderly, who are usually more sensitive than younger adults to the effects of pentoxifylline.

Other medicines—Although certain medicines should not be used together at all, in other cases two different medicines may be used together even if an interaction might occur. In these cases, your doctor may want to change the dose, or other precautions may be necessary. When you are taking pentoxifylline, it is important that your health care professional know if you are taking any other prescription or nonprescription (over-the-counter [OTC]) medicine, or if you smoke tobacco.

Other medical problems—The presence of other medical problems may affect the use of pentoxifylline. Make sure you tell your doctor if you have any other medical problems, especially:

- Any condition in which there is a risk of bleeding (e.g., recent stroke)—Pentoxifylline may make the condition worse
- Kidney disease or
- Liver disease—The chance of side effects may be increased

Proper Use of This Medicine

Swallow the tablet whole. Do not crush, break, or chew it before swallowing.

Pentoxifylline should be taken with meals to lessen the chance of stomach upset. Taking an antacid with the medicine may also help.

Dosing—The dose of pentoxifylline will be different for different patients. *Follow your doctor's orders or the directions on the label.* The following information includes only the average doses of pentoxifylline. *If your dose is different, do not change it* unless your doctor tells you to do so.

- For *oral* dosage form (extended-release tablets):
  - —For peripheral vascular disease (circulation problems):
    - Adults—400 milligrams (mg) two to three times a day, taken with meals.
    - Children—Use must be determined by your doctor.

Missed dose—If you miss a dose of this medicine, take it as soon as possible. However, if it is almost time for your next dose, skip the missed dose and go back to your regular dosing schedule. Do not double doses.

Storage—To store this medicine:

- Keep out of the reach of children.
- Store away from heat and direct light.
- Do not store in the bathroom, near the kitchen sink, or in other damp places. Heat or moisture may cause the medicine to break down.
- Do not keep outdated medicine or medicine no longer needed. Be sure that any discarded medicine is out of the reach of children.

Precautions While Using This Medicine

It may take several weeks for this medicine to work. If you feel that pentoxifylline is not working, do not stop taking it on your own. Instead, check with your doctor.

Smoking tobacco may worsen your condition since nicotine may further narrow your blood vessels. Therefore, it is best to avoid smoking.

Side Effects of This Medicine

Along with its needed effects, a medicine may cause some unwanted effects. Although not all of these side effects may occur, if they do occur they may need medical attention.

Check with your doctor as soon as possible if any of the following side effects occur:

Rare

Chest pain; irregular heartbeat

Signs and symptoms of overdose (in the order in which they may occur)

Drowsiness; flushing; faintness; unusual excitement; convulsions (seizures)

Other side effects may occur that usually do not need medical attention. These side effects may go away during treatment as your body adjusts to the medicine. However, check with your doctor if any of the following side effects continue or are bothersome:

Less common

Dizziness; headache; nausea or vomiting; stomach discomfort

Other side effects not listed above may also occur in some patients. If you notice any other effects, check with your doctor.

Revised: 07/13/93
Interim revision: 08/05/97

PERGOLIDE Systemic

A commonly used brand name in the U.S. and Canada is Permax.

Description

Pergolide (PER-go-lide) belongs to the group of medicines known as ergot alkaloids. It is used with levodopa or with carbidopa and levodopa combination to treat people who have Parkinson's disease. It works by stimulating certain parts of the central nervous system (CNS) that are involved in this disease.

Pergolide is available only with your doctor's prescription, in the following dosage form:

Oral

- Tablets (U.S. and Canada)

Before Using This Medicine

In deciding to use a medicine, the risks of taking the medicine must be weighed against the good it will do. This is a decision you and your doctor will make. For pergolide, the following should be considered:

Allergies—Tell your doctor if you have ever had any unusual or allergic reaction to pergolide or other ergot medicines such as ergotamine. Also tell your health care professional if you are allergic to any other substances, such as foods, preservatives, or dyes.

Pregnancy—Studies have not been done in pregnant women. However, pergolide has not been shown to cause birth defects or other problems in animal studies.

Breast-feeding—This medicine may stop milk from being produced.

Children—Studies on this medicine have been done only in adult patients, and there is no specific information about its use in children.

Older adults—This medicine has been tested and has not been shown to cause different side effects or problems in older people than it does in younger adults.

Other medicines—Although certain medicines should not be used together at all, in other cases 2 different medicines may be used together even if an interaction might occur. In these cases, your doctor may want to change the dose, or other precautions may be necessary. When you are taking pergolide, it is especially important that your health care professional know if you are taking any other prescription or nonprescription (over-the-counter [OTC]) medicine.

Other medical problems—The presence of other medical problems may affect the use of pergolide. Make sure you tell your doctor if you have any other medical problems, especially:

- Heart disease or
- Mental problems (history of)—Pergolide may make the condition worse

Proper Use of This Medicine

If pergolide upsets your stomach, it may be taken with meals. If stomach upset continues, check with your doctor.

Dosing—The dose of pergolide will be different for different patients. *Follow your doctor's orders or the directions on the label.* The following information includes only the average doses of pergolide. *If your dose is different, do not change it* unless your doctor tells you to do so.

The number of tablets that you take depends on the strength of the medicine. Also, *the number of doses you take each day, the time allowed between doses, and the length of time you take the medicine depend on the medical problem for which you are taking pergolide.*

- For *oral* dosage form (tablets):
  —Adults: 50 micrograms a day for the first two days. The dose may be increased every three days as needed. However, the usual dose is not more than 5000 micrograms.

Missed dose—If you miss a dose of this medicine, take it as soon as you remember it. However, if it is almost time for your next dose, skip the missed dose and go back to your regular dosing schedule. Do not double doses.

Storage—To store this medicine:

- Keep out of the reach of children.
- Store away from heat and direct light.
- Do not store in the bathroom, near the kitchen sink, or in other damp places. Heat or moisture may cause the medicine to break down.
- Do not keep outdated medicine or medicine no longer needed. Be sure that any discarded medicine is out of the reach of children.

Precautions While Using This Medicine

It is important that your doctor check your progress at regular visits, to make sure that this medicine is working and to check for unwanted effects.

This medicine may cause some people to become drowsy, dizzy, or less alert than they are normally. *Make sure you know how you react to this medicine before you drive, use machines, or do anything else that could be dangerous if you are dizzy or are not alert.*

Dizziness, lightheadedness, or fainting may occur after the first doses of pergolide, especially when you get up from a lying or sitting position. Getting up slowly may help. Taking the first dose at bedtime or when you are able to lie down may also lessen problems. If the problem continues or gets worse, check with your doctor.

Pergolide may cause dryness of the mouth. For temporary relief, use sugarless candy or gum, melt bits of ice in your mouth, or use a saliva substitute. However, if your mouth continues to feel dry for more than 2 weeks, check with your medical doctor or dentist. Continuing dryness of the mouth may increase the chance of dental disease, including tooth decay, gum disease, and fungus infections.

It may take several weeks for pergolide to work. Do not stop taking this medicine or reduce the amount you are taking without first checking with your doctor.

Side Effects of This Medicine

Along with its needed effects, a medicine may cause some unwanted effects. Although not all of these side effects may occur, if they do occur they may need medical attention.

Check with your doctor immediately if any of the following side effects occur:

Rare

Chest pain (severe); convulsions (seizures); fainting; fast heartbeat; headache (severe or continuing); increased sweating; nausea and vomiting (continuing or severe); nervousness; unexplained shortness of breath; vision changes, such as blurred vision or temporary blindness; weakness (sudden)

Also, check with your doctor as soon as possible if any of the following side effects occur:

More common

Confusion; hallucinations (seeing, hearing, or feeling things that are not there); pain or burning while urinating; uncontrolled movements of the body, such as the face, tongue, arms, hands, head, and upper body

Less common

High blood pressure

Other side effects may occur that usually do not need medical attention. These side effects may go away during treatment as your body adjusts to the medicine. However, check with your doctor if any of the following side effects continue or are bothersome:

More common

Abdominal or stomach pain; constipation; dizziness or lightheadedness, especially when getting up from a lying or sitting position; drowsiness; lower back pain; nausea; runny nose; weakness

Less common

Chills; diarrhea; dryness of mouth; loss of appetite; swelling of the face; vomiting

Other side effects not listed above may also occur in some patients. If you notice any other effects, check with your doctor.

Revised: 03/19/93

PERMETHRIN Topical

A commonly used brand name in the U.S. and Canada is Nix Cream Rinse.

Description

Permethrin (per-METH-rin) is used to treat head lice infections. It acts by destroying both the lice and their eggs.

This medicine is available in the following dosage form:

Topical

- Lotion (U.S. and Canada)

Before Using This Medicine

If you are using this medicine without a prescription, carefully read any precautions on the label. For topical permethrin, the following should be considered:

Allergies—Tell your doctor if you have ever had any unusual or allergic reaction to permethrin; to other synthetic pyrethroids, such as those found in household insecticides; to pyrethrins or chrysanthemums; or to veterinary insecticides containing permethrin. Also tell your health care professional if you are allergic to any other substances, such as preservatives or dyes.

Pregnancy—Permethrin has not been studied in pregnant women. However, this medication has not been shown to cause birth defects or other problems in animal studies.

Breast-feeding—It is not known whether permethrin passes into the breast milk. However, animal studies have shown that permethrin can cause tumors. Be sure you have discussed the risks and benefits of the medicine with your doctor.

Children—Studies on this medicine have been done only in adult patients, and there is no specific information comparing use of topical permethrin in children with use in other age groups.

Older adults—Many medicines have not been studied specifically in older people. Therefore, it may not be known whether they work exactly the same way they do in younger adults or if they cause different side effects or problems in older people. There is no specific information comparing use of topical permethrin in the elderly with use in other age groups.

Other medicines—Although certain medicines should not be used together at all, in other cases two different medicines may be used together even if an interaction might occur. In these cases, your doctor may want to change the dose, or other precautions may be necessary. Tell your health care professional if you are using any other prescription or nonprescription (over-the-counter [OTC]) medicine that is to be applied to the hair and scalp.

Other medical problems—The presence of other medical problems may affect the use of topical permethrin. Make sure you tell your doctor if you have other medical problems, especially:

- Severe inflammation of the scalp—Use of permethrin may make the condition worse

Proper Use of This Medicine

Keep this medicine away from the eyes. If you accidentally get some in your eyes, flush them thoroughly with water at once.

Permethrin lotion comes in a container that holds only one treatment. Use as much of the medicine as you need and discard any remaining lotion properly.

To use:

- Shampoo the hair and scalp using regular shampoo.
- Thoroughly rinse and towel dry the hair and scalp.
- Allow hair to air dry for a few minutes.
- Shake the permethrin lotion well before applying.
- Thoroughly wet the hair and scalp with the permethrin lotion. Be sure to cover the areas behind the ears and on the back of the neck also. Allow the lotion to remain in place for 10 minutes.
- Then, rinse the hair and scalp thoroughly and dry with a clean towel.
- When the hair is dry, you may want to comb the hair with a fine-toothed comb to remove any remaining nits (eggs) or nit shells.

Head lice can be easily transferred from one person to another by direct contact with clothing, hats, scarves, bedding, towels, washcloths, hairbrushes and combs, or hairs from infected persons. Therefore, *all members of your household should be examined for head lice and should receive treatment if they are found to be infected.* If you have any questions about this, check with your doctor.

Dosing—*Follow your doctor's orders or the directions on the label.* The following information includes only the average dose of permethrin. *If your dose is different, do not change it* unless your doctor tells you to do so.

- For *topical* dosage form (lotion):
  - —For head lice:
    - Adults and children 2 years of age and older—Apply to the hair and scalp one time.
    - Children up to 2 years of age—Use and dose must be determined by your doctor.

Storage—To store this medicine:

- Keep out of the reach of children.
- Store away from heat and direct light.
- Keep this medicine from freezing. Do not refrigerate.
- Do not keep outdated medicine or medicine no longer needed. Be sure that any discarded medicine is out of the reach of children.

Precautions While Using This Medicine

To prevent reinfection or spreading of the infection to other people, good health habits are required. These include the following:

- Machine wash all clothing (including hats, scarves, and coats), bedding, towels, and washcloths in very hot water and dry them by using the hot cycle of a dryer for at least 20 minutes. Clothing or bedding that cannot be washed should be dry cleaned or sealed in an airtight plastic bag for 2 weeks.
- Shampoo all wigs and hairpieces.
- Wash all hairbrushes and combs in very hot soapy water (above 130 °F) for 5 to 10 minutes and do not share them with other people.
- Clean the house or room by thoroughly vacuuming upholstered furniture, rugs, and floors.
- Wash all toys in very hot soapy water (above 130 °F) for 5 to 10 minutes or seal in an airtight plastic bag for 2 weeks. This is especially important for stuffed toys used on the bed.

Side Effects of This Medicine

Along with its needed effects, a medicine may cause some unwanted effects. Although not all of these side effects

may occur, if they do occur they may need medical attention.

Check with your doctor if any of the following side effects continue or are bothersome:

Less common or rare

Burning, itching, numbness, rash, redness, stinging, swelling, or tingling of the scalp

Other side effects not listed above may also occur in some patients. If you notice any other effects, check with your doctor.

Revised: 07/25/94

PERPHENAZINE AND AMITRIPTYLINE Systemic

Some commonly used brand names are:

In the U.S.—

Etrafon
Etrafon-A
Etrafon-Forte
Triavil

Generic name product may also be available.

In Canada—

Elavil Plus
Etrafon
Etrafon-A
Etrafon-D
Etrafon-F
PMS Levazine
Triavil

Description

Perphenazine (per-FEN-a-zeen) and amitriptyline (a-mee-TRIP-ti-leen) combination is used to treat certain mental and emotional conditions.

This combination is available only with your doctor's prescription, in the following dosage form:

Oral

- Tablets (U.S. and Canada).

Before Using This Medicine

In deciding to use a medicine, the risks of taking the medicine must be weighed against the good it will do. This is a decision you and your doctor will make. For perphenazine and amitriptyline combination, the following should be considered:

Allergies—Tell your doctor if you have ever had any unusual or allergic reaction to perphenazine (e.g., Trilafon) or other phenothiazines (such as acetophenazine [e.g., Tindal], chlorpromazine [e.g., Thorazine], fluphenazine [e.g., Prolixin], mesoridazine [e.g., Serentil], prochlorperazine [e.g., Compazine], promazine [e.g., Sparine], promethazine [e.g., Phenergan], thioridazine [e.g., Mellaril], trifluoperazine [e.g., Stelazine], triflupromazine [e.g., Vesprin], trimeprazine [e.g., Temaril]) or to amitriptyline (e.g., Elavil) or other tricyclic antidepressants (such as amoxapine [e.g., Asendin], clomipramine [e.g., Anafranil], desipramine [e.g., Pertofrane], doxepin [e.g., Sinequan], imipramine [e.g., Tofranil], nortriptyline [e.g., Aventyl], protriptyline [e.g., Vivactil], trimipramine [e.g., Surmontil]). Also tell your health care professional if you are allergic to any other substances, such as foods, preservatives, or dyes.

Pregnancy—Studies have not been done in pregnant women. However, perphenazine and amitriptyline combination has not been shown to cause birth defects in animal studies. Side effects such as jaundice and muscle tremors have occurred in some newborn babies when their mothers received other phenothiazines during pregnancy.

Breast-feeding—Perphenazine and amitriptyline combination passes into the breast milk and may cause drowsiness and other unwanted effects in nursing babies.

Children—Certain side effects, such as muscle spasms of the face, neck, and back, tic-like or twitching movements, inability to move the eyes, twisting of the body, or weakness of the arms and legs, are more likely to occur in children, who are usually more sensitive than adults to some of the side effects of perphenazine and amitriptyline combination.

Older adults—Confusion, vision problems, dizziness or fainting, drowsiness, dryness of mouth, constipation, problems in urinating, trembling of the hands and fingers, and symptoms of tardive dyskinesia (such as uncontrolled movements of the mouth, tongue, jaw, arms, and/or legs) are especially likely to occur in elderly patients. Older patients are usually more sensitive than younger adults to the effects of perphenazine and amitriptyline combination.

Other medicines—Although certain medicines should not be used together at all, in other cases 2 different medicines may be used together even if an interaction might occur. In these cases, your doctor may want to change the dose, or other precautions may be necessary. When you are taking perphenazine and amitriptyline combination, it is especially important that your health care professional know if you are taking any of the following:

- Amphetamines or
- Appetite suppressants (diet pills) or
- Medicine for asthma or other breathing problems or
- Medicine for colds, sinus problems, or hay fever or other allergies (including nose drops and sprays)—Using these medicines with perphenazine and amitriptyline combination may increase the risk of serious effects on the heart

- Antithyroid agents (medicine for overactive thyroid) or
- Cimetidine (e.g., Tagamet) or
- Methyldopa (e.g., Aldomet) or
- Metoclopramide (e.g., Reglan) or
- Metyrosine (e.g., Demser) or
- Pemoline (e.g., Cylert) or
- Pimozide (e.g., Orap) or
- Promethazine (e.g., Phenergan) or
- Rauwolfia alkaloids (alseroxylon [e.g., Rauwiloid], deserpidine [e.g., Harmonyl], rauwolfia serpentina [e.g., Raudixin], reserpine [e.g., Serpasil]) or
- Trimeprazine (e.g., Temaril)—Taking these medicines with perphenazine and amitriptyline combination may increase the risk of serious side effects

- Central nervous system (CNS) depressants (medicines that cause drowsiness)—Taking these medicines with perphen-

azine and amitriptyline combination may increase the CNS depressant effects
- Epinephrine (e.g., Adrenalin)—Severe low blood pressure (hypotension) and fast heartbeat may occur if epinephrine is used with perphenazine and amitriptyline combination
- Levodopa (e.g., Dopar)—Perphenazine may prevent levodopa from working properly in the treatment of Parkinson's disease
- Lithium (e.g., Lithane)—The amount of medicine you need to take may change
- Metrizamide—When this dye is used for myelograms during the use of perphenazine and amitriptyline combination, there is an increased risk of seizures
- Monoamine oxidase (MAO) inhibitors (furazolidone [e.g., Furoxone], isocarboxazid [e.g., Marplan], phenelzine [e.g., Nardil], procarbazine [e.g., Matulane], selegiline [e.g., Eldepryl], tranylcypromine [e.g., Parnate])—Taking amitriptyline while you are taking or within 2 weeks of taking monoamine oxidase (MAO) inhibitors may cause sudden high body temperature, extremely high blood pressure, and severe convulsions; however, sometimes certain of these medicines may be used together under close supervision by your doctor

Other medical problems—The presence of other medical problems may affect the use of perphenazine and amitriptyline combination. Make sure you tell your doctor if you have any other medical problems, especially:
- Alcohol abuse—Certain side effects such as heat stroke may be more likely to occur
- Asthma (history of) or other lung disease or
- Bipolar disorder (manic-depressive illness) or
- Blood disease or
- Breast cancer or
- Difficult urination or
- Enlarged prostate or
- Epilepsy or other seizure disorders or
- Glaucoma or
- Heart or blood vessel disease or
- Mental illness (severe) or
- Parkinson's disease or
- Stomach or intestinal problems—Perphenazine and amitriptyline combination may make the condition worse
- Kidney disease or
- Liver disease—Higher blood levels of perphenazine and amitriptyline may occur, increasing the chance of side effects
- Overactive thyroid—Perphenazine and amitriptyline combination may cause an increased chance of serious effects on the heart
- Reye's syndrome—There may be an increased chance of unwanted effects on the liver

Proper Use of This Medicine

To lessen stomach upset, take this medicine immediately after meals or with food, unless your doctor has told you to take it on an empty stomach.

Do not take more of this medicine and do not take it more often than your doctor ordered. This is particularly important for elderly patients, since they are more sensitive to the effects of this medicine.

Sometimes perphenazine and amitriptyline combination must be taken for several weeks before its full effect is reached.

Dosing—The dose of perphenazine and amitriptyline combination will be different for different patients. *Follow your doctor's orders or the directions on the label.* The following information includes only the average doses of perphenazine and amitriptyline combination. *If your dose is different, do not change it* unless your doctor tells you to do so.

The number of tablets that you take depends on the strength of the medicine. Also, *the number of doses you take each day, the time allowed between doses, and the length of time you take the medicine depend on your special needs.*

- For *oral* dosage form (tablets):
  —For certain mental and emotional conditions:
  - Adults—At first, 1 tablet taken three or four times a day. Your doctor may increase your dose if needed.
  - Children—Use and dose must be determined by your doctor.

Missed dose—If you miss a dose of this medicine, take it as soon as possible. However, if it is within 2 hours of your next dose, skip the missed dose and go back to your regular dosing schedule. Do not double doses.

Storage—To store this medicine:
- Keep out of the reach of children. Overdose of perphenazine and amitriptyline combination is especially dangerous in young children.
- Store away from heat and direct light.
- Do not store in the bathroom, near the kitchen sink, or in other damp places. Heat or moisture may cause the medicine to break down.
- Do not keep outdated medicine or medicine no longer needed. Be sure that any discarded medicine is out of the reach of children.

Precautions While Using This Medicine

Your doctor should check your progress at regular visits to allow dose adjustments and help reduce side effects.

Do not stop taking this medicine without first checking with your doctor. Your doctor may want you to reduce gradually the amount you are taking before stopping completely. This is to prevent side effects and to prevent your condition from becoming worse.

Do not take this medicine within two hours of taking antacids or medicine for diarrhea. Taking these products too close together may make this medicine less effective.

This medicine will add to the effects of alcohol and other CNS depressants (medicines that cause drowsiness). Some examples of CNS depressants are antihistamines or medicine for hay fever, other allergies, or colds; sedatives, tranquilizers, or sleeping medicine; prescription pain medicine or narcotics barbiturates; medicine for seizures; or anesthetics, including some dental anesthetics. *Check with your doctor before taking any of the above while you are using this medicine.*

Before having any kind of surgery, dental treatment, or emergency treatment, tell the medical doctor or dentist in charge that you are taking this medicine. Taking perphenazine and amitriptyline combination together with medicines that are used during surgery or dental or emergency treatments may increase the CNS depressant effects.

This medicine may cause some people to become drowsy or less alert than they are normally, especially during the first few weeks of treatment. Even if this medicine is taken only at bedtime, it may cause some people to feel drowsy or less alert on arising. *Make sure you know how you react to this medicine before you drive, use machines, or do anything else that could be dangerous if you are not alert.*

Dizziness, lightheadedness, or fainting may occur, especially when you get up from a lying or sitting position. Getting up slowly may help. If the problem continues or gets worse, check with your doctor.

This medicine may make you sweat less, causing your body temperature to increase. *Use extra care not to become overheated during exercise or hot weather while you are taking this medicine,* since overheating may result in heat stroke. Also, hot baths or saunas may make you feel dizzy or faint.

Perphenazine and amitriptyline combination may cause dryness of the mouth. For temporary relief, use sugarless gum or candy, melt bits of ice in your mouth, or use a saliva substitute. However, if your mouth continues to feel dry for more than 2 weeks, check with your medical doctor or dentist. Continuing dryness of the mouth may increase the chance of dental disease, including tooth decay, gum disease, and fungus infections.

Perphenazine may cause your skin to be more sensitive to sunlight than it is normally. Exposure to sunlight, even for brief periods of time, may cause a skin rash, itching, redness or other discoloration of the skin, or a severe sunburn. When you begin taking this medicine:

- Stay out of direct sunlight, especially between the hours of 10:00 a.m. and 3:00 p.m., if possible.
- Wear protective clothing, including a hat. Also, wear sunglasses.
- Apply a sun block product that has a skin protection factor (SPF) of at least 15. Some patients may require a product with a higher SPF number, especially if they have a fair complexion. If you have any questions about this, check with your health care professional.
- Apply a sun block lipstick that has an SPF of at least 15 to protect your lips.
- Do not use a sunlamp or tanning bed or booth.

If you have a severe reaction from the sun, check with your doctor.

Side Effects of This Medicine

Along with its needed effects, perphenazine (included in this combination medicine) can sometimes cause serious side effects. Tardive dyskinesia (a movement disorder) may occur and may not go away after you stop using the medicine. Signs of tardive dyskinesia include fine, worm-like movements of the tongue, or other uncontrolled movements of the mouth, tongue, cheeks, jaw, or arms and legs. Other serious but rare side effects may also occur. These include severe muscle stiffness, fever, unusual tiredness or weakness, fast heartbeat, difficult breathing, increased sweating, loss of bladder control, and seizures (neuroleptic malignant syndrome). *You and your doctor should discuss the good this medicine will do as well as the risks of taking it.*

Stop taking this medicine and get emergency help immediately if any of the following side effects occur:

Rare

Convulsions (seizures); difficulty in breathing; fast heartbeat; fever; high or low blood pressure; increased sweating; loss of bladder control; muscle stiffness (severe); unusual tiredness or weakness; unusually pale skin

Also, check with your doctor as soon as possible if any of the following side effects occur:

More common

Blurred vision or any change in vision; difficulty in speaking or swallowing; fainting; inability to move eyes; lip smacking or puckering; loss of balance control; mask-like face; muscle spasms, especially of face, neck, and back; nervousness, restlessness, or need to keep moving; puffing of cheeks; rapid or fine, worm-like movements of tongue; shuffling walk; stiffness of arms and legs; trembling and shaking of fingers and hands; tic-like or twitching movements; twisting movements of body; uncontrolled chewing movements; uncontrolled movements of arms or legs; weakness of arms and legs

Less common

Confusion; constipation; difficult urination; eye pain; hallucinations (seeing, hearing, or feeling things that are not there); increased skin sensitivity to sun; shakiness; slow pulse or irregular heartbeat

Rare

Abdominal or stomach pain; aching muscles or joints; back or leg pain; fever and chills; hair loss; hot, dry skin or lack of sweating; irritability; loss of appetite; muscle weakness or twitching; nausea, vomiting, or diarrhea; nosebleeds; prolonged, painful, inappropriate penile erection; ringing, buzzing, or other unexplained noises in ears; skin discoloration; skin rash and itching; sore throat and fever; swelling of face and tongue; swelling of testicles; unusual bleeding or bruising; yellow eyes or skin

Symptoms of overdose

Agitation; confusion; convulsions (seizures); drowsiness (severe); enlarged pupils; fast, slow, or irregular heartbeat; fever; hallucinations (seeing, hearing, or feeling things that are not there); shortness of breath or troubled breathing; unusual tiredness or weakness (severe); vomiting (severe)

Other side effects may occur that usually do not need medical attention. These side effects may go away during treatment as your body adjusts to the medicine. However,

check with your doctor if any of the following side effects continue or are bothersome:

More common

Decreased sweating; dizziness; drowsiness; dryness of mouth; headache; increased appetite for sweets; nasal congestion; tiredness or weakness (mild); unpleasant taste; weight gain (unusual)

Less common

Changes in menstrual period; decreased sexual ability; heartburn; increased sweating; swelling or pain in breasts or unusual secretion of milk

After you stop using this medicine, your body may need time to adjust. The length of time this takes depends on the amount of medicine you are using and how long you used it. During this time, check with your doctor if you notice any of the following symptoms:

Dizziness; nausea or vomiting; stomach pain; trembling of fingers and hands; symptoms of tardive dyskinesia, including lip smacking or puckering, puffing of cheeks, rapid or fine, worm-like movements of tongue, uncontrolled chewing movements, or uncontrolled movements of arms or legs

Other side effects may occur if the medicine is stopped suddenly or stopped after long-term treatment. Check with your doctor if you notice any of the following symptoms:

Diarrhea; headache; irritability; restlessness; trouble in sleeping, with vivid dreams; unusual excitement

Other side effects not listed above may also occur in some patients. If you notice any other effects, check with your doctor.

Revised: 01/27/92
Interim revision: 08/09/94

PHENAZOPYRIDINE Systemic

Some commonly used brand names are:

In the U.S.—

Azo-Standard	Pyridiate
Baridium	Pyridium
Eridium	Urodine
Geridium	Urogesic
Phenazodine	Viridium

Generic name product may also be available.

In Canada—

Phenazo	Pyridium

Description

Phenazopyridine (fen-az-oh-PEER-i-deen) is used to relieve the pain, burning, and discomfort caused by infection or irritation of the urinary tract. It is not an antibiotic and will not cure the infection itself.

In the U.S., phenazopyridine is available only with your doctor's prescription. In Canada, it is available without a prescription. It is available in the following dosage form:

Oral

- Tablets (U.S. and Canada)

Before Using This Medicine

In deciding to use a medicine, the risks of taking the medicine must be weighed against the good it will do. This is a decision you and your doctor will make. For phenazopyridine, the following should be considered:

Allergies—Tell your doctor if you have ever had any unusual or allergic reaction to phenazopyridine. Also tell your health care professional if you are allergic to any other substances, such as foods, preservatives, or dyes.

Pregnancy—Phenazopyridine has not been studied in pregnant women. However, phenazopyridine has not been shown to cause birth defects in animal studies.

Breast-feeding—It is not known whether phenazopyridine passes into the breast milk. However, phenazopyridine has not been reported to cause problems in nursing babies.

Children—Although there is no specific information comparing use of phenazopyridine in children with use in other age groups, it is not expected to cause different side effects or problems in children than it does in adults.

Older adults—Many medicines have not been studied specifically in older people. Therefore, it may not be known whether they work exactly the same way they do in younger adults. Although there is no specific information comparing use of phenazopyridine in the elderly with use in other age groups, this medicine is not expected to cause different side effects or problems in older people than it does in younger adults.

Other medicines—Although certain medicines should not be used together at all, in other cases two different medicines may be used together even if an interaction might occur. In these cases, your doctor may want to change the dose, or other precautions may be necessary. Tell your health care professional if you are taking any other prescription or nonprescription (over-the-counter [OTC]) medicine.

Other medical problems—The presence of other medical problems may affect the use of phenazopyridine. Make sure you tell your doctor if you have any other medical problems, especially:

- Glucose-6-phosphate dehydrogenase (G6PD) deficiency or
- Hepatitis or
- Kidney disease—The chance of side effects may be increased.

Proper Use of This Medicine

This medicine is best taken with food or after eating a meal or a snack to lessen stomach upset.

Do not use any leftover medicine for future urinary tract problems without first checking with your doctor. An infection may require additional medicine.

Dosing—The dose of phenazopyridine will be different for different patients. *Follow your doctor's orders or the directions on the label.* The following information includes only the average doses of phenazopyridine. *If your dose is different, do not change it* unless your doctor tells you to do so.

- For *oral* dosage form (tablets):
  - —For relieving pain, burning, and discomfort in the urinary tract:
    - Adults and teenagers—200 milligrams (mg) three times a day.
    - Children—The dose is based on body weight and must be determined by your doctor. The usual dose is 4 mg per kilogram (kg) (about 1.8 mg per pound) of body weight three times a day.

Missed dose—If you miss a dose of this medicine, take it as soon as you remember. However, if it is almost time for your next dose, skip the missed dose and go back to your regular dosing schedule. Do not double doses.

Storage—To store this medicine:

- Keep out of the reach of children.
- Store away from heat and direct light.
- Do not store this medicine in the bathroom, near the kitchen sink, or in other damp places. Heat or moisture may cause the medicine to break down.
- Do not keep outdated medicine or medicine no longer needed. Be sure that any discarded medicine is out of the reach of children.

Precautions While Using This Medicine

Check with your doctor if symptoms such as bloody urine, difficult or painful urination, frequent urge to urinate, or sudden decrease in the amount of urine appear or become worse while you are taking this medicine.

Phenazopyridine causes the urine to turn reddish orange. This is to be expected while you are using it. This effect is harmless and will go away after you stop taking the medicine. Also, the medicine may stain clothing.

For *patients who wear soft contact lenses:*

- It is best not to wear soft contact lenses while being treated with this medicine. Phenazopyridine may cause discoloration or staining of contact lenses. It may not be possible to remove the stain.

For *diabetic patients:*

- This medicine may cause false test results with urine sugar tests and urine ketone tests. If you have any questions about this, check with your health care professional, especially if your diabetes is not well controlled.

Before you have any medical tests, tell the person in charge that you are taking this medicine. The results of some tests may be affected by this medicine.

Side Effects of This Medicine

Along with its needed effects, a medicine may cause some unwanted effects. Although not all of these side effects may occur, if they do occur they may need medical attention.

Check with your doctor as soon as possible if any of the following side effects occur:

Rare

Blue or blue-purple color of skin; fever and confusion; shortness of breath, tightness in chest, wheezing, or troubled breathing; skin rash; sudden decrease in the amount of urine; swelling of face, fingers, feet, and/or lower legs; unusual tiredness or weakness; weight gain; yellow eyes or skin

Other side effects may occur that usually do not need medical attention. These side effects may go away during treatment as your body adjusts to the medicine. However, check with your doctor if any of the following side effects continue or are bothersome:

Less common or rare

Dizziness; headache; indigestion; stomach cramps or pain

Other side effects not listed above may also occur in some patients. If you notice any other effects, check with your doctor.

Revised: 06/08/92
Interim revision: 08/24/94

PHENOTHIAZINES Systemic

Some commonly used brand names are:

In the U.S.—

Compa-Z[9]
Compazine[9]
Compazine Spansule[9]
Cotranzine[9]
Levoprome[5]
Mellaril[13]
Mellaril Concentrate[13]
Mellaril-S[13]
Ormazine[2]
Permitil[3]
Permitil Concentrate[3]
Primazine[10]
Prolixin[3]
Prolixin Concentrate[3]
Prolixin Decanoate[3]
Prolixin Enanthate[3]
Prozine-50[10]
Serentil[4]
Serentil Concentrate[4]
Sparine[10]
Stelazine[14]
Stelazine Concentrate[14]
Thorazine[2]
Thorazine Concentrate[2]
Thorazine Spansule[2]
Thor-Prom[2]
Tindal[1]
Trilafon[7]
Trilafon Concentrate[7]
Ultrazine-10[9]
Vesprin[15]

In Canada—

Apo-Fluphenazine[3]
Apo-Perphenazine[7]
Apo-Thioridazine[13]
Apo-Trifluoperazine[14]
Chlorpromanyl-5[2]
Chlorpromanyl-20[2]
Chlorpromanyl-40[2]
Dartal[11]
Largactil[2]
Largactil Liquid[2]
Largactil Oral Drops[2]
Majeptil[12]

Mellaril[13]
Modecate[3]
Modecate Concentrate[3]
Moditen Enanthate[3]
Moditen HCl[3]
Moditen HCl-H.P.[3]
Neuleptil[6]
Novo-Chlorpromazine[2]
Novo-Flurazine[14]
Novo-Ridazine[13]
Nozinan[5]
Nozinan Liquid[5]
Nozinan Oral Drops[5]
PMS Perphenazine[7]
PMS Prochlorperazine[9]
PMS Thioridazine[13]
PMS Trifluoperazine[14]
Prorazin[9]
Solazine[14]
Stelazine[14]
Stelazine Concentrate[14]
Stemetil[9]
Stemetil Liquid[9]
Permitil[3]
Piportil L_4[8]
Serentil[4]
Terfluzine[14]
Terfluzine Concentrate[14]
Trilafon[7]
Trilafon Concentrate[7]

Note: For quick reference, the following phenothiazines are numbered to match the corresponding brand names.

This information applies to the following medicines:

1. Acetophenazine (a-set-oh-FEN-a-zeen)†
2. Chlorpromazine (klor-PROE-ma-zeen)‡§
3. Fluphenazine (floo-FEN-a-zeen)‡
4. Mesoridazine (mez-oh-RID-a-zeen)
5. Methotrimeprazine (meth-oh-trim-EP-ra-zeen)
6. Pericyazine (pair-ee-SYE-a-zeen)*
7. Perphenazine (per-FEN-a-zeen)‡§
8. Pipotiazine (pip-oh-TYE-a-zeen)*
9. Prochlorperazine (proe-klor-PAIR-a-zeen)‡§
10. Promazine (PROE-ma-zeen)‡§
11. Thiopropazate (thye-oh-PROE-pa-zayt)*
12. Thioproperazine (thye-oh-proe-PAIR-a-zeen)*
13. Thioridazine (thye-oh-RID-a-zeen)‡
14. Trifluoperazine (trye-floo-oh-PAIR-a-zeen)‡
15. Triflupromazine (trye-floo-PROE-ma-zeen)†

Note: This information does *not* apply to Ethopropazine, Promethazine, Propiomazine, and Trimeprazine.

*Not commercially available in the U.S.
†Not commercially available in Canada.
‡Generic name product may also be available in the U.S.
§Generic name product may also be available in Canada.

Description

Phenothiazines (FEE-noe-THYE-a-zeens) are used to treat nervous, mental, and emotional disorders. Some are used also to control anxiety or agitation in certain patients, severe nausea and vomiting, severe hiccups, and moderate to severe pain in some hospitalized patients. Chlorpromazine is also used in the treatment of certain types of porphyria, and with other medicines in the treatment of tetanus. Phenothiazines may also be used for other conditions as determined by your doctor.

Phenothiazines are available only with your doctor's prescription in the following dosage forms:

Oral

Acetophenazine
- Tablets (U.S.)

Chlorpromazine
- Extended-release capsules (U.S.)
- Oral concentrate (U.S. and Canada)
- Syrup (U.S. and Canada)
- Tablets (U.S. and Canada)

Fluphenazine
- Elixir (U.S. and Canada)
- Oral solution (U.S.)
- Tablets (U.S. and Canada)

Mesoridazine
- Oral solution (U.S.)
- Tablets (U.S. and Canada)

Methotrimeprazine
- Oral solution (Canada)
- Syrup (Canada)
- Tablets (Canada)

Pericyazine
- Capsules (Canada)
- Oral solution (Canada)

Perphenazine
- Oral solution (U.S. and Canada)
- Syrup (Canada)
- Tablets (U.S. and Canada)

Prochlorperazine
- Extended-release capsules (U.S.)
- Syrup (U.S. and Canada)
- Tablets (U.S. and Canada)

Promazine
- Tablets (U.S.)

Thiopropazate
- Tablets (Canada)

Thioproperazine
- Tablets (Canada)

Thioridazine
- Oral solution (U.S. and Canada)
- Oral suspension (U.S. and Canada)
- Tablets (U.S. and Canada)

Trifluoperazine
- Oral solution (U.S. and Canada)
- Syrup (Canada)
- Tablets (U.S. and Canada)

Parenteral

Chlorpromazine
- Injection (U.S. and Canada)

Fluphenazine
- Injection (U.S. and Canada)

Mesoridazine
- Injection (U.S.)

Methotrimeprazine
- Injection (U.S. and Canada)

Perphenazine
- Injection (U.S. and Canada)

Pipotiazine
- Injection (Canada)

Prochlorperazine
- Injection (U.S. and Canada)

Promazine
- Injection (U.S. and Canada)

Trifluoperazine
- Injection (U.S. and Canada)

Triflupromazine
- Injection (U.S.)

Rectal

Chlorpromazine
- Suppositories (U.S. and Canada)

Prochlorperazine
- Suppositories (U.S. and Canada)

Before Using This Medicine

In deciding to use a medicine, the risks of taking the medicine must be weighed against the good it will do. This is a decision you and your doctor will make. For phenothiazines, the following should be considered:

Allergies—Tell your doctor if you have ever had any unusual or allergic reaction to phenothiazines. Also tell your health care professional if you are allergic to any other substances, such as foods, preservatives, or dyes.

Pregnancy—Although studies have not been done in pregnant women, some side effects, such as jaundice and muscle tremors and other movement disorders, have occurred in a few newborns whose mothers received phenothiazines close to the time of delivery. Studies in animals have shown that chlorpromazine and trifluoperazine, given in doses many times the usual human dose, may cause birth defects.

Breast-feeding—Phenothiazines pass into the breast milk and may cause drowsiness and a greater chance of unusual muscle movement in the nursing baby.

Children—Certain side effects, such as muscle spasms of the face, neck, and back, tic-like or twitching movements, inability to move the eyes, twisting of the body, or weakness of the arms and legs, are more likely to occur in children, especially those with severe illness or dehydration. Children are usually more sensitive than adults to some of the side effects of phenothiazines.

Older adults—Constipation, dizziness or fainting, drowsiness, dryness of mouth, trembling of the hands and fingers, and symptoms of tardive dyskinesia (such as rapid, worm-like movements of the tongue or any other uncontrolled movements of the mouth, tongue, or jaw, and/or arms and legs) are especially likely to occur in elderly patients, who are usually more sensitive than younger adults to the effects of phenothiazines.

Other medicines—Although certain medicines should not be used together at all, in other cases 2 different medicines may be used together even if an interaction might occur. In these cases, your doctor may want to change the dose, or other precautions may be necessary. When you are taking phenothiazines, it is especially important that your health care professional know if you are taking any of the following:

- Amantadine (e.g., Symmetrel) or
- Antihypertensives (high blood pressure medicine) or
- Bromocriptine (e.g., Parlodel) or
- Deferoxamine (e.g., Desferal) or
- Diuretics (water pills) or
- Levobunolol (e.g., Betagan) or
- Medicine for heart disease or
- Metipranolol (e.g., OptiPranolol)
- Nabilone (e.g., Cesamet) (with high doses) or
- Narcotic pain medicine or
- Nimodipine (e.g., Nimotop) or
- Other antipsychotics (medicine for mental illness) or
- Pentamidine (e.g., Pentam) or
- Pimozide (e.g., Orap)
- Promethazine (e.g., Phenergan) or
- Trimeprazine (e.g., Temaril)—Severe low blood pressure may occur
- Antidepressants (medicine for depression)—The risk of serious side effects may be increased
- Antithyroid agents (medicine for overactive thyroid) or
- Central nervous system (CNS) depressants (medicines that cause drowsiness)—There may be an increased chance of blood problems
- Epinephrine (e.g., Adrenalin)—Severe low blood pressure and fast heartbeat may occur
- Levodopa (e.g., Dopar)—Phenothiazines may prevent levodopa from working properly in the treatment of Parkinson's disease
- Lithium (e.g., Lithane, Lithizine)—The amount of medicine you need to take may change
- Methyldopa (e.g., Aldomet) or
- Metoclopramide (e.g., Reglan) or
- Metyrosine (e.g. Demser) or
- Pemoline (e.g., Cylert) or
- Rauwolfia alkaloids (alseroxylon [e.g., Rauwiloid], deserpidine [e.g., Harmonyl], rauwolfia serpentina [e.g., Raudixin], reserpine [e.g., Serpasil])—Taking these medicines with phenothiazines may increase the chance and severity of certain side effects
- Metrizamide—When this dye is used for myelograms, the risk of seizures may be increased

Other medical problems—The presence of other medical problems may affect the use of phenothiazines. Make sure you tell your doctor if you have any other medical problems, especially:

- Alcohol abuse—Certain side effects such as heat stroke may be more likely to occur
- Blood disease or
- Breast cancer or
- Difficult urination or
- Enlarged prostate or
- Glaucoma or
- Heart or blood vessel disease or
- Lung disease or
- Parkinson's disease or
- Seizure disorders or
- Stomach ulcers—Phenothiazines may make the condition worse
- Liver disease—Higher blood levels of phenothiazines may occur, increasing the chance of side effects
- Reye's syndrome—There may be an increased chance of unwanted effects on the liver

Proper Use of This Medicine

For patients taking this medicine *by mouth:*

- This medicine may be taken with food or a full glass (8 ounces) of water or milk to reduce stomach irritation.
- *If your medicine comes in a dropper bottle,* measure each dose with the special dropper provided with your prescription and dilute it in 1/2 a glass (4 ounces) of orange or grapefruit juice or water.
- If you are taking the *extended-release capsule form* of this medicine, each dose should be swallowed whole. Do not break, crush, or chew before swallowing.

For patients using the *suppository form* of this medicine:

- If the suppository is too soft to insert, chill it in the refrigerator for 30 minutes or run cold water over it before removing the foil wrapper.
- To insert the suppository: First remove the foil wrapper and moisten the suppository with cold water. Lie down on your side and use your finger to push the suppository well up into the rectum.

Do not take more of this medicine and do not take it more often than your doctor ordered. This is particularly important for children or elderly patients, since they may react very strongly to this medicine.

Sometimes this medicine must be taken for several weeks before its full effect is reached when it is used to treat mental and emotional conditions.

Dosing—The dose of phenothiazines will be different for different patients. *Follow your doctor's orders or the directions on the label.* The following information includes only the average doses of phenothiazines. *If your dose is different, do not change it* unless your doctor tells you to do so.

The number of capsules, tablets, or teaspoonfuls of elixir, solution, suspension, or syrup that you take, or the number of injections you receive or suppositories that you use, depends on the strength of the medicine. Also, *the number of doses you use each day, the time allowed between doses, and the length of time you take the medicine depend on the medical problem for which you are taking phenothiazines.*

For acetophenazine

- For *oral* dosage form (tablets):
  - —For nervous, mental, or emotional disorders:
    - Adults and teenagers—20 milligrams (mg) three times a day. Your doctor may change your dose if needed.
    - Children up to 12 years of age—Dose must be determined by your doctor.

For chlorpromazine

- For *oral extended-release capsule* dosage form:
  - —For nervous, mental, or emotional disorders:
    - Adults—30 to 300 milligrams (mg) one to three times a day. Your doctor may increase your dose if needed. However, the dose is usually not more than 1000 mg a day.
    - Children—This dosage form is not recommended for use in children.
- For *oral concentrate, syrup, or tablet* dosage forms:
  - —For nervous, mental, or emotional disorders:
    - Adults and teenagers—At first, 10 to 25 mg two to four times a day. Your doctor may increase your dose if needed. However, the dose is usually not more than 1000 mg a day.
    - Children up to 6 months of age—Dose must be determined by your doctor.
    - Children 6 months of age and older—Dose is based on body weight or size, and must be determined by your doctor. The usual dose is 0.55 mg per kilogram (kg) (0.25 mg per pound) of body weight, every four to six hours.
  - —For nausea and vomiting:
    - Adults and teenagers—10 to 25 mg every four hours as needed.
    - Children up to 6 months of age—Dose must be determined by your doctor.
    - Children 6 months of age and older—Dose is based on body weight or size, and must be determined by your doctor. The usual dose is 0.55 mg per kg (0.25 mg per pound) of body weight, every four to six hours.
  - —For sedation before surgery:
    - Adults and teenagers—25 to 50 mg two to three hours before surgery.
    - Children—Dose is based on body weight or size, and must be determined by your doctor. The usual dose is 0.55 mg per kg (0.25 mg per pound) of body weight, two or three hours before surgery.
  - —For treatment of hiccups:
    - Adults and teenagers—25 to 50 mg three or four times a day.
    - Children—Dose must be determined by your doctor.
  - —For porphyria:
    - Adults and teenagers—25 to 50 mg three or four times a day.
    - Children—Use and dose must be determined by your doctor.
- For *injection* dosage form:
  - —For severe nervous, mental, or emotional disorders:
    - Adults—At first, 25 to 50 mg, injected into a muscle. The dose may be repeated in one hour, and every three to twelve hours thereafter. Your doctor may increase your dose if needed.
    - Children up to 6 months of age—Dose must be determined by your doctor.
    - Children 6 months of age and over—Dose is based on body weight or size and must be determined by your doctor. The usual dose is 0.55 mg per kg (0.25 mg per pound) of body weight, injected into a muscle every six to eight hours as needed.
  - —For nausea and vomiting:
    - Adults—At first, 25 mg injected into a muscle. The dose may be increased to 25 to 50 mg every three to four hours if needed.
    - Children up to 6 months of age—Dose must be determined by your doctor.
    - Children 6 months of age and over—Dose is based on body weight or size and must be determined by your doctor. The usual dose is 0.55 mg per kg (0.25 mg per pound) of body weight, injected into a muscle every six to eight hours as needed.
  - —For nausea and vomiting during surgery:
    - Adults—At first, 12.5 mg injected into a muscle. The dose may be repeated if needed. Or, up to 25 mg, diluted and injected slowly into a vein.
    - Children—Dose is based on body weight or size and must be determined by your doctor. The usual dose is 0.275 mg per kg (0.125 mg per pound) of body weight, injected into a muscle, or diluted and injected slowly into a vein.
  - —For sedation before surgery:
    - Adults—12.5 to 25 mg, injected into a muscle one or two hours before surgery.

• Children—Dose is based on body weight and must be determined by your doctor. The usual dose is 0.55 mg per kg (0.25 mg per pound) of body weight, injected into a muscle one to two hours before surgery.

—For treatment of hiccups:

• Adults—25 to 50 mg, injected into a muscle three or four times a day. Or, 25 to 50 mg diluted and injected slowly into a vein.

• Children—Dose must be determined by your doctor.

—For porphyria:

• Adults—25 mg injected into a muscle every six or eight hours.

• Children—Dose must be determined by your doctor.

—For tetanus:

• Adults—25 to 50 mg, injected into a muscle three or four times a day. Or, 25 to 50 mg, diluted and injected slowly into a vein. Your doctor may increase your dose if needed.

• Children—Dose is based on body weight and must be determined by your doctor. The usual dose is 0.55 mg per kg (0.25 mg per pound) of body weight, injected into a muscle every six to eight hours. Or, 0.55 mg per kg (0.25 mg per pound) of body weight, diluted and injected slowly into a vein.

• For *rectal* dosage form (suppositories):

—For nausea and vomiting:

• Adults and teenagers—50 to 100 mg, inserted into the rectum every six to eight hours as needed.

• Children up to 6 months of age—Dose must be determined by your doctor.

• Children 6 months of age and over—Dose is based on body weight and must be determined by your doctor. The usual dose is 1 mg per kg (0.45 mg per pound) of body weight, inserted into the rectum every six to eight hours as needed.

For fluphenazine

• For *oral* dosage form (elixir, solution, or tablets):

—For nervous, mental, or emotional disorders:

• Adults—At first, 2.5 to 10 milligrams (mg) a day, taken in smaller doses every six to eight hours during the day. Your doctor may increase your dose if needed. However, the dose is usually not more than 20 mg a day.

• Children—0.25 to 0.75 mg one to four times a day.

• Older adults—1 to 2.5 mg a day. Your doctor may increase your dose if needed.

• For *long-acting decanoate injection* dosage form:

—For nervous, mental, or emotional disorders:

• Adults—At first, 12.5 to 25 mg, injected into a muscle or under the skin every one to three weeks. Your doctor may increase your dose if needed. However, the dose is usually not more than 100 mg.

• Children 5 to 12 years of age—3.125 to 12.5 mg, injected into a muscle or under the skin every one to three weeks.

• Children 12 years of age and over—At first, 6.25 to 18.75 mg a week, injected into a muscle or under the skin. Your doctor may increase your dose if needed. However, the dose is usually not more than 25 mg every one to three weeks.

• For *long-acting enanthate injection* dosage form:

—For nervous, mental, or emotional disorders:

• Adults and teenagers—25 mg, injected into a muscle or under the skin every one to three weeks. Your doctor may increase your dose if needed. However, the dose is usually not more than 100 mg.

• Children up to 12 years of age—Dose must be determined by your doctor.

• For *short-acting hydrochloride injection* dosage form:

—For nervous, mental, or emotional disorders:

• Adults and teenagers—1.25 to 2.5 mg, injected into a muscle every six to eight hours. Your doctor may increase your dose if needed. However, the dose is usually not more than 10 mg a day.

• Children up to 12 years of age—Dose must be determined by your doctor.

• Older adults—1 to 2.5 mg a day, injected into a muscle. Your doctor may increase your dose if needed.

For mesoridazine

• For *oral* dosage form (solution or tablets):

—For nervous, mental, or emotional disorders:

• Adults and teenagers—30 to 150 milligrams (mg), taken in smaller doses two or three times during the day.

• Children up to 12 years of age—Dose must be determined by your doctor.

• For *injection* dosage form:

—For nervous, mental, or emotional disorders:

• Adults and teenagers—25 mg injected into a muscle. The dose may be repeated in thirty to sixty minutes if needed.

• Children up to 12 years of age—Dose must be determined by your doctor.

For methotrimeprazine

• For *oral* dosage form (solution, syrup, or tablets):

—For nervous, mental, or emotional disorders:

• Adults and teenagers—At first, 6 to 75 milligrams (mg) a day, taken in smaller doses two or three times a day with meals. Your doctor may increase your dose if needed.

• Children—Dose is based on body weight and must be determined by your doctor. At first, the usual dose is 0.25 mg per kilogram (kg) (0.11 mg per pound) of body weight a day, taken in smaller doses two or three times a day with meals. Your doctor may increase your dose if needed.

—For pain:

• Adults and teenagers—At first, 6 to 25 mg a day, taken in smaller doses three times a day with meals. For more severe pain, 50 to 75 mg a day, taken in smaller doses two or three times a day with meals. Your doctor may increase your dose if needed.

• Children—Dose is based on body weight and must be determined by your doctor. At first, the usual dose is 0.25 mg per kg (0.11 mg per pound) of body weight a day, taken in smaller doses two or three times a day with meals. Your doctor may increase your dose if needed. However, the dose is usually not more than 40 mg a day.

—For sedation before surgery:

• Adults and teenagers—At first, 6 to 25 mg a day, taken in smaller doses three times a day with meals. Your doctor may increase your dose if needed.

• Children—Dose is based on body weight and must be determined by your doctor. At first, the usual dose is 0.25 mg per kg (0.11 mg per pound) of body weight a day, taken in smaller doses two or three times a day with meals. Your doctor may increase your dose if needed. However, the dose is usually not more than 40 mg a day.

• For *injection* dosage form:

—For nervous, mental, or emotional disorders:

• Adults and teenagers—At first, 10 to 20 mg, injected into a muscle every four to six hours. Your doctor may increase your dose if needed.

• Children—Dose must be determined by your doctor.

—For pain:

• Adults and teenagers—At first, 2.5 to 20 mg, injected into a muscle. Your doctor may increase your dose if needed.

• Children—Dose is based on body weight and must be determined by your doctor. The usual dose is 0.062 to 0.125 mg per kg (0.028 to 0.057 mg per pound) of body weight, injected into a muscle.

• Older adults—At first, 5 to 10 mg injected into a muscle every four to six hours. Your doctor may increase your dose if needed.

—For sedation before surgery:

• Adults and teenagers—2 to 20 mg, injected into a muscle forty-five minutes to three hours before surgery.

• Children—Dose must be determined by your doctor.

For pericyazine

• For *oral* dosage form (capsules or solution):

—For nervous, mental, or emotional disorders:

• Adults—At first, 5 to 20 milligrams (mg) taken in the morning, and 10 to 40 mg taken in the evening. Your doctor may change your dose if needed.

• Children 5 years of age and over—2.5 to 10 mg taken in the morning, and 5 to 30 mg taken in the evening.

• Older adults—At first, 5 mg a day. Your doctor may increase your dose if needed. However, the dose is usually not more than 30 mg a day.

For perphenazine

• For *oral solution* dosage form:

—For nervous, mental, or emotional disorders in hospitalized patients:

• Adults and teenagers—8 to 16 milligrams (mg) two to four times a day.

• Children up to 12 years of age—Dose must be determined by your doctor.

• For *oral syrup* dosage form:

—For nervous, mental, or emotional disorders:

• Adults and teenagers—2 to 16 mg two to four times a day.

• Children up to 12 years of age—Dose must be determined by your doctor.

—For nausea and vomiting:

• Adults and teenagers—2 to 4 mg two to four times a day.

• Children up to 12 years of age—Dose must be determined by your doctor.

• For *oral tablet* dosage form:

—For nervous, mental, or emotional disorders:

• Adults and teenagers—4 to 16 mg two to four times a day.

• Children up to 12 years of age—Dose must be determined by your doctor.

—For nausea and vomiting:

• Adults and teenagers—8 to 16 mg a day, taken in smaller doses during the day. Your doctor will lower your dose as soon as possible.

• Children up to 12 years of age—Dose must be determined by your doctor.

• For *injection* dosage form:

—For nervous, mental, or emotional disorders:

• Adults and teenagers—5 to 10 mg injected into a muscle every six hours. Hospitalized patients may need higher doses.

• Children up to 12 years of age—Dose must be determined by your doctor.

—For nausea and vomiting:

• Adults and teenagers—At first, 5 mg injected into a muscle, or diluted and injected slowly into a vein. Your doctor may increase your dose if needed.

• Children up to 12 years of age—Dose must be determined by your doctor.

For pipotiazine

- For *injection* dosage form:
  - —For nervous, mental, or emotional disorders:
    - Adults and teenagers—At first, 50 to 100 milligrams (mg) injected into a muscle.Your doctor may increase your dose if needed. However, the dose is usually not more than 150 mg every four weeks.
    - Children up to 12 years of age—Dose must be determined by your doctor.

For prochlorperazine

- For *oral syrup* dosage form:
  - —For nervous, mental, or emotional disorders:
    - Adults and teenagers—At first, 5 to 10 milligrams (mg) three or four times a day.Your doctor may increase your dose if needed. However, the dose is usually not more than 150 mg a day.
    - Children up to 2 years of age—Dose must be determined by your doctor.
    - Children 2 to 12 years of age—2.5 mg two or three times a day.
  - —For nausea and vomiting:
    - Adults and teenagers—5 to 10 mg three or four times a day.
    - Children—Dose is based on body weight and must be determined by your doctor. The usual dose is 2.5 mg taken one to three times a day. For children 2 to 5 years of age, the dose is usually not more than 20 mg a day. For children 6 to 12 years of age, the dose is usually not more than 25 mg a day.
  - —For anxiety:
    - Adults and teenagers—5 mg three or four times a day. This dose is usually not taken for longer than twelve weeks.
    - Children—Dose must be determined by your doctor.
- For *oral extended-release capsule* dosage form:
  - —For nervous, mental, or emotional disorders:
    - Adults and teenagers—At first, 5 to 10 mg every three or four hours. Your doctor may increase your dose if needed. However, the dose is usually not more than 150 mg a day.
    - Children—This dosage form is not recommended for use in children.
  - —For nausea and vomiting:
    - Adults and teenagers—15 to 30 mg once a day in the morning, or 10 mg taken every twelve hours. Your doctor may increase your dose if needed. However, the dose is usually not more than 40 mg a day.
    - Children—This dosage form is not recommended for use in children.
  - —For anxiety:
    - Adults and teenagers—15 mg once a day in the morning, or 10 mg taken every twelve hours. This dose is usually not taken for longer than twelve weeks.
    - Children—This dosage form is not recommended for use in children.
- For *oral tablet* dosage form:
  - —For nervous, mental, or emotional disorders:
    - Adults and teenagers—5 to 10 mg three or four times a day. Your doctor may increase your dose if needed. However, the dose is usually not more than 150 mg a day.
    - Children—The tablet dosage form is often not suitable for use in children. The syrup dosage form is usually recommended.
  - —For nausea and vomiting:
    - Adults and teenagers—5 to 10 mg three or four times a day.
    - Children—The tablet dosage form is often not suitable for use in children. The syrup dosage form is usually recommended.
  - —For anxiety:
    - Adults and teenagers—5 mg three or four times a day. This dose is usually not taken for longer than twelve weeks.
    - Children—The tablet dosage form is often not suitable for use in children. The syrup dosage form is usually recommended.
- For *injection* dosage form:
  - —For nervous, mental, or emotional disorders:
    - Adults and teenagers—At first, 10 to 20 mg injected into a muscle. The dose may be repeated every two to four hours if needed for up to four doses. Later, the dose is usually 10 to 20 mg every four to six hours. However, the dose is usually not more than 200 mg a day.
    - Children up to 2 years of age—Dose must be determined by your doctor.
    - Children 2 to 12 years of age—Dose is based on body weight and must be determined by your doctor. The usual dose is 0.132 mg per kilogram (kg) (0.06 mg per pound) of body weight, injected into a muscle. However, the dose for children 2 to 5 years of age is usually not more than 20 mg a day. The dose for children 6 to 12 years of age is usually not more than 25 mg a day.
  - —For nausea and vomiting:
    - Adults and teenagers—5 to 10 mg, injected into a muscle every three to four hours as needed. Or, 2.5 to 10 mg injected slowly into a vein. The dose is usually not more than 40 mg a day.
    - Children up to 2 years of age—Dose must be determined by your doctor.
    - Children 2 to 12 years of age—Dose is based on body weight and must be determined by your doctor. The usual dose is 0.132 mg per kg (0.06 mg per pound) of body weight, injected into a muscle. However, the dose for children 2 to 5 years of age is usually not more than 20 mg a

day. The dose for children 6 to 12 years of age is usually not more than 25 mg a day.

—For nausea and vomiting in surgery:

• Adults and teenagers—5 to 10 mg, injected into a muscle. Or, up to 20 mg injected slowly into a vein. The dose is usually not more than 40 mg a day.

• Children—Dose must be determined by your doctor.

—For anxiety:

• Adults and teenagers—5 to 10 mg injected into a muscle every three to four hours. Or, 2.5 to 10 mg injected slowly into a vein. The dose is usually not more than 40 mg a day.

• Children up to 2 years of age—Dose must be determined by your doctor.

• Children 2 to 12 years of age—Dose is based on body weight and must be determined by your doctor. The usual dose is 0.132 mg per kg (0.06 mg per pound) of body weight, injected into a muscle. However, the dose for children 2 to 5 years of age is usually not more than 20 mg a day. The dose for children 6 to 12 years of age is usually not more than 25 mg a day.

• For *rectal* dosage form (suppositories):

—For nervous, mental, or emotional disorders:

• Adults and teenagers—10 mg inserted into the rectum three or four times a day. Your doctor may increase your dose if needed.

• Children—Dose must be determined by your doctor.

—For nausea and vomiting:

• Adults and teenagers—25 mg inserted into the rectum two times a day.

• Children up to 2 years of age—Dose must be determined by your doctor.

• Children 2 to 12 years of age—Dose is based on body weight and must be determined by your doctor. The usual dose is 2.5 mg inserted into the rectum one to three times a day. The dose in children 2 to 5 years of age is usually not more than 20 mg a day. The dose for children 6 to 12 years of age is usually not more than 25 mg a day.

For promazine

• For *oral* dosage form (tablets):

—For nervous, mental, or emotional disorders:

• Adults—10 to 200 milligrams (mg) every four to six hours.

• Children up to 12 years of age—Dose must be determined by your doctor.

• Children 12 years of age and over—10 to 25 mg every four to six hours.

• For *injection* dosage form:

—For nervous, mental, or emotional disorders:

• Adults—At first, 50 to 150 mg injected into a muscle, or diluted and injected into a vein. Later, 10 to 200 mg, injected into a muscle or vein, every four to six hours.

• Children up to 12 years of age—Dose must be determined by your doctor.

• Children 12 years of age and over—10 to 25 mg, injected into a muscle, every four to six hours.

For thiopropazate

• For *oral* dosage form (tablets):

—For nervous, mental, or emotional disorders:

• Adults and teenagers—At first, 10 milligrams (mg) three times a day. Your doctor may increase your dose if needed. However, the dose is usually not more than 100 mg a day.

• Children—Dose must be determined by your doctor.

For thioproperazine

• For *oral* dosage form (tablets):

—For nervous, mental, or emotional disorders:

• Adults and teenagers—At first, 5 milligrams (mg) a day. Your doctor may increase your dose if needed.

• Children—Dose must be determined by your doctor.

For thioridazine

• For *oral* dosage form (suspension, solution, or tablets):

—For nervous, mental, or emotional disorders:

• Adults and teenagers—At first, 25 to 100 milligrams (mg) three times a day. Your doctor may increase your dose if needed. However, the dose is usually not more than 800 mg a day.

• Children up to 2 years of age—Dose must be determined by your doctor.

• Children 2 to 12 years of age—Dose is based on body weight or size and must be determined by your doctor. The usual dose is 10 to 25 mg two or three times a day.

For trifluoperazine

• For *oral* dosage form (solution, syrup, or tablets):

—For nervous, mental, or emotional disorders:

• Adults and teenagers—At first, 2 to 5 milligrams (mg) two times a day. Your doctor may increase your dose if needed. However, the dose is usually not more than 40 mg a day.

• Children up to 6 years of age—Dose must be determined by your doctor.

• Children 6 years of age and over—1 mg one or two times a day.

—For anxiety:

• Adults and teenagers—1 to 2 mg a day. Your doctor may increase your dose if needed. However, the dose is usually not more than 6 mg a day, and is usually not taken for longer than twelve weeks.

• Children—Dose must be determined by your doctor.

- For *injection* dosage form:
    - —For nervous, mental, or emotional disorders:
        - Adults and teenagers—1 to 2 mg, injected into a muscle every four to six hours as needed. However, the dose is usually not more than 10 mg a day.
        - Children up to 6 years of age—Dose must be determined by your doctor.
        - Children 6 years of age and over—1 mg injected into a muscle one or two times a day.

For triflupromazine

- For *injection* dosage form:
    - —For nervous, mental, or emotional disorders:
        - Adults and teenagers—60 milligrams (mg) injected into a muscle as needed. However, the dose is usually not more than 150 mg a day.
        - Children up to $2^1/_2$ years of age—Dose must be determined by your doctor.
        - Children $2^1/_2$ years of age and over—Dose is based on body weight and must be determined by your doctor. The usual dose is 0.2 to 0.25 mg per kilogram (kg) (0.09 to 0.11 mg per pound) of body weight, injected into a muscle. However, the dose is usually not more than 10 mg a day.
    - —For nausea and vomiting:
        - Adults and teenagers—5 to 15 mg injected into a muscle every four hours, or 1 mg injected into a vein as needed. Your doctor may increase your dose if needed. However, the dose is usually not more than 60 mg a day injected into a muscle, or 3 mg a day injected into a vein.
        - Children up to $2^1/_2$ years of age—Dose must be determined by your doctor.
        - Children $2^1/_2$ years of age and over—Dose is based on body weight and must be determined by your doctor. The usual dose is 0.2 to 0.25 mg per kg (0.09 to 0.11 mg per pound) of body weight, injected into a muscle. However, the dose is usually not more than 10 mg a day.

Missed dose—If you miss a dose of this medicine and your dosing schedule is:

- One dose a day: Take the missed dose as soon as possible. Then go back to your regular dosing schedule. However, if you do not remember the missed dose until the next day, skip it and go back to your regular dosing schedule. Do not double doses.
- More than one dose a day: If you remember within an hour or so of the missed dose, take it right away. However, if you do not remember until later, skip the missed dose and go back to your regular dosing schedule. Do not double doses.

If you have any questions about this, check with your doctor.

Storage—To store this medicine:

- Keep out of the reach of children.
- Store away from heat and direct light.
- Do not store the capsule or tablet form of this medicine in the bathroom, near the kitchen sink, or in other damp places. Heat or moisture may cause the medicine to break down.
- Keep the liquid form of this medicine from freezing.
- Do not keep outdated medicine or medicine no longer needed. Be sure that any discarded medicine is out of the reach of children.

Precautions While Using This Medicine

Your doctor should check your progress at regular visits, especially during the first few months of treatment with this medicine. This will allow your dosage to be changed if necessary to meet your needs.

Do not stop taking this medicine without first checking with your doctor. Your doctor may want you to reduce gradually the amount you are taking before stopping completely. This is to prevent side effects and to keep your condition from becoming worse.

Do not take this medicine within two hours of taking antacids or medicine for diarrhea. Taking these products too close together may make this medicine less effective.

This medicine will add to the effects of alcohol and other CNS depressants (medicines that slow down the nervous system, possibly causing drowsiness). Some examples of CNS depressants are antihistamines or medicine for hay fever, other allergies, or colds; sedatives, tranquilizers, or sleeping medicine; prescription pain medicine or narcotics; barbiturates; medicine for seizures; muscle relaxants; or anesthetics, including some dental anesthetics. *Check with your doctor before taking any of the above while you are using this medicine.*

Before using any prescription or over-the-counter (OTC) medicine for colds or allergies, check with your doctor. These medicines may increase the chance of heat stroke or other unwanted effects, such as dizziness, dry mouth, blurred vision, and constipation, while you are taking a phenothiazine.

Before you have any medical tests, tell the medical doctor in charge that you are taking this medicine. The results of some tests (such as electrocardiogram [ECG] readings, certain pregnancy tests, the metyrapone test, and urine bilirubin tests) may be affected by this medicine.

Before having any kind of surgery, dental treatment, or emergency treatment, tell the medical doctor or dentist in charge that you are using this medicine.

This medicine may cause some people to become drowsy or less alert than they are normally. Even if this medicine is taken only at bedtime, it may cause some people to feel drowsy or less alert on arising. *Make sure you know how you react to this medicine before you drive, use machines, or do anything else that could be dangerous if you are not alert.*

Phenothiazines may cause blurred vision, difficulty in reading, or other changes in vision, especially during the first few weeks of treatment. Do not drive, use machines, or do anything else that could be dangerous if you are not able to see well. *If the problem continues or gets worse, check with your doctor.*

Dizziness, lightheadedness, or fainting may occur, especially when you get up from a lying or sitting position. Getting up slowly may help. If the problem continues or gets worse, check with your doctor.

This medicine may make you sweat less, causing your body temperature to increase. *Use extra care not to become overheated during exercise or hot weather while you are taking this medicine*, since overheating may result in heat stroke. Also, hot baths or saunas may make you feel dizzy or faint while you are taking this medicine.

This medicine may also make you more sensitive to cold temperatures. Dress warmly during cold weather. Be careful during prolonged exposure to cold, such as in winter sports or swimming in cold water.

Phenothiazines may cause dryness of the mouth. For temporary relief, use sugarless candy or gum, melt bits of ice in your mouth, or use a saliva substitute. However, if your mouth continues to feel dry for more than 2 weeks, check with your medical doctor or dentist. Continuing dryness of the mouth may increase the chance of dental disease, including tooth decay, gum disease, and fungus infections.

Phenothiazines may cause your skin to be more sensitive to sunlight than it is normally. Exposure to sunlight, even for brief periods of time, may cause a skin rash, itching, redness or other discoloration of the skin, or a severe sunburn. When you begin taking this medicine:

- Stay out of direct sunlight, especially between the hours of 10:00 a.m. and 3:00 p.m., if possible.
- Wear protective clothing, including a hat. Also, wear sunglasses.
- Apply a sun block product that has a skin protection factor (SPF) of at least 15. Some patients may require a product with a higher SPF number, especially if they have a fair complexion. If you have any questions about this, check with your health care professional.
- Apply a sun block lipstick that has an SPF of at least 15 to protect your lips.
- Do not use a sunlamp or tanning bed or booth.

If you have a severe reaction from the sun, check with your doctor.

Phenothiazines may cause your eyes to be more sensitive to sunlight than they are normally. Exposure to sunlight over a period of time (several months to years) may cause blurred vision, change in color vision, or difficulty in seeing at night. When you go out during the daylight hours, even on cloudy days, wear sunglasses that block ultraviolet (UV) light. Ordinary sunglasses may not protect your eyes. If you have any questions about the kind of sunglasses to wear, check with your medical doctor or eye doctor.

If you are taking a liquid form of this medicine, avoid getting it on your skin or clothing because it may cause a skin rash or other irritation.

If you are receiving this medicine by injection:

- The effects of the long-acting injection form of this medicine may last for up to 12 weeks. *The precautions and side effects information for this medicine applies during this time.*

Side Effects of This Medicine

Along with their needed effects, phenothiazines can sometimes cause serious side effects. Tardive dyskinesia (a movement disorder) may occur and may not go away after you stop using the medicine. Signs of tardive dyskinesia include fine, worm-like movements of the tongue, or other uncontrolled movements of the mouth, tongue, cheeks, jaw, or arms and legs. Other serious but rare side effects may also occur. These include severe muscle stiffness, fever, unusual tiredness or weakness, fast heartbeat, difficult breathing, increased sweating, loss of bladder control, and seizures (neuroleptic malignant syndrome). *You and your doctor should discuss the good this medicine will do as well as the risks of taking it.*

Stop taking this medicine and check with your doctor immediately if any of the following side effects occur:

Rare

Convulsions (seizures); difficult or fast breathing; fast heartbeat or irregular pulse; fever; high or low blood pressure; increased sweating; loss of bladder control; muscle stiffness (severe); unusually pale skin; unusual tiredness or weakness

Check with your doctor immediately if any of the following side effects occur:

More common

Lip smacking or puckering; puffing of cheeks; rapid or fine, worm-like movements of tongue; uncontrolled chewing movements; uncontrolled movements of arms or legs

Also, check with your doctor as soon as possible if any of the following side effects occur:

More common

Blurred vision, change in color vision, or difficulty in seeing at night; difficulty in speaking or swallowing; fainting; inability to move eyes; loss of balance control; mask-like face; muscle spasms (especially of face, neck, and back); restlessness or need to keep moving; shuffling walk; stiffness of arms or legs; tic-like or twitching movements; trembling and shaking of hands and fingers; twisting movements of body; weakness of arms and legs

Less common

Difficulty in urinating; skin rash; sunburn (severe)

Rare

Abdominal or stomach pains; aching muscles and joints; confusion; fever and chills; hot, dry skin or lack of sweating; muscle weakness; nausea, vomiting, or diarrhea; painful, inappropriate penile erection (continuing); skin discoloration (tan or blue-gray); skin itching (severe); sore throat and fever; unusual bleeding or bruising; yellow eyes or skin

Other side effects may occur that usually do not need medical attention. These side effects may go away during treatment as your body adjusts to the medicine. However,

check with your doctor if any of the following side effects continue or are bothersome:

More common

Constipation; decreased sweating; dizziness; drowsiness; dryness of mouth; nasal congestion

Less common

Changes in menstrual period; decreased sexual ability; increased sensitivity of skin to sunlight (skin rash, itching, redness or other discoloration of skin, or severe sunburn); swelling or pain in breasts; unusual secretion of milk; weight gain (unusual)

After you stop using this medicine, your body may need time to adjust. The length of time this takes depends on the amount of medicine you are using and how long you used it. During this time, check with your doctor if you notice dizziness, nausea and vomiting, stomach pain, trembling of the fingers and hands, or any of the following symptoms of tardive dyskinesia:

Lip smacking or puckering; puffing of cheeks; rapid or fine, worm-like movements of tongue; uncontrolled chewing movements; uncontrolled movements of arms or legs

Although not all of the side effects listed above have been reported for all of these medicines, they have been reported for at least one of them. However, since all of the phenothiazines are very similar, any of the above side effects may occur with any of these medicines.

Other side effects not listed above may also occur in some patients. If you notice any other effects, check with your doctor.

Additional Information

Once a medicine has been approved for marketing for a certain use, experience may show that it is also useful for other medical problems. Although these uses are not included in product labeling, phenothiazines are used in certain patients with the following medical conditions:

- Chronic neurogenic pain (certain continuing pain conditions)
- Huntington's chorea (hereditary movement disorder)

Other than the above information, there is no additional information relating to proper use, precautions, or side effects for these uses.

Revised: 03/16/92
Interim revision: 08/23/94

PHENOXYBENZAMINE Systemic

A commonly used brand name in the U.S. is Dibenzyline.

Description

Phenoxybenzamine (fen-ox-ee-BEN-za-meen) belongs to the general class of medicines called antihypertensives. It is used to treat high blood pressure (hypertension) due to a disease called pheochromocytoma.

Phenoxybenzamine blocks the effects of certain chemicals in the body. When these chemicals are present in large amounts, they cause high blood pressure.

Phenoxybenzamine may also be used for other conditions as determined by your doctor.

Phenoxybenzamine is available only with your doctor's prescription, in the following dosage form:

Oral

- Capsules (U.S.)

Before Using This Medicine

In deciding to use a medicine, the risks of taking the medicine must be weighed against the good it will do. This is a decision you and your doctor will make. For phenoxybenzamine, the following should be considered:

Allergies—Tell your doctor if you have ever had any unusual or allergic reaction to phenoxybenzamine. Also, tell your health care professional if you are allergic to any other substances, such as foods, preservatives, or dyes.

Pregnancy—Phenoxybenzamine has not been studied in pregnant women or animals. Make sure your doctor knows if you are pregnant or if you may become pregnant before taking phenoxybenzamine.

Breast-feeding—It is not known whether phenoxybenzamine passes into breast milk. However, this medicine has not been reported to cause problems in nursing babies.

Children—Although there is no specific information about the use of phenoxybenzamine in children, it is not expected to cause different side effects or problems in children than it does in adults.

Older adults—Dizziness or lightheadedness may be more likely to occur in the elderly, who are more sensitive to the effects of phenoxybenzamine. In addition, phenoxybenzamine may reduce tolerance to cold temperatures in elderly patients.

Other medicines—Although certain medicines should not be used together at all, in other cases two different medicines may be used together even if an interaction might occur. In these cases, your doctor may want to change the dose, or other precautions may be necessary. Tell your health care professional if you are taking any other prescription or nonprescription (over-the-counter [OTC]) medicine.

Other medical problems—The presence of other medical problems may affect the use of phenoxybenzamine. Make sure you tell your doctor if you have any other medical problems, especially:

- Angina (chest pain) or
- Heart or blood vessel disease—Some kinds may be worsened by phenoxybenzamine
- Kidney disease—Effects may be increased
- Lung infection—Symptoms such as stuffy nose may be worsened

• Recent heart attack or stroke—Lowering blood pressure may make problems resulting from stroke or heart attack worse

Proper Use of This Medicine

To help you remember to take your medicine, try to get into the habit of taking it at the same time each day.

Dosing—The dose of phenoxybenzamine will be different for different patients. *Follow your doctor's orders or the directions on the label.* The following information includes only the average doses of phenoxybenzamine. *If your dose is different, do not change it* unless your doctor tells you to do so.

- For *oral* dosage form (capsules):
  - —For high blood pressure caused by pheochromocytoma:
    - Adults—At first, 10 milligrams (mg) two times a day. Then, your doctor may increase your dose to 20 to 40 mg two or three times a day.
    - Children—Dose is based on body weight and must be determined by your doctor. The usual starting dose is 0.2 mg per kilogram (kg) (0.09 mg per pound) of body weight taken once a day. Then, your doctor may increase your dose to 0.4 to 1.2 mg per kg (0.18 to 0.55 mg per pound) of body weight a day. This is divided into three or four doses.

Missed dose—If you miss a dose of this medicine, take it as soon as you remember. However, if it is almost time for your next dose, skip the missed dose and go back to your regular dosing schedule. Do not double doses.

Storage—To store this medicine:

- Keep out of the reach of children.
- Store away from heat and direct light.
- Do not store in the bathroom, near the kitchen sink, or in other damp places. Heat or moisture may cause the medicine to break down.
- Do not keep outdated medicine or medicine no longer needed. Be sure that any discarded medicine is out of the reach of children.

Precautions While Using This Medicine

It is important that your doctor check your progress at regular visits to make sure that this medicine is working properly and to check for unwanted effects.

Do not take other medicines unless they have been discussed with your doctor. This especially includes over-the-counter (nonprescription) medicines for appetite control, asthma, colds, cough, hay fever, or sinus problems, since they may interfere with the effects of this medicine.

Phenoxybenzamine may cause some people to become dizzy, drowsy, or less alert than they are normally. This is more likely to happen when you begin to take it or when you increase the amount of medicine you are taking. *Make sure you know how you react to this medicine before you drive, use machines, or do anything else that could be dangerous if you are dizzy or not alert.*

Dizziness, lightheadedness, or fainting may occur, especially when you get up from a lying or sitting position. Getting up slowly may help, but if the problem continues or gets worse, check with your doctor.

The dizziness, lightheadedness, or fainting is also more likely to occur if you drink alcohol, stand for a long time, exercise, or if the weather is hot. *While you are taking this medicine, be careful in the amount of alcohol you drink. Also, use extra care during exercise or hot weather or if you must stand for a long time.*

Before having any kind of surgery (including dental surgery) or emergency treatment, *tell the medical doctor or dentist in charge that you are using this medicine.*

Phenoxybenzamine may cause dryness of the mouth, nose, and throat. For temporary relief of mouth dryness, use sugarless candy or gum, melt bits of ice in your mouth, or use a saliva substitute. However, if dry mouth continues for more than 2 weeks, check with your medical doctor or dentist. Continuing dryness of the mouth may increase the chance of dental disease, including tooth decay, gum disease, and fungus infections.

Side Effects of This Medicine

In rats and mice, phenoxybenzamine has been found to increase the risk of development of malignant tumors. It is not known if phenoxybenzamine increases the chance of tumors in humans.

Along with its needed effects, a medicine may cause some unwanted effects. The following side effects may go away as your body adjusts to the medicine. However, check with your doctor if any of these effects continue or are bothersome:

More common

Dizziness or lightheadedness, especially when getting up from a lying or sitting position; fast heartbeat; pinpoint pupils; stuffy nose

Less common

Confusion; drowsiness; dryness of mouth; headache; lack of energy; sexual problems in males; unusual tiredness or weakness

Other side effects not listed above may also occur in some patients. If you notice any other effects, check with your doctor.

Additional Information

Once a medicine has been approved for marketing for a certain use, experience may show that it is also useful for other medical problems. Although this use is not included in product labeling, phenoxybenzamine is used in certain patients with the following medical condition:

- Benign prostatic hypertrophy

Other than the above information, there is no additional information relating to proper use, precautions, or side effects for this use.

Revised: 09/20/92
Interim revision: 07/20/94

PHENTOLAMINE AND PAPAVERINE Intracavernosal

Some commonly used brand names for phentolamine are:

In the U.S.—
Regitine
Generic name product may also be available.

In Canada—
Regitine
Generic name product may also be available.

Description

Phentolamine (fen-TOLE-a-meen) given by injection causes blood vessels to expand, thereby increasing blood flow. When it is used in combination with papaverine (pa-PAV-er-een), another medicine that has this effect, and is injected into the penis (intracavernosal), it increases blood flow to the penis, which results in an erection. This combination is used to treat some men who are impotent.

This medicine should not be used as a sexual aid by men who are not impotent. If the medicine is not used properly, permanent damage to the penis and loss of the ability to have erections could result.

Phentolamine and papaverine are available only with your doctor's prescription, in the following dosage form:

Parenteral
- Injection (U.S. and Canada)

Before Using This Medicine

In deciding to use a medicine, the risks of taking the medicine must be weighed against the good it will do. This is a decision you and your doctor will make. For papaverine and phentolamine, the following should be considered:

Allergies—Tell your doctor if you have ever had any unusual or allergic reaction to papaverine or phentolamine. Also tell your health care professional if you are allergic to any other substances, such as foods, preservatives, or dyes.

Older adults—Many medicines have not been studied specifically in older people. Therefore, it may not be known whether they work exactly the same way they do in younger adults or if they cause different side effects or problems in older people. Although there is no specific information comparing the use of phentolamine and papaverine for impotence in the elderly, it is not expected to cause different side effects or problems in older people than it does in younger adults.

Other medicines—Although certain medicines should not be used together at all, in other cases two different medicines may be used together even if an interaction might occur. In these cases, your doctor may want to change the dose, or other precautions may be necessary. Tell your health care professional if you are taking any other prescription or nonprescription (over-the-counter [OTC]) medicine.

Other medical problems—The presence of other medical problems may affect the use of papaverine and phentolamine. Make sure you tell your doctor if you have any other medical problems, especially:

- Bleeding problems—These conditions increase the risk of bleeding at the place of injection
- Liver disease—Papaverine can cause liver damage when it is given in ways that allow it to get into the bloodstream (by mouth or by injection into a muscle, a vein, or an artery); when papaverine is given by intracavernosal injection, liver damage is much less likely because the medicine enters the bloodstream very slowly
- Priapism (history of) or
- Sickle cell disease—Patients with these conditions have an increased risk of priapism (erection lasting longer than 4 hours) while using papaverine and phentolamine

Proper Use of This Medicine

To give the injection:

- Cleanse the injection site with alcohol. Using a sterile needle, *inject the medicine slowly and directly into the base of the penis as instructed by your doctor. It should not be injected just under the skin.* The injection is usually not painful, although you may feel some tingling in the tip of your penis. If the injection is very painful or you notice bruising or swelling at the place of injection, that means you are injecting the medicine under the skin. Stop, withdraw the needle, and reposition it properly before continuing with the injection.
- After you have completed the injection, put pressure on the place of injection to prevent bruising. Then massage your penis as instructed by your doctor. This helps the medicine spread to all parts of the penis, so that it will work better.

This medicine usually begins to work in about 10 minutes. You should attempt intercourse within 2 hours after injecting the medicine.

Dosing—The dose of phentolamine will be different for different patients. *Follow your doctor's orders or the directions on the label.* The following information includes only the average doses of phentolamine. *If your dose is different, do not change it* unless your doctor tells you to do so.

- For *injection* dosage form:
  —For the treatment of impotence:
    - Adults—First, add one milliliter (mL) of sterile water for injection to the phentolamine powder. Second, mix 0.5 to 1 milligram (mg) (0.1 to 0.2 mL) of phentolamine injection with 30 to 60 mg of papaverine injection in your syringe. Inject this medicine very slowly into the area of your penis as directed by your doctor. Allow one or two minutes to completely inject the dose. Do not inject more than one dose in a day. Also, do not use this medicine more than two days in a row or more than three times a week.

Storage—To store this medicine:
- Keep out of the reach of children.
- Store away from heat and direct light.
- Keep the medicine from freezing.

Precautions While Using This Medicine

Use the injection exactly as directed by your doctor. Do not use more of it and do not use it more often than ordered. If too much is used, the erection may become so strong that it lasts too long and does not reverse when it should. This condition is called priapism, and it can be very dangerous. If the effect is not reversed, the blood supply to the penis may be cut off and permanent damage may occur.

Contact your doctor immediately if the erection lasts for longer than 4 hours or if it becomes painful. This may be a sign of priapism and must be treated right away to prevent permanent damage.

If you notice bleeding at the site when you inject the medicine, put pressure on the spot until the bleeding stops. If it doesn't stop, check with your doctor.

It is important for you to examine your penis regularly. Check with your doctor if you find a lump where the medicine has been injected or if you notice that your penis is becoming curved. These may be signs that unwanted tissue is growing (called fibrosis), which should be seen by your doctor.

Side Effects of This Medicine

Along with its needed effects, a medicine may cause some unwanted effects. Although not all of these side effects may occur, if they do occur they may need medical attention.

Check with your doctor immediately if the following side effects occur:

Rare

Erection continuing for more than 4 hours, or painful erection

Check with your doctor as soon as possible if the following side effects occur:

Rare

Dizziness; lumps in the penis

Other side effects may occur that usually do not need medical attention. These side effects may go away during treatment as your body adjusts to the medicine. However, check with your doctor if any of the following side effects continue or are bothersome:

Less common or rare

Bruising or bleeding at place of injection; burning (mild) along penis; difficulty in ejaculating; swelling at place of injection

Phentolamine and papaverine injected into the penis may cause tingling at the tip of the penis. This is no cause for concern.

Other side effects not listed above may also occur in some patients. If you notice any other effects, check with your doctor.

Revised: 09/20/92
Interim revision: 06/07/94

PHENYLEPHRINE Nasal

Some commonly used brand names are:

In the U.S.

Alconefrin Nasal Drops 12
Alconefrin Nasal Drops 25
Alconefrin Nasal Drops 50
Alconefrin Nasal Spray 25
Doktors
Duration
Neo-Synephrine Nasal Drops
Neo-Synephrine Nasal Jelly
Neo-Synephrine Nasal Spray
Neo-Synephrine Pediatric Nasal Drops
Nostril Spray Pump
Nostril Spray Pump Mild
Rhinall
Rhinall-10 Children's Flavored Nose Drops
Vicks Sinex

Generic name product may also be available.

In Canada

Neo-Synephrine Nasal Drops
Neo-Synephrine Nasal Spray

Description

Phenylephrine (fen-ill-EF-rin) is used for the temporary relief of congestion or stuffiness in the nose caused by hay fever or other allergies, colds, or sinus trouble. It may also be used in ear infections to relieve congestion.

This medicine may also be used for other conditions as determined by your doctor.

This medicine is available without a prescription; however, your doctor may have special instructions on the proper use or dose for your medical condition.

Phenylephrine is available in the following dosage forms:

Nasal
- Nasal jelly (U.S.)
- Nasal drops (U.S. and Canada)
- Nasal spray (U.S. and Canada)

Before Using This Medicine

If you are using this medicine without a prescription, carefully read and follow any precautions on the label. For nasal phenylephrine, the following should be considered:

Allergies—Tell your doctor if you have ever had any unusual or allergic reaction to phenylephrine or to any other nasal decongestant. Also tell your health care professional if you are allergic to any other substances, such as foods, preservatives, or dyes.

Pregnancy—Nasal phenylephrine may be absorbed into the body. However, nasal phenylephrine has not been shown to cause birth defects or other problems in humans.

Breast-feeding—Nasal phenylephrine may be absorbed into the body. However, it is not known whether phenylephrine passes into the breast milk. This medicine has not been reported to cause problems in nursing babies.

Children—Children may be especially sensitive to the effects of nasal phenylephrine. This may increase the chance of side effects during treatment.

Older adults—Many medicines have not been studied specifically in older people. Therefore, it may not be known whether they work exactly the same way they do in younger adults or if they cause different side effects or problems in older people. There is no specific information comparing use of nasal phenylephrine in the elderly with use in other age groups.

Other medicines—Although certain medicines should not be used together at all, in other cases two different medicines may be used together even if an interaction might occur. In these cases, your doctor may want to change the dose, or other precautions may be necessary. Tell your health care professional if you are using any other prescription or nonprescription (over-the-counter [OTC]) medicine.

Other medical problems—The presence of other medical problems may affect the use of nasal phenylephrine. Make sure you tell your doctor if you have any other medical problems, especially:

- Diabetes mellitus (sugar diabetes) or
- Heart or blood vessel disease or
- High blood pressure or
- Overactive thyroid—Nasal phenylephrine may make the condition worse

Proper Use of This Medicine

To use the *nose drops:*

- Blow your nose gently. Tilt the head back while standing or sitting up, or lie down on a bed and hang head over the side. Place the drops into each nostril and keep the head tilted back for a few minutes to allow the medicine to spread throughout the nose.
- Rinse the dropper with hot water and dry with a clean tissue. Replace the cap right after use.
- To avoid spreading the infection, do not use the container for more than one person.

To use the *nose spray:*

- Blow your nose gently. With the head upright, spray the medicine into each nostril. Sniff briskly while squeezing the bottle quickly and firmly. For best results, spray once or twice into each nostril and wait 3 to 5 minutes to allow the medicine to work. Then, blow your nose gently and thoroughly. Repeat until the complete dose is used.
- Rinse the tip of the spray bottle with hot water, taking care not to suck water into the bottle, and dry with a clean tissue. Replace the cap right after use.
- To avoid spreading the infection, do not use the container for more than one person.

To use the *nose jelly:*

- Blow your nose gently. Wash your hands before applying the medicine. With your finger, place a small amount of jelly (about the size of a pea) up each nostril. Sniff it well back into the nose.
- Wipe the tip of the tube with a clean, damp tissue and replace the cap right after use.

Use this medicine only as directed. Do not use more of it, do not use it more often, and do not use it for longer than 3 days without first checking with your doctor. To do so may make your runny or stuffy nose worse and may also increase the chance of side effects.

Dosing—The dose of nasal phenylephrine will be different for different patients. *Follow your doctor's orders or the directions on the label.* The following information includes only the average doses of nasal phenylephrine. *If your dose is different, do not change it* unless your doctor tells you to do so.

- For stuffy nose:
  - —For *nose jelly* dosage form:
    - Adults—Use a small amount in the nose every three or four hours as needed.
    - Children—Use is not recommended.
  - —For *nose drops* dosage form:
    - Adults and children 12 years of age and older—Use two or three drops of a 0.25 to 0.5% solution in the nose every four hours as needed.
    - Children 6 to 12 years of age—Use two or three drops of a 0.25% solution in the nose every four hours as needed.
    - Children 2 to 6 years of age—Use two or three drops of a 0.125 or 0.16% solution in the nose every four hours as needed.
    - Children up to 2 years of age—Use and dose must be determined by your doctor.
  - —For *nose spray* dosage form:
    - Adults and children 12 years of age and older—Use two or three sprays of a 0.25 to 0.5% solution in the nose every four hours as needed.
    - Children 6 to 12 years of age—Use two or three sprays of a 0.25% solution in the nose every four hours as needed.
    - Children up to 6 years of age—Use and dose must be determined by your doctor.

Missed dose—If you are using this medicine on a regular schedule and you miss a dose, use it right away if you remember within an hour or so of the missed dose. However, if you do not remember until later, skip the missed dose and go back to your regular dosing schedule. Do not double doses.

Storage—To store this medicine:

- Keep out of the reach of children.
- Store away from heat and direct light.
- Keep the medicine from freezing.
- Do not keep outdated medicine or medicine no longer needed. Be sure that any discarded medicine is out of the reach of children.

Side Effects of This Medicine

Along with its needed effects, a medicine may cause some unwanted effects. Although not all of these side effects may occur, if they do occur they may need medical attention.

When this medicine is used for short periods of time at low doses, side effects usually are rare. However, check with your doctor as soon as possible if any of the following occur:

Increase in runny or stuffy nose

Symptoms of too much medicine being absorbed into the body

Fast, irregular, or pounding heartbeat; headache or dizziness; increased sweating; nervousness; paleness; trembling; trouble in sleeping

Note: The above side effects are more likely to occur in children because there is a greater chance that too much of this medicine may be absorbed into the body.

Other side effects may occur that usually do not need medical attention. These side effects may go away during treatment as your body adjusts to the medicine. However, check with your health care professional if any of the following side effects continue or are bothersome:

Burning, dryness, or stinging of inside of nose

Other side effects not listed above may also occur in some patients. If you notice any other effects, check with your health care professional.

Revised: 05/16/94

PHENYLEPHRINE Ophthalmic

Some commonly used brand names are:

In the U.S.—

Ak-Dilate
Ak-Nefrin
Dilatair
I-Phrine
Isopto Frin
Mydfrin
Neo-Synephrine
Ocugestrin
Ocu-Phrin Sterile Eye Drops
Ocu-Phrin Sterile Ophthalmic Solution
Phenoptic
Prefrin Liquifilm
Relief Eye Drops for Red Eyes

Generic name product may be available.

In Canada—

Ak-Dilate
Minims Phenylephrine
Mydfrin
Prefrin Liquifilm
Spersaphrine

Description

Ophthalmic phenylephrine (fen-ill-EF-rin) in strengths of 2.5 and 10% is used to dilate (enlarge) the pupil. It is used before eye examinations, before and after eye surgery, and to treat certain eye conditions. In the U.S., these preparations are available only with your doctor's prescription.

Ophthalmic phenylephrine in the strength of 0.12% is used to relieve redness due to minor irritations of the eye, such as those caused by allergy, dust, smoke, wind, and other irritants. This preparation is available without a prescription; however, your doctor may have special instructions on the proper use of phenylephrine for your eye problem.

Phenylephrine is available in the following dosage form:

Ophthalmic

- Ophthalmic solution (eye drops) (U.S. and Canada)

Before Using This Medicine

In deciding to use a medicine, the risks of using the medicine must be weighed against the good it will do. This is a decision you and your doctor will make. For phenylephrine, the following should be considered:

Allergies—Tell your doctor if you have ever had any unusual or allergic reaction to phenylephrine or to sulfites. Also tell your health care professional if you are allergic to any other substances, such as preservatives.

Pregnancy—Ophthalmic phenylephrine may be absorbed into the body. However, studies on effects in pregnancy have not been done in either humans or animals.

Breast-feeding—Ophthalmic phenylephrine may be absorbed into the mother's body. However, it is not known whether phenylephrine passes into breast milk. Although most medicines pass into breast milk in small amounts, many of them may be used safely while breast-feeding. Mothers who are using this medicine and who wish to breast-feed should discuss this with their doctor.

Children—Children may be especially sensitive to the effects of phenylephrine. This may increase the chance of side effects during treatment. In addition, the 10% strength is not recommended for use in infants. Also, the 2.5 and 10% strengths are not recommended for use in low birth weight infants.

Older adults—Repeated use of 2.5 or 10% phenylephrine may increase the chance of problems during treatment with this medicine. In addition, heart and blood vessel problems have occurred more often in elderly patients than in younger adults.

Other medicines—Although certain medicines should not be used together at all, in other cases two different medicines may be used together even if an interaction might occur. In these cases, your doctor may want to change the dose, or other precautions may be necessary. Tell your health care professional if you are using any other prescription or nonprescription (over-the-counter [OTC]) medicine.

Other medical problems—The presence of other medical problems may affect the use of phenylephrine. Make sure you tell your doctor if you have any other medical problems, especially:

- Diabetes mellitus (sugar diabetes) or
- Heart or blood vessel disease or
- High blood pressure—The 2.5 and 10% strengths of phenylephrine may make the condition worse

- Idiopathic orthostatic hypotension (a certain kind of low blood pressure)—Use of this medicine may cause a large increase in blood pressure to occur

Proper Use of This Medicine

Do not use if the solution turns brown or becomes cloudy.

To use:

- First, wash your hands. Tilt the head back and, pressing your finger gently on the skin just beneath the lower eyelid, pull the lower eyelid away from the eye to make a space. Drop the medicine into this space. Let go of the eyelid and gently close the eyes. Do not blink. Keep the eyes closed and apply pressure to the inner corner of the eye with your finger for 2 or 3 minutes to allow the medicine to be absorbed by the eye.
- Immediately after using the eye drops, wash your hands to remove any medicine that may be on them.
- To keep the medicine as germ-free as possible, do not touch the applicator tip to any surface (including the eye). Also, keep the container tightly closed.

For patients using the *2.5 or 10% eye drops:*

- *It is very important that you use this medicine only as directed.* Do not use more of it and do not use it more often than your doctor ordered. To do so may increase the chance of too much medicine being absorbed into the body and the chance of side effects. *This is especially important when this medicine is used in children or in patients with heart disease or high blood pressure,* since high doses of this medicine may cause an irregular heartbeat and an increase in blood pressure.

Dosing—The dose of ophthalmic phenylephrine will be different for different patients. *Follow your doctor's orders or the directions on the label.* The following information includes only the average doses of ophthalmic phenylephrine. *If your dose is different, do not change it* unless your doctor tells you to do so.

- For *ophthalmic solution (eye drops)* dosage form:
  - —For eye redness:
    - Adults and children—Use one drop of 0.12% solution every three or four hours as needed.
  - —For eye exams:
    - Adults and children—Use one drop of 2.5% solution. Depending on the eye test to be done, it will take from fifteen minutes to one or two hours for the medicine to work before you can have the eye test.
  - —For use before eye surgery:
    - Adults and teenagers—Use one drop of 2.5 or 10% solution thirty to sixty minutes before the start of eye surgery.
    - Children—Use one drop of 2.5% solution thirty to sixty minutes before the start of eye surgery.
  - —For certain eye conditions:
    - Adults and teenagers—Depending on the eye condition being treated, your doctor may tell you to use one drop of 2.5 or 10% solution in the eye from once a day to three times a day.
    - Children—Depending on the eye condition being treated, your doctor may tell you to use one drop of 2.5% solution in the eye from once a day to three times a day.

Missed dose—If you are using the 2.5 or 10% eye drops and you miss a dose of this medicine, apply it as soon as possible. However, if it is almost time for your next dose, skip the missed dose and go back to your regular dosing schedule. Do not double doses.

Storage—To store this medicine:

- Keep out of the reach of children.
- Store away from heat and direct light.
- Keep the medicine from freezing.
- Do not keep outdated medicine or medicine no longer needed. Be sure that any discarded medicine is out of the reach of children.

Precautions While Using This Medicine

If eye pain or change in vision occurs or if redness or irritation of the eye continues, gets worse, or lasts for more than 72 hours, stop using the medicine and check with your doctor.

For patients using the *2.5 or 10% eye drops:*

- After you apply this medicine to your eyes, your pupils will become unusually large. This will cause your eyes to become more sensitive to light than they are normally. *When you go out during the daylight hours, even on cloudy days, wear sunglasses that block ultraviolet (UV) light to protect your eyes from sunlight and other bright lights.* Ordinary sunglasses may not protect your eyes. If you have any questions about the kind of sunglasses to wear, check with your doctor. Also, if this effect continues for longer than 12 hours after you have stopped using this medicine, check with your doctor.

Side Effects of This Medicine

Along with its needed effects, a medicine may cause some unwanted effects. Although not all of these side effects may occur, if they do occur they may need medical attention.

Check with your doctor as soon as possible if any of the following side effects occur:

Symptoms of too much medicine being absorbed into the body—Less common with 10% solution; rare with 2.5% or weaker solution

Dizziness; fast, irregular, or pounding heartbeat; increased sweating; increase in blood pressure; paleness; trembling

Other side effects may occur that usually do not need medical attention. These side effects may go away during treatment as your body adjusts to the medicine. However,

check with your doctor if any of the following side effects continue or are bothersome:

More common with 2.5 or 10% solution

Burning or stinging of eyes; headache or browache; sensitivity of eyes to light; watering of eyes

Less common

Eye irritation not present before use of this medicine

Other side effects not listed above may also occur in some patients. If you notice any other effects, check with your doctor.

Revised: 07/14/95

PHENYLPROPANOLAMINE Systemic†

Some commonly used brand names are:

In the U.S.—

- Acutrim 16 Hour
- Acutrim Late Day
- Acutrim II Maximum Strength Control
- Dexatrim Maximum Strength Caplets
- Dexatrim Maximum Strength Capsules
- Dexatrim Maximum Strength Tablets
- Diet-Aid Maximum Strength
- Efed II Yellow
- Phenyldrine
- Prolamine
- Propagest

Generic name product may also be available.

Another commonly used name is PPA.

†Not commercially available in Canada.

Description

Phenylpropanolamine (fen-ill-proe-pa-NOLE-a-meen), commonly known as PPA, is used as a nasal decongestant or as an appetite suppressant. It acts on many different parts of the body. PPA produces effects that may be helpful or harmful. This depends on a patient's individual condition and response and the amount of medicine taken.

Phenylpropanolamine clears nasal congestion (stuffy nose) by narrowing or constricting the blood vessels. However, this same action may cause an increase in blood pressure in patients who have hypertension (high blood pressure).

Phenylpropanolamine also decreases appetite. However, the way PPA and similar medicines do this is unclear. Stimulation of the central nervous system (CNS) may be a major reason. Phenylpropanolamine in combination with dieting, exercise, and changes in eating habits can help obese patients lose weight. However, this appetite-reducing effect is only temporary, and is useful only for the first few weeks of dieting until new eating habits are established.

Phenylpropanolamine has caused serious side effects (even death) when too much was taken.

There are a number of products on the market that contain only phenylpropanolamine. Other products contain PPA along with added ingredients. The information that follows is for PPA alone. There may be additional information for the combination products. Read the label of the product you are using. If you have questions or if you want more information about the other ingredients, check with your health care professional.

Some preparations containing PPA are available only with your doctor's prescription. Others are available without a prescription; however, your doctor may have special instructions on the proper use of this medicine.

Phenylpropanolamine is available in the following dosage forms:

Oral

- Capsules (U.S.)
- Extended-release capsules (U.S.)
- Tablets (U.S.)
- Extended-release tablets (U.S.)

Before Using This Medicine

If you are taking this medicine without a prescription, carefully read and follow any precautions on the label. For phenylpropanolamine, the following should be considered:

Allergies—Tell your doctor if you have ever had any unusual or allergic reaction to phenylpropanolamine or to amphetamine, dextroamphetamine, ephedrine, epinephrine, isoproterenol, metaproterenol, methamphetamine, norepinephrine, phenylephrine, pseudoephedrine, or terbutaline. Also tell your health care professional if you are allergic to any other substances, such as foods, preservatives, or dyes.

Pregnancy—Phenylpropanolamine has not been shown to cause birth defects in humans. However, women who take phenylpropanolamine in the weeks following delivery may be more likely to suffer mental or mood changes.

Breast-feeding—Phenylpropanolamine has not been reported to cause problems in nursing babies.

Children—Mental changes may be more likely to occur in young children taking phenylpropanolamine than in adults. Phenylpropanolamine should not be used for weight control in children under the age of 12 years. Children 12 to 18 years old should not take phenylpropanolamine for weight control unless its use is ordered and supervised by a doctor.

Older adults—Many medicines have not been studied specifically in older people. Therefore, it may not be known whether they work exactly the same way they do in younger adults or if they cause different side effects or problems in older people. There is no specific information comparing use of phenylpropanolamine in the elderly with use in other age groups.

Other medicines—Although certain medicines should not be used together at all, in other cases 2 different medicines may be used together even if an interaction might occur. In these cases, your doctor may want to change the dose, or other precautions may be necessary. When you are taking phenylpropanolamine, it is especially important that your health care professional know if you are taking any of the following:

- Amantadine (e.g., Symmetrel) or
- Amphetamines or
- Caffeine (e.g., NoDoz) or
- Chlophedianol (e.g., Ulone) or
- Cocaine or
- Medicine for asthma or other breathing problems or
- Methylphenidate (e.g., Ritalin) or
- Nabilone (e.g., Cesamet) or
- Other appetite suppressants (diet pills) or
- Other medicine for colds, sinus problems, or hay fever or other allergies (including nose drops or sprays) or
- Pemoline (e.g., Cylert)—Using these medicines while taking phenylpropanolamine may cause severe nervousness, irritability, trouble in sleeping, or possibly irregular heartbeat or seizures
- Beta-blockers (acebutolol [e.g., Sectral], atenolol [e.g., Tenormin], betaxolol [e.g., Kerlone], carteolol [e.g., Cartrol], labetalol [e.g., Normodyne], metoprolol [e.g., Lopressor], nadolol [e.g., Corgard], oxprenolol [e.g., Trasicor], penbutolol [e.g., Levatol], pindolol [e.g., Visken], propranolol [e.g., Inderal], sotalol [e.g., Sotacor], timolol [e.g., Blocadren])—Taking these medicines with phenylpropanolamine may cause serious high blood pressure (hypertension) and other effects on the heart
- Digitalis glycosides (heart medicine)—Changes in the rhythm of your heart may occur
- Monoamine oxidase (MAO) inhibitors (furazolidone [e.g., Furoxone], isocarboxazid [e.g., Marplan], phenelzine [e.g., Nardil], procarbazine [e.g., Matulane], selegiline [e.g., Eldepryl], tranylcypromine [e.g., Parnate])—Taking phenylpropanolamine while you are taking or within 2 weeks of taking MAO inhibitors may cause sudden high body temperature, extremely high blood pressure, and severe convulsions; at least 14 days should be allowed between stopping treatment with one medicine and starting treatment with the other
- Rauwolfia alkaloids (alseroxylon [e.g., Rauwiloid], deserpidine [e.g., Harmonyl], rauwolfia serpentina [e.g., Raudixin], reserpine [e.g., Serpasil])—Phenylpropanolamine may not work properly when taken with rauwolfia alkaloids

Other medical problems—The presence of other medical problems may affect the use of phenylpropanolamine. Make sure you tell your doctor if you have any other medical problems, especially:

- Diabetes mellitus (sugar diabetes)—Use of phenylpropanolamine may cause an increase in blood glucose levels
- Enlarged prostate or
- Glaucoma or
- High blood pressure—Use of phenylpropanolamine may make the condition worse
- Heart or blood vessel disease (including a history of heart attack or stroke) or
- Overactive thyroid—Serious effects on the heart may occur
- Mental illness, history of—Use of phenylpropanolamine may cause the mental illness to return

Proper Use of This Medicine

For patients taking an *extended-release form* of this medicine:

- Swallow the capsule or tablet whole. Do not crush, break, or chew before swallowing.
- Take with a full glass (at least 8 ounces) of water.
- If taking only one dose of this medicine a day, take it in the morning around 10 a.m.

Take phenylpropanolamine (PPA) only as directed. Do not take more of it, do not take it more often, and do not take it for a longer time than directed. To do so may increase the chance of side effects.

For patients taking this medicine *as an appetite suppressant:*

- *Do not take this medicine for longer than a few weeks without your doctor's permission.*

If PPA causes trouble in sleeping, take the last dose for each day a few hours before bedtime.

Dosing—The dose of phenylpropanolamine will be different for different patients. *Follow your doctor's orders or the directions on the label.* The following information includes only the average doses of phenylpropanolamine. *If your dose is different, do not change it* unless your doctor tells you to do so.

The number of capsules or tablets that you take depends on the strength of the medicine. Also, *the number of doses you take each day, the time allowed between doses, and the length of time you take the medicine depend on the medical problem for which you are taking phenylpropanolamine.*

- For appetite control:
  - For *oral* dosage forms (capsules and tablets):
    - Adults—25 mg three times a day. Do not take more than 75 mg in twenty-four hours.
    - Children 12 to 18 years of age—Use and dose must be determined by your doctor.
    - Children up to 12 years of age—Use is not recommended.
  - For *long-acting* dosage forms (extended-release capsules and tablets):
    - Adults—75 mg taken once a day in the morning around 10 a.m.
    - Children 12 to 18 years of age—Use and dose must be determined by your doctor.
    - Children up to 12 years of age—Use is not recommended.
- For stuffy nose:
  - For *capsule and tablet* dosage forms:
    - Adults and children 12 to 18 years of age—25 mg every four hours as needed. Do not take more than 150 mg in twenty-four hours.
    - Children 6 to 12 years of age—12.5 mg every four hours as needed. Do not take more than 75 mg in twenty-four hours.
    - Children 2 to 6 years of age—6.25 mg every four hours as needed. Do not take more than 37.5 mg in twenty-four hours.
    - Children up to 2 years of age—Use and dose must be determined by your doctor.

—For *extended-release capsule* dosage form:
- Adults—75 mg every twelve hours.
- Children—Use and dose must be determined by your doctor.

Missed dose—For patients taking phenylpropanolamine *for nasal congestion:* If you miss a dose, take it as soon as possible. However, if it is within 2 hours (or 12 hours for extended-release forms) of your next dose, skip the missed dose and go back to your regular dosing schedule. Do not double doses.

Storage—To store this medicine:
- Keep out of the reach of children.
- Store away from heat and direct light.
- Do not store in the bathroom, near the kitchen sink, or in other damp places. Heat or moisture may cause the medicine to break down.
- Do not keep outdated medicine or medicine no longer needed. Be sure that any discarded medicine is out of the reach of children.

Precautions While Using This Medicine

Do not drink large amounts of caffeine-containing coffee, tea, or colas while you are taking this medicine. To do so may cause unwanted effects.

This medicine may cause some people to become dizzy. *Make sure you know how you react to this medicine before you drive, use machines, or do anything else that could be dangerous if you are dizzy or not alert.*

For patients taking this medicine *for nasal congestion:*
- *If cold symptoms do not improve within 7 days or if you also have a high fever, check with your doctor.* These signs may mean that you have other medical problems.

Side Effects of This Medicine

Along with its needed effects, a medicine may cause some unwanted effects. Although not all of these side effects may occur, if they do occur they may need medical attention.

Check with your doctor as soon as possible if any of the following side effects occur:

Rare

Headache (severe); increased blood pressure; painful or difficult urination; tightness in chest

Early symptoms of overdose

Abdominal or stomach pain; fast, pounding, or irregular heartbeat; headache (severe); increased sweating not caused by exercise; nausea and vomiting (severe); nervousness (severe); restlessness (severe)

Late symptoms of overdose

Confusion; convulsions (seizures); fast breathing; fast and irregular pulse; hallucinations (seeing, hearing, or feeling things that are not there); hostile behavior; muscle trembling

Other side effects may occur that usually do not need medical attention. These side effects may go away during treatment as your body adjusts to the medicine. However, check with your doctor if any of the following side effects continue or are bothersome:

Less common—more common with high doses

Dizziness; dryness of nose or mouth; false sense of well-being; headache (mild); nausea (mild); nervousness (mild); restlessness (mild); trouble in sleeping

Other side effects not listed above may also occur in some patients. If you notice any other effects, check with your doctor.

Additional Information

Once a medicine has been approved for marketing for a certain use, experience may show that it is also useful for other medical problems. Although this use is not included in product labeling, phenylpropanolamine is used in certain patients with the following medical condition:
- Urinary stress incontinence (loss of bladder control when you cough, sneeze, or laugh)

Other than the above information, there is no additional information relating to proper use, precautions, or side effects for this use.

Revised: 06/21/94

PHOSPHATES Systemic

Some commonly used brand names are:

In the U.S.—

K-Phos M. F.[2]
K-Phos Neutral[2]
K-Phos No. 2[2]
K-Phos Original[1]
Neutra-Phos[2]
Neutra-Phos-K[1]
Uro-KP-Neutral[2]

In Canada—

Uro-KP-Neutral[2]

Note: For quick reference, the following phosphates are numbered to match the corresponding brand names.

This information applies to the following medicines:

1. Potassium Phosphates (poe-TASS-ee-um FOS-fates)‡§
2. Potassium and Sodium (SOE-dee-um) Phosphates
3. Sodium Phosphates†‡

†Not commercially available in Canada.
‡Generic name product may also be available in the U.S.
§Generic name product may also be available in Canada.

Description

Phosphates are used as dietary supplements for patients who are unable to get enough phosphorus in their regular diet, usually because of certain illnesses or diseases. Phosphate is the drug form (salt) of phosphorus. Some phosphates are used to make the urine more acid, which helps treat certain urinary tract infections. Some phosphates are used to prevent the formation of calcium stones in the urinary tract.

Injectable phosphates are to be administered only by or under the supervision of your health care professional. Some of these oral preparations are available only with a prescription. Others are available without a prescription; however, your health care professional may have special instructions on the proper dose of this medicine for your medical condition. You should take phosphates only under the supervision of your health care professional.

Phosphates are available in the following dosage forms:

Oral

Potassium Phosphates
- Capsules for solution (U.S.)
- Powder for solution (U.S.)
- Tablets for solution (U.S.)

Potassium and Sodium Phosphates
- Capsules for solution (U.S.)
- Powder for solution (U.S.)
- Tablets for solution (U.S. and Canada)

Parenteral

Potassium Phosphates
- Injection (U.S. and Canada)

Sodium Phosphates
- Injection (U.S.)

Importance of Diet

For good health, it is important that you eat a balanced and varied diet. Follow carefully any diet program your health care professional may recommend. For your specific dietary vitamin and/or mineral needs, ask your health care professional for a list of appropriate foods. If you think that you are not getting enough vitamins and/or minerals in your diet, you may choose to take a dietary supplement.

The best dietary sources of phosphorus include dairy products, meat, poultry, fish, and cereal products.

The daily amount of phosphorus needed is defined in several different ways.

For U.S.—
- Recommended Dietary Allowances (RDAs) are the amount of vitamins and minerals needed to provide for adequate nutrition in most healthy persons. RDAs for a given nutrient may vary depending on a person's age, sex, and physical condition (e.g., pregnancy).
- Daily Values (DVs) are used on food and dietary supplement labels to indicate the percent of the recommended daily amount of each nutrient that a serving provides. DV replaces the previous designation of United States Recommended Daily Allowances (USRDAs).

For Canada—
- Recommended Nutrient Intakes (RNIs) are used to determine the amounts of vitamins, minerals, and protein needed to provide adequate nutrition and lessen the risk of chronic disease.

Normal daily recommended intakes for phosphorus are generally defined as follows:

Persons	U.S. (mg)	Canada (mg)
Infants and children		
Birth to 3 years of age	300–800	150–350
4 to 6 years of age	800	400
7 to 10 years of age	800	500–800
Adolescent and adult males	800–1200	700–1000
Adolescent and adult females	800–1200	800–850
Pregnant females	1200	1050
Breast-feeding females	1200	1050

Before Using This Medicine

In deciding to use a medicine, the risks of taking the medicine must be weighed against the good it will do. This is a decision you and your health care professional will make. For phosphates the following should be considered:

Allergies—Tell your health care professional if you have ever had any unusual or allergic reaction to potassium, sodium, or phosphates. Also, tell your health care professional if you are allergic to any other substances, such as foods, preservatives, or dyes.

Pregnancy—It is especially important that you are receiving enough vitamins and minerals when you become pregnant and that you continue to receive the right amount of vitamins and minerals throughout your pregnancy. The healthy growth and development of the fetus depend on a steady supply of nutrients from the mother. However, taking large amounts of a dietary supplement in pregnancy may be harmful to the mother and/or fetus and should be avoided.

Breast-feeding—It is especially important that you receive the right amount of vitamins and minerals so that your baby will also get the vitamins and minerals needed to grow properly. However, taking large amounts of a dietary supplement while breast-feeding may be harmful to the mother and/or baby and should be avoided.

Children—Problems in children have not been reported with intake of normal daily recommended amounts. However, use of enemas that contain phosphates in children has resulted in high blood levels of phosphorus.

Older adults—Problems in older adults have not been reported with intake of normal daily recommended amounts.

Other medicines—Although certain medicines should not be used together at all, in other cases two different medicines may be used together even if an interaction might occur. In these cases, your health care professional may want to change the dose, or other precautions may be necessary. When you are taking phosphates, it is especially important that your health care professional know if you are taking any of the following:
- Amiloride (e.g., Midamor) or
- Angiotensin-converting enzyme (ACE) inhibitors (benazepril [e.g., Lotensin], captopril [e.g., Capoten], enalapril [e.g., Vasotec], fosinopril [e.g., Monopril], lisinopril [e.g., Zestril, Prinivil], quinapril [e.g., Accupril], ramipril [e.g., Altace]) or

- Cyclosporine or
- Digitalis glycosides (heart medicine) or
- Heparin (e.g., Panheprin), with long-term use, or
- Medicine for inflammation or pain (except narcotics) or
- Other potassium-containing medicine or
- Salt substitutes, low-salt foods, or milk or
- Spironolactone (e.g., Aldactone) or
- Triamterene (e.g., Dyrenium)—Use with potassium-containing phosphates may increase the risk of hyperkalemia (too much potassium in the blood), possibly leading to serious side effects
- Antacids—Use with phosphates may prevent the phosphate from working properly
- Calcium-containing medicine, including antacids and calcium supplements—Use with phosphates may prevent the phosphate from working properly; calcium deposits may form in tissues
- Corticosteroids (cortisone-like medicine)—Use with sodium-containing phosphates may increase the risk of swelling
- Phosphate-containing medications, other, including phosphate enemas—Use with sodium or potassium phophates may cause high blood levels of phosphorus which may increase the chance of side effects
- Sodium-containing medicines (other)—Use with sodium phosphates may cause your body to retain (keep) water

Other medical problems—The presence of other medical problems may affect the use of phosphates. Make sure you tell your health care professional if you have any other medical problems, especially:

- Burns, severe or
- Heart disease or
- Pancreatitis (inflammation of the pancreas) or
- Rickets or
- Softening of bones or
- Underactive parathyroid glands—Sodium- or potassium-containing phosphates may make these conditions worse
- Dehydration or
- Underactive adrenal glands—Potassium-containing phosphates may increase the risk of hyperkalemia (too much potassium in the blood)
- Edema (swelling in feet or lower legs or fluid in lungs) or
- High blood pressure or
- Liver disease or
- Toxemia of pregnancy—Sodium-containing phosphates may make these conditions worse
- High blood levels of phosphate (hyperphosphatemia)—Use of phosphates may make this condition worse
- Infected kidney stones—Phosphates may make this condition worse
- Kidney disease—Sodium-containing phosphates may make this condition worse; potassium-containing phosphates may increase the risk of hyperkalemia (too much potassium in the blood)
- Myotonia congenita—Potassium-containing phosphates may increase the risk of hyperkalemia (too much potassium in the blood), and make this condition worse

Proper Use of This Medicine

For patients taking the *tablet form* of this medicine:

- *Do not swallow the tablet.* Before taking, dissolve the tablet in 3/4 to 1 glass (6 to 8 ounces) of water. Let the tablet soak in water for 2 to 5 minutes and then stir until completely dissolved.

For patients using the *capsule form* of this medicine:

- *Do not swallow the capsule.* Before taking, mix the contents of 1 capsule in one-third glass (about 2 1/2 ounces) of water or juice or the contents of 2 capsules in two-thirds glass (about 5 ounces) of water and stir well until dissolved.

For patients using the *powder form* of this medicine:

- Add the entire contents of 1 bottle (2 1/4 ounces) to enough warm water to make 1 gallon of solution *or* the contents of one packet to enough warm water to make 1/3 of a glass (about 2.5 ounces) of solution. Shake the container for 2 or 3 minutes or until all the powder is dissolved.
- Do not dilute solution further.
- This solution may be chilled to improve the flavor; do not allow it to freeze.
- Discard unused solution after 60 days.

Take this medicine immediately after meals or with food to lessen possible stomach upset or laxative action.

To help prevent kidney stones, *drink at least a full glass (8 ounces) of water every hour during waking hours,* unless otherwise directed by your health care professional.

Take this medicine only as directed. Do not take more of it and do not take it more often than recommended on the label, unless otherwise directed by your health care professional.

Dosing—The dose of these single or combination medicines will be different for different patients. *Follow your health care professional's orders or the directions on the label.* The following information includes only the average doses of these medicines. *If your dose is different, do not change it* unless your health care professional tells you to do so.

The number of teaspoonfuls or ounces of prepared solution that you drink depends on the equivalent amount of phophorus contained in the product. Also, *the number of doses you take each day, the time allowed between doses, and the length of time you take the medicine depend on the medical problem for which you are taking the single or combination medicine.*

For potassium phosphates

- For *tablets for oral solution* dosage form:
  - —To replace phosphorus lost by the body or to make the urine more acid or to prevent the formation of kidney stones in the urinary tract:
    - Adults and teenagers—The equivalent of 228 milligrams (mg) of phosphorus (2 tablets) dissolved in six to eight ounces of water four times a day, with meals and at bedtime.
  - —To replace phosphorus lost by the body:
    - Children over 4 years of age—The equivalent of 228 mg of phosphorus (2 tablets) dissolved in six to eight ounces of water four times a day, with meals and at bedtime.
    - Children up to 4 years of age—The dose must be determined by your doctor.

- For *capsules for oral solution* dosage form:
  —To replace phosphorus lost by the body:
  - Adults, teenagers, and children over 4 years of age—The equivalent of 250 mg of phosphorus (contents of 1 capsule) dissolved in two and one-half ounces of water or juice four times a day, after meals and at bedtime.
  - Children up to 4 years of age—Dose must be determined by your doctor.
- For *powder for oral solution* dosage form:
  —To replace phosphorus lost by the body:
  - Adults, teenagers, and children over 4 years of age—The equivalent of 250 mg of phosphorus dissolved in two and one-half ounces of water four times a day, after meals and at bedtime.
  - Children up to 4 years of age—Dose must be determined by your doctor.

For potassium and sodium phosphates

- For *tablets for oral solution* dosage form:
  —To replace phosphorus lost by the body or to make the urine more acid or to prevent the fomation of kidney stones in the urinary tract:
  - Adults and teenagers—The equivalent of 250 milligrams (mg) of phosphorus dissolved in eight ounces of water four times a day, after meals and at bedtime.

  —To replace phosphorus lost by the body:
  - Children over 4 years of age—The equivalent of 250 mg of phosphorus dissolved in eight ounces of water four times a day, after meals and at bedtime.
  - Children up to 4 years of age—Dose must be determined by your doctor.
- For *capsules for oral solution* dosage form:
  —To replace phosphorus lost by the body:
  - Adults, teenagers, and children over 4 years of age—The equivalent of 250 mg of phosphorus (the contents of 1 capsule) dissolved in two and one-half ounces of water or juice four times a day, after meals and at bedtime.
  - Children up to 4 years of age—Dose must be determined by your doctor.
- For *powder for oral solution* dosage form:
  —To replace phosphorus lost by the body:
  - Adults, teenagers, and children over 4 years of age—The equivalent of 250 mg of phosphorus dissolved in two and one-half ounces of water four times a day, after meals and at bedtime.
  - Children up to 4 years of age—Dose must be determined by your doctor.
- For *tablets for oral solution* dosage form:
  —To replace phosphorus lost by the body:
  - Adults, teenagers, and children over 4 years of age—The equivalent of 250 mg of phosphorus (1 tablet) dissolved in eight ounces of water four times a day.
  - Children up to 4 years of age—Dose must be determined by your doctor.

Missed dose—If you miss a dose of this medicine, take it as soon as possible. However, if it is within 1 or 2 hours of your next dose, skip the missed dose and go back to your regular dosing schedule. Do not double doses.

Storage—To store this medicine:
- Keep out of the reach of children.
- Store away from heat and direct light.
- Do not store the capsule, tablet, or powder form of this medicine in the bathroom, near the kitchen sink, or in other damp places. Heat or moisture may cause the medicine to break down.
- Keep the liquid form of this medicine from freezing.
- Do not keep outdated medicine or medicine no longer needed. Be sure that any discarded medicine is out of the reach of children.

Precautions While Using This Medicine

Your health care professional should check your progress at regular visits to make sure that this medicine does not cause unwanted effects.

Do not take iron supplements within 1 to 2 hours of taking this medicine. To do so may keep the iron from working properly.

For patients taking potassium phosphate-containing medicines:
- Check with your health care professional before starting any strenuous physical exercise, especially if you are out of condition and are taking other medication. Exercise and certain medicines may increase the amount of potassium in the blood.

For patients on a *potassium-restricted diet:*
- This medicine may contain a large amount of potassium. If you have any questions about this, check with your health care professional.
- Do not use salt substitutes and low-salt milk unless told to do so by your health care professional. They may contain potassium.

For patients on a sodium-restricted diet:
- This medicine may contain a large amount of sodium. If you have any questions about this, check with your health care professional.

Side Effects of This Medicine

Along with its needed effects, a medicine may cause some unwanted effects. Although not all of these side effects may occur, if they do occur they may need medical attention.

Check with your health care professional as soon as possible if any of the following side effects occur:

Less common or rare

Confusion; convulsions (seizures); decrease in amount of urine or in frequency of urination; fast, slow, or irregular heartbeat; headache or dizziness; increased thirst; muscle cramps; numbness, tingling, pain, or weakness in hands or feet; numbness or tingling around lips;

shortness of breath or troubled breathing; swelling of feet or lower legs; tremor; unexplained anxiety; unusual tiredness or weakness; weakness or heaviness of legs; weight gain

Other side effects may occur that usually do not need medical attention. These side effects may go away during treatment as your body adjusts to the medicine. However, check with your health care professional if any of the following side effects continue or are bothersome:

Diarrhea; nausea or vomiting; stomach pain

Other side effects not listed above may also occur in some patients. If you notice any other effects, check with your health care professional.

Revised: 04/16/92
Interim revision: 08/30/94; 07/18/95

PHYSOSTIGMINE Ophthalmic†

Some commonly used brand names in the U.S. are Eserine Salicylate, Eserine Sulfate, and Isopto Eserine.

Generic name product may also be available in the U.S.

†Not commercially available in Canada.

Description

Physostigmine (fi-zoe-STIG-meen) is used to treat certain types of glaucoma.

This medicine is available only with your doctor's prescription, in the following dosage forms:

Ophthalmic
- Ophthalmic ointment (U.S.)
- Ophthalmic solution (eye drops) (U.S.)

Before Using This Medicine

In deciding to use a medicine, the risks of taking the medicine must be weighed against the good it will do. This is a decision you and your doctor will make. For physostigmine, the following should be considered:

Allergies—Tell your doctor if you have ever had any unusual or allergic reaction to physostigmine. Also tell your health care professional if you are allergic to any other substances, such as preservatives.

Pregnancy—Ophthalmic physostigmine may be absorbed into the body. However, studies on effects in pregnancy have not been done in either humans or animals.

Breast-feeding—Ophthalmic physostigmine may be absorbed into the mother's body. However, physostigmine has not been reported to cause problems in nursing babies.

Children—Although there is no specific information comparing use of this medicine in children with use in other age groups, it is not expected to cause different side effects or problems in children than it does in adults.

Older adults—Many medicines have not been studied specifically in older people. Therefore, it may not be known whether they work exactly the same way they do in younger adults or if they cause different side effects or problems in older people. Although there is no specific information comparing use of physostigmine in the elderly with use in other age groups, it is not expected to cause different side effects or problems in older people than it does in younger adults.

Other medicines—Although certain medicines should not be used together at all, in other cases two different medicines may be used together even if an interaction might occur. In these cases, your doctor may want to change the dose, or other precautions may be necessary. Tell your health care professional if you are using any other prescription or nonprescription (over-the-counter [OTC]) medicine.

Other medical problems—The presence of other medical problems may affect the use of physostigmine. Make sure you tell your doctor if you have any other medical problems, especially:
- Eye disease or problems (other)—Physostigmine may make the condition worse

Proper Use of This Medicine

To use the *ophthalmic solution (eye drops) form* of this medicine:
- Do not use if the solution becomes discolored.
- First, wash your hands. With the middle finger, apply pressure to the inside corner of the eye (and continue to apply pressure for 1 or 2 minutes after the medicine has been placed in the eye). Tilt the head back and with the index finger of the same hand, pull the lower eyelid away from the eye to form a pouch. Drop the medicine into the pouch and gently close the eyes. Do not blink. Keep the eyes closed for 1 or 2 minutes to allow the medicine to be absorbed.
- Immediately after using the eye drops, wash your hands to remove any medicine that may be on them.
- To keep the medicine as germ-free as possible, do not touch the applicator tip to any surface (including the eye). Also, keep the container tightly closed.

To use the *ointment form* of this medicine:
- First, wash your hands. Pull the lower eyelid away from the eye to form a pouch. Squeeze a thin strip of ointment into the pouch. A 1-cm (approximately 1/3-inch) strip of ointment is usually enough unless otherwise directed by your doctor. Gently close the eyes and keep them closed for 1 or 2 minutes to allow the medicine to be absorbed.
- Immediately after using the eye ointment, wash your hands to remove any medicine that may be on them.
- To keep the medicine as germ-free as possible, do not touch the applicator tip to any surface (including the eye). After using the eye ointment, wipe the tip

of the ointment tube with a clean tissue and keep the tube tightly closed.

Use this medicine only as directed. Do not use more of it and do not use it more often than your doctor ordered. To do so may increase the chance of too much medicine being absorbed into the body and the chance of side effects.

Dosing—The dose of ophthalmic physostigmine will be different for different patients. *Follow your doctor's orders or the directions on the label.* The following information includes only the average doses of ophthalmic physostigmine. *If your dose is different, do not change it* unless your doctor tells you to do so.

The number of doses you use each day, the time allowed between doses, and the length of time you use the medicine depend on the medical problem for which you are using ophthalmic physostigmine.

- For glaucoma:
  - —For *ophthalmic ointment* dosage form:
    - Adults and children—Use in each eye one to three times a day.
  - —For *ophthalmic solution (eye drops)* dosage form:
    - Adults and children—One drop in each eye up to four times a day.

Missed dose—If you miss a dose of this medicine and your dosing schedule is:

- One dose a day—Apply the missed dose as soon as possible. However, if you do not remember the missed dose until the next day, skip the missed dose and go back to your regular dosing schedule. Do not double doses.
- More than one dose a day—Apply the missed dose as soon as possible. However, if it is almost time for your next dose, skip the missed dose and go back to your regular dosing schedule. Do not double doses.

Storage—To store this medicine:

- Keep out of the reach of children.
- Store away from heat and direct light.
- Keep the medicine from freezing.
- Do not keep outdated medicine or medicine no longer needed. Be sure that any discarded medicine is out of the reach of children.

Precautions While Using This Medicine

Your doctor should check your eye pressure at regular visits.

For a short time after you apply this medicine, your vision may be blurred or there may be a change in your near or distant vision, especially at night. *Make sure your vision is clear before you drive, use machines, or do anything else that could be dangerous if you are not able to see well.*

Side Effects of This Medicine

Along with its needed effects, a medicine may cause some unwanted effects. Although not all of these side effects may occur, if they do occur they may need medical attention.

Check with your doctor as soon as possible if any of the following side effects occur:

Symptoms of too much medicine being absorbed into the body

Increased sweating; loss of bladder control; muscle weakness; nausea, vomiting, diarrhea, or stomach cramps or pain; shortness of breath, tightness in chest, or wheezing; slow or irregular heartbeat; unusual tiredness or weakness; watering of mouth

Other side effects may occur that usually do not need medical attention. These side effects may go away during treatment as your body adjusts to the medicine. However, check with your doctor if any of the following side effects continue or are bothersome:

More common

Blurred vision or change in near or distant vision; eye pain

Less common

Burning, redness, stinging, or other eye irritation; headache or browache; twitching of eyelids; watering of eyes

Other side effects not listed above may also occur in some patients. If you notice any other effects, check with your doctor.

Revised: 07/01/93

PILOCARPINE Ophthalmic

Some commonly used brand names are:

In the U.S.—

Adsorbocarpine
Akarpine
Isopto Carpine
Ocu-Carpine
Ocusert Pilo-20
Ocusert Pilo-40
Pilagan
Pilocar
Pilopine HS
Piloptic-1/2
Piloptic-1
Piloptic-2
Piloptic-3
Piloptic-4
Piloptic-6
Pilostat

Generic name product may be available.

In Canada—

Isopto Carpine
Minims Pilocarpine
Miocarpine
Ocusert Pilo-20
Ocusert Pilo-40
Pilopine HS
Pilostat
P.V. Carpine Liquifilm
Spersacarpine

Description

Pilocarpine (pye-loe-KAR-peen) is used to treat glaucoma and other eye conditions.

This medicine is available only with your doctor's prescription, in the following dosage forms:

Ophthalmic

- Ocular system (eye insert) (U.S. and Canada)
- Ophthalmic gel (eye gel) (U.S. and Canada)
- Ophthalmic solution (eye drops) (U.S. and Canada)

Before Using This Medicine

In deciding to use a medicine, the risks of taking the medicine must be weighed against the good it will do. This is a decision you and your doctor will make. For pilocarpine, the following should be considered:

Allergies—Tell your doctor if you have ever had any unusual or allergic reaction to pilocarpine. Also tell your health care professional if you are allergic to any other substances, such as preservatives.

Pregnancy—Ophthalmic pilocarpine may be absorbed into the body. However, studies on effects in pregnancy have not been done in either humans or animals.

Breast-feeding—Ophthalmic pilocarpine may be absorbed into the body. However, it is not known whether pilocarpine passes into the breast milk. Although most medicines pass into breast milk in small amounts, many of them may be used safely while breast-feeding. Mothers who are using this medicine and who wish to breast-feed should discuss this with their doctor.

Children—Although there is no specific information comparing use of this medicine in children with use in other age groups, pilocarpine is not expected to cause different side effects or problems in children than it does in adults.

Older adults—Many medicines have not been studied specifically in older people. Therefore, it may not be known whether they work exactly the same way they do in younger adults or if they cause different side effects or problems in older people. Although there is no specific information comparing use of pilocarpine in the elderly with use in other age groups, this medicine is not expected to cause different side effects or problems in older people than it does in younger adults.

Other medicines—Although certain medicines should not be used together at all, in other cases two different medicines may be used together even if an interaction might occur. In these cases, your doctor may want to change the dose, or other precautions may be necessary. Tell your health care professional if you are using any other prescription or nonprescription (over-the-counter [OTC]) medicine.

Other medical problems—The presence of other medical problems may affect the use of pilocarpine. Make sure you tell your doctor if you have any other medical problems, especially:

- Asthma or
- Eye disease or problems (other)—Pilocarpine may make the condition worse

Proper Use of This Medicine

To use the *eye drop form* of pilocarpine:

- First, wash your hands. Tilt the head back and, pressing your finger gently on the skin just beneath the lower eyelid, pull the lower eyelid away from the eye to make a space. Drop the medicine into this space. Let go of the eyelid and gently close the eyes. Do not blink. Keep the eyes closed and apply pressure to the inner corner of the eye with your finger for 1 or 2 minutes to allow the medicine to be absorbed by the eye.
- Immediately after using the eye drops, wash your hands to remove any medicine that may be on them.
- To keep the medicine as germ-free as possible, do not touch the applicator tip to any surface (including the eye). Also, keep the container tightly closed.

To use the *eye gel form* of pilocarpine:

- First, wash your hands. Tilt the head back and, pressing your finger gently on the skin just beneath the lower eyelid, pull the lower eyelid away from the eye to make a space. Squeeze a thin strip of gel into this space. A 1 1/2-cm (approximately 1/2-inch) strip of gel is usually enough, unless you have been told by your doctor to use a different amount. Let go of the eyelid and gently close the eyes. Keep the eyes closed for 1 or 2 minutes to allow the medicine to be absorbed by the eye.
- Immediately after using the eye gel, wash your hands to remove any medicine that may be on them.
- To keep the medicine as germ-free as possible, do not touch the applicator tip to any surface (including the eye). After using the eye gel, wipe the tip of the gel tube with a clean tissue and keep the tube tightly closed.

To use the *eye insert form* of pilocarpine:

- This medicine usually comes with patient directions. Read them carefully before using this medicine.
- If you think this medicine unit may be damaged, do not use it. If you have any questions about this, check with your health care professional.
- If the unit seems to be releasing too much medicine into your eye, remove it and replace with a new unit. If you have any questions about this, check with your doctor.

Use this medicine only as directed. Do not use more of it and do not use it more often than your doctor ordered. To do so may increase the chance of too much medicine being absorbed into the body and the chance of side effects.

Dosing—The dose of ophthalmic pilocarpine will be different for different patients. *Follow the doctor's orders or the directions on the label.* The following information includes only the average doses of ophthalmic pilocarpine. *If your dose is different, do not change it unless your doctor tells you to do so.*

The number of doses you use each day, the time allowed between doses, and the length of time you use the medicine depend on the medical problem for which you are using ophthalmic pilocarpine.

- For *eye drop* dosage form:
  - —For chronic glaucoma:
    - Adults and children—One drop one to four times a day.

—For acute angle-closure glaucoma:
- Adults and children—One drop every five to ten minutes for three to six doses. Then one drop every one to three hours until eye pressure is reduced.

- For *eye gel* dosage form:
  —For glaucoma:
  - Adults and teenagers—Use once a day at bedtime.
  - Children—Use and dose must be determined by your doctor.

- For *eye insert* dosage form:
  —For glaucoma:
  - Adults and children—Insert one ocular system every seven days.
  - Infants—Use and dose must be determined by your doctor.

Missed dose—
- For patients using the *eye drop form* of pilocarpine: If you miss a dose of this medicine, use it as soon as possible. However, if it is almost time for your next dose, skip the missed dose and go back to your regular dosing schedule. Do not double doses.
- For patients using the *eye gel form* of pilocarpine: If you miss a dose of this medicine, use it as soon as possible. However, if you do not remember the missed dose until the next day, skip the missed dose and go back to your regular dosing schedule. Do not double doses.
- For patients using the *eye insert form* of pilocarpine: If you forget to replace the eye insert at the proper time, replace it as soon as possible. Then go back to your regular dosing schedule.

Storage—To store this medicine:
- Keep out of the reach of children.
- Store away from heat and direct light.
- Store the eye system form of this medicine in the refrigerator. However, keep the medicine from freezing.
- Store the 5-gram size of the gel form of this medicine in the refrigerator. Store the 3.5-gram size at room temperature. Also, keep both sizes of the gel form of this medicine from freezing.
- Keep the solution form of this medicine from freezing.
- Do not keep outdated medicine or medicine no longer needed. Be sure that any discarded medicine is out of the reach of children.

Precautions While Using This Medicine

Your doctor should check your eye pressure at regular visits.

For patients using the *eye drop or gel form* of this medicine:
- For a short time after you use this medicine, your vision may be blurred or there may be a change in your near or far vision, especially at night. *Make sure your vision is clear before you drive, use machines, or do anything else that could be dangerous if you are not able to see well.*

For patients using the *eye insert form* of this medicine:
- For the first several hours after you insert this unit in the eye, your vision may be blurred or there may be a change in your near or far vision, especially at night. Therefore, insert this unit in the eye at bedtime, unless otherwise directed by your doctor. If this unit is inserted in the eye at any other time of the day, *make sure your vision is clear before you drive, use machines, or do anything else that could be dangerous if you are not able to see well.*

Side Effects of This Medicine

Along with its needed effects, a medicine may cause some unwanted effects. Although not all of these side effects may occur, if they do occur they may need medical attention.

Check with your doctor as soon as possible if any of the following side effects occur:

Symptoms of too much medicine being absorbed into the body

Increased sweating; muscle tremors; nausea, vomiting, or diarrhea; troubled breathing or wheezing; watering of mouth

Less common or rare

Eye pain

Other side effects may occur that usually do not need medical attention. These side effects may go away during treatment as your body adjusts to the medicine. However, check with your doctor if any of the following side effects continue or are bothersome:

More common

Blurred vision or change in near or far vision; decrease in night vision

Less common

Eye irritation; headache or browache

Other side effects not listed above may also occur in some patients. If you notice any other effects, check with your doctor.

Revised: 06/21/95

PILOCARPINE Systemic†

A commonly used brand name in the U.S. is Salagen.

†Not commercially available in Canada.

Description

Pilocarpine (pye-loe-KAR-peen) tablets are used to treat dryness of the mouth and throat caused by a decrease in the amount of saliva that may occur after radiation treatment for cancer of the head and neck. This medicine may help you speak without having to sip liquids. It may also help with chewing, tasting, and swallowing. This medicine may reduce your need for other oral comfort agents, such as hard candy, sugarless gum, or artificial saliva agents.

This medicine is available only with your doctor's prescription, in the following dosage form:

Oral

- Tablets (U.S.)

Before Using This Medicine

In deciding to use a medicine, the risks of using the medicine must be weighed against the good it will do. This is a decision you and your doctor will make. For pilocarpine, the following should be considered:

Allergies—Tell your doctor if you have ever had any unusual or allergic reaction to pilocarpine taken by mouth or used in the eye. Also tell your health care professional if you are allergic to any other substances, such as foods, preservatives, or dyes.

Pregnancy—Pilocarpine has not been studied in pregnant women. However, studies in animals have shown that pilocarpine, when given in very high doses, may cause birth defects. Before using this medicine, make sure your doctor knows if you are pregnant or if you may become pregnant.

Breast-feeding—It is not known whether pilocarpine passes into the breast milk. However, this medicine has not been reported to cause problems in nursing babies.

Children—Studies on this medicine have been done only in adult patients and there is no specific information comparing use of pilocarpine in children with use in other age groups.

Older adults—This medicine has been tested and has not been shown to cause different side effects or problems in older people than it does in younger adults.

Other medicines—Although certain medicines should not be used together at all, in other cases two different medicines may be used together even if an interaction might occur. In these cases, your doctor may want to change the dose, or other precautions may be necessary. When you are using pilocarpine, it is especially important that your health care professional know if you are taking any of the following:

- Amantadine (e.g., Symmetrel) or
- Anticholinergics (medicine for abdominal or stomach spasms or cramps) or
- Antidepressants (medicine for depression) or
- Antidyskinetics (medicine for Parkinson's disease or other conditions affecting control of muscles) or
- Antihistamines or
- Antipsychotics (medicine for mental illness) or
- Buclizine (e.g., Bucladin) or
- Carbamazepine (e.g., Tegretol) or
- Cyclizine (e.g., Marezine) or
- Cyclobenzaprine (e.g., Flexeril) or
- Disopyramide (e.g., Norpace) or
- Flavoxate (e.g., Urispas) or
- Ipratropium (e.g., Atrovent) or
- Meclizine (e.g., Antivert) or
- Methylphenidate (e.g., Ritalin) or
- Orphenadrine (e.g., Norflex) or
- Oxybutynin (e.g., Ditropen) or
- Procainamide (e.g., Pronestyl) or
- Promethazine (e.g., Phenergan) or
- Quinidine (e.g., Quinidex) or
- Trimeprazine (e.g., Temaril)—Pilocarpine may reduce the effect of these medicines or these medicines may reduce the effects of pilocarpine
- Antimyasthenics (ambenonium [e.g., Mytelase], neostigmine [e.g., Prostigmin], pyridostigmine [Mestinon]) or
- Beta-adrenergic blocking agents (acebutolol [e.g., Sectral], atenolol [e.g., Tenormin], betaxolol [e.g., Kerlone], carteolol [e.g., Cartrol], labetalol [e.g., Normodyne], metoprolol [e.g., Lopressor], nadolol [e.g., Corgard], oxprenolol [e.g., Trasicor], penbutolol [e.g., Levatol], pindolol [e.g., Visken], propranolol [e.g., Inderal], sotalol [e.g., Sotacor], timolol [e.g., Blocadren]) or
- Bethanecol (e.g., Urecholine) or
- Ophthalmic beta-adrenergic blocking agents (betaxolol [e.g., Betoptic], carteolol [e.g., Ocupress], levobunolol [e.g., Betagan], metipranolol [e.g., OptiPranolol], timolol [e.g., Timoptic])—Pilocarpine may increase the side effects of these medicines
- Carbachol (e.g., Isopto Carbachol) or
- Demecarium (e.g., Humorsol) or
- Echothiophate (e.g., Phospholine Iodide) or
- Isoflurophate (e.g., Floropryl) or
- Physostigmine (e.g., Isopto Eserine) or
- Pilocarpine (ophthalmic) (e.g., Isopto Carpine)—Pilocarpine may increase the effects of these ophthalmic glaucoma medicines

Other medical problems—The presence of other medical problems may affect the use of pilocarpine. Make sure you tell your doctor if you have any other medical problems, especially:

- Asthma, bronchitis, or other breathing problems, or
- Gallbladder problems or
- Glaucoma, angle closure, or
- Heart or blood vessel disease or
- Iritis (inflammation of the iris [colored part] of the eye) or
- Kidney problems or
- Mental problems—Pilocarpine may make the condition worse
- Retinal detachment, tendency for, or
- Retinal disease—Pilocarpine may increase the risk of a detached retina

Proper Use of This Medicine

Take this medicine only as directed. Do not take it more often and do not take a larger dose than directed. To do so may increase the chance of side effects.

It is important that you visit your dentist regularly even though this medicine may make your dry mouth feel better. Having a dry mouth condition makes you more likely to have dental and other mouth problems.

Dosing—The dose of pilocarpine will be different for different patients. *Follow your doctor's orders or the directions on the label.* The following information includes only the average dose of pilocarpine. *If your dose is different, do not change it* unless your doctor tells you to do so.

- For *oral* dosage form (tablets):
  - —For dryness of mouth and throat:
    - Adults—5 milligrams (mg) three times a day.
    - Children—Use and dose must be determined by your doctor.

Missed dose—If you miss a dose of this medicine, take it as soon as possible. However, if it is almost time for your next dose, skip the missed dose and go back to your regular dosing schedule. Do not double doses.

Storage—To store this medicine:
- *Keep out of the reach of children.*
- Store away from heat and direct light.
- Do not store in the bathroom, near the kitchen sink, or in other damp places. Heat or moisture may cause the medicine to break down.
- Do not keep outdated medicine or medicine no longer needed. Be sure that any discarded medicine is out of the reach of children.

Precautions While Using This Medicine

This medicine may cause difficulty in reading or other vision problems, especially at night. It may also cause some people to become dizzy or lightheaded. *Make sure you know how you react to this medicine before you drive, use machines, or do anything else that could be dangerous if you are not alert or able to see well.* If these reactions are especially bothersome, check with your doctor.

This medicine may cause you to sweat more than is usual. *If you do, it is important that you drink extra liquids to offset this sweating so you do not lose too much fluid and become dehydrated.* Check with your doctor if you are not sure how much extra liquid to drink or if you cannot drink as much liquid as you should.

Side Effects of This Medicine

Along with its needed effects, a medicine may cause some unwanted effects. Although not all of these side effects may occur, if they do occur they may need medical attention.

Check with your doctor as soon as possible if any of the following side effects occur:

Symptoms of overdose

Chest pain; confusion; diarrhea (continuing or severe); fainting; fast, slow, or irregular heartbeat (continuing or severe); headache (continuing or severe); nausea or vomiting (continuing or severe); shortness of breath or troubled breathing; stomach cramps or pain; tiredness or weakness (continuing or severe); trembling or shaking (continuing or severe); trouble seeing (continuing or severe)

Other side effects may occur that usually do not need medical attention. These side effects may go away during treatment as your body adjusts to the medicine. However, check with your doctor if any of the following side effects continue or are bothersome:

More common

Sweating

Less common or rare

Chills; diarrhea; dizziness; fast heartbeat; headache; holding more body water; indigestion; nausea; nosebleeds; passing urine more often; redness of face or feeling of warmth; runny nose; swelling of face, fingers, ankles, or feet; trembling or shaking; trouble swallowing; trouble seeing; unusual weak feeling; voice change; vomiting

Other side effects not listed above may also occur in some patients. If you notice any other effects, check with your doctor.

Developed: 01/17/95
Interim revision: 03/15/95

PIMOZIDE Systemic

A commonly used brand name in the U.S. and Canada is Orap.

Description

Pimozide (PIM-oh-zide) is used to treat the symptoms of Tourette's syndrome. It is meant only for patients with severe symptoms who cannot take or have not been helped by other medicine.

Pimozide works in the central nervous system to help control the vocal outbursts and uncontrolled, repeated movements of the body (tics) that interfere with normal life. It will not completely cure the tics, but will help to reduce their number and severity.

Pimozide may also be used for other conditions as determined by your doctor.

This medicine is available only with your doctor's prescription, in the following dosage form:

Oral
- Tablets (U.S. and Canada)

Before Using This Medicine

In deciding to use a medicine, the risks of taking the medicine must be weighed against the good it will do. This is a decision you and your doctor will make. For pimozide, the following should be considered:

Allergies—Tell your doctor if you have ever had any unusual or allergic reaction to pimozide, haloperidol, loxapine, molindone, phenothiazines, or thioxanthenes. Also tell your health care professional if you are allergic to any other substances, such as foods, preservatives, or dyes.

Pregnancy—Studies in rats and rabbits given more than the usual human dose of pimozide have shown fewer pregnancies, slowed development of the fetus, and toxic effects in the mother and fetus.

Breast-feeding—It is not known whether pimozide passes into breast milk.

Children—Children are especially sensitive to the effects of pimozide. This may increase the chance of side effects during treatment. Pimozide should not be used in children for any medical problem other than Tourette's syndrome.

Older adults—Constipation, dizziness or fainting, drowsiness, dryness of mouth, and trembling of the hands and fingers, and symptoms of tardive dyskinesia (such as rapid, worm-like movements of the tongue or any other uncontrolled movements of the mouth, tongue, or jaw, and/or arms and legs) may be especially likely to occur in the elderly, who are usually more sensitive than younger adults to the effects of pimozide.

Other medicines—Although certain medicines should not be used together at all, in other cases 2 different medicines may be used together even if an interaction might occur. In these cases, your doctor may want to change the dose, or other precautions may be necessary. When you are taking pimozide, it is especially important that your health care professional know if you are taking any of the following:

- Amoxapine (e.g., Asendin) or
- Methyldopa (e.g., Aldomet) or
- Metoclopramide (e.g., Reglan) or
- Metyrosine (e.g., Demser) or
- Promethazine (e.g., Phenergan) or
- Rauwolfia alkaloids (alseroxylon [e.g., Rauwiloid], deserpidine [e.g., Harmonyl], rauwolfia serpentina [e.g., Raudixin], reserpine [e.g., Serpasil]) or
- Trimeprazine (e.g., Temaril)—Taking these medicines with pimozide may increase the chance of serious side effects
- Amphetamines or
- Methylphenidate (e.g., Ritalin) or
- Pemoline (e.g., Cylert)—Taking these medicines with pimozide may cover up the cause of tics
- Anticholinergics (medicine for abdominal or stomach spasms or cramps)—Taking these medicines with pimozide may cause an increased chance of certain side effects, such as dryness of mouth, constipation, and unusual excitement
- Antipsychotics (medicine for mental illness) or
- Disopyramide (e.g., Norpace) or
- Maprotiline (e.g., Ludiomil) or
- Procainamide (e.g., Pronestyl) or
- Quinidine (e.g., Quinidex) or
- Tricyclic antidepressants (medicine for depression)—Taking these medicines with pimozide may increase the chance of serious effects on the rhythm of your heart
- Central nervous system (CNS) depressants—Using these medicines with pimozide may increase the CNS depressant effects

Other medical problems—The presence of other medical problems may affect the use of pimozide. Make sure you tell your doctor if you have any other medical problems, especially:

- Breast cancer (history of) or
- Heart disease—Pimozide may make the condition worse
- Kidney disease or
- Liver disease—Higher blood levels of pimozide may occur, increasing the chance of side effects
- Tics other than those caused by Tourette's syndrome—Pimozide should not be used because of the risk of serious side effects

Proper Use of This Medicine

Use pimozide only as directed by your doctor. Do not use more of it, do not use it more often, and do not use it for a longer time than your doctor ordered. To do so may increase the chance of side effects.

Dosing—The dose of pimozide will be different for different patients. *Follow your doctor's orders or the directions on the label.* The following information includes only the average doses of pimozide. *If your dose is different, do not change it* unless your doctor tells you to do so.

The number of tablets that you take depends on the strength of the medicine. Also, *the number of doses you take each day, the time allowed between doses, and the length of time you take the medicine depend on the medical problem for which you are using pimozide.*

- For *oral* dosage form (tablets):
  - —Adults and adolescents: To start, 1 to 2 milligrams (mg) a day. Your doctor may increase your dose if needed. However, the dose is usually not more than 10 mg a day.
  - —Children up to 12 years of age: Dose must be determined by the doctor.

Missed dose—If you miss a dose of this medicine, take it as soon as possible. Then take any remaining doses for that day at regularly spaced times. Do not double doses.

Storage—To store this medicine:

- Keep out of the reach of children.
- Store away from heat and direct light.
- Do not store in the bathroom, near the kitchen sink, or in other damp places. Heat or moisture may cause the medicine to break down.
- Do not keep outdated medicine or medicine no longer needed. Be sure that any discarded medicine is out of the reach of children.

Precautions While Using This Medicine

Your doctor should check your progress at regular visits, especially during the first few months of treatment with this medicine. The amount of pimozide you take may be changed often to meet the needs of your condition and to help avoid unwanted effects.

Do not suddenly stop taking this medicine without first checking with your doctor. Your doctor may want you to reduce gradually the amount you are taking before stopping completely. This will allow your body time to adjust and help to avoid worsening of your medical condition.

This medicine will add to the effects of alcohol and other CNS depressants (medicines that slow down the nervous system, possibly causing drowsiness). Some examples of CNS depressants are antihistamines or medicine for hay fever, other allergies, or colds; sedatives, tranquilizers, or sleeping medicine; prescription pain medicine or narcotics; barbiturates; medicine for seizures; muscle relaxants; or anesthetics, including some dental anesthetics. *Check with your doctor before taking any of the above while you are using this medicine.*

This medicine may cause some people to become drowsy or less alert or to have blurred vision or muscle stiffness, especially as the amount of medicine is increased. Even if you take pimozide at bedtime, you may feel drowsy or less alert on arising. *Make sure you know how you react to this medicine before you drive, use machines, or do anything else that could be dangerous if you are not alert or able to see well or if you do not have good muscle control.*

Although not a problem for many patients, dizziness, lightheadedness, or fainting may occur, especially when you get up from a sitting or lying position. Getting up slowly may help. If the problem continues or gets worse, check with your doctor.

Before having any kind of surgery, dental treatment, or emergency treatment, tell the medical doctor or dentist in charge that you are using this medicine. Taking pimozide together with medicines that are used during surgery or dental or emergency treatment may increase the CNS depressant effects.

Pimozide may cause dryness of the mouth. For temporary relief, use sugarless gum or candy, melt bits of ice in your mouth, or use a saliva substitute. However, if your mouth continues to feel dry for more than 2 weeks, check with your medical doctor or dentist. Continuing dryness of the mouth may increase the chance of dental disease, including tooth decay, gum disease, and fungus infections.

Side Effects of This Medicine

Along with its needed effects, pimozide can sometimes cause serious side effects. Tardive dyskinesia (a movement disorder) may occur and may not go away after you stop using the medicine. Signs of tardive dyskinesia include fine, worm-like movements of the tongue, or other uncontrolled movements of the mouth, tongue, cheeks, jaw, or arms and legs. Other serious but rare side effects may also occur. These include severe muscle stiffness, fever, unusual tiredness or weakness, fast heartbeat, difficult breathing, increased sweating, loss of bladder control, and seizures (neuroleptic malignant syndrome). *You and your doctor should discuss the good this medicine will do as well as the risks of taking it.*

Stop taking pimozide and get emergency help immediately if any of the following side effects occur:

Rare

Convulsions (seizures); difficult or fast breathing; fast heartbeat or irregular pulse; fever (high); high or low (irregular) blood pressure; increased sweating; loss of bladder control; muscle stiffness (severe); tiredness or weakness; unusually pale skin

Symptoms of overdose

Drowsiness or dizziness (severe); muscle trembling, jerking, or stiffness (severe); troubled breathing (severe); uncontrolled movements (severe); unusual tiredness or weakness (severe)

Check with your doctor as soon as possible if any of the following side effects occur:

More common

Difficulty in speaking or swallowing; loss of balance control; mask-like face; mood or behavior changes; restlessness or need to keep moving; shuffling walk; slowed movements; stiffness of arms and legs; trembling and shaking of fingers and hands

Less common or rare

Inability to move eyes; increased blinking or spasms of eyelid; lip smacking or puckering; muscle spasms, especially of the face, neck, or back; puffing of cheeks; rapid or worm-like movements of tongue; sore throat and fever; uncontrolled chewing movements; uncontrolled twisting movements of neck, trunk, arms, or legs; unusual bleeding or bruising; unusual facial expressions or body positions; yellow eyes or skin

Other side effects may occur that usually do not need medical attention. These side effects may go away during treatment as your body adjusts to the medicine. However, check with your doctor if any of the following side effects continue or are bothersome:

More common

Blurred vision or other vision problems; constipation; dizziness, lightheadedness, or fainting (especially when getting up from a lying or sitting position); drowsiness; dryness of mouth; skin rash, itching, or discoloration; swelling or soreness of breasts; unusual secretion of milk

Less common

Decreased sexual ability; diarrhea; headache; loss of appetite and weight; mental depression; nausea or vomiting; swelling of the face

After you stop using pimozide, it may still produce some side effects that need attention. During this period of time, check with your doctor as soon as possible if you notice any of the following side effects:

Lip smacking or puckering; puffing of cheeks; rapid or worm-like movements of the tongue; uncontrolled chewing movements; uncontrolled movements of the arms and legs

Other side effects not listed above may also occur in some patients. If you notice any other effects, check with your doctor.

Revised: 04/16/93

PIPERAZINE Systemic

A commonly used brand name in Canada is Entacyl.
Generic name product may be available in the U.S.

Description

Piperazine (PI-per-a-zeen) belongs to the family of medicines called anthelmintics (ant-hel-MIN-tiks). Anthelmintics are used in the treatment of worm infections.

Piperazine is used to treat:
- common roundworms (ascariasis) and
- pinworms (enterobiasis; oxyuriasis).

Piperazine works by paralyzing the worms. They are then passed in the stool.

Piperazine is available only with your doctor's prescription, in the following dosage forms:

Oral
- Granules for oral solution (Canada)
- Oral suspension (Canada)
- Tablets (U.S.)

Before Using This Medicine

In deciding to use a medicine, the risks of taking the medicine must be weighed against the good it will do. This is a decision you and your doctor will make. For piperazine, the following should be considered:

Allergies—Tell your doctor if you have ever had any unusual or allergic reaction to piperazine or ethylenediamine. Also tell your health care professional if you are allergic to any other substances, such as foods, preservatives, or dyes.

Pregnancy—Piperazine has not been studied in pregnant women. Piperazine has not been shown to cause birth defects or other problems in animal studies. However, piperazine, taken by mouth, may be changed within the body into a substance that may cause cancer. Before taking piperazine, make sure your doctor knows if you are pregnant or if you may become pregnant.

Breast-feeding—It is not known whether piperazine passes into breast milk. Although most medicines pass into breast milk in small amounts, many of them may be used safely while breast-feeding. Mothers who are taking this medicine and who wish to breast-feed should discuss this with their doctor.

Children—Children may be especially sensitive to the effects of piperazine. This may increase the chance of side effects during treatment.

Older adults—Many medicines have not been studied specifically in older people. Therefore, it may not be known whether they work exactly the same way they do in younger adults or if they cause different side effects or problems in older people. There is no specific information comparing use of piperazine in the elderly with use in other age groups.

Other medicines—Although certain medicines should not be used together at all, in other cases two different medicines may be used together even if an interaction might occur. In these cases, your doctor may want to change the dose, or other precautions may be necessary. When you are taking piperazine, it is especially important that your health care professional know if you are taking any of the following:

- Phenothiazines (acetophenazine [e.g., Tindal], chlorpromazine [e.g., Thorazine], fluphenazine [e.g., Prolixin], mesoridazine [e.g., Serentil], perphenazine[e.g., Trilafon], prochlorperazine [e.g., Compazine], promazine [e.g., Sparine], promethazine [e.g., Phenergan], thioridazine [e.g., Mellaril], trifluoperazine [e.g., Stelazine], triflupromazine [e.g., Vesprin], trimeprazine [e.g., Temaril])—Taking piperazine and a phenothiazine together may increase the risk of convulsions (seizures)
- Pyrantel (e.g., Antiminth)—Taking piperazine and pyrantel together may decrease the effects of piperazine

Other medical problems—The presence of other medical problems may affect the use of piperazine. Make sure you tell your doctor if you have any other medical problems, especially:

- Kidney disease or
- Liver disease—Patients with kidney or liver disease may have an increased chance of side effects
- Seizure disorder, especially a history of epilepsy—Piperazine may make the condition worse

Proper Use of This Medicine

No special preparations or other steps (for example, special diet, fasting, other medicines, laxatives, or enemas) are necessary before, during, or immediately after you take piperazine.

Piperazine may be taken with or without food or on a full or empty stomach. However, if your doctor tells you to take the medicine a certain way, take it exactly as directed.

For patients taking the *granules for oral solution form* of piperazine:
- Dissolve the contents of 1 packet of granules in 57 mL (about 2 ounces) of water, milk, or fruit juice.
- Be sure to drink all of the liquid to get the full dose of medicine.

Take this medicine only as directed. Do not take more of it and do not take it more often than your doctor ordered. To do so may increase the chance of serious side effects.

To help clear up your infection completely, *take this medicine in regularly spaced doses as ordered by your doctor.* In some infections, a second treatment with this medicine may be required to clear up the infection completely. *Do not miss any doses.*

For patients taking piperazine for *pinworms:*
- Pinworms may be easily passed from one person to another, especially among persons in the same household. Therefore, all household members may have to be treated at the same time to prevent their infection or reinfection.

Dosing—The dose of piperazine will be different for different patients. *Follow your doctor's orders or the directions on the label.* The following information includes only the average doses of piperazine. *If your dose is different, do not change it* unless your doctor tells you to do so.

The number of tablets or teaspoonfuls of solution or suspension of the medicine that you take depends on the strength of the medicine. Also, *the number of doses you take each day, the time allowed between doses, and the length of time you take the medicine depend on the medical problem for which you are taking piperazine.*

- For *granules for oral solution* dosage form:
  - —For common roundworms or pinworms:
    - Adults and teenagers—2 grams three times a day for one day. Treatment may need to be repeated in two weeks.
    - Children—Dose is based on age and/or body weight. Treatment may need to be repeated in two weeks.
      - —Up to 2 years of age: Dose must be determined by your doctor.
      - —2 to 8 years of age: 2 grams once a day for one day.
      - —8 to 14 years of age: 2 grams two times a day for one day.
- For *oral suspension* dosage form:
  - —For common roundworms or pinworms:
    - Adults and teenagers—1.8 grams every four hours for a total of three doses in one day. Treatment may need to be repeated in two weeks.
    - Children—Dose is based on age. Treatment may need to be repeated in two weeks.
      - —Up to 2 years of age: 600 milligrams (mg) every four hours for a total of three doses in one day.
      - —2 to 8 years of age: 1.2 grams every six hours for a total of two doses in one day.
      - —8 to 14 years of age: 1.2 grams every four hours for a total of three doses in one day.
- For *tablet* dosage form:
  - —For common roundworms:
    - Adults and teenagers—3.5 grams (piperazine hexahydrate) per day for two days in a row. Treatment may need to be repeated in one week.
    - Children—Dose is based on body weight and must be determined by your doctor. However, the usual dose is 75 mg (piperazine hexahydrate) per kilogram (34 mg per pound) of body weight per day for two days in a row. Treatment may need to be repeated in one week.
  - —For pinworms:
    - Adults and children—Dose is based on body weight and must be determined by your doctor. However, the usual dose is 65 mg (piperazine hexahydrate) per kilogram (29.5 mg per pound) of body weight per day for seven days in a row. Treatment may need to be repeated in one week.

Missed dose—If you miss a dose of this medicine, take it as soon as possible. However, if it is almost time for your next dose, skip the missed dose and go back to your regular dosing schedule. Do not double doses.

Storage—To store this medicine:
- Keep out of the reach of children. Overdose of piperazine is very dangerous in young children.
- Store away from heat and direct light.
- Do not store in the bathroom, near the kitchen sink, or in other damp places. Heat or moisture may cause the medicine to break down.
- Keep the liquid form of this medicine from freezing.
- Do not keep outdated medicine or medicine no longer needed. Be sure that any discarded medicine is out of the reach of children.

Precautions While Using This Medicine

It is important that your doctor check your progress after treatment. This is to make sure that the infection is cleared up completely, and to allow your doctor to check for any unwanted effects.

If your symptoms do not improve after you have taken this medicine for the full course of treatment, or if they become worse, check with your doctor.

For patients taking piperazine for *pinworms:*
- In some patients, pinworms may return after treatment with piperazine. Washing (not shaking) all bedding and nightclothes (pajamas) after treatment may help to prevent this.

Side Effects of This Medicine

Along with its needed effects, a medicine may cause some unwanted effects. Although not all of these side effects may occur, if they do occur they may need medical attention.

Check with your doctor immediately if any of the following side effects occur:

Rare

Blurring of vision; clumsiness; crawling or tingling feeling of the skin; fever; irregular, twisting movement, especially of the face, arms, and legs; joint pain; skin rash or itching

Other side effects may occur that usually do not need medical attention. These side effects may go away during treatment as your body adjusts to the medicine. However, check with your doctor if any of the following side effects continue or are bothersome:

Less common

Abdominal or stomach cramps or pain; diarrhea; dizziness; drowsiness; headache; muscle weakness; nausea or vomiting; tremors

Other side effects not listed above may also occur in some patients. If you notice any other effects, check with your doctor.

Revised: 11/21/96

PLAGUE VACCINE Systemic†

†Not commercially available in Canada.

Description

Plague vaccine is an active immunizing agent used to prevent infection by plague bacteria. It works by causing your body to produce its own protection (antibodies) against the disease.

Plague is a serious disease that can cause death. It is caused by a germ called *Yersinia pestis*, and is spread most often by infected rodents and by the bites of infected fleas. Plague may also be spread by close person-to-person contact with infected persons (such as occurs with persons living in the same household) who may carry plague bacteria in their nose and throat. Some infected persons do not appear to be sick, but they can still spread the germ to others.

If you are traveling to plague-infected areas of Africa, Asia, Latin America, or the western third of the United States, plague vaccine may help prevent plague infection. However, plague vaccine does not provide 100% protection. Therefore, it is very important to avoid contact with domestic and wild animals that may be infected, even if you have received the vaccine. To reduce your chance of getting plague from the bites of infected fleas, use insect repellent on exposed parts of your body, such as legs and ankles. Also apply DEET or another insecticide to clothes and outer bedding according to manufacturers' directions.

Plague vaccine is to be administered only by or under the supervision of a doctor. It is available in the following dosage form:

Parenteral
- Injection (U.S.)

Before Receiving This Vaccine

In deciding to use a medicine, the risks of taking the medicine must be weighed against the good it will do. This is a decision you and your doctor will make. For plague vaccine, the following should be considered:

Allergies—Tell your doctor if you have ever had any unusual or allergic reaction to plague vaccine. Also tell your health care professional if you are allergic to any other substances, such as foods, preservatives, or dyes.

Pregnancy—Studies on the effects of plague vaccine in pregnancy have not been done in either humans or animals.

Breast-feeding—This vaccine has not been reported to cause problems in nursing babies.

Children and teenagers—Studies on plague vaccine have been done only in adult patients between the ages of 18 and 61, and there is no specific information comparing use of plague vaccine in children and teenagers younger than 18 years of age with use in other age groups. Although there is no specific information comparing use of plague vaccine in children and teenagers younger than 18 years of age with use in other age groups, this vaccine is not expected to cause different side effects or problems in children or teenagers than it does in adults.

Older adults—Studies on plague vaccine have been done only in adult patients between the ages of 18 and 61, and there is no specific information comparing use of plague vaccine in persons 61 years of age and older with use in other age groups. Although there is no specific information comparing use of plague vaccine in the elderly with use in other age groups, this vaccine is not expected to cause different side effects or problems in older people than it does in younger adults.

Other medicines—Although certain medicines should not be used together at all, in other cases two different medicines may be used together even if an interaction might occur. In these cases, your doctor may want to change the dose, or other precautions may be necessary. Tell your health care professional if you are taking any other prescription or nonprescription (over-the-counter [OTC]) medicine.

Other medical problems—The presence of other medical problems may affect the use of plague vaccine. Make sure you tell your doctor if you have any other medical problems, especially:
- Previous sensitivity reaction to plague vaccine—Use of plague vaccine is not recommended
- Severe illness with fever—The symptoms of the condition may be confused with the side effects of the vaccine

Proper Use of This Vaccine

Dosing—The dose of plague vaccine will be different for different patients. The following information includes only the average doses of plague vaccine.
- For *injection* dosage form:
  —For prevention of plague:
  - Adults, teenagers, and children—The first dose, injected into a muscle, followed by a second dose 1 to 3 months later and a third dose 5 to 6 months after the second dose.

To get the best possible protection against plague, you should complete the vaccine dosing schedule before you travel to areas where you may be exposed to plague.

If you will be traveling regularly to parts of the world where plague is a problem, you should get a booster (repeat) dose of the vaccine every 6 months.

Side Effects of This Vaccine

Along with its needed effects, a vaccine may cause some unwanted effects. Although not all of these side effects may occur, if they do occur they may need medical attention.

Get emergency help immediately if any of the following side effects occur:

Rare
Difficulty in breathing or swallowing; hives; itching, especially of soles or palms; reddening of skin, especially

around ears; swelling of eyes, face, or inside of nose; unusual tiredness or weakness (sudden and severe)

Other side effects may occur that usually do not need medical attention. However, check with your doctor if any of the following side effects continue or are bothersome:

More common

Fever; general feeling of discomfort or illness; headache; joint pain; muscle pain; nausea and/or vomiting; pain, redness, or swelling at place of injection; swollen glands

Other side effects not listed above may also occur in some patients. If you notice any other effects, check with your doctor.

Developed: 02/23/96

PLICAMYCIN Systemic†

A commonly used brand name in the U.S. is Mithracin.

Another commonly used name is mithramycin.

†Not commercially available in Canada.

Description

Plicamycin (plye-ka-MYE-sin) belongs to the group of medicines known as antineoplastics. It may be used to treat certain types of cancer. It is also used to treat hypercalcemia or hypercalciuria (too much calcium in the blood or urine) that may occur with some types of cancer.

Plicamycin may also be used for other conditions as determined by your doctor.

Plicamycin is to be administered by or under the immediate care of your doctor. It is available only with a prescription, in the following dosage form:

Parenteral

- Injection (U.S.)

Before Receiving This Medicine

Plicamycin is a very strong medicine. In addition to its helpful effects in treating your medical problem, it has side effects that could be very serious. Before you receive this medicine, be sure that you have discussed its use with your doctor.

In deciding to use a medicine, the risks of taking the medicine must be weighed against the good it will do. This is a decision you and your doctor will make. For plicamycin, the following should be considered:

Allergies—Tell your doctor if you have ever had any unusual or allergic reaction to plicamycin. Also tell your health care professional if you are allergic to any other substances, such as foods, preservatives, or dyes.

Pregnancy—Plicamycin is not recommended for use during pregnancy. There is a possibility that it may be harmful to the fetus.

Breast-feeding—It is not known whether plicamycin passes into the breast milk.

Children—Studies on this medicine have not been done in children; however, plicamycin can cause serious side effects in any patient. Therefore, it is especially important that you discuss with the child's doctor the good that this medicine may do as well as the risks of using it.

Older adults—Many medicines have not been studied specifically in older people. Therefore, it may not be known whether they work exactly the same way they do in younger adults or if they cause different side effects or problems in older people. There is no specific information comparing use of plicamycin in the elderly with use in other age groups.

Other medicines—Although certain medicines should not be used together at all, in other cases two different medicines may be used together even if an interaction might occur. In these cases, your doctor may want to change the dose, or other precautions may be necessary. Tell your health care professional if you are taking *any* other medicines or are having x-ray treatments.

Other medical problems—The presence of other medical problems may affect the use of plicamycin. Make sure you tell your doctor if you have any other medical problems, especially:

- Bleeding problems—Use of plicamycin may increase the risk of bleeding
- Blood disease or
- Kidney disease or
- Liver disease—Use of plicamycin may make these conditions worse
- Chickenpox (including recent exposure) or
- Herpes zoster (shingles)—Use of plicamycin may make your reaction to either of these conditions worse

Proper Use of This Medicine

Plicamycin sometimes causes nausea, vomiting, and loss of appetite. However, it is very important that you continue to receive the medicine, even if you begin to feel ill. If you have any questions about this, check with your doctor.

Dosing—The dose of plicamycin will be different for different patients. The dose is based on body weight and will be determined by your doctor. *Follow your doctor's orders.* The following information includes only the average doses of plicamycin.

- For *injection* dosage form:
  - To treat cancer:
    - Adults and children—The dose that is used may depend on a number of things, including what the medicine is being used for, the patient's weight, and whether or not other medicines are also being taken. *If you are receiving plicamycin at home, follow your doctor's orders or the directions on the label.* If you have any questions about the proper dose of plicamycin, ask your doctor.

—To treat hypercalcemia or hypercalciuria (too much calcium in the blood or urine):
  - Adults—The dose is based on body weight and must be determined by your doctor. At first, the usual dose is 15 to 25 micrograms (mcg) per kg (6.8 to 11.4 mcg per pound) of body weight a day, injected slowly into a vein. The dose is given over a period of four to six hours once a day for three to four days. Your doctor may repeat the treatment if needed.
  - Children—Dose must be determined by your doctor.

Precautions After Receiving This Medicine

It is very important that your doctor check your progress daily while you are receiving plicamycin to make sure that this medicine does not cause unwanted effects.

Your doctor may want you to follow a low-calcium, low–vitamin D diet. If you have any questions about this, check with your doctor.

Do not take aspirin or large amounts of any other preparations containing aspirin, other salicylates, or acetaminophen without first checking with your doctor. These medicines may increase the effects of plicamycin.

While you are being treated with plicamycin, and after you stop treatment with it, *do not have any immunizations (vaccinations) without your doctor's approval.* Plicamycin may lower your body's resistance and there is a chance you might get the infection the immunization is meant to prevent. In addition, other persons living in your household should not take or have recently taken oral polio vaccine since there is a chance they could pass the polio virus on to you. Also, avoid other persons who have taken oral polio vaccine. Do not get close to them, and do not stay in the same room with them for very long. If you cannot take these precautions, you should consider wearing a protective face mask that covers the nose and mouth.

Plicamycin can lower the number of white blood cells in your blood temporarily, increasing the chance of getting an infection. It can also lower the number of platelets, which are necessary for proper blood clotting. If this occurs, there are certain precautions your doctor may ask you to take, especially when your blood count is low, to reduce the risk of infection of bleeding:

- If you can, avoid people with infections. *Check with your doctor immediately* if you think you are getting an infection or if you get a fever or chills.
- *Check with your doctor immediately* if you notice any unusual bleeding or bruising.
- Be careful when using a regular toothbrush, dental floss, or toothpick. Your medical doctor, dentist, or nurse may recommend other ways to clean your teeth and gums. Check with your medical doctor before having any dental work done.
- Do not touch your eyes or the inside of your nose unless you have just washed your hands and have not touched anything else in the meantime.
- Be careful not to cut yourself when you are using sharp objects such as a safety razor or fingernail or toenail cutters.
- Avoid contact sports or other situations where bruising or injury could occur.

Side Effects of This Medicine

Along with its needed effects, a medicine may cause some unwanted effects. Although not all of these side effects may occur, if they do occur they may need medical attention.

Check with your doctor or nurse immediately if any of the following side effects occur:

Less common

Muscle and abdominal cramps

Symptoms of overdose

Bloody or black, tarry stools; flushing or redness or swelling of face; nosebleed; skin rash or small red spots on skin; sore throat and fever; unusual bleeding or bruising; vomiting of blood; yellow eyes or skin

Other side effects may occur that usually do not need medical attention. These side effects may go away during treatment as your body adjusts to the medicine. However, check with your doctor if any of the following side effects continue or are bothersome:

More common

Diarrhea; irritation or soreness of mouth; loss of appetite; nausea or vomiting—may occur 1 to 2 hours after the injection is started and continue for 12 to 24 hours

Less common

Drowsiness; fever; headache; mental depression; pain, redness, soreness, or swelling at place of injection; unusual tiredness or weakness

After you stop using plicamycin, it may still produce some side effects that need attention. During this period of time check with your doctor if you notice any of the following side effects:

Bloody or black, tarry stools; nosebleed; sore throat and fever; unusual bleeding or bruising; vomiting of blood

Other side effects not listed above may also occur in some patients. If you notice any other effects, check with your doctor.

Additional Information

Once a medicine has been approved for marketing for a certain use, experience may show that it is also useful for other medical problems. Although this use is not included in product labeling, plicamycin is used in certain patients with the following medical condition:

- Paget's disease of the bone

Other than the above information, there is no additional information relating to proper use, precautions, or side effects for these uses.

Revised: 09/14/92
Interim revision: 08/02/94

PNEUMOCOCCAL VACCINE POLYVALENT Systemic

Some commonly used brand names are:

In the U.S.—
- Pneumovax 23
- Pnu-Imune 23

In Canada—
- Pneumovax 23

Description

Pneumococcal (NEU-mo-KOK-al) vaccine polyvalent is an active immunizing agent used to prevent infection by pneumococcal bacteria. It works by causing your body to produce its own protection (antibodies) against the disease.

The following information applies only to the polyvalent 23 pneumococcal vaccine. Other polyvalent pneumococcal vaccines may be available in countries other than the U.S.

Pneumococcal infection can cause serious problems, such as pneumonia, which affects the lungs; meningitis, which affects the brain; bacteremia, which is a severe infection in the blood; and possibly death. These problems are more likely to occur in older adults and persons with certain diseases or conditions that make them more susceptible to a pneumococcal infection or more apt to develop serious problems from a pneumococcal infection.

Immunization against pneumococcal disease is recommended for:

- older adults, especially those 50 years of age and older.
- adults and children 2 years of age or older with chronic illnesses.
- persons with human immunodeficiency virus (HIV) infection, either with or without symptoms.
- persons with spleen problems or without spleens and persons who are to have their spleens removed.
- persons with sickle cell disease.
- persons who are waiting for organ transplants.
- persons who will be treated with x-rays or cancer medicines.
- persons in nursing homes and orphanages.
- persons who will be traveling outside the U.S. and who have certain diseases or conditions that make them more susceptible to pneumococcal infection or more likely to develop serious problems from pneumococcal infection.
- persons who are bedridden.

Immunization against pneumococcal infection is not recommended for infants and children younger than 2 years of age, because these persons cannot produce enough antibodies to the vaccine to protect them against a pneumococcal infection.

Pneumococcal vaccine is usually given only once to each person. Additional injections are not given, except in special cases, because of the possibility of more frequent and more severe side effects.

This vaccine is to be administered only by or under the supervision of your doctor or other health care professional. It is available in the following dosage form:

Parenteral
- Injection (U.S. and Canada)

Before Receiving This Vaccine

In deciding to use a medicine, the risks of taking the medicine must be weighed against the good it will do. This is a decision you and your doctor will make. For pneumococcal vaccine, the following should be considered:

Allergies—Tell your doctor if you have ever had any unusual or allergic reaction to pneumococcal vaccine. Also tell your health care professional if you are allergic to any other substances, such as preservatives (especially thimerosal).

Pregnancy—Studies on effects in pregnancy have not been done in either humans or animals. However, if the vaccine is needed, it should be given after the first three months of pregnancy and only to women who have certain diseases or conditions that make them more susceptible to a pneumococcal infection or more likely to develop serious problems from a pneumococcal infection.

Breast-feeding—It is not known whether pneumococcal vaccine passes into the breast milk. Although most medicines pass into breast milk in small amounts, many of them may be used safely while breast-feeding. Mothers who are receiving this vaccine and who wish to breast-feed should discuss this with their doctor.

Children—Use of pneumococcal vaccine is not recommended in infants and children younger than 2 years of age. In children 2 years of age and older, this vaccine is not expected to cause different side effects or problems than it does in adults.

Older adults—Many medicines have not been studied specifically in older people. Therefore, it may not be known whether they work exactly the same way they do in younger adults. Although there is no specific information comparing use of pneumococcal vaccine in the elderly with use in other age groups, this vaccine is not expected to cause different side effects or problems in older people than it does in younger adults.

Other medicines—Although certain medicines should not be used together at all, in other cases two different medicines may be used together even if an interaction might occur. In these cases, your doctor may want to change the dose, or other precautions may be necessary. Before you receive pneumococcal vaccine, it is especially important that your health care professional know if you have received any of the following:

- Pneumococcal vaccine injection of any kind in the past—May increase the chance and severity of side effects

Other medical problems—The presence of other medical problems may affect the use of pneumococcal vaccine.

Make sure you tell your doctor if you have any other medical problems, especially:

- Severe illness with fever—The symptoms of the illness may be confused with possible side effects of the vaccine
- Thrombocytopenic purpura (blood disorder)—Use of pneumococcal vaccine may make the condition worse

Proper Use of This Vaccine

Dosing—The dose of pneumococcal vaccine will be different for different patients. The following information includes only the average doses of pneumococcal vaccine.

- For *injection* dosage form:
  —For prevention of pneumococcal pneumonia:
    - Adults and children 2 years of age and older—One dose injected under the skin or into a muscle.
    - Children up to 2 years of age—Use is not recommended.

Precautions After Receiving This Vaccine

If you have more than one doctor, be sure they all know that you have received pneumococcal vaccine polyvalent 23 so that they can put the information in your medical records. *This vaccine is usually given only once* to each person, except in special cases.

Side Effects of This Vaccine

Along with its needed effects, a medicine may cause some unwanted effects. Although not all of these side effects may occur, if they do occur they may need medical attention.

Get emergency help immediately if any of the following side effects occur:

Symptoms of allergic reaction
Difficulty in breathing or swallowing; hives; itching, especially of feet or hands; reddening of skin, especially around ears; swelling of eyes, face, or inside of nose; unusual tiredness or weakness (sudden and severe)

Check with your doctor as soon as possible if the following side effect occurs:

Rare
Fever over 102 °F (39 °C)

Other side effects may occur that usually do not need medical attention. However, check with your doctor if any of the following side effects continue or are bothersome:

More common
Redness, soreness, hard lump, swelling, or pain at place of injection

Less common or rare
Aches or pain in joints or muscles; fever of 101 °F (38.3 °C) or less; skin rash; swollen glands; unusual tiredness or weakness; vague feeling of bodily discomfort

Side effects may be more common and more severe if this is not the first time you have received pneumococcal vaccine. Check with your doctor as soon as possible if you do have a severe reaction.

Other side effects not listed above may also occur in some patients. If you notice any other effects, check with your doctor.

Revised: 07/12/94

PODOPHYLLUM Topical†

Some commonly used brand names in the U.S. are Podocon-25 and Podofin.

†Not commercially available in Canada.

Description

Podophyllum (pode-oh-FILL-um) is used to remove benign (not cancer) growths, such as certain kinds of warts. It works by destroying the tissue of the growth.

A few hours after podophyllum is applied to a wart, the wart becomes blanched (loses all color). In 24 to 48 hours, the medicine causes death of the tissue. After about 72 hours, the wart begins to slough or come off and gradually disappears.

Podophyllum is usually applied only in a doctor's office because it is a poison and can cause serious side effects if not used properly. However, your doctor may ask you to apply this medicine at home. If you do apply it at home, be sure you understand exactly how to use it.

Podophyllum is available only with your doctor's prescription, in the following dosage form:

Topical
- Topical solution (U.S.)

Before Using This Medicine

In deciding to use a medicine, the risks of using the medicine must be weighed against the good it will do. This is a decision you and your doctor will make. For podophyllum, the following should be considered:

Allergies—Tell your doctor if you have ever had any unusual or allergic reaction to podophyllum or benzoin. Also tell your health care professional if you are allergic to any other substances, such as preservatives or dyes.

Pregnancy—Topical podophyllum is absorbed through the skin. It should not be used during pregnancy, since it may cause birth defects or other harmful effects in the fetus.

Breast-feeding—Topical podophyllum is absorbed through the skin. However, it is not known whether topical podophyllum passes into breast milk. Although most medicines pass into breast milk in small amounts, many of them may be used safely while breast-feeding. Mothers who are using this medicine and who wish to breast-feed should discuss this with their doctor.

Children—Although there is no specific information comparing use of topical podophyllum in children with use in other age groups, this medicine is not expected to cause different side effects or problems in children than it does in adults.

Older adults—Many medicines have not been studied specifically in older people. Therefore, it may not be known whether they work exactly the same way they do in younger adults. Although there is no specific information comparing use of topical podophyllum in the elderly with use in other age groups, this medicine is not expected to cause different side effects or problems in older people than it does in younger adults.

Other medicines—Although certain medicines should not be used together at all, in other cases two different medicines may be used together even if an interaction might occur. In these cases, your doctor may want to change the dose, or other precautions may be necessary. Tell your health care professional if you are using any other prescription or nonprescription (over-the-counter [OTC]) medicine.

Other medical problems—The presence of other medical problems may affect the use of podophyllum. Make sure you tell your doctor if you have any other medical problems, especially:

- Crumbling or bleeding warts or warts that have recently had surgery on them—Using podophyllum on these warts may increase the chance of absorption of the medicine through the skin

Proper Use of This Medicine

Podophyllum is a poison. Keep it away from the mouth because it is harmful if swallowed.

Also, *keep podophyllum away from the eyes and other mucous membranes,* such as the inside of the nose, mouth, or vagina. This medicine may cause severe irritation. If you get some in your eyes, immediately flush the eyes with water for 15 minutes. If you get some on your normal skin, thoroughly wash the skin with soap and water to remove the medicine. However, if this medicine contains tincture of benzoin, it may be removed more easily from the skin by swabbing with rubbing alcohol.

This medicine may contain alcohol and therefore may be flammable. *Do not use near heat, near open flame, or while smoking.*

Use podophyllum only as directed. Do not use more of it, do not use it more often, and do not use it for a longer time than your doctor ordered. To do so may increase the chance of too much medicine being absorbed into the body and the chance of side effects.

Do not use podophyllum on moles or birthmarks. To do so may cause severe irritation.

Also, *do not apply this medicine to crumbling or bleeding warts or to warts that have recently had surgery on them.* To do so may increase the chance of absorption through the skin.

To use:

- Podophyllum can cause severe irritation of normal skin. Therefore, apply petrolatum around the affected area before you apply podophyllum, and/or apply talcum powder to the treated area immediately after you apply podophyllum. This is to prevent the medicine from spreading to the normal skin.
- Use a toothpick or a cotton-tipped or glass applicator to apply this medicine. Apply 1 drop at a time, allowing time for drying between drops, until the affected area is covered.
- After podophyllum is applied, allow it to remain on the affected area for 1 to 6 hours as directed by your doctor. Then, remove the medicine by thoroughly washing the affected area with soap and water. If this medicine contains tincture of benzoin, it may be removed more easily by swabbing the affected area with rubbing alcohol. However, this may be more irritating than washing with soap and water.
- Immediately after applying this medicine, wash your hands to remove any medicine that may be on them.

Dosing—The dose of topical podophyllum will be different for different patients. *Follow your doctor's orders or the directions on the label.* The following information includes only the average doses of topical podophyllum. *If your dose is different, do not change it unless your doctor tells you to do so.*

- For *topical solution* dosage form:
  - —For venereal warts:
    - Adults and children—Apply to the affected area(s) of the skin and leave on the skin for one to six hours. Treatment may be repeated every week for up to six weeks.
  - —For other warts or benign growths:
    - Adults and children—Apply to the affected area(s) of the skin once a day.

Missed dose—If you miss a dose of this medicine, apply it as soon as possible. Then go back to your regular dosing schedule.

Storage—To store this medicine:

- Keep out of the reach of children.
- Store away from heat and direct light.
- Do not store in the bathroom, near the kitchen sink, or in other damp places. Heat or moisture may cause the medicine to break down.
- Do not keep outdated medicine or medicine no longer needed. Be sure that any discarded medicine is out of the reach of children.

Side Effects of This Medicine

Along with its needed effects, a medicine may cause some unwanted effects. Although not all of these side effects may occur, if they do occur they may need medical attention.

Check with your doctor immediately if any of the following side effects occur:

Early symptoms of too much medicine being absorbed into the body

Abdominal or stomach pain; clumsiness or unsteadiness; confusion; decreased or loss of reflexes; diarrhea (may be severe and continuing); excitement, irritability, or nervousness; hallucinations (seeing, hearing, or feeling things that are not there); muscle weakness; nausea or vomiting; sore throat and fever; unusual bleeding or bruising

Late symptoms of too much medicine being absorbed into the body

Constipation; convulsions (seizures); difficult or painful urination; difficulty in breathing; dizziness or lightheadedness, especially when getting up from a lying or sitting position; drowsiness; fast heartbeat; numbness, tingling, pain, or weakness in hands or feet (may not occur for about 2 weeks after medicine is used); pain in upper abdomen or stomach (mild, dull, and continuing)

Also, check with your doctor as soon as possible if any of the following side effects occur:

Burning, redness, or other irritation of affected area; skin rash or itching

Other side effects not listed above may also occur in some patients. If you notice any other effects, check with your doctor.

Revised: 08/15/94; 08/19/97

POLIOVIRUS VACCINE Systemic

Some commonly used brand names are:

In the U.S.—

Ipol[2] Orimune[3]

Other commonly used names are:

enhanced-potency IPV[2]
IPV[1]
N-IPV[2]
OPV[3]
Sabin vaccine[3]
Salk vaccine[1]
TOPV[3]

Note: For quick reference, the following poliovirus vaccines are numbered to match the corresponding brand names.

This information applies to the following medicines:

1. Poliovirus Vaccine Inactivated‡§
2. Poliovirus Vaccine Inactivated Enhanced Potency‡§
3. Poliovirus Vaccine Live Oral§

‡Generic name product may also be available in the U.S.
§Generic name product may also be available in Canada.

Description

Poliovirus (POE-lee-oh VYE-russ) vaccine is an active immunizing agent used to prevent poliomyelitis (polio). It works by causing your body to produce its own protection (antibodies) against the virus that causes polio.

There are two types of polio vaccine that are given by injection, poliovirus vaccine inactivated (IPV) and poliovirus vaccine inactivated enhanced potency (enhanced-potency IPV). The type of vaccine that is given by mouth is called poliovirus vaccine live oral (OPV).

Polio is a very serious infection that causes paralysis of the muscles, including the muscles that enable you to walk and breathe. A polio infection may leave a person unable to breathe without the help of an iron lung, unable to walk without leg braces, or confined to a wheelchair. There is no cure for polio.

Immunization against polio is recommended for all infants from age 6 to 12 weeks, all children, all adolescents up to 18 years of age, and certain adults, including:

- Persons traveling outside the U.S. to countries where polio is uncontrolled, whether or not they have been vaccinated against polio in the past.
- All adults who may be exposed to polio, whether or not they have been vaccinated against polio in the past.
- Adults who have not been vaccinated or who have not had the complete series of vaccinations against polio and who live in households in which children are to be given the oral polio vaccine (OPV).
- Employees in day-care centers and group homes for children, such as orphanages.
- Employees in medical facilities, such as hospitals and doctors' offices.
- Laboratory workers handling samples that may contain polioviruses.

Immunization against polio is not recommended for infants younger than 6 weeks of age, because antibodies they received from their mothers before birth may interfere with the effectiveness of the vaccine. Infants who were immunized against polio before 6 weeks of age should receive the complete series of polio immunization.

This vaccine is to be administered only by or under the supervision of your doctor or other health care professional. It is available in the following dosage forms:

Oral

- Oral solution (U.S. and Canada)

Parenteral

- Injection (U.S. and Canada)

Before Receiving This Vaccine

For a while after you are immunized, there is a very small risk (1 in 5 million) that any persons living in your household who have not yet been immunized against polio or who have or had an immune deficiency condition may develop poliomyelitis (polio) from being around you. Talk to your doctor if you have any questions about this.

In deciding to use a medicine, the risks of taking the medicine must be weighed against the good it will do. This is a decision you and your doctor will make. For polio vaccine, the following should be considered:

Allergies—Tell your doctor if you have ever had any unusual or allergic reaction to polio vaccine or to neomycin, penicillin, polymyxin B, or streptomycin. The polio vaccines available in the U.S. may contain neomycin, polymyxin B, and/or streptomycin. The polio vaccines available in Canada may contain neomycin, penicillin, polymyxin B, and/or streptomycin. Also tell your health

care professional if you are allergic to any other substances, such as foods, preservatives, or dyes.

Diet—Make certain your health care professional knows if you are on any special diet, such as a low-sugar diet, because the oral solution form of polio vaccine may be given to you on a sugar cube.

Pregnancy—Studies on effects in pregnancy have not been done in either humans or animals. However, this vaccine has not been shown to cause birth defects or other problems in humans. Although it is not recommended for all pregnant women, polio vaccine is given to pregnant women at great risk of catching polio.

Breast-feeding—Polio vaccine has not been reported to cause problems in nursing babies.

Children—Use is not recommended for infants up to 6 weeks of age. For infants and children 6 weeks of age and older, polio vaccine is not expected to cause different side effects or problems than it does in adults.

Older adults—Many medicines have not been studied specifically in older people. Therefore, it may not be known whether they work exactly the same way they do in younger adults. Although there is no specific information comparing use of polio vaccine in the elderly with use in other age groups, this vaccine is not expected to cause different side effects or problems in older persons than it does in younger adults.

Other medicines—Although certain medicines should not be used together at all, in other cases two different medicines may be used together even if an interaction might occur. In these cases, your doctor may want to change the dose, or other precautions may be necessary. Before you receive polio vaccine, it is especially important that your health care professional know if you are receiving or have received any of the following:

- Cancer medicines or
- Corticosteroids (e.g., cortisone-like medicines) or
- Radiation therapy—May reduce the useful effect of the vaccine

Other medical problems—The presence of other medical problems may affect the use of polio vaccine. Make sure you tell your doctor if you have any other medical problems, especially:

- Diarrhea or
- Virus infection or
- Vomiting—The condition may reduce the useful effect of the vaccine
- Fever or
- Illness (moderate or severe) or
- Weakness (severe)—The symptoms of the condition may be confused with possible side effects of the vaccine
- Immune deficiency condition (or family history of)—The condition may increase the chance of side effects of the vaccine

Proper Use of This Vaccine

Dosing—The dose of polio vaccine will be different for different patients. The following information includes only the average doses of polio vaccine.

- For prevention of polio:
  - —For *enhanced-potency IPV injection* dosage form:
    - Adults and children 6 years of age and older—One dose is given at your first visit, then a second dose is given four to eight weeks later. A third dose is given six to twelve months after the second dose. The doses are injected under the skin.
    - Infants and children 6 weeks to 6 years of age—One dose is given at your first visit, then a second dose is given four to eight weeks later. A third dose is given six to twelve months after the second dose. A booster dose is given at four to six years of age only if the third dose was given before the child's fourth birthday. The doses are injected under the skin.
  - —For *IPV injection* dosage form:
    - Adults and children 18 years of age and older—One dose is given every four to eight weeks for a total of three doses. A fourth dose is given six to twelve months after the third dose. The doses are injected under the skin.
    - Children 6 weeks to 18 years of age—One dose is given every four to eight weeks for a total of three doses. A fourth dose is given six to twelve months after the third dose. A booster dose is given at four to six years of age only if the fourth dose was given before the child's fourth birthday. Booster doses are given every five years until the child is eighteen years of age. The doses are injected under the skin.
  - —For *OPV oral* dosage form:
    - Adults and children 18 years of age and older—Use and dose must be determined by your doctor.
    - Infants and children 6 weeks to 18 years of age—One dose is given at your first visit, then a second dose is given six to eight weeks later. A third dose is given eight to twelve months after the second dose. A booster dose is given at four to six years of age only if the third dose was given before the child's fourth birthday. The doses are taken by mouth.

Precautions After Receiving This Vaccine

Tell your doctor that you have received this vaccine if you are to receive any other live virus vaccines within 1 month after receiving this vaccine.

Side Effects of This Vaccine

In very rare instances (approximately 1 case in 3.2 million doses), healthy persons who have taken the oral vaccine (OPV) and healthy persons who are close contacts of adults or children who have taken OPV have been infected by the polio virus and have become paralyzed. No paralysis caused by polio infection has occurred with the injected vaccine (IPV) since 1955.

Along with its needed effects, a vaccine may cause some unwanted effects. Although not all of these side effects

may occur, if they do occur they may need medical attention.

Get emergency help immediately if any of the following side effects occur:

Symptoms of allergic reaction

Difficulty in breathing or swallowing; hives; itching, especially of feet or hands; reddening of skin, especially around ears; swelling of eyes, face, or inside of nose; unusual tiredness or weakness (sudden and severe)

Other side effects may occur that usually do not need medical attention. However, check with your doctor if any of the following side effects continue or are bothersome:

Less common

Fever over 101.3 °F (38.5 °C) (with injection); itching or skin rash (with injection); redness, soreness, hard lump, tenderness, or pain at the place of injection (with injection)

Other side effects not listed above may also occur in some patients. If you notice any other effects, check with your doctor.

Revised: 07/12/94

POLYETHYLENE GLYCOL AND ELECTROLYTES Local

Some commonly used brand names are:

In the U.S.—

Co-Lav
Colovage
Colyte
Colyte-flavored
Go-Evac
GoLYTELY
NuLYTELY
NuLYTELY, Cherry Flavor
OCL

In Canada—

Colyte
GoLYTELY
Klean-Prep
Peglyte

Description

The polyethylene glycol (pol-ee-ETH-i-leen GLYE-col) (PEG) and electrolytes solution is used to clean the colon (large bowel or lower intestine) before certain tests or surgery of the colon. The PEG-electrolyte solution is usually taken by mouth. However, sometimes it is given in the hospital through a nasogastric tube (a tube inserted through the nose).

The PEG-electrolyte solution acts like a laxative. It causes liquid stools or mild diarrhea. In this way, it flushes all solid material from the colon, so the doctor can have a clear view of the colon.

The PEG-electrolyte solution is available only with your doctor's prescription. It is available in the following dosage forms:

Oral

- Oral solution (U.S. and Canada)
- Powder for oral solution (U.S. and Canada)

Before Using This Medicine

In deciding to use a medicine, the risks of taking the medicine must be weighed against the good it will do. This is a decision you and your doctor will make. For the PEG-electrolyte solution, the following should be considered:

Allergies—Tell your doctor if you have ever had any unusual or allergic reaction to PEG. Also tell your health care professional if you are allergic to any other substances, such as foods, preservatives, or dyes.

Pregnancy—Studies on effects in pregnancy have not been done in either humans or animals. Before taking the PEG-electrolyte solution or having a colon examination, make sure your doctor knows if you are pregnant.

Breast-feeding—It is not known whether PEG-electrolyte solution passes into breast milk. Although most medicines pass into breast milk in small amounts, many of them may be used safely while breast-feeding. Mothers who are taking this medicine and who wish to breast-feed should discuss this with their doctor.

Children—Although there is no specific information comparing use of PEG-electrolyte solution in children with use in other age groups, this medicine is not expected to cause different side effects or problems in children than it does in adults.

Older adults—This medicine has been tested and has not been shown to cause different side effects or problems in older people than it does in younger adults.

Other medicines—Although certain medicines should not be used together at all, in other cases two different medicines may be used together even if an interaction might occur. In these cases, your doctor may want to change the dose, or other precautions may be necessary. Tell your health care professional if you are taking any of the following:

- Any other oral medicines—Any medicines taken within 1 hour of the PEG-electrolyte solution may be flushed from the body and not have an effect

Other medical problems—The presence of other medical problems may affect the use of PEG-electrolyte solution. Make sure you tell your doctor if you have any other medical problems, especially:

- Blockage or obstruction of the intestine or
- Paralytic ileus or
- Perforated bowel or
- Toxic colitis or
- Toxic megacolon—PEG-electrolyte solution may make these conditions worse; in some cases the colon may rip open or tear

Proper Use of This Medicine

Your doctor may have special instructions for you, depending on the type of test you are going to have. If you have not received such instructions or if you do not understand them, check with your doctor in advance.

Take the PEG-electrolyte solution exactly as directed. Otherwise, the test you are going to have may not work and may have to be done again.

It will take close to 3 hours to drink all of the PEG-electrolyte solution. The first bowel movement may start an hour or so after you start drinking the solution. *Continue drinking all the solution to get the best results,* unless otherwise directed by your doctor.

Do not eat anything for at least 3 hours before taking the PEG-electrolyte solution. If you do so, the colon may not get completely clean. If you are drinking the PEG-electrolyte solution the evening before the test, you may drink clear liquids (e.g., water, ginger ale, decaffeinated cola, decaffeinated tea, broth, gelatin) up until the time of the test. However, check first with your doctor.

For patients *using the powder form of this medicine:*
- *The powder must be mixed with water before it is used.* Add lukewarm water to the fill mark on the bottle.
- *Shake well* until all the ingredients are dissolved.
- Do not add any other ingredients, such as flavoring, to the solution.
- After you mix the solution, you must use it within 48 hours.

Dosing—*Follow your doctor's orders or the directions on the label.* The following information includes only the usual amount taken of PEG-electrolyte solution. *If your dose is different, do not change it* unless your doctor tells you to do so:
- For cleaning the colon:
  - —For *oral* dosage forms (oral solution and powder for oral solution):
    - Adults and teenagers—Drink one full glass (8 ounces) of the PEG-electrolyte solution *rapidly* every ten minutes. If you sip small amounts of the solution, it will not work as well.
    - Children—The amount of PEG-electrolyte solution taken is based on body weight and must be determined by your doctor. It is usually 25 to 40 milliliters (mL) per kilogram (kg) (11.3 to 18.2 mL per pound) of body weight per hour.

Storage—To store this medicine:
- Keep out of the reach of children.
- Store away from heat and direct light.
- Store the solution in the refrigerator to improve the taste. However, keep the medicine from freezing.
- Do not keep any leftover solution. Be sure that any discarded medicine is out of the reach of children.

Side Effects of This Medicine

Along with its needed effects, a medicine may cause some unwanted effects. Although not all of these side effects may occur, if they do occur they may need medical attention.

Check with your doctor as soon as possible if the following side effect occurs:

Rare
Skin rash

Other side effects may occur that usually do not need medical attention. These side effects may go away as your body adjusts to the medicine. However, check with your health care professional if any of the following side effects continue or are bothersome:

More common
Bloating; nausea

Less common
Abdominal or stomach cramps; irritation of the anus; vomiting

Other side effects not listed above may also occur in some patients. If you notice any other effects, check with your health care professional.

Revised: 08/15/95

POTASSIUM IODIDE Systemic

Some commonly used brand names are:

In the U.S.—
Pima
Generic name product may also be available.

In Canada—
Thyro-Block*

Other commonly used names are KI and SSKI.

*Not commercially available in the U.S.; however, potassium iodide tablets are available to government and public health organizations for use in radiation emergencies.

Description

Potassium iodide (poe-TAS-ee-um EYE-oh-dide) is used to treat overactive thyroid and to protect the thyroid gland from the effects of radiation from inhaled or swallowed radioactive iodine. It may be used before and after administration of medicine containing radioactive iodine or after accidental exposure to radioactive iodine (for example, from nuclear power plant accidents that involved release of radioactivity to the environment). It may also be used for other problems as determined by your doctor.

Potassium iodide is taken by mouth. It may be taken as an oral solution, syrup, uncoated tablet, or enteric-coated tablet. However, the enteric-coated tablet form may cause serious side effects and its use is generally not recommended.

Some brands of the oral solution are available without a prescription. Use them only as directed by state or local public health authorities in case of a radiation emergency. Other forms and strengths of potassium iodide are available only with your doctor's prescription.

Potassium iodide is available in the following dosage forms:

Oral
- Enteric-coated tablets (U.S.)
- Oral solution (U.S.)
- Syrup (U.S.)
- Tablets (Canada)

Before Using This Medicine

In deciding to use a medicine, the risks of taking the medicine must be weighed against the good it will do. This is a decision you and your doctor will make. For potassium iodide, the following should be considered:

Allergies—Tell your doctor if you have ever had any unusual or allergic reaction to potassium iodide, iodine, or iodine-containing foods. Also tell your health care professional if you are allergic to any substances, such as foods, preservatives, or dyes.

Pregnancy—Taking potassium during pregnancy may cause thyroid problems or goiter in the newborn infant.

Breast-feeding—Potassium iodide passes into the breast milk and may cause skin rash and thyroid problems in nursing babies.

Children—Potassium iodide may cause skin rash and thyroid problems in infants.

Older adults—Many medicines have not been studied specifically in older people. Therefore, it may not be known whether they work exactly the same way they do in younger adults. Although there is no specific information comparing use of potassium iodide in the elderly with use in other age groups, this medicine is not expected to cause different side effects or problems in older people than in younger adults.

Other medicines—Although certain medicines should not be used together at all, in other cases two different medicines may be used together even if an interaction might occur. In these cases, your doctor may want to change the dose, or other precautions may be necessary. When you are taking potassium iodide, it is especially important that your health care professional know if you are taking any of the following:

- Amiloride (e.g., Midamor) or
- Spironolactone (e.g., Aldactone) or
- Triamterene (e.g., Dyrenium)—Use of these medicines with potassium iodide may increase the amount of potassium in the blood and increase the chance of side effects
- Antithyroid agents (medicine for overactive thyroid) or
- Lithium (e.g., Lithane)—Use of these medicines with potassium iodide may increase the chance of side effects

Other medical problems—The presence of other medical problems may affect the use of potassium iodide. Make sure you tell your doctor if you have any other medical problems, especially:

- High blood levels of potassium (hyperkalemia) or
- Myotonia congenita or
- Tuberculosis—Potassium iodine may make these conditions worse
- Kidney disease—May cause an increase of potassium in the blood
- Overactive thyroid (unless you are taking this medicine for this medical problem)—Prolonged use of potassium iodine may be harmful to the thyroid gland

Proper Use of This Medicine

For patients taking this medicine for *radiation exposure:*

- Take this medicine only when directed to do so by state or local public health authorities.
- Take this medicine once a day for 10 days, unless otherwise directed by public health authorities. *Do not take more of it and do not take it more often than directed.* Taking more of the medicine will not protect you better and may result in a greater chance of side effects.

If potassium iodide upsets your stomach, *take it after meals or with food or milk* unless otherwise directed by your doctor. If stomach upset (nausea, vomiting, stomach pain, or diarrhea) continues, check with your doctor.

For patients taking the *oral solution form* of this medicine:

- This medicine is to be taken by mouth even if it comes in a dropper bottle.
- Do not use if solution turns brownish yellow.
- Take potassium iodide in a full glass (8 ounces) of water or in fruit juice, milk, or broth to improve the taste and lessen stomach upset. Be sure to drink all of the liquid to get the full dose of medicine.
- If crystals form in potassium iodide solution, they may be dissolved by warming the closed container of solution in warm water and then gently shaking the container.

For patients taking the *uncoated tablet form* of this medicine:

- Before taking, dissolve each tablet in 1/2 glass (4 ounces) of water or milk. Be sure to drink all of the liquid to get the full dose of medicine.

Dosing—The dose of potassium iodide will be different for different patients. *Follow your doctor's orders or the directions on the label.* The following information includes only the average doses of potassium iodide. *If your dose is different, do not change it* unless your doctor tells you to do so.

The amount of solution or syrup or the number of tablets you take depends on the strength of the medicine. Also, *the number of doses you take each day, the time allowed between doses, and the length of time you take the medicine depend on the medical problem for which you are taking potassium iodide.*

- For *solution* dosage form:
  - —To treat overactive thyroid (hyperthyroidism):
    - Adults and teenagers—250 milligrams (mg) (0.25 milliliters [mL]) three times a day.
    - Children—Use and dose must be determined by your doctor.

—To protect the thyroid gland against radiation exposure:
- Adults and teenagers—100 to 150 mg (0.1 to 0.15 mL) twenty-four hours before receiving or being exposed to radioactive iodine. Then, once a day for three to ten days after receiving or being exposed to radioactive iodine.
- Children up to 1 year of age—65 mg (0.065 mL) once a day for ten days after receiving or being exposed to radioactive iodine.
- Children 1 year of age or older—130 mg (0.13 mL) once a day for ten days after receiving or being exposed to radioactive iodine.

- For *syrup* dosage form:

—To protect the thyroid gland against radiation exposure:
- Adults and teenagers—100 to 150 mg (about 1.5 to 2.3 mL) twenty-four hours before receiving or being exposed to radioactive iodine. Then, once a day for three to ten days after receiving or being exposed to radioactive iodine.
- Children up to 1 year of age—65 mg (1 mL) once a day for ten days after receiving or being exposed to radioactive iodine.
- Children 1 year of age or older—130 mg (2 mL) once a day for ten days after receiving or being exposed to radioactive iodine.

- For *tablet* dosage form:

—To protect the thyroid gland against radiation exposure:
- Adults and teenagers—100 to 150 mg twenty-four hours before receiving or being exposed to radioactive iodine. Then, once a day for three to ten days after receiving or being exposed to radioactive iodine.
- Children up to 1 year of age—65 mg once a day for ten days after receiving or being exposed to radioactive iodine.
- Children 1 year of age and older—130 mg a day for ten days after receiving or being exposed to radioactive iodine.

Missed dose—If you miss a dose of this medicine, take it as soon as possible. However, if it is almost time for your next dose, skip the missed dose and go back to your regular dosing schedule. Do not double doses.

Storage—To store this medicine:
- Keep out of the reach of children.
- Store away from heat and direct light.
- Do not store the tablet form of this medicine in the bathroom, near the kitchen sink, or in other damp places. Heat or moisture may cause the medicine to break down.
- Keep the oral liquid forms of this medicine from freezing. Do not refrigerate.
- Do not keep outdated medicine or medicine no longer needed. Be sure that any discarded medicine is out of the reach of children.

Precautions While Using This Medicine

Your doctor should check your progress at regular visits to make sure that this medicine does not cause unwanted effects.

For patients on a low-potassium diet:
- *This medicine contains potassium.* Check with your health care professional before you take this medicine.

Side Effects of This Medicine

Along with its needed effects, a medicine may cause some unwanted effects. Although not all of these side effects may occur, if they do occur they may need medical attention. When this medicine is used for a short time at low doses, side effects usually are rare.

Check with your doctor as soon as possible if any of the following side effects occur:

Less common

Hives; joint pain; swelling of arms, face, legs, lips, tongue, and/or throat; swelling of lymph glands

With long-term use

Burning of mouth or throat; confusion; headache (severe); increased watering of mouth; irregular heartbeat; metallic taste; numbness, tingling, pain or weakness in hands or feet; soreness of teeth and gums; sores on skin; symptoms of head cold; unusual tiredness; weakness or heaviness of legs

Other side effects may occur that usually do not need medical attention. These side effects may go away during treatment as your body adjusts to the medicine. However, check with your doctor if any of the following side effects continue or are bothersome:

Less common

Diarrhea; nausea or vomiting; stomach pain

Other side effects not listed above may also occur in some patients. If you notice any other effects, check with your doctor.

Additional Information

Once a medicine has been approved for marketing for a certain use, experience may show that it is also useful for other medical problems. Although these uses are not included in product labeling, potassium iodide is used in certain patients with the following medical conditions:
- To prepare the thyroid gland before a thyroid operation
- Iodine deficiency
- Certain skin conditions caused by fungus

In addition to the above information, for patients taking this medicine for a fungus infection:
- *Keep taking it for the full course of treatment,* even if you begin to feel better after a few days. This will help clear up your infection completely. *Do not miss any doses.*

Other than the above information, there is no additional information relating to proper use, precautions, or side effects for these uses.

Revised: 04/14/92
Interim revision: 08/26/94

POTASSIUM SUPPLEMENTS Systemic

Some commonly used brand names are:

In the U.S.—

Cena-K[5]
Effer-K[4]
Gen-K[5]
Glu-K[6]
K-8[5]
K+ 10[5]
Kaochlor 10%[5]
Kaochlor S-F 10%[5]
Kaon[6]
Kaon-Cl[5]
Kaon-Cl-10[5]
Kaon-Cl 20% Liquid[5]
Kato[5]
Kay Ciel[5]
Kaylixir[6]
K+ Care[5]
K+ Care ET[2]
K-Dur[5]
K-Electrolyte[2]
K-G Elixir[6]
K-Ide[2,5]
K-Lease[5]
K-Lor[5]
Klor-Con 8[5]
Klor-Con 10[5]
Klor-Con/EF[2]
Klor-Con Powder[5]
Klor-Con/25 Powder[5]
Klorvess[3]
Klorvess Effervescent Granules[3]
Klorvess 10% Liquid[5]
Klotrix[5]
K-Lyte[2]
K-Lyte/Cl[3]
K-Lyte/Cl 50[3]
K-Lyte/Cl Powder[5]
K-Lyte DS[4]
K-Norm[5]
Kolyum[7]
K-Sol[5]
K-Tab[5]
K-Vescent[2]
Micro-K[5]
Micro-K 10[5]
Micro-K LS[5]
Potasalan[5]
Rum-K[5]
Slow-K[5]
Ten-K[5]
Tri-K[9]
Twin-K[8]

In Canada—

Apo-K[5]
K-10[5]
Kalium Durules[5]
Kaochlor-10[5]
Kaochlor-20[5]
Kaon[6]
KCL 5%[5]
K-Dur[5]
K-Long[5]
K-Lor[5]
K-Lyte[2]
K-Lyte/Cl[5]
K-Med 900[5]
Micro-K[5]
Micro-K 10[5]
Neo-K[3]
Potassium-Rougier[6]
Potassium-Sandoz[3]
Roychlor-10%[5]
Slow-K[5]

Another commonly used name for trikates is potassium triplex.

Note: For quick reference, the following potassium supplements are numbered to match the corresponding brand names.

This information applies to the following:

1. Potassium Acetate (poe-TAS-ee-um AS-a-tate)‡†
2. Potassium Bicarbonate (bi-KAR-bo-nate)‡
3. Potassium Bicarbonate and Potassium Chloride (KLOR-ide)
4. Potassium Bicarbonate and Potassium Citrate (SIH-trayt)†
5. Potassium Chloride‡§
6. Potassium Gluconate (GLOO-ko-nate)‡
7. Potassium Gluconate and Potassium Chloride†
8. Potassium Gluconate and Potassium Citrate†
9. Trikates (TRI-kates)†

†Not commercially available in Canada.
‡Generic name product may be available in the U.S.
§Generic name product may be available in Canada.

Description

Potassium is needed to maintain good health. Although a balanced diet usually supplies all the potassium a person needs, potassium supplements may be needed by patients who do not have enough potassium in their regular diet or have lost too much potassium because of illness or treatment with certain medicines.

There is no evidence that potassium supplements are useful in the treatment of high blood pressure.

Lack of potassium may cause muscle weakness, irregular heartbeat, mood changes, or nausea and vomiting.

Injectable potassium is administered only by or under the supervision of your doctor. Some forms of oral potassium may be available in stores without a prescription. Since too much potassium may cause health problems, you should take potassium supplements only if directed by your doctor. Potassium supplements are available with your doctor's prescription in the following dosage forms:

Oral

Potassium Bicarbonate
- Tablets for solution (U.S. and Canada)

Potassium Bicarbonate and Potassium Chloride
- Powder for solution (U.S. and Canada)
- Tablets for solution (U.S. and Canada)

Potassium Bicarbonate and Potassium Citrate
- Tablets for solution (U.S.)

Potassium Chloride
- Extended-release capsules (U.S. and Canada)
- Solution (U.S. and Canada)
- Powder for solution (U.S. and Canada)
- Powder for suspension (U.S.)
- Extended-release tablets (U.S. and Canada)

Potassium Gluconate
- Elixir (U.S. and Canada)
- Tablets (U.S.)

Potassium Gluconate and Potassium Chloride
- Solution (U.S.)
- Powder for solution (U.S.)

Potassium Gluconate and Potassium Citrate
- Solution (U.S.)

Trikates
- Solution (U.S.)

Parenteral

Potassium Acetate
- Injection (U.S.)

Potassium Chloride
- Concentrate for injection (U.S. and Canada)

Importance of Diet

For good health, it is important that you eat a balanced and varied diet. Follow carefully any diet program your health care professional may recommend. For your specific dietary vitamin and/or mineral needs, ask your health care professional for a list of appropriate foods.

The following table includes some potassium-rich foods.

Food (amount)	Milligrams of potassium	Milli-equivalents of potassium
Acorn squash, cooked (1 cup)	896	23
Potato with skin, baked (1 long)	844	22
Spinach, cooked (1 cup)	838	21
Lentils, cooked (1 cup)	731	19
Kidney beans, cooked (1 cup)	713	18
Split peas, cooked (1 cup)	710	18
White navy beans, cooked (1 cup)	669	17
Butternut squash, cooked (1 cup)	583	15
Watermelon (1/16)	560	14
Raisins (1/2 cup)	553	14
Yogurt, low-fat, plain (1 cup)	531	14

Food (amount)	Milligrams of potassium	Milli-equivalents of potassium
Orange juice, frozen (1 cup)	503	13
Brussel sprouts, cooked (1 cup)	494	13
Zucchini, cooked, sliced (1 cup)	456	12
Banana (medium)	451	12
Collards, frozen, cooked (1 cup)	427	11
Cantaloupe (1/4)	412	11
Milk, low-fat 1% (1 cup)	348	9
Broccoli, frozen, cooked (1 cup)	332	9

The daily amount of potassium needed is defined in several different ways.

For U.S.—

- Recommended Dietary Allowances (RDAs) are the amount of vitamins and minerals needed to provide for adequate nutrition in most healthy persons. RDAs for a given nutrient may vary depending on a person's age, sex, and physical condition (e.g., pregnancy).
- Daily Values (DVs) are used on food and dietary supplement labels to indicate the percent of the recommended daily amount of each nutrient that a serving provides. DV replaces the previous designation of United States Recommended Daily Allowances (USRDAs).

For Canada—

- Recommended Nutrient Intakes (RNIs) are used to determine the amounts of vitamins, minerals, and protein needed to provide adequate nutrition and lessen the risk of chronic disease.

Because lack of potassium is rare, there is no RDA or RNI for this mineral. However, it is thought that 1600 to 2000 mg (40 to 50 milliequivalents [mEq]) per day for adults is adequate.

Remember:

- The total amount of potassium that you get every day includes what you get from food *and* what you may take as a supplement. Read the labels of processed foods. Many foods now have added potassium.
- Your total intake of potassium should not be greater than the recommended amounts, unless ordered by your doctor. In some cases, too much potassium may cause muscle weakness, confusion, irregular heartbeat, or difficult breathing.

Before Using This Medicine

In deciding to use a medicine, the risks of taking the medicine must be weighed against the good it will do. This is a decision you and your doctor will make. For potassium supplements, the following should be considered:

Allergies—Tell your doctor if you have ever had any unusual or allergic reaction to potassium preparations. Also tell your doctor and pharmacist if you are allergic to any other substances, such as foods, preservatives, or dyes.

Pregnancy—Potassium supplements have not been shown to cause problems in humans.

Breast-feeding—Potassium supplements pass into breast milk. However, this medicine has not been reported to cause problems in nursing babies.

Children—Although there is no specific information comparing use of potassium supplements in children with use in other age groups, they are not expected to cause different side effects or problems in children than they do in adults.

Older adults—Many medicines have not been studied specifically in older people. Therefore, it may not be known whether they work exactly the same way they do in younger adults. Although there is no specific information comparing use of potassium supplements in the elderly with use in other age groups, they are not expected to cause different side effects or problems in older people than they do in younger adults.

Older adults may be at a greater risk of developing high blood levels of potassium (hyperkalemia).

Other medicines—Although certain medicines should not be used together at all, in other cases two different medicines may be used together even if an interaction might occur. In these cases, your doctor may want to change the dose, or other precautions may be necessary. When you are taking potassium supplements, it is especially important that your doctor and pharmacist know if you are taking any of the following:

- Amantadine (e.g., Symmetrel) or
- Anticholinergics (medicine for abdominal or stomach spasms or cramps) or
- Antidepressants (medicine for depression) or
- Antidyskinetics (medicine for Parkinson's disease or other conditions affecting control of muscles) or
- Antihistamines or
- Antipsychotic medicine (medicine for mental illness) or
- Buclizine (e.g., Bucladin) or
- Carbamazepine (e.g., Tegretol) or
- Cyclizine (e.g., Marezine) or
- Cyclobenzaprine (e.g., Flexeril) or
- Disopyramide (e.g., Norpace) or
- Flavoxate (e.g., Urispas) or
- Ipratropium (e.g., Atrovent) or
- Meclizine (e.g., Antivert) or
- Methylphenidate (e.g., Ritalin) or
- Orphenadrine (e.g., Norflex) or
- Oxybutynin (e.g., Ditropan) or
- Procainamide (e.g., Pronestyl) or
- Promethazine (e.g., Phenergan) or
- Quinidine (e.g., Quinidex) or
- Trimeprazine (e.g., Temaril)—Use with potassium supplements may cause or worsen certain stomach or intestine problems

- Angiotensin-converting enzyme (ACE) inhibitors (benazepril [e.g., Lotensin], captopril [e.g., Capoten], enalapril [e.g., Vasotec], fosinopril [e.g., Monotril], lisinopril [e.g., Prinivil, Zestril], quinapril [e.g., Accupril], ramipril [e.g., Altace]) or
- Amiloride (e.g., Midamor) or
- Beta-adrenergic blocking agents (acebutolol [e.g., Sectral], atenolol [e.g., Tenormin], betaxolol [e.g., Kerlone], carteolol [e.g., Cartrol], labetalol [e.g., Normodyne], metoprolol [e.g., Lopressor], nadolol [e.g., Corgard], oxprenolol [e.g., Trasicor], penbutolol [e.g., Levatol], pindolol

[e.g., Visken], propranolol [e.g., Inderal], sotalol [e.g., Sotacor], timolol [e.g., Blocadren]) or
- Heparin (e.g., Panheprin) or
- Inflammation or pain medicine (except narcotics) or
- Potassium-containing medicines (other) or
- Salt substitutes, low-salt foods, or milk or
- Spironolactone (e.g., Aldactone) or
- Triamterene (e.g., Dyrenium)—Use with potassium supplements may further increase potassium blood levels, which may cause or worsen heart problems
- Digitalis glycosides (heart medicine)—Use with potassium supplements may make heart problems worse
- Thiazide diuretics (water pills)—If you have been taking a potassium supplement and a thiazide diuretic together, stopping the thiazide diuretic may cause hyperkalemia (high blood levels of potassium)

Other medical problems—The presence of other medical problems may affect the use of potassium supplements. Make sure you tell your doctor if you have any other medical problems, especially:
- Addison's disease (underactive adrenal glands) or
- Dehydration (excessive loss of body water, continuing or severe)
- Diabetes mellitus or
- Kidney disease—Potassium supplements may increase the risk of hyperkalemia (high blood levels of potassium), which may worsen or cause heart problems in patients with these conditions
- Diarrhea (continuing or severe)—The loss of fluid in combination with potassium supplements may cause kidney problems, which may increase the risk of hyperkalemia (high blood levels of potassium)
- Heart disease—Potassium supplements may make this condition worse
- Intestinal or esophageal blockage—Potassium supplements may damage the intestines
- Stomach ulcer—Potassium supplements may make this condition worse

Proper Use of This Medicine

For patients taking the *liquid form* of this medicine:
- This medicine *must be diluted* in at least one-half glass (4 ounces) of cold water or juice to reduce its possible stomach-irritating or laxative effect.
- If you are on a salt (sodium)-restricted diet, check with your doctor before using tomato juice to dilute your medicine. Tomato juice has a high salt content.

For patients taking the *soluble granule, soluble powder, or soluble tablet form* of this medicine:
- This medicine must be completely dissolved in at least one-half glass (4 ounces) of cold water or juice to reduce its possible stomach-irritating or laxative effect.
- Allow any ''fizzing'' to stop before taking the dissolved medicine.
- If you are on a salt (sodium)-restricted diet, check with your doctor before using tomato juice to dilute your medicine. Tomato juice has a high salt content.

For patients taking the *extended-release tablet form* of this medicine:
- Swallow the tablets whole with a full (8-ounce) glass of water. Do not chew or suck on the tablet.
- Some tablets may be broken or crushed and sprinkled on applesauce or other soft food. However, check with your doctor or pharmacist first, since this should not be done for most tablets.
- If you have trouble swallowing tablets or if they seem to stick in your throat, check with your doctor. When this medicine is not properly released, it can cause irritation that may lead to ulcers.

For patients taking the *extended-release capsule form* of this medicine:
- Do not crush or chew the capsule. Swallow the capsule whole with a full (8-ounce) glass of water.
- Some capsules may be opened and the contents sprinkled on applesauce or other soft food. However, check with your doctor or pharmacist first, since this should not be done for most capsules.

Take this medicine immediately after meals or with food to lessen possible stomach upset or laxative action.

Take this medicine only as directed by your doctor. Do not take more of it, do not take it more often, and do not take it for a longer time than your doctor ordered. *This is especially important if you are also taking both diuretics (water pills) and digitalis medicines for your heart.*

Dosing—The dose of these single or combination medicines will be different for different patients. *Follow your doctor's orders or the directions on the label.* The following information includes only the average dose of these medicines. *If your dose is different, do not change it* unless your doctor tells you to do so.

The number of ounces of solution that you drink, or the number of tablets or capsules you take, depends on the strength of the medicine. Also, *the number of doses you take each day, the time allowed between doses, and the length of time you take the medicine depend on the medical problem for which you are taking the single or combination medicine.*

For potassium bicarbonate
- For *oral* dosage form (tablets for solution):
  - —To prevent potassium loss or replace potassium lost by the body:
    - Adults and teenagers—25 to 50 milliequivalents (mEq) dissolved in one-half to one glass of cold water, taken one or two times a day. Your doctor may change the dose if needed. However, most people will not take more than 100 mEq a day.
    - Children—Dose must be determined by your doctor.

For potassium bicarbonate and potassium chloride
- For *oral* dosage form (granules for solution):
  - —To prevent potassium loss or replace potassium lost by the body:
    - Adults and teenagers—20 milliequivalents (mEq) dissolved in one-half to one glass of cold water, taken one or two times a day. Your doctor may change the dose if needed. However, most people will not take more than 100 mEq a day.

- Children—Dose must be determined by your doctor.

- For *oral* dosage form (tablets for solution):
  —To prevent potassium loss or replace potassium lost by the body:
  - Adults and teenagers—20, 25, or 50 mEq dissolved in one-half to one glass of cold water, taken one or two times a day. Your doctor may change the dose if needed. However, most people will not take more than 100 mEq a day.
  - Children—Dose must be determined by your doctor.

For potassium bicarbonate and potassium citrate

- For *oral* dosage form (tablets for solution):
  —To prevent potassium loss or replace potassium lost by the body:
  - Adults and teenagers—25 or 50 milliequivalents (mEq) dissolved in one-half to one glass of cold water, taken one or two times a day. Your doctor may change the dose if needed. However, most people will not take more than 100 mEq a day.
  - Children—Dose must be determined by your doctor.

For potassium chloride

- For *oral* dosage form (extended-release capsules):
  —To replace potassium lost by the body:
  - Adults and teenagers—40 to 100 milliequivalents (mEq) a day, divided into two or three smaller doses during the day. Your doctor may change the dose if needed. However, most people will not take more than 100 mEq a day.

  —To prevent potassium loss:
  - Adults and teenagers—16 to 24 mEq a day, divided into two or three smaller doses during the day. Your doctor may change the dose if needed. However, most people will not take more than 100 mEq a day.
  - Children—Dose must be determined by your doctor.

- For *oral* dosage form (liquid for solution):
  —To prevent potassium loss or replace potassium lost by the body:
  - Adults and teenagers—20 mEq mixed into one-half glass of cold water or juice, taken one to four times a day. Your doctor may change the dose if needed. However, most people will not take more than 100 mEq a day.
  - Children—Dose is based on body weight and must be determined by your doctor. The usual dose is 1 to 3 mEq of potassium per kilogram (kg) (0.45 to 1.36 mEq per pound) of body weight taken in smaller doses during the day. The solution should be well mixed in water or juice.

- For *oral* dosage form (powder for solution):
  —To prevent potassium loss or replace potassium lost by the body:
  - Adults and teenagers—15 to 25 mEq dissolved in four to six ounces of cold water, taken two or four times a day. Your doctor may change the dose if needed. However, most people will not take more than 100 mEq a day.
  - Children—Dose is based on body weight and must be determined by your doctor. The usual dose is 1 to 3 mEq per kg (0.45 to 1.36 mEq per pound) of body weight taken in smaller doses during the day. The solution should be mixed into water or juice.

- For *oral* dosage form (powder for suspension):
  —To prevent potassium loss or replace potassium lost by the body:
  - Adults and teenagers—20 mEq dissolved in two to six ounces of cold water, taken one to five times a day. Your doctor may change the dose if needed. However, most people will not take more than 100 mEq a day.
  - Children—Dose must be determined by your doctor.

- For *oral* dosage form (extended-release tablets):
  —To prevent potassium loss or replace potassium lost by the body:
  - Adults and teenagers—6.7 to 20 mEq taken three times a day. However, most people will not take more than 100 mEq a day.
  - Children—Dose must be determined by your doctor.

For potassium gluconate

- For *oral* dosage form (liquid for solution):
  —To prevent potassium loss or replace potassium lost by the body:
  - Adults and teenagers—20 milliequivalents (mEq) mixed into one-half glass of cold water or juice, taken two to four times a day. Your doctor may change the dose if needed. However, most people will not take more than 100 mEq a day.
  - Children—Dose is based on body weight and must be determined by your doctor. The usual dose is 2 to 3 mEq per kilogram (kg) (0.9 to 1.36 mEq per pound) of body weight a day, taken in smaller doses during the day. The solution should be completely mixed into water or juice.

- For *oral* dosage form (tablets):
  —To prevent potassium loss or replace potassium lost by the body:
  - Adults and teenagers—5 to 10 mEq taken two to four times a day. However, most people will not take more than 100 mEq a day.
  - Children—Dose must be determined by your doctor.

For potassium gluconate and potassium chloride

- For *oral* dosage form (liquid for solution):
  —To prevent potassium loss or replace potassium lost by the body:
  - Adults and teenagers—20 milliequivalents (mEq) diluted in 2 tablespoonfuls or more of cold water or juice, taken two to four times a day. Your doctor may change the dose if needed.

However, most people will not take more than 100 mEq a day.

• Children—Dose is based on body weight and must be determined by your doctor. The usual dose is 2 to 3 mEq per kilogram (kg) (0.9 to 1.36 mEq per pound) of body weight taken in smaller doses during the day. The solution should be well mixed into water or juice.

• For *oral* dosage form (powder for solution):

—To prevent potassium loss or replace potassium lost by the body:

• Adults and teenagers—20 mEq mixed in 2 tablespoonfuls or more of cold water or juice taken two to four times a day. Your doctor may change the dose if needed. However, most people will not take more than 100 mEq a day.

• Children—Dose is based on body weight and must be determined by your doctor. The usual dose is 2 to 3 mEq per kg (0.9 to 1.36 mEq per pound) of body weight taken in smaller doses during the day. The solution should be well mixed into water or juice.

For potassium gluconate and potassium citrate

• For *oral* dosage form (liquid for solution):

—To prevent potassium loss or replace potassium lost by the body:

• Adults and teenagers—20 milliequivalents (mEq) mixed into one-half glass of cold water or juice, taken two to four times a day. Your doctor may change the dose if needed. However, most people will not take more than 100 mEq a day.

• Children—Dose is based on body weight and must be determined by your doctor. The usual dose is 2 to 3 mEq per kg (0.9 to 1.36 mEq per pound) of body weight taken in smaller doses during the day. The solution should be well mixed into water or juice.

For trikates

• For *oral* dosage form (liquid for solution):

—To prevent potassium loss or replace potassium lost by the body:

• Adults and teenagers—15 milliequivalents (mEq) mixed into one-half glass of cold water or juice, taken three or four times a day. Your doctor may change the dose if needed. However, most people will not take more than 100 mEq a day.

• Children—Dose is based on body weight and must be determined by your doctor. The usual dose is 2 to 3 mEq per kilogram (kg) (0.9 to 1.36 mEq per pound) of body weight taken in smaller doses during the day. The solution should be well mixed into water or juice.

Missed dose—If you miss a dose of this medicine and remember within 2 hours, take the missed dose right away with food or liquids. Then go back to your regular dosing schedule. However, if you do not remember until later, skip the missed dose and go back to your regular dosing schedule. Do not double doses.

Storage—To store this medicine:

- Keep out of the reach of children.
- Store away from heat and direct light.
- Do not store in the bathroom, near the kitchen sink, or in other damp places. Heat or moisture may cause the medicine to break down.
- Keep the liquid form of this medicine from freezing.
- Do not keep outdated medicine or medicine no longer needed. Be sure that any discarded medicine is out of the reach of children.

Precautions While Using This Medicine

Your doctor should check your progress at regular visits to make sure the medicine is working properly and that possible side effects are avoided. Laboratory tests may be necessary.

Do not use salt substitutes, eat low-sodium foods, especially some breads and canned foods, or drink low-sodium milk unless you are told to do so by your doctor, since these products may contain potassium. It is important to read the labels carefully on all low-sodium food products.

Check with your doctor before starting any physical exercise program, especially if you are out of condition and are taking any other medicine. Exercise and certain medicines may increase the amount of potassium in the blood.

Check with your doctor at once if you notice blackish stools or other signs of stomach or intestinal bleeding. This medicine may cause such a condition to become worse, especially when taken in tablet form.

Side Effects of This Medicine

Along with its needed effects, a medicine may cause some unwanted effects. Although not all of these side effects may occur, if they do occur they may need medical attention.

Stop taking this medicine and check with your doctor immediately if any of the following side effects occur:

Less common

Confusion; irregular or slow heartbeat; numbness or tingling in hands, feet, or lips; shortness of breath or difficult breathing; unexplained anxiety; unusual tiredness or weakness; weakness or heaviness of legs

Also, check with your doctor if any of the following side effects occur:

Rare

Abdominal or stomach pain, cramping, or soreness (continuing); chest or throat pain, especially when swallowing; stools with signs of blood (red or black color)

Other side effects may occur that usually do not need medical attention. These side effects may go away during treatment as your body adjusts to the medicine. However, check with your doctor if any of the following side effects continue or are bothersome:

More common

Diarrhea; nausea; stomach pain, discomfort, or gas (mild); vomiting

Sometimes you may see what appears to be a whole tablet in the stool after taking certain extended-release potassium chloride tablets. This is to be expected. Your body has absorbed the potassium from the tablet and the shell is then expelled.

Other side effects not listed above may also occur in some patients. If you notice any other effects, check with your doctor.

Revised: 07/16/92
Interim revision: 07/11/95

PRALIDOXIME Systemic

A commonly used brand name in the U.S. and Canada is Protopam Chloride.

Generic name product may also be available in the U.S.

Other commonly used names are 2-PAM and 2-PAM chloride.

Description

Pralidoxime (pra-li-DOX-eem) is used together with another medicine called atropine to treat poisoning caused by organic phosphorus pesticides (e.g., diazinon, malathion, mevinphos, parathion, and sarin) and by organophosphate chemicals (''nerve gases'') used in chemical warfare. Pralidoxime is also used to treat overdose of medicines, such as ambenonium, neostigmine, and pyridostigmine, that are used to treat myasthenia gravis. Poisoning with these chemicals or medicines causes your muscles, including the muscles that help you breathe, to become weak. Pralidoxime is used to help you get back strength in your muscles.

Pralidoxime is to be given only by or under the direct supervision of a doctor or trained military personnel. It is available in the following dosage form:

Parenteral
- Injection (U.S. and Canada)

Before Using This Medicine

In deciding to use a medicine, the risks of taking the medicine must be weighed against the good it will do. This is a decision you and your doctor will make. For pralidoxime, the following should be considered:

Allergies—Tell your doctor if you have ever had any unusual or allergic reaction to pralidoxime. Also tell your health care professional if you are allergic to any other substances, such as foods, preservatives, or dyes.

Pregnancy—Studies on effects in pregnancy have not been done in either humans or animals.

Breast-feeding—It is not known whether pralidoxime passes into breast milk. Although most medicines pass into breast milk in small amounts, many of them may be used safely while breast-feeding. Mothers who are taking this medicine and who wish to breast-feed should discuss this with their doctor.

Children—Although there is no specific information comparing use of pralidoxime in children with use in other age groups, this medicine is not expected to cause different side effects or problems in children than it does in adults.

Older adults—Many medicines have not been studied specifically in older people. Therefore it may not be known whether they work exactly the same way they do in younger adults or if they cause different side effects or problems in older people. There is no information comparing use of pralidoxime in the elderly with use in other age groups.

Other medicines—Although certain medicines should not be used together at all, in other cases two different medicines may be used together even if an interaction might occur. In these cases, your doctor may want to change the dose, or other precautions may be necessary. When you are using pralidoxime, it is especially important that your health care professional know if you are taking any of the following:

- Aminophylline (e.g., Somophyllin) or
- Caffeine (e.g., NoDoz) or
- Theophylline (e.g., Theo-Dur, Somophyllin-T)—These medicines may make the effects of the poisoning worse

Other medical problems—The presence of other medical problems may affect the use of pralidoxime. Make sure you tell your doctor if you have any other medical problems, especially:

- Kidney disease—The effects of this medicine may be increased
- Myasthenia gravis—This medicine may make the condition worse

Proper Use of This Medicine

For patients using the pralidoxime auto-injector (automatic injection device):

- You will be trained to use the pralidoxime auto-injector by a medic or other trained military personnel. You will also be told the conditions under which it should be used. The auto-injector also comes with patient directions. Read them carefully before you actually need to use this medicine. Then, when an emergency arises, you will know how to inject the pralidoxime.
- It is important that you do not remove the safety cap on the auto-injector until you are ready to use it. This prevents spillage of the medicine from the device during storage and handling.
- To use the pralidoxime auto-injector:
  —Remove the gray safety cap.
  —Place the black tip of the device on the thigh, with the injector pointed straight at the thigh.
  —Press hard into the thigh until the auto-injector functions. Hold in place for several seconds. Remove the auto-injector and dispose of it as directed.
  —Massage the injected area for 10 seconds.

Use this medicine only as directed. *Do not use more of it and do not use it more often than your doctor or medic ordered.* Do not use more than recommended on the label unless otherwise directed by your doctor or medic.

Dosing—The dose of pralidoxime will be different for different patients. *Follow your doctor's or medic's orders or the directions on the label.* The following information includes only the average doses of pralidoxime.

- For *injection* dosage form:
  - —For treatment of organic phosphorus pesticide poisoning:
    - Adults and teenagers—The usual dose is 1 to 2 grams injected into a vein. The dose may be repeated after one hour, and then every eight to twelve hours if muscle weakness continues.
    - Children—The dose is based on body weight and must be determined by your doctor. It is usually 25 to 50 milligrams (mg) per kilogram (kg) (11.35 to 22.7 mg per pound) of body weight injected into a vein. The dose may be repeated after one hour, and then every eight to twelve hours if muscle weakness continues.
  - —For treatment of organic phosphorus chemical (''nerve gas'') poisoning:
    - Adults—The usual dose is 600 mg injected into a muscle. The dose may be repeated fifteen minutes after the first dose and again fifteen minutes after the second dose, if needed.
    - Children—Dose must be determined by your doctor.
  - —For treatment of overdose of medicines used to treat myasthenia gravis:
    - Adults and teenagers—At first, the dose is 1 to 2 grams injected into a vein. Then, the dose is 250 mg injected into a vein every five minutes.
    - Children—Dose must be determined by your doctor.

Storage—To store this medicine:
- Keep out of the reach of children.
- Store away from heat and direct light.
- Keep the medicine from freezing. Do not refrigerate.
- Do not keep outdated medicine or medicine no longer needed. Be sure that any discarded medicine is out of the reach of children.

Precautions While Using This Medicine

This medicine will add to the effects of CNS depressants (medicines that may make you drowsy or less alert). Some examples of CNS depressants are antihistamines or medicine for hay fever, other allergies, or colds; sedatives, tranquilizers, or sleeping medicine; prescription pain medicine or narcotics; barbiturates; medicine for seizures; muscle relaxants; or anesthetics, including some dental anesthetics. Check with your doctor before taking any of the above while you are using this medicine.

Side Effects of This Medicine

Along with its needed effects, a medicine may cause some unwanted effects. Although not all of these side effects may occur, if they do occur they may need medical attention.

Check with your doctor as soon as possible if any of the following side effects occur:

More common

Blurred or double vision; difficulty in focusing your eyes; difficulty in speaking; difficult or rapid breathing; dizziness; fast heartbeat; muscle stiffness or weakness; pain at the place of injection (after injection into a muscle)

Other side effects may occur that usually do not need medical attention. These side effects may go away during treatment as your body adjusts to the medicine. However, check with your doctor if any of the following side effects continue or are bothersome:

More common

Drowsiness; headache; nausea

Other side effects not listed above may also occur in some patients. If you notice any other effects, check with your doctor.

Additional Information

Once a medicine has been approved for marketing for a certain use, experience may show that it is also useful for other medical problems. Although this use is not included in product labeling, pralidoxime has been used in some patients to treat poisoning caused by certain carbamate pesticides.

Other than the above information, there is no additional information relating to proper use, precautions, or side effects for this use.

Developed: 04/01/96

PRAZIQUANTEL Systemic†

A commonly used brand name in the U.S. is Biltricide.

†Not commercially available in Canada.

Description

Praziquantel (pray-zi-KWON-tel) belongs to the family of medicines called anthelmintics (ant-hel-MIN-tiks). Anthelmintics are used in the treatment of worm infections.

Praziquantel is used to treat blood fluke infections. These are also known as snail fever, schistosomiasis (shis-toe-soe-MYE-a-siss), or bilharziasis (bil-har-ZYE-a-siss). Praziquantel may also be used for other worm infections as determined by your doctor. However, it will not work for pinworms or other roundworms.

Praziquantel works by causing severe spasms and paralysis of the worms' muscles. Some kinds of worms are then passed in the stool. However, you may not notice them since they are sometimes completely destroyed in the intestine.

Praziquantel is available only with your doctor's prescription, in the following dosage form:

Oral

- Tablets (U.S.)

Before Using This Medicine

In deciding to use a medicine, the risks of taking the medicine must be weighed against the good it will do. This is a decision you and your doctor will make. For praziquantel, the following should be considered:

Allergies—Tell your doctor if you have ever had any unusual or allergic reaction to praziquantel. Also tell your health care professional if you are allergic to any other substances, such as foods, preservatives, or dyes.

Pregnancy—Studies have not been done in humans. Studies in rats and rabbits given up to 40 times the usual human dose have not shown that praziquantel causes birth defects. However, praziquantel has been shown to cause a greater chance of miscarriage in rats given 3 times the human dose.

Breast-feeding—Praziquantel passes into the breast milk. You should stop breast-feeding on the day you begin taking praziquantel. Do not restart breast-feeding until 72 hours after treatment is completed. During this time the breast milk should be squeezed out or sucked out with a breast pump and thrown away.

Children—This medicine has been tested in a limited number of children 4 years of age or older and, in effective doses, has not been reported to cause different side effects or problems in children over 4 years of age than it does in adults.

Older adults—Many medicines have not been studied specifically in older people. Therefore, it may not be known whether they work exactly the same way they do in younger adults or if they cause different side effects or problems in older people. There is no specific information comparing use of praziquantel in the elderly with use in other age groups.

Other medicines—Although certain medicines should not be used together at all, in other cases two different medicines may be used together even if an interaction might occur. In these cases, your doctor may want to change the dose, or other precautions may be necessary. Tell your health care professional if you are taking any other prescription or nonprescription (over-the-counter [OTC]) medicine.

Other medical problems—The presence of other medical problems may affect the use of praziquantel. Make sure you tell your doctor if you have any other medical problems, especially:

- Liver disease—Patients with moderate to severe liver disease may have an increased chance of side effects
- Worm cysts in the eye—The death of worm cysts in the eye caused by praziquantel may cause damage to the eyes

Proper Use of This Medicine

No special preparations (for example, special diets, fasting, other medicines, laxatives, or enemas) are necessary before, during, or immediately after taking praziquantel.

Praziquantel has a bitter taste that may cause gagging or vomiting. The bitter taste may be more noticeable if the tablets are held in the mouth or chewed. Therefore, *do not chew praziquantel tablets.* Swallow them whole with a small amount of liquid during meals.

To help clear up your infection completely, *take this medicine exactly as directed by your doctor for the full time of treatment. Do not miss any doses.*

Dosing—The dose of praziquantel will be different for different patients. *Follow your doctor's orders or the directions on the label.* The following information includes only the average doses of praziquantel. *If your dose is different, do not change it* unless your doctor tells you to do so.

The number of doses you take each day, the time allowed between doses, and the length of time you take the medicine depend on the medical problem for which you are taking praziquantel.

- For the treatment of clonorchiasis (Chinese or Oriental liver fluke) and opisthorchiasis (liver flukes):
  - —Adults and children 4 years of age and older: Dose is based on body weight and will be determined by your doctor. This dose is taken three times a day for one day.
  - —Children up to 4 years of age: Dose must be determined by the doctor.
- For the treatment of schistosomiasis:
  - —Adults and children 4 years of age and older: Dose is based on body weight and will be determined by your doctor. This dose is taken two or three times a day for one day.
  - —Children up to 4 years of age: Dose must be determined by the doctor.

Missed dose—If you do miss a dose of this medicine, take it as soon as possible. However, if it is almost time for your next dose, skip the missed dose and go back to your regular dosing schedule. Do not double doses.

Storage—To store this medicine:

- Keep out of the reach of children.
- Store away from heat and direct light.
- Do not store in the bathroom, near the kitchen sink, or in other damp places. Heat or moisture may cause the medicine to break down.
- Do not keep outdated medicine or medicine no longer needed. Be sure that any discarded medicine is out of the reach of children.

Precautions While Using This Medicine

It is important that your doctor check your progress after treatment. This is to make sure that the infection is cleared up completely.

If your symptoms do not improve after you have taken this medicine for the full time of treatment, or if they become worse, check with your doctor.

This medicine may cause some people to become dizzy, drowsy, or less alert than they are normally. If any of these side effects occur, *do not drive, use machines, or do anything else that could be dangerous if you are dizzy or are not alert* while you are taking praziquantel and for 24 hours after you stop taking it.

Side Effects of This Medicine

Along with its needed effects, a medicine may cause some unwanted effects. The following side effects may go away during treatment as your body adjusts to the medicine. However, check with your doctor if any of the following side effects continue or are bothersome:

More common

Abdominal or stomach cramps or pain; bloody diarrhea; dizziness; drowsiness; fever; headache; increased sweating; loss of appetite; general feeling of discomfort or illness; nausea or vomiting

Less common

Skin rash, hives, or itching

Other side effects not listed above may also occur in some patients. If you notice any other effects, check with your doctor.

Additional Information

Once a medicine has been approved for marketing for a certain use, experience may show that it is also useful for other medical problems. Although these uses are not included in product labeling, praziquantel is used in certain patients with the following medical conditions:

- Some kinds of fluke infections
- Some kinds of tapeworm infections

Other than the above information, there is no additional information relating to proper use, precautions, or side effects for these uses.

Revised: 03/23/93

PRAZOSIN Systemic

A commonly used brand name in the U.S. and Canada is Minipress. Generic name product may also be available.

Description

Prazosin (PRA-zoe-sin) belongs to the general class of medicines called antihypertensives. It is used to treat high blood pressure (hypertension).

High blood pressure adds to the work load of the heart and arteries. If it continues for a long time, the heart and arteries may not function properly. This can damage the blood vessels of the brain, heart, and kidneys, resulting in a stroke, heart failure, or kidney failure. High blood pressure may also increase the risk of heart attacks. These problems may be less likely to occur if blood pressure is controlled.

Prazosin works by relaxing blood vessels so that blood passes through them more easily. This helps to lower blood pressure.

Prazosin may also be used for other conditions as determined by your doctor.

Prazosin is available only with your doctor's prescription, in the following dosage forms:

Oral

- Capsules (U.S.)
- Tablets (Canada)

Before Using This Medicine

In deciding to use a medicine, the risks of taking the medicine must be weighed against the good it will do. This is a decision you and your doctor will make. For prazosin, the following should be considered:

Allergies—Tell your doctor if you have ever had any unusual or allergic reaction to prazosin, doxazosin, or terazosin. Also tell your health care professional if you are allergic to any other substance, such as foods, preservatives, or dyes.

Pregnancy—Limited use of prazosin to control high blood pressure in pregnant women has not shown that prazosin causes birth defects or other problems. Studies in animals given many times the highest recommended human dose of prazosin also have not shown that prazosin causes birth defects. However, in rats given many times the highest recommended human dose, lower birth weights were seen.

Breast-feeding—Prazosin passes into breast milk in small amounts. However, it has not been reported to cause problems in nursing babies.

Children—Studies on this medicine have been done only in adult patients, and there is no specific information comparing use of prazosin in children with use in other age groups.

Older adults—Dizziness, lightheadedness, or fainting (especially when getting up from a lying or sitting position) may be more likely to occur in the elderly, who are more sensitive to the effects of prazosin. In addition, prazosin may reduce tolerance to cold temperatures in elderly patients.

Other medicines—Although certain medicines should not be used together at all, in other cases two different medicines may be used together even if an interaction might occur. In these cases, your doctor may want to change the dose, or other precautions may be necessary. Tell your health care professional if you are taking any other prescription or nonprescription (over-the-counter [OTC]) medicine.

Other medical problems—The presence of other medical problems may affect the use of prazosin. Make sure you tell your doctor if you have any other medical problems, especially:

- Angina (chest pain) or
- Heart disease (severe)—Prazosin may make these conditions worse
- Kidney disease—Possible increased sensitivity to the effects of prazosin

Proper Use of This Medicine

For patients *taking this medicine for high blood pressure:*

- In addition to the use of the medicine your doctor has prescribed, treatment for your high blood pressure may include weight control and care in the types of foods you eat, especially foods high in sodium. Your doctor will tell you which of these are most important for you. You should check with your doctor before changing your diet.
- Many patients who have high blood pressure will not notice any signs of the problem. In fact, many may feel normal. It is very important that you *take your medicine exactly as directed* and that you keep your appointments with your doctor even if you feel well.
- Remember that prazosin will not cure your high blood pressure but it does help control it. Therefore, you must continue to take it as directed if you expect to lower your blood pressure and keep it down. *You may have to take high blood pressure medicine for the rest of your life.* If high blood pressure is not treated, it can cause serious problems such as heart failure, blood vessel disease, stroke, or kidney disease.

To help you remember to take your medicine, try to get into the habit of taking it at the same time each day.

Dosing—The dose of prazosin will be different for different patients. *Follow your doctor's orders or the directions on the label.* The following information includes only the average doses of prazosin. *If your dose is different, do not change it* unless your doctor tells you to do so.

The number of capsules or tablets that you take depends on the strength of the medicine.

- For *oral* dosage form (capsules or tablets):
  - —For high blood pressure:
    - Adults—At first, 0.5 or 1 milligram (mg) two or three times a day. Then, your doctor will slowly increase your dose to 6 to 15 mg a day. This is divided into two or three doses.
    - Children—Dose is based on body weight and must be determined by your doctor. The usual dose is 50 to 400 micrograms (mcg) (0.05 to 0.4 mg) per kilogram of body weight (22.73 to 181.2 mcg per pound [0.023 to 0.18 mg per pound]) a day. This is divided into two or three doses.

Missed dose—If you miss a dose of this medicine, take it as soon as possible. However, if it is almost time for your next dose, skip the missed dose and go back to your regular dosing schedule. Do not double doses.

Storage—To store this medicine:

- Keep out of the reach of children.
- Store away from heat and direct light.
- Do not store in the bathroom, near the kitchen sink, or in other damp places. Heat or moisture may cause the medicine to break down.
- Do not keep outdated medicine or medicine no longer needed. Be sure that any discarded medicine is out of the reach of children.

Precautions While Using This Medicine

It is important that your doctor check your progress at regular visits to make sure that this medicine is working properly.

For patients *taking this medicine for high blood pressure:*

- *Do not take other medicines unless they have been discussed with your doctor.* This especially includes over-the-counter (nonprescription) medicines for appetite control, asthma, colds, cough, hay fever, or sinus problems, since they may tend to make prazosin less effective.

Dizziness, lightheadedness, or sudden fainting may occur after you take this medicine, especially when you get up from a lying or sitting position. These effects are more likely to occur when you take the first dose of this medicine. Taking the first dose at bedtime may prevent problems. However, *be especially careful if you need to get up during the night.* These effects may also occur with any doses you take after the first dose. Getting up slowly may help lessen this problem. *If you feel dizzy, lie down so that you do not faint.* Then sit for a few moments before standing to prevent the dizziness from returning.

The dizziness, lightheadedness, or fainting is more likely to occur if you drink alcohol, stand for a long time, exercise, or if the weather is hot. *While you are taking this medicine, be careful to limit the amount of alcohol you drink. Also, use extra care during exercise or hot weather or if you must stand for a long time.*

Prazosin may cause some people to become drowsy or less alert than they are normally. *Make sure you know how you react to this medicine before you drive, use machines, or do anything else that could be dangerous if you are dizzy, drowsy, or are not alert.* After you have taken several doses of this medicine, these effects should lessen.

Side Effects of This Medicine

Along with its needed effects, a medicine may cause some unwanted effects. Although not all of these side effects may occur, if they do occur they may need medical attention.

Check with your doctor as soon as possible if any of the following side effects occur:

More common

Dizziness or lightheadedness, especially when getting up from a lying or sitting position; fainting (sudden)

Less common

Loss of bladder control; pounding heartbeat; swelling of feet or lower legs

Rare
Chest pain; painful inappropriate erection of penis (continuing); shortness of breath

Other side effects may occur that usually do not need medical attention. These side effects may go away during treatment as your body adjusts to the medicine. However, check with your doctor if any of the following side effects continue or are bothersome:

More common
Drowsiness; headache; lack of energy

Less common
Dryness of mouth; nervousness; unusual tiredness or weakness

Rare
Frequent urge to urinate; nausea

Other side effects not listed above may also occur in some patients. If you notice any other effects, check with your doctor.

Additional Information

Once a medicine has been approved for marketing for a certain use, experience may show that it is also useful for other medical problems. Although these uses are not included in product labeling, prazosin is used in certain patients with the following medical conditions:

- Congestive heart failure
- Ergot alkaloid poisoning
- Pheochromocytoma
- Raynaud's disease
- Benign enlargement of the prostate

For patients taking this medicine for *benign enlargement of the prostate*:

- Prazosin will not shrink the size of your prostate, but it does help to relieve the symptoms.

Other than the above information, there is no additional information relating to proper use, precautions, or side effects for these uses.

Revised: 08/02/94

PRAZOSIN AND POLYTHIAZIDE Systemic†

A commonly used brand name in the U.S. is Minizide.

†Not commercially available in Canada.

Description

Prazosin (PRA-zoe-sin) and polythiazide (pol-i-THYE-a-zide) combination is used in the treatment of high blood pressure (hypertension).

High blood pressure adds to the workload of the heart and arteries. If it continues for a long time, the heart and arteries may not function properly. This can damage the blood vessels of the brain, heart, and kidneys resulting in a stroke, heart failure, or kidney failure. High blood pressure may also increase the risk of heart attacks. These problems may be less likely to occur if blood pressure is controlled.

Prazosin works by relaxing blood vessels so that blood passes through them more easily. The polythiazide in this combination is a thiazide diuretic (water pill) that helps to reduce the amount of water in the body by increasing the flow of urine. Both of these actions help to lower blood pressure.

This medicine is available only with your doctor's prescription, in the following dosage form:

Oral
- Capsules (U.S.)

Before Using This Medicine

In deciding to use a medicine, the risks of taking the medicine must be weighed against the good it will do. This is a decision you and your doctor will make. For prazosin and polythiazide, the following should be considered:

Allergies—Tell your doctor if you have ever had any unusual or allergic reaction to prazosin, sulfonamides (sulfa drugs), bumetanide, furosemide, acetazolamide, dichlorphenamide, methazolamide, or any of the thiazide diuretics. Also tell your health care professional if you are allergic to any other substance, such as foods, preservatives, or dyes.

Pregnancy—When polythiazide (contained in this combination medicine) is used during pregnancy, it may cause side effects including jaundice, blood problems, and low potassium in the newborn infant. The combination of prazosin and polythiazide has not been shown to cause birth defects.

Breast-feeding—Polythiazide passes into breast milk. Prazosin passes into breast milk in small amounts. However, prazosin and polythiazide combination has not been reported to cause problems in nursing babies.

Children—Although there is no specific information about the use of this medicine in children, it is not expected to cause different side effects or problems in children than it does in adults. However, extra caution may be necessary in infants with jaundice, because these medicines can make the condition worse.

Older adults—Dizziness, lightheadedness, or fainting or symptoms of too much potassium loss may be more likely to occur in the elderly, who are more sensitive to the effects of prazosin and polythiazide. In addition, this medicine may reduce tolerance to cold temperatures in elderly patients.

Other medicines—Although certain medicines should not be used together at all, in other cases two different medicines may be used together even if an interaction might occur. In these cases, your doctor may want to change the dose, or other precautions may be necessary. When you

are taking prazosin and polythiazide, it is especially important that your health care professional know if you are taking any of the following:

- Cholestyramine or
- Colestipol—Use with thiazide diuretics may prevent the diuretic from working properly; take the diuretic at least 1 hour before or 4 hours after cholestyramine or colestipol
- Digitalis glycosides (heart medicine)—Polythiazide may cause low potassium in the blood, which can lead to symptoms of digitalis toxicity
- Lithium (e.g., Lithane)—Risk of lithium overdose, even at usual doses, may be increased

Other medical problems—The presence of other medical problems may affect the use of prazosin and polythiazide. Make sure you tell your doctor if you have any other medical problems, especially:

- Angina (chest pain) or
- Heart disease (severe)—Prazosin may make these conditions worse
- Diabetes mellitus (sugar diabetes)—Polythiazide may increase the amount of sugar in the blood
- Gout (history of) or
- Lupus erythematosus (history of) or
- Pancreatitis (inflammation of the pancreas)—Thiazide diuretics may make these conditions worse
- Kidney disease—Effects of this combination medicine may be increased because of increased sensitivity to the effects of prazosin and slower removal of polythiazide from the body. If kidney disease is severe, polythiazide may not work
- Liver disease—If polythiazide causes loss of too much water from the body, liver disease can become much worse

Proper Use of This Medicine

In addition to the use of the medicine your doctor has prescribed, treatment for your high blood pressure may include weight control and care in the types of foods you eat, especially foods high in sodium. Your doctor will tell you which of these are most important for you. You should check with your doctor before changing your diet.

Many patients who have high blood pressure will not notice any signs of the problem. In fact, many may feel normal. It is very important that you *take your medicine exactly as directed* and that you keep your appointments with your doctor even if you feel well.

Remember that this medicine will not cure your high blood pressure but it does help control it. Therefore, you must continue to take it as directed if you expect to lower your blood pressure and keep it down. *You may have to take high blood pressure medicine for the rest of your life.* If high blood pressure is not treated, it can cause serious problems such as heart failure, blood vessel disease, stroke, or kidney disease.

This medicine may cause you to have an unusual feeling of tiredness when you begin to take it. You may also notice an increase in the amount of urine or in your frequency of urination. After taking the medicine for a while, these effects should lessen.

It is best to plan your dose or doses according to a schedule that will least affect your personal activities and sleep. Ask your health care professional to help you plan the best time to take this medicine.

To help you remember to take your medicine, try to get into the habit of taking it at the same time each day.

Dosing—The dose of prazosin and polythiazide combination will be different for different patients. *Follow your doctor's orders or the directions on the label.* The following information includes only the average doses of prazosin and polythiazide combination. *If your dose is different, do not change it* unless your doctor tells you to do so.

The number of capsules that you take depends on the strength of the medicine.

- For *oral* dosage form (capsules):
  - —For high blood pressure:
    - Adults—1 capsule two or three times a day.
    - Children—Dose must be determined by your doctor.

Missed dose—If you miss a dose of this medicine, take it as soon as possible. However, if it is almost time for your next dose, skip the missed dose and go back to your regular dosing schedule. Do not double doses.

Storage—To store this medicine:

- Keep out of the reach of children.
- Store away from heat and direct light.
- Do not store in the bathroom, near the kitchen sink, or in other damp places. Heat or moisture may cause the medicine to break down.
- Do not keep outdated medicine or medicine no longer needed. Be sure that any discarded medicine is out of the reach of children.

Precautions While Using This Medicine

It is important that your doctor check your progress at regular visits to make sure this medicine is working properly.

Do not take other medicines unless they have been discussed with your doctor. This especially includes over-the-counter (nonprescription) medicine for appetite control, asthma, colds, cough, hay fever, or sinus problems, since they may tend to increase your blood pressure.

This medicine may cause a loss of potassium from your body.

- To help prevent this, your doctor may want you to:

  —eat or drink foods that have a high potassium content (for example, orange or other citrus fruit juices), or

  —take a potassium supplement, or

  —take another medicine to help prevent the loss of the potassium in the first place.

- It is very important to follow these directions. Also, it is important not to change your diet on your own. This is more important if you are already on a special diet (as for diabetes), or if you are taking a potassium supplement or a medicine to reduce potassium loss.

Extra potassium may not be necessary and, in some cases, too much potassium could be harmful.

Check with your doctor if you become sick and have severe or continuing vomiting or diarrhea. These problems may cause you to lose additional water and potassium.

Dizziness, lightheadedness, or sudden fainting may occur after you take this medicine, especially when you get up from a lying or sitting position. These effects are more likely to occur when you take the first dose of this medicine. Taking the first dose at bedtime may prevent problems. However, *be especially careful if you need to get up during the night.* These effects may also occur with any doses you take after the first dose. Getting up slowly may help lessen this problem. *If you feel dizzy, lie down so that you do not faint.* Then sit for a few moments before standing to prevent the dizziness from returning.

Make sure you know how you react to this medicine before you drive, use machines, or do anything else that could be dangerous if you are dizzy or are not alert. After you have taken several doses of this medicine, these effects should lessen.

The dizziness, lightheadedness, or fainting is also more likely to occur if you drink alcohol, stand for a long time, exercise, or if the weather is hot. *While you are taking this medicine, be careful to limit the amount of alcohol you drink. Also, use extra care during exercise or hot weather or if you must stand for a long time.*

For *diabetic patients*:

- Polythiazide (contained in this combination medicine) may raise blood sugar levels. While you are using this medicine, be especially careful in testing for sugar in your blood or urine. If you have any questions about this, check with your doctor.

Some people who take this medicine may become more sensitive to sunlight than they are normally. Exposure to sunlight, even for brief periods of time, may cause a skin rash, itching, redness or other discoloration of the skin, or a severe sunburn. When you begin taking this medicine:

- Stay out of direct sunlight, especially between the hours of 10:00 a.m. and 3:00 p.m., if possible.
- Wear protective clothing, including a hat and sunglasses.
- Apply a sun block product that has a skin protection factor (SPF) of at least 15. Some patients may require a product with a higher SPF number, especially if they have a fair complexion. If you have any questions about this, check with your health care professional.
- Do not use a sunlamp or tanning bed or booth.
- Apply a sun block lipstick that has an SPF of at least 15 to protect your lips.

If you have a severe reaction from the sun, check with your doctor.

Side Effects of This Medicine

Along with its needed effects, a medicine may cause some unwanted effects. Although not all of these side effects may occur, if they do occur they may need medical attention.

Check with your doctor as soon as possible if any of the following side effects occur, especially since some of them may mean that your body is losing too much potassium:

Signs and symptoms of too much potassium loss

Dryness of mouth (severe); increased thirst; irregular heartbeat (continuing); mood or mental changes; muscle cramps or pain; nausea or vomiting; unusual tiredness or weakness; weak pulse

Signs and symptoms of too much sodium loss

Confusion; convulsions; decreased mental activity; irritability; muscle cramps; unusual tiredness or weakness

More common

Dizziness or lightheadedness, especially when getting up from a lying or sitting position; sudden fainting

Less common

Inability to control urination; irregular heartbeat; pounding heartbeat; swelling of feet or lower legs; weight gain

Rare

Black, tarry stools; blood in urine or stools; chest pain; cough or hoarseness; fever or chills; joint pain; lower back or side pain; painful or difficult urination; painful, inappropriate erection of penis, continuing; pinpoint red spots on skin; shortness of breath; skin rash or hives; stomach pain (severe) with nausea and vomiting; unusual bleeding or bruising; yellow eyes or skin

Other side effects may occur that usually do not need medical attention. These side effects may go away during treatment as your body adjusts to the medicine. However, check with your doctor if any of the following side effects continue or are bothersome:

Less common

Decreased sexual ability; diarrhea; drowsiness; headache; increased sensitivity of skin to sunlight; lack of energy; loss of appetite; nervousness; stomach upset or pain

Rare

Frequent urge to urinate; nausea

Other side effects not listed above may also occur in some patients. If you notice any other effects, check with your doctor.

Revised: 07/21/92
Interim revision: 07/20/94

PRIMAQUINE Systemic

Generic name product may be available in the U.S. and Canada.

Description

Primaquine (PRIM-a-kween) belongs to the group of medicines called antiprotozoals. It is used in the treatment of malaria.

Primaquine is available only with your doctor's prescription, in the following dosage form:

Oral

- Tablets (U.S. and Canada)

Before Using This Medicine

In deciding to use a medicine, the risks of taking the medicine must be weighed against the good it will do. This is a decision you and your doctor will make. For primaquine, the following should be considered:

Allergies—Tell your doctor if you have ever had any unusual or allergic reaction to primaquine or iodoquinol (e.g., Yodoxin). Also tell your health care professional if you are allergic to any other substances, such as foods, preservatives, or dyes.

Pregnancy—Primaquine is not recommended for use during pregnancy.

Breast-feeding—It is not known if primaquine is excreted in breast milk. However, primaquine has not been reported to cause problems in nursing babies.

Children—Although there is no specific information comparing use of primaquine in children with use in other age groups, this medicine is not expected to cause different side effects or problems in children than it does in adults.

Older adults—Many medicines have not been studied specifically in older people. Therefore, it may not be known whether they work exactly the same way they do in younger adults or if they cause different side effects or problems in older people. There is no specific information comparing use of primaquine in the elderly with use in other age groups.

Other medicines—Although certain medicines should not be used together at all, in other cases two different medicines may be used together even if an interaction might occur. In these cases, your doctor may want to change the dose, or other precautions may be necessary. When you are taking primaquine it is especially important that your health care professional know if you are taking any of the following:

- Acetohydroxamic acid (e.g., Lithostat) or
- Antidiabetics, oral (diabetes medicine you take by mouth) or
- Dapsone or
- Furazolidone (e.g., Furoxone) or
- Methyldopa (e.g., Aldomet) or
- Nitrofurantoin (e.g., Furadantin) or
- Procainamide (e.g., Pronestyl) or
- Quinacrine (e.g., Atabrine) or
- Quinidine (e.g., Quinidex) or
- Quinine (e.g., Quinamm) or
- Sulfonamides (sulfa medicine) or
- Sulfoxone (e.g., Diasone) or
- Vitamin K (e.g., AquaMEPHYTON, Synkayvite)—Taking these medicines with primaquine may increase the chance of side effects affecting the blood

Other medical problems—The presence of other medical problems may affect the use of primaquine. Make sure you tell your doctor if you have any other medical problems, especially:

- Family or personal history of favism or hemolytic anemia or
- Glucose-6-phosphate dehydrogenase (G6PD) deficiency or
- Nicotinamide adenine dinucleotide (NADH) methemoglobin reductase deficiency—Patients with any of these medical problems who take primaquine may have an increased chance of side effects affecting the blood

Proper Use of This Medicine

If this medicine upsets your stomach, it may be taken with meals or antacids. If stomach upset (nausea, vomiting, or stomach pain) continues, check with your doctor.

If you are taking primaquine for malaria, *keep taking it for the full time of treatment* to help prevent or completely clear up the infection. *Do not miss any doses.*

Dosing—The dose of primaquine will be different for different patients. *Follow your doctor's orders or the directions on the label.* The following information includes only the average doses of primaquine. *If your dose is different, do not change it* unless your doctor tells you to do so.

The number of tablets that you take depends on the strength of the medicine. Also, *the number of doses you take each day, the time allowed between doses, and the length of time you take the medicine depend on the medical problem for which you are taking primaquine.*

- For the *treatment of malaria*:
  —Adults and older children: 26.3 mg of primaquine phosphate (which equals 15 mg of primaquine base) once a day for fourteen days.
  —Younger children: Dose is based on body weight and must be determined by the doctor.

Missed dose—If you do miss a dose of this medicine, take it as soon as possible. However, if it is almost time for your next dose, skip the missed dose and go back to your regular dosing schedule. Do not double doses.

Storage—To store this medicine:

- Keep out of the reach of children.
- Store away from heat and direct light.
- Do not store in the bathroom, near the kitchen sink, or in other damp places. Heat or moisture may cause the medicine to break down.
- Do not keep outdated medicine or medicine no longer needed. Be sure that any discarded medicine is out of the reach of children.

Precautions While Using This Medicine

Your doctor should check your progress at regular visits to make sure that primaquine is not causing blood problems.

Side Effects of This Medicine

Along with its needed effects, a medicine may cause some unwanted effects. Although not all of these side effects may occur, if they do occur they may need medical attention.

Check with your doctor immediately if any of the following side effects occur:

More common
Back, leg, or stomach pains; dark urine; fever; loss of appetite; pale skin; unusual tiredness or weakness

Less common
Bluish fingernails, lips, or skin; dizziness or lightheadedness; difficulty breathing

Rare
Sore throat and fever

Other side effects may occur that usually do not need medical attention. These side effects may go away during treatment as your body adjusts to the medicine. However, check with your doctor if any of the following side effects continue or are bothersome:

More common
Nausea or vomiting; stomach pain or cramps

Other side effects not listed above may also occur in some patients. If you notice any other effects, check with your doctor.

Additional Information

Once a medicine has been approved for marketing for a certain use, experience may show that it is also useful for other medical problems. Although this use is not included in product labeling, primaquine is used in certain patients with the following medical condition:

- *Pneumocystis carinii* pneumonia (PCP)

Other than the above information, there is no additional information relating to proper use, precautions, or side effects for this use.

Revised: 01/19/93

PRIMIDONE Systemic

Some commonly used brand names are:

In the U.S.—
Myidone
Mysoline
Generic name product may also be available.

In Canada—
Apo-Primidone
Mysoline
PMS Primidone
Sertan
Generic name product may also be available.

Description

Primidone (PRYE-mih-done) belongs to the group of medicines called anticonvulsants. It is used in the treatment of epilepsy to manage certain types of seizures. Primidone may be used alone or in combination with other anticonvulsants. It acts by controlling nerve impulses in the brain.

Primidone is available only with your doctor's prescription, in the following dosage forms:

Oral
- Suspension (U.S.)
- Tablets (U.S. and Canada)
- Chewable tablets (Canada)

Before Using This Medicine

In deciding to use a medicine, the risks of taking the medicine must be weighed against the good it will do. This is a decision you and your doctor will make. For primidone, the following should be considered:

Allergies—Tell your doctor if you have ever had any unusual or allergic reaction to primidone or to any barbiturate medicine (for example, amobarbital, butabarbital, pentobarbital, phenobarbital, secobarbital). Also tell your health care professional if you are allergic to any other substances, such as foods, preservatives, or dyes.

Pregnancy—Although most mothers who take medicine for seizure control deliver normal babies, there are reports of increased birth defects when these medicines are used during pregnancy. Newborns whose mothers were taking primidone during pregnancy have been reported to have bleeding problems. It is not definitely known if any of these medicines are the cause of such problems.

Breast-feeding—Primidone passes into the breast milk and may cause unusual drowsiness in nursing babies. It may be necessary for you to take another medicine or to stop breast-feeding during treatment. Be sure you have discussed the risks and benefits of the medicine with your doctor.

Children—Unusual excitement or restlessness may occur in children, who are usually more sensitive than adults to these effects of primidone.

Older adults—Unusual excitement or restlessness may occur in elderly patients, who are usually more sensitive than younger adults to these effects of primidone.

Other medicines—Although certain medicines should not be used together at all, in other cases 2 different medicines may be used together even if an interaction might occur. In these cases, your doctor may want to change the dose, or other precautions may be necessary. When you are taking primidone it is especially important that your health care professional know if you are taking any of the following:

- Adrenocorticoids (cortisone-like medicines) or
- Anticoagulants (blood thinners)—Use with primidone may decrease the effects of these medications, and the amount of medicine you need to take may change

- Central nervous system (CNS) depressants (medicine that causes drowsiness)—Using these medicines with primidone may increase the CNS and other depressant effects
- Oral contraceptives (birth control pills) containing estrogen—Primidone may decrease the effectiveness of these oral contraceptives, and you may need to change to a different type of birth control
- Other anticonvulsants (seizure medicine)—A change in the pattern of seizures may occur; close monitoring of blood levels of both medications is recommended. Use of valproic acid with primidone may cause increased CNS depression and other serious side effects
- Monoamine oxidase (MAO) inhibitors (furazolidone [e.g., Furoxone], isocarboxazid [e.g., Marplan], phenelzine [e.g., Nardil], procarbazine [e.g., Matulane], selegiline [e.g., Eldepryl], tranylcypromine [e.g., Parnate])—Taking primidone while you are taking or within 2 weeks of taking monoamine oxidase (MAO) inhibitors may prolong the effects of primidone and may change the pattern of seizures

Other medical problems—The presence of other medical problems may affect the use of primidone. Make sure you tell your doctor if you have any other medical problems, especially:

- Asthma, emphysema, or chronic lung disease—Primidone may cause serious problems in breathing
- Hyperactivity (in children) or
- Kidney disease or
- Liver disease—Primidone may make the condition worse
- Porphyria—Primidone should not be used when this medical problem exists because it may make the condition worse

Proper Use of This Medicine

Take primidone every day in regularly spaced doses as ordered by your doctor. This will provide the proper amount of medicine needed to prevent seizures.

Dosing—The dose of primidone will be different for different patients. *Follow your doctor's orders or the directions on the label.* The following information includes only the average doses of primidone. *If your dose is different, do not change it* unless your doctor tells you to do so.

The number of tablets or teaspoonfuls of suspension that you take depends on the strength of the medicine. Also, *the number of doses you take each day, the time allowed between doses, and the length of time you take the medicine depend on your special needs.*

- For *oral* dosage forms (chewable tablets, tablets or suspension):
  —For epilepsy:
    - Adults, teenagers, and children 8 years of age or older—At first, 100 or 125 milligrams (mg) once a day at bedtime. Your doctor may increase your dose if needed. However, the dose is usually not more than 2000 mg a day.
    - Children up to 8 years of age—At first, 50 mg once a day at bedtime. Your doctor may increase your dose if needed.

Missed dose—If you miss a dose of this medicine, take it as soon as possible. However, if it is within an hour of your next dose, skip the missed dose and go back to your regular dosing schedule. Do not double doses.

Storage—To store this medicine:

- Keep out of the reach of children.
- Store away from heat and direct light.
- Do not store the tablet form of this medicine in the bathroom, near the kitchen sink, or in other damp places. Heat or moisture may cause the medicine to break down.
- Keep the liquid form of this medicine from freezing.
- Do not keep outdated medicine or medicine no longer needed. Be sure that any discarded medicine is out of the reach of children.

Precautions While Using This Medicine

It is very important that your doctor check your progress at regular visits, especially during the first few months of treatment with primidone. This will allow your doctor to adjust the amount of medicine you are taking to meet your needs.

If you have been taking primidone regularly for several weeks, you should not suddenly stop taking it. Your doctor may want you to reduce gradually the amount you are taking before stopping completely.

Before you have any medical tests, tell the medical doctor in charge that you are taking this medicine. The results of some tests (such as the metyrapone and phentolamine tests) may be affected by this medicine.

Before having any kind of surgery, dental treatment, or emergency treatment, tell the medical doctor or dentist in charge that you are using this medicine.

This medicine will add to the effects of alcohol and other CNS depressants (medicines that cause drowsiness). Some examples of CNS depressants are antihistamines or medicine for hay fever, other allergies, or colds; sedatives, tranquilizers, or sleeping medicine; prescription pain medicine or narcotics; barbiturates; medicine for seizures; muscle relaxants; or anesthetics, including some dental anesthetics. *Check with your doctor before taking any of the above while you are using this medicine.*

Primidone may cause some people to become dizzy, lightheaded, drowsy, or less alert than they are normally. Even if taken at bedtime, it may cause some people to feel drowsy or less alert on arising. *Make sure you know how you react to this medicine before you drive, use machines, or do anything else that could be dangerous if you are dizzy or are not alert.*

Oral contraceptives (birth control pills) containing estrogen may not work properly if you take them while you are taking primidone. Unplanned pregnancies may occur. You should use a different or additional means of birth control while you are taking primidone. If you have any questions about this, check with your health care professional.

Side Effects of This Medicine

Along with its needed effects, a medicine may cause some unwanted effects. Although not all of these side effects may occur, if they do occur they may need medical attention.

Check with your doctor if any of the following side effects occur:

Less common
Unusual excitement or restlessness (especially in children and in the elderly)

Rare
Skin rash; unusual tiredness or weakness

Symptoms of overdose
Confusion; continuous, uncontrolled back-and-forth and/or rolling eye movements; double vision; shortness of breath or troubled breathing

Other side effects may occur that usually do not need medical attention. These side effects may go away during treatment as your body adjusts to the medicine. However, check with your doctor if any of the following side effects continue or are bothersome:

More common
Clumsiness or unsteadiness; dizziness

Less common
Decreased sexual ability; drowsiness; loss of appetite; mood or mental changes; nausea or vomiting

Other side effects not listed above may also occur in some patients. If you notice any other effects, check with your doctor.

Additional Information

Once a medicine has been approved for marketing for a certain use, experience may show that it is also useful for other medical problems. Although this use is not included in product labeling, primidone is used in certain patients with the following medical conditions:

- Essential tremor

Other than the above information, there is no additional information relating to proper use, precautions, or side effects for these uses.

Revised: 01/27/92
Interim revision: 08/16/94

PROBENECID Systemic

Some commonly used brand names are:

In the U.S.—
Benemid
Probalan
Generic name product may also be available.

In Canada—
Benemid
Benuryl

Description

Probenecid (proe-BEN-e-sid) is used in the treatment of chronic gout or gouty arthritis. These conditions are caused by too much uric acid in the blood. The medicine works by removing the extra uric acid from the body. Probenecid does not cure gout, but after you have been taking it for a few months it will help prevent gout attacks. This medicine will help prevent gout attacks only as long as you continue to take it.

Probenecid is also used to prevent or treat other medical problems that may occur if too much uric acid is present in the body.

Probenecid is sometimes used with certain kinds of antibiotics to make them more effective in the treatment of infections.

Probenecid is available only with your doctor's prescription, in the following dosage form:

Oral
- Tablets (U.S. and Canada)

Before Using This Medicine

In deciding to use a medicine, the risks of taking the medicine must be weighed against the good it will do. This is a decision you and your doctor will make. For probenecid, the following should be considered:

Allergies—Tell your doctor if you have ever had any unusual or allergic reaction to probenecid. Also tell your health care professional if you are allergic to any other substances, such as foods, preservatives, or dyes.

Pregnancy—Probenecid has not been shown to cause birth defects or other problems in humans.

Breast-feeding—Probenecid has not been reported to cause problems in nursing babies.

Children—Probenecid has been tested in children 2 to 14 years of age for use together with antibiotics. It has not been shown to cause different side effects or problems than it does in adults. Studies on the effects of probenecid in patients with gout have been done only in adults. Gout is very rare in children.

Older adults—Many medicines have not been studied specifically in older people. Therefore, it may not be known whether they work exactly the same way they do in younger adults. There is no specific information comparing use of probenecid in the elderly with use in other age groups.

Other medicines—Although certain medicines should not be used together at all, in other cases two different medicines may be used together even if an interaction might occur. In these cases, your doctor may want to change the dose, or other precautions may be necessary. When you are taking probenecid, it is especially important that your health care professional know if you are taking any of the following:

- Antineoplastics (cancer medicine)—The chance of serious side effects may be increased
- Aspirin or other salicylates—These medicines may keep probenecid from working properly for treating gout, depending on the amount of aspirin or other salicylate that you take and how often you take it
- Heparin—Probenecid may increase the effects of heparin, which increases the chance of side effects

- Indomethacin (e.g., Indocin) or
- Ketoprofen (e.g., Orudis) or
- Methotrexate (e.g., Mexate)—Probenecid may increase the blood levels of these medicines, which increases the chance of side effects
- Medicine for infection, including tuberculosis or virus infection—Probenecid may increase the blood levels of many of these medicines. In some cases, this is a desired effect and probenecid may be used to help the other medicine work better. However, the chance of side effects is sometimes also increased
- Nitrofurantoin (e.g., Furadantin)—Probenecid may keep nitrofurantoin from working properly
- Zidovudine (e.g., AZT, Retrovir)—Probenecid increases the blood level of zidovudine and may allow lower doses of zidovudine to be used. However, the chance of side effects is also increased

Other medical problems—The presence of other medical problems may affect the use of probenecid. Make sure you tell your doctor if you have any other medical problems, especially:

- Blood disease or
- Cancer being treated by antineoplastics (cancer medicine) or radiation (x-rays) or
- Kidney disease or stones (or history of) or
- Stomach ulcer (history of)—The chance of side effects may be increased

Proper Use of This Medicine

If probenecid upsets your stomach, it may be taken with food. If this does not work, an antacid may be taken. If stomach upset (nausea, vomiting, or loss of appetite) continues, check with your doctor.

For patients taking probenecid *for gout:*

- After you begin to take probenecid, gout attacks may continue to occur for a while. However, if you take this medicine regularly as directed by your doctor, the attacks will gradually become less frequent and less painful than before. After you have been taking probenecid for several months, they may stop completely.
- This medicine will help prevent gout attacks but it will not relieve an attack that has already started. *Even if you take another medicine for gout attacks, continue to take this medicine also.* If you have any questions about this, check with your doctor.

For patients taking probenecid *for gout or to help remove uric acid from the body:*

- When you first begin taking probenecid, the amount of uric acid in the kidneys is greatly increased. This may cause kidney stones or other kidney problems in some people. To help prevent this, your doctor may want you to drink at least 10 to 12 full glasses (8 ounces each) of fluids each day, or to take another medicine to make your urine less acid. It is important that you follow your doctor's instructions very carefully.

Dosing—The dose of probenecid will be different for different patients. *Follow your doctor's orders or the directions on the label.* The following information includes only the average doses of probenecid. *If your dose is different, do not change it* unless your doctor tells you to do so.

- *For treating gout or removing uric acid from the body:*
  - —Adults: 250 mg (one-half of a 500-mg tablet) two times a day for about one week, then 500 mg (one tablet) two times a day for a few weeks. After this, the dose will depend on the amount of uric acid in your blood or urine. Most people need 2, 3, or 4 tablets a day, but some people may need higher doses.
  - —Children: It is not likely that probenecid will be needed to treat gout or to remove uric acid from the body in children. If a child needs this medicine, however, the dose would have to be determined by the doctor.
- *For helping antibiotics work better:*
  - —Adults: The amount of probenecid will depend on the condition being treated. Sometimes, only one dose of 2 tablets is needed. Other times, the dose will be 1 tablet four times a day.
  - —Children: The dose will have to be determined by the doctor. It depends on the child's weight, as well as on the condition being treated. Older children and teenagers may need the same amount as adults.

Missed dose—If you are taking probenecid regularly and you miss a dose, take the missed dose as soon as possible. However, if you do not remember until it is almost time for the next dose, skip the missed dose and go back to your regular dosing schedule. Do not double doses.

Storage—To store this medicine:

- Keep out of the reach of children.
- Store away from heat and direct light.
- Do not store this medicine in the bathroom, near the kitchen sink, or in other damp places. Heat or moisture may cause the medicine to break down.
- Do not keep outdated medicine or medicine no longer needed. Be sure that any discarded medicine is out of the reach of children.

Precautions While Using This Medicine

If you will be taking probenecid for more than a few weeks, your doctor should check your progress at regular visits.

Before you have any medical tests, tell the person in charge that you are taking this medicine. The results of some tests may be affected by probenecid.

For *diabetic patients:*

- Probenecid may cause false test results with copper sulfate urine sugar tests (Clinitest®), but not with glucose enzymatic urine sugar tests (Clinistix®). If you have any questions about this, check with your health care professional.

For patients taking probenecid *for gout or to help remove uric acid from the body:*

- Taking aspirin or other salicylates may lessen the effects of probenecid. This will depend on the dose of aspirin or other salicylate that you take, and on how often you take it. Also, drinking too much alcohol may increase the amount of uric acid in the blood and lessen the effects of this medicine. Therefore, *do not take aspirin or other salicylates or drink alcoholic beverages while taking this medicine*, unless you have first checked with your doctor.

Side Effects of This Medicine

Along with its needed effects, a medicine may cause some unwanted effects. Although not all of these side effects may occur, if they do occur they may need medical attention.

The following side effects may mean that you are having an allergic reaction to this medicine. *Check with your doctor immediately* if any of the following side effects occur:

Rare

Fast or irregular breathing; puffiness or swellings of the eyelids or around the eyes; shortness of breath, troubled breathing, tightness in chest, or wheezing; changes in the skin color of the face occurring together with any of the other side effects listed here; or skin rash, hives, or itching occurring together with any of the other side effects listed here

Also, check with your doctor as soon as possible if any of the following side effects occur:

Less common

Bloody urine; difficult or painful urination; lower back or side pain (especially if severe or sharp); skin rash, hives, or itching (occurring without other signs of an allergic reaction)

Rare

Cloudy urine; cough or hoarseness; fast or irregular breathing; fever; pain in back and/or ribs; sores, ulcers, or white spots on lips or in mouth; sore throat and fever with or without chills; sudden decrease in the amount of urine; swelling of face, fingers, feet, and/or lower legs; swollen and/or painful glands; unusual bleeding or bruising; unusual tiredness or weakness; yellow eyes or skin; weight gain

Other side effects may occur that usually do not need medical attention. These side effects may go away during treatment as your body adjusts to the medicine. However, check with your doctor if any of the following side effects continue or are bothersome:

More common

Headache; joint pain, redness, or swelling; loss of appetite; nausea or vomiting (mild)

Less common

Dizziness; flushing or redness of face (occurring without any signs of an allergic reaction); frequent urge to urinate; sore gums

Other side effects not listed above may also occur in some patients. If you notice any other effects, check with your doctor.

Revised: 09/01/92

PROBENECID AND COLCHICINE Systemic

Some commonly used brand names are:

In the U.S.—

ColBenemid
Col-Probenecid
Proben-C

Generic name product may also be available.

Description

Probenecid (proe-BEN-e-sid) and colchicine (KOL-chi-seen) combination is used to treat gout or gouty arthritis.

The probenecid in this medicine helps to prevent gout attacks by removing extra uric acid from the body. The colchicine in this medicine also helps to prevent gout attacks. Although colchicine may also be used to relieve an attack of gout, this requires more colchicine than this combination medicine contains. Probenecid and colchicine combination does not cure gout. This medicine will help prevent gout attacks only as long as you continue to take it.

Probenecid and colchicine combination is available only with your doctor's prescription, in the following dosage form:

Oral

- Tablets (U.S.)

Before Using This Medicine

In deciding to use a medicine, the risks of taking the medicine must be weighed against the good it will do. This is a decision you and your doctor will make. For probenecid and colchicine combination, the following should be considered:

Allergies—Tell your doctor if you have ever had any unusual or allergic reaction to probenecid or to colchicine. Also tell your health care professional if you are allergic to any other substances, such as foods, preservatives, or dyes.

Pregnancy—Probenecid has not been shown to cause birth defects or other problems in humans. Although studies with colchicine have not been done in pregnant women, some reports have suggested that use of colchicine during pregnancy can cause harm to the fetus. Also, studies in animals have shown that colchicine causes birth defects. Therefore, do not begin taking this medicine during pregnancy, and do not become pregnant while taking it, unless you have first discussed this problem with your doctor. Also, check with your doctor immediately if you suspect that you have become pregnant while taking this medicine.

Breast-feeding—This medicine has not been reported to cause problems in nursing babies.

Children—Studies on this combination medicine have been done only in adult patients, and there is no specific information about its use in children.

Older adults—Elderly people are especially sensitive to the effects of colchicine. This may increase the chance of side effects during treatment.

There is no specific information comparing use of probenecid in the elderly with use in other age groups.

Other medicines—Although certain medicines should not be used together at all, in other cases two different medicines may be used together even if an interaction might occur. In these cases, your doctor may want to change the dose, or other precautions may be necessary. When you are taking probenecid and colchicine combination, it is especially important that your health care professional know if you are taking any of the following:

- Amphotericin B by injection (e.g., Fungizone) or
- Antineoplastics (cancer medicine) or
- Antithyroid agents (medicine for overactive thyroid) or
- Azathioprine (e.g., Imuran) or
- Cyclophosphamide (e.g., Cytoxan) or
- Flucytosine (e.g., Ancobon) or
- Ganciclovir (e.g., Cytovene) or
- Interferon (e.g., Intron A, Roferon-A) or
- Mercaptopurine (e.g., Purinethol) or
- Methotrexate (e.g., Mexate) or
- Phenylbutazone (e.g., Butazolidin) or
- Plicamycin (e.g., Mithracin) or
- Zidovudine (e.g., AZT, Retrovir)—Taking any of these medicines together with colchicine may increase the chance of serious side effects. Also, the chance of serious side effects may be increased when antineoplastics (cancer medicine), methotrexate, phenylbutazone, or zidovudine are taken together with probenecid
- Aspirin or other salicylates, including bismuth subsalicylate (e.g., Pepto-Bismol)—These medicines may keep probenecid from working properly for treating gout, depending on the amount of aspirin or other salicylate that you take and how often you take it
- Heparin—Probenecid may increase the effects of heparin, which increases the chance of side effects
- Indomethacin (e.g., Indocin) or
- Ketoprofen (e.g., Orudis)—Probenecid may increase the blood levels of these medicines, which increases the chance of side effects
- Medicine for infection, including tuberculosis or virus infection—Probenecid may increase the blood levels of many of these medicines, which may increase the chance of side effects. Also, the chance of serious side effects may be increased when some of these medicines are taken together with colchicine
- Nitrofurantoin (e.g., Furadantin)—Probenecid may keep nitrofurantoin from working properly

Other medical problems—The presence of other medical problems may affect the use of probenecid and colchicine combination. Make sure you tell your doctor if you have any other medical problems, especially:

- Alcohol abuse or
- Blood disease or
- Cancer being treated by antineoplastics (cancer medicine) or radiation (x-rays) or
- Heart disease (severe) or
- Intestinal disease (severe) or
- Kidney disease or stones (or history of) or
- Liver disease or
- Stomach ulcer or other stomach problems (or history of)—The chance of serious side effects may be increased

Proper Use of This Medicine

If this medicine upsets your stomach, it may be taken with food. If this does not work, an antacid may be taken. If stomach upset (nausea, vomiting, loss of appetite, or stomach pain) continues, check with your doctor.

Take this medicine only as directed by your doctor. Do not take more of it and do not take it more often than your doctor ordered. The colchicine in this combination medicine may cause serious side effects if too much is taken.

After you begin to take this medicine, gout attacks may continue to occur for a while. However, if you take this medicine regularly as directed by your doctor, the attacks will gradually become less frequent and less painful than before. After you have been taking this medicine for several months, they may stop completely.

This medicine will help prevent gout attacks but it will not relieve an attack that has already started. *Even if you take another medicine for gout attacks, continue to take this medicine also.*

When you first begin taking this medicine, the amount of uric acid in the kidneys is greatly increased. This may cause kidney stones or other kidney problems in some people. To help prevent this, your doctor may want you to drink at least 10 to 12 full glasses (8 ounces each) of fluids each day, or to take another medicine to make your urine less acid. It is important that you follow your doctor's instructions very carefully.

Dosing—The dose of probenecid and colchicine combination will be different for different patients. *Follow your doctor's orders or the directions on the label.* The following information includes only the average doses of this medicine. *If your dose is different, do not change it* unless your doctor tells you to do so.

- For *oral* dosage form (tablets):
  - —For preventing gout attacks:
    - Adults—One tablet a day for one week, then one tablet twice a day. If you are still having a lot of gout attacks a month after you start taking two tablets a day, your doctor may direct you to increase the dose.
    - Children—Dose must be determined by your doctor.

Missed dose—If you miss a dose of this medicine, take it as soon as possible. However, if it is almost time for your next dose, skip the missed dose and go back to your regular dosing schedule. Do not double doses.

Storage—To store this medicine:

- Keep out of the reach of children.
- Store away from heat and direct light.
- Do not store this medicine in the bathroom, near the kitchen sink, or in other damp places. Heat or moisture may cause the medicine to break down.
- Do not keep outdated medicine or medicine no longer needed. Be sure that any discarded medicine is out of the reach of children.

Precautions While Using This Medicine

Your doctor should check your progress at regular visits while you are taking this medicine.

Before you have any medical tests, tell the person in charge that you are taking this medicine. The results of some tests may be affected by probenecid or by colchicine.

For *diabetic patients:*

- The probenecid in this combination medicine may cause false test results with copper sulfate urine sugar tests (e.g., Clinitest®), but not with glucose enzymatic urine sugar tests (e.g., Clinistix®). If you have any questions about this, check with your health care professional.

Taking aspirin or other salicylates may lessen the effects of the probenecid in this combination medicine. This will depend on the dose of aspirin or other salicylate that you take, and on how often you take it. Also, drinking large amounts of alcoholic beverages may increase the chance of stomach problems and may increase the amount of uric acid in your blood. *Therefore, do not take aspirin or other salicylates or drink alcoholic beverages while you are taking this medicine,* unless you have first checked with your doctor.

For patients taking 4 tablets or more of this medicine a day:

- *Stop taking this medicine immediately and check with your doctor as soon as possible if severe diarrhea, nausea or vomiting, or stomach pain occurs while you are taking this medicine.*

Side Effects of This Medicine

Along with its needed effects, a medicine may cause some unwanted effects. Although not all of these side effects may occur, if they do occur they may need medical attention.

The following side effects may mean that you are having an allergic reaction to this medicine. *Check with your doctor immediately* if any of the following side effects occur:

Rare

Fast or irregular breathing; puffiness or swelling of the eyelids or around the eyes; shortness of breath, troubled breathing, tightness in chest, or wheezing; changes in the skin color of the face occurring together with any of the other side effects listed here; or skin rash, hives, or itching occurring together with any of the other side effects listed here

Also check with your doctor immediately if any of the following side effects occur:

Symptoms of overdose

Bloody urine; burning feeling in stomach, throat, or skin; convulsions (seizures); diarrhea (severe or bloody); fever; mood or mental changes; muscle weakness (severe); nausea or vomiting (severe and continuing); sudden decrease in amount of urine; troubled or difficult breathing

Also, check with your doctor as soon as possible if any of the following side effects occur:

Less common

Difficult or painful urination; lower back or side pain (especially if severe or sharp); skin rash, hives, or itching (occurring without other signs of an allergic reaction)

Rare

Black or tarry stools; cloudy urine; cough or hoarseness; fast or irregular breathing; numbness, tingling, pain, or weakness in hands or feet; pinpoint red spots on skin; sores, ulcers, or white spots on lips or in mouth; sore throat, fever, and chills; sudden decrease in the amount of urine; swelling of face, fingers, feet, and/or lower legs; swollen and/or painful glands; unusual bleeding or bruising; unusual tiredness or weakness; yellow eyes or skin; weight gain

Other side effects may occur that usually do not need medical attention. These side effects may go away during treatment as your body adjusts to the medicine. However, check with your doctor if any of the following side effects continue or are bothersome:

More common

Diarrhea (mild); headache; loss of appetite; nausea or vomiting (mild); stomach pain

Less common

Dizziness; flushing or redness of face (occurring without any signs of an allergic reaction); frequent urge to urinate; sore gums; unusual loss of hair

Other side effects not listed above may also occur in some patients. If you notice any other effects, check with your doctor.

Revised: 09/09/92
Interim revision: 08/27/94

PROBUCOL Systemic*

Some commonly used brand names are:

In Canada—
Lorelco

Other—
Bifenabid
Lesterol
Lurselle
Panesclerina
Superlipid

*Not commerically available in the U.S.

Description

Probucol (PROE-byoo-kole) is used to lower levels of cholesterol (a fat-like substance) in the blood. This may help prevent medical problems caused by cholesterol clogging the blood vessels.

Probucol is available only with your doctor's prescription, in the following dosage form:

Oral

- Tablets (Canada)

Before Using This Medicine

In deciding to use a medicine, the risks of taking the medicine must be weighed against the good it will do. This is a decision you and your doctor will make. For probucol, the following should be considered:

Allergies—Tell your doctor if you have ever had any unusual or allergic reaction to probucol. Also tell your health care professional if you are allergic to any other substances, such as foods, preservatives, or dyes.

Diet—Before prescribing medicine for your condition, your doctor will probably try to control your condition by prescribing a personal diet for you. Such a diet may be low in fats, sugars, and/or cholesterol. Many people are able to control their condition by carefully following their doctor's orders for proper diet and exercise. Medicine is prescribed only when additional help is needed and is effective only when a schedule of diet and exercise is properly followed.

Also, this medicine is less effective if you are greatly overweight. It may be very important for you to go on a reducing diet. However, check with your doctor before going on any diet.

Make certain your health care professional knows if you are on a low-sodium, low-sugar, or any other special diet.

Pregnancy—Probucol has not been studied in pregnant women. However, it has not been shown to cause birth defects or other problems in rats or rabbits.

Breast-feeding—It is not known whether probucol passes into the breast milk. However, this medicine is not recommended for use during breast-feeding because it may cause unwanted effects in nursing babies.

Children—There is no specific information about the use of probucol in children. However, use is not recommended in children under 2 years of age since cholesterol is needed for normal development.

Older adults—Many medicines have not been studied specifically in older people. Therefore, it may not be known whether they work exactly the same way they do in younger adults or if they cause different side effects or problems in older people. There is no specific information comparing use of probucol in the elderly with use in other age groups.

Other medicines—Although certain medicines should not be used together at all, in other cases two different medicines may be used together even if an interaction might occur. In these cases, your doctor may want to change the dose, or other precautions may be necessary. Tell your health care professional if you are taking any other prescription or nonprescription (over-the-counter [OTC]) medicine.

Other medical problems—The presence of other medical problems may affect the use of probucol. Make sure you tell your doctor if you have any other medical problems, especially:

- Gallbladder disease or gallstones or
- Heart disease—Probucol may make these conditions worse
- Liver disease—Higher blood levels of probucol may result, which may increase the chance of side effects

Proper Use of This Medicine

Many patients who have high cholesterol levels will not notice any signs of the problem. In fact, many may feel normal. *Take this medicine exactly as directed by your doctor, even though you may feel well.* Try not to miss any doses and do not take more medicine than your doctor ordered.

Remember that this medicine will not cure your condition but it does help control it. Therefore, you must continue to take it as directed if you expect to keep your cholesterol levels down.

Follow carefully the special diet your doctor gave you. This is the most important part of controlling your condition, and is necessary if the medicine is to work properly.

This medicine works better when taken with meals.

Dosing—The dose of probucol will be different for different patients. *Follow your doctor's orders or the directions on the label.* The following information includes only the average doses of probucol. *If your dose is different, do not change it* unless your doctor tells you to do so:

- The number of tablets that you take depends on the strength of the medicine.
- For *oral* dosage form (tablets):
  - —Adults: 500 milligrams two times a day taken with the morning and evening meals.
  - —Children:
    - Up to 2 years of age—Use is not recommended.
    - 2 years of age and over—Dose must be determined by your doctor.

Missed dose—If you miss a dose of this medicine, take it as soon as possible. However, if it is almost time for your next dose, skip the missed dose and go back to your regular dosing schedule. Do not double doses.

Storage—To store this medicine:

- Keep out of the reach of children.
- Store away from heat and direct light.
- Do not store in the bathroom, near the kitchen sink, or in other damp places. Heat or moisture may cause the medicine to break down.
- Do not keep outdated medicine or medicine no longer needed. Be sure that any discarded medicine is out of the reach of children.

Precautions While Using This Medicine

It is very important that your doctor check your progress at regular visits. This will allow your doctor to see if the medicine is working properly to lower your cholesterol levels and to decide if you should continue to take it.

Do not stop taking this medicine without first checking with your doctor. When you stop taking this medicine, your blood fat levels may increase again. Your doctor may want you to follow a special diet to help prevent this.

Side Effects of This Medicine

Along with its needed effects, a medicine may cause some unwanted effects. Although not all of these side effects may occur, if they do occur they may need medical attention.

Check with your doctor as soon as possible if any of the following side effects occur:

More common

Dizziness or fainting; fast or irregular heartbeat

Rare

Swellings on face, hands, or feet, or in mouth; unusual bleeding or bruising; unusual tiredness or weakness

Other side effects may occur that usually do not need medical attention. These side effects may go away during treatment as your body adjusts to the medicine. However, check with your doctor if any of the following side effects continue or are bothersome:

More common

Bloating; diarrhea; nausea and vomiting; stomach pain

Less common

Headache; numbness or tingling of fingers, toes, or face

Other side effects not listed above may also occur in some patients. If you notice any other effects, check with your doctor.

Revised: 04/13/93
Interim revision: 06/28/95; 08/18/97

PROCAINAMIDE Systemic

Some commonly used brand names are:

In the U.S.—

Procan SR	Pronestyl
Promine	Pronestyl-SR

Generic name product may also be available.

In Canada—

Procan SR	Pronestyl-SR
Pronestyl	

Generic name product may also be available.

Description

Procainamide (proe-KANE-a-mide) is used to correct irregular heartbeats to a normal rhythm and to slow an overactive heart. This allows the heart to work more efficiently. Procainamide produces its beneficial effects by slowing nerve impulses in the heart and reducing sensitivity of heart tissues.

Procainamide is available only with your doctor's prescription, in the following dosage forms:

Oral

- Capsules (U.S. and Canada)
- Tablets (U.S.)
- Extended-release tablets (U.S. and Canada)

Parenteral

- Injection (U.S. and Canada)

Before Using This Medicine

In deciding to use a medicine, the risks of taking the medicine must be weighed against the good it will do. This is a decision you and your doctor will make. For procainamide, the following should be considered:

Allergies—Tell your doctor if you have ever had any unusual or allergic reaction to procainamide, procaine, or any other ''caine-type'' medicine. Also tell your health care professional if you are allergic to any other substance, such as foods, preservatives, or dyes.

Pregnancy—Procainamide has not been studied in pregnant women. However, it has been used in some pregnant women and has not been shown to cause problems. Before taking this medicine, make sure your doctor knows if you are pregnant or if you may become pregnant.

Breast-feeding—Procainamide passes into breast milk.

Children—Procainamide has been used in a limited number of children. In effective doses, the medicine has not been shown to cause different side effects or problems than it does in adults.

Older adults—Dizziness or lightheadedness is more likely to occur in the elderly, who are usually more sensitive to the effects of this medicine.

Other medicines—Although certain medicines should not be used together at all, in other cases two different medicines may be used together even if an interaction might occur. In these cases, your doctor may want to change the dose, or other precautions may be necessary. When you are taking procainamide, it is especially important that your health care professional know if you are taking any of the following:

- Antiarrhythmics (medicines for heart rhythm problems), other—Effects on the heart may be increased
- Antihypertensives (high blood pressure medicine)—Effects on blood pressure may be increased
- Antimyasthenics (ambenonium [e.g., Mytelase], neostigmine [e.g., Prostigmin], pyridostigmine [e.g., Mestinon])—Effects may be blocked by procainamide
- Pimozide (e.g., Orap)—May increase the risk of heart rhythm problems

Other medical problems—The presence of other medical problems may affect the use of procainamide. Make sure you tell your doctor if you have any other medical problems, especially:

- Asthma—Possible allergic reaction
- Kidney disease or
- Liver disease—Effects may be increased because of slower removal of procainamide from the body
- Lupus erythematosus (history of)—Procainamide may cause the condition to become active
- Myasthenia gravis—Procainamide may increase muscle weakness

Proper Use of This Medicine

Take procainamide exactly as directed by your doctor, even though you may feel well. Do not take more medicine than ordered.

Procainamide should be taken with a glass of water on an empty stomach 1 hour before or 2 hours after meals so that it will be absorbed more quickly. However, to lessen stomach upset, your doctor may want you to take the medicine with food or milk.

For patients taking the *extended-release tablets:*

- Swallow the tablet whole without breaking, crushing, or chewing it.

This medicine works best when there is a constant amount in the blood. *To help keep the amount constant, do not miss any doses. Also, it is best to take the doses at evenly spaced times day and night.* For example, if you are to take 6 doses a day, the doses should be spaced about 4 hours apart. If this interferes with your sleep or other daily activities, or if you need help in planning the best times to take your medicine, check with your health care professional.

Dosing—The dose of procainamide will be different for different patients. *Follow your doctor's orders or the directions on the label.* The following information includes only the average doses of procainamide. *If your dose is different, do not change it* unless your doctor tells you to do so.

The number of capsules or tablets that you take depends on the strength of the medicine.

- For *regular (short-acting) oral* dosage forms (capsules or tablets):
  - —For atrial arrhythmias (fast or irregular heartbeat):
    - Adults—500 milligrams (mg) to 1000 mg (1 gram) every four to six hours.
    - Children—12.5 mg per kilogram (5.68 mg per pound) of body weight four times a day.
  - —For ventricular arrhythmias (fast or irregular heartbeat):
    - Adults—50 mg per kilogram (22.73 mg per pound) of body weight per day divided into eight doses taken every three hours.
    - Children—12.5 mg per kilogram (5.68 mg per pound) of body weight four times a day.
- For *long-acting oral* dosage form (extended-release tablets):
  - —For atrial arrhythmias (fast or irregular heartbeat):
    - Adults—1000 mg (1 gram) every six hours.
    - Children—Use is not recommended.
  - —For ventricular arrhythmias (fast or irregular heartbeat):
    - Adults—50 mg per kilogram (22.73 mg per pound) of body weight per day divided into four doses taken every six hours.
- For *injection* dosage form:
  - —For arrhythmias (fast or irregular heartbeat):
    - Adults—
      - —*First few doses:* May be given intramuscularly (into the muscle) at 50 mg per kilogram (22.73 mg per pound) of body weight per day in divided doses every three hours; or may be given intravenously (into the vein) by slowly injecting 100 mg (mixed in fluid) every five minutes or infusing 500 to 600 mg (mixed in fluid) over a twenty-five to thirty minute period.
      - —*Doses after the first few doses:* 2 to 6 mg (mixed in fluid) per minute infused into the vein.
    - Children—Dose must be determined by your doctor.

Missed dose—If you miss a dose of this medicine and remember within 2 hours (4 hours if you are taking the long-acting tablets), take it as soon as possible. However, if you do not remember until later, skip the missed dose and go back to your regular dosing schedule. Do not double doses.

Storage—To store this medicine:

- Keep out of the reach of children.
- Store away from heat and direct light.
- Do not store in the bathroom, refrigerator, near the kitchen sink, or in other damp places. Moisture usually present in these areas may cause the medicine to break down. Keep the container tightly closed and store in a dry place.
- Do not keep outdated medicine or medicine no longer needed. Be sure that any discarded medicine is out of the reach of children.

Precautions While Using This Medicine

It is important that your doctor check your progress at regular visits to make sure the medicine is working properly. This will allow necessary changes in the amount of medicine you are taking, which also may help reduce side effects.

Do not stop taking this medicine without first checking with your doctor. Stopping it suddenly may cause a serious change in the activity of your heart. Your doctor may want you to reduce gradually the amount you are taking before stopping completely.

Before having any kind of surgery (including dental surgery) or emergency treatment, tell the medical doctor or dentist in charge that you are taking this medicine.

Your doctor may want you to carry a medical identification card or bracelet stating that you are taking this medicine.

Dizziness or lightheadedness may occur, especially in elderly patients and when large doses are used. *Elderly patients should use extra care to avoid falling. Make sure you know how you react to this medicine before you drive, use machines, or do anything else that could be dangerous if you are dizzy or are not alert.*

Tell the doctor in charge that you are taking this medicine before you have any medical tests. The results of some tests may be affected by this medicine.

Side Effects of This Medicine

Along with its needed effects, a medicine may cause some unwanted effects. Although not all of these side effects may occur, if they do occur they may need medical attention.

Check with your doctor as soon as possible if any of the following side effects occur:

Less common
Fever and chills; joint pain or swelling; pains with breathing; skin rash or itching

Rare
Confusion; fever or sore mouth, gums, or throat; hallucinations (seeing, hearing, or feeling things that are not there); mental depression; unusual bleeding or bruising; unusual tiredness or weakness

Signs and symptoms of overdose
Confusion; decrease in urination; dizziness (severe) or fainting; drowsiness; fast or irregular heartbeat; nausea and vomiting

Other side effects may occur that usually do not need medical attention. These side effects may go away during treatment as your body adjusts to the medicine. However, check with your doctor if any of the following side effects continue or are bothersome:

More common
Diarrhea; loss of appetite

Less common
Dizziness or lightheadedness

The medicine in the extended-release tablets is contained in a special wax form (matrix). The medicine is slowly released, after which the wax matrix passes out of the body. Sometimes it may be seen in the stool. This is normal and is no cause for concern.

Other side effects not listed above may also occur in some patients. If you notice any other effects, check with your doctor.

Revised: 08/04/93

PROCARBAZINE Systemic

Some commonly used brand names are:

In the U.S.
Matulane

In Canada
Natulan

Description

Procarbazine (pro-KAR-ba-zeen) belongs to the group of medicines known as alkylating agents. It is used to treat some kinds of cancer.

Procarbazine is thought to interfere with the growth of cancer cells which are eventually destroyed. It also blocks the action of a chemical substance in the central nervous system called monoamine oxidase (MAO), but this is probably not related to its effect against cancer. Since the growth of normal body cells may also be affected by procarbazine, other effects will also occur. Some of these may be serious and must be reported to your doctor. Other effects, like hair loss, may not be serious but may cause concern. Some effects may not occur for months or years after the medicine is used.

Before you begin treatment with procarbazine, you and your doctor should talk about the good this medicine will do as well as the risks of using it.

Procarbazine is available only with your doctor's prescription, in the following dosage form:

Oral
- Capsules (U.S. and Canada)

Before Using This Medicine

In deciding to use a medicine, the risks of taking the medicine must be weighed against the good it will do. This is a decision you and your doctor will make. For procarbazine, the following should be considered:

Allergies—Tell your doctor if you have ever had any unusual or allergic reaction to procarbazine.

Pregnancy—Tell your doctor if you are pregnant or if you intend to have children. This medicine may cause birth defects or premature birth if either the male or female is taking it at the time of conception or if it is taken during pregnancy. Procarbazine causes birth defects frequently in animals. In addition, many cancer medicines may cause sterility which could be permanent. Although sterility has not been reported with this medicine, procarbazine does affect production of sperm and the possibility should be kept in mind.

Be sure that you have discussed this with your doctor before taking this medicine. It is best to use some kind of birth control while you are taking procarbazine. Tell your doctor right away if you think you have become pregnant while taking procarbazine.

Breast-feeding—Tell your doctor if you are breast-feeding or if you intend to breast-feed during treatment with this medicine. Because procarbazine may cause serious side effects, breast-feeding is generally not recommended while you are taking it.

Children—Although there is no specific information about the use of procarbazine in children, it is not expected to cause different side effects or problems in children than it does in adults.

Older adults—Side effects may be more likely to occur in elderly patients, who are usually more sensitive to the effects of procarbazine.

Other medicines—Although certain medicines should not be used together at all, in other cases two different medicines may be used together even if an interaction might occur. In these cases, your doctor may want to change the dose, or other precautions may be necessary. When you are taking procarbazine, it is especially important that your health care professional know if you are taking any of the following:

- Amantadine (e.g., Symmetrel) or
- Anticholinergics (medicine to help reduce stomach acid and for abdominal or stomach spasms or cramps) or
- Antidiabetics, oral (diabetes medicine you take by mouth) or
- Antidyskinetics (medicine for Parkinson's disease or other conditions affecting control of muscles) or
- Antihistamines or
- Antipsychotics (medicine for mental illness) or
- Buclizine (e.g., Bucladin) or
- Central nervous system (CNS) depressants or
- Cyclizine (e.g., Marezine) or
- Disopyramide (e.g., Norpace) or
- Flavoxate (e.g., Urispas) or
- Insulin or
- Ipratropium (e.g., Atrovent) or
- Meclizine (e.g., Antivert) or
- Orphenadrine (e.g., Norflex) or
- Oxybutynin (e.g., Ditropen) or
- Procainamide (e.g., Pronestyl) or
- Promethazine (e.g., Phenergan) or
- Quinidine (e.g., Quinidex) or
- Trimeprazine (e.g., Temaril)—Effects of these medicines may be increased by procarbazine
- Amphetamines or
- Appetite suppressants (diet pills) or
- Dextromethorphan (e.g., Delsym) or
- Levodopa (e.g., Dopar) or
- Medicine for asthma or other breathing problems or
- Medicine for colds, sinus problems, or hay fever or other allergies (including nose drops or sprays) or
- Methyldopa (e.g., Aldomet) or
- Methylphenidate (e.g., Ritalin) or
- Narcotic pain medicine—Taking any of these medicines while you are taking or within 2 weeks of taking procarbazine may cause a severe high blood pressure reaction
- Amphotericin B by injection (e.g., Fungizone) or
- Antithyroid agents (medicine for overactive thyroid) or
- Azathioprine (e.g., Imuran) or
- Chloramphenicol (e.g., Chloromycetin) or
- Colchicine or
- Flucytosine (e.g., Ancobon) or
- Interferon (e.g., Intron A, Roferon-A) or
- Plicamycin (e.g., Mithracin) or
- Zidovudine (e.g., Retrovir) or
- If you have ever been treated with x-rays or cancer medicines—Procarbazine may increase the effects of these medicines or radiation therapy on the blood
- Buspirone (e.g., BuSpar)—Risk of increased blood pressure
- Carbamazepine (e.g., Tegretol) or
- Cyclobenzaprine (e.g., Flexeril) or
- Maprotiline (e.g., Ludiomil) or
- Monoamine oxidase (MAO) inhibitors (furazolidone [e.g., Furoxone], isocarboxazid [e.g., Marplan], pargyline [e.g., Eutonyl], phenelzine [e.g., Nardil], procarbazine [e.g., Matulane], tranylcypromine [e.g., Parnate]) or
- Tricyclic antidepressants (amitriptyline [e.g., Elavil], amoxapine [e.g., Asendin], clomipramine [e.g., Anafranil], desipramine [e.g., Pertofrane], doxepin [e.g., Sinequan], imipramine [e.g., Tofranil], nortriptyline [e.g., Aventyl], protriptyline [e.g., Vivactil], trimipramine [e.g., Surmontil])—Taking procarbazine while you are taking or within 2 weeks of taking any of these medicines may cause a severe high blood pressure reaction
- Cocaine—Use of cocaine while you are taking or within 2 weeks of taking procarbazine may cause a severe high blood pressure reaction
- Fluoxetine (e.g., Prozac)—Taking this medicine while you are taking or within 2 weeks of taking procarbazine may cause a severe high blood pressure reaction or may lead to confusion, agitation, restlessness, and stomach problems
- Guanadrel (e.g., Hylorel) or
- Guanethidine (e.g., Ismelin) or
- Rauwolfia alkaloids (alseroxylon [e.g., Rauwiloid], deserpidine [e.g., Harmonyl], rauwolfia serpentina [e.g., Raudixin], reserpine [e.g., Serpasil])—Taking these medicines while you are taking or within 1 week of taking procarbazine may cause a severe high blood pressure reaction

Other medical problems—The presence of other medical problems may affect the use of procarbazine. Make sure you tell your doctor if you have any other medical problems, especially:

- Alcoholism
- Angina (chest pain) or
- Heart or blood vessel disease or
- Heart attack or stroke (recent)—Lowered blood pressure caused by procarbazine may make problems associated with some of these conditions worse
- Chickenpox (including recent exposure) or
- Herpes zoster (shingles)—Risk of severe disease affecting other parts of the body
- Diabetes mellitus (sugar diabetes)—Procarbazine may change the amount of diabetes medicine needed
- Epilepsy—Procarbazine may change the seizures
- Headaches (severe or frequent)—You may not realize when a severe headache is caused by a dangerous reaction to procarbazine
- Infection—Procarbazine can reduce immunity to infection
- Kidney disease—Effects may be increased because of slower removal of procarbazine from the body
- Liver disease—Procarbazine can cause severe liver disease to become much worse
- Mental illness (or history of)—Some cases of mental illness may be worsened
- Overactive thyroid—Increased risk of dangerous reaction to procarbazine
- Parkinson's disease—May be worsened
- Pheochromocytoma—Blood pressure may be affected

Proper Use of This Medicine

Use this medicine only as directed by your doctor. Do not use more or less of it and do not use it more often than your doctor ordered. The exact amount of medicine you need has been carefully worked out. Taking too much may increase the chance of side effects while taking too little may not improve your condition.

Procarbazine is sometimes given together with certain other medicines. If you are using a combination of medicines, make sure that you take each one at the right time and do not mix them. Ask your health care professional to help you plan a way to take your medicines at the right times.

Procarbazine commonly causes nausea and vomiting. Even if you begin to feel ill, *do not stop using this medicine without first checking with your doctor.* Ask your health care professional for ways to lessen these effects.

If you vomit shortly after taking a dose of procarbazine, check with your doctor. You will be told whether to take the dose again or to wait until the next scheduled dose.

Dosing—The dose of procarbazine will be different for different patients. The dose that is used may depend on a number of things, including what the medicine is being used for, the patient's weight, and whether or not other medicines are also being taken. *If you are taking procarbazine at home, follow your doctor's orders or the directions on the label.* If you have any questions about the proper dose of procarbazine, ask your doctor.

Missed dose—If you miss a dose of this medicine and you remember it within a few hours, take it as soon as you remember it. However, if several hours have passed or if it is almost time for the next dose, skip the missed dose and go back to your regular dosing schedule and check with your doctor. Do not double doses.

Storage—To store this medicine:

- Keep out of the reach of children.
- Store away from heat and direct light.
- Do not store in the bathroom, near the kitchen sink, or in other damp places. Heat or moisture may cause the medicine to break down.
- Do not keep outdated medicine or medicine no longer needed. Be sure that any discarded medicine is out of the reach of children.

Precautions While Using This Medicine

It is very important that your doctor check your progress at regular visits to make sure that this medicine is working properly and to check for unwanted effects.

Check with your doctor or hospital emergency room immediately if severe headache, stiff neck, chest pains, fast heartbeat, or nausea and vomiting occur while you are taking this medicine. These may be symptoms of a serious high blood pressure reaction that should have a doctor's attention.

When taken with certain foods, drinks, or other medicines, procarbazine can cause very dangerous reactions such as sudden high blood pressure. To avoid such reactions, *obey the following rules of caution:*

- Do not eat foods that have a high tyramine content (most common in foods that are aged or fermented to increase their flavor), such as cheeses, yeast or meat extracts, fava or broad bean pods, smoked or pickled meat, poultry, or fish, fermented sausage (bologna, pepperoni, salami, and summer sausage) or other unfresh meat, or any overripe fruit. If a list of these foods and beverages is not given to you, ask your health care professional to provide one.
- Do not drink alcoholic beverages or alcohol-free or reduced-alcohol beer or wine.
- Do not eat or drink large amounts of caffeine-containing food or beverages, such as chocolate, coffee, tea, or cola.
- Do not take any other medicine unless approved or prescribed by your doctor. This especially includes over-the-counter (OTC) or nonprescription medicine such as that for colds (including nose drops or sprays), cough, asthma, hay fever, appetite control; "keep awake" products; or products that make you sleepy.

After you stop using this medicine you must continue to obey the rules of caution concerning food, drink, and other medication for at least 2 weeks since procarbazine may continue to react with certain foods or other medicines for up to 14 days after you stop taking it.

This medicine will add to the effects of alcohol and other CNS depressants (medicines that slow down the nervous system, possibly causing drowsiness). Some examples of CNS depressants are antihistamines or medicine for hay fever, other allergies, or colds; sedatives, tranquilizers, or sleeping medicine; prescription pain medicine or narcotics; barbiturates; medicine for seizures; muscle relaxants; or anesthetics, including some dental anesthetics. *Check with your doctor before taking any of the above while you are using this medicine.*

This medicine may cause some people to become drowsy or less alert than they are normally. Make sure you know how you react to this medicine before you drive, use machines, or do anything else that could be dangerous if you are not alert.

While you are being treated with procarbazine, and after you stop treatment with it, *do not have any immunizations (vaccinations) without your doctor's approval.* Procarbazine may lower your body's resistance and there is a chance you might get the infection the immunization is meant to prevent. In addition, other persons living in your household should not take or should not have recently taken oral polio vaccine since there is a chance they could pass the polio virus on to you. Also, avoid persons who have taken oral polio vaccine. Do not get close to them and do not stay in the same room with them for very long. If you cannot take these precautions, you should consider wearing a protective face mask that covers the nose and mouth.

Procarbazine can lower the number of white blood cells in your blood temporarily, increasing the chance of getting an infection. It can also lower the number of platelets, which are necessary for proper blood clotting. If this occurs, there are certain precautions you can take, especially when your blood count is low, to reduce the risk of infection or bleeding:

- If you can, avoid people with infections. *Check with your doctor immediately* if you think you are getting an infection or if you get a fever or chills, cough or hoarseness, lower back or side pain, or painful or difficult urination.
- *Check with your doctor immediately* if you notice any unusual bleeding or bruising; black, tarry stools; blood in urine or stools; or pinpoint red spots on your skin.
- Be careful when using a regular toothbrush, dental floss, or toothpick. Your medical doctor, dentist, or nurse may recommend other ways to clean your teeth and gums. Check with your medical doctor before having any dental work done.
- Do not touch your eyes or the inside of your nose unless you have just washed your hands and have not touched anything else in the meantime.
- Be careful not to cut yourself when you are using sharp objects such as a safety razor or fingernail or toenail cutters.
- Avoid contact sports or other situations where bruising or injury could occur.

For *diabetic patients*:

- Procarbazine may affect blood sugar levels. While you are using this medicine, be especially careful in testing for sugar in your blood or urine.

If you are going to have surgery (including dental surgery) or emergency treatment tell the medical doctor or dentist in charge that you are using this medicine or have used it within the past 2 weeks.

Your doctor may want you to carry an identification card stating that you are using this medicine.

Side Effects of This Medicine

Along with their needed effects, medicines like procarbazine can sometimes cause unwanted effects such as blood problems, loss of hair, high blood pressure reactions, and other side effects. These and others are described below. Also, because of the way these medicines act on the body, there is a chance that they might cause other unwanted effects that may not occur until months or years after the medicine is used. These delayed effects may include certain types of cancer, such as leukemia. Discuss these possible effects with your doctor.

Although not all of these side effects may occur, if they do occur they may need medical attention.

Stop taking this medicine and check with your doctor immediately if the following side effects occur. If your doctor is not available, go to the nearest hospital emergency room.

Rare

Chest pain (severe); enlarged pupils of eyes; fast or slow heartbeat; headache (severe); increased sensitivity of eyes to light; increased sweating (possibly with fever or cold, clammy skin); stiff or sore neck

Check with your doctor immediately if any of the following side effects occur:

Less common

Black, tarry stools; blood in urine or stools; bloody vomit; cough or hoarseness; fever or chills; lower back or side pain; painful or difficult urination; pinpoint red spots on skin; unusual bleeding or bruising

Check with your doctor as soon as possible if any of the following side effects occur:

More common

Confusion; convulsions (seizures); cough; hallucinations (seeing, hearing, or feeling things that are not there); missing menstrual periods; shortness of breath; thickening of bronchial secretions; tiredness or weakness (continuing)

Less common

Diarrhea; sores in mouth and on lips; tingling or numbness of fingers or toes; unsteadiness or awkwardness; yellow eyes or skin

Rare

Fainting; skin rash, hives, or itching; wheezing

Other side effects may occur that usually do not need medical attention. These side effects may go away during treatment as your body adjusts to the medicine. Also, your health care professional may be able to tell you about ways to prevent or reduce some of these side effects. Check with your health care professional if any of the following side effects continue or are bothersome or if you have any questions about them:

More common

Drowsiness; muscle or joint pain; muscle twitching; nausea and vomiting; nervousness; nightmares; trouble in sleeping; unusual tiredness or weakness

Less common

Constipation; darkening of skin; difficulty in swallowing; dizziness or lightheadedness when getting up from a lying or sitting position; dry mouth; feeling of warmth and redness in face; headache; loss of appetite; mental depression

This medicine may cause a temporary loss of hair in some people. After treatment with procarbazine has ended, normal hair growth should return.

Other side effects not listed above may also occur in some patients. If you notice any other effects, check with your doctor.

Revised: August 1990
Interim revision: 08/05/93; 06/30/94

PROGESTERONE INTRAUTERINE DEVICE (IUD)†

A commonly used brand name in the U.S. is Progestasert.

†Not commercially available in Canada.

Description

A progesterone intrauterine device (proe-JES-ter-one IN-tra-YOU-ta-rin de-VICE) (also called an IUD) is inserted by a health care professional into a woman's uterus as a contraceptive (birth control method).

The progesterone IUD works by causing changes in the uterus that help to prevent pregnancy. The fertilization of the woman's egg with her partner's sperm is less likely with an IUD in place, but it can occur. Even so, the IUD makes it harder for the fertilized egg to become attached to the uterus walls, making it hard to become pregnant. The hormone, progesterone, released from the IUD is believed to improve the effects of the device. After the IUD is removed, most women trying to become pregnant can become pregnant.

Studies have shown that pregnancy can occur in up to 2 of each 100 women using a progesterone IUD during the first year of use. Other birth control methods such as not having intercourse, taking birth control pills (the Pill), or having surgery to become sterile are as effective or more effective. Methods that do not work as well include using condoms, diaphragms, vaginal sponges, or spermicides. Discuss with your health care professional what your options are for birth control and the risks and benefits of each method.

IUDs do not protect a woman from sexually transmitted diseases (STDs), including human immunodeficiency virus (HIV) or acquired immunodeficiency syndrome (AIDS). The use of latex (rubber) condoms or abstinence (not having intercourse) is recommended for protection from these diseases.

Your lifestyle will determine how safe and reliable the progesterone IUD will be for you. Problems that may occur with use of an IUD are far less likely to occur in women who have a long-term relationship with one sexual partner. Also, it is important that your sexual partner not have any other sexual partners. If you or your partner has more than one sexual partner it increases *your* chance of getting an infection in the vagina. If an infection is present in the vagina or uterus when the IUD is in the uterus it may make an infection more serious. *If your lifestyle changes while you are using an IUD or you get or are exposed to a sexually transmitted disease, call your health care professional.*

Progesterone IUDs are available only from your doctor or other authorized health care professional in the following form:

Intrauterine

- Progesterone Intrauterine Device (U.S.)

Before Receiving This Device

In deciding whether to use a progesterone IUD as a method of birth control, you need to consider the risks of using it as well as the good it can do. This is a decision you, your sexual partner, and your health care professional will make. For progesterone IUDs, the following should be considered:

Pregnancy—IUD use is not recommended during pregnancy or if you plan to become pregnant in the near future. It is also not recommended in women who have had a pregnancy develop outside of the uterus (ectopic pregnancy).

There is a rare chance that a woman can become pregnant with the IUD in the uterus. If this happens, it is recommended that the IUD be removed or that the pregnancy be ended within the first 3 months. If the pregnancy continues, removing the IUD decreases the chance of a problem developing. However, whether the IUD is removed or not, some problems can occur. Some of these problems include miscarriage, premature labor and delivery, infection, and, very rarely, death of the mother.

Your health care professional will help you decide on the proper time to begin using an IUD after delivering a baby. Sometimes problems can occur if you start using the IUD too soon after delivery. These problems include having the IUD move out of place or having it press into the walls of the uterus or the cervix (opening to the uterus). These problems may harm the cervix or uterus, causing pain or unusual uterine bleeding. *Call your health care professional immediately* if you have any problems.

Breast-feeding—The progesterone IUD has not been shown to cause problems in nursing babies and its use is recommended for those women needing contraception while breast-feeding.

Teenagers—Sexually active teenagers are strongly encouraged to use a contraceptive method that protects them against sexually transmitted diseases (STDs).

Teenagers who have not had children usually have more side effects than teenagers or adults who have had children. In teenagers who have not had children, the IUD may move out of place. This may harm the uterus or cervix. Abdominal pain and increased menstrual bleeding also are more common in teenagers than in women who are older and have had children.

Other medical problems—The presence of other medical problems may affect the use of progesterone IUDs. Make sure you tell your health care professional if you have any other medical problems, especially:

- Abnormal uterus—May decrease the IUD's ability to prevent pregnancy or may increase the chance of problems, such as the IUD moving out of the uterus or pressing through the cervix or uterus
- Acquired immunodeficiency syndrome (AIDS), autoimmune diseases, treatable cancer, suspected or known cancer of the uterus or cervix, or any other condition that

may decrease the ability of the body to fight infection—These conditions may increase the chance of a vaginal infection occurring with the use of an IUD

- Blood disorders or
- Uterine bleeding problems, especially heavy bleeding during periods or bleeding between periods—At the time of insertion, use of a progesterone IUD can make uterine bleeding worse, although this lessens with continued use. Also, heavy uterine bleeding may cause the IUD to move out of place
- Diabetes, insulin-dependent or
- Heart defect—If an infection occurs during use of an IUD, the infection may become worse and/or be harder to treat in these patients
- Ectopic pregnancy (pregnancy not in the uterus), history of—The chance of an ectopic pregnancy may be increased if contraception fails during IUD use
- Fainting (history of) or
- Slow heartbeat (history of)—The chance of problems may be increased when, or soon after, the IUD is inserted
- Infection in the vagina or uterus or
- Recent infected abortion or
- Sexually transmitted disease in the last 12 months—Use of an IUD may make an infection worse
- Surgery involving the uterus or fallopian tubes—Certain surgeries of the uterus or the fallopian tubes may increase the chance of problems if an IUD is present in the uterus. Also, if contraception fails, the chance of an ectopic pregnancy may be higher

Proper Use of This Device

IUDs come with patient information. *You must understand this information.* You should keep a copy for reference. *Be sure you understand possible problems with the progesterone IUD, especially side effects, risks, and warning signs of trouble.*

Spermicides such as contraceptive foams or creams are not needed to prevent pregnancy with a properly placed progesterone IUD.

It is important that you check for the IUD threads every month (if not more often) especially after each menstrual period. Feeling the IUD threads near the cervix lets you know that the progesterone IUD is still in place.

To check for the IUD threads:

- Wash your hands thoroughly.
- Squat and, using your middle finger, find the cervix high in the vagina.
- The IUD threads should hang down from the cervix.
- *Do not pull on the threads.*

Dosing—*Follow your health care professional's orders to schedule the proper time to remove and replace your progesterone IUD, usually at 12 months.* You and your health care professional may choose to replace it sooner or begin a new method of birth control.

- For preventing pregnancy:
  - —For progesterone dosage form:
    - Adults and teenagers—One device inserted into the vagina by a health care professional and replaced within 12 months of use.

Precautions While Using This Device

It is very important to keep all medical appointments with your health care professional during the first year of IUD use. This will allow the health care professional to make sure that the device is still in place and working properly.

Check with your medical doctor if you plan to have surgery of the uterus or fallopian tubes. Your doctor may remove your IUD before the surgery or help you choose another type of treatment.

Tell your doctor immediately if you think that the IUD has moved out of place. Do not try to put the IUD back into place inside the uterus. Do not try to remove the IUD.

Although IUDs are very reliable, there is a rare chance that the IUD may fail to protect some people from becoming pregnant. Very rarely a pregnancy can occur outside of the uterus; this is called an ectopic pregnancy. It can be hard to tell if an ectopic pregnancy has occurred. Unlike a normal pregnancy in the uterus, which stops the menstrual period, some people can still have a menstrual period with an ectopic pregnancy. These women may not think they are pregnant.

Notify your doctor immediately if you feel many of the following changes that can occur with a pregnancy: Enlarged or tender breasts, lack of or unusual menstrual period, lower abdominal pain or cramping (possibly severe), sore abdomen, unusual tiredness or weakness, unusual uterine bleeding (in some cases, very heavy).

If you think you are pregnant or if you miss a period while you are using the IUD, tell your health care professional. Until your doctor is able to see you, use another birth control method, such as condoms, to prevent pregnancy just in case you are not pregnant.

Also, notify your doctor and use another birth control method, such as condoms, if:

- you have unusual uterine bleeding;
- you are exposed to or get a sexually transmitted disease (STD);
- you feel the tip of the IUD at the cervix or you or your partner feels pain during sexual intercourse;
- you cannot find the threads from the IUD or think that the thread length is different;
- you or your sexual partner's lifestyle changes and one or both of you have more than one sexual partner;
- you have unusual or severe lower abdominal pain or cramping, possibly with a fever; or
- you develop vaginal discharge or sores in the vaginal area.

You can use other products in the vagina, such as tampons or condoms, while you are using a progesterone IUD.

After you stop using this device, you may become pregnant. The contraceptive effect of a progesterone IUD is usually reversible. If you stop using an IUD and still do not want to become pregnant, you should begin using another contraceptive method immediately to prevent pregnancy.

Side Effects of This Device

Along with its needed effects, a progesterone IUD may cause some unwanted effects. Although not all of these side effects may occur, if any do occur they may need medical attention.

Get emergency help immediately if any of the following side effects occur:

Rare

Abdominal pain or cramping (severe); faintness, dizziness, or sharp pain at time of IUD insertion; uterine bleeding (heavy or unexpected)

Check with your health care professional immediately if any of the following side effects occur:

More common

Abdominal pain or cramping on insertion (continuing); unusual spotting or uterine bleeding between periods; unusual uterine bleeding on insertion (continuing)

Rare

Abdominal pain, continuous (dull or aching), fever, odorous vaginal discharge, unusual tiredness or weakness, and any unusual uterine bleeding

Other side effects not listed above may also occur in some patients. If you notice any other effects, check with your health care professional.

Developed: 12/04/95

PROGESTINS—For Contraceptive Use Systemic

Some commonly used brand names are:

In the U.S.—

Depo-Provera Contraceptive Injection[2]	NORPLANT[1]
	Nor-QD[3]
Micronor[3]	Ovrette[4]

In Canada—

Micronor[3]	NORPLANT[1]

Another commonly used name for norethindrone is norethisterone.

Note: For quick reference, the following progestins are numbered to match the corresponding brand names.

This information applies to the following medicines:

1. Levonorgestrel (LEE-voe-nor-jes-trel)
2. Medroxyprogesterone (me-DROX-ee-proe-JES-te-rone)†
3. Norethindrone (nor-eth-IN-drone)
4. Norgestrel (nor-JES-trel)†

†Not commercially available in Canada.

Description

Progestins (proe-JESS-tins) are hormones.

The low dose progestins for contraception are used to prevent pregnancy. Progestins can prevent fertilization by preventing a woman's egg from fully developing.

Also, progestins cause changes at the opening of the uterus, such as thickening of the cervical mucus. This makes it hard for the partner's sperm to reach the egg. The fertilization of the woman's egg with her partner's sperm is less likely to occur while she is taking, receiving, or using a progestin, but it can occur. Even so, the progestins make it harder for the fertilized egg to become attached to the walls of the uterus, making it difficult to become pregnant.

No contraceptive method is 100 percent effective. *Studies show that fewer than 1 of each 100 women become pregnant during the first year of use when correctly receiving the injection on time or when using the implant capsules. In addition, fewer than 10 of each 100 women correctly taking progestins by mouth for contraception become pregnant during the first year of use.* Other birth control methods, such as taking combination estrogen-progestin birth control pills (the Pill) or having surgery to become sterile, are as effective or more effective. Methods that do not work as well include using condoms, diaphragms, or spermicides. Discuss with your health care professional what your options are for birth control.

Progestins are available only with your doctor's prescription, in the following dosage forms:

Oral

Norethindrone

- Tablets (U.S. and Canada)

Norgestrel

- Tablets (U.S.)

Subdermal

Levonorgestrel

- Implant capsules (U.S. and Canada)

Parenteral

Medroxyprogesterone

- Injection (U.S.)

Before Using This Medicine

In deciding to use a medicine, the risks of taking the medicine must be weighed against the good it will do. If you are using progestins for contraception you should understand how their benefits and risks compare to those of other birth control methods. This is a decision you, your sexual partner, and your doctor will make. For progestins, the following should be considered:

Allergies—Tell your doctor if you have ever had any unusual or allergic reaction to progestins. Also tell your health care professional if you are allergic to any other substances, such as foods, preservatives, or dyes.

Diet—Make certain your health care professional knows if you are on any special diet, such as a low-sodium or low-sugar diet.

Pregnancy—Low dose progestins for contraception that have been used during pregnancy have not caused problems. However, in some cases, smaller-than-normal babies were born to women who received a progestin during pregnancy. Progesterone has not caused problems and is sometimes used in a few patients to treat a certain type of infertility.

Breast-feeding—Although progestins pass into the breast milk, low doses of progestins have not been shown to cause problems in nursing babies. Low-dose progestins for contraception are recommended for nursing mothers when contraception is desired.

Teenagers—Progestins have been used by teenagers and have not been shown to cause different side effects or problems than they do in adults. You must take progestin contraceptives every day in order for them to work. Progestins do not protect against sexually transmitted diseases, a risk factor for teenagers.

Older adults—This medicine has been tested and has not been shown to cause different side effects or problems in older people than it does in younger adults.

Other medicines—Although certain medicines should not be used together at all, in other cases two different medicines may be used together even if an interaction might occur. In these cases, your doctor may want to change the dose, or other precautions may be necessary. When you are taking a progestin, it is especially important that your health care professional know if you are taking any of the following:

- Aminoglutethimide (e.g., Cytadren) or
- Carbamazepine (e.g., Tegretol) or
- Phenobarbital or
- Phenytoin (e.g., Dilantin) or
- Rifabutin (e.g., Mycobutin) or
- Rifampin (e.g., Rifadin, Rimactane)—These medicines may decrease the effects of progestins and increase your chance of pregnancy, so use of a second form of birth control is recommended

Other medical problems—The presence of other medical problems may affect the use of progestins. Make sure you tell your doctor if you have any other medical problems, especially:

- Asthma or
- Epilepsy (or history of) or
- Heart or circulation problems or
- Kidney disease (severe) or
- Migraine headaches—Progestins may cause fluid build-up and may cause these conditions to become worse
- Bleeding problems, undiagnosed, such as blood in urine or changes in vaginal bleeding—May make diagnosis of these problems more difficult
- Breast disease (such as breast lumps or cysts) (history of)—May make this condition worse in certain types of diseases that do not react in a positive way to progestins
- Central nervous system (CNS) disorders, such as mental depression (or history of) or
- Diabetes mellitus (sugar diabetes)—May cause a mild increase in your blood sugar and a need to change the amount of medicine you take for diabetes
- High blood cholesterol—Effects of progestins may cause these conditions or may make these conditions worse
- Liver disease—Effects of some progestins may be increased and may worsen this condition
- Other conditions that increase the chances for osteoporosis (brittle bones)—Since it is possible that certain doses of progestins may cause temporary thinning of the bones by changing your hormone balance, it is important that your doctor know if you have an increased risk of osteoporosis. Some things that can increase your risk for having osteoporosis include cigarette smoking, abusing alcohol, taking or drinking large amounts of caffeine, and having a family history of osteoporosis or easily broken bones. Some medicines, such as glucocorticoids (cortisone-like medicines) or anticonvulsants (seizure medicine), can also cause thinning of the bones. However, it is thought that progestins can help protect against osteoporosis in postmenopausal women

Proper Use of This Medicine

To make the use of a progestin as safe and reliable as possible, you should understand how and when to take it and what effects may be expected. Progestins for contraception usually come with patient directions. Read them carefully before taking or using this medicine.

Progestins do not protect a woman from sexually transmitted diseases (STDs), including human immunodeficiency virus (HIV), or acquired immunodefiency syndrome (AIDS). The use of latex (rubber) condoms or abstinence is recommended for protection from these diseases.

Take this medicine only as directed by your doctor. Do not take more of it and do not take it for a longer time than your doctor ordered. To do so may increase the chance of side effects. Try to take the medicine at the same time each day to reduce the possibility of side effects and to allow it to work better.

When using the levonorgestrel subdermal dosage form:

- For insertion:

  —Six implant capsules are inserted under the skin of your upper arm by a health care professional. This usually takes about 15 minutes. No pain will be felt from the insertion process because you will receive a small injection from your doctor of a medicine that will numb your arm.

- For care of insertion site:

  —Keep the gauze wrap on for 24 hours after the insertion. Then, you should remove it. The sterile strips of tape should be left over the area for 3 days.

  —Be careful not to bump the site or get that area wet for at least 3 days after the procedure. Do not do any heavy lifting for 24 hours. Swelling and bruising are common for a few days.

- For contraceptive protection:

  —Full protection from pregnancy begins within 24 hours, if the insertion is done within 7 days of the beginning of your menstrual period. Otherwise, use another birth control method for the rest of your first cycle. Protection using this method lasts for 5 years or until removal, whichever comes first.

- For removal:

  —The implant capsules need to be removed after 5 years. However, you may have them removed by a health care professional at any time before that.

  —Keep a gauze wrap on for 24 hours after the removal. The sterile strips of tape underneath the gauze wrap should be left over the area for 3 days.

Be careful not to bump the site or get that area wet until the area is healed.

—If you want to continue using this form of birth control, your health care professional may insert new implant capsules in the same area as the old ones were or into the other arm.

—If the implant capsules are hard to remove, your health care professional may want you to return another day before the removal process is completed.

When using medroxyprogesterone injection dosage form for contraception:

- Your injection is given by a health care professional *every* 3 months (13 weeks).
- To stop using medroxyprogesterone injection for contraception, simply do not have another injection.
- Full protection from pregnancy begins immediately if you receive the first injection within the first 5 days of your menstrual period or within 5 days after delivering a baby if you will not be breast-feeding. If you are going to breast-feed, you may have to wait for 6 weeks from your delivery date before receiving your first injection. If you follow this schedule, you do not need to use another form of birth control. Protection from that one injection ends at 3 months (13 weeks). You will need another injection every 3 months (13 weeks) to have full protection from becoming pregnant. However, if the injection is given later than 5 days from the first day of your last menstrual period, you will need to use another method of birth control as directed by your doctor.

When using an oral progestin dosage form:

- Take a tablet every 24 hours each day of the year. Taking the medicine at the same time each day helps to reduce the possibility of side effects and makes it work as expected. Taking your tablet 3 hours late is almost the same as missing a dose and can cause the medicine to not work properly.
- Make sure you never run out of tablets by keeping an extra supply of tablets on hand and using it next. Replace the extra supply on a regular schedule.
- Keep the tablets in the container in which you received them. The tablets will keep well when kept dry and at room temperature (light will fade some tablet colors but will not change the tablets' effect). Also, most containers help you to keep track of your dosage schedule.
- Your doctor has prescribed this medicine only for you after studying your health record and the results of your physical examination. Use of the tablets by other persons may be dangerous because of differences in health and body make-up. Therefore, *do not give your birth control tablets to anyone else, and do not take tablets prescribed for someone else.* Also, check with your doctor before taking any leftover birth control tablets from an old prescription, especially after a pregnancy. This medicine may be dangerous if your health has changed since your last physical examination.
- Full protection from pregnancy begins 3 weeks after you begin taking the medicine for the first time. You should *use a second method of birth control for at least the first 3 weeks to ensure full protection.* You are not fully protected if you miss pills. The chances of your getting pregnant are greater with each pill that is missed.

Dosing—*Follow your doctor's orders or the directions on the label.* Also, follow your health care professional's orders to schedule the proper time to remove the implant capsules or receive an injection of progestins for contraception. You and your health care professional may choose to replace the implant capsules sooner or begin a new method of birth control. The following information includes only the average doses of these medicines. *If your dose is different, do not change it* unless your doctor tells you to do so.

For levonorgestrel

- For *subdermal* dosage form (implant):
  —For preventing pregnancy:
    - Adults and teenagers—Six implant capsules (a total dose of 216 milligrams [mg]) inserted under the skin of the upper arm in a fan-like pattern.

For medroxyprogesterone

- For *injection* dosage form:
  —For preventing pregnancy:
    - Adults and teenagers—150 milligrams (mg) injected into a muscle in the upper arm or in the buttocks every three months (13 weeks).

For norethindrone

- For *oral* dosage form (tablets):
  —For preventing pregnancy:
    - Adults and teenagers—0.35 milligrams (mg) every day at the same time beginning on the first day of your menstrual cycle whether menstrual bleeding begins or not. The first day of your menstrual cycle can be figured out by counting 28 days from the first day of your last menstrual cycle.

For norgestrel

- For *oral* dosage form (tablets):
  —For preventing pregnancy:
    - Adults and teenagers—75 micrograms (mcg) every day at the same time beginning on the first day of your menstrual cycle whether menstrual bleeding occurs or not. The first day of your menstrual cycle can be figured out by counting 28 days from the first day of your last menstrual cycle.

Missed dose—

- For *oral* dosage form (tablets): When you miss 1 day's dose of oral tablets or are 3 hours or more late in taking your dose, many doctors recommend that you take the missed dose immediately, continue your normal schedule, and use another method of contraception for 2 days. If you miss 2 doses, then take one tablet immediately, continue your normal schedule, and use another method of birth control for 7 days.

This is different from what is done after a person misses a dose of birth control tablets that contain more than one hormone.

- For *injection* dosage form: If you miss having your next injection and it has been longer than 13 weeks since your last injection, your doctor may want you to stop receiving the medicine. Use another method of birth control until your period begins or until your doctor determines that you are not pregnant.
- If your doctor has other directions, follow that advice.

Any time you miss a menstrual period within 45 days after a missed or delayed dose you will need to be tested for a possible pregnancy.

Storage—To store this medicine:

- Keep out of the reach of children.
- Store away from heat.
- Do not store in the bathroom, near the kitchen sink, or in other damp places. Heat or moisture may cause the medicine to break down.
- Keep the medicine from freezing. Do not refrigerate.
- Keep the injectable form of this medicine from freezing.
- Do not keep outdated medicine or medicine no longer needed. Be sure that any discarded medicine is out of the reach of children.

Precautions While Using This Medicine

It is very important that your health care professional check your progress at regular visits. This will allow your dosage to be adjusted to your changing needs, and will allow any unwanted effects to be detected. These visits are usually every 12 months when you are taking progestins by mouth for birth control. If you are receiving the medroxyprogesterone injection for contraception, a physical exam is only needed every 12 months, but you need an injection every 3 months (13 weeks). If you are using the levonorgestrel implant capsules, your doctor will want to check the area where they were placed within 30 days after they are put into or removed from your arm. After that, a visit every 12 months usually is all that is needed.

Vaginal bleeding of various amounts may occur between your regular menstrual periods during the first 3 months of use. This is not unusual and does not mean you should stop the medicine. This is sometimes called spotting when the bleeding is slight, or breakthrough bleeding when it is heavier. If this occurs, continue on your regular dosing schedule. *Check with your doctor:*

- If vaginal bleeding continues for an unusually long time.
- If your menstrual period has not started within 45 days of your last period.

Missed menstrual periods may occur. *If you suspect a pregnancy, you should call your doctor immediately.*

If you are scheduled for any laboratory tests, tell your health care professional that you are taking a progestin. Progestins can change certain test results.

Use a second method of birth control while using medicines that reduce the effectiveness of progestins for contraception. Also, continue to use another method of birth control until you have your next injection of medroxyprogesterone for contraception. If you are using the oral tablets or implant capsules, continue using a back-up method of birth control for a full cycle (or 4 weeks) after stopping those medicines that affect contraception to ensure full protection. Sometimes your doctor may use these medicines with progestins for contraception but will give you special directions to follow to make sure your progestin is working properly. The following medicines might reduce the effectiveness of progestins for contraception:

Aminoglutethimide (e.g., Cytadren)
Carbamazepine (e.g., Tegretol)
Phenobarbital
Phenytoin (e.g., Dilantin)
Rifabutin (e.g., Mycobutin)
Rifampin (e.g., Rifadin)

Side Effects of This Medicine

Along with its needed effects, a medicine may cause some unwanted effects. Although not all of these side effects may occur, if they do occur they may need medical attention.

Check with your doctor as soon as possible if any of the following side effects occur:

More common

Changes in uterine bleeding (increased amounts of menstrual bleeding occurring at regular monthly periods; lighter uterine bleeding between menstrual periods; heavier uterine bleeding between regular monthly periods; or stopping of menstrual periods)

Less common

Mental depression; skin rash; unexpected or increased flow of breast milk

Other side effects may occur that usually do not need medical attention. These side effects may go away during treatment as your body adjusts to the medicine. However, check with your doctor if any of the following side effects continue or are bothersome:

More common

Abdominal pain or cramping; swelling of face, ankles, or feet; mild headache; mood changes; nervousness; pain or irritation at place of injection or place where implant capsules were inserted; unusual tiredness or weakness; weight gain

Less common

Acne; breast pain or tenderness; brown spots on exposed skin, possibly long-lasting; hot flashes; loss or gain of body, facial, or scalp hair; loss of sexual desire; nausea; trouble in sleeping

Not all of the side effects listed above have been reported for each of these medicines, but they have been reported for at least one of them. All of the progestins are similar, so any of the above side effects may occur with any of these medicines.

After you stop using this medicine, your body may need time to adjust. The length of time this takes depends on the amount of medicine you were using and how long you used it. During this period of time check with your doctor if you notice the following side effect:

Delayed return to fertility

Other side effects not listed above may also occur in some patients. If you notice any other effects, check with your doctor.

Revised: 08/08/95
Interim revision: 06/26/96

PROGESTINS—For Noncontraceptive Use Systemic

Some commonly used brand names are:

In the U.S.—

Amen[3]	Hy/Gestrone[1]
Aygestin[5]	Hylutin[1]
Curretab[3]	Megace[4]
Cycrin[3]	Prodrox[1]
Depo-Provera[3]	Pro-Span[1]
Gesterol 50[6]	Provera[3]
Gesterol LA 250[1]	

In Canada—

Colprone[2]	Norlutate[5]
Depo-Provera[3]	PMS-Progesterone[6]
Megace[4]	Provera[3]

Another commonly used name for norethindrone is norethisterone.

Note: For quick reference, the following progestins are numbered to match the corresponding brand names.

This information applies to the following medicines:

1. Hydroxyprogesterone (hye-drox-ee-proe-JES-te-rone)†‡
2. Medrogestone (me-droe-JES-tone)*
3. Medroxyprogesterone (me-DROX-ee-proe-JES-te-rone)‡
4. Megestrol (me-JES-trole)‡
5. Norethindrone (nor-eth-IN-drone)
6. Progesterone (proe-JES-ter-one)‡

*Not commercially available in the U.S.
†Not commercially available in Canada.
‡Generic name product may be available in the U.S.

Description

Progestins (proe-JESS-tins) are hormones. They are used by both men and women for different purposes.

Progestins are prescribed for several reasons:

- To properly regulate the menstrual cycle. Progestins work by causing changes in the uterus. After the amount of progestins in the blood drops, the lining of the uterus begins to come off and bleeding occurs (menstrual period). Progestins help other hormones start and stop the menstrual cycle.
- To treat a condition called endometriosis or unusual and heavy bleeding of the uterus (dysfunctional uterine bleeding) by starting or stopping the menstrual cycle.
- To help treat cancer of the breast, kidney, or uterus. Progestins help change the cancer cell's ability to react to other hormones and proteins that cause tumor growth. In this way, progestins can stop the growth of a tumor.
- To test the body's production of certain hormones such as estrogen.
- To treat loss of appetite and severe weight or muscle loss in patients with acquired immunodeficiency syndrome (AIDS) by causing certain proteins to be produced that cause increased appetite and weight gain.

Progestins may also be used for other conditions as determined by your doctor.

Depending on how much and which progestin you use or take, a progestin can have different effects. For instance, high doses of progesterone are necessary for some women to continue a pregnancy while other progestins in low doses can prevent a pregnancy from occurring. Other effects include causing weight gain, increasing body temperature, developing the milk-producing glands for breast-feeding, and relaxing the uterus to maintain a pregnancy. Progestins can help other hormones work properly.

Progestins may help to prevent anemia (low iron in blood), too much menstrual blood loss, and cancer of the uterus.

Progesterone (a naturally produced hormone in pregnancy) is sometimes used to treat a certain type of infertility that is caused when the body does not produce enough progesterone to support a pregnancy.

Progestins are available only with your doctor's prescription, in the following dosage forms:

Oral

Medrogestone
- Tablets (Canada)

Medroxyprogesterone
- Tablets (U.S. and Canada)

Megestrol
- Oral suspension (U.S.)
- Tablets (U.S. and Canada)

Norethindrone
- Tablets (U.S. and Canada)

Parenteral

Hydroxyprogesterone
- Injection (U.S.)

Medroxyprogesterone
- Injection (U.S. and Canada)

Progesterone
- Injection (U.S. and Canada)

Vaginal

Progesterone
- Suppositories

Before Using This Medicine

In deciding to use a medicine, the risks of taking the medicine must be weighed against the good it will do. This is

a decision you and your health care professional will make. For progestins, the following should be considered:

Allergies—Tell your doctor if you have ever had any unusual or allergic reaction to progestins. Also tell your health care professional if you are allergic to any other substances, such as foods, preservatives, or dyes.

Diet—Make certain your health care professional knows if you are on any special diet, such as a low-sodium or low-sugar diet.

Pregnancy—Progesterone, a natural hormone that the body makes during pregnancy, has not caused problems. In fact, it is sometimes used in a few patients to treat a certain type of infertility that is caused when the body does not produce enough natural progesterone to support a pregnancy.

Other progestins have not been studied in pregnant women. Be sure to tell your doctor if you become pregnant while using any of the progestins. It is best to use some kind of birth control method while you are receiving progestins in high doses. High doses of progestins are not recommended for use during pregnancy since there have been some reports that they may cause birth defects in the genitals (sex organs) of a male fetus. Also, some of these progestins may cause male-like changes in a female fetus and female-like changes in a male fetus, but these problems usually can be reversed. Low doses of progestins, such as those doses used for contraception, have not caused major problems when used accidentally during pregnancy, but small (low birth weight) babies have occurred in some cases.

Breast-feeding—Although progestins pass into the breast milk, they have not been shown to cause problems in nursing babies. However, progestins may change the quality or amount (increase or decrease) of the mother's breast milk. It may be necessary for you to take another medicine or to stop breast-feeding during treatment. Be sure you have discussed the risks and benefits of the medicine with your doctor.

Children—Although there is no specific information comparing use of progestins in children with use in other age groups, this medicine is not expected to cause different side effects or problems in children than it does in adults.

Teenagers—Although there is no specific information comparing use of progestins in teenagers with use in other age groups, this medicine is not expected to cause different side effects or problems in teenagers than it does in adults.

Older adults—This medicine has been tested and has not been shown to cause different side effects or problems in older people than it does in younger adults.

Other medicines—Although certain medicines should not be used together at all, in other cases two different medicines may be used together even if an interaction might occur. In these cases, your doctor may want to change the dose, or other precautions may be necessary. When you are taking a progestin, it is especially important that your health care professional know if you are taking any of the following:

- Aminoglutethimide (e.g., Cytadren) or
- Carbamazepine (e.g., Tegretol) or
- Phenobarbital or
- Phenytoin (e.g., Dilantin) or
- Rifabutin (e.g., Mycobutin) or
- Rifampin (e.g., Rifadin, Rimactane)—These medicines may decrease the effects of progestins and increase the chance of pregnancy, so use of a second form of birth control is recommended

Other medical problems—The presence of other medical problems may affect the use of progestins. Make sure you tell your doctor if you have any other medical problems, especially:

- Asthma or
- Epilepsy (or history of) or
- Heart or circulation problems or
- Kidney disease (severe) or
- Migraine headaches—Progestins may cause fluid build-up and may cause these conditions to become worse
- Bleeding problems, undiagnosed, such as blood in urine or changes in vaginal bleeding—May make diagnosis of these problems more difficult
- Blood clots (or history of) or
- Stroke (or history of) or
- Varicose veins—May have greater chance of causing blood clots if these conditions are already present when high doses of progestins are taken
- Breast disease (such as breast lumps or cysts) (history of)—May make this condition worse in certain types of diseases that do not react in a positive way to progestins
- Central nervous system (CNS) disorders, such as mental depression (or history of) or
- High blood cholesterol—Effects of progestins may cause these conditions, or may make these conditions worse
- Diabetes mellitus (sugar diabetes)—May cause an increase in your blood sugar and a change in the amount of medicine you take for diabetes; progestins in high doses are more likely to cause this problem
- Liver disease—Effects of progestins may be increased and may make this condition worse
- Other conditions that increase the chances for osteoporosis (brittle bones)—Since it is possible that certain doses of progestins may cause temporary thinning of the bones by changing your hormone balance, it is important that your doctor know if you have an increased risk of osteoporosis. Some things that can increase your risk for having osteoporosis include cigarette smoking, abusing alcohol, taking or drinking large amounts of caffeine, and having a family history of osteoporosis or easily broken bones. Some medicines, such as glucocorticoids (cortisone-like medicines) or anticonvulsants (seizure medicine), can also cause thinning of the bones. However, it is thought that progestins can help protect against osteoporosis in postmenopausal women

Proper Use of This Medicine

To make the use of a progestin as safe and reliable as possible, you should understand how and when to take it and what effects may be expected. Progestins usually come with patient directions. Read them carefully before taking or using this medicine.

Take this medicine only as directed by your doctor. Do not take more of it and do not take it for a longer time than your doctor ordered. To do so may increase the chance of side effects. Try to take the medicine at the same time each day to reduce the possibility of side effects and to allow it to work better.

Progestins are often given together with certain medicines. If you are using a combination of medicines, make sure that you take each one at the proper time and do not mix them. Ask your health care professional to help you plan a way to remember to take your medicines at the right times.

Dosing—The dose of these medicines will be different for different patients. *Follow your doctor's orders or the directions on the label.* The following information includes only the average doses of these medicines. *If your dose is different, do not change it* unless your doctor tells you to do so.

The number of tablets, injections, or suppositories that you take, receive, or use depends on the strength of the medicine. Also, *the number of doses you take or use each day, the time allowed between doses, and the length of time you take or use the medicine depend on the medical problem for which you are taking progestins.*

For hydroxyprogesterone

- For *injection* dosage form:
  - —For controlling unusual and heavy bleeding of the uterus (dysfunctional uterine bleeding) or treating the problem of not having menstrual cycles over a period of time (amenorrhea):
    - Adults and teenagers—375 milligrams (mg) injected into a muscle as a single dose.
  - —For preparing the uterus for the menstrual period and to see if you are producing estrogen:
    - Adults and teenagers—125 to 250 mg injected into a muscle as a single dose on day ten of the menstrual cycle (counting from the first day of the last menstrual cycle). May be repeated every seven days if needed.

For medrogestone

- For *oral* dosage form (tablets):
  - —For preparing the uterus for the menstrual period, controlling unusual and heavy bleeding of the uterus (dysfunctional uterine bleeding), or treating the problem of not having menstrual cycles over a period of time (amenorrhea):
    - Adults and teenagers—5 to 10 milligrams (mg) a day for ten to fourteen days each month as directed by your doctor.

For medroxyprogesterone

- For *oral* dosage form (tablets):
  - —For controlling unusual and heavy bleeding of the uterus (dysfunctional uterine bleeding) or treating the problem of not having menstrual cycles over a period of time (amenorrhea):
    - Adults and teenagers—5 to 10 milligrams (mg) a day for five to ten days as directed by your doctor.
  - —For preparing the uterus for the menstrual period:
    - Adults and teenagers—10 mg daily for five or ten days as directed by your doctor.
  - —For hormone therapy during female menopause:
    - Adults—When taking estrogen each day on day one through twenty-five: Oral, 5 to 10 mg of medroxyprogesterone daily for ten to fourteen or more days each month as directed by your doctor. Or, your doctor may want you to take 2.5 mg a day without stopping. Your doctor will help decide the number of tablets that is best for you and when to take them.
- For *injection* dosage form:
  - —For treating cancer of the kidneys or uterus:
    - Adults and teenagers—At first, 400 to 1000 milligrams (mg) injected into a muscle as a single dose once a week. Then, your doctor may lower your dose to 400 mg or more once a month.

For megestrol

- For *oral* dosage form (suspension):
  - —For treating loss of appetite (anorexia), and loss of muscle (cachexia) or weight caused by acquired immunodeficiency syndrome (AIDS):
    - Adults and teenagers—800 milligrams (mg) a day for the first month. Then your doctor may want you to take 400 or 800 mg a day for three more months.
- For *oral* dosage form (tablets):
  - —For treating cancer of the breast:
    - Adults and teenagers—160 mg a day as a single dose or in divided doses for two or more months.
  - —For treating cancer of the uterus:
    - Adults and teenagers—40 to 320 mg a day for two or more months.

For norethindrone

- For *oral* dosage form (tablets):
  - —For controlling unusual and heavy bleeding of the uterus (dysfunctional uterine bleeding) or treating the problem of not having menstrual cycles over a period of time (amenorrhea):
    - Adults and teenagers—2.5 to 10 milligrams (mg) a day from day five through day twenty-five (counting from the first day of the last menstrual cycle). Or, your doctor may want you to take the medicine only for five to ten days as directed.
  - —For treating endometriosis:
    - Adults and teenagers—At first, 5 mg a day for two weeks. Then, your doctor may increase your dose slowly up to 15 mg a day for six to nine months. Let your doctor know if your menstrual period starts. Your doctor may want you to take more of the medicine or may want you to stop taking the medicine for a short period of time.

For progesterone

- For *injection* dosage form:
  - —For controlling unusual and heavy bleeding of the uterus (dysfunctional uterine bleeding) or treating

the problem of not having menstrual cycles over a period of time (amenorrhea):

- Adults and teenagers—5 to 10 milligrams (mg) injected into a muscle a day for six to ten days. Or, your doctor may want you to receive 100 or 150 mg injected into a muscle as a single dose. Sometimes your doctor may want you first to take another hormone called estrogen. If your menstrual period starts, your doctor will want you to stop taking the medicine.

- For *suppositories* dosage form (vaginal):
  —For maintaining a pregnancy (at ovulation and at the beginning of pregnancy):
  - Adults and teenagers—25 mg to 100 mg (one suppository) inserted into the vagina one or two times a day beginning near the time of ovulation. Your doctor may want you to receive the medicine for up to eleven weeks.

Missed dose—If you miss a dose of this medicine, take the missed dose as soon as possible. However, if it is almost time for your next dose, skip the missed dose and go back to your regular dosing schedule. Do not double doses.

Storage—To store this medicine:

- Keep out of the reach of children.
- Store away from heat.
- Do not store in the bathroom, near the kitchen sink, or in any other damp places. Heat or moisture may cause the medicine to break down.
- Keep the injectable form of this medicine from freezing.
- Do not keep outdated medicine or medicine no longer needed. Be sure that any discarded medicine is out of the reach of children.

Precautions While Using This Medicine

It is very important that your doctor check your progress at regular visits. This will allow your dosage to be adjusted to your changing needs, and will allow any unwanted effects to be detected. These visits will usually be every 6 to 12 months, but some doctors require them more often.

Vaginal bleeding of various amounts may occur between your regular menstrual periods during the first 3 months of use. This is sometimes called spotting when slight, or breakthrough bleeding when heavier. If this should occur, continue on your regular dosing schedule. *Check with your doctor:*

- If vaginal bleeding continues for an unusually long time.
- If your menstrual period has not started within 45 days of your last period.

Missed menstrual periods may occur. *If you suspect a pregnancy, you should stop taking this medicine immediately and call your doctor.* Your doctor will let you know if you should continue taking the progestin.

If you are scheduled for any laboratory tests, tell your health care professional that you are taking a progestin. Progestins can change certain test results.

In some patients, tenderness, swelling, or bleeding of the gums may occur. Brushing and flossing your teeth carefully and regularly and massaging your gums may help prevent this. See your dentist regularly to have your teeth cleaned. Check with your medical doctor or dentist if you have any questions about how to take care of your teeth and gums, or if you notice any tenderness, swelling, or bleeding of your gums.

You will need to use a birth control method while taking progestins for noncontraceptive use if you are fertile and sexually active.

Side Effects of This Medicine

Along with their needed effects, progestins used in high doses sometimes cause some unwanted effects such as blood clots, heart attacks, and strokes, or problems of the liver and eyes. Although these effects are rare, some of them can be very serious and cause death. It is not clear if these problems are due to the progestin. They may be caused by the disease or condition for which progestins are being used.

The following side effects may be caused by blood clots. Although not all of these side effects may occur, if they do occur they need immediate medical attention. *Get emergency help immediately* if any of the following side effects occur:

Rare

Symptoms of blood clotting problems, usually severe or sudden, such as, headache or migraine; loss of or change in speech, coordination, or vision; numbness of or pain in chest, arm or leg; unexplained shortness of breath

Also, check with your doctor as soon as possible if any of the following side effects occur:

More common

Changes in uterine bleeding (increased amounts of menstrual bleeding occurring at regular monthly periods; lighter uterine bleeding between menstrual periods; heavier uterine bleeding between regular monthly periods; or stopping of menstrual periods); symptoms of hyperglycemia (dry mouth; frequent urination; loss of appetite; unusual thirst)

Less common

Mental depression; skin rash; unexpected or increased flow of breast milk

Other side effects may occur that usually do not need medical attention. These side effects may go away during treatment as your body adjusts to the medicine. However, check with your doctor if any of the following side effects continue or are bothersome:

More common

Abdominal pain or cramping; swelling of face, ankles, or feet; mild blood pressure increase; mild headache; mood changes; nervousness; pain or irritation at place of injection site; unusual tiredness or weakness; weight gain

Less common

Acne; breast pain or tenderness; brown spots on exposed skin, possibly long-lasting; hot flashes; loss or gain of body, facial, or scalp hair; loss of sexual desire; nausea; trouble in sleeping

Not all of the side effects listed above have been reported for each of these medicines, but they have been reported for at least one of them. All of the progestins are similar, so any of the above side effects may occur with any of these medicines.

After you stop using this medicine, your body may need time to adjust. The length of time this takes depends on the amount of medicine you were using and how long you used it. During this period of time check with your doctor if you notice the following side effect:

Delayed return to fertility

Other side effects not listed above may also occur in some patients. If you notice any other effects, check with your doctor.

Additional Information

Once a medicine has been approved for marketing for a certain use, experience may show that it is also useful for other medical problems. Although these uses are not included in product labeling, progestins are used in certain patients with the following medical conditions:

- Carcinoma of the prostate
- Corpus luteum insufficiency
- Endometrial hyperplasia
- Polycystic ovary syndrome
- Precocious puberty

Other than the above information, there is no additional information relating to proper use, precautions, or side effects for these uses.

Revised: 08/08/95
Interim revision: 09/19/95; 06/26/96

PROPAFENONE Systemic

A commonly used brand name in the U.S. and Canada is Rythmol.

Description

Propafenone (proe-pa-FEEN-none) belongs to the group of medicines known as antiarrhythmics. It is used to correct irregular heartbeats to a normal rhythm.

Propafenone produces its helpful effects by slowing nerve impulses in the heart and making the heart tissue less sensitive.

There is a chance that propafenone may cause new or make worse existing heart rhythm problems when it is used. Since similar medicines have been shown to cause severe problems in some patients, propafenone is only used to treat serious heart rhythm problems. Discuss this possible effect with your doctor.

This medicine is available only with your doctor's prescription, in the following dosage form:

Oral

- Tablets (U.S. and Canada)

Before Using This Medicine

In deciding to use a medicine, the risks of taking the medicine must be weighed against the good it will do. This is a decision you and your doctor will make. For propafenone, the following should be considered:

Allergies—Tell your doctor if you have ever had any unusual or allergic reaction to propafenone. Also tell your health care professional if you are allergic to any other substances, such as foods, preservatives, or dyes.

Pregnancy—Propafenone has not been studied in pregnant women. Although this medicine has not been shown to cause birth defects in animal studies, it has been shown to reduce fertility in monkeys, dogs, and rabbits. In addition, in rats it caused decreased growth in the infant and deaths of mothers and infants. Before taking propafenone, make sure your doctor knows if you are pregnant or if you may become pregnant.

Breast-feeding—Propafenone passes into breast milk. However, this medicine has not been reported to cause problems in nursing babies.

Children—Propafenone can cause serious side effects in any patient. Therefore, it is especially important that you discuss with the child's doctor the good that this medicine may do as well as the risks of using it.

Older adults—Many medicines have not been studied specifically in older people. Therefore, it may not be known whether they work exactly the same way they do in younger adults or if they cause different side effects or problems in older people. There is no specific information comparing use of propafenone in the elderly with use in other age groups.

Other medicines—Although certain medicines should not be used together at all, in other cases two different medicines may be used together even if an interaction might occur. In these cases, your doctor may want to change the dose, or other precautions may be necessary. When you are taking propafenone it is especially important that your health care professional know if you are taking either of the following:

- Digoxin (e.g., Lanoxin) or
- Warfarin (e.g., Coumadin)—Effects of these medicines may be increased when used with propafenone

Other medical problems—The presence of other medical problems may affect the use of propafenone. Make sure you tell your doctor if you have any other medical problems, especially:

- Asthma or
- Bronchitis or

- Emphysema—Propafenone can increase trouble in breathing
- Bradycardia (unusually slow heartbeat)—There is a risk of further decreased heart function
- Congestive heart failure—Propafenone may make this condition worse
- Kidney disease or
- Liver disease—Effects of propafenone may be increased because of slower removal from the body
- Recent heart attack—Risk of irregular heartbeat may be increased
- If you have a pacemaker—Propafenone may interfere with the pacemaker and require more careful follow-up by the doctor

Proper Use of This Medicine

Take propafenone exactly as directed by your doctor, even though you may feel well. Do not take more or less of it than your doctor ordered.

This medicine works best when there is a constant amount in the blood. *To help keep the amount constant, do not miss any doses. Also, it is best to take each dose at evenly spaced times day and night.* For example, if you are to take 3 doses a day, doses should be spaced about 8 hours apart. If you need help in planning the best times to take your medicine, check with your health care professional.

Dosing—The dose of propafenone will be different for different patients. *Follow your doctor's orders or the directions on the label.* The following information includes only the average doses of propafenone. *If your dose is different, do not change it* unless your doctor tells you to do so:

- The number of tablets that you take depends on the strength of the medicine.
- For *oral* dosage forms (tablets):
  —Adults: 150 milligrams every eight hours; may be increased to 225 milligrams every eight hours or 300 mg every twelve hours; up to 300 mg every eight hours.

Missed dose—If you miss a dose of propafenone and remember within 4 hours, take it as soon as possible. However, if you do not remember until later, skip the missed dose and go back to your regular dosing schedule. Do not double doses.

Storage—To store this medicine:

- Keep out of the reach of children.
- Store away from heat and direct light.
- Do not store in the bathroom, near the kitchen sink, or in other damp places. Heat or moisture may cause the medicine to break down.
- Do not keep outdated medicine or medicine no longer needed. Be sure that any discarded medicine is out of the reach of children.

Precautions While Using This Medicine

It is important that your doctor check your progress at regular visits to make sure the medicine is working properly. This will allow changes to be made in the amount of medicine you are taking, if necessary.

Your doctor may want you to carry a medical identification card or bracelet stating that you are using this medicine.

Before having any kind of surgery (including dental surgery) or emergency treatment, tell the medical doctor or dentist in charge that you are taking this medicine.

Propafenone may cause some people to become dizzy or lightheaded. Make sure you know how you react to this medicine before you drive, use machines, or do anything else that could be dangerous if you are dizzy.

Side Effects of This Medicine

Along with its needed effects, a medicine may cause some unwanted effects. Although not all of these side effects may occur, if they do occur they may need medical attention.

Check with your doctor as soon as possible if any of the following side effects occur:

More common
Fast or irregular heartbeat

Less common
Chest pain; shortness of breath; swelling of feet or lower legs

Rare
Fever or chills; joint pain; low blood pressure; slow heartbeat; trembling or shaking

Other side effects may occur that usually do not need medical attention. These side effects may go away during treatment as your body adjusts to the medicine. However, check with your doctor if any of the following side effects continue or are bothersome:

More common
Change in taste or bitter or metallic taste; dizziness

Less common
Blurred vision; constipation or diarrhea; dryness of mouth; headache; nausea and/or vomiting; skin rash; unusual tiredness or weakness

Other side effects not listed above may also occur in some patients. If you notice any other effects, check with your doctor.

Revised: 10/07/92

PROPIOMAZINE Systemic†

A commonly used brand name in the U.S. is Largon.

†Not commercially available in Canada.

Description

Propiomazine (proe-pee-OH-ma-zeen) is used to produce sleepiness or drowsiness and to relieve anxiety before or during surgery or certain procedures. It is also used with analgesics (pain medicine) during labor to produce drowsiness and relieve anxiety.

Propiomazine is given only by or under the immediate supervision of a medical doctor or dentist trained to use this medicine. If you will be receiving propiomazine during surgery, your doctor or anesthesiologist will give you the medicine and closely follow your progress.

Propiomazine is available in the following dosage form:

Parenteral

- Injection (U.S.)

Before Receiving This Medicine

In deciding to use a medicine, the risks of taking the medicine must be weighed against the good it will do. This is a decision you and your doctor will make. For propiomazine, the following should be considered:

Allergies—Tell your doctor if you have ever had any unusual or allergic reaction to propiomazine or to other phenothiazines (such as acetophenazine, chlorpromazine, fluphenazine, mesoridazine, perphenazine, prochlorperazine, promazine, promethazine, thioridazine, trifluoperazine, triflupromazine, trimeprazine). Also tell your health care professional if you are allergic to any other substances, such as foods, preservatives, or dyes.

Pregnancy—Propiomazine has not been shown to cause problems in pregnant women.

Breast-feeding—Propiomazine has not been reported to cause problems in nursing babies.

Children—Although there is no specific information comparing use of propiomazine in children with use in other age groups, this medicine is not expected to cause different side effects or problems in children than it does in adults.

Older adults—Many medicines have not been studied specifically in older people. Therefore, it may not be known whether they work exactly the same way they do in younger adults or if they cause different side effects or problems in older people. There is no specific information comparing use of propiomazine in the elderly with use in other age groups.

Other medicines—Although certain medicines should not be used together at all, in other cases 2 different medicines may be used together even if an interaction might occur. In these cases, your doctor may want to change the dose, or other precautions may be necessary. When you are taking propiomazine, it is especially important that your health care professional know if you are taking any of the following:

- Central nervous system (CNS) depressants (medicine that causes drowsiness) or
- Tricyclic antidepressants (medicine for depression)—Taking these medicines with propiomazine will cause an increase in CNS depressant effects

Proper Use of This Medicine

Dosing—The dose of propiomazine will be different for different patients. Your doctor will decide on the right amount for you. The dose will depend on:

- Your age;
- Your general physical condition;
- The kind of surgery you are having; and
- Other medicines you are taking or will receive before and during surgery or labor.

Precautions After Receiving This Medicine

For patients going home within 24 hours after receiving propiomazine:

- Propiomazine may cause some people to feel drowsy, tired, or weak for up to one or two days after it has been given. It may also cause problems with coordination and one's ability to think. Therefore, *do not drive, use machines, or do other things that could be dangerous if you are not alert* until the effects of the medicine have disappeared or until the day after receiving propiomazine, whichever period of time is longer.
- *Do not drink alcoholic beverages or take other CNS depressants (medicines that slow down the nervous system, possibly causing drowsiness) for about 24 hours after you have received propiomazine, unless otherwise directed by your doctor.* To do so may add to the effects of the medicine. Some examples of CNS depressants are antihistamines or medicine for hay fever, other allergies, or colds; other sedatives, tranquilizers, or sleeping medicine; prescription pain medicine or narcotics; medicine for seizures; and muscle relaxants.

Side Effects of This Medicine

Along with its needed effects, a medicine may cause some unwanted effects. Although not all of these side effects may occur, if they do occur they may need medical attention.

Check with your doctor immediately if any of the following side effects occur:

Rare

Convulsions (seizures); difficult or unusually fast breathing; fast or irregular heartbeat or pulse; fever (high); high or low blood pressure; loss of bladder control; muscle stiffness (severe); unusual increase in sweating; unusually pale skin; unusual tiredness or weakness

Also, check with your doctor as soon as possible if the following side effect occurs:

Redness, swelling, or pain at place of injection

Other side effects may occur that usually do not need medical attention. The following side effects may go away as the effects of propiomazine wear off. However, check with your doctor if any of the following side effects continue or are bothersome:

More common

Dizziness; drowsiness (prolonged); dryness of mouth

Less common

Confusion; diarrhea; nausea or vomiting; restlessness; skin rash; stomach pain

Other side effects not listed above may also occur in some patients. If you notice any other effects, check with your doctor.

Revised: 04/16/93
Interim revision: 07/26/94

PSEUDOEPHEDRINE Systemic

Some commonly used brand names are:

In the U.S.—

- Cenafed
- Chlor-Trimeton Non-Drowsy Decongestant 4 Hour
- Decofed
- Dorcol Children's Decongestant Liquid
- Drixoral Non-Drowsy Formula
- Efidac/24
- Genaphed
- Halofed
- Halofed Adult Strength
- Myfedrine
- Novafed
- PediaCare Infants' Oral Decongestant Drops
- Pseudo
- Pseudogest
- Sudafed
- Sudafed Liquid, Children's
- Sudafed 12 Hour
- Sufedrin

Generic name product may also be available.

In Canada—

- Balminil Decongestant Syrup
- Benylin Decongestant
- Eltor 120
- Maxenal
- Robidrine
- Sudafed
- Sudafed 12 Hour

Generic name product may also be available.

Description

Pseudoephedrine (soo-doe-e-FED-rin) is used to relieve nasal or sinus congestion caused by the common cold, sinusitis, and hay fever and other respiratory allergies. It is also used to relieve ear congestion caused by ear inflammation or infection.

Some of these preparations are available only with your doctor's prescription. Others are available without a prescription; however, your doctor may have special instructions on the proper dose of pseudoephedrine for your medical condition.

Pseudoephedrine is available in the following dosage forms:

Oral

- Capsules (Canada)
- Extended-release capsules (U.S. and Canada)
- Oral solution (U.S.)
- Syrup (U.S. and Canada)
- Tablets (U.S. and Canada)
- Extended-release tablets (U.S. and Canada)

Before Using This Medicine

If you are taking this medicine without a prescription, carefully read and follow any precautions on the label. For pseudoephedrine, the following should be considered:

Allergies—Tell your doctor if you have ever had any unusual or allergic reaction to pseudoephedrine or similar medicines, such as albuterol, amphetamines, ephedrine, epinephrine, isoproterenol, metaproterenol, norepinephrine, phenylephrine, phenylpropanolamine, or terbutaline. Also tell your health care professional if you are allergic to any other substances, such as foods, preservatives, or dyes.

Pregnancy—Studies on birth defects have not been done in humans. Pseudoephedrine has not been shown to cause birth defects in animal studies. However, studies in animals have shown that pseudoephedrine causes a reduction in average weight, length, and rate of bone formation in the animal fetus.

Breast-feeding—Pseudoephedrine passes into breast milk and may cause unwanted effects in nursing babies (especially newborn and premature babies).

Children—Pseudoephedrine may be more likely to cause side effects in infants, especially newborn and premature infants, than in older children and adults.

Older adults—Many medicines have not been studied specifically in older people. Therefore, it may not be known whether they work exactly the same way they do in younger adults or if they cause different side effects or problems in older people. There is no specific information comparing use of pseudoephedrine in the elderly with use in other age groups.

Other medicines—Although certain medicines should not be used together at all, in other cases two different medicines may be used together even if an interaction might occur. In these cases, your doctor may want to change the dose, or other precautions may be necessary. When you are taking pseudoephedrine, it is especially important that your health care professional knows if you are taking any of the following:

- Beta-blockers (acebutolol [e.g., Sectral], atenolol [e.g., Tenormin], betaxolol [e.g., Kerlone], bisoprolol [e.g., Zebeta], carteolol [e.g., Cartrol], labetalol [e.g., Normodyne], metoprolol [e.g., Lopressor], nadolol [e.g., Corgard], oxprenolol [e.g., Trasicor], penbutolol [e.g., Levatol], pindolol [e.g., Visken], propranolol [e.g., Inderal], sotalol [e.g., Sotacor], timolol [e.g., Blocadren])—Pseudoephedrine may decrease the effect of these medicines; also, taking pseudoephedrine with beta-blockers may increase the chance of side effects

• Cocaine—Using cocaine with pseudoephedrine may increase the effects of either one of these medicines on the heart and increase the chance of side effects

• Monoamine oxidase (MAO) inhibitors (furazolidone [e.g., Furoxone], isocarboxazid [e.g., Marplan], phenelzine [e.g., Nardil], procarbazine [e.g., Matulane], selegiline [e.g., Eldepryl], tranylcypromine [e.g., Parnate])—Taking pseudoephedrine while you are taking or within 2 weeks of taking monoamine oxidase (MAO) inhibitors may increase the chance of serious side effects

Other medical problems—The presence of other medical problems may affect the use of pseudoephedrine. Make sure you tell your doctor if you have any other medical problems, especially:

- Diabetes mellitus (sugar diabetes)
- Enlarged prostate or
- Heart or blood vessel disease or
- High blood pressure—Pseudoephedrine may make the condition worse
- Overactive thyroid

Proper Use of This Medicine

For patients taking *pseudoephedrine extended-release capsules:*

- Swallow the capsule whole. However, if the capsule is too large to swallow, you may mix the contents of the capsule with jam or jelly and swallow without chewing.
- Do not crush or chew before swallowing.

For patients taking *pseudoephedrine extended-release tablets:*

- Swallow the tablet whole.
- Do not break, crush, or chew before swallowing.

To help prevent trouble in sleeping, *take the last dose of pseudoephedrine for each day a few hours before bedtime.* If you have any questions about this, check with your doctor.

Take this medicine only as directed. Do not take more of it, do not take it more often, and do not take it for a longer period of time than recommended on the label (usually 7 days), unless otherwise directed by your doctor. To do so may increase the chance of side effects.

Dosing—The dose of pseudoephedrine will be different for different patients. *Follow your doctor's orders or the directions on the label.* The following information includes only the average doses of pseudoephedrine. *If your dose is different, do not change it* unless your doctor tells you to do so.

The number of capsules, tablets, or teaspoonfuls of solution or syrup that you take each day depends on the strength of the medicine. Also, the time between doses depends on whether you are taking a short-acting or long-acting form of pseudoephedrine.

• For nasal or sinus congestion:

—For *regular (short-acting) oral* dosage form (capsules, oral solution, syrup, or tablets):

• Adults and children 12 years of age and older—60 milligrams (mg) every four to six hours. Do not take more than 240 mg in twenty-four hours.

• Children 6 to 12 years of age—30 mg every four to six hours. Do not take more than 120 mg in twenty-four hours.

• Children 2 to 6 years of age—15 mg every four to six hours. Do not take more than 60 mg in twenty-four hours.

• Children up to 2 years of age—Use and dose must be determined by your doctor.

—For *long-acting oral* dosage form (extended-release capsules or extended-release tablets):

• Adults and children 12 years of age and older—120 mg every 12 hours, or 240 mg every 24 hours. Do not take more than 240 mg in twenty-four hours.

• Children up to 12 years of age—Use is not recommended.

Missed dose—If you miss a dose of this medicine and you remember within an hour or so of the missed dose, take it right away. However, if you do not remember until later, skip the missed dose and go back to your regular dosing schedule. Do not double doses.

Storage—To store this medicine:

- Keep out of the reach of children.
- Store away from heat and direct light.
- Do not store the capsule or tablet form of this medicine in the bathroom, near the kitchen sink, or in other damp places. Heat or moisture may cause the medicine to break down.
- Keep the liquid form of this medicine from freezing.
- Do not keep outdated medicine or medicine no longer needed. Be sure that any discarded medicine is out of the reach of children.

Precautions While Using This Medicine

If symptoms do not improve within 7 days or if you also have a high fever, check with your doctor since these signs may mean that you have other medical problems.

Side Effects of This Medicine

Along with its needed effects, a medicine may cause some unwanted effects. Although not all of these side effects may occur, if they do occur they may need medical attention.

Check with your doctor as soon as possible if any of the following side effects occur:

Rare—more common with high doses

Convulsions (seizures); hallucinations (seeing, hearing, or feeling things that are not there); irregular or slow heartbeat; shortness of breath or troubled breathing

Symptoms of overdose

Convulsions (seizures); fast breathing; hallucinations (seeing, hearing, or feeling things that are not there); increase in blood pressure; irregular heartbeat (continuing); shortness of breath or troubled breathing (severe or continuing); slow or fast heartbeat (severe or continuing); unusual nervousness, restlessness, or excitement

Other side effects may occur that usually do not need medical attention. These side effects may go away during treatment as your body adjusts to the medicine. However, check with your health care professional if any of the following side effects continue or are bothersome:

More common

Nervousness; restlessness; trouble in sleeping

Less common

Difficult or painful urination; dizziness or lightheadedness; fast or pounding heartbeat; headache; increased sweating; nausea or vomiting; trembling; troubled breathing; unusual paleness; weakness

Other side effects not listed above may also occur in some patients. If you notice any other effects, check with your health care professional.

Revised: 04/19/94

PYRANTEL Oral

Some commonly used brand names are:

In the U.S.—

Antiminth

Reese's Pinworm Medicine

Generic name product may also be available.

In Canada—

Combantrin

Description

Pyrantel (pi-RAN-tel) belongs to the family of medicines called anthelmintics (ant-hel-MIN-tiks). Anthelmintics are used in the treatment of worm infections.

Pyrantel is used to treat:

- common roundworms (ascariasis);
- pinworms (enterobiasis; oxyuriasis); and
- more than one worm infection at a time.

This medicine may also be used for other worm infections as determined by your doctor.

Pyrantel works by paralyzing the worms. They are then passed in the stool.

Pyrantel is available in the following dosage forms:

Oral

- Oral suspension (U.S. and Canada)
- Tablets (Canada)

Before Using This Medicine

In deciding to use a medicine, the risks of taking the medicine must be weighed against the good it will do. This is a decision you and your doctor will make. For pyrantel, the following should be considered:

Allergies—Tell your doctor if you have ever had any unusual or allergic reaction to pyrantel. Also tell your health care professional if you are allergic to any other substances, such as foods, preservatives, or dyes.

Pregnancy—Studies have not been done in pregnant women. However, pyrantel has not been reported to cause birth defects or other problems in animal studies.

Breast-feeding—Only small amounts of pyrantel are absorbed into the body. Pyrantel has not been reported to cause problems in nursing babies.

Children—This medicine has been tested in a limited number of children 2 years of age or older and, in effective doses, has not been reported to cause different side effects or problems in children than it does in adults.

Older adults—Many medicines have not been studied specifically in older people. Therefore, it may not be known whether they work exactly the same way they do in younger adults or if they cause different side effects or problems in older people. There is no specific information comparing use of pyrantel in the elderly with use in other age groups.

Other medicines—Although certain medicines should not be used together at all, in other cases two different medicines may be used together even if an interaction might occur. In these cases, your doctor may want to change the dose, or other precautions may be necessary. When you are taking pyrantel, it is especially important that your health care professional know if you are taking any of the following:

- Piperazine (e.g., Entacyl)—Using pyrantel and piperazine together may decrease the effectiveness of pyrantel

Proper Use of This Medicine

No special preparations (for example, special diets, fasting, other medicines, laxatives, or enemas) are necessary before, during, or immediately after you take pyrantel.

For patients taking pyrantel *oral suspension:*

- Use a specially marked measuring spoon or other device to measure each dose accurately. The average household teaspoon may not hold the right amount of liquid.

To help clear up your infection completely, *take this medicine exactly as directed by your doctor.* In some infections a second dose of this medicine may be required to clear up the infection completely.

For patients taking pyrantel for *pinworms:*

- Pinworms may be easily passed from one person to another, especially among persons in the same household. Therefore, all household members may have to be treated at the same time to prevent their infection or reinfection. Also, all household members may have to be treated again in 2 to 3 weeks to clear up the infection completely.

Dosing—The dose of pyrantel will be different for different patients. *Follow your doctor's orders or the directions on the label.* The following information includes only the average doses of pyrantel. *If your dose is different, do not change it* unless your doctor tells you to do so.

The number of tablets or teaspoonfuls of suspension that you take depends on the strength of the medicine. Also, *the number of doses you take each day, the time allowed between doses, and the length of time you take the medicine depend on the medical problem for which you are taking pyrantel.*

- For *oral* dosage forms (oral suspension or tablets):
  —Adults and children 2 years of age and older: Dose is based on body weight and will be determined by your doctor. It is taken as a single dose and may need to be repeated in two to three weeks.

Storage—To store this medicine:
- Keep out of the reach of children.
- Store away from heat and direct light.
- Keep the liquid form of this medicine from freezing.
- Do not keep outdated medicine or medicine no longer needed. Be sure that any discarded medicine is out of the reach of children.

Precautions While Using This Medicine

If your symptoms do not improve within a few days, or if they become worse, check with your doctor.

This medicine may cause some people to become dizzy, drowsy, or less alert than they are normally. *Make sure you know how you react to this medicine before you drive, use machines, or do anything else that could be dangerous if you are dizzy or are not alert.* If these reactions are especially bothersome, check with your doctor.

For patients taking pyrantel for *pinworms:*
- In some patients, pinworms may return after treatment with pyrantel. Washing (not shaking) all bedding and nightclothes (pajamas) after treatment may help to prevent this.
- Some doctors may also recommend other measures to help keep your infection from returning. If you have any questions about this, check with your doctor.

Side Effects of This Medicine

Along with its needed effects, a medicine may cause some unwanted effects. Although not all of these side effects may occur, if they do occur they may need medical attention.

Check with your doctor as soon as possible if any of the following side effects occur:

Rare
Skin rash

Other side effects may occur that usually do not need medical attention. These side effects may go away during treatment as your body adjusts to the medicine. However, check with your doctor if any of the following side effects continue or are bothersome:

Less common
Abdominal or stomach cramps or pain; diarrhea; dizziness; drowsiness; headache; loss of appetite; nausea or vomiting; trouble in sleeping

Other side effects not listed above may also occur in some patients. If you notice any other effects, check with your doctor.

Additional Information

Once a medicine has been approved for marketing for a certain use, experience may show that it is also useful for other medical problems. Although this use is not included in product labeling, pyrantel is used in certain patients with the following medical condition:
- Hookworm infection

For patients taking this medicine for *hookworm infection:*
- Anemia (iron-poor blood) may occur in patients with hookworm infections. Therefore, your doctor may want you to take iron supplements to help clear up the anemia. If so, it is important to take iron every day while you are being treated for hookworms. Do not miss any doses. Your doctor may also want you to keep taking iron supplements for up to 6 months after you stop taking pyrantel. If you have any questions about this, check with your doctor.

Other than the above information, there is no additional information relating to proper use, precautions, or side effects for this use.

Revised: 01/19/93

PYRAZINAMIDE Systemic

Some commonly used brand names in Canada are pms-Pyrazinamide and Tebrazid.

Description

Pyrazinamide (peer-a-ZIN-a-mide) belongs to the family of medicines called anti-infectives. It is used, along with other medicines, to treat tuberculosis (TB).

To help clear up your tuberculosis (TB) completely, you must keep taking this medicine for the full time of treatment, even if you begin to feel better. This is very important. It is also important that you do not miss any doses.

Pyrazinamide is available only with your doctor's prescription, in the following dosage form:

Oral
- Tablets (U.S. and Canada)

Before Using This Medicine

In deciding to use a medicine, the risks of taking the medicine must be weighed against the good it will do. This is a decision you and your doctor will make. For pyrazinamide, the following should be considered:

Allergies—Tell your doctor if you have ever had any unusual or allergic reaction to pyrazinamide or to ethionamide (e.g., Trecator-SC), isoniazid (e.g., INH, Nydrazid), or niacin (e.g., Nicobid, nicotinic acid). Also tell your health care professional if you are allergic to any other substances, such as foods, preservatives, or dyes.

Pregnancy—Studies on effects in pregnancy have not been done in either humans or animals.

Breast-feeding—Pyrazinamide passes into the breast milk in small amounts.

Children—Pyrazinamide has been used in children and, in effective doses, has not been reported to cause different side effects or problems in children than it does in adults.

Older adults—Many medicines have not been studied specifically in older people. Therefore, it may not be known whether they work exactly the same way they do in younger adults. Although there is no specific information comparing pyrazinamide in the elderly with use in other age groups, this medicine is not expected to cause different side effects or problems in older people than it does in younger adults.

Other medicines—Although certain medicines should not be used together at all, in other cases two different medicines may be used together even if an interaction might occur. In these cases, your doctor may want to change the dose, or other precautions may be necessary. Tell your health care professional if you are taking any other prescription or nonprescription (over-the-counter [OTC]) medicine.

Other medical problems—The presence of other medical problems may affect the use of pyrazinamide. Make sure you tell your doctor if you have any other medical problems, especially:

- Gout (history of)—Pyrazinamide may worsen or cause a gout attack in patients with a history of gout
- Liver disease (severe)—Patients with severe liver disease who take pyrazinamide may have an increase in side effects

Proper Use of This Medicine

To help clear up your TB completely, *it is important that you keep taking this medicine for the full time of treatment,* even if you begin to feel better after a few weeks. *It is important that you do not miss any doses.*

Dosing—The dose of pyrazinamide will be different for different patients. *Follow your doctor's orders or the directions on the label.* The following information includes only the average doses of pyrazinamide. *If your dose is different, do not change it* unless your doctor tells you to do so.

- For *oral* dosage form (tablets):
  —For tuberculosis (TB):
    - Adults and children—Dose is based on body weight. The usual dose is 15 to 30 milligrams (mg) of pyrazinamide per kilogram (kg) (6.8 to 13.6 mg per pound) of body weight once a day; or 50 to 70 mg per kg (22.7 to 31.8 mg per pound) two times a week or three times a week, depending on the schedule your doctor chooses for you. This medicine must be taken along with other medicines used to treat TB.

Missed dose—If you do miss a dose of this medicine, take it as soon as possible. However, if it is almost time for your next dose, skip the missed dose and go back to your regular dosing schedule. Do not double doses.

Storage—To store this medicine:

- Keep out of the reach of children.
- Store away from heat and direct light.
- Do not store in the bathroom, near the kitchen sink, or in other damp places. Heat or moisture may cause the medicine to break down.
- Do not keep outdated medicine or medicine no longer needed. Be sure that any discarded medicine is out of the reach of children.

Precautions While Using This Medicine

It is very important that your doctor check your progress at regular visits.

If your symptoms do not improve within 2 to 3 weeks, or if they become worse, check with your doctor.

For diabetic patients:

- *This medicine may cause false test results with urine ketone tests.* Check with your doctor before changing your diet or the dosage of your diabetes medicine.

Side Effects of This Medicine

Along with its needed effects, a medicine may cause some unwanted effects. Although not all of these side effects may occur, if they do occur they may need medical attention.

Check with your doctor immediately if any of the following side effects occur:

More common

Pain in large and small joints

Rare

Loss of appetite; pain and swelling of joints, especially big toe, ankle, and knee; tense, hot skin over affected joints; unusual tiredness or weakness; yellow eyes or skin

Other side effects may occur that usually do not need medical attention. These side effects may go away during treatment as your body adjusts to the medicine. However, check with your doctor if any of the following side effects continue or are bothersome:

Rare

Itching; skin rash

Other side effects not listed above may also occur in some patients. If you notice any other effects, check with your doctor.

Revised: 08/15/97

PYRETHRINS AND PIPERONYL BUTOXIDE Topical

Some commonly used brand names are:

In the U.S.—

A-200 Gel Concentrate	Pyrinyl
A-200 Shampoo Concentrate	R & C
Barc	Rid
Blue	Tisit
Licetrol	Tisit Blue
Pronto Lice Killing Shampoo Kit	Tisit Shampoo
	Triple X

In Canada—

R & C

Description

Medicine containing pyrethrins (pye-REE-thrins) is used to treat head, body, and pubic lice infections. This medicine is absorbed by the lice and destroys them by acting on their nervous systems. It does not affect humans in this way. The piperonyl butoxide (pye-PEER-i-nil byoo-TOX-ide) is included to make the pyrethrins more effective in killing the lice. This combination medicine is known as a pediculicide (pe-DIK-yoo-li-side).

This medicine is available without a prescription; however, your doctor may have special instructions on the proper use of this medicine for your medical condition.

Pyrethrins and piperonyl butoxide combination medicine is available in the following dosage forms:

Topical

- Gel (U.S.)
- Solution shampoo (U.S. and Canada)
- Topical solution (U.S.)

Before Using This Medicine

If you are using this medicine without a prescription, carefully read and follow any precautions on the label. For pyrethrins and piperonyl butoxide combination, the following should be considered:

Allergies—Tell your doctor if you have ever had any unusual or allergic reaction to pyrethrins, piperonyl butoxide, ragweed, chrysanthemum plants, or kerosene or other petroleum products. Also tell your health care professional if you are allergic to any other substances, such as preservatives or dyes.

Pregnancy—Pyrethrins and piperonyl butoxide may be absorbed through the skin. However, this medicine has not been shown to cause birth defects or other problems in humans when used on the skin.

Breast-feeding—Pyrethrins and piperonyl butoxide combination may be absorbed through the mother's skin. It is not known whether pyrethrins and piperonyl butoxide combination passes into the breast milk. Although most medicines pass into breast milk in small amounts, many of them may be used safely while breast-feeding. Mothers who are using this medicine and who wish to breast-feed should discuss this with their doctor.

Children—Although there is no specific information comparing use of pyrethrins and piperonyl butoxide combination in children with use in other age groups, this medicine is not expected to cause different side effects or problems in children than it does in adults.

Older adults—Many medicines have not been studied specifically in older people. Therefore, it may not be known whether they work exactly the same way they do in younger adults. Although there is no specific information comparing use of pyrethrins and piperonyl butoxide combination medicine in the elderly with use in other age groups, this medicine is not expected to cause different side effects or problems in older people than it does in younger adults.

Other medical problems—The presence of other medical problems may affect the use of pyrethrins and piperonyl butoxide combination. Make sure you tell your doctor if you have any other medical problems, especially:

- Inflammation of the skin (severe)—Use of pyrethrins and piperonyl butoxide combination may make the condition worse

Proper Use of This Medicine

Pyrethrins and piperonyl butoxide combination medicine usually comes with patient directions. Read them carefully before using this medicine.

Use this medicine only as directed. Do not use more of it and do not use it more often than recommended on the label. To do so may increase the chance of absorption through the skin and the chance of side effects.

Keep pyrethrins and piperonyl butoxide combination medicine away from the mouth and do not inhale it. This medicine is harmful if swallowed or inhaled.

To lessen the chance of inhaling this medicine, apply it in a well-ventilated room (for example, one with free flowing air or with a fan turned on).

Keep this medicine away from the eyes and other mucous membranes, such as the inside of the nose, mouth, or vagina, because it may cause irritation. If you accidentally get some in your eyes, flush them thoroughly with water at once.

Do not apply this medicine to the eyelashes or eyebrows. If they become infected with lice, check with your doctor.

To use the *gel or solution form* of this medicine:

- Apply enough medicine to thoroughly wet the dry hair and scalp or skin. Allow the medicine to remain on the affected areas for exactly 10 minutes.
- Then, thoroughly wash the affected areas with warm water and soap or regular shampoo. Rinse thoroughly and dry with a clean towel.

To use the *shampoo form* of this medicine:

- Apply enough medicine to thoroughly wet the dry hair and scalp or skin. Allow the medicine to remain on the affected areas for exactly 10 minutes.

- Then use a small amount of water and work shampoo into the hair and scalp or skin until a lather forms. Rinse thoroughly and dry with a clean towel.

After rinsing and drying, use a nit removal comb (special fine-toothed comb, usually included with this medicine) to remove the dead lice and eggs (nits) from hair.

Immediately after using this medicine, wash your hands to remove any medicine that may be on them.

This medicine should be used again in 7 to 10 days after the first treatment in order to kill any newly hatched lice.

Lice can easily move from one person to another by close body contact. This can happen also by direct contact with such things as clothing, hats, scarves, bedding, towels, washcloths, hairbrushes and combs, or the hair of infected persons. Therefore, *all members of your household should be examined for lice and receive treatment if they are found to be infected.*

To use this medicine for *pubic (crab) lice:*

- Your sexual partner may also need to be treated, since the infection may spread to persons in close contact. If your partner is not being treated or if you have any questions about this, check with your doctor.

Dosing—The dose of pyrethrins and piperonyl butoxide combination will be different for different patients. *Follow your doctor's orders or the directions on the label.* The following information includes only the average doses of pyrethrins and piperonyl butoxide combination. *If your dose is different, do not change it* unless your doctor tells you to do so.

- For *topical* dosage forms (gel, solution shampoo, and topical solution):
  - —For head, body, or pubic lice:
    - Adults and children—Use one time, then repeat one time in seven to ten days.

Storage—To store this medicine:

- Keep out of the reach of children.
- Store away from heat and direct light.
- Keep the medicine from freezing.
- Do not keep outdated medicine or medicine no longer needed. Be sure that any discarded medicine is out of the reach of children.

Precautions While Using This Medicine

To prevent reinfection or spreading of the infection to other people, good health habits are also required. These include the following:

- For *head lice*

  —Machine wash all clothing (including hats, scarves, and coats), bedding, towels, and washcloths in very hot water and dry them by using the hot cycle of a dryer for at least 20 minutes. Clothing or bedding that cannot be washed should be dry-cleaned or sealed in a plastic bag for 2 weeks.

  —Shampoo all wigs and hairpieces.

  —Wash all hairbrushes and combs in very hot soapy water (above 130 °F) for 5 to 10 minutes and do not share them with other people.

  —Clean the house or room by thoroughly vacuuming upholstered furniture, rugs, and floors.

- For *body lice*

  —Machine wash all clothing, bedding, towels, and washcloths in very hot water and dry them by using the hot cycle of a dryer for at least 20 minutes. Clothing or bedding that cannot be washed should be dry-cleaned or sealed in a plastic bag for 2 weeks.

  —Clean the house or room by thoroughly vacuuming upholstered furniture, rugs, and floors.

- For *pubic lice*

  —Machine wash all clothing (especially underwear), bedding, towels, and washcloths in very hot water and dry them by using the hot cycle of a dryer for at least 20 minutes. Clothing or bedding that cannot be washed should be dry-cleaned or sealed in a plastic bag for 2 weeks.

  —Scrub toilet seats frequently.

Side Effects of This Medicine

Along with its needed effects, a medicine may cause some unwanted effects. Although not all of these side effects may occur, if they do occur they may need medical attention.

Check with your doctor as soon as possible if any of the following side effects occur:

Less common or rare

Skin irritation not present before use of this medicine; skin rash or infection; sneezing (sudden attacks of); stuffy or runny nose; wheezing or difficulty in breathing

Other side effects not listed above may also occur in some patients. If you notice any other effects, check with your health care professional.

Revised: 07/26/93
Interim revision: 02/18/94

PYRIDOXINE (Vitamin B_6) Systemic

Some commonly used brand names are:

In the U.S.—

Beesix
Doxine
Nestrex
Pyri
Rodex
Vitabee 6

Generic name product may also be available.

In Canada—

Generic name product is available.

Description

Vitamins (VYE-ta-mins) are compounds that you *must* have for growth and health. They are needed in small amounts only and are usually available in the foods that you eat. Pyridoxine (peer-i-DOX-een) (vitamin B_6) is necessary for normal breakdown of proteins, carbohydrates, and fats.

Some conditions may increase your need for pyridoxine. These include:

- Alcoholism
- Burns
- Diarrhea
- Dialysis
- Heart disease
- Intestinal problems
- Liver disease
- Overactive thyroid
- Stress, long-term illness, or serious injury
- Surgical removal of stomach

In addition, infants receiving unfortified formulas such as evaporated milk may need additional pyridoxine.

Increased need for pyridoxine should be determined by your health care professional.

Lack of pyridoxine may lead to anemia (weak blood), nerve damage, seizures, skin problems, and sores in the mouth. Your doctor may treat these problems by prescribing pyridoxine for you.

Claims that pyridoxine is effective for treatment of acne and other skin problems, alcohol intoxication, asthma, hemorrhoids, kidney stones, mental problems, migraine headaches, morning sickness, and menstrual problems, or to stimulate appetite or milk production have not been proven.

Injectable pyridoxine is given by or under the supervision of a health care professional. Other forms of pyridoxine are available without a prescription.

Pyridoxine is available in the following dosage forms:

Oral

- Extended-release capsules (U.S.)
- Tablets (U.S. and Canada)
- Extended-release tablets (U.S.)

Parenteral

- Injection (U.S. and Canada)

Importance of Diet

For good health, it is important that you eat a balanced and varied diet. Follow carefully any diet program your health care professional may recommend. For your specific dietary vitamin and/or mineral needs, ask your health care professional for a list of appropriate foods. If you think that you are not getting enough vitamins and/or minerals in your diet, you may choose to take a dietary supplement.

Pyridoxine is found in various foods, including meats, bananas, lima beans, egg yolks, peanuts, and whole-grain cereals. Pyridoxine is not lost from food during ordinary cooking, although some other forms of vitamin B_6 are.

Vitamins alone will not take the place of a good diet and will not provide energy. Your body also needs other substances found in food such as protein, minerals, carbohydrates, and fat. Vitamins themselves often cannot work without the presence of other foods.

The daily amount of pyridoxine needed is defined in several different ways.

For U.S.—

- Recommended Dietary Allowances (RDAs) are the amount of vitamins and minerals needed to provide for adequate nutrition in most healthy persons. RDAs for a given nutrient may vary depending on a person's age, sex, and physical condition (e.g., pregnancy).
- Daily Values (DVs) are used on food and dietary supplement labels to indicate the percent of the recommended daily amount of each nutrient that a serving provides. DV replaces the previous designation of United States Recommended Daily Allowances (USRDAs).

For Canada—

- Recommended Nutrient Intakes (RNIs) are used to determine the amounts of vitamins, minerals, and protein needed to provide adequate nutrition and lessen the risk of chronic disease.

Normal daily recommended intakes for pyridoxine are generally defined as follows:

- Infants and children—
  Birth to 3 years of age: 0.3 to 1 milligram (mg).
  4 to 6 years of age: 1.1 mg.
  7 to 10 years of age: 1.4 mg.
- Adolescent and adult males—1.7 to 2 mg.
- Adolescent and adult females—1.4 to 1.6 mg.
- Pregnant females—2.2 mg.
- Breast-feeding females—2.1 mg.

Before Using This Dietary Supplement

If you are taking this dietary supplement without a prescription, carefully read and follow any precautions on the label. For pyridoxine, the following should be considered:

Allergies—Tell your health care professional if you have ever had any unusual or allergic reaction to pyridoxine. Also tell your health care professional if you are allergic to any other substances, such as foods, preservatives, or dyes.

Pregnancy—It is especially important that you are receiving enough vitamins when you become pregnant and that you continue to receive the right amount of vitamins throughout your pregnancy. The healthy growth and development of the fetus depend on a steady supply of nutrients from the mother. However, excessive doses of pyridoxine taken during pregnancy may cause the infant to become dependent on pyridoxine.

Breast-feeding—It is especially important that you receive the right amounts of vitamins so that your baby will also get the vitamins needed to grow properly. You should also check with your health care professional if you are giving your baby an unfortified formula. In that case, the baby must get the vitamins needed some other way. However, taking large amounts of a dietary supplement while breast-feeding may be harmful to the mother and/or baby and should be avoided.

Children—Problems in children have not been reported with intake of normal daily recommended amounts.

Older adults—Problems in older adults have not been reported with intake of normal daily recommended amounts.

Medicines or other dietary supplements—Although certain medicines or dietary supplements should not be used together at all, in other cases they may be used together even if an interaction might occur. In these cases, your health care professional may want to change the dose, or other precautions may be necessary. When you are taking pyridoxine, it is especially important that your health care professional know if you are taking the following:

- Levodopa (e.g., Larodopa)—Use with pyridoxine may prevent the levodopa from working properly

Proper Use of This Dietary Supplement

Dosing—The amount of pyridoxine needed to meet normal daily recommended intakes will be different for different individuals. The following information includes only the average amounts of pyridoxine.

- For *oral* dosage forms (capsules, tablets, oral solution):
  - —To prevent deficiency, the amount taken by mouth is based on normal daily recommended intakes:
    - Adult and teenage males—1.7 to 2 milligrams (mg) per day.
    - Adult and teenage females—1.4 to 1.6 mg per day.
    - Pregnant females—2.2 mg per day.
    - Breast-feeding females—2.1 mg per day.
    - Children 7 to 10 years of age—1.4 mg per day.
    - Children 4 to 6 years of age—1.1 mg per day.
    - Children birth to 3 years of age—0.3 to 1 mg per day.
  - —To treat deficiency:
    - Adults, teenagers, and children—Treatment dose is determined by prescriber for each individual based on the severity of deficiency.

To use the *extended-release capsule form* of this dietary supplement:

- Swallow the capsule whole.
- Do not crush, break, or chew before swallowing.
- If the capsule is too large to swallow, you may mix the contents of the capsule with jam or jelly and swallow without chewing.

To use the *extended-release tablet form* of this dietary supplement:

- Swallow the tablet whole.
- Do not crush, break, or chew before swallowing.

Missed dose—If you miss taking a vitamin for 1 or more days there is no cause for concern, since it takes some time for your body to become seriously low in vitamins. However, if your health care professional has recommended that you take this vitamin, try to remember to take it as directed every day.

Storage—To store this dietary supplement:

- Keep out of the reach of children.
- Store away from heat and direct light.
- Do not store the capsule or tablet form of this medicine in the bathroom, near the kitchen sink, or in other damp places. Heat or moisture may cause the dietary supplement to break down.
- Do not keep outdated dietary supplements or those no longer needed. Be sure that any discarded medicine is out of the reach of children.

Side Effects of This Dietary Supplement

Along with its needed effects, a dietary supplement may cause some unwanted effects. Although pyridoxine does not usually cause any side effects at usual doses, check with your health care professional as soon as possible if you notice either of the following side effects:

With large doses

Clumsiness; numbness of hands or feet

Also check with your health care professional if you notice any other unusual effects while you are taking pyridoxine.

Revised: 09/21/92
Interim revision: 08/22/94; 05/01/95

PYRIMETHAMINE Systemic

A commonly used brand name in the U.S. and Canada is Daraprim.

Description

Pyrimethamine (peer-i-METH-a-meen) is an antiprotozoal (an-tee-proe-toe-ZOE-al) medicine. Antiprotozoals work by killing protozoa (tiny, one-celled animals) or preventing their growth. Some protozoa are parasites that can cause many different kinds of infections in the body.

This medicine is used with one or more other medicines to treat malaria and toxoplasmosis (tok-soe-plaz-MOE-siss). This medicine may also be used for other problems as determined by your doctor.

Pyrimethamine is available only with your doctor's prescription, in the following dosage form:

Oral

- Tablets (U.S. and Canada)

Before Using This Medicine

In deciding to use a medicine, the risks of taking the medicine must be weighed against the good it will do. This is

a decision you and your doctor will make. For pyrimethamine, the following should be considered:

Allergies—Tell your doctor if you have ever had any unusual or allergic reaction to pyrimethamine. Also tell your health care professional if you are allergic to any other substances, such as foods, preservatives, or dyes.

Pregnancy—Studies in humans have not shown that pyrimethamine causes birth defects. Also, use in pregnant women has not shown pyrimethamine to cause birth defects. However, use is not generally recommended during the first 3 to 4 months of pregnancy. Studies in animals have shown that pyrimethamine may cause birth defects, anemia, or other problems, especially when given in large doses.

Breast-feeding—Pyrimethamine passes into the breast milk. However, problems in nursing babies have not been reported.

Children—Pyrimethamine has been used in children and, in effective doses, has not been shown to cause different side effects or problems in children than it does in adults.

Older adults—Many medicines have not been studied specifically in older people. Therefore, it may not be known whether they work exactly the same way they do in younger adults or if they cause different side effects or problems in older people. There is no specific information comparing use of pyrimethamine in the elderly with use in other age groups.

Other medicines—Although certain medicines should not be used together at all, in other cases two different medicines may be used together even if an interaction might occur. In these cases, your doctor may want to change the dose, or other precautions may be necessary. When you are taking pyrimethamine, it is especially important that your health care professional know if you are taking any of the following:

- Amphotericin B by injection (e.g., Fungizone) or
- Antineoplastics (cancer medicine) or
- Antithyroid agents (medicine for overactive thyroid) or
- Azathioprine (e.g., Imuran) or
- Chloramphenicol (e.g., Chloromycetin) or
- Colchicine or
- Cyclophosphamide (e.g., Cytoxan) or
- Flucytosine (e.g., Ancobon) or
- Ganciclovir (e.g., Cytovene) or
- Interferon (e.g., Intron A, Roferon-A) or
- Mercaptopurine (e.g., Purinethol) or
- Methotrexate (e.g., Mexate) or
- Plicamycin (e.g., Mithracin) or
- Zidovudine (e.g., AZT, Retrovir)—Use of these medicines together with pyrimethamine may increase the chance of side effects affecting the blood

Other medical problems—The presence of other medical problems may affect the use of pyrimethamine. Make sure you tell your doctor if you have any other medical problems, especially:

- Anemia or other blood problems—High doses of pyrimethamine may make these conditions worse
- Liver disease—Patients with liver disease may have an increased chance of side effects
- Seizure disorders, such as epilepsy—High doses of pyrimethamine may increase the chance of convulsions (seizures)

Proper Use of This Medicine

Keep this medicine out of the reach of children. Overdose is especially dangerous.

If this medicine upsets your stomach or causes vomiting, it may be taken with meals or a snack.

If you are taking this medicine to *treat malaria*, take the number of tablets your doctor told you to take (up to 3) once, as a single dose, along with other medicine your doctor gave you. If you develop a fever and are not near a medical facility, and are taking this medicine to treat what you think may possibly be malaria, take the number of tablets your doctor told you to take (up to 3) once, as a single dose.

This medicine works best when you take it on a regular schedule. If you are to take 2 doses a day, one dose may be taken with breakfast and the other one with the evening meal. *Make sure that you do not miss any doses.* If you have any questions about this, check with your health care professional.

Dosing—The dose of pyrimethamine will be different for different patients. *Follow your doctor's orders or the directions on the label.* The following information includes only the average doses of pyrimethamine. *If your dose is different, do not change it* unless your doctor tells you to do so.

The number of doses you take each day, the time allowed between doses, and the length of time you take the medicine depend on the medical problem for which you are taking pyrimethamine.

- For the treatment of *malaria*:
  —Adults and adolescents: 75 milligrams of pyrimethamine together with 1.5 grams of sulfadoxine as a single dose. These 2 medicines may also be taken with other medicine. This will be determined by your doctor.

  —Children: Dose is based on body weight and will be determined by the doctor. Pyrimethamine taken together with other medicines.
- For the treatment of *toxoplasmosis*:
  —Adults and adolescents: 25 to 200 milligrams of pyrimethamine taken together with other medicines for several weeks. The proper dose for you must be determined by the doctor.

  —Children: Dose is based on body weight and must be determined by the doctor.

Missed dose—If you do miss a dose of this medicine, take it as soon as possible. This will help to keep you taking your medicine on a regular schedule. However, if it is almost time for your next dose, skip the missed dose and go back to your regular dosing schedule. Do not double doses.

Storage—To store this medicine:

- Keep out of the reach of children. Overdose is very dangerous.
- Store away from heat and direct light.
- Do not store in the bathroom, near the kitchen sink, or in other damp places. Heat or moisture may cause the medicine to break down.
- Do not keep outdated medicine or medicine no longer needed. Be sure that any discarded medicine is out of the reach of children.

Precautions While Using This Medicine

It is very important that your doctor check you at regular visits for any blood problems that may be caused by this medicine, especially if you will be taking this medicine in high doses for toxoplasmosis.

If your symptoms do not improve within a few days or if they become worse, check with your doctor.

If this medicine causes anemia, your doctor may want you to take leucovorin (e.g., folinic acid, Wellcovorin) to help clear up the anemia. If so, it is important to take the leucovorin every day while you are taking this medicine. Do not miss any doses.

Pyrimethamine, especially in high doses, may cause blood problems. These problems may result in a greater chance of certain infections, slow healing, and bleeding of the gums. Therefore, you should be careful when using regular toothbrushes, dental floss, and toothpicks. Dental work should be delayed until your blood counts have returned to normal. Check with your medical doctor or dentist if you have any questions about proper oral hygiene (mouth care) during treatment.

Side Effects of This Medicine

Along with its needed effects, a medicine may cause some unwanted effects. Although not all of these side effects may occur, if they do occur they may need medical attention.

Check with your doctor immediately if any of the following side effects occur:

More common with high doses

Change in or loss of taste; fever and sore throat; soreness, swelling, or burning of tongue; unusual bleeding or bruising; unusual tiredness or weakness

Rare

Skin rash

Symptoms of overdose

Abdominal or stomach pain; convulsions (seizures); increased excitability; vomiting (severe and continuing)

Other side effects may occur that usually do not need medical attention. These side effects may go away during treatment as your body adjusts to the medicine. However, check with your doctor if either of the following side effects continues or is bothersome:

More common with high doses

Diarrhea; loss of appetite; nausea; vomiting

Other side effects not listed above may also occur in some patients. If you notice any other effects, check with your doctor.

Additional Information

Once a medicine has been approved for marketing for a certain use, experience may show that it is also useful for other medical problems. Although these uses are not included in product labeling, pyrimethamine is used in certain patients with the following medical conditions:

- Isosporiasis (treatment and prevention)
- *Pneumocystis carinii* pneumonia (treatment)

For patients taking this medicine for *Pneumocystis carinii* pneumonia:

- Pyrimethamine is used in combination with other medicines for mild to moderate pneumonia in patients who cannot take standard treatment.

Other than the above information, there is no additional information relating to proper use, precautions, or side effects for these uses.

Revised: 01/19/93

PYRITHIONE Topical

Some commonly used brand names are:

In the U.S.—

- Danex
- DHS Zinc Dandruff Shampoo
- Head & Shoulders Antidandruff Cream Shampoo Normal to Dry Formula
- Head & Shoulders Antidandruff Cream Shampoo Normal to Oily Formula
- Head & Shoulders Antidandruff Lotion Shampoo Normal to Dry Formula
- Head & Shoulders Antidandruff Lotion Shampoo Normal to Oily Formula
- Head & Shoulders Antidandruff Lotion Shampoo 2 in 1 (Complete Dandruff Shampoo plus Conditioner in One) Formula
- Head & Shoulders Dry Scalp Conditioning Formula Lotion Shampoo
- Head & Shoulders Dry Scalp Regular Formula Lotion Shampoo
- Head & Shoulders Dry Scalp 2 in 1 (Dry Scalp Shampoo Plus Conditioner in One) Formula Lotion Shampoo
- Sebex
- Sebulon
- Zincon Dandruff Lotion Shampoo
- ZNP Bar Shampoo
- ZNP Shampoo

In Canada—

- Dan-Gard
- Sebulon

Description

Pyrithione (peer-i-THYE-one) is used to help control the symptoms of dandruff and seborrheic dermatitis of the scalp.

This medicine is available without a prescription; however, your doctor may have special instructions on the proper use of this medicine for your medical condition.

Pyrithione is available in the following dosage forms:

Topical
- Bar shampoo (U.S.)
- Cream shampoo (U.S.)
- Lotion shampoo (U.S. and Canada)

Before Using This Medicine

If you are using this medicine without a prescription, carefully read and follow any precautions on the label. For pyrithione, the following should be considered:

Allergies—Tell your doctor if you have ever had any unusual or allergic reaction to pyrithione. Also tell your health care professional if you are allergic to any other substances, such as preservatives or dyes.

Pregnancy—Pyrithione has not been shown to cause birth defects or other problems in humans.

Breast-feeding—Pyrithione has not been reported to cause problems in nursing babies.

Children—Although there is no specific information comparing use of pyrithione in children with use in other age groups, this medicine is not expected to cause different side effects or problems in children than it does in adults.

Older adults—Many medicines have not been studied specifically in older people. Therefore, it may not be known whether they work exactly the same way they do in younger adults. Although there is no specific information comparing use of pyrithione in the elderly with use in other age groups, this medicine is not expected to cause different side effects or problems in older people than it does in younger adults.

Other medicines—Although certain medicines should not be used together at all, in other cases two different medicines may be used together even if an interaction might occur. In these cases, your doctor may want to change the dose, or other precautions may be necessary. Tell your health care professional if you are using any other topical prescription or nonprescription (over-the-counter [OTC]) medicine that is to be applied to the same area of the skin.

Proper Use of This Medicine

For best results, use this medicine at least 2 times a week or as directed by your doctor.

To use:
- Before applying this shampoo, wet the hair and scalp with lukewarm water.
- Apply enough shampoo to the scalp to work up a lather and rub in well, then rinse.
- Apply the shampoo again and rinse thoroughly.

Keep this medicine away from the eyes. If you should accidentally get some in your eyes, flush them thoroughly with water.

Dosing—The dose of pyrithione will be different for different patients. *Follow your doctor's orders or the directions on the label.* The following information includes only the average dose of pyrithione. *If your dose is different, do not change it* unless your doctor tells you to do so:

- For *topical* dosage forms (bar shampoo, cream shampoo, and lotion shampoo):
  - —For dandruff and seborrheic dermatitis of the scalp:
    - Adults and children—Use as a shampoo on the scalp 2 times a week.

Missed dose—If you miss a dose of this medicine, use it as soon as possible. However, if it is almost time for your next dose, skip the missed dose and go back to your regular dosing schedule.

Storage—To store this medicine:
- Keep out of the reach of children.
- Store away from heat and direct light.
- Keep the medicine from freezing.
- Do not keep outdated medicine or medicine no longer needed. Be sure that any discarded medicine is out of the reach of children.

Precautions While Using This Medicine

If your condition does not get better after regular use of this medicine, or if it gets worse, check with your doctor.

Side Effects of This Medicine

Along with its needed effects, a medicine may cause some unwanted effects. Although not all of these side effects may occur, if they do occur they may need medical attention.

Check with your doctor as soon as possible if the following side effect occurs:

Less common or rare
Irritation of skin

Other side effects not listed above may also occur in some patients. If you notice any other effects, check with your health care professional.

Revised: 07/26/93

PYRVINIUM Oral*

A commonly used brand name in Canada is Vanquin.

Another commonly used name is viprynium.

*Not commercially available in the U.S.

Description

Pyrvinium (peer-VIN-ee-um) is used to treat pinworms (enterobiasis). It will not work for other types of worm infections (for example, roundworms or tapeworms).

Pyrvinium is available only with your doctor's prescription, in the following dosage forms:

Oral

- Oral suspension (Canada)

Before Using This Medicine

In deciding to use a medicine, the risks of taking the medicine must be weighed against the good it will do. This is a decision you and your doctor will make. For pyrvinium, the following should be considered:

Allergies—Tell your doctor if you have ever had any unusual or allergic reaction to pyrvinium. Also tell your health care professional if you are allergic to any other substances, such as foods, preservatives, or dyes.

Pregnancy—Pyrvinium has not been studied in pregnant women or animals. However, pyrvinium has not been reported to cause birth defects or other problems in humans.

Breast-feeding—Pyrvinium has not been reported to cause problems in nursing babies.

Children—Pyrvinium has been studied in children and, in effective doses, has not been reported to cause different side effects or problems in children than it does in adults. However, because of limited experience, caution is recommended in children weighing less than 10 kilograms (22 pounds). Older children are more likely to have stomach upset after receiving large doses.

Older adults—Many medicines have not been studied specifically in older people. Therefore, it may not be known whether they work exactly the same way they do in younger adults. Although there is no specific information comparing use of pyrvinium in the elderly with use in other age groups, this medicine is not expected to cause different side effects or problems in older people than it does in younger adults.

Other medicines—Although certain medicines should not be used together at all, in other cases two different medicines may be used together even if an interaction might occur. In these cases, your doctor may want to change the dose, or other precautions may be necessary. Tell your health care professional if you are taking any other prescription or nonprescription (over-the-counter [OTC]) medicine.

Other medical problems—The presence of other medical problems may affect the use of pyrvinium. Make sure you tell your doctor if you have any other medical problems, especially:

- Inflammatory bowel disease—Patients with inflammatory bowel disease may have an increased chance of side effects

Proper Use of This Medicine

No special preparations (for example, special diets, fasting, other medicines, laxatives, or enemas) are necessary before, during, or immediately after you take pyrvinium.

Use a specially marked measuring spoon or other device to measure each dose accurately. The average household teaspoon may not hold the right amount of liquid.

Pinworms may be easily passed from one person to another, especially among persons in the same household. Therefore, all household members may have to be treated at the same time to prevent their infection or reinfection. Also, all household members may have to be treated again in 2 to 3 weeks to clear up the infection completely. Make sure each family member takes the correct amount, since the dose may be different for each person.

To help clear up your infection completely, *take this medicine exactly as directed by your doctor.* Read the instructions on the label and follow them carefully. The amount of medicine you need is based on your weight. You must take the exact amount if the medicine is going to work. A second course of pyrvinium is usually required to clear up the infection completely.

Dosing—The dose of pyrvinium will be different for different patients. *Follow your doctor's orders or the directions on the label.* The following information includes only the average doses of pyrvinium. *If your dose is different, do not change it* unless your doctor tells you to do so.

- For the *oral suspension* dosage form:
  —Adults and children: Dose is based on body weight and will be determined by your doctor. It is taken as a single dose and is repeated in 2 to 3 weeks.

Storage—To store this medicine:

- Keep out of the reach of children.
- Store away from heat and direct light.
- Do not store in the bathroom, near the kitchen sink, or in other damp places. Heat or moisture may cause the medicine to break down.
- Do not freeze oral suspension.
- Do not keep outdated medicine or medicine no longer needed. Be sure that any discarded medicine is out of the reach of children.

Precautions While Using This Medicine

If your symptoms do not improve within a few days, or if they become worse, check with your doctor.

Pyrvinium may cause your skin to be more sensitive to sunlight than it is normally. Exposure to sunlight, even for brief periods of time, may cause a skin rash, itching, redness or other discoloration of the skin, or a severe sunburn. For a day or two after taking this medicine:

- Stay out of direct sunlight, especially between the hours of 10:00 a.m. and 3:00 p.m., if possible.
- Wear protective clothing, including a hat. Also, wear sunglasses.
- Apply a sun block product that has a skin protection factor (SPF) of at least 15. Some patients may require a product with a higher SPF number, especially if they have a fair complexion. If you have any questions about this, check with your health care professional.
- Apply a sunblock lipstick that has an SPF of at least 15 to protect your lips.
- Do not use a sunlamp or tanning bed or booth.

If you have a severe reaction from the sun, check with your doctor.

In some patients, pinworms may return after treatment with pyrvinium. Washing (not shaking) all bedding and nightclothes (pajamas) after treatment may help to prevent this. Some doctors may also recommend other measures to help keep your infection from returning. If you have any questions about this, check with your doctor.

Side Effects of This Medicine

Along with its needed effects, a medicine may cause some unwanted effects. Although not all of these side effects may occur, if they do occur they may need medical attention.

Check with your doctor as soon as possible if the following side effect occurs:

Rare

Skin rash

Other side effects may occur that usually do not need medical attention. These side effects may go away during treatment as your body adjusts to the medicine. However, check with your doctor if any of the following side effects continue or are bothersome:

Rare

Diarrhea; increased sensitivity of skin to sunlight; nausea and vomiting; stomach cramps

This medicine is a dye and will *color your stools red*. This color is not harmful and will disappear in a few days. Pyrvinium may also stain clothing red. If vomiting occurs, the vomit will be red in color.

Other side effects not listed above may also occur in some patients. If you notice any other effects, check with your doctor.

Revised: 01/19/93

QUINACRINE Systemic

A commonly used brand name in the U.S. and Canada is Atabrine. Another commonly used name is mepacrine.

Description

Quinacrine (KWIN-a-kreen) is used to treat giardiasis (jee-ar-DYE-a-siss), a protozoal infection of the intestinal tract. This medicine may also be used for other conditions as determined by your doctor.

Quinacrine is available only with your doctor's prescription, in the following dosage form:

Oral

- Tablets (U.S. and Canada)

Before Using This Medicine

In deciding to use a medicine, the risks of taking the medicine must be weighed against the good it will do. This is a decision you and your doctor will make. For quinacrine, the following should be considered:

Allergies—Tell your doctor if you have ever had any unusual or allergic reaction to quinacrine. Also tell your health care professional if you are allergic to any other substances, such as foods, preservatives, or dyes.

Pregnancy—Use of quinacrine to treat giardiasis in a pregnant woman should be delayed until after delivery as long as the woman is not experiencing symptoms of the disease.

Breast-feeding—Quinacrine is excreted in breast milk. However, quinacrine has not been reported to cause problems in nursing babies.

Children—Quinacrine can cause serious side effects in any patient. Therefore, it is especially important that you discuss with the child's doctor the good that this medicine may do as well as the risks of using it.

Older adults—Many medicines have not been studied specifically in older people. Therefore, it may not be known whether they work exactly the same way they do in younger adults. Although there is no specific information comparing use of quinacrine in the elderly with use in other age groups, this medicine is not expected to cause different side effects or problems in older people than it does in younger adults.

Other medicines—Although certain medicines should not be used together at all, in other cases two different medicines may be used together even if an interaction might occur. In these cases, your doctor may want to change the dose, or other precautions may be necessary. When you are taking quinacrine, it is especially important that your health care professional know if you are taking any of the following:

- Primaquine—Use with quinacrine may increase the chance of side effects from primaquine

Other medical problems—The presence of other medical problems may affect the use of quinacrine. Make sure you tell your doctor if you have any other medical problems, especially:

- Mental illness (severe) (history of)—Quinacrine may cause mood or other mental changes in some patients
- Porphyria—Quinacrine may make porphyria worse
- Psoriasis—Quinacrine may cause an attack of psoriasis or make psoriasis worse

Proper Use of This Medicine

Quinacrine is best taken after meals with a full glass (8 ounces) of water, tea, or fruit juice, unless otherwise directed by your doctor.

For patients *unable to swallow tablets or unable to tolerate bitter taste:*

- The tablets may be crushed and mixed with jam, honey, or chocolate syrup or placed in empty gelatin capsules to cover up the bitter taste. Be sure to take all the food so that you get the full dose of medicine.

To help clear up your infection completely, *keep taking quinacrine for the full time of treatment,* even if you begin to feel better after a few days. If you stop taking this medicine too soon, your symptoms may return. *Do not miss any doses.*

Dosing—The dose of quinacrine will be different for different patients. *Follow your doctor's orders or the directions on the label.* The following information includes only the average doses of quinacrine. *If your dose is different, do not change it* unless your doctor tells you to do so.

- For the *tablet* dosage form:
  —Adults and older children: 100 milligrams three times a day for five to seven days.
  —Younger children: Dose is based on body weight and will be determined by the doctor. The dose is taken three times a day for five to seven days.

Missed dose—If you do miss a dose of this medicine, take it as soon as possible. However, if it is almost time for your next dose, skip the missed dose and go back to your regular dosing schedule. Do not double doses.

Storage—To store this medicine:

- Keep out of the reach of children.
- Store away from heat and direct light.
- Do not store in the bathroom, near the kitchen sink, or in other damp places. Heat or moisture may cause the medicine to break down.
- Do not keep outdated medicine or medicine no longer needed. Be sure that any discarded medicine is out of the reach of children.

Precautions While Using This Medicine

It is important that your doctor check your progress at different times. This is to check whether or not the infection is cleared up completely.

If your symptoms do not improve within a few days, or if they become worse, check with your doctor.

Quinacrine may cause some people to become dizzy. *Make sure you know how you react to this medicine before you drive, use machines, or do anything else that could be dangerous if you are dizzy or are not alert.* If this reaction is especially bothersome, check with your doctor.

Side Effects of This Medicine

Along with its needed effects, a medicine may cause some unwanted effects. Although not all of these side effects may occur, if they do occur they may need medical attention. When this medicine is used for a short time, side effects are not generally serious. However, if this medicine is used for a long time and/or in high doses, other more serious side effects may occur.

Check with your doctor immediately if any of the following side effects occur:

Less common

Hallucinations (seeing, hearing, or feeling things that are not there); irritability; mood or other mental changes; nervousness; nightmares; skin rash, redness, itching, or peeling

Symptoms of overdose

Convulsions (seizures); fainting; irregular heartbeat

Other side effects may occur that usually do not need medical attention. These side effects may go away during treatment as your body adjusts to the medicine. However, check with your doctor if any of the following side effects continue or are bothersome:

More common

Abdominal or stomach cramps; diarrhea; dizziness; headache; loss of appetite; nausea or vomiting

Quinacrine is a dye-like medicine and commonly causes *yellow discoloration of the skin or urine*. This side effect is only *temporary* and will go away when you stop taking this medicine.

Other side effects not listed above may also occur in some patients. If you notice any other effects, check with your doctor.

Additional Information

Once a medicine has been approved for marketing for a certain use, experience may show that it is also useful for other medical problems. Although this use is not included in product labeling, quinacrine is used in certain patients with the following medical condition:

- Discoid lupus erythematosus

Other than the above information, there is no additional information relating to proper use, precautions, or side effects for this use.

Revised: 02/01/93

QUINIDINE Systemic

Some commonly used brand names are:

In the U.S.—

Cardioquin
Cin-Quin
Duraquin
Quinaglute Dura-tabs
Quinalan
Quinidex Extentabs
Quinora

Generic name product may also be available.

In Canada—

Apo-Quinidine
Cardioquin
Novoquinidin
Quinaglute Dura-tabs
Quinate
Quinidex Extentabs

Generic name product may also be available.

Description

Quinidine (KWIN-i-deen) is used to correct certain irregular heartbeats to a normal rhythm and to slow an overactive heart. The injection dosage form is also used to treat malaria.

Quinidine acts directly on the heart tissues to make them less responsive. It also slows impulses along special nerve networks to the heart. This allows the heart to work more efficiently.

Do not confuse this medicine with *quinine*, which, although related, has different medical uses.

Quinidine is available only with your doctor's prescription, in the following dosage forms:

Oral

- Capsules (U.S.)
- Tablets (U.S. and Canada)
- Extended-release tablets (U.S. and Canada)

Parenteral

- Injection (U.S. and Canada)

Before Using This Medicine

In deciding to use a medicine, the risks of taking the medicine must be weighed against the good it will do. This is a decision you and your doctor will make. For quinidine, the following should be considered:

Allergies—Tell your doctor if you have ever had any unusual or allergic reaction to quinidine or quinine. Also tell your health care professional if you are allergic to any other substance, such as foods, preservatives, or dyes.

Pregnancy—Studies on effects in pregnancy have not been done in either humans or animals. However, a closely related medicine, quinine, has been shown to cause birth defects of the nervous system, fingers, and toes, and decreased hearing in the infant. Quinine also may cause contractions of the uterus.

Breast-feeding—Quinidine passes into breast milk. However, it has not been reported to cause problems in nursing babies.

Children—Studies on this medicine have been done only in adult patients, and there is no specific information comparing use of quinidine in children with use in other age groups. Use of the extended-release tablets in children is not recommended.

Older adults—Many medicines have not been studied specifically in older people. Therefore, it may not be

known whether they work exactly the same way they do in younger adults. Although there is no specific information comparing use of quinidine in the elderly with use in other age groups, this medicine is not expected to cause different side effects or problems in older people than it does in younger adults.

Other medicines—Although certain medicines should not be used together at all, in other cases two different medicines may be used together even if an interaction might occur. In these cases, your doctor may want to change the dose, or other precautions may be necessary. When you are taking quinidine, it is especially important that your health care professional knows if you are taking any of the following:

- Anticoagulants (blood thinners)—Risk of bleeding may be increased
- Other heart medicine (especially digoxin)—Effects on the heart may be increased
- Pimozide (e.g., Orap)—Risk of heart rhythm problems may be increased
- Urinary alkalizers (medicine that makes the urine less acid, such as acetazolamide [e.g., Diamox], calcium- and/or magnesium-containing antacids, dichlorphenamide [e.g., Daranide], methazolamide [e.g., Neptazane], potassium or sodium citrate and/or citric acid, sodium bicarbonate [baking soda])—Effects may be increased because levels of quinidine in the body may be increased

Other medical problems—The presence of other medical problems may affect the use of quinidine. Make sure you tell your doctor if you have any other medical problems, especially:

- Asthma or emphysema—Possible allergic reaction
- Blood disease
- Infection
- Kidney disease or
- Liver disease—Effects may be increased because of slower removal of quinidine from the body
- Myasthenia gravis—Muscle weakness may be increased
- Overactive thyroid
- Psoriasis

Proper Use of This Medicine

Take quinidine with a full glass (8 ounces) of water on an empty stomach 1 hour before or 2 hours after meals so that it will be absorbed more quickly. However, to lessen stomach upset, your doctor may want you to take the medicine with food or milk.

For patients taking the *extended-release tablet* form of this medicine:

- Swallow the tablets whole.
- Do not break, crush, or chew before swallowing.

Take quinidine exactly as directed by your doctor even though you may feel well. Do not take more medicine than ordered and do not miss any doses.

Dosing—The dose of quinidine will be different for different patients. *Follow your doctor's orders or the directions on the label.* The following information includes only the average doses of quinidine. *If your dose is different, do not change it* unless your doctor tells you to do so.

The number of capsules or tablets that you take depends on the strength of the medicine. Also, *the number of doses you take each day, the time allowed between doses, and the length of time you take the medicine depend on the medical problem for which you are taking quinidine.* When you first begin to take quinidine for irregular heartbeat, you may need to take a higher number of doses each day. This depends on what type of irregular heartbeat you have and will be determined by your doctor.

- For *regular (short-acting) oral* dosage forms (capsules and tablets):
  - —For irregular heartbeat:
    - Adults—200 to 650 milligrams (mg) two to four times a day.
    - Children—6 to 8.25 mg per kilogram (kg) (2.73 to 3.75 mg per pound) of body weight five times a day.
- For *long-acting oral* dosage forms (tablets):
  - —For irregular heartbeat:
    - Adults—300 to 660 mg every six to twelve hours.
    - Children—Use is not recommended.
- For *injection* dosage form:
  - —For irregular heartbeat:
    - Adults—400 to 600 mg injected into the muscle every two hours. Or, 600 to 800 mg in a solution and injected into a vein.
    - Children—Dose must be determined by your doctor.
  - —For malaria:
    - Adults—10 mg per kg (4.54 mg per pound) of body weight in a solution and injected slowly into a vein over one to two hours. Then, 0.02 mg per kg (0.009 mg per pound) of body weight per minute is given. Or, 12 to 24 mg per kg (5.45 to 10.91 mg per pound) of body weight in a solution and injected slowly into a vein over a four hour period every eight hours.
    - Children—Dose must be determined by your doctor.

Missed dose—If you miss a dose of this medicine and remember within 2 hours of the missed dose, take it as soon as possible. However, if you do not remember until later, skip the missed dose and go back to your regular dosing schedule. Do not double doses.

Storage—To store this medicine:

- Keep out of the reach of children.
- Store away from heat and direct light.
- Do not store in the bathroom, near the kitchen sink, or in other damp places. Heat or moisture may cause the medicine to break down.
- Do not keep outdated medicine or medicine no longer needed. Be sure that any discarded medicine is out of the reach of children.

Precautions While Using This Medicine

It is very important that your doctor check your progress at regular visits to make sure that the quinidine is working properly and does not cause unwanted effects.

Do not stop taking this medicine without first checking with your doctor, to avoid possible worsening of your condition.

Before having any kind of surgery (including dental surgery) or emergency treatment, tell the medical doctor or dentist in charge that you are taking this medicine.

Your doctor may want you to carry a medical identification card or bracelet stating that you are using this medicine.

Some people who are unusually sensitive to this medicine may have side effects after the first dose or first few doses. Check with your doctor right away if the following side effects occur: breathing difficulty, changes in vision, dizziness, fever, headache, ringing in ears, or skin rash.

Side Effects of This Medicine

Along with its needed effects, a medicine may cause some unwanted effects. Although not all of these side effects may occur, if they do occur they may need medical attention.

Check with your doctor immediately if any of the following side effects occur:

Less common

Blurred vision or any change in vision; dizziness, lightheadedness, or fainting; fever; headache (severe); ringing or buzzing in the ears or any loss of hearing; skin rash, hives, or itching; wheezing, shortness of breath, or troubled breathing

Rare

Fast heartbeat; unusual bleeding or bruising; unusual tiredness or weakness

Other side effects may occur that usually do not need medical attention. These side effects may go away during treatment as your body adjusts to the medicine. However, check with your doctor if any of the following side effects continue or are bothersome:

More common

Bitter taste; diarrhea; flushing of skin with itching; loss of appetite; nausea or vomiting; stomach pain or cramping

Less common

Confusion

Other side effects not listed above may also occur in some patients. If you notice any other effects, check with your doctor.

Revised: 03/24/94

QUININE Systemic

In the U.S.—

Generic name product may be available.

In Canada—

Generic name product may be available.

Description

Quinine (KWYE-nine) is used to treat malaria. This medicine is usually given with one or more other medicines for malaria.

Quinine may also be used for other problems as determined by your doctor. Do not confuse quinine with *quinidine*, a different medicine that is used for heart problems.

Quinine is available only with your doctor's prescription in the following dosage forms:

Oral

- Capsules (U.S. and Canada)
- Tablets (U.S.)

Before Using This Medicine

In deciding to use a medicine, the risks of taking the medicine must be weighed against the good it will do. This is a decision you and your doctor will make. For quinine, the following should be considered:

Allergies—Tell your doctor if you have ever had any unusual or allergic reaction to quinine, quinidine (e.g., Quinidex), or to dietary items that contain quinine, such as tonic water or bitter lemon. Also tell your health care professional if you are allergic to any other substances, such as foods, preservatives, or dyes.

Pregnancy—Quinine has been used for the treatment of malaria in pregnant women. Treatment is important because if a pregnant woman gets malaria, there is an increased chance of premature births, stillbirths, and abortion. However, quinine has been shown to cause birth defects in rabbits and guinea pigs and has also been shown to cause rare birth defects, stillbirths, and other problems in humans. In addition, quinine has been shown to cause miscarriage when taken in large amounts.

Breast-feeding—Quinine passes into the breast milk in small amounts. However, this medicine has not been reported to cause problems in nursing babies.

Children—This medicine has been used to treat malaria in children and, in effective doses, has not been shown to cause different side effects or problems in children than it does in adults.

Older adults—Many medicines have not been studied specifically in older people. Therefore, it may not be known whether they work exactly the same way they do in younger adults or if they cause different side effects or problems in older people. There is no specific information comparing use of quinine in the elderly with use in other age groups.

Other medicines—Although certain medicines should not be used together at all, in other cases two different med-

icines may be used together even if an interaction might occur. In these cases, your doctor may want to change the dose, or other precautions may be necessary. When you are taking quinine, it is especially important that your health care professional know if you are taking the following:

- Mefloquine (e.g., Larium)—Use of mefloquine with quinine may increase the chance of side effects

Other medical problems—The presence of other medical problems may affect the use of quinine. Make sure you tell your doctor if you have any other medical problems, especially:

- Blackwater fever, history of, or
- Glucose-6-phosphate dehydrogenase (G6PD) deficiency or
- Purpura, or history of (purplish or brownish red discoloration of skin)—Patients with a history of blackwater fever, G6PD deficiency, or purpura may have an increased risk of side effects affecting the blood
- Heart disease—Quinine can cause side effects of the heart, usually at higher doses
- Hypoglycemia—Quinine may cause low blood sugar
- Myasthenia gravis—Quinine may increase muscle weakness in patients with myasthenia gravis

Proper Use of This Medicine

Take this medicine only as directed. Do not take more of it, do not take it more often, and do not take it for a longer time than recommended on the label, unless otherwise directed by your doctor. To do so may increase the chance of side effects.

Take this medicine with or after meals to lessen possible stomach upset, unless otherwise directed by your doctor. If you are to take this medicine at bedtime, take it with a snack or with a glass of water, milk, or other beverage.

For patients *taking quinine for malaria:*

- To help clear up your infection completely, *keep taking this medicine for the full time of treatment,* even if you begin to feel better after a few days. If you stop taking this medicine too soon, your symptoms may return. *Do not miss any doses.*

Dosing—The dose of quinine will be different for different patients. *Follow your doctor's orders or the directions on the label.* The following information includes only the average dose of quinine. *If your dose is different, do not change it* unless your doctor tells you to do so.

The number of capsules or tablets that you take depends on the strength of the medicine. Also, *the number of doses you take each day, the time allowed between doses, and the length of time you take the medicine depend on the medical problem for which you are taking quinine.*

- For treatment of *malaria:*
  - —Adults and older children: 600 to 650 mg every eight hours for at least three days. This medicine must be taken with other medicine to treat malaria.
  - —Younger children: Dose must be determined by the doctor.

Missed dose—If you do miss a dose of this medicine, take it as soon as possible. However, if it is almost time for your next dose, skip the missed dose and go back to your regular dosing schedule. Do not double doses.

Storage—To store this medicine:

- Keep out of the reach of children.
- Store away from heat and direct light.
- Do not store in the bathroom, near the kitchen sink, or in other damp places. Heat or moisture may cause the medicine to break down.
- Do not keep outdated medicine or medicine no longer needed. Be sure that any discarded medicine is out of the reach of children.

Precautions While Using This Medicine

Quinine may cause blurred vision or a change in color vision. *Make sure you know how you react to this medicine before you drive, use machines, or do anything else that could be dangerous if you are not able to see well.* If these reactions are especially bothersome, check with your doctor.

Side Effects of This Medicine

Along with its needed effects, a medicine may cause some unwanted effects. Although not all of these side effects may occur, if they do occur they may need medical attention.

Check with your doctor immediately if any of the following side effects occur:

Rare

Anxiety; back, leg, or stomach pains; cold sweats; cool, pale skin; fever and chills; headache; increased hunger; loss of appetite; muscle aches; nausea and vomiting; nervousness; pale skin; pale stools; shakiness; skin rash, redness, hives, or itching; sore throat and fever; stomach pain; sweating; unusual bleeding or bruising; unusual tiredness or weakness; wheezing, shortness of breath, or difficult breathing; yellow skin and eyes

Signs and symptoms of overdose

Blindness; confusion; convulsions (seizures); decreased vision; irregular heartbeat; lightheadedness

Other side effects may occur that usually do not need medical attention. These side effects may go away during treatment as your body adjusts to the medicine. However, check with your doctor if any of the following side effects continue or are bothersome:

More common

Abdominal or stomach cramps or pain; blurred vision or change in color vision; diarrhea; headache (severe); nausea and vomiting; ringing or buzzing in ears or loss of hearing (usually temporary)

Other side effects not listed above may also occur in some patients. If you notice any other effects, check with your doctor.

Additional Information

Once a medicine has been approved for marketing for a certain use, experience may show that it is also useful for other medical problems. Although these uses are not included in product labeling, quinine is used in certain patients with the following medical conditions:

- Babesiosis (infection caused by parasites)
- Nighttime leg cramps

Other than the above information, there is no additional information relating to proper use, precautions, or side effects for these uses.

Revised: 02/23/93
Interim revision: 06/23/95

RABIES IMMUNE GLOBULIN Systemic

Some commonly used brand names in the U.S. and Canada are Hyperab and Imogam.

Generic name product may also be available.

Other commonly used names are HRIG and RIG.

Description

Rabies immune globulin (RAY-beez im-MUNE GLOB-yoo-lin) is used along with rabies vaccine to prevent infection caused by the rabies virus. Rabies immune globulin works by giving your body the antibodies it needs to protect it against the rabies virus. This is called passive protection. This passive protection lasts long enough to protect your body until your body can produce its own antibodies against the rabies virus.

Rabies immune globulin is given to persons who have been exposed (for example, by a bite, scratch, or lick) to an animal that is known, or thought, to have rabies. This is called post-exposure prophylaxis. Rabies immune globulin is used only in persons who have never before received the rabies vaccine.

Rabies infection is a serious, and often fatal, infection. In the U.S., rabies in wild animals, especially raccoons, skunks, and bats, accounts for most cases of rabies passed on to humans, pets, and other domestic animals. In Canada, the animals most often infected with rabies are foxes, skunks, bats, dogs, and cats. Horses, swine, and cattle also have been known to become infected with rabies. In much of the rest of the world, including Latin America, Africa, and Asia, dogs account for most cases of rabies passed on to humans.

If you are being (or will be) treated for a possible rabies infection while traveling outside of the U.S. or Canada, contact your doctor as soon as you return to the U.S. or Canada, since it may be necessary for you to have additional treatment.

Rabies immune globulin is to be administered only by or under the supervision of your doctor or other health care professional. It is available in the following dosage form:

Parenteral

- Injection (U.S. and Canada)

Before Receiving This Medicine

In deciding to use a medicine, the risks of using the medicine must be weighed against the good it will do. This is a decision you and your doctor will make. For rabies immune globulin, the following should be considered:

Allergies—Tell your doctor if you have ever had any unusual or allergic reaction to rabies immune globulin or any other kind of human immune globulin. Also tell your health care professional if you are allergic to any other substances, such as foods, thimerosal or other preservatives, or dyes.

Pregnancy—Studies on effects in pregnancy have not been done in either humans or animals. However, the use of rabies immune globulin in pregnant women has not been reported to cause problems.

Breast-feeding—Rabies immune globulin has not been reported to cause problems in nursing babies.

Children—Although there is no specific information comparing use of rabies immune globulin in children with use in other age groups, this medicine is not expected to cause different side effects or problems in children than it does in adults.

Older adults—Many medicines have not been studied specifically in older people. Therefore, it may not be known whether they work exactly the same way they do in younger adults or if they cause different side effects or problems in older people. There is no specific information comparing use of rabies immune globulin in the elderly with use in other age groups.

Other medical problems—The presence of other medical problems may affect the use of rabies immune globulin. Make sure you tell your doctor if you have any other medical problems, especially:

- Immunoglobulin A (IgA) deficiencies—Rabies immune globulin may cause an allergic reaction to occur

Proper Use of This Medicine

Dosing—The dose of rabies immune globulin will be different for different patients. The following information includes only the average dose of rabies immune globulin.

- *For injection* dosage form:
  - —For preventing rabies infection:
    - Adults and children—The dose is based on body weight and must be determined by your doctor. The usual dose is 20 International Units (IU) per kilogram (kg) (9.1 IU per pound) of body weight. This medicine is injected into the buttocks (gluteal) muscle and may also be injected around the areas of any wounds caused by the animal with rabies. This medicine is usually used on the first day of your rabies treatment along with the first dose of rabies vaccine. If this medicine is not used on the first day, it may be used any day up through the seventh day of your rabies treatment.

Side Effects of This Medicine

Along with its needed effects, a medicine may cause some unwanted effects. The following side effects may occur, but usually do not need medical attention. However, check with your doctor if any of the following side effects continue or are bothersome:

Less common

Fever; pain, soreness, tenderness, or stiffness of the muscles at the place(s) of injection—may last for several hours after the injection(s)

Other side effects not listed above may also occur in some patients. If you notice any other effects, check with your doctor.

Developed: 08/31/94

RABIES VACCINE Systemic

Some commonly used brand names are:

In the U.S.—

Imovax[2] Imovax I.D.[2]

Other commonly used names are:

HDCV[2] RVA[1]

Note: For quick reference, the following rabies vaccines are numbered to match the corresponding brand names.

This information applies to the following vaccines:

1. Rabies Vaccine Adsorbed†‡
2. Rabies Vaccine, Human Diploid Cell§

†Not commercially available in Canada.
‡Generic name product may also be available in the U.S.
§Generic name product may also be available in Canada.

Description

Rabies (RAY-beez) Vaccine is an active immunizing agent used to prevent infection caused by the rabies virus. The vaccine works by causing your body to produce its own protection (antibodies) against the rabies virus.

Rabies vaccine is used in two ways. Rabies vaccine is given to persons who have been exposed (for example, by a bite, scratch, or lick) to a animal that is known, or thought, to have rabies. This is called post-exposure prophylaxis. Rabies vaccine may also be given ahead of time to persons who have a high risk of getting infected with rabies virus. These persons include veterinarians, animal handlers, travelers who will spend more than 1 month in countries having a high rate of rabies infection, and persons who live, work, or take vacations in wild areas of the country where they are likely to come into contact with wild animals. This is called pre-exposure prophylaxis.

Rabies infection is a serious, and often fatal, infection. In the U.S., rabies in wild animals, especially raccoons, skunks, and bats, accounts for most cases of rabies passed on to humans, pets, and other domestic animals. In Canada, the animals most often infected with rabies are foxes, skunks, bats, dogs, and cats. Horses, swine, and cattle also have been known to become infected with rabies. In much of the rest of the world, including Latin America, Africa, and Asia, dogs account for most cases of rabies passed on to humans.

If you are being (or will be) treated for a possible rabies infection while traveling outside of the U.S. or Canada, contact your doctor as soon as you return to the U.S. or Canada, since it may be necessary for you to have additional treatment.

This vaccine is to be administered only by or under the supervision of your doctor or other health care professional. It is available in the following dosage form:

Parenteral

- Injection (U.S. and Canada)

Before Receiving This Vaccine

In deciding to use a vaccine, the risks of using the vaccine must be weighed against the good it will do. This is a decision you and your doctor will make. For rabies vaccine, the following should be considered:

Allergies—Tell your doctor if you have ever had any unusual or allergic reaction to rabies vaccine, or to cow (bovine) serum, human albumin, kanamycin, monkey proteins, neomycin, polymyxin B, or thimerosal, since some of these may also be present in the vaccine. Also tell your health care professional if you are allergic to any other substances, such as foods, preservatives, or dyes.

Pregnancy—Studies on effects in pregnancy have not been done in either humans or animals. However, the use of rabies vaccine in pregnant women has not been reported to cause problems.

Breast-feeding—Rabies vaccine has not been reported to cause problems in nursing babies.

Children—This vaccine is not expected to cause different side effects or problems in children than it does in adults.

Older adults—Many vaccines have not been studied specifically in older people. Therefore, it may not be known whether they work exactly the same way they do in younger adults or if they cause different side effects or problems in older people. There is no specific information comparing use of rabies vaccine in the elderly with use in other age groups.

Other medicines—Although certain medicines should not be used together at all, in other cases two different medicines may be used together even if an interaction might occur. In these cases, your doctor may want to change the dose, or other precautions may be necessary. While you are receiving rabies vaccine, it is especially important that your health care professional know if you are taking any of the following:

- Cancer medicines or
- Corticosteroids (i.e., cortisone-like medicines) or
- Medicine to prevent malaria, such as chloroquine (Aralen), hydroxychloroquine (Plaquenil), or mefloquine (Lariam), or
- Radiation therapy—These treatments may reduce the useful effect of the vaccine

Other medical problems—The presence of other medical problems may affect the use of rabies vaccine. Make sure you tell your doctor if you have any other medical problems, especially:

- Illness, severe, with fever—The symptoms of the condition may be confused with the possible side effects of the vaccine
- Immune deficiency condition (or family history of)—May decrease the useful effects of the vaccine

Proper Use of This Vaccine

In order for rabies vaccine to work properly, *it is very important that you do not miss any doses.* Keep your appointments with your doctor.

Dosing—The dose of rabies vaccine will be different for different patients. The number of injections and the time between injections depend on the reason for which you are receiving rabies vaccine.

For rabies vaccine adsorbed

- For *injection* dosage form:
  - —For post-exposure prophylaxis if you have never received rabies vaccine before:
    - Adults and children—One dose on the first day, then one dose three, seven, fourteen, and twenty-eight days later for a total of five doses. The vaccine is injected into the muscle (deltoid) in the upper arm. Very young or small children may have the vaccine injected into the upper leg (thigh) muscle. On the first day, you will also receive an injection of another medicine (rabies immune globulin).
  - —For post-exposure prophylaxis if you have received rabies vaccine before:
    - Adults and children—One dose on the first day, then one dose three days later for a total of two doses. The vaccine is injected into the muscle (deltoid) in the upper arm. Very young or small children may have the vaccine injected into the upper leg (thigh) muscle.
  - —For pre-exposure prophylaxis if you have never received rabies vaccine before:
    - Adults and children—One dose on the first day, then one dose seven and twenty-one or twenty-eight days later for a total of three doses. The vaccine is injected into the muscle (deltoid) in the upper arm. Very young or small children may have the vaccine injected into the upper leg (thigh) muscle.
  - —For pre-exposure prophylaxis if you have received rabies vaccine before (also known as a booster dose):
    - Adults and children—One dose injected into the muscle (deltoid) in the upper arm. Very young or small children may have the vaccine injected into the upper leg (thigh) muscle.

For rabies vaccine, human diploid cell

- For *injection* dosage form:
  - —For post-exposure prophylaxis if you have never received rabies vaccine before:
    - Adults and children—One dose on the first day, then one dose three, seven, fourteen, and twenty-eight days later for a total of five doses. The vaccine is injected into the muscle (deltoid) in the upper arm. Very young or small children may have the vaccine injected into the upper leg (thigh) muscle. On the first day, you will also receive an injection of another medicine (rabies immune globulin).
  - —For post-exposure prophylaxis if you have received rabies vaccine before:
    - Adults and children—One dose on the first day, then one dose three days later for a total of two doses. The vaccine is injected into the muscle (deltoid) in the upper arm. Very young or small children may have the vaccine injected into the upper leg (thigh) muscle.
  - —For pre-exposure prophylaxis if you have never received rabies vaccine before:
    - Adults and children—One dose on the first day, then one dose seven and twenty-one or twenty-eight days later for a total of three doses. The vaccine is injected into, or under the skin of, the muscle (deltoid) in the upper arm. Very young or small children may have the vaccine injected into the upper leg (thigh) muscle.
  - —For pre-exposure prophylaxis if you have received rabies vaccine before (also known as a booster dose):
    - Adults and children—One dose injected into, or under the skin of, the muscle (deltoid) in the upper arm. Very young or small children may have the vaccine injected into the upper leg (thigh) muscle.

Missed dose—If you miss a dose of this vaccine, *contact your doctor as soon as possible.*

Precautions While Receiving This Vaccine

This vaccine may cause some people to become dizzy. Make sure you know how you react to this vaccine before you drive, use machines, or do anything else that could be dangerous if you are dizzy.

Side Effects of This Vaccine

Along with its needed effects, a vaccine may cause some unwanted effects. Although not all of these side effects may occur, if they do occur they may need medical attention.

Check with your doctor as soon as possible if either of the following side effects occur:

Rare

Hives or skin rash

Other side effects may occur that usually do not need medical attention. These side effects may go away during treatment as your body adjusts to the vaccine. However, check with your doctor if any of the following side effects continue or are bothersome:

More common

Chills; dizziness; fever; general feeling of discomfort or illness; headache; itching, pain, redness, or swelling at the place of injection; muscle or joint aches; nausea; stomach or abdomen pain; tiredness or weakness

Other side effects not listed above may also occur in some patients. If you notice any other effects, check with your doctor.

Developed: 08/31/94

RADIOPAQUE AGENTS Diagnostic

This information applies to the following medicines:

1. Diatrizoates (dye-a-tri-ZOE-ates)
2. Iodipamide (eye-oh-DI-pa-mide)
3. Iohexol (eye-oh-HEX-ole)
4. Iopamidol (eye-oh-PA-mi-dole)
5. Iothalamate (eye-oh-thal-A-mate)
6. Ioversol (eye-oh-VER-sole)
7. Ioxaglate (eye-OX-a-glate)
8. Metrizamide (me-TRI-za-mide)

Description

Radiopaque agents are drugs used to help diagnose certain medical problems. They contain iodine, which absorbs x-rays. Depending on how they are given, radiopaque agents build up in a particular area of the body. The resulting high level of iodine allows the x-rays to make a ''picture'' of the area.

The radiopaque agents are used in the diagnosis of:

- Biliary tract problems—Diatrizoates, Iodipamide, Iohexol, Iothalamate
- Blood vessel diseases—Diatrizoates, Iohexol, Iopamidol, Iothalamate, Ioversol, Ioxaglate, Metrizamide
- Blood vessel diseases of the brain—Diatrizoates, Iohexol, Iopamidol, Iothalamate, Ioversol, Ioxaglate
- Blood vessel diseases of the heart—Diatrizoates, Iohexol, Iopamidol, Iothalamate, Ioversol, Ioxaglate, Metrizamide
- Brain diseases and tumors—Diatrizoates, Iohexol, Iopamidol, Iothalamate, Ioversol, Ioxaglate, Metrizamide
- Breast lesions—Diatrizoates
- Heart disease—Diatrizoates, Iohexol, Iopamidol, Iothalamate, Ioversol, Ioxaglate, Metrizamide
- Impaired flow of cerebrospinal fluid in brain—Iohexol, Iopamidol, Metrizamide
- Kidney diseases—Diatrizoates, Iothalamate, Ioversol, Ioxaglate
- Joint diseases—Diatrizoates, Iohexol, Iothalamate, Ioxaglate, Metrizamide
- Liver diseases—Diatrizoates, Iohexol, Iothalamate, Ioversol, Ioxaglate
- Pancreas disease—Diatrizoates, Iohexol, Iothalamate, Ioversol, Ioxaglate
- Spinal disk diseases—Diatrizoates
- Spleen diseases—Diatrizoates, Iothalamate
- Stomach and intestinal problems—Diatrizoates, Iohexol
- Urinary tract problems—Diatrizoates, Iohexol, Iopamidol, Iothalamate, Ioversol, Ioxaglate, Metrizamide

Radiopaque agents are taken by mouth or given by enema or injection. X-rays are then used to check if there are any problems with the stomach, intestines, kidneys, or other parts of the body.

Some radiopaque agents, such as iohexol, iopamidol, and metrizamide are given by injection into the spinal canal. X-rays are then used to help diagnose problems or diseases in the head, spinal canal, and nervous system.

The doses of radiopaque agents will be different for different patients and depend on the type of test. The strength of the solution is determined by how much iodine it contains. Different tests will require a different strength and amount of solution depending on the age of the patient, the contrast needed, and the x-ray equipment used.

Radiopaque agents are to be used only by or under the direct supervision of a doctor.

Before Having This Test

In deciding to use a diagnostic test, any risks of the test must be weighed against the good it will do. This is a decision you and your doctor will make. Also, test results may be affected by other things. For radiopaque agents, the following should be considered:

Allergies—Tell your doctor if you have ever had any unusual or allergic reaction to iodine, to products containing iodine (for example, iodine-containing foods such as seafood, cabbage, kale, rape [turnip-like vegetable], turnips, or iodized salt), or to any radiopaque agent. Also tell your doctor if you are allergic to any other substance, such as sulfites or other preservatives.

Pregnancy—Studies have not been done in humans with most of the radiopaque agents. However, iohexol, iopamidol, iothalamate, ioversol, ioxaglate, and metrizamide have not been shown to cause birth defects or other problems in animal studies. Some of the radiopaque agents, such as diatrizoates have, on rare occasions, caused hypothyroidism (underactive thyroid) in the baby when they were taken late in the pregnancy. Also, x-rays of the abdomen are usually not recommended during pregnancy. This is to avoid exposing the fetus to radiation. Be sure you have discussed this with your doctor.

Breast-feeding—Although some of these radiopaque agents pass into the breast milk, they have not been shown to cause problems in nursing babies. However, it may be necessary for you to stop breast-feeding temporarily after receiving a radiopaque agent. Be sure you have discussed this with your doctor.

Children—Children, especially those with other medical problems, may be especially sensitive to the effects of radiopaque agents. This may increase the chance of side effects.

Older adults—Elderly people are especially sensitive to the effects of radiopaque agents. This may increase the chance of side effects.

Other medical problems—The presence of other medical problems may affect the use of radiopaque agents. Make sure you tell your doctor if you have any other medical problems, especially:

- Asthma, hay fever, or other allergies (history of)—If you have a history of these conditions, the risk of having a

reaction, such as an allergic reaction to the radiopaque agent, is greater
- Diabetes mellitus (sugar diabetes)—There is a greater risk of having kidney problems
- High blood pressure (severe) or
- Pheochromocytoma (PCC)—Injection of the radiopaque agent may cause a dangerous rise in blood pressure
- Kidney disease (severe)—More serious kidney problems may develop; also, the radiopaque agent may build up in the body and cause side effects
- Liver disease—The radiopaque agent may build up in the body and cause side effects
- Multiple myeloma (bone cancer)—Serious kidney problems may develop in patients with this condition
- Overactive thyroid—A sudden increase in symptoms, such as fast heartbeat or palpitations, unusual tiredness or weakness, nervousness, excessive sweating, or muscle weakness may occur
- Sickle cell disease—The radiopaque agent may promote the formation of abnormal blood cells

Preparation For This Test

Your doctor may have special instructions for you in preparation for your test. He or she might prescribe a special diet or use of a laxative, depending on the type of test. If you have not received such instructions or if you do not understand them, check with your doctor in advance.

For some tests your doctor may tell you not to eat for several hours before having the test. This is to prevent any food from coming back up and entering your lungs during the test. You may be allowed to drink small amounts of clear liquids; however, check first with your doctor.

Precautions After Having This Test

Make sure your doctor knows if you are planning to have any thyroid tests in the near future. Even after several weeks or months the results of the thyroid test may be affected by the iodine in this agent.

Side Effects of This Medicine

Along with their needed effects, radiopaque agents can sometimes cause serious effects such as severe allergic reactions or heart problems. These effects may occur almost immediately or a few minutes after the radiopaque agent is given. Although these serious side effects appear only rarely, your health care professional will be prepared to give you immediate medical attention if needed. If you have any questions about this, check with your doctor.

Check with your doctor as soon as possible if the following side effects occur:

With injection into the spinal canal

Rare

Hallucinations (seeing hearing, or feeling things that are not there); paralysis of one side of body or of legs and arms

Other side effects may occur that usually do not need medical attention. These side effects may go away as your body adjusts to this agent. However, check with your doctor if any of the following side effects continue or are bothersome:

With oral or rectal use

Less common

Diarrhea or laxative effect

With injection into a vein or an artery

More common

Unusual warmth and flushing of skin

Less common

Chills; dizziness or lightheadedness; headache; nausea or vomiting; pain or burning at the place of injection; sweating; unusual or metallic taste; unusual thirst

With injection into the spinal canal

More common

Backache; dizziness; headache (mild to moderate); nausea and vomiting (mild to moderate); stiffness of neck

Less common or rare

Difficult urination; drowsiness; headache (severe); increased sensitivity of eyes to light; increased sweating; loss of appetite; ringing or buzzing in ears; unusual tiredness or weakenss

Not all of the side effects listed above have been reported for each of these agents, but they have been reported for at least one of them. There are some similarities among these agents, so many of the above side effects may occur with any of them.

Other side effects not listed above may also occur in some patients. If you notice any other effects, check with your doctor.

Revised: August 1990
Interim revision: 05/23/94

RADIOPAQUE AGENTS Diagnostic, Local

This information applies to the following medicines:
1. Diatrizoate and Iodipamide (dye-a-tri-ZOE-ate and eye-oh-DI-pa-mide)
2. Diatrizoates
3. Iohexol (eye-oh-HEX-ole)
4. Iothalamate (eye-oh-thal-A-mate)
5. Ioxaglate (eye-OX-a-glate)

Description

Radiopaque agents are drugs used to help diagnose certain medical problems. They contain iodine, which blocks x-rays. Depending on how the radiopaque agent is given, it localizes or builds up in certain areas of the body. The resulting high level of iodine allows the x-rays to make a "picture" of the area.

The areas of the body in which the radiopaque agent localizes will appear white on the x-ray film. This creates the needed distinction, or contrast, between one organ and other tissues. The contrast will help the doctor see any special conditions that may exist in that organ or part of the body.

The local radiopaque agents are used in the diagnosis of:

- Urinary tract diseases—Diatrizoates, Iohexol, Iothalamate
- Uterus and fallopian tube diseases—Diatrizoate and Iodipamide, Diatrizoates, Iohexol, Ioxaglate

A catheter or syringe is used to put the solution of the radiopaque agent into the bladder or ureters to help diagnose problems or diseases of the kidneys or other areas of the urinary tract. It may also be placed into the uterus and fallopian tubes to help diagnose problems or disease of those organs. After the test is done, the patient expels most of the solution by urinating (after bladder or ureter studies) or from the vagina (after uterine or fallopian tube studies).

Radiopaque agents are classified by their osmolality (a measure of concentration). There are high- and low-osmolality contrast agents. Low-osmolality agents are newer and more expensive than the high-osmolality ones. For most patients, a high-osmolality contrast agent is a good and safe choice. However, some patients are considered to be at a greater risk of having severe reactions to a radiopaque agent. Patients at risk are those who have had a severe reaction to radiopaque agents in the past. Also, patients with asthma or a history of allergies may be at a greater risk of severe reactions. For these patients, a low-osmolality contrast agent may be chosen. If you have any questions about this, check with the radiologist.

The doses of radiopaque agents will be different for different patients and depend on the type of test. The strength of the solution is determined by how much iodine it contains. Different tests will require a different strength and amount of solution depending on the age of the patient, the contrast needed, and the x-ray equipment used. Also, for tests of the kidneys and other areas of the urinary tract, the amount of solution to be used depends on the size of the bladder.

Radiopaque agents are to be used only by or under the supervision of a doctor in radiology or a radiologist.

Before Having This Test

In deciding to use a diagnostic test, any risks of the test must be weighed against the good it will do. This is a decision you and your doctor will make. Also, test results may be affected by other things. For radiopaque agents the following should be considered:

Allergies—Tell your doctor if you have ever had any unusual or allergic reaction to iodine, to products containing iodine (for example, iodine-containing foods, such as seafoods, cabbage, kale, rape [turnip-like vegetable], turnips, or iodized salt), or to other radiopaque agents. Also tell your doctor if you are allergic to any other substances, such as sulfites or other preservatives.

Pregnancy—Studies on effects in pregnancy when radiopaque agents are instilled into the bladder or ureters have not been done in women. Studies in animals have been done only with iothalamate, which has not been shown to cause birth defects or other problems.

Diagnostic tests of the uterus and fallopian tubes using radiopaque agents are not recommended during pregnancy or for at least 6 months after a pregnancy has ended. The test may cause other problems, such as infection in the uterus.

Also, radiopaque agents containing iodine have, on rare occasions, caused hypothyroidism (underactive thyroid) in the baby when they were injected into the amniotic sac late in the pregnancy. In addition, x-rays of the abdomen during pregnancy may have harmful effects on the fetus. Make sure your doctor knows if you are pregnant or if you suspect that you may be pregnant when you are to receive this radiopaque agent.

Breast-feeding—Although small amounts of radiopaque agents are absorbed into the body and may pass into the breast milk, these agents have not been shown to cause problems in nursing babies. However, it may be necessary for you to stop breast-feeding temporarily after receiving a radiopaque agent. Be sure you have discussed this with your doctor.

Children—Although there is no specific information comparing use of radiopaque agents in children with use in other age groups, these agents are not expected to cause different side effects or problems in children than they do in adults when used in the bladder or ureters. There is no specific information about the use of radiopaque agents in children for studies of the uterus or fallopian tubes.

Older adults—Many medicines have not been studied specifically in older people. Therefore, it may not be known whether they work exactly the same way they do in younger adults. Although there is no specific information comparing use of radiopaque agents for instillation into the bladder or ureters or into the uterus and fallopian tubes in the elderly with use in other age groups, these agents are not expected to cause different side effects or problems in older people than they do in younger adults.

Other medical problems—The presence of other medical problems may affect the use of radiopaque agents. Make sure you tell your doctor if you have any other medical problems, especially:

- Asthma, hay fever, or other allergies (history of) or
- Reaction to a skin test for allergies or to penicillins—If you have a history of these conditions, there is a greater chance of having a reaction, such as an allergic reaction, to the radiopaque agent
- Enlarged prostate or
- Kidney disease (severe)—There may be blockage that makes it difficult or impossible to put the solution of the radiopaque agent into the bladder or ureters
- Genital tract infection or
- Urinary tract infection—The risk of complications is greater in patients with these conditions
- Pelvic inflammatory disease (severe)—The condition may be aggravated by this test

Preparation for This Test

Your doctor may have special instructions for you in preparation for your test, such as the need for a special diet or for a laxative, enema, or vaginal douche, depending on the kind of test you are having done. If you have not received such instructions or if you do not understand them, check with your doctor in advance.

For your comfort and for best test results, you may be instructed to urinate just before the procedure.

Precautions After Having This Test

Make sure your doctor knows if you are planning to have any thyroid tests in the near future. Even after several weeks the results of the thyroid test may be affected by the iodine in this agent.

Side Effects of This Medicine

Along with its needed effects, radiopaque agents can cause serious side effects such as allergic reactions. These effects may occur almost immediately or a few minutes after the radiopaque agent is given. Although these serious side effects appear only rarely, your health care professional will be prepared to give you immediate medical attention if needed. If you have any questions about this, check with your doctor.

Check with your health care professional immediately if any of the following side effects occur:

Less common

Abdominal or stomach pain and discomfort (severe); backache

Other side effects may occur that usually do not need medical attention. These side effects should go away as the effects of the radiopaque agent wear off. However, check with your doctor if any of the following side effects continue or are bothersome:

More common

Abdominal or stomach pain and discomfort (mild)

Less common

Chills; fever; nausea and vomiting

Other side effects not listed above may also occur in some patients. If you notice any other effects, check with your doctor.

Revised: August 1990
Interim revision: 05/23/94; 04/24/95

RADIOPHARMACEUTICALS Diagnostic

This information applies to the following medicines when used for diagnosis:

1. Ammonia N 13 (a-MOE-nya)
2. Cyanocobalamin Co 57 (sye-an-oh-koe-BAL-a-min)
3. Ferrous Citrate Fe 59 (FER-us SI-trate)
4. Fludeoxyglucose F 18 (flu-dee-ox-ee-GLOO-kose)
5. Gallium Citrate Ga 67 (GAL-ee-um)
6. Indium In 111 Oxyquinoline (IN-dee-um ox-i-KWIN-oh-leen)
7. Indium In 111 Pentetate (PEN-te-tate)
8. Indium In 111 Pentetreotide
9. Indium In 111 Satumomab Pendetide
10. Iobenguane, Radioiodinated
11. Iodohippurate Sodium I 123 (eye-oh-doe-HIP-yoor-ate SOE-dee-um)
12. Iodohippurate Sodium I 131
13. Iofetamine I 123 (eye-oh-FET-a-meen)
14. Iothalamate Sodium I 125 (eye-oh-thal-A-mate)
15. Krypton Kr 81m (KRIP-tonn)
16. Radioiodinated Albumin (ray-dee-oh-EYE-oh-din-nay-ted al-BYOO-min)
17. Rubidium Rb 82 (roo-BID-ee-um)
18. Sodium Chromate Cr 51 (KROE-mate)
19. Sodium Iodide I 123 (EYE-oh-dyed)
20. Sodium Iodide I 131
21. Sodium Pertechnetate Tc 99m (per-TEK-ne-tate)
22. Technetium Tc 99m Albumin (tek-NEE-see-um al-BYOO-min)
23. Technetium Tc 99m Albumin Aggregated
24. Technetium Tc 99m Albumin Colloid
25. Technetium Tc 99m Bicisate (bye-SIS-ate)
26. Technetium Tc 99m Disofenin (DYE-so-fen-in)
27. Technetium Tc 99m Exametazime (ex-a-MET-a-zeem)
28. Technetium Tc 99m Gluceptate (gloo-SEP-tate)
29. Technetium Tc 99m Lidofenin (lye-doe-FEN-in)
30. Technetium Tc 99m Mebrofenin (ME-bro-fen-in)
31. Technetium Tc 99m Medronate (ME-droe-nate)
32. Technetium Tc 99m Mertiatide (meer-TYE-a-tide)
33. Technetium Tc 99m Oxidronate (OX-i-dron-ate)
34. Technetium Tc 99m Pentetate (PEN-te-tate)
35. Technetium Tc 99m Pyrophosphate (peer-oh-FOS-fate)
36. Technetium Tc 99m (Pyro- and trimeta-) Phosphates
37. Technetium Tc 99m Sestamibi (SES-ta-mi-bi)
38. Technetium Tc 99m Succimer (SUX-sim-mer)
39. Technetium Tc 99m Sulfur Colloid
40. Technetium Tc 99m Teboroxime (te-boe-ROX-eem)
41. Thallous Chloride Tl 201 (THA-luss KLOR-ide)
42. Xenon Xe 127 (ZEE-non)
43. Xenon Xe 133

Description

Radiopharmaceuticals (ray-dee-oh-far-ma-SOO-ti-kals) are agents used to diagnose certain medical problems or treat certain diseases. They may be given to the patient in several different ways. For example, they may be given by mouth, given by injection, or placed into the eye or into the bladder.

These radiopharmaceuticals are used in the diagnosis of:

- Abscess and infection—Gallium Citrate Ga 67, Indium In 111 Oxyquinoline
- Biliary tract blockage—Technetium Tc 99m Disofenin, Technetium Tc 99m Lidofenin, Technetium Tc 99m Mebrofenin
- Blood volume studies—Radioiodinated Albumin, Sodium Chromate Cr 51
- Blood vessel diseases—Sodium Pertechnetate Tc 99m
- Blood vessel diseases of the brain—Ammonia N 13, Iofetamine I 123, Technetium Tc 99m Bicisate, Technetium Tc 99m Exametazime, Xenon Xe 133
- Bone diseases—Technetium Tc 99m Medronate, Technetium Tc 99m Oxidronate, Technetium Tc 99m Pyrophosphate, Technetium Tc 99m (Pyro- and trimeta-) Phosphates

- Bone marrow diseases—Sodium Chromate Cr 51, Technetium Tc 99m Albumin Colloid, Technetium Tc 99m Sulfur Colloid
- Brain diseases and tumors—Fludeoxyglucose F 18, Indium In 111 Pentetreotide, Iofetamine I 123, Sodium Pertechnetate Tc 99m, Technetium Tc 99m Exametazime, Technetium Tc 99m Gluceptate, Technetium Tc 99m Pentetate
- Cancer; tumors—Fludeoxyglucose F 18, Gallium Citrate Ga 67, Indium In 111 Pentetreotide, Indium In 111 Satumomab Pendetide, Radioiodinated Iobenguane
- Disorders of iron metabolism and absorption—Ferrous Citrate Fe 59
- Heart disease—Ammonia N 13, Fludeoxyglucose F 18, Rubidium Rb 82, Sodium Pertechnetate Tc 99m, Technetium Tc 99m Albumin, Technetium Tc 99m Sestamibi, Technetium Tc 99m Teboroxime, Thallous Chloride Tl 201
- Heart muscle damage (infarct)—Ammonia N 13, Fludeoxyglucose F 18, Rubidium Rb 82, Technetium Tc 99m Pyrophosphate, Technetium Tc 99m (Pyro- and trimeta-) Phosphates, Technetium Tc 99m Sestamibi, Technetium Tc 99m Teboroxime, Thallous Chloride Tl 201
- Impaired flow of cerebrospinal fluid in brain—Indium In 111 Pentetate
- Kidney diseases—Iodohippurate Sodium I 123, Iodohippurate Sodium I 131, Iothalamate Sodium I 125, Technetium Tc 99m Gluceptate, Technetium Tc 99m Mertiatide, Technetium Tc 99m Pentetate, Technetium Tc 99m Succimer
- Liver diseases—Ammonia N 13, Fludeoxyglucose F 18, Technetium Tc 99m Albumin Colloid, Technetium Tc 99m Disofenin, Technetium Tc 99m Lidofenin, Technetium Tc 99m Mebrofenin, Technetium Tc 99m Sulfur Colloid
- Lung diseases—Krypton Kr 81m, Technetium Tc 99m Albumin Aggregated, Technetium Tc 99m Pentetate, Xenon Xe 127, Xenon Xe 133
- Parathyroid diseases; parathyroid cancer—Technetium Tc 99m Sestamibi, Thallous Chloride Tl 201
- Pernicious anemia; improper absorption of vitamin B_{12} from intestines—Cyanocobalamin Co 57
- Red blood cell diseases—Sodium Chromate Cr 51
- Salivary gland diseases—Sodium Pertechnetate Tc 99m
- Spleen diseases—Sodium Chromate Cr 51, Technetium Tc 99m Albumin Colloid, Technetium Tc 99m Sulfur Colloid
- Stomach and intestinal bleeding—Sodium Chromate Cr 51, Sodium Pertechnetate Tc 99m, Technetium Tc 99m (Pyro- and trimeta-) Phosphates, Technetium Tc 99m Sulfur Colloid
- Stomach problems—Technetium Tc 99m Sulfur Colloid
- Tear duct blockage—Sodium Pertechnetate Tc 99m
- Thyroid diseases; thyroid cancer—Fludeoxyglucose F 18, Indium In 111 Pentetreotide, Radioiodinated Iobenguane, Sodium Iodide I 123, Sodium Iodide I 131, Sodium Pertechnetate Tc 99m, Technetium Tc 99m Sestamibi
- Urinary bladder diseases—Sodium Pertechnetate Tc 99m

Radiopharmaceuticals are radioactive agents. However, when small amounts are used, the radiation your body receives is very low and is considered safe. When larger amounts of these agents are given to treat disease, there may be different effects on the body.

When radiopharmaceuticals are used to help diagnose medical problems, only small amounts are given to the patient. The radiopharmaceutical then passes through, or is taken up by, an organ of the body (which organ depends on what radiopharmaceutical is used and how it has been given). Then the radioactivity is detected, and pictures are produced, by special imaging equipment. These pictures allow the nuclear medicine doctor to study how the organ is working and to detect cancer or tumors that may be present in the organ.

Some radiopharmaceuticals are used in larger amounts to treat certain kinds of cancer and other diseases. In those cases, the radioactive agent is taken up in the cancerous area and destroys the affected tissue. *The information that follows applies only to radiopharmaceuticals when used in small amounts to diagnose medical problems.*

The dosages of radiopharmaceuticals that are used to diagnose medical problems will be different for different patients and depend on the type of test. The amount of radioactivity of a radiopharmaceutical is expressed in units called becquerels or curies. Radiopharmaceutical dosages given may be as small as 0.185 megabecquerels (5 microcuries) or as high as 1295 megabecquerels (35 millicuries). The radiation received from these dosages may be about the same as, or even less than, the radiation received from an x-ray study of the same organ.

Radiopharmaceuticals are to be given only by or under the direct supervision of a doctor with specialized training in nuclear medicine.

Before Having This Test

In deciding to use a diagnostic test, any risks of the test must be weighed against the good it will do. This is a decision you and your doctor will make. Also, test results may be affected by other things. For radiopharmaceuticals, the following should be considered:

Allergies—If you will be receiving albumin in the form of radioiodinated albumin, technetium Tc 99m albumin aggregated, technetium Tc 99m albumin colloid, or technetium Tc 99m albumin for your test, tell your doctor if you have ever had any unusual or allergic reaction to products containing human serum albumin. Also tell your doctor if you are allergic to any other substance, such as foods, preservatives, or dyes.

Pregnancy—Radiopharmaceuticals usually are not recommended for use during pregnancy. This is to avoid exposing the fetus to radiation. Some radiopharmaceuticals may be used for diagnostic tests in pregnant women, but it is necessary to inform your doctor if you are pregnant so the doctor may reduce the radiation dose to the baby. This is especially important with radiopharmaceuticals that contain radioactive iodine, which can go to the baby's thyroid gland and, in high enough amounts, may cause thyroid damage. Be sure you have discussed this with your doctor.

Breast-feeding—Some radiopharmaceuticals pass into the breast milk and may expose the baby to radiation. If you must receive a radiopharmaceutical, it may be necessary for you to stop breast-feeding for some time after receiving it. Be sure you have discussed this with your doctor.

Children—For most radiopharmaceuticals, the amount of radiation used for a diagnostic test is very low and considered safe. However, be sure you have discussed with your doctor the benefit versus the risk of exposing your child to radiation.

Older adults—Many medicines have not been studied specifically in older people. Therefore, it may not be known whether they work exactly the same way they do in younger adults or if they cause different side effects or problems in older people. Although there is no specific information comparing use of most radiopharmaceuticals in the elderly with use in other age groups, problems would not be expected to occur. However, it is a good idea to check with your doctor if you notice any unusual effects after receiving a radiopharmaceutical.

Other medicines—Although certain medicines should not be used together at all, in other cases two different medicines may be used together even if an interaction might occur. In these cases, your doctor may want to change the dose, or other precautions may be necessary. When you are going to receive a radiopharmaceutical, it is especially important that your doctor know if you are taking any other prescription or nonprescription (over-the-counter [OTC]) medicine.

In addition, if you will be receiving radioactive iodine (sodium iodide I 123, sodium iodide I 131) or sodium pertechnetate Tc 99m for a thyroid test, it is especially important that your doctor know if you have been taking iodine through other medicine or foods. For example, the results of your test may be affected if:

- You are taking iodine-containing medicines, including certain multivitamins and cough syrups.
- You eat large amounts of iodine-containing foods, such as iodized salt, seafood, cabbage, kale, rape (turnip-like vegetable), or turnips.
- You have had an x-ray test recently for which you were given a special dye that contained iodine.

Other medical problems—The presence of other medical problems may affect the use of radiopharmaceuticals. Make sure you tell your doctor if you have any other medical problems.

Preparation for This Test

The nuclear medicine doctor may have special instructions for you in preparation for your test. For example, before some tests you must fast for several hours, or the results of the test may be affected. For other tests you should drink plenty of liquids. If you do not understand the instructions you receive or if you have not received any instructions, check with the nuclear medicine doctor in advance.

Precautions After Having This Test

There are usually no special precautions to observe for radiopharmaceuticals when they are used in small amounts for diagnosis.

Some radiopharmaceuticals may accumulate in your bladder. Therefore, to increase the flow of urine and lessen the amount of radiation to your bladder, your doctor may instruct you to drink plenty of liquids and urinate often after certain tests.

For patients receiving *radioactive iodine (iodohippurate sodium I 123, iodohippurate sodium I 131, iofetamine I 123, iothalamate I 125, radioiodinated albumin, or radioiodinated iobenguane)*:

- Make sure your doctor knows if you are planning to have any future thyroid tests. Even after several weeks, the results of the thyroid test may be affected by the iodine solution that may be given before the radiopharmaceutical.

Side Effects of This Medicine

Along with its needed effects, a medicine may cause some unwanted effects. When radiopharmaceuticals are used in very small doses to study an organ of the body, side effects are rare and usually involve an allergic reaction. These effects may occur almost immediately or a few minutes after the radiopharmaceutical is given. It may be helpful to note the time when you first notice any side effect. Your doctor, nuclear medicine physician and/or technologist, or nurse will be prepared to give you immediate medical attention if needed.

Check with your doctor or nurse immediately if any of the following side effects occur:

Rare

Chills; difficulty breathing; drowsiness (severe); fainting; fast heartbeat; fever; flushing or redness of skin; headache (severe); nausea or vomiting; skin rash, hives, or itching; stomach pain; swelling of throat, hands, or feet

Other side effects not listed above may also occur in some patients. If you notice any other effects, note the time when they start and check with your doctor.

Revised: 08/30/94

RAUWOLFIA ALKALOIDS Systemic

Some commonly used brand names are:

In the U.S.—

Harmonyl[1]	Rauverid[2]
Raudixin[2]	Serpalan[3]
Rauval[2]	Wolfina[2]

In Canada—

Novoreserpine[3]	Serpasil[3]
Reserfia[3]	

Note: For quick reference, the following rauwolfia alkaloids are numbered to match the corresponding brand names.

This information applies to the following medicines:

1. Deserpidine (de-SER-pi-deen)†
2. Rauwolfia Serpentina (rah-WOOL-fee-a ser-pen-TEE-na)†‡
3. Reserpine (re-SER-peen)‡

†Not commercially available in Canada.
‡Generic product may also be available in the U.S.

Description

Rauwolfia alkaloids belong to the general class of medicines called antihypertensives. They are used to treat high blood pressure (hypertension).

High blood pressure adds to the workload of the heart and arteries. If it continues for a long time, the heart and arteries may not function properly. This can damage the blood vessels of the brain, heart, and kidneys, resulting in a stroke, heart failure, or kidney failure. High blood pressure may also increase the risk of heart attacks. These problems may be less likely to occur if blood pressure is controlled.

Rauwolfia alkaloids work by controlling nerve impulses along certain nerve pathways. As a result, they act on the heart and blood vessels to lower blood pressure.

Rauwolfia alkaloids may also be used to treat other conditions as determined by your doctor.

These medicines are available only with your doctor's prescription, in the following dosage forms:

Oral

Deserpidine
- Tablets (U.S.)

Rauwolfia Serpentina
- Tablets (U.S.)

Reserpine
- Tablets (U.S. and Canada)

Before Using This Medicine

In deciding to use a medicine, the risks of taking the medicine must be weighed against the good it will do. This is a decision you and your doctor will make. For rauwolfia alkaloids, the following should be considered:

Allergies—Tell your doctor if you have ever had any unusual or allergic reaction to rauwolfia alkaloids. Also tell your health care professional if you are allergic to any other substance, such as foods, preservatives, or dyes.

Pregnancy—Rauwolfia alkaloids have not been studied in pregnant women. However, too much use of rauwolfia alkaloids during pregnancy may cause unwanted effects (difficult breathing, low temperature, loss of appetite) in the baby. In rats, use of rauwolfia alkaloids during pregnancy causes birth defects and in guinea pigs decreases newborn survival rates. Before taking this medicine, make sure your doctor knows if you are pregnant or if you may become pregnant.

Breast-feeding—Rauwolfia alkaloids pass into breast milk and may cause unwanted effects (difficult breathing, low temperature, loss of appetite) in infants of mothers taking large doses of this medicine. Be sure you have discussed this with your doctor before taking this medicine.

Children—Although there is no specific information comparing use of rauwolfia alkaloids in children with use in other age groups, rauwolfia alkaloids are not expected to cause different side effects or problems in children than they do in adults.

Older adults—Many medicines have not been studied specifically in older people. Therefore, it may not be known whether they work exactly the same way they do in younger adults. Although there is no specific information comparing use of rauwolfia alkaloids in the elderly with use in other age groups, dizziness or drowsiness may be more likely to occur in the elderly, who are more sensitive to the effects of rauwolfia alkaloids.

Other medicines—Although certain medicines should not be used together at all, in other cases two different medicines may be used together even if an interaction might occur. In these cases, your doctor may want to change the dose, or other precautions may be necessary. When you are taking rauwolfia alkaloids, it is especially important that your health care professional know if you are taking any of the following:

- Monoamine oxidase (MAO) inhibitors (furazolidone [e.g., Furoxone], isocarboxazid [e.g., Marplan], phenelzine [e.g., Nardil], procarbazine [e.g., Matulane], selegiline [e.g., Eldepryl], tranylcypromine [e.g., Parnate])—Taking a rauwolfia alkaloid while you are taking or within 2 weeks of taking MAO inhibitors may increase the risk of central nervous system depression or may cause a severe high blood pressure reaction

Other medical problems—The presence of other medical problems may affect the use of rauwolfia alkaloids. Make sure you tell your doctor if you have any other medical problems, especially:

- Allergies or other breathing problems such as asthma—Rauwolfia alkaloids can cause breathing problems
- Epilepsy
- Gallstones or
- Stomach ulcer or
- Ulcerative colitis—Rauwolfia alkaloids increase activity of the stomach, which may make the condition worse
- Heart disease—Rauwolfia alkaloids can cause heart rhythm problems or slow heartbeat
- Kidney disease—Some patients may not do well when blood pressure is lowered by rauwolfia alkaloids
- Mental depression (or history of)—Rauwolfia alkaloids cause mental depression

- Parkinson's disease—Rauwolfia alkaloids can cause parkinsonism-like effects
- Pheochromocytoma

Proper Use of This Medicine

For patients taking this medicine *for high blood pressure*:

- In addition to the use of the medicine your doctor has prescribed, treatment for your high blood pressure may include weight control and care in the types of foods you eat, especially foods high in sodium. Your doctor will tell you which of these are most important for you. You should check with your doctor before changing your diet.
- Many patients who have high blood pressure will not notice any signs of the problem. In fact, many may feel normal. It is very important that you *take your medicine exactly as directed* and that you keep your appointments with your doctor even if you feel well.
- Remember that this medicine will not cure your high blood pressure but it does help control it. Therefore, you must continue to take it as directed if you expect to lower your blood pressure and keep it down. *You may have to take high blood pressure medicine for the rest of your life.* If high blood pressure is not treated, it can cause serious problems such as heart failure, blood vessel disease, stroke, or kidney disease.

To help you remember to take your medicine, try to get into the habit of taking it at the same time each day.

This medicine is sometimes given together with certain other medicines. If you are using a combination of drugs, make sure that you take each medicine at the proper time and do not mix them. Ask your health care professional to help you plan a way to remember to take your medicines at the right times.

If this medicine upsets your stomach, it may be taken with meals or milk. If stomach upset (nausea, vomiting, stomach cramps or pain) continues or gets worse, check with your doctor.

Dosing—The dose of these medicines will be different for different patients. *Follow your doctor's orders or the directions on the label.* The following information includes only the average doses of these medicines. *If your dose is different, do not change it* unless your doctor tells you to do so.

The number of tablets that you take depends on the strength of the medicine.

For deserpidine

- For *oral* dosage form (tablets):
  - —For high blood pressure:
    - Adults—250 to 500 micrograms (mcg) a day. This may be taken as a single dose or divided into two doses.
    - Children—Dose must be determined by your doctor.

For rauwolfia serpentina

- For *oral* dosage form (tablets):
  - —For high blood pressure:
    - Adults—50 to 200 milligrams (mg) a day. This may be taken as a single dose or divided into two doses.
    - Children—Dose must be determined by your doctor.

For reserpine

- For *oral* dosage form (tablets):
  - —For high blood pressure:
    - Adults—100 to 250 micrograms (mcg) a day.
    - Children—Dose is based on body weight and must be determined by your doctor. The usual dose is 5 to 20 mcg per kilogram (kg) (2.27 to 9.1 mcg per pound) of body weight a day. This may be taken as a single dose or divided into two doses.

Missed dose—If you miss a dose of this medicine, do not take the missed dose at all and do not double the next one. Instead, go back to your regular dosing schedule.

Storage—To store this medicine:

- Keep out of the reach of children.
- Store away from heat and direct light.
- Do not store in the bathroom, near the kitchen sink, or in other damp places. Heat or moisture may cause the medicine to break down.
- Do not keep outdated medicine or medicine no longer needed. Be sure that any discarded medicine is out of the reach of children.

Precautions While Using This Medicine

It is important that your doctor check your progress at regular visits to make sure that this medicine is working properly.

For patients taking this medicine *for high blood pressure*:

- *Do not take other medicines unless they have been discussed with your doctor.* This especially includes over-the-counter (nonprescription) medicines for appetite control, asthma, colds, cough, hay fever, or sinus problems, since they may tend to increase your blood pressure.

Before having any kind of surgery (including dental surgery) or emergency treatment, *tell the medical doctor or dentist in charge that you are taking this medicine.*

In some patients, this medicine may cause mental depression. *Tell your doctor right away:*

- if you or anyone else notices unusual changes in your mood.
- if you start having early-morning sleeplessness or unusually vivid dreams or nightmares.

This medicine will add to the effects of alcohol and other CNS depressants (medicines that slow down the nervous system, possibly causing drowsiness). Some examples of CNS depressants are antihistamines or medicine for hay fever, other allergies, or colds; sedatives, tranquilizers, or sleeping medicine; prescription pain medicine or narcotics; barbiturates; medicine for seizures; muscle relaxants; or anesthetics, including some dental anesthetics. *Check with your doctor before taking any of the above while you are using this medicine.*

This medicine may cause some people to become drowsy or less alert than they are normally. This is more likely to happen when you begin to take it or when you increase the amount of medicine you are taking. *Make sure you know how you react to this medicine before you drive, use machines, or do anything else that could be dangerous if you are not alert.*

This medicine may cause dryness of the mouth. For temporary relief, use sugarless candy or gum, melt bits of ice in your mouth, or use a saliva substitute. However, if dry mouth continues for more than 2 weeks, check with your medical doctor or dentist. Continuing dryness of the mouth may increase the chance of dental disease, including tooth decay, gum disease, and fungus infections.

This medicine often causes stuffiness in the nose. However, do not use nasal decongestant medicines without first checking with your health care professional.

Side Effects of This Medicine

Suggestions that rauwolfia alkaloids may increase the risk of breast cancer occurring later have not been proven. However, rats and mice given 100 to 300 times the human dose had an increased number of tumors.

Along with its needed effects, a medicine may cause some unwanted effects. Although not all of these side effects may occur, if they do occur they may need medical attention.

Check with your doctor immediately if any of the following side effects occur:

Less common
: Drowsiness or faintness; impotence or decreased sexual interest; lack of energy or weakness; mental depression or inability to concentrate; nervousness or anxiety; vivid dreams or nightmares or early-morning sleeplessness

Check with your doctor as soon as possible if any of the following side effects occur:

More common
: Dizziness

Less common
: Black, tarry stools; bloody vomit; chest pain; headache; irregular heartbeat; shortness of breath; slow heartbeat; stomach cramps or pain

Rare
: Painful or difficult urination; skin rash or itching; stiffness; trembling and shaking of hands and fingers; unusual bleeding or bruising

Signs and symptoms of overdose
: Dizziness or drowsiness (severe); flushing of skin; pinpoint pupils of eyes; slow pulse

Other side effects may occur that usually do not need medical attention. These side effects may go away during treatment as your body adjusts to the medicine. However, check with your doctor if any of the following side effects continue or are bothersome:

More common
: Diarrhea; dryness of mouth; loss of appetite; nausea and vomiting; stuffy nose

Less common
: Swelling of feet and lower legs

After you stop using this medicine, it may still produce some side effects that need attention. During this period of time *check with your doctor immediately* if you notice any of the following side effects:

Drowsiness or faintness; impotence or decreased sexual interest; irregular or slow heartbeat; lack of energy or weakness; mental depression or inability to concentrate; nervousness or anxiety; vivid dreams or nightmares or early-morning sleeplessness

Other side effects not listed above may also occur in some patients. If you notice any other effects, check with your doctor.

Additional Information

Once a medicine has been approved for marketing for a certain use, experience may show that it is also useful for other medical problems. Although this use is not included in product labeling, reserpine is used in certain patients with the following medical condition:

- Raynaud's disease

Other than the above information, there is no additional information relating to proper use, precautions, or side effects for this use.

Revised: 07/28/92
Interim revision: 07/20/94

RAUWOLFIA ALKALOIDS AND THIAZIDE DIURETICS Systemic

Some commonly used brand names are:

In the U.S.—

Demi-Regroton[5]
Diupres[4]
Diurese-R[10]
Diurigen with Reserpine[4]
Diutensen-R[8]
Enduronyl[2]
Enduronyl Forte[2]
Hydropine[7]
Hydropine H.P.[7]
Hydropres[6]
Hydrosine[6]
Hydrotensin[6]
Mallopres[6]
Metatensin[10]
Naquival[10]
Oreticyl[1]
Oreticyl Forte[1]
Rauzide[3]
Regroton[5]
Renese-R[9]
Salazide[7]
Salutensin[7]
Salutensin-Demi[7]

In Canada—

Dureticyl[2]
Hydropres[6]
Salutensin[7]

Note: For quick reference, the following rauwolfia alkaloids and thiazide diuretics are numbered to match the corresponding brand names.

This information applies to the following medicines:

1. Deserpidine (de-SER-pi-deen) and Hydrochlorothiazide (hye-droe-klor-oh-THYE-a-zide)†
2. Deserpidine and Methyclothiazide (meth-i-kloe-THYE-a-zide)‡
3. Rauwolfia Serpentina (rah-WOOL-fee-a ser-pen-TEE-na) and Bendroflumethiazide (ben-droe-floo-meth-EYE-a-zide)†
4. Reserpine (re-SER-peen) and Chlorothiazide (klor-oh-THYE-a-zide)†‡
5. Reserpine and Chlorthalidone (klor-THAL-i-done)†
6. Reserpine and Hydrochlorothiazide‡
7. Reserpine and Hydroflumethiazide (hye-droe-floo-meth-EYE-a-zide)‡
8. Reserpine and Methyclothiazide†
9. Reserpine and Polythiazide (pol-i-THYE-a-zide)†
10. Reserpine and Trichlormethiazide (trye-klor-meth-EYE-a-zide)†‡

†Not commercially available in Canada.
‡Generic name product may also be available in the U.S.

Description

Rauwolfia alkaloid and thiazide diuretic combinations are used in the treatment of high blood pressure (hypertension).

High blood pressure adds to the workload of the heart and arteries. If it continues for a long time, the heart and arteries may not function properly. This can damage the blood vessels of the brain, heart, and kidneys, resulting in a stroke, heart failure, or kidney failure. High blood pressure may also increase the risk of heart attacks. These problems may be less likely to occur if blood pressure is controlled.

Rauwolfia alkaloids work by controlling nerve impulses along certain nerve pathways. As a result, they act on the heart and blood vessels to lower blood pressure. Thiazide diuretics help to reduce the amount of water in the body by increasing the flow of urine. This also helps to lower blood pressure.

These medicines are available only with your doctor's prescription, in the following dosage forms:

Oral

Deserpidine and Hydrochlorothiazide
- Tablets (U.S.)

Deserpidine and Methyclothiazide
- Tablets (U.S. and Canada)

Rauwolfia Serpentina and Bendroflumethiazide
- Tablets (U.S.)

Reserpine and Chlorothiazide
- Tablets (U.S.)

Reserpine and Chlorthalidone
- Tablets (U.S.)

Reserpine and Hydrochlorothiazide
- Tablets (U.S. and Canada)

Reserpine and Hydroflumethiazide
- Tablets (U.S. and Canada)

Reserpine and Methyclothiazide
- Tablets (U.S.)

Reserpine and Polythiazide
- Tablets (U.S.)

Reserpine and Trichlormethiazide
- Tablets (U.S.)

Before Using This Medicine

In deciding to use a medicine, the risks of taking the medicine must be weighed against the good it will do. This is a decision you and your doctor will make. For rauwolfia alkaloids and thiazide diuretics, the following should be considered:

Allergies—Tell your doctor if you have ever had any unusual or allergic reaction to sulfonamides (sulfa drugs), thiazide diuretics (water pills), or rauwolfia alkaloids. Also tell your health care professional if you are allergic to any other substance, such as foods, preservatives, or dyes.

Pregnancy—Too much use of thiazide diuretics (contained in this combination medicine) during pregnancy may cause unwanted effects including jaundice, blood problems, and low potassium in the baby. Too much use of rauwolfia alkaloids may cause difficult breathing, low temperature, and loss of appetite in the baby. This medicine has not been shown to cause birth defects in humans. In rats, use of rauwolfia alkaloids during pregnancy decreases newborn survival rates. Be sure that you have discussed this with your doctor before taking this medicine.

Breast-feeding—Rauwolfia alkaloids pass into breast milk and may cause unwanted effects (difficult breathing, low temperature, loss of appetite) in infants of mothers taking it in large doses. Thiazide diuretics also pass into breast milk. Be sure you have discussed this with your doctor before taking this medicine.

Children—Although there is no specific information comparing use of these medicines in children with use in other age groups, these medicines are not expected to cause different side effects or problems in children than they do in adults.

Older adults—Many medicines have not been studied specifically in older people. Therefore, it may not be known whether they work exactly the same way they do in younger adults. Although there is no specific information comparing use of rauwolfia alkaloid and thiazide diuretic combinations in the elderly with use in other age groups, this medicine is not expected to cause different side effects or problems in older people than it does in younger adults. However, drowsiness, dizziness, or faintness or symptoms of too much potassium loss may be more likely to occur in the elderly, who are more sensitive to the effects of rauwolfia alkaloids and thiazide diuretics.

Other medicines—Although certain medicines should not be used together at all, in other cases two different medicines may be used together even if an interaction might occur. In these cases, your doctor may want to change the dose, or other precautions may be necessary. When you are taking rauwolfia alkaloids and thiazide diuretics, it is especially important that your health care professional know if you are taking any of the following:

- Cholestyramine or
- Colestipol—Use with thiazide diuretics may prevent the diuretic from working properly; take the diuretic at least 1 hour before or 4 hours after cholestyramine or colestipol
- Digitalis glycosides (heart medicine)—Thiazide diuretics may cause low potassium in the blood, which can lead to symptoms of digitalis toxicity

- Lithium (e.g., Lithane)—Risk of lithium overdose, even at usual doses, may be increased
- Monoamine oxidase (MAO) inhibitors (furazolidone [e.g., Furoxone], isocarboxazid [e.g., Marplan], phenelzine [e.g., Nardil], procarbazine [e.g., Matulane], selegiline [e.g., Eldepryl], tranylcypromine [e.g., Parnate])—Taking a rauwolfia alkaloid while you are taking or within 2 weeks of taking MAO inhibitors may increase the risk of central nervous system depression or may cause a severe high blood pressure reaction

Other medical problems—The presence of other medical problems may affect the use of rauwolfia alkaloids and thiazide diuretics. Make sure you tell your doctor if you have any other medical problems, especially:

- Allergies or other breathing problems such as asthma—Rauwolfia alkaloids can cause breathing problems
- Diabetes mellitus (sugar diabetes)—Thiazide diuretics may change the amount of diabetes medicine needed
- Epilepsy
- Gallstones or
- Stomach ulcer or
- Ulcerative colitis—Rauwolfia alkaloids increase activity of the stomach, which may make the condition worse
- Gout (history of)—Thiazide diuretics may increase the amount of uric acid in the blood, which can lead to gout
- Heart disease—Rauwolfia alkaloids can cause heart rhythm problems or slow heartbeat
- Kidney disease—Some patients may not do well when blood pressure is lowered by this medicine. If kidney disease is severe, thiazide diuretics may not work
- Liver disease—If thiazide diuretics cause loss of too much water from the body, liver disease can become much worse
- Lupus erythematosus (history of)—Thiazide diuretics may worsen the condition
- Mental depression (or history of)—Rauwolfia alkaloids cause mental depression
- Pancreatitis (inflammation of pancreas)
- Parkinson's disease—Rauwolfia alkaloids can cause parkinsonism-like effects
- Pheochromocytoma

Proper Use of This Medicine

In addition to the use of the medicine your doctor has prescribed, treatment for your high blood pressure may include weight control and care in the types of foods you eat, especially foods high in sodium. Your doctor will tell you which of these are most important for you. You should check with your doctor before changing your diet.

Many patients who have high blood pressure will not notice any signs of the problem. In fact, many may feel normal. It is very important that you *take your medicine exactly as directed* and that you keep your appointments with your doctor even if you feel well.

Remember that this medicine will not cure your high blood pressure but it does help control it. Therefore, you must continue to take it as directed if you expect to lower your blood pressure and keep it down. *You may have to take high blood pressure medicine for the rest of your life.* If high blood pressure is not treated, it can cause serious problems such as heart failure, blood vessel disease, stroke, or kidney disease.

This medicine may cause you to have an unusual feeling of tiredness when you begin to take it. You may also notice an increase in the amount of urine or in your frequency of urination. After you have taken the medicine for a while, these effects should lessen. In general, to keep the increase in urine from affecting your sleep:

- If you are to take a single dose a day, take it in the morning after breakfast.
- If you are to take more than one dose a day, take the last dose no later than 6 p.m., unless otherwise directed by your doctor.

However, it is best to plan your dose or doses according to a schedule that will least affect your personal activities and sleep. Ask your health care professional to help you plan the best time to take this medicine.

To help you remember to take your medicine, try to get into the habit of taking it at the same time each day.

If this medicine upsets your stomach, it may be taken with meals or milk. If stomach upset (nausea, vomiting, stomach pain or cramps) continues, check with your doctor.

Dosing—The dose of these medicines will be different for different patients. *Follow your doctor's orders or the directions on the label.* The following information includes only the average doses of these medicines. *If your dose is different, do not change it* unless your doctor tells you to do so.

For deserpidine and hydrochlorothiazide combination

- For *oral* dosage form (tablets):
  - —For high blood pressure:
    - Adults—1 tablet two times a day.
    - Children—Dose must be determined by your doctor.

For deserpidine and methyclothiazide combination

- For *oral* dosage form (tablets):
  - —For high blood pressure:
    - Adults—One-half to 1 tablet a day.
    - Children—Dose must be determined by your doctor.

For rauwolfia serpentina and bendroflumethiazide combination

- For *oral* dosage form (tablets):
  - —For high blood pressure:
    - Adults—1 to 4 tablets a day.
    - Children—Dose must be determined by your doctor.

For reserpine and chlorothiazide combination

- For *oral* dosage form (tablets):
  - —For high blood pressure:
    - Adults—1 or 2 tablets one or two times a day.
    - Children—Dose must be determined by your doctor.

For reserpine and chlorthalidone combination
- For *oral* dosage form (tablets):
  - —For high blood pressure:
    - Adults—1 or 2 tablets once a day.
    - Children—Dose must be determined by your doctor.

For reserpine and hydrochlorothiazide combination
- For *oral* dosage form (tablets):
  - —For high blood pressure:
    - Adults—1 tablet one to four times a day.
    - Children—Dose must be determined by your doctor.

For reserpine and hydroflumethiazide combination
- For *oral* dosage form (tablets):
  - —For high blood pressure:
    - Adults—1 tablet one or two times a day.
    - Children—Dose must be determined by your doctor.

For reserpine and methyclothiazide combination
- For *oral* dosage form (tablets):
  - —For high blood pressure:
    - Adults—1 to 4 tablets a day.
    - Children—Dose must be determined by your doctor.

For reserpine and polythiazide combination
- For *oral* dosage form (tablets):
  - —For high blood pressure:
    - Adults—One-half to 2 tablets a day.
    - Children—Dose must be determined by your doctor.

For reserpine and trichlormethiazide combination
- For *oral* dosage form (tablets):
  - —For high blood pressure:
    - Adults—1 or 2 tablets a day. This may be taken as a single dose or divided into smaller doses.
    - Children—Dose must be determined by your doctor.

Missed dose—If you miss a dose of this medicine, take it as soon as possible. However, if it is almost time for your next dose, skip the missed dose and go back to your regular dosing schedule. Do not double doses.

Storage—To store this medicine:
- Keep out of the reach of children.
- Store away from heat and direct light.
- Do not store in the bathroom, near the kitchen sink, or in other damp places. Heat or moisture may cause the medicine to break down.
- Do not keep outdated medicine or medicine no longer needed. Be sure that any discarded medicine is out of the reach of children.

Precautions While Using This Medicine

It is important that your doctor check your progress at regular visits to make sure that this medicine is working properly.

Do not take other medicines unless they have been discussed with your doctor. This especially includes over-the-counter (nonprescription) medicines for appetite control, asthma, colds, cough, hay fever, or sinus problems, since they may tend to increase your blood pressure.

Before having any kind of surgery (including dental surgery), or emergency treatment, *tell the medical doctor or dentist in charge that you are taking this medicine.*

This medicine may cause a loss of potassium from your body.
- To help prevent this, your doctor may want you to:
  - —eat or drink foods that have a high potassium content (for example, orange or other citrus fruit juices), or
  - —take a potassium supplement, or
  - —take another medicine to help prevent the loss of the potassium in the first place.
- It is very important to follow these directions. Also, it is important not to change your diet on your own. This is more important if you are already on a special diet (as for diabetes), or if you are taking a potassium supplement or a medicine to reduce potassium loss. Extra potassium may not be necessary and, in some cases, too much potassium could be harmful.

Check with your doctor if you become sick and have severe or continuing vomiting or diarrhea. These problems may cause you to lose additional water and potassium.

This medicine may cause some people to become drowsy or less alert than they are normally. This is more likely to happen when you begin to take it or when you increase the amount of medicine you are taking. *Make sure you know how you react to this medicine before you drive, use machines, or do anything else that could be dangerous if you are not alert.*

Dizziness, lightheadedness, or fainting may occur, especially when you get up from a lying or sitting position. This is more likely to occur in the morning. Getting up slowly may help. When you get up from lying down, sit on the edge of the bed with your feet dangling for 1 or 2 minutes. Then stand up slowly. If the problem continues or gets worse, check with your doctor.

The dizziness, lightheadedness, or fainting is also more likely to occur if you drink alcohol, stand for a long time, exercise, or if the weather is hot. *While you are taking this medicine, be careful to limit the amount of alcohol you drink. Also, use extra care during exercise or hot weather or if you must stand for a long time.*

In some patients, this medicine may cause mental depression. *Tell your doctor right away:*
- if you or anyone else notices unusual changes in your moods.
- if you start having early-morning sleeplessness or unusually vivid dreams or nightmares.

This medicine will add to the effects of alcohol and other CNS depressants (medicines that slow down the nervous system, possibly causing drowsiness). Some examples of CNS depressants are antihistamines or medicine for hay fever, other allergies, or colds; sedatives, tranquilizers, or sleeping medicine; prescription pain medicine or narcotics; barbiturates; medicine for seizures; muscle relaxants; or anesthetics, including dental anesthetics. *Check with your doctor before taking any of the above while you are taking this medicine.*

For *diabetic patients*:

- This medicine may raise blood sugar levels. While you are using this medicine, be especially careful in testing for sugar in your urine. If you have any questions about this, check with your doctor.

Some people who take this medicine may become more sensitive to sunlight than they are normally. Exposure to sunlight, even for brief periods of time, may cause severe sunburn; skin rash, redness, itching, or discoloration; or vision changes. When you begin taking this medicine:

- Stay out of direct sunlight, especially between the hours of 10:00 a.m. and 3:00 p.m., if possible.
- Wear protective clothing, including a hat and sunglasses.
- Apply a sun block product that has a skin protection factor (SPF) of at least 15. Some patients may require a product with a higher SPF number, especially if they have a fair complexion. If you have any questions about this, check with your health care professional.
- Do not use a sunlamp or tanning bed or booth.

If you have a severe reaction from the sun, check with your doctor.

This medicine often causes stuffiness in the nose. However, do not use nasal decongestant medicines without first checking with your health care professional.

This medicine may cause dryness of the mouth. For temporary relief, use sugarless candy or gum, melt bits of ice in your mouth, or use a saliva substitute. However, if dry mouth continues for more than 2 weeks, check with your medical doctor or dentist. Continuing dryness of the mouth may increase the chance of dental disease, including tooth decay, gum disease, and fungus infections.

Side Effects of This Medicine

Suggestions that rauwolfia alkaloids may increase the risk of breast cancer occurring later have not been proven. However, rats and mice given 100 to 300 times the human dose had an increased risk of tumors.

Along with its needed effects, a medicine may cause some unwanted effects. Although not all of these side effects may occur, if they do occur they may need medical attention.

Check with your doctor immediately if any of the following side effects occur:

Less common

Drowsiness or faintness; impotence or decreased sexual interest; lack of energy or weakness; mental depression or inability to concentrate; nervousness or anxiety; vivid dreams or nightmares or early-morning sleeplessness

Check with your doctor as soon as possible if any of the following side effects occur:

Less common

Black, tarry stools; bloody vomit; chest pain; headache; irregular or slow heartbeat; joint pain; shortness of breath

Rare

Painful or difficult urination; skin rash or itching; sore throat and fever; stiffness; stomach pain (severe) with nausea and vomiting; trembling and shaking of hands and fingers; unusual bleeding or bruising; yellow eyes or skin

Symptoms of too much potassium loss or overdose

Dry mouth; increased thirst; muscle cramps or pain; nausea or vomiting

Other signs and symptoms of overdose

Dizziness or drowsiness, severe; flushing of skin; pinpoint pupils of eyes; slow pulse

Other side effects may occur that usually do not need medical attention. These side effects may go away during treatment as your body adjusts to the medicine. However, check with your doctor if any of the following side effects continue or are bothersome:

More common

Diarrhea; dizziness, especially when getting up from a lying or sitting position; loss of appetite; stuffy nose

After you stop using this medicine, it may still produce some side effects that need attention. During this period of time *check with your doctor immediately* if you notice any of the following side effects:

Drowsiness or faintness; impotence or decreased sexual interest; irregular or slow heartbeat; lack of energy or weakness; mental depression or inability to concentrate; nervousness or anxiety; vivid dreams or nightmares or early-morning sleeplessness

Other side effects not listed above may also occur in some patients. If you notice any other effects, check with your doctor.

Revised: 09/22/92
Interim revision: 07/20/94

RESERPINE, HYDRALAZINE, AND HYDROCHLOROTHIAZIDE Systemic

Some commonly used brand names are:

In the U.S.—

Cam-Ap-Es	Ser-Ap-Es
Cherapas	Serpazide
Ser-A-Gen	Tri-Hydroserpine
Seralazide	Unipres

Generic name product may also be available.

In Canada—

Ser-Ap-Es

Description

Reserpine (re-SER-peen), hydralazine (hye-DRAL-a-zeen), and hydrochlorothiazide (hye-droe-KLOR-oh-THYE-a-zide) combinations are used to treat high blood pressure (hypertension).

High blood pressure adds to the workload of the heart and arteries. If it continues for a long time, the heart and arteries may not function properly. This can damage the blood vessels of the brain, heart, and kidneys, resulting in a stroke, heart failure, or kidney failure. High blood pressure may also increase the risk of heart attacks. These problems may be less likely to occur if blood pressure is controlled.

Reserpine works by controlling nerve impulses along certain nerve pathways. As a result, it acts on the heart and blood vessels to lower blood pressure. Hydralazine works by relaxing blood vessels and increasing the supply of blood to the heart while reducing its work load. Hydrochlorothiazide is a thiazide diuretic (water pill) that helps to reduce the amount of water in the body by increasing the flow of urine. This also helps to lower blood pressure.

This medicine is available only with your doctor's prescription, in the following dosage form:

Oral

- Tablets (U.S. and Canada)

Before Using This Medicine

In deciding to use a medicine, the risks of taking the medicine must be weighed against the good it will do. This is a decision you and your doctor will make. For reserpine, hydralazine, and hydrochlorothiazide, the following should be considered:

Allergies—Tell your doctor if you have ever had any unusual or allergic reaction to hydralazine, sulfonamides (sulfa drugs), thiazide diuretics (water pills), or rauwolfia alkaloids. Also tell your health care professional if you are allergic to any other substances, such as foods, preservatives, or dyes.

Pregnancy—Too much use of reserpine and hydrochlorothiazide during pregnancy may cause unwanted effects (jaundice, blood problems, low potassium, difficult breathing, low temperatures, and loss of appetite) in the baby. In rats, rauwolfia alkaloids (like reserpine) decrease newborn survival rates.

Studies with hydralazine have not been done in humans. However, studies in mice have shown that hydralazine causes birth defects (cleft palate, defects in head and face bones); these birth defects may also occur in rabbits, but do not occur in rats. Be sure that you have discussed this with your doctor before taking this medicine.

Breast-feeding—Reserpine passes into breast milk and may cause unwanted effects (difficult breathing, low temperature, loss of appetite) in infants of mothers taking large doses of it. Hydrochlorothiazide also passes into breast milk. Be sure you have discussed this with your doctor before taking this medicine.

Children—Although there is no specific information comparing use of this medicine in children with use in other age groups, this medicine is not expected to cause different side effects or problems in children than it does in adults.

Older adults—Many medicines have not been studied specifically in older people. Therefore, it may not be known whether they work exactly the same way they do in younger adults. Although there is no specific information comparing use of reserpine, hydralazine, and hydrochlorothiazide combination in the elderly with use in other age groups, this medicine is not expected to cause different side effects or problems in older people than it does in younger adults. However, drowsiness, dizziness, or faintness, or symptoms of too much potassium loss may be more likely to occur in the elderly, who are usually more sensitive to the effects of this medicine. Also, this medicine may reduce tolerance to cold temperatures in elderly patients.

Other medicines—Although certain medicines should not be used together at all, in other cases two different medicines may be used together even if an interaction might occur. In these cases, your doctor may want to change the dose, or other precautions may be necessary. When you are taking this medicine, it is especially important that your health care professional know if you are taking any of the following:

- Cholestyramine or
- Colestipol—Use with thiazide diuretics may prevent the diuretic from working properly; take the diuretic at least 1 hour before or 4 hours after cholestyramine or colestipol
- Diazoxide (e.g., Proglycem)—Effect on blood pressure may be increased
- Digitalis glycosides (heart medicine)—Hydrochlorothiazide may cause low potassium in the blood, which can lead to symptoms of digitalis toxicity
- Lithium (e.g., Lithane)—Risk of lithium overdose, even at usual doses, may be increased
- Monoamine oxidase (MAO) inhibitors (furazolidone [e.g., Furoxone], isocarboxazid [e.g., Marplan], phenelzine [e.g., Nardil], procarbazine [e.g., Matulane], selegiline [e.g., Eldepryl], tranylcypromine [e.g., Parnate])—Taking a rauwolfia alkaloid while you are taking or within 2 weeks of taking MAO inhibitors may increase the risk of central nervous system depression or may cause a severe high blood pressure reaction

Other medical problems—The presence of other medical problems may affect the use of this medicine. Make sure you tell your doctor if you have any other medical problems, especially:

- Allergies or other breathing problems such as asthma—Reserpine can cause breathing problems
- Diabetes mellitus (sugar diabetes)—Hydrochlorothiazide may change the amount of diabetes medicine needed
- Epilepsy
- Gallstones or
- Stomach ulcer or
- Ulcerative colitis—Reserpine increases activity of the stomach, which may make the condition worse
- Gout (history of)—Hydrochlorothiazide may increase the amount of uric acid in the blood, which can lead to gout
- Heart disease—Reserpine can cause heart rhythm problems or slow heartbeat. Lowering blood pressure may worsen some conditions
- Kidney disease—Some patients may not do well when blood pressure is lowered by this medicine. Effects of hydralazine may be increased because of slower removal from the body. If kidney disease is severe, hydrochlorothiazide may not work
- Liver disease—If hydrochlorothiazide causes loss of too much water from the body, liver disease can become much worse
- Lupus erythematosus (history of)—Hydrochlorothiazide may worsen the condition
- Mental depression (or history of)—Reserpine causes mental depression
- Pancreatitis (inflammation of pancreas)
- Parkinson's disease—Reserpine can cause parkinsonism-like effects
- Pheochromocytoma
- Stroke (recent)—Lowering blood pressure may make problems resulting from this condition worse

Proper Use of This Medicine

In addition to the use of the medicine your doctor has prescribed, treatment for your high blood pressure may include weight control and care in the types of foods you eat, especially foods high in sodium. Your doctor will tell you which of these are most important for you. You should check with your doctor before changing your diet.

Many patients who have high blood pressure will not notice any signs of the problem. In fact, many may feel normal. It is very important that you *take your medicine exactly as directed* and that you keep your appointments with your doctor even if you feel well.

Remember that this medicine will not cure your high blood pressure but it does help control it. Therefore, you must continue to take it as directed if you expect to lower your blood pressure and keep it down. *You may have to take high blood pressure medicine for the rest of your life.* If high blood pressure is not treated, it can cause serious problems such as heart failure, blood vessel disease, stroke, or kidney disease.

This medicine may cause you to have an unusual feeling of tiredness when you begin to take it. You may also notice an increase in the amount of urine or in your frequency of urination. After you have taken the medicine for a while, these effects should lessen. In general, to keep the increase in urine from affecting your sleep:

- If you are to take a single dose a day, take it in the morning after breakfast.
- If you are to take more than one dose a day, take the last dose no later than 6 p.m., unless otherwise directed by your doctor.

However, it is best to plan your dose or doses according to a schedule that will least affect your personal activities and sleep. Ask your health care professional to help you plan the best time to take this medicine.

To help you remember to take your medicine, try to get into the habit of taking it at the same time each day.

If this medicine upsets your stomach, it may be taken with meals or milk. If stomach upset (nausea, vomiting, stomach pain or cramps) continues, check with your doctor.

Dosing—The dose of reserpine, hydralazine, and hydrochlorothiazide combination will be different for different patients. *Follow your doctor's orders or the directions on the label.* The following information includes only the average doses of reserpine, hydralazine, and hydrochlorothiazide combination. *If your dose is different, do not change it* unless your doctor tells you to do so.

- For *oral* dosage form (tablets):
  —For high blood pressure:
    - Adults—1 or 2 tablets three times a day.
    - Children—Use and dose must be determined by your doctor.

Missed dose—If you miss a dose of this medicine, take it as soon as possible. However, if it is almost time for your next dose, skip the missed dose and go back to your regular dosing schedule. Do not double doses.

Storage—To store this medicine:

- Keep out of the reach of children.
- Store away from heat and direct light.
- Do not store in the bathroom, near the kitchen sink, or in other damp places. Heat or moisture may cause the medicine to break down.
- Do not keep outdated medicine or medicine no longer needed. Be sure that any discarded medicine is out of the reach of children.

Precautions While Using This Medicine

It is important that your doctor check your progress at regular visits to make sure that this medicine is working properly.

Do not take other medicines unless they have been discussed with your doctor. This especially includes over-the-counter (nonprescription) medicines for appetite control, asthma, colds, cough, hay fever, or sinus problems, since they may tend to increase your blood pressure.

Before having any kind of surgery (including dental surgery), or emergency treatment, *make sure the medical doctor or dentist in charge knows that you are taking this medicine.*

This medicine may cause some people to have headaches or to feel dizzy or drowsy. *Make sure you know how you react to this medicine before you drive, use machines, or do anything else that could be dangerous if you are dizzy or are not alert.*

Dizziness, lightheadedness, or fainting may occur, especially when you get up from a lying or sitting position. This is more likely to occur in the morning. *Getting up slowly may help.* When you get up from lying down, sit on the edge of the bed with your feet dangling for 1 or 2 minutes. Then stand up slowly. If the problem continues or gets worse, check with your doctor.

The dizziness, lightheadedness, or fainting is also more likely to occur if you drink alcohol, stand for a long time, exercise, or if the weather is hot. *While you are taking this medicine, be careful to limit the amount of alcohol you drink. Also, use extra care during exercise or hot weather or if you must stand for a long time.*

In some patients, this medicine may cause mental depression. *Tell your doctor right away:*

- if you or anyone else notices unusual changes in your mood.
- if you start having early-morning sleeplessness or unusually vivid dreams or nightmares.

This medicine will add to the effects of alcohol and other CNS depressants (medicines that slow down the nervous system, possibly causing drowsiness). Some examples of CNS depressants are antihistamines or medicine for hay fever, other allergies, or colds; sedatives, tranquilizers, or sleeping medicine; prescription pain medicine or narcotics; barbiturates; medicine for seizures; muscle relaxants; or anesthetics, including dental anesthetics. *Check with your doctor before taking any of the above while you are taking this medicine.*

This medicine may cause a loss of potassium from your body.

- To help prevent this, your doctor may want you to:
  - —eat or drink foods that have a high potassium content (for example, orange or other citrus fruit juices), or
  - —take a potassium supplement, or
  - —take another medicine to help prevent the loss of the potassium in the first place.
- It is very important to follow these directions. Also, it is important not to change your diet on your own. This is more important if you are already on a special diet (as for diabetes), or if you are taking a potassium supplement or a medicine to reduce potassium loss. Extra potassium may not be necessary and, in some cases, too much potassium could be harmful.

Check with your doctor if you become sick and have severe or continuing nausea, vomiting, or diarrhea. These problems may cause you to lose additional water and potassium.

For *diabetic patients:*

- This medicine may raise blood sugar levels. While you are using this medicine, be especially careful in testing for sugar in your urine. If you have any questions about this, check with your doctor.

Some people who take this medicine may become more sensitive to sunlight than they are normally. Exposure to sunlight, even for brief periods of time, may cause severe sunburn; skin rash, redness, itching, or discoloration; or vision changes. When you begin taking this medicine:

- Stay out of direct sunlight, especially between the hours of 10:00 a.m. and 3:00 p.m., if possible.
- Wear protective clothing, including a hat and sunglasses.
- Apply a sun block product that has a skin protection factor (SPF) of at least 15. Some patients may require a product with a higher SPF number, especially if they have a fair complexion. If you have any questions about this, check with your health care professional.
- Do not use a sunlamp or tanning bed or booth.

If you have a severe reaction from the sun, check with your doctor.

This medicine often causes stuffiness in the nose. However, do not use nasal decongestant medicines without first checking with your health care professional.

This medicine may cause dryness of the mouth. For temporary relief, use sugarless candy or gum, melt bits of ice in your mouth, or use a saliva substitute. However, if dry mouth continues for more than 2 weeks, check with your medical doctor or dentist. Continuing dryness of the mouth may increase the chance of dental disease, including tooth decay, gum disease, and fungus infections.

Side Effects of This Medicine

Suggestions that rauwolfia alkaloids may increase the risk of breast cancer occurring later have not been proven. However, rats and mice given 100 to 300 times the human dose had an increased number of tumors.

Along with its needed effects, a medicine may cause some unwanted effects. Although not all of these side effects may occur, if they do occur they may need medical attention.

Check with your doctor immediately if any of the following side effects occur:

More common

General feeling of discomfort or illness or weakness

Less common

Drowsiness or faintness; impotence or decreased sexual interest; lack of energy or weakness; mental depression or inability to concentrate; nervousness or anxiety; vivid dreams or nightmares or early-morning sleeplessness

Check with your doctor as soon as possible if any of the following side effects occur:

Signs and symptoms of too much potassium loss

Dryness of mouth; increased thirst; irregular heartbeat; mood or mental changes; muscle cramps or pain; weak pulse

Signs and symptoms of too much sodium loss
Confusion; convulsions; decreased mental activity; irritability; muscle cramps; unusual tiredness or weakness

Less common
Black, tarry stools; blisters on skin; bloody vomit; chest pain; fever and sore throat; headache; irregular heartbeat; joint pain; numbness, tingling, pain, or weakness in hands or feet; shortness of breath; skin rash or itching; slow heartbeat; stomach cramps or pain; swelling of lymph glands

Rare
Lower back or side pain; painful or difficult urination; stiffness; stomach pain (severe) with nausea and vomiting; trembling and shaking of hands and fingers; unusual bleeding or bruising; yellow eyes or skin

Signs and symptoms of overdose
Dizziness or drowsiness (severe); dryness of mouth; flushing of skin; increased thirst; muscle cramps or pain; nausea or vomiting (severe); pinpoint pupils of eyes; slow pulse

Other side effects may occur that usually do not need medical attention. These side effects may go away during treatment as your body adjusts to the medicine. However, check with your doctor if any of the following side effects continue or are bothersome:

More common
Diarrhea; dizziness, especially when getting up from a lying or sitting position; loss of appetite; nausea or vomiting; stuffy nose

Less common
Constipation; flushing or redness of skin; increased sensitivity of skin to sunlight; swelling of feet and lower legs; watering or irritated eyes

After you stop using this medicine, it may still produce some side effects that need attention. During this period of time *check with your doctor immediately* if you notice any of the following side effects:

Drowsiness or faintness; general feeling of discomfort or illness or weakness; impotence or decreased sexual interest; irregular heartbeat; mental depression or inability to concentrate; nervousness or anxiety; vivid dreams or nightmares or early-morning sleeplessness

Other side effects not listed above may also occur in some patients. If you notice any other effects, check with your doctor.

Revised: 09/22/92
Interim revision: 07/20/94

RESORCINOL Topical

A commonly used brand name in the U.S. is RA.

Description

Resorcinol (re-SOR-si-nole) is used to treat acne, seborrheic dermatitis, eczema, psoriasis, and other skin disorders. It is also used to treat corns, calluses, and warts.

Resorcinol works by helping to remove hard, scaly, or roughened skin.

Some of these preparations are available only with your doctor's prescription. Others are available without a prescription; however, your doctor may have special instructions on the proper use of resorcinol for your medical condition.

Resorcinol is available in the following dosage forms:

Topical
- Lotion (U.S.)
- Ointment (U.S. and Canada)

Before Using This Medicine

If you are using this medicine without a prescription, carefully read and follow any precautions on the label. For resorcinol, the following should be considered:

Allergies—Tell your doctor if you have ever had any unusual or allergic reaction to resorcinol. Also tell your health care professional if you are allergic to any other substances, such as preservatives or dyes.

Pregnancy—Resorcinol may be absorbed through the mother's skin. However, topical resorcinol has not been shown to cause birth defects or other problems in humans.

Breast-feeding—This medicine may be absorbed through the mother's skin. However, topical resorcinol has not been reported to cause problems in nursing babies.

Children—Resorcinol may be absorbed through the skin and should not be used on large areas of the bodies of infants and children. In addition, resorcinol should not be used on wounds, since doing so may cause a blood disease called methemoglobinemia.

Older adults—Many medicines have not been studied specifically in older people. Therefore, it may not be known whether they work exactly the same way they do in younger adults. Although there is no specific information comparing use of resorcinol in the elderly with use in other age groups, this medicine is not expected to cause different side effects or problems in older people than it does in younger adults.

Other medicines—Although certain medicines should not be used together at all, in other cases two different medicines may be used together even if an interaction might occur. In these cases, your doctor may want to change the dose, or other precautions may be necessary. Tell your health care professional if you are using any other prescription or nonprescription (over-the-counter [OTC]) medicine.

Proper Use of This Medicine

It is very important that you use this medicine only as directed. Do not use more of it, do not use it more often, and do not use it for a longer time than your doctor ordered. To do so may increase the chance of absorption through the skin and the chance of resorcinol poisoning.

Apply enough resorcinol to cover the affected areas, and rub in gently.

Immediately after using this medicine, wash your hands to remove any medicine that may be on them.

Keep this medicine away from the eyes. If you should accidentally get some in your eyes, flush them thoroughly with water.

Dosing—The dose of resorcinol will be different for different patients. *Follow your doctor's orders or the directions on the label.* The following information includes only the average doses of resorcinol. *If your dose is different, do not change it* unless your doctor tells you to do so.

- For *lotion* dosage form:
  - —For acne, seborrheic dermatitis, eczema, or psoriasis:
    - Adults and children—Use as needed.
- For *ointment* dosage form:
  - —For acne, seborrheic dermatitis, eczema, psoriasis, corns, calluses, or warts:
    - Adults and children—Use and dose must be determined by the doctor.

Missed dose—If you miss a dose of this medicine, apply it as soon as possible. However, if it is almost time for your next dose, skip the missed dose and go back to your regular dosing schedule. Do not double doses.

Storage—To store this medicine:

- Keep out of the reach of children.
- Store away from heat and direct light.
- Keep the medicine from freezing.
- Do not keep outdated medicine or medicine no longer needed. Be sure that any discarded medicine is out of the reach of children.

Precautions While Using This Medicine

When using resorcinol, do not use any of the following preparations on the same affected area as this medicine, unless otherwise directed by your doctor:

Abrasive soaps or cleansers
Alcohol-containing preparations
Any other topical acne preparation or preparation containing a peeling agent (for example, benzoyl peroxide, salicylic acid, sulfur, or tretinoin [vitamin A acid])
Cosmetics or soaps that dry the skin
Medicated cosmetics
Other topical medicine for the skin

To use any of the above preparations on the same affected area as resorcinol may cause severe irritation of the skin.

This medicine may darken light-colored hair.

Side Effects of This Medicine

Along with its needed effects, a medicine may cause some unwanted effects. Although not all of these side effects may occur, if they do occur they may need medical attention.

Check with your doctor as soon as possible if any of the following side effects occur:

Less common or rare

Skin irritation not present before use of this medicine

Symptoms of resorcinol poisoning

Diarrhea, nausea, stomach pain, or vomiting; dizziness; drowsiness; headache (severe or continuing); nervousness or restlessness; slow heartbeat, shortness of breath, or troubled breathing; sweating; unusual tiredness or weakness

Other side effects may occur that usually do not need medical attention. These side effects may go away during treatment as your body adjusts to the medicine. However, check with your doctor if the following side effect continues or is bothersome:

More common

Redness and peeling of skin (may occur after a few days)

Other side effects not listed above may also occur in some patients. If you notice any other effects, check with your doctor.

Revised: 07/26/93

RESORCINOL AND SULFUR Topical

Some commonly used brand names are:

In the U.S.—

Acnomel Acne Cream
Bensulfoid Cream
Clearasil Adult Care Medicated Blemish Cream
Clearasil Adult Care Medicated Blemish Stick
Night Cast Special Formula Mask-lotion
Rezamid Acne Treatment
Sulforcin

In Canada—

Acne-Aid Gel
Acnomel Cake
Acnomel Cream
Acnomel Vanishing Cream
Rezamid Lotion

Description

Resorcinol and sulfur (re-SOR-si-nole and SUL-fur) combination is used to treat acne and similar skin conditions.

This medicine is available without a prescription; however, your doctor may have special instructions on the proper use of this medicine for your medical condition.

Resorcinol and sulfur combination is available in the following dosage forms:

Topical

- Cake (Canada)
- Cream (U.S. and Canada)
- Gel (Canada)

- Lotion (U.S. and Canada)
- Stick (U.S.)

Before Using This Medicine

If you are using this medicine without a prescription, carefully read and follow any precautions on the label. For resorcinol and sulfur combination, the following should be considered:

Allergies—Tell your doctor if you have ever had any unusual or allergic reaction to resorcinol or sulfur. Also tell your health care professional if you are allergic to any other substances, such as preservatives or dyes.

Pregnancy—Resorcinol may be absorbed through the mother's skin. However, topical resorcinol and sulfur combination has not been shown to cause birth defects or other problems in humans.

Breast-feeding—Resorcinol may be absorbed through the mother's skin. However, topical resorcinol and sulfur combination has not been reported to cause problems in nursing babies.

Children—Resorcinol may be absorbed through the skin and should not be used on large areas of the bodies of infants and children. In addition, resorcinol should not be used on wounds, since doing so may cause a blood disease called methemoglobinemia.

Older adults—Many medicines have not been studied specifically in older people. Therefore, it may not be known whether they work exactly the same way they do in younger adults or if they cause different side effects or problems in older people. There is no specific information comparing use of resorcinol and sulfur in the elderly with use in other age groups.

Other medicines—Although certain medicines should not be used together at all, in other cases two different medicines may be used together even if an interaction might occur. In these cases, your doctor may want to change the dose, or other precautions may be necessary. Tell your health care professional if you are using any other prescription or nonprescription (over-the-counter [OTC]) medicine.

Proper Use of This Medicine

Use this medicine only as directed. Do not use more of it and do not use it more often than recommended on the label, unless otherwise directed by your doctor. To do so may increase the chance of absorption through the skin and the chance of resorcinol poisoning.

Before using this medicine, wash the affected areas thoroughly and gently pat dry. Then apply a small amount to the affected areas and spread on gently, but do not rub in.

Immediately after using this medicine, wash your hands to remove any medicine that may be on them.

Keep this medicine away from the eyes. If you should accidentally get some in your eyes, flush them thoroughly with water.

Dosing—The dose of resorcinol and sulfur combination will be different for different patients. *Follow your doctor's orders or the directions on the label.* The following information includes only the average doses of resorcinol and sulfur combination. *If your dose is different, do not change it* unless your doctor tells you to do so.

- For acne and similar skin conditions:
  - —For *cake* dosage form:
    - Adults and children—Use two or three times a day.
  - —For *cream* dosage form:
    - Adults and children—Use one to three times a day.
  - —For *gel and stick* dosage forms:
    - Adults and children—Use as needed.
  - —For *lotion* dosage form:
    - Adults and children—Use two times a day.

Missed dose—If you miss a dose of this medicine, apply it as soon as possible. However, if it is almost time for your next dose, skip the missed dose and go back to your regular dosing schedule. Do not double doses.

Storage—To store this medicine:

- Keep out of the reach of children.
- Store away from heat and direct light.
- Keep the medicine from freezing.
- Do not keep outdated medicine or medicine no longer needed. Be sure that any discarded medicine is out of the reach of children.

Precautions While Using This Medicine

When using resorcinol and sulfur combination, do not use any of the following preparations on the same affected area as this medicine, unless otherwise directed by your doctor:

Abrasive soaps or cleansers
Alcohol-containing preparations
Any other topical acne preparation or preparation containing a peeling agent (for example, benzoyl peroxide, salicylic acid, or tretinoin [vitamin A acid])
Cosmetics or soaps that dry the skin
Medicated cosmetics
Other topical medicine for the skin

To use any of the above preparations on the same affected area as this medicine may cause severe irritation of the skin.

Do not use any topical mercury-containing preparation, such as ammoniated mercury ointment, on the same affected area as this medicine. To do so may cause a foul odor, may be irritating to the skin, and may stain the skin black. If you have any questions about this, check with your health care professional.

This medicine (depending on the product you are using) may darken light-colored hair. If you have any questions about this, check with your health care professional.

Side Effects of This Medicine

Along with its needed effects, a medicine may cause some unwanted effects. Although not all of these side effects may occur, if they do occur they may need medical attention.

Check with your doctor as soon as possible if the following side effect occurs:

Less common or rare

Skin irritation not present before use of this medicine

Symptoms of resorcinol poisoning

Diarrhea, nausea, stomach pain, or vomiting; dizziness; drowsiness; headache (severe or continuing); nervousness or restlessness; slow heartbeat, shortness of breath, or troubled breathing; sweating; unusual tiredness or weakness

Other side effects may occur that usually do not need medical attention. However, check with your health care professional if the following side effects continue or are bothersome:

More common

Redness and peeling of skin (may occur after a few days)

Less common

Unusual dryness of skin

Other side effects not listed above may also occur in some patients. If you notice any other effects, check with your health care professional.

Revised: 07/26/93

RH_O(D) IMMUNE GLOBULIN Systemic

Some commonly used brand names are:

In the U.S.—

Gamulin Rh
HypRho-D Full Dose
HypRho-D Mini-Dose
MICRhoGAM
Mini-Gamulin Rh
RhoGAM

In Canada—

HypRho-D Full Dose
WinRho SD

Other commonly used names are anti-D gammaglobulin; anti-D (Rh_o) immunoglobulin; anti-Rh immunoglobulin; anti-Rh_o(D); D(Rh_o) immune globulin; RhD immune globulin; Rh immune globulin; Rh-IG; and Rh_o(D) immune human globulin.

Description

Rh_o(D) immune globulin is used to prevent your body from interacting with any of your baby's blood that may get into your blood system while you are pregnant or during the delivery of your baby. If your blood type is Rh_o(D) negative and your baby's blood type is Rh_o(D) positive, your body may produce a defense (antibodies) against Rh_o(D) positive blood. These antibodies usually will not cause a problem if this is your first pregnancy, unless you have had a blood transfusion in the past and have already developed these antibodies. However, if you have other Rh_o(D) positive babies in the future, these antibodies may try to destroy the blood of the future babies. If this occurs, it is a very serious condition. Babies born with this condition may need to have their blood replaced.

Rh_o(D) immune globulin may also be used if you have recently received a transfusion that contained Rh_o(D) positive blood and your blood type is Rh_o(D) negative.

Rh_o(D) immune globulin is to be administered only by or under the supervision of your doctor or other health care professional. It is available in the following dosage form:

Parenteral

- Injection (U.S. and Canada)

Before Using This Medicine

In deciding to use a medicine, the risks of using the medicine must be weighed against the good it will do. This is a decision you and your doctor will make. For Rh_o(D) immune globulin, the following should be considered:

Allergies—Tell your doctor if you have ever had any unusual or allergic reaction to Rh_o(D) immune globulin, any other kind of human immune globulin, or to thimerosal. Also tell your health care professional if you are allergic to any other substances, such as foods, preservatives, or dyes.

Pregnancy— Studies on effects in pregnancy have not been done in either humans or animals. However, this medicine has been used in pregnant women and has not been shown to cause birth defects or other problems.

Breast-feeding—Rh_o(D) immune globulin has not been reported to cause problems in nursing babies.

Children—Studies on this medicine have been done only in adult patients and there is no specific information comparing use of Rh_o(D) immune globulin in children with use in other age groups.

Other medical problems—The presence of other medical problems may affect the use of Rh_o(D) immune globulin. Make sure you tell your doctor if you have any other medical problems, especially:

- Immunoglobulin A (IgA) deficiencies—Rh_o(D) immune globulin may cause an allergic reaction to occur

Proper Use of This Medicine

Dosing—The dose of Rh_o(D) immune globulin will be different for different patients. The following information includes only the average dose of Rh_o(D) immune globulin.

- *For injection* dosage form:
  - —To prevent your body from producing antibodies against Rh_o(D) positive blood:
    - Adults and children—One or more injections, depending on how much Rh_o(D) positive blood has gotten into your blood system. The medicine may be used during your pregnancy, within 72 hours after your baby is born, at the end of an incomplete pregnancy (abortion, miscarriage), or after a transfusion. The medicine is usually injected into a muscle, although it may be injected into a vein.

Side Effects of This Medicine

Along with its needed effects, a medicine may cause some unwanted effects. The following side effects may occur and usually do not need medical attention. However, check with your doctor if either of the following side effects continue or are bothersome:

Less common

Fever; soreness at the place of injection

Other side effects not listed above may also occur in some patients. If you notice any other effects, check with your doctor.

Developed: 08/31/94
Interim revision: 06/02/95

RIBAVIRIN Systemic

Some commonly used brand names are:

In the U.S.—
Virazole

In Canada—
Virazole

Other—
Virazid

Another commonly used name is tribavirin.

Description

Ribavirin (rye-ba-VYE-rin) is used to treat severe virus pneumonia in infants and young children. It is given by oral inhalation (breathing in the medicine as a fine mist through the mouth), using a special nebulizer (sprayer) attached to an oxygen hood or tent or face mask.

This medicine may also be used for other virus infections as determined by your doctor. However, it will not work for certain viruses, such as the common cold.

Ribavirin is to be administered only by or under the immediate supervision of your doctor, in the following dosage form:

Inhalation
- For inhalation solution (U.S. and Canada)

Before Receiving This Medicine

In deciding to use a medicine, the risks of taking the medicine must be weighed against the good it will do. This is a decision you and your doctor will make. For ribavirin, the following should be considered:

Allergies—Tell your doctor if you or your child has ever had any unusual or allergic reaction to ribavirin for inhalation. Also tell your health care professional if you or your child is allergic to any other substances, such as foods, preservatives, or dyes.

Pregnancy—Ribavirin for inhalation is not usually prescribed for teenagers or adults. However, women who are pregnant or may become pregnant may be exposed to ribavirin that is given off in the air if they spend time at the patient's bedside while ribavirin is being given. Although studies have not been done in humans, ribavirin has been shown to cause birth defects and other problems in certain animal studies. Be sure you have discussed this with your doctor.

Breast-feeding—Ribavirin for inhalation is not usually prescribed for teenagers or adults. However, ribavirin passes into the breast milk of animals and has been shown to cause problems in nursing animals and their young.

Children—This medicine has been tested in children, and, when used as it should be and in effective doses, has not been shown to cause serious side effects or problems.

Older adults—Ribavirin for inhalation is not usually prescribed for use in elderly patients.

Proper Use of This Medicine

To help clear up your infection completely, *ribavirin must be given for the full time of treatment,* even if you or your child begins to feel better after a few days. Also, this medicine works best when there is a constant amount in the lungs. To help keep the amount constant, ribavirin must be given on a regular or continuous schedule.

Dosing—The dose of ribavirin will be different for different patients. *Follow your doctor's orders or the directions.* The following information includes only the average doses of ribavirin. *If your dose is different, do not change it* unless your doctor tells you to do so.

- For the *inhalation* dosage form:
  —For treatment of respiratory syncytial virus (RSV) infection:
  - Adults and teenagers—Dose has not been determined since this medicine is not usually prescribed for teenagers or adults.
  - Infants and children—Dose must be determined by the doctor.

Side Effects of This Medicine

Along with its needed effects, a medicine may cause some unwanted effects. The following side effects may go away during treatment as your body adjusts to the medicine. However, check with your doctor if any of the following side effects continue or are bothersome:

Rare

Headache; itching, redness, or swelling of eye; skin rash or irritation

Other side effects not listed above may also occur in some patients. If you notice any other effects, check with your doctor.

Additional Information

Once a medicine has been approved for marketing for a certain use, experience may show that it is also useful for other medical problems. Although these uses are not included in product labeling, ribavirin is used in certain patients with the following medical conditions:

- Influenza A and B (given by aerosol inhalation)
- Lassa fever (either given orally or by injection)

For patients taking this medicine by mouth or injection for *Lassa fever*:

- *Check with your doctor immediately* if any of the following side effects occur:
  More common
  Unusual tiredness and weakness
- Other side effects may occur that usually do not need medical attention. The following side effects may go away during treatment as your body adjusts to the medicine. However, check with your doctor if any of the following side effects continue or are bothersome:
  Less common
  Headache; loss of appetite; nausea; trouble in sleeping; unusual tiredness or weakness

Other than the above information, there is no additional information relating to proper use, precautions, or side effects for these uses.

Revised: 02/23/93
Interim revision: 06/08/94

RIBOFLAVIN (Vitamin B_2) Systemic

Generic name product is available in the U.S. and Canada.

Description

Vitamins (VYE-ta-mins) are compounds that you *must* have for growth and health. They are needed in small amounts only and are usually available in the foods that you eat. Riboflavin (RYE-boe-flay-vin) (vitamin B_2) is needed to help break down carbohydrates, proteins, and fats. It also makes it possible for oxygen to be used by your body.

Lack of riboflavin may lead to itching and burning eyes, sensitivity of eyes to light, sore tongue, itching and peeling skin on the nose and scrotum, and sores in the mouth. Your doctor may treat this condition by prescribing riboflavin for you.

Some conditions may increase your need for riboflavin. These include:

- Alcoholism
- Burns
- Cancer
- Diarrhea (continuing)
- Fever (continuing)
- Illness (continuing)
- Infection
- Intestinal diseases
- Liver disease
- Overactive thyroid
- Serious injury
- Stress (continuing)
- Surgical removal of stomach

In addition, riboflavin may be given to infants with high blood levels of bilirubin (hyperbilirubinemia).

Increased need for riboflavin should be determined by your health care professional.

Claims that riboflavin is effective for treatment of acne, some kinds of anemia (weak blood), migraine headaches, and muscle cramps have not been proven.

Oral forms of riboflavin are available without a prescription. If you take more than you need, it will simply be lost from your body.

Riboflavin is available in the following dosage form:

Oral
- Tablets (U.S. and Canada)

Importance of Diet

For good health, it is important that you eat a balanced and varied diet. Follow carefully any diet program your health care professional may recommend. For your specific dietary vitamin and/or mineral needs, ask your health care professional for a list of appropriate foods. If you think that you are not getting enough vitamins and/or minerals in your diet, you may choose to take a dietary supplement.

Riboflavin is found in various foods, including milk and dairy products, fish, meats, green leafy vegetables, and whole grain and enriched cereals and bread. It is best to eat fresh fruits and vegetables whenever possible since they contain the most vitamins. Food processing may destroy some of the vitamins, although little riboflavin is lost from foods during ordinary cooking.

Vitamins alone will not take the place of a good diet and will not provide energy. Your body also needs other substances found in food such as protein, minerals, carbohydrates, and fat. Vitamins themselves often cannot work without the presence of other foods.

The daily amount of riboflavin needed is defined in several different ways.

For U.S.—
- Recommended Dietary Allowances (RDAs) are the amount of vitamins and minerals needed to provide for adequate nutrition in most healthy persons. RDAs for a given nutrient may vary depending on a person's age, sex, and physical condition (e.g., pregnancy).
- Daily Values (DVs) are used on food and dietary supplement labels to indicate the percent of the recommended daily amount of each nutrient that a serving provides. DV replaces the previous designation of

United States Recommended Daily Allowances (USRDAs).

For Canada—

- Recommended Nutrient Intakes (RNIs) are used to determine the amounts of vitamins, minerals, and protein needed to provide adequate nutrition and lessen the risk of chronic disease.

Normal daily recommended intakes for riboflavin are generally defined as follows:

Persons	U.S. (mg)	Canada (mg)
Infants and children		
Birth to 3 years of age	0.4–0.8	0.3–0.7
4 to 6 years of age	1.1	0.9
7 to 10 years of age	1.2	1–1.3
Adolescent and adult males	1.4–1.8	1–1.6
Adolescent and adult females	1.2–1.3	1–1.1
Pregnant females	1.6	1.1–1.4
Breast-feeding females	1.7–1.8	1.4–1.5

Before Using This Dietary Supplement

If you are taking this dietary supplement without a prescription, carefully read and follow any precautions on the label. For riboflavin, the following should be considered:

Allergies—Tell your health care professional if you are allergic to any substances, such as foods, preservatives, or dyes.

Pregnancy—It is especially important that you are receiving enough vitamins when you become pregnant and that you continue to receive the right amounts of vitamins throughout your pregnancy. The healthy growth and development of the fetus depend on a steady supply of nutrients from the mother. However, taking large amounts of a dietary supplement in pregnancy may be harmful to the mother and/or fetus and should be avoided.

Breast-feeding—It is especially important that you receive the right amounts of vitamins so that your baby will also get the vitamins needed to grow properly. However, taking large amounts of a dietary supplement while breast-feeding may be harmful to the mother and/or baby and should be avoided.

Children—Problems in children have not been reported with intake of normal daily recommended amounts.

Older adults—Problems in older adults have not been reported with intake of normal daily recommended amounts.

Other medicines or dietary supplements—Although certain medicines or dietary supplements should not be used together at all, in other cases two different medicines or dietary supplements may be used together even if an interaction might occur. In these cases, your health care professional may want to change the dose, or other precautions may be necessary. Tell your health care professional if you are taking any other dietary supplements or prescription or nonprescription (over-the-counter [OTC]) medicine.

Proper Use of This Dietary Supplement

Dosing—The amount of riboflavin needed to meet normal daily recommended intakes will be different for different patients. The following information includes only the average amounts of riboflavin.

- For *oral* dosage form (tablets):
  - —To prevent deficiency, the amount taken by mouth is based on normal daily recommended intakes:

    For the U.S.

    - Adults and teenage males—1.4 to 1.8 milligrams (mg) per day.
    - Adults and teenage females—1.2 to 1.3 mg per day.
    - Pregnant females—1.6 mg per day.
    - Breast-feeding females—1.7 to 1.8 mg per day.
    - Children 7 to 10 years of age—1.2 mg per day.
    - Children 4 to 6 years of age—1.1 mg per day.
    - Children birth to 3 years of age—0.4 to 0.8 mg per day.

    For Canada

    - Adults and teenage males—1 to 1.6 mg per day.
    - Adults and teenage females—1 to 1.1 mg per day.
    - Pregnant females—1.1 to 1.4 mg per day.
    - Breast-feeding females—1.4 to 1.5 mg per day.
    - Children 7 to 10 years of age—1 to 1.3 mg per day.
    - Children 4 to 6 years of age—0.9 mg per day.
    - Children birth to 3 years of age—0.3 to 0.7 mg per day.
  - —To treat deficiency:
    - Adults and teenagers—Treatment dose is determined by prescriber for each individual based on the severity of deficiency.

Missed dose—If you miss taking a vitamin for 1 or more days there is no cause for concern, since it takes some time for your body to become seriously low in vitamins. However, if your health care professional has recommended that you take this vitamin, try to remember to take it as directed every day.

Storage—To store this dietary supplement:

- Keep out of the reach of children.
- Store away from heat and direct light.
- Do not store in the bathroom, near the kitchen sink, or in other damp places. Heat or moisture may cause the dietary supplement to break down.
- Do not keep outdated dietary supplements or those no longer needed. Be sure that any discarded dietary supplement is out of the reach of children.

Side Effects of This Dietary Supplement

Along with its needed effects, a dietary supplement may cause some unwanted effects. Riboflavin may cause urine to have a more yellow color than normal, especially if large doses are taken. This is to be expected and is no cause for alarm. Usually, however, riboflavin does not cause any side effects. Check with your health care professional if you notice any other unusual effects while you are using it.

Revised: 08/22/92
Interim revision: 07/29/94; 05/01/95

RIFABUTIN Systemic

A commonly used brand name in the U.S. and Canada is Mycobutin.

Description

Rifabutin (rif-a-BUE-tin) is used to help prevent *Mycobacterium avium* complex (MAC) disease from causing disease throughout the body in patients with advanced human immunodeficiency virus (HIV) infection. MAC is an infection caused by two similar bacteria, *Mycobacterium avium* and *Mycobacterium intracellulare*. *Mycobacterium avium* is more common in patients with HIV infection. MAC may also occur in other patients whose immune system is not working properly. Symptoms of MAC in people with acquired immunodeficiency syndrome (AIDS) include fever, night sweats, chills, weight loss, and weakness. Rifabutin will not work for colds, flu, or most other infections.

Rifabutin is available only with your doctor's prescription, in the following dosage form:

Oral
- Capsules (U.S. and Canada)

Before Using This Medicine

In deciding to use a medicine, the risks of taking the medicine must be weighed against the good it will do. This is a decision you and your doctor will make. For rifabutin, the following should be considered:

Allergies—Tell your doctor if you have ever had any unusual or allergic reaction to rifabutin or rifampin. Also tell your health care professional if you are allergic to any other substances, such as foods, preservatives, or dyes.

Pregnancy—Rifabutin has not been studied in pregnant women. However, studies in animals have shown that rifabutin causes birth defects. Before you take this medicine, make sure your doctor knows if you are pregnant or if you may become pregnant.

Breast-feeding—It is not known whether rifabutin passes into the breast milk. However, if your baby does not have the AIDS virus, there is a chance that you could pass the virus to your baby by breast-feeding. Talk to your doctor first if you are thinking about breast-feeding your baby.

Children—Studies on this medicine have only been done in adult patients, and there is no specific information comparing use of rifabutin in children with use in other age groups. However, studies are being done to determine the best dose for children.

Older adults—Many medicines have not been studied specifically in older people. Therefore, it may not be known whether they work exactly the same way they do in younger adults. Although there is no specific information comparing use of rifabutin in the elderly with use in other age groups, this medicine is not expected to cause different side effects or problems in older people than it does in younger adults.

Other medicines—Although certain medicines should not be used together at all, in other cases two different medicines may be used together even if an interaction might occur. In these cases, your doctor may want to change the dose, or other precautions may be necessary. When you are taking rifabutin, it is especially important that your health care professional know if you are taking any of the following:

- Zidovudine (e.g., AZT, Retrovir)—Use of rifabutin with zidovudine may lower the amount of zidovudine in the blood

Other medical problems—The presence of other medical problems may affect the use of rifabutin. Make sure you tell your doctor if you have any other medical problems, especially:

- Active tuberculosis—Patients with active tuberculosis (TB) who need to take rifabutin *must* also take other medicines to cure their TB. Rifabutin used alone may cause TB germs to develop a resistance to other medicines. This may make future treatment of TB very difficult

Proper Use of This Medicine

Rifabutin may be taken on an empty stomach (either 1 hour before or 2 hours after a meal). However, if this medicine upsets your stomach, you may want to take it with food.

For *patients unable to swallow capsules:*
- The contents of the capsules may be mixed with applesauce. Be sure to take all the food to get the full dose of medicine.

To help prevent MAC disease, *it is very important that you keep taking this medicine for the full time of treatment*. You may have to take it every day for many months. *It is important that you do not miss any doses.*

Dosing—The dose of rifabutin may be different for different patients. *Follow your doctor's orders or the directions on the label.* The following information includes only the average doses of rifabutin. *If your dose is different, do not change it* unless your doctor tells you to do so.

• For *oral* dosage forms (capsules):
—For the prevention of *Mycobacterium avium* complex (MAC):
  • Adults and teenagers—300 milligrams (mg) once a day, or 150 mg two times a day.
  • Children—Use and dose must be determined by your doctor.

Missed dose—If you miss a dose of this medicine, take it as soon as possible. However, if it is almost time for your next dose, skip the missed dose and go back to your regular dosing schedule. Do not double doses. *If this medicine is taken on an irregular schedule, side effects may occur more often and may be more serious than usual.* If you have any questions about this, check with your health care professional.

Storage—To store this medicine:
- Keep out of the reach of children.
- Store away from heat and direct light.
- Do not store in the bathroom, near the kitchen sink, or in other damp places. Heat or moisture may cause the medicine to break down.
- Do not keep outdated medicine or medicine no longer needed. Be sure that any discarded medicine is out of the reach of children.

Precautions While Using This Medicine

It is very important that your doctor check your progress at regular visits.

Rifabutin will cause your urine, stool, saliva, skin, sputum, sweat, and tears to turn reddish orange to reddish brown. This is to be expected while you are taking this medicine. This effect may cause soft contact lenses to become permanently discolored. Standard cleaning solutions may not take out all the discoloration. Therefore, *it is best not to wear soft contact lenses while taking this medicine.* Hard contact lenses are not discolored by rifabutin. If you have any questions about this, check with your doctor.

Side Effects of This Medicine

Along with its needed effects, a medicine may cause some unwanted effects. Although not all of these side effects may occur, if they do occur they may need medical attention.

Check with your doctor immediately if any of the following side effects occur:

More common
Skin rash

Rare
Change in taste; eye pain; fever and sore throat; joint pain; loss of vision; muscle pain; yellow skin

Other side effects may occur that usually do not need medical attention. These side effects may go away during treatment as your body adjusts to the medicine. However, check with your doctor if any of the following side effects continue or are bothersome:

More common
Nausea; vomiting

This medicine commonly causes reddish orange to reddish brown discoloration of urine, stools, saliva, skin, sputum, sweat, and tears. This side effect does not usually need medical attention. However, tears that have been discolored by this medicine may also discolor soft contact lenses (see *Precautions While Using This Medicine*).

Other side effects not listed above may also occur in some patients. If you notice any other effects, check with your doctor.

Revised: 06/22/94

RIFAMPIN Systemic

Some commonly used brand names are:

In the U.S.—
Rifadin
Rifadin IV
Rimactane

In Canada—
Rifadin
Rimactane
Rofact

Another commonly used name is rifampicin.

Description

Rifampin (rif-AM-pin) is used to treat certain bacterial infections.

Rifampin is used with other medicines to treat tuberculosis (TB). Rifampin is also taken by itself by patients who may carry meningitis bacteria in their nose and throat (without feeling sick) and may spread these bacteria to others. This medicine may also be used for other problems as determined by your doctor. However, rifampin will not work for colds, flu, or other virus infections.

To help clear up your tuberculosis (TB) completely, you must keep taking this medicine for the full time of treatment, even if you begin to feel better. This is very important. It is also important that you do not miss any doses.

Rifampin is available only with your doctor's prescription, in the following dosage forms:

Oral
• Capsules (U.S. and Canada)

Parenteral
• Injection (U.S.)

Before Using This Medicine

In deciding to use a medicine, the risks of taking the medicine must be weighed against the good it will do. This is a decision you and your doctor will make. For rifampin, the following should be considered:

Allergies—Tell your doctor if you have ever had any unusual or allergic reaction to rifampin. Also tell your health

care professional if you are allergic to any other substances, such as foods, preservatives, or dyes.

Pregnancy—Pregnant women with tuberculosis (TB) should be treated with TB medicines, including rifampin. Rifampin can rarely cause bleeding in newborn babies and mothers when it was taken during the last weeks of pregnancy. Studies in rats and mice have shown that rifampin given in high doses causes birth defects, usually backbone problems (spina bifida) and cleft palate.

Breast-feeding—Rifampin passes into the breast milk. However, rifampin has not been reported to cause problems in nursing babies.

Children—This medicine has been tested in children and, in effective doses, has not been shown to cause different side effects or problems in children than it does in adults.

Older adults—Many medicines have not been studied specifically in older people. Therefore, it may not be known whether they work exactly the same way they do in younger adults. Although there is no specific information comparing use of rifampin in the elderly with use in other age groups, this medicine is not expected to cause different side effects or problems in older people than it does in younger adults.

Other medicines—Although certain medicines should not be used together at all, in other cases two different medicines may be used together even if an interaction might occur. In these cases, your doctor may want to change the dose, or other precautions may be necessary. When you are taking rifampin, it is especially important that your health care professional know if you are taking any of the following:

- Acetaminophen (e.g., Tylenol) (with long-term, high-dose use) or
- Amiodarone (e.g., Cordarone) or
- Anabolic steroids (nandrolone [e.g., Anabolin], oxandrolone [e.g., Anavar], oxymetholone [e.g., Anadrol], stanozolol [e.g., Winstrol]) or
- Androgens (male hormones) or
- Antithyroid agents (medicine for overactive thyroid) or
- Carbamazepine (e.g., Tegretol) or
- Carmustine (e.g., BiCNU) or
- Chloroquine (e.g., Aralen) or
- Dantrolene (e.g., Dantrium) or
- Daunorubicin (e.g., Cerubidine) or
- Disulfiram (e.g., Antabuse) or
- Divalproex (e.g., Depakote) or
- Etretinate (e.g., Tegison) or
- Gold salts (medicine for arthritis) or
- Hydroxychloroquine (e.g., Plaquenil) or
- Isoniazid (e.g., INH, Nydrazid) or
- Mercaptopurine (e.g., Purinethol) or
- Methotrexate (e.g., Mexate) or
- Methyldopa (e.g., Aldomet) or
- Naltrexone (e.g., Trexan) (with long-term, high-dose use) or
- Phenothiazines (acetophenazine [e.g., Tindal], chlorpromazine [e.g., Thorazine], fluphenazine [e.g., Prolixin], mesoridazine [e.g., Serentil], perphenazine [e.g., Trilafon], prochlorperazine [e.g., Compazine], promazine [e.g., Sparine], promethazine [e.g., Phenergan], thioridazine [e.g., Mellaril], trifluoperazine [e.g., Stelazine], triflupromazine [e.g., Vesprin], trimeprazine [e.g., Temaril]) or
- Plicamycin (e.g., Mithracin) or
- Valproic acid (e.g., Depakene)—These medicines may increase the chance of liver damage if taken with rifampin
- Anticoagulants (blood thinners) or
- Aminophylline (e.g., Somophyllin) or
- Antidiabetics, oral (diabetes medicine you take by mouth), or
- Chloramphenicol or
- Corticosteroids (cortisone-like medicine) or
- Digitalis glycosides (heart medicine) or
- Disopyramide (e.g., Norpace) or
- Fluconazole (e.g., Diflucan) or
- Human immunodeficiency virus (HIV) protease inhibitors (medicines for the treatment of HIV infection) or
- Itraconazole (e.g., Sporanox) or
- Ketoconazole (e.g., Nizoral) or
- Methadone (e.g., Dolophine) or
- Mexiletine (e.g., Mexitil) or
- Oxtriphylline (e.g., Choledyl) or
- Quinidine (e.g., Quinidex) or
- Theophylline (e.g., Theo-dur, Somophyllin-T) or
- Tocainide (e.g., Tonocard) or
- Verapamil (e.g., Calan)—Rifampin may decrease the effects of these medicines
- Estramustine (e.g., EMCYT) or
- Estrogens (female hormones) or
- Oral contraceptives (birth control pills) containing estrogen or
- Phenytoin (e.g., Dilantin)—Rifampin may decrease the effects of these medicines. If you are taking oral contraceptives, this may increase the chance of pregnancy. These medicines may also increase the chance of liver damage if taken with rifampin

Other medical problems—The presence of other medical problems may affect the use of rifampin. Make sure you tell your doctor if you have any other medical problems, especially:

- Alcohol abuse (or history of) or
- Liver disease—There may be an increased chance of side effects affecting the liver in patients with a history of alcohol abuse or liver disease

Proper Use of This Medicine

Rifampin is best taken with a full glass (8 ounces) of water on an empty stomach (either 1 hour before or 2 hours after a meal). However, if this medicine upsets your stomach, your doctor may want you to take it with food.

For *patients unable to swallow capsules:*

- Contents of the capsules may be mixed with applesauce or jelly. Be sure to take all the food to get the full dose of medicine.
- Your pharmacist can prepare an oral liquid form of this medicine if needed. The liquid form may be kept at room temperature or in the refrigerator. Follow the directions on the label. Shake the bottle well before using. Do not use after the expiration date on the label. The medicine may not work properly after that date. In addition, use a specially marked measuring spoon or other device to measure each dose accurately. The average household teaspoon may not hold the right amount of liquid.

To help clear up your tuberculosis (TB) completely, it is very important that you keep taking this medicine for the full time of treatment, even if you begin to feel better after a few weeks. You may have to take it every day for as long as 1 to 2 years or more. *It is important that you do not miss any doses.*

Dosing—The dose of rifampin will be different for different patients. *Follow your doctor's orders or the directions on the label.* The following information includes only the average doses of rifampin. *If your dose is different, do not change it* unless your doctor tells you to do so.

The number of capsules that you take depends on the strength of the medicine. Also, *the number of doses you take each day, the time allowed between doses, and the length of time you take the medicine depend on the medical problem for which you are taking rifampin.*

- For *oral* dosage form (capsules) and *injection* dosage form:
  - —For the treatment of tuberculosis (TB):
    - Adults and older children—600 milligrams (mg) once a day. Your doctor may instruct you to take 600 mg two times a week or three times a week. Rifampin must be taken with other medicines to treat tuberculosis.
    - Infants and children—Dose is based on body weight and will be determined by your doctor. Rifampin is usually taken once a day. Your doctor may instruct you to take rifampin two times a week or three times a week. Rifampin must be taken with other medicines to treat tuberculosis.
  - —For the treatment of patients in contact with the meningitis bacteria:
    - Adults and older children—600 mg two times a day for two days.
    - Infants and children—Dose is based on body weight and will be determined by your doctor. The medicine is taken twice a day for two days.

Missed dose—If you do miss a dose of this medicine, take it as soon as possible. However, if it is almost time for your next dose, skip the missed dose and go back to your regular dosing schedule. Do not double doses. *If this medicine is taken on an irregular schedule, side effects may occur more often and may be more serious than usual.* If you have any questions about this, check with your health care professional.

Storage—To store the capsule form of this medicine:
- Keep out of the reach of children.
- Store away from heat and direct light.
- Do not store in the bathroom, near the kitchen sink, or in other damp places. Heat or moisture may cause the medicine to break down.
- Do not keep outdated medicine or medicine no longer needed. Be sure that any discarded medicine is out of the reach of children.

Precautions While Using This Medicine

It is very important that your doctor check your progress at regular visits.

If your symptoms do not improve within 2 to 3 weeks, or if they become worse, check with your doctor.

Oral contraceptives (birth control pills) containing estrogen may not work properly if you take them while you are taking rifampin. Unplanned pregnancies may occur. You should use a different means of birth control while you are taking rifampin. If you have any questions about this, check with your health care professional.

Liver problems may be more likely to occur if you drink alcoholic beverages regularly while you are taking this medicine. Also, the regular use of alcohol may keep this medicine from working properly. Therefore, *you should not drink alcoholic beverages while you are taking this medicine.*

If this medicine causes you to feel very tired or very weak or causes a loss of appetite, nausea, or vomiting, stop taking it and check with your doctor immediately. These may be early warning signs of more serious problems that could develop later.

Rifampin will cause the urine, stool, saliva, sputum, sweat, and tears to turn reddish orange to reddish brown. This is to be expected while you are taking this medicine. This effect may cause soft contact lenses to become permanently discolored. Standard cleaning solutions may not take out all the discoloration. Therefore, *it is best not to wear soft contact lenses while taking this medicine.* Hard contact lenses are not discolored by rifampin. If you have any questions about this, check with your doctor.

Rifampin can lower the number of white blood cells in your blood temporarily, increasing the chance of getting an infection. It can also lower the number of platelets, which are necessary for proper blood clotting. These problems may result in a greater chance of getting certain infections, slow healing, and bleeding of the gums. Be careful when using a regular toothbrush, dental floss, or a toothpick. Dental work should be delayed until your blood counts have returned to normal. Check with your medical doctor or dentist if you have any questions about proper oral hygiene (mouth care) during treatment.

Before you have any medical tests, tell the doctor in charge that you are taking this medicine. The results of some tests may be affected by this medicine.

Side Effects of This Medicine

Along with its needed effects, a medicine may cause some unwanted effects. Although not all of these side effects may occur, if they do occur they may need medical attention.

Check with your doctor immediately if any of the following side effects occur:

Less common

Chills; difficult breathing; dizziness; fever; headache; itching; muscle and bone pain; shivering; skin rash and redness

Rare

Bloody or cloudy urine; greatly decreased frequency of urination or amount of urine; loss of appetite; nausea or vomiting; sore throat; unusual bleeding or bruising; unusual tiredness or weakness; yellow eyes or skin

Signs and symptoms of overdose
Itching over the whole body; mental changes; reddish orange color of skin, mouth, and eyeballs; swelling around the eyes or the whole face

Other side effects may occur that usually do not need medical attention. These side effects may go away during treatment as your body adjusts to the medicine. However, check with your doctor if any of the following side effects continue or are bothersome:

More common
Diarrhea; stomach cramps

Less common
Sore mouth or tongue

This medicine commonly causes reddish-orange to reddish-brown discoloration of urine, stool, saliva, sputum, sweat, and tears. This side effect does not usually need medical attention.

Other side effects not listed above may also occur in some patients. If you notice any other effects, check with your doctor.

Additional Information

Once a medicine has been approved for marketing for a certain use, experience may show that it is also useful for other medical problems. Although these uses are not included in product labeling, rifampin is used in certain patients with the following medical conditions:

- Atypical mycobacterial infections, such as *Mycobacterium avium* complex (MAC)
- Leprosy (Hansen's disease)
- Prevention of *Haemophilus influenzae* infection
- Treatment of serious staphylococcal infections

Other than the above information, there is no additional information relating to proper use, precautions, or side effects for these uses.

Revised: 08/15/97

RIFAMPIN AND ISONIAZID Systemic†

A commonly used brand name in the U.S. is Rifamate.

Another commonly used name is rifampicin and isoniazid.

†Not commercially available in Canada.

Description

Rifampin and isoniazid (rif-AM-pin and eye-soe-NYE-a-zid) is a combination antibiotic and anti-infective medicine. This combination medication is used to treat tuberculosis (TB). It may be taken alone or with one or more other medicines for TB.

To help clear up your tuberculosis (TB) infection completely, you must keep taking this medicine for the full time of treatment, even if you begin to feel better. This is very important. It is also important that you do not miss any doses.

Rifampin and isoniazid combination is available only with your doctor's prescription, in the following dosage form:

Oral
- Capsules (U.S.)

Before Using This Medicine

In deciding to use a medicine, the risks of taking the medicine must be weighed against the good it will do. This is a decision you and your doctor will make. For rifampin and isoniazid combination, the following should be considered:

Allergies—Tell your doctor if you have ever had any unusual or allergic reaction to ethionamide (e.g., Trecator-SC), pyrazinamide, niacin (e.g., Nicobid, nicotinic acid), rifampin (e.g., Rifadin), rifabutin (e.g., Mycobutin), or isoniazid (e.g., INH, Nydrazid). Also tell your health care professional if you are allergic to any other substances, such as foods, preservatives, or dyes.

Pregnancy—Pregnant women with tuberculosis (TB) should be treated with TB medicines, including isoniazid and rifampin. Rifampin and isoniazid combination has not been shown to cause birth defects or other problems in humans. However, rifampin rarely caused bleeding in newborn babies and mothers when it was taken during the last weeks of pregnancy. Also, studies in rats and mice have shown that rifampin given in high doses causes birth defects, usually backbone problems (spina bifida) and cleft palate.

Breast-feeding—Rifampin and isoniazid both pass into the breast milk. However, rifampin and isoniazid have not been reported to cause problems in nursing babies.

Children—Rifampin and isoniazid combination is not recommended for use in children.

Older adults—Liver problems are more likely to occur in patients over 50 years of age who are taking isoniazid-containing medicines.

Other medicines—Although certain medicines should not be used together at all, in other cases two different medicines may be used together even if an interaction might occur. In these cases, your doctor may want to change the dose, or other precautions may be necessary. When you are taking rifampin and isoniazid combination, it is especially important that your health care professional knows if you are taking any of the following:

- Acetaminophen (e.g., Tylenol) (with long-term, high-dose use) or
- Alfentanil (e.g., Alfenta) or
- Amiodarone (e.g., Cordarone) or
- Anabolic steroids (nandrolone [e.g., Anabolin], oxandrolone [e.g., Anavar], oxymetholone [e.g., Anadrol], stanozolol [e.g., Winstrol]) or
- Androgens (male hormones) or
- Antithyroid agents (medicine for overactive thyroid) or

- Carbamazepine (e.g., Tegretol) or
- Carmustine (e.g., BiCNU) or
- Chloroquine (e.g., Aralen) or
- Dantrolene (e.g., Dantrium) or
- Daunorubicin (e.g., Cerubidine) or
- Disulfiram (e.g., Antabuse) or
- Divalproex (e.g., Depakote) or
- Etretinate (e.g., Tegison) or
- Gold salts (medicine for arthritis) or
- Hydroxychloroquine (e.g., Plaquenil) or
- Mercaptopurine (e.g., Purinethol) or
- Methyldopa (e.g., Aldomet) or
- Naltrexone (e.g., Trexan) (with long-term, high-dose use) or
- Phenothiazines (acetophenazine [e.g., Tindal], chlorpromazine [e.g., Thorazine], fluphenazine [e.g., Prolixin], mesoridazine [e.g., Serentil], perphenazine [e.g., Trilafon], prochlorperazine [e.g., Compazine], promazine [e.g., Sparine], promethazine [e.g., Phenergan], thioridazine [e.g., Mellaril], trifluoperazine [e.g., Stelazine], triflupromazine [e.g., Vesprin], trimeprazine [e.g., Temaril]) or
- Plicamycin (e.g., Mithracin) or
- Valproic acid (e.g., Depakene)—These medicines may increase the chance of liver damage if taken with rifampin and isoniazid combination

- Aminophylline (e.g., Somophyllin) or
- Anticoagulants (blood thinners) or
- Antidiabetics, oral (diabetes medicine you take by mouth) or
- Chloramphenicol or
- Corticosteroids (cortisone-like medicine) or
- Digitalis glycosides (heart medicine) or
- Disopyramide (e.g., Norpace) or
- Estramustine (e.g., EMCYT) or
- Fluconazole (e.g., Diflucan) or
- Human immunodeficiency virus (HIV) protease inhibitors (medicines for the treatment of HIV infection) or
- Itraconazole (e.g., Sporanox) or
- Ketoconazole (e.g., Nizoral) or
- Methadone (e.g., Dolophine) or
- Methotrexate (e.g., Mexate) or
- Mexiletine (e.g., Mexitil) or
- Oxtriphylline (e.g., Choledyl) or
- Quinidine (e.g., Quinidex) or
- Theophylline (e.g., Theo-dur, Somophyllin-T) or
- Tocainide (e.g., Tonocard) or
- Verapamil (e.g., Calan)—Rifampin and isoniazid combination may decrease the effects of these medicines
- Disulfiram (e.g., Antabuse)—This medicine may increase the chance of liver damage and side effects, such as dizziness, lack of coordination, irritability, and inability to sleep
- Estrogens (female hormones) or
- Oral contraceptives (birth control pills) containing estrogen or
- Phenytoin (e.g., Dilantin)—Rifampin and isoniazid combination may decrease the effects of these medicines. If you are taking oral contraceptives, this may increase the chance of pregnancy. These medicines may also increase the chance of liver damage if taken with rifampin and isoniazid combination

Other medical problems—The presence of other medical problems may affect the use of rifampin and isoniazid combination. Make sure you tell your doctor if you have any other medical problems, especially:

- Alcohol abuse (or history of) or
- Liver disease—There may be an increased chance of getting hepatitis if you take this medicine and drink alcohol daily
- Convulsive disorders such as seizures or epilepsy—Rifampin and isoniazid combination may increase the frequency of seizures (convulsions) in some patients
- Kidney disease (severe)—There may be an increased chance of side effects in patients with severe kidney disease

Proper Use of This Medicine

If this medicine upsets your stomach, take it with food. Antacids may also help. However, do not take aluminum-containing antacids within 1 hour of the time you take rifampin and isoniazid combination. They may keep this medicine from working properly.

To help clear up your tuberculosis (TB) completely, it is very important that you keep taking this medicine for the full time of treatment, even if you begin to feel better after a few weeks. You may have to take it every day for as long as 1 to 2 years or more. *It is important that you do not miss any doses.*

Your doctor may also want you to take pyridoxine (e.g., Hexa-Betalin, vitamin B_6) every day to help prevent or lessen some of the side effects of isoniazid. If it is needed, *it is very important to take pyridoxine every day along with this medicine. Do not miss any doses.*

Dosing—The dose of rifampin and isoniazid combination will be different for different patients. *Follow your doctor's orders or the directions on the label.* The following information includes only the average doses of rifampin and isoniazid combination. *If your dose is different, do not change it* unless your doctor tells you to do so.

- For the *oral* dosage form (capsules):
  - —For the treatment of tuberculosis:
    - Adults and older children—600 milligrams (mg) of rifampin and 300 mg of isoniazid once a day.
    - Children—This combination medicine is not recommended for use in children.

Missed dose—If you do miss a dose of this medicine, take it as soon as possible. However, if it is almost time for your next dose, skip the missed dose and go back to your regular dosing schedule. Do not double doses. *If rifampin and isoniazid combination is taken on an irregular schedule, side effects may occur more often and may be more serious than usual.* If you have any questions about this, check with your health care professional.

Storage—To store this medicine:

- Keep out of the reach of children.
- Store away from heat and direct light.
- Do not store in the bathroom, near the kitchen sink, or in other damp places. Heat or moisture may cause the medicine to break down.

- Do not keep outdated medicine or medicine no longer needed. Be sure that any discarded medicine is out of the reach of children.

Precautions While Using This Medicine

It is very important that your doctor check your progress at regular visits. In addition, you should check with your doctor immediately if blurred vision or loss of vision, with or without eye pain, occurs during treatment. He or she may want you to have your eyes checked by an ophthalmologist (eye doctor).

If your symptoms do not improve within 2 to 3 weeks, or if they become worse, check with your doctor.

Oral contraceptives (birth control pills) containing estrogen may not work properly if you take them while you are taking rifampin and isoniazid combination. Unplanned pregnancies may occur. You should use a different means of birth control while you are taking this medicine. If you have any questions about this, check with your health care professional.

Liver problems may be more likely to occur if you drink alcoholic beverages regularly while you are taking this medicine. Also, the regular use of alcohol may keep this medicine from working properly. Therefore, *you should strictly limit the amount of alcoholic beverages you drink while you are taking this medicine.*

Certain foods such as cheese (Swiss or Cheshire) or fish (tuna, skipjack, or Sardinella) may rarely cause reactions in some patients taking isoniazid-containing medicines. Check with your doctor if redness or itching of the skin, hot feeling, fast or pounding heartbeat, sweating, chills or clammy feeling, headache, or lightheadedness occurs after eating these foods while you are taking this medicine.

This medicine will cause the urine, stool, saliva, sputum, sweat, and tears to turn reddish-orange to reddish-brown. This is to be expected while you are taking this medicine. This effect may cause soft contact lenses to become permanently discolored. Standard cleaning solutions may not take out all the discoloration. Therefore, *it is best not to wear soft contact lenses while taking this medicine.* This condition will return to normal once you stop taking this medicine. Hard contact lenses are not discolored by this medicine. If you have any questions about this, check with your doctor.

If this medicine causes you to feel very tired or very weak; or causes clumsiness; unsteadiness; a loss of appetite; nausea; numbness, tingling, burning, or pain in the hands and feet; or vomiting, stop taking it and check with your doctor immediately. These may be early warning symptoms of more serious liver or nerve problems that could develop later.

Rifampin and isoniazid combination may cause blood problems. These problems may result in a greater chance of certain infections, slow healing, and bleeding of the gums. Therefore, you should be careful when using regular toothbrushes, dental floss, and toothpicks. Dental work should be delayed until your blood counts have returned to normal. Check with your medical doctor or dentist if you have any questions about proper oral hygiene (mouth care) during treatment.

Side Effects of This Medicine

Along with its needed effects, a medicine may cause some unwanted effects. Although not all of these side effects may occur, if they do occur they may need medical attention.

Check with your doctor immediately if any of the following side effects occur:

More common

Clumsiness or unsteadiness; dark urine; loss of appetite; nausea and vomiting; numbness, tingling, burning, or pain in hands and feet; unusual tiredness or weakness; yellow eyes or skin

Less common

Chills; difficult breathing; dizziness; fever; headache; itching; muscle and bone pain; shivering; skin rash and redness

Rare

Bloody or cloudy urine; blurred vision or loss of vision, with or without eye pain; convulsions (seizures); depression; greatly decreased frequency of urination or amount of urine; mood or mental changes; sore throat; unusual bleeding or bruising

Other side effects may occur that usually do not need medical attention. These side effects may go away during treatment as your body adjusts to the medicine. However, check with your doctor if any of the following side effects continue or are bothersome:

More common

Diarrhea; stomach pain or upset

Less common

Sore mouth or tongue

This medicine commonly causes reddish orange to reddish brown discoloration of urine, stool, saliva, sputum, sweat, and tears. This side effect does not usually require medical attention.

Dark urine and yellowing of the eyes or skin (signs of liver problems) are more likely to occur in patients 50 years of age and older.

Other side effects not listed above may also occur in some patients. If you notice any other effects, check with your doctor.

Revised: 08/15/97

RIFAMPIN, ISONIAZID, AND PYRAZINAMIDE Systemic†

A commonly used brand name in the U.S. is Rifater.

†Not commercially available in Canada.

Description

Rifampin, isoniazid, and pyrazinamide (rif-AM-pin, eye-soe-NYE-a-zid, and peer-a-ZIN-a-mide) is a combination anti-infective medicine. This combination medicine is used to treat tuberculosis (TB). It may be taken alone or with one or more of other medicines for TB.

To help clear up your tuberculosis (TB) completely, you must keep taking this medicine for the full time of treatment, even if you begin to feel better. This is very important. It is also important that you do not miss any doses.

Rifampin, isoniazid, and pyrazinamide combination is available only with your doctor's prescription, in the following dosage form:

Oral

- Tablets (U.S.)

Before Using This Medicine

In deciding to use a medicine, the risks of taking the medicine must be weighed against the good it will do. This is a decision you and your doctor will make. For rifampin, isoniazid, and pyrazinamide combination, the following should be considered:

Allergies—Tell your doctor if you have ever had any unusual or allergic reaction to ethionamide (e.g., Trecator-SC), pyrazinamide, niacin (e.g., Nicobid, nicotinic acid), rifampin (e.g., Rifadin), rifabutin (e.g., Mycobutin), or isoniazid (e.g., INH, Nydrazid). Also tell your health care professional if you are allergic to any other substances, such as foods, preservatives, or dyes.

Pregnancy—Pregnant women with tuberculosis (TB) should be treated with TB medicines, including isoniazid, pyrazinamide, and rifampin. Rifampin, isoniazid, and pyrazinamide combination has not been shown to cause birth defects or other problems in humans. However, rifampin can rarely cause bleeding in newborn babies and mothers when taken during the last weeks of pregnancy. Also, studies in rats and mice have shown that rifampin given in high doses causes birth defects, usually backbone problems (spina bifida) and cleft palate.

Breast-feeding—Rifampin, isoniazid, and pyrazinamide pass into the breast milk. However, rifampin, isoniazid, and pyrazinamide have not been reported to cause problems in nursing babies.

Children—Rifampin, isoniazid, and pyrazinamide combination may not be appropriate for use in children and adolescents up to 15 years of age.

Older adults—Liver problems are more likely to occur in patients over 50 years of age who are taking isoniazid-containing medicines.

Other medicines—Although certain medicines should not be used together at all, in other cases two different medicines may be used together even if an interaction might occur. In these cases, your doctor may want to change the dose, or other precautions may be necessary. When you are taking rifampin, isoniazid, and pyrazinamide combination, it is especially important that your health care professional know if you are taking any of the following:

- Acetaminophen (e.g., Tylenol) (with long-term, high-dose use) or
- Alfentanil (e.g., Alfenta) or
- Amiodarone (e.g., Cordarone) or
- Anabolic steroids (nandrolone [e.g., Anabolin], oxandrolone [e.g., Anavar], oxymetholone [e.g., Anadrol], stanozolol [e.g., Winstrol]) or
- Androgens (male hormones) or
- Antithyroid agents (medicine for overactive thyroid) or
- Carbamazepine (e.g., Tegretol) or
- Carmustine (e.g., BiCNU) or
- Chloroquine (e.g., Aralen) or
- Dantrolene (e.g., Dantrium) or
- Daunorubicin (e.g., Cerubidine) or
- Divalproex (e.g., Depakote) or
- Etretinate (e.g., Tegison) or
- Gold salts (medicine for arthritis) or
- Hydroxychloroquine (e.g., Plaquenil) or
- Mercaptopurine (e.g., Purinethol) or
- Methyldopa (e.g., Aldomet) or
- Naltrexone (e.g., Trexan) (with long-term, high-dose use) or
- Phenothiazines (acetophenazine [e.g., Tindal], chlorpromazine [e.g.,Thorazine], fluphenazine [e.g., Prolixin], mesoridazine [e.g., Serentil], perphenazine [e.g., Trilafon], prochlorperazine [e.g., Compazine], promazine [e.g., Sparine], promethazine [e.g., Phenergan], thioridazine [e.g., Mellaril], trifluoperazine [e.g., Stelazine], triflupromazine [e.g., Vesprin], trimeprazine [e.g., Temaril]) or
- Plicamycin (e.g., Mithracin) or
- Valproic acid (e.g., Depakene)—These medicines may increase the chance of liver damage if taken with rifampin, isoniazid, and pyrazinamide combination
- Aminophylline (e.g., Somophyllin) or
- Anticoagulants (blood thinners) or
- Antidiabetics, oral (diabetes medicines you take by mouth) or
- Chloramphenicol or
- Corticosteroids (cortisone-like medicine) or
- Digitalis glycosides (heart medicine) or
- Disopyramide (e.g., Norpace) or
- Estramustine (e.g., Emcyt) or
- Fluconazole (e.g., Diflucan) or
- Human immunodeficiency virus (HIV) protease inhibitors (medicines for the treatment of HIV infection) or
- Itraconazole (e.g., Sporanox) or
- Ketoconazole (e.g., Nizoral) or
- Methadone (e.g., Dolophine) or
- Methotrexate (e.g., Mexate) or
- Mexiletine (e.g., Mexitil) or
- Oxtriphylline (e.g., Choledyl) or
- Quinidine (e.g., Quinidex) or
- Theophylline (e.g., Theo-Dur, Somophyllin-T) or
- Tocainide (e.g., Tonocard) or
- Verapamil (e.g., Calan)—Rifampin, isoniazid, and pyrazinamide combination may decrease the effects of these medicines

- Disulfiram (e.g., Antabuse)—This medicine may increase the chance of liver damage and side effects, such as dizziness, lack of coordination, irritability, and inability to sleep
- Estrogens (female hormones) or
- Oral contraceptives (birth control pills) containing estrogen or
- Phenytoin (e.g., Dilantin)—Rifampin, isoniazid, and pyrazinamide combination may decrease the effects of these medicines. If you are taking oral contraceptives, this may increase the chance of pregnancy. These medicines may also increase the chance of liver damage if taken with rifampin, isoniazid, and pyrazinamide combination

Other medical problems—The presence of other medical problems may affect the use of rifampin, isoniazid, and pyrazinamide combination. Make sure you tell your doctor if you have any other medical problems, especially:

- Alcohol abuse (or history of) or
- Liver disease—There may be an increased chance of getting hepatitis if you take this medicine and drink alcohol daily
- Convulsive disorders such as seizures or epilepsy—Rifampin, isoniazid, and pyrazinamide combination may increase the frequency of convulsions (seizures) in some patients
- Gout (history of)—Rifampin, isoniazid, and pyrazinamide combination may worsen or cause a gout attack in patients with a history of gout
- Kidney disease (severe)—There may be an increased chance of side effects in patients with severe kidney disease

Proper Use of This Medicine

If this medicine upsets your stomach, take it with food. Antacids may also help. However, do not take aluminum-containing antacids within 1 hour of the time you take rifampin, isoniazid, and pyrazinamide combination. They may keep this medicine from working properly.

To help clear up your tuberculosis (TB) completely, it is very important that you keep taking this medicine for the full time of treatment, even if you begin to feel better after a few weeks. *It is important that you do not miss any doses.*

Your doctor may also want you to take pyridoxine (e.g., Hexa-Betalin, vitamin B_6) every day to help prevent or lessen some of the side effects of isoniazid. If it is needed, *it is very important to take pyridoxine every day along with this medicine. Do not miss any doses.*

Dosing—The dose of rifampin, isoniazid, and pyrazinamide combination will be different for different patients. *Follow your doctor's orders or the directions on the label.* The following information includes only the average doses of rifampin, isoniazid, and pyrazinamide combination. *If your dose is different, do not change it* unless your doctor tells you to do so.

- For *oral* dosage form (tablets):
  - —For the treatment of tuberculosis:
    - Adults and teenagers over 15 years of age weighing 44 kilograms (kg) (97 pounds) or less—4 tablets once a day.
    - Adults and teenagers over 15 years of age weighing between 45 and 54 kg (99 and 119 pounds)—5 tablets once a day.
    - Adults and teenagers over 15 years of age weighing 55 kg (121 pounds) or more—6 tablets once a day.
    - Children up to 15 years of age—This medicine is not recommended for this age group.

Missed dose—If you miss a dose of this medicine, take it as soon as possible. However, if it is almost time for your next dose, skip the missed dose and go back to your regular dosing schedule. Do not double doses. *If rifampin, isoniazid, and pyrazinamide combination is taken on an irregular schedule, side effects may occur more often and may be more serious than usual.* If you have any questions about this, check with your health care professional.

Storage—To store this medicine:

- Keep out of the reach of children.
- Store away from heat and direct light.
- Do not store in the bathroom, near the kitchen sink, or in other damp places. Heat or moisture may cause the medicine to break down.
- Do not keep outdated medicine or medicine no longer needed. Be sure that any discarded medicine is out of the reach of children.

Precautions While Using This Medicine

It is very important that your doctor check your progress at regular visits. In addition, you should *check with your doctor immediately if blurred vision or loss of vision, with or without eye pain, occurs during treatment.* He or she may want you to have your eyes checked by an ophthalmologist (eye doctor).

If your symptoms do not improve within 2 to 3 weeks, or if they become worse, check with your doctor.

Oral contraceptives (birth control pills) containing estrogen may not work properly if you take them while you are taking rifampin, isoniazid, and pyrazinamide combination. Unplanned pregnancies may occur. You should use a different method of birth control while you are taking this medicine. If you have any questions about this, check with your health care professional.

Liver problems may be more likely to occur if you drink alcoholic beverages regularly while you are taking this medicine. Also, the regular use of alcohol may keep this medicine from working properly. Therefore, *you should strictly limit the amount of alcoholic beverages you drink while you are taking this medicine.*

Certain foods such as cheese (Swiss or Cheshire) or fish (tuna, skipjack, or Sardinella) may rarely cause reactions in some patients taking isoniazid-containing medicines. Check with your doctor if redness or itching of the skin, hot feeling, fast or pounding heartbeat, sweating, chills or clammy feeling, headache, or lightheadedness occurs while you are taking this medicine.

This medicine will cause the urine, stool, saliva, sputum, sweat, and tears to turn reddish orange to reddish brown. This is to be expected while you are taking this medicine. This effect may cause soft contact lenses to become permanently discolored. Standard cleaning solutions may not take out all the discoloration. Therefore, *it is best not to wear soft contact lenses while taking this medicine*. Hard contact lenses are not discolored by this medicine. This condition will return to normal once you stop taking this medicine. If you have any questions about this, check with your health care professional.

If this medicine causes you to feel very tired or very weak; or causes clumsiness; unsteadiness; a loss of appetite; nausea; numbness, tingling, burning, or pain in the hands and feet; or vomiting, stop taking it and check with your doctor immediately. These may be early warning symptoms of more serious liver or nerve problems that could develop later.

Rifampin, isoniazid, and pyrazinamide combination may cause blood problems. These problems may result in a greater chance of certain infections, slow healing, and bleeding of the gums. Therefore, you should be careful when using regular toothbrushes, dental floss, and toothpicks. Dental work should be delayed until your blood counts have returned to normal. Check with your medical doctor or dentist if you have any questions about proper oral hygiene (mouth care) during treatment.

For diabetic patients: This medicine *may cause false test results with urine ketone tests*. Check with your doctor before changing your diet or the dosage of your diabetes medicine.

Side Effects of This Medicine

Along with its needed effects, a medicine may cause some unwanted effects. Although not all of these side effects may occur, if they do occur they may need medical attention.

Check with your doctor immediately if any of the following side effects occur:

More common

Clumsiness or unsteadiness; dark urine; loss of appetite; nausea and vomiting; numbness, tingling, burning, or pain in hands and feet; pain in large and small joints; unusual tiredness or weakness; yellow eyes or skin

Less common

Chills; difficulty in breathing; dizziness; fever; headache; itching; muscle and bone pain; redness of skin; shivering; skin rash

Rare

Bloody or cloudy urine; blurred vision or loss of vision, with or without eye pain; convulsions (seizures); greatly decreased frequency of urination or amount of urine; mental depression; mood or mental changes; sore throat; unusual bleeding or bruising

Other side effects may occur that usually do not need medical attention. These side effects may go away during treatment as your body adjusts to the medicine. However, check with your doctor if any of the following side effects continue or are bothersome:

More common

Diarrhea; stomach pain

Less common

Sore mouth or tongue

This medicine commonly causes urine, stool, saliva, sputum, sweat, and tears to turn reddish orange to reddish brown. This side effect does not usually require medical attention.

Dark urine and yellowing of the eyes or skin (signs of liver problems) caused by isoniazid are more likely to occur in patients 50 years of age and older.

Other side effects not listed above may also occur in some patients. If you notice any other effects, check with your doctor.

Developed: 08/15/97

RILUZOLE Systemic†

A commonly used brand name in the U.S. is Rilutek.

†Not commercially available in Canada.

Description

Riluzole (RIL-yoo-zole) is used to treat patients with amyotrophic lateral sclerosis (ALS), also known as Lou Gehrig's disease. Riluzole is not a cure for ALS, but it may extend survival in the early stages of the disease, and/or may extend the time until a tracheostomy may be needed.

Riluzole is available only with your doctor's prescription, in the following dosage form:

Oral

- Tablets (U.S.)

Before Using This Medicine

In deciding to use a medicine, the risks of taking the medicine must be weighed against the good it will do. This is a decision you and your doctor will make. For riluzole, the following should be considered:

Allergies—Tell your doctor if you have ever had any unusual or allergic reaction to riluzole. Also tell your health care professional if you are allergic to any other substances, such as foods, preservatives, or dyes.

Pregnancy—Studies with riluzole have not been done in pregnant women. Some unwanted effects have been reported in animal studies. Before taking this medicine, make sure your doctor knows if you are pregnant or if you may become pregnant.

Breast-feeding—Riluzole has been shown to pass into the milk of nursing animals. It may also pass into human milk and may cause unwanted effects in nursing babies. It may be necessary for you to stop breast-feeding during treatment. Be sure you have discussed the risks and benefits of the medicine with your doctor.

Children—Studies on this medicine have been done only in adult patients, and there is no specific information comparing use of riluzole in children with use in other age groups.

Older adults—Many medicines have not been studied specifically in older people. Therefore, it may not be known whether they work exactly the same way they do in younger adults. Although there is no specific information comparing use of riluzole in the elderly with use in other age groups, this medicine has been used in elderly patients and is not expected to cause different side effects or problems in older people than it does in younger adults.

Other medicines—Although certain medicines should not be used together at all, in other cases two different medicines may be used together even if an interaction might occur. In these cases, your doctor may want to change the dose, or other precautions may be necessary. Tell your doctor and pharmacist if you are taking any other prescription or nonprescription (over-the-counter [OTC]) medicine.

Other medical problems—The presence of other medical problems may affect the use of riluzole. Make sure you tell your doctor if you have any other medical problems, especially:

- Kidney disease or
- Liver disease—Higher blood levels of riluzole may occur, increasing the chance of side effects

Proper Use of This Medicine

Riluzole should be taken on a regular basis and at the same time of the day (for example, in the morning and the evening).

Riluzole should be taken on an empty stomach. Take this medicine at least one hour before meals or two hours after meals.

Dosing—The dose of riluzole will be different for different patients. *Follow your doctor's orders or the directions on the label.* The following information includes only the average doses of riluzole. *If your dose is different, do not change it* unless your doctor tells you to do so.

- For *oral* dosage form (tablets):
  - For ALS:
    - Adults—Oral, 50 milligrams (mg) every twelve hours.
    - Children up to 18 years of age—Use and dose must be determined by your doctor.

Missed dose—If you miss a dose of this medicine, skip the missed dose and go back to your regular dosing schedule. Do not double doses.

Storage—To store this medicine:

- Keep out of the reach of children.
- Store away from heat and bright light.
- Do not store in the bathroom, near the kitchen sink, or in other damp places. Heat or moisture may cause the medicine to break down.
- Do not keep outdated medicine or medicine no longer needed. Be sure that any discarded medicine is out of the reach of children.

Precautions While Using This Medicine

If you become ill with a fever, report this to your doctor promptly. Fever may be a sign of infection.

This medicine may cause dizziness or drowsiness. *Make sure you know how you react to this medicine before you drive, use machines, or do anything else that could be dangerous if you are dizzy or are not alert.*

Avoid drinking alcoholic beverages. It is not known if drinking alcohol while taking riluzole may cause liver problems.

Side Effects of This Medicine

Along with its needed effects, a medicine may cause some unwanted effects. Although not all of these side effects may occur, if they do occur they may need medical attention.

Check with your doctor as soon as possible if any of the following side effects occur:

More common

Diarrhea; nausea; vomiting; worsening of some symptoms of ALS, including spasticity and tiredness or weakness

Less common

Difficulty in breathing; increased cough; pneumonia

Rare

Bloody or cloudy urine, frequent urge to urinate, or painful or difficult urination; convulsions (seizures); fast or pounding heartbeat; fever, chills, or continuing sores in mouth; hypertension (high blood pressure); increased thirst, irregular heartbeat, mood or mental changes, or muscle cramps, pain, or weakness; lack of coordination; lack of energy; mental depression; pain, tenderness, bluish color, or swelling of foot or leg; redness, scaling, or peeling of the skin; swelling of eyelids, mouth, lips, tongue, and/or throat; swelling of face; trouble in swallowing; yellow eyes or skin

Other side effects may occur that usually do not need medical attention. These side effects may go away during treatment as your body adjusts to the medicine. However, check with your doctor if any of the following side effects continue or are bothersome:

More common

Abdominal pain or gas; dizziness; drowsiness; loss of appetite; numbness or tingling around the mouth

Less common

Back or muscle pain or stiffness; constipation; general feeling of discomfort or illness; hair loss; headache; irritation or soreness of mouth; runny nose; skin rash or itching; trouble in sleeping

This medicine may also cause the following side effect that your doctor will watch for:

More common

Liver problems

Other side effects not listed above may also occur in some patients. If you notice any other effects, check with your doctor.

Developed: 07/30/96

RIMANTADINE Systemic†

A commonly used brand name in the U.S. in Flumadine.

†Not commercially available in Canada.

Description

Rimantadine (ri-MAN-ta-deen) is an antiviral. It is used to prevent or treat certain influenza (flu) infections (type A). It may be given alone or along with flu shots. Rimantadine will not work for colds, other types of flu, or other virus infections.

Rimantadine is available only with your doctor's prescription, in the following dosage forms:

Oral
- Syrup (U.S.)
- Tablets (U.S.)

Before Using This Medicine

In deciding to use a medicine, the risks of taking the medicine must be weighed against the good it will do. This is a decision you and your doctor will make. For rimantadine, the following should be considered:

Allergies—Tell your doctor if you have ever had any unusual or allergic reaction to rimantadine or amantadine. Also tell your health care professional if you are allergic to any other substances, such as foods, preservatives, or dyes.

Pregnancy—Studies have not been done in humans. However, studies in some animals have shown that rimantadine is harmful to the fetus and causes birth defects.

Breast-feeding—It is not known if rimantadine passes into breast milk. Although most medicines pass into breast milk in small amounts, many of them may be used safely while breast-feeding. Mothers who are taking this medicine and who wish to breast-feed should discuss this with their doctor.

Children—This medicine has been tested in children over one year of age and has not been shown to cause different side effects or problems in these children than it does in adults. There is no specific information comparing the use of rimantadine in children under one year of age with use in other age groups.

Older adults—Elderly people are especially sensitive to the effects of rimantadine. Difficulty in sleeping, difficulty in concentrating, dizziness, headache, nervousness, and weakness may be especially likely to occur. Stomach pain, nausea, vomiting, and loss of appetite may also occur.

Other medicines—Although certain medicines should not be used together at all, in other cases two different medicines may be used together even if an interaction might occur. In these cases, your doctor may want to change the dose, or other precautions may be necessary. Tell your health care professional if you are taking any other prescription or nonprescription (over-the-counter [OTC]) medicine.

Other medical problems—The presence of other medical problems may affect the use of rimantadine. Make sure you tell your doctor if you have any other medical problems, especially:

- Epilepsy or other seizures (history of)—Rimantadine may increase the frequency of convulsions (seizures) in patients with a seizure disorder
- Kidney disease—Rimantadine is removed from the body by the kidneys; patients with severe kidney disease will need to receive a lower dose of rimantadine
- Liver disease—Patients with severe liver disease may need to receive a lower dose of rimantadine

Proper Use of This Medicine

Talk to your doctor about the *possibility of getting a flu shot* if you have not had one yet.

This medicine is *best taken before exposure, or as soon as possible after exposure,* to people who have the flu.

To help keep yourself from getting the flu, *keep taking this medicine for the full time of treatment.*

If you already have the flu, *continue taking this medicine for the full time of treatment even if you begin to feel better after a few days.* This will help to clear up your infection completely. If you stop taking this medicine too soon, your symptoms may return. This medicine should be taken for at least 5 to 7 days.

This medicine works best when there is a constant amount in the blood. *To help keep the amount constant, do not miss any doses. Also, it is best to take the doses at evenly spaced times day and night.*

If you are using the oral liquid form of rimantadine, use a specially marked measuring spoon or other device to measure each dose accurately. The average household teaspoon may not hold the right amount of liquid.

Dosing—The dose of rimantadine will be different for different patients. *Follow your doctor's orders or the directions on the label.* The following information includes only the average doses of rimantadine. Your dose may be different if you have kidney disease or liver disease. *If your dose is different, do not change it* unless your doctor tells you to do so.

- For *oral* dosage forms (syrup, tablets):
  - —For the prevention or treatment of flu:
    - Elderly adults—100 milligrams (mg) once a day.
    - Adults and children 10 years of age and older—100 mg two times a day.
    - Children up to 10 years of age—5 mg per kilogram (2.3 mg per pound) of body weight once a day. Children in this age group should not receive more than 150 mg a day.

Missed dose—If you do miss a dose of this medicine, take it as soon as possible. This will help to keep a constant amount of medicine in the blood. However, if it is almost time for your next dose, skip the missed dose and go back to your regular dosing schedule. Do not double doses.

Storage—To store this medicine:

- Keep out of the reach of children.
- Store away from heat and direct light.
- Keep the syrup form of this medicine from freezing.
- Do not keep outdated medicine or medicine no longer needed. Be sure that any discarded medicine is out of the reach of children.

Precautions While Using This Medicine

This medicine may cause some people to become dizzy or confused, or to have trouble concentrating. *Make sure you know how you react to this medicine before you drive, use machines, or do anything else that could be dangerous if you are dizzy or confused.* If these reactions are especially bothersome, check with your doctor.

If your symptoms do not improve within a few days, or if they become worse, check with your doctor.

Side Effects of This Medicine

Along with its needed effects, a medicine may cause some unwanted effects. Although not all of these side effects may occur, if they do occur they may need medical attention.

Side effects may occur that usually do not need medical attention. These side effects may go away during treatment as your body adjusts to the medicine. However, check with your doctor if any of the following side effects continue or are bothersome:

Less common

Difficulty in concentrating; dizziness; dryness of mouth; headache; loss of appetite; nausea; nervousness; stomach pain; trouble in sleeping; unusual tiredness; vomiting

Other side effects not listed above may also occur in some patients. If you notice any other effects, check with your doctor.

Developed: 03/29/94

RISPERIDONE Systemic

A commonly used brand name in the U.S. and Canada is Risperdal.

Description

Risperidone (ris-PER-i-done) is used to treat psychotic disorders, such as schizophrenia.

Risperidone is available only with your doctor's prescription, in the following dosage form:

Oral

- Tablets (U.S. and Canada)

Before Using This Medicine

In deciding to use a medicine, the risks of taking the medicine must be weighed against the good it will do. This is a decision you and your doctor will make. For risperidone, the following should be considered:

Allergies—Tell your doctor if you have ever had any unusual or allergic reaction to risperidone. Also tell your health care professional if you are allergic to any other substances, such as foods, preservatives, or dyes.

Pregnancy—Studies with risperidone have not been done in pregnant women. Some unwanted effects have been reported in animal studies, but the risk to human babies is not clear. Before taking this medicine, make sure your doctor knows if you are pregnant or if you may become pregnant.

Breast-feeding—Risperidone has been shown to pass into the milk of nursing animals. It may also pass into human milk and may cause unwanted effects, such as behavior changes, in nursing babies. It may be necessary for you to take another medicine or to stop breast-feeding during treatment. Be sure you have discussed the risks and benefits of the medicine with your doctor.

Children—Studies on this medicine have been done only in adult patients, and there is no specific information comparing use of risperidone in children with use in other age groups.

Older adults—Elderly people may be especially sensitive to the effects of risperidone. This may increase the chance of side effects during treatment.

Other medicines—Although certain medicines should not be used together at all, in other cases two different medicines may be used together even if an interaction might occur. In these cases, your doctor may want to change the dose, or other precautions may be necessary. When you are taking risperidone, it is especially important that your health care professional know if you are taking any of the following:

- Antihypertensives (high blood pressure medicine) or
- Central nervous system (CNS) depressants (medicine that makes you drowsy or less alert) or
- Tricyclic antidepressants (medicine for depression)—Risperidone may add to the effects of these medicines, causing unwanted effects
- Bromocriptine (e.g., Parlodel) or
- Levodopa (e.g., Dopar, Larodopa) or
- Pergolide (e.g., Permax)—Risperidone may interfere with the effects of these medicines.
- Carbamazepine (e.g., Epitol, Tegretol) or
- Clozapine (e.g., Clozaril)—These medicines may affect the blood levels of risperidone. Your doctor may need to change your dose of risperidone

Other medical problems—The presence of other medical problems may affect the use of risperidone. Make sure you tell your doctor if you have any other medical problems, especially:

- Brain tumor or

- Drug overdose or
- Intestinal obstruction or
- Reye's syndrome—Risperidone may mask the signs and symptoms of these conditions
- Breast cancer or
- Heart or blood vessel problems or
- Parkinson's disease—Risperidone may make these conditions worse
- Drug abuse or dependence, history of—Because risperidone is a new medicine, it is not known if it could become habit-forming, causing mental or physical dependence
- Epilepsy or other seizure disorders—Risperidone may increase the risk of seizures
- Kidney disease or
- Liver disease—Higher blood levels of risperidone may occur, increasing the chance of side effects

Proper Use of This Medicine

Take this medicine only as directed by your doctor to benefit your condition as much as possible. Do not take more of it, do not take it more often, and do not take it for a longer time than your doctor ordered.

Dosing—The dose of risperidone will be different for different patients. *Follow your doctor's orders or the directions on the label.* The following information includes only the average doses of risperidone. *If your dose is different, do not change it* unless your doctor tells you to do so.

- For *oral* dosage form (tablets):
  - —For schizophrenia:
    - Adults—At first, 1 milligram (mg) two times a day. Your doctor may increase your dose as needed. However, the dose is usually not more than 16 mg a day.
    - Children up to 18 years of age—Use and dose must be determined by the doctor.
    - Older adults—At first, 0.5 mg two times a day. Your doctor may increase your dose as needed. However, the dose is usually not more than 3 mg a day.

Missed dose—If you miss a dose of this medicine, take it as soon as possible. However, if it is almost time for your next dose, skip the missed dose and go back to your regular dosing schedule. Do not double doses.

Storage—To store this medicine:

- Keep out of the reach of children.
- Store away from heat and direct light.
- Do not store in the bathroom, near the kitchen sink, or in other damp places. Heat or moisture may cause the medicine to break down.
- Do not keep outdated medicine or medicine no longer needed. Be sure that any discarded medicine is out of the reach of children.

Precautions While Using This Medicine

Your doctor should check your progress at regular visits, especially during the first few months of treatment with this medicine. This will allow your dosage to be changed if necessary to meet your needs.

Do not stop taking this medicine without first checking with your doctor. Your doctor may want you to reduce gradually the amount you are taking before stopping completely. This is to prevent side effects and to keep your condition from becoming worse.

This medicine may add to the effects of alcohol and other CNS depressants (medicine that makes you drowsy or less alert). Some examples of CNS depressants are antihistamines or medicine for hay fever, other allergies, or colds; sedatives, tranquilizers, or sleeping medicine; prescription pain medicine or narcotics; barbiturates; medicine for seizures; muscle relaxants; or anesthetics, including some dental anesthetics. *Check with your doctor before taking any of the above while you are using this medicine.*

Before having any kind of surgery, dental treatment, or emergency treatment, tell the medical doctor or dentist in charge that you are using this medicine. Taking risperidone together with medicines that are used during surgery, dental, or emergency treatments may increase the CNS depressant effects.

This medicine may cause blurred vision, dizziness, or drowsiness. *Make sure you know how you react to this medicine before you drive, use machines, or do anything else that could be dangerous if you are not alert or able to see clearly.*

Dizziness, lightheadedness, or fainting may occur, especially when you get up from a lying or sitting position. Getting up slowly may help. If the problem continues or gets worse, check with your doctor.

Risperidone may cause your skin to be more sensitive to sunlight than it is normally. Exposure to sunlight, even for brief periods of time, may cause a skin rash, itching, redness or other discoloration of the skin, or a severe sunburn. When you begin taking this medicine:

- Stay out of direct sunlight, especially between the hours of 10:00 a.m. and 3:00 p.m., if possible.
- Wear protective clothing, including a hat. Also, wear sunglasses.
- Apply a sun block product that has a skin protection factor (SPF) of at least 15. Some patients may require a product with a higher SPF number, especially if they have a fair complexion. If you have any questions about this, check with your health care professional.
- Apply a sun block lipstick that has an SPF of at least 15 to protect your lips.
- Do not use a sunlamp or tanning bed or booth.

If you have a severe reaction from the sun, check with your doctor.

Risperidone may cause dryness of the mouth. For temporary relief, use sugarless candy or gum, melt bits of ice in your mouth, or use a saliva substitute. However, if your mouth continues to feel dry for more than 2 weeks, check with your medical doctor or dentist. Continuing dryness of the mouth may increase the chance of dental disease, including tooth decay, gum disease, and fungus infections.

This medicine may make you sweat less, causing your body temperature to increase. Use extra care not to become overheated during exercise or hot weather while you are taking this medicine, since overheating may result in heatstroke. Also, hot baths or saunas may make you feel dizzy or faint while you are taking this medicine.

Side Effects of This Medicine

Along with its needed effects, risperidone can sometimes cause serious side effects. Tardive dyskinesia (a movement disorder) may occur and may not go away after you stop using the medicine. Signs of tardive dyskinesia include fine, worm-like movements of the tongue, or other uncontrolled movements of the mouth, tongue, cheeks, jaw, or arms and legs. Other serious but rare side effects may also occur. These include neuroleptic malignant syndrome (NMS), which may cause severe muscle stiffness, fever, severe tiredness or weakness, fast heartbeat, difficult breathing, increased sweating, loss of bladder control, or seizures. *You and your doctor should discuss the good this medicine will do as well as the risks of taking it.*

Stop taking risperidone and get emergency help immediately if any of the following side effects occur:

Rare

Convulsions (seizures), difficult or fast breathing, fast heartbeat or irregular pulse, fever (high), high or low blood pressure, increased sweating, loss of bladder control, muscle stiffness (severe), unusually pale skin, unusual tiredness or weakness (severe)

Check with your doctor immediately if any of the following side effects occur:

More common

Difficulty in speaking or swallowing; inability to move eyes; muscle spasms of face, neck, and back; twisting movements of body

Rare

Lip smacking or puckering; prolonged, painful, inappropriate erection of the penis; puffing of cheeks; rapid or worm-like movements of tongue; uncontrolled chewing movements; uncontrolled movements of arms and legs

Check with your doctor as soon as possible if any of the following side effects occur:

More common

Anxiety or nervousness; changes in vision, including blurred vision; decreased sexual desire or performance; dizziness; loss of balance control; mask-like face; menstrual changes; mood or mental changes, including aggressive behavior, agitation, difficulty in concentration, and memory problems; problems in urination or increase in amount of urine; restlessness or need to keep moving (severe); shuffling walk; skin rash or itching; stiffness or weakness of arms or legs; tic-like or twitching movements; trembling and shaking of fingers and hands; trouble in sleeping

Less common

Back pain; chest pain; seborrhea; unusual secretion of milk

Rare

Extreme thirst; increased blinking or spasms of eyelid; loss of appetite; talking, feeling, and acting with excitement and activity you cannot control; uncontrolled twisting movements of neck, trunk, arms, or legs; unusual bleeding or bruising; unusual facial expressions or body positions

Other side effects may occur that usually do not need medical attention. These side effects may go away during treatment as your body adjusts to the medicine. However, check with your doctor if any of the following side effects continue or are bothersome:

More common

Constipation, coughing, diarrhea, drowsiness, dryness of mouth, headache, heartburn, increased dream activity, increased length of sleep, nausea, runny nose, sore throat, unusual tiredness or weakness, weight gain

Less common

Darkening of skin color, dry skin, increased sensitivity of the skin to sun, increased watering of mouth, joint pain, stomach pain, vomiting, weight loss

Some side effects, such as uncontrolled movements of the mouth, tongue, and jaw, or uncontrolled movements of arms and legs, may occur after you have stopped taking this medicine. If you notice any of these effects, check with your doctor as soon as possible.

Other side effects not listed above may also occur in some patients. If you notice any other effects, check with your doctor.

Developed: 08/15/95

RITODRINE Systemic

Some commonly used brand names are:

In the U.S.—

Yutopar

Generic name product is available.

In Canada—

Yutopar

Yutopar S.R.

Description

Ritodrine (RI-toe-dreen) is used to stop premature labor. It is available only with your doctor's prescription and is to be administered only by or under the supervision of your doctor.

Ritodrine is available in the following dosage forms:

Oral

- Extended-release capsules (Canada)
- Tablets (Canada)

Parenteral

- Injection (U.S. and Canada)

Before Using This Medicine

In deciding to use a medicine, the risks of taking the medicine must be weighed against the good it will do. This is

a decision you and your doctor will make. For ritodrine, the following should be considered:

Allergies—Tell your doctor if you have ever had any unusual or allergic reaction to ritodrine or sulfites. Also tell your health care professional if you are allergic to any other substances, such as foods, preservatives, or dyes.

Other medicines—Although certain medicines should not be used together at all, in other cases two different medicines may be used together even if an interaction might occur. In these cases, your doctor may want to change the dose, or other precautions may be necessary. When you are taking or receiving ritodrine, it is especially important that your health care professional know if you are taking any of the following:

- Beta-adrenergic blocking agents (acebutolol [e.g., Sectral], atenolol [e.g., Tenormin], betaxolol [e.g., Kerlone], bisoprolol [e.g., Zebeta], carteolol [e.g., Cartrol], labetalol [e.g., Normodyne], metoprolol [e.g., Lopressor], nadolol [e.g., Corgard], oxprenolol [e.g., Trasicor], penbutolol [e.g., Levatol], pindolol [e.g., Visken], propranolol [e.g., Inderal], sotalol [e.g., Sotacor], timolol [e.g., Blocadren])—Ritodrine may be less effective if it is used with any of these medicines
- Corticosteroids (cortisone-like medicines)—These medicines are often given together to the mother to help her baby's lungs develop. If you are taking corticosteroids, your dose may need to be changed if ritodrine is also taken or injected. Sometimes the combination of these medicines increases the chance of side effects occurring in the mother.
- Medicine for asthma or breathing problems—Because these products have some effects that are similar to those of ritodrine, the chance of side effects developing is increased when these medicines are used with ritodrine

Other medical problems—The presence of other medical problems may affect the use of ritodrine. Make sure you tell your doctor if you have any other medical problems, especially:

- Diabetes mellitus (sugar diabetes)—Ritodrine may make this condition worse
- Heart or blood vessel disease or
- Overactive thyroid, uncontrolled—Use of ritodrine may cause serious effects on the heart, including irregular heartbeat
- High blood pressure (hypertension), uncontrolled, or
- Migraine headaches (or history of)—Ritodrine may make these conditions worse. Rarely, use of ritodrine during a migraine headache may cause problems with blood circulation in the brain

Proper Use of This Medicine

Dosing—The dose of ritodrine will be different for different women. *Follow your doctor's orders or the directions on the label.* The following information includes only the average doses of ritodrine. *If your dose is different, do not change it* unless your doctor tells you to do so. The injection form of this medicine will be given to you by your health care professional.

- For *oral* dosage form (extended-release capsules):
  —Adults: In the first twenty-four hours after the doctor stops your intravenous ritodrine, your dose may be as high as 40 milligrams (mg) every eight hours. After that, the dose is usually 40 mg taken every eight to twelve hours. Your doctor may want you to take oral ritodrine up until it is time for you to deliver your baby or until your 37th week of pregnancy.
- For *oral* dosage form (tablets):
  —Adults: In the first twenty-four hours after the doctor stops your intravenous ritodrine, your dose may be as high as 10 mg every two hours. After that, the dose is usually 10 to 20 mg every four to six hours. Your doctor may want you to take oral ritodrine up until it is time for you to deliver your baby or until your 37th week of pregnancy.
- For *injection* dosage form:
  —Adults: 50 to 350 micrograms per minute, injected into a vein.

Missed dose—If you miss an oral dose of this medicine and remember within an hour or so of the missed dose, take it right away. However, if you do not remember until later, skip the missed dose and go back to your regular dosing schedule. Do not double doses.

Storage—To store this medicine:

- Keep out of the reach of children.
- Store away from heat and direct light.
- Do not store in the bathroom, near the kitchen sink, or in other damp places. Heat or moisture may cause the medicine to break down.
- Do not keep outdated medicine or medicine no longer needed. Be sure that any discarded medicine is out of the reach of children.

Precautions While Using This Medicine

Check with your doctor right away if your contractions begin again or your water breaks.

Do not take other medicines unless they have been discussed with your doctor. This especially includes over-the-counter (nonprescription) medicines for appetite control, asthma, colds, cough, hay fever, or sinus problems since they may increase the unwanted effects of this medicine.

Side Effects of This Medicine

Along with its needed effects, a medicine may cause some unwanted effects. Although not all of these side effects may occur, if they do occur they may need medical attention.

Tell your health care professional immediately if either of the following side effects occurs while you are receiving this medicine:

More common

Chest pain or tightness; shortness of breath—rare with oral form

Check with your health care professional as soon as possible if the following side effects occur:

More common

Blurred vision; dizziness or lightheadedness; drowsiness; dry mouth; flushed and dry skin; fast or irregular heartbeat—rare with oral form; fruit-like breath odor; increased urination; loss of appetite; nausea; severe pounding or racing heartbeat—rare with oral form;

sleepiness; stomachache; tiredness; troubled breathing (rapid and deep); unusual thirst; vomiting

Rare

Sore throat or fever; yellow eyes or skin

Symptoms of overdose

Fast or irregular heartbeat (severe); nausea or vomiting (severe); nervousness or trembling (severe); shortness of breath (severe)

Other side effects may occur that usually do not need medical attention. These side effects may go away during treatment as your body adjusts to the medicine. However, check with your doctor if any of the following side effects continue or are bothersome:

More common

Headache; reddened skin; trembling

Less common or rare

Anxiety; emotional upset; jitteriness, nervousness, or restlessness; skin rash

After you stop using this medicine, your body may need time to adjust. The length of time this takes depends on the amount of medicine you were using and how long you used it. During this period of time check with your doctor if you notice the following side effect:

Shortness of breath

Other side effects not listed above may also occur in some patients. If you notice any other effects, check with your doctor.

Revised: 06/28/96

ROPIVACAINE Parenteral-Local

A commonly used brand name in the U.S. and Canada is Naropin.

Description

Ropivacaine (roe-PIV-a-kane) is a local anesthetic (an-ess-THET-ik) given by injection to cause loss of feeling before and during surgery or labor and delivery. It does not cause loss of consciousness.

Ropivacaine is given only by or under the immediate supervision of a medical doctor, or by a specially trained nurse, in the doctor's office or in a hospital. It is available in the following dosage form:

Parenteral

- Injection (U.S. and Canada)

Before Using This Medicine

In deciding to use a medicine, the risks of using the medicine must be weighed against the good it will do. This is a decision you and your health care professional will make. For ropivacaine, the following should be considered:

Allergies—Tell your health care professional if you have ever had an unusual or allergic reaction to ropivacaine or any other local anesthetic.

Pregnancy—Ropivacaine has not been shown to cause birth defects in humans.

Use of ropivacaine during labor and delivery may rarely cause unwanted effects. This medicine may increase the length of labor by making it more difficult for the mother to bear down (push). It may also cause unwanted effects in the fetus or newborn baby. Before receiving ropivacaine for labor and delivery, you should discuss with your doctor the good the medicine will do as well as the risks of receiving it.

Breast-feeding—It is not known whether ropivacaine passes into breast milk. However, this medicine has not been reported to cause problems in nursing babies.

Children—Studies on this medicine have been done only in adolescents and adults, and there is no specific information comparing use of ropivacaine in children with use in other age groups.

Older adults—Many medicines have not been specifically studied in older people. Therefore, it may not be known whether they work exactly the same way they do in younger adults or if they cause different side effects or problems in older people. There is no specific information comparing use of ropivacaine in the elderly with use in other age groups. Based on information about similar medicines, it is expected that elderly people will be more sensitive than younger adults to the effects of ropivacaine. This may increase the chance of side effects.

Other medicines—Although certain medicines should not be used together at all, in other cases two different medicines may be used together even if an interaction might occur. In these cases, your medical doctor or nurse may want to change the dose, or other precautions may be necessary. Tell your health care professional if you are taking any other prescription or nonprescription (over-the-counter [OTC]) medicine.

Other medical problems—The presence of other medical problems may affect the use of ropivacaine. Make sure you tell your health care professional if you have any other medical problems, especially:

- Heart disease—This medicine may make your condition worse
- Kidney disease or
- Liver disease—Side effects may be more likely in patients with kidney disease or liver disease

Proper Use of This Medicine

Dosing—The dose of ropivacaine will be different for different patients. Your health care professional will decide on the right amount for you, depending on:

- Your age;
- Your general physical condition;
- The reason the medicine is being given; and
- Other medicines you are taking or will receive before or after ropivacaine is given.

Precautions After Receiving This Medicine

For patients going home before the numbness or loss of feeling caused by ropivacaine wears off:

- During the time that the injected area feels numb, serious injury can occur without your knowing it. Be especially careful to avoid injury until the medicine wears off or feeling returns to the area.

Side Effects of This Medicine

Along with its needed effects, a medicine may cause some unwanted effects. Although not all of these side effects may occur, if they do occur they may need medical attention. While you are in the hospital or in your doctor's office, your medical doctor or nurse will carefully follow the effects of any medicine you have received. However, some effects may not be noticed until later.

Check with your doctor immediately if any of the following side effects occur:

Less common or rare

Burning or prickling sensation; fever; itching

Check with your doctor as soon as possible if any of the following side effects occur:

Less common or rare

Back pain; difficulty urinating; headache; pain

Other side effects not listed above may occur in some patients. If you notice any other effects, check with your doctor.

Developed: 08/18/97

RUBELLA AND MUMPS VIRUS VACCINE LIVE Systemic†

A commonly used brand name in the U.S. is BIAVAX II.

†Not commercially available in Canada.

Description

Rubella (rue-BELL-a) and mumps virus vaccine live is an active immunizing agent used to prevent infection by the rubella and mumps viruses. It works by causing your body to produce its own protection (antibodies) against the virus.

Rubella (also known as German measles) is a serious infection that causes miscarriages, stillbirths, or birth defects in unborn babies when pregnant women get the disease.

Mumps is an infection that can cause serious problems, such as encephalitis and meningitis, which affect the brain. In addition, adolescent boys and men are very susceptible to a condition called orchitis, which causes pain and swelling in the testicles and scrotum and, in rare cases, sterility. Also, mumps infection can cause spontaneous abortion in women during the first 3 months of pregnancy.

While immunization against rubella and mumps is recommended for all persons 12 months of age and older, it is especially important for women of childbearing age and persons traveling outside the U.S.

If rubella and mumps virus vaccine live is to be given to a child, the child should be at least 12 months of age. This is to make sure the vaccine is effective. In a child less than 12 months of age, antibodies from the mother may prevent the vaccine from working.

This vaccine is to be administered only by or under the supervision of your doctor or other health care professional. It is available in the following dosage form:

Parenteral

- Injection (U.S.)

Before Receiving This Vaccine

In deciding to use a medicine, the risks of taking the medicine must be weighed against the good it will do. This is a decision you and your doctor will make. For rubella and mumps virus vaccine live, the following should be considered:

Allergies—Tell your doctor if you have ever had any unusual or allergic reaction to rubella and mumps virus vaccine live, to the antibiotic neomycin, or to gelatin. Also tell your health care professional if you are allergic to any other substances, such as preservatives.

Pregnancy—Tell your doctor if you are pregnant or if you may become pregnant within 3 months after receiving this vaccine. Although adequate studies have not been done in either humans or animals and problems have not been shown to occur, use of rubella and mumps virus vaccine live during pregnancy, or becoming pregnant within 3 months after receiving rubella and mumps virus vaccine live, is not recommended. Rubella vaccine virus crosses the placenta. However, the Centers for Disease Control and Prevention monitored more than 200 women who received the vaccine within 3 months before or after becoming pregnant and those women gave birth to normal babies. Mumps vaccine virus may infect the placenta, although the vaccine has not been shown to infect the fetus or to cause birth defects.

Breast-feeding—Rubella vaccine virus may pass into breast milk. However, this vaccine has not been reported to cause problems in nursing babies.

Children—Use of this vaccine is not recommended for infants younger than 12 months of age. Children who received the vaccine when younger than 12 months of age should receive another dose of vaccine at 12 to 15 months of age.

Other medicines—Although certain medicines should not be used together at all, in other cases two different medicines may be used together even if an interaction might occur. In these cases, your doctor may want to change the dose, or other precautions may be necessary. Before you receive rubella and mumps virus vaccine live, it is especially important that your health care professional know if you have received any of the following:

- Cancer medicines or
- X-ray treatment—May reduce the useful effect of the vaccine

Other medical problems—The presence of other medical problems may affect the use of rubella and mumps virus vaccine live. Make sure you tell your doctor if you have any other medical problems, especially:

- Immune deficiency condition (or family history of)—Condition may increase the chance and severity of side effects of the vaccine and/or may decrease the useful effects of the vaccine
- Severe illness with fever—The symptoms of the condition may be confused with the possible side effects of the vaccine

Proper Use of This Vaccine

Dosing—The following information includes only the average dose of rubella and mumps virus vaccine live.

- For *injection* dosage form:
  - —For prevention of rubella and mumps:
    - Adults and children 12 months of age and older—One dose injected under the skin.
    - Children up to 12 months of age—Use is not recommended.

Precautions After Receiving This Vaccine

Do not become pregnant for 3 months after receiving rubella and mumps virus vaccine live without first checking with your doctor. There may be a chance that this vaccine can cause birth defects.

Tell your doctor that you have received this vaccine:

- If you are to receive blood products or immune globulins within 14 days of receiving this vaccine
- If you are to receive this vaccine within 3 months of receiving blood products or immune globulin
- If you are to receive a tuberculin skin test within 4 to 6 weeks after receiving this vaccine. The results of the test may be affected by this vaccine.

Side Effects of This Vaccine

Along with its needed effects, a vaccine may cause some unwanted effects. Although not all of these side effects may occur, if they do occur they may need medical attention.

Get emergency help immediately if any of the following side effects occur:

Symptoms of allergic reaction—rare

Difficulty in breathing or swallowing; hives; itching, especially of feet or hands; reddening of skin, especially around ears; swelling of eyes, face, or inside of nose; unusual tiredness or weakness (sudden and severe)

Check with your doctor as soon as possible if any of the following side effects occur:

Less common

Pain or tenderness of eyes

Rare

Bruising or purple spots on skin; confusion; fever over 103 °F (39.4 °C); headache (severe or continuing); irritability; pain, numbness, or tingling of hands, arms, legs, or feet; pain, tenderness, or swelling in testicles and scrotum; stiff neck; vomiting

Other side effects may occur that usually do not need medical attention. However, check with your doctor if any of the following side effects continue or are bothersome:

More common

Burning or stinging at place of injection; skin rash; swelling of glands in neck

Less common

Aches or pain in joints; headache (mild); itching, swelling, redness, tenderness, or hard lump at place of injection; nausea; runny nose; sore throat; vague feeling of bodily discomfort

The above side effects (especially aches or pain in joints) are more likely to occur in adults, particularly women.

Other side effects not listed above may also occur in some patients. If you notice any other effects, check with your doctor.

Developed: 4/29/97

RUBELLA VIRUS VACCINE LIVE Systemic

A commonly used brand name in the U.S. and Canada is Meruvax II.

Generic name product may also be available.

Description

Rubella (rue-BELL-a) virus vaccine live is an active immunizing agent used to prevent infection by the rubella virus. It works by causing your body to produce its own protection (antibodies) against the virus infection.

Rubella (also known as German measles) is a serious infection that causes miscarriages, stillbirths, or birth defects in unborn babies when pregnant women get the disease. While immunization against rubella is recommended for everyone, it is especially important for women of child-bearing age.

Immunization against rubella is also important for employees in medical facilities, adolescents and adult men, persons traveling outside the U.S., and all children 12 months of age and older, including school-aged children.

Immunization against rubella is not recommended for infants less than 12 months of age, because antibodies they received from their mothers before birth may interfere with the effectiveness of the vaccine. Children who were immunized against rubella before 12 months of age should be immunized again.

You can be considered immune to rubella only if you received rubella vaccine on or after your first birthday and have the medical record to prove it, or if you have had a blood test showing immunity to rubella. A past history of having a rubella infection does not prove immunity, because the signs of rubella infection are not reliable enough to be certain that you have had the disease.

Since vaccination with rubella vaccine may not provide protection for everyone, you may want to ask your doctor to check your immunity to the rubella virus 6 to 8 weeks following your vaccination. This may be especially important if you are a woman of child-bearing age who is likely to become pregnant in the future.

This vaccine is to be administered only by or under the supervision of your doctor or other health care professional. It is available in the following dosage form:

Parenteral

- Injection (U.S. and Canada)

Before Receiving This Vaccine

In deciding to use a medicine, the risks of taking the medicine must be weighed against the good it will do. This is a decision you and your doctor will make. For rubella vaccine, the following should be considered:

Allergies—Tell your doctor if you have ever had any unusual or allergic reaction to rubella vaccine, the antibiotic neomycin, or to gelatin. Also tell your health care professional if you are allergic to any other substances, such as preservatives.

Pregnancy—Tell your doctor if you are pregnant or if you may become pregnant within 3 months after receiving this vaccine. Vaccination during pregnancy or within 3 months of pregnancy is not recommended.

Breast-feeding—Rubella vaccine may pass into the breast milk. However, studies have not shown that this causes any problems.

Children—Use is not recommended for infants less than 12 months of age. This medicine has been tested in older infants and children and, in effective doses, has not been shown to cause different side effects or problems than it does in adults.

Other medicines—Although certain medicines should not be used together at all, in other cases two different medicines may be used together even if an interaction might occur. In these cases, your doctor may want to change the dose, or other precautions may be necessary. Before you receive rubella vaccine, it is especially important that your health care professional know if you have received any of the following:

- Cancer medicines or
- Corticosteroids (e.g., cortisone-like medicines) or
- Radiation therapy—May reduce the useful effect of the vaccine

Other medical problems—The presence of other medical problems may affect the use of rubella vaccine. Make sure you tell your doctor if you have any other medical problems, especially:

- Immune deficiency condition (or family history of)—Condition may increase the chance and severity of side effects of the vaccine and/or may decrease the useful effects of the vaccine
- Severe illness with fever—The symptoms of the condition may be confused with the possible side effects of the vaccine

Proper Use of This Vaccine

Dosing—The dose of rubella vaccine will be different for different patients. The following information includes only the average dose of rubella vaccine.

- For *injection* dosage form:
  - —For prevention of rubella:
    - Adults and children 12 months of age and older—One dose injected under the skin.
    - Children up to 12 months of age—Use is not recommended.

Precautions After Receiving This Vaccine

Do not become pregnant for 3 months after receiving rubella vaccine without first checking with your doctor. There is a chance that this vaccine may cause birth defects.

Tell your doctor that you have received this vaccine:

- if you are to receive a tuberculin skin test within 4 to 6 weeks after receiving this vaccine. The results of the test may be affected by this vaccine.
- if you are to receive blood transfusions or other blood products within 2 weeks after receiving this vaccine.
- if you are to receive gamma globulin or other immune globulins within 2 weeks after receiving this vaccine.

Side Effects of This Vaccine

Along with its needed effects, a vaccine may cause some unwanted effects. Although not all of these side effects may occur, if they do occur they may need medical attention.

Get emergency help immediately if any of the following side effects occur:

Symptoms of allergic reaction

Difficulty in breathing or swallowing; hives; itching, especially of feet or hands; reddening of skin, especially around ears; swelling of eyes, face, or inside of nose; unusual tiredness or weakness (sudden and severe)

Check with your doctor as soon as possible if any of the following side effects occur:

Less common

Pain or tenderness of eyes

Rare

Bruising or purple spots on skin; confusion; convulsions (seizures); headache (severe or continuing); pain, numbness, or tingling of hands, arms, legs, or feet; stiff neck; unusual irritability; vomiting

Other side effects may occur that usually do not need medical attention. However, check with your doctor if any of the following side effects continue or are bothersome:

More common

Burning or stinging at place of injection; skin rash; swelling of glands in neck

Less common

Aches or pain in joints; headache (mild), sore throat, runny nose, or fever; itching, swelling, redness, tenderness, or hard lump at place of injection; nausea; vague feeling of bodily discomfort

The above side effects (especially aches or pain in joints) are more likely to occur in adults, particularly women.

Some of the above side effects may not occur until 1 to 4 weeks after immunization and usually last less than 1 week. Aches or pain in joints may not occur until 1 to 10 weeks after immunization, and usually lasts less than 1 week. Check with your doctor if this side effect continues or is bothersome.

Other side effects not listed above may also occur in some patients. If you notice any other effects, check with your doctor.

Revised: 07/23/97

SALICYLATES Systemic

Some commonly used brand names are:

In the U.S.—

Acuprin 81[1]
Amigesic[8]
Anacin Caplets[2]
Anacin Maximum Strength[2]
Anacin Tablets[2]
Anaflex 750[8]
Arthritis Pain Ascriptin[3]
Arthritis Pain Formula[3]
Arthritis Strength Bufferin[3]
Arthropan[5]
Aspergum[1]
Aspirin Regimen Bayer Adult Low Dose[1]
Aspirin Regimen Bayer Regular Strength Caplets[1]
Aspir-Low[1]
Aspirtab[1]
Aspirtab-Max[1]
Backache Caplets[7]
Bayer Children's Aspirin[1]
Bayer Select Maximum Strength Backache Pain Relief Formula[7]
Bufferin Caplets[3]
Bufferin Tablets[3]
Buffex[3]
Buffinol[3]
Buffinol Extra[3]
Cama Arthritis Pain Reliever[3]
CMT[6]
Cope[4]
Disalcid[8]
Doan's Regular Strength Tablets[7]
Easprin[1]
Ecotrin Caplets[1]
Ecotrin Tablets[1]
Empirin[1]
Extended-release Bayer 8-Hour[1]
Extra Strength Bayer Arthritis Pain Formula Caplets[1]
Extra Strength Bayer Aspirin Caplets[1]
Extra Strength Bayer Aspirin Tablets[1]
Extra Strength Bayer Plus Caplets[3]
Gensan[2]
Genuine Bayer Aspirin Caplets[1]
Genuine Bayer Aspirin Tablets[1]
Halfprin[1]
Healthprin Adult Low Strength[1]
Healthprin Full Strength[1]
Healthprin Half-Dose[1]
Magan[7]
Magnaprin[3]
Marthritic[8]
Maximum Strength Arthritis Foundation Safety Coated Aspirin[1]
Maximum Strength Ascriptin[3]
Maximum Strength Doan's Analgesic Caplets[7]
Mobidin[7]
Mono-Gesic[8]
Norwich Aspirin[1]
P-A-C Revised Formula[2]
Regular Strength Ascriptin[3]
Salflex[8]
Salsitab[8]
Sloprin[1]
St. Joseph Adult Chewable Aspirin[1]
Tricosal[6]
Trilisate[6]
ZORprin[1]

In Canada#—

Anacin[2]
Anacin Extra Strength[2]
Antidol[2]
Apo-Asa[1]
Apo-ASEN[1]
Arco Pain Tablet[2]
Arthrisin[1]
Artria S.R.[1]
Aspergum[1]
Aspirin Caplets[1]
Aspirin Children's Tablets[1]
Aspirin, Coated[1]
Aspirin Plus Stomach Guard Extra Strength[3]
Aspirin Plus Stomach Guard Regular Strength[3]
Aspirin Tablets[1]
Astone[2]
Astrin[1]
Bufferin Caplets[3]
Bufferin Extra Strength Caplets[3]
C2[2]
Calmine[2]
C2 Buffered[4]
Coryphen[1]
Disalcid[8]
Doan's Backache Pills[7]
Dodd's Extra Strength[9]
Dodd's Pills[9]
Dolomine[2]
Entrophen Caplets[1]
Entrophen Extra Strength[1]
Entrophen 15 Maximum Strength Tablets[1]
Entrophen 10 Super Strength Caplets[1]
Entrophen Tablets[1]
Gin Pain Pills[9]
Headache Tablet[1]
Herbopyrine[2]
Instantine[2]
Kalmex[2]
Nervine[2]
Novasen[1]
Novasen Sp.C[1]
Pain Aid[2]
PMS-ASA[1]
Sero-Gesic[7]
217 Strong[2]
217[2]
Tri-Buffered ASA[3]
Trilisate[6]

Other commonly used names are:

acetylsalicylic acid[1]
ASA[1]#
choline magnesium trisalicylate[6]
salicylsalicylic acid[8]

Note: For quick reference, the following salicylates are numbered to match the corresponding brand names.

This information applies to the following medicines:

1. Aspirin (AS-pir-in)‡§#
2. Aspirin and Caffeine (kaf-EEN)‡
3. Buffered Aspirin‡#**
4. Buffered Aspirin and Caffeine#
5. Choline Salicylate (KOE-leen sa-LI-si-late)†
6. Choline and Magnesium (mag-NEE-zhum) Salicylates‡
7. Magnesium Salicylate
8. Salsalate (SAL-sa-late)‡
9. Sodium Salicylate‡

†Not commercially available in Canada.
‡Generic name product may be available in the U.S.
§Generic name product may be available in Canada.
#*Aspirin* is a brand name in Canada; acetylsalicylic acid is the generic name. ASA, a commonly used designation for aspirin (or acetylsalicylic acid) in both the U.S. and Canada, is the term used in Canadian product labeling.
**Some of the buffered aspirin products may be identified on the label as Aspirin (ASA), Alumina, and Magnesia or as Aspirin, Alumina, and Magnesium Oxide.

Description

Salicylates are used to relieve pain and reduce fever. Most salicylates are also used to relieve some symptoms caused by arthritis (rheumatism), such as swelling, stiffness, and joint pain. However, they do not cure arthritis and will help you only as long as you continue to take them.

Aspirin may also be used to lessen the chance of heart attack, stroke, or other problems that may occur when a blood vessel is blocked by blood clots. Aspirin helps prevent dangerous blood clots from forming. However, this effect of aspirin may increase the chance of serious bleeding in some people. Therefore, aspirin should be used for this purpose only when your doctor decides, after studying your medical condition and history, that the danger of blood clots is greater than the risk of bleeding. *Do not take aspirin to prevent blood clots or a heart attack unless it has been ordered by your doctor.*

Salicylates may also be used for other conditions as determined by your doctor.

The caffeine present in some of these products may provide additional relief of headache pain or faster pain relief.

Some salicylates are available only with your medical doctor's or dentist's prescription. Others are available without a prescription; however, your medical doctor or dentist may have special instructions on the proper dose of these medicines for your medical condition.

These medicines are available in the following dosage forms:

Oral

Aspirin

- Tablets (U.S. and Canada)
- Chewable tablets (U.S. and Canada)

- Chewing gum tablets (U.S. and Canada)
- Delayed-release (enteric-coated) tablets (U.S. and Canada)
- Extended-release tablets (U.S. and Canada)

Aspirin and Caffeine
- Capsules (Canada)
- Tablets (U.S. and Canada)

Buffered Aspirin
- Tablets (U.S. and Canada)

Buffered Aspirin and Caffeine
- Tablets (U.S. and Canada)

Choline Salicylate
- Oral solution (U.S.)

Choline and Magnesium Salicylates
- Oral solution (U.S.)
- Tablets (U.S. and Canada)

Magnesium Salicylate
- Tablets (U.S. and Canada)

Salsalate
- Capsules (U.S.)
- Tablets (U.S. and Canada)

Sodium Salicylate
- Tablets (Canada)
- Delayed-release (enteric-coated) tablets (U.S.)

Rectal

Aspirin
- Suppositories (U.S. and Canada)

Before Using This Medicine

If you are taking this medicine without a prescription, carefully read and follow any precautions on the label. For salicylates, the following should be considered:

Allergies—Tell your doctor if you have ever had any unusual or allergic reaction to aspirin or other salicylates, including methyl salicylate (oil of wintergreen), or to any of the following medicines:

Diclofenac (e.g., Voltaren)
Diflunisal (e.g., Dolobid)
Etodolac (e.g., Lodine)
Fenoprofen (e.g., Nalfon)
Floctafenine (e.g., Idarac)
Flurbiprofen, oral (e.g., Ansaid)
Ibuprofen (e.g., Motrin)
Indomethacin (e.g., Indocin)
Ketoprofen (e.g., Orudis)
Ketorolac (e.g., Toradol)
Meclofenamate (e.g., Meclomen)
Mefenamic acid (e.g., Ponstel)
Nabumetone (e.g., Relafen)
Naproxen (e.g., Naprosyn)
Oxaprozin (e.g., Daypro)
Oxyphenbutazone (e.g., Tandearil)
Phenylbutazone (e.g., Butazolidin)
Piroxicam (e.g., Feldene)
Sulindac (e.g., Clinoril)
Suprofen (e.g., Suprol)
Tenoxicam (e.g., Mobiflex)
Tiaprofenic acid (e.g., Surgam)
Tolmetin (e.g., Tolectin)
Zomepirac (e.g., Zomax)

Also tell your health care professional if you are allergic to any other substances, such as foods, preservatives, or dyes.

Diet—Make certain your health care professional knows if you are on a low-sodium diet. Regular use of large amounts of sodium salicylate (as for arthritis) can add a large amount of sodium to your diet. Sodium salicylate contains 46 mg of sodium in each 325-mg tablet and 92 mg of sodium in each 650-mg tablet.

Pregnancy—Salicylates have not been shown to cause birth defects in humans. Studies on birth defects in humans have been done with aspirin but not with other salicylates. However, salicylates caused birth defects in animal studies.

Some reports have suggested that too much use of aspirin late in pregnancy may cause a decrease in the newborn's weight and possible death of the fetus or newborn infant. However, the mothers in these reports had been taking much larger amounts of aspirin than are usually recommended. Studies of mothers taking aspirin in the doses that are usually recommended did not show these unwanted effects. However, there is a chance that regular use of salicylates late in pregnancy may cause unwanted effects on the heart or blood flow in the fetus or in the newborn infant.

Use of salicylates, especially aspirin, during the last 2 weeks of pregnancy may cause bleeding problems in the fetus before or during delivery or in the newborn infant. Also, too much use of salicylates during the last 3 months of pregnancy may increase the length of pregnancy, prolong labor, cause other problems during delivery, or cause severe bleeding in the mother before, during, or after delivery. *Do not take aspirin during the last 3 months of pregnancy unless it has been ordered by your doctor.*

Studies in humans have not shown that caffeine (present in some aspirin products) causes birth defects. However, studies in animals have shown that caffeine causes birth defects when given in very large doses (amounts equal to those present in 12 to 24 cups of coffee a day).

Breast-feeding—Salicylates pass into the breast milk. Although salicylates have not been reported to cause problems in nursing babies, it is possible that problems may occur if large amounts are taken regularly, as for arthritis (rheumatism).

Caffeine passes into the breast milk in small amounts.

Children—*Do not give aspirin or other salicylates to a child or a teenager with a fever or other symptoms of a virus infection, especially flu or chickenpox, without first discussing its use with your child's doctor.* This is very important because salicylates may cause a serious illness called Reye's syndrome in children and teenagers with fever caused by a virus infection, especially flu or chickenpox.

Some children may need to take aspirin or another salicylate regularly (as for arthritis). However, your child's doctor may want to stop the medicine for a while if a fever or other symptoms of a virus infection occur. Discuss this with your child's doctor, so that you will know ahead of time what to do if your child gets sick.

Children who do not have a virus infection may also be more sensitive to the effects of salicylates, especially if they have a fever or have lost large amounts of body fluid because of vomiting, diarrhea, or sweating. This may increase the chance of side effects during treatment.

Older adults—Elderly people are especially sensitive to the effects of salicylates. This may increase the chance of side effects during treatment.

Other medicines—Although certain medicines should not be used together at all, in other cases two different medicines may be used together even if an interaction might occur. In these cases, your doctor may want to change the dose, or other precautions may be necessary. When you are taking a salicylate, it is especially important that your health care professional know if you are taking any of the following:

- Anticoagulants (blood thinners) or
- Carbenicillin by injection (e.g., Geopen) or
- Cefamandole (e.g., Mandol) or
- Cefoperazone (e.g., Cefobid) or
- Cefotetan (e.g., Cefotan) or
- Dipyridamole (e.g., Persantine) or
- Divalproex (e.g., Depakote) or
- Heparin or
- Inflammation or pain medicine, except narcotics, or
- Pentoxifylline (e.g., Trental) or
- Plicamycin (e.g., Mithracin) or
- Ticarcillin (e.g., Ticar) or
- Valproic acid (e.g., Depakene)—Taking these medicines together with a salicylate, especially aspirin, may increase the chance of bleeding
- Antidiabetics, oral (diabetes medicine you take by mouth)—Salicylates may increase the effects of the antidiabetic medicine; a change in dose may be needed if a salicylate is taken regularly
- Ciprofloxacin (e.g., Cipro) or
- Enoxacin (e.g., Penetrex) or
- Itraconazole (e.g., Sporanox) or
- Ketoconazole (e.g., Nizoral) or
- Lomefloxacin (e.g., Maxaquin) or
- Norfloxacin (e.g., Noroxin) or
- Ofloxacin (e.g., Floxin) or
- Tetracyclines (medicine for infection), taken by mouth—Buffered aspirin, choline and magnesium salicylates, and magnesium salicylate may keep these medicines from working properly if taken too close to them
- Methotrexate (e.g., Mexate) or
- Vancomycin (e.g., Vancocin)—The chance of serious side effects may be increased
- Probenecid (e.g., Benemid)—Salicylates can keep probenecid from working properly for treating gout
- Sulfinpyrazone (e.g., Anturane)—Salicylates can keep sulfinpyrazone from working properly for treating gout; also, taking a salicylate, especially aspirin, with sulfinpyrazone may increase the chance of bleeding
- Urinary alkalizers (medicine that makes the urine less acid, such as acetazolamide [e.g., Diamox], calcium- and/or magnesium-containing antacids, dichlorphenamide [e.g., Daranide], methazolamide [e.g., Neptazane], potassium or sodium citrate and/or citric acid, sodium bicarbonate [baking soda])—These medicines may make the salicylate less effective by causing it to be removed from the body more quickly

Other medical problems—The presence of other medical problems may affect the use of salicylates. Make sure you tell your doctor if you have any other medical problems, especially:

- Anemia or
- Overactive thyroid or
- Stomach ulcer or other stomach problems—Salicylates may make your condition worse
- Asthma, allergies, and nasal polyps (history of) or
- Glucose-6-phosphate dehydrogenase (G6PD) deficiency or
- High blood pressure (hypertension) or
- Kidney disease or
- Liver disease—The chance of side effects may be increased.
- Gout—Salicylates can make this condition worse and can also lessen the effects of some medicines used to treat gout
- Heart disease—The chance of some side effects may be increased. Also, the caffeine present in some aspirin products can make some kinds of heart disease worse
- Hemophilia or other bleeding problems—The chance of bleeding may be increased, especially with aspirin

Proper Use of This Medicine

Take this medicine after meals or with food (except for enteric-coated capsules or tablets and aspirin suppositories) to lessen stomach irritation.

Take tablet or capsule forms of this medicine with a full glass (8 ounces) of water. Also, do not lie down for about 15 to 30 minutes after swallowing the medicine. This helps to prevent irritation that may lead to trouble in swallowing.

For patients taking *aspirin (including buffered aspirin and/or products containing caffeine):*

- *Do not use any product that contains aspirin if it has a strong, vinegar-like odor.* This odor means the medicine is breaking down. If you have any questions about this, check with your health care professional.
- If you are to take any medicine that contains aspirin within 7 days after having your tonsils removed, a tooth pulled, or other dental or mouth surgery, be sure to swallow the aspirin whole. Do not chew aspirin during this time.
- Do not place any medicine that contains aspirin directly on a tooth or gum surface. This may cause a burn.
- There are several different forms of aspirin or buffered aspirin tablets. If you are using:

  —chewable aspirin tablets, they may be chewed, dissolved in liquid, crushed, or swallowed whole.

  —delayed-release (enteric-coated) aspirin tablets, they must be swallowed whole. Do not crush them or break them up before taking.

  —extended-release (long-acting) aspirin tablets, check with your pharmacist as to how they should be taken. Some may be broken up (but must not be crushed) before swallowing if you cannot swallow them whole. Others should not be broken up and must be swallowed whole.

To use *aspirin suppositories:*
- If the suppository is too soft to insert, chill it in the refrigerator for 30 minutes or run cold water over it before removing the foil wrapper.
- To insert the suppository: First remove the foil wrapper and moisten the suppository with cold water. Lie down on your side and use your finger to push the suppository well up into the rectum.

To take *choline and magnesium salicylates (e.g., Trilisate) oral solution:*
- The liquid may be mixed with fruit juice just before taking.
- Drink a full glass (8 ounces) of water after taking the medicine.

To take *enteric-coated sodium salicylate tablets:*
- The tablets must be swallowed whole. Do not crush them or break them up before taking.

Unless otherwise directed by your medical doctor or dentist:
- Do not take more of this medicine than recommended on the label, to lessen the chance of side effects.
- Children up to 12 years of age should not take this medicine more than 5 times a day.

When used for arthritis (rheumatism), this medicine must be taken regularly as ordered by your doctor in order for it to help you. Up to 2 to 3 weeks or longer may pass before you feel the full effects of this medicine.

Dosing—The dose of these medicines will be different for different patients. *Follow your doctor's orders or the directions on the label.* The following information includes only the average doses of these medicines. *If your dose is different, do not change it* unless your doctor tells you to do so.

The number of capsules or tablets or teaspoonfuls of solution that you take depends on the strength of the medicine. Also, *the number of doses you take each day, the time allowed between doses, and the length of time you take the medicine depend on whether you are taking a long-acting or a short-acting form of the medicine and the medical problem for which you are taking the salicylate.*

For aspirin
- For *short-acting tablet, chewable tablet, and delayed-release (enteric-coated) tablet oral* dosage forms:
  —For pain or fever:
  - Adults and teenagers—325 to 500 milligrams (mg) every three or four hours, 650 mg every four to six hours, or 1000 mg every six hours as needed.
  - Children up to 2 years of age—Dose must be determined by your doctor.
  - Children 2 to 4 years of age—160 mg every four hours as needed.
  - Children 4 to 6 years of age—240 mg every four hours as needed.
  - Children 6 to 9 years of age—320 to 325 mg every four hours as needed.
  - Children 9 to 11 years of age—320 to 400 mg every four hours as needed.
  - Children 11 to 12 years of age—320 to 480 mg every four hours as needed.

  —For arthritis:
  - Adults and teenagers—A total of 3600 to 5400 mg a day, divided into several smaller doses.
  - Children—A total of 80 to 100 mg per kilogram (kg) (32 to 40 mg per pound) of body weight a day, divided into several smaller doses.

  —For preventing a heart attack, stroke, or other problems caused by blood clots:
  - Adults—Most people will take 81, 162.5, or 325 mg a day or 325 mg every other day. Some people taking aspirin to prevent a stroke may need as much as 1000 mg a day.
  - Children—Use and dose must be determined by your doctor.
- For *chewing gum tablet* dosage form:
  —For pain:
  - Adults and teenagers—2 tablets every four hours as needed.
  - Children up to 3 years of age—Dose must be determined by your doctor.
  - Children 3 to 6 years of age—1 tablet (227 mg) up to three times a day.
  - Children 6 to 12 years of age—1 or 2 tablets (227 mg each) up to four times a day.
- For *long-acting oral* dosage forms (extended-release tablets):
  —For pain:
  - Adults and teenagers—1 or 2 tablets twice a day.
  - Children—The long-acting aspirin tablets are too strong for use in children.

  —For arthritis:
  - Adults and teenagers—1 or 2 tablets twice a day, at first. Your doctor will then adjust your dose as needed.
  - Children—The long-acting aspirin tablets are too strong for use in children.
- For *rectal* dosage form (suppositories):
  —For pain or fever:
  - Adults and teenagers—325 to 650 mg every four hours as needed.
  - Children up to 2 years of age—Dose must be determined by your doctor.
  - Children 2 to 4 years of age—160 mg every four hours as needed.
  - Children 4 to 6 years of age—240 mg every four hours as needed.
  - Children 6 to 9 years of age—325 mg every four hours as needed.
  - Children 9 to 11 years of age—325 to 400 mg every four hours as needed.

• Children 11 to 12 years of age—325 to 480 mg every four hours as needed.

—For arthritis:

• Adults and teenagers—A total of 3600 to 5400 mg a day, divided into several smaller doses.

• Children—A total of 80 to 100 mg per kilogram (kg) (32 to 40 mg per pound) of body weight a day, divided into several smaller doses.

For aspirin and caffeine

• For *oral capsule* dosage form:

—For pain or fever:

• Adults and teenagers—325 to 500 milligrams (mg) of aspirin every three or four hours, 650 mg of aspirin every four to six hours, or 1000 mg of aspirin every six hours as needed.

• Children up to 6 years of age—Aspirin and caffeine capsules are too strong for use in children up to 6 years of age.

• Children 6 to 9 years of age—325 mg every four hours as needed.

• Children 9 to 12 years of age—325 to 400 mg every four hours as needed.

—For arthritis:

• Adults and teenagers—A total of 3600 to 5400 mg of aspirin a day, divided into several smaller doses.

• Children—A total of 80 to 100 mg per kilogram (kg) (32 to 40 mg per pound) of body weight a day, divided into several smaller doses.

—For preventing a heart attack, stroke, or other problems caused by blood clots:

• Adults—325 mg a day or every other day. People who take smaller doses of aspirin will have to use a different product. Some people taking aspirin to prevent a stroke may need as much as 1000 mg a day.

• Children—Use and dose must be determined by your doctor.

• For *oral tablet* dosage form:

—For pain or fever:

• Adults and teenagers—325 to 500 mg of aspirin every three or four hours, 650 mg of aspirin every four to six hours, or 1000 mg of aspirin every six hours as needed.

• Children up to 9 years of age—Aspirin and caffeine tablets are too strong for use in children up to 9 years of age.

• Children 9 to 12 years of age—325 to 400 mg every four hours as needed.

—For arthritis:

• Adults and teenagers—A total of 3600 to 5400 mg of aspirin a day, divided into several smaller doses.

• Children—A total of 80 to 100 mg per kg (32 to 40 mg per pound) of body weight a day, divided into several smaller doses.

—For preventing a heart attack, stroke, or other problems caused by blood clots:

• Adults—325 mg a day or every other day. People who take smaller doses of aspirin will have to use a different product. Some people taking aspirin to prevent a stroke may need as much as 1000 mg a day.

• Children—Use and dose must be determined by your doctor.

For buffered aspirin

• For *oral* dosage form (tablets):

—For pain or fever:

• Adults and teenagers—325 to 500 milligrams (mg) of aspirin every three or four hours, 650 mg of aspirin every four to six hours, or 1000 mg of aspirin every six hours as needed.

• Children up to 2 years of age—Dose must be determined by your doctor.

• Children 2 to 4 years of age—One-half of a 325-mg tablet every four hours as needed.

• Children 4 to 6 years of age—Three-fourths of a 325-mg tablet every four hours as needed.

• Children 6 to 9 years of age—One 325-mg tablet every four hours as needed.

• Children 9 to 11 years of age—One or one and one-fourth 325-mg tablets every four hours as needed.

• Children 11 to 12 years of age—One or one and one-half 325-mg tablets every four hours as needed.

—For arthritis:

• Adults and teenagers—A total of 3600 to 5400 mg of aspirin a day, divided into several smaller doses.

• Children—A total of 80 to 100 mg per kilogram (kg) (32 to 40 mg per pound) of body weight a day, divided into several smaller doses.

—For preventing a heart attack, stroke, or other problems caused by blood clots:

• Adults—325 mg a day or every other day. People who take smaller doses of aspirin will have to use a different product. Some people taking aspirin to prevent a stroke may need as much as 1000 mg a day.

• Children—Use and dose must be determined by your doctor.

For buffered aspirin and caffeine

• For *oral* dosage form (tablets):

—For pain or fever:

• Adults and teenagers—325 or 421 milligrams (mg) of aspirin every three or four hours, 650 mg of aspirin every four to six hours, or 842 mg of aspirin every six hours as needed.

• Children up to 2 years of age—Dose must be determined by your doctor.

• Children 2 to 4 years of age—One-half of a 325-mg tablet every four hours as needed.

• Children 4 to 6 years of age—Three-fourths of a 325-mg tablet every four hours as needed.

• Children 6 to 9 years of age—One 325-mg or 421-mg tablet every four hours as needed.

• Children 9 to 11 years of age—One or one and one-fourth 325-mg tablets every four hours as needed.

• Children 11 to 12 years of age—One or one and one-half 325-mg tablets, or one 421-mg tablet, every four hours as needed.

—For arthritis:

• Adults and teenagers—A total of 3600 to 5400 mg of aspirin a day, divided into several smaller doses.

• Children—A total of 80 to 100 mg per kilogram (kg) (32 to 40 mg per pound) of body weight a day, divided into several smaller doses.

—For preventing a heart attack, stroke, or other problems caused by blood clots:

• Adults—162.5 or 325 mg (one-half or one 325-mg tablet) a day or 325 mg every other day. People who need smaller doses of aspirin will have to use a different product. Some people taking aspirin to prevent a stroke may need as much as 1000 mg a day.

• Children—Use and dose must be determined by your doctor.

For choline salicylate

• For *oral* dosage form (oral solution):

—For pain or fever:

• Adults and teenagers—One-half or three-fourths of a teaspoonful every three hours, one-half or one teaspoonful every four hours, or one or one and one-half teaspoonfuls every six hours as needed.

• Children up to 2 years of age—Dose must be determined by your doctor.

• Children 2 to 4 years of age—1.25 milliliters (mL) (one-fourth of a teaspoonful) every four hours as needed. This amount should be measured by a special dropper or measuring spoon.

• Children 4 to 6 years of age—1.66 mL every four hours as needed. This amount should be measured by a special dropper or measuring spoon.

• Children 6 to 11 years of age—2.5 mL (one-half of a teaspoonful) every four hours as needed. This amount should be measured by a special measuring spoon.

• Children 11 to 12 years of age—2.5 to 3.75 mL (one-half to three-fourths of a teaspoonful) every four hours as needed. This amount should be measured by a special measuring spoon.

—For arthritis:

• Adults—A total of five and one-half to eight teaspoonfuls a day, divided into several smaller doses.

• Children—A total of 0.6 to 0.7 mL per kilogram (kg) (0.25 to 0.28 mL per pound) of body weight a day, divided into several smaller doses.

For choline and magnesium salicylates

• For *oral* dosage forms (oral solution or tablets):

—For pain or fever:

• Adults and teenagers—A total of 2000 to 3000 milligrams (mg) a day, divided into two or three doses.

• Children weighing up to 37 kilograms (kg) (about 89 pounds)—A total of 50 mg per kg (20 mg per pound) of body weight a day, divided into two doses.

• Children weighing more than 37 kg (90 pounds or more)—2200 mg a day, divided into two doses.

—For inflammation or arthritis:

• Adults and teenagers—A total of 3000 mg a day, divided into two or three doses, to start. Your doctor will then adjust your dose as needed.

• Children weighing up to 37 kg (about 89 pounds)—A total of 50 mg per kg (20 mg per pound) of body weight a day, divided into two doses.

• Children weighing more than 37 kg (90 pounds or more)—2200 mg a day, divided into two doses.

For magnesium salicylate

• For *oral* dosage form (tablets):

—For pain:

• Adults and teenagers—2 regular-strength tablets every four hours, up to a maximum of 12 tablets a day, or 2 extra-strength tablets every eight hours, up to a maximum of 8 tablets a day.

• Children—Dose must be determined by your doctor.

For salsalate

• For *oral* dosage forms (capsules or tablets):

—For arthritis:

• Adults and teenagers—500 to 1000 milligrams (mg) two or three times a day, to start. Your doctor will then adjust your dose as needed.

• Children—Dose must be determined by your doctor.

For sodium salicylate

• For *oral* dosage forms (tablets or delayed-release [enteric-coated] tablets):

—For pain or fever:

• Adults and teenagers—325 or 650 milligrams (mg) every four hours as needed.

• Children up to 6 years of age—This medicine is too strong for use in children younger than 6 years of age.

• Children 6 years of age and older—325 mg every four hours as needed.

—For arthritis:

• Adults and teenagers—A total of 3600 to 5400 mg a day, divided into several smaller doses.

• Children—A total of 80 to 100 mg per kilogram (kg) (32 to 40 mg per pound) of body weight a day, divided into several smaller doses.

Missed dose—If your medical doctor or dentist has ordered you to take this medicine according to a regular schedule and you miss a dose, take it as soon as you remember. However, if it is almost time for your next dose, skip the missed dose and go back to your regular dosing schedule. Do not double doses.

Storage—To store this medicine:

- Keep out of the reach of children. Overdose is very dangerous in young children.
- Store away from heat and direct light.
- Do not store tablets or capsules in the bathroom, near the kitchen sink, or in other damp places. Heat or moisture may cause the medicine to break down.
- Keep liquid forms of this medicine from freezing.
- Store aspirin suppositories in a cool place. It is usually best to keep them in the refrigerator, but keep them from freezing.
- Do not keep outdated medicine or medicine no longer needed. Be sure that any discarded medicine is out of the reach of children.

Precautions While Using This Medicine

Check the labels of all nonprescription (over-the-counter [OTC]) and prescription medicines you now take. If any contain aspirin or other salicylates (including bismuth subsalicylate [e.g., Pepto-Bismol] or any shampoo or skin medicine that contains salicylic acid or any other salicylate), check with your health care professional. Taking or using them together with this medicine may cause an overdose.

If you will be taking salicylates for a long time (more than 5 days in a row for children or 10 days in a row for adults) or in large amounts, *your doctor should check your progress at regular visits.*

Check with your medical doctor or dentist:

- If you are taking this medicine to relieve pain and the pain lasts for more than 10 days (5 days for children) or if the pain gets worse, if new symptoms occur, or if redness or swelling is present. These could be signs of a serious condition that needs medical or dental treatment.
- If you are taking this medicine to bring down a fever, and the fever lasts for more than 3 days or returns, if the fever gets worse, if new symptoms occur, or if redness or swelling is present. These could be signs of a serious condition that needs treatment.
- If you are taking this medicine for a sore throat, and the sore throat is very painful, lasts for more than 2 days, or occurs together with or is followed by fever, headache, skin rash, nausea, or vomiting.
- If you are taking this medicine regularly, as for arthritis (rheumatism), and you notice a ringing or buzzing in your ears or severe or continuing headaches. These are often the first signs that too much salicylate is being taken. Your doctor may want to change the amount of medicine you are taking every day.

For patients taking *aspirin to lessen the chance of heart attack, stroke, or other problems caused by blood clots:*

- *Take only the amount of aspirin ordered by your doctor.* If you need a medicine to relieve pain, a fever, or arthritis, your doctor may not want you to take extra aspirin. It is a good idea to discuss this with your doctor, so that you will know ahead of time what medicine to take.
- *Do not stop taking this medicine for any reason without first checking with the doctor who directed you to take it.*

Taking certain other medicines together with a salicylate may increase the chance of unwanted effects. The risk will depend on how much of each medicine you take every day, and on how long you take the medicines together. If your doctor directs you to take these medicines together on a regular basis, follow his or her directions carefully. However, *do not take any of the following medicines together with a salicylate for more than a few days, unless your doctor has directed you to do so and is following your progress*:

Acetaminophen (e.g., Tylenol)
Diclofenac (e.g., Voltaren)
Diflunisal (e.g., Dolobid)
Etodolac (e.g., Lodine)
Fenoprofen (e.g., Nalfon)
Floctafenine (e.g., Idarac)
Flurbiprofen, oral (e.g., Ansaid)
Ibuprofen (e.g., Motrin)
Indomethacin (e.g., Indocin)
Ketoprofen (e.g., Orudis)
Ketorolac (e.g., Toradol)
Meclofenamate (e.g., Meclomen)
Mefenamic acid (e.g., Ponstel)
Nabumetone (e.g., Relafen)
Naproxen (e.g., Naprosyn)
Oxaprozin (e.g., Daypro)
Phenylbutazone (e.g., Butazolidin)
Piroxicam (e.g., Feldene)
Sulindac (e.g., Clinoril)
Tenoxicam (e.g., Mobiflex)
Tiaprofenic acid (e.g., Surgam)
Tolmetin (e.g., Tolectin)

For *diabetic patients:*

- False urine sugar test results may occur if you are regularly taking large amounts of salicylates, such as:

  —*Aspirin:* 8 or more 325-mg (5-grain), or 4 or more 500-mg or 650-mg (10-grain), or 3 or more 800-mg (or higher strength), doses a day.

  —*Buffered aspirin or*
  —*Sodium salicylate:* 8 or more 325-mg (5-grain), or 4 or more 500-mg or 650-mg (10-grain), doses a day.

  —*Choline salicylate:* 4 or more teaspoonfuls (each teaspoonful containing 870 mg) a day.

—*Choline and magnesium salicylates:* 5 or more 500-mg tablets or teaspoonfuls, 4 or more 750-mg tablets, or 2 or more 1000-mg tablets, a day.

—*Magnesium salicylate:* 7 or more regular-strength, or 4 or more extra-strength, tablets a day.

—*Salsalate:* 4 or more 500-mg doses, or 3 or more 750-mg doses, a day.

- Smaller doses or occasional use of salicylates usually will not affect urine sugar tests. However, check with your health care professional (especially if your diabetes is not well-controlled) if:

  —you are not sure how much salicylate you are taking every day.

  —you notice any change in your urine sugar test results.

  —you have any other questions about this possible problem.

Do not take aspirin for 5 days before any surgery, including dental surgery, unless otherwise directed by your medical doctor or dentist. Taking aspirin during this time may cause bleeding problems.

For patients taking *buffered aspirin, choline and magnesium salicylates (e.g., Trilisate), or magnesium salicylate (e.g., Doan's):*

- Buffered aspirin, choline and magnesium salicylates, or magnesium salicylate can keep many other medicines, especially some medicines used to treat infections, from working properly. This problem can be prevented by not taking the 2 medicines too close together. Ask your health care professional how long you should wait between taking a medicine for infection and taking buffered aspirin, choline and magnesium salicylates, or magnesium salicylate.

If you are taking a laxative containing cellulose, take the salicylate at least 2 hours before or after you take the laxative. Taking these medicines too close together may lessen the effects of the salicylate.

For patients taking this medicine by mouth:

- Stomach problems may be more likely to occur if you drink alcoholic beverages while being treated with this medicine, especially if you are taking it in high doses or for a long time. Check with your doctor if you have any questions about this.

For patients using *aspirin suppositories:*

- Aspirin suppositories may cause irritation of the rectum. Check with your doctor if this occurs.

Salicylates may interfere with the results of some medical tests. Before you have any medical tests, tell the doctor in charge if you have taken any of these medicines within the past week. If possible, it is best to check with the doctor first, to find out whether the medicine may be taken during the week before the test.

For patients taking one of the products that contain *caffeine:*

- Caffeine may interfere with the result of a test that uses adenosine (e.g., Adenocard) or dipyridamole (e.g., Persantine) to help find out how well your blood is flowing through certain blood vessels. Therefore, you should not have any caffeine for at least 8 to 12 hours before the test.

If you think that you or anyone else may have taken an overdose, get emergency help at once. Taking an overdose of these medicines may cause unconsciousness or death. Signs of overdose include convulsions (seizures), hearing loss, confusion, ringing or buzzing in the ears, severe drowsiness or tiredness, severe excitement or nervousness, and fast or deep breathing.

Side Effects of This Medicine

Along with its needed effects, a medicine may cause some unwanted effects. When this medicine is used for short periods of time at low doses, side effects usually are rare. Although not all of the following side effects may occur, if they do occur they may need medical attention.

Get emergency help immediately if any of the following side effects occur:

Any loss of hearing; bloody urine; confusion; convulsions (seizures); diarrhea (severe or continuing); difficulty in swallowing; dizziness, lightheadedness, or feeling faint (severe); drowsiness (severe); excitement or nervousness (severe); fast or deep breathing; flushing, redness, or other change in skin color; hallucinations (seeing, hearing, or feeling things that are not there); increased sweating; increased thirst; nausea or vomiting (severe or continuing); shortness of breath, troubled breathing, tightness in chest, or wheezing; stomach pain (severe or continuing); swelling of eyelids, face, or lips; unexplained fever; uncontrollable flapping movements of the hands (especially in elderly patients); vision problems

Symptoms of overdose in children

Changes in behavior; drowsiness or tiredness (severe); fast or deep breathing

Also, check with your doctor as soon as possible if any of the following side effects occur:

Less common or rare

Abdominal or stomach pain, cramping, or burning (severe); bloody or black, tarry stools; headache (severe or continuing); ringing or buzzing in ears (continuing); skin rash, hives, or itching; unusual tiredness or weakness; vomiting of blood or material that looks like coffee grounds

Other side effects may occur that usually do not need medical attention. These side effects may go away during treatment as your body adjusts to the medicine. However, check with your health care professional if any of the following side effects continue or are bothersome:

More common

Abdominal or stomach cramps, pain, or discomfort (mild to moderate); heartburn or indigestion; nausea or vomiting

Less common
Trouble in sleeping, nervousness, or jitters (only for products containing caffeine)

Other side effects not listed above may also occur in some patients. If you notice any other effects, check with your doctor.

Revised: August 1990
Interim revision: 07/25/95

SALICYLIC ACID Topical

Some commonly used brand names are:

In the U.S.—

Antinea
Buf-Puf Acne Cleansing Bar with Vitamin E
Calicylic Creme
Clearasil Clearstick Maximum Strength Topical Solution
Clearasil Clearstick Regular Strength Topical Solution
Clearasil Double Textured Pads Maximum Strength
Clearasil Double Textured Pads Regular Strength
Clearasil Medicated Deep Cleanser Topical Solution
Clear Away
Clear by Design Medicated Cleansing Pads
Compound W Gel
Compound W Liquid
Duofilm
Duoplant Topical Solution
Freezone
Gordofilm
Hydrisalic
Ionax Astringent Skin Cleanser Topical Solution
Ionil Plus Shampoo
Ionil Shampoo
Keralyt
Keratex Gel
Lactisol
Listerex Golden Scrub Lotion
Listerex Herbal Scrub Lotion
Mediplast
Noxzema Anti-Acne Gel
Noxzema Anti-Acne Pads Maximum Strength
Noxzema Anti-Acne Pads Regular Strength
Occlusal-HP Topical Solution
Occlusal Topical Solution
Off-Ezy Topical Solution Corn & Callus Remover Kit
Off-Ezy Topical Solution Wart Removal Kit
Oxy Clean Medicated Cleanser
Oxy Clean Medicated Pads Maximum Strength
Oxy Clean Medicated Pads Regular Strength
Oxy Clean Medicated Pads Sensitive Skin
Oxy Night Watch Maximum Strength Lotion
Oxy Night Watch Sensitive Skin Lotion
Paplex
Paplex Ultra
Propa pH Medicated Acne Cream Maximum Strength
Propa pH Medicated Cleansing Pads Maximum Strength
Propa pH Medicated Cleansing Pads Sensitive Skin
Propa pH Perfectly Clear Skin Cleanser Topical Solution Normal/Combination Skin
Propa pH Perfectly Clear Skin Cleanser Topical Solution Oily Skin
Propa pH Perfectly Clear Skin Cleanser Topical Solution Sensitive Skin Formula
P&S
Salac
Salacid
Sal-Acid Plaster
Salactic Film Topical Solution
Sal-Clens Plus Shampoo
Sal-Clens Shampoo
Saligel
Salonil
Sal-Plant Gel Topical Solution
Sebucare
Stri-Dex Dual Textured Pads Maximum Strength
Stri-Dex Dual Textured Pads Regular Strength
Stri-Dex Dual Textured Pads Sensitive Skin
Stri-Dex Maximum Strength Pads
Stri-Dex Regular Strength Pads
Stri-Dex Super Scrub Pads
Trans-Plantar
Trans-Ver-Sal
Verukan-HP Topical Solution
Verukan Topical Solution
Viranol
Viranol Ultra
Wart-Off Topical Solution
X-Seb

Generic name product may also be available.

In Canada—

Compound W Gel
Compound W Liquid
Cuplex Gel
Occlusal-HP Topical Solution
Occlusal Topical Solution
Oxy Clean Extra Strength Medicated Pads
Oxy Clean Extra Strength Cleanser Topical Solution
Oxy Clean Medicated Soap
Oxy Clean Regular Strength Medicated Cleanser Topical Solution
Oxy Clean Regular Strength Medicated Pads
Oxy Clean Sensitive Skin Cleanser Topical Solution
Oxy Clean Sensitive Skin Pads
Oxy Night Watch Night Time Acne Medication Extra Strength Lotion
Oxy Night Watch Night Time Acne Medication Regular Strength Lotion
Oxy Sensitive Skin Vanishing Formula Lotion
Salac
Tersac Cleansing Gel
Trans-Ver-Sal

Description

Salicylic acid (sal-i-SILL-ik AS-id) is used to treat many skin disorders, such as acne, dandruff, psoriasis, seborrheic dermatitis of the skin and scalp, calluses, corns, common warts, and plantar warts, depending on the dosage form and strength of the preparation.

Some of these preparations are available only with your doctor's prescription. Others are available without a prescription; however, your doctor may have special instructions on the proper use of salicylic acid for your medical condition.

Salicylic acid is available in the following dosage forms:

Topical
- Cream (U.S.)
- Gel (U.S. and Canada)
- Lotion (U.S. and Canada)
- Ointment (U.S.)
- Pads (U.S. and Canada)
- Plaster (U.S. and Canada)
- Shampoo (U.S.)
- Soap (U.S. and Canada)
- Topical solution (U.S. and Canada)

Before Using This Medicine

If you are using this medicine without a prescription, carefully read and follow any precautions on the label. For salicylic acid, the following should be considered:

Allergies—Tell your doctor if you have ever had any unusual or allergic reaction to salicylic acid. Also tell your health care professional if you are allergic to any other substances, such as preservatives or dyes.

Pregnancy—This medicine may be absorbed through the mother's skin. Salicylic acid has not been studied in pregnant women. However, studies in animals have shown that salicylic acid causes birth defects when given orally in doses about 6 times the highest dose recommended for topical use in humans. Before using this medicine, make sure your doctor knows if you are pregnant or if you may become pregnant, especially if you will be using salicylic acid on large areas of your body.

Breast-feeding—Salicylic acid may be absorbed through the mother's skin. However, topical salicylic acid has not been reported to cause problems in nursing babies.

Children—Young children may be at increased risk of unwanted effects because of increased absorption of salicylic acid through the skin. Also, young children may be more likely to get skin irritation from salicylic acid. Salicylic acid should not be applied to large areas of the body, used for long periods of time, or used under occlusive dressing (air-tight covering, such as kitchen plastic wrap) in infants and children.

Older adults—Elderly people are more likely to have age-related blood vessel disease. This may increase the chance of problems during treatment with this medicine.

Other medicines—Although certain medicines should not be used together at all, in other cases two different medicines may be used together even if an interaction might occur. In these cases, your doctor may want to change the dose, or other precautions may be necessary. Tell your health care professional if you are using any other prescription or nonprescription (over-the-counter [OTC]) medicine.

Other medical problems—The presence of other medical problems may affect the use of salicylic acid, especially if you are using a 5% or stronger salicylic acid preparation. Make sure you tell your doctor if you have any other medical problems, especially:

- Blood vessel disease
- Diabetes mellitus (sugar diabetes)—Use of this medicine may cause severe redness or ulceration, especially on the hands or feet
- Inflammation, irritation, or infection of the skin—Use of this medicine may cause severe irritation if applied to inflamed, irritated, or infected area of the skin

Proper Use of This Medicine

It is very important that you use this medicine only as directed. Do not use more of it, do not use it more often, and do not use it for a longer time than recommended on the label, unless otherwise directed by your doctor. To do so may increase the chance of absorption through the skin and the chance of salicylic acid poisoning.

If your doctor has ordered an occlusive dressing (airtight covering, such as kitchen plastic wrap) to be applied over this medicine, make sure you know how to apply it. Since an occlusive dressing will increase the amount of medicine absorbed through your skin and the possibility of salicylic acid poisoning, use it only as directed. If you have any questions about this, check with your doctor.

Keep this medicine away from the eyes and other mucous membranes, such as the mouth and inside of the nose. If you should accidentally get some in your eyes or on other mucous membranes, immediately flush them with water for 15 minutes.

To use the *cream, lotion, or ointment form* of salicylic acid:

- Apply enough medicine to cover the affected area, and rub in gently.

To use the *gel form* of salicylic acid:

- Before using salicylic acid gel, apply wet packs to the affected areas for at least 5 minutes. If you have any questions about this, check with your health care professional.
- Apply enough gel to cover the affected areas, and rub in gently.

To use the *pad form* of salicylic acid:

- Wipe the pad over the affected areas.
- Do not rinse off medicine after treatment.

To use the *plaster form* of salicylic acid for warts, corns, or calluses:

- This medicine comes with patient instructions. Read them carefully before using.
- *Do not use this medicine on irritated skin or on any area that is infected or reddened. Also, do not use this medicine if you are a diabetic or if you have poor blood circulation.*
- *Do not use this medicine on warts with hair growing from them or on warts on the face, in or on the genital (sex) organs, or inside the nose or mouth. Also do not use on moles or birthmarks.* To do so may cause severe irritation.
- Wash the area to be treated and dry thoroughly. Warts may be soaked in warm water for 5 minutes before drying.
- Cut the plaster to fit the wart, corn, or callus and apply.
- For corns and calluses:
  —Repeat every 48 hours as needed for up to 14 days, or as directed by your doctor, until the corn or callus is removed.
  —Corns or calluses may be soaked in warm water for 5 minutes to help in their removal.
- For warts:
  —Depending on the product, either:
    - Apply plaster and repeat every 48 hours as needed, or
    - Apply plaster at bedtime, leave in place for at least 8 hours, remove plaster in the morning, and repeat every 24 hours as needed.

  —Repeat for up to 12 weeks as needed, or as directed by your doctor, until wart is removed.
- If discomfort gets worse during treatment or continues after treatment, or if the wart spreads, check with your doctor.

To use the *shampoo form* of salicylic acid:

- Before applying this medicine, wet the hair and scalp with lukewarm water. Apply enough medicine to work up a lather and rub well into the scalp for 2 or 3 minutes, then rinse. Apply the medicine again and rinse thoroughly.

To use the *soap form* of salicylic acid:

- Work up a lather with the soap, using hot water, and scrub the entire affected area with a washcloth or facial sponge or mitt.
- If you are to use this soap in a foot bath, work up rich suds in hot water and soak the feet for 10 to 15 minutes. Then pat dry without rinsing.

To use the *topical solution form* of salicylic acid for acne:

- Wet a cotton ball or pad with the topical solution and wipe the affected areas.
- Do not rinse off medicine after treatment.

To use the *topical solution form* of salicylic acid for warts, corns, or calluses:

- This medicine comes with patient instructions. Read them carefully before using.
- *This medicine is flammable. Do not use it near heat or open flame or while smoking.*
- *Do not use this medicine on irritated skin or on any area that is infected or reddened. Also, do not use this medicine if you are a diabetic or if you have poor blood circulation.*
- *Do not use this medicine on warts with hair growing from them or on warts on the face, in or on the genital (sex) organs, or inside the nose or mouth. Also do not use on moles or birthmarks.* To do so may cause severe irritation.
- Avoid breathing in the vapors from the medicine.
- Wash the area to be treated and dry thoroughly. Warts may be soaked in warm water for 5 minutes before drying.
- Apply the medicine one drop at a time to completely cover each wart, corn, or callus. Let dry.
- For warts—Repeat one or two times a day as needed for up to 12 weeks, or as directed by your doctor, until wart is removed.
- For corns and calluses—Repeat one or two times a day as needed for up to 14 days, or as directed by your doctor, until the corn or callus is removed.
- Corns and calluses may be soaked in warm water for 5 minutes to help in their removal.
- If discomfort gets worse during treatment or continues after treatment, or if the wart spreads, check with your doctor.

Unless your hands are being treated, wash them immediately after applying this medicine to remove any medicine that may be on them.

Dosing—The dose of salicylic acid will be different for different patients. *Follow your doctor's orders or the directions on the label.* The following information includes only the average doses of salicylic acid. *If your dose is different, do not change it* unless your doctor tells you to do so.

- For *cream* dosage form:
  - —For corns and calluses:
    - Adults and children—Use the 2 to 10% cream as needed. Use the 25 to 60% cream one time every three to five days.
- For *gel* dosage form:
  - —For acne:
    - Adults and children—Use the 0.5 to 5% gel one time a day.
  - —For psoriasis:
    - Adults and children—Use the 5% gel one time a day.
  - —For common warts:
    - Adults and children—Use the 5 to 26% gel one time a day.
- For *lotion* dosage form:
  - —For acne:
    - Adults and children—Use the 1 to 2% lotion one to three times a day.
  - —For dandruff and antiseborrhic dermatitis of the scalp:
    - Adults and children—Use the 1.8 to 2% lotion on the scalp one or two times a day.
- For *ointment* dosage form:
  - —For acne:
    - Adults and children—Use the 3 to 6% ointment as needed.
  - —For psoriasis and seborrheic dermatitis:
    - Adults and children—Use the 3 to 10% ointment as needed.
  - —For common warts:
    - Adults and children—Use the 3 to 10% ointment as needed. Use the 25 to 60% ointment one time every three to five days.
- For *pads* dosage form:
  - —For acne:
    - Adults and children—Use one to three times a day.
- For *plaster* dosage form:
  - —For corns, calluses, common warts, or plantar warts:
    - Adults and children—Use one time a day or one time every other day.
- For *shampoo* dosage form:
  - —For dandruff or seborrheic dermatitis of the scalp:
    - Adults and children—Use on the scalp one or two times a week.
- For *soap* dosage form:
  - —For acne:
    - Adults and children—Use as needed.
- For *topical solution* dosage form:
  - —For acne:
    - Adults and children—Use the 0.5 to 2% topical solution one to three times a day.
  - —For common warts and plantar warts:
    - Adults and children—Use the 5 to 27% topical solution one or two times a day.
  - —For corns and calluses:
    - Adults and children—Use the 12 to 27% topical solution one or two times a day.

Missed dose—If you miss a dose of this medicine, apply it as soon as possible. However, if it is almost time for your next dose, skip the missed dose and go back to your regular dosing schedule.

Storage—To store this medicine:
- Keep out of the reach of children.
- Store away from heat and direct light.
- Keep the medicine from freezing.
- Do not keep outdated medicine or medicine no longer needed. Be sure that any discarded medicine is out of the reach of children.

Precautions While Using This Medicine

When using salicylic acid, do not use any of the following preparations on the same affected area as this medicine, unless otherwise directed by your doctor:

Abrasive soaps or cleansers
Alcohol-containing preparations
Any other topical acne preparation or preparation containing a peeling agent (for example, benzoyl peroxide, resorcinol, sulfur, or tretinoin [vitamin A acid])
Cosmetics or soaps that dry the skin
Medicated cosmetics
Other topical medicine for the skin

To use any of the above preparations on the same affected area as salicylic acid may cause severe irritation of the skin.

Side Effects of This Medicine

Along with its needed effects, a medicine may cause some unwanted effects. Although not all of these side effects may occur, if they do occur they may need medical attention.

Check with your doctor as soon as possible if any of the following side effects occur:

Less common or rare
Skin irritation not present before use of this medicine (moderate or severe)

Symptoms of salicylic acid poisoning
Confusion; dizziness; headache (severe or continuing); rapid breathing; ringing or buzzing in ears (continuing)

Other side effects may occur that usually do not need medical attention. However, check with your doctor if any of the following side effects continue or are bothersome:

More common
Skin irritation not present before use of this medicine (mild); stinging

Other side effects not listed above may also occur in some patients. If you notice any other effects, check with your health care professional.

Revised: 07/26/93

SALICYLIC ACID AND SULFUR Topical

Some commonly used brand names are:

In the U.S.—

Acno
Acnotex
Aveeno Cleansing Bar
Creamy SS Shampoo
Fostex Regular Strength Medicated Cleansing Bar
Fostex Regular Strength Medicated Cleansing Cream (for face and scalp)
Meted Maximum Strength Anti-Dandruff Shampoo with Conditioners
Night Cast Regular Formula Mask-lotion
Pernox Lemon Medicated Scrub Cleanser
Pernox Lotion Lathering Abradant Scrub Cleanser
Pernox Lotion Lathering Scrub Cleanser
Pernox Regular Medicated Scrub Cleanser
Sastid (AL) Scrub
Sastid Plain Shampoo and Acne Wash
Sastid Soap
Sebasorb Liquid
Sebex
Sebulex Antiseborrheic Treatment and Conditioning Shampoo
Sebulex Antiseborrheic Treatment Shampoo
Sebulex Cream Medicated Shampoo
Sebulex Medicated Dandruff Shampoo with Conditioners
Sebulex Regular Medicated Dandruff Shampoo
Therac Lotion
Vanseb Cream Dandruff Shampoo
Vanseb Lotion Dandruff Shampoo

Generic name product may also be available.

In Canada—

Aveeno Acne Bar
Fostex Medicated Cleansing Bar
Fostex Medicated Cleansing Cream (for face and scalp)
Fostex Medicated Cleansing Liquid
Meted Maximum Strength Anti-Dandruff Shampoo with Conditioners
Night Cast R
Pernox Lemon Medicated Scrub Cleanser
Pernox Regular Medicated Scrub Cleanser
Sastid Soap
Sebulex Conditioning Suspension Shampoo
Sebulex Lotion Shampoo
Sebulex Medicated Shampoo
Sulsal Soap

Description

Salicylic acid (sal-i-SILL-ik AS-id) and sulfur (SUL-fur) combination is used to treat acne and other skin disorders and dandruff and other scalp disorders, such as seborrheic dermatitis.

This medicine is available without a prescription; however, your doctor may have special instructions on the proper use of this medicine for your medical condition.

Salicylic acid and sulfur combination is available in the following dosage forms:

Topical
- Cleansing cream (U.S. and Canada)
- Lotion (U.S. and Canada)
- Cleansing lotion (U.S. and Canada)
- Cream shampoo (U.S. and Canada)
- Lotion shampoo (U.S. and Canada)
- Suspension shampoo (U.S. and Canada)
- Bar soap (U.S. and Canada)
- Cleansing suspension (U.S. and Canada)
- Topical suspension (U.S.)

Before Using This Medicine

If you are using this medicine without a prescription, carefully read and follow any precautions on the label. For salicylic acid and sulfur combination, the following should be considered:

Allergies—Tell your doctor if you have ever had any unusual or allergic reaction to salicylic acid or sulfur. Also tell your health care professional if you are allergic to any other substances, such as preservatives or dyes.

Pregnancy—Salicylic acid and sulfur combination has not been studied in pregnant women. However, for the individual medicines:

- *Salicylic acid*—Salicylic acid may be absorbed through the mother's skin. Studies with topical salicylic acid have not been done in humans. However, studies in animals have shown that salicylic acid causes birth defects when given orally in doses about 6 times the highest dose recommended for topical use in humans.
- *Sulfur*—Topical sulfur has not been shown to cause birth defects or other problems in humans.

Before using this medicine, make sure your doctor knows if you are pregnant or if you may become pregnant.

Breast-feeding—Salicylic acid may be absorbed through the mother's skin. However, topical salicylic acid and sulfur combination has not been reported to cause problems in nursing babies.

Children—Young children may be at increased risk of unwanted effects because of increased absorption of salicylic acid through the skin. Products containing salicylic acid should not be applied to large areas of the body or used for long periods of time in infants and children.

Older adults—Many medicines have not been studied specifically in older people. Therefore, it may not be known whether they work exactly the same way they do in younger adults or if they cause different side effects or problems in older people. There is no specific information comparing use of salicylic acid and sulfur combination in the elderly with use in other age groups.

Other medicines—Although certain medicines should not be used together at all, in other cases two different medicines may be used together even if an interaction might occur. In these cases, your doctor may want to change the dose, or other precautions may be necessary. Tell your health care professional if you are using any other topical prescription or nonprescription (over-the-counter [OTC]) medicine that is to be applied to the same area of the skin.

Proper Use of This Medicine

Use this medicine only as directed. Do not use more of it and do not use it more often than recommended on the label, unless otherwise directed by your doctor.

Immediately after using this medicine, wash your hands to remove any medicine that may be on them.

Keep this medicine away from the eyes. If you should accidentally get some in your eyes, flush them thoroughly with water.

To use the *skin cleanser form* of this medicine:

- After wetting the skin, apply this medicine with your fingertips or a wet sponge and rub in gently to work up a lather. Then rinse thoroughly and pat dry.

To use the *lotion or topical suspension form* of this medicine:

- Apply a small amount of this medicine to the affected areas, and rub in gently.

To use the *shampoo form* of this medicine:

- Wet the hair and scalp with lukewarm water. Then apply enough medicine to work up a lather and rub into the scalp. Continue rubbing the lather into the scalp for several minutes or allow it to remain on the scalp for about 5 minutes, depending on the product being used, then rinse. Apply the medicine again and rinse thoroughly.

To use the *bar soap form* of this medicine:

- After wetting the skin, use this medicine to wash the face and other affected areas. Then rinse thoroughly and pat dry.

Dosing—The dose of salicylic acid and sulfur combination will be different for different patients. *Follow your doctor's orders or the directions on the label.* The following information includes only the average doses of salicylic acid and sulfur combination. *If your dose is different, do not change it* unless your doctor tells you to do so.

- For acne or oily skin:
  - —For *bar soap and cleansing cream* dosage forms:
    - Adults and children—Use on the skin two or three times a day.
  - —For *cleansing suspension, lotion, and topical suspension* dosage forms:
    - Adults and children—Use on the skin one or two times a day.
  - —For *cleansing lotion* dosage form:
    - Adults and children—Use on the skin one to three times a day.
- For dandruff and seborrheic dermatitis of the scalp:
  - —For *cream shampoo, lotion shampoo, and suspension shampoo* dosage forms:
    - Adults and children—Use on the scalp one or two times a week.

Missed dose—If you miss a dose of this medicine, apply or use it as soon as possible. However, if it is almost time for your next dose, skip the missed dose and go back to your regular dosing schedule.

Storage—To store this medicine:

- Keep out of the reach of children.
- Store away from heat and direct light.
- Keep the medicine from freezing.
- Do not keep outdated medicine or medicine no longer needed. Be sure that any discarded medicine is out of the reach of children.

Precautions While Using This Medicine

When using salicylic acid and sulfur combination medicine, do not use any of the following preparations on the same affected area as this medicine, unless otherwise directed by your doctor:

- Abrasive soaps or cleansers
- Alcohol-containing preparations
- Any other topical acne preparation or preparation containing a peeling agent (for example, benzoyl peroxide, resorcinol, or tretinoin [vitamin A acid])
- Cosmetics or soaps that dry the skin
- Medicated cosmetics
- Other topical medicine for the skin

To use any of the above preparations on the same affected area as salicylic acid and sulfur combination medicine may cause severe irritation of the skin.

Do not use any topical mercury-containing preparation, such as ammoniated mercury ointment, on the same affected area as this medicine. To do so may cause a foul odor, may be irritating to the skin, and may stain the skin black. If you have any questions about this, check with your health care professional.

Taking large doses of aspirin or other salicylates (including diflunisal) while using topical salicylic acid (contained in this medicine) may lead to overdose. If you have any questions about this, check with your health care professional.

Side Effects of This Medicine

Along with its needed effects, a medicine may cause some unwanted effects. Although not all of these side effects may occur, if they do occur they may need medical attention.

Check with your doctor as soon as possible if the following side effect occurs:

- Skin irritation not present before use of this medicine

Other side effects may occur that usually do not need medical attention. However, check with your health care professional if the following side effects continue or are bothersome:

- Redness and peeling of skin (may occur after a few days); unusual dryness of skin

Other side effects not listed above may also occur in some patients. If you notice any other effects, check with your health care professional.

Revised: 07/26/93

SALICYLIC ACID, SULFUR, AND COAL TAR Topical

Some commonly used brand names are:

In the U.S.—

- Sebex-T Tar Shampoo
- Sebutone
- Vanseb-T

In Canada—

- Sebutone

Description

Salicylic acid (sal-i-SILL-ik AS-id), sulfur (SUL-fur), and coal tar combination is used to treat dandruff, seborrheic dermatitis, and psoriasis of the scalp.

This medicine is available without a prescription; however, your doctor may have special instructions on the proper use of this medicine for your medical condition.

Salicylic acid, sulfur, and coal tar combination is available in the following dosage forms:

Topical

- Cream shampoo (U.S.)
- Lotion shampoo (U.S. and Canada)

Before Using This Medicine

If you are using this medicine without a prescription, carefully read and follow any precautions on the label. For salicylic acid, sulfur, and coal tar combination, the following should be considered:

Allergies—Tell your doctor if you have ever had any unusual or allergic reaction to salicylic acid, sulfur, or coal tar. Also tell your health care professional if you are allergic to any other substances, such as preservatives or dyes.

Pregnancy—Salicylic acid, sulfur, and coal tar combination has not been studied in pregnant women. However, for the individual medicines:

- *Salicylic acid*—Salicylic acid may be absorbed through the mother's skin. Studies with topical salicylic acid have not been done in humans. However, studies in animals have shown that salicylic acid causes birth defects when given orally in doses about 6 times the highest dose recommended for topical use in humans.
- *Sulfur*—Sulfur has not been shown to cause birth defects or other problems in humans.
- *Coal tar*—Studies with coal tar on effects in pregnancy have not been done in either humans or animals.

Breast-feeding—Salicylic acid may be absorbed through the mother's skin. However, topical salicylic acid, sulfur, and coal tar combination has not been reported to cause problems in nursing babies.

Children—Young children may be at increased risk of unwanted effects because of increased absorption of salicylic acid through the skin. Medicines containing salicylic acid should not be applied to large areas of the body or used for long periods of time in infants and children.

Older adults—Many medicines have not been studied specifically in older people. Therefore, it may not be known whether they work exactly the same way they do in younger adults or if they cause different side effects or problems in older people. There is no specific information

comparing use of salicylic acid, sulfur, and coal tar combination medicine in the elderly with use in other age groups.

Other medicines—Although certain medicines should not be used together at all, in other cases two different medicines may be used together even if an interaction might occur. In these cases, your doctor may want to change the dose, or other precautions may be necessary. Tell your health care professional if you are using any other topical prescription or nonprescription (over-the-counter [OTC]) medicine that is to be applied to the same area of the skin.

Proper Use of This Medicine

Use this medicine only as directed. Do not use it more often than recommended on the label, unless otherwise directed by your doctor.

Keep this medicine away from the eyes. If you should accidentally get some in your eyes, flush them thoroughly with water.

Before using this medicine, wet the hair and scalp with lukewarm water. Then apply a generous amount to the scalp and work up a rich lather. Rub the lather into the scalp for 5 minutes, then rinse. Apply the medicine again and rinse thoroughly.

Immediately after using this medicine, wash your hands to remove any medicine that may be on them.

Dosing—The dose of salicylic acid, sulfur, and coal tar combination will be different for different patients. *Follow your doctor's orders or the directions on the label.* The following information includes only the average doses of salicylic acid, sulfur, and coal tar combination. *If your dose is different, do not change it* unless your doctor tells you to do so.

- For dandruff, seborrheic dermatitis, and psoriasis of the scalp:
  - —For *cream shampoo and lotion shampoo* dosage forms:
    - Adults and children—Use on the scalp one or two times a week.

Missed dose—If you miss a dose of this medicine, apply it as soon as possible. However, if it is almost time for your next dose, skip the missed dose and go back to your regular dosing schedule.

Storage—To store this medicine:
- Keep out of the reach of children.
- Store away from heat and direct light.
- Keep the medicine from freezing.
- Do not keep outdated medicine or medicine no longer needed. Be sure that any discarded medicine is out of the reach of children.

Precautions While Using This Medicine

Do not use any topical mercury-containing preparation, such as ammoniated mercury ointment, on the same affected area as this medicine. To do so may cause a foul odor, may be irritating to the skin, and may stain the skin black. If you have any questions about this, check with your health care professional.

This medicine may temporarily discolor blond, bleached, or tinted hair.

Side Effects of This Medicine

In animal studies, coal tar (contained in this combination medicine) has been shown to increase the chance of skin cancer.

Along with its needed effects, a medicine may cause some unwanted effects. Although not all of these side effects may occur, if they do occur they may need medical attention.

Check with your doctor as soon as possible if the following side effect occurs:

Skin irritation not present before use of this medicine

Other side effects not listed above may also occur in some patients. If you notice any other effects, check with your health care professional.

Revised: 07/26/93

SELEGILINE Systemic

Some commonly used brand names are:

In the U.S.—

Eldepryl

Generic name product may also be available in the U.S.

In Canada—

Eldepryl
Novo-selegiline
SD Deprenyl

Other commonly used names are deprenil and deprenyl.

Description

Selegiline (seh-LEDGE-ah-leen) is used in combination with levodopa or levodopa and carbidopa combination to treat Parkinson's disease, sometimes called shaking palsy or paralysis agitans. This medicine works to increase and extend the effects of levodopa, and may help to slow the progress of Parkinson's disease.

Selegiline is available only with your doctor's prescription, in the following dosage form:

Oral
- Capsules (U.S.)
- Tablets (U.S. and Canada)

Before Using This Medicine

In deciding to use a medicine, the risks of taking the medicine must be weighed against the good it will do. This is a decision you and your doctor will make. For selegiline, the following should be considered:

Allergies—Tell your doctor if you have ever had any unusual or allergic reaction to selegiline. Also tell your

health care professional if you are allergic to any other substances, such as foods, preservatives, or dyes.

Pregnancy—Selegiline has not been studied in pregnant women. However, this medicine has not been shown to cause birth defects or other problems in animal studies.

Breast-feeding—It is not known whether selegiline passes into the breast milk.

Children—Studies on this medicine have been done only in adult patients and there is no specific information about its use in children. Therefore, be sure to discuss with your doctor the use of this medicine in children.

Older adults—In studies done to date that included elderly people, selegiline did not cause different side effects or problems in older people than it did in younger adults.

Other medicines—Although certain medicines should not be used together at all, in other cases 2 different medicines may be used together even if an interaction might occur. In these cases, your doctor may want to change the dose, or other precautions may be necessary. When you are taking selegiline, it is especially important that your health care professional know if you are taking any of the following:

- Antidepressants, tricyclic (amitriptyline [e.g., Elavil], amoxapine [e.g., Asendin], clomipramine [e.g., Anafranil], desipramine [e.g., Norpramin], doxepin [e.g., Sinequan], imipramine [e.g., Tofranil], nortriptyline [e.g., Pamelor], protriptyline [e.g., Vivactil], trimipramine [e.g., Surmontil]) or
- Fluoxetine (e.g., Prozac) or
- Fluvoxamine (e.g., Luvox) or
- Meperidine (e.g., Demerol) or
- Nefazodone (e.g., Serzone) or
- Paroxetine (e.g., Paxil) or
- Sertraline (e.g., Zoloft) or
- Venlafaxine (e.g., Effexor)—Using these medicines together may increase the chance of serious side effects

Other medical problems—The presence of other medical problems may affect the use of selegiline. Make sure you tell your doctor if you have any other medical problems, especially:

- Stomach ulcer (history of)—Selegiline may make the condition worse

Proper Use of This Medicine

Take this medicine only as directed by your doctor. Do not take more of it, do not take it more often, and do not take it for a longer time than your doctor ordered.

Dosing—The dose of selegiline will be different for different patients. Your doctor will determine the proper dose of selegiline for you. *Follow your doctor's orders or the directions on the label.*

For the treatment of Parkinson's disease, the usual dose of selegiline is 5 mg two times a day, taken with breakfast and lunch. Some patients may need less than this.

Missed dose—If you miss a dose of this medicine, take it as soon as possible. However, if you do not remember the missed dose until late afternoon or evening, skip the missed dose and go back to your regular dosing schedule. Do not double doses.

Storage—To store this medicine:

- Keep out of the reach of children.
- Store away from heat and direct light.
- Do not store in the bathroom, near the kitchen sink, or in other damp places. Heat or moisture may cause the medicine to break down.
- Do not keep outdated medicine or medicine no longer needed. Be sure that any discarded medicine is out of the reach of children.

Precautions While Using This Medicine

When selegiline is taken at doses of 10 mg or less per day for the treatment of Parkinson's disease, there are no restrictions on food or beverages you eat or drink. However, the chance exists that dangerous reactions, such as sudden high blood pressure, may occur if doses higher than those used for Parkinson's disease are taken with certain foods, beverages, or other medicines. These foods, beverages, and medicines include:

- Foods that have a high tyramine content (most common in foods that are aged or fermented to increase their flavor), such as cheeses; fava or broad bean pods; yeast or meat extracts; smoked or pickled meat, poultry, or fish; fermented sausage (bologna, pepperoni, salami, summer sausage) or other fermented meat; sauerkraut; or any overripe fruit. If a list of these foods and beverages is not given to you, ask your health care professional to provide one.
- Alcoholic beverages or alcohol-free or reduced-alcohol beer and wine.
- Large amounts of caffeine-containing food or beverages such as coffee, tea, cola, or chocolate.
- Any other medicine unless approved or prescribed by your doctor. This especially includes nonprescription (over-the-counter [OTC]) medicine, such as that for colds (including nose drops or sprays), cough, asthma, hay fever, and appetite control; "keep awake" products; or products that make you sleepy.

Also, for at least 2 weeks after you stop taking this medicine, these foods, beverages, and other medicines may continue to react with selegiline if it was taken in doses higher than those usually used for Parkinson's disease.

Check with your doctor or hospital emergency room immediately if severe headache, stiff neck, chest pains, fast heartbeat, or nausea and vomiting occur while you are taking this medicine. These may be symptoms of a serious side effect that should have a doctor's attention.

Dizziness, lightheadedness, or fainting may occur, especially when you get up from a lying or sitting position. Getting up slowly may help. If the problem continues or gets worse, check with your doctor.

Selegiline may cause dryness of the mouth. For temporary relief, use sugarless candy or gum, melt bits of ice in your mouth, or use a saliva substitute. However, if your mouth continues to feel dry for more than 2 weeks, check with your medical doctor or dentist. Continuing dryness of the mouth may increase the chance of dental disease, including tooth decay, gum disease, and fungus infections.

Side Effects of This Medicine

When you start taking selegiline in addition to levodopa or carbidopa and levodopa combination, you may experience an increase in side effects. If this occurs, your doctor may gradually reduce the amount of levodopa or carbidopa and levodopa combination you take.

Along with its needed effects, a medicine may cause some unwanted effects. Although not all of these side effects may occur, if they do occur they may need medical attention.

Stop taking this medicine and get emergency help immediately if any of the following side effects occur:

Symptoms of unusually high blood pressure (caused by reaction of higher than usual doses of selegiline with restricted foods or medicines)

Chest pain (severe); enlarged pupils; fast or slow heartbeat; headache (severe); increased sensitivity of eyes to light; increased sweating (possibly with fever or cold, clammy skin); nausea and vomiting (severe); stiff or sore neck

Check with your doctor as soon as possible if any of the following side effects occur:

More common

Increase in unusual movements of body; mood or other mental changes

Less common or rare

Bloody or black, tarry stools; severe stomach pain; or vomiting of blood or material that looks like coffee grounds; difficulty in speaking; loss of balance control; uncontrolled movements, especially of face, neck, and back; restlessness or desire to keep moving; or twisting movements of body; difficult or frequent urination; dizziness or lightheadedness, especially when getting up from a lying or sitting position; hallucinations (seeing, hearing, or feeling things that are not there); irregular heartbeat; lip smacking or puckering, puffing of cheeks, rapid or worm-like movements of tongue, uncontrolled chewing movements, uncontrolled movements of arms and legs; swelling of feet or lower legs; wheezing, difficulty in breathing, or tightness in chest

Symptoms of overdose

Agitation or irritability; chest pain; convulsions (seizures); difficulty opening mouth or lockjaw; dizziness (severe) or fainting; fast or irregular pulse (continuing); high fever; high or low blood pressure; increased sweating (possibly with fever or cold, clammy skin); severe spasm where the head and heels are bent backward and the body arched forward; troubled breathing

Other side effects may occur that usually do not need medical attention. These side effects may go away during treatment as your body adjusts to the medicine. However, check with your doctor if any of the following side effects continue or are bothersome:

More common

Abdominal or stomach pain; dizziness or feeling faint; dryness of mouth; nausea or vomiting; trouble in sleeping

Less common or rare

Anxiety, nervousness, or restlessness; blurred or double vision; body ache or back or leg pain; burning of lips, mouth, or throat; chills; constipation or diarrhea; drowsiness; headache; heartburn; high or low blood pressure; inability to move; slow or difficult urination; frequent urge to urinate; increased sensitivity of skin to light; increased sweating; irritability (temporary); loss of appetite or weight loss; memory problems; muscle cramps or numbness of fingers or toes; pounding or fast heartbeat; red, raised, or itchy skin; ringing or buzzing in ears; slowed movements; uncontrolled closing of eyelids; taste changes; unusual feeling of well-being; unusual tiredness or weakness

With doses higher than 10 mg a day

Clenching, gnashing, or grinding teeth; sudden jerky movements of body

Other side effects not listed above may also occur in some patients. If you notice any other effects, check with your doctor.

Revised: 09/30/92
Interim revision: 03/28/95; 08/21/96

SELENIUM SULFIDE Topical

Some commonly used brand names are:

In the U.S.—

Exsel Lotion Shampoo
Glo-Sel
Head & Shoulders Intensive Treatment Conditioning Formula Dandruff Lotion Shampoo
Head & Shoulders Intensive Treatment Regular Formula Dandruff Lotion Shampoo
Head & Shoulders Intensive Treatment 2 in 1 (Persistent Dandruff Shampoo plus Conditioner in One) Formula Dandruff Lotion Shampoo
Selsun
Selsun Blue Dry Formula
Selsun Blue Extra Conditioning Formula
Selsun Blue Extra Medicated Formula
Selsun Blue Oily Formula
Selsun Blue Regular Formula

Generic name product may also be available.

In Canada—

Selsun
Selsun Blue
Selsun Blue Extra Conditioning Formula
Versel Lotion

Description

Selenium sulfide (se-LEE-nee-um SUL-fide) 1% and 2.5% strengths are used on the scalp to help control the symptoms of dandruff and seborrheic dermatitis.

Selenium sulfide 2.5% strength is used also on the body to treat tinea versicolor (a type of fungus infection of the skin).

In the United States, the 2.5% strength is available only with your doctor's prescription. The 1% strength is available without a prescription; however, your doctor may have special instructions on the proper use of this medicine for your medical problem.

Selenium sulfide is available in the following dosage form:

Topical

- Lotion (U.S. and Canada)

Before Using This Medicine

If you are using this medicine without a prescription, carefully read and follow any precautions on the label. For selenium sulfide, the following should be considered:

Allergies—Tell your doctor if you have ever had any unusual or allergic reaction to selenium sulfide. Also tell your health care professional if you are allergic to any other substances, such as preservatives or dyes.

Pregnancy—

- *For use on the scalp:* Selenium sulfide has not been shown to cause birth defects or other problems in humans.
- *For use on the body:* Selenium sulfide should not be used if you are pregnant or if you may become pregnant. The medicine may be absorbed into your body and may affect your baby.

Breast-feeding—Selenium sulfide has not been reported to cause problems in nursing babies.

Children—There is no specific information comparing use of selenium sulfide in infants and children with use in other age groups; however, this medicine is not expected to cause different side effects or problems in children than it does in adults.

Older adults—Many medicines have not been studied specifically in older people. Therefore, it may not be known whether they work exactly the same way they do in younger adults. Although there is no specific information comparing use of selenium sulfide in the elderly with use in other age groups, this medicine is not expected to cause different side effects or problems in older people than it does in younger adults.

Other medicines—Although certain medicines should not be used together at all, in other cases two different medicines may be used together even if an interaction might occur. In these cases, your doctor may want to change the dose, or other precautions may be necessary. Tell your health care professional if you are using any other topical prescription or nonprescription (over-the-counter [OTC]) medicine that is to be applied to the same area of the skin.

Other medical problems—The presence of other medical problems may affect the use of selenium sulfide. Make sure you tell your doctor if you have any other medical problems, especially:

- Blistered, raw, or oozing areas on your scalp or body—Use of this medicine on these areas may increase the chance of absorption through the skin

Proper Use of This Medicine

If you are using the 2.5% strength of selenium sulfide: Use this medicine only as directed. Do not use it more often than recommended on the label, unless otherwise directed by your doctor.

If you are using the 1% strength of selenium sulfide: For best results, use this medicine at least 2 times a week or as directed by your doctor.

To use selenium sulfide for *dandruff or seborrheic dermatitis of the scalp:*

- Before using this medicine, wet the hair and scalp with lukewarm water.
- Apply enough medicine (1 or 2 teaspoonfuls) to the scalp to work up a lather. Allow the lather to remain on the scalp for 2 to 3 minutes, then rinse.
- Apply the medicine again and rinse well.
- If this medicine is used on light or blond, gray, or chemically treated (bleached, tinted, permanent-waved) hair, rinse your hair well for at least 5 minutes after using the medicine to lessen the chance of hair discoloration.
- After treatment, wash your hands well.

To use selenium sulfide for *tinea versicolor of the body:*

- Apply the medicine to the affected areas of your body, except for your face and genitals (sex organs).
- Work up a lather using a small amount of water.
- Allow the medicine to remain on your skin for 10 minutes.
- Rinse your body well to remove all the medicine.

Do not use this medicine if blistered, raw, or oozing areas are present on your scalp or the area of your body that is to be treated, unless otherwise directed by your doctor.

Keep this medicine away from the eyes. If you should accidentally get some in your eyes, flush them thoroughly with water.

Dosing—The dose of selenium sulfide will be different for different patients. *Follow your doctor's orders or the directions on the label.* The following information includes only the average doses of selenium sulfide. *If your dose is different, do not change it* unless your doctor tells you to do so.

- For *lotion* dosage form:
  - —For dandruff or seborrheic dermatitis:
    - Adults and children—If you are using the 1% lotion, use on the scalp two times a week. If you are using the 2.5% lotion, use on the scalp two times a week for two weeks, then use one time a week or less often.
    - Infants—Use and dose must be determined by your doctor.
  - —For tinea versicolor:
    - Adults and children—Use the 2.5% lotion on the body one time a day for seven days.
    - Infants—Use and dose must be determined by your doctor.

Missed dose—If you miss a dose of this medicine, use it as soon as possible. However, if it is almost time for your next dose, skip the missed dose and go back to your regular dosing schedule.

Storage—To store this medicine:
- Keep out of the reach of children.
- Store away from heat and direct light.
- Keep the medicine from freezing.
- Do not keep outdated medicine or medicine no longer needed. Be sure that any discarded medicine is out of the reach of children.

Precautions While Using This Medicine

If your condition does not get better after regular use of this medicine, or if it gets worse, check with your doctor.

Side Effects of This Medicine

Along with its needed effects, a medicine may cause some unwanted effects. Although not all of these side effects may occur, if they do occur they may need medical attention.

Check with your doctor as soon as possible if the following side effect occurs:

Less common or rare
Skin irritation

Other side effects may occur that usually do not need medical attention. Check with your health care professional if any of the following side effects continue or are bothersome:

More common
Unusual dryness or oiliness of hair or scalp

Less common
Increase in normal hair loss

Other side effects not listed above may also occur in some patients. If you notice any other effects, check with your health care professional.

Revised: 07/26/93

SELENIUM SUPPLEMENTS Systemic

Some commonly used brand names are:

In the U.S.—
Sele-Pak[1]
Selepen[1]

Note: For quick reference, the following selenium supplements are numbered to match the corresponding brand names.

This information applies to the following:
1. Selenious Acid (se-LEE-nee-us as-id)†‡
2. Selenium (se-LEE-nee-um)‡§

†Not commercially available in Canada.
‡Generic name product may also be available in the U.S.
§Generic name product may also be available in Canada.

Description

Selenium supplements are used to prevent or treat selenium deficiency.

The body needs selenium for normal growth and health. Selenium is needed for certain enzymes that help with normal body functions.

Lack of selenium may lead to changes in fingernails, muscle weakness, and heart problems.

Selenium deficiency in the United States is rare. Patients receiving total parenteral nutrition (TPN) for long periods of time may need selenium. Selenium deficiency is a problem in areas of the world where the soil contains little selenium.

Although selenium is being used to prevent certain types of cancer, there is not enough information to show that this is effective.

Injectable selenium is given by or under the supervision of a health care professional. Other forms of selenium are available without a prescription.

Selenium supplements are available as part of a multivitamin/mineral complex or alone in the following dosage forms:

Oral
Selenium
- Tablets (U.S. and Canada)

Parenteral
Selenious Acid
- Injection (U.S.)

Importance of Diet

For good health, it is important that you eat a balanced and varied diet. Follow carefully any diet program your health care professional may recommend. For your specific dietary vitamin and/or mineral needs, ask your health care professional for a list of appropriate foods. If you think that you are not getting enough vitamins and/or minerals in your diet, you may choose to take a dietary supplement.

Selenium is found in seafood, liver, lean red meat, and grains grown in soil that is rich in selenium.

The daily amount of selenium needed is defined in several different ways.

For U.S.—
- Recommended Dietary Allowances (RDAs) are the amount of vitamins and minerals needed to provide for adequate nutrition in most healthy persons. RDAs for a given nutrient may vary depending on a person's age, sex, and physical condition (e.g., pregnancy).
- Daily Values (DVs) are used on food and dietary supplement labels to indicate the percent of the recommended daily amount of each nutrient that a serving provides. DV replaces the previous designation of United States Recommended Daily Allowances (USRDAs).

For Canada—
- Recommended Nutrient Intakes (RNIs) are used to determine the amounts of vitamins, minerals, and protein needed to provide adequate nutrition and lessen the risk of chronic disease.

Normal daily recommended intakes for selenium are generally defined as follows:

- Infants and children—
  Birth to 3 years of age: 10 to 20 micrograms (mcg) per day.
  4 to 6 years of age: 20 mcg per day.
  7 to 10 years of age: 30 mcg per day.
- Adolescent and adult males—40 to 70 mcg per day.
- Adolescent and adult females—45 to 55 mcg per day.
- Pregnant females—65 mcg per day.
- Breast-feeding females—75 mcg per day.

Before Using This Dietary Supplement

If you are taking this dietary supplement without a prescription, carefully read and follow any precautions on the label. For selenium supplements, the following should be considered:

Allergies—Tell your health care professional if you have ever had any unusual or allergic reaction to selenious acid or selenium. Also tell your health care professional if you are allergic to any other substances, such as foods, preservatives, or dyes.

Pregnancy—It is especially important that you are receiving enough vitamins and minerals when you become pregnant and that you continue to receive the right amount of vitamins and minerals throughout your pregnancy. The healthy growth and development of the fetus depend on a steady supply of nutrients from the mother. However, taking large amounts of a dietary supplement in pregnancy may be harmful to the mother and/or fetus and should be avoided.

Studies in animals have shown that selenium causes birth defects when given in large doses.

Breast-feeding—It is important that you receive the right amounts of vitamins and minerals so that your baby will also get the vitamins and minerals needed to grow properly. However, taking large amounts of a dietary supplement while breast-feeding may be harmful to the mother and/or baby and should be avoided.

Children—Problems in children have not been reported with intake of normal daily recommended amounts.

Older adults—Problems in older adults have not been reported with intake of normal daily recommended amounts.

Medicines or dietary supplements—Although certain medicines should not be used together at all, in other cases or dietary supplements may be used together even if an interaction might occur. In these cases, your doctor may want to change the dose, or other precautions may be necessary. Tell your health care professional if you are taking any other dietary supplement or any nonprescription (over-the-counter [OTC]) or prescription medicine.

Other medical problems—The presence of other medical problems may affect the use of selenium supplements. Make sure you tell your health care professional if you have any other medical problems, especially:

- Kidney problems or
- Stomach problems—These conditions may cause higher blood levels of selenium, which may increase the chance of unwanted effects

Proper Use of This Dietary Supplement

Dosing—The amount of selenium needed to meet normal daily recommended intakes will be different for different patients. The following information includes only the average amounts of selenium.

- For *oral* dosage form (tablets):
  - —To prevent deficiency, the amount taken by mouth is based on normal daily recommended intakes:
    - Adults and teenage males—40 to 70 micrograms (mcg) per day.
    - Adults and teenage females—45 to 55 mcg per day.
    - Pregnant females—65 mcg per day.
    - Breast-feeding females—75 mcg per day.
    - Children 7 to 10 years of age—30 mcg per day.
    - Children 4 to 6 years of age—20 mcg per day.
    - Children birth to 3 years of age—10 to 20 mcg per day.
  - —To treat deficiency:
    - Adults, teenagers, and children—Treatment dose is determined by prescriber for each individual based on severity of deficiency.

Missed dose—If you miss taking selenium supplements for one or more days there is no cause for concern, since it takes some time for your body to become seriously low in selenium. However, if your health care professional has recommended that you take selenium, try to remember to take it as directed every day.

Storage—To store this dietary supplement:

- Keep out of the reach of children.
- Store away from heat and direct light.
- Do not store in the bathroom, near the kitchen sink, or in other damp places. Heat or moisture may cause the dietary supplement to break down.
- Keep the dietary supplement from freezing. Do not refrigerate.
- Do not keep outdated dietary supplement or those no longer needed. Be sure that any discarded dietary supplement is out of the reach of children.

Side Effects of This Dietary Supplement

Along with its needed effects, a dietary supplement may cause some unwanted effects. Although selenium supplements have not been reported to cause any side effects, check with your health care professional immediately if any of the following side effects occur as a result of an overdose:

Symptoms of overdose

Diarrhea; fingernail weakening; garlic odor of breath and sweat; hair loss; irritability; itching of skin; metallic taste; nausea and vomiting; unusual tiredness and weakness

Other side effects not listed above may also occur in some individuals. If you notice any other effects, check with your health care professional.

Revised: 04/16/92
Interim revision: 06/06/92; 08/15/94; 05/01/95

SERTRALINE Systemic

A commonly used brand name in the U.S. and Canada is Zoloft.

Description

Sertraline (SER-tral-leen) is used to treat mental depression.

This medicine is available only with your doctor's prescription, in the following dosage form:

Oral
- Capsules (Canada)
- Tablets (U.S.)

Before Using This Medicine

In deciding to use a medicine, the risks of taking the medicine must be weighed against the good it will do. This is a decision you and your doctor will make. For sertraline, the following should be considered:

Allergies—Tell your doctor if you have ever had any unusual or allergic reaction to sertraline. Also tell your health care professional if you are allergic to any other substances, such as foods, preservatives, or dyes.

Pregnancy—Studies have not been done in pregnant women. However, studies in animals have shown that sertraline may cause delayed development and decreased survival rates of offspring when given in doses many times the usual human dose. Before taking this medicine, make sure your doctor knows if you are pregnant or if you may become pregnant.

Breast-feeding—It is not known whether sertraline is excreted in breast milk.

Children—Studies on this medicine have been done only in adult patients, and there is no specific information comparing use of sertraline in children with use in other age groups.

Older adults—In studies done to date that have included elderly people, sertraline did not cause different side effects or problems in older people than it did in younger adults.

Other medicines—Although certain medicines should not be used together at all, in other cases two different medicines may be used together even if an interaction might occur. In these cases, your doctor may want to change the dose, or other precautions may be necessary. When you are taking sertraline, it is especially important that your health care professional know if you are taking any of the following:

- Digitoxin (e.g., Crystodigin) or
- Warfarin (e.g., Coumadin)—Higher or lower blood levels of these medicines or sertraline may occur, which may increase the chance of unwanted effects; your doctor may need to change the dose of either these medicines or sertraline
- Monoamine oxidase (MAO) inhibitors (furazolidone [e.g., Furoxone], isocarboxazid [e.g., Marplan], phenelzine [e.g., Nardil], procarbazine [e.g., Matulane], selegiline [e.g., Eldepryl], tranylcypromine [e.g., Parnate])—Taking sertraline while you are taking or within 2 weeks of taking MAO inhibitors may cause confusion, agitation, restlessness, stomach or intestinal symptoms, sudden high body temperature, extremely high blood pressure, and severe convulsions; at least 14 days should be allowed between stopping treatment with one medicine and starting treatment with the other

Other medical problems—The presence of other medical problems may affect the use of sertraline. Make sure you tell your doctor if you have any other medical problems, especially:

- Drug abuse or dependence (or history of)—Because sertraline is a new drug, it is not known if it could become habit-forming, causing mental or physical dependence
- Kidney disease, severe, or
- Liver disease—Higher blood levels of sertraline may occur, increasing the chance of side effects

Proper Use of This Medicine

Take this medicine only as directed by your doctor, to benefit your condition as much as possible. Do not take more of it, do not take it more often, and do not take it for a longer time than your doctor ordered.

You may have to take sertraline for up to 4 weeks or longer before you begin to feel better. Your doctor should check your progress at regular visits during this time.

This medicine should always be taken at the same time in relation to meals and snacks to make sure that it is absorbed in the same way.

Dosing—The dose of sertraline will be different for different patients. *Follow your doctor's orders or the directions on the label.* The following information includes only the average doses of sertraline. *If your dose is different, do not change it* unless your doctor tells you to do so.

- The number of capsules or tablets that you take depends on the strength of the medicine and the medical problem for which you are taking sertraline.
- For *oral* dosage forms (capsules or tablets):
  —Adults: To start, usually 50 milligrams once a day, taken either in the morning or evening. Your doctor may gradually increase your dose if needed.

—Children: Dose must be determined by the doctor.

—Older adults: To start, usually 12.5 to 25 milligrams once a day, taken either in the morning or evening. Your doctor may gradually increase your dose if needed.

Missed dose—Because sertraline may be given to different patients at different times of the day, you and your doctor should discuss what to do about any missed doses.

Storage—To store this medicine:

- Keep out of the reach of children.
- Store away from heat and direct light.
- Do not store in the bathroom, near the kitchen sink, or in other damp places. Heat or moisture may cause the medicine to break down.
- Do not keep outdated medicine or medicine no longer needed. Be sure that any discarded medicine is out of the reach of children.

Precautions While Using This Medicine

It is important that your doctor check your progress at regular visits, to allow for changes in your dose and to help reduce any side effects.

This medicine could possibly add to the effects of alcohol and other CNS depressants (medicines that slow down the nervous system, possibly causing drowsiness). Some examples of CNS depressants are antihistamines or medicine for hay fever, other allergies, or colds; sedatives, tranquilizers, or sleeping medicine; prescription pain medicine or narcotics; barbiturates; medicine for seizures; muscle relaxants; or anesthetics, including some dental anesthetics. *Check with your doctor before taking any of the above while you are using this medicine.*

This medicine may cause some people to become drowsy. *Make sure you know how you react to sertraline before you drive, use machines, or do anything else that could be dangerous if you are not alert.*

This medicine may cause dryness of the mouth. For temporary relief, use sugarless gum or candy, melt bits of ice in your mouth, or use a saliva substitute. However, if your mouth continues to feel dry for more than 2 weeks, check with your medical doctor or dentist. Continuing dryness of the mouth may increase the chance of dental disease, including tooth decay, gum disease, and fungus infections.

Side Effects of This Medicine

Along with its needed effects, a medicine may cause some unwanted effects. Although not all of these side effects may occur, if they do occur they may need medical attention.

Check with your doctor as soon as possible if any of the following side effects occur:

Less common or rare

Fast talking and excited feelings or actions that are out of control; fever; skin rash, hives, or itching

Other side effects may occur that usually do not need medical attention. These side effects may go away during treatment as your body adjusts to the medicine. However, check with your doctor if any of the following side effects continue or are bothersome:

More common

Decreased appetite or weight loss; decreased sexual drive or ability; diarrhea; drowsiness; dryness of mouth; headache; nausea; stomach or abdominal cramps, gas, or pain; tiredness or weakness; tremor; trouble in sleeping

Less common

Anxiety, agitation, nervousness or restlessness; changes in vision, including blurred vision; constipation; fast or irregular heartbeat; flushing or redness of skin, with feeling of warmth or heat; increased appetite; vomiting

Other side effects not listed above may also occur in some patients. If you notice any other effects, check with your doctor.

Revised: 03/19/93

SEVOFLURANE Inhalation-Systemic

Some commonly used brand names are:

In the U.S.—
Ultane

In Canada—
Sevorane

Description

Sevoflurane (see-voe-FLOO-rane) belongs to the group of medicines known as general anesthetics (an-ess-THET-iks). Sevoflurane is used to cause general anesthesia (loss of consciousness) before and during surgery. It is inhaled (breathed in). Although sevoflurane can be used by itself, combinations of anesthetics are often used together. This helps produce more effective anesthesia in some patients.

General anesthetics are given only by or under the immediate supervision of a doctor trained to use them. If you will be receiving a general anesthetic during your surgery, your anesthesiologist or nurse anesthetist will give you the medicine and closely follow your progress.

Sevoflurane is available in the following dosage form:

- Inhalation (U.S. and Canada)

Before Receiving This Medicine

In deciding to use a medicine, the risks of taking the medicine must be weighed against the good it will do. This is a decision you and your doctor will make. For sevoflurane, the following should be considered:

Allergies—Tell your doctor if you have or anyone in your family has ever had any unusual or allergic reaction to an anesthetic. Also tell your doctor if you are allergic to any other substances, such as foods, preservatives, or dyes.

Pregnancy—Sevoflurane has not been studied in pregnant women.

Breast-feeding—It is not known whether sevoflurane passes into breast milk. However, your doctor may want you to stop breast-feeding for about 24 hours after you receive the medicine.

Children—Sevoflurane has been tested in children. Sevoflurane may cause children to become agitated (excited) when it is used to start anesthesia when they are awake. Also, children receiving sevoflurane during surgery may become agitated as they awaken after surgery.

Older adults—Sevoflurane has been tested and does not cause different side effects in older people than in younger adults. However, older people usually need smaller amounts than younger people. Your doctor will consider your age in deciding on the right amount of sevoflurane for you.

Other medicines—Although certain medicines should not be used together at all, in other cases 2 different medicines may be used together even if an interaction might occur. In these cases, your doctor may want to change the dose, or other precautions may be necessary. When you are receiving an inhalation anesthetic, it is especially important that your doctor know if you are taking *any* other prescription or nonprescription (over-the-counter [OTC]) medicine including any of the following:

- Aminoglycosides (e.g., amikacin, gentamicin, kanamycin, netilmicin, tobramycin) or
- Capreomycin (e.g., Capastat) or
- Clindamycin (e.g., Cleocin) or
- Lincomycin (e.g., Lincocin) or
- Polymyxins—Use of these medicines with sevoflurane may increase the effects of sevoflurane

Your doctor should be aware of any "street drugs" you are taking also.

Other medical problems—The presence of other medical problems may affect the use of sevoflurane. Make sure you tell your doctor if you have any other medical problems, especially:

- Diseases that can cause muscle weakness, such as familial periodic paralysis, muscular dystrophy, myasthenia gravis, or myasthenic syndrome—Weakness may be increased
- Head injury—Sevoflurane may make this condition worse
- Kidney disease—Sevoflurane may make this condition worse
- Liver disease—The effects of sevoflurane may be increased
- Malignant hyperthermia, during or shortly after receiving an anesthetic (history of, or a family history of)—This side effect may occur again
- Portwine stain—Sevoflurane may interfere with the laser treatment to remove portwine stain

Proper Use of This Medicine

Dosing—The dose of sevoflurane will be different for different patients. Your doctor will decide on the right amount for you, depending on:

- Your age.
- Your general physical condition.
- The kind of surgery being performed.
- Other medications you are taking or will receive before and during surgery.

Precautions After Receiving This Medicine

For patients going home within 24 hours after receiving this medicine:

- Sevoflurane may cause some people to feel drowsy, tired, or weak for a while after they receive it. It may also cause problems with coordination and ability to think. Therefore, for about 24 hours (or longer if necessary) after receiving sevoflurane, *do not drive, operate moving machinery, or do anything else that could be dangerous if you are not alert.*
- Unless otherwise directed by your doctor or dentist, *do not drink alcoholic beverages or take other CNS depressants (medicines that may make you drowsy or less alert) for about 24 hours after you have received sevoflurane.* Taking these medicines or drinking alcoholic beverages may add to the effects of sevoflurane. Some examples of CNS depressants are antihistamines or medicine for hay fever, other allergies, or colds; other sedatives, tranquilizers, or sleeping medicine, prescription pain medicine or narcotics; barbiturates; medicine for seizures; and muscle relaxants.

Side Effects of This Medicine

Along with its needed effects, a medicine may cause some unwanted effects. Although not all of these side effects may occur, if they do occur they may need medical attention. While you are receiving and recovering from an inhalation anesthetic like sevoflurane, your health care professional will closely follow its effects. However, some effects may not be noticed until later.

The following side effects should go away as the effects of sevoflurane wear off. However, check with your doctor if any of them continue or are bothersome:

More common
Cough (increased); dizziness; drowsiness; increased amount of saliva; nausea; shivering; vomiting

Less common
Headache

Other side effects may occur in some patients. If you notice any other effects, check with your doctor.

Developed: 06/28/96

SILICONE OIL 5000 CENTISTOKES Parenteral-Local†

A commonly used brand name in the U.S. is AdatoSil 5000.
Another commonly used name is polydimethylsiloxane.

†Not commercially available in Canada.

Description

Silicone (SIL-i-kone) oil 5000 centistokes (SEN-ti-stokes) is used during eye surgery to prevent or treat a very serious eye problem called a detached retina. It is injected into the back area of the eye to hold the retina in place while it is healing. This product is usually left in the eye for up to 1 year or longer before it is removed during surgery.

Silicone oil 5000 centistokes is administered only by, or under the immediate supervision of, your doctor. It is available in the following dosage form:

Parenteral-Local
- Injection (U.S.)

Before Receiving This Product

In deciding to receive a medicine, the risks of receiving the medicine must be weighed against the good it will do. This is a decision you and your doctor will make. For silicone oil, the following should be considered:

Allergies—Tell your doctor if you have ever had any unusual or allergic reaction to silicone oil.

Pregnancy—Silicone oil has not been shown to cause birth defects or other problems in humans.

Breast-feeding—Silicone oil has not been reported to cause problems in nursing babies.

Children—This product has been tested in children and has not been shown to cause different side effects or problems in children than it does in adults.

Older adults—This product has been tested and has not been shown to cause different side effects or problems in older people than it does in younger adults.

Other medical problems—The presence of other medical problems may affect the use of silicone oil. Make sure you tell your doctor if you have any other medical problems, especially:

- Intraocular lens (IOL) replacement—Silicone oil can chemically react with IOLs made with silicone, causing a decrease in vision

Proper Use of This Product

Dosing—The following information includes only the usual procedure for administering silicone oil.

- For *injection* dosage form:
  - —For detached retina:
    - Adults and children—Silicone is injected into the back area of the eye during surgery to hold the retina in place while it is healing. It is usually left in the eye for up to 1 year or longer before it is removed during surgery.

Precautions Before Receiving This Product

Discuss with your doctor the possible side effects that may be caused by this product. Some of them may be serious or long-term.

Precautions After Receiving This Product

It is very important that your doctor check your progress at regular visits.

Side Effects of This Product

Along with its needed effects, a medicine may cause some unwanted effects. Although not all of these side effects may occur, if they do occur they may need medical attention.

Check with your doctor immediately if any of the following side effects occur:

More common

Abdominal pain; blurred vision or other change in vision not present before treatment, or returning or getting worse after treatment; eye pain; eye redness; headache; nausea or vomiting; swelling of eye; tearing

Less common

Seeing floaters or light flashes

Rare

Sensitivity to light

Other side effects not listed above may also occur in some patients. If you notice any other effects, check with your doctor.

Developed: 02/27/96

SILVER SULFADIAZINE Topical

Some commonly used brand names are:

In the U.S.—

Flint SSD
Sildimac
Silvadene
SSD
SSD AF
Thermazene

In Canada—

Flamazine

Description

Silver sulfadiazine (SILL-ver sul-fa-DYE-a-zeen), a sulfa medicine, is used to prevent and treat bacterial or fungus infections. It works by killing the fungus or bacteria.

Silver sulfadiazine cream is applied to the skin and/or burned area(s) to prevent and treat bacterial or fungus infections that may occur in burns. This medicine may also be used for other problems as determined by your doctor.

Other medicines are used along with this medicine for burns. Patients with severe burns or burns over a large area of the body must be treated in a hospital.

Silver sulfadiazine is available only with your doctor's prescription, in the following dosage form:

Topical
- Cream (U.S. and Canada)

Before Using This Medicine

In deciding to use a medicine, the risks of using the medicine must be weighed against the good it will do. This is

a decision you and your doctor will make. For silver sulfadiazine, the following should be considered:

Allergies—Tell your doctor if you have ever had any unusual or allergic reaction to silver sulfadiazine or to any of the following medicines:

- Acetazolamide (e.g., Diamox)
- Antidiabetics, oral (diabetes medicine you take by mouth)
- Dichlorphenamide (e.g., Daranide)
- Furosemide (e.g., Lasix)
- Methazolamide (e.g., Neptazane)
- Sulfonamides, other (sulfa medicine)
- Thiazide diuretics (water pills)

Also tell your health care professional if you are allergic to any other substances, such as preservatives or dyes.

Pregnancy—Studies have not been done in humans. However, sulfa medicines may increase the chance of liver problems in newborn infants. Silver sulfadiazine has not been shown to cause birth defects or other problems in studies in rabbits treated with 3 to 10 times the usual amount of silver sulfadiazine.

Breast-feeding—It is not known whether silver sulfadiazine applied to the skin and/or burns passes into the breast milk. However, silver sulfadiazine may be absorbed into the body when used on skin and/or burns. Sulfa medicines given by mouth do pass into the breast milk. They may cause liver problems, anemia (iron-poor blood), and other unwanted effects in nursing babies, especially those with glucose-6-phosphate dehydrogenase deficiency (lack of G6PD enzyme). Therefore, caution is recommended when using this medicine in nursing women.

Children—Use is not recommended in premature or newborn infants up to 1 month of age. Sulfa medicines may cause liver problems in these infants. Although there is no specific information comparing use of silver sulfadiazine in older infants and children with use in other age groups, this medicine is not expected to cause different side effects or problems in older infants and children than it does in adults.

Older adults—Many medicines have not been studied specifically in older people. Therefore, it may not be known whether they work exactly the same way they do in younger adults or if they cause different side effects or problems in older people. There is no specific information comparing use of silver sulfadiazine in the elderly with use in other age groups.

Other medicines—Although certain medicines should not be used together at all, in other cases two different medicines may be used together even if an interaction might occur. In these cases, your doctor may want to change the dose, or other precautions may be necessary. When you are taking silver sulfadiazine, it is especially important that your health care professional know if you are taking any of the following:

- Collagenase (e.g., Santyl) or
- Papain (e.g., Panafil) or
- Sutilains (e.g., Travase)—Silver sulfadiazine may prevent these enzymes from working properly

Other medical problems—The presence of other medical problems may affect the use of silver sulfadiazine. Make sure you tell your doctor if you have any other medical problems, especially:

- Blood problems or
- Glucose-6-phosphate dehydrogenase deficiency (lack of G6PD enzyme)—Use of this medicine may cause blood problems or make them worse
- Kidney disease or
- Liver disease—In persons with these conditions, use may result in higher blood levels of this medicine; a smaller dose may be needed
- Porphyria—Use of this medicine may result in a severe attack of porphyria

Proper Use of This Medicine

This medicine should not be used on premature or newborn infants up to 1 month of age, unless otherwise directed by your doctor. It may cause liver problems in these infants.

To use:

- Before applying this medicine, cleanse the affected area(s). Remove dead or burned skin and other debris.
- Wear a sterile glove to apply this medicine. Apply a thin layer (about 1/16 inch) of silver sulfadiazine to the affected area(s). Keep the affected area(s) covered with the medicine at all times.
- If this medicine is rubbed off the affected area(s) by moving around or if it is washed off during bathing, showering, or the use of a whirlpool bath, reapply the medicine.
- After this medicine has been applied, the treated area(s) may be covered with a dressing or left uncovered as desired.

To help clear up your skin and/or burn infection completely, *keep using silver sulfadiazine for the full time of treatment.* You should keep using this medicine until the burned area has healed or is ready for skin grafting. *Do not miss any doses.*

Dosing—The dose of silver sulfadiazine will be different for different patients. *Follow your doctor's orders or the directions on the label.* The following information includes only the average doses of silver sulfadiazine. *If your dose is different, do not change it* unless your doctor tells you to do so.

- For *topical* dosage form (cream):
  - —For burn wound infections:
    - Adults and children 1 month of age and older—Use one or two times a day.
    - Premature and newborn infants up to 1 month of age—Use and dose must be determined by the doctor.

Missed dose—If you miss a dose of this medicine, apply it as soon as possible. However, if it is almost time for your next dose, skip the missed dose and go back to your regular dosing schedule.

Storage—To store this medicine:

- Keep out of the reach of children.
- Store away from heat and direct light.
- Keep the medicine from freezing.

- Do not keep outdated medicine or medicine no longer needed. Be sure that any discarded medicine is out of the reach of children.

Precautions While Using This Medicine

It is important that your doctor check your progress at regular visits.

If your skin infection or burn does not improve within a few days or weeks (for more serious burns or burns over larger areas), or if it becomes worse, check with your doctor.

This medicine may rarely stain skin brownish gray.

Side Effects of This Medicine

Along with its needed effects, a medicine may cause some unwanted effects. Although not all of these side effects may occur, if they do occur they may need medical attention.

Check with your doctor as soon as possible if the following side effect occurs:

Rare
Increased sensitivity of skin to sunlight, especially in patients with burns on large areas

Other side effects may occur that usually do not need medical attention. These side effects may go away during treatment as your body adjusts to the medicine. However, check with your doctor if any of the following side effects continue or are bothersome:

More common
Burning feeling on treated area(s)

Less common or rare
Brownish-gray skin discoloration; itching or skin rash

Other side effects not listed above may also occur in some patients. If you notice any other effects, check with your doctor.

Revised: 07/26/93

SIMETHICONE Oral

Some commonly used brand names are:

In the U.S.—

Extra Strength Gas-X
Extra Strength Maalox Anti-Gas
Flatulex
Gas Relief
Gas-X
Genasyme
Maalox Anti-Gas
Maximum Strength Gas Relief
Maximum Strength Mylanta Gas Relief
Maximum Strength Phazyme
My Baby Gas Relief Drops
Mylanta Gas
Mylanta Gas Relief
Mylicon Drops
Phazyme
Phazyme-95

Generic name product may also be available.

In Canada—

Extra Strength Maalox GRF Gas Relief Formula
Maalox GRF Gas Relief Formula
Ovol
Ovol-40
Ovol-80
Phazyme Drops
Phazyme-95
Phazyme-125

Description

Simethicone (si-METH-i-kone) is used to relieve the painful symptoms of too much gas in the stomach and intestines.

Simethicone may also be used for other conditions as determined by your doctor.

Simethicone is available without a prescription; however, your doctor may have special instructions on the proper use and dose for your medical problem. It is available in the following dosage forms:

Oral
- Capsules (U.S. and Canada)
- Oral suspension (U.S. and Canada)
- Tablets (U.S.)
- Chewable tablets (U.S. and Canada)

Before Using This Medicine

In deciding to use a medicine, the risks of taking the medicine must be weighed against the good it will do. This is a decision you and your doctor will make. For simethicone, the following should be considered:

Allergies—Tell your doctor if you have ever had any unusual or allergic reaction to simethicone. Also tell your health care professional if you are allergic to any other substances, such as foods, preservatives, or dyes.

Diet—Avoid foods that seem to increase gas. Chew food thoroughly and slowly. Reduce air swallowing by avoiding fizzy, carbonated drinks. Do not smoke before meals. Develop regular bowel habits and exercise regularly. Make certain your health care professional knows if you are on a low-sodium, low-sugar, or any other special diet. Most medicines contain more than their active ingredient.

Pregnancy—Simethicone is not absorbed into the body and is not likely to cause problems.

Breast-feeding—Simethicone has not been reported to cause problems in nursing babies.

Children—This medicine has been tested in children and, in effective doses, has not been shown to cause different side effects or problems than it does in adults.

Older adults—Many medicines have not been studied specifically in older people. Therefore, it may not be known whether they work exactly the same way they do in younger adults. There is no specific information comparing use of simethicone in the elderly with use in other age groups.

Proper Use of This Medicine

For effective use of simethicone:

- Follow your doctor's instructions if this medicine was prescribed.
- Follow the manufacturer's package directions if you are treating yourself.

Take this medicine after meals and at bedtime for best results.

For patients taking the *chewable tablet* form of this medicine:

- It is important that you chew the tablets thoroughly before you swallow them. This is to allow the medicine to work faster and more completely.

For patients taking the *oral liquid* form of this medicine:

- This medicine is to be taken by mouth even if it comes in a dropper bottle. The amount you should take is to be measured with the specially marked dropper or measuring spoon.

Dosing—The dose of simethicone will be different for different patients. *Follow your doctor's orders or the directions on the label.* The following information includes only the average doses of simethicone. *If your dose is different, do not change it* unless your doctor tells you to do so.

- For symptoms of too much gas:
  - —For *oral* dosage forms (capsules or tablets):
    - Adults and teenagers—Usual dose is 60 to 125 milligrams (mg) four times a day, after meals and at bedtime. The dose should not be more than 500 mg in twenty-four hours.
    - Children—Dose must be determined by the doctor.
  - —For *oral* dosage form (chewable tablets):
    - Adults and teenagers—Usual dose is 40 to 125 mg four times a day, after meals and at bedtime or the dose may be 150 mg three times a day, after meals. The dose should not be more than 500 mg in twenty-four hours.
    - Children—Dose must be determined by the doctor.
  - —For *oral* dosage form (suspension):
    - Adults and teenagers—Usual dose is 40 to 95 mg four times a day, after meals and at bedtime. The dose should not be more than 500 mg in twenty-four hours.
    - Children—Dose must be determined by the doctor.

Missed dose—If you must take this medicine regularly and you miss a dose, take it as soon as possible. However, if it is almost time for your next dose, skip the missed dose and go back to your regular dosing schedule. Do not double doses.

Storage—To store this medicine:

- Keep out of the reach of children.
- Store away from heat and direct light.
- Do not store the capsule or tablet form of this medicine in the bathroom, near the kitchen sink, or in other damp places. Heat or moisture may cause the medicine to break down.
- Keep the liquid form of this medicine from freezing.
- Do not keep outdated medicine or medicine no longer needed. Be sure that any discarded medicine is out of the reach of children.

Side Effects of This Medicine

There have not been any common or important side effects reported with this medicine. However, if you notice any side effects, check with your doctor.

Additional Information

Once a medicine has been approved for marketing for a certain use, experience may show that it is also useful for other medical problems. Although these uses are not included in product labeling, simethicone is used in certain patients before the following tests:

- Before a gastroscopy
- Before a radiography of the bowel

Other than the above information, there is no additional information relating to proper use, precautions, or side effects for these uses.

Revised: 06/16/93
Interim revision: 06/21/95

SINCALIDE Diagnostic

A commonly used brand name in the U.S. and Canada is Kinevac.

Description

Sincalide (SIN-ka-lide) belongs to the group of medicines known as diagnostic aids. Diagnostic aids are used to help diagnose certain medical problems. Sincalide is given by injection before tests are done to check if the gallbladder and pancreas are working properly and to help diagnose other problems of these organs.

The doses of sincalide will be different for different patients and depend on the weight of the patient and on the type of test.

Sincalide is used only under the supervision of a doctor. It is available in the following dosage form:

Parenteral

- Powder for injection (U.S. and Canada)

Before Having This Test

In deciding to use a diagnostic test, any risks of the test must be weighed against the good it will do. This is a decision you and your doctor will make. Also, test results may be affected by other things. For sincalide, the following should be considered:

Allergies—Tell your doctor if you have ever had any unusual or allergic reaction to sincalide. Also tell your health

care professional if you are allergic to any other substances, such as foods, preservatives, or dyes.

Pregnancy—Sincalide has not been studied in pregnant women. Studies in animals have not shown that sincalide causes birth defects or other problems. However, sincalide may cause abortion or premature labor if given to a pregnant woman toward the end of the pregnancy. Be sure you have discussed this with your doctor.

Breast-feeding—It is not known whether sincalide passes into the breast milk. Although most medicines pass into breast milk in small amounts, many of them may be used safely while breast-feeding. Mothers who are receiving this diagnostic test and who wish to breast-feed should discuss this with their doctor.

Children—Studies on this medicine have been done only in adult patients, and there is no specific information comparing use of sincalide in children with use in other age groups.

Older adults—Many medicines have not been studied specifically in older people. Therefore, it may not be known whether they work exactly the same way they do in younger adults or if they cause different side effects or problems in older people. There is no specific information comparing use of sincalide in the elderly with use in other age groups.

Other medicines—Although certain medicines should not be used together at all, in other cases two different medicines may be used together even if an interaction might occur. In these cases, your doctor may want to change the dose, or other precautions may be necessary. Tell your health care professional if you are taking any other prescription of nonprescription (over-the-counter [OTC]) medicine.

Other medical problems—The presence of other medical problems may affect the use of sincalide. Make sure you tell your doctor if you have any other medical problems, especially:

- Blockage of the intestines or
- Gallbladder stones—Sincalide may make these conditions worse

Preparation For This Test

Your doctor may have special instructions for you in preparation for your test. If you have not received instructions or if you do not understand them, check with your doctor in advance.

Side Effects of This Medicine

Along with its needed effects, sincalide may cause some unwanted effects. Although not all of these side effects may occur, if they do occur they may need medical attention.

Check with your health care professional as soon as possible if any of the following side effects occur:

Less common or rare

Dizziness, fainting, or lightheadedness; increase in blood pressure; shortness of breath; skin rash

Other side effects may occur that usually do not need medical attention. These side effects should go away as the effects of the medicine wear off. However, check with your health care professional if any of the following side effects continue or are bothersome:

More common

Abdominal or stomach pain, cramps, or discomfort; nausea

Less common or rare

Diarrhea; dizziness; flushing or redness of skin; headache; increased sweating; numbness; sneezing; urge to have bowel movement; vomiting

Other side effects not listed above may also occur in some patients. If you notice any other effects, check with your health care professional.

Developed: 02/27/95

SKELETAL MUSCLE RELAXANTS Systemic

Some commonly used brand names are:

In the U.S.—

Carbacot[5]
EZE-DS[3]
Maolate[2]
Paraflex[3]
Parafon Forte DSC[3]
Relaxazone[3]
Remular[3]
Remular-S[3]
Robaxin[5]
Robaxin-750[5]
Skelaxin[4]
Skelex[5]
Soma[1]
Strifon Forte DSC[3]
Vanadom[1]

In Canada—

Robaxin[5]
Robaxin-750[5]
Soma[1]

Note: For quick reference, the following skeletal muscle relaxants are numbered to match the corresponding brand names.

This information applies to the following medicines:

1. Carisoprodol (kar-eye-soe-PROE-dole)‡
2. Chlorphenesin (klor-FEN-e-sin)†
3. Chlorzoxazone (klor-ZOX-a-zone)†‡
4. Metaxalone (me-TAX-a-lone)†
5. Methocarbamol (meth-oh-KAR-ba-mole)‡

This information does *not* apply to Baclofen, Cyclobenzaprine, Dantrolene, Diazepam, or Orphenadrine.

†Not commercially available in Canada.
‡Generic name product may also be available in the U.S.

Description

Skeletal muscle relaxants are used to relax certain muscles in your body and relieve the stiffness, pain, and discomfort caused by strains, sprains, or other injury to your muscles. However, these medicines do not take the place of rest, exercise or physical therapy, or other treatment that your doctor may recommend for your medical problem. Methocarbamol also has been used to relieve some of the muscle problems caused by tetanus.

Skeletal muscle relaxants act in the central nervous system (CNS) to produce their muscle relaxant effects. Their actions in the CNS may also produce some of their side effects.

In the U.S., these medicines are available only with your doctor's prescription. In Canada, some of these medicines are available without a prescription.

These medicines are available in the following dosage forms:

Oral

Carisoprodol
- Tablets (U.S. and Canada)

Chlorphenesin
- Tablets (U.S.)

Chlorzoxazone
- Tablets (U.S.)

Metaxalone
- Tablets (U.S.)

Methocarbamol
- Tablets (U.S. and Canada)

Parenteral

Methocarbamol
- Injection (U.S. and Canada)

Before Using This Medicine

In deciding to use a medicine, the risks of taking the medicine must be weighed against the good it will do. This is a decision you and your doctor will make. For the skeletal muscle relaxants, the following should be considered:

Allergies—Tell your doctor if you have ever had any unusual or allergic reaction to any of the skeletal muscle relaxants or to carbromal, mebutamate, meprobamate (e.g., Equanil), or tybamate. Also tell your health care professional if you are allergic to any other substances, such as foods, preservatives, or dyes.

Pregnancy—Although skeletal muscle relaxants have not been shown to cause birth defects or other problems, studies on birth defects have not been done in pregnant women. Studies in animals with metaxalone have not shown that it causes birth defects.

Breast-feeding—Carisoprodol passes into the breast milk and may cause drowsiness or stomach upset in nursing babies. It is not known whether chlorphenesin, chlorzoxazone, metaxalone, or methocarbamol passes into the breast milk. However, these medicines have not been reported to cause problems in nursing babies.

Children—Studies with the skeletal muscle relaxants have been done only in adult patients, and there is no specific information comparing use of these medicines in children with use in other age groups. However, carisoprodol and chlorzoxazone have been used in children. They have not been reported to cause different side effects or problems in children than they do in adults.

Older adults—Many medicines have not been tested in older people. Therefore, it may not be known whether they work exactly the same way they do in younger adults or if they cause different side effects or problems in older people. There is no specific information about the use of skeletal muscle relaxants in the elderly.

Other medicines—Although certain medicines should not be used together at all, in other cases two different medicines may be used together even if an interaction might occur. In these cases, your doctor may want to change the dose, or other precautions may be necessary. When you are taking a skeletal muscle relaxant, it is especially important that your health care professional know if you are taking any of the following:

- Alcohol or
- Central nervous system (CNS) depressants or
- Tricyclic antidepressants (amitriptyline [e.g., Elavil], amoxapine [e.g., Asendin], clomipramine [e.g., Anafranil], desipramine [e.g., Pertofrane], doxepin [e.g., Sinequan], imipramine [e.g., Tofranil], nortriptyline [e.g., Aventyl], protriptyline [e.g., Vivactil], trimipramine [e.g., Surmontil])—The chance of side effects may be increased

Other medical problems—The presence of other medical problems may affect the use of a skeletal muscle relaxant. Make sure you tell your doctor if you have any other medical problems, especially:

- Allergies, history of, or
- Blood disease caused by an allergy or reaction to any other medicine, history of, or
- Drug abuse or dependence, or history of, or
- Kidney disease or
- Liver disease or
- Porphyria—Depending on which of the skeletal muscle relaxants you take, the chance of side effects may be increased; your doctor can choose a muscle relaxant that is less likely to cause problems
- Epilepsy—Convulsions may be more likely to occur if methocarbamol is given by injection

Proper Use of This Medicine

Chlorzoxazone, metaxalone, or methocarbamol tablets may be crushed and mixed with a little food or liquid if needed to make the tablets easier to swallow.

Dosing—The dose of these medicines will be different for different patients. *Follow your doctor's orders or the directions on the label.* The following information includes only the average doses of these medicines. *If your dose is different, do not change it* unless your doctor tells you to do so.

For carisoprodol

- For *oral* dosage form (tablets):
  - —For relaxing stiff, sore muscles:
    - Adults and teenagers—350 milligrams (mg) four times a day.
    - Children up to 5 years of age—Dose must be determined by your doctor.
    - Children 5 to 12 years of age—6.25 mg per kilogram (2.5 mg per pound) of body weight four times a day.

For chlorphenesin

- For *oral* dosage form (tablets):
  - —For relaxing stiff, sore muscles:
    - Adults and teenagers—800 milligrams (mg) three times a day, at first. Your doctor may decrease your dose after you begin to feel better.
    - Children—Use and dose must be determined by your doctor.

For chlorzoxazone

- For *oral* dosage form (tablets):
  - —For relaxing stiff, sore muscles:
    - Adults and teenagers—500 milligrams (mg) three or four times a day.
    - Children—125 to 500 mg three or four times a day, depending on the child's size and weight.

For metaxalone

- For *oral* dosage form (tablets):
  - —For relaxing stiff, sore muscles:
    - Adults and teenagers—800 milligrams (mg) three or four times a day.
    - Children—Use and dose must be determined by your doctor.

For methocarbamol

- For *oral* dosage form (tablets):
  - —For relaxing stiff, sore muscles:
    - Adults and teenagers—1500 milligrams (mg) four times a day, at first. Your doctor may decrease your dose after you begin to feel better.
    - Children—Use and dose must be determined by your doctor.
- For *injection* dosage form:
  - —For relaxing stiff, sore muscles:
    - Adults and teenagers—1 to 3 grams a day, injected into a muscle or a vein. This total daily dose may be divided into smaller amounts that are given several times a day, especially when the medicine is injected into a muscle.
    - Children—Use and dose must be determined by your doctor.

Missed dose—If you miss a dose of this medicine and remember within an hour or so of the missed dose, take it right away. But if you do not remember until later, skip the missed dose and go back to your regular dosing schedule. Do not double doses.

Storage—To store this medicine:

- Keep out of the reach of children.
- Store away from heat and direct light.
- Do not store this medicine in the bathroom, near the kitchen sink, or in other damp places. Heat or moisture may cause the medicine to break down.
- Do not keep outdated medicine or medicine no longer needed. Be sure that any discarded medicine is out of the reach of children.

Precautions While Using This Medicine

If you will be taking this medicine for a long time (for example, more than a few weeks), your doctor should check your progress at regular visits.

This medicine will add to the effects of alcohol and other CNS depressants (medicines that slow down the nervous system, possibly causing drowsiness). Some examples of CNS depressants are antihistamines or medicine for hay fever, other allergies, or colds; sedatives, tranquilizers, or sleeping medicine; prescription pain medicine or narcotics; barbiturates; medicine for seizures; other muscle relaxants; or anesthetics, including some dental anesthetics. *Do not drink alcoholic beverages, and check with your doctor before taking any of the medicines listed above, while you are using this medicine.*

Skeletal muscle relaxants may cause blurred vision or clumsiness or unsteadiness in some people. They may also cause some people to feel drowsy, dizzy, lightheaded, faint, or less alert than they are normally. *Make sure you know how you react to this medicine before you drive, use machines, or do anything else that could be dangerous if you are dizzy or are not alert, well-coordinated, and able to see well.*

For *diabetic patients:*

- Metaxalone (e.g., Skelaxin) may cause false test results with one type of test for sugar in your urine. If your urine sugar test shows an unusually large amount of sugar, or if you have any questions about this, check with your health care professional. This is especially important if your diabetes is not well controlled.

Side Effects of This Medicine

Along with its needed effects, a medicine may cause some unwanted effects. Although not all of these side effects may occur, if they do occur they may need medical attention.

Check with your doctor as soon as possible if any of the following side effects occur:

Less common

Fainting; fast heartbeat; fever; hive-like swellings (large) on face, eyelids, mouth, lips, and/or tongue; mental depression; shortness of breath, troubled breathing, tightness in chest, and/or wheezing; skin rash, hives, itching, or redness; slow heartbeat (methocarbamol injection only); stinging or burning of eyes; stuffy nose and red or bloodshot eyes

Rare

Blood in urine; bloody or black, tarry stools; convulsions (seizures) (methocarbamol injection only); cough or hoarseness; fast or irregular breathing; lower back or side pain; muscle cramps or pain (not present before treatment or more painful than before treatment); painful or difficult urination; pain, tenderness, heat, redness, or swelling over a blood vessel (vein) in arm or leg (methocarbamol injection only); pinpoint red spots on skin; puffiness or swelling of the eyelids or around the eyes; sores, ulcers, or white spots on lips or in mouth; sore throat and fever with or without chills; swollen and/or painful glands; unusual bruising or bleeding; unusual tiredness or weakness; vomiting of blood or material that looks like coffee grounds; yellow eyes or skin

Other side effects may occur that usually do not need medical attention. These side effects may go away during treatment as your body adjusts to the medicine. However, check with your doctor if any of the following side effects continue or are bothersome:

More common

Blurred or double vision or any change in vision; dizziness or lightheadedness; drowsiness

Less common or rare

Abdominal or stomach cramps or pain; clumsiness or unsteadiness; confusion; constipation; diarrhea; excitement, nervousness, restlessness, or irritability; flushing or redness of face; headache; heartburn; hiccups; muscle weakness; nausea or vomiting; pain or peeling of skin at place of injection (methocarbamol only); trembling; trouble in sleeping; uncontrolled movements of eyes (methocarbamol injection only)

Although not all of the side effects listed above have been reported for all of these medicines, they have been reported for at least one of them. However, since all of these skeletal muscle relaxants have similar effects, it is possible that any of the above side effects may occur with any of these medicines.

In addition to the other side effects listed above, chlorzoxazone may cause your urine to turn orange or reddish purple. Methocarbamol may cause your urine to turn black, brown, or green. This effect is harmless and will go away when you stop taking the medicine. However, if you have any questions about this, check with your doctor.

Other side effects not listed above may also occur in some patients. If you notice any other effects, check with your doctor.

Revised: 08/11/95

SODIUM BENZOATE AND SODIUM PHENYLACETATE Systemic†

A commonly used brand name in the U.S. is Ucephan.

†Not commercially available in Canada.

Description

Sodium benzoate (SOE-dee-um BEN-zo-ate) and sodium phenylacetate (fen-ill-AH-seh-tate) combination is used to treat a condition caused by too much ammonia in the blood (hyperammonemia). This medicine works by causing less ammonia to be produced by the body.

Ammonia is formed from the breakdown of protein in the body. If the ammonia cannot be removed by the body, then a buildup may cause serious unwanted effects.

Sodium benzoate and sodium phenylacetate combination is available only with your doctor's prescription in the following dosage form:

Oral

- Oral solution (U.S.)

Before Using This Medicine

In deciding to use a medicine, the risks of taking the medicine must be weighed against the good it will do. This is a decision you and your doctor will make. For sodium benzoate and sodium phenylacetate combination, the following should be considered:

Allergies—Tell your doctor if you have ever had any unusual or allergic reaction to sodium benzoate or sodium phenylacetate. Also tell your health care professional if you are allergic to any other substances, such as foods, preservatives, or dyes.

Pregnancy—Sodium benzoate and sodium phenylacetate combination has not been studied in pregnant women or animals.

Breast-feeding—It is not known whether sodium benzoate and sodium phenylacetate combination passes into the breast milk. Although most medicines pass into breast milk in small amounts, many of them may be used safely while breast-feeding. Mothers who are taking this medicine and who wish to breast-feed should discuss this with their doctor.

Children—Sodium benzoate and sodium phenylacetate may cause serious unwanted effects if given to infants of low birthweight.

Older adults—Many medicines have not been studied specifically in older people. Therefore, it may not be known whether they work exactly the same way they do in younger adults or if they cause different side effects or problems in older people. There is no specific information comparing the use of sodium benzoate and sodium phenylacetate in the elderly with use in other age groups.

Other medicines—Although certain medicines should not be used together at all, in other cases two different medicines may be used together even if an interaction might occur. In these cases, your doctor may want to change the dose, or other precautions may be necessary. When you are taking sodium benzoate and sodium phenylacetate combination, it is especially important that your health care professional know if you are taking the following:

- Penicillins—Use with penicillins may keep the sodium benzoate and sodium phenylacetate combination from working properly

Other medical problems—The presence of other medical problems may affect the use of sodium benzoate and sodium phenylacetate combination. Make sure you tell your doctor if you have any other medical problems, especially:

- Edema (swelling) or
- Heart disease or
- Kidney disease or
- Toxemia of pregnancy—Increased retention of water may make these conditions worse

Proper Use of This Medicine

This medicine should be added to infant formula or milk and given immediately after mixing. Sodium benzoate and sodium phenylacetate should not be mixed with other beverages (especially acidic beverages such as tea or coffee), since they may cause the medicine to separate out.

Take this medicine with meals.

It is important that you follow any special instructions from your doctor, such as following a low protein diet. If you have any questions about this, check with your doctor.

Dosing—The dose of this combination medicine will be different for different patients. *Follow your doctor's orders or the directions on the label.* The following information includes only the average dose of this combination medicine. *If your dose is different, do not change it* unless your doctor tells you to do so.

- For *oral* dosage form (solution):
  - —Treatment of too much ammonia in the blood:
    - Adults and children—The dose is based on body weight and must be determined by the doctor. It is usually 2.5 milliliters (mL) per kilogram (1.1 mL per pound) a day, given in three to six divided doses. The dose is usually no more than 100 mL a day.

Missed dose—If you miss a dose of this medicine, take it as soon as possible. However, if it is almost time for your next dose, skip the missed dose and go back to your regular dosing schedule. Do not double doses.

Storage—To store this medicine:
- Keep out of the reach of children.
- Store away from heat and direct light.
- Do not store in the bathroom, near the kitchen sink, or in other damp places. Heat or moisture may cause the medicine to break down.
- Keep the medicine from freezing. Do not refrigerate.
- Do not keep outdated medicine or medicine no longer needed. Be sure that any discarded medicine is out of the reach of children.

Precautions While Using This Medicine

Your doctor should check your progress at regular visits to make sure that this medicine is working properly.

Side Effects of This Medicine

Along with its needed effects, a medicine may cause some unwanted effects. Although not all of these side effects may occur, if they do occur they may need medical attention.

Stop taking this medicine and get emergency help immediately if any of the following side effects occur:

Symptoms of overdose

Continual vomiting; feeling of faintness; rapid fall in blood pressure; shortness of breath or troubled breathing; unusual drowsiness; unusual irritability

Other side effects may occur that usually do not need medical attention. These side effects may go away during treatment as your body adjusts to the medicine. However, check with your doctor if either of the following side effects continue or are bothersome:

More common

Nausea or vomiting

Other side effects not listed above may also occur in some patients. If you notice any other effects, check with your doctor.

Revised: 07/15/93

SODIUM BICARBONATE Systemic

Some commonly used brand names are:

In the U.S.—

- Arm and Hammer Pure Baking Soda
- Bell/ans
- Citrocarbonate
- Soda Mint

Generic name product may also be available.

In Canada—

- Citrocarbonate

Generic name product may also be available.

Description

Sodium bicarbonate (SOE-dee-um bye-KAR-boe-nate), also known as baking soda, is used to relieve heartburn, sour stomach, or acid indigestion by neutralizing excess stomach acid. When used for this purpose, it is said to belong to the group of medicines called antacids. It may be used to treat the symptoms of stomach or duodenal ulcers. Sodium bicarbonate is also used to make the blood and urine more alkaline in certain conditions.

Antacids should not be given to young children (up to 6 years of age) unless prescribed by their doctor. Since children cannot usually describe their symptoms very well, a doctor should check the child before giving this medicine. The child may have a condition that needs other treatment. If so, antacids will not help and may even cause unwanted effects or make the condition worse.

Sodium bicarbonate for oral use is available without a prescription; however, your doctor may have special instructions on the proper use and dose for your medical problem. Sodium bicarbonate is available in the following dosage forms:

Oral
- Effervescent powder (U.S. and Canada)
- Oral powder (U.S. and Canada)
- Tablets (U.S. and Canada)

Parenteral
- Injection (U.S. and Canada)

Before Using This Medicine

If you are taking this medicine without a prescription, carefully read and follow any precautions on the label. For sodium bicarbonate, the following should be considered:

Allergies—Tell your doctor if you have ever had any unusual or allergic reaction to sodium bicarbonate. Also tell your health care professional if you are allergic to any other substances, such as foods, preservatives, or dyes.

Pregnancy—Sodium bicarbonate is absorbed by the body and although it has not been shown to cause problems, the chance always exists. In addition, medicines containing sodium should usually be avoided if you tend to retain (keep) body water.

Breast-feeding—It is not known whether sodium bicarbonate passes into the breast milk. However, this medicine has not been reported to cause problems in nursing babies.

Children—Antacids should not be given to young children (up to 6 years of age) unless prescribed by a physician. This medicine may not help and may even worsen some conditions, so make sure that your child's problem should be treated with this medicine before you use it.

Older adults—Many medicines have not been studied specifically in older people. Therefore, it may not be known whether they work exactly the same way they do in younger adults or if they cause different side effects or problems in older people. There is no specific information comparing use of sodium bicarbonate in the elderly with use in other age groups.

Other medicines—Although certain medicines should not be used together at all, in other cases two different medicines may be used together even if an interaction might occur. In these cases, your doctor may want to change the dose, or other precautions may be necessary. When you are taking sodium bicarbonate, it is especially important that your health care professional know if you are taking any of the following:

- Ketoconazole (e.g., Nizoral) or
- Tetracyclines (medicine for infection) taken by mouth—Use with sodium bicarbonate may result in lower blood levels of these medicines, possibly decreasing their effectiveness
- Mecamylamine (e.g., Inversine)—Use with sodium bicarbonate may increase the effects of mecamylamine
- Methenamine (e.g., Mandelamine)—Use with sodium bicarbonate may reduce the effects of methenamine

Other medical problems—The presence of other medical problems may affect the use of sodium bicarbonate. Make sure you tell your doctor if you have any other medical problems, especially:

- Appendicitis or
- Intestinal or rectal bleeding—Oral forms of sodium bicarbonate may make these conditions worse
- Edema (swelling of feet or lower legs) or
- Heart disease or
- High blood pressure (hypertension)
- Kidney disease or
- Liver disease or
- Problems with urination or
- Toxemia of pregnancy—Sodium bicarbonate may cause the body to retain (keep) water, which may make these conditions worse

Proper Use of This Medicine

For safe and effective use of sodium bicarbonate:

- Follow your doctor's instructions if this medicine was prescribed.
- Follow the manufacturer's package directions if you are treating yourself.

For patients *taking this medicine for a stomach ulcer:*

- *Take it exactly as directed and for the full time of treatment as ordered by your doctor,* to obtain maximum relief of your symptoms.
- Take it 1 and 3 hours after meals and at bedtime for best results, unless otherwise directed by your doctor.

Dosing—The dose of sodium bicarbonate will be different for different patients. *Follow your doctor's orders or the directions on the label.* The following information includes only the average doses of this medicine. *If your dose is different, do not change it* unless your doctor tells you to do so.

The number of teaspoonfuls of powder or of tablets you take depends on the strength of the medicine. *Also, the number of doses you take each day, the time allowed between doses, and the length of time you take the medicine depends on the medical problem for which you are taking sodium bicarbonate.*

- For *sodium bicarbonate* effervescent powder:
  - —To relieve heartburn or sour stomach:
    - Adults and teenagers—3.9 to 10 grams (1 to 2 1/2 teaspoonfuls) in a glass of cold water after meals. However, the dose is usually not more than 19.5 grams (5 teaspoonfuls) a day.
    - Children up to 6 years of age—Dose must be determined by your doctor.
    - Children 6 to 12 years of age—1 to 1.9 grams (1/4 to 1/2 teaspoonful) in a glass of cold water after meals.
- For *sodium bicarbonate* powder:
  - —To relieve heartburn or sour stomach:
    - Adults and teenagers—One-half teaspoonful in a glass of water every two hours. Your doctor may change the dose if needed.
    - Children—Dose must be determined by your doctor.
  - —To make the urine more alkaline (less acidic):
    - Adults and teenagers—One teaspoonful in a glass of water every four hours. Your doctor may change the dose if needed. However, the dose is usually not more than 4 teaspoonfuls a day.
    - Children—Dose must be determined by your doctor.
- For *sodium bicarbonate* tablets:
  - —To relieve heartburn or sour stomach:
    - Adults and teenagers—325 milligrams (mg) to 2 grams one to four times a day.
    - Children up to 6 years of age—Dose must be determined by your doctor.
    - Children 6 to 12 years of age—The dose is 520 mg. The dose may be repeated in thirty minutes.

—To make the urine more alkaline (less acidic):

- Adults and teenagers—At first, four grams, then 1 to 2 grams every four hours. However, the dose is usually not more than 16 grams a day.
- Children—The dose is based on body weight and must be determined by your doctor. The usual dose is 23 to 230 mg per kilogram (kg) (10.5 to 105 mg per pound) of body weight a day. Your doctor may change the dose if needed.

Missed dose—If you must take this medicine regularly and you miss a dose, take it as soon as possible. However, if it is almost time for your next dose, skip the missed dose and go back to your regular dosing schedule. Do not double doses.

Storage—To store this medicine:

- Keep out of the reach of children.
- Store away from heat and direct light.
- Do not store the powder or tablet form of this medicine in the bathroom, near the kitchen sink, or in other damp places. Heat or moisture may cause the medicine to break down.
- Do not keep outdated medicine or medicine no longer needed. Be sure that any discarded medicine is out of the reach of children.

Precautions While Using This Medicine

If this medicine has been ordered by your doctor and if you will be taking it regularly for a long time, your doctor should check your progress at regular visits. This is to make sure the medicine does not cause unwanted effects.

Do not take sodium bicarbonate:

- *Within 1 to 2 hours of taking other medicine by mouth.* To do so may keep the other medicine from working properly.
- *For a long period of time.* To do so may increase the chance of side effects.

For patients on a *sodium-restricted diet*:

- This medicine contains a large amount of sodium. If you have any questions about this, check with your health care professional.

For patients *taking this medicine as an antacid*:

- *Do not take this medicine if you have any signs of appendicitis* (such as stomach or lower abdominal pain, cramping, bloating, soreness, nausea, or vomiting). Instead, check with your doctor as soon as possible.
- *Do not take this medicine with large amounts of milk or milk products.* To do so may increase the chance of side effects.
- *Do not take sodium bicarbonate for more than 2 weeks* or if the problem comes back often. Instead, check with your doctor. Antacids should be used only for occasional relief, unless otherwise directed by your doctor.

Side Effects of This Medicine

Along with its needed effects, a medicine may cause some unwanted effects. Although the following side effects occur very rarely when this medicine is taken as recommended, they may be more likely to occur if it is taken:

- In large doses.
- For a long time.
- By patients with kidney disease.

Check with your doctor as soon as possible if any of the following side effects occur:

Frequent urge to urinate; headache (continuing); loss of appetite (continuing); mood or mental changes; muscle pain or twitching; nausea or vomiting; nervousness or restlessness; slow breathing; swelling of feet or lower legs; unpleasant taste; unusual tiredness or weakness

Other side effects may occur that usually do not need medical attention. These side effects may go away during treatment as your body adjusts to the medicine. However, check with your doctor if any of the following side effects continue or are bothersome:

Less common

Increased thirst; stomach cramps

Other side effects not listed above may also occur in some patients. If you notice any other effects, check with your doctor.

Revised: 02/03/92
Interim revision: 08/10/94

SODIUM FLUORIDE Systemic

Some commonly used brand names are:

In the U.S.—

Fluoritab
Fluorodex
Flura
Flura-Drops
Flura-Loz
Karidium
Luride
Luride Lozi-Tabs
Luride-SF Lozi-Tabs
Pediaflor
Pharmaflur
Pharmaflur 1.1
Pharmaflur df
Phos-Flur

Generic name product may also be available.

In Canada—

Flozenges
Fluor-A-Day
Fluoritabs
Fluorosol
Karidium
PDF
Pedi-Dent
Solu-Flur

Generic name product may be available.

Description

Fluoride has been found to be helpful in reducing the number of cavities in the teeth. It is usually present naturally in drinking water. However, some areas of the country do not have a high enough level in the water to prevent cavities. To make up for this, extra fluorides may be added to the diet. Some children may require both dietary fluorides and topical fluoride treatments by the dentist. Use of a fluoride toothpaste or rinse may be helpful as well.

Taking fluorides does not replace good dental habits. These include eating a good diet, brushing and flossing teeth often, and having regular dental checkups.

Fluoride may also be used for other conditions as determined by your health care professional.

This medicine is available only with a prescription, in the following dosage forms:

Oral

- Lozenges (U.S. and Canada)
- Oral solution (U.S. and Canada)
- Tablets (U.S. and Canada)
- Chewable tablets (U.S. and Canada)

Importance of Diet

For good health, it is important that you eat a balanced and varied diet. Follow carefully any diet program your health care professional may recommend. For your specific dietary vitamin and/or mineral needs, ask your health care professional for a list of appropriate foods. If you think that you are not getting enough vitamins and/or minerals in your diet, you may choose to take a dietary supplement.

People get needed fluoride from fish, including the bones, tea, and drinking water that has fluoride added to it. Food that is cooked in water containing fluoride or in Teflon-coated pans also provides fluoride. However, foods cooked in aluminum pans provide less fluoride.

The daily amount of fluoride needed is defined in several different ways.

For U.S.—

- Recommended Dietary Allowances (RDAs) are the amount of vitamins and minerals needed to provide for adequate nutrition in most healthy persons. RDAs for a given nutrient may vary depending on a person's age, sex, and physical condition (e.g., pregnancy).
- Daily Values (DVs) are used on food and dietary supplement labels to indicate the percent of the recommended daily amount of each nutrient that a serving provides. DV replaces the previous designation of United States Recommended Daily Allowances (USRDAs).

For Canada—

- Recommended Nutrient Intakes (RNIs) are used to determine the amounts of vitamins, minerals, and protein needed to provide adequate nutrition and lessen the risk of chronic disease.

There is no RDA or RNI for fluoride. Daily recommended intakes for fluoride are generally defined as follows:

- Infants and children—
  Birth to 3 years of age: 0.1 to 1.5 milligrams (mg).
  4 to 6 years of age: 1 to 2.5 mg.
  7 to 10 years of age: 1.5 to 2.5 mg.
- Adolescents and adults—1.5 to 4 mg.

Remember:

- The total amount of fluoride you get every day includes what you get from the foods and beverages that you eat and what you may take as a supplement.
- This total amount *should not* be greater than the above recommendations, unless ordered by your health care professional. Taking too much fluoride can cause serious problems to the teeth and bones.

Before Using This Medicine

In deciding to use a medicine, the risks of taking the medicine must be weighed against the good it will do. This is a decision you and your health care professional will make. For sodium fluoride, the following should be considered:

Allergies—Tell your health care professional if you are allergic to any other substances, such as foods, preservatives, or dyes.

Pregnancy—It is especially important that you are receiving enough vitamins and minerals when you become pregnant and that you continue to receive the right amount of vitamins and minerals throughout your pregnancy. The healthy growth and development of the fetus depend on a steady supply of nutrients from the mother. However, taking large amounts of a dietary supplement in pregnancy may be harmful to the mother and/or fetus and should be avoided. Sodium fluoride occurs naturally in water and has not been shown to cause problems in infants of mothers who drank fluoridated water or took appropriate doses of supplements.

Breast-feeding—It is especially important that you receive the right amounts of vitamins and minerals so that your baby will also get the vitamins and minerals needed to grow properly. However, taking large amounts of a dietary supplement while breast-feeding may be harmful to the mother and/or baby and should be avoided. Small amounts of sodium fluoride pass into breast milk.

Children—Problems in children have not been reported with intake of normal daily recommended amounts. Doses of sodium fluoride that are too large or are taken for a long time may cause bone problems and teeth discoloration in children.

Older adults—Problems in older adults have not been reported with intake of normal daily recommended amounts. Older people are more likely to have joint pain, kidney problems, or stomach ulcers which may be made worse by taking large doses of sodium fluoride. You should check with your health care professional.

Other medicines—Although certain medicines or dietary supplements should not be used together at all, in other cases they may be used together even if an interaction might occur. In these cases, your health care professional may want to change the dose, or other precautions may be necessary. Tell your health care professional if you are taking/using any other prescription or nonprescription (over-the-counter [OTC]) medicine.

Other medical problems—The presence of other medical problems may affect the use of sodium fluoride. Make sure you tell your health care professional if you have any other medical problems, especially:

- Brown, white, or black discoloration of teeth or
- Joint pain or
- Kidney problems (severe) or
- Stomach ulcer—Sodium fluoride may make these conditions worse

Proper Use of This Medicine

Take this medicine only as directed by your health care professional. Do not take more of it and do not take it more often than ordered. Taking too much fluoride over a period of time may cause unwanted effects.

For individuals taking the *chewable tablet form* of this medicine:

- Tablets should be chewed or crushed before they are swallowed.
- This medicine works best if it is taken at bedtime, after the teeth have been thoroughly brushed. Do not eat or drink for at least 15 minutes after taking sodium fluoride.

For individuals taking the *oral liquid form* of this medicine:

- This medicine is to be taken by mouth even though it comes in a dropper bottle. The amount to be taken is to be measured with the specially marked dropper.
- *Always store this medicine in the original plastic container.* Fluoride will affect glass and should not be stored in glass containers.
- This medicine may be dropped directly into the mouth or mixed with cereal, fruit juice, or other food. However, if this medicine is mixed with foods or beverages that contain calcium, the amount of sodium fluoride that is absorbed may be reduced.

Dosing—The dose of sodium fluoride will be different for different individuals. *Follow your health care professional's orders or the directions on the label.* The following information includes only the average doses of sodium fluoride. *If your dose is different, do not change it* unless your health care professional tells you to do so.

The amount of solution or the number of lozenges or tablets you take depends on the strength of the medicine. Also, *the number of doses you take each day, the time allowed between doses, and the length of time you take the medicine depend on the medical problem for which you are taking sodium fluoride.*

- For *oral* dosage form (lozenges, solution, tablets, or chewable tablets):
  - —To prevent cavities in the teeth (where there is not enough fluoride in the water):
    - Children—Dose is based on the amount of fluoride in drinking water in your area. Dose is also based on the child's age and must be determined by your health care professional.

Missed dose—If you miss a dose of this medicine, take it as soon as you remember. However, if it is almost time for the next dose, skip the missed dose and go back to your regular dosing schedule. Do not double doses. If you have any questions about this, check with your health care professional.

Storage—To store this medicine:

- Keep out of the reach of children, since overdose is especially dangerous in children.
- Store away from heat and direct light.
- Do not store in the bathroom, near the kitchen sink, or in other damp places. Heat or moisture may cause the medicine to break down.
- Protect the oral liquid from freezing.
- Do not keep outdated medicine or medicine no longer needed. Be sure that any discarded medicine is out of the reach of children.

Precautions While Using This Medicine

The level of fluoride present in the water is different in different parts of the U.S. If you move to another area, check with a health care professional in the new area as soon as possible to see if this medicine is still needed or if the dose needs to be changed. Also, check with your health care professional if you change infant feeding habits (e.g., breast-feeding to infant formula), drinking water (e.g., city water to nonfluoridated bottled water), or filtration (e.g., tap water to filtered tap water).

Do not take calcium supplements or aluminum hydroxide–containing products and sodium fluoride at the same time. It is best to space doses of these two products 2 hours apart, to get the full benefit from each medicine.

Inform your health care professional as soon as possible if you notice white, brown, or black spots on the teeth. These are signs of too much fluoride in children when it is given during periods of tooth development.

Side Effects of This Medicine

Along with its needed effects, a medicine may cause some unwanted effects. Although not all of these side effects may occur, if they do occur they may need medical attention.

Check with your health care professional as soon as possible if any of the following side effects occur:

Sores in mouth and on lips (rare)

Sodium fluoride in drinking water or taken as a supplement does not usually cause any side effects. However, *taking an overdose of fluoride may cause serious problems.*

Stop taking this medicine and check with your health care professional immediately if any of the following side effects occur, as they may be symptoms of severe overdose:

Black, tarry stools; bloody vomit; diarrhea; drowsiness; faintness; increased watering of mouth; nausea or vomiting; shallow breathing; stomach cramps or pain; tremors; unusual excitement; watery eyes; weakness

Check with your health care professional as soon as possible if the following side effects occur, as some may be early symptoms of possible chronic overdose:

Pain and aching of bones; stiffness; white, brown, or black discoloration of teeth—occur only during periods of tooth development in children

Other side effects not listed above may also occur in some individuals. If you notice any other effects, check with your health care professional.

Revised: 07/17/92
Interim revision: 08/07/95

SODIUM IODIDE Systemic†

A commonly used brand name in the U.S. is Iodopen.
Generic name product may also be available.

†Not commercially available in Canada.

Description

Sodium iodide (SOE-dee-um EYE-oh-dide) is used to prevent or treat iodine deficiency.

The body needs iodine for normal growth and health. For patients who are unable to get enough iodine in their regular diet or who have a need for more iodine, sodium iodide may be necessary. Iodine is needed so that your thyroid gland can function properly.

Iodine deficiency in the United States is rare because iodine is added to table salt. Most people get enough salt from the foods they eat, without adding salt to their meals. Iodine deficiency is a problem in other areas of the world.

Lack of iodine may lead to thyroid problems, mental problems, hearing loss, and goiter.

Injectable sodium iodide is administered only by or under the supervision of a health care professional. Some multivitamin/mineral preparations that contain sodium iodide are available without your health care professional's prescription.

Sodium iodide is available in the following dosage forms:

Oral
- Sodium iodide is available orally as part of a multivitamin/mineral combination.

Parenteral
- Injection (U.S.)

Importance of Diet

For good health, it is important that you eat a balanced and varied diet. Follow carefully any diet program your health care professional may recommend. For your specific dietary vitamin and/or mineral needs, ask your health care professional for a list of appropriate foods. If you think that you are not getting enough vitamins and/or minerals in your diet, you may choose to take a dietary supplement.

Iodine is found in various foods, including seafood, small amounts of iodized salt, and vegetables grown in iodine-rich soils. Iodine-containing mist from the ocean is another important source of iodine, since iodine is absorbed by the skin. Iodized salt provides 76 micrograms (mcg) of iodine per gram of salt.

The daily amount of iodine needed is defined in several different ways.

For U.S.—
- Recommended Dietary Allowances (RDAs) are the amount of vitamins and minerals needed to provide for adequate nutrition in most healthy persons. RDAs for a given nutrient may vary depending on a person's age, sex, and physical condition (e.g., pregnancy).
- Daily Values (DVs) are used on food and dietary supplement labels to indicate the percent of the recommended daily amount of each nutrient that a serving provides. DV replaces the previous designation of United States Recommended Daily Allowances (USRDAs).

For Canada—
- Recommended Nutrient Intakes (RNIs) are used to determine the amounts of vitamins, minerals, and protein needed to provide adequate nutrition and lessen the risk of chronic disease.

Normal daily recommended intakes in mcg for iodine are generally defined as follows:

Persons	U.S. (mcg)	Canada (mcg)
Infants and children		
Birth to 3 years of age	40–70	30–65
4 to 6 years of age	90	85
7 to 10 years of age	120	95–125
Adolescent and adult males	150	125–160
Adolescent and adult females	150	110–160
Pregnant females	175	135–185
Breast-feeding females	200	160–210

Before Using This Dietary Supplement

If you are taking this dietary supplement without a prescription, carefully read and follow any precautions on the label. For sodium iodide, the following should be considered:

Allergies—Tell your health care professional if you have ever had any unusual or allergic reaction to iodine, iodine-containing foods, or sodium iodide. Also tell your health care professional if you are allergic to any other substances, such as foods, preservatives, or dyes.

Pregnancy—It is especially important that you are receiving enough vitamins and minerals when you become pregnant and that you continue to receive the right amount of vitamins and minerals throughout your pregnancy. The healthy growth and development of the fetus depend on a steady supply of nutrients from the mother. A deficiency of iodine in the mother may cause nerve or growth problems for the fetus. However, high doses of sodium iodide may cause thyroid problems or goiter in the newborn infant.

Breast-feeding—It is important that you receive the right amounts of vitamins and minerals so that your baby will also get the vitamins and minerals needed to grow properly. Taking high doses of sodium iodide may cause skin rash and thyroid problems in nursing babies.

Children—Problems in children have not been reported with intake of normal daily recommended amounts. However, high doses of sodium iodide may cause skin rash and thyroid problems in infants.

Older adults—Problems in older adults have not been reported with intake of normal daily recommended amounts.

Other medicines or dietary supplements—Although certain medicines or dietary supplements should not be used together at all, in other cases they may be used together even if an interaction might occur. In these cases, your health care professional may want to change the dose, or other precautions may be necessary. When you are taking sodium iodide, it is especially important that your health care professional know if you are taking any of the following:

- Antithyroid agents (medicine for overactive thyroid)—These medicines may prevent sodium iodide from working properly
- Iodine-containing preparations, other—Use of these preparations with sodium iodide may increase blood levels of iodine, which may increase the chance of side effects
- Lithium (e.g., Lithane)—Use of this medicine with sodium iodide may increase the chance of side effects

Other medical problems—The presence of other medical problems may affect the use of sodium iodide. Make sure you tell your health care professional if you have any other medical problems, especially:

- Kidney disease—Use of sodium iodide may increase the amount of iodine in the blood and increase the chance of side effects
- Thyroid disease—This condition may increase the chance of side effects of sodium iodide
- Tuberculosis—Use of sodium iodide may make this condition worse

Proper Use of This Dietary Supplement

Dosing—The amount of iodine needed to meet normal daily recommended intakes will be different for different individuals. The following information includes only the average amounts of iodine.

- For *oral* dosage form (as part of a multivitamin/mineral supplement):
  - —To prevent deficiency, the amount taken by mouth is based on normal daily recommended intakes:

For the U.S.

- Adults and teenagers—150 micrograms (mcg) per day.
- Pregnant females—175 mcg per day.
- Breast-feeding females—200 mcg per day.
- Children 7 to 10 years of age—120 mcg per day.
- Children 4 to 6 years of age—90 mcg per day.
- Children birth to 3 years of age—40 to 70 mcg per day.

For Canada

- Adult and teenage males—125 to 160 mcg per day.
- Adult and teenage females—110 to 160 mcg per day.
- Pregnant females—135 to 185 mcg per day.
- Breast-feeding females—160 to 210 mcg per day.
- Children 7 to 10 years of age—95 to 125 mcg per day.
- Children 4 to 6 years of age—85 mcg per day.
- Children birth to 3 years of age—30 to 65 mcg per day.

—To treat deficiency:

- Adults, teenagers, and children—Treatment dose is determined by prescriber for each individual based on severity of deficiency.

Missed dose—If you miss taking sodium iodide for one or more days there is no cause for concern, since it takes some time for your body to become seriously low in iodine. However, if your health care professional has recommended that you take iodine try to remember to use it as directed every day.

Storage—To store this dietary supplement:

- Keep out of the reach of children.
- Store away from heat and direct light.
- Do not store in the bathroom, near the kitchen sink, or in other damp places. Heat or moisture may cause the medicine to break down.
- Keep the medicine from freezing. Do not refrigerate.
- Do not keep outdated medicine or medicine no longer needed. Be sure that any discarded medicine is out of the reach of children.

Precautions While Using This Dietary Supplement

Many other products contain iodine. For example, iodine is absorbed through the skin from some skin cleansers (e.g., povidone-iodine). It may be especially important that infants and small children not receive large amounts of iodine. Check with your health care professional before using any other products that contain iodine while you are using sodium iodide.

Side Effects of This Dietary Supplement

Along with its needed effects, a dietary supplement may cause some unwanted effects. Although not all of these side effects may occur, if they do occur they may need medical attention. When this dietary supplement is used at low doses, side effects are rare.

Check with your health care professional as soon as possible if any of the following side effects occur:

Less common

Hives; joint pain; swelling of arms, face, legs, lips, tongue, and/or throat; swelling of lymph glands

With long-term use

Burning of mouth or throat; headache (severe); increased watering of mouth; metallic taste; skin sores; soreness of teeth and gums; stomach irritation

Other side effects not listed above may also occur in some individuals. If you notice any other effects, check with your health care professional.

Additional Information

Once a product has been approved for marketing for a certain use, experience may show that it is also useful for other medical problems. Although this use is not included in product labeling, injections of sodium iodide are used in certain patients with the following medical condition:

- Thyrotoxicosis crisis (severe overactive thyroid)

Other than the above information, there is no additional information relating to proper use, precautions, or side effects for this use.

Revised: 02/26/92
Interim revision: 08/19/94; 06/19/95

SODIUM IODIDE I 131 Therapeutic

Description

Sodium iodide (EYE-oh-dyed) I 131, also called radioactive iodine or radioiodide, is a radiopharmaceutical (ray-dee-oh-far-ma-SOO-ti-kal). Radiopharmaceuticals are radioactive agents, which may be used to diagnose some diseases by studying the function of the body's organs or to treat certain diseases.

Sodium iodide I 131 is used to treat an overactive thyroid gland and certain kinds of thyroid cancer. It is taken up mainly by the thyroid gland. In the treatment of hyperactive thyroid gland, radiation from the radioactive iodine damages the thyroid gland to bring its activity back down to normal. Larger doses of radioiodide are usually used after thyroid cancer surgery to destroy any remaining diseased thyroid tissue or to destroy thyroid cancer that has spread to other tissues.

When very small doses are given, a measure of the radioactivity taken up by the gland helps your doctor decide whether your thyroid gland is working properly. Also, an image of the organ on paper or a computer printout can be provided.

The information that follows applies only to the use of sodium iodide I 131 in treating an overactive or cancerous thyroid gland.

Sodium iodide I 131 is to be given only by or under the direct supervision of a doctor with specialized training in nuclear medicine or radiation oncology. It is available in the following dosage forms:

Oral

- Capsules (U.S. and Canada)
- Solution (U.S. and Canada)

Before Using This Medicine

In deciding to use a medicine, the risks of taking the medicine must be weighed against the good it will do. This is a decision you and your doctor will make. For sodium iodide I 131, the following should be considered:

Diet—If you eat large amounts of iodine-containing foods, such as iodized salt and seafoods, or cabbage, kale, rape (turnip-like vegetable), or turnips, the iodine contained in these foods will reduce the amount of this radiopharmaceutical that your thyroid gland will accept. Avoid these foods for at least 2 to 4 weeks weeks before the treatment with radioiodide.

Pregnancy—Sodium iodide I 131 should not be used during pregnancy. This is to avoid exposing the fetus to radiation. Also, it may cause the newborn baby to have an underactive thyroid gland. A pregnancy test should be done prior to treatment with radioactive iodine if pregnancy is a possibility. Be sure you have discussed this with your doctor.

Breast-feeding—Sodium iodide I 131 passes into the breast milk and may cause unwanted effects, such as underactive thyroid, in the nursing baby. If you must receive this radiopharmaceutical, it will be necessary for you to stop breast-feeding several weeks before treatment. Be sure you have discussed this with your doctor.

Children—Sodium iodide I 131 has been used in children and has not been shown to cause different side effects or problems than it does in adults. However, vomiting may more difficult to manage in younger children.

Older adults—Sodium iodide I 131 has been used in older people and has not been shown to cause different side effects or problems in older people than it does in younger adults.

Other medicines/tests—Tell your doctor if you have had an x-ray test recently for which you were given a radiopaque agent that contained iodine. The iodine contained in the radiopaque agent will reduce the amount of sodium iodide I 131 that your thyroid gland will accept. Also, tell your doctor if you are taking any other prescription or nonprescription (over-the-counter [OTC]) medicine.

Other medical problems—The presence of other medical problems may affect the use of sodium iodide I 131. Make sure you tell your doctor if you have any other medical problems, especially:

- Diarrhea or
- Vomiting—The radioactive iodine will be present in the diarrhea and vomit and will put you and others at a higher risk of radiation contamination; also, some of the dose will be lost, making the treatment less effective
- Kidney disease—Kidney disease may cause the radioiodide to stay in the body longer than usual, which may increase the risk of side effects
- If you have heart disease and are receiving sodium iodide I 131 to treat an overactive thyroid—The radiation may worsen the thyroid condition if antithyroid medicine and/or beta-blockers, such as propranolol, are not given before and after treatment

Proper Use of This Medicine

Your doctor may have special instructions for you to get ready for your treatment. If you have not received such instructions or you do not understand them, check with your doctor ahead of time.

Dosing—The doses of radiopharmaceuticals will be different for different patients and for the different types of treatments. The amount of radioactivity of a radiopharmaceutical is expressed in units called becquerels or curies. The usual adult dose of radioiodide to treat an overactive thyroid gland is 148 to 370 megabecquerels (4 to 10 millicuries). The usual amount of radioiodide to treat cancer of the thyroid is much larger, 1.1 to 7.4 gigabecquerels (30 to 200 millicuries). The dose you receive depends on your size and age. The amount of radiation received by specific areas of the body to treat a disease is many times higher than that received from any diagnostic test, such as x-rays and nuclear medicine scans. Doses may need to be repeated, depending on the kind of disease you have and how your body is responding to treatment.

Precautions After Using This Medicine

There are no special precautions when this medicine is used in very small doses to help study the function of the thyroid. However, if you are receiving sodium iodide I 131 for an overactive thyroid or cancer of the thyroid, your doctor may tell you to *follow some or all of these guidelines for 48 to 96 hours* after receiving the medicine, to help reduce the chance of contaminating other persons:

- *Do not kiss anyone, or handle or use another person's eating or drinking utensils, toothbrush, or bathroom glass.*
- *Do not have sex.*
- *Do not sit close to others, especially pregnant women, and do not hold children in your lap for long periods of time.*
- Sleep alone.
- *Wash the tub and sink after each use (including after brushing teeth).*
- *Wash your hands after using or cleaning the toilet.*
- Use a separate towel and washcloth.
- Wash your clothes, bed linens, and eating utensils separately.
- Sodium iodide I 131 is passed in the urine. To prevent contamination of your home, *flush the toilet twice after you urinate.*

To increase the flow of urine and lessen the amount of radioactive iodine in your body, drink plenty of liquids and urinate often.

If you were treated with sodium iodide I 131 for an overactive thyroid, your doctor may want to check the level of thyroid hormone in your blood every 2 to 3 months during the first year, and once a year thereafter. This is to make sure that your thyroid has not become underactive.

Side Effects of This Medicine

Studies have not shown that sodium iodide I 131 increases the chance of cancer or other long-term problems. When used to treat an overactive thyroid gland, sodium iodide I 131 may cause the patient to have an underactive thyroid gland after treatment. The thyroid gland may become underactive even several years after treatment for hyperthyroidism. Before receiving this medicine, be sure you have discussed its use with your doctor.

Along with its needed effects, a medicine may cause some unwanted effects. Although not all of these side effects may occur, if they do occur they may need medical attention.

When this medicine is used in very small doses to help study the function of the gland, side effects are rare. However, check with your doctor as soon as possible if any of the following side effects occur after treatment for overactive thyroid or cancer of the thyroid:

After treatment of overactive thyroid

Symptoms of an underactive thyroid

Changes in menstrual periods; clumsiness; coldness; drowsiness; dry, puffy skin; headache; listlessness; muscle aches; thinning of hair (temporary)—may occur 2 to 3 months after treatment; unusual tiredness or weakness; weight gain

Rare

After treatment of overactive thyroid

Excessive sweating; fast heartbeat; fever; palpitations; unusual irritability; unusual tiredness

After treatment of cancer of the thyroid

Black, tarry stools; blood in urine or stools; cough or hoarseness; fever or chills; lower back or side pain; painful or difficult urination; pinpoint red spots on skin; unusual bleeding or bruising

Other side effects may occur that usually do not need medical attention. These side effects may go away during treatment as your body adjusts to the medicine. However,

check with your doctor if any of the following side effects continue or are bothersome:

Less common

After treatment of overactive thyroid or cancer of the thyroid

Neck tenderness or swelling; sore throat

After treatment of cancer of the thyroid

Loss of taste (temporary); nausea and vomiting (temporary); tenderness of salivary glands

Other side effects not listed above may also occur in some patients. If you notice any other effects, check with your doctor.

Revised: 07/15/96

SODIUM PHENYLBUTYRATE Systemic†

A commonly used brand name in the U.S. is Buphenyl.

†Not commercially available in Canada.

Description

Sodium phenylbutyrate (SOE-dee-um fen-il-BYOO-ti-rate) is used to help treat a deficiency of enzymes that help remove ammonia from your body.

Ammonia is formed from the breakdown of protein in the body. If the ammonia cannot be removed by the body, then a buildup may cause serious unwanted effects. This medicine works by helping to reduce high levels of ammonia in the blood.

Sodium phenylbutyrate is available only with your doctor's prescription, in the following dosage forms:

Oral

- Powder for solution (U.S.)
- Tablets (U.S.)

Before Using This Medicine

In deciding to use a medicine, the risks of taking the medicine must be weighed against the good it will do. This is a decision you and your doctor will make. For sodium phenylbutyrate, the following should be considered:

Allergies—Tell your doctor if you have ever had any unusual or allergic reaction to sodium phenylbutyrate. Also tell your health care professional if you are allergic to any other substances, such as foods, preservatives, or dyes.

Pregnancy—Studies on effects in pregnancy have not been done in either humans or animals.

Breast-feeding—It is not known whether sodium phenylbutyrate passes into breast milk.

Children—This medicine has been reported to cause unwanted side effects in children. Also, nerve problems and brain damage associated with your condition may continue to worsen despite treatment.

Older adults—Many medicines have not been studied specifically in older people. Therefore, it may not be known whether they work exactly the same way they do in younger adults or if they cause different side effects or problems in older people. There is no specific information comparing the use of sodium phenylbutyrate in the elderly with use in other age groups.

Other medicines—Although certain medicines should not be used together at all, in other cases two different medicines may be used together even if an interaction might occur. In these cases, your doctor may want to change the dose, or other precautions may be necessary. When you are taking sodium phenylbutyrate, it is especially important that your health care professional know if you are taking the following:

- Probenecid—Probenecid may increase the effects of sodium phenylbutyrate

Other medical problems—The presence of other medical problems may affect the use of sodium phenylbutyrate. Make sure you tell your doctor if you have any other medical problems, especially:

- Edema (swelling) or
- Heart disease or
- Kidney disease, severe—Increased retention of water may make these conditions worse
- Kidney disease or
- Liver disease—Higher blood levels of sodium phenylbutyrate may result and increase the risk of side effects

Proper Use of This Medicine

For patients taking the *powder* form of this medicine:

- Sodium phenylbutyrate should be mixed with solid food or a liquid. However, it should not be mixed with acidic beverages such as coffee, tea, or grapefruit, orange, or tomato juice.

Take this medicine with meals or feedings.

It is important that you follow any special instructions from your doctor, such as following a low-protein diet. Also, your doctor may recommend that you take amino acid supplements. If you have any questions about this, check with your doctor.

Dosing—The dose of sodium phenylbutyrate will be different for different patients. *Follow your doctor's orders or the directions on the label.* The following information includes only the average doses of sodium phenylbutyrate. *If your dose is different, do not change it* unless your doctor tells you to do so.

- For too much ammonia in the body:
  - —For *oral* dosage form (powder for solution):
    - Adults, teenagers, and children weighing 20 kilograms (kg) (44 pounds) or more—The dose is based on body size and must be determined by your doctor. It is usually given four to six times

a day with meals or feedings. The dose is usually not more than 20 grams a day.

• Children weighing up to 20 kg (44 pounds)—The dose is based on body weight. The usual dose is 450 to 600 milligrams (mg) per kg (205 to 273 mg per pound) of body weight a day. The dose is given four to six times a day with meals or feedings. The dose is usually not more than 20 grams a day.

For *oral* dosage form (tablets):

• Adults, teenagers, and children weighing 20 kg (44 pounds) or more—The dose is based on body size and must be determined by your doctor. It is usually given three times a day with meals or feedings. The dose is usually not more than 20 grams (40 tablets) a day.

• Children weighing up to 20 kg (44 pounds)—Use of the tablets is not recommended.

Missed dose—If you miss a dose of this medicine, take it as soon as possible. It is important to take the full amount every day as prescribed by your doctor.

Storage—To store this medicine:

- Keep out of the reach of children.
- Store away from heat and direct light.
- Do not store in the bathroom, near the kitchen sink, or in other damp places. Heat or moisture may cause the medicine to break down. However, a strong, musty odor is normal for your medicine.
- Keep the medicine from freezing. Do not refrigerate.
- Keep container tightly closed.
- Do not keep outdated medicine or medicine no longer needed. Be sure that any discarded medicine is out of the reach of children.

Precautions While Using This Medicine

Your doctor should check your progress at regular visits to make sure that this medicine is working properly.

Side Effects of This Medicine

Along with its needed effects, a medicine may cause some unwanted effects. Although not all of these side effects may occur, if they do occur they may need medical attention.

Check with your doctor as soon as possible if any of the following side effects occur:

More common

Change in frequency of breathing; lack of or irregular menstruation; mood or mental changes; muscle pain or twitching; nausea or vomiting; nervousness or restlessness; lower back, side, or stomach pain; swelling of feet or lower legs; unpleasant taste; unusual tiredness or weakness

Less common

Chills; fever; joint pain; sore throat; unusual bleeding or bruising

Rare

Convulsions (seizures); dizziness; dryness of mouth; fast, slow, or irregular heartbeat; increased blood pressure; increased thirst; irritability; muscle cramps; rectal bleeding; swelling of face; unusual weight gain; weak pulse

Other side effects may occur that usually do not need medical attention. These side effects may go away during treatment as your body adjusts to the medicine. However, check with your doctor if any of the following side effects continue or are bothersome:

Less common

Changes in taste; decreased appetite; strong body odor

Rare

Abdominal or stomach pain; constipation; fainting; headache; mental depression; skin rash

Other side effects not listed above may also occur in some patients. If you notice any other effects, check with your doctor.

Developed: 08/07/97

SODIUM PHOSPHATE P 32 Therapeutic

Description

Sodium phosphate (SOE-dee-um FOS-fate) P 32 is a radiopharmaceutical (ray-dee-oh-far-ma-SOO-ti-kal). Radiopharmaceuticals are radioactive agents that may be used to treat certain diseases or to study the activity of the body's organs.

Sodium phosphate P 32 is used to treat certain kinds of cancer. In this case, the radioactive agent builds up in the cancerous area and destroys the affected tissue. This radiopharmaceutical may also be used for other conditions as determined by your doctor.

Sodium phosphate P 32 is to be given only by or under the direct supervision of a doctor with specialized training in nuclear medicine. It is available in the following dosage form:

Parenteral

• Solution (U.S. and Canada)

Before Using This Medicine

In deciding to use a medicine, the risks of taking the medicine must be weighed against the good it will do. This is a decision you and your doctor will make. For sodium phosphate P 32, the following should be considered:

Allergies—Tell your doctor if you have ever had any unusual or allergic reaction to sodium phosphate P 32. Also tell your doctor if you are allergic to any other substances, such as foods, preservatives, or dyes.

Pregnancy—Studies have not been done in either humans or animals. However, to avoid exposing the fetus to radiation, sodium phosphate P 32 is not recommended for use during pregnancy. Be sure you have discussed this with your doctor.

Breast-feeding—Sodium phosphate may pass into the breast milk. If you must receive this radiopharmaceutical, it will be necessary for you to stop breast-feeding during treatment. Be sure you have discussed this with your doctor.

Children—Studies on this medicine have been done only in adult patients, and there is no specific information about its use in children. However, children are especially sensitive to the effects of radiation. This may increase the chance of side effects during and after treatment.

Older adults—Older adults are especially sensitive to the effects of radiation. This may increase the chance of side effects during and after treatment.

Other medicines—Although certain medicines should not be used together at all, in other cases two different medicines may be used together even if an interaction might occur. In these cases, your doctor may want to change the dose, or other precautions may be necessary. When you are receiving sodium phosphate P 32, it is especially important that your doctor know if you are taking any other prescription or nonprescription (over-the-counter [OTC]) medicine.

Other medical problems—The presence of other medical problems may affect the use of sodium phosphate P 32. Make sure you tell your doctor if you have any other medical problems.

Proper Use of This Medicine

Your doctor may have special instructions for you in preparation for your treatment. If you do not understand them or if you have not received such instructions, check with your doctor in advance.

Dosing—The doses of radiopharmaceuticals will be different for different patients and for the different types of treatments. The amount of radioactivity of a radiopharmaceutical is expressed in units called becquerels or curies. Usual adult doses of sodium phosphate P 32 range from 37 megabecquerels (1 millicurie) to 185 megabecquerels (5 millicuries). The dose you receive depends on your size, age, and blood test measurements (blood counts). The amount of radiation received by the body to treat a disease is many times higher than from any diagnostic test, such as x-rays and nuclear medicine scans. Repeated doses may be necessary, depending on the kind of disease you have and how your body is responding to treatment.

Side Effects of This Medicine

Along with its needed effects, a medicine may cause some unwanted effects. When sodium phosphate P 32 is used at recommended doses, side effects usually are rare. However, blood problems, such as anemia or a decrease in the number of white blood cells, may occur in some patients.

Also, the following side effects may occur in patients with bone cancer receiving sodium phosphate P 32 for the relief of bone pain:

More common

Diarrhea, fever, nausea, vomiting

Other side effects not listed above may also occur in some patients. If you notice any other effects, check with your doctor.

Revised: 07/16/93

SPECTINOMYCIN Systemic

A commonly used brand name in the U.S. and Canada is Trobicin.

Description

Spectinomycin (spek-ti-noe-MYE-sin) is used to treat most types of gonorrhea. It is given by injection into a muscle. It is sometimes given with other medicines for gonorrhea and related infections.

Spectinomycin may be used in patients who are allergic to penicillins, cephalosporins, or probenecid (e.g., Benemid). This medicine is also used to treat recent sexual partners of patients who have gonorrhea. However, spectinomycin will not work for gonorrhea of the throat, syphilis, colds, flu, or other virus infections.

Spectinomycin is available only with your doctor's prescription, in the following dosage form:

Parenteral

- Injection (U.S. and Canada)

Before Receiving This Medicine

In deciding to use a medicine, the risks of taking the medicine must be weighed against the good it will do. This is a decision you and your doctor will make. For spectinomycin, the following should be considered:

Allergies—Tell your doctor if you have ever had any unusual or allergic reaction to spectinomycin. Also tell your health care professional if you are allergic to any other substances, such as foods, preservatives, or dyes.

Pregnancy—Studies have not been done in humans. However, spectinomycin has been recommended for the treatment of gonorrhea and related infections in pregnant patients who are allergic to penicillins, cephalosporins, or probenecid (e.g., Benemid). In addition, studies in animals have not shown that spectinomycin causes birth defects or other problems.

Breast-feeding—It is not known if spectinomycin passes into breast milk. However, spectinomycin has not been reported to cause problems in nursing babies.

Children—This medicine has been used in a limited number of children. In effective doses, the medicine has not been shown to cause different side effects or problems than it does in adults. However, use in infants is not recommended.

Older adults—Many medicines have not been studied specifically in older people. Therefore, it may not be known whether they work exactly the same way they do in younger adults. Although there is no specific information comparing use of spectinomycin in the elderly with use in other age groups, this medicine is not expected to cause different side effects or problems in older people than it does in younger adults.

Other medicines—Although certain medicines should not be used together at all, in other cases two different medicines may be used together even if an interaction might occur. In these cases, your doctor may want to change the dose, or other precautions may be necessary. Tell your health care professional if you are taking any other prescription or nonprescription (over-the-counter [OTC]) medicine.

Proper Use of This Medicine

Spectinomycin is given by injection into a muscle. To help clear up your gonorrhea completely, usually only one dose is needed. However, in some infections a second dose of this medicine may be required.

Gonorrhea and related infections are spread by having sex with an infected partner. Therefore, it may be desirable that the male sexual partner wear a condom (prophylactic) during intercourse to prevent infection. Also, it may be necessary for your partner to be treated at the same time you are being treated. This will help to avoid passing the infection back and forth.

Dosing—The dose of spectinomycin will be different for different patients. The following information includes only the average doses of spectinomycin.

- For *cervical, rectal, or urethral gonorrhea*:
  - —Adults and children 45 kilograms of body weight (99 pounds) and over: 2 grams injected into a muscle as a single dose.
  - —Children up to 45 kilograms of body weight (99 pounds): 40 milligrams per kilogram of body weight injected into a muscle as a single dose.
  - —Infants: Use is not recommended.

Precautions After Receiving This Medicine

If your symptoms do not improve within a few days, or if they become worse, check with your doctor.

This medicine may cause some people to become dizzy. *Make sure you know how you react to this medicine before you drive, use machines, or do anything else that could be dangerous if you are dizzy.* If this reaction is especially bothersome, check with your doctor.

Side Effects of This Medicine

Along with its needed effects, a medicine may cause some unwanted effects. Although not all of these side effects may occur, if they do occur they may need medical attention.

Check with your doctor as soon as possible if any of the following side effects occur:

Rare

Chills or fever; itching or redness of the skin

Other side effects may occur that usually do not need medical attention. These side effects may go away during treatment as your body adjusts to the medicine. However, check with your doctor if any of these effects continue or are bothersome:

Less common

Dizziness; nausea and vomiting; pain at the place of injection; stomach cramps

Other side effects not listed above may also occur in some patients. If you notice any other effects, check with your doctor.

Revised: 02/23/93

SPERMICIDES Vaginal

Some commonly used brand names are:

In the U.S.—

Advantage 24[2]
Because[2]
Conceptrol Contraceptive Inserts[2]
Conceptrol Gel[2]
Delfen[2]
Emko[2]
Emko Pre-Fil[2]
Encare[2]
Gynol II Extra Strength Contraceptive Jelly[2]
Gynol II Original Formula Contraceptive Jelly[2]
Koromex Cream[3]
Koromex Crystal Clear Gel[2]
Koromex Foam[2]
Koromex Jelly[2]
K-Y Plus[2]
Ortho-Creme[2]
Ortho-Gynol[3]
Ramses Crystal Clear Gel[2]
Semicid[2]
Shur-Seal[2]
VCF[2]

In Canada—

Advantage 24[2]
Delfen[2]
Emko[2]
Encare[2]
Ortho-Gynol[3]
Pharmatex[1]
Ramses Contraceptive Foam[2]

Note: For quick reference, the following spermicides are numbered to match the corresponding brand names.

This information applies to the following medicines:

1. Benzalkonium Chloride (benz-al-KOE-nee-um KLOR-ide)*
2. Nonoxynol 9 (no-NOX-i-nole nine)
3. Octoxynol 9 (awk-TOX-i-nole nine)

*Not commercially available in the U.S.

Description

Vaginal spermicides are a type of contraceptive (birth control). These products are inserted into the vagina *before* any genital contact occurs or sexual intercourse begins. They work by damaging and killing sperm in the vagina.

Therefore, the sperm are not able to travel from the vagina into the uterus and fallopian tubes, where fertilization usually takes place.

Vaginal spermicides when used alone are much less effective in preventing pregnancy than birth control pills or the IUD or spermicides used with another form of birth control, such as cervical caps, condoms, or diaphragms. *Studies have shown that when spermicides are used alone, pregnancy usually occurs in 21 of each 100 women during the first year of spermicide use.* The number of pregnancies is reduced when spermicides are used with another method, especially the condom. Discuss with a doctor what your options are for birth control and the risks and benefits of each method.

Laboratory studies have shown that nonoxynol 9 kills or stops the growth of the AIDS virus (HIV) and herpes simplex I and II viruses. It was also shown to be effective against other types of organisms that cause gonorrhea, chlamydia, syphilis, trichomoniasis, and other sexually transmitted diseases (venereal disease, VD, STDs). Benzalkonium chloride also killed the AIDS virus in laboratory studies. Although this has *not* been proven in *human* studies, some scientists *believe* that if spermicides are put into the vagina or on the inside and outside of a latex (rubber) condom, they *may* kill these germs before they are able to come in contact with the vagina or rectum (lower bowel).

The most effective way to protect yourself against STDs (such as AIDS) is by abstinence (not having sexual intercourse) or by having one partner who you can be sure is not already infected or is not going to get an STD. However, if either of these methods is not likely or possible, using latex (rubber) condoms with a spermicide is the best way of protecting yourself.

The use of a spermicide is recommended even when you are using nonbarrier methods of birth control such as birth control pills (the Pill) or intrauterine devices (IUDs), since these do not offer any protection from STDs.

The safety of using spermicides in the rectum (lower bowel), anus, or rectal area is not known. However, no side effects or problems have been reported that are different from those reported for use in the vagina.

Vaginal spermicides are available without a prescription, in the following dosage forms:

Vaginal

Benzalkonium chloride

- Suppositories (Canada)

Nonoxynol 9

- Cream (U.S. and Canada)
- Film (U.S.)
- Foam (U.S. and Canada)
- Gel (U.S. and Canada)
- Jelly (U.S.)
- Suppositories (U.S. and Canada)

Octoxynol 9

- Cream (U.S.)
- Jelly (U.S. and Canada)

Before Using This Medicine

In deciding to use vaginal spermicides, the risks of using them must be weighed against the good they will do. This is a decision you and possibly your doctor will make. The following information may help you in making your decision:

Allergies—If you have ever had any unusual or allergic reaction to benzalkonium chloride, nonoxynol 9, or octoxynol 9, it is best to check with your doctor before using vaginal spermicides.

Pregnancy—Many studies have shown that the use of vaginal spermicides does not increase the risk of birth defects or miscarriage.

Breast-feeding—It is not known if vaginal spermicides pass into breast milk in humans. However, their use has not been reported to cause problems in nursing babies.

Teenagers—These products have been used by teenagers and have not been shown to cause different side effects or problems than they do in adults. However, some younger users may need extra counseling and information on the importance of using spermicides exactly as they are supposed to be used so they will work properly.

Other medicines—If you are using this medicine without a prescription, carefully read and follow any precautions on the label. For spermicides, the following should be considered:

- Salicylates used on the skin (e.g., some types of ointments for muscle aches) or
- Sulfonamides (sulfa medicine) for use in the vagina or
- Chemicals or substances such as aluminum, citrate, cotton, dressings, hydrogen peroxide, iodides, lanolin, nitrates, permanganates, some forms of silver, soaps, detergents, or tartrates—Benzalkonium chloride may not work if it comes in direct contact with these as well as many other chemicals
- Vaginal douches and rectal or vaginal cleansing products—For spermicides to work properly to prevent pregnancy, they must stay in contact with the sperm in the vagina for at least 6 or 8 hours (depending upon which brand of spermicide you use) after sexual intercourse. *Vaginal douching is not necessary after use of these medicines.* Douching too soon (even with just water) may stop the spermicide from working. Also, washing or rinsing the vaginal or rectal area may also make the spermicide ineffective in helping to prevent sexually transmitted diseases

Medical problems—The presence of certain medical problems may affect the use of vaginal spermicides. Since in some cases spermicides should not be used, check with your doctor if you have any of the following:

- Allergies, irritations, or infections of the genitals—Using vaginal spermicides may cause moderate to severe irritation in these conditions. Also, benzalkonium suppositories may be less effective in women with vaginal infections
- Conditions or medical problems where it is important that pregnancy does not occur—Vaginal spermicides when used alone are much less effective than birth control pills or the IUD or spermicides used with another form of birth control such as cervical caps, condoms, or diaphragms. Discuss with your doctor what your options are for birth control and the risks and benefits of each method
- Recent childbirth or abortion or

- Toxic shock syndrome (history of)—Cervical caps or diaphragms should not be used in these cases because there is an increased chance of developing toxic shock syndrome
- Sores on the genitals (sex organs) or
- Irritation of the vagina—It is not known whether spermicides can cause breaks in the skin that could increase the chances of getting a sexually transmitted disease, especially AIDS. Discuss this with a doctor if you have any questions

If you develop any medical problem or begin using any new medicine (prescription or nonprescription) while you are using this medicine, you may want to check with your doctor.

Proper Use of This Medicine

Make sure you carefully read and follow the directions that come with each spermicide product. Each product may have different directions for using the product. The directions tell you how much to use, how long you must wait before having intercourse, and how long you must leave it in the vagina after intercourse. *Vaginal douching is not needed or advised after using these medicines.* When using a spermicide, douching within 6 to 8 hours after the last sexual intercourse (even with just water) may stop the spermicide from working properly. Also, washing or rinsing the vaginal or rectal area may wash the spermicide away before it has had time to work properly.

Cervical caps and diaphragms are not recommended for use during your menstrual period because of an increased chance of developing toxic shock syndrome. Your doctor may advise you to use condoms with a spermicide instead during your menstrual periods when protection is needed.

For proper use of spermicide when used alone:

- Follow directions carefully to make sure the spermicide is properly placed in the vagina. The spermicide should be inserted deep into the vagina, directly on the cervix (opening to the uterus).
- Use the correct amount, according to the product directions.
- Use another dose for *each* act of intercourse.
- After you have applied or inserted the spermicide, wait the correct amount of time before having intercourse so that the spermicide can begin to work.
- If you do not have intercourse within half an hour, read the product directions to see if you need to apply more spermicide.

For proper use of spermicide with cervical caps, condoms, or diaphragms:

- *Make sure the directions for the spermicide you choose state that it is safe for use with latex cervical caps, condoms, or diaphragms.* If the directions do not say the spermicide is safe to use with latex products, the spermicide may cause cervical caps, condoms, or diaphragms to weaken and leak or cause condoms to break during intercourse.
- If there is a leak or break during intercourse, it may be a good idea for the female partner to immediately place more spermicide in the vagina.
- *If you need an extra lubricant, make sure it is a water-based product safe for use with cervical caps, condoms, or diaphragms.* Spermicides, especially gels and jellies, provide some lubrication during sexual intercourse.
- Oil-based products such as hand, face, or body cream; petroleum jelly; cooking oils or shortenings; or baby oil should *not* be used because they weaken the latex rubber. (Even some products that easily rinse away with water are oil-based and should not be used.) Use of oil-based products increases the chances of the condom breaking during sexual intercourse. These products can also cause the rubber in cervical caps or diaphragms to break down faster and wear out sooner.

For patients using spermicides with a cervical cap:

- *To be most effective at preventing pregnancy, the cervical cap must always be used with a spermicide.* Both must be used every time you have sexual intercourse.
- Before inserting the cervical cap, inspect it for holes, tears, or cracks. If there are holes or defects, the cervical cap will not work effectively, even with a spermicide. It must be replaced.
- Before you put the cervical cap over the cervix (opening to the uterus), a spermicide cream, foam, gel, or jelly should be put into the cup of the cervical cap. Follow the manufacturer's directions on how long before sexual intercourse you may apply the spermicide. Fill the cervical cap one-third full with spermicide.
- To insert the cervical cap, squeeze the rim between your thumb and forefinger so that it is narrow enough to fit into the vagina. While in a comfortable position, push the cervical cap as deeply into the vagina as it will go. Release the rim and press it into place around the cervix with your finger. The rim should be round again and be directly on the cervix. The cervical cap is held onto the cervix by suction.
- Some doctors may recommend that you put more spermicide into the vagina each time you repeat sexual intercourse using a cervical cap. You should also check to make sure the cervical cap is in the proper position on the cervix before and after each time you have intercourse. You may wear the cervical cap for up to 48 hours (2 days).
- *Do not remove the cervical cap if it has been less than 8 hours since the last time you had sexual intercourse.* For the cervical cap to be most effective at preventing pregnancy, it must remain in the vagina for at least 8 hours after sexual intercourse.
- To remove the cervical cap, use 1 or 2 fingers to push the rim away from the cervix. This will break the suction seal with the cervix. Then gently pull the cervical cap out of the vagina. *Call your doctor if you have trouble removing the cervical cap.*

For patients using spermicides with condoms:

- Condoms do not have to be used with spermicides, but the spermicide may provide a back-up birth control method in case the condom breaks or leaks.

- Spread some spermicide on the outside of the condom, after it is unrolled over the penis. It is even more important that the female partner also use a spermicide inside the vagina.
- Each time you repeat intercourse, a new condom must be used. *Condoms should never be reused.* Spermicide should also be applied to the outside of the new condom. The female partner must also put more spermicide in the vagina each time she has intercourse.

For patients using spermicides with a diaphragm:

- *To be most effective at preventing pregnancy, diaphragms must always be used with a spermicide.* Some women may choose to insert a diaphragm every night, to avoid the chance of unprotected sexual intercourse and unplanned pregnancy happening.
- Inspect the diaphragm for holes by holding it up to a light. If there are holes or defects, the diaphragm will not work effectively, even with a spermicide. It must be replaced.
- Before you put the diaphragm over the cervix (opening to the uterus), a spermicide cream, foam, gel, or jelly should be put into the cup of the diaphragm. Follow the manufacturer's directions on how much spermicide to use and how long before sexual intercourse you may apply the spermicide. Also, spread some spermicide all around the rim of the diaphragm that will be touching the cervix. Some doctors also advise spreading more spermicide on the outside of the cup of the diaphragm.
- To insert the diaphragm, squeeze the rim between your thumb and forefinger so that it is narrow enough to fit into the vagina. While in a comfortable position, push the diaphragm as deeply into the vagina as it will go. (Some women use a special applicator that makes it easier to insert the diaphragm.) Release the rim. The diaphragm rim should be round again and be directly on the cervix.
- Each time you repeat sexual intercourse, you should put more spermicide into the vagina. *Do not remove the diaphragm if it has been less than 6 or 8 hours (depending upon which brand of spermicide you use) since the last sexual intercourse.* For the diaphragm to be most effective at preventing pregnancy, it must remain in the vagina for at least 6 or 8 hours (depending upon which brand of spermicide you use) after sexual intercourse. Be careful not to move the diaphragm out of place while you are applying more spermicide.
- Do not wear the diaphragm for more than 24 hours, since doing so increases the risk of getting toxic shock syndrome or a urinary tract (bladder) infection.
- To remove the diaphragm, hook one finger over the rim nearest the front. Pull the diaphragm downward and out of the vagina. *Call your doctor if you have trouble removing the diaphragm.*

Dosing—*Follow your doctor's orders or the directions on the label.* The following information includes the usual way that spermicides are used.

For benzalkonium chloride

- For preventing pregnancy:
  - —For *vaginal suppositories* dosage form:
    - Adults and teenagers:
      - —For use alone: One suppository inserted into the vagina at least ten minutes but not longer than four hours before each time you have sexual intercourse.
      - —For use with a diaphragm: After the diaphragm with spermicide has been placed into the vagina, insert one suppository at least ten minutes, but not longer than four hours, before each time you have sexual intercourse. Also, insert another suppository before sexual intercourse if six hours have passed since you inserted the diaphragm.

For nonoxynol 9

- For preventing pregnancy:
  - —For *vaginal cream* dosage form:
    - Adults and teenagers:
      - —For use alone: One applicatorful of a 5% cream inserted into the vagina just before each time you have sexual intercourse.
      - —For use with a diaphragm: One applicatorful of a 2 or 5% cream inserted into the cup of the diaphragm. Spread more spermicide along the rim of the diaphragm. Insert the diaphragm into the vagina just before, but not longer than six hours before, sexual intercourse. Also, insert one applicatorful just before each time you have intercourse or if six hours have passed since you inserted the diaphragm.
  - —For *vaginal film* dosage form:
    - Adults and teenagers—One film inserted into the vagina from five to fifteen minutes (but not longer than one and one-half hours) before each time you have sexual intercourse.
  - —For *vaginal foam* dosage form:
    - Adults and teenagers:
      - —For use alone: One applicatorful inserted into the vagina just before, but not longer than one hour before, each time you have sexual intercourse.
      - —For use with a diaphragm: One applicatorful inserted into either the vagina or into the cup of the diaphragm, depending on the product. Spread more spermicide along the rim of the diaphragm. Insert the diaphragm into the vagina just before, but not longer than one hour before, sexual intercourse. Also, insert another applicatorful into the vagina just before, but not longer than one hour before, each time you have sexual intercourse.

—For *vaginal gel* dosage form:

- Adults and teenagers:

  —For use alone: One applicatorful of a 3.5, 4, or 5% gel inserted into the vagina before each time you have sexual intercourse. The 3.5% gel may be used up to twenty-four hours before each act of intercourse. The 4% gel may be used up to one hour before each act of intercourse. The 5% gel must be used just before intercourse.

  —For use with a diaphragm: One or two teaspoonfuls (depending on the product) or the contents of one packet of gel is placed into the cup of the diaphragm. Spread more spermicide along the rim of the diaphragm. Insert the diaphragm into the vagina just before, or up to six hours before, sexual intercourse. Also, insert another applicatorful or the contents of one packet into the vagina before each time you have sexual intercourse or if six hours have passed since you inserted the diaphragm.

—For *vaginal jelly* dosage form:

- Adults and teenagers:

  —For use alone: One applicatorful of 2.2 or 3% jelly inserted into the vagina just before each time you have sexual intercourse. The contraceptive effect of the 2.2 or 3% jelly will last one hour.

  —For use with a diaphragm: One applicatorful or two teaspoonfuls of jelly (depending on the product) placed into the cup of the diaphragm. Spread more spermicide along the rim of the diaphragm. Insert the diaphragm into the vagina just before, but not longer than six hours before, sexual intercourse. Also, insert another applicatorful before each time you have sexual intercourse or if six hours have passed since you inserted the diaphragm.

—For *vaginal suppositories* dosage form:

- Adults and teenagers:

  —For use alone: One suppository inserted into the vagina from ten to fifteen minutes (depending on the product) before, but not longer than one hour before, each time you have sexual intercourse.

- Adults and teenagers:

  —For use with a diaphragm: After the diaphragm with spermicide has been placed into the vagina, insert one suppository into the vagina from ten to fifteen minutes (depending on the product) before, but not longer than one hour before, sexual intercourse. Also, insert another suppository before each time you have sexual intercourse or if six hours have passed since you have inserted the diaphragm.

For octoxynol 9

- For preventing pregnancy:

  —For *vaginal cream* dosage form:

  - Adults and teenagers:

    —For use with a diaphragm: Two teaspoonfuls placed into the cup of the diaphragm. Spread more spermicide along the rim of the diaphragm. Insert the diaphragm into the vagina just before, but not longer than six hours before, sexual intercourse. Also, insert one applicatorful of the vaginal cream just before each time you have sexual intercourse or if six hours have passed since you inserted the diaphragm.

  —For *vaginal jelly* dosage form:

  - Adults and teenagers:

    —For use with a diaphragm: One applicatorful placed into the cup of the diaphragm. Spread more spermicide along the rim of the diaphragm. Insert the diaphragm into the vagina just before, but not longer than six hours before, sexual intercourse. Also, insert another applicatorful just before each time you have sexual intercourse or if six hours have passed since you inserted the diaphragm.

Storage—To store this medicine:

- Keep out of the reach of children.
- Store away from heat and direct light.
- Do not store in the bathroom, near the kitchen sink, or in other damp places. Heat or moisture may cause the medicine to break down.
- Do not refrigerate.
- Do not keep outdated products or products no longer needed. Be sure that any discarded products are out of the reach of children.

Precautions While Using This Medicine

During use of spermicides, either partner may notice burning, stinging, warmth, itching, or other irritation of the skin, sex organs, anus, or rectum. Using a weaker strength of vaginal spermicide or one with different ingredients may be necessary. If you are using benzalkonium chloride suppositories, it may help to wet them before they are inserted into the vagina. If any of these effects continue after you have changed products, you may have an allergy to these products or an infection, and should contact a doctor as soon as possible.

Side Effects of This Medicine

Along with its needed effects, a medicine may cause some unwanted effects. Although not all of these side effects may occur, if they do occur they may need medical attention.

Check with a doctor *immediately* if any of the following side effects occur:

Rare

Signs of toxic shock syndrome—for cervical caps or diaphragms

Chills; confusion; dizziness; fever; lightheadedness; muscle aches; sunburn-like skin rash that is followed by peeling of the skin; unusual redness of the inside of the nose, mouth, throat, vagina, or insides of the eyelids

Also, check with a doctor as soon as possible if any of the following side effects occur:

Rare

For females and males

Skin rash, redness, irritation, or itching that does not subside or go away within a short period of time

For females only

Cloudy or bloody urine; increased frequency of urination; pain in the bladder or lower abdomen; pain on urination; thick, white, or curd-like vaginal discharge—with use of cervical caps or diaphragms only; vaginal irritation, redness, rash, dryness, or whitish discharge

Other side effects may occur that usually do not need medical attention. However, check with a doctor if any of the following side effects continue or are bothersome:

Less common

Vaginal discharge (temporary)—for creams, foams, and suppositories; vaginal dryness or odor

Other side effects not listed above may also occur in some people. If you notice any other effects, check with your doctor.

Revised: 07/28/93
Interim revision: 06/30/94; 08/16/97

SPIRAMYCIN Systemic*

Some commonly used brand names are:

In Canada—

Rovamycine

Other—

Provamicina
Rovamycina
Rovamycine
Rovamycine-250
Rovamycine-500
Spiramycine Coquelusédal

*Not commercially available in the U.S.

Description

Spiramycin (speer-a-MYE-sin) is used to treat many kinds of infections. It is often used to treat toxoplasmosis in pregnant women since this medicine decreases the chance that the unborn baby will get the infection. This medicine may also be used for other problems as determined by your doctor. It will not work for colds, flu, or other virus infections.

Spiramycin is available only with your doctor's prescription, in the following dosage forms:

Oral

Spiramycin

- Capsules (Canada)
- Tablets (France, Germany, Italy, Mexico, Spain)

Parenteral

Spiramycin Adipate

- Injection (France)

Rectal

Spiramycin Adipate

- Suppository (France)

Before Using This Medicine

In deciding to use a medicine, the risks of taking the medicine must be weighed against the good it will do. This is a decision you and your doctor will make. For spiramycin, the following should be considered:

Allergies—Tell your doctor if you have ever had any unusual or allergic reaction to spiramycin, or any related medicines, such as erythromycin, azithromycin, clarithromycin, troleandomycin, dirithromycin, or josamycin. Also tell your health care professional if you are allergic to any other substances, such as foods, preservatives, or dyes.

Pregnancy—Spiramycin is used to treat toxoplasmosis in pregnant women since this medicine decreases the chance that the unborn baby will get the infection. If the unborn baby is already infected with toxoplasmosis, spiramycin does not treat the infection. This medicine has not been found to cause birth defects or other problems in humans.

Breast-feeding—Spiramycin passes into the breast milk. However, spiramycin has not been shown to cause problems in nursing babies to date.

Children—This medicine has been tested in children and, in effective doses, has not been shown to cause different side effects or problems in children than it does in adults.

Older adults—Many medicines have not been studied specifically in older people. Therefore, it may not be known whether they work exactly the same way they do in younger adults or if they cause different side effects or problems in older people. There is no specific information comparing use of spiramycin in the elderly with use in other age groups.

Other medicines—Although certain medicines should not be used together at all, in other cases two different medicines may be used together even if an interaction might occur. In these cases, your doctor may want to change the dose, or other precautions may be necessary. Tell your health care professional if you are taking any other prescription or nonprescription (over-the-counter [OTC]) medicine.

Other medical problems—The presence of other medical problems may affect the use of spiramycin. Make sure you tell your doctor if you have any other medical problems, especially:

- Liver disease or
- Obstruction of the bile ducts—Liver disease or obstruction of the bile ducts may increase the chance of side effects

Proper Use of This Medicine

Spiramycin is *best taken on an empty stomach.*

To help clear up your infection completely, *keep taking this medicine for the full time of treatment,* even if you begin to feel better after a few days. If you stop taking this medicine too soon, your symptoms may return.

This medicine works best when there is a constant amount in the blood. *To help keep the amount constant, do not miss any doses. Also, it is best to take the doses at evenly spaced times day and night.* If this interferes with your sleep or other daily activities, or if you need help in planning the best times to take your medicine, check with your health care professional.

For patients using *spiramycin suppositories:*

- First remove the foil wrapper and moisten the suppository with cold water. Lie down on your side and use your finger to push the suppository well up into the rectum.

Dosing—The dose of spiramycin will be different for different patients. *Follow your doctor's orders or the directions on the label.* The following information includes only the average doses of spiramycin. *If your dose is different, do not change it* unless your doctor tells you to do so.

The number of capsules or tablets that you take or the number of suppositories that you use depends on the strength of the medicine. Also, *the number of doses you take each day, the time allowed between doses, and the length of time you take the medicine depend on the medical problem for which you are taking spiramycin.*

- For *oral* dosage forms (capsules or tablets):
  —For treatment of infections:
    - Adults and teenagers—1 to 2 grams (3,000,000 to 6,000,000 International Units [IU]) two times a day, or 500 mg to 1 gram (1,500,000 to 3,000,000 IU) three times a day. For severe infections, the dose is 2 to 2.5 grams (6,000,000 to 7,500,000 IU) two times a day.
    - Children weighing 20 kilograms (kg) (44 pounds) or more—Dose is based on body weight. The usual dose is 25 mg (75,000 IU) per kg (11.4 mg per pound) of body weight two times a day, or 17 mg (51,000 IU) per kg (7.7 mg per pound) of body weight three times a day.
- For *injection* dosage form:
  —For treatment of infections:
    - Adults and teenagers—500 mg (1,500,000 IU) injected slowly into a vein every eight hours. For severe infections, the dose is 1 gram (3,000,000 IU) injected slowly into a vein every eight hours.
    - Children—Use and dose must be determined by your doctor.
- For *rectal* dosage form (suppository):
  —For treatment of infections:
    - Adults and children 12 years of age and over—Two or three 750 mg (1,950,000 IU) suppositories per day.
    - Children up to 12 years of age—Two or three 500 mg (1,300,000 IU) suppositories per day.
    - Newborns—Dose is based on body weight. The usual dose is one 250 mg (650,000 IU) suppository per 5 kg (250 mg suppository per 11 pounds) of body weight once a day.

Missed dose—If you miss a dose of this medicine, take it as soon as possible. This will help to keep a constant amount of medicine in the blood. However, if it is almost time for your next dose, skip the missed dose and go back to your regular dosing schedule. Do not double dose.

Storage—To store this medicine:

- Keep out of the reach of children.
- Store away from heat and direct light.
- Do not store the tablet form of spiramycin in the bathroom, near the kitchen sink, or in other damp places. Heat or moisture may cause the medicine to break down.
- Do not keep outdated medicine or medicine no longer needed. Be sure that any discarded medicine is out of the reach of children.

Precautions While Using This Medicine

If your symptoms do not improve within a few days, or if they become worse, check with your doctor.

Side Effects of This Medicine

Along with its needed effects, a medicine may cause some unwanted effects. Although not all of these side effects may occur, if they do occur they may need medical attention.

Check with your doctor immediately if any of the following side effects occur:

Less common

Skin rash and itching, unusual bleeding or bruising

Rare–with spiramycin injection only

Pain at site of injection

Rare

Bloody stools, chest pain, fever, heartburn, irregular heartbeat, nausea, recurrent fainting, stomach pain and tenderness, vomiting, yellow eyes or skin

Other side effects may occur that usually do not need medical attention. These side effects may go away during treatment as your body adjusts to the medicine. However, check with your doctor if any of the following side effects continue or are bothersome:

Less common

Diarrhea

Other side effects not listed above may also occur in some patients. If you notice any other effects, check with your doctor.

Developed: 05/28/96

STAVUDINE Systemic†

A commonly used brand name in the U.S. is Zerit.
Another commonly used name is d4T.

†Not commercially available in Canada.

Description

Stavudine (STAV-yoo-deen) (also known as d4T) is used in the treatment of the infection caused by the human immunodeficiency virus (HIV). HIV is the virus responsible for acquired immune deficiency syndrome (AIDS).

Stavudine (d4T) will not cure or prevent HIV infection or AIDS; however, it helps to keep HIV from reproducing and appears to slow down the destruction of the immune system. This may help delay the development of problems usually related to AIDS or HIV disease. Stavudine will not keep you from spreading HIV to other people. People who receive this medicine may continue to have the problems usually related to AIDS or HIV disease.

Stavudine may cause some serious side effects, including peripheral neuropathy. Symptoms of peripheral neuropathy include tingling, burning, numbness, and pain in the hands or feet. *Check with your doctor if any new health problems or symptoms occur while you are taking stavudine.*

Stavudine is available only with your doctor's prescription, in the following dosage form:

Oral
- Capsules (U.S.)

Before Using This Medicine

In deciding to use a medicine, the risks of taking the medicine must be weighed against the good it will do. This is a decision you and your doctor will make. For stavudine, the following should be considered:

Allergies—Tell your doctor if you have ever had any unusual or allergic reaction to stavudine. Also tell your health care professional if you are allergic to any other substances, such as foods, preservatives, or dyes.

Pregnancy—Stavudine has not been studied in pregnant women. However, studies in animals have shown that stavudine causes birth defects when given in very high doses. Before taking this medicine, make sure your doctor knows if you are pregnant or if you may become pregnant.

Breast-feeding—It is not known whether stavudine passes into the breast milk. However, if your baby does not already have the AIDS virus, there is a chance that you could pass it to your baby by breast-feeding. Talk to your doctor first if you are thinking about breast-feeding your baby.

Children—Studies on this medicine have been done only in adult patients, and there is no specific information comparing use of stavudine in children with use in other age groups.

Older adults—Stavudine has not been studied specifically in older people. Therefore, it is not known whether it causes different side effects or problems in the elderly than it does in younger adults.

Other medicines—Although certain medicines should not be used together at all, in other cases two different medicines may be used together even if an interaction might occur. In these cases, your doctor may want to change the dose, or other precautions may be necessary. When you are taking stavudine, it is especially important that your health care professional know if you are taking any of the following:

- Chloramphenicol (e.g., Chloromycetin) or
- Cisplatin (e.g., Platinol) or
- Dapsone (e.g., Avlosulfon) or
- Didanosine (e.g. ddI, Videx) or
- Ethambutol (e.g., Myambutol) or
- Ethionamide (e.g., Trecator-SC) or
- Hydralazine (e.g., Apresoline) or
- Isoniazid (e.g., Nydrazid) or
- Lithium (e.g., Eskalith, Lithobid) or
- Metronidazole (e.g., Flagyl) or
- Nitrofurantoin (e.g., Macrodantin) or
- Phenytoin (e.g., Dilantin) or
- Vincristine (e.g., Oncovin) or
- Zalcitabine (e.g. ddC, HIVID)—Use of these medicines with stavudine may increase the chance of peripheral neuropathy (tingling, burning, numbness, or pain in your hands or feet)

Other medical problems—The presence of other medical problems may affect the use of stavudine. Make sure you tell your doctor if you have any other medical problems, especially:

- Alcohol abuse, active or a history of, or
- Liver disease—Stavudine may make liver disease worse in patients with liver disease, active alcohol abuse, or a history of alcohol abuse
- Kidney disease—Patients with kidney disease may have an increased chance of side effects
- Peripheral neuropathy—Stavudine may make this condition worse

Proper Use of This Medicine

Take this medicine exactly as directed by your doctor. Do not take more of it, do not take it more often, and do not take it for a longer time than your doctor ordered. Also, do not stop taking this medicine without checking with your doctor first.

Keep taking stavudine for the full time of treatment, even if you begin to feel better.

This medicine works best when there is a constant amount in the blood. *To help keep the amount constant, do not miss any doses.* If you need help in planning the best times to take your medicine, check with your health care professional.

Only take medicine that your doctor has prescribed specifically for you. Do not share your medicine with others.

Dosing—The dose of stavudine will be different for different patients. *Follow your doctor's orders or the direc-*

tions on the label. The following information includes only the average doses of stavudine. Your dose may be different if you have kidney disease. *If your dose is different, do not change it* unless your doctor tells you to do so:

- For *oral* dosage form (capsules):
  - —For treatment of HIV infection:
    - Adults and teenagers weighing 60 kilograms (kg) (132 pounds) or more—40 milligrams (mg) two times a day.
    - Adults and teenagers weighing up to 60 kg (132 pounds)—30 mg two times a day.
    - Children—Use and dose must be determined by your doctor.

Missed dose—If you miss a dose of this medicine, take it as soon as possible. However, if it is almost time for your next dose, skip the missed dose and go back to your regular dosing schedule. Do not double doses.

Storage—To store this medicine:

- Keep out of the reach of children.
- Store away from heat and direct light.
- Do not store in the bathroom, near the kitchen sink, or in other damp places. Heat or moisture may cause the medicine to break down.
- Do not keep outdated medicine or medicine no longer needed. Be sure that any discarded medicine is out of the reach of children.

Precautions While Using This Medicine

It is very important that your doctor check your progress at regular visits.

Do not take any other medicines without checking with your doctor first. To do so may increase the chance of side effects from stavudine.

HIV may be acquired from or spread to other people through infected body fluids, including blood, vaginal fluid, or semen. *If you are infected, it is best to avoid any sexual activity involving an exchange of body fluids with other people. If you do have sex, always wear (or have your partner wear) a condom (''rubber'').* Only use condoms made of latex, and *use them every time you have vaginal, anal, or oral sex.* The use of a spermicide (such as nonoxynol-9) may also help prevent transmission of HIV if it is not irritating to the vagina, rectum, or mouth. Spermicides have been shown to kill HIV in lab tests. Do not use oil-based jelly, cold cream, baby oil, or shortening as a lubricant—these products can cause the condom to break. Lubricants without oil, such as *K-Y Jelly*, are recommended. Women may wish to carry their own condoms. Birth control pills and diaphragms will help protect against pregnancy, but they will not prevent someone from giving or getting the AIDS virus. *If you inject drugs*, get help to stop. *Do not share needles or equipment with anyone.* In some cities, more than half of the drug users are infected, and sharing even 1 needle or syringe can spread the virus. If you have any questions about this, check with your health care professional.

Side Effects of This Medicine

Along with its needed effects, a medicine may cause some unwanted effects. Although not all of these side effects may occur, if they do occur they may need medical attention.

Check with your doctor immediately if any of the following side effects occur:

More common

Tingling, burning, numbness, or pain in the hands or feet

Less common

Fever; joint pain; muscle pain; skin rash

Rare

Nausea and vomiting; stomach pain (severe); unusual tiredness or weakness

Other side effects may occur that usually do not need medical attention. These side effects may go away during treatment as your body adjusts to the medicine. However, check with your doctor if any of the following side effects continue or are bothersome:

Less common

Diarrhea; difficulty in sleeping; headache; lack of strength or energy; loss of appetite

Other side effects not listed above may also occur in some patients. If you notice any other effects, check with your doctor.

Developed: 11/28/94

STREPTOZOCIN Systemic

A commonly used brand name in the U.S. and Canada is Zanosar.

Description

Streptozocin (strep-toe-ZOE-sin) belongs to the group of medicines known as alkylating agents. It is used to treat cancer of the pancreas.

Streptozocin seems to interfere with the growth of cancer cells, which are eventually destroyed. It also directly affects the way the pancreas works. Since the growth of normal body cells may also be affected by streptozocin, other effects will also occur. Some of these may be serious and must be reported to your doctor. Other effects may not be serious but may cause concern. Some effects may not occur for months or years after the medicine is used.

Before you begin treatment with streptozocin, you and your doctor should talk about the good this medicine will do as well as the risks of using it.

Streptozocin is to be given only by or under the immediate supervision of your doctor. It is available in the following dosage form:

Parenteral

- Injection (U.S. and Canada)

Before Using This Medicine

In deciding to use a medicine, the risks of taking the medicine must be weighed against the good it will do. This is a decision you and your doctor will make. For streptozocin, the following should be considered:

Allergies—Tell your doctor if you have ever had any unusual or allergic reaction to streptozocin.

Pregnancy—Tell your doctor if you are pregnant or if you intend to have children. There is a chance that this medicine may cause birth defects if either the male or the female is receiving it at the time of conception or if it is taken during pregnancy. Studies in rats and rabbits have shown that streptozocin causes birth defects or miscarriage. In addition, many cancer medicines may cause sterility which could be permanent. Although this has not been reported with this medicine, the possibility should be kept in mind.

Be sure that you have discussed this with your doctor before receiving this medicine. It is best to use some kind of birth control while you are receiving streptozocin. Tell your doctor right away if you think you have become pregnant while receiving streptozocin.

Breast-feeding—Tell your doctor if you are breast-feeding or if you intend to breast-feed during treatment with this medicine. Because streptozocin may cause serious side effects, breast-feeding is generally not recommended while you are receiving it.

Children—There is no specific information comparing use of streptozocin in children with use in other age groups.

Older adults—Many medicines have not been studied specifically in older people. Therefore, it may not be known whether they work exactly the same way they do in younger adults or if they cause different side effects or problems in older people. There is no specific information comparing use of streptozocin in the elderly with use in other age groups.

Other medicines—Although certain medicines should not be used together at all, in other cases two different medicines may be used together even if an interaction might occur. In these cases, your doctor may want to change the dose, or other precautions may be necessary. When you are receiving streptozocin, it is especially important that your health care professional know if you are taking any of the following:

- Anti-infectives by mouth or by injection (medicine for infection) or
- Carmustine (e.g., BiCNU) or
- Cisplatin (e.g., Platinol) or
- Combination pain medicine containing acetaminophen and aspirin (e.g., Excedrin) or other salicylates (with large amounts taken regularly) or
- Cyclosporine (e.g., Sandimmune) or
- Deferoxamine (e.g., Desferal) (with long-term use) or
- Gold salts (medicine for arthritis) or
- Inflammation or pain medicine except narcotics or
- Lithium (e.g., Lithane) or
- Methotrexate (e.g., Mexate) or
- Penicillamine (e.g., Cuprimine) or
- Plicamycin (e.g., Mithracin) or
- Tiopronin (e.g., Thiola)—Increased risk of harmful effects on the kidney
- Phenytoin (e.g., Dilantin)—May interfere with the effects of streptozocin

Other medical problems—The presence of other medical problems may affect the use of streptozocin. Make sure you tell your doctor if you have any other medical problems, especially:

- Chickenpox (including recent exposure) or
- Herpes zoster (shingles)—Risk of severe disease affecting other parts of the body
- Diabetes mellitus (sugar diabetes)—May be worsened
- Infection—Streptozocin can decrease your body's ability to fight infection
- Kidney disease or
- Liver disease—Effects of streptozocin may be increased because of slower removal from the body

Proper Use of This Medicine

While you are receiving streptozocin, your doctor may want you to drink extra fluids so that you will pass more urine. This will help prevent kidney problems and keep your kidneys working well.

This medicine usually causes nausea and vomiting, which may be severe. However, it is very important that you continue to receive the medicine, even if you begin to feel ill. Ask your health care professional for ways to lessen these effects.

Dosing—The dose of streptozocin will be different for different patients. The dose that is used may depend on a number of things, including what the medicine is being used for, the patient's size, and whether or not other medicines are also being taken. *If you are receiving streptozocin at home, follow your doctor's orders or the directions on the label.* If you have any questions about the proper dose of streptozocin, ask your doctor.

Precautions While Using This Medicine

It is very important that your doctor check your progress at regular visits to make sure that this medicine is working properly and to check for any unwanted effects.

While you are being treated with streptozocin, and after you stop treatment with it, *do not have any immunizations (vaccinations) without your doctor's approval.* Streptozocin may lower your body's resistance and there is a chance you might get the infection the immunization is meant to prevent. In addition, other people living in your household should not take oral polio vaccine since there is a chance they could pass the polio virus on to you. Also, avoid persons who have recently taken oral polio vaccine. Do not get close to them and do not stay in the same room with them for very long. If you cannot take these precautions, you should consider wearing a protective face mask that covers the nose and mouth.

If streptozocin accidentally seeps out of the vein into which it is injected, it may damage some tissues and cause scarring. *Tell the health care professional right away if you notice redness, pain, or swelling at the place of injection.*

Side Effects of This Medicine

Along with their needed effects, medicines like streptozocin can sometimes cause unwanted effects such as kidney problems and other side effects. These and others are described below. Also, because of the way these medicines act on the body, there is a chance that they might cause other unwanted effects that may not occur until months or years after the medicine is used. These delayed effects may include certain types of cancer, such as leukemia. Streptozocin has been shown to cause tumors (some cancerous) in animals. Discuss these possible effects with your doctor.

Although not all of these side effects may occur, if they do occur they may need medical attention.

Check with your health care professional immediately if any of the following side effects occur shortly after the medicine is given:

Less common

Anxiety, nervousness, or shakiness; chills, cold sweats, or cool, pale skin; drowsiness or unusual tiredness or weakness; fast pulse; headache; pain or redness at place of injection; unusual hunger

Check with your doctor immediately if the following side effects occur any time while you are being treated with this medicine:

Rare

Black, tarry stools; blood in urine or stools; cough or hoarseness; fever or chills; lower back or side pain; painful or difficult urination; pinpoint red spots on skin; unusual bleeding or bruising

Check with your health care professional as soon as possible if any of the following side effects occur:

More common

Swelling of feet or lower legs; unusual decrease in urination

Other side effects may occur that usually do not need medical attention. These side effects may go away during treatment as your body adjusts to the medicine. Also, your health care professional may be able to tell you about ways to prevent or reduce some of these side effects. Check with your health care professional if any of the following side effects continue or are bothersome or if you have any questions about them:

More common

Nausea and vomiting (usually occurs within 2 to 4 hours after receiving dose and may be severe)

Less common

Diarrhea

After you stop receiving streptozocin, your body may need time to adjust. The length of time this takes depends on the amount of medicine you were using and how long you used it. During this period of time, check with your doctor if you notice either of the following side effects:

More common

Decrease in urination; swelling of feet or lower legs

Other side effects not listed above may also occur in some patients. If you notice any other effects, check with your doctor.

Revised: 08/26/92
Interim revision: 06/30/94

STRONTIUM CHLORIDE Sr 89 Therapeutic

A commonly used brand name in the U.S. and Canada is Metastron.

Description

Strontium chloride Sr 89 (STRON-shee-um KLOR-ide) is a radiopharmaceutical (ray-dee-oh-far-ma-SOO-ti-kal). Radiopharmaceuticals are radioactive agents that may be used to diagnose some diseases by studying the function of the body's organs or to treat certain diseases.

Strontium chloride Sr 89 is used to help relieve the bone pain that may occur with certain kinds of cancer. The radioactive strontium is taken up in the bone cancer area and gives off radiation that helps provide relief of pain.

Strontium chloride Sr 89 is to be given only by or under the direct supervision of a doctor with specialized training in nuclear medicine or radiation oncology. It is available in the following dosage form:

Parenteral

- Injection (U.S. and Canada)

Before Using This Medicine

In deciding to use a medicine, the risks of receiving the medicine must be weighed against the good it will do. This is a decision you and your doctor will make. For strontium chloride Sr 89, the following should be considered:

Allergies—Tell your doctor if you have ever had any unusual or allergic reaction to bone tumor–seeking medicines, like strontium chloride Sr 89. Also tell your doctor if you are allergic to any other substances, such as foods, preservatives, or dyes.

Pregnancy—Studies have not been done in either humans or animals. However, to avoid exposing the fetus to radiation, strontium chloride Sr 89 is not recommended for use during pregnancy. Be sure you have discussed this with your doctor.

Breast-feeding—Strontium chloride Sr 89 may pass into the breast milk. If you must receive this radiopharmaceutical, it will be necessary for you to stop breast-feeding. Be sure you have discussed this with your doctor.

Children—Studies on this medicine have been done only in adult patients, and there is no specific information about its use in children.

Older adults—Strontium chloride Sr 89 has been used in older people and has not been shown to cause different side effects or problems in older people than it does in younger adults.

Other medicines—Although certain medicines should not be used together at all, in other cases two different medicines may be used together even if an interaction might occur. In these cases, your doctor may want to change the dose, or other precautions may be necessary. When you are receiving strontium chloride Sr 89, it is especially important that your doctor know if you are taking any of the following:

- Calcium-containing medicines—These medicines may keep the strontium chloride Sr 89 from being taken up by the bone
- If you have ever been treated with x-rays or cancer medicines—Cancer medicines or radiation therapy may increase the harmful effects of strontium chloride Sr 89 on the bone marrow

Other medical problems—The presence of other medical problems may affect the use of strontium chloride Sr 89. Make sure you tell your doctor if you have any other medical problems.

Proper Use of This Medicine

Your doctor may have special instructions for you to follow to get ready for your treatment. If you do not understand them or if you have not received such instructions, check with your doctor in advance.

If you have a problem controlling your bladder, tell your doctor before receiving strontium chloride Sr 89. Special precautions will need to be taken to prevent contamination of clothing, bed linen, and the environment.

Dosing—The doses of radiopharmaceuticals will be different for different patients and for the different types of treatments. The amount of radioactivity of a radiopharmaceutical is expressed in units called becquerels or curies. The usual adult dose of strontium chloride Sr 89 is 148 megabecquerels (4 millicuries). The dose you receive depends on your size, age, and blood test measurements (blood counts). The amount of radiation received by specific areas of the body to treat a disease is many times higher than from any diagnostic test, such as x-rays and nuclear medicine scans. Repeated doses may be necessary, depending on the kind of disease you have and how your body is responding to treatment.

Precautions After Using This Medicine

It is very important that your doctor check your progress at regular visits to make sure that this medicine is working properly and to check for unwanted effects. You may need to have blood tests done regularly.

Follow these guidelines for 1 week after receiving strontium chloride Sr 89, to help reduce the chance of contaminating other persons or the environment:

- *Use a normal toilet, if available, instead of a urinal.*
- *Strontium chloride Sr 89 is passed in the urine and feces. To prevent contamination of your home environment, flush the toilet twice after using.*
- *Wipe any spilled urine with a tissue and flush it away.*
- *Wash your hands after using or cleaning the toilet.*
- Wash your clothes and bed linens immediately if they become soiled with your urine or blood. Wash them separately from other clothes.
- *If you cut yourself, wash away any spilled blood.*

Strontium chloride Sr 89 can temporarily lower the number of white blood cells in your blood, increasing the chance of getting an infection. It can also lower the number of platelets, which are necessary for proper blood clotting. If *your blood count becomes abnormally low*, there are certain precautions you can take, to reduce the risk of infection or bleeding, such as:

- With abnormally low white blood cell counts:

  —If you can, avoid people with infections. *Check with your doctor immediately* if you think you are getting an infection or if you get a fever or chills, cough or hoarseness, lower back or side pain, or painful or difficult urination.

  —Be careful when using a regular toothbrush, dental floss, or toothpick. Your medical doctor, dentist, or nurse may recommend other ways to clean your teeth and gums. Check with your medical doctor before having any dental work done.

  —Do not touch your eyes or the inside of your nose unless you have just washed your hands and have not touched anything else in the meantime.
- With abnormally low platelet blood counts:

  —Be careful not to cut yourself when you are using sharp objects such as a safety razor or fingernail or toenail cutters.

  —Avoid contact sports or other situations where bruising or injury could occur.

Side Effects of This Medicine

Along with its needed effects, a medicine may cause some unwanted effects. When strontium chloride Sr 89 is used at recommended doses, side effects usually are rare. However, blood problems, such as a decrease in the number of white blood cells or platelets, may occur in some patients.

Check with your doctor immediately if any of the following side effects occur:

Rare

Black, tarry stools; blood in urine or stools; cough or hoarseness; fever or chills; lower back or side pain; painful or difficult urination; pinpoint red spots on skin; unusual bleeding or bruising

Other side effects may occur that usually do not need medical attention. These side effects may go away after treatment as your body adjusts to the medicine. Check with your doctor if any of the following side effects continue or are bothersome or if you have any questions about them:

More common

Flushing; increase in bone pain

Other side effects not listed above may also occur in some patients. If you notice any other effects, check with your doctor.

Revised: 06/23/94
Interim revision: 05/18/95

SUCCIMER Systemic†

A commonly used brand name in the U.S. is Chemet.
Other commonly used names are dimercaptosuccinic acid and DMSA.

†Not commercially available in Canada.

Description

Succimer (SUX-i-mer) is used to remove excess lead from the body. It is used to treat acute lead poisoning, especially in small children.

Succimer combines with lead in the bloodstream. The combination of lead and succimer is then removed from the body by the kidneys. By removing the excess lead, the medicine lessens damage to various organs and tissues of the body.

Oral

Capsules (U.S.)

Before Using This Medicine

In deciding to use a medicine, the risks of taking the medicine must be weighed against the good it will do. This is a decision you and your doctor will make. For succimer, the following should be considered:

Allergies—Tell your doctor if you have ever had any unusual or allergic reaction to succimer. Also, tell your health care professional if you are allergic to any other substances, such as foods, preservatives, or dyes.

Pregnancy—Studies have not been done in humans. However, some studies in animals have shown that succimer causes birth defects.

Breast-feeding—It is not known whether succimer is excreted in breast milk.

Children—This medicine has been tested in children over the age of 1 year and, in effective doses, has not been shown to cause different side effects or problems than it does in adults.

Older adults—Many medicines have not been studied specifically in older people. Therefore, it may not be known whether they work exactly the same way they do in younger adults or if they cause different side effects or problems in older people. There is no specific information comparing use of succimer in the elderly with use in other age groups.

Other medical problems—The presence of other medical problems may affect the use of succimer. Make sure you tell your doctor if you have any other medical problems, especially:

- Dehydration or
- Kidney disease—Higher blood levels of succimer may result and your doctor may need to change your dose

Proper Use of This Medicine

Children who have too much lead in their bodies should be removed from the lead-containing environment (for example, home, school, or other areas where the child has been exposed to lead) until the lead has been removed from the environment.

Your doctor may want to put your child in the hospital while he or she is receiving succimer. This will allow the doctor to check your child's condition while the lead can be removed from the child's environment.

When opening your bottle of succimer, you may notice an unpleasant odor. However, this is a normal odor for these capsules and does not affect the medicine's working properly.

If the capsules cannot be swallowed, the contents of the capsule may be sprinkled on food and eaten immediately. The contents may also be given on a spoon and followed by a fruit drink.

Dosing—The dose of succimer will be different for different patients. *Follow your doctor's orders or the directions on the label.*

- For the *oral* dosage form (capsules):
  - —For treatment of lead poisoning:
    - For adults and children 12 years of age and older—Dose is based on body weight. The usual dose is 10 milligrams (mg) of succimer per kilogram (4.5 mg per pound) of body weight every eight hours for five days.
    - For children up to 12 years of age—Dose is based on body weight. The usual dose is 10 mg of succimer per kilogram (4.5 mg per pound) of body weight every eight hours for five days. The same dose is then given every twelve hours for the next fourteen days, for a total of nineteen days of therapy.

Missed dose—If you miss a dose of this medicine, take it as soon as possible. However, if it is almost time for your next dose, skip the missed dose and go back to your regular dosing schedule. Do not double doses.

Storage—To store this medicine:

- Keep out of the reach of children.
- Store away from heat and direct light.
- Do not store in the bathroom, near the kitchen sink, or in other damp places. Heat or moisture may cause the medicine to break down.
- Keep the medicine from freezing. Do not refrigerate.

- Do not keep outdated medicine or medicine no longer needed. Be sure that any discarded medicine is out of the reach of children.

Precautions While Using This Medicine

It is important that your doctor check your progress at regular visits to make sure that this medicine is working properly and to prevent unwanted effects. Certain blood and urine tests must be done regularly to make sure you are taking the correct dose of succimer.

Side Effects of This Medicine

Along with its needed effects, a medicine may cause some unwanted effects. Although not all of these side effects may occur, if they do occur they may need medical attention.

Check with your doctor as soon as possible if the following side effect occurs:

Less common

Fever and chills

Other side effects may occur that usually do not need medical attention. These side effects may go away during treatment as your body adjusts to the medicine. However, check with your doctor if any of the following side effects continue or are bothersome:

More common

Diarrhea; loose stools; loss of appetite; nausea and vomiting; skin rash

Succimer may cause your urine, sweat, and feces to have an unpleasant odor.

Other side effects not listed above may also occur in some patients. If you notice any other effects, check with your doctor.

Revised: 06/22/93

SUCRALFATE Oral

Some commonly used brand names are:

In the U.S.—

Carafate

Generic name product may also be available.

In Canada—

Sulcrate

Description

Sucralfate (soo-KRAL-fate) is used to treat and prevent duodenal ulcers. This medicine may also be used for other conditions as determined by your doctor.

Sucralfate works by forming a ''barrier'' or ''coating'' over the ulcer. This protects the ulcer from the acid of the stomach, allowing it to heal. Sucralfate contains an aluminum salt.

This medicine is available only with your doctor's prescription, in the following dosage form:

Oral

- Oral suspension (U.S. and Canada)
- Tablets (U.S. and Canada)

Before Using This Medicine

In deciding to use a medicine, the risks of taking the medicine must be weighed against the good it will do. This is a decision you and your doctor will make. For sucralfate, the following should be considered:

Allergies—Tell your doctor if you have ever had any unusual or allergic reaction to sucralfate. Also, tell your health care professional if you are allergic to any other substances, such as foods, preservatives, or dyes.

Pregnancy—Studies have not been done in humans. However, sucralfate has not been shown to cause birth defects or other problems in animal studies.

Breast-feeding—Sucralfate has not been shown to cause problems in nursing babies.

Children—This medicine has been tested in a limited number of children. In effective doses, the medicine has not been shown to cause different side effects or problems than it does in adults.

Older adults—Many medicines have not been studied specifically in older people. Therefore, it may not be known whether they work exactly the same way they do in younger adults. Although there is no specific information comparing the use of sucralfate in the elderly with use in other age groups, this medicine is not expected to cause different side effects or problems in older people than it does in younger adults.

Other medicines—Although certain medicines should not be used together at all, in other cases two different medicines may be used together even if an interaction might occur. In these cases, your doctor may want to change the dose, or other precautions may be necessary. When you are taking sucralfate, it is especially important that your health care professional know if you are taking the following:

- Ciprofloxacin or
- Digoxin or
- Norfloxacin or
- Ofloxacin or
- Phenytoin or
- Theophylline—Sucralfate may prevent these medicines from working properly

Other medical problems—The presence of other medical problems may affect the use of sucralfate. Make sure you

tell your doctor if you have any other medical problems, especially:

- Gastrointestinal tract obstruction disease—Sucralfate may bind with other foods and drugs and cause obstruction of the gastrointestinal tract
- Kidney failure—Use may lead to a toxic increase of aluminum blood levels

Proper Use of This Medicine

Sucralfate is best taken with water on an empty stomach 1 hour before meals and at bedtime, unless otherwise directed by your doctor.

Take this medicine for the full time of treatment, even if you begin to feel better. Also, it is important that you keep your doctor's appointments for check-ups so that your doctor will be better able to tell you when to stop taking this medicine.

Dosing—The dose of sucralfate will be different for different patients. *Follow your doctor's orders or the directions on the label.* The following information includes only the average doses of sucralfate. *If your dose is different, do not change it* unless your doctor tells you to do so.

The number of tablets or teaspoonfuls of suspension that you take depends on the strength of the medicine. Also, *the number of doses you take each day, the time allowed between doses, and the length of time you take the medicine depend on the medical problem for which you are taking sucralfate.*

- For *oral* dosage form (suspension):
  - —To treat duodenal ulcers:
    - Adults and teenagers—One gram four times a day, one hour before each meal and at bedtime. Some people may take two grams two times a day, when they wake up and at bedtime on an empty stomach.
    - Children—Dose must be determined by your doctor.
- For *oral* dosage form (tablets):
  - —To treat duodenal ulcers:
    - Adults and teenagers—One gram four times a day, one hour before each meal and at bedtime.
    - Children—Dose must be determined by your doctor.
  - —To prevent duodenal ulcers:
    - Adults and teenagers—One gram two times a day on an empty stomach.
    - Children—Dose must be determined by your doctor.

Missed dose—If you miss a dose of this medicine, take it as soon as possible. However, if it is almost time for your next dose, skip the missed dose and go back to your regular dosing schedule. Do not double doses.

Storage—To store this medicine:

- Keep out of the reach of children.
- Store away from heat and direct light.
- Do not store in the bathroom, near the kitchen sink, or in other damp places. Heat or moisture may cause the medicine to break down.
- Keep the liquid form of this medicine from freezing. Do not refrigerate.
- Do not keep outdated medicine or medicine no longer needed. Be sure that any discarded medicine is out of the reach of children.

Precautions While Using This Medicine

Antacids may be taken with sucralfate to help relieve any stomach pain, unless your doctor has told you not to use them. *However, antacids should not be taken within 30 minutes before or after sucralfate.* Taking these medicines too close together may keep sucralfate from working properly.

Side Effects of This Medicine

Along with its needed effects, a medicine may cause some unwanted effects. Some side effects may occur that usually do not need medical attention. These side effects may go away during treatment as your body adjusts to the medicine. *Check with your doctor immediately* if any of the following side effects occur:

Signs of aluminum toxicity
Drowsiness; convulsions (seizures)

Check with your doctor as soon as possible if any of the following side effects continue or are bothersome:

More common
Constipation

Less common or rare
Backache; diarrhea; dizziness or lightheadedness; dryness of mouth; indigestion; nausea; skin rash, hives, or itching; stomach cramps or pain

Other side effects not listed above may also occur in some patients. If you notice any other effects, check with your doctor.

Additional Information

Once a medicine has been approved for marketing for a certain use, experience may show that it is also useful for other medical problems. Although these uses are not included in product labeling, sucralfate is used in certain patients with the following medical conditions:

- Gastric ulcers
- Gastroesophageal reflux disease (a condition in which stomach acid washes back into the esophagus)
- Stomach or intestinal ulcers resulting from stress or trauma damage or from damage caused by medication used to treat rheumatoid arthritis

Other than the above information, there is no additional information relating to proper use, precautions, or side effects for these uses.

Revised: 03/24/92
Interim revision: 08/17/94; 07/26/96

SULCONAZOLE Topical†

A commonly used brand name in the U.S. is Exelderm.

†Not commercially available in Canada.

Description

Sulconazole (sul-KON-a-zole) is used to treat infections caused by a fungus. It works by killing the fungus or preventing its growth.

Sulconazole is applied to the skin to treat the following:

- ringworm of the body (tinea corporis);
- ringworm of the foot (tinea pedis; athlete's foot);
- ringworm of the groin (tinea cruris; jock itch);
- ''sun fungus'' (tinea versicolor; pityriasis versicolor).

Sulconazole may also be used for other conditions as determined by your doctor.

Topical sulconazole is available only with your doctor's prescription in the following dosage forms:

Topical

- Cream (U.S.)
- Solution (U.S.)

Before Using This Medicine

In deciding to use a medicine, the risks of taking the medicine must be weighed against the good it will do. This is a decision you and your doctor will make. For sulconazole, the following should be considered:

Allergies—Tell your doctor if you have ever had any unusual or allergic reaction to sulconazole or other antifungals such as miconazole (e.g., Micatin) or econazole (e.g., Spectazole). Also tell your health care professional if you are allergic to any other substances such as foods, preservatives, or dyes.

Pregnancy—Topical sulconazole has not been studied in pregnant women. However, studies in animals have shown that sulconazole when taken by mouth causes unwanted effects such as death of the fetus or difficult labor. Before you use this medicine, make sure your doctor knows if you are pregnant or if you may become pregnant.

Breast-feeding—It is not known whether topical sulconazole passes into the breast milk. Although most medicines pass into breast milk in small amounts, many of them may be used safely while breast-feeding. Mothers who are using this medicine and who wish to breast-feed should discuss this with their doctor.

Children—Studies on this medicine have been done only in adult patients, and there is no specific information comparing use of sulconazole in children with use in other age groups.

Older adults—Many medicines have not been studied specifically in older people. Therefore, it may not be known whether they work exactly the same way they do in younger adults. Although there is no specific information comparing use of topical sulconazole in the elderly with use in other age groups, this medicine is not expected to cause different side effects or problems in older people than it does in younger adults.

Other medicines—Although certain medicines should not be used together at all, in other cases two different medicines may be used together even if an interaction might occur. In these cases, your doctor may want to change the dose, or other precautions may be necessary. Tell your health care professional if you are using any other topical prescription or nonprescription (over-the-counter [OTC]) medicine that is to be applied to the same area of the skin.

Proper Use of This Medicine

Apply enough sulconazole to cover the affected and surrounding skin areas, and rub in gently.

Keep this medicine away from the eyes.

When sulconazole is used to treat certain types of fungus infections of the skin, occlusive dressing (airtight covering, such as kitchen plastic wrap) should *not* be applied over the medicine. To do so may irritate the skin. *Do not apply an airtight covering over this medicine unless you have been directed to do so by your doctor.*

To help clear up your infection completely, *it is very important that you keep using sulconazole for the full time of treatment,* even if your symptoms begin to clear up after a few days. Since fungus infections may be very slow to clear up, you may have to continue using this medicine every day for several weeks or more. If you stop using this medicine too soon, your symptoms may return.

Do not miss any doses.

Dosing—The dose of sulconazole will be different for different patients. *Follow your doctor's orders or the directions on the label.* The following information includes only the average doses of topical sulconazole. *If your dose is different, do not change it* unless your doctor tells you to do so.

The number of doses you use each day, the time allowed between doses, and the length of time you use the medicine depend on the medical problem for which you are using topical sulconazole.

- For *topical cream* dosage form:
  - —For ringworm of the body or ringworm of the groin or ''sun fungus'':
    - Adults—Use one or two times a day for at least three weeks.
    - Children—Use and dose must be determined by your doctor.
  - —For athlete's foot:
    - Adults—Use two times a day for at least four weeks.
    - Children—Use and dose must be determined by your doctor.

- For *topical solution* dosage form:
  - —For ringworm of the body or ringworm of the groin or "sun fungus":
    - Adults—Use one or two times a day for at least three weeks.
    - Children—Use and dose must be determined by your doctor.

Missed dose—If you miss a dose of this medicine, apply it as soon as possible. However, if it is almost time for your next dose, skip the missed dose and go back to your regular dosing schedule.

Storage—To store this medicine:
- Keep out of the reach of children.
- Store away from heat and direct light.
- Keep the medicine from freezing. Do not refrigerate.
- Do not keep outdated medicine or medicine no longer needed. Be sure that any discarded medicine is out of the reach of children.

Precautions While Using This Medicine

If your skin problem does not improve within 4 to 6 weeks or if it becomes worse, check with your doctor.

To help clear up your infection completely and to help make sure it does not return, good health habits are also required. The following measures will help reduce chaffing and irritation and will also help keep the area cool and dry:

- For patients using sulconazole for *ringworm of the groin (tinea cruris; jock itch):*
  - —Avoid wearing underwear that is tight-fitting or made from synthetic materials (for example, rayon or nylon). Instead, wear loose-fitting, cotton underwear.
- For patients using sulconazole for *ringworm of the foot (tinea pedis; athlete's foot):*
  - —Carefully dry the feet, especially between the toes, after bathing.
  - —Avoid wearing socks made from wool or synthetic materials (for example, rayon or nylon). Instead wear clean, cotton socks and change them daily or more often if the feet sweat a lot.
  - —Wear sandals or other well-ventilated shoes.
- For patients using sulconazole for *ringworm of the body (tinea corporis):*
  - —Carefully dry yourself after bathing.
  - —Avoid too much heat and humidity if possible.
  - —Wear well-ventilated, loose-fitting clothing.

If you have any questions about these measures, check with your health care professional.

Side Effects of This Medicine

Along with its needed effects, a medicine may cause some unwanted effects. Although not all of these side effects may occur, if they do occur they may need medical attention.

Check with your doctor as soon as possible if any of the following side effects occur:

Less common

Burning or stinging, itching, redness of the skin, or other signs of irritation not present before use of this medicine

Other side effects not listed above may also rarely occur. If you notice any other effects, check with your doctor.

Additional Information

Once a medicine has been approved for marketing for a certain use, experience may show that it is also useful for other medical problems. Although this use is not included in product labeling, sulconazole is used in certain patients with the following medical condition:

- Cutaneous candidiasis

Other than the above information, there is no additional information relating to proper use, precautions, or side effects for this use.

Developed: 03/29/94

SULFADOXINE AND PYRIMETHAMINE Systemic

A commonly used brand name in the U.S. and Canada is Fansidar.

Description

Sulfadoxine (sul-fa-DOX-een), a sulfa medicine, and pyrimethamine (peer-i-METH-a-meen) combination is used to treat malaria. This medicine may also be used to prevent malaria in people who are living in, or will be traveling to, an area where there is a chance of getting malaria. Sulfadoxine and pyrimethamine combination may also be taken with other medicines for malaria, or may be used for other problems as determined by your doctor.

Since sulfadoxine and pyrimethamine combination may cause some serious side effects, it is usually used only to prevent or treat serious malaria infections in areas where it is known that other medicines may not work.

This medicine is available only with your doctor's prescription, in the following dosage form:

Oral

- Tablets (U.S. and Canada)

Before Using This Medicine

In deciding to use a medicine, the risks of taking the medicine must be weighed against the good it will do. This is a decision you and your doctor will make. For sulfadoxine and pyrimethamine combination, the following should be considered:

Allergies—Tell your doctor if you have ever had any unusual or allergic reaction to sulfa medicines, furosemide (e.g., Lasix) or thiazide diuretics (water pills), oral antidiabetics (diabetes medicine you take by mouth), glaucoma medicine you take by mouth (acetazolamide [e.g., Diamox], dichlorphenamide [e.g., Daranide], methazolamide [e.g., Neptazane]), or pyrimethamine (e.g., Daraprim). Also tell your health care professional if you are allergic to any other substances, such as foods, preservatives, or dyes.

Pregnancy—Studies have not been done in pregnant women. However, use is not recommended during pregnancy. Studies in rats have shown that sulfadoxine and pyrimethamine combination may cause birth defects and anemia. Also, women who travel to an area where there is a chance of getting malaria, and who may be taking sulfadoxine and pyrimethamine combination, should not become pregnant.

Breast-feeding—Sulfadoxine and pyrimethamine pass into the breast milk. This medicine is not recommended for use during breast-feeding. It may cause liver problems, anemia, and other unwanted effects in nursing babies.

Children—Sulfadoxine and pyrimethamine combination should not be used in infants up to 2 months of age.

Older adults—Many medicines have not been studied specifically in older people. Therefore, it may not be known whether they work exactly the same way they do in younger adults or if they cause different side effects or problems in older people. There is no specific information comparing use of sulfadoxine and pyrimethamine combination in the elderly with use in other age groups.

Other medicines—Although certain medicines should not be used together at all, in other cases two different medicines may be used together even if an interaction might occur. In these cases, your doctor may want to change the dose, or other precautions may be necessary. When you are taking sulfadoxine and pyrimethamine combination, it is especially important that your health care professional know if you are taking any of the following:

- Acetaminophen (e.g., Tylenol) (with long-term, high-dose use) or
- Amiodarone (e.g., Cordarone) or
- Anabolic steroids (dromostanolone [e.g., Drolban], ethylestrenol [e.g., Maxibolin], nandrolone [e.g., Anabolin], oxandrolone [e.g., Anavar], oxymetholone [e.g., Anadrol], stanozolol [e.g., Winstrol]) or
- Androgens (male hormones) or
- Carbamazepine (e.g., Tegretol) or
- Carmustine (e.g., BiCNU) or
- Chloroquine (e.g., Aralen) or
- Dantrolene (e.g., Dantrium) or
- Daunorubicin (e.g., Cerubidine) or
- Disulfiram (e.g., Antabuse) or
- Divalproex (e.g., Depakote) or
- Estrogens (female hormones) or
- Etretinate (e.g., Tegison) or
- Gold salts (medicine for arthritis) or
- Hydroxychloroquine (e.g., Plaquenil) or
- Naltrexone (e.g., Trexan) (with long-term, high-dose use) or
- Oral contraceptives (birth control pills) containing estrogen or
- Other anti-infectives by mouth or by injection (medicine for infection) or
- Phenothiazines (acetophenazine [e.g., Tindal], chlorpromazine [e.g., Thorazine], fluphenazine [e.g., Prolixin], mesoridazine [e.g., Serentil], perphenazine [e.g., Trilafon], prochlorperazine [e.g., Compazine], promazine [e.g., Sparine], promethazine [e.g., Phenergan], thioridazine [e.g., Mellaril], trifluoperazine [e.g., Stelazine], triflupromazine [e.g., Vesprin], trimeprazine [e.g., Temaril]) or
- Phenytoin (e.g., Dilantin) or
- Valproic acid (e.g., Depakene)—Use of sulfadoxine and pyrimethamine combination with these medicines may increase the chance of side effects affecting the liver
- Acetohydroxamic acid (e.g., Lithostat) or
- Amphotericin B by injection (e.g., Fungizone) or
- Antidiabetics, oral (diabetes medicine you take by mouth) or
- Antineoplastics (cancer medicine) or
- Azathioprine (e.g., Imuran) or
- Chloramphenicol (e.g., Chloromycetin) or
- Colchicine or
- Cyclophosphamide (e.g., Cytoxan) or
- Dapsone or
- Flucytosine (e.g., Ancobon) or
- Furazolidone (e.g., Furoxone) or
- Ganciclovir (e.g., Cytovene) or
- Interferon (e.g., Intron A, Roferon-A) or
- Nitrofurantoin (e.g., Furadantin) or
- Primaquine or
- Procainamide (e.g., Pronestyl) or
- Quinidine (e.g., Quinidex) or
- Quinine (e.g., Quinamm) or
- Sulfoxone (e.g., Diasone) or
- Vitamin K (e.g., AquaMEPHYTON, Synkayvite) or
- Zidovudine (e.g., AZT, Retrovir)—Use of sulfadoxine and pyrimethamine combination with these medicines may increase the chance of side effects affecting the blood
- Antithyroid agents (medicine for overactive thyroid) or
- Mercaptopurine (e.g., Purinethol) or
- Methotrexate (e.g., Mexate) or
- Methyldopa (e.g., Aldomet) or
- Plicamycin (e.g., Mithracin)—Use of sulfadoxine and pyrimethamine combination with these medicines may increase the chance of side effects affecting the liver and the blood

Other medical problems—The presence of other medical problems may affect the use of sulfadoxine and pyrimethamine combination. Make sure you tell your doctor if you have any other medical problems, especially:

- Anemia or other blood problems—Patients with these problems may have an increase in side effects involving the blood
- Kidney disease or
- Liver disease—Patients with kidney and/or liver disease may have an increased chance of side effects
- Porphyria—This medicine may cause an attack of porphyria
- Seizure disorders, such as epilepsy—High doses of this medicine may increase the chance of convulsions (seizures)

Proper Use of This Medicine

Do not give this medicine to infants under 2 months of age unless otherwise directed by your doctor. Also, *keep this medicine out of the reach of children.* Overdose is especially dangerous in children.

Sulfa-containing medicines are best taken with a full glass (8 ounces) of water. Several additional glasses of water should be taken every day, unless otherwise directed by your doctor. Drinking extra water will help to prevent some unwanted effects (e.g., kidney stones) of this medicine. If this medicine upsets your stomach or causes vomiting, it may be taken with meals or a snack.

For patients taking this medicine *to prevent malaria:*

- Your doctor may want you to start taking this medicine 1 to 2 weeks before you travel to an area where there is a chance of getting malaria. This will help you to see how you react to the medicine. Also, it will allow time for your doctor to change your medicine if you have a reaction to this medicine.
- Also, you should keep taking this medicine while you are in the area and for 4 weeks after you leave the area. No medicine will protect you completely from malaria. However, to protect you as completely as possible, *it is important that you keep taking this medicine for the full time your doctor ordered.* Also, if fever develops during your travels or within 2 months after you leave the area, *check with your doctor immediately.*
- This medicine works best when you take it on a regular schedule. For example, if you are to take it once a week, it is best to take it on the same day each week. *Do not miss any doses.* If you have any questions about this, check with your health care professional.

For patients taking this medicine *to treat malaria:*

- To help clear up your infection completely, *take this medicine exactly as directed by your doctor.*

For patients taking this medicine *to self-treat presumptive malaria:*

- After you take this medicine to self-treat presumptive malaria, you should continue to take your other medicine for malaria once a week.

Dosing—The dose of sulfadoxine and pyrimethamine combination will be different for different patients. *Follow your doctor's orders or the directions on the label.* The following information includes only the average doses of sulfadoxine and pyrimethamine combination. *If your dose is different, do not change it* unless your doctor tells you to do so.

- For *treatment* of malaria:
  - —Adults and teenagers: 3 tablets as a single dose on the third day of quinine therapy.
  - —Children: Dose is based on body weight and must be determined by your doctor.
- For *self-treatment of presumed malaria*:
  - —Adults and teenagers: 3 tablets as a single dose when you get a fever and medical care is not available.
  - —Children: Dose is based on body weight and must be determined by your doctor. The dose may range from 1/4 tablet to 3 tablets taken as a single dose.
- For *prevention* of malaria:
  - —Adults and teenagers: 1 tablet once every seven days, or 2 tablets once every fourteen days.
  - —Children: Dose is based on body weight and must be determined by your doctor. The dose may range from 1/2 tablet to 3/4 tablet taken once every seven days, or 1/4 tablet to 1 1/2 tablets taken once every fourteen days.

Missed dose—For patients taking this medicine *to prevent malaria:* If you do miss a dose of this medicine, take it as soon as possible. This will help to keep you taking your medicine on a regular schedule. However, if it is almost time for your next dose, skip the missed dose and go back to your regular dosing schedule. Do not double doses.

Storage—To store this medicine:

- Keep out of the reach of children. Overdose of sulfadoxine and pyrimethamine combination is very dangerous in children.
- Store away from heat and direct light.
- Do not store in the bathroom, near the kitchen sink, or in other damp places. Heat or moisture may cause the medicine to break down.
- Do not keep outdated medicine or medicine no longer needed. Be sure that any discarded medicine is out of the reach of children.

Precautions While Using This Medicine

If this medicine causes skin rash, itching, redness, sores in the mouth or on the genitals (sex organs), or sore throat, check with your doctor immediately. These may be early warning signs of more serious skin or related problems that could develop later.

Malaria is spread by mosquitoes. If you are living in, or will be traveling to, an area where there is a chance of getting malaria, the following mosquito-control measures will help to prevent infection:

- If possible, sleep under mosquito netting to avoid being bitten by malaria-carrying mosquitoes.
- Wear long-sleeved shirts or blouses and long trousers to protect your arms and legs, especially from dusk through dawn when mosquitoes are out.
- Apply mosquito repellant to uncovered areas of the skin from dusk through dawn when mosquitoes are out.

For patients taking this medicine *to prevent malaria:*

- *It is very important that your doctor check your progress at regular visits.* This medicine may cause blood problems, especially if it is taken for a long time.
- If this medicine causes anemia, your doctor may want you to take leucovorin (e.g., folinic acid, Wellcovorin) to help clear up the anemia. If so, it is important to take the leucovorin every day while you are taking this medicine. Do not miss any doses.
- Sulfadoxine and pyrimethamine combination may cause blood problems. These problems may result in

a greater chance of certain infections, slow healing, and bleeding of the gums. Therefore, you should be careful when using regular toothbrushes, dental floss, and toothpicks. Dental work should be delayed until your blood counts have returned to normal. Check with your medical doctor or dentist if you have any questions about proper oral hygiene (mouth care) during treatment.

- Sulfadoxine and pyrimethamine combination may cause your skin to be more sensitive to sunlight than it is normally. Exposure to sunlight, even for brief periods of time, may cause a skin rash, itching, redness or other discoloration of the skin, or a severe sunburn. When you begin taking this medicine:

  —Stay out of direct sunlight, especially between the hours of 10:00 a.m. and 3:00 p.m., if possible.

  —Wear protective clothing, including a hat. Also, wear sunglasses.

  —Apply a sun block product that has a skin protection factor (SPF) of at least 15. Some patients may require a product with a higher SPF number, especially if they have a fair complexion. If you have any questions about this, check with your health care professional.

  —Apply a sun block lipstick that has an SPF of at least 15 to protect your lips.

  —Do not use a sunlamp or tanning bed or booth.

  If you have a severe reaction from the sun, check with your doctor.

For patients taking this medicine *to self-treat presumed malaria:*

- Seek medical help as soon as possible, especially if your symptoms do not improve within 48 hours.

Side Effects of This Medicine

Along with its needed effects, a medicine may cause some unwanted effects. Although not all of these side effects may occur, if they do occur they may need medical attention.

Check with your doctor immediately if any of the following side effects occur:

More common

Change in or loss of taste; fever and sore throat; skin rash; soreness, redness, swelling, burning, or stinging of tongue; unusual bleeding or bruising; unusual tiredness or weakness

Less common

Aching of joints and muscles; redness, blistering, peeling, or loosening of skin; yellow eyes or skin

Rare

Blood in urine; lower back pain; pain or burning while urinating; swelling of front part of neck

Symptoms of overdose

Bleeding or bruising (severe); clumsiness or unsteadiness; convulsions (seizures); loss of appetite (severe); sore throat and fever (severe); tiredness or weakness (severe); trembling; vomiting (severe)

Also, check with your doctor as soon as possible if the following side effect occurs:

More common

Increased sensitivity of skin to sunlight

Other side effects may occur that usually do not need medical attention. These side effects may go away during treatment as your body adjusts to the medicine. However, check with your doctor if any of the following side effects continue or are bothersome:

More common

Diarrhea; headache; nausea or vomiting; nervousness; stomach pain

Other side effects not listed above may also occur in some patients. If you notice any other effects, check with your doctor.

Additional Information

Once a medicine has been approved for marketing for a certain use, experience may show that it is also useful for other medical problems. Although this use is not included in product labeling, sulfadoxine and pyrimethamine combination is used in certain patients with the following medical condition:

- Isosporiasis (prevention)

Other than the above information, there is no additional information relating to proper use, precautions, or side effects for this use.

Revised: 02/23/93

SULFAPYRIDINE Systemic

A commonly used brand name in Canada is Dagenan.

Generic name product may also be available in the U.S. and Canada.

Description

Sulfapyridine (sul-fa-PEER-i-deen) is a sulfa medicine. It is used to help control dermatitis herpetiformis (Duhring's disease), a skin problem. It may also be used for other problems as determined by your doctor. However, this medicine will not work for any kind of infection as other sulfa medicines do.

This medicine may cause some serious side effects. *Before using this medicine, be sure to talk to your doctor about these problems, as well as the good this medicine will do.*

Sulfapyridine is available only with your doctor's prescription, in the following dosage form:

Oral

- Tablets (U.S. and Canada)

Before Using This Medicine

In deciding to use a medicine, the risks of taking the medicine must be weighed against the good it will do. This is

a decision you and your doctor will make. For sulfapyridine, the following should be considered:

Allergies—Tell your doctor if you have ever had any unusual or allergic reaction to sulfa medicines, furosemide (e.g., Lasix) or thiazide diuretics (water pills), oral antidiabetics (diabetes medicine you take by mouth), glaucoma medicine you take by mouth (acetazolamide [e.g., Diamox], dichlorphenamide [e.g., Daranide], methazolamide [e.g., Neptazane]), or pyrimethamine (e.g., Daraprim). Also tell your health care professional if you are allergic to any other substances, such as foods, preservatives, or dyes.

Pregnancy—Studies have not been done in humans. Studies in rats and mice have shown that some sulfa medicines, given by mouth in high doses, cause birth defects, including cleft palate and bone problems. In addition, sulfa medicines may cause liver problems in newborn infants. Therefore, use is not recommended during pregnancy.

Breast-feeding—Sulfapyridine passes into the breast milk. This medicine may cause liver problems in nursing babies. In addition, it may cause blood problems in nursing babies with glucose-6-phosphate dehydrogenase (G6PD) deficiency (lack of G6PD enzyme). Therefore, use is not recommended in nursing women.

Children—Use of this medicine is not recommended since dermatitis herpetiformis usually does not occur in children.

Older adults—Many medicines have not been studied specifically in older people. Therefore, it may not be known whether they work exactly the same way they do in younger adults or if they cause different side effects or problems in older people. There is no specific information comparing the use of sulfapyridine in the elderly with use in other age groups.

Other medicines—Although certain medicines should not be used together at all, in other cases two different medicines may be used together even if an interaction might occur. In these cases, your doctor may want to change the dose, or other precautions may be necessary. When you are taking sulfapyridine, it is especially important that your health care professional know if you are taking any of the following:

- Acetaminophen (e.g., Tylenol) (with long-term, high-dose use) or
- Amiodarone (e.g., Cordarone) or
- Anabolic steroids (nandrolone [e.g., Anabolin], oxandrolone [e.g., Anavar], oxymetholone [e.g., Anadrol], stanozolol [e.g., Winstrol]) or
- Androgens (male hormones) or
- Antithyroid agents (medicine for overactive thyroid) or
- Carbamazepine (e.g., Tegretol) or
- Carmustine (e.g., BiCNU) or
- Chloroquine (e.g., Aralen) or
- Dantrolene (e.g., Dantrium) or
- Daunorubicin (e.g., Cerubidine) or
- Disulfiram (e.g., Antabuse) or
- Divalproex (e.g., Depakote) or
- Estrogens (female hormones) or
- Etretinate (e.g., Tegison) or
- Gold salts (medicine for arthritis) or
- Hydroxychloroquine (e.g., Plaquenil) or
- Mercaptopurine (e.g., Purinethol) or
- Naltrexone (e.g., Trexan) (with long-term, high-dose use) or
- Oral contraceptives (birth control pills) containing estrogen or
- Other anti-infectives by mouth or by injection (medicine for infection) or
- Phenothiazines (acetophenazine [e.g., Tindal], chlorpromazine [e.g., Thorazine], fluphenazine [e.g., Prolixin], mesoridazine [e.g., Serentil], perphenazine [e.g., Trilafon], prochlorperazine [e.g., Compazine], promazine [e.g., Sparine], promethazine [e.g., Phenergan], thioridazine [e.g., Mellaril], trifluoperazine [e.g., Stelazine], triflupromazine [e.g., Vesprin], trimeprazine [e.g., Temaril]) or
- Plicamycin (e.g., Mithracin) or
- Valproic acid (e.g., Depakene)—Use of sulfapyridine with these medicines may increase the chance of side effects affecting the liver

- Acetohydroxamic acid (e.g., Lithostat) or
- Dapsone or
- Furazolidone (e.g., Furoxone) or
- Nitrofurantoin (e.g., Furadantin) or
- Primaquine or
- Procainamide (e.g., Pronestyl) or
- Quinidine (e.g., Quinidex) or
- Quinine (e.g., Quinamm) or
- Sulfoxone (e.g., Diasone) or
- Vitamin K (e.g., AquaMEPHYTON, Synkayvite)—Use of sulfapyridine with these medicines may increase the chance of side effects affecting the blood

- Anticoagulants (blood thinners) or
- Ethotoin (e.g., Peganone) or
- Mephenytoin (e.g., Mesantoin)—Use of sulfapyridine with these medicines may increase the chance of side effects of these medicines

- Antidiabetics, oral (diabetes medicine you take by mouth)—Use of oral antidiabetics with sulfapyridine may increase the chance of side effects affecting the blood and/or the side effects or oral antidiabetics

- Methotrexate (e.g., Mexate)—Use of methotrexate with sulfapyridine may increase the chance of side effects affecting the liver and/or the side effects of methotrexate

- Methyldopa (e.g., Aldomet)—Use of methyldopa with sulfapyridine may increase the chance of side effects affecting the liver and/or the blood

- Phenytoin (e.g., Dilantin)—Use of phenytoin with sulfapyridine may increase the chance of side effects affecting the liver and/or the side effects of phenytoin

Other medical problems—The presence of other medical problems may affect the use of sulfapyridine. Make sure you tell your doctor if you have any other medical problems, especially:

- Blood problems or
- Glucose-6-phosphate dehydrogenase deficiency (lack of G6PD enzyme)—Patients with these problems may have an increase in side effects affecting the blood

- Kidney disease or
- Liver disease—Patients with kidney disease or liver disease may have an increased chance of side effects

- Porphyria—Use of sulfapyridine may cause an attack of porphyria

Proper Use of This Medicine

Each dose of sulfapyridine should be taken with a full glass (8 ounces) of water. Several additional glasses of water should be taken every day, unless otherwise directed by your doctor. Drinking extra water will help to prevent some unwanted effects (e.g., kidney stones) of the sulfa medicine.

For patients taking sulfapyridine *for dermatitis herpetiformis:*

- Your doctor may want you to follow a strict, gluten-free diet.
- You may have to use this medicine regularly for 6 months to a year before you can reduce the dose of sulfapyridine or stop it altogether. If you have any questions about this, check with your doctor.

Dosing—The dose of sulfapyridine will be different for different patients. *Follow your doctor's orders or the directions on the label.* The following information includes only the average doses of sulfapyridine. Your dose may be different if you have kidney disease. *If your dose is different, do not change it* unless your doctor tells you to do so.

- For *dermatitis herpetiformis*:
  —Adults and adolescents: 250 milligrams to 1 gram four times a day until improvement occurs. After improvement has occurred, the dose should then be reduced by 250 to 500 milligrams every three days until there are no symptoms; that dose should be taken once daily.
  —Children: Use is not recommended, because children usually do not get this condition.

Missed dose—For patients taking sulfapyridine *for dermatitis herpetiformis:* You may skip a missed dose if this does not make your symptoms return or get worse. If your symptoms do return or get worse, take the missed dose as soon as possible. Then go back to your regular dosing schedule.

Storage—To store this medicine:

- Keep out of the reach of children.
- Store away from heat and direct light.
- Do not store in the bathroom, near the kitchen sink, or in other damp places. Heat or moisture may cause the medicine to break down.
- Do not keep outdated medicine or medicine no longer needed. Be sure that any discarded medicine is out of the reach of children.

Precautions While Using This Medicine

It is very important that your doctor check your progress at regular visits. This medicine may cause blood problems, especially if it is taken for a long time.

If your symptoms do not improve within a few days, or if they become worse, check with your doctor.

Sulfapyridine may cause blood problems. These problems may result in a greater chance of certain infections, slow healing, and bleeding of the gums. Therefore, you should be careful when using regular toothbrushes, dental floss, and toothpicks. Dental work should be delayed until your blood counts have returned to normal. Check with your medical doctor or dentist if you have any questions about proper oral hygiene (mouth care) during treatment.

Sulfapyridine may cause your skin to be more sensitive to sunlight than it is normally. Exposure to sunlight, even for brief periods of time, may cause a skin rash, itching, redness or other discoloration of the skin, or a severe sunburn. When you begin taking this medicine:

- Stay out of direct sunlight, especially between the hours of 10:00 A.M. and 3:00 P.M., if possible.
- Wear protective clothing, including a hat. Also, wear sunglasses.
- Apply a sun block product that has a skin protection factor (SPF) of at least 15. Some patients may require a product with a higher SPF number, especially if they have a fair complexion. If you have any questions about this, check with your health care professional.
- Apply a sun block lipstick that has an SPF of at least 15 to protect your lips.
- Do not use a sunlamp or tanning bed or booth.

You may still be more sensitive to sunlight or sunlamps for many months after stopping this medicine. *If you have a severe reaction from the sun, check with your doctor.*

Tell the doctor in charge that you are taking this medicine before you have any medical tests. The results of the bentiromide (e.g., Chymex) test for pancreas function are affected by this medicine.

Side Effects of This Medicine

Along with its needed effects, a medicine may cause some unwanted effects. Although not all of these side effects may occur, if they do occur they may need medical attention.

Check with your doctor immediately if any of the following side effects occur:

More common
Fever; headache (continuing); itching; skin rash

Less common
Aching of joints and muscles; difficulty in swallowing; pale skin; redness, blistering, peeling, or loosening of skin; sore throat; unusual bleeding or bruising; unusual tiredness or weakness; yellow eyes or skin

Rare
Blood in urine; lower back pain; pain or burning while urinating; swelling of front part of neck

Also, check with your doctor as soon as possible if the following side effect occurs:

More common
Increased sensitivity of skin to sunlight

Other side effects may occur that usually do not need medical attention. These side effects may go away during treatment as your body adjusts to the medicine. However, check with your doctor if any of the following side effects continue or are bothersome:

More common
Diarrhea; loss of appetite; nausea or vomiting

Other side effects not listed above may also oc[illegible] patients. If you notice any other effects, c[illegible] doctor.

Additional Information

Once a medicine has been approved for marketing for a certain use, experience may show that it is also useful for other medical problems. Although these uses are not included in product labeling, sulfapyridine is used in certain patients with the following medical conditions:

- Pemphigoid
- Pyoderma gangrenosum
- Subcorneal pustular dermatitis

Other than the above information, there is no additional information relating to proper use, precautions, or side effects for these uses.

Revised: 02/01/93

SULFASALAZINE Systemic

Some commonly used brand names are:

In the U.S.—

Azulfidine	Azulfidine EN-Tabs

Generic name product may also be available.

In Canada—

PMS-Sulfasalazine	Salazopyrin EN-Tabs
PMS-Sulfasalazine E.C.	S.A.S.-500
Salazopyrin	S.A.S. Enteric-500

Generic name product may also be available.

Other commonly used names are salazosulfapyridine, salicylazosulfapyridine, and sulphasalazine.

Description

Sulfasalazine (sul-fa-SAL-a-zeen), a sulfa medicine, is used to prevent and treat inflammatory bowel disease, such as ulcerative colitis. It works inside the bowel by helping to reduce the inflammation and other symptoms of the disease. Sulfasalazine is sometimes given with other medicines to treat inflammatory bowel disease.

Sulfasalazine is available only with your doctor's prescription, in the following dosage forms:

Oral

- Capsules (Canada)
- Oral suspension (Canada)
- Tablets (U.S. and Canada)
- Enteric-coated tablets (U.S. and Canada)

Rectal

- Enema (Canada)

Before Using This Medicine

In deciding to use a medicine, the risks of taking the medicine must be weighed against the good it will do. This is a decision you and your doctor will make. For sulfasalazine, the following should be considered:

Allergies—Tell your doctor if you have ever had any unusual or allergic reaction to any of the sulfa medicines, furosemide (e.g., Lasix) or thiazide diuretics (water pills), oral antidiabetics (diabetes medicine you take by mouth), glaucoma medicine you take by mouth (for example, acetazolamide [e.g., Diamox], dichlorphenamide [e.g., Daranide], methazolamide [e.g., Neptazane]), or salicylates (for example, aspirin). Also tell your health care professional if you are allergic to any other substances, such as foods, preservatives, or dyes.

Pregnancy—Sulfasalazine has not been studied in pregnant women. However, reports on women who took sulfasalazine during pregnancy have not shown that it causes birth defects or other problems. In addition, sulfasalazine has not been shown to cause birth defects in studies in rats and rabbits given doses of up to 6 times the human dose.

Breast-feeding—Sulfa medicines pass into the breast milk in small amounts and have been shown to cause unwanted effects in nursing babies with glucose-6-phosphate dehydrogenase (G6PD) deficiency. It may be necessary for you to take another medicine or to stop breast-feeding during treatment. Be sure you have discussed the risks and benefits of the medicine with your doctor.

Children—Sulfasalazine should not be used in children up to 2 years of age because it may cause brain problems. However, sulfasalazine has not been shown to cause different side effects or problems in children over the age of 2 years than it does in adults.

Older adults—This medicine has been tested and has not been shown to cause different side effects or problems in older people than it does in younger adults.

Other medicines—Although certain medicines should not be used together at all, in other cases two different medicines may be used together even if an interaction might occur. In these cases, your doctor may want to change the dose, or other precautions may be necessary. When you are taking sulfasalazine, it is especially important that your health care professional know if you are taking any of the following:

- Acetaminophen (e.g., Tylenol) (with long-term, high-dose use) or
- Amiodarone (e.g., Cordarone) or
- Anabolic steroids (nandrolone [e.g., Anabolin], oxandrolone [e.g., Anavar], oxymetholone [e.g., Anadrol], stanozolol [e.g., Winstrol]) or
- Androgens (male hormones) or
- Antithyroid agents (medicine for overactive thyroid) or
- Carbamazepine (e.g., Tegretol) or
- Carmustine (e.g., BiCNU) or
- Chloroquine (e.g., Aralen) or
- Dantrolene (e.g., Dantrium) or
- Daunorubicin (e.g., Cerubidine) or
- Disulfiram (e.g., Antabuse) or
- Divalproex (e.g., Depakote) or
- Estrogens (female hormones) or
- Etretinate (e.g., Tegison) or
- Gold salts (medicine for arthritis) or

- Hydroxychloroquine (e.g., Plaquenil) or
- Mercaptopurine (e.g., Purinethol) or
- Naltrexone (e.g., ReVia) (with long-term, high-dose use) or
- Oral contraceptives (birth control pills) containing estrogen or
- Other anti-infectives by mouth or by injection (medicine for infection) or
- Phenothiazines (acetophenazine [e.g., Tindal], chlorpromazine [e.g., Thorazine], fluphenazine [e.g., Prolixin], mesoridazine [e.g., Serentil], perphenazine [e.g., Trilafon], prochlorperazine [e.g., Compazine], promazine [e.g., Sparine], promethazine [e.g., Phenergan], thioridazine [e.g., Mellaril], trifluoperazine [e.g., Stelazine], triflupromazine [e.g., Vesprin], trimeprazine [e.g., Temaril]) or
- Plicamycin (e.g., Mithracin) or
- Valproic acid (e.g., Depakene)—Use of sulfasalazine with these medicines may increase the chance of side effects affecting the liver
- Acetohydroxamic acid (e.g., Lithostat) or
- Dapsone or
- Furazolidone (e.g., Furoxone) or
- Nitrofurantoin (e.g., Furadantin) or
- Primaquine or
- Procainamide (e.g., Pronestyl) or
- Quinidine (e.g., Quinidex) or
- Quinine (e.g., Quinamm) or
- Sulfoxone (e.g., Diasone) or
- Vitamin K (e.g., AquaMEPHYTON, Synkayvite)—Use of sulfasalazine with these medicines may increase the chance of side effects affecting the blood
- Anticoagulants (blood thinners) or
- Ethotoin (e.g., Peganone) or
- Mephenytoin (e.g., Mesantoin)—Use of sulfasalazine with these medicines may increase the chance of side effects of these medicines
- Antidiabetics, oral (diabetes medicine you take by mouth)—Use of oral antidiabetics with sulfasalazine may increase the chance of side effects affecting the blood and/or the side effects or oral antidiabetics
- Methotrexate (e.g., Mexate)—Use of methotrexate with sulfasalazine may increase the chance of side effects affecting the liver and/or the side effects of methotrexate
- Methyldopa (e.g., Aldomet)—Use of methyldopa with sulfasalazine may increase the chance of side effects affecting the liver and/or the blood
- Phenytoin (e.g., Dilantin)—Use of phenytoin with sulfasalazine may increase the chance of side effects affecting the liver and/or the side effects of phenytoin

Other medical problems—The presence of other medical problems may affect the use of sulfasalazine. Make sure you tell your doctor if you have any other medical problems, especially:

- Blood problems or
- Glucose-6-phosphate dehydrogenase deficiency (lack of G6PD enzyme)—Patients with these problems may have an increase in side effects affecting the blood
- Kidney disease or
- Liver disease—Patients with kidney disease or liver disease may have an increased chance of side effects
- Porphyria—Use of sulfasalazine may cause an attack of porphyria

Proper Use of This Medicine

Do not give sulfasalazine to infants and children up to 2 years of age, unless otherwise directed by your doctor. It may cause brain problems.

Sulfasalazine is best taken right after meals or with food to lessen stomach upset. If stomach upset continues or is bothersome, check with your doctor.

Each dose of sulfasalazine should also be taken with a full glass (8 ounces) of water. Several additional glasses of water should be taken every day, unless otherwise directed by your doctor. Drinking extra water will help to prevent some unwanted effects of the sulfa medicine.

For patients taking the *oral suspension* form of this medicine:

- Use a specially marked measuring spoon or other device to measure each dose accurately. The average household teaspoon may not hold the right amount of liquid.

For patients taking the *enteric-coated tablet* form of this medicine:

- Swallow tablets whole. Do not break or crush.

Keep taking this medicine for the full time of treatment, even if you begin to feel better after a few days. *Do not miss any doses.*

Dosing—The dose of sulfasalazine will be different for different patients. *Follow your doctor's orders or the directions on the label.* The following information includes only the average doses of sulfasalazine. *If your dose is different, do not change it* unless your doctor tells you to do so.

The number of tablets or teaspoonfuls of oral suspension that you take depends on the strength of the medicine. Also, *the number of doses you take each day, the time allowed between doses, and the length of time you take the medicine depend on the medical problem for which you are taking sulfasalazine.*

- For prevention or treatment of inflammatory bowel disease:
  —For *oral* dosage form (capsules):
  - Adults, teenagers, and children 2 years of age and over—Your doctor will have you start with a small dose and then determine a schedule for you to increase your dose gradually.
  - Infants and children up to 2 years of age—Use is not recommended.

  —For *oral* dosage forms (oral suspension, tablets, enteric-coated tablets):
  - Adults and teenagers—To start, 500 milligrams (mg) to 1000 mg (1 gram) every six to eight hours. Your doctor may then decrease the dose to 500 mg every six hours. Later, your doctor may change your dose as needed.
  - Children 2 years of age and over—Dose is based on body weight and must be determined by your doctor.

    —To start, the dose is usually:
    - 6.7 to 10 mg per kilogram (kg) (3.05 [illegible] 4.55 mg per pound) of body weight [illegible] four hours or

- 10 to 15 mg per kg (4.55 to 6.82 mg per pound) of body weight every six hours or
- 13.3 to 20 mg per kg (6.05 to 9.09 mg per pound) of body weight every eight hours.

—Then, the dose is usually 7.5 mg per kg (3.41 mg per pound) of body weight every six hours.

- Infants and children up to 2 years of age—Use is not recommended.

—For *rectal* dosage form (enema):

- Adults and teenagers—3 grams (1 unit), used rectally as directed, every night.
- Children 2 years of age and over—Dose must be determined by your doctor.
- Infants and children up to 2 years of age—Use is not recommended.

Missed dose—If you do miss a dose of this medicine, take it as soon as possible. However, if it is almost time for your next dose, skip the missed dose and go back to your regular dosing schedule. Do not double doses.

Storage—To store this medicine:

- Keep out of the reach of children.
- Store away from heat and direct light.
- Do not store the capsule or tablet form of this medicine in the bathroom, near the kitchen sink, or in other damp places. Heat or moisture may cause the medicine to break down.
- Keep the oral liquid and enema forms of this medicine from freezing.
- Do not keep outdated medicine or medicine no longer needed. Be sure that any discarded medicine is out of the reach of children.

Precautions While Using This Medicine

It is very important that your doctor check your progress at regular visits. This medicine may cause blood problems, especially if it is taken for a long time.

If your symptoms (including diarrhea) do not improve within 1 or 2 months, or if they become worse, check with your doctor.

Sulfasalazine may cause blood problems. These problems may result in a greater chance of certain infections, slow healing, and bleeding of the gums. Therefore, you should be careful when using regular toothbrushes, dental floss, and toothpicks. Dental work should be delayed until your blood counts have returned to normal. Check with your medical doctor or dentist if you have any questions about proper oral hygiene (mouth care) during treatment.

Sulfasalazine may cause your skin to be more sensitive to sunlight than it is normally. Exposure to sunlight, even for brief periods of time, may cause a skin rash, itching, redness or other discoloration of the skin, or a severe sunburn. When you begin taking this medicine:

- Stay out of direct sunlight, especially between the hours of 10:00 a.m. and 3:00 p.m., if possible.
- Wear protective clothing, including a hat. Also, wear sunglasses.
- Apply a sun block product that has a skin protection factor (SPF) of at least 15. Some patients may require a product with a higher SPF number, especially if they have a fair complexion. If you have any questions about this, check with your health care professional.
- Apply a sun block lipstick that has an SPF of at least 15 to protect your lips.
- Do not use a sunlamp or tanning bed or booth.

If you have a severe reaction from the sun, check with your doctor.

This medicine may also cause some people to become dizzy. *Make sure you know how you react to this medicine before you drive, use machines, or do anything else that could be dangerous if you are dizzy.* If this reaction is especially bothersome, check with your doctor.

Before you have any medical tests, tell the doctor in charge that you are taking this medicine. The results of the bentiromide (e.g., Chymex) test for pancreas function are affected by this medicine.

Side Effects of This Medicine

Along with its needed effects, a medicine may cause some unwanted effects. Although not all of these side effects may occur, if they do occur they may need medical attention.

Check with your doctor immediately if any of the following side effects occur:

More common

Aching of joints; headache (continuing); itching; skin rash

Less common or rare

Aching of joints and muscles; back, leg, or stomach pains; bloody diarrhea; bluish fingernails, lips, or skin; chest pain; cough; difficult breathing; difficulty in swallowing; fever and sore throat; general feeling of discomfort or illness; loss of appetite; pale skin; redness, blistering, peeling, or loosening of skin; unusual bleeding or bruising; unusual tiredness or weakness; yellow eyes or skin

Also, check with your doctor as soon as possible if the following side effect occurs:

More common

Increased sensitivity of skin to sunlight

Other side effects may occur that usually do not need medical attention. These side effects may go away during treatment as your body adjusts to the medicine. However, check with your doctor if any of the following side effects continue or are bothersome:

More common

Abdominal or stomach pain or upset; diarrhea; loss of appetite; nausea or vomiting

In some patients this medicine may also cause the urine or skin to become orange-yellow. This side effect does not need medical attention.

Other side effects not listed above may also occur in some patients. If you notice any other effects, check with your doctor.

Additional Information

Once a medicine has been approved for marketing for a certain use, experience may show that it is also useful for other medical problems. Although these uses are not included in product labeling, sulfasalazine is used in certain patients with the following medical conditions:

- Ankylosing spondylitis
- Rheumatoid arthritis

Other than the above information, there is no additional information relating to proper use, precautions, or side effects for these uses.

Revised: 04/07/95

SULFINPYRAZONE Systemic

Some commonly used brand names are:

In the U.S.—
Anturane

Generic name product may also be available.

In Canada—
Anturan
Apo-Sulfinpyrazone
Novopyrazone

Description

Sulfinpyrazone (sul-fin-PEER-a-zone) is used in the treatment of chronic gout (gouty arthritis), which is caused by too much uric acid in the blood. The medicine works by removing the extra uric acid from the body. Sulfinpyrazone does not cure gout, but after you have been taking it for a few months it may help prevent gout attacks. This medicine will help prevent gout attacks only as long as you continue to take it.

Sulfinpyrazone is sometimes used to prevent or treat other medical problems that may occur if too much uric acid is present in the body.

Sulfinpyrazone may also be used for other conditions as determined by your doctor.

Sulfinpyrazone is available only with your doctor's prescription, in the following dosage forms:

Oral
- Capsules (U.S.)
- Tablets (U.S. and Canada)

Before Using This Medicine

In deciding to use a medicine, the risks of taking the medicine must be weighed against the good it will do. This is a decision you and your doctor will make. For sulfinpyrazone, the following should be considered:

Allergies—Tell your doctor if you have ever had any unusual or allergic reaction to sulfinpyrazone or to aspirin, oxyphenbutazone (e.g., Tandearil), or phenylbutazone (e.g., Butazolidin), or other anti-inflammatory analgesics (medicines used for pain and/or inflammation). Also tell your health care professional if you are allergic to any other substances, such as foods, preservatives, or dyes.

Pregnancy—Sulfinpyrazone has not been reported to cause problems in humans.

Breast-feeding—It is not known whether sulfinpyrazone passes into the breast milk.

Children—Studies on this medicine have been done only in adult patients, and there is no specific information comparing use of sulfinpyrazone in children with use in other age groups.

Older adults—Many medicines have not been studied specifically in older people. Therefore, it may not be known whether they work exactly the same way they do in younger adults or if they cause different side effects or problems in older people. There is no specific information comparing use of sulfinpyrazone in the elderly with use in other age groups.

Other medicines—Although certain medicines should not be used together at all, in other cases two different medicines may be used together even if an interaction might occur. In these cases, your doctor may want to change the dose, or other precautions may be necessary. When you are taking sulfinpyrazone, it is especially important that your health care professional know if you are taking any of the following:

- Anticoagulants (blood thinners) or
- Carbenicillin by injection (e.g., Geopen) or
- Cefamandole (e.g., Mandol) or
- Cefoperazone (e.g., Cefobid) or
- Cefotetan (e.g., Cefotan) or
- Dipyridamole (e.g., Persantine) or
- Divalproex (e.g., Depakote) or
- Heparin (e.g., Panheprin) or
- Inflammation or pain medicine, except narcotics, or
- Moxalactam (e.g., Moxam) or
- Pentoxifylline (e.g., Trental) or
- Plicamycin (e.g., Mithracin) or
- Ticarcillin (e.g., Ticar) or
- Valproic acid (e.g., Depakene)—Use of these medicines together with sulfinpyrazone may increase the chance of bleeding
- Antineoplastics (cancer medicine)—The chance of serious side effects may be increased
- Aspirin or other salicylates, including bismuth subsalicylate (e.g., Pepto Bismol)—These medicines may keep sulfinpyrazone from working properly in treating gout, depending on the amount of aspirin or other salicylate that you take and how often you take it. Taking sulfinpyrazone and aspirin together may also increase the chance of bleeding
- Nitrofurantoin (e.g., Furadantin)—Sulfinpyrazone may keep nitrofurantoin from working properly

Other medical problems—The presence of other medical problems may affect the use of sulfinpyrazone. Make sure

you tell your doctor if you have any other medical problems, especially:

- Blood disease (or history of) or
- Cancer being treated by antineoplastics (cancer medicine) or radiation (x-rays) or
- Kidney stones (or history of) or other kidney disease or
- Stomach ulcer or other stomach or intestinal problems (or history of)—The chance of serious side effects may be increased; also, sulfinpyrazone may not work properly for treating gout if some kinds of kidney disease are present

Proper Use of This Medicine

If sulfinpyrazone upsets your stomach, it may be taken with food. If this does not work, an antacid may be taken. If stomach upset (nausea, vomiting, or stomach pain) continues, check with your doctor.

In order for sulfinpyrazone to help you, it must be taken regularly as ordered by your doctor.

When you first begin taking sulfinpyrazone, the amount of uric acid in the kidneys is greatly increased. This may cause kidney stones in some people. To help prevent this, your doctor may want you to drink at least 10 to 12 full glasses (8 ounces each) of fluids each day, or to take another medicine to make your urine less acid. *It is important that you follow your doctor's instructions very carefully.*

For patients taking sulfinpyrazone for *gout:*

- After you begin to take sulfinpyrazone, gout attacks may continue to occur for a while. However, if you take this medicine regularly as directed by your doctor, the attacks will gradually become less frequent and less painful. After you have been taking sulfinpyrazone for several months, they may stop completely.
- Sulfinpyrazone helps to prevent gout attacks. It will not relieve an attack that has already started. *Even if you take another medicine for gout attacks, continue to take this medicine also.*

Dosing—The dose of sulfinpyrazone will be different for different patients. *Follow your doctor's orders or the directions on the label.* The following information includes only the average doses of sulfinpyrazone. *If your dose is different, do not change it* unless your doctor tells you to do so.

- *For treating gout or removing uric acid from the body:*

  —Adults: The starting dose of sulfinpyrazone is usually 100 mg or 200 mg a day (one-half of a 100-mg tablet two times a day, one 100-mg tablet one or two times a day, or one 200-mg capsule or tablet once a day). Then, the dose is usually increased by 100 mg or 200 mg every few days, up to 800 mg a day. Starting with a low dose and increasing the dose gradually helps prevent kidney stones and other side effects. After a while, the dose may be changed again, depending on the amount of uric acid in your blood or urine.

  —Children: It is not likely that sulfinpyrazone will be needed to treat gout or remove uric acid from the body in children. However, if a child needs this medicine, the dose would have to be determined by the doctor.

Missed dose—If you miss a dose of this medicine, take it as soon as possible. However, if is almost time for your next dose, skip the missed dose and go back to your regular dosing schedule. Do not double doses.

Storage—To store this medicine:

- Keep out of the reach of children.
- Store away from heat and direct light.
- Do not store this medicine in the bathroom, near the kitchen sink, or in other damp places. Heat or moisture may cause the medicine to break down.
- Do not keep outdated medicine or medicine no longer needed. Be sure that any discarded medicine is out of the reach of children.

Precautions While Using This Medicine

Your doctor should check your progress at regular visits to make sure that this medicine does not cause unwanted effects.

Before you have any medical tests, tell the person in charge that you are taking this medicine. The results of some tests may be affected by sulfinpyrazone.

For patients taking sulfinpyrazone for *gout or to help remove uric acid from the body:*

- Taking aspirin or other salicylates may lessen the effects of sulfinpyrazone. This will depend on the dose of aspirin or other salicylate that you take, and on how often you take it. Also, drinking too much alcohol may increase the amount of uric acid in the blood and lessen the effects of sulfinpyrazone. Therefore, *do not take aspirin or other salicylates or drink alcoholic beverages while taking this medicine,* unless you have first checked with your doctor.

Side Effects of This Medicine

Along with its needed effects, a medicine may cause some unwanted effects. Although not all of these side effects may occur, if they do occur they may need medical attention.

Check with your doctor immediately if any of the following side effects occur:

Rare

Shortness of breath, troubled breathing, tightness in chest, and/or wheezing; sores, ulcers, or white spots on lips or in mouth; sore throat and fever with or without chills; swollen and/or painful glands; unusual bleeding or bruising

Symptoms of overdose

Clumsiness or unsteadiness; convulsions (seizures); diarrhea; nausea or vomiting (severe or continuing); stomach pain (severe or continuing); difficulty in breathing

Also, check with your doctor as soon as possible if any of the following side effects occur:

More common

Lower back and/or side pain; painful urination (possibly with blood)

Less common
Skin rash
Rare
Bloody or black, tarry stools; fever; increased blood pressure; pinpoint red spots on skin; sudden decrease in amount of urine; swelling of face, fingers, feet, and/or lower legs; unusual tiredness or weakness; vomiting of blood or material that looks like coffee grounds; weight gain

Other side effects may occur that usually do not need medical attention. These side effects may go away during treatment as your body adjusts to the medicine. However, check with your doctor if any of the following side effects continue or are bothersome:

More common
Joint pain, redness, and/or swelling; nausea or vomiting; stomach pain

Other side effects not listed above may also occur in some patients. If you notice any other effects, check with your doctor.

Revised: 01/19/93

SULFONAMIDES Ophthalmic

Some commonly used brand names are:

In the U.S.—

Ak-Sulf[1]	Sodium Sulamyd[1]
Bleph-10[1]	Spectro-Sulf[1]
Cetamide[1]	Steri-Units Sulfacetamide[1]
Gantrisin[2]	Sulf-10[1]
Isopto-Cetamide[1]	Sulfair[1]
I-Sulfacet[1]	Sulfair 10[1]
Ocu-Sul-10[1]	Sulfair 15[1]
Ocu-Sul-15[1]	Sulfair Forte[1]
Ocu-Sul-30[1]	Sulfamide[1]
Ocusulf-10[1]	Sulten-10[1]
Ophthacet[1]	

In Canada—

Ak-Sulf[1]	Isopto-Cetamide[1]
Bleph-10[1]	Sodium Sulamyd[1]
Cetamide[1]	Sulfex[1]

Another commonly used name for sulfisoxazole is sulfafurazole.

Note: For quick reference, the following sulfonamides are numbered to match the corresponding brand names.

This information applies to the following medicines:
1. Sulfacetamide (sul-fa-SEE-ta-mide)‡
2. Sulfisoxazole (sul-fi-SOX-a-zole)

‡Generic name product may may also be available in the U.S.

Description

Sulfonamides (sul-FON-a-mides) or sulfa medicines belong to the family of medicines called anti-infectives. Sulfonamide ophthalmic preparations are used to treat infections of the eye.

Sulfonamides are available only with your doctor's prescription, in the following dosage forms:

Ophthalmic
Sulfacetamide
- Ophthalmic ointment (U.S. and Canada)
- Ophthalmic solution (eye drops) (U.S. and Canada)

Sulfisoxazole
- Ophthalmic ointment (U.S.)
- Ophthalmic solution (eye drops) (U.S.)

Before Using This Medicine

In deciding to use a medicine, the risks of using the medicine must be weighed against the good it will do. This is a decision you and your doctor will make. For sulfonamide ophthalmic preparations, the following should be considered:

Allergies—Tell your doctor if you have ever had any unusual or allergic reaction to any of the sulfa medicines; furosemide (e.g., Lasix) or thiazide diuretics (water pills); oral antidiabetics (diabetes medicine you take by mouth); or glaucoma medicine you take by mouth (for example, acetazolamide [e.g., Diamox], dichlorphenamide [e.g., Daranide], or methazolamide [e.g., Neptazane]). Also tell your health care professional if you are allergic to any other substances, such as preservatives.

Pregnancy—Sulfonamide ophthalmic preparations have not been shown to cause birth defects or other problems in humans.

Breast-feeding—Sulfonamide ophthalmic preparations have not been reported to cause problems in nursing babies.

Children—Studies on sulfonamide ophthalmic preparations have been done only in adult patients, and there is no specific information comparing use in children with use in other age groups.

Older adults—Many medicines have not been studied specifically in older people. Therefore, it may not be known whether they work exactly the same way they do in younger adults or if they cause different side effects or problems in older people. There is no specific information comparing use of sulfonamides in the elderly with use in other age groups.

Other medicines—Although certain medicines should not be used together at all, in other cases two different medicines may be used together even if an interaction might occur. In these cases, your doctor may want to change the dose, or other precautions may be necessary. When you are taking sulfonamide ophthalmic preparations, it is especially important that your health care professional know if you are using any of the following:

- Silver preparations, such as silver nitrate or mild silver protein for the eye—Sulfonamide ophthalmic preparations should not be used with silver ophthalmic preparations, since a chemical reaction may occur.

Proper Use of This Medicine

For patients using the *eye drop form* of sulfonamides:
- The bottle is only partially full to provide proper drop control.

- To use:
  —First, wash your hands. Then tilt the head back and pull the lower eyelid away from the eye to form a pouch. Drop the medicine into the pouch and gently close the eyes. Do not blink. Keep the eyes closed for 1 or 2 minutes to allow the medicine to come into contact with the infection.
  —If you think you did not get the drop of medicine into your eye properly, use another drop.
  —To keep the medicine as germ-free as possible, do not touch the applicator tip to any surface (including the eye). Also, keep the container tightly closed.

For patients using the *eye ointment form* of sulfonamides:
- To use:
  —First, wash your hands. Then pull the lower eyelid away from the eye to form a pouch. Squeeze a thin strip of ointment into the pouch. A 1.25- to 2.5-cm (approximately 1/2- to 1-inch) strip of ointment is usually enough unless otherwise directed by your doctor. Gently close the eyes and keep them closed for 1 or 2 minutes to allow the medicine to come into contact with the infection.
  —To keep the medicine as germ-free as possible, do not touch the applicator tip to any surface (including the eye). After using sulfonamides eye ointment, wipe the tip of the ointment tube with a clean tissue and keep the tube tightly closed.

To help clear up your infection completely, *keep using this medicine for the full time of treatment,* even if your symptoms have disappeared. *Do not miss any doses.*

Dosing—The dose of ophthalmic sulfonamides will be different for different patients. *Follow your doctor's orders or the directions on the label.* The following information includes only the average doses of ophthalmic sulfonamides. *If your dose is different, do not change it* unless your doctor tells you to do so.

The number of doses you use each day, the time allowed between doses, and the length of time you use the medicine depend on the medical problem for which you are using ophthalmic sulfonamides.

For sulfacetamide
- For eye infections:
  —For *ophthalmic* dosage forms (ointment):
    - Adults and adolescents—Use four times a day and at bedtime.
    - Children—Use and dose must be determined by your doctor.

  —For *ophthalmic* dosage forms (solution):
    - Adults and adolescents—One drop every one to three hours during the day and less often during the night.
    - Children—Use and dose must be determined by your doctor.

For sulfisoxazole
- For eye infections:
  —For *ophthalmic* dosage forms (ointment):
    - Adults and children—Use one to three times a day and at bedtime.

  —For *ophthalmic* dosage forms (solution):
    - Adults and adolescents—One drop three or more times a day.
    - Children—
      —Infants up to 2 months of age: Use and dose must be determined by your doctor.
      —Infants and children 2 months of age and older: One drop three or more times a day.

Missed dose—If you miss a dose of this medicine, apply it as soon as possible. However, if it is almost time for your next dose, skip the missed dose and go back to your regular dosing schedule.

Storage—To store this medicine:
- Keep out of the reach of children.
- Store away from heat and direct light.
- Keep sulfacetamide eye drops in a cool place. Keep all dosage forms of these medicines from freezing.
- Do not keep outdated medicine or medicine no longer needed. Be sure that any discarded medicine is out of the reach of children.

Precautions While Using This Medicine

After application, eye ointments usually cause your vision to blur for a few minutes.

After application of this medicine to the eye, occasional stinging or burning may be expected.

If your symptoms do not improve within a few days, or if they become worse, check with your doctor.

Side Effects of This Medicine

Along with its needed effects, a medicine may cause some unwanted effects. Although not all of these side effects may occur, if they do occur they may need medical attention.

Check with your doctor as soon as possible if any of the following side effects occur:

More common

Itching, redness, swelling, or other sign of irritation not present before use of this medicine

Other side effects not listed above may also occur in some patients. If you notice any other effects, check with your doctor.

Revised: 07/01/93

SULFONAMIDES Systemic

Some commonly used brand names are:

In the U.S.—

Gantanol[3]
Gantrisin[4]
Thiosulfil Forte[2]
Urobak[3]

In Canada—

Apo-Sulfamethoxazole[3]
Apo-Sulfisoxazole[4]
Novo-Soxazole[4]
Sulfizole[4]

Note: For quick reference, the following sulfonamides are numbered to match the corresponding brand names.

This information applies to the following medicines:

1. Sulfadiazine (sul-fa-DYE-a-zeen)‡§
2. Sulfamethizole (sul-fa-METH-a-zole)†
3. Sulfamethoxazole (sul-fa-meth-OX-a-zole)§
4. Sulfisoxazole (sul-fi-SOX-a-zole)‡

†Not commercially available in Canada.
‡Generic name product may also be available in the U.S.
§Generic name product may also be available in Canada.

Description

Sulfonamides (sul-FON-a-mides) or sulfa medicines are used to treat infections. They will not work for colds, flu, or other virus infections.

Sulfonamides are available only with your doctor's prescription, in the following dosage forms:

Oral

Sulfadiazine
- Tablets (U.S. and Canada)

Sulfamethizole
- Tablets (U.S.)

Sulfamethoxazole
- Tablets (U.S. and Canada)

Sulfisoxazole
- Oral suspension (U.S.)
- Syrup (U.S.)
- Tablets (U.S. and Canada)

Before Using This Medicine

In deciding to use a medicine, the risks of taking the medicine must be weighed against the good it will do. This is a decision you and your doctor will make. For sulfonamides, the following should be considered:

Allergies—Tell your doctor if you have ever had any unusual or allergic reaction to sulfa medicines, furosemide (e.g., Lasix) or thiazide diuretics (water pills), oral antidiabetics (diabetes medicine you take by mouth), glaucoma medicine you take by mouth (for example, acetazolamide [e.g., Diamox], dichlorphenamide [e.g., Daranide], or methazolamide [e.g., Neptazane]). Also tell your health care professional if you are allergic to any other substances, such as foods, preservatives, or dyes.

Pregnancy—Studies have not been done in pregnant women. However, studies in mice, rats, and rabbits have shown that some sulfonamides cause birth defects, including cleft palate and bone problems. Sulfonamides are not recommended for use at the time of labor and delivery. These medicines may cause unwanted effects in the baby.

Breast-feeding—Sulfonamides pass into the breast milk. This medicine is not recommended for use during breast-feeding. It may cause liver problems, anemia, and other unwanted effects in nursing babies, especially those with glucose-6-phosphate dehydrogenase (G6PD) deficiency.

Children—Sulfonamides should not be given to infants under 2 months of age unless directed by the child's doctor, because they may cause unwanted effects.

Older adults—Elderly people are especially sensitive to the effects of sulfonamides. Severe skin problems and blood problems may be more likely to occur in the elderly. These problems may also be more likely to occur in patients who are taking diuretics (water pills) along with this medicine.

Other medicines—Although certain medicines should not be used together at all, in other cases two different medicines may be used together even if an interaction might occur. In these cases, your doctor may want to change the dose, or other precautions may be necessary. When you are taking sulfonamides, it is especially important that your health care professional knows if you are taking any of the following:

- Acetaminophen (e.g., Tylenol) (with long-term, high-dose use) or
- Amiodarone (e.g., Cordarone) or
- Anabolic steroids (nandrolone [e.g., Anabolin], oxandrolone [e.g., Anavar], oxymetholone [e.g., Anadrol], stanozolol [e.g., Winstrol]) or
- Androgens (male hormones) or
- Antithyroid agents (medicine for overactive thyroid) or
- Carbamazepine (e.g., Tegretol) or
- Carmustine (e.g., BiCNU) or
- Chloroquine (e.g., Aralen) or
- Dantrolene (e.g., Dantrium) or
- Daunorubicin (e.g., Cerubidine) or
- Disulfiram (e.g., Antabuse) or
- Divalproex (e.g., Depakote) or
- Estrogens (female hormones) or
- Etretinate (e.g., Tegison) or
- Gold salts (medicine for arthritis) or
- Hydroxychloroquine (e.g., Plaquenil) or
- Mercaptopurine (e.g., Purinethol) or
- Naltrexone (e.g., Trexan) (with long-term, high-dose use) or
- Oral contraceptives (birth control pills) containing estrogens or
- Other anti-infectives by mouth or by injection (medicine for infection) or
- Phenothiazines (acetophenazine [e.g., Tindal], chlorpromazine [e.g., Thorazine], fluphenazine [e.g., Prolixin], mesoridazine [e.g., Serentil], perphenazine [e.g., Trilafon], prochlorperazine [e.g., Compazine], promazine [e.g., Sparine], promethazine [e.g., Phenergan], thioridazine [e.g., Mellaril], trifluoperazine [e.g., Stelazine], triflupromazine [e.g., Vesprin], trimeprazine [e.g., Temaril]) or
- Plicamycin (e.g., Mithracin) or
- Valproic acid (e.g., Depakene)—Use of sulfonamides with these medicines may increase the chance of side effects affecting the liver
- Acetohydroxamic acid (e.g., Lithostat) or
- Dapsone or
- Furazolidone (e.g., Furoxone) or
- Nitrofurantoin (e.g., Furadantin) or

- Primaquine or
- Procainamide (e.g., Pronestyl) or
- Quinidine (e.g., Quinidex) or
- Quinine (e.g., Quinamm) or
- Sulfoxone (e.g., Diasone) or
- Vitamin K (e.g., AquaMEPHYTON, Synkayvite)—Use of sulfonamides with these medicines may increase the chance of side effects affecting the blood
- Anticoagulants (blood thinners) or
- Ethotoin (e.g., Peganone) or
- Mephenytoin (e.g., Mesantoin)—Use of sulfonamides with these medicines may increase the chance of side effects of these medicines
- Antidiabetics, oral (diabetes medicine you take by mouth)—Use of oral antidiabetics with sulfonamides may increase the chance of side effects affecting the blood and/or the side effects of oral antidiabetics
- Methenamine (e.g., Mandelamine)—Use of this medicine with sulfonamides may increase the chance of side effects of sulfonamides
- Methotrexate (e.g., Mexate) or
- Phenytoin (e.g., Dilantin)—Use of these medicines with sulfonamides may increase the chance of side effects affecting the liver and/or the side effects of these medicines
- Methyldopa (e.g., Aldomet)—Use of methyldopa with sulfonamides may increase the chance of side effects affecting the liver and/or the blood

Other medical problems—The presence of other medical problems may affect the use of sulfonamides. Make sure you tell your doctor if you have any other medical problems, especially:

- Anemia or other blood problems or
- Glucose-6-phosphate dehydrogenase (G6PD) deficiency—Patients with these problems may have an increase in side effects affecting the blood
- Kidney disease or
- Liver disease—Patients with kidney and/or liver disease may have an increased chance of side effects
- Porphyria—This medicine may bring on an attack of porphyria

Proper Use of This Medicine

Sulfonamides should not be given to infants less than 2 months of age unless directed by the patient's doctor because sulfonamides may cause serious unwanted effects.

Sulfonamides are best taken with a full glass (8 ounces) of water. Several additional glasses of water should be taken every day, unless otherwise directed by your doctor. Drinking extra water will help to prevent some unwanted effects of sulfonamides.

For patients taking the *oral liquid form* of this medicine:

- Use a specially marked measuring spoon or other device to measure each dose accurately. The average household teaspoon may not hold the right amount of liquid.

To help clear up your infection completely, *keep taking this medicine for the full time of treatment,* even if you begin to feel better after a few days. If you stop taking this medicine too soon, your symptoms may return.

This medicine works best when there is a constant amount in the blood or urine. *To help keep the amount constant, do not miss any doses. Also, it is best to take the doses at evenly spaced times day and night.* If you need help in planning the best times to take your medicine, check with your health care professional.

Dosing—The dose of these medicines will be different for different patients. *Follow your doctor's orders or the directions on the label.* The following information includes only the average doses of these medicines. *If your dose is different, do not change it* unless your doctor tells you to do so.

For sulfadiazine

- For *tablet* dosage form:
  - —For bacterial or protozoal infections:
    - Adults and teenagers—2 to 4 grams for the first dose, then 1 gram every four to six hours.
    - Children up to 2 months of age—Use is not recommended.
    - Children 2 months of age and older—Dose is based on body weight. The usual dose is 75 milligrams (mg) per kilogram (kg) (34 mg per pound) of body weight for the first dose, then 37.5 mg per kg (17 mg per pound) of body weight every six hours, or 25 mg per kg (11.4 mg per pound) of body weight every four hours.

For sulfamethizole

- For *tablet* dosage form:
  - —For bacterial infections:
    - Adults and teenagers—500 milligrams (mg) to 1 gram every six to eight hours.
    - Children up to 2 months of age—Use is not recommended.
    - Children 2 months of age and older—Dose is based on body weight. The usual dose is 7.5 to 11.25 mg per kilogram (kg) (3.4 to 5.1 mg per pound) of body weight every six hours.

For sulfamethoxazole

- For *tablet* dosage form:
  - —For bacterial or protozoal infections:
    - Adults and teenagers—2 to 4 grams for the first dose, then 1 to 2 grams every eight to twelve hours.
    - Children up to 2 months of age—Use and dose must be determined by your doctor.
    - Children 2 months of age and older—Dose is based on body weight. The usual dose is 50 to 60 milligrams (mg) per kilogram (kg) (22.7 to 27.3 mg per pound) of body weight for the first dose, then 25 to 30 mg per kg (11.4 to 13.6 mg per pound) of body weight every twelve hours.

For sulfisoxazole

- For *suspension, syrup, or tablet* dosage forms:
  - —For bacterial or protozoal infections:
    - Adults and teenagers—2 to 4 grams for the first dose, then 750 milligrams (mg) to 1.5 grams every four hours; or 1 to 2 grams every six hours.
    - Children up to 2 months of age—Use and dose must be determined by your doctor.

• Children 2 months of age and older—Dose is based on body weight. The usual dose is 75 mg per kilogram (kg) (34 mg per pound) of body weight for the first dose, then 25 mg per kg (11.4 mg per pound) of body weight every four hours, or 37.5 mg per kg (17 mg per pound) of body weight every six hours.

Missed dose—If you miss a dose of this medicine, take it as soon as possible. This will help to keep a constant amount of medicine in the blood or urine. However, if it is almost time for your next dose, skip the missed dose and go back to your regular dosing schedule. Do not double doses.

Storage—To store this medicine:

- Keep out of the reach of children.
- Store away from heat and direct light.
- Do not store the tablet form of this medicine in the bathroom, near the kitchen sink, or in other damp places. Heat or moisture may cause the medicine to break down.
- Keep the oral liquid forms of this medicine from freezing.
- Do not keep outdated medicine or medicine no longer needed. Be sure that any discarded medicine is out of the reach of children.

Precautions While Using This Medicine

It is very important that your doctor check your progress at regular visits. This medicine may cause blood problems, especially if it is taken for a long time.

If your symptoms do not improve within a few days, or if they become worse, check with your doctor.

Sulfonamides may cause blood problems. These problems may result in a greater chance of certain infections, slow healing, and bleeding of the gums. Therefore, you should be careful when using regular toothbrushes, dental floss, and toothpicks. Dental work should be delayed until your blood counts have returned to normal. Check with your medical doctor or dentist if you have any questions about proper oral hygiene (mouth care) during treatment.

Sulfonamides may cause your skin to be more sensitive to sunlight than it is normally. Exposure to sunlight, even for brief periods of time, may cause a skin rash, itching, redness or other discoloration of the skin, or a severe sunburn. When you begin taking this medicine:

- Stay out of direct sunlight, especially between the hours of 10:00 a.m. and 3:00 p.m., if possible.
- Wear protective clothing, including a hat. Also, wear sunglasses.
- Apply a sun block product that has a skin protection factor (SPF) of at least 15. Some patients may require a product with a higher SPF number, especially if they have a fair complexion. If you have any questions about this, check with your health care professional.
- Apply a sun block lipstick that has an SPF of at least 15 to protect your lips.
- Do not use a sunlamp or tanning bed or booth.

If you have a severe reaction from the sun, check with your doctor.

This medicine may also cause some people to become dizzy. *Make sure you know how you react to this medicine before you drive, use machines, or do anything else that could be dangerous if you are dizzy or are not alert.* If this reaction is especially bothersome, check with your doctor.

Side Effects of This Medicine

Along with its needed effects, a medicine may cause some unwanted effects. Although not all of these side effects may occur, if they do occur they may need medical attention.

Check with your doctor immediately if any of the following side effects occur:

More common

Itching; skin rash

Less common

Aching of joints and muscles; difficulty in swallowing; pale skin; redness, blistering, peeling, or loosening of skin; sore throat and fever; unusual bleeding or bruising; unusual tiredness or weakness; yellow eyes or skin

Rare

Abdominal or stomach cramps and pain (severe); abdominal tenderness; blood in urine; diarrhea (watery and severe), which may also be bloody; greatly increased or decreased frequency of urination or amount of urine; increased thirst; lower back pain; mood or mental changes; pain or burning while urinating; swelling of front part of neck

Note: Some of the above side effects (severe abdominal or stomach cramps and pain, and watery and severe diarrhea, which may also be bloody) may also occur up to several weeks after you stop taking any of these medicines.

Also, check with your doctor as soon as possible if the following side effect occurs:

More common

Increased sensitivity of skin to sunlight

Other side effects may occur that usually do not need medical attention. These side effects may go away during treatment as your body adjusts to the medicine. However, check with your doctor if any of the following side effects continue or are bothersome:

More common

Diarrhea; dizziness; headache; loss of appetite; nausea or vomiting; tiredness

Other side effects not listed above may also occur in some patients. If you notice any other effects, check with your doctor.

Revised: 08/25/95

SULFONAMIDES Vaginal

Some commonly used brand names are:

In the U.S.—

AVC[1]
Sulfa-Gyn[3]
Sulnac[3]
Sultrin[3]
Trysul[3]
V.V.S.[3]
Vagitrol[1]

In Canada—

AVC[2]
Sultrin[3]

Another commonly used name for triple sulfa is sulfathiazole, sulfacetamide, and sulfabenzamide.

Note: For quick reference, the following vaginal sulfonamides are numbered to match the corresponding brand names.

This information applies to the following medicines:

1. Sulfanilamide (sul-fa-NILL-a-mide)‡
2. Sulfanilamide, Aminacrine (am-in-AK-rin), and Allantoin (al-AN-toyn)*
3. Triple Sulfa (TRI-pel SUL-fa)‡

*Not commercially available in the U.S.
‡Generic name product may be available in the U.S.

Description

Sulfonamides (sul-FON-a-mides), or sulfa medicines, are used to treat bacterial infections. They work by killing bacteria or preventing their growth.

Vaginal sulfonamides are used to treat bacterial infections. These medicines may also be used for other problems as determined by your doctor.

Vaginal sulfonamides are available only with your doctor's prescription, in the following dosage forms:

Vaginal
- Sulfanilamide
  - Cream (U.S.)
  - Suppositories (U.S.)
- Sulfanilamide, Aminacrine, and Allantoin
  - Cream (Canada)
  - Suppositories (Canada)
- Triple Sulfa
  - Cream (U.S. and Canada)
  - Tablets (U.S.)

Before Using This Medicine

In deciding to use a medicine, the risks of using the medicine must be weighed against the good it will do. This is a decision you and your doctor will make. For vaginal sulfonamides, the following should be considered:

Allergies—Tell your doctor if you have ever had any unusual or allergic reaction to any of the sulfa medicines, furosemide (e.g., Lasix) or thiazide diuretics (water pills), oral antidiabetics (diabetes medicine you take by mouth), or glaucoma medicine you take by mouth (for example, acetazolamide [e.g., Diamox], dichlorphenamide [e.g., Daranide], or methazolamide [e.g., Neptazane]). Also tell your health care professional if you are allergic to any other substances, such as foods, preservatives, or dyes.

Pregnancy—Studies have not been done in humans. However, vaginal sulfonamides are absorbed through the vagina into the bloodstream and appear in the bloodstream of the fetus. Studies in rats and mice given high doses by mouth have shown that certain sulfonamides cause birth defects.

Breast-feeding—Vaginal sulfonamides are absorbed through the vagina into the bloodstream and pass into the breast milk. Use is not recommended in nursing mothers. Vaginal sulfonamides may cause liver problems in nursing babies. These medicines may also cause anemia in nursing babies with glucose-6-phosphate dehydrogenase (G6PD) deficiency.

Children—Studies on this medicine have been done only in adult patients and there is no specific information comparing the use of vaginal sulfonamides in children with use in other age groups.

Older adults—Many medicines have not been studied specifically in older people. Therefore, it may not be known whether they work exactly the same way they do in younger adults or if they cause different side effects or problems in older people. There is no specific information comparing the use of vaginal sulfonamides in the elderly with use in other age groups.

Other medicines—Although certain medicines should not be used together at all, in other cases two different medicines may be used together even if an interaction might occur. In these cases, your doctor may want to change the dose, or other precautions may be necessary. Tell your health care professional if you are taking or using any other prescription or nonprescription (over-the-counter [OTC]) medicine.

Other medical problems—The presence of other medical problems may affect the use of vaginal sulfonamides. Make sure you tell your doctor if you have any other medical problems, especially:

- Glucose-6-phosphate dehydrogenase (G6PD) deficiency—Anemia (a blood problem) can occur if sulfonamides are used
- Kidney disease
- Porphyria—Sulfonamides can cause porphyria attacks

Proper Use of This Medicine

Vaginal sulfonamides usually come with patient directions. Read them carefully before using this medicine.

This medicine is usually inserted into the vagina with an applicator. However, if you are pregnant, check with your doctor before using the applicator.

To help clear up your infection completely, *it is very important that you keep using this medicine for the full time of treatment*, even if your symptoms begin to clear up after a few days. If you stop using this medicine too soon, your symptoms may return. *Do not miss any doses.* Also, *do not stop using this medicine if your menstrual period starts during the time of treatment.*

Dosing—The dose of these medicines will be different for different patients. *Follow your doctor's orders or the directions on the label.* The following information includes only the average doses of these medicines. *If your dose is* *different, do not change it* unless your doctor tells you to do so.

For sulfanilamide

- For *vaginal cream* dosage form:
  - —For bacterial infections:
    - Adults and teenagers—One applicatorful (approximately 6 grams) inserted into the vagina one or two times a day for thirty days. Use when you wake up and/or just before you go to bed.
    - Children—Dose must be determined by your doctor.
- For *vaginal suppositories* dosage form:
  - —For bacterial infections:
    - Adults and teenagers—One suppository inserted into the vagina one or two times a day for thirty days. Use when you wake up and/or just before you go to bed.
    - Children—Dose must be determined by your doctor.

For sulfanilamide, aminacrine, and allantoin

- For *vaginal cream* dosage form:
  - —For bacterial infections:
    - Adults and teenagers—One applicatorful (approximately 6 grams) inserted into the vagina one or two times a day. Use when you wake up and/or just before you go to bed.
    - Children—Dose must be determined by your doctor.
- For *vaginal suppositories* dosage form:
  - —For bacterial infections:
    - Adults and teenagers—One suppository inserted into the vagina one or two times a day for thirty days. Use when you wake up and/or just before you go to bed.
    - Children—Dose must be determined by your doctor.

For triple sulfa

- For *vaginal cream* dosage form:
  - —For bacterial infections:
    - Adults and teenagers—At first, one applicatorful (approximately 4 to 5 grams) inserted into the vagina two times a day for four to six days. Then, your doctor may lower your dose to one-half to one-quarter applicatorful two times a day. Use when you wake up and just before you go to bed.
    - Children—Dose must be determined by your doctor.
- For *vaginal tablets* dosage form:
  - —For bacterial infections:
    - Adults and teenagers—One tablet inserted into the vagina two times a day for ten days. Use when you wake up and just before you go to bed.
    - Children—Dose must be determined by your doctor.

Missed dose—If you miss a dose of this medicine, insert it as soon as possible. However, if it is almost time for your next dose, skip the missed dose and go back to your regular dosing schedule.

Storage—To store this medicine:

- Keep out of the reach of children.
- Store away from heat and direct light.
- Do not store the vaginal tablet or vaginal suppository form of this medicine in the bathroom, near the kitchen sink, or in other damp places. Heat or moisture may cause the medicine to break down.
- Keep the vaginal cream and vaginal suppository forms of this medicine from freezing.
- Do not keep outdated medicine or medicine no longer needed. Be sure that any discarded medicine is out of the reach of children.

Precautions While Using This Medicine

If your symptoms do not improve within a few days, or if they become worse, check with your doctor.

Vaginal medicines usually will slowly work their way out of the vagina during treatment. Also, aminacrine-containing vaginal sulfonamides may stain underclothing. To keep the medicine from soiling or staining your clothing, a sanitary napkin may be worn. Minipads, clean paper tissues, or paper diapers may also be used. However, the use of tampons is not recommended since they may soak up too much of the medicine. In addition, tampons may be more likely to slip out of the vagina if you use them during treatment with this medicine.

To help clear up your infection completely and to help make sure it does not return, good health habits are also required.

- Wear cotton panties (or panties or pantyhose with cotton crotches) instead of synthetic (for example, nylon or rayon) underclothes.
- Wear only freshly washed underclothes.

If you have any questions about this, check with your health care professional.

Many vaginal infections are spread by sexual intercourse. The male sexual partner may carry the fungus or other organism in his reproductive tract. Therefore, it may be desirable that your partner wear a condom (prophylactic) during intercourse to keep the infection from returning. Also, it may be necessary for your partner to be treated at the same time you are being treated to avoid passing the infection back and forth. In addition, *do not stop using this medicine if you have intercourse during treatment.*

Some patients who use vaginal medicines may prefer to use a douche for cleansing purposes before inserting the next dose of medicine. Some doctors recommend a vinegar and water or other douche. However, others do not recommend douching at all. If you do use a douche, *do not overfill the vagina with douche solution.* To do so may force the solution up into the uterus (womb) and may cause inflammation or infection. Also, *do not douche if you are pregnant since this may harm the fetus.* If you have any questions about this or which douche products are best for you, check with your health care professional.

Side Effects of This Medicine

Studies in rats have shown that long-term use of sulfonamides may cause cancer of the thyroid gland. In addition, studies in rats have shown that sulfonamides may increase the chance of goiters (noncancerous tumors of the thyroid gland).

Along with its needed effects, a medicine may cause some unwanted effects. Although not all of these side effects may occur, if they do occur they may need medical attention.

Check with your doctor immediately if any of the following side effects occur:

Less common

Itching, burning, skin rash, redness, swelling, or other sign of irritation not present before use of this medicine

Other side effects may occur that usually do not need medical attention. These side effects may go away during treatment as your body adjusts to the medicine. However, check with your doctor if either of the following side effects continues or is bothersome:

Less common or rare

Rash or irritation of penis of sexual partner

Other side effects not listed above may also occur in some patients. If you notice any other effects, check with your doctor.

Revised: 07/22/92
Interim revision: 06/15/94; 07/31/95

SULFONAMIDES AND PHENAZOPYRIDINE Systemic

Some commonly used brand names are:

In the U.S.—

Azo Gantanol[1]
Azo Gantrisin[2]
Azo-Sulfamethoxazole[1]
Azo-Sulfisoxazole[2]
Azo-Truxazole[2]
Sul-Azo[2]

In Canada—

Azo Gantrisin[2]

Note: For quick reference, the following sulfonamides and phenazopyridine combinations are numbered to match the corresponding brand names.

This information applies to the following medicines:

1. Sulfamethoxazole (sul-fa-meth-OX-a-zole) and Phenazopyridine (fen-az-oh-PEER-i-deen)†‡
2. Sulfisoxazole (sul-fi-SOX-a-zole) and Phenazopyridine‡

†Not commercially available in Canada.
‡Generic name product may also be available in the U.S.

Description

Sulfonamides and phenazopyridine, combination products containing a sulfa medicine and a urinary pain reliever, are used to treat infections of the urinary tract and to help relieve the pain, burning, and irritation of these infections.

Sulfonamides and phenazopyridine combinations are available only with your doctor's prescription, in the following dosage forms:

Oral

Sulfamethoxazole and Phenazopyridine
- Tablets (U.S.)

Sulfisoxazole and Phenazopyridine
- Tablets (U.S. and Canada)

Before Using This Medicine

In deciding to use a medicine, the risks of taking the medicine must be weighed against the good it will do. This is a decision you and your doctor will make. For sulfonamides and phenazopyridine, the following should be considered:

Allergies—Tell your doctor if you have ever had any unusual or allergic reaction to any of the sulfa medicines, furosemide (e.g., Lasix) or thiazide diuretics (water pills), oral antidiabetics (diabetes medicine you take by mouth), glaucoma medicine you take by mouth (for example, acetazolamide [e.g., Diamox], dichlorphenamide [e.g., Daranide], or methazolamide [e.g., Neptazane]), or phenazopyridine (e.g., Pyridium). Also tell your health care professional if you are allergic to any other substances, such as foods, preservatives, or dyes.

Pregnancy—Studies have not been done in humans. Studies in mice, rats, and rabbits have shown that some sulfonamides cause birth defects, including cleft palate and bone problems. In addition, sulfa medicines may cause liver problems in newborn infants. Therefore, use is not recommended during pregnancy. Phenazopyridine has not been shown to cause birth defects in animal studies.

Breast-feeding—Sulfonamides pass into the breast milk. This medicine is not recommended for use during breast-feeding. It may cause liver problems, anemia, and other unwanted effects in nursing babies, especially those with glucose-6-phosphate dehydrogenase (G6PD) deficiency.

Children—This medicine has been tested in a limited number of children 12 years of age or older. In effective doses, the medicine has not been shown to cause different side effects or problems in children than it does in adults.

Older adults—Elderly people are especially sensitive to the effects of sulfonamides. Severe skin problems and blood problems may be more likely to occur in the elderly. These problems may also be more likely to occur in patients who are taking diuretics (water pills) along with this medicine.

Other medicines—Although certain medicines should not be used together at all, in other cases two different medicines may be used together even if an interaction might occur. In these cases, your doctor may want to change the dose, or other precautions may be necessary. When you are taking sulfonamides and phenazopyridine, it is especially important that your health care professional know if you are taking any of the following:

- Acetaminophen (e.g., Tylenol) (with long-term, high-dose use) or

- Amiodarone (e.g., Cordarone) or
- Anabolic steroids (nandrolone [e.g., Anabolin], oxandrolone [e.g., Anavar], oxymetholone [e.g., Anadrol], stanozolol [e.g., Winstrol]) or
- Androgens (male hormones) or
- Antithyroid agents (medicine for overactive thyroid) or
- Carbamazepine (e.g., Tegretol) or
- Carmustine (e.g., BiCNU) or
- Chloroquine (e.g., Aralen) or
- Dantrolene (e.g., Dantrium) or
- Daunorubicin (e.g., Cerubidine) or
- Disulfiram (e.g., Antabuse) or
- Divalproex (e.g., Depakote) or
- Estrogens (female hormones) or
- Etretinate (e.g., Tegison) or
- Gold salts (medicine for arthritis) or
- Hydroxychloroquine (e.g., Plaquenil) or
- Mercaptopurine (e.g., Purinethol) or
- Naltrexone (e.g., Trexan) (with long-term, high-dose use) or
- Oral contraceptives (birth control pills) containing estrogen or
- Other anti-infectives by mouth or by injection (medicine for infection) or
- Phenothiazines (acetophenazine [e.g., Tindal], chlorpromazine [e.g., Thorazine], fluphenazine [e.g., Prolixin], mesoridazine [e.g., Serentil], perphenazine [e.g., Trilafon], prochlorperazine [e.g., Compazine], promazine [e.g., Sparine], promethazine [e.g., Phenergan], thioridazine [e.g., Mellaril], trifluoperazine [e.g., Stelazine], triflupromazine [e.g., Vesprin], trimeprazine [e.g., Temaril]) or
- Plicamycin (e.g., Mithracin) or
- Valproic acid (e.g., Depakene)—Use of sulfonamides and phenazopyridine combination with these medicines may increase the chance of side effects affecting the liver

- Acetohydroxamic acid (e.g., Lithostat) or
- Dapsone or
- Furazolidone (e.g., Furoxone) or
- Nitrofurantoin (e.g., Furadantin) or
- Primaquine or
- Procainamide (e.g., Pronestyl) or
- Quinidine (e.g., Quinidex) or
- Quinine (e.g., Quinamm) or
- Sulfoxone (e.g., Diasone) or
- Vitamin K (e.g., AquaMEPHYTON, Synkayvite)—Use of sulfonamides and phenazopyridine combination with these medicines may increase the chance of side effects affecting the blood
- Anticoagulants (blood thinners) or
- Ethotoin (e.g., Peganone) or
- Heparin or
- Mephenytoin (e.g., Mesantoin)—Use of sulfonamides and phenazopyridine combination with these medicines may increase the chance of side effects of these medicines

- Antidiabetics, oral (diabetes medicine you take by mouth)—Use of oral antidiabetics with sulfonamides and phenazopyridine combination may increase the chance of side effects affecting the blood and/or the side effects of oral antidiabetics

- Methenamine (e.g., Mandelamine) or
- Methenamine-containing medicines (e.g., Urised)—Use of these medicines with sulfonamides and phenazopyridine combination may increase the chance of side effects of the sulfonamides

- Methotrexate (e.g., Mexate)—Use of methotrexate with sulfonamides and phenazopyridine combination may increase the chance of side effects affecting the liver and/or the side effects of methotrexate

- Methyldopa (e.g., Aldomet)—Use of methyldopa with sulfonamides and phenazopyridine combination may increase the chance of side effects affecting the liver and/or the blood

- Phenytoin (e.g., Dilantin)—Use of phenytoin with sulfonamides and phenazopyridine combination may increase the chance of side effects affecting the liver and/or the side effects of phenytoin

Other medical problems—The presence of other medical problems may affect the use of sulfonamides and phenazopyridine. Make sure you tell your doctor if you have any other medical problems, especially:

- Anemia or other blood problems or
- Glucose-6-phosphate dehydrogenase deficiency (lack of G6PD enzyme)—Patients with these problems may have an increase in side effects affecting the blood

- Hepatitis or other liver disease or
- Kidney disease—Patients with kidney disease or liver disease may have an increased chance of side effects

- Porphyria—Use of sulfonamides may bring on an attack of porphyria

Proper Use of This Medicine

Sulfonamides and phenazopyridine combinations are best taken with a full glass (8 ounces) of water. Several additional glasses of water should be taken every day, unless otherwise directed by your doctor. Drinking extra water will help to prevent some unwanted effects (e.g., kidney stones) of the sulfonamide. This medicine may be taken with meals or following meals if it upsets your stomach.

To help clear up your infection completely, *keep taking this medicine for the full time of treatment,* even if you begin to feel better after a few days. If you stop taking this medicine too soon, your symptoms may return.

This medicine works best when there is a constant amount in the urine. *To help keep the amount constant, do not miss any doses. Also, it is best to take the doses at evenly spaced times, day and night.* For example, if you are to take 4 doses a day, the doses should be spaced about 6 hours apart. If this interferes with your sleep or other daily activities, or if you need help in planning the best times to take your medicine, check with your health care professional.

Dosing—The dose of sulfonamides and phenazopyridine combination may be different for different patients. *Follow your doctor's orders or the directions on the label.* The following information includes only the average doses of sulfonamides and phenazopyridine combination. Your dose may be different if you have kidney disease. *If your dose is different, do not change it* unless your doctor tells you to do so.

- For *sulfamethoxazole and phenazopyridine combination*:

  —Adults and children 12 years of age and older: 2 grams of sulfamethoxazole and 400 mg of phenazopyridine for the first dose, then 1 gram of sulfamethoxazole and 200 mg of phenazopyridine every twelve hours for up to two days.

—Children up to 12 years of age: This medication is not recommended.

- For *sulfisoxazole and phenazopyridine combination*:

  —Adults and children 12 years of age and older: 2 to 3 grams of sulfisoxazole and 200 to 300 mg of phenazopyridine for the first dose, then 1 gram of sulfisoxazole and 100 mg of phenazopyridine every twelve hours for up to two days.

  —Children up to 12 years of age: This medication is not recommended.

Missed dose—If you miss a dose of this medicine, take it as soon as possible. This will help to keep a constant amount of medicine in the urine. However, if it is almost time for your next dose, skip the missed dose and go back to your regular dosing schedule. Do not double doses.

Storage—To store this medicine:

- Keep out of the reach of children.
- Store away from heat and direct light.
- Do not store in the bathroom, near the kitchen sink, or in other damp places. Heat or moisture may cause the medicine to break down.
- Do not keep outdated medicine or medicine no longer needed. Be sure that any discarded medicine is out of the reach of children.

Precautions While Using This Medicine

If your symptoms do not improve within a few days, or if they become worse, check with your doctor.

Sulfonamides may cause blood problems. These problems may result in a greater chance of certain infections, slow healing, and bleeding of the gums. Therefore, you should be careful when using regular toothbrushes, dental floss, and toothpicks. Dental work should be delayed until your blood counts have returned to normal. Check with your medical doctor or dentist if you have any questions about proper oral hygiene (mouth care) during treatment.

Sulfonamides may cause your skin to be more sensitive to sunlight than it is normally. Exposure to sunlight, even for brief periods of time, may cause a skin rash, itching, redness or other discoloration of the skin, or a severe sunburn. When you begin taking this medicine:

- Stay out of direct sunlight, especially between the hours of 10:00 a.m. and 3:00 p.m., if possible.
- Wear protective clothing, including a hat. Also, wear sunglasses.
- Apply a sun block product that has a skin protection factor (SPF) of at least 15. Some patients may require a product with a higher SPF number, especially if they have a fair complexion. If you have any questions about this, check with your health care professional.
- Apply a sun block lipstick that has an SPF of at least 15 to protect your lips.
- Do not use a sunlamp or tanning bed or booth.

If you have a severe reaction, check with your doctor.

This medicine may also cause some people to become dizzy. *Make sure you know how you react to this medicine before you drive, use machines, or do anything else that could be dangerous if you are dizzy or are not alert.* If this reaction is especially bothersome, check with your doctor.

This medicine causes the urine to turn reddish orange. This is to be expected while you are using this medicine and is not harmful. Also, the medicine may stain clothing. If you have any questions about removing the stain, check with your health care professional.

For diabetic patients:

- *This medicine may cause false test results with some urine sugar tests and urine ketone tests.* Check with your doctor before changing your diet or the dosage of your diabetes medicine.

Side Effects of This Medicine

Along with its needed effects, a medicine may cause some unwanted effects. Although not all of these side effects may occur, if they do occur they may need medical attention.

Check with your doctor immediately if any of the following side effects occur:

More common

Itching; skin rash

Less common

Aching of joints and muscles; blue or blue-purple discoloration of skin; difficulty in swallowing; pale skin; redness, blistering, peeling, or loosening of skin; shortness of breath; sore throat and fever; unusual bleeding or bruising; unusual tiredness or weakness; yellow eyes or skin

Rare

Blood in urine; greatly increased or decreased frequency of urination or amount of urine; increased thirst; lower back pain; pain or burning while urinating; swelling of front part of neck

In addition to the side effects listed above, check with your doctor as soon as possible if the following side effect occurs:

More common

Increased sensitivity of skin to sunlight

Other side effects may occur that usually do not need medical attention. These side effects may go away during treatment as your body adjusts to the medicine. However, check with your doctor if any of the following side effects continue or are bothersome:

More common

Diarrhea; dizziness; headache; loss of appetite; nausea or vomiting; tiredness

Less common

Indigestion; stomach cramps or pain

This medicine causes the urine to become reddish orange. This side effect does not require medical attention.

Other side effects not listed above may also occur in some patients. If you notice any other effects, check with your doctor.

Revised: 02/01/93

SULFONAMIDES AND TRIMETHOPRIM Systemic

Some commonly used brand names are:

In the U.S.—

Bactrim[2]	Septra DS[2]
Bactrim DS[2]	Septra I.V.[2]
Bactrim I.V.[2]	Septra Pediatric[2]
Bactrim Pediatric[2]	Sulfatrim[2]
Cofatrim Forte[2]	Sulfatrim-DS[2]
Cotrim[2]	Sulfatrim Pediatric[2]
Cotrim DS[2]	Sulfatrim S/S[2]
Cotrim Pediatric[2]	Sulfatrim Suspension[2]
Septra[2]	

In Canada—

Apo-Sulfatrim[2]	Novo-Trimel D.S.[2]
Apo-Sulfatrim DS[2]	Nu-Cotrimox[2]
Bactrim[2]	Nu-Cotrimox DS[2]
Bactrim DS[2]	Roubac[2]
Coptin[1]	Septra[2]
Coptin 1[1]	Septra DS[2]
Novo-Trimel[2]	

Other commonly used names are:

Cotrimazine[1]	SMZ-TMP[2]
Cotrimoxazole[2]	

Note: For quick reference, the following sulfonamide and trimethoprim combinations are numbered to match the corresponding brand names.

This information applies to the following medicines:

1. Sulfadiazine (sul-fa-DYE-a-zeen) and Trimethoprim (trye-METH-oh-prim)*
2. Sulfamethoxazole (sul-fa-meth-OX-a-zole) and Trimethoprim‡

*Not commercially available in the U.S.
‡Generic name product may also be available in the U.S.

Description

Sulfonamide (sul-FON-ah-mide) and trimethoprim combinations are used to prevent and treat infections. Sulfadiazine and trimethoprim combination is used to treat urinary tract infections. Sulfamethoxazole and trimethoprim combination is used to treat infections, such as bronchitis, middle ear infection, urinary tract infection, and traveler's diarrhea. It is also used for the prevention and treatment of *Pneumocystis carinii* pneumonia (PCP). These medicines will not work for colds, flu, or other virus infections. They may also be used for other conditions as determined by your doctor.

Sulfonamide and trimethoprim combinations are available only with your doctor's prescription, in the following dosage forms:

Oral

Sulfadiazine and Trimethoprim
- Oral suspension (Canada)
- Tablets (Canada)

Sulfamethoxazole and Trimethoprim
- Oral suspension (U.S. and Canada)
- Tablets (U.S. and Canada)

Parenteral

Sulfamethoxazole and Trimethoprim
- Injection (U.S. and Canada)

Before Using This Medicine

In deciding to use a medicine, the risks of taking the medicine must be weighed against the good it will do. This is a decision you and your doctor will make. For sulfonamide and trimethoprim combinations, the following should be considered:

Allergies—Tell your doctor if you have ever had any unusual or allergic reaction to sulfa medicines, furosemide (e.g., Lasix) or thiazide diuretics (water pills), oral antidiabetics (diabetes medicine you take by mouth), glaucoma medicine you take by mouth (for example, acetazolamide [e.g., Diamox], dichlorphenamide [e.g., Daranide], methazolamide [e.g., Neptazane]), or trimethoprim (e.g., Trimpex). Also tell your health care professional if you are allergic to any other substances, such as foods, preservatives (e.g., sulfites), or dyes.

Pregnancy—Sulfamethoxazole and trimethoprim combination has not been reported to cause birth defects or other problems in humans. However, studies in mice, rats, and rabbits have shown that some sulfonamides cause birth defects, including cleft palate and bone problems. Studies in rabbits have also shown that trimethoprim causes birth defects, as well as a decrease in the number of successful pregnancies. Sulfonamides are not recommended for use at the time of labor and delivery because these medicines may cause unwanted effects in the baby.

Breast-feeding—Sulfonamides and trimethoprim pass into the breast milk. These medicines are not recommended for use during breast-feeding. They may cause liver problems, anemia, and other unwanted effects in nursing babies, especially those with glucose-6-phosphate dehydrogenase (G6PD) deficiency.

Children—Sulfadiazine and trimethoprim combination should not be given to infants less than 3 months of age. Sulfamethoxazole and trimethoprim combination should not be given to infants less than 2 months of age unless directed by the child's doctor. These combinations may cause unwanted effects. In special situations, sulfamethoxazole and trimethoprim combination may be given to infants less than 2 months of age.

Older adults—Elderly people are especially sensitive to the effects of sulfonamide and trimethoprim combinations. Severe skin problems and blood problems may be more likely to occur in the elderly. These problems may also be more likely to occur in patients who are taking diuretics (water pills) along with this medicine.

Other medicines—Although certain medicines should not be used together at all, in other cases two different medicines may be used together even if an interaction might occur. In these cases, your doctor may want to change the dose, or other precautions may be necessary. When you are taking sulfonamide and trimethoprim combinations, it is especially important that your health care professional know if you are taking any of the following:

- Acetaminophen (e.g., Tylenol) (with long-term, high-dose use) or
- Amiodarone (e.g., Cordarone) or
- Anabolic steroids (nandrolone [e.g., Anabolin], oxandrolone [e.g., Anavar], oxymetholone [e.g., Anadrol], stanozolol [e.g., Winstrol]) or
- Androgens (male hormones) or

- Antithyroid agents (medicine for overactive thyroid) or
- Carbamazepine (e.g., Tegretol) or
- Carmustine (e.g., BiCNU) or
- Chloroquine (e.g., Aralen) or
- Dantrolene (e.g., Dantrium) or
- Daunorubicin (e.g., Cerubidine) or
- Disulfiram (e.g., Antabuse) or
- Divalproex (e.g., Depakote) or
- Estrogens (female hormones) or
- Etretinate (e.g., Tegison) or
- Gold salts (medicine for arthritis) or
- Mercaptopurine (e.g., Purinethol) or
- Naltrexone (e.g., Trexan) (with long-term, high-dose use) or
- Oral contraceptives (birth control pills) containing estrogens or
- Other anti-infectives by mouth or by injection (medicine for infection) or
- Phenothiazines (acetophenazine [e.g., Tindal], chlorpromazine [e.g., Thorazine], fluphenazine [e.g., Prolixin], mesoridazine [e.g., Serentil], perphenazine [e.g., Trilafon], prochlorperazine [e.g., Compazine], promazine [e.g., Sparine], promethazine [e.g., Phenergan], thioridazine [e.g., Mellaril], trifluoperazine [e.g., Stelazine], triflupromazine [e.g., Vesprin], trimeprazine [e.g., Temaril]) or
- Plicamycin (e.g., Mithracin) or
- Valproic acid (e.g., Depakene)—Use of sulfonamide and trimethoprim combinations with these medicines may increase the chance of side effects affecting the liver

- Acetohydroxamic acid (e.g., Lithostat) or
- Furazolidone (e.g., Furoxone) or
- Nitrofurantoin (e.g., Furadantin) or
- Primaquine or
- Procainamide (e.g., Pronestyl) or
- Quinidine (e.g., Quinidex) or
- Quinine (e.g., Quinamm) or
- Sulfoxone (e.g., Diasone)—Use of sulfonamide and trimethoprim combinations with these medicines may increase the chance of side effects affecting the blood

- Anticoagulants (blood thinners) or
- Ethotoin (e.g., Peganone) or
- Mephenytoin (e.g., Mesantoin) or
- Methotrexate (e.g., Mexate) or
- Phenytoin (e.g., Dilantin)—Use of sulfonamide and trimethoprim combinations with these medicines may increase the chance of side effects of these medicines

- Antidiabetics, oral (diabetes medicine you take by mouth)—Use of oral antidiabetics with sulfonamide and trimethoprim combinations may increase the chance of side effects affecting the blood and/or the side effects of the oral antidiabetics

- Methenamine (e.g., Mandelamine)—Use of methenamine with sulfonamide and trimethoprim combinations may increase the chance of side effects of the sulfonamide

- Methyldopa (e.g., Aldomet)—Use of methyldopa with sulfonamide and trimethoprim combinations may increase the chance of side effects affecting the liver and/or the blood

Other medical problems—The presence of other medical problems may affect the use of sulfonamide and trimethoprim combinations. Make sure you tell your doctor if you have any other medical problems, especially:

- Anemia or other blood problems or
- Glucose-6-phosphate dehydrogenase (G6PD) deficiency—Patients with these problems may have an increase in side effects affecting the blood

- Kidney disease or
- Liver disease—Patients with kidney and/or liver disease may have an increased chance of side effects

- Porphyria—This medicine may bring on an attack of porphyria

Proper Use of This Medicine

Sulfadiazine and trimethoprim combination should not be given to infants less than 3 months of age, and sulfamethoxazole and trimethoprim combination should not be given to infants less than 2 months of age unless directed by the child's doctor. These medicines may cause unwanted effects in the baby. In special situations, sulfamethoxazole and trimethoprim combination may be given to infants less than 2 months of age.

Sulfonamide and trimethoprim combinations are best taken with a full glass (8 ounces) of water. Several additional glasses of water should be taken every day, unless otherwise directed by your doctor. Drinking extra water will help to prevent some unwanted effects of sulfonamides.

For patients taking the *oral liquid form* of this medicine:

- Use a specially marked measuring spoon or other device to measure each dose accurately. The average household teaspoon may not hold the right amount of liquid.

To help clear up your infection completely, *keep taking this medicine for the full time of treatment,* even if you begin to feel better after a few days. If you stop taking this medicine too soon, your symptoms may return.

This medicine works best when there is a constant amount in the blood or urine. *To help keep the amount constant, do not miss any doses. Also, it is best to take the doses at evenly spaced times day and night.* If you need help in planning the best times to take your medicine, check with your health care professional.

Dosing—The dose of these medicines will be different for different patients. *Follow your doctor's orders or the directions on the label.* The following information includes only the average doses of these medicines. *If your dose is different, do not change it* unless your doctor tells you to do so.

The number of tablets or teaspoonfuls of suspension that you take depends on the strength of the medicine. Also, *the number of doses you take each day, the time allowed between doses, and the length of time you take the medicine depend on the medical problem for which you are taking sulfonamide and trimethoprim combinations.*

For sulfadiazine and trimethoprim combination

- For *oral* dosage forms (suspension, tablets):
  —For bacterial infections:
  - Adults and teenagers—820 milligrams (mg) of sulfadiazine and 180 mg of trimethoprim once a day.
  - Infants less than 3 months of age—Use is not recommended.

• Infants 3 months of age and older and children up to 12 years of age—Dose is based on body weight. The usual dose is 7 mg of sulfadiazine and 1.5 mg of trimethoprim per kilogram (kg) (3.2 mg of sulfadiazine and 0.7 mg of trimethoprim per pound) of body weight every twelve hours.

For sulfamethoxazole and trimethoprim combination

• For *oral* dosage forms (suspension, tablets):

—For bacterial infections:

• Adults and children 40 kilograms (kg) of body weight (88 pounds) and over—800 milligrams (mg) of sulfamethoxazole and 160 mg of trimethoprim every twelve hours.

• Infants less than 2 months of age—Use is not recommended.

• Infants 2 months of age and older and children up to 40 kg of weight (88 pounds)—Dose is based on body weight. The usual dose is 20 to 30 mg of sulfamethoxazole and 4 to 6 mg of trimethoprim per kg (9.1 to 13.6 mg of sulfamethoxazole and 1.8 to 2.7 mg of trimethoprim per pound) of body weight every twelve hours.

—For the treatment of *Pneumocystis carinii* pneumonia (PCP):

• Adults and children older than 2 months—Dose is based on body weight. The usual dose is 18.75 to 25 mg of sulfamethoxazole and 3.75 to 5 mg of trimethoprim per kg (8.5 to 11.4 mg of sulfamethoxazole and 1.7 to 2.3 mg of trimethoprim per pound) of body weight every six hours.

—For the prevention of *Pneumocystis carinii* pneumonia (PCP):

• Adults and teenagers—800 mg of sulfamethoxazole and 160 mg of trimethoprim once a day.

• Infants and children 4 weeks of age and older—Dose is based on body size and must be determined by your doctor. There are several dosing regimens available that your doctor may choose from. One dosing regimen is 375 mg of sulfamethoxazole and 75 mg of trimethoprim per square meter of body surface two times a day, three times a week on consecutive days (e.g., Monday, Tuesday, Wednesday).

• For *injection* dosage form:

—For bacterial infections:

• Adults and children older than 2 months—The usual total daily dose is 40 to 50 mg of sulfamethoxazole and 8 to 10 mg of trimethoprim per kg (18.2 to 22.7 mg of sulfamethoxazole and 3.6 to 4.5 mg of trimethoprim per pound) of body weight. This total daily dose may be divided up and injected into a vein every six, eight, or twelve hours.

• Infants less than 2 months of age—Use is not recommended.

—For the treatment of *Pneumocystis carinii* pneumonia (PCP):

• Adults and children older than 2 months—The usual dose is 18.75 to 25 mg of sulfamethoxazole and 3.75 to 5 mg of trimethoprim per kg (8.5 to 11.4 mg of sulfamethoxazole and 1.7 to 2.3 mg of trimethoprim per pound) of body weight. This is injected into a vein every six hours.

• Infants less than 2 months of age—Use is not recommended.

Missed dose—If you miss a dose of this medicine, take it as soon as possible. This will help to keep a constant amount of medicine in the blood or urine. However, if it is almost time for your next dose, skip the missed dose and go back to your regular dosing schedule. Do not double doses.

Storage—To store this medicine:

- Keep out of the reach of children.
- Store away from heat and direct light.
- Do not store the tablet form of this medicine in the bathroom, near the kitchen sink, or in other damp places. Heat or moisture may cause the medicine to break down.
- Keep the oral liquid form of this medicine from freezing.
- Do not keep outdated medicine or medicine no longer needed. Be sure that any discarded medicine is out of the reach of children.

Precautions While Using This Medicine

It is very important that your doctor check your progress at regular visits. This medicine may cause blood problems, especially if it is taken for a long time.

If your symptoms do not improve within a few days, or if they become worse, check with your doctor.

Sulfonamide and trimethoprim combinations may cause blood problems. These problems may result in a greater chance of certain infections, slow healing, and bleeding of the gums. Therefore, you should be careful when using regular toothbrushes, dental floss, and toothpicks. Dental work should be delayed until your blood counts have returned to normal. Check with your medical doctor or dentist if you have any questions about proper oral hygiene (mouth care) during treatment.

Sulfonamide and trimethoprim combinations may cause your skin to be more sensitive to sunlight than it is normally. Exposure to sunlight, even for brief periods of time, may cause a skin rash, itching, redness or other discoloration of the skin, or a severe sunburn. When you begin taking this medicine:

- Stay out of direct sunlight, especially between the hours of 10:00 a.m. and 3:00 p.m., if possible.
- Wear protective clothing, including a hat. Also, wear sunglasses.
- Apply a sun block product that has a skin protection factor (SPF) of at least 15. Some patients may require a product with a higher SPF number, especially if they have a fair complexion. If you have any ques-

tions about this, check with your health care professional.
- Apply a sun block lipstick that has an SPF of at least 15 to protect your lips.
- Do not use a sunlamp or tanning bed or booth.

If you have a severe reaction from the sun, check with your doctor.

This medicine may also cause some people to become dizzy. *Make sure you know how you react to this medicine before you drive, use machines, or do anything else that could be dangerous if you are dizzy or are not alert.* If this reaction is especially bothersome, check with your doctor.

Side Effects of This Medicine

Along with its needed effects, a medicine may cause some unwanted effects. Although not all of these side effects may occur, if they do occur they may need medical attention.

Check with your doctor immediately if any of the following side effects occur:

More common
Itching; skin rash

Less common
Aching of joints and muscles; difficulty in swallowing; pale skin; redness, blistering, peeling, or loosening of skin; sore throat and fever; unusual bleeding or bruising; unusual tiredness or weakness; yellow eyes or skin

Rare
Abdominal or stomach cramps and pain (severe); abdominal or stomach tenderness; anxiety; blood in urine; bluish fingernails, lips, or skin; confusion; diarrhea (watery and severe), which may also be bloody; difficult breathing; drowsiness; fever; general feeling of illness; greatly increased or decreased frequency of urination or amount of urine; hallucinations; headache, severe; increased thirst; lower back pain; mental depression; nausea; nervousness; pain at site of injection; pain or burning while urinating; stiff neck and/or back; swelling of front part of neck

Note: Some of the above side effects (severe abdominal or stomach cramps and pain, and watery and severe diarrhea, which may also be bloody) may also occur up to several weeks after you stop using any of these medicines.

Also, check with your doctor as soon as possible if the following side effect occurs:

More common
Increased sensitivity of skin to sunlight

Other side effects may occur that usually do not need medical attention. These side effects may go away during treatment as your body adjusts to the medicine. However, check with your doctor if any of the following side effects continue or are bothersome:

More common
Diarrhea; dizziness; headache; loss of appetite; nausea or vomiting; tiredness

Other side effects not listed above may also occur in some patients. If you notice any other effects, check with your doctor.

Additional Information

Once a medicine has been approved for marketing for a certain use, experience may show that it is also useful for other medical problems. Although these uses are not included in product labeling, sulfamethoxazole and trimethoprim combination is used in certain patients for the following medical conditions:

- Bile infections
- Bone and joint infections
- Sexually transmitted diseases, such as gonorrhea
- Sinus infections
- Toxoplasmosis (prevention of)
- Urinary tract infections (prevention of)
- Whipple's disease

Other than the above information, there is no additional information relating to proper use, precautions, or side effects for these uses.

Revised: 03/01/96

SULFUR Topical

Some commonly used brand names are:

In the U.S.—

Cuticura Ointment	Fostril Lotion
Finac	Lotio Alsulfa
Fostex Regular Strength Medicated Cover-Up	Sulpho-Lac

Generic name product may also be available.

In Canada—

Fostex CM	Fostril Cream

Generic name product may also be available.

Description

Sulfur (SUL-fur) is used to treat many kinds of skin disorders. Sulfur cream, lotion, ointment, and bar soap are used to treat acne. Sulfur ointment is used to treat seborrheic dermatitis and scabies. Sulfur may also be used for other conditions as determined by your doctor.

Some of these preparations are available only with your doctor's prescription. Others are available without a prescription; however, your doctor may have special instructions on the proper use of sulfur for your medical condition.

Sulfur is available in the following dosage forms:

Topical
- Cream (U.S. and Canada)
- Lotion (U.S.)
- Ointment (U.S.)
- Bar soap (U.S. and Canada)

Before Using This Medicine

If you are using this medicine without a prescription, carefully read and follow any precautions on the label. For topical sulfur preparations, the following should be considered:

Allergies—Tell your doctor if you have ever had any unusual or allergic reaction to sulfur. Also tell your health care professional if you are allergic to any other substances, such as preservatives or dyes.

Pregnancy—Topical sulfur has not been shown to cause birth defects or other problems in humans.

Breast-feeding—Topical sulfur has not been reported to cause problems in nursing babies.

Children—Although there is no specific information comparing use of this medicine in children with use in other age groups, this medicine is not expected to cause different side effects or problems in children than it does in adults.

Older adults—Many medicines have not been studied specifically in older people. Therefore, it may not be known whether they work exactly the same way they do in younger adults or if they cause different side effects or problems in older people. Although there is no specific information comparing use of sulfur in the elderly with use in other age groups, this medicine is not expected to cause different side effects or problems in older people than it does in younger adults.

Other medicines—Although certain medicines should not be used together at all, in other cases two different medicines may be used together even if an interaction might occur. In these cases, your doctor may want to change the dose, or other precautions may be necessary. Tell your health care professional if you are using any other topical prescription or nonprescription (over-the-counter [OTC]) medicine that is to be applied to the same area of the skin.

Proper Use of This Medicine

Use this medicine only as directed. Do not use it more often and do not use it for a longer period of time than recommended on the label, unless otherwise directed by your doctor.

Keep this medicine away from the eyes. If you should accidentally get some in your eyes, flush them thoroughly with water.

To use the *cream or lotion form* of this medicine:

- Before applying the medicine, wash the affected areas with soap and water and dry thoroughly. Then apply enough medicine to cover the affected areas and rub in gently.

To use the *ointment form* of this medicine for *seborrheic dermatitis:*

- Before applying the medicine, wash the affected areas with soap and water and dry thoroughly. Then apply enough medicine to cover the affected areas and rub in gently.

To use the *ointment form* of this medicine for *scabies:*

- Before applying the medicine, wash your entire body with soap and water and dry thoroughly.
- At bedtime, apply enough medicine to cover your entire body from the neck down and rub in gently. Leave the medicine on your body for 24 hours.
- Before applying the medicine again, you may wash your entire body.
- 24 hours after the last treatment with this medicine, it is important that you thoroughly wash your entire body again.

To use the *soap form* of this medicine:

- Work up a rich lather with the soap, using warm water. Wash the affected areas and rinse thoroughly. Apply again, and rub in gently for a few minutes. Remove excess lather with a towel or tissue without rinsing.

Dosing—The dose of topical sulfur will be different for different patients. *Follow your doctor's orders or the directions on the label.* The following information includes only the average doses of topical sulfur. *If your dose is different, do not change it* unless your doctor tells you to do so.

- For acne:
  - —For *cream and bar soap* dosage forms:
    - Adults and children—Use on the skin as needed.
  - —For *lotion* dosage form:
    - Adults and children—Use two or three times a day.
  - —For *ointment* dosage form:
    - Adults and children—Use the 0.5% ointment on the skin as needed.
- For seborrheic dermatitis:
  - —For *ointment* dosage form:
    - Adults and children—Use the 5 to 10% ointment one or two times a day.
- For scabies:
  - —For *ointment* dosage form:
    - Adults and children—Use the 6% ointment each night for three nights.

Missed dose—If you miss a dose of this medicine, use it as soon as possible. However, if it is almost time for your next dose, skip the missed dose and go back to your regular dosing schedule.

Storage—To store this medicine:

- Keep out of the reach of children.
- Store away from heat and direct light.
- Keep the cream, lotion, and ointment forms of this medicine from freezing.
- Do not keep outdated medicine or medicine no longer needed. Be sure that any discarded medicine is out of the reach of children.

Precautions While Using This Medicine

When using sulfur, do not use any of the following preparations on the same affected area as this medicine, unless otherwise directed by your doctor:

Abrasive soaps or cleansers

Alcohol-containing preparations
Any other topical acne preparation or preparation containing a peeling agent (for example, benzoyl peroxide, resorcinol, salicylic acid, or tretinoin [vitamin A acid])
Cosmetics or soaps that dry the skin
Medicated cosmetics
Other topical medicine for the skin

To use any of the above preparations on the same affected area as sulfur may cause severe irritation of the skin.

Do not use any topical mercury-containing preparation, such as ammoniated mercury ointment, on the same area as this medicine. To do so may cause a foul odor, may be irritating to the skin, and may stain the skin black. If you have any questions about this, check with your health care professional.

Side Effects of This Medicine

Along with its needed effects, a medicine may cause some unwanted effects. Although not all of these side effects may occur, if they do occur they may need medical attention.

Check with your doctor as soon as possible if the following side effect occurs:

Skin irritation not present before use of this medicine

Other side effects may occur that usually do not need medical attention. However, check with your health care professional if the following side effect continues or is bothersome:

Redness and peeling of skin (may occur after a few days)

Other side effects not listed above may also occur in some patients. If you notice any other effects, check with your health care professional.

Revised: 10/28/93

SULFURATED LIME Topical

Some commonly used brand names are:

In the U.S.—
Vlemasque
Generic name product may also be available.

In Canada—
Vlemasque

Another commonly used name is Vleminckx's solution.

Description

Sulfurated (SUL-fur-ay-ted) lime is used to treat acne, scabies, and other skin disorders, such as seborrheic dermatitis and pustular infections.

This medicine is available without a prescription; however, your doctor may have special instructions on the proper use of this medicine for your medical problem.

Sulfurated lime is available in the following dosage forms:

Topical
- Mask (U.S. and Canada)
- Topical solution (U.S.)

Before Using This Medicine

If you are using this medicine without a prescription, carefully read and follow any precautions on the label. For sulfurated lime, the following should be considered:

Allergies—Tell your doctor if you have ever had any unusual or allergic reaction to sulfurated lime. Also tell your health care professional if you are allergic to any other substances, such as preservatives or dyes.

Pregnancy—Sulfurated lime has not been shown to cause birth defects or other problems in humans.

Breast-feeding—Sulfurated lime has not been reported to cause problems in nursing babies.

Children—Although there is no specific information comparing use of sulfurated lime in children with use in other age groups, this medicine is not expected to cause different side effects or problems in children than it does in adults.

Older adults—Many medicines have not been studied specifically in older people. Therefore, it may not be known whether they work exactly the same way they do in younger adults or if they cause different side effects or problems in older people. There is no specific information comparing use of sulfurated lime in the elderly with use in other age groups.

Other medicines—Although certain medicines should not be used together at all, in other cases two different medicines may be used together even if an interaction might occur. In these cases, your doctor may want to change the dose, or other precautions may be necessary. Tell your health care professional if you are using any other topical prescription or nonprescription (over-the-counter [OTC]) medicine that is to be applied to the same area of the skin.

Proper Use of This Medicine

Use this medicine only as directed. Do not use more of it, do not use it more often, and do not use it for a longer period of time than recommended on the label, unless otherwise directed by your doctor.

Keep this medicine away from the eyes. If you should accidentally get some in your eyes, flush them thoroughly with water.

To use the *topical solution form* of sulfurated lime for wet dressings, as a soak, or in a bath:

- Sulfurated lime solution must be diluted before you use it on your skin for wet dressings, as a soak, or in a bath. The directions may say to dilute to 1:9 or 1:32. To dilute to 1:9 means that for every 1 part of sulfurated lime you add 9 parts of water. (If you are using cupfuls, for example, you would add 9 cupfuls of water to 1 cupful of sulfurated lime.) In the same

way, if the directions say 1:32, for every 1 part of sulfurated lime you add 32 parts of water. Make sure you understand exactly how you should use this solution. If you have any questions about this, check with your health care professional.
- Before diluting and/or applying this solution, remove all jewelry and metallic ornaments, since the solution may discolor metals. Also, avoid getting this solution on metal spoons or bath fixtures.

To use the *mask form* of sulfurated lime:
- Apply a generous amount of this medicine over the entire face and neck, unless otherwise directed by your doctor.
- Allow the medicine to remain on the affected areas for 20 to 25 minutes.
- Remove the medicine with lukewarm water, using a gentle circular motion. Then, pat the skin dry.

Dosing—The dose of sulfurated lime will be different for different patients. *Follow your doctor's orders or the directions on the label.* The following information includes only the average doses of sulfurated lime. *If your dose is different, do not change it* unless your doctor tells you to do so.
- For *mask* dosage form:
  - —For acne:
    - Adults and children—Use once a day.
- For *topical solution* dosage form:
  - —For acne, seborrheic dermatitis, and pustular infections:
    - Adults and children—Use as a diluted solution (1:32 to 1:9) one or two times a day.
  - —For scabies:
    - Adults and children—Use as a diluted solution (1:9) one or two times a day for three days.

Missed dose—If you miss a dose of this medicine, apply it as soon as possible. However, if it is almost time for your next dose, skip the missed dose and go back to your regular dosing schedule.

Storage—To store this medicine:
- Keep out of the reach of children.
- Store away from heat and direct light.
- Keep the medicine from freezing.
- Do not keep outdated medicine or medicine no longer needed. Be sure that any discarded medicine is out of the reach of children.

Precautions While Using This Medicine

When using sulfurated lime, do not use any of the following preparations on the same affected area as this medicine, unless otherwise directed by your doctor:

Abrasive soaps or cleansers
Alcohol-containing preparations
Any other topical acne preparation or preparation containing a peeling agent (for example, benzoyl peroxide, resorcinol, salicylic acid, sulfur, or tretinoin [vitamin A acid])
Cosmetics or soaps that dry the skin
Medicated cosmetics
Other topical medicine for the skin

To use any of the above preparations on the same affected area as sulfurated lime may cause severe irritation of the skin.

Do not use any topical mercury-containing preparation, such as ammoniated mercury ointment on the same affected area as this medicine. To do so may cause a foul odor, may be irritating to the skin, and may stain the skin black. If you have any questions about this, check with your doctor.

Side Effects of This Medicine

Along with its needed effects, a medicine may cause some unwanted effects. Although not all of these side effects may occur, if they do occur they may need medical attention.

Check with your doctor as soon as possible if the following side effect occurs:

Skin irritation not present before use of this medicine

Other side effects may occur that usually do not need medical attention. However, check with your health care professional if the following side effects continue or are bothersome:

Redness and peeling of skin (may occur after a few days); unusual dryness of skin

Other side effects not listed above may also occur in some patients. If you notice any other effects, check with your health care professional.

Revised: 09/28/93

SUMATRIPTAN Systemic

A commonly used brand name in the U.S. and Canada is Imitrex.

Description

Sumatriptan (soo-ma-TRIP-tan) is used to treat severe migraine headaches. Many people find that their headaches go away completely after they take sumatriptan. Other people find that their headaches are much less painful, and that they are able to go back to their normal activities even though their headaches are not completely gone. Sumatriptan often relieves other symptoms that occur together with a migraine headache, such as nausea, vomiting, sensitivity to light, and sensitivity to sound.

Sumatriptan is not an ordinary pain reliever. It will not relieve any kind of pain other than migraine headaches. This medicine is usually used for people whose headaches are not relieved by acetaminophen, aspirin, or other pain relievers.

Sumatriptan injection is also used to treat cluster headaches.

Sumatriptan has caused serious side effects in some people, especially people who have heart or blood vessel disease. Be sure that you discuss with your doctor the risks of using this medicine as well as the good that it can do.

Sumatriptan is available only with your doctor's prescription, in the following dosage forms:

Oral
- Tablets (U.S. and Canada)

Parenteral
- Injection (U.S. and Canada)

Before Using This Medicine

In deciding to use a medicine, the risks of using the medicine must be weighed against the good it will do. This is a decision you and your doctor will make. For sumatriptan, the following should be considered:

Allergies—Tell your doctor if you have ever had any unusual or allergic reaction to sumatriptan. Also tell your health care professional if you are allergic to any other substances, such as foods, preservatives, or dyes.

Pregnancy—Sumatriptan has not been studied in pregnant women. However, in some animal studies, sumatriptan caused harmful effects to the fetus. These unwanted effects usually occurred when sumatriptan was given in amounts that were large enough to cause harmful effects in the mother.

Breast-feeding—Sumatriptan passes into human breast milk. Breast-feeding mothers should discuss the risks and benefits of this medicine with their doctors.

Children—Studies on this medicine have been done only in patients 18 years of age or older, and there is no specific information comparing use of sumatriptan in children with use in other age groups.

Older adults—This medicine has been tested in a limited number of patients between 60 and 65 years of age. It did not cause different side effects or problems in these patients than it did in younger adults. However, there is no specific information comparing use of sumatriptan in patients older than 65 years of age with use in younger adults.

Other medicines—Although certain medicines should not be used together at all, in other cases two different medicines may be used together even if an interaction might occur. In these cases, your doctor may want to change the dose, or other precautions may be necessary. Tell your health care professional if you are taking any other prescription or nonprescription (over-the-counter [OTC]) medicine, especially other prescription medicine for migraine headaches, or if you smoke tobacco.

When you are taking sumatriptan, it is especially important that your health care professional know if you are taking the following:
- Monoamine oxidase (MAO) inhibitors (furazolidone [e.g., Furoxone]; isocarboxazid [e.g., Marplan], phenelzine [e.g., Mardil], procarbazine [e.g., Matulane], selegiline [e.g., Eldepryl], tranylcyromine [e.g., Parnate])—Taking sumatriptan while you are taking or within 2 weeks of taking MAO inhibitors may cause sudden high body temperature, extremely high blood pressure and severe convulsions; at least 14 days should be allowed between stopping treatment with one medicine and starting treatment with the other.

Other medical problems—The presence of other medical problems may affect the use of sumatriptan. Make sure you tell your doctor if you have any other medical problems, especially:
- Angina (chest pain) or
- Fast or irregular heartbeat or
- Heart or blood vessel disease or
- High blood pressure or
- Kidney disease or
- Liver disease or
- Stroke (history of)—The chance of side effects may be increased. Heart or blood vessel disease and high blood pressure sometimes do not cause any symptoms, so some people do not know that they have these problems. Before deciding whether you should use sumatriptan, your doctor may need to do some tests to make sure that you do not have any of these conditions.

Proper Use of This Medicine

Do not use sumatriptan for a headache that is different from your usual migraines. Instead, check with your doctor.

To relieve your migraine as soon as possible, use sumatriptan as soon as the headache pain begins. Even if you get warning signals of a coming migraine (an aura), you should wait until the headache pain starts before using sumatriptan. Using sumatriptan during the aura probably will not prevent the headache from occurring. However, even if you do not use sumatriptan until your migraine has been present for several hours, the medicine will still work.

Lying down in a quiet, dark room for a while after you use this medicine may help relieve your migraine.

If you are not much better in 1 or 2 hours after an injection of sumatriptan, or in 2 to 4 hours after a tablet is taken, *do not use any more of this medicine for the same migraine.* A migraine that is not relieved by the first dose of sumatriptan probably will not be relieved by a second dose, either. Ask your doctor ahead of time about other medicine to be taken if sumatriptan does not work. After taking the other medicine, check with your doctor as soon as possible. Headaches that are not relieved by sumatriptan are sometimes caused by conditions that need other treatment. However, even if sumatriptan does not relieve one migraine, it may still relieve the next one.

If you feel much better after a dose of sumatriptan, but your headache comes back or gets worse after a while, you may use more sumatriptan. However, *use this medicine only as directed by your doctor. Do not use more of it, and do not use it more often, than directed.* Using too much sumatriptan may increase the chance of side effects.

Your doctor may direct you to take another medicine to help prevent headaches. *It is important that you follow your doctor's directions, even if your headaches continue to occur.* Headache-preventing medicines may take several weeks to start working. Even after they do start working, your headaches may not go away completely. However, your headaches should occur less often, and they should be less severe and easier to relieve. This can reduce the amount of sumatriptan or pain relievers that you need. If you do not notice any improvement after several weeks of headache-preventing treatment, check with your doctor.

For patients taking *sumatriptan tablets:*

- Sumatriptan tablets are to be swallowed whole with a full glass of water. *Do not break, crush, or chew the tablets before swallowing them.*

For patients using *sumatriptan injection:*

- This medicine comes with patient directions. *Read them carefully before using the medicine,* and check with your health care professional if you have any questions.
- Your health care professional will teach you how to inject yourself with the medicine. *Be sure to follow the directions carefully. Check with your health care professional if you have any problems using the medicine.*
- After you have finished injecting the medicine, be sure to follow the precautions in the patient directions about safely discarding the empty cartridge and the needle. Always return the empty cartridge and needle to their container before discarding them. Do not throw away the autoinjector unit, because refills are available.

Dosing—The dose of sumatriptan will be different for different patients. *Follow your doctor's orders or the directions on the label.* The following information includes only the average doses of sumatriptan. *If your dose is different, do not change it* unless your doctor tells you to do so.

- For *oral* dosage form (tablets):
  - —For migraine headaches:
    - Adults—25 to 100 mg as a single dose. If the migraine comes back after being relieved, another dose may be taken two hours after the last dose. *Do not take more than 300 mg in any twenty-four-hour period.* If you are taking the tablets after using an injection, do not take more than 200 mg in a twenty-four-hour period.
    - Children—Use and dose must be determined by your doctor.
- For *parenteral* dosage form (injection):
  - —For migraine or cluster headaches:
    - Adults—One 6-mg injection. One more 6-mg dose may be injected, if necessary, if the migraine comes back after being relieved. However, the second injection should not be given any sooner than one hour after the first one. *Do not use more than two 6-mg injections in a twenty-four-hour period (one day).* However, some people may be directed to use no more than two 6-mg doses in a forty-eight-hour period (two days).
    - Children—Use and dose must be determined by your doctor.

Storage—To store this medicine:

- Keep out of the reach of children since overdose is especially dangerous in children.
- Store away from heat and direct light.
- Do not store tablets in the bathroom, near the kitchen sink, or in other damp places. Heat or moisture may cause the medicine to break down.
- Keep the injection form of sumatriptan from freezing.
- Do not keep outdated medicine or medicine no longer needed. Be sure that any discarded medicine is out of the reach of children.

Precautions While Using This Medicine

Check with your doctor if you have used sumatriptan for three headaches, and have not had good relief. Also, check with your doctor if your migraine headaches are worse, or if they are occurring more often, than before you started using sumatriptan.

Drinking alcoholic beverages can make headaches worse or cause new headaches to occur. People who suffer from severe headaches should probably avoid alcoholic beverages, especially during a headache.

Some people feel drowsy or dizzy during or after a migraine, or after taking sumatriptan to relieve a migraine. As long as you are feeling drowsy or dizzy, *do not drive, use machines, or do anything else that could be dangerous if you are dizzy or are not alert.*

Side Effects of This Medicine

Along with its needed effects, a medicine may cause some unwanted effects. Most side effects of sumatriptan are milder and occur less often with the tablets than with the injection. Although not all of these side effects may occur, if they do occur they may need medical attention.

Stop using this medicine and check with your doctor immediately if any of the following side effects occur:

Rare

Chest pain (severe); fast or irregular breathing; puffiness or swelling of eyelids, area around the eyes, face, or lips; shortness of breath, troubled breathing, or wheezing

Check with your doctor right away if any of the following side effects continue for more than 1 hour. Even if they go away in less than 1 hour, *check with your doctor before using any more sumatriptan if any of the following side effects occur:*

Less common

Chest pain (mild); heaviness, tightness, or pressure in chest and/or neck

Also check with your doctor as soon as possible if any of the following side effects occur:

Less common

Difficulty in swallowing; pounding heartbeat; skin rash, hives, itching, or bumps on skin

Other side effects may occur that usually do not need medical attention. Some of the following effects, such as nausea, vomiting, drowsiness, dizziness, and general feeling of illness or tiredness, often occur during or after a migraine, even when sumatriptan has not been used. Most of the side effects caused by sumatriptan go away within a short time (less than 1 hour after an injection or 2 hours after a tablet). However, check with your doctor if any of the following side effects continue or are bothersome:

More common

Burning, pain, or redness at place of injection; discomfort in jaw, mouth, tongue, throat, nose, or sinuses; dizziness; drowsiness; feeling of burning, warmth, heat, numbness, tightness, or tingling; feeling cold, "strange," or weak; flushing; lightheadedness; muscle aches, cramps, or stiffness; nausea or vomiting

Less common or rare

Anxiety; general feeling of illness or tiredness; vision changes

Other side effects not listed above may also occur in some patients. If you notice any other effects, check with your doctor.

Revised: 3/27/97

SUNSCREEN AGENTS Topical

Some commonly used brand names are:

In the U.S.—

A-Fil[25]
Aquaderm Sunscreen Moisturizer[41]
Aquaray Sunscreen[34]
Bain de Soleil All Day For Kids[30]
Bain de Soleil All Day Sunfilter[31]
Bain de Soleil Mega Tan[26]
Bain de Soleil Orange Gelee[33]
Bain de Soleil Sand Buster[33]
Bain de Soleil SPF + Color[26]
Bain de Soleil Tropical Deluxe[33]
Banana Boat Active Kids Sunblock[34]
Banana Boat Baby Sunblock[34]
Banana Boat Dark Tanning[45, 51]
Banana Boat Faces Sensitive Skin Sunblock[34]
Banana Boat Protective Tanning[45]
Banana Boat Sport Sunblock[34]
Banana Boat Sunblock[42]
Banana Boat Sunscreen[49]
Blistex Daily Conditioning Treatment for Lips[49]
Blistex Medicated Lip Conditioner[49]
Blistex Regular[49]
Blistex Ultraprotection[10]
Bullfrog Body[29]
Bullfrog Extra Moisturizing[29]
Bullfrog For Kids[29]
Bullfrog Original Concentrated[29]
Bullfrog Sport[28]
Bullfrog Sunblock[41]
Catrix Correction[20]
Catrix Lip Saver[41]
Chap-et Sun Ban Lip Conditioner[49]
Chap Stick[51]
Chap Stick Sunblock[49]
Chap Stick Sunblock Petroleum Jelly Plus[49]
Coppertone All Day Protection[12, 27, 41]
Coppertone Kids Sunblock[12, 27]
Coppertone Lipkote Lip Balm[41]
Coppertone Moisturizing Sunscreen[41]
Coppertone Moisturizing Suntan[8, 41]
Coppertone Sport[34]
Coppertone Sport Ultra Sweatproof[41]
Coppertone Tan Magnifier Gel,[32, 52, 56]
Coppertone Waterbabies Sunblock[27]
Curel Everyday Sun Protection[41]
Dermsol[34]
DML Facial Moisturizer Cream[41]
Durascreen[34]
DuraScreen[37]
Eclipse Lip & Face Protectant [49]
Eclipse Original Suncreen[16]
Eucerin Dry Skin Care Daily Facial[39]
Formula 405 Solar[2, 32, 49]
Hawaiian Baby Faces Sunblock[22]
Hawaiian Tropic Baby Faces[19]
Hawaiian Tropic Baby Faces Sunblock[28]
Hawaiian Tropic Dark Tanning[45, 52]
Hawaiian Tropic Dark Tanning with Sunscreen[20]
Hawaiian Tropic Just For Kids[10, 28]
Hawaiian Tropic Land Sport[33]
Hawaiian Tropic Plus[19, 23]
Hawaiian Tropic Plus Sunblock[23]
Hawaiian Tropic Protective Tanning Dry[9, 53]
Hawaiian Tropic Protective Tanning[49]
Hawaiian Tropic Self-tanning Sunblock[41]
Hawaiian Tropic Sport Sunblock[28, 29]
Hawaiian Tropic Sunblock[10, 28]
Hawaiian Tropic Water Sport[44]
Herpecin-L Cold Sore[51]
Johnson's Baby Sunblock Extra Protection[38]
Johnson's Baby Sunblock[38]
Johnson's No More Tears Baby Sunblock[55]
Maxafil Cream[17]
Mentholatum Lip Balm[51]
Neutrogena Chemical-Free Sunblocker[54]
Neutrogena Deep Glow[32]
Neutrogena Intensified Day Moisture[46]
Neutrogena Light Glow[32]
Neutrogena Lip Moisturizer[41]
Neutrogena Moisture Untinted & with Sheer Tint[41]
Neutrogena No Stick Sunscreen[12]
Neutrogena Sunblock[18, 21, 34]
Nivea Sun[34]
Noxzema Moisturizer[46]
Oil of Olay Daily UV Protectant Beauty Fluid[46]
Oil of Olay Daily UV Protectant[46]
Oil of Olay Moisture Replenishment[46, 52]
PreSun Active Clear[34]
PreSun For Kids[34]
PreSun Lip Protector[49]
PreSun Moisturizing[49]
PreSun Moisturizing Sunscreen with Keri[34, 49]
PreSun Sensitive Skin[34]
PreSun Spray Mist[34, 47]
Presun Spray Mist for Kids[35]
Q.T. Quick Tanning[32]
Ray Block[49]
Shade Oil-Free Gel[13]
Shade Sunblock[12, 27]
Shade Sunblock Oil-Free[34]
Shade UVA Guard[6]
Shade Waterproof Sunblock[27]
Softsense Skin Essential Everyday UV Protectant[41]
Solbar PF[41]
Solbar PF Liquid[29, 41]
Solbar PF Ultra[29]
Solbar Plus[7]
Solex A15 Clear[49]
Stay Moist Moisturizing Lip Conditioner[49]
Sundown Sport Sunblock[55]
Sundown Sunblock[38]
Sundown Sunscreen[40]
TI Screen Baby Natural[54]
TI Screen[27, 34, 41]
Total Eclipse Moisturizing Skin Lotion[48]
Total Eclipse Oily and Acne Prone Skin Sunscreen[15]
Tropical Blend Dark Tanning[8, 41, 49]
Tropical Blend Dry Oil[8, 14]
Vaseline Extra Defense for Hand and Body[41]
Vaseline Intensive Care Active Sport[41]
Vaseline Intensive Care Baby Moisturizing Sunblock[38, 54]
Vaseline Intensive Care Blockout Moisturizing[36, 38]
Vaseline Intensive Care Lip Therapy[41]
Vaseline Intensive Care Moisturizing Sunblock[34, 41]
Vaseline Intensive Care Moisturizing Sunscreen[33]
Vaseline Moisturizing Sunscreen[41]
Vaseline Ultraviolet Daily Defense for Hand and Body[41]
Waterbabies Little Licks[34]
Waterbabies Sunblock[12, 41]

In Canada—

Bain de Soleil All Day Sunblock[30]
Bain de Soleil Long Lasting For Kids[30]
Bain de Soleil Long Lasting Sport Sunblock[31]
Bain de Soleil Long Lasting Sunblock[30]
Bain de Soleil Long Lasting Sunfilter[31]
Bain de Soleil Mega Tan[26]
Bain de Soleil Orange Gelee[33]
Bain de Soleil SPF + Color[29]
Blistex Medicated Lip Conditioner[49]
Blistex Medicated Lip Conditioner with Sunscreen[24]
Blistex Sunblock[49]
Blistex Ultraprotection[10]
Can Screen 400 Sunscreen[6]
Chap Stick Sunblock Lip Balm[49]
Coppertone Dark Tanning[8]
Coppertone Lipkote[41]
Coppertone Sport[34]
Coppertone Waterbabies Sunblock[27]
Coppertone Waterproof Sunblock Lotion[11]
Johnson's Baby Sunblock Extra Protection[38]
Johnson's Baby Sunblock[38]
Johnson's No More Tears Baby Sunblock[55]
Ombrelle Sunscreen[6]
Photoplex Plus Sunscreen[3]
Pond's Daily Replenishing Moisturizer[46, 52]
Presun Clear[5]
Presun Creamy Sundown Sunscreen[49]
Presun[1]
Presun Sunscreen[5, 34, 49]
Presun Sunscreen for Kids[5, 34]
Shade Waterproof Sunblock[27]
Solbar Liquid[32]
Solbar[50]
Solbar Plus[50]
Solbar Shield[34]
Sundown Broad Spectrum Sunblock[38]
Sundown[43]
Sundown Sunscreen[41]
TI - UVA - B Sunscreen[41]
Tropical Blend Waterproof[49]
Vaseline Baby Sunblock[55]
Vaseline Broad Spectrum Sunblock[4]
Vaseline Intensive Care Baby Sunblock[38]
Vaseline Kids Sunblock[34, 41]
Vaseline Lip Therapy[41]
Vaseline Sports Sunblock[41]
Vaseline Sports Sunscreen[41]
Vaseline Sunblock[34, 35, 41]
Vaseline Sunscreen[41]
Waterbabies Sunblock[12, 41]

Note: For quick reference, the following sunscreen agents are numbered to match the corresponding brand names.

This information applies to the following medicines:

1. Aminobenzoic (a-mee-noe-ben-ZOE-ik) Acid, Padimate (PAD-i-mate) O, and Oxybenzone (ox-i-BEN-zone)
2. Aminobenzoic Acid and Titanium Dioxide (tye-TANE-ee-um dye-OX-ide)
3. Avobenzone (a-voe-BENZ-one), Octocrylene (OK-toe-kri-leen), Octyl Salicylate (OK-til sal-i-SIL-ate), and Oxybenzone
4. Avobenzone and Octyl Methoxycinnamate (OK-til meth-ox-ee-SIN-a-mate)
5. Avobenzone, Octyl Methoxycinnamate, Octyl Salicylate, and Oxybenzone
6. Avobenzone, Octyl Methoxycinnamate, and Oxybenzone
7. Dioxybenzone (dye-ox-i-BEN-zone), Oxybenzone, and Padimate O
8. Homosalate (hoe-mo-SAL-ate)
9. Homosalate, Menthyl Anthranilate (MEN-thil AN-thra-ni-late), and Octyl Methoxycinnamate
10. Homosalate, Menthyl Anthranilate, Octyl Methoxycinnamate, Octyl Salicylate, and Oxybenzone
11. Homosalate, Octocrylene, Octyl Methoxycinnamate, and Oxybenzone
12. Homosalate, Octyl Methoxycinnamate, Octyl Salicylate, and Oxybenzone
13. Homosalate, Octyl Methoxycinnamate, and Oxybenzone
14. Homosalate and Oxybenzone
15. Lisadimate (lis-AD-i-mate), Oxybenzone, and Padimate O
16. Lisadimate and Padimate O
17. Menthyl Anthranilate
18. Menthyl Anthranilate, Octocrylene, and Octyl Methoxycinnamate
19. Menthyl Anthranilate, Octocrylene, Octyl Methoxycinnamate, and Oxybenzone
20. Menthyl Anthranilate and Octyl Methoxycinnamate
21. Menthyl Anthranilate, Octyl Methoxycinnamate, and Octyl Salicylate
22. Menthyl Anthranilate, Octyl Methoxycinnamate, Octyl Salicylate, and Oxybenzone
23. Menthyl Anthranilate, Octyl Methoxycinnamate, and Oxybenzone
24. Menthyl Anthranilate and Padimate O
25. Menthyl Anthranilate and Titanium Dioxide
26. Octocrylene and Octyl Methoxycinnamate
27. Octocrylene, Octyl Methoxycinnamate, Octyl Salicylate, and Oxybenzone
28. Octocrylene, Octyl Methoxycinnamate, Octyl Salicylate, Oxybenzone, and Titanium Dioxide
29. Octocrylene, Octyl Methoxycinnamate, and Oxybenzone
30. Octocrylene, Octyl Methoxycinnamate, Oxybenzone, and Titanium Dioxide
31. Octocrylene, Octyl Methoxycinnamate, and Titanium Dioxide
32. Octyl Methoxycinnamate
33. Octyl Methoxycinnamate and Octyl Salicylate
34. Octyl Methoxycinnamate, Octyl Salicylate, and Oxybenzone
35. Octyl Methoxycinnamate, Octyl Salicylate, Oxybenzone, and Padimate O
36. Octyl Methoxycinnamate, Octyl Salicylate, Oxybenzone, Padimate O, and Titanium Dioxide
37. Octyl Methoxycinnamate, Octyl Salicylate, Oxybenzone, Phenylbenzimidazole (FEN-il benz-i-MI-da-zole), and Titanium Dioxide
38. Octyl Methoxycinnamate, Octyl Salicylate, Oxybenzone, and Titanium Dioxide
39. Octyl Methoxycinnamate, Octyl Salicylate, Phenylbenzimidazole, and Titanium Dioxide
40. Octyl Methoxycinnamate, Octyl Salicylate, and Titanium Dioxide
41. Octyl Methoxycinnamate and Oxybenzone
42. Octyl Methoxycinnamate, Oxybenzone, and Padimate O
43. Octyl Methoxycinnamate, Oxybenzone, Padimate O, and Titanium Dioxide
44. Octyl Methoxycinnamate, Oxybenzone, and Titanium Dioxide
45. Octyl Methoxycinnamate and Padimate O
46. Octyl Methoxycinnamate and Phenylbenzimidazole
47. Octyl Salicylate
48. Octyl Salicylate and Padimate O
49. Oxybenzone and Padimate O
50. Oxybenzone and Roxadimate (rox-AD-i-mate)
51. Padimate O
52. Phenylbenzimidazole
53. Phenylbenzimidazole and Sulisobenzone (sul-i-soe-BEN-zone)
54. Titanium Dioxide
55. Titanium Dioxide and Zinc Oxide (zink OX-ide)
56. Trolamine Salicylate (TROLE-a-meen sal-i-SIL-ate)

Description

Sunscreen agents are used to prevent sunburn. Limiting your exposure to the sun and using sunscreen agents when in the sun may help prevent early wrinkling and skin cancer. There are two kinds of sunscreen agents: chemical and physical. Chemical sunscreen agents protect you from the sun by absorbing the ultraviolet (UV) and visible sun rays, while physical sunscreen agents reflect, scatter, absorb, or block these rays.

Sunscreen agents often contain more than one ingredient. For example, products may contain one ingredient that provides protection against the ultraviolet A (UVA) sun rays and another ingredient that protects you from the ultraviolet B (UVB) sun rays, which are more likely to cause sunburn than the UVA sun rays. Ideally, coverage should include protection against both UVA and UVB sun rays.

The sun protection factor (SPF) that you find on the label of these products tells you the minimum amount of UVB sunlight that is needed with that product to produce redness on sunscreen-protected skin as compared with unprotected skin. Sunscreen products with high SPFs will provide more protection against the sun.

Sunscreen agents are available in the following dosage forms:

Topical

Aminobenzoic Acid, Padimate O, and Oxybenzone combination
- Lotion (Canada)

Aminobenzoic Acid and Titanium Dioxide combination
- Cream (U.S.)

Avobenzone, Octocrylene, Octyl Salicylate, and Oxybenzone combination
- Lotion (Canada)

Avobenzone and Octyl Methoxycinnamate combination
- Lotion (Canada)

Avobenzone, Octyl methoxycinnamate, Octyl Salicylate, and Oxybenzone combination
- Cream (Canada)
- Gel (Canada)

Avobenzone, Octyl Methoxycinnamate, and Oxybenzone combination
- Lotion (U.S. and Canada)
- Spray (Canada)

Dioxybenzone, Oxybenzone, and Padimate O combination
- Cream (U.S.)

Homosalate
- Lotion (U.S.)
- Oil (U.S. and Canada)
- Spray (U.S.)

Homosalate, Menthyl Anthranilate, and Octyl Methoxycinnamate combination
- Oil (U.S.)

Homosalate, Menthyl Anthranilate, Octyl Methoxycinnamate, Octyl Salicylate, and Oxybenzone combination
- Lip Balm (U.S. and Canada)
- Lotion (U.S.)

Homosalate, Octocrylene, Octyl Methoxycinnamate, and Oxybenzone combination
- Lotion (Canada)

Homosalate, Octyl Methoxycinnamate, Octyl Salicylate, and Oxybenzone combination
- Lotion (U.S. and Canada)
- Stick (U.S.)

Homosalate, Octyl Methoxycinnamate, and Oxybenzone combination
- Gel (U.S.)

Homosalate and Oxybenzone combination
- Spray (U.S.)

Lisadimate, Oxybenzone, and Padimate O combination
- Lotion (U.S.)

Lisadimate and Padimate O combination
- Lotion (U.S.)

Menthyl Anthranilate
- Cream (U.S.)

Menthyl Anthranilate, Octocrylene, and Octyl Methoxycinnamate combination
- Cream (U.S.)

Menthyl Anthranilate, Octocrylene, Octyl Methoxycinnamate, and Oxybenzone combination
- Gel (U.S.)

Menthyl Anthranilate and Octyl Methoxycinnamate combination
- Cream (U.S.)
- Lotion (U.S.)

Menthyl Anthranilate, Octyl Methoxycinnamate, and Octyl Salicylate combination
- Cream (U.S.)

Menthyl Anthranilate, Octyl Methoxycinnamate, Octyl Salicylate, and Oxybenzone combination
- Lotion (U.S.)

Menthyl Anthranilate, Octyl Methoxycinnamate, and Oxybenzone combination
- Gel (U.S.)
- Lip Balm (U.S.)
- Lotion (U.S.)

Menthyl Anthranilate and Padimate O combination
- Lip Balm (Canada)

Menthyl Anthranilate and Titanium Dioxide combination
- Cream (U.S.)

Octocrylene and Octyl Methoxycinnamate combination
- Lotion (U.S. and Canada)

Octocrylene, Octyl Methoxycinnamate, Octyl Salicylate, and Oxybenzone combination
- Lotion (U.S. and Canada)

Octocrylene, Octyl Methoxycinnamate, Octyl Salicylate, Oxybenzone, and Titanium Dioxide combination
- Lotion (U.S.)

Octocrylene, Octyl Methoxycinnamate, and Oxybenzone combination
- Cream (U.S.)
- Gel (U.S.)
- Lotion (U.S. and Canada)

Octocrylene, Octyl Methoxycinnamate, Oxybenzone, and Titanium Dioxide combination
- Lotion (U.S. and Canada)

Octocrylene, Octyl Methoxycinnamate, and Titanium Dioxide combination
- Lotion (U.S. and Canada)

Octyl Methoxycinnamate
- Gel (Canada)
- Lotion (U.S.)

Octyl Methoxycinnamate and Octyl Salicylate combination
- Gel (U.S. and Canada)
- Lotion (U.S.)
- Oil (U.S.)

Octyl Methoxycinnamate, Octyl Salicylate, and Oxybenzone combination
- Cream (U.S. and Canada)
- Gel (U.S.)
- Lotion (U.S. and Canada)
- Spray (U.S.)
- Stick (U.S.)

Octyl Methoxycinnamate, Octyl Salicylate, Oxybenzone, and Padimate O combination
- Lotion (Canada)
- Spray (U.S.)

Octyl Methoxycinnamate, Octyl Salicylate, Oxybenzone, Padimate O, and Titanium Dioxide combination
- Lotion (U.S.)

Octyl Methoxycinnamate, Octyl Salicylate, Oxybenzone, Phenylbenzimidazole, and Titanium Dioxide combination
- Lotion (U.S.)

Octyl Methoxycinnamate, Octyl Salicylate, Oxybenzone, and Titanium Dioxide combination
- Cream (Canada)
- Lotion (U.S. and Canada)

Octyl Methoxycinnamate, Octyl Salicylate, Phenylbenzimidazole, and Titanium Dioxide combination
- Lotion (U.S.)

Octyl Methoxycinnamate, Octyl Salicylate, and Titanium Dioxide combination
- Lotion (U.S.)

Octyl Methoxycinnamate and Oxybenzone combination
- Cream (U.S.)
- Gel (U.S.)
- Lip Balm (U.S. and Canada)
- Lotion (U.S. and Canada)
- Stick (U.S. and Canada)

Octyl Methoxycinnamate, Oxybenzone, and Padimate O combination
- Lotion (U.S.)

Octyl Methoxycinnamate, Oxybenzone, Padimate O, and Titanium Dioxide combination
- Stick (Canada)

Octyl Methoxycinnamate, Oxybenzone, and Titanium Dioxide combination
- Lotion (U.S.)

Octyl Methoxycinnamate and Padimate O combination
- Oil (U.S.)

Octyl Methoxycinnamate and Phenylbenzimidazole combination
- Cream (U.S.)
- Lotion (U.S. and Canada)

Octyl Salicylate
- Spray (U.S.)

Octyl Salicylate and Padimate O combination
- Lotion (U.S.)

Oxybenzone and Padimate O combination
- Cream (Canada)
- Lip Balm (U.S. and Canada)
- Lotion (U.S. and Canada)
- Oil (U.S. and Canada)
- Stick (U.S.)

Oxybenzone and Roxadimate combination
- Cream (Canada)
- Lotion (Canada)

Padimate O
- Lip Balm (U.S. and Canada)
- Lotion (U.S.)
- Oil (U.S.)

Phenylbenzimidazole
- Gel (U.S.)
- Lotion (U.S. and Canada)

Phenylbenzimidazole and Sulisobenzone combination
- Gel (U.S.)

Titanium Dioxide
- Lotion (U.S.)

Titanium Dioxide and Zinc Oxide combination
- Lotion (U.S. and Canada)

Trolamine Salicylate
- Oil (U.S.)

Before Using This Product

If you are using this medicine without a prescription, carefully read and follow any precautions on the label. For sunscreen agents, the following should be considered:

Allergies—Tell your doctor if you have ever had any unusual or allergic reaction to any of the sunscreen agents. Also tell your health care professional if you are allergic to artificial sweeteners (e.g., saccharin [Sweet and Low]); anesthetics (e.g., benzocaine [Americaine], procaine [Novocaine], tetracaine [Pontocaine]); oral antidiabetics (diabetes medicine you take by mouth); hair dyes containing aniline or paraphenylenediamine; sulfa medicines; thiazide diuretics (a certain type of water pill); cinnamon derivatives used in flavorings, medicines, perfumes, or toothpastes; or to any other substances, such as foods or preservatives.

Pregnancy—Studies on effects in pregnancy have not been done in either humans or animals.

Breast-feeding—Sunscreen agents have not been reported to cause problems in nursing babies.

Children—Infants under 6 months of age should be kept out of the sun. Sunscreen agents should not be used on infants under 6 months of age because of increased chance of side effects. Children 6 months of age and older should be kept out of the sun or have limited exposure to the sun. Sunscreen agents with a sun protection factor (SPF) of at least 15 should be applied during exposure to the sun. Lotion sunscreen products are preferred for use in children. Alcohol-based sunscreen products should be avoided because they can cause irritation.

Older adults—It is believed that the elderly, who spend little time in the sun and use sunscreen agents frequently, may be at risk for vitamin D deficiency (which may result in bone disease and fracture), although this has not been proven. To help you get enough vitamin D, it is recommended that you eat food rich in vitamin D, such as fortified milk or fatty fish. Your doctor may also advise you to take vitamin D supplements. Check with your doctor about this.

Other medicines—Although certain medicines and products should not be used together at all, in other cases two different medicines or products may be used together even if an interaction may occur. In these cases, your doctor may want to change the dose, or other precautions may be necessary. Tell your health care professional if you are using any prescription or nonprescription (over-the-counter [OTC]) medicine or other product that is to be applied to the same area of the skin.

Other medical problems—The presence of other medical problems may affect the use of sunscreen agents. Make sure you tell your health care professional if you have any other medical problems, especially:

- Skin conditions or diseases, especially those caused or worsened by exposure to light—Worsening of skin condition may occur

Proper Use of This Product

Sunscreen agents are for external use only. These products usually come with patient directions. Read them carefully before using any product.

In choosing the sunscreen product, you may consider the following:

• *Type of Activity*—Take precautions when you are in places of higher elevations (mountains) or on reflective surfaces (concrete, sand, snow, or water), as these may increase the likelihood of sun damage to the skin. Use a sunscreen with ultraviolet A/ultraviolet B (UVA/UVB) coverage and with a sun protection factor (SPF) of 15 or higher. Activities that make you sweat, such as outdoor jobs (gardeners, construction workers), outdoor sports (tennis) or exercise, prolonged sunbathing, or watersports such as swimming, waterskiing, or windsurfing, may result in the removal of the sunscreen agent from the skin. Use a water-resistant or waterproof sunscreen agent with SPF of 15 or more. When possible, also wear a hat, long-sleeved shirt, long pants, and UV-opaque sunglasses. Wearing UV-opaque sunglasses when you are in the sun is also necessary because the sun rays can cause cataracts.

• *Age*—Do not use sunscreen agents on infants less than 6 months of age. For children 6 months of age and older, use a lotion form of sunscreen with SPF of 15 or higher. Avoid using alcohol-based sunscreen products for this age group.

• *Site of application*—For the ear and nose, use a physical sunscreen agent. For the lips, use a gel-based lip sunscreen or lip balm.

• *Skin condition*—If your skin is dry, use a cream or lotion form of sunscreen agent. If your skin is oily, use an alcohol or gel-based sunscreen. Avoid using alcohol-based sunscreens on eczematous or inflamed skin.

Skin Type (complexion)	*Appropriate Sunscreen Agent*
Very fair—Always burns easily; rarely tans	Use SPF 20 to 30
Fair—Always burns easily; tans minimally	Use SPF 12 to 20
Light—Burns moderately; tans gradually (light brown)	Use SPF 8 to 12
Medium—Burns minimally; always tans well (moderate brown)	Use SPF 4 to 8
Dark—Rarely burns; tans profusely (dark brown)	Use SPF 2 to 4

Before every exposure to the sun, apply an appropriate sunscreen product that protects you against ultraviolet sun rays. For maximum sun protection, sunscreens should be applied uniformly and thickly to all exposed skin surfaces (including the lips, using lip sunscreen or lip balm). Sunscreen products containing aminobenzoic acid, lisadimate, padimate O, or roxadimate should be applied 1 to 2 hours before sun exposure. Other sunscreen products should be applied 30 minutes before sun exposure, unless otherwise directed by the package instructions. Lip sunscreens should be applied 45 to 60 minutes before sun exposure.

Because most sunscreens are easily removed from the skin, you should reapply these products liberally every 1 to 2 hours for adequate protection. You should reapply sunscreen especially after swimming or heavy perspiration. Lip sunscreens should be reapplied liberally at least once every hour while you are in the sun and also before and after swimming, after eating and drinking, and during other activities that remove it from the lips.

Keep sunscreen products *away from the eyes.*

Some sunscreen agents contain *alcohol and are flammable. Do not use near heat, near open flame, or while smoking.*

Dosing—*Follow your doctor's orders or the directions on the label.* The following information includes only the average dose of sunscreen agents.

• For *topical* dosage forms (cream, gel, lotion, lip balm, oil, spray, and stick):
  —For sunburn (prevention):
    • Adults and children 6 months of age and older—Apply liberally and evenly to exposed area(s) of skin (including the lips, using lip sunscreen or lip balm) before sun exposure. Reapply when needed.
    • Children under 6 months of age—Use is not recommended.

Storage—To store this product:
• Keep out of the reach of children.
• Store away from heat and direct light.
• Keep the product from freezing. Do not refrigerate.
• Do not keep outdated sunscreen product no longer needed. Be sure that any discarded sunscreen product is out of the reach of children.

Precautions While Using This Product

If rash or irritation develops, stop using the sunscreen and check with your doctor.

Sunscreen agents containing aminobenzoic acid, lisadimate, padimate O, or roxadimate may discolor and stain light-colored fabrics yellow.

In addition to using sunscreen agents, it is advisable to minimize exposure to the sun from *10 a.m. to 2 p.m. (11 a.m. to 3 p.m. daylight savings time)* when the sun is at its strongest. Take extra precautions also on cloudy or overcast days and around reflective surfaces such as concrete, sand, snow, or water, since these surfaces can reflect the sun's damaging rays. Wear protective clothing including a hat, long-sleeved shirt, and long pants. Sunglasses also should be worn to avoid sun damage to the eyes (cataract formation). Avoid sunlamps and tanning parlors because these can damage the skin and eyes as direct sunlight can.

Side Effects of This Product

Along with its needed effects, sunscreen products may cause some unwanted effects. Although not all of these side effects may occur, if they do occur they may need medical attention.

Check with your doctor as soon as possible if any of the following side effects occur:

Rare

Acne; burning, itching, or stinging of skin; early appearance of redness or swelling of skin; late appearance of rash with or without weeping blisters that become crusted, especially in sun-exposed areas, and may extend to unexposed areas of skin; pain in hairy areas; pus in the hair follicles

Other side effects may occur that usually do not need medical attention. These side effects may go away during treatment as your body adjusts to the product. However,

check with your doctor if any of the following side effects continue or are bothersome:

More common

Drying or tightening of skin

Other side effects not listed above may also occur in some patients. If you notice any other effects, check with your doctor.

Developed: 04/02/96

TACRINE Systemic†

A commonly used brand name in the U.S. is Cognex.
Other commonly used names are THA and tetrahydroaminoacridine.

†Not commercially available in Canada.

Description

Tacrine (TA-crin) is used to treat the symptoms of mild to moderate Alzheimer's disease. Tacrine will not cure Alzheimer's disease, and it will not stop the disease from getting worse. However, tacrine can improve thinking ability in some patients with Alzheimer's disease.

In Alzheimer's disease, many chemical changes take place in the brain. One of the earliest and biggest changes is that there is less of a chemical messenger called acetylcholine (ACh). ACh helps the brain to work properly. Tacrine slows the breakdown of ACh, so it can build up and have a greater effect. However, as Alzheimer's disease gets worse, there will be less and less ACh, so tacrine may not work as well.

Tacrine may cause liver problems. You must have blood tests regularly while taking this medicine to see if the medicine is affecting your liver.

This medicine is available only with your doctor's prescription, in the following dosage form:

Oral

- Capsules (U.S.)

Before Using This Medicine

In deciding to use a medicine, the risks of taking the medicine must be weighed against the good it will do. This is a decision you and your doctor will make. For tacrine the following should be considered:

Allergies—Tell your doctor if you have ever had any unusual or allergic reaction to tacrine or to wound antiseptics (e.g., Akrinol, Panflavin, Monacrin). Also tell your health care professional if you are allergic to any other substances, such as foods, preservatives, or dyes.

Pregnancy—Studies on effects in pregnancy have not been done in either humans or animals.

Breast-feeding—It is not known whether tacrine passes into breast milk. However, use of tacrine is not recommended in nursing mothers.

Older adults—Studies on tacrine have been done only in middle-aged and older patients. Information on the effects of tacrine is based on these patients.

Other medicines—Although certain medicines should not be used together at all, in other cases two different medicines may be used together even if an interaction might occur. In these cases, your doctor may want to change the dose, or other precautions may be necessary. When you are taking tacrine, it is especially important that your health care professional know if you are taking any of the following:

- Cimetidine (e.g., Tagamet)—Cimetidine may cause higher blood levels of tacrine, which may increase the chance of side effects
- Inflammation or pain medicine, except narcotics—Stomach irritation may be increased
- Neuromuscular blocking agents (medicines used in surgery to relax muscles)—Tacrine may increase the effects of these medicines; your doctor may change the dose of tacrine before you have surgery
- Smoking tobacco—Smoking may cause lower blood levels of tacrine, which may decrease the effects of tacrine; if you smoke, your doctor may need to change the dose of tacrine
- Theophylline (e.g., Theo-Dur, Uniphyl)—Tacrine may cause higher blood levels of theophylline, which may increase the chance of side effects; your doctor may need to change the dose of theophylline

Other medical problems—The presence of other medical problems may affect the use of tacrine. Make sure you tell your doctor if you have any other medical problems, especially:

- Asthma (or history of) or
- Heart problems, including slow heartbeat or hypotension (low blood pressure), or
- Intestinal blockage or
- Liver disease (or history of) or
- Parkinson's disease or
- Stomach ulcer (or history of) or
- Urinary tract blockage or difficult urination—Tacrine may make these conditions worse
- Brain disease, other, or
- Epilepsy or history of seizures or
- Head injury with loss of consciousness—Tacrine may cause seizures

Proper Use of This Medicine

Take this medicine only as directed by your doctor. Do not take more or less of it, and do not take it more or less often than your doctor ordered. Taking too much may increase the chance of side effects, while taking too little may not improve your condition.

Tacrine is best taken on an empty stomach (1 hour before or 2 hours after meals). However, if this medicine upsets your stomach, your doctor may want you to take it with food.

Tacrine seems to work best when it is taken at regularly spaced times, usually four times a day.

Dosing—The dose of tacrine will be different for different patients. *Follow your doctor's orders or the directions on the label.* The following information includes only the average doses of tacrine. *If your dose is different, do not change it* unless your doctor tells you to do so.

- For *oral* dosage form (capsules):
  - —For treatment of Alzheimer's disease:
    - Adults—To start, 10 milligrams (mg) four times a day. Your doctor may increase your dose gradually if you are doing well on this medicine and your liver tests are normal. However, the dose is usually not more than 40 mg four times a day.

Missed dose—If you miss a dose of this medicine, take it as soon as possible. However, if it is within 2 hours of your next dose, skip the missed dose and go back to your regular dosing schedule. Do not double doses.

Storage—To store this medicine:
- Keep out of the reach of children.
- Store away from heat and direct light.
- Do not store in the bathroom, near the kitchen sink, or in other damp places. Heat or moisture may cause the medicine to break down.
- Do not keep outdated medicine or medicine no longer needed. Be sure that any discarded medicine is out of the reach of children.

Precautions While Using This Medicine

It is important that your doctor check your progress at regular visits. Also, you must have your blood tested every other week for at least 16 weeks when you first start using tacrine to see if this medicine is affecting your liver. If all of the blood tests are normal, you will still need regular testing, but then your doctor may decide to do the tests less often.

Tell your doctor if your symptoms get worse, or if you notice any new symptoms.

Before you have any kind of surgery, dental treatment, or emergency treatment, tell the medical doctor or dentist in charge that you are taking this medicine. Taking tacrine together with medicines that are sometimes used during surgery or dental or emergency treatments may increase the effects of these medicines.

Tacrine may cause some people to become dizzy, clumsy, or unsteady. Make sure you know how you react to this medicine before you do anything that could be dangerous if you are dizzy, clumsy, or unsteady.

Do not stop taking this medicine or decrease your dose without first checking with your doctor. Stopping this medicine suddenly or decreasing the dose by a large amount may cause mental or behavior changes.

If you think you or someone else may have taken an overdose of tacrine, get emergency help at once. Taking an overdose of tacrine may lead to seizures or shock. Some signs of shock are large pupils, irregular breathing, and fast weak pulse. Other signs of an overdose are severe nausea and vomiting, increasing muscle weakness, greatly increased sweating, and greatly increased watering of the mouth.

Side Effects of This Medicine

Along with its needed effects, a medicine may cause some unwanted effects. Some side effects will have signs or symptoms that you can see or feel. Your doctor may watch for others by doing certain tests

Tacrine may cause some serious side effects, including liver problems. You and your doctor should discuss the good this medicine will do as well as the risks of receiving it.

Check with your doctor as soon as possible if any of the following side effects occur:

More common

Clumsiness or unsteadiness; diarrhea; loss of appetite; nausea; vomiting

Less common

Fainting; fast or pounding heartbeat; fever; high or low blood pressure; skin rash; slow heartbeat

Rare

Aggression, irritability, or nervousness; change in stool color; convulsions (seizures); cough, tightness in chest, troubled breathing, or wheezing; stiffness of arms or legs, slow movement, or trembling and shaking of hands and fingers; trouble in urinating; yellow eyes or skin

Symptoms of overdose

Convulsions (seizures); greatly increased sweating; greatly increased watering of mouth; increasing muscle weakness; low blood pressure; nausea (severe); shock (fast weak pulse, irregular breathing, large pupils); slow heartbeat; vomiting (severe)

This medicine may also cause the following side effect that your doctor will watch for:

More common

Liver problems

Other side effects may occur that usually do not need medical attention. These side effects may go away during treatment as your body adjusts to the medicine. However, check with your doctor if any of the following side effects continue or are bothersome:

More common

Abdominal or stomach pain or cramping; dizziness; headache; indigestion; muscle aches or pain

Less common

Belching; fast breathing; flushing of skin; general feeling of discomfort or illness; increased sweating; increased urination; increased watering of eyes; increased watering of mouth; runny nose; swelling of feet or lower legs; trouble in sleeping

Other side effects not listed above may also occur in some patients. If you notice any other effects, check with your doctor.

Developed: 08/05/94
Interim revision: 08/24/95

TACROLIMUS Systemic

A commonly used brand name in the U.S. and Canada is Prograf.

Description

Tacrolimus (ta-KROE-li-mus) belongs to a group of medicines known as immunosuppressive agents. It is used to lower the body's natural immunity in patients who receive organ (for example, kidney, liver, pancreas, lung, and heart) transplants.

When a patient receives an organ transplant, the body's white blood cells will try to get rid of (reject) the transplanted organ. Tacrolimus works by preventing the white blood cells from getting rid of the transplanted organ.

Tacrolimus may also be used for other indications, as determined by your doctor.

Tacrolimus is a very strong medicine. It can cause side effects that can be very serious, such as kidney problems. It may also reduce the body's ability to fight infections. You and your doctor should talk about the good this medicine will do as well as the risks of using it.

Tacrolimus is available only with your doctor's prescription, in the following dosage forms:

Oral
- Capsules (U.S. and Canada)

Parenteral
- Injection (U.S. and Canada)

Before Using This Medicine

In deciding to use a medicine, the risks of taking the medicine must be weighed against the good it will do. This is a decision you and your doctor will make. For tacrolimus, the following should be considered:

Allergies—Tell your health care professional if you have ever had any unusual or allergic reaction to tacrolimus. Also, if you will be receiving this medicine by injection, tell your health care professional if you are allergic to any other substances, such as castor oil.

Pregnancy—Some women have become pregnant and had babies while receiving tacrolimus after an organ transplantation. Some of the newborn babies had temporary kidney problems after birth. Some babies were born prematurely.

Breast-feeding—Tacrolimus passes into breast milk. There is a chance that it causes the same side effects in the baby that it does in the mother. It may be necessary for you to stop breast-feeding during treatment.

Children—This medicine does not cause different types of side effects or problems in children than it does in adults, although some side effects may occur more or less often than they do in adult patients.

Older adults—There is no specific information comparing the use of tacrolimus in the elderly with the use in other age groups. Tacrolimus is not expected to cause different side effects or problems in older people than it does in younger adults. However, older patients may need lower doses of tacrolimus.

Dental—The effects of tacrolimus may cause increased infections and delayed healing. Dental work, whenever possible, should be completed prior to beginning this medicine.

Other medicines—Although certain medicines should not be used together at all, in other cases two different medicines may be used together even if an interaction might occur. In these cases, your doctor may want to change the dose, or other precautions may be necessary. When you are taking tacrolimus, it is especially important that your health care professional knows if you are taking any of the following:

- Amiloride or
- Spironolactone (e.g., Aldactone) or
- Triamterene (e.g., Dyrenium)—Since both tacrolimus and these medicines increase the amount of potassium in the body, potassium levels could become too high
- Cyclosporine (e.g., Neoral)—May increase the effects of tacrolimus by increasing the amount of this medicine in the body; may cause kidney problems
- Danazol (e.g., Danocrine) or
- Erythromycins (medicine for infection) or
- Fluconazole (e.g., Diflucan) or
- Itraconazole (e.g., Sporanox) or
- Ketoconazole (e.g., Nizoral)—May increase the effects of tacrolimus by increasing the amount of this medicine in the body
- Rifampin (e.g., Rifadin)—May decrease the effects of tacrolimus by decreasing the amount of this medicine in the body

Other medical problems—The presence of other medical problems may affect the use of tacrolimus. Make sure you tell your doctor if you have any other medical problems, especially:

- Cancer—Tacrolimus can make this condition worse
- Chickenpox (including recent exposure) or
- Herpes zoster (shingles)—Risk of severe disease affecting other parts of the body
- Diabetes mellitus (sugar diabetes)—Tacrolimus can increase the amount of sugar in the blood
- Hepatitis or
- Kidney disease or
- Liver disease, other—Tacrolimus can have harmful effects on the kidney in patients with these conditions; a lower dose of tacrolimus may be needed in patients with these conditions
- Hyperkalemia (high amount of potassium in the blood) or
- Nervous system problems—Tacrolimus can make these conditions worse
- Infection—Tacrolimus decreases the body's ability to fight infection

Proper Use of This Medicine

Take this medicine only as directed by your doctor. Do not take more or less of it and do not take it more often than your doctor ordered. The exact amount of medicine you need has been carefully worked out. Taking too much may increase the chance of side effects, while taking too little may lead to rejection of your transplanted organ.

To help you remember to take your medicine, try to get into the habit of taking it at the same time each day. This will also help tacrolimus work better by keeping a constant amount in the blood.

Absorption of this medicine may be changed if you change your diet. This medicine should be taken consistently with respect to meals. You should not change the type or amount of food you eat unless you discuss it with your health care professional.

Do not stop taking this medicine without first checking with your doctor. You may have to take medicine for the rest of your life to prevent your body from rejecting the transplant.

Dosing—The dose of tacrolimus will be different for different patients. *Follow your doctor's orders or the directions on the label.* The following information includes only the average doses of tacrolimus. *If your dose is different, do not change it* unless your doctor tells you to do so.

The number of capsules that you take depends on the strength of the medicine in the capsule and the dose prescribed by your doctor. Also, *the number of doses you take each day, the time allowed between doses, and the length of time you take the medicine depend on the medical problem for which you are taking tacrolimus.*

- For *oral* dosage form (capsules):
  —Adults, teenagers, or children—Dose is based on body weight. The usual dose is 0.1 to 0.3 milligrams (mg) per kilogram (kg) (0.045 to 0.14 mg per pound) of body weight a day.
- For *injection* dosage form:
  —Adults, teenagers or children—Dose is based on body weight. The usual dose is 0.01 to 0.05 mg per kg (0.0045 to 0.0227 mg per pound) of body weight a day.

Missed dose—If you miss a dose of tacrolimus and remember it within 12 hours, take the missed dose as soon as you remember. However, if it is almost time for the next dose, skip the missed dose, go back to your regular dosing schedule, and check with your doctor. Do not double doses.

Storage—To store this medicine:
- Keep out of the reach of children.
- Store away from heat and direct light.
- Do not store in the bathroom, near the kitchen sink, or in other damp places.
- Do not keep outdated medicine or medicine no longer needed. Be sure that any discarded medicine is out of reach of children.

Precautions While Using This Medicine

It is very important that your doctor check your progress at regular visits. Your doctor will want to do laboratory tests to make sure that tacrolimus is working properly and to check for unwanted effects.

While you are taking tacrolimus, it is important to maintain good dental hygiene and see a dentist regularly for teeth cleaning.

Raw oysters or other shellfish may contain bacteria that can cause serious illness, and possibly death. This is more likely to be a problem if these foods are eaten by patients with certain medical conditions. Even eating oysters from "clean" water or good restaurants does not guarantee that the oysters do not contain the bacteria. Symptoms of this infection include sudden chills, fever, nausea, vomiting, blood poisoning, and sometimes death. Eating raw shellfish is not a problem for most healthy people; however, patients with the following conditions may be at greater risk: cancer, immune disorders, organ transplantation, long-term corticosteroid use (as for asthma, arthritis, or organ transplantation), liver disease (including viral hepatitis), excess alcohol intake (2-3 drinks or more per day), diabetes, stomach problems (including previous stomach surgery and low stomach acid), and hemochromatosis (an iron disorder). *Do not eat raw oysters or other shellfish while you are taking tacrolimus. Be sure oysters and shellfish are fully cooked.*

While you are being treated with tacrolimus, and after you stop treatment with it, *it is important to see your doctor about the immunizations (vaccinations) you should receive. Do not get any immunizations without your doctor's approval.* Tacrolimus lowers your body's resistance. For some immunizations, there is a chance you might get the infection the immunization is meant to prevent. For other immunizations, it may be especially important to receive the immunization to prevent a disease. In addition, other persons living in your house should not take oral poliovirus vaccine since there is a chance they could pass the poliovirus on to you. Also, avoid persons who have recently taken oral poliovirus vaccine. Do not get close to them, and do not stay in the same room with them for very long. If you cannot take these precautions, you should consider wearing a protective face mask that covers the nose and mouth.

Treatment with tacrolimus may also increase the chance of getting other infections. If you can, avoid people with colds or other infections. If you think you are getting a cold or other infection, check with your doctor.

Tacrolimus is not available in all countries. *If you are traveling to another country, be sure you will have a supply of your medicine.*

Grapefruits and grapefruit juice may increase the effects of tacrolimus by increasing the amount of this medicine in the body. *You should not eat grapefruit or drink grapefruit juice while you are taking this medicine.*

Side Effects of This Medicine

Along with its needed effects, a medicine may cause some unwanted effects. Some side effects will have signs or symptoms that you can see or feel. Your doctor will watch for others by doing certain tests.

Also, because of the way tacrolimus acts on the body, there is a chance that it may cause effects that may not occur until years after the medicine is used. These delayed effects may include certain types of cancer, such as lymphomas or skin cancers.

Check with your doctor or nurse immediately if any of the following side effects occur:

More common

Abdominal pain; abnormal dreams; agitation; anxiety; chills; confusion; convulsions (seizures); diarrhea; dizziness; fever and sore throat; flu-like symptoms; frequent urination; hallucinations (seeing or hearing things that are not there); headache; infection; itching; loss of appetite; loss of energy or weakness; mental depression; muscle trembling or twitching; nausea; nervousness; pale skin; shortness of breath; skin rash; swelling of feet or lower legs; tingling; trembling and shaking of hands; trouble in sleeping; unusual bleeding or bruising; unusual tiredness or weakness; vomiting

Less common

Blurred vision; chest pain; increased sensitivity to pain; muscle cramps; numbness or pain in legs; ringing in ears; sweating

Rare

Flushing of face or neck; general feeling of discomfort or illness; weight loss; wheezing

This medicine may also cause the following side effects that your doctor will watch for:

More common

Hyperkalemia (too much potassium in the blood); hypomagnesemia (not enough magnesium in the blood); kidney problems

Less common

Hyperlipidemia (high cholesterol); hypertension (high blood pressure)

Other side effects not listed above may also occur in some patients. If you notice any other effects, check with your doctor.

Additional Information

Once a medicine has been approved for marketing for a certain use, experience may show that it is also useful for other medical problems. Although not specifically included in the product labeling, tacrolimus is used in certain patients with the following medical conditions:

- Bone marrow transplantation
- Uveitis, severe, refractory (an eye condition)

For patients receiving bone marrow transplantation, tacrolimus may work by preventing the cells from the transplanted bone marrow from attacking the cells of the patient. The dose of tacrolimus for patients receiving bone marrow transplantation is based on body weight. The usual dose is 0.12 to 0.3 mg per kg (0.05 to 0.14 mg per pound) of body weight a day for patients taking tacrolimus by mouth, and 0.04 to 0.1 mg per kg (0.018 to 0.045 mg per pound) of body weight a day for patients receiving tacrolimus by injection.

The dose of tacrolimus for patients with severe, refractory uveitis is based on body weight. For severe, refractory uveitis, the usual dose is 0.1 to 0.15 mg per kg (0.045 to 0.068 mg per pound) of body weight a day.

Other than the above information, there is no additional information relating to proper use, precautions, or side effects for these uses.

Developed: 08/14/97

TAMOXIFEN Systemic

Some commonly used brand names are:

In the U.S.—

Nolvadex

In Canada—

Alpha-Tamoxifen
Med Tamoxifen
Nolvadex
Nolvadex-D
Novo-Tamoxifen
Tamofen
Tamone
Tamoplex

Description

Tamoxifen (ta-MOX-i-fen) is a medicine that blocks the effects of the hormone estrogen in the body. It is used to treat breast cancer in women or men.

The exact way that tamoxifen works against cancer is not known but it may be related to the way it blocks the effects of estrogen on the body.

Before you begin treatment with tamoxifen, you and your doctor should talk about the good this medicine will do as well as the risks of using it.

Tamoxifen is available only with your doctor's prescription, in the following dosage forms:

Oral

- Tablets (U.S. and Canada)
- Enteric-coated tablets (Canada)

Before Using This Medicine

In deciding to use a medicine, the risks of taking the medicine must be weighed against the good it will do. This is a decision you and your doctor will make. For tamoxifen, the following should be considered:

Allergies—Tell your doctor if you have ever had any unusual or allergic reaction to tamoxifen.

Pregnancy—Tell your doctor if you are pregnant or if you intend to become pregnant. Tamoxifen use in women has been shown to cause miscarriages, birth defects, death of the fetus, and vaginal bleeding. Studies in rats and rabbits have also shown that tamoxifen causes miscarriages, death of the fetus, and slowed learning. Studies in animals have also shown that tamoxifen may cause some of the same problems as an estrogen called diethylstilbestrol (DES). DES causes genital tract problems and, rarely, an increased risk of cancer of the cervix or vagina in daughters of women who took it during their pregnancy; it is not known whether tamoxifen causes these same problems.

Be sure that you have discussed this with your doctor before taking this medicine. It is best to use some kind of birth control while you are taking tamoxifen and for about two months after you stop taking it. However, do not use oral contraceptives (''the Pill'') since they may interfere with this medicine. Tell your doctor right away if you think you have become pregnant while taking tamoxifen.

Breast-feeding—Because this medicine may cause serious side effects, breast-feeding is generally not recommended while you are taking it.

Older adults—Many medicines have not been studied specifically in older people. Therefore, it may not be known whether they work exactly the same way they do in younger adults. Although there is no specific information comparing use of tamoxifen in the elderly with use in other age groups, this medicine is not expected to cause different side effects or problems in older people than it does in younger adults.

Other medicines—Although certain medicines should not be used together at all, in other cases two different medicines may be used together even if an interaction might occur. In these cases, your doctor may want to change the dose, or other precautions may be necessary. Tell your health care professional if you are taking any other prescription or nonprescription (over-the-counter [OTC]) medicine.

Other medical problems—The presence of other medical problems may affect the use of tamoxifen. Make sure you tell your doctor if you have any other medical problems, especially:

- Cataracts or other eye problems—Tamoxifen may also cause these problems
- High cholesterol levels in the blood—Tamoxifen can increase cholesterol levels

Proper Use of This Medicine

Use this medicine only as directed by your doctor. Do not use more or less of it, and do not use it more often than your doctor ordered. The exact amount of medicine you need has been carefully worked out. Taking too much may increase the chance of side effects, while taking too little may not improve your condition.

For patients taking *enteric-coated tamoxifen tablets:*

- The tablets must be swallowed whole. Do not crush them or break them up before taking.

Tamoxifen sometimes causes mild nausea and vomiting. However, it may have to be taken for several weeks or months to be effective. Even if you begin to feel ill, *do not stop using this medicine without first checking with your doctor.* Ask your health care professional for ways to lessen these effects.

If you vomit shortly after taking a dose of tamoxifen, check with your doctor. You will be told whether to take the dose again or to wait until the next scheduled dose.

Dosing—The dose of tamoxifen will be different for different patients. *Follow your doctor's orders or the directions on the label.* The following information includes only the average doses of tamoxifen. *If your dose is different, do not change it* unless your doctor tells you to do so.

- For *oral* dosage forms (tablets or enteric-coated tablets):
  —For breast cancer in women or men:
    - Adults—10 to 20 milligrams (mg) two times a day, in the morning and evening.

Missed dose—If you miss a dose of this medicine, do not take the missed dose at all and do not double the next one. Instead, go back to your regular dosing schedule and check with your doctor.

Storage—To store this medicine:

- Keep out of the reach of children.
- Store away from heat and direct light.
- Do not store in the bathroom, near the kitchen sink, or in other damp places. Heat or moisture may cause the medicine to break down.
- Do not keep outdated medicine or medicine no longer needed. Be sure that any discarded medicine is out of the reach of children.

Precautions While Using This Medicine

It is very important that your doctor check your progress at regular visits to make sure that this medicine is working properly and to check for unwanted effects.

For women: Tamoxifen may make you more fertile. It is best to use some type of birth control while you are taking it. However, do not use oral contraceptives (the ''Pill'') since they may change the effects of tamoxifen. Tell your doctor right away if you think you have become pregnant while taking this medicine.

For patients taking *enteric-coated tamoxifen tablets:*

- If you are also taking an antacid, take this medicine at least 1 or 2 hours before or after taking the antacid. Taking the two medicines too close together may cause the enteric coating to dissolve too early. This may increase the risk of unwanted effects from tamoxifen.

Side Effects of This Medicine

Along with its needed effects, a medicine may cause some unwanted effects. Some side effects will have signs or symptoms that you can see or feel. Your doctor will watch for others by doing certain tests.

Also, because of the way this medicine acts on the body, there is a chance that it might cause other unwanted effects that may not occur until months or years after the medicine is used. Tamoxifen has been reported to increase the chance of cancer of the uterus (womb) in some women taking it. It also causes liver cancer in rats. In addition, tamoxifen has been reported to cause cataracts and other eye problems. Discuss these possible effects with your doctor.

Check with your doctor as soon as possible if any of the following side effects occur:

For both females and males

Less common or rare

Blurred vision; confusion; pain or swelling in legs; shortness of breath; weakness or sleepiness; yellow eyes or skin

For females only

Less common or rare

Change in vaginal discharge; pain or feeling of pressure in pelvis; vaginal bleeding

This medicine may also cause the following side effect that your doctor will watch for:

For both females and males

Less common or rare

Cataracts in the eyes or other eye problems; liver problems

Other side effects may occur that usually do not need medical attention. These side effects may go away during treatment as your body adjusts to the medicine. Also, your health care professional may be able to tell you about ways to prevent or reduce some of these side effects. Check with your health care professional if any of the following side effects continue or are bothersome or if you have any questions about them:

For both females and males

Less common

Bone pain; headache; nausea and/or vomiting (mild); skin rash or dryness

For females only

More common

Hot flashes; weight gain

Less common

Changes in menstrual period; itching in genital area; vaginal discharge

For males only

Less common

Impotence or decreased sexual interest

Other side effects not listed above may also occur in some patients. If you notice any other effects, check with your doctor.

Revised: 08/12/94

TERAZOSIN Systemic

A commonly used brand name in the U.S. and Canada is Hytrin.

Description

Terazosin (ter-AY-zoe-sin) is used to treat high blood pressure (hypertension).

High blood pressure adds to the work load of the heart and arteries. If it continues for a long time, the heart and arteries may not function properly. This can damage the blood vessels of the brain, heart, and kidneys, resulting in a stroke, heart failure, or kidney failure. High blood pressure may also increase the risk of heart attacks. These problems may be less likely to occur if blood pressure is controlled.

Terazosin helps to lower blood pressure by relaxing blood vessels so that blood passes through them more easily.

Terazosin is also used to treat benign enlargement of the prostate (benign prostatic hyperplasia [BPH]). Benign enlargement of the prostate is a problem that can occur in men as they get older. The prostate gland is located below the bladder. As the prostate gland enlarges, certain muscles in the gland may become tight and get in the way of the tube that drains urine from the bladder. This can cause problems in urinating, such as a need to urinate often, a weak stream when urinating, or a feeling of not being able to empty the bladder completely.

Terazosin helps relax the muscles in the prostate and the opening of the bladder. This may help increase the flow of urine and/or decrease the symptoms. However, terazosin will not help shrink the prostate. The prostate may continue to grow. This may cause the symptoms to become worse over time. Therefore, even though terazosin may lessen the problems caused by enlarged prostate now, surgery still may be needed in the future.

Terazosin is available only with your doctor's prescription, in the following dosage form:

Oral

- Tablets (U.S. and Canada)

Before Using This Medicine

In deciding to use a medicine, the risks of taking the medicine must be weighed against the good it will do. This is a decision you and your doctor will make. For terazosin, the following should be considered:

Allergies—Tell your doctor if you have ever had any unusual or allergic reaction to terazosin, prazosin, or doxazosin. Also tell your health care professional if you are allergic to any other substances, such as foods, preservatives, or dyes.

Pregnancy—Studies have not been done in humans. Studies in animals given many times the highest recommended human dose have not shown that terazosin causes birth defects. However, these studies have shown a decrease in successful pregnancies.

Breast-feeding—It is not known whether terazosin passes into breast milk. Although most medicines pass into breast milk in small amounts, many of them may be used safely while breast-feeding. Mothers who are taking this medicine and who wish to breast-feed should discuss this with their doctor.

Children—Studies on this medicine have been done only in adult patients, and there is no specific information comparing use of terazosin in children with use in other age groups.

Older adults—Dizziness, lightheadedness, or fainting (especially when getting up from a lying or sitting position) may be more likely to occur in the elderly, who are more sensitive to the effects of terazosin.

Other medicines—Although certain medicines should not be used together at all, in other cases two different medicines may be used together even if an interaction might occur. In these cases, your doctor may want to change the dose, or other precautions may be necessary. Tell your health care professional if you are taking any other prescription or nonprescription (over-the-counter [OTC]) medicine.

Other medical problems—The presence of other medical problems may affect the use of terazosin. Make sure you tell your doctor if you have any other medical problems, especially:

- Angina (chest pain)—Terazosin may make this condition worse
- Heart disease (severe)—Terazosin may make this condition worse
- Kidney disease—Possible increased sensitivity to the effects of terazosin

Proper Use of This Medicine

For patients *taking this medicine for high blood pressure:*

- In addition to the use of the medicine your doctor has prescribed, treatment for your high blood pressure may include weight control and care in the types of foods you eat, especially foods high in sodium. Your doctor will tell you which of these are most important for you. You should check with your doctor before changing your diet.
- Many patients who have high blood pressure will not notice any signs of the problem. In fact, many may feel normal. It is very important that you *take your medicine exactly as directed* and that you keep your appointments with your doctor even if you feel well.
- Remember that terazosin will not cure your high blood pressure but it does help control it. Therefore, you must continue to take it as directed if you expect to lower your blood pressure and keep it down. *You may have to take high blood pressure medicine for the rest of your life.* If high blood pressure is not treated, it can cause serious problems such as heart failure, blood vessel disease, stroke, or kidney disease.

For patients *taking this medicine for benign enlargement of the prostate:*

- Remember that terazosin will not shrink the size of your prostate but it does help to relieve the symptoms.
- It may take up to 6 weeks before your symptoms get better.

To help you remember to take your medicine, try to get into the habit of taking it at the same time each day.

Dosing—The dose of terazosin will be different for different patients. *Follow your doctor's orders or the directions on the label.* The following information includes only the average doses of terazosin. *If your dose is different, do not change it* unless your doctor tells you to do so.

The number of tablets that you take depends on the strength of the medicine.

- For *oral* dosage form (tablets):
  - —For benign enlargement of the prostate:
    - Adults—At first, 1 milligram (mg) taken at bedtime. Then, 5 to 10 mg once a day.
  - —For high blood pressure:
    - Adults—At first, 1 mg taken at bedtime. Then, 1 to 5 mg once a day.
    - Children—Use and dose must be determined by your doctor.

Missed dose—If you miss a dose of this medicine, take it as soon as possible the same day. However, if you do not remember the missed dose until the next day, skip the missed dose and go back to your regular dosing schedule. Do not double doses.

Storage—To store this medicine:

- Keep out of the reach of children.
- Store away from heat and direct light.
- Do not store in the bathroom, near the kitchen sink, or in other damp places. Heat or moisture may cause the medicine to break down.
- Do not keep outdated medicine or medicine no longer needed. Be sure that any discarded medicine is out of the reach of children.

Precautions While Using This Medicine

It is important that your doctor check your progress at regular visits to make sure that this medicine is working properly.

For patients *taking this medicine for high blood pressure:*

- *Do not take other medicines unless they have been discussed with your doctor.* This especially includes over-the-counter (nonprescription) medicines for appetite control, asthma, colds, cough, hay fever, or sinus problems, since they may tend to increase your blood pressure.

Dizziness, lightheadedness, or sudden fainting may occur after you take this medicine, especially when you get up from a lying or sitting position. These effects are more likely to occur when you take the first dose of this medicine. Taking the first dose at bedtime may prevent problems. However, *be especially careful if you need to get up during the night.* These effects may also occur with any doses you take after the first dose. Getting up slowly may help lessen this problem. *If you feel dizzy, lie down so that you do not faint.* Then sit for a few moments before standing to prevent the dizziness from returning.

The dizziness, lightheadedness, or fainting is more likely to occur if you drink alcohol, stand for long periods of time, exercise, or if the weather is hot. *While you are taking this medicine, be careful to limit the amount of alcohol you drink. Also, use extra care during exercise or hot weather or if you must stand for long periods of time.*

Terazosin may cause some people to become drowsy or less alert than they are normally. *Make sure you know how you react to this medicine before you drive, use machines, or do anything else that could be dangerous if you are dizzy, drowsy, or are not alert.* After you have taken several doses of this medicine, these effects should lessen.

Side Effects of This Medicine

Along with its needed effects, a medicine may cause some unwanted effects. Although not all of these side effects may occur, if they do occur they may need medical attention.

Check with your doctor as soon as possible if any of the following side effects occur:

More common
Dizziness

Less common
Chest pain; dizziness or lightheadedness when getting up from a lying or sitting position; fainting (sudden); fast or irregular heartbeat; pounding heartbeat; shortness of breath; swelling of feet or lower legs

Rare
Weight gain

Other side effects may occur that usually do not need medical attention. These side effects may go away during treatment as your body adjusts to the medicine. However, check with your doctor if any of the following side effects continue or are bothersome:

More common
Headache; unusual tiredness or weakness

Less common
Back or joint pain; blurred vision; drowsiness; nausea and vomiting; stuffy nose

Other side effects not listed above may also occur in some patients. If you notice any other effects, check with your doctor.

Revised: 06/26/92
Interim revision: 07/08/94

TERBINAFINE Systemic*

A commonly used brand name in Canada is Lamisil.

*Not commercially available in the U.S.

Description

Terbinafine (ter-BIN-a-feen) belongs to the group of medicines called antifungals. It is used to treat fungus infections of the scalp, body, groin (jock itch), feet (athlete's foot), fingernails, and toenails.

Terbinafine is available only with your doctor's prescription, in the following dosage form:

Oral
- Tablets (Canada)

Before Using This Medicine

In deciding to use a medicine, the risks of taking the medicine must be weighed against the good it will do. This is a decision you and your doctor will make. For terbinafine, the following should be considered:

Allergies—Tell your doctor if you have ever had any unusual or allergic reaction to terbinafine. Also tell your health care professional if you are allergic to any other substances, such as foods, preservatives, or dyes.

Pregnancy—Terbinafine has not been studied in pregnant women. Before taking any medicine, make sure your doctor knows if you are pregnant or if you may become pregnant.

Breast-feeding—Terbinafine passes into breast milk. Mothers who are taking this medicine and wish to breast-feed should discuss this with their doctor.

Children—Studies on this medicine have been done only in adult patients, and there is no specific information comparing use of terbinafine in children with use in other age groups.

Older adults—Many medicines have not been studied specifically in older people. Therefore, it may not be known whether they work exactly the same way they do in younger adults or if they cause different side effects or problems in older people. There is no specific information comparing use of terbinafine in the elderly with use in other age groups.

Other medicines—Although certain medicines should not be used together at all, in other cases two different medicines may be used together even if an interaction might occur. In these cases, your doctor may want to change the dose, or other precautions may be necessary. When you are taking terbinafine, it is especially important that your health care professional know if you are taking any of the following:

- Acetaminophen (e.g., Tylenol) (with long-term, high-dose use) or
- Amiodarone (e.g., Cordarone) or
- Anabolic steroids (nandrolone [e.g., Anabolin], oxandrolone [e.g., Anavar], oxymetholone [e.g., Anadrol], stanozolol [e.g., Winstrol]) or
- Androgens (male hormones) or
- Antithyroid agents (medicine for overactive thyroid) or
- Carmustine (e.g., BiCNU) or
- Chloroquine (e.g., Aralen) or
- Dantrolene (e.g., Dantrium) or
- Daunorubicin (e.g., Cerubidine) or
- Estrogens (female hormones) or
- Etretinate (e.g., Tegison) or
- Gold salts (medicine for arthritis) or
- Hydroxychloroquine (e.g., Plaquenil) or
- Mercaptopurine (e.g., Purinethol) or
- Methotrexate (e.g., Mexate) or
- Methyldopa (e.g., Aldomet) or
- Naltrexone (e.g., Trexan) (with long-term, high-dose use) or
- Other anti-infectives by mouth or by injection (medicine for infection) or

- Phenothiazines (acetophenazine [e.g., Tindal], chlorpromazine [e.g., Thorazine], fluphenazine [e.g., Prolixin], mesoridazine [e.g., Serentil], perphenazine [e.g., Trilafon], prochlorperazine [e.g., Compazine], promazine [e.g., Sparine], promethazine [e.g., Phenergan], thioridazine [e.g., Mellaril], trifluoperazine [e.g., Stelazine], triflupromazine [e.g., Vesprin], trimeprazine [e.g., Temaril]) or
- Plicamycin (e.g., Mithracin)—Use of these medicines with terbinafine may increase the chance of side effects affecting the liver
- Azole antifungals (fluconazole [e.g., Diflucan], itraconazole [e.g., Sporanox], ketoconazole [e.g., Nizoral]) or
- Chloramphenicol (e.g., Chloromycetin) or
- Cimetidine (e.g., Tagamet) or
- Clarithromycin (e.g., Biaxin) or
- Diltiazem (e.g., Cardizem) or
- Erythromycins (e.g., EES, E-Mycin) or
- Isoniazid (e.g., INH, Nydrazid) or
- Quinine (e.g., Quinamm) or
- Ranitidine (e.g., Zantac) or
- Verapamil (e.g., Calan)—Use of these medicines with terbinafine may increase the chance of side effects of terbinafine
- Carbamazepine (e.g., Tegretol) or
- Corticosteroids (cortisone-like medicine) or
- Griseofulvin (e.g., Fulvicin, Grisovin) or
- Phenobarbital (e.g., Luminal) or
- Phenylbutazone (e.g., Butazolidin) or
- Primidone (e.g., Mysoline) or
- Rifampin (e.g., Rifadin)—Use of these medicines with terbinafine may prevent terbinafine from working properly
- Disulfiram (e.g., Antabuse) or
- Divalproex (e.g., Depakote) or
- Oral contraceptives (birth control pills) containing estrogen or
- Valproic acid (e.g., Depakene)—Use of these medicines with terbinafine may increase the chance of side effects of terbinafine, especially those affecting the liver
- Phenytoin (e.g., Dilantin)—Use of this medicine with terbinafine may prevent terbinafine from working properly and may increase the chance of side effects affecting the liver

Other medical problems—The presence of other medical problems may affect the use of terbinafine. Make sure you tell your doctor if you have any other medical problems, especially:

- Alcohol abuse (or history of) or
- Kidney disease or
- Liver disease—These conditions may increase the chance of side effects caused by terbinafine

Proper Use of This Medicine

Terbinafine may be taken with food or on an empty stomach.

To help clear up your infection completely, *it is very important that you keep taking this medicine for the full time of treatment,* even if your symptoms begin to clear up or you begin to feel better after a few days. Since fungus infections may be very slow to clear up, you may need to take this medicine for several weeks or months. If you stop taking this medicine too soon, your symptoms may return.

This medicine works best when there is a constant amount in the blood. *To help keep the amount constant, do not miss any doses. Also, it is best to take the doses at the same times every day.* If you need help in planning the best time to take your medicine, check with your health care professional.

Dosing—The dose of terbinafine may be different for different patients. *Follow your doctor's orders or the directions on the label.* The following information includes only the average doses of terbinafine. Your dose may be different if you have kidney or liver disease. *If your dose is different, do not change it* unless your doctor tells you to do so.

The number of tablets that you take depends on the strength of the medicine. Also, *the length of time you take the medicine depends on the medical problem for which you are taking terbinafine.*

- For *oral* dosage form (tablets):
  - —For onychomycosis (fungus infections of the fingernails or toenails):
    - Adults and teenagers—125 milligrams (mg) two times a day or 250 mg once a day for 6 weeks to 3 months.
    - Children—Use and dose must be determined by the doctor.
  - —For tinea corporis (ringworm of the body):
    - Adults and teenagers—125 mg two times a day or 250 mg once a day for 2 to 4 weeks.
    - Children—Use and dose must be determined by the doctor.
  - —For tinea cruris (ringworm of the groin; jock itch):
    - Adults and teenagers—125 mg two times a day or 250 mg once a day for 2 to 4 weeks.
    - Children—Use and dose must be determined by the doctor.
  - —For tinea pedis (ringworm of the foot; athlete's foot):
    - Adults and teenagers—125 mg two times a day or 250 mg once a day for 2 to 6 weeks.
    - Children—Use and dose must be determined by the doctor.

Missed dose—If you miss a dose of this medicine, take it as soon as possible. This will help to keep a constant amount of medicine in the blood. However, if it is almost time for your next dose, skip the missed dose and go back to your regular dosing schedule. Do not double doses.

Storage—To store this medicine:

- Keep out of the reach of children.
- Store away from heat and direct light.
- Do not store this medicine in the bathroom, near the kitchen sink, or in other damp places. Heat or moisture may cause the medicine to break down.
- Do not keep outdated medicine or medicine no longer needed. Be sure that any discarded medicine is out of the reach of children.

Precautions While Using This Medicine

It is important that your doctor check your progress at regular visits. This will allow your doctor to check for any unwanted effects.

If your symptoms do not improve within a few weeks (or months for onychomycosis), or if they become worse, check with your doctor.

Liver problems may be more likely to occur if you drink alcoholic beverages while you are taking this medicine. Therefore, you should not drink alcoholic beverages while you are taking this medicine.

Side Effects of This Medicine

Along with its needed effects, a medicine may cause some unwanted effects. Although not all of these effects may occur, if they do occur they may need medical attention.

Check with your doctor immediately if any of the following side effects occur:

Less common
Skin rash or itching

Rare
Aching joints and muscles; dark urine; difficulty in swallowing; fever, chills, or sore throat; loss of appetite; pale skin; pale stools; redness, blistering, peeling, or loosening of skin; unusual bleeding or bruising; unusual tiredness or weakness; yellow skin or eyes

Other side effects may occur that usually do not need medical attention. These side effects may go away during treatment as your body adjusts to the medicine. However, check with your doctor if any of the following side effects continue or are bothersome:

More common
Diarrhea; nausea and vomiting; stomach pain (mild)

Less common
Change of taste or loss of taste

Other side effects not listed above may also occur in some patients. If you notice any other effects, check with your doctor.

Developed: 06/22/95

TERBINAFINE Topical†

A commonly used brand name in the U.S. is Lamisil.

†Not commercially available in Canada.

Description

Terbinafine (TER-bin-a-feen) is used to treat infections caused by a fungus. It works by killing the fungus or preventing its growth.

Terbinafine is applied to the skin to treat:
- ringworm of the body (tinea corporis);
- ringworm of the foot (interdigital and plantar tinea pedis; athlete's foot); and
- ringworm of the groin (tinea cruris; jock itch).

Terbinafine is available only with your doctor's prescription, in the following dosage form:

Topical
- Cream (U.S.)

Before Using This Medicine

In deciding to use a medicine, the risks of using the medicine must be weighed against the good it will do. This is a decision you and your doctor will make. For terbinafine, the following should be considered:

Allergies—Tell your doctor if you have ever had any unusual or allergic reaction to terbinafine. Also tell your health care professional if you are allergic to any other substances, such as foods, preservatives, or dyes.

Pregnancy—Terbinafine has not been studied in pregnant women. However, terbinafine has not been shown to cause birth defects or other problems in animal studies.

Breast-feeding—Oral terbinafine passes into the breast milk. It is not known whether topical terbinafine passes into breast milk. Although most medicines pass into breast milk in small amounts, many of them may be used safely while breast-feeding. Mothers who are using this medicine and who wish to breast-feed should discuss this with their doctor. Nursing mothers should not apply topical terbinafine to the breasts.

Children—Studies on this medicine have been done only in adult patients, and there is no specific information comparing use of terbinafine in children under the age of 12 with use in other age groups.

Older adults—Many medicines have not been studied specifically in older people. Therefore, it may not be known whether they work exactly the same way they do in younger adults. Although there is no specific information comparing use of terbinafine in the elderly with use in other age groups, this medicine is not expected to cause different side effects or problems in older people than it does in younger adults.

Other medicines—Although certain medicines should not be used together at all, in other cases two different medicines may be used together even if an interaction might occur. In these cases, your doctor may want to change the dose, or other precautions may be necessary. Tell your health care professional if you are using any other topical prescription or nonprescription (over-the-counter [OTC]) medicine that is to be applied to the same area of the skin.

Other medical problems—The presence of other medical problems may affect the use of terbinafine. Make sure you tell your doctor if you have any other medical problems, especially:
- Fungus infection of the nails—condition may decrease the effect of terbinafine

Proper Use of This Medicine

Apply enough terbinafine to cover the affected and surrounding skin areas and rub in gently.

Keep this medicine away from the eyes, nose, mouth, and other mucous membranes.

Do not apply an occlusive dressing (airtight covering, such as a tight bandage or plastic kitchen wrap) over this medicine unless you have been directed to do so by your doctor.

Dosing—The dose of terbinafine will be different for different patients. *Follow your doctor's orders or the directions on the label.* The following information includes only the average doses of terbinafine. *If your dose is different, do not change it* unless your doctor tells you to do so.

The number of doses you use each day, the time allowed between doses, and the length of time you use the medicine depend on the medical problem for which you are using terbinafine.

- For *topical* dosage form (cream):
  - —For tinea corporis or tinea cruris:
    - Adults and children 12 years of age and over—Use one or two times a day.
    - Infants and children up to 12 years of age—Use and dose must be determined by your doctor.
  - —For tinea pedis:
    - Adults and children 12 years of age and over—Use two times a day.
    - Infants and children up to 12 years of age—Use and dose must be determined by your doctor.

To help clear up your infection completely, it *is very important that you keep using terbinafine for the full time of treatment,* even if your symptoms begin to clear up after a few days. Since fungus infections may be very slow to clear up, you may have to continue using this medicine every day for several weeks or more. If you stop using this medicine too soon, your symptoms may return. *Do not miss any doses.*

Missed dose—If you do miss a dose of this medicine, apply it as soon as possible. However, if it is almost time for your next dose, skip the missed dose and go back to your regular dosing schedule.

Storage—To store this medicine:

- Keep out of the reach of children.
- Store away from heat and direct light.
- Keep the medicine from freezing.
- Do not keep outdated medicine or medicine no longer needed. Be sure that any discarded medicine is out of the reach of children.

Precautions While Using This Medicine

If your skin problem does not improve within 4 weeks, or if it becomes worse, check with your doctor.

To help clear up your infection completely and to help make sure it does not return, good health habits are also needed. The following measures will help reduce chafing and irritation and will also help keep the area cool and dry.

- *For patients using terbinafine for ringworm of the body:*
  - —Carefully dry yourself after bathing.
  - —Avoid too much heat and humidity if possible. Try to keep moisture from building up on affected areas of the body.
  - —Wear well-ventilated, loose-fitting clothing.
  - —Use a bland, absorbent powder (for example, talcum powder) once or twice a day. Be sure to use the powder after terbinafine cream has been applied and has disappeared into the skin.
- *For patients using terbinafine for ringworm of the groin*:
  - —Avoid wearing underwear that is tight-fitting or made from synthetic (man-made) materials (for example, rayon or nylon). Instead, wear loose-fitting, cotton underwear.
  - —Use a bland, absorbent powder (for example, talcum powder) on the skin. It is best to use the powder between the times you use terbinafine.
- *For patients using terbinafine for ringworm of the foot*:
  - —Carefully dry the feet, especially between the toes, after bathing.
  - —Avoid wearing socks made from wool or synthetic materials (for example, rayon or nylon). Instead, wear clean, cotton socks and change them daily or more often if the feet sweat a lot.
  - —Wear sandals or well-ventilated shoes (for example, shoes with holes).
  - —Use a bland, absorbent powder (for example, talcum powder) between the toes, on the feet, and in socks and shoes once or twice a day. It is best to use the powder between the times you use terbinafine.

If you have any questions about these measures, check with your health care professional.

Side Effects of This Medicine

Along with its needed effects, a medicine may cause some unwanted effects. Although not all of these side effects may occur, if they do occur they may need medical attention.

Check with your health care professional as soon as possible if any of the following side effects occur:

Rare

Redness, itching, burning, blistering, swelling, oozing, or other signs of skin irritation not present before use of this medicine

Other side effects not listed above may also occur in some patients. If you notice any other effects, check with your doctor.

Revised: 07/29/93
Interim revision: 08/19/97

TESTOLACTONE Systemic†

A commonly used brand name in the U.S. is Teslac.

†Not commercially available in Canada.

Description

Testolactone (tess-toe-LAK-tone) belongs to the general group of medicines called antineoplastics. It is used to treat some cases of breast cancer in females.

Testolactone is available only with your doctor's prescription, in the following dosage form:

Oral
- Tablets (U.S.)

Before Using This Medicine

In deciding to use a medicine, the risks of taking the medicine must be weighed against the good it will do. This is a decision you and your doctor will make. For testolactone, the following should be considered:

Allergies—Tell your doctor if you have ever had any unusual or allergic reaction to testolactone.

Pregnancy—Studies have not been done in humans. However, studies in rats at doses 2.5 to 7.5 times the human dose have shown that testolactone causes an increase in the number of fetus and infant deaths and abnormal growth.

Breast-feeding—It is not known whether testolactone passes into breast milk. However, this medicine has not been reported to cause problems in nursing babies.

Older adults—Many medicines have not been studied specifically in older people. Therefore, it may not be known whether they work exactly the same way they do in younger adults or if they cause different side effects or problems in older people. There is no specific information comparing use of testolactone in the elderly with use in other age groups.

Other medicines—Although certain medicines should not be used together at all, in other cases two different medicines may be used together even if an interaction might occur. In these cases, your doctor may want to change the dose, or other precautions may be necessary. Tell your health care professional if you are taking any other prescription or nonprescription (over-the-counter [OTC]) medicine.

Other medical problems—The presence of other medical problems may affect the use of testolactone. Make sure you tell your doctor if you have any other medical problems, especially:
- Heart or kidney disease

Proper Use of This Medicine

Use this medicine only as directed by your doctor. Do not use more or less of it, and do not use it more often than your doctor ordered. The exact amount of medicine you need has been carefully worked out. Taking too much may increase the chance of side effects, while taking too little may not improve your condition.

Testolactone sometimes causes nausea and vomiting. However, it may have to be taken for several weeks or months to be effective. Even if you begin to feel ill, *do not stop using this medicine without first checking with your doctor.* Ask your health care professional for ways to lessen these effects.

If you vomit shortly after taking a dose of testolactone, check with your doctor. You will be told whether to take the dose again or to wait until the next scheduled dose.

Dosing—The dose of testolactone will be different for different patients. The dose that is used may depend on a number of things, including what the medicine is being used for and whether or not other medicines are also being taken. *If you are taking testolactone at home, follow your doctor's orders or the directions on the label.* If you have any questions about the proper dose of testolactone, ask your doctor.

Missed dose—If you miss a dose of this medicine, take it as soon as you remember. However, if it is almost time for the next dose, skip the missed dose and go back to your regular dosing schedule. Do not double doses. If you miss two or more doses in a row, check with your doctor.

Storage—To store this medicine:
- Keep out of the reach of children.
- Store away from heat and direct light.
- Do not store in the bathroom, near the kitchen sink, or in other damp places. Heat or moisture may cause the medicine to break down.
- Do not keep outdated medicine or medicine no longer needed. Be sure that any discarded medicine is out of the reach of children.

Precautions While Using This Medicine

It is very important that your doctor check your progress at regular visits to make sure that this medicine is working properly and to check for unwanted effects.

Side Effects of This Medicine

Along with its needed effects, a medicine may cause some unwanted effects. Although not all of these side effects may occur, if they do occur they may need medical attention.

Check with your doctor as soon as possible if the following side effect occurs:

Less common
Numbness or tingling of fingers, toes, or face

Other side effects may occur that usually do not need medical attention. These side effects may go away during treatment as your body adjusts to the medicine. Also, your health care professional may be able to tell you about ways to prevent or reduce some of these side effects. Check with your health care professional if any of the

following side effects continue or are bothersome or if you have any questions about them:

Less common

Diarrhea; loss of appetite; nausea or vomiting; pain or swelling in feet or lower legs; swelling or redness of tongue

Other side effects not listed above may also occur in some patients. If you notice any other effects, check with your doctor.

Revised: 08/04/92
Interim revision: 06/30/94

TETANUS IMMUNE GLOBULIN Systemic

A commonly used brand name in the U.S. is BayTet.
Generic name product may also be available.
Another commonly used name is TIG.

Description

Tetanus immune globulin (TET-n-us im-MUNE GLOB-yoo-lin) is used to prevent tetanus infection (also known as lockjaw). Tetanus is a serious illness that causes convulsions (seizures) and severe muscle spasms that can be strong enough to cause bone fractures of the spine. Tetanus causes death in 30 to 40 percent of cases.

In recent years, two thirds of all tetanus cases have been in persons 50 years of age and older. A tetanus infection in the past does not make you immune to tetanus in the future.

Tetanus immune globulin works by giving your body the antibodies it needs to protect it against tetanus infection. This is called passive protection. This passive protection lasts long enough to protect your body until your body can produce its own antibodies against tetanus.

Tetanus immune globulin is to be administered only by or under the supervision of your doctor or other health care professional. It is available in the following dosage form:

Parenteral

- Injection (U.S. and Canada)

Before Receiving This Medicine

In deciding to use a medicine, the risks of using the medicine must be weighed against the good it will do. This is a decision you and your doctor will make. For tetanus immune globulin, the following should be considered:

Allergies—Tell your doctor if you have ever had any unusual or allergic reaction to tetanus immune globulin.

Pregnancy—Studies on effects in pregnancy have not been done in either humans or animals. However, there is no reason to suspect that tetanus immune globulin causes problems in pregnant women.

Breast-feeding—Tetanus immune globulin has not been reported to cause problems in nursing babies.

Children—Although there is no specific information comparing use of tetanus immune globulin in children with use in other age groups, this medicine is not expected to cause different side effects or problems in children than it does in adults.

Older adults—Many medicines have not been studied specifically in older people. Therefore, it may not be known whether they work exactly the same way they do in younger adults or if they cause different side effects or problems in older people. There is no specific information comparing use of tetanus immune globulin in the elderly with use in other age groups. However, there is no evidence that the effects of tetanus immune globulin in older adults differ from those in younger persons.

Other medical problems—The presence of other medical problems may affect the use of tetanus immune globulin. Make sure you tell your doctor if you have any other medical problems.

Proper Use of This Medicine

Dosing—The dose of tetanus immune globulin will be different for different patients. The following information includes only the average dose of tetanus immune globulin.

- For *injection* dosage form:
  - —For preventing tetanus infection:
    - Adults and children—250 units injected into a muscle.

Side Effects of This Medicine

Along with its needed effects, a medicine may cause some unwanted effects. Although not all of these side effects may occur, if they do occur they may need medical attention.

Check with your doctor immediately if any of the following side effects occur:

Rare

Difficulty in breathing or swallowing; hives; itching, especially of soles or palms; reddening of skin, especially around ears; swelling of eyes, face, or inside of nose; unusual tiredness or weakness, sudden and severe

Other side effects not listed above may also occur in some patients. If you notice any other effects, check with your doctor.

Developed: 06/27/97

TETANUS TOXOID Systemic

Description

Tetanus (TET-n-us) Toxoid is used to prevent tetanus (also known as lockjaw). Tetanus is a serious illness that causes convulsions (seizures) and severe muscle spasms that can be strong enough to cause bone fractures of the spine. Tetanus causes death in 30 to 40 percent of cases.

Immunization against tetanus is recommended for all infants 6 to 8 weeks of age and older, all children, and all adults. Immunization against tetanus consists first of a series of either 3 or 4 injections, depending on which type of tetanus toxoid you receive. In addition, it is very important that you get a booster injection every 10 years for the rest of your life. Also, if you get a wound that is unclean or hard to clean, you may need an emergency booster injection if it has been more than 5 years since your last booster. In recent years, two-thirds of all tetanus cases have been in persons 50 years of age and older. A tetanus infection in the past does not make you immune to tetanus in the future.

This vaccine is to be administered only by or under the supervision of your doctor or other health care professional. It is available in the following dosage form:

Parenteral
- Injection (U.S. and Canada)

Before Receiving This Vaccine

In deciding to receive this vaccine, the risks of receiving the vaccine must be weighed against the good it will do. This is a decision you and your doctor will make. For tetanus toxoid, the following should be considered:

Allergies—Tell your doctor if you have ever had any unusual or allergic reaction to tetanus toxoid. Also tell your health care professional if you are allergic to any other substances, such as preservatives (especially thimerosal).

Pregnancy—This vaccine has not been shown to cause birth defects or other problems in humans. Vaccination of a pregnant woman can prevent her newborn baby from getting tetanus at birth.

Breast-feeding—Tetanus toxoid has not been reported to cause problems in nursing babies.

Children—Use is not recommended for infants up to 6 weeks of age. For infants and children 6 weeks of age and older, tetanus toxoid is not expected to cause different side effects or problems than it does in adults.

Older adults—This vaccine is not expected to cause different side effects or problems in older people than it does in younger adults. However, the vaccine may be slightly less effective in older persons than in younger adults.

Other medicines—Although certain medicines should not be used together at all, in other cases two different medicines may be used together even if an interaction might occur. In these cases, your doctor may want to change the dose, or other precautions may be necessary. Before you receive tetanus toxoid, it is especially important that your health care professional know if you are using any prescription or nonprescription (over-the-counter [OTC]) medicine.

Other medical problems—The presence of other medical problems may affect the use of tetanus toxoid. Make sure you tell your doctor if you have any other medical problems, especially:

- A severe reaction or a fever greater than 103 °F (39.4 °C) following a previous dose of tetanus toxoid—May increase the chance of side effects with future doses of tetanus toxoid; be sure your doctor knows about this before you receive the next dose of tetanus toxoid
- Bronchitis, pneumonia, or other illness involving lungs or bronchial tubes, or
- Severe illness with fever—Possible side effects from tetanus toxoid may be confused with the symptoms of the condition

Proper Use of This Vaccine

Dosing—The dose of tetanus toxoid will be different for different patients. The following information includes only the average doses of tetanus toxoid.

- For *injection* dosage forms:
  - —For prevention of tetanus (lockjaw):
    - Adults, children, and infants 6 weeks of age and older—One dose is given at your first visit, then a second dose is given four to eight weeks later. Depending on the product given, you may receive a third dose four to eight weeks after the second dose, and a fourth dose six to twelve months after that; or you may receive a third dose six to twelve months after the second dose. Everyone should receive a booster dose every ten years. The doses are injected under the skin or into a muscle. In addition, if you get a wound that is unclean or hard to clean, you may need an emergency booster injection if it has been more than 5 years since your last booster dose.

Side Effects of This Vaccine

Along with its needed effects, a vaccine may cause some unwanted effects. Although not all of these side effects may occur, if they do occur they may need medical attention.

Get emergency help immediately if any of the following side effects occur:

Symptoms of allergic reaction

Difficulty in breathing or swallowing; hives; itching, especially of feet or hands; reddening of skin, especially around ears; swelling of eyes, face, or inside of nose; unusual tiredness or weakness (sudden and severe)

Check with your doctor as soon as possible if any of the following side effects occur:

Rare

Confusion; convulsions (seizures); fever over 103 °F (39.4 °C); headache (severe or continuing); sleepiness (excessive); swelling, blistering, or pain at place of injection (severe or continuing); swelling of glands in armpit; unusual irritability; vomiting (severe or continuing)

Other side effects may occur that usually do not need medical attention. However, check with your doctor if any of the following side effects continue or are bothersome:

More common

Redness or hard lump at place of injection

Less common

Chills, fever, irritability, or unusual tiredness; pain, tenderness, itching, or swelling at place of injection; skin rash

Other side effects not listed above may also occur in some patients. If you notice any other effects, check with your doctor.

Revised: 07/12/94

TETRACYCLINE PERIODONTAL FIBERS Dental†

A commonly used brand name in the U.S. is Actisite.

†Not commercially available in Canada.

Description

Tetracycline periodontal fibers (tet-ra-SYE-kleen pare-ee-o-DON-tal FI-bers) are used to help treat periodontal disease (a disease of your gums). Periodontal disease is caused by bacteria growing beneath the gum line. Tetracycline works by keeping the number of bacteria from growing. Lowering the amount of bacteria helps to reduce inflammation and swelling in your mouth, and the amount of bleeding around the teeth. Tetracycline fibers are placed in the inflamed mouth areas by your dentist after he or she has thoroughly cleaned your teeth.

Tetracycline periodontal fibers are available only from your dentist, in the following dosage form:

Dental

- Periodontal fibers (U.S.)

Before Using This Medicine

In deciding to use a medicine, the risks of using the medicine must be weighed against the good it will do. This is a decision you and your dentist will make. For tetracycline periodontal fibers, the following should be considered:

Allergies—Tell your dentist if you have ever had any unusual or allergic reaction to tetracycline or any other tetracycline medicine (such as doxycycline, demeclocycline, oxytetracycline, or minocycline). Also tell your dentist if you are allergic to any other substances, such as foods, preservatives, or dyes.

Pregnancy—Studies on the effects in pregnancy have not been done in either humans or animals.

Breast-feeding—It is not known whether the tetracycline from tetracycline periodontal fibers passes into the breast milk.

Children—Studies on this medicine have been done only in adult patients, and there is no specific information comparing use of this medicine in children with use in other age groups.

Older adults—Many medicines have not been studied specifically in older people. Therefore, it may not be known whether they work exactly the same way they do in younger adults or if they cause different side effects or problems in older people. There is no specific information comparing use of this medicine in the elderly with use in other age groups.

Proper Use of This Medicine

When tetracycline periodontal fibers are in place in your mouth, *try to avoid any actions that may knock the fibers loose*. For example:

- Do not chew hard, crusty, or sticky foods, or chewing gum.
- Do not brush or floss near any treated areas, but continue to clean the other teeth.
- Do not use a dental spray device (e.g., Water-Pik).
- Do not probe or pick at the fibers with your tongue, toothpicks, or fingers.

Dosing—The amount of tetracycline periodontal fibers that will be put in your gums will be determined by your dentist. The number of teeth that need treatment and the depth of the pockets in your gums will determine the amount of fiber that is used.

Precautions While Using This Medicine

Check with your dentist right away if the fibers become loose or fall out before your next dental visit.

Check with your dentist right away if you have pain or swelling or other problems in the treated areas.

It is very important that your dentist check your progress and remove the tetracycline periodontal fibers after ten days. Do not miss any dental appointments.

Side Effects of This Medicine

Along with its needed effects, a medicine may cause some unwanted effects. Although not all of these side effects may occur, if they do occur they may need medical attention.

Check with your dentist immediately if any of the following side effects occur:

Rare

Gum redness, swelling, and pain in the areas of treatment; tongue pain and redness

Other side effects may occur that usually do not need medical attention. These side effects may go away during treatment as your body adjusts to the medicine. However,

check with your dentist if any of the following side effects continue or are bothersome:

More common

Discomfort in the area where the fibers have been placed; redness in the area where the fibers were removed

Rare

Staining of the tongue; white patches on tongue or in mouth

Other side effects not listed above may also occur in some patients. If you notice any other effects, check with your dentist.

Developed: 12/15/94

TETRACYCLINES Ophthalmic

Some commonly used brand names are:

In the U.S.—

Achromycin[2]
Aureomycin[1]

In Canada—

Achromycin[2]
Aureomycin[1]

Note: For quick reference, the following tetracyclines are numbered to match the corresponding brand names.

This information applies to the following medicines:

1. Chlortetracycline (klor-te-tra-SYE-kleen)
2. Tetracycline (te-tra-SYE-kleen)

Description

Tetracyclines belong to the family of medicines called antibiotics. Tetracycline ophthalmic preparations are used to treat infections of the eye. They may also be used along with other medicines that are taken by mouth for infections of the eye.

Tetracyclines are available only with your doctor's prescription, in the following dosage forms:

Ophthalmic

Chlortetracycline
- Ophthalmic ointment (U.S. and Canada)

Tetracycline
- Ophthalmic ointment (U.S. and Canada)
- Ophthalmic suspension (eye drops) (U.S.)

Before Using This Medicine

In deciding to use a medicine, the risks of using the medicine must be weighed against the good it will do. This is a decision you and your doctor will make. For tetracycline ophthalmic preparations, the following should be considered:

Allergies—Tell your doctor if you have ever had any unusual or allergic reaction to tetracycline or chlortetracycline or to any related antibiotics, such as demeclocycline (e.g., Declomycin), doxycycline (e.g., Vibramycin), methacycline (e.g., Rondomycin), minocycline (e.g., Minocin), or oxytetracycline (e.g., Terramycin). Also tell your health care professional if you are allergic to any other substances, such as preservatives.

Pregnancy—Tetracycline ophthalmic preparations have not been shown to cause birth defects or other problems in humans.

Breast-feeding—Tetracycline ophthalmic preparations have not been reported to cause problems in nursing babies.

Children—Although there is no specific information comparing use of ophthalmic tetracyclines in children with use in other age groups, they are not expected to cause different side effects or problems in children than they do in adults.

Older adults—Many medicines have not been studied specifically in older people. Therefore, it may not be known whether they work exactly the same way they do in younger adults or if they cause different side effects or problems in older people. There is no specific information comparing use of tetracyclines in the elderly with use in other age groups.

Other medicines—Although certain medicines should not be used together at all, in other cases two different medicines may be used together even if an interaction might occur. In these cases, your doctor may want to change the dose, or other precautions may be necessary. Tell your health care professional if you are using any other prescription or nonprescription (over-the-counter [OTC]) medicine that is to be used in the eye.

Proper Use of This Medicine

For patients using the *eye drop form* of tetracyclines:

- The bottle is only partially full to provide proper drop control.
- To use:

—First, wash your hands. Then tilt the head back and pull the lower eyelid away from the eye to form a pouch. Drop the medicine into the pouch and gently close the eyes. Do not blink. Keep the eyes closed for 1 or 2 minutes to allow the medicine to come into contact with the infection.

—If you think you did not get the drop of medicine into your eye properly, use another drop.

—To keep the medicine as germ-free as possible, do not touch the applicator tip to any surface (including the eye). Also, keep the container tightly closed.

For patients using the *eye ointment form* of tetracyclines:

- To use:

—First, wash your hands. Then pull the lower eyelid away from the eye to form a pouch. Squeeze a thin strip of ointment into the pouch. A 1-cm (approximately 1/3-inch) strip of ointment is usually enough unless otherwise directed by your doctor. Gently close the eyes and keep them closed for 1 or 2 minutes to allow the medicine to come into contact with the infection.

—To keep the medicine as germ-free as possible, do not touch the applicator tip to any surface (including the eye). After using tetracyclines eye ointment, wipe the tip of the ointment tube with a clean tissue and keep the tube tightly closed.

To help clear up your infection completely, *keep using this medicine for the full time of treatment,* even if your symptoms have disappeared. *Do not miss any doses.*

Dosing—The dose of ophthalmic tetracyclines will be different for different patients. *Follow your doctor's orders or the directions on the label.* The following information includes only the average doses of ophthalmic tetracyclines. *If your dose is different, do not change it unless your doctor tells you to do so.*

The number of doses you use each day, the time allowed between doses, and the length of time you use the medicine depend on the medical problem for which you are using ophthalmic tetracyclines.

- For eye infections:
  - —For *ophthalmic ointment* dosage forms:
    - Adults and children—Use every two to four hours.
  - —For *ophthalmic suspension* dosage form:
    - Adults and children—One drop every six to twelve hours.

Missed dose—If you miss a dose of this medicine, apply it as soon as possible. However, if it is almost time for your next application, skip the missed dose and go back to your regular dosing schedule.

Storage—To store this medicine:

- Keep out of the reach of children.
- Store away from heat and direct light.
- Keep the medicine from freezing.
- Do not keep outdated medicine or medicine no longer needed. Be sure that any discarded medicine is out of the reach of children.

Precautions While Using This Medicine

After application, this medicine usually causes your vision to blur for a few minutes.

If your symptoms do not improve within a few days, or if they become worse, check with your doctor.

Side Effects of This Medicine

There have not been any common or important side effects reported with this medicine. However, if you notice any unusual effects, check with your doctor.

Revised: 07/01/93

TETRACYCLINES Systemic

Some commonly used brand names are:

In the U.S.—

Achromycin[5]	Monodox[2]
Achromycin V[5]	Panmycin[5]
Declomycin[1]	Robitet[5]
Doryx[2]	Sumycin[5]
Doxi Film[2]	Terramycin[4]
Doxy[2]	Tetracyn[5]
Doxy-Caps[2]	Tija[4]
Dynacin[3]	Vibramycin[2]
Minocin[3]	Vibra-Tabs[2]

In Canada—

Achromycin[5]	Minocin[3]
Achromycin V[5]	Novodoxylin[2]
Apo-Doxy[2]	Novotetra[5]
Apo-Tetra[5]	Nu-Tetra[5]
Declomycin[1]	Tetracyn[5]
Doryx[2]	Vibramycin[2]
Doxycin[2]	Vibra-Tabs[2]

Note: For quick reference, the following tetracyclines are numbered to match the corresponding brand names.

This information applies to the following medicines:

1. Demeclocycline (dem-e-kloe-SYE-kleen)
2. Doxycycline (dox-i-SYE-kleen)‡
3. Minocycline (mi-noe-SYE-kleen)‡
4. Oxytetracycline (ox-i-te-tra-SYE-kleen)‡
5. Tetracycline (te-tra-SYE-kleen)‡

‡Generic name product may also be available in the U.S.

Description

Tetracyclines are used to treat infections and to help control acne. Demeclocycline and doxycycline may also be used for other problems as determined by your doctor. Tetracyclines will not work for colds, flu, or other virus infections.

Tetracyclines are available only with your doctor's prescription, in the following dosage forms:

Oral

- Demeclocycline
  - Capsules (U.S.)
  - Tablets (U.S. and Canada)
- Doxycycline
  - Capsules (U.S. and Canada)
  - Delayed-release capsules (U.S. and Canada)
  - Oral suspension (U.S.)
  - Tablets (U.S. and Canada)
- Minocycline
  - Capsules (U.S. and Canada)
  - Oral suspension (U.S.)
  - Tablets (U.S.)
- Oxytetracycline
  - Capsules (U.S.)
- Tetracycline
  - Capsules (U.S. and Canada)
  - Oral suspension (U.S. and Canada)
  - Tablets (U.S. and Canada)

Parenteral
- Doxycycline
  - Injection (U.S. and Canada)
- Minocycline
  - Injection (U.S.)
- Oxytetracycline
  - Injection (U.S.)
- Tetracycline
  - Injection (U.S. and Canada)

Before Using This Medicine

In deciding to use a medicine, the risks of taking the medicine must be weighed against the good it will do. This is a decision you and your doctor will make. For tetracyclines, the following should be considered:

Allergies—Tell your doctor if you have ever had any unusual or allergic reaction to any of the tetracyclines or combination medicines containing a tetracycline. Also tell your health care professional if you are allergic to any other substances, such as foods, preservatives, or dyes. In addition, if you are going to be given oxytetracycline or tetracycline by injection, tell your doctor if you have ever had an unusual or allergic reaction to "caine-type" anesthetics.

Pregnancy—Use is not recommended during the last half of pregnancy. Tetracyclines may cause the unborn infant's teeth to become discolored and may slow down the growth of the infant's teeth and bones if they are taken during that time. In addition, liver problems may occur in pregnant women, especially those receiving high doses by injection into a vein.

Breast-feeding—Use is not recommended since tetracyclines pass into the breast milk. They may cause the nursing baby's teeth to become discolored and may slow down the growth of the baby's teeth and bones. They may also cause increased sensitivity of nursing babies' skin to sunlight and fungus infections of the mouth and vagina. In addition, minocycline may cause dizziness, lightheadedness, or unsteadiness in nursing babies.

Children—Tetracyclines may cause permanent discoloration of teeth and slow down the growth of bones. These medicines should not be given to children up to 8 years of age unless directed by the child's doctor.

Older adults—Many medicines have not been studied specifically in older people. Therefore, it may not be known whether they work exactly the same way they do in younger adults or if they cause different side effects or problems in older people. There is no specific information comparing use of tetracyclines in the elderly with use in other age groups.

Other medicines—Although certain medicines should not be used together at all, in other cases two different medicines may be used together even if an interaction might occur. In these cases, your doctor may want to change the dose, or other precautions may be necessary. When you are taking tetracyclines, it is especially important that your health care professional know if you are taking any of the following:

- Antacids or
- Calcium supplements such as calcium carbonate or
- Cholestyramine (e.g., Questran) or
- Choline and magnesium salicylates (e.g., Trilisate) or
- Colestipol (e.g., Colestid) or
- Iron-containing medicine or
- Laxatives (magnesium-containing) or
- Magnesium salicylate (e.g., Magan)—Use of these medicines with tetracyclines may decrease the effect of tetracyclines
- Oral contraceptives (birth control pills) containing estrogen—Use of birth control pills with tetracyclines may decrease the effect of the birth control pills and increase the chance of unwanted pregnancy

Other medical problems—The presence of other medical problems may affect the use of tetracyclines. Make sure you tell your doctor if you have any other medical problems, especially:

- Diabetes insipidus (water diabetes)—Demeclocycline may make the condition worse
- Kidney disease (does not apply to doxycycline or minocycline)—Patients with kidney disease may have an increased chance of side effects
- Liver disease—Patients with liver disease may have an increased chance of side effects if they use doxycycline or minocycline

Proper Use of This Medicine

Do not give tetracyclines to infants or children up to 8 years of age unless directed by your doctor. Tetracyclines may cause permanently discolored teeth and other problems in this age group.

Do not take milk, milk formulas, or other dairy products within 1 to 2 hours of the time you take tetracyclines (except doxycycline and minocycline) by mouth. They may keep this medicine from working properly.

If this medicine has changed color or tastes or looks different, has become outdated (old), has been stored incorrectly (too warm or too damp area or place), do not use it. To do so may cause *serious side effects*. Discard the medicine. If you have any questions about this, check with your health care professional.

Tetracyclines should be taken with a full glass (8 ounces) of water to prevent irritation of the esophagus (tube between the throat and stomach) or stomach. In addition, most tetracyclines (except doxycycline and minocycline) are best taken on an empty stomach (either 1 hour before or 2 hours after meals). However, if this medicine upsets your stomach, your doctor may want you to take it with food.

For patients taking the *oral liquid form* of this medicine:

- Use a specially marked measuring spoon or other device to measure each dose accurately. The average household teaspoon may not hold the right amount of liquid.
- Do not use after the expiration date on the label since the medicine may not work properly after that date. Check with your pharmacist if you have any questions about this.

For patients taking *doxycycline or minocycline:*

- These medicines may be taken with food or milk if they upset your stomach.

• Swallow the capsule (with enteric-coated pellets) form of doxycycline whole. Do not break or crush.

To help clear up your infection completely, *keep taking this medicine for the full time of treatment,* even if you begin to feel better after a few days. If you stop taking this medicine too soon, your symptoms may return.

This medicine works best when there is a constant amount in the blood or urine. *To help keep the amount constant, do not miss any doses. Also, it is best to take the doses at evenly spaced times day and night.* For example, if you are to take 4 doses a day, the doses should be spaced about 6 hours apart. If this interferes with your sleep or other daily activities, or if you need help in planning the best times to take your medicine, check with your health care professional.

Dosing—The dose of these medicines will be different for different patients. *Follow your doctor's orders or the directions on the label.* The following information includes only the average doses of these medicines. *If your dose is different, do not change it* unless your doctor tells you to do so.

The number of capsules, tablets, or teaspoonfuls of suspension that you take depends on the strength of the medicine. Also, *the number of doses you take each day, the time allowed between doses, and the length of time you take the medicine depend on the medical problem for which you are taking a tetracycline.*

For demeclocycline

• For *oral* dosage forms (capsules, tablets):

—For bacterial or protozoal infections:

• Adults and teenagers—150 milligrams (mg) every six hours; or 300 mg every twelve hours.

• Infants and children up to 8 years of age—Tetracyclines are usually not used in young children because tetracyclines can permanently stain teeth.

• Children 8 years of age and older—Dose is based on body weight. The usual dose is 1.65 to 3.3 mg per kilogram (kg) (0.8 to 1.5 mg per pound) of body weight every six hours; or 3.3 to 6.6 mg per kg (1.5 to 3 mg per pound) of body weight every twelve hours.

For doxycycline

• For *oral* dosage forms (capsules, suspension, and tablets):

—For bacterial or protozoal infections:

• Adults and children over 45 kilograms (kg) of body weight (99 pounds)—100 milligrams (mg) every twelve hours the first day, then 100 to 200 mg once a day or 50 to 100 mg every twelve hours.

• Infants and children up to 8 years of age—Tetracyclines are usually not used in young children because tetracyclines can permanently stain teeth.

• Children 45 kg of body weight (99 pounds) and less—Dose is based on body weight. The usual dose is 2.2 mg per kg (1 mg per pound) of body weight the first day, then 2.2 to 4.4 mg per kg (1 to 2 mg per pound) of body weight once a day; or 1.1 to 2.2 mg per kg (0.5 to 1 mg per pound) of body weight every twelve hours.

—For the prevention of malaria:

• Adults and teenagers—100 mg once a day. You should take the first dose one or two days before travel to an area where malaria may occur, continue taking the medicine every day throughout travel, and for four weeks after you leave the malarious area.

• Children over 8 years of age—Dose is based on body weight. The usual dose is 2 mg per kg (0.9 mg per pound) of body weight once a day. You should take the first dose one or two days before travel to an area where malaria may occur, continue taking the medicine every day throughout travel, and for four weeks after you leave the malarious area.

• Infants and children up to 8 years of age—Tetracyclines are usually not used in young children because tetracyclines can permanently stain teeth.

• For *injection* dosage form:

—For bacterial or protozoal infections:

• Adults and children over 45 kg of body weight (99 pounds)—200 mg injected into a vein once a day; or 100 mg injected into a vein every twelve hours the first day, then 100 to 200 mg injected into a vein once a day. Another dose is 50 to 100 mg every twelve hours.

• Infants and children up to 8 years of age—Tetracyclines are usually not used in young children because tetracyclines can permanently stain teeth.

• Children 45 kg of body weight (99 pounds) and less—Dose is based on body weight. The usual dose is 4.4 mg per kg (2 mg per pound) of body weight injected into a vein once a day; or 2.2 mg per kg (1 mg per pound) of body weight injected into a vein every twelve hours the first day, then 2.2 to 4.4 mg per kg (1 to 2 mg per pound) of body weight once a day, or 1.1 to 2.2 per kg (0.5 to 1 mg per pound) of body weight every twelve hours.

For minocycline

• For *oral* dosage forms (capsules, suspension, and tablets):

—For bacterial or protozoal infections:

• Adults and teenagers—200 milligrams (mg) at first, then 100 mg every twelve hours; or 100 to 200 mg at first, then 50 mg every six hours.

• Infants and children up to 8 years of age—Tetracyclines are usually not used in young children because tetracyclines can permanently stain teeth.

• Children 8 years of age and over—Dose is based on body weight. The usual dose is 4 mg per kilogram (kg) (1.8 mg per pound) of body weight at first, then 2 mg per kg (0.9 mg per pound) of body weight every twelve hours.

- For *injection* dosage form:
  —For bacterial or protozoal infections:
  - Adults and teenagers—200 mg at first, then 100 mg every twelve hours, injected into a vein.
  - Infants and children up to 8 years of age—Tetracyclines are usually not used in young children because tetracyclines can permanently stain teeth.
  - Children 8 years of age and over—Dose is based on body weight. The usual dose is 4 mg per kg (1.8 mg per pound) of body weight at first, then 2 mg per kg (0.9 mg per pound) of body weight every twelve hours, injected into a vein.

For oxytetracycline

- For *oral* dosage form (capsules):
  —For bacterial or protozoal infections:
  - Adults and teenagers—250 to 500 milligrams (mg) every six hours.
  - Infants and children up to 8 years of age—Tetracyclines are usually not used in young children because tetracyclines can permanently stain teeth.
  - Children 8 years of age and over—Dose is based on body weight. The usual dose is 6.25 to 12.5 mg per kilogram (kg) (2.8 to 5.7 mg per pound) of body weight every six hours.
- For *injection* dosage form (muscle injection):
  —For bacterial or protozoal infections:
  - Adults and teenagers—100 mg every eight hours; or 150 mg every twelve hours; or 250 mg once a day, injected into a muscle.
  - Infants and children up to 8 years of age—Tetracyclines are usually not used in young children because tetracyclines can permanently stain teeth.
  - Children 8 years of age and over—Dose is based on body weight. The usual dose is 5 to 8.3 mg per kg (2.3 to 3.8 mg per pound) of body weight every eight hours; or 7.5 to 12.5 mg per kg (3.4 to 5.7 mg per pound) of body weight every twelve hours, injected into a muscle.
- For *injection* dosage form (vein injection):
  —For bacterial or protozoal infections:
  - Adults and teenagers—250 to 500 mg injected into a vein every twelve hours.
  - Infants and children up to 8 years of age—Tetracyclines are usually not used in young children because tetracyclines can permanently stain teeth.
  - Children 8 years of age and over—Dose is based on body weight. The usual dose is 5 to 10 mg per kg (2.3 to 4.5 mg per pound) of body weight, injected into a vein, every twelve hours.

For tetracycline

- For *oral* dosage forms (capsules, suspension, and tablets):
  —For bacterial or protozoal infections:
  - Adults and teenagers—250 to 500 milligrams (mg) every six hours; or 500 mg to 1 gram every twelve hours.
  - Infants and children up to 8 years of age—Tetracyclines are usually not used in young children because tetracyclines can permanently stain teeth.
  - Children 8 years of age and over—Dose is based on body weight. The usual dose is 6.25 to 12.5 mg per kilogram (kg) (2.8 to 5.7 mg per pound) of body weight every six hours; or 12.5 to 25 mg per kg (5.7 to 11.4 mg per pound) of body weight every twelve hours.
- For *injection* dosage form:
  —For bacterial or protozoal infections:
  - Adults and teenagers—100 mg every eight hours; or 150 mg every twelve hours; or 250 mg once a day, injected into a muscle.
  - Infants and children up to 8 years of age—Tetracyclines are usually not used in young children because tetracyclines can permanently stain teeth.
  - Children 8 years of age and over—Dose is based on body weight. The usual dose is 5 to 8.3 mg per kg (2.3 to 3.8 mg per pound) of body weight every eight hours; or 7.5 to 12.5 mg per kg (3.4 to 5.7 mg per pound) of body weight every twelve hours, injected into a muscle.

Missed dose—If you miss a dose of this medicine, take it as soon as possible. This will help to keep a constant amount of medicine in the blood or urine. However, if it is almost time for your next dose, skip the missed dose and go back to your regular dosing schedule. Do not double doses.

Storage—To store this medicine:

- Keep out of the reach of children.
- Store away from heat and direct light.
- Do not store the capsule or tablet form of this medicine in the bathroom, near the kitchen sink, or in other damp places. Heat or moisture may cause the medicine to break down.
- Keep the oral liquid forms of this medicine from freezing.
- Do not keep outdated medicine or medicine no longer needed. Be sure that any discarded medicine is out of the reach of children.

Precautions While Using This Medicine

If your symptoms do not improve within a few days (or a few weeks or months for acne patients), or if they become worse, check with your doctor.

Do not take antacids; calcium supplements such as calcium carbonate; *choline and magnesium salicylates combination (e.g., Trilisate); magnesium salicylate (e.g., Magan); magnesium-containing laxatives* such as Epsom salt; *or sodium bicarbonate* (baking soda) within 1 to 2 hours of the time you take any of the tetracyclines by mouth. In addition, *do not take iron preparations* (including vitamin preparations that contain iron) within 2 to 3 hours of the time you take tetracyclines by mouth. To do so may keep this medicine from working properly.

Oral contraceptives (birth control pills) containing estrogen may not work properly if you take them while you are taking tetracyclines. Unplanned pregnancies may occur. You should use a different or additional means of birth control while you are taking tetracyclines. If you have any questions about this, check with your health care professional.

Before having surgery (including dental surgery) with a general anesthetic, tell the medical doctor or dentist in charge that you are taking a tetracycline. This does not apply to doxycycline, however.

Tetracyclines may cause your skin to be more sensitive to sunlight than it is normally. Exposure to sunlight, even for brief periods of time, may cause a skin rash, itching, redness or other discoloration of the skin, or a severe sunburn. When you begin taking this medicine:

- Stay out of direct sunlight, especially between the hours of 10:00 a.m. and 3:00 p.m., if possible.
- Wear protective clothing, including a hat. Also, wear sunglasses.
- Apply a sun block product that has a skin protection factor (SPF) of at least 15. Some patients may require a product with a higher SPF number, especially if they have a fair complexion. If you have any questions about this, check with your health care professional.
- Apply a sun block lipstick that has an SPF of at least 15 to protect your lips.
- Do not use a sunlamp or tanning bed or booth.

You may still be more sensitive to sunlight or sunlamps for 2 weeks to several months or more after stopping this medicine. *If you have a severe reaction, check with your doctor.*

For patients taking *minocycline:*

- Minocycline may also cause some people to become dizzy, lightheaded, or unsteady. *Make sure you know how you react to this medicine before you drive, use machines, or do anything else that could be dangerous if you are dizzy or are not alert.* If these reactions are especially bothersome, check with your doctor.

Side Effects of This Medicine

Along with its needed effects, a medicine may cause some unwanted effects. In some infants and children, tetracyclines may cause the teeth to become discolored. Even though this may not happen right away, check with your doctor as soon as possible if you notice this effect or if you have any questions about it.

For all tetracyclines

More common

Increased sensitivity of skin to sunlight (rare with minocycline)

Rare

Abdominal pain; bulging fontanel (soft spot on head) of infants; headache; loss of appetite; nausea and vomiting; yellowing skin; visual changes

For demeclocycline only

Less common

Greatly increased frequency of urination or amount of urine; increased thirst; unusual tiredness or weakness

For minocycline only

Less common

Pigmentation (darker color or discoloration) of skin and mucous membranes

Other side effects may occur that usually do not need medical attention. These side effects may go away during treatment as your body adjusts to the medicine. However, check with your doctor if any of the following side effects continue or are bothersome:

For all tetracyclines

More common

Cramps or burning of the stomach; diarrhea; nausea or vomiting

Less common

Itching of the rectal or genital (sex organ) areas; sore mouth or tongue

For minocycline only

More common

Dizziness, lightheadedness, or unsteadiness

In some patients tetracyclines may cause the tongue to become darkened or discolored. This effect is only temporary and will go away when you stop taking this medicine.

Other side effects not listed above may also occur in some patients. If you notice any other effects, check with your doctor.

Additional Information

Once a medicine has been approved for marketing for a certain use, experience may show that it is also useful for other medical problems. Although these uses are not included in product labeling, tetracyclines are used in certain patients with the following medical conditions:

- Syndrome of inappropriate antidiuretic hormone (SIADH) (for demeclocycline)
- Traveler's diarrhea (for doxycyline)
- Lyme disease (for doxycycline and tetracycline)

For patients taking this medicine for *SIADH:*

- Some doctors may prescribe demeclocycline for certain patients who retain (keep) more body water than usual. Although demeclocycline works like a diuretic (water pill) in these patients, it will not work that way in other patients who may need a diuretic.

For patients taking this medicine for *traveler's diarrhea:*

- Some doctors may prescribe doxycycline by mouth to help prevent or treat traveler's diarrhea. It is usually given daily for three weeks to prevent traveler's diarrhea. If you have any questions about this, check with your doctor.

Other than the above information, there is no additional information relating to proper use, precautions, or side effects for these uses.

Revised: 08/30/92
Interim revision: 03/18/94; 05/26/94; 04/19/95; 07/24/96

TETRACYCLINES Topical

Some commonly used brand names are:

In the U.S.—

Aureomycin[1]
Achromycin[3]
Meclan[2]
Topicycline[3]

In Canada—

Achromycin[3]
Aureomycin[1]

Note: For quick reference, the following tetracyclines are numbered to match the corresponding brand names.

This information applies to the following medicines:

1. Chlortetracycline (klor-te-tra-SYE-kleen)
2. Meclocycline (me-kloe-SYE-kleen)
3. Tetracycline (te-tra-SYE-kleen)

Description

Tetracyclines belong to the family of medicines called antibiotics. The topical ointment forms are used to treat infections of the skin. Meclocycline cream and the topical liquid form of tetracycline are used to help control acne. They may be used alone or with one or more other medicines that are applied to the skin or taken by mouth for acne.

Topical ointment forms of the tetracyclines are available without a prescription; however, your doctor may have special instructions on the proper use of these medicines for your medical problem. Meclocycline cream and the topical liquid form of tetracycline are available only with your doctor's prescription.

Topical tetracycline is available in the following dosage forms:

Topical

Chlortetracycline
- Ointment (U.S. and Canada)

Meclocycline
- Cream (U.S.)

Tetracycline
- Ointment (U.S. and Canada)
- Topical solution (U.S.)

Before Using This Medicine

In deciding to use a medicine, the risks of using the medicine must be weighed against the good it will do. This is a decision you and your doctor will make. For topical tetracyclines, the following should be considered:

Allergies—Tell your doctor if you have ever had any unusual or allergic reaction to topical tetracyclines or to any related antibiotics, such as chlortetracycline for the eye (e.g., Aureomycin); demeclocycline (e.g., Declomycin); doxycycline (e.g., Vibramycin); methacycline (e.g., Rondomycin); minocycline (e.g., Minocin); oxytetracycline (e.g., Terramycin); or tetracycline by mouth or by injection (e.g., Achromycin). In addition, if you are to use the cream form of meclocycline, tell your doctor if you have ever had any unusual or allergic reaction to formaldehyde. Also tell your health care professional if you are allergic to any other substances, such as preservatives or dyes.

Pregnancy—Studies have not been done in humans. In studies in rats and rabbits, chlortetracycline and tetracycline topical preparations have not been shown to cause birth defects or other problems. However, studies in rabbits have shown meclocycline to cause a slight delay in bone formation.

Breast-feeding—It is not known whether tetracycline topical preparations pass into breast milk. Although most medicines pass into breast milk in small amounts, many of them may be used safely while breast-feeding. Mothers who are using any of these medicines and who wish to breast-feed should discuss this with their doctor.

Children—Tetracycline topical solution has been tested on a limited number of children 11 years of age or older and has not been shown to cause different side effects or problems in children than it does in adults. Although there is no specific information about the use of topical chlortetracycline or topical meclocycline in children, they are not expected to cause different side effects or problems in children than they do in adults.

Older adults—Many medicines have not been tested in older people. Therefore, it may not be known whether they work exactly the same way they do in younger adults or if they cause different side effects or problems in older people. There is no specific information about the use of topical tetracyclines in the elderly.

Other medicines—Although certain medicines should not be used together at all, in other cases two different medicines may be used together even if an interaction might occur. In these cases, your doctor may want to change the dose, or other precautions may be necessary. When you are using topical tetracyclines, it is important that your health care professional knows if you are using any other topical prescription or nonprescription (over-the-counter [OTC]) medicine that is to be applied to the same area of the skin.

Proper Use of This Medicine

For patients using the *cream form or topical liquid form* of this medicine for acne:

- The cream or topical liquid form of this medicine will not cure your acne. However, to help keep your acne under control, *keep using this medicine for the full time of treatment,* even if your symptoms begin to clear up after a few days. You may have to continue using this medicine every day for months or even longer in some cases. If you stop using this medicine too soon, your symptoms may return. *It is important that you do not miss any doses.*

For patients using the *cream form* of this medicine for acne:

- Do not get this medicine on your clothing since it may stain.
- Before applying this medicine, thoroughly wash the affected area with warm water and soap, rinse well, and pat dry.
- To use:

  —Apply a thin film of medicine, using enough to cover the affected area lightly. *You should apply the medicine to the whole area usually affected by acne, not just to the pimples themselves.* This will help keep new pimples from breaking out.

—Do not get this medicine in the eyes, nose, mouth, or on other mucous membranes. Spread the medicine away from these areas when applying.

For patients using the *topical liquid form* of this medicine for acne:

- Do not get this medicine on your clothing since it may stain.
- This medicine usually comes with patient instructions. Read these instructions carefully before using this medicine.
- The liquid form contains alcohol and is flammable. *Do not use near heat, near open flame, or while smoking.*
- Do not use after the expiration date on the label. The medicine may not work properly. Check with your pharmacist if you have any questions about this.
- The presence of the floating plastic plug in the liquid means that the medicine has been mixed properly. *Do not remove the plastic plug.*
- It is important that you do not use this medicine more often than your doctor ordered. It may cause your skin to become too dry or irritated.
- Before applying this medicine, thoroughly wash the affected area with warm water and soap, rinse well, and pat dry. After washing or shaving, it is best to wait 30 minutes before applying this medicine. The alcohol in it may irritate freshly washed or shaved skin.
- You should avoid washing the acne-affected areas too often. This may dry your skin and make your acne worse. Washing with a mild, bland soap 2 or 3 times a day should be enough, unless you have oily skin. If you have any questions about this, check with your doctor.
- To use:

  —This medicine comes in a bottle with an applicator tip that may be used to apply the medicine directly to the skin. Use the applicator with a dabbing motion instead of a rolling motion (not like a roll-on deodorant, for example). Tilt the bottle and press the tip firmly against your skin. If needed, you can make the medicine flow faster from the applicator tip by slightly increasing the pressure against the skin. If the medicine flows too fast, use less pressure.

  —Apply a generous amount of medicine, using enough so that the skin feels wet all over. After applying the medicine with the applicator, use your fingertips to spread the medicine around evenly and rub it into your skin. A second coat may be needed to completely cover the affected areas. Be sure to wash the medicine off your hands afterward.

  —*You should apply the medicine to the whole area usually affected by acne, not just to the pimples themselves.* This will help keep new pimples from breaking out.

  —Since this medicine contains alcohol, it will sting or burn. Therefore, *do not get this medicine in the eyes, nose, mouth, or on other mucous membranes.* Spread the medicine away from these areas when applying. If this medicine does get in the eyes, wash them out immediately, but carefully, with large amounts of cool tap water. If your eyes still burn or are painful, check with your doctor.
- The bottle contains about an 8-week supply of medicine if used only on the face and neck or about a 4-week supply if used on the face and neck plus other affected areas.

For patients using the *topical ointment form* of this medicine:

- To help clear up your infection completely, *keep using this medicine for the full time of treatment,* even if your symptoms begin to clear up after a few days. If you stop using this medicine too soon, your symptoms may return. *Do not miss any doses.*
- Do not get this medicine on your clothing since it may stain.
- If you are using this medicine without a prescription, do not use it to treat deep wounds, puncture wounds, or serious burns without first checking with your health care professional.
- Do not get this medicine in the eyes.
- Before applying this medicine, thoroughly wash the affected area with warm water and soap, rinse well, and dry completely.
- After applying this medicine, you may cover the treated area with a gauze dressing if you wish.

Dosing—The dose of these medicines will be different for different patients. *Follow your doctor's orders or the directions on the label.* The following information includes only the average doses of these medicines. *If your dose is different, do not change it* unless your doctor tells you to do so.

For chlortetracycline

- For *ointment* dosage form:
  - —For skin infections:
    - Adults and children—Use one or two times a day.

For meclocycline

- For *cream* dosage form:
  - —For acne:
    - Adults and children—Use two times a day, morning and evening.

For tetracycline

- For *ointment* dosage form:
  - —For skin infections:
    - Adults and children—Use one or two times a day.
- For *topical solution* dosage form:
  - —For acne:
    - Adults and children over 11 years of age—Use two times a day, morning and evening.

- Infants and children up to 11 years of age—Use and dose must be determined by the doctor.

Missed dose—If you miss a dose of this medicine, apply it as soon as possible. However, if it is almost time for your next dose, skip the missed dose and go back to your regular dosing schedule.

Storage—To store this medicine:
- Keep out of the reach of children.
- Store away from heat and direct light.
- Keep the medicine from freezing.
- Do not keep outdated medicine or medicine no longer needed. Be sure that any discarded medicine is out of the reach of children.

Precautions While Using This Medicine

For patients using either the *cream form or the topical liquid form* of this medicine for acne:
- Some people may notice improvement in their acne within 4 to 6 weeks. However, if there is no improvement in your acne after you have used this medicine for 6 to 8 weeks or if it becomes worse, check with your health care professional. The treatment of acne may take up to 8 to 12 weeks before full improvement is seen.
- If your doctor has ordered another medicine to be applied to the skin along with this medicine, it is best to wait at least 1 hour before you apply the second medicine. This may help keep your skin from becoming too irritated. Also, if the medicines are used too close together, they may not work properly.
- The liquid form of this medicine may also cause the skin to become unusually dry, even with normal use. If this occurs, check with your doctor.
- This medicine may cause faint yellowing of the skin, especially around hair roots. This may be more easily seen in people with light complexions. The color may be removed by washing. However, the medicine should be left on the skin as long as possible. Do not wash immediately after applying the medicine. To do so will keep the medicine from working properly. If the yellow color is bothersome during the daytime, the medicine may be applied after school or work and again at bedtime, unless otherwise directed by your doctor.
- Treated areas of the skin may glow bright yellow under ''black'' (ultraviolet or UV) light such as that used in some discos. To help reduce or avoid this, apply the medicine later in the evening or wash it off before exposure to ''black'' light.
- You may continue to use cosmetics (make-up) while you are using this medicine for acne. However, it is best to use only ''water-base'' cosmetics. Also, it is best not to use cosmetics too heavily or too often. They may make your acne worse. If you have any questions about this, check with your doctor.

For patients using the *topical ointment form* of this medicine:
- If your skin infection does not improve within 2 weeks, or if it becomes worse, check with your health care professional.

Side Effects of This Medicine

Along with its needed effects, a medicine may cause some unwanted effects. Although not all of these side effects may occur, if they do occur they may need medical attention.

Check with your doctor as soon as possible if any of the following side effects occur:

Less common

Pain, redness, swelling, or other sign of irritation not present before use of this medicine

Other side effects may occur that usually do not need medical attention. These side effects may go away during treatment as your body adjusts to the medicine. However, check with your doctor if any of the following side effects continue or are bothersome:

More common—For topical liquid form only

Dry or scaly skin; stinging or burning feeling

More common—For cream and topical liquid forms only

Faint yellowing of the skin, especially around hair roots

Other side effects not listed above may also occur in some patients. If you notice any other effects, check with your doctor.

Revised: 10/27/93

THEOPHYLLINE, EPHEDRINE, GUAIFENESIN, AND PHENOBARBITAL Systemic†

Some commonly used brand names are:

In the U.S.—

Bronkolixir	Guiaphed
Bronkotabs	Mudrane GG

†Not commercially available in Canada.

Description

Theophylline, ephedrine, guaifenesin, and phenobarbital (fee-noe-BAR-bi-tal) combination is used to treat the symptoms of bronchial asthma, chronic bronchitis, emphysema, and other lung diseases. This medicine relieves cough, wheezing, shortness of breath, and troubled breathing. It works by opening up the bronchial tubes (air passages) of the lungs and increasing the flow of air through them.

Some of these preparations are available only with your doctor's prescription. Others are available without a prescription; however, your doctor may have special instructions on the proper use of this medicine for your medical condition.

Theophylline, ephedrine, guaifenesin, and phenobarbital combination is available in the following dosage forms:

Oral
- Elixir (U.S.)
- Tablets (U.S.)

Before Using This Medicine

If you are taking this medicine without a prescription, carefully read and follow any precautions on the label. For theophylline, ephedrine, guaifenesin, and phenobarbital combination medicine, the following should be considered:

Allergies—Tell your doctor if you have ever had any unusual or allergic reaction to aminophylline, caffeine, dyphylline, oxtriphylline, theobromine, or theophylline; ephedrine or medicines like ephedrine such as albuterol, amphetamines, epinephrine, isoproterenol, metaproterenol, norepinephrine, phenylephrine, phenylpropanolamine, pseudoephedrine, or terbutaline; or phenobarbital or other barbiturates. Also tell your health care professional if you are allergic to any other substances, such as foods, preservatives, or dyes.

Diet—Make certain your health care professional knows if you are on any special diet, such as a low-sodium or low-sugar diet or a high-protein, low-carbohydrate or low-protein, high-carbohydrate diet. A high-protein, low-carbohydrate diet may decrease the effects of theophylline; a low-protein, high-carbohydrate diet may increase the effects of theophylline.

Avoid eating or drinking large amounts of caffeine-containing foods or beverages, such as chocolate, cocoa, tea, coffee, and cola drinks, because they may increase the central nervous system (CNS) stimulant effects of theophylline.

Also, eating charcoal broiled foods every day while taking theophylline may keep this medicine from working properly.

Pregnancy—Studies with theophylline on birth defects has not been done in humans. However, some studies in animals have shown that theophylline causes birth defects when given in doses many times the human dose. Also, use of theophylline during pregnancy may cause unwanted effects such as fast heartbeat, jitteriness, irritability, gagging, vomiting, and breathing problems in the newborn infant.

Studies with ephedrine on birth defects have not been done in either humans or animals.

Phenobarbital taken during pregnancy has been shown to increase the chance of birth defects in humans. Also, taking phenobarbital regularly during the last 3 months of pregnancy may cause the baby to become dependent on the medicine. This may lead to withdrawal side effects in the baby after birth. In addition, one study in humans has suggested that phenobarbital taken during pregnancy may increase the chance of brain tumors in the baby.

Guaifenesin has not been shown to cause birth defects or other problems in humans.

Breast-feeding—Theophylline, ephedrine, and phenobarbital pass into the breast milk and may cause unwanted effects such as drowsiness, irritability, fretfulness, or trouble in sleeping in babies of mothers taking this medicine. Guaifenesin has not been reported to cause problems in nursing babies.

Children—Newborn infants may be especially sensitive to the effects of theophylline, ephedrine, guaifenesin, and phenobarbital combination medicine. This may increase the chance of side effects during treatment.

Older adults—Elderly people 55 years of age or older may be especially sensitive to the effects of theophylline, ephedrine, guaifenesin, and phenobarbital combination medicine. This may increase the chance of side effects during treatment.

Other medicines—Although certain medicines should not be used together at all, in other cases two different medicines may be used together even if an interaction might occur. In these cases, your doctor may want to change the dose, or other precautions may be necessary. When you are taking theophylline, ephedrine, guaifenesin, and phenobarbital combination medicine, it is especially important that your health care professional know if you are taking any of the following:

- Anticoagulants (blood thinners) or
- Corticosteroids (cortisone-like medicines) or
- Corticotropin—The effects of these medicines may be decreased by the phenobarbital in this combination medicine
- Beta-blockers (acebutolol [e.g., Sectral], atenolol [e.g., Tenormin], betaxolol [e.g., Betoptic, Kerlone], bisoprolol [e.g., Zebeta], carteolol [e.g., Cartrol], labetalol [e.g., Normodyne], levobunolol [e.g., Betagan], metoprolol [e.g., Lopressor], nadolol [e.g., Corgard], oxprenolol [e.g., Trasicor], penbutolol [e.g., Levatol], pindolol [e.g., Visken], propranolol [e.g., Inderal], sotalol [e.g., Sotacor], timolol [e.g., Blocadren, Timoptic])—Use of these medicines with this combination medicine may prevent either the beta-blocker or this combination medicine from working properly
- Central nervous system (CNS) depressants—The effects of these medicines or the phenobarbital in this combination medicine may be increased
- Cimetidine (e.g., Tagamet) or
- Ciprofloxacin (e.g., Cipro) or
- Erythromycin (e.g., E-Mycin) or
- Nicotine chewing gum (e.g., Nicorette) or
- Norfloxacin (e.g., Noroxin) or
- Ranitidine (e.g., Zantac) or
- Troleandomycin (e.g., TAO)—These medicines may increase the effects of theophylline
- Cocaine or
- Ergoloid mesylates (e.g., Hydergine) or
- Ergotamine (e.g., Gynergen)—The effects of these medicines on the heart and blood vessels may be increased by ephedrine
- Digitalis glycosides (heart medicine)—Use of digitalis glycosides with this combination medicine may increase the chance of irregular heartbeat
- Monoamine oxidase (MAO) inhibitors (furazolidone [e.g., Furoxone], isocarboxazid [e.g., Marplan], phenelzine

[e.g., Nardil], procarbazine [e.g., Matulane], tranylcypromine [e.g., Parnate])—Taking ephedrine while you are taking or within 2 weeks of taking monoamine oxidase (MAO) inhibitors may increase the chance of serious side effects
- Oral contraceptives (birth control pills) containing estrogen—Phenobarbital may decrease the birth control effects of these medicines; use of another method of birth control may be necessary while you are taking this combination medicine
- Phenytoin—The effects of phenytoin may be decreased by theophylline
- Smoking tobacco or marijuana—If you smoke or have smoked (tobacco or marijuana) regularly within the last 2 years, the amount of medicine you need may vary, depending on how much and how recently you have smoked

Other medical problems—The presence of other medical problems may affect the use of theophylline, ephedrine, guaifenesin, and phenobarbital combination medicine. Make sure you tell your doctor if you have any other medical problems, especially:

- Alcohol abuse or
- Fever or
- Liver disease or
- Respiratory infections, such as influenza (flu)—The effects of theophylline may be increased
- Diabetes mellitus (sugar diabetes)—Ephedrine may make the condition worse; your doctor may need to change the dose of your diabetes medicine
- Diarrhea—The absorption of theophylline may be decreased; therefore, the effects of this medicine may be decreased
- Enlarged prostate or
- Heart or blood vessel disease or
- High blood pressure or
- Hyperactivity (in children) or
- Stomach ulcer (or history of) or other stomach problems or
- Underactive adrenal gland—This combination medicine may make the condition worse
- Fibrocystic breast disease—Symptoms of this disease may be increased by theophylline
- Kidney disease—The effects of phenobarbital may be increased
- Overactive thyroid—The effects of theophylline may be decreased
- Pain—Phenobarbital may cause unusual excitement in the presence of pain
- Porphyria (or history of)—Phenobarbital may make the symptoms of this disease worse

Proper Use of This Medicine

This medicine works best when taken with a glass of water on an empty stomach (either 30 minutes to 1 hour before meals or 2 hours after meals) since that way it will get into the blood sooner. However, in some cases your doctor may want you to take this medicine with meals or right after meals to lessen stomach upset. If you have any questions about how you should be taking this medicine, check with your doctor.

Take this medicine only as directed. Do not take more of it and do not take it more often than recommended on the label, unless otherwise directed by your doctor. To do so may increase the chance of serious side effects. Also, if too much is taken, the phenobarbital in this medicine may become habit-forming.

In order for this medicine to help your medical problem, it must be taken every day in regularly spaced doses as recommended. This is necessary to keep a constant amount of this medicine in the blood. To help keep the amount constant, do not miss any doses.

Dosing—The dose of theophylline, ephedrine, guaifenesin, and phenobarbital combination will be different for different patients. *Follow your doctor's orders or the directions on the label.* The following information includes only the average doses of theophylline, ephedrine, guaifenesin, and phenobarbital combination. *If your dose is different, do not change it* unless your doctor tells you to do so.

The number of tablets or teaspoonfuls of elixir that you take depends on the strength of the medicine. Also, *the number of doses you take each day, the time allowed between doses, and the length of time you take the medicine depend on the medical problem for which you are taking theophylline, ephedrine, guaifenesin, and phenobarbital combination.*

- For symptoms of bronchial asthma, chronic bronchitis, emphysema, or other lung disease:
  - —For *elixir* dosage form:
    - Adults—10 milliliters (mL) (2 teaspoonfuls) four times a day or 15 mL (3 teaspoonfuls) three or four times a day, depending on which product you are taking.
    - Children—Dose must be determined by your doctor.
  - —For *tablet* dosage form:
    - Adults—One tablet four or five times a day or one or two tablets three or four times a day, depending on which product you are taking.
    - Children—Dose must be determined by your doctor.

Missed dose—If you miss a dose of this medicine, take it as soon as possible. However, if it is almost time for your next dose, skip the missed dose and go back to your regular dosing schedule. Do not double doses.

Storage—To store this medicine:

- Keep out of the reach of children.
- Store away from heat and direct light.
- Do not store the tablet form of this medicine in the bathroom, near the kitchen sink, or in other damp places. Heat or moisture may cause the medicine to break down.
- Keep the liquid form of this medicine from freezing.
- Do not keep outdated medicine or medicine no longer needed. Be sure that any discarded medicine is out of the reach of children.

Precautions While Using This Medicine

The theophylline in this medicine may add to the central nervous system (CNS) stimulant effects of caffeine-containing foods or beverages such as chocolate, cocoa, tea, coffee, and cola drinks. *Avoid eating or drinking large amounts of these foods or beverages while taking this medicine.* If you have any questions about this, check with your doctor.

The phenobarbital in this medicine will add to the effects of alcohol and other CNS depressants (medicines that slow down the nervous system, possibly causing drowsiness). Some examples of CNS depressants are antihistamines or medicine for hay fever, other allergies, or colds; sedatives, tranquilizers, or sleeping medicine; prescription pain medicine or narcotics; other barbiturates; medicine for seizures; muscle relaxants; or anesthetics, including some dental anesthetics. *Check with your doctor before taking any of the above while you are using this medicine.*

Do not eat charcoal-broiled foods every day while taking this medicine since these foods may keep the medicine from working properly.

Check with your doctor at once if you develop symptoms of influenza (flu) or a fever, since either of these may increase the chance of side effects with this medicine.

Also, *check with your doctor if diarrhea occurs* because the dose of this medicine may need to be changed.

This medicine may cause some people to become dizzy, lightheaded, drowsy, or less alert than they are normally. *Make sure you know how you react to this medicine before you drive, use machines, or do anything else that could be dangerous if you are dizzy or are not alert.*

Side Effects of This Medicine

Along with its needed effects, a medicine may cause some unwanted effects. Although not all of these side effects may occur, if they do occur they may need medical attention.

Check with your doctor as soon as possible if any of the following side effects occur:

Less common

Heartburn and/or vomiting

Symptoms of overdose

Bloody or black, tarry stools; chest pain; convulsions (seizures); diarrhea; dizziness or lightheadedness; fast, pounding, or irregular heartbeat; hallucinations (seeing, hearing, or feeling things that are not there); increase or decrease in blood pressure; irritability; loss of appetite; mood or mental changes; muscle twitching; nausea (continuing or severe) or vomiting; stomach cramps or pain; trembling; trouble in sleeping; unusual tiredness or weakness; vomiting blood or material that looks like coffee grounds

Other side effects may occur that usually do not need medical attention. These side effects may go away during treatment as your body adjusts to the medicine. However, check with your health care professional if any of the following side effects continue or are bothersome:

More common

Drowsiness; headache; nausea; nervousness or restlessness

Less common

Difficult or painful urination; feeling of warmth; flushing or redness of face

Other side effects not listed above may also occur in some patients. If you notice any other effects, check with your doctor.

Revised: October 1990
Interim revision: 09/02/94

THEOPHYLLINE, EPHEDRINE, AND HYDROXYZINE Systemic†

Some commonly used brand names are:

In the U.S.—

Ami Rax
Hydrophed
Marax
Marax-DF
Theomax DF

Generic name product may also be available.

†Not commercially available in Canada.

Description

Theophylline (thee-OFF-i-lin), ephedrine (e-FED-rin), and hydroxyzine (hye-DROX-i-zeen) combination medicine is used to treat the symptoms of bronchial asthma, chronic bronchitis, emphysema, and other lung diseases. This medicine relieves cough, wheezing, shortness of breath, and troubled breathing. It works by opening up the bronchial tubes (air passages) of the lungs and increasing the flow of air through them.

This medicine is available only with your doctor's prescription, in the following dosage forms:

Oral

- Syrup (U.S.)
- Tablets (U.S.)

Before Using This Medicine

In deciding to use a medicine, the risks of taking the medicine must be weighed against the good it will do. This is a decision you and your doctor will make. For theophylline, ephedrine, and hydroxyzine combination medicine, the following should be considered:

Allergies—Tell your doctor if you have ever had any unusual or allergic reaction to aminophylline, caffeine, dyphylline, oxtriphylline, theobromine, or theophylline; ephedrine or medicines like ephedrine such as albuterol, amphetamines, epinephrine, isoproterenol, metaproterenol, norepinephrine, phenylephrine, phenylpropanolamine, pseudoephedrine, or terbutaline; or hydroxyzine. Also tell your health care professional if you are allergic to any other substances, such as foods, preservatives, or dyes.

Diet—Make certain your health care professional knows if you are on any special diet, such as a low-sodium or low-sugar diet or a high-protein, low-carbohydrate or low-protein, high-carbohydrate diet. A high-protein, low-carbohydrate diet may decrease the effects of theophylline; a low-protein, high-carbohydrate diet may increase the effects of theophylline.

Avoid eating or drinking large amounts of caffeine-containing foods or beverages, such as chocolate, cocoa, tea, coffee, and cola drinks, because they may increase the central nervous system (CNS) stimulant effects of theophylline.

Also, eating charcoal broiled foods every day while taking theophylline may keep this medicine from working properly.

Pregnancy—Studies with theophylline on birth defects have not been done in humans. However, some studies in animals have shown that theophylline causes birth defects when given in doses many times the human dose. Also, use of theophylline during pregnancy may cause unwanted effects such as fast heartbeat, jitteriness, irritability, gagging, vomiting, and breathing problems in the newborn infant.

Studies with ephedrine on birth defects have not been done in either humans or animals.

Hydroxyzine is not recommended during the first months of pregnancy because it has been shown to cause birth defects in rats when given in doses up to many times the usual human dose.

Breast-feeding—Theophylline and ephedrine pass into the breast milk and may cause unwanted effects such as irritability, fretfulness, or trouble in sleeping in babies of mothers taking this medicine. Hydroxyzine has not been reported to cause problems in nursing babies.

Children—Theophylline, ephedrine, and hydroxyzine combination medicine is not recommended for use in children up to 2 years of age. Although there is no specific information about the use of theophylline, ephedrine, and hydroxyzine combination medicine in children 2 years of age and older, it is not expected to cause different side effects or problems in these children than it does in adults.

Older adults—Elderly people 55 years of age or older may be especially sensitive to the effects of theophylline, ephedrine, and hydroxyzine combination medicine. This may increase the chance of side effects during treatment.

Other medicines—Although certain medicines should not be used together at all, in other cases two different medicines may be used together even if an interaction might occur. In these cases, your doctor may want to change the dose, or other precautions may be necessary. When you are taking theophylline, ephedrine, and hydroxyzine combination medicine, it is especially important that your health care professional know if you are taking any of the following:

- Beta-blockers (acebutolol [e.g., Sectral], atenolol [e.g., Tenormin], betaxolol [e.g., Betoptic, Kerlone], bisoprolol [e.g., Zebeta], carteolol [e.g., Cartrol], labetalol [e.g., Normodyne], levobunolol [e.g., Betagan], metoprolol [e.g., Lopressor], nadolol [e.g., Corgard], oxprenolol [e.g., Trasicor], penbutolol [e.g., Levatol], pindolol [e.g., Visken], propranolol [e.g., Inderal], sotalol [e.g., Sotacor], timolol [e.g., Blocadren, Timoptic])—Use of these medicines with this combination medicine may prevent either the beta-blocker or this medicine from working properly
- Central nervous system (CNS) depressants—The effects of these medicines or hydroxyzine may be increased
- Cimetidine (e.g., Tagamet) or
- Ciprofloxacin (e.g., Cipro) or
- Erythromycin (e.g., E-Mycin) or
- Nicotine chewing gum (e.g., Nicorette) or
- Norfloxacin (e.g., Noroxin) or
- Ranitidine (e.g., Zantac) or
- Troleandomycin (e.g., TAO)—These medicines may increase the effects of theophylline
- Cocaine or
- Ergoloid mesylates (e.g., Hydergine) or
- Ergotamine (e.g., Gynergen)—The effects of these medicines on the heart and blood vessels may be increased by ephedrine
- Digitalis glycosides (heart medicine)—Use of these medicines with ephedrine may increase the chance of irregular heartbeat
- Monoamine oxidase (MAO) inhibitors (furazolidone [e.g., Furoxone], isocarboxazid [e.g., Marplan], phenelzine [e.g., Nardil], procarbazine [e.g., Matulane], tranylcypromine [e.g., Parnate])—Taking ephedrine while you are taking or within 2 weeks of taking monoamine oxidase (MAO) inhibitors may increase the chance of serious side effects
- Phenytoin—The effects of phenytoin may be decreased by theophylline
- Smoking tobacco or marijuana—If you smoke or have smoked (tobacco or marijuana) regularly within the last 2 years, the amount of medicine you need may vary, depending on how much and how recently you have smoked

Other medical problems—The presence of other medical problems may affect the use of theophylline, ephedrine, and hydroxyzine combination medicine. Make sure you tell your doctor if you have any other medical problems, especially:

- Alcohol abuse or
- Fever or
- Liver disease or
- Respiratory infections, such as influenza (flu)—The effects of theophylline may be increased
- Diabetes mellitus (sugar diabetes)—Ephedrine may make the condition worse; your doctor may need to change the dose of your diabetes medicine
- Diarrhea—The absorption of theophylline may be decreased; therefore, the effects of this medicine may be decreased
- Enlarged prostate or
- Heart or blood vessel disease or
- High blood pressure or
- Stomach ulcer (or history of) or other stomach problems—This combination medicine may make the condition worse
- Fibrocystic breast disease—Symptoms of this disease may be increased by theophylline
- Overactive thyroid—The effects of theophylline may be decreased

Proper Use of This Medicine

This medicine works best when taken with a glass of water on an empty stomach (either 30 minutes to 1 hour before meals or 2 hours after meals) since that way it will get into the blood sooner. However, in some cases your doctor may want you to take this medicine with meals or right after meals to lessen stomach upset. If you have any questions about how you should be taking this medicine, check with your doctor.

Take this medicine only as directed. Do not take more of it and do not take it more often than your doctor ordered. To do so may increase the chance of serious side effects.

In order for this medicine to help your medical problem, it must be taken every day in regularly spaced doses as ordered by your doctor. This is necessary to keep a constant amount of this medicine in the blood. To help keep the amount constant, do not miss any doses.

Dosing—The dose of theophylline, ephedrine, and hydroxyzine combination will be different for different patients. *Follow your doctor's orders or the directions on the label.* The following information includes only the average doses of theophylline, ephedrine, and hydroxyzine combination. *If your dose is different, do not change it* unless your doctor tells you to do so.

- For symptoms of bronchial asthma, chronic bronchitis, emphysema, or other lung disease:
  - —For *syrup* dosage form:
    - Adults—20 milliliters (mL) (4 teaspoonfuls) two to four times a day.
    - Children 5 years of age and over—5 mL (1 teaspoonful) three or four times a day.
    - Children 2 to 5 years of age—2.5 to 5 mL (1/2 to 1 teaspoonful) three or four times a day.
    - Children up to 2 years of age—Use is not recommended.
  - —For *tablet* dosage form:
    - Adults—One tablet two to four times a day.
    - Children 5 years of age and over: One-half tablet two to four times a day.
    - Children up to 5 years of age: Use is not recommended.

Missed dose—If you miss a dose of this medicine, take it as soon as possible. However, if it is almost time for your next dose, skip the missed dose and go back to your regular dosing schedule. Do not double doses.

Storage—To store this medicine:
- Keep out of the reach of children.
- Store away from heat and direct light.
- Do not store the tablet form of this medicine in the bathroom, near the kitchen sink, or in other damp places. Heat or moisture may cause the medicine to break down.
- Keep the syrup form of this medicine from freezing.
- Do not keep outdated medicine or medicine no longer needed. Be sure that any discarded medicine is out of the reach of children.

Precautions While Using This Medicine

The theophylline in this medicine may add to the central nervous system stimulant effects of caffeine-containing foods or beverages such as chocolate, cocoa, tea, coffee, and cola drinks. *Avoid eating or drinking large amounts of these foods or beverages while taking this medicine.* If you have any questions about this, check with your doctor.

The hydroxyzine in this medicine will add to the effects of alcohol and CNS depressants (medicines that slow down the nervous system, possibly causing drowsiness). Some examples of CNS depressants are antihistamines or medicine for hay fever, other allergies, or colds; sedatives, tranquilizers, or sleeping medicine; prescription pain medicine or narcotics; barbiturates; medicine for seizures; muscle relaxants; or anesthetics, including dental anesthetics. *Check with your doctor before taking any of the above while you are taking this medicine.*

Do not eat charcoal-broiled foods every day while taking this medicine since these foods may keep the medicine from working properly.

Check with your doctor at once if you develop symptoms of influenza (flu) or a fever, since either of these may increase the chance of side effects with this medicine.

Also, *check with your doctor if diarrhea occurs* because the dose of this medicine may need to be changed.

This medicine may cause some people to become dizzy, lightheaded, drowsy, or less alert than they are normally. *Make sure you know how you react to this medicine before you drive, use machines, or do anything else that could be dangerous if you are dizzy or are not alert.*

Side Effects of This Medicine

Along with its needed effects, a medicine may cause some unwanted effects. Although not all of these side effects may occur, if they do occur they may need medical attention.

Check with your doctor as soon as possible if any of the following side effects occur:

Less common

Heartburn and/or vomiting

Symptoms of overdose

Bloody or black, tarry stools; chest pain; convulsions (seizures); diarrhea; dizziness or lightheadedness; fast, pounding, or irregular heartbeat; hallucinations (seeing, hearing, or feeling things that are not there); increase or decrease in blood pressure; irritability; loss of appetite; mood or mental changes; muscle twitching; nausea (continuing or severe) or vomiting; stomach cramps or pain; trembling; trouble in sleeping; unusual tiredness or weakness; vomiting blood or material that looks like coffee grounds

Other side effects may occur that usually do not need medical attention. These side effects may go away during treatment as your body adjusts to the medicine. However,

check with your doctor if any of the following side effects continue or are bothersome:

More common

Drowsiness; headache; nausea; nervousness or restlessness

Less common

Difficult or painful urination; feeling of warmth; flushing or redness of face

Other side effects not listed above may also occur in some patients. If you notice any other effects, check with your doctor.

Revised: October 1990
Interim revision: 09/02/94

THEOPHYLLINE, EPHEDRINE, AND PHENOBARBITAL Systemic†

Some commonly used brand names are:

In the U.S.—

Tedrigen
Theodrine
Theofedral
Theophedrital
Theotal

Generic name product may also be available.

†Not commercially available in Canada.

Description

Theophylline (thee-OFF-i-lin), ephedrine (e-FED-rin), and phenobarbital (fee-noe-BAR-bi-tal) combination is used to treat the symptoms of bronchial asthma, asthmatic bronchitis, and other lung diseases. This medicine relieves cough, wheezing, shortness of breath, and troubled breathing. It works by opening up the bronchial tubes (air passages) of the lungs and increasing the flow of air through them.

Some preparations of this medicine are available only with your doctor's prescription. Others are available without a prescription; however, your doctor may have special instructions on the proper dose of this medicine for your medical condition.

Theophylline, ephedrine, and phenobarbital combination is available in the following dosage forms:

Oral

- Tablets (U.S.)

Before Using This Medicine

If you are taking this medicine without a prescription, carefully read and follow any precautions on the label. For theophylline, ephedrine, and phenobarbital combination medicine, the following should be considered:

Allergies—Tell your doctor if you have ever had any unusual or allergic reaction to aminophylline, caffeine, dyphylline, oxtriphylline, theobromine, or theophylline; to ephedrine or medicines like ephedrine such as albuterol, amphetamines, epinephrine, isoproterenol, metaproterenol, norepinephrine, phenylephrine, phenylpropanolamine, pseudoephedrine, or terbutaline; or to phenobarbital or other barbiturates. Also tell your health care professional if you are allergic to any other substances, such as foods, preservatives, or dyes.

Diet—Make certain your health care professional knows if you are on any special diet, such as a low-sodium or low-sugar diet or a high-protein, low-carbohydrate or low-protein, high-carbohydrate diet. A high-protein, low-carbohydrate diet may decrease the effects of theophylline; a low-protein, high-carbohydrate diet may increase the effects of theophylline.

Avoid eating or drinking large amounts of caffeine-containing foods or beverages, such as chocolate, cocoa, tea, coffee, and cola drinks, because they may increase the central nervous system (CNS) stimulant effects of theophylline.

Also, eating charcoal broiled foods every day while taking theophylline may keep this medicine from working properly.

Pregnancy—Studies with theophylline on birth defects have not been done in humans. However, some studies in animals have shown that theophylline causes birth defects when given in doses many times the human dose. Also, use of theophylline during pregnancy may cause unwanted effects such as fast heartbeat, jitteriness, irritability, gagging, vomiting, and breathing problems in the newborn infant.

Studies with ephedrine on birth defects have not been done in either humans or animals.

Phenobarbital taken during pregnancy has been shown to increase the chance of birth defects in humans. Also, taking phenobarbital regularly during the last 3 months of pregnancy may cause the baby to become dependent on the medicine. This may lead to withdrawal side effects in the baby after birth. In addition, one study in humans has suggested that phenobarbital taken during pregnancy may increase the chance of brain tumors in the baby.

Breast-feeding—Theophylline, ephedrine, and phenobarbital pass into the breast milk and may cause unwanted effects such as drowsiness, irritability, fretfulness, or trouble in sleeping in nursing babies of mothers taking this medicine.

Children—Newborn infants may be especially sensitive to the effects of theophylline, ephedrine, and phenobarbital combination medicine. This may increase the chance of side effects during treatment.

Older adults—Elderly people 55 years of age or older may be especially sensitive to the effects of theophylline, ephedrine, and phenobarbital combination medicine. This may increase the chance of side effects during treatment.

Other medicines—Although certain medicines should not be used together at all, in other cases two different medicines may be used together even if an interaction might occur. In these cases, your doctor may want to change the

dose, or other precautions may be necessary. When you are taking theophylline, ephedrine, and phenobarbital combination medicine, it is especially important that your health care professional know if you are taking any of the following:

- Anticoagulants (blood thinners) or
- Corticosteroids (cortisone-like medicines) or
- Corticotropin—The effects of these medicines may be decreased by phenobarbital
- Beta-blockers (acebutolol [e.g., Sectral], atenolol [e.g., Tenormin], betaxolol [e.g., Betoptic, Kerlone], bisoprolol [e.g., Zebeta], carteolol [e.g., Cartrol], labetalol [e.g., Normodyne], levobunolol [e.g., Betagan], metoprolol [e.g., Lopressor], nadolol [e.g., Corgard], oxprenolol [e.g., Trasicor], penbutolol [e.g., Levatol], pindolol [e.g., Visken], propranolol [e.g., Inderal], sotalol [e.g., Sotacor], timolol [e.g., Blocadren, Timoptic])—Use of these medicines with this combination medicine may prevent either the beta-blocker or this combination medicine from working properly
- Central nervous system (CNS) depressants—The effects of these medicines or phenobarbital may be increased
- Cimetidine (e.g., Tagamet) or
- Ciprofloxacin (e.g., Cipro) or
- Erythromycin (e.g., E-Mycin) or
- Nicotine chewing gum (e.g., Nicorette) or
- Norfloxacin (e.g., Noroxin) or
- Ranitidine (e.g., Zantac) or
- Troleandomycin (e.g., TAO)—These medicines may increase the effects of theophylline
- Cocaine or
- Ergoloid mesylates (e.g., Hydergine) or
- Ergotamine (e.g., Gynergen)—The effects of these medicines on the heart and blood vessels may be increased by ephedrine
- Digitalis glycosides (heart medicine)—Use of digitalis glycosides with this combination medicine may increase the chance of irregular heartbeat
- Monoamine oxidase (MAO) inhibitors (furazolidone [e.g., Furoxone], isocarboxazid [e.g., Marplan], phenelzine [e.g., Nardil], procarbazine [e.g., Matulane], tranylcypromine [e.g., Parnate])—Taking ephedrine while you are taking or within 2 weeks of taking monoamine oxidase (MAO) inhibitors may increase the chance of serious side effects
- Oral contraceptives (birth control pills) containing estrogen—Phenobarbital may decrease the birth control effects of these medicines; use of another method of birth control may be necessary while you are taking this combination medicine
- Phenytoin—The effects of phenytoin may be decreased by theophylline
- Smoking tobacco or marijuana—If you smoke or have smoked (tobacco or marijuana) regularly within the last 2 years, the amount of medicine you need may vary, depending on how much and how recently you have smoked

Other medical problems—The presence of other medical problems may affect the use of theophylline, ephedrine, and phenobarbital combination medicine. Make sure you tell your doctor if you have any other medical problems, especially:

- Alcohol abuse or
- Fever or
- Liver disease or
- Respiratory infections, such as influenza (flu)—The effects of theophylline may be increased
- Diabetes mellitus (sugar diabetes)—Ephedrine may make the condition worse; your doctor may need to change the dose of your diabetes medicine
- Diarrhea—The absorption of theophylline may be decreased; therefore, the effects of this medicine may be decreased
- Enlarged prostate or
- Heart or blood vessel disease or
- High blood pressure or
- Hyperactivity (in children) or
- Stomach ulcer (or history of) or other stomach problems or
- Underactive adrenal gland—This combination medicine may make the condition worse
- Fibrocystic breast disease—Symptoms of this disease may be increased by theophylline
- Kidney disease—The effects of phenobarbital may be increased
- Overactive thyroid—The effects of theophylline may be decreased
- Pain—Phenobarbital may cause unusual excitement in the presence of pain
- Porphyria (or history of)—Phenobarbital may make the symptoms of this disease worse

Proper Use of This Medicine

This medicine works best when taken with a glass of water on an empty stomach (either 30 minutes to 1 hour before meals or 2 hours after meals) since that way it will get into the blood sooner. However, in some cases your doctor may want you to take this medicine with meals or right after meals to lessen stomach upset. If you have any questions about how you should be taking this medicine, check with your doctor.

Take this medicine only as directed. Do not take more of it and do not take it more often than recommended on the label, unless otherwise directed by your doctor. To do so may increase the chance of serious side effects. Also, if too much is taken, the phenobarbital in this medicine may become habit-forming.

In order for this medicine to help your medical problem, it must be taken every day in regularly spaced doses as recommended. This is necessary to keep a constant amount of this medicine in the blood. To help keep the amount constant, do not miss any doses.

Dosing—The dose of theophylline, ephedrine, and phenobarbital combination will be different for different patients. *Follow your doctor's orders or the directions on the label.* The following information includes only the average doses of theophylline, ephedrine, and phenobarbital combination. *If your dose is different, do not change it* unless your doctor tells you to do so.

The number of tablets that you take depends on the strength of the medicine. Also, *the number of doses you take each day, the time allowed between doses, and the length of time you take the medicine depend on the medical problem for which you are taking theophylline, ephedrine, and phenobarbital combination.*

- For *oral* dosage form (tablets):
  —For symptoms of bronchial asthma, chronic bronchitis, emphysema, or other lung disease:
    - Adults—One or two tablets every four hours.
    - Children 6 to 12 years of age—One-half to one tablet every four hours.
    - Children up to 6 years of age—Dose must be determined by your doctor.

Missed dose—If you miss a dose of this medicine, take it as soon as possible. However, if it is almost time for your next dose, skip the missed dose and go back to your regular dosing schedule. Do not double doses.

Storage—To store this medicine:
- Keep out of the reach of children.
- Store away from heat and direct light.
- Do not store the tablet form of this medicine in the bathroom, near the kitchen sink, or in other damp places. Heat or moisture may cause the medicine to break down.
- Do not keep outdated medicine or medicine no longer needed. Be sure that any discarded medicine is out of the reach of children.

Precautions While Using This Medicine

The theophylline in this medicine may add to the central nervous system stimulant effects of caffeine-containing foods or beverages such as chocolate, cocoa, tea, coffee, and cola drinks. *Avoid eating or drinking large amounts of these foods or beverages while taking this medicine.* If you have any questions about this, check with your doctor.

The phenobarbital in this combination medicine will add to the effects of alcohol and other CNS depressants (medicines that slow down the nervous system, possibly causing drowsiness). Some examples of CNS depressants are antihistamines or medicine for hay fever, other allergies, or colds; sedatives, tranquilizers, or sleeping medicine; prescription pain medicine or narcotics; other barbiturates; medicine for seizures; muscle relaxants; or anesthetics, including some dental anesthetics. *Check with your doctor before taking any of the above while you are using this medicine.*

Do not eat charcoal-broiled foods every day while taking this medicine since these foods may keep the medicine from working properly.

Check with your doctor at once if you develop symptoms of influenza (flu) or a fever since either of these may increase the chance of side effects with this medicine. Also, *check with your doctor if diarrhea occurs* because the dose of this medicine may need to be changed.

This medicine may cause some people to become dizzy, lightheaded, drowsy, or less alert than they are normally. *Make sure you know how you react to this medicine before you drive, use machines, or do anything else that could be dangerous if you are dizzy or are not alert.*

Side Effects of This Medicine

Along with its needed effects, a medicine may cause some unwanted effects. Although not all of these side effects may occur, if they do occur they may need medical attention.

Check with your doctor as soon as possible if any of the following side effects occur:

Less common

Heartburn and/or vomiting

Symptoms of overdose

Bloody or black, tarry stools; chest pain; convulsions (seizures); diarrhea; dizziness or lightheadedness; fast, pounding, or irregular heartbeat; hallucinations (seeing, hearing, or feeling things that are not there); increase or decrease in blood pressure; irritability; loss of appetite; mood or mental changes; muscle twitching; nausea (continuing or severe) or vomiting; stomach cramps or pain; trembling; trouble in sleeping; unusual tiredness or weakness; vomiting blood or material that looks like coffee grounds

Other side effects may occur that usually do not need medical attention. These side effects may go away during treatment as your body adjusts to the medicine. However, check with your health care professional if any of the following side effects continue or are bothersome:

More common

Drowsiness; headache; nausea; nervousness or restlessness

Less common

Difficult or painful urination; feeling of warmth; flushing or redness of face

Other side effects not listed above may also occur in some patients. If you notice any other effects, check with your doctor.

Revised: October 1990
Interim revision: 09/02/94

THEOPHYLLINE AND GUAIFENESIN Systemic†

Some commonly used brand names are:

In the U.S.—

Asbron G
Asbron G Inlay-Tabs
Bronchial
Broncomar GG
Ed-Bron G
Elixophyllin-GG
Equibron G
Glyceryl-T
Mudrane GG-2
Quibron
Quibron-300
Slo-Phyllin GG
Synophylate-GG
Theolate
Uni-Bronchial

Generic name product may also be available.

Another commonly used name is theophylline and glyceryl guaiacolate.

†Not commercially available in Canada.

Description

Theophylline (thee-OFF-i-lin) and guaifenesin (gwye-FEN-e-sin) combination is used to treat the symptoms of bronchial asthma, chronic bronchitis, emphysema, and other lung diseases. This medicine relieves cough, wheezing, shortness of breath, and troubled breathing. It works by opening up the bronchial tubes (air passages) of the lungs and increasing the flow of air through them.

This medicine is available only with your doctor's prescription, in the following dosage forms:

Oral

- Capsules (U.S.)
- Elixir (U.S.)
- Oral solution (U.S.)
- Syrup (U.S.)
- Tablets (U.S.)

Before Using This Medicine

In deciding to use a medicine, the risks of taking the medicine must be weighed against the good it will do. This is a decision you and your doctor will make. For theophylline and guaifenesin combination medicine, the following should be considered:

Allergies—Tell your doctor if you have ever had any unusual or allergic reaction to aminophylline, caffeine, dyphylline, oxtriphylline, theobromine, or theophylline. Also tell your health care professional if you are allergic to any other substances, such as foods, preservatives, or dyes.

Diet—Make certain your health care professional knows if you are on any special diet, such as a low-sodium or low-sugar diet or a high-protein, low-carbohydrate or low-protein, high-carbohydrate diet. A high-protein, low-carbohydrate diet may decrease the effects of theophylline; a low-protein, high-carbohydrate diet may increase the effects of theophylline.

Avoid eating or drinking large amounts of caffeine-containing foods or beverages, such as chocolate, cocoa, tea, coffee, and cola drinks, because they may increase the central nervous system (CNS) stimulant effects of theophylline.

Also, eating charcoal broiled foods every day while taking theophylline may keep this medicine from working properly.

Pregnancy—Studies on birth defects have not been done in humans. However, some studies in animals have shown that theophylline causes birth defects when given in doses many times the human dose. Also, use of theophylline during pregnancy may cause unwanted effects such as fast heartbeat, jitteriness, irritability, gagging, vomiting, and breathing problems in the newborn infant. Guaifenesin has not been shown to cause birth defects or other problems in humans.

Breast-feeding—Theophylline passes into the breast milk and may cause irritability, fretfulness, or trouble in sleeping in babies of mothers taking this medicine. Guaifenesin has not been reported to cause problems in nursing babies.

Children—The side effects of theophylline are more likely to occur in newborn infants, who are usually more sensitive to the effects of this medicine.

Although there is no specific information about the use of guaifenesin in children, it is not expected to cause different side effects or problems in children than it does in adults.

Older adults—The side effects of theophylline are more likely to occur in elderly patients 55 years of age and older, who are usually more sensitive than younger adults to the effects of this medicine.

Although there is no specific information about the use of guaifenesin in the elderly, it is not expected to cause different side effects or problems in older people than it does in younger adults.

Other medicines—Although certain medicines should not be used together at all, in other cases two different medicines may be used together even if an interaction might occur. In these cases, your doctor may want to change the dose, or other precautions may be necessary. When you are taking theophylline and guaifenesin combination medicine, it is especially important that your health care professional know if you are taking any of the following:

- Beta-blockers (acebutolol [e.g., Sectral], atenolol [e.g., Tenormin], betaxolol [e.g., Betoptic, Kerlone], bisoprolol [e.g., Zebeta], carteolol [e.g., Cartrol], labetalol [e.g., Normodyne], levobunolol [e.g., Betagan], metoprolol [e.g., Lopressor], nadolol [e.g., Corgard], oxprenolol [e.g., Trasicor], penbutolol [e.g., Levatol], pindolol [e.g., Visken], propranolol [e.g., Inderal], sotalol [e.g., Sotacor], timolol [e.g., Blocadren, Timoptic])—Use of these medicines with theophylline may prevent either the beta-blocker or theophylline from working properly
- Cimetidine (e.g., Tagamet) or
- Ciprofloxacin (e.g., Cipro) or
- Erythromycin (e.g., E-Mycin) or
- Nicotine chewing gum (e.g., Nicorette) or
- Norfloxacin (e.g., Noroxin) or
- Ranitidine (e.g., Zantac) or
- Troleandomycin (e.g., TAO)—These medicines may increase the effects of theophylline
- Phenytoin (e.g., Dilantin)—The effects of phenytoin may be decreased by theophylline
- Smoking tobacco or marijuana—If you smoke or have smoked (tobacco or marijuana) regularly within the last 2 years, the amount of medicine you need may vary, depending on how much and how recently you have smoked

Other medical problems—The presence of other medical problems may affect the use of theophylline and guaifenesin combination medicine. Make sure you tell your doctor if you have any other medical problems, especially:

- Alcohol abuse or
- Fever or
- Liver disease or
- Respiratory infections, such as influenza (flu)—The effects of theophylline may be increased
- Diarrhea—The absorption of theophylline may be decreased; therefore, the effects of this medicine may be decreased
- Enlarged prostate or
- Heart disease or

- High blood pressure or
- Stomach ulcer (or history of) or other stomach problems—Theophylline may make the condition worse
- Fibrocystic breast disease—Symptoms of this disease may be increased by theophylline
- Overactive thyroid—The effects of theophylline may be decreased

Proper Use of This Medicine

This medicine works best when taken with a glass of water on an empty stomach (either 30 minutes to 1 hour before meals or 2 hours after meals) since that way it will get into the blood sooner. However, in some cases your doctor may want you to take this medicine with meals or right after meals to lessen stomach upset. If you have any questions about how you should be taking this medicine, check with your doctor.

Take this medicine only as directed. Do not take more of it, do not take it more often, and do not take it for a longer time than your doctor ordered. To do so may increase the chance of serious side effects.

In order for this medicine to help your medical problem, it must be taken every day in regularly spaced doses as ordered by your doctor. This is necessary to keep a constant amount of this medicine in the blood. To help keep the amount constant, do not miss any doses.

Dosing—When you are taking theophylline and guaifenesin combination, it is very important that you get the exact amount of medicine that you need. The dose of this medicine will be different for different patients. Your doctor will determine the proper dose of the theophylline and guaifenesin combination for you. *Follow your doctor's orders or the directions on the label.*

After you begin taking theophylline and guaifenesin combination, it is very important that your doctor check your blood level of theophylline at regular intervals to find out if your dose of theophylline and guaifenesin combination needs to be changed. *Do not change your dose of theophylline and guaifenesin combination* unless your doctor tells you to do so.

The number of capsules or tablets or teaspoonfuls of elixir, solution, or syrup that you take depends on the strength of the medicine.

Missed dose—If you miss a dose of this medicine, take it as soon as possible. However, if it is almost time for your next dose, skip the missed dose and go back to your regular dosing schedule. Do not double doses.

Storage—To store this medicine:

- Keep out of the reach of children.
- Store away from heat and direct light.
- Do not store the capsule or tablet form of this medicine in the bathroom, near the kitchen sink, or in other damp places. Heat or moisture may cause the medicine to break down.
- Keep the liquid form of this medicine from freezing.
- Do not keep outdated medicine or medicine no longer needed. Be sure that any discarded medicine is out of the reach of children.

Precautions While Using This Medicine

Your doctor should check your progress at regular visits, especially for the first few weeks after you begin taking this medicine. A blood test may be taken to help your doctor decide whether the dose of this medicine should be changed.

The theophylline in this medicine may add to the central nervous system stimulant effects of caffeine-containing foods or beverages such as chocolate, cocoa, tea, coffee, and cola drinks. *Avoid eating or drinking large amounts of these foods or beverages while taking this medicine.* If you have any questions about this, check with your doctor.

Do not eat charcoal-broiled foods every day while taking this medicine since these foods may keep the medicine from working properly.

Check with your doctor at once if you develop symptoms of influenza (flu) or a fever since either of these may increase the chance of side effects with this medicine.

Also, *check with your doctor if diarrhea occurs* because the dose of this medicine may need to be changed.

Side Effects of This Medicine

Along with its needed effects, a medicine may cause some unwanted effects. Although not all of these side effects may occur, if they do occur they may need medical attention.

Check with your doctor as soon as possible if any of the following side effects occur:

Less common

Heartburn and/or vomiting

Symptoms of overdose of theophylline

Bloody or black, tarry stools; confusion or change in behavior; convulsions (seizures); diarrhea; dizziness or lightheadedness; fast breathing; fast, pounding, or irregular heartbeat; flushing or redness of face; headache; increased urination; irritability; loss of appetite; muscle twitching; nausea (continuing or severe) or vomiting; stomach cramps or pain; trembling; trouble in sleeping; unusual tiredness or weakness; vomiting blood or material that looks like coffee grounds

Other side effects may occur that usually do not need medical attention. These side effects may go away during treatment as your body adjusts to the medicine. However, check with your doctor if any of the following side effects continue or are bothersome:

More common

Nausea; nervousness or restlessness

Other side effects not listed above may also occur in some patients. If you notice any other effects, check with your doctor.

Revised: October 1990
Interim revision: 09/02/94

THIABENDAZOLE Systemic†

A commonly used brand name in the U.S is Mintezol.

†Not commercially available in Canada.

Description

Thiabendazole (thye-a-BEN-da-zole) belongs to the family of medicines called anthelmintics (ant-hel-MIN-tiks). Anthelmintics are medicines used in the treatment of worm infections.

Thiabendazole is used to treat:

- creeping eruption (cutaneous larva migrans);
- pork worms (trichinosis);
- threadworms (strongyloidiasis); and
- visceral larva migrans (toxocariasis).

This medicine may also be used for other worm infections as determined by your doctor.

Thiabendazole is available only with your doctor's prescription, in the following dosage forms:

Oral

- Chewable tablets (U.S.)
- Oral suspension (U.S.)

Before Using This Medicine

In deciding to use a medicine, the risks of taking the medicine must be weighed against the good it will do. This is a decision you and your doctor will make. For thiabendazole, the following should be considered:

Allergies—Tell your doctor if you have ever had any unusual or allergic reaction to thiabendazole. Also tell your health care professional if you are allergic to any other substances, such as foods, preservatives, or dyes.

Pregnancy—Studies have not been done in humans. In addition, thiabendazole has not been shown to cause birth defects or other problems in studies in rabbits, rats, and mice given 2½ to 15 times the usual human dose. However, another study in mice given 10 times the usual human dose has shown that thiabendazole causes cleft palate (a split in the roof of the mouth) and bone defects.

Breast-feeding—It is not known whether thiabendazole passes into human breast milk. However, this medicine has not been reported to cause problems in nursing babies.

Children—This medicine has been tested in children over 13.6 kg of body weight (30 pounds). In effective doses, it has not been reported to cause different side effects or problems in children than it does in adults.

Older adults—Many medicines have not been studied specifically in older people. Therefore, it may not be known whether they work exactly the same way they do in younger adults or if they cause different side effects or problems in older people. There is no specific information comparing use of thiabendazole in the elderly with use in other age groups.

Other medicines—Although certain medicines should not be used together at all, in other cases two different medicines may be used together even if an interaction might occur. In these cases, your doctor may want to change the dose, or other precautions may be necessary. When you are taking thiabendazole, it is especially important that your health care professional know if you are taking any of the following:

- Theophylline—Patients taking thiabendazole and theophylline together may have an increased chance of theophylline side effects

Other medical problems—The presence of other medical problems may affect the use of thiabendazole. Make sure you tell your doctor if you have any other medical problems, especially:

- Kidney disease or
- Liver disease—Patients with kidney and/or liver disease may have an increased chance of side effects

Proper Use of This Medicine

No special preparations (for example, special diets, fasting, other medicines, laxatives, or enemas) are necessary before, during, or immediately after treatment with thiabendazole.

Thiabendazole is best taken after meals (breakfast and evening meal). This helps to prevent some common side effects such as nausea, vomiting, dizziness, or loss of appetite.

Doctors may also prescribe a corticosteroid (a cortisone-like medicine) for certain patients with *pork worms (trichinosis)*, especially for those with severe symptoms. This is to help reduce the inflammation caused by the pork worm larvae. If your doctor prescribes these 2 medicines together, it is important to take the corticosteroid along with thiabendazole. Take them exactly as directed by your doctor. Do not miss any doses.

For patients taking the *oral liquid form* of thiabendazole:

- Use a specially marked measuring spoon or other device to measure each dose accurately. The average household teaspoon may not hold the right amount of liquid.

For patients taking the *chewable tablet form* of thiabendazole:

- Tablets should be chewed or crushed before they are swallowed.

To help clear up your infection completely, *take this medicine exactly as directed by your doctor for the full time of treatment.* In some patients a second course of this medicine may be required to clear up the infection completely. *Do not miss any doses.*

Dosing—The dose of thiabendazole will be different for different patients. *Follow your doctor's orders or the directions on the label.* The following information includes only the average doses of thiabendazole. *If your dose is different, do not change it* unless your doctor tells you to do so.

The number of tablets or teaspoonfuls of suspension that you take depends on the strength of the medicine. Also, *the number of doses you take each day, the time allowed between doses, and the length of time you take the medicine depend on the medical problem for which you are taking thiabendazole.*

- For *oral* dosage forms (oral suspension or tablets):
  —Adults and children over 13.6 kilograms (30 pounds) of body weight:
- For *cutaneous larva migrans* and *strongyloidiasis*: Dose is based on body weight and will be determined by your doctor. The dose is taken two times a day for two days.
- For *trichinosis*: Dose is based on body weight and will be determined by your doctor. The dose is taken two times a day for two to four days.
- For *visceral larva migrans*: Dose is based on body weight and will be determined by your doctor. The dose is taken two times a day for five to seven days.
  —Children up to 13.6 kilograms (30 pounds) of body weight: Dose must be determined by the doctor.

Missed dose—If you do miss a dose of this medicine, take it as soon as possible. However, if it is almost time for your next dose, skip the missed dose and go back to your regular dosing schedule. Do not double doses.

Storage—To store this medicine:

- Keep out of the reach of children.
- Store away from heat and direct light.
- Do not store the chewable tablet form of this medicine in the bathroom, near the kitchen sink, or in other damp places. Heat or moisture may cause the medicine to break down.
- Keep the oral liquid form of this medicine from freezing.
- Do not keep outdated medicine or medicine no longer needed. Be sure that any discarded medicine is out of the reach of children.

Precautions While Using This Medicine

It is important that your doctor check your progress at regular visits. This is to make sure that the infection is cleared up completely.

Thiabendazole may cause blurred vision or yellow vision. It may also cause some people to become dizzy, drowsy, or less alert than they are normally. *Make sure you know how you react to this medicine before you drive, use machines, or do anything else that could be dangerous if you are dizzy or are not alert or able to see well.* If these reactions are especially bothersome, check with your doctor.

Good health habits are required to help prevent reinfection. These include the following:

- For creeping eruption (cutaneous larva migrans) or visceral larva migrans (toxocariasis):
  —Keep dogs and cats off beaches and bathing areas.
  —Treat household pets for worms (deworm) regularly.
  —Cover children's sandboxes when not being used.

  These measures help to prevent contamination of the sand or soil by worm larvae from the animals' wastes. This helps to keep children from picking up the larvae when they put their hands in their mouths after touching contaminated sand or soil.
- For pork worms (trichinosis):
  —Cook all pork, pork-containing products, and game at not less than 140 °F (60 °C) until well done (not pink in the center) before eating. This will kill any trichinosis larvae that may be in the meat.

Side Effects of This Medicine

Along with its needed effects, a medicine may cause some unwanted effects. Although not all of these side effects may occur, if they do occur they may need medical attention.

Check with your doctor immediately if any of the following side effects occur:

More common

Confusion; diarrhea (severe); hallucinations (seeing, hearing, and feeling things that are not there); irritability; loss of appetite; nausea and vomiting (severe); numbness or tingling in the hands or feet

Less common

Skin rash or itching

In addition to the side effects mentioned above, check with your doctor as soon as possible if any of the following side effects occur:

Rare

Aching of joints and muscles; blurred or yellow vision; chills; convulsions (seizures); dark urine; fever; lower back pain; pain or burning while urinating; pale stools; redness, blistering, peeling, or loosening of skin; unusual feeling in the eyes; unusual tiredness or weakness; yellow eyes and skin

Other side effects may occur that usually do not need medical attention. These side effects may go away during treatment as your body adjusts to the medicine. However, check with your doctor if any of the following side effects continue or are bothersome:

More common

Dizziness; drowsiness; dryness of eyes and mouth; headache; ringing or buzzing in the ears

This medicine may cause the urine to have an asparagus-like or other unusual odor while you are taking it and for about 24 hours after you stop taking it. This side effect does not need medical attention.

Other side effects not listed above may also occur in some patients. If you notice any other effects, check with your doctor.

Additional Information

Once a medicine has been approved for marketing for a certain use, experience may show that it is also useful for other medical problems. Although these uses are not in-

cluded in product labeling, thiabendazole is used in certain patients with the following medical conditions:
- Capillariasis
- Dracunculiasis
- Trichostrongyliasis

Other than the above information, there is no additional information relating to proper use, precautions, or side effects for these uses.

Revised: 02/01/93

THIABENDAZOLE Topical*†

*Not commercially available in the U.S.
†Not commercially available in Canada.

Description

Thiabendazole (thye-a-BEN-da-zole) belongs to the family of medicines called anthelmintics (ant-hel-MIN-tiks). Anthelmintics are medicines used in the treatment of worm infections.

Thiabendazole topical preparations are used to treat a skin disease called cutaneous larva migrans (creeping eruption). Cutaneous larva migrans is caused by dog and cat hookworm larvae. These larvae cause slowly moving burrows or tunnels in the skin. This may result in itching, redness, or inflammation around the end of the burrows or tunnels.

Thiabendazole is available only with your doctor's prescription, in the following dosage form:

Topical
- Topical suspension

Before Using This Medicine

In deciding to use a medicine, the risks of using the medicine must be weighed against the good it will do. This is a decision you and your doctor will make. For topical thiabendazole, the following should be considered:

Allergies—Tell your doctor if you have ever had any unusual or allergic reaction to thiabendazole. Also tell your health care professional if you are allergic to any other substances, such as preservatives or dyes.

Pregnancy—Thiabendazole may be absorbed through the skin. However, thiabendazole topical preparations have not been shown to cause birth defects or other problems in humans.

Breast-feeding—Thiabendazole may be absorbed through the mother's skin. However, thiabendazole topical preparations have not been shown to cause problems in nursing babies.

Children—Although there is no specific information comparing the use of thiabendazole in children with use in other age groups, this medicine is not expected to cause different side effects or problems in children than it does in adults.

Older adults—Many medicines have not been studied specifically in older people, Therefore, it may not be known whether they work exactly the same way they do in younger adults. Although there is no specific information comparing the use of thiabendazole in the elderly with use in other age groups, this medicine is not expected to cause different side effects or problems in older people than it does in younger adults.

Other medicines—Although certain medicines should not be used together at all, in other cases two different medicines may be used together even if an interaction might occur. In these cases, your doctor may want to change the dose, or other precautions may be necessary. Tell your health care professional if you are using any other topical prescription or nonprescription (over-the-counter [OTC]) medicine that is to be applied to the same area of the skin.

Proper Use of This Medicine

Apply thiabendazole directly to, and about 5 to 7.5 cm (2 to 3 inches) around, the slowly moving end of each burrow or tunnel being made by the larva of the worm in the skin.

To help clear up your infection completely, *use this medicine exactly as directed by your doctor for the full time of treatment. Do not miss any doses.*

Dosing—The dose of topical thiabendazole will be different for different patients. *Follow your doctor's orders or the directions on the label.* The following information includes only the average doses of topical thiabendazole. *If your dose is different, do not change it* unless your doctor tells you to do so.

- For *topical* dosage form (suspension):
  —For cutaneous larva migrans:
    - Adults and children—Use two to four times a day for two to seven days.

Missed dose—If you miss a dose of this medicine, apply it as soon as possible. However, if it is almost time for your next dose, skip the missed dose and go back to your regular dosing schedule.

Storage—To store this medicine:
- Keep out of the reach of children.
- Store away from heat and direct light.
- Keep the medicine from freezing.
- Do not keep outdated medicine or medicine no longer needed. Be sure that any discarded medicine is out of the reach of children.

Precautions While Using This Medicine

If your skin problem does not improve within a few days, or if the burrow or tunnel continues to get longer, check with your doctor.

Side Effects of This Medicine

There have not been any common or important side effects reported with this medicine when used on the skin. However, if you notice any side effects, check with your doctor.

Revised: 09/28/93
Interim revision: 05/31/94

THIAMINE (Vitamin B_1) Systemic

Some commonly used brand names are:

In the U.S.—

Biamine

Generic name product may also be available.

In Canada—

Betaxin
Bewon

Generic name product may also be available.

Description

Vitamins (VYE-ta-mins) are compounds that you *must* have for growth and health. They are needed in small amounts only and are usually available in the foods that you eat. Thiamine (THYE-a-min) (vitamin B_1) is needed for the breakdown of carbohydrates.

Some conditions may increase your need for thiamine. These include:

- Alcoholism
- Burns
- Diarrhea (continuing)
- Fever (continuing)
- Illness (continuing)
- Intestinal disease
- Liver disease
- Overactive thyroid
- Stress (continuing)
- Surgical removal of stomach

Also, the following groups of people may have a deficiency of thiamine:

- Patients using an artificial kidney (on hemodialysis)
- Individuals who do heavy manual labor on a daily basis

Increased need for thiamine should be determined by your health care professional.

Lack of thiamine may lead to a condition called beriberi. Signs of beriberi include loss of appetite, constipation, muscle weakness, pain or tingling in arms or legs, and possible swelling of feet or lower legs. In addition, if severe, lack of thiamine may cause mental depression, memory problems, weakness, shortness of breath, and fast heartbeat. Your health care professional may treat this by prescribing thiamine for you.

Thiamine may also be used for other conditions as determined by your health care professional.

Claims that thiamine is effective for treatment of skin problems, chronic diarrhea, tiredness, mental problems, multiple sclerosis, nerve problems, and ulcerative colitis (a disease of the intestines), or as an insect repellant or to stimulate appetite have not been proven.

Injectable thiamine is administered only by or under the supervision of your health care professional. Other forms of thiamine are available without a prescription.

Thiamine is available in the following dosage forms:

Oral
- Elixir (Canada)
- Tablets (U.S. and Canada)

Parenteral
- Injection (U.S. and Canada)

Importance of Diet

For good health, it is important that you eat a balanced and varied diet. Follow carefully any diet program your health care professional may recommend. For your specific dietary vitamin and/or mineral needs, ask your health care professional for a list of appropriate foods. If you think that you are not getting enough vitamins and/or minerals in your diet, you may choose to take a dietary supplement.

Thiamine is found in various foods, including cereals (whole-grain and enriched), peas, beans, nuts, and meats (especially pork and beef). Some thiamine in foods is lost with cooking.

Vitamins alone will not take the place of a good diet and will not provide energy. Your body also needs other substances found in food such as protein, minerals, carbohydrates, and fat. Vitamins themselves often cannot work without the presence of other foods.

The daily amount of thiamine needed is defined in several different ways.

For U.S.—

- Recommended Dietary Allowances (RDAs) are the amount of vitamins and minerals needed to provide for adequate nutrition in most healthy persons. RDAs for a given nutrient may vary depending on a person's age, sex, and physical condition (e.g., pregnancy).
- Daily Values (DVs) are used on food and dietary supplement labels to indicate the percent of the recommended daily amount of each nutrient that a serving

provides. DV replaces the previous designation of United States Recommended Daily Allowances (USRDAs).

For Canada—

- Recommended Nutrient Intakes (RNIs) are used to determine the amounts of vitamins, minerals, and protein needed to provide adequate nutrition and lessen the risk of chronic disease.

Normal daily recommended intakes in milligrams (mg) for thiamine are generally defined as follows:

Persons	U.S. (mg)	Canada (mg)
Infants and children		
Birth to 3 years of age	0.3–0.7	0.3–0.6
4 to 6 years of age	0.9	0.7
7 to 10 years of age	1	0.8–1
Adolescent and adult males	1.2–1.5	0.8–1.3
Adolescent and adult females	1–1.1	0.8–0.9
Pregnant females	1.5	0.9–1
Breast-feeding females	1.6	1–1.2

Before Using This Dietary Supplement

If you are taking this dietary supplement without a prescription, carefully read and follow any precautions on the label. For thiamine, the following should be considered:

Allergies—Tell your health care professional if you have ever had any unusual or allergic reaction to thiamine. Also tell your health care professional if you are allergic to any other substances, such as foods, preservatives, or dyes.

Pregnancy—It is especially important that you are receiving enough vitamins when you become pregnant and that you continue to receive the right amount of vitamins throughout your pregnancy. The healthy growth and development of the fetus depend on a steady supply of nutrients from the mother. However, taking large amounts of a dietary supplement in pregnancy may be harmful to the mother and/or fetus and should be avoided.

Breast-feeding—It is especially important that you receive the right amounts of vitamins so that your baby will also get the vitamins needed to grow properly. However, taking large amounts of a dietary supplement while breast-feeding may be harmful to the mother and/or baby and should be avoided.

Children—Problems in children have not been reported with intake of normal daily recommended amounts.

Older adults—Problems in older adults have not been reported with intake of normal daily recommended amounts. Studies have shown that older adults may have lower blood levels of thiamine than younger adults. Your health care professional may recommend that you take a vitamin supplement that contains thiamine.

Medicines or other dietary supplements—Although certain medicines or dietary supplements should not be used together at all, in other cases they may be used together even if an interaction might occur. In these cases, your health care professional may want to change the dose, or other precautions may be necessary. Tell your health care professional if you are taking any other dietary supplement or prescription or nonprescription (over-the-counter [OTC]) medicine.

Proper Use of This Dietary Supplement

Dosing—The amount of thiamine needed to meet normal daily recommended intakes will be different for different individuals. The following information includes only the average amounts of thiamine.

- For *oral* dosage forms (tablets, oral solution):
  - —To prevent deficiency, the amount taken by mouth is based on normal daily recommended intakes:

    For the U.S.
    - Adult and teenage males—1.2 to 1.5 milligrams (mg) per day.
    - Adult and teenage females—1 to 1.1 mg per day.
    - Pregnant females—1.5 mg per day.
    - Breast-feeding females—1.6 mg per day.
    - Children 7 to 10 years of age—1 mg per day.
    - Children 4 to 6 years of age—0.9 mg per day.
    - Children birth to 3 years of age—0.3 to 0.7 mg per day.

    For Canada
    - Adult and teenage males—0.8 to 1.3 mg per day.
    - Adult and teenage females—0.8 to 0.9 mg per day.
    - Pregnant females—0.9 to 1 mg per day.
    - Breast-feeding females—1 to 1.2 mg per day.
    - Children 7 to 10 years of age—0.8 to 1 mg per day.
    - Children 4 to 6 years of age—0.7 mg per day.
    - Children birth to 3 years of age—0.3 to 0.6 mg per day.
  - —To treat deficiency:
    - Adults and teenagers—Treatment dose is determined by prescriber for each individual based on the severity of deficiency. The following dosage has been established: Beriberi—Oral, 5 to 10 mg three times a day.
    - Children—Treatment dose is determined by prescriber for each individual based on the severity of deficiency. The following dosage has been established: Beriberi—Oral, 10 a day.

Missed dose—If you miss taking a vitamin for 1 or more days there is no cause for concern, since it takes some time for your body to become seriously low in vitamins. However, if your health care professional has recommended that you take this vitamin, try to remember to take it as directed every day.

Storage—To store this dietary supplement:

- Keep out of the reach of children.
- Store away from heat and direct light.
- Do not store in the bathroom, near the kitchen sink, or in other damp places. Heat or moisture may cause the dietary supplement to break down.

- Keep the oral liquid form of this dietary supplement from freezing.
- Do not keep outdated dietary supplements or those no longer needed. Be sure that any discarded dietary supplement is out of the reach of children.

Side Effects of This Dietary Supplement

Along with its needed effects, a dietary supplement may cause some unwanted effects. Although not all of these side effects may occur, if they do occur they may need medical attention.

Check with your health care professional immediately if any of the following side effects occur:

Rare—Soon after receiving injection only

Coughing; difficulty in swallowing; hives; itching of skin; swelling of face, lips, or eyelids; wheezing or difficulty in breathing

Other side effects not listed above may also occur in some individuals. If you notice any other effects, check with your health care professional.

Additional Information

Once a medicine or dietary supplement has been approved for marketing for a certain use, experience may show that it is also useful for other medical problems. Although this use is not included in product labeling, thiamine is used in certain patients with the following medical conditions:

- Enzyme deficiency diseases such as encephalomyelopathy, maple syrup urine disease, pyruvate carboxylase, and hyperalaninemia

Other than the above information, there is no additional information relating to proper use, precautions, or side effects for these uses.

Revised: 06/24/92
Interim revision: 07/29/94; 05/26/95

THIETHYLPERAZINE Systemic

Some commonly used brand names are:

In the U.S.—
Norzine
Torecan

In Canada—
Torecan

Description

Thiethylperazine (thye-eth-il-PER-a-zeen) is a phenothiazine medicine. It is used to treat nausea and vomiting.

This medicine is available only with your doctor's prescription in the following dosage forms:

Oral
- Tablets (U.S. and Canada)

Parenteral
- Injection (U.S. and Canada)

Rectal
- Suppositories (U.S.)

Before Using This Medicine

In deciding to use a medicine, the risks of taking the medicine must be weighed against the good it will do. This is a decision you and your doctor will make. For thiethylperazine, the following should be considered:

Allergies—Tell your doctor if you have ever had any unusual or allergic reaction to thiethylperazine or other phenothiazine medicines. Also tell your health care professional if you are allergic to any other substances, such as foods, preservatives, or dyes.

Pregnancy—Thiethylperazine is not recommended during pregnancy. Other phenothiazine medicines have been reported to cause unwanted effects, such as jaundice and muscle tremors and other movement disorders, in newborn babies whose mothers took these medicines during pregnancy.

Breast-feeding—It is not known if thiethylperazine passes into the breast milk. However, thiethylperazine is not recommended for use during breast-feeding because there is the chance that it may cause unwanted effects in nursing babies.

Children—Children are usually more sensitive than adults to the effects of phenothiazine medicines such as thiethylperazine. Certain side effects, such as muscle spasms of the face, neck, and back, tic-like or twitching movements, inability to move the eyes, twisting of the body, or weakness of the arms and legs, are more likely to occur in children, especially those with severe illness or dehydration.

Older adults—Elderly patients are usually more sensitive to the effects of phenothiazine medicines such as thiethylperazine. Confusion; difficult or painful urination; dizziness; drowsiness; feeling faint; or dryness of mouth, nose, or throat may be more likely to occur in elderly patients. Also, nightmares or unusual excitement, nervousness, restlessness, or irritability may be more likely to occur in elderly patients. In addition, uncontrolled movements may be more likely to occur in elderly patients taking thiethylperazine.

Other medicines—Although certain medicines should not be used together at all, in other cases two different medicines may be used together even if an interaction might occur. In these cases, your doctor may want to change the dose, or other precautions may be necessary. When you are taking thiethylperazine, it is especially important that your health care professional know if you are taking any of the following:

- Amoxapine (e.g., Asendin) or
- Antipsychotics (medicine for mental illness) or
- Methyldopa (e.g., Aldomet) or
- Metoclopramide (e.g., Reglan) or
- Metyrosine (e.g., Demser) or
- Pemoline (e.g., Cylert) or
- Pimozide (e.g., Orap) or

- Promethazine (e.g., Phenergan) or
- Rauwolfia alkaloids (alseroxylon [e.g., Rauwiloid], deserpidine [e.g., Harmonyl], rauwolfia serpentina [e.g., Raudixin], reserpine [e.g., Serpasil]) or
- Trimeprazine (e.g., Temaril)—Side effects of these medicines, such as uncontrolled body movements, may become more severe and frequent if they are used together with thiethylperazine
- Central nervous system (CNS) depressants (medicine that causes drowsiness) or
- Tricyclic antidepressants (medicine for depression)—CNS depressant effects of these medicines or thiethylperazine, such as drowsiness, may be increased in severity; also, taking maprotiline or tricyclic antidepressants may cause some side effects of these medicines, such as dryness of mouth, to become more severe
- Contrast agents, injected into spinal canal—If you are having an x-ray test of the head, spinal canal, or nervous system for which you are going to receive an injection into the spinal canal, thiethylperazine may increase your chance of having seizures
- Epinephrine—Side effects, such as low blood pressure and fast or racing heartbeat, may occur more often or may be more severe
- Levodopa—When used together with thiethylperazine, the levodopa may not work as it should
- Quinidine—Unwanted effects on the heart may occur or become more severe

Other medical problems—The presence of other medical problems may affect the use of thiethylperazine. Make sure you tell your doctor if you have any other medical problems, especially:

- Alcohol abuse—This medicine, if taken together with alcohol, may lower the blood pressure and cause CNS depressant effects, such as severe drowsiness
- Asthma attack or
- Other lung diseases—Thiethylperazine may cause secretions to become thick so that it might be difficult to cough them up, for example, during an asthma attack
- Blood disease or
- Heart or blood vessel disease—These medicines may cause more serious conditions to develop
- Difficult urination or
- Enlarged prostate—This medicine may cause urinary problems to get worse
- Glaucoma—This medicine may cause an increase in inner eye pressure
- Liver disease—Thiethylperazine may accumulate in the body, increasing the chance of side effects, such as muscle spasms
- Parkinson's disease or
- Seizure disorders—The chance of thiethylperazine causing seizures or uncontrolled movements is greater when these conditions are present

Proper Use of This Medicine

Thiethylperazine is used only to relieve or prevent nausea and vomiting. *Use it only as directed. Do not use more of it and do not use it more often than your doctor ordered.* To do so may increase the chance of side effects.

For patients *taking this medicine by mouth:*

- This medicine may be taken with food or a full glass (8 ounces) of water or milk to reduce stomach irritation.

For patients using the *suppository form of this medicine:*

- To insert suppository: First, remove foil wrapper and moisten the suppository with cold water. Lie down on your side and use your finger to push the suppository well up into the rectum. If the suppository is too soft to insert, chill it in the refrigerator for 30 minutes or run cold water over it before removing the foil wrapper.

Dosing—The dose of thiethylperazine will be different for different patients. *Follow your doctor's orders or the directions on the label.* The following information includes only the average doses of thiethylperazine. *If your dose is different, do not change it* unless your doctor tells you to do so.

The number of doses you take each day, the time allowed between doses, and the length of time you take the medicine depend on the medical problem for which you are taking thiethylperazine.

- For nausea and vomiting:
  - —For *oral* dosage form (tablets):
    - Adults—10 milligrams (mg) one to three times a day.
    - Children—Use and dose must be determined by your doctor.
  - —For *injection* dosage form:
    - Adults—10 mg one to three times a day, injected into a muscle.
    - Children—Use and dose must be determined by your doctor.
  - —For *rectal* dosage form (suppositories):
    - Adults—10 mg one to three times a day.
    - Children—Use and dose must be determined by your doctor.

Missed dose—If you are taking this medicine regularly and you miss a dose, take it as soon as possible. However, if it is almost time for your next dose, skip the missed dose and go back to your regular dosing schedule. Do not double doses.

Storage—To store this medicine:

- Keep out of the reach of children, since overdose may be very dangerous in children.
- Store away from heat and direct light.
- Do not store the tablet form of this medicine in the bathroom medicine cabinet, near the kitchen sink, or in other damp places. Heat or moisture may cause the medicine to break down.
- Do not keep outdated medicine or medicine no longer needed. Be sure that any discarded medicine is out of the reach of children.

Precautions While Using This Medicine

If you are going to be taking this medicine for a long time, your doctor should check your progress at regular visits, especially during the first few months of treatment with this medicine. This will allow your dosage to be changed if necessary to meet your needs.

Thiethylperazine will add to the effects of alcohol and other CNS depressants (medicines that slow down the nervous system, possibly causing drowsiness). Some examples of CNS depressants are antihistamines or medicine for hay fever, other allergies, or colds; sedatives, tranquilizers, or sleeping medicine; prescription pain medicine or narcotics; barbiturates; medicine for seizures; muscle relaxants; or anesthetics, including some dental anesthetics. *Check with your doctor before taking any of the above while you are using this medicine.*

This medicine may cause some people to have blurred vision or to become dizzy, lightheaded, drowsy, or less alert than they are normally. *Make sure you know how you react to this medicine before you drive, use machines, or do anything else that could be dangerous if you are dizzy or are not alert or able to see well.*

Dizziness, lightheadedness, or fainting may occur, especially when you get up from a lying or sitting position. Getting up slowly may help. If the problem continues or gets worse, check with your doctor.

When using thiethylperazine on a regular basis, make sure your doctor knows if you are taking large amounts of aspirin or other salicylates at the same time (as for arthritis or rheumatism). Effects of too much aspirin, such as ringing in the ears, may be covered up by this medicine.

Thiethylperazine may cause dryness of the mouth, nose, and throat. For temporary relief of mouth dryness, use sugarless candy or gum, melt bits of ice in your mouth, or use a saliva substitute. However, if your mouth continues to feel dry for more than 2 weeks, check with your medical doctor or dentist. Continuing dryness of the mouth may increase the chance of dental disease, including tooth decay, gum disease, and fungus infections.

Side Effects of This Medicine

Along with its needed effects, a medicine may cause some unwanted effects. Although not all of these side effects may occur, if they do occur they may need medical attention.

Check with your doctor immediately if any of the following side effects occur:

Less common or rare

Lip smacking or puckering; puffing of cheeks; rapid or fine, worm-like movements of tongue; uncontrolled chewing movements; uncontrolled movements of arms or legs

Also, check with your doctor as soon as possible if any of the following side effects occur:

Less common or rare

Abdominal or stomach pains; aching muscles and joints; blurred vision, change in color vision, or difficulty in seeing at night; confusion (especially in the elderly); convulsions (seizures); difficulty in speaking or swallowing; fast heartbeat; fever and chills; inability to move eyes; loss of balance control; mask-like face; muscle spasms (especially of face, neck, and back); nausea, vomiting, or diarrhea; shuffling walk; skin itching (severe); sore throat and fever; stiffness of arms or legs; swelling of arms, hands, and face; tic-like or twitching movements; trembling and shaking of hands and fingers; twisting movements of body; unusual bleeding or bruising; unusual tiredness or weakness; weakness of arms and legs; yellow eyes or skin

Other side effects may occur that usually do not need medical attention. These side effects may go away during treatment as your body adjusts to the medicine. However, check with your doctor if any of the following side effects continue or are bothersome:

More common

Drowsiness or dizziness

Less common or rare

Constipation; decreased sweating; dryness of mouth, nose and throat; feeling faint; fever; headache; lightheadedness; nightmares (continuing); ringing or buzzing in ears; skin rash; unusual excitement, nervousness, restlessness, or irritability

Other side effects not listed above may also occur in some patients. If you notice any other effects, check with your doctor.

Revised: 06/17/93

THIOGUANINE Systemic

A commonly used brand name in Canada is Lanvis.

Generic name product available in the U.S.

Description

Thioguanine (thye-oh-GWON-een) belongs to the group of medicines known as antimetabolites. It is used to treat some kinds of cancer.

Thioguanine interferes with the growth of cancer cells, which are eventually destroyed. Since the growth of normal body cells may also be affected by thioguanine, other effects will also occur. Some of these may be serious and must be reported to your doctor. Other effects may not be serious but may cause concern. Some effects may not occur for months or years after the medicine is used.

Before you begin treatment with thioguanine, you and your doctor should talk about the good this medicine will do as well as the risks of using it.

Thioguanine is available only with your doctor's prescription, in the following dosage form:

Oral

- Tablets (U.S. and Canada)

Before Using This Medicine

In deciding to use a medicine, the risks of taking the medicine must be weighed against the good it will do. This is

a decision you and your doctor will make. For thioguanine, the following should be considered:

Allergies—Tell your doctor if you have ever had any unusual or allergic reaction to thioguanine.

Pregnancy—Tell your doctor if you are pregnant or if you intend to have children. There is a chance that this medicine may cause birth defects if either the male or female is taking it at the time of conception or if it is taken during pregnancy. In addition, many cancer medicines may cause sterility which could be permanent. Although this has not been reported with this medicine, the possibility should be kept in mind.

Be sure that you have discussed this with your doctor before taking this medicine. It is best to use some kind of birth control while you are taking thioguanine. Tell your doctor right away if you think you have become pregnant while taking thioguanine.

Breast-feeding—Tell your doctor if you are breast-feeding or if you intend to breast-feed during treatment with this medicine. Because thioguanine may cause serious side effects, breast-feeding is generally not recommended while you are receiving it.

Children—Although there is no specific information about the use of thioguanine in children, it is not expected to cause different side effects or problems in children than it does in adults.

Older adults—Many medicines have not been tested in older people. Therefore, it may not be known whether they work exactly the same way they do in younger adults or if they cause different side effects or problems in older people. There is no specific information about the use of thioguanine in the elderly.

Other medicines—Although certain medicines should not be used together at all, in other cases two different medicines may be used together even if an interaction might occur. In these cases, your doctor may want to change the dose, or other precautions may be necessary. When you are taking thioguanine, it is especially important that your health care professional know if you are taking any of the following:

- Antithyroid agents (medicine for overactive thyroid) or
- Azathioprine (e.g., Imuran) or
- Chloramphenicol (e.g., Chloromycetin) or
- Colchicine or
- Flucytosine (e.g., Ancobon) or
- Interferon (e.g., Intron A, Roferon-A) or
- Plicamycin (e.g., Mithracin) or
- Zidovudine (e.g., Retrovir) or
- If you have ever been treated with x-rays or cancer medicines—Thioguanine may increase the effects of these medicines or radiation therapy on the blood

- Probenecid (e.g., Benemid) or
- Sulfinpyrazone (e.g., Anturane)—Thioguanine may increase the concentration of uric acid in the blood, which these medicines are used to lower

Other medical problems—The presence of other medical problems may affect the use of thioguanine. Make sure you tell your doctor if you have any other medical problems, especially:

- Chickenpox (including recent exposure) or
- Herpes zoster (shingles)—Risk of severe disease affecting other parts of the body
- Gout (history of) or
- Kidney stones (history of)—Thioguanine may increase levels of uric acid in the body, which can cause gout or kidney stones

- Infection—Thioguanine can reduce immunity to infection
- Kidney disease or
- Liver disease—Effects may be increased because of slower removal of thioguanine from the body

Proper Use of This Medicine

Take this medicine only as directed by your doctor. Do not take more or less of it, and do not take it more often than your doctor ordered. The exact amount of medicine you need has been carefully worked out. Taking too much may increase the chance of side effects, while taking too little may not improve your condition.

Thioguanine is sometimes given together with certain other medicines. If you are using a combination of medicines, make sure that you take each one at the right time and do not mix them. Ask your health care professional to help you plan a way to take your medicine at the right times.

While you are using thioguanine, your doctor may want you to drink extra fluids so that you will pass more urine. This will help prevent kidney problems and keep your kidneys working well.

Thioguanine sometimes causes nausea and vomiting. However, it is very important that you continue to take this medicine, even if you begin to feel ill. *Do not stop taking this medicine without first checking with your doctor.* Ask your health care professional for ways to lessen these effects.

If you vomit shortly after taking a dose of thioguanine, check with your doctor. You will be told whether to take the dose again or to wait until the next scheduled dose.

Dosing—The dose of thioguanine will be different for different patients. The dose that is used may depend on a number of things, including what the medicine is being used for, the patient's weight, and whether or not other medicines are also being taken. *If you are taking thioguanine at home, follow your doctor's orders or the directions on the label.* If you have any questions about the proper dose of thioguanine, ask your doctor.

Missed dose—If you miss a dose of this medicine, do not take the missed dose at all and do not double the next one. Instead, go back to your regular dosing schedule and check with your doctor.

Storage—To store this medicine:

- Keep out of the reach of children.
- Store away from heat and direct light.
- Do not store in the bathroom, near the kitchen sink, or in other damp places. Heat or moisture may cause the medicine to break down.

- Do not keep outdated medicine or medicine no longer needed. Be sure that any discarded medicine is out of the reach of children.

Precautions While Using This Medicine

It is very important that your doctor check your progress at regular visits to make sure that this medicine is working properly and to check for unwanted effects.

While you are being treated with thioguanine, and after you stop treatment with it, *do not have any immunizations (vaccinations) without your doctor's approval.* Thioguanine may lower your body's resistance and there is a chance you might get the infection the immunization is meant to prevent. Other people living in your household should not take or should not have recently taken oral polio vaccine since there is a chance they could pass the polio virus on to you. Also, avoid other persons who have taken oral polio vaccine. Do not get close to them and do not stay in the same room with them for very long. If you cannot take these precautions, you should consider wearing a protective face mask that covers the nose and mouth.

Thioguanine can lower the number of white blood cells in your blood temporarily, increasing the chance of getting an infection. It can also lower the number of platelets, which are necessary for proper blood clotting. If this occurs, there are certain precautions you can take, especially when your blood count is low, to reduce the risk of infection or bleeding:

- If you can, avoid people with infections. *Check with your doctor immediately* if you think you are getting an infection or if you get a fever or chills, cough or hoarseness, lower back or side pain, or painful or difficult urination.
- *Check with your doctor immediately* if you notice any unusual bleeding or bruising; black, tarry stools; blood in urine or stools; or pinpoint red spots on your skin.
- Be careful when using a regular toothbrush, dental floss, or toothpick. Your medical doctor, dentist, or nurse may recommend other ways to clean your teeth and gums. Check with your medical doctor before having any dental work done.
- Do not touch your eyes or the inside of your nose unless you have just washed your hands and have not touched anything else in the meantime.
- Be careful not to cut yourself when you are using sharp objects such as a safety razor or fingernail or toenail cutters.
- Avoid contact sports or other situations where bruising or injury could occur.

Side Effects of This Medicine

Along with their needed effects, medicines like thioguanine can sometimes cause unwanted effects such as blood problems and other side effects. These and others are described below. Also, because of the way these medicines act on the body, there is a chance that they might cause other unwanted effects that may not occur until months or years after the medicine is used. These delayed effects may include certain types of cancer, such as leukemia. Discuss these possible effects with your doctor.

Although not all of these side effects may occur, if they do occur they may need medical attention.

Check with your doctor immediately if any of the following side effects occur:

Less common

Black, tarry stools; blood in urine or stools; cough or hoarseness; fever or chills; lower back or side pain; painful or difficult urination; pinpoint red spots on skin; unusual bleeding or bruising

Check with your doctor as soon as possible if any of the following side effects occur:

Less common

Joint pain; swelling of feet or lower legs; unsteadiness when walking

Rare

Sores in mouth and on lips; yellow eyes or skin

Other side effects may occur that usually do not need medical attention. These side effects may go away during treatment as your body adjusts to the medicine. Also, your health care professional may be able to tell you about ways to prevent or reduce some of these side effects. Check with your health care professional if any of the following side effects continue or are bothersome or if you have any questions about them:

Less common

Diarrhea; loss of appetite; nausea and vomiting; skin rash or itching

After you stop taking thioguanine, it may still produce some side effects that need attention. During this period of time, check with your doctor if you notice any of the following side effects:

Black, tarry stools; blood in urine or stools; cough or hoarseness; fever or chills; lower back or side pain; painful or difficult urination; pinpoint red spots on skin; unusual bleeding or bruising

Other side effects not listed above may also occur in some patients. If you notice any other effects, check with your doctor.

Revised: 09/90
Interim revision: 08/11/93; 07/05/94

THIOTEPA Systemic

Generic name product available in the U.S. and Canada.

Description

Thiotepa (thye-oh-TEP-a) belongs to the group of medicines called alkylating agents. It is used to treat some kinds of cancer.

Thiotepa interferes with the growth of cancer cells, which are eventually destroyed. Since the growth of normal body cells may also be affected by thiotepa, other effects will also occur. Some of these may be serious and must be reported to your doctor. Other effects, like hair loss, may not be serious but may cause concern. Some effects do not occur for months or years after the medicine is used.

Before you begin treatment with thiotepa, you and your doctor should talk about the good this medicine will do as well as the risks of using it.

Thiotepa is to be administered only by or under the immediate supervision of your doctor. It is available in the following dosage form:

Parenteral
- Injection (U.S. and Canada)

Before Using This Medicine

In deciding to use a medicine, the risks of taking the medicine must be weighed against the good it will do. This is a decision you and your doctor will make. For thiotepa, the following should be considered:

Allergies—Tell your doctor if you have ever had any unusual or allergic reaction to thiotepa.

Pregnancy—Tell your doctor if you are pregnant or if you intend to have children. There is a chance that this medicine may cause birth defects if either the male or female is using it at the time of conception or if it is used during pregnancy. Studies have shown that thiotepa causes birth defects in humans. In addition, many cancer medicines may cause sterility which could be permanent. Although this is uncommon with this medicine, the possibility should be kept in mind.

Be sure that you have discussed this with your doctor before using this medicine. It is best to use some kind of birth control while you are receiving thiotepa. Tell your doctor right away if you think you have become pregnant while receiving thiotepa.

Breast-feeding—Tell your doctor if you intend to breast-feed. Because this medicine may cause serious side effects, breast-feeding is generally not recommended while you are receiving it. It is not known whether thiotepa passes into the breast milk.

Children—There is no specific information about the use of thiotepa in children.

Older adults—Many medicines have not been tested in older people. Therefore, it may not be known whether they work exactly the same way they do in younger adults or if they cause different side effects or problems in older people. There is no specific information about the use of thiotepa in the elderly.

Other medicines—Although certain medicines should not be used together at all, in other cases two different medicines may be used together even if an interaction might occur. In these cases, your doctor may want to change the dose, or other precautions may be necessary. When you are receiving thiotepa, it is especially important that your health care professional know if you are taking any of the following:

- Antithyroid agents (medicine for overactive thyroid) or
- Azathioprine (e.g., Imuran) or
- Chloramphenicol (e.g., Chloromycetin) or
- Colchicine or
- Flucytosine (e.g., Ancobon) or
- Interferon (e.g., Intron A, Roferon-A) or
- Plicamycin (e.g., Mithracin) or
- Zidovudine (e.g., Retrovir) or
- If you have ever been treated with x-rays or cancer medicines—Thiotepa may increase the effects of these medicines or radiation therapy on the blood
- Probenecid (e.g., Benemid) or
- Sulfinpyrazone (e.g., Anturane)—Thiotepa may increase the concentration of uric acid in the blood, which these medicines are used to lower

Other medical problems—The presence of other medical problems may affect the use of thiotepa. Make sure you tell your doctor if you have any other medical problems, especially:

- Chickenpox (including recent exposure) or
- Herpes zoster (shingles)—Risk of severe disease affecting other parts of the body
- Gout (history of) or
- Kidney stones (history of)—Thiotepa may increase levels of uric acid in the body, which can cause gout or kidney stones
- Infection—Thiotepa can reduce immunity to infection
- Kidney disease or
- Liver disease—Effects may be increased because of slower removal of thiotepa from the body

Proper Use of This Medicine

While you are using thiotepa, your doctor may want you to drink extra fluids so that you will pass more urine. This will help prevent kidney problems and keep your kidneys working well.

Thiotepa sometimes causes nausea, vomiting, and loss of appetite. However, it is very important that you continue to receive the medicine, even if you begin to feel ill. Ask your health care professional for ways to lessen these effects.

Dosing—The dose of thiotepa will be different for different patients. The dose that is used may depend on a number of things, including what the medicine is being used for, the patient's weight, and whether or not other medicines are also being taken. *If you are receiving thiotepa at home, follow your doctor's orders or the directions on* *the label.* If you have any questions about the proper dose of thiotepa, ask your doctor.

Precautions While Using This Medicine

It is very important that your doctor check your progress at regular visits to make sure that this medicine is working properly and to check for unwanted effects.

Before having any kind of surgery, including dental surgery, make sure the medical doctor or dentist in charge knows that you are taking this medicine.

While you are being treated with thiotepa, and after you stop treatment with it, *do not have any immunizations (vaccinations) without your doctor's approval.* Thiotepa may lower your body's resistance and there is a chance you might get the infection the immunization is meant to prevent. Other people living in your household should not take or should not have recently taken oral polio vaccine since there is a chance they could pass the polio virus on to you. Also, avoid other persons who have taken oral polio vaccine. Do not get close to them and do not stay in the same room with them for very long. If you cannot take these precautions, you should consider wearing a protective face mask that covers the nose and mouth.

Thiotepa can lower the number of white blood cells in your blood temporarily, increasing the chance of getting an infection. It can also lower the number of platelets, which are necessary for proper blood clotting. If this occurs, there are certain precautions you can take, especially when your blood count is low, to reduce the risk of infection or bleeding:

- If you can, avoid people with infections. *Check with your doctor immediately* if you think you are getting an infection or if you get a fever or chills, cough or hoarseness, lower back or side pain, or painful or difficult urination.
- *Check with your doctor immediately* if you notice any unusual bleeding or bruising; black, tarry stools; blood in urine or stools; or pinpoint red spots on your skin.
- Be careful when using a regular toothbrush, dental floss, or toothpick. Your medical doctor, dentist, or nurse may recommend other ways to clean your teeth and gums. Check with your medical doctor before having any dental work done.
- Do not touch your eyes or the inside of your nose unless you have just washed your hands and have not touched anything else in the meantime.
- Be careful not to cut yourself when you are using sharp objects such as a safety razor or fingernail or toenail cutters.
- Avoid contact sports or other situations where bruising or injury could occur.

Side Effects of This Medicine

Along with their needed effects, medicines like thiotepa can sometimes cause unwanted effects such as blood problems, loss of hair, and other side effects. These and others are described below. Also, because of the way these medicines act on the body, there is a chance that they might cause other unwanted effects that may not occur until months or years after the medicine is used. These delayed effects may include certain types of cancer, such as leukemia. Discuss these possible effects with your doctor.

Although not all of these side effects may occur, if they do occur they may need medical attention.

Check with your doctor or nurse immediately if any of the following side effects occur:

Less common

Black, tarry stools; blood in urine or stools; cough or hoarseness; fever or chills; lower back or side pain; painful or difficult urination; pinpoint red spots on skin; unusual bleeding or bruising

Rare

Skin rash; tightness of throat; wheezing

Check with your health care professional as soon as possible if any of the following side effects occur:

Less common

Joint pain; pain at place of injection or instillation; swelling of feet or lower legs

Rare

Sores in mouth and on lips

Other side effects may occur that usually do not need medical attention. These side effects may go away during treatment as your body adjusts to the medicine. Also, your health care professional may be able to tell you about ways to prevent or reduce some of these side effects. Check with your health care professional if any of the following side effects continue or are bothersome or if you have any questions about them:

Less common

Dizziness; hives; loss of appetite; missing menstrual periods; nausea and vomiting

This medicine may cause a temporary loss of hair in some people. After treatment with thiotepa has ended, normal hair growth should return.

After you stop receiving thiotepa, it may still produce some side effects that need attention. During this period of time, check with your doctor if you notice any of the following:

Black, tarry stools; blood in urine or stools; cough or hoarseness; fever or chills; lower back or side pain; painful or difficult urination; pinpoint red spots on skin; unusual bleeding or bruising

Other side effects not listed above may also occur in some patients. If you notice any other effects, check with your doctor.

Revised: 09/90
Interim revision: 08/11/93; 07/05/94

THIOXANTHENES Systemic

Some commonly used brand names are:

In the U.S.—

Navane[3]
Taractan[1]
Thiothixene HCl Intensol[3]

In Canada—

Fluanxol[2]
Fluanxol Depot[2]
Navane[3]

Note: For quick reference, the following thioxanthenes are numbered to match the corresponding brand names.

This information applies to the following medicines:

1. Chlorprothixene (klor-proe-THIX-een)†
2. Flupenthixol (floo-pen-THIX-ole)*
3. Thiothixene (thye-oh-THIX-een)‡

*Not commercially available in the U.S.
†Not commercially available in Canada.
‡Generic name product may also be available in the U.S.

Description

This medicine belongs to the family of medicines known as thioxanthenes (thye-oh-ZAN-theens). It is used in the treatment of nervous, mental, and emotional conditions. Improvement in such conditions is thought to result from the effect of the medicine on nerve pathways in specific areas of the brain.

Thioxanthene medicines are available only with your doctor's prescription, in the following dosage forms:

Oral

Chlorprothixene
- Suspension (U.S.)
- Tablets (U.S.)

Flupenthixol
- Tablets (Canada)

Thiothixene
- Capsules (U.S. and Canada)
- Solution (U.S.)

Parenteral

Chlorprothixene
- Injection (U.S.)

Flupenthixol
- Injection (Canada)

Thiothixene
- Injection (U.S.)

Before Using This Medicine

In deciding to use a medicine, the risks of taking the medicine must be weighed against the good it will do. This is a decision you and your doctor will make. For thioxanthenes, the following should be considered:

Allergies—Tell your doctor if you have ever had any unusual or allergic reaction to thioxanthene or to phenothiazine medicines. Also tell your health care professional if you are allergic to any other substances, such as foods, preservatives, or dyes.

Pregnancy—Studies have not been done in pregnant women. Although animal studies have not shown that thioxanthenes cause birth defects, the studies have shown that these medicines cause a decrease in fertility and fewer successful pregnancies.

Breast-feeding—It is not known if thioxanthenes pass into the breast milk. However, similar medicines for nervous, mental, or emotional conditions do pass into breast milk and may cause drowsiness and increase the risk of other problems in the nursing baby. Be sure you have discussed the risks and benefits of this medicine with your doctor.

Children—Certain side effects, such as muscle spasms of the face, neck, and back, tic-like or twitching movements, inability to move the eyes, twisting of the body, or weakness of the arms and legs, are more likely to occur in children, who are usually more sensitive than adults to the side effects of thioxanthenes.

Older adults—Constipation, dizziness or fainting, drowsiness, dryness of mouth, trembling of the hands and fingers, and symptoms of tardive dyskinesia (such as rapid, worm-like movements of the tongue or any other uncontrolled movements of the mouth, tongue, or jaw, and/or arms and legs) are especially likely to occur in elderly patients, who are usually more sensitive than younger adults to the effects of thioxanthenes.

Other medicines—Although certain medicines should not be used together at all, in other cases 2 different medicines may be used together even if an interaction might occur. In these cases, your doctor may want to change the dose, or other precautions may be necessary. When you are taking thioxanthenes, it is especially important that your health care professional know if you are taking any of the following:

- Amoxapine (e.g., Asendin) or
- Methyldopa (e.g., Aldomet) or
- Metoclopramide (e.g., Reglan) or
- Metyrosine (e.g., Demser) or
- Other antipsychotics (medicine for mental illness) or
- Pemoline (e.g., Cylert) or
- Pimozide (e.g., Orap) or
- Promethazine (e.g., Phenergan) or
- Rauwolfia alkaloids (alseroxylon [e.g., Rauwiloid], deserpidine [e.g., Harmonyl], rauwolfia serpentina [e.g., Raudixin], reserpine [e.g., Serpasil]) or
- Trimeprazine (e.g., Temaril)—Taking these medicines with thioxanthenes may increase the chance and severity of certain side effects
- Central nervous system (CNS) depressants (medicine that causes drowsiness) or
- Tricyclic antidepressants (medicine for depression)—Taking these medicines with thioxanthenes may add to the CNS depressant effects
- Epinephrine (e.g., Adrenalin)—Severe low blood pressure (hypotension) and fast heartbeat may occur if epinephrine is used with thioxanthenes
- Levodopa (e.g., Sinemet)—Thioxanthenes may keep levodopa from working properly in the treatment of Parkinson's disease
- Quinidine (e.g., Quinidex)—Unwanted effects on your heart may occur

Other medical problems—The presence of other medical problems may affect the use of thioxanthenes. Make sure

you tell your doctor if you have any other medical problems, especially:

- Alcohol abuse—Drinking alcohol will add to the central nervous system (CNS) depressant effects of thioxanthenes
- Blood disease or
- Enlarged prostate or
- Glaucoma or
- Heart or blood vessel disease or
- Lung disease or
- Parkinson's disease or
- Stomach ulcers or
- Urination problems—Thioxanthenes may make the condition worse
- Liver disease—Higher blood levels of thioxanthenes may occur, increasing the chance of side effects
- Reye's syndrome—The risk of liver problems may be increased
- Seizure disorders—The risk of seizures may be increased

Proper Use of This Medicine

This medicine may be taken with food or a full glass (8 ounces) of water or milk to reduce stomach irritation.

For patients taking *thiothixene oral solution:*

- This medicine must be diluted before you take it. Just before taking, measure the dose with the specially marked dropper. Mix the medicine with a full glass of water, milk, tomato or fruit juice, soup, or carbonated beverage.

Do not take more of this medicine or take it more often than your doctor ordered. This is particularly important when this medicine is given to children, since they may react very strongly to its effects.

Sometimes this medicine must be taken for several weeks before its full effect is reached.

Dosing—The dose of these medicines will be different for different patients. *Follow your doctor's orders or the directions on the label.* The following information includes only the average doses of these medicines. *If your dose is different, do not change it* unless your doctor tells you to do so.

The number of capsules or tablets or the amount of liquid that you take depends on the strength of the medicine. Also, the number of doses you take each day, the time allowed between doses, and the length of time you take the medicine depend on the medical problem for which you are taking thioxanthenes.

For chlorprothixene

- For treatment of psychosis:
  - —*Oral* dosage forms (suspension or tablets):
    - Adults and teenagers—25 to 50 milligrams (mg) three or four times a day.
    - Children 6 to 12 years of age—10 to 25 mg three or four times a day.
    - Children up to 6 years of age—Use and dose must be determined by your doctor.
  - —*Injection* dosage form:
    - Adults and teenagers—25 to 50 mg, injected into a muscle, three or four times a day.
    - Children up to 12 years of age—Use and dose must be determined by your doctor.

For flupenthixol

- For treatment of psychosis:
  - —*Oral* dosage form (tablets):
    - Adults—To start, 1 milligram (mg) three times a day. Your doctor may increase your dose if needed, depending on your condition.
    - Children— Use and dose must be determined by your doctor.
  - —*Long-acting injection* dosage form:
    - Adults—To start, 20 to 40 milligrams (mg) injected into a muscle. Your doctor will determine whether your dose needs to be changed, depending on your condition.
    - Children—Use and dose must be determined by your doctor.

For thiothixene

- For treatment of psychosis:
  - —*Oral* dosage forms (capsules and solution):
    - Adults and teenagers—To start, 2 milligrams (mg) three times a day, or 5 mg two times a day. Your doctor may increase your dose if needed. However, the dose is usually not more than 60 mg a day.
    - Children up to 12 years of age—Use and dose must be determined by your doctor.
  - —*Injection* dosage form:
    - Adults and teenagers—4 milligrams (mg), injected into a muscle, two to four times a day. Your doctor may increase your dose if needed. However, the dose is usually not more than 30 mg a day.
    - Children up to 12 years of age—Use and dose must be determined by your doctor.

Missed dose—If you miss a dose of this medicine, take it as soon as possible. However, if it is within 2 hours of your next dose, skip the missed dose and go back to your regular dosing schedule. Do not double doses.

Storage—To store this medicine:

- Keep out of the reach of children.
- Store away from heat and direct light.
- Do not store the capsule or tablet form of this medicine in the bathroom, near the kitchen sink, or in other damp places. Heat or moisture may cause the medicine to break down.
- Keep the liquid form of this medicine from freezing.
- Do not keep outdated medicine or medicine no longer needed. Be sure that any discarded medicine is out of the reach of children.

Precautions While Using This Medicine

Your doctor should check your progress at regular visits. This will allow the dosage of the medicine to be adjusted when necessary and also will reduce the possibility of side effects.

Do not stop taking this medicine without first checking with your doctor. Your doctor may want you to gradually reduce the amount you are taking before stopping completely. This is to prevent side effects and to prevent your condition from becoming worse.

This medicine will add to the effects of alcohol and other CNS depressants (medicines that slow down the nervous system, possibly causing drowsiness). Some examples of CNS depressants are antihistamines or medicine for hay fever, other allergies, or colds; sedatives, tranquilizers, or sleeping medicine; prescription pain medicine or narcotics; barbiturates; medicine for seizures; muscle relaxants; or anesthetics, including some dental anesthetics. *Check with your doctor before taking any such depressants while you are using this medicine.*

Do not take this medicine within an hour of taking antacids or medicine for diarrhea. Taking them too close together may make this medicine less effective.

Before having any kind of surgery, dental treatment, or emergency treatment, tell the medical doctor or dentist in charge that you are using this medicine. Taking thioxanthenes together with medicines that are used during surgery or dental or emergency treatments may increase the CNS depressant effects.

This medicine may cause some people to become drowsy or less alert than they are normally, especially during the first few weeks the medicine is being taken. Even if you take this medicine only at bedtime, you may feel drowsy or less alert on arising. *Make sure you know how you react to this medicine before you drive, use machines, or do anything else that could be dangerous if you are not alert.*

Dizziness, lightheadedness, or fainting may occur while you are taking this medicine, especially when you get up from a lying or sitting position. Getting up slowly may help. If the problem continues or gets worse, check with your doctor.

This medicine may make you sweat less, causing your body temperature to increase. *Use extra care not to become overheated during exercise or hot weather while you are taking this medicine,* since overheating may result in heat stroke. Also, hot baths or saunas may make you feel dizzy or faint while you are taking this medicine.

Thioxanthenes may cause your skin to be more sensitive to sunlight than it is normally. Exposure to sunlight, even for brief periods of time, may cause a skin rash, itching, redness or other discoloration of the skin, or a severe sunburn. When you begin taking this medicine:

- Stay out of direct sunlight, especially between the hours of 10:00 a.m. and 3:00 p.m., if possible.
- Wear protective clothing, including a hat. Also, wear sunglasses.
- Apply a sun block product that has a skin protection factor (SPF) of at least 15. Some patients may require a product with a higher SPF number, especially if they have a fair complexion. If you have any questions about this, check with your health care professional.
- Apply a sun block lipstick that has an SPF of at least 15 to protect your lips.
- Do not use a sunlamp or tanning bed or booth.

If you have a severe reaction from the sun, check with your doctor.

This medicine may cause dryness of the mouth. For temporary relief, use sugarless gum or candy, melt bits of ice in your mouth, or use a saliva substitute. However, if your mouth continues to feel dry for more than 2 weeks, check with your medical doctor or dentist. Continuing dryness of the mouth may increase the chance of dental disease, including tooth decay, gum disease, and fungus infections.

If you are taking a liquid form of this medicine, *try to avoid spilling it on your skin or clothing.* Skin rash and irritation have been caused by similar medicines.

If you are receiving this medicine by injection:

- The effects of the long-acting injection form of this medicine may last for up to 3 weeks. *The precautions and side effects information for this medicine applies during this period of time.*

Side Effects of This Medicine

Along with their needed effects, thioxanthenes can sometimes cause serious side effects. Tardive dyskinesia (a movement disorder) may occur and may not go away after you stop using the medicine. Signs of tardive dyskinesia include fine, worm-like movements of the tongue, or other uncontrolled movements of the mouth, tongue, cheeks, jaw, or arms and legs. Other serious but rare side effects may also occur. Some of these side effects, including severe muscle stiffness, fever, unusual tiredness or weakness, fast heartbeat, difficult breathing, increased sweating, loss of bladder control, and seizures, may be the sign of a condition called neuroleptic malignant syndrome. *You and your doctor should discuss the good this medicine will do as well as the risks of taking it.*

Although not all of these side effects may occur, if they do occur they may need medical attention.

Stop taking this medicine and get emergency help immediately if any of the following side effects occur:

Rare

Convulsions (seizures); difficulty in breathing; fast heartbeat; high fever; high or low (irregular) blood pressure; increased sweating; loss of bladder control; muscle stiffness (severe); unusually pale skin; unusual tiredness

Also, check with your doctor as soon as possible if any of the following side effects occur:

More common

Difficulty in talking or swallowing; inability to move eyes; lip smacking or puckering; loss of balance control; mask-like face; muscle spasms, especially of the neck and back; puffing of cheeks; rapid or worm-like movements of tongue; restlessness or need to keep moving (severe); shuffling walk; stiffness of arms and legs; trembling and shaking of fingers and hands; twisting movements of body; uncontrolled chewing movements; uncontrolled movements of the arms and legs

Less common
Blurred vision or other eye problems; difficult urination; fainting; skin discoloration; skin rash

Rare
Hot, dry skin or lack of sweating; increased blinking or spasms of eyelid; muscle weakness; sore throat and fever; uncontrolled twisting movements of neck, trunk, arms, or legs; unusual bleeding or bruising; unusual facial expressions or body positions; yellow eyes or skin

Symptoms of overdose
Difficulty in breathing (severe); dizziness (severe); drowsiness (severe); muscle trembling, jerking, stiffness, or uncontrolled movements (severe); small pupils; unusual excitement; unusual tiredness or weakness (severe)

Other side effects may occur that usually do not need medical attention. These side effects may go away during treatment as your body adjusts to the medicine. However, check with your doctor if any of the following side effects continue or are bothersome:

More common
Constipation; decreased sweating; dizziness, lightheadedness, or fainting; drowsiness (mild); dryness of mouth; increased appetite and weight; increased sensitivity of skin to sunlight (skin rash, itching, redness or other discoloration of skin, or severe sunburn); stuffy nose

Less common
Changes in menstrual period; decreased sexual ability; swelling of breasts (in males and females); unusual secretion of milk

After you stop taking this medicine your body may need time to adjust, especially if you took this medicine in high doses or for a long time. If you stop taking it too quickly, the following withdrawal effects may occur and should be reported to your doctor:

Dizziness; nausea and vomiting; stomach pain; trembling of fingers and hands; uncontrolled, continuing movements of mouth, tongue, or jaw

Although not all of the side effects listed above have been reported for all thioxanthenes, they have been reported for at least one of them. However, since these medicines are very similar, any of the above side effects may occur with any of them.

Other side effects not listed above may also occur in some patients. If you notice any other effects, check with your doctor.

Revised: 06/17/93

THROMBOLYTIC AGENTS Systemic

Some commonly used brand names are:

In the U.S.—

Abbokinase[4]	Eminase[2]
Abbokinase Open-Cath[4]	Kabikinase[3]
Activase[1]	Streptase[3]

In Canada—

Abbokinase[4]	Eminase[2]
Abbokinase Open-Cath[4]	Kabikinase[3]
Activase rt-PA[1]	Streptase[3]

Other commonly used names are:

Anisoylated plasminogen-streptokinase activator complex[2]	Tissue-type plasminogen activator (recombinant)[1]
	t-PA[1]
APSAC[2]	rt-PA[1]

Note: For quick reference, the following thrombolytic agents are numbered to match the corresponding brand names.

This information applies to the following medicines:

1. Alteplase, Recombinant (AL-ti-plase)
2. Anistreplase (an-EYE-strep-lase)
3. Streptokinase (strep-toe-KYE-nase)
4. Urokinase (yoor-oh-KYE-nase)

Description

Thrombolytic agents are used to dissolve blood clots that have formed in certain blood vessels. These medicines are usually used when a blood clot seriously lessens the flow of blood to certain parts of the body.

Thrombolytic agents are also used to dissolve blood clots that form in tubes that are placed into the body. The tubes allow treatments (such as dialysis or injections into a vein) to be given over a long period of time.

These medicines are to be given only by or under the direct supervision of a doctor.

These medicines are available in the following dosage forms:

Parenteral

Alteplase, Recombinant
- Injection (U.S. and Canada)

Anistreplase
- Injection (U.S. and Canada)

Streptokinase
- Injection (U.S. and Canada)

Urokinase
- Injection (U.S. and Canada)

Before Receiving This Medicine

In deciding to use a medicine, the risks of using the medicine must be weighed against the good it will do. This is a decision you and your doctor will make. For thrombolytic agents, the following should be considered:

Allergies—Tell your doctor if you have ever had any unusual or allergic reaction to alteplase, anistreplase, streptokinase, or urokinase. Also tell your health care professional if you are allergic to any other substances, such as foods, preservatives, or dyes.

Pregnancy—Tell your doctor if you are pregnant or if you have recently had a baby.

There is a slight chance that use of a thrombolytic agent during the first five months of pregnancy may cause a miscarriage. However, both streptokinase and urokinase have been used in pregnant women and have not been reported to cause this problem. Also, studies in pregnant women (for streptokinase) and studies in animals (for urokinase) have not shown that these medicines cause either miscarriage or harm to the fetus (including birth defects). Studies on birth defects with alteplase and anistreplase have not been done in either pregnant women or animals.

Breast-feeding—It is not known whether thrombolytic agents pass into the breast milk. Although most medicines pass into breast milk in small amounts, many of them may be used safely while breast-feeding. Mothers who are taking any of these medicines and who wish to breast-feed should discuss this with their doctor.

Children—These medicines have been tested in children and, in effective doses, have not been shown to cause different side effects or problems than they do in adults.

Older adults—The need for treatment with a thrombolytic agent (instead of other kinds of treatment) may be increased in elderly patients with blood clots. However, the chance of bleeding may also be increased. It is especially important that you discuss the use of this medicine with your doctor.

Other medicines—Although certain medicines should not be used together at all, in other cases two different medicines may be used together even if an interaction might occur. In these cases, your doctor may want to change the dose, or other precautions may be necessary. Before you receive a thrombolytic agent, it is especially important that your doctor know if you are taking any of the following:

- Anticoagulants (blood thinners) or
- Aspirin or
- Cefamandole (e.g., Mandol) or
- Cefoperazone (e.g., Cefobid) or
- Cefotetan (e.g., Cefotan) or
- Divalproex (e.g., Depakote) or
- Enoxaparin (e.g., Lovenox) or
- Heparin or
- Indomethacin (e.g., Indocin) or
- Inflammation or pain medicine (except narcotics) or
- Phenylbutazone (e.g., Butazolidin) or
- Plicamycin (e.g., Mithracin) or
- Sulfinpyrazone (e.g., Anturane) or
- Ticlopidine (e.g., Ticlid) or
- Valproic acid (e.g., Depakene)—The chance of bleeding may be increased

Also, tell your doctor if you have had an injection of anistreplase or streptokinase within the past year. If you have, these medicines may not work properly if they are given to you again. Your doctor may decide to use alteplase or urokinase instead.

Other medical problems or recent childbirth—The presence of other medical problems or recent delivery of a child may affect the use of thrombolytic agents. Make sure you tell your doctor if you have any other medical problems, especially:

- Blood disease, bleeding problems, or a history of bleeding in any part of the body or
- Brain disease or tumor or
- Colitis or stomach ulcer (or history of) or
- Heart or blood vessel disease or
- High blood pressure or
- Liver disease (severe) or
- Stroke (or history of) or
- Tuberculosis (TB) (active)—The chance of serious bleeding may be increased
- Streptococcal (''strep'') infection (recent)—Anistreplase or streptokinase may not work properly after a streptococcal infection; your doctor may decide to use a different thrombolytic agent

Also, tell your doctor if you have recently had any of the following conditions:

- Falls or blows to the body or head or any other injury or
- Injections into a blood vessel or
- Placement of any tube into the body or
- Surgery, including dental surgery—The chance of serious bleeding may be increased

If you have recently had a baby, use of these medicines may cause serious bleeding.

Proper Use of This Medicine

Dosing—The dose of these medicines will be different for different patients. The dose you receive will depend on the medicine you receive and will be based on the condition for which you are receiving the medicine. In some cases, the dose will also depend on your body weight.

Precautions While Receiving This Medicine

Thrombolytic agents can cause bleeding that usually is not serious. However, serious bleeding may occur in some people. *To help prevent serious bleeding, carefully follow any instructions given by your health care professional. Also, move around as little as possible, and do not get out of bed on your own, unless your health care professional tells you it is all right to do so.*

Side Effects of This Medicine

Along with its needed effects, a medicine may cause some unwanted effects. Although not all of these side effects may occur, if they do occur they may need medical attention.

Tell your health care professional immediately if any of the following side effects occur:

More common

Bleeding or oozing from cuts, gums, or around the place of injection; fever

Less common or rare

Bruising; changes in facial skin color; confusion; double vision; fast or irregular breathing; flushing or redness of skin; headache (mild); muscle pain (mild); nausea; shortness of breath, troubled breathing, tightness in chest, and/or wheezing; skin rash, hives, or itching; swelling of eyes, face, lips, or tongue; trouble in speaking; weakness in arms or legs

Symptoms of bleeding inside the body

Abdominal or stomach pain or swelling; back pain or backaches; blood in urine; bloody or black, tarry stools; constipation; coughing up blood; dizziness; headaches (sudden, severe, or continuing); joint pain, stiffness, or swelling; muscle pain or stiffness (severe or continuing); nosebleeds; unexpected or unusually heavy bleeding from vagina; vomiting of blood or material that looks like coffee grounds

Other side effects not listed above may also occur in some patients. If you notice any other effects, check with your doctor.

Revised: 09/01/94
Interim revision: 08/07/97

THYROID HORMONES Systemic

Some commonly used brand names are:

In the U.S.—

Armour Thyroid[5]
Cytomel[2]
Levo-T[1]
Levothroid[1]
Levoxyl[1]
Synthroid[1]
Thyrar[5]
Thyroid Strong[5]
Thyrolar[3]
Westhroid[5]

In Canada—

Cytomel[2]
Eltroxin[1]
PMS-Levothyroxine Sodium[1]
Synthroid[1]

Note: For quick reference, the following thyroid hormones are numbered to match the corresponding brand names.

This information applies to the following medicines:

1. Levothyroxine (lee-voe-thye-ROX-een)‡
2. Liothyronine (lye-oh-THYE-roe-neen)‡
3. Liotrix (LYE-oh-trix)†
4. Thyroglobulin (thye-roe-GLOB-yoo-lin)*†
5. Thyroid (THYE-roid)‡§

Note: This information does *not* apply to Thyrotropin.

*Not commercially available in the U.S.
†Not commercially available in Canada.
‡Generic name product may also be available in the U.S.
§Generic name product may also be available in Canada.

Description

Thyroid medicines belong to the general group of medicines called hormones. They are used when the thyroid gland does not produce enough hormone. They are also used to help decrease the size of enlarged thyroid glands (known as goiter) and to treat thyroid cancer.

These medicines are available only with your doctor's prescription, in the following dosage forms:

Oral
- Levothyroxine
  - Tablets (U.S. and Canada)
- Liothyronine
  - Tablets (U.S. and Canada)
- Liotrix
  - Tablets (U.S.)
- Thyroglobulin
  - Tablets
- Thyroid
  - Tablets (U.S. and Canada)

Parenteral
- Levothyroxine
  - Injection (U.S. and Canada)

Before Using This Medicine

In deciding to use a medicine, the risks of taking the medicine must be weighed against the good it will do. This is a decision you and your doctor will make. For thyroid hormones, the following should be considered:

Allergies—Tell your doctor if you have ever had any unusual or allergic reaction to thyroid hormones. Also tell your health care professional if you are allergic to any other substances, such as foods, preservatives, or dyes.

Pregnancy—Use of proper amounts of thyroid hormone during pregnancy has not been shown to cause birth defects or other problems. However, your doctor may want you to change your dose while you are pregnant. This will make regular visits to your doctor important.

Breast-feeding—Use of proper amounts of thyroid hormones by mothers has not been shown to cause problems in nursing babies.

Children—Thyroid hormones have been tested in children and have not been shown to cause different side effects or problems in children than they do in adults.

Older adults—This medicine has been tested and has not been shown to cause different side effects or problems in older people than it does in younger adults. However, a different dose may be needed in the elderly. Therefore, it is important to take the medicine only as directed by the doctor.

Other medicines—Although certain medicines should not be used together at all, in other cases two different medicines may be used together even if an interaction might occur. In these cases, your doctor may want to change the dose, or other precautions may be necessary. When you are taking thyroid hormones, it is especially important that your health care professional know if you are taking any of the following:

- Amphetamines
- Anticoagulants (blood thinners)
- Appetite suppressants (diet pills)
- Cholestyramine (e.g., Questran)
- Colestipol (e.g., Colestid)
- Medicine for asthma or other breathing problems
- Medicine for colds, sinus problems, or hay fever or other allergies (including nose drops or sprays)

Other medical problems—The presence of other medical problems may affect the use of thyroid hormones. Make sure you tell your doctor if you have any other medical problems especially:

- Diabetes mellitus (sugar diabetes)
- Hardening of the arteries
- Heart disease
- High blood pressure

- Overactive thyroid (history of)
- Underactive adrenal gland
- Underactive pituitary gland

Proper Use of This Medicine

Use this medicine only as directed by your doctor. Do not use more or less of it, and do not use it more often than your doctor ordered. Your doctor has prescribed the exact amount your body needs and if you take different amounts, you may experience symptoms of an overactive or underactive thyroid. Take it at the same time each day to make sure it always has the same effect.

If your condition is due to a lack of thyroid hormone, you may have to take this medicine for the rest of your life. It is very important that you *do not stop taking this medicine without first checking with your doctor.*

Dosing—The dose of these medicines will be different for different patients. *Follow your doctor's orders or the directions on the label.* The following information includes only the average doses of these medicines. *If your dose is different, do not change it* unless your doctor tells you to do so.

The number of tablets that you take depends on the strength of the medicine. The amount of thyroid hormone that you need to take every day depends on the results of your thyroid tests. However, treatment is usually started with lower doses that are increased a little at a time until you are taking the full amount. This helps prevent side effects.

For levothyroxine

- For *oral* dosage form (tablets):
  - —For replacing the thyroid hormone:
    - Adults and teenagers—At first, 0.0125 to 0.05 milligrams (mg) once a day. Then, your doctor may increase your dose a little at a time to 0.075 to 0.125 mg a day. The dose is usually no higher than 0.15 mg once a day.
    - Children less than 6 months of age—The dose is based on body weight and must be determined by your doctor. The usual dose is 0.025 to 0.05 mg once a day.
    - Children 6 months to 12 months of age—The dose is based on body weight and must be determined by your doctor. The usual dose is 0.05 to 0.075 mg once a day.
    - Children 1 to 5 years of age—The dose is based on body weight and must be determined by your doctor. The usual dose is 0.075 to 0.1 mg once a day.
    - Children 6 to 10 years of age—The dose is based on body weight and must be determined by your doctor. The usual dose is 0.1 to 0.15 mg once a day.
    - Children over 10 years of age—The dose is based on body weight and must be determined by your doctor. The usual dose is 0.15 to 0.2 mg once a day.
- For *injection* dosage form:
  - —For replacing the thyroid hormone:
    - Adults and teenagers—50 to 100 micrograms (mcg) injected into a muscle or into a vein once a day. People with very serious conditions caused by too little thyroid hormone may need higher doses.
    - Children less than 6 months of age—The dose is based on body weight and must be determined by your doctor. The usual dose is 0.019 to 0.038 mg once a day.
    - Children 6 months to 12 months of age—The dose is based on body weight and must be determined by your doctor. The usual dose is 0.038 to 0.056 mg once a day.
    - Children 1 to 5 years of age—The dose is based on body weight and must be determined by your doctor. The usual dose is 0.056 to 0.075 mg once a day.
    - Children 6 to 10 years of age—The dose is based on body weight and must be determined by your doctor. The usual dose is 0.075 to 0.113 mg once a day.
    - Children over 10 years of age—The dose is based on body weight and must be determined by your doctor. The usual dose is 0.113 to 0.15 mg once a day.

For liothyronine sodium

- For *oral* dosage form (tablets):
  - —For replacing the thyroid hormone:
    - Adults and teenagers—At first, 25 micrograms (mcg) a day. Some patients with very serious conditions caused by too little thyroid hormone may need to take only 2.5 to 5 mcg a day at first. Also, some patients with heart disease or the elderly may need lower doses at first. Then, your doctor may increase your dose a little at a time to up to 50 mcg a day if needed. Your doctor may want you to divide your dose into smaller amounts that are taken two or more times a day.
  - —For treating a large thyroid gland (goiter):
    - Adults—At first, 5 mcg a day. Some patients with heart disease or the elderly may need lower doses at first. Then, your doctor may increase your dose a little at a time to 50 to 100 mcg a day.

For liotrix (levothyroxine and liothyronine combination)

- For *oral* dosage form (tablets):
  - —For replacing the thyroid hormone:
    - Adults, teenagers, and children—At first, 50 micrograms (mcg) of levothyroxine and 12.5 mcg of liothyronine once a day. Some people with very serious conditions caused by too little thyroid hormone may need only 12.5 mcg of levothyroxine and 3.1 mcg of liothyronine once a day. Also, some elderly patients may need lower doses at first. Then, your doctor may want to increase

your dose a little at a time to up to 100 mcg of levothyroxine and 25 mcg of liothyronine.

For thyroglobulin
- For *oral* dosage form (tablets):
  - —For replacing the thyroid hormone:
    - Adults, teenagers, and children—At first, 32 milligrams (mg) a day. Some people with very serious conditions caused by too little thyroid hormone may need to take only 16 to 32 mg a day at first. Then, the doctor may want you to increase your dose a little at a time to 65 to 160 mg a day.

For thyroid
- For *oral* dosage form (tablets):
  - —For replacing thyroid hormone:
    - Adults, teenagers, and children—60 milligrams (mg) a day. Some people with very serious conditions caused by too little thyroid hormone may need to take only 15 mg a day at first. Also, some elderly patients may need lower doses at first. Then, your doctor may want you to increase your dose a little at a time to 60 to 120 mg a day.

Missed dose—If you miss a dose of this medicine, take it as soon as possible. However, if it is almost time for your next dose, skip the missed dose and go back to your regular dosing schedule. Do not double doses. If you miss 2 or more doses in a row or if you have any questions about this, check with your doctor.

Storage—To store this medicine:
- Keep out of the reach of children.
- Store away from heat and direct light.
- Do not store in the bathroom, near the kitchen sink, or in other damp places. Heat or moisture may cause the medicine to break down.
- Do not keep outdated medicine or medicine no longer needed. Be sure that any discarded medicine is out of the reach of children.

Precautions While Using This Medicine

It is very important that your doctor check your progress at regular visits, to make sure that this medicine is working properly.

If you have certain kinds of heart disease, this medicine may cause chest pain or shortness of breath when you exert yourself. If these occur, do not overdo exercise or physical work. If you have any questions about this, check with your doctor.

Before having any kind of surgery (including dental surgery) or emergency treatment, *tell the medical doctor or dentist in charge that you are taking this medicine.*

Do not take any other medicine unless prescribed by your doctor. Some medicines may increase or decrease the effects of thyroid on your body and cause problems in controlling your condition. Also, thyroid hormones may change the effects of other medicines.

Side Effects of This Medicine

Along with its needed effects, a medicine may cause some unwanted effects. Although not all of these side effects may occur, if they do occur they may need medical attention.

Check with your doctor as soon as possible if any of the following side effects occur since they may indicate an overdose or an allergic reaction:

Rare

Headache (severe) in children; skin rash or hives

Signs and symptoms of overdose

Chest pain; fast or irregular heartbeat; shortness of breath

For patients taking this medicine for underactive thyroid:
- This medicine usually takes several weeks to have a noticeable effect on your condition. Until it begins to work, you may experience no change in your symptoms. Check with your doctor if the following symptoms continue:

  Clumsiness; coldness; constipation; dry, puffy skin; listlessness; muscle aches; sleepiness; tiredness; weakness; weight gain

Other effects may occur if the dose of the medicine is not exactly right. These side effects will go away when the dose is corrected. Check with your doctor if any of the following symptoms occur:

Changes in appetite; changes in menstrual periods; diarrhea; fever; hand tremors; headache; increased sensitivity to heat; irritability; leg cramps; nervousness; sweating; trouble in sleeping; vomiting; weight loss

Other side effects not listed above may also occur in some patients. If you notice any other effects, check with your doctor.

Revised: 05/22/92
Interim revision: 07/25/94; 01/08/95; 06/26/96

TICLOPIDINE Systemic

A commonly used brand name in the U.S. and Canada is Ticlid.

Generic name product may be available.

Description

Ticlopidine (tye-KLOE-pi-deen) is used to lessen the chance of having a stroke. It is given to people who have already had a stroke and to people with certain medical problems that may lead to a stroke. Because ticlopidine can cause serious side effects, especially during the first 3 months of treatment, it is used mostly for people who cannot take aspirin to prevent strokes.

A stroke may occur when a blood vessel in the brain is blocked by a blood clot. Ticlopidine reduces the chance that a harmful blood clot will form, by preventing certain cells in the blood from clumping together. This effect of ticlopidine may also increase the chance of serious bleeding in some people.

This medicine is available only with a doctor's prescription in the following dosage form:

Oral

- Tablets (U.S. and Canada)

Before Using This Medicine

In deciding to use a medicine, the risks of taking the medicine must be weighed against the good it will do. This is a decision you and your doctor will make. For ticlopidine, the following should be considered:

Allergies—Tell your doctor if you have ever had any unusual or allergic reaction to ticlopidine. Also tell your health care professional if you are allergic to any other substances, such as foods, preservatives, or dyes.

Pregnancy—Studies with ticlopidine have not been done in pregnant women. This medicine did not cause birth defects in animal studies. However, it caused other unwanted effects in animal studies when it was given in amounts that were large enough to cause harmful effects in the mother.

Breast-feeding—It is not known whether ticlopidine passes into the breast milk.

Children—There is no specific information comparing use of ticlopidine in children with use in other age groups.

Older adults—This medicine has been tested and has not been shown to cause different side effects or problems in older people than it does in younger adults.

Other medicines—Although certain medicines should not be used together at all, in other cases two different medicines may be used together even if an interaction might occur. In these cases, your doctor may want to change the dose, or other precautions may be necessary. When you are taking ticlopidine, it is especially important that your health care professional know if you are taking any of the following:

- Anticoagulants (blood thinners) or
- Carbenicillin by injection (e.g., Geopen) or
- Dipyridamole (e.g., Persantine) or
- Divalproex (e.g., Depakote) or
- Heparin (e.g., Hepalean, Liquaemin) or
- Inflammation or pain medicine, except narcotics, or
- Pentoxifylline (e.g., Trental) or
- Plicamycin (e.g., Mithracin) or
- Sulfinpyrazone (e.g., Anturane) or
- Ticarcillin (e.g., Ticar) or
- Valproic acid (e.g., Depakene)—The chance of serious bleeding may be increased

Other medical problems—The presence of other medical problems may affect the use of ticlopidine. Make sure you tell your doctor if you have any other medical problems, especially:

- Blood clotting problems, such as hemophilia and von Willebrand's disease, or
- Liver disease (severe) or
- Stomach ulcers—The chance of serious bleeding may be increased
- Blood disease—The chance of serious side effects may be increased
- Kidney disease (severe)—Ticlopidine is removed from the body more slowly when the kidneys are not working properly. This may increase the chance of side effects

Proper Use of This Medicine

Ticlopidine should be taken with food. This increases the amount of medicine that is absorbed into the body. It may also lessen the chance of stomach upset.

Take this medicine only as directed by your doctor. Ticlopidine will not work properly if you take less of it than directed. Taking more ticlopidine than directed may increase the chance of serious side effects without increasing the helpful effects.

Dosing—*Follow your doctor's orders or the directions on the label.* The following dose was used, and found effective, in studies. However, some people may need a different dose. *If your dose is different, do not change it* unless your doctor tells you to do so:

- For *oral* dosage form (tablets):
  - —For prevention of strokes:
    - Adults—1 tablet (250 mg) two times a day, with food.
    - Children—It is not likely that ticlopidine would be used to help prevent strokes in children. If a child needs this medicine, however, the dose would have to be determined by the doctor.

Missed dose—If you miss a dose of this medicine, take it as soon as possible. However, if it is almost time for your next dose, skip the missed dose and go back to your regular dosing schedule. Do not double doses.

Storage—To store this medicine:

- Keep out of the reach of children.
- Store away from heat and direct light.
- Do not store in the bathroom, near the kitchen sink, or in other damp places. Heat or moisture may cause the medicine to break down.
- Do not keep outdated medicine or medicine no longer needed. Be sure that any discarded medicine is out of the reach of children.

Precautions While Using This Medicine

It is very important that blood tests be done before treatment is started with ticlopidine, and repeated every 2 weeks for the first 3 months of treatment with ticlopidine. The tests are needed to find out whether certain side effects are occurring. Finding these side effects early helps to prevent them from becoming serious. Your doctor will arrange for the blood tests to be done. *Be sure that you do not miss any appointments for these tests.* You will probably not need to have your blood tested so often after the first 3 months of treatment, because the side effects are less likely to occur after that time.

Tell all medical doctors, dentists, nurses, and pharmacists you go to that you are taking this medicine. Ticlopidine may increase the risk of serious bleeding during an operation or some kinds of dental work. Therefore, treatment may have to be stopped about 10 days to 2 weeks before the operation or dental work is done.

Ticlopidine may cause serious bleeding, especially after an injury. Sometimes, bleeding inside the body can occur without your knowing about it. Ask your doctor whether there are certain activities you should avoid while taking this medicine (for example, sports that can cause injuries). *Also, check with your doctor immediately if you are injured while being treated with this medicine.*

Check with your doctor immediately if you notice any of the following side effects:
- Bruising or bleeding, especially bleeding that is hard to stop. Bleeding inside the body sometimes appears as bloody or black, tarry stools, or faintness.
- Any sign of infection, such as fever, chills, or sore throat.
- Sores, ulcers, or white spots in the mouth.

After you stop taking ticlopidine, the chance of bleeding may continue for 1 or 2 weeks. During this period of time, continue to follow the same precautions that you followed while you were taking the medicine.

Side Effects of This Medicine

Along with its needed effects, a medicine may cause some unwanted effects. Although not all of these side effects may occur, if they do occur they may need medical attention.

Check with your doctor immediately if any of the following side effects occur:

Less common or rare
Abdominal or stomach pain (severe) or swelling; back pain; blistering, peeling, or loosening of the skin or lips or mucous membranes (moist lining of many body cavities, including the mouth, lips, inside of nose, anus, and vagina); blood in eyes; blood in urine; bloody or black, tarry stools; bruising or purple areas on skin; coughing up blood; decreased alertness; dizziness; fever, chills, or sore throat; headache (severe or continuing); joint pain or swelling; nosebleeds; paralysis or problems with coordination; pinpoint red spots on skin; red lesions on the skin, often with a purple center; red, thickened, or scaly skin; sores, ulcers, or white spots in mouth; stammering or other difficulty in speaking; unusually heavy bleeding or oozing from cuts or wounds; unusually heavy or unexpected menstrual bleeding; vomiting of blood or material that looks like coffee grounds

Also, check with your doctor as soon as possible if any of the following side effects occur:

More common
Skin rash

Less common or rare
General feeling of discomfort or illness; hives or itching of skin; ringing or buzzing in ears; yellow eyes or skin

Other side effects may occur that usually do not need medical attention. These side effects may go away during treatment as your body adjusts to the medicine. However, check with your doctor if any of the following side effects continue or are bothersome:

More common
Abdominal or stomach pain (mild); diarrhea; indigestion; nausea

Less common
Bloating or gas; dizziness; vomiting

Other side effects not listed above may also occur in some patients. If you notice any other effects, check with your doctor.

Revised: 07/26/96
Interim revision: 08/05/97

TIOPRONIN Systemic†

Some commonly used brand names are:

In the U.S.—
Thiola

Other—
Capen
Captimer
Epatiol
Mucolysin
Sutilan
Thiosol
Tioglis
Vincol

†Not commercially available in Canada.

Description

Tiopronin (tye-oh-PRO-nin) is used to prevent kidney stones, which may develop due to too much cystine in the urine (cystinuria). This medicine works by removing the extra cystine from the body.

In addition to the helpful effects of this medicine, it has side effects that can be very serious. Before you take tiopronin, be sure that you have discussed its use with your doctor.

Tiopronin is available only with your doctor's prescription, in the following dosage form:

Oral
- Tablets (U.S.)

Before Using This Medicine

In deciding to use a medicine, the risks of taking the medicine must be weighed against the good it will do. This is a decision you and your doctor will make. For tiopronin, the following should be considered:

Allergies—Tell your doctor if you have ever had any unusual or allergic reaction to penicillamine or tiopronin. Also tell your health care professional if you are allergic to any other substances, such as foods, preservatives, or dyes.

Diet—It is important that you follow any special instructions from your doctor, such as following a low-methionine diet. Methionine is found in animal proteins such as milk, eggs, cheese, and fish. Also, make certain your health care professional knows if you are on any special diet, such as a low-sodium or low-sugar diet.

Pregnancy—Studies have not been done in humans. However, studies in animals have shown that tiopronin may cause problems during pregnancy and harmful effects on the fetus.

Breast-feeding—Tiopronin may pass into the breast milk. This medicine is not recommended during breast-feeding because it may cause unwanted effects in nursing babies.

Children—Although there is no specific information comparing use of tiopronin in children with use in other age groups, this medicine is not expected to cause different side effects or problems in children than it does in adults.

Older adults—Many medicines have not been studied specifically in older people. Therefore, it may not be known whether they work exactly the same way they do in younger adults or if they cause different side effects or problems in older people. Although there is no specific information comparing the use of tiopronin in the elderly with use in other age groups, this medicine is not expected to cause different side effects or problems in older people than it does in younger adults.

Other medicines—Although certain medicines should not be used together at all, in other cases two different medicines may be used together even if an interaction might occur. In these cases, your doctor may want to change the dose, or other precautions may be necessary. Tell your health care professional if you are taking any other prescription or nonprescription (over-the-counter [OTC]) medicine.

Other medical problems—The presence of other medical problems may affect the use of tiopronin. Make sure you tell your doctor if you have any other medical problems, especially:

- Blood problems (or a history of) or
- Kidney disease (or a history of) or
- Liver disease—Tiopronin may make these conditions worse

Proper Use of This Medicine

Take this medicine on an empty stomach (at least 30 minutes before meals or 2 hours after meals).

You should drink 2 full glasses (8 ounces each) of water with each meal and at bedtime. You should also drink another 2 full glasses during the night.

It is important that you follow any special instructions from your doctor, such as following a low-methionine diet. Methionine is found in animal proteins such as milk, eggs, cheese, and fish. If you have any questions about this, check with your doctor.

Take this medicine regularly as directed. Do not stop taking it without first checking with your doctor, since stopping the medicine and then restarting it may increase the chance of side effects.

Dosing—The dose of tiopronin will be different for different patients. *Follow your doctor's orders or the directions on the label.* The following information includes only the average doses of tiopronin. *If your dose is different, do not change it* unless your doctor tells you to do so.

- For *oral* dosage form (tablets):
  - —To prevent kidney stones:
    - Adults—To start, 800 milligrams (mg) a day, divided into three doses. Your doctor may change your dose if needed.
    - Children up to 9 years of age—Dose must be determined by your doctor.
    - Children 9 years and older—Dose is based on body weight and must be determined by your doctor. The usual dose to start is 15 mg per kilogram (kg) (6.8 mg per pound) of body weight a day, divided into three doses. Your doctor may change your dose if needed.

Missed dose—If you miss a dose of this medicine, take it as soon as possible. However, if it is almost time for your next dose, skip the missed dose and go back to your regular dosing schedule. Do not double doses.

Storage—To store this medicine:
- Keep out of the reach of children.
- Store away from heat and direct light.
- Do not store in the bathroom, near the kitchen sink, or in other damp places. Heat or moisture may cause the medicine to break down.
- Do not keep outdated medicine or medicine no longer needed. Be sure that any discarded medicine is out of the reach of children.

Precautions While Using This Medicine

Your doctor should check your progress at regular visits to make sure that this medicine is working properly and does not cause unwanted effects.

Side Effects of This Medicine

Along with its needed effects, a medicine may cause some unwanted effects. Although not all of these side effects may occur, if they do occur they may need medical attention.

Check with your doctor immediately if any of the following side effects occur:

More common

Yellow skin or eyes

Less common

Muscle pain; sore throat and fever; unusual bleeding or bruising

Check with your doctor as soon as possible if any of the following side effects occur:

More common

Pain, swelling, or tenderness of the skin; skin rash, hives or itching; ulcers or sores in mouth

Less common

Bloody or cloudy urine; chills; difficulty in breathing; high blood pressure; hoarseness; joint pain; swelling of feet or lower legs; tenderness of glands; unusual bleeding

Rare

Chest pain; cough; difficulty in chewing, talking, or swallowing; double vision; general feeling of discomfort, illness, or weakness; muscle weakness; spitting up blood; swelling of lymph glands

Other side effects may occur that usually do not need medical attention. These side effects may go away during treatment as your body adjusts to the medicine. However, check with your doctor if any of the following side effects continue or are bothersome:

More common

Abdominal or stomach pain; bloating or gas; diarrhea or soft stools; loss of appetite; nausea and vomiting; warts; wrinkling or peeling or unusually dry skin

Less common

Changes in taste or smell

Other side effects not listed above may also occur in some patients. If you notice any other effects, check with your doctor.

Revised: 05/19/92
Interim revision: 08/09/94

TIZANIDINE Systemic†

A commonly used brand name in the U.S. is Zanaflex.

†Not commercially available in Canada.

Description

Tizanidine (tye-ZAN-i-dine) is used to help relax certain muscles in your body. It relieves the spasms, cramping, and tightness of muscles caused by medical problems such as multiple sclerosis or certain injuries to the spine. Tizanidine does not cure these problems, but it may allow other treatment, such as physical therapy, to be more helpful in improving your condition.

Tizanidine acts on the central nervous system (CNS) to produce its muscle relaxant effects. Its actions on the CNS may also cause some of the medicine's side effects.

This medicine is available only with your doctor's prescription, in the following dosage form:

Oral

- Tablets (U.S.)

Before Using This Medicine

In deciding to use a medicine, the risks of taking the medicine must be weighed against the good it will do. This is a decision you and your doctor will make. For tizanidine, the following should be considered:

Allergies—Tell your doctor if you have ever had any unusual or allergic reaction to tizanidine. Also tell your health care professional if you are allergic to any other substances, such as foods, preservatives, or dyes.

Pregnancy—Tizanidine has not been studied in pregnant women. However, studies in animals have shown that tizanidine causes birth defects and other pregnancy problems. Before taking this medicine, make sure your doctor knows if you are pregnant or if you become pregnant.

Breast-feeding—Tizanidine may pass into the breast milk. However, this medicine has not been reported to cause problems in nursing babies.

Children—Studies on this medicine have been done only in adult patients, and there is no specific information comparing use of tizanidine in children with use in other age groups.

Older adults—Studies in older adults show that tizanidine stays in the body a little longer than it does in younger adults. Your doctor will consider this when deciding on your doses.

Other medicines—Although certain medicines should not be used together at all, in other cases two different medicines may be used together even if an interaction might occur. In these cases, your doctor may want to change the dose, or other precautions may be necessary. When you are taking tizanidine, it is especially important that your health care professional know if you are taking any of the following:

- Antihypertensives (high blood pressure medicine)—Severe low blood pressure may occur
- Oral contraceptives (birth control pills)—The chance of side effects may be increased
- Phenytoin—Tizanidine may increase the blood levels of phenytoin, which increases the chance of serious side effects

Other medical problems—The presence of other medical problems may affect the use of tizanidine. Make sure you tell your doctor if you have any other medical problems, especially:

- Kidney disease or
- Liver disease—The chance of side effects may be increased; higher blood levels of tizanidine may result and a smaller dose may be needed

Proper Use of This Medicine

Take this medicine only as directed. Do not take more of it and do not take it more often than recommended on the label, unless otherwise directed by your doctor. To do so may increase the chance of side effects.

Dosing—The dose of tizanidine will be different for different patients. *Follow your doctor's orders or the directions on the label.* The following information includes only the average doses of tizanidine. *If your dose is different, do not change it* unless your doctor tells you to do so.

- For *oral* dosage form (tablets):
  - —For muscle relaxation:
    - Adults—The dose is 8 milligrams (mg) every six to eight hours as needed. No more than 36 mg should be taken within a twenty-four-hour period.
    - Children—Use and dose must be determined by your doctor.

Missed dose—If you miss a dose of this medicine, and you remember within an hour or so of the missed dose, take it as soon as you remember. However, if you do not remember until later, skip the missed dose and go back to your regular dosing schedule. Do not double doses.

Storage—To store this medicine:

- Keep out of the reach of children.
- Store away from heat and direct light.
- Do not store in the bathroom, near the kitchen sink, or in other damp places. Heat or moisture may cause the medicine to break down.
- Do not keep outdated medicine or medicine no longer needed. Be sure that any discarded medicine is out of the reach of children.

Precautions While Using This Medicine

Your doctor should check your progress at regular visits, especially during the first few weeks of treatment with this medicine. During this time the amount of medicine you are taking may have to be changed often to meet your individual needs.

Do not suddenly stop taking this medicine. Unwanted effects may occur if the medicine is stopped suddenly. Check with your doctor for the best way to reduce gradually the amount you are taking before stopping completely.

This medicine will add to the effects of alcohol and other CNS depressants (medicines that make you drowsy or less alert). Some examples of CNS depressants are antihistamines or medicine for hay fever, other allergies, or colds; sedatives, tranquilizers, or sleeping medicine; prescription pain medicine or narcotics; barbiturates; medicine for seizures; other muscle relaxants; or anesthetics, including some dental anesthetics. *Check with your doctor before taking any of the above while you are using tizanidine.*

This medicine may cause dizziness, drowsiness, lightheadedness, clumsiness or unsteadiness, or vision problems in some people. *Make sure you know how you react to this medicine before you drive, use machines, or do anything else that could be dangerous if you are not alert, well-coordinated, and able to see well.*

Tizanidine may cause dryness of the mouth. For temporary relief, use sugarless candy or gum, melt bits of ice in your mouth, or use a saliva substitute. However, if dry mouth continues for more than 2 weeks, check with your medical doctor or dentist. Continuing dryness of the mouth may increase the chance of dental disease, including tooth decay, gum disease, and fungus infections.

Dizziness, lightheadedness, or fainting may occur when you get up suddenly from a lying or sitting position. Getting up slowly may help lessen this problem.

Side Effects of This Medicine

Along with its needed effects, a medicine may cause some unwanted effects. Although not all of these side effects may occur, if they do occur they may need medical attention.

Check with your doctor as soon as possible if any of the following side effects occur:

More common

Fever; loss of appetite; nausea and/or vomiting; nervousness; pain or burning while urinating; sores on the skin; tingling, burning, or prickling sensations; yellow eyes or skin

Less common

Black, tarry stools; bloody vomit; blurred vision; chills or sore throat; coldness; convulsions (seizures); cough; dry, puffy skin; eye pain; fainting; irregular heartbeat; kidney stones; seeing things that are not there; unusual tiredness or weakness; weight gain

Other side effects may occur that usually do not need medical attention. These side effects may go away during treatment as your body adjusts to the medicine. However, check with your doctor if any of the following side effects continue or are bothersome:

More common

Anxiety; back pain; constipation; depression; diarrhea; difficulty in speaking; dizziness or lightheadedness, especially when getting up from a lying or sitting position; drowsiness; dry mouth; heartburn; increased sweating; increased muscle spasms or tone; muscle weakness; pain or burning in throat; runny nose; skin rash; sleepiness; stomach pain; uncontrolled movements of the body

Less common

Difficulty swallowing; dry skin; joint or muscle pain or stiffness; loss of hair; migraine headache; mood changes; neck pain; swelling of feet or lower legs; swollen area that feels warm and tender; trembling or shaking; unusual feeling of well-being; weight loss

Other side effects not listed above may also occur in some patients. If you notice any other effects, check with your doctor.

Developed: 08/12/97

TOBRAMYCIN Ophthalmic

A commonly used brand name in the U.S. and Canada is Tobrex. Generic name product may also be available in the U.S.

Description

Ophthalmic tobramycin (toe-bra-MYE-sin) is used in the eye to treat bacterial infections of the eye. Tobramycin works by killing bacteria.

Ophthalmic tobramycin may be used alone or with other medicines for eye infections. Either the drops or ointment form of this medicine may be used alone during the day. In addition, both forms may be used together, with the drops being used during the day and the ointment at night.

Tobramycin ophthalmic preparations are available only with your doctor's prescription, in the following dosage forms:

Ophthalmic

- Ophthalmic ointment (U.S. and Canada)
- Ophthalmic solution (eye drops) (U.S. and Canada)

Before Using This Medicine

In deciding to use a medicine, the risks of using the medicine must be weighed against the good it will do. This is a decision you and your doctor will make. For ophthalmic tobramycin, the following should be considered:

Allergies—Tell your doctor if you have ever had any unusual or allergic reaction to ophthalmic tobramycin or to any related medicines, such as amikacin (e.g., Amikin), gentamicin (e.g., Garamycin), kanamycin (e.g., Kantrex), neomycin (e.g., Mycifradin), netilmicin (e.g., Netromycin), streptomycin, or tobramycin by injection (e.g., Nebcin). Also tell your health care professional if you are allergic to any other substances, such as preservatives.

Pregnancy—Studies have not been done in humans. However, tobramycin ophthalmic preparations have not been shown to cause birth defects or other problems in animals given high doses.

Breast-feeding—Tobramycin ophthalmic preparations may be absorbed into the eye. However, tobramycin is unlikely to pass into the breast milk in large amounts and little would be absorbed by the infant. Therefore, this medicine is unlikely to cause serious problems in nursing babies.

Children—This medicine has been tested in children and, in effective doses, has not been shown to cause different side effects or problems than it does in adults.

Older adults—Many medicines have not been studied specifically in older people. Therefore, it may not be known whether they work exactly the same way they do in younger adults or if they cause different side effects or problems in older people. There is no specific information comparing use of ophthalmic tobramycin in the elderly with use in other age groups.

Other medicines—Although certain medicines should not be used together at all, in other cases two different medicines may be used together even if an interaction might occur. In these cases, your doctor may want to change the dose, or other precautions may be necessary. Tell your health care professional if you are using any other prescription or nonprescription (over-the-counter [OTC]) medicine that is to be used in the eye.

Proper Use of This Medicine

For patients using tobramycin *ophthalmic solution (eye drops):*

- The bottle is only partially full to provide proper drop control.
- To use:
  - — First, wash your hands. Tilt the head back and with the index finger of one hand, press gently on the skin just beneath the lower eyelid and pull the lower eyelid away from the eye to make a space. Drop the medicine into this space. Let go of the eyelid and gently close the eyes. Do not blink. Keep the eyes closed for 1 or 2 minutes, to allow the medicine to come into contact with the infection.
  - —If you think you did not get the drop of medicine into your eye properly, use another drop.
  - —To keep the medicine as germ-free as possible, do not touch the applicator tip to any surface (including the eye). Also, keep the container tightly closed.
- If your doctor ordered two different ophthalmic solutions to be used together, wait at least 5 minutes between the times you apply the medicines. This will help to keep the second medicine from "washing out" the first one.

For patients using tobramycin *ophthalmic ointment (eye ointment):*

- To use:
  - —First, wash your hands. Tilt the head back and with the index finger of one hand, press gently on the skin just beneath the lower eyelid and pull the lower eyelid away from the eye to make a space. Squeeze a thin strip of ointment into this space. A 1.25-cm (approximately 1/2-inch) strip of ointment is usually enough unless otherwise directed by your doctor. Let go of the eyelid and gently close the eyes and keep them closed for 1 or 2 minutes, to allow the medicine to come into contact with the infection.
  - —To keep the medicine as germ-free as possible, do not touch the applicator tip to any surface (including the eye). After using tobramycin eye ointment, wipe the tip of the ointment tube with a clean tissue and keep the tube tightly closed.

To help clear up your eye infection completely, *keep using tobramycin for the full time of treatment,* even if your symptoms have disappeared. *Do not miss any doses.*

Dosing—The dose of ophthalmic tobramycin will be different for different patients. *Follow your doctor's orders or the directions on the label.* The following information includes only the average dose of ophthalmic tobramycin. *If your dose is different, do not change it* unless your doctor tells you to do so.

The number of doses you use each day, the time allowed between doses, and the length of time you use the medicine depend on the medical problem for which you are using ophthalmic tobramycin.

- For *ophthalmic ointment* dosage forms:
  - —For mild to moderate infections:
    - Adults and children—Use every eight to twelve hours.
  - —For severe infections:
    - Adults and children—Use every three to four hours until improvement occurs.
- For *ophthalmic solution (eye drops)* dosage forms:
  - —For mild to moderate infections:
    - Adults and children—One drop every four hours.

—For severe infections:
  • Adults and children—One drop every hour until improvement occurs.

Missed dose—If you miss a dose of this medicine, use it as soon as possible. However, if it is almost time for your next dose, skip the missed dose and go back to your regular dosing schedule.

Storage—To store this medicine:
- Keep out of the reach of children.
- Store away from heat and direct light.
- Keep the medicine from freezing.
- Do not keep outdated medicine or medicine no longer needed. Be sure that any discarded medicine is out of the reach of children.

Precautions While Using This Medicine

If your eye infection does not improve within a few days, or if it becomes worse, check with your doctor.

Side Effects of This Medicine

Along with its needed effects, a medicine may cause some unwanted effects. Although not all of these side effects may occur, if they do occur they may need medical attention.

Check with your doctor immediately if any of the following side effects occur:

Less common
  Itching, redness, swelling, or other sign of eye or eyelid irritation not present before use of this medicine

Symptoms of overdose
  Increased watering of the eyes; itching, redness, or swelling of the eyes or eyelids

Other side effects may occur that usually do not need medical attention. These side effects may go away during treatment as your body adjusts to the medicine. However, check with your doctor if either of the following side effects continues or is bothersome:

Less common
  Burning or stinging of the eyes

Eye ointments usually cause your vision to blur for a few minutes after application.

Other side effects not listed above may also occur in some patients. If you notice any other effects, check with your doctor.

Revised: 07/01/93
Interim revision: 09/30/93

TOCAINIDE Systemic

A commonly used brand name in the U.S. and Canada is Tonocard.

Description

Tocainide (toe-KAY-nide) belongs to the group of medicines known as antiarrhythmics. It is used to correct irregular heartbeats to a normal rhythm.

Tocainide produces its helpful effects by slowing nerve impulses in the heart and making the heart tissue less sensitive.

Tocainide is available only with your doctor's prescription, in the following dosage form:

Oral
  • Tablets (U.S. and Canada)

Before Using This Medicine

In deciding to use a medicine, the risks of taking the medicine must be weighed against the good it will do. This is a decision you and your doctor will make. For tocainide, the following should be considered:

Allergies—Tell your doctor if you have ever had any unusual or allergic reaction to tocainide or anesthetics. Also tell your health care professional if you are allergic to any other substances, such as foods, preservatives, or dyes.

Pregnancy—Tocainide has not been shown to cause birth defects or other problems in humans. Studies in animals have shown that high doses of tocainide may increase the possibility of death in the animal fetus.

Breast-feeding—Tocainide may pass into breast milk. Mothers who are taking this medicine and who wish to breast-feed should discuss this with their doctor.

Children—Studies on this medicine have been done only in adult patients and there is no specific information comparing use of tocainide in children with use in other age groups.

Older adults—Dizziness or lightheadedness may be more likely to occur in the elderly, who are usually more sensitive to the effects of tocainide.

Other medicines—Although certain medicines should not be used together at all, in other cases two different medicines may be used together even if an interaction might occur. In these cases, your doctor may want to change the dose, or other precautions may be necessary. Tell your health care professional if you are taking any other prescription or nonprescription (over-the-counter [OTC]) medicine.

Other medical problems—The presence of other medical problems may affect the use of tocainide. Make sure you tell your doctor if you have any other medical problems, especially:
- Congestive heart failure—Tocainide may make this condition worse
- Kidney disease or
- Liver disease—Effects may be increased because of slower removal of tocainide from the body

Proper Use of This Medicine

Take tocainide exactly as directed by your doctor, even though you may feel well. Do not take more medicine than ordered.

If tocainide upsets your stomach, your doctor may advise you to take it with food or milk.

This medicine works best when there is a constant amount in the blood. *To help keep the amount constant, do not miss any doses. Also, it is best to take the doses at evenly spaced times day and night.* For example, if you are to take 3 doses a day, the doses should be spaced about 8 hours apart. If this interferes with your sleep or other daily activities, or if you need help in planning the best times to take your medicine, check with your health care professional.

Dosing—The dose of tocainide will be different for different patients. *Follow your doctor's orders or the directions on the label.* The following information includes only the average doses of tocainide. *If your dose is different, do not change it* unless your doctor tells you to do so.

The number of tablets that you take depends on the strength of the medicine.

- For *oral* dosage form (tablets):
  - —For irregular heartbeat:
    - Adults—At first, 400 milligrams (mg) every eight hours. Then, your doctor may increase your dose up to 600 mg three times a day.
    - Children—Use and dose must be determined by your doctor.

Missed dose—If you miss a dose of tocainide and remember within 4 hours, take it as soon as possible. Then go back to your regular dosing schedule. However, if you do not remember until later, skip the missed dose and go back to your regular dosing schedule. Do not double doses.

Storage—To store this medicine:

- Keep out of the reach of children.
- Store away from heat and direct light.
- Do not store in the bathroom, near the kitchen sink, or in other damp places. Heat or moisture may cause the medicine to break down.
- Do not keep outdated medicine or medicine no longer needed. Be sure that any discarded medicine is out of the reach of children.

Precautions While Using This Medicine

It is important that your doctor check your progress at regular visits to make sure the medicine is working properly. This will allow changes to be made in the amount of medicine you are taking, if necessary.

Your doctor may want you to carry a medical identification card or bracelet stating that you are using this medicine.

Tocainide may cause some people to become dizzy, lightheaded, or less alert than they are normally. *Make sure you know how you react to this medicine before you drive, use machines, or do anything else that could be dangerous if you are dizzy or are not alert.*

Before having any kind of surgery (including dental surgery) or emergency treatment, tell the medical doctor or dentist in charge that you are taking this medicine.

Side Effects of This Medicine

Along with its needed effects, a medicine may cause some unwanted effects. Although not all of these side effects may occur, if they do occur they may need medical attention.

Check with your doctor as soon as possible if any of the following side effects occur:

Less common

Trembling or shaking

Rare

Blisters on skin; cough or shortness of breath; fever or chills; irregular heartbeats; peeling or scaling of skin; skin rash (severe); sores in mouth; unusual bleeding or bruising

Other side effects may occur that usually do not need medical attention. These side effects may go away during treatment as your body adjusts to the medicine. However, check with your doctor if any of the following side effects continue or are bothersome:

More common

Dizziness or lightheadedness; loss of appetite; nausea

Less common

Blurred vision; confusion; headache; nervousness; numbness or tingling of fingers and toes; skin rash; sweating; vomiting

Other side effects not listed above may also occur in some patients. If you notice any other effects, check with your doctor.

Revised: 08/21/96

TOLNAFTATE Topical

Some commonly used brand names are:

In the U.S.—

Aftate for Athlete's Foot Aerosol Spray Liquid
Aftate for Athlete's Foot Aerosol Spray Powder
Aftate for Athlete's Foot Gel
Aftate for Athlete's Foot Sprinkle Powder
Aftate for Jock Itch Aerosol Spray Powder
Aftate for Jock Itch Gel
Aftate for Jock Itch Sprinkle Powder
Genaspore Cream
NP-27 Cream
NP-27 Powder
NP-27 Solution
NP-27 Spray Powder
Tinactin Aerosol Liquid
Tinactin Aerosol Powder
Tinactin Antifungal Deodorant Powder Aerosol
Tinactin Cream
Tinactin Jock Itch Cream
Tinactin Jock Itch Spray Powder
Tinactin Powder
Tinactin Solution
Ting Antifungal Cream
Ting Antifungal Powder
Ting Antifungal Spray Liquid
Ting Antifungal Spray Powder
Zeasorb-AF Powder

Generic name product may also be available.

In Canada—

Pitrex Cream	Tinactin Jock Itch Cream
Tinactin Aerosol Liquid	Tinactin Plus Aerosol Powder
Tinactin Aerosol Powder	Tinactin Plus Powder
Tinactin Cream	Tinactin Powder
Tinactin Jock Itch Aerosol Powder	Tinactin Solution

Description

Tolnaftate (tole-NAF-tate) belongs to the group of medicines called antifungals. It is used to treat some types of fungus infections. It may also be used together with medicines taken by mouth for fungus infections.

Tolnaftate is available without a prescription; however, your doctor may have special instructions on the proper use of tolnaftate for your medical problem.

Tolnaftate is available in the following dosage forms:

Topical

- Aerosol powder (U.S. and Canada)
- Aerosol solution (U.S. and Canada)
- Cream (U.S. and Canada)
- Gel (U.S.)
- Powder (U.S. and Canada)
- Topical solution (U.S. and Canada)

Before Using This Medicine

If you are taking this medicine without a prescription, carefully read and follow any precautions on the label. For tolnaftate, the following should be considered:

Allergies—Tell your doctor if you have ever had any unusual or allergic reaction to tolnaftate. Also tell your health care professional if you are allergic to any other substances, such as preservatives or dyes.

Pregnancy—Tolnaftate topical preparations have not been shown to cause birth defects or other problems in humans.

Breast-feeding—Tolnaftate topical preparations have not been reported to cause problems in nursing babies.

Children—Tolnaftate should not be used on children up to 2 years of age, unless otherwise directed by your doctor. Although there is no specific information comparing use of tolnaftate in children 2 years of age and older with use in other age groups, this medicine is not expected to cause different side effects or problems in children 2 years of age and older than it does in adults.

Older adults—Many medicines have not been studied specifically in older people. Therefore, it may not be known whether they work exactly the same way they do in younger adults or if they cause different side effects or problems in older people. There is no specific information comparing use of tolnaftate in the elderly with use in other age groups.

Other medicines—Although certain medicines should not be used together at all, in other cases two different medicines may be used together even if an interaction might occur. In these cases, your doctor may want to change the dose, or other precautions may be necessary. Tell your health care professional if you are using any other topical prescription or nonprescription (over-the-counter [OTC]) medicine that is to be applied to the same area of the skin.

Proper Use of This Medicine

Before applying tolnaftate, wash the affected area and dry thoroughly. Then apply enough medicine to cover the affected area.

Keep this medicine away from the eyes.

For patients using the *powder form* of this medicine:

- If the powder is used on the feet, sprinkle it between toes, on feet, and in socks and shoes.

For patients using the *aerosol powder form* of this medicine:

- Shake well before using.
- From a distance of 6 to 10 inches, spray the powder on the affected areas. If it is used on the feet, spray it between toes, on feet, and in socks and shoes.
- Do not inhale the powder.
- Do not use near heat, near open flame, or while smoking.

For patients using the *solution form* of this medicine:

- If tolnaftate solution becomes a solid, it may be dissolved by warming the closed container of medicine in warm water.

For patients using the *aerosol solution form* of this medicine:

- Shake well before using.
- From a distance of 6 inches, spray the solution on the affected areas. If it is used on the feet, spray between toes and on feet.
- Do not inhale the vapors from the spray.
- Do not use near heat, near open flame, or while smoking.

To help clear up your infection completely, *keep using this medicine for 2 weeks after burning, itching, or other symptoms have disappeared,* unless otherwise directed by your doctor. *Do not miss any doses.*

Dosing—The dose of tolnaftate will be different for different patients. *Follow your doctor's orders or the directions on the label.* The following information includes only the average dose of tolnaftate. *If your dose is different, do not change it* unless your doctor tells you to do so.

- For *topical* dosage forms (aerosol powder, aerosol solution, cream, gel, powder, or topical solution):
  - —For fungus infections:
    - Adults and children 2 years of age and over—Apply to the affected area(s) of the skin two times a day.
    - Children up to 2 years of age—Use is not recommended except under the advice and supervision of your doctor.

Missed dose—If you miss a dose of this medicine, apply it as soon as possible. Then go back to your regular dosing schedule.

Storage—To store this medicine:
- Keep out of the reach of children.
- Store away from heat and direct light.
- Do not store the powder form of this medicine in the bathroom, near the kitchen sink, or in other damp places. Heat or moisture may cause the medicine to break down.
- Keep the medicine from freezing.
- Do not puncture, break, or burn the aerosol powder or aerosol solution container.
- Do not keep outdated medicine or medicine no longer needed. Be sure that any discarded medicine is out of the reach of children.

Precautions While Using This Medicine

If your skin problem does not improve within 4 weeks, or if it becomes worse, check with your health care professional.

To help prevent reinfection after the period of treatment with this medicine, the powder or spray powder form of this medicine may be used each day after bathing and carefully drying the affected area.

Side Effects of This Medicine

Along with its needed effects, a medicine may cause some unwanted effects. Although not all of these side effects may occur, if they do occur they may need medical attention.

Check with your health care professional as soon as possible if the following side effect occurs:

Skin irritation not present before use of this medicine

When you apply the aerosol solution form of this medicine, a mild temporary stinging may be expected.

Other side effects not listed above may also occur in some patients. If you notice any other effects, check with your health care professional.

Revised: 11/05/91
Interim revision: 08/10/94

TORSEMIDE Systemic†

A commonly used brand name in the U.S. is Demadex.

†Not commercially available in Canada.

Description

Torsemide (TORE-se-mide) belongs to the group of medicines called loop diuretics. Torsemide is given to help reduce the amount of water in the body in certain conditions, such as congestive heart failure, severe liver disease (cirrhosis), or kidney disease. It works by acting on the kidneys to increase the flow of urine.

Torsemide is also used to treat high blood pressure (hypertension). High blood pressure adds to the work load of the heart and arteries. If it continues for a long time, the heart and arteries may not function properly. This can damage the blood vessels of the brain, heart, and kidneys, resulting in a stroke, heart failure, or kidney failure. High blood pressure may also increase the risk of heart attacks. These problems may be less likely to occur if blood pressure is controlled.

Torsemide is available only with your doctor's prescription, in the following dosage forms:

Oral
- Tablets (U.S.)

Parenteral
- Injection (U.S.)

Before Using This Medicine

In deciding to use a medicine, the risks of taking the medicine must be weighed against the good it will do. This is a decision you and your doctor will make. For torsemide, the following should be considered:

Allergies—Tell your doctor if you have ever had any unusual or allergic reaction to bumetanide, ethacrynic acid, furosemide, sulfonamides (sulfa drugs), or thiazide diuretics (water pills). Also, tell your health care professional if you are allergic to any other substances, such as foods, preservatives, or dyes.

Pregnancy—Studies have not been done in pregnant women. In general, diuretics are not useful for normal swelling of feet and hands that occurs during pregnancy. Diuretics should not be taken during pregnancy unless recommended by your doctor.

Breast-feeding—It is not known whether torsemide passes into breast milk. Although most medicines pass into breast milk in small amounts, many of them may be used safely while breast-feeding. Mothers who are taking this medicine and who wish to breast-feed should discuss this with their doctor.

Children—Studies on this medicine have been done only in adult patients, and there is no specific information comparing use of torsemide in children with use in other age groups.

Older adults—Many medicines have not been studied specifically in older people. Therefore, it may not be known whether they work exactly the same way they do in younger adults. Although there is no specific information comparing use of torsemide in the elderly with use in other age groups, this medicine is not expected to cause different side effects or problems in older people than it does in younger adults.

Other medicines—Although certain medicines should not be used together at all, in other cases two different medicines may be used together even if an interaction might occur. In these cases, your doctor may want to change the dose, or other precautions may be necessary. When you

are taking torsemide, it is especially important that your health care professional know if you are taking any of the following:

- Acetazolamide (e.g., Diamox) or
- Alcohol or
- Amphotericin B by injection (e.g., Fungizone) or
- Azlocillin (e.g., Azlin) or
- Capreomycin (e.g., Capastat) or
- Carbenicillin by injection (e.g., Geopen) or
- Corticosteroids (cortisone-like medicine) or
- Corticotropin (ACTH) or
- Dichlorphenamide (e.g., Daranide) or
- Diuretics (water pills) or
- Insulin or
- Laxatives (with overdose or chronic misuse) or
- Methazolamide (e.g., Neptazane) or
- Mezlocillin (e.g., Mezlin) or
- Piperacillin (e.g., Pipracil) or
- Salicylates or
- Sodium bicarbonate (e.g., baking soda) or
- Ticarcillin (e.g., Ticar) or
- Ticarcillin and clavulanate (e.g., Timentin) or
- Vitamin B_{12} (e.g., AlphaRedisol, Rubramin-PC) (when used in megaloblastic anemia) or
- Vitamin D—Use of these medicines with torsemide may increase the chance of potassium loss
- Aldesleukin (e.g., Proleukin) or
- Anti-infectives by mouth or by injection (medicine for infection) or
- Carmustine (e.g., BiCNU) or
- Cisplatin (e.g., Platinol) or
- Combination pain medicine containing acetaminophen and aspirin (e.g., Excedrin) or other salicylates (with large amounts taken regularly) or
- Cyclosporine (e.g., Sandimmune) or
- Deferoxamine (e.g., Desferal) (with long-term use) or
- Gold salts (medicine for arthritis) or
- Inflammation or pain medicine, except narcotics, or
- Methotrexate (e.g., Mexate) or
- Penicillamine (e.g., Cuprimine) or
- Pentamidine (e.g., Pentam 300) or
- Plicamycin (e.g., Mithracin) or
- Streptozocin (e.g., Zanosar) or
- Tiopronin (e.g., Thiola)—Use of these medicines with torsemide may increase the chance of kidney damage
- Anticoagulants (blood thinners)—Torsemide may decrease the effects of these medicines
- Lithium (e.g., Lithane)—Use of lithium with torsemide may increase the chance of kidney damage; also, the chance of side effects of lithium may be increased

Other medical problems—The presence of other medical problems may affect the use of torsemide. Make sure you tell your doctor if you have any other medical problems, especially:

- Diabetes mellitus (sugar diabetes)—Torsemide may increase the amount of sugar in the blood
- Gout or
- Hearing problems—Torsemide may make these conditions worse
- Heart attack (recent)—Use of torsemide after a recent heart attack may make this condition worse
- Kidney disease (severe) or
- Liver disease—Higher blood levels of torsemide may occur, which may increase the chance of side effects

Proper Use of This Medicine

This medicine may cause you to have an unusual feeling of tiredness when you begin to take it. You may also notice an increase in the amount of urine or in your frequency of urination. After you have taken the medicine for a while, these effects should lessen.

It is best to plan your dose or doses according to a schedule that will least affect your personal activities and sleep. Ask your health care professional to help you plan the best time to take this medicine.

To help you remember to take your medicine, try to get into the habit of taking it at the same time each day.

For patients taking this medicine for *high blood pressure:*

- In addition to the use of the medicine your doctor has prescribed, treatment for your high blood pressure may include weight control and care in the types of foods you eat, especially foods high in sodium. Your doctor will tell you which of these are most important for you. You should check with your doctor before changing your diet.
- Many patients who have high blood pressure will not notice any signs of the problem. In fact, many may feel normal. It is very important that you *take your medicine exactly as directed* and that you keep your appointments with your doctor even if you feel well.
- Remember that this medicine will not cure your high blood pressure but it does help control it. Therefore, you must continue to take it as directed if you expect to lower your blood pressure and keep it down. *You may have to take high blood pressure medicine for the rest of your life.* If high blood pressure is not treated, it can cause serious problems, such as heart failure, blood vessel disease, stroke, or kidney disease.

Dosing—The dose of torsemide will be different for different patients. *Follow your doctor's orders or the directions on the label.* The following information includes only the average doses of torsemide. *If your dose is different, do not change it* unless your doctor tells you to do so.

The number of tablets that you take depends on the strength of the medicine. Also, *the length of time you take the medicine depends on the medical problem for which you are taking torsemide.*

- For *oral* dosage form (tablets):
  - —For lowering the amount of water in the body:
    - Adults—Dose is usually 5 to 20 milligrams (mg) once a day. However, your doctor may increase your dose as needed.
    - Children—Use and dose must be determined by your doctor.
  - —For high blood pressure:
    - Adults—5 to 10 mg once a day.
    - Children—Use and dose must be determined by your doctor.

- For *injection* dosage form:
  —For lowering the amount of water in the body:
  - Adults—Dose is usually 5 to 20 mg injected into a vein once a day. However, your doctor may increase your dose as needed.
  - Children—Use and dose must be determined by your doctor.

Missed dose—If you miss a dose of this medicine, take it as soon as possible. However, if it is almost time for your next dose, skip the missed dose and go back to your regular dosing schedule. Do not double doses.

Storage—To store this medicine:
- Keep out of the reach of children.
- Store away from heat and direct light.
- Do not store in the bathroom, near the kitchen sink, or in other damp places. Heat or moisture may cause the medicine to break down.
- Keep the medicine from freezing. Do not refrigerate.
- Do not keep outdated medicine or medicine no longer needed. Be sure that any discarded medicine is out of the reach of children.

Precautions While Using This Medicine

It is important that your doctor check your progress at regular visits to make sure that this medicine is working properly.

This medicine may cause a loss of potassium from your body:
- To help prevent this, your doctor may want you to:
  —eat or drink foods that have a high potassium content (for example, orange or other citrus fruit juices), or
  —take a potassium supplement, or
  —take another medicine to help prevent the loss of the potassium in the first place.
- It is very important to follow these directions. Also, it is important not to change your diet on your own. This is more important if you are already on a special diet (as for diabetes) or if you are taking a potassium supplement or a medicine to reduce potassium loss. Extra potassium may not be necessary and, in some cases, too much potassium could be harmful.

To prevent the loss of too much water and potassium, tell your doctor if you become sick, especially with severe or continuing nausea and vomiting or diarrhea.

Before having any kind of surgery (including dental surgery) or emergency treatment, make sure the medical doctor or dentist in charge knows that you are taking this medicine.

Dizziness, lightheadedness, or fainting may occur, especially when you get up from a lying or sitting position. This is more likely to occur in the morning. *Getting up slowly may help.* When you get up from lying down, sit on the edge of the bed with your feet dangling for 1 or 2 minutes. Then stand up slowly. If the problem continues or gets worse, check with your doctor.

The dizziness, lightheadedness, or fainting is also more likely to occur if you drink alcohol, stand for long periods of time, or exercise, or if the weather is hot. *While you are taking this medicine, be careful to limit the amount of alcohol you drink. Also, use extra care during exercise or hot weather or if you must stand for long periods of time.*

For *diabetic patients:*
- This medicine may affect blood sugar levels. While you are using this medicine, be especially careful in testing for sugar in your blood or urine.

For patients taking this medicine for *high blood pressure:*
- *Do not take other medicines unless they have been discussed with your doctor.* This especially includes over-the-counter (nonprescription) medicines for appetite control, asthma, colds, cough, hay fever, or sinus problems, since they may tend to increase your blood pressure.

Side Effects of This Medicine

Along with its needed effects, a medicine may cause some unwanted effects. Although not all of these side effects may occur, if they do occur they may need medical attention.

Check with your doctor as soon as possible if any of the following side effects occur:

Less common

Dryness of mouth; fast or irregular heartbeat; increased thirst; mood or mental changes; muscle pain or cramps; nausea or vomiting; unusual tiredness or weakness

Rare

Black, tarry stools; dizziness when getting up from a sitting or lying position; ringing or buzzing in the ears or any hearing loss; skin rash

Other side effects may occur that usually do not need medical attention. These side effects may go away during treatment as your body adjusts to the medicine. However, check with your doctor if any of the following side effects continue or are bothersome:

More common

Constipation; dizziness; headache; stomach upset

Developed: 02/15/95
Interim revision: 08/01/95

TRAMADOL Systemic†

A commonly used brand name in the U.S. is Ultram.

†Not commercially available in Canada.

Description

Tramadol (TRA-ma-dole) is used to relieve pain, including pain after surgery. The effects of tramadol are similar to those of narcotic analgesics. Although tramadol is not a narcotic, it may become habit-forming, causing mental or physical dependence.

Tramadol is available only with your doctor's prescription, in the following dosage form:

Oral

- Tablets (U.S.)

Before Using This Medicine

In deciding to use a medicine, the risks of taking the medicine must be weighed against the good it will do. This is a decision you and your doctor will make. For tramadol, the following should be considered:

Allergies—Tell your doctor if you have ever had any unusual or allergic reaction to tramadol or narcotic analgesics. Also tell your healthcare professional if you are allergic to any other substances, such as foods, preservatives, or dyes.

Pregnancy—Although studies on birth defects have not been done in pregnant women, tramadol has not been reported to cause birth defects. In animal studies, there were drug-related birth defects observed. Studies done in animals given very high (toxic) doses resulted in lower than normal birth weights and some deaths in the fetuses and birth defects in some of the newborns.

Breast-feeding—Tramadol passes into breast milk and may cause unwanted effects in nursing babies. It may be necessary for you to take another medicine or to stop breast-feeding during treatment. Be sure you have discussed the risks and benefits of the medicine with your doctor.

Children—There is no specific information on the relationship of age to the effects of tramadol in patients less than 16 years of age.

Older adults—Studies in older adults show that tramadol stays in the body a little longer than it does in younger adults. Your doctor will consider this when deciding on your doses.

Other medicines—Although certain medicines should not be used together at all, in other cases two different medicines may be used together even if an interaction might occur. In these cases, your doctor may want to change the dose, or other precautions may be necessary. When you are taking tramadol, it is especially important that your health care provider know if you are taking any of the following:

- Carbamazepine (e.g., Tegretol)—May decrease the effects of tramadol by decreasing the amount of medicine in the body
- Central nervous system (CNS) depressants (medicines that cause drowsiness)—Using these medicines with tramadol may increase the chance of serious side effects or increase the risk of convulsions (seizures)
- Monoamine oxidase (MAO) inhibitors (furazolidone [e.g., Furoxone], isocarboxazid [e.g., Marplan], phenelzine [e.g., Nardil], procarbazine [e.g., Matulane], selegiline [e.g., Eldepryl], tranylcypromine [e.g., Parnate])—The chance of convulsions (seizures) may be increased

Other medical problems—The presence of other medical problems may affect the use of tramadol. Make sure you tell your doctor if you have any other medical problems, especially:

- Abdominal or stomach conditions (severe)—Tramadol may hide signs of other medical conditions
- Alcohol or drug abuse, or history of—May increase the serious side effects of tramadol
- Head injury—Tramadol can hide signs of other medical conditions
- Kidney disease or
- Liver disease—The chance of side effects may be increased
- Seizures—The chance of convulsions (seizures) may be increased

Proper Use of This Medicine

If you think that this medicine is not working as well after you have been taking it for a few weeks, *do not increase the dose.* Instead, check with your medical doctor or dentist.

Dosing—The dose of tramadol will be different for different patients. *Follow your doctor's orders or the directions on the label.* The following information includes only the average doses of tramadol. *If your dose is different, do not change it* unless your doctor tells you to do so.

The number of doses you take each day, the time allowed between doses, and the length of time you take the medicine depend on the medical problem for which you are taking tramadol.

Take this medicine only as directed. Do not take more of it, do not take it more often, and do not take it for a longer time than your doctor ordered. Using too much of this medicine increases the chance of unwanted effects.

- For pain:
  - —For *oral* dosage form (tablets):
    - Adults—One to two 50-milligram (mg) tablets every six hours as needed. Your doctor may want you to take 2 tablets for the first dose if you are having severe pain. This helps the medicine start working a little faster.
    - Children up to 16 years of age—Use and dose must be determined by your doctor.

Missed dose—If your medical doctor or dentist has directed you to take this medicine according to a regular schedule and you miss a dose of this medicine, take it as soon as possible. However, if it is almost time for your next dose, skip the missed dose and go back to your regular dosing schedule. Do not double doses.

Storage—To store this medicine:

- Keep out of the reach of children.
- Store away from heat and direct light.
- Do not store tramadol tablets in the bathroom, near the kitchen sink, or in other damp places. Heat or moisture may cause the medicine to break down.
- Do not keep outdated medicine or medicine no longer needed. Be sure that any discarded medicine is out of the reach of children.

Precautions While Using This Medicine

This medicine will add to the effects of alcohol and other CNS depressants (medicine that causes drowsiness). Some examples of CNS depressants are antihistamines or medicine for hay fever, other allergies, or colds; sedatives, tranquilizers, or sleeping medicine; prescription pain medicine or narcotics; barbiturates; medicine for seizures; muscle relaxants; or anesthetics, including some dental anesthetics. *Do not drink alcoholic beverages, and check with your medical doctor or dentist before taking any of the medicines listed above while you are using this medicine.*

This medicine may cause some people to become drowsy, dizzy, or lightheaded. *Make sure you know how you react to this medicine before you drive, use machines, or do anything else that could be dangerous if you are dizzy or are not alert.*

Dizziness, lightheadedness, or fainting may occur, especially when you get up suddenly from a lying or sitting position. Getting up slowly may help lessen this problem.

Nausea or vomiting may occur, especially after the first couple of doses. This effect may go away if you lie down for awhile. However, if nausea or vomiting continues, check with your medical doctor or dentist. Lying down for a while may also help relieve some other side effects, such as dizziness or lightheadedness, that may occur.

Before having any kind of surgery (including dental surgery) or emergency treatment, tell the medical doctor or dentist in charge that you are taking this medicine. Taking tramadol together with medicines that are used during surgery or dental or emergency treatments may cause increased side effects.

If you think you or someone else may have taken an overdose of tramadol, get emergency help at once. Signs of an overdose include convulsions (seizures) and pinpoint pupils of the eyes.

Side Effects of This Medicine

Along with its needed effects, a medicine may cause some unwanted effects. Although not all of these side effects may occur, if they do occur they may need medical attention.

Get emergency help immediately if any of the following symptoms of overdose occur:

Convulsions (seizures); difficulty in breathing; pin-pointed pupils of the eyes

Also, check with your doctor as soon as possible if any of the following side effects occur:

Less common

Blurred vision; difficult urination; frequent urge to urinate

Rare

Blisters under the skin; change in walking and balance; convulsions (seizures); dizziness or lightheadedness when getting up from a lying or sitting position; fainting; fast heartbeat; loss of memory; numbness, tingling, pain, or weakness in hands or feet; seeing, hearing, or feeling things that are not there; severe redness, swelling, and itching of the skin; shortness of breath; trembling and shaking of hands or feet; trouble performing routine tasks

Other side effects may occur that usually do not need medical attention. These side effects may go away during treatment as your body adjusts to the medicine. However, check with your doctor if any of the following side effects continue or are bothersome:

Less common

Abdominal or stomach pain; anxiety; confusion; constipation; diarrhea; dizziness; dry mouth; excessive gas; flushing or redness of the skin; general feeling of bodily discomfort; headache; heartburn; hot flashes; itching; loss of appetite; loss of strength or energy; nausea; nervousness; skin rash; sleepiness; sweating; trouble in sleeping; unusual feeling of excitement; vomiting

After you stop using this medicine, your body may need time to adjust. The length of time this takes depends on the amount of medicine you were using and how long you used it. During this period of time check with your doctor if you notice any of the following side effects:

Anxiety; body aches; diarrhea; fast heartbeat; fever, runny nose, or sneezing; gooseflesh; high blood pressure; increased sweating; increased yawning; loss of appetite; nausea or vomiting; nervousness, restlessness or irritability; shivering or trembling; stomach cramps; trouble in sleeping; unusually large pupils; weakness

Other side effects not listed above may also occur in some patients. If you notice any other effects, check with your doctor.

Developed: 07/15/96

TRAZODONE Systemic

Some commonly used brand names are:

In the U.S.—

Desyrel
Trialodine
Trazon

Generic name product may also be available.

In Canada—

Desyrel

Description

Trazodone (TRAZ-oh-done) belongs to the group of medicines known as antidepressants or "mood elevators." It is used to relieve mental depression and depression that sometimes occurs with anxiety.

Trazodone is available only with your doctor's prescription, in the following dosage form:

Oral

- Tablets (U.S. and Canada)

Before Using This Medicine

In deciding to use a medicine, the risks of taking the medicine must be weighed against the good it will do. This is a decision you and your doctor will make. For trazodone, the following should be considered:

Allergies—Tell your doctor if you have ever had any unusual or allergic reaction to trazodone. Also tell your health care professional if you are allergic to any other substances, such as foods, preservatives, or dyes.

Pregnancy—Studies have not been done in pregnant women. However, studies in animals have shown that trazodone causes birth defects and a decrease in the number of successful pregnancies when given in doses many times larger than human doses.

Breast-feeding—Trazodone passes into breast milk.

Children—Studies on this medicine have been done only in adult patients, and there is no specific information comparing use of trazodone in children with use in other age groups.

Older adults—Drowsiness, dizziness, confusion, vision problems, dryness of mouth, and constipation may be more likely to occur in the elderly, who are usually more sensitive to the effects of trazodone.

Other medicines—Although certain medicines should not be used together at all, in other cases two different medicines may be used together even if an interaction might occur. In these cases, your doctor may want to change the dose, or other precautions may be necessary. When you are taking trazodone, it is especially important that your health care professional know if you are taking any of the following:

- Antihypertensives (high blood pressure medicine)—Taking these medicines with trazodone may result in low blood pressure (hypotension); the amount of medicine you need to take may change
- Central nervous system (CNS) depressants (medicine that causes drowsiness) or
- Tricyclic antidepressants (medicine for depression)—Taking these medicines with trazodone may add to the CNS depressant effects

Other medical problems—The presence of other medical problems may affect the use of trazodone. Make sure you tell your doctor if you have any other medical problems, especially:

- Alcohol abuse (or history of)—Drinking alcohol with trazodone will increase the central nervous system (CNS) depressant effects
- Heart disease—Trazodone may make the condition worse
- Kidney disease or
- Liver disease—Higher blood levels of trazodone may occur, increasing the chance of side effects

Proper Use of This Medicine

To lessen stomach upset and to reduce dizziness and lightheadedness, take this medicine with or shortly after a meal or light snack, even for a daily bedtime dose, unless your doctor has told you to take it on an empty stomach.

Take trazodone only as directed by your doctor, to benefit your condition as much as possible.

Sometimes trazodone must be taken for up to 4 weeks before you begin to feel better, although most people notice improvement within 2 weeks.

Dosing—The dose of trazodone will be different for different patients. *Follow your doctor's orders or the directions on the label.* The following information includes only the average doses of trazodone. *If your dose is different, do not change it* unless your doctor tells you to do so:

- Adults—Oral, to start, 50 milligrams per dose taken three times a day, or 75 milligrams per dose taken two times a day. Your doctor may increase your dose if needed.
- Children 6 to 18 years of age—Oral. Your doctor will tell you what dose to take based on your body weight.
- Children up to 6 years of age—Dose must be determined by the doctor.
- Elderly patients—Oral, to start, 25 milligrams per dose taken three times a day. Your doctor may increase your dose if needed.

Missed dose—If you miss a dose of this medicine, take it as soon as possible. However, if it is within 4 hours of your next dose, skip the missed dose and go back to your regular dosing schedule. Do not double doses.

Storage—To store this medicine:

- Keep out of the reach of children.
- Store away from heat and direct light.
- Do not store in the bathroom, near the kitchen sink, or in other damp places. Heat or moisture may cause the medicine to break down.
- Do not keep outdated medicine or medicine no longer needed. Be sure that any discarded medicine is out of the reach of children.

Precautions While Using This Medicine

It is very important that your doctor check your progress at regular visits. This will allow your doctor to check the medicine's effects and to change the dose if needed.

Do not stop taking this medicine without first checking with your doctor. To prevent a possible return of your medical problem, your doctor may want you to reduce gradually the amount of medicine you are using before you stop completely.

Before having any kind of surgery, dental treatment, or emergency treatment, tell the medical doctor or dentist in charge that you are using this medicine. Taking trazodone together with medicines that are used during surgery or dental or emergency treatments may increase the CNS depressant effects.

This medicine will add to the effects of alcohol and other CNS depressants (medicines that slow down the nervous system, possibly causing drowsiness). Some examples of CNS depressants are antihistamines or medicine for hay fever, other allergies, or colds; sedatives, tranquilizers, or sleeping medicine; prescription pain medicine or narcotics; barbiturates; medicine for seizures; muscle relaxants; or anesthetics, including some dental anesthetics. *Check with your doctor before taking any of the above while you are using this medicine.*

This medicine may cause some people to become drowsy or less alert than they are normally. *Make sure you know how you react to this medicine before you drive, use machines, or do anything else that could be dangerous if you are not alert.*

Dizziness, lightheadedness, or fainting may occur, especially when you get up from a lying or sitting position. Getting up slowly may help. If this problem continues or gets worse, check with your doctor.

Trazodone may cause dryness of the mouth. For temporary relief, use sugarless gum or candy, melt bits of ice in your mouth, or use a saliva substitute. However, if your mouth continues to feel dry for more than 2 weeks, check with your medical doctor or dentist. Continuing dryness of the mouth may increase the chance of dental disease, including tooth decay, gum disease, and fungus infections.

Side Effects of This Medicine

Along with its needed effects, a medicine may cause some unwanted effects. Although not all of these side effects may occur, if they do occur they may need medical attention.

Stop taking this medicine and check with your doctor immediately if the following side effect occurs:

Rare

Painful, inappropriate erection of the penis, continuing

Also, check with your doctor as soon as possible if any of the following side effects occur:

Less common

Confusion; muscle tremors

Rare

Fainting; fast or slow heartbeat; skin rash; unusual excitement

Symptoms of overdose

Drowsiness; loss of muscle coordination; nausea and vomiting

Other side effects may occur that usually do not need medical attention. These side effects may go away during treatment as your body adjusts to the medicine. However, check with your doctor if any of the following side effects continue or are bothersome:

More common

Dizziness or lightheadedness; drowsiness; dryness of mouth (usually mild); headache; nausea and vomiting; unpleasant taste

Less common

Blurred vision; constipation; diarrhea; muscle aches or pains; unusual tiredness or weakness

Other side effects not listed above may also occur in some patients. If you notice any other effects, check with your doctor.

Revised: 01/13/93
Interim revision: 01/19/95

TRETINOIN Topical

Some commonly used brand names are:

In the U.S.—

Avita
Renova
Retin-A
Retin-A MICRO

In Canada—

Renova
Retin-A
Retisol-A
Stieva-A
Stieva-A Forte
Vitamin A Acid
Vitinoin

Other commonly used names are retinoic acid and vitamin A acid.

Description

Tretinoin (TRET-i-noyn) is used to treat acne. It works partly by keeping skin pores clear.

One of the tretinoin creams is used to treat fine wrinkles, dark spots, or rough skin on the face caused by damaging rays of the sun. It works by lightening the skin, replacing older skin with newer skin, and by slowing down the way the body removes skin cells that may have been harmed by the sun. Tretinoin works best when used within a skin care program that includes protecting the treated skin from the sun. However, it does not completely or permanently erase these skin problems or greatly improve more obvious changes in the skin, such as deep wrinkles caused by sun or the natural aging process.

Tretinoin may also be used to treat other skin diseases as determined by your doctor.

Tretinoin is available only with your doctor's prescription, in the following dosage forms:

Topical
- Cream (U.S. and Canada)
- Gel (U.S. and Canada)
- Topical solution (U.S. and Canada)

Before Using This Medicine

In deciding to use a medicine, the risks of using the medicine must be weighed against the good it will do. This is a decision you and your doctor will make. For tretinoin, the following should be considered:

Allergies—Tell your doctor if you have ever had any unusual or allergic reaction to acitretin, etretinate, isotretinoin, tretinoin, or vitamin A preparations. Also tell your health care professional if you are allergic to any other substances, such as preservatives or dyes.

Pregnancy—Tretinoin has not been studied in pregnant women. Topical tretinoin is not recommended during pregnancy. Topical tretinoin has been shown to cause delayed bone development in some animal fetuses. Before using this medicine, make sure your doctor knows if you are pregnant or if you may become pregnant.

Breast-feeding—It is not known whether tretinoin passes into the breast milk. Mothers who are using this medicine and who wish to breast-feed should discuss this with their doctors.

Children—Studies on this medicine have been done only in adult patients, and there is no specific information comparing use of this medicine in children with use in other age groups. Children are unlikely to have skin problems due to the sun. In older children treated for acne, tretinoin is not expected to cause different side effects or problems than it does in other age groups.

Older adults—Many medicines have not been studied specifically in older people. Therefore, it may not be known whether they work exactly the same way they do in younger adults or if they cause different side effects or problems in older people. There is no specific information comparing use of tretinoin in patients 50 years of age and older with use in other age groups.

Other medicines—Although certain medicines should not be used together at all, in other cases two different medicines may be used together even if an interaction might occur. In these cases, your doctor may want to change the dose, or other precautions may be necessary. Tell your health care professional if you are using any other topical prescription or nonprescription (over-the-counter [OTC]) medicine that is to be applied to the same area of the skin. When you are using topical tretinoin, it is especially important that your health care professional know if you are taking any of the following:

- Acitretin (e.g., Soriatane)
- Etretinate (e.g., Tegison)
- Tretinoin, oral (e.g., Vesanoid)—May increase chance of getting severe dryness or redness of skin

Other medical problems—The presence of other medical problems may affect the use of tretinoin. Make sure you tell your doctor if you have any other medical problems, especially:

- Dermatitis, seborrheic or
- Eczema or
- Sunburn—Use of this medicine may cause or increase the irritation associated with these problems

Proper Use of This Medicine

It is very important that you use this medicine only as directed. Do not use more of it, do not use it more often, and do not use it for a longer time than your doctor ordered. To do so may cause irritation of the skin.

Do not apply this medicine to windburned or sunburned skin or on open wounds.

Do not use this medicine in or around the eyes or lips, or inside of the nose. Spread the medicine away from these areas when applying. If the medicine accidentally gets on these areas, wash with water at once.

This medicine usually comes with patient directions. Read them carefully before using the medicine.

Before applying tretinoin, wash the skin with a mild soap or cleanser and warm water by using the tips of your fingers. Then gently pat dry. Do not scrub your face with a sponge or washcloth. *Wait 20 to 30 minutes before applying this medicine to make sure the skin is completely dry.* Applying tretinoin to wet skin can irritate the skin.

To use the *cream or gel form* of this medicine:
- Apply just enough medicine to very lightly cover the affected areas, and rub in gently but well. A pea-sized amount is enough to cover the whole face.

To use the *solution form* of this medicine:
- Using your fingertips, a gauze pad, or a cotton swab, apply enough tretinoin solution to cover the affected areas. If you use a gauze pad or a cotton swab for applying the medicine, avoid getting it too wet. This will help prevent the medicine from running into areas not intended for treatment.

After applying the medicine, wash your hands to remove any medicine that might remain on them.

Dosing—The dose of topical tretinoin will be different for different patients. *Follow your doctor's orders or the directions on the label.* The following information includes only the average dose of topical tretinoin. *If your dose is different, do not change it* unless your doctor tells you to do so.

- For *topical* dosage forms (cream, gel, or solution):
  —For acne:
  - Adults and teenagers—Apply to the affected area(s) of the skin once a day, at bedtime.
- For *cream* dosage form (brand name *Renova* only):
  —For fine wrinkles, dark spots, or rough skin caused by the sun:
  - Adults up to 50 years of age—Apply to the affected area(s) of the skin once a day, at bedtime.
  - Adults 50 years of age and older—Use and dose must be determined by your doctor.

Missed dose—If you miss a dose of this medicine, skip the missed dose and go back to your regular dosing schedule. Do not double doses.

Storage—To store this medicine:
- Keep out of the reach of children.
- Store away from heat and direct light. The gel product is flammable and should be kept away from fire or excessive heat.
- Keep the medicine from freezing.
- Do not keep outdated medicine or medicine no longer needed. Be sure that any discarded medicine is out of the reach of children.

Precautions While Using This Medicine

During the first 3 weeks you are using tretinoin, your skin may become irritated. Also, your acne may seem to get worse before it gets better. It may take longer than 12 weeks before you notice full improvement of your acne, even if you use the medicine every day. Check with your health care professional at any time skin irritation becomes severe or if your acne does not improve within 8 to 12 weeks.

Your should avoid washing the skin treated with tretinoin for at least 1 hour after applying it.

Avoid using any topical medicine on the same area within 1 hour before or after using tretinoin. Otherwise, tretinoin may not work properly or skin irritation might occur.

Unless your doctor tells you otherwise, it is especially important to avoid using the following skin products on the same area as tretinoin:
- Any other topical acne product or skin product containing a peeling agent (such as benzoyl peroxide, resorcinol, salicylic acid, or sulfur)
- Hair products that are irritating, such as permanents or hair removal products
- Skin products that cause sensitivity to the sun, such as those containing spices or limes
- Skin products containing a large amount of alcohol, such as astringents, shaving creams, or after-shave lotions
- Skin products that are too drying or abrasive, such as some cosmetics, soaps, or skin cleansers

Using these products along with tretinoin may cause mild to severe irritation of the skin. Although skin irritation can occur, some doctors sometimes allow benzoyl peroxide to be used with tretinoin to treat acne. Usually tretinoin is applied at night so that it does not cause a problem with any other topical products that you might use during the day. Check with your doctor before using topical medicines with tretinoin.

During the first 6 months of use, *avoid overexposing the treated areas to sunlight, wind, or cold weather.* The skin will be more prone to sunburn, dryness, or irritation, especially during the first 2 or 3 weeks. However, you should not stop using this medicine unless the skin irritation becomes too severe. *Do not use a sunlamp.*

To help tretinoin work properly, regularly use sunscreen or sublocking lotions with a sun protection factor (SPF) of at least 15. Also, wear protective clothing and hats, and apply creams, lotions, or moisturizers often.

Check with your doctor at any time your skin becomes too dry and irritated. Your health care professional can help you choose the right skin products for you to reduce skin dryness and irritation and may include the following:
- For patients using tretinoin for the treatment of acne:
  —Regular use of water-based creams or lotions helps to reduce skin irritation or dryness that may be caused by the use of tretinoin.
- For patients using tretinoin for the treatment of fine wrinkling, dark spots, and rough skin caused by the sun:
  —This medicine should be used as *part of an ongoing program to avoid further damage* to your skin from the sun. This program includes staying out of the sun when possible or wearing proper clothing or hats to protect your skin from sunlight.
  —Regular use of oil-based creams or lotions helps to reduce skin irritation or dryness caused by the use of tretinoin.

Side Effects of This Medicine

In some animal studies, tretinoin has been shown to cause skin tumors to develop faster when the treated area is exposed to ultraviolet light (sunlight or artificial sunlight from a sunlamp). Other studies have not shown the same result and more studies need to be done. It is not known if tretinoin causes skin tumors to develop faster in humans.

Along with its needed effects, a medicine may cause some unwanted effects. Although not all of these side effects may occur, if they do occur they may need medical attention.

Check with your doctor as soon as possible if any of the following side effects occur:

More common

Burning feeling or stinging skin (severe); lightening of skin of treated area, unexpected; peeling of skin (severe); redness of skin (severe); unusual dryness of skin (severe)

Rare

Darkening of treated skin

Other side effects may occur that usually do not need medical attention. These side effects may go away during treatment as your body adjusts to the medicine. However, check with your doctor if any of the following side effects continue or are bothersome:

More common

Burning feeling, stinging, or tingling of skin (mild)—lasting for a short time after first applying the medicine; chapping or slight peeling of skin (mild); redness of skin (mild); unusual dryness of skin (mild); unusually warm skin (mild)

The side effects will go away after you stop using tretinoin. On the rare chance that your skin color changes, this effect may last for several months before your skin color returns to normal.

Other side effects not listed above may also occur in some patients. If you notice any other effects, check with your doctor.

Additional Information

Once a medicine has been approved for marketing for a certain use, experience may show that it is also useful for other medical problems. Although this use is not included in product labeling, tretinoin is used in certain patients with the following medical conditions:

- Keratosis follicularis (skin disorder of small, red bumps)
- Verruca plana (flat warts)

Other than the above information, there is no additional information relating to its proper use, precautions, or side effects for these uses.

Revised: 08/20/97

TRIENTINE Systemic†

A commonly used brand name in the U.S. is Syprine.

Another commonly used name is trien.

†Not commercially available in Canada.

Description

Trientine (TRYE-en-teen) is used to treat Wilson's disease, a disease in which there is too much copper in the body.

This medicine combines with excess copper in the body and may prevent your body from absorbing the copper in the foods you eat. Removing copper from the body prevents damage to the liver, brain, and other organs. The combination of copper and trientine is then easily removed by the kidneys and it passes from the body in urine.

Trientine is available only with your doctor's prescription, in the following dosage form:

Oral

- Capsules (U.S.)

Before Using This Medicine

In deciding to use a medicine, the risks of taking the medicine must be weighed against the good it will do. This is a decision you and your doctor will make. For trientine, the following should be considered:

Pregnancy—Trientine has not been shown to cause birth defects or other problems in humans. However, it has been shown to cause birth defects in rats.

Breast-feeding—It is not known whether trientine passes into the breast milk. This medicine has not been reported to cause problems in nursing babies.

Children—Anemia is especially likely to occur in children during treatment with trientine.

Older adults—Many medicines have not been studied specifically in older people. Therefore, it may not be known whether they work exactly the same way they do in younger adults or if they cause different side effects or problems in older people. There is no specific information comparing use of trientine in the elderly with use in other age groups.

Other medicines—Although certain medicines should not be used together at all, in other cases two different medicines may be used together even if an interaction might occur. In these cases, your doctor may want to change the dose, or other precautions may be necessary. When you are taking trientine, it is especially important that your health care professional know if you are taking:

- Copper supplements or
- Iron supplements or other medicine containing minerals (contained in some vitamin combination products)—Use of these medicines with trientine may decrease the effects of trientine; iron supplements or other medicines containing minerals should be given 2 hours before or after trientine

Other medical problems—The presence of other medical problems may affect the use of trientine. Make sure you tell your doctor if you have any other medical problems, especially:

- Iron-deficiency—Trientine may make this condition worse

Proper Use of This Medicine

Take trientine with water. The capsule should be swallowed whole. It must not be opened, crushed, or chewed.

Take this medicine on an empty stomach (at least 1 hour before or 2 hours after meals) and at least 1 hour before or after any other medicine, food, or milk. This will allow trientine to be better absorbed by your body.

Trientine will not cure Wilson's disease, but it will help remove the excess copper from your body. Therefore, *you must continue to take this medicine regularly, as directed. You may have to take trientine for the rest of your life.* If Wilson's disease is not treated continually, it can cause severe liver damage and can cause death. *Do not stop taking this medicine without first checking with your doctor.*

It is very important for you to follow any special instructions from your doctor, such as following a low-copper diet. You may need to avoid foods known to be high in copper, such as chocolate, mushrooms, liver, molasses, broccoli, cereals enriched with copper, shellfish, organ meats, and nuts. If you have any questions about this, check with your doctor.

Take this medicine only as directed by your doctor. Do not take more or less of it and do not take it more often than your doctor ordered. If too much is used, it may increase the chance of side effects.

Dosing—The dose of trientine will be different for different patients. *Follow your doctor's orders or the directions on the label.*

- For *oral* dosage form (capsules):
  —For Wilson's disease:
    - Adults and teenagers—The usual dose is 750 milligrams (mg) to 1.25 grams a day. The dose may be divided into two to four smaller doses.
    - Children—The usual dose is 500 to 750 mg a day. The dose may be divided into two to four smaller doses.

Missed dose—If you miss a dose of this medicine, double the next dose. Do not make up more than one missed dose at a time.

Storage—To store this medicine:

- Keep out of the reach of children.
- Store sealed, unopened bottles of trientine in the refrigerator, but not in the freezer. Before opening a sealed bottle, let it stand at room temperature for about 6 hours. Keep it at room temperature after opening it.
- Do not store in the bathroom, near the kitchen sink, or in other damp places. Heat or moisture may cause the medicine to break down.
- Do not keep outdated medicine or medicine no longer needed. Be sure that any discarded medicine is out of the reach of children.

Precautions While Using This Medicine

Your doctor should check your progress at regular visits to make sure trientine is working properly and to check for unwanted effects. Laboratory tests may be needed. This will allow your doctor to change your dose, if necessary.

During the first month of treatment, you may need to take your temperature each night. *Tell your doctor if you develop a fever or skin rash.*

Do not take copper or iron preparations or any other mineral supplements within 2 hours of taking trientine. This includes any vitamin preparation that contains minerals.

If a capsule breaks open and the contents touch your skin, wash the area right away with water. Trientine may cause a rash.

Side Effects of This Medicine

Along with its needed effects, a medicine may cause some unwanted effects. Although not all of these side effects may occur, if they do occur they may need medical attention.

Check with your doctor as soon as possible if any of the following side effects occur:

More common—Symptoms of anemia
Unusually pale skin; unusual tiredness

Note: The above signs of anemia are more likely to occur in children, menstruating women, and pregnant women, who usually need more iron than other patients. If these signs appear during trientine treatment, your doctor will need to do some tests.

Rare
Fever; general feeling of discomfort, illness, or weakness; joint pain; skin rash, blisters, hives, or itching; swollen glands

Other side effects not listed above may also occur in some patients. If you notice any other effects, check with your doctor.

Revised: 09/17/92
Interim revision: 04/29/94

TRIFLURIDINE Ophthalmic

A commonly used brand name in the U.S. and Canada is Viroptic. Another commonly used name is trifluorothymidine.

Description

Trifluridine (trye-FLURE-i-deen) ophthalmic preparations are used to treat virus infections of the eye.

Trifluridine is available only with your doctor's prescription, in the following dosage form:

Ophthalmic
- Ophthalmic solution (eye drops) (U.S. and Canada)

Before Using This Medicine

In deciding to use a medicine, the risks of using the medicine must be weighed against the good it will do. This is a decision you and your doctor will make. For trifluridine, the following should be considered:

Allergies—Tell your doctor if you have ever had any unusual or allergic reaction to trifluridine. Also tell your health care professional if you are allergic to any other substances, such as preservatives.

Pregnancy—Studies have not been done in humans. When injected into developing chick embryos, trifluridine has been shown to cause birth defects. However, studies in rats and rabbits have not shown that trifluridine causes birth defects, although it did cause delayed bone formation in rats and rabbits and death in unborn rabbits.

Breast-feeding—It is unlikely that trifluridine, used in the eyes, is absorbed into the mother's body and passes into the breast milk. In addition, trifluridine has not been reported to cause problems in nursing babies.

Children—Although there is no specific information comparing the use of trifluridine in children with use in other age groups, it is not expected to cause different side effects or problems in children than it does in adults.

Older adults—Many medicines have not been studied specifically in older people. Therefore, it may not be

known whether they work exactly the same way they do in younger adults or if they cause different side effects or problems in older people. There is no specific information comparing the use of trifluridine in the elderly with use in other age groups.

Other medicines—Although certain medicines should not be used together at all, in other cases two different medicines may be used together even if an interaction might occur. In these cases, your doctor may want to change the dose, or other precautions may be necessary. Tell your health care professional if you are using any other prescription or nonprescription (over-the-counter [OTC]) medicine that is to be used in the eye.

Proper Use of This Medicine

The bottle is only partially full to provide proper drop control.

To use:

- First, wash your hands. Then tilt the head back and pull the lower eyelid away from the eye to form a pouch. Drop the medicine into the pouch and gently close the eyes. Do not blink. Keep the eyes closed for 1 or 2 minutes to allow the medicine to come into contact with the infection.
- If you think you did not get the drop of medicine into your eye properly, use another drop.
- To keep the medicine as germ-free as possible, do not touch the applicator tip to any surface (including the eye). Also, keep the container tightly closed.

Do not use this medicine more often or for a longer time than your doctor ordered. To do so may cause problems in the eyes. If you have any questions about this, check with your doctor.

To help clear up your infection completely, *keep using this medicine for the full time of treatment,* even if your symptoms have disappeared. *Do not miss any doses.*

Dosing—The dose of ophthalmic trifluridine will be different for different patients. *Follow your doctor's orders or the directions on the label.* The following information includes only the average doses of ophthalmic trifluridine. *If your dose is different, do not change it unless your doctor tells you to do so.*

The number of doses you use each day, the time allowed between doses, and the length of time you use the medicine depend on the medical problem for which you are using ophthalmic trifluridine.

- For *ophthalmic solution* dosage forms:
  - —For virus eye infection:
    - Adults and children—One drop every two hours while you are awake. After healing has occurred, the dose may be reduced for seven more days to one drop every four hours (at least 5 doses a day) while you are awake.

Missed dose—If you miss a dose of this medicine, apply it as soon as possible. However, if it is almost time for your next dose, skip the missed dose and go back to your regular dosing schedule.

Storage—To store this medicine:

- Keep out of the reach of children.
- Store in the refrigerator because heat will cause this medicine to break down. However, keep the medicine from freezing. Follow the directions on the label.
- Do not keep outdated medicine or medicine no longer needed. Be sure that any discarded medicine is out of the reach of children.

Precautions While Using This Medicine

It is very important that you keep your appointment with your doctor. If your symptoms become worse, check with your doctor sooner.

Side Effects of This Medicine

Along with its needed effects, a medicine may cause some unwanted effects. Although not all of these side effects may occur, if they do occur they may need medical attention.

Check with your doctor as soon as possible if any of the following side effects occur:

Rare

Blurred vision or other change in vision; dryness of eye; irritation of eye; itching, redness, swelling, or other sign of irritation not present before use of this medicine

Other side effects may occur that usually do not need medical attention. These side effects may go away during treatment as your body adjusts to the medicine. However, check with your doctor if either of the following side effects continues or is bothersome:

More common

Burning or stinging

Other side effects not listed above may also occur in some patients. If you notice any other effects, check with your doctor.

Revised: 07/01/93

TRILOSTANE Systemic†

A commonly used brand name in the U.S. is Modrastane.

†Not commercially available in Canada.

Description

Trilostane (TRYE-loe-stane) is used in the treatment of Cushing's syndrome. It is normally used in short-term treatment until permanent therapy is possible.

In Cushing's syndrome, the adrenal gland overproduces steroids. Although steroids are important for various functions of the body, too much can cause problems. Trilostane reduces the amount of steroids produced by the adrenal gland.

Trilostane is available only with your doctor's prescription, in the following dosage form:

Oral

- Capsules (U.S.)

Before Using This Medicine

In deciding to use a medicine, the risks of taking the medicine must be weighed against the good it will do. This is a decision you and your doctor will make. For trilostane, the following should be considered:

Allergies—Tell your doctor if you have ever had any unusual or allergic reaction to trilostane. Also tell your health care professional if you are allergic to any other substance, such as foods, preservatives, or dyes.

Pregnancy—Use of trilostane is not recommended during pregnancy. It has been shown to cause serious problems, including miscarriage, in humans. Trilostane has also been shown to cause birth defects in animals.

Breast-feeding—It is not known whether trilostane passes into breast milk. However, this medicine has not been reported to cause problems in nursing babies.

Children—There is no specific information about the use of trilostane in children.

Older adults—Many medicines have not been tested in older people. Therefore, it may not be known whether they work exactly the same way they do in younger adults or if they cause different side effects or problems in older people. There is no specific information about the use of trilostane in the elderly.

Other medicines—Although certain medicines should not be used together at all, in other cases two different medicines may be used together even if an interaction might occur. In these cases, your doctor may want to change the dose, or other precautions may be necessary. When you are taking trilostane, it is especially important that your health care professional know if you are taking any other prescription or nonprescription (over-the-counter [OTC]) medicine.

Other medical problems—The presence of other medical problems may affect the use of trilostane. Make sure you tell your doctor if you have any other medical problems, especially:

- Infection or
- Injury (recent serious)—Trilostane may weaken the body's normal defenses
- Kidney disease
- Liver disease

Proper Use of This Medicine

Take trilostane only as directed by your doctor. Do not take more or less of it, and do not take it more often than your doctor ordered.

Dosing—The dose of trilostane will be different for different patients. *Follow your doctor's orders or the directions on the label.* The following information includes only the average doses of trilostane. *If your dose is different, do not change it* unless your doctor tells you to do so.

- For *oral* dosage form (capsules):
  - —For Cushing's syndrome:
    - Adults—To start, 30 milligrams (mg) four times a day. Your doctor may increase the dose every three to four days as needed. However, the dose is usually not more than 90 mg four times a day.
    - Children—Dose must be determined by your doctor.

Missed dose—If you miss a dose of this medicine, take it as soon as possible. However, if it is almost time for your next dose, skip the missed dose and go back to your regular dosing schedule. Do not double doses.

Storage—To store this medicine:

- Keep out of the reach of children.
- Store away from heat and direct light.
- Do not store in the bathroom, near the kitchen sink, or in other damp places. Heat or moisture may cause the medicine to break down.
- Do not keep outdated medicine or medicine no longer needed. Be sure that any discarded medicine is out of the reach of children.

Precautions While Using This Medicine

It is very important that your doctor check your progress at regular visits to make sure that trilostane is working properly and does not cause unwanted effects.

Check with your doctor right away if you get an injury, infection, or illness of any kind. This medicine may weaken your body's normal defenses.

Before having any kind of surgery (including dental surgery) or emergency treatment, tell the medical doctor or dentist in charge that you are taking trilostane.

Your doctor may want you to carry a medical identification card or wear a bracelet stating that you are taking this medicine.

Side Effects of This Medicine

Along with its needed effects, a medicine may cause some unwanted effects. Although not all of these side effects may occur, if they do occur they may need medical attention.

Check with your doctor as soon as possible if any of the following side effects occur:

Rare

Darkening of skin; drowsiness or tiredness; loss of appetite; mental depression; skin rash; vomiting

Other side effects may occur that usually do not need medical attention. These side effects may go away during treatment as your body adjusts to the medicine. However, check with your health care professional if any of the following side effects continue or are bothersome:

More common

Diarrhea; stomach pain or cramps

Less common

Aching muscles; belching or bloating; burning mouth or nose; dizziness or lightheadedness; fever; flushing; headache; increase in salivation; nausea; watery eyes

Other side effects not listed above may also occur in some patients. If you notice any other effects, check with your doctor.

Revised: 09/90
Interim revision: 07/05/94

TRIMETHOBENZAMIDE Systemic†

Some commonly used brand names are:

In the U.S.—

Arrestin	T-Gen
Benzacot	Ticon
Bio-Gan	Tigan
Stemetic	Tiject-20
Tebamide	Triban
Tegamide	Tribenzagan

Generic name product may also be available.

†Not commercially available in Canada.

Description

Trimethobenzamide (trye-meth-oh-BEN-za-mide) is used to treat nausea and vomiting.

This medicine is available only with your doctor's prescription in the following dosage forms:

Oral
- Capsules (U.S.)

Parenteral
- Injection (U.S.)

Rectal
- Suppositories (U.S.)

Before Using This Medicine

In deciding to use a medicine, the risks of taking the medicine must be weighed against the good it will do. This is a decision you and your doctor will make. For trimethobenzamide, the following should be considered:

Allergies—Tell your doctor if you have ever had any unusual or allergic reaction to trimethobenzamide, or if you are allergic or sensitive to benzocaine or other local anesthetics (the suppository form of this medicine contains benzocaine). Also tell your health care professional if you are allergic to any other substances, such as foods, preservatives, or dyes.

Pregnancy—Studies have not been done in pregnant women. However, although studies in animals have not shown that trimethobenzamide causes birth defects, it has been shown to increase the chance of a miscarriage.

Breast-feeding—It is not known whether trimethobenzamide passes into breast milk. Although most medicines pass into breast milk in small amounts, many of them may be used safely while breast-feeding. Mothers who are taking this medicine and who wish to breast-feed should discuss this with their doctor.

Children—This medicine should not be used to treat nausea and vomiting in children unless otherwise directed by your doctor. Some side effects may be more serious in children.

Older adults—Many medicines have not been studied specifically in older people. Therefore, it may not be known whether they work exactly the same way they do in younger adults or if they cause different side effects or problems in older people. There is no specific information comparing use of trimethobenzamide in the elderly with use in other age groups.

Other medicines—Although certain medicines should not be used together at all, in other cases 2 different medicines may be used together even if an interaction might occur. In these cases, your doctor may want to change the dose, or other precautions may be necessary. When you are using trimethobenzamide, it is especially important that your health care professional know if you are taking any of the following:

- Central nervous system (CNS) depressants (medicine that causes drowsiness) or
- Tricyclic antidepressants (medicine for depression)—Taking these medicines with trimethobenzamide may cause increased CNS depressant or other serious effects

Other medical problems—The presence of other medical problems may affect the use of trimethobenzamide. Make sure you tell your doctor if you have any other medical problems, especially:

- High fever or
- Intestinal infection—Using trimethobenzamide may result in serious side effects

Proper Use of This Medicine

Do not use this medicine to treat nausea and vomiting in children unless otherwise directed by your doctor. If you are giving this medicine to a child, be especially careful not to give more than is prescribed since side effects may be more serious in children.

Trimethobenzamide is used only to relieve or prevent nausea and vomiting. Use it only as directed. Do not use more of it and do not use it more often than your doctor ordered. To do so may increase the chance of side effects.

To insert the *rectal suppository form* of this medicine:

- First, remove foil wrapper and moisten the suppository with cold water. Lie down on your side and use your finger to push the suppository well up into the rectum. If the suppository is too soft to insert, chill it in the refrigerator for 30 minutes or run cold water over it before removing the foil wrapper.
- Wash your hands with soap and water.

Dosing—The dose of trimethobenzamide will be different for different patients. *Follow your doctor's orders or the directions on the label.* The following information includes only the average doses of trimethobenzamide. *If your dose is different, do not change it* unless your doctor tells you to do so.

The number of capsules that you take, or suppositories that you use, depends on the strength of the medicine. Also, *the number of doses you take each day, the time allowed between doses, and the length of time you take the medicine depend on the medical problem for which you are taking trimethobenzamide.*

- For *oral* dosage form (capsules):
  - —For nausea and vomiting:
    - Adults and children 12 years of age and older—250 milligrams (mg) three or four times a day as needed.
    - Children—Dose is based on body weight and must be determined by your doctor. The usual dose is 15 mg per kilogram (6.8 mg per pound). The dose is usually not more than 200 mg three or four times a day as needed.
- For *rectal* dosage form (suppositories):
  - —For nausea and vomiting:
    - Adults and children 12 years of age and older—200 mg three or four times a day as needed.
    - Children—Dose is based on body weight and must be determined by your doctor. The usual dose is 15 mg per kilogram (6.8 mg per pound). The dose is usually not more than 200 mg three or four times a day as needed.
- For *injection* dosage form:
  - —For nausea and vomiting:
    - Adults and children 12 years of age and older—200 mg three or four times a day as needed, injected into a muscle.
    - Children—Dose must be determined by your doctor.

Missed dose—If you must use this medicine regularly and you miss a dose, use it as soon as possible. However, if it is almost time for your next dose, skip the missed dose and go back to your regular dosing schedule. Do not double doses.

Storage—To store this medicine:

- Keep out of the reach of children.
- Store away from heat and direct light.
- Do not store the capsule form of this medicine in the bathroom, near the kitchen sink, or in other damp places. Heat or moisture may cause the medicine to break down.
- Do not keep outdated medicine or medicine no longer needed. Be sure that any discarded medicine is out of the reach of children.

Precautions While Using This Medicine

Trimethobenzamide will add to the effects of alcohol and other CNS depressants (medicines that slow down the nervous system, possibly causing drowsiness). Some examples of CNS depressants are antihistamines or medicine for hay fever, other allergies, or colds; sedatives, tranquilizers, or sleeping medicine; prescription pain medicine or narcotics; barbiturates; medicine for seizures; muscle relaxants; or anesthetics, including some dental anesthetics. *Check with your doctor before taking any of the above while you are using this medicine.*

This medicine may cause some people to become dizzy, lightheaded, drowsy, or less alert than they are normally. *Make sure you know how you react to this medicine before you drive, use machines, or do anything else that could be dangerous if you are dizzy or are not alert.*

When using trimethobenzamide on a regular basis, make sure your doctor knows if you are taking large amounts of aspirin or other salicylates at the same time (as for arthritis or rheumatism). Effects of too much aspirin, such as ringing in the ears, may be covered up by this medicine.

Side Effects of This Medicine

Along with its needed effects, a medicine may cause some unwanted effects. Although not all of these side effects may occur, if they do occur they may need medical attention.

Check with your doctor as soon as possible if any of the following side effects occur:

Rare

Body spasm, with head and heels bent backward and body bowed forward; convulsions (seizures); mental depression; shakiness or tremors; skin rash; sore throat and fever; unusual tiredness; vomiting (severe or continuing); yellow eyes or skin

Other side effects may occur that usually do not need medical attention. These side effects may go away during treatment as your body adjusts to the medicine. However,

check with your doctor if any of the following side effects continue or are bothersome:

More common

Drowsiness

Less common

Blurred vision; diarrhea; dizziness; headache; muscle cramps

Other side effects not listed above may also occur in some patients. If you notice any other effects, check with your doctor.

Revised: 05/12/93

TRIMETHOPRIM Systemic

Some commonly used brand names are:

In the U.S.—

Proloprim Trimpex

Generic name product may also be available.

In Canada

Proloprim

Description

Trimethoprim (trye-METH-oh-prim) is used to treat infections of the urinary tract. It may also be used for other problems as determined by your doctor. It will not work for colds, flu, or other virus infections.

Trimethoprim is available only with your doctor's prescription, in the following dosage form:

Oral

- Tablets (U.S. and Canada)

Before Using This Medicine

In deciding to use a medicine, the risks of taking the medicine must be weighed against the good it will do. This is a decision you and your doctor will make. For trimethoprim, the following should be considered:

Allergies—Tell your doctor if you have ever had any unusual or allergic reaction to trimethoprim. Also tell your health care professional if you are allergic to any other substances, such as foods, preservatives, or dyes.

Pregnancy—Studies have not been done in humans. Studies in rats have shown that trimethoprim causes birth defects. Studies in rabbits have shown that trimethoprim causes a decrease in the number of successful pregnancies. However, in the few reports where trimethoprim was taken by pregnant women, trimethoprim has not been reported to cause birth defects or other problems in humans.

Breast-feeding—Trimethoprim passes into the breast milk. However, this medicine has not been reported to cause serious problems in nursing babies.

Children—This medicine has been used in a limited number of children 2 months of age or older, and tested in children 12 years of age or older. In effective doses, the medicine has not been shown to cause different side effects or problems in children than it does in adults.

Older adults—Elderly people may be more sensitive to the effects of trimethoprim. Blood problems may be more likely to occur in elderly patients who are taking diuretics (water pills) along with this medicine.

Other medicines—Although certain medicines should not be used together at all, in other cases two different medicines may be used together even if an interaction might occur. In these cases, your doctor may want to change the dose, or other precautions may be necessary. When you are taking trimethoprim, it is especially important that your health care professional know if you are taking any of the following:

- Anticonvulsants (seizure medicine) or
- Methotrexate (e.g., Mexate) or
- Pyrimethamine (e.g., Daraprim) or
- Triamterene (e.g., Dyrenium)—Use of these medicines with trimethoprim may increase the chance of side effects affecting the blood

Other medical problems—The presence of other medical problems may affect the use of trimethoprim. Make sure you tell your doctor if you have any other medical problems, especially:

- Anemia—Patients with anemia may have an increased chance of side effects affecting the blood
- Kidney disease—Patients with kidney disease may have an increased chance of side effects

Proper Use of This Medicine

Do not give this medicine to infants or children under 12 years of age unless otherwise directed by your doctor.

Trimethoprim may be taken on an empty stomach or, if it upsets your stomach, it may be taken with food.

To help clear up your infection completely, *keep taking this medicine for the full time of treatment* even if you begin to feel better after a few days. If you stop taking this medicine too soon, your symptoms may return.

This medicine works best when there is a constant amount in the body. *To help keep the amount constant, do not miss any doses. Also, it is best to take the doses at evenly spaced times day and night.* For example, if you are to take 2 doses a day, the doses should be spaced about 12 hours apart. If this interferes with your sleep or other daily activities, or if you need help in planning the best times to take your medicine, check with your health care professional.

Dosing—The dose of trimethoprim will be different for different patients. *Follow your doctor's orders or the directions on the label.* The following information includes only the average doses of trimethoprim. Your dose may be different if you have kidney disease. *If your dose is different, do not change it* unless your doctor tells you to do so.

The number of tablets that you take depends on the strength of the medicine. Also, *the number of doses you take each day, the time allowed between doses, and the length of time you take the medicine depend on the medical problem for which you are taking trimethoprim.*

- For the *treatment of urinary tract infections:*
  —Adults and children 12 years of age and older: 100 milligrams every twelve hours for ten days, or 200 milligrams once a day for ten days.
  —Children up to 12 years of age: Dose must be determined by the doctor.

Missed dose—If you do miss a dose of this medicine, take it as soon as possible. This will help to keep a constant amount of medicine in the body. However, if it is almost time for your next dose, skip the missed dose and go back to your regular dosing schedule. Do not double doses.

Storage—To store this medicine:

- Keep out of the reach of children.
- Store away from heat and direct light.
- Do not store in the bathroom, near the kitchen sink, or in other damp places. Heat or moisture may cause the medicine to break down.
- Do not keep outdated medicine or medicine no longer needed. Be sure that any discarded medicine is out of the reach of children.

Precautions While Using This Medicine

It is important that your doctor check your progress at regular visits if you will be taking this medicine for a long time. This will allow your doctor to check for any unwanted effects that may be caused by this medicine.

If your symptoms do not improve within a few days, or if they become worse, check with your doctor.

If this medicine causes anemia, your doctor may want you to take folic acid (a vitamin) every day to help clear up the anemia. If so, it is important to take folic acid every day along with this medicine; do not miss any doses.

Trimethoprim may cause blood problems. These problems may result in a greater chance of certain infections, slow healing, and bleeding of the gums. Therefore, you should be careful when using regular toothbrushes, dental floss, and toothpicks. Dental work should be delayed until your blood counts have returned to normal. Check with your medical doctor or dentist if you have any questions about proper oral hygiene (mouth care) during treatment.

Side Effects of This Medicine

Along with its needed effects, a medicine may cause some unwanted effects. Although not all of these side effects may occur, if they do occur they may need medical attention.

Check with your doctor immediately if any of the following side effects occur:

Rare

Bluish fingernails, lips, or skin; difficult breathing; headache; general feeling of discomfort or illness; nausea; neck stiffness; pale skin; skin rash or itching; sore throat and fever; unusual bleeding or bruising; unusual tiredness or weakness; signs of Stevens-Johnson syndrome, such as aching joints and muscles; redness, blistering, peeling, or loosening of skin; unusual tiredness or weakness

Other side effects may occur that usually do not need medical attention. These side effects may go away during treatment as your body adjusts to the medicine. However, check with your doctor if any of the following side effects continue or are bothersome:

Less common

Diarrhea; headache; loss of appetite; nausea or vomiting; stomach cramps or pain

Other side effects not listed above may also occur in some patients. If you notice any other effects, check with your doctor.

Additional Information

Once a medicine has been approved for marketing for a certain use, experience may show that it is also useful for other medical problems. Although these uses are not included in product labeling, trimethoprim is used in certain patients for the following medical conditions:

- Prevention of urinary tract infections
- Treatment of *Pneumocystis carinii* pneumonia (PCP)

For patients taking this medicine for *prevention of urinary tract infections*:

- Your doctor may have prescribed this medicine to *prevent* infections of the urinary tract. It is usually given once a day and may be given for a long time for this purpose. If you have any questions about this, check with your doctor.

Other than the above information, there is no additional information relating to proper use, precautions, or side effects for these uses.

Revised: 02/23/93

TRIMETREXATE Systemic

A commonly used brand name in the U.S. and Canada is NeuTrexin.

Description

Trimetrexate (tre-me-TREX-ate) is used, together with leucovorin (loo-koe-VOR-in), to treat *Pneumocystis* (noo-moe-SISS-tis) *carinii* pneumonia (PCP), a very serious kind of pneumonia. This kind of pneumonia occurs commonly in patients whose immune system is not working normally, such as cancer patients, transplant patients, and patients with acquired immune deficiency syndrome (AIDS).

Trimetrexate may cause some serious, even life-threatening, side effects. To prevent these effects, *you must take another medicine, leucovorin, together with trimetrexate*, and for three days after you stop receiving trimetrexate. Before you begin treatment with trimetrexate, you and your doctor should talk about the good this medicine will do as well as the risks of using it.

Trimetrexate is to be administered only by or under the immediate supervision of your doctor. It is available in the following dosage form:

Parenteral

- Injection (U.S. and Canada)

Before Receiving This Medicine

In deciding to use a medicine, the risks of using the medicine must be weighed against the good it will do. This is a decision you and your doctor will make. For trimetrexate, the following should be considered:

Allergies—Tell your doctor if you have ever had any unusual or allergic reaction to trimetrexate, methotrexate, or leucovorin. Also tell your health care professional if you are allergic to any other substances, such as foods, preservatives, or dyes.

Pregnancy—Use of trimetrexate during pregnancy should be avoided whenever possible since trimetrexate has caused birth defects and death of the fetus in animal studies. The use of birth control is recommended during trimetrexate therapy. Tell your doctor immediately if you think you may be pregnant or if you need advice about birth control.

Breast-feeding—It is not known if trimetrexate passes into breast milk. However, breast-feeding should be stopped during treatment with this medicine because trimetrexate may cause serious unwanted effects in nursing babies.

Children—This medicine has been tested in a limited number of children younger than 18 years of age. Trimetrexate can cause serious side effects in any patient. However, in effective doses, the medicine did not cause different side effects or problems in the few children who received it than it does in adults.

Older adults—Many medicines have not been studied specifically in older people. Therefore, it may not be known whether they work exactly the same way they do in younger adults or if they cause different side effects or problems in older people. There is no specific information comparing use of trimetrexate in the elderly with use in other age groups.

Other medicines—Although certain medicines should not be used together at all, in other cases two different medicines may be used together even if an interaction might occur. In these cases, your doctor may want to change the dose, or other precautions may be necessary. When you are taking trimetrexate, it is especially important that your health care professional know if you are taking any of the following:

- Acetaminophen (e.g., Tylenol) (with long-term, high-dose use) or
- Amiodarone (e.g., Cordarone) or
- Anabolic steroids (nandrolone [e.g., Anabolin], oxandrolone [e.g., Anavar], oxymetholone [e.g., Anadrol], stanozolol [e.g., Winstrol]) or
- Androgens (male hormones) or
- Carbamazepine (e.g., Tegretol) or
- Chloroquine (e.g., Aralen) or
- Dantrolene (e.g., Dantrium) or
- Daunorubicin (e.g., Cerubidine) or
- Estrogens (female hormones) or
- Etretinate (e.g., Tegison) or
- Hydroxychloroquine (e.g., Plaquenil) or
- Methyldopa (e.g., Aldomet) or
- Naltrexone (e.g., Trexan) (with long-term, high-dose use) or
- Phenothiazines (acetophenazine [e.g., Tindal], chlorpromazine [e.g., Thorazine], fluphenazine [e.g., Prolixin], mesoridazine [e.g., Serentil], perphenazine [e.g., Trilafon], prochlorperazine [e.g., Compazine], promazine [e.g., Sparine], promethazine [e.g., Phenergan], thioridazine [e.g., Mellaril], trifluoperazine [e.g., Stelazine], triflupromazine [e.g., Vesprin], trimeprazine [e.g., Temaril]) or
- Phenytoin (e.g., Dilantin)—Use of these medicines while you are taking trimetrexate may decrease the breakdown of trimetrexate in the liver and increase the chance of trimetrexate side effects

- Alcohol or
- Cimetidine (e.g., Tagamet) or
- Diltiazem (e.g., Cardizem) or
- Erythromycins (medicine for infection) or
- Isoniazid (e.g., INH, Nydrazid) or
- Quinine (e.g., Quinamm) or
- Ranitidine (e.g., Zantac) or
- Verapamil (e.g., Calan)—Use of these medicines with trimetrexate may increase the chance of trimetrexate side effects

- Amphotericin B by injection (e.g., Fungizone) or
- Antineoplastics (cancer medicine) or
- Azathioprine (e.g., Imuran) or
- Colchicine or
- Cyclophosphamide (e.g., Cytoxan) or
- Flucytosine (e.g., Ancobon) or
- Ganciclovir (e.g., Cytovene) or
- Interferon (e.g., Intron A, Roferon-A) or
- Zidovudine (e.g., AZT, Retrovir)—Receiving trimetrexate while you are using these medicines may make side effects affecting the blood worse

- Cisplatin (e.g., Platinol) or
- Combination pain medicine containing acetaminophen and aspirin (e.g., Excedrin) or other salicylates (with large amounts taken regularly) or
- Cyclosporine (e.g., Sandimmune) or
- Deferoxamine (e.g., Desferal) (with long-term use) or
- Foscarnet (e.g., Foscavir) or
- Inflammation or pain medicine (except narcotics) or
- Lithium (e.g., Lithane) or
- Penicillamine (e.g., Cuprimine) or
- Streptozocin (e.g., Zanosar) or
- Tiopronin (e.g., Thiola)—Use of these medicines while you are taking trimetrexate may decrease the elimination of trimetrexate through the kidneys and increase the chance of trimetrexate toxicity

- Antithyroid agents (medicine for overactive thyroid) or
- Carmustine (e.g., BiCNU) or
- Chloramphenicol (e.g., Chloromycetin) or
- Disulfiram (e.g., Antabuse) or
- Divalproex (e.g., Depakote) or
- Gold salts (medicine for arthritis) or
- Mercaptopurine (e.g., Purinethol) or
- Methotrexate (e.g., Mexate) or
- Oral contraceptives (birth control pills) containing estrogen or
- Other anti-infectives by mouth or by injection (medicine for infection) or
- Plicamycin (e.g., Mithracin) or
- Valproic acid (e.g., Depakene)—Use of these medicines with trimetrexate may increase the chance of side effects from trimetrexate

Other medical problems—The presence of other medical problems may affect the use of trimetrexate. Make sure you tell your doctor if you have any other medical problems, especially:

- Anemia or
- Low platelet count or
- Low white blood cell count—Trimetrexate may make any blood diseases that you have worse
- Kidney disease or
- Liver disease—Kidney or liver disease may increase the chance of side effects from trimetrexate

Proper Use of This Medicine

When you take *leucovorin:*

- *Leucovorin must be taken with trimetrexate* to help prevent very serious, possibly life-threatening, unwanted effects. Leucovorin should be taken during trimetrexate treatment and for 3 days after trimetrexate is stopped.
- *Take oral leucovorin exactly as directed by your doctor.* Do not take more of it, do not take it more often, and do not take it for a longer time than your doctor ordered. Also, do not stop taking this medicine without checking with your doctor first.
- Oral leucovorin works best when there is a constant amount in the blood. *To help keep the amount constant, do not miss any doses.* If you need help in planning the best times to take your medicine, check with your health care professional.
- If you vomit shortly after taking an oral dose of leucovorin, check with your doctor. You will be told whether to take the dose again or to wait until the next scheduled dose.

Dosing—The doses of trimetrexate and of leucovorin will be different for different patients. *Follow your doctor's orders or the directions on the label.* The following information includes only the average doses of trimetrexate and leucovorin. *If your doses are different, do not change them* unless your doctor tells you to do so.

For trimetrexate

- For the treatment of *Pneumocystis carinii* pneumonia:
  —For *injection* dosage form:
    - Adults—45 milligrams per square meter of body surface area (mg/m^2) injected into a vein once a day for twenty-one days. Your doctor will check your blood counts and may change your dose based on these counts.
    - Children and teenagers—Use and dose must be determined by your doctor.

For leucovorin

- For the prevention of serious side effects of trimetrexate in the treatment of *Pneumocystis carinii* pneumonia:
  —For the *oral or injection* dosage forms:
    - Adults—20 milligrams per square meter of body surface area (mg/m^2) taken by mouth or injected into a vein every six hours for twenty-four days. Your doctor will check your blood counts and may change your dose based on these counts.
    - Children and teenagers—Use and dose must be determined by your doctor.

Missed dose—If you miss a dose of leucovorin, take it as soon as possible. This will help to keep a constant amount of medicine in the blood. However, if it is almost time for your next dose, skip the missed dose and go back to your regular dosing schedule. Do not double doses.

Storage—To store leucovorin:

- Keep out of the reach of children.
- Store away from heat and direct light.
- Do not store in the bathroom, near the kitchen sink, or in other damp places. Heat or moisture may cause the medicine to break down.
- Do not keep outdated medicine or medicine no longer needed. Be sure that any discarded medicine is out of the reach of children.

Precautions While Receiving This Medicine

If your symptoms do not improve within a few days, or if they become worse, check with your doctor.

It is very important that your doctor check your progress at regular visits to make sure that this medicine is working properly and to check for unwanted effects.

Trimetrexate can lower the number of white blood cells in your blood temporarily, increasing your chance of getting an infection. It can also lower the number of platelets, which are necessary for proper blood clotting. If this occurs, there are certain precautions you can take, especially when your blood count is low, to reduce the risk of infection or bleeding:

- If you can, avoid people with infections. *Check with your doctor immediately* if you think you are getting an infection or if you get a fever or chills, cough or hoarseness, lower back or side pain, or painful or difficult urination.
- *Check with your doctor immediately* if you notice any unusual bleeding or bruising; black, tarry stools; blood in urine or stools; or pinpoint red spots on your skin.
- Be careful when using a regular toothbrush, dental floss, or toothpick. Your medical doctor, dentist, or nurse may recommend other ways to clean your teeth and gums. Check with your medical doctor before having any dental work done.

• Be careful not to cut yourself when you are using sharp objects such as a safety razor or fingernail or toenail cutters.

Side Effects of This Medicine

Along with its needed effects, a medicine may cause some unwanted effects. Although not all of these side effects may occur, if they do occur they may need medical attention.

Check with your doctor immediately if any of the following side effects occur:

More common

Fever and sore throat

Less common

Black, tarry stools; blood in urine or stools; fever; mouth sores or ulcers; pinpoint red spots on skin; skin rash and itching; unusual bleeding or bruising; unusual tiredness or weakness

Other side effects may occur that usually do not need medical attention. These side effects may go away during treatment as your body adjusts to the medicine. However, check with your doctor if any of the following side effects continue or are bothersome:

Less common

Confusion; nausea and vomiting; stomach pain

Other side effects not listed above may also occur in some patients. If you notice any other effects, check with your doctor.

Developed: 04/15/94
Revised: 07/14/95
Interim revision: 06/20/96

TRIOXSALEN Systemic

A commonly used brand name in the U.S. and Canada is Trisoralen. Another commonly used name is trioxysalen.

Description

Trioxsalen (trye-OX-sa-len) belongs to the group of medicines called psoralens. It is used along with ultraviolet light (found in sunlight and some special lamps) in a treatment called psoralen plus ultraviolet light A (PUVA) to treat vitiligo, a disease in which skin color is lost. Trioxsalen may also be used for other conditions as determined by your doctor.

Trioxsalen is available only with your doctor's prescription, in the following dosage form:

Oral

• Tablets (U.S. and Canada)

Before Using This Medicine

Trioxsalen is a very strong medicine that increases the skin's sensitivity to sunlight. In addition to causing serious sunburns if not properly used, it has been reported to increase the chance of skin cancer and cataracts. Also, like too much sunlight, PUVA can cause premature aging of the skin. Therefore, trioxsalen should be used only as directed and it should *not* be used simply for suntanning. Before using this medicine, be sure that you have discussed its use with your doctor.

In deciding to use a medicine, the risks of taking the medicine must be weighed against the good it will do. This is a decision you and your doctor will make. For trioxsalen, the following should be considered:

Allergies—Tell your doctor if you have ever had any unusual or allergic reaction to trioxsalen. Also tell your health care professional if you are allergic to any other substances, such as preservatives or dyes.

Pregnancy—Studies have not been done in either humans or animals.

Breast-feeding—Trioxsalen has not been reported to cause problems in nursing babies.

Children—Although there is no specific information comparing use of trioxsalen in children with use in other age groups, this medicine is not expected to cause different side effects or problems in children than it does in adults.

Older adults—Many medicines have not been studied specifically in older people. Therefore, it may not be known whether they work exactly the same way they do in younger adults or if they cause different side effects or problems in older people. There is no specific information comparing use of trioxsalen in the elderly with use in other age groups.

Other medicines—Although certain medicines should not be used together at all, in other cases two different medicines may be used together even if an interaction might occur. In these cases, your doctor may want to change the dose, or other precautions may be necessary. Tell your health care professional if you are using any other prescription or nonprescription (over-the-counter [OTC]) medicine.

Other medical problems—The presence of other medical problems may affect the use of trioxsalen. Make sure you tell your doctor if you have any other medical problems, especially:

• Allergy to sunlight (family history of) or
• Lupus erythematosus or
• Porphyria or
• Other conditions that make you more sensitive to light—This medicine will make the condition worse
• Eye problems, such as cataracts or loss of the lens of the eyes—Use of this medicine may make your cataracts or other eye problems worse; having no lens in your eye may increase the side effects of this medicine
• Heart or blood vessel disease (severe)—The heat from the light treatment may make the condition worse
• Infection or
• Stomach problems—Use of this medicine may make the condition worse
• Melanoma or other skin cancer (history of) or

- Recent treatment with x-rays or cancer medicines or plans to have x-rays in the near future—May increase your chance of skin cancer

Proper Use of This Medicine

This medicine may take several weeks or months to help your condition. *Do not increase the amount of trioxsalen you are taking or spend extra time in the sunlight or under an ultraviolet lamp.* This will not make the medicine act any more quickly and may result in a serious burn.

If this medicine upsets your stomach, it may be taken with meals or milk.

Dosing—The dose of trioxsalen will be different for different patients. *Follow your doctor's orders or the directions on the label.* The following information includes only the average doses of trioxsalen. *If your dose is different, do not change it* unless your doctor tells you to do so.

The number of doses you take each day, the time allowed between doses, and the length of time you take the medicine depend on the medical problem for which you are taking trioxsalen.

- For *oral* dosage form (tablets):
  - —For vitiligo:
    - Adults and children 12 years of age and over—20 to 40 milligrams (mg) taken two to four hours before ultraviolet light A (UVA) exposure. This treatment (trioxsalen and UVA) is given two or three times a week with the treatments spaced at least forty-eight hours apart.
    - Children up to 12 years of age—Dose must be determined by your doctor.
  - —For increasing tolerance to sunlight or increasing color of the skin:
    - Adults and children 12 years of age and over—20 to 40 mg taken two hours before ultraviolet light A (UVA) exposure. This treatment (trioxsalen and UVA) is given two or three times a week with the treatments spaced at least forty-eight hours apart.
    - Children up to 12 years of age—Dose must be determined by your doctor.

Missed dose—If you are late in taking, or miss taking, a dose of this medicine, notify your doctor so your light treatment can be rescheduled. Remember that exposure to sunlight or ultraviolet light must take place 2 to 4 hours *after* you take the medicine or it will not work. If you have any questions about this, check with your doctor.

Storage—To store this medicine:

- Keep out of the reach of children.
- Store away from heat and direct light.
- Do not store in the bathroom, near the kitchen sink, or in other damp places. Heat or moisture may cause the medicine to break down.
- Do not keep outdated medicine or medicine no longer needed. Be sure that any discarded medicine is out of the reach of children.

Precautions While Using This Medicine

Your doctor should check your progress at regular visits to make sure this medicine is working and that it does not cause unwanted effects. Eye examinations should be included.

This medicine increases the sensitivity of your skin and lips to sunlight. Therefore, *exposure to the sun, even through window glass or on a cloudy day, could cause a serious burn.* If you must go out during the daylight hours:

- *Before each treatment, cover your skin for at least 24 hours* by wearing protective clothing, such as long-sleeved shirts, full-length slacks, wide-brimmed hat, and gloves. In addition, *protect your lips with a special sun block lipstick that has a skin protection factor of at least 15.* Check with your doctor before using sun block products on other parts of your body before a treatment, since sun block products should not be used on the areas of your skin that are to be treated.
- *After each treatment, cover your skin for at least 8 hours* by wearing protective clothing. In addition, use a sun block product that has a skin protection factor of at least 15 on your lips and on those areas of your body that cannot be covered.

If you have any questions about this, check with your health care professional.

Your skin may continue to be sensitive to sunlight for some time after treatment with this medicine. Use extra caution for at least 48 hours following each treatment if you plan to spend any time in the sun. Do not sunbathe during this time.

For 24 hours after you take each dose of trioxsalen, your eyes should be protected during daylight hours with special wraparound sunglasses that totally block or absorb ultraviolet light (ordinary sunglasses are not adequate). This is to prevent cataracts. Your doctor will tell you what kind of sunglasses to use. These glasses should be worn even in indirect light, such as light coming through window glass or on a cloudy day.

Eating certain foods while you are taking trixosalen may increase your skin's sensitivity to sunlight. To help prevent this, avoid eating limes, figs, parsley, parsnips, mustard, carrots, and celery while you are being treated with this medicine.

This medicine may cause your skin to become dry or itchy. *However, check with your doctor before applying anything to your skin to treat this problem.*

Side Effects of This Medicine

Along with its needed effects, a medicine may cause some unwanted effects. Although not all of these side effects may occur, if they do occur they may need medical attention.

Check with your doctor immediately if you think you have taken an overdose or if any of the following side effects occur, since they may indicate a serious burn:

Blistering and peeling of skin; reddened, sore skin; swelling, especially of feet or lower legs

Other side effects may occur that usually do not need medical attention. These side effects may go away during treatment as your body adjusts to the medicine. However, check with your doctor if any of the following side effects continue for more than 48 hours or are bothersome:

More common

Itching of skin; nausea

Less common

Dizziness; headache; mental depression; nervousness; trouble in sleeping

There is an increased risk of developing skin cancer after use of trioxsalen. You should check your body regularly and show your doctor any skin sores that do not heal, new skin growths, and skin growths that have changed in the way they look or feel.

Premature aging of the skin may occur as a result of prolonged trioxsalen therapy. This effect is permanent and is similar to what happens when a person sunbathes for long periods of time.

Other side effects not listed above may also occur in some patients. If you notice any other effects, check with your doctor.

Additional Information

Once a medicine has been approved for marketing for a certain use, experience may show that it is also useful for other medical problems. Although this use is not included in product labeling, trioxsalen is used in certain patients with the following medical condition:

- Psoriasis

Other than the above information, there is no additional information relating to proper use, precautions, or side effects for this use.

Revised: 07/25/94

TROPICAMIDE Ophthalmic

Some commonly used brand names are:

In the U.S.—

I-Picamide
Mydriacyl
Mydriafair
Ocu-Tropic
Opticyl
Spectro-Cyl
Tropicacyl

Generic name product may also be available.

In Canada—

Minims Tropicamide
Mydriacyl
Tropicacyl

Description

Tropicamide (troe-PIK-a-mide) is used to dilate (enlarge) the pupil so that the doctor can see into the back of your eye. It is used before eye examinations, such as cycloplegic refraction and examination of the fundus of the eye. Tropicamide may also be used before and after eye surgery.

This medicine is available only with your doctor's prescription, in the following dosage form:

Ophthalmic

- Ophthalmic solution (eye drops) (U.S. and Canada)

Before Using This Medicine

In deciding to use a medicine, the risks of taking the medicine must be weighed against the good it will do. This is a decision you and your doctor will make. For tropicamide, the following should be considered:

Allergies—Tell your doctor if you have ever had any unusual or allergic reaction to tropicamide. Also tell your health care professional if you are allergic to any other substances, such as preservatives.

Pregnancy—Studies on effects in pregnancy have not been done in either humans or animals.

Breast-feeding—Tropicamide has not been reported to cause problems in nursing babies.

Children—Infants and young children and children with blond hair or blue eyes may be especially sensitive to the effects of tropicamide. This may increase the chance or severity of some of the side effects during treatment.

Older adults—Elderly people are especially sensitive to the effects of tropicamide. This may increase the chance of side effects during treatment.

Other medicines—Although certain medicines should not be used together at all, in other cases two different medicines may be used together even if an interaction might occur. In these cases, your doctor may want to change the dose, or other precautions may be necessary. Tell your health care professional if you are using any other prescription or nonprescription (over-the-counter [OTC]) medicine.

Other medical problems—The presence of other medical problems may affect the use of tropicamide. Make sure you tell your doctor if you have any other medical problems, especially:

- Brain damage (in children) or
- Down's syndrome (mongolism) (in children and adults) or
- Glaucoma or
- Spastic paralysis (in children)—Tropicamide may make the condition worse

Proper Use of This Medicine

To use:

- First, wash your hands. Tilt the head back and, pressing your finger gently on the skin just beneath the lower eyelid, pull the lower eyelid away from the eye to make a space. Drop the medicine into this space. Let go of the eyelid and gently close the eyes. Do not blink. Keep the eyes closed and apply pressure to the inner corner of the eye with your finger for 2 or 3 minutes to allow the medicine to be absorbed by the eye. *This is especially important in infants.*

- Immediately after using the eye drops, wash your hands to remove any medicine that may be on them. If you are using the eye drops for an infant or child, be sure to wash the infant's or child's hands also, and do not let any of the medicine get in the infant's or child's mouth.
- To keep the medicine as germ-free as possible, do not touch the applicator tip to any surface (including the eye). Also, keep the container tightly closed.

Use this medicine only as directed. Do not use more of it and do not use it more often than your doctor ordered. To do so may increase the chance of too much medicine being absorbed into the body and the chance of side effects.

Dosing—The dose of tropicamide will be different for different patients. *Follow your doctor's orders or the directions on the label.* The following information includes only the average doses of tropicamide. If your dose is different, do not change it unless your doctor tells you to do so.

- For *ophthalmic solution (eye drops)* dosage form:
  - —For cycloplegic refraction (eye examination):
    - Adults—One drop of 1% solution, repeated once in five minutes.
    - Children—One drop of 0.5 to 1% solution, repeated once in five minutes.
  - —For examination of fundus of eye:
    - Adults and children—One drop of 0.5% solution fifteen to twenty minutes before examination.

Precautions While Using This Medicine

After this medicine is applied to your eyes:

- Your pupils will become unusually large and you will have blurring of vision, especially for close objects. *Make sure your vision is clear before you drive, use machines, or do anything else that could be dangerous if you are not able to see well.*
- Your eyes will become more sensitive to light than they are normally. When you go out during the daylight hours, even on cloudy days, *wear sunglasses that block ultraviolet (UV) light to protect your eyes from sunlight and other bright lights.* Ordinary sunglasses may not protect your eyes. If you have any questions about the kind of sunglasses to wear, check with your doctor.
- If these effects continue for longer than 24 hours after the medicine is used, check with your doctor.

Side Effects of This Medicine

Along with its needed effects, a medicine may cause some unwanted effects. Although not all of these side effects may occur, if they do occur they may need medical attention.

Check with your doctor as soon as possible if any of the following side effects occur:

Symptoms of too much medicine being absorbed into the body

Clumsiness or unsteadiness; confusion; fast heartbeat; flushing or redness of face; hallucinations (seeing, hearing, or feeling things that are not there); increased thirst or dryness of mouth; skin rash; slurred speech; swollen stomach in infants; unusual behavior, especially in children; unusual drowsiness, tiredness, or weakness

Other side effects may occur that usually do not need medical attention. These side effects may go away during treatment as your body adjusts to the medicine. However, check with your doctor if any of the following side effects continue or are bothersome:

More common

Blurred vision; headache; sensitivity of eyes to light; stinging of the eye when the medicine is applied

Other side effects not listed above may also occur in some patients. If you notice any other effects, check with your doctor.

Revised: 07/14/95

TUBERCULIN, PURIFIED PROTEIN DERIVATIVE (PPD) Injection

Some commonly used brand names are:

In the U.S.—

Aplisol
Aplitest
Tuberculin PPD TINE TEST
Tubersol

In Canada—

Tubersol

Description

Tuberculin (too-BER-kyu-lin), purified protein derivative (PPD) is used as a test to help diagnose tuberculous infection.

How the test is done: Tuberculin PPD is injected into the surface layers of the skin. If the test is positive, a reaction will be seen at and around the place of injection or puncture. If the test is given using an injection, this reaction is usually a hard, raised area with clear margins. If the test is given using the puncture devices, the reaction is usually a swollen area at the puncture site. Forty-eight to 72 hours after administration of the injection the size of the reaction is measured and recorded and the results of the test are studied.

Tuberculin PPD is to be used only by or under the supervision of a doctor. It is available in the following dosage forms:

Parenteral

- Injection (U.S. and Canada)
- Multiple-puncture device (U.S.)

Before Having This Test

In deciding to use a diagnostic test, the risks of the test must be weighed against the good it will do. This is a decision you and your doctor will make. For tuberculin PPD, the following should be considered:

Allergies—Tell your doctor if you have ever had any unusual or allergic reaction to tuberculin PPD. Also tell your health care professional if you are allergic to any other substances, such as foods, preservatives, or dyes.

Pregnancy—Studies on the effects in pregnancy have not been done in either humans or animals. However, pregnancy may affect your reaction to the test. Before you receive tuberculin PPD, make sure your doctor knows if you are pregnant or if you may become pregnant.

Breast-feeding—It is not known whether tuberculin PPD passes into the breast milk. However, tuberculin PPD has not been reported to cause problems in nursing babies.

Children—Although there is no specific information comparing use of tuberculin PPD in children with use in other age groups, this diagnostic test is not expected to cause different side effects or problems in children than it does in adults.

Older adults—Reactions to tuberculin PPD in older patients may be more likely to develop slowly and may not reach the peak effect until after 72 hours.

Other medicines—Although certain medicines should not be used together at all, in other cases two different medicines may be used together even if an interaction might occur. In these cases, your doctor may want to change the dose, or other precautions may be necessary. Tell your health care professional if you are taking any other prescription or non prescription (over-the-counter [OTC]) medicine, including steroids.

Other medical problems—The presence of other medical problems may affect the use of tuberculin PPD. Make sure you tell your doctor if you have any other medical problems, especially:

- Positive tuberculin reaction (previous)—The reaction to tuberculin PPD may be severe, possibly causing sores on the skin where the test is given

Side Effects of This Test

Along with its needed effects, a medicine may cause some unwanted effects. Although not all of these side effects may occur, if they do occur they may need medical attention.

Rare

Skin rash or itching; redness, blistering, peeling, or loosening of the skin

Other side effects may occur that usually do not need medical attention. However, check with your doctor if any of the following side effects continue or are bothersome:

Less common

Pain; redness at the site of injection; sores at and around the place of injection

Other side effects not listed above may also occur in some patients. If you notice any other effects, check with your doctor.

Developed: 08/01/95

TYPHOID Vi POLYSACCHARIDE VACCINE Systemic†

A commonly used brand name in the U.S. is Typhim Vi.

†Not commercially available in Canada.

Description

Typhoid (TYE-foid) fever is a serious disease that can cause death. It is caused by a germ called *Salmonella typhi*, and is spread most often through infected food or water. Typhoid may also be spread by close person-to-person contact with infected persons (such as occurs with persons living in the same household). Some infected persons do not appear to be sick, but they can still spread the germ to others.

Typhoid fever is very rare in the U.S. and other areas of the world that have good water and sewage (waste) systems. However, it is a problem in parts of the world that do not have such systems. If you are traveling to certain countries or remote (out-of-the-way) areas, typhoid vaccine will help protect you from typhoid fever. The U.S. Centers for Disease Control (CDC) currently recommend caution in the following areas of the world:

- Africa
- Asia
- Latin America

Typhoid vaccine given by injection helps prevent typhoid fever, but does not provide 100% protection. Therefore, it is very important to avoid infected persons and food and water that may be infected, even if you have received the vaccine.

To get the best possible protection against typhoid, you should receive the vaccine at least 1 week before you travel to areas where you may be exposed to typhoid.

If you will be traveling regularly to parts of the world where typhoid is a problem, you should get a booster (repeat) dose of the vaccine every 2 years.

Typhoid vaccine is to be used only by or under the supervision of a doctor. It is available in the following dosage form:

Parenteral

- Injection (U.S.)

Before Receiving This Vaccine

In deciding to use a medicine, the risks of taking the medicine must be weighed against the good it will do. This is a decision you and your doctor will make. For typhoid Vi polysaccharide vaccine, the following should be considered:

Allergies—Tell your doctor if you have ever had any unusual or allergic reaction to typhoid vaccine. Also tell your health care professional if you are allergic to any other substances, such as preservatives.

Pregnancy—Studies on effects in pregnancy have not been done in either humans or animals.

Breast-feeding—This vaccine has not been reported to cause problems in nursing babies.

Children—Typhoid Vi polysaccharide vaccine is not recommended for infants and children younger than 2 years of age. For children 2 years of age and over, this vaccine is not expected to cause different side effects or problems than it does in adults.

Older adults—Many medicines have not been studied specifically in older people. Therefore, it may not be known whether they work exactly the same way they do in younger adults. Although there is no specific information comparing use of typhoid vaccine in the elderly with use in other age groups, this vaccine is not expected to cause different side effects or problems in older people than it does in younger adults.

Other medicines—Although certain medicines should not be used together at all, in other cases two different medicines may be used together even if an interaction might occur. In these cases, your doctor may want to change the dose, or other precautions may be necessary. Tell your health care professional if you are taking any other prescription or nonprescription (over-the-counter [OTC]) medicine.

Other medical problems—The presence of other medical problems may affect the use of typhoid vaccine. Make sure you tell your doctor if you have any other medical problems, especially:

- Previous sensitivity reaction to typhoid vaccine—Use of typhoid vaccine is not recommended
- Severe illness with fever—The symptoms of the condition may be confused with the side effects of the vaccine

Proper Use of This Vaccine

Dosing—The dose of typhoid Vi polysaccharide vaccine is the same for all patients 2 years of age and older. For infants and children up to two years of age, the use of typhoid Vi polysaccharide vaccine is not recommended.

- For *injection* dosage form:
  - —For prevention of typhoid fever:
    - Adults and children 2 years of age and older—One dose injected into a muscle.
    - Children up to 2 years of age—Use is not recommended.

Side Effects of This Vaccine

Along with its needed effects, a vaccine may cause some unwanted effects. Although not all of these side effects may occur, if they do occur they may need medical attention. *It is very important that you tell your doctor about any side effects that occur after a dose of typhoid vaccine,* even though the side effect may have gone away without treatment. Some types of side effects may mean that you should not receive any more doses of typhoid vaccine.

Get emergency help immediately if any of the following side effects occur:

Rare

Difficulty in breathing or swallowing; hives; itching, especially of feet or hands; reddening of skin, especially around ears; swelling of eyes, face, or inside of nose; unusual tiredness or weakness (sudden and severe)

Other side effects may occur that usually do not need medical attention. However, check with your doctor if any of the following side effects continue or are bothersome:

More common

Fever; general feeling of discomfort or illness; headache; muscle pain; pain, redness, or swelling at place of injection

Other side effects not listed above may also occur in some patients. If you notice any other effects, check with your doctor.

Developed: 08/01/95

UNDECYLENIC ACID, COMPOUND Topical

Some commonly used brand names are:

In the U.S.—

- Caldesene Medicated Powder
- Cruex Antifungal Cream
- Cruex Antifungal Powder
- Cruex Antifungal Spray Powder
- Decylenes Powder
- Desenex Antifungal Cream
- Desenex Antifungal Liquid
- Desenex Antifungal Ointment
- Desenex Antifungal Penetrating Foam
- Desenex Antifungal Powder
- Desenex Antifungal Spray Powder
- Gordochom Solution

In Canada—

- Cruex Aerosol Powder
- Cruex Cream
- Cruex Powder
- Desenex Aerosol Powder
- Desenex Foam
- Desenex Ointment
- Desenex Powder
- Desenex Solution

Description

Compound undecylenic acid (un-de-sill-ENN-ik AS-id) belongs to the group of medicines called antifungals. It is used to treat some types of fungus infections. However, compound undecylenic acid generally has been replaced by newer and more effective medicines for the treatment of fungus infections.

Compound undecylenic acid is available without a prescription; however, your doctor may have special instructions on the proper use of this medicine for your medical condition.

Compound undecylenic acid is available in the following dosage forms:

Topical

- Aerosol foam (U.S. and Canada)
- Aerosol powder (U.S. and Canada)
- Cream (U.S. and Canada)
- Ointment (U.S. and Canada)
- Powder (U.S. and Canada)
- Solution (U.S. and Canada)

Before Using This Medicine

If you are taking this medicine without a prescription, carefully read and follow any precautions on the label. For compound undecylenic acid, the following should be considered:

Allergies—Tell your doctor if you have ever had any unusual or allergic reaction to compound undecylenic acid. Also tell your health care professional if you are allergic to any other substances, such as preservatives or dyes.

Pregnancy—Compound undecylenic acid topical preparations have not been shown to cause birth defects or other problems in humans.

Breast-feeding—Compound undecylenic acid topical preparations have not been reported to cause problems in nursing babies.

Children—Compound undecylenic acid should not be used on children up to 2 years of age, unless otherwise directed by your doctor. Although there is no specific information comparing use of compound undecylenic acid topical preparations in children 2 years of age and older with use in other age groups, this medicine is not expected to cause different side effects or problems in children 2 years of age and older than it does in adults.

Older adults—Many medicines have not been studied specifically in older people. Therefore, it may not be known whether they work exactly the same way they do in younger adults or if they cause different side effects or problems in older people. There is no specific information comparing use of compound undecylenic acid in the elderly with use in other age groups.

Other medicines—Although certain medicines should not be used together at all, in other cases two different medicines may be used together even if an interaction might occur. In these cases, your doctor may want to change the dose, or other precautions may be necessary. Tell your health care professional if you are using any other topical prescription or nonprescription (over-the-counter [OTC]) medicine that is to be applied to the same area of the skin.

Proper Use of This Medicine

Before applying compound undecylenic acid, wash the affected and surrounding areas, and dry thoroughly. Then apply enough medicine to cover these areas.

Keep this medicine away from the eyes.

For patients using the *cream form* of this medicine:

- Apply cream generously to affected and surrounding areas. Rub in well.
- Do not use on pus-containing sores or on badly broken skin.

For patients using the *powder form* of this medicine:

- If the powder is used on the feet, sprinkle it between toes, on feet, and in socks and shoes.

For patients using the *aerosol powder or aerosol foam form* of this medicine:

- From a distance of 4 to 6 inches, spray the affected and surrounding areas. If the medicine is used on the feet, spray it between the toes also. The powder may also be sprayed in socks and shoes.
- Do not use this medicine around the eyes, nose, or mouth.
- Do not inhale the aerosol.
- Do not use near heat, near open flame, or while smoking.

To help clear up your infection completely, *keep using this medicine for 2 weeks after burning, itching, or other symptoms have disappeared,* unless otherwise directed by your doctor. *Do not miss any doses.*

Dosing—The dose of topical compound undecylenic acid will be different for different patients. *Follow your doctor's orders or the directions on the label.* The following information includes only the average doses of topical compound undecylenic acid. *If your dose is different, do not change it unless your doctor tells you to do so.*

- For fungus infections:
  —For *aerosol foam, aerosol powder, ointment, powder,* or *solution* dosage forms:
  - Adults and children 2 years of age and over—Apply to the affected area(s) of the skin two times a day.

- Children up to 2 years of age—Use is not recommended.

—For *cream* dosage form:

- Adults and children—Apply to the affected area(s) of the skin as often as necessary.

Missed dose—If you miss a dose of this medicine, apply it as soon as possible. Then go back to your regular dosing schedule.

Storage—To store this medicine:

- Keep out of the reach of children.
- Store away from heat and direct light.
- Do not store the powder form of this medicine in the bathroom, near the kitchen sink, or in other damp places. Heat or moisture may cause the medicine to break down.
- Keep the aerosol foam, aerosol powder, cream, ointment, and solution forms of this medicine from freezing.
- Do not puncture, break, or burn the aerosol foam or powder container.
- Do not keep outdated medicine or medicine no longer needed. Be sure that any discarded medicine is out of the reach of children.

Precautions While Using This Medicine

If your skin problem does not improve within 4 weeks, or if it becomes worse, check with your health care professional.

To help prevent reinfection after the period of treatment with this medicine, the powder or spray powder form of this medicine may be used each day after bathing and careful drying.

Side Effects of This Medicine

Along with its needed effects, a medicine may cause some unwanted effects. Although not all of these side effects may occur, if they do occur they may need medical attention.

Check with your health care professional as soon as possible if the following side effect occurs:

Skin irritation not present before use of this medicine

Other side effects not listed above may also occur in some patients. If you notice any other effects, check with your health care professional.

Revised: 07/25/94

UROFOLLITROPIN Systemic

Some commonly used brand names are:

In the U.S.—

Fertinex   Metrodin

In Canada—

Fertinorm HP   Metrodin

Other commonly used names are follicle-stimulating hormone, FSH, and urofollitrophin.

Description

Urofollitropin (yoor-oh-fol-li-TROE-pin) is a fertility drug that is identical to the hormone called follicle-stimulating hormone (FSH) that is produced naturally by the pituitary gland.

FSH is primarily responsible for stimulating growth of the ovarian follicle, which includes the developing egg, the cells surrounding the egg that produce the hormones needed to support a pregnancy, and the fluid around the egg. As the ovarian follicle grows, an increasing amount of the hormone estrogen (ES-troe-jen) is produced by the cells in the follicle and released into the bloodstream. Estrogen causes the endometrium (lining of the uterus) to thicken before ovulation occurs. The higher blood levels of estrogen will also provide a cue to the hypothalamus and pituitary gland to slow the production and release of FSH.

Another pituitary hormone, luteinizing hormone (LH), also helps to increase the amount of estrogen produced by the follicle cells. However, the main function of LH is to cause ovulation. The sharp rise in the blood level of LH that triggers ovulation is sometimes called the LH surge. After ovulation, the group of hormone-producing follicle cells become what is called the corpus luteum and will produce estrogen and large amounts of another hormone, progesterone (proe-JES-ter-one). Progesterone causes the endometrium to mature so that it can support the egg after it is fertilized. If implantation of a fertilized egg does not occur, the levels of estrogen and progesterone decrease and the endometrium sloughs off (e.g., menstruation occurs).

Urofollitropin is usually given in combination with human chorionic gonadotropin (hCG). The actions of hCG are almost identical to those of LH. It is given to simulate the natural LH surge. This results in predictable ovulation.

Urofollitropin is often used in women who have low levels of FSH and too-high levels of LH. Women with polycystic ovary syndrome usually have hormone levels such as this and are treated with urofollitropin to make up for the low amounts of FSH. Many women being treated with urofollitropin have already tried clomiphene (e.g., Serophene) and have not been able to conceive yet. Urofollitropin may also be used to cause the ovary to produce several follicles, which can then be harvested for use in gamete intrafallopian transfer (GIFT) or *in vitro* fertilization (IVF).

Urofollitropin is to be given only by or under the supervision of your doctor. It is available in the following dosage form:

Parenteral

- Injection (U.S. and Canada)

Before Receiving This Medicine

In deciding to use a medicine, the risks of taking the medicine must be weighed against the good it will do. This is

a decision you and your doctor will make. For urofollitropin, the following should be considered:

Allergies—Tell your doctor if you have ever had any unusual or allergic reaction to urofollitropin. Also tell your health care professional if you are allergic to any other substances, such as foods, preservatives, or dyes.

Pregnancy—If you become pregnant as a result of using this medicine, there is an increased chance of a multiple pregnancy.

Other medicines—Although certain medicines should not be used together at all, in other cases two different medicines may be used together even if an interaction might occur. In these cases, your doctor may want to change the dose, or other precautions may be necessary. Tell your health care professional if you are taking any other prescription or nonprescription (over-the-counter [OTC]) medicine.

Other medical problems—The presence of other medical problems may affect the use of urofollitropin. Make sure you tell your doctor if you have any other medical problems, especially:

- Cyst on ovary—Urofollitropin can cause further growth of cysts on the ovary
- Unusual vaginal bleeding—Some irregular vaginal bleeding is a sign that the endometrium is growing too rapidly, possibly of endometrial cancer, or some hormone imbalances; the increases in estrogen production caused by urofollitropin can make these problems worse. If a hormonal imbalance is present, it should be treated before the beginning of menotropins therapy

Proper Use of This Medicine

Dosing—The dose of urofollitropin will be different for different patients. *Follow your doctor's orders or the directions on the label.* The following information includes only the average doses of urofollitropin. *If your dose is different, do not change it* unless your doctor tells you to do so.

- For *injection* dosage form:
  - —For becoming pregnant while having a condition called polycystic ovary syndrome:
    - Adults—75 Units injected under the skin or into a muscle once a day for seven or more days. Usually, another medicine called chorionic gonadotropin (hCG) will be given the day after the last dose. If needed, your doctor may then increase your dose of urofollitropin to 150 Units a day for another seven or more days. Higher doses may be prescribed by your doctor.
  - —For becoming pregnant while using other pregnancy methods (assisted reproductive technology [ART]):
    - Adults—150 Units injected under the skin or into a muscle once a day. Your treatment will probably begin on Day 2 or Day 3 after your menstrual period begins. Usually, another medicine called chorionic gonadotropin (hCG) will be given the day after the last dose.

Precautions While Receiving This Medicine

It is very important that your doctor check your progress at regular visits to make sure that the medicine is working properly and to check for unwanted effects. Your doctor will likely want to monitor the development of the ovarian follicle(s) by measuring the amount of estrogen in your bloodstream and by checking the size of the follicle(s) with ultrasound examinations.

If your doctor has asked you to record your basal body temperature (BBT) daily, make sure that you do this every day. It is important that intercourse take place around the time of ovulation to give you the best chance of becoming pregnant.

Side Effects of This Medicine

Along with its needed effects, a medicine may cause some unwanted effects. Although not all of these side effects may occur, if they do occur they may need medical attention.

Check with your doctor as soon as possible if any of the following side effects occur:

More common

Abdominal or pelvic pain; bloating (mild); redness, pain, or swelling at the injection site

Less common or rare

Abdominal or stomach pain (severe); bloating (moderate to severe); decreased amount of urine; feeling of indigestion; fever and chills; nausea, vomiting, or diarrhea (continuing or severe); pelvic pain (severe); shortness of breath; skin rash or hives; swelling of lower legs; weight gain (rapid)

Other side effects may occur that usually do not need medical attention. These side effects may go away during treatment as your body adjusts to the medicine. However, check with your doctor if any of the following side effects continue or are bothersome:

Less common or rare

Breast tenderness; diarrhea (mild); nausea; vomiting

After you stop using this medicine, your body may need time to adjust. The length of time this takes depends on the amount of medicine you were using and how long you used it. During this period of time check with your doctor if you notice any of the following side effects:

Abdominal or stomach pain (severe); bloating (moderate to severe); decreased amount of urine; feeling of indigestion; nausea, vomiting, or diarrhea (continuing or severe); pelvic pain (severe); shortness of breath; swelling of lower legs; weight gain (rapid)

Other side effects not listed above may also occur in some patients. If you notice any other effects, check with your doctor.

Revised: 07/08/92
Interim revision: 06/30/94; 08/07/97

URSODIOL Systemic

Some commonly used brand names are:

In the U.S.—
Actigall

In Canada—
Ursofalk

Other commonly used names are ursodeoxycholic acid and UDCA.

Description

Ursodiol (ur-so-DYE-ole) is used in the treatment of gallstone disease. It is taken by mouth to dissolve the gallstones.

Ursodiol is used in patients with gallstones who do not need to have their gallbladders removed or in those in whom surgery should be avoided because of other medical problems. However, ursodiol works only in those patients whose gallstones are made of cholesterol and works best when these stones are small and of the ''floating'' type.

Ursodiol is also used to help prevent gallstones in patients who are on rapid weight-loss programs.

Ursodiol is available only with your doctor's prescription, in the following dosage form:

Oral
- Capsules (U.S. and Canada)

Before Using This Medicine

In deciding to use a medicine, the risks of taking the medicine must be weighed against the good it will do. This is a decision you and your doctor will make. For ursodiol, the following should be considered:

Allergies—Tell your doctor if you have ever had any unusual or allergic reaction to ursodiol or other products containing bile acids.

Diet—It is thought that body weight and the kind of diet the patient follows may affect how fast the stones dissolve and whether new stones will form. However, check with your doctor before going on any diet.

Pregnancy—Ursodiol has not been studied in pregnant women. However, ursodiol has not been shown to cause birth defects or other problems in animal studies.

Breast-feeding—It is not known whether ursodiol passes into the breast milk. Although most medicines pass into breast milk in small amounts, many of them may be used safely while breast-feeding. Mothers who are taking this medicine and who wish to breast-feed should discuss this with their doctor.

Children—Although there is no specific information comparing use of ursodiol in children with use in other age groups, this medicine is not expected to cause different side effects or problems in children than it does in adults.

Older adults—Many medicines have not been studied specifically in older people. Therefore, it may not be known whether they work exactly the same way they do in younger adults. Although there is no specific information comparing use of ursodiol in the elderly with use in other age groups, this medicine is not expected to cause different side effects or problems in older people than it does in younger adults.

Other medicines—Although certain medicines should not be used together at all, in other cases two different medicines may be used together even if an interaction might occur. In these cases, your doctor may want to change the dose, or other precautions may be necessary. Tell your health care professional if you are taking any other prescription or nonprescription (over-the-counter [OTC]) medicine.

Other medical problems—The presence of other medical problems may affect the use of ursodiol. Make sure you tell your doctor if you have any other medical problems, especially:

- Biliary tract problems or
- Pancreatitis (inflammation of pancreas)—These conditions may make it necessary to have surgery since treatment with ursodiol would take too long

Proper Use of This Medicine

Take ursodiol with meals for best results, unless otherwise directed by your doctor.

Take ursodiol for the full time of treatment, even if you begin to feel better. If you stop taking this medicine too soon, the gallstones may not dissolve as fast or may not dissolve at all.

Dosing—The dose of ursodiol will be different for different patients. *Follow your doctor's orders or the directions on the label.* The following information includes only the average doses of ursodiol. *If your dose is different, do not change it unless your doctor tells you to do so.*

The number of capsules that you take depends on the strength of the medicine. Also, *the number of doses you take each day, the time allowed between doses, and the length of time you take the medicine depend on the medical problem for which you are taking ursodiol.*

- For *oral* dosage form (capsules):
  —For gallstone disease:
    - Adults and children 12 years of age and older—The dose is based on body weight and must be determined by your doctor. The usual dose is 8 to 10 milligrams (mg) per kilogram (kg) (3.6 to 4.5 mg per pound) of body weight a day, divided into two or three doses. Each dose is usually taken with a meal.
    - Children up to 12 years of age—Use and dose must be determined by your doctor.

  —For prevention of gallstones during rapid weight loss:
    - Adults—Oral, 300 mg two times a day.
    - Children up to 12 years of age—Use and dose must be determined by your doctor.

Missed dose—If you miss a dose of this medicine, take it as soon as possible or double your next dose.

Storage—To store this medicine:

- Keep out of the reach of children.
- Store away from heat and direct light.
- Do not store in the bathroom, near the kitchen sink, or in other damp places. Heat or moisture may cause the medicine to break down.
- Do not keep outdated medicine or medicine no longer needed. Be sure that any discarded medicine is out of the reach of children.

Precautions While Using This Medicine

It is important that your doctor check your progress at regular visits. Laboratory tests will have to be done every few months while you are taking this medicine to make sure that the gallstones are dissolving and your liver is working properly.

Do not take aluminum-containing antacids (e.g., ALternaGEL, Maalox) while taking ursodiol. To do so may keep ursodiol from working properly. Before using an antacid, check with your health care professional.

Check with your doctor immediately if severe abdominal or stomach pain, especially toward the upper right side, or severe nausea and vomiting occur. These symptoms may mean that you have other medical problems or that your gallstone condition needs your doctor's attention.

Side Effects of This Medicine

Along with its needed effects, a medicine may cause some unwanted effects. The following side effects may go away during treatment as your body adjusts to the medicine. However, check with your doctor if any of the following side effects continue or are bothersome:

More common

Back pain; diarrhea

Less common or rare

Constipation; dizziness; hair loss; heartburn; nausea; vomiting

Other side effects not listed above may also occur in some patients. If you notice any other effects, check with your doctor.

Additional Information

Once a medicine has been approved for marketing for a certain use, experience may show that it is also useful for other medical problems. Although these uses are not included in product labeling, ursodiol is used in certain patients with the following medical conditions:

- Chronic liver disease
- Liver transplant (to help reduce the risk of rejection)

There is no additional information relating to proper use, precautions, or side effects for these uses.

Revised: 08/08/97

VALACYCLOVIR Systemic†

A commonly used brand name in the U.S. is Valtrex.

†Not commercially available in Canada.

Description

Valacyclovir (val-ay-SYE-kloe-veer) is used to treat the symptoms of herpes zoster (also known as shingles), a herpes virus infection of the skin. In your body, valacyclovir becomes the anti-herpes medicine, acyclovir. Although valacyclovir will not cure herpes zoster, it does help relieve the pain and discomfort and helps the sores heal faster.

Valacyclovir is available only with your doctor's prescription, in the following dosage form:

Oral
- Tablets (U.S.)

Before Using This Medicine

In deciding to use a medicine, the risks of taking the medicine must be weighed against the good it will do. This is a decision you and your doctor will make. For valacyclovir, the following should be considered:

Allergies—Tell your doctor if you have ever had any unusual or allergic reaction to valacyclovir or acyclovir. Also tell your health care professional if you are allergic to any other substances, such as foods, sulfites or other preservatives, or dyes.

Pregnancy—Adequate and well-controlled studies in humans have not been done with valacyclovir or acyclovir. However, acyclovir has been used in pregnant women and has not been reported to cause birth defects or other problems.

Breast-feeding—It is not known whether valacyclovir passes into the breast milk. Acyclovir does pass into breast milk and has not been reported to cause problems in nursing babies.

Children—Studies on this medicine have been done only in adult patients. There is no specific information comparing use of valacyclovir in children with use in other age groups.

Older adults—Valacyclovir has been used in the elderly and has not been shown to cause different side effects or problems in older people than it does in younger adults.

Other medicines—Although certain medicines should not be used together at all, in other cases two different medicines may be used together even if an interaction might occur. In these cases, your doctor may want to change your dose or other precautions may be necessary. Tell your health care professional if you are taking any other prescription or nonprescription (over-the-counter [OTC]) medicine.

Other medical problems—The presence of other medical problems may affect the use of valacyclovir. Make sure you tell your doctor if you have any other medical problems, especially:

- Bone marrow transplantation or
- Human immunodefiency virus (HIV) infection, advanced, or
- Kidney transplantation—Patients with these medical problems may have an increased risk of severe side effects
- Kidney disease—Kidney disease may increase blood levels of this medicine, increasing the chance of side effects

Proper Use of This Medicine

Valacyclovir works best *if it is used within 48 hours after the symptoms of shingles* (for example, pain, burning, or blisters) *begin to appear.*

Valacyclovir may be taken with meals.

Keep taking valacyclovir for the full time of treatment, even if your symptoms begin to clear up after a few days. *Do not miss any doses.* However, *do not use this medicine more often or for a longer time than your doctor ordered.*

Dosing—The dose of valacyclovir will be different for different patients. *Follow your doctor's orders or the directions on the label.* The following information includes only the average doses of valacyclovir. Your dose may be different if you have kidney disease. *If your dose is different, do not change it* unless your doctor tells you to do so.

- For *oral* dosage form (tablets):
  - —For treatment of shingles:
    - Adults—1 gram three times a day for seven days.
    - Children—Use and dose must be determined by your doctor.

Missed dose—If you miss a dose of this medicine, take it as soon as possible. However, if it is almost time for your next dose, skip the missed dose and go back to your regular dosing schedule. Do not double doses.

Storage—To store this medicine:
- Keep out of the reach of children.
- Store away from heat and direct light.
- Do not store the tablets in the bathroom, near the kitchen sink, or in other damp places. Heat or moisture may cause the medicine to break down.
- Do not keep outdated medicine or medicine no longer needed. Be sure that any discarded medicine is out of the reach of children.

Precautions While Using This Medicine

If your symptoms do not improve within a few days, or if they become worse, check with your doctor.

The areas affected by shingles should be kept as clean and dry as possible. Also, wear loose-fitting clothing to avoid irritating the sores (blisters).

Side Effects of This Medicine

Along with its needed effects, a medicine may cause some unwanted effects. The following side effects may go away during treatment as your body adjusts to the medicine. However, check with your doctor if any of these side effects continue or are bothersome:

More common
Headache, nausea

Less common
Constipation, diarrhea, dizziness, loss of appetite, stomach pain, unusual tiredness or weakness, vomiting

Other side effects not listed above may also occur in some patients. If you notice any other effects, check with your doctor.

Developed: 05/28/96

VALPROIC ACID Systemic

Some commonly used brand names are:

In the U.S.—
Depacon[2]
Depakene[2]
Depakote[1]
Depakote Sprinkle[1]

In Canada—
Alti-Valproic[3]
Depakene[3]
Deproic[3]
Dom-Valproic[3]
Epival[1]
Med Valproic[3]
Novo-Valproic[3]
Penta-Valproic[3]
pms-Valproic Acid[3]
pms-Valproic Acid E.C.[3]

Note: for quick reference, the following medicines are numbered to match the corresponding brand names.

This information applies to the following medicines:
1. Divalproex (dye-VAL-pro-ex)
2. Valproate Sodium (val-PRO-ate SO-dee-um)†
3. Valproic Acid (val-PRO-ic acid)‡

†Not commercially available in Canada.
‡Generic name product may also be available in the U.S.

Description

Valproic acid, valproate sodium, and divalproex belong to the group of medicines called anticonvulsants. They are used to control certain types of seizures in the treatment of epilepsy. Valproic acid, valproate sodium, and divalproex may be used alone or with other seizure medicine. Divalproex is also used to treat the manic phase of bipolar disorder (manic-depressive illness), and to help prevent migraine headaches.

Divalproex and valproate sodium form valproic acid in the body. Therefore, the following information applies to all of these medicines.

These medicines are available only with your doctor's prescription, in the following dosage forms:

Oral
Divalproex
- Delayed-release capsules (U.S.)
- Delayed-release tablets (U.S. and Canada)

Valproic Acid
- Capsules (U.S. and Canada)
- Syrup (U.S. and Canada)

Parenteral
Valproate Sodium
- Injection (U.S.)

Before Using This Medicine

In deciding to use a medicine, the risks of taking the medicine must be weighed against the good it will do. This is a decision you and your doctor will make. For valproic acid, valproate sodium, and divalproex, the following should be considered:

Allergies—Tell your doctor if you have ever had any unusual or allergic reaction to valproic acid, valproate sodium, or divalproex. Also tell your health care professional if you are allergic to any other substances, such as foods, preservatives, or dyes.

Pregnancy—Valproic acid, valproate sodium, and divalproex have been reported to cause birth defects when taken by the mother during the first 3 months of pregnancy. Also, animal studies have shown that valproic acid, valproate sodium, and divalproex cause birth defects when taken in doses several times greater than doses used in humans. However, these medicines may be necessary to control seizures in some pregnant patients. Be sure you have discussed this with your doctor.

Breast-feeding—Valproic acid, valproate sodium, and divalproex pass into the breast milk, but their effect on the nursing baby is not known. It may be necessary for you to take another medicine or to stop breast-feeding during treatment with valproic acid, valproate sodium, or divalproex. Be sure you have discussed the risks and benefits of this medicine with your doctor.

Children—Abdominal or stomach cramps, nausea or vomiting, tiredness or weakness, and yellow eyes or skin may be especially likely to occur in children, who are usually more sensitive to the effects of these medicines. Children up to 2 years of age, those taking more than one medicine for seizure control, and children with certain other medical problems may be more likely to develop serious side effects.

Older adults—Elderly people are especially sensitive to the effects of these medicines. This may increase the chance of side effects during treatment. The dose of this medicine may be lower for older adults.

Other medicines—Although certain medicines should not be used together at all, in other cases two different medicines may be used together even if an interaction might occur. In these cases, your doctor may want to change the dose, or other precautions may be necessary. When you are taking valproic acid, valproate sodium, or divalproex, it is especially important that your health care professional knows if you are taking any of the following:

- Acetaminophen (e.g., Tylenol) (with long-term, high-dose use) or
- Amiodarone (e.g., Cordarone) or

- Anabolic steroids (nandrolone [e.g., Anabolin], oxandrolone [e.g., Anavar], oxymetholone [e.g., Anadrol], stanozolol [e.g., Winstrol]) or
- Androgens (male hormones) or
- Barbiturates or
- Carbamazepine (e.g., Tegretol) or
- Carmustine (e.g., BiCNU) or
- Dantrolene (e.g., Dantrium) or
- Daunorubicin (e.g., Cerubidine) or
- Disulfiram (e.g., Antabuse) or
- Estrogens (female hormones) or
- Etretinate (e.g., Tegison) or
- Gold salts (medicine for arthritis) or
- Mercaptopurine (e.g., Purinethol) or
- Methotrexate (e.g., Mexate) or
- Methyldopa (e.g., Aldomet) or
- Naltrexone (e.g., Trexan) (with long-term, high-dose use) or
- Phenothiazines (acetophenazine [e.g., Tindal], chlorpromazine [e.g., Thorazine], fluphenazine [e.g., Prolixin], mesoridazine [e.g., Serentil], perphenazine [e.g., Trilafon], prochlorperazine [e.g., Compazine], promazine [e.g., Sparine], promethazine [e.g., Phenergan], thioridazine [e.g., Mellaril], trifluoperazine [e.g., Stelazine], triflupromazine [e.g., Vesprin], trimeprazine [e.g., Temaril]) or
- Plicamycin (e.g., Mithracin)—There is an increased risk of serious side effects to the liver
- Central nervous system (CNS) depressants (medicine that causes drowsiness) or
- Tricyclic antidepressants (medicine for depression)—There may be an increase in CNS depressant effects
- Carbenicillin by injection (e.g., Geopen) or
- Dipyridamole (e.g., Persantine) or
- Inflammation or pain medicine, except narcotics, or
- Pentoxifylline (e.g., Trental) or
- Sulfinpyrazone (e.g., Anturane) or
- Ticarcillin (e.g., Ticar)—Valproic acid, valproate sodium, or divalproex may increase the chance of bleeding because of decreased blood clotting ability; the potential of aspirin, medicine for inflammation or pain, or sulfinpyrazone to cause stomach ulcer and bleeding may also increase the chance of bleeding in patients taking valproic acid, valproate sodium, or divalproex
- Heparin—There is an increased risk of side effects that may cause bleeding
- Mefloquine—The amount of valproic acid, valproate sodium, or divalproex that you need to take may change
- Other anticonvulsants (medicine for seizures)—There is an increased risk of seizures or other unwanted effects

Other medical problems—The presence of other medical problems may affect the use of these medicines. Make sure you tell your doctor if you have any other medical problems, especially:

- Blood disease or
- Brain disease or
- Kidney disease—There is an increased risk of serious side effects
- Liver disease—Valproic acid, valproate sodium, or divalproex may make the condition worse

Proper Use of This Medicine

For patients taking *the capsule form* of valproic acid:

- Swallow the capsule whole without chewing, crushing, or breaking. This is to prevent irritation of the mouth or throat.

For patients taking *the delayed-release capsule form* of divalproex:

- Swallow the capsule whole, or sprinkle the contents on a small amount of soft food such as applesauce or pudding and swallow without chewing.

For patients taking *the delayed-release tablet form* of divalproex:

- Swallow the tablet whole without chewing, breaking, or crushing. This is to prevent damage to the special coating that helps lessen irritation of the stomach.

For patients taking *the syrup form* of valproic acid:

- The syrup may be mixed with any liquid or added to food for a better taste.

For patients taking the oral dosage forms of vaproic acid and divalproex:

- These medicines may be taken with meals or snacks to reduce stomach upset.

This medicine must be taken exactly as directed by your doctor to prevent seizures and lessen the possibility of side effects.

Dosing—The dose of valproic acid, valproate sodium, or divalproex will be different for different patients. *Follow your doctor's orders or the directions on the label.* The following information includes only the average doses of valproic acid, valproate sodium, or divalproex. *If your dose is different, do not change it* unless your doctor tells you to do so.

The number of capsules or tablets or teaspoonfuls of syrup that you take or the number of injections you receive depends on the strength of the medicine. Also, *the number of doses you take each day, the time allowed between doses, and the length of time you take the medicine depend on the medical problem for which you are using valproic acid, valproate sodium, or divalproex.*

- If valproic acid or divalproex is the only medicine you are taking for seizures:

  —Adults and adolescents: Dose is based on body weight. The usual dose is 5 to 15 milligrams (mg) per kilogram (kg) (2.3 to 6.9 mg per pound) of body weight to start. Your doctor may increase your dose gradually every week by 5 to 10 mg per kg of body weight if needed. However, the dose is usually not more than 60 mg per kg of body weight a day. If the total dose a day is greater than 250 mg, it is usually divided into smaller doses and taken two or more times during the day.

  —Children 1 to 12 years of age: Dose is based on body weight. The usual dose is 15 to 45 mg per kg (6.9 to 20.7 mg per pound) of body weight to start. The doctor may increase the dose gradually every week by 5 to 10 mg per kg of body weight if needed.

- If you are taking more than one medicine for seizures:

  —Adults and adolescents: Dose is based on body weight. The usual dose is 10 to 30 mg per kg (4.6 to 13.8 mg per pound) of body weight to start. Your doctor may increase your dose gradually every week by 5 to 10 mg per kg of body weight if needed. If the total dose a day is greater than 250 mg, it is usually divided into smaller doses and taken two or more times during the day.

—Children 1 to 12 years of age: Dose is based on body weight. The usual dose is 30 to 100 mg per kg (13.8 to 45.5 mg per pound) of body weight.

- If you are using valproate sodium for seizures because you temporarily cannot take oral medication:

—Adults, adolescents, and children: Dose is based on body weight, and will be determined by your doctor. The dose is injected into a vein.

- If you are taking divalproex for treatment of mania:
  —Adults: At first, 750 mg a day, usually divided into smaller doses and taken two or more times during the day. Your doctor may increase your dose if needed.
  —Children: Use and dose must be determined by your doctor.
- If you are taking divalproex for prevention of migraine headaches:
  —Adults: At first, 250 mg two times a day. Your doctor may increase your dose if needed. However, the dose is usually not more than 1000 mg a day.
  —Children: Use and dose must be determined by your doctor.

Missed dose—If you miss a dose of this medicine, and your dosing schedule is:

- One dose a day—Take the missed dose as soon as possible. However, if you do not remember until the next day, skip the missed dose and go back to your regular dosing schedule. Do not double doses.
- Two or more doses a day—If you remember within 6 hours of the missed dose, take it right away. Then take the rest of the doses for that day at equally spaced times. Do not double doses.

If you have any questions about this, check with your doctor.

Storage—To store this medicine:

- Keep out of the reach of children.
- Store away from heat and direct light.
- Do not store the capsule or tablet form of this medicine in the bathroom, near the kitchen sink, or in other damp places. Heat or moisture may cause the medicine to break down.
- Keep the syrup form of this medicine from freezing.
- Do not keep outdated medicine or medicine no longer needed. Be sure that any discarded medicine is out of the reach of children.

Precautions While Using This Medicine

Your doctor should check your progress at regular visits, especially for the first few months you take this medicine. This is necessary to allow dose adjustments and to reduce any unwanted effects.

Do not stop taking this medicine without first checking with your doctor. Your doctor may want you to gradually reduce the amount you are taking before stopping completely.

Before you have any medical tests, tell the doctor in charge that you are taking this medicine. The results of the metyrapone and thyroid function tests may be affected by this medicine.

Before having any kind of surgery, dental treatment, or emergency treatment, tell the medical doctor or dentist in charge that you are taking this medicine. Valproic acid, valproate sodium, or divalproex may change the time it takes your blood to clot, which may increase the chance of bleeding. Also, taking valproic acid, valproate sodium, or divalproex together with medicines that are used during surgery or dental or emergency treatments may increase the CNS depressant effects.

Valproic acid, valproate sodium, and divalproex will add to the effects of alcohol and other CNS depressants (medicines that make you drowsy or less alert). Some examples of CNS depressants are antihistamines or medicine for hay fever, other allergies, or colds; sedatives, tranquilizers, or sleeping medicine; prescription pain medicine or narcotics; barbiturates; medicine for seizures; muscle relaxants; or anesthetics, including some dental anesthetics. *Check with your doctor before taking any of the above while you are using this medicine.*

For diabetic patients:

- This medicine may interfere with urine tests for ketones and give false-positive results.

Your doctor may want you to carry a medical identification card or bracelet stating that you are taking this medicine.

This medicine may cause some people to become drowsy or less alert than they are normally. *Make sure you know how you react to this medicine before you drive, use machines, or do anything else that could be dangerous if you are drowsy or not alert.*

Side Effects of This Medicine

Along with its needed effects, a medicine may cause some unwanted effects. Although not all of these side effects may occur, if they do occur they may need medical attention.

Check with your doctor as soon as possible if any of the following side effects occur:

Less common

Abdominal or stomach cramps (severe); behavioral, mood, or mental changes; continuous, uncontrolled back-and-forth and/or rolling eye movements; double vision; increase in seizures; loss of appetite; nausea or vomiting (continuing); spots before eyes; swelling of face; tiredness and weakness; unusual bleeding or bruising; yellow eyes or skin

Other side effects may occur that usually do not need medical attention. These side effects may go away during treatment as your body adjusts to the medicine. However, check with your doctor if any of the following side effects continue or are bothersome:

More common

Abdominal or stomach cramps (mild); change in menstrual periods; diarrhea; hair loss; indigestion; loss of appetite; nausea and vomiting; trembling of hands and arms; unusual weight loss or gain

Less common or rare

Clumsiness or unsteadiness; constipation; dizziness; drowsiness; headache; skin rash; unusual excitement, restlessness, or irritability

Other side effects not listed above may also occur in some patients. If you notice any other effects, check with your doctor.

Revised: 08/15/97

VANCOMYCIN Oral

A commonly used brand name in the U.S. and Canada is Vancocin.

Description

Vancomycin (van-koe-MYE-sin) belongs to the family of medicines called antibiotics. Antibiotics are medicines used in the treatment of infections caused by bacteria.

Vancomycin is taken by mouth to treat a certain type of diarrhea or colitis (an inflammation of the large intestine) caused by a certain type of bacteria. Vancomycin will not work for colds, flu, or other virus infections. Vancomycin may also be used for other conditions as determined by your doctor.

Vancomycin is available only with your doctor's prescription, in the following dosage forms:

Oral

- Capsules (U.S. and Canada)
- Oral solution (U.S.)

Before Using This Medicine

In deciding to use a medicine, the risks of taking the medicine must be weighed against the good it will do. This is a decision you and your doctor will make. For oral vancomycin, the following should be considered:

Allergies—Tell your doctor if you have ever had any unusual or allergic reaction to oral vancomycin. Also tell your health care professional if you are allergic to any other substances, such as foods, preservatives, or dyes.

Pregnancy—Studies with oral vancomycin have not been done in either humans or animals.

Breast-feeding—Vancomycin passes into the breast milk. However, when taken by mouth, only small amounts of vancomycin are absorbed into the mother's body. In addition, vancomycin is not absorbed very much from the digestive tract (stomach and intestines) of the nursing infant.

Children—Although there is no specific information comparing use of oral vancomycin in children with use in other age groups, this medicine is not expected to cause different side effects or problems in children than it does in adults.

Older adults—Many medicines have not been studied specifically in older people. Therefore, it may not be known whether they work exactly the same way they do in younger adults. Although there is no specific information comparing use of oral vancomycin in the elderly with use in other age groups, this medicine is not expected to cause different side effects or problems in older people than it does in younger adults.

Other medicines—Although certain medicines should not be used together at all, in other cases two different medicines may be used together even if an interaction might occur. In these cases, your doctor may want to change the dose, or other precautions may be necessary. When you are taking oral vancomycin, it is especially important that your health care professional know if you are taking any of the following:

- Cholestyramine (e.g., Questran) or
- Colestipol (e.g., Colestid)—Use of these medicines with oral vancomycin may decrease the effects of oral vancomycin; oral vancomycin and these medicines should be taken several hours apart

Other medical problems—The presence of other medical problems may affect the use of oral vancomycin. Make sure you tell your doctor if you have any other medical problems, especially:

- Kidney disease, severe, or
- Other inflammatory bowel disorders—Patients with these medical problems may have an increased chance of side effects

Proper Use of This Medicine

For patients taking the *oral liquid form* of vancomycin:

- Use a specially marked measuring spoon or other device to measure each dose accurately. The average household teaspoon may not hold the right amount of liquid.
- Do not use after the expiration date on the label. The medicine may not work properly after that date. Check with your pharmacist if you have any questions about this.

To help clear up your colitis completely, *keep taking this medicine for the full time of treatment,* even if you begin to feel better after a few days. If you stop taking this medicine too soon, your symptoms may return. *Do not miss any doses.*

Dosing—The dose of oral vancomycin will be different for different patients. *Follow your doctor's orders or the directions on the label.* The following information includes only the average doses of oral vancomycin. *If your dose is different, do not change it* unless your doctor tells you to do so.

The number of capsules or teaspoonfuls of solution that you take depends on the strength of the medicine. Also, *the number of doses you take each day, the time allowed between doses, and the length of time you take the medicine depend on the medical problem for which you are taking oral vancomycin.*

- For *oral* dosage forms (capsules, oral solution):
  —For treatment of colitis or severe diarrhea:
    - Adults and teenagers—125 to 500 milligrams (mg) every six hours for five to ten days.
    - Children—Dose is based on body weight and must be determined by the doctor. The usual dose is 10 mg per kilogram (kg) of body weight (4.5 mg per pound), up to 125 mg. This dose is taken every six hours for five to ten days.

Missed dose—If you miss a dose of this medicine, take it as soon as possible. However, if it is almost time for your next dose, skip the missed dose and go back to your regular dosing schedule. Do not double doses.

Storage—To store this medicine:
- Keep out of the reach of children.
- Store away from heat and direct light.
- Do not store the capsule form of this medicine in the bathroom, near the kitchen sink, or in other damp places. Heat or moisture may cause the medicine to break down.
- Store the oral liquid form of vancomycin in the refrigerator because heat will cause this medicine to break down. However, keep the medicine from freezing. Follow the directions on the label.
- Do not keep outdated medicine or medicine no longer needed. Be sure that any discarded medicine is out of the reach of children.

Precautions While Using This Medicine

It is important that your doctor check your progress during and after treatment. This is to make sure that the colitis is cleared up completely.

If the symptoms of your colitis do not improve within a few days, or if they become worse, check with your doctor.

If your doctor orders cholestyramine or colestipol for your colitis, do not take vancomycin by mouth within 3 to 4 hours of taking either of these medicines. To do so may keep vancomycin from working properly.

If you are taking this medicine for diarrhea caused by other antibiotics, do not take any other diarrhea medicine without first checking with your health care professional. Medicines for diarrhea may make your diarrhea worse or make it last longer.

Side Effects of This Medicine

Along with its needed effects, a medicine may cause some unwanted effects. Although not all of these side effects may occur, if they do occur they may need medical attention.

Check with your doctor immediately if the following side effect occurs:

Rare
Skin rash

Other side effects may occur that usually do not need medical attention. These side effects may go away during treatment as your body adjusts to the medicine. However, check with your doctor if any of the following side effects continue or are bothersome:

More common
Bitter or unpleasant taste; mouth irritation; nausea or vomiting

Other side effects not listed above may also occur in some patients. If you notice any other effects, check with your doctor.

Revised: 08/10/94

VANCOMYCIN Systemic

Some commonly used brand names are:

In the U.S.—
Lyphocin
Vancocin
Vancoled

Generic name product may also be available.

In Canada—
Vancocin

Description

Vancomycin (van-koe-MYE-sin) belongs to the family of medicines called antibiotics. Antibiotics are medicines used in the treatment of infections caused by bacteria. They work by killing bacteria or preventing their growth. Vancomycin will not work for colds, flu, or other virus infections.

Vancomycin is used to treat infections in many different parts of the body. It is sometimes given with other antibiotics. Vancomycin is also used in patients with heart valve disease (e.g., rheumatic fever) or prosthetic (artificial) heart valves who are allergic to penicillin. This medicine is used to prevent endocarditis (inflammation of the lining of the heart) in these patients who are having dental work or surgery done on the upper respiratory tract (for example, nose or throat). Vancomycin may also be used for other conditions as determined by your doctor.

Vancomycin given by injection is usually used for serious infections in which other medicines may not work. However, this medicine may also cause some serious side effects, including damage to your hearing and kidneys. These side effects may be more likely to occur in elderly patients. You and your doctor should talk about the good this medicine will do as well as the risks of receiving it.

Vancomycin is available only with your doctor's prescription, in the following dosage form:

Parenteral
- Injection (U.S. and Canada)

Before Receiving This Medicine

In deciding to use a medicine, the risks of taking the medicine must be weighed against the good it will do. This is a decision you and your doctor will make. For vancomycin, the following should be considered:

Allergies—Tell your doctor if you have ever had any unusual or allergic reaction to vancomycin. Also tell your health care professional if you are allergic to any other substances, such as foods, preservatives, or dyes.

Pregnancy—Vancomycin has not been reported to cause hearing loss or kidney damage in the infants of women given vancomycin during their second or third trimesters of pregnancy. It has also not been reported to cause birth defects in animal studies.

Breast-feeding—Vancomycin passes into breast milk. However, this medicine has not been reported to cause problems in nursing babies.

Children—Vancomycin can cause serious side effects in any patient. Therefore, it is especially important that you discuss with the child's doctor the good that this medicine will do as well as the risks of using it.

Older adults—Elderly people may be especially sensitive to the effects of vancomycin. This may increase the chance of hearing or kidney damage.

Other medicines—Although certain medicines should not be used together at all, in other cases two different medicines may be used together even if an interaction might occur. In these cases, your doctor may want to change the dose, or other precautions may be necessary. When you are receiving vancomycin, it is especially important that your health care professional knows if you are taking any of the following:

- Aminoglycosides by injection (amikacin [e.g., Amikin], gentamicin [e.g., Garamycin], kanamycin [e.g., Kantrex], neomycin [e.g., Mycifradin], netilmicin [e.g., Netromycin], streptomycin, tobramycin [e.g., Nebcin]) or
- Amphotericin B by injection (e.g., Fungizone) or
- Bacitracin by injection or
- Bumetanide by injection (e.g., Bumex) or
- Capreomycin (e.g., Capastat) or
- Cisplatin (e.g., Platinol) or
- Cyclosporine (e.g., Sandimmune) or
- Ethacrynic acid by injection (e.g., Edecrin) or
- Furosemide by injection (e.g., Lasix) or
- Paromomycin (e.g., Humatin) or
- Polymyxins, especially colistimethate (e.g., Coly-Mycin M) and polymyxin B (e.g., Aerosporin) or
- Streptozocin (e.g., Zanosar)—Use of these medicines with vancomycin may increase the chance of side effects

Other medical problems—The presence of other medical problems may affect the use of vancomycin. Make sure you tell your doctor if you have any other medical problems, especially:

- Kidney disease or
- Loss of hearing, or deafness, history of—Patients with kidney disease or a history of hearing loss or deafness may have an increased chance of side effects

Proper Use of This Medicine

Some medicines given by injection may sometimes be given at home to patients who do not need to be in the hospital for the full time of treatment. If you are receiving this medicine at home, *make sure you clearly understand and carefully follow your doctor's instructions.*

To help clear up your infection completely, *vancomycin must be given for the full time of treatment,* even if you begin to feel better after a few days. Also, this medicine works best when there is a constant amount in the blood or stool. To help keep the amount constant, vancomycin must be given on a regular schedule.

Dosing—The dose of vancomycin will be different for different patients. *Follow your doctor's orders or the directions on the label.* The following information includes only the average doses of vancomycin. *If your dose is different, do not change it* unless your doctor tells you to do so.

- For *injection* dosage form:
  - —For the prevention of heart infection in patients who have heart valve problems and are allergic to penicillin:
    - Adults and teenagers—1 gram injected into a vein one hour before dental work or surgery, and 1 gram injected into a vein 8 hours after the first dose.
    - Children—20 milligrams (mg) per kilogram (kg) (9.1 mg per pound) of body weight injected into a vein one hour before a dental procedure or surgery, and 20 mg per kg (9.1 mg per pound) of body weight injected into a vein 8 hours after the first dose.
  - —For treatment of bacterial infections:
    - Adults and teenagers—7.5 mg per kg (3.4 mg per pound) of body weight, or 500 mg, injected into a vein every six hours; or 15 mg per kg (6.8 mg per pound) of body weight, or 1 gram, injected into a vein every twelve hours.
    - Children—10 mg per kg (4.5 mg per pound) of body weight injected into a vein every six hours; or 20 mg per kg (9.1 mg per pound) of body weight injected into a vein every twelve hours.
    - Newborns and infants 1 week to 1 month of age—15 mg per kg (6.8 mg per pound) of body weight injected into a vein at first, then 10 mg per kg (4.5 mg per pound) of body weight injected into a vein every eight hours.
    - Newborns up to 1 week of age—15 mg per kg (6.8 mg per pound) of body weight injected into a vein at first, then 10 mg per kg (4.5 mg per pound) of body weight injected into a vein every twelve hours.

Side Effects of This Medicine

Along with its needed effects, a medicine may cause some unwanted effects. Although not all of these side effects may occur, if they do occur they may need medical attention.

Check with your health care professional immediately if any of the following side effects occur:

Less common

Change in the frequency of urination or amount of urine; difficulty in breathing; drowsiness; increased thirst; loss of appetite; nausea or vomiting; weakness

Rare

Loss of hearing; ringing or buzzing or a feeling of fullness in the ears

Note: The above side effects may also occur up to several weeks after you stop receiving this medicine.

Symptoms of "red-neck syndrome"—Rare

Chills or fever; fainting; fast heartbeat; itching; nausea or vomiting; rash or redness of the face, base of neck, upper body, back, and arms; tingling; unpleasant taste

Note: Symptoms of the "red-neck syndrome" are more common when vancomycin is given by direct or rapid injection.

The above side effects, except the "red-neck syndrome," are more likely to occur in the elderly, who are usually more sensitive to the effects of vancomycin.

Other side effects not listed above may also occur in some patients. If you notice any other effects, check with your doctor.

Revised: 09/20/92
Interim revision: 03/28/94; 03/28/95

VASOPRESSIN Systemic

Some commonly used brand names are:

In the U.S.—

Pitressin

Generic name product may also be available.

In Canada—

Pitressin

Pressyn

Description

Vasopressin (vay-soe-PRESS-in) is a hormone naturally produced by your body. It is necessary to maintain good health. Lack of vasopressin causes your body to lose too much water.

Vasopressin is used to control the frequent urination, increased thirst, and loss of water associated with diabetes insipidus (water diabetes).

Vasopressin also may be used for other conditions as determined by your doctor.

This medicine is available only with your doctor's prescription, in the following dosage form:

Parenteral

- Injection (U.S. and Canada)

Before Receiving This Medicine

In deciding to use a medicine, the risks of taking the medicine must be weighed against the good it will do. This is a decision you and your doctor will make. For vasopressin, the following should be considered:

Allergies—Tell your doctor if you have ever had any unusual or allergic reaction to vasopressin. Also tell your health care professional if you are allergic to any other substances, such as foods, preservatives, or dyes.

Pregnancy—Vasopressin has not been shown to cause birth defects or other problems in humans.

Breast-feeding—Vasopressin has not been reported to cause problems in nursing babies.

Children—Children may be especially sensitive to the effects of vasopressin. This may increase the chance of side effects during treatment.

Older adults—Many medicines have not been studied specifically in older people. Therefore, it may not be known whether they work exactly the same way they do in younger adults or if they cause different side effects or problems in older people. Although there is no specific information comparing the use of vasopressin in the elderly with use in other age groups, the elderly may be more sensitive to its effects.

Other medicines—Although certain medicines should not be used together at all, in other cases two different medicines may be used together even if an interaction might occur. In these cases, your doctor may want to change the dose, or other precautions may be necessary. Tell your health care professional if you are taking any other prescription or nonprescription (over-the-counter [OTC]) medicine.

Other medical problems—The presence of other medical problems may affect the use of vasopressin. Make sure you tell your doctor if you have any other medical problems, especially:

- Asthma or
- Epilepsy or
- Heart disease or
- Kidney disease or
- Migraine headaches—If fluid retention (keeping more body water) caused by vasopressin occurs too fast, these conditions may be worsened
- Heart or blood vessel disease—Vasopressin can cause chest pain or a heart attack; it can also increase blood pressure

Proper Use of This Medicine

Use this medicine only as directed. Do not use more of it and do not use it more often than your doctor ordered. To do so may increase the chance of side effects.

Dosing—The dose of vasopressin will be different for different patients. *Follow your doctor's orders or the directions on the label.* The following information includes only the average doses of vasopressin. *If your dose is different, do not change it* unless your doctor tells you to do so.

- For *injection* dosage form:
  —For controlling water loss when urinating too often (diabetes insipidus):
    - Adults and teenagers—5 to 10 Units injected into a muscle or under the skin two or three times a day as needed.
    - Children—2.5 to 10 Units injected into a muscle or under the skin three or four times a day.

Missed dose—If you miss a dose of this medicine, use it as soon as possible. However, if it is almost time for your next dose, skip the missed dose and go back to your regular dosing schedule. Do not double doses.

Storage—To store this medicine:
- Keep out of the reach of children.
- Store away from heat and direct light.
- Keep from freezing.
- Do not keep outdated medicine or medicine no longer needed. Be sure that any discarded medicine is out of the reach of children.

Side Effects of This Medicine

Along with its needed effects, a medicine may cause some unwanted effects. Although not all of these effects may occur, if they do occur they may need medical attention.

Check with your doctor immediately if any of the following side effects occur since they may be signs or symptoms of an allergic reaction or overdose:

Rare

Chest pain; coma; confusion; convulsions (seizures); drowsiness; fever; headache (continuing); problems with urination; redness of skin; skin rash, hives, or itching; swelling of face, feet, hands, or mouth; weight gain; wheezing or troubled breathing

Other side effects may occur that usually do not need medical attention. These side effects may go away during treatment as your body adjusts to the medicine. However, check with your doctor if any of the following side effects continue or are bothersome:

Less common

Abdominal or stomach cramps; belching; diarrhea; dizziness or lightheadedness; increased sweating; increased urge for bowel movement; nausea or vomiting; pale skin; passage of gas; "pounding" in head; trembling; white-colored area around mouth

Other side effects not listed above may also occur in some patients. If you notice any other effects, check with your doctor.

Revised: 08/26/93
Interim revision: 06/30/94

VENLAFAXINE Systemic

A commonly used brand name in the U.S. and Canada is Effexor.

Description

Venlafaxine (ven-la-FAX-een) is used to treat mental depression.

This medicine is available only with your doctor's prescription, in the following dosage form:

Oral
- Tablets (U.S. and Canada)

Before Using This Medicine

In deciding to use a medicine, the risks of taking the medicine must be weighed against the good it will do. This is a decision you and your doctor will make. For venlafaxine, the following should be considered:

Allergies—Tell your doctor if you have ever had any unusual or allergic reaction to venlafaxine. Also tell your health care professional if you are allergic to any other substances, such as foods, preservatives, or dyes.

Pregnancy—Studies have not been done in pregnant women. However, studies in animals have shown that venlafaxine may cause decreased survival rates of offspring, when given in doses many times the usual human dose. Before taking this medicine, make sure your doctor knows if you are pregnant or if you may become pregnant.

Breast-feeding—It is not known whether venlafaxine passes into breast milk. Although most medicines pass into breast milk in small amounts, many of them may be used safely while breast-feeding. Mothers who are taking this medicine and who wish to breast-feed should discuss this with their doctor.

Children—Studies on this medicine have been done only in adult patients, and there is no specific information comparing use of venlafaxine in children with use in other age groups.

Older adults—In studies done to date that have included elderly people, venlafaxine did not cause different side effects or problems in older people than it did in younger adults.

Other medicines—Although certain medicines should not be used together at all, in other cases two different medicines may be used together even if an interaction might occur. In these cases, your doctor may want to change the dose, or other precautions may be necessary. When you are taking venlafaxine, it is especially important that your health care professional know if you are taking the following:

- Monoamine oxidase (MAO) inhibitors (furazolidone [e.g., Furoxone], isocarboxazid [e.g., Marplan], phenelzine [e.g., Nardil], procarbazine [e.g., Matulane], selegiline [e.g., Eldepryl], tranylcypromine [e.g., Parnate])—Taking venlafaxine while you are taking or within 2 weeks of taking MAO inhibitors may cause confusion, agitation, restlessness, stomach or intestinal symptoms, sudden high body temperature, extremely high blood pressure, and severe convulsions; up to 14 days should be allowed between stopping treatment with one medicine and starting treatment with the other

Other medical problems—The presence of other medical problems may affect the use of venlafaxine. Make sure you tell your doctor if you have any other medical problems, especially:

- Drug abuse or dependence (or history of)—Because venlafaxine is a new medicine, it is not known if it could become habit-forming, causing mental or physical dependence
- Heart disease or
- High or low blood pressure—Venlafaxine may make these conditions worse
- Kidney disease (severe) or
- Liver disease (severe)—Higher blood levels of venlafaxine may occur, increasing the chance of side effects
- Seizures (history of)—The risk of seizures may be increased

Proper Use of This Medicine

Take this medicine only as directed by your doctor to benefit your condition as much as possible. Do not take more of it, do not take it more often, and do not take it for a longer time than your doctor ordered.

You may have to take venlafaxine for up to 4 weeks or longer before you begin to feel better. Your doctor should check your progress at regular visits during this time.

Venlafaxine should be taken with food or on a full stomach to lessen the chance of stomach upset. However, if your doctor tells you to take the medicine a certain way, take it exactly as directed.

Dosing—The dose of venlafaxine will be different for different patients. *Follow your doctor's orders or the directions on the label.* The following information includes only the average doses of venlafaxine. *If your dose is different, do not change it* unless your doctor tells you to do so.

The number of tablets that you take depends on the strength of the medicine. Also, *the number of doses you take each day, the time allowed between doses, and the length of time you take the medicine depend on your special needs.*

- *For oral* dosage form (tablets):
  - —For mental depression:
    - Adults—At first, 75 milligrams (mg) a day, taken in smaller doses two or three times during the day.Your doctor may increase your dose if needed. However, the dose is usually not more than 375 mg a day.
    - Children up to 18 years of age—Use and dose must be determined by your doctor.

Missed dose—If you miss a dose of this medicine, take it as soon as possible. However, if it is within 2 hours of your next dose, skip the missed dose and go back to your regular dosing schedule. Do not double doses.

Storage—To store this medicine:

- Keep out of the reach of children.
- Store away from heat and direct light.
- Do not store in the bathroom, near the kitchen sink, or in other damp places. Heat or moisture may cause the medicine to break down.
- Keep the medicine from freezing. Do not refrigerate.
- Do not keep outdated medicine or medicine no longer needed. Be sure that any discarded medicine is out of the reach of children.

Precautions While Using This Medicine

It is important that your doctor check your progress at regular visits, to allow for changes in your dose and to help reduce any side effects.

Do not stop taking this medicine without first checking with your doctor. Your doctor may want you to gradually reduce the amount you are taking before stopping completely. This is to decrease the chance of side effects.

This medicine could possibly add to the effects of alcohol and other CNS depressants (medicines that may make you drowsy or less alert). Some examples of CNS depressants are antihistamines or medicine for hay fever, other allergies, or colds; sedatives, tranquilizers, or sleeping medicine; prescription pain medicine or narcotics; barbiturates; medicine for seizures; muscle relaxants; or anesthetics, including some dental anesthetics. *Check with your doctor before taking any of the above while you are using this medicine.*

Venlafaxine may cause some people to become drowsy or have blurred vision. *Make sure you know how you react to this medicine before you drive, use machines, or do anything else that could be dangerous if you are not alert or able to see clearly.*

Dizziness, lightheadedness, or fainting may occur, especially when you get up from a lying or sitting position. Getting up slowly may help. If this problem continues or gets worse, check with your doctor.

This medicine may cause dryness of the mouth. For temporary relief, use sugarless gum or candy, melt bits of ice in your mouth, or use a saliva substitute. However, if your mouth continues to feel dry for more than 2 weeks, check with your medical doctor or dentist. Continuing dryness of the mouth may increase the chance of dental disease, including tooth decay, gum disease, and fungus infections.

Side Effects of This Medicine

Along with its needed effects, a medicine may cause some unwanted effects. Although not all of these side effects may occur, if they do occur they may need medical attention.

Check with your doctor as soon as possible if any of the following side effects occur:

More common

Changes in vision, such as blurred vision; decrease in sexual desire or ability; headache

Less common

Chest pain; fast or pounding heartbeat; itching or skin rash; mood or mental changes; problems in urinating; ringing or buzzing in ears

Rare
Convulsions (seizures); lightheadedness or fainting; lockjaw; menstrual changes; swelling of feet or lower legs; talking, feeling, and acting with excitement and activity you cannot control; trouble in breathing

Symptoms of overdose
Extreme drowsiness; extreme tiredness or weakness

This medicine may also cause the following side effect that your doctor will watch for:

Less common
High blood pressure

Other side effects may occur that usually do not need medical attention. These side effects may go away during treatment as your body adjusts to the medicine. However, check with your doctor if any of the following side effects continue or are bothersome:

More common
Abnormal dreams; anxiety or nervousness; change in your sense of taste; chills; constipation; diarrhea; dizziness; drowsiness; dryness of mouth; heartburn; increased sweating; loss of appetite; nausea; runny nose; stomach pain or gas; tingling, burning, or prickly sensations; tremor; trouble in sleeping; unusual tiredness or weakness; vomiting; weight loss

Less common
Twitching; yawning

After you stop using this medicine, your body may need time to adjust. The length of time this takes depends on the amount of medicine you were using and how long you used it. During this period of time check with your doctor if you notice any of the following side effects:

Dizziness; headache; nausea; nervousness; trouble in sleeping; unusual tiredness or weakness

Other side effects not listed above may also occur in some patients. If you notice any other effects, check with your doctor.

Developed: 05/24/95

VIDARABINE Ophthalmic

A commonly used brand name in the U.S. and Canada is Vira-A. Other commonly used names are arabinoside and ara-A.

Description

Vidarabine (vye-DARE-a-been) ophthalmic preparations are used to treat virus infections of the eye.

Vidarabine is available only with your doctor's prescription, in the following dosage form:

Ophthalmic
- Ophthalmic ointment (U.S. and Canada)

Before Using This Medicine

In deciding to use a medicine, the risks of using the medicine must be weighed against the good it will do. This is a decision you and your doctor will make. For vidarabine, the following should be considered:

Allergies—Tell your doctor if you have ever had any unusual or allergic reaction to vidarabine. Also tell your health care professional if you are allergic to any other substances, such as preservatives.

Pregnancy—Studies have not been done in humans. Studies in rats and rabbits have shown that vidarabine, given by injection, causes birth defects. In addition, studies in rabbits have shown that vidarabine, applied as a 10% ointment to the skin, may cause birth defects or other problems. However, these doses are much higher than those used in the eyes of humans. Therefore, the chance that vidarabine ophthalmic ointment would cause birth defects or other problems in humans is very small.

Breast-feeding—It is not known whether vidarabine, applied to the eyes, is absorbed into the body and passes into the breast milk. Although most medicines pass into breast milk in small amounts, many of them may be used safely while breast-feeding. Mothers who are taking this medicine and who wish to breast-feed should discuss this with their doctor.

Children—Although there is no specific information comparing use of vidarabine in children with use in other age groups, it is not expected to cause different side effects or problems in children than it does in adults.

Older adults—Many medicines have not been studied specifically in older people. Therefore, it may not be known whether they work exactly the same way they do in younger adults or if they cause different side effects or problems in older people. There is no specific information comparing use of vidarabine in the elderly with use in other age groups.

Other medicines—Although certain medicines should not be used together at all, in other cases two different medicines may be used together even if an interaction might occur. In these cases, your doctor may want to change the dose, or other precautions may be necessary. Tell your health care professional if you are using any other prescription or nonprescription (over-the-counter [OTC]) medicine in your eyes.

Proper Use of This Medicine

To use:
- First, wash your hands. Then pull the lower eyelid away from the eye to form a pouch. Squeeze a thin strip of ointment into the pouch. A 1.25-cm (approximately 1/2-inch) strip of ointment is usually enough unless otherwise directed by your doctor. Gently close the eyes and keep them closed for 1 or 2 minutes to allow the medicine to come into contact with the infection.
- To keep the medicine as germ-free as possible, do not touch the applicator tip to any surface (including

the eye). After using vidarabine eye ointment, wipe the tip of the ointment tube with a clean tissue and keep the tube tightly closed.

Do not use this medicine more often or for a longer time than your doctor ordered. To do so may cause problems in the eyes. If you have any questions about this, check with your doctor.

To help clear up your infection completely, *keep using this medicine for the full time of treatment,* even if your symptoms have disappeared. *Do not miss any doses.*

Dosing—The dose of ophthalmic vidarabine will be different for different patients. *Follow your doctor's orders or the directions on the label.* The following information includes only the average doses of ophthalmic vidarabine. *If your dose is different, do not change it* unless your doctor tells you to do so.

The number of doses you use each day, the time allowed between doses, and the length of time you use the medicine depend on the medical problem for which you are using ophthalmic vidarabine.

- For *ophthalmic ointment* dosage forms:
  - —For virus eye infection:
    - Adults and children—Use in each eye every three hours (five times a day). After healing has occurred, the dose may be reduced to two times a day for seven days more.

Missed dose—If you miss a dose of this medicine, apply it as soon as possible. However, if it is almost time for your next dose, skip the missed dose and go back to your regular dosing schedule.

Storage—To store this medicine:

- Keep out of the reach of children.
- Store away from heat and direct light.
- Keep the medicine from freezing.
- Do not keep outdated medicine or medicine no longer needed. Be sure that any discarded medicine is out of the reach of children.

Precautions While Using This Medicine

After application, eye ointments usually cause your vision to blur for a few minutes.

It is very important that you keep your appointments with your doctor. If your symptoms become worse, check with your doctor sooner.

This medicine may cause your eyes to become more sensitive to light than they are normally. Wearing sunglasses and avoiding too much exposure to bright light may help lessen the discomfort.

Side Effects of This Medicine

Along with its needed effects, a medicine may cause some unwanted effects. Although not all of these side effects may occur, if they do occur they may need medical attention.

Check with your doctor as soon as possible if any of the following side effects occur:

Increased sensitivity of eyes to light; itching, redness, swelling, pain, burning, or other sign of irritation not present before use of this medicine

Other side effects may occur that usually do not need medical attention. These side effects may go away during treatment as your body adjusts to the medicine. However, check with your doctor if either of the following side effects continues or is bothersome:

Excess flow of tears; feeling of something in the eye

Other side effects not listed above may also occur in some patients. If you notice any other effects, check with your doctor.

Revised: 07/01/93

VINBLASTINE Systemic

Some commonly used brand names are:

In the U.S.—

Velban
Velsar

Generic name product may also be available.

In Canada—

Velbe

Description

Vinblastine (vin-BLAS-teen) belongs to the group of medicines known as antineoplastic agents. It is used to treat some kinds of cancer as well as some noncancerous conditions.

Vinblastine interferes with the growth of cancer cells, which are eventually destroyed. Since the growth of normal body cells may also be affected by vinblastine, other effects will also occur. Some of these may be serious and must be reported to your doctor. Other effects, such as hair loss, may not be serious but may cause concern. Some effects do not occur for months or years after the medicine is used.

Before you begin treatment with vinblastine, you and your doctor should talk about the good this medicine will do as well as the risks of using it.

Vinblastine is to be administered only by or under the immediate supervision of your doctor. It is available in the following dosage form:

Parenteral

- Injection (U.S. and Canada)

Before Using This Medicine

In deciding to use a medicine, the risks of taking the medicine must be weighed against the good it will do. This is a decision you and your doctor will make. For vinblastine, the following should be considered:

Allergies—Tell your doctor if you have ever had any unusual or allergic reaction to vinblastine.

Pregnancy—Tell your doctor if you are pregnant or if you intend to have children. This medicine may cause birth defects if either the male or female is taking it at the time of conception or if it is taken during pregnancy. In addition, many cancer medicines may cause sterility which could be permanent. Although sterility has not been reported with this medicine, vinblastine may interfere with production of sperm and the possibility should be kept in mind.

Be sure that you have discussed this with your doctor before receiving this medicine. It is best to use some kind of birth control while you are receiving vinblastine. Tell your doctor right away if you think you have become pregnant while receiving vinblastine.

Breast-feeding—Tell your doctor if you are breast-feeding or if you intend to breast-feed during treatment with this medicine. Because vinblastine may cause serious side effects, breast-feeding is generally not recommended while you are receiving it.

Children—This medicine has been tested in children and has not been shown to cause different side effects or problems than it does in adults.

Older adults—Many medicines have not been tested in older people. Therefore, it may not be known whether they work exactly the same way they do in younger adults or if they cause different side effects or problems in older people. There is no specific information about the use of vinblastine in the elderly.

Other medicines—Although certain medicines should not be used together at all, in other cases two different medicines may be used together even if an interaction might occur. In these cases, your doctor may want to change the dose, or other precautions may be necessary. When you are receiving vinblastine, it is especially important that your health care professional know if you are taking any of the following:

- Amphotericin B by injection (e.g., Fungizone) or
- Antithyroid agents (medicine for overactive thyroid) or
- Azathioprine (e.g., Imuran) or
- Chloramphenicol (e.g., Chloromycetin) or
- Colchicine or
- Flucytosine (e.g., Ancobon) or
- Interferon (e.g., Intron A, Roferon-A) or
- Plicamycin (e.g., Mithracin) or
- Zidovudine (e.g., Retrovir) or
- If you have ever been treated with x-rays or cancer medicines—Vinblastine may increase the effects of these medicines or radiation therapy on the blood

- Probenecid (e.g., Benemid) or
- Sulfinpyrazone (e.g., Anturane)—Vinblastine may increase the concentration of uric acid in the blood, which these medicines are used to lower

Other medical problems—The presence of other medical problems may affect the use of vinblastine. Make sure you tell your doctor if you have any other medical problems, especially:

- Chickenpox (including recent exposure) or
- Herpes zoster (shingles)—Risk of severe disease affecting other parts of the body

- Gout (history of) or
- Kidney stones (history of)—Vinblastine may increase levels of uric acid in the body, which can cause gout or kidney stones

- Infection—Vinblastine can reduce immunity to infection

- Liver disease—Effects may be increased because of slower removal of vinblastine from the body

Proper Use of This Medicine

Vinblastine is sometimes given together with certain other medicines. If you are using a combination of medicines, it is important that you receive each one at the proper time. If you are taking some of these medicines by mouth, ask your health care professional to help you plan a way to take them at the right times.

While you are using this medicine, your doctor may want you to drink extra fluids so that you will pass more urine. This will help prevent kidney problems and keep your kidneys working well.

Vinblastine sometimes causes nausea and vomiting. However, it is very important that you continue to receive the medicine, even if you begin to feel ill. Ask your health care professional for ways to lessen these effects.

Dosing—The dose of vinblastine will be different for different patients. The dose that is used may depend on a number of things, including what the medicine is being used for, the patient's weight or size, and whether or not other medicines are also being taken. *If you are receiving vinblastine at home, follow your doctor's orders or the directions on the label.* If you have any questions about the proper dose of vinblastine, ask your doctor.

Precautions While Using This Medicine

It is very important that your doctor check your progress at regular visits to make sure that this medicine is working properly and to check for unwanted effects.

While you are being treated with vinblastine, and after you stop treatment with it, *do not have any immunizations (vaccinations) without your doctor's approval.* Vinblastine may lower your body's resistance and there is a chance you might get the infection the immunization is meant to prevent. Other people living in your household should not take oral polio vaccine since there is a chance they could pass the polio virus on to you. Also, avoid persons who have taken oral polio vaccine. Do not get close to them, and do not stay in the same room with them for very long. If you cannot take these precautions, you should consider wearing a protective face mask that covers the nose and mouth.

Vinblastine can temporarily lower the number of white blood cells in your blood, increasing the chance of getting an infection. It can also lower the number of platelets,

which are necessary for proper blood clotting. If this occurs, there are certain precautions you can take, especially when your blood count is low, to reduce the risk of infection or bleeding:

- If you can, avoid people with infections. *Check with your doctor immediately* if you think you are getting an infection or if you get a fever or chills, cough or hoarseness, lower back or side pain, or painful or difficult urination.
- *Check with your doctor immediately* if you notice any unusual bleeding or bruising; black, tarry stools; blood in urine or stools; or pinpoint red spots on your skin.
- Be careful when using a regular toothbrush, dental floss, or toothpick. Your medical doctor, dentist, or nurse may recommend other ways to clean your teeth and gums. Check with your medical doctor before having any dental work done.
- Do not touch your eyes or the inside of your nose unless you have just washed your hands and have not touched anything else in the meantime.
- Be careful not to cut yourself when you are using sharp objects such as a safety razor or fingernail or toenail cutters.
- Avoid contact sports or other situations where bruising or injury could occur.

If vinblastine accidentally seeps out of the vein into which it is injected, it may damage the skin and cause some scarring. *Tell the doctor or nurse right away if you notice redness, pain, or swelling at the place of injection.*

Side Effects of This Medicine

Along with their needed effects medicines like vinblastine can sometimes cause unwanted effects such as blood problems, loss of hair, and other side effects. These and others are described below. Also, because of the way these medicines act on the body, there is a chance that they might cause other unwanted effects that may not occur until months or years after the medicine is used. These delayed effects may include certain types of cancer, such as leukemia. Discuss these possible effects with your doctor.

Although not all of these side effects may occur, if they do occur they may need medical attention.

Check with your doctor or nurse immediately if any of the following side effects occur:

Less common

Cough or hoarseness; fever or chills; lower back or side pain; painful or difficult urination; pain or redness at place of injection

Rare

Black, tarry stools; blood in urine or stools; pinpoint red spots on skin; unusual bleeding or bruising

Check with your health care professional as soon as possible if any of the following side effects occur:

Less common

Joint pain; sores in mouth and on lips; swelling of feet or lower legs

Rare

Difficulty in walking; dizziness; double vision; drooping eyelids; headache; jaw pain; mental depression; numbness or tingling in fingers and toes; pain in fingers and toes; pain in testicles; weakness

Other side effects may occur that usually do not need medical attention. These side effects may go away during treatment as your body adjusts to the medicine. Also, your health care professional may be able to tell you about ways to prevent or reduce some of these side effects. Check with your health care professional if any of the following side effects continue or are bothersome or if you have any questions about them:

Less common

Muscle pain; nausea and vomiting

This medicine often causes a temporary loss of hair. After treatment with vinblastine has ended, or sometimes even during treatment, normal hair growth should return.

Other side effects not listed above may also occur in some patients. If you notice any other effects, check with your doctor.

Revised: 09/90
Interim revision: 08/02/93; 07/05/94

VINCRISTINE Systemic

Some commonly used brand names are:

In the U.S.—

Oncovin
Vincrex
Vincasar PFS

Generic name product may also be available.

In Canada—

Oncovin

Description

Vincristine (vin-KRIS-teen) belongs to the group of medicines known as antineoplastic agents. It is used to treat some kinds of cancer as well as some noncancerous conditions.

Vincristine interferes with the growth of cancer cells, which are eventually destroyed. Since the growth of normal body cells may also be affected by vincristine, other effects will also occur. Some of these may be serious and must be reported to your doctor. Other effects, such as hair loss, may not be serious but may cause concern. Some effects may not occur for months or years after the medicine is used.

Before you begin treatment with vincristine, you and your doctor should talk about the good this medicine will do as well as the risks of using it.

Vincristine is to be administered only by or under the immediate supervision of your doctor. It is available in the following dosage form:

Parenteral
- Injection (U.S. and Canada)

Before Using This Medicine

In deciding to use a medicine, the risks of taking the medicine must be weighed against the good it will do. This is a decision you and your doctor will make. For vincristine, the following should be considered:

Allergies—Tell your doctor if you have ever had any unusual or allergic reaction to vincristine.

Pregnancy—Tell your doctor if you are pregnant or if you intend to have children. There is a chance that this medicine may cause birth defects if either the male or female is taking it at the time of conception or if it is taken during pregnancy. Vincristine causes birth defects and death of the fetus in animals. In addition, many cancer medicines may cause sterility, which could be permanent. Although sterility has not been reported with this medicine, the possibility should be kept in mind.

Be sure that you have discussed this with your doctor before receiving this medicine. It is best to use some kind of birth control while you are receiving vincristine. Tell your doctor right away if you think you have become pregnant while receiving vincristine.

Breast-feeding—Tell your doctor if you are breast-feeding or if you intend to breast-feed during treatment with this medicine. Because vincristine may cause serious side effects, breast-feeding is generally not recommended while you are receiving it.

Children—This medicine has been tested in children and has not been shown to cause different side effects or problems than it does in adults.

Older adults—Nervous system effects may be more likely to occur in the elderly, who are usually more sensitive to the effects of vincristine.

Other medicines—Although certain medicines should not be used together at all, in other cases two different medicines may be used together even if an interaction might occur. In these cases, your doctor may want to change the dose, or other precautions may be necessary. When you are receiving vincristine, it is especially important that your health care professional know if you are taking any of the following:

- Probenecid (e.g., Benemid) or
- Sulfinpyrazone (e.g., Anturane)—Vincristine may increase the concentration of uric acid in the blood, which these medicines are used to lower
- If you have ever been treated with x-rays or cancer medicines—Vincristine may increase the effects of these medicines or radiation therapy on the blood

Other medical problems—The presence of other medical problems may affect the use of vincristine. Make sure you tell your doctor if you have any other medical problems, especially:

- Chickenpox (including recent exposure) or
- Herpes zoster (shingles)—Risk of severe disease affecting other parts of the body
- Gout (history of) or
- Kidney stones (history of)—Vincristine may increase levels of uric acid in the body, which can cause gout or kidney stones
- Infection—Vincristine can reduce immunity to infection
- Liver disease—Effects may be increased because of slower removal of vincristine from the body
- Nerve or muscle disease—May be worsened

Proper Use of This Medicine

Vincristine is often given together with certain other medicines. If you are using a combination of medicines, it is important that you receive each one at the proper time. If you are taking some of these medicines by mouth, ask your health care professional to help you plan a way to take them at the right times.

While you are using this medicine, it may be necessary to drink extra fluids so that you will pass more urine. This will help prevent kidney problems and keep your kidneys working well. Ask your doctor if this is necessary for you.

This medicine sometimes causes nausea and vomiting. However, it is very important that you continue to receive the medicine, even if you begin to feel ill. Ask your health care professional for ways to lessen these effects.

Vincristine frequently causes constipation and stomach cramps. Your doctor may want you to take a laxative. However, do not decide to take these medicines on your own without first checking with your doctor.

Dosing—The dose of vincristine will be different for different patients. The dose that is used may depend on a number of things, including what the medicine is being used for, the patient's weight or size, and whether or not other medicines are also being taken. *If you are receiving vincristine at home, follow your doctor's orders or the directions on the label.* If you have any questions about the proper dose of vincristine, ask your doctor.

Precautions While Using This Medicine

It is very important that your doctor check your progress at regular visits to make sure that vincristine is working properly and to check for unwanted effects.

While you are being treated with vincristine, and after you stop treatment with it, *do not have any immunizations (vaccinations) without your doctor's approval.* Vincristine may lower your body's resistance and there is a chance you might get the infection the immunization is meant to prevent. Other people living in your household should not take or should not have recently taken oral polio vaccine since there is a chance they could pass the polio virus on to you. Also, avoid other persons who have taken oral polio vaccine. Do not get close to them, and do not stay in the same room with them for very long. If you cannot take these precautions, you should consider wearing a protective face mask that covers the nose and mouth.

If vincristine accidentally seeps out of the vein into which it is injected, it may damage some tissues and cause scarring. *Tell the doctor or nurse right away if you notice redness, pain, or swelling at the place of injection.*

Side Effects of This Medicine

Along with their needed effects, medicines like vincristine can sometimes cause unwanted effects such as blood problems, nervous system problems, loss of hair, and other side effects. These and others are described below. Also, because of the way these medicines act on the body, there is a chance that they might cause other unwanted effects that may not occur until months or years after the medicine is used. These delayed effects may include certain types of cancer, such as leukemia. Discuss these possible effects with your doctor.

Although not all of these side effects may occur, if they do occur they may need medical attention.

Check with your doctor or nurse immediately if the following side effects occur:

Less common

Pain or redness at place of injection

Rare

Black, tarry stools; blood in urine or stools; cough or hoarseness; fever or chills; pinpoint red spots on skin; unusual bleeding or bruising

Check with your health care professional as soon as possible if any of the following side effects occur:

More common

Blurred or double vision; constipation; difficulty in walking; drooping eyelids; headache; jaw pain; joint pain; lower back or side pain; numbness or tingling in fingers and toes; pain in fingers and toes; pain in testicles; stomach cramps; swelling of feet or lower legs; weakness

Less common

Agitation; bed-wetting; confusion; convulsions (seizures); decrease or increase in urination; dizziness or lightheadedness when getting up from a lying or sitting position; hallucinations (seeing, hearing, or feeling things that are not there); lack of sweating; loss of appetite; mental depression; painful or difficult urination; trouble in sleeping; unconsciousness

Rare

Sores in mouth and on lips

Other side effects may occur that usually do not need medical attention. These side effects may go away during treatment as your body adjusts to the medicine. Also, your health care professional may be able to tell you about ways to prevent or reduce some of these side effects. Check with your health care professional if any of the following side effects continue or are bothersome or if you have any questions about them:

Less common

Bloating; diarrhea; loss of weight; nausea and vomiting; skin rash

This medicine often causes a temporary loss of hair. After treatment with vincristine has ended, or sometimes even during treatment, normal hair growth should return.

Other side effects not listed above may also occur in some patients. If you notice any other effects, check with your doctor.

Revised: 09/90
Interim revision: 08/11/93; 07/05/94

VITAMIN A Systemic

A commonly used brand name in the U.S. and Canada is Aquasol A.

Another commonly used name is retinol.

Generic name product may also be available in the U.S. and Canada.

Description

Vitamins (VYE-ta-mins) are compounds that you *must* have for growth and health. They are needed in small amounts only and are usually available in the foods that you eat. Vitamin A is needed for night vision and for growth of skin, bones, and male and female reproductive organs. In pregnant women vitamin A is necessary for the growth of a healthy fetus.

Lack of vitamin A may lead to a rare condition called night blindness (problems seeing in the dark), as well as dry eyes, eye infections, skin problems, and slowed growth. Your health care professional may treat these problems by prescribing vitamin A for you.

Some conditions may increase your need for vitamin A. These include:

- Diarrhea
- Eye diseases
- Intestine diseases
- Infections (continuing or chronic)
- Measles
- Pancreas disease
- Stomach removal
- Stress (continuing)

In addition, infants receiving unfortified formula may need vitamin A supplements.

Vitamin A absorption will be decreased in any condition in which fat is poorly absorbed.

Increased need for vitamin A should be determined by your health care professional.

Claims that vitamin A is effective for treatment of conditions such as acne or lung diseases, or for treatment of eye problems, wounds, or dry or wrinkled skin not caused by lack of vitamin A have not been proven. Although vitamin A is being used to prevent certain types of cancer, some experts feel there is not enough information to show that this is effective, particularly in well-nourished individuals.

Injectable vitamin A is given by or under the supervision of a health care professional. Other forms of vitamin A are available without a prescription.

Vitamin A is available in the following dosage forms:

Oral
- Capsules (U.S. and Canada)
- Oral solution (U.S.)
- Tablets (U.S.)

Parenteral
- Injection (U.S.)

Importance of Diet

For good health, it is important that you eat a balanced and varied diet. Follow carefully any diet program your health care professional may recommend. For your specific dietary vitamin and/or mineral needs, ask your health care professional for a list of appropriate foods. If you think that you are not getting enough vitamins and/or minerals in your diet, you may choose to take a dietary supplement.

Vitamin A is found in various foods including yellow-orange fruits and vegetables; dark green, leafy vegetables; vitamin A-fortified milk; liver; and margarine. Vitamin A comes in two different forms, retinols and beta-carotene. Retinols are found in foods that come from animals (meat, milk, eggs). The form of vitamin A found in plants is called beta-carotene (which is converted to vitamin A in the body). Food processing may destroy some of the vitamins. For example, freezing may reduce the amount of vitamin A in foods.

Vitamins alone will not take the place of a good diet and will not provide energy. Your body needs other substances found in food, such as protein, minerals, carbohydrates, and fat. Vitamins themselves often cannot work without the presence of other foods. For example, small amounts of fat are needed so that vitamin A can be absorbed into the body.

The daily amount of vitamin A needed is defined in several different ways.

For U.S.—
- Recommended Dietary Allowances (RDAs) are the amount of vitamins and minerals needed to provide for adequate nutrition in most healthy persons. RDAs for a given nutrient may vary depending on a person's age, sex, and physical condition (e.g., pregnancy).
- Daily Values (DVs) are used on food and dietary supplement labels to indicate the percent of the recommended daily amount of each nutrient that a serving provides. DV replaces the previous designation of United States Recommended Daily Allowances (USRDAs).
- Normal daily recommended intakes in the United States for vitamin A are generally defined according to age or condition and to the form of vitamin A as follows:

Age or Condition	Form of Vitamin A		
	RE or mcg of Retinol	Amount in Units as Retinol	Amount in Units as a Combination of Retinol and Beta-carotene*
Infants and children			
Birth to 3 years	375–400	1250–1330	1875–2000
4 to 6 years	500	1665	2500
7 to 10 years	700	2330	3500
Teenage and adult males	1000	3330	5000
Teenage and adult females	800	2665	4000
Pregnant females	800	2665	4000
Breast-feeding females	1200–1300	4000–4330	6000–6500

*Based on 1980 Recommended Dietary Allowances (RDAs) for vitamin A in the diet that is a combination of retinol and beta-carotene.

For Canada—
- Recommended Nutrient Intakes (RNIs) are used to determine the amounts of vitamins, minerals, and protein needed to provide adequate nutrition and lessen the risk of chronic disease.
- Normal daily recommended intakes in Canada for vitamin A are generally defined according to age or condition and to the form of vitamin A as follows:

Age or Condition	Form of Vitamin A		
	RE or mcg of Retinol	Amount in Units as Retinol	Amount in Units as a Combination of Retinol and Beta-carotene*
Infants and children			
Birth to 3 years	400	1330	2000
4 to 6 years	500	1665	2500
7 to 10 years	700–800	2330–2665	3500
Teenage and adult males	1000	3330	5000
Teenage and adult females	800	2665	4000
Pregnant females	900	2665–3000	4000–4500
Breast-feeding females	1200	4000	6000

*Based on 1980 U.S. Recommended Dietary Allowances (RDAs) for vitamin A in the diet that is a combination of retinol and beta-carotene.

In the past, the RDA and RNI for vitamin A have been expressed in Units. This term Units has been replaced by retinol equivalents (RE) or micrograms (mcg) of retinol, with 1 RE equal to 1 mcg of retinol. This was done to better describe the two forms of vitamin A, retinol and beta-carotene. One RE of vitamin A is equal to 3.33 Units of retinol and 10 Units of beta-carotene. Some products available have not changed their labels and continue to be labeled in Units.

Before Using This Dietary Supplement

If you are taking this dietary supplement without a prescription, carefully read and follow any precautions on the label. For vitamin A, the following should be considered:

Allergies—Tell your health care professional if you have ever had any unusual or allergic reaction to vitamin A. Also tell your health care professional if you are allergic to any other substances, such as foods, preservatives, or dyes.

Pregnancy—It is especially important that you are receiving enough vitamins when you become pregnant and that you continue to receive the right amount of vitamins throughout your pregnancy. The healthy growth and development of the fetus depend on a steady supply of nutrients from the mother.

However, taking too much vitamin A (more than 1800 RE [6000 Units]) during pregnancy can also cause harmful effects such as birth defects or slow or reduced growth in the child.

Breast-feeding—It is especially important that you receive the right amounts of vitamins so that your baby will also get the vitamins needed to grow properly. However, taking large amounts of a dietary supplement while breast-feeding may be harmful to the mother and/or baby and should be avoided.

Children—Problems in children have not been reported with intake of normal daily recommended amounts. However, side effects from high doses and/or prolonged use of vitamin A are more likely to occur in young children than adults.

Older adults—Problems in older adults have not been reported with intake of normal daily recommended amounts. However, some studies have shown that the elderly may be at risk of high blood levels of vitamin A with long-term use.

Dental—High doses and/or prolonged use of vitamin A may cause bleeding from the gums; dry or sore mouth; or drying, cracking, or peeling of the lips.

Medicines or other dietary supplements—Although certain medicines or dietary supplements should not be used together at all, in other cases they may be used together even if an interaction might occur. In these cases, your health care professional may want to change the dose, or other precautions may be necessary. When you are taking vitamin A, it is especially important that your health care professional know if you are taking any of the following:

- Etretinate or
- Isotretinoin (e.g., Accutane)—Use with vitamin A may cause high blood levels of vitamin A, which may increase the chance of side effects

Other medical problems—The presence of other medical problems may affect the use of vitamin A. Make sure you tell your health care professional if you have any other medical problems, especially:

- Alcohol abuse (or history of) or
- Liver disease—Vitamin A use may make liver problems worse
- Kidney disease—May cause high blood levels of vitamin A, which may increase the chance of side effects

Proper Use of This Dietary Supplement

Dosing—The amount of vitamin A needed to meet normal daily recommended intakes will be different for different individuals. The following information includes only the average amounts of vitamin A. The combination of retinol and beta-carotene in the diet is based on 1980 U.S. Recommended Dietary Allowances (RDAs).

- For *oral* dosage form (capsules, tablets, oral solution):

—To prevent deficiency, the amount taken by mouth is based on normal daily recommended intakes:

For the U.S.

- Adult and teenage males—1000 retinol equivalents (RE) (3330 Units of retinol or 5000 Units as a combination of retinol and beta-carotene) per day.
- Adult and teenage females—800 RE (2665 Units of retinol or 4000 Units as a combination of retinol and beta-carotene) per day.
- Pregnant females—800 RE (2665 Units of retinol or 4000 Units as a combination of retinol and beta-carotene) per day.
- Breast-feeding females—1200 to 1300 RE (4000 to 4330 Units of retinol or 6000 to 6500 Units as a combination of retinol and beta-carotene) per day.
- Children 7 to 10 years of age—700 RE (2330 Units of retinol or 3500 Units as a combination of retinol and beta-carotene) per day.
- Children 4 to 6 years of age—500 RE (1665 Units of retinol or 2500 Units as a combination of retinol and beta-carotene) per day.
- Children birth to 3 years of age—375 to 400 RE (1250 to 1330 Units of retinol or 1875 to 2000 Units as a combination of retinol and beta-carotene) per day.

For Canada

- Adult and teenage males—1000 RE (3330 Units of retinol or 5000 Units as a combination of retinol and beta-carotene) per day.
- Adult and teenage females—800 RE (2665 Units of retinol or 4000 Units as a combination of retinol and beta-carotene) per day.
- Pregnant females—900 RE (2665 to 3000 Units of retinol or 4000 to 4500 Units as a combination of retinol and beta-carotene) per day.
- Breast-feeding females—1200 RE (4000 Units of retinol or 6000 Units as a combination of retinol and beta-carotene) per day.
- Children 7 to 10 years of age—700 to 800 RE (2330 to 2665 Units of retinol or 3500 Units as a combination of retinol and beta-carotene) per day.

- Children 4 to 6 years of age—500 RE (1665 Units of retinol or 2500 Units as a combination of retinol and beta-carotene) per day.
- Children birth to 3 years of age—400 RE (1330 Units or 2000 Units as a combination of retinol and beta-carotene) per day.

—To treat deficiency:

- Adults and teenagers—Treatment dose is determined by prescriber for each individual based on severity of deficiency. The following dose has been determined for xerophthalmia (eye disease): Oral, 7500 to 15,000 RE (25,000 to 50,000 Units) a day.
- Children—Treatment dose is determined by prescriber for each individual based of severity of deficiency. The following doses have been determined:
  —For measles—
  - Children 6 months to 1 year of age: Oral, 30,000 RE (100,000 Units) as a single dose.
  - For children 1 year of age and older: Oral, 60,000 RE (200,000 Units) as a single dose.

  —Xerophthalmia (eye disease)—
  - Children 6 months to 1 year of age: Oral, 30,000 RE (100,000 Units) as a single dose, the same dose being repeated the next day and again at 4 weeks.
  - Children 1 year of age and older: Oral, 60,000 RE (200,000 Units) as a single dose, the same dose being repeated the next day and again at 4 weeks.

Note: Vitamin A is used in measles and xerophthalmia only when vitamin A deficiency is a problem as determined by your health care professional. Vitamin A deficiency occurs in malnutrition or in certain disease states.

Missed dose—If you miss taking a vitamin for one or more days there is no cause for concern, since it takes some time for your body to become seriously low in vitamins. However, if your health care professional has recommended that you take this vitamin, try to remember to take it as directed every day.

For individuals taking the *oral liquid form* of vitamin A:

- This preparation is to be taken by mouth even though it comes in a dropper bottle.
- This dietary supplement may be dropped directly into the mouth or mixed with cereal, fruit juice, or other food.

Storage—To store this dietary supplement:

- Keep out of the reach of children.
- Store away from heat and direct light.
- Do not store in the bathroom, near the kitchen sink or in other damp places. Heat or moisture may cause the dietary supplement to break down.
- Keep the oral liquid form of this dietary supplement from freezing.
- Do not keep outdated dietary supplements or those no longer needed. Be sure that any discarded dietary supplement is out of the reach of children.

Precautions While Using This Dietary Supplement

Vitamin A is stored in the body; therefore, when you take more than the body needs, it will build up in the body. This may lead to poisoning and even death. Problems are more likely to occur in:

- Adults taking 7500 RE (25,000 Units) a day for 8 months in a row, or 450,000 RE (1,500,000 Units) all at once; or
- Children taking 5400 RE (18,000 Units) to 15,000 RE (50,000 Units) a day for several months in a row, or 22,500 RE (75,000 Units) to 105,100 RE (350,000 Units) all at once.
- Pregnant women taking more than 1800 RE (6000 Units) a day.

Remember that the total amount of vitamin A you get every day includes what you get from foods that you eat and what you take as a supplement.

Side Effects of This Dietary Supplement

Along with its needed effects, a dietary supplement may cause some unwanted effects. Vitamin A does not usually cause any side effects at normal recommended doses. *However, taking large amounts of vitamin A over a period of time may cause some unwanted effects that can be serious. Check with your health care professional immediately* if any of the following side effects occur, since they may be signs of sudden overdose:

Bleeding from gums or sore mouth; bulging soft spot on head (in babies); confusion or unusual excitement; diarrhea; dizziness or drowsiness; double vision; headache (severe); irritability (severe); peeling of skin, especially on lips and palms; vomiting (severe)

Check with your health care professional as soon as possible if any of the following side effects occur, since they may also be signs of gradual overdose:

Bone or joint pain; convulsions (seizures); drying or cracking of skin or lips; dry mouth; fever; general feeling of discomfort or illness or weakness; headache; increased sensitivity of skin to sunlight; increase in frequency of urination, especially at night, or in amount of urine; irritability; loss of appetite; loss of hair; stomach pain; unusual tiredness; vomiting; yellow-orange patches on soles of feet, palms of hands, or skin around nose and lips

Other side effects not listed above may also occur in some individuals. If you notice any other effects, check with your health care professional.

Revised: 07/29/94
Interim revision: 05/26/95

VITAMIN B_{12} Systemic

Some commonly used brand names are:

In the U.S.—

Alphamin[2]	Hydroxy-Cobal[2]
Cobex[1]	LA-12[2]
Cobolin-M[1]	Neuroforte-R[1]
Crystamine[1]	Primabalt[1]
Crysti-12[1]	Rubesol-1000[1]
Cyanoject[1]	Rubramin PC[1]
Cyomin[1]	Shovite[1]
Hydrobexan[2]	Vibal[1]
Hydro-Cobex[2]	Vibal LA[2]
Hydro-Crysti-12[2]	Vitabee 12[1]

In Canada—

Anacobin[1]	Bedoz[1]

Note: For quick reference, the following supplements are numbered to match the corresponding brand names.

This information applies to the following:

1. Cyanocobalamin (sye-an-oh-koe-BAL-a-min)‡§
2. Hydroxocobalamin (hye-drox-oh-koe-BAL-a-min)†‡

†Not commercially available in Canada.
‡Generic name product may also be available in the U.S.
§Generic name product may be available in Canada.

Description

Vitamins (VYE-ta-mins) are compounds that you *must* have for growth and health. They are needed in small amounts only and are usually available in the foods that you eat. Vitamin B_{12} is necessary for healthy blood. Cyanocobalamin and hydroxocobalamin are man-made forms of vitamin B_{12}.

Some people have a medical problem called pernicious anemia in which vitamin B_{12} is not absorbed from the intestine. Others may have a badly diseased intestine or have had a large part of their stomach or intestine removed, so that vitamin B_{12} cannot be absorbed. These people need to receive vitamin B_{12} by injection.

Some conditions may increase your need for vitamin B_{12}. These include:

- Alcoholism
- Anemia, hemolytic
- Fever (continuing)
- Genetic disorders such as homocystinuria and/or methylmalonic aciduria
- Intestine diseases
- Infections (continuing or chronic)
- Kidney disease
- Liver disease
- Pancreas disease
- Stomach disease
- Stress (continuing)
- Thyroid disease
- Worm infections

In addition, persons that are strict vegetarians or have macrobiotic diets may need vitamin B_{12} supplements.

Increased need for vitamin B_{12} should be determined by your health care professional.

Lack of vitamin B_{12} may lead to anemia (weak blood), stomach problems, and nerve damage. Your health care professional may treat this by prescribing vitamin B_{12} for you.

Claims that vitamin B_{12} is effective for treatment of various conditions such as aging, allergies, eye problems, slow growth, poor appetite or malnutrition, skin problems, tiredness, mental problems, sterility, thyroid disease, and nerve diseases have not been proven. Many of these treatments involve large and expensive amounts of vitamins.

Injectable vitamin B_{12} is given by or under the supervision of a health care professional. Some strengths of oral vitamin B_{12} are available only with your health care professional's prescription. Others are available without a prescription.

Vitamin B_{12} is available in the following dosage forms:

Oral

Cyanocobalamin
- Extended-release tablets (U.S.)
- Tablets (U.S. and Canada)

Parenteral

Cyanocobalamin
- Injection (U.S. and Canada)

Hydroxocobalamin
- Injection (U.S.)

Importance of Diet

For good health, it is important that you eat a balanced and varied diet. Follow carefully any diet program your health care professional may recommend. For your specific dietary vitamin and/or mineral needs, ask your health care professional for a list of appropriate foods. If you think that you are not getting enough vitamins and/or minerals in your diet, you may choose to take a dietary supplement.

Vitamin B_{12} is found in various foods, including fish, egg yolk, milk, and fermented cheeses. It is *not* found in any vegetables. Ordinary cooking probably does not destroy the vitamin B_{12} in food.

Vitamins alone will not take the place of a good diet and will not provide energy. Your body also needs other substances found in food, such as protein, minerals, carbohydrates, and fat. Vitamins themselves often cannot work without the presence of other foods.

The daily amount of vitamin B_{12} needed is defined in several different ways.

For U.S.—

- Recommended Dietary Allowances (RDAs) are the amount of vitamins and minerals needed to provide for adequate nutrition in most healthy persons. RDAs for a given nutrient may vary depending on a person's age, sex, and physical condition (e.g., pregnancy).
- Daily Values (DVs) are used on food and dietary supplement labels to indicate the percent of the recommended daily amount of each nutrient that a serving

provides. DV replaces the previous designation of United States Recommended Daily Allowances (USRDAs).

For Canada—
- Recommended Nutrient Intakes (RNIs) are used to determine the amounts of vitamins, minerals, and protein needed to provide adequate nutrition and lessen the risk of chronic disease.

Normal daily recommended intakes in micrograms (mcg) for vitamin B_{12} are generally defined as follows:

Persons	U.S. (mcg)	Canada (mcg)
Infants and children		
Birth to 3 years of age	0.3–0.7	0.3–0.4
4 to 6 years of age	1	0.5
7 to 10 years of age	1.4	0.8–1
Adolescent and adult males	2	1–2
Adolescent and adult females	2	1–2
Pregnant females	2.2	2–3
Breast-feeding females	2.6	1.5–2.5

Before Using This Dietary Supplement

If you are taking this dietary supplement without a prescription, carefully read and follow any precautions on the label. For vitamin B_{12}, the following should be considered:

Allergies—Tell your health care professional if you have ever had any unusual or allergic reaction to vitamin B_{12}. Also, tell your health care professional if you are allergic to any other substances, such as foods, preservatives, or dyes.

Pregnancy—It is especially important that you are receiving enough vitamins when you become pregnant and that you continue to receive the right amount of vitamins throughout your pregnancy. Healthy fetal growth and development depend on a steady supply of nutrients from mother to fetus. However, taking large amounts of a dietary supplement in pregnancy may be harmful to the mother and/or fetus and should be avoided.

You may need vitamin B_{12} supplements if you are a strict vegetarian (vegan-vegetarian). Too little vitamin B_{12} can cause harmful effects such as anemia or nervous system injury.

Breast-feeding—It is especially important that you receive the right amounts of vitamins so that your baby will also get the vitamins needed to grow properly. If you are a strict vegetarian, your baby may not be getting the vitamin B_{12} needed. However, taking large amounts of a dietary supplement while breast-feeding may be harmful to the mother and/or baby and should be avoided.

Children—Problems in children have not been reported with intake of normal daily recommended amounts.

Older adults—Problems in older adults have not been reported with intake of normal daily recommended amounts.

Medicines or other dietary supplements—Although certain medicines or dietary supplement should not be used together at all, in other cases they may be used together even if an interaction might occur. In these cases, your health care professional may want to change the dose, or other precautions may be necessary. Tell your health care professional if you are taking any other dietary supplement or any prescription or nonprescription (over-the-counter [OTC]) medicine.

Other medical problems—The presence of other medical problems may affect the use of vitamin B_{12}. Make sure you tell your health care professional if you have any other medical problems, especially:
- Leber's disease (an eye disease)—Vitamin B_{12} may make this condition worse

Proper Use of This Dietary Supplement

Dosing—The amount of vitamin B_{12} needed to meet normal daily recommended intakes will be different for different individuals. The following information includes only the average amounts of vitamin B_{12}.
- For *oral* dosage form (tablets or extended-release tablets):
  —To prevent deficiency, the amount taken by mouth is based on normal daily recommended intakes:
  For the U.S.
  - Adults and teenagers—2 micrograms (mcg) per day.
  - Pregnant females—2.2 mcg per day.
  - Breast-feeding females—2.6 mcg per day.
  - Children 7 to 10 years of age—1.4 mcg per day.
  - Children 4 to 6 years of age—1 mcg per day.
  - Children birth to 3 years of age—0.3 to 0.7 mcg per day.

  For Canada
  - Adults and teenagers—1 to 2 mcg per day.
  - Pregnant females—2 to 3 mcg per day.
  - Breast-feeding females—1.5 to 2.5 mcg per day.
  - Children 7 to 10 years of age—0.8 to 1 mcg per day.
  - Children 4 to 6 years of age—0.5 mcg per day.
  - Children birth to 3 years of age—0.3 to 0.4 mcg per day.

  —To treat deficiency:
  - Adults, teenagers, and children—Treatment dose is determined by prescriber for each individual based on the severity of deficiency.

For patients receiving vitamin B_{12} by injection for pernicious anemia or if part of the stomach or intestine has been removed:
- You will have to receive treatment for the rest of your life. You must continue to receive vitamin B_{12} even if you feel well, in order to prevent future problems.

Missed dose—If you miss taking a vitamin for one or more days there is no cause for concern, since it takes some time for your body to become seriously low in vitamins. However, if your health care professional has recommended that you take this vitamin, try to remember to take it as directed.

Storage—To store this dietary supplement:
- Keep out of the reach of children.
- Store away from heat and direct light.
- Do not store in the bathroom, near the kitchen sink, or in other damp places. Heat or moisture may cause the dietary supplement to break down.
- Do not keep outdated dietary supplement or those no longer needed. Be sure that any discarded dietary supplement is out of the reach of children.

Side Effects of This Dietary Supplement

Along with its needed effects, a dietary supplement may cause some unwanted effects. Cyanocobalamin or hydroxocobalamin does not usually cause any side effects. *However, check with your health care professional immediately* if any of the following side effects occur:

Rare—soon after receiving injection only
Skin rash or itching; wheezing

Check with your health care professional as soon as possible if either of the following side effects continues or is bothersome:

Less common
Diarrhea; itching of skin

Other side effects not listed above may also occur in some individuals. If you notice any other effects, check with your health care professional.

Revised: 01/29/92
Interim revision: 06/02/92; 06/19/95

VITAMIN D and Related Compounds Systemic

Some commonly used brand names are:

In the U.S.—

Calciferol[5]
Calciferol Drops[5]
Calcijex[3]
Calderol[2]
DHT[4]
DHT Intensol[4]
Drisdol[5]
Drisdol Drops[5]
Hytakerol[4]
Rocaltrol[3]

In Canada—

Calciferol[5]
Calcijex[3]
Drisdol[5]
Hytakerol[4]
One-Alpha[1]
Ostoforte[5]
Radiostol Forte[5]
Rocaltrol[3]

Note: For quick reference, the following vitamin D and related compounds are numbered to match the corresponding brand names.

This information applies to the following:
1. Alfacalcidol (al-fa-KAL-si-dol)*
2. Calcifediol (kal-si-fe-DYE-ole)†
3. Calcitriol (kal-si-TRYE-ole)
4. Dihydrotachysterol (dye-hye-droh-tak-ISS-ter-ole)
5. Ergocalciferol (er-goe-kal-SIF-e-role)‡§

*Not commercially available in the U.S.
†Not commercially available in Canada.
‡Generic name product may be available in the U.S.
§Generic name product may be available in Canada.

Description

Vitamins (VYE-ta-mins) are compounds that you *must* have for growth and health. They are needed in small amounts only and are available in the foods that you eat. Vitamin D is necessary for strong bones and teeth.

Lack of vitamin D may lead to a condition called rickets, especially in children, in which bones and teeth are weak. In adults it may cause a condition called osteomalacia, in which calcium is lost from bones so that they become weak. Your doctor may treat these problems by prescribing vitamin D for you. Vitamin D is also sometimes used to treat other diseases in which calcium is not used properly by the body.

Ergocalciferol is the form of vitamin D used in vitamin supplements.

Some conditions may increase your need for vitamin D. These include:
- Alcoholism
- Intestine diseases
- Kidney disease
- Liver disease
- Pancreas disease
- Surgical removal of stomach

In addition, individuals and breast-fed infants who lack exposure to sunlight, as well as dark-skinned individuals, may be more likely to have a vitamin D deficiency. Increased need for vitamin D should be determined by your health care professional.

Alfacalcidol, calcifediol, calcitriol, and dihydrotachysterol are forms of vitamin D used to treat hypocalcemia (not enough calcium in the blood). Alfacalcidol, calcifediol, and calcitriol are also used to treat certain types of bone disease that may occur with kidney disease in patients who are undergoing kidney dialysis.

Claims that vitamin D is effective for treatment of arthritis and prevention of nearsightedness or nerve problems have not been proven. Some psoriasis patients may benefit from vitamin D supplements; however, controlled studies have not been performed.

Injectable vitamin D is given by or under the supervision of a health care professional. Some strengths of ergocalciferol and all strengths of alfacalcidol, calcifediol, calcitriol, and dihydrotachysterol are available only with your doctor's prescription. Other strengths of ergocalciferol are available without a prescription. However, it may be a good idea to check with your health care professional before taking vitamin D on your own. *Taking large amounts over long periods may cause serious unwanted effects.*

Vitamin D and related compounds are available in the following dosage forms:

Oral

- Alfacalcidol
  - Capsules (Canada)
  - Oral solution (Canada)
- Calcifediol
  - Capsules (U.S.)
- Calcitriol
  - Capsules (U.S. and Canada)
  - Oral solution (Canada)
- Dihydrotachysterol
  - Capsules (U.S. and Canada)
  - Oral solution (U.S.)
  - Tablets (U.S.)
- Ergocalciferol
  - Capsules (U.S. and Canada)
  - Oral solution (U.S. and Canada)
  - Tablets (U.S. and Canada)

Parenteral

- Calcitriol
  - Injection (U.S. and Canada)
- Ergocalciferol
  - Injection (U.S. and Canada)

Importance of Diet

For good health, it is important that you eat a balanced and varied diet. Follow carefully any diet program your health care professional may recommend. For your specific dietary vitamin and/or mineral needs, ask your health care professional for a list of appropriate foods. If you think that you are not getting enough vitamins and/or minerals in your diet, you may choose to take a dietary supplement.

Vitamin D is found naturally only in fish and fish-liver oils. However, it is also found in milk (vitamin D–fortified). Cooking does not affect the vitamin D in foods. Vitamin D is sometimes called the "sunshine vitamin" since it is made in your skin when you are exposed to sunlight. If you eat a balanced diet and get outside in the sunshine at least 1.5 to 2 hours a week, you should be getting all the vitamin D you need.

Vitamins alone will not take the place of a good diet and will not provide energy. Your body also needs other substances found in food such as protein, minerals, carbohydrates, and fat. Vitamins themselves often cannot work without the presence of other foods. For example, fat is needed so that vitamin D can be absorbed into the body.

The daily amount of vitamin D needed is defined in several different ways.

For U.S.—

- Recommended Dietary Allowances (RDAs) are the amount of vitamins and minerals needed to provide for adequate nutrition in most healthy persons. RDAs for a given nutrient may vary depending on a person's age, sex, and physical condition (e.g., pregnancy).
- Daily Values (DVs) are used on food and dietary supplement labels to indicate the percent of the recommended daily amount of each nutrient that a serving provides. DV replaces the previous designation of United States Recommended Daily Allowances (USRDAs).

For Canada—

- Recommended Nutrient Intakes (RNIs) are used to determine the amounts of vitamins, minerals, and protein needed to provide adequate nutrition and lessen the risk of chronic disease.

In the past, the RDA and RNI for vitamin D have been expressed in Units (U). This term has been replaced by micrograms (mcg) of vitamin D.

Normal daily recommended intakes in mcg and Units are generally defined as follows:

Persons	U.S. (mcg)	U.S. Units	Canada (mcg)	Canada Units
Infants and children				
Birth to 3 years of age	7.5–10	300–400	5–10	200–400
4 to 6 years of age	10	400	5	200
7 to 10 years of age	10	400	2.5–5	100–200
Adolescents and adults	5–10	200–400	2.5–5	100–200
Pregnant and breast-feeding females	10	400	5–7.5	200–300

Remember:

- The total amount of each vitamin that you get every day includes what you get from the foods that you eat *and* what you may take as a supplement.
- Your total amount should not be greater than the RDA or RNI, unless ordered by your doctor. *Taking too much vitamin D over a period of time may cause harmful effects.*

Before Using This Dietary Supplement

If you are taking this dietary supplement without a prescription, carefully read and follow any precautions on the label. For vitamin D and related compounds, the following should be considered:

Allergies—Tell your health care professional if you have ever had any unusual or allergic reaction to alfacalcidol, calcifediol, calcitriol, dihydrotachysterol, or ergocalciferol. Also, tell your health care professional if you are allergic to any other substances, such as foods, preservatives, or dyes.

Pregnancy—It is especially important that you are receiving enough vitamin D when you become pregnant and that you continue to receive the right amounts of vitamins throughout your pregnancy. The healthy growth and development of the fetus depend on a steady supply of nutrients from the mother.

You may need vitamin D supplements if you are a strict vegetarian (vegan-vegetarian) and/or have little exposure to sunlight and do not drink vitamin D-fortified milk.

Taking too much alfacalcidol, calcifediol, calcitriol, dihydrotachysterol, or ergocalciferol can also be harmful to the fetus. Taking more than your health care professional has recommended can cause your baby to be more sensitive than usual to its effects, can cause problems with a gland called the parathyroid, and can cause a defect in the baby's heart.

Breast-feeding—It is especially important that you receive the right amounts of vitamins so that your baby will also get the vitamins needed to grow properly. Infants who are totally breast-fed and have little exposure to the sun may require vitamin D supplementation. However, taking large amounts of a dietary supplement while breast-feeding may be harmful to the mother and/or baby and should be avoided.

Only small amounts of alfacalcidol, calcifediol, calcitriol, or dihydrotachysterol pass into breast milk and these amounts have not been reported to cause problems in nursing babies.

Children—Problems in children have not been reported with intake of normal daily recommended amounts. Some studies have shown that infants who are totally breast-fed, especially with dark-skinned mothers, and have little exposure to sunlight may be at risk of vitamin D deficiency. Your health care professional may prescribe a vitamin/mineral supplement that contains vitamin D. Some infants may be sensitive to even small amounts of alfacalcidol, calcifediol, calcitriol, dihydrotachysterol, or ergocalciferol. Also, children may show slowed growth when receiving large doses of alfacalcidol, calcifediol, calcitriol, dihydrotachysterol, or ergocalciferol for a long time.

Older adults—Problems in older adults have not been reported with intake of normal daily recommended amounts. Studies have shown that older adults may have lower blood levels of vitamin D than younger adults, especially those who have little exposure to sunlight. Your health care professional may recommend that you take a vitamin supplement that contains vitamin D.

Medicines or other dietary supplements—Although certain medicines or dietary supplements should not be used together at all, in other cases they may be used together even if an interaction might occur. In these cases, your health care professional may want to change the dose, or other precautions may be necessary. When you are taking vitamin D and related compounds, it is especially important that your health care professional know if you are taking any of the following:

- Antacids containing magnesium—Use of these products with any vitamin D–related compound may result in high blood levels of magnesium, especially in patients with kidney disease
- Calcium-containing preparations or
- Thiazide diuretics (water pills)—Use of these preparations with vitamin D may cause high blood levels of calcium and increase the chance of side effects
- Vitamin D and related compounds, other—Use of vitamin D with a related compound may cause high blood levels of vitamin D and increase the chance of side effects.

Other medical problems—The presence of other medical problems may affect the use of vitamin D and related compounds. Make sure you tell your health care professional if you have any other medical problems, especially:

- Heart or blood vessel disease—Alfacalcidol, calcifediol, calcitriol, or dihydrotachysterol may cause hypercalcemia (high blood levels of calcium), which may make these conditions worse
- Kidney disease—High blood levels of alfacalcidol, calcifediol, calcitriol, dihydrotachysterol, or ergocalciferol may result, which may increase the chance of side effects
- Sarcoidosis—May increase sensitivity to alfacalcidol, calcifediol, calcitriol, dihydrotachysterol, or ergocalciferol and increase the chance of side effects

Proper Use of This Dietary Supplement

For use as a dietary supplement:

- *Do not take more than the recommended daily amount.* Vitamin D is stored in the body, and taking too much over a period of time can cause poisoning and even death.

If you have any questions about this, check with your health care professional.

For individuals taking the *oral liquid form* of this dietary supplement:

- This preparation should be taken by mouth even though it comes in a dropper bottle.
- This dietary supplement may be dropped directly into the mouth or mixed with cereal, fruit juice, or other food.

While you are taking alfacalcidol, calcifediol, calcitriol, or dihydrotachysterol, your health care professional may want you to follow a special diet or take a calcium supplement. Be sure to follow instructions carefully. If you are already taking a calcium supplement or any medicine containing calcium, make sure your health care professional knows.

Dosing—The dose of these vitamin D and related compounds will be different for different patients. *Follow your doctor's orders or the directions on the label.* The following information includes only the average doses of these medicines. *If your dose is different, do not change it* unless your health care professional tells you to do so.

The number of milliliters (mL) of solution that you take, or the number of capsules or tablets you take, depends on the strength of the medicine. Also, *the number of doses you take each day, the time allowed between doses, and the length of time you take the medicine depend on the medical problem for which you are taking the combination medicine.*

For alfacalcidol

- To treat diseases in which calcium is not used properly by the body or to treat bone disease in kidney patients undergoing kidney dialysis:
  - —For *oral* dosage form (capsules):
    - Adults and teenagers—At first, 1 microgram (mcg) a day. Your doctor may change your dose if needed. However, most people will take not more than 3 mcg a day.
  - —For *oral* dosage form (solution):
    - Adults and teenagers—At first, 1 mcg a day. Your doctor may change your dose if needed. However, most people will take not more than 3 mcg a day.
    - Children—0.25 mcg a day.

For calcifediol

- To treat diseases in which calcium is not used properly by the body or to treat bone disease in kidney patients undergoing kidney dialysis:
  —For *oral* dosage form (capsules):
  - Adults, teenagers, and children over 10 years of age—At first, 300 to 350 micrograms (mcg) a week, taken in divided doses either once a day or every other day. Your doctor may change your dose if needed.
  - Children up to 2 years of age—20 to 50 mcg a day.
  - Children 2 to 10 years of age—50 mcg a day.

For calcitriol

- To treat diseases in which calcium is not used properly by the body or to treat bone disease in kidney patients undergoing kidney dialysis:
  —For *oral* dosage form (capsules and solution):
  - Adults, teenagers, and children—At first, 0.25 micrograms (mcg) a day. Your doctor may change your dose if needed.

  —For *injection* dosage form:
  - Adults and teenagers—At first, 0.5 mcg injected into a vein three times a week. Your doctor may change your dose if needed.
  - Children—Use and dose must be determined by your doctor.

For dihydrotachysterol

- To treat diseases in which calcium is not used properly by the body:
  —For *oral* dosage forms (capsules, solution, or tablets):
  - Adults and teenagers—At first, 100 micrograms (mcg) to 2.5 milligrams (mg) a day. Your doctor may change your dose if needed.
  - Children—At first, 1 to 5 mg a day. Your doctor may change your dose if needed.

For ergocalciferol

- For *oral* dosage forms (capsules, tablets, oral solution):
  —The amount of vitamin D to meet normal daily recommended intakes will be different for different individuals. The following information includes only the average amounts of vitamin D.

  —To prevent deficiency, the amount taken by mouth is based on normal daily recommended intakes:

  For the U.S.
  - Adults and teenagers: 5 to 10 micrograms (mcg) (200 to 400 Units) per day.
  - Pregnant and breast-feeding females: 10 mcg (400 Units) per day.
  - Children 4 to 10 years of age: 10 mcg (400 Units) per day.
  - Children birth to 3 years of age: 7.5 to 10 mcg (300 to 400 Units) per day.

  For Canada
  - Adults and teenagers: 2.5 to 5 mcg (100 to 200 Units) per day.
  - Pregnant and breast-feeding females: 5 to 7.5 mcg (200 to 300 Units) per day.
  - Children 7 to 10 years of age: 2.5 to 5 mcg (100 to 200 Units) per day.
  - Children 4 to 6 years of age: 5 mcg (200 Units) per day.
  - Children birth to 3 years of age: 5 to 10 mcg (200 to 400 Units) per day.

  —To treat deficiency:
  - Adults, teenagers, and children: Treatment dose is determined by prescriber for each individual based on severity of deficiency.

  —To treat diseases in which calcium and phosphate are not used properly by the body:
  - Adults and teenagers: At first, 1000 to 500,000 Units a day. The doctor may change your dose if needed.
  - Children: At first, 1000 to 200,000 Units a day. The doctor may change your dose if needed.

Missed dose—
- *For use as a dietary supplement:* If you miss taking a dietary supplement for one or more days there is no cause for concern, since it takes some time for your body to become seriously low in vitamins. However, if your health care professional has recommended that you take this dietary supplement, try to remember to take it as directed every day.
- If you are taking this medicine for a reason other than as a dietary supplement and you miss a dose and your dosing schedule is:

  —One dose every other day: Take the missed dose as soon as possible if you remember it on the day it should be taken. However, if you do not remember the missed dose until the next day, take it at that time. Then skip a day and start your dosing schedule again. Do not double doses.

  —One dose a day: Take the missed dose as soon as possible. Then go back to your regular dosing schedule. However, if you do not remember the missed dose until the next day, skip the missed dose and go back to your regular dosing schedule. Do not double doses.

  —More than one dose a day: Take the missed dose as soon as possible. Then go back to your regular dosing schedule. However, if it is almost time for your next dose, skip the missed dose and go back to your regular dosing schedule. Do not double doses.

If you have any questions about this, check with your health care professional.

Storage—To store this dietary supplement:
- Keep out of the reach of children.
- Store away from heat and direct light.

- Do not store in the bathroom, near the kitchen sink, or in other damp places. Heat or moisture may cause the dietary supplement to break down.
- Keep the oral liquid form of the dietary supplement from freezing.
- Do not keep outdated dietary supplements or those no longer needed. Be sure that any discarded dietary supplement is out of the reach of children.

Precautions While Using This Dietary Supplement

For individuals taking vitamin D *without a prescription:*

- Vitamin D is stored in the body; therefore, when you take more than the body needs, it will build up in the body. This may lead to poisoning. Problems are more likely to occur in:

  —Adults taking 20,000 to 80,000 Units a day and more for several weeks or months.

  —Children taking 2,000 to 4,000 Units a day for several months.
- Remember that the total amount of vitamin D you get every day includes what you get from foods that you eat and what you take as a supplement.

If you are taking this medicine for a reason other than as a dietary supplement, *your doctor should check your progress at regular visits* to make sure that it does not cause unwanted effects.

Do not take any nonprescription (over-the-counter [OTC]) medicine or dietary supplement that contains calcium, phosphorus, or vitamin D while you are taking any of these dietary supplements unless you have been told to do so by your health care professional. The extra calcium, phosphorus, or vitamin D may increase the chance of side effects.

Do not take antacids or other medicines containing magnesium while you are taking any of these medicines. Taking these medicines together may cause unwanted effects.

Side Effects of This Dietary Supplement

Along with its needed effects, a dietary supplement may cause some unwanted effects. Alfacalcidol, calcifediol, calcitriol, dihydrotachysterol, and ergocalciferol do not usually cause any side effects when taken as directed. However, *taking large amounts over a period of time may cause some unwanted effects that can be serious.*

Check with your doctor immediately if any of the following effects occur:

Late symptoms of severe overdose

High blood pressure; irregular heartbeat; stomach pain (severe)

Check with your health care professional as soon as possible if any of the following effects occur:

Early symptoms of overdose

Constipation (especially in children or adolescents); diarrhea; dryness of mouth; headache (continuing); increased thirst; increase in frequency of urination, especially at night, or in amount of urine; loss of appetite; metallic taste; nausea or vomiting (especially in children or adolescents); unusual tiredness or weakness

Late symptoms of overdose

Bone pain; cloudy urine; drowsiness; increased sensitivity of eyes to light or irritation of eyes; itching of skin; mood or mental changes; muscle pain; nausea or vomiting; weight loss

Other side effects not listed above may also occur in some individuals. If you notice any other effects, check with your health care professional.

Revised: 08/03/92
Interim revision: 08/18/92; 08/17/95

VITAMIN E Systemic

Some commonly used brand names are:

In the U.S.—

- Amino-Opti-E
- Aquasol E
- E-Complex-600
- E-200 I.U. Softgels
- E-1000 I.U. Softgels
- E-400 I.U. in a Water Soluble Base
- E-Vitamin Succinate
- Liqui-E
- Pheryl-E
- Vita Plus E

Generic name product may be available.

In Canada—

- Aquasol E
- Webber Vitamin E

Generic name product may be available.

Another commonly used name is alpha tocopherol.

Description

Vitamins (VYE-ta-mins) are compounds that you *must* have for growth and health. They are needed in only small amounts and are available in the foods that you eat. Vitamin E prevents a chemical reaction called oxidation, which can sometimes result in harmful effects in your body. It is also important for the proper function of nerves and muscles.

Some conditions may increase your need for vitamin E. These include:

- Intestine disease
- Liver disease
- Pancreas disease
- Surgical removal of stomach

Increased need for vitamin E should be determined by your health care professional.

Infants who are receiving a formula that is not fortified with vitamin E may be likely to have a vitamin E deficiency. Also, diets high in polyunsaturated fatty acids may increase your need for vitamin E.

Claims that vitamin E is effective for treatment of cancer and for prevention or treatment of acne, aging, loss of hair, bee stings, liver spots on the hands, bursitis, diaper rash, frostbite, stomach ulcer, heart attacks, labor pains, certain blood diseases, miscarriage, muscular dystrophy, poor posture, sexual impotence, sterility, infertility, menopause, sunburn, and lung damage from air pollution have not been proven. Although vitamin E is being used to prevent certain types of cancer, there is not enough information to show that this is effective.

Lack of vitamin E is extremely rare, except in people who have a disease in which it is not absorbed into the body.

Vitamin E is available without a prescription in the following dosage forms:

Oral

- Capsules (U.S. and Canada)
- Oral solution (U.S. and Canada)
- Tablets (U.S.)
- Chewable tablets (U.S.)

Importance of Diet

For good health, it is important that you eat a balanced and varied diet. Follow carefully any diet program your health care professional may recommend. For your specific dietary vitamin and/or mineral needs, ask your health care professional for a list of appropriate foods. If you think that you are not getting enough vitamins and/or minerals in your diet, you may choose to take a dietary supplement.

Vitamin E is found in various foods including vegetable oils (corn, cottonseed, soybean, safflower), wheat germ, whole-grain cereals, and green leafy vegetables. Cooking and storage may destroy some of the vitamin E in foods.

Vitamin supplements alone will not take the place of a good diet and will not provide energy. Your body also needs other substances found in food such as protein, minerals, carbohydrates, and fat. Vitamins themselves often cannot work without the presence of other foods. For example, small amounts of fat are needed so that vitamin E can be absorbed into the body.

The daily amount of vitamin E needed is defined in several different ways.

For U.S.—

- Recommended Dietary Allowances (RDAs) are the amount of vitamins and minerals needed to provide for adequate nutrition in most healthy persons. RDAs for a given nutrient may vary depending on a person's age, sex, and physical condition (e.g., pregnancy).
- Daily Values (DVs) are used on food and dietary supplement labels to indicate the percent of the recommended daily amount of each nutrient that a serving provides. DV replaces the previous designation of United States Recommended Daily Allowances (USRDAs).

For Canada—

- Recommended Nutrient Intakes (RNIs) are used to determine the amounts of vitamins, minerals, and protein needed to provide adequate nutrition and lessen the risk of chronic disease.

Vitamin E is available in various forms, including *d-* or *dl*-alpha tocopheryl acetate, *d-* or *dl*-alpha tocopherol, and *d-* or *dl*-alpha tocopheryl acid succinate. In the past, the RDA for vitamin E have been expressed in Units. This term has been replaced by alpha tocopherol equivalents (alpha-TE) or milligrams (mg) of *d*-alpha tocopherol. One Unit is equivalent to 1 mg of *dl*-alpha tocopherol acetate or 0.6 mg *d*-alpha tocopherol. Most products available in stores continue to be labeled in Units.

Normal daily recommended intakes in milligrams (mg) of alpha tocopherol equivalents (mg alpha-TE) and Units for vitamin E are generally defined as follows:

Persons	U.S.		Canada	
	mg alpha-TE	Units	mg alpha-TE	Units
Infants and children				
Birth to 3 years of age	3–6	5–10	3–4	5–6.7
4 to 6 years of age	7	11.7	5	8.3
7 to 10 years of age	7	11.7	6–8	10–13
Adolescent and adult males	10	16.7	6–10	10–16.7
Adolescent and adult females	8	13	5–7	8.3–11.7
Pregnant females	10	16.7	8–9	13–15
Breast-feeding females	11–12	18–20	9–10	15–16.7

Before Using This Dietary Supplement

If you are taking this dietary supplement without a prescription, carefully read and follow any precautions on the label. For vitamin E, the following should be considered:

Allergies—Tell your health care professional if you have ever had any unusual or allergic reaction to vitamin E. Also, tell your health care professional if you are allergic to any other substances, such as foods, preservatives, or dyes.

Pregnancy—It is especially important that you are receiving enough vitamins when you become pregnant and that you continue to receive the right amount of vitamins throughout your pregnancy. The healthy growth and development of the fetus depend on a steady supply of nutrients from the mother. However, taking large amounts of a dietary supplement during pregnancy may be harmful and should be avoided.

Breast-feeding—It is especially important that you receive the right amounts of vitamins so that your baby will also get the vitamins needed to grow properly. You should also check with your health care professional if you are giving your baby an unfortified formula. In that case, the baby must get the vitamins needed some other way. However, taking large amounts of a dietary supplement while breast-feeding may be harmful to the mother and/or baby and should be avoided.

Children—Problems in children have not been reported with intake of normal daily recommended amounts. You should check with your health care professional if you are giving your baby an unfortified formula. In that case, the baby must get the vitamins needed some other way. Some studies have shown that premature infants may have low levels of vitamin E. Your health care professional may recommend a vitamin E supplement.

Older adults—Problems in older adults have not been reported with intake of normal daily recommended amounts.

Medicines or other dietary supplements—Although certain medicines or dietary supplements should not be used together at all, in other cases they may be used together even if an interaction might occur. In these cases, your health care professional may want to change the dose, or other precautions may be necessary. Tell your health care professional if you are taking any other prescription or nonprescription (over-the-counter [OTC]) medicine.

Other medical problems—The presence of other medical problems may affect the use of vitamin E. Make sure you tell your health care professional if you have any other medical problems, especially:

- Bleeding problems—Vitamin E, when taken in doses greater than 800 Units a day for long periods of time, may make this condition worse

Proper Use of This Dietary Supplement

Dosing—The amount of vitamin E needed to meet normal daily recommended intakes will be different for different individuals. The following information includes only the average amounts of vitamin E.

- For *oral solution* dosage form:
  - —To prevent the following deficiencies in infants:
    - Infants receiving a formula high in polyunsaturated fatty acids—15 to 25 Units per day or 7 Units per 32 ounces of formula.
    - Infants with certain colon problems—15 to 25 Units per kilogram (kg) (6.8 to 11 Units per pound) of body weight per day. The water-soluble form of vitamin E must be used.
    - Infants of normal birthweight—5 Units per 32 ounces of formula.
- For *oral* dosage forms (capsules, tablets, oral solution):
  - —To prevent deficiency for individuals (other than infants), the amount taken by mouth is based on normal daily recommended intakes:

    For the U.S.
    - Adult and teenage males—10 milligrams (mg) of alpha tocopherol equivalents (mg alpha-TE) or 16.7 Units per day.
    - Adult and teenage females—8 mg alpha-TE or 13 Units per day.
    - Pregnant females—10 mg alpha-TE or 16.7 Units per day.
    - Breast-feeding females—11 to 12 mg alpha-TE or 18 to 20 Units per day.
    - Children 4 to 10 years of age—7 mg alpha-TE or 11.7 Units per day.
    - Children birth to 3 years of age—3 to 6 mg alpha-TE or 5 to 10 Units per day.

    For Canada
    - Adult and teenage males—6 to 10 mg alpha-TE or 10 to 16.7 Units per day.
    - Adult and teenage females—5 to 7 mg alpha-TE or 8.3 to 11.7 Units per day.
    - Pregnant females—8 to 9 mg alpha-TE or 13 to 15 Units per day.
    - Breast-feeding females—9 to 10 mg alpha-TE or 15 to 16.7 Units per day.
    - Children 7 to 10 years of age—6 to 8 mg alpha-TE or 10 to 13 Units per day.
    - Children 4 to 6 years of age—5 mg alpha-TE or 8.3 Units per day.
    - Children birth to 3 years of age—3 to 4 mg alpha-TE or 5 to 6.7 Units per day.
  - —To treat deficiency:
    - Adults, teenagers, and children—Treatment dose is determined by prescriber for each individual based on the severity of deficiency.

For individuals taking the *oral liquid form of this dietary supplement:*

- This preparation should be taken by mouth even though it comes in a dropper bottle.
- This dietary supplement may be dropped directly into the mouth or mixed with cereal, fruit juice, or other food.

Missed dose—If you miss taking a vitamin for one or more days there is no cause for concern, since it takes some time for your body to become seriously low in vitamins. However, if your health care professional has recommended that you take this vitamin, try to remember to take it as directed every day.

Storage—To store this dietary supplement:

- Keep out of the reach of children.
- Store away from heat and direct light.
- Do not store in the bathroom, near the kitchen sink, or in other damp places. Heat or moisture may cause the dietary supplement to break down.
- Keep the oral liquid form of this dietary supplement from freezing.
- Do not keep outdated dietary supplements or those no longer needed. Be sure that any discarded dietary supplement is out of the reach of children.

Side Effects of This Dietary Supplement

Along with its needed effects, a dietary supplement may cause some unwanted effects. When used for short periods of time at recommended doses, vitamin E usually does not cause any side effects. However, check with your health care professional as soon as possible if any of the following side effects occur:

With doses greater than 400 Units a day and long-term use

Blurred vision; diarrhea; dizziness; headache; nausea or stomach cramps; unusual tiredness or weakness

Other side effects not listed above may also occur in some individuals. If you notice any other effects, check with your health care professional.

Revised: 06/22/93
Interim revision: 07/20/94; 05/26/95

VITAMIN K Systemic

Some commonly used brand names are:

In the U.S.—

AquaMEPHYTON[2]
Konakion[2]
Mephyton[2]
Synkayvite[1]

Note: For quick reference, the following medicines are numbered to match the corresponding brand names.

Another commonly used name is phytomenadione.

This information applies to the following medicines:

1. Menadiol (men-a-DYE-ole)†
2. Phytonadione (fye-toe-na-DYE-one)§

†Not commercially available in Canada.
§Generic name product may also be available in Canada.

Description

Vitamins (VYE-ta-mins) are compounds that you *must* have for growth and health. They are needed in only small amounts and are usually available in the foods that you eat. Vitamin K is necessary for normal clotting of the blood.

Vitamin K is found in various foods including green leafy vegetables, meat, and dairy products. If you eat a balanced diet containing these foods, you should be getting all the vitamin K you need. Little vitamin K is lost from foods with ordinary cooking.

Lack of vitamin K is rare but may lead to problems with blood clotting and increased bleeding. Your doctor may treat this by prescribing vitamin K for you.

Vitamin K is routinely given to newborn infants to prevent bleeding problems.

This medicine is available only with your doctor's prescription, in the following dosage forms:

Oral
- Menadiol
  - Tablets (U.S.)
- Phytonadione
  - Tablets (U.S.)

Parenteral
- Menadiol
  - Injection (U.S.)
- Phytonadione
  - Injection (U.S. and Canada)

Before Using This Medicine

In deciding to use a medicine, the risks of taking the medicine must be weighed against the good it will do. This is a decision you and your doctor will make. For vitamin K, the following should be considered:

Allergies—Tell your doctor if you have ever had any unusual or allergic reaction to vitamin K. Also tell your health care professional if you are allergic to any other substances, such as foods, preservatives, or dyes.

Pregnancy—Vitamin K has not been reported to cause birth defects or other problems in humans.

Breast-feeding—Vitamin K taken by the mother has not been reported to cause problems in nursing babies. You should also check with your doctor if you are giving your baby an unfortified formula. In that case, the baby must get the vitamins needed some other way.

Children—Children may be especially sensitive to the effects of vitamin K, especially menadiol. This may increase the chance of side effects during treatment.

Older adults—Many medicines have not been tested in older people. Therefore, it may not be known whether they work exactly the same way they do in younger adults or if they cause different side effects or problems in older people. There is no specific information about the use of vitamin K in the elderly.

Other medicines—Although certain medicines should not be used together at all, in other cases two different medicines may be used together even if an interaction might occur. In these cases, your doctor may want to change the dose, or other precautions may be necessary. When you are taking vitamin K, it is especially important that your health care professional know if you are taking any of the following:

- Acetohydroxamic acid (e.g., Lithostat) or
- Antidiabetics, oral (diabetes medicine you take by mouth) or
- Dapsone or
- Furazolidone (e.g., Furoxone) or
- Methyldopa (e.g., Aldomet) or
- Nitrofurantoin (e.g., Furadantin) or
- Primaquine or
- Procainamide (e.g., Pronestyl) or
- Quinidine (e.g., Quinidex) or
- Quinine (e.g., Quinamm) or
- Sulfonamides (sulfa medicine) or
- Sulfoxone (e.g., Diasone)—The chance of a serious side effect may be increased, especially with menadiol
- Anticoagulants (blood thinners)—Vitamin K decreases the effects of these medicines and is sometimes used to treat bleeding caused by anticoagulants; however, anyone receiving an anticoagulant should not take any supplement that contains vitamin K (alone or in combination with

other vitamins or nutrients) unless it has been ordered by their doctor

Other medical problems—The presence of other medical problems may affect the use of vitamin K. Make sure you tell your doctor if you have any other medical problems, especially:

- Cystic fibrosis or
- Diarrhea (prolonged) or
- Intestinal problems—These conditions may interfere with absorption of vitamin K into the body when it is taken by mouth; higher doses may be needed, or the medicine may have to be injected
- Glucose-6-phosphate dehydrogenase (G6PD) deficiency or
- Liver disease—The chance of unwanted effects may be increased

Proper Use of This Medicine

Take this medicine only as directed by your doctor. Do not take more or less of it, do not take it more often, and do not take it for a longer time than your doctor ordered. To do so may cause serious unwanted effects such as blood clotting problems.

Your doctor should check your progress at regular visits. A blood test must be taken regularly to see how fast your blood is clotting. This will help your doctor decide how much medicine you need.

Dosing—The dose of these medicines will be different for different patients. *Follow your doctor's orders or the directions on the label.* The following information includes only the average doses of these medicines. *If your dose is different, do not change it* unless your doctor tells you to do so.

The number of tablets or injections that you take depends on the strength of the medicine. Also, *the number of doses you take each day, the time allowed between doses, and the length of time you take the medicine depend on the medical problem for which you are taking the medicine.*

For menadiol

- For *oral* dosage form (tablets):
  —For problems with blood clotting or increased bleeding, or for dietary supplementation:
  - Adults and children—The usual dose is 5 to 10 milligrams (mg) a day.
- For *injection* dosage form:
  —For problems with blood clotting or increased bleeding, or for dietary supplementation:
  - Adults and children—The usual dose is 5 to 15 mg, injected into a muscle or under the skin, one or two times a day.

For phytonadione

- For *oral* dosage form (tablets):
  —For problems with blood clotting or increased bleeding, or for dietary supplementation:
  - Adults and teenagers—The usual dose is 2.5 to 25 milligrams (mg). The dose may be repeated after twelve to forty-eight hours, if needed.
  - Children—The usual dose is 5 to 10 mg.
- For *injection* dosage form:
  —For problems with blood clotting or increased bleeding, or for dietary supplementation:
  - Adults and teenagers receiving solid food—The usual dose is 2 to 25 mg, injected into a muscle or under the skin. The dose may be repeated, if needed.
  - Adults and teenagers receiving total parenteral nutrition (TPN)—The usual dose is 5 to 10 mg, injected into a muscle, once a week.
  - Children receiving solid food—The usual dose is 5 to 10 mg injected into a muscle or under the skin.
  - Children receiving TPN—The usual dose is 2 to 5 mg, injected into a muscle, once a week.
  - Infants receiving solid food—The usual dose is 1 to 2 mg injected into a muscle or under the skin.
  - Infants receiving milk substitutes or breast milk—The dose is based on the amount of vitamin K in the infant's diet and must be determined by your doctor.

  —For prevention of bleeding in newborns: The usual dose is 0.5 to 1 mg, injected into a muscle or under the skin, right after delivery. The dose may be repeated after six to eight hours, if needed.

Missed dose—If you miss a dose of this medicine, take it as soon as possible. However, if it is almost time for your next dose, skip the missed dose and go back to your regular dosing schedule. Do not double doses. *Tell your doctor about any doses you miss.*

Storage—To store this medicine:

- Keep out of the reach of children.
- Store away from heat and direct light.
- Do not store in the bathroom, near the kitchen sink, or in other damp places. Heat or moisture may cause the medicine to break down.
- Do not keep outdated medicine or medicine no longer needed. Be sure that any discarded medicine is out of the reach of children.

Precautions While Using This Medicine

Tell all medical doctors and dentists you go to that you are taking this medicine.

Always check with your health care professional before you start or stop taking any other medicine. This includes any nonprescription (over-the-counter [OTC]) medicine, even aspirin. Other medicines may change the way this medicine affects your body.

Side Effects of This Medicine

Along with its needed effects, a medicine may cause some unwanted effects. Although vitamin K does not usually cause side effects that need medical attention, check with your doctor if any of the following side effects continue or are bothersome:

Less common

Flushing of face; redness, pain, or swelling at place of injection; unusual taste

Other side effects not listed above may also occur in some patients. If you notice any other effects, check with your doctor.

Revised: August 1990
Interim revision: 07/20/94

VITAMINS AND FLUORIDE Systemic

Some commonly used brand names are:

In the U.S.—

Adeflor[1]	Poly-Vi-Flor[1]
Cari-Tab[2]	Tri-Vi-Flor[2]
Mulvidren-F[1]	Vi-Daylin/F[1]

In Canada—

Adeflor[1]	Tri-Vi-Flor[2]
Poly-Vi-Flor[1]	

Note: For quick reference, the following vitamins and fluoride combinations are numbered to match the corresponding brand names.

This information applies to the following medicines:

1. Multiple Vitamins and Fluoride
2. Vitamins A, D, and C and Fluoride

Description

This medicine is a combination of vitamins and fluoride. Vitamins are used when the daily diet does not include enough of the vitamins needed for good health.

Fluoride has been found to be helpful in reducing the number of cavities in the teeth. It is usually present naturally in drinking water. However, some areas of the country do not have a high enough level of fluoride in the water. To make up for this, extra fluorides may be added to the diet. Some children may require both dietary fluorides and fluoride treatments by the dentist. Use of a fluoride toothpaste or rinse may be helpful, as well.

Taking fluorides does not replace good dental habits. These include eating a good diet, brushing and flossing teeth frequently, and having regular dental checkups.

This medicine is available only with your medical doctor's or dentist's prescription, in the following dosage forms:

Oral

- Oral solution (U.S. and Canada)
- Chewable Tablets (U.S. and Canada)

Before Using This Dietary Supplement

In deciding to use a dietary supplement, the risks of taking the dietary supplement must be weighed against the good it will do. This is a decision you and your medical doctor or dentist will make. For multiple vitamins and fluoride, the following should be considered:

Allergies—Tell your medical doctor or dentist if you have ever had any unusual or allergic reactions to fluoride. Also, tell your medical doctor, dentist, and pharmacist if you are allergic to any other substances, such as foods, preservatives, or dyes.

Pregnancy—Fluoride occurs naturally in water and has not been shown to cause problems in infants of mothers who drank fluoridated water or took recommended doses of supplements.

Breast-feeding—Small amounts of fluoride pass into breast milk; however, problems have not been documented with normal intake.

Children—Doses of fluoride that are too large or are taken for a long time may cause bone problems and teeth discoloration in children.

Older adults—This dietary supplement has not been shown to cause different side effects or problems in older people than it does in younger adults.

Medicines or other dietary supplements—Although certain medicines or dietary supplements should not be used together at all, in other cases they may be used together even if an interaction might occur. In these cases, your medical doctor or dentist may want to change the dose, or other precautions may be necessary. When you are taking multiple vitamins and fluoride it is especially important that your medical doctor or dentist, and pharmacist know if you are taking any of the following:

- Anticoagulants, coumarin- or indandione-derivative (blood thinners)—Use with vitamin K (in the multiple vitamins and fluoride preparations) may prevent the anticoagulant from working properly
- Iron supplements—Use with vitamin E (in the multiple vitamins and fluoride preparation) may prevent the iron supplement from working properly
- Vitamin D and related compounds—Use with vitamin D (in the multiple vitamins and fluoride preparations) may cause high blood levels of vitamin D, which may increase the chance of side effects

Other medical problems—The presence of other medical problems may affect the use of multiple vitamins and fluoride. Make sure you tell your medical doctor or dentist if you have any other medical problems, especially:

- Dental fluorosis (teeth discoloration)—Fluorides may make this condition worse

Proper Use of This Dietary Supplement

Take this dietary supplement only as directed by your medical doctor or dentist. Do not take more of it and do not take it more often than ordered. Taking too much fluoride and some vitamins (especially vitamins A and D) over a period of time may cause unwanted effects.

Do not take multiple vitamins and fluoride products at the same time as taking foods that contain calcium. It is best to space them 1 to 2 hours apart, to get the full benefit from the medicine.

For patients taking the *chewable tablet form* of this dietary supplement:

- Tablets should be chewed or crushed before they are swallowed.
- This dietary supplement works best if it is taken at bedtime, after the teeth have been thoroughly brushed.

For patients taking the *oral liquid form of* this dietary supplement:

- This dietary supplement is to be taken by mouth even though it comes in a dropper bottle. The amount to be taken is to be measured with the specially marked dropper.
- *Always store this dietary supplement in the original plastic container.* It has been designed to give you the correct dose. Also, fluoride will interact with glass and should not be stored in glass containers.
- This dietary supplement may be dropped directly into the mouth or mixed with cereal, fruit juice, or other food.

Missed dose—If you miss a dose of this dietary supplement, take it as soon as you remember. However, if it is almost time for the next dose, skip the missed dose and go back to your regular dosing schedule. Do not double doses.

Storage—To store this dietary supplement:

- Keep this dietary supplement out of the reach of children, since overdose is especially dangerous in children.
- Store away from heat and direct light.
- Do not store in the bathroom, near the kitchen sink, or in other damp places. Heat or moisture may cause the dietary supplement to break down.
- Protect the oral solution from freezing.
- Do not keep outdated dietary supplements or those no longer needed. Be sure that any discarded dietary supplement is out of the reach of children.

Precautions While Using This Dietary Supplement

The level of fluoride present in the water is different in different parts of the country. If you move to another area, check with a medical doctor or dentist in the new area as soon as possible to see if this medicine is still needed or if the dose needs to be changed. Also, check with your medical doctor or dentist if you change infant feeding habits (e.g., breast-feeding to infant formula), drinking water (e.g., city water to nonfluoridated bottled water), or filtering systems (e.g., tap water to filtered tap water).

Inform your medical doctor or dentist as soon as possible if you notice white, brown, or black spots on the teeth. These are signs of too much fluoride.

Side Effects of This Dietary Supplement

Along with its needed effects, a dietary supplement may cause some unwanted effects. Although not all of these side effects may occur, if they do occur they may need medical attention.

When the correct amount of this dietary supplement is used, side effects usually are rare. However, *taking an overdose of fluoride may cause serious problems.*

Stop taking this dietary supplement and check with your medical doctor immediately if any of the following side effects occur, as they may be signs of severe fluoride overdose:

Black, tarry stools; bloody vomit; diarrhea; drowsiness; faintness; increased watering of mouth; nausea or vomiting; shallow breathing; stomach cramps or pain; tremors; unusual excitement; watery eyes; weakness

Check with your medical doctor or dentist as soon as possible if the following side effects occur, as some may be early signs of possible chronic fluoride overdose:

Pain and aching of bones; skin rash; sores in the mouth and on the lips; stiffness; white, brown, or black discoloration of teeth

Other side effects not listed above may also occur in some patients. If you notice any other effects, check with your medical doctor or dentist.

Revised: September 1990
Interim revision: 08/21/92

XYLOMETAZOLINE Nasal

Some commonly used brand names are:

In the U.S.—

Chlorohist-LA	Otrivin Nasal Drops
Neo-Synephrine II Long Acting Nasal Spray Adult Strength	Otrivin Nasal Spray
Neo-Synephrine II Long Acting Nose Drops Adult Strength	Otrivin Pediatric Nasal Drops

Generic name product may also be available.

In Canada—

Otrivin Nasal Drops	Otrivin Pediatric Nasal Spray
Otrivin Nasal Spray	Otrivin With Metered-Dose Pump
Otrivin Pediatric Nasal Drops	

Description

Xylometazoline (zye-loe-met-AZ-oh-leen) is used for the temporary relief of congestion or stuffiness in the nose caused by hay fever or other allergies, colds, or sinus trouble.

This medicine may also be used for other conditions as determined by your doctor.

This medicine is available without a prescription; however, your doctor may have special instructions on the proper use or dose for your medical condition.

Xylometazoline is available in the following dosage forms:

Nasal
- Nasal drops (U.S. and Canada)
- Nasal spray (U.S. and Canada)

Before Using This Medicine

If you are using this medicine without a prescription, carefully read and follow any precautions on the label. For xylometazoline, the following should be considered:

Allergies—Tell your doctor if you have ever had any unusual or allergic reaction to xylometazoline or to any of the other nasal decongestants. Also tell your health care professional if you are allergic to any other substances, such as foods, preservatives, or dyes.

Pregnancy—Xylometazoline may be absorbed into the body. However, xylometazoline has not been shown to cause birth defects or other problems in humans.

Breast-feeding—Xylometazoline may be absorbed into the body. However, xylometazoline has not been reported to cause problems in nursing babies.

Children—Children may be especially sensitive to the effects of xylometazoline. This may increase the chance of side effects during treatment.

Older adults—Many medicines have not been studied specifically in older people. Therefore, it may not be known whether they work exactly the same way they do in younger adults or if they cause different side effects or problems in older people. There is no specific information comparing use of xylometazoline in the elderly with use in other age groups.

Other medicines—Although certain medicines should not be used together at all, in other cases two different medicines may be used together even if an interaction might occur. In these cases, your doctor may want to change the dose, or other precautions may be necessary. Tell your health care professional if you are taking any other prescription or nonprescription (over-the-counter [OTC]) medicine.

Other medical problems—The presence of other medical problems may affect the use of xylometazoline. Make sure you tell your doctor if you have any other medical problems, especially:
- Diabetes mellitus (sugar diabetes)
- Heart or blood vessel disease or
- High blood pressure—Xylometazoline may make the condition worse
- Overactive thyroid

Proper Use of This Medicine

To use the *nose drops*:
- Blow your nose gently. Tilt the head back while standing or sitting up. Place the drops into each nostril and immediately bend head forward toward the knees for a few seconds to allow the medicine to spread throughout the nose.
- Rinse the dropper with hot water and dry with a clean tissue. Replace the cap right after use.

To use the *nose spray*:
- Blow your nose gently. With the head upright, spray the medicine into each nostril. Sniff briskly while squeezing the bottle quickly and firmly. For best results, spray once into each nostril, wait 3 to 5 minutes to allow the medicine to work, then blow your nose gently and thoroughly. Repeat until the complete dose is used.
- Rinse the tip of the spray bottle with hot water taking care not to suck water into the bottle, and dry with a clean tissue. Replace the cap right after use.

To avoid spreading the infection, do not use the container for more than one person.

Use this medicine only as directed. Do not use more of it, do not use it more often, and do not use it for longer than 3 days, unless otherwise directed by your doctor. To do so may make your runny or stuffy nose worse and may also increase the chance of side effects.

Dosing—The dose of nasal xylometazoline will be different for different patients. *Follow your doctor's orders or the directions on the label.* The following information includes only the average doses of nasal xylometazoline. *If your dose is different, do not change it* unless your doctor tells you to do so.

- For stuffy nose:
  - —For *nose drops* dosage form:
    - Adults and children 12 years of age and older—Use two or three drops of a 0.05 to 0.1% solution in each nostril every eight to ten hours as needed.

• Children 2 to 12 years of age—Use two or three drops of a 0.05% solution in each nostril every eight to ten hours as needed.

• Children up to 2 years of age—Use and dose must be determined by your doctor.

—For *nose spray* dosage form:

• Adults and children 12 years of age and older—Use two or three sprays of a 0.05 to 0.1% solution in each nostril every eight to ten hours as needed.

• Children up to 12 years of age—Use and dose must be determined by your doctor.

Missed dose—If you miss a dose of this medicine and you remember within an hour or so of the missed dose, use it right away. However, if you do not remember until later, skip the missed dose and go back to your regular dosing schedule. Do not double doses.

Storage—To store this medicine:

- Keep out of the reach of children.
- Store away from heat and direct light.
- Keep the medicine from freezing.
- Do not keep outdated medicine or medicine no longer needed. Be sure that any discarded medicine is out of the reach of children.

Side Effects of This Medicine

Along with its needed effects, a medicine may cause some unwanted effects. Although not all of these side effects may occur, if they do occur they may need medical attention.

When this medicine is used for short periods of time at low doses, side effects usually are rare. However, check with your doctor as soon as possible if any of the following occur:

Increase in runny or stuffy nose

Symptoms of too much medicine being absorbed into the body

Blurred vision; headache or lightheadedness; nervousness; pounding, irregular, or fast heartbeat; trouble in sleeping

Other side effects may occur that usually do not need medical attention. These side effects may go away during treatment as your body adjusts to the medicine. However, check with your health care professional if any of the following side effects continue or are bothersome:

Burning, dryness, or stinging of inside of nose; sneezing

Other side effects not listed above may also occur in some patients. If you notice any other effects, check with your health care professional.

Revised: 05/16/94

YELLOW FEVER VACCINE Systemic

A commonly used brand name in the U.S. is YF-Vax.
Generic name product may be available in Canada.

Description

Yellow Fever Vaccine is used to prevent infection by the yellow fever virus. It works by causing your body to produce its own protection (antibodies) against the virus.

Vaccination against yellow fever is recommended for all persons 9 months of age and older who are traveling to or living in areas of Africa, South America, or other countries where there is yellow fever infection and for people who are traveling to countries that require yellow fever immunization (certificate of vaccination). It is also needed by other people who might come into contact with the yellow fever virus.

Infants 6 to 9 months of age and pregnant women should be vaccinated only if they must travel to areas where there is an epidemic of yellow fever and they cannot be protected from mosquito bites.

Infants 4 to 6 months of age may be vaccinated only if there is a high risk of getting yellow fever infection.

Vaccination against yellow fever is not recommended for infants younger than 4 months of age because they have an increased chance of getting serious side effects from the vaccine.

The certificate of vaccination for yellow fever is valid for 10 years beginning 10 days after the first vaccination, or on the date of the second vaccination if within 10 years of the first injection.

Yellow fever vaccine is given only at authorized Yellow Fever Vaccination Centers. The location of these centers can be obtained from your state, province, and local health departments.

The vaccine is available in the following dosage form:

Parenteral

- Injection (U.S. and Canada)

Before Using This Medicine

In deciding to use a medicine, the risks of taking the medicine must be weighed against the good it will do. This is a decision you and your doctor will make. For yellow fever vaccine, the following should be considered:

Allergies—Tell your doctor if you have ever had any unusual or allergic reaction to yellow fever vaccine. Also tell your doctor if you are allergic to any other substances, such as foods (especially eggs and chicken), preservatives, or dyes. The yellow fever vaccine available in the U.S. and Canada is grown in chick embryo cell culture so it may contain egg or chicken protein.

If you are allergic to eggs or chicken, your doctor may have to do a skin test before giving you the vaccine. However, if you need the vaccine because of international travel requirements, not because you are traveling to a country where there is a high risk of getting yellow fever, you may ask your doctor for a waiver letter stating the reason why you cannot be vaccinated.

Pregnancy—Yellow fever vaccine may cause birth defects. Therefore, it is not recommended for use in pregnant women, especially in the first 3 months of pregnancy, unless they are at high risk of getting yellow fever. Pregnant women who have not already been immunized are generally advised to postpone their travel and vaccination until after giving birth.

If travel to high-risk areas cannot be postponed, pregnant women should be vaccinated. The chance of getting serious problems from infection with yellow fever in those areas is much greater than the chance of getting a serious side effect from the vaccine for both the mother and the fetus.

However, a pregnant woman who needs the vaccine because of international travel requirements, not because she is traveling to a country where there is a high risk of getting yellow fever, may ask the doctor for a waiver letter (official-looking on letterhead stationery) stating why she cannot be vaccinated.

Breast-feeding—Yellow fever vaccine has not been shown to cause problems in nursing babies.

Children—Yellow fever vaccine is recommended for children 9 months of age or older if they are traveling to, or living in, areas where there is yellow fever infection, or if they are traveling to areas that require yellow fever immunization (certificate of vaccination). In special cases, such as high-risk exposure, yellow fever vaccine may be given to children 4 to 9 months of age. However, the vaccine is not recommended for infants younger than 4 months of age, because of an increased chance of serious side effects.

Other medicines—Although certain medicines should not be used together at all, in other cases two different medicines may be used together even if an interaction might occur. In these cases, your doctor may want to change the dose, or other precautions may be necessary. Before you receive yellow fever vaccine, it is especially important that your doctor know if you have received any of the following:

- Treatment with x-rays or medicines that may lower the body's protection against infection such as those used for organ transplants (e.g., cyclosporine), cancer medicines, or corticosteroids—May decrease the useful effect of yellow fever vaccine

Other medical problems—The presence of other medical problems may affect the use of yellow fever vaccine. Make sure you tell your doctor if you have any other medical problems, especially:

- Immune deficiency condition (or family history of)—The condition may decrease the useful effect of the vaccine or may increase the risk and severity of side effects
- Serious illness with fever—The symptoms of the illness may be confused with the possible side effects of the vaccine

Side Effects of This Medicine

Along with its needed effects, a vaccine may cause some unwanted effects. Although not all of these side effects may occur, if they do occur they may need medical attention.

Get emergency help immediately if any of the following side effects occur:

Rare

Confusion; convulsions (seizures); coughing; difficulty in breathing or swallowing; fast heartbeat; feeling of burning, crawling, or tingling of skin; nervousness or irritability; reddening of skin; severe headache; skin rash or itching; sneezing; stiff neck; throbbing in the ears; unusual tiredness or weakness; vomiting

Other side effects may occur that usually do not need medical attention. These side effects may go away during treatment as your body adjusts to the medicine. However, check with your doctor if any of the following side effects continue or are bothersome:

Less common

Low fever; mild headache; muscle pain; pain at place of injection

Other side effects not listed above may also occur in some patients. If you notice any other effects, check with your doctor.

Developed: 11/22/93

YOHIMBINE Systemic

Some commonly used brand names are:

In the U.S.—

Actibine	Yocon
Aphrodyne	Yohimar
Baron-X	Yohimex
Dayto Himbin	Yoman
Prohim	Yovital
Thybine	

Generic name product may also be available.

In Canada—

PMS-Yohimbine	Yocon

Generic name product may also be available.

Description

Yohimbine (yo-HIM-been) is used to treat men who are impotent (not able to have sex). It is taken by mouth to help produce erections.

The way yohimbine works is not known for sure. It is thought, however, to work by increasing the body's production of certain chemicals that help produce erections. It does not work in all men who are impotent.

Yohimbine is available only with your doctor's prescription, in the following dosage form:

Oral

- Tablets (U.S. and Canada)

Before Using This Medicine

In deciding to use a medicine, the risks of taking the medicine must be weighed against the good it will do. This is a decision you and your doctor will make. For yohimbine, the following should be considered:

Allergies—Tell your doctor if you have ever had any unusual or allergic reaction to yohimbine or any of the rauwolfia alkaloids, such as deserpidine (e.g, Harmonyl), rauwolfia serpentina (e.g., Raudixin), or reserpine (e.g., Serpalan). Also tell your health care professional if you are allergic to any other substances, such as foods, preservatives, or dyes.

Older adults—Many medicines have not been studied specifically in older people. Therefore, it may not be known whether they work exactly the same way they do in younger adults. Although there is no specific information comparing use of yohimbine in the elderly with use in other age groups, this medicine has been used in some elderly patients and has not been shown to cause different side effects or problems in older people than it does in younger adults.

Other medicines—Although certain medicines should not be used together at all, in other cases two different medicines may be used together even if an interaction might occur. In these cases, your doctor may want to change the dose, or other precautions may be necessary. Tell your health care professional if you are taking any other prescription or nonprescription (over-the-counter [OTC]) medicine.

Other medical problems—The presence of other medical problems may affect the use of yohimbine. Make sure you tell your doctor if you have any other medical problems, especially:

- Angina pectoris or
- Depression or
- Other psychiatric illness or
- Heart disease or
- High blood pressure or
- Kidney disease—Yohimbine may make these conditions worse
- Liver disease—Effects of yohimbine may be increased because of slower removal from the body

Proper Use of This Medicine

This medicine usually begins to work about 2 to 3 weeks after you begin to take it.

Dosing—The dose of yohimbine will be different for different patients. *Follow your doctor's orders or the directions on the label.* The following information includes only the average doses of yohimbine. *If your dose is different, do not change it* unless your doctor tells you to do so.

The number of tablets that you take depends on the strength of the medicine.

- For *oral* dosage form (tablets):
  - —For treating impotence:
    - Adults—5.4 to 6 milligrams (mg) three times a day.

Missed dose—If you miss a dose of this medicine, take it as soon as possible. However, if it is almost time for your next dose, skip the missed dose and go back to your regular dosing schedule. Do not double doses.

Storage—To store this medicine:
- Keep out of the reach of children.
- Store away from heat and direct light.
- Do not store in the bathroom, near the kitchen sink, or in other damp places. Heat or moisture may cause the medicine to break down.
- Keep the medicine from freezing. Do not refrigerate.
- Do not keep outdated medicine or medicine no longer needed. Be sure that any discarded medicine is out of the reach of children.

Precautions While Using This Medicine

It is important that your doctor check your progress at regular visits to make sure that this medicine is working properly.

Use yohimbine exactly as directed by your doctor. Do not use more of it and do not use it more often than ordered. If too much is used, the risk of side effects such as fast heartbeat and high blood pressure is increased.

Side Effects of This Medicine

Along with its needed effects, a medicine may cause some unwanted effects. Although not all of these side effects may occur, if they do occur they may need medical attention.

Check with your doctor as soon as possible if any of the following side effects occur:

Less common

Fast heartbeat; increased blood pressure

Other side effects may occur that usually do not need medical attention. These side effects may go away during treatment as your body adjusts to the medicine. However, check with your doctor if any of the following side effects continue or are bothersome:

Less common

Dizziness; headache; irritability; nervousness or restlessness

Rare

Nausea and vomiting; skin flushing; sweating; tremor

Other side effects not listed above may also occur in some patients. If you notice any other effects, check with your doctor.

Revised: 10/24/92
Interim revision: 07/05/94

ZAFIRLUKAST Systemic†

A commonly used brand name in the U.S. is Accolate.

†Not commercially available in Canada.

Description

Zafirlukast (za-FIR-loo-kast) is used by patients with mild-to-moderate asthma to decrease the symptoms of asthma and the number of acute asthma attacks. However, this medicine should not be used to relieve an asthma attack that has already started.

This medicine is available only with your doctor's prescription, in the following dosage form:

Oral

- Tablets (U.S.)

Before Using This Medicine

In deciding to use a medicine, the risks of taking the medicine must be weighed against the good it will do. This is a decision you and your doctor will make. For zafirlukast, the following should be considered:

Allergies—Tell your doctor if you have ever had any unusual or allergic reaction to zafirlukast.

Pregnancy—Zafirlukast has not been studied in pregnant women. Studies in animals have shown that this medicine causes problems only when given in doses many times higher than the usual human dose.

Breast-feeding—Zafirlukast passes into breast milk and may cause unwanted effects in nursing babies. Breast-feeding is not recommended while you are taking zafirlukast.

Children—Studies on this medicine have been done only in adult patients and there is no specific information comparing use of zafirlukast in children up to 12 years of age with use in other age groups.

Older adults—In studies, mild to moderate respiratory tract infections were more likely to occur in patients 55 years of age or older taking zafirlukast. It is not known whether these infections were caused by taking zafirlukast or by other factors.

Other medicines—Although certain medicines should not be used together at all, in other cases two different medicines may be used together even if an interaction might occur. In these cases, your doctor may want to change the dose, or other precautions may be necessary. When you are taking zafirlukast, it is especially important that your health care professional know if you are taking any of the following:

- Astemizole (e.g., Hismanal) or
- Carbamazepine (e.g., Tegretol) or
- Cisapride (e.g., Propulsid) or
- Cyclosporine (e.g., Sandimmune) or
- Felodipine (e.g., Plendil) or
- Isradipine (e.g., DynaCirc) or
- Nicardipine (e.g., Cardene) or
- Nifedipine (e.g., Procardia, Adalat) or
- Nimodipine (e.g., Nimotop) or
- Phenytoin (e.g., Dilantin) or
- Tolbutamide (e.g., Orinase) or
- Warfarin (e.g., Coumadin)—Zafirlukast may increase the effects of these medicines

Proper Use of This Medicine

Zafirlukast is used to prevent asthma attacks. It is not used to relieve an attack that has already started. For relief of an asthma attack that has already started, you should use another medicine. If you do not have another medicine to use for an attack or if you have any questions about this, check with your health care professional.

Food may change the amount of zafirlukast that is absorbed. For this reason, it should be taken on an empty stomach, 1 hour before or 2 hours after a meal.

Dosing—The dose of this medicine will be different for different patients. *Follow your doctor's orders or the directions on the label.* The following information includes only the average doses of zafirlukast. *If your dose is different, do not change it* unless your doctor tells you to do so.

- For *oral* dosage form (tablets):
  - —For asthma:
    - Adults and children 12 years of age and older—20 milligrams (mg) two times a day, on an empty stomach, at least 1 hour before or 2 hours after meals.
    - Children up to 12 years of age—Use and dose must be determined by your doctor.

Missed dose—If you miss a dose of this medicine, take it as soon as possible. However, if it is almost time for your next dose, skip the missed dose and go back to your regular dosing schedule. Do not double doses.

Storage—To store this medicine:

- Keep out of the reach of children.
- Store away from heat and direct light.
- Do not store in the bathroom, near the kitchen sink, or in other damp places. Heat or moisture may cause the medicine to break down.
- Do not keep outdated medicine or medicine no longer needed. Be sure that any discarded medicine is out of the reach of children.

Precautions While Using This Medicine

To work properly, zafirlukast must be taken every day at regularly spaced times, even if your asthma seems better.

You may be taking other medicines for asthma along with zafirlukast. Do not stop taking or reduce the dose of the other medicines, even if your asthma seems better, unless you are told to do so by your doctor.

Side Effects of This Medicine

Along with its needed effects, a medicine may cause some unwanted effects. The following side effects may go away during treatment as your body adjusts to the medicine. However, check with your doctor if any of the following side effects continue or are bothersome:

Less common

Headache; nausea

Developed: 07/18/97

ZALCITABINE Systemic

A commonly used brand name in the U.S. and Canada is HIVID. Another commonly used name is ddC.

Description

Zalcitabine (zal-SITE-a-been) (also known as ddC) is used in the treatment of the infection caused by the human immunodeficiency virus (HIV). HIV is the virus that causes acquired immune deficiency syndrome (AIDS).

Zalcitabine (ddC) will not cure or prevent HIV infection or AIDS; however, it helps keep HIV from reproducing and appears to slow down the destruction of the immune system. This may help delay the development of problems usually related to AIDS or HIV disease. Zalcitabine will not keep you from spreading HIV to other people. People who receive this medicine may continue to have other problems usually related to AIDS or HIV disease.

Zalcitabine may cause some serious side effects, including peripheral neuropathy (a problem involving the nerves). Symptoms of peripheral neuropathy include tingling, burning, numbness, or pain in the hands or feet. Zalcitabine may also cause pancreatitis (inflammation of the pancreas). Symptoms of pancreatitis include stomach pain, and nausea and vomiting. *Check with your doctor if any new health problems or symptoms occur while you are taking zalcitabine.*

Zalcitabine is available only with your doctor's prescription, in the following dosage form:

Oral

- Tablets (U.S. and Canada)

Before Using This Medicine

In deciding to use a medicine, the risks of taking the medicine must be weighed against the good it will do. This is a decision you and your doctor will make. For zalcitabine, the following should be considered:

Allergies—Tell your doctor if you have ever had any unusual or allergic reaction to zalcitabine. Also tell your health care professional if you are allergic to any other substances, such as foods, preservatives, or dyes.

Pregnancy—Zalcitabine has not been studied in pregnant women. However, studies in animals have shown that zalcitabine causes birth defects when given in very high doses. Before taking this medicine, make sure your doctor knows if you are pregnant or if you may become pregnant.

Breast-feeding—It is not known whether zalcitabine passes into the breast milk. However, if your baby does not already have the AIDS virus, there is a chance that you could pass it to your baby by breast-feeding. Talk to your doctor first if you are thinking about breast-feeding your baby.

Children—Zalcitabine can cause serious side effects in any patient. Therefore, it is especially important that you discuss with your child's doctor the good that this medicine may do as well as the risks of using it. Your child must be seen frequently and your child's progress carefully followed by the doctor while the child is taking zalcitabine.

Older adults—Zalcitabine has not been studied specifically in older people. Therefore, it is not known whether it causes different side effects or problems in the elderly than it does in younger adults.

Other medicines—Although certain medicines should not be used together at all, in other cases two different medicines may be used together even if an interaction might occur. In these cases, your doctor may want to change the dose, or other precautions may be necessary. When you are taking zalcitabine, it is especially important that your health care professional know if you are taking any of the following:

- Alcohol or
- Asparaginase (e.g., Elspar) or
- Azathioprine (e.g., Imuran) or
- Estrogens (female hormones) or
- Furosemide (e.g., Lasix) or
- Methyldopa (e.g., Aldomet) or
- Pentamidine by injection (e.g., Pentam, Pentacarinat) or
- Sulfonamides (e.g., Bactrim, Septra) or
- Sulindac (e.g., Clinoril) or
- Tetracyclines or
- Thiazide diuretics (water pills) (e.g., Diuril, Hydrodiuril) or
- Valproic acid (e.g., Depakote)—Use of these medicines with zalcitabine may increase the chance of pancreatitis (inflammation of the pancreas)
- Aminoglycosides by injection (amikacin [e.g., Amikin], gentamicin [e.g., Garamycin], kanamycin [e.g., Kantrex], neomycin [e.g., Mycifradin], netilmicin [e.g., Netromycin], streptomycin, tobramycin [e.g., Nebcin]) or
- Amphotericin B (e.g., Fungizone) or
- Foscarnet (e.g., Foscavir)—Use of these medicines with zalcitabine may increase the chance of side effects
- Antacids, aluminum-, and/or magnesium-containing (e.g., Maalox, Mylanta)—Use of antacids with zalcitabine may decrease the absorption of zalcitabine; antacids and zalcitabine should not be taken at the same time
- Chloramphenicol (e.g., Chloromycetin) or
- Cisplatin (e.g., Platinol) or
- Dapsone (e.g., Avlosulfon) or

- Didanosine (e.g., Videx, ddI) or
- Ethambutol (e.g., Myambutol) or
- Ethionamide (e.g., Trecator-SC) or
- Hydralazine (e.g., Apresoline) or
- Isoniazid (e.g., Nydrazid) or
- Lithium (e.g., Eskalith, Lithobid) or
- Metronidazole (e.g., Flagyl) or
- Nitrous oxide or
- Phenytoin (e.g., Dilantin) or
- Stavudine (e.g., Zerit, d4T) or
- Vincristine (e.g., Oncovin)—Use of these medicines with zalcitabine may increase the chance of peripheral neuropathy (tingling, burning, numbness, or pain in your hands or feet)

- Cimetidine (e.g., Tagamet) or
- Probenecid (e.g., Benemid)—Use of these medicines with zalcitabine may increase the chance of side effects of zalcitabine

- Nitrofurantoin (e.g., Furadantin, Macrodantin)—Use of nitrofurantoin with zalcitabine may increase the chance of side effects, including peripheral neuropathy (tingling, burning, numbness, or pain in your hands or feet) and pancreatitis (inflammation of the pancreas)

Other medical problems—The presence of other medical problems may affect the use of zalcitabine. Make sure you tell your doctor if you have any other medical problems, especially:

- Alcohol abuse or
- Increased blood triglycerides (or a history of) or
- Pancreatitis (or a history of)—Patients with these medical problems may be at increased risk of pancreatitis (inflammation of the pancreas)

- Alcohol abuse, history of, or
- Liver disease—Zalcitabine may make liver disease worse in patients with liver disease or a history of alcohol abuse

- Kidney disease—Patients with kidney disease may have an increased chance of side effects

- Peripheral neuropathy—Zalcitabine may make this condition worse

Proper Use of This Medicine

Take this medicine exactly as directed by your doctor. Do not take more of it, do not take it more often, and do not take it for a longer time than your doctor ordered. Also, do not stop taking this medicine without checking with your doctor first.

Keep taking zalcitabine for the full time of treatment, even if you begin to feel better.

This medicine works best when there is a constant amount in the blood. *To help keep the amount constant, do not miss any doses.* If you need help in planning the best times to take your medicine, check with your health care professional.

Only take medicine that your doctor has prescribed specifically for you. Do not share your medicine with others.

Dosing—The dose of zalcitabine will be different for different patients. *Follow your doctor's orders or the directions on the label.* The following information includes only the average doses of zalcitabine. Your dose may be different if you have kidney disease. *If your dose is different, do not change it* unless your doctor tells you to do so:

- For *oral* dosage form (tablets):
  - —For treatment of HIV infection:
    - Adults and children 13 years of age and older—0.75 milligrams (mg), together with 200 mg of zidovudine, every eight hours; or 0.75 mg alone every eight hours.
    - Children up to 12 years of age—Use and dose must be determined by your doctor.

Missed dose—If you miss a dose of this medicine, take it as soon as possible. However, if it is almost time for your next dose, skip the missed dose and go back to your regular dosing schedule. Do not double doses.

Storage—To store this medicine:

- Keep out of the reach of children.
- Store away from heat and direct light.
- Do not store in the bathroom, near the kitchen sink, or in other damp places. Heat or moisture may cause the medicine to break down.
- Do not keep outdated medicine or medicine no longer needed. Be sure that any discarded medicine is out of the reach of children.

Precautions While Using This Medicine

It is very important that your doctor check your progress at regular visits.

Do not take any other medicines without checking with your doctor first. To do so may increase the chance of side effects from zalcitabine.

HIV may be acquired from or spread to other people through infected body fluids, including blood, vaginal fluid, or semen. *If you are infected, it is best to avoid any sexual activity involving an exchange of body fluids with other people. If you do have sex, always wear (or have your partner wear) a condom (''rubber'').* Only use condoms made of latex, and *use them every time you have vaginal, anal, or oral sex.* The use of a spermicide (such as nonoxynol-9) may also help prevent transmission of HIV if it is not irritating to the vagina, rectum, or mouth. Spermicides have been shown to kill HIV in lab tests. Do not use oil-based jelly, cold cream, baby oil, or shortening as a lubricant—these products can cause the condom to break. Lubricants without oil, such as *K-Y Jelly*, are recommended. Women may wish to carry their own condoms. Birth control pills and diaphragms will help protect against pregnancy, but they will not prevent someone from giving or getting the AIDS virus. *If you inject drugs*, get help to stop. *Do not share needles or equipment with anyone.* In some cities, more than half of the drug users are infected, and sharing even 1 needle or syringe can spread the virus. If you have any questions about this, check with your health care professional.

Side Effects of This Medicine

Along with its needed effects, a medicine may cause some unwanted effects. Although not all of these side effects

may occur, if they do occur they may need medical attention.

Check with your doctor immediately if any of the following side effects occur:

More common
Tingling, burning, numbness, or pain in the hands, arms, feet, or legs

Less common
Fever; joint pain; muscle pain; skin rash; ulcers in the mouth and throat

Rare
Fever and sore throat; nausea and vomiting; stomach pain (severe); yellow eyes or skin

Other side effects may occur that usually do not need medical attention. These side effects may go away during treatment as your body adjusts to the medicine. However, check with your doctor if any of the following side effects continue or are bothersome:

Less common
Diarrhea; headache

Other side effects not listed above may also occur in some patients. If you notice any other effects, check with your doctor.

Revised: 02/01/95

ZIDOVUDINE Systemic

Some commonly used brand names are:

In the U.S.—
Retrovir

In Canada—
Apo-Zidovudine
Novo-AZT
Retrovir

Another commonly used name is AZT.

Description

Zidovudine (zye-DOE-vue-deen) (also known as AZT) is used, alone or together with zalcitabine (ddC), in the treatment of the infection caused by the human immunodeficiency virus (HIV). HIV is the virus responsible for acquired immune deficiency syndrome (AIDS). Zidovudine is used to slow the progression of disease in patients infected with HIV who have advanced symptoms, early symptoms, or no symptoms at all. This medicine also is used to help prevent pregnant women who have HIV from passing the virus to their babies during pregnancy and at birth.

Zidovudine will not cure or prevent HIV infection or AIDS; however, it helps keep HIV from reproducing and appears to slow down the destruction of the immune system. This may help delay the development of problems usually related to AIDS or HIV disease. Zidovudine will not keep you from spreading HIV to other people. People who receive this medicine may continue to have the problems usually related to AIDS or HIV disease.

Zidovudine may cause some serious side effects, including bone marrow problems. Symptoms of bone marrow problems include fever, chills, or sore throat; pale skin; and unusual tiredness or weakness. These problems may require blood transfusions or temporarily stopping treatment with zidovudine. *Check with your doctor if any new health problems or symptoms occur while you are taking zidovudine.*

Zidovudine is available only with your doctor's prescription, in the following dosage forms:

Oral
- Capsules (U.S. and Canada)
- Syrup (U.S. and Canada)

Parenteral
- Injection (U.S. and Canada)

Before Using This Medicine

In deciding to use a medicine, the risks of taking the medicine must be weighed against the good it will do. This is a decision you and your doctor will make. For zidovudine, the following should be considered:

Allergies—Tell your doctor if you have ever had any unusual or allergic reaction to zidovudine. Also tell your health care professional if you are allergic to any other substances, such as foods, preservatives, or dyes.

Pregnancy—Zidovudine crosses the placenta. Studies in pregnant women have not been completed. However, zidovudine has been shown to decrease the chance of passing HIV to your baby during pregnancy and at birth. Zidovudine has not been shown to cause birth defects in studies in rats and rabbits given this medicine by mouth in doses many times larger than the human dose.

Breast-feeding—It is not known whether zidovudine passes into the breast milk. However, if your baby does not have the AIDS virus, there is a chance that you could pass it to your baby by breast-feeding. Talk to your doctor first if you are thinking about breast-feeding your baby.

Children—Zidovudine can cause serious side effects in any patient. Therefore, it is especially important that you discuss with your child's doctor the good that this medicine may do as well as the risks of using it. Your child must be carefully followed, and frequently seen, by the doctor while he or she is taking zidovudine.

Older adults—Zidovudine has not been studied specifically in older people. Therefore, it is not known whether it causes different side effects or problems in the elderly than it does in younger adults.

Other medicines—Although certain medicines should not be used together at all, in other cases 2 different medicines may be used together even if an interaction might occur. In these cases, your doctor may want to change the dose, or other precautions may be necessary. When you are taking zidovudine, it is especially important that your health care professional know if you are taking any of the following:

- Amphotericin B by injection (e.g., Fungizone) or
- Antineoplastics (cancer medicine) or
- Antithyroid agents (medicine for overactive thyroid) or
- Azathioprine (e.g., Imuran) or
- Chloramphenicol (e.g., Chloromycetin) or
- Colchicine or
- Cyclophosphamide (e.g., Cytoxan) or
- Flucytosine (e.g., Ancobon) or
- Ganciclovir (e.g., Cytovene) or
- Interferon (e.g., Intron A, Roferon-A) or
- Mercaptopurine (e.g., Purinethol) or
- Methotrexate (e.g., Mexate) or
- Plicamycin (e.g., Mithracin)—Caution should be used if these medicines and zidovudine are used together; taking zidovudine while you are using or receiving these medicines may make anemia and other blood problems worse
- Clarithromycin (e.g., Biaxin)—Clarithromycin may decrease the amount of zidovudine in the blood
- Probenecid (e.g., Benemid)—Probenecid may increase the amount of zidovudine in the blood, increasing the chance of side effects

Other medical problems—The presence of other medical problems may affect the use of zidovudine. Make sure you tell your doctor if you have any other medical problems, especially:

- Anemia or other blood problems—Zidovudine may make these conditions worse
- Liver disease—Patients with liver disease may have an increase in side effects from zidovudine
- Low amounts of folic acid or vitamin B_{12} in the blood—Zidovudine may worsen anemia caused by a decrease of folic acid or vitamin B_{12}

Proper Use of This Medicine

Patient information sheets about zidovudine are available. Read this information carefully.

Take this medicine exactly as directed by your doctor. Do not take more of it, do not take it more often, and do not take it for a longer time than your doctor ordered. Also, do not stop taking this medicine without checking with your doctor first.

Keep taking zidovudine for the full time of treatment, even if you begin to feel better.

For patients using *zidovudine syrup:*

- Use a specially marked measuring spoon or other device to measure each dose accurately. The average household teaspoon may not hold the right amount of liquid.

This medicine works best when there is a constant amount in the blood. *To help keep the amount constant, do not miss any doses.* If you need help in planning the best times to take your medicine, check with your health care professional.

Dosing—The dose of zidovudine will be different for different patients. *Follow your doctor's orders or the directions on the label.* The following information includes only the average doses of zidovudine. *If your dose is different, do not change it* unless your doctor tells you to do so.

- For the treatment of HIV infection:
  - —For *oral* dosage forms (capsules and syrup):
    - Adults and teenagers—100 milligrams (mg) every four hours for a total of 500 or 600 mg a day; or 200 mg of zidovudine together with 0.75 mg of zalcitabine every eight hours.
    - Children 3 months to 12 years of age—Dose is based on body size and must be determined by your doctor.
  - —For *injection* dosage form:
    - Adults and teenagers—Dose is based on body weight and must be determined by your doctor. The usual dose is 1 to 2 mg per kilogram (kg) (0.45 to 0.9 mg per pound) of body weight, injected slowly into a vein every four hours around the clock. The injection dosage form is given until you can take zidovudine by mouth.
    - Children 3 months to 12 years of age—Dose is based on body size and must be determined by your doctor.
- To help prevent pregnant women from passing HIV to their babies during pregnancy and at birth:
  - —For *capsule* dosage form:
    - Pregnant women (after 14 weeks of pregnancy, up to the start of labor)—100 milligrams (mg) five times a day until the start of labor.
  - —For *syrup* dosage form:
    - Pregnant women (after 14 weeks of pregnancy, up to the start of labor)—100 milligrams (mg) five times a day until the start of labor.
    - Newborn infants—Dose is based on body weight and must be determined by your doctor. The usual dose of syrup is 2 mg per kilogram (kg) (0.9 mg per pound) of body weight every six hours starting within twelve hours of birth and continuing through six weeks of age.
  - —For *injection* dosage form:
    - Pregnant women (during labor and delivery)—Dose is based on body weight and must be determined by your doctor. The usual dose is 2 milligrams (mg) per kilogram (kg) (0.9 mg per pound) of body weight infused into a vein over the first hour, followed by 1 mg per kg (0.45 mg per pound of body weight) infused into a vein each hour until the umbilical cord is clamped.
    - Newborn infants—If the infant is unable to receive zidovudine syrup, the injection form may be used instead. Dose is based on body weight and must be determined by your doctor. The usual dose is 1.5 mg per kilogram (kg) (0.7 mg per pound) of body weight every six hours.

Missed dose—If you do miss a dose of this medicine, take it as soon as possible. However, if it is almost time for your next dose, skip the missed dose and go back to your regular dosing schedule. Do not double doses.

Storage—To store this medicine:

- Keep out of the reach of children.
- Store away from heat and direct light.
- Do not store capsule in the bathroom, near the kitchen sink, or in other damp places. Heat or moisture may cause the medicine to break down.
- Do not keep outdated medicine or medicine no longer needed. Be sure that any discarded medicine is out of the reach of children.

Precautions While Using This Medicine

It is very important that your doctor check your progress at regular visits. This medicine may cause blood problems.

Do not take any other medicines without checking with your doctor first. To do so may increase the chance of side effects from zidovudine.

Zidovudine may cause blood problems. These problems may result in a greater chance of certain infections and slow healing. Therefore, you should be careful when using regular toothbrushes, dental floss, and toothpicks not to damage your gums. Check with your medical doctor or dentist if you have any questions about proper oral hygiene (mouth care) during treatment.

HIV may be acquired from or spread to other people through infected body fluids, including blood, vaginal fluid, or semen. *If you are infected, it is best to avoid any sexual activity involving an exchange of body fluids with other people. If you do have sex, always wear (or have your partner wear) a condom (''rubber'').* Only use condoms made of latex, and *use them every time you have vaginal, anal, or oral sex.* The use of a spermicide (such as nonoxynol-9) may also help prevent the spread of HIV if it is not irritating to the vagina, rectum, or mouth. Spermicides have been shown to kill HIV in lab tests. Do not use oil-based jelly, cold cream, baby oil, or shortening as a lubricant—these products can cause the condom to break. Lubricants without oil, such as *K-Y Jelly*, are recommended. Women may wish to carry their own condoms. Birth control pills and diaphragms will help protect against pregnancy, but they will not prevent someone from giving or getting the AIDS virus. *If you inject drugs*, get help to stop. *Do not share needles with anyone.* In some cities, more than half of the drug users are infected, and sharing even 1 needle can spread the virus. If you have any questions about this, check with your health care professional.

Side Effects of This Medicine

Along with its needed effects, a medicine may cause some unwanted effects. Although not all of these side effects may occur, if they do occur they may need medical attention.

Check with your doctor immediately if any of the following side effects occur:

More common

Fever, chills, or sore throat; pale skin; unusual tiredness or weakness

Note: The above side effects may also occur up to weeks or months after you stop taking this medicine.

Rare

Abdominal discomfort; confusion; convulsions (seizures); general feeling of discomfort; loss of appetite; mood or mental changes; muscle tenderness and weakness; nausea

Other side effects may occur that usually do not need medical attention. These side effects may go away during treatment as your body adjusts to the medicine. However, check with your doctor if any of the following side effects continue or are bothersome:

More common

Headache (severe); muscle soreness; nausea; trouble in sleeping

Less common

Bluish-brown colored bands on nails

Other side effects not listed above may also occur in some patients. If you notice any other effects, check with your doctor.

Additional Information

Once a medicine has been approved for marketing for a certain use, experience may show that it is also useful for other medical problems. Although this use is not included in product labeling, zidovudine is used in certain patients with the following medical condition:

- Human immunodeficiency virus (HIV) infection due to occupational exposure (possible prevention of)

Other than the above information, there is no additional information relating to proper use, precautions, or side effects for this use.

Revised: 06/22/94
Interim revision: 01/11/95

ZINC SUPPLEMENTS Systemic

Some commonly used brand names are:

In the U.S.—

Orazinc[2, 3]
Verazinc[3]
Zinc-220[3]
Zinc 15[3]
Zinca-Pak[3]
Zincate[3]

In Canada—

PMS Egozinc[3]

Note: For quick reference, the following zinc supplements are numbered to match the corresponding brand names.

This information applies to the following:
1. Zinc Chloride (zink KLOR-ide)†‡
2. Zinc Gluconate (GLOO-coh-nate)‡§
3. Zinc Sulfate (SUL-fate)‡

†Not commercially available in Canada.
‡Generic name product may also be available in the U.S.
§Generic name product may also be available in Canada.

Description

Zinc supplements are used to prevent or treat zinc deficiency.

The body needs zinc for normal growth and health. For patients who are unable to get enough zinc in their regular diet or who have a need for more zinc, zinc supplements may be necessary. They are generally taken by mouth but some patients may have to receive them by injection.

Zinc supplements may be used for other conditions as determined by your health care professional.

Lack of zinc may lead to poor night vision and wound-healing, a decrease in sense of taste and smell, a reduced ability to fight infections, and poor development of reproductive organs.

Some conditions may increase your need for zinc. These include:

- Acrodermatitis enteropathica (a lack of absorption of zinc from the intestine)
- Alcoholism
- Burns
- Diabetes mellitus (sugar diabetes)
- Down's syndrome
- Eating disorders
- Intestine diseases
- Infections (continuing or chronic)
- Kidney disease
- Liver disease
- Pancreas disease
- Sickle cell disease
- Skin disorders
- Stomach removal
- Stress (continuing)
- Thalassemia
- Trauma (prolonged)

In addition, premature infants may need additional zinc.

Increased need for zinc should be determined by your health care professional.

Claims that zinc is effective in preventing vision loss in the elderly have not been proven. Zinc has not been proven effective in the treatment of porphyria.

Injectable zinc is given by or under the supervision of a health care professional. Other forms of zinc are available without a prescription.

Zinc supplements are available in the following dosage forms:

Oral

Zinc Gluconate
- Lozenges (U.S.)
- Tablets (U.S. and Canada)

Zinc Sulfate
- Capsules (U.S.)
- Tablets (U.S. and Canada)
- Extended-release tablets (U.S.)

Parenteral

Zinc Chloride
- Injection (U.S.)

Zinc Sulfate
- Injection (U.S.)

Importance of Diet

For good health, it is important that you eat a balanced and varied diet. Follow carefully any diet program your health care professional may recommend. For your specific dietary vitamin and/or mineral needs, ask your health care professional for a list of appropriate foods. If you think that you are not getting enough vitamins and/or minerals in your diet, you may choose to take a dietary supplement.

Zinc is found in various foods, including lean red meats, seafoods (especially herring and oysters), peas, and beans. Zinc is also found in whole grains; however, large amounts of whole-grains have been found to decrease the amount of zinc that is absorbed. Additional zinc may be added to the diet through treated (galvanized) cookware. Foods stored in uncoated tin cans may cause less zinc to be available for absorption from food.

The daily amount of zinc needed is defined in several different ways.

For U.S.—

- Recommended Dietary Allowances (RDAs) are the amount of vitamins and minerals needed to provide for adequate nutrition in most healthy persons. RDAs for a given nutrient may vary depending on a person's age, sex, and physical condition (e.g., pregnancy).
- Daily Values (DVs) are used on food and dietary supplement labels to indicate the percent of the recommended daily amount of each nutrient that a serving provides. DV replaces the previous designation of United States Recommended Daily Allowances (USRDAs).

For Canada—

- Recommended Nutrient Intakes (RNIs) are used to determine the amounts of vitamins, minerals, and protein needed to provide adequate nutrition and lessen the risk of chronic disease.

Normal daily recommended intakes in milligrams (mg) for zinc are generally defined as follows:

Persons	U.S. (mg)	Canada (mg)
Infants and children		
Birth to 3 years of age	5–10	2–4
4 to 6 years of age	10	5
7 to 10 years of age	10	7–9
Adolescent and adult males	15	9–12
Adolescent and adult females	12	9
Pregnant females	15	15
Breast-feeding females	16–19	15

Before Using This Dietary Supplement

If you are taking this dietary supplement without a prescription, carefully read and follow any precautions on the label. For zinc supplements, the following should be considered:

Allergies—Tell your health care professional if you are allergic to any substances, such as foods, preservatives, or dyes.

Pregnancy—It is especially important that you are receiving enough vitamins and minerals when you become pregnant and that you continue to receive the right amount of vitamins and minerals throughout your pregnancy. The healthy growth and development of the fetus depend on a steady supply of nutrients from the mother. There is evidence that low blood levels of zinc may lead to problems in pregnancy or defects in the baby. However, taking large amounts of a dietary supplement in pregnancy may be harmful to the mother and/or fetus and should be avoided.

Breast-feeding—It is important that you receive the right amounts of vitamins and minerals so that your baby will also get the vitamins and minerals needed to grow properly. However, taking large amounts of a dietary supplement while breast-feeding may be harmful to the mother and/or baby and should be avoided.

Children—Problems in children have not been reported with intake of normal daily recommended amounts.

Older adults—Problems in older adults have not been reported with intake of normal daily recommended amounts. There is some evidence that the elderly may be at risk of becoming deficient in zinc due to poor food selection, decreased absorption of zinc by the body, or medicines that decrease absorption of zinc or increase loss of zinc from the body.

Medicines or other dietary supplements—Although certain medicines or dietary supplements should not be used together at all, in other cases they may be used together even if an interaction might occur. In these cases, your health care professional may want to change the dose, or other precautions may be necessary. When you are taking zinc supplements, it is especially important that your health care professional know if you are taking any of the following:

- Copper supplements or
- Tetracycline (medicine for infection)—Use with zinc supplements may cause these copper supplements or tetracycline to be less effective; zinc supplements should be given at least 2 hours after copper supplements, or tetracycline

Other medical problems—The presence of other medical problems may affect the use of zinc supplements. Make sure you tell your health care professional if you have any other medical problems, especially:

- Copper deficiency—Zinc supplements may make this condition worse

Proper Use of This Dietary Supplement

Dosing—The amount of zinc needed to meet normal daily recommended intakes will be different for different individuals. The following information includes only the average amounts of zinc.

- For *oral* dosage form (capsules, lozenges, tablets, extended-release tablets):
  —To prevent deficiency, the amount taken by mouth is based on normal daily recommended intakes (Note that the normal daily recommended intakes are expressed as an actual amount of zinc. The dosage form [e.g., zinc gluconate, zinc sulfate] has a different strength):

  For the U.S.
  - Adult and teenage males—15 milligrams (mg) per day.
  - Adult and teenage females—12 mg per day.
  - Pregnant females—15 mg per day.
  - Breast-feeding females—16 to 19 mg per day.
  - Children 4 to 10 years of age—10 mg per day.
  - Children birth to 3 years of age—5 to 10 mg per day.

  For Canada
  - Adult and teenage males—9 to 12 mg per day.
  - Adult and teenage females—9 mg per day.
  - Pregnant females—15 mg per day.
  - Breast-feeding females—15 mg per day.
  - Children 7 to 10 years of age—7 to 9 mg per day.
  - Children 4 to 6 years of age—5 mg per day.
  - Children birth to 3 years of age—2 to 4 mg per day.

  —To treat deficiency:
  - Adults, teenagers, and children—Treatment dose is determined by prescriber for each individual based on severity of deficiency.

Zinc supplements are most effective if they are taken at least 1 hour before or 2 hours after meals. However, if zinc supplements cause stomach upset, they may be taken with a meal. You should tell your health care professional if you are taking your zinc supplement with meals.

Missed dose—If you miss taking zinc supplements for one or more days there is no cause for concern, since it takes some time for your body to become seriously low in zinc. However, if your health care professional has recommended that you take zinc, try to remember to take it as directed every day.

Storage—To store this dietary supplement:
- Keep out of the reach of children.
- Store away from heat and direct light.
- Do not store in the bathroom, near the kitchen sink, or in other damp places. Heat or moisture may cause the dietary supplement to break down.
- Keep the dietary supplement from freezing. Do not refrigerate.
- Do not keep outdated dietary supplements or those no longer needed. Be sure that any discarded dietary supplement is out of the reach of children.

Precautions While Using This Dietary Supplement

When zinc combines with certain foods it may not be absorbed into your body and it will do you no good. If you are taking zinc, the following foods should be avoided or taken 2 hours after you take zinc:
- Bran
- Fiber-containing foods
- Phosphorus-containing foods such as milk or poultry
- Whole-grain breads and cereals

Do not take zinc supplements and copper, iron, or phosphorus supplements at the same time. It is best to space doses of these products 2 hours apart, to get the full benefit from each dietary supplement.

Side Effects of This Dietary Supplement

Along with its needed effects, a dietary supplement may cause some unwanted effects. Although not all of these side effects may occur, if they do occur they may need medical attention.

Check with your health care professional as soon as possible if any of the following side effects occur:

Rare—With large doses
Chills; continuing ulcers or sores in mouth or throat; fever; heartburn; indigestion; nausea; sore throat; unusual tiredness or weakness

Symptoms of overdose
Chest pain; dizziness; fainting; shortness of breath; vomiting; yellow eyes or skin

Other side effects not listed above may also occur in some individuals. If you notice any other effects, check with your health care professional.

Additional Information

Once a medicine or dietary supplement has been approved for marketing for a certain use, experience may show that it is also useful for other medical problems. Although this use is not included in product labeling, zinc supplements are used in certain patients with the following medical condition:
- Wilson's disease (a disease of too much copper in the body)

Other than the above information, there is no additional information relating to proper use, precautions, or side effects for this use.

Revised: 02/03/92
Interim revision: 08/21/92; 05/26/95

ZOLPIDEM Systemic†

A commonly used brand name in the U.S. is Ambien.

†Not commercially available in Canada.

Description

Zolpidem (ZOLE-pi-dem) belongs to the group of medicines called central nervous system (CNS) depressants (medicines that slow down the nervous system). Zolpidem is used to treat insomnia (trouble in sleeping). In general, when sleep medicines are used every night for a long time, they may lose their effectiveness. In most cases, sleep medicines should be used only for short periods of time, such as 1 or 2 days, and generally for no longer than 1 or 2 weeks.

This medicine is available only with your doctor's prescription, in the following dosage form:

Oral
- Tablets (U.S.)

Before Using This Medicine

Sleep medicines may cause a special type of memory loss or ''amnesia''. When this occurs, a person does not remember what has happened during the several hours between use of the medicine and the time when its effects wear off. This is usually not a problem since most people fall asleep after taking the medicine. In most instances, memory problems can be avoided by taking zolpidem only when you are able to get a full night's sleep (7 to 8 hours) before you need to be active again. Be sure to talk to your doctor if you think you are having memory problems.

In deciding to use a medicine, the risks of taking the medicine must be weighed against the good it will do. This is a decision you and your doctor will make. For zolpidem, the following should be considered:

Allergies—Tell your doctor if you have ever had any unusual or allergic reaction to zolpidem. Also tell your health care professional if you are allergic to any other substances, such as foods, preservatives, or dyes.

Pregnancy—Zolpidem has not been studied in pregnant women. However, studies in pregnant animals have shown that zolpidem slows down the development of the offspring when given to the mother in doses many times the human dose. Before taking this medicine, make sure your doctor knows if you are pregnant or if you may become pregnant.

Breast-feeding—Although zolpidem passes into breast milk, it has not been reported to cause problems in nursing babies.

Children—Studies on this medicine have been done only in adult patients, and there is no specific information comparing use of zolpidem in children with use in other age groups.

Older adults—Confusion and falling are more likely to occur in the elderly, who are usually more sensitive than younger adults to the effects of zolpidem.

Other medicines—Although certain medicines should not be used together at all, in other cases two different medicines may be used together even if an interaction might occur. In these cases, your doctor may want to change the dose, or other precautions may be necessary. When you are taking zolpidem, it is especially important that your health care professional know if you are taking any of the following:

- Other central nervous system (CNS) depressants (medicines that cause drowsiness) or
- Tricyclic antidepressants (amitriptyline [e.g., Elavil], amoxapine [e.g., Asendin], clomipramine [e.g., Anafranil], desipramine [e.g., Pertofrane], doxepin [e.g., Sinequan], imipramine [e.g., Tofranil], nortriptyline [e.g., Aventyl], protriptyline [e.g., Vivactil], trimipramine [e.g., Surmontil])—The CNS depressant effects of either these medicines or zolpidem may be increased, possibly leading to unwanted effects

Other medical problems—The presence of other medical problems may affect the use of zolpidem. Make sure you tell your doctor if you have any other medical problems, especially:

- Alcohol abuse (or history of) or
- Drug abuse or dependence (or history of)—Dependence on zolpidem may develop
- Emphysema, asthma, bronchitis, or other chronic lung disease or
- Mental depression or
- Sleep apnea (temporary stopping of breathing during sleep)—Zolpidem may make these conditions worse
- Kidney disease or
- Liver disease—Higher blood levels of zolpidem may result, increasing the chance of side effects

Proper Use of This Medicine

Take this medicine only as directed by your doctor. Do not take more of it, do not take it more often, and do not take it for a longer time than your doctor ordered. If too much is taken, it may become habit-forming (causing mental or physical dependence).

Take zolpidem just before going to bed, when you are ready to go to sleep. This medicine works very quickly to put you to sleep.

Do not take this medicine when your schedule does not permit you to get a full night's sleep (7 to 8 hours). If you must wake up before this, you may continue to feel drowsy and may experience memory problems, because the effects of the medicine have not had time to wear off.

Zolpidem may be taken with or without food or on a full or empty stomach. It may work faster if you take it on an empty stomach. However, if your doctor tells you to take the medicine a certain way, take it exactly as directed.

Dosing—The dose of zolpidem will be different for different patients. *Follow your doctor's orders or the directions on the label.* The following information includes only the average doses of zolpidem. *If your dose is different, do not change it* unless your doctor tells you to do so.

The number of tablets that you take depends on the strength of the medicine.

- For *oral* dosage form (tablets):
  - —For the treatment of insomnia (trouble in sleeping):
    - Adults—10 milligrams (mg) at bedtime.
    - Older adults—5 mg at bedtime.
    - Children up to 18 years of age—Use and dose must be determined by the doctor.

Missed dose—If you miss a dose of this medicine, skip the missed dose and go back to your regular dosing schedule. Do not double doses.

Storage—To store this medicine:

- Keep out of the reach of children.
- Store away from heat and direct light.
- Do not store in the bathroom, near the kitchen sink, or in other damp places. Heat or moisture may cause the medicine to break down.
- Do not keep outdated medicine or medicine no longer needed. Be sure that any discarded medicine is out of the reach of children.

Precautions While Using This Medicine

If you think you need to take zolpidem for more than 7 to 10 days, be sure to discuss it with your doctor. Insomnia that lasts longer than this may be a sign of another medical problem.

This medicine will add to the effects of alcohol and other CNS depressants (medicines that slow down the nervous system, possibly causing drowsiness). Some examples of CNS depressants are antihistamines or medicine for hay fever, other allergies, or colds; sedatives, tranquilizers, or sleeping medicine; prescription pain medicine or narcotics; barbiturates; medicine for seizures; muscle relaxants; or anesthetics, including some dental anesthetics. *Check with your doctor before taking any of the above while you are using this medicine.*

This medicine may cause some people, especially older persons, to become drowsy, dizzy, lightheaded, clumsy or unsteady, or less alert than they are normally. Even though zolpidem is taken at bedtime, it may cause some people to feel drowsy or less alert on arising. Also, this medicine may cause double vision or other vision problems. *Make sure you know how you react to zolpidem before you drive, use machines, or do anything else that could be dangerous if you are dizzy, or are not alert or able to see well.*

If you develop any unusual and strange thoughts or behavior while you are taking zolpidem, be sure to discuss it with your doctor. Some changes that have occurred in people taking this medicine are like those seen in people who drink alcohol and then act in a manner that is not normal. Other changes may be more unusual and extreme, such as confusion, hallucinations (seeing, hearing, or feeling things that are not there), and unusual excitement, nervousness, or irritability.

If you will be taking zolpidem for a long time, do not stop taking it without first checking with your doctor. Your doctor may want you to reduce gradually the amount you are taking before stopping completely. Stopping this medicine suddenly may cause withdrawal side effects.

After taking zolpidem for insomnia, you may have difficulty sleeping (rebound insomnia) for the first few nights after you stop taking it.

If you think you or someone else may have taken an overdose of this medicine, get emergency help at once. Taking an overdose of zolpidem or taking alcohol or other CNS depressants with zolpidem may lead to breathing problems and unconsciousness. Some signs of an overdose are severe drowsiness, severe nausea or vomiting, staggering, and troubled breathing.

Side Effects of This Medicine

Along with its needed effects, a medicine may cause some unwanted effects. Although not all of these side effects may occur, if they do occur they may need medical attention.

Check with your doctor as soon as possible if any of the following side effects occur:

Less common

Clumsiness or unsteadiness; confusion—more common in older adults; mental depression

Rare

Dizziness, lightheadedness, or fainting; falling—more common in older adults; fast heartbeat; hallucinations (seeing, hearing, or feeling things that are not there); skin rash; swelling of face; trouble in sleeping; unusual excitement, nervousness, or irritability; wheezing or difficulty in breathing

Symptoms of overdose

Clumsiness or unsteadiness (severe); dizziness (severe); double vision or other vision problems; drowsiness (severe); nausea (severe); troubled breathing; slow heartbeat; vomiting (severe)

Other side effects may occur that usually do not need medical attention. These side effects may go away during treatment as your body adjusts to the medicine. However, check with your doctor if any of the following side effects continue or are bothersome:

Less common

Abdominal or stomach pain; daytime drowsiness; diarrhea; double vision or other vision problems; drugged feelings; dryness of mouth; general feeling of discomfort or illness; headache; memory problems; nausea; nightmares or unusual dreams; vomiting

After you stop using this medicine, your body may need time to adjust. The length of time this takes depends on the amount of medicine you were using and how long you used it. During this time check with your doctor if you notice any of the following side effects:

Abdominal or stomach cramps or discomfort; agitation, nervousness, or feelings of panic; convulsions (seizures); flushing; lightheadedness; muscle cramps; nausea; sweating; tremors; uncontrolled crying; unusual tiredness or weakness; vomiting; worsening of mental or emotional problems

Other side effects not listed above may also occur in some patients. If you notice any other effects, check with your doctor.

Developed: 06/29/94

Glossary

Abdomen—The body area between the chest and pelvis.

Abortifacient—Agent that causes abortion.

Abrade—Scrape or rub away the outer cover or layer of a part.

Absorption—Passing of substances into or across tissues of the body, for example, digested food into the blood from the small intestine, or poisons through the skin.

Achlorhydria—Absence of acid that normally would be found in the stomach.

Acidic—1. Refers to sharp, sour taste. 2. Having a pH of less than 7.

Acidifier, urinary—Medicine that makes the urine more acidic.

Acidosis—Too much acidity or loss of alkalinity in the body fluids and tissues.

Acne—Inflammatory condition of sebaceous glands and hair follicles of the face, neck, and upper back, marked by red raised areas, pimples, and cysts.

Acromegaly—Enlargement of the face, body, hands, and feet because of too much growth hormone.

Acute—Describes a condition that begins suddenly, often has severe symptoms, and usually lasts a short time.

Added fiber—In food labeling, at least 2.5 grams of more fiber per serving than reference food.

Addison's disease—Disease caused by not enough secretion of corticosteroid hormones by the adrenal glands; causes weakness, salt loss, and low blood pressure.

Adhesion—The abnormal connecting of tissue, holding parts together that are normally separate.

Adjunct —An additional or secondary treatment that is helpful but may not be necessary for treatment of a particular condition; not effective for that condition if used alone.

Adjuvant—1. A substance added to or used with another substance to assist its action. 2. Something that assists or enhances the effectiveness of medical treatment.

Adrenal cortex—Outer layer of tissue of the adrenal gland, which produces corticosteroid hormones.

Adrenal glands—Two organs located next to the kidneys. They produce the hormones epinephrine (adrenaline) and norepinephrine and corticosteroid (cortisone-like) hormones.

Adrenaline—*See* Epinephrine.

Adrenal medulla—Inner part of the adrenal gland, which produces epinephrine (adrenaline) and norepinephrine.

Adrenocorticoids—*See* Corticosteroids.

Adverse effect—Symptom produced by a drug or therapy that is harmful to the patient.

Aerosol—Suspension of very small liquid or solid particles in compressed gas. Drugs in aerosol form are dispensed in the form of a mist by releasing the gas.

African sleeping sickness—*See* Trypanosomiasis, African.

Agent—A force or substance able to cause a change.

Agoraphobia—Fear of public places or open spaces.

Agranulocytosis—Disease marked by a severe decrease in the number of granulocytes normally present in the blood. Also called *granulocytopenia*.

AIDS (acquired immunodeficiency syndrome)—Disease caused by human immunodeficiency virus (HIV). The disease results in a breakdown of the body's immune system, which makes a person more likely to get some other infections and some forms of cancer.

Alcohol-abuse deterrent—Medicine used to help alcoholics avoid the use of alcohol.

Alkaline—Having a pH of more than 7. Opposite of acidic.

Alkalizer, urinary—Medicine that makes the urine more alkaline.

Alkalosis—Too much alkalinity or loss of acidity in the body fluids and tissues.

Allergy—Abnormal, high sensitivity to particular substances that are ordinarily harmless; common reactions include hives, itching, sneezing, stuffy nose, and swelling of mucous membranes.

Alopecia—Loss or absence of hair from areas where it normally is present.

Altitude sickness agent—Medicine used to prevent or lessen some of the effects of high altitude on the body.

Alzheimer's disease—Progressive disorder of thinking and other mental processes, usually beginning in late middle age.

Amino acid—One of a large group of organic compounds that contain nitrogen; they are the building blocks of protein and also the end product of protein digestion.

Aminoglycosides—A class of chemically related antibiotics used to treat some serious types of bacterial infections.

Ampul—Small sealed glass or plastic container holding sterile solution, usually for injection. Also, *ampule*.

Anabolic steroid—Any of a group of compounds resembling testosterone that aid in the building of body tissues.

Analgesic—Medicine that relieves pain.

Anaphylaxis—Sudden, life-threatening allergic reaction.

Androgen—Hormone such as testosterone, that promotes male characteristics, such as a deep voice and beard growth.

Anemia—Reduction, to below normal, of hemoglobin in the blood.

Anesthesiologist—A physician who is qualified to give an anesthetic and other medicines to a patient before and during surgery.

Anesthetic—Medicine that causes a loss of feeling or sensation, especially of pain, sometimes through loss of consciousness.

Aneurysm—Abnormal dilatation or saclike swelling of an artery, vein, or the heart.

Angina—Pain, tightness, or feeling of heaviness in the chest, due to a lack of oxygen supply for the heart muscle. The pain may be felt in the left shoulder, jaw, or arm instead of or in addition to the chest. Symptoms often occur during exercise.

Angioedema—Condition marked by hives and continuing swelling of areas of the skin.

Anorexia—Loss of appetite for food.

Anoxia—Absence of oxygen. (The term is sometimes incorrectly used for hypoxia.)

Antacid—Medicine used to neutralize excess acid in the stomach.

Antagonist—Drug or other substance that blocks or works against the action of another.

Anthelmintic—Medicine used to destroy or expel intestinal worms.

Antiacne agent—Medicine used to treat acne.

Antianemic—Agent that prevents or corrects anemia.

Antianginal—Medicine used to prevent or treat angina attacks.

Antianxiety agent—Medicine used to treat excessive nervousness, tension, or anxiety.

Antiarrhythmic—Medicine used to treat irregular heartbeats.

Antiasthmatic—Medicine used to treat asthma.

Antibacterial—Medicine that kills or slows the growth of bacteria.

Antibiotic—Medicine used to treat infections.

Antibody—Special kind of blood protein that helps the body fight infection.

Antibulimic—Medicine used to treat bulimia.
Anticholelithic—Medicine used to dissolve gallstones.
Anticoagulant—Medicine used to prevent the clotting of blood.
Anticonvulsant—Medicine used to prevent or treat convulsions (seizures).
Antidepressant—Medicine used to treat mental depression.
Antidiabetic agent—Medicine used to control blood sugar levels in patients with diabetes mellitus (sugar diabetes).
Antidiarrheal—Medicine used to treat diarrhea.
Antidiuretic—Medicine used to decrease urine output (for example, in patients with diabetes insipidus).
Antidiuretic hormone—*See* Vasopressin.
Antidote—Medicine used to prevent or treat harmful effects of another medicine or a poison.
Antidyskinetic—Medicine used to help treat the loss of muscle control caused by certain diseases or by some other medicines.
Antidysmenorrheal—Medicine used to treat menstrual cramps.
Antiemetic—Medicine used to prevent or treat nausea and vomiting.
Antiendometriotic—Medicine used to treat endometriosis.
Antienuretic—Medicine used to help prevent bedwetting.
Antifibrotic—Medicine used to treat fibrosis.
Antiflatulent—Medicine used to help relieve excess gas in the stomach or intestines.
Antifungal—Medicine used to treat infections caused by a fungus.
Antiglaucoma agent—Medicine used to treat glaucoma.
Antigout agent—Medicine used to prevent or relieve gout attacks.
Antihemorrhagic—Medicine used to prevent or help stop serious bleeding.
Antihistamine—Medicine used to prevent or relieve the symptoms of allergies (such as hay fever).
Antihypercalcemic—Medicine used to help lower the amount of calcium in the blood.
Antihyperlipidemic—Medicine used to help lower high levels of lipids in the blood.
Antihyperphosphatemic—Medicine used to help lower the amount of phosphate in the blood.
Antihypertensive—Medicine used to help lower high blood pressure.
Antihyperuricemic—Medicine used to prevent or treat gout or other medical problems caused by too much uric acid in the blood.
Antihypocalcemic—Medicine used to increase calcium blood levels in patients with too little calcium.
Antihypoglycemic—Medicine used to increase blood sugar levels in patients with low blood sugar.
Antihypokalemic—Medicine used to increase potassium blood levels in patients with too little potassium.
Anti-infective—Medicine used to treat infection.
Anti-inflammatory—Medicine used to relieve pain, swelling, and other symptoms of inflammation.
Anti-inflammatory, nonsteroidal—An anti-inflammatory medicine that is not a cortisone-like medicine.
Anti-inflammatory, steroidal—A cortisone-like anti-inflammatory medicine.
Antimetabolite—Medicine that interferes with the normal processes within cells, preventing their growth.
Antimuscarinic—Medicine used to block the effects of a certain chemical in the body; often used to reduce smooth muscle spasms, especially abdominal or stomach cramps or spasms.
Antimyasthenic—Medicine used to treat myasthenia gravis.
Antimyotonic—Medicine used to prevent or relieve night-time leg cramps or muscle spasms.
Antineoplastic—Medicine used to treat cancer.
Antineuralgic—Medicine used to treat nerve pain (neuralgia).
Antioxidant—Nutrient that protects tissues of the body against oxygen damage. The antioxidants are vitamins A, betacarotene, C, and E.
Antiprotozoal—Medicine used to treat infections caused by protozoa.
Antipruritic—Medicine used to prevent or relieve itching.
Antipsoriatic—Medicine used to treat psoriasis.
Antipsychotic—Medicine used to treat certain mental and emotional conditions, including psychosis.
Antipyretic—Medicine used to reduce fever.
Antirheumatic—Medicine used to treat arthritis (rheumatism).
Antirosacea—Medicine used to treat rosacea.
Antiseborrheic—Medicine used to treat dandruff and seborrhea.
Antiseptic—Medicine that stops the growth of germs; used on the surface of the skin to prevent infections in cuts, scrapes, and wounds.
Antispasmodic—Medicine used to reduce smooth muscle spasms (for example, stomach, intestinal, or urinary tract spasms).
Antispastic—Medicine used to treat muscle spasms.
Antithyroid agent—Medicine used to treat an overactive thyroid gland.
Antitremor agent—Medicine used to treat tremors (trembling or shaking).
Antitubercular—Medicine used to treat tuberculosis (TB).
Antitussive—Medicine used to relieve cough.
Antiulcer agent—Medicine used to treat stomach and duodenal ulcers.
Antivertigo agent—Medicine used to prevent dizziness (vertigo).
Antiviral—Medicine used to treat infections caused by a virus.
Anus—The opening at the end of the digestive tract through which waste matter (feces) passes out of the body.
Anxiety—An emotional state with apprehension, worry, or tension in reaction to real or imagined danger or dread; accompanied by sweating, increased pulse, trembling, weakness, and fatigue.
Apnea—Temporary absence of breathing.
Apoplexy—*See* Stroke.
Appendicitis—Inflammation of the appendix.
Appetite stimulant—Medicine used to help increase the desire for food.
Appetite suppressant—Medicine used in weight control programs to help decrease the desire to eat.
Arrhythmia—Abnormal heart rhythm.
Arteritis, temporal—Inflammatory disease of arteries, usually of the head or eyes; occurs in older people.
Arthralgia—Pain in a joint.
Arthritis, rheumatoid—Chronic disease, mainly of the joints, marked by pain and swelling.
Ascites—Accumulation of fluid in the abdominal cavity.
Asthma—Disease marked by inflammation with constriction of the bronchial tubes (air passages). The constricted airways result in wheezing and difficult breathing. Attacks may be brought on by allergens, virus infection, cold air, or exercise.
Atherosclerosis—Common disease of the arteries in which artery walls thicken and harden.
Avoid—To keep away from deliberately.
Bacteremia—Presence of bacteria in the blood.
Bacterium—Tiny, one-celled organism. Different types of bacteria are responsible for a number of diseases and infections.
Bancroft's filariasis—Disease transmitted by mosquitoes in which an infection with the filarial worm occurs; affects the lymph system, producing inflammation.
Basophil—One type of white blood cell; plays a role in allergic reactions.

Beriberi—Disorder caused by too little vitamin B_1 (thiamine), marked by an accumulation of fluid in the body, extreme weight loss, inflammation of nerves, or paralysis.
Bile—Thick fluid produced by the liver and stored in the gallbladder; helps in the digestion of fats.
Bile duct—Tube which carries bile from the liver to the gallbladder, or from the gallbladder to the intestine.
Bilharziasis—*See* Schistosomiasis.
Biliary—Relating to bile, the bile duct, or the gallbladder.
Bilirubin—The bile pigment that is orange-colored or yellow; an excess in the blood may cause jaundice.
Bipolar disorder—Severe mental illness marked by repeated episodes of depression and mania. Also called *manic-depressive illness*.
Bisexual—One who is sexually attracted to both sexes.
Black fever—*See* Leishmaniasis, visceral.
Bone marrow—Soft material filling the cavities of bones; concerned with blood cells and platelet production.
Bone marrow depression—Condition in which the production of red blood cells, leukocytes, or platelets by the red bone marrow is decreased.
Bone resorption inhibitor—Medicine used to prevent or treat certain types of bone disorders, such as Paget's disease of the bone; helps prevent bone loss.
Bowel disease, inflammatory, suppressant—Medicine used to treat certain intestinal disorders, such as colitis.
Bradycardia—Slow heart rate, usually less than 60 beats per minute in adults.
Bronchitis—Inflammation of the bronchial tubes (air passages) of the lungs.
Bronchodilator—Medicine used to open up the bronchial tubes (air passages) of the lungs to increase the flow of air through them.
Buccal—Relating to the cheek. A buccal medicine is taken by placing it between the cheek and the gum and letting it slowly dissolve.
Bulimia—Disturbance in eating behavior marked by bouts of excessive eating followed by self-induced vomiting and diarrhea, hard exercise, or fasting.
Bulk—In nutrition, fiber that absorbs water while in the intestine and swells the stool.
Bursa—Small fluid-filled sac that helps reduce friction; located between body parts that move over one another (such as in a joint) .
Bursitis—Inflammation of a bursa.
Calorie—Unit of heat that measures the energy value of food.
Calorie free—In food labeling, fewer than 5 calories per serving.
Candidiasis of the mouth—Overgrowth of the yeast *Candida* in the mouth marked by white patches on the tongue or inside the mouth. Also called *thrush* or *white mouth*.
Candidiasis of the vagina—Yeast infection of the vagina caused by the yeast *Candida;* associated with itching, burning, and a curd-like white discharge.
Canker sore—Acute, painful ulcer inside the mouth.
Carbohydrate—Any one of a large group of compounds from plants, including sugars and starches, that contain only carbon, hydrogen, and oxygen. Carbohydrates are a source of energy for animals and humans.
Carbon dioxide—A colorless gas. In the body, it is a final product in the breakdown of foods and is breathed out of the body through the lungs.
Cardiac—Relating to the heart.
Cardiac arrhythmia—*See* Arrhythmia.
Cardiac load–reducing agent—Medicine used to ease the workload of the heart by allowing the blood to flow through the blood vessels more easily.
Cardiotonic—Medicine used to improve the strength and efficiency of the heart.
Caries, dental—Tooth decay, sometimes causing pain, leading to tooth damage. Also called *cavities*.
Cartilage—Type of connective tissue; it is elastic and softer than bone and makes up a part of the skeleton.
Cataract—A cloudiness in the lens of the eye that impairs vision or causes blindness.
Catheter—Tube inserted into a small opening in the body so that fluids can be put in or taken out.
Caustic—1. Burning or corrosive. 2. Substance that is irritating and destructive to living tissue.
Cavity—1. Hollow space within the body. 2. Hole in a tooth caused by dental caries.
Central nervous system—Part of the nervous system that is composed of the brain and spinal cord.
Cerebral—Relating to the brain.
Cerebral palsy—Permanent disorder of motor weakness and loss of coordination due to damage to the brain.
Cervix—Lower end or necklike opening of the uterus to the vagina.
Chemotherapy—Treatment of illness or disease by chemical agents. The term most commonly refers to the use of drugs to treat cancer.
Chickenpox—*See* Varicella.
Chlamydia—A family of microorganisms that cause a variety of diseases in humans. One form is commonly transmitted by sexual contact. Infection can be transmitted to the baby during the birth process.
Cholesterol—Fatlike substance made by the liver but also absorbed from the diet; found only in animal tissues. Too much blood cholesterol is associated with several potential health risks, especially atherosclerosis (hardening of the arteries).
Cholesterol free—In food labeling, less than 2 milligrams of cholesterol and 2 grams or less of saturated fat per serving.
Chromosome—The structure in the cell nucleus that contains the DNA; in humans, there are normally 46.
Chronic—Describes a condition of long duration, which is often of gradual onset and may involve very slow changes.
Cirrhosis—Chronic liver disease marked by destruction of its cells and abnormal tissue growth, resulting in abnormal function.
Clitoris—Small, erectile organ that is part of the female external sex organs.
CNS—*See* Central nervous system.
Cold sores—*See* Herpes simplex.
Colic—Waves of sudden severe abdominal pain, which are usually separated by relatively pain-free intervals.
Colitis—Inflammation of the colon (large bowel).
Collagen—A tough connective tissue protein found in bone, skin, tendons, and ligaments.
Colony stimulating factor—Protein that stimulates the production of one or more kinds of cells made in the bone marrow.
Colostomy—Operation in which part of the colon (large bowel) is brought through the abdominal wall to create an artificial opening. The contents of the intestine are passed out of the body through the opening.
Coma—Sleeplike state from which the patient cannot be aroused.
Coma, hepatic—Disturbances in alertness and mental function caused by severe liver disease.
Compliance—The extent to which a patient's behavior yields to or agrees with medical advice.
Component—Any ingredient that helps make up a substance.
Compound—Substance made up of two or more units, elements, ingredients, or parts.

Condom—Thin sheath or cover, made of latex (rubber) or animal intestine, that is worn over the penis during sexual intercourse to prevent pregnancy. Condoms made of latex (rubber) are also used to prevent infection.

Congestive heart failure—Condition of inadequate blood flow caused by the inability of the heart to pump strongly enough; characterized by breathlessness and edema.

Conjugated estrogens—A mixture of naturally occurring estrogens.

Conjunctiva—Delicate mucous membrane covering the front of the eye and the inside of the eyelid.

Conjunctivitis—Inflammation of the conjunctiva.

Connective tissue—Material of the body that joins and supports other tissue and body parts; includes skin, bone, and tendons.

Constriction—Squeezing together and becoming narrower or smaller, such as constriction of blood vessels or eye pupils.

Contagious disease—Most often refers to disease that can be transmitted from one person to another. May also refer to disease that can be transmitted from an animal to a person.

Contamination—The introduction of germs or unclean material into or on normally sterile substances or objects.

Contraceptive—Medicine or device used to prevent pregnancy.

Contraction—A shortening or tightening, as in the normal function of muscles.

Convulsion—*See* Seizure.

Corrosive—Causing slow wearing away by a destructive agent.

Corticosteroids—Group of cortisone-like hormones that are secreted by the adrenal cortex and are critical to the body. The two major groups of corticosteroids are glucocorticoids, which affect fat and body metabolism, and mineralocorticoids, which regulate salt/water balance. Also called *adrenocorticoids*.

Cortisol—Natural hormone produced by the adrenal cortex, important for carbohydrate, protein, and fat metabolism and for the normal response to stress; synthetic cortisol (hydrocortisone) is used to treat inflammations, allergies, collagen diseases, rheumatic disorders, and adrenal failure.

Cot death—*See* Sudden infant death syndrome (SIDS).

Cowpox—*See* Vaccinia.

Creutzfeldt-Jakob disease—Rare disease, probably caused by a slow-acting virus that affects the brain and nervous system.

Crib death—*See* Sudden infant death syndrome (SIDS).

Criteria—Standards on which a judgment or decision is based.

Crohn's disease—A chronic inflammatory disease of the digestive tract, usually the lower small intestine.

Croup—Inflammation and blockage of the larynx (voice box) in young children, which causes a barking cough.

Crystalluria—Crystals in the urine.

Cushing's syndrome—Condition caused by too much cortisone-like hormone, leading to weight gain, round face, and high blood pressure.

Cycloplegia—Paralysis of certain eye muscles; can be caused by medication for certain eye tests.

Cycloplegic—Medicine used to induce cycloplegia.

Cyst—Abnormal sac or closed cavity filled with liquid or semisolid matter.

Cystic—Marked by cysts.

Cystic fibrosis—Hereditary disease of children and young adults which mainly affects the lungs. Exocrine glands do not function normally, and excess mucus is produced.

Cystine—An amino acid found in most proteins; it is released by the breakdown of the protein.

Cystitis, interstitial—Inflammation of the bladder that occurs mainly in women and is associated with pain, frequent urge to urinate, and burning urination.

Cytomegalovirus—One of a group of viruses. One form may be transmitted sexually or by infected blood and can cause death in patients with weakened immune systems.

Cytoplasm—The contents of a cell outside the nucleus.

Cytotoxic agent—Chemical that kills cells or stops cell division; used to treat cancer.

Daily Value (DV)—Value used on food and dietary supplement labels to indicate the percent of the recommended daily amount of each nutrient that a serving provides. DV takes the place of USRDA (United States Recommended Daily Allowance).

Decongestant, nasal—Medicine used to help relieve nasal congestion (stuffy nose).

Decongestant, ophthalmic—Medicine used in the eye to relieve redness, burning, itching, or other eye irritation.

Decubitus ulcer—Bedsore; damage to the skin and underlying tissues caused by constant pressure.

Dental—Related to the teeth and gums.

Depression, mental—Condition marked by deep sadness; associated with lack of any pleasurable interest in life. Other symptoms include disturbances in sleep, appetite, and concentration, and difficulty in performing day-to-day tasks.

Dermatitis herpetiformis—Skin disease marked by sores that develop suddenly and intense itching.

Dermatitis, seborrheic—Type of eczema found on the scalp and face.

Dermatomyositis—Inflammatory disorder, mainly of the skin and muscle fibers.

Diabetes insipidus—Disorder in which the patient produces large amounts of dilute urine and is constantly thirsty. Also called *water diabetes*.

Diabetes mellitus—Disorder in which the body does not produce enough insulin or else the body tissues are unable to use the insulin present. This leads to hyperglycemia. Also called *sugar diabetes*.

Diagnose—Find out the cause or nature of a disorder. This often includes physical examination, laboratory tests, or other tests.

Diagnostic procedure—A process carried out to determine the cause or nature of a condition, disease, or disorder.

Dialysis, renal—Process using mechanical or other means to remove waste materials or poisons from the blood when the kidneys are not working well.

Dietary fiber—The part of food that cannot be broken down and digested; recommended as part of a balanced diet.

Dietary supplement—Nutrient eaten or taken into the body in addition to the usual food.

Digestant—Agent that will help in digestion.

Diplopia—Awareness of two images of a single object at one time; double vision.

Discharge—1. Material that is released and flows away from an organ or body part. 2. Release of electrical energy by a nerve cell.

Disintegration—The process of breaking down into small pieces. In nutrition, a measure of how fast a vitamin tablet or capsule breaks into small pieces in stomach fluids.

Dissolution—The breaking down of a substance into its separate parts. In nutrition, a measure of how fast a vitamin tablet or capsule dissolves once it has been swallowed.

Diuretic—Medicine used to increase the amount of urine produced by helping the kidneys get rid of water and salt.

Diverticulitis—Inflammation of a diverticulum in the intestinal tract.

Diverticulum—Sac or pouch opening from a canal or cavity, such as the gut or bladder.

DNA—Deoxyribonucleic acid; the genetic material that controls heredity. DNA is found chiefly in the cell nucleus.

Down syndrome—Disorder associated with the presence of an extra chromosome 21. Patients with Down syndrome are mentally retarded and are marked physically by a round head, flat nose, slightly slanted eyes, and short stature. Formerly called *mongolism.*

Drug interaction—The action of one drug upon another when taken close together; depending on the drugs and the patient's medical condition, may be harmful to the patient.

Duct—Tube or channel, especially one that serves to carry secretions from a gland.

Dumdum fever—*See* Leishmaniasis, visceral.

Duodenal ulcer—Open sore in that part of the small intestine closest to the stomach.

Duodenum—First of the three parts of the small intestine.

Dyskinesia—Refers to abnormal, involuntary movement or having difficulty in performing voluntary movement.

Dyspnea—Shortness of breath; difficult breathing.

Eczema—Inflammation of the skin, marked by itching and rash, and often including blisters that weep and become crusted.

Edema—Swelling of body tissue due to accumulation of excess fluids.

Eighth-cranial-nerve disease—Disease of the eighth cranial nerve, which serves the inner ear; results in dizziness, loss of balance, impaired hearing, nausea, or vomiting.

Electrolyte—In medical use, chemicals (ions) in body fluids that are needed for normal functioning of the body. Body electrolytes include bicarbonate, chloride, sodium, potassium, etc.

Element—In chemistry, a simple substance that cannot be broken down into simpler substances by chemical means; made up of atoms of only one kind.

Embolism—Sudden blocking of a blood vessel by a blood clot or other substances carried by the blood.

Embryo—In humans, a developing fertilized egg within the uterus (womb) from about two to eight weeks after fertilization.

Emergency—Extremely serious unexpected or sudden happening or situation that calls for immediate action.

Emetic—Substance used to cause vomiting; used in some cases of drug overdose and poisonings.

Emollient—Substance that soothes and softens, such as an emollient lotion.

Emphysema—Lung condition in which the air spaces are enlarged and damaged, causing poor exchange of oxygen and carbon dioxide during the process of breathing in and out.

Encephalitis—Inflammation of the brain.

Encephalopathy—Any degenerative disease of the brain; caused by many different medical conditions.

Endemic—Refers to a disease that is always present in a human community.

Endocarditis—Inflammation of the lining of the heart, leading to fever, heart murmurs, and heart failure.

Endocrine gland—A gland that has no duct, but releases its secretion directly into the blood or lymph.

Endometriosis—Condition in which material similar to the lining of the uterus (womb) appears at other sites, usually within the pelvic cavity, causing pain or bleeding.

Enema—Solution introduced into the rectum and colon to help empty the bowel, give nutrients or medicine, or help x-ray the lower intestines.

Enteric coating—Special coating on tablets that allows them to pass through the stomach unchanged. The tablets are broken up in the intestine and absorbed.

Enteritis—Inflammation of the small intestine, usually causing diarrhea.

Enuresis—Urinating while asleep (bedwetting).

Enzyme—One of a type of protein produced by cells. Enzymes usually bring about or speed up normal chemical body reactions.

Eosinophil—One type of white blood cells; plays a role in allergic reactions and in fighting parasite infections.

Eosinophilia—Condition in which the number of eosinophils in the blood is abnormally high.

Epidemic—Refers to a disease that is present in a community only occasionally, but affects a large number of people when it is present.

Epidural space—Area in the spinal column into which medicines (usually for pain) can be administered.

Epilepsy—Any of a group of brain disorders featuring sudden attacks of seizures or other symptoms.

Epinephrine—Hormone secreted by the adrenal gland. It stimulates the heart, constricts blood vessels, and relaxes some smooth muscles. Also called *adrenaline.*

EPO—*See* Erythropoietin.

Ergot alkaloids—A class of medicines that cause narrowing of blood vessels; used to treat migraine headaches, and to reduce bleeding in childbirth.

Erythropoietin—Hormone, secreted by the kidney, that controls the production of red blood cells by the bone marrow; also available as a synthetic drug (EPO).

Esophagus—The part of the digestive tract that connects the pharynx to the stomach.

Estrogen—Principal female sex hormone necessary for the normal sexual development of the female; during the menstrual cycle, its actions help prepare for possible pregnancy.

Excessive—Describes an amount or degree that is more than what is proper, usual, or normal.

Excrete—To throw off or eliminate waste material from the body, blood, or organs.

Exocrine gland—Any gland that discharges its secretion through a duct directly on the skin or other surface but not into the blood.

Exophthalmic goiter—*See* Graves' disease.

Exophthalmos—Thrusting forward of the eyeballs in their sockets giving the appearance of the eyes sticking out too far; commonly associated with hyperthyroidism.

Expectorant—Medicine used to help remove mucus or phlegm in the lungs by coughing or spitting it up.

Expel—To force out.

Extrapyramidal symptoms—Movement disorders occurring with certain diseases or with use of certain drugs, including trembling and shaking of hands and fingers, twisting movements of the body, shuffling walk, and stiffness of arms or legs.

Familial Mediterranean fever—Inherited condition involving inflammation of the lining of the chest, abdomen, and joints. Also called *recurrent polyserositis.*

Fasciculation—Small, repeated contraction of a few muscle fibers, which is visible through the skin; muscular twitching.

Fat—An energy-rich organic compound that occurs naturally in animals and plants. Fats are an essential nutrient for humans.

Fat free—In food labeling, less than 0.5 grams of fat per serving.

Fatty acid—One of the basic organic compounds that make up lipids.

Favism—Inherited condition resulting from sensitivity to broad (fava) beans; marked by fever, vomiting, diarrhea, and acute destruction of red blood cells.

Feces—Solid waste left after food is digested; passed out of the intestine through the anus. Also called *stool.*

Fertility—Ability to bring about the start of pregnancy or produce offspring.

Fertilization—Union of an ovum with a sperm.

Fetal—Relating to the fetus.

Fetus—In humans, a developing baby within the uterus (womb) from about the beginning of the third month of pregnancy.

Fewer calories—In food labeling, at least 25 percent fewer calories per serving than the reference food.

Fiber—The carbohydrate material of food that cannot be digested. Fiber adds bulk to the diet.

Fibrocystic—Having benign (noncancerous) tumors of connective tissue.

Fibroid tumor—A noncancerous tumor of the uterus formed of fibrous or fully developed connective tissue.

Fibrosis—Scarring and thickening of connective tissue causing it to tighten and become less flexible.

Fistula—Abnormal tubelike passage connecting two internal organs or one that leads from an abscess or internal organ to the body surface.

Flatulence—Excessive amount of gas in the stomach or intestine.

Flu—*See* Influenza.

Flushing—Temporary redness of the face and/or neck.

Folic acid—A vitamin of the B complex. Lack of folic acid may lead to anemia.

Follicle—Small secretory sac, pouch, or cavity.

Food Guide Pyramid—An eating plan developed by Health and Human Services and the Department of Agriculture that describes the basic food groups. It serves as a guide for having a proper diet.

Fungus—Any of a group of simple organisms, including molds and yeasts.

Fungus infection—Infection caused by a fungus. Some common fungus infections are tinea pedis (athlete's foot), tinea capitis (ringworm of the scalp), tinea cruris (ringworm of the groin or jock itch), and mouth or vaginal candidiasis (yeast infections).

Gait—Manner of walk.

Gamma globulin—The portion of the blood that contains most of the antibodies associated with the body's ability to fight infection.

Gastric—Relating to the stomach.

Gastric acid secretion inhibitor—Medicine used to decrease the amount of acid produced by the stomach.

Gastroenteritis—Inflammation of the stomach and intestine.

Gastroesophageal reflux—Backward flow of stomach contents into the esophagus. The condition is often characterized by "heartburn."

Generic—General in nature; relating to an entire group or class. In relation to medicines, the general name of a drug substance; not owned by one specific group as would be true for a trademark or brand name.

Genetics—The study of genes and their passing on of a quality or trait from parent to offspring.

Genital—1. Relating to the organs concerned with reproduction; the sexual organs. 2. Relating to reproduction.

Genital warts—Small growths found on the genitals or around the anus; caused by a virus. The disease may be transmitted by sexual contact.

Geriatric—Relating to aged persons.

Gilles de la Tourette syndrome—*See* Tourette's disorder.

Gingiva—Gums.

Gingival hyperplasia—Excessive growth of the gums.

Gingivitis—Inflammation of the gums.

Glandular fever—*See* Mononucleosis.

Glaucoma—Condition of abnormally high pressure in the eye; may lead to loss of vision if not treated.

Glomeruli—Clusters of capillaries in the kidney that act as filters of the blood.

Glomerulonephritis—Inflammation of the glomeruli of the kidney not directly caused by infection.

Glucose—A simple sugar. In living organisms, it is formed by the breakdown of carbohydrates and is the chief source of energy.

Glucose-6-phosphate dehydrogenase (G6PD) deficiency—Lack of or reduced amounts of an enzyme (glucose-6-phosphate dehydrogenase) that helps the breakdown of certain sugar compounds in the body.

Gluten—Type of protein found primarily in wheat and rye.

Goiter—Enlargement of the thyroid gland that causes the neck to swell; usually results from a lack of iodine or overactivity of the thyroid gland.

Gonadotropin—Any hormone that stimulates the activities of the ovaries or testes.

Gonorrhea—An infectious disease, usually transmitted by sexual contact. It causes infection in the genital organs in both men and women, and may result in disease in other parts of the body.

Good source of fiber—In food labeling, 2.5 grams to 4.9 grams of fiber per serving.

Gout—Disease in which uric acid deposits in the joints and kidneys, leading to arthritis and kidney stones.

Granulation—Small, fleshy outgrowths on the healing surface of a wound or ulcer; a normal stage in healing.

Granulocyte—One type of white blood cells.

Granulocytopenia—*See* Agranulocytosis.

Granuloma—A granular growth or mass produced in response to chronic infection, inflammation, a foreign body, or to unknown causes.

Graves' disease—Enlargement of the thyroid gland (goiter) and overproduction of thyroid hormones, causing fast heart beat, tremor, sweating, and weight loss. Also called *exophthalmic goiter.*

Groin—The area between the abdomen and thigh.

Guillain-Barré syndrome—Nerve disease marked by sudden numbness and weakness in the limbs that may progress to paralysis; recovery usually follows.

Gynecomastia—Excessive development of the breast tissue in the male.

Hair follicle—Sheath of tissue surrounding a hair root.

Hansen's disease—*See* Leprosy.

Hartnup disease—Hereditary disease in which the body has trouble processing certain chemicals, leading to mental retardation, rough skin, and problems with muscle coordination.

Healthy—1. Food labeling term that may be used if the food is low in fat and saturated fat and a serving does not contain more than 480 milligrams of sodium or more than 95 milligrams of cholesterol. The food must also meet requirements of 10% DV per serving of vitamin A, vitamin C, calcium, iron, protein, and fiber. 2. Being in a state of physical, mental, and social wellness.

Heart attack—*See* Myocardial infarction.

Helicobacter pylori—Organism that has been associated with gastritis and certain ulcers.

Hematologic—Relating to the blood.

Hematuria—Presence of blood or red blood cells in the urine.

Heme—A blood pigment containing iron; a component of hemoglobin.

Hemoglobin—Iron-containing substance found in red blood cells that transports oxygen from the lungs to the tissues of the body.

Hemolytic anemia—Type of anemia resulting from breakdown of red blood cells.

Hemophilia—Hereditary disease marked by delayed blood clotting, leading to uncontrolled bleeding even after minor injuries. Generally, only males have the disease.

Hemorrhoids—Enlarged veins in the walls of the anus. Also called *piles*.

Hepatic—Relating to the liver.

Hepatitis—Inflammation of the liver.

Hernia, hiatal—Condition in which the stomach passes partly into the chest cavity through the opening for the esophagus in the diaphragm.

Herpes simplex—The virus that causes "cold sores," small, painful blisters, on the lips. Infection may extend around the mouth and nose. In the case of genital herpes, the genitals (sex organs) are infected.

Herpes zoster—An infectious disease usually marked by pain and blisters along one nerve, often on the face, chest, stomach, or back. The infection is caused by the same virus that causes chickenpox. Also called *shingles*.

Heterosexual—One who is sexually attracted to persons of the opposite sex.

High blood pressure—*See* Hypertension.

High fiber—In food labeling, 5 grams or more of fiber per serving. (Foods making high-fiber claims must meet the definition for low fat, or the level of total fat must appear next to the high-fiber claim.)

Hirsutism—Excessive hair growth or the growth of hair in unusual places, especially in women.

HIV (human immunodeficiency virus)—Virus that causes AIDS.

Hives—*See* Urticaria.

Hoarseness—Gruff, husky, quality of the voice.

Hodgkin's disease—Malignant condition marked by swelling of the lymph nodes, with weight loss and fever.

Homosexual—One who is sexually attracted to persons of the same sex.

Hormone—Substance produced in one part of the body (such as a gland), which then passes into the bloodstream and travels to other organs or tissues, where it carries out its effect.

Hot flashes—Sensations of heat of the face, neck, and upper body, often accompanied by sweating and flushing; commonly associated with menopause.

Hydrocortisone—*See* Cortisol.

Hyperactivity—Abnormally increased activity and shortened attention span.

Hypercalcemia—Abnormally high amount of calcium in the blood.

Hypercalciuria—Abnormally high amount of calcium in the urine.

Hypercholesterolemia—Excessive amount of cholesterol in the blood.

Hyperglycemia—Abnormally high amount of glucose in the blood.

Hyperkalemia—Abnormally high amount of potassium in the blood.

Hyperkeratosis—Overgrowth or thickening of the outer layer of the skin.

Hyperlipidemia—General term for an abnormally high level of any or all of the lipids in the blood.

Hyperphosphatemia—Abnormally high amount of phosphate in the blood.

Hypersensitivity—An excessive response by the body to a foreign substance.

Hypertension—Blood pressure in the arteries (blood vessels) that is higher than normal for the patient's age group. Hypertension may lead to a number of serious health problems. Also called *high blood pressure*.

Hyperthermia—Abnormally high body temperature.

Hyperthyroidism—Excessive secretion of thyroid hormones by the thyroid gland, causing thyrotoxicosis.

Hypocalcemia—Abnormally low amount of calcium in the blood.

Hypoglycemia—Abnormally low amount of glucose in the blood.

Hypokalemia—Abnormally low amount of potassium in the blood.

Hypotension, orthostatic—Excessive fall in blood pressure that occurs when standing or upon standing up.

Hypothalamus—Area of the brain that controls many body functions, including body temperature, certain metabolic and endocrine processes, and some activities of the nervous system.

Hypothermia—Abnormally low body temperature.

Hypothyroidism—Condition caused by thyroid hormone deficiency, which results in a decrease in metabolism.

Hypoxia—Broad term meaning intake of oxygen or its use by the body is inadequate.

Ileostomy—Operation in which the ileum is brought through the abdominal wall to create an artificial opening. The contents of the intestine are discharged through the opening.

Ileum—Last of the three portions of the small intestine.

Immune—Having protection against infectious disease.

Immune deficiency condition—Lack of immune response to protect against infectious disease.

Immune system—Complex network of the body that defends against foreign substances or organisms that may harm the body.

Immunity—The body's ability to resist disease and infection.

Immunizing agent, active—Agent that causes the body to produce its own antibodies for protection against certain infections or substances.

Immunocompromised—Decreased natural immunity caused by certain medicines, diseases, genetic disorders, or use of immunosuppressants.

Immunosuppressant—Medicine that reduces the body's natural immunity.

Impair—To decrease, weaken, or damage, usually because of injury or disease.

Impairment—Decrease in strength or ability, often because of illness or injury (for example, hearing impairment).

Impetigo—Contagious bacterial skin infection common in babies and children in which skin redness develops into blisters that break and form a thick crust.

Implant—1. Special form of medicine, often a small pellet or rod, that is inserted into the body or beneath the skin so that the medicine will be released continuously over a period of time. 2. To insert or graft material or an object into a body site. 3. Material or an object inserted into a body site, such as a lens implant or a breast implant. 4. Action of a fertilized ovum becoming attached or embedded in the uterus.

Impotence—Difficulty or inability of a male to have or maintain an erection of the penis.

Incontinence—Inability to control natural passage of urine or of bowel movements.

Induce—To cause or bring about.

Infertility—Refers to the inability of a woman to become pregnant or of a man to cause pregnancy.

Inflammation—Pain, redness, swelling, and heat in a part of the body, usually in response to injury or illness.

Inflammatory bowel disease—Irritation of the intestinal tract.

Influenza—Highly contagious respiratory virus infection, marked by coughing, headache, chills, fever, muscle pain, and general weakness. Also called *flu*.

Ingredient—One of the parts or substances that make up a mixture or compound.

Inhalation—1. Act of drawing in the breath or drawing air into the lungs. 2. Medicine that is used when breathed (inhaled) into the lungs. Some inhalations work locally in the lungs, while others produce their effects elsewhere in the body.

Inhalator—Device used to help patient breathe in air, anesthetics, or other gases, or medicial mists or vapors.

Inhibitor—Substance that prevents a process or reaction.

Inner ear—Inner portion of the ear; a liquid filled system of cavities and ducts that make up the organs of hearing and balance.

Inorganic—Being made up of matter that is not living and has never lived.

Insomnia—Inability to sleep or remain asleep.

Insulin—Hormone that increases the efficiency with which the body uses sugar. Injections of insulin are used in the treatment and control of diabetes mellitus (sugar diabetes).

Interferon—Substance produced by cells infected with a virus, which stops the growth and the spread of the virus; may also have effects on cells fighting cancer.

Intra-amniotic—Within the sac that contains the fetus and amniotic fluid.

Intra-arterial—Within an artery.

Intracavernosal—Into the corpus cavernosa (cavities in the penis that, when filled with blood, produce an erection).

Intracavitary—Into a body cavity (for example, the chest cavity or bladder).

Intramuscular—Into a muscle.

Intrauterine device (IUD)—Small plastic or metal device placed in the uterus (womb) to prevent pregnancy.

Intravenous—Into a vein.

Ion—Atom or group of atoms carrying an electric charge.

Irrigation—Washing of a body cavity or wound with a stream of sterile water or a solution of a medicine.

Ischemia—Condition caused by inadequate blood flow to a part of the body; usually caused by constriction or blocking of blood vessels that supply the part of the body affected.

Jaundice—Yellowing of the eyes and skin due to excess bilirubin in the blood.

Jock itch—Ringworm of the groin.

Kala-azar—*See* Leishmaniasis, visceral.

Kaposi's sarcoma—Malignant tumor of blood vessels; often appears in the skin. One form occurs in immunocompromised patients, for example, transplant recipients and AIDS patients.

Keratin—Tough protein substance found in hair, nails, and the outer layer of the skin.

Keratolytic—Medicine used to soften thickened or hardened areas of the skin, such as warts.

Ketoacidosis—Type of acidosis associated with diabetes.

Lactation—Secretion of breast milk.

Lactose—A sugar found in milk.

Larva—The immature form of life of some insects and other animal groups that hatch from eggs.

Larynx—Organ that serves as a passage for air from the pharynx to the lungs; it contains the vocal cords.

Laxative—Natural or synthetic substances used to encourage bowel movements.

Laxative, bulk-forming—Laxative that acts by absorbing liquid and swelling to form a soft, bulky stool. The bowel is then stimulated normally by the presence of the bulky mass.

Laxative, hyperosmotic—Laxative that acts by drawing water into the bowel from surrounding body tissues. This provides a soft stool mass and increased bowel action.

Laxative, lubricant—Laxative that acts by coating the bowel and the stool mass with a waterproof film. This keeps moisture in the stool. The stool remains soft and its passage is made easier.

Laxative, stimulant—Laxative that acts directly on the intestinal wall. The direct stimulation increases the muscle contractions that move the stool mass along. Also called *contact laxative.*

Laxative, stool softener—Laxative that acts by helping liquids mix into the stool and prevent dry, hard stool masses. The stool remains soft and its passage is made easier. Also called *emollient laxative.*

Lean—Food labeling term for seafood or game meat, meals, and main dishes. May be used if a serving contains less than 10 grams of total fat, 4.5 grams or less of saturated fat, and less than 95 milligrams of cholesterol. Seafood and game meat must meet these criteria per 100 grams of food. Meals and main dishes must meet these criteria per 100 grams of food and per labeled serving.

Legionnaires' disease—Lung infection caused by a certain bacterium.

Leishmaniasis, visceral—Tropical disease, transmitted by sandfly bites, which causes liver and spleen enlargement, anemia, weight loss, and fever. Also called *black fever, Dumdum fever,* or *kala-azar.*

Lennox-Gastaut syndrome—Type of childhood epilepsy.

Leprosy—Chronic infectious disease marked by skin lesions. It is slowly progressive and leads to loss of feeling, tissue destruction, and deformity. Also called *Hansen's disease.*

Lesion—A defined area of diseased or injured tissue.

Less cholesterol—In food labeling, at least 25 percent less cholesterol and 2 grams or less of saturated fat per serving than the reference food.

Less fat—In food labeling, at least 25 percent less fat per serving than the reference food.

Less saturated fat—In food labeling, at least 25 percent less fat per serving than the reference food.

Less sodium—In food labeling, at least 25 percent less sodium per serving than the reference food.

Less sugar—In food labeling, at least 25 percent less sugar per serving than the reference food.

Leukemia—Malignant disease of the blood and bone marrow in which too many white blood cells are produced; results in anemia, bleeding, and low resistance to infections.

Leukocyte—White blood cell.

Leukoderma—*See* Vitiligo.

Leukopenia—Abnormally low number of leukocytes in the blood.

Ligament—Tough, fibrous tissue that connects one bone to another or supports organs.

Lipid—Term applied generally to fat or fatlike substances not soluble in water.

Local effect—Affecting only the area to which something is being applied.

Long-acting—Refers to a medicine that is made up in a special way so that it is slowly released in the body; the medicine's effect lasts longer than usual.

Low calorie—In food labeling, 40 calories or less per serving. However, for small servings (30 grams or less or 2 tablespoons or less), low calorie is 40 calories or less per 50 grams of the food.

Low cholesterol—In food labeling, 20 milligrams or less of cholesterol and 2 grams or less of saturated fat per serving. However, for small servings (30 grams or less or 2 tablespoons or less), low cholesterol is 20 milligrams or less of cholesterol per 50 grams of the food and 2 grams or less of saturated fat per serving.

Low fat—In food labeling, 3 grams or less of fat per serving. However, for small servings (30 grams or less or 2 tablespoons or less), low fat is 3 grams or less of fat per 50 grams of the food.

Low saturated fat—One gram or less of fat per serving and not more than 15 percent of calories from saturated fatty acids.
Low sodium—In food labeling, 140 milligrams or less of sodium per serving. However, for small servings (30 grams or less or 2 tablespoons or less), low sodium is 140 milligrams or less of sodium per 50 grams of the food.
Lozenge—A dry, medicated tablet or disk to be placed in the mouth and allowed to dissolve slowly. Also called *troche*.
Lugol's solution—Deep brown liquid containing iodine and potassium iodide.
Lupus—*See* Lupus erythematosus, systemic.
Lupus erythematosus, systemic—Chronic inflammatory disease most often affecting the skin, joints, and various internal organs. Also called *lupus* or *SLE* (systemic lupus erythematosus).
Lymph—Fluid that bathes the tissues. It is formed in tissue spaces in all parts of the body and circulated by the lymphatic system.
Lymphatic system—Network of vessels that conveys lymph from the spaces between the cells of the body back to the bloodstream.
Lymph node—A small rounded body found at intervals along the lymphatic system. The nodes act as filters for the lymph by keeping bacteria and other foreign particles from entering the bloodstream. They also produce lymphocytes.
Lymphocyte—Any of a number of white blood cells found in the blood, lymph, and lymphatic tissues. They are involved in immunity.
Lymphoma—Malignant tumors that arise in lymph nodes or the tissue where lymphocytes are formed.
Lyse—To cause breakdown. In cells, damage or rupture of the membrane results in destruction of the cell.
Macrobiotic—Vegetarian diet consisting mostly of whole grains.
Malaria—Tropical blood infection caused by protozoa; symptoms include chills, fever, sweats, headaches, and anemia. Malaria is spread to humans by the bite of an infected mosquito.
Malignant—Becoming continually worse if untreated; cancerous.
Malnutrition—Condition caused by unbalanced or insufficient diet.
Mammogram—X-ray picture of the breast.
Mania—Mental state in which fast talking and excited feelings or actions are out of control.
Mast cells—Cells in the connective tissue that store histamine; they release substances that bring about inflammation and produce signs of allergic reactions.
Mastocytosis—Accumulation of too many mast cells in tissues.
Mediate—To bring about or accomplish indirectly.
Megavitamin therapy—Taking very large doses of vitamins to prevent or treat certain medical problems.
Melanoma—Highly malignant cancer tumor, usually occurring on the skin.
Meniere's disease—Disease affecting the inner ear that is characterized by ringing in the ears, nausea, dizziness, and progessive hearing loss.
Meningitis—Inflammation of the tissues that surround the brain and spinal cord.
Menopause—The time in a woman's life when the ovaries no longer produce an egg cell at regular times and menstruation stops.
Metabolism—Sum of all physical and chemical changes that occur in cells to maintain growth and function, including building-up processes, breaking-down processes, and energy changes.
Methemoglobin—Substance formed when hemoglobin has been oxidized; in this form, hemoglobin cannot act as an oxygen carrier.
Methemoglobinemia—Presence of methemoglobin in the blood.
Microorganism—Any organism too small to be seen by the naked eye.
Middle ear—Chamber of the ear lying behind the eardrum and containing the three bones that conduct sound.
Migraine—Throbbing headache, usually affecting one side of the head; often accompanied by nausea, vomiting, and sensitivity to light.
Mineral—One of many elements needed in small amounts for many body functions, including blood clotting, muscle movement, and fluid balance.
Miotic—Medicine used in the eye that causes the pupil to constrict (become smaller).
Mongolism—*See* Down syndrome.
Mono—*See* Mononucleosis.
Monoclonal—Derived from a single cell; related to production of drugs by genetic engineering, such as monoclonal antibodies.
Mononucleosis—Infectious viral disease occurring mostly in adolescents and young adults, marked by fever, sore throat, swelling of the lymph nodes in the neck and armpits, and by severe fatigue. Also called *mono* or *glandular fever*.
More fiber—*See* Added fiber.
Motility—Ability to move without outside aid, force, or cause.
Motor—Relating to structures that bring about movement, such as nerves and muscles.
Mucolytic—Medicine that breaks down or dissolves mucus.
Mucosal—Relating to mucous membrane.
Mucous membrane—Moist layer of tissue surrounding or lining many body structures and cavities, including the mouth, lips, inside of nose, anus, and vagina.
Mucus—Thick fluid produced by the mucous membranes and glands.
Multiple sclerosis (MS)—Chronic, inflammatory nerve disease marked by weakness, unsteadiness, shakiness, and speech and vision problems.
Myalgia—Tenderness or pain in a muscle or muscles.
Myasthenia gravis—Chronic disease marked by abnormal weakness, and sometimes paralysis, of certain muscles.
Mydriatic—Medicine used in the eye that causes the pupil to dilate (become larger).
Myelogram—X-ray picture of the spinal cord.
Myeloma, multiple—Cancerous bone marrow disease.
Myocardial infarction—Interruption of blood supply to the heart, leading to sudden, severe chest pain, and damage to the heart muscle. Also called *heart attack*.
Myocardial reinfarction prophylactic—Medicine used to help prevent additional heart attacks in patients who have already had one attack.
Myotonia congenita—Hereditary muscle disorder marked by difficulty in relaxing a muscle or releasing a grip after any strong effort.
Narcolepsy—Extreme tendency to fall asleep suddenly.
Nasal—Relating to the nose.
Nasogastric (NG) tube—Tube that is inserted through the nose, down the throat, and into the stomach. It may be used to remove fluid or gas from the stomach or to give medicine, fluid, or nutrients to the patient.
Nebulizer—Instrument that administers liquid in the form of a fine spray.
Necrosis—Death of tissue, cells, or a part of a structure or organ, surrounded by healthy parts.
Neoplasm—New and abnormal growth of tissue in or on a part of the body, in which the multiplication of cells is uncontrolled and progressive. Also called *tumor*.
Nephron—Unit of the kidney that contributes to formation of urine by filtering the blood, adding substances to the fluid formed, and removing substances from it.

Neuralgia—Severe stabbing or throbbing pain along the course of one or more nerves.

Neuralgia, trigeminal—Severe burning or stabbing pain along certain nerves in the face. Also called *tic douloureux.*

Neural tube defects—Severe, abnormal conditions resulting when the nerve tract in the fetus fails to close fully. *See* Spina bifida.

Neuritis, optic—Disease of the nerves in the eye.

Neuritis, peripheral—Inflammation of terminal nerves or the nerve endings, usually associated with pain, muscle wasting, and loss of reflexes.

Neutropenia—Abnormally small number of neutrophils in the blood.

Neutrophil—The most common type of granulocyte; important in the body's protection against infection.

Nit—Egg of a louse.

No added sugar—In food labeling, no sugars added to food during processing or packing. This includes ingredients that contain sugars, for example, fruit juices, applesauce, or dried fruit.

No sugar added—*See* No added sugar.

Nodule—Small, rounded mass, lump, or swelling.

Nonsuppurative—Not discharging pus.

NSAID (nonsteroidal anti-inflammatory drug)—*See* Anti-inflammatory, nonsteroidal.

Nucleus—The part of the cell that contains the chromosomes.

Nutrient—Food substance that provides a source of energy or aids in growth and repair. Nutrients include carbohydrates, fats, proteins, minerals, and vitamins.

Nutrition—1. Study of food and drink relating to the building of sound bodies and promoting health. 2. All the body processes that are part of taking in food and using it.

Nutrition Labeling and Education Act (NLEA) of 1990—The law that required the Food and Drug Administration to develop new labeling requirements for foods and dietary supplements.

Nystagmus—Rapid, rhythmic, involuntary movements of the eyeball; may be from side to side, up and down, or around.

Obesity—Excess accumulation of fat in the body along with an increase in body weight that exceeds the healthy range for the body's frame.

Obstetrics—Field of medicine concerned with the care of women during pregnancy and childbirth.

Obstruction—Something that blocks or closes up a passage or structure.

Occlusive dressing—Dressing (such as plastic kitchen wrap) that completely cuts off air to the skin.

Occult—Concealed, hidden, or of unknown cause; cannot be seen by the human eye; detectable only by microscope or chemical testing, as for occult blood in the stools or feces.

Ophthalmic—Relating to the eye.

Opioid—1. Any synthetic narcotic with opium-like actions; not derived from opium. 2. Natural chemicals that produce opium-like effects by acting at the same cell sites where opium exerts action.

Oral—Relating to the mouth.

Orchitis—Inflammation of the testis.

Organic—1. In nutrition, a term used to describe plants that have been treated with animal or vegetable fertilizers instead of chemicals. 2. In chemistry, refers to substances that contain carbon.

Organism—Any individual living thing; may consist of a single cell or may be made up of many cells.

Osteitis deformans—*See* Paget's disease.

Osteomalacia—Softening of the bones due to lack of vitamin D.

Osteoporosis—Loss of calcium from bone tissue, leaving bones brittle and easy to fracture.

OTC (over the counter)—Refers to medicine or devices available without a prescription.

Otic—Relating to the ear.

Otitis media—Inflammation of the middle ear.

Ototoxicity—Having a harmful effect on the organs or nerves of the ear concerned with hearing and balance.

Ovary—Female sex organ that produces egg cells and sex hormones.

Overactive thyroid—*See* Hyperthyroidism.

Ovulation—Process by which an ovum is released from the ovary. In human menstruating females, this usually occurs once a month.

Ovum—Mature female sex or reproductive cell, or egg cell. It is capable of developing into a new organism if fertilized.

Oxidize—To lose electrons or to combine with oxygen.

Paget's disease—Chronic bone disease, marked by thickening of the bones and severe pain. Also called *osteitis deformans.*

Palpitation—Rapid, forceful, or throbbing heart beat.

Pancreatitis—Inflammation of the pancreas.

Pancytopenia—Reduction in the number of red cells, all types of white cells, and platelets in the blood.

Paralysis agitans—*See* Parkinson's disease.

Parathyroid glands—Four small bodies situated beside the thyroid gland; secrete parathyroid hormone that regulates calcium and phosphorus metabolism.

Parenteral—Most often refers to injecting a medicine into the body using a needle.

Parkinsonism—*See* Parkinson's disease.

Parkinson's disease—Brain disease marked by tremor (shaking), stiffness, and difficulty in moving. Also called *Parkinsonism, paralysis agitans,* or *shaking palsy.*

Patent ductus arteriosus (PDA)—Condition in babies in which an important fetal blood vessel fails to close as it should, resulting in faulty circulation and serious health problems.

Pediculicide—Medicine that kills lice.

Pediculosis—Infestation of the body, pubis (genital region), or scalp with lice.

Pellagra—Disease caused by too little niacin, which results in scaly skin, diarrhea, and mental depression.

Pemphigus—Skin disease marked by successive outbreaks of blisters.

Peptic ulcer—Open sore in the esophagus, stomach, or duodenum.

Peritoneum—Membrane sac lining the abdominal wall and covering the liver, stomach, spleen, gallbladder, and intestines.

Peritonitis—Inflammation of the peritoneum.

Peyronie's disease—Dense, fiber-like growth in the penis, which can be felt as an irregular hard lump, and which usually causes bending and pain when the penis is erect.

pH—Symbol used to express degree of acidity or alkalinity of a solution on a scale of 0 to 14; below 7 is acidic and above 7 is alkaline.

Pharynx—Space just behind the mouth that serves as a passageway for food from the mouth to the esophagus and for air from the nose and mouth to the larynx.

Phenol—Substance used as a preservative for some injectable medicines.

Pheochromocytoma—Tumor of the adrenal medulla.

Phlebitis—Inflammation of a vein.

Phlegm—Thick mucus produced in the respiratory passages.

Piles—*See* Hemorrhoids.

Pituitary gland—Pea-sized body located at the base of the brain. It produces a number of hormones that are essential to normal body growth and functioning.

Placebo—Medicine that, unknown to the patient, has no active medicinal substance; its use may relieve or improve a condition because the patient believes it will. Also called *sugar pill.*

Plaque, dental—Mixture of saliva, bacteria, and carbohydrates that forms on the teeth, leading to caries (cavities) and gum disease.

Platelet—Small, disk-shaped body found in the blood. Platelets play an important role in blood clotting.

Platelet aggregation inhibitor—Medicine used to help prevent the platelets in the blood from clumping together. This effect reduces the chance of heart attack or stroke in certain patients.

Pledget—Small mass of gauze or cotton used to apply or absorb fluids or keep out air.

Pleura—Membrane covering the lungs and lining the chest cavity.

Pneumococcal—Relating to certain bacteria that cause pneumonia.

Pneumocystis carinii—Organism that causes pneumocystis carinii pneumonia.

Pneumocystis carinii pneumonia—A lung infection of infants and weakened persons, including those with AIDS or those receiving drugs that weaken the immune system.

Polymorphous light eruption—A skin problem in certain people, which results from exposure to sunlight.

Polymyalgia rheumatica—A rheumatic disease, most common in elderly patients, which causes aching and stiffness in the shoulders and hips.

Polyp—Tumor or mass of tissue attached with a stalk or broad base; found in cavities such as the nose, uterus, or rectum.

Porphyria—A group of uncommon, usually inherited diseases of defective porphyrin metabolism.

Porphyrin—One of a number of pigments occurring in living organisms throughout nature (for example, as constituents in heme, chlorophyll, vitamin B_{12} and certain enzymes).

Potency—The strength of a medicine, chemical, or vitamin that will bring about a certain effect.

Preservative—Substance added to a product to destroy or prevent the growth of microorganisms.

Prevent—To stop or to keep from happening.

Priapism—Prolonged abnormal, painful erection of the penis.

Proctitis—Inflammation of the rectum.

Progesterone—Natural steroid hormone responsible for preparing the uterus for pregnancy. If fertilization occurs, progesterone's actions carry on or maintain the pregnancy.

Progestin—A natural or synthetic hormone that has progesterone-like actions.

Progressive—In medicine, advancing, as an illness or condition, from bad to worse.

Prolactin—Hormone secreted by the pituitary gland that stimulates and maintains milk flow in women following childbirth.

Prolactinoma—A pituitary tumor; results in secretion of excess prolactin.

Prophylactic—1. Agent or medicine used to prevent the occurrence of a specific condition. 2. Condom.

Prostate—Gland surrounding the neck of the male urethra just below the base of the bladder. It secretes a fluid that constitutes a major portion of the semen.

Prosthesis—Any artificial substitute for a missing body part.

Protein—One of a class of compounds that contain carbon, hydrogen, nitrogen, oxygen, and sometimes other elements. Proteins make up the greatest part of plant and animal tissue. They are a source of energy for animals and humans.

Protozoa—Tiny, one-celled animals; some cause diseases in humans.

Psoralen—Chemical found in plants and used in certain perfumes and medicines. Exposure to a psoralen and then to sunlight may increase the risk of severe burning.

Psoriasis—Chronic skin disease marked by itchy, scaly, red patches.

Psychosis—Severe mental illness marked by loss of contact with reality, often involving delusions, hallucinations, and disordered thinking.

Puberty—Period in life during which sexual organs mature, making reproduction possible.

Pulmonary—Relating to the lungs.

Puncture—Wound or opening made by piercing with a pointed object or instrument.

Purity—Free from contamination.

Purpura—Skin rash or spots marked by bleeding into the skin; may be caused by defects in the capillaries or a decreased number of platelets.

PUVA—Treatment for psoriasis by use of a psoralen, such as methoxsalen or trioxsalen, and long-wave ultraviolet light.

Rachischisis—*See* Spina bifida.

Radiation—General term for any form of energy moving in all directions from a common center, including radioactive elements and x-ray tubes.

Radiopaque agent—Substance that makes it easier to see an area of the body with x-rays. Radiopaque agents are used to help diagnose a variety of medical problems.

Radiopharmaceutical—Radioactive agent used to diagnose certain medical problems or treat certain diseases.

Raynaud's syndrome—Condition marked by numbness, tingling, and color change (white, blue, then red) in the fingers when they are exposed to cold.

Recommended Dietary Allowances (RDAs)—In the U.S., the amount of vitamins and minerals needed to provide for adequate nutrition in most healthy persons. RDAs for a given nutrient may vary depending on a person's age, sex, and physical condition (for example, pregnancy).

Recommended Nutrient Intakes (RNIs)—In Canada, values used to determine the amounts of vitamins, minerals, and protein needed to provide adequate nutrition and lessen the risk of chronic disease.

Rectal—Relating to the rectum.

Reduced calories—*See* Fewer calories.

Reduced cholesterol—*See* Less cholesterol.

Reduced fat—*See* Less fat.

Reduced saturated fat—*See* Less saturated fat.

Reduced sodium—*See* Less sodium.

Reduced sugar—*See* Less sugar.

Reference food—A basic food item. In food labeling, reference food is compared against the same food that has had something added to it or taken away from it.

Relapse—To fall back into illness after recovery has begun.

Renal—Relating to the kidneys.

Reproduction—Process that gives rise to new individuals of the same kind.

Reye's syndrome—Serious disease affecting the liver and brain that sometimes occurs after a virus infection, such as influenza or chickenpox. It occurs most often in young children and teenagers. The first sign of Reye's syndrome is usually severe, prolonged vomiting.

Rheumatic heart disease—Heart disease marked by scarring and chronic inflammation of the heart and its valves, occurring after rheumatic fever.

Rhinitis—Inflammation of the mucous membrane inside the nose.

Rickets—Bone disease usually caused by too little vitamin D, resulting in soft and malformed bones.

Rigidity—Lacking the ability to bend or be bent; stiffness.

Ringworm—*See* Tinea.
Risk—The possibility of injury or of suffering harm.
River blindness—Tropical disease produced by infection with worms of the Onchocerca type. The condition usually causes severe itching and may cause blindness.
Rosacea—Skin disease of the face, usually in middle-aged and older persons. Also called *adult acne.*
Saliva—Liquid secreted into the mouth by salivary glands; breaks down starch and moistens food for easy swallowing.
Sarcoidosis—Chronic disorder marked by enlarged lymph nodes in many parts of the body and inflammation, often in the muscles, eye, lungs, liver, and spleen.
Saturated fat—In chemistry, a fat that has all of the possible hydrogen atoms present on the carbon atoms and no double or triple bonds between the carbon atoms.
Saturated fat free—In food labeling, less than 0.5 grams of fat and less than 0.5 grams trans fatty acid per serving.
Scabicide—Medicine used to treat scabies (itch mite) infection.
Scabies—Contagious dermatitis caused by a mite burrowing into the skin; marked by tiny skin eruptions and severe itching.
Schistosomiasis—Tropical infection in which worms enter the skin from infested water and settle in the bladder or intestines, causing inflammation and scarring. Also called *bilharziasis.*
Schizophrenia—Severe mental disorder in which thinking, mood, and behavior are disturbed.
Scintigram—Image obtained by photographing emissions made by a radiopharmaceutical introduced into the body.
Scleroderma—Chronic disease first seen as hardening, thickening, and shrinking of the skin; later, certain organs also are affected.
Scotoma—Area of decreased vision or total loss of vision in a part of the visual field; a blind spot.
Scrotum—Sac that holds the testes (male sex glands).
Scurvy—Disease caused by a deficiency of vitamin C (ascorbic acid), marked by bleeding gums, bleeding beneath the skin, and body weakness.
Sebaceous gland—Skin gland that secretes sebum.
Seborrhea—Skin condition caused by the excess release of sebum from the sebaceous glands, accompanied by dandruff and oily skin.
Sebum—Fatty secretion produced by sebaceous (oil) glands of the skin.
Secretion—1. Process in which a gland in the body or on the surface of the body releases a substance for use. 2. The substance released by the gland.
Sedative-hypnotic—Medicine used to treat excessive nervousness, restlessness, or insomnia.
Sedation—A profoundly relaxed or calmed state.
Seizure—A sudden attack, usually referring to contractions of muscles as seen in epilepsy or other disorders.
Semen—Fluid released from the penis at sexual climax. It is made up of sperm suspended in secretions from the reproductive tract.
Sensory—Relating to the senses (smell, taste, hearing, sight, and touch).
Severe—Of a great degree, such as very serious pain or distress.
Shaking palsy—*See* Parkinson's disease.
Shingles—*See* Herpes zoster.
Shock—Severe disruption of cellular metabolism associated with reduced blood volume and blood pressure too low to supply adequate blood to the tissues.
Short-acting—Refers to a medicine that is effective for a short amount of time.
Shunt—Surgical connection used to transfer blood or other fluid from one part of the body to another.
SIADH (secretion of inappropriate antidiuretic hormone) syndrome—Disease caused by excess production of antidiuretic hormone; the body retains (keeps) more fluid than normal.
Sickle cell anemia—Hereditary disorder that mainly affects blacks; caused by abnormal hemoglobin. The name comes from the sickle-shaped red blood cells found in the blood of patients.
Sinusitis—Inflammation of a sinus.
Sjögren's syndrome—Condition usually occurring in older women, marked by dry eyes, dry mouth, and inflamed salivary glands.
Skeletal muscle relaxant—Medicine used to relax certain muscles and help relieve the pain and discomfort caused by strains, sprains, or other injury to the muscles.
Skeleton—The bony framework of the body that supports the soft tissues and organs.
SLE—*See* Lupus erythematosus, systemic.
Sodium fluoride—Mineral often found in drinking water that makes teeth stronger and helps prevent cavities.
Sodium free—In food labeling, less than 5 milligrams of sodium per serving.
Soluble—Able to be dissolved in a fluid.
Spasticity—Increase in normal muscular tone, causing stiff, awkward movements.
Spastic paralysis—Paralysis marked by muscle rigidity or spasticity in the part of the body that is paralyzed.
Sperm—Mature male reproductive or sex cell. When a sperm fertilizes an ovum, a new organism begins developing.
Spermicide—Substance that kills sperm.
Spina bifida—Birth defect in which the infant's spinal cord is partially exposed through a hole in the backbone. Also called *rachischisis.*
Stenosis—Abnormal narrowing of a canal or duct of the body.
Sterility—1. Inability to produce offspring. 2. The state of being free of living microorganisms.
Stimulant, respiratory—Medicine used to stimulate breathing.
Stomatitis—Inflammation of the mucous membrane of the mouth.
Stool—*See* Feces.
Strength—In nutrition, the measure of a vitamin's health value.
Streptokinase—Enzyme that dissolves blood clots.
Stroke—Very serious event in which blood flow to the brain is stopped; an artery to the brain may become clogged by a blood clot or it may burst and cause hemorrhage. Stroke can affect speech, memory, and behavior, and may result in paralysis. Also called *apoplexy.*
Stye—Infection of one or more sebaceous glands of the eyelid, marked by swelling.
Subcutaneous—Under the skin.
Sublingual—Under the tongue. A sublingual medicine is taken by placing it under the tongue and letting it slowly dissolve.
Sudden infant death syndrome (SIDS)—Sudden death of an apparently well infant from an unknown cause; death usually occurs during sleep. Also called *crib death* or *cot death.*
Sugar diabetes—*See* Diabetes mellitus.
Sugar free—In food labeling, less than 0.5 grams of sugar per serving.
Sugar pill—*See* Placebo.
Sulfite—Type of preservative; causes allergic reactions, such as asthma, in sensitive patients.
Sunscreen—Substance, usually a cream or lotion, that blocks ultraviolet light and helps prevent sunburn when applied to the skin.
Suppository—Mass of medicated material shaped for insertion into the rectum, vagina, or urethra; solid at room temperature but melts at body temperature.
Suppressant—Medicine that stops an action or condition.

Suspension—A form of medicine in which the drug is mixed with a liquid but is not dissolved in it. When left standing, particles settle at the bottom of the liquid and the top portion turns clear. When shaken it is ready for use.

Symptom—Outward sign of a disease or disorder.

Syncope—Sudden loss of consciousness due to inadequate blood flow to the brain; fainting.

Synthetic—A substance that is manufactured rather than occurring naturally.

Syphilis—An infectious disease, usually transmitted by sexual contact. The three stages of the disease may be separated by months or years.

Syringe—Device used to inject liquids into the body, remove material from a part of the body, or wash out a body cavity.

Systemic—Having general effects throughout the body; applies to most medicines when taken by mouth or given by injection.

Tachycardia—Abnormal rapid beating of the heart, usually at a rate over 100 beats per minute in adults.

Tardive dyskinesia—Slow, involuntary movements, often of the tongue, lips, or arms, usually brought on by certain drugs.

TB—*See* Tuberculosis.

Temporomandibular joint (TMJ)—Hinge that connects the lower jaw to the skull.

Tendinitis—Inflammation of a tendon.

Tendon—Band of tough tissue that attaches a muscle to bone.

Teratogenic—Causing abnormal development in an embryo or fetus, resulting in birth defects.

Testicle—Male sex organ that produces sperm and testosterone.

Testosterone—Principal male sex hormone.

Tetany—Condition marked by spasm and twitching of the muscles, particularly those of the hands, feet, and face; caused by a decrease in the calcium ion concentration in the blood.

Therapeutic—Relating to the treatment of a specific condition.

Thimerosal—Chemical used as a preservative in some medicines, and as an antiseptic and disinfectant.

Thrombolytic agent—Substance that dissolves blood clots.

Thrombophlebitis—Inflammation of a vein accompanied by the formation of a blood clot.

Thrombus—Blood clot that obstructs a cavity of the heart or a blood vessel.

Thrush—*See* Candidiasis of the mouth.

Thyroid gland—Gland in the lower front of the neck. It releases thyroid hormones, which control body metabolism.

Thyrotoxicosis—Condition resulting from excessive amounts of thyroid hormones in the blood, causing increased metabolism, fast heartbeat, tremors, nervousness, and increased sweating.

Tic—Repeated involuntary movement or spasm of a muscle.

Tic douloureux—*See* Neuralgia, trigeminal.

Tinea—Fungus infection of the surface of the skin, particularly the scalp, feet, and nails. Also called *ringworm.*

Tinnitus—Ringing in the ears.

Tone—The slight, continuous tension present in resting muscles.

Topical—Refers to local effects, especially of medicine applied directly to the skin.

Tourette's disorder—Rare condition beginning in childhood, marked by tics and other unnecessary movements and barks, sniffs, or grunts (may be swearing). Also called *Gilles de la Tourette syndrome.*

Toxemia—Blood poisoning caused by bacterial production of toxins.

Toxemia of pregnancy—Condition occurring in pregnant women marked by hypertension, edema, excess protein in the urine, convulsions, and possibly coma.

Toxic—Poisonous; related to or caused by a toxin or poison.

Toxin—A substance produced by an animal or plant that is poisonous to another organism.

Toxoplasmosis—Disease caused by a blood protozoan, usually transmitted to humans from cats or by eating raw meat; generally the symptoms are mild and self-limited.

Tracheostomy—A surgical opening through the throat into the trachea (windpipe) to bypass an obstruction to breathing.

Tranquilizer—Medicine that produces a calming effect. It is used to relieve mental anxiety and tension.

Transdermal—A means of administering medicine into the body by use of skin patches or disks, or ointment; medicine contained in the patch or disk or the ointment is absorbed through the skin.

Transmit—In medicine, to pass or spread infection or disease from one person to another.

Trichomoniasis—Infection of the vagina resulting in inflammation of genital tissues and discharge. It can be passed to and from males.

Triglyceride—A molecular form in which fats are present in food and the body; triglycerides are stored in the body as fat.

Troche—*See* Lozenge.

Trypanosome fever—*See* Trypanosomiasis, African.

Trypanosomiasis, African—Tropical disease, transmitted by tsetse fly bites, which causes fever, headache, and chills, followed by enlarged lymph nodes and anemia. Months or even years later, the disease affects the central nervous system, causing drowsiness and lethargy, coma, and death. Also called *African sleeping sickness.*

Tuberculosis (TB)—Infectious disease which may affect any organ but most commonly the lungs; symptoms include fever, night sweats, weight loss, and spitting up blood.

Tumor—Abnormal growth or enlargement in or on a part of the body.

Tyramine—Chemical present in many foods and beverages. Its structure and action in the body are similar to epinephrine.

Ulcer—Open sore or break in the skin or mucous membrane; often fails to heal and is accompanied by inflammation.

Ulcerative colitis—Chronic, recurrent inflammation and ulceration of the colon.

Ulceration—1. Formation or development of an ulcer. 2. Condition of an area marked with ulcers loosely associated with one another.

Ultraviolet rays—Invisible radiation having a wavelength shorter than that of visible light but longer than that of x-rays.

Underactive thyroid—*See* Hypothyroidism.

Ureter—Tube through which urine passes from the kidney to the bladder.

Urethra—Tube through which urine passes from the bladder to the outside of the body.

Uric acid—Product of protein metabolism, excreted in the urine.

Urticaria—An eruption of itching wheals on the skin. Also called *hives.*

USRDA—Labeling term formerly used to indicate how much of a nutrient a serving provided. This term is now stated as Daily Value (DV).

Uterus—Hollow organ in the female in which the fetus develops until birth.

Vaccine—Preparation of microorganisms given to protect against the disease that they cause.

Vaccinia—The skin and sometimes body reactions associated with smallpox vaccine. Also called *cowpox.*

Vagina—Passage in the female leading from the cervix of the uterus to the outside of the body.

Vaginal—Relating to the vagina.

Varicella—Very infectious virus disease marked by fever and itchy rash that develops into blisters and then scabs. Also called *chickenpox.*

Vasoconstrictor—Medicine or enzyme that causes smooth muscles of blood vessels to contract, raising blood pressure.

Vascular—Relating to the blood vessels.

Vasodilator—Medicine that dilates the blood vessels, permitting increased blood flow.

Vasopressin—A hormone whose actions increase the absorption of water by the kidney and constrict small blood vessels. Also called *antidiuretic hormone, ADH*.

Ventricular fibrillation—Life-threatening condition of fine, quivering, irregular movements of many muscle fibers of certain heart muscle; replaces the normal heart beat and interrupts pumping function.

Ventricle—A small cavity, such as one of the two lower chambers of the heart or one of the several cavities of the brain.

Vertigo—Sensation of motion, usually whirling, or dizziness, either of oneself or of one's surroundings.

Very low sodium—In food labeling, 35 milligrams or less of sodium per serving. However, for small servings (30 grams or less or 2 tablespoons or less), very low sodium is 35 milligrams or less of sodium per 50 grams of the food.

Veterinary—Relating to animals and their diseases and treatment.

Virus—Any of a group of simple microbes too small to be seen by a light microscope. They can grow and reproduce only in living cells. Many cause diseases in humans, including the common cold.

Vitamin—Any of a group of substances, needed in small amounts only, for growth and health. Vitamins are usually found naturally in food, but may also be man-made.

Vitamin, natural—A vitamin that comes from natural sources such as plants.

Vitamin, synthetic—A vitamin that does not come from natural sources, but instead is man-made.

Vitamins, fat-soluble—Vitamins that can be dissolved in fat (vitamins A, D, E, K). They are stored in fat tissue.

Vitamins, water-soluble—Vitamins that can be dissolved in water (vitamin C and the B-complex vitamins). They are stored in small amounts by the body.

Vitiligo—Condition in which some areas of skin lose pigment and turn white. Also called *leukoderma.*

von Willebrand's disease—Hereditary blood disease in which blood clotting is delayed, leading to excessive bleeding even after minor injuries.

Water diabetes—*See* Diabetes insipidus.

Water pill—*See* Diuretic.

Wheal—Temporary, small, raised area of the skin, usually accompanied by itching or burning; welt.

Wheezing—A whistling sound made when there is difficulty in breathing.

White mouth—*See* Candidiasis of the mouth.

Wilson's disease—Inborn defect in the body's ability to process copper. Too much copper may accumulate and lead to jaundice, cirrhosis, mental retardation, or symptoms like those of Parkinson's disease.

Without added sugar—*See* No added sugar.

Zollinger-Ellison syndrome—Disorder in which a tumor of the pancreas causes the stomach to produce too much acid, leading to ulcers.

Appendix I

INTRODUCTORY VERSION PATIENT EDUCATION LEAFLETS

In an effort to provide consumers with information and to help health care professionals counsel their patients on medicines that are newly available, USP creates Introductory Version Patient Education Leaflets. In order to make these leaflets available as soon as possible after a drug is marketed, the introductory leaflets are not produced through the full DI review process. Instead, they contain information based primarily on the FDA-approved manufacturer's package insert which may also be reviewed by selected members of appropriate USP DI Advisory Panels. The manufacturer of the drug is also given an opportunity to comment.

Introductory Version Patient Education Leaflets are meant to fill the immediate need for information on a temporary basis until a full monograph for a given drug has been developed and gone through the complete review process. Once the monograph is final, the corresponding leaflet will be revised accordingly and released as a final USP DI Patient Drug Education Leaflet.

The following selection of Introductory Version Patient Education Leaflets is provided to supply information on medicines whose monographs are currently under development. Additional introductory leaflets are published in the monthly USP DI Update as they are developed.

Acarbose (Oral)
Amphotericin B Lipid Complex (Injection)
Amifostine (Injection)
Anastrozole (Oral)
Baclofen (Injection)
Betaine (Oral)
Bicalutamide (Oral)
Bismuth Subsalicylate, Metronidazole, and Tetracycline (For H. pylori—Oral)
Brimonidine (Ophthalmic)
Cabergoline (Oral)
Calcitonin (Nasal)
Calcium Acetate (Oral)
Ceftibuten (Oral)
Clonidine (Injection)
Dexfenfluramine (Oral)
Donepezil (Oral)
Fexofenadine (Oral)
Fluticasone (Inhalation)
Fluticasone (Nasal)
Fluvoxamine (Oral)
Glatiramer Acetate (Injection)
Glimepiride (Oral)
Histrelin (Injection)
Imiquimod (Topical)
Indinavir (Oral)
Insulin Lispro (Injection)
Interferon, Beta-1a (Injection)
Interferon, Beta-1b (Injection)
Ipratropium and Albuterol (Inhalation-Local)
Losartan and Hydrochlorothiazide (Oral)
Miglitol (Oral)
Mirtazapine (Oral)
Nefazodone (Oral)
Nelfinavir (Oral)
Nevirapine (Oral)
Nicotine (Nasal)
Olanzapine (Oral)
Pegaspargase (Injection)
Pentosan (Oral)
Porfimer (Injection)
Pramipexole (Oral)
Protease Inhibitors (Oral)
- Indinavir (Oral)
- Ritonavir (Oral)
- Saquinavir (Oral)

Ranitidine Bismuth Citrate (Oral)
Rimexolone (Ophthalmic)
Sparfloxacin (Oral)
Teniposide (Injection)
Tiludronate (Oral)
Topiramate (Oral)
Topotecan (Injection)
Tretinoin (Oral)
Troglitazone (Oral)
Vinorelbine (Injection)
Zileuton (Oral)

USP DI® Patient Education Leaflets™—Introductory Version*

Acarbose (Oral)

A commonly used brand name is *Precose*.

ABOUT YOUR MEDICINE

Acarbose (AK-ar-bose) is used to treat a type of diabetes mellitus (sugar diabetes).

If any of the information in this leaflet causes you special concern or if you want additional information about your medicine and its use, check with your doctor, nurse, or pharmacist. **Remember, keep this and all other medicines out of the reach of children and never share your medicines with others.**

BEFORE USING

Tell your doctor, nurse, and pharmacist if you . . .

- are allergic to any medicine, either prescription or nonprescription (OTC);
- are pregnant or intend to become pregnant while using this medicine;
- are breast-feeding;
- are taking any other prescription or nonprescription (OTC) medicine, especially activated charcoal, medicine for digestion that contains amylase or pancreatin, corticosteroids (cortisone-like medicine), or diuretics (water pills);
- have any other medical problems, especially cirrhosis of the liver, kidney disease, or problems with digestion or other intestinal problems.

PROPER USE

Follow carefully the special meal plan your doctor gave you. This is the most important part of controlling your condition, and is needed for acarbose to work properly. Also, exercise regularly and test for sugar in your blood or urine as directed.

In order for acarbose to work properly, it must be taken at the beginning of each main meal. It is important that you do not miss any doses. However, if you finish a meal and have forgotten to take the medicine, do not take the missed dose. Instead, take the next dose at the beginning of your next meal, as scheduled. **Do not double doses.**

PRECAUTIONS

Your doctor will want to check your progress at regular visits, especially during the first several weeks of treatment.

Acarbose does not cause hypoglycemia (low blood sugar). However, low blood sugar can occur if you delay or miss a meal or snack, exercise more than usual, cannot eat because of nausea or vomiting, or drink alcohol. It can also occur when other medicines that can lower blood sugar are taken with acarbose.

Symptoms of low blood sugar include abdominal or stomach pain (mild); anxiety; chills (continuing); cold sweats; confusion; convulsions (seizures); cool, pale skin; difficulty in thinking; drowsiness; excessive hunger; fast heartbeat; headache (continuing); nausea or vomiting (continuing); nervousness; shakiness; unconsciousness; unsteady walk; unusual tiredness or weakness; or vision changes.

If symptoms of low blood sugar occur, **eat or drink glucose tablets or gel, fruit juice, or honey to relieve the symptoms. Table sugar (sucrose) or regular (non-diet) soft drinks will not work and should not be used.** Also, check your blood for low blood sugar. **Get to your doctor or a hospital right away if symptoms do not improve.**

Someone should call for emergency help immediately if severe symptoms such as convulsions (seizures) or unconsciousness occur. Do not force food or drink because this could cause choking from not swallowing correctly.

High blood sugar symptoms may occur if you skip a dose of acarbose, if you overeat or do not follow your meal plan, if you have a fever or infection, or do not exercise as much as usual.

Symptoms of high blood sugar include blurred vision; drowsiness; flushed, dry skin; fruit-like breath odor; increased urination; loss of appetite; nausea or vomiting; stomachache; tiredness; troubled breathing (fast and deep); or unusual thirst. **If symptoms of high blood sugar occur, check your blood sugar level, then call your doctor for instructions.**

POSSIBLE SIDE EFFECTS

Side Effects That Should Be Reported To Your Doctor Immediately

Rare—Yellow eyes or skin

Side Effects That Usually Do Not Require Medical Attention

These possible side effects may go away during treatment; however, if they continue or are bothersome, check with your doctor, nurse, or pharmacist.

More common—Abdominal or stomach pain; bloated feeling or gas; diarrhea

Other side effects not listed above may also occur in some patients. If you notice any other effects, check with your doctor, nurse, or pharmacist.

***This leaflet has been developed by the USP based primarily on labeling provided by the manufacturer at the time of its approval. This information is intended for use as a temporary educational aid until the drug has been assessed by USP advisory panels. The information does not cover all possible uses, actions, precautions, side effects, or interactions of this medicine. It is not intended as medical advice for individual problems.**

Acarbose (Oral) 911835

USP DI® Patient Education Leaflets™—Introductory Version*

Amphotericin B Lipid Complex (Injection)

A commonly used brand name is *ABELCET*.

ABOUT YOUR MEDICINE

Amphotericin (am-foe-TER-i-sin) **B lipid complex** is an antifungal. It is used to treat aspergillosis, a serious fungal infection.

If any of the information in this leaflet causes you special concern or if you want additional information about your medicine and its use, check with your doctor, nurse, or pharmacist. **Remember, keep this and all other medicines out of the reach of children and never share your medicines with others.**

BEFORE RECEIVING THIS MEDICINE

Tell your doctor, nurse, and pharmacist if you . . .

- are allergic to any medicine, either prescription or nonprescription (OTC);
- are pregnant or intend to become pregnant while using this medicine;
- are breast-feeding;
- are taking any other prescription or nonprescription (OTC) medicine;
- have any other medical problems, especially kidney disease;
- have ever been treated with x-rays or cancer medicine.

POSSIBLE SIDE EFFECTS

Side Effects That Should Be Reported To Your Doctor Immediately

More common—Fever and chills; headache; nausea and vomiting

Less common—Difficulty in breathing; sore throat and fever; unusual bleeding or bruising; unusual tiredness or weakness

Rare—Increased or decreased urination

Side Effects That Usually Do Not Require Medical Attention

These possible side effects may go away during treatment; however, if they continue or are bothersome, check with your doctor, nurse, or pharmacist.

More common—Diarrhea; loss of appetite; stomach pain

Other side effects not listed above may also occur in some patients. If you notice any other effects, check with your doctor, nurse, or pharmacist.

***This leaflet has been developed by the USP based primarily on labeling provided by the manufacturer at the time of its approval. This information is intended for use as a temporary educational aid until the drug has been assessed by USP advisory panels. The information does not cover all possible uses, actions, precautions, side effects, or interactions of this medicine. It is not intended as medical advice for individual problems.**

Amphotericin B Lipid Complex (Injection) 911766

USP DI® Patient Education Leaflets™—Introductory Version*

Amifostine (Injection)

A commonly used brand name is *Ethyol*.

ABOUT YOUR MEDICINE

Amifostine (am-i-FOS-teen) is used to lessen some of the harmful effects of cisplatin (a cancer medicine).

If any of the information in this leaflet causes you special concern or if you want additional information about your medicine and its use, check with your doctor, nurse, or pharmacist.

BEFORE RECEIVING THIS MEDICINE

Tell your doctor, nurse, and pharmacist if you . . .

- are allergic to any medicine, either prescription or nonprescription (OTC);
- are pregnant or intend to become pregnant while using this medicine;
- are breast-feeding;
- are using any other prescription or nonprescription (OTC) medicine, especially medicines that lower blood pressure;
- have any other medical problems, especially low blood pressure.

PROPER USE

This medicine may cause severe nausea and vomiting. Your doctor will prescribe medicine before and during your treatment that will lessen these effects.

POSSIBLE SIDE EFFECTS

Side Effects That Should Be Reported To Your Doctor

More common—Nausea or vomiting

Rare—Dizziness; muscle cramps; tingling, burning, or prickly sensations

Side Effects That Usually Do Not Require Medical Attention

These possible side effects may go away during treatment; however, if they continue or are bothersome, check with your doctor, nurse, or pharmacist.

Less common or rare—Chills; feeling of warmth; flushing or redness of skin, especially on face and neck; sleepiness (excessive); skin rash

Other side effects not listed above may also occur in some patients. If you notice any other effects, check with your doctor, nurse, or pharmacist.

***This leaflet has been developed by the USP based primarily on labeling provided by the manufacturer at the time of its approval. This information is intended for use as a temporary educational aid until the drug has been assessed by USP advisory panels. The information does not cover all possible uses, actions, precautions, side effects, or interactions of this medicine. It is not intended as medical advice for individual problems.**

Amifostine (Injection) 915847

USP DI® Patient Education Leaflets™—Introductory Version*

Anastrozole (Oral)

A commonly used brand name is *Arimidex*.

ABOUT YOUR MEDICINE

Anastrozole (an-ASS-troh-zole) belongs to the group of medicines called antineoplastics. It is used to treat breast cancer.

If any of the information in this leaflet causes you special concern or if you want additional information about your medicine and its use, check with your doctor, nurse, or pharmacist. **Remember, keep this and all other medicines out of the reach of children and never share your medicines with others.**

BEFORE USING

Tell your doctor, nurse, and pharmacist if you . . .

- are allergic to any medicine, either prescription or nonprescription (OTC);
- are pregnant or intend to become pregnant while using this medicine;
- are breast-feeding;
- are using any other prescription or nonprescription (OTC) medicine;
- have any other medical problems.

PROPER USE

Take this medicine only as directed by your doctor. Do not use more or less of it, and do not use it more often than your doctor ordered.

Anastrozole sometimes causes nausea, vomiting, and diarrhea. However, it is very important that you continue to use the medicine, even if you begin to feel ill. Ask your doctor, nurse, or pharmacist for ways to lessen these effects.

If you do miss a dose of this medicine, do not take the missed dose at all and do not double the next one. Instead, go back to your regular dosing schedule and check with your doctor.

PRECAUTIONS

It is important that your doctor check your progress at regular visits to make sure this medicine is working properly and to check for unwanted effects.

POSSIBLE SIDE EFFECTS

Side Effects That Should Be Reported To Your Doctor Immediately

More common—Chest pain; shortness of breath

Other Side Effects That Should Be Reported To Your Doctor

Less common—Cough or hoarseness; difficult or painful urination; fever or chills; increased blood pressure; lower back or side pain; pain, tenderness, bluish color, or swelling of foot or leg; sore throat; unusual tiredness or weakness; vaginal bleeding (unexpected and heavy)

Side Effects That Usually Do Not Require Medical Attention

These possible side effects may go away during treatment; however, if they continue or are bothersome, check with your doctor, nurse, or pharmacist.

More common—Bone pain; diarrhea; dizziness; dry mouth; feeling of warmth; flushing or redness of skin, especially on face and neck; headache; hot flashes; nausea or vomiting; skin rash; stomach pain; sweating

Less common—Breast pain; dryness of the vagina; itching of skin; joint pain; loss of hair; muscle pain; numbness or tingling of hands or feet; stuffy nose; weight gain

Other side effects not listed above may also occur in some patients. If you notice any other effects, check with your doctor, nurse, or pharmacist.

***This leaflet has been developed by the USP based primarily on labeling provided by the manufacturer at the time of its approval. This information is intended for use as a temporary educational aid until the drug has been assessed by USP advisory panels. The information does not cover all possible uses, actions, precautions, side effects, or interactions of this medicine. It is not intended as medical advice for individual problems.**

Anastrozole (Oral) 915814

USP DI® Patient Education Leaflets™—Introductory Version*

Baclofen (Injection)

A commonly used brand name is *Lioresal*.

ABOUT YOUR MEDICINE

Baclofen (BAK-loh-fen) is used to help relax certain muscles in your body. It relieves the spasms, cramping, and tightness of muscles caused by medical problems such as multiple sclerosis, cerebral palsy, or certain injuries to the spine. Baclofen does not cure these problems, but it may allow other treatment, such as physical therapy, to be more helpful in improving your condition.

Baclofen is given only by or under the direct supervision of your doctor.

If any of the information in this leaflet causes you special concern or if you want additional information about your medicine and its use, check with your doctor, nurse, or pharmacist. **Remember, keep this and all other medicines out of the reach of children and never share your medicines with others.**

BEFORE USING

Tell your doctor, nurse, and pharmacist if you . . .

- are allergic to any medicine, either prescription or nonprescription (OTC);
- are pregnant or intend to become pregnant while using this medicine;
- are breast-feeding;
- are taking any other prescription or nonprescription (OTC) medicine, especially other CNS depressants;
- have any other medical problems, especially kidney disease, mental illness, or spinal lesions.

PRECAUTIONS

Your doctor should check your progress at regular visits, especially for the first few weeks after you begin using this medicine. During this time, the amount of medicine you are using may have to be changed often to meet your individual needs.

This medicine will add to the effects of alcohol and other CNS depressants (medicines that may make you drowsy or less alert). **Check with your doctor before taking any such depressants while using this medicine.**

This medicine may cause drowsiness, dizziness, vision problems, or clumsiness or unsteadiness in some people. **Make sure you know how you react to this medicine before you drive, use machines, or do other jobs that require you to be alert, well-coordinated, and able to see well.**

This medicine may cause dryness of the mouth. For temporary relief, use sugarless gum or candy, melt bits of ice in your mouth, or use a saliva substitute. However, if dry mouth continues for more than 2 weeks, check with your medical doctor or dentist. Continuing dryness of the mouth may increase the chance of dental disease, including tooth decay, gum disease, and fungus infections.

Dizziness, lightheadedness, or fainting may occur, especially when you get up from a lying or sitting position. Getting up slowly may help lessen this problem.

POSSIBLE SIDE EFFECTS

Side Effects That Should Be Reported To Your Doctor

More common—Blurred or double vision; convulsions (seizures); fainting; fever, chest pain, or cough; hallucinations; muscle weakness; shortness of breath or troubled breathing

Less common or rare—Bloody or dark urine; high blood pressure (hypertension); mental depression or other mood changes; ringing or buzzing in ears

Side Effects That Usually Do Not Require Medical Attention

These possible side effects may go away during treatment; however, if they continue or are bothersome, check with your doctor, nurse, or pharmacist.

More common—Clumsiness or unsteadiness; constipation; diarrhea; difficult urination; dizziness or lightheadedness, especially when getting up from a lying or sitting position; dry mouth; headache; itching of skin; numbness or tingling of hands or feet; sleepiness; slurring of speech or other speech problems; swelling of ankles, feet, or lower legs; trembling or shaking; trouble in sleeping; unusual weakness, especially muscle weakness

Less common—Decrease in sexual ability or interest in sex; frequent urge to urinate

Other side effects not listed above may also occur in some patients. If you notice any other effects, check with your doctor, nurse, or pharmacist.

Some side effects may occur after you have stopped using this medicine. **Check with your doctor immediately** if any of the following side effects occur:

Convulsions (seizures); flushing of face; hallucinations; headache; high blood pressure (hypertension); increased sweating; muscle spasms; slow heartbeat

---

***This leaflet has been developed by the USP based primarily on labeling provided by the manufacturer at the time of its approval. This information is intended for use as a temporary educational aid until the drug has been assessed by USP advisory panels. The information does not cover all possible uses, actions, precautions, side effects, or interactions of this medicine. It is not intended as medical advice for individual problems.**

Baclofen (Injection) 914786

USP DI® Patient Education Leaflets™—Introductory Version*

Betaine (Oral)

A commonly used brand name is *Cystadane*.

ABOUT YOUR MEDICINE

Betaine (BAY-ta-een) is used to treat a lack of or defect in certain enzymes that cause too much homocysteine in the urine.

If any of the information in this leaflet causes you special concern or if you want additional information about your medicine and its use, check with your doctor, nurse, or pharmacist. **Remember, keep this and all other medicines out of the reach of children and never share your medicines with others.**

BEFORE USING

Tell your doctor, nurse, and pharmacist if you . . .

- are allergic to any medicine, either prescription or nonprescription (OTC);
- are pregnant or intend to become pregnant while using this medicine;
- are breast-feeding;
- are taking any other prescription or nonprescription (OTC) medicine;
- have any other medical problems.

PROPER USE

Betaine powder should be mixed with 4 to 6 ounces of water until completely dissolved. Do not use if the powder does not dissolve completely or gives a colored solution.

Take this medicine with meals.

It is important that you follow any special instructions from your doctor, such as taking folic acid, pyridoxine (vitamin B_6), and vitamin B-12 supplements.

Replace cap tightly after use to protect the powder from moisture.

If you miss a dose of this medicine, take it as soon as possible. However, if it is almost time for your next dose, skip the missed dose and go back to your regular dosing schedule. Do not double doses.

PRECAUTIONS

Your doctor should check your progress at regular visits to make sure that this medicine is working properly.

POSSIBLE SIDE EFFECTS

Side Effects That Usually Do Not Require Medical Attention

These possible side effects may go away during treatment; however, if they continue or are bothersome, check with your doctor, nurse, or pharmacist.

Rare—Diarrhea; nausea; stomach upset

Other side effects not listed above may also occur in some patients. If you notice any other effects, check with your doctor, nurse, or pharmacist.

***This leaflet has been developed by the USP based primarily on labeling provided by the manufacturer at the time of its approval. This information is intended for use as a temporary educational aid until the drug has been assessed by USP advisory panels. The information does not cover all possible uses, actions, precautions, side effects, or interactions of this medicine. It is not intended as medical advice for individual problems.**

Betaine (Oral) 912190

USP DI® Patient Education Leaflets™—Introductory Version*

Bicalutamide (Oral)

A commonly used brand name is *Casodex*.

ABOUT YOUR MEDICINE

Bicalutamide (bye-ka-LOO-ta-mide) is used with another medicine to treat cancer of the prostate gland.

If any of the information in this leaflet causes you special concern or if you want additional information about your medicine and its use, check with your doctor, nurse, or pharmacist. **Remember, keep this and all other medicines out of the reach of children and never share your medicines with others.**

BEFORE USING

Discuss with your doctor the possible side effects that may be caused by this medicine. Some of them may be serious and/or long-term.

Tell your doctor, nurse, and pharmacist if you . . .

- are allergic to any medicine, either prescription or nonprescription (OTC);
- intend to have children;
- are taking any other prescription or nonprescription (OTC) medicine;
- have any other medical problems, especially liver disease.

PROPER USE

Take this medicine exactly as directed by your doctor, at the same time each day. Bicalutamide may be taken with food or on an empty stomach.

Bicalutamide is used together with another medicine. **It is very important that the two medicines be used as directed. Follow your doctor's instructions very carefully about when to use these medicines.**

Bicalutamide in combination therapy sometimes causes unwanted effects such as hot flashes or decreased sexual ability. You may also have difficulty in urinating when you first begin to take it. However, it is very important that you continue to take the medicine, even if you have side effects or you begin to feel better. **Do not stop taking this medicine without first checking with your doctor.**

If you vomit shortly after taking a dose of bicalutamide, check with your doctor. You will be told whether to take the dose again or to wait until the next scheduled dose.

If you miss a dose of this medicine, take it as soon as possible. However, if you do not remember until the next day, skip the missed dose and go back to your regular dosing schedule. Do not double doses.

PRECAUTIONS

It is very imporant that your doctor check your progress at regular visits to make sure that this medicine is working properly.

POSSIBLE SIDE EFFECTS

Side Effects That Should Be Reported To Your Doctor

More common—High blood pressure; itching of skin; mental depression; skin rash; swelling of face, fingers, feet, or lower legs; unusual tiredness or weakness

Rare—Yellow eyes or skin

Side Effects That Usually Do Not Require Medical Attention

These possible side effects may go away during treatment; however, if they continue or are bothersome, check with your doctor, nurse, or pharmacist.

More common—Constipation; diarrhea; "hot flashes" (sudden sweating and feelings of warmth); nausea

Less common—Anxiety; bloated feeling or gas; confusion; drowsiness; impotence or decrease in sexual desire; indigestion; loss of appetite; muscle pain or weakness; nervousness; numbness or tingling in hands or feet; swelling and tenderness of breasts; vomiting

Other side effects not listed above may also occur in some patients. If you notice any other effects, check with your doctor, nurse, or pharmacist.

***This leaflet has been developed by the USP based primarily on labeling provided by the manufacturer at the time of its approval. This information is intended for use as a temporary educational aid until the drug has been assessed by USP advisory panels. The information does not cover all possible uses, actions, precautions, side effects, or interactions of this medicine. It is not intended as medical advice for individual problems.**

Bicalutamide (Oral) 911846

USP DI® Patient Education Leaflets™—Introductory Version*

Bismuth Subsalicylate, Metronidazole, and Tetracycline (For *H. pylori*—Oral)

A commonly used brand name is *Helidac Therapy*.

ABOUT YOUR MEDICINE

Bismuth subsalicylate (BIS-muth sub-sa-LIS-a-late), **metronidazole** (me-troe-NI-da-zole), and **tetracycline** (tet-ra-SYE-kleen) are taken together with an H2-blocker to treat ulcers related to infection with the *H. pylori* organism (germ).

If any of the information in this leaflet causes you special concern or if you want additional information about your medicine and its use, check with your doctor, nurse, or pharmacist. **Remember, keep this and all other medicines out of the reach of children and never share your medicines with others.**

BEFORE USING

This medicine should not be used in infants, children under 8 years of age, children or adolescents with symptoms of a virus infection, or pregnant women unless otherwise directed by your doctor.

Tell your doctor, nurse, and pharmacist if you . . .

- are allergic to any medicine, either prescription or nonprescription (OTC);
- **are pregnant or intend to become pregnant while using this medicine;**
- are breast-feeding;
- are taking **any** other prescription or nonprescription (OTC) medicine;
- have any other medical problems, especially liver or kidney problems.

PROPER USE

Take this medicine exactly as directed. This medicine comes with patient information. **Read the instructions carefully. Keep taking this medicine for the full time of treatment,** even if you begin to feel better. If you stop taking it too soon or miss taking even one pill, your symptoms may return.

Each dose of this medicine (4 pills) should be taken 4 times a day, with meals and at bedtime, for 14 days. The 2 bismuth subsalicylate tablets should be chewed and swallowed. The metronidazole tablet and the tetracycline capsule should be taken with a full glass (8 ounces) of water to prevent irritation of the stomach or esophagus. The individual products contained in this package should not be used alone or for other purposes.

Do not take antacids or sodium bicarbonate (baking soda) within 1 to 2 hours of the time you take this medicine. Also, do not take iron or zinc preparations, including vitamins, within 2 to 3 hours of the time you take this medicine.

Do not give this medicine to infants or children under 8 years of age, unless directed by your child's doctor. It may cause permanently discolored teeth and other problems in this age group. **Do not give this medicine to a child or a teenager with symptoms of a virus infection, especially flu or chickenpox, unless otherwise directed by your child's doctor.**

If you miss a dose of this medicine, skip the missed dose and go back to your regular dosing schedule. Do not double doses. If you miss more than 4 doses, check with your doctor.

PRECAUTIONS

Do not drink alcoholic beverages or use other alcohol-containing preparations while taking this medicine and for at least one day after stopping it. To do so may cause unwanted effects.

Oral contraceptives (birth control pills) containing estrogen may not work properly if you take them while you are taking this medicine. Unplanned pregnancies may occur. **You should use a different or additional means of birth control while you are taking this medicine.**

This medicine should not be used by pregnant women because it may cause problems in the fetus or in newborn infants. Also, liver problems may be more likely to occur in the mother. **Check with your doctor as soon as possible if you suspect you are pregnant.**

Check the labels of all prescription and nonprescription (OTC) medicines you now take. Using other salicylate-containing products while taking this medicine may lead to overdose. Check with your doctor or pharmacist.

This medicine may cause some people to become dizzy or lightheaded. **Make sure you know how you react before you drive, use machines, or do anything that could be dangerous if you are dizzy or are not alert.**

This medicine may cause your skin to be more sensitive to sunlight than it is normally. When you begin taking this medicine, avoid too much sun and do not use a sunlamp. If you work or play outdoors, use a full-protection suncreen. **If you have a severe reaction, check with your doctor.**

POSSIBLE SIDE EFFECTS

Side Effects That Should Be Reported To Your Doctor Immediately

Less common—Numbness, tingling, pain, or weakness of hands or feet

Rare—Convulsions (seizures)

Side Effects That Should Be Reported To Your Doctor

More common—Abdominal pain; black or tarry stools; diarrhea; increased sensitivity of skin to sunlight; nausea

Less common—Any vaginal irritation, discharge, or dryness not present before use of this medicine; clumsiness or unsteadiness; dizziness; fever or sore throat; loss of appetite; mood or mental changes; rectal irritation; skin rash, hives, or itching; stomach and back pain (severe); vomiting

Rare—Headache; nervousness; trouble in sleeping; unusual tiredness or weakness; visual changes; yellow skin

Side Effects That Usually Do Not Require Medical Attention

These possible side effects may go away during treatment; however, if they continue or are bothersome, check with your doctor, nurse, or pharmacist.

More common—Constipation; dark tongue or grayish black stools; dark urine; dry mouth; metal taste in mouth

Other side effects not listed above may also occur in some patients. If you notice any other effects, check with your doctor, nurse, or pharmacist.

***This leaflet has been developed by the USP based primarily on labeling provided by the manufacturer at the time of its approval. This information is intended for use as a temporary educational aid until the drug has been assessed by USP advisory panels. The information does not cover all possible uses, actions, precautions, side effects, or interactions of this medicine. It is not intended as medical advice for individual problems.**

USP DI® Patient Education Leaflets™—Introductory Version*

Brimonidine (Ophthalmic)

A commonly used brand name is *Alphagan*.

ABOUT YOUR MEDICINE

Brimonidine (bri-MOE-ni-deen) is used to treat glaucoma. It is also used in patients without glaucoma who have an increase in eye pressure.

If any of the information in this leaflet causes you special concern or if you want additional information about your medicine and its use, check with your doctor, nurse, or pharmacist. **Remember, keep this and all other medicines out of the reach of children and never share your medicines with others.**

BEFORE USING

Tell your doctor, nurse, and pharmacist if you . . .

- are allergic to any medicine, either prescription or nonprescription (OTC);
- are pregnant or intend to become pregnant while using this medicine;
- are breast-feeding;
- are taking any other prescription or nonprescription (OTC) medicine, especially MAO inhibitors;
- have any other medical problems, especially heart or blood vessel disease.

PROPER USE

If your doctor ordered two different eye drops to be used together, wait at least 10 minutes between the times you apply the medicines. This will help to keep the second medicine from "washing out" the first one.

To use the eye drops:

- First, wash your hands. Tilt the head back and, pressing your finger gently on the skin just beneath the lower eyelid, pull the lower eyelid away from the eye to make a space. Drop the medicine into this space. Let go of the eyelid and gently close the eyes. Do not blink. Keep the eyes closed and apply pressure to the inner corner of the eye with your finger for 1 or 2 minutes to allow the medicine to be absorbed by the eye.
- If you think you did not get the drop of medicine into your eye properly, use another drop.
- To keep the medicine as germ-free as possible, do not touch the applicator tip to any surface (including the eye), and keep the container tightly closed.

Use this medicine only as directed. Do not use more of it and do not use it more often than directed. To do so may increase the chance of absorption into the body and the chance of unwanted effects.

If you are using this medicine regularly and you miss a dose, use it as soon as possible. However, if it is almost time for your next dose, skip the missed dose and go back to your regular dosing schedule. Do not double doses.

PRECAUTIONS

It is important that your doctor check your progress at regular visits. This is to make sure the medicine is working properly.

This medicine may cause some people to become dizzy, drowsy, or tired. **Make sure you know how you react to this medicine before you drive, use machines, or do anything else that could be dangerous if you are not alert.**

This medicine may cause your eyes to become more sensitive to light than they are normally. Wearing sunglasses and avoiding too much exposure to bright light may help lessen the discomfort.

POSSIBLE SIDE EFFECTS

Side Effects That Should Be Reported To Your Doctor Immediately

Less common—Fainting

Other Side Effects That Should Be Reported to Your Doctor

More common—Blood in eyes; headache; redness of eyes or inner lining of eyelids; swelling of eye or eyelid; tearing of eyes

Less common—Blurred vision or other change in vision; dizziness; eye pain or ache; feeling of something in the eye; increased blood pressure; mental depression; muscle pain; nausea; runny or stuffy nose; sneezing; vomiting

Side Effects That Usually Do Not Require Medical Attention

These possible side effects may go away during treatment; however, if they continue or are bothersome, check with your doctor, nurse, or pharmacist.

More common—Burning or stinging; drowsiness; dryness of mouth; eye discomfort; tiredness

Less common—Anxiety; change in taste; crusting in corner of eye or on eyelid; discoloration of eyeball; eye dryness; muscle weakness; paleness of eye or inner lining of eyelid; pounding heartbeat; sensitivity of eyes to light; trouble in sleeping

Other side effects not listed above may also occur in some patients. If you notice any other effects, check with your doctor, nurse, or pharmacist.

***This leaflet has been developed by the USP based primarily on labeling provided by the manufacturer at the time of its approval. This information is intended for use as a temporary educational aid until the drug has been assessed by USP advisory panels. The information does not cover all possible uses, actions, precautions, side effects, or interactions of this medicine. It is not intended as medical advice for individual problems.**

Brimonidine (Ophthalmic) 912237

USP DI® Patient Education Leaflets™—Introductory Version*

Cabergoline (Oral)

A commonly used brand name is *Dostinex*.

ABOUT YOUR MEDICINE

Cabergoline (ca-BER-goe-leen) is a medicine used to treat different types of medical problems that occur when too much prolactin hormone is produced. It can be used to treat certain menstrual problems, fertility problems in men and women, and pituitary prolactinomas (tumors of the pituitary gland).

If any of the information in this leaflet causes you special concern or if you want additional information about your medicine and its use, check with your doctor, nurse, or pharmacist. **Remember, keep this and all other medicines out of the reach of children and never share your medicines with others.**

BEFORE USING

Tell your doctor, nurse, and pharmacist if you . . .

- are allergic to any medicine, either prescription or nonprescription (OTC);
- are pregnant or intend to become pregnant while using this medicine;
- are breast-feeding;
- are taking any other prescription or nonprescription (OTC) medicine;
- have any other medical problems, especially high blood pressure (history of or pregnancy-induced) or liver problems.

PROPER USE

If you miss a dose of this medicine, take the missed dose if you remember it within 1 or 2 days. However, if you do not remember until it is almost time for your next dose, check with your doctor to see if you can double your dose.

PRECAUTIONS

It is important that your doctor check your progress at regular visits while you are taking this medicine.

This medicine may cause some people to become drowsy, dizzy, or less alert than they are normally. **Make sure you know how you react to this medicine before you drive, use machines, or do other jobs that require you to be alert.**

Dizziness, lightheadedness, or fainting may occur, especially when you get up from a lying or sitting position. Getting up slowly may help.

Tell your doctor right away if you think you have become pregnant. You and your doctor should discuss whether you should continue to take this medicine during pregnancy.

Check with your doctor right away if you have symptoms of fainting, hallucinations, lightheadedness, stuffy nose, or racing heart.

POSSIBLE SIDE EFFECTS

Side Effects That Should Be Reported To Your Doctor

More common—Abdominal pain; sensation that you are moving in space or that objects are moving around you (vertigo)

Rare—Changes in vision; difficulty in concentrating; dizziness or fainting when getting up suddenly from a lying or sitting position; loss of appetite; swelling of hands, ankles, feet, or lower legs; unusually fast heartbeat; weight gain or loss

Side Effects That Usually Do Not Require Medical Attention

These possible side effects may go away during treatment; however, if they continue or are bothersome, check with your doctor, nurse, or pharmacist.

More common—Constipation; dizziness; nausea or stomach discomfort; weakness

Less common—Burning, itching, or stinging of the skin; diarrhea; dry mouth or toothache; gas; general feeling of discomfort or illness; hot flashes; mental depression; muscle or joint pain; runny nose; sleepiness; sore throat; trouble in sleeping; vomiting

Other side effects not listed above may also occur in some patients. If you notice any other effects, check with your doctor, nurse, or pharmacist.

***This leaflet has been developed by the USP based primarily on labeling provided by the manufacturer at the time of its approval. This information is intended for use as a temporary educational aid until the drug has been assessed by USP advisory panels. The information does not cover all possible uses, actions, precautions, side effects, or interactions of this medicine. It is not intended as medical advice for individual problems.**

USP DI® Patient Education Leaflets™—Introductory Version*

Calcitonin (Nasal)

A commonly used brand name is *Miacalcin*.

ABOUT YOUR MEDICINE

Calcitonin (kal-si-TOE-nin) is used to treat women with postmenopausal osteoporosis (bone loss). It is used together with calcium and vitamin D.

If any of the information in this leaflet causes you special concern or if you want additional information about your medicine and its use, check with your doctor, nurse, or pharmacist. **Remember, keep this and all other medicines out of the reach of children and never share your medicines with others.**

BEFORE USING

Tell your doctor, nurse, and pharmacist if you . . .

- are allergic to any medicine, either prescription or nonprescription (OTC);
- are taking any other prescription or nonprescription (OTC) medicine;
- have any other medical problems.

PROPER USE

This medicine usually comes with patient directions. **Read them carefully before using this medicine.** If you have any questions about using the pump spray, ask your doctor, nurse, or pharmacist.

Use this medicine only as directed by your doctor. Do not use more of it and do not use if more often or for a longer time than directed.

To prepare this medicine:

- If your medicine and its pump were not already assembled by the pharmacist, carefully follow the instructions provided.
- **Before you use a new bottle of calcitonin spray, the spray pump will need to be primed (started).** If your pharmacist assembled the unit for you, check to see if it has already been primed by pumping the unit once. If a full spray comes out, the unit has already been primed; if not, you must prime the pump.
- To prime, hold the bottle upright and away from you, then pump it several times until you see a faint spray.
- **Do not prime the pump again before each daily use.**

To use the nose spray:

- Before using the spray, blow your nose gently.
- Keeping your head in an upright position, carefully place the nozzle into one nostril.
- Press the pump toward the bottle one time. **Do not spray more than once.**
- **Do not inhale.**
- To keep the nosepiece clean, wipe it with a clean tissue and replace the dust cap after use.

If you miss a dose of this medicine, use it as soon as possible. However, if it is almost time for your next dose, skip the missed dose and go back to your regular dosing schedule. Do not double doses.

Once the pump has been used, the bottle may be kept at room temperature until the medicine is gone (2 weeks).

PRECAUTIONS

It is important that your doctor check your progress at regular visits to make sure that this medicine is working and to check for unwanted effects.

POSSIBLE SIDE EFFECTS

Side Effects That Should Be Reported To Your Doctor

More common—Crusting, white patches, or sores inside nose; dryness, itching, redness, swelling, tenderness, or other signs of nasal irritation not present before use of this medicine; nosebleeds; runny nose

Less common—Breathing difficulty or wheezing (severe); bloody or cloudy urine or any problems with urination; chest pain; chills, cough, dizziness; ear congestion or pain; frequent urge to urinate or painful urination; headache (severe or continuing); hoarseness or voice changes; sneezing and other symptoms of head cold; swollen glands; fever, or sore throat

Signs of allergic reaction—*Rare*—Skin rash, hives, or itching

Side Effects That Usually Do Not Require Medical Attention

These possible side effects may go away during treatment; however, if they continue or are bothersome, check with your doctor, nurse, or pharmacist.

More common—Back pain; headache; joint pain

Less common or rare—Abdominal pain; constipation; diarrhea; dry, itching, or burning eyes; flushing; mental depression; muscle pain; nausea; stomach upset; tearing of eyes; unusual tiredness or weakness

Other side effects not listed above may also occur in some patients. If you notice any other effects, check with your doctor, nurse, or pharmacist.

***This leaflet has been developed by the USP based primarily on labeling provided by the manufacturer at the time of its approval. This information is intended for use as a temporary educational aid until the drug has been assessed by USP advisory panels. The information does not cover all possible uses, actions, precautions, side effects, or interactions of this medicine. It is not intended as medical advice for individual problems.**

Calcitonin (Nasal) 914108

USP DI® Patient Education Leaflets™—Introductory Version*

Calcium Acetate (Oral)

A commonly used brand name is *PhosLo*.

ABOUT YOUR MEDICINE

Calcium acetate (KAL-see-um ASS-a-tate) is used to treat hyperphosphatemia (too much phosphate in the blood) in patients with kidney disease.

If any of the information in this leaflet causes you special concern or if you want additional information about your medicine and its use, check with your doctor, nurse, or pharmacist. **Remember, keep this and all other medicines out of the reach of children and never share your medicines with others.**

BEFORE USING

Tell your doctor, nurse, and pharmacist if you . . .

- are allergic to any medicine, either prescription or nonprescription (OTC);
- are pregnant or intend to become pregnant while using this medicine;
- are breast-feeding;
- are taking any other prescription or nonprescription (OTC) medicine, especially digitalis glycosides (heart medicine), other calcium-containing products, or tetracyclines (medicine for infection);
- have any other medical problems, especially hypercalcemia (high blood levels of calcium).

If you have any questions about this, check with your doctor, nurse, or pharmacist.

PROPER USE

Take this medicine with meals. Follow carefully any diet program your doctor may recommend. Also, avoid antacids unless otherwise directed by your doctor.

Take this medicine only as directed by your doctor. Do not take more of it and do not take it more often than directed.

If you miss a dose of this medicine, skip the missed dose and go back to your regular schedule. Do not double doses.

PRECAUTIONS

Your doctor should check your progress at regular visits, especially during the first few months of treatment with this medicine since your dose may have to be adjusted. This is to make sure the medicine is working properly and does not cause unwanted effects.

Do not take other calcium-containing products or eat excessive amounts of calcium-containing foods while you are taking this medicine. Hypercalcemia (too much calcium in the blood) may result if too much calcium is taken.

POSSIBLE SIDE EFFECTS

Side Effects That Should Be Reported To Your Doctor Immediately

Less common—Signs of severe hypercalcemia, such as loss of awareness or sensibility, mental confusion and excitement, or unconsciousness

Other Side Effects That Should Be Reported To Your Doctor

Less common—Signs of mild hypercalcemia, such as constipation, loss of appetite, nausea, or vomiting

Rare—Itching

Other side effects not listed above may also occur in some patients. If you notice any other effects, check with your doctor, nurse, or pharmacist.

***This leaflet has been developed by the USP based primarily on labeling provided by the manufacturer at the time of its approval. This information is intended for use as a temporary educational aid until the drug has been assessed by USP advisory panels. The information does not cover all possible uses, actions, precautions, side effects, or interactions of this medicine. It is not intended as medical advice for individual problems.**

Calcium Acetate (Oral) 914913

USP DI® Patient Education Leaflets™—Introductory Version*

Ceftibuten (Oral)

A commonly used brand name is *Cedax*.

ABOUT YOUR MEDICINE

Ceftibuten (sef-ti-BYOO-ten) is used to treat bacterial infections. However, it will not work for colds, flu, or other viral infections.

If any of the information in this leaflet causes you special concern or if you want additional information about your medicine and its use, check with your doctor, nurse, or pharmacist. **Remember, keep this and all other medicines out of the reach of children and never share your medicines with others.**

BEFORE USING

Discuss with your doctor the possible side effects of this medicine. Some of them may be serious.

Tell your doctor, nurse, and pharmacist if you . . .

- are allergic to any medicine, either prescription or nonprescription (OTC);
- are pregnant or intend to become pregnant while using this medicine;
- are breast-feeding;
- are taking **any** other prescription or nonprescription (OTC) medicine;
- have any other medical problems, especially intestinal disease (such as colitis), kidney disease, or stomach disease.

PROPER USE

To help clear up your infection completely, **keep taking this medicine for the full time of treatment** even if you begin to feel better after a few days.

The oral suspension form of ceftibuten should be taken on an empty stomach (either 2 hours before or 1 hour after a meal).

This medicine works best when there is a constant amount in the blood. **To help keep the amount constant, do not miss any doses.** If you need help in planning the best times to take your medicine, check with your doctor, nurse, or pharmacist.

If you do miss a dose of this medicine, take it as soon as possible. However, if it is almost time for your next dose, skip the missed dose and go back to your regular dosing schedule. **Do not double doses.**

PRECAUTIONS

If your symptoms do not improve within a few days, or if they become worse, check with your doctor.

Diabetics:

- **This medicine may cause false test results with some urine sugar tests.** Check with your doctor before changing your diet or the dosage of your diabetes medicine.
- The oral suspension form of ceftibuten contains sucrose (1 gram per teaspoon).

If diarrhea occurs, do not take any diarrhea medicine without first checking with your doctor or pharmacist. Diarrhea medicines may make your diarrhea worse or last longer.

This medicine must not be given to other people or used for other infections unless you are otherwise directed by your doctor.

POSSIBLE SIDE EFFECTS

Side Effects That Should Be Reported To Your Doctor Immediately

Rare—Blood in urine or stools; difficult or painful urination; difficulty in speaking; fever, chills, or sore throat; mood or mental changes; redness, tenderness, itching, burning, or peeling of skin; skin rash or hives; wheezing or troubled breathing; yellow eyes or skin

Other Side Effects That Should Be Reported To Your Doctor

Less common—Abdominal pain; bloated feeling, gas, or indigestion; constipation; diarrhea or loose stools; headache; nausea or vomiting; sore mouth or tongue; vaginal itching and discharge

Other side effects not listed above may also occur in some patients. If you notice any other effects, check with your doctor, nurse, or pharmacist.

***This leaflet has been developed by the USP based primarily on labeling provided by the manufacturer at the time of its approval. This information is intended for use as a temporary educational aid until the drug has been assessed by USP advisory panels. The information does not cover all possible uses, actions, precautions, side effects, or interactions of this medicine. It is not intended as medical advice for individual problems.**

Ceftibuten (Oral) 915166

USP DI® Patient Education Leaflets™—Introductory Version*

Clonidine (Injection)

A commonly used brand name is *Duraclon*.

ABOUT YOUR MEDICINE

Clonidine (KLOE-ni-deen) injection is used with injected pain medicine to treat pain in cancer patients.

Clonidine is to be started under the immediate supervision of your doctor. After your doctor has seen how you respond to clonidine, you may be able to receive this medicine at home.

If any of the information in this leaflet causes you special concern or if you want additional information about your medicine and its use, check with your doctor, nurse, or pharmacist. **Remember, keep this and all other medicines out of the reach of children and never share your medicines with others.**

BEFORE RECEIVING THIS MEDICINE

Tell your doctor, nurse, and pharmacist if you . . .

- are allergic to any medicine, either prescription or nonprescription (OTC);
- are pregnant or intend to become pregnant while using this medicine;
- are breast-feeding;
- are using any other prescription or nonprescription (OTC) medicine, especially anticoagulants (blood thinners), beta-blockers, calcium channel blockers, or digitalis glycosides (heart medicine);
- have any other medical problems, especially bleeding problems, an infection at the place of injection or catheter (tube), or heart problems.

PROPER USE

Clonidine is given continuously as an epidural infusion (run around the spinal cord) using an infusion pump. The pump and its tube should be checked regularly to make sure the clonidine has not stopped accidentally. The injection or catheter site should also be checked regularly for signs of infection.

If you are using this medicine at home, make sure you understand exactly how to use it.

Tell your doctor immediately if you think the clonidine has stopped for any reason.

PRECAUTIONS

This medicine may add to the effects of alcohol and other CNS depressants (medicines that may make you drowsy or less alert). Check with your doctor before taking any such depressants while you are using this medicine.

Dizziness, lightheadedness, or fainting may occur, especially when you get up from a lying or sitting position. Getting up slowly may help.

This medicine may cause some people to become drowsy or less alert than they are normally. **Make sure you know how you react to this medicine before you drive, use machines, or do other jobs that require you to be alert.**

POSSIBLE SIDE EFFECTS

Side Effects That Should Be Reported To Your Doctor

More common—Dizziness, lightheadedness, or fainting; slow heartbeat

Less common—Chest pain; difficult, slow, or shallow breathing; fast heartbeat; hallucinations; sleepiness (excessive); fever; mental depression; vomiting

Side Effects That Usually Do Not Require Medical Attention

These possible side effects may go away during treatment; however, if they continue or are bothersome, check with your doctor, nurse, or pharmacist.

More common—Anxiety; confusion; dry mouth; nausea; sleepiness

Less common—Constipation; ringing, buzzing, or other unexplained noises in the ears; sweating; weakness

Other side effects not listed above may also occur in some patients. If you notice any other effects, check with your doctor, nurse, or pharmacist.

If clonidine is suddenly stopped, check with your doctor immediately. If you notice any of the following symptoms, report them to your doctor: agitation, headache, nervousness, pounding heartbeat, or shaking and trembling.

***This leaflet has been developed by the USP based primarily on labeling provided by the manufacturer at the time of its approval. This information is intended for use as a temporary educational aid until the drug has been assessed by USP advisory panels. The information does not cover all possible uses, actions, precautions, side effects, or interactions of this medicine. It is not intended as medical advice for individual problems.**

Clonidine (Injection) 915596

USP DI® Patient Education Leaflets™—Introductory Version*

Dexfenfluramine (Oral)

A commonly used brand name is *Redux*.

ABOUT YOUR MEDICINE

Dexfenfluramine (dex-fen-FLURE-a-meen) has been used with a reduced-calorie diet to help cause and maintain weight loss in patients being treated for obesity.

Dexfenfluramine may cause very serious heart valve problems, with no signs of the problem at first. Because of this serious side effect, dexfenfluramine was taken off the market in September 1997. This information is being made available since some patients may still have this medicine at home.

Doctors can do special tests to see if heart valve damage has occurred with this medicine, even in patients with no symptoms. If you have been taking dexfenfluramine, contact your doctor for advice.

Remember, keep this and all other medicines out of the reach of children and never share your medicines with others.

BEFORE USING

Discuss with your doctor the possible side effects of this medicine. Some of them may be serious.

Tell your doctor, nurse, and pharmacist if you . . .

- are allergic to any medicine, either prescription or nonprescription (OTC);
- are pregnant or intend to become pregnant while using this medicine;
- are breast-feeding;
- are taking any other prescription or nonprescription (OTC) medicine, especially fluoxetine, fluvoxamine, MAO inhibitors, nefazodone, paroxetine, sertraline, or venlafaxine;
- have any other medical problems, especially eating disorders or lung problems.

PROPER USE

Take this medicine only as directed by your doctor. Do not take more of it, do not take it more often, and do not take it for a longer time than your doctor ordered.

Follow a reduced-calorie diet while taking dexfenfluramine. Also, take this medicine with meals.

If you miss a dose of this medicine, take it as soon as possible. However, if it is almost time for your next dose, skip the missed dose and go back to your regular dosing schedule. Do not double doses.

PRECAUTIONS

Tell your doctor right away if exercise becomes more difficult for you. This may be a sign of a very serious unwanted effect called primary pulmonary hypertension or of a very serious unwanted effect on your heart valves.

This medicine may cause false-positive results in some urine tests for amphetamine use. If you have a urine test for drug use, tell the tester that you are taking this medicine.

This medicine may add to the effects of alcohol and other CNS depressants (medicines that make you drowsy or less alert). **Check with your doctor before taking any such depressants while you are using this medicine.**

This medicine may cause some people to become dizzy or drowsy or to have changes in vision. **Make sure you know how you react to this medicine before you drive, use machines, or do other jobs that require you to be alert or able to see well.**

POSSIBLE SIDE EFFECTS

Side Effects That Should Be Reported To Your Doctor Immediately

Rare—Awareness of heartbeat; fast or irregular heartbeat; swelling of face or neck

Rare—Signs of primary pulmonary hypertension or severe heart valve damage—Chest pain; decreased ability to exercise; fainting; swelling of feet or lower legs; trouble in breathing

Other Side Effects That Should Be Reported To Your Doctor

Less common—Changes in vision; mental depression; nausea and vomiting; painful menstrual periods

Side Effects That Usually Do Not Require Medical Attention

These possible side effects may go away during treatment; however, if they continue or are bothersome, check with your doctor, nurse, or pharmacist.

More common—Diarrhea; drowsiness; dry mouth; unusual weakness

Less common—Abdominal pain; anxiety or nervousness; chills; dizziness; feeling of constant movement of self or surroundings; headache; increased thirst; increased urination; trouble in sleeping

Other side effects not listed above may also occur in some patients. If you notice any other effects, check with your doctor, nurse, or pharmacist.

After you stop using this medicine your body may need time to adjust. Check with your doctor if you notice abdominal pain, diarrhea, dizziness, high blood pressure, mood or mental changes, nausea, trouble in sleeping, or vomiting.

***This leaflet has been developed by the USP based primarily on labeling provided by the manufacturer at the time of its approval. This information is intended for use as a temporary educational aid until the drug has been assessed by USP advisory panels. The information does not cover all possible uses, actions, precautions, side effects, or interactions of this medicine. It is not intended as medical advice for individual problems.**

Dexfenfluramine (Oral) 910923

USP DI® Patient Education Leaflets™—Introductory Version*

Donepezil (Oral)

A commonly used brand name is *Aricept*.

ABOUT YOUR MEDICINE

Donepezil (doe-NEP-pe-zil) is used to treat the symptoms of mild to moderate Alzheimer's disease. Donepezil will not cure Alzheimer's disease, and it will not stop the disease from getting worse. However, it can improve thinking ability in some patients.

If any of the information in this leaflet causes you special concern or if you want additional information about your medicine and its use, check with your doctor, nurse, or pharmacist. **Remember, keep this and all other medicines out of the reach of children and never share your medicines with others.**

BEFORE USING

Tell your doctor, nurse, and pharmacist if you . . .

- are allergic to any medicine, either prescription or nonprescription (OTC);
- are pregnant or intend to become pregnant while using this medicine;
- are breast-feeding;
- are taking any other prescription or nonprescription (OTC) medicine, especially carbamazepine, dexamethasone, ketoconazole, phenobarbital, phenytoin, quinidine, or rifampin;
- have any other medical problems, especially asthma or obstructive lung disease, difficult urination, heart problems, liver disease, seizures, stomach ulcers, or urinary tract blockage.

PROPER USE

Take this medicine exactly as directed by your doctor. Do not take more of it and do not take it more often than your doctor ordered. Taking more of the medicine will not protect you better and may result in a greater chance of side effects.

It is important that your doctor check your progress at regular visits, to allow for changes in your dose and to help reduce any side effects.

This medicine works best if it is taken at bedtime. Donepezil may be taken with or without food.

If you miss a dose of this medicine, skip the missed dose and go back to your regular dosing schedule. Do not double doses.

PRECAUTIONS

It is very important that your doctor check your progess at regular visits. If your symptoms get worse, check with your doctor.

Before having any kind of surgery or dental or emergency treatment, tell the medical doctor or dentist in charge that you are using this medicine.

Donepezil may cause some people to become dizzy or unsteady. **Make sure you know how you react to this medicine before you do anything that could be dangerous if you are dizzy or unsteady.**

If you think that you or anyone else may have taken an overdose of this medicine, get emergency help at once. Taking an overdose of donepezil may lead to seizures, severe nausea, slow heartbeat, irregular breathing, vomiting, increased muscular weakness, greatly increased sweating, and greatly increased watering of the mouth.

POSSIBLE SIDE EFFECTS

Side Effects That Should Be Reported To Your Doctor

More common—Diarrhea; dizziness; fatigue; headache; nausea; pain; trouble in sleeping; vomiting

Less common—Abnormal dreams; loss of appetite; mental depression; muscle cramps; unusual bleeding or bruising

Rare—Drowsiness; fainting; frequent urination; joint pain, stiffness, or swelling

Signs of overdose—Convulsions (seizures); greatly increased sweating; greatly increased watering of mouth; increasing muscle weakness; low blood pressure; nausea (severe); shock (fast weak pulse, irregular breathing, large pupils); slow heartbeat; vomiting (severe)

Other side effects not listed above may also occur in some patients. If you notice any other effects, check with your doctor, nurse, or pharmacist.

***This leaflet has been developed by the USP based primarily on labeling provided by the manufacturer at the time of its approval. This information is intended for use as a temporary educational aid until the drug has been assessed by USP advisory panels. The information does not cover all possible uses, actions, precautions, side effects, or interactions of this medicine. It is not intended as medical advice for individual problems.**

USP DI® Patient Education Leaflets™—Introductory Version*

Fexofenadine (Oral)

A commonly used brand name is *Allegra.*

ABOUT YOUR MEDICINE

Fexofenadine (fex-oh-FEN-a-deen) is used to relieve or prevent the symptoms of hay fever.

If any of the information in this leaflet causes you special concern or if you want additional information about your medicine and its use, check with your doctor, nurse, or pharmacist. **Remember, keep this and all other medicines out of the reach of children and never share your medicines with others.**

BEFORE USING

Tell your doctor, nurse, and pharmacist if you . . .

- are allergic to any medicine, either prescription or nonprescription (OTC);
- are pregnant or intend to become pregnant;
- are breast-feeding;
- are taking any other prescription or nonprescription (OTC) medicine;
- have any other medical problems, especially kidney disease.

PROPER USE

Fexofenadine is used to relieve or prevent the symptoms of your medical problem. Take it only as directed. Do not take more of it and do not take it more often than your doctor ordered. To do so may increase the chance of side effects.

If you must take this medicine regularly and you miss a dose, take it as soon as possible. However, if it is almost time for your next dose, skip the missed dose and go back to your regular dosing schedule. Do not double doses.

POSSIBLE SIDE EFFECTS

Side Effects That Usually Do Not Require Medical Attention

These possible side effects may go away during treatment; however, if they continue or are bothersome, check with your doctor, nurse, or pharmacist.

Less common or rare—Drowsiness; painful menstrual periods; stomach upset; symptoms of cold or flu; unusual tiredness

Other side effects not listed above may also occur in some patients. If you notice any other effects, check with your doctor, nurse, or pharmacist.

***This leaflet has been developed by the USP based primarily on labeling provided by the manufacturer at the time of its approval. This information is intended for use as a temporary educational aid until the drug has been assessed by USP advisory panels. The information does not cover all possible uses, actions, precautions, side effects, or interactions of this medicine. It is not intended as medical advice for individual problems.**

Fexofenadine (Oral) 911970

USP DI® Patient Education Leaflets™—Introductory Version*

Fluticasone (Inhalation)

A commonly used brand name is *Flovent*.

ABOUT YOUR MEDICINE

Fluticasone (floo-TIK-a-sone) is used regularly to help prevent the symptoms of asthma. It will not relieve an attack that has already started. Fluticasone is a cortisone-like medicine.

If any of the information in this leaflet causes you special concern or if you want additional information about your medicine and its use, check with your doctor, nurse, or pharmacist. **Remember, keep this and all other medicines out of the reach of children and never share your medicines with others.**

BEFORE USING

Discuss with your doctor the possible side effects that may be caused by this medicine. Some of them may be serious or long-term.

Tell your doctor, nurse, and pharmacist if you . . .

- are allergic to any medicine, either prescription or nonprescription (OTC);
- are pregnant or intend to become pregnant while using this medicine;
- are breast-feeding;
- are taking any other prescription or nonprescription (OTC) medicine;
- have any other medical problems, especially herpes simplex infection of the eye, tuberculosis of the lungs, or any untreated infection caused by bacteria or by a fungus, parasite, or virus.

PROPER USE

This medicine comes with patient directions. **Read them carefully before using this medicine.**

This medicine will not relieve an asthma attack that has already started. However, your doctor may want you to continue using this medicine at the usual time, even if you use another medicine to relieve an asthma attack.

Use this medicine only as directed. Do not use more of it and do not use it more often than your doctor ordered. To do so may increase the chance of side effects.

In order for this medicine to help you, it must be used every day in regularly spaced doses as ordered by your doctor. Do not stop treatment even if you are feeling better unless told to do so by your doctor.

Gargling and rinsing your mouth with water after each dose may help prevent yeast infection in your mouth or throat. However, do not swallow the water after rinsing.

If you miss a dose of this medicine, use it as soon as possible. However, if it is almost time for your next dose, skip the missed dose and go back to your regular dosing schedule. Do not double doses.

PRECAUTIONS

Check with your doctor if you go through a period of unusual stress or have an asthma attack that does not improve with a bronchodilator.

Your doctor may want you to carry a medical identification card stating that you are using this medicine.

Tell the doctor in charge that you are using this medicine before having any kind of surgery (including dental surgery) or emergency treatment.

Avoid exposure to chicken pox or measles. If exposed, contact your doctor immediately.

POSSIBLE SIDE EFFECTS

Side Effects That Should Be Reported To Your Doctor Immediately

Rare—Hives; shortness of breath; skin rash; swelling of face, lips, or eyelids; tightness in chest; troubled breathing; wheezing

Side Effects That Usually Do Not Require Medical Attention

More common—Creamy white, curd-like patches in mouth or throat; general feeling of illness or weakness; headache; hoarseness or other voice changes; muscle soreness; nausea; pain in nasal passages; runny or stuffy nose; trouble in sleeping

Other side effects not listed above may also occur in some patients. If you notice any other effects, check with your doctor, nurse, or pharmacist.

***This leaflet has been developed by the USP based primarily on labeling provided by the manufacturer at the time of its approval. This information is intended for use as a temporary educational aid until the drug has been assessed by USP advisory panels. The information does not cover all possible uses, actions, precautions, side effects, or interactions of this medicine. It is not intended as medical advice for individual problems.**

Fluticasone (Inhalation) 910934

USP DI® Patient Education Leaflets™—Introductory Version*

Fluticasone (Nasal)

A commonly used brand name is *Flonase*.

ABOUT YOUR MEDICINE

Fluticasone (floo-TIK-a-sone) is a nasal corticosteroid (kor-ti-koh-STER-oid) (cortisone-like medicine). It belongs to the family of medicines called steroids. It is sprayed into the nose to help relieve the stuffy nose, irritation, and discomfort of hay fever and other nasal allergies.

If any of the information in this leaflet causes you special concern or if you want additional information about your medicine and its use, check with your doctor, nurse, or pharmacist. **Remember, keep this and all other medicines out of the reach of children and never share your medicines with others.**

BEFORE USING

Children using this medicine should have their progress checked by their doctor at regular visits. Also, if used in high doses or too often, this medicine may get into the bloodstream through the lining of the nose and may affect growth. It is important to follow your doctor's directions carefully.

Tell your doctor, nurse, and pharmacist if you . . .

- are allergic to any medicine, either prescription or nonprescription (OTC);
- are pregnant or intend to become pregnant while using this medicine;
- are breast-feeding;
- are taking any other prescription or nonprescription (OTC) medicine;
- have any other medical problems.

PROPER USE

Before using this medicine, clear the nasal passages by blowing your nose. Then, with the nosepiece inserted into the nostril, aim the spray toward the inner corner of the eye.

In order for this medicine to help you, it must be used regularly as ordered by your doctor. This medicine usually begins to work in about 1 week, but up to 3 weeks may pass before you feel its full effects.

Use this medicine only as directed. Do not use more of it and do not use it more often than your doctor ordered. To do so may increase the chance of unwanted effects.

Check with your doctor before using this medicine for nasal problems other than the one for which it was prescribed, since it should not be used on many types of nasal infections.

If you miss a dose of this medicine and remember within an hour or so, use it right away. However, if you do not remember until later, skip the missed dose and go back to your regular dosing schedule. Do not double doses.

PRECAUTIONS

If you will be using this medicine for more than a few weeks, your doctor should check your progress at regular visits.

Check with your doctor:

—if signs of a nose, sinus, or throat infection occur.

—if your symptoms do not improve within 3 weeks.

—if your condition gets worse.

POSSIBLE SIDE EFFECTS

Side Effects That Should Be Reported To Your Doctor

More common—Bloody mucus or unexplained nosebleeds; headache; sore throat

Less common—Cough; dizziness; hives; nausea or vomiting; runny or stuffy nose; sores inside nose

Rare—Eye pain or gradual loss of vision; shortness of breath, troubled breathing, or wheezing; skin rash; swelling of eyelids, face, or lips; white patches inside nose or throat

Side Effects That Usually Do Not Require Medical Attention

These possible side effects may go away during treatment; however, if they continue or are bothersome, check with your doctor, nurse, or pharmacist.

More common—Burning, dryness, or other irritation inside the nose

Less common—Bad taste in mouth; dryness of mouth; sneezing

Other side effects not listed above may also occur in some patients. If you notice any other effects, check with your doctor, nurse, or pharmacist.

***This leaflet has been developed by the USP based primarily on labeling provided by the manufacturer at the time of its approval. This information is intended for use as a temporary educational aid until the drug has been assessed by USP advisory panels. The information does not cover all possible uses, actions, precautions, side effects, or interactions of this medicine. It is not intended as medical advice for individual problems.**

Fluticasone (Nasal) 910821

USP DI® Patient Education Leaflets™—Introductory Version*

Fluvoxamine (Oral)

A commonly used brand name is *Luvox*.

ABOUT YOUR MEDICINE

Fluvoxamine (floo-VOX-uh-meen) is used to treat obsessive-compulsive disorder (OCD).

If any of the information in this leaflet causes you special concern or if you want additional information about your medicine and its use, check with your doctor, nurse, or pharmacist. **Remember, keep this and all other medicines out of the reach of children and never share your medicines with others.**

BEFORE USING

Tell your doctor, nurse, and pharmacist if you . . .

- are allergic to any medicine, either prescription or nonprescription (OTC);
- are pregnant or intend to become pregnant while using this medicine;
- are breast-feeding;
- are taking any other prescription or nonprescription (OTC) medicine, especially alprazolam, astemizole, carbamazepine, clozapine, diazepam, diltiazem, lithium, MAO inhibitors, methadone, metoprolol, midazolam, propranolol, terfenadine, theophylline, triazolam, tricyclic antidepressants, tryptophan, or warfarin;
- have any other medical problems, especially liver problems, or a recent heart attack or unstable heart disease;
- smoke cigarettes.

PROPER USE

Take this medicine only as directed by your doctor, to benefit your condition as much as possible. Do not take more of it, do not take it more often, and do not take it for a longer time than your doctor ordered.

If you miss a dose of this medicine and you are taking:

- One dose a day—Skip the missed dose and go back to your regular dosing schedule.
- Two doses a day—Take the missed dose as soon as possible. However, if it is almost time for your next dose, skip the missed dose and go back to your regular dosing schedule. Do not double doses.

PRECAUTIONS

It is important that your doctor check your progress at regular visits, to allow for changes in your dose and to help reduce any side effects.

This medicine may add to the effects of alcohol and other CNS depressants (medicines that make you drowsy). **Check with your doctor before taking any such depressants while you are using this medicine.**

This medicine may cause some people to become dizzy or drowsy, or to have blurred vision. **Make sure you know how you react to this medicine before you drive, use machines, or do other jobs that require you to be alert.**

This medicine may cause dryness of the mouth. For temporary relief, use sugarless gum or candy, melt bits of ice in your mouth, or use a saliva substitute. However, if your mouth feels dry for more than 2 weeks, check with your medical doctor or dentist. Continuing dryness of the mouth may increase the chance of dental disease, including tooth decay, gum disease, and fungus infections.

POSSIBLE SIDE EFFECTS

Side Effects That Should Be Reported To Your Doctor Immediately

Rare—Convulsions (seizures)

Other Side Effects That Should Be Reported To Your Doctor

More common—Diarrhea; dizziness; nervousness; twitching or jerking movements; unusual tiredness or weakness

Less common or rare—Agitation; behavior, mood, or mental changes; blurred vision; decreased sexual drive or ability; fast or pounding heartbeat; problems in urination; skin rash or hives; talking, feeling, and acting with excitement and activity that you cannot control; tremor; troubled breathing; vomiting

Side Effects That Usually Do Not Require Medical Attention

These possible side effects may go away during treatment; however, if they continue or are bothersome, check with your doctor, nurse, or pharmacist.

More common—Constipation; drowsiness; dry mouth; headache; nausea; runny nose; trouble in sleeping

Less common—Anxiety; change in sense of taste; chills; feeling flushed, warm, or hot; increased sweating; increased thirst; leg cramps; loss of appetite; muscle pain; sore throat; stomach pain or gas; trouble in swallowing; weight loss; yawning

Other side effects not listed above may also occur in some patients. If you notice any other effects, check with your doctor, nurse, or pharmacist.

***This leaflet has been developed by the USP based primarily on labeling provided by the manufacturer at the time of its approval. This information is intended for use as a temporary educational aid until the drug has been assessed by USP advisory panels. The information does not cover all possible uses, actions, precautions, side effects, or interactions of this medicine. It is not intended as medical advice for individual problems.**

Fluvoxamine (Oral) 910639

USP DI® Patient Education Leaflets™—Introductory Version*

Glatiramer Acetate (Injection)

A commonly used brand name is *Copaxone*.

ABOUT YOUR MEDICINE

Glatiramer acetate (gla-TEER-a-meer ASS-a-tate) is used in the treatment of multiple sclerosis (MS). It will not cure MS, but it may reduce the frequency of relapses in patients with the relapsing-remitting form of MS.

If any of the information in this leaflet causes you special concern or if you want additional information about your medicine and its use, check with your doctor, nurse, or pharmacist. **Remember, keep this and all other medicines out of the reach of children and never share your medicines with others.**

BEFORE USING

Tell your doctor, nurse, and pharmacist if you . . .

- are allergic to any medicine, either prescription or nonprescription (OTC);
- are pregnant or intend to become pregnant while using this medicine;
- are breast-feeding;
- are taking any other prescription or nonprescription (OTC) medicine;
- have any other medical problems.

PROPER USE

This medicine comes with patient directions. It is very important that you read and understand this information. Also, your doctor or nurse will teach you how to prepare the injection and how to inject yourself. **Be certain that you understand these directions, and follow them carefully.**

Glatiramer acetate comes in brown vials and **must be stored in the freezer.** The sterile water used to prepare this medicine for injection comes in clear vials and may be stored at room temperature.

Needles, syringes, and vials should be used for only one injection. Put all used needles, syringes, and vials in a covered container that the needles cannot punch through, such as an empty liquid laundry detergent container. **Keep the container tightly closed and out of the reach of children.** When the container is full, throw it away as directed by your doctor and the laws of your state.

If you miss a dose of this medicine, use it as soon as possible. However, if you do not remember until the next day, skip the missed dose and go back to your regular dosing schedule. Do not double doses.

PRECAUTIONS

If you will be taking this medicine regularly for a long time, your doctor should check your progress at regular visits.

Do not change your dose or dosing schedule without first checking with your doctor. Do not stop using this medicine without first checking with your doctor.

Before you have a Papanicolaou (Pap) smear (or test), tell the doctor or nurse in charge that you are using this medicine. The results of the test may be affected by this medicine.

POSSIBLE SIDE EFFECTS

Side Effects That Should Be Reported To Your Doctor Immediately

Get emergency help immediately if these symptoms become severe.

More common—Chest pain; difficulty in breathing; dizziness; flushing; hives; pain at place of injection (severe); pounding heartbeat; sweating; uncomfortable changes in your general health

Less common—Continuous, uncontrolled back-and-forth or rolling eye movements; eye pain or tenderness or any change in vision; throat spasms

Other Side Effects That Should Be Reported To Your Doctor

These possible side effects may go away during treatment; however, if they continue or are bothersome, check with your doctor, nurse, or pharmacist.

More common—Anxiety or nervousness; confusion or unusual excitement; coughing or other bronchial irritation; migraine headaches; mood or mental changes; muscle pain; nausea; neck pain; racing heartbeat; skin rash or itching; swelling of face, hands, feet, or lower legs; swelling of lymph glands; vaginal discharge (thick, white, or curd-like); vomiting

Less common—Abdominal or stomach discomfort; any sign of infection, such as fever, chills, or sore throat; back pain; diarrhea; ear pain; frequent urge to urinate; loss of appetite; menstrual changes; pain; purple or red spots on skin; speech problems

Rare—Blood in urine; fast breathing; high blood pressure; impotence or decreased interest in sex; sores, ulcers, or white spots in mouth or throat

Side Effects That Usually Do Not Require Medical Attention

These possible side effects may go away during treatment; however, if they continue or are bothersome, check with your doctor, nurse, or pharmacist.

More common—Hard lump, redness, swelling, pain, itching, purple spot, tenderness, or warmth at place of injection; runny nose; tremor; unusual tiredness or weakness; weight gain

Other side effects not listed above may occur in some patients. If you notice any other effects, check with your doctor, nurse, or pharmacist.

***This leaflet has been developed by the USP based primarily on labeling provided by the manufacturer at the time of its approval. This information is intended for use as a temporary educational aid until the drug has been assessed by USP advisory panels. The information does not cover all possible uses, actions, precautions, side effects, or interactions of this medicine. It is not intended as medical advice for individual problems.**

Glatiramer Acetate (Injection) 914345

USP DI® Patient Education Leaflets™—Introductory Version*

Glimepiride (Oral)

A commonly used brand name is *Amaryl*.

ABOUT YOUR MEDICINE

Glimepiride (glye-MEP-i-ride) is an oral antidiabetic (diabetes medicine you take by mouth). It is used to treat a certain type of diabetes mellitus (sugar diabetes) called non-insulin-dependent diabetes mellitus (NIDDM) or Type II diabetes.

Glimepiride is also used in combination with insulin to treat NIDDM in people whose diabetes cannot be controlled with diet and exercise and an oral antidiabetic.

If any of the information in this leaflet causes you special concern or if you want additional information about your medicine and its use, check with your doctor, nurse, or pharmacist. **Remember, keep this and all other medicines out of the reach of children and never share your medicines with others.**

BEFORE USING

Tell your doctor, nurse, and pharmacist if you . . .

- are allergic to any medicine, either prescription or nonprescription (OTC);
- are pregnant or intend to become pregnant while using this medicine;
- are breast feeding;
- are taking any other prescription or nonprescription (OTC) medicine, especially beta-blockers;
- have any other medical problems, especially diabetic ketoacidosis (ketones in the blood) or kidney disease.

PROPER USE

This medicine should be taken with breakfast or the first morning meal.

Take this medicine only as directed. Do not take more or less of it than your doctor ordered, and take it at the same time every day.

Follow carefully the special meal plan your doctor gave you and exercise regularly. Also, test for sugar in your blood or urine as directed.

PRECAUTIONS

Your doctor will want to check your progress at regular visits, especially during the first few weeks that you take this medicine.

Eat or drink something containing sugar and check with your doctor right away if mild symptoms of low blood sugar (hypoglycemia) appear. Good sources of sugar are glucose tablets or gel, fruit juice, corn syrup, honey, regular (non-diet) soft drinks, or sugar dissolved in water. It is a good idea to check your blood sugar to confirm that it is low.

Someone should call for emergency help immediately if severe symptoms such as convulsions (seizures) or unconsciousness occur. Under these conditions diabetics should not eat or drink anything. There is a chance that they could choke from not swallowing correctly.

Symptoms of low blood sugar include abdominal or stomach pain (mild); anxious feeling; chills (continuing); cold sweats; confusion; convulsions (seizures); cool pale skin; difficulty in thinking; drowsiness; excessive hunger; fast heartbeat; headache (continuing); nausea or vomiting (continuing); nervousness; shakiness; unconsciousness; unsteady walk; unusual tiredness or weakness; or vision changes. **These symptoms may occur if you** delay or miss a meal or snack, exercise much more than usual, cannot eat because of nausea and vomiting, or drink a significant amount of alcohol. **Tell someone to take you to your doctor or to a hospital right away if the symptoms do not improve after drinking or eating a sweet food.**

POSSIBLE SIDE EFFECTS

Side Effects That Should Be Reported To Your Doctor Immediately

Less common—Convulsions (seizures), unconsciousness

Other Side Effects That Should Be Reported To Your Doctor

Less common—Low blood sugar, including anxious feeling, behavior change similar to being drunk, blurred vision, cold sweats, confusion, cool pale skin, difficulty in concentrating, drowsiness, excessive hunger, fast heartbeat, headache, nausea, nervousness, nightmares, restless sleep, shakiness, slurred speech, unusual tiredness or weakness

Rare—Blurred vision or difficulty in focusing eyes; depression; dizziness; headache; skin redness, itching, or rash; swelling or puffiness of face, ankles, or hands

Side Effects That Usually Do Not Require Medical Attention

These possible side effects may go away during treatment; however, if they continue or are bothersome, check with your doctor, nurse, or pharmacist.

Less common or rare—Abdominal or stomach pain; diarrhea; vomiting

Other side effects not listed above may also occur in some patients. If you notice any other effects, check with your doctor, nurse, or pharmacist.

***This leaflet has been developed by the USP based primarily on labeling provided by the manufacturer at the time of its approval. This information is intended for use as a temporary educational aid until the drug has been assessed by USP advisory panels. The information does not cover all possible uses, actions, precautions, side effects, or interactions of this medicine. It is not intended as medical advice for individual problems.**

Glimepiride (Oral) 911890

USP DI® Patient Education Leaflets™—Introductory Version*

Histrelin (Injection)

A commonly used brand name is *Supprelin*.

ABOUT YOUR MEDICINE

Histrelin (HISS-tra-lyn) is used to treat unusually early sexual development in children.

If any of the information in this leaflet causes you special concern or if you want additional information about your medicine and its use, check with your doctor, nurse, or pharmacist. **Remember, keep this and all other medicines out of the reach of children and never share your medicines with others.**

BEFORE USING

Discuss with your doctor the possible side effects that may be caused by this medicine. Some of them may be serious and/or long-term.

Tell your doctor, nurse, and pharmacist if you . . .

- are allergic to any medicine, either prescription or nonprescription (OTC);
- are pregnant or intend to become pregnant while using this medicine;
- are breast-feeding;
- are taking any other prescription or nonprescription (OTC) medicine;
- have any other medical problems.

PROPER USE

Histrelin comes with patient directions. Read these instructions carefully.

Use this medicine only as directed by your doctor. Do not use more or less of it, and do not use it more often than your doctor ordered. The exact amount of medicine you need has been carefully worked out. Using too much may increase the chance of side effects, while using too little may not improve your condition.

Use a new vial each day with each injection. Do not save any solution that is left in the vial. Throw it away.

Before using this medicine, make sure you understand:

- How to prepare the injection.
- Proper use of disposable syringes.
- How to give the injection.
- How long the injection is stable.
- How to rotate the injections by using a different area of the body each day.

If you have any questions about any of this, check with your doctor, nurse, or pharmacist.

It is important that this medicine is injected at the same time every day. Skipping doses may lead to the return of early sexual development. This may result in growth problems later on if growth occurs too quickly and too early.

Do not stop using this medicine without first checking with your doctor.

If you miss a dose of this medicine, use it as soon as possible. However, if it is almost time for your next dose, skip the missed dose and go back to your regular dosing schedule.

PRECAUTIONS

It is very important that your doctor check your progress at regular visits, especially while you are using the medicine. Your doctor will need to continue to check your progress after you stop using the medicine. This is because sexual development may slow down or stop after treatment with histrelin has ended.

POSSIBLE SIDE EFFECTS

Side Effects That Should Be Reported To Your Doctor Immediately

Less common—Convulsions; fainting; eye problems; unusual mood or behavior changes

Rare—Fast heartbeat; skin rash, itching or swelling (other than at place of injection); trouble in swallowing or breathing

Other Side Effects That Should Be Reported To Your Doctor

More common—Breast soreness; chest or ear congestion; chills; cough; diarrhea; dizziness or lightheadedness; frequent urination; headache; joint pain; loss of bladder control; loss of hearing; muscle soreness; nausea; redness, swelling, or itching at place of injection (severe or continuing); runny nose; vaginal bleeding, dryness, or discharge; vomiting

Less common—Constipation; increased thirst; unusual tiredness or weakness

Side Effects That Usually Do Not Require Medical Attention

These possible side effects may go away during treatment; however, if they continue or are bothersome, check with your doctor, nurse, or pharmacist.

More common—Irritation, redness, or swelling at place of injection (mild); loss of appetite

Other side effects not listed above may also occur in some patients. If you notice any other effects, check with your doctor, nurse, or pharmacist.

***This leaflet has been developed by the USP based primarily on labeling provided by the manufacturer at the time of its approval. This information is intended for use as a temporary educational aid until the drug has been assessed by USP advisory panels. The information does not cover all possible uses, actions, precautions, side effects, or interactions of this medicine. It is not intended as medical advice for individual problems.**

USP DI® Patient Education Leaflets™—Introductory Version*

Imiquimod (Topical)

A commonly used brand name is *Aldara*.

ABOUT YOUR MEDICINE

Imiquimod (i-MIK-wi-mod) is used to treat external warts around the genital and rectal areas. It is not used on warts inside the vagina, penis, or rectum.

If any of the information in this leaflet causes you special concern or if you want additional information about your medicine and its use, check with your doctor, nurse, or pharmacist. **Remember, keep this and all other medicines out of the reach of children and never share your medicines with others.**

BEFORE USING

Tell your doctor, nurse, or pharmacist if you . . .

- are allergic to any medicine, either prescription or nonprescription (OTC);
- are pregnant or intend to become pregnant while using this medicine;
- are breast-feeding;
- are taking any other prescription or nonprescription (OTC) medicine, especially topical medicines;
- have any other medical problems, especially sores in the genital area, or have had recent surgery on or near the wart area.

PROPER USE

Wash your hands before and after using this medicine. Avoid getting this medicine in your eyes.

Use this medicine only as directed by your doctor. Do not use more of it, do not use it more often, and do not use it for a longer time than directed. Throw out any unused cream from the single-dose packet.

Do not bandage, wrap, or apply any occulsive dressing over this medicine, unless otherwise directed by your doctor. To do so may irritate the skin. If you must cover the area, use only cotton gauze dressings and wear cotton underclothes.

If you miss a dose of this medicine, apply it as soon as possible. Then go back to your regular dosing schedule.

PRECAUTIONS

If you notice severe skin irritation, check with your doctor. It may be necessary for you to reduce the number of times a day that you use the medicine or to stop using the medicine for a short time until your skin is less irritated.

Avoid having genital, oral, or anal sex while the cream is on your skin. Make sure you wash the cream off your skin before you engage in **any** sexual activity. Also, this medicine contains oils that can weaken latex (rubber) condoms, diaphragms, or cervical caps causing them not to work properly to prevent pregnancy.

Do not use any other skin product on the same skin area on which you use this medicine, unless directed by your doctor.

POSSIBLE SIDE EFFECTS

Side Effects That Should Be Reported To Your Doctor

More common—Blisters on skin; itching in genital or other skin areas; open sores or scabs on skin; redness of skin (severe); scaling

Signs of too much medicine being absorbed into the body—Flu-like symptoms, including diarrhea, fatigue, fever, headache, muscle pain

Side Effects That Usually Do Not Require Medical Attention

These possible side effects may go away during treatment; however, if they continue or are bothersome, check with your doctor, nurse, or pharmacist.

More common—Burning or stinging of skin (mild); flaking of skin; rash; redness of skin (mild); soreness or tenderness of skin (mild); swelling at place of application

Less common—Lightening of the treated skin

Other side effects not listed above may also occur in some patients. If you notice any other effects, check with your doctor, nurse, or pharmacist.

***This leaflet has been developed by the USP based primarily on labeling provided by the manufacturer at the time of its approval. This information is intended for use as a temporary educational aid until the drug has been assessed by USP advisory panels. The information does not cover all possible uses, actions, precautions, side effects, or interactions of this medicine. It is not intended as medical advice for individual problems.**

Imiquimod (Topical) 915111

USP DI® Patient Education Leaflets™—Introductory Version*

Indinavir (Oral)

A commonly used brand name is *Crixivan*.

ABOUT YOUR MEDICINE

Indinavir (in-DIN-a-veer) is a protease inhibitor. It is used alone or in combination with other medicines to treat patients who are infected with the human immunodeficiency virus (HIV).

HIV is the virus that causes acquired immune deficiency syndrome (AIDS). This medicine appears to slow down the destruction of the immune system caused by HIV. This may help slow down the progress of HIV disease and the serious infections that occur with AIDS. However, this medicine will not cure or prevent HIV infection, and it will not keep you from spreading the virus to other people. Patients who are taking this medicine may continue to have the problems usually related to AIDS or HIV disease.

If any of the information in this leaflet causes you special concern or if you want additional information about your medicine and its use, check with your doctor, nurse, or pharmacist. **Remember, keep this and all other medicines out of the reach of children and never share your medicines with others.**

BEFORE USING

Discuss with your doctor the possible side effects that may be caused by this medicine. Some of them may be serious.

Tell your doctor, nurse, and pharmacist if you . . .

- are allergic to any medicine, either prescription or nonprescription (OTC);
- are pregnant or intend to become pregnant while using this medicine;
- are breast-feeding;
- are taking any other prescription or nonprescription (OTC) medicine, especially astemizole, cisapride, midazolam, rifampin, terfenadine, terfenadine-containing medicines, or triazolam;
- have any other medical problems, especially alcohol abuse (or history of), or kidney or liver disease.

PROPER USE

Take this medicine exactly as directed by your doctor. Do not take more of it, do not take it more often, and do not take it for a longer time than directed. Also, do not stop taking this medicine without first checking with your doctor.

Keep taking this medicine for the full time of treatment, even if you begin to feel better after a few days.

Indinavir should be taken with water 1 hour before or 2 hours after a meal. However, it may be taken with other liquids (such as skim milk, juice, coffee, or tea) or with a light meal.

Drink plenty of water or other liquids every day, unless otherwise directed by your doctor. Drinking extra water will help to prevent some unwanted effects this medicine has on the kidneys.

This medicine works best when there is a constant amount in the blood. **To help keep the amount constant, do not miss any doses.** If you need help in planning the best times to take your medicine, check with your doctor, nurse, or pharmacist.

If you do miss a dose of this medicine, and remember within 2 hours, take it right away. However, if you do not remember until later, skip the missed dose and go back to your regular dosing schedule. **Do not double doses.**

Indinavir capsules are sensitive to moisture. Carefully follow any directions for storage that are on the bottle.

PRECAUTIONS

It is very important that your doctor check your progress at regular visits.

Do not take any other medicines without first checking with your doctor. To do so may increase the chance of serious side effects.

POSSIBLE SIDE EFFECTS

Side Effects That Should Be Reported To Your Doctor Immediately

Less common—Back pain (severe); rash

Rare—Yellow eyes or skin

Side Effects That Usually Do Not Require Medical Attention

These possible side effects may go away during treatment; however, if they continue or are bothersome, check with your doctor, nurse, or pharmacist.

More common—Abdominal or stomach pain; change in taste; diarrhea; dizziness; dry mouth; dry skin; headache; loss of appetite; nausea; sore throat; tiredness or weakness; trouble in sleeping; vomiting

Other side effects not listed above may also occur in some patients. If you notice any other effects, check with your doctor, nurse, or pharmacist.

***This leaflet has been developed by the USP based primarily on labeling provided by the manufacturer at the time of its approval. This information is intended for use as a temporary educational aid until the drug has been assessed by USP advisory panels. The information does not cover all possible uses, actions, precautions, side effects, or interactions of this medicine. It is not intended as medical advice for individual problems.**

Indinavir (Oral)—913819

USP DI® Patient Education Leaflets™—Introductory Version*

Insulin Lispro (Injection)

A commonly used brand name is *Humalog*.

ABOUT YOUR MEDICINE

Insulin lispro (IN-su-lin LYE-sproe) is a type of insulin. Like other types of insulin, it is used to control diabetes mellitus (sugar diabetes). Diabetes mellitus is a condition in which the body does not make enough insulin or does not properly use the insulin it makes. Insulin lispro works faster than other types of insulin, therefore, you may have to use insulin lispro in combination with another type of insulin to keep your blood glucose (sugar) under control.

If any of the information in this leaflet causes you special concern or if you want additional information about your medicine and its use, check with your doctor, nurse, or pharmacist. **Remember, keep this and all other medicines out of the reach of children and never share your medicines with others.**

BEFORE USING

Tell your doctor, nurse, and pharmacist if you . . .

- are allergic to any medicine, either prescription or nonprescription (OTC);
- are pregnant or intend to become pregnant while using this medicine;
- are breast-feeding;
- are taking **any** other prescription or nonprescription (OTC) medicine;
- have **any** other medical problems.

PROPER USE

Each package of insulin lispro contains a patient information sheet. Read this sheet carefully. Follow directions for proper storage.

Follow carefully the special meal plan your doctor gave you and exercise regularly. Also, test for sugar in your blood or urine as directed.

PRECAUTIONS

Your doctor will want to check your progress at regular visits, especially during the first few weeks that you take this medicine.

Drinking alcohol while you are using insulin lispro may cause you to have dangerously low blood sugar. Avoid alcoholic beverages until you have discussed this with your doctor.

If mild symptoms of hypoglycemia (low blood sugar) appear, eat or drink something containing sugar and check with your doctor right away. Good sources of sugar are glucose tablets or gel, fruit juice, corn syrup, honey, regular (non-diet) soft drinks, or sugar cubes or sugar dissolved in water. It is a good idea to check your blood sugar to confirm that it is low.

If severe symptoms such as convulsions (seizures) or unconsciousness occur, someone should call for emergency medical help immediately. Under these conditions diabetic patients should not eat or drink anything. There is a chance that they could choke from not swallowing correctly. Glucagon is also used in emergency situations such as unconsciousness. Have a glucagon kit available, along with a syringe and needle. Make sure you and people in your household know how and when to prepare and use it.

Symptoms of low blood sugar can include: behavior change similar to being drunk; blurred vision; cold sweats; confusion; convulsions (seizures); depression; difficulty in concentrating; dizziness or lightheadedness; drowsiness; excessive hunger; fast heartbeat; feeling anxious; headache; irritability or abnormal behavior; nervousness; nightmares or restless sleep; shakiness; slurred speech; tingling in the hands, feet, lips, or tongue; or unconsciousness.

These symptoms may occur if you take too much insulin lispro or insulin, delay or miss a meal or snack, exercise much more than usual, cannot eat because of nausea and vomiting, or drink a significant amount of alcohol. **Tell someone to take you to your doctor or to a hospital right away if the symptoms do not improve after drinking or eating a sweet food.**

Symptoms of hyperglycemia (high blood sugar) can include: drowsiness; dry mouth; flushed, dry skin; fruit-like breath odor; increased urination; ketones in urine; loss of appetite; nausea or vomiting; troubled breathing (rapid and deep); unconsciousness; or unusual thirst.

Symptoms of high blood sugar may occur if you do not take enough insulin lispro or insulin, skip a dose of insulin lispro or insulin, overeat or do not follow your meal plan, have a fever or infection, or do not exercise as much as usual.

If symptoms of high blood sugar appear, check with your doctor right away.

POSSIBLE SIDE EFFECTS

Side Effects That Should Be Reported To Your Doctor Immediately

Less common—Convulsions (seizures); unconsciousness

Other Side Effects That Should Be Reported To Your Doctor

More common—Hypoglycemia (low blood sugar)

Less common or rare—Depression of the skin at place of injection; dryness of mouth; fast or weak pulse; increased thirst; irregular heartbeat; itching, redness or swelling at place of injection; mood or mental changes; muscle cramps or pain; nausea or vomiting; shortness of breath; skin rash or itching over the whole body; sweating; thickening of the skin at place of injection; unusual tiredness or weakness; wheezing

Other side effects not listed above may also occur in some patients. If you notice any other effects, check with your doctor nurse, or pharmacist.

***This leaflet has been developed by the USP based primarily on labeling provided by the manufacturer at the time of its approval. This information is intended for use as a temporary educational aid until the drug has been assessed by USP advisory panels. The information does not cover all possible uses, actions, precautions, side effects, or interactions of this medicine. It is not intended as medical advice for individual problems.**

Insulin Lispro (Injection) 911948

USP DI® Patient Education Leaflets™—Introductory Version*

Interferon Beta-1a (Injection)

A commonly used brand name is *Avonex*.

ABOUT YOUR MEDICINE

Interferon (in-ter-FEER-on) **beta-1a** is injected into a muscle to treat multiple sclerosis. It will not cure MS, but it may reduce the frequency of relapses in patients with the relapsing-remitting form of MS.

If any of the information in this leaflet causes you special concern or if you want additional information about your medicine and its use, check with your doctor, nurse, or pharmacist. **Remember, keep this and all other medicines out of the reach of children and never share your medicines with others.**

BEFORE USING

Tell your doctor, nurse, and pharmacist if you . . .

- are allergic to any medicine, either prescription or nonprescription (OTC);
- **are pregnant or intend to become pregnant while using this medicine;**
- are breast-feeding;
- are taking **any** other prescription or nonprescription (OTC) medicine;
- have any other medical problems, especially heart disease, mental depression, or seizure disorder.

PROPER USE

If you are injecting this medicine yourself, **use it exactly as directed.**

Each package of this medicine contains a patient instruction sheet. Read this sheet carefully and make sure you understand:

- How to prepare and give the injection.
- Proper use of disposable syringes.
- How long the injection is stable.

If you have any questions about any of this, check with your doctor, nurse, or pharmacist.

If you miss a dose of this medicine, use it as soon as possible. Then go back to your regular schedule, but do not give two injections within two days of each other.

PRECAUTIONS

It is very important that your doctor check your progress at regular visits.

This medicine commonly causes a flu-like reaction, with aching muscles, fever and chills, headache, and tiredness or weakness. **Follow your doctor's instructions carefully about when to take acetaminophen.**

If you or anyone else notices unusual changes in your mood, especially thoughts of suicide, **tell your doctor right away.**

POSSIBLE SIDE EFFECTS

Side Effects That Should Be Reported To Your Doctor Immediately

Less common—Seizures (convulsions); thoughts of suicide

Other Side Effects That Should Be Reported To Your Doctor

More common—Flu-like symptoms, including chills, diarrhea, fever, headache, joint pain, muscle aches, nausea, unusual tiredness or weakness; unusual bleeding or bruising

Less common—Abdominal pain; allergic reaction (coughing; difficulty in swallowing; hives or itching; swelling of face, lips, or eyelids; wheezing or difficulty in breathing); chest pain; clumsiness or unsteadiness; dizziness; fainting; flushing; hair loss; loss of hearing; pain or discharge from the vagina; pain or redness at place of injection; runny or stuffy nose, sneezing, or sore throat; skin irritation or rash not present before use of this medicine; speech problems

Rare—General feeling of discomfort or illness; loss of appetite; painful blisters on trunk of body, also known as "shingles"; painful cold sores or blisters on lips, nose, eyes, or genitals

Side Effects That Usually Do Not Require Medical Attention

These possible side effects may go away during treatment; however, if they continue or are bothersome, check with your doctor, nurse, or pharmacist.

Less common—Heartburn; trouble in sleeping

Other side effects not listed above may also occur in some patients. If you notice any other effects, check with your doctor, nurse, or pharmacist.

***This leaflet has been developed by the USP based primarily on labeling provided by the manufacturer at the time of its approval. This information is intended for use as a temporary educational aid until the drug has been assessed by USP advisory panels. The information does not cover all possible uses, actions, precautions, side effects, or interactions of this medicine. It is not intended as medical advice for individual problems.**

Interferon Beta-1a (Injection) 914549

USP DI® Patient Education Leaflets™—Introductory Version*

Interferon, Beta–1b (Injection)

A commonly used brand name is *Betaseron*.

ABOUT YOUR MEDICINE

Interferon (in-ter-FEER-on) **beta-1b** is injected subcutaneously (under the skin) to treat multiple sclerosis.

If any of the information in this leaflet causes you special concern or if you want additional information about your medicine and its use, check with your doctor, nurse, or pharmacist. **Remember, keep this and all other medicines out of the reach of children and never share your medicines with others.**

BEFORE USING

Tell your doctor, nurse, and pharmacist if you . . .

- are allergic to any medicine, either prescription or nonprescription (OTC);
- are pregnant or intend to become pregnant while using this medicine;
- are breast-feeding;
- are taking **any** other prescription or nonprescription (OTC) medicine;
- have any other medical problems, especially mental problems (or history of).

PROPER USE

If you are injecting this medicine yourself, **use it exactly as directed.**

Each package of this medicine contains a patient instruction sheet. Read this sheet carefully and make sure you understand:

- How to prepare and give the injection.
- Proper use of disposable syringes.
- How long the injection is stable.

If you have any questions about any of this, check with your doctor, nurse, or pharmacist.

Do not inject the medicine into a spot that is red, painful, or hard.

If you miss a dose of this medicine, use it as soon as you remember. Then, do not inject the next dose until 48 hours later. If you have any questions about this, check with your doctor.

PRECAUTIONS

It is very important that your doctor check your progress at regular visits.

This medicine commonly causes a flu-like reaction, with aching muscles, fever and chills, and headache. **Follow your doctor's instructions carefully about taking your temperature, and how much and when to take acetaminophen.** Using beta interferon at night may make these effects less bothersome.

In some patients this medicine may cause mental depression. **Tell your doctor right away** if you or anyone else notices unusual changes in your mood, especially thoughts of suicide.

POSSIBLE SIDE EFFECTS

Side Effects That Should Be Reported To Your Doctor Immediately

Less common—Mental depression

Other Side Effects That Should Be Reported To Your Doctor

More common—Aching muscles; fever or chills; headache; sweating; weakness

Less common—Pain or redness at place of injection; shortness of breath; unusually fast or irregular heartbeat

Side Effects That Usually Do Not Require Medical Attention

These possible side effects may go away during treatment; however, if they continue or are bothersome, check with your doctor, nurse, or pharmacist.

More common—Anxiety; constipation; diarrhea; dizziness; early, late, or painful menstrual periods or spotting between periods; stomach pain

Less common—Breast pain; confusion; nervousness; tiredness

Other side effects not listed above may also occur in some patients. If you notice any other effects, check with your doctor, nurse, or pharmacist.

***This leaflet has been developed by the USP based primarily on labeling provided by the manufacturer at the time of its approval. This information is intended for use as a temporary educational aid until the drug has been assessed by USP advisory panels. The information does not cover all possible uses, actions, precautions, side effects, or interactions of this medicine. It is not intended as medical advice for individual problems.**

USP DI® Patient Education Leaflets™—Introductory Version*

Ipratropium and Albuterol (Inhalation)

A commonly used brand name is *Combivent*.

ABOUT YOUR MEDICINE

Ipratropium (i-pra-TROE-pee-um) and **albuterol** (al-BYOO-ter-ol) combination is a bronchodilator (medicine that opens up narrowed breathing passages). It is taken by inhalation to help control the coughing, wheezing, shortness of breath, and troubled breathing caused by lung diseases, such as asthma, chronic bronchitis, and emphysema.

If any of the information in this leaflet causes you special concern or if you want additional information about your medicine and its use, check with your doctor, nurse, or pharmacist. **Remember, keep this and all other medicines out of the reach of children and never share your medicines with others.**

BEFORE USING

Tell your doctor, nurse, and pharmacist if you...

- are allergic to any medicine, either prescription or nonprescription (OTC);
- are allergic to soya lecithin, soybean protein, or other legumes, such as peanuts;
- are pregnant or intend to become pregnant while using this medicine;
- are breast-feeding;
- are taking any other prescription or nonprescription (OTC) medicine;
- have any other medical problems, especially glaucoma, heart or blood vessel disease, or high blood pressure.

PROPER USE

It is very important that you use ipratropium and albuterol combination only as directed. Do not use more of it and do not use it more often than directed. To do so may increase the chance of serious side effects.

This medicine usually comes with patient directions. Read them carefully before using this medicine. If you do not understand the directions or you are not sure how to use the inhaler, ask your doctor, nurse, or pharmacist to show you how to use it.

Keep the spray away from the eyes because this medicine may cause irritation or blurred vision. This is especially important for people with glaucoma. Closing your eyes while you are inhaling this medicine may help keep it out of your eyes.

If you use ipratropium and albuterol combination regularly and you miss a dose, use it as soon as possible. Then use any remaining doses for that day at regularly spaced intervals.

PRECAUTIONS

Check with your doctor at once if difficulty in breathing continues after using a dose of this medicine or if your condition gets worse.

POSSIBLE SIDE EFFECTS

Side Effects That Should Be Reported To Your Doctor

Rare—Shortness of breath or wheezing; skin rash or hives; swelling of the face, lips, eyelids, mouth, or throat

Side Effects That Usually Do Not Require Medical Attention

These possible side effects may go away during treatment; however, if they continue or are bothersome, check with your doctor, nurse, or pharmacist.

Less common—Cough; headache; nausea

Rare—Changes in taste; chest discomfort or pain; dizziness; dry mouth; fast or irregular heartbeat; nervousness; trembling

Other side effects not listed above may also occur in some patients. If you notice any other effects, check with your doctor, nurse, or pharmacist.

***This leaflet has been developed by the USP based primarily on labeling provided by the manufacturer at the time of its approval. This information is intended for use as a temporary educational aid until the drug has been assessed by USP advisory panels. The information does not cover all possible uses, actions, precautions, side effects, or interactions of this medicine. It is not intended as medical advice for individual problems.**

Ipratropium and Albuterol (Inhalation) 912725

USP DI® Patient Education Leaflets™—Introductory Version*

Losartan and Hydrochlorothiazide (Oral)

A commonly used brand name is *Hyzaar*.

ABOUT YOUR MEDICINE

Losartan (loe-SAR-tan) and **hydrochlorothiazide** (hye-droe-klor-oh-THYE-a-zide) combination is used to treat high blood pressure.

If any of the information in this leaflet causes you special concern or if you want additional information about your medicine and its use, check with your doctor, nurse, or pharmacist. **Remember, keep this and all other medicines out of the reach of children and never share your medicines with others.**

BEFORE USING

Tell your doctor, nurse, and pharmacist if you . . .

- are allergic to any medicine, either prescription or nonprescription (OTC);
- **are pregnant or intend to become pregnant while using this medicine;**
- are breast-feeding;
- are taking any other prescription or nonprescription (OTC) medicine, especially barbiturates, cholestyramine, colestipol, corticosteroids, gestodene, insulin, ketoconazole, lithium, narcotics, nonsteroidal anti-inflammatory drugs (NSAIDs), oral antidiabetic agents, potassium-containing supplements or salt substitutes containing potassium, sulfaphenazole, or troleandomycin;
- have any other medical problems, especially kidney or liver disease.

PROPER USE

Even if you feel well and do not notice any signs of your medical problem, **take this medicine exactly as directed.**

This medicine may be taken with or without food.

If you miss a dose of this medicine, take it as soon as possible. However, if it is almost time for your next dose, skip the missed dose and go back to your regular dosing schedule. Do not double doses.

PRECAUTIONS

If you think that you may have become pregnant, check with your doctor immediately. Use of this medicine, especially during the second and third trimesters (after the first three months) of pregnancy, may cause serious injury or even death to the unborn child.

Dizziness or lightheadedness may occur, especially after the first dose of this medicine or if you are dehydrated. Make sure you know how you react to this medicine before you drive, use machines, or do other things that require you to be alert and clearheaded.

Dizziness, lightheadedness, or fainting may occur if you exercise or if the weather is hot. Use extra care during exercise or hot weather.

Check with your doctor if you become sick while taking this medicine, especially with severe or continuing vomiting or diarrhea. These conditions may cause you to lose too much water, possibly causing low blood pressure.

Avoid alcoholic beverages until you have discussed their use with your doctor. Alcohol may increase the low blood pressure effect and the possibility of dizziness and fainting.

POSSIBLE SIDE EFFECTS

Side Effects That Should Be Reported To Your Doctor

Less common—Dizziness; upper respiratory infection, with symptoms such as cough, fever, or sore throat

Rare—Pounding heartbeat; skin rash; swelling of feet and lower legs

Side Effects That Usually Do Not Require Medical Attention

These possible side effects may go away during treatment; however, if they continue or are bothersome, check with your doctor, nurse, or pharmacist.

Less common—Back pain; stomach pain

Rare—Cough; sinus problems

Other side effects not listed above may also occur in some patients. If you notice any other effects, check with your doctor, nurse, or pharmacist.

***This leaflet has been developed by the USP based primarily on labeling provided by the manufacturer at the time of its approval. This information is intended for use as a temporary educational aid until the drug has been assessed by USP advisory panels. The information does not cover all possible uses, actions, precautions, side effects, or interactions of this medicine. It is not intended as medical advice for individual problems.**

Losartan and Hydrochlorothiazide (Oral) 910810

USP DI® Patient Education Leaflets™—Introductory Version*

Miglitol (Oral)

A commonly used brand name is *Glyset*.

ABOUT YOUR MEDICINE

Miglitol (MIG-li-tol) is used to treat a type of diabetes mellitus (sugar diabetes).

If any of the information in this leaflet causes you special concern or if you want additional information about your medicine and its use, check with your doctor, nurse, or pharmacist. **Remember, keep this and all other medicines out of the reach of children and never share your medicines with others.**

BEFORE USING

Tell your doctor, nurse, and pharmacist if you . . .

- are allergic to any medicine, either prescription or nonprescription (OTC);
- are pregnant or intend to become pregnant while using this medicine;
- are breast-feeding;
- are taking any other prescription or nonprescription (OTC) medicine especially activated charcoal, propranolol, ranitidine, or medicine for digestion that contains amylase or pancreatin;
- have any other medical problems, especially kidney disease, or problems with digestion or other intestinal problems.

PROPER USE

Follow carefully the special meal plan your doctor gave you. This is the most important part of controlling your condition, and is necessary if the medicine is to work properly. Also, exercise regularly and test for sugar in your blood or urine as directed. **It is important that you do not miss any doses.**

In order for miglitol to work properly, it must be taken at the beginning of each main meal. However, if you finish a meal and have forgotten to take the medicine, do not take the missed dose. Instead, take the next dose at the beginning of your next meal, as scheduled. **Do not double doses.**

Your doctor will want to check your progress at regular visits, especially during the first few weeks you take this medicine.

Miglitol does not cause hypoglycemia (low blood sugar). However, low blood sugar can occur if you delay or miss a meal or snack, exercise more than usual, cannot eat because of nausea or vomiting, or drink a significant amount of alcohol. It can also occur when other medicines that can lower blood sugar are taken with miglitol.

Symptoms of low blood sugar include anxiety; behavior change similar to being drunk; blurred vision; cold sweats; confusion; convulsions (seizures); cool, pale skin; difficulty in thinking; drowsiness; excessive hunger; fast heartbeat; headache; nausea; nervousness; nightmares; shakiness; slurred speech; trouble in sleeping; unconsciousness; or unusual tiredness or weakness.

If symptoms of low blood sugar occur, **eat or drink glucose tablets or gel, fruit juice, or honey to relieve the symptoms. Table sugar (sucrose) or regular (nondiet) soft drinks will not work and should not be used.** Also, check your blood for low blood sugar. **Get to a doctor or a hospital right away if the symptoms do not improve.**

Someone should call for emergency help immediately if severe symptoms such as convulsions (seizures) or unconsciousness occur. Do not force food or drink because one could choke from not swallowing correctly.

Hyperglycemia (high blood sugar) may occur if you skip a dose of your medicine, overeat or do not follow your meal plan, have a fever or infection, or do not exercise as much as usual.

Symptoms of high blood sugar include blurred vision; drowsiness; dry mouth; flushed, dry skin; fruit-like breath odor; increased urination; loss of appetite; nausea or vomiting; stomach ache; tiredness; troubled breathing (rapid and deep); unconsciousness; or unusual thirst. **If symptoms of high blood sugar occur, check your blood sugar level, then call your doctor for instructions.**

POSSIBLE SIDE EFFECTS

Side Effects That Usually Do Not Require Medical Attention

These possible side effects may go away during treatment; however, if they continue or are bothersome, check with your doctor, nurse, or pharmacist.

More common—Abdominal or stomach pain; bloated stomach or gas; diarrhea

Less common—Skin rash

Other side effects not listed above may also occur in some patients. If you notice any other effects, check with your doctor, nurse, or pharmacist.

***This leaflet has been developed by the USP based primarily on labeling provided by the manufacturer at the time of its approval. This information is intended for use as a temporary educational aid until the drug has been assessed by USP advisory panels. The information does not cover all possible uses, actions, precautions, side effects, or interactions of this medicine. It is not intended as medical advice for individual problems.**

USP DI® Patient Education Leaflets™—Introductory Version*

Mirtazapine (Oral)

A commonly used brand name is *Remeron*.

ABOUT YOUR MEDICINE

Mirtazapine (mir-TAZ-a-peen) is used to treat mental depression.

If any of the information in this leaflet causes you special concern or if you want additional information about your medicine and its use, check with your doctor, nurse, or pharmacist. **Remember, keep this and all other medicines out of the reach of children and never share your medicines with others.**

BEFORE USING

Tell your doctor, nurse, and pharmacist if you . . .

- are allergic to any medicine, either prescription or nonprescription (OTC);
- are pregnant or intend to become pregnant while using this medicine;
- are breast-feeding;
- are taking any other prescription or nonprescription (OTC) medicine, especially MAO inhibitors;
- have any other medical problems, especially liver disease.

PROPER USE

Take this medicine only as directed by your doctor in order to improve your condition as much as possible. Do not take more of it and do not take it more often than your doctor ordered.

Mirtazapine may be taken with or without food, on a full or an empty stomach. Follow your doctor's instructions.

PRECAUTIONS

It is important that your doctor check your progress at regular visits, to allow for changes in your dose and help reduce any side effects.

Mirtazapine should not be taken with MAO inhibitors (e.g., furazolidone, isocarboxazid, phenelzine, procarbazine, selegiline, or tranylcypromine) or sooner than 14 days after stopping an MAO inhibitor. To do so may increase the chance of serious side effects.

This medicine will add to the effects of alcohol and other CNS depressants (medicines that may make you drowsy or less alert). **Check with your doctor before taking any CNS depressants while you are taking this medicine.**

Mirtazapine may cause drowsiness or trouble in thinking. **Make sure you know how you react to this medicine before you drive, use machines, or do other jobs that require you to be alert and clearheaded.**

Dizziness, lightheadedness, or fainting may occur, especially when you get up from a lying or sitting position. Getting up slowly may help. If this problem continues or gets worse, check with your doctor.

This medicine may cause dryness of the mouth. For temporary relief, use sugarless gum or candy, melt bits of ice in your mouth, or use a saliva substitute. However, if your mouth feels dry for more than 2 weeks, check with your medical doctor or dentist. Continuing dryness of the mouth may increase the chance of dental disease, including tooth decay, gum disease, and fungus infections.

POSSIBLE SIDE EFFECTS

Side Effects That Should Be Reported To Your Doctor Immediately

Rare—Convulsions (seizures); mouth sores; sore throat, chills, or fever

Other Side Effects That Should Be Reported To Your Doctor

Less common—Decreased or increased movement; mood or mental changes; shortness of breath; swelling of feet or ankles

Rare—Decreased sexual ability; menstrual pain; missing menstrual periods

Side Effects That Usually Do Not Require Medical Attention

These possible side effects may go away during treatment; however, if they continue or are bothersome, check with your doctor, nurse, or pharmacist.

More common—Constipation; dizziness; drowsiness; dry mouth; increased appetite; weight gain

Less common—Abdominal pain; abnormal dreams; back pain; dizziness or fainting when getting up suddenly from a lying or sitting position; frequent urge to urinate; increased sensitivity to touch and pain; increased thirst; low blood pressure; muscle pain; nausea; sense of constant movement of self or surroundings; trembling or shaking; vomiting; weakness

Other side effects not listed above may also occur in some patients. If you notice any other effects, check with your doctor, nurse, or pharmacist.

***This leaflet has been developed by the USP based primarily on labeling provided by the manufacturer at the time of its approval. This information is intended for use as a temporary educational aid until the drug has been assessed by USP advisory panels. The information does not cover all possible uses, actions, precautions, side effects, or interactions of this medicine. It is not intended as medical advice for individual problems.**

Mirtazapine (Oral) 912157

USP DI® Patient Education Leaflets™—Introductory Version*

Nefazodone (Oral)

A commonly used brand name is *Serzone*.

ABOUT YOUR MEDICINE

Nefazodone (ne-FAZ-oh-done) is used to treat mental depression.

If any of the information in this leaflet causes you special concern or if you want additional information about your medicine and its use, check with your doctor, nurse, or pharmacist. **Remember, keep this and all other medicines out of the reach of children and never share your medicines with others.**

BEFORE USING

Tell your doctor, nurse, and pharmacist if you . . .

- are allergic to any medicine, either prescription or nonprescription (OTC);
- are pregnant or intend to become pregnant while using this medicine;
- are breast-feeding;
- are taking any other prescription or nonprescription (OTC) medicine, especially alprazolam, astemizole, digoxin, haloperidol, MAO inhibitors, terfenadine, or triazolam;
- have any other medical problems, especially heart disease or circulation problems, or liver disease.

PROPER USE

Take this medicine only as directed by your doctor. You may have to take this medicine for several weeks before you begin to feel better. Your doctor should check your progress at regular visits during this time.

If you miss a dose of this medicine, take it as soon as possible. However, if it is almost time for your next dose, skip the missed dose and go back to your regular dosing schedule. Do not double doses.

PRECAUTIONS

It is important that your doctor check your progress at regular visits, to allow for changes in your dose and help reduce any side effects.

This medicine may add to the effects of alcohol and other CNS depressants (medicines that may make you drowsy or less alert). **Check with your doctor before taking any such depressants while you are using this medicine.**

This medicine may cause some people to become dizzy or drowsy, or to have blurred vision or other vision changes. **Make sure you know how you react to this medicine before you drive, use machines, or do other jobs that require you to be alert or able to see well.**

Dizziness, lightheadedness, or fainting may occur, especially when you get up from a lying or sitting position. Getting up slowly may help. If this problem continues or gets worse, check with your doctor.

This medicine may cause dryness of the mouth. For temporary relief, use sugarless gum or candy, melt bits of ice in your mouth, or use a saliva substitute. However, if your mouth feels dry for more than 2 weeks, check with your medical doctor or dentist. Continuing dryness of the mouth may increase the chance of dental disease, including tooth decay, gum disease, and fungus infections.

POSSIBLE SIDE EFFECTS

Side Effects That Should Be Reported To Your Doctor

More common—Agitation; blurred vision or other changes in vision; confusion; dizziness or lightheadedness

Less common—Clumsiness or unsteadiness; difficult or frequent urination; difficulty concentrating; memory problems; skin rash or itching

Side Effects That Usually Do Not Require Medical Attention

These possible side effects may go away during treatment; however, if they continue or are bothersome, check with your doctor, nurse, or pharmacist.

More common—Constipation; drowsiness; dry mouth; nausea; tiredness or weakness; trouble in sleeping

Less common—Burning, prickling, or tingling sensations; change in your sense of taste; decrease in sex drive; diarrhea; feeling of warmth or flushing; headache; heartburn; increased appetite; ringing in ears; strange dreams; vomiting

Other side effects not listed above may also occur in some patients. If you notice any other effects, check with your doctor, nurse, or pharmacist.

***This leaflet has been developed by the USP based primarily on labeling provided by the manufacturer at the time of its approval. This information is intended for use as a temporary educational aid until the drug has been assessed by USP advisory panels. The information does not cover all possible uses, actions, precautions, side effects, or interactions of this medicine. It is not intended as medical advice for individual problems.**

Nefazodone (Oral) 910730

USP DI® Patient Education Leaflets™—Introductory Version*

Nelfinavir (Oral)

A commonly used brand name is *Viracept*.

ABOUT YOUR MEDICINE

Nelfinavir (nel-FIN-a-veer) is a protease inhibitor. It is used alone or in combination with other medicines to treat patients who are infected with the human immunodeficiency virus (HIV).

HIV is the virus that causes acquired immune deficiency syndrome (AIDS). This medicine appears to slow down the destruction of the immune system caused by HIV. This may help slow down the progress of HIV disease and the serious infections that occur with AIDS. However, this medicine will not cure or prevent HIV infection, and it will not keep you from spreading the virus to other people. Patients who are taking this medicine may continue to have the problems usually related to AIDS or HIV disease.

If any of the information in this leaflet causes you special concern or if you want additional information about your medicine and its use, check with your doctor, nurse, or pharmacist. **Remember, keep this and all other medicines out of the reach of children and never share your medicines with others.**

BEFORE USING

Tell your doctor, nurse, and pharmacist if you . . .

- are allergic to any medicine, either prescription or nonprescription (OTC);
- are pregnant or intend to become pregnant while using this medicine;
- are breast-feeding;
- are using any other prescription or nonprescription (OTC) medicine, especially astemizole, cisapride, midazolam, oral contraceptives, rifabutin, rifampin, terfenadine, terfenadine-containing medicines, or triazolam;
- have any other medical problems, especially liver disease.

PROPER USE

Nelfinavir should be taken with food.

This medicine works best when there is a constant amount in the blood. **To help keep the amount constant, do not miss any doses.** If you need help in planning the best times to take your medicine, check with your doctor, nurse, or pharmacist.

If you do miss a dose of this medicine, take it as soon as possible. However, if it is almost time for your next dose, skip the missed dose and go back to your regular dosing schedule. **Do not double doses.**

PRECAUTIONS

It is very important that your doctor check your progress at regular visits.

If diarrhea occurs, do not take any diarrhea medicine without first checking with your doctor or pharmacist. Diarrhea medicines may make your diarrhea worse or last longer.

Oral contraceptives (birth control pills) containing estrogen may not work properly if you take them while you are taking nelfinavir. Unplanned pregnancies may occur. Use different or additional birth control while using this medicine.

This medicine must not be given to other people or used for other infections unless you are otherwise directed by your doctor.

POSSIBLE SIDE EFFECTS

Side Effects That Should Be Reported To Your Doctor

More common—Diarrhea

Less common—Gas; nausea; skin rash

Other side effects not listed above may also occur in some patients. If you notice any other effects, check with your doctor, nurse, or pharmacist.

***This leaflet has been developed by the USP based primarily on labeling provided by the manufacturer at the time of its approval. This information is intended for use as a temporary educational aid until the drug has been assessed by USP advisory panels. The information does not cover all possible uses, actions, precautions, side effects, or interactions of this medicine. It is not intended as medical advice for individual problems.**

Nelfinavir (Oral) 915213

USP DI® Patient Education Leaflets™—Introductory Version*

Nevirapine (Oral)

A commonly used brand name is *Viramune.*

ABOUT YOUR MEDICINE

Nevirapine (na-VEER-a-peen) is used to treat patients who are infected with the human immunodeficiency virus (HIV). HIV is the virus that causes acquired immunodeficiency syndrome (AIDS). This medicine is taken together with other medicines, such as zidovudine (AZT), to treat HIV infection. These medicines seem to slow down the progress of HIV disease. However, this medicine will not cure HIV infection, and it will not keep you from spreading the virus to other people.

If any of the information in this leaflet causes you special concern or if you want additional information about your medicine and its use, check with your doctor, nurse, or pharmacist. **Remember, keep this and all other medicines out of the reach of children and never share your medicines with others.**

BEFORE USING

Tell your doctor, nurse, and pharmacist if you . . .

- are allergic to any medicine, either prescription or nonprescription (OTC);
- are pregnant or intend to become pregnant while using this medicine;
- are breast-feeding;
- are taking any other prescription or nonprescription (OTC) medicine, especially oral contraceptives (birth control pills); protease inhibitors, such as indinavir, ritonavir, or saquinavir; rifabutin; or rifampin;
- have any other medical problems.

PROPER USE

Take this medicine exactly as directed by your doctor. Do not take more of it, do not take it more often, and do not take it for a longer time than your doctor ordered. Also, do not stop taking this medicine without first checking with your doctor.

Keep taking this medicine for the full time of treatment, even if you begin to feel better.

This medicine may be taken with or without food.

This medicine works best when there is a constant amount in the blood. **To help keep the amount constant, do not miss any doses.** If you need help in planning the best time to take your medicine, check with your doctor, nurse, or pharmacist.

If you do miss a dose of this medicine, take it as soon as possible. However, if it is almost time for the next dose, skip the missed dose and go back to your regular dosing schedule. Do not double doses.

Only take medicine that your doctor has prescribed specifically for you. **Do not share your medicine with others.**

PRECAUTIONS

It is important that your doctor check your progress at regular visits.

Do not take any other medicines without first checking with your doctor.

Oral contraceptives (birth control pills) containing estrogen may not work properly if you take them while you are taking this medicine. Unplanned pregnancies may occur. Use different or additional birth control while using this medicine.

POSSIBLE SIDE EFFECTS

Side Effects That Should Be Reported To Your Doctor Immediately

More common—Skin rash
Less common—Fever
Rare—Yellow eyes or skin

Side Effects That Usually Do Not Require Medical Attention

These possible side effects may go away during treatment; however, if they continue or are bothersome, check with your doctor, nurse, or pharmacist.

Less common—Headache; nausea

Other side effects not listed above may also occur in some patients. If you notice any other effects, check with your doctor, nurse, or pharmacist.

***This leaflet has been developed by the USP based primarily on labeling provided by the manufacturer at the time of its approval. This information is intended for use as a temporary educational aid until the drug has been assessed by USP advisory panels. The information does not cover all possible uses, actions, precautions, side effects, or interactions of this medicine. It is not intended as medical advice for individual problems.**

USP DI® Patient Education Leaflets™—Introductory Version*

Nicotine (Nasal)

A commonly used brand name is *Nicotrol NS*.

ABOUT YOUR MEDICINE

Nicotine (NIK-o-teen) in a nasal spray is used to help you stop smoking. It may be used for up to 3 months. It is best to use nicotine nasal spray while taking part in a stop-smoking program that includes education, counseling, or psychological support.

If any of the information in this leaflet causes you special concern or if you want additional information about your medicine and its use, check with your doctor, nurse, or pharmacist. **Remember, keep this and all other medicines out of the reach of children and never share your medicines with others.**

BEFORE USING

Tell your doctor, nurse, and pharmacist if you . . .

- are allergic to any medicine, either prescription or nonprescription (OTC);
- are pregnant or intend to become pregnant while using this medicine;
- are breast-feeding;
- are taking any other prescription or nonprescription (OTC) medicine, especially alpha-blockers, beta-blockers, insulin, or theophylline;
- have **any** other medical problems.

PROPER USE

Nicotine nasal spray usually comes with patient directions. **Read the directions carefully before using this medicine.**

It is important to participate in a stop-smoking program during treatment. To do so may make it easier for you to stop smoking.

Use of nicotine nasal spray may be gradually reduced by using only one-half of a dose at a time or skipping doses by not using the spray every hour. You may also keep track of the number of doses and use fewer each day, or set a date to stop using nicotine nasal spray.

PRECAUTIONS

Do not smoke during treatment with nicotine nasal spray because of the risk of nicotine overdose.

Nicotine should not be used during pregnancy. If there is a possibility you might become pregnant, you may want to use some type of birth control. **If you think that you may have become pregnant, check with your doctor immediately.**

Nicotine nasal spray must be kept out of the reach of children and pets. Even very small amounts of nicotine may cause problems in children. If a child uses nicotine nasal spray, contact your doctor or poison control center at once.

During the first week of use, you may have a hot, peppery feeling in the back of the throat or nose; coughing; runny nose; sneezing; or watery eyes. **Do not stop using this medicine. If you continue to use nicotine nasal spray regularly, you should adjust to these effects. If these effects do not lessen after 1 week, check with your doctor.**

Do not use nicotine nasal spray for longer than 3 months. To do so may result in physical dependence on the nicotine.

Avoid contact with the skin, mouth, eyes, and ears. If even a small amount of nicotine nasal spray comes into contact with the skin, mouth, eyes, or ears, the affected area should be immediately rinsed with water only.

POSSIBLE SIDE EFFECTS

Side Effects That Should Be Reported To Your Doctor

More common—Feelings of dependence; joint pain; shortness of breath; swelling of gums, mouth, or tongue; tightness in chest; tingling in arms, legs, hands, or feet

Less common—Confusion; difficulty in swallowing; dryness or pain in throat; fast or irregular heartbeat; muscle pain; nasal blister or sore; numbness of nose or mouth; tingling, burning, or prickly sensations in nose, mouth, or head

Rare—Blood-containing blisters on skin; difficulty in speaking; loss of memory; migraine headaches; skin rash; swelling of feet or lower legs; wheezing

Side Effects That Usually Do Not Require Medical Attention

These possible side effects may go away during treatment; however, if they continue or are bothersome, check with your doctor, nurse, or pharmacist.

More common—Back pain; constipation; cough; headache; hot, peppery feeling in the back of the throat or nose; indigestion; nausea; runny nose; sneezing; watery eyes

Less common—Acne; change in sense of smell or taste; dryness, burning, itching, or irritation of the eyes; earache; flushing of face; gas; hoarseness; itching; menstrual problems; nosebleed; sinus problems; soreness of teeth and gums; stuffy nose

Other side effects not listed above may also occur in some patients. If you notice any other effects, check with your doctor, nurse, or pharmacist.

***This leaflet has been developed by the USP based primarily on labeling provided by the manufacturer at the time of its approval. This information is intended for use as a temporary educational aid until the drug has been assessed by USP advisory panels. The information does not cover all possible uses, actions, precautions, side effects, or interactions of this medicine. It is not intended as medical advice for individual problems.**

Nicotine (Nasal) 911992

USP DI® Patient Education Leaflets™—Introductory Version*

Olanzapine (Oral)

A commonly used brand name is *Zyprexa*.

ABOUT YOUR MEDICINE

Olanzapine (oh-LAN-za-peen) is used to treat psychotic disorders, such as schizophrenia.

If any of the information in this leaflet causes you special concern or if you want additional information about your medicine and its use, check with your doctor, nurse, or pharmacist. **Remember, keep this and all other medicines out of the reach of children and never share your medicines with others.**

BEFORE USING

Discuss with your doctor the possible side effects of this medicine. Some may be serious and/or permanent. For example, tardive dyskinesia (a movement disorder) may occur and may not go away after you stop using the medicine.

Tell your doctor, nurse, and pharmacist if you . . .

- are allergic to any medicine, either prescription or nonprescription (OTC);
- are pregnant or intend to become pregnant while using this medicine;
- are breast-feeding;
- are taking **any** other prescription or nonprescription (OTC) medicine;
- have **any** other medical problems.

PROPER USE

Take this medicine only as directed by your doctor in order to improve your condition as much as possible. Do not take more of it and do not take it more often than your doctor ordered.

Olanzapine may be taken with or without food, on a full or an empty stomach. Follow your doctor's instructions.

PRECAUTIONS

It is important that your doctor check your progress at regular visits, to allow for changes in your dose and help reduce any side effects.

This medicine may add to the effects of alcohol and other CNS depressants (medicines that may make you drowsy or less alert). **Check with your doctor before taking any CNS depressants while you are taking this medicine.**

Olanzapine may cause drowsiness, trouble in thinking, trouble in controlling movements, or trouble in seeing clearly. **Make sure you know how you react to this medicine before you drive, use machines, or do other jobs that require you to be alert, well-coordinated, or able to think or see well.**

This medicine may make it more difficult for your body to cool itself down. **Use care not to become overheated during exercise or hot weather** since overheating may result in heat stroke.

Dizziness, lightheadedness, or fainting may occur, especially when you get up from a lying or sitting position. Getting up slowly may help. If this problem continues or gets worse, check with your doctor.

POSSIBLE SIDE EFFECTS

Side Effects That Should Be Reported To Your Doctor Immediately

More common—Difficulty swallowing; stiff arms or legs; trembling and shaking of hands and fingers

Less common—Chest pain; inability to move eyes; lip smacking or puckering; muscle spasms of face, neck, and back; rapid or worm-like movements of tongue; twitching movements; uncontrolled chewing movements; uncontrolled movements of arms or legs

Rare—Confusion; mental or physical sluggishness; swelling of face; trouble in breathing

Other Side Effects That Should Be Reported To Your Doctor

More common—Agitation; behavior problems; restlessness or need to keep moving

Less common—Fever; flu-like symptoms; mood or mental changes; swelling of ankles or feet

Rare—Changes in menstrual period

Side Effects That Usually Do Not Require Medical Attention

These possible side effects may go away during treatment; however, if they continue or are bothersome, check with your doctor, nurse, or pharmacist.

More common—Constipation; dizziness; dizziness or fainting when getting up suddenly from a lying or sitting position; drowsiness; dry mouth; headache; runny nose; vision problems; weakness; weight gain

Less common—Abdominal pain; fast heartbeat; increased appetite; increased cough; joint pain; loss of bladder control; low blood pressure; muscle tension; nausea; sore throat; stuttering; thirst; trouble in sleeping; trouble in speaking or slurred speech; vomiting; watering of mouth; weight loss

Other side effects not listed above may also occur in some patients. If you notice any other effects, check with your doctor, nurse, or pharmacist.

***This leaflet has been developed by the USP based primarily on labeling provided by the manufacturer at the time of its approval. This information is intended for use as a temporary educational aid until the drug has been assessed by USP advisory panels. The information does not cover all possible uses, actions, precautions, side effects, or interactions of this medicine. It is not intended as medical advice for individual problems.**

Olanzapine (Oral) 913728

USP DI® Patient Education Leaflets™—Introductory Version*

Pegaspargase (Injection)

A commonly used brand name is *Oncaspar*.

ABOUT YOUR MEDICINE

Pegaspargase (peg-AS-par-jase) is used to treat some kinds of cancer.

If any of the information in this leaflet causes you special concern or if you want additional information about your medicine and its use, check with your doctor, nurse, or pharmacist.

BEFORE USING

Discuss with your doctor the possible side effects that may be caused by this medicine. Some of them may be serious and/or long-term.

Tell your doctor, nurse, and pharmacist if you . . .

- are allergic to any medicine, either prescription or nonprescription (OTC);
- are pregnant or intend to have children;
- are breast-feeding;
- are taking **any** other prescription or nonprescription (OTC) medicine;
- have any other medical problems, especially chicken pox (including recent exposure), herpes zoster (shingles), infection, liver disease, or pancreatitis (inflammation of the pancreas);
- have ever been treated with x-rays or cancer medicines.

PROPER USE

While you are using this medicine, your doctor may want you to drink extra fluids so that you will pass more urine. This will help prevent kidney problems and keep your kidneys working well.

This medicine often causes nausea, vomiting, and loss of appetite. However, it is very important that you continue to receive the medicine, even if you begin to feel ill. After several doses, your stomach upset should lessen. Ask your doctor, nurse, or pharmacist for ways to lessen these effects.

PRECAUTIONS

It is very important that your doctor check your progress at regular visits to make sure this medicine is working properly and to check for unwanted effects.

While you are being treated with pegaspargase, and after you stop treatment with it, **do not have any immunizations (vaccinations) without your doctor's approval.**

POSSIBLE SIDE EFFECTS

Side Effects That Should Be Reported To Your Doctor Immediately

More common—Fever or chills; joint pain; puffy face; skin rash or itching; stomach pain (severe) with nausea and vomiting; trouble in breathing

Rare—Headache (severe); inability to move arm or leg; unusual bleeding or bruising

Other Side Effects That Should Be Reported To Your Doctor

Less common—Confusion; drowsiness; frequent urination; hallucinations; lower back or side pain; mental depression; nervousness; pain at place of injection; sores in mouth or on lips; swelling of feet or lower legs; unusual thirst; unusual tiredness

Rare—Convulsions (seizures); pain in lower legs

Side Effects That Usually Do Not Require Medical Attention

These possible side effects may go away during treatment; however, if they continue or are bothersome, check with your doctor, nurse, or pharmacist.

More common—Headache (mild); loss of appetite; nausea or vomiting; stomach cramps; weight loss

Other side effects not listed above may also occur in some patients. If you notice any other effects, check with your doctor, nurse, or pharmacist.

After you stop receiving pegaspargase, it may still produce some side effects that need attention. During this time, **check with your doctor or nurse immediately** if any of the following side effects occur: headache (severe); inability to move arm or leg; stomach pain (severe) with nausea and vomiting.

***This leaflet has been developed by the USP based primarily on labeling provided by the manufacturer at the time of its approval. This information is intended for use as a temporary educational aid until the drug has been assessed by USP advisory panels. The information does not cover all possible uses, actions, precautions, side effects, or interactions of this medicine. It is not intended as medical advice for individual problems.**

Pegaspargase (Injection) 910184

USP DI® Patient Education Leaflets™—Introductory Version*

Pentosan (Oral)

A commonly used brand name is *Elmiron*.

ABOUT YOUR MEDICINE

Pentosan (PEN-toe-san) is used to relieve the symptoms of the bladder condition called interstitial cystitis.

If any of the information in this leaflet causes you special concern or if you want additional information about your medicine and its use, check with your doctor, nurse, or pharmacist. **Remember, keep this and all other medicines out of the reach of children and never share your medicines with others.**

BEFORE USING

Tell your doctor, nurse, and pharmacist if you . . .

- are allergic to any medicine, either prescription or nonprescription (OTC);
- are pregnant or intend to become pregnant while using this medicine;
- are breast-feeding;
- are taking any other prescription or nonprescription (OTC) medicine, especially alteplase, aspirin (high doses), coumarin anticoagulants, heparin, or streptokinase;
- have any other medical problems, especially blockage or obstruction of the intestine, blood or blood vessel disease or other blood problems, polyps, or stomach ulcer.

PROPER USE

Take this medicine on an empty stomach (at least 1 hour before or 2 hours after meals) and at least 1 hour before or after any other food, milk, or medicine. **Also, always take it with a full glass (8 ounces) of water.**

If you miss a dose of this medicine, take it as soon as possible. However, if it is almost time for your next dose, skip the missed dose and go back to your regular dosing schedule. Do not double doses.

PRECAUTIONS

This medicine may increase the risk of serious bleeding. Before having any kind of surgery or dental or emergency treatment, tell the medical doctor or dentist in charge that you are using this medicine.

POSSIBLE SIDE EFFECTS

Side Effects That Should Be Reported To Your Doctor

Rare—Fever, chills, or sore throat; itching; skin rash or hives; trouble in breathing; unusual bleeding or bruising; unusual tiredness or weakness

Side Effects That Usually Do Not Require Medical Attention

These possible side effects may go away during treatment; however, if they continue or are bothersome, check with your doctor, nurse, or pharmacist.

Less common—Abdominal pain; diarrhea; dizziness; hair loss; headache; nausea; skin rash; stomach upset

Rare—Bleeding gums; constipation; difficulty in swallowing; dryness or pain in throat; gas; heartburn; increased sensitivity to sunlight; loss of appetite; nosebleeds; pain on swallowing; ringing in the ears; runny nose; sores in mouth or on lips; vision problems; vomiting

Other side effects not listed above may also occur in some patients. If you notice any other effects, check with your doctor, nurse, or pharmacist.

***This leaflet has been developed by the USP based primarily on labeling provided by the manufacturer at the time of its approval. This information is intended for use as a temporary educational aid until the drug has been assessed by USP advisory panels. The information does not cover all possible uses, actions, precautions, side effects, or interactions of this medicine. It is not intended as medical advice for individual problems.**

USP DI® Patient Education Leaflets™—Introductory Version*

Porfimer (Injection)

A commonly used brand name is *Photofrin*.

ABOUT YOUR MEDICINE

Porfimer (POR-fi-mer) is used to treat cancer of the esophagus.

If any of the information in this leaflet causes you special concern or if you want additional information about your medicine and its use, check with your doctor, nurse, or pharmacist.

BEFORE RECEIVING THIS MEDICINE

Tell your doctor, nurse, and pharmacist if you . . .

- are allergic to any medicine, either prescription or nonprescription (OTC);
- are pregnant or intend to become pregnant while using this medicine;
- are breast-feeding;
- are using any other prescription or nonprescription (OTC) medicine;
- have any other medical problems, especially porphyria or tumors in the lung or throat.

PROPER USE

Treatment with porfimer occurs in three steps. First, the medicine is injected into your body. Over the next two days, the medicine leaves most of the healthy tissue, but stays in the cancer cells. Then, a laser light is directed at the site of the cancer that triggers the medicine to destroy the cancer cells. About two days after the light is applied, your doctor will surgically remove the parts of the cancer that have been destroyed.

PRECAUTIONS

It is very important that your doctor check your progress at regular visits to make sure this medicine is working properly and to check for unwanted effects.

While you are being treated with porfimer, and for at least 30 days after you stop treatment with it, your skin will be sensitive to sunlight and to bright indoor lights, such as dental lights, operating room lights, and unshaded light bulbs. You should avoid exposing your skin to direct sunlight and bright indoor lights during this time. Ultraviolet sunscreens will not protect your skin from sunlight or bright indoor lights.

Before exposing yourself to sunlight or bright indoor lights, you should test how a small portion of your skin reacts to sunlight for 10 minutes. Wait 24 hours, and if the exposed part of your skin is not blistered, red, or swollen, you can slowly increase your exposure to sunlight and bright indoor lights. If a reaction does occur, wait another 2 weeks, then test your sensitivity to sunlight again.

During treatment with this medicine, and for at least 30 days after you stop treatment with it, your eyes may be sensitive to sunlight, bright indoor lights, or car headlights. Only certain sunglasses can protect your eyes during this time. Check with your doctor about which sunglasses you should use.

POSSIBLE SIDE EFFECTS

Side Effects That Should Be Reported To Your Doctor Immediately

More common—Chest pain; difficulty in swallowing; fast or irregular heartbeat; shortness of breath or troubled breathing

Less common—Abdominal or stomach pain (severe); nausea or vomiting (severe); swelling of neck

Other Side Effects That Should Be Reported To Your Doctor

More common—Blood in stools; bloody vomit; cloudy or bloody urine; cough; difficult, burning, or painful urination; fever; frequent urge to urinate; swelling of the face, feet, or lower legs; unusual tiredness or weakness; unusual weight gain; wheezing; white patches on tongue or in mouth

Less common—Yellow eyes or skin

Side Effects That Usually Do Not Require Medical Attention

These possible side effects may go away during treatment; however, if they continue or are bothersome, check with your doctor, nurse, or pharmacist.

More common—Blistering, redness, or swelling of skin; constipation; trouble in sleeping

Less common—Double vision; increased sensitivity of eyes to light; weakness

Other side effects not listed above may also occur in some patients. If you notice any other effects, check with your doctor, nurse, or pharmacist.

After you stop using this medicine, your body may need time to adjust. Check with your doctor if you notice that your skin is blistered, red, or swollen; or if your eyes are more sensitive to the sun, bright lights, or car headlights.

***This leaflet has been developed by the USP based primarily on labeling provided by the manufacturer at the time of its approval. This information is intended for use as a temporary educational aid until the drug has been assessed by USP advisory panels. The information does not cover all possible uses, actions, precautions, side effects, or interactions of this medicine. It is not intended as medical advice for individual problems.**

Porfimer (Injection) 915870

USP DI® Patient Education Leaflets™—Introductory Version*

Pramipexole (Oral)

A commonly used brand name is *Mirapex*.

ABOUT YOUR MEDICINE

Pramipexole (pra-mi-PEX-ole) is used to treat Parkinson's disease. It may be used alone, or in combination with levodopa or other medicines to treat this disease.

If any of the information in this leaflet causes you special concern or if you want additional information about your medicine and its use, check with your doctor, nurse, or pharmacist. **Remember, keep this and all other medicines out of the reach of children and never share your medicines with others.**

BEFORE USING

Tell your doctor, nurse, and pharmacist if you . . .

- are allergic to any medicine, either prescription or nonprescription (OTC);
- are pregnant or intend to become pregnant while using this medicine;
- are breast-feeding;
- are using any other prescription or nonprescription (OTC) medicine, especially cimetidine, diltiazem, haloperidol, metoclopramide, phenothiazines, quinidine, quinine, ranitidine, thioxanthenes, triamterene, or verapamil;
- have any other medical problems, especially kidney disease.

PROPER USE

Take this medicine only as directed by your doctor, to benefit your condition as much as possible. Do not take more or less of it, and do not take it more or less often than your doctor ordered.

Pramipexole may be taken with food to lessen stomach upset.

If you miss a dose of this medicine, take it as soon as possible. However, if it is almost time for your next dose, skip the missed dose and go back to your regular dosing schedule. Do not double doses.

PRECAUTIONS

It is important that your doctor check your progress at regular visits, especially for the first few months you take pramipexole. Your doctor will need to adjust your dosage gradually to find the best level of medicine for your condition.

This medicine may add to the effects of alcohol and other CNS depressants (medicines that may make you drowsy or less alert). **Check with your doctor before taking any CNS depressants while you are taking this medicine.**

This medicine may cause some people to become drowsy. **Make sure you know how you react to this medicine before you drive, use machines, or do other jobs that could be dangerous if you are dizzy, drowsy, or not alert.**

Dizziness, lightheadedness, or fainting may occur, especially when you get up from a lying or sitting position. Getting up slowly may help. If the problem continues or gets worse, check with your doctor.

Pramipexole may cause dryness of the mouth. For temporary relief, use sugarless gum or candy, melt bits of ice in your mouth, or use a saliva substitute. However, if your mouth continues to feel dry for more than 2 weeks, check with your medical doctor or dentist. Continuing dryness of the mouth may increase the chance of dental disease, including tooth decay, gum disease, and fungus infections.

Do not stop taking pramipexole without first checking with your doctor. To do so may increase the chance of serious side effects. Your doctor may want you to reduce gradually the amount you are using before stopping completely.

POSSIBLE SIDE EFFECTS

Side Effects That Should Be Reported To Your Doctor

More common—Dizziness, lightheadedness, or fainting, especially when standing up; drowsiness; hallucinations (more common in older adults); nausea; trouble in sleeping

Less common—Confusion; changes in vision; dizziness (continuing); frequent urination; memory problems; mood or mental changes; muscle or joint pain; unusual tiredness or weakness

Side Effects That Usually Do Not Require Medical Attention

These possible side effects may go away during treatment; however, if they continue or are bothersome, check with your doctor, nurse, or pharmacist.

More common—Constipation; dry mouth

Less common—Decreased sexual drive or ability; increased sweating; loss of appetite; trouble in swallowing; weight loss

Other side effects not listed above may also occur in some patients. If you notice any other effects, check with your doctor, nurse, or pharmacist.

***This leaflet has been developed by the USP based primarily on labeling provided by the manufacturer at the time of its approval. This information is intended for use as a temporary educational aid until the drug has been assessed by USP advisory panels. The information does not cover all possible uses, actions, precautions, side effects, or interactions of this medicine. It is not intended as medical advice for individual problems.**

USP DI® Patient Education Leaflets™—Introductory Version*

Protease Inhibitors (Oral)

Including Indinavir□; Ritonavir□; Saquinavir□.
Some commonly used brand names are *Crixivan, Norvir, and Invirase.*

ABOUT YOUR MEDICINE

Indinavir (in-DIN-a-veer), **ritonavir** (ri-TOE-na-veer), and **saquinavir** (sa-KWIN-a-veer) are protease inhibitors. They are used alone or in combination with other medicines to treat patients who are infected with the human immunodeficiency virus (HIV).

HIV is the virus that causes acquired immune deficiency syndrome (AIDS). This medicine appears to slow down the destruction of the immune system caused by HIV. This may help slow down the progress of HIV disease and the serious infections that occur with AIDS. However, this medicine will not cure or prevent HIV infection, and it will not keep you from spreading the virus to other people. Patients who are taking this medicine may continue to have the problems usually related to AIDS or HIV disease.

If any of the information in this leaflet causes you special concern or if you want additional information about your medicine and its use, check with your doctor, nurse, or pharmacist. **Remember, keep this and all other medicines out of the reach of children and never share your medicines with others.**

BEFORE USING

Discuss with your doctor the possible side effects that may be caused by this medicine. Some of them may be serious.

Tell your doctor, nurse, and pharmacist if you . . .

- are allergic to any medicine, either prescription or nonprescription (OTC);
- are pregnant or intend to become pregnant while using this medicine;
- are breast-feeding;
- are taking **any** other prescription or nonprescription (OTC) medicine;
- have any other medical problems, especially liver disease.

PROPER USE

Take this medicine exactly as directed by your doctor. Do not take more of it, do not take it more often, and do not take it for a longer time than directed. Also, do not stop taking this medicine without first checking with your doctor.

Keep taking this medicine for the full time of treatment, even if you begin to feel better after a few days.

Make sure you carefully read and follow the instructions that come with each product. For best results . . .

- **Indinavir** should be taken with water 1 hour before or 2 hours after a meal. However, it may be taken with other liquids (such as skim milk, juice, coffee, or tea) or with a light meal. Drink plenty of water or other liquids every day, unless otherwise directed by your doctor. Drinking extra water will help to prevent some unwanted effects this medicine has on the kidneys.
- **Ritonavir** should be taken with food. To improve the taste, the oral solution form may be mixed with chocolate milk or a liquid nutritional supplement. Use a specially marked measuring spoon or other device to measure each dose accurately since the average household teaspoon may not hold the right amount of liquid. Be sure to drink it within 1 hour of mixing.
- **Saquinavir** should be taken within 2 hours after a full meal.

This medicine works best when there is a constant amount in the blood. **To help keep the amount constant, do not miss any doses.** If you need help in planning the best times to take your medicine, check with your doctor, nurse, or pharmacist.

If you do miss a dose of this medicine, take it as soon as possible. However if it is almost time for your next dose, skip the missed dose and go back to your regular dosing schedule. **Do not double doses.**

Indinavir capsules are sensitive to moisture. Ritonavir capsules should be refrigerated and protected from light. Carefully follow any directions for storage that are on the bottle.

PRECAUTIONS

It is very important that your doctor check your progress at regular visits.

Do not take any other medicines without first checking with your doctor. To do so may increase the chance of serious side effects.

For patients taking ritonavir:

- **Oral contraceptives (birth control pills) containing estrogen may not work properly if you take them while you are taking this medicine.** Unplanned pregnancies may occur. **Use different or additional birth control while taking this medicine.**
- Use of tobacco products may make this medicine less effective.

POSSIBLE SIDE EFFECTS

Side Effects That Should Be Reported To Your Doctor Immediately

Less common—Back pain (severe--indinavir); numbness, burning, or tingling in hands or feet (ritonavir and saquinavir); rash (indinavir); tingling sensation around mouth (ritonavir)

Rare—Yellow eyes or skin (indinavir)

Side Effects That Usually Do Not Require Medical Attention

These possible side effects may go away during treatment; however, if they continue or are bothersome, check with your doctor, nurse, or pharmacist.

More common—Abdominal or stomach pain; change in taste; diarrhea; dizziness (indinavir); dry mouth (indinavir); headache; loss of appetite; nausea; tiredness or weakness; trouble in sleeping (indinavir); vomiting

Other side effects not listed above may also occur in some patients. If you notice any other effects, check with your doctor, nurse, or pharmacist.

***This leaflet has been developed by the USP based primarily on labeling provided by the manufacturer at the time of its approval. This information is intended for use as a temporary educational aid until the drug has been assessed by USP advisory panels. The information does not cover all possible uses, actions, precautions, side effects, or interactions of this medicine. It is not intended as medical advice for individual problems.**

Protease Inhibitors (Oral) 911981

USP DI® Patient Education Leaflets™—Introductory Version*

Ranitidine Bismuth Citrate (Oral)

A commonly used brand name is *Tritec.*

ABOUT YOUR MEDICINE

Ranitidine bismuth citrate (ra-NIT-ti-deen BIS-muth SI-trate) is used to treat active duodenal ulcers associated with infection caused by the *H. pylori* organism. It is used in combination with an antibiotic called clarithromycin. This medicine should not be taken alone for the treatment of ulcers.

If any of the information in this leaflet causes you special concern or if you want additional information about your medicine and its use, check with your doctor, nurse, or pharmacist. **Remember, keep this and all other medicines out of the reach of children and never share your medicines with others.**

BEFORE USING

Tell your doctor, nurse, and pharmacist if you . . .

- are allergic to any medicine, either prescription or nonprescription (OTC);
- are pregnant or intend to become pregnant while using this medicine;
- are breast-feeding;
- are taking **any** other prescription or nonprescription (OTC) medicine;
- have any other medical problems, especially acute porphyria or kidney disease.

PROPER USE

Take this medicine for the full time of treatment, even if you begin to feel better. It is important to see your doctor regularly to determine if the combination of ranitidine bismuth citrate and clarithromycin is working properly to cure the infection causing your ulcer.

This medicine may be taken with or without food.

If you miss a dose of this medicine, take it as soon as possible. However, if it is almost time for your next dose, skip the missed dose and go back to your regular dosing schedule. Do not double doses.

PRECAUTIONS

The results of dipstick tests for protein in the urine may be affected by this medicine. While you are taking ranitidine bismuth citrate, testing with sulfosalicylic acid is recommended.

POSSIBLE SIDE EFFECTS

Side Effects That Should Be Reported To Your Doctor Immediately

Rare—Allergic reaction (fast or irregular breathing, puffiness or swelling around face, shortness of breath, skin rash)

Side Effects That Should Be Reported to Your Doctor

More common—Diarrhea; headache

Less common—Dizziness; itching; nausea; trouble in sleeping; vomiting

Rare—Constipation; stomach pain

Side Effects That Usually Do Not Require Medical Attention

These possible side effects may go away during treatment; however, if they continue or are bothersome, check with your doctor, nurse, or pharmacist.

More common—Change in sense of taste

Less common—Darkening of the tongue or stools

Other side effects not listed above may also occur in some patients. If you notice any other effects, check with your doctor, nurse, or pharmacist.

***This leaflet has been developed by the USP based primarily on labeling provided by the manufacturer at the time of its approval. This information is intended for use as a temporary educational aid until the drug has been assessed by USP advisory panels. The information does not cover all possible uses, actions, precautions, side effects, or interactions of this medicine. It is not intended as medical advice for individual problems.**

Ranitidine Bismuth Citrate (Oral) 913579

USP DI® Patient Education Leaflets™—Introductory Version*

Rimexolone (Ophthalmic)

A commonly used brand name is *Vexol.*

ABOUT YOUR MEDICINE

Rimexolone (ri-MEKS-oh-lone) is an ophthalmic corticosteroid (kor-ti-koh-STER-oid) (cortisone-like medicine). It is used to treat a certain eye condition known as anterior uveitis. It is also used after eye surgery to reduce inflammation (redness and swelling).

If any of the information in this leaflet causes you special concern or if you want additional information about your medicine and its use, check with your doctor, nurse, or pharmacist. **Remember, keep this and all other medicines out of the reach of children and never share your medicines with others.**

BEFORE USING

Tell your doctor, nurse, and pharmacist if you . . .

- are allergic to any medicine, either prescription or nonprescription (OTC);
- are pregnant or intend to become pregnant while using this medicine;
- are breast-feeding;
- are taking any other prescription or nonprescription (OTC) medicine;
- have any other medical problems, especially cataracts, glaucoma, herpes infection of the eye, tuberculosis of the eye (active or history of), or any other eye infection.

PROPER USE

For patients who wear contact lenses:

- Do not apply this medicine while you are wearing contact lenses, because it may increase the chance of getting an eye infection. Also, ask your eye doctor how long to wait after applying this medicine before inserting your contact lenses. You may be told not to wear contact lenses at all during treatment and for a day or two after treatment has ended.
- Always shake the container very well just before applying the eye drops.

To use:

- First, wash your hands. Tilt the head back and, pressing your finger gently on the skin just beneath the lower eyelid, pull the lower eyelid away from the eye to make a space. Drop the medicine into this space. Let go of the eyelid and gently close the eyes. Do not blink. Keep the eyes closed and apply pressure to the inner corner of the eye with your finger for 1 or 2 minutes to allow the medicine to come into contact with the irritation. If you think you did not get the drop of medicine into your eye properly, use another drop.
- After using the medicine, wash your hands to remove any medicine that may be on them.
- To keep the medicine as germ-free as possible, do not touch the applicator tip to any surface (including the eye), and keep the container tightly closed.

Do not use this medicine more often or for a longer time than your doctor ordered. To do so may increase the chance of side effects, especially in children 2 years of age or younger.

Do not use any leftover medicine for future eye problems without first checking with your doctor. This medicine should not be used if certain kinds of infections are present.

If you miss a dose of this medicine, apply it as soon as possible. However, if it is almost time for your next dose, skip the missed dose.

PRECAUTIONS

An eye doctor should check your eyes at regular visits while you are using this medicine to make sure it does not cause unwanted effects. Also, if your eye condition does not improve, or if it gets worse, check with your doctor.

POSSIBLE SIDE EFFECTS

Side Effects That Should Be Reported To Your Doctor

Less common or rare—Blurred vision or other change in vision; change in taste; discharge, crusting, or sticky feeling of the eye; discoloration of the eye; dryness of the eye; eye pain or discomfort; feeling of something in the eye; headache or browache; increased sensitivity of eyes to light; runny or stuffy nose; sore throat; tearing, redness, itching, swelling, or other sign of irritation of the eye; unusual tiredness or weakness

Other side effects not listed above may also occur in some patients. If you notice any other effects, check with your doctor, nurse, or pharmacist.

***This leaflet has been developed by the USP based primarily on labeling provided by the manufacturer at the time of its approval. This information is intended for use as a temporary educational aid until the drug has been assessed by USP advisory panels. The information does not cover all possible uses, actions, precautions, side effects, or interactions of this medicine. It is not intended as medical advice for individual problems.**

Rimexolone (Ophthalmic) 910832

USP DI® Patient Education Leaflets™—Introductory Version*

Sparfloxacin (Oral)

A commonly used brand name is *Zagam*.

ABOUT YOUR MEDICINE

Sparfloxacin (spar-FLOX-a-sin) is used in adults to treat bacterial infections that make bronchitis worse and cause pneumonia. It will not work for colds, flu, or other virus infections.

This medicine should not be used by children.

If any of the information in this leaflet causes you special concern or if you want additional information about your medicine and its use, check with your doctor, nurse, or pharmacist. **Remember, keep this and all other medicines out of the reach of children and never share your medicines with others.**

BEFORE USING

Discuss with your doctor the possible side effects of this medicine. Some of them may be serious.

Tell your doctor, nurse, and pharmacist if you . . .

- are allergic to any medicine, either prescription or nonprescription (OTC);
- are pregnant or intend to become pregnant while using this medicine;
- are breast-feeding;
- are using **any** other prescription or nonprescription (OTC) medicine;
- have any other medical problems, especially heart or kidney disease, or sensitivity to light.

PROPER USE

Sparfloxacin may be taken with food, milk, or caffeine-containing products. If you are taking antacids or multivitamins while you are taking this medicine, take them at least 2 hours after you take sparfloxacin.

To help clear up your infection completely, **keep taking this medicine for the full time of treatment,** even if you begin to feel better after a few days.

This medicine works best when there is a constant amount in the blood. **To help keep the amount constant, do not miss any doses.** If you need help in planning the best times to take your medicine, check with your doctor, nurse, or pharmacist.

If you do miss a dose of this medicine, take it as soon as possible. However, if it is almost time for your next dose, skip the missed dose and go back to your regular dosing schedule. **Do not double doses.**

PRECAUTIONS

If your symptoms of infection do not improve within a few days, or if they become worse, check with your doctor.

If diarrhea occurs, do not take any diarrhea medicine without first checking with your doctor or pharmacist. Diarrhea medicines may make your diarrhea worse or last longer.

During treatment with this medicine and for 5 days after treatment has stopped, avoid too much sun, direct or indirect (such as through window glass or on a cloudy day).

This medicine must not be given to other people or used for other infections or problems unless you are otherwise directed by your doctor.

POSSIBLE SIDE EFFECTS

Side Effects That Should Be Reported To Your Doctor Immediately

More common—Blisters on skin; burning or itching of skin; skin rash or redness; sunburn (severe)

Rare—Abdominal or stomach cramps and pain (severe); abdominal tenderness; confusion; diarrhea (watery and severe), which may also be bloody; feeling restless; fever; hallucinations; pain, swelling, or tenderness in legs, shoulders, or hands; trembling or shaking

Other Side Effects That Should Be Reported To Your Doctor

These possible side effects may go away during treatment; however, if they continue or are bothersome, check with your doctor, nurse, or pharmacist.

Less common—Abdominal or stomach pain or discomfort (mild); changes in taste; diarrhea (mild); dizziness; drowsiness; headache; lightheadedness; nausea or vomiting; nervousness; vaginal itching and discharge

Note: Severe abdominal stomach cramps and pain, and watery and severe diarrhea, which may also be bloody, may also occur up to several weeks after you stop using this medicine.

Other side effects not listed above may also occur in some patients. If you notice any other effects, check with your doctor, nurse, or pharmacist.

***This leaflet has been developed by the USP based primarily on labeling provided by the manufacturer at the time of its approval. This information is intended for use as a temporary educational aid until the drug has been assessed by USP advisory panels. The information does not cover all possible uses, actions, precautions, side effects, or interactions of this medicine. It is not intended as medical advice for individual problems.**

USP DI® Patient Education Leaflets™—Introductory Version*

Teniposide (Injection)

A commonly used brand name is *Vumon*.

ABOUT YOUR MEDICINE

Teniposide (ten-i-POE-side) belongs to the group of medicines called antineoplastics. Teniposide injection is used along with other medicines to treat acute lymphoblastic leukemia (ALL).

If any of the information in this leaflet causes you special concern or if you want additional information about your medicine and its use, check with your doctor, nurse, or pharmacist.

BEFORE USING

Discuss with your doctor the possible side effects that may be caused by this medicine. Some of them may be serious and/or long-term.

Tell your doctor, nurse, and pharmacist if you . . .

- are allergic to any medicine, either prescription or nonprescription (OTC);
- are pregnant or intend to have children;
- are breast-feeding;
- are taking any other prescription or nonprescription (OTC) medicine, especially salicylates, sulfamethizole, or tolbutamide;
- have any other medical problems, especially chickenpox (including recent exposure), herpes zoster (shingles), or infection;
- have ever been treated with x-rays or cancer medicines.

PROPER USE

Teniposide often causes nausea and vomiting, which usually are not severe. However, it is very important that you continue to receive the medicine, even if you begin to feel ill. Ask your doctor, nurse, or pharmacist for ways to lessen these effects.

PRECAUTIONS

It is very important that your doctor check your progress at regular visits to make sure that teniposide is working properly and to check for unwanted effects.

While you are being treated with teniposide, and after you stop treatment, **do not have any immunizations (vaccinations) without your doctor's approval.**

Teniposide can temporarily lower the number of white blood cells in your blood, increasing the chance of getting an infection. It can also lower the number of platelets, which are necessary for proper blood clotting. If this occurs:

- Avoid people with infections.
- Be careful when using a regular toothbrush, dental floss, or toothpick.
- Do not touch your eyes or the inside of your nose unless you have just washed your hands and have not touched anything else in the meantime.
- Be careful not to cut, bruise, or injure yourself.

POSSIBLE SIDE EFFECTS

Side Effects That Should Be Reported To Your Doctor Immediately

Less common—Black, tarry stools; blood in urine or stools; cough or hoarseness; fever or chills; flushing of face; sudden hives or itching of skin; lower back or side pain; painful or difficult urination; pinpoint red spots on skin; shortness of breath; unusual bleeding or bruising; unusually fast heartbeat

Rare—Pain or redness at place of injection

Other Side Effects That Should Be Reported To Your Doctor

More common—Sores in mouth or on lips

Side Effects That Usually Do Not Require Medical Attention

These possible side effects may go away during treatment; however, if they continue or are bothersome, check with your doctor, nurse, or pharmacist.

More common—Diarrhea; nausea and vomiting

Less common—Skin rash

This medicine often causes a temporary loss of hair. After treatment with teniposide has ended, normal hair growth should return.

Other side effects not listed above may also occur in some patients. If you notice any other effects, check with your doctor, nurse, or pharmacist.

***This leaflet has been developed by the USP based primarily on labeling provided by the manufacturer at the time of its approval. This information is intended for use as a temporary educational aid until the drug has been assessed by USP advisory panels. The information does not cover all possible uses, actions, precautions, side effects, or interactions of this medicine. It is not intended as medical advice for individual problems.**

Teniposide (Injection) 919338

USP DI® Patient Education Leaflets™—Introductory Version*

Tiludronate (Oral)

A commonly used brand name is *Skelid*.

ABOUT YOUR MEDICINE

Tiludronate (tye-LOO-droh-nate) is used to treat Paget's disease of the bone.

If any of the information in this leaflet causes you special concern or if you want additional information about your medicine and its use, check with your doctor, nurse, or pharmacist. **Remember, keep this and all other medicines out of the reach of children and never share your medicines with others.**

BEFORE USING

Tell your doctor, nurse, and pharmacist if you . . .

- are allergic to any medicine, either prescription or nonprescription (OTC);
- are pregnant or intend to become pregnant while using this medicine;
- are breast-feeding;
- are taking **any** other prescription or nonprescription (OTC) medicine, especially antacids or other medicines containing aluminum or magnesium, aspirin or other salicylates or salicylate-containing medicines, or dietary supplements (including calcium);
- have any other medical problems, especially kidney disease, or problems with digestion or other intestinal problems.

PROPER USE

Take tiludronate with a full glass (6 to 8 ounces) of plain water on an empty stomach.

It is important that you eat a well-balanced diet with an adequate amount of calcium and vitamin D (found in milk or other dairy products). However, do not take any beverages (including mineral water), dietary supplements, food, or other medicines at least 2 hours before or after taking tiludronate. To do so may keep this medicine from working properly.

If you miss a dose of this medicine, take it as soon as possible. However, if it is almost time for your next dose, skip the missed dose and go back to your regular dosing schedule. Do not double doses.

POSSIBLE SIDE EFFECTS

Side Effects That Should Be Reported To Your Doctor

More common—Chest pain; chills; cough; ear congestion or pain; hoarseness or voice changes; nasal congestion; runny nose; sneezing; sore throat

Less common—Increased blood pressure; swelling of face, feet, or lower legs; unusual weight gain

Side Effects That Usually Do Not Require Medical Attention

These possible side effects may go away during treatment; however, if they continue or are bothersome, check with your doctor, nurse, or pharmacist.

More common—Back pain; diarrhea; general feeling of body discomfort; headache; nausea; stomach upset

Less common—Joint pain; dizziness; dryness or pain in throat; gas; red or irritated eyes; skin rash; vomiting

Other side effects not listed above may also occur in some patients. If you notice any other effects, check with your doctor, nurse, or pharmacist.

***This leaflet has been developed by the USP based primarily on labeling provided by the manufacturer at the time of its approval. This information is intended for use as a temporary educational aid until the drug has been assessed by USP advisory panels. The information does not cover all possible uses, actions, precautions, side effects, or interactions of this medicine. It is not intended as medical advice for individual problems.**

Tiludronate (Oral) 914516

USP DI® Patient Education Leaflets™—Introductory Version*

Topiramate (Oral)

A commonly used brand name is *Topamax*.

ABOUT YOUR MEDICINE

Topiramate (toe-PYRE-a-mate) is used to help control some types of seizures in the treatment of epilepsy. This medicine cannot cure epilepsy and will only work to help control seizures for as long as you continue to take it.

If any of the information in this leaflet causes you special concern or if you want additional information about your medicine and its use, check with your doctor, nurse, or pharmacist. **Remember, keep this and all other medicines out of the reach of children and never share your medicines with others.**

BEFORE USING

Tell your doctor, nurse, and pharmacist if you . . .

- are allergic to any medicine, either prescription or nonprescription (OTC);
- are pregnant or intend to become pregnant while using this medicine;
- are breast-feeding;
- are taking any other prescription or nonprescription (OTC) medicine, especially CNS depressants, digoxin, or contraceptives, certain oral medicines for glaucoma, or other anticonvulsants;
- have any other medical problems, especially kidney disease, kidney stones (history of), liver disease, or if you are receiving hemodialysis.

PROPER USE

Take this medicine as directed by your doctor in order to improve your condition as much as possible. Do not take more or less of it, and do not take it more or less often than your doctor ordered.

Topiramate may be taken with or without food, on a full or an empty stomach. Swallow the tablets whole, without breaking, crushing, or chewing them. The bitter taste may be more noticeable if the tablets are held in the mouth or chewed.

If you miss a dose of this medicine, take it as soon as possible. However, if it is almost time for your next dose, skip the missed dose and go back to your regular dosing schedule. Do not double doses.

PRECAUTIONS

It is important that your doctor check your progress at regular visits, especially for the first few months you take topiramate. This is necessary to allow dose adjustments and to reduce any unwanted effects.

Topiramate will add to the effects of alcohol and other CNS depressants (medicines that slow down the nervous system, possibly causing drowsiness). **Check with your doctor before taking any CNS depressants while you are taking this medicine.**

This medicine may cause blurred vision, double vision, clumsiness, unsteadiness, dizziness, drowsiness, or trouble in thinking. **Make sure you know how you react to this medicine before you drive, use machines, or do other jobs that require you to be alert, well-coordinated, or able to think or see well.**

Oral contraceptives (birth control pills) containing estrogen may not work properly if you take them while you are taking this medicine. Unplanned pregnancies may occur. You should use a different or additional means of birth control while you are using topiramate. If you have any questions about this, check with your doctor or pharmacist.

Do not stop using this medicine without first checking with your doctor. Stopping the medicine suddenly may cause your seizures to return or occur more often. Your doctor may want you to reduce gradually the amount you are using before stopping completely.

POSSIBLE SIDE EFFECTS

Side Effects That Should Be Reported To Your Doctor Immediately

More common—Clumsiness or unsteadiness; confusion; continuous, uncontrolled back-and-forth or rolling eye movements; dizziness; double vision or other vision problems; loss of balance; memory problems; menstrual changes; menstrual pain; mental depression or other mood or mental changes; speech and language problems; trouble in concentrating; unusual anxiety, nervousness, or irritability

Less common—Fever, chills, or sore throat; skin rash or itching

Rare—Blood in urine; eye pain; nosebleeds; redness and swelling of the gums; swelling; trouble in hearing

Side Effects That Usually Do Not Require Medical Attention

These possible side effects may go away during treatment; however, if they continue or are bothersome, check with your doctor, nurse, or pharmacist.

More common—Abdominal pain; back or chest pain; breast pain; burning, prickling, or tingling sensations; constipation; drowsiness; indigestion; loss of appetite; nausea; tremors; unusual tiredness or weakness; weight loss

Less common—Body odor; dry mouth; hot flashes; increased sweating; leg pain; muscle aches or pain

Other side effects not listed above may also occur in some patients. If you notice any other effects, check with your doctor, nurse, or pharmacist.

***This leaflet has been developed by the USP based primarily on labeling provided by the manufacturer at the time of its approval. This information is intended for use as a temporary educational aid until the drug has been assessed by USP advisory panels. The information does not cover all possible uses, actions, precautions, side effects, or interactions of this medicine. It is not intended as medical advice for individual problems.**

Topiramate (Oral) 913580

USP DI® Patient Education Leaflets™—Introductory Version*

Topotecan (Injection)

A commonly used brand name is *Hycamtin*.

ABOUT YOUR MEDICINE

Topotecan (toe-poe-TEE-kan) belongs to the group of medicines called antineoplastics. It is used to treat cancer of the ovaries.

If any of the information in this leaflet causes you special concern or if you want additional information about your medicine and its use, check with your doctor, nurse, or pharmacist.

BEFORE USING

Discuss with your doctor the possible side effects of this medicine. Some of them may be serious or long-term.

Tell your doctor, nurse, and pharmacist if you . . .

- are allergic to any medicine, either prescription or nonprescription (OTC);
- are pregnant or intend to become pregnant while using this medicine;
- are breast-feeding;
- are using any other prescription or nonprescription (OTC) medicine, especially cisplatin or filgrastim;
- have any other medical problems, especially kidney disease.

PROPER USE

This medicine often causes nausea and vomiting. However, it is very important that you continue to receive the medicine, even if you have discomfort or begin to feel ill. Ask your doctor, nurse, or pharmacist for other ways to lessen these effects.

PRECAUTIONS

It is very important that your doctor check your progress at regular visits to make sure this medicine is working properly and to check for unwanted effects.

POSSIBLE SIDE EFFECTS

Side Effects That Should Be Reported To Your Doctor Immediately

More common—Troubled breathing

Other Side Effects That Should Be Reported To Your Doctor

More common—Black, tarry stools; blood in urine or stools; cough or hoarseness; difficult or painful urination; fever or chills; lower back or side pain; pinpoint red spots on skin; sores in mouth or on lips; unusual bleeding or bruising; unusual tiredness or weakness

Side Effects That Usually Do Not Require Medical Attention

These possible side effects may go away during treatment; however, if they continue or are bothersome, check with your doctor, nurse, or pharmacist.

More common—Abdominal pain; constipation; diarrhea; headache; loss of appetite; nausea or vomiting; numbness, burning, or tingling in hands or feet; weakness in arms or legs

This medicine may cause a temporary loss of hair. After treatment, normal growth should return.

Other side effects not listed above may also occur in some patients. If you notice any other effects, check with your doctor, nurse, or pharmacist.

***This leaflet has been developed by the USP based primarily on labeling provided by the manufacturer at the time of its approval. This information is intended for use as a temporary educational aid until the drug has been assessed by USP advisory panels. The information does not cover all possible uses, actions, precautions, side effects, or interactions of this medicine. It is not intended as medical advice for individual problems.**

Topotecan (Injection) 915858

USP DI® Patient Education Leaflets™—Introductory Version*

Tretinoin (Oral)

A commonly used brand name is *Vesanoid*.

ABOUT YOUR MEDICINE

Tretinoin (TRET-i-noyn) is used to treat a form of leukemia.

If any of the information in this leaflet causes you special concern or if you want additional information about your medicine and its use, check with your doctor, nurse, or pharmacist. **Remember, keep this and all other medicines out of the reach of children and never share your medicines with others.**

BEFORE USING

Discuss with your doctor the possible side effects that may be caused by this medicine. Some of them may be serious or long-term.

Tretinoin can cause serious birth defects and other problems in babies born to mothers who take the medicine during pregnancy. Women who are able to become pregnant must use effective birth control during treatment with this medicine, and for a month after treatment is finished. However, no one form of birth control is 100% effective. Therefore, **two different types of birth control must be used at the same time.** Be sure that you have discussed with your doctor the problems that may occur if you become pregnant while taking this medicine, as well as the best kinds of birth control to use.

Because tretinoin might cause serious side effects in nursing babies, **mothers must stop breast-feeding before starting treatment.**

Tell your doctor, nurse, and pharmacist if you . . .

- are allergic to any medicine, either prescription or nonprescription (OTC);
- **are pregnant or may become pregnant while using this medicine;**
- **are breast-feeding;**
- are taking **any** other prescription or nonprescription (OTC) medicine, especially cimetidine, cyclosporine, diltiazem, erythromycin, glucocorticoids (cortisone-like medicines), ketoconazole, pentobarbital, phenobarbital, or rifampin;
- have **any** other medical problems.

PROPER USE

Take this medicine only as directed by your doctor. Do not take more or less of it and do not take it more often than your doctor ordered.

If you miss a dose of this medicine, take it as soon as possible. However, if you do not remember the missed dose until it is almost time for your next dose, check with your doctor.

PRECAUTIONS

It is very important that your doctor check your progress at regular visits to make sure this medicine is working properly and check for unwanted effects.

Fever, headache, tiredness, and weakness may occur during treatment. **It is very important that you continue taking the medicine, even if it makes you feel ill.** However, **check with your doctor right away, if you get a fever or a severe headache,** because these effects sometimes mean that a more serious side effect is occurring. Also, **check with your doctor right away if bone pain, breathing problems, discomfort or pain in chest, nausea and vomiting, vision problems, or weight gain occurs during treatment.**

POSSIBLE SIDE EFFECTS

Side Effects That Should Be Reported To Your Doctor Immediately

More common—Bone pain; discomfort or pain in chest; fever; shortness of breath, troubled breathing, tightness in chest, or wheezing; weight gain

Less common—Convulsions (seizures); difficulty in speaking, slow speech, or inability to speak; feeling of heaviness in chest; inability to move arms, legs, or muscles of face; pain in back or left arm

Other Side Effects That Should Be Reported To Your Doctor

More common—Cracked lips; coughing, sneezing, sore throat, or stuffy or runny nose; crusting, redness, pain, or sores in mouth or nose; decreased urination; earache or feeling of fullness in ear; irregular heartbeat; mental depression; skin rash; swelling of abdomen, face, fingers, hands, feet, or lower legs

Less common—Cramping or pain in stomach (severe); difficult or painful urination; drowsiness (severe and continuing); hallucinations; hearing loss; heartburn, indigestion, or nausea (severe and continuing); mood, mental, or personality changes; pain in lower back or side; swollen area that feels warm and tender; yellow eyes or skin

Side Effects That Usually Do Not Require Medical Attention

These possible side effects may go away during treatment; however, if they continue or are bothersome, check with your doctor, nurse, or pharmacist.

More common—Anxiety; confusion; constipation; diarrhea; dizziness; dryness of skin, mouth, or nose; feeling of burning, crawling, or tingling in skin; flushing; general feeling of discomfort or illness; hair loss; indigestion; itching of skin; loss of appetite; muscle pain; shivering; trouble in sleeping; weight loss

Other side effects not listed above may also occur in some patients. If you notice any other effects, check with your doctor, nurse, or pharmacist.

***This leaflet has been developed by the USP based primarily on labeling provided by the manufacturer at the time of its approval. This information is intended for use as a temporary educational aid until the drug has been assessed by USP advisory panels. The information does not cover all possible uses, actions, precautions, side effects, or interactions of this medicine. It is not intended as medical advice for individual problems.**

Tretinoin (Oral) 911915

USP DI® Patient Education Leaflets™—Introductory Version*

Troglitazone (Oral)

A commonly used brand name is *Rezulin*.

ABOUT YOUR MEDICINE

Troglitazone (TROE-glit-a-zone) is used to treat a certain type of diabetes mellitus (sugar diabetes) called non-insulin-dependent diabetes mellitus (NIDDM) or Type II diabetes. It may be used alone, with insulin, or with a type of oral diabetes medicine called sulfonylureas.

If any of the information in this leaflet causes you special concern or if you want additional information about your medicine and its use, check with your doctor, nurse, or pharmacist. **Remember, keep this and all other medicines out of the reach of children and never share your medicines with others.**

BEFORE USING

Tell your doctor, nurse, and pharmacist if you . . .

- are allergic to any medicine, either prescription or nonprescription (OTC);
- are pregnant or intend to become pregnant while using this medicine;
- are breast-feeding;
- are using any other prescription or nonprescription (OTC) medicine, especially cholestyramine, terfenadine, or medicines containing ethinyl estradiol or norethindrone;
- have any other medical problems, especially diabetic ketoacidosis (ketones in the blood), heart disease, or insulin-dependent (Type I) diabetes mellitus.

PROPER USE

Follow carefully the special meal plan your doctor gave you. This is the most important part of controlling your condition, and is necessary if the medicine is to work properly. Also, exercise regularly and test for sugar in your blood or urine as directed.

This medicine should be taken with a meal.

If you miss a dose of this medicine, and you remember it the same day, take it with the next meal. However, if you do not remember it until the next day, skip the missed dose and go back to your regular dosing schedule. Do not double doses.

PRECAUTIONS

Your doctor will want to check your progress at regular visits, especially during the first few weeks you take this medicine.

This medicine does not cause hypoglycemia (low blood sugar). However, low blood sugar can occur when troglitazone is taken with other medicines, such as insulin or sulfonylureas, that can lower blood sugar. Low blood sugar can also occur if you delay or miss a meal or snack, exercise more than usual, drink alcohol, or cannot eat because of nausea or vomiting.

Symptoms of low blood sugar include anxiety; behavior change similar to being drunk; blurred vision; cold sweats; confusion; convulsions (seizures); cool, pale skin; difficulty in thinking; drowsiness; excessive hunger; fast heartbeat; headache (continuing); nausea; nervousness; nightmares; restless sleep; shakiness; slurred speech; unconsciousness; or unusual tiredness or weakness.

If symptoms of low blood sugar occur, **eat glucose tablets or gel, corn syrup, honey, or sugar cubes; or drink fruit juice, non-diet soft drink, or sugar dissolved in water to relieve the symptoms.** Also, check your blood for low blood sugar. **Get to a doctor or a hospital right away if the symptoms do not improve.**

Someone should call for emergency help immediately if severe symptoms such as convulsions (seizures) or unconsciousness occur. Do not force food or drink because one could choke from not swallowing correctly.

Hyperglycemia (high blood sugar) may occur if you skip a dose of your medicine, overeat or do not follow your meal plan, have a fever or infection, or do not exercise as much as usual.

Symptoms of high blood sugar include blurred vision; drowsiness; dry mouth; flushed, dry skin; fruit-like breath odor; increased urination; ketones in urine; loss of appetite; nausea or vomiting; stomach discomfort; tiredness; troubled breathing (rapid and deep); unconsciousness; or unusual thirst.

If symptoms of high blood sugar occur, check your blood sugar level, then call your doctor for instructions.

POSSIBLE SIDE EFFECTS

Side Effects That Should Be Reported To Your Doctor

More common—General feeling of pain, or back pain; infection

Less common—Increased or painful urination; swelling of feet or lower legs

Rare—Yellow eyes or skin

Side Effects That Usually Do Not Require Medical Attention

These possible side effects may go away during treatment; however, if they continue or are bothersome, check with your doctor, nurse, or pharmacist.

More common—Dizziness; headache; unusual tiredness or weakness

Less common—Diarrhea; sore throat; stuffy nose

Other side effects not listed above may also occur in some patients. If you notice any other effects, check with your doctor, nurse, or pharmacist.

***This leaflet has been developed by the USP based primarily on labeling provided by the manufacturer at the time of its approval. This information is intended for use as a temporary educational aid until the drug has been assessed by USP advisory panels. The information does not cover all possible uses, actions, precautions, side effects, or interactions of this medicine. It is not intended as medical advice for individual problems.**

Troglitazone (Oral) 914527

USP DI® Patient Education Leaflets™—Introductory Version*

Vinorelbine (Injection)

A commonly used brand name is *Navelbine*.

ABOUT YOUR MEDICINE

Vinorelbine (vi-NOR-el-been) belongs to the group of medicines known as antineoplastic agents. It is used to treat lung cancer.

If any of the information in this leaflet causes you special concern or if you want additional information about your medicine and its use, check with your doctor, nurse, or pharmacist.

BEFORE USING

Discuss with your doctor the possible side effects that may be caused by this medicine. Some of them may be serious and/or long-term.

Tell your doctor, nurse, and pharmacist if you . . .

- are allergic to any medicine, either prescription or nonprescription (OTC);
- are pregnant or intend to have children;
- are breast-feeding;
- are taking **any** other prescription or nonprescription (OTC) medicine;
- have any other medical problems, especially chicken pox (including recent exposure), herpes zoster (shingles), infection, liver disease, lung disease, or nerve or muscle disease;
- have ever been treated with radiation or cancer medicines.

PROPER USE

While you are using this medicine, it may be necessary to drink extra fluids so that you will pass more urine. This will help prevent kidney problems and keep your kidneys working well.

This medicine sometimes causes nausea and vomiting. However, it is very important that you continue to receive the medicine, even if you begin to feel ill. Ask your doctor, nurse, or pharmacist for ways to lessen these effects.

Vinorelbine often causes constipation. Your doctor may want you to take a laxative; however, do not decide to take laxatives on your own without first checking with your doctor.

PRECAUTIONS

It is very important that your doctor check your progress at regular visits to make sure that vinorelbine is working properly and to check for unwanted effects.

While you are being treated with vinorelbine, and after you stop treatment, **do not have any immunizations (vaccinations) without your doctor's approval.**

POSSIBLE SIDE EFFECTS

Side Effects That Should Be Reported To Your Doctor Immediately

More common—Redness, pain, or swelling at place of injection

Less common—Cough or hoarseness; fever or chills; lower back or side pain; painful or difficult urination

Rare—Black, tarry stools; blood in urine or stools; pinpoint red spots on skin; unusual bleeding or bruising

Other Side Effects That Should Be Reported To Your Doctor

More common—Constipation; numbness or tingling in fingers and toes; sores in mouth and on lips

Less common—Chest pain; jaw pain; joint pain; muscle pain; shortness of breath

Rare—Agitation; confusion; convulsions (seizures); dizziness; hallucinations; loss of appetite; mental depression; trouble in sleeping

Side Effects That Usually Do Not Require Medical Attention

These possible side effects may go away during treatment; however, if they continue or are bothersome, check with your doctor, nurse, or pharmacist.

More common—Diarrhea; nausea and vomiting; unusual tiredness

Less common—Skin rash

This medicine often causes a temporary loss of hair. After treatment with vinorelbine has ended, or sometimes even during treatment, normal hair growth should return.

Other side effects not listed above may also occur in some patients. If you notice any other effects, check with your doctor, nurse, or pharmacist.

***This leaflet has been developed by the USP based primarily on labeling provided by the manufacturer at the time of its approval. This information is intended for use as a temporary educational aid until the drug has been assessed by USP advisory panels. The information does not cover all possible uses, actions, precautions, side effects, or interactions of this medicine. It is not intended as medical advice for individual problems.**

Vinorelbine (Injection) 910640

USP DI® Patient Education Leaflets™—Introductory Version*

Zileuton (Oral)

A commonly used brand name is *Zyflo*.

ABOUT YOUR MEDICINE

Zileuton (zye-LOO-ton) is used to prevent the symptoms of asthma.

If any of the information in this leaflet causes you special concern or if you want additional information about your medicine and its use, check with your doctor, nurse, or pharmacist. **Remember, keep this and all other medicines out of the reach of children and never share your medicines with others.**

BEFORE USING

Tell your doctor, nurse, and pharmacist if you . . .

- are allergic to any medicine, either prescription or nonprescription (OTC);
- are pregnant or intend to become pregnant while using this medicine;
- are breast-feeding;
- are taking any other prescription or nonprescription (OTC) medicine, especially astemizole, beta-blockers, cisapride, cyclosporine, felodipine, isradipine, nicardipine, nifedipine, nimodipine, terfenadine or terfenadine-containing medicines, theophylline, or warfarin;
- have any other medical problems, especially alcohol abuse (or history of) or liver disease.

PROPER USE

Zileuton is used to prevent asthma attacks. **It is not used to relieve an attack that has already started.**

In order for this medicine to work properly, it must be used every day in regularly spaced doses as directed by your doctor. Do not stop treatment even if you are feeling better unless told to do so by your doctor.

Your doctor should check your progress at regular visits to make sure that this medicine is working properly and to run liver enzyme tests.

If you miss a dose of this medicine, use it as soon as possible. However, if it is almost time for your next dose, skip the missed dose and go back to your regular dosing schedule. Do not double doses.

PRECAUTIONS

This medicine may be used with other asthma medicines. **Do not stop taking the other medicines or reduce the amount you are taking even if your asthma seems better, unless you are told to do so by your doctor.**

Check with your doctor:

- If you need more inhalations (puffs) than usual of a fast-acting bronchodilator to relieve a severe asthma attack.
- If you need more than the maximum number of prescribed bronchodilator puffs per day.

POSSIBLE SIDE EFFECTS

Side Effects That Should Be Reported To Your Doctor

Rare—Flu-like symptoms; itching; nausea; pain in upper abdomen; unusual tiredness or sleepiness; yellow eyes or skin

Side Effects That Usually Do Not Require Medical Attention

These possible side effects may go away during treatment; however, if they continue or are bothersome, check with your doctor, nurse, or pharmacist.

More common—Stomach upset

Other side effects not listed above may also occur in some patients. If you notice any other effects, check with your doctor, nurse, or pharmacist.

***This leaflet has been developed by the USP based primarily on labeling provided by the manufacturer at the time of its approval. This information is intended for use as a temporary educational aid until the drug has been assessed by USP advisory panels. The information does not cover all possible uses, actions, precautions, side effects, or interactions of this medicine. It is not intended as medical advice for individual problems.**

Zileuton (Oral) 915790

Appendix II

ADDITIONAL PRODUCTS AND USES

The following information is new information not included in the text of this book. It has not gone through the USP DI review process. Refer to the Glossary for definitions of medical and technical terms.

GENERIC NAME (*Brand name*)	DOSAGE FORM(S)	USE	COMMENTS
Acebutolol Hydrochloride (Generic [U.S.])	Capsules	Antihypertensive	Available generically
Acenocoumarol (*Sintrom* [Canada])	Tablets	Anticoagulant	For general information that may apply to all coumarin-derivative anticoagulants, see *Anticoagulants (Systemic)*
Acitretin (*Soriatane* [Canada])	Capsules	Antipsoriatic	Canadian drug product
Acyclovir (Generic [U.S.])	Capsules Tablets	Antiviral	Available generically
Albendazole (*Albenza* [U.S.])	Tablets	Anthelmintic	Available in the U.S.
Alendronate (*Fosamax* [U.S.])	Tablets	Bone resorption inhibitor (osteoporosis prophylactic)	Additional FDA-approved use
Aminosalicylic Acid (*Paser* [U.S.])	Granules	Antibacterial (antimycobacterial), for tuberculosis	For general information that may apply to this product see *Aminosalicylate Sodium (Systemic)*
Amlexanox (*Aphthasol* [U.S.])	Oral Paste	Antiulcer agent, for mouth ulcers	U.S. drug product
Amoxicillin (*Amoxil* [U.S.]; Generic [U.S.]) (*Trimox* [U.S.]; *Wymox* [U.S.]) (*Polymox* [U.S.])	 Capsules Oral Suspension Chewable Tablets Capsules Oral Suspension Oral Suspension	Antiulcer agent, for duodenal ulcer associated with *Helicobacter pylori* infection; for concurrent use with clarithromycin and lansoprazole; or for patients allergic or intolerant to clarithromycin, for concurrent use with lansoprazole	Additional FDA-approved uses
Amphotericin B Cholesteryl Sulfate Complex (*Amphotec* [U.S.])	Injection	Antifungal	U.S. drug product
Amsacrine (*Amsa P-D* [Canada])	Injection	Antineoplastic, for leukemia	Canadian drug product
Anagrelide (*Agrylin* [U.S.])	Capsules	Platelet reducing agent	U.S. drug product
Anileridine (*Leritine* [Canada])	Tablets Injection	Analgesic, for moderate to severe pain	An opioid analgesic For general information that may apply to all opioid analgesics, see *Narcotic Analgesics—For Pain Relief (Systemic)*
Azelastine Hydrochloride (*Astelin* [U.S.])	Nasal Solution	Antihistamine (nasal), for seasonal allergic rhinitis	U.S. drug product
Azithromycin (*Zithromax* [U.S.])	for Oral Suspension	Antibacterial	Additional dosage form
Benzoyl Peroxide (*Triaz* [U.S.])	Gel Cleansing Lotion	Antiacne agent (topical); Keratolytic (topical)	Additional brand name product; Rx

Additional Products and Uses *(continued)*

GENERIC NAME (*Brand name*)	DOSAGE FORM(S)	USE	COMMENTS
Benzydamine Hydrochloride (*Tantum* [Canada])	Oral Topical Solution	Analgesic (oral-local), for mouth and throat pain	Canadian drug product
Betamethasone Dipropionate (*Occlucort* [Canada])	Lotion	Corticosteroid (topical); Anti-inflammatory, steroidal (topical), for skin disorders	Canadian brand name product
Betamethasone Disodium Phosphate (*Betnesol* [Canada])	Dental Pellets	Corticosteroid (topical); Anti-inflammatory (steroidal), for mouth ulcers	Dosage form available in Canada; for use in the mouth For general information that may apply to this medication see *Corticosteroids—Medium to Very High Potency (Topical)*
Betaxolol Hydrochloride (*Betoptic S* [Canada])	Ophthalmic Suspension	Antiglaucoma agent (ophthalmic)	Available in Canada
Budesonide (*Entocort* [Canada])	Extended-release Capsules	Anti-inflammatory (steroidal), for Crohn's disease	Additional dosage form
Budesonide		Anti-inflammatory (steroidal), nasal; Corticosteroid (nasal), for inflammation or nasal problems caused by allergy	
(*Rhinocort Nasal Inhaler* [U.S.])	Nasal Aerosol		Additional dosage form
(*Rhinocort Aqua* [Canada])	Nasal Solution	To prevent return of nasal polyps, after surgery	Additional use
(*Rhinocort Turbuhaler* [Canada])	Nasal Powder	To prevent return of nasal polyps, after surgery	Additional use
Budesonide (*Entocort* [Canada])	Tablets for Suspension	Inflammatory suppressant, for bowel disease	Additional dosage form
Bufexamac (*Norfemac* [Canada]; *Parfenac* [Canada])	Cream Ointment	Anti-inflammatory (nonsteroidal), for skin or rectal inflammation	Canadian drug product
Bupropion Hydrochloride (*Wellbutrin SR* [U.S.]; *Zyban* [U.S.])	Extended-release Tablets	Antidepressant; Smoking cessation adjunct	Additional dosage form; additional FDA-approved use
Butenafine Hydrochloride (*Mentax* [U.S.])	Cream	Antifungal, for athlete's foot	U.S. drug product
Caffeine (*Chewable NoDoz* [U.S.])	Chewable Tablets	Central nervous system stimulant, for fatigue (feeling very tired) or sleepiness	Additional dosage form Tablets should be chewed well before swallowing
Calcium Acetate (Generic [U.S.])	Tablets	Antihyperphosphatemic, for lowering blood phosphate levels	Available generically
Carbidopa and Levodopa (*Nu-Levocarb* [Canada])	Tablets	Antidyskinetic, for Parkinson's disease	Additional brand name product
Carboxymethylcellulose	Ophthalmic Solution	Protectant (ophthalmic); Artificial tears	Additional brand name products; OTC
(*Celluvisc* [U.S.])			
(*Refresh Plus* [U.S.])			Brand name change—formerly *Cellufresh*

Additional Products and Uses *(continued)*

GENERIC NAME (*Brand name*)	DOSAGE FORM(S)	USE	COMMENTS
Cefaclor (*Ceclor CD* [U.S.])	Extended-release Tablets	Antibacterial	Additional dosage form
Cefprozil (*Cefzil* [U.S.])	Oral Suspension Tablets	Antibacterial, for acute sinusitis	Additional FDA-approved use
Cefuroxime Axetil (*Ceftin* [U.S.])	Oral Suspension Tablets	Antibacterial, for certain types of gonorrhea, Lyme disease, or acute sinusitis	Additional FDA-approved uses
Cervical Cap, Cavity-rim (*Prentif* [U.S.])		Contraceptive	Cervical cap should be left in place a minimum of 8 hours after last act of intercourse. May be left in place for 48 hours after initial insertion Additional contraceptive cream or jelly is not necessary prior to repeat acts of intercourse. However, proper cervical cap placement should be confirmed before and after each act of intercourse
Cetirizine Hydrochloride (*Zyrtec* [U.S.])	Syrup Tablets	Antihistamine, for rhinitis and urticaria	Syrup is additional dosage form; additional brand name product
Chloramphenicol (*Diochloram* [Canada])	Ophthalmic Ointment Ophthalmic Solution	Antibacterial (ophthalmic)	Additional brand name product
Chlorhexidine Gluconate (Generic [U.S.])	Oral Rinse	Antibacterial (dental), for gingivitis	Available generically
Choline Salicylate and Cetyl-dimethyl-benzyl-ammonium Chloride (*Teejel* [Canada])	Gel	Analgesic (oral-local), for teething or mouth pain	Contains 39% alcohol Should not be used by patients who cannot take other salicylates
Clarithromycin (*Biaxin* [U.S.])	Tablets	Antiulcer agent, for duodenal ulcer associated with *Helicobacter pylori* infection; for concurrent use with omeprazole, with ranitidine bismuth citrate, or with amoxicillin and lansoprazole	Additional FDA-approved uses
Clioquinol and Flumethasone Pivalate (*Locacorten Vioform* [Canada])	Cream Ointment	Antibacterial-antifungal-corticosteroid (topical), for skin inflammation, infection, and itching	Canadian combination product For general information that may apply to this combination, see *Clioquinol and Hydrocortisone (Topical)*
Clioquinol and Flumethasone Pivalate (*Locacorten Vioform* [Canada])	Otic Solution	Antibacterial-antifungal-corticosteroid (otic), for ear infections	Canadian combination product For general information that may apply to all otic corticosteroids, see *Corticosteroids (Otic)*
Clobazam (*Frisium* [Canada])	Tablets	Anticonvulsant	Canadian drug product
Clobetasol Propionate (*Cormax* [U.S.])	Ointment	Corticosteroid (topical); Anti-inflammatory, steroidal (topical), for skin disorders	Additional brand name product
(Generic [U.S.])			Available generically

Additional Products and Uses *(continued)*

GENERIC NAME (*Brand name*)	DOSAGE FORM(S)	USE	COMMENTS
Condom, female, polyurethane (*Reality* [U.S.])		Contraceptive	U.S. product; OTC; caution should be taken not to use after the expiration date The closed ring of the device is put into place against the pubic bone of the vagina by using the index finger; the open ring plus about one inch of the device stays outside of the vagina; caution should be taken not to twist the device The product is removed by squeezing and twisting the outer ring to keep sperm inside the condom and pulling gently; should not be flushed down toilet A new condom must be used with each act of sexual intercourse; lubricant may be added; a male condom should not be used with the female condom because the female condom may not stay in place or work as well Estimated one year pregnancy rate is 21 to 26%
Condom, male, polyurethane (*Avanti* [U.S.]; *Avanti Super Thin* [U.S.])		Contraceptive	Product is made of polyurethane; OTC; caution should be taken not to use after the expiration date Oil or water-based lubricants may be used; caution should be taken not to twist the condom; directions to apply or remove these condoms are the same as for latex condoms. For general information that may apply to all condoms, see *Condoms*
Cromolyn Sodium (*Nasalcrom* [U.S.])	Nasal Solution	Antihistamine (nasal); Antiallergic (nasal)	Available OTC
Cyproterone Acetate (*Androcur* [Canada])	Injection Tablets	Antineoplastic, for prostate cancer	Canadian drug product
Debrisoquine Sulfate (*Declinax* [Canada])	Tablets	Antihypertensive	Canadian drug product
Desmopressin (*DDAVP* [U.S.])	Tablets	Antidiuretic, for diabetes insipidus	Additional dosage form
Desoximetasone (Generic [U.S.])	Ointment	Corticosteroid (topical); Anti-inflammatory, steroidal (topical), for skin disorders	Available generically
Dexamethasone Sodium Phosphate (*Dexacort Turbinaire* [U.S.])	Nasal Aerosol	Anti-inflammatory (steroidal), nasal; Corticosteroid (nasal), for inflammation or nasal problems caused by allergy	Brand name change—formerly *Decadron Turbinaire*
Diclofenac Sodium and Misoprostol (*Arthrotec* [Canada])	Tablets (enteric-coated)	Antirheumatic	Canadian combination product
Diethylamine Salicylate (*Algesal* [Canada])	Cream	Analgesic (topical), for muscle and joint pain	Caution required in patients who cannot take other salicylates
Diflorasone Diacetate (*Psorcon* [U.S.])	Cream	Corticosteroid (topical); Anti-inflammatory, steroidal (topical), for skin disorders	Additional brand name product
Dihydroergotamine Mesylate (*Migranal* [Canada])	Nasal Solution	Vascular headache suppressant, for migraine headaches	Additional dosage form in Canada
Dipivefrin Hydrochloride (*AKPro* [U.S.]; *DPE* [Canada])	Ophthalmic Solution	Antiglaucoma agent (ophthalmic)	Additional brand name products

Additional Products and Uses *(continued)*

GENERIC NAME (*Brand name*)	DOSAGE FORM(S)	USE	COMMENTS
Dipyridamole and Aspirin (*Asasantine* [Canada])	Capsules	Platelet aggregation inhibitor	For general information that may apply to this combination, see *Dipyridamole (Therapeutic)* and *Salicylates (Systemic)*
Docusate Sodium (*Colace* [U.S.])	Enema	Laxative, for constipation	Additional OTC product
Domperidone (*Motilium* [Canada])	Tablets	Stomach and intestine stimulant; Antiemetic, drug-related	Canadian drug product
Enalapril Maleate and Hydrochlorothiazide (*Vaseretic* [Canada])	Tablets	Antihypertensive	Canadian brand name product
Epirubicin Hydrochloride		Antineoplastic, for several kinds of cancer	Canadian drug product
(*Pharmorubicin PFS* [Canada])	Injection		
(*Pharmorubicin RDF* [Canada])	for Injection		
Erythromycin	Topical:	Antiacne agent (topical)	
(*E/Gel* [U.S.]; *Emgel* [U.S.])	Gel		Additional brand name products
(*Theramycin Z* [U.S.]; *Erythro-Statin* [U.S.])	Solution		
(Generic [U.S.])	Gel		Available generically
Estradiol (*Alora* [U.S.])	Transdermal System	Estrogen	Additional brand name product
Etodolac (*Lodine* [U.S.])	Capsules Tablets	Analgesic; Antirheumatic	Additional FDA-approved use
(*Lodine XL* [U.S.])	Extended-release Tablets	Antirheumatic	Additional dosage form
Etoposide	Injection	Antineoplastic, for several kinds of cancer	
(*Toposar* [U.S.])			Additional brand name product
(Generic [U.S.])			Available generically
Etoposide Phosphate (*Etopophos* [U.S.])	for Injection	Antineoplastic, for cancer of the testicles or lung cancer	Additional dosage form For additional information, see *Etoposide (Systemic)*
Famciclovir	Tablets	Antiviral	
(*Famvir* [U.S.])		For genital herpes	Additional FDA-approved use
(*Famvir* [Canada])		For herpes zoster and genital herpes	Available in Canada
Famotidine (*Mylanta-AR* [U.S.])	Tablets	Antiulcer agent, for gastric and duodenal ulcers and for heartburn	Additional OTC brand name product
Flunisolide (*Nasarel* [U.S.])	Nasal Solution	Anti-inflammatory (steroidal), nasal; Corticosteroid (nasal), for inflammation or nasal problems caused by allergy	Additional brand name product
Fluocinonide (Generic [U.S.])	Ointment	Corticosteroid (topical); Anti-inflammatory, steroidal (topical), for skin disorders	Available generically

Additional Products and Uses *(continued)*

GENERIC NAME (*Brand name*)	DOSAGE FORM(S)	USE	COMMENTS
Fluocinonide, Procinonide, and Ciprocinonide (*Trisyn* [Canada])	Cream	Corticosteroid (topical); Anti-inflammatory (steroidal), for skin disorders	For general information that may apply to all topical corticosteroids, see *Corticosteroids—Medium to Very High Potency (Topical)*
Fluoxetine Hydrochloride (*Prozac* [U.S. and Canada])	Capsules Oral Solution	Antibulimic	Additional FDA-approved use Additional use in Canada (capsules only)
Flurbiprofen Sodium (Generic [U.S.])	Ophthalmic Solution	Anti-inflammatory (nonsteroidal) ophthalmic, for eye inflammation	Available generically
Fluspirilene (*Imap* [Canada]; *Imap Forte* [Canada])	Injection	Antipsychotic	Canadian drug product
Fluticasone Propionate (*Flonase* [Canada])	Nasal Suspension	Anti-inflammatory (steroidal), nasal; Corticosteroid (nasal), for inflammation or nasal problems caused by allergy	Additional dosage form For general information that may apply to all nasal corticosteroids, see *Corticosteroids (Nasal)*
Fluvoxamine Maleate (*Luvox* [Canada])	Tablets	Antiobsessional agent, for treatment of obsessive-compulsive disorder Antidepressant	Canadian drug product
Foscarnet (*Foscavir* [U.S.])	Injection	Antiviral, for certain types of herpes simplex infections	Additional FDA-approved use
Framycetin Sulfate (*Soframycin* [Canada])	Ophthalmic Ointment Ophthalmic Solution	Antibacterial (ophthalmic), for eye infections	Canadian drug product Belongs to the group of *Streptomyces*-derived antibiotics (including neomycin, paromomycin, kanamycin)
Framycetin Sulfate (*Sofra-Tulle* [Canada])	Impregnated Gauze	Antibacterial (topical), for skin or burn infections	Canadian drug product Belongs to the group of *Streptomyces*-derived antibiotics (including neomycin, paromomycin, kanamycin)
Framycetin Sulfate and Gramicidin (*Soframycin* [Canada])	Ointment	Antibacterial (topical), for skin or burn infections	Canadian combination product
Framycetin Sulfate, Gramicidin, and Dexamethasone (*Sofracort Eye-Ear Drops* and *Sofracort Eye-Ear Ointment* [Canada])	Ophthalmic Ointment Ophthalmic Solution	Antibacterial-corticosteroid (ophthalmic), for eye infections	Canadian combination product
Framycetin Sulfate, Gramicidin, and Dexamethasone (*Sofracort Eye-Ear Drops* and *Sofracort Eye-Ear Ointment* [Canada])	Otic Ointment Otic Solution	Antibacterial-corticosteroid (otic), for ear infections	Canadian combination product
Fusidic Acid (*Fucidin* [Canada])	for Injection Oral Suspension Tablets	Antibacterial (systemic), for infections in many different parts of the body	Canadian drug product

Additional Products and Uses *(continued)*

GENERIC NAME (*Brand name*)	DOSAGE FORM(S)	USE	COMMENTS
Fusidic Acid (*Fucidin* [Canada])	Cream Impregnated Gauze Ointment	Antibacterial (topical), for skin or burn infections	Canadian drug product
Ganciclovir (*Cytovene* [Canada])	Capsules	Antiviral, for cytomegalovirus	Additional dosage form in Canada
Gemfibrozil (Generic [U.S.])	Tablets	Antihyperlipidemic	Available generically
Glyburide (Generic [U.S. and Canada])	Tablets	Antidiabetic agent	Available generically
Gonadorelin Acetate (*Lutrepulse* [U.S.])	for Injection	Hormone, for treatment of infertility	Additional FDA-approved use Intended for use only with *Lutrepulse* pump
Goserelin Acetate (*Zoladex* [U.S. and Canada])	Implants	Hormone, for treatment of endometriosis Antineoplastic, for breast cancer (U.S. only)	Additional FDA-approved uses; also approved in Canada
Hydrochlorothiazide (*Microzide* [U.S.])	Capsules	Antihypertensive	Additional dosage form
Hydrocortisone (*Anusol-HC 2.5%* [U.S.]; *Prevex HC* [Canada])	Cream	Corticosteroid (topical); Anti-inflammatory, steroidal (topical), for skin disorders	U.S. and Canadian brand name products
Hydrocortisone Acetate (*Gynecort 10* [U.S.]; *Lanacort 10* [U.S.])	Cream	Corticosteroid (topical); Anti-inflammatory, steroidal (topical), for skin disorders	Additional brand name products; OTC
Hydrocortisone Buteprate (*Pandel* [U.S.])	Cream	Corticosteroid (topical); Anti-inflammatory, steroidal (topical), for skin disorders	U.S. drug product
Hydrocortisone Butyrate (*Locoid* [U.S.])	Topical Solution	Corticosteroid (topical); Anti-inflammatory, steroidal (topical), for skin disorders	Additional dosage form
Hydrocortisone and Acetic Acid	Otic Solution	Corticosteroid-antiseptic (otic); Anti-inflammatory, steroidal (otic), for ear infections with inflammation	
(*Acetasol HC* [U.S.]; *Otomycet HC* [U.S.]; *Vasotate HC* [U.S.])			Additional brand name products
(Generic [U.S.])			Available generically
Hydrocortisone and Urea (*Sential* [Canada])	Cream	Corticosteroid (topical); Anti-inflammatory, steroidal (topical), for skin disorders	Canadian brand name product For general information that may apply to this medication, see *Corticosteroids—Low Potency (Topical)*
Hydroxyurea (Generic [U.S.])	Capsules	Antineoplastic	Available generically
Hyoscyamine Sulfate (*Levbid* [U.S.])	Extended-release Tablets	Anticholinergic, to reduce spasms in irritable bowel syndrome, urinary tract disorders, and peptic ulcer	Additional dosage form; additional brand name product

Additional Products and Uses *(continued)*

GENERIC NAME (*Brand name*)	DOSAGE FORM(S)	USE	COMMENTS
Indapamide (Generic [U.S.])	Tablets	Antihypertensive; Diuretic	Available generically
Indium In 111 Imciromab Pentetate (*Myoscint* [U.S.])	Injection	Diagnostic aid, for cardiac imaging	U.S. drug product
Insulin Lispro (*Humalog* [Canada])	Injection	Antidiabetic agent	Available in Canada
Interferon Alfa-2b, Recombinant (*Intron A* [U.S.])	for Injection	Hepatitis treatment; Antineoplastic, for melanoma	Additional FDA-approved uses
Interferon, Alfa-2b, Recombinant (*Intron A* [Canada])	Injection	Antineoplastic, for leukemia or skin cancer Hepatitis treatment	Additional HPB-approved uses
	for Injection		Additional dosage form in Canada
Ipratropium Bromide (*Atrovent* [U.S.])	Nasal Solution	Anticholinergic (nasal), for rhinorrhea (runny nose) caused by certain conditions	Available in the U.S.
Isosorbide Dinitrate (*Coradur* [Canada])	Extended-release Tablets	Antianginal	Canadian brand name product
Isotretinoin (*Isotrex* [Canada])	Gel	Antiacne agent (topical)	Canadian brand name product
Ivermectin (*Stromectol* [U.S.])	Tablets	Anthelmintic, for intestinal threadworm and river blindness	U.S. drug product
Ketorolac Tromethamine (*Acular* [U.S.])	Ophthalmic Solution	Anti-inflammatory, nonsteroidal (ophthalmic), for inflammation following cataract surgery	Additional FDA-approved use
Ketotifen Fumarate (*Zaditen* [Canada])	Syrup Tablets	Antiallergic (systemic); Asthma prophylactic in children	Canadian drug product
Lansoprazole (*Prevacid* [U.S.])	Delayed-release Capsules	Gastric acid secretion inhibitor; Antiulcer agent, for gastric ulcer or healed duodenal ulcer, or for concurrent use with clairithromycin or with amoxicillin and clarithromycin	Additional FDA-approved uses
Leuprolide Acetate		Hormone-like agent	Additional FDA-approved uses; additional brand name products
(*Lupron Depot-Ped* [U.S.])	for Injection	For treatment of premature puberty	
(*Lupron for Pediatric Use* [U.S.])	Injection		
(*Lupron Depot-3 Month 11.25 mg* [U.S.])	for Injection	For treatment of anemia and endometriosis	
Levobunolol Hydrochloride	Ophthalmic Solution	Antiglaucoma agent	
(*AKBeta* [U.S.])			Additional brand name product
(Generic [U.S.])			Available generically
Levocabastine (*Livostin* [Canada])	Nasal Suspension	Antihistamine (nasal); Antiallergic (nasal)	Canadian drug product

Additional Products and Uses *(continued)*

GENERIC NAME (*Brand name*)	DOSAGE FORM(S)	USE	COMMENTS
Levodopa and Benserazide (*Prolopa* [Canada])	Capsules	Antidyskinetic, for symptoms of Parkinson's disease	Canadian drug product
Liothyronine Sodium (*Triostat* [U.S.])	Injection	Thyroid hormone	Additional dosage form
Lodoxamide Tromethamine (*Alomide* [Canada])	Ophthalmic Solution	Mast cell stabilizer (ophthalmic); Antiallergic (ophthalmic)	Available in Canada
Loperamide Hydrochloride (*Apo-Loperamide Caplets* [Canada])	Tablets	Antidiarrheal	Additional brand name product; OTC
Loratadine (*Claritin* [U.S.])	Syrup Tablets	Antihistaminic, for rhinitis and urticaria	Additional FDA-approved use (uticaria)
(*Claritin Redi-Tabs* [U.S.])	Tablets		Additional brand name tablets are rapidly disintegrating
Loratadine and Pseudoephedrine (*Claritin-D 12 Hour* [U.S.]; *Claritin-D 24-Hour* [U.S.])	Extended-release Tablets	Antihistamine, for rhinitis	Brand name changes
Megestrol (*Megace OS* [Canada])	Oral Suspension	Progestational agent	Additional brand name product
Melphalan Hydrochloride (*Alkeran* [U.S.])	for Injection	Antineoplastic, for multiple myeloma	Additional dosage form
Methyldopa (*Nu-Medopa* [Canada])	Tablets	Antihypertensive	Canadian brand name product
Metoprolol Tartrate (*Nu-Metop* [Canada])	Tablets	Antianginal; Antihypertensive; Myocardial reinfarction prophylactic	Canadian brand name product
Metronidazole and Nystatin (*Flagystatin* [Canada])	Vaginal Cream Vaginal Suppositories Vaginal Tablets	Antiprotozoal-antifungal (vaginal), for yeast infections or trichomoniasis	Canadian combination product
Moclobemide (*Manerex* [Canada])	Tablets	Antidepressant	Canadian drug product
Morphine Sulfate (*Kadian* [U.S. and Canada])	Extended-release Capsules	Analgesic	Additional dosage form in the U.S. Additional brand name product in Canada
Mupirocin Calcium (*Bactroban Nasal* [U.S.])	Nasal Ointment	Antibacterial, nasal	Additional dosage form
Nafarelin Acetate (*Synarel* [U.S.])	Nasal Solution	Hormone-like agent for treatment of premature puberty	Additional FDA-approved use
Naproxen (*Naprelan* [U.S.])	Extended-release Tablets	Analgesic; Antigout agent; Anti-inflammatory; Antidysmenorrheal; Antirheumatic	Additional dosage form in the U.S.
Nefazodone (*Serzone* [Canada])	Tablets	Antidepressant	Canadian drug product

Additional Products and Uses *(continued)*

GENERIC NAME (*Brand name*)	DOSAGE FORM(S)	USE	COMMENTS
Neomycin and Polymyxin B Sulfates and Gramicidin (*Triple Antibiotic* [U.S.])	Ophthalmic Solution	Antibiotic, ophthalmic	Additional brand name product
Nicardipine Hydrochloride (*Cardene SR* [U.S.])	Extended-release Tablets	Antihypertensive	Additional dosage form
Nicotinamide (*Papulex* [Canada])	Gel	Antiacne agent (topical)	Canadian drug product
Nicotine (*NicoDerm CQ* [U.S.])	Transdermal System	Smoking cessation adjunct	Brand name change; available OTC
(*Nicotrol* [U.S.])			Available OTC
Nilutamide (*Anandron* [Canada])	Tablets	Antineoplastic, for prostate cancer	Canadian drug product
Nystatin (*Nystop* [U.S.])	Topical Powder	Antifungal	Additional brand name product
Ofloxacin (*Ocuflox* [U.S. and Canada])	Ophthalmic Solution	Antibacterial (ophthalmic), for corneal ulcers	Additional FDA-approved use Canadian drug product
Olopatadine Hydrochloride (*Patanol* [U.S.])	Ophthalmic Solution	Antihistamine (ophthalmic); Mast cell stabilizer (ophthalmic); Antiallergic, for conjunctivitis	U.S. drug product
Omeprazole (*Prilosec* [U.S.])	Delayed-release Capsules	Gastric acid secretion inhibitor/antiulcer agent, for treatment of heartburn and symptoms of gastroesophageal reflux	Additional FDA-approved uses
		Antiulcer agent, for duodenal ulcer associated with *Helicobacter pylori* infection; for concurrent use with clarithromycin	
(*Losec* [Canada])	Delayed-release Tablets	Antiulcer agent, for duodenal ulcer associated with *Helicobacter pylori* infection; for concurrent use with amoxicillin or clarithromycin	Additional use in Canada
Ondansetron (*Zofran* [Canada])	Oral Solution	Antiemetic	Additional dosage form
Oxaprozin (*Daypro* [Canada])	Tablets	Anti-inflammatory, nonsteroidal	Available in Canada
Oxybutynin Chloride (Generic [U.S.])	Syrup	Antispasmodic, for the urinary tract	Available generically
Oxycodone Hydrochloride (*OxyContin SR* [U.S.])	Extended-release Tablets	Analgesic	Additional dosage form
Oxymetazoline Hydrochloride (*Nasal Decongestant Spray* [U.S.])	Nasal Solution (nasal spray)	Decongestant (nasal)	Additional brand name product; OTC
Oxymetazoline Hydrochloride (*Visine L.R.* [Canada])	Ophthalmic Solution	Decongestant (ophthalmic)	Available in Canada

Additional Products and Uses *(continued)*

GENERIC NAME (*Brand name*)	DOSAGE FORM(S)	USE	COMMENTS
Permethrin (*Elimite* [U.S.]; *Nix Dermal Cream* [Canada])	Cream	Scabicide, for scabies	Additional brand name products
(*Nix Creme Rinse* [U.S. and Canada])	Lotion	Pediculicide, for head lice	OTC in U.S.; formerly Rx Available in Canada Note—Permethrin 0.5% is used also as a repellent in the form of a contact spray for clothing (not skin) to prevent the bites of ixodid ticks. The bites of ixodid ticks infected with *Borrelia burgdorferi* cause Lyme disease
Phenylephrine Hydrochloride (*Dionephrine* [Canada]; *Neofrin* [U.S.])	Ophthalmic Solution	Mydriatic; Decongestant (ophthalmic)	Additional brand name products
Pizotyline Malate (*Sandomigran* [Canada]; *Sandomigran DS* [Canada])	Tablets	Migraine headache preventive	Dosage should be decreased gradually over 2-weeks before stopping the medicine completely, to prevent rebound headache
Podofilox (*Condylox* [U.S.])	Gel Topical Solution	Cytotoxic (topical), for venereal warts	U.S. drug product
Polymyxin B Sulfate (*Aerosporin* [U.S.])	for Ophthalmic Solution	Antibacterial, for certain eye infections	U.S. drug product
Prednicarbate (*Dermatop* [U.S.])	Cream	Anti-inflammatory (steroidal), topical, and antipruritic, topical, for skin disorders	U.S. drug product
Pyrithione (*Theraplex Z* [U.S.])	Lotion Shampoo	Antiseborrheic (topical), for dandruff and other scalp disorders	Additional brand name product
Rifampin (Generic [U.S.])	Capsules	Antibacterial, for tuberculosis	Available generically
Risperidone (*Risperdal* [U.S.])	Oral Solution	Antipsychotic	Additional dosage form
Salicylic Acid and Sulfur (*Diasporal Cream* [U.S.])	Cream	Antiacne agent (topical)	Additional brand name product; additional dosage form; OTC
Saquinavir (*Invirase* [Canada])	Capsules	Antiviral, for HIV infection and AIDS	Canadian drug product
Selegiline Hydrochloride (*Carbex* [U.S.])	Tablets	Antidyskinetic, for Parkinson's disease (treatment adjunct)	Additional brand name
(Generic [U.S.])			Available generically
Sermorelin Acetate (*Geref* [U.S.])	for Injection	Growth hormone releasing hormone; Diagnostic aid, for growth hormone deficiency	U.S. drug product
Simethicone (*Degas* [U.S.])	Chewable Tablets	Antiflatulent, for treatment of excess gas in the intestines	Additional brand name product
Somatropin, Recombinant (*Humatrope* [U.S.]; *Nutropin* [U.S.]; *Nutropin AQ* [U.S.]; *Serostim* [U.S.])	Injection	Growth hormone	Additional brand name products Hemodialysis patients should receive somatropin at night just before going to sleep or at least 3 to 4 hours after hemodialysis; chronic cycling peritoneal dialysis patients should receive somatropin in the morning after having completed dialysis; chronic ambulatory peritoneal dialysis patients should receive somatropin in the evening at the time of the overnight exchange

Additional Products and Uses *(continued)*

GENERIC NAME (*Brand name*)	DOSAGE FORM(S)	USE	COMMENTS
Stavudine (*Zerit* [Canada])	Capsules	Antiviral, for HIV infection and AIDS	Available in Canada
Sulfasalazine (*Azulfidine EN-tabs* [U.S.])	Tablets (enteric-coated)	Antirheumatic	Additional FDA-approved use
Sumatriptan (*Imitrex* [Canada])	Nasal Spray	Antimigraine agent	Additional dosage form
Technetium Tc 99m Arcitumomab (*CEA-Scan* [U.S.])	Injection	Diagnostic aid, for cancer of the colon or rectum	U.S. drug product
Technetium Tc 99m Nofetumomab Merpentan (*Verluma* [U.S.])	Injection	Diagnostic aid, for lung cancer	U.S. drug product
Teniposide (*Vumon* [U.S. and Canada])	Injection	Antineoplastic, for several kinds of cancer	U.S. and Canadian drug product
Terbinafine (*Lamisil* [U.S.])	Tablets	Antifungal	Available in the U.S.
Terfenadine (Generic [U.S.])	Tablets	Antihistamine, for rhinitis	Available generically
Thiotepa (*Thioplex* [U.S.])	for Injection	Antineoplastic, for several kinds of cancer	Additional brand name product
Timolol Hemihydrate (*Betimol* [U.S.])	Ophthalmic Solution	Antiglaucoma agent (ophthalmic)	Additional dosage form; additional brand name product
Timolol Maleate		Antiglaucoma agent	
(*Beta-Tim* [Canada]; *Med Timolol* [Canada]; *Novo-Timol* [Canada]; *Nu-Timolol* [Canada]; *Timodal* [Canada])	Ophthalmic Solution		Additional brand name products
(Generic [U.S.])			Available generically
(*Timoptic-XE* [U.S. and Canada])	Ophthalmic Gel-forming Solution		Additional dosage form
Tioconazole (*Trosyd Dermal Cream* [Canada])	Cream	Antifungal (topical), for treatment of ringworm of the body, jock itch, athlete's foot, sun fungus, or other skin fungus infections	Canadian drug product
Tobramycin (*AKTob* [U.S.])	Ophthalmic Solution	Antibacterial (ophthalmic), for eye infections	Additional brand name product
Triamcinolone Acetonide (*Nasacort* [U.S.])	Nasal Aerosol	Anti-inflammatory (steroidal), nasal; Corticosteroid (nasal), for rhinitis	Additional FDA-approved pediatric use
(*Nasacort AQ* [U.S.])	Nasal Solution		Additional dosage form and additional brand name product
Triamcinolone Acetonide (Generic [U.S.])	Dental Paste	Corticosteroid (dental), for discomfort and redness of some mouth and gum problems	Available generically

Additional Products and Uses *(continued)*

GENERIC NAME (*Brand name*)	DOSAGE FORM(S)	USE	COMMENTS
Triethanolamine Salicylate (*Myoflex* [Canada]; *Royflex* [Canada])	Cream	Analgesic (topical), for muscle and joint pain	Should not be used by patients who cannot take other salicylates
Valacyclovir	Tablets	Antiviral	
(*Valtrex* [U.S.])		For genital herpes	Additional FDA-approved use
(*Valtrex* [Canada])		For herpes zoster and genital herpes	Available in Canada
Vindesine Sulfate (*Eldisine* [Canada])	for Injection	Antineoplastic, for leukemia	Canadian drug product
Warfarin (*Coumadin* [U.S.])	Tablets	Anticoagulant, to prevent blood clots after heart valve replacement; to reduce risk after heart attack, of death, another heart attack, and stroke and certain other conditions caused by blood clots	Additional FDA-approved uses
	for Injection		Additional dosage form
Xylometazoline Hydrochloride (*Inspire* [U.S.])	Nasal Spray	Decongestant, nasal	Additional brand name product
Zidovudine (*Retrovir* [U.S.])	Tablets	Antiviral, for HIV infection and AIDS	Additional dosage form
Zopiclone (*Imovane* [Canada])	Tablets	Sedative-hypnotic, for trouble in sleeping	Canadian drug product

Appendix III

POISON CONTROL CENTER LISTING

The following is a list of emergency telephone numbers of poison control centers, as of April 1997. Center names in **bold print** are Certified Regional Poison Centers. Source: American Association of Poison Control Centers.

ALABAMA

Alabama Poison Center, Tuscaloosa
Area: Alabama state
408 Paul W. Bryant Dr., Suite D
Tuscaloosa, AL 35401
(205) 345-0600; (800) 462-0800 (AL only)

Regional Poison Control Center
Area: Alabama state
The Children's Hospital of Alabama
1600 Seventh Ave. South
Birmingham, AL 35233
(205) 933-4050; (205) 939-9201; (800) 292-6678

ALASKA

Anchorage Poison Control Center
Area: Alaska state
Providence Alaska Medical Center
3600 Providence Dr., P.O. Box 196604
Anchorage, AK 99516-6604
(907) 261-3193; (800) 478-3193

ARIZONA

Arizona Poison and Drug Information Center
Area: Arizona state, except Phoenix
Arizona Health Sciences Center, Room 1156
1501 N. Campbell Ave.
Tucson, AZ 85724
(520) 626-6016 ; (800) 322-0101 (AZ only)

Samaritan Regional Poison Center
Area: Maricopa County (Phoenix)
Good Samaritan Regional Medical Center
1111 E. McDowell Rd., Ancillary I
Phoenix, AZ 85006
(602) 253-3334; (800) 362-0101 (AZ only)

ARKANSAS

Arkansas Poison and Drug Information Center
Area: Arkansas state
University of Arkansas for Medical Sciences
4301 West Markham - Slot 522
Little Rock, AR 72205
(800) 376-4766

Southern Poison Center, Inc.
Area: Eastern Arkansas
847 Monroe Ave., Suite 230
Memphis, TN 38163
(901) 528-6048

CALIFORNIA

California Poison Control System—Fresno Division
Area: Central California
Valley Children's Hospital
3151 N. Millbrook, IN31
Fresno, CA 93703
(800) 876-4766 (CA only)

California Poison Control System—Sacramento Division
Area: Northeastern California
UCDMC—HSF Room 1024
2315 Stockton Blvd.
Sacramento, CA 95817
(800) 876-4766 (CA only)

California Poison Control System—San Diego Division
Area: San Diego County and Imperial County
UCSD Medical Center
200 West Arbor Dr.
San Diego, CA 92103-8925
(800) 876-4766 (CA only)

California Poison Control System—San Francisco Division
Area: San Francisco Bay area
San Francisco General Hospital
1001 Potrero Ave., Building 80, Room 230
San Francisco, CA 94110
(800) 876-4766 (CA only)

COLORADO

Rocky Mountain Poison and Drug Center
Area: Colorado state
8802 E. Ninth Ave.
Denver, CO 80220-6800
(303) 629-1123; (800) 332-3073 (CO only)

CONNECTICUT

Connecticut Poison Control Center
Area: Connecticut state
University of Connecticut Health Center
263 Farmington Ave.
Farmington, CT 06030-5365
(800) 343-2722 (CT only)

DELAWARE

The Poison Control Center
Area: Delaware state
3600 Market St., Suite 220
Philadelphia, PA 19104-2641
(215) 386-2100; (800) 722-7112

DISTRICT OF COLUMBIA

National Capital Poison Center
Area: Washington, DC and surrounding metro area
3201 New Mexico Ave., NW, Suite #310
Washington, DC 20016
(202) 625-3333

FLORIDA

Florida Poison Information Center—Jacksonville
Area: Northern and eastern coastal areas of Florida
655 West Eighth St.
Jacksonville, FL 32209
(904) 549-4480; (800) 282-3171 (FL only)

Florida Poison Information Center—Miami
Area: Miami and surrounding metro counties
University of Miami, Department of Pediatrics
P.O. Box 016960 (R-131)
Miami, FL 33101
(305) 585-5253; (800) 282-3171 (FL only)

Florida Poison Information Center—Tampa
Area: Tampa and surrounding metro counties
Tampa General Hospital
P.O. Box 1289
Tampa, FL 33601
(813) 253-4444; (800) 282-3171 (FL only)

GEORGIA

Georgia Poison Center
Area: Georgia state
Grady Memorial Hospital
80 Butler St., SE, P.O. Box 26066
Atlanta, GA 30335-3801
(404) 616-9000; (800) 282-5846 (GA only)

HAWAII

Hawaii Poison Center
1319 Punahou St.
Honolulu, HI 96813
(808) 941-4411

IDAHO

Rocky Mountain Poison and Drug Center
Area: Idaho state
8802 E. Ninth Ave.
Denver, CO 80220-6800
(303) 629-1123; (800) 860-0620 (ID only)

ILLINOIS

Illinois Poison Control Center
Area: Illinois state
222 S. Riverside Plaza, Suite 1900
Chicago, IL 60606
(800) 942-5969 (IL only)

INDIANA

Indiana Poison Center
Area: Indiana state
Methodist Hospital of Indiana
I-65 & 21st St., P.O. Box 1367
Indianapolis, IN 46206-1367
(317) 929-2323; (800) 382-9097 (IN only)

IOWA

McKennan Poison Center
Area: Northwestern Iowa
P.O. Box 5045, 800 E. 21st St.
Sioux Falls, SD 57117-5045
(605) 322-3894; (800) 952-0123

St. Luke's Poison Center
Area: Iowa state
St. Luke's Regional Medical Center
2720 Stone Park Blvd.
Sioux City, IA 51104
(712) 277-2222; (800) 352-2222

KANSAS

Mid-America Poison Control Center
Area: Kansas state
University of Kansas Medical Center
3901 Rainbow Blvd., Room B-400
Kansas City, KS 66160-7231
(913) 588-6633; (800) 332-6633 (KS only)

KENTUCKY

Kentucky Regional Poison Center
Medical Towers South, Suite 572
234 East Gray St.
Louisville, KY 40202
(502) 589-8222

LOUISIANA

Louisiana Drug and Poison Information Center
Area: Louisiana state
Northeast Louisiana University, School of Pharmacy
Monroe, LA 71209-6430
(800) 256-9822 (LA only)

MAINE

Maine Poison Control Center
Area: Maine state
Maine Medical Center, Department of Emergency Medicine
22 Bramhall St.
Portland, ME 04102
(207) 871-2950; (800) 442-6305 (ME only)

MARYLAND

Maryland Poison Center
Area: Maryland state
20 N. Pine St.
Baltimore, MD 21201
(410) 706-7701; (800) 492-2414 (MD only)

National Capital Poison Center
Area: Washington, DC and surrounding metro area
3201 New Mexico Ave., NW, Suite #310
Washington, DC 20016
(202) 625-3333

MASSACHUSETTS

Massachusetts Poison Control System
Area: Massachusetts state
Children's Hospital
300 Longwood Ave.
Boston, MA 02115
(617) 232-2120; (800) 682-9211

MICHIGAN

Blodgett Regional Poison Center
Area: Eastern Michigan and peninsula
1840 Wealthy, SE
Grand Rapids, MI 49506-2968
(800) 764-7661 (MI only)

Children's Hospital of Michigan Poison Control Center
Area: Southeastern and thumb area of Michigan
4160 John R., Suite 425
Detroit, MI 48201
(313) 745-5711; (800) 764-7661 (MI only)

MINNESOTA

Hennepin Regional Poison Center
Area: Minneapolis and surrounding counties
Hennepin County Medical Center
701 Park Ave.
Minneapolis, MN 55415
(612) 347-3141

Minnesota Regional Poison Center
Area: Eastern metro area of Twin Cities, greater Minnesota
8100 34th Ave. S., P.O. Box 1309
Minneapolis, MN 55440-1309
(612) 221-2113; (800) 222-1222 (MN only)

North Dakota Poison Information Center
Area: Northwestern Minnesota
MeritCare Medical Center
720 Fourth St. North
Fargo, ND 58122
(701) 234-5575; (800) 732-2200 (MN only)

MISSISSIPPI

Mississippi Regional Poison Control Center
Area: Mississippi state
University of Mississippi Medical Center
2500 North State St.
Jackson, MS 39216
(601) 354-7660

Southern Poison Center, Inc.
Area: Northern Mississippi
847 Monroe Ave., Suite 230
Memphis, TN 38163
(901) 528-6048

MISSOURI

Cardinal Glennon Children's Hospital Regional Poison Center
Area: Missouri state
1465 S. Grand Blvd.
St. Louis, MO 63104
(314) 772-5200; (800) 366-8888 (MO only)

Children's Mercy Hospital Poison Control Center
Area: Western Missouri
2401 Gillham Rd.
Kansas City, MO 64108
(816) 234-3430

MONTANA

Rocky Mountain Poison and Drug Center
Area: Montana state
8802 E. Ninth Ave.
Denver, CO 80220-6800
(303) 629-1123; (800) 525-5042 (MT only)

NEBRASKA

The Poison Center
Area: Nebraska state
8301 Dodge St.
Omaha, NE 68114
(402) 354-5555; (800) 955-9119 (NE only)

NEVADA

Rocky Mountain Poison and Drug Center
Area: Nevada state
8802 E. Ninth Ave.
Denver, CO 80220-6800
(303) 629-1123; (800) 446-6179 (NV only)

NEW HAMPSHIRE

New Hampshire Poison Information Center
Area: New Hampshire state
Dartmouth-Hitchcock Medical Center
One Medical Center Drive
Lebanon, NH 03756
(603) 650-8000; (800) 562-8236 (NH only)

NEW JERSEY

New Jersey Poison Information and Education System
Area: New Jersey state
201 Lyons Ave.
Newark, NJ 07112
(800) 764-7661 (NJ only)

NEW MEXICO

New Mexico Poison and Drug Information Center
Area: New Mexico state
University of New Mexico
Health Science Center Library, Room 125
Albuquerque, NM 87131-1076
(505) 272-2222; (800) 432-6866 (NM only)

NEW YORK

Central New York Poison Control Center
Area: Central New York
750 East Adams St.
Syracuse, NY 13210
(315) 476-4766; (800) 252-5655 (NY only)

Finger Lakes Poison Center
Area: Finger Lakes region of New York
University of Rochester Medical Center
601 Elmwood Ave., Box 321, Room G-3275
Rochester, NY 14642
(716) 275-3232; (800) 333-0542 (NY only)

Hudson Valley Regional Poison Center
Area: Eastern New York from New York City to Canada
Phelps Memorial Hospital Center
701 North Broadway
Sleepy Hollow, NY 10591-1096
(914) 366-3030; (800) 336-6997 (NY only)

Long Island Regional Poison Control Center
Area: Long Island
Winthrop University Hospital
259 First St.
Mineola, NY 11501
(516) 542-2323

New York City Poison Control Center
Area: New York City
New York City Department of Health
455 First Ave., Room 123
New York, NY 10016
(212) POISONS; (212) 340-4494

Western New York Regional Poison Control Center
Area: Western New York
219 Bryant St.
Buffalo, NY 14222
(716) 878-7654; (800) 888-7655 (NY western regions only)

NORTH CAROLINA

Carolinas Poison Center
Area: North Carolina state
Carolinas Medical Center
1012 S. Kings Dr., Suite 206, P.O. Box 32861
Charlotte, NC 28232-2861
(704) 355-4000; (800) 848-6946 (NC only)

WNC Poison Control Center
Area: Western North Carolina
St. Joseph's Hospital
428 Biltmore Ave., Box 60
Asheville, NC 28801
(704) 255-4490; (800) 542-4225 (NC only)

NORTH DAKOTA

North Dakota Poison Information Center
Area: North Dakota state
MeritCare Medical Center
720 Fourth St. North
Fargo, ND 58122
(701) 234-5575; (800) 732-2200 (ND only)

OHIO

Central Ohio Poison Center
Area: Central Ohio
700 Children's Dr.
Columbus, OH 43205-2696
(614) 228-1323; (800) 682-7625 (OH only)

Cincinnati Drug and Poison Information Center
Area: Southwestern Ohio
231 Bethesda Ave., M.L. 144
Cincinnati, OH 45267-0144
(513) 558-5111; (800) 872-5111 (OH only)

Greater Cleveland Poison Control Center
Area: Cleveland and surrounding metro area
11100 Euclid Ave.
Cleveland, OH 44106-6010
(216) 231-4455; (888) 234-4455 (OH only)

Medical College of Ohio Poison and Drug Information Center
Area: Toledo and surrounding metro areas
3000 Arlington Ave.
Toledo, OH 43614
(419) 381-3897; (800) 589-3897 (419 and 517 area codes only)

OKLAHOMA

Oklahoma Poison Control Center
Area: Oklahoma state
940 NE 13th St., Room 3N118
Oklahoma City, OK 73104
(405) 271-5454; (800) 764-7661 (OK only)

OREGON

Oregon Poison Center
Area: Oregon state
Oregon Health Sciences University
3181 SW Sam Jackson Park Rd., CB550
Portland, OR 97201
(503) 494-8968; (800) 452-7165 (OR only)

PENNSYLVANIA

Central Pennsylvania Poison Center
Area: Central Pennsylvania
Pennsylvania State University Hospital
Milton S. Hershey Medical Center
Hershey, PA 17033
(717) 531-6111; (800) 521-6110 (PA only)

Pittsburgh Poison Center
Area: Western Pennsylvania
3705 Fifth Ave.
Pittsburgh, PA 15213
(412) 681-6669

The Poison Control Center
Area: Southeastern Pennsylvania and Lehigh Valley
3600 Market St., Suite 220
Philadelphia, PA 19104-2641
(215) 386-2100; (800) 722-7112

RHODE ISLAND

Rhode Island Poison Center
Area: Rhode Island state
593 Eddy St.
Providence, RI 02903
(401) 444-5727

SOUTH CAROLINA

Palmetto Poison Center
Area: South Carolina state
College of Pharmacy
University of South Carolina
Columbia, SC 29208
(803) 777-1117; (800) 922-1117 (SC only)

SOUTH DAKOTA

McKennan Poison Center
Area: South Dakota state
P.O. Box 5045, 800 E. 21st St.
Sioux Falls, SD 57117-5045
(605) 322-3894; (800) 952-0123

St. Luke's Poison Center
Area: Southeastern South Dakota
St. Luke's Regional Medical Center
2720 Stone Park Blvd.
Sioux City, IA 51104
(712) 277-2222; (800) 352-2222

TENNESSEE

Middle Tennessee Poison Center
Area: Middle Tennessee state
The Center for Clinical Toxicology
501 Oxford House, 1161 21st Ave. South
Nashville, TN 37232-4632
(615) 936-2034; (800) 288-9999 (TN only)

Southern Poison Center, Inc.
Area: Western and eastern Tennessee
847 Monroe Ave., Suite 230
Memphis, TN 38163
(901) 528-6048; (800) 288-9999 (TN only)

TEXAS

Central Texas Poison Center
Area: Central Texas
Scott and White Memorial Hospital
2401 South 31st St.
Temple, TX 76508
(817) 724-7401; (800) 764-7661 (TX only)

North Texas Poison Center
Area: Northern Texas
5201 Harry Hines Blvd., P.O. Box 35926
Dallas, TX 75235
(800) 764-7661 (TX only)

South Texas Poison Center
Area: Southern Texas
University of Texas Health Science Center
7703 Floyd Curl Dr., Room 146, Forensic Science Bldg.
San Antonio, TX 78284-7849
(800) 764-7661 (TX only)

Southeast Texas Poison Center
Area: Southeastern Texas
The University of Texas Medical Branch
301 University Blvd.
Galveston, TX 77555-1175
(409) 765-1420; (800) 764-7661 (TX only)

Texas Panhandle Poison Center
Area: Amarillo and surrounding area
1501 S. Coulter, P.O. Box 1110
Amarillo, TX 79175
(800) 764-7661 (TX only)

West Texas Regional Poison Center
Area: Western Texas
4815 Alameda Ave.
El Paso, TX 79905
(800) 764-7661 (TX only)

UTAH

Utah Poison Control Center
Area: Utah state
410 Chipeta Way, Suite 230
Salt Lake City, UT 84108
(801) 581-2151; (800) 456-7707 (UT only)

VERMONT

Vermont Poison Center
Area: Vermont state
Fletcher Allen Health Care
111 Colchester Ave.
Burlington, VT 05401
(802) 658-3456

VIRGINIA

Blue Ridge Poison Center
Area: Central western Virginia
University of Virginia Medical Center, Box 67
Charlottesville, VA 22901
(804) 924-5543; (800) 451-1428 (VA only)

National Capital Poison Center
Area: Washington, DC and surrounding metro area
3201 New Mexico Ave., NW, Suite #310
Washington, DC 20016
(202) 625-3333

Virginia Poison Center
Area: Eastern and central Virginia
Medical College of Virginia Hospital
P.O. Box 980522, 401 N. 12th St.
Richmond, VA 23298-0522
(804) 828-4780; (800) 522-6337 (VA only)

WASHINGTON

Washington Poison Center
Area: Washington state
155 NE 100th St., Suite #400
Seattle, WA 98125-8012
(206) 526-2121; (800) 732-6985 (WA only)

WEST VIRGINIA

West Virginia Poison Center
Area: West Virginia state
3110 MacCorkle Ave., SE
Charleston, WV 25304
(304) 348-4211; (800) 642-3625 (WV only)

WISCONSIN

Children's Hospital of Wisconsin Poison Center
Area: Eastern Wisconsin
P.O. Box 1997
Milwaukee, WI 53201
(414) 266-2222; (800) 815-8855 (WI only)

University of Wisconsin Hospital Regional Poison Center
Area: Western Wisconsin
600 Highland Ave., Room F6/133 CSC
Madison, WI 53792
(608) 262-3702; (800) 815-8855 (WI only)

WYOMING

The Poison Center
Area: Wyoming state
8301 Dodge St.
Omaha, NE 68114
(402) 390-5555; (800) 955-9119 (WY only)

Appendix IV

USP PEOPLE 1995–2000

OFFICERS

President: Jane E. Henney, M.D., Albuquerque, NM
Treasurer: John T. Fay, Jr., Ph.D., San Clemente, CA
Past President: Mark Novitch, M.D., Washington, DC
Secretary: Jerome A. Halperin, Rockville, MD

BOARD OF TRUSTEES

Edwin D. Bransome, Jr., M.D., *Trustee, Medical Sciences*, Augusta, GA
William H. Campbell, Ph.D., *Trustee, Pharmaceutical Sciences*, Chapel Hill, NC
Jordan L. Cohen, Ph.D., *Trustee, Pharmaceutical Sciences*, Lexington, KY
Jean Paul Gagnon, Ph.D., *Trustee, At Large*, Kansas City, MO
Edward L. Langston, M.D., R.Ph., *Trustee, Medical Sciences*, Moline, IL
Joseph A. Mollica, Ph.D., *Trustee, At Large*, Princeton, NJ
Grace Powers Monaco, J.D., *Trustee, Public*, King George, VA
Edward Zalta, M.D., *Trustee, At Large*, Newport Beach, CA

GENERAL COMMITTEE OF REVISION

Loyd V. Allen, Jr., Ph.D., Edmond, OK
Thomas J. Ambrosio, Ph.D., Somerville, NJ
Ann B. Amerson, Pharm.D., Lexington, KY
Gordon L. Amidon, Ph.D., Ann Arbor, MI
Gregory E. Amidon, Ph.D., Kalamazoo, MI
Larry Augsburger, Ph.D., Baltimore, MD
Henry L. Avallone, Titusville, NJ
Leonard C. Bailey, Ph.D., Piscataway, NJ
Jorge R. Barrio, Ph.D., Los Angeles, CA
Gregory B. Bennett, Ph.D., East Hanover, NJ
Terrence F. Blaschke, M.D., Stanford, CA
Judy P. Boehlert, Ph.D., Park Ridge, NJ
James C. Boylan, Ph.D., Abbott Park, IL
R. Edward Branson, Ph.D., Brookville, MD
William H. Briner, Durham, NC
Harry G. Brittain, Ph.D., Maplewood, NJ
Paul M. Bummer, Ph.D., Lexington, KY
Stephen R. Byrn, Ph.D., West Lafayette, IN
Peter R. Byron, Ph.D., Richmond, VA
Ronald J. Callahan, Ph.D., Boston, MA
Herbert S. Carlin, D.Sc., Califon, NJ
Culley C. Carson III, M.D., Chapel Hill, NC
Lester Chafetz, Ph.D., Kansas City, MO
Yie W. Chien, Ph.D., Piscataway, NJ
Henry M. Chilton, Pharm.D., Winston-Salem, NC
Zak T. Chowhan, Ph.D., Hunt Valley, MD
Sebastian G. Ciancio, D.D.S., Buffalo, NY
Patricia E. Cole, Ph.D., M.D., Smithtown, NY
David S. Cooper, M.D., Baltimore, MD
Murray S. Cooper, Ph.D., Islamorada, FL
William A. Craig, M.D., Madison, WI
Stephanie Y. Crawford, Ph.D., Chicago, IL
Edward M. Croom, Jr., Ph.D., University, MS
Ian E. Davidson, Ph.D., M.B.A., Kansas City, MO
Leon Ellenbogen, Ph.D., Madison, NJ
Hans Fisher, Ph.D., New Brunswick, NJ
Edward A. Fitzgerald, Ph.D., Rockville, MD
Everett Flanigan, Ph.D., Bradley, IL
Thomas S. Foster, Pharm.D., Lexington, KY
C. David Fox, Ph.D., Rouses Point, NY
Sylvan G. Frank, Ph.D., Columbus, OH
David O. Freedman, M.D., Birmingham, AL
Joseph F. Gallelli, Ph.D., Bethesda, MD
Barry D. Garfinkle, Ph.D., West Point, PA
Robert L. Garnick, Ph.D., South San Francisco, CA
John Christian Gillin, M.D., San Diego, CA
Douglas D. Glover, M.D., R.Ph., Morgantown, WV
Alan M. Goldberg, Ph.D., Baltimore, MD
Dennis K.J. Gorecki, Ph.D., Saskatoon, SK
Robert M. Guthrie, M.D., Columbus, OH
Samir A. Hanna, Ph.D., Lawrenceville, NJ
Stanley L. Hem, Ph.D., West Lafayette, IN
Evelyn V. Hess, M.D., F.A.C.P., M.A.C.R., Cincinnati, OH
Joy Hochstadt, Ph.D., New York, NY
Richard D. Johnson, Ph.D., Pharm D., Kansas City, MO
H. Thomas Karnes, Ph.D., Richmond, VA
David B. Katague, Ph.D., Rockville, MD
Rosalyn C. King, Pharm.D., M.P.H., Silver Spring, MD
Gordon L. Klein, M.D., M.P.H., Galveston, TX
Harvey G. Klein, M.D., Bethesda, MD
Joseph E. Knapp, Ph.D., Pittsburgh, PA
Michael S. Korczynski, Ph.D., Baltimore, MD
Helen F. Krause, M.D., Pittsburgh, PA
Paul Kucera, Ph.D., Warwick, NY
Pauline M. Lacroix, Ph.D., Nepean, ON
V. Cory Langston, D.V.M., Ph.D. Diplomate ACVCP, Mississippi State, MS
Thomas P. Layloff, Ph.D., St. Louis, MO
Patricia D. Leinbach, Ph.D., Rockville, MD
John W. Levchuk, Ph.D., Rockville, MD
Robert D. Lindeman, M.D., Albuquerque, NM
Charles H. Lochmüller, Ph.D., Durham, NC
Hugh E. Lockhart, Ph.D., East Lansing, MI
Edward G. Lovering, Ph.D., Nepean, ON
Catherine M. MacLeod, M.D., Chicago, IL
Carol S. Marcus, Ph.D., M.D., Torrance, CA
Joan C. May, Ph.D., Rockville, MD
Michael Mayersohn, Ph.D., Tucson, AZ
Keith M. McErlane, Ph.D., Vancouver, BC
Thomas Medwick, Ph.D., Piscataway, NJ
Robert F. Morrissey, Ph.D., New Brunswick, NJ
Terry E. Munson, Fairfax, VA
Steven L. Nail, Ph.D., West Lafayette, IN
Harold S. Nelson, M.D., Denver, CO
David W. Newton, Ph.D., Winchester, VA
Sharon J. Northup, Ph.D., M.B.A., Washington, DC
Samuel W. Page, Ph.D., Washington, DC
Garnet E. Peck, Ph.D., West Lafayette, IN
Robert V. Petersen, Ph.D., Salt Lake City, UT
Rosemary C. Polomano, Ph.D., M.S.N., R.N., Pottstown, PA
Ronald E. Reid, Ph.D., Vancouver, BC
Thomas P. Reinders, Pharm.D., Richmond, VA
Christopher T. Rhodes, Ph.D., West Kingston, RI
Jim E. Riviere, D.V.M., Ph.D., Raleigh, NC
George A. Robertson, Ph.D., Frederick, MD
Joseph R. Robinson, Ph.D., Madison, WI
Lary A. Robinson, M.D., Tampa, FL
Harold N. Rode, Ph.D., Ottawa, ON
Dan M. Roden, M.D., Nashville, TN
David B. Roll, Ph.D., Salt Lake City, UT
Thomas W. Rosanske, Ph.D., Kansas City, MO
Theodore J. Roseman, Ph.D., Lincolnshire, IL
Peter C. Ruenitz, Ph.D., Athens, GA
Gordon D. Schiff, M.D., Chicago, IL
Paul L. Schiff, Jr., Ph.D., Pittsburgh, PA
Sally S. Seaver, Ph.D., Concord, MA
Ralph F. Shangraw, Ph.D., Baltimore, MD
Eli Shefter, Ph.D., La Jolla, CA
Eric B. Sheinin, Ph.D., Rockville, MD
Robert L. Siegle, M.D., San Antonio, TX
Edward B. Silberstein, M.D., Cincinnati, OH
Marilyn Dix Smith, Ph.D., Dayton, NJ

E. John Staba, Ph.D., Minneapolis, MN
Thomas E. Starzl, M.D., Ph.D., Pittsburgh, PA
Robert S. Stern, M.D., Boston, MA
James T. Stewart, Ph.D., Athens, GA
Scott V.W. Sutton, Ph.D., Fort Worth, TX
Dennis P. Swanson, M.S., Pittsburgh, PA
Henry S.I. Tan, Ph.D., Cincinnati, OH
Thomas D. Thomson, Ph.D., V.M.D., Greenfield, IN
Clarence T. Ueda, Pharm D., Ph.D., Omaha, NE
Huib J.M. van de Donk, Ph.D., Bilthoven, The Netherlands
Stanley van den Noort, M.D., Irvine, CA
Joseph C. Veltri, Pharm.D., Salt Lake City, UT
Robert E. Vestal, M.D., Boise, ID
Irving W. Wainer, Ph.D., Washington, D.C.
Philip D. Walson, M.D., Columbus, OH
Elliott T. Weisman, Philadelphia, PA
Paul F. White, Ph.D., M.D., Dallas, TX
Richard J. Whitley, M.D., Birmingham, AL
Robert J. Wolfangel, Ph.D., St. Louis, MO
Manfred E. Wolff, Ph.D., Laguna Beach , CA
Marie Linda A. Workman, Ph.D., R.N., Bay Village, OH
Wesley E. Workman, Ph.D., St. Charles, MO
Timothy J. Wozniak, Ph.D., Indianapolis, IN
Dale Eric Wurster, Ph.D., Iowa City, IA
John W. Yarbro, M.D., Columbia, MO
Lynn C. Yeoman, Ph.D., Houston, TX
Thom J. Zimmerman, M.D., Ph.D., Louisville, KY

EXECUTIVE COMMITTEE OF REVISION

Jerome A. Halperin, *Chair*
Lester Chafetz, Ph.D.
Joseph F. Gallelli, Ph.D.
Gordon L. Klein, M.D., M.P.H.
Robert D. Lindeman, M.D.
Carol S. Marcus, Ph.D., M.D.
Joseph R. Robinson, Ph.D.

DIVISION OF INFORMATION DEVELOPMENT EXECUTIVE COMMITTEE

Robert E. Vestal, M.D., *Chair*
Ann B. Amerson, Pharm.D.
James C. Boylan, Ph.D.
Herbert S. Carlin, D. Sc.
Culley C. Carson III, M.D.
Sebastian G. Ciancio, D.D.S.
Evelyn V. Hess, M.D., F.A.C.P., M.A.C.R.
V. Cory Langston, D.V.M., Ph.D. Diplomate ACVCP
Catherine M. MacLeod, M.D.
Rosemary C. Polomano, Ph.D., M.S.N., R.N.
Thomas P. Reinders, Pharm.D.
Dan M. Roden, M.D.
Gordon D. Schiff, M.D.
Robert S. Stern, M.D.
Joseph C. Veltri, Pharm.D.

DIVISION OF STANDARDS DEVELOPMENT EXECUTIVE COMMITTEE

Thomas P. Layloff, Ph.D., *Chair*
Gregory E. Amidon, Ph.D.
Judy P. Boehlert, Ph.D.
James C. Boylan, Ph.D.
William H. Briner
Herbert S. Carlin, D.Sc.
Zak T. Chowhan, Ph.D.
Everett Flanigan, Ph.D.
Thomas S. Foster, Pharm.D.
Robert L. Garnick, Ph.D.
Dennis K.J. Gorecki, Ph.D.
Stanley L. Hem, Ph.D.
Joseph E. Knapp, Ph.D.
Paul Kucera, Ph.D.
Edward G. Lovering, Ph.D.
Thomas Medwick, Ph.D.
Sharon J. Northup, Ph.D., M.B.A.
Ralph F. Shangraw, Ph.D.
James T. Stewart, Ph.D.
Henry S.I. Tan, Ph.D.
Elliott T. Weisman

DRUG NOMENCLATURE COMMITTEE

Herbert S. Carlin, D.Sc., *Chair*
Ann B. Amerson, Pharm.D.
Lester Chafetz, Ph.D.
Stephanie Y. Crawford, Ph.D.
Everett Flanigan, Ph.D.
Douglas D. Glover, M.D., R.Ph.
Richard D. Johnson, Ph.D., Pharm D.
Edward G. Lovering, Ph.D.
Rosemary C. Polomano, Ph.D., M.S.N., R.N.
Thomas P. Reinders, Pharm.D.
Eric B. Sheinin, Ph.D.
Thomas D. Thomson, Ph.D., V.M.D.
Philip D. Walson, M.D.

DIVISION OF DRUG INFORMATION ADVISORY PANELS

Members who serve as Chairs are listed first.

The information presented in this text represents an ongoing review of the drugs contained herein and represents a consensus of various viewpoints expressed. The individuals listed below have served on the USP Advisory Panels for the 1996–1997 revision period and have contributed to the development of the 1998 USP DI database. Such listing does not imply that these individuals have reviewed all of the material in this text or that they individually agree with all statements contained herein.

Anesthesiology

Paul F. White, Ph.D., *Chair*, M.D., Dallas, TX; Charles J. Coté, M.D., Chicago, IL; Peter S.A. Glass, M.D., Durham, NC; Michele E. Gold, Ph.D., C.R.N.A., Beverly Hills, CA; Frederick J. Goldstein, Ph.D., Philadelphia, PA; Thomas K. Henthorn, M.D., Chicago, IL; Michael B. Howie, M.D., Columbus, OH; Robert J. Hudson, M.D., Winnipeg, MB; Scott D. Kelley, M.D., San Francisco, CA; Susan K. Palmer, M.D., Aurora, CO; Carl E. Rosow, M.D., Ph.D., Boston, MA; Mark A. Schumacher, Ph.D., M.D., San Francisco, CA; Peter S. Sebel, Ph.D., Atlanta, GA; Mehernoor F. Watcha, M.D., Dallas, TX; Matthew B. Weinger, M.D., San Diego, CA; Richard B. Weiskopf, M.D., San Francisco, CA; David H. Wong, Pharm.D., M.D., Long Beach, CA

Blood and Blood Products

Harvey G. Klein, M.D., *Chair*, Bethesda, MD; James P. AuBuchon, M.D., Lebanon, NH; Morris A. Blajchman, M.D., Hamilton, Ontario; Marcela Contreras, M.D., London, England; Alfred J. Grindon, M.D., Atlanta, GA; Douglas A. Kennedy, Ph.D., Ottawa, Ontario; Craig M. Kessler, M.D., Washington, DC; Jukka Koistinen, M.D., Ph.D., Helsinki, Finland; Volker Kretschmer, M.D., Ph.D., Marburg, Germany; Margot S. Kruskall, M.D., Boston, MA; Naomi L.C. Luban, M.D., Washington, DC; Jay E. Menitove, M.D., Kansas City, MO; Paul M. Ness, M.D., Baltimore, MD; Henk W. Reesink, M.D., Ph.D., Amsterdam, The Netherlands; William T. Sawyer, M.S., Chapel Hill, NC; Karen A. Skalla, RN, MSN, AOCN, Brownsville, VT; Ronald G. Strauss, M.D., Iowa City, IA

Cardiovascular and Renal Drugs

Dan M. Roden, M.D., *Chair*, Nashville, TN; Jonathan Abrams, M.D., Albuquerque, NM; Joseph S. Alpert, M.D., Tucson, AZ; Jerry L. Bauman, Pharm.D., Chicago, IL; Ellen D. Burgess, M.D., Calgary, Alberta; James H. Chesebro, M.D., New York, NY; Moses Chow, Pharm.D., Hartford, CT; Joseph Cinanni, M.D., Ottawa, Ontario; Peter B. Corr, Ph.D., St. Louis, MO; David J. Driscoll, M.D., Rochester, MN; Dwain L. Eckberg, M.D., Richmond, VA; Andrew E. Epstein, M.D., Birmingham, AL; Arthur M. Feldman, M.D., Ph.D., Pittsburgh, PA; Michael P. Frenneaux, M.D., Wales, England; William H. Frishman, M.D., Bronx, NY; Edward D. Frohlich, M.D., New Orleans, LA; Donald B. Hunninghake, M.D., Minneapolis, MN; Joseph L. Izzo, Jr., M.D., Buffalo, NY; Norman M. Kaplan, M.D., Dallas, TX; Peter R. Kowey, M.D., Wynnewood, PA; Joseph Loscalzo, M.D., Ph.D., Boston, MA; Patrick A. McKee, M.D., Oklahoma City, OK; Juan Carlos Prieto, M.D., Santiago, Chile; Jane F. Schultz, R.N., M.S.N., Hayfield, MN; Alexander M.M. Shepherd, M.D., San Antonio, TX; Burton E. Sobel, M.D., Burlington, VT; Raymond L. Woosley, M.D., Ph.D., Washington, DC

Children and Medicines (Ad Hoc)

Janice M. Ozias, Ph.D., *Chair*, Austin, TX; Anna Birna Almarsdottir, Ph.D., Copenhagen, Denmark; Pilar Aramburuzabala, Ph.D., Segovia, Spain; Roger Bibace, Ph.D., Worcester, MA; Renée R. Jenkins, M.D., Washington, DC; Margo Kroshus, B.S.N., Rochester, MN; Colleen Lum Lung, R.N., Englewood, CO; Carolyn H. Lund, R.N., San Francisco, CA; Robert O'Brien, Ph.D., Chevy Chase, MD; Robert H. Pantell, M.D., San Francisco, CA; Susan Schneider, M.P.H., Bethesda, MD; Bernard A. Sorofman, Ph.D., Iowa City, IA; Wayne A. Yankus, M.D., Midland Park, NJ

Clinical Toxicology/Substance Abuse

Joseph C. Veltri, Pharm.D., *Chair*, Salt Lake City, UT; Neal L. Benowitz, M.D., San Francisco, CA; Usoa E. Busto, Pharm.D., Toronto, Ontario; Timothy R. Dring, Woodbridge, NJ; David J. George, Ph.D., Madison, NJ; Edward P. Krenzelok, Pharm.D., Pittsburgh, PA; David C. Lewis, M.D., Providence, RI; Michael Montagne, Ph.D., Boston, MA; Claudio A. Naranjo, M.D., North York, Ontario; Edward J. Otten, M.D., Cincinnati, OH; Paul Pentel, M.D., Minneapolis, MN; Lorie G. Rice, San Francisco, CA; Elizabeth J. Scharman, Pharm.D., Charleston, WV; Michael W. Shannon, M.D., Boston, MA; Rose Ann G. Soloway, RN, MSEd, ABAT, Washington, DC; Anthony C. Tommasello, M.S., Baltimore, MD; Theodore G. Tong, Pharm.D., Tucson, AZ; Alison M. Trinkoff, ScD, RN, Baltimore, MD; William A. Watson, Pharm.D., Kansas City, MO; Julian White, M.D., North Adelaide, Australia

Consumer Interest/Health Education

Gordon D. Schiff, M.D., *Chair*, Chicago, IL; Michael J. Ackerman, Ph.D., Bethesda, MD; Frank J. Ascione, Pharm.D., Ph.D., Ann Arbor, MI; Roger Bibace, Ph.D., Worcester, MA; Allan H. Bruckheim, M.D., Harrison, NY; Mary E. Carman, Ottawa, Ontario; Margaret A. Charters, Ph.D., Syracuse, NY; Laura J. Cranston, Fairfax Station, VA; Jennifer Cross, San Francisco, CA; David A. Danielson, Watertown, MA; Sandra M. Fabregas, R.Ph., San Juan, PR; Sophia Jones-Redmond, Chicago, IL; Louis H. Kompare, Franklin, TN; Margo Kroshus, B.S.N., Rochester, MN; Bruce L. Lambert, Ph.D., Chicago, IL; Arthur Levin, New York, NY; Roberto Lopez Linares, Lima, Peru; Janet M. Manuel, Halifax, Nova Scotia; Frederick S. Mayer, R.Ph., M.P.H, San Rafael, CA; Jacqueline D. McLeod, New York, NY; Charles Medawar, London, England; Nancy Milio, Ph.D., Chapel Hill, NC; Michael A. Moné, Frankfort, KY; Janet Ohene-Frempong, Philadelphia, PA; James C. Wohlleb, Little Rock, AR

Critical Care Medicine

Catherine M. MacLeod, M.D., *Chair*, Chicago, IL; Robert A. Balk, M.D., Chicago, IL; Philip S. Barie, M.D., New York, NY; Thomas P. Bleck, M.D., Charlottesville, VA; Eugene Y. Cheng, M.D., Milwaukee, WI; Susan S. Fish, Pharm.D., Boston, MA; Edgar R. Gonzalez, Pharm.D., Richmond, VA; Angela M. Hadbavny, Pharm.D., Pittsburgh, PA; John W. Hoyt, M.D., Pittsburgh, PA; Louis J. Ling, M.D., Minneapolis, MN; Sheldon A. Magder, M.D., Montreal, Quebec; Daniel A. Notterman M.D., Princeton, NJ; Sharon D. Peters, M.D., St. John's, Newfoundland; Domenic A. Sica, M.D., Richmond, VA; George A. Skowronski, New South Wales, Australia; Martin G. Tweeddale, Ph.D., M.B., Vancouver, British Columbia

Dentistry

Sebastian G. Ciancio, D.D.S., *Chair*, Buffalo, NY; B. Ellen Byrne, D.D.S., Ph.D., Richmond, VA; Barbara R. Clark, Pharm.D., Kansas City, MO; Frederick Curro, D.M.D., Ph.D., Jersey City, NJ; Tommy W. Gage, D.D.S., Ph.D., Dallas, TX; Daniel A. Haas, D.D.S., Ph.D., Toronto, Ontario; Richard E. Hall, D.D.S., Ph.D., Buffalo, NY; John T. Hamilton, Ph.D., London, Ontario; Angelo J. Mariotti, D.D.S., Ph.D., Columbus, OH; Linda C. Niessen, D.M.D., Dallas, TX; Clarence L. Trummel, D.D.S., Farmington, CT; Joel M. Weaver II, D.D.S., Ph.D., Columbus, OH; Clifford W. Whall, Jr., Ph.D., Chicago, IL; Raymond P. White, Jr., D.D.S., Ph.D., Chapel Hill, NC; Richard L. Wynn, Ph.D., Baltimore, MD; John A. Yagiela, D.D.S., Ph.D., Los Angeles, CA

Dermatology

Robert S. Stern, M.D., *Chair*, Boston, MA; Beatrice B. Abrams, Ph.D., East Hanover, NJ; Richard D. Baughman, M.D., Lebanon, NH; Mary-Margaret Chren, M.D., Tiburon, CA; Diane M. Cooper, Ph.D., R.N., Bay Pines, FL; Ponciano D. Cruz, M.D., Dallas, TX; Vincent Falanga, M.D., Miami, FL; James J. Ferry, Ph.D., Kalamazoo, MI; Vincent C. Ho, M.D., Vancouver, British Columbia; Donald P. Lookingbill, M.D., Jacksonville, FL; Stuart Maddin, M.D., Vancouver, British Columbia; Milton Orkin, M.D., Minneapolis, MN; Amy S. Paller, M.D., Chicago, IL; Jean-Claude Roujeau, M.D., Paris, France; Neil H. Shear, M.D., Toronto, Ontario; Celia A. Viets, M.D., Ottawa, Ontario; Dennis P. West, Ph.D., Chicago, IL

Diagnostic Agents—Nonradioactive

Robert L. Siegle, M.D., *Chair*, San Antonio, TX; Leonard M. Baum, R.Ph., Princeton, NJ; Martin J. K. Blomley, M.B., London, England; Robert C. Brasch, M.D., San Francisco, CA; Olivier Clement, M.D., Ph.D., Paris, France; Sachiko T. Cochran, M.D., Los Angeles, CA; Kathryn L. Grant, Pharm.D., Tucson, AZ; Kenneth D. Hopper, M.D., Hershey, PA; Fred T. Lee, Jr., M.D., Madison, WI; Robert F. Mattrey, M.D., San Diego, CA; James A. Nelson, M.D., Seattle, WA; Jovitas Skucas, M.D., Rochester, NY; Gerald L. Wolf, Ph.D., M.D., Charlestown, MA

Drug Utilization Review

Terrence F. Blaschke, M.D., *Chair*, Stanford, CA; David M. Angaran, R.Ph., Columbus, OH; Edward P. Armstrong, Pharm.D., Tucson, AZ; Jim L. Blackburn, Pharm.D., Saskatoon, Saskatchewan; Catherine E. Burley, M.D., Fayetteville, GA; Patricia J. Byrns, M.D., Chicago, IL; Elizabeth A. Chrischilles, Ph.D., Iowa City, IA; Theodore M. Collins, R.Ph., Madison, WI; Robert P. Craig, Pharm.D., Scottsdale, AZ; W. Gary Erwin, Pharm.D., Philadelphia, PA; Stan N. Finklestein, M.D., Cambridge, MA; Catherine A. Harrington, Pharm.D., Ph.D., Fairfax, VA; Joel W. Hay, Ph.D., Los Angeles, CA; Mark L. Horn, M.D., New York, NY; Judith K. Jones, M.D., Ph.D., Arlington, VA; Michael L. Kelly, R.Ph., Jackson, MS; Duane M. Kirking, Pharm.D., Ph.D., Ann Arbor, MI; Ann M. Koeniguer, R.Ph., Summerfield, NC; David Lee, M.D., Arlington, VA; Gary M. Levine, R.Ph., St. Louis, MO; Gladys Peachey, RN, MEd, MHSc, Dundas, Ontario; Eleanor M. Perfetto, Ph.D., Chester Springs, PA; T. Donald Rucker, Ph.D., River Forest, IL; Daniel W. Saylak, D.O., Bryan, TX; Fredrica E. Smith, M.D., Los Alamos, NM; Brian L. Strom, M.D., Philadelphia, PA; Ilene H. Zuckerman, Pharm.D., Batimore, MD

Endocrinology

David S. Cooper, M.D., *Chair*, Baltimore, MD; Robert L. Barbieri, M.D., Wellesley, MA; Stuart J. Brink, M.D., Waltham, MA; R. Keith Campbell, Pharm.D., Pullman, WA; Ernesto Canalis, M.D., Hartford, CT; Betty J. Dong, Pharm.D., San Francisco, CA; Shereen Ezzat, M.D., Toronto, Ontario; Lawrence A. Frohman, M.D., Chicago, IL; Steven R. Goldring, M.D., Boston, MA; Jerome M. Hershman, M.D., Los Angeles, CA; Robert G. Josse, M.B., Toronto, Ontario; Michael M. Kaplan, M.D., West Bloomfield, MI; Selna Kaplan, M.D., Ph.D., San Francisco, CA; Marvin E. Levin, M.D., Chesterfield, MO; Marvin M. Lipman, M.D., Scarsdale, NY; Daniel J. Marante, M.D., Miami, FL; Barbara J. Maschak-Carey, RN, Philadelphia, PA; Shlomo Melmed, M.D., Los Angeles, CA; Ronald P. Monsaert, M.D., Danville, PA; John E. Morley, M.B., B.Ch., St. Louis, MO; Paul Saenger, M.D.,

Bronx, NY; Mary Lee Vance, M.D., Charlottesville, VA; Leonard Wartofsky, M.D., Washington, DC

Family Practice

Robert M. Guthrie, M.D., *Chair*, Columbus, OH; John A. Brose, D.O., Athens, OH; Mark E. Clasen, M.D., Ph.D., Dayton, OH; Yves Gariepy, Ste-Foy, Quebec; Sloan Karver, M.D., Wyomissing, PA; Joseph A. Lieberman III, M.D., Wilmington, DE; Charles D. Ponte, Pharm.D., Morgantown, WV; John W. Robinson, M.D., Salt Lake City, UT; Jack M. Rosenberg, Pharm.D., Ph.D., Hillsdale, NJ; Jorge E. Sanchez, M.D., San Salvador, El Salvador; John E. Thornburg, D.O., Ph.D., East Lansing, MI; Richard A. Wherry, M.D., Dahlonega, GA; Theodore L. Yarboro, Sr., M.D., M.P.H., Sharon, PA

Gastroenterology

Gordon L. Klein, M.D., *Chair*, Galveston, TX; Karl E. Anderson, M.D., Galveston, TX; Paul Bass, Ph.D., Madison, WI; Adrian M. Di Bisceglie, M.D., St. Louis, MO; Jack A. DiPalma, M.D., Mobile, AL; Thomas Q. Garvey III, M.D., Potomac, MD; Flavio Habal, M.D., Ph.D., Toronto, Ontario; Eric G. Hassall, M.D., Vancouver, British Columbia; Alan F. Hofmann, M.D., La Jolla, CA; Paul E. Hyman, M.D., Orange, CA; Agnes V. Klein, M.D., Ottawa, Ontario; James H. Lewis, M.D., Washington, DC; Bernard Mehl, D.P.S., New York, NY; Joel E. Richter, M.D., Cleveland, OH; William J. Snape, Jr., M.D., Long Beach, CA; C. Noel Williams, M.D., Halifax, Nova Scotia; Hyman J. Zimmerman, M.D., Bethesda, MD

Geriatrics

Robert E. Vestal, M.D., *Chair*, Boise, ID; Darrell R. Abernethy, M.D., Washington, DC; Mark H. Beers, M.D., West Point, PA; Robert A. Blouin, Pharm.D., Lexington, KY; S. George Carruthers, M.D., London, Ontario; Martin J. Connolly, M.D., Cheshire, England; Madeline Feinberg, Pharm.D., Silver Spring, MD; Jerry H. Gurwitz, M.D., Worcester, MA; Geri R. Hall, Ph.D., ARNP, CS, Scottsdale, AZ; Martin D. Higbee, Pharm.D., Tucson, AZ; Brian B. Hoffman, M.D., Palo Alto, CA; Barbara A. Liu, M.D., North York, Ontario; Ann Miller, Morro Bay, CA; Paul A. Mitenko, M.D., Nanaimo, British Columbia; Janice B. Schwartz, M.D., Chicago, IL; Joanne G. Schwartzerg, M.D., Chicago, IL; William Simonson, Pharm.D., Portland, OR; Daniel S. Sitar, Ph.D., Winnipeg, Manitoba; Alastair J.J. Wood, M.D., Nashville, TN; Carla Zeilman, Pharm.D., Albuquerque, NM

Hematologic and Oncologic Disease

John W. Yarbro, M.D., Ph.D., *Chair*, Columbia, MO; Joseph S. Bailes, M.D., Dallas, TX; Laurence H. Baker, D.O., Ann Arbor, MI; Edward Braud, M.D., Springfield, IL; Donald C. Doll, M.D., Columbia, MO; Ross C. Donehower, M.D., Baltimore, MD; Jan M. Ellerhorst-Ryan, R.N., Cincinnati, OH; Martha Harczy, M.D., Ottawa, Ontario; David T. Harris, M.D., Wynnewood, PA; Connie Henke Yarbro, R.N., Columbia, MO; Charles Hoppel, M.D., Cleveland, OH; B. J. Kennedy, M.D., Minneapolis, MN; Barnett S. Kramer, M.D., Bethesda, MD; Celeste Lindley, Pharm.D., Chapel Hill, NC; Michael J. Mastrangelo, M.D., Philadelphia, PA; Paulette Mehta, M.D., Gainesville, FL; Perry D. Nisen, M.D., Ph.D., Abbott Park, IL; David S. Rosenthal, M.D., Cambridge, MA; Roy L. Silverstein, M.D., New York, NY; Ellen L. Stovall, Silver Spring, MD; Samuel G. Taylor, M.D., Chicago, IL; Raymond B. Weiss, M.D., Rockville, MD

Infectious Disease Therapy

William A. Craig, M.D., *Chair*, Madison, WI; P. Joan Chesney, M.D., Memphis, TN; C. Glenn Cobbs, M.D., Birmingham, AL; Courtney V. Fletcher, Pharm.D., Minneapolis, MN; Frederick G. Hayden, M.D., Charlottesville, VA; Carol A. Kauffman, M.D., Ann Arbor, MI; Marc LeBel, Pharm.D., Ste-Foy, Quebec; S. Ragnar Norrby, M.D., Ph.D., Lund, Sweden; Laszlo Palkonyay, M.D, Ottawa, Ontario; Douglas D. Richman, M.D., La Jolla, CA; Xavier Saez-Llorens, M.D., Miami, FL; Roy T. Steigbigel, M.D., Stony Brook, NY; Richard J. Whitley, M.D., Birmingham, AL

International Health

Rosalyn C. King, Pharm.D., M.P.H., *Chair*, Silver Spring, MD; Eugenie Brown, Pharm.D., Kingston, Jamaica; Laura Ceron, Pharm.D., Lima, Peru; Albin Chaves Matamoros, M.D., San Jose, Costa Rica; Gabriel Daniel, Washington, DC; Enrique Fefer, Ph.D., Rockville, MD; Peter H.M. Fontilus, Netherlands Antilles; Reginald F. Gipson, M.D., M.P.H., Atlanta, GA; Mariatou Tala Jallow, Pharm.D., Banjul, The Gambia; Mohan P. Joshi, M.D., Kathmandu, Nepal; David E. Kuhl, Pharm.D., Albuquerque, NM; Richard O. Laing, M.D., Boston, MA; Thomas Lapnet-Moustapha, Pharm.D., Yaounde, Cameroon; Denise Leclerc, Ph.D., Montreal, Quebec; Aissatou Lo, Dakar, Senegal; David Ofori-Adjei, M.D., Accra, Ghana; Dr. S. Ofosu-Amaah, Legon, Accra, Ghana; James Rankin, Arlington, VA; Dennis Ross-Degnan, Boston, MA; Budiono Santoso, M.D., Ph.D., Yogyakarta, Indonesia; Fela Viso Gurovich, Ph.D., Mexico City, Mexico; Krisantha Weerasuriya, M.D., Colombo, Sri Lanka; Albert I. Wertheimer, Ph.D., West Point, PA

Medication Counseling Behavior Guidelines (Ad Hoc)

Frank J. Ascione, Pharm.D., Ph.D., *Chair*, Ann Arbor, MI; John E. Arradondo, M.D., Nashville, TN; Candace Barnett, Atlanta, GA; Allan H. Bruckheim, M.D., Harrison, NY; Mark E. Clasen, M.D., Ph.D., Dayton, OH; Frederick Curro, D.M.D., Ph.D., Jersey City, NJ; Robin DiMatteo, Ph.D., Riverside, CA; Diane B. Ginsburg, Austin, TX; Denise Grimes, Jackson, MI; Richard Herrier, Tucson, AZ; Barry Kass, R.Ph., Boston, MA; Thomas Kellenberger, Pharm.D., Montvale, NJ; Alice Kimball, Darnestown, MD; Patricia A. Kramer, B.Sc., Bismarck, ND; Patricia Kummeth, Rochester, MN; Ken Leibowitz, Philadelphia, PA; Colleen Lum Lung, R.N., Englewood, CO; Louise Matte, B.Sc., B.Pharm., Montreal, Quebec; Amy Outlaw, Pharm.D., Stone Mountain, GA; Constance Pavlides, R.N., Rockville, MD; Scotti Russell, Richmond, VA; Lisa Tedesco, Ph.D., Ann Arbor, MI

Neurology

Stanley van den Noort, M.D., *Chair*, Irvine, CA; A. Leland Albright, M.D., Pittsburgh, PA; Elizabeth U. Blalock, M.D., Anaheim, CA; Mitchell F. Brin, M.D., New York, NY; Louis R. Caplan, M.D., Boston, MA; James C. Cloyd, Pharm.D., Minneapolis, MN; David M. Dawson, M.D., West Roxbury, MA; Mark J. Fisher, M.D., Los Angeles, CA; Kathleen M. Foley, M.D., New York, NY; Robert A. Gross, M.D., Ph.D., Rochester, NY; Stanley Hashimoto, M.D., Vancouver, British Columbia; William C. Koller, M.D., Ph.D., Kansas City, KS; Ilo E. Leppik, M.D., Minneapolis, MN; Ira T. Lott, M.D., Orange, CA; T.J. Murray, M.D., Halifax, Nova Scotia; Judith A. Paice, Ph.D., R.N., Chicago, IL; Richard D. Penn, M.D., Chicago, IL; Roger J. Porter, M.D., Philadelphia, PA; Neil H. Raskin, M.D., San Francisco, CA; James F. Toole, M.D., Winston-Salem, NC; Howard L. Weiner, M.D., Boston, MA

Nursing Practice

Rosemary C. Polomano, Ph.D., M.S.N., R.N., *Chair*, Pottstown, PA; Bonnie J. Adamson, R.N., London, Ontario; Ramona A. Benkert, M.S.N., R.N., Plymouth, MI; Mecca S. Cranley, Ph.D., R.N., Buffalo, NY; Linda Felver, Ph.D., R.N., Portland, OR; Hector Hugo Gonzalez, Ph.D., R.N., San Antonio, TX; Theodore L. Goodfriend, M.D., Madison, WI; Ada K. Jacox, R.N., Ph.D., Detroit, MI; Daisy M. Jones, R.N., Chicago, IL; Patricia Kummeth, Rochester, MN; Ida S. Martinson, Ph.D., R.N., Hung Hom, Hong Kong; Ginette A. Pepper, Ph.D., R.N., Denver, CO; Geraldine A. Peterson, M.A., R.N., Potomac, MD; Linda C. Pugh, Ph.D., R.N., Hershey, PA; Sharon S. Rising, M.S.N., Chesire, CT; April H. Vallerand, Ph.D., R.N., Manalapan, NJ

Nutrition and Electrolytes

Robert D. Lindeman, M.D., *Chair*, Albuquerque, NM; Jeffrey P. Baker, M.D., Toronto, Ontario; Connie W. Bales, Ph.D., R.D., Durham, NC; Dennis M. Bier, M.D., Houston, TX; Gladys Block, Ph.D., Berkeley, CA; Karim Anton Calis, Pharm.D., M.P.H., Rockville, MD; David F. Driscoll, Ph.D., Boston, MA; P.W.F. Fischer, Ph.D., Ottawa, Ontario; Dr. Nigel Gericke, Cape Town, South Africa; Walter H. Glinsmann, M.D., Washington, DC; Helen A. Guthrie, Ph.D., Ft. Myers, FL; John N. Hathcock, Ph.D., Washington, DC; Leslie M. Klevay, M.D., Grand Forks, ND; Linda S. Knox, Ph.D., R.N., Philadelphia, PA; Bonnie Liebman, M.S., Washington, DC; Sohrab Mobarhan, M.D., Maywood, IL; Robert M. Russell, M.D., Boston, MA; Harold H. Sandstead, M.D., Galveston, TX; Benjamin Torun, M.D., Ph.D., Miami, FL; Carlos A. Vaamonde, M.D., Miami, FL; Stanley Wallach, M.D., New York, NY

Obstetrics and Gynecology

Douglas D. Glover, M.D., *Chair*, Morgantown, WV; Rudi Ansbacher, M.D., Ann Arbor, MI; James E. Axelson, Ph.D., Aldergrove, British Columbia; Augusto Bondani, M.D., Ph.D., Mexico City, Mexico; Florence Comite, M.D., New Haven, CT; Stephen H. Cruikshank, M.D., Dayton, OH; Marilynn C. Frederiksen, M.D., Chicago, IL; L. Wayne Hess, M.D., Columbia, MO; Art Jacknowitz, Pharm.D., Morgantown, WV; William J. Ledger, M.D., New York, NY; Andre-Marie Leroux, M.D., Ottawa, Ontario; William A. Nahhas, M.D., Dayton, OH; Warren N. Otterson, M.D., Bulverde, TX; Anne Pastuszak, Ph.D., Toronto, Ontario; Johanna F. Perlmutter, M.D., Boston, MA; Richard H. Reindollar, M.D., Boston, MA; Ronald J. Ruggiero, Pharm.D., San Francisco, CA; Pamela Shrock, Ph.D., Roslyn Harbor, NY; G. Millard Simmons, Jr., M.D., Morgantown, WV; Phillip G. Stubblefield, M.D., Boston, MA; Raul G. Toledo, M.D., San Salvador, El Salvador

Ophthalmology

Thom J. Zimmerman, M.D., *Chair*, Louisville, KY; Steven R. Abel, Pharm.D., Indianapolis, IN; Jules L. Baum, M.D., Wellesley Hills, MA; Lee R. Duffner, M.D., Golden Beach, FL; Forrest Ellis, M.D., Indianapolis, IN; David L. Epstein, M.D., Durham, NC; Robert Fechtner, M.D., Louisville, KY; Allan J. Flach, Pharm.D., M.D., Corte Madera, CA; Frederick T. Fraunfelder, M.D., Portland, OR; Gary N. Holland, M.D., Los Angeles, CA; David A. Lee, M.D., Los Angeles, CA; Vincent H.L. Lee, Ph.D., Los Angeles, CA; Joel S. Mindel, M.D., Ph.D., New York, NY; Steven M. Podos, M.D., New York, NY; Graham E. Trope, M.B., Ph.D., Toronto, Ontario; Roberto Warman, M.D., Miami, FL; Kirk R. Wilhelmus, M.D., Houston, TX

Otorhinolaryngology

Helen F. Krause, M.D., *Chair*, Pittsburgh, PA; Robert E. Brummett, Ph.D., Portland, OR; Linda J. Gardiner, M.D., Fort Myers, FL; Cedric F. Grigg, PhC, DBA, Victor, NY; Julianna Gulya, M.D., Washington, DC; James A. Hadley, M.D., Rochester, NY; David B. Hom, M.D., Minneapolis, MN; Donald C. Lanza, M.D., Philadelphia, PA; Richard L. Mabry, M.D., Dallas, TX; Scott C. Manning, M.D., Seattle, WA; Lawrence J. Marentette, M.D., Ann Arbor, MI; Robert A. Mickel, M.D., Ph.D., San Francisco, CA; Arnold M. Noyek, M.D., Toronto, Ontario; Randal A. Otto, M.D., San Antonio, TX; Leonard P. Rybak, M.D., Ph.D., Springfield, IL; Randal S. Weber, M.D., Philadelphia, PA

Outcomes and Cost-Effectiveness (Ad Hoc)

Elizabeth A. Chrischilles, Ph.D., *Co-chair*, Iowa City, IA; Stan N. Finklestein, M.D., *Co-chair*, Cambridge, MA; Jerome L. Avorn, M.D., Boston, MA; Lisa A. Bero, Ph.D., San Francisco, CA; Robert S. Epstein M.D., Montvale, NJ; Steven F. Finder, M.D., M.B.A., San Antonio, TX; Deborah A. Freund, Ph.D., Bloomington, IN; Gordon H. Guyatt, M.D., Hamilton, Ontario; Abraham G. Hartzema, Pharm.D., Ph.D., Chapel Hill, NC; Joel W. Hay, Ph.D., Los Angeles, CA; Paul C. Langley, Ph.D, Denver, CO; Kathleen N. Lohr, Ph.D., Research Triangle Park, NC; Nicolaas Otten, Pharm.D, Ottawa, Ontario; A. David Paltiel, Ph.D, New Haven, CT; Eleanor M. Perfetto, Ph.D., Chester Springs, PA; Kevin A. Schulman, M.D., M.B.A., Washington, DC; Kathleen A. Weis, Dr.P.H., NP, Rockville, MD

Parasitic and Tropical Disease

David O. Freedman, M.D., *Chair*, Birmingham, AL; Prof. Tomas D. Arias, Ph.D., Panama City, Panama; Michele Barry, M.D., New Haven, CT; Frank J. Bia, M.D., New Haven, CT; P. Das Gupta, M.D., New Delhi, India; Philip R. Fischer, M.D., Salt Lake City, UT; Eduardo Gotuzzo, M.D., Lima, Peru; M. Gail Hill, Ph.D., RN, CRNP, Birmingham, AL; Dennis D. Juranek, M.D., Atlanta, GA; Jay S. Keystone, M.D., Toronto, Ontario; Dennis E. Kyle, Ph.D., Washington, DC; Sornchai Looareesuwan, M.D., Bangkok, Thailand; Douglas W. MacPherson, M.D., Hamilton, Ontario; Edward K. Markell, M.D., Ph.D., Berkeley, CA; Philippa A. McDonald, M.D., Ottawa, Ontario; Richard Pearson, M.D., Charlottesville, VA; Prof. Dr. Heonir Rocha, Salvador Bahia, Brazil; Peter D. Walzer, M.D., Cincinnati, OH; A. Clinton White, Jr., M.D., Houston, TX

Pediatric Anesthesiology (Ad Hoc)

Charles J. Coté, M.D., *Chair*, Chicago, IL; J. Michael Badgwell, M.D., Lubbock, TX; Barbara W. Brandom, M.D., Pittsburgh, PA; Ryan Cook, M.D., Pittsburgh, PA; John J. Downes, M.D., Philadelphia, PA; Dennis M. Fisher, M.D., San Francisco, CA; John E. Forestner, M.D., Fort Worth, TX; Helen W. Karl, M.D., Seattle, WA; Harry G.G. Kingston, M.D., Portland, OR; Anne Marie Lynn, M.D., Seattle, WA; Robert J. Mamlok, M.D., Lubbock, TX; Mark Shriner, M.D., Philadelphia, PA; Victoria Simpson, M.D., Ph.D., Denver, CO; Mehernoor F. Watcha, M.D., Dallas, TX

Pediatrics

Philip D. Walson, M.D., *Chair*, Columbus, OH; Cheston M. Berlin, Jr., M.D., Hershey, PA; Nancy Jo Braden, M.D., Phoenix, AZ; George S. Goldstein, M.D., Briarcliff Manor, NY; Russell J. Hopp, D.O., Omaha, NE; Ralph E. Kauffman, M.D., Kansas City, MO; Joan M. Korth-Bradley, Pharm.D., Ph.D., Philadelphia, PA; Richard D. Leff, Pharm.D., Shawnee Mission, KS; Carolyn H. Lund, R.N., San Francisco, CA; Maureen C. Maguire, R.N., Baltimore, MD; Mark A. Riddle, M.D., Baltimore, MD; Emilio J. Sanz, M.D., Ph.D., Tenerife, Spain; Wayne Snodgrass, M.D., Galveston, TX; Stephen P. Spielberg, M.D., Ph.D., Blue Bell, PA; Jose Teran, M.D., Quito, Ecuador; Robert M. Ward, M.D., Salt Lake City, UT; Sumner J. Yaffe, M.D., Bethesda, MD

Pharmacy Practice

Thomas P. Reinders, Pharm.D., *Chair*, Richmond, VA; Hannes Enlund, Ph.D., Kuopio, Finland; Donald J. Filibeck, Pharm.D., Dublin, OH; Ned E. Heltzer, M.S., Philadelphia, PA; Frederick Klein, Montvale, NJ; Calvin H. Knowlton, Ph.D., Lumberton, NJ; Patricia A. Kramer, B.Sc., Bismarck, ND; Diane Lamarre, Saint Lambert, Quebec; Shirley P. McKee, B.Sc., Houston, TX; Eucharia E. Nnadi-Okolo, Ph.D., Washington, DC; John E. Ogden, M.S., Burke, VA; Henry A. Palmer, Ph.D., Storrs, CT; Roger P. Potyk, Pharm.D., San Antonio, TX; Betsy L. Sleath, Ph.D., Chapel Hill, NC; William E. Smith, Pharm.D., Richmond, VA; Craig S. Stern, Pharm.D., Northridge, CA; Linda S. Tyler, Pharm.D., Salt Lake City, UT; John H. Vandel, R.Ph., Torrington, WY; Joan H. Veal, Rockville, MD; Mary Ann Wagner, Alexandria, VA; Glenn Y. Yokoyama, Pharm.D., Pasadena, CA

Psychiatric Disease

John Christian Gillin, M.D., *Chair*, San Diego, CA; Ross J. Baldessarini, M.D., Belmont, MA; R.H. Belmaker, M.D., Beersheva, Israel; Alex A. Cardoni, M.S. Pharm., Hartford, CT; Paula J. Clayton, M.D., Minneapolis, MN; Larry Ereshefsky, Pharm.D., San Antonio, TX; W. Edwin Fann, M.D., Houston, TX; Jan Fawcett, M.D., Chicago, IL; John Feighner, M.D., San Diego, CA; Burton J. Goldstein, M.D., Williams Island, FL; Clarice Gorenstein, Ph.D., Sao Paulo, Brazil; Paul Grof, M.D., Ottawa, Ontario; Russell T. Joffe, M.D., Hamilton, Ontario; Nancy E. Johnston, R.N., Thornhill, Ontario; Stephen R. Marder, M.D., Los Angeles, CA; Stuart A. Montgomery, M.D., London, England; Andrew A. Nierenberg, M.D., Boston, MA; Fred Quitkin, M.D., New York, NY; Ruth Robinson, Saskatoon, Saskatchewan; Matthew V. Rudorfer, M.D., Rockville, MD; Carl Salzman, M.D., Boston, MA; Colette F. Strnad, Ph.D., Ottawa, Ontario; Karen A. Theesen, Pharm.D., Omaha, NE; Thomas W. Uhde, M.D., Detroit, MI; George E. Woody, M.D., Philadelphia, PA

Pulmonary Disease/Allergy

Harold S. Nelson, M.D., *Chair*, Denver, CO; John A. Anderson, M.D., Detroit, MI; Emil J. Bardana, M.D., Portland, OR; I. Leonard Bernstein, M.D., Cincinnati, OH; Alexander G. Chuchalin, M.D., Ph.D., Moscow, Russia; Nicholas J. Gross, M.D., Ph.D., Hines, IL; Karen Huss, DNSc, R.N., Potomac, MD; Elliot Israel, M.D., Boston, MA; John W. Jenne, M.D., Sandia Park, NM; H. William Kelly, Pharm.D., Albuquerque, NM; James P. Kemp, M.D., San Diego, CA; Bennie C. McWilliams, Jr., M.D., Albuquerque, NM; Shirley Murphy, M.D., Albuquerque, NM; Thomas F. Myers, M.D., Maywood, IL; Gary S. Rachelefsky, M.D., Los Angeles, CA; Joe Reisman, M.D., Toronto, Ontario; Robert E. Reisman, M.D., Williamsville, NY; Albert L. Sheffer, M.D., Boston, MA; Paul C. Stillwell, M.D., San Diego, CA; Stanley J. Szefler, M.D., Denver, CO; Virginia S. Taggart, Bethesda, MD; David G. Tinkleman, M.D., Denver, CO; John H. Toogood, M.D., London, Ontario; Martin D. Valentine, M.D., Baltimore, MD; Sally E. Wenzel, M.D., Denver, CO

Radiopharmaceuticals

Carol S. Marcus, Ph.D., M.D., *Chair*, Torrance, CA; J.D. Bernardy, J.D., Lexington, MA; Dik Blok, Pharm.D., Leiden, The Netherlands; Capt William H. Briner, Durham, NC; Melissa P. Brown, Bethesda, MD; Janet F. Eary, M.D., Seattle, WA; David L. Gilday, M.D., Toronto, Ontario; Don Lyster, Ph.D., Vancouver, British Columbia; John

G. McAfee, M.D., Chevy Chase, MD; James A. Ponto, M.S., Iowa City, IA; Mark H. Rotman, Pharm.D., M.S., Middletown, MD; Carl Seidel, M.S., Denton, TX; Barry A. Siegel, M.D., St. Louis, MO; Edward B. Silberstein, M.D., Cincinnati, OH; Roberta A. Strohl, RN, MN, Baltimore, MD; James B. Stubbs, Ph.D., Roswell, GA; Dennis P. Swanson, M.S., Pittsburgh, PA; Andrew T. Taylor, M.D., Atlanta, GA; Mathew L. Thakur, Ph.D., Philadelphia, PA; Ann Warbick-Cerone, Ottawa, Ontario; John H. Waterman, MS, Arlington Heights, IL; Robert G. Wolfangel, Ph.D., St. Louis, MO

Rheumatology-Clinical Immunology
Evelyn V. Hess, M.D., *Chair*, Cincinnati, OH; Donato Alarcon-Segovia, M.D., Mexico City, Mexico; John Baum, M.D., Rochester, NY; David H. Campen, M.D., Santa Clara, CA; Paul Emery, M.D., Leeds, England; Daniel E. Furst, M.D., Seattle, WA; Jean G. Gispen, M.D., Oxford, MS; Esther Gonzales-Pares, M.D., San Juan, PR; Donna J. Hawley, R.N., Ed.D., Wichita, KS; Israeli A. Jaffe, M.D., New York, NY; Daniel J. Lovell, M.D., M.P.H., Cincinnati, OH; Walter P. Maksymowych, M.D., Edmonton, Alberta; Donald R. Miller, Pharm.D., Fargo, ND; Ivan G. Otterness, Ph.D., Groton, CT; Robert L. Rubin, Ph.D., La Jolla, CA; Lee S. Simon, M.D., Boston, MA; Daniel J. Stechschulte, M.D., Kansas City, KS; Michael E. Weinblatt, M.D., Boston, MA; Michael H. Weisman, M.D., San Diego, CA; William S. Wilke, M.D., Cleveland, OH; David E. Yocum, M.D., Tucson, AZ

Surgical Drugs and Devices
Lary A. Robinson, M.D., *Chair*, Tampa, FL; Kay A. Ball, M.S.A., R.N., Lewis Center, OH; Alan R. Dimick, M.D., Birmingham, AL; H. Kim Lyerly, M.D., Durham, NC; Henry J. Mann, Pharm.D., Minneapolis, MN; Joseph A. Moylan, M.D., Miami, FL; Ronald Lee Nichols, M.D., New Orleans, LA; Hiram C. Polk, Jr., M.D., Louisville, KY; Robert P. Rapp, Pharm.D., Lexington, KY; Ronald Rubin, M.D., West Newton, MA

Therapeutic Information Management
Ann B. Amerson, Pharm.D., *Chair*, Lexington, KY; Marie A. Abate, Pharm.D., Morgantown, WV; Wesley G. Byerly, Pharm.D., Winston-Salem, NC; Teresa Dowling, Pharm.D., Wilmington, DE; Thomas M. Gesell, Pharm.D., Abbott Park, IL; Stephen R. Kaplan, M.D., Buffalo, NY; Ossy M.J. Kasilo, Ph.D., Harare, Zimbabwe; Aishah A. Latiff, Ph.D., Penang Malaysia; Leslie A. Lenert, M.D., Stanford, CA; Dr. Hubert G.M. Leufkens, Utrecht, The Netherlands; M. Laurie Mashford, M.D., Victoria, Australia; Louise Matte, B.Sc., B.Pharm., Montreal, Quebec; Kurt A. Proctor, Ph.D., Alexandria, VA; Carol A. Romano, Ph.D., R.NC., Bethesda, MD; Cedric M. Smith, M.D., Buffalo, NY; Gary H. Smith, Pharm.D., Baltimore, MD; Dennis F. Thompson, Pharm.D., Oklahoma City, OK; William G. Troutman, Pharm.D., Albuquerque, NM; Gordon J. Vanscoy, Pharm.D., Irwin, PA; Valentin A. Vinogradov, M.D., Ph.D., Moscow, Russia; Lee A. Wanke, Seattle, WA; Antonio Carlos Zanini, M.D., Ph.D., Sao Paulo, Brazil

Transplant Immunology
Thomas E. Starzl, M.D., Ph.D., *Chair*, Pittsburgh, PA; Clyde F. Barker, M.D., Philadelphia, PA; Gilbert J. Burckart, Pharm.D., Pittsburgh, PA; Paul M. Colombani, M.D., Baltimore, MD; Allan P. Donner, Ph.D., London, Ontario; Robert A. Good, Ph.D., M.D., St. Petersburg, FL; Carl C. Groth, M.D., Ph.D., Huddinge, Sweden; John A. Hansen, M.D., Seattle, WA; Roger L. Jenkins, M.D., Boston, MA; John R. Lake, M.D., San Francisco, CA; Leonard Makowka, M.D., Ph.D., Los Angeles, CA; Suzanne V. McDiarmid, M.D., Los Angeles, CA; Charles Miller, M.D., New York, NY; Ali Naji, M.D., Ph.D., Philadelphia, PA; David H. Sachs, M.D., Boston, MA; Joseph A. Tami, Pharm.D., Carlsbad, CA; Angus W. Thomson, Ph.D., Pittsburgh, PA; Raman Venkataramanan, Ph.D., Pittsburgh, PA; Professor Roger Williams, CBE, London, England

Urology
Culley C. Carson III, M.D., *Chair*, Chapel Hill, NC; John A. Belis, M.D., Hershey, PA; B.J. Reid Czarapata, CRNP, Rockville, MD; Sam D. Graham, Jr., M.D., Atlanta, GA; Mireille Gregoire, M.D., Quebec, Quebec; Wayne Hellstrom, M.D., New Orleans, LA; Joseph M. Khoury, M.D., Chapel Hill, NC; Marguerite C. Lippert, M.D., Charlottesville, VA; Michael G. Mawhinney, Ph.D., Morgantown, WV; Nelson Rodrigues Netto, Jr., M.D., Sao Paulo, Brazil; Mariano Rosello-Barbera, M.D., Palma de Mallorca, Spain; Randall G. Rowland, M.D., Ph.D., Indianapolis, IN; J. Patrick Spirnak, M.D., Cleveland, OH; William F. Tarry, M.D., Morgantown, WV; Chris M. Teigland, M.D., Charlotte, NC; Robert M. Weiss, M.D., New Haven, CT

Veterinary Medicine
V. Cory Langston, D.V.M., Ph.D., *Chair*, Mississippi State, MS; Michael D. Apley, D.V.M., Ph.D., Ames, IA; Gordon W. Brumbaugh, D.V.M., Ph.D., College Station, TX; Thomas J. Burkgren, D.V.M., M.B.A., Perry, IA; Cynthia T. Culmo, R.Ph., Austin, TX; Lloyd E. Davis, Ph.D., D.V.M., Champaign, IL; Patricia M. Dowling, D.V.M., M.S., Saskatoon, Saskatchewan; Stuart D. Forney, M.S., Fort Collins, CO; Antoinette D. Jernigan, D.V.M., Ph.D., Groton, CT; Mark G. Papich, D.V.M., Raleigh, NC; Thomas E. Powers, D.V.M., Ph.D., Columbus, OH; Jim E. Riviere, D.V.M., Ph.D., Raleigh, NC; Charles R. Short, D.V.M., Ph.D., Baton Rouge, LA; Hector Sumano Lopez, D.V.M., Ph.D., Mexico City, Mexico; Jeffrey R. Wilcke, D.V.M., Blacksburg, VA

Division of Information Development Additional Contributors

The information presented in the USP DI data base represents ongoing review and the consensus of various viewpoints expressed. In addition to the individuals listed below, many schools, associations, pharmaceutical companies, and governmental agencies have provided comment or otherwise contributed to the development of the 1998 USP DI data base. Such listing does not imply that these individuals have reviewed all of the material in the database or that they individually agree with all statements contained herein.

Lori J. Acuncius, Pharm.D., Hines, IL
S. Adami, M.D., Verona, Italy
Z.R. Aisanov, M.D., Ph.D., Moscow, Russia
Linda Albrecht, Berlin, Germany
Louis M. Aledort, M.D., New York, NY
Cara Alfaro, Pharm.D., San Antonio, TX
Harunobu Amagase, Ph.D., Mission Viejo, CA
Stephen W. Anderson, M.D., Atlanta, GA
David Apgar, Pharm.D., Tucson, AZ
Louis V. Avioli, M.D., St. Louis, MO
Dennis V.C. Awang, Ph.D., Ottawa, Ontario
Maria R. Baer, M.D., Buffalo, NY
Philip L. Ballard, M.D., Philadelphia, PA
Patsy Barnett, Pharm.D., Birmingham, AL
Dennis Bartholomeev, M.D., Biloxi, MS
LuAnne Barron, Birmingham, AL
Mark Batshaw, M.D., Philadelphia, PA
Robert W. Beightol, Pharm.D., Roanoke, VA
Maria Bell, M.D., Shreveport, LA
Les Benet, Ph.D., San Francisco, CA
N.J. Benevenga, Madison, WI
William M. Bennett, M.D., Portland, OR
Tim Benstrad, M.D., Halifax, Nova Scotia
Wilma L.F. Bergfeld, M.D., Cleveland, OH
Bruno A. Bernard, Clichy Cedex, France
Erik Berntorp, M.D., Malmo, Sweden
Joseph Betz, Ph.D., Washington, DC
Joseph Biederman, M.D., Boston, MA

Richard E. Blackwell, M.D., Birmingham, AL
Robert Blaser, M.S., Boston, MA
Mark Blumenthal, Austin, TX
Henry G. Bone III, M.D., Detroit, MI
William Bonnez, M.D., Rochester, NY
Bertha A. Bouroncle, M.D., Columbus, OH
Barry Boyd, D.M.D., M.D., Buffalo, NY
Peter R. Bradley, Havant Hampshire, England
Wayne Bradley, Duluth, GA
Michael Brodsky, M.D., Orange, CA
Murray Brown, D.V.M., Gainesville, FL
Myron Brown, D.V.M., Shawnee Mission, KS
Todd Brown, M.P.H., Boston, MA
Saul Brusilow, M.D., Baltimore, MD
Gina Caliendo, Pharm.D., New York, NY
Bruce Carr, M.D., Dallas, TX
Kyong-Mi Chang, M.D., La Jolla, CA
Bruce D. Cheson, M.D., Bethesda, MD
R.E. Coleman, Sheffield, England
Jackson Como, Pharm.D., Birmingham, AL
James W. Cooper, Ph.D., Athens, GA
Clinton N. Corder, Ph.D., M.D., Oklahoma City, OK
Lawrence Corey, M.D., Seattle, WA
James Correia, Ph.D., N. Billerica, MA
Arthur L. Craigmill, Ph.D., Davis, CA
Philip E. Cryer, M.D., St. Louis, MO
Frederick J. Curley, Worcester, MA
Horace G. Cutler, Ph.D., Athens, GA
Pamela B. Davis, M.D., Ph.D., Cleveland, OH
Thomas D. DeCillis, North Port, FL
Vincent L. DeQuattro, M.D., Los Angeles, CA
Jonathan W. DeVries, Ph.D., Minneapolis, MN
Louis Diamond, Ph.D., Denver, CO
Virgil C. Dias, Pharm.D., Brooksfield, CT
James E. Doherty, M.D., Little Rock, AR
R. Gordon Douglas, M.D., Rahway, NJ
Brian O.L. Duke, M.D., Lancaster, England
James A. Duke, Fulton, MD
Michael S. Dunn, M.D., Toronto, Ontario
Sue Duran, R.Ph., M.S., Auburn University, AL
Lawrence H. Einhorn, M.D., Indianapolis, IN
Avi I. Einzig M.D., Bronx, NY
Gary W. Elmer, M.D, Seattle, WA
Fran Ertl, Long Beach, CA
James O. Ertle, M.D., Hinsdale, IL
Elihu H. Estey, M.D., Houston, TX
Daniel Evans, M.D., Hershey, PA
Ronnie Fass, M.D., Tucson, AZ
William Feldman, M.D., Toronto, Ontario
Clara Fenger, D.V.M., Lexington, KY
M. Brian Fennerty, M.D., Portland, OR
Greg C. Flaker, M.D., Columbia, MO
William A. Gahl, M.D., Bethesda, MD
Jose P.B. Gallardo, R.Ph., Iowa City, IA
Charlotte A. Gaydos, M.S., Dr.Ph., Baltimore, MD
Bruce G. Gellin, M.D., M.P.H., Bethesda, MD
Anne A. Gershon, M.D., New York, NY
George P. Giacoia, M.D., Bethesda, MD
Ray W. Gifford, Jr., M.D., Cleveland, OH
Robert Gibson, Pharm.D., Petaluma, CA
Joseph Glajch, Ph.D., N. Billerica, MA
W. Paul Glezen, M.D., Houston, TX
Michael Goldstein, M.D., Salt Lake City, UT
Maj. John D. Grabenstein, M.S., Chapel Hill, NC
David Y. Graham, M.D., Houston, TX
Gilman D. Grave, M.D., Bethesda, MD
Roy Greengrass, M.D., Durham, NC
Jack M. Gwaltney, Jr., M.D., Charlottesville, VA
Steven Hadler, M.D., Atlanta, GA
John J. Halperin, M.D., Manhasset, NY
Margaret R. Hammerschlag, M.D., Brooklyn, NY
Ada Hamosh, M.D., M.P.H., Baltimore, MD
Nina Han, Pharm.D., Chicago, IL
Steven T. Harris, M.D., San Francisco, CA
C.A. Harwood, MBChB, Nepean, Ontario
David W. Hawkins, Pharm.D., Augusta, GA
Amy M. Heck, Pharm.D., Bethesda, MD
Alfred D. Heggie, M.D., Cleveland, OH
Christopher Hendel, M.S., Burlington, VT
Jack E. Henningfield, Ph.D., Baltimore, MD
Basil I. Hirschowitz, M.D., Birmingham, AL
David D. Ho, M.D., New York, NY
M.E. Hoar, Springfield, MA
Patrick Hoffman, Ph.D., Hunt Valley, MD
Richard A. Holmes, M.D., N. Billerica, MA
William Hopkins, Pharm.D., Atlanta, GA
Richard B. Hornick, M.D., Orlando, FL
Peter J. Houghton, B.Pharm, Ph.D., London, England
Lawrence M. Hurvitz, M.D., Sarasota, FL
B. Thomas Hutchinson, M.D., Boston, MA
J. Thomas Hutton, M.D., Lubbock, TX
John Iazzetta, Pharm.D., Toronto, Ontario
Rodney D. Ice, Ph.D., Atlanta, GA
Michael Ihrig, Eschborn, Germany
Laurence S. Jacobs, M.D., Rochester, NY
Robert Jacobson, M.D., Carville, LA
Henry D. Jampel, M.D., Baltimore, MD
Ann L. Janer, Auburn, AL
Joseph Jankovic, M.D., Houston, TX
Cynda A. Johnson, M.D., Kansas City, KS
Lawrence F. Johnson, M.D., Bethesda, MD
Leslye D. Johnson, Ph.D., Bethesda, MD
Alan H. Jobe, M.D., Torrance, CA
William S. Jordan, M.D., Bethesda, MD
Burton Kallman, Ph.D., Newport Beach, CA
Henry J. Kaminski, M.D., Cleveland, OH
Lily Kao, M.D., Oakland, CA
Jonathan E. Kaplan, M.D., Atlanta, GA
Carol K. Kasper, M.D., Los Angeles, CA
Samuel Katz, M.D., Durham, NC
John J. Kavanagh, M.D., Houston, TX
Riitta Kekomäki, M.D., Ph.D., Helsinki, Finland
Larry Kien, M.D., Ph.D., Columbus, OH
Charles Kilo, M.D., St. Louis, MO
Betsy King, B.S., Denton, TX
Charles H. King, M.D., Cleveland, OH
A. Douglas Kinghorn, Ph.D., Chicago, IL
Wendy Klein-Schwartz, Baltimore, MD
Alan Knight, M.D., North York, Ontario
Michael R. Knowles, M.D., Chapel Hill, NC
Sandra Knowles, B.Sc.Phm., Toronto, Ontario
Stephen Krane, M.D., Boston, MA
Vicki L. Kraus, R.N., Iowa City, IA
Eric H. Kraut, M.D., Columbus, OH
Paul Kucera, Ph.D., Pearl River, NY
Paul B. Kuehn, Ph.D., Woodinville, WA
Robert Kuhn, Pharm.D., Lexington, KY
Roger Kurlan, M.D., Rochester, MN
Thomas L. Kurt, M.D., Dallas, TX
John R. LaMontagne, M.D., Bethesda, MD
Larry Lawson, Springville, UT
P.D. Leathwood, LaTour de Peilz, Switzerland
Christine A. Lee, M.D., London, England
William Lee, M.D., Dallas, TX
Claire Leonard, M.D., Salt Lake City, UT
Herbert Lepor, M.D., New York, NY
Robert L. Lesser, M.D., New Haven, CT
Angelo Licata, M.D., Ph.D., Cleveland, OH
Franklin C. Lowe, M.D., New York, NY
Michael L. Macknin, M.D., Cleveland, OH
Robert D. Madoff, M.D., St. Paul, MN
Louis A. Magnarelli, Ph.D., New Haven, CT
Howard I. Maibach, M.D., San Francisco, CA
Claude Mailhot, Montreal, Quebec
Joseph L. Malone, M.D., Bethesda, MD
Laxmaiah Manchikanti, M.D., Paducah, KY
Prof. P.M. Mannucci, Milano, Italy
Alan J. Margolis, M.D., Bolinas, CA
Maurie Markman, M.D., Cleveland, OH
James G. Marks, Jr., M.D., Hershey, PA
Patricia Marshik, Pharm.D., Albuquerque, NM
David H. Martin, M.D., New Orleans, LA
Iris P. Masucci, Pharm.D., Bethesda, MD
Ruben Matalon, M.D., Galveston, TX
Micheline Mathews-Roth, M.D., Boston, MA
Jennifer Mawhinney, M.D., Columbus, OH
David Mayer, Oakland, CA
Jack R. McCormack, Pharm.D., Little Rock, AR
Norman L. McElroy, San Jose, CA
Edward J. McGuire, M.D., Ann Arbor, MI
Herbert Y. Meltzer, M.D., Cleveland, OH
E. Messing, M.D., Madison, WI
Boyd E. Metzger, M.D., Chicago, IL
Peter Mirtschin, Tanunda, South Australia

Daniel Mishell, M.D., Los Angeles, CA
Lynne M. Mofenson, M.D., Bethesda, MD
Mark Molitch, M.D., Chicago, IL
Kathleen Moltz, M.D., Waltham, MA
Garreth A. Moore, D.V.M., Blacksburg, VA
Richard Moore, M.D., Baltimore, MD
Ricardo Alberto Moreno, Ph.D., Sao Paulo, Brazil
Grant Morrow III, M.D., Columbus, OH
Marvin Moser, M.D., White Plains, NY
Edward A. Mortimer, Jr., M.D., Cleveland, OH
Robert Murphy, M.D., Chicago, IL
Robert Naclerio, M.D., Chicago, IL
Ernesto Navarro Marin, M.D., San Salvador, El Salvador
Serpil Nebioglu, Ph.D., Tandogan-Ankara, Turkey
Kenneth H. Neldner, M.D., Lubbock, TX
Robert P. Nelson, Jr., M.D., Charleston, SC
H.A.W. Neil, Oxford, England
David Nierenberg, M.D., Lebanon, NH
John Gordon Nutt, M.D., Portland, OR
Edward J. O'Connell, M.D., Rochester, MN
Elise Olsen, M.D., Durham, NC
Walter Orenstein, M.D., Atlanta, GA
Jerry Overman, Pharm.D., San Antonio, TX
Judith M. Ozbun, R.Ph., M.S., Fargo, ND
Dennis Pabis, Pharm.D., San Antonio, TX
Ariel Pablos-Mendez, M.D., M.P.H., New York, NY
David Pantalone, Pittsburgh, PA
Robert C. Park, M.D., Washington, DC
Lawrence C. Parish, M.D., Philadelphia, PA
Frank Patrick, M.D., Philadelphia, PA
Herbert Patrick, M.D., Philadelphia, PA
Steve Piechota, Pharm.D., Waterbury, CT
Man-Chiu Poon, M.D., Calgary, Alberta
Daniel H. Polk, M.D., Torrance, CA
Lisa Profeta-Fernandez, Pharm.D., New York, NY
Antonio Ramirez Amaya, M.D., San Salvador, El Salvador
Nixa Ramos, Arecibo, PR
Vesa Rasi, M.D., Ph.D., Helsinki, Finland
James E. Rasmussen, M.D., Ann Arbor, MI
Lee B. Reichman, M.D., M.P.H., Newark, NJ
Michael F. Rein, M.D., Charlottesville, VA
Alfred J. Remillard, Pharm.D., Saskatoon, Saskatchewan
Ann Richards, Pharm.D., San Antonio, TX
Matthew Riddle, Jr., M.D., Portland, OR
Robert A. Rizza, M.D., Rochester, MN
Harold R. Roberts, M.D., Chapel Hill, NC
Mario Rodrigues Louz, Ph.D., Sao Paulo Brazil
Prof. Dr. Von Erhard Roeder, Bonn-Endenich, Germany
Gerald Salen, M.D., New York, NY
Evelyn Salerno, Pharm.D., Hialeah, FL
Belinda Sartor, M.D., Shreveport, LA
Irwin A. Schaffer, M.D., Cleveland, OH
Peter Schantz, M.D., Atlanta, GA
Paul L. Schiff, Jr., Ph.D., Pittsburgh, PA
Delia Scholes, Ph.D., Seattle, WA
David E. Schteingart, M.D., Ann Arbor, MI
Volker Schulz, M.D., Berlin, Germany
George S. Schuster, D.D.S., Ph.D., Augusta, GA
Jane R. Schwebke, M.D., Birmingham, AL
Charles F. Seifert, Pharm.D., Rapid City, SD
Alan Shalita, M.D., Brooklyn, NY
Allen F. Shaughnessy, Pharm.D., Harrisburg, PA
Yvonne M. Shevchuk, Pharm.D., Saskatoon, Saskatchewan
Leonard Sigal, M.D., New Brunswick, NJ
David E. Silverstone, M.D., New Haven, CT
Patricia Simone, M.D., Atlanta, GA
Ethel Siris, M.D., New York, NY
Gail Skowron, M.D., Providence, RI
Barry H. Smith, M.D. Ph.D., New York, NY
Geralynn B. Smith, Detroit, MI
Samuel Smith, M.D., Baltimore, MD
Elliott M. Sogol, Ph.D., Research Triangle Park, NC
Fabio Soldati, Lugano, Switzerland
Sunil K. Sood, M.D., New Hyde Park, NY
A.A. Spectrum, Gardena, CA
Leon Speroff, M.D., Portland, OR
Stanley M. Spinola, M.D., Indianapolis, IN
Joan Stachnik, Chicago, IL
Allen C. Steere, M.D., Boston, MA
Sidney J. Stohs, Ph.D., Omaha, NE
David C. Stuhr, Denver, CO
Jay Sullivan, M.D., Memphis, TN
Linda Gore Sutherland, Pharm.D., Laramie, WY
Struan K. Sutherland, M.D., Melbourne, Victoria, Australia
Lynn M. Taussig, M.D., Denver, CO
Daniel Thiebeaud, M.D., Lausanne, Switzerland
Ron Tringali, M.S., Hershey, PA
Anthony T. Tu, Fort Collins, CO
Mendel Tuchman, M.D., Minneapolis, MN
Arthur O. Tucker, Ph.D., Dover, DE
Stephen K. Tyring, M.D., Ph.D., Galveston, TX
Wulf Utian, M.D., Ph.D., Cleveland, OH
Dolores Vicencio, Mexico City, Mexico
Donald G. Vidt, M.D., Cleveland, OH
Paul A. Volberding, M.D., San Francisco, CA
William Warner, Ph.D., New York, NY
John C. Watson, M.D., M.P.H., Atlanta, GA
Robert S. Weinstein, M.D., Little Rock, AR
Stuart R. Weiss, M.D., San Diego, CA
Timothy E. Welty, Pharm.D., Cincinnati, OH
John White, Pharm.D., Spokane, WA
Craig C. Williams, R.Ph., Flagstaff, AZ
K.A. Winship, London, England
Robert G. Wolfangel, Ph.D., St. Louis, MO
G. Frederick Wooten, Jr., M.D., Charlottesville, VA
Seth W. Wright, M.D., Nashville, TN
J. Richard Wuest, Pharm.D., Cincinnati, OH
Johji Yamahara, Kyoto, Japan
Robert Yarchoan, M.D., Bethesda, MD
Mark Yorra, M.P.H., Boston, MA
Mona Zarifa, M.D., Rockville, MD
Jonathan M. Zenilman, M.D., Baltimore, MD
Xiaorini Zhang, M.D., Geneva, Switzerland
Frederic J. Zucchero, M.A., R.Ph., Chesterfield, MO

HEADQUARTERS STAFF

DIVISION OF INFORMATION DEVELOPMENT

Director: Keith W. Johnson
Assistant Director: Georgie M. Cathey
Administrative Staff: Jaime A. Ramirez *(Administrative Assistant)*, Maureen Rawson, Mayra L. Rios, Milagro M. Welter
Senior Drug Information Specialists: Ann Corken *(Supervisor and Nutrition Information Coordinator)*, Nancy Lee Dashiell *(Supervisor)*, Angela Méndez Mayo *(Supervisor* and *Spanish Publications Coordinator)*
Drug Information Specialists: Katherine M. Bennett, Susan Braun, Robin S. Isham-Schermerhorn, Jymeann King, Esther Klein, Denise S. Penn, Bridget Petry, Kathleen M. Phelan, Daniel W. Seyoum, Susan M. Sromek, Susanne Streety, Robyn C. Tyler, Ronald T. Wassel *(Supervisor)*, Joyce P. Weaver
Drug Utilization Review Program Director: Thomas R. Fulda
Medical Information Specialists: Syed R. Ahmad, Joyce Carpenter, Rosaly Correa de Araujo, Fay Menacker, Monique Parr, Jenny J. Tao, Lisa L. Wei
Veterinary Drug Information Specialists: Kathryn Meyer, Amy Neal
Manager, Strategic Planning and Patient Education Programs: Stacy M. Hartranft
Coordinator, USP Dictionary: Jean R. Canada
Computer/Database Applications: Bernard G. Silverstein *(Manager, Database Development)*, Anna Poker, Darcy Schwartz
Consumer Information Development: Diana M. Blais *(Manager)*, Bandana Das *(Assistant)*, Marilyn L. Foster *(Associate)*, Lauren E. O'Connor *(Assistant)*, Janet E. Schmidt *(Associate)*, Patricia Tschirhart-Spangler
Editors: Anne M. Lawrence *(Coordinator)*, Anne Adams, Carol N. Hankin, Sakti P. Mukherjee, Toni Tyson, Deborah F. Zimmer
Library Services: Florence A. Hogan *(Manager)*, Terri Rikhy *(Associate)*, Madeleine Welsch *(Assistant)*
International Programs: Nancy L. Blum *(Coordinator)*, Kirill A. Burimski *(Russia Project Coordinator)*
Research Associate: Maria C. Robie
Research Assistant: AnnaMarie J. Sibik
Consultants: Sandra Lee Boyer, Patricia J. Bush, David W. Hughes, Muriel Lippman, Marcelo Vernengo
Medical Consultants: William P. Baker, M.D., Ph.D.; Donald R. Bennett, M.D., Ph.D.; Carol Proudfit, Ph.D.; Joseph H. Smith, M.D.; Walter L. Way, M.D.
Scholar in Residence: James Blackburn, Saskatoon, Saskatchewan
Student Interns: Jason Abfier, Georgetown University, School of Medicine; Mustafa Farouq, Mansoura University, Egypt; Peggy Kaproth, University of Minnesota, College of Pharmacy; Ana Mata, Universidad Salvadorena Alberto Masferrer, El Salvador; Medha Sasane, University of North Carolina, School of Pharmacy; Vasilisa Sazonov, University of Ljubljana, Slovenia
Visiting Scholars: Marja Airaksinen, Finland; Lyubov Boulkina, Russia; Jane Strang, Australia

USP ADMINISTRATIVE STAFF

Executive Vice President: Jerome A. Halperin
Senior Vice President and General Counsel: Joseph G. Valentino
Vice President, External Affairs: Jacqueline L. Eng
Vice President, Division of Information Technology: Joseph Knudson
Senior Vice President, Business Operations and Development: J. Robert Strang
Director, Personnel: Arlene Bloom
Director, Finance: Abe Brauner
Director, Fulfillment/Facilities: Drew J. Lutz
Legal: Ken Alexander *(Associate Legal Counsel for Business Affairs)*, Kim Keller Reid *(Staff Attorney)*, Jennifer Devine *(Staff Attorney)*

DIVISION OF STANDARDS DEVELOPMENT

Vice President and Director: Lee T. Grady
Assistant Directors: Charles H. Barnstein *(Revision)*, Barbara B. Hubert *(DSD)*
Senior Scientists: Roger Dabbah, V. Srinivasan, William W. Wright
Scientists: Frank P. Barletta, Vivian A. Gray, W. Larry Paul, Todd L. Cecil
Senior Scientific Associates: Gabriel I. Giancaspro, Terry H. Mainprize, Claudia C. Okeke
Manager, Standards Technical Editing: Keith A. Seabaugh
Senior Technical Editors: Ann K. Ferguson, Melissa M. Smith
Senior Translator: Maria T. Gil-Montero
Supervisor of Administration: Anju K. Malhotra
Support Staff: Gerald L. Anderson, Angela M. Healey, Cecilia Luna, Nurilya U. Ivanov
Drug Research and Testing Laboratory: Richard F. Lindauer *(Director)*
Reference Standards Operations: Robert H. King *(Director)*
Hazard Communications: Linda Shear
Consultants: J. Joseph Belson, Martin Golden, Aubrey S. Outschoorn

MARKETING

Vice President: Mark A. Sohasky
Category Manager, Drug & Therapeutic Information: Joan April
Category Manager, Drug Standards & Practitioner Reporting: Charlotte McKamy
Senior Account Manager, Electronic Products: Susan Williams
Account Manager, Electronic Products: Mary Dougherty
Marketing Associate: Matthew Valleskey
Technical Support Specialist: Ric Blackman

PRODUCTION SERVICES

Production Manager, Information Products: A. V. Precup
Production Coordinators: Susan J. Detwiler, Harriet S. Nathanson
Product Development Specialist: Jo-Ann Marshall
Consultants: Mary Coe and Suzanne Peake, Indexing; Ken Mendel, Data Programming
Also Contributing: Doreen Conrad and Michelle Wulffaert of Editech Services, Inc., Production Coordinators; Doris Mullen and Michael Spencer of Editech Services, Inc., Proofreading
Production Manager, Standards Products: Sandra F. Boynton
Senior Editorial Associates: Jesusa D. Cordova, Margaret Kay
Editorial Associates: Ellen Elovitz, Keith Gentile, Suzanne Thren
Desktop Publishing Staff: Susan L. Entwistle *(Supervisor/ Applications Analyst)*, Lauren Taylor Davis, Deborah James, M. T. Samahon, Donna Singh, Micheline Tranquille

PRODUCT DEVELOPMENT

Manager, Electronic Products: Linda M. Guard
Coordinator, Electronic Products: Kelly C. Modzelewski
Applications Analyst, SGML: Laurie J. Manning
Software Engineer: Anthony M. Gray
FOSI Development: Deborah R. Connelly

CREATIVE SERVICES

Derik Rice *(Senior Project Manager)*, Cristy González and Elayne Peterson *(Project Managers)*, Tia C. Morfessis and Randy White *(Senior Designers)*, Rodney Warren *(Designer)*, Larry Lawrence *(Project Assistant)*

PRACTITIONER REPORTING PROGRAMS

Vice President, Practitioner Reporting Programs: Diane D. Cousins
Manager, Program Development: Shawn C. Becker
Manager, Program Operations: Anne Paula Thompson
Analyst Coder Specialist: Rita F. Calnan
Administrative Assistant: Elida B. Amezquita
Coordinator, Data Utilization: Ilze E. Mohseni
Nurse Associate WATS: M. Susan Zmuda
Data Entry Specialist II: Lata Rao
Staff Assistant: Lynn K. Murdock
Program Assistant: Michele R. Balser

MEMBERS OF THE UNITED STATES PHARMACOPEIAL CONVENTION

as of September, 1997

U.S. Colleges and Schools of Medicine

Albany Medical College, Albany, NY: Daniel S. Stein, M.D.
Boston University School of Medicine, Boston, MA: J. Worth Estes, M.D.
Brown University School of Medicine, Providence, RI: Edward Hawrot, Ph.D.
Case Western Reserve University School of Medicine, Cleveland, OH: Charles L. Hoppel, M.D.
Columbia University College of Physicians and Surgeons, New York, NY: Brian F. Hoffman, M.D.
Creighton University School of Medicine, Omaha, NE: Peter W. Abel, Ph.D.
Duke University Medical Center School of Medicine, Durham, NC: James C. McAllister III, M.S.
East Carolina University School of Medicine, Greenville, NC: Donald W. Barnes, Ph.D.
East Tennessee State University James H. Quillen College of Medicine, Johnson City, TN: Peter J. Rice, Ph.D.
Emory University School of Medicine, Atlanta, GA: Yung-Fong Sung, M.D.
Georgetown University School of Medicine, Washington, DC: Arthur Raines, Ph.D.
Harvard Medical School, Boston, MA: David E. Golan, M.D., Ph.D.
Howard University College of Medicine, Washington, DC: Robert E. Taylor, M.D., Ph.D.
Indiana University School of Medicine, Indianapolis, IN: D. Craig Brater, M.D.
Johns Hopkins University School of Medicine, Baltimore, MD: E. Robert Feroli, Pharm.D.
Louisiana State University School of Medicine, New Orleans, LA: Paul L. Kirkendol, Ph.D.
Loyola University of Chicago Stritch School of Medicine, Maywood, IL: Stanley A. Lorens, Ph.D.
Marshall University School of Medicine, Huntington, WV: John L. Szarek, Ph.D.
Mayo Medical School, Rochester, MN: James J. Lipsky, M.D.
Medical College of Ohio, Toledo, OH: Robert D. Wilkerson, Ph.D.
Medical College of Pennsylvania and Hahnemann University School of Medicine, Philadelphia, PA: Edward J. Barbieri, Ph.D.
Medical College of Wisconsin, Milwaukee, WI: Garrett J. Gross, Ph.D.
Meharry Medical College School of Medicine, Nashville, TN: Dolores Shockley, Ph.D.
Mount Sinai School of Medicine, New York, NY: Christopher P. Cardozo, M.D.
New York Medical College, Valhalla, NY: Mario A. Inchiosa, Jr., Ph.D.
Northwestern University Medical School, Chicago, IL: Marilynn C. Frederiksen, M.D.
Oregon Health Sciences University School of Medicine, Portland, OR: Hall Downes, M.D., Ph.D.
Ponce School of Medicine, Ponce, PR: Arthur L. Hupka, Ph.D.
Rush Medical College, Chicago, IL: Paul G. Pierpaoli, M.S.
St. Louis University Health Sciences Center School of Medicine, St. Louis, MO: Alvin H. Gold, Ph.D.
Stanford University School of Medicine, Stanford, CA: Leslie A. Lenert, M.D.
SUNY at Buffalo School of Medicine and Biomedical Sciences, Buffalo, NY: Cedric M. Smith, M.D.
SUNY Health Science Center at Syracuse, Syracuse, NY: Oliver M. Brown, Ph.D.
Temple University School of Medicine, Philadelphia, PA: Ronald J. Tallarida, Ph.D.
The Bowman Gray School of Medicine of Wake Forest University, Winston-Salem, NC: Jack W. Strandhoy, Ph.D.
The Medical College of Georgia School of Medicine, Augusta, GA: David W. Hawkins, Pharm.D.
The Ohio State University College of Medicine, Columbus, OH: Robert M. Guthrie, M.D.
The Pennsylvania State University College of Medicine, Hershey, PA: Cheston M. Berlin, Jr., M.D.
The University of Iowa College of Medicine, Iowa City, IA: John E. Kasik, M.D., Ph.D.
The University of Michigan Medical School, Ann Arbor, MI: Edward F. Domino, Ph.D.
The University of Mississippi Medical Center, Jackson, MS: George W. Moll, Jr., M.D., Ph.D.
Tufts University School of Medicine, Boston, MA: John M. Mazzullo, M.D.
Tulane University School of Medicine, New Orleans, LA: Floyd R. Domer, Ph.D.
Uniformed Services University of the Health Sciences, Bethesda, MD: Louis R. Cantilena, M.D., Ph.D.
University of Alabama School of Medicine, Birmingham, AL: Robert B. Diasio, M.D.
University of California, Davis School of Medicine, Davis, CA: Larry G. Stark, Ph.D.
University of California, San Diego School of Medicine, La Jolla, CA: Harold J. Simon, M.D., Ph.D.
University of California, San Francisco School of Medicine, San Francisco, CA: Mark A. Schumacher, Ph.D., M.D.
University of Chicago Pritzker School of Medicine, Chicago, IL: Patrick Horn, M.D.
University of Cincinnati College of Medicine, Cincinnati, OH: Leonard T. Sigell, Ph.D.
University of Colorado School of Medicine, Denver, CO: Alan S. Hollister, M.D., Ph.D.
University of Connecticut Health Center School of Medicine, Farmington, CT: Paul F. Davern, M.B.A.
University of Florida College of Medicine, Gainesville, FL: Lal C. Garg, Ph.D.
University of Hawaii John A. Burns School of Medicine, Honolulu, HI: Bert K.B. Lum, Ph.D., M.D.
University of Illinois at Chicago School of Medicine, Chicago, IL: Lawrence Isaac, Ph.D.
University of Kansas Medical Center School of Medicine, Kansas City, KS: Harold N. Godwin, M.S.
University of Louisville School of Medicine, Louisville, KY: Peter P. Rowell, Ph.D.
University of Massachusetts Medical School, Worcester, MA: Glenn R. Kershaw, M.D.
University of Medicine and Dentistry of New Jersey-New Jersey Medical School, Newark, NJ: Mohamed S. Abdel-Rahman, Ph.D.
University of Medicine and Dentistry of New Jersey-Robert Wood Johnson Medical School, New Brunswick, NJ: Richard D. Huhn, M.D.
University of Missouri-Columbia School of Medicine, Columbia, MO: John W. Yarbro, M.D.
University of Missouri-Kansas City School of Medicine, Kansas City, MO: Paul G. Cuddy, Pharm.D.
University of Nebraska College of Medicine, Omaha, NE: Manuchair Ebadi, Ph.D.
University of Nevada School of Medicine, Reno, NV: John Q. Adams, Pharm.D.
University of New Mexico School of Medicine, Albuquerque, NM: Jane E. Henney, M.D.
University of North Carolina School of Medicine, Chapel Hill, NC: Culley C. Carson, M.D.
University of North Dakota School of Medicine, Grand Forks, ND: David W. Hein, Ph.D.
University of Oklahoma College of Medicine, Oklahoma City, OK: Patrick A. McKee, M.D.
University of Pennsylvania School of Medicine, Philadelphia, PA: Marilyn E. Hess, Ph.D.
University of Rochester School of Medicine and Dentistry, Rochester, NY: Ira Shoulson, M.D.
University of South Florida College of Medicine, Tampa, FL: Joseph J. Krzanowski, Ph.D.
University of Tennessee, Memphis College of Medicine, Memphis, TN: Murray Heimberg, M.D., Ph.D.
University of Texas Health Science Center at San Antonio Medical School, San Antonio, TX: Alexander M.M. Shepherd, M.D., Ph.D.
University of Texas Houston Medical School, Houston, TX: Timothy P. Bohan, M.D., Ph.D.
University of Texas Southwestern Medical Center at Dallas, Dallas, TX: Paul F. White, Ph.D., M.D.
University of Washington School of Medicine, Seattle, WA: Georgiana K. Ellis, M.D.
Vanderbilt University School of Medicine, Nashville, TN: Dan M. Roden, M.D.
Virginia Commonwealth University/Medical College of Virginia School of Medicine, Richmond, VA: Aron H. Lichtman, Ph.D.
Wayne State University School of Medicine, Detroit, MI: Deborah G. May, M.D.
West Virginia University Robert C. Byrd Health Sciences Center, Morgantown, WV: Douglas D. Glover, M.D., R.Ph.
Wright State University School of Medicine, Dayton, OH: Robert L. Koerker, Ph.D.
Yale University School of Medicine, New Haven, CT: Florence Comite, M.D.

State Medical Societies

Alaska State Medical Association, Anchorage, AK: Keith M. Brownsberger, M.D.
California Medical Association, San Francisco, CA: Rene H. Bravo, M.D.

Connecticut State Medical Society, New Haven, CT: James E. O'Brien, M.D., Ph.D.
Florida Medical Association, Jacksonville, FL: Robert E. Windom, M.D.
Idaho Medical Association, Boise, ID: Lawrence L. Knight, M.D.
Illinois State Medical Society, Chicago, IL: Albino T. Bismonte, M.D.
Indiana State Medical Association, Indianapolis, IN: Daria Schooler, M.D., R.Ph.
Kansas Medical Society, Topeka, KS: James L. Early, M.D.
Kentucky Medical Association, Louisville, KY: Ellsworth C. Seeley, M.D.
Louisiana State Medical Society, Metairie, LA: Merlin H. Allen, M.D.
Massachusetts Medical Society, Waltham, MA: Errol Green, M.D.
Medical and Chirurgical Faculty of the State of Maryland, Baltimore, MD: Margaret N. Burri, M.A.
Medical Association of Georgia, Atlanta, GA: Edwin D. Bransome, M.D.
Medical Association of the State of Alabama, Montgomery, AL: James R. Reed, M.D., Ph.D.
Medical Society of Delaware, Wilmington, DE: Michael J. Pasquale, M.D.
Medical Society of New Jersey, Lawrenceville, NJ: Joseph N. Micale, M.D.
Medical Society of the District of Columbia, Washington, DC: Kim A. Bullock, M.D.
Medical Society of the State of New York, Lake Success, NY: Richard Blum, M.D.
Medical Society of Virginia, Richmond, VA: Boyd M. Clements, M.D.
Michigan State Medical Society, East Lansing, MI: Douglas D. Notman, M.D.
Mississippi State Medical Association, Jackson, MS: William A. Causey, M.D.
Missouri State Medical Association, Jefferson City, MO: C.C. Swarens
Nebraska Medical Association, Lincoln, NE: Fred H. Ayers, M.D.
New Hampshire Medical Society, Concord, NH: Belinda L. Castor, M.D.
North Carolina Medical Society, Raleigh, NC: Don C. Chaplin, M.D.
North Dakota Medical Association, Bismarck, ND: William W. Barnes, M.D.
Ohio State Medical Association, Columbus, OH: Janet K. Bixel, M.D.
Oklahoma State Medical Association, Oklahoma City, OK: Clinton N. Cordon, M.D., Ph.D.
Pennsylvania Medical Society, Harrisburg, PA: Benjamin Calesnick, M.D.
South Carolina Medical Association, Columbia, SC: Frank R. Ervin, M.D.
South Dakota State Medical Association, Sioux Falls, SD: Thomas C. Johnson, M.D.
State Medical Society of Wisconsin, Madison, WI: Melvin Rosen, M.D., Ph.D.
Tennessee Medical Association, Nashville, TN: John J. Ingram, M.D.
Texas Medical Association, Austin, TX: John E. Presley, M.D.
Utah Medical Association, Salt Lake City, UT: Douglas E. Rollins, M.D., Ph.D.
Washington State Medical Association, Seattle, WA: William O. Robertson, M.D.
West Virginia State Medical Association, Charleston, WV: Kevin W. Yingling, M.D., F.A.C.P., R.Ph.
Wyoming Medical Society, Inc., Cheyenne, WY: Richard W. Johnson, Jr.

U.S. Colleges and Schools of Pharmacy

Auburn University School of Pharmacy, Auburn, AL: Kenneth N. Barker, Ph.D.
Butler University College of Pharmacy and Health Sciences, Indianapolis, IN: Jayesh Vora, Ph.D.
Campbell University School of Pharmacy, Buies Creek, NC: Antoine Al-Achi, Ph.D.
Creighton University School of Pharmacy and Allied Health Professions, Omaha, NE: Kenneth R. Keefner, Ph.D.
Drake University College of Pharmacy and Health Sciences, Des Moines, IA: Sidney Finn, Ph.D.
Duquesne University School of Pharmacy, Pittsburgh, PA: Lawrence H. Block, Ph.D.
Ferris State University College of Pharmacy, Big Rapids, MI: Kenneth J. McMullen
Florida A&M University College of Pharmacy and Pharmaceutical Sciences, Tallahassee, FL: Seth Y. Ablordeppey, Ph.D.
Idaho State University College of Pharmacy, Pocatello, ID: Eugene I. Isaacson, Ph.D.
Long Island University Arnold & Marie Schwartz College of Pharmacy and Health Sciences, Brooklyn, NY: Jack Rosenberg, Pharm.D., Ph.D.
Massachusetts College of Pharmacy and Allied Health Sciences, Boston, MA: Sumner M. Robinson, Ph.D.
Medical University of South Carolina College of Pharmacy, Charleston, SC: Jaymin C. Shah, Ph.D.
Mercer University Southern School of Pharmacy, Atlanta, GA: J. Grady Strom, Jr., Ph.D.
Midwestern University Chicago College of Pharmacy, Downers Grove, IL: Mary W.L. Lee, Pharm.D.
North Dakota State University College of Pharmacy, Fargo, ND: Jagdish Singh, Ph.D.
Northeast Louisiana University School of Pharmacy, Monroe, LA: William M. Bourn, Ph.D.
Northeastern University School of Pharmacy, Boston, MA: Mehdi Boroujerdi, Ph.D.
NOVA Southeastern University College of Pharmacy, North Miami Beach, FL: William D. Hardigan, Ph.D.
Ohio Northern University College of Pharmacy, Ada, OH: Metta Lou Henderson, Ph.D.
Oregon State University College of Pharmacy, Corvallis, OR: John H. Block, Ph.D.
Philadelphia College of Pharmacy and Science, Philadelphia, PA: Alfonso R. Gennaro, Ph.D.
Purdue University School of Pharmacy, West Lafayette, IN: Stephen R. Byrn, Ph.D.
Rutgers-The State University of New Jersey College of Pharmacy, Piscataway, NJ: Leonard C. Bailey, Ph.D.
Samford University School of Pharmacy, Birmingham, AL: Hilmer (Tony) A. McBride, Ph.D.
Shenandoah University School of Pharmacy, Winchester, VA: David W. Newton, Ph.D.
South Dakota State University College of Pharmacy, Brookings, SD: Chandradhar Dwivedi, Ph.D.
Southwestern Oklahoma State University School of Pharmacy, Weatherford, OK: Keith W. Reichmann, Ph.D.
St John's University College of Pharmacy and Allied Health Professions, Jamaica, NY: Thomas H. Wiser, Pharm.D.
St. Louis College of Pharmacy, St. Louis, MO: John W. Zuzack, Ph.D.
Temple University School of Pharmacy, Philadelphia, PA: Reza Fassihi, Ph.D.
Texas Southern University College of Pharmacy and Health Sciences, Houston, TX: William B. Harrell, Ph.D.
Texas Tech University School of Pharmacy, Amarillo, TX: Arthur A. Nelson, Ph.D.
The Ohio State University College of Pharmacy, Columbus, OH: Sylvan G. Frank, Ph.D.
The University of Arizona College of Pharmacy, Tucson, AZ: Michael Mayersohn, Ph.D.
The University of Georgia College of Pharmacy, Athens, GA: Stuart Feldman, Ph.D.
University at Buffalo School of Pharmacy, Buffalo, NY: Howard Forman, Pharm.D.
University of Arkansas for Medical Sciences College of Pharmacy, Little Rock, AR: Jonathan J. Wolfe, Ph.D.
University of California San Francisco, School of Pharmacy, San Francisco, CA: Emil T. Lin, Ph.D.
University of Cincinnati College of Pharmacy, Cincinnati, OH: Henry S.I. Tan, Ph.D.
University of Colorado School of Pharmacy, Denver, CO: Louis Diamond, Ph.D.
University of Connecticut School of Pharmacy, Storrs, CT: Michael C. Gerald, Ph.D.
University of Florida College of Pharmacy, Gainesville, FL: Michael A. Schwartz, Ph.D.
University of Houston College of Pharmacy, Houston, TX: Mustafa F. Lokhandwala, Ph.D.
University of Illinois College of Pharmacy, Chicago, IL: John F. Fitzloff, Ph.D.
University of Iowa College of Pharmacy, Iowa City, IA: Gilbert S. Banker, Ph.D.
University of Kansas School of Pharmacy, Lawrence, KS: John Stobaugh, Ph.D.
University of Kentucky College of Pharmacy, Lexington, KY: Paul M. Bummer, Ph.D.
University of Maryland at Baltimore School of Pharmacy, Baltimore, MD: Larry Augsburger, Ph.D.
University of Michigan School of Pharmacy, Ann Arbor, MI: Duane M. Kirking, Ph.D.
University of Minnesota College of Pharmacy, Minneapolis, MN: James C. Cloyd, Pharm.D.
University of Mississippi School of Pharmacy, University, MS: Alan B Jones, Ph.D.
University of Missouri-Kansas City School of Pharmacy, Kansas City, MO: William A. Watson, Pharm.D.
University of Montana School of Pharmacy and Allied Health Professions, Missoula, MT: Todd G. Cochran, Ph.D.
University of Nebraska College of Pharmacy, Omaha, NE: Clarence T. Ueda, Pharm D., Ph.D.
University of New Mexico College of Pharmacy, Albuquerque, NM: William M. Hadley, Ph.D.
University of North Carolina School of Pharmacy, Chapel Hill, NC: Richard J. Kowalsky, Pharm.D.
University of Oklahoma College of Pharmacy, Oklahoma City, OK: Loyd V. Allen, Jr., Ph.D.
University of Pittsburgh School of Pharmacy, Pittsburgh, PA: Dennis P. Swanson, M.S.
University of Puerto Rico, Medical Sciences Campus School of Pharmacy, San Juan, PR: Ilia I. Oquendo, Ph.D.
University of Rhode Island College of Pharmacy, Kingston, RI: Hossein Zia, Ph.D.

University of South Carolina College of Pharmacy, Columbia, SC: Bozena B. Michniak, Ph.D.
University of Southern California School of Pharmacy, Los Angeles, CA: Robert T. Koda, Pharm.D., Ph.D.
University of Tennessee College of Pharmacy, Memphis, TN: Dick R. Gourley, Pharm.D.
University of Texas College of Pharmacy, Austin, TX: James T. Doluisio, Ph.D.
University of the Pacific School of Pharmacy, Stockton, CA: Ravindra Vasavada, Ph.D.
University of Toledo College of Pharmacy, Toledo, OH: Paul W. Erhardt, Ph.D.
University of Utah College of Pharmacy, Salt Lake City, UT: David B. Roll, Ph.D.
University of Washington School of Pharmacy, Seattle, WA: Danny D. Shen, Ph.D.
University of Wisconsin School of Pharmacy, Madison, WI: Melvin H. Weinswig, Ph.D.
University of Wyoming School of Pharmacy, Laramie, WY: Kenneth F. Nelson, Ph.D.
Virginia Commonwealth University/Medical College of Virginia School of Pharmacy, Richmond, VA: Susanna Wu-Pong, Ph.D.
Washington State University College of Pharmacy, Pullman, WA: Mahmoud M. Abdel-Monem, Ph.D.
Wayne State University College of Pharmacy and Allied Health Professions, Detroit, MI: Craig K. Svennson, Pharm.D., Ph.D.
West Virginia University School of Pharmacy, Morgantown, WV: Arthur I. Jacknowitz, Pharm.D.
Western University of Health Sciences School of Pharmacy, Pomona, Ca: Krishna Kumar, Ph.D.
Wilkes University School of Pharmacy, Wilkes-Barre, PA: Arthur H. Kibbe, Ph.D.
Xavier University of Louisiana College of Pharmacy, New Orleans, LA: Merrill A. Patin, Pharm.D.

State Pharmacy Associations

Alabama Pharmacy Association, Montgomery, AL: David L. Laven, R.Ph.
Arizona Pharmacy Association, Tempe, AZ: Edward P. Armstrong, Ph.D.
Arkansas Pharmacists Association, Little Rock, AR: Leslee J. Falls, Pharm.D.
California Pharmacists Association, Sacramento, CA: R. David Lauper, Pharm.D.
Colegio de Farmaceuticos de Puerto Rico, San Juan, PR: Felix G. Mendez, R.Ph.
Colorado Pharmacists Association, Inc., Denver, CO: Thomas G. Arthur, R.Ph., M.S.A.
Connecticut Pharmacists Association, Rocky Hill, CT: Henry A. Palmer, Ph.D.
Delaware Pharmaceutical Society, Wilmington, DE: Kenneth Musto, Jr., R.Ph.
Florida Pharmacy Association, Tallahassee, FL: Michael A. Mone, B.S., J.D.
Georgia Pharmacy Association, Inc., Atlanta, GA: Larry L. Braden, R.Ph.
Hawaii Pharmaceutical Association, Honolulu, HI: Gerry K. Fujii, Pharm.D.
Illinois Pharmacists Association, Chicago, IL: Ronald Gottrich, R.Ph.
Iowa Pharmacists Association, Des Moines, IA: Lloyd E. Matheson, Ph.D.
Kansas Pharmacists Association, Topeka, KS: Ravi Gadi, Pharm.D., M.S.
Kentucky Pharmacists Association, Frankfort, KY: Robert L. Barnett, R.Ph.
Louisiana Pharmacists Association, Baton Rouge, LA: Christee G. Atwood
Maine Pharmacy Association, Bangor, ME: Stanley Stewart, R.Ph.
Maryland Pharmacists Association, Baltimore, MD: Nicholas C. Lykos
Massachusetts Pharmacists Association, Waltham, MA: Harold B. Sparr, R.Ph.
Michigan Pharmacists Association, Lansing, MI: Patrick L. McKercher, Ph.D.
Minnesota Pharmacists Association, St. Paul, MN: Mary S. Hayney, Pharm.D.
Mississippi Pharmacists Association, Jackson, MS: Dinah G. Jordan
Missouri Pharmacy Association, Jefferson City, MO: George L. Oestreich, R.Ph., M.P.A.
Montana State Pharmaceutical Association, Helena, MT: James Marmar, R.Ph.
Nebraska Pharmacists Association, Lincoln, NE: Leland C. Lucke
Nevada Pharmacists Association, Reno, NV: Herbert R. Bohner
New Hampshire Pharmacists Association, Concord, NH: Elizabeth A. Gower, R.Ph.
New Jersey Pharmacists Association, Robbinsville, NJ: Steven H. Zlotnick, Pharm.D.
North Carolina Pharmaceutical Association, Chapel Hill, NC: Alfred H. Mebane, R.Ph.
North Dakota Pharmaceutical Association, Bismarck, ND: William J. Grosz, Sc.D.
Ohio Pharmacists Association, Dublin, OH: Amelia S. Bennett
Oklahoma Pharmaceutical Association, Oklahoma City, OK: Carl D. Lyons
Oregon State Pharmacists Association, Salem, OR: Charles F. Gress
Pennsylvania Pharmacists Association, Harrisburg, PA: Edward J. Bechtel, R.Ph.
Pharmaceutical Society of the State of New York, Albany, NY: Bruce Moden, R.Ph.
Rhode Island Pharmacists Association, Pawtucket, RI: Margot B. Kreplick, R.Ph.
South Carolina Pharmacy Association, Columbia, SC: James R. Bracewell
South Dakota Pharmaceutical Association, Pierre, SD: Galen D. Jordre
Tennessee Pharmacists Association, Nashville, TN: Roger L. Davis, Pharm.D.
Texas Pharmacy Association, Austin, TX: Eric H. Frankel, Pharm.D.
Utah Pharmaceutical Association, Orem, UT: C. Neil Jensen, R.Ph.
Vermont Pharmacists Association, Richmond, VT: Frederick H. Dobson III, Ph.D., R.Ph.
Virginia Pharmacy Association, Richmond, VA: Marianne R. Rollings, R.Ph.
Washington State Pharmacists Association, Renton, WA: Rodney D. Shafer, R.Ph.
Washington, D.C. Pharmaceutical Association, Washington, DC: James F. Harris, R.Ph.
Wisconsin Pharmacists Association, Madison, WI: Judith E. Thompson, R.Ph., M.S.
Wyoming Pharmacists Association, Powell, WY: William H. Rathburn, R.Ph.

National and State Professional and Scientific Organizations

Academy of Managed Care Pharmacy, Alexandria, VA: Darlene M. Mednick, R.Ph.
American Academy of Family Physicians, Washington, DC: Roger R. Tobias, M.D.
American Academy of Nurse Practitioners, Austin, TX: Jan Towers, Ph.D., NP-C
American Academy of Ophthalmology, San Francisco, CA: Joel S. Mindel, M.D., Ph.D.
American Academy of Pediatrics, Elk Grove Village, IL: Ralph E. Kauffman, M.D.
American Academy of Physician Assistants, Alexandria, VA: Greg P. Thomas, PA-C, M.P.H.
American Association of Colleges of Nursing, Washington, DC: Barbara A. Durand, Ed.D.
American Association of Colleges of Osteopathic Medicine, Chevy Chase, MD: Anthony J. Silvagni, D.O., Pharm.D.
American Association of Colleges of Pharmacy, Alexandria, Va: Richard P. Penna, Pharm.D.
American Association of Critical-Care Nurses, Aliso Viejo, CA: Barbara Johnston, Ph.D., R.N.
American Association of Dental Schools, Washington, DC: Gary E. Jeffers, D.M.D., M.S.
American Association of Pharmaceutical Scientists, Alexandria, Va: Richard A. Soltero, Ph.D.
American Association of Pharmacy Technicians, Inc., Greensboro, NC: Alice T. Foust
American Association of Poison Control Centers, Washington, DC: Toby L. Litovitz, M.D.
American Chemical Society, Washington, DC: Norman C. Jamieson, Ph.D.
American College of Cardiology, Bethesda, MD: Bertram Pitt, M.D.
American College of Chest Physicians, Northbrook, IL: Irwin Ziment, M.D.
American College of Clinical Pharmacy, Kansas City, MO: Mary H.H. Chandler, Pharm.D.
American College of Obstetricians and Gynecologists, Washington, D.C.: Rudi Ansbacher, M.D.
American College of Radiology, Reston, Va: Bruce L. McClennan, M.D.
American College of Rheumatology, Atlanta, GA: Daniel E. Furst, M.D.
American Dental Association, Chicago, IL: Clifford W. Whall, Jr., Ph.D.
American Dietetic Association, Chicago, IL: Mary K. Russell, R.D., L.D.N., C.N.S.D.
American Geriatrics Society, New York, NY: Jerry Gurwitz, M.D.
American Medical Association, Chicago, IL: Joseph W. Cranston, Ph.D.
American Nurses Association, Inc. Washington, DC: Divina Grossman, Ph.D., R.N., ARNP, CS
American Optometric Association, St. Louis, MO: Jimmy D. Bartlett, O.D.
American Pharmaceutical Association, Washington, DC: Lowell J. Anderson
American Podiatric Medical Association, Bethesda, MD: Pamela J. Colman, DPM
American Psychiatric Association, Washington, DC: Deborah A. Zarin, M.D.
American Public Health Association, Washington, DC: J. Warren Salmon, Ph.D.
American Society for Clinical Pharmacology and Therapeutics, Norristown, PA: William J. Mroczek, M.D.

American Society for Parenteral and Enteral Nutrition, Silver Spring, MD: Jay Mirtallo, R.Ph.
American Society for Pharmacology and Experimental Therapeutics, Bethesda, MD: Kenneth L. Dretchen, Ph.D.
American Society for Quality Control, Milwaukee, WI: George L. Schorn, R.Ph.
American Society of Anesthesiologists, Park Ridge, IL: John R. Moyers, M.D.
American Society of Clinical Oncology, Alexandria, Va: Joseph S. Bailes, M.D.
American Society of Consultant Pharmacists, Alexandria, VA: Milton S. Moskowitz, R.Ph, FASCP
American Society of Health-System Pharmacists, Bethesda, MD: Charles E. Myers, M.S., M.B.A.
American Type Culture Collection, Rockville, MD: Raymond H. Cypess, D.V.M., Ph.D.
American Veterinary Medical Association, Schaumburg, IL: Jack W. Oliver, D.V.M., Ph.D.
AOAC International, Gaithersburg, MD: Thomas P. Layloff, Ph.D.
Association of American Veterinary Medical Colleges, Washington, DC: Lester M. Crawford, Ph.D., D.V.M.
Drug Information Association, Ambler, PA: Judith Weissinger, Ph.D.
Federation of State Medical Boards, Euless, TX: Dale L. Austin, M.A.
Intravenous Nurses' Society, Cambridge, MA: Mary Alexander, CRNI
National Association of Boards of Pharmacy, Park Ridge, IL: Carmen A. Catizone, M.S., R.Ph.
National Community Pharmacists Association (formerly NARD), Alexandria, VA: Louis A. Mitchell, P.D.
National Pharmaceutical Association, Washington, DC: Barry Bleidt, Ph.D., Pharm.D., R.Ph.
Oncology Nursing Society, Pittsburgh, PA: Mary Garlick Roll, R.N., M.S.

Governmental Bodies

Centers for Disease Control and Prevention, Atlanta, GA: John A. Becher
Department of Veterans Affairs Veterans Health Administration, Washington, DC: John E. Ogden
FDA Center for Biologics Evaluation and Research, Rockville, MD: Elaine C. Esber, M.D.
FDA Center for Devices and Radiological Health, Rockville, MD: Elizabeth D. Jacobson, Ph.D.
FDA Center for Drug Evaluation and Research, Rockville, MD: Roger L. Williams, M.D.
FDA Center for Veterinary Medicine, Rockville, MD: Richard H. Teske, D.V.M.
Health Canada, Tunney's Pasture, ON: Keith Bailey, D.Phil.
Health Care Financing Administration, Washington, DC: Grant Bagley, M.D.
Ministerio de Sanidad Y Consumo (Ministry of Health, Spain), Madrid, Spain: Federico Plaza, Farmaceutico
National Institute of Standards and Technology, Gaithersburg, MD: Thomas E. Gills
National Institutes of Health, Bethesda, MD: Joseph F. Gallelli, Ph.D.
Russian Center for Pharmaceutical and Medical Technical Information (PHARMEDINFO), Moscow, Russia: Galina Shashkova
Therapeutic Goods Administration of Australia, Woden, ACT: John Cable, Ph.D.
United States Agency for International Development, Washington, DC: Anthony Boni
United States Air Force, Andrews AFB, MD: James H. Young, BSPH/MSSM
United States Army Office of the Surgeon General, Falls Church, VA: Bruce A. Nelson, R.Ph.
United States Food and Drug Administration, Rockville, MD: Mary K. Pendergast, LLM
United States Navy Bureau of Medicine and Surgery, Washington, DC: David R. Woker, R.Ph.

Health Science and other Foreign Organizations and Pharmacopeias

Asociacion Farmaceutica Mexicana, A.C., Mexico, D.F.: Jose Manuel Cardenas Gutierrez, O.F.B.
Association of Faculties of Pharmacy of Canada, Vancouver, BC: Dennis K.J. Gorecki, Ph.D.
British Pharmacopoeia Commission, London, UK: Robert C. Hutton, Ph.D.
Canadian Association of University Schools of Nursing, Ottawa, ON: Wendy McBride
Canadian Nurses Association, Ottawa, ON: Gladys Peachey, R.N., B.N., M.Ed., M.H.Sc.
Canadian Pharmaceutical Association, Ottawa, ON: Leroy C. Fevang, M.B.A.
Committee on the Pharmacopeia of Japan, Tokyo, Japan: Mitsuru Uchiyama, Ph.D.
Federation Internationale Pharmaceutique, Hague, The Netherlands: Daan Crommelin, Ph.D.
National Academy of Medicine (Academia Nacional de Medicina de Mexico), Colonia Doctores, Mex: Fermin Valenzuela, M.D.
Pan American Health Organization, Washington, DC: Enrique Fefer, Ph.D.
Permanent Commission of the Mexican United States Pharmacopeia, Mexico: Q. Ma del Carmen Becerril, Chemist

Consumer Organizations and Individuals Representing Public Interests

American Cancer Society, Atlanta, Ga: Harmon J. Eyre, M.D.
American Diabetes Association, Alexandria, VA: Lawrence Blonde, M.D.
American Heart Association, Dallas, TX: Rodman D. Starke, M.D.
Arthritis Foundation, Atlanta, GA: Marianne H. Kaple, M.Ed.
Asthma and Allergy Foundation of America, Washington, DC: Mary E. Worstell, M.P.H.
Center for Science in the Public Interest, Washington, DC: Bonnie F. Liebman, M.S.
Citizens for Public Action on Blood Pressure and Cholesterol, Inc., Bethesda, MD: Gerald J. Wilson, M.A., M.B.A.
Consumer's Union, Yonkers, NY: Marvin M. Lipman, M.D.
National Organization for Rare Disorders, New Fairfield, CT: Michael Langan

Domestic, Foreign, and International Manufacturers, Trade, and Affiliated Associations

American Association of Health Plans, Washington, DC: Clyde R. Cooper, Pharm.D.
Animal Health Institute, Alexandria, Va: Richard A. Carnevale, V.M.D.
Council for Responsible Nutrition, Washington, DC: V. Annette Dickinson, Ph.D.
Generic Pharmaceutical Industry Association, Washington, DC: Alice E. Till, Ph.D.
Health Industry Manufacturers Association, Washington, DC: Dee G. Simons, M.A.
International Federation of Pharmaceutical Manufacturers Association, Geneva, Switzerland: Richard Arnold, Ph.D.
International Pharmaceutical Excipients Council, Wayne, NJ: David R. Schoneker, M.S.
Joint Commission on Accreditation of Healthcare Organizations, Oakbrook Terrace, IL: Jerod M. Loeb, Ph.D.
National Association of Pharmaceutical Manufacturers, Garden City, NY: Loren R. Gelber, Ph.D.
National Pharmaceutical Alliance, Alexandria, VA: Gary L. Yingling, M.S., J.D.
National Wholesale Druggists' Association, Reston, VA: John M. Hammond
Nonprescription Drug Manufacturers Association, Washington, DC: R. William Soller, Ph.D.
Nonprescription Drug Manufacturers Association of Canada, Ottawa, ON: David S. Skinner
Parenteral Drug Association, Bethesda, MD: Russell E. Madsen, M.S.
Pharmaceutical Research and Manufacturers of America, Washington, DC: Maurice Q. Bectel, D.Sc.
The Cosmetic, Toiletry and Fragrance Association, Washington, DC: Gerald N. McEwen, Ph.D., J.D.
The National Association of Chain Drug Stores, Alexandria, VA: Leonard J. DeMino
World Federation of Proprietary Medicine Manufacturers, London: Jerome A. Reinstein, Ph.D.

Members at Large

Clement Bezold, Ph.D., Alexandria, VA
Lester Chafetz, Ph.D., Kansas City, MO
Thomas S. Foster, Pharm.D., Lexington, KY
Alan H. Kaplan, J.D., Washington, DC
Jay S. Keystone, M.D., Toronto, ON
Carol S. Marcus, Ph.D., M.D., Torrance, CA
Maurice L. Mashford, M.D., Parkville, Victoria
David Ofori-Adjei, M.D., FRCP, Accra, Ghana
Thomas F. Patton, Ph.D., St. Louis, MO
Gordon D. Schiff, M.D., Chicago, IL
Ralph F. Shangraw, Ph.D., Baltimore, MD
Robert E. Vestal, M.D., Boise, ID

Ex Officio Members

Donald R. Bennett, M.D., Ph.D., Downers Grove, IL
John V. Bergen, Ph.D., Wayne, PA
James C. Boylan, Ph.D., Abbott Park, IL
J. Richard Crout, M.D., Bethesda, MD
James T. Doluisio, Ph.D., Austin, TX
Arthur Hull Hayes, Jr., M.D., New Rochelle, NY

Honorary Members

George F. Archambault, Pharm.D., J.D., Bethesda, MD
William M. Heller, Ph.D., Stuart, FL
William J. Kinnard, Ph.D., Baltimore, MD
Frederick Mahaffey, Pharm.D., Bolivar, MO
Lloyd C. Miller, Ph.D., Escondidio, CA
John H. Moyer, M.D., D.Sc., Palmyra, PA
John A. Owen, Jr., M.D., Charlottesville, VA
Paul Parker, Pharm.D., Lexington, KY

Committee Member(s)

Eileen Hemphill, Washington, DC